Langenscheidt's New College Spanish Dictionary

Spanish-English
English-Spanish

LANGENSCHEIDT
NEW YORK · BERLIN · MUNICH · VIENNA · ZURICH

Langenscheidt's New College Spanish Dictionary

Original Title: Smart Diccionario Español-Inglés, English-Spanish

Printed in Germany

Preface

The creation of a dictionary is the result of a long process which consists principally of observing the slow evolution of a language, especially of its vocabulary, and bringing to each edition the new terminology and usage adapted by that language. Once these have been incorporated into the ocean of words built up over centuries, they become a part of the whole like a glass of water poured into the sea.

Langenscheidt's New College Spanish Dictionary is a bilingual dictionary which has been written and structured according to the latest developments in the two languages. The reader will find a large number of easy-to-understand definitions, oriented toward explaining and clarifying meaning and usage.

The **New College Spanish Dictionary** places special emphasis on the living, spoken language. It lists a large number of colloquialisms and slang terms that have become part of the general conversation and literature of our time. This is an effective aid to the user in understanding everyday conversation, contemporary writing, comics, the press, and, in general, all informal and colloquial language.

Technical, literary, formal and academic language form the largest part of the dictionary entries, as corresponds to their importance in the language. The **New College Spanish Dictionary** also incorporates the differences between British and American English and in addition, includes the national and regional variants of Spanish as spoken in Latin America.

In conclusion, the **New College Spanish Dictionary** is characterized by two special qualities which make it exceptional: on the one hand, the clarity of the definitions, based on the didactic purpose of serving speakers of both English and Spanish effectively and on the other, the large number of entries, definitions and usage examples provided, which aid the reader in understanding and dealing with a wide variety of language contexts and situations.

THE EDITORS

Prólogo

Crear un diccionario resulta una larga labor que consiste principalmente en observar la lenta evolución de la lengua y muy especialmente de su léxico, y aportar en cada nuevo trabajo aquellos nuevos usos que se han descubierto y que, una vez incorporados al océano de las palabras acrisoladas siglo tras siglo, quedan perdidos como el agua en un vaso vertida al mar.

Langenscheidt's New College Spanish Dictionary es un diccionario bilingüe, escrito y estructurado según los últimos desarrollos producidos en ambas lenguas. El lector encontrará en él multitud de explicaciones fáciles de entender, encaminadas a precisar y aclarar significados, usos y dificultades de la lengua inglesa.

Es fundamental el tratamiento que en el **New College Spanish Dictionary** se hace de la lengua viva. Contiene la lista de entradas de un buen número de términos de argot y de la lengua de la calle que han alcanzado un uso generalizado en las conversaciones y en la literatura de nuestra época. Esta característica ayudará eficazmente a comprender el idioma conversacional y a traducir la narrativa actual, los comics, la prensa y, en suma, todo lo que, por pertenecer a un ámbito familiar o coloquial, tradicionalmente ignorado por los diccionarios, puede dejarnos sin comprender un texto o una situación.

El lenguaje técnico, el literario, el de cortesías formales y el usual académico tienen la más alta representación como corresponde estadísticamente a su peso específico y numérico dentro de la lengua. Del mismo modo, el **New College Spanish Dictionary** incorpora las diferencias entre el inglés británico y el americano y reúne todas las precisiones, correspondencias y entradas propias del español utilizado en América Latina.

El **New College Spanish Dictionary** tiene, en conclusión, dos cualidades que le hacen excepcional: por un lado, la claridad de planteamientos que viene dada, en gran parte, por su intención didáctica de servir eficazmente a los lectores de habla española y, por otro, la riqueza de entradas, precisiones de uso y correspondencias que ayudan al consultante a captar y comprender gran variedad de contextos y situaciones.

LOS EDITORES

First Part

Spanish-English

Contents

Materias

Directions for the Use of the Dictionary

Advertencias para facilitar la consulta del diccionario

La idea principal, en cuanto a la sección español-inglés, a la hora de redactarla, ha sido la siguiente: facilitar al consultante el término inglés que puede necesitar en un momento determinado. Nos pareció conveniente incluir muchas entradas y ser muy concisos, para evitar la repetición de informaciones dadas en la sección inglés-español, que es a donde el consultante debe recurrir para aclarar más a fondo dudas sobre la lengua inglesa. Veamos unos ejemplos que ilustrarán esta característica de nuestra obra:

The main idea in the preparation of the Spanish-English section was the following: to make the English terms that the reader needs at a particular moment easily accessible. For this reason, a wide number of entries are included and these are kept short and concise in order to avoid repetition of information given in the English-Spanish section, which is the section the user should refer to to clarify further doubts regarding the English language. Some examples which illustrate this characteristic of the dictionary follow:

plantilla *s.f.* **1** insole (zapato), sole (calcetín) ... **3** staff, payroll (nómina). **4** *DEP.* squad, team.
platero, -a *s.m.* y *f.* **1** silversmith (orfebre). **2** jeweller (joyero).
pontón *s.m.* **1** lighter (barco). **2** pontoon (puente). **3** float (de hidroavión).
publicar *v.t.* **1** to publicize, to make public (anunciar). **2** to divulge, to reveal (revelar). **3** to publish (editar).

Queda constancia de las distintas correspondencias adecuadas a las diferentes categorías gramaticales, incluso cuando podría pensarse, por ser así en español, que serviría la misma:

The different definitions corresponding to different grammatical categories should be noted, as opposed to what one might expect in Spanish:

palurdo, -a *adj.* **1** (*desp.*) rustic, uncouth. || *s.m.* y *m.* **2** (*desp.*) bumpkin, yokel.

También en esta sección hemos incluido registros de uso:

In this section, we have also included usage registers:

poblacho *s.m.* (*desp.*) dump, hole.
potable ... **2** (*fam.*) acceptable, passable (aceptable),

tecnicismos:

technical vocabulary:

plaqueta ... *BIOL.* blood platelet.
páramo ... *GEOG.* moor,

diferenciación entre el inglés de uno y otro lado del Atlántico:

differences between American and British English:

paidología *s.f.* (*brit.*) paedology, (*EE.UU.*) pedology.
pañal *s.m.* **1** (*brit.*) nappy, (*EE.UU.*) diaper.
pantalón *s.m.* **1** (*brit.*) trousers, (*EE.UU.*) pants,

sustantivos compuestos, ya sea de los que coinciden con la traducción de sus componentes del español al inglés, como los que tienen su correspondencia propia:

compound nouns, including those which coincide with a word-for-word translation from Spanish as well as those which do not:

potable ... agua –, drinking water.
pantalón ... – vaquero, jeans.
palabra ... – de rey, word of honour.
presencial ... testigo –, eyewitness.
propiciatorio, -a ... víctima propiciatoria, scapegoat.

locuciones y modismos, propios de los distintos usos del término español culto, coloquial, familiar, etc.:

idioms and slang expressions as they occur in formal, colloquial and familiar Spanish:

pábulo ... dar – a, (*fig.*) to fuel; to give encouragement (to).
plata ... hablar en plata, (*fig.*) to speak frankly, to put it bluntly.
palmo ... dejar a uno con un – de narices, (*fig.* y fam.) to leave someone crestfallen.
plumero ... vérsele a uno el –, (*fig.* y fam.) to see through someone, to see what someone's thinking.

Por otra parte, y además de tecnicismos, palabras propias de la lengua de la calle, términos usados por los periodistas o los comentaristas deportivos o los que aparecen en la lengua a raíz del constante desarrollo tecnológico, es muy importante en este diccionario la inclusión, como entrada, de términos usados en América Latina, así como acepciones de palabras comunes a los dos ámbitos geográficos que tienen, además, otros usos en esa área lingüística.

On the other hand, and in addition to technical vocabulary, street jargon, sports and media terminology and those words which reflect the constant technological development, this dictionary includes, as headwords, words specific to Latin America as well as those terms shared by both Spain and Latin America but which have different meanings in different linguistic regions.

pochada *s.m.* **1** (*Am.*) vast amount, (*fam.*) pile, (*fam.*) heap (cantidad). **2** (*Am.*) puncture (pinchazo).
puntudo, -a *adj.* **1** (*Am.*) sharp, pointed (puntiagudo). **2** (*Am.*) (*fig.*) faultfinding (crítico).
pollero, -a ... || *s.f.* (*Am.*) skirt (falda).
punchar ... (*Am.*) *ZOOL.* spotted cavy.
plata ... 2 (*Am.*) (*fam.*) money.
páramo ... **3** (*Am.*) high grassland ... **5** (*Am.*) drizzle (llovizna).

Esperamos que estas breves instrucciones acerca de cómo utilizar este diccionario sirvan de ayuda para que el consultante de nuestra obra vea con claridad su estructura interna, su riqueza de planteamientos y el tipo de datos que en ella puede encontrar. En definitiva, deseamos que **Langenscheidt's New College Spanish Dictionary** le sea de gran utilidad, pues éste ha sido nuestro objetivo a lo largo de toda su elaboración.

We hope that these brief instructions on the use of the dictionary assist the user in understanding clearly the internal structure, the variety of terminology and the type of information which can be found in it. Finally, we hope that **Langenscheidt's New College Spanish Dictionary** proves to be of great benefit to the reader, whose satisfaction has been our primary goal in the preparation of this work.

Abbreviations used in this dictionary

Abreviaturas usadas en este diccionario

AER. *aeronáutica* aeronautics
adj. *adjetivo* adjective
adv. *adverbio* adverb
AGR. *agricultura* agriculture
Am. *América Latina* Latin America
ANAT. *anatomía* anatomy
ANTR. *antropología* anthropology
arc. *arcaísmo* archaism
ARQ. *arquitectura* architecture
ART. *bellas artes* fine arts
art. *artículo* article
ASTR. *astronomía* astronomy
ASTRON. *astronáutica* astronautics
atr. *atributo, atributivo* attributive
BIOL. *biología* biology
BIOQ. *bioquímica* biochemistry
BOT. *botánica* botany
brit. *inglés británico* British English
c. *contable* countable
card. *cardinal* cardinal
COM. *comercio* commerce
comp. *comparativo* comparative
conj. *conjunción* conjunction
contr. *contracción* contraction
cuant. *cuantificador* quantifier
def. *definido* definite
DEP. *deportes* sport
DER. *derecho* law
DER. MAR. *derecho marítimo* maritime law
desp. *despectivo* derogatory
ECOL. *ecología* ecology
ECON. *economía* economy
EE.UU. *americanismo* American English
ELEC. *electricidad* electricity
ELECTR. *electrónica* electronics
euf. *eufemismo* euphemism
f. *género femenino* feminine gender
fam. *familiar* (*lenguaje*) informal language
fig. *figuradamente/figurado* figurative
FIL. *filosofía* philosophy
FILOL. *filología* philology
FON. *fonética* phonetics
form. *formal* (*nivel de lengua*) formal language
FOT. *fotografía* photography
GAST. *gastronomía* gastronomy
GEOG. *geografía* geography
GEOL. *geología* geology
GEOM. *geometría* geometry
ger. *gerundio* gerund
GRAM. *gramática* grammar
HIST. *historia* history
hum. *humorístico* humorous
i. *intransitivo* intransitive
imp. *impersonal* impersonal
ind. *indefinido* indefinite
indic. *indicativo* indicative
INF. *informática* computer science
int. *intensificador* intensifier
interj. *interjección* interjection
interr. *interrogativo* interrogative
inv. *invariable* invariable
irr. *irregular* irregular
juv. *juvenil* (*lenguaje*) juvenile language
LIT. *literatura* literature
lit. *literario* literary
LOG. *lógica* logic
m. *masculino* masculine
MAR. *marina/marítimo* marine/maritime
MAT. *matemáticas* mathematics
MEC. *mecánica* mechanics
MED. *medicina* medicine
MET. *metalurgia* metallurgy
MIL. *militar* military
MIN. *minería* mining
MUS. *música* music
n.c. *nombre contable* countable noun
num. *numeral* numeral
o.d. *objeto directo* direct object
OPT. *óptica* optics
ord. *ordinal* ordinal
pers. *personal* personal
pl. *plural* plural
POL. *política* politics
pos. *posesivo* possessive
p.p. *participio pasado* past participle
prep. *preposición* preposition
pres. *presente* present
pred. *predicativo* predicative
pret. *pretérito* preterite

pron.	*pronombre/pronominal* pronoun/pronominal	*s.i.*	*sustantivo incontable* uncountable noun
pron. rel.	*pronombre relativo* relative pronoun	*sing.*	*singular* singular
PSIC.	*psicología* psychology	*suj.*	*sujeto* subject
PSIQ.	*psiquiatría* psychiatry	*super.*	*superlativo* superlative
p.u.	*poco usado* little used	*t.*	*transitivo* transitive
QUIM.	*química* chemistry	*TEC.*	*tecnología, tecnicismo* technology
r.	*reflexivo* reflexive	*TV*	*televisión* television
RAD.	*radio* radio	*v.*	*verbo* verb
REL.	*religión* religion	*v. i.*	*verbo intransitivo* intransitive verb
rel.	*relativo* relative	*v.pron.*	*verbo pronominal* pronominal verb
RET.	*retórica* rhetoric	*v.t.*	*verbo transitivo* transitive verb
s.	*sustantivo* noun	*vulg.*	*vulgarismo/vulgar* vulgarism/vulgar
s.c.	*sustantivo contable* countable noun	*ZOOL.*	*zoología* zoology

The Pronunciation of Spanish

La pronunciación del español

Accentuation

1. If the word ends in a vowel, or in *n* or *s*, the penultimate syllable is stressed: *espada, biblioteca, hablan, telefonean, edificios.*
2. If the word ends in a consonant other than *n* or *s*, the last syllable is stressed: *dificultad, hablar, laurel, niñez.*
3. If the word is to be stressed in any way contrary to rules **1** and **2**, an acute accent is written over the stressed vowel: *rubí, máquina, crímenes, carácter, continúa, autobús.*
4. **Diphthongs and syllable division.** Of the 5 vowels, *a e o* are considered "strong", *i* and *u* "weak":
   a) A combination of weak + strong forms a diphthong, the stress falling on the stronger element: *reina, baile, cosmonauta, tiene, bueno.*
   b) A combination of weak + weak forms a diphthong, the stress falling on the second element: *viuda, ruido.*
   c) Two strong vowels together remain as two distinct syllables, the stress falling according to rules **1** and **2**: *ma/estro, atra/er.*
   d) Any word having a vowel combination not stressed according to these rules bears an accent: *traído, oído, baúl, río.*

Value of the letters

Since the pronunciation of Spanish is (in contrast with English) adequately represented by orthography, the Spanish headwords have not been provided with a transcription in the I.P.A. alphabet, except in a very few cases of recent loan-words whose spelling and pronunciation are not in accord. The sounds of Spanish are described below, each with its corresponding I.P.A. symbol.

The pronunciation described is that of educated Castilian, and does NOT refer to that of certain Spanish provinces or of Spanish America (although a few outstanding features of the latter's pronunciation are mentioned).

It should be further realized that is it impossible to explain adequately the sounds of one language in terms of another; what is said below is no more than a very approximate guide.

Vowels

Spanish vowels are clearly and sharply pronounced, and single vowels are free from the tendency to diphtongization which is noticeable in English. When they are in an unstressed position they are relaxed only very slightly, again in striking contrast to English. Stressed vowels are more open and short before *rr* (compare *parra* with *para*, *perro* with *pero*).

a [a] Not so short as in English *fat*, nor so long as in English *father*: *paz, pata.*

e [e] Like *e* in English *they* (but without the following sound of *y*): *grande, pelo.* A shorter sound when followed by a consonant in the same syllable, like *e* in English *get*: *España, renta.*

i [i] Like *i* in English *machine*, though somewhat shorter: *pila, rubi.*

o [o] Not so short as in English *hot*, nor so lang as in English *November*: *solo*, *esposa*. A shorter sound when followed by a consonant in the same syllable, like *o* in English *hot*: *costra*, *bomba*.

u [u] Like *oo* in English *food*: *puro*, *luna*. Silent after *q* and in *gue*, *gui*, unless marked with a diaeresis (*antigüedad*, *argüir*).

y [i] when a vowel (in the conjunction *y* "and" and at the end of a word), is pronounced like *i*.

Diphthongs

ai [aj] like *i* in English *right*: *baile*, *vaina*.

ei [ej] like *ey* in English *they*: *reina*, *peine*.

oi [oj] like *oy* in English *boy*: *boina*, *oigo*.

au [aw] like *ou* in English *rout*: *causa*, *áureo*.

eu [ew] Like the vowel sounds in English *may-you*, without the sound of the *y*: *deuda*, *reuma*.

Semiconsonants

i, y [j] like *y* in English *yes*: *yeso*, *tiene*; in some cases in S. Am. this *y* is pronounced like the *s* [ʒ] in English *measure*: *mayo*, *yo*.

u [w] like *w* in English *water*: *huevo*, *agua*.

Consonants

b, v These two letters represent the same value in Spanish. There are two distinct pronunciations:

[b] 1. At the start of the breath-group and after *m*, *n* the sound is plosive like English *b*: *batalla*, *venid*; *tromba*, *invierno*.

[β] 2. In all other positions the sound is a bilabial fricative, unknown in English, in which the lips do not quite meet: *estaba*, *cueva*, *de Vigo*.

c [k] 1. *c* before *a*, *o*, *u* or a consonant is like English *k*: *caló*, *cobre*.

[θ] 2. *c* before *e*, *i* is like English *th* in *thin*: *cédula*, *cinco*. In *S.Am.* this is pronounced like English voiceless *s* in *chase* [s].

N.B. In words like *acción*, both types of *c*-sound are heard [kθ].

ch [tʃ] like English *ch* in *church*: *mucho*, *chocho*.

d Three distinct pronunciations:

[d] 1. At the start of the breath-group and after *l*, *n*, the sound is plosive like English *d*: *doy*, *aldea*, *conde*.

[ð] 2. Between vowels and after consonants other than *l*, *n* the sound is relaxed and approaches English voiced *th* [ð] in *this*: *codo*, *guardar*; in parts of Spain it is further relaxed and even disappears, particularly in the *-ado* ending.

3. In final position, this type 2 is further relaxed or altogether omitted: *usted*, *Madrid*.

f [f] like English *f*: *fuero*, *flor*.

g Three distinct pronunciations:

[x] 1. Before *e*, *i* is the same of the Spanish *j* (below): *coger*, *general*.

[g] 2. At the start of the breath-group and after *n*, the sound is that of English *g* in *get*: *Granada*, *rango*.

[γ] 3. In other positions the sound is as in 2 above, but with no more than a close approximation of the vocal organs: *agua*, *guerra*.

N.B. In the group *gue*, *gui* the *u* is silent (*guerra*, *guindar*) unless marked with the diaeresis (*antigüedad*, *argüir*). In the group *gua* all letters are sounded.

h [–] always silent: *honor*, *buhardilla*.

j [x] A strong guttural sound not found in English, but like the *ch* in Scots *loch*, Welsh *bach*, German *Achtung*: *jota*, *ejercer*. Silent at the end of the word: *reloj*.

k	[k]	like English *k*: *kilogramo*, *kerosene*.
l	[l]	like English *l*: *león*, *pala*.
ll	[ʎ]	approximating to English *lli* in *million*: *millón*, *calle*. In *S.Am.* like the *s* [ʒ] in English *measure*.
m	[m]	like English *m*: *mano*, *como*.
n	[n]	like English *n*: *nono*, *pan*; except before *v*, when the group is pronounced like *mb*: *enviar*, *invadir*.
ñ	[ɲ]	approximating to English *ni* in *onion*: *paño*, *ñoño*.
p	[p]	like English *p*, but without the slight aspiration which follows it: *Pepe*, *copa*. Silent in *septiembre*, *séptimo*.
q	[k]	like English *k*; always in combination with *u*, which is silent: *que*, *quiosco*.
r	[r]	a single trill stronger than any *r* in English, but like Scots *r*: *caro*, *querer*. Somewhat relaxed in final position. Pronounced like *rr* at the start of a word and after *l*, *n*, *s*: *rata*.
rr	[rr]	strongly trilled: *carro*, *hierro*.
s	[s]	voiceless *s*, like *s* in English *chase*: *rosa*, *soso*. But before a voiced consonant (*b*, *d*, hard *g*, *l*, *m*, *n*) is a
	[z]	voiced *s*, like English *s* in *rose*: *desde*, *mismo*, *asno*. Before "impure *s*" in recent loan-words, an extra *e*-sound is inserted in pronunciation: *e-sprint*, *e-stand*.
t	[t]	like English *t*, but without the slight aspiration which follows it: *patata*, *tope*.
v	[–]	see *b*.
w	[–]	found in a few recent loan-words only; usually pronouncd like an English *v* or like Spanish *b*, *v*: *wáter*.
x	[gs]	like English *gs* in *big sock*: *máximo*, *examen*. Before a consonant like English *s* in *chase*: *extraño*, *mixto*.
z	[θ]	like English *th* in *thin*: *Zote*, *zumbar*. In *S.Am.* like English voiceless *s* in *chase*.

The Spanish Alphabet

a [a], b [be], c [θe], ch [tʃe], d [de], e [e], f ['efe], g [x̣e], h ['atʃe], i [i], j ['x̣ota], k [ka], l ['ele], ll ['eʎe], m ['eme], n ['ene], ñ ['eɲe], o [o], p [pe], q [ku], r ['ere], rr ['erre], s ['ese], t [te], u [u], v ['uβe], x ['ekis], y [i'γrheγa], z ['θeta] *or* ['θeða].

The letters are of the feminine gender: "Madrid se escribe con una *m* mayúscula."

a, A *s.f.* **1** a, A (primera letra del alfabeto español). || *prep.* **2** to (dirección): *voy a París = I'm going to Paris.* **3** in, at (lugar): *llegar al hotel = to arrive at the hotel; llegar a Londres = to arrive in London.* **4** at (tiempo): *a las dos = at two o'clock; al final = at the end.* **5** to (marca intervalos y distancia): *de seis a siete = from six to seven; de esquina a esquina = from corner to corner.* **6** to (seguida de infinitivo): *vamos a comer = we are going to eat.* **7** to (marca una orden o decisión): *¡a la calle! = to the street!* **8** by, on, in (modo de hacer algo): *a pie = on foot; en avion = by plane; a sangre fría = in cold blood.* **9** on (al): *al salir = on leaving.* **10** to (complemento indirecto): *me lo dieron = they gave it to me.* **11** (distancia, sin traducir): *está a 10 km de aquí = it's 10 km from here.* **12** at (precio): *galletas a 100 pesetas = biscuits at 100 pesetas.* **13** a, per (frecuencia): *dos veces al mes = twice a month; tres veces por semana = three times a week.* || **14 – casa,** home. **15 – no ser por,** were it not for. **16 – que,** I bet: *a que no vienen = I bet they don't come.* **17 – tiempo,** on time. **18 – ver,** let's see.

abacería *s.f.* grocer's, grocery store.

abacial *adj.* REL. abbatial.

ábaco *s.m.* abacus.

abacorar *v.t.* (Am.) to pester, to harass (acosar).

abad *s.m.* REL. abbot.

abadejo *s.m.* **1** cod (bacalao). **2** firecrest (ave).

abadengo, -a *adj.* REL. abbatial.

abadesa *s.f.* REL. abbess.

abadía *s.f.* **1** REL. abbey (edificio). **2** abbacy (oficio).

abajeño, -a *adj.* **1** (Am.) lowland. || *s.m.* y *f.* **2** lowlander.

abajo *adv.* **1** below: *hay gente abajo = there are people below.* **2** down, downwards (dirección): *vamos abajo = let's go down.* **3** downstairs (en casa): *los que viven abajo = those who live downstairs.* || **4 aquí –,** down here. **5 desde –,** from below. **6 la parte de –,** the lower part. **7 más –,** below. **8 por –,** underneath.

abalanzar *v.t.* **1** to fling, to hurl (lanzar con violencia). **2** to balance (equilibrar). || *v.pron.* **3** to throw oneself (echarse).

abalaustrado, -a *adj.* balustered.

abalear *v.t.* **1** AGR. to winnow. **2** (Am.) to shoot, to fire (disparar). **3** (Am.) to wound with a bullet (herir con bala).

abaleo *s.m.* **1** winnowing (acción de abalear). **2** hayfork (herramienta).

abalorio *s.m.* **1** bead (cuentecilla). **2** beads (conjunto de cuentecillas).

abaluartar *v.t.* to fortify with a bulwark.

abanderado *s.m.* MIL. standard bearer.

abanderamiento *s.m.* MAR. registering.

abanderar *v.t.* MAR. to register (matricular un barco).

abandonado, -a *adj.* **1** abandoned. **2** neglected (jardín). **3** derelict (casa). **4** deserted (lugar).

abandonar *v.t.* **1** to abandon (dejar desamparado). **2** DEP. to pull out, to retire (de una competición). **3** to give up (renunciar). **4** to stop, to give up (desistir). || *pron.* **5** to give in (dejar de oponer resistencia). **6** to slacken (aflojar en el rendimiento). **7** to give in to (entregar la voluntad).

abandonismo *s.m.* defeatism.

abandonista *adj./s.m.* y *f.* defeatist.

abandono *s.m.* **1** abandonment (acción de abandonar). **2** DEP. withdrawal. **3** giving up (acción de dejar): *el abandono de mis estudios = the giving up of my studies.* **4** neglect, moral abandon (de uno mismo). **5** dereliction (de una casa). **6** neglect (de un jardín). || **7 con –,** carelessly; without care (sin cuidado).

abanicar *v.t.* **1** to fan. || *v.pron.* **2** to fan oneself.

abanico *s.m.* **1** fan. **2** (fig.) saber (sable). **3** (fig.) gamma, range (surtido).

abaniqueo *s.m.* fanning.

abaniquería *s.f.* fan shop.

abanto *s.m.* **1** ZOOL. African vulture (ave). || *adj.* **2** cowardly (toro).

abaratamiento *s.m.* price reduction.

abaratar *v.t.* to lower, to reduce (rebajar el precio).

abarcamiento *s.m.* embracing.

abarcar *v.t.* **1** to embrace (rodear con los brazos). **2** to cover, to embrace (comprender). **3** to undertake (muchos trabajos). **4** to be able to see (poder ver). **5** (Am.) to monopolize, to corner (acaparar).

abarrancar *v.t.* y *v.pron.* to get bogged down (atascarse).

abarrancadero *s.m.* jam (atascadero).

abarrotamiento *s.m.* filling, stowing.

abarrotar o **embarrotar** *v.t.* **1** MAR. to stow. **2** to fill up (llenar).

abastecer *v.t.* y *v.pron.* to supply, to provide.

abastecedor, -ora *s.m.* y *f.* supplier.

abastecimiento *s.m.* supplying, provision.

abastero *s.m.* (Am.) cattle trader (comprador de reses).

abasto *s.m.* **1** supply (provisión). **2** (Am.) supplies (víveres). || **3 dar – a,** to supply.

abatanar *v.t.* to beat (golpear).

abatatado, -a *adj.* **1** (Am.) ashamed (avergonzado). **2** (Am.) upset (turbado).

abate *s.m.* REL. father (clérigo).

abatible *adj.* folding, reclining.

abatidero *s.m.* drain.

abatido, -a *adj.* **1** downcast, dejected (desanimado). **2** humble (humilde). **3** contemptible, mean (despreciable). **4** COM. depreciated (depreciado).

abatimiento *s.m.* **1** demolition (acción de abatir). **2** dejection, depression (desánimo).

abatir *v.t.* y *v.pron.* **1** to demolish, to pull down (derribar). **2** to humiliate (humillar). **3** to discourage, to lose heart (desalentar). || *v.t.* **4** to take down (bajar). || *v.i.* **5** MAR. to change course (apartarse un barco de su rumbo). || *v.pron.* **6** to swoop, to dive (aves).
abdicación *s.f.* abdication.
abdicar *v.t.* **1** to abdicate (reyes). **2** to relinquish (renunciar). **3** to give up, to abandon (abandonar una idea, creencia, etc.).
abdomen *s.m.* ANAT. abdomen.
abdominal *adj.* abdominal.
abducción *s.f.* **1** abduction. **2** abduction (rapto).
abductor *s.m.* **1** ANAT. abductor. **2** abductor (raptor).
abecé *s.m.* **1** alphabet (abecedario). **2** (fig.) rudiments (rudimentos).
abecedario *s.m.* **1** alphabet (alfabeto). **2** spelling book (libro).
abedul *s.m.* birch (árbol).
abeja *s.f.* **1** bee. || **2 — carpintera,** carpenter bee. **3 — machiega, maesa** o **maestra,** queen bee. **4 — obrera,** worker. **5 — reina,** queen bee.
abejarrón *s.m.* bumble bee.
abejaruco *s.m.* bee-eater (ave).
abejero, -a *s.m.* y *f.* **1** beekeeper, apiarist. || *s.m.* **2** bee-eater (ave).
abejón *s.m.* **1** drone (zángano). **2** bumble bee (abejorro).
abejorreo *s.m.* buzz, buzzing (zumbido).
abejorro *s.m.* **1** bumble bee (abejarrón). **2** cockchafer (insecto coleóptero). **3** pest, nuisance (persona molesta).
aberración *s.f.* aberration.
aberrante *adj.* aberrant.
abertura *s.f.* **1** opening (boquete). **2** hole (agujero). **3** crack (grieta). **4** fissure (hendidura). **5** wide valley, pass (valle ancho). **6** aperture (del diafragma). **7** (fig.) openness.
abetal o **abetar** *s.m.* fir wood.
abeto *s.m.* **1** fir (árbol). || **2 — blanco,** silver fir.
abierto, -a *adj.* **1** open: *ventana abierta = open window.* **2** open, frank (franco). **3** sincere (sincero). **4** clear (claro). **5** open, clear (raso, llano). **6** DEP. open (competiciones). || **7 — de par en par,** wide-open. **8 sonidos abiertos,** GRAM. open sounds.
abigarrado, -a *adj.* **1** motley (mezcla rara). **2** multicoloured (de muchos colores). **3** heterogeneous (heterogéneo).
abigarrar *v.t.* to paint in many colours.
abisal *adj.* **1** abysmal (abismal). **2** abyssal (lo más profundo del mar).
abisinio, -a *adj.* y *s.* Abyssinian.
abismal *adj.* abysmal.
abismar *v.t.* **1** to throw into an abyss (sumir algo en un abismo). || *v.pron.* **2** to sink (sumergirse). **3** to become absorbed (en estudios, etc.). **4** (Am.) to be amazed o surprised (admirarse).
abismo *s.m.* **1** abyss (profundidad inmensa). **2** hell (infierno). **3** depths (cosa inmensa e incomprensible). || **4 hay un — entre nuestras ideas,** there's a world of difference between our ideas.
abjuración *s.f.* abjuration.
abjurar *v.t.* to abjure, to forswear.
ablación *s.f.* **1** MED. ablation. **2** GEOL. ablation, erosion.
ablandar *v.t.* y *v.pron.* to soften (poner blando). **2** to mitigate (mitigar). || *v.t.* **3** to loosen (laxar). || *v.i.* **4** to slacken (lluvia). **5** to warm up (hacer menos frío). || *v.i.* y *v.pron.* **6** to drop (viento).
ablativo *s.m.* GRAM. ablative: *ablativo absoluto = ablative absolute.*
ablución *s.f.* ablution.
abnegación *s.f.* abnegation, self-denial.
abnegadamente *adv.* with abnegation.
abnegado, -a *adj.* unselfish.
abnegar *v.t.* **1** to abnegate. || *v.pron.* **2** to deny oneself.
abocado, -a *adj.* smooth (vino).
abocar *v.i.* **1** to bring one's mouth nearer (ir a dar con la boca). **2** to enter (entrar). || *v.t.* y *v.pron.* **3** to move nearer (aproximar). || *v.t.* **4** to pour (verter). || *v.pron.* **5** to meet (reunirse).
abocinado, -a *adj.* trumpet-shaped (atrompetado).
abocinar *v.t.* **1** to shape like a trumpet (dar forma de bocina). **2** to fall flat on one's face (caer de bruces).
abochornar *v.t.* **1** to get close (producir bochorno). **2** to blush (sonrojar). || *v.t.* **3** to become parched (las plantas).
abofetear *v.t.* to slap.
abogacía *s.f.* legal profession.
abogado, -a *s.m.* y *f.* **1** DER. lawyer, solicitor (licenciado en derecho). **2** mediator (intercesor). **3** patron saint (santo protector). || **4 — del diablo,** Devil's advocate. **5 — del estado,** public prosecutor.
6 — de secano, shady lawyer.
abogar *v.i.* **1** DER. to defend (defender). || **2 — por,** to plead for.
abolengo *s.m.* ancestry.
abolición *s.f.* abolition.
abolicionismo *s.m.* abolitionism.
abolicionista *adj./s.m.* y *f.* abolitionist.
abolir *v.t.* to abolish.
abolsarse *v.pron.* to get baggy.
abollado, -a *adj.* dented.
abolladura *s.f.* dent.
abollar *v.t.* to dent.
abollón *s.m.* large dent.
abombar *v.t.* **1** to make convex (dar forma convexa). **2** to daze, to stun (aturdir). || *v.i.* **3** to bang (dar a la bomba). || *v.pron.* **4** to bulge (tomar la forma convexa). **5** to rot (pudrirse). **6** to be tipsy (estar un poco borracho).
abominable *adj.* abominable.
abominación *s.f.* abomination.
abominar *v.t.* **1** to abominate, to detest (odiar). **2** to curse (maldecir).
abonado, -a *adj.* **1** AGR. fertilized: *terreno abonado = fertilized land.* **2** paid (acreditado). || *s.m.* y *f.* **3** subscriber (de teléfono, club, etc.). **4** season ticket holder (de teatro, ferrocarril, etc.).
abonanzar *v.i.* to calm down (calmarse el tiempo).
abonar *v.t.* **1** to pay (pagar). **2** to pay off (pagar una parte del pago total). **3** to credit (en las cuentas corrientes). **4** AGR. to fertilize. **5** to vouch for (salir fiador). **6** to guarantee (dar por seguro). **7** to accredit (acreditar). || *v.pron.* **8** subscribe (inscribir).
abono *s.m.* **1** AGR. fertilizer (fertilizante). **2** season ticket (para el teatro, tren, etc.). **3** credit (en los bancos). **4** subscription (a una revista, etc.).
abordaje *s.m.* **1** MAR. boarding. **2** (fig.) approach.
abordable *adj.* attainable, approachable.
abordar *v.t.* e *i.* **1** MAR. to board (a un enemigo). **2** MAR. to come alongside (juntarse una embarcación a otra). **3** MAR. to collide (chocar). || *v.t.* **4** MAR. to dock (atracar). **5** to get down to (empezar a tratar una cuestión). **6** to tackle (emprender algo difícil). **7** to approach (acercarse). || *v.i.* **8** to dock (tomar puerto).
aborigen *adj.* y *s.m.* y *f.* aboriginal, native.
aborrascarse *v.pron.* to blow up a storm, to get stormy.
aborrecer *v.t.* **1** to loathe, to detest (odiar). **2** ZOOL. to abandon. || *v.t.* y *v.pron.* **3** to annoy (hartar). **4** to anger (enfadar). **5** to bore (aburrir).
aborrecible *adj.* loathesome, detestable.
aborrecimiento *s.m.* **1** loathing, hatred (odio). **2** annoyance (fastidio).
aborregarse *v.pron.* to cloud over (el cielo).
abortar *v.t.* e *i.* **1** MED. to miscarry (malparir). **2** to abort (voluntariamente). || *v.i.* **3** to fail (fallar).
abortivo, -a *adj.* abortive.
aborto *s.m.* **1** MED. miscarriage (malparto). **2** abortion (voluntario). **3** (fig.) failure (fallo).
abotagamiento *s.m.* swelling, lump.
abotargado, -a *adj.* swollen.
abotagarse o **abotargarse** *v.pron.* to swell up, to become swollen.
abotonar *v.t.* y *v.pron.* **1** to button up, to do up (abrochar). || *v.i.* **2** BOT. to bud. || *v.t.* **3** (Am.) to adulate (adular).
abovedar o **embovedar** *v.t.* ARQ. to arch, to vault.
abracadabra *s.m.* abracadabra.
abracadabrante *adj.* strange, wierd, unusual.
abrasador, -ora *adj.* burning, scorching.
abrasar *v.t.* y *v.pron.* **1** to burn (quemar). **2** to dry up (plantas). || *v.t.* **3** to squander, to waste (malgastar). **4** to shame, to fill with shame (avergonzar). || *v.pron.* **5** to burn (quemarse). **6** (fig.) to burn (estar vivamente agitado por una pasión).
abrasión *s.m.* **1** abrasion, graze. || **2 — marina,** marine erosion.
abrasivo, -a *adj.* y *s.m.* abrasivo.
abrazadera *s.f.* clasp.
abrazar *v.t.* y *v.pron.* to embrace (ceñir con los brazos). || *v.t.* **2** to envelop, to enclose (rodear ciñendo). **3** to include (incluir). **4** to adopt, to embrace (una

doctrina). **5** to take charge (encargarse de algo).
abrazo *s.m.* **1** embrace, hug. || **2 un –,** best wishes (en las cartas).
abrecartas *s.m.* letter opener.
abrelatas *s.m.* tin opener, can opener.
abrevadero *s.m.* water trough, watering place.
abrevar *v.t.* **1** to water (dar de beber). **2** to soak (remojar). **3** to sate, to satiate (saciar).
abreviadamente *adv.* briefly, in short.
abreviado, -a *adj.* **1** brief (breve). **2** shortened (un texto). **3** abbreviated (palabra).
abreviar *v.t.* **1** to abbreviate (palabras). **2** to cut short (acortar). **3** to reduce (reducir). **4** to accelerate (acelerar). **5** to hurry up (apresurar).
abreviatura *s.f.* abbreviation.
abridor *s.m.* opener: *abridor de latas = tin opener can opener.*
abrigado, -a *adj.* **1** wrapped up (persona). **2** sheltered, protected (lugar).
abrigar *v.t.* y *v.pron.* **1** to shelter, to take shelter (resguardar del mal tiempo). **2** to wrap up (con abrigo). || *v.t.* **3** to help, to protect (amparar). **4** to hold (opinión). **5** to have (una idea).
abrigo *s.m.* **1** overcoat (prenda). **2** shelter (refugio). **3** (fig.) shelter, protection (protección). **4** haven (para los barcos). **5** help, support (amparo). || **6 estar al – de,** to be free from.
abril *s.m.* **1** April (mes). || *s.pl.* **2** youth, salad days. || **3 estar hecho un –,** to look beautiful.
abrillantar *v.t.* **1** to cut (labrar las piedras preciosas). **2** to polish (sacar brillo). **3** to embellish, to enhance (dar brillantez a un acto).
abrir *v.t.* **1** to open (puerta, boca, negocio, cuenta, ventana, fuego, botella, etc.). **2** to build (construir). **3** to open out (extender lo plegado). **4** to unblock, to clear (desobstruir). **5** to turn on (el agua). **6** to open (dar comienzo a un plazo). **7** to open (inaugurar). **8** to lead, to head (ir en cabeza). **9** to sink (un pozo). **10** MED. to open up, to cut open. **11** to engrave (grabar). **12** to whet (el apetito). || *v.t.* y *v.pron.* **13** to reveal (dejar al descubierto). **14** to split open (rajar, hender). **15** to unstick, to open (despegar). **16** to rip (rasgar). || **17** to clear up (despejarse la atmósfera). || *v.i.* y *v.pron.* **18** to open (flores). || *v.pron.* **19** to get wider, to open out (ensancharse). **20** to split open (agrietarse). **21** to open up, to relax (relajarse). **22** to be open, to be frank (manifestarse sincero). || **23 – con llave,** to unlock. **24 en un – y cerrar de ojos,** in the twinkling of an eye.
abrochar *v.t.* y *pron.* **1** to button up, to do up, to fasten (cerrar). || *v.t.* **2** (Am.) to reproach, to tell off (reprochar). **3** (Am.) to grab (agarrar). || *v.r.* **4** to lock together (en una pelea).
abrogar *v.t.* to annul, to abrogate (anular).
abrojal *s.m.* BOT. thistle patch.
abrojero *s.m.* (Am.) V. **abrojo.**
abrojo *s.m.* **1** BOT. thistle. **2** MIL. caltrop. || *s.pl.* **3** MAR. reef.
abrumador, -a *adj.* **1** tiresome, tiring (calor, trabajo). **2** crushing, overwhelming, humiliating (victoria). **3** overwhelming (mayoría).
abrumadoramente *adv.* overwhelmingly, crushingly.
abrumar *v.t.* **1** to overwhelm, to crush (oprimir). **2** to overwhelm (agobiar con atenciones, etc.). **3** to exhaust (producir gran molestia). || *v.pron.* **4** to get foggy o misty.
abrupto, -a *adj.* **1** steep, sheer (escarpado). **2** (fig.) abrupt.
absceso *s.m.* MED. abscess.
abscisa *s.f.* MAT. abscissa.
absentismo o **ausentismo** *s.m.* absenteeism.
ábside *s.m.* y *f.* **1** ARQ. apse. **2** ASTR. apsis.
absolución *s.f.* **1** REL. absolution. **2** DER. acquittal.
absolutamente *adv.* **1** absolutely, completely. || **2 – nada,** nothing at all.
absolutismo *s.m.* absolutism.
absolutista *adj./s.m.* y *f.* absolutist.
absoluto, -a *adj.* **1** absolute: *poder absoluto = absolute power.* **2** (fig.) domineering (dominante). **3** absolute, unlimited (ilimitado). || **4 en –, a)** not at all (de ninguna manera); **b)** absolutely (de un modo total). **5 una mayoría –,** an absolute majority.
absolutorio, -a *adj.* *fallo absolutorio = verdict of not guilty.*
absolver *v.t.* **1** DER. to acquit, to clear (confirmar la inocencia). **2** REL. to forgive, to absolve (perdonar). **3** to free, to release (liberar).
absorbente *adj.* **1** absorbent. **2** (fig.) absorbing, fascinating (interesante). || *s.m.* **3** absorbent.
absorber *v.t.* **1** to absorb (captar). **2** to absorb, to attract (atraer la atención). **3** to take up, to absorb (consumir): *el trabajo me absorbe mucho mi tiempo = work takes up a lot of my time.*
absorbible *adj.* absorbable.
absorción *s.f.* **1** absorbtion. || **2 absorción atmosférica,** atmospheric absorption.
absorto, -a *adj.* **1** absorbed (con el pensamiento fijo). **2** absorbed, captivated, amazed (que queda admirado ante una cosa).
abstemio, -a *adj.* **1** abstemious, tee-total. || *s.m.* **2** teetotaller, abstainer.
abstención *s.f.* abstention.
abstencionismo *s.m.* abstentionism, non-participation.
abstencionista *adj.* y *s.m.* y *f.* abstentionist.
abstenerse *v.pron.* **1** to abstain, to refrain (prescindir de algo). **2** POL. to abstain. || **3 – de,** to abstain from.
abstinencia *s.f.* **1** abstinence. **2** REL. fasting, fast (de comer).
abstinente *adj.* abstinent.
abstracción *s.f.* **1** abstraction (hecho y resultado de abstraer). **2** abstraction (modo de pensar). **3** absorption, engrossment (concentración).
abstracto, -a *adj.* abstract: *arte abstracto = abstract art.*
abstraer *v.t.* **1** to abstract. **2** to consider separately (separar mentalmente). || *v.pron.* **3** to be absorbed (abismarse en los pensamientos).
abstraído, -a *adj.* **1** absorbed (absorto). **2** absentminded (distraído).
abstruso, -a *adj.* abstruse.
absuelto, -a *adj.* **1** DER. acquitted. **2** REL. absolved, forgiven.
absurdamente *adv.* absurdly.
absurdo, -a *adj.* **1** absurd, illogical (carente de lógica). **2** absurd, ridiculous (ridículo). || *s.m.* **3** absurdity. || **4 reducción al –,** reduction to absurdity.
abubilla *s.f.* hoopoe (ave).
abuchear *v.t.* to boo, to jeer.
abucheo *s.m.* booing, jeering.
abuela *s.f.* **1** grandmother. || **2 no tener –,** to blow one's own trumpet.
abuelo *s.m.* **1** grandfather. || *s.m.pl.* **2** grandparents.
abulia *s.f.* lack of willpower.
abúlico, -a *adj.* weak-willed, (fam.) spineless.
abultamiento *s.m.* **1** bulkiness (bulto). **2** increase (incremento). **3** exaggeration (exageración).
abultar *v.i.* **1** to be bulky (presentar un cierto bulto). || *v.t.* **2** to exaggerate (exagerar).
abundamiento *s.m.* **1** abundance. || **2 a mayor –,** furthermore (además).
abundancia *s.f.* **1** abundance, plenty. || **2 cuerno de la –,** horn of plenty. **3 en –,** in abundance.
abundante *adj.* abundant, plentiful.
abundar *v.t.* **1** to abound, to be plentiful (haber gran cantidad). **2** to share: *abundar en la opinión de alguien = to share someone's opinion.*
aburguesarse *v.pron.* to become bourgeois o middle class.
aburrarse *v.pron.* (Am.) to become brutalized (embrutecerse).
aburrición *s.f.* (Am.) unfriendliness (antipatía).
aburridamente *adv.* (Am.) boringly, tediously.
aburrido, -a *adj.* **1** bored: *estar aburrido = to be bored.* **2** boring: *ser aburrido = to be boring.* **3** sick, fed up (harto).
aburrimiento *s.m.* boredom, tedium.
aburrir *v.t.* **1** to bore (causar aburrimiento). **2** to tire (hartar). || *v.pron.* **3** to be bored, to get bored. **4** to get o be tired (cansarse).
abusar *v.i.* **1** to abuse, to overuse (usar excesivamente). **2** to abuse, to go over the top (tratar con rigor injusto). **3** to take advantage, to abuse (aprovechar): *abusar de alguien más débil = to take advantage of someone weaker.*
abusivamente *adv.* improperly.

abusivo, -a *adj.* **1** improper (impropio). **2** excessive, outrageous (excesivo): *precios abusivos = excessive prices.*
abuso *s.m.* **1** abuse (acción que no se considera legal o normal). **2** betrayal (de la amistad, confianza, etc.).
abusón, -ona *adj.* **1** selfish, greedy (avaricioso). **2** abusive (que abusa). || *s.m.* y *f.* **3** selfish o greedy person (egoísta). **4** abusive person (persona que abusa).
abyección *s.f.* abjection, abjectness, wretchedness.
abyecto, -a *adj.* abject, wretched.
acá *adv.* **1** here, over here: *ven acá = come here.* || **2 — y allá,** here and there. **3 desde entonces —,** since then. **4 más —,** nearer. **5 muy —,** very near.
acabado, -a *adj.* **1** completed, finished (terminado). **2** perfect (perfecto). **3** finished (producto). **4** worn out (cansado). || *s.m.* **5** finish (de un coche, etc.).
acabar *v.t.* **1** to put the finishing touches to (perfeccionar): *voy a acabar el cuadro = I'm going to put the finishing touches to the painting.* || *v.t.* y *v.pron.* **2** to finish, to conclude (terminar algo): *he acabado el libro = I've finished the book.* || *v.i.* **3** to end (finalizar). **4** to die (morirse). **5** to run out (agotarse). || **6** to end up (con gerundio): *acabé comprándolo = I ended up buying it.* || **7 — bien,** to turn out all right. **8 — con,** to finish with; to end with: *han acabado con sus estudios = they've finished with their studies.* **9 — de,** to have just: *acaba de llover = it's just rained.* **10 — mal,** to come to a bad end. **11 — por,** finally; in the end: *acabó por hacerlo = she finally did it.* **12 no acabo de entenderlo,** I just can't understand it. **13 para — de arreglarlo,** to top it all; on top of everything. **14 ¡se acabó!,** well, that's that.
acabe *s.m.* (Am.) end (fin).
acabóse *s.m.* limit, last straw, end (colmo).
acacia *s.f.* acacia (árbol y madera).
academia *s.f.* **1** academy: *academia militar = military academy.* **2** academy school: *academia privada = private school.* || **3 — de baile,** dancing school. **4 — de música,** conservatoire; music school.
academicismo *s.m.* academicism.
académico, -a *adj.* **1** academic. || *s.m.* y *f.* **2** academician, member of an academy.
acaecer *v.i.* to happen, to occur.
acaecimiento *s.m.* occurrence.
acalorar *v.t.* **1** to make hot, to warm up (producir calor). **2** to excite.
acaloradamente *adv.* excitedly, excitedly.
acaloramiento *s.m.* **1** heat (calor). **2** enthusiasm, eagerness, keenness, passion (pasión).
acalorar *v.t.* **1** to make hot, to warm up (producir calor). **2** to excite, to arouse (enardecer). || *v.pron.* **3** to get tired, to be worn out (fatigarse). **4** to get worked up, to get heated (exaltarse).
acallar *v.t.* **1** to quieten, to silence (hacer callar). **2** to calm down (calmar los ánimos).
acampanado, -a *adj.* bell-shaped.
acampar *v.i.* y *v.pron.* to camp, to camp out.
acanalado, -a *adj.* **1** grooved. **2** corrugated (hierro). **3** ARQ. fluted.
acanalar *v.t.* **1** to groove (hacer estrías). **2** ARQ. to flute.
acanelado, -a *adj.* **1** cinnamon-flavoured (con sabor a canela). **2** cinnamon-coloured (con color de canela).
acantilado *s.m.* cliff.
acantilar *v.t.* y *v.pron.* MAR. to go aground (encallar).
acanto *s.m.* BOT. y ARQ. acanthus.
acantonar *v.t.* y *v.pron.* MIL. to billet, to quarter.
acaparador, -a *adj.* **1** acquisitive. || *s.m.* y *f.* **2** hoarder.
acaparamiento *s.m.* hoarding.
acaparar *v.t.* **1** COM. to monopolize, to corner (monopolizar). **2** to hoard (comida, existencias).
acaracolado, -a *adj.* spiral, twisting.
acaramelar *v.t.* **1** to coat o cover with caramel (cubrir). || *v.pron.* **2** (fam.) to be an angel, to be a darling (mostrarse muy galante).
acariciar *v.t.* **1** to caress (hacer caricias). **2** to stroke (rozar con suavidad). **3** (fig.) to cherish (proyectos, ideas, etc.).
acarrear *v.t.* **1** to carry, to haul, to transport (transportar). **2** to cause, to lead to (causar).
acarreo *s.m.* **1** carrying, transporting (acción de acarrear). **2** transport costs (coste del transporte).
acartonarse *v.pron.* **1** to start looking like cardboard. **2** (fig.) to become wizened (personas muy ancianas).
acaso *s.m.* **1** accident, chance (suceso casual). || *adv.* **2** perhaps, maybe: *acaso me vaya mañana = perhaps I'll go tomorrow.* || **3 al —,** to chance. **4 por si —,** just in case.
acatamiento *s.m.* **1** respect (de las leyes). **2** reverence (reverencia).
acatar *v.t.* to respect, to observe (respetar).
acatarrarse *v.pron.* to catch o get a cold.
acaudalado, -a *adj.* wealthy, rich (rico).
acaudalar *v.t.* to accumulate, to acquire.
acaudillar *v.t.* **1** MIL. to send (mandar). **2** POL. to lead, to head (conducir, guiar). **3** to be in charge (estar al mando).
acceder *v.i.* to accede, to assent.
accesible *adj.* **1** accessible (lugares). **2** attainable (objetivos). **3** approachable (personas).
accesión *s.f.* **1** assent, agreement (acción de acceder). **2** DER. accession. **3** MED. attack. **4** POL. accession (al poder). **5** accessory (accesorio).
accésit *s.m.* consolation prize.
acceso *s.m.* **1** access, entry (camino de entrada). **2** approach (avión). **3** way, approach (acción de aproximarse). **4** MED. attack, fit (ataque). **5** outburst, fit (de violencia, enfado, etc.).
accesorio, -a *adj.* **1** accessory. || *s.m.* **2** accessory (que se puede cambiar). || *s.pl.* **3** spare parts (para coches). **4** props (del teatro).
accidentado, -a *adj.* **1** rough, uneven (superficie). **2** hilly (terreno). **3** injured (herido). **4** damaged (tren, coche, etc.). **5** troubled, agitated, eventful (vida). **6** eventful (vacaciones, viaje). **7** upset (turbado).
accidental *adj.* **1** accidental. **2** unexpected, circumstantial (circunstancial). || *s.m.* **3** MUS. accidental.
accidentalmente *adv.* accidentally, by chance.
accidentarse *v.pron.* to have an accident.
accidente *s.m.* **1** accident (suceso fortuito): *sufrir un accidente = to have an accident.* **2** GEOG. roughness, hilliness (de terreno). **3** unevenness (de superficie). **4** MED. faint. **5** MUS. accidental. **6** GRAM. accidence. || **7 — de carretera,** road accident. **8 por —,** by accident.
acción *s.f.* **1** action (hecho y resultado de hacer): *acción militar = military action.* **2** act, deed (acto): *buena acción = good deed.* **3** MIL. action, engagement. **4** gesture (ademán). **5** FIN. share: *acción ordinaria = ordinary share.* **6** DER. shares, stocks. || **9 — de gracias,** thanksgiving. **10 hombre de —,** man of action. **11 mala —,** evil deed.
accionar *v.t.* **1** MEC. to work, to drive (dar movimiento). || *v.i.* **2** to gesticulate (hacer gestos).
accionariado *s.m.* FIN. shareholders.
accionista *s.m.* y *f.* FIN. shareholder.
acebo *s.m.* BOT. holly tree (árbol).
acebuche *s.m.* BOT. wild olive tree.
acechanza *s.m.* observing, watching.
acechar *v.t.* to observe, to watch.
acecho *s.m.* watching, observing.
acedía *s.f.* **1** acidity, sorness (propiedad de acedo). **2** MED. heartburn. **3** abrasiveness (aspereza en el trato). **4** ZOOL. plaice (pez).
acedo, -a *adj.* acidic, sour.
aceitada *s.f.* olive oil cake (torta).
aceitar *v.t.* to add oil.
aceite *s.m.* **1** oil. || **2 — de oliva,** olive oil. **3 — de motor,** motor oil. **4 — lubricante,** lubricating oil. **5 — vegetal,** vegetable oil. **6 echar — al fuego,** to add fuel to the fire.
aceitera *s.f.* oil bottle.
aceitero, -a *adj.* **1** oil. || *s.m.* **2** oil dealer.
aceitoso, -a *adj.* oily.
aceituna *s.f.* olive.
aceitunado, -a *adj.* olive, olive-coloured.
aceitunero, -a *s.m.* y *f.* **1** olive seller (vendedor). **2** olive picker (persona que recoge aceitunas). **3** olive picking season (época de la recolección).
aceituno *s.m.* olive tree (olivo).
aceleración *s.f.* acceleration.
aceleradamente *adv.* quickly, fast.
acelerado, -a *adj.* quick, fast.
acelerador, -ora *adj.* **1** accelerating. || *s.m.* **2** accelerator.

acelerar *v.t.* y *v.pron.* to accelerate, to speed up.
acelga *s.f.* BOT. chard, beet (planta).
acémila *s.f.* 1 mula (mula). 2 (fig.) dolt, ass (persona ruda).
acendrado, -a *adj.* 1 pure (puro). 2 clean (limpio). 3 refined (refinado).
acendradamente *adv.* purely.
acendrar *v.t.* 1 to purify (purificar). 2 to clean (limpiar). 3 to refine (metales).
acento *s.m.* 1 GRAM. accent (signo ortográfico). 2 stress, emphasis (mayor intensidad al pronunciar). 3 accent (modulación de la voz o tono peculiar): *acento gallego = Galician accent.*
acentuación *s.f.* accentuation.
acentuadamente *adv.* clearly.
acentuar *v.t.* 1 to put an accent on, to accent (escrito). 2 to stress (hablado). 3 to emphasize (enfatizar). || *v.pron.* 4 to become more important (tomar importancia).
acepción *s.f.* GRAM. meaning, sense (significado).
aceptabilidad *s.f.* acceptability.
aceptable *adj.* acceptable.
aceptablemente *adv.* acceptably.
aceptación *s.f.* 1 acceptance (acción de aceptar). 2 success (éxito).
aceptante *adj.* 1 accepting || *s.m.* y *f.* 2 acceptor.
aceptar *v.t.* 1 to accept (recibir). 2 to approve (aprobar). 3 to agree (acordar): *acepto hacerlo = I agree to do it.* 4 COM. to accept (obligarse al pago de una letra).
acequia *s.f.* irrigation ditch o channel (canal).
acera *s.f.* 1 pavement (para peatones). 2 row (fila).
acerado, -a *adj.* 1 steel (de acero). 2 strong (fuerte). 3 biting, mordant (mordaz).
acerar *v.t.* 1 to turn into steel (convertir en acero). 2 to coat with steel, to steel (dar un baño de acero). || *v.t.* y *v.pron.* 3 to strengthen (fortalecer).
acerbamente *adv.* bitterly, harshly, acerbically.
acerbidad *s.f.* acerbity, harshness, bitterness.
acerbo, -a *adj.* 1 bitter, sour (de sabor). 2 (fig.) cruel, harsh (cruel).
acerca *adv.* about, concerning: *un documental acerca de la droga = a documentary about drugs.*
acercamiento *s.m.* 1 approach: *el acercamiento de las vacaciones = the approach of the holidays.* 2 (fig.) reconciliation (entre personas). 3 POL. rapprochement.
acercar *v.t.* 1 to bring near (poner cerca). 2 to give, to pass (pasar): *acércame la botella = pass me the bottle.* || *v.pron.* 3 to draw near, to come near (estar próxima a suceder una cosa): *se acerca el día de la boda = the day of the wedding is drawing near.* 4 to approach (aproximarse): *nos acercamos al pueblo = we're approaching the village.*
acería o **acerería** *s.f.* steelworks (fábrica).
acerico *s.m.* pin cushion (para agujas y alfileres).
acero *s.m.* 1 steel (metal). 2 sword (espada). 3 (fig.) steel, bravery (valor). || 4 — **inoxidable,** stainless steel. 5 **tener buenos aceros,** to be made of steel.
acérrimamente *adv.* steadfastly, staunchly, firmly.
acérrimo, -a *adj.* steadfast, staunch, firm.
acertadamente *adv.* correctly.
acertado, -a *adj.* 1 right, correct (correcto). 2 clever, wise (sabio, listo). 3 fitting, apt (apto). 4 well-aimed, accurate (tiro). 5 good (bueno). 6 well-thought-out (plan, táctica, estrategia).
acertante *s.m.* y *f.* 1 winner (ganador). || *adj.* 2 winning.
acertar *v.t.* 1 to hit (diana). 2 to be correct, to guess (adivinar). || *v.t.* e *i.* 3 to find (encontrar). 4 to find out (averiguar). 5 to be successful, to succeed (hacer algo con acierto). || *v.i.* 6 BOT. to do well (plantas). || 7 — **a,** to happen to: *acerté a encontrarlo = I happened to find it.* 8 — **con,** to hit on: *han acertado con el regalo perfecto = they've hit on the perfect present.*
acertijo *s.m.* riddle, puzzle.
acervo *s.m.* 1 pile, heap (montón). 2 common property (bienes comunes).
acetato *s.m.* acetate.
acético, -a *adj.* acetic.
acetileno *s.m.* acetylene.
acetona *s.f.* acetone.
aciago, a *adj.* fateful, ill-fated (infausto).
acíbar *s.m.* 1 BOT. aloe. 2 bitterness (amargura).
acicalado, -a *adj.* 1 polished (metales). 2 smart, neat (persona).
acicalamiento *s.m.* 1 polishing (de metales). 2 dressing up (persona).
acicalar *v.t.* 1 to clean (limpiar). 2 to polish, to burnish (bruñir). || *v.t.* y *v.pron.* 3 to decorate, to adorn (adornar).
acicate *s.m.* 1 spur (espuela). 2 incentive, spur (incentivo).
acidez *s.f.* acidity.
acidia *s.f.* laziness, idleness (pereza).
acidificar *v.t.* y *v.pron.* to acidify.
acidímetro *s.m.* acidimeter.
ácido, -a *adj.* 1 sour, bitter, acid. || *s.m.* 2 acid. || 3 — **acético,** acetic acid. 4 — **bórico,** boric acid. 5 — **cianhídrico,** hydrocyanic acid. 6 — **clorhídrico,** hydro chloric acid. 7 — **fórmico,** formic acid. 8 — **nítrico,** nitric acid. 9 — **sulfúrico,** sulphuric acid. 10 — **úrico,** uric acid.
acidosis *s.f.* MED. acidosis.
acídulo, -a *adj.* acidulous.
acierto *s.m.* 1 skill, ability (habilidad). 2 common sense, prudence (prudencia). 3 coincidence (casualidad). 4 success (éxito). 5 correct answer (respuesta correcta). 6 good hit (buen tiro). 7 good idea (buena idea). 8 wisdom (sabiduría).
ácimo, -a *adj.* unleavened.
acimut o **azimut** *s.m.* ASTR. azimuth.
aclamación *s.f.* 1 acclamation, acclaim. 2 applause (aplauso).
aclamar *v.t.* 1 to acclaim, to applaud (aplaudir). 2 to hail (conferir algún honor por voz común). 3 to name (nombrar).
aclaración *s.f.* 1 clarification, explanation (explicación). 2 rinse, rinsing (de la ropa). 3 clearing up (del tiempo).
aclarado *s.m.* rinse (de la ropa).
aclarar *v.t.* y *v.pron.* 1 to clarify, to explain (explicar). 2 to clear away (para dejar espacio libre). || *v.pron.* 3 to rinse (la ropa). 4 to explain (explicar). || *v.i.* 5 to clear up (disipar las nubes). 6 to break (amanecer). 7 to clear (purificarse un líquido).
aclaratorio, -a *adj.* explanatory.
aclimatación *s.f.* acclimatization.
aclimatar *v.t.* 1 to acclimatize, to adapt. || *v.pron.* 2 to become acclimatized, to adapt oneself.
acmé *s.m.* acme.
acné *s.m.* MED. acne.
acobardar *v.t.* y *v.pron.* to frighten, to scare (causar miedo).
acodado, -a *adj.* bent, elbowed.
acodar *v.t.* y *v.pron.* 1 to lean, to rest (apoyar). || *v.t.* 2 to bend (doblar).
acogedor, -a *adj.* 1 cosy, snug (casa). 2 friendly, warm (persona, ambiente).
acoger *v.t.* 1 to welcome (admitir en su casa o compañía). 2 to accept, to receive. || *v.t.* y *v.pron.* 3 to give refuge (refugiar). 4 to shelter, to protect (proteger). 5 to agree (estar de acuerdo con opiniones). || *v.pron.* 6 to take refuge (en un pretexto).
acogida *adj.* 1 welcome, greeting, reception (recibimiento). 2 agreement, acceptance (aceptación). 3 withdrawal (retirada).
acogido *s.m.* 1 resident (persona pobre que vive en establecimientos benéficos). || *adj.* 2 welcomed.
acogotar *v.t.* 1 to kill with a rabbit punch (matar con golpes en el cogote). 2 to dominate (dominar).
acolchado, -a *adj.* padded, quilted.
acolchar o **colchar** *v.t.* to pad, to quilt.
acólito *s.m.* 1 REL. acolyte. 2 (fig.) acolyte, follower.
acometedor, -a *adj.* 1 aggressive (agresivo). 2 enterprising (emprendedor).
acometer *v.t.* 1 to attack, to assail (atacar). 2 to undertake (emprender). 3 to try (intentar). 4 to overcome (sobrevenir). 5 to join (empalmar).
acometida *s.f.* 1 attack, offensive (ataque). 2 connection (de cables, cañerías, etc.).
acometividad *s.f.* 1 aggression (agresión). 2 enterprise, energy (brío).
acomodable *adj.* adaptable.
acomodación *s.f.* accomodation, adaptation (proceso de adaptación).
acomodado, -a *adj.* 1 comfortable, well-off (de buena posición económica). 2 reasonable (precio). 3 suitable (apto). 4 arranged, tidy (colocado).

acomodador, -a *s.m.* y *f.* usher (hombre), usherette (mujer) (en un espectaculo).
acomodamiento *s.m.* 1 suitability (comodidad). 2 agreement (acuerdo).
acomodar *v.t.* 1 to adjust (ajustar). 2 to adapt (adaptar). 3 to arrange (arreglar). 4 to place, to order (ordenar). 5 to supply, to provide (proveer). 6 to give work (dar empleo). 7 to seat, to show to a seat (colocar en sus sitios en un espectáculo). || *v.pron.* 8 to agree, to come to an agreement (avenirse).
acomodo *s.m.* 1 job, post (empleo). 2 convenience (conveniencia). 3 (Am.) bribe (soborno).
acompañado, -a *adj.* 1 accompanied: *estar acompañado = to be accompanied.* 2 busy (concurrido). || *s.m.* 3 aid, assistant (ayudante).
acompañanta *s.f.* companion.
acompañante *adj.* 1 accompanying. || *s.m.* 2 companion. 3 MUS. accompanist.
acompañamiento *s.m.* 1 accompaniment (acción de acompañar). 2 company, retinue (la gente que acompaña). 3 MUS. accompaniment. 4 extras (en el teatro). 5 wedding party (en una boda).
acompañar *v.t.* y *v.pron.* 1 to accompany, to go with (ir en compañía). 2 to take: *acompañar a casa = to take home.* 3 to accompany, to go with (ir una cosa junto con otra). 4 MUS. to accompany. || *v.t.* 5 to share (participar en los sentimientos de otro). || **6 te acompaño en el sentimiento,** please accept my condolences.
acompasadamente *adv.* 1 MUS. rhythmically. 2 calmly, deliberately (pausadamente). 3 slowly (lentamente).
acompasado, -a *adj.* 1 MUS. rhythmic. 2 calm, deliberate (pausado). 3 slow, steady (lento).
acompasar o **compasar** *v.t.* 1 MUS. to mark the rhythm of. 2 MAT, to measure with a compass. 3 to keep in time (mantener el ritmo).
acomplejar *v.t.* 1 to give a complex (producir un complejo). || *v.pron.* 2 to have a complex (padecer un complejo).
aconchabamiento *s.m.* grouping o ganging together.
aconchabarse *v.pron.* to plot, to gang up, to conspire.
acondicionado, -a *adj.* 1 equipped: *bien acondicionado = well equipped; mal acondicionado = badly equipped.* || 2 **aire —,** air conditioning.
acondicionador *s.m.* conditioner: *acondicionador de aire = air conditioning.*
acondicionamiento *s.m.* conditioning.
acondicionar *v.t.* y *v.pron.* 1 to arrange (organizar). 2 to prepare (preparar). 3 to condition (el aire). || *v.t.* 4 to create an atmosphere (crear un ambiente propicio).
acongojadamente *adv.* distressingly, upsettingly.
acongojante *adj.* distresing, upsetting.
acongojar *v.t.* 1 to distress, to upset. || *v.pron.* 2 to become distressed, to get upset.
aconsejable *adj.* 1 advisable: *es aconsejable no fumar = it's advisable not to smoke.* 2 sensible (sensato).
aconsejar *v.t.* 1 to advise (dar consejo). || *v.pron.* 2 to take advice (tomar consejo).
acontecer *v.i.* to happen, to occur.
acontecimiento *s.m.* event.
acopiar *v.t.* 1 to gather, to collect (recoger). 2 to store, to stock (almacenar).
acopio *s.m.* 1 collecting, gathering (acción de recoger). 2 storing, stocking (acción de almacenar).
acoplado, -a *adj.* 1 matched. || *s.m.* 2 (Am.) trailer (vehículo).
acoplamiento *s.m.* 1 MEC. joint, coupling (pieza). 2 joining, coupling (acción de acoplar). 3 ELEC. connection. 4 assembly (montaje).
acoplar *v.t.* 1 to couple, to join (encajar). 2 to combine (combinar). 3 ELEC. to connect. 4 to yoke (caballos, bueyes, etc.). 5 to couple (tren) || *v.t.* y *v.pron.* 6 ZOOL. to mate (unión sexual de animales). || *v.pron.* 7 to get attached to, to take a liking to (encariñarse mutuamente).
acoquinamiento *s.m.* intimidation, coercion.
acoquinar *v.t.* 1 to intimidate, to hassle. || *v.pr.* 2 to be intimidated.
acorazado, -a *adj.* 1 armour-plated, armored. || *s.m.* 2 MAR. battleship.
acorazamiento *s.m.* armour-plating.
acorazar *v.t.* to armour-plate, to armour.
acorchado, -a *adj.* cork-like.
acorchamiento *s.m.* sponginess.
acorcharse *v.pron.* 1 to become spongy (ponerse esponjoso). 2 to go numb (insensibilizarse).
acordado, -a *adj.* agreed: *lo acordado = that which has been agreed.*
acordar *v.t.* 1 to agree (decidir de común acuerdo). 2 to resolve, to sort out (resolver). 3 to reconcile, to consiliate (conciliar). 4 MUS. to tune (afinar). || *v.t.* y *v.pron.* 5 to remember, to recall (recordar).
acorde *adj.* 1 in agreement, agreed (conforme): *estamos acordes = we're in agreement.* 2 MUS. in harmony, in tune. || *s.m.* 3 MUS. chord.
acordeón *s.m.* MUS. accordion.
acordeonista *s.m.* y *f.* accordionist.
acordonado, -a *adj.* 1 ribbed (superficies). 2 cordoned-off (sitio). 3 milled (moneda).
acordonamiento *s.m.* 1 ribbing (de ropa). 2 cordoning-off (de policía). 3 milling (de monedas).
acordonar *v.t.* 1 to tie up, to lace up (zapatos). 2 to mill (monedas). 3 to surround (rodear de gente). 4 to cordon off (un sitio).
acorralar *v.t.* y *v.pron.* 1 to corral, to round up (encerrar el ganado). || *v.t.* 2 to corner (reducir a estrechos límites a alguien). 3 to intimidate (acobardar).
acortamiento *s.m.* 1 shortening (acción de acortar). 2 reduction (acción de reducir).
acortar *v.t.* 1 to shorten (la longitud). 2 to reduce (reducir). 3 to shorten (un texto). || *v.pron.* 4 to be shy (quedarse corto en hablar).
acosado, -a *adj.* hounded, hunted.
acosar *v.t.* 1 to pursue, to harry (perseguir). 2 to bother, to pester (importunar).
acoso *s.m.* 1 pursuit. 2 (fig.) pestering, hounding.
acostar *v.t.* 1 to put to bed (meter en la cama). 2 MAR. to come alongside. || *v.i.* y *v.pron.* 3 to lean (inclinarse). || *v.i.* 4 MAR. to reach land (llegar a la costa). || *v.pron.* 5 to go to bed (irse a la cama). 5 (Am.) to give birth (dar a luz).
acostumbradamente *adv.* usually, normally.
acostumbrar *v.i.* 1 to be in the habit (tener costumbre). || *v.t.* y *v.pron.* 2 to get accustomed, to get into the habit, to get used to: *me he acostumbrado a trabajar = I've got used to working.*
acotación *s.f.* 1 note (note). 2 marginal note (nota en el margen). 3 comment (comentario). 4 stage direction (en el teatro). 5 elevation mark (topografía).
acotar *v.t.* 1 to demarcate, to delimit (señalar límites). 2 to annotate (anotar). 3 to lop (árbol). 4 to accept (aceptar). || *v.pron.* 5 to reach safety (ponerse a salvo).
acracia *s.f.* anarchy.
ácrata *adj./s.m.* y *f.* anarchist.
acre *adj.* 1 acrid (olor). 2 bitter, sour (sabor). 3 acre (medida). 4 biting, mordant (mordaz).
acremente *adv.* bitterly.
acrecentador, -a *adj.* rising, increasing.
acrecentamiento *s.m.* rise, increase.
acrecentar *v.t.* y *v.pron.* 1 to rise, to increase (aumentar). || *v.t.* 2 to improve (mejorar).
acrecimiento *s.m.* DER. accretion.
acreditado, -a *adj.* 1 reputable (fama de bueno): *un abogado acreditado = a reputable lawyer.* 2 accredited (embajador).
acreditar *v.t.* y *v.pron.* 1 to do credit to (hacer digno de crédito). 2 to prove (probar). 3 to add to the reputation of (dar fama o crédito). || *v.t.* 4 to accredit (embajador). 5 to vouch for (avalar). 6 to authorize (autorizar). 7 COM. to credit.
acreedor, -a *adj.* 1 deserving, worthy (de mérito). || *s.m.* 2 COM. creditor.
acribillar *v.t.* 1 to riddle, to pepper (abrir muchos agujeros o hacer muchas heridas): *acribillar a balazos = to riddle with bullets.* 2 to pester, to bug (molestar).
acrimonia *s.f.* 1 acridness, pungency (olor). 2 bitterness (sabor). 3 (fig.) acrimony, bitterness.
acrisolar *v.t.* 1 to purify (metales). 2 to perfect (perfeccionar). || *v.t.* y *v.pron.* 3 to prove, to test (probar).

acritud *s.f.* **1** acridness, pungency (olor). **2** bitterness (sabor). **3** bitterness, sharpness (de carácter).
acrobacia *s.f.* acrobatics.
acróbata *s.m.* y *f.* acrobat.
acrofobia *s.f.* acrophobia.
acrópolis *s.f.* Acropolis.
acróstico, -a *adj./s.m.* y *f.* acrostic.
acta *s.f.* **1** minutes, record (relación escrita). || **2 levantar –,** to take the minutes.
actinia *s.f.* ZOOL. sea anemone.
actitud *s.f.* **1** position, posture, pose (postura del cuerpo). **2** attitude (disposición de ánimo): *actitud agresiva = aggressive attitude.*
activamente *adv.* actively.
activar *v.t.* **1** to activate: *activar un mecanismo = to activate a mechanism.* **2** to quicken (acelerar).
actividad *s.f.* **1** activity: *actividad en la calle = activity in the street.* **2** active (activo): *estar en actividad = to be active.*
activista *s.m.* y *f.* activist.
activo, -a *adj.* **1** active (que obra). **2** active, lively (animado). **3** GRAM. active: *voz activa = active voice.* **4** busy (ocupado). **5** GEOL. active. || *s.m.* **6** COM. assets. || **7 estar en –,** MIL. to be on active service.
acto *s.m.* **1** act, action (acción). **2** act (teatro). **3** ceremony, function (ceremonia): *acto de clausura = closing ceremony.* || **4 – seguido,** immediately afterwards. **5 en el –,** on the spot. **6 salón de actos,** assembly hall.
actor *s.m.* **1** actor (teatro, cine). **2** DER. plaintiff.
actriz *s.f.* actress.
actuación *s.f.* **1** performance: *la actuación del grupo = the performance of the group.* **2** behaviour, conduct (conducta). **3** action (acción).
actual *adj.* **1** present, present-day (de hoy): *moda actual = present-day fashion.* **2** topical, current (problema, cuestión).
actualidad *s.f.* **1** present (tiempo presente): *en la actualidad = at the present.* **2** current importance (cosa del momento): *un problema de actualidad = a problem of current importance.* || **3 en la –,** nowadays, at the moment, at the present time.
actualización *s.f.* modernization.
actualizar *v.t.* to modernize, to bring up to date.
actuante *adj.* **1** acting. || *s.m.* y *f.* **2** performer.
actuar *v.i.* **1** to act, to perform (teatro, cine). **2** to operate, to work (funcionar). **3** MUS. to perform. **4** DER. to take proceedings.
actuario *s.m.* DER. actuary.
acuarela *s.f.* ART. watercolour (pintura).
acuarelista *s.m.* y *f.* watercolourist.
acuario *s.m.* **1** aquarium (para peces). **2** ASTR. Aquarius.
acuartelado, -a *adj.* HIST. quartered.
acuartelamiento *s.m.* **1** MIL. quartering, billeting (tropas). **2** quartering (de un escudo).
acuartelar *v.t.* y *v.pron.* **1** MIL. to quarter, to billet (tropas). || *v.t.* **2** to divide into quarters (dividir en cuarteles).
acuático, -a *adj.* aquatic: *esquí acuático = water skiing.*
acucia *s.f.* **1** haste (prisa). **2** desire, longing (deseo).
acuciadamente *adv.* **1** hastily (de prisa). **2** longingly (con anhelo).
acuciamiento *s.m.* **1** stimulation (estímulo). **2** desire (deseo).
acuciante *adj.* urgent.
acuciar *v.t.* **1** to urge, to press (estimular). **2** to long for (anhelar).
acuclillarse *v.pron.* to squat down (ponerse en cuclillas).
acuchillado, -a *adj.* **1** slashed (ropa). **2** hardened, experienced (persona).
acuchillador, -a *adj.* **1** slashing. || *s.m.* **2** knifer, stabber (persona). **3** floor dresser (que acuchilla los suelos).
acuchillamiento *s.m.* surfacing (de los suelos de madera).
acuchillar *v.t.* **1** to knife, to stab (apuñalar). **2** to surface (alisar). **3** to slash (ropa).
acudir *v.i.* **1** to turn up, to go along (ir a un sitio). **2** to go (ir). **3** to come (venir). **4** to turn to someone (recurrir a alguien). **5** to use, to make use of (valerse de algo).
acueducto *s.m.* aquaduct.
acuerdo *s.m.* **1** agreement, resolution (resolución). **2** agreement, pact (pacto). **3** agreement, understanding (entendimiento): *tenemos un acuerdo mutuo = we have a mutual understanding.* **4** harmony (armonía). **5** advice, opinion (consejo, opinión). || **6 ¡de –!,** O.K.; alright. **7 de – con,** in accordance with. **8 estar de –,** to agree. **9 llegar a un –,** to come to an agreement. **10 ponerse de –,** to come to an agreement.
acuilmarse *v.pron.* (Am.) to be sad (entristecerse).
acullá *adv.* over there.
acumulable *adj.* accumulative.
acumulación *s.f.* accumulation.
acumulador, -a *adj.* **1** accumulative. || *s.m.* **2** acumulator.
acumular *v.t.* y *v.pron.* **1** to accumulate, to amass (amontonar). **2** to blame, to impute (culpar). **3** to gather, to collect (recoger). **4** to join (unir).
acumulativamente *adv.* accumulatively.
acumulativo, -a *adj.* accumulative.
acunar *v.t.* to rock (mecer en la cuna).
acuñar *v.t.* **1** to mint, to coin (fabricar monedas). **2** to wedge (meter cuñas).
acuoso, -a *adj.* **1** watery (abundante en agua). **2** juicy (jugoso).
acupuntura *s.f.* acupuncture.
acurrucarse *v.pron.* **1** to huddle up (debido al frío). **2** to shrink (por miedo).
acusación *s.f.* accusation.
acusado, -a *adj.* **1** DER. accused. || *s.m.* y *f.* **2** DER. accused, defendant.
acusador, -a *adj.* **1** accusing. || *s.m.* y *f.* **2** accuser.
acusar *v.t.* **1** to accuse (imputar): *acusar de asesinato = to accuse of murder.* **2** to acknowledge (avisar el recibo de algo). **3** DER. to charge (resumir en un juicio). **4** to blame (culpar). **5** to show (mostrar): *acusar dolor = to show pain.* || *v.t.* y *v.pron.* **6** to report (denunciar). **7** to confess (confesar).
acusativo *s.m.* GRAM. accusative.
acusatorio, -a *adj.* accusatory.
acuse *s.m.* acknowledgement: *acuse de recibo = acknowledgement of receipt.*
acusica *s.m.* y *f.* sneak, snitch, telltale.
acusón *s.m.* y *f.* V. **acusica.**
acústica *s.f.* acoustics.
acústico, -a *adj.* acoustic.
acutángulo, -a *adj.* acute-angled.
achacable *adj.* attributable.
achacar *v.t.* **1** to attribute (atribuir). **2** to put on, to lay on (culpa, responsabilidad, etc.).
achacosamente *adv.* weakly.
achacoso, -a *adj.* sickly (enfermizo).
achancharse *v.pron.* (Am.) to get lazy (apoltronarse).
achantar *v.t.* **1** to squash, to flatten (apabullar). || *v.pron.* **2** to hide away (esconderse). **3** to back down (achicarse). **4** (Am.) to stay, to linger (detenerse).
achaparrado, -a *adj.* **1** tubby, plump (rechoncho). **2** squat, stocky (bajo y grueso).
achaque *s.m.* **1** complaint, ailment (enfermedad habitual). **2** vice (vicio). **3** fault (defecto). **4** excuse (excusa). **5** pretext (pretexto). **6** apearance (apariencia). **7** reputation (reputación). **8** fine (multa).
achatar *v.t.* y *v.pron.* to squash, to flatten (aplastar).
achicar *v.t.* y *v.pron.* to reduce, to make smaller (reducir). **2** to humiliate (humillar). || *v.t.* **3** to drain (una mina). **4** to bale out (un barco).
achicoria *s.f.* BOT. chicory.
achicharrar o **chicharrar** *v.t.* y *v.pron.* **1** to burn (quemar). **2** to overheat (calentar demasiado). **3** to overcook (asar o cocer demasiado). || *v.t.* **4** to bother, to pester (importunar).
achique *s.m.* **1** MAR. baling (un barco). **2** draining (una mina).
acholado *adj.* (Am.) intimidated, frightened (acobardado).
achuchar *v.t.* **1** to squash, to flatten (aplastar). **2** to push (empujar). **3** to squeeze (estrujar). **4** to set on, to urge on (perros).
achuchón *s.m.* **1** push, shove (empujón). **2** squashing (aplastamiento).
achucutado, -a *adj.* withered (marchito).
achumado, -a *adj.* (Am.) drunk (borracho).
adagio *s.m.* **1** adage, proverb (máxima). **2** MUS. adagio.
adalid *s.m.* leader.
adamascado, -a *adj.* damask.
adamascar *v.t.* to damask.

adamismo *s.m.* Adamism.
adamita *s.m.* y *f.* Adamite.
adán *s.m.* 1 sloven (descuidado). 2 apathetic person (apático). 3 indifferent person (persona indiferente).
adaptable *adj.* adaptable.
adaptación *s.f.* adaptation.
adaptado, -a *adj.* integrated.
adaptador, -a *adj.* 1 adapting. || *s.m.* 2 adapter.
adaptar *v.t.* 1 to adapt (acomodar). 2 to adjust (ajustar). 3 to agree, to come to an agreement (avenirse). || *v.pron.* 4 to adapt oneself.
adarga *s.f.* shield (escudo).
adecentar *v.t.* 1 to make decent (poner decente). 2 to decorate (adornar). || *v.pron.* 3 to make oneself decent.
adecuación *s.f.* adequacy, suitability.
adecuadamente *adv.* adequately, suitably.
adecuado, -a *adj.* 1 adequate (suficiente). 2 appropriate, suitable (apto).
adecuar *v.t.* to adapt, to make suitable.
adefesio *s.m.* 1 absurdity (disparate). 2 extravagance (extravagancia). 3 ridiculous person (persona ridícula). 4 ridiculous thing (cosa ridícula). 5 ridiculous clothes (ropa ridícula).
adelantado, -a *adj.* 1 advanced (niño). 2 early (temprano). 3 fast (reloj): *estar adelantado = to be fast.* 4 advanced (desarrollado). || *s.m.* 5 HIS. governor (gobernador). || **6 por –,** in advance.
adelantamiento *s.m.* 1 advance (adelanto). 2 overtaking (en coche). 3 progress (progreso). 4 promotion (promoción).
adelantar *v.t.* y *v.pron.* 1 to move forward (mover hacia adelante). 2 to put forward (reloj). 3 to anticipate (anticipar). || *v.t.* 4 to speed up, to quicken (acelerar). 5 to advance, to pay in advance (dinero). || *v.i.* y *v.pron.* 5 to overtake (pasar delante de algo o alguien): *adelantar un coche = to overtake a car.* 6 to improve (mejorar). 7 to progress (progresar). 8 to get ahead, to outstrip (aventajar).
adelante *adv.* 1 forward (hacia adelante): *ir adelante = to go forward.* 2 further (más allá): *ir un poco más adelante = to go a little further.* || *interj.* 3 ¡adelante!, **a)** come in! (¡pase!); **b)** MIL. forward!; **c)** carry on! (¡siga!) || **4 en –; hoy en –,** from now on. **5 llevar –,** to carry out. **6 más –,** later on (luego). **7 salir –,** to get by/on.
adelanto *s.m.* 1 advance, improvement (avance): *los adelantos técnicos = the technical advances.* 2 progress, advancement (progreso). 3 advance, loan (anticipo). 4 DEP. lead: *un adelanto de diez segundos = a lead of ten seconds.*
adelfa *s.f.* BOT. rosebay, oleander.
adelgazamiento *s.m.* slimming, weight loss.
adelgazante *adj.* slimming.
adelgazar *v.t.* y *v.pron.* 1 to make thin, to thin (poner delgado). || *v.i.* 2 to slim, to lose weight (perder peso). 3 to get thin (enflaquecer). || *v.t.* 4 to purify (depurar). 5 to sutilize (sutilizar).
ademán *s.m.* 1 expression, look (de la cara). 2 gesture (con las manos). 3 posture (postura). 4 attitude (actitud). || *s.m.pl.* 5 manners (modales). || **6 en – de,** as if to. **7 hacer – de,** to make as if to; to look as if to: *hicieron ademán de disparar = they looked as if they were going to fire.*
además *adv.* 1 besides, moreover, furthermore, in addition: *y además fui al teatro = and moreover I went to the theatre.* || **2 – de eso,** on top of that; besides that.
adenitis *s.f.* MED. adenoids.
adentrarse *v.pron.* 1 to go inside (entrar). 2 to go deeper (profundizar). 3 to go deeply (penetrar).
adentro *adv.* 1 inside: *vamos adentro = let's go inside.* || *s.m.pl.* 2 heart (corazón): *en mis adentros = in my heart.* || **3 decir para sus adentros,** to say to oneself. **4 mar –,** out to sea. **5 tierra –,** inland.
adepto, -a *adj.* 1 supporting, in favour. || *s.m.* 2 follower, supporter.
aderezado, -a *adj.* favourable.
aderezar *v.t.* 1 to cook (guisar). 2 to season (condimentar). 3 to prepare (preparar). 4 to direct, to run (dirigir). || *v.t.* y *v.pron.* 5 to decorate (adornar). 6 to beautify (hermosear).
aderezo *s.m.* 1 seasoning (condimento). 2 set of jewels (juego de joyas). 3 decoration (adorno). 4 preparation (preparación).
adeudar *v.t.* 1 to owe (tener deudas). || *v.pron.* 2 to get into debt, to run into debt (endeudarse).
adeudo *s.m.* 1 debt (deuda). 2 duty (en las aduanas). 3 debit (banco).
adherencia *s.f.* 1 sticking (accion de pegar), adherence (acción de adherir). 2 roadholding ability (de coches). 3 adhesion (adhesión).
adherente *s.m.* y *f.* 1 adherent, follower. || *adj.* 2 adherent.
adherir *v.i.* y *v.pron.* 1 to adhere, to stick (pegar). 2 to adhere, to follow (partido, idea, doctrina).
adhesión *s.f.* 1 adhesion (adherencia). 2 support, adherence (a un partido, doctrina, etc.).
adhesivo, -a *adj.* 1 adhesive, sticky. || *s.m.* 2 adhesive.
ad hoc *adj.* ad hoc.
ad hominem *adv.* y *adj.* ad hominem: *argumento and hominem = ad hominem argument.*
adicción *s.f.* adiction.
adición *s.f.* 1 MAT. addition. 2 addition (hecho y resultado de añadir). 3 sum (suma).
adicional *adj.* additional.
adicionar *v.t.* 1 MAT. to add, to add up (sumar). 2 to add (añadir).
adicto, -a *adj.* 1 fond, attached (aficionado): *adicto a = fond of/attached to.* || *s.m.* y *f.* 2 supporter, follower (adepto). 3 addict (drogas).
adiestrable *adj.* trainable.
adiestrado, -a *adj.* 1 trained (animales). 2 trained, instructed (personas).
adiestrador, -a *s.m.* y *f.* 1 trainer (de animales). 2 trainer, instructor (de personas).
adiestramiento *s.m.* 1 training (de animales). 2 training, instructing (de personas).
adiestrar *v.t.* y *v.pron.* 1 to train (animales). 2 to train, to instruct (personas). 3 to teach (enseñar). || *v.t.* 4 to guide (guiar).
adinerado *adj.* wealthy, rich (rico).
adintelado, -a *adj.* ARQ. flat: *arco adintelado = flat arch.*
adiós *interj.* 1 good-bye, bye, bye-bye. || *s.m.* 2 good-bye, farewell. || **3 decir –,** to say good-bye.
adiposidad *s.f.* MED. obesity, (p.u.) adiposity.
adiposo, -a *adj.* fat, obese, (p.u.) adipose.
aditamento *s.m.* addition.
aditivo, -a *adj.* y *s.m.* additive.
adivinación *s.f.* 1 solution (solución). 2 guessing (acción de adivinar). 3 divination, prophecy (profecía).
adivinanza *s.f.* riddle, puzzle (acertijo).
adivinar *v.t.* 1 to predict, to prophecy (predecir). 2 to unravel, to solve (un enigma). 3 to guess (acertar). 4 to guess (intuir). 5 to read (los pensamientos).
adivinatorio, -a *adj.* divinatory.
adivino, -a *s.m.* y *f.* fortune-teller.
adjetivación *s.f.* use as an adjective.
adjetivar *v.t.* 1 GRAM. to use adjectively. 2 to describe (calificar). || *v.pron.* 3 to use as an adjective (dar valor de adjetivo).
adjetivo *s.m.* 1 adjectival. || *s.m.* 2 adjective.
adjudicación *s.f.* 1 DER. adjudication. 2 award (acción de conceder).
adjudicar *v.t.* 1 DER. to adjudicate. 2 to sell (en una subasta). 3 to award (en un concurso). 3 to distribute (distribuir). || *v.pron.* 4 to appropriate something (apropiarse de algo). 5 to win (triunfar).
adjuntar *v.t.* 1 to enclose (en una carta): *te adjunto mi dirección = I enclose my address.* 2 to attach (a un documento).
adjuntía *s.f.* assistant.
adjunto, -a *adj.* 1 attached (que está unido). 2 enclosed (en una carta). 3 assistant: *profesor adjunto = assistant teacher.* || *s.m.* 4 assistant.
adlátere *s.m.* assistant.
ad libitum *adv.* ad libitum.
ad limina *adv.* ad limina.
ad litteram o **ad pedem litterae** *adv.* ad litteram.
administración *s.f.* 1 administration (acción de administrar). 2 running administration (gestión). 3 management (directores). || **4 consejo de –,** board of directors.
administrador, -a *adj.* 1 administrating. || *s.m.* y *f.* 2 administrator. 3 manager (de una granja, finca, etc.). || **4 – de correos,** postmaster.

administrativamente *adv.* administratively.
administrar *v.t.* 1 to administer, to manage (regir). 2 REL. to administer (los sacramentos, medicinas). 3 to give (dar).
administrativo, -a *adj.* 1 administrative, managerial. || *s.m.* 2 office worker.
admirable *adj.* admirable.
admirablemente *adv.* admirably.
admiración *s.f.* 1 admiration (acción de admirar): *causar admiración = to inspire admiration.* 2 GRAM. exclamation mark (signo ortográfico). 3 wonder, surprise (sorpresa).
admirador, -a *s.m.* y *f.* admirer.
admirar *v.t.* 1 to admire: *te admiro mucho = I admire you a lot.* 2 to surprise (sorprender). 3 to respect (respetar). || *v.pron.* 4 to be amazed, to be astonished (maravillarse).
admirativamente *adv.* admiringly.
admirativo, -a *adj.* admiring.
admisibilidad *s.f.* admissibility.
admisible *adj.* admissible, acceptable.
admisión *s.f.* 1 admission. 2 acceptance (aceptación). 3 MEC. intake.
admitir *v.t.* 1 to admit, to accept (aceptar): *admito que soy imbécil = I admit that I'm stupid.* 2 to permit, to allow (permitir). 3 to recognize (reconocer).
admonición *s.f.* warning, admonition, rebuke.
admonitor *s.m.* admonisher, rebuker.
admonitorio, -a *adj.* warning: *voz admonitoria = warning voice.*
adobado, -a *adj.* marinated.
adobamiento *s.m.* marinating.
adobar *v.t.* 1 to cook (cocinar). 2 to marinate (carne). 3 to tan (curtir las pieles). 4 to prepare (preparar).
adobe *s.m.* adobe.
adocenado *adj.* 1 ordinary, common (corriente). 2 (Am.) ignorant, thick (inculto).
adocenar *v.t.* 1 to divide into dozens (ordenar por docenas). || *v.t.* y *v.pron.* 2 (fam.) to become a stick-in-the-mud (estancarse).
adoctrinamiento *s.m.* indoctrination.
adoctrinar o **doctrinar** *v.t.* to indoctrinate.
adolecer *v.i.* 1 to be ill. || *v.pron.* 2 to feel sorry, to pity, to feel pity (condolerse).
adolescencia *s.f.* adolescence.
adolescente *adj.* y *s.m.* y *f.* adolescent.
adonde *conj.* where.
adónde *adv.interr.* where?
adondequiera *adv.* wherever, (p.u.) wheresoever.
adonis *s.m.* Adonis.
adopción *s.f.* adoption.
adoptable *adj.* adoptable.
adoptante *adj.* y *s.m.* y *f.* adopting.
adoptar *v.t.* to adopt: *adoptar la costumbre = to adopt the custom.*
adoptivo, -a *adj.* 1 adopted, adoptive (hijo). 2 adoptive (padres). || 3 **patria adoptiva,** country of adoption.
adoquín *s.m.* 1 paving stone (para pavimentos). 2 (fam.) dunce, dope, dolt (persona torpe).
adoquinado, -a *adj.* 1 paved. || *s.m.* 2 paving.
adoquinar *v.t.* to pave.
adorable *adj.* adorable.
adoración *s.f.* 1 adoration, worship (de Dios o personas). || 2 REL. **— de los Reyes,** Epiphany.
adorador, -a *adj.* 1 adoring, worshipping. || *s.m.* y *f.* 2 adorer, worshipper.
adorar *v.t.* 1 to adore, to worship. 2 REL. to worship (reverenciar). || *v.pron.* 3 to pray (rezar).
adormecedor, -a *adj.* soporific.
adormecer *v.t.* 1 to send to sleep (causar sueño). 2 to calm (calmar). || *v.pron.* 3 to get sleepy, to fall asleep (empezar a dormirse).
adormecimiento *s.m.* sleepiness, drowsiness.
adormidera *s.f.* BOT. poppy.
adormilarse *v.pron.* to doze, to drowse.
adornado, -a *adj.* 1 decorated, adornado (decorado). 2 garnished (comida).
adornamiento *s.m.* adornment, decoration.
adornar *v.t.* y *v.prn.* 1 to adorn, to decorate (decorar). 2 to garnish (la comida). || *v.t.* 3 to endow (dotar de grandes cualidades).
adorno *s.m.* 1 adornment, decoration. 2 garnishing (de comida).
adosar *v.t.* to lean (apoyar).
adquirente *adj.* 1 acquiring (acción de adquirir). 1 buying, purchasing (acción de comprar). || *s.m.* 3 buyer, purchaser (comprador).
adquirible *adj.* acquirable.
adquirir *v.t.* 1 to acquire, to obtain (obtener). 2 to purchase, to buy (comprar). 3 to incorporate (incorporar).
adquisición *s.f.* 1 acquisition. 2 purchase (compra).
adquisitivo, -a *adj.* 1 acquisitive. || 2 **poder —,** purchasing power.
adrede *adv.* onpurpose, deliberately.
adrenalina *s.f.* adrenalin.
adscribir *v.t.* 1 to assign, to attach (asignar). 2 to attribute (atribuir). || *v.t.* y *v.pron.* 3 to appoint, to assign (destinar).
adscripción *s.f.* 1 appointment (destino). 2 attribution (atribución).
adscrito, -a *adj.* appointed (destinado).
aduana *s.f.* 1 customs. || 2 **oficial de —,** customs officer.
aduanero, -a *adj.* 1 customs. || 2 *s.m.* y *f.* customs officer.
aducción *s.f.* adduction.
aducir *v.t.* to adduce.
aductor, -a *adj.* 1 ANAT. adductive. || *s.m.* 2 ANAT. adductor.
adueñarse *v.pron.* to take possession.
adulación *s.f.* adulation.
adulador, -a *adj.* 1 adulating. || *s.m.* y *f.* 2 adulator.
adulante *adj.* adulating.
adular *v.t.* to adulate.
adulatorio, -a *adj.* adulating.
adúltera *s.f.* adultress.
adulteración *s.f.* adulteration.
adulterante *adj.* adulterating.
adulterar *v.t.* 1 to adulterate (falsificar). || *v.i.* 2 to commit adultery (cometer adulterio).
adulterio *s.m.* 1 adultery (sexual). 2 adulteration (falsificación).
adúltero, -a *adj.* 1 adulterous. || 2 *s.m.* y *f.* adulterer.
adulto, -a *adj.* 1 adult, grown-up. || *s.m.* y *f.* 2 adult, grown-up.
adusto, -a *adj.* 1 serious (serio). 2 austere (austero). 3 burnt (quemado).
advenedizo, -a *adj.* 1 foreign (desconocido). 2 upstart (nuevo rico). || *s.m.* y *f.* 3 upstart (nuevo rico). 4 stranger (desconocido).
advenimiento *s.m.* 1 arrival, coming (llegada). 2 REL. advent. 3 accession (al trono).
adventicio *adj.* adventitious.
adventismo *s.m.* adventism.
adverbial *adj.* adverbial.
adverbialización *s.f.* adverbialization.
adverbializar *v.t.* to use as an adverb.
adverbialmente *adv.* adverbially.
adverbio *s.m.* adverb.
adversamente *adv.* adversely.
adversario *s.m.* y *adj.* 1 opposing. || *s.m.* y *f.* 2 adversary, opponent.
adversativo, -a *adj.* GRAM. adversative.
adversidad *s.f.* adversity, setback (contrariedad).
adverso, -a *adj.* 1 adverse (un resultado, situación). 2 bad (suerte). 3 opposite, facing (opuesto).
advertencia *s.f.* 1 warning (aviso). 2 piece of advice (consejo). 3 note (nota). 4 fore word (en un libro).
advertidamente *adv.* knowingly.
advertido, -a *adj.* 1 warned (avisado). 2 wary (que no ignora los peligros).
advertimiento *s.m.* warning.
advertir *v.t.* 1 to warn (avisar). 2 to advise (aconsejar). 3 to notice (notar). 4 to feel (sentir). || *v.t.* e *i.* 4 to observe (observar). || *v.i.* 5 to attend (atender).
adviento *s.m.* REL. Advent.
advocación *s.f.* REL. dedication, name.
advocar *v.t.* to advocate.
adyacencia *s.f.* adjacency.
adyacente *adj.* adjacent.
aéreo, -a *adj.* 1 aerial, air: *tráfico aéreo = air traffic.* 2 flimsy, light (ligero). 3 subtle (sutil). 4 illusory (ilusorio).
aero *prefijo* aero-.
aerodinámica *s.f.* aerodynamics.
aerodinámico, -a *adj.* 1 aerodynamic. 2 streamlined (coche, tren, etc.).
aeródromo *s.m.* aerodrome, airfield.
aerolito *s.m.* meteorite.
aerómetro *s.m.* aerometer.
aeromodelismo *s.m.* aeroplane modelling, aeromodelling.
aeromotor *s.m.* aeromotor.
aeronauta *s.m.* aeronaut.
aeronáutica *s.f.* aeronautics.
aeronáutico, -a *adj.* aeronautical.
aeronave *s.m.* airship.
aeroplano *s.m.* aeroplane.

aeropuerto *s.m.* airport.
aerosol *s.m.* aerosol.
aerostación *s.f.* balloon-flying.
aerostática *s.f.* aerostatics.
aerostático, -a *adj.* aerostatic.
aeróstato *s.m.* aerostat.
aerovía *s.f.* airway.
afabilidad *s.f.* affability, pleasantness.
afabilísimo *adj.* extremely affable o pleasant.
afable *adj.* affable, pleasant.
afablemente *adv.* affably, pleasantly.
afamado, -a *adj.* famous.
afamar *v.t.* 1 to make famous. || *v.pron.* 2 to become famous.
afán *s.m.* 1 hard work, toil (trabajo excesivo). 2 enthusiasm, eagerness (entusiasmo). 3 urge, longing (anhelo). 4 desire (deseo). || **5 con —,** enthusiastically. **6 el — de,** the desire for. **7 poner —,** to give everything.
afanadamente *adv.* enthusiastically, eagerly.
afanar *v.i.* y *v.pron.* 1 to labour, to toil (trabajar corporalmente). || *v.t.* 2 to work hard (trabajar mucho). 3 (fam.) to swipe, to pinch (hurtar). 4 to pester, to bother (importunar). || *v.pron.* 5 to give everything, to strive (esforzarse).
afanoso, -a *adj.* 1 tough, hard (trabajo, tarea). 2 enthusiastic, eager (entusiasta). 3 worried (preocupado). 4 industrious (carácter).
afasia *s.f.* aphasia.
afear *v.t.* y *v.pron.* 1 to make ugly (poner feo). || *v.t.* 2 to censure, to tell off (censurar).
afección *s.f.* 1 MED. illness, disease (enfermedad). 2 affection (cariño). 3 affect (afecto). 4 propensity (propensión).
afectable *adj.* affectable.
afectación *s.f.* affectation.
afectadamente *adv.* affectedly.
afectado, -a *adj.* 1 affected (con artificio). 2 upset (perturbado). || **3 estar — de los riñones,** MED. to have kidney trouble.
afectar *v.t.* 1 to be affected (comportarse con artificio). 2 to affect (tener afecto): *su muerte me afectó mucho = his death affected me a lot.* 3 to pretend (fingir). 4 to concern, to affect (atañer). 5 to damage (dañar). || *v.t.* y *v.pron.* 6 to cause a sensation (causar sensación).
afectividad *s.f.* affectivity.
afectivo, -a *adj.* affective.
afecto, -a *adj.* 1 affectionate (cariñoso). || *s.m.* 2 affection, liking (cariño). || **3 — a,** fond of. **4 — a,** DER. subject to. **4 — de,** MED. suffering from.
afectuosamente *adv.* affectionately.
afectuosidad *s.f.* affection.
afectuoso, -a *adj.* affectionate.
afeitado *s.m.* shave.
afeitadora *s.f.* razor, shaver.
afeitar *v.t.* 1 to shave. || 2 *v.pron.* to have a shave, to shave.
afeite *s.m.* make up, cosmetics (cosmético).
afelpado, -a *adj.* plush, velvety.
afelpar *v.t.* to make plush (como felpa o terciopelo).
afeminación *s.f.* effeminacy.
afeminadamente *adv.* affinately.
afeminado, -a *adj.* 1 effeminate. || *s.m.* 2 effeminate person.
afeminamiento *s.m.* effeminacy.
afeminar *v.t.* y *v.pron.* to become effeminate.
aferradamente *adv.* stubbornly, (fam.) pig-headedly.
aferrado, -a *adj.* stubborn, (fam.) pig-headed.
aferramiento *s.m.* 1 grasping (acción de agarrar). 2 anchoring (acción de anclar). 3 (fig.) obstinacy, stubbornness, pigheadedness.
aferrar *v.t.* e *i.* 1 to grab (asir). || *v.i.* 2 MAR. to anchor (anclar). || *v.i.* y *v.pron.* 3 to stick to (insistir). || *v.pron.* 4 to take in (las velas).
afgano, -a *adj.* y *s.m.* y *f.* Afghan.
afianzamiento *s.m.* 1 FIN. guarantee, security. 2 DER. surety. 3 strengthening (refuerzo). 4 consolidation (consolidación).
afianzar *v.t.* 1 to guarantee (dar fianza). || *v.t.* y *v.pron.* 2 to grasp, to clutch (agarrar). 3 to hold (sujetar). 4 to stick to, to cling to (sostener firmemente una opinión).
afición *s.f.* 1 fondness, liking (amor a algo). 2 inclination (inclinación). 3 DEP. fans, public (amantes). 4 fondness (cariño). 5 hobby, pastime (pasatiempo). || **6 por —,** as a hobby. **7 tener — a,** to be fond of; to like.
aficionadamente *adv.* enthusiastically, keenly.
aficionado, -a *adj.* 1 enthusiastic (entusiasta). 2 fond, keen: *aficionado a los toros = fond of bullfighting.* || *s.m.* y *f.* 3 fan, supporter (del cine, teatro, deportes). 4 lover (amante): *aficionado a la ópera = opera-lover.*
aficionar *v.t.* y *v.pron.* to become fond, to take a liking: *aficionarse a la música = to become fond of music.*
afijo, -a *adj.* 1 GRAM. affixed. || 2 GRAM. affix.
afilado, -a *adj.* 1 sharp: *una navaja afilada = a sharp knife.* 2 pointed (puntiagudo). 3 high-pitched (voz).
afilador *s.m.* 1 knife-grinder (persona). 2 sharpener (utensilio). 3 strop (correa).
afiladura *s.f.* sharpening (acción de afilar).
afilar *v.t.* 1 to sharpen (cuchillo, lapicero). 2 to strop (afeitadora). || *v.pron.* 3 to get thin (adelgazarse).
afiliación *s.f.* affiliation.
afiliado, -a *adj.* 1 affiliated: *afiliado a un club = affiliated to a club.* 2 member: *los países afiliados = the member countries.* || *s.m.* y *f.* 2 member, affiliate.
afiliar *v.t.* y *v.pron.* to become affiliated, to become a member.
afilón *s.m.* 1 strop (correa). 2 sharpener (chaira).
afín *adj.* 1 adjacent (adyacente). 2 similar (semejante). 3 related (emparentado). || *s.m.* 4 relations, relatives (parientes).
afinación *s.f.* 1 MUS. tuning. 2 refining (afinado). 3 completion (acción de completar).
afinador *s.m.* 1 MUS. tuning key (llave). 2 MUS. tuner (persona).
afinamiento *s.m.* 1 MUS. tuning. 2 refining (depuración). 3 polishing, refining (de una persona).
afinar *v.t.* y *v.pron.* 1 MUS. to tune. 2 TEC. to refine (depurar). 3 to refine, to polish (perfeccionar). 4 to purify (purificar). 5 to complete (completar). 6 to sing in tune (al cantar). 7 to play in tune (al tocar).
afincar *v.i.* y *v.pron.* 1 to settle (fijar residencia). 2 to buy property (fincar).
afinidad *s.f.* 1 affinity, similarity (semejanza). 2 relationship, kinship (relación de parentesco). 3 QUIM. affinity.
afirmación *s.f.* affirmation, assertion.
afirmado *s.m.* road surface.
afirmante *adj.* asserting, affirming.
afirmar *v.t.* 1 to affirm, to state (asegurar). 2 to ratify (ratificar). || *v.t.* y *v.pron.* 3 to make firm, to secure (dar firmeza).
afirmativamente *adv.* affirmatively.
afirmativo, -a *adj.* affirmative.
aflicción *s.f.* affliction, sorrow, sadness (tristeza).
aflictivo, -a *adj.* grievous, distressing.
afligidamente *adv.* sadly.
afligir *v.t.* y *v.pron.* to afflict, to distress.
aflojar *v.t.* 1 to loosen (corbata, cuerda, tuerca, nudo, etc.). 2 to slacken, to get slack (soltar o entregar de mala gana). || *v.i.* 3 to weaken (perder fuerza). 4 to relent, to give in (ceder).
aflorar *v.i.* 1 to crop out, to appear (aparecer). 2 to arise (surgir). 3 to break out (brotar).
afluencia *s.f.* 1 flow (acción de afluir). 2 plenty, abundance (abundancia). 3 verbosity (verbosidad). 4 flow (movimiento de gente).
afluente *adj.* 1 flowing (que afluye). 2 fluent, eloquent (de palabra). || *s.m.* 3 tributary.
afluir *v.i.* 1 to flock (concurrir en gran número). 2 to flow (ríos).
aflujo *s.m.* MED. afflux.
afonía *s.f.* MED. loss of voice, (p.u.) aphony (falta de voz).
afónico, -a *adj.* hoarse, (p.u.) aphonic: *estar afónico = to be hoarse.*
aforado, -a *adj.* privileged.
aforamiento *s.m.* 1 gauging, measuring (acción de medir). 2 evaluation (evaluación). 3 assessment (en aduanas).
aforar *v.t.* 1 to grant a privilege (dar fueros). 2 to value (valuar). 3 to gauge, to measure (medir). 4 to calculate (calcular).
aforismo *s.m.* aphorism.
aforo *s.m.* 1 gauging, measuring (acción de medir). 2 valuation (acción de valuar). 3 calculation (acción de calcular). 4 capacity (capacidad).

afortunadamente *adv.* fortunately, luckily.
afortunado, -a *adj.* 1 fortunate, lucky (con buena suerte). 2 happy (feliz).
afrancesado, -a *adj.* 1 francophile, (desp.) frenchified. || *s.m.* y *f.* 2 francophile, (desp.) frenchified-person.
afrenta *s.f.* 1 shame, disgrace (vergüenza). 2 affront, insult (ofensa).
afrentar *v.t.* 1 to shame, to disgrace (causar afrenta). 2 to humiliate (humillar). 3 to insult, to affront (insultar). 4 to offend (ofender). || *v.pron.* 3 to be ashamed (avergonzarse).
afrentosamente *adv.* insultingly, offensively.
afrentoso, -a *adj.* insulting, offensive.
africado, -a *adj.* GRAM. affricative.
africanismo *s.m.* Africanism.
africanista *adj./s.m.* y *f.* Africanist.
africanizar *v.t.* to Africanize.
afrodisiaco, -a o **afrodisíaco, -a** *adj.* y *s.m.* aphrodisiaco.
afrodita *s.f.* Aphrodite.
afrontar *v.t.* e *i.* 1 to place opposite (poner enfrente). || *v.t.* 2 to bring face to face (carear). 3 to face up to (hacer frente).
afta *s.f.* MED. aphtha.
afuera *adv.* 1 outside, out: *vamos afuera = let's go outside.* || *s.f.pl.* 2 outskirts, suburbs. || *interj.* 3 get out!; out!
afuetear *v.t.* (Am.) to whip (azotar).
afusilar *v.t.* (Am.) to shoot (fusilar).
agachado, -a *adj.* 1 bent (inclinado o doblado). 2 (Am.) sly, cunning (astuto). 3 (Am.) servile (servil).
agachar *v.t.* e *i.* 1 to bend, to bow (inclinar una parte del cuerpo). || *v.pron.* 2 to bend down, to stoop (encogerse). 3 to squat, to crouch (en cuclillas). 4 to lie low, to go into hiding (estar ocultado cierto tiempo). 5 (Am.) to give in, to submit (someterse). 6 (Am.) to keep maliciously quiet (callar con malicia). || 7 (Am.) **agacharse con algo,** to pinch, to make off with (robar).
agalla *s.f.* 1 BOT. gall (excrecencia). 2 gill (branquia de los peces). 3 guts (valor). 4 (Am.) greed (codicia). || *s.pl.* 5 tonsils (amígdalas). || 6 **tener agallas,** to be daring.
ágape *s.m.* 1 HIST. love feast. 2 feast, banquet (banquete).
agarrada *s.f.* row, quarrel (riña).
agarradera *s.f.* 1 (Am.) handle (agarradero). 2 influence (influencia).
agarradero *s.m.* 1 handle (mango). 2 help, influence (amparo).
agarrado, -a *adj.* mean, tight (tacaño).
agarrar *v.t.* y *v.pron.* 1 to grab, to seize (asir). || *v.t.* 2 to catch an illness (contraer una enfermedad). 3 BOT. to take root (arraigar). 4 to stick (quedar adherido). || *v.pron.* 5 to quarrel, to row (reñir).
agarrotado, -a *adj.* 1 tied, bound (atado). 2 stiff (rígido). 3 seized up, broken (motor).
agarrotamiento *s.m.* 1 tying, binding (acción de atar). 2 strangling, garrotting (acción de estrangular). 3 seizing up (de un motor).
agarrotar *v.t.* 1 to tie up, to bind (atar). 2 to garrotte (criminal). 3 to torment, to dispirit (oprimir moralmente) || *v.pron.* 4 to stiffen, to tighten, to go stiff (ponerse rígido un miembro). 5 to seize up (un motor).
agasajador, -a *adj.* welcoming, warm.
agasajar *v.t.* 1 to put up (hospedar). 2 to treat well (tratar bien).
agasajo *s.m.* good treatment, warm hospitality.
ágata *s.f.* agate.
agazapar *v.t.* 1 to grab (agarrar). || *v.pron.* 2 to hide (esconderse).
agencia *s.f.* 1 agency (oficina para gestiones, etc.): *agencia de viajes = travel agency.* 2 office (oficina): *agencia de patentes = patents office.* || 3 **— de prensa,** news agency. 4 **— de publicidad,** publishing agency.
agenciar *v.t.* e *i.* 1 to manage (gestionar). || *v.t.* y *v.pron.* 2 to procure (conseguir algo con diligencia).
agenda *s.f.* 1 agenda (libro de memorias). 2 diary (cuadernillo de uso diario).
agente *s.m.* 1 agent (persona): *agente secreto = secret agent.* 2 QUIM. agent. || 3 **— de cambio y de bolsa,** stockbroker. 4 **— de policía,** policeman. 5 **— fiscal,** tax inspector.
agigantado, -a *adj.* huge, enormous, gigantic.
agigantar *v.t.* y *v.pron.* 1 to enlarge, to increase enormously. || *v.pron.* 2 to be encouraged (crecerse en ánimo)
ágil *adj.* agile, nimble.
agilidad *s.f.* agility, nimbleness.
agilizar *v.t.* to make agile.
ágilmente *adv.* agilely, nimbly.
agitación *s.f.* 1 agitation, shaking (de líquidos, máquinas, etc.). 2 movement, hustle (en la calle). 3 roughness (del mar). 4 roll (de un barco). 5 waving (de telas, banderas, etc.). 6 POL. restlessness.
agitador, -a *s.m.* 1 MEC. shaker, agitator. 2 agitator (persona).
agitar *v.t.* y *v.pron.* 1 to shake (sacudir): *agitar una botella = to shake a bottle.* 2 to agitate, to disturb (turbar). || *v t.* 3 to agitate, to rouse (alborotar). 4 to wave (bandera, mano, pañuelo).
aglomeración *s.f.* aglomeration, mass.
aglomerado, -a *adj.* 1 crowded together. || *s.m.* 2 agglomerate (combustible).
aglomerante *s.m.* binding substance.
aglomerar *v.t.* y *v.pron.* 1 to pile, to amass (amontonar). 2 to agglomerate, to crowd together (juntar).
aglutinación *s.f.* agglutination.
aglutinate *adj.* y *s.* agglutinant.
aglutinar *v.t.* y *r.* to agglutinate.
aglutinativo, -a *adj.* MED. agglutinative.
agnosticismo *s.m.* agnosticism.
agnóstico, -a *adj.* y *s.* agnostic.
agobiado, -a *adj.* 1 tired, exhausted (fatigado). 2 weighed down (una carga).
agobiante *adj.* 1 oppressive (calor). 2 tiring, exhausting, backbreaking, tiresome (trabajo, niño, etc.). 3 overwhelming (dolor).
agobiar *v.t.* y *r.* 1 to weigh down (una carga). 2 to exhaust (calor, trabajo, niño). 3 to overwhelm (dolor, responsabilidad).
agolpamiento *s.m.* 1 crowd, throng (gente). 2 pile, heap (cosas).
agolparse *v.pron.* 1 to throng, to crowd together (gente). 2 to pile up, to amass (cosas).
agonía *s.f.* 1 agony (dolor grave). 2 death throes (antes de la muerte). 3 longing, desire (deseo). 4 knell, toll (toque de campana).
agónico *adj.* 1 dying: *estar agónico = to be dying.* 2 death (muerte).
agonizante *adj.* 1 dying. || *s.m.* y *f.* 2 dying person.
agonizar *v.i.* to be dying (estar muriéndose).
ágora *s.f.* agora.
agorafobia *s.f.* agoraphobia.
agorero, -a *adj.* 1 ominous, of ill-omen: ave agorera = bird of ill-omen. 2 prophetic (profético). || *s.m.* y *f.* 3 prophet, soothsayer.
agostamiento *adj.* withering.
agostar *v.t.* y *r.* 1 to dry up, to wither (secarse). || *v.t.* 2 to plough in August (labrar la tierra). || *v.i.* 3 to graze, to pasture (pastar).
agosto *s.m.* 1 August (mes). || 2 **hacer uno su —,** to make one's fortune.
agotado, -a *adj.* 1 exhausted, worn out (persona). 2 sold out (cosas).
agotador, -a *adj.* tiring, exhausting.
agotamiento *s.m.* exhaustion, tiredness.
agotar *v.t.* 1 to exhaust (fatigar). 2 to empty (vaciar). 3 to exhaust (recursos, paciencia, tema, tierra). || *v.pron.* 4 to exhaust oneself (cansarse). 5 to run out (existencias).
agracejo *s.m.* 1 BOT. berberry. 2 unripe grape (uva no madurada).
agraciadamente *adv.* attractively, prettily.
agraciado, -a *adj.* 1 pretty, attractive (atractivo). 2 graceful (elegante). || 3 **salir —,** to be the winner.
agraciar *v.t.* 1 to award (premiar). 2 to pardon (dar merced). 3 to grace (dar gracia). 4 to make beautiful (dar belleza).
agradable *adj.* nice, pleasant.
agradablemente *adv.* pleasantly, nicely.
agradar *v.i.* 1 to please, to be pleasing to (complacer). || *v.pron.* 2 to be pleased. 3 to like each other (gustarse).
agradecer *v.t.* 1 to thank (mostrar gratitud). 2 to be grateful (sentir gratitud): *te lo agradezco mucho = I'm very grateful to you for it.* || *v.pron.* 3 to be welcome.
agradecido, -a *adj.* grateful: *estoy muy agradecido = I'm very grateful.*
agradecimiento *s.m.* gratitude, gratefulness.
agrado *s.m.* 1 friendliness, affability (afabilidad). 2 pleasure (complacencia).

3 liking, taste (gusto): *de mi agrado = to my liking.*
agrandamiento *s.m.* expansion, enlargement.
agrandar *v.t.* 1 to enlarge, to make bigger. || *v.pron.* 2 to get bigger.
agrario, -a *adj.* agrarian, agricultural.
agravamiento *s.m.* 1 worsening, aggravation.
agravante *s.m.* y *f.* unpleasant circumstances.
agravar *v.t.* 1 to increase the weight (aumentar el peso). 2 to overwhelm, to weigh down (oprimir con tributos). 3 to aggravate (hacer más grave). || *v.t.* y *v.pron.* 4 to worsen, to get worse (aumentar la gravedad).
agraviante *adj.* 1 insulting, offensive. || *s.m.* 2 insulter.
agraviar *v.t.* 1 to insult (insultar). 2 to offend (ofender). 3 DER. to wrong (perjudicar). || *v.r.* 4 to take offence.
agravio *s.m.* 1 offence, insult (ofensa). 2 slight, affront (afrenta). 3 wrong, injury (perjuicio). || 4 **deshacer agravios,** to get revenge.
agravioso, -a *adj.* insulting, offensive.
agraz *s.m.* 1 unripe grape (uva sin madurar). 2 sour grape juice (zumo). 3 bitterness (amargura).
agrazón *s.m.* 1 wild grape (uva silvestre). 2 BOT. gooseberry bush (grosellero). 3 (fig.) annoyance.
agredir *v.t.* to attack, to assault.
agregación *s.f.* aggregation.
agregado, -a *s.m.* y *f.* 1 aggregate (conjunto). 2 assistant (adjunto).
agregar *v.t.* 1 to add (añadir). 2 to join (juntar). 3 to amass (reunir). 4 to appoint (destinar). || *v.pron.* 5 to be added.
agresión *s.f.* aggression.
agresivamente *adv.* aggressively.
agresividad *s.f.* aggresiveness.
agresivo *adj.* aggressive.
agresor *s.m.* y *f.* aggressor.
agreste *adj.* 1 rural (campestre). 2 rough, uncouth (tosco).
agriado, -a *adj.* 1 rural (campestre). 2 rough, uncouth (tosco).
agriado, -a *adj.* (Am.) resentful (resentido).
agriar *v.t.* y *v.pron.* 1 to turn sour (poner agrio). 2 to irritate (irritar).
agricultor, -a *s.m.* y *f.* 1 farmer. || *adj.* 2 agricultural.
agricultura *s.f.* agriculture, farming.
agridulce *adj.* bittersweet.
agridulcemente *adv.* bittersweetly.
agrietamiento *s.m.* cracking.
agrietar *v.t.* y *v.pron.* to crack.
agriamente *adv.* sourly, bitterly.
agrio *adj.* 1 sour, bitter (sabor). 2 (fig.) sharp, bitter (persona). 3 rough (áspero). || *s.m.pl.* 4 citrus fruits.
agrisado, -a *adj.* grey.
agro *s.m.* agriculture.
agronomía *s.f.* agronomy.
agronómico, -a *adj.* agronomic, agronomical.
agrónomo, -a *s.m.* y *f.* 1 agronomist. || *adj.* 2 agricultural.
agropecuario *adj.* agricultural, farming.
agrupable *adj.* able to be grouped.
agrupación *s.f.* 1 group (grupo). 2 MUS. group. 3 grouping (acción de agrupar). 4 association (asociación).
agrupar *v.t.* 1 to group, to group together. || *v.pron.* 2 to form a group, to group together.
agua *s.f.* 1 water (líquido). 2 tide (marea). 3 leak (abertura en un barco). || *pl.* 4 rain (lluvia). 5 waters (las del río o mar). 6 waters (aguas medicinales). 7 wake (que deja atrás un buque). 8 water (de una piedra). || 9 **— abajo,** downstream. 10 **— arriba,** upstream. 11 **— bendita,** holy water. 11 **— blanda,** soft water. 12 **— de colonia,** eau de cologne. 13 **— de azahar,** orange-flower water. 14 **— de Seltz,** soda water. 15 **— de socorro,** emergency baptism. 16 **— dulce,** fresh water. 17 **— dura,** hard water. 18 **— fuerte,** nitric acid. 19 **— mineral,** mineral water. 20 **— natural,** tapwater. 21 **— oxigenada,** oxygenated water. 22 **— pesada,** heavy water. 23 **— potable,** drinking water. 24 **— regia,** aqua regia. 25 **— salada,** salt water. 26 **— termal,** spring water. 27 **aguas jurisdiccionales,** territorial waters. 28 **aguas mayores,** high tides. 29 **aguas muertas,** neap tide. 30 **aguas residuales,** sewage. 31 **aguas territoriales,** territorial waters. 32 **— pasada, no mueve molino,** it's no use crying over spilt milk. 33 **bailar el — a uno,** to dance attendance on someone. 34 **bañarse en — de rosas,** to see everything through rose-coloured glasses. 35 **cubrir aguas,** to put the roof on. 36 **echarse al —,** to take the plunge. 37 **estar con el — al cuello,** to be up to the neck. 38 **estar entre dos aguas,** to be in two minds. 39 **hacer —,** MAR. to leak. 40 **hacerse la boca —,** to make one's mouth water. 41 **llevar uno el — a su molino,** to take care of number one. 42 **tomar las aguas,** to take the waters. 43 **volver las aguas por donde solían ir,** to be the same as ever.
aguacate *s.m.* 1 BOT. avocado (árbol). 2 avocado pear (fruto). 3 (Am.) dope, fool (persona floja).
aguacero *s.m.* heavy shower (chubasco).
aguacil *s.m.* V. alguacil.
aguador, -a *s.m.* y *f.* 1 water carrier (transportador). 2 water seller (vendedor).
aguaducho *s.m.* 1 water stall (puesto). 2 aquaduct (acueducto). 3 noria, waterwheel (noria).
aguafiestas *s.m.* y *f.* wet blanket, killjoy.
aguafuerte *s.f.* 1 nitric acid (ácido). || *s.m.* 2 etching (lámina).
aguamanil *s.m.* 1 water jug (jarro). 2 washstand (palanganero).
aguamarina *s.f.* aquamarine.
aguantable *adj.* tolerable.
aguantaderas *s.f.pl.* tolerance, patience: *tener aguantaderas = to be tolerant.*
aguantar *v.t.* 1 to bear, to stick, to stand, to endure (soportar): *no lo aguanto más = I can't stand it any longer.* 2 to hold back (contener). 3 to hold (sujetar). 4 to last (durar). 5 to swallow (insultos). 6 to tolerate (tolerar). || *v.pron.* 7 to keep quiet (callar). 8 to hold oneself back (reprimirse).
aguar *v.t.* 1 to water down, to dilute (diluir). 2 to spoil (estropear). || *v.pron.* 3 to be flooded (llenarse de agua un lugar).
aguardar *v.t., i.* y *pron.* to wait for, to await (esperar).
aguardentoso *adj.* 1 alcoholic. 2 hoarse, husky (voz).
aguardiente *s.m.* aguardiente, liquor.
aguarrás *s.m.* turpentine, (fam.) turps.
agudeza *s.f.* 1 vivacity (viveza). 2 wit, humour (ingenio). 3 sharpness (perspicacia de los sentidos). 4 witticism (dicho ingenioso). 5 sharpness, acuteness (de dolores).
agudizar *v.t.* 1 to sharpen (hacer agudo). || *v.pron.* 2 to intensify (intensificarse). 3 to worsen, to get worse (agravarse).
agudo, -a *adj.* 1 sharp (afilado). 2 witty, funny (gracioso). 3 sharp, acute (perspicaz). 4 acute (dolores). 5 high (sonido). 6 keen (sentidos). 7 GRAM. oxytone. 8 shrewd, clever (listo).
agüero *s.m.* 1 omen, presage (presagio). 2 prediction (predicción).
aguerrido, -a *adj.* hardened.
aguijón *s.m.* 1 goad (aguijada). 2 sting (de los insectos). 3 spine (de las plantas). 4 (fig.) spur (estímulo).
aguijonear *v.t.* 1 to goad (picar con el aguijón). 2 to spur (estimular).
águila *s.f.* 1 eagle (ave). 2 eagle (insignia). 3 eagle (moneda). 4 genius (genio). 5 ASTR. aquila, eagle. || 6 **— imperial,** imperial eagle. 7 **— real,** golden eagle. 8 **— ratonera,** buzzard.
aguileña *s.f.* BOT. columbine.
aguileño, -a *adj.* 1 ANAT. aquiline (nariz). 2 sharp-featured (cara).
aguilón *s.m.* 1 ZOOL. large eagle (águila grande). 2 jib (brazo de grúa).
aguilucho *s.m.* ZOOL. eaglet (pollo del águila).
aguinaldo *s.m.* Christmas present (regalo de Navidad).
aguja *s.f.* 1 needle (de coser, tocadiscos). 2 hand (de reloj, brújula, indicador). 3 ARQ. steeple, spire (de una torre). 4 ZOOL. needlefish (pez). 5 hatpin (de sombrero). 6 ANAT. rib (costilla). || *pl.* 7 points (riel movible). || 8 **— de media,** knitting needle. 9 **buscar una — en un pajar,** to look for a needle in a haystack.
agujazo *s.m.* prick, jab.
agujerear *v.t.* 1 to make holes. 2 to perforate (perforar).
agujero *s.m.* 1 hole (abertura). 2 needle maker (fabricante). 3 needle seller (vendedor). 4 pin cushion (alfiletero).
agujetas *s.f.pl.* stiffness; **tener —,** to be stiff.
agusanarse *v.pron.* to get maggoty.
agustinismo *s.m.* Augustinism.
agustino, -a *adj./s.m.*y *f.* Augustinian.

aguzar *v.t.* 1 to sharpen (sacar punta o filo). 2 to spur (estimular). 3 (fig.) to sharpen (afinar los sentidos).

¡ah! *interj.* ah!

aherrojar *v.t.* 1 to shackle (con grilletes). 2 to oppress (oprimir).

ahí *adv.* 1 there: *ahí está = there it is.* || **2 por —, a)** that way (en esa dirección); **b)** more or less (más o menos); **c)** around: *he estado por ahí = I've been around.*

ahijada *s.f.* goddaughter.

ahijado *s.m.* godson.

ahijar *v.t.* 1 to adopt (adoptar). || *v.i.* 2 to have children (tener hijos). 3 BOT. to shoot, to sprout (retoñar).

ahincadamente *adv.* insistently.

ahínco *s.m.* 1 effort (esfuerzo). 2 insistence (empeño). 3 enthusiasm, keenness (entusiasmo). 4 earnestness (diligencia).

ahíto *adj.* 1 full, full up (lleno). 2 fed up, tired (harto).

ahogado, -a *adj.* 1 drowned (en agua). 2 suffocated (por falta de aire). 3 stuffy (una habitación). 4 pent-up (emoción). 5 muffled, smothered (ruido, grito). || **6 verse —,** to be in a jam, to be in a tight spot.

ahogamiento *s.m.* 1 drowning (agua). 2 suffocation (aire).

ahogar *v.t.* y *v.pron.* 1 to drown (en el agua). 2 to put out, extinguish (apagar). 3 to soak (plantas, por exceso de agua). 4 to choke (plantas, por estar muy juntas). || *v.t.* e *i.* 5 to oppress (oprimir). 6 to tire, to wear out (fatigar). || **7 to be crushed (carecer de espacio).**

ahogo *s.m.* 1 tight spot (aprieto). 2 anguish, distress (congoja). 3 tightness of the chest. 4 scarcity (escasez). 5 haste (prisa).

ahondamiento *s.m.* deepening.

ahondar *v.t.* 1 to deepen (hacer más hondo). 2 to excavate, to dig (excavar). || *v.t.* e *i.* 3 to go deeply into, to probe (escudriñar).

ahora *adv.* 1 now: *ahora mismo = right now.* 2 soon (pronto). || *conj.* 2 now then, on the other hand, now: *ahora, yo pienso... = on the other hand, I think...* || **3 — bien, a)** but (pero); **b)** on the other hand (por otra parte). **4 ¡— vengo!,** coming! **5 desde —,** from now on. **5 hasta —,** up till now (hasta la fecha). **6 ¡hasta —!,** see you soon! (hasta luego). **7 por —,** at the moment.

ahorcar *v.t.* 1 to hang (colgar). 2 to block (en el dómino). 3 to give up (abandonar). || *v.pron.* 4 to hang oneself (colgarse).

ahorita *adv.* right now.

ahormar *v.t.* 1 to persuade (persuadir). 2 to break in (zapatos). 3 to wear in (ropa). 4 to adjust (ajustar).

ahornar *v.t.* to put in an oven (enhornar).

ahorrar *v.t.* y *pron.* 1 to save: *ahorrarse tiempo = to save time; ahorrar dinero = to save money.* 2 to avoid (evitar). || *v.t.* 3 to free (un esclavo).

ahorratividad *s.f.* thriftiness.

ahorrativo, -a *adj.* thrifty.

ahorro *s.m.* 1 saving (acción de ahorrar). 2 saving (cantidad ahorrada): *el ahorro nacional = the national saving.* 3 (fig.) saving: *el tiempo ahorrado = the time saved.* || *pl.* 4 savings.

ahuecar *v.t.* 1 to hollow out (poner hueco). 2 to soften (poner más blando). 3 to deepen (la voz). || *v.i.* 4 (fam.) to beat it (irse). || *v.pron.* 5 to become conceited (engreírse).

ahumado, -a *adj.* 1 smoked (carne, pescado). 2 smoky (sabor, ventana). || *s.m.* 3 smoking.

ahumar *v.t.* 1 to smoke (poner al humo). 2 to fill with smoke (llenar de humo). || *v.i.* 3 to smoke (echar humo). || *v.pron.* 4 to taste smoky (saber a humo). 5 to blacken (ennegrecerse). 6 to get drunk (emborracharse).

ahuyentar *v.t.* 1 to drive away (hacer huir). || *v.pron.* 2 to flee, to run away (huir).

airadamente *adv.* angrily, crossly.

airado, -a *adj.* 1 angry, cross, annoyed (enfadado). 2 seething, violent (violento). 3 inmoral, loose (inmoral).

airar *v.t.* 1 to anger (enfadar). || *v.pron.* 2 to get angry.

aire *s.m.* 1 air: *aire fresco = fresh air.* 2 draught (viento). 3 air, atmosphere (atmósfera). 4 appearance (aspecto). 5 likeness (parecido). 6 poise, grace (garbo). 7 air, tune (canción). 8 movement, air (movimiento). || **9 al — libre,** in the open air. **10 darse —,** to put on airs. **11 estar de buen —,** to be in a good mood. **12 estar de mal —,** to be in a bad mood. **13 estar en el —,** to be in the air. **14 mudar** o **cambiar de aires,** to have a change of air.

aireación *s.f.* ventilation.

aireado, -a *adj.* ventilated.

airear *v.t.* 1 to air (ropa). 2 to ventilate, to air (ventilar). 3 to air (un asunto, idea, tema, etc.). || *v.t.* 4 to reveal (hacer público). || *v.pron.* 5 to catch a cold (resfriarse).

airosamente *adv.* elegantly, gracefully (con elegancia).

airoso, -a *adj.* 1 draughty (habitación). 2 windy (ventoso). 3 ventilated (ventilado). 4 elegant, graceful (elegante).

aislable *adj.* isolable.

aislacionismo *s.m.* isolationism.

aislacionista *adj./s.m.* y *f.* isolationist.

aisladamente *adv.* alone.

aislado, -a *adj.* 1 isolated (pueblo, casa, etc.). 2 alone (solo).

aislador, -a *adj.* 1 ELEC. insolating. || *s.m.* 2 ELEC. insolator.

aislamiento *s.m.* 1 isolation. 2 ELEC. insulation.

aislante *s.m.* ELEC. insulator.

aislar *v.t.* 1 to isolate. 2 ELEC. to insulate. || *v.pron.* 2 to isolate oneself. 3 to seclude oneself (retirar de la vida).

ajar *v.t.* 1 to crumple (vestidos, telas, etc.). 2 to offend (ofender). 3 to humiliate (humillar). || *v.pron.* 4 to get old, to age (envejecer).

ajardinado, -a *adj.* landscaped.

ajardinar *v.t.* to landscape.

ajedrecista *s.m.* y *f.* chess player.

ajedrez *s.m.* chess.

ajenjo *s.m.* 1 BOT. wormwood (planta). 2 absinthe (bebida).

ajeno, -a *adj.* 1 someone else's, other people's (perteneciente a otro): *una casa ajena = someone else's house.* 2 free from (libre de algo): *ajeno de preocupaciones = free from worries.* 3 alien, foreign (alienado). 4 unaware of (inconsciente de algo). 5 outside (fuera). 6 not in keeping (no conforme).

ajetrear *v.t.* 1 (Am.) to tire out (cansar). || *v.pron.* 2 to tire oneself out (cansarse). 3 to rush around (moverse mucho). 4 to be busy (estar ocupado).

ajetreo *s.m.* 1 tiredness (cansancio). 2 bustle, hustle (actividad). 3 rush (prisa). 4 hard work (mucho trabajo).

ajo *s.m.* 1 garlic (planta y diente). 2 intrigue (intriga). 3 swearword (palabrota). || **4 diente de —,** clove of garlic. **5 soltar ajos,** to swear.

ajonje o **ajonjo** *s.m.* birdlime.

ajonjolí *s.m.* BOT. sesame.

ajuar *s.m.* 1 furnishings (conjunto de muebles). 2 trousseau (de novia).

ajumarse *v.pron.* to get drunk (emborracharse).

ajustadamente *adv.* 1 correctly (correctamente). 2 tightly (ropa).

ajustado, -a *adj.* 1 correct, right (correcto). 2 tight: *una camisa ajustada = a tight shirt.* 3 adjusted (resultado de ajustar).

ajustador, -a *adj.* 1 adjuster. || *s.m.* 2 tight waistcoat (jubón ajustado). 3 fitter (operario).

ajustamiento *s.m.* V. **ajuste.**

ajustar *v.t.* y *pron.* 1 to fit (encajar). 2 to adapt (adapt). 3 to adjust (regular). 4 to arrange, to sort out (arreglar). || *v.t.* 5 to settle (concertar). 6 to pay, to settle (liquidar el importe de una cuenta). 7 to contract, to engage (contratar). 8 to fix (un precio). 9 (Am.) to be (cumplir años). || *v.pron.* 10 to adapt oneself (adaptarse). 11 to conform (conformar). 12 to come to an agreement (llegar a un acuerdo). || **13 — cuentas,** to settle accounts.

ajuste *s.m.* 1 adjustment (acción de ajustar). 2 fitting (ropa). 3 agreement (acuerdo). 4 hiring, taking on (acción de contratar). 5 FIN. settlement. 6 fixing (de precios). 7 TEC. fitting (ensamblaje). 8 arrangement (arreglo).

ajusticiado, -a *s.m.* y *f.* executed person.

ajusticiamiento *s.m.* execution.

ajusticiar *v.t.* to execute.

al *contr.* 1 when, on (con infinitivo): *al levantarme = on getting up when I got up.* || **2 al mediodía,** at midday. **3 al menos,** at least.

ala *s.f.* 1 wing (de aves, aviones, insectos). 2 brim (de sombrero). 3 eaves (del tejado). 4 wing (parte lateral de una casa). **5** wing, flank (flanco). **6** MIL. flank, wing. **7** DEP. wing. **8** POL. wing. || **9 ahuecar el –,** to beat it (marcharse). **10 cortar a uno las alas,** to clip someone's wings.

alabanza *s.f.* praise: *en alabanza de = in praise of.*

alabar *v.t.* **1** to praise. || *v.pron.* **2** to boast (vanagloriarse).

alabarda *s.f.* halberd.

alabardero, -a *s.m.* y *f.* **1** HIST. halberdier. **2** paid applauder (en el teatro).

alabastro *s.m.* alabaster.

alacena *s.m.* built-in cupboard.

alacrán *s.m.* **1** scorpion (insecto). **2** toadfish (pejesapo).

alado, -a *adj.* **1** winged, flying (con alas). **2** (fig.) swift, winged, quick, rapid (rápido).

alagar *v.t.* to flood.

alambicadamente *adv.* subtly.

alambicado, -a *adj.* **1** distilled (destilado). **2** subtle (sutil).

alambicamiento *s.m.* **1** distillation (destilación). **2** sutlety (sutileza).

alambicar *v.t.* **1** to distil (destilar). **2** to scrutinize (examinar). **3** to sutilize (hablar o escribir con sutileza).

alambrada *s.f.* **1** wire netting (reja). **2** wire fence (valla). **3** MIL. barbed-wire entanglement.

alambrado *s.m.* **1** wire netting (reja). **2** wire fence (valla). **3** ELEC. wiring.

alambrar *v.t.* **1** to wire (cercar con alambre). || *v.i.* **2** to clear up (despejarse el cielo).

alambre *s.m.* wire (hilo): **alambre de espino,** barbed wire.

alameda *s.f.* **1** boulevard (avenida). **2** BOT. poplar grove.

álamo *s.m.* poplar (árbol y madera).

alancear *v.t.* **1** to spear (dar lanzadas). **2** to reprimand (zaherir).

alano, -a *adj./s.m.*y *f.* mastiff (perro).

alar *s.m.* **1** eaves (alero de tejado). **2** pavement (acera).

alarde *s.m.* **1** display, show (ostentación). **2** MIL. review, parade.

alardear *v.i.* **1** to show off, to boast.

alargadera *s.f.* **1** TEC. extensión. **2** QUIM. adapter.

alargador *adj.* lenghtening.

alargamiento *s.m.* **1** lenghtening, extension. **2** prolongation (de tiempo).

alargar *v.t.* y *v.pron.* **1** to lengthen (dar más longitud). **2** to stretch (estirar). **3** to prolong (prolongar). **4** to put off (tratar con detenimiento). || *v.t.* **5** to pass, to give (dar). **6** to stretch (el cuello). **7** to spin out (discurso, historia, chiste).

alarido *s.m.* **1** scream, yell (grito). **2** war cry (grito de guerra).

alarife *s.m.* **1** bricklayer (albañil). **2** master builder (maestro de obras).

alarma *s.f.* **1** alarm (señal o aviso). **2** alarm (inquietud, susto). || **3 dar la –,** to give the alarm. **4 falsa –,** false alarm.

alarmado, -a *adj.* alarmed.

alarmante *adj.* alarming.

alarmar *v.t.* **1** to alarm (dar la alarma). **2** to alarm (asustar). **3** MIL. to call to arms. || *v.pron.* **3** to be o get alarmed.

alarmista *s.m.* y *f.* **1** alarmist. || *adj.* **2** alarming, alarmist.

alazán o **alazano** *adj.* y *s.* sorrel (caballo).

alba *s.f.* dawn, daybreak: *al alba = at dawn.*

albacea *s.m.* y *f.* **1** executor (hombre). **2** executrix (mujer).

albahaca *s.f.* basil.

albaicín *s.m.* hilly district.

albanés, -esa *adj./s.m.*y *f.* Albanian.

albañil *s.m.* bricklayer, mason.

albañilería *s.f.* bricklaying.

albarán *s.m.* invoice (recibo).

albarca *s.f.* **1** sandal (albarca). **2** clog (zueco).

albarda *s.f.* packsaddle (aparejo).

albardero, -a *s.m.* y *f.* saddle maker.

albardilla *s.f.* **1** saddle (silla). **2** ARQ. coping. **3** lard (capa de tocino).

albardón *s.m.* **1** packsaddle (aparejo). **2** ARQ. coping.

albaricoque *s.m.* apricot.

albaricoquero *s.m.* apricot tree.

albatros *s.m.* ZOOL. albatross.

albear *v.i.* to whiten (blanquear).

albedrío *s.m.* **1** liberty (libertad). **2** whim, caprice (capricho).

alberca *s.f.* tank (depósito de agua).

albergar *v.t.* y *pron.* **1** to give shelter (dar albergue). **2** to take shelter (recibir albergue).

albergue *s.m.* **1** shelter, refuge (refugio). **2** lodgings (lugar de hospedaje). **3** orphanage (para huérfanos). **4** lair, den (para animales). || **5 – de jóvenes,** youth hostel.

albinismo *s.m.* albinismo.

albino, -a *adj./s.m.*y *f.* albino.

albo *adj.* white (blanco).

albóndiga o **almóndiga** *s.f.* meatball.

albor *s.m.* **1** whiteness (blancura). **2** beginning (principio). || *pl.* **3** daylight, dawn light (luz del alba). **4** youth (juventud).

alborada *s.f.* **1** daybreak, dawn (alba). **2** MIL. reveille (toque militar). **3** MUS. aubade.

alborear *v.i.* to dawn (amanecer).

albornoz *s.m.* bathrobe (bata).

alborotadamente *adv.* noisily.

alborotadizo, -a *adj.* excitable, jumpy.

alborotado, -a *adj.* **1** excited (excitado). **2** reckless (aturdido). **3** noisy (ruidoso).

alborotador, -a *adj.* **1** noisy, rowdy (ruidoso). **2** rebellious (rebelde). || *s.m.* y *f.* **3** rebel (rebelde). **4** troublemaker (agitador).

alborotar *v.t.* y *pron.* **1** to make a noise, to make a racket (hacer ruido). **2** to incite, to rouse (sublevar). **3** to trouble, to disturb (inquietar). **4** to excite (excitar). || *v.pron.* **5** to get rough (encresparse el mar).

alboroto *s.m.* **1** din, racket (estrépito). **2** uproar, disturbance (jaleo). **3** rebellion (rebelión). **4** mutiny (motín). **5** scare (sobresalto). || *pl.* **6** (Am.) popcorn (palomitas de maíz).

alborozadamente *adv.* jubilantly, joyfully.

alborozado, -a *adj.* jubilant, overjoyed.

alborozar *v.t.* **1** to make happy, to fill with joy. || *v.pron.* **2** to be overjoyed.

alborozo *s.m.* joy, jubilation.

albricias *s.f.pl.* **1** reward (recompensa, regalo). || **2 ¡albricias!,** fantastic!, great!

albufera *s.f.* lagoon.

álbum *s.m.* album.

albumen *s.m.* BOT. albumen.

albúmina *s.f.* QUIM. albumin.

albur *s.m.* **1** dace (pez). **2** risk, chance (azar).

alcachofa *s.f.* **1** artichoke (planta). **2** nozzle (colador de ducha, etc.).

alcahuete *s.m.* y *f.* **1** drop-curtain (telón). **2** go-between (persona que concierta o encubre). **3** pimp, procurer (correveidile).

alcahuetear *v.i.* **1** to procure, to pimp (ser chulo de prostitutas). **2** to act as a go-between (concertar).

alcaide *s.m.* governor.

alcaldada *s.f.* abuse of authority.

alcalde *s.m.* **1** mayor (de un ayuntamiento). **2** DER. justice of the peace.

alcaldía *s.f.* **1** mayorality (oficio). **2** mayor's office (oficina).

álcali *s.m.* **1** QUIM. alkali. || **2 álcali volátil,** ammonia.

alcalinidad *s.f.* QUIM. alkalinity.

alcalino, -a *adj.* QUIM. alkaline.

alcaloide *adj.* y *s.* QUIM. alkaloid.

alcance *s.m.* **1** reach (acción de alcanzar). **2** reach (distancia): *estar al alcance = to be within reach.* **3** pursuit, chase (persecución). **4** deficit (saldo deudor). **5** importance (importancia). **6** consequence (consecuencia). **7** stop-press (noticias de última hora). **8** MIL. range (distancia a que llega el tiro de un arma). || **9 al – del oído,** within earshot. **10 al – de la voz,** within call.

alcancía *s.f.* moneybox, (fam.) piggy bank (hucha).

alcanfor *s.m.* camphor.

alcantarilla *s.f.* **1** sewer, drain (cloaca). **2** small bridge (puentecillo).

alcantarillado *s.m.* drains, drainage system.

alcantarillar *v.t.* to lay drains.

alcanzado, -a *adj.* **1** in debt (endeudado). **2** in need (necesitado).

alcanzar *v.t.* **1** to catch up with, to catch (unirse al que va delante). **2** to reach (tocar o coger lo que está alejado). **3** to perceive (percibir). **4** to get, to manage (conseguir). **5** to be enough (ser suficiente). **6** to live at the same time as (ser contemporáneo). **7** to know (saber). **8** to understand (entender). **9** to hit (una bala). **10** to see (ver).

alcaparra *s.f.* **1** BOT. caper (planta). **2** caper (botón de la flor).

alcaparrón *s.m.* BOT. caper.

alcaraván *s.m.* stone curlew (ave).

alcarraza *s.f.* jar, jug (vasija).

alcarria *s.f.* barren highland.

alcatraz *s.m.* 1 gannet (ave). 2 BOT. arum (planta).
alcaudón *s.m.* shrike (ave).
alcayata *s.f.* hook (escarpia).
alcazaba *s.f.* citadel.
alcázar *s.m.* 1 fortress, citadel (fortaleza). 2 royal palace (palacio real). 3 MAR. quarter-deck.
alce *s.m.* 1 ZOOL. moose, elk. 2 cut (naipes). 3 (Am.) collecting, gathering (acción de recoger la caña).
alcista *s.m.* y *f.* FIN. speculator, (fam.) bull.
alcoba *s.f.* 1 bedroom (dormitorio). 2 box (caja).
alcohol *s.m.* 1 alcohol. || 2 **— absoluto,** pure alcohol. 3 **— amílico,** amylic alcohol. 4 **— metílico,** methylated spirits.
alcohólico -a *adj./s.m.y f.* alcoholic.
alcoholismo *s.m.* alcoholism.
alcoholizado *s.m.* y *f.* alcoholic.
alcoholizar *v.t.* to alcoholize (mezclar con alcohol).
alcor *s.m.* hill (colina).
alcornoque *s.m.* 1 cork oak (árbol y madera). 2 idiot, dope (persona ignorante).
alcotán *s.m.* ZOOL. lanner (ave).
alcurnia *s.f.* lineage, ancestry (linaje).
aldaba *s.f.* 1 doorknocker (para llamar). 2 bolt, latch (para cerrar). || *pl.* 3 influence.
aldabón *s.m.* large doorknocker.
aldabonazo *s.m.* bang, knock.
aldea *s.f.* hamlet, small village.
aldeano *adj.* 1 rustic (rústico). 2 hamlet, village (de aldea). || *s.m.* y *f.* 3 villager.
aldehuela *s.f.* hamlet.
aldeorrio o **aldeorro** *s.m.* rural backwater.
aleación *s.f.* alloy.
aleatorio *adj.* lucky, fortuitous.
aleccionar *v.t.* 1 to teach (enseñar). 2 to instruct (instruir).
aledaño *adj.* 1 bordering, adjacent (contiguo). || *s.m.* 2 limit, border (límite). || *pl.* 3 surrounding area.
alegación *s.f.* 1 DER. allegation. 2 assertion (aserción).
alegar *v.t.* 1 to allege (citar algo que sirve de prueba). 2 DER. to plead, to put forward (aportar razones en favor de su caso). 3 (Am.) to argue, to dispute (discutir).
alegato *s.m.* 1 DER. plea (escrito). 2 declaration, statement (declaración).
alegoría *s.f.* allegory.
alegóricamente *adv.* allegorically.
alegórico *adj.* allegorical.
alegorización *s.f.* allegorization.
alegorizar *v.t.* allegorize.
alegrar *v.t.* 1 to cheer up, to make happy (causar alegría): *me alegraron = they cheered me up.* 2 to make beautiful (hermosear). 3 to liven up (avivar). 4 to poke (avivar el fuego). 5 to rouse (toro). 6 to scrape (legrar). || *v.pron.* 7 to be glad, to be pleased (sentir alegría): *me alegro que hayas venido = I'm glad you've come.* 8 to get merry (achisparse). 9 to cheer up (animarse).
alegre *adj.* 1 happy, cheerful (feliz). 2 cheerful (de temperamento). 3 lively, fun (divertido). 4 bright (color, tiempo). 5 lively (música). 6 good, cheering (noticia). 7 frivolous (frívolo). 8 immoral (inmoral). 9 tipsy, merry (achispado).
alegremente *adv.* happily, cheerfully.
alegreto *adj.* y *s.* MUS. allegretto.
alegría *s.f.* 1 joy, happiness (felicidad). 2 cheerfulness (de buen humor). 3 brightness (colores, tiempo, etc.). 4 BOT. sesame (ajonjolí). || *pl.* 5 festivities. || 6 **saltar de —,** to jump for joy.
alegro, -a *adj.* y *s.* MUS. allegro.
alegrón *s.m.* extreme happiness (alegría muy intensa).
alejandrino *s.m.* y *f.* Alexandrine.
alejar *v.t.* 1 to move away (colocar más lejos). 2 to keep away (mantener lejos). || *v.pron.* 3 to go away (irse). 4 to move away (colocar más lejos).
alelar *v.t.* 1 to stun, to bewilder. || *v.pron.* 2 to be stunned, to be bewildered.
alelí *s.f.* BOT. wallflower (planta).
aleluya *interj.* 1 hallelujah. || *s.m.* 2 Easter time (tiempo pascual). 3 witticism (dicho ingenioso). || *s.f.* 4 BOT. wood sorrel (planta). 5 joy (alegría). 6 doggerel (verso despreciable). 7 daub (pintura despreciable).
alemán, -ana *adj. s.m.* y *f.* German.
alentado, -a *adj.* 1 brave (valiente). 2 proud (orgulloso).
alentar *v.i.* 1 to breathe (respirar). || *v.t.* y *pron.* 2 to encourage, to cheer (animar).
alerce *s.m.* larch (árbol y madera).
alergia *s.f.* allergy.
alérgico, -a *adj.* allergic: *alérgico al polvo = allergic to the dust.*
alero *s.m.* 1 eaves (borde del tejado). 2 mudguard (de los coches).
alerón *s.m.* aileron (de un avión).
alerta *adv.* 1 alertly, watchfully. || *adj.* 2 alert, watchful. || *interj.* 3 look out!, careful! || 4 **estar —,** to be on the alert.
alertado, -a *p.p.* 1 de **alertar.** || *adj.* 2 alerted.
alertamente *adv.* alertly.
alertar *v.t.* 1 to alert (poner alerta). || *v.pron.* 2 to suspect (sospechar).
aleta *s.f.* 1 fin (de pez). 2 flipper (de foca, etc.). 3 wing (ala). 4 wing (de coche). 5 blade (de hélice).
aletargar *v.t.* 1 to make lethargic (producir letargo). || *v.pron.* 2 to be feel lethargic (padecer letargo).
aletazo *s.m.* 1 wingbeat (de aves). 2 flick (de peces).
aletear *v.i.* 1 to flap its wings (aves). 2 to move its fins (peces).
aleteo *s.m.* 1 flapping (aves). 2 flicking (peces). 3 beating (corazón).
alevín *s.m.* 1 small fish, fry (cría del pez). 2 beginner (principiante).
alevosía *s.f.* 1 treachery (traición). 2 caution (antes de un delito).
alevoso o **aleve** *adj.* 1 treacherous. || *s.m.* 2 traitor.
alexia *s.f.* MED. alexia.
alfa *s.f.* 1 alpha (letra griega). || 2 **partículas —,** FIS. alpha particles. 3 **rayos —,** FIS. alpha rays.
alfabéticamente *adv.* alphabetically.
alfabético, -a *adj.* alphabetical.
alfabetizado, -a *adj.* literate.
alfabetizar *v.t.* 1 to put in alphabetical order (ordenar). 2 to teach to read and write (enseñar a leer y escribir).
alfabeto, -a *s.m.* y *f.* alphabet.
alfaguara *s.m.* spring (manantial).
alfalfa *s.f.* BOT. alfalfa.
alfanje *s.m.* 1 swordfish (pez espada). 2 cutlass (sable corvo).
alfarería *s.f.* 1 pottery (arte del alfarero). 2 pottery shop (tienda). 3 pottery workshop (lugar de fabricación).
alfarero *s.m.* potter.
alfarje *s.m.* oil-stone (piedra).
alféizar *s.m.* ARQ. embrasure, splay.
alfeñique *s.m.* weakling (persona débil).
alférez *s.m.* 1 standard bearer (abanderado). 2 subaltern (oficial). || 3 **— de fragata,** midshipman. 4 **— de navío,** sublieutenant.
alfil *s.m.* bishop (ajedrez).
alfiler *s.m.* 1 pin (clavillo). 2 brooch, pin (joya). *s.pl.* 3 pin money (dinero). || 4 **estar prendido con alfileres,** to be wobbly.
alfombra *s.f.* 1 carpet (para el suelo). 2 rug, mat (alfombrilla).
alfombrado, -a *adj. p.p.* 1 de **alfombrar.** || 2 carpeting.
alfombrar *v.t.* to carpet.
alfombrilla *s.f.* rug, mat.
alforja *s.f.* 1 saddlebag (bolsa doble). 2 provisions (provisiones).
alga *s.f.* BOT. alga.
algarabía *s.f.* 1 Arabic (lengua árabe). 2 gibberish, gobbledygook (lenguaje incomprensible). 3 racket (griterío). 4 BOT. broom.
algarada *s.f.* uproar, din (alboroto).
algarroba *s.f.* 1 BOT. vetch (planta). 2 vetch seed (semilla). 3 carob bean (fruto).
algarrobal *s.m.* 1 vetch plantation (de algarroba). 2 carob tree plantation (de algarrobo).
algarrobilla *s.f.* 1 alga (alga). 2 vetch (algarroba).
algarrobo *s.m.* carob tree (árbol).
álgebra *s.f.* MAT. algebra.
algebraico, -a *adj.* algebraic.
algebrista *s.m.* y *f.* algebraist.
algidez *s.f.* MED. algidity.
álgido, -a *adj.* 1 cold, icy; (p.u.) algid. || 2 **punto —,** critical moment.
algo *pron.indef.* 1 something: *comer algo = to eat something; es algo diferente = it's something different.* 2 anything (negativo o interrogativo): *¿quieres algo? = do you want anything?* || *adv.* 3 rather, quite, somewhat: *es algo caro = it's somewhat expensive.* || 4 **— es —,** it's better than nothing. 5 **tomar —,** to have a drink.
algodón *s.m.* 1 cotton (tejido): *hecho de algodón = made of cotton.* 2 BOT. cotton plant (planta). 3 MED. swab. || 4 **— hi-**

drófilo, cotton wool. 5 — **pólvora,** guncotton. 6 **estar criado entre algodones,** to be mollycoddled.
algodonal *s.m.* cotton plantation.
algodonar *v.t.* to pack with cotton wool.
algodoncillo *s.m.* BOT. milkweed.
algodonero, -a *adj.* 1 cotton. || *s.m.* 2 BOT. cotton plant (planta). || *s.m.* y *f.* 3 cotton dealer (vendedor). 4 cotton worker (obrero).
algodonoso, -a *adj.* cottony.
algoritmo *s.m.* MAT. algorism.
alguacil o **aguacil** DER. bailiff.
alguacilillo *s.m.* alguazil (toros).
alguien *pron.indef.* 1 someone, somebody: *alguien viene = someone is coming.* 2 anyone, anybody (interrogativo): *¿alguien fuma? = does anyone smoke?* || 3 **ser —,** to be someone.
algún *adj.* (apócope de **alguno**) 1 any, some: *algún día = some day.* || 2 — **tanto,** a bit; a little (un poco).
alguno, -a *adj.* 1 some (afirmativo): *compré algunos discos = I bought some records.* 2 any (interrogativo): *¿quieres alguno? = do you want any?* 3 a few (unos pocos, bastante): *hemos tenido algunos problemas = we've had a few problems.* || *pron.indef.* 4 one (singular): *alguno de nosotros = one of us.* 5 some (plural). 6 someone, somebody (alguien). || 7 — **que otro,** a few; one or two.
alhaja *s.f.* 1 jewel (joya). 2 decoration (adorno). 3 (fig.) treasure, jewel (cosa muy valiosa). 4 (fig.) treasure (persona).
alhajado, -a *adj.* rich, wealthy.
alhajar *v.t.* 1 to furnish (amueblar). 2 to adorn with jewels (enjoyar).
alharaca *s.f.* y *pl.* fuss.
alhelí o **alelí** *s.m.* 1 BOT. wallflower. || 2 — **de Mahón,** Virginia stock.
alhóndiga *s.f.* corn exchange.
aliado, -a *adj.* 1 allied. || *s.m.* y *f.* 2 ally.
alianza *s.f.* 1 alliance (convenio, unión). 2 engagement ring (anillo de compromiso).
aliar *v.t.* 1 to ally (concordar). || *v.pron.* 2 to form an alliance (formar una alianza).
alias *adv.* 1 alias (por otro nombre). || *s.m.* 2 alias.
alicaído, -a *adj.* 1 weak (débil). 2 sad (triste). 3 depressed (desalentado). 4 drooping (con alas caídas).
alicatar *v.t.* to tile.
alicates *s.m.pl.* pliers.
aliciente *s.m.* 1 incentive, inducement (incentivo). 2 spur, stimulus (estímulo). 3 attraction (atracción).
alícuota *adj.* aliquot.
alienable *adj.* alienable.
alienación *s.f.* alienation.
alienado, -a *adj.* 1 insane, demented (demente). || *s.m.* y *f.* 2 lunatic.
alienar *v.t.* to alienate.
alienígena *adj./s.m.* y *f.* alien.
alienismo *s.m.* alienism.
aliento *s.m.* 1 breath (aire expulsado). 2 breathing (acción de alentar, respiración). 3 courage, bravery (valentía). 4 encouragement (ánimo). || 5 **de un —,** in one breath. 6 **mal —,** bad breath.
aligeramiento *s.m.* 1 lightenning (de un peso). 2 alleviation (alivio).
aligerar *v.t.* y *pron.* 1 to lighten (quitar peso). || *v.t.* 2 to quicken (acelerar). 3 to put back, to difer (diferir).
alijo *s.m.* 1 unloading (de un barco). 2 contraband (contrabando).
alimaña *s.f.* vermin, pest.
alimentación *s.f.* 1 food (comida). 2 feeding (acción de alimentar). 3 TEC. feed: *bomba de alimentación = feed pump.*
alimentante *adj.* nourishing.
alimentar *v.t.* y *pron.* 1 to feed (dar alimento). || *v.t.* 2 to supply (suministrar). 3 TEC. to feed (dar energía). 4 to feed (fomentar vicios, etc.). 5 to maintain, to support (a una familia).
alimenticio *adj.* 1 nourishing (que alimenta). 2 food: *valor alimenticio = food value.*
alimento *s.m.* 1 food (comida). 2 (fig.) food. 3 encouragement (ánimo). 4 fuel (para las pasiones). || *s.pl.* 5 DER. alimony.
alimoche *s.m.* ZOOL. African vulture (ave).
alimón *m.adv.* **al -,** together.
alineación *s.f.* 1 TEC. alignment: *fuera de alineación = out of alignment.* 2 DEP. line-up.
alineado, -a *adj.* aligned: *país no alineado = non-aligned country.*
alinear *v.t.* 1 to align, to line up (poner en línea). 2 MIL. to form up. || *v.pron.* 3 to line up (poner en línea). 4 MIL. to fall in.
aliñar *v.t.* 1 to decorate, to adorn (aderezar). 2 to govern (gobernar). 3 to administer (administrar). 4 to season (condimentar). 5 to dress (ensaladas). 6 (Am.) to set (arreglar los huesos).
aliño *s.m.* 1 adornment (adorno). 2 preparation (preparación). 3 seasoning (condimento). 4 dressing (de ensaladas).
alioli *s.m.* garlic and oil sauce.
alisar *v.t.* 1 to smooth (poner liso). 2 to smooth (el pelo). || *s.m.* 3 alder grove (sitio con alisos).
aliseda, alisal o **alisar** *s.f.* alder grove.
alisios *adj.* 1 trade: *los vientos alisios = the trade winds.* || *s.m.pl.* 2 trade winds.
aliso *s.m.* alder (árbol).
alistado, -a *adj.* 1 MIL. enlisted. 2 enrolled (inscrito).
alistamiento *s.m.* 1 MIL. enlistment. 2 enrollment (en un colegio, etc.).
alistar *v.t.* 1 to put on a list (poner en lista). 2 MIL. to recruit, to enlist. 3 to prepare (preparar). 4 to take up (espabilar). || *v.i.* 5 to wake up, to liven up (espabilarse). || *v.pron.* 6 MIL. to join up, to enlist (como soldado). 7 to enrol (inscribirse). 8 (Am.) to get ready (arreglarse).
aliteración *s.f.* alliteration.
aliviadero *s.m.* overflow channel.
aliviar *v.t.* 1 MED. to alleviate, to relieve (dolores). 2 to lighten (aligerar). 3 to quicken (avivar el paso). 4 to help (ayudar). || *v.pron.* 5 to diminish (disminuir). 6 to get better, to improve (mejorar).
alivio *s.m.* 1 relief, alleviation: *¡qué alivio! = what a relief!* 2 lightenning (de una carga). 3 MED. relief.
aljaba *s.f.* quiver (caja para flechas).
aljibe *s.m.* 1 tank, cistern (cisterna). 2 MAR. tanker (barco).
aljofaina *s.f.* washbasin (jofaina).
aljófar *s.m.* pearl (perla).
alma *s.f.* 1 soul. 2 spirit, heart (espíritu). 3 soul, person (individuo). 4 crux, heart (parte principal de una cosa): *el alma del problema = the crux of the problem.* 5 scaffold pole (madero vertical). 6 (fig.) heart and soul, lifeblood (lo que vitaliza o da fuerza a una cosa). 7 MUS. sound post. 8 hollow (hueco). || 9 — **de cántaro,** insensitive person. 10 — **de Dios,** good soul. 11 **doler el —,** to be weary. 12 **encomendar el —,** to commend one's soul to God. 13 **entregar el —,** to pass away. 14 **estar con el — en un hilo,** to have one's heart in one's mouth. 15 **no tener —,** to have a heart of stone.
almacén *s.m.* 1 warehouse (para guardar mercancías). 2 store, department store (tienda grande). 3 magazine (en las imprentas).
almacenaje *s.m.* 1 storage (almacenamiento). 2 storage charges (gastos).
almacenamiento *s.m.* storage.
almacenar *v.t.* 1 to store, to put into store (guardar). 2 to collect, to keep (reunir muchas cosas).
almacenero *s.m.* warehouseman.
almacenista *s.m.* warehouse owner.
almácigo *s.m.* 1 BOT. mastic tree (árbol). 2 nursery (semillero).
almadraba *s.f.* 1 tunny net (red). 2 tunny-fishing ground (lugar).
almadreña o **madreña** *s.f.* clog (zueco).
almanaque *s.m.* almanac.
almazara *s.f.* oil mill (molino de aceite).
almeja *s.f.* clam.
almena *s.f.* battlements.
almenado, -a *adj.* battlemented.
almenar *v.t.* to construct battlements.
almenara *s.f.* 1 beacon (fuego hecho como señal). 2 candelabra (candelero).
almendra *s.f.* 1 BOT. almond. 2 pebble (piedra pequeña). 3 cut-glass drop (diamante en forma de almendra). || 4 — **amarga,** bitter almond. 5 — **dulce,** sweet almond.
almendrada *s.f.* almond milk shake (bebida).
almendrado, -a *adj.* 1 almond-shaped. || *s.m.* 2 macaroon.
almendral *s.m.* almond orchard.
almendrero *s.m.* BOT. almond tree (árbol).
almendrilla *s.f.* gravel (piedra machacada).
almendro *s.m.* almond tree (árbol).
almendruco *s.m.* green almond.

almete *s.m.* helmet (casco).
almiar *s.m.* AGR. haystack (pajar).
almíbar *s.m.* 1 syrup. || **2 estar hecho un –,** to be sweet.
almibarado, -a *adj.* syrupy.
almibarar *v.t.* 1 to cover with syrup (cubrir). 2 to use sweet words (efectuar dulzura).
almidón *s.m.* starch.
almidonado, -a *adj.* starched.
almidonar *v.t.* to starch.
almimbar *s.m.* mimbar, minbar.
alminar *s.m.* minaret.
almiranta *s.f.* MAR. viceadmiral's ship (barco).
almirantazgo *s.m.* admiralty.
almirante *s.m.* MIL. admiral.
almirez *s.m.* mortar (mortero).
almizcle *s.m.* musk.
almizcleño, -a *adj.* musky.
almohada *s.f.* 1 pillow (de la cama). 2 cushion (para sentarse). || **3 consultar con la –,** to sleep on it.
almohadazo *s.m.* blow with a cushion.
almohadilla *s.f.* 1 small cushion (cojín pequeño). 2 cushion (de la voluta del capitel jónico). 3 hardness pad (de un sillar).
almohadillado, -a *adj.* padded.
almohadillar *v.t.* to pad (acolchar).
almohadón *s.m.* pillowcase, pillowslip (funda).
almóndiga o **almondiguilla** *s.f.* meatball.
almoneda *s.f.* 1 auction (subasta). 2 sale (venta de objetos a poco precio).
almorrana *s.f.* MED. piles, haemorrhoids.
almorzar *v.i.* 1 to have lunch. || *v.t.* 2 to have for lunch.
almuecín o **almuédano** *s.m.* REL. muezzin.
almuerzo *s.m.* 1 lunch (al mediodía). 2 breakfast (desayuno).
alocado, -a *adj.* 1 mad, crazy (loco). 2 irresponsible (falto de cordura).
alocución *s.f.* allocution.
áloe, aloe o **aloes** *s.m.* 1 BOT. aloe. 2 MED. aloes.
alojado, -a *adj.* 1 housed. || 2 (Am.) guest, lodger (invitado).
alojamiento *s.m.* 1 lodgings, accommodation (lugar). 2 MIL. billeting (acción). 3 billet, quarters (lugar).
alojar *v.t.* 1 to lodge, to accommodate (hospedar). 2 MIL. to quarter, to billet. || *v.pron.* 3 to lodge, to be accommodated. 4 MIL. to be billeted, to be quartered. 5 to lodge (encajar).
alondra *s.f.* ZOOL. lark (ave).
alopecia *s.f.* MED. alopecia.
alpaca *s.f.* alpaca.
alpargata *s.f.* canvas sandal.
alpargatería *s.f.* 1 sandal factory (fábrica). 2 sandal shop (tienda).
alpestre *adj.* 1 Alpine (alpino). 2 wild (silvestre).
alpinismo *s.m.* climbing, mountaineering.
alpinista *s.m.* y *f.* climber, mountaineer.
alpino *adj.* Alpine.
alpiste *s.m.* 1 BOT. canary grass (planta). 2 birdseed (semilla).
alquería *s.f.* 1 farm (granja). 2 farmstead (conjunto de casas).
alquilable *adj.* rentable, for rent.
alquilar *v.t.* 1 to rent (casa, piso, televisión). 2 to hire (coche). 3 to charter (avión, barco).
alquiler *s.m.* 1 renting, hiring (acción de alquilar). 2 rent, hire charge (precio). || **3 de –,** for rent. **4 pagar el –,** to pay the rent.
alquimia *s.f.* alchemy.
alquímico, -a *adj.* alchemic.
alquimista *s.m.* y *f.* alchemist.
alquitrán *s.m.* 1 tar. || **2 – mineral,** coal tar.
alrededor *adv.* 1 around, round, about (en círculo): *alrededor de la ciudad = around the city.* 2 about, around (con aproximación): *alrededor de cien = about a hundred.* || *s.m.pl.* 3 surroundings (contornos).
alta *s.f.* 1 enrollment (ingreso). 2 MED. discharge. || **3 dar de –,** to discharge. **4 darse de –,** MIL. to enrol.
altamente *adv.* highly, extremely.
altanería *s.f.* 1 height (altura). 2 pride (orgullo). 3 falconry (caza con aves).
altanero, -a *adj.* 1 arrogant, haughty (arrogante). 2 proud (orgulloso).
altar *s.m.* 1 REL. altar. || **2 – mayor,** high altar.
altavoz *s.m.* speaker, loudspeaker.
alterabilidad *s.f.* changeability.
alterable *adj.* changeable.
alteración *s.f.* 1 alteration. 2 MED. deterioration. 3 dispute, quarrel (riña).
alteradizo, -a *adj.* changeable.
alterante *adj.* changing.
alterar *v.t.* y *pron.* 1 to change, to alter (cambiar). 2 to adulterate, to spoil (adulterar). 3 to change for the worse (empeorar). 4 to upset, to disturb (producir un trastorno).
altercado *s.m.* altercation, quarrel, row.
altercador, -a *adj.* 1 argumentative. || *s.m.* y *f.* 2 argumentative person.
altercante *adj.* argumentative, captious.
altercar *v.i.* to argue, to quarrel.
alter ego *s.m.* alter ego.
alternación *s.f.* alternation.
alternadamente *adv.* alternately.
alternado, -a *adj.* alternate.
alternador *s.m.* ELEC. alternator.
alternancia *s.f.* alternation.
alternante *adj.* alternating.
alternar *v.t.* 1 to alternate (por turno). || *v.i.* 2 to alternate (por turnos). 3 to take turns, to change (hacer cambios). 4 to vary (variar). 5 to mix, to associate, to go around (tener amistad con personas muy consideradas). || *v.pron.* 6 to take turns.
alternativa *s.f.* 1 alternation (alternación). 2 alternative, option (opción). 3 shift work (trabajo por turnos). 4 AGR. rotation.
alternativamente *adv.* alternately.
alternativo *s.m.* y *adj.* alternating.
alterno, -a *adj.* 1 alternating (alternativo). 2 BOT. alternate. || **3 corriente alterna,** alternating current.
alteza *s.f.* 1 height (altura). 2 sublimity (sublimidad). || **3 Alteza,** Highness (tratamiento).
altibajos *s.m.pl.* 1 bumps, ups and downs (de un terreno). 2 (fig.) ups and downs.
altillo *s.m.* 1 hill (cerro). 2 boot (maletero). 3 (Am.) attic (desván).
altipampa *s.f.* high plateau.
altiplanicie *s.f.* high plateau.
altísimo *adj.* 1 very high. || **2 El Altísimo,** the Almighty.
altisonante o **altísono** *adj.* high-sounding, pompous.
altitud *s.f.* altitude, height.
altivamente *adv.* arrogantly, haughtily.
altivecer *v.t.* to be haughty.
altivez o **altiveza** *s.f.* arrogance, haughtiness.
altivo, -a *adj. arrogant, haughty.*
alto, -a *adj.* 1 **tall (persona, árbol).** 2 high, tall (edificio). 3 high (montaña, precio, puesto, muro, río, etc.). 4 upper (piso, planta). 5 high (voz). 6 loud (fuerte): *la música está muy alta = the music is very loud.* 7 late (hora). 8 MUS. sharp (nota). 9 MUS. alto (instrumento o voz). 10 difficult (difícil). 11 deep, profound (profundo). 12 noble (noble). || *s.m.* 13 height (altura). || *adv.* 14 high up (en un lugar elevado). 15 loud, loudly (con voz fuerte): *cantar muy alto = to sing very loudly.* || **16 alta sociedad,** high society. **17 clase alta,** upper class. **18 desde lo –,** from the top. **19 pasar por –,** to ignore.
altozano *s.m.* 1 hillock (pequeña elevación). 2 (Am.) parvis (atrio).
altramuz *s.m.* lupin (planta).
altruismo *s.m.* altruism.
altruista *adj.* 1 altruistic. || *s.m.* y *f.* 2 altruist.
altura *s.f.* 1 height, altitude (elevación sobre la tierra). 2 height (altura). 3 MAT. height. 4 GEOG. latitude. 5 summit (cumbre). || *s.pl.* 6 heaven (cielo). || **7 a estas alturas,** at this stage; at this time. **8 estar a la – de algo,** to be equal to something. **9 tomar –,** to climb.
alubia *s.f.* kidney bean.
alucinación *s.f.* hallucination.
alucinadamente *adv.* (fam.) amazingly, incredibly.
alucinado, -a *adj.* amazed (pasmado): *estar o quedar alucinado = to be amazed.*
alucinador *adj.* hallucinatory.
alucinamiento *s.m.* hallucination.
alucinante *adj.* 1 hallucinatory. 2 (fam.) amazing, incredible (impresionante).
alucinar *v.t.* 1 to hallucinate (por drogas, etc.). 2 to deceive (engañar). 3 (fam.) to be amazed (estar pasmado). || *v.pron.* 4 to delude oneself.
alucinógeno *s.m.* 1 hallucinogen. || *adj.* 2 hallucinogenic.
alud *s.m.* avalanche (de nieve).
aludir *v.i.* to allude.
alumbrado *adj.* 1 lit up, lighted. || *s.m.* y *f.* 2 REL. illuminist. || *s.m.* 3 lighting (conjunto de luces).

alumbrar *v.i.* 1 to shed light (lucir). || *v.t.* 2 to illuminate, to light (iluminar). 3 to give light (dar luz). 4 to restore the sight of (dar vista al ciego). 5 to teach (enseñar). 6 to give birth (dar a luz). 7 to hit (golpear). || *v.pron.* 8 (fam.) to get sloshed (emborracharse).
alúmina *s.f.* QUIM. alumina.
aluminio *s.m.* aluminium.
alumnado *s.m.* student body.
alumno, -a *s.m.* y *f.* 1 pupil (de colegio). 2 student (de universidad).
alunizar *v.i.* to land on the moon.
alusión *s.f.* allusion, reference.
aluvial *adj.* alluvial.
aluvión *s.m.* flood (inundación).
alveolado *adj.* honeycombed.
alveolar *adj.* alveolar.
alvéolo o **alveolo** *s.m.* 1 cell (celdilla). 2 ANAT. alveolus.
alza *s.f.* 1 price rise (subida de precio). 2 MIL. sight (de un arma). 3 sluice gate (de una presa). || **4 en –,** rising. **5 estar en –,** to rise.
alzacuello *s.m.* collar, (fam.) dog collar.
alzada *s.f.* 1 height (altura de un caballo). 2 summer grazing (lugar de pastos para el verano).
alzado *adj.* 1 fixed (precio). 2 fraudulent (fraudulento). 3 (Am.) insolent (insolente). 4 (Am.) on heat (encelo).
alzamiento *s.m.* 1 lifting, raising (acción de alzar). 2 bid (puja). 3 rebellion, revolt (sublevación). 4 rise, increase (de precios).
alzar *v.t.* 1 to raise, to lift (levantar). 2 to steal, to lift (robar). 3 to gather in (la cosecha). 4 to gather (los pliegos). || *v.t.* e *i.* 5 REL. to elevate (la hostia). || *v.pron.* 6 POL. to revolt, to rise (sublevarse). 7 DER. to make an appeal (apelar). 8 COM. to go fraudulantly bankrupt (quebrar fraudulentamente). 9 to stick out (sobresalir).
allá *adv.* 1 there, over there (lugar). 2 long ago, back (tiempo): *allá en verano = back in the summer.* || **3 en el más –,** in the beyond. **4 más –,** further on. **5 más – de,** beyond. **6 por –,** there or thereabouts.
allanamiento *s.m.* 1 levelling, flattening (acción de allanar). 2 DER. submission. || **3 – de morada,** housebreaking.
allanar *v.t.* 1 to level, to flatten (poner llano). 2 to overcome (vencer una dificultad). 3 to pacify (pacificar). 4 to burgle, to break into (una casa). || *v.pron.* 5 to submit, to agree (conformarse).
allegado, -a *adj.* 1 immediate (inmediato). || *s.m.* y *f.* 2 relative, relation (pariente). 3 supporter (partidario).
allegamiento *s.m.* gathering, collecting.
allegar *v.t.* 1 to gather, to collect (reunir). 2 to add (añadir). || *v.i.* 3 to arrive (llegar). || *v.pron.* 4 to agree (ponerse de acuerdo).
allende *adv.* 1 over there (de la parte de allá). 2 beyond (más allá de). 3 besides (además).
allí *adv.* 1 there, over there (en o a aquel lugar). 2 then (entonces). || **3 – dentro,** in there. **4 por –,** that way.
ama *s.m.* 1 owner of the house (dueña de la casa). 2 lady of the house (señora de la casa). 3 owner (dueña). 4 mistress (mujer, respeto de los criados). 5 house keeper (criada de una casa). || **6 – de cría** o **de leche,** wet nurse. **7 – de llaves** o **de gobierno,** housekeeper. **8 – seca,** nurse.
amabilidad *s.f.* 1 kindness. 2 amiability (afabilidad).
amabilísimo *adj.* very friendly.
amable *adj.* 1 kind, pleasant (afable). 2 friendly, nice (simpático). 3 loveable (que merece ser amado).
amablemente *adv.* kindly.
amachinarse *v.pron.* (Am.) to live together (amancebarse).
amacho, -a *adj.* (Am.) strong, vigorous (vigoroso).
amado, -a *adj.* 1 beloved. || *s.m.* y *f.* 2 lover.
amadrinar *v.t.* 1 to yoke (caballerías). 2 to sponsor (apadrinar).
amaestrar *v.t.* 1 to train (adiestrar). 2 to teach (enseñar).
amagar *v.t.* 1 to threaten (amenazar). 2 to show signs (hacer intención de hacer o decir algo). 3 MED. to appear the first signs. 4 DEP. to feint. || *v.pron.* 5 to hide away (esconderse).
amago *s.m.* 1 first signs, symptom (principio de algo). 2 threat (amenaza). 3 DEP. feint.
amainar *v.t.* 1 MAR. to take in (las velas). || *v.i.* 2 to slacken, to drop (viento). 3 (fig.) to moderate, to ease off (perder intensidad).
amaine *s.m.* 1 MAR. taking in (velas). 2 slackening (viento). 3 calming down, abating (emociones, etc.).
amalgama *s.f.* amalgam.
amalgamación *s.f.* amalgamation.
amalgamador *s.m.* y *f.* amalgamator.
amalgamamiento *s.m.* amalgamation.
amalgamar *v.t.* to amalgamate.
amamantar *v.t.* to suckle, to breast-feed.
amancebamiento *s.m.* living together.
amancebarse *v.pron.* to live together.
amanecer *s.m.* 1 dawn, daybreak. || *v.i.* 2 to dawn, to get light (comenzar el día). 3 to appear (aparecer). 4 to find oneself at dawn (estar en un lugar al comenzar el día).
amanecida *s.f.* dawn, daybreak.
amaneradamente *adv.* affectedly.
amanerado, -a *adj.* affected, mannered.
amaneramiento *s.m.* affectation.
amanerarse *v.pron.* to become affected.
amanita *s.f.* BOT. amanito.
amansar *v.t.* 1 to tame (domesticar). 2 to calm (calmar).
amante *adj.* 1 loving. || *s.m.* y *f.* 2 lover. || *s.pl.* 3 lovers.
amanuense *s.m.* scribe (escribiente).
amañar *v.t.* 1 to do skilfully (disponer con maña). || *v.pron.* 2 to be skilful.
amapola *s.f.* BOT. poppy (planta).
amar *v.t.* to love (querer): *te amo = I love you.*
amaranto *s.m.* BOT. amaranth (planta).
amaraje *s.m.* landing.
amarar *v.i.* to land on the sea.
amargamente *adv.* bitterly.
amargar *v.t.* 1 to sour, to make bitter (poner amargo). 2 to embitter (una relación, persona). 3 to spoil (estropear). 4 to grieve (apenar). || *v.i.* 5 to taste bitter (tener sabor amargo). || *v.pron.* 6 to become bitter, (cosa). 7 to embitter, to become embittered (persona).
amargo, -a *adj.* 1 bitter, sour. 2 (fig.) bitter: *una experiencia amarga = a bitter experience.* 3 harsh, unpleasant (desapacible). || *s.m.* 4 bitterness (amargor). 5 bitters (licor).
amargor *s.m.* bitterness.
amargosamente *adv.* bitterly.
amargoso, -a *adj.* bitter.
amargura *s.f.* 1 bitterness (amargor). 2 grief, distress (pena).
amarillear *v.i.* to go yellow, to turn yellow (ponerse amarillo).
amarillecer *v.i.* to go o turn yellow.
amarillento, -a *adj.* 1 yellowish (color). 2 sallow (piel).
amarillejo *adj.* 1 yellowish (color). 2 sallow (piel).
amarilleo *s.m.* yellowing.
amarillez *s.f.* 1 yellowness (color). 2 sallowness (piel).
amarillo, -a *adj.* 1 yellow. || *s.m.* 2 yellow.
amarilloso *adj.* yellowish.
amarra *s.f.* 1 MAR. cable, mooring line (cuerda). 2 martingale (correa de caballo). || *s.pl.* 3 influence, connections (influencia).
amarradero *s.m.* 1 MAR. bollard (poste). 2 mooring (lugar donde se ata el barco). 3 mooring ring (argolla).
amarrado, -a *adj.* tied (atado).
amarraje *s.m.* mooring charge (impuesto).
amarrar *v.t.* 1 MAR. to moor, to tie up. 2 to fasten (sujetar).
amarre *s.m.* MAR. mooring.
amartelar *v.t.* 1 to make jealous (dar celos). 2 to make fall in love (enamorar). || *v.pron.* 3 to fall in love (enamorarse).
amartillar *v.t.* 1 to hammer (martillar). 2 to cock (un arma).
amasado, -a *adj.* doughy.
amasar *v.t.* 1 to knead (pan). 2 to mix (mezclar). 3 to amass (dinero).
amasijo *s.m.* 1 kneading (acción de amasar el pan). 2 mixture (mezcla). 3 job, task (tarea). 4 plot (confabulación).
amateur *adj.* y *s.m.* y *f.* amateur.
amatista *s.f.* amethyst.
amatorio, -a *adj.* love, (p.u.) amatory.
amazacotado, -a *adj.* 1 heavy (pesado). 2 shapeless (confuso). 3 out of proportion (desproporcionado).
amazona *s.f.* 1 HIST. amazon. 2 rider, horsewoman (que monta a caballo).
amazónico, -a o **amazonio, -a** *adj.* Amazon.
ambages *s.m.pl.* beating about the bush.

ámbar *s.m.* amber.
ambarino *adj.* amber.
ambición *s.f.* ambition.
ambicionar *v.t.* to strive after, to persue.
ambiciosamente *adv.* ambitiously.
ambicioso, -a *adj.* 1 ambitious. || *s.m.* y *f.* 2 ambitious person.
ambidextro, -a o **ambidiestro, -a** *adj.* ambidextrous.
ambientación *s.f.* 1 orientation (orientación). 2 atmosphere (ambiente). 3 setting (en el teatro, cine).
ambiental *adj.* environmental.
ambientar *v.t.* 1 to create an atmosphere (crear ambiente). 2 to set (tener lugar).
ambiente *adj.* 1 surrounding. || *s.m.* 2 atmosphere (aire que rodea los cuerpos). 3 (fig.) atmosphere (de un bar, ciudad, etc.). || 4 **medio —,** environment.
ambiguamente *adv.* ambiguously.
ambigüedad *s.f.* ambiguity.
ambiguo, -a *adj.* 1 ambiguous (no muy claro). 2 doubtful (dudoso).
ámbito *s.m.* 1 ambit, field (espacio encerrado). 2 atmosphere (ambiente).
ambliopía *s.f.* amblyopia.
ambos *adj.pl.* both: *ambos estudian = they both study.*
ambrosía *s.f.* ambrosia.
ambulancia *s.f.* 1 ambulance (vehículo). 2 field hospital (hospital ambulante). || 3 **— de correos,** post-office coach.
ambular *v.i.* to wander around.
ambulante *adj.* 1 travelling: *vendedor ambulante = travelling salesman.* 2 strolling (actor, músico). 3 walking (que anda).
ambulatorio *adj.* 1 ambulatory. || *s.m.* 2 MED. clinic.
ameba o **amiba** *s.f.* ZOOL. amoeba.
amedrentar *v.t.* 1 to terrify, to scare (atemorizar). || *v.pron.* 2 to be terrified, to be scared.
amén *s.m.* 1 REL. amen. || *interj.* 2 amen! || 3 **en un —,** in a trice.
amenaza *s.f.* threat.
amenazador, -a *adj.* threatening.
amenazadoramente *adv.* threateningly.
amenazante *adj.* threatening.
amenazar *v.t.* to threaten, to menace: *amenazar de muerte = to threaten with death.* || *v.t.* e *i.* 2 to presage (presagiar).
amenguamiento *s.m.* diminishing, lessening.
amenguar *v.t.* e *i.* 1 to reduce, to dimin ish (acortar). || *v.t.* 2 to dishonour (deshonrar).
amenidad *s.f.* pleasantness, amenity.
amenizar *v.t.* 1 to make more pleasant (hacer más agradable). 2 to liven up (avivar). 3 to make more interesting (hacer más interesante).
ameno, -a *adj.* 1 pleasant, nice (agradable). 2 entertaining (entretenido). 3 charming (placentero).
amenorrea *s.f.* MED. amenorrhoea.
americana *s.f.* jacket, coat.
americanismo *s.m.* Americanism.
americanista *s.m.* y *f.* Americanist.
americanización *s.f.* Americanization.
americanizar *v.t.* to Americanize.
americano *adj.* y *s.m.* y *f.* American.
amerindio *adj.* 1 Amerindian. || *s.m.* y *f.* 2 Amerind.
amerizaje *s.m.* landing.
amerizar *v.i.* to land on the sea.
ametralladora *s.f.* machine gun.
ametrallar *v.t.* to machine-gun.
amianto *s.m.* asbestos.
amiba *s.f.* amoeba.
amiga *s.f.* 1 friend. 2 girlfriend (novia).
amigable *adj.* amicable, friendly.
amigablemente *adv.* amicably.
amigacho *s.m.* y *f.* chum, pal, mate.
amigar *v.t.* 1 to make friends.
amigazo *s.m.* y *f.* great friend.
amígdala *s.f.* ANAT. tonsil.
amigdalitis *s.m.* tonsillitis.
amigo *s.m.* 1 friendly (amistoso). 2 fond: *ser amigo de los caballos = to be fond of the horses.* || *s.m.* 3 friend: *amigo íntimo = close friend.* 4 boyfriend (novio). 5 lover (amante). || 6 **hacerse amigos,** to make friends.
amigote *s.m.* old mate, old friend.
amilanado, -a *adj.* frightened, scared.
amilanamiento *s.m.* fear (miedo).
amilanar *v.t.* 1 to scare, to frighten (atemorizar). || *v.pron.* 2 to be discouraged (desanimar). 3 to be intimidated (acobardar).
aminorar o **minorar** *v.t.* to diminish, to get smaller.
amistad *s.f.* 1 friendship. || *s.pl.* 2 friends. || 3 **hacer las amistades,** to make it up.
amistar *v.t.* 1 to make friends. || *v.pron.* 2 to make it up (reconciliar). 3 to become friends (hacerse amigos).
amistosamente *adv.* amicably.
amistoso, -a *adj.* friendly, amicable.
amito *s.m.* REL. amice.
amnesia *s.f.* amnesia, loss of memory.
amnésico, -a *adj.* 1 amnesic. || *s.m.* y *f.* 2 amnesiac.
amniótico, -a *adj.* ANAT. amniotic.
amnistía *s.f.* amnesty.
amnistiar *v.t.* to amnesty, to give amnesty.
amo *s.m.* 1 master. 2 master of the house (dueño de la casa). 3 owner (propietario). 4 head of the family (cabeza de familia). 5 foreman (capataz). 6 boss (jefe). ||
7 **ser el —,** to be the boss.
amodorrado, -a *adj.* drowsy, sleepy (con sueño).
amodorramiento *s.m.* drowsiness, sleepiness (sueño).
amodorrarse *v.pron.* 1 to get sleepy (empezar a tener sueño). 2 to go to sleep (dormirse).
amohinar *v.t.* 1 to annoy, to irritate (molestar). || *v.pron.* 2 to get annoyed (enfadarse).
amojamiento *s.m.* wizening, drying up.
amojamar *v.t.* 1 to dry and salt (pescado). || *v.pron.* 2 to become wizened (apergaminarse).
amolar *v.t.* 1 to sharpen, to grind (afilar un cuchillo, etc.). 2 (fig.) to get on some, one's nerves (molestar).
amoldamiento *s.m.* fitting, adaption, adjustment (ajuste).
amoldar *v.t.* 1 to mould. 2 (fig.) to mould, to shape (el comportamiento, etc.). || *v.pron.* 3 to adapt oneself (adaptarse).
amonedado, -a *adj.* (Am.) rich (rico).
amonedar *v.t.* to coin, to mint.
amonestación *s.f.* 1 warning (advertencia). 2 reprimand, rebuke (reprensión). 3 piece of advice (consejo). 4 REL. marriage banns.
amonestar *v.t.* 1 to warn (advertir). 2 to advise (aconsejar). 3 to reprove, to admonish (reprender). 4 REL. to publish the banns (anunciar una boda).
amoniacal *adj.* QUIM. ammoniacal.
amoniaco *s.m.* 1 QUIM. ammonia. || *adj.* 2 QUIM. ammoniac.
amontillado *s.m.* amontillado (jerez).
amontonadamente *adv.* in a pile o heap.
amontonador *adj.* 1 heaping. || *s.f.* 2 heaping machine (máquina).
amontonamiento *s.m.* 1 piling, heaping (acción). 2 hoarding (de riquezas). 3 collection (de datos). 4 crowding (de personas).
amontonar *v.t.* 1 to pile up, to heap (poner en un montón). 2 to bank up (nieve, nubes). 3 to gather, to collect (datos, etc.). 4 (Am.) to insult (insultar). || 5 *v.pron.* to pile up, to get piled up (ponerse en un montón). 6 to drift (nieve). 7 to accumulate (acumularse). 8 to crowd together (gente).
amor *s.m.* 1 love. 2 devotion (devoción). 3 lover (amante). 4 love (persona amada). || 5 **— con — se paga,** one good turn deserves another. 6 **— pasajero,** passing fancy. 7 **— propio,** self-respect; self-esteem. 8 **hacer el —,** to make love. 9 **por el — de Dios,** for God's sake; for the love of God.
amoral *adj.* amoral.
amoralidad *s.f.* amorality.
amoralismo *s.m.* amoralism.
amoratarse *v.pron.* (Am.) 1 to turn purple (ponerse color morado). 2 to get bruised (contusionarse).
amorcillo *s.m.* 1 flirtation. 2 Cupid (figura).
amordazamiento *s.m.* 1 gagging (de personas). 2 muzzling (de perros). 3 (fig.) silencing (de la prensa, etc.).
amordazar *v.t.* 1 to gag (a una persona). 2 to muzzle (a un perro). 3 (fig.) to silence (la prensa, etc.).
amorfo, -a *adj.* amorphous.
amoroso, -a *adj.* 1 loving, affectionate, tender (tierno). 2 (fig.) workable (la tierra). 3 (fig.) MET. malleable. 4 (fig.) mild (el tiempo). || 5 **en tono —,** in an affectionate tone.
amortajar *v.t.* to shroud.
amortiguación *s.f.* 1 deadening, muffling (del sonido). 2 subduing, dimming (de la luz). 3 damping (de un golpe). 4 toning down (de colores).

amortiguador *s.m.* 1 MEC. shock-absorber. 2 buffer (tren). 3 ELEC. damper. 4 dimmer (de una luz). || *adj.* 5 muffling, deadening.
amortiguar *v.t.* 1 to deaden, to muffle (sonido). 2 to dim, to subdue (la luz). 3 to cushion (un golpe). 4 to absorb (choque). 5 to soften, to tone down (color). 6 ELEC. to dampen. || *v.pron.* 7 (Am.) to wither (marchitarse). 8 to get depressed (deprimirse).
amortizable *adj.* 1 COM. redeemable.
amortización *s.f.* 1 DER. amortization. 2 COM. redemption. 3 abolition (de un empleo).
amortizar *v.t.* 1 DER. to amortize. 2 COM. to redeem. 3 to pay off, to repay (un préstamo, etc.).
amoscarse *v.pron.* (fam.) to get cross, to get angry (enfadarse).
amostazar *v.t.* 1 to make cross, to make angry (enfadar). || *v.pron.* 2 to get cross, to get angry (enfadarse). 3 (Am.) to blush (sonrojarse). 4 (Am.) to get embarrassed (avergonzarse).
amotinado *s.m.* 1 MIL. mutineer. 2 rebel (rebelde). || *adj.* 3 mutinous. 4 rebelious (rebelde).
amotinador *adj.* V. **amotinado.**
amotinamiento *s.m.* 1 riot (disturbio). 2 POL. uprising, insurrection. 3 MIL. mutiny (en un barco, etc.).
amotinar *v.t.* 1 to stir up, to incite a mutiny (incitar un amotinamiento). || *v.pron.* 2 to riot (alborotarse). 3 POL. to rise up, to revolt (rebelarse). 4 to mutiny (en un barco, etc.).
amover *v.t.* to dismiss, to remove (despedir de un empleo).
amparar *v.t.* 1 to protect (proteger). 2 to shelter (de los elementos). 3 to help (ayudar). || *v.pron.* 4 to seek protection (buscar protección). 5 to seek help (buscar ayuda). 6 to protect oneself (protegerse). 7 to defend oneself (defenderse).
amperaje *s.m.* ELEC. amperage.
amperímetro *s.m.* ELEC. ammeter.
amperio *s.m.* ELEC. ampere, amp.
ampliable *adj.* which can be enlarged, enlargeable.
ampliación *s.f.* 1 extension, enlargement (de una casa, etc.). 2 enlargement (de una foto). 3 expansion (expansión). 4 amplification (amplificación).
ampliadora *s.f.* enlarger (para las fotos).
ampliar *v.t.* 1 to enlarge, to extend (hacer más grande). 2 to enlarge (una foto). 3 to amplify (sonido).
amplificación *s.f.* 1 amplification (sonido). 2 (Am.) enlargement (de fotos).
amplificador *s.m.* ELEC. amplifier.
amplificar *v.t.* 1 ELEC. to amplify. 2 (Am.) to enlarge (una foto).
amplio, -a *adj.* 1 spacious (con mucho espacio). 2 extensive (investigación, etc.). 3 ample, wide (poderes). 4 broad, wide (ancho).
amplitud *s.f.* 1 spaciousness (espacio). 2 extent (de daños, conocimiento, etc.). 3 expanse, size (de un terreno, etc.).
ampo *s.m.* 1 whiteness (blancura). 2 snowflake (copo de nieve).
ampolla *s.f.* 1 MED. blister. 2 flask, bottle (frasco).
ampolleta *s.f.* 1 phial, small bottle (botella pequeña). 2 hourglass (reloj). 3 bulb (de un termómetro, etc.).
ampulosidad *s.f.* bombast, pomposity.
ampuloso, -a *adj.* bombastic, pompous.
amputación *s.f.* MED. amputation.
amputado, -a *adj.* MED. amputated.
amputar *v.t.* MED. to amputate.
amueblar *v.t.* to furnish.
amularse *v.pron.* 1 to get angry (enfadarse). || *v.i.* 2 to be sterile (ser estéril).
amuleto *s.m.* amulet, charm.
amura *s.f.* MAR. 1 width, beam. || 2 **cambiar de —,** MAR. to go about, to tack.
amurallar *v.t.* to wall, to wall in.
anabaptismo *s.m.* REL. anabaptism.
anacarado, -a *adj.* mother-of-pearl.
anacardo *s.m.* cashew (fruto seco).
anacoluto *s.m.* GRAM. anacoluthon.
anaconda *s.f.* ZOOL. anaconda (serpiente).
anacoreta *s.f.* anachorite.
anacreóntico, -a *adj.* anacreontic.
anacrónico, -a *adj.* anachronistic.
anacronismo *s.m.* anachronism.
ánade *s.m.* ZOOL. mallard (pato).
anadón *s.m.* duckling (patito).
anaerobio *adj.* 1 BIOL. anaerobic. || *s.m.* 2 BIOL. anaerobe.
anafase *adj.* BIOL. anaphase.
anáfora *s.f.* anaphora (repetición).
anafrodisia *s.f.* anaphrodisia.
anagogia o **anagoge** *s.f.* REL. anagoge, anagogy.
anagrama *s.f.* anagram.
anal *adj.* anal.
analectas *s.f.pl.* analects, analecta, florilegium.
anales *s.m.pl.* anals.
analfabetismo *s.m.* illiteracy.
analfabeto, -a *s.m.* y *f.* illiterate.
analgesia *s.f.* MED. analgesia.
analgésico *s.m.* y *adj.* MED. analgesic.
análisis *s.m.* 1 analysis. 2 MED. test: *análisis de sangre = blood test.* 3 MED. analysis: *análisis de orina = urine analysis.*
analista *s.m.* y *f.* 1 analyst (el que hace análisis). 2 annalist (el que escribe anales).
analítico, -a *adj.* analytic, analytical.
analizador *s.m.* 1 FIS. analyser. || *adj.* 2 analysing, analyzing.
analizar *v.t.* to analyse, to analyze.
analogía *s.f.* 1 analogy. 2 similarity (semejanza).
analógico, -a *adj.* GRAM. analogical.
análogo, -a *adj.* similar, analogous.
ananá o **ananás** *s.m.* BOT. pineapple (piña).
anapesto *s.m.* anapest.
anaquel *s.m.* shelf.
anaquelería *s.f.* shelves (pl.), shelving.
anaranjado, -a *adj.* 1 orange (coloured). || *s.m.* orange (colour).
anarquía *s.f.* anarchy.
anárquicamente *adv.* anarchistically.
anárquico, -a *adj.* anarchic.
anarquismo *s.m.* anarchism.
anarquista *adj./s.m.* y *f.* anarchist.
anatema *s.m.* REL. anathema.
anatomía *s.f.* 1 anatomy (ciencia). 2 anatomy (cuerpo).
anatómico, -a *adj.* anatomic, anatomical.
anatomista *s.m.* y *f.* anatomist.
anatomizar *v.t.* e *i.* to anatomize, to dissect.
anca *s.f.* 1 haunch (parte posterior lateral de un caballo). 2 rump (parte posterior superior). || 3 **ancas de rana,** frog's legs.
ancestral *adj.* ancestral.
ancianidad *s.f.* old age.
anciano, -a *adj.* 1 old, elderly, aged (de edad). || *s.m.* 2 old man, elderly man. || *s.f.* 3 old woman, elderly woman.
ancla *s.f.* 1 MAR. anchor. || 2 **echar anclas,** MAR. to drop anchor.
anclaje *s.m.* MAR. anchorage.
anclar *v.t.* MAR. to anchor, to drop anchor.
áncora *s.f.* 1 MAR. anchor. || **— de protección,** last hope (última esperanza).
ancho, -a *adj.* 1 broad, wide. 2 full (falda). 3 thick (espeso). 4 too wide (demasiado ancho). 5 satisfied, smug (satisfecho). || *s.m.* 6 width, breadth (anchura). 7 guage (ferrocarril). || 8 **estar a sus anchas,** to be comfortable. 9 **quedarse tan ancho,** to behave as if nothing has happened.
anchoa *s.f.* ZOOL. anchovy (pez).
anchura *s.f.* 1 width, breadth. 2 (fig.) freedom (libertad). 3 (fig.) ease, comfort (comodidad).
andada *s.f.* (Am.) long walk (paseo largo).
andaderas *s.f.pl.* baby walker.
andalucismo *s.m.* 1 Andalusian word (palabra). 2 Andalusian expression (expresión). 3 love of things typical of Andalusia (afición a las cosas andaluzas).
andaluz, -a *adj./s.m.* y *f.*Andalusian.
andamio *s.m.* 1 TEC. scaffolding. 2 stage, platform (tablado).
andana *s.f.* 1 row, line (fila). || 2 **llamarse —,** to go back on one's word.
andanada *s.f.* 1 MIL. broadside. 2 big rocket (fuegos artificiales). 3 (fig.) telling off, reprimand (reprimenda). || 4 (Am.) **por andanadas,** in abundance (en abundancia).
andante *adv.* 1 MUS. andante. || *s.m.* 2 errant: *caballero andante = knight-errant.*
andantino *adv.* y *s.m.* MUS. andantino.
andanza *s.f.* 1 fortune, fate (destino). || 2 **andanzas,** achievements (logros).
andar *v.i.* 1 to walk (caminar). 2 to move (moverse). 3 to work (funcionar): *la radio no anda = the radio doesn't work.* 4 to go, to run, to work (una máquina). 5 to be: *anda por aquí = she's around here.* 6 to pass (el tiempo). || *v.t.* 7 to walk. 8 to cover, to travel (cubrir distancias). || *v.pron.* 9 to leave, to go away (irse). || 10 *interj.* **¡anda!,** come on! (para animar); you're joking! (descon-

fianza); my word! (admiración). **11 — a caballo,** to ride (on horseback). **12 — a golpes,** to fight. **13 — bien de salud,** to be in good health. **14 — con cuidado,** to be careful. **15 — con rodeos,** to beat about the bush. **16 — de puntillas,** to tiptoe; to walk on tip-toes. **17 — mal de la cabeza,** not to be right in the head. **18 — tras,** to be after. **19 andarse con bromas,** to joke; to make jokes.

andariego, -a *s.m.* y *f.* 1 wanderer, rover (errante). 2 keen walker (que le gusta andar). || *adj.* 3 fond of walking (que le gusta andar). 4 wandering, roving (errante).

andarín, -ina *s.m.* y *f.* 1 walker. || **2 es muy —,** he is keen on walking.

andas *s.f.* 1 stretcher (camilla). 2 litter, sedan chair (silla de manos). 3 bier (féretro).

andén *s.m.* 1 platform (de estación). 2 hard shoulder (de autopista). 3 quarside (muelle).

andino, -a *adj.* Andean, of the Andes.

andorrano, -a *adj./s.m.* y *f.* Andorran.

andrajo *s.m.* 1 rag, tatter (trozo de ropa vieja). 2 good-for-nothing (sinvergüenza). || **3 estar en andrajos,** to be in rags.

andrajoso, -a *adj.* ragged.

andrino V. **endrino.**

androceo *s.m.* BOT. androecium.

andurrial *s.m.* 1 (Am.) muddy place, quagmire (sitio fangoso). || **2 andurriales,** out-of-the-way place (paraje alejado).

anécdota *s.f.* anecdote.

anecdótico, -a *adj.* anecdotal, anecdotic.

anecdotario *s.m.* collection of anecdotes.

anegable *adj.* subject to flooding.

anegadizo, -a *adj.* 1 subject to flooding, frequently flooded. 2 heavier than water (más pesado que el agua).

anegar *v.t.* 1 to drown (ahogar). 2 to flood (inundar). 3 (fig.) to destroy (destrozar). || *v.pron.* 4 to drown (ahogarse). 5 to flood, to be flooded (inundarse). 6 MAR. to sink (hundirse).

anejo, -a *adj.* 1 attached, dependent (dependiente). || *s.m.* 2 ARQ. annex (de un edificio).

anemia *s.f.* MED. anaemia, anemia.

anémico, -a *adj.* MED. anaemic, anemic.

anemómetro *s.m.* FIS. anemometer.

anémona o **anémone** *s.f.* 1 BOT. anemone (planta). || 2 ZOOL. **anémona de mar,** sea anemone.

anemoscopio *s.m.* wind direction indicator.

anestesia *s.f.* MED. anaesthesia.

anestesiar *v.t.* MED. to anaesthetize.

anestésico, -a *s.m.* y *adj.* MED. anaesthetic.

aneurisma *s.m.* MED. aneurysm, aneurism.

anexión *s.f.* annexation.

anexionar o **anexar** *v.t.* to annex.

anexionismo *s.m.* annexationism, annexionism.

anexionista *adj./s.m.* y *f.* annexationist, annexionist.

anexo, -a *adj.* 1 ARQ. attached, annexed (edificio). 2 attached (documento). || *s.m.* 3 ARQ. annex, annexe (de un edificio). 4 annex, annexe, appendix (de un libro). || 5 ANAT. adnexa.

anfibio *adj.* 1 amphibious. || *s.m.* 2 amphibian.

anfibolita *s.f.* MIN. amphibolite.

anfiteatro *s.m.* amphitheatre.

anfitrión *s.m.* y *f.* host (hombre); hostess (mujer).

ánfora *s.f.* amphora (cántaro).

angarillas *s.f. pl.* 1 stretcher (camilla). 2 panniers (para los caballos). 3 portable platform (para transportar cosas a mano).

ángel *s.m.* 1 angel: *ángel de la guardia = guardian angel.* 2 charm (encanto). || **3 — caído,** fallen angel.

angélica *s.f.* BOT. angelica.

angelical *adj.* angelic, angelical.

angélico, -a *adj.* 1 angelic, angelical. || *s.m.* 2 little angel, cherub.

angelito *s.m.* 1 little angel, cherub. || **2 que duermas con los angelitos,** sleep well.

angelote *s.m.* 1 chubby child (niño gordo). 2 angel (estatua). 3 ZOOL. angelfish (pez). 4 BOT. type of clover (especie de trébol).

ángelus *s.m.* angelus.

angina *s.f.* 1 MED. angina. 2 ANAT. tonsil. || **3 angina de pecho,** angina pectoris. **4 tener anginas,** to have a sore throat.

angioma *s.m.* MED. angioma.

angiospermas *s.f. pl.* BOT. angiospermae.

angiospermo, -a *adj.* BOT. angiospermus.

anglicanism *s.m.* REL. anglicanism.

anglicanizar *v.t.* to anglicize.

anglicano, -a *adj./s.m.* y *f.* REL. anglican: *La Iglesia Anglicana = The Church of England; The Anglican Church.*

anglicismo *s.m.* anglicism.

anglicista *s.m.* y *f.* anglicist.

anglo *adj.* 1 anglian. || *s.m.* y *f.* angle, anglian.

angloamericano, -a *adj./s.m.* y *f.* Angloamerican.

anglófilo, -a *adj./s.m.* y *f.* anglophile.

anglófobo *adj./s.m.* y *f.* anglophobe.

anglosajón *adj./s.m.* y *f.* Anglo-Saxon.

angostamente *adv.* narrowly.

angostar *vot.* 1 to narrow (estrechar). || *v.pron.* 2 to narrow, to get narrower (estrecharse).

angosto, -a *adj.* narrow (estrecho).

angostura *s.f.* 1 narrowness (estrechez). 2 narrow part (parte estrecha). 3 GEOG. narrow pass (entre montañas).

anguila *s.f.* 1 ZOOL. eel (pez). || **2 anguila de mar,** ZOOL. conger eel (pez).

angula *s.f.* ZOOL. elver (cría de la anguila).

angular *adj.* 1 angular. || *s.m.* 2 TEC. angle iron. || **3 piedra —,** ARQ. cornerstone.

angularidad *s.f.* angularity.

ángulo *s.m.* 1 MAT. angle: *ángulo agudo = acute angle.* 2 corner (esquina). 3 curve, bend (curva). 4 TEC. angle iron (angular). || **5 — facial,** ANAT. facial angle. **6 desde este —,** (fig.), from this angle. **7 formar — con,** to be at an angle to.

angurria *s.f.* 1 MED. strangury. 2 (Am.) starvation, hunger (hambre). 3 (Am.) stinginess, miserliness, meanness (tacañería).

angustia *s.f.* 1 anguish, distress (psíquico). 2 anguish (físico). || **3 dar angustias a,** to trouble; to distress.

angustiadamente *adv.* distressedly, with anguish.

angustiado, -a *adj.* 1 anguished, distressed (psíquico). 2 narrow (estrecho). 3 worried, (preocupado).

angustiar *v.t.* 1 to cause anguish to, to distress. 2 to worry (preocupar). || *v.pron.* 3 to become distressed. 4 to get anxious, to worry (preocuparse).

angustioso, -a *adj.* 1 distressing (una situación, etc.). 2 agonizing (una espera, etc.). 3 anguished, distressed (angustiado). || **4 un momento angustioso,** a moment of anguish.

anhelante *adj.* 1 panting, out of breath, gasping (jadeante). 2 longing, eager (deseoso).

anhelar *v.i.* 1 to pant, to gasp (jadear). || *v.pron.* 2 (fig.) to long o yearn for (desear que pase algo).

anhelo *s.m.* 1 panting, gasping (jadeo). 2 (fig.) yearning, craving (deseo). || 3 anhelos, aspirations (aspiraciones).

anhídrido *s.m.* QUIM. anhydride.

anidar *v.t.* 1 to take in, to shelter (acoger). || *v.i.* y *pron.* 2 to nest, to make one's nest (las aves).

anilina *s.f.* aniline.

anilla *s.f.* 1 ring (anillo). 2 curtain ring (de cortinas). 3 ring (de un ave).

anillo *s.m.* 1 ring: *anillo de boda = wedding ring.* 2 ARQ. annulet (de una columna). 3 ZOOL. annulus (de un gusano). 4 BOT. ring (árbol). || **5 — de compromiso,** engagement ring. **6 sentar como el — al dedo,** it's just what the doctor ordered.

ánima *s.f.* 1 soul (alma). 2 bore (de un cañón). 3 soul in purgatory (alma que se purifica en el purgatorio).

animación *s.f.* 1 animation (acción de animar). 2 life (de una persona). 3 liveliness (de una situación, etc.). 4 movement, bustle, activity (en la calle, etc.). 5 animation (cine). 6 starting (puesta en marcha).

animadamente *adv.* in a lively way.

animado, -a *adj.* 1 lively, full of life (una fiesta, etc.). 2 busy, lively, bustling (una calle, etc.). 3 encouraged, inspired (inspirado). || **4 dibujos animados,** cartoons.

animador *adj.* 1 encouraging, inspiring (que inspira). || *s.m.* y *f.* 2 entertainer (en un bar, etc.).

animadversión *s.f.* ill-will.

animal *s.m.* 1 animal. 2 (fig.) brute, animal (bruto). || *adj.* 3 animal. 4 (fig.) rough, brutish, stupid, daft (bruto).

animalada *s.f.* 1 gross language (grosería). 2 gluttonous behaviour (gula). || 3 **decir animaladas,** to be crude/vulgar.
animalidad *s.f.* animality.
animar *v.t.* 1 to animate, to give life (dar vida). 2 to encourage (a una persona). 3 to liven up, to enliven (una fiesta, etc.). 4 to brighten up (un sitio, etc.). 5 to cheer up (a una persona deprimida). || *v.pron.* 6 to pluck up courage (cobrar ánimo). 7 to liven up, to get livelier (una fiesta, etc.). 8 to cheer up (una persona deprimida). 9 to decide (decidirse). || 10 **anímate!,** cheer up! (para dar ánimos); make up your mind! (decídete). 11 **te animas?,** do you fancy it?
anímico, -a *adj.* psychic.
animismo *s.m.* animism.
animista *adj.* 1 animistic. || 2 *s.m.* y *f.* animist.
ánimo *s.m.* 1 mind (mente). 2 soul (alma). 3 spirit (espíritu). 4 courage, pluck (valor). 5 energy (energía). 6 intention: *con ánimo de = with the intention of* (intención). || 7 **ánimo!,** come on! (en deporte, etc.). 8 **dar ánimos a,** to encourage. 9 **estado de –,** state of mind. 10 **estar sin –,** to be in low spirits.
animosidad *s.f.* animosity, enmity (antipatía).
animoso *adj.* 1 brave, daring (valiente). 2 determined (decidido).
aniñadamente *adv.* childishly.
aniñado, -a *adj.* childish.
aniñarse *v.pron.* to become childish.
aniquilar *v.t.* 1 annihilate, to wipe out, to destroy. 2 to overwhelm, to overcome (anonadar). || *v.pron.* 3 to deteriorate (la salud).
anís *s.m.* 1 BOT. anise, aniseed. 2 anis, anisette (bebida). 3 (Am.) strength, energy (energía). || 4 **estar hecho un –,** (Am.) to be dressed up to the nines.
anisete *s.m.* anisette.
aniversario *s.m.* y *adj.* aniversary.
ano *s.m.* ANAT. anus.
anoche *adv.* 1 last night, yesterday evening. || 2 **antes de –,** the night before last.
anochecer *v.i.* 1 to get dark. 2 to arrive at night (llegar al anochecer). || *s.m.* 3 nightfall, dusk. || 4 **al –,** at nightfall; at dusk.
anochecida *s.f.* nightfall, dusk.
anochecido *adv.* night, dark.
anodinia *s.f.* MED. anodynia.
anodino, -a *adj.* 1 MED. anodyne. 2 insignificant (insignificante). 3 uninteresting, anodyne (sin interés).
ánodo *s.m.* ELEC. anode.
anomalía *s.f.* anomaly.
anómalo, -a *adj.* anomalous.
anonadación *s.f.* o **anonadamiento** *s.m.* annihilation, destruction (aniquilación).
anonadar *v.t.* 1 to annihilate, to destroy (aniquilar). 2 to overwhelm, to overcome (apocar).
anónimo *adj.* 1 anonymous. || *s.m.* 2 anonimity (anonimato). 3 anonymous person (persona). 4 anonymous letter (carta). 5 anonymous work (obra).
anónimo, -a *adj.* anonymous.
anorak *s.m.* anorak.
anorexia *s.f.* MED. anorexia.
anormal *adj.* 1 abnormal. || *s.m.* y *f.* 2 abnormal person, mentally deficient person.
anormalidad *s.f.* abnormality.
anquilosamiento *s.m.* MED. anchylosis, ankylosis.
anquilosar *v.t.* 1 to anchylose, to ankylose. || *v.pron.* 2 to anchylose.
ansia *s.f.* 1 anxiety (ansiedad). 2 fear, anguish (temor). 3 MED. nervous tension. || 4 **ansias,** MED. sick-feeling; nausea.
ansiar *v.t.* to long for, to yearn for.
ansiedad *s.f.* 1 anxiety, worry (preocupación). 2 MED. nervous tension, anxiety.
ansiosamente *adv.* 1 longingly. 2 anxiously (con inquietud).
ansioso, -a *adj.* 1 anxious, worried (inquieto). 2 eager (deseoso). 3 MED. nervously tense, anxious.
anta *s.m.* 1 ZOOL. emu, moose. 2 (Am.) ZOOL. tapir.
antagónico, -a *adj.* antagonistic.
antagonismo *s.m.* antagonism.
antagonista *adj.* 1 antagonistic, antagonist. || *s.m.* y *f.* 2 antagonist.
antaño *adv.* 1 long ago, formerly (hace mucho tiempo). 2 last year (el año pasado).
antártico *s.m.* y *adj.* antarctic.
ante *s.m.* 1 ZOOL. elk, moose. 2 suede (piel). 3 ZOOL. buffalo (búfalo). 4 (Am.) ZOOL. tapir.
ante *prep.* 1 before, in the presence of (una persona). 2 in the face of (el enemigo, un peligro, etc.). 3 with regard to (un asunto). || 4 **– esta posibilidad,** in view of this possibility. 5 **– todo,** above all.
anteanoche *adv.* the night o evening before last.
anteayer *adv.* the day before yesterday.
antebrazo *s.m.* ANAT. forearm.
antecámera *s.f.* antechamber, anteroom, lobby (vestíbulo).
antecedente *s.m.* 1 GRAM. antecedent. || *adj.* 2 previous, preceding (previo). || 3 **antecedentes,** record; background. 4 **antecedentes penales,** criminal record.
anteceder *v.t.* to precede, to go before.
antecesor, -a *adj.* 1 preceding, former (anterior). || *s.m.* 2 predecessor. 3 ancestor, forefather (antepasado).
antedecir *v.t.* to predict, to foretell.
antediluviano, -a *adj.* 1 antediluvian, before the flood. 2 antiquated (anticuado).
antelación *s.f.* 1 precedence, priority (prioridad). || 2 **con –,** in advance, beforehand.
antemano *adv.* || **de –,** beforehand.
antena *s.f.* 1 feeler, antenna. 2 RAD. aerial, antenna.
anteojera *s.f.* 1 blinker (para los caballos). 2 glasses case (estuche para gafas).
anteojo *s.m.* 1 telescope. || *s.m.pl.* 2 opera glasses (para la ópera). 3 binoculars (prismáticos). 4 blinkers (para los caballos). 5 glasses (gafas).
antepasado *s.m.* 1 ancestor, forefather (ascendiente). || *adj.* 2 before last, previous (previo).
antepecho *s.m.* 1 guardrail, handrail (en un puente, edificio, etc.). 2 ledge, sill (de una ventana). 3 MIL. breastwork (pieza de la guarnición de las caballerías).
anteponer *v.t.* 1 to place in front. 2 (fig.) to prefer (preferir). || *v.pron.* 3 to be in front (estar delante). 4 (fig.) to overcome (vencer).
antepuerta *s.f.* 1 storm door (de una casa). 2 second gate, inner door (de una fortaleza).
antepuerto *s.m.* MAR. outer harbour.
anterior *adj.* 1 front, fore, anterior (parte, pata, etc.). 2 preceding, previous, former (previo).
anterioridad *s.f.* 1 anteriority (de tiempo). 2 priority (prioridad). || 3 **con –,** before, previously (antes); beforehand, in advance (con antelación).
anteriormente *adv.* 1 before, previously (antes). 2 beforehand, in advance (con antelación).
antes *adv.* 1 before: *una semana antes = a week before.* 2 first (primero). 3 earlier: *le vi antes = I saw him earlier.* 4 rather, better: *antes muerto que esclavo = better dead than enslaved.* || *conj.* 5 on the contrary (más bien). || *adj.* 6 before, previous: *el día antes = the day before; the previous day.* || 7 **– hoy que mañana,** the sooner the better (cuanto antes mejor). 8 **mucho –,** a long time before.
anti- (prefijo) anti-.
antiaéreo, -a *adj.* 1 anti-aircraft. || *s.m.* 2 anti-aircraft gun (cañón).
antibiótico *s.m.* MED. antibiotic.
anticiclón *s.m.* anticyclone.
anticipación *s.f.* 1 bringing forward (de una fecha, etc.). 2 anticipation, prediction (predicción). 3 COM. advance.
anticipadamente *adv.* in advance.
anticipado, -a *adj.* 1 advance, in advance. || 2 **pago –,** advance payment.
anticipante *adj.* bringing foreward, advancing.
anticipar *v.t.* 1 to bring foreward, to advance (una fecha, etc.). 2 to predict, to foretell (predicar). 3 to pay in advance (dinero). 4 (fig.) to anticipate (prever). || *v.pron.* 5 to be early (llegar temprano). 6 to anticipate, to be one step ahead (de un rival, etc.). 7 to be premature, to be born prematurely (un bebé). 8 to anticipate (adivinar).
anticipo *s.m.* 1 beginning: *fue el anticipo del fin = it was the beginning of the end.* 2 COM. advance (dinero anticipado). 3 COM. loan (préstamo). 4 DER. retaining fee.

anticlerical *adj./s.m.* y *f.* anticlerical.
anticlericalismo *s.m.* anticlericalism.
anticlímax *s.m.* anticlimax.
anticlinal *s.m.* 1 (Am.) watershed. 2 GEOL. anticline.
anticonceptivo *adj.* y *s.m.* 1 contraceptive. || **2 métodos anticonceptivos,** birth control methods. **3 píldora —,** contraceptive pill; (fam.) the pill.
anticongelante *s.m.* antifreeze (solución).
anticuado, -a *adj.* 1 out-of-date, antiquated, obsolete (una máquina, etc.). 2 outdated, out of fashion (fuera de moda). 3 antiquated, old-fashioned (una persona). || **4 quedarse —,** to go out of fashion.
anticuar *v.t.* 1 to declare out-of-date. || *v.pron.* 2 to go out of fashion (la ropa, etc.). 3 to become obsolete (una máquina, etc.).
anticuario *s.m.* 1 antique dealer (vendedor). 2 antique shop (tienda).
antídoto *s.m.* MED. antidote.
antiespasmódico, -a *adj.* y *s.m.* MED. antispasmodic.
antiestético, -a *adj.* unsightly, offensive (to the eye), ugly.
antifaz *s.m.* 1 mask (máscara). 2 veil (velo).
antífona *s.f.* REL. antiphon.
antígeno *s.m.* MED. antigen.
antigualla *s.f.* 1 antique. 2 has-been (persona). 3 old news, old hat (noticia, información, etc.).
antiguamente *adv.* 1 before, formerly (antes). 2 in the olden days (en la antigüedad).
antigubernamental *adj.* anti-government.
antigüedad *s.f.* 1 seniority. 2 antiquity, age (cualidad). || 3 *s.f.pl.* antiques (objetos antiguos). || **4 tienda de antigüedades,** antique shop.
antiguo, -a *adj.* 1 antique (objeto). 2 old (viejo). 3 former (anterior). 4 old-fashioned, out-of-date (pasado de moda). || **5 — testamento,** REL. Old Testament. **6 desde muy —,** from time immemorial.
antílope *s.m.* ZOOL. antelope.
antinatural *adj.* unnatural.
antinomia *s.f.* antinomy.
antinómico, -a *adj.* antinomic, antinomical.
antioxidante *adj.* 1 anti-rust, rustproof. || *s.m.* 2 rustproofing.
antipapa *s.m.* antipope.
antipapista *s.m.* y *f.* antipapist.
antiparras *s.f. pl.* (fam.) specs, glasses.
antipatía *s.f.* antipathy, unfriendliness.
antipirético *adj.* y *s.m.* MED. antipyretic.
antípoda *adj.* 1 antipodal. || *s.m.* 2 antipode.
antiquísimo, -a *adj.* very old, ancient.
antisemita *adj.* 1 anti-semetic. || *s.m.* y *f.* 2 anti-semite.
antisemítico, -a *adj.* anti-semitic.
antisemitismo *s.m.* anti-semitism.
antisepsia *s.f.* MED. antisepsis.
antiséptico, -a *adj.* y *s.m.* MED. antiseptic.
anti-social *adj.* antisocial.
antítesis *s.f.* antithesis.
antitético, -a *adj.* antithetic(al).
antojadizo, -a *adj.* 1 whimsical capricious (caprichoso). 2 unpredictable, fickle (cambiadizo).
antojado *adj.* longing, eager.
antojarse *v.pron.* to take a fancy to, to want. 2 to have a mind: *se me antoja ver la película = I have a mind to see the film.*
antojo *s.m.* 1 whim, fancy, caprice. 2 sudden craving (de una mujer embarazada). 3 birthmark (mancha en la piel). || **4 cada uno a su —,** each to his own. **5 vivir a su —,** to live one's own life.
antología *s.f.* anthology.
antónimo *s.m.* antonym.
antonomasia *s.f.* antonomasia.
antonomástico, -a *adj.* antonomastic.
antorcha *s.f.* 1 torch. 2 (fig.) guiding light (persona). || **3 — a soplete,** blowlamp.
antracita *s.f.* MIN. anthracite.
ántrax *s.m.* MED. anthrax.
antro *s.m.* 1 cavern. || **2 — de corrupción,** den of iniquity.
antropocéntrico, -a *adj.* antropocentric.
antropocentrismo *s.m.* antropocentrism.
antropofagia *s.f.* cannibalism.
antropófago *s.m.* 1 cannibal. || *adj.* 2 man-eating, cannibalistic.
antropoide *adj.* anthropoid.
antropoideo *s.m.* anthropoid.
antropología *s.f.* anthropology.
antropológico, -a *adj.* anthropological.
antropólogo, -a *s.m.* y *f.* anthropologist.
antropometría *s.f.* anthropometry.
antropomorfismo *s.m.* anthropomorphism.
antropomorfo *adj.* 1 anthropomorphous. || *s.m.* y *f.* 2 anthropomorph.
antroponimia *s.f.* anthroponymy.
anual *adj.* annual.
anualidad *s.f.* 1 annuity, annual payment (pago). 2 annual event (acontecimiento).
anualmente *adv.* annually, yearly.
anuario *s.m.* yearbook, annual (libro).
anubarrado, -a *adj.* cloud, overcast.
anudadura *s.m.* 1 knotting. 2 fastening, tying (de cordones, etc.). 3 tying (de corbata). 4 knot (nudo).
anudar *v.t.* 1 to knot, to lie in a knot (una cuerda, etc.). 2 to tie (la corbata). 3 to tie, to fasten (los cordones, etc.). 4 to begin (empezar). || *v.pron.* 5 to get into knots, to get tied up (enredarse). 6 BOT. to remain stunted (no crecer). || **7 anudarse la voz,** to get a lump in one's throat.
anuencia *s.f.* consent.
anulación *s.f.* 1 annulment, cancellation (de un acontecimiento). 2 annulment, invalidation (de un contrato). 3 annulment (de un testamento).
anular *adj.* 1 annular, ring-shaped. || *s.m.* 2 ring-finger (dedo).
anular *v.t.* 1 DER. to repeal, to revoke. 2 to annul, to cancel (un acontecimiento, etc.). 3 to overule (una decisión). 4 DEP. to disallow (un tanto). 5 MAT. to cancel out.
anulativo, -a *adj.* annulling, cancelling.
anunciación *s.f.* 1 announcement (anuncio). 2 REL. annunciation.
anunciador *s.m.* y *f.* 1 announce. 2 advertiser (en un periódico).
anunciante *s.m.* y *f.* advertiser.
anunciar *v.t.* 1 to announce (una noticia, etc.). 2 to tell, to announce (contar). 3 to advertise (en un periódico, etc.).
anuncio *s.m.* 1 announcement (de una noticia). 2 advertisement (en un periódico, etc.).
anuria *s.f.* MED. anury.
anverso *s.m.* obverse.
anzuelo *s.m.* hook (de pescar).
añadido, -a *adj.* 1 added. || *s.m.* 2 hairpiece (de cabello).
añadidura *s.f.* 1 addition (en un texto). 2 piece added on (de un vestido, etc.).
añadir *v.t.* 1 to add. 2 to increase (aumentar). || *v.pron.* 3 to make additions (a un texto).
añagaza *s.f.* 1 hunting, decoy (en la caza). 2 (fig.) lure, bait.
añalejo *s.m.* REL. liturgical calender.
añal *adj.* 1 yearly, annual (acontecimiento, etc.). 2 year-old (edad). || *s.m.* 3 year-old animal, yearling (animal de un año).
añejo, -a *adj.* 1 old (viejo). 2 mellow, mature (vino).
añicos *s.m. pl.* 1 bits, pieces, fragments (trozos). || **2 estar hecho —,** (fig.) to be worn out. **3 hacer —,** to smash (cristal, etc.); to tear to pieces (papel).
añil *s.m.* 1 BOT. indigo plant (planta). 2 indigo (color).
año *s.m.* 1 year: *el año pasado = last year.* || *s.m.pl.* 2 days: *en aquellos años = in those days.* || **3 — luz,** ASTR. light year. **4 — económico,** fiscal o financial year. **5 — Nuevo,** New Year. **6 — tras —,** year after year; year in year out. **7 Feliz — Nuevo!,** Happy New Year! **8 en los años sesenta,** in the sixties. **9 ¿cuántos años tienes?,** how old are you? **10 tener muchos años,** to be very old.
añojal *s.m.* break, strip of land (terreno).
añojo *s.m.* yearling (de un año).
añoranza *s.f.* 1 longing, yearning. 2 nostalgia (nostalgia).
añorar *v.t.* 1 to long for (desear). 2 to grieve (por un muerto). || *v.i.* 3 to yearn, to pine for.
aorta *s.f.* ANAT. aorta.
apabullar *v.t.* 1 to squash, to flatten (aplastar). 2 (fig. y fam.) to silence (callar).
apacentamiento *s.m.* 1 grazing (acción). 2 pasture (pasto).
apacentar *v.t.* 1 to pasture, to graze. 2 (fig.) to feed (el intelecto). 3 to gratify, to satisfy (deseos, etc.). || *v.pron.* 4 to pasture, to graze.
apacibilidad *s.f.* 1 gentleness, even temper (de carácter). 2 calmness (del tiempo).

apacible *adj.* 1 gentle, mild, placid (de carácter). 2 calm, peaceful (de vida). 3 calm (tiempo, mar).
apaciguar *v.t.* 1 to calm (down), to quieten down (a una persona). 2 to relieve, to soothe (un dolor). || *v.pron.* 3 to calm down, MAR. to become calm. 4 to die down (una tormenta). 5 to calm down, to quieten down (personas).
apache *s.m.* apache.
apadrinador *adj.* 1 sponsoring. || *s.m.* y *f.* 2 sponsor.
apadrinamiento *s.m.* sponsorship, sponsoring (de un deportista, escritor, etc.).
apadrinar *v.t.* 1 to be godfather to (ser padrino de). 2 to be best man (en una boda). 3 to sponsor (patrocinar). 4 to support (apoyar).
apagable *adj.* extinguishable.
apagado, -a *adj.* 1 extinguished, that is out (un fuego). 2 dull, lifeless (color). 3 weak (voz). 4 muffled (ruido). || 5 **cal –,** slaked lime.
apagador *s.m.* 1 MUS. damper (del piano). 2 extinguisher (para apagar).
apagar *v.t.* 1 to put out, to extinguish (un fuego, incendio). 2 to turn o switch off (una luz, una radio). 3 to deaden, to muffle (sonido). 4 to quench (thirst). 5 to soften (color). 6 MUS. to damp, to mute (sonido). || *v.pron.* 7 to go out (un fuego). 8 to go out (una luz). 9 to fade away (sonido).
apagón *s.m.* blackout.
apaisado, -a *adj.* oblong.
apalabrar *v.t.* to make a verbal agreement on, to agree to.
apalancamiento *s.m.* leverage.
apalancar *v.t.* 1 to lever up, to move (levantar). 2 to lever open (abrir).
apaleamiento *s.m.* 1 threshing (del grano). 2 beating (de una alfombra). 3 beating, thrashing (de una persona).
apalear *v.t.* 1 to thresh (el grano). 2 to beat (una alfombra). 3 to beat, to thrash (a una persona).
apandillar *v.t.* 1 to form into a gang (formar una pandilla). || *v.pron.* 2 to band together, to form a gang.
apañado, -a *adj.* 1 skillful, handy (habilidoso). 2 suitable (conveniente). || **estamos apañados,** we're done fo; we've had it.
apañamiento *s.m.* repairing, mending.
apañar *v.t.* 1 to patch, to repair (unos pantalones, etc.). 2 to suit (convenir). 3 to wrap up (abrigar). 4 to pick up (coger). 5 (fam.) to rip off, to have away (robar). || *v.pron.* 6 to fix things, to arrange things. || 7 **apañárselas,** to manage, to get by: *me las apañaré = I'll get by.*
apaño *s.m.* 1 repair, mend (arreglo). 2 skill (habilidad). 3 mistress (concubina).
aparador *s.m.* 1 sideboard (mueble). 2 workshop (taller). 3 shopwindow (escaparate).
aparato *s.m.* 1 set (de radio, etc.). 2 device (dispositivo). 3 (fam.) phone (teléfono). 4 ANAT. system: *aparato digestivo = digestive system.* 5 bandage (vendaje). 6 FIS. apparatus. || 7 **ponerse al aparato,** (fam.) to come to the phone.
aparatosidad *s.f.* showiness, ostentation.
aparatoso, -a *adj.* 1 showy, ostentatious (vistoso). 2 spectacular: *un accidente aparatoso = a spectacular accident.* 3 pompous (pomposo).
aparcamiento *s.m.* 1 parking (acción de aparcar). 2 car park (lugar). 3 lay-by (en la carretera).
aparcar *v.t.* e *i.* to park.
aparcería *s.f.* partnership.
aparcero, -a *s.m.* y *f.* 1 tenant farmer. 2 part owner (copropietario). 3 (Am.) companion (compañero).
apareamiento *s.m.* 1 pairing off, matching up (de cosas). 2 mating (animales).
aparear *v.t.* 1 to match up (cosas). 2 to mate (animales). 3 to make equal (hacer igual). || *v.pron.* 4 to mate (animales). 5 to match (cosas).
aparecer *v.i.* 1 to appear. 2 to be, to appear (en una lista, etc.). 3 (fam.) to show up, to turn up (una persona, cosa): *hoy no ha aparecido el cartero = the postman hasn't shown up today.* || *v.pron.* 4 to appear.
aparecido *s.m.* ghost (fantasma).
aparejado, -a *adj.* 1 fit, ready (preparado). 2 suitable (apropiado).
aparejador, -ora *s.m.* y *f.* 1 quantity surveyor (ayudante del arquitecto). 2 MAR. rigger.
aparejar *v.t.* 1 to get ready, to prepare (preparar). 2 to saddle (un caballo). 3 MAR. to fit out, to rig (un barco). || *v.pron.* 4 to get ready (prepararse). 5 (Am.) to mate (aparear).
aparejo *s.m.* 1 preparation (preparación). 2 equipment, gear (conjunto de cosas). 3 MAR. rigging (jarcia). 4 TEC. block and tackle (sistema de poleas).
aparentador,-a *s.m.* y *f.* 1 pretender, to pretend. || *adj.* 2 who pretends.
aparentar *v.t.* 1 to feign (fingir). 2 to look, to seem to be (edad): *no aparenta los años que tiene = she doesn't look her age.* || *v.pron.* 3 to show off (presumir).
aparente *adj.* 1 apparent. 2 visible, apparent (visible). 3 evident (patente).
aparentemente *adv.* apparently.
aparición *s.f.* apparition.
apariencia *s.f.* 1 appearance, aspect (aspecto). || 2 **juzgar por las apariencias,** to judge by appearences.
apartadamente *adv.* apart.
apartadero *s.m.* 1 lay-by (en una carretera). 2 siding (para los trenes).
apartado, -a *adj.* 1 separated (separado). 2 isolated, remote (un pueblo, etc.). 3 aloof, solitary (persona). || *s.m.* 4 paragraph, section (párrafo). || 5 **– de correos,** post-office box.
apartamento *s.m.* flat.
apartar *v.t.* 1 to separate, to part (dos personas que se riñen). 2 to put aside (dejar a un lado). 3 (fam.) to begin, to start (empezar). 4 MIN. to extract (extraer). 5 to dissuade, to put off (disuadir). || *v.pron.* 6 to go away, to leave (marcharse). 7 to part, to separate (separarse). 8 to move aside (quitarse de en medio). 9 to cut oneself off (del mundo, etc.). 10 to wander off, to go off (un tema). 11 to stray from, to go off (un camino).
aparte *adv.* 1 separated. 2 aside, apart: *poner aparte = to put aside.* 3 besides (además). 4 separately (por separado). || 5 **– de,** apart from; besides. 6 **dejando –,** leaving aside; not to mention.
apasionadamente *adv.* passionately.
apasionado, -a *adj.* 1 passionate. 2 biassed, prejudiced (parcial). 3 interested (interesado).
apasionar *v.t.* 1 to fill with passion, to excite (excitar). || *v.pron.* 2 to get excited, to get worked up (excitarse). 3 to become interested (interesarse). 4 to fall madly in love (enamorarse locamente).
apatía *s.f.* apathy, in difference.
apático, -a *adj.* 1 apathetic, indifferent. 2 listless (perezoso).
apátrida *adj.* 1 stateless. || *s.m.* y *f.* 2 a stateless person.
apeadero *s.m.* 1 stopping place (lugar de descanso en el camino). 2 mounting block (poyo). 3 halt (ferrocarril).
apeamiento *s.m.* 1 dismounting (de un caballo). 2 getting off (de un tren, autobús, etc.). 3 getting out (de un coche).
apear *v.t.* 1 to help down (ayudar a bajar de un caballo). 2 to take down, to get down (bajar un objeto). 3 to help out (de un coche). 4 to hobble (trabar un caballo). || *v.pron.* 5 to dismount, to get off (de un caballo). 6 to get off (un tren, autobús, etc.). 7 to get out (de un coche). 8 (fig. y fam.) to back down (de una confrontación).
apechar o **apechugar** *v.t.* 1 to push with one's chest (empujar con el pecho). 2 (fig. y fam.) to shoulder (un trabajo, responsabilidades, etc.). 3 to face up to (las consecuencias).
apedreamiento *s.m.* stoning (castigo).
apedrear *v.t.* 1 to throw stones at (lanzar piedras). 2 to stone to death (matar a pedradas). || *v.pron.* 3 to be damaged by hail (cosechas).
apego *s.m.* 1 affection (cariño). 2 interest (interés). || 3 **tener – a,** to be fond of.
apelable *adj.* DER. appealable.
apelación *s.f.* 1 DER. appeal. 2 consultation (entre médicos). || 3 **sin –,** irremediable (sin arreglo).
apelante *adj./s.m.* y *f.* DER. appellant.
apelar *v.i.* 1 DER. to appeal. 2 (fig.) to appeal. 3 to resort to (recurrir).
apelativo *adj.* y *s.m.* appellative.
apelmazar *v.t.* to compress (compactar).
apelotonar *v.t.* 1 to roll into a ball (hacer una bola de algo). || *v.pron.* 2 to go lumpy. 3 to form balls (la lana, etc.).
apellidar *v.t.* 1 to call by someone's surname (llamar por su apellido). || *v.pron.* 2 to be called (llamarse).
apellido *s.m.* surname.

apenar *v.t.* 1 to cause grief (causar pena). || *v.pron.* 2 to be grieved (sentir pena).
apenas *adv.* 1 hardly. 2 with difficulty (con dificultad). || 3 **apenas... cuando...,** no sooner... than...
apencar *v.i.* 1 (fam.) to take on, to shoulder (un trabajo, responsabilidad, etc.). 2 to face, to put up with (aceptar).
apéndice *s.m.* ANAT. appendix.
apendicitis *s.f.* MED. appendicitis.
apendicular *adj.* appendicular.
apensionado, -a adj. (Am.) sad, unhappy (triste).
apeo *s.m.* 1 surveying (de tierras). 2 ARQ. propping up (con puntales). 3 support (apoyo, puntal). 4 scaffolding (andamios).
apepsia *s.f.* MED. apepsy.
apercepción *s.f.* preparation (preparación).
apercibimiento *s.m.* 1 warning (aviso). 2 preparation (preparación).
apercibir *v.t.* 1 to prepare, to get ready (preparar). 2 to provide (proveer). 3 to realize (darse cuenta). 4 to warn (advertir). || *v.pron.* 5 to get ready (prepararse).
apergaminado, -a *adj.* 1 parchment-like. 2 (fig.) wizened (la cara, etc.).
apergaminarse *v.r.* (fig. y fam.) to become wizened or wrinkled (la cara, etc.).
aperitivo *s.m.* aperitive.
apero *s.m.* 1 agricultural equipment (conjunto de implementos para trabajar la tierra). 2 tools, equipment (herramientas). || *s.m.* 3 (Am.) riding outfit (útiles de montar a caballo).
apertura *s.f.* 1 opening (de una sesión, etc.). 2 beginning (comienzo).
apesadumbrar *v.t.* 1 to trouble, to upset (entristecer). || *v.pron.* 2 to get upset (entristecerse).
apestar *v.i.* 1 to stink, to smell (oler mal). || *v.t.* 2 to infect with the plague (infectar con la peste).
apetecedor *adj.* tempting.
apetecer *v.t.* 1 to long for, to crave (desear que ocurra algo). || *v.i.* 2 to tempt, to take one's fancy (causar deseo, apetito).
apetecible *adj.* tempting, attractive.
apetencia *s.f.* longing, craving, desire (deseo).
apetito *s.m.* appetite.
apetitoso, -a *adj.* 1 appetizing tempting. 2 (fig. y fam.) tempting, attractive (atractivo).
apiadar *v.t.* 1 to move to pity (causar pena). || *v.pron.* 2 to take pity, to pity (sentir pena).
ápice *s.m.* 1 apex, point, tip (extremo). 2 crux (de un problema, etc.). || 3 **ni un –,** not an ounce.
apícola *adj.* apicultural (de las abejas).
apicultor *s.m.* y *f.* beekeeper.
apilamiento *s.m.* piling up, heaping.
apilar *v.t.* y *pron.* to pile up, to heap up.
apilonar V. **apilar.**
apiñado, -a *adj.* crammed, packed (apretado).
apiñamiento *s.m.* cramming, jamming.
apiñar *v.t.* 1 to pile up (amontonar). 2 to jam, to cram (apretar). || *v.pron.* 3 to pack together, to crowd together (la gente).
apiparse *v.pron.* (fam.) to scoff, to guzzle (la comida).
apisonadora *s.f.* MEC. steamroller.
apisonamiento *s.m.* 1 rolling (con una apisonadora). 2 ramming (con un pisón).
apisonar *v.t.* 1 to roll, to roll flat (con la apisonadora). 2 to ram (con el pisón).
aplacamiento *s.m.* appeasement, calming, placating.
aplacar *v.t.* 1 to appease, to placate, to calm (calmar). 2 to quench (la sed). 3 to satisfy (el hambre). || *v.pron.* 4 to calm down (calmarse).
aplanamiento *s.m.* smoothing, levelling, flattening.
aplanador *adj.* 1 smoothing, levelling, flattening. || *s.f.* 2 leveller (máquina). || 3 **– de calles,** (Am.) layabout, idler (perezoso).
aplanar *v.t.* 1 to smooth, to level, to flatten (allanar). 2 (fig. y fam.) to knock out (pasmar). || *v.pron.* 3 to collapse, to fall down (un edificio).
aplastamiento *s.m.* 1 squashing, flattening, crushing. 2 (fig.) crushing (de argumentos, etc.).
aplastante *adj.* (fig.) crushing (victoria, etc.).
aplastar *v.t.* 1 to squash, to flatten, to crush. 2 (fig.) to crush, to destroy (un argumento, etc.). || *v.pron.* 3 to be crushed o squashed o flattened. 4 (Am.) to collapse (en un sillón, etc.).
aplaudir *v.t.* e *i.* to applaud, to clap.
aplauso *s.m.* applause.
aplazamiento *s.m.* 1 postponement. 2 deferment (de un pago).
aplazar *v.t.* to postpone, to put off (posponer).
aplicación *s.f.* 1 application. 2 puting into practice/action (un plan, etc.). 3 use, application (uso). 4 (Am.) request (petición).
aplicable *adj.* applicable.
aplicar *v.t.* 1 to apply (un medicamento, etc.). 2 to put into effect (una ley). || *v.pron.* 3 to work hard (trabajar). 4 to devote oneself (a hacer algo). 5 to be used (usarse). 6 to come into effect (entrar en vigor).
aplique *s.m.* wall lamp (lámpara).
aplomo *s.m.* aplomb.
apocado, -a *adj.* timid (tímido).
apocalipsis *s.m.* apocalypse.
apocalíptico, -a *adj.* apocalyptic(al).
apocamiento *s.m.* 1 timidness (timidez). 2 lowliness (bajeza).
apocar *v.t.* 1 to make smaller, to diminish (disminuir). 2 (fig.) to belittle (humillar). 3 to intimidate. || *v.pron.* 4 (fig.) to humble oneself (humillarse). 5 to feel humble (sentirse humillado).
apocopar *v.t.* GRAM. to apocopate.
apócope *s.f.* GRAM. apocopation.
apócrifo *adj.* apocryphal.
apoderado *s.m.* 1 agent, representative (representante). 2 manager (de un deportista). 3 businessman (empresario).
apoderamiento *s.m.* 1 empowering (acción de apoderar). 2 seizure (acción de apoderarse).
apodar *v.t.* to nickname (dar un apodo).
apodo *s.m.* nickname.
apófisis *s.f.* ANAT. apophysis.
apofonía *s.f.* ablaut.
apogeo *s.m.* 1 ASTR. apogee. 2 (fig.) summit, height, peak: *está en el apogeo de su carrera = she is at the peak of her career.*
apolillar *v.t.* 1 to eat, to make holes in (la polilla). || 2 (Am.) **estar apolillando,** to be taking a nap (durmiendo).
apolíneo, -a *adj.* apollonian.
apolítico, -a *adj.* apolitical.
apologético, -a *adj.* apologetic.
apología *s.f.* vindication, apology.
apológico, -a *adj.* apological.
apólogo *s.m.* apologue.
apoltronarse *v.pron.* to become lazy o idle (vago).
apoplejía *s.f.* MED. apoplexy.
apoplético, -a *adj.* y *s.m.* apoplectic.
apoquinar *v.t.* to pay cash.
aporreado, -a *p.p.* 1 de **aporrear.** || *adj.* 2 cudgelled.
aporrear *v.t.* to beat, to pound on: *aporrear la puerta = to pound on the door.*
aportación *s.f.* contribution (normalmente de dinero).
aportar *v.t.* 1 to contribute (con dinero). 2 to bring, to present (pruebas o similar en un caso o discusión).
aporte *s.m.* supply, contribution: *aporte de vitaminas = supply of vitamins.*
aposentamiento *s.m.* lodging.
aposentar *v.t.* y *pron.* to settle down: *se aposentaron felizmente en el interior = they finally settled down happily inland.*
aposento *s.m.* room, apartment, lodging.
aposición *s.f.* apposition.
apósito *s.m.* MED. bandage.
aposta *adv.* on purpose.
apostador, -a *s.m.* y *f.* punter, better.
apostar *v.t.* 1 to bet: *apostar mucho dinero al mismo caballo = to bet a lot of money on one horse.* || *v.t.* y *pron.* 2 to station, to post, to take a position (poner para vigilar): *me aposté en la ventana y esperé = I took a position by the window and waited.*
apostasía *s.f.* REL. apostasy.
apóstata *s.m.* y *f.* REL. apostate.
apostatar *v.i.* REL. to apostatize.
a posteriori *adv.* a posteriori.
apostilla *s.f.* marginal note, annotation.
apóstol *s.m.* apostle.
apostolado *s.m.* apostolate.
apostólico, -a *adj.* apostolic.
apostrofar *v.t.* 1 to apostrophize. || 2 to scold (regañar).
apóstrofo *s.m.* apostrophe.
apostura *s.f.* handsomeness, good looks.
apotema *s.f.* GEOM. apothem.
apoteosis *s.f.* apotheosis.

apoyar *v.t.* **1** to support, to lean (físicamente). **2** to back up, to support (en un plan, idea, etc.). **3** to confirm, to uphold. **4** MIL. to reinforce (reforzar).
apoyatura *s.f.* basis, foundation.
apoyo *s.m.* **1** support (físico). **2** basis, fundation (de una teoría o parecido). **3** protection; approval (protección).
apreciable *adj.* **1** worthy, estimable (persona). **2** considerable, noticeable (una cantidad, cifra, actitud, acción): *una apreciable suma de dinero = a considerable sum of money.*
apreciación *s.f.* appraisal, appreciation.
apreciar *v.t.* **1** to assess, to value (poner precio). **2** esteem; to like, to be fond of (caer bien). **3** to observe, to notice (percibir). **4** to appreciate (una obra de arte o similar).
aprecio *s.m.* **1** esteem, regard (estima hacia una persona). **2** valuation, appraisal (en términos monetarios).
aprehender *v.t.* **1** to apprehend, to detain, to seize (coger). **2** to apprehend, to understand (entender).
aprehensión *s.f.* **1** apprehension, capture (captura). **2** comprehension, understanding (acto de entender algo). **3** fear, apprehension (temor).
aprehensivo, -a *adj.* apprehensive.
apremiante *adj.* urgent, pressing.
apremiantemente *adv.* urgently.
apremiar *v.t.* to press (a alguien para hacer algo): *las circunstancias nos apremian = the situation presses us.*
apremio *s.m.* **1** pressure, urgency. **2** DER. judicial order, writ.
aprender *v.t.* to learn: *aprendí a leer a los 3 años = I learned how to read when I was three.*
aprendiz, -iza *s.m.* y *f.* apprentice.
aprendizaje *s.m.* **1** apprenticeship. **2** learning.
aprensión *s.f.* **1** apprehension, dread (temor). **2** odd idea (idea tonta).
aprensivo, -a *adj.* apprehensive, nervous, worried.
apresamiento *s.m.* capture, seizure.
apresar *v.t.* **1** to capture, to seize (especialmente un barco). **2** to grasp, to clutch (un animal, especialmente): *el tigre apresó al pequeño cervatillo = the tiger clutched the small deer.* **3** to take prisoner (tomar prisionero a alguien).
aprestar *v.t.* y *pron.* to get ready, to prepare.
apresuradamente *adv.* hurriedly, in a hurry.
apresurado, -a *p.p.* **1** de **apresurar.** || *adj.* **2** hasty, hurried.
apresuramiento *s.m.* hurry, haste.
apresurar *v.t.* y *pron.* to hurry: *me apresuré a darle las gracias = I hurried to thank him.*
apretadamente *adv.* tightly, closely.
apretado, -a *p.p.* **1** de **apretar.** || *adj.* **2** cramped (con poco espacio). **3** difícil, dangerous (peligroso). **4** dense, thick (compacto). **5** tight (fuertemente ensamblado): *a very tight screw = un tornillo muy apretado.* **6** contested (reñido, especialmente en el contexto deportivo).
apretar *v.t.* **1** to tighten (un objeto apretable). **2** to hug, to squeeze (contra uno mismo). **3** to press: *un profesor que nos aprieta mucho = a teacher that presses us a lot.* **4** to squash, to squeeze (aplastar). || *v.t.* e *i.* **5** to urge (urgir). **6** to pinch, to be too tight: *me aprietan los zapatos = my shoes are too tight.* || *v.i.* **7** to get worse, to get more severe: *el calor aprieta = the heat is getting worse.* || *v.pron.* **8** to huddle together (apretarse unos contra otros).
apretón *s.m.* **1** squeeze, pressure, crush (físico). **2** difficulty, jam, fix (dificultad seria). **3** cramp (dolor, especialmente en el estómago).
apretujar *v.t.* **1** to squeeze, to press hard. || *v.pron.* **2** to cram, to crowd (agolparse).
aprieto *s.m.* difficulty, jam, fix: *estar en un aprieto = to be in a fix.*
a priori *adv.* (form.) a priori.
apriorismo *s.m.* apriorism.
apriorista *s.m.* y *f.* deductive, aprioristic.
aprisa *adv.* quickly, swiftly.
aprisco *s.m.* sheepfold, pen.
aprisionar *v.t.* **1** to put into prison. **2** to capture (coger).
aprobación *s.f.* approval, consent: *doy mi aprobación = I grant my approval.*
aprobado, -a *p.p.* **1** de **aprobar.** || *adj.* **2** approved. || *s.m.* **3** pass mark (nota académica).
aprobar *v.t.* **1** to approve, to consent. **2** to pass (asignatura).
apropiación *s.f.* appropiation.
apropiadamente *adv.* appropriately, fittingly.
apropiado, -a *p.p.* **1** de **apropiar.** || *adj.* **2** suitable, appropriate, fitting.
apropiar *v.t.* **1** (Am.) to earmark, to assign. || *v.pron.* **2** to take, to appropriate seize.
aprovechable *adj.* useful, usable.
aprovechadamente *adv.* profitably.
aprovechado, -a *p.p.* **1** de **aprovechar.** || *adj.* **2** opportunistic.
aprovechamiento *s.m.* exploitation (de cualquier cosa).
aprovechar *v.t.* **1** to use, to take advantage of. || *v.i.* **2** to improve, to progress (progresar). || *v.pron.* **3** to avail oneself of.
aprovisionamiento *s.m.* supplying, supply.
aprovisionar *v.t.* to supply.
aproximación *s.f.* approximation.
aproximadamente *adv.* approximately.
aproximado, -a *p.p.* **1** de **aproximar.** || *adj.* **2** near, close, next.
aproximar *v.t.* **1** to bring near. || *v.pron.* **2** to come near.
aptitud *s.m.* aptitude, ability.
apto, -a *adj.* **1** apt, fit. **2** able, competent (capaz).
apuesta V. **apuesto, -a.**
apuestamente *adv.* smartly, attractively.
apuesto, -a *adj.* **1** good-looking. || *s.f.* **2** bet.
apuntador, -ora *s.m.* y *f.* prompter (en el teatro).
apuntalamiento *s.m.* propping, bracing.
apuntalar *v.t.* to prop up.
apuntar *v.t.* **1** to aim (con arma). **2** to point (señalar, normalmente con el dedo). **3** to note (escribir). **4** to hint, to suggest (sugerir, una solución, por ejemplo). **5** to sketch (bosquejar). **6** to mend, to darn (coser muy ligeramente). **7** to enter (reflejar un dato, un punto, etc.). **8** to sharpen (sacar punta). || *v.i.* **9** to begin to show, to appear gradually (el sol, la barba, etc.). || *v.pron.* **10** to get sour (agriarse, el vino o parecido). **11** to get tight (emborracharse).
apunte *s.m.* **1** note (escrito). **2** COM. entry (de algún artículo o producto). **3** prompter (dado, por el apuntador, en el teatro).
apuñalar *v.t.* to knife, to stab.
apuñalear *v.t.* (Am.) to knife.
apuradamente *adv.* with difficulty: *lo he hecho apuradamente = I've done it with difficulty.*
apurado, -a *p.p.* **1** de **apurar.** || *adj.* **2** hurried, rushed, in a hurry.
apurar *v.t.* **1** to finish up: *apura el vaso de vino = finish up your glass of wine.* **2** (Am.) to hurry (darse prisa). **3** to force; to rush: *hazlo sin apurar a tu pobre hermano = do it without rushing your poor brother.* || *v.pron.* **4** to worry, to fret: *no te apures = don't worry.*
apuro *s.m.* difficulty, jam (normalmente económica).
aquejar *v.t.* **1** to afflict (enfermedad). **2** to distress, to grieve (afligir).
aquel, aquella, aquello *adj.* **1** that, that... over there: *aquel hombre no es el policía = that man is not the policeman.* || *pron.* **2** that, that one: *este coche es bonito pero aquél es mejor = this car is nice, but that one is better.* || *s.m.* **3** attraction: *tiene un aquél difícil de definir = she has an attraction difficult to define.*
aquelarre *s.m.* witches' sabbath.
aquí *adv.* **1** here: *here comes the doctor = aquí llega el doctor.* **2** now: *aquí comienza la película = now the film starts.* **3** at this point (en un relato): *y aquí se echó a llorar al recordarlo = and at this point he burst out crying.* || **4 — y allí,** here and there.
aquiescencia *s.f.* acquiescence.
aquiescente *adj.* aquiescent.
aquietar *v.t.* y *pron.* to calm, to soothe.
aquilatar *v.t.* **1** to appraise (los quilates de una joya). **2** to weigh up, to test (comprobar). **3** to improve (mejorar).
árabe *adj.* **1** Arabian. || *s.m.* y *f.* **2** Arab.
arábigo, -a o **arábico, -a** *adj.* **1** arabic. || *s.m.* **2** Arabic.
arabismo *s.m.* arabism.
arabista *s.m.* y *f.* Arabist.
arabizar *v.t.* to arabize.
arable *adj.* (Am.) arable.
arácnido, -a *adj.* ZOOL. arachnid, arachnidam.
arada *s.f.* AGR. plowing.

arado *p.p.* 1 de **arar.** || *s.m.* 2 (brit.) plough; (EE.UU.) plow (instrumento).
aragonés, -esa *adj./s.m.* y *f.* Aragonese.
arancel *s.m.* customs tariff, duty.
arancelario, -a *adj.* pertaining to tariffs, tariff: *protección arancelaria = tariff protection.*
arándano *s.m.* BOT. bilberry, whortleberry.
arandela *s.f.* MEC. washer.
arandillo *s.m.* ZOOL. marsh warble.
aranzada *s.f.* a land measure.
araña *s.f.* 1 ZOOL. spider. 2 chandelier (candelabro). 3 BOT. love-in-the-mist. 4 resourceful person. || **5 — de mar,** ZOOL. spider crab.
arañar *v.t.* y *pron.* 1 to scratch (cuerpo). || *v.t.* 2 to scrape together (especialmente dinero). 3 to scratch (una superficie).
arañazo *s.m.* scratch.
arar *v.t.* 1 AGR. to plough. 2 to crumple, to wrinkle (arrugar).
arbitraje *s.m.* 1 arbitration (especialmente antes de una huelga). 2 DEP. refereeing, umpiring.
arbitramento o **arbitramiento** *s.m.* arbitration.
arbitrar *v.t.* 1 to arbitrate (juzgar). 2 to allot, to assign (medios, recursos, etc.). || *v.t.* e *i.* 3 DEP. to umpire.
arbitrariamente *adv.* arbitrarily.
arbitrariedad *s.f.* arbitrary act.
arbitrario, -a *adj.* arbitrary.
arbitrio *s.m.* 1 will, free will. 2 means, expedient (medios). || *s.m.pl.* 3 municipal taxes.
arbitrista *s.m.* y *f.* utopic planner or schemer, idealist.
árbitro *s.m.* 1 DEP. referee, umpire. 2 arbitrator (en cuestiones comerciales).
árbol *s.m.* 1 BOT. tree. 2 MEC. axle. 3 MAR. mast.
arboladura *s.f.* MAR. masting, mast and yards.
arboleda *s.f.* grove, wooded land.
arboledo *s.m.* woodland.
arbolista *s.m.* arborist.
arbollón *s.m.* abollón sewer, drain.
arborecer *s.m.* to grow into a tree.
arbóreo, -a *adj.* BOT. arboreal.
arbusto *s.m.* shrub, bush.
arca *s.m.* 1 chest (donde guardar cosas). || *s.f.pl.* 2 coffers (donde se guarda el dinero). || **3 — de agua,** water tank. **4 — de la alianza,** REL. Ark of the Covenant. **5 — de Noé,** Noah's Ark.
arcabucero *s.m.* HIST. 1 harquebusier. 2 harquebus marker.
arcabuz *s.m.* harquebus.
arcada *s.f.* retch (antes de vomitar).
arcaduz *s.m.* 1 pipe, conduit. 2 harquebus marker.
arcaico, -a *adj.* archaic.
arcaísmo, -a *s.m.* archaism.
arcaizar *v.t.* to archaize.
arcángel *s.m.* REL. archangel.
arcano, -a *adj.* 1 arcane. || *s.m.* 2 arcanum.
arce *s.m.* BOT. maple tree.
arcediano *s.m.* REL. archdeacon.
arcén *s.m.* 1 border, brim, edge. 2 curbstone (de un pozo).
arcilla *s.f.* clay.
arcilloso, -a *adj.* clayey, clay-like.
arcipreste *s.m.* REL. archpriest.
arciprestazgo *s.m.* archpriesthood.
arco *s.m.* 1 bow. 2 GEOM. arc. 3 ARQ. arch. 4 DEP. goal.
archicofradía *s.f.* REL. brotherhood.
archidiócesis *s.f.* archdiocese.
archiducal *adj.* archducal.
archiduque *s.m.* archduke.
archiduquesa *s.f.* archduchess.
archiducado *s.m.* archduchy, archdukedom.
archimandita *s.m.* archimandrite.
archipiélago *s.m.* GEOG. archipelago.
archivador *s.m.* letter file, filing cabinet.
archivador, -a *adj.* 1 filing. || *s.m.* y *f.* 2 archivist. 3 filing clerk. || *s.f.* 4 school notebook.
archivar *v.t.* 1 to file (ordenar). 2 to shelve (una idea, plan, proyecto, etc.).
archivero, -a *s.m.* y *f.* archivist.
archivo *s.m.* 1 archives, records. 2 (fig.) soul of discretion (persona que guarda un secreto muy bien).
arder *v.i.* 1 to burn. 2 to glow (resplandecer). 3 to burn (arder con alguna pasión o similar). || *v.t.* 4 to burn, to scorch (abrasar). || *v.pron.* 5 to spoil, to rot (estropearse por excesivo calor).
ardid *s.m.* stratagem, trick, artifice.
ardiente *adj.* 1 burning (quemando). 2 glowing, shining (que brilla). 3 passionate, ardent (pasión).
ardientemente *adv.* ardently, passionately, fervently: *he deseado eso ardientemente = I have wanted that passionately.*
ardilla *s.f.* ZOOL. squirrel.
ardor *s.m.* 1 warmth (de calor). 2 MED. burning sensation: *ardor de estómago = heartburn.* 3 (fig.) ardour, eagerness, zeal (celo).
ardoroso, -a *adj.* burning, ardent, vehement, eager, zealous.
arduamente *adv.* arduously.
arduo, -a *adj.* ardous, hard, difficult.
área *s.f.* 1 GEOM. area. 2 area (tipo de medida). 3 zone, area: *en este área no hay bares = in this zone there are no bars.*
arena *s.f.* 1 sand. 2 bullring (de la plaza de toros). 3 (fig.) arena (política, especialmente).
arenero *s.m.* sandbox.
arenga *s.f.* harangue, speech, address.
arenilla *s.f.* MED. stone (en el riñón).
arenisco *s.m.* sandy.
arenoso, -a *adj.* sandy.
arenque *s.m.* ZOOL. herring.
aréola *s.f.* areola.
areómetro *s.m.* MEC. areometer, hydrometer.
areópago *s.m.* aeropagus.
arete *s.m.* earring.
argamasa *s.f.* mortar.
argelino, -a *adj./s.m.* y *f.* algerian, algerine.
argénteo, -a *adj.* silvery, silver-white.
argentería *s.f.* embroidery in gold or silver.
argentinismo *s.m.* argentinism.
argiro, -a *adj.* argive.
argolla *s.f.* shackles.
argón *s.m.* QUIM. argón.
argot *s.m.* slang, jargon.
argucia *s.f.* sophistry, subtlety.
argüir *v.i.* 1 to argue. || *v.t.* 2 to reproach, to accuse (acusar). 3 to deduce, to infer (deducir).
argumentación *s.f.* argumentation.
argumentar *v.t.* to argue, to dispute, to reason.
argumento *s.m.* 1 argument. 2 plot (de una novela o similar).
aria *s.f.* MUS. aria.
aridez *s.f.* aridity, aridness.
árido, -a *adj.* 1 arid, dry (especialmente el terreno). 2 dull, uninteresting: *un tema muy árido = a very uninteresting topic.*
aries *s.m.* ASTR. aries.
ariete *s.m.* 1 HIST. battering ram. 2 DEP. centre forward (delantero centro).
arillero *s.m.* (Am.) the poorer quarter of a city.
ario, -a *adj.* aryan.
arisco, -a *adj.* unsociable, surly, shy.
arista *s.f.* 1 edge (borde). 2 GEOM. edge.
aristocracia *s.f.* aristocracy.
aristócrata *s.m.* y *f.* aristocrat.
aristocrático, -a *adj.* aristocratic.
aristotélico, -a *adj./s.m.* y *f.* aristotelian.
aristotelismo *s.m.* FIL. aristotelianism.
aritmética *s.f.* arithmetic.
aritmético, -a *adj.* 1 arithmetical. || *s.m.* y *f.* 2 arithmetician.
aritmómetro *s.m.* TEC. arithmometer, calculating machine.
arlequín *s.m.* harlequin.
arlequinado, -a *adj.* 1 parti-coloured (ropa).
arma *s.f.* 1 arm, weapon. 2 MIL. division, corps. || *s.f.pl.* 3 MIL. troops. 4 means (medios): *las armas para luchar contra la pobreza son los libros = the means to fight against poverty are books.* || **5 — blanca,** bladed weapon. **6 — de fuego,** firearm.
armada *s.f.* MAR. 1 navy, naval forces. 2 fleet (flota).
armadía *s.f.* raft, float.
armadillo *s.m.* ZOOL. armadillo.
armado, -a *p.p.* 1 de **armar.** || *adj.* 2 armed.
armador, -a *s.m.* y *f.* MAR. 1 shipowner. 2 shipbuilder.
armadura *s.f.* 1 HIST. armour. 2 frame (de algunos objetos).
armamento *s.m.* weaponry.
armar *v.t.* 1 to arm, to provide with arms. 2 to prime (preparar un arma para el disparo, especialmente las antiguas). 3 to assemble (poner distintos elementos juntos). 4 to fit out, to equip (equipar, especialmente en un contexto militar). || *v.t.* y *pron.* 5 to prepare (disponer). 6 to cause (follón o similar). || **7 armarla,** to make trouble, to start a row. **8 armarse de valor/paciencia,** to

gather up one's courage/to arm oneself with patience.
armario *s.m.* press, wardrove, cabinet, closet.
armatoste *s.m.* contraption: *vaya armatoste = what a contraption.*
armazón *s.m.* frame, framework, skeleton.
armella *s.f.* eyebolt.
armenio, -a *adj.* armenian.
armería *s.f.* 1 gunsmith's shop. 2 MIL. armory.
armero, -a *s.m.* y *f.* gunsmith.
armiño *s.m.* ZOOL. ermine.
armisticio *s.m.* armistice.
armónicamente *adj.* harmonically.
armonio *s.m.* harmonium.
armoniosamente *adv.* harmoniously.
armonioso, -a *adj.* harmonious.
armonizable *adj.* harmonizable.
armonización *s.f.* harmonization.
armonizar o **harmonizar** *v.i.* to harmonize.
árnica *s.f.* BOT. arnica.
aro *s.m.* 1 hoop. 2 (Am.) ring, wedding ring. 3 BOT. arum. || 4 **entrar por el —,** to have no other choice, to have no choice.
aroma *s.m.* 1 scent, aroma. 2 bouquet (de vinos).
aromático, -a *adj.* aromatic.
aromatizar *v.t.* to aromatize, to perfume, to scent.
arpa *s.m.* 1 MUS. harp. || 2 **tocar el —,** (Am.) to steal.
arpegio *s.m.* MUS. arpeggio.
arpillera *s.f.* burlap, sackcloth.
arponear o **arponar** *v.t.* to harpoon.
arponero *s.m.* 1 harpoon maker. 2 bow maker.
arquear *v.t.* y *pron.* 1 to arch, to curve (un objeto o parte del cuerpo). || *v.t.* 2 to gauge (medir la capacidad de un barco). 3 to beat (batir lana).
arqueo *s.m.* 1 arching, curving (curvatura). 2 MAT. gauging (medición de la capacidad de un barco). 3 COM. audit.
arqueología *s.f.* archaeology.
arqueológico, -a *adj.* archaeological.
arqueólogo, -a *s.m.* y *f.* archaeologist.
arquería *s.f.* arcade.
arquero *s.m.* 1 HIST. archer. 2 DEP. goalkeeper (portero).
arqueta *s.f.* small coffer.
arquetipo *s.m.* archetype.
arquiepiscopal *adj.* REL. archiepiscopal.
arquitecto, -a *s.m.* y *f.* architect.
arquitectónico, -a *adj.* architectonic.
arquitectura *s.f.* architecture.
arquitectural *adj.* architectural.
arquitrabe *s.m.* ARQ. architrave.
arrabal *s.m.* suburb.
arrabalero, -a *adj.* 1 suburban. 2 uncouth, coarse (burdo).
arracimarse *v.pron.* to cluster, to bunch.
arraclán *s.m.* BOT. alder buckthorn.
arraigado, -a *p.p.* 1 de **arraigar.** || *adj.* 2 well-rooted, deep-rooted (en un lugar).
arraigar *v.i.* y *pron.* 1 to take root (plantas o similares). 2 DER. to post bail, to post bond. || *v.t.* 3 to fix, to establish (fijar). || *v.pron.* 4 to settle down, to become deeply rooted, to take hold (una persona, una característica, una tradición, etc.).
arraigo *s.m.* 1 rooting (de plantas). 2 hold, influence: *tengo mucho arraigo sobre él = I've got quite a hold over him.*
arramblar *v.t.* y *pron.* 1 to cover with sand (después de una inundación o crecida). || *v.t.* 2 to sweep away (arrastrar). 3 to make off with: *el tío arrambló con toda la cerveza = the bloke made of with all the beer.*
arrancada *s.f.* sudden burst, burst of speed.
arrancar *v.t.* 1 to uproot, to pull up. 2 to pull away, to snatch (apartar): *la música nos arrancó de nuestros asientos = the music pulled us away from our seats.* || *v.t.* e *i.* 3 to start, to start up (un vehículo). || *v.i.* 4 to originate, to stem (una idea, un proyecto, etc.): *la teoría arranca de los estudios de John Lavern = the theory stems from the studies by John Lavern.* || *v.i.* y *pron.* 5 to start, to break (a hacer algo): *ella se arrancó a cantar = she broke into a song.*
arranque *s.m.* 1 uprooting (acción de arrancar). 2 starting, jolting (de un vehículo). 3 fit, outburst (arrebato). 4 start, beginning (comienzo de algo).
arras *s.f.pl.* 1 coins given by the bridegroom to the bride as a symbol. 2 pledge (prenda).
arrasado, -a *adj.* satin-like, satiny.
arrasar *v.t.* 1 to level, to flatten, to smooth (un terreno). 2 to raze, to devastate (destruir totalmente). 3 to fill to the brim (llenar hasta arriba). || *v.t.* y *pron.* 4 to fill with tears (llenarse de lágrimas los ojos). || *v.i.* y *pron.* 5 to clear (despejarse de nubes el cielo).
arrastrar *v.t.* 1 to drag (algo, físicamente). 2 to convince, to win over, to carry away (entusiasmar con palabras o ejemplo). 3 to play decidedly (en las cartas). || *v.pron.* 4 to humiliate oneself, to crawl, to grovel.
arrastre *s.m.* 1 pulling, dragging. || 2 **estar uno para el —,** to be useless, to be washed-up.
¡arre! *interj.* giddyap, get up.
¡arrea! *interj.* my God, geepers.
arrear *v.t.* 1 to drive (ganado). 2 to urge on, to hurry: *no me arrees tanto = don't urge me on in that way.*
arrebatadamente *adv.* 1 thoughtlessly, carelessly (sin cuidado). 2 hastily (con prisa).
arrebatado, -a *p.p.* 1 de **arrebatar.** || *adj.* 2 impetuous (característica personal). 3 very bright, blazing (de color).
arrebatador, -a *adj.* 1 captivating, charming (de gran belleza, especialmente mujeres): *está arrebatadora = she's truly captivating.* 2 violent (violento).
arrebatar *v.t.* 1 to snatch, to seize (quitar con fuerza). || *v.t.* y *pron.* 2 to move, to stir: *su discurso nos arrebató de una manera impresionante = his speech stirred us in an impressive way.* || *v.pron.* 3 to get carried away, to be seized (por una pasión).
arrebato *s.m.* 1 fit, rage, fury. 2 rapture.
arrebol *s.m.* red glow.
arrebujadamente *adv.* confusedly.
arrebujar *v.t.* 1 to throw in a heap, to leave in a mess (especialmente objetos que se pueden doblar, como ropa, libros, etc.). || *v.pron.* 2 to wrap oneself up, to bundle oneself up (por el frío, especialmente).
arrechar *v.t.* y *pron.* (Am.) to make an effort, to try hard.
arrechucho *s.m.* fit, attack: *le dio un arrechucho = he got a fit.*
arreciar *v.i.* y *pron.* to grow worse, to get more severe (especialmente un fenómeno natural, como tormenta, lluvia, etc.).
arrecife *s.m.* 1 GEOL. reef (en el mar). 2 stone-paved road.
arredramiento *s.m.* backing out, fright, intimidation.
arredrar *v.t.* y *pron.* to frighten away, to scare away.
arregladamente *adv.* regularly, in an orderly way.
arreglado, -a *p.p.* 1 de **arreglar.** || *adj.* 2 neat, tidy (ordenado). 3 made up (maquillado, especialmente mujeres). 4 fixed, mended (reparado). 5 reasonable (especialmente, hablando de precios).
arreglar *v.t.* 1 to fix, to mend (reparar). 2 to range, to put in the right order. 3 to resolve, to settle (problema, dificultad, etc.). || 4 **arreglárselas,** to manage whatever the situation (salir adelante como buenamente sea).
arreglo *s.m.* 1 arrangement. 2 repair, mending (reparación). 3 solution (de un problema). 4 MUS. arrangement. || 5 **con — a,** according to, in accordance with.
arrellanarse *v.pron.* to sit back comfortably, to lounge.
arremangado, -a *p.p.* 1 de **arremangar.** || *adj.* 2 with one's sleeves rolled up.
arremangar V. **remangar.**
arremeter *v.i.* to attack, to rush.
arremetida *s.f.* attack, assault.
arremolinarse *v.pron.* 1 to mill about, to crowd about. 2 to swirl, to eddy (el agua).
arrendador, -a *s.m.* y *t.* tenant.
arrendajo *s.m.* 1 ZOOL. jay. 2 (fig.) aper, mimic.
arrendamiento *s.m.* rental, rent, hire.
arrendar *v.t.* to rent out, to let.
arrendatario, -a *adj.* 1 renting. || *s.m.* y *f.* 2 tenant.
arreo *s.m.* 1 ornament (adorno). || *s.pl.* 2 harness, trappings (para los caballos).
arrepentimiento *s.m.* repentance, regret.
arrepentirse *v.pron.* 1 to repent, to regret: *se arrepintió al final = he repented at the end.* 2 to be sorry (sentirlo).
arrestado, -a *p.p.* 1 de **arrestar.** || *adj.* 2 arrested (detenido). 3 bol, daring (atrevido).

arrestar *v.t.* 1 to arrest, to detain. || *v.pron.* 2 to rush boldly, not to be afraid at all.
arresto *s.m.* 1 arrest. 2 MIL. confinement (arresto militar). 3 daring, boldness (valentía).
arrevesado, -a *adj.* (Am.) complicated, intricate.
arrianismo *s.m.* arianism.
arriar *v.t.* MAR. to lower, to haul down (las velas).
arriba *adv.* 1 above: *ella no sabe quién vive arriba = she doesn't know who lives above.* 2 upstairs (en una casa): *come upstairs to help me = ven arriba para ayudarme.* 3 above, abovementioned (arriba citado). || 4 **de — abajo,** from top to bottom.
arribar *v.i.* 1 to arrive, to land (en barco).
arribista *s.m.* arriviste, upstart, social climber.
arriendo *s.m.* rent, renting.
arriero *s.m.* muleteer.
arriesgado, -a *adj.* 1 risky, dangerous. 2 daring, bold, rash.
arriesgar *v.t.* y *pron.* to take the risk, to take a risk, to risk: *no te arriesgues a perderlo todo = don't take the risk of losing everything.*
arrimadero *s.m.* support, prop.
arrimar *v.t.* y *pron.* 1 to bring near: *arrima una silla = bring a chair near.* || *v.t.* 2 to put aside, to shelve (arrinconar un plan, proyecto, etc.). || *v.pron.* 3 to lean (apoyarse). 4 to seek protection (buscar protección). 5 (Am.) to shack up, to live together (vivir amancebados).
arrimón *s.m.* loafer, idler.
arrinconar *v.t.* 1 to put away, to leave in a corner. 2 to corner, to pursue (perseguir hasta un rincón). 3 to abandon, to neglect (no hacer caso). || *v.pron.* 4 to withdraw, to retreat (aislarse).
arritmia *s.f.* MED. arrhythmia.
arrítmico, -a *adj.* 1 MED. arrhythmic. 2 lack of rythm.
arroba *s.f.* 1 arroba (Spanish measurement). || 2 **echar por arrobas,** to exaggerate.
arrobado, -a *p.p.* 1 de **arrobar.** || *adj.* 2 ecstatic, enraptured.
arrobar *v.t.* y *pron.* to enchant, to enrapture; to become enraptured.
arrobo *s.m.* ecstasy, rapture.
arrodillamiento o **arrodilladura** *s.m.* o *s.f.* kneeling.
arrodillar *v.t.* y *pron.* to kneel down.
arrogación *s.f.* arrogation.
arrogancia *s.f.* arrogance.
arrogante *adj.* arrogant.
arrogantemente *adv.* arrogantly.
arrogar *v.t.* 1 to arrogate, to assume (atribuirse algún derecho). 2 to adopt (una postura o similar). || *v.pron.* 2 to arrogate oneself (derecho o similar).
arrojadamente *adv.* daringly, boldly, resolutely.
arrojadizo, -a *adj.* for throwing, easily thown, that can be thrown (especialmente un arma).
arrojado, -a *adj.* bold, intrepid, dashing, rash.
arrojo *s.m.* 1 boldness, rashness, resolutness.
arrollador *s.m.* 1 rolling, winding. 2 violent, sweeping.
arrollar *v.t.* 1 to carry away (quitar de enmedio). 2 to trample, to run over (atropellar). 3 (fig.) to defeat easily.
arropamiento *s.m.* wrapping up, bundling up.
arropar *v.t.* 1 to tuck in (típico movimiento de meter bien la ropa de la cama). 2 (fig.) to protect: *su hermano mayor siempre le arropa = his elder brother always protects him.*
arrostrar *v.t.* 1 to face (up to), confront. || *v.pron.* 2 to face (up to), stand up to.
arroyo *s.m.* 1 stream, brook. 2 (fig.) gutter (como sitio donde va gente perdida). || 3 **poner en el — a alguien,** to put someone on the street, to turn out of the house.
arroyuelo *s.m.* rill, small brook.
arroz *s.m.* rice.
arrozal *s.m.* rice field, rice paddy.
arrufianado, -a *adj.* like a scoundrel, looking like a rascal.
arruga *s.f.* wrinkle, crease, crumple, rumple.
arrugamiento *s.m.* wrinkling, creasing, crumpling.
arrugar *v.t.* 1 to wrinkle, to line (la cara). 2 to crease (ropa). 3 to crumple (papel o similar). 4 (Am.) to bother, to annoy. || *v.pron.* 5 to coil up, to shrink (encogerse). 6 to get afraid, not to dare: *el pobrecillo se arrugó cuando vio a la policía = the poor fellow got very afraid when he saw the police.* || 7 **— la frente/el ceño/el entrecejo,** to knit one's brow (con sentido de enfado).
arruinador, -ora *adj.* ruining (por ejemplo, negocio).
arruinamiento *s.m.* ruin, ruination.
arrullador, -ora *adj.* 1 cooing. 2 lulling.
arrullar *v.t.* 1 to coo, to lull, to sing to sleep. 2 (fig.) to court (los enamorados).
arrullo *s.m.* cooing, lullaby.
arrumaco *s.m.* caress, show of affection.
arrumbar *v.t.* 1 to put aside, to put away, to cast aside, to lay aside. 2 to abandon, to neglect (cosa o persona).
arsenal *s.m.* 1 MAR. navy yard, shipyard. 2 MIL. arsenal.
arsénico *s.m.* arsenic.
arte *s.m.* 1 art (cualquiera de ellos). 2 skill (habilidad): *este hombre tiene un arte especial para cocinar = this man has a very special skill for cooking.* || 3 **malas artes,** trickery.
artefacto *s.m.* device, appliance.
artemisa *s.f.* BOT. mugwort, sagebrush.
arteramente *adv.* craftily, cunningly, slyly.
arteria *s.f.* ANAT. artery.
arterial *adj.* arterial.
arteriola *s.f.* ANAT. arteriole.
arteriosclerosis *s.f.* arteriosclerosis.
artero, -a *adj.* cunning, artful, crafty, sly.
artesa *s.f.* trough, kneading trough.
artesanado *s.m.* ARQ. craftsmanship, artisanship, artisanry.
artesanía *s.f.* craftsmanship.
artesano *s.m.* craftsman.
artesiano, -a *adj.* artesian.
artesón *s.m.* kitchen tub.
artesonado, -a *p.p.* 1 de **artesonar.** || *adj.* 2 coffered (techos). || *s.m.* 3 ARQ. coffering.
ártico, -a *adj.* arctic.
articulación *s.f.* 1 FON. articulation (de sonidos). 2 ANAT. articulation, joint.
articulado, -a *p.p.* 1 de **articular.** || *adj.* 2 articulate (lenguaje). || *s.m.* 3 DER. articles (de una ley): *el articulado está muy bien escrito = the articles are very well written.*
articular *v.t.* 1 to enunciate, to articulate (palabras). 2 DER. to divide into articles (una ley). 3 to join (unir un mecanismo que está en piezas).
articulatorio, -a *adj.* enunciatory, having to do with pronunciation.
articulista *s.m.* y *f.* writer of articles.
artículo *s.m.* 1 PER. article. 2 GRAM. article. 3 DER. article. 4 item, thing (especialmente desde el punto de vista del comercio). || 5 **— de fe,** REL. article of faith. 6 **— de la muerte,** one's last breath, one's last moments. 7 **— de primera necesidad,** basic commodity. 8 **— determinado,** GRAM. determinate article. 9 **— indeterminado,** GRAM. indeterminate article.
artífice *s.m.* 1 artificer, craftsman, artist. 2 maker.
artificial *adj.* artificial.
artificiero *s.m.* artificer.
artificio *s.m.* device, contrivance.
artificioso, -a *adj.* cunning, crafty.
artilugio *s.m.* contraption, worthless mechanical contrivance.
artillería *s.f.* artillery.
artillero *s.m.* gunner, artilleryman.
artimaña *s.f.* 1 trick, stratagem. 2 trap, snare.
artista *s.m.* y *f.* artist.
artístico, -a *adj.* artistic.
artrítico, -a *adj./s.m.* y *f.* arthritic.
artritis *s.f.* arthritis.
artritismo *s.m.* arthritism.
artrosis *s.f.* arthrosis.
arzobispado *s.m.* archbishopric.
arzobispal *adj.* archiepiscopal.
arzobispo *s.m.* archbishop.
as *s.m.* 1 ace (naipe o dado). 2 ace, star (experto).
asa *s.f.* handle, grip.
asado, -a *p.p.* 1 de **asar.** || *adj.* 2 cooked (con muchísimo calor). || *s.m.* 3 GAST. roasted meat.
asaetear *v.t.* to shoot, to hit (con un arco).
asainetado, -a *adj.* funny, comical (parecido a un sainete).
asalariado, -a *adj.* 1 salaried. || *s.m.* y *f.* 2 wage-earner.

asaltante *s.m.* y *f.* attacker, assailant.
asaltar *v.t.* **1** to attack, to assault. **2** to overtake (de repente, una duda, un pensamiento, un temor, etc.). **3** to rob: *asaltar un banco = to rob a bank.*
asalto *s.m.* **1** assault, attack. **2** DEP. round (en el boxeo). **3** DEP. bout (en la esgrima). **4** robbery (robo).
asamblea *s.f.* assembly, meeting.
asambleísta *s.f.* member of an assembly.
asaz *adv.* quite, too (demasiado).
asbesto *s.m.* asbestos.
ascendencia *s.f.* ancestry, line of ancestors.
ascendente *adj.* ascending, upward.
ascender *v.i.* **1** to ascend, to rise. **2** to be promoted (en el trabajo, ejército, etc.). **3** to amount to (cantidad): *todo asciende a 24.000 pesetas = everything amounts to 24.000 pesetas.*
ascendiente *s.m.* **1** influence: *tiene ascendiente sobre mí = he has influence over me.* || *s.m.* y *f.* **2** ancestor (antepasado).
ascensión *s.f.* **1** ascension, rise. || **2 la Ascensión,** REL. the Ascension.
ascensional *adj.* ascensional.
ascensionista *s.m.* y *f.* balloonist.
ascenso *s.m.* **1** promotion (especialmente en el trabajo). **2** ascent, rise.
ascensor *s.m.* lift, elevator.
ascensorista *s.m.* y *f.* elevator operator.
asceta *s.m.* y *f.* ascetic.
ascético, -a *adj.* ascetic.
ascetismo *s.m.* asceticism.
asco *s.m.* **1** disgust, revulsion. **2** disgusting thing, revolting thing (cosa concreta). **3** (fig.) fear (miedo). || **4 estar hecho un –,** to be filthy, to be covered in dirt. **5 hacer ascos,** to turn up one's nose. **6 ser un –,** to be disgusting, to be worthless.
ascua *s.f.* **1** ember. || **2 arrimar el – a su sardina,** to look out for number one. **3 – de oro,** glittering object. **4 estar en ascuas,** to be on edge.
aseadamente *adv.* cleanly, neatly.
aseado, -a *adj.* clean, neat.
asear *v.t.* y *pron.* **1** to wash. **2** to clean (limpiar).
asechanza *s.f.* trap, snare.
asechar *v.t.* to trap, to snare.
asediar *v.t.* **1** to besiege, to lay siege to. **2** (fig.) to pester, to bother.
asedio *s.m.* siege, blockade. **2** (fig.) nuisance, annoyance.
asegurado, -a *adj.* **1** insured. || *s.m.* y *f.* **2** policyhalder.
asegurador, -ora *adj.* **1** insuring (de seguros de todo tipo). || *s.m.* y *f.* **2** insurance company.
aseguramiento *s.m.* **1** securing; security. **2** insurance.
asegurar *v.t.* **1** to secure (sujetar). **2** to assure, to reassure: *te aseguro que no te miento = I assure you I'm not lying to you.* **3** to insure (a través de compañía de seguros). || *v.pron.* **4** to insure oneself (contra incendios, accidentes, etc.). **5** to make sure: *asegúrate de que todo está cerrado = make sure that everything is locked.*
asemejar *v.t.* y *pron.* to liken, to compare, to be like: *esto casi se asemeja a la guerra = this is like the war.*
asenso *s.m.* assent, approbation.
asentada o **sentada** *s.f.* sitting.
asentaderas *s.f.pl.* buttocks.
asentado, -a *p.p.* **1** de **asentar.** || *adj.* **2** sensible (de carácter): *un hombre serio y asentado = a serious and sensible man.* **3** stable, established (negocio, empresa, etc.).
asentador *s.m.* **1** razor strop. **2** wholesale provider.
asentamiento *s.m.* assent.
asentar *v.t.* **1** to note, to write down. **2** to suppose, to take it for granted (dar por sabido). **3** to fix (fijar, un precio). || *v.pron.* **4** to settle down (como colonos). **5** to alight (posarse).
asentimiento *s.m.* consent, assent.
asentir *v.i.* to assent, to agree.
aseo *s.m.* **1** cleanliness. **2** washroom (lugar).
asepsia *s.f.* asepsis.
aséptico, -a *adj.* aseptic.
asequible *adj.* accessible, obtainable, reachable.
aserradero *s.m.* sawmill.
aserrado, -a *p.p.* **1** de **aserrar.** || *adj.* **2** serrated.
asertivo, -a *adj.* assertive.
aserto, -a *s.m.* y *f.* assertion, affirmation, statement.
aserradero *s.m.* sawmill.
aserrar *v.t.* to saw.
aserrín o **serrín** *s.m.* sawdust.
asesinar *v.t.* to murder, to assassinate.
asesinato *s.m.* murder, assassination.
asesino *s.m.* y *f.* **1** killer, murderer, assassin. || *adj.* **2** murderous.
asesor, -ora *s.m.* y *f.* adviser, assessor.
asesoramiento *s.m.* advice, counsel.
asesorar *v.t.* to counsel, to advise.
asesoría *s.f.* consultanting office.
asestar *v.t.* to deal, to deliver (un golpe).
aseveración *s.f.* asseveration, assertion.
aseverar *v.t.* to asseverate, assert.
aseverativo, -a *adj.* asseverative, assertive.
asexual *adj.* asexual.
asfaltado, -a *p.p.* **1** de **asfaltar.** || *adj.* **2** covered in asphalt, asphalted.
asfaltar *v.t.* to asphalt.
asfáltico, -a *adj.* asphaltic.
asfalto *s.m.* asphalt.
asfixia *s.f.* asphyxia, asphyxiation.
asfixiar *v.t.* **1** to asphyxiate, to smother. **2** to suffocate, to be asphyxiated.
así *adv.* **1** this way, like this: *se hace así = it's done like this.* || *conj.* **2** therefore (por lo tanto). **3** so: *estoy cansado, así que no puedo ayudarte ahora = I'm tired so I can't help you now.* || **4 –, –,** so so, not too well. **5 – como –,** any which way, any way. **6 – que,** when, at the time: *así que llegue, házmelo saber = when he arrives, let me know.*
asiático, -a *adj.* Asiatic, Asian. || *s.m.* y *f.* Asian.
asidero *s.m.* **1** handle, hold. **2** occasion, pretext.
asiduamente *adv.* assiduously.
asiduidad *s.f.* assiduity, frequency.
asiduo, -a *adj.* assiduous, frequent.
asiento *s.m.* **1** seat. **2** COM. entry (apunte de mercancías recibidas o cosas de ese estilo). **3** maturity (del carácter). **4** ARQ. settling.
asignación *s.f.* **1** allotment (de dinero o especie). **2** allowance (de dinero).
asignado, -a *adj.* assigned.
asignatario, -a *s.m.* y *f.* (Am.) DER. legatee, heir.
asignatura *s.f.* subject or course of study.
asilar *v.t.* **1** to give shelter (dar protección). **2** to give political asylum (dar asilo político). || *v.pron.* **3** to take shelter (protegerse). **4** to seek political asylum (buscar asilo político).
asilo *s.m.* **1** shelter (refugio). **2** residence (especialmente para los ancianos).
asimetría *s.f.* asymmetry.
asimétrico, -a *adj.* asymmetric.
asimiento *s.m.* **1** grasping, holding. **2** (fig.) attachment (afecto).
asimilable *adj.* assimilable.
asimilación *s.f.* assimilation.
asimilar *v.t.* **1** to assimilate. || *v.pron.* **2** to be similar.
asimilativo, -a *adj.* assimilative.
asimismo o **así mismo** *adv.* in like manner, likewise, also.
asir *v.t.* **1** to grasp, to seize. **2** to grab on (agarrarse, especialmente cuando se va uno a caer). || *v.i.* **3** to take root (plantas).
asistencia *s.f.* **1** attendance (a un espectáculo, clase, etc.). **2** aid, assistance (ayuda médica o de socorro).
asistenta *s.f.* charwoman, maid, home help.
asistente *adj.* **1** attending. || *s.m.* y *f.* **2** attendant, assistant. **3** MIL. aid. || *s.f.* **4** home help.
asistir *v.i.* **1** to be present, to attend (a espectáculo, clase, etc.). || *v.t.* **2** to help, to work (especialmente como criada por horas). **3** to accompany (acompañar).
asma *s.f.* asthma.
asmático, -a *adj., s.m.* y *f.* asthmatic.
asnal *adj.* donkey-like, asinine.
asno, -a *s.m.* y *f.* **1** ZOOL. ass, donkey, jack-ass. **2** (fig.) jack-ass (persona).
asociación *s.f.* association, partnership.
asociado, -a *p.p.* **1** de **asociar.** || *adj.* **2** associated. || *s.m.* y *f.* **3** member (de una asociación).
asociativo, -a *adj.* associative.
asolador, -a *adj.* ravaging, destroying.
asolar *v.t.* **1** to ravage, to destroy. **2** to parch, to scorch (plantas, por la acción del sol).
asomar *v.i.* **1** to appear, to be visible: *ya asoman los dientes del pequeño = the baby's teeth are beggining to be visible.* || *v.t.* **2** to show (especialmente la cara por algún lugar). || *v.pron.* **3** to lean out (normalmente, por la ventana o similar).

asombrar *v.t.* 1 to amaze, to astonish. 2 to shade (dar sombra). || *v.pron.* 3 to be amazed, to be astonished.
asombro *s.m.* amazement, astonishment.
asombro *s.m.* 1 fright. 2 amazement, astonishment.
asombrosamente *adv.* amazingly, aston ishingly.
asombroso, -a *adj.* amazing, astonishing.
asomo *s.m.* 1 suspicion (sospecha). 2 trace, least: *ni asomo de duda = not a trace of a doubt.* || 3 **ni por asomo,** not at all, no way, not by a long shot.
asonancia *s.f.* FON. assonance.
asonante *adj.* FON. assonant.
aspa *s.f.* 1 X-shaped cross. 2 vane, blade, sail (de molino). 3 MAT. multiplication sign.
aspaviento *s.m.* exaggerated behavior, theatricality.
aspecto *s.m.* aspect, appearance, looks.
ásperamente *adv.* roughly, harshly, rudely.
aspereza *s.f.* 1 roughness, ruggedness (de una superficie cualquiera). 2 harshness (en el trato humano o social). 3 sourness, bitterness (en el gusto o sabor).
áspero, -a *adj.* 1 rough, rugged (superficie). 2 harsh (en el trato). 3 sour, bitter (en el gusto o sabor).
asperón *s.m.* sardstone, grindstone.
aspersión *s.f.* aspersion, sprinkling.
aspid o **aspide** *s.m.* ZOOL. asp, aspic.
aspillera *s.f.* loophole.
aspiración *s.f.* 1 inhalation, breathing in (respiración hacia dentro). 2 suction (succión). 3 aspiration, desire (anhelo). 4 FON. aspiration.
aspirador, -a *s.m.* o *f.* vacuum cleaner.
aspirante *s.m.* y *f.* candidate (candidato).
aspirar *v.t.* 1 to inhale, to breath in (inspirar). 2 to suck, to draw in (succionar). 3 to aspire, to desire, to long for (desear). 4 FON. aspirate.
aspirina *s.f.* aspirin.
asqueado, -a *p.p.* 1 de **asquear.** || *adj.* 2 sickened: *estoy asqueado de la avaricia de los hombres = I am sickened by men's greediness.*
asquear *v.t.* 1 to nauseate, to disgust. || *v.i.* 2 to be sickening, to be disgusting.
asquerosamente *adv.* disgustingly, repulsively.
asquerosidad *s.f.* 1 filth (suciedad). 2 (fig.) vileness (vileza).
asqueroso, -a *adj.* loathsome, dirty, filthy, sickening/nauseous.
asta *s.f.* 1 horn. 2 shaft (de una lanza u otros instrumentos alargados). 3 flagpole, flastaff (de la bandera). || 4 **a media —,** at half mast.
astenia *s.f.* MED. asthenia.
asténico, -a *adj.* without any energy, without strength.
asterisco *s.m.* asterisk.
asterismo *s.m.* ASTR. group of planets.
asteroide *s.m.* ASTR. asteroid.
astigmático, -a *adj.* astigmatic.
astigmatismo *s.m.* astigmatism.
astilla *s.f.* splinter, fragment, chip.
astillar *v.t.* to chip, to splinter, to destroy, to break into pieces.
astillero *s.m.* MAR. shipyard, dockyard.
astracán *s.m.* astrakhan.
astral *adj.* astral.
astricción *s.f.* astriction.
astringente *adj.* astringent.
astringir o **astiñir** *v.t.* 1 to contract, to astringe. 2 (fig.) to constrain, to bind.
astro *s.m.* 1 ASTR. heavenly body, star. 2 (fig.) star, celebrity.
astrofísica *s.f.* astrophysics.
astrolabio *s.m.* astrolabe.
astrología *s.f.* astrology.
astrológico, -a *adj.* astrological.
astrólogo, -a *adj.* 1 astrologic, astrological. || *s.m.* y *f.* 2 astrologer.
astronauta *s.m.* astronaut.
astronáutica *s.f.* astronautics.
astronave *s.f.* spaceship.
astronomía *s.f.* astronomy.
astronómicamente *adv.* astronomically.
astronómico, -a *adj.* 1 astronomic. 2 (fig.) astronomical, enormous.
astrónomo *s.m.* astronomer.
astucia *s.f.* 1 astuteness, cunning. 2 trick, artifice.
astutamente *adv.* astutely, cleverly, shrewdly.
asturiano, -a *adj.* y *s.m.* y *f.* from Asturias.
astuto, -a *adj.* astute, cunning, sly, crafty, clewer.
asueto *s.m.* brief vacation, day off, school holiday.
asumir *v.t.* to assume, to take on: *no sabe asumir sus responsabilidades = he is unable to assume his own responsibilities.*
asunción *s.f.* assumption.
asunto *s.m.* 1 matter, topic. 2 affair, concern (tema de cierta preocupación). 3 love affair (affaire amoroso).
asustadizo, -a *adj.* easily frightened, scary, skittish.
asustar *v.t.* 1 to frighten, to scare. || *v.pron.* 2 to be frightened, to be scared.
atacante *adj.* attacking, assaulting.
atacar *v.t.* 1 to attack. 2 to refute, to contradict (refutar). 3 to criticize (criticar).
atadero *s.m.* tie fastener, hook, loop.
atado, -a *adj.* 1 spiritless, irresolute. || *s.m.* y *f.* 2 pack bundle.
atado, -a *p.p.* 1 de **atar.** || *adj.* 2 tied. 3 rigged (unas elecciones o similar): *todo está bien atado = everything is rigged (to our advantage).*
atadura *s.f.* 1 tying, binding (acción). 2 bond, tied (hecho concreto). 3 (fig.) hindrance, restriction: *ataduras sociales = social hindrances.*
atajar *v.t.* 1 to stop, to intercept: *atajaron las críticas = they stopped the criticism.* 2 to parry (parar, un golpe). || *v.i.* 3 to take a short cut (coger un atajo). || *v.pron.* 4 (Am.) to get drunk (emborracharse).
atajo *s.m.* 1 short cut (en el camino). 2 (fig.) short cut, quick method (de hacer las cosas).
atalaya *s.f.* 1 ARQ. watch tower. 2 (fig.) vantage point (sitio desde donde uno contempla con claridad el desarrollo de algún acontecimiento).
atañer *v.imp.* to concern, to respect, to regard.
ataque *s.m.* 1 attack, assault (especialmente de tipo militar). 2 MED. attack.
atar *v.t.* 1 to tie, to bind; to fasten. || *v.pron.* 2 (fig.) to be joined in wedlock (casarse, para siempre). || 3 **— corto,** to keep on a close rein. 4 **no — ni desatar,** to get nowhere.
atardecer *v.i.* 1 to get dark. || *s.m.* 2 dusk.
atarear *v.t.* 1 to assign work to. || *v.pron.* 2 to busy oneself, to occupy oneself (ocuparse).
atascadero *s.m.* 1 mudhole. 2 difficulty, obstruction, blind alley, dead end.
atascamiento *s.m.* blockage, obstruction.
atasco *s.m.* blockage, obstruction.
ataúd *s.m.* coffin.
ataviar *v.t.* to adorn, to deck out.
atávico, -a *adj.* atavistic.
atavío *s.m.* 1 decoration, adornment. 2 (fig.) dress, attire.
atavismo *s.m.* atavism.
ateísmo *s.m.* FIL. atheism.
atemorizar *v.t.* 1 to frighten, to terrify. || *v.pron.* 2 to be frightened, to be terrified.
atemperar *v.t.* to temper, to moderate: *debes atemperar tu apetito = you must moderate your appetite.*
atenazar *v.t.* 1 to hold down, to immobolize (inmovilizar). 2 to torment; to grip: *me atenazó el miedo = fear gripped me.*
atención *s.f.* 1 attention, care, heed. 2 kindness (amabilidad). || *s.pl.* 3 duties, responsabilities (deberes). || 4 **—!** (your) attention, please. 5 **en — a,** bearing in mind, in view of.
atender *v.t.* e *i.* 1 to pay attention to (hacer caso). 2 to take care of (cuidar). 3 to comply with (satisfacer). || *v.t.* 4 to wait for (esperar).
ateneo *s.m.* athenaeum.
atenerse *v.pron.* to abide by, to adhere to.
ateniense *adj./s.m.* y *f.* athenian.
atentado, -a *p.p.* 1 de **atentar.** || *s.m.* 2 DER. illegal act (en contra de alguna ley). 3 attempt (intento, de matar).
atentamente *adv.* attentively, politely.
atentar *v.t.* 1 to commit an illegal act. || *v.i.* 2 to try to kill somebody (intentar matar a alguien): *atentaron contra mi vida en 1980 = they tried to kill me in 1980.*
atentatorio, -a *adj.* threat (contra la moral o la ley).
atento, -a *adj.* 1 observant, attentive. 2 corteous, considerate: *es un chico muy atento = he is a very corteous boy.*
atenuación *s.f.* attenuation, diminishing.

atenuador, -a *adj.* 1 attenuating. || *s.m.* 2 attenuator.
atenuante *adj.* attenuating, palliative.
atenuar *v.t.* to attenuate, to extenuate, to diminish.
ateo, -a *adj.* 1 atheistic. || *s.m.* y *f.* 2 atheist.
aterciopelado, -a *adj.* velvety.
aterirse *v.pron.* to be frozen, to be numb with cold (de frío).
aterrar *v.t.* to terrify, to frighten: *la idea de la muerte no me aterra = the thought of death does not terrify me.*
aterrizaje *s.m.* AER. landing, touchdown.
aterrizar *v.t.* to land, to touch down.
aterrorizar *v.t.* to frighten, to terrorize.
atesorar *v.t.* 1 to store up, to hoard. 2 (fig.) to posses (virtues).
atestación *s.f.* attestation.
atestado, -a *p.p.* 1 de **atestar.** || *adj.* 2 full up, up to the brim: *el estadio estaba atestado de gente = the stadium was up to the brim with people.* || *s.m.* 3 DER. affidavit.
atestamiento *s.m.* stuffing, cramming.
atestar *v.t.* 1 to stuff (llenar hasta más no poder). 2 to witness (ser testigo de). || *v.pron.* 3 to stuff oneself (llenarse, de comida y bebida).
atestiguar *v.t.* to attest, to witness.
atestiguación *s.f.* attestation, providing testimony.
atezado, -a *adj.* tanned, dark-skinned.
atiborrar *v.t.* 1 to cram (la cabeza de ideas, el estómago de comida, etc.). || *v.pron.* 2 to stuff oneself (llenarse, normalmente de comida).
ático *s.m.* ARQ. attic, garret.
atildado, -a *adj.* neat, elegant.
atildamiento *s.m.* 1 GRAM. putting of tildes, putting of. 2 neatness (pulcritud en el aspecto personal).
atildar *v.t.* to spruce up.
atinar *v.t.* 1 to find, to locate. 2 to hit upon, to discover.
atinado, -a *adj.* 1 sensible, wise, sound. 2 apt, fitting, relevant.
atinadamente *adv.* prudently, sensibly.
atinente *adj.* relevant, pertinent.
atiplado, -a *adj.* 1 high-pitched, shrill (voz).
atiplar *v.t.* 1 to raise the pitch of (la voz o un instrumento). || *v.pron.* 2 to rise in pitch (un sonido).
atirantar *v.t.* to tighten, to make taut.
atisbar *v.t.* to peep, to spy, to observe.
atisbo *s.m.* inkling: *ni atisbo del problema = not an inteling about the problem.*
atizar *v.t.* 1 to stir, to poke (específicamente un fuego de leña o carbón). 2 to hit, to strike (golpear).
atizador *s.m.* poker (instrumento).
atlántico *s.m.* atlantic.
atlas *s.m.* GEOG. atlas, book of maps.
atleta *s.m.* y *f.* athlete.
atlético, -a *adj.* athletic.
atletismo *s.m.* athletics.
atmósfera *s.f.* atmosphere.
atmosférico, -a *adj.* atmospheric.
atocinarse *v.pron.* 1 to get het up (enfadarse). 2 to fall madly in love (enamorarse locamente). 3 to get disgustingly fat (coger peso).
atolón *s.m.* atoll.
atolondradamente *adv.* impulsively, recklessly.
atolondramiento *s.m.* recklessness, rashness.
atolondrado, -a *adj.* impulsive, reckless, rash.
atolladero *s.m.* V. **atascadero.**
atomicidad *s.f.* atomicity.
atomismo *s.m.* atomism.
atomista *s.m.* FIL. atomist.
atomización *s.f.* atomization.
atomizar *v.t.* to atomize.
átomo *s.m.* FIS. atom.
atonal *adj.* atonal.
atonalidad *s.f.* atonality.
atonía *s.f.* atony.
atónito, -a *adj.* amazed, astounded, astonished.
átono, -a *adj.* GRAM. atonic.
atontamiento *s.m.* confusion, bewilderment.
atontar *v.t.* to confuse, to bewilder.
atoramiento *s.m.* obstruction, blockage.
atorar *v.t.* 1 to obstruct, to clog. 2 to choke.
atormentadamente *adv.* tormentedly, distressedly.
atormentar *v.t.* 1 to torment (atormentar). 2 to plague (molestar continuamente): *no me atormentes más, vete = don't plague me any more, go.*
atornillador *s.m.* screwdriver.
atornillamiento *s.m.* screwing.
atornillar *v.t.* to screw in, to screw on.
atortolar *v.t.* 1 to shake up, to confuse. || *v.pron.* 2 to fall in love.
atosigamiento *s.m.* urging, pressing.
atosigar *v.t.* 1 to poison. 2 (fig.) to press, to rush. || *v.pron.* 3 to get flustered.
atrabiliario, -a *adj.* cranky, peevish.
atracada *s.f.* MAR. docking, berthing.
atracadero *s.m.* pier, dock.
atracador, -a *s.m.* y *f.* gangster, hold-up man; hold-up woman.
atracar *v.t.* y *pron.* 1 to hold up. 2 to gorge (con comida). || *v.t.* e *i.* 3 MAR. to moor.
atracción *s.f.* attraction.
atraco *s.m.* robbery, holdup.
atracón *s.m.* overeating, gorging, big feed.
atractivo, -a *adj.* 1 attractive. || *s.m.* 2 attractiveness, attraction.
atraer *v.t.* to attract, to draw.
atragantarse *v.pron.* 1 to choke. 2 to take a strong dislike towards: *se me han atragantado las matemáticas = I have taken a strong dislike to Maths.*
atrancar *v.t.* 1 to bar, to bolt (una puerta o ventana, especialmente). || *v.i.* 2 to take long steps (andar a pasos largos).
atrapar *v.t.* to catch, to trap: *te atrapé = I caught you.*
atrás *adv.* 1 back, behind: *se quedaron atrás = they stayed behind.* 2 back, ago (en el tiempo): *tiempo atrás = some time ago.* || *interj.* 3 get back.
atrasado, -a *p.p.* 1 de **atrasar.** || *adj.* 2 behind (en los estudios). 3 slow (reloj). 4 delayed (con retraso en la llegada o salida). 5 backward (intelectual, económica, socialmente, etc.).
atrasar *v.t.* y *pron.* 1 to delay. 2 to put back (especialmente el reloj). || *v.i.* 3 to be slow (reloj): *este reloj se atrasa = this watch is slow.* || *v.pron.* 4 to be delayed, to be late.
atraso *s.m.* 1 delay, slowness, tardiness. || *s.pl.* 2 back payment (de dinero).
atravesado, -a *p.p.* 1 de **atravesar.** || *adj.* 2 (fig.) wicked (malo).
atravesar *v.t.* 1 to pierce (el cuerpo, una superficie, etc.). 2 to cross, to go through: *atravesamos la ciudad en 10 minutos = we went through the city in ten minutes.* || *v.pron.* 3 to get in the way, to block one's way: *se me atravesó un coche malamente = a car blocked my way in a stupid way.* 4 not to be able to stand (no aguantar a alguien): *lo siento, pero se me ha atravesado Juan = I'm sorry but I can't stand Juan.*
atrayente *adj.* attractive.
atreverse *v.pron.* to dare: *¿a que no te atreves a tirarte desde aquí = I'm sure you won't dare to dive from here.*
atrevidamente *adv.* daringly, boldly, impudently, brazenly.
atrevido, -a *adj.* 1 daring, bold. 2 forward, impudent, cheeky.
atrevimiento *s.m.* 1 daring, boldness. 2 forwardness, effrontery, impudente.
atribución *s.f.* attribution.
atribuible *adj.* attributable.
atribular *v.t.* 1 to distress, to afflict. || *v.pron.* 2 to become distressed.
atributivo, -a *adj.* attributive.
atributo *s.m.* attribute.
atril *s.m.* music stand, reading desk, lectern.
atrincheramiento *s.m.* entrenchment.
atrincherar *v.t.* 1 to entrench, to surround with trenches. || *v.pron.* 2 to entrench oneself, to dig in.
atrio *s.m.* ARQ. porch, entrance.
atrocidad *s.f.* atrocity, outrage.
atrofia *s.f.* atrophy.
atrofiar *v.t.* e *i.* 1 to atrophy, to diminish. || *v.pron.* 2 to suffer atrophy.
atronador, -a *adj.* thundering, deafening.
atronar *v.t.* to thunder, to deafen.
atropellar *v.t.* 1 to knock down, to run over. 2 to bully, to abuse (atacar los derechos de otros). || *v.pron.* 3 to act too hastily (no poner cuidado en cómo actúa uno).
atropelladamente *adv.* hastily, hurriedly.
atropello *s.m.* 1 attack, assault. 2 (fig.) violation, abuse.
atropina *s.f.* CHEM. atropine.
atroz *adj.* 1 atrocious. 2 enormous, huge.
atrozmente *adv.* atrociously.
attrezzo *s.m.* attrezzo (en el teatro o similar).

atuendo *s.m.* 1 dress. 2 pomp, ostentation.
atufar *v.i.* to stink, to smell bad.
atún *s.m.* ZOOL. tuna, tunny.
atunero, -a *s.m.* y *f.* 1 tunny dealer. || 2 *s.m.* tunny fisher.
aturdidamente *adv.* thoughtlessly, recklessly.
aturdimiento *s.m.* confusion, bewilderment.
aturullar *v.t.* 1 to baffle, to bewilder. || *v.pron.* 2 to become flustered, to become bewildered.
atusar *v.t.* to slick, to smooth (los bigotes, el pelo, etc.).
audacia *s.f.* audacity, boldness.
audaz *adj.* audacious, bold.
audazmente *adv.* audaciously, boldly.
audible *adj.* audible.
audición *s.f.* hearing, audition.
audiencia *s.f.* 1 hearing. 2 DER. high court. 3 PER. readership (los que leen un periódico determinado).
audífono *s.m.* hearing aid, earphone, headphone.
audiómetro *s.m.* audiometer.
audiovisual *adj.* audiovisual.
auditivo, -a *adj.* auditive.
auditor *s.m.* adviser, counselor.
auditoría *s.f.* FIN. auditing.
auditorio *s.m.* 1 auditorium (lugar). 2 audience (gente).
auge *s.m.* 1 acme, culmination. 2 ASTR. apogee.
augur *s.m.* augur.
augural *adj.* augural.
augurar *v.t.* to augur, to predict, to foretell.
augurio *s.m.* augury, omen.
augusto, -a *adj.* august.
aula *s.f.* classroom, lecture hall.
aulaga *s.f.* BOT. furze, gorse.
áulico, -a *adj.* 1 aulic, courtly. || *s.m.* y *f.* 2 courtier.
aullar *v.i.* to howl.
aullido *s.m.* howl, wail.
aumentar *v.t.* e *i.* 1 to increase, to augment. || *v.t.* 2 FOT. to enlarge. 3 to magnify (hacerse más grande). 4 RAD. to amplify.
aumentativo, -a *adj.* augmentative.
aumento *s.m.* 1 increase. 2 FOT. enlargement. 3 RAD. amplification. 4 magnification (agrandamiento, normalmente de una imagen o similar).
aun *adv.* even, even though: *aun sabiendo el idioma lo pasarás mal = even though you may speak the language you'll have a difficult time.*
aún *adv.* still, yet.
aunar *v.t.* 1 to join, to unite: *aunar esfuerzos = to unite our efforts.* || *v.pron.* 2 to join together, unite.
aunque *conj.* although, though: *aunque eres grande no sabes jugar bien = although you are big you can't play very well.*
¡aupa! o **¡upa!** *interj.* up!, get up!
aupar *v.t.* to lift, to help up, give a leg up.
aura *s.f.* aura.
áureo, -a *adj.* golden, gold, aureous.
aureola *s.f.* 1 aureole, halo, circular stain. 2 (fig.) fame, aureole.
aurícula *s.f.* auricle.
auricular *adj.* 1 aural. || *s.m.* 2 receiver (del teléfono).
aurífero, -a *adj.* auriferous, gold-bearing.
auriga *s.f.* HIST. charioteer.
aurora *s.f.* 1 dawn. 2 (fig.) beginning, dawn: *la aurora de una nueva época = the beginning of a new time.*
auscultación *s.f.* auscultation.
auscultar *v.t.* MED. to auscultate, to listen (para diagnóstico).
ausencia *s.f.* 1 absence. 2 lack.
ausentarse *v.pron.* to absent oneself.
ausente *adj.* 1 absent. 2 absent-minded (distraído).
ausentismo *s.m.* absenteeism.
auspiciar *v.t.* to auspicate, to foretell.
auspicio *s.m.* auspice, omen.
austeridad *s.f.* austerity.
austero, -a *adj.* austere.
austral *adj.* austral, southern.
australiano, -a *adj./s.m.* y f. Australian.
austriaco, -a *adj./s.m.* y f. Austrian.
austro *s.m.* south wind.
autarquía *s.f.* ECON. autarchy, self-sufficiency.
autárquico, -a *adj.* autarchic.
auténticamente *adv.* authentically.
autenticar *v.t.* to authenticate.
autenticidad *s.f.* authenticity.
auténtico, -a *adj.* authentic, genuine.
autentificar *v.t.* to authenticate.
autillo *s.m.* ZOOL. tawny owl (ave nocturna).
autismo *s.m.* PSIQ. autism.
autista *adj.* autistic.
auto *s.m.* 1 car. || *prefijo* 2 auto-, self-. || 3 **— sacramental,** LIT. eucharistic play. || 4 **-de fe,** auto-da-fé.
autobiografía *s.f.* autobiography.
autobiográfico, -a *adj.* autobiographical.
autobombo *s.m.* self-glorification, self praise, self promotion.
autobús *s.m.* bus, omnibus, autobus.
autocar *s.m.* coach, autocar, bus.
autoclave *s.f.* autoclave; pressure cooker.
autocracia *s.f.* autocracy.
autócrata *s.m.* y *f.* autocrat.
autóctono, -a *adj.* 1 native, indigenous. || 2 *s.m.* y *f.* native.
autodeterminación *s.f.* self-determination.
autodidacta *adj.* self-taught.
autógeno, -a *adj.* autogenous.
autogestión *s.f.* self-management.
autogiro *s.m.* autogiro.
autografía *s.f.* autography.
autografiar *v.i.* to sign an autograph.
autógrafo, -a *adj.* 1 autograph. || 2 *s.m.* y *f.* autograph.
autointoxicación *s.f.* autointoxication.
autómata *s.m.* automaton.
automáticamente *adv.* automatically.
automático, -a *adj.* automatic.
automatismo *s.m.* automatism.
automatizar *v.t.* to automatize.
automoción *s.f.* automobile.
automotor *s.m.* self-propelled vehicle.
automotriz *adj.* self-propelled.
automóvil *adj.* y *s.m.* automobile.
automovilismo *s.m.* automobilism, motoring.
automovilista *s.m.* y *f.* 1 driver, motorist.
automovilístico, -a *adj.* automobile.
autonomía *s.f.* POL. autonomy, self-government.
autónomo, -a *adj.* autonomous, autonomic.
autonomista *s.m.* y *f.* autonomist.
autopista *s.f.* expressway, motorway.
autopsia *s.f.* autopsy.
autor, -ora *s.m.* y *f.* author, anthoress, writer.
autoridad *s.f.* 1 authority. 2 expert (en alguna materia).
autoritario, -a *adj.* 1 authoritarian, imperious. || *s.m.* y *f.* 2 authoritarian, despot.
autoritarismo *s.m.* authoritarianism.
autorización *s.f.* authorization.
autorizadamente *adv.* authoritatively.
autorizado, -a *adj.* authorized, official.
autorizar *v.t.* to authorize.
autorretrato *s.m.* self-portrait.
autoservicio *s.m.* self-service.
autosugestión *s.f.* autosuggestion.
auxiliar *v.t.* 1 to help. || *adj.* 2 auxiliary. 3 GRAM. auxiliary. || *s.m.* y *f.* 4 junior clerk (administrativo). 5 assistant.
auxilio *s.m.* help, aid, relief, assistance.
aval *s.m.* endorsement, guarantee.
avalancha *s.f.* avalanche.
avalar *v.t.* to endorse, to guarantee.
avalorar *v.t.* to value, to appraise.
avance *s.m.* 1 advance (en el espacio). 2 COM. balance sheet, estimate (de cuentas). 3 TV. preview. 4 MIL. attack.
avanzada o **avanzadilla** *s.f.* MIL. scout, patrol.
avanzado, -a *p.p.* 1 de **avanzar.** || *adj.* 2 advanced. || *s.f.* 3 MIL. outpost.
avanzar *v.t.* y *pron.* to advance.
avaricia *s.f.* avarice, greediness.
avaricioso, -a o **avariento, -a** *adj.* 1 avaricious, miserly, greedly. || *s.m.* y *f.* 2 miser, greedy person.
avaro, -a *adj.* 1 avaricious, miserly, greedy. || *s.m.* y *f.* 2 miser, greedy person.
avasallamiento *s.m.* subjugation.
avasallar *v.t.* to subdue.
ave *s.m.* bird.
avecinarse *pron.* to come near: *se avecinan malos tiempos = bad times are coming near.*
avefría *s.f.* lapwing.
avejentar *v.t.* y *pron.* to age prematurely.
avellana *s.f.* BOT. hazelnut.
avellanar *v.t.* 1 to countersink. || *v.pron.* 2 to shrivel.
avellano *s.m.* BOT. hazel, hazel tree, filbert.
avemaría *s.f.* REL. Ave Maria, Hail Mary.
avena *s.f.* AGR. oat, oats.
avenencia *s.f.* agreement, compromise.

avenido, -a *p.p.* 1 de **avenir.** || **2 bien –,** in agreement, happy together. **3 mal –,** in disagreement.
avenimiento *s.m.* reconciliation, conciliation, agreement.
avenir *v.i.* 1 to happen, to occur. || *v.pron.* 2 to be happy together, to harmonize.
aventajar *v.t.* 1 to excell (a todos los demás). 2 to improve (mejorar).
aventajado, -a *p.p.* 1 de **aventajar.** || *adj.* 2 outstanding (especialmente en los estudios).
aventar *v.t.* AGR. to winnow.
aventura *s.f.* 1 adventure. 2 hazard, chance, risk.
aventurado, -a *adj.* venturesome, risky.
aventurar *v.t.* 1 to risk, to venture, to hazard. || *v.pron.* 2 to take a risk, to dare.
aventurero, -a *adj.* 1 adventurous. || *s.m.* 2 adventurer. || *s.f.* 3 adventuress.
avergonzar *v.t.* 1 to make (someone) ashamed, to make (someone) blush. || *v.pron.* 2 to be ashamed: *me avergüenzo de ser analfabeto = I am ashamed of being illiterate.*
avería *s.f.* damage, spoliage; breakdown.
averiarse *v.pron.* to become damaged, to break down.
averiguación *s.f.* inquiry, ascertainment.
averiguar *v.t.* 1 to ascertain. 2 to investigate, to enquire (investigar).
averno, -a *s.m.* y *f.* 1 avernus. 2 foet, hell.
aversión *s.f.* aversion, dislike, loathing.
avestruz *s.f.* ZOOL. ostrich.
avetoro *s.m.* bittern.
avezar *v.t.* to accustom.
avezado, -a *p.p.* 1 de **avezar.** || *adj.* 2 accostumed.
aviación *s.f.* 1 aviation. 2 aviation corps, air force.
aviador, -a *s.m.* y *f.* pilot.
aviar *v.t.* 1 to prepare. 2 to equip, to supply (especialmente comida).
avícola *adj.* bird-rearing.
avicultor, -a *s.m.* y *f.* poultry breeder, chicken farmer.
avicultura *s.f.* aviculture.
ávidamente *adv.* avidly, eagerly.
avidez *s.f.* avidity, greed.
ávido, -a *adj.* avid, greedy.
avieso, -a *adj.* malicious, pervers.
avinagrado, -a *adj.* bitter, sour, (fig.) crabby (persona).
avinagrar *v.t.* 1 to sour, to make sour. || *v.pron.* 2 to turn sour.
avío *s.m.* supplies, provisions (comida, normalmente).
avión *s.m.* airplane, plane, aircraft.
avioneta *s.f.* light airplane.
avisado, -a *p.p.* 1 de **avisar.** || *adj.* 2 prudent, discreet.
avisar *v.t.* to inform, to notify.
aviso *s.m.* 1 notification, notice (un escrito). 2 warning (advertencia).
avispa *s.f.* ZOOL. wasp.
avispado, -a *adj.* keen-witted, clever, smart.
avispero *s.m.* honeycomb.
avistar *v.t.* 1 to sight, to make out. || *v.pron.* 2 to meet.
avitaminosis *s.f.* avitaminosis.
avituallamiento *s.m.* provisioning, victualing.
avituallar *v.t.* to provision, victual.
avivador, -a *adj.* enlivening, stirring up.
avivar *v.t.* to spur on.
avizor, -a *adj.* 1 watching. || **2 ojo –,** on the lookout, with one's eyes open.
avutarda *s.f.* ZOOL. great bustard.
avizorar *v.t.* to watch, to spy on.
avoceta *s.f.* ZOOL. avocet.
axial o **axil** *adj.* axial.
axila *s.f.* asilla, armpit.
axiología *s.f.* axiology.
axioma *s.m.* axiom.
axiomático, -a *adj.* axiomatic.
axis *s.m.* axis.
¡ay! *interj.* ¡ay!
ayer *adv.* y *s.m.* yesterday.
ayo *s.m.* tutor.
ayuda *s.f.* help, assistance, aid.
ayudante *s.m.* y *f.* assistant, aide.
ayudantía *s.f.* 1 assistantship. 2 adjutancy.
ayudar *v.t.* to help, to assist, to aid.
ayunar *v.i.* to fast, to go without.
ayuno *s.m.* fast, fasting.
ayuntamiento *s.m.* 1 POL. town hall. 2 joining (juntarse). || **3 – carnal,** sexual intercourse.
ayuntar *v.t.* 1 to join, to unite. || *v.pron.* 2 to have sexual intercourse.
azabache *s.m.* jet.
azacán, -a *adj.* 1 menial, drudging. || *s.m.* y *f.* drudge.
azacanear *v.i.* to toil, to slave.
azada *s.f.* hoe.
azadón *s.m.* large hoe.
azafata *s.f.* 1 airline stewardess, hostess. 2 (Am.) tray.
azafate *s.m.* flat wicker basket.
azafrán *s.m.* BOT. saffron.
azafranal *s.m.* saffron plantation.
azahar *s.m.* orange blossom.
azalea *s.f.* azalea.
azamboa *s.f.* BOT. kind of citron.
azar *s.m.* 1 chance. || **2 juegos de azar,** games of chance.
azararse *v.pron.* to get troubled, to get rattled, to get flustered.
azaroso, -a *adj.* misfortunate, unlucky, risky.
ázimo *adj.* unleavened.
azimut *s.m.* acimut.
azogar *v.t.r.* to quicksilver, to silver (espejos).
azogue *s.m.* MIN. mercury, quicksilver.
azor *s.m.* goshawk.
azoramiento *s.m.* 1 alarm. 2 embarrassment, confusion, fluster. 3 excitement.
azorante *adj.* alarming, starling, confusing.
azotaina *s.f.* flogging, spanking.
azotar *v.t.* y *pron.* 1 to beat (golpear repetidamente). 2 to flog, to whip (con látigo o parecido).
azote *s.m.* 1 whip (objeto). 2 spanking (típico de niños). 3 (fig.) scourge (persona).
azotea *s.f.* flat roof.
azteca *adj.* aztec.
azúcar *s.m.* sugar.
azucarar *v.t.* 1 to sugar. 2 GAST. to coat or ice with sugar.
azucarera *s.f.* 1 sugar bowl. 2 sugar factory.
azucarillo *s.m.* spongy sugar bar.
azucena *s.f.* BOT. Madonna lily, white lily.
azufrado, -a *p.p.* 1 de **azufrar.** || *adj.* 2 sulfureous (como color o componente).
azufrar *v.t.* to sulfur.
azufre *s.f.* QUIM. sulphur, brimstone.
azul *s.m.* y *adj.* blue.
azulado, -a *adj.* blue, bluish.
azulejo *s.m.* glazed tile.
azulino, -a *adj.* bluish.
azur *s.m.* y *adj.* azure.
azuzar *v.t.* 1 to set (the dogs) on. 2 to incite.

b, B *s.f.* b, B (segunda letra del alfabeto español)
baba *s.f.* 1 saliva, spittle. 2 BIOL. slime. || **3 caérsele a uno la –,** (fig.) to be stupid.
babada *s.f.* BIOL. kneecap.
babaza *s.f.* 1 BIOL. slime. 2 ZOOL. slug.
babear *v.i.* to slaver.
babel *s.f.* 1 chaos, bedlam. 2 **Babel** Babel. 3 **Torre de Babel,** Tower of Babel.
babera *s.f.* beaver.
babero *s.m.* bib.
Babia *s.* **estar en –,** to daydream.
babieca *adj.* stupid.
babilla *s.f.* BIOL. kneecap.
bable *s.m.* Asturian dialect.
babor *s.m.* port.
babosa *s.f.* 1 slug. 2 onion.
babucha *s.f.* slipper.
baby *s.m.* child's overall.
baca *s.f.* luggage rack.
bacalada *s.f.* cured cod.
bacalao *s.m.* 1 ZOOL. cod. || **2 cortar el –,** to have the last word, to be the boss.
bacanal *adj.* bacchanalian.
bacante *s.m.* 1 bacchante. 2 (fig.) drunken woman.
bacará o **bacarrá** *s.m.* 1 baccarat.
bacía *s.f.* shaving bowl.
bacilar *adj.* bacillary.
bacilo *s.m.* germ, microbe.
bacín *s.m.* 1 chamberpot, (fam.) potty. 2 (person) bastard, wretch.
bacina *s.f.* begging bowl.
bacinada *s.f.* (también **bacinero, bacinera, bacineta, bacinete, bacinica** y **bacinilla**) chamberpot.
bacteria *s.f.* BIOL. germ, bacterium.
bactericida *adj.* 1 germ killing. || *s.f.* 2 germicide.
bacteriología *s.f.* bacteriology.
bacteriólogo, -a *s.m.* y *f.* bacteriologist.
báculo *s.m.* 1 stick, walking stick. 2 (fig.) comfort. || **3 báculo pastoral,** bishop's staff.
bache *s.m.* 1 hole, pothole. || **2 – de aire,** air pocket.
bachear *v.t.* to repair the potholes.
bachiller *s.m.* a person who has passed the school-leaving exam.
bachillerato *s.m.* school-leaving certificate.
bachillería *s.f.* nonsense, prattle.
badajada *s.f.* 1 chime (de campana). 2 gossip, chitchat.
badajo *s.m.* 1 clapper (de campana). 2 gossip, (fam.) chatterbox.
badal *s.m.* steak.
badana *s.f.* 1 tanned hide. || **2 zurrar la –,** (fam.) to tan someone's hide.
badea *s.m.* 1 melon, watermelon or cucumber of poor quality. 2 (person.) weakling. 3 in substantial thing.
badén *s.m.* 1 hollow, depression. 2 irrigation channel.
bafle *s.m.* MUS. speaker.
baga *s.f.* 1 linseed pod. 2 halter, rope (de caballos).
bagaje *s.m.* MIL. equipment. 2 luggage, baggage. 3 pack animal.
bagar *v.i.* to go to seed (lino).
bagatela *s.f.* trinket, bagatelle.
bagre *s.m.* 1 catfish. || 2 *adj.* ugly woman. 3 clever, astute.
bagual *adj.* 1 uncouth, rude. || 2 *s.m.* wild horse.
¡bah! *interj.* bah!
baharí *s.m.* sparrowhawk.
bahía *s.f.* GEOG. bay.
bailador *s.m.* 1 dancer. 2 (fam.) thief.
bailar *v.t.* e *i.* 1 to dance. 2 (fig.) to jump around.
bailable *adj.* music that you can dance to, catchy.
bailarín, -ina *s.m.* y *f.* ballet dancer, ballerina (mujer).
baile *s.m.* 1 dance. || **2 – clásico,** ballet. **3 – de San Vito,** St. Vitus' dance.
bailotear *v.i.* to dance around.
bailoteo *s.m.* dancing around.
baivel *s.m.* bevel.
baja *s.m.* 1 drop, fall (en precio, en temperatura). 2 MIL. casualty. 3 MIL. slump. || **4 darse de –,** to go sick, to retire.
bajá *s.m.* governor (de Turquía).
bajada *s.f.* 1 slope. 2 descent.
bajalato *s.m.* governor (de Turquía).
bajamar *s.f.* low tide, low water.
bajar *v.t.* 1 to lower. 2 to take down (un objeto). 3 to help down (una persona). 4 to drop. 5 to turn down (radio, gas, luz, etc.). 6 to go down, to come down (escaleras, montañas, calles, etc.). 7 (fig.) to humiliate. || 8 *v.i.* to go down, to come down. 9 to get out (de coches), to get off (de aviones, de trenes, etc.).
bajareque *s.m.* 1 shack, hut. 2 adobe wall.
bajel *s.m.* MAR. ship.
bajera *s.f.* 1 lower leaves (de la planta del tabaco). 2 blanket (para caballos).
bajeza *s.f.* meanness, small-mindedness.
bajial *s.m.* lowland.
bajío *s.m.* sandbank.
bajista *adj.* (fam.) bear (cuando en la Bolsa se venden más acciones de las que se compran).
bajo, -a *adj.* 1 low (montaña, agua, etc.). 2 short (persona). 3 soft, low (voz, sonido). 4 humble (persona). 5 pale (color). 6 base (metal). 7 ground floor (edificio). 8 vulgar, common (persona). 9 MAR. sandbank 10 hem (ropa). || *adv.* 11 below. 12 softly, quietly (hablar, cantar). 13 *prep.* under, underneath.
bajón *s.m.* 1 fall, drop (precio, etc.). 2 worsening (salud).
bajuno, -a *adj.* 1 despicable, contemptible. 2 worthless.
bajura *s.f.* 1 lowness, smallness. || **2 pesca de –,** MAR. coastal fishing.
bala *s.f.* MIL. 1 bullet. 2 sweet. || **3 – fría,** spent bullet. **4 – perdida,** stray bullet. **5 – rasa,** low shot. **6 – roja,** tra-

cer bullet. 7 **como una –,** like a shot. 8 **ni a –,** no way.
balacera *s.f.* (Am.) shoot-out.
balada *s.f.* ballad.
baladí *adj.* 1 insignificant, worthless, trivial.
baladrón, -a *adj.* boastful.
baladronada *s.f.* boast, brag.
bálago *s.m.* 1 AGR. thatch. 2 soapsuds.
balalaica *s.f.* balalaika.
balance *s.m.* 1 rocking, swinging. 2 (fig.) hesitation. 3 COM. balance.
balancear *v.t.* 1 to balance. || *v.i.* 2 to swing, to rock. 3 (fig.) to hesitate, to waver.
balanceo *s.m.* rocking, swinging.
balancín *s.m.* 1 balance beam. 2 swingletree (de carros y diligencias). 3 balancing pole (de volatinero). 4 swing (columpio). 5 AGR. yoke.
balandra *s.f.* MAR. sloop.
balandrán *s.m.* cassock.
balandro *s.m.* MAR. small sloop.
bálano o **balano** *s.m.* 1 ANAT. glans penis. 2 acorn barnacle.
balanza *s.f.* 1 scales. 2 COM. balance. 3 **– de pagos,** balance of payments. 4 **en –,** in the balance.
balanzón *s.m.* container, vessel.
balar *v.i.* 1 to baa, to bleat. || 2 **– por una cosa,** to dream of getting something.
balarrasa *s.m.* imprudent.
balasto *s.i.* ballast.
balaustra *s.f.* pomegranate tree.
balaustrado, -a o **balaustral** *adj.* bannister, balustraded.
balaustre *s.m.* bannister, balustrade.
balay *s.m.* wicker basket.
balazo *s.m.* 1 shot. 2 bullet wound.
balbucir o **balbucear** *v.i.* to stammer, to stutter.
balbuciente *adj.* stammering, stuttering.
balcánico, -a *adj.* Balkan.
balcón *s.m.* 1 balcony. 2 railing.
balconada *s.f.* row of balconies.
balconaje *s.m.* row of balconies.
balconcillo *s.m.* 1 gallery (teatro). 2 seat (plaza de toros). 3 cliff-top path.
balda *s.f.* 1 shelf. 2 knocker (de una puerta).
baldado, -a *adj.* crippled, disabled.
baldadura *s.f.* disability.
baldamiento *s.m.* disablement.
baldar *v.t.* 1 to cripple, to disable. 2 to trump (en cartas). 3 to cause somebody problems. 4 to leave something unfinished. 5 to bend, to twist.
balde *s.m.* 1 bucket. || 2 **de –,** for nothing, free. 3 **en –,** in vain. 4 **estar en –,** to be in the way, to be out of work.
baldear *v.t.* to swill, to wash down.
baldeo *s.m.* swilling.
baldíamente *adv.* 1 uselessly. 2 without guard.
baldío, -a *adj.* 1 AGR. uncultivated. 2 without foundation. 3 idle, lazy.
baldón *s.m.* 1 insult, affront. 2 shame, disgrace.
baldonar o **baldonear** *v.t.* to insult, to affront.
baldosa *s.f.* paving stone.
baldosar *v.t.* to pave.
baldosín *s.m.* floor tile.
balea *s.f.* brush, broom.
balear *adj.* 1 Balearic. 2 Balearic dialect. || *v.t.* 3 (Am.) to shoot, to fire.
baleo *s.m.* 1 doormat. 2 fan. 3 small brush. 4 shoot-out.
balerío, -a *s.m.* y *f.* round of bullets.
balero *s.m.* 1 bullet mould. 2 toy.
balido *s.m.* baa, bleat.
balín *s.m.* pellet, small bullet.
balística *s.f.* ballistics.
baliza *s.f.* 1 MAR. buoy. 2 AER. beacon.
balizar *v.t.* to mark.
balneario, -a *adj.* 1 medicinal, thermal. || *s.c.* 2 spa.
balompié *s.m.* DEP. football.
balompédico, -a *adj.* football.
balón *s.m.* 1 ball, football. 2 balloon. 3 COM. bale.
baloncesto *s.m.* DEP. basketball.
balonmano *s.m.* DEP. handball.
balonvolea *s.m.* DEP. volleyball.
balsa *s.f.* 1 pond. 2 MAR. raft. 3 BOT. balsa wood.
balsadero, -a *s.m.* y *f.* ferry.
balsamina *s.f.* BOT. balsam.
bálsamo *s.m.* 1 balsam. || 2 **ser – una cosa,** to be a comfort.
balsámico, -a *adj.* balsamic.
balsear *v.t.* to cross (en balsa).
báltico, -a *s.f.* 1 Baltic. *adj.* 2 Baltic.
baluarte *s.m.* 1 bastion. 2 (fig.) defence.
ballena *s.f.* 1 whale. 2 whalebone (de las camisas).
ballenato *s.m.* calfwhale.
ballenero *s.m.* MAR. whaler, whaling ship.
ballesta *s.f.* 1 HIST. crossbow. 2 MEC. spring.
ballestero *s.m.* HIST. crossbowman.
ballestilla *s.f.* 1 beam. 2 sign (cartas). 3 ASTR. device for measuring the height of the stars.
ballet *s.m.* ballet.
bamba *s.f.* 1 bun (con relleno). 2 hanging scaffolding.
bambalina *s.f.* fly (teatro).
bambochada *s.f.* painting of drunken scenes.
bamboche *s.m.* plump person with a fat, red face.
bambolear *v.i.* to sway, to reel, to roll.
bamboleo *s.m.* swaying, reeling, rolling.
bambú *s.f.* bamboo.
banal *adj.* banal, trivial.
banalidad *s.f.* banality, triviality.
banalmente *adv.* banally, trivially.
banana *s.f.* banana, banana tree.
bananar *s.m.* banana plantation.
banasta *s.f.* large basket.
banca *s.f.* 1 COM. banking. 2 bench. 3 stall. 4 card game.
bancal *s.m.* AGR. plot patch.
bancario, -a *adj.* banking, bank.
bancarrota *s.f.* 1 bankruptsy. 2 failure.
banco *s.m.* 1 FIN. bank. 2 bench (de sentarse). 3 MAR. shoal, bank. 4 sandbank. 5 GEOL. stratum.
banda *s.f.* 1 strip, band. 2 sash, ribbon (en vestidos). 3 side (de carretera, barco, montaña, etc.) 4 band, gang (de gente, de soldados) 5 POL. party. 6 flock (de pájaros). 7 MUS. band, group. 8 RAD. band. 9 **cerrarse uno en banda,** to be obstinate.
bandada *s.f.* 1 flock (de pájaros). 2 mob, crowd (de gente).
bandazo *s.m.* lurch, violent roll.
bandear *v.t.* 1 to change sides. || *v.pron.* 2 to look after oneself, to look after number one. || *v.t.* y *v.pron.* 3 to swing, to move to and fro.
bandeja *s.f.* tray.
bandera *s.f.* 1 flag, banner. 2 band (militar). || 3 **– blanca,** white flag. 4 **– negra,** skull and crossbones. 5 **a banderas desplegadas,** openly, freely. 6 **arriar –,** to strike the flag.
bandería *s.f.* band, faction: *no quiero más banderías en mi partido = I don't want any more factions in my party.*
banderilla *s.f.* 1 banderilla. 2 **– de fuego,** banderilla with fireworks. 3 **clavar/plantar/poner una –,** to satirize, to taunt.
banderillazo *s.m.* hit, strike (con la banderilla).
banderillear *v.t.* to stick the banderilla in the neck of the bull.
banderillero *s.m.* banderillero.
banderín *s.m.* small flag, pennant.
bandidaje o **bandolerismo** *s.m.* banditry.
bando *s.m.* 1 edict, order. 2 party, side.
bandola *s.f.* MUS. mandolin.
bandoleón or **bandoneón** *s.m.* MUS. large accordion.
bandolero, -a *s.m.* y *f.* 1 bandoleer. || *s.m.* 2 bandit, outlaw.
bandolín *s.c.* MUS. mandolin.
bandurria *s.f.* MUS. bandurria.
banjo *s.m.* banjo.
banquero *s.m.* banker.
banqueta *s.f.* stool.
banquete *s.m.* banquet, feast: *¡vaya banquete! = what a banquet!*
banquetear *v.t.*e i. to banquet.
banquillo *s.m.* DER. prisoner's seat, dock.
bantú *s.m.* y *f.* 1 Bantu. || *adj.* 2 Bantu.
bañador *s.m.* swimming costume, swimsuit.
bañar *v.t.* 1 to bathe. 2 to cover. 3 to bathe (sol), to bathe (luz). || *v.pron.* 4 to bath. 5 to swim, to bathe (mar).
bañero, -a *s.m.* y *f.* 1 livesaver. || 2 *s.f.* bath, bathtub.
bañista *s.m.* y *f.* bather, swimmer.
baño *s.m.* 1 bath. 2 bathroom. 3 bath, bathtub. 4 coat (of paint). || *pl.* 5 spa, baths. 6 **baño de María,** steaming.
baobab *s.c.* BOT. baobab.
baptisterio *s.m.* 1 baptist(e)ry. 2 font.
baquear *v.i.* to float.
baquelita *s.f.* bakelite.
baqueta *s.c.* 1 drumsticks. 2 BOT. jonquil. 3 MIL. ramrod. || 4 **correr baquetas,** to run the gauntlet. 5 **tratar a –,** to treat cruelly.
baquetazo *s.m.* hit, strike (de una baqueta).
baqueteado, -a *adj.* experienced.

baquetear *v.t.* **1** to make someone run the gauntlet. **2** to hassle, to annoy.
baqueteo *s.m.* nuisance, bind.
baquetero *s.m.* ramrod holder.
báquico, -a *adj.* bacchanalian, Bacchic.
baquio *s.m.* foot (de la poesía clásica).
bar *s.m.* **1** bar. **2** FIS. bar.
barahúnda *s.f.* din, racket.
baraja *s.f.* **1** pack of cards. || **2 jugar con dos barajas,** to cheat, to play dirty.
barajar *v.t.* **1** to shuffle (cartas). **2** (fig.) to mix up, to jumble up. **3** to catch (en el aire). **4** to whittle (madera).
barajada or **barajadura** *s.f.* shuffle.
baranda *s.f.* **1** balustrade (de balcón). **2** cushion (de billar). **3** boss, chief.
barandado *adj.* balustraded.
barandajo or **barandaje** *s.m.* railing, balustrade.
barandal *s.m.* **1** bar (de una balaustrada). **2** balustrade.
barandilla *s.f.* **1** balustrade. **2** bannister (de una escalera). **3** side (de un carro). **4** wooden bridge.
baratador, -a *s.m.* y *f.* dealer.
baratar or **baratear** *v.t.* to lower, reduce (precios).
baratería *s.f.* fraud, bribery.
baratija *s.f.* trinket.
baratillero, -a *s.m.* y *f.* secondhand dealer.
baratillo *s.m.* **1** cheap goods. **2** flea-market.
barato, -a *adj.* **1** cheap, inexpensive. || *s.c.* **2** bargain sale. **3** money given by winning gamblers. || *adv.* **4** cheaply, cheap, inexpensively. || **5 irse de —,** to get off scot-free. **6 echar a —,** to shun. || *s.i.* **7** cheapness. **8** change.
Báratro *s.m.* hell.
baratura *s.f.* cheapness.
baraúnda *s.f.* din, racket.
baraustar *v.t.* **1** to fire, shoot. **2** to deflect.
barba *s.f.* **1** chin. **2** beard. **3** tuft (de cabras). || **4** *s.pl.* BOT. roots. **5** gills (de pez). **6** actor of old man's parts. || **7 barba honrada,** respected person. **8 hacer la —,** to have a shave, to shave. **9 hacer la — a uno,** to annoy, to flatter. **10 a — regalada,** plentifully. **11 por —,** per head. **12 en mis barbas,** in my presence, face to face.
barbacana *s.f.* barbican.
barbacoa *s.f.* **1** bed. **2** roast meat. **3** barbecue. **4** loft.
barbado, -a *adj.* **1** bearded. || *s.m.* **2** BOT. seedling.
barbar *v.i.* **1** to grow a beard. **2** BOT. to take root.
barbaridad *s.f.* **1** barbarity. **2** atrocity. **3** exaggeration. **4** enormous quantity. || **5 ¡qué —!,** (fam.) how terrible!
barbáricamente *adv.* barbarically.
barbarie *s.f.* barbarity, barbarism, cruelty.
barbarismo *s.m.* **1** barbarity, savagery. **2** incorrect use of foreign or Spanish words.
barbarizar *v.t.* e *i.* to barbarize, to corrupt.
bárbaro, -a *adj.* **1** HIST. barbarian. **2** cruel, barbarous, savage (fig.). **3** (fam.) fantastic, tremendous. **4** (fam.) uncouth, rough.
barbear *v.t.* to shave.
barbechar *v.t.* to plough (antes de sembrar).
barbecho *s.m.* **1** fallow land. **2** ploughing. **3** ploughed land. **4 firmar en barbecho,** to sign something without looking.
barbería *s.f.* barber's, hairdresser's.
barbero *s.m.* **1** hairdresser, barber. **2** fawner, flatterer.
barbián, -ana *adj.* **1** bold, daring. **2** (desp.) forward, brazen.
barbicano, -a *adj.* white-bearded, grey-bearded.
barbilampiño *adj.* beardless, smooth-faced.
barbilindo or **barbilucio** *adj.* **1** flash, dapper, well-dressed. || *s.m.* **2** candy, fop.
barbilla *s.f.* **1** chin. || *s.c.pl.* **2** lightly-bearded person.
barbillera *s.f.* o **barboquejo** o **barbuquejo** *s.m.* chin strap.
barbitonto, -a *adj.* stupid-looking, stupid-faced.
barbitúrico *adj.* y *s.m.* hypnotic drug.
barbo *s.m.* **1** barbel. **2** barbo de mar, red mullet.
barbón *s.m.* **1** bearded man. **2** ZOOL. billy goat. **3** BOT. bearded vine shoot.
barbotar o **barbotear** *v.i.* to mumble, to mutter.
barbudo, -a *adj.* long-bearded, bushy-bearded.
barbulla *s.f.* uproar, rumpous.
barbullar *v.i.* to chatter, to babble.
barca *s.f.* small boat.
barcada *s.f.* **1** boatload. **2** trip.
barcaje *s.m.* **1** boat-charge. **2** transport by boat.
barcarola *s.f.* barcarole.
barcaza *s.f.* barge, lighter.
barcia *s.f.* chaff.
barcino, -a o **barceno, -a** *adj.* **1** white, brown, reddish (aplicado a animales de estos colores). **2** POL. party-swapper.
barco *s.m.* **1** boat, ship. **2** GEOL. small ravine, gully.
barda *s.f.* **1** thatch. **2** hedge, fence. **3** storm cloud.
bardaguera *s.f.* BOT. osier.
bardal *s.m.* thatched wall.
bardana *s.f.* burdock.
bardo *s.m.* bard.
baremo *s.m.* **1** scale. **2** ready reckoner.
barí *adj.* excellent.
barimetría *s.f.* measure of gravity.
bario *s.m.* barium.
barisfera *s.f.* FIS. Barysphere.
barita *s.f.* barium sulphate.
barítono *s.m.* baritone.
barjuleta *s.f.* rucksack.
barloventear *v.i.* **1** MAR. to tack. **2** (fig.) to roam, to wander.
barlovento *s.m.* windward.
barman *s.m.* barman.
barniz *s.m.* **1** varnish. **2** (fig.) vague idea, smattering.
barnizar *v.t.* to varnish, to gloss.
barógrafo *s.m.* barograph.
barométrico, -a *adj.* barometric.
barómetro *s.m.* **1** barometer. || **2 — de mercurio,** mercury barometer. **3 — de aneroide,** aneroid barometer. **4 — registrador,** barograph.
barón *s.m.* baron.
baronía *s.f.* barony.
barquero, -a *s.m.* y *f.* boatman (hombre), boatwoman (mujer).
barquía *s.f.* skiff.
barquilla *s.f.* **1** mold (para hacer pasteles). **2** small boat. **3** basket (de un globo). **4** MAR. log.
barquillero, -a *s.m.* y *f.* wafer seller.
barquillo *s.m.* wafer, cornet
barquín *s.m.* large bellows.
barquinazo *s.m.* bump, jolt.
barquinera *s.f.* large bellows
barquino *s.m.* wineskin.
barra *s.f.* **1** bar. **2** MEC. lever. **3** ingot, bar (de oro o plata). **4** DER. bar, rail. **5** counter (de un bar). **6** MAR. sandbank. **7** bar (de jabón). **8** loaf of bread. || **9 llevar a uno a la —,** to take someone to court. **10 sin pararse en barras,** to stop at nothing.
barrabás *s.m.* **1** evil person. || *adj.* **2** cheeky, naughty.
barrabasada *s.f.* thoughtless action.
barraca *s.f.* **1** shack, hut. **2** thatched cottage (en Valencia y Murcia).
barracón *s.m.* large shack, cabin.
barrado, -a *adj.* striped.
barragán *s.m.* **1** wool cloth. **2** woollen overcoat. **2** single man (hombre soltero).
barragana *s.f.* concubine.
barranca *s.f.* ravine, gorge.
barrancal *s.m.* area full of ravines.
barranco *s.m.* **1** ravine, gorge. **2** rill. **3** (fig.) problem, fix.
barrancoso, -a *adj.* full of ravines.
barranquera *s.f.* ravine, gully.
barraquero, -a *s.m.* y *f.* shack-builder.
barreda *s.f.* barrier, wooden fence.
barredero, -a *s.m.* y *f.* **1** sweeping. || *s.f.* **2** brush. **3** street-cleaning machine, road sweeper.
barrena *s.f.* **1** drill. **2** AER. **en barrena,** spin.
barrenar *v.t.* **1** to drill. **2** MAR. to scuttle. **3** to spoil (los planes de alguien). **4** to break the law.
barrendero, -a *s.m.* y *f.* street-sweeper.
barrenero *s.m.* driller.
barrenillo *s.m.* **1** lava. **2** tree disease.
barreno *s.m.* **1** large drill. **2** bore-hole. **3** blast-hole. **4** MAR. **dar barreno,** to scuttle.
barreño, -a *s.m.* y *f.* large bowl, container.
barrer *v.t.* **1** to sweep. **2** (fam.) to take everything, lock, stock and barrel. || **3 — hacia dentro,** to look after number one.
barrera *s.f.* **1** barrier, fence. **2** fence (en una plaza de toros). **3 barrera del so-**

nido, sound barrier. **4** clay-pit. **5** crockery, cupboard.
barrero *s.m.* **1** potter. **2** clay-pit. **3** mire, bog.
barriada *s.f.* **1** district, area. **2** part of a district.
barrial *s.m.* mire, bog.
barrica *s.f.* barrel (de tamaño medio).
barricada *s.f.* **1** barricade. **2** POL. hide-out. **3** riot.
barriga *s.f.* **1** stomach, belly. **2** bulge (de una pared). **3** bulge (de una botella).
barrigón, -ona *adj.* chubby, potbellied.
barrigudo, -a *adj.* chubby, potbellied.
barriguera *s.f.* girth.
barril *s.m.* **1** barrel, cask. **2** earthenware mug.
barrilero *s.m.* cooper.
barrilete *s.m.* **1** MEC. clamp. **2** chamber (de una pistola). **3** barrel, cask.
barrio *s.m.* **1** district, area, suburb. **2** hamlet, settlement. || **3 el otro –,** eternity.
barrizal *s.m.* mire, bog.
barro *s.m.* **1** mud. **2** clay. **3** worthless object. **4** ANAT. pimple, spot. || **5 tener uno – a mano,** to have money.
barroco, -a *adj.* **1** baroque. || *s.m.* **2** ART. baroque.
barroquismo *s.m.* **1** baroque. **2** (desp.) in bad taste.
barroso, -a *adj.* **1** muddy, muddy-coloured. **2** ANAT. spotty.
barrote *s.m.* thick bar.
barrueco *s.m.* imperfect pearl.
barruntar *v.t.* to foresee.
barrunto *s.m.* suspicion, premonition, sign.
bartola *loc. adv.* **la bartola,** carelessly.
bartulear o **bartular** *v.i.* to think over, to mull over, to ponder.
bártulos *s.m.pl.* **1** everyday things. || **2 liar/preparar los –,** to get ready, to prepare oneself (para un viaje o similar).
barullero, -a *adj./s.m.* y *f.* complicated, confused, disorganized.
barullo *s.m.* disturbance, uproar.
barzón *s.m.* **1** wander, stroll. **2** BOT. saddle tree. **3** MAR. ring.
barzonear *v.i.* to wander about, to stroll around.
basa *s.f.* ARQ. base (de una columna).
basáltico, -a *adj.* basaltic.
basalto *s.m.* MIN. basalt.
basamento *s.m.* ARQ. base.
basanita *s.f.* basalt.
basar *v.t.* **1** to base. || *v.pron.* **2** to be based upon.
basca *s.f.* **1** MED. nausea, sick feeling. **2** fit of temper, tantrum. **3** impetus.
bascosidad *s.f.* dirt.
báscula *s.f.* scales, weighing machine.
basculador *s.m.* tilter.
bascular *v.i.* to swing.
base *s.f.* **1** base. **2** POL. power base. || **3 – de operaciones,** base camp. **4 – imponible,** taxable income. **5 – militar,** military base.
basicidad *s.f.* basicity.
básico, -a *adj.* basic.
basidio *s.m.* BIOL. cell.
basílica *s.f.* **1** basilica. **2** large church.
basilisco *s.m.* **1** basilisk. || **2 estar hecho un –,** to be irritated.
basquear *v.i.* **1** to be nauseous, to feel sick. || *v.t.* **2** to make someone sick.
bastante *adj.* **1** enough, sufficient. || *adv.* **2** enough, sufficiently.
bastar *v.i.* y *pron.* **1** to be enough, to be sufficient: *bastan 600 pesetas para entrar en el zoo = 600 pesetas are enough to get into the zoo.* || *v.i.* **2** to be abundant.
bastardear *v.i.* to bastardize, to debase.
bastardía *s.f.* bastardry, baseness.
bastardilla *adj./s.f.* italic letter.
baste *s.m.* **1** tacking. || **2** cushion (caballos).
bastear *v.t.* to sew, to tack.
bastero *s.m.* saddle-maker or seller.
basteza *s.f.* roughness, coarseness.
bastidor *s.m.* **1** frame. **2** wing (teatro). **3** MEC. axle. **4** entre bastidores, in private.
bastilla *s.f.* hem.
bastimentar *v.t.* to provision, to supply.
bastimento *s.m.* **1** provision, supply. **2** MAR. boat.
bastión *s.m.* bastion, fortress.
basto, -a *adj.* **1** rough, coarse. **2** rude, uncouth (persona). || **3 ¡basta!,** that's enough, stop it! || *s.c.* **4** saddle. || *s.pl.* **5** clubs (palo de la baraja). **6** stitch.
bastón *s.m.* **1** walking stick. **2** (fig.) control. **3** vertical bar. || **4 empuñar uno el –,** to take over, to take command.
bastoncillo *s.c.* **1** narrow stripe. **2** ear cleaner, cotton bud.
bastonear *v.t.* **1** to hit, beat (con un palo). **2** to stir (vino).
bastonera *s.f.* umbrella stand.
bastonero *s.m.* **1** stick-maker or seller. **2** dance director. **3** warder, gaoler (de prisiones).
basura *s.f.* rubbish, refuse.
basurero *s.m.* **1** dustman, refuse collector (persona). **2** rubbish dump (lugar).
bata *s.f.* **1** dressing gown. **2** MED. white coat.
batacazo *s.m.* thud, bump, thump.
batahola, bataola o **tabaola** *s.f.* uproar, din, rumpus.
batalla *s.f.* **1** MIL. battle. **2** HIST. joust. **3** aggitation (mental). **4** seat (de la silla de montar) **5** MEC. wheelbase. || **6 – campal,** pitched batlle. **7 perder la –,** to lose the battle.
batallar *v.i.* **1** to battle, to fight. **2** to argue, to dispute. **3** to hesitate, to waver.
batallón, -ona *adj.* **1** problematical. || *s.m.* **2** MIL. battalion.
batán *s.m.* fulling hammer.
batanar o **batanear** *v.t.* **1** TEC. to full. **2** (fam.) to hit, to beat.
batanero *s.m.* fuller.
bataola *s.f.* racket, uproar, din.
batata *s.f.* BOT. yam, sweet potato.
bate *s.m.* baseball bat.
bateador, -a *s.m.* y *f.* batter.
batear *v.i.* to bat.
batea *s.f.* **1** tray. **2** bowl. **3** MAR. small boat. **4** low-sided wagon, cart.
batel *s.m.* small boat.
batelero, -a *s.m.* y *f.* boatman (hombre), boatwoman (mujer).
batería *s.f.* **1** MIL. battery. **2** MIL. fortification works. **3** MUS. drums. **4** ELEC. battery. **5** footlights (teatro). **6** kitchen utensils. || *s.m.* **7** MUS. drummer (persona). || **8 en –,** parallel parking.
batiburrillo, batiborrillo o **baturrillo** *s.m.* pot-pourri, hotchpotch.
batida *s.f.* **1** beating, beat. **2** search, combing (de la policía).
batidera *s.f.* **1** MEC. concrete mixer. **2** MEC. panel cutter.
batidero *s.m.* **1** banging, knocking. **2** uneven, bumpy ground. **3** MAR. strengthening, reinforcement.
batido, -a *adj.* **1** well-trodden path. **2** shot silk. || *s.m.* **3** dough (de pasteles). **4** milk shake (de chocolate, vainilla, etc.).
batidor, -a *s.m.* y *f.* **1** mixer, beater. **2** MIL. scout. **3** outriders (caballería). **4** beater (cacería). **5** large-toothed comb. **6** batidor de oro o plata, goldsmith or silversmith.
batiente *s.m.* **1** frame (de puerta, ventana). **2** damper (de un piano). **3** gun carriage wheel-guard. || **4 reír a mandíbula –,** to laugh heartily, to split one's sides laughing.
batihoja *s.m.* smith (que lamina metales).
batimetría *s.f.* MAR. bathometry.
batímetro *s.m.* MAR. bathometre.
batimiento *s.m.* beating.
batín *s.m.* short dressing gown.
batintín *s.m.* gong.
batir *v.t.* **1** to beat. **2** to beat, to whisk (al cocinar). **3** to demolish, to knock down (casas). **4** to take down (tienda de campaña). **5** to beat (el sol, el aire, la lluvia, etc.). **6** to hammer, to beat (metales). **7** to mint (monedas). **8** to adjust (resmas de papel). **9** to stalk (animales). **10** MIL. to reconnoitre. **11** MIL. to attack, to combat. || **12 – una marca** o **record,** to break a record.
batíscafo *s.m.* bathysphere.
batista *s.f.* batiste.
batracio, -a *s.m.* y *f.* batrachian.
batuda *s.f.* leaps, jumps.
batuta *s.f.* **1** MUS. baton. **2** llevar uno la batuta, to be in command, to be the boss.
baúl *s.m.* **1** trunk, chest. **2** ANAT. stomach, belly. || **3 – mundo,** large trunk. **4 henchir** o **llenar el –,** to eat a lot.
bausán, -ana *s.m.* y *f.* **1** dummy. **2** idiot, fool. **3** lazybones, loafer.
bautismal *adj.* baptismal.
bautismo *s.m.* **1** baptism. || **2 romper a uno el –,** to hit someone over the head.
bautista *s.m.* **1** baptist. **2 El Bautista,** St. John the Baptist.
bautisterio o **baptisterio** *s.m.* baptist(e)ry.
bautizar *v.t.* **1** to baptise, to christen. **2** to water, to dilute (vino).
bautizo *s.m.* baptism, christening.
bauxita *s.f.* MIN. bauxite.
baya *s.f.* berry.
bayadera *s.f.* Indian dancer and singer.

bayal *adj.* **1** long-stalked. || *s.m.* **2** lever.
bayeta *s.f.* **1** dish cloth. **2** baize.
bayoneta *s.f.* **1** bayonet. || **2 a la –,** to fight with fixed bayonets. **3 calar la –,** to fix bayonets.
bayonetazo *s.m.* **1** bayonet thrust, wound.
baza *s.f.* **1** trick (cartas). **2** (fig.) opportunity. || **3 hacer –,** to prosper, to thrive. **4 meter –,** to butt in. **5 no dejar meter –,** not to let someone get a word in edgeways.
bazar *s.m.* bazaar.
bazo, -a *adj.* **1** reddish. || *s.m.* **2** ANAT. spleen.
bazoca o **bazuca** *s.f.* bazooka.
bazofia *s.f.* **1** rubbish, left-overs. **2** nonsense, rubbish.
bazucar o **bazuquear** *v.t.* to shake.
bazuqueo *s.m.* shaking.
be *s.c.* **1 be por be,** meticulously. **2** baa (sound of sheep).
beatería *s.f.* false piety, cant.
beaterio *s.m.* beguine convent.
beatificación *s.f.* beatification.
beatificar *v.t.* to beatify.
beatífico, -a *adj.* beatific.
beatísimo *s.m.* beatism.
beatitud *s.f.* **1** beatitude. **2** eternal happiness, blessedness.
beato, -a *adj.* **1** content, happy. **2** REL. blessed. **3** *adj./s.m.* y *f.* canting, hypocritical (desp.).
bebé *s.m.* baby.
bebedero, -a *adj.* **1** drinkable. || *s.m.* **2** drinking trough. **3** spout (of jugs, etc.).
bebedor, -a *s.m.* y *f.* **1** drinker. || *adj.* **2** hard-drinking.
beber *v.t.* **1** to drink. **2** to toast. || *s.m.* **3** drink.
bebible *adj.* drinkable.
bebido, -a *adj.* **1** half-drunky, merry. || *s.f.* **2** drink, alcoholic drink.
bebistrajo *s.m.* **1** unpleasant drink. **2** strange mixture (de bebida): *siempre estás tomando bebistrajos = you're always drinking strange mixtures.*
beca *s.f.* **1** insignia (de estudiante). **2** grant (dinero). **3** sash (adorno de vestimenta).
becado, -a *s.m.* y *f.* grant holder.
becario, -a *s.m.* y *f.* grant holder.
becerra *s.f.* **1** yearling calf. **2** dragon (planta).
becerrada *s.f.* bullfight (con becerros).
becerrillo *s.m.* calfskin.
becerro *s.m.* **1** yearling calf. **2** calfskin. **3** REL. cartulary, register. || **4** (fig.) **– de oro,** golden calf, money. **5** ZOOL. **– marino,** seal.
becuadro *s.m.* MUS. natural sign.
bechamel *s.f.* GAST. bechamel, white sauce.
bedel *s.m.* **1** porter, beadle. **2** watchman, guard.
beduino, -a *adj./s.m.* y *f.* Bedouin.
befa *s.f.* jibe, taunt.
befar *v.i.* to taunt, to jeer.
befo, -a *adj.* **1** ANAT. thick-lipped. **2** ANAT. knock-kneed. || *s.m.* **3** lip (de animales).
begonia *s.f.* BOT. begonia.
behaviorismo *s.m.* PSIC. behaviourism.
beige *adj.* **1** beige. || *s.m.* **2** beige.
béisbol *s.m.* DEP. baseball.
bejín *s.m.* **1** BOT. fungus. **2** temperamental person, turbulent person. **3** crybaby.
bejuco *s.m.* liana.
bejuquear *v.t.* to thrash, to beat.
bejuquillo *s.m.* gold necklace.
bel *s.m.* FIS. Bel.
beldad *s.f.* **1** beauty. **2** beautiful woman.
beldar o **bieldar** *v.t.* AGR. to winnow (con rastrillo o bieldo).
belduque *s.m.* large, sharp knife.
belén *s.m.* **1** Bethlehem. **2** nativity scene. **3** (fig.) chaos, mess, madhouse. **4** risky business.
beleño *s.m.* BOT. henbane.
belesa *s.f.* BOT. leadwort.
belez o **belezo** *s.m.* **1** pot, container. **2** household furnishing. **3** vat (para vino o aceite).
belfo, -a *adj.* **1** thick-lipped. || *s.m.* **2** lip.
belicista *adj.* **1** militaristic, war-loving. || *s.m.* y *f.* **2** militarist, warmonger.
bélico, -a *adj.* bellicose, warlike.
belicosidad *s.f.* bellicosity, aggressiveness.
belicoso, -a *adj.* bellicose, warlike, aggressive.
beligerancia *s.f.* **1** belligerancy. || **2 conceder/dar – a uno,** to give credit to someone.
beligerante *adj.* belligerant, aggressive.
beligero, -a *adj.* bellicose.
belio *s.m.* FIS. Bel.
bellacada *s.f.* dirty trick, mean thing.
bellaco, -a *adj.* **1** evil, wicked. **2** cunning, sly. || *s.m.* y *f.* **3** rouge, scoundrel.
belladona *s.f.* BOT. belladona, deadly nightshade.
bellamente *adv.* beautifully.
bellaquear *v.i.* **1** to play a mean trick, to cheat. **2** to rear (caballos).
bellaquería *s.f.* **1** mean trick, dirty trick. **2** slyness, cunning.
belleza *s.f.* **1** beauty. || **2 decir bellezas,** to speak elegantly. **3 una –,** a beautiful woman. **4 crema de –,** beauty cream. **5 concurso de –,** beauty contest.
bellido, -a *adj.* beautiful, (mujer), handsome, (hombre).
bello, -a *adj.* beautiful, lovely, pretty.
bellota *s.f.* **1** BOT. acorn. **2** tassle (en pasamanería, etc.). **3** MAR. **bellota de mar,** sea urchin.
bellote *s.m.* large nail.
bellotear *v.i.* to eat acorns.
bellotero, -a *s.m.* y *f.* **1** acorn-gatherer or seller. **2** acorn season. **3** acorn crop. **4** acorn tree.
bemol *s.m.* y *adj.* **1** MUS. flat. || **2 tener bemoles/tres bemoles,** to be hard, difficult.
bemolado, -a *adj.* MUS. flat.
ben *s.m.* BOT. horseradish.
benceno *s.m.* QUIM. benzene.
bencina *s.f.* QUIM. benzine.
bendecir *v.t.* **1** to praise. **2** to consecrate. **3** to bless.
bendición *s.f.* **1** blessing, benediction. || **2 echar la –,** to give one's blessing to someone. **3 hacer con – algo,** to do something gladly. **4 ser una –,** to be saintly, very good.
bendito, -a *adj.* **1** saintly, holy. **2** lucky, fortunate. **3** simple, simple-minded. || *s.m.* y *f.* **4** saint.
benedictino, -a *adj./s.m.* y *f.* **1** Benedictine. || *s.m.* **2** benedictine (bebida).
benefactor, -a *adj.* **1** beneficent. || *s.m.* y *f.* **2** benefactor.
beneficencia *s.f.* **1** welfare. **2** charity.
beneficiado, -a *p.p.* **1** de **beneficiar.** || *adj.* **2** benefitted.
beneficial *adj.* of ecclesiastical benefices.
beneficiar *v.t.* **1** to benefit, to be of benefit. **2** AGR. to cultivate. **3** to work, exploit (minas). **4** to process (minerales). **5** to sell at a discount. **6** to cut into pieces (animales).
beneficiario, -a *s.m.* y *f.* beneficiary.
beneficio *s.m.* **1** benefit. **2** COM. profit. **3** AGR. cultivation. **4** extraction (de las minas). **5** benefit, charity performance. || **6 a – de,** for the benefit of. **7 a – de inventario,** with reservations.
beneficioso, -a *adj.* beneficial, profitable.
benéfico, -a *adj.* beneficent, charitable.
benemérito, -a *adj.* **1** meritorius, worthy. || **2 la Benemérita,** The Civil Guard.
beneplácito *s.m.* approval, consent.
benevolencia *s.f.* benevolence, kindliness.
benévolo, -a *adj.* kind, benevolent.
bengala *s.f.* **1** flare. **2** BOT. rattan. **3** military badge.
benignidad *s.f.* kindliness, mildness, benignity.
benigno, -a *adj.* **1** kindly, benign. **2** mild (tiempo). || **3 tumor –,** benign tumour.
benjamín, -ina *s.m.* y *f.* **1** youngest son or daughter. || *s.m.* **2** small Champagne bottle.
bentos *s.m.* BIOL. benthos.
benzoico, -a *adj.* QUIM. benzoic.
benzol *s.m.* QUIM. benzol.
beodo, -a *adj.* **1** drunk. || *s.m.* y *f.* **2** drunk, drunkard.
berberecho *s.m.* cockle.
berberís *s.m.* BOT. barberry, berberry.
bérbero o **bérberos** *s.m.* BOT. barberry, berberry.
berbiquí *s.m.* carpenter's brace.
berenjena *s.f.* aubergine, eggplant.
berenjenal *s.m.* **1** aubergine field. || **2 meterse uno en buen/en mal/en un –,** to get into a mess.
bergamonte, bergamota o **bergamoto** *s.c.* BOT. bergamot.
bergante *s.m.* rogue, scoundrel.
bergantín *s.m.* MAR. brig, brigantine.
beri-beri *s.f.* MED. beriberi.
berilio *s.m.* QUIM. beryllium.
berilo *s.m.* MIN. beryl.
berkelio *s.m.* berkelium.
berlanga *s.f.* three of a kind (naipes).
berlina *s.f.* **1** two-seater car. || **2 en –,** in ridicule.

berlinés, -esa *adj.* 1 of/from Berlin. || *s.m.* y *f.* 2 Berliner.
berlinga *s.f.* stick.
bermejear *v.i.* to be reddish.
bermejo, -a *adj.* reddish.
bermellón *s.m.* vermilion.
berrear *v.i.* 1 ZOOL. to low. 2 to shout, to bellow. 3 MUS. to sing off key.
berrenchín *s.m.* 1 ZOOL. breath of the wild boar. 2 (fam.) temper, rage.
berrendo, -a *adj.* 1 two-coloured, two-toned. 2 mottled (toro).
berreo *s.m.* howl, screech.
berrera *s.f.* o **berro** *s.m.* watercress.
berrido *s.m.* 1 ZOOL. lowing. 2 howling, bellowing (de persona). 3 MUS. screeching, howling.
berrinche *s.m.* tantrum, rage.
berrocal *s.m.* rocky area, place.
berroqueña *adj.* granite.
berrueco *s.m.* 1 MED. tumour of the eye. 2 GEOG. crag.
berza *s.f.* cabbage.
berzal *s.m.* cabbage patch, field.
besamanos *s.m.pl.* 1 royal audience. 2 hand kissing.
besamel o **besamela** *s.f.* GAST. bechamel.
besana *s.f.* 1 first furrow. 2 AGR. ploughed field.
besar *v.t.* 1 to kiss. 2 (fig.) to touch, to brush against. || *v.pron.* 3 to stumble, to trip.
beso *s.m.* 1 kiss. 2 trip, fall (fig.) || 3 **– de Judas,** kiss of Judas. 4 **– de paz,** kiss of peace. 5 **comerse a uno a besos,** to smother someone with kisses.
bestia *s.f.* 1 beast, animal. 2 (fam.) brute, idiot. || 3 **¡qué –!,** what a brute!
bestial *adj.* 1 beastly, bestial. 2 (fam.) fantastic, terrific.
bestialidad *s.f.* bestiality, beastliness.
bestializarse *v.pron.* to become an animal, beast.
bestiario *s.m.* 1 bestiary. 2 HIST. gladiator.
best-seller *s.m.* best seller.
besucón, -ona *adj.* 1 fond of kissing. || *s.m.* y *f.* 2 person fond of kissing.
besugo *s.m.* sea bream.
besuguera *s.f.* 1 fish pan (para cocinar). 2 MAR. fishing boat.
besuquear *v.t.* to smother with kisses.
besuqueo *s.m.* kissing, necking.
beta *s.f.* GRAM. 1 beta. 2 piece of rope or string. 3 **rayos beta,** beta rays.
betarraga o **betarrata** *s.f.* BOT. beetroot.
betón *s.m.* mixture of cement and small stones.
betuminoso, -a *adj.* bituminous.
betún *s.m.* QUIM. bitumen, asphalt. 2 shoe polish. 3 TEC. lute. 4 **– de Judea** o **judaico,** asphalt.
betunería *s.f.* 1 shoe polish factory. 2 shoe polish shop. 3 shoeshine shop.
betunero *s.m.* 1 shoe polish-maker or seller. 2 bootblack, shoeshine boy.
bezo *s.m.* 1 thick lip. 2 MED. proud flesh.
bi *prefijo* bi.
biberón *s.m.* feeding bottle.
biblia *s.f.* REL. Bible.
bíblico, -a *adj.* biblical.
bibliofilia *s.f.* bibliophilism.
bibliófilo, -a *s.m.* y *f.* bibliophile.
bibliografía *s.f.* bibliography.
bibliográfico, -a *adj.* bibliographic, bibliographical.
bibliógrafo, -a *s.m.* y *f.* bibliographer.
bibliología *s.f.* bibliology.
bibliomanía *s.f.* bibliomania.
bibliómano, -a *s.m.* y *f.* bibliomaniac.
biblioteca *s.f.* 1 library. 2 book collection. 3 bookcase. 4 index. 5 **– circulante,** mobile library.
bibliotecario, -a *s.m.* y *f.* librarian.
bicarbonato *s.m.* QUIM. bicarbonate.
bicéfalo, -a *adj.* two-headed.
bíceps *s.m.* ANAT. biceps.
bicerra *s.f.* mountain goat.
bicicleta *s.f.* bicycle.
biciclo *s.m.* velocipede.
bicoca *s.f.* bargain.
bicorne *adj.* two-horned.
bicornio *s.m.* two-cornered hat.
bicho *s.m.* 1 small animal. 2 (fam.) bug. 3 beast. 4 (fam.) bull. 5 odd-looking person. || 6 **mal –,** rouge, villain. 7 **matar el –,** to drink spirits.
bidé *s.m.* bidet.
bidente *s.m.* two-forked hoe.
bidón *s.m.* 1 tin, can. 2 drum (grande), oildrum.
biela *s.f.* connecting rod.
bielda *s.f.* AGR. winnowing fork.
bieldar *v.i.* AGR. to winnow.
bieldo o **bielgo** *s.m.* 1 pitchfork. 2 AGR. winnowing fork.
bien *s.m.* 1 good. 2 benefit. || *s.pl.* 3 goods. || *adv.* 4 well. || 5 **cantar –,** to sing well. 6 **si –,** while, although. 7 **tener uno a –** o **por –,** to see fit to. 8 **bienes de fortuna,** profits. 9 **bienes gananciales,** goods acquired during a marriage. 10 **bienes nullis,** ownerless. 11 **bienes raíces,** real estate. 12 **bienes inmuebles,** real estate. 13 **bienes de consumo y uso,** consumer goods. 14 **bienes de producción,** production goods.
bienal *adj.* biennial.
bienandanza *s.f.* happiness.
bienaventurado, -a *adj.* 1 happy, fortunate. 2 REL. blessed.
bienaventuranza *s.f.* REL. bliss, blessedness. 2 prosperity, happiness. || *pl.* 3 the Beatitudes.
bienestar *s.m.* 1 well-being. 2 comfort. 3 peace, satisfaction.
bienhablado, -a *adj.* well-spoken.
bienhechor, -a *adj.* 1 beneficial, beneficent. || *s.m.* y *f.* 2 benefactor.
bienio *s.m.* two-year period, biennium.
bienllegado, -a *adj.* safely-arrived.
bienmandado, -a *adj.* obedient.
bienoliente *adj.* pleasant-smelling, fragrant.
bienquerer *v.t.* to be fond of, to like.
bienquistar *v.t.* to reconcile, to bring people together.
bienvenido, -a *adj.* welcome.
bienvivir *v.i.* to live comfortably, to lead a decent life.
bies *s.m.* bias.
bifásico, -a *adj.* ELEC. two-phase.
bífero, -a *adj.* BOT. biannual, biennial.
bífido, -a *adj.* BOT. bifid.
biforme *adj.* with two forms.
bifronte *adj.* double-faced.
bifurcación *s.f.* (fam.) bifurcation (p.u.), junction, fork.
bifurcado, -a *adj.* forked.
bifurcarse *v.pron.* to bifurcate (p.u.), to fork, to branch.
bigamia *s.f.* bigamy.
bígamo, -a *s.m.* y *f.* 1 bigamist. || *adj.* 2 bigamous.
bigardear *v.i.* to wander about, to roam around.
bigardía *s.f.* taunt, jibe.
bigardo, -a *s.m.* y *f.* loafer, idler.
bígaro *s.m.* winkle.
bigarrado, -a *adj.* mottled.
bigornia *s.f.* two-headed anvil.
bigote *s.m.* 1 moustache. 2 rule (en tipografía). 3 tap hole (de un horno). || *s.m.pl.* 4 flames. || 5 **tener uno bigotes,** to be steadfast, firm. 6 **no tener malos bigotes,** to be beautiful. 7 **de bigotes,** fantastic, terrific.
bigotera *s.f.* 1 moustache support. 2 moustache (en el labio después de beber). 3 folding seat (en coches). 4 bow compass. 5 toe cap (de zapato). || 6 **pegar a uno una –,** to cheat, swindle someone.
bigotudo, -a *adj.* big-moustached.
bigudí *s.m.* hair-curler.
bikini *s.m.* bikini.
bilabial *adj./s.f.* FON. bilabial.
bilateral *adj.* bilateral.
bilingüe *adj.* bilingual.
bilingüismo *s.m.* bilingualism.
bilioso, -a *adj.* bilious.
bilis *s.f.* 1 bile. || 2 **echar** o **segregar –,** to be irritated.
bilítero, -a *adj.* two-lettered, double-lettered.
bilocación *s.f.* being in two places at once.
bilocarse *v.pron.* to be in two different places at the same time.
billar *s.m.* 1 billiards. 2 billiard room.
billetaje *s.m.* wad of tickets, tickets.
billete *s.m.* 1 note, brief letter. 2 ticket. 3 FIN. banknote. 4 HIST. billet. || 5 **– kilométrico,** roundabout ticket. 6 **– de ida,** single ticket. 7 **– de ida y vuelta,** return ticket. 8 **– amoroso,** love letter. 9 **sacar un –,** to buy a ticket.
billetero *s.m.* wallet.
billón *s.m.* 1 (brit.) billion. 2 (EE.UU.) trillion.
billonésimo -a *adj./*s.m. y *f.* 1 (brit.) billionth. 2 (EE.UU.) trillionth.
bimensual *adj.* twice-monthly, fortnightly.
bimestral *adj.* two-monthly, bimonthly.
bimestre *adj.* two-monthly, bimonthly. || *s.c.* 2 two months.
bimetalismo *s.m.* bimetallism.
binar *v.t.* 1 to plough a second time. 2 to hoe a second time. 3 to celebrate mass twice in a day.

binario *adj.* binary.
binóculo *s.m.* 1 binoculars. 2 opera glasses. 3 pince-nez.
binomio *s.m.* MAT. binomial.
binza *s.f.* 1 BIOL. membrane. 2 skin (de una cebolla).
biodinámica *s.f.* biodynamics.
bioelemento *s.m.* bioelement.
biogenético, -a *adj.* biogenetic.
biografía *s.f.* biography.
biografiar *v.t.* to write a biography.
biográfico, -a *adj.* biographic, biographical.
biógrafo, -a *s.m.* y *f.* biographer.
biología *s.f.* biology.
biológico, -a *adj.* biological.
biólogo, -a *s.m.* y *f.* biologist.
biombo *s.m.* folding screen.
biomecánica *s.f.* biomechanics.
biopsia *s.f.* MED. biopsy.
biopsíquico, -a *adj.* biopsychic.
bioquímica *s.f.* 1 biochemistry. || *s.c.* 2 biochemist. || *adj.* 3 biochemical.
biosfera *s.f.* biosphere.
biotipo *s.m.* biotype.
bióxido *s.m.* dioxide.
bipartidismo *s.m.* bipartitism.
bípedo, -a o **bípede** *adj./s.m. f.* biped.
biplano *s.m.* biplane.
biquini o **bikini** *s.m.* bikini.
birlar *v.t.* 1 to throw a second time. 2 to take away. 3 to swindle, cheat. 4 to kill or knock down with one blow.
birlo *s.m.* 1 ball, bowl. 2 thief, robber.
birlibirloque *loc. adv.* **por arte de —,** as if by magic.
birlocha *s.f.* kite.
birmano, -a *adj./s.m.* y *f.* Burmese.
birrefringencia *s.f.* FIS. birefringence.
birrefringente *adj.* FIS. birefringent.
birreme *s.i.* MAR. bireme.
birreta *s.f.* biretta.
birrete *s.m.* 1 biretta. 2 cap. 3 bonnet.
birretina *s.f.* MIL. Hussar's cap.
birria *s.f.* 1 useless, worthless thing. 2 (fam.) monstrosity. 3 rubbish. 4 mania, fixed idea.
bis *adv.* 1 twice. 2 MUS. encore.
bisabuelo, -a *s.m.* y *f.* great-grandfather. (hombre) 1 great-grandmother (mujer). || *s.m.pl.* 2 great-grandparents.
bisagra *s.f.* hinge.
bisbisar o **bisbisear** *v.t.* to mumble, to mutter.
bisecar *v.t.* MAT. bisect.
bisección *s.f.* MAT. bisection.
bisector, -triz *adj.* 1 bisecting. || *s.m.* y *f.* 2 bisector, bisectrix.
bisel *s.m.* bevel, bevel edge.
biselado, -a *adj.* bevelled.
biselador, -ora *s.m.* y *f.* beveller.
biselar *v.t.* to bevel.
bisemanal *adj.* bi-weekly, twice-weekly.
bisexual *adj.* bisexual.
bisiesto *adj.* 1 bisextile. 2 **año —,** leap year.
bismuto *s.i.* QUIM. bismuth.
bisnieto, -a o **biznieto, -a** *s.m.* (*f.*) great-grandson (*m.*); great-granddaughter. || *s.m.pl.* great-grandchildren.
bisojo, -a *adj.* cross-eyed, squinting.
bisonte *s.m.* bison.
bisoñada o **bisoñería** *s.f.* naive mistake.
bisoñé *s.m.* toupee.
bistec *s.m.* steak, beefsteak.
bistorta *s.f.* BOT. bistort.
bisturí *s.m.* MED. scalpel, bistoury.
bisulco, -a *adj.* ZOOL. cloven-hoofed, bisulcate.
bisulfito *s.m.* bisulphate.
bisutería *s.f.* imitation jewellery.
bita *s.f.* bitt, bollard.
bitácora *s.f.* binnacle.
bitoque *s.m.* 1 spigot, bung. 2 MED. cannula. 3 drain. 4 tap.
bitor *s.m.* ZOOL. bittern.
bituminoso, -a o **betuminoso, -a** *adj.* bituminous.
bivalvo, -a *adj.* BIOL. bivalve.
bizantinismo *s.m.* Byzantinism.
bizantino, -a *adj./s.m.* y *f.* Byzantine.
bizarría *s.f.* 1 courage, bravery. 2 generosity. 3 dash.
bizarro, -a *adj.* 1 courageous, brave. 2 generous. 3 dashing.
bizaza o **biaza** *s.f.* leather bag.
bizcar *v.i.* to be cross-eyed, to squint.
bizco, -a *adj.* 1 cross-eyed. || *s.m.* y *f.* 2 a cross-eyed person.
bizcochada *s.f.* 1 milk and sponge soup. 2 bread roll.
bizcochar *v.t.* 1 to make sponge. 2 to rebake bread.
bizcochero *s.m.* biscuit tin, barrel.
bizcocho *s.m.* 1 sponge. 2 sponge cake. 3 TEC. bisket ware. 4 **— borracho,** rum baba.
bizma *s.f.* poultice.
bizmar *v.t.* to poultice.
biznaga *s.c.* BOT. bishop's weed.
biznieto *s.m.* 1 great-grandson. || *s.f.* 2 great-granddaughter.
bizquear *v.i.* to squint, to be cross-eyed
bizquera *s.f.* squint.
blanco, -a *adj.* 1 white (color). 2 white-skinned (gente). || *s.m.* 3 target. 4 white patch (de un animal). 5 gap (entre dos objetos). 6 blank space (espacio en blanco). 7 interval, interlude (teatro o similar). 8 aim, goal (objetivo). 9 ancient Spanish coin. 10 dominó. || 11 **arma blanca,** knife. 12 **blanca morfea,** type of leprosy. 13 **— de España,** whiting. 14 **— de huevo,** egg-white. 15 **— de plomo,** white lead. 16 **estar en —,** to understand nothing. 17 **estar sin blanca, no tener blanca,** to be broke, skint. 18 **en —,** blank. 19 **guante —, con guante —,** with withe gloves. 20 **lo — del ojo,** the white of the eye. 21 **pasar la noche en —,** to have a sleepless night. 22 **votar en —,** to spoil one's vote.
blancura o **blancor** *s.m.* o *f.* whiteness.
blancuzco, -a *adj.* whitish.
blandamente *adv.* softly, gently.
blandear *v.i.* 1 to weaken. || *v.t.* 2 to convince. 3 to brandish (un arma).
blandengue *adj.* 1 soft, feeble. || *s.m.* y *f.* 2 weakling, softie.
blandicia o **blandeza** *s.f.* 1 softness. 2 adulation, flattery.
blandir *v.t.* 1 to brandish (arma). || *v.i.* y *pron.* 2 to rock, to swing.
blando, -a *adj.* 1 soft. 2 tender (carne o similar). 3 weak. 4 cowardly. 5 flat. || *adv.* 6 softly, gently.
blanducho, -a *adj.* 1 soft. 2 (desp.) flabby.
blandura *s.f.* 1 softness, gentleness. 2 blandishment, flattery. 3 mildness (tiempo).
blanduzco, -a *adj.* softish.
blanqueadora *s.f.* whitener, bleacher.
blanqueamiento *s.m.* whitening, bleaching.
blanquear *v.t.* 1 to whiten. 2 to whitewash. 3 to bleach. || *v.i.* 4 to appear white. 5 to turn white, to whiten.
blanquecedor *s.m.* metal blancher.
blanquecer *v.t.* 1 to blanch (metales). 2 to whiten.
blanquecino, -a *adj.* whitish.
blanquición *s.f.* blanching (metales).
blanquillo, -a *adj.* 1 whitish. 2 white bread.
blasfemar *v.i.* 1 to blaspheme. 2 (fig.) to curse, to swear.
blasfemia *s.f.* 1 blasphemy. 2 (fig.) curse, oath.
blasfemo, -a *adj.* 1 blasphemous. || *s.m.* y *f.* 2 blasphemer.
blasón *s.m.* 1 coat of arms. 2 heraldry. 3 armorial bearings. 4 (fig.) glory, fame.
blasonador, -a *adj.* boaster, show-off.
blasonar *v.i.* 1 to boast, to brag || *v.t.* 2 to emblazon.
blasonería *s.f.* boasting, bragging.
blastodermo *s.m.* BIOL. blastoderm.
blástula *s.f.* BIOL. blastula.
bledo *s.m.* BOT. blite. || 2 **no dársele a uno un — de una cosa,** not to give a damn, not to care two hoots. 3 **no valer** o **no importar un — una cosa,** to be unimportant.
blefaritis *s.f.* MED. blepharitis.
blenda *s.f.* MIN. blende.
blenorragia *s.f.* MED. blennorrhagia.
blenorrea *s.f.* MED. blennorrhoea.
blinda *s.f.* 1 beam. 2 MIL. trench board.
blindaje *s.m.* 1 MIL. armour plating. 2 MIL. blindage.
blindar *v.t.* to armour, to armour-plate.
bloc *s.m.* pad, writing pad, note-book.
blocao *s.m.* blockhouse.
blondo, -a *adj.* blond, fair.
bloque *s.m.* 1 block. 2 concrete bench. 3 block of houses. 4 TEC. cylinder block. 5 POL. bloc.
bloquear *v.t.* 1 to block. 2 MIL. to besiege. 3 FIN. to freeze, to block. 4 MEC. to jam, to block.
bloqueo *s.m.* 1 MIL. blockade. 2 FIN. freezing, blocking. || 3 **romper, forzar el —,** to run the blockade.
blues *s.m.* MUS. blues.
bluff *s.m.* 1 bluff. || 2 **hacer un —,** to bluff.
blusa *s.f.* 1 blouse. 2 overalls, smock.
blusón *s.m.* long shirt, blouse.
boa *s.f.* 1 ZOOL. boa. 2 boa (ropa).
boardilla *s.f.* attic, garret.

boato *s.m.* show, showiness, ostentation.
bobada *s.f.* 1 silly, foolish thing. || **2 decir una –,** to say something stupid. **3 ¡qué –!,** how stupid!
bobalicón *adj.* 1 idiotic, very stupid. || *s.c.* 2 idiot, clot.
bobamente *adv.* stupidly, foolishly.
bobático, -a *adj.* silly, foolish.
bobear *v.i.* 1 to say silly things, to talk nonsense. 2 to be silly, to fool around.
bobería *s.f.* silly, foolish thing, stupidity.
bóbilis *adv.* 1 for nothing, free. 2 (fam.) without lifting a finger.
bobillo *s.m.* glass jug, pitcher.
bobina *s.f.* 1 bobbin. 2 FOT. reel, spool. 3 ELEC. coil.
bobo, -a *adj.* 1 silly, foolish, stupid. || *s.m.* y *f.* 2 fool, idiot. 3 bufoon, clown (theatre). 4 MAR. fish. 5 BOT. bush. || **6 – de Coria,** village idiot. **7 a los bobos se les aparece la madre de Dios,** fortune favours fools.
boca *s.f.* 1 ANAT. mouth. 2 ZOOL. pincer (de crustáceos). 3 GEOG. mouth (de un río, por ejemplo). 4 MIL. muzzle (de un arma). 5 entrance, opening (en un espacio, edificio, etc.). 6 (fig.) mouth, person: *hay demasiadas bocas que alimentar = there are too many mouths to feed.* 7 edge, cutting edge (filo de ciertos objetos). 8 bouquet (sabor del vino). || **9 a –,** by word of mouth. **10 a – de cañón,** at close range, at point blank. **11 a – de jarro/a bocajarro, a)** at close range, at point blank; **b)** pointblank; without any warning, bluntly: *me dijo que no quería saber de mí a boca de jarro = he said pointblank that he didn't want to have anything to do with me.* **12 a – llena,** frankly, openly. **13 abrir –,** to whet the appetite. **14 andar de – en –,** to be the talk of the town. **15 andar en – de alguien,** to be the subject of gossip. **16 a pedir de –,** exactly as one pleases, according to one's wish; like a dream. **17 blando de –,** sensitive to the bit (caballerías). **18 – abajo, a)** on one's stomach, face down, face downward; **b)** on the wrong side (un escrito). **19 – arriba, a)** on one's back, face up, face upward; **b)** on the right side (un escrito). **20 – de dragón,** BOT. snapdragon. **21 – de escorpión,** wicked tongue, evil tongue (de una persona). **22 – de fuego,** firearm. **23 – del estómago, a)** pit of the stomach; **b)** ANAT. cardiac opening. **24 – de lobo,** pitch dark, pitch black. **25 – de riego,** hydrant. **26 – de verdades,** frank person, outspoken person. **27 calentársele a uno la –, a)** to get worked up; **b)** to talk too much. **28 callar la –,** to shut up, to be quiet. **29 callar la – a alguien,** to shut someone up. **30 cerrar la – a alguien,** to silence someone, to leave someone speechless. **31 con la – abierta,** open-mouthed, dumbfounded. **32 de –,** doubtful, not very true. **33 de – en –,** from mouth to mouth. **34 decir una cosa con la – chica,** to say something without really meaning it. **35 despegar la –,** to open one's mouth, to talk: *el tipo ese no despega la boca para nada = that fellow doesn't talk at all.* **36 duro de –,** insensitive to the bit (caballerías). **37 hablar por – de ganso,** to repeat what one has heard, to say what one is told. **38 hablar por – de otro,** to adopt another person's opinions, to express someone else's opinions. **39 hacer –,** to whet the appetite. **40 hacer la – a una caballería,** to accustom a horse to the bit. **41 írsele la – a uno,** to talk too much, to say things one was not supposed to say. **42 mentir con toda la –,** to lie in everything one says. **43 meterse en la – del lobo,** to step into the lion's den, to go into danger. **44 no abrir uno la –,** to keep silent. **45 no caérsele a uno de la – alguna cosa,** to mention continuously. **46 no decir uno esta – es mía,** not to open one's mouth, not to say boo, not to speak a word. **47 quitar a alguien de la – alguna cosa,** to say something before anybody else, to speak first. **48 quitarse uno algo de la –,** not to eat something to give it to another person. **49 tapar la – a alguien,** to silence someone, to shut someone's mouth. **50 traer en – a alguien,** to mention someone at all times. **51 traer siempre en la – una cosa,** to mention something repeatedly, to talk about something at all times.
bocacalle *s.f.* 1 intersection, entrance (a una calle). || **2 la primera –,** the first turning.
bocacha *s.c.* 1 (euf.) loudmouth. 2 MIL. blunderbuss.
bocadear *v.t.* to divide into pieces.
bocadillo *s.m.* 1 roll. 2 narrow ribbon.
bocado *s.f.* 1 mouthful, bite. 2 piece, bit. 3 bridle, bit (de los caballos). || **4 – de Adán,** Adam's apple. **5 buen –,** profit. **6 – sin hueso,** easy job, sinecure. **7 contarle a uno los bocados,** to give someone a bite to eat. **8 no haber para un –,** to be in short supply.
bocajarro *loc. sdv.* **a bocajarro** *adv.* 1 at point-blank range. 2 to say something without warning.
bocal *s.m.* jug, pitcher.
bocamanga *s.f.* 1 cuff. || **2 una carta en la –,** a card up one's sleeve.
bocanada *s.f.* 1 mouthful, swallow. 2 puff (de humo, de viento). || **3 – de aire o de viento,** a gust, rush of wind.
bocarte *s.m.* 1 young sardine. 2 MIN. ore crusher. 3 stone-cutter's hammer.
bocateja *s.f.* first tile (del alero del tejado).
bocaza(s) *adj.* loud mouth.
bocazo *s.m.* dud explosion.
bocel *s.m.* 1 ARQ. torus. || **2 cuarto –,** quarter round.
bocelar *v.t.* to make mouldings on.
bocera *s.f.* moustache, smear on the lips.
boceto *s.m.* sketch, outline, design.
bocezar *v.i.* to move the lips (animales).
bocina *s.f.* 1 horn (de coche). 2 megaphone. 3 MUS. horn. 4 speaker. 5 MAR. whelk. 6 ASTR. Ursa Minor (Osa menor).
bocinar *v.i.* 1 to sound one's horn. 2 MUS. to play the horn.
bocinero *s.m.* hornblower.
bocio *s.m.* goitre.
bocón, -ona *adj.* 1 loud-mouthed. || *s.m.* y *f.* 2 loud mouth, braggart.
bocoy *s.m.* cask.
bocudo, -a *adj.* loud-mouthed.
bocha *s.f.* 1 bowl. || *s.f.pl.* 2 DEP. bowls.
boche *s.m.* small hole.
bochinche *s.m.* row, din, riot.
bochinchero, -a *adj.* rowdy.
bochorno *s.m.* 1 sultry, stifling atmosphere. 2 hot summer breeze. 3 blush, hot flush. 4 embarrassment.
bochornoso, -a *adj.* 1 sultry, stifling, stuffy. 2 shameful (fig.).
boda *s.f.* 1 wedding, marriage. || **2 bodas de diamante,** diamond wedding. **3 bodas de oro,** golden wedding. **4 bodas de plata,** silver wedding.
bodega *s.f.* 1 wine cellar. 2 vine crop. 3 wine shop. 4 granary. 5 cellar. 6 MAR. hold.
bodegón *s.m.* 1 cheap restaurant. 2 inn, tavern. 3 ART. still life.
bodegonero, -a o **bodeguero, -a** *s.m.* y *f.* owner (de un bodegón).
bodijo o **bodorrio** *s.m.* 1 unequal marriage, mis-match. 2 quiet wedding.
bodón *s.m.* 1 pond, pool (que se seca en el verano).
bodoque *s.m.* 1 pellet, ball (tirado desde ballesta). 2 MED. lump. 3 (fam.) dunce, dolt.
bodoquera *s.f.* 1 pellet mould. 2 blowpipe.
bodrio *s.m.* 1 soup. 2 hotchpotch (comida). 3 (fig.) muddle, mess, mix-up.
bóer *adj./s.m.* y *f.* HIST. Boer.
bofe *s.m.* 1 ZOOL. lung. 2 light. || **3 echar uno el – o los bofes,** to overwork, to slog away.
bofetada *s.f.* 1 slap. 2 (fig.) punch.
bofetón *s.m.* hard slap, punch.
boga *s.f.* 1 rowing. 2 fashion, vogue. || *s.c.* 3 MAR. rower.
bogada *s.f.* stroke (de un remo).
bogar *v.i.* to row.
bogavante *s.c.* 1 stroke. 2 ZOOL. lobster.
bogatono, -a *adj./s.m.* y *f.* of or from Bogotá.
bohardilla *s.f.* attic, garret.
bohemio, -a o **bohemo, -a** *adj./s.m.* y *f.* 1 Bohemian. 2 gypsy.
bohena *s.f.* ANAT. lung.
bohordo *m.* scape, stem.
bohío *s.m.* cabin, shack.
boicot o **boicoteo** *s.m.* boycott.
boicotear *v.t.* to boycott.
boina *s.f.* beret.
boira *s.f.* fog.
boite *s.f.* dance hall, nightclub.
boj o **boje** *s.m.* 1 box (árbol). 2 boxwood (madera).
bojar *v.t.* 1 to measure the perimeter of an island, cape, etc.

bojeo o **bojo** *s.m.* 1 measurement of the perimeter of an island, cape, etc. 2 coasting.

bol *s.m.* 1 bowl. 2 MAR. net, dragnet. || 3 **bol arménico** o **de Armenia,** Armenian bole.

bola *s.f.* 1 ball. 2 slam (en el bridge, etc.). 3 large, round kite. || 4 lie, **contar bolas,** to tell lies. 5 **— de cristal,** crystall ball. 6 **— de nieve,** snowball. 7 **dejar que ruede la —,** to let things take there course. 8 **estar como — de billar,** to be as bald as a coot. 9 **escurrir la —,** to escape, to run away.

bolardo *s.m.* bollard.

bolazo *s.m.* 1 hit, blow. 2 silly remark. 3 lie. || 4 **de —,** hastily.

bolchevique *adj.* POL. 1 Bolshevik. || *s.m.* y *f.* 2 Bolshevik.

bolcheviquismo o **bolchevismo** *s.m.* POL. Bolshevism.

boleadoras *s.f.pl.* bolas.

bolear *v.t.* 1 to throw. || *v.i.* 2 to play dirty. 3 to lie, to tell lies.

boleo *s.m.* 1 throwing. || 2 **a —,** without thinking, unthinkingly.

bolero, -a *adj.* 1 lying, fibbing. || *s.m.* 2 bolero (baile). 3 *s.m.* y *f.* bolero dancer. 4 *s.m.* bolero (chaqueta).

boleta *s.f.* 1 ticket. 2 MIL. pass, permit. 3 voucher.

boletería *s.f.* (Am.) ticket office.

boletero, -a *s.m.* y *f.* ticket seller.

boletín *s.m.* 1 bulletin. 2 journal, review. 3 ticket. 4 form.

boleto *s.m.* ticket.

boliche *s.m.* 1 jack (en el juego). 2 skittles, bowls (juego). 3 cup-and-ball (juguete). 4 bad-quality tobacco. 5 small furnace. 6 small fry (fish).

bólido *s.m.* 1 FIS. meteorite. 2 racing car.

bolígrafo *s.m.* 1 pen, ball-point pen.

bolillo *s.m.* 1 bobbin. 2 fetlock (de caballo). || *s.m.pl.* 3 toffee bars.

bolina *s.f.* 1 bowline. MAR. 2 sounding line. || 3 MAR. **navegar** o **ir de —,** to sail close to the wind.

bolineador, -a *adj.* sailing close to the wind.

bolinear *v.i.* to sail close to the wind.

bolinero *adj.* 1 sailing close to the wind. 2 troublemaker.

bolo *s.m.* 1 skittle, ninepin. 2 slam (naipes). 3 dunce, dimwit. 4 MED. large pill. || *s.m.pl.* 5 skittles. || 6 **— alimenticio,** alimentary bolus. 7 **echar uno a rodar los bolos,** to cause a fight, to create a disturbance.

bolonio *s.m.* dunce, dimwit.

bolsa *s.f.* 1 bag. 2 purse (para dinero). 3 crease (ropa). 4 COM. stock market, stock exchange. 5 wealth. 6 grant (education). 7 MIN. pocket. || 8 **— de corporales,** stock file. 9 **— de comercio,** Commodity Exchange. 10 **— negra,** black market. 11 **— de trabajo,** employment exchange. 12 **— de agua caliente,** hotwater bottle. 13 **— de la compra,** shopping bag. 14 **— de papel,** paper bag. 15 **— de aire,** air pocket. 16 **— para tabaco,** tobacco pouch. 17 **jugar la —,** to play the market. 18 **¡la — o la vida!,** your money or your life!

bolsear o **bolsiquear** *v.t.* to pick pockets.

bolsero, -a *s.m.* y *f.* purse-maker or purseseller.

bolsillo *s.m.* 1 pocket. 2 purse (money). || 3 **consultar uno con el —,** to check if one has enough money. 4 **de —,** pocket, pocket-size. 5 **meterse a uno en el —,** to have someone eating out of one's hand. 6 **no echarse uno nada en el —,** not to take advantage of something. 7 **rascarse el —,** to pay up. 8 **tener uno en el — a otro,** to have someone in one's pocket.

bolsín *s.m.* street market (de la Bolsa).

bolsiquear *v.t.* to pick pockets.

bolsista *s.m.* y *f.* 1 FIN. stockbroker. 2 (fam.) pickpocket.

bolso *s.m.* 1 purse. 2 bag. || 3 **— de mano,** handbag.

bolsón *s.m.* 1 satchel (para la escuela). 2 handbag (para mujeres). 3 MIN. lump of ore. 4 (fam.) fool, dimwit.

bollar *v.t.* 1 to emboss. 2 to dent.

bollería *s.f.* pastry shop, baker's.

bollero, -a *s.m.* y *f.* baker.

bollo *s.m.* 1 bun, roll. 2 dent. 3 MED. lump, swelling. 4 puff (en ropa). || 5 **armarse** o **hacerse un —,** to cause a rumpus, to make a fuss.

bollón *s.m.* 1 stud. 2 stud earring.

bollonado *adj.* studded.

bomba *s.f.* 1 MIL. bomb. 2 TEC. pump. 3 globe, glass (de lámparas). 4 MUS. slide. 5 bombshell (noticia bomba). 6 poetry. 7 drunkenness. || 8 **— atómica** o **nuclear,** atomic bomb, nuclear bomb. 9 **— de alimentación,** feed pump. 10 **— de cobalto,** cobalt bomb. 11 **— de mano,** hand grenade, grenade. 12 **— neumática,** pneumatic pump. 13 **— de aire,** air pump. 14 **— aspirante,** suction pump. 15 **— de bicicleta,** bicycle pump. 16 **— de humo,** smoke bomb. 17 **— de incendios,** fire engine. 18 **— fétida,** stink bomb. 19 **— de profundidad,** depth charge. 20 **— de relojería,** time bomb. 21 **caer como una —,** (fig.) to burst like a bomb, to surprise. 22 **pasarlo —,** to have a great time, to have a whale of a time.

bombacho, -a *adj.* y *s.m.* baggy trousers.

bombarda *s.f.* 1 MIL. bombard. 2 MUS. bombardon.

bombardear *v.t.* to bombard, to shell.

bombardero *s.m.* 1 gunboat. 2 bomber (avión). || *adj.* 3 bombing, bomber.

bombardino *s.m.* MUS. saxhorn.

bombardón *s.m.* MUS. bombardon.

bombear *v.t.* 1 MIL. to shell, to bomb. 2 to lob (a ball). 3 to pump (liquids). 4 (fig.) to blow one's own trumpet.

bombeo *s.m.* 1 bulge. 2 camber (carretera). 3 convexity.

bombero *s.m.* 1 fireman. 2 **cuerpo de bomberos,** firebrigade.

bombilla *s.f.* 1 ELEC. bulb. 2 MAR. lantern. 3 pipe (para beber mate). 4 **— de flash,** flash bulb.

bombillo *s.m.* 1 MAR. small pump. 2 TEC. U-bend. 3 pipette.

bombín *s.m.* bowler hat.

bombo *s.m.* 1 MUS. large drum. 2 drummer. 3 MAR. barge. 4 lottery drum. 5 exaggerated praise, flattery. || 6 **dar —,** to make a song and dance about something, (fam.). 7 **darse —,** to blow one's own trumpet. 8 **sin bombos ni platillos,** without a song and dance, quietly.

bombón *s.m.* 1 sweet, chocolate. 2 (fam.) beauty, cracker (mujer guapísima).

bombona *s.f.* 1 gas bottle, cylinder. 2 carboy.

bombonera *s.f.* 1 chocolate tin, box. 2 cosy place.

bombonería *s.f.* sweetshop.

bonachón, -ona *adj./s.m.* y *f.* honest, easy-going, candid.

bonancible *adj.* calm, settled.

bonanza *s.f.* MAR. 1 calm, fair weather. 2 COM. bonanza, boom. 3 MIN. rich vein of ore. || 4 **ir en —,** MAR. to sail with the wind.

bondad *s.f.* 1 goodness, kindliness, kindness. || 2 **tenga la — de,** be so kind as to, be kind enough to.

bondadoso, -a *adj.* good, kind, kindly.

bonete *s.c.* 1 REL. biretta, hat. 2 lay priest. 3 sweet jar. 4 bonnet. MIL. 5 ZOOL. reticulum. || 6 **bravo —,** fool, idiot. 7 **gran —,** important and influential person. 8 **a tente —,** determinedly, doggedly. 9 **tirarse los bonetes,** to bicker, to quarrel.

bonetería *s.f.* hat factory.

bonetero, -a *s.m.* y *f.* 1 hatter. || *s.m.* 2 BOT. spindle tree.

bongó *s.m.* bongo.

boniato o **buniato** *s.m.* sweet potato.

bonificación *s.f.* 1 rise, improvement. 2 bonus. 3 discount.

bonificar *v.t.* 1 AGR. to improve, to better. 2 COM. to discount.

bonitamente *adv.* 1 nicely. 2 cunningly.

bonitera *s.f.* 1 tuna fishing. 2 tuna fishing season.

bonito, -a *adj.* 1 pretty, nice. || *s.m.* 2 MAR. tuna.

bono *s.m.* 1 voucher. 2 FIN. bond.

bonzo *s.m.* Bonze.

boñiga *s.f.* cow dung.

boñigo *s.m.* cow pat.

boom *s.m.* ECON. boom: *el boom de la construcción = the building boom.*

boomerang *s.m.* boomerang.

boqueada *s.f.* 1 last gasp, breath. || 2 **dar las últimas boqueadas,** to be at death's door, to breath one's last.

boquear *v.t.* 1 to utter, to pronounce. || *v.i.* 2 to gasp, to gape. 3 (fig.) to be on one's last legs, to be at death's door.

boquera *s.f.* 1 AGR. sluice. 2 hayloft window. 3 MED. lip sore, ulcer.

boquerón *s.m.* 1 ZOOL. anchovy. 2 wide opening, hole.

boquete *s.m.* 1 narrow entrance, opening. 2 breach.

boquiabierto, -a *adj.* 1 open-mouthed. 2 amazed, agog.

boquilla *s.f.* 1 MUS. mouthpiece. 2 cigarette holder. 3 mouthpiece (de pipa). 4 filter tip (de cigarrillo). 5 AGR. sluice. 6 mortice. 7 bracket, clasp. 8 burner (lám-

paras, etc.). **9** nozzle (de medias, etc.). || **10 de –,** as a joke, in jest.
boquillero, -a *adj./s.m.* y *f.* rogue, charlatan.
boquín *s.m.* rough cloth.
bora *s.m.* bora.
bórax *s.m.* borax.
borbollar o **borbollear** *v.i.* to bubble, to boil.
borbollón *s.m.* **1** bubbling. || **2 a borbollones,** gushingly.
borbollonear *v.i.* to bubble, to boil.
bobónico, -a *adj.* Bourbon.
borbor *s.i.* bubbling.
borborigno *s.m.* rumbling.
borboritar *v.i.* to bubble.
borbotar o **borbotear** *v.i.* to bubble.
borboteo *s.m.* bubbling.
borbotón *s.m.* **1** bubbling. **2 a borbotones,** gushingly.
borceguí *s.m.* **1** half boot. **2** laced boot.
borda *s.f.* **1** gunwale. **2** MAR. mainsail. **3** shack, cabin. **4 echar** o **tirar algo por la –,** to throw something overboard. **5 motor de fuera –,** outboard motor.
bordada *s.f.* **1** MAR. tack. **2 dar bordadas,** to tack.
bordado, -a *adj.* **1** embroided. **2** finished. || *s.m.* **3** embroidery, needlework.
bordador, -a *s.m.* **1** embroiderer. || *s.f.* **2** embroideress.
bordadura *s.f.* needlework, embroidery.
bordar *v.t.* **1** to embroider. **2** to do something perfectly.
borde *s.m.* **1** edge. **2** border. **3** side (de carreteras). **4** rim, lip (de tazas, vasijas, etc.). **5** MAR. board. **6** hem (de vestidos). || **7 al – de,** on the brink, verge of. **8 – del mar,** seaside. **9** bastard.
bordear *v.t.* **1** to border. **2** to skirt. || *v.i.* MAR. **3** to tack.
bordillo *s.m.* kerb.
bordo *s.m.* **1** MAR. side, board. **2** MAR. tack. **3 a –,** on board. **4 dar bordos,** MAR. to tack. **5 de alto –,** big ship. **6 ir a –,** to go on board. **7 persona de alto –,** distinguished person.
bordón *s.m.* **1** pilgrim's staff. **2** guide. **3** LIT. refrain. **4** MUS. bass string. **5** omission (en imprenta). **6** youngest child. **7** (fam.) pet saying.
bordoncillo *s.c.* pet saying.
bordonear *v.t.* **1** MUS. to strum. || *v.i.* **2** to wander, roam.
bordonería *s.f.* strumming.
bordura *s.f.* bordure.
boreal *adj.* **1** northern. || **2 aurora –,** aurora borealis.
bóreas *s.m.* boreas, north wind.
borgoña *s.m.* **1** GEOG. Burgundy. **2** burgundy (wine).
bórico *adj.* boric, boracic.
borla *s.f.* **1** tassel. || **2 tomar uno la –,** to graduate as a doctor.
borne *s.m.* ELEC. terminal.
bornear *v.t.* **1** to turn, to twist. **2** to place, to allign. || *v.i.* **3** to swing at nchor. || *v.pron.* **4** to warp (madera).
boro *s.m.* QUIM. boron.
borona *s.f.* **1** millet. **2** corn, maize. **3** corn bread.
borra *s.f.* **1** lamb. **2** coarse wool. **3** flock. **4** fluff. **5** sediment. **6** padding (relleno).
borrachear *v.i.* to get drunk.
borrachera *s.f.* **1** drunkenness. **2** spree, binge. || **3 ir de –,** to go on a binge/ spree.
borrachín, -ina *s.m.* y *f.* drunkard, wino, sot.
borracho, -a *adj.* **1** drunk: *borracho como una cuba = drunk as a lord.* || *s.m.* y *f.* **2** drunk, drunkard. || **3 bizcocho –,** GAST. rum baba.
borrador *s.m.* **1** first draft, rough draft. **2** sketch pad. **3** COM. daybook. **4** rubber, board duster.
borradura *s.f.* crossing-out.
borraja *s.f.* **1** BOT. borage. || **2 quedar algo en agua de borrajas,** to come to nothing.
borrajear o **borronear** *v.t.* **1** to doodle. **2** to scribble.
borrar *v.t.* **1** to rub out, to erase, to wipe out. **2** to cross out. || *v.t.* y *pron.* **3** to fade, to disappear: *el recuerdo se ha borrado de mi mente = the memory has disappeared from my mind.*
borrasca *s.f.* **1** storm, squall. **2** orgy. **3** danger, hazard.
borrascoso, -a *adj.* **1** stormy, squally. **2** (fig.) stormy.
borrasquero, -a *adj.* wild, rowdy.
borregada *s.f.* flock of lambs.
borrego o **borro, -a** *s.m.* y *f.* **1** lamb (de uno o dos años). **2** dope, fool. || *adj.* **3** foolish.
borreguero, -a *s.c.* shepherd (de ovejas).
borreguil *adj.* **1 vivir, estar en una situación –,** to vegetate, to stagnate. **2 tener un espíritu –,** to follow the crowd.
borrica *s.f.* **1** she-donkey, donkey. **2** silly woman (fam.).
borricada *s.f.* **1** drove of asses. **2** silly thing, nonsense.
borrico *s.m.* **1** donkey, ass. **2** (fam.) fool, ass, dunce. **3** trestle table, sawhorse.
borrón *s.m.* **1** smudge, blot. **2** (fig.) blemish, stain. **3** TEC. first draft, rough draft. **4** sketch pad. || **5 – y cuenta nueva,** let's start again, let's forget about it.
borronear *v.t.* **1** to scribble. **2** to doodle.
borroso, -a *adj.* **1** blurred, fuzzy. **2** muddy.
boscaje *s.m.* **1** wood, grove. **2** ART. woodland scene.
boscoso, -a *adj.* wooded: *zona boscosa = wooded area.*
bosque *s.m.* **1** wood, forest. **2** (fig.) beard. || **3 – maderable,** timber-yielding.
bosquejar *v.t.* **1** to sketch, to make an outline. **2** to make a rough model. **3** to outline (un plan, proyecto, medida, etc.).
bosquejo *s.m.* **1** sketch, outline. **2** rough model. **3** outline.
bosquete *s.m.* grove, copse.
bostezar *v.i.* to yawn.
bostezo *s.m.* yawn.
bota *s.f.* **1** boot. **2** wineskin. **3** barrel. **4** liquid measure (516 litres). || **5 – de montar,** riding boots. **6 morir con las botas puestas,** to die with one's boots on. **7 ponerse uno las botas,** to have one's fill, to strike it rich.
botador *s.m.* **1** MAR. pole. **2** nail-puller. **3** shooting stick. **4** spendthrift.
botadura *s.f.* MAR. launching.
botafuego *s.m.* **1** MIL. linstock. **2** quick-tempered person.
botafumeiro *s.m.* incense burner, censer.
botalón *s.c.* MAR. boom.
botana *s.c.* **1** patch. **2** stopper. **3** plaster. **4** scar.
botánico, -a *adj.* **1** botanic, botanical. || *s.m.* y *f.* **2** botanist. || *s.f.* **3** Botany.
botanista *s.m.* y *f.* botanist.
botar *v.t.* **1** to throw, to fling. **2** MAR. to launch. **3** MAR. to turn the helm. || *v.i.* **4** to bounce (pelota). **5** to buck. **6** to rebound.
botarate *s.m.* y *f.* **1** fool, dolt, idiot. **2** spendthrift.
bote *s.m.* **1** tin, can. **2** pot, jar. **3** bounce (de pelota). **4** MAR. boat. **5** box (para propinas). || **6 – de remos,** rowing boat. **7 – salvavidas,** lifeboat. **8 darse el –,** to scram, to beat it. || **9 dar un –,** to jump. **10 estar de – en –,** to be packed out. **11 estar en el –,** to be in the bag. **12 pegar un –,** to start with surprise. **13 tener a uno en el –,** to have someone in one's pocket.
botella *s.f.* **1** bottle. || *adj.* y *s.f.* **2** sinecure, soft job. || **3 – de Leyden,** Leyden jar. **4 en –,** bottled. **5 – termos,** thermos flask.
botellero *s.m.* **1** bottle rack. **2** bottle maker. **3** bottle seller.
botellín *s.m.* small bottle.
botero *s.c.* **1** wineskin maker. **2** shoe maker. **3** MAR. skipper, captain.
botica *s.f.* **1** chemist's, pharmacy. **2** medicines. **3 hay de todo como en –,** there is everything under the sun.
boticario, -a *s.m.* y *f.* chemist, pharmacist.
botijero, -a *s.m.* y *f.* **1** jug maker. **2** jug seller.
botijo, -a *s.m.* y *f.* earthenware jug, pitcher.
botillería *s.f.* refreshment stall, drinks stand.
botillo *s.m.* small wineskin.
botín, -ina *s.m.* **1** ankle boot, bootee. || *s.m.* **2** MIL. plunder, booty, loot.
botinería *s.f.* shoe shop, cobbler's.
botinero, -a *s.m.* y *f.* shoe maker or seller.
botiquín *s.m.* **1** medicine cabinet, chest. **2** first-aid kit.
boto *s.m.* **1** riding boot. **2** wineskin. || *adj.* **3** dim, dense.
botón *s.m.* **1** button. **2** BOT. bud. **3** door knob, door handle. **4** RAD. knob. **5** tip (en esgrima). **6** MUS. key. || **7 – de fuego,** ignipuncture. **8 – de oro,** buttercup. **9 – de muestra,** sample.
botonadura *s.f.* buttons, set of buttons.
botonería *s.f.* button shop.

botonero, -a *s.m.* y *f.* 1 button seller. 2 button maker.
botones *s.m.pl.* 1 buttons, bellboy 2 messenger, errandboy.
botulismo *s.m.* botulism, food poisoning.
boulevard *s.m.* boulevard.
bouquet *s.m.* bouquet.
boutique *s.f.* boutique.
bóveda *s.f.* 1 ARQ. vault. 2 crypt. 3 **– celeste,** vault of heaven, celestial vault. 4 **– claustral,** cloister vault. 5 **– craneal,** cranial cavity. 6 **– de cañón,** barrel vault. 7 **– palatina,** roof of the mouth, palate. 8 **– por artista,** cloister vault.
bovedilla *s.f.* 1 small vault. 2 curved part of the stern. 3 MAR. space between the beams of roofs.
bóvido *adj.* 1 bovine. || *s.m.pl.* 2 ZOOL. bovines.
bovino, -a *adj.* 1 bovine. || *s.m.pl.* 2 bovines.
boxeador *s.m.* boxer.
boxear *v.i.* to box.
boxeo *s.m.* DEP. boxing.
boya *s.f.* 1 MAR. buoy. 2 float (de una red).
boyante *adj.* 1 MAR. buoyant. 2 prosperous. 3 content: *está boyante estos días = she's content these days.* 4 (vulg.) easily managed.
boyar *v.i.* to float.
boyero, -a *s.m.* y *f.* 1 oxherd. || *s.f.* 2 ox pen.
bozal *s.m.* 1 learner, novice. 2 pure negro. 3 fool, idiot.
bozo *s.m.* 1 down. 2 ANAT. mouth. 3 halter (de caballos).
bracamarte *s.m.* sword.
braceada *s.f.* frenetic moving of the arms.
braceador, -a *adj.* high-stepping.
braceaje *s.m.* 1 minting (monedas). 2 MAR. depth.
bracear *v.i.* 1 to swing one's arms. 2 to swim, to do the front crawl. 3 to struggle, to fight. 4 to step high (de caballos).
bracero, -a *s.m.* y *f.* 1 labourer, worker. 2 helper.
bráctea *s.f.* BOT. bract.
braga *s.f.* 1 rope, guy. 2 nappy. || *s.pl.* 3 knickers, panties (mujeres).
bragado, -a *adj.* 1 tough, hard. 2 evil, wicked (desp.).
bragazas *s.m.* henpecked husband.
braguero *s.m.* MED. truss.
bragueta *s.f.* fly.
braguetazo *s.m.* 1 marriage of convenience, (fam.). 2 **dar un braguetazo,** to marry into money.
G**brahmán, bracmán** o **brahmín** *s.m.* Brahman, Brahmin.
brahmanismo *s.m.* REL. Brahmanism, Brahminism.
bramar *v.i.* 1 to bellow, to roar (toros). 2 to low (vacas). 3 to trumpet (elefantes). 4 to bawl, to bellow (fig.). 5 to howl, to roar (el mar, viento, etc.).
bramido *s.m.* 1 bellowing, roaring (toros). 2 lowing (vacas). 3 trumpeting (elefantes). 4 bawling, bellowing (fig.). 5 howling, roaring (el mar, viento, etc.): *me encanta escuchar el bramido del viento = I love listening to the howling of the wind.*
brandy *s.m.* brandy, cognac.
branquia *s.f.* gill.
braña *s.f.* meadow, pasture.
brasa *s.f.* 1 ember, hot coal. || 2 **a la –,** braised.
brasero *s.m.* 1 brazier. 2 stake (hoguera). 3 earth (en casa).
brasil *s.m.* 1 BOT. brazilwood. || 2 **palo –,** brazil.
brasileño, -a o **brasilero, -a** *adj./s.m.* y *f.* Brazilian.
bravata *s.f.* 1 boasting, bragging. || 2 **echar bravatas,** to boast, to brag.
bravear *v.i.* to boast, to brag, to show off.
braveza *s.f.* 1 bravery. 2 ferocity. 3 fury (de los elementos).
bravío, -a *adj.* 1 wild, fierce. 2 BOT. wild. 3 coarse, rough. || *s.m.* 4 ferocity, savageness.
bravo, -a *adj.* 1 brave, fearless. 2 fierce (animal). 3 excellent, marvellous. 4 boastful. 5 rough (mar). 6 angry (enojado). 7 brave (toro). 8 rugged (paisaje). || *interj.* 9 **¡–!,** well done!, fantastic!
bravonel *adj.* 1 boastful. || *s.m.* 2 show-off, braggart.
bravucón, -ona *adj.* 1 boastful, big-headed. || *s.m.* y *f.* 2 boaster, show-off, big head.
bravuconada o **bravuconería** *s.f.* 1 boasting, showing off. 2 boast, brag.
bravura *s.f.* 1 wildness, fierceness (de los animales). 2 bravery, courage. 3 boasting, bragging (bravata).
braza *s.c.* 1 MAR. fathom. 2 MAR. brace. || 3 **– de espalda,** backstroke. 4 **– de mariposa,** butterfly stroke. 5 **nadar a la –,** to do the breaststroke.
brazada *s.f.* 1 movement of the arms. 2 stroke (de un nadador o de un remo). 3 fathom (medida).
brazal *s.m.* 1 brassard (armadura). 2 armband. 3 irrigation channel.
brazalete *s.m.* 1 armband. 2 bracelet. 3 brassard (armadura).
brazo *s.m.* 1 ANAT. arm. 2 ZOOL. foreleg. 3 arm (de las sillas). 4 arm (de las balanzas, tocadiscos, palancas, anclas, etc.). 5 BOT. branch, limb. || *pl.* 6 protectors. 7 workers, hands. || 8 **– de cruz,** limb of the cross. 8 **– de gitano,** swiss roll. 9 **– de mar,** arm of the sea. 10 **– de río,** branch of a river. 11 **– real, secular** o **seglar,** secular arm. 12 **a – partido,** hand to hand (sin armas), for all one is worth (con gran empeño). 13 **con los brazos abiertos,** with open arms. 14 **cruzarse de brazos,** to fold one's arms. 15 **dar uno su – a torcer,** to give in. 16 **hecho un – de mar,** dressed to kill, dressed up to the nines. 17 **ser el – derecho de uno,** to be someone's right-hand man.
brazuelo *s.m.* ZOOL. shoulder.
brea *s.f.* 1 pitch, tar. || 2 **– mineral,** mineral pitch. 3 **– líquida,** tar.
brear *v.t.* 1 to insult, to abuse. 2 to beat up, to thrash. 3 to ill-treat (maltratar).
brebaje o **brebajo** *s.m.* 1 concoction, brew. 2 MAR. grog.
breca *s.f.* 1 bleak (albur). 2 sea bream (pagel).
brecol, bracolera o **brócuIi** *s.m.* o *f.* BOT. broccoli.
brecha *s.f.* 1 MIL. breach, gap. 2 opening, gap (en una pared o muro). 3 MED. wound. || 4 **abrir –,** to make a breach. 5 **batir en –,** to batter. 6 **estar uno siempre en la –,** to be always in the thick of it. 7 **montar la –,** to go through the breach.
brega *s.f.* 1 fight, struggle. 2 row, quarrel (riña). 3 trick, practical joke (burla).
bregar *v.i.* 1 to fight, to struggle. 2 to overwork, to slog away. 3 to row, to quarrel. || *v.t.* 4 to knead (amasar).
breña *s.f.* scrub, brush.
breñal o **breñar** *s.m.* scrub, brush.
bresca *s.f.* honeycomb.
brescar *v.t.* to uncap (las colmenas).
brete *s.m.* 1 shackles, fetters. 2 (fig.) tight spot, corner. || 3 **estar en un –,** to be in a corner, a tight spot.
bretón, -ona *adj./s.m.* y *f.* 1 Breton. || *s.m.* 2 BOT. tree cabbage.
breva *s.c.* 1 BOT. early fig. 2 BOT. early acorn (bellota). 3 flattened cigar (puro). 4 (fam.) stroke of luck. | 5 (fam.) **es una –,** it's a piece of cake. 6 **¡no caerá esa –!,** no such luck!
breval *adj.* fig-bearing.
breve *adj.* 1 short, brief. 2 GRAM. short. || 3 **en –,** shortly, before long, so on. || *s.m.* REL. 4 papal brief. 5 MUS. breve.
brevedad *s.f.* 1 brevity, shortness. || 2 **con –,** briefly, concisely. 3 **con la mayor –,** as so on as possible. 4 **para mayor –,** to be brief.
breviario *s.m.* 1 REL. breviary. 2 compendium.
brezal *s.m.* moor, heath.
brezo *s.m.* BOT. heather.
briba o **bribia** *s.i.* 1 idle life, tramp's life. || 2 **andar** o **echarse uno a la –,** to idle around, to loaf about.
bribón, -ona *adj.* 1 roguish, rascally. 2 idle, lazy. || *s.m.* y *f.* 3 rogue, rascal. 4 tramp, beggar (mendigo).
bribonada *s.f.* 1 dirty trick. 2 roguishness (cualidad de bibrón).
bribonear *v.i.* 1 to loaf about, to idle around. 2 to be a rogue, rascal. 3 to play dirty trick.
bribonería *s.f.* 1 roguishness. 2 idle life, tramp's life.
bribonesco, -a *adj.* roguish, rascally.
bricolage *s.m.* do-it-yourself.
brida *s.f.* 1 bridle, rein. 2 MED. bride. 3 TEC. clamp. 4 flange (de un tubo). || 5 **a toda –,** at full speed, flat out.
bridge *s.m.* bridge.
bridón *s.m.* 1 small bridle, snaffle. 2 MIL. bridoon. 3 steed (caballo).
brigada *s.f.* 1 MIL. brigade. 2 gang, squad (de trabajadores). 3 squad (de

policías). || 4 **— móvil,** flying squad. 5 **general de —,** brigadier.
brigadier *s.m.* brigadier.
brillante *adj.* 1 brilliant, bright, shining. 2 (fig.) brilliant. 3 shining (superficie). 4 sparkling, brilliant (conversación). 5 bright (colores). 6 brilliant (compañía). 7 sparkling (joyas). 8 brilliant (estudiante). || *s.m.* 9 diamond.
brillantemente *adv.* brilliantly, brightly.
brillantez *s.f.* brilliance, brightness.
brillantina *s.f.* brilliantine.
brillar *v.i.* 1 to shine (en general). 2 to sparkle (los ojos). 3 to glow (de felicidad). 4 to sparkle, to shine (joyas, luna, estrellas, etc.). 5 to shine (en conversación). 6 to blaze (llamas). 7 (fig.) to stand out, to shine out (en estudios).
brillo *s.m.* 1 brilliance, brightness, shine, sparkle. 2 lustre, shine (de superficies). 3 (fig.) brilliance. || 4 **sacar — a,** to polish, to shine.
brincar *v.i.* 1 to jump. 2 to jump up and down (niños). 3 to gambol (ovejas, etc.). 4 to omit, to miss out. 5 (fig.) to get angry. || 6 (fam.) **está que brinca,** he's hopping mad.
brinco *s.m.* 1 jump, leap, hop. || 2 **a brincos,** by fits and starts. 3 **de un —,** with one leap. 4 **en un —,** in no time at all.
brincotear *v.i.* 1 to jump up and down.
brindar *v.i.* 1 to toast, to drink a toast. || *v.t.* 2 to offer, to present. 3 **— el toro a alguien,** to dedicate the bull to someone. || *v.pron.* 4 to offer oneself.
brindis *s.m.* 1 toast. 2 dedication ceremony (en los toros). || 3 **echar un —,** to toast, to drink a toast.
brío *s.m.* 1 spirit, dash, brio. 2 energy, verve. 3 daring. 4 elegance. 5 determination, resolution. || 7 **hombre de bríos,** a man of spirit. 6 **cortar los bríos a uno,** to clip someone's wings.
brioso, -a *adj.* 1 spirited, dashing. 2 energetic. 3 daring. 4 elegant. 5 determined, resolute.
briozoo *s.m.* BOT. bryozoan, bryozoon.
briqueta *s.f.* briquette.
brisa *s.f.* breeze.
briscado, -a *adj.* 1 brocaded. || *s.m.* 2 brocade-work.
briscar *v.t.* to brocade.
británico, -a *adj./s.m.* y *f.* British.
britano, -a *adj.* 1 British. || *s.m.* y *f.* 2 HIST. Briton.
brizna *s.f.* 1 strand, filament. 2 blade (de hierba). 3 string (de judía). 4 piece, bit (trozo).
briznoso, -a *adj.* drizzly.
broca *s.f.* 1 MEC. bit, drill. 2 tack (de zapatos). 3 reel, bobbin (de bordadora).
brocado *s.m.* 1 brocade. || *adj.* 2 brocaded.
brocal *s.m.* 1 curb (de un pozo). 2 mouth, rim. 3 edge, border (de un escudo).
brocatel *s.m.* 1 brocatelle (tela). 2 brocatello (mármol).
brocearse *v.r.* to dry up, to run out (una mina).
brocha *s.f.* 1 paintbrush. 2 shaving brush (de afeitar). || 3 **de — gorda,** painter and decorator (de casa); dauber (mal pintor).
brochada *adj.* 1 brocaded. || *s.f.* 2 brushstroke.
brochazo *s.m.* brushstroke.
broche *s.m.* 1 brooch. 2 clip, fastener.
broma *s.f.* 1 joke, prank: *no te lo tomes a broma = don't take it as a joke.* 2 ZOOL. shipworm (molusco). 3 fun, merriment: *lo dije en broma = I said it in fun.*
bromar o **abromar** *v.t.* to gnaw.
bromatología *s.f.* bromatology.
bromazo *s.m.* stupid joke, unpleasant trick.
bromear *v.i.* to joke.
bromista *s.m.* y *f.* 1 joker. 2 practical joker. || *adj.* 3 fond of joking.
bromo *s.m.* QUIM. bromine.
bromuro *s.m.* 1 bromide. || 2 **— de plata,** bromide paper.
bronca *s.f.* 1 quarrel, row. 2 telling-off, ticking-off. 3 boos, jeers (protestas). || 4 **armar una —,** to create a row, to make a big fuss: *se armó una bronca = there was a tremendous row.* 5 **buscar —,** to look for trouble. 6 **dar una —,** to hiss, to boo. 7 **echar una —,** to give a telling-off, a ticking-off.
bronce *s.m.* 1 MET. bronze. 2 bronze (estatua). 3 copper coin. || 4 **ser un —** o **de —,** to work like a horse.
bronceado *adj.* 1 bronze, bronze-coloured. 2 sunburnt, tanned (tostado). || *s.m.* 3 suntan, tan. 4 TEC. bronzing.
broncear *v.t.* 1 TEC. to bronze. 2 to suntan, to tan (sol).
bronco, -a *adj.* 1 coarse, rough. 2 brittle (metales). 3 harsh, gruff (sonido, voz). 4 gruff, surly (carácter).
bronconeumonía *s.f.* MED. bronchopneumonia.
bronquedad *s.f.* 1 coarseness, roughness. 2 MET. brittleness. 3 harshness, gruffness (sonido, voz). 4 gruffness, surliness (carácter).
bronquial *adj.* ANAT. bronchial.
bronquio *s.m.* ANAT. bronchus.
bronquitis *s.f.* MED. bronchitis.
broquel *s.m.* 1 shield. 2 (fig.) shield.
broquelarse *v.r.* 1 to shield oneself. 2 (fig.) to protect/defend/shield oneself.
brotar *v.i.* 1 BOT. to germinate, to sprout. 2 to sprout, to bud (raíces). 3 (fig.) to sprout. 4 to flow, to gush (agua). 5 to rise (ríos). 6 MED. to appear, to break out. 7 to flow (lágrimas). 8 to produce, to throw out (renuevos). 9 to break out (protestaciones). || *v.t.* 10 to produce.
brote *s.m.* 1 BOT. 1 bud, shoot. 2 budding (brotadura). 3 rise (de fiebre). 4 MED. appearance, outbreak. 5 outbreak (de huelgas, etc.). 6 welling-up (de lágrimas). 7 (fig.) outbreak.
broza *s.f.* 1 dead leaves. 2 rubbish (desperdicio). 3 thicket, undergrowth (maleza). 4 (fig.) nonsense, rubbish. 4 printer's brush (imprenta).
bruces *s.m.pl.* 1 lips. || 2 **caer de —,** to fall flat on one's face, to fall headlong. 3 **de —,** face down.
bruja *s.f.* 1 witch. 2 ZOOL. barn owl. 3 (fig.) hag, witch.
brujear *v.i.* to practise witchcraft.
brujería *s.f.* 1 witchcraft, sorcery. 2 magic, black magic.
brujo *s.m.* 1 wizard, sorcerer. 2 witch doctor (en las tribus).
brújula *s.f.* 1 compass. || 2 **perder la —,** to lose one's bearings.
brujulear *v.t.* 1 to turn over (cartas). 2 to guess (fam.). 3 to investigate. 4 to scheme, to plot (tramar).
brujuleo *s.i.* 1 (fam.) guessing.
brulote *s.m.* 1 MAR. fire-ship. 2 swear word (palabrota).
bruma *s.f.* 1 mist. 2 sea mist (en el mar).
brumal *adj.* wintry, wintery.
brumo *s.m.* white wax.
brumoso, -a *adj.* misty.
bruno, -a *adj.* 1 dark brown. || *s.m.* 2 BOT. black plum.
bruñido, -a *s.m.* y *f.* 1 polishing. || *adj.* 2 polished.
bruñidor, -a *s.m.* y *f.* polisher.
bruñir *v.t.* 1 to polish, to shine. 2 to make up. 3 (Am.) to annoy, to pester.
bruscamente *adv.* 1 suddenly, abruptly, brusquely.
brusco, -a *adj.* 1 abrupt, sudden. 2 sharp (cambio de temperatura, curva). 3 sharp, brusque (de carácter).
brusquedad *s.f.* 1 abruptness, brusqueness (persona). 2 brusqueness, suddenness (de cosas).
brutal *adj.* 1 brutal, brutish. 2 (fam.) fantastic, terrific. 3 (fam.) enormous, huge.
brutalidad *s.f.* 1 brutality, savagery. 2 stupidity. 3 stupid, cruel action.
brutalmente *adv.* brutally.
bruteza *s.f.* 1 brutality. 2 stupidity.
bruto, -a *adj.* 1 stupid, thick. 2 ignorant. 3 brutal, brutish. 4 rough, coarse (tosco). 5 uncut (diamante, piedra). 6 crude (petróleo, hierro). || *s.m.* y *f.* 7 beast (animal). 8 (*fig.*) brute, beast. || 9 **peso —,** gross weight. 10 **producto —,** ECON. gross product. 11 **producto nacional —,** ECON. gross national product.
bruza *s.f.* 1 horse brush (para caballos). 2 printer's brush (en imprenta).
bruzar *v.t.* to brush.
bubónico, -a *adj.* 1 MED. bubonic. || 2 **peste bubónica,** bubonic plague.
bucal *adj.* ANAT. buccal, oral.
bucanero *s.m.* buccaneer.
búcaro *s.m.* 1 odoriferous clay (arcilla). 2 vase, jar.
buccino *s.m.* ZOOL. whelk.
bucear *v.i.* 1 to swim under water. 2 to work as a diver. 3 (fig.) to explore, to delve into.
bucéfalo *s.m.* (fig. y fam.) dolt, idiot.
bucle *s.m.* curl, ringlet.
bucólico, -a *adj.* 1 bucolic, pastoral. || *s.f.* 2 bucolic, pastoral poem (poesía). 3 (fam.) food, grub.

buchada *s.f.* mouthful.
buche *s.m.* **1** craw, crop (de aves). **2** maw (de animales). **3** (fam.) stomach, belly. **4** mouthful (de líquido). **5** pucker, bag (en la ropa). **6** (fig.) bosom,
inner secrets. **7** newly-born, donkey (borrico). || **8 llenarse el –,** to fill one's belly.
buchón, -ona *adj.* **1** portbellied (barrigón). || **2 paloma buchona,** ponter (pigeon).
budín *s.m.* pudding, pie.
budión *s.c.* ZOOL. wrasse.
budismo *s.m.* REL. buddhism.
budista *s.m.* y *f.* REL. buddhist.
buen *adj.* apócope de **bueno.**
buenamente *adv.* **1** effortlessly, easily. **2** simply. **3** willingly.
buenaventura *s.f.* **1** good luck, fortune (suerte). **2** fortune. || **3 decir** o **echar la – a alguien,** to tell someone's fortune.
bueno, -a *adj.* **1** good (persona o cosa). **2** kind, benevolent (de buen corazón). **3** healthy: *este niño no está bueno últimamente = this child is not very healthy lately.* **4** of good quality, of a good make (especialmente hablando de un producto u objeto). **5** fit, proper, suitable: *no es bueno sacar dinero de la Bolsa ahora = it's not suitable to get the money out of the Stock Exchange nowadays.* **6** good, fair (tiempo atmosférico). **7** funny (divertido): *eso sí que es bueno = that's funny indeed.* **8** considerable: *una buena cantidad de cerveza = a considerable amount of beer.* **9** innocent, naive (bonachón). || *adv.* **10** enough (basta): *bueno, no me des tantos besos = enough, don't kiss me so much.* || **11 de buenas a primeras,** all of a sudden.
buey *s.m.* **1** ox, bullock. || **2 buey marino,** seacow.
bufa *s.f.* **1** joke. **2** drunkenness. || *adj.* **3** drunk.
bufador *s.m.* GEOL. fissure, crack.
búfalo *s.m.* ZOOL. buffalo.
bufanda *s.f.* scarf.
bufar *v.i.* **1** to snort (toro). **2** to spit (gato). || **3 – de rabia,** to snort with rage.
bufete *s.m.* **1** writing desk. **2** lawyer's office. **3** lawyer's practise. || **4 abrir –,** to set up a legal practise.
buffet *s.m.* **1** sideboard. **2** buffet (de comida).
bufido *s.m.* **1** snort (toro). **2** hiss (gato). **3** (fig.) snort.
bufo, -a *adj.* **1** comic, ridiculous, farcical. **2** comic (opera). || **3 opera –,** comic opera. || *s.m.* **4** clown, buffoon. **5** comic-opera singer. || *s.f.* **6** buffoonery.
bufón *adj.* **1** comical, farcical. || *s.m.* **2** buffoon, clown. **3** HIST. jester.
bufonada *s.f.* buffonery, clowning.
bufonearse *v.r.* **1** to play the clown. **2** to make fun of, to laugh at (burlarse de).
bufonesco, -a *adj.* comical, funny, farcical.
buganvilla *s.f.* BOT. bougainvillea.
bugle *s.m.* MUS. bugle.
buglosa *s.f.* BOT. bugloss.
buharda *s.f.* dormer window.
buhardilla, bohardilla o **boardilla** *s.f.* attic, garret.
buharro *s.m.* ZOOL. scops owl.
buhedera *s.f.* opening, hole.
buhedo *s.m.* pond, pool.
buhero *s.m.* owl-keeper.
búho *s.m.* **1** ZOOL. owl. **2** (fig.) recluse, hermit.
buhonería *s.f.* **1** pedlar's goods (objetos). **2** peddling.
buhonero *s.m.* pedlar, hawker.
buido, -a *adj.* **1** sharp (afilado). **2** grooved (acanalado).
buitre *s.m.* ZOOL. **1** vulture. **2 gran – de las Indias,** condor.
buitrero, -a *s.m.* y *f.* vulture hunter.
buitrón *s.m.* fish trap.
buje *s.m.* axle box, bushing.
bujería *s.f.* trinket, knick-knack.
bujía *s.f.* **1** MEC. spark plug. **2** candle (vela). **3** ELEC. candle power.
bula *s.f.* **1** papal bull (del papa). **2** bulla (medalla romana). **3** seal (sello). || **4 no poder con la –,** to be done in.
bulario *s.m.* papal bulls.
bulbo *s.m.* BOT. bulb.
bulboso, -a *adj.* bulbous.
bulldog *s.m.* bulldog.
bulerías *s.f.pl.* bulerias.
buleto *s.m.* papal brief.
bulevar *s.c.* boulevard.
búlgaro, -a *adj./s.m.* y *f.* Bulgarian.
bulo *s.m.* hoax, false news.
bulto *s.m.* **1** size, volume (volumen). **2** shape, form (forma). **3** vague shape, form (forma confusa). **4** bundle, parcel (fardo). **5** bump (chichón). **6** MED. swelling, lump. **7** ART. statue, sculpture. || **8 a –,** roughly, broadly. **9 buscar a uno el –,** to pester, hassle someone. **10 escurrir uno el –,** to avoid, dodge something. **11 poner de – una cosa,** to exaggerate. **12 ser de –,** to be obvious.
bulla *s.f.* **1** racket, din, uproar, noise. **2** crowd, mob. || **3 meter** o **armar –,** to make a racket, etc.
bullanga *s.f.* **1** racket, uproar. **2** disturbance, riot (tumulto).
bullanguero, -a *adj.* **1** noisy, riotous. || *s.m.* y *f.* **2** noisy person. **3** rioter,troublemaker.
bulldozer *s.m.* bulldozer.
bullicio *s.m.* **1** din, racket, uproar (ruido). **2** bustle. **3** riot, confusion.
bullicioso, -a *adj.* **1** noisy, rowdy. **2** busy, bustling. **3** riotous.
bullir *v.i.* **1** to boil. **2** to bubble (a borbotones). **3** to swarm (insectos). **4** (fig.) to boil. **5** to bustle about (agitarse). || *v.t.* **6** to move, to stir. || *v.pron.* **7** to move, to budge.
bumerán *s.m.* boomerang.
bungalow *s.m.* bungalow.
buniato *s.m.* BOT. sweet potato.
búnker *s.m.* **1** bunker. **2** bunker (golf). **3** shelter (contra bombas). || **4 estar en el –,** to be bunkered.
buñolería *s.f.* doughnut shop.
buñolero, -a *s.m.* y *f.* doughnut seller/ maker.
buñuelo *s.m.* **1** doughnut. **2** mess, botched-up job.
buque *s.m.* **1** boat, ship. **2** hull (casco). **3** tonnage, capacity (capacidad). || **4 – carguero,** cargo ship o freighter. **5 – costero,** coaster. **6 – de desembarco,** landing craft. **7 – de guerra,** warship. **8 – insignia,** flagship. **9 – de pasajeros,** passenger ship. **10 – de ruedas,** paddle steamer. **11 – de vapor,** steam ship. **12 – de vela,** sailing ship. **13 – escuela,** training ship. **14 – nodriza,** mother ship. **15 ir en buque,** to go by boat.
buqué *s.m.* bouquet.
burbuja *s.f.* bubble. || **2 hacer burbujas,** to bubble, to make bubbles.
burbujeante *adj.* bubbly, fizzy.
burbujear *v.i.* to bubble.
burbujeo *s.m.* bubbling.
burda *s.f.* **1** MAR. backstay. || *adj.* **2** rough, coarse.
burdégano *s.m.* ZOOL. hinny.
burdel *s.m.* brothel.
burdo, -a *adj.* **1** rough (tosco). **2** clumsy (torpe).
bureta *s.f.* burette.
burga *s.f.* hot spring.
burgado *s.m.* snail.
burgo *s.m.* hamlet.
burgomaestre *s.m.* burgomaster, mayor.
burgués, -a *adj.* **1** middle-class, bourgeois. || *s.m.* y *f.* **2** middle-class person, bourgeois.
burguesía *s.f.* middle-class, bourgeois.
buriel *adj.* dark red.
buril *s.m.* burin.
burilada o **buriladura** *s.f.* burin stroke.
burilar *v.t.* to chisel, to engrave (con un buril).
burla *s.f.* **1** taunt, jibe. **2** joke (broma). **3** trick, hoax (engaño). || **4 – burlando,** without realising. **5 de burlas,** in fun. **6 entre burlas y veras,** half jokingly. **7 gastar burlas,** to play tricks. **8 hacer – de,** to make fun of, to mock.
burladero *s.m.* refuge.
burlador, -a *s.m.* y *f.* **1** mocker. **2** hoaxer, joker. || **3** *m.* seducer, libertine, Don Juan. || *adj.* **4** mocking.
burlar *v.t.* **1** to fool, to deceive, to trick. **2** to deceive (a una mujer). **3** to outwit (chasquear). **4** to flout the laws (burlar las leyes). **5** to frustrate. || *v.pron.* **6** make fun of, to ridicule. **7** to joke.
burlería *s.f.* **1** fun, mockery. **2** trick, hoax. **3** tall story (historia difícil de creer).
burlesco, -a *adj.* **1** burlesque. **2** (fig.) comic, funny.
burlete *s.m.* draught excluder.
burlón, -a *adj.* **1** mocking, joking. || *s.m.* y *f.* **2** joker, leg-puller.
buró *s.m.* bureau, writing desk.
burocracia *s.f.* **1** civil service. **2** (desp.) bureaucracy.
burócrata *s.m.* y *f.* **1** civil servant. **2** (desp.) bureaucrat.
burocrático, -a *adj.* bureaucratic.

burrada *s.f.* 1 drove of donkeys. 2 (fam.) stupid thing, nonsense. 3 silly or stupid remark (necedad). || 4 **decir burradas,** to talk nonsense. 5 **una –,** an enormous amount, a lot: *cuesta una burrada = it costs an enormous amount.*
burrajo, -a *adj.* foolish, stupid.
burrero *s.m.* donkey driver.
burro *s.m.* 1 donkey. 2 (fig.) idiot, ass. 3 hard worker. 4 TEC. sawhorse. 5 brute, lout (tosco). || 6 **– de carga,** person who does the donkey work, hard worker. 7 **caerse del –,** to back down, to admit one's mistake. 8 **no ver tres en un –,** to be as blind as a bat.
bursátil *adj.* stock-exchange, financial.
burujo *s.m.* 1 cattle cake (comida de los animales). 2 lump.
burujón *s.m.* lump, bump.
bus *s.m.* bus.
busca *s.f.* 1 hunt, search. 2 group of hunters. || 3 **en – de,** in search of.
buscador, -a *s.m.* y *f.* 1 searcher. || *adj.* 2 searching, seeking. || 3 **– de oro,** gold prospector.
buscapié *s.m.* feeler, hint.
buscapiés *s.m.* firecracker.
buscapleitos *s.m.* y *f.* troublemaker.
buscar *v.t.* 1 to look for, to search for. 2 to seek (ayuda, amistad, consejo). 3 to look up (consultar). 4 to look for, to ask for (buscar problemas, dificultades, etc.). || *v.i.* 5 to look, to hunt. || *v.pron.* 6 **buscarle tres pies al gato,** to quibble, to split. 7 **buscársela,** to ask for it, to look for trouble. || *v.pron.* 8 **buscarse la vida,** to look after oneself, to earn one's living. 9 **– una aguja en un pajar,** to look for a needle in a hay-stack. 10 **ir a –,** to pick up, to fetch.
buscarruidos *s.m.* y *f.* troublemaker, rabble-rouser.
buscavidas *s.m.* y *f.* 1 busybody, nosey parker. 2 hustler (persona habilidosa para encontrar medios de subsistencia). 3 social climber (ambicioso).
busco *s.m.* threshold.
buscón, -ona *s.m.* y *f.* 1 searcher. 2 thief (ladrón). 3 crook (estafador). 4 prostitute. || *adj.* 5 thieving.
busilis *s.m.* 1 snag, hitch. 2 core (el punto central). || 3 **ahí está el –,** there's the catch. 4 **dar en el –,** to put one's finger on the problem.
búsqueda *s.i.* hunt, search.
busto *s.m.* bust.
butaca *s.f.* 1 armchair, easy chair. 2 seat (teatro). || *s.pl.* 3 stalls (teatro).
butacón *s.m.* large armchair.
butano *s.m.* 1 QUIM. butane. 2 butane gas (gas butano). 3 **una bombona de butano,** a butane cylinder.
butifarra *s.c.* Catalan sausage.
butírico *adj.* QUIM. buryric.
butiro *s.i.* 1 butter.
buzamiento *s.c.* GEOL. dip.
buzar *v.i.* GEOL. to dip.
buzo *s.c.* 1 diver. || 2 **campana de –,** diving bell.
buzón *s.c.* 1 letter box, post box. 2 canal, sluice (canal). 3 stopper, plug (tapón). 4 drain, sewer (sumidero).

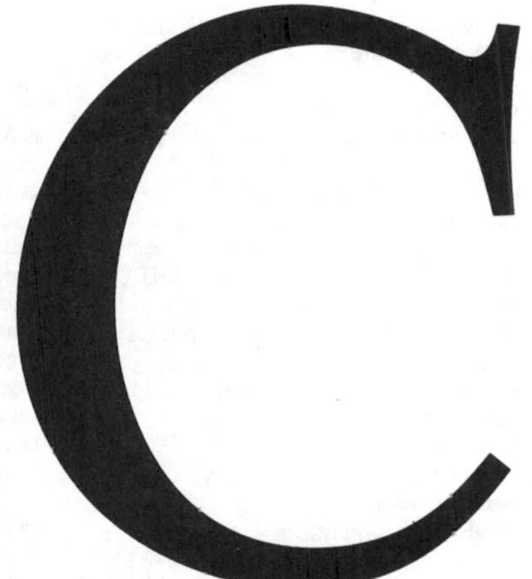

c, C *s.c.* 1 c, C, (tercera letra del alfabeto español). 2 100 (numeración romana).
¡ca! *interj.* come off it!
cabal *adj.* 1 right, proper. 2 complete, perfect. || 3 **no estar en sus cabales,** to be mad, to be out of one's mind.
cábala *s.f.* 1 supposition, guess. 2 cabala.
cabalmente *adv.* completely, perfectly.
cabalístico, -a *adj.* cabalistic.
cabalgadura *s.f.* 1 mount. 2 beast of burden. 3 troop of riders.
cabalgar *v.intr.* 1 to ride. 2 to mount.
cabalgata *s.f.* 1 group of riders. 2 mounted procession.
caballa *s.f.* mackerel.
caballada *s.f.* 1 team of horses. 2 (Am.) stupid thing.
caballar *adj.* equine.
caballeresco, -a *adj.* knightly, chivalric.
caballerete *s.m.* young show-off.
caballería *s.f.* 1 mount. 2 MIL. cavalry. 3 HIST. chivalry, knighthood. || 4 **— andante,** knight errantry. 5 **andarse en —,** to overdo compliments.
caballeriza *s.f.* 1 stable. 2 stable hands.
caballerizo *s.m.* groom.
caballero *s.m.* 1 rider. 2 gentleman. 3 HIST. knight. 4 sir (término de tratamiento). 5 **— andante,** knight errant. 6 **armar —,** to dub a knight.
caballerosidad *s.f.* gentlemanliness.
caballeroso, -a *adj.* gentlemanly.
caballete *s.m.* 1 ridge (tejado). 2 bridge (nariz). 3 easel (pintura).
caballista *s.m.* horseman.
caballito *s.m.* 1 rocking horse. || *pl.* 2 carousel. || 3 **— del diablo,** dragonfly.
caballo *s.m.* 1 horse. 2 knight (ajedrez). 3 queen (naipe). || 4 **— de agua,** sea horse. 5 **— de batalla,** main point. 6 **— de Frisa,** mace. 7 **— del diablo,** dragonfly. 8 **— de vapor,** horsepower. 9 **a mata —,** flat out.
caballón *s.m.* ridge.
cabaña *s.f.* 1 hut, shack. 2 complete herd (ganado). 3 (Am.) cattle-breeding ranch.
cabañal *s.m.* cattle track.
cabañero, -a *s.m.* y *f.* shepherd.
cabaret *s.m.* cabaret.
cabaretera *s.f.* 1 cabaret dancer. 2 nightclub hostess.
cabás *s.m.* satchel.
cabe *prep.* next to, near to.
cabecear *v.i.* 1 to shake the head. 2 to nod (sueño). 3 MAR. to pitch. 4 to slip (mercancías). || 5 to strengthen (vinc). 6 to bind (coser). 7 (Am.) to top cigars.
cabeceo *s.m.* 1 nodding of head. 2 shaking of head. 3 MAR. pitching. 4 slipping (mercancías).
cabecera *s.f.* 1 head. 2 headboard (cama). 3 POL. administrative centre. 4 heading (libro).
cabecilla *s.m.* y *f.* ringleader.
cabellera *s.f.* 1 head of hair. 2 wig. 3 ASTR. luminous comet tail.
cabello *s.m.* 1 hair. || 2 **— merino,** woolly hair. 3 **— de angel,** vermicelli cake.
cabelludo, -a *adj.* hairy, shaggy.
caber *v.i.* 1 to fit. 2 to befall. 3 to be possible.
cabero, -a *adj.* last.
cabestrante *s.m.* capstan.
cabestrillo *s.m.* sling.
cabestro *s.m.* 1 halter. 2 bell-ox.
cabeza *s.f.* 1 head. 2 chief. 3 talent, intellect. 4 origin (de una cosa). 5 administrative centre (de un territorio). || 6 **— de chorlito,** dimwit. 7 **— de puente,** bridgehead. 8 **— de turco,** scapegoat. 9 **alzar —,** to be on the mend. 10 **bajar la —,** to conform. 11 **dar de —,** to go bust. 12 **dar en la — a uno,** to annoy. 13 **de —,** very worried. 14 **llenar a uno la — de viento,** to praise down to the ground. 15 **ir — abajo,** to go downhill. 16 **írsele a uno la —,** to feel giddy. 17 **metérsele a uno en la — alguna cosa,** to get into one's head. 18 **no levantar —,** to be hard-pressed. 19 **perder la —,** to lose one's head. 20 **quitar de la —,** to dissuade. 21 **sentar —,** to come to one's senses. 22 **tocado de la —,** to be weak in the head.
cabezada *s.f.* 1 butt. 2 nod (sueño).
cabezal *s.m.* 1 bolster. 2 head-strap (caballos).
cabezalero, -a *s.c.* DER. executor.
cabezo *s.m.* 1 peak. 2 MAR. reef.
cabezota *s.m.* 1 big head. || *s.m.* y *f.* 2 pigheaded person.
cabezudo, -a *adj.* 1 bigheaded. 2 stubborn. 3 heady (vino).
cabezuela *s.f.* BOT. head.
cabida *s.f.* 1 space, room, capacity. 2 area.
cabildear *v.i.* 1 to lobby. 2 to intrigue.
cabildeo *s.m.* 1 lobbying. 2 intriguing.
cabildo *s.m.* 1 REL. chapter. 2 POL. town council.
cabillo *s.m.* tip (planta).
cabina *s.f.* cabin.
cabio *s.m.* rafter.
cabizbajo, -a *adj.* downcast.
cabizcaído, -a *adj.* downcast.
cable *s.m.* 1 cable, rope. 2 cable length (medida). || 3 **echar un —,** to lend a hand.
cablegrafiar *v.i.* to cable.
cablegrama *s.f.* cable, cablegram.
cablero *s.m.* cable ship.
cabo *s.m.* 1 end. 2 GEOG. cape. 3 bit, butt. 4 thread, strand. 5 MIL. corporal. || 6 **— suelto,** loose end. 7 **al —,** finally. 8 **atar cabos,** to tie up the loose ends. 9 **de — a rabo,** from beginning to end. 10 **estar al — de la calle,** to be in the know. 11 **llevar a — una cosa,** to carry through.
cabotaje *s.m.* coastal traffic, coastal trading.
cabra *s.f.* 1 she-goat, nanny goat. || 2 **— montés,** wild goat. 3 **como una —,** mad, crazy. 4 **la — tira al monte,** a leopard can't change its spots.
cabrear *v.t.* 1 to annoy. || *v.pron.* 2 to get angry.

cabrería *s.f.* goat pen.
cabrerizo, -a *adj.* 1 goatish. 2 goatherd.
cabrero *s.c.* 1 goatherd. || *adj.* 2 (Am.) bad-tempered.
cabrestrante o **cabestrante** *s.m.* capstan, winch.
cabrilla *s.f.* workbench (carpintería).
cabrillear *v.i.* 1 to ripple (mar). 2 to shimmer (luz).
cabrilleo *s.m.* rippling.
cabrío, -a *adj.* goatish.
cabriola *s.f.* 1 skip, leap. 2 somersault.
cabriolé *s.m.* cabriolet.
cabritilla *s.f.* kidskin.
cabrito *s.m.* kid.
cabrón *s.m.* 1 male goat. 2 cuckold. 3 (vulg.) bastard.
cacahual o **cacaotal** *s.m.* cocoa plantation.
cacahuete *s.m.* peanut, monkey nut.
cacao *s.m.* 1 cocoa tree. 2 cocoa.
cacaraña *s.f.* pockmark.
cacarear *v.i.* 1 to cackle. 2 to crow. || *v.t.* 3 to boast about.
cacareo *s.m.* 1 cackling. 2 crowing, boasting.
cacatúa *s.f.* cockatoo.
cacear *v.t.* to ladle.
cacera *s.f.* irrigation ditch.
cacería *s.f.* 1 hunting, shooting. 2 animals bagged.
cacerola *s.f.* saucepan.
cacique *s.c.* 1 (Am.) chief. 2 political boss.
caciquil *adj.* of a chief.
caciquismo *s.m.* 1 power of a chief. 2 despotism.
caco *s.m.* 1 thief. 2 coward.
cacofonía *s.f.* cacophony.
cacofónico, -a *adj.* rackety.
cachar *v.t.* 1 to smash. 2 to saw grainwise. 3 to plough.
cacharpas *s.f.pl.* (Am.) junk.
cacharrazo o (Am.) **cachetada** *s.m.* o *f.* whack.
cacharrería *s.f.* pot shop.
cacharrero, -a *s.m.* y *f.* pot seller.
cacharro *s.m.* 1 pot. 2 (desp.) crock.
cachava *s.f.* stick.
cachaza *s.f.* 1 calmness, phlegm, forbearance. 2 rum.
cachazudo, -a *adj.* 1 calm, phlegmatic. || *s.m.* y *f.* 2 phlegmatic person.
cachear *v.t.* to frisk.
cacheo *s.m.* frisking.
cachera *s.f.* 1 woollen garment. 2 artificial spur (riñas de gallos). 3 (Am.) cow's skull. 4 (Am.) whore.
cachete *s.m.* 1 slap, whack. 2 chubby cheek. 3 dagger. 4 (Am.) favour, help. || 5 **dar un —,** (Am.) to lend a hand.
cachetero *s.c.* 1 dagger. 2 stabber (tauromaquia). 3 the final nail in the coffin.
cachetudo, -a *adj.* 1 chubby-cheeked.
cachicán *s.m.* 1 AGR. foreman. || *adj.* 2 crafty.
cachipolla *s.f.* mayfly.
cachiporra *s.f.* 1 truncheon. || *adj.* 2 (Am.) boastful.
cachiporrazo *s.m.* truncheon blow.
cachivache *s.m.* 1 pot, utensil. 2 good-for-nothing.
cacho *s.m.* 1 bit, crumb. 2 (Am.) horn. 3 (Am.) dice holder. 4 dice game. || *adj.* 5 bent.
cachón *s.m.* breaker.
cachondearse *v.pron.* to treat things as a joke.
cachondeo *s.m.* fooling about.
cachondez *s.f.* randiness.
cachondo, -a *adj.* 1 ZOOL. on heat. 2 (vulg.) randy (brit.), horny (EE.UU.).
cachorrillo *s.m.* pocket revolver.
cachorro *s.m.* 1 pup, puppy. 2 pocket revolver.
cachucha *s.f.* 1 cap. 2 boat. 3 popular dance (Andalucía).
cachudo, -a *adj.* long-horned.
cachuela *s.f.* 1 gizzard. 2 stew.
cada *adj.* each.
cadalso *s.m.* 1 platform. 2 scaffold.
cadarzo *s.m.* silk floss.
cadáver *s.m.* corpse.
cadena *s.f.* 1 chain. 2 succession. 3 bond. || 4 **— de montañas,** mountain range. 5 **— perpetua,** life imprisonment. 6 **— de fabricación,** production line. 7 **— en —,** chain reaction.
cadencia *s.f.* 1 cadence. 2 rhythm. 3 MUS. cadenza.
cadenciado, -a *adj.* cadenced, rhythmical.
cadencioso, -a *adj.* cadenced, rhythmical.
cadenero *s.m.* 1 surveyor. 2 (Am.) chained horse.
cadeneta *s.f.* 1 chain stitch. 2 flourish (cabecera de libro). 3 **— de papel,** paper chain.
cadenilla *s.f.* small chain.
cadente *adj.* 1 ruinous. 2 cadenced.
cadera *s.f.* hip.
cadetada *s.f.* thoughtless act.
cadete *s.m.* 1 cadet. 2 (Am.) errand boy.
cadí *s.m.* magistrate (juez musulmán).
cadmio *s.m.* cadmium.
cadozo *s.m.* whirlpool.
caducar *v.i.* 1 to become senile. 2 to expire. 3 to wear out.
caduceo *s.m.* caduceum.
caducidad *s.f.* expiry.
caducifolio, -a *adj.* deciduous.
caduco, -a *adj.* 1 very old. 2 perishable.
caduquez *s.f.* senility.
caedizo, -a *adj.* unstable, weak.
caer *v.i.* 1 to fall. 2 to befall. 3 to decline (autoridad, etc.). 4 to be situated. 5 to suit (una prenda de vestir). 6 to die. || 7 **estar una cosa al —,** to be about to happen. 8 **— bien una cosa,** to create a good effect. 9 **— bien una persona,** to create a good impression. 10 **— muy bajo,** to come right down in the world. 11 **¡ya caigo!,** now I understand!
caído, -a *adj.* 1 fallen. 2 crestfallen. 3 drooping (cabeza).
caimiento *s.m.* 1 fall, falling. 2 decline.
café *s.m.* 1 coffee. 2 café. || 3 **— cantante,** music café. 4 **— teatro,** night spot.
cafeína *s.f.* caffeine.
cafetal *s.m.* coffee plantation.
cafetalero, -a *adj.* 1 coffee. || *s.m.* y *f.* 2 coffee grower.
cafetera *s.f.* coffee pot.
cafetería *s.f.* 1 café, coffee house. 2 buffet bar (estación de trenes).
cafetero, -a *adj.* 1 coffee. || *s.m.* y *f.* 2 coffee grower. 3 café owner.
cafetín *s.m.* small café.
cafeto *s.m.* coffee tree.
cafre *adj.* 1 Kaffir. 2 cruel, savage. 3 coarse, uncouth.
caftán *s.m.* caftan.
cagada *s.f.* 1 (vulg.) shit. 2 (fig.) balls-up.
cagadero *s.m.* bog, (vulg.) loo (brit.), john (EE.UU.).
cagafierro *s.m.* iron slag.
cagajón *s.m.* horse dung.
cagalera *s.f.* (vulg.) the shits, the runs.
cagar *v.i.* 1 (vulg.) to shit, (vulg.) to have a shit. || *v.t.* 2 (vulg.) to balls up, (vulg.) to make a balls of.
cagarruta *s.f.* sheep dirt.
dagatorio *s.m.* (vulg.) bog.
caguama *s.f.* 1 ZOOL. green turtle. 2 shell (de esta tortuga).
cagueta *s.m.* y *f.* coward.
cahíz *s.m.* grain measure.
cahizada *s.f.* measure of land.
caíd *s.m.* kaid.
caimán *s.m.* 1 caiman. 2 crafty person.
cairel *s.m.* 1 wig. 2 fringe.
caito *s.m.* (Am.) coarse wool.
caja *s.c.* 1 box. 2 coffin. 3 MUS. case. 4 body (coche). 5 COM. cashdesk. 6 stock (arma de fuego). 7 drum (instrumento). || 8 **— de ahorros,** savings bank. 9 **— del cuerpo,** thorax. 10 **— del tambor/— del tímpano,** eardrum. 11 **— de música,** musical box. 12 **— de reclutamiento,** recruiting office. 13 **— registradora,** till. 14 **— fuerte,** safe. 15 **despedir/echar a uno a cajas destempladas,** to send someone packing. 16 **entrar en —,** to be called up.
cajero, -a *s.m.* y *f.* cashier.
cajetilla *s.f.* 1 cigarette packet. 2 (Am.) dandy, dude.
cajetín *s.m.* 1 small box. 2 rubber stamp.
cajista *s.m.* y *f.* typesetter.
cajo *s.m.* edging (libro).
cajón *s.m.* 1 big box. 2 drawer. 3 COM. stall. 4 (Am.) ravine. || 5 **— de sastre,** hotchpotch. 6 muddle-headed person. 7 **ser de — una cosa,** to be quite common.
cajonería *s.f.* drawers.
cal *s.f.* 1 lime. || 2 **— anhidra/viva,** quicklime. 3 **— muerta,** slaked lime. 4 **— hidráulica,** cement.
cala *s.f.* 1 cove. 2 slice (fruta). 3 plug. 4 suppository. 5 MAR. hold.
calabacear *v.i.* (fam.) to flunk.
calabacero, -a *s.m.* y *f.* pumpkin seller. || *s.f.* 2 pumpkin plant.
calabacín *s.m.* 1 marrow. 2 blockhead.
calabacino *s.m.* hollow gourd.
calabaza *s.f.* 1 pumpkin. 2 gourd. 3 head. 4 blockhead. || 5 **dar calabazas,** to fail (examen). 6 to jilt (boda).
calabobos *s.m.* drizzle.
calabozo *s.m.* cell, dungeon.
calabriada *s.f.* mix-up.
calabriar *v.t.* to mix up.
calabrote *s.m.* MAR. cable.
calada *s.f.* 1 soaking. 2 swoop (ave de rapiña). 3 drag (de cigarrillo).

calado *s.m.* **1** drawnwork (costura). **2** draught (barco). **3** depth (mar).
calador *s.m.* **1** sounder. **2** MED. probe.
caladura *s.f.* **1** slicing. **2** soaking.
calafate *s.m.* shipwright.
calafateador *s.m.* shipwright.
calafatear *v.t.* to seal.
calafateo *s.m.* sealing.
calamar *s.m.* squid.
calambre *s.m.* cramp.
calambuco *s.m.* BOT. calaba.
calambur *s.m.* pun.
calamento *s.m.* calamint.
calamidad *s.f.* calamity.
calamiforme *adj.* cane-shaped.
calamina *s.f.* calamine.
calamita *s.f.* **1** lodestone. **2** compass.
cálamo *s.m.* **1** cane. **2** pen. || **3 — currente,** off the cuff.
calamocha *s.f.* yellow ochre.
calamón *s.m.* **1** ORN. purple gallinule. **2** round-headed nail.
calamorra *adj.* **1** woolly-faced (oveja). || *s.f.* **2** (fam.) nut.
calamorrada *s.f.* (fam.) head butt.
calandrar *v.t.* TEC. to dress in a calender.
calandria *s.f.* **1** ORN. lark. **2** TEC. calender, mangle. **3** hypochondriac.
calaña *s.f.* **1** sample. **2** nature. **3** fan.
calañés *s.m.* **1** wide-brimmed hat.
cálao *s.m.* ORN. hornbill.
calar *v.t.* **1** to penetrate. **2** to perforate. **3** to do drawn work (costura). **4** to slice (fruta). **5** to fix (bayoneta). **6** to size up (intenciones, secreto). **7** MAR. to lower. **8** MAR. to draw (profundidad). || *v.pron.* **9** to pull right down (sombrero). **10** to get soaked. || **11** to stall (motor). **12** ORN. to swoop.
calavera *s.f.* **1** skull. **2** (desp.) flirt, loose liver.
calaverada *s.f.* crazy act.
calaverar *v.i.* to live it up.
calboche *s.m.* chestnut roaster.
calcado *s.m.* tracing.
calcáneo *s.m.* calcaneum.
calcañal o **calcañar** o **calcaño** *s.m.* heel.
calcar *v.t.* **1** to trace. **2** to copy.
calcáreo, -a *adj.* lime.
calce *s.m.* **1** steel tyre. **2** shim. **3** wedge.
calcedonia *s.f.* chalcedony.
calceta *s.f.* **1** stocking. **2** shackle.
calcetear *v.i.* to knit.
calcetería *s.f.* **1** knitting (acto). **2** knitwear shop.
calcetero, -a *s.m.* y *f.* **1** knitwear worker. **2** knitwear salesman.
calcetín *s.m.* sock.
cálcico, -a *adj.* **1** calcic. **2** QUIM. calcic.
calcificación *s.f.* QUIM. calcifying.
calcificar *v.t.* y *v.i.* to calcify.
calcina *s.f.* concrete.
calcinación *s.f.* QUIM. calcination.
calcinamiento *s.m.* calcination.
calcinar *v.t.* to calcine.
calcio *s.m.* QUIM. calcium.
calco *s.m.* **1** traced copy. **2** tracing paper. || **3 — lingüístico,** calque.
calcografía *s.f.* chalcography.
calcografiar *v.t.* to do copperplate engraving.
calcógrafo *s.m.* copperplate engraver.
calcomanía o **calcamonía** *s.f.* decalcomania.
calcopirita *s.f.* copper pyrite.
calculable *adj.* MAT. calculable.
calculador, -a *s.f.* **1** calculator. || *adj.* **2** calculating.
calcular *v.t.* to calculate.
calculatorio, -a *adj.* calculatory.
calculista *s.c.* designer.
cálculo *s.c.* **1** calculation. **2** MAT. calculus.
calculoso *adj.* containing gravel.
calda *s.f.* **1** heating. || **2** *pl.* hot springs.
caldario *s.m.* spa.
caldeamiento *s.m.* TEC. heating.
caldear *v.t.* to heat up.
caldeo *s.i.* warming.
caldera *s.f.* **1** boiler. **2** crater. || **3 — de vapor,** MEC. steam boiler.
calderada *s.f.* TEC. boiler contents.
calderería *s.f.* TEC. boiler-making.
calderero *s.m.* TEC. boiler-maker.
caldereta *s.f.* **1** small boiler. **2** holy-water vessel. **3** GAST. lamb stew. **4** GAST. fish soup: *me encanta la caldereta = I love fish soup.*
calderilla *s.f.* **1** holy-water vessel. **2** loose change: *¿tienes calderilla? = have you got any loose change?*
caldero *s.m.* metal pot.
calderón *s.m.* **1** large pot. **2** MUS. pause.
caldo *s.m.* **1** stock. **2** salad dressing. || **3 — de cultivo,** culture medium: *una casa llena de libros es el mejor caldo de cultivo para los hijos = a house full of books is the best culture medium for children.*
caldoso, -a *adj.* with a lot of stock.
cale *s.m.* smack.
calé *s.m.* y *f.* gypsy.
calecer *v.i.* to heat up.
calefacción *s.f.* **1** heating. || **2 — central,** central heating.
calefactor *s.c.* heating installer.
caleidoscopio o **calidoscopio** *s.m.* kaleidoscope.
calendar *v.t.* to date (documento).
calendario *s.m.* **1** calendar. || **2 — juliano,** Julian calendar. **3 — gregoriano,** Gregorian calendar. **4 — perpetuo,** lifelong calendar.
calendarista *s.m.* y *f.* calendar-maker.
calendas *s.f.pl.* calends.
calentador *s.m.* heater.
calentamiento *s.m.* heating.
calentar *v.t.* **1** to heat. **2** to hit. **3** to speed up. || *v.pron.* **4** to get heated up.
calentón *s.m.* warming up.
calentura *s.f.* high temperature.
calenturiento, -a *adj.* **1** MED. feverish: *me siento calenturiento = I feel feverish.* **2** (fig.) heated.
calenturón *s.m.* MED. high fever.
caleño, -a *adj.* limey.
calepino *s.m.* Latin dictionary.
calera *s.c.* **1** limestone quarry. **2** lime kiln.
calesa *s.f.* buggy.
calesero *s.m.* landau driver.
calesín *s.m.* covered chaise.
caleta *s.f.* cove, inlet.
caletre *s.m.* (fam.) brains.
calibración *s.f.* calibration.
calibrador *s.m.* calibrator.
calibrar *v.t.* **1** to calibrate. **2** to gauge.
calibre *s.m.* **1** calibre. **2** size. **3** importance.
calicanto *s.m.* masonry.
caliche *s.m.* **1** chip of whitewash. **2** crack. **3** (Am.) saltpetre.
calidad *s.f.* **1** quality. **2** position. **3** stipulation (contrato). || **4 a — de que,** provided that. **5 en — de,** in the capacity of.
cálido, -a *adj.* hot.
calidoscópico, -a *adj.* kaleidoscopic.
calientapiés *s.m.* foot-warmer.
caliente *adj.* **1** hot. **2** heated. || **3 en —,** straightaway.
califa *s.m.* HIST. caliph.
califato *s.m.* HIST. caliphate.
calífero, -a *adj.* lime.
calificable *adj.* qualifiable.
calificación *s.f.* **1** qualification. **2** mark.
calificado, -a *adj.* **1** qualified. **2** authorized.
calificador, -a *adj.* qualifying.
calificar *v.t.* **1** to qualify. **2** to mark (examen). **3** to ennoble.
calificativo, -a *adj.* qualifying.
californiano, -a *adj.* Californian.
calígine *s.f.* **1** darkness, mist. **2** sultry weather.
caligrafía *s.f.* calligraphy.
caligrafiar *v.t.* to write beautifully.
caligráfico, -a *adj.* calligraphic.
calígrafo, -a *s.m.* y *f.* calligrapher.
calilla *s.f.* (Am.) nuisance.
calima o **calina** *s.f.* haze.
calimba *s.f.* (Am.) branding-iron.
calimoso, -a o **calinoso, -a** *adj.* hazy.
cáliz *s.m.* **1** chalice. **2** BOT. calyx.
caliza *s.f.* **1** limestone. || **2 — lenta,** dolomite.
calma *s.f.* **1** calm. **2** inactivity. **3** calmness. || **4 — chicha,** dead calm. **5 en —,** calm (mar).
calmante *adj.* **1** shooting. || *s.m.* **2** sedative.
calmar *v.t.* **1** to calm. || *v.pron* **2** to become calm.
calmo, -a *adj.* **1** fallow (terreno). **2** resting.
calmoso *adj.* **1** calm. **2** sluggish.
caló *s.m.* **1** gypsy language. **2** slang.
calología *s.f.* aesthetics.
calón *s.m.* **1** fathometer. **2** fishing-net support.
calor *s.m.* **1** heat. **2** warmth. **3** fervour. || **4 — canicular,** stifling heat.
caloría *s.f.* calory.
calórico, -a *adj.* caloric.
calorífero, -a *adj.* heat-producing.
calorificación *s.f.* calorification.
calorífico, -a *adj.* calorific.
calorífugo, -a *adj.* **1** heat-resistant. **2** non-inflammable.
calorimetría *s.f.* calorimetry.
calorímetro *s.m.* calorimeter.
calostro *s.m.* colostrum.
caloyo *s.m.* **1** new-born lamb. **2** kid.
calumnia *s.f.* slander.
calumniar *v.t.* to slander.
calumnioso, -a *adj.* slanderous.
calva *s.f.* bald patch.
calvario *s.m.* **1** Calvary. **2** series of adversities.

calvero *s.m.* 1 clearing. 2 claypit.
calvicie *s.f.* baldness.
calvinismo *s.m.* Calvinism.
calvinista *adj.* 1 Calvinistic. || *s.c.* 2 Calvinist.
calvo, -a *adj.* 1 bald. 2 barren (terreno).
calza *s.f.* 1 stocking. 2 distinguishing ribbon (animales). 3 chock, wedge.
calzada *s.f.* road.
calzadera *s.f.* thick lace (abarcas).
calzado, -a *adj.* 1 wearing shoes. || *s.m.* 2 footwear.
calzador *s.m.* shoehorn.
calzadura *s.f.* putting on shoes.
calzar *v.t.* 1 to put on shoes. 2 to wedge, chock. 3 to take (escopeta). 4 to underlay (imprenta). 5 (Am.) to fill (diente). 6 (Am.) to sign (escrito). 7 (Am.) AGR. to earth up. || 8 **— poco,** to be a little thick. 9 **calzarse a uno,** to dominate someone. 10 **calzarse uno alguna cosa,** to get something.
calzo *s.m.* 1 chock, wedge. 2 fulcrum. || *pl.* 3 legs (caballo).
calzón *s.m.* 1 shorts. 2 three-piece suite.
calzonazos o **calzorras** *s.m.* wimp.
calzoncillos *s.m.* underpants.
calzoneras *s.f.pl.* (Am.) side-fastening trousers.
calzonudo, -a *adj.* (Am.) wimpish.
callada *s.f.* 1 silence. || 2 **dar la — por respuesta,** to say nothing.
callado, -a *adj.* 1 quiet. 2 reserved.
callahuaya *s.m.* (Am.) herb-doctor.
callandico *adv.* stealthily.
callandito, -a *adv.* stealthily.
callar *v.i.* 1 to keep quiet. || *v.t.* 2 not to mention. || 3 **¡calla!,** you don't say! 4 **calla callando,** on the quiet. 5 **al buen — llaman Sancho,** mind what you say.
calle *s.f.* 1 street. 2 lane. || 3 **el hombre de la —,** the man in the street.
calleja *s.f.* alley.
callejear *v.i.* to wander around the streets.
callejeo *s.m.* wandering around the streets.
callejero, -a *adj.* 1 street. 2 fond of street wandering. || *s.m.* 3 street-guide.
callejón *s.m.* 1 alleyway. || 2 **— sin salida,** cul-de-sac. 3 impasse.
callejuela *s.f.* 1 alley. 2 pretext.
callicida *s.f.* corn remover.
callista *s.m.* y *f.* chiropodist.
callo *s.m.* 1 corn. 2 callosity. || *pl.* 3 tripe.
callosidad *s.f.* callosity.
calloso, -a *adj.* hard-skinned.
cama *s.f.* 1 bed. || 2 **— turca,** day bed. 3 **caer en —,** to fall ill. 4 **estar en —/guardar —/hacer —,** to be confined to bed, to stay in bed.
camada *s.f.* 1 litter. 2 gang (ladrones). 3 GEOL. layer.
camafeo *s.m.* cameo.
camal *s.m.* 1 halter. 2 (Am.) abattoir.
camaleón *s.m.* chameleon.
camama *s.f.* lie.
camamila o **camomila** *s.f.* camomile.
camándula *s.f.* 1 rosary. 2 slyness.
camandulear *v.i.* 1 to feign devotion. 2 to be hypocritical.
camandulería *s.f.* hypocrisy.
camandulero, -a *adj.* hypocritical.
cámara *s.f.* 1 room. 2 chamber. 3 MAR. cabin. 4 OPT. camera. 5 granary. 6 inner tube (rueda). 7 ANAT. cavity. 8 cameraman. || *pl.* 9 MED. diarrhoea. || 10 **— frigorífica,** refrigeration chamber. 11 **— mortuoria,** funeral chamber. 12 **— oscura,** camera obscura. 13 **— fotográfica,** camera. 14 **de —,** in-waiting. 15 **música de —,** chamber music. 16 **— de gas,** gas chamber. 17 **— lenta,** slow motion.
camarada *s.m.* y *f.* comrade.
camaradería *s.f.* comradeship.
camaraje *s.m.* granary rent.
camaranchón *s.m.* lumber room.
camarera *s.f.* 1 waitress. 2 maid. || 3 **— mayor,** lady-in-waiting.
camarero *s.m.* 1 waiter. || 2 **— mayor,** gentleman-in-waiting.
camarilla *s.f.* coterie.
camarín *s.m.* 1 REL. image space. 2 dressing room (teatro). 3 closet.
camarlengo *s.m.* papal chamberlain.
camarón *s.m.* 1 shrimp. 2 (Am.) timber cart. 3 (Am.) tip.
camaronero, -a *s.m.* y *f.* shrimp seller.
camarote *s.m.* birth, cabin.
camarotero *s.m.* cabin attendant.
camastro *s.m.* rickety bed.
camastrón, -a *adj.* cunning.
camastronería *s.f.* cunning.
cambado, -a *adj.* (Am.) bow-legged.
cambalache *s.m.* bartering.
cambalachear *v.t.* to barter.
cambar *v.t.* (Am.) to bend.
cámbaro *s.m.* crab.
cambera *s.c.* crab net.
cambiante *adj.* changing, changeable.
cambiar *v.t.* 1 to change. 2 to exchange. || *v.i.* 3 to veer (viento). || *v.pron.* 4 to change one's clothes.
cambiavía *s.m.* (Am.) switchman.
cambio *s.m.* 1 change. 2 exchange rate. 3 barter. || 4 **— democrático,** shift to democracy. 5 **libre —,** free trade. 6 **en —,** on the other hand.
cambista *s.m.* y *f.* money-changer.
cambrón *s.m.* bramble.
cambronal *s.m.* bramble bushes.
cambucho *s.m.* (Am.) 1 cornet. 2 basket. 3 den.
camelar *v.t.* to cajole.
camelia *s.f.* camellia.
camelista *s.m.* y *f.* cajoler.
camelote *s.m.* camlet.
camellero *s.m.* camel herd.
camello *s.m.* camel.
camellón *s.m.* ridge.
cameraman *s.m.* cameraman.
camerino *s.m.* dressing room.
camero, -a *adj.* full-sized (de cama).
camilla *s.f.* 1 stretcher. 2 round table.
camillero, -a *s.m.* y *f.* stretcher-bearer.
caminante *s.m.* y *f.* 1 walker. 2 traveller.
caminar *v.i.* 1 to walk. 2 to progress. || *v.t.* 3 to cover.
caminata *s.f.* hike.
caminero, -a *adj.* of the road.
camino *s.m.* 1 road. 2 way. 3 means. || 4 **— de cabaña,** cattle track. 5 **— de herradura,** bridle path. 6 **— de hierro,** railway. 7 **— de Santiago,** Milky Way. 8 **— de sirga,** towpath. 9 **— real,** national highway. 10 **— trillado,** (fam.) the beaten track. 11 **— vecinal,** municipal road. 12 **abrir —,** to make headway. 13 **de —,** on the way. 14 **ir cada cual por su —,** to go one's own way. 15 **ir fuera de —,** to take a wrong turning. 16 **llevar —,** to be justifiable. 17 **ponerse en —,** to start out.
camión *s.m.* lorry.
camionaje *s.m.* haulage.
camionero, -a *s.m.* y *f.* lorry driver.
camioneta *s.f.* van.
camisa *s.f.* 1 shirt. 2 covering. 3 slough (culebra). || 4 **— de fuerza,** straightjacket. 5 **meterse uno en — de once varas,** to meddle in other people's business. 6 **no llegarle a uno la — al cuerpo,** to be dead scared.
camisería *s.f.* shirt shop.
camisero, -a *s.m.* y *f.* shirt maker.
camiseta *s.f.* 1 vest. 2 T-shirt.
camisola *s.f.* team shirt.
camisolín *s.m.* dicky.
camisón *s.m.* 1 nightgown. 2 (Am.) dress.
camón *s.m.* 1 portable throne. 2 balcony. || 3 **— de vidrios,** glass partition.
camorra *s.f.* row.
camorrear *v.i.* to row, to quarrel, to argue.
camorrero, -a *adj.* quarrelsome.
camorrista *adj.* quarrelsome.
camote *s.m.* (Am.) 1 sweet potato. 2 bulb. 3 infatuation. 4 lover. 5 lie. 6 fool. 7 ANAT. calf. 8 weal.
campa *adj.* treeless.
campal *adj.* 1 country. 2 pitched (battle).
campamento *s.m.* 1 camp. 2 camping.
campana *s.f.* 1 bell. || 2 **— de buzo,** diving bell. 3 **echar las campanas al vuelo,** to shout from the rooftops, to be over come with joy. 4 **oír uno campanas y no saber dónde,** to get hold of the wrong end of the stick.
campanada *s.f.* peal.
campanario *s.m.* belfry.
campanear *v.i.* to peal.
campaneo *s.m.* pealing.
campanero, -a *s.m.* y *f.* bell ringer.
campaniforme *adj.* bell-shaped.
campanil *adj.* 1 bell (metal). || *s.c.* 2 belfry.
campanilla *s.f.* 1 handbell. 2 bubble. 3 uvula. 4 bell flower. || 5 **de campanillas,** eminent.
campanillazo *s.m.* loud ring.
campanillear *v.i.* to ring.
campanilleo *s.m.* ringing.
campano *s.m.* 1 cowbell. 2 big glass.
campanología *s.f.* bell-ringing.
campanólogo, -a *s.m.* y *f.* professional bell-ringer.
campante *adj.* 1 outstanding. 2 self-satisfied.
campanudo, -a *adj.* 1 bell-shaped. 2 pompous.
campánula *s.f.* bell flower.
campaña *s.f.* 1 plain. 2 campaign. || 3 **— electoral,** election campaign.
campar *v.i.* 1 to stand out. 2 to camp. || 3 **— por sus respetos,** to act independently.
campeador *adj.* y *s.m.* champion.

campear *v.i.* 1 to go to pasture. 2 to become green (sembrado). 3 to stand out. 4 MIL. to be in the field.
campechanía *s.f.* openness.
campechano, -a *adj.* down-to-earth.
campeche *s.m.* BOT. campeachy-wood.
campeón, -ona *s.m.* y *f.* champion.
campeonato *s.m.* championship.
campero, -a *adj.* 1 country. 2 outdoor. || *s.f.* 3 tight jacket.
campesino, -a *adj.* 1 country. || *s.m.* y *f.* farmer.
campestre *adj.* country.
camping *s.m.* 1 campsite. || 2 **— gas,** gas bottle.
campiña *s.f.* open land.
campo *s.m.* 1 countryside. 2 field. 3 DEP. ground. || 4 **— de concentración,** concentration camp. 5 **— eléctrico,** electric field. 6 **— gravitatorio terrestre,** Earth's gravitational field. 7 **— magnético,** magnetic field. 8 **— santo,** graveyard. 9 **Campos Elíseos,** Elysian Fields. 10 **a — traviesa,** across country. 11 **levantar el —,** to raise camp.
camposanto *s.m.* graveyard.
campus *s.m.* campus.
camuflaje *s.m.* camouflage.
camuflar *v.t.* to camouflage.
camuñas *s.f.pl.* 1 seeds. 2 **el Camuñas,** the Bogeyman.
can *s.m.* 1 dog. 2 trigger (arma de fuego). 3 ARQ. corbel. || 4 **Can Mayor,** Canis Major. 5 **Can Menor,** Canis Minor.
cana *s.f.* 1 grey hair. || 2 **echar una — al aire,** to let one's hair down. 3 **peinar canas una persona,** to be getting on.
canáceo, -a *adj.* cannaceous.
canadiense *adj./s.m.* y *f.* Canadian.
canal *s.m.* y *f.* 1 canal. 2 channel. 3 narrow valley. 4 conduit. 5 cleaned carcass. 6 ARQ. fluting. || 7 **abrir en —,** to cut right down the middle.
canalado, -a *adj.* fluted.
canaladura *s.f.* flute.
canaleja *s.f.* mill spout.
canalete *s.m.* paddle.
canalización *s.f.* channelling.
canalizar *v.t.* to channel.
canalizo *s.m.* 1 MAR. narrow channel.
canalón *s.m.* 1 roof gutter. || *pl.* 2 ravioli.
canalla *s.f.* 1 rabble. || *s.m.* 2 good-for-nothing.
canallada *s.f.* rotten trick.
canallesco, -a *adj.* rotten.
canana *s.f.* cartridge belt.
canapé *s.m.* 1 divan. 2 GAST. canapé.
canariera *s.f.* canary cage.
canario, -a *adj.* 1 from the Canary Islands. || *s.m. y* f. 2 canary.
canasta *s.f.* 1 wicker basket. 2 canasta.
canastada *s.f.* basketful.
canastero, -a *s.m.* y *f.* wicker basket maker.
canastilla *s.m.* 1 layette. 2 small basket.
canastillero, -a *s.m.* y *f.* wicker tray maker.
canastillo *s.m.* wicker tray.
canasto o **canastro** *s.m.* 1 large basket. || 2 **¡canastos!,** (fam.) good heavens!
cáncamo *s.m.* eyebolt.
cancamurria *s.f.* (fam.) the blues.
cancamusa *s.f.* trick.
cancán o **can can** *s.m.* cancan.
cáncano *s.m.* louse.
cancel *s.m.* 1 storm door. 2 (Am.) partition.
cancela *s.f.* lattice gate.
cancelación *s.f.* cancellation.
cancelar *v.t.* to cancel.
cancelaria *s.f.* papal chancery.
cancelario *s.m.* university chancellor.
cáncer *s.m.* cancer.
cancerado, -a *adj.* cancerous.
cancerar *v.pron.* to get cancer.
cancerbero o **cerbero** *s.m.* 1 strict watchman. 2 goalkeeper (fútbol).
cancerígeno, -a *adj.* cancer-producing.
canceroso, -a *adj.* cancerous.
canciller *s.m.* chancellor.
cancilleresco, -a *adj.* chancellery.
cancillería *s.f.* chancellery.
canción *s.f.* 1 song. || 2 **— de cuna,** lullaby. 3 **volver a la misma —,** to repeat the same old story.
cancionero *s.m.* song book.
cancionista *s.m.* y *f.* songwriter.
cancro *s.m.* 1 cancer. 2 canker.
cancroide *s.m.* cancroid tumour.
cancha *s.f.* 1 DEP. ground. 2 widest part (río). 3 (Am.) knack. 4 (Am.) popcorn. || *interj.* 5 clear the way! || 6 **dar — a uno,** to give someone an advantage.
canchero, -a *adj.* talented.
candado *s.m.* padlock.
cande o **candi** *adj.* crystallized.
candeal o **candial** *adj.* white (pan).
candela *s.f.* 1 candle power. 2 candle. 3 candlestick. 4 light.
candelabro *s.m.* candelabrum.
candelada *s.f.* bonfire.
candelaria *s.f.* 1 Candlemas. 2 BOT. great mullein.
candelejón *adj.* (Am.) naïve.
candelero *s.m.* 1 candlestick. 2 oil lamp. 3 MAR. stanchion. || 4 **en el —,** in a position of authority.
candelilla *s.f.* (Am.) glow-worm.
candencia *s.f.* incandescence.
candente *adj.* incandescent.
cándidamente *adv.* innocently.
candidato, -a *s.m.* y *f.* candidate.
candidez *s.f.* innocence.
cándido, -a *adj.* simple.
candiel *s.m.* egg sweet.
candil *s.m.* 1 oil lamp. 2 ZOOL. tine.
candileja *s.f.* 1 oil lamp reservoir. 2 oil lamp. || *pl.* 3 footlights (teatro).
candiota *adj.* 1 Candiot. || *s.c.* 2 wine cask.
candiotero *s.m.* cooper.
candongo, -a *s.m.* y *f.* shirker.
candonguear *v.i.* to shirk work.
candongueo *s.m.* shirking.
candonguero, -a *adj.* 1 crafty. 2 lazy.
candor *s.m.* 1 pure whiteness. 2 innocence.
candoroso, -a *adj.* innocent.
caneca *s.f.* earthenware glass.
canecillo *s.m.* corbel.
canela *s.f.* 1 cinnamon. 2 (fam.) peach.
canelado, -a *adj.* cinnamon-flavoured.
canelero *s.m.* cinnamon tree.
canelón *s.m.* 1 icicle. 2 curled fringe (pelo).
canesú *s.m.* decorative fancing.
caney *s.c.* (Am.) 1 river bend. 2 hut.
cangilón *s.m.* bucket.
cangrejera *s.f.* nest of crabs.
cangrejero, -a *s.m.* y *f.* crab seller.
cangrejo *s.m.* 1 crab. 2 MAR. gaff. || 3 **— de mar,** crab. 4 **— de río,** crayfish.
cangrena *s.f.* gangrene.
canguelo *s.m.* (fam.) wind up.
canguro *s.m.* kangaroo.
caníbal *s.m.* y *f.* cannibal.
canibalismo *s.m.* cannibalism.
canica *s.f.* marble.
canicie *s.f.* grey hair.
canícula *s.f.* 1 dog days. 2 ASTR. Sirius.
canicular *adj.* canicular.
canicularío *s.m.* dog keeper.
cánido, -a *adj.* canine.
canijo, -a *adj.* sickly.
canil *s.m.* dog bread.
canilla *s.f.* 1 long bone. 2 barrel tap. 3 bobbin (tejer). 4 weft pirn (tejido).
canillera *s.f.* 1 greave. 2 (Am.) cowardice.
canillero *s.m.* bunghole.
canilludo, -a *adj.* (Am.) long-legged.
canino, -a *adj.* 1 canine. || *s.m.* 2 canine tooth. || *s.f.* dog excrement.
caninez *s.f.* ravenous hunger.
canje *s.m.* exchange.
canjeable *adj.* exchangeable.
canjear *v.t.* to exchange.
cannáceo, -a *adj.* cannaceous.
canoso, -a *adj.* white-haired.
canoa *s.f.* 1 canoe. 2 (Am.) canal.
canódromo *s.m.* dog track.
canon *s.* 1 canon. 2 FIN. levy. 3 canon (parte de la misa).
canónico, -a *adj.* REL. canonical: *derecho canónico = canonic law.*
canóniga *s.f.* pre-lunch nap.
canónigo *s.c.* REL. canon.
canonista *s.m.* y *f.* expert in canon law.
canonizable *adj.* worthy of canonizing.
canonización *s.i.* canonization.
canonizar *v.t.* to canonize.
canonjía *s.c.* 1 canonry. 2 cushy job.
canoro, -a *adj.* tuneful.
cansado, -a *adj.* tired.
cansancio *s.m.* tiredness.
cansar *v.t.* to tire.
cansino, -a *adj.* tiring.
cantable *adj.* singable.
cantador, -a *s.m.* y *f.* singer.
cantal *s.m.* boulder.
cantaletear *v.t.* 1 to make fun of. 2 to chant.
cantante *s.m.* y *f.* singer.
cantar *v.t.* 1 to sing. 2 to chant. || *s.m.* 3 song. || 4 **— de plano,** to tell all. 5 **— de gesta,** epic poem. 6 **eso es otro —,** that's another kettle of fish.
cántara *s.f.* 1 pitcher. 2 liquid measure.
cantarada *s.f.* pitcher contents.
cantarela *s.f.* 1 treble string. 2 chantarelle (hongo).
cantarera *s.f.* pottery stand.
cantarería *s.f.* 1 pottery. 2 pottery shop.
cantarero, -a *s.m.* y *f.* 1 pot dealer. 2 potter.
cantarín, -a *adj.* song-loving.

cántaro *s.m.* 1 pitcher. || 2 **a cántaros,** (fam.) bucketfuls.
cantata *s.f.* MUS. cantata.
cantatriz *s.f.* female singer.
cantautor, -a *adj.* composer-cum-singer.
cantazo *s.m.* blow with a stone.
cante *s.m.* 1 singing. || 2 **— hondo/— jondo/— flamenco,** gypsy singing.
cantear *v.t.* to border.
cantera *s.f.* 1 quarry. 2 talent.
cantería *s.f.* stonework.
cantero *s.m.* 1 stonemason. 2 brittle end. 3 plot (terreno).
cántico *s.m.* canticle.
cantidad *s.f.* 1 quantity. || 2 **— de movimiento,** momentum.
cantiga o **cántiga** *s.f.* carol.
cantil *s.m.* ledge.
cantilena *s.f.* chant.
cantillo *s.m.* small pebble.
cantimplora *s.f.* water bottle.
cantina *s.f.* 1 canteen. 2 refreshment room. 3 wine cellar. 4 lunch box.
cantinela *s.f.* chant.
cantinero, -a *s.m.* y *f.* canteen-keeper.
cantizal *s.m.* stony area.
canto *s.m.* 1 singing. 2 song. 3 edge. 4 pebble.
cantón *s.m.* 1 corner. 2 canton.
cantonal *adj.* cantonal.
cantonar *v.t.* to billet.
cantonear *v.i.* to loaf around.
cantonero, -a *s.m.* y *f.* 1 loafer. 2 corner-plate. 3 corner table.
cantor, -a *s.m.* y *f.* singer.
cantoral *s.m.* choir book.
canturrear *v.i.* to hum.
canturreo *s.m.* humming.
canturriar *v.i.* to hum.
cánula *s.f.* cannula.
canutero *s.m.* 1 pincushion. 2 (Am.) pen barrel.
canutillo *s.m.* small tube.
canuto *s.m.* 1 small tube. 2 (Am.) pen barrel.
caña *s.f.* 1 BOT. stem. 2 long bone. 3 leg (bota). 4 marrow (hueso). 5 glass. 6 tipstock (arma de fuego). 7 shaft (columna). || 8 **— de azúcar,** sugar cane.
cañada *s.f.* 1 ravine. 2 cattle track.
cañadú o **cañadulce** o **cañaduz** *s.f.* sugar cane.
cañal o **cañaveral** *s.m.* reedbed.
cañamar *s.m.* sugar-cane plantation.
cañamazo *s.m.* 1 burlap. 2 sketch.
cañamelar *s.c.* sugar-cane plantation.
cañameño, -a *adj.* hempen.
cañamiel *s.f.* sugar cane.
cáñamo *s.m.* hemp.
cañamón *s.m.* hempseed.
cañamoncillo *s.m.* mixing sand.
cañariego, -a *adj.* migrating.
cañavera *s.f.* reed grass.
cañería *s.f.* piping.
cañero, -a *adj.* 1 cane. || *s.m.* y *f.* 2 plumber.
cañista *s.m.* y *f.* hurdle maker.
cañivano, -a *adj.* hollow.
cañiza *adj.* 1 long-grained. || *s.f.* 2 canvas.
cañizo *s.m.* AGR. hurdle.
caño *s.m.* 1 tube. 2 spout. 3 sewer. 4 navigation channel.
cañón *s.m.* 1 long tube. 2 barrel (arma de fuego). 3 quill (pluma). 4 GEOL. canyon. 5 MIL. cannon.
cañonazo *s.m.* cannon shot.
cañonear *v.t.* to shell.
cañoneo *s.m.* shelling.
cañonera *s.f.* embrasure.
cañonería *s.f.* 1 cannonry. 2 pipework (órgano).
cañonero *s.m.* gunboat.
cañucela *s.f.* reed pen.
cañutazo *s.m.* hearsay.
cañutería *s.f.* 1 piping. 2 embroidery.
cañutero *s.m.* pincushion.
cañutillo *s.m.* 1 small pipe. 2 bugle (de bordar).
cañuto *s.m.* 1 internode. 2 short tube.
caoba *s.m.* mahogany.
caos *s.m.* chaos.
caótico, -a *adj.* chaotic.
capa *s.f.* 1 cape. 2 coat. 3 layer (mineral). 4 pretext. 5 colour (animal). || 6 **— aguadera,** waterproof cape. 7 **— pluvial,** pontificial cape. 8 **de — caída,** going through a bad patch. 9 **hacer de su — un sayo,** to do as one pleases in one's own affairs.
capacidad *s.f.* capacity.
capacitación *s.f.* enabling.
capacitado, -a *adj.* qualified.
capacitar *v.t.* to capacitate.
capachero, -a *s.m.* basket maker.
capacho, -a *s.m.* y *f.* basket.
capar *v.t.* to castrate.
caparazón *s.m.* 1 shell. 2 covering. 3 nosebag.
caparra *s.f.* 1 ZOOL. tick. 2 earnest (dinero).
caparrón *s.m.* 1 bud. 2 bean.
caparrosa *s.f.* 1 vitriol. || 2 **— azul,** blue vitriol. 3 **— blanco,** white vitriol. 4 **— verde,** copperas.
capataz *s.m.* foreman.
capaz *adj.* able.
capazo *s.m.* large basket.
capciosidad *s.f.* captiousness.
capcioso, -a *adj.* captious.
capea *s.f.* 1 waving the cape (tauromaquia). 2 amateur bullfight.
capear *v.t.* 1 to steal a cape. 2 to wave the cape. 3 to trick. 4 MAR. to ride out the storm.
capelo *s.m.* 1 cardinal's hat. 2 cardinalate.
capellada *s.f.* toe piece.
capellán *s.m.* chaplain.
capellanía *s.f.* chaplaincy.
capeón *s.m.* young bull.
capero *s.m.* 1 priest. 2 hallstand.
caperuza *s.f.* hood.
capialzado, -a *adj.* splayed.
capialzar *v.t.* to splay.
capicúa *s.m.* 1 reversible number. 2 palindrome.
capilar *adj.* hair.
capilaridad *s.f.* capillarity.
capilla *s.f.* 1 cowl. 2 chapel. 3 choir. 4 proof sheet (imprimir). || 5 **— ardiente,** funeral chapel. 6 **estar en —,** to be on death row. 7 **hacer capillas,** to fragment.
capillejo *s.m.* bonnet.
capillero *s.m.* churchwarden.
capilleta *s.f.* tiny chapel.
capillo *s.m.* 1 baby's bonnet. 2 hood. 3 toe-piece support. 4 rabbit net. 5 wax strainer.
capirotazo *s.m.* click.
capirote *s.m.* 1 mozetta. 2 hood.
capirucho *s.m.* cowl.
capisayo *s.m.* 1 bishop's gown. 2 vest.
capital *adj.* 1 capital. || *s.f.* 2 capital.
capitalidad *s.f.* capital status.
capitalismo *s.m.* capitalism.
capitalización *s.f.* capitalization.
capitalizar *v.t.* to capitalize.
capitalmente *adv.* seriously.
capitán *s.m.* 1 captain. || 2 **— general,** field marshall.
capitana *s.f.* captain's wife.
capitanear *v.t.* to captain.
capitanía *s.f.* 1 captaincy. || 2 **— general,** commander's jurisdiction.
capitel *s.m.* ARCH. capital.
capitolio *s.m.* 1 capitol. 2 (fam.) palace.
capitonné *s.m.* removal lorry.
capítula *s.f.* REL. chapter.
capitulación *s.f.* 1 capitulation. || *pl.* 2 marriage articles.
capitular *adj.* 1 chapter. || *v.t.* 2 to pact. 3 to decree. || *v.i.* 4 to capitulate.
capítulo *s.m.* 1 chapter. 2 charge.
capó o **capota** *s.m.* o *f.* bonnet (coche).
capón *adj.* 1 castrated. || *s.m.* 2 capon. 3 bundle of vines. 4 rap on the head.
caponar *v.t.* to tie up vines.
caporal *s.m.* 1 corporal. 2 foreman.
capota *s.f.* bonnet (sombrero femenino).
capotar *v.i.* to nose over.
capotazo *s.m.* pass (tauromaquia).
capote *s.m.* 1 cloak. 2 cape. 3 scowl. 4 heavy sky. || 5 **echar un —,** to lend a hand.
capotear *v.t.* 1 to use the cape (tauromaquia). 2 to fool. 3 to dodge.
capoteo *s.m.* using the cape.
Capricornio *s.m.* Capricorn.
capricho *s.m.* 1 whim. 2 caprice.
caprichosamente *adv.* whimsically.
caprichoso, -a *adj.* whimsical.
caprichudo, -a *adj.* whimsical.
caprino, -a *adj.* goat.
cápsula *s.f.* 1 cap. 2 capsule. || 3 **— espacial,** space capsule.
capsular *adj.* capsular.
captación *s.f.* securing.
captar *v.t.* 1 to captivate. 2 to collect. 3 to receive.
captura *s.f.* capture.
capturar *v.t.* to capture.
capuana *s.f.* thrashing.
capucha *s.f.* 1 hood. 2 circumflex.
capuchina *s.f.* 1 nasturtium. 2 oil lamp.
capuchino, -a *s.m.* y *f.* Capuchin.
capullo *s.m.* 1 bud. 2 cocoon. 3 prepuce.
capuz *s.m.* hood.
caquexia *s.f.* cachexia.
caqui *s.m.* 1 kaki. 2 khaki.
cara *s.f.* 1 face. 2 side. || 3 **dar la —,** to face the consequences of one's actions. 4 **de —,** opposite. 5 **echar en —,** to reproach. 6 **hacer —,** to confront.
caraba *s.c.* (fam.) the end.
carabela *s.f.* MAR. caravel.

carabina *s.f.* 1 carbine. 2 chaperon. || 3 **ser una cosa la — de Ambrosio,** to be useless.
carabinazo *s.m.* carbine shot.
carabinero *s.m.* carabineer.
cárabo *s.m.* tawny owl.
caracol *s.m.* 1 snail. 2 snail shell. 3 curl (pelo). || 4 **¡caracoles!,** good heavens!
caracola *s.f.* spiral shell.
caracolear *v.i.* to prance in circles (caballo).
carácter *s.m.* 1 character. 2 characteristic. || 3 **con — de,** in the role of.
característica *s.f.* characteristic.
característico, -a *adj.* 1 characteristic. || *s.m.* y *f.* 2 character actor.
caracterización *s.f.* characterization.
caracterizado, -a *adj.* distinguished.
caracterizar *v.t.* 1 to characterize. || *v.pron.* 2 to dress up (actor).
caracú *s.m.* (Am.) 1 marrow bone. 2 marrow.
caracha o **carache** *s.m.* mange.
caradura *s.m.* y *f.* (desp.) swine.
caramanchel *s.m.* 1 MAR. hatchway covering. 2 attic. 3 canteen. 4 stall. 5 dugout.
¡caramba! *interj.* good grief!
carambanado, -a *adj.* icicle-shaped.
carámbano *s.m.* icicle.
carambola *s.f.* 1 cannon. 2 chance. 3 trick.
caramelizar *v.t.* to caramelize.
caramelo *s.m.* sweet.
caramillo *s.m.* 1 flageolet. 2 rustic flute. 3 untidy heap. 4 piece of gossip.
caramilloso, -a *adj.* fussy.
carantamaula *s.f.* 1 ugly mask. 2 (fam.) ugly person.
carantoña *s.f.* 1 ugly person. || *pl.* 2 cajolery.
carantoñero, -a *adj.* cajoling.
carapacho *s.m.* 1 tortoise shell. 2 (Am.) shellfish stew.
¡carape! *interj.* good grief!
carasol *s.m.* suntrap.
carátula *s.f.* 1 mask. 2 the stage (teatro). 3 cover (libro). 4 title page.
caravana *s.f.* 1 caravan. 2 stream (tráfico). || *pl.* (Am.) 3 long earrings.
caravanero *s.m.* caravan guide.
caravasar *s.c.* caravanserai.
caray *interj.* good grief!
carbodinamita *s.f.* QUIM. carbodynamite.
carbol *s.m.* phenol.
carbón *s.m.* 1 coal. 2 carbon. 3 charcoal. || 4 **— animal,** animal charcoal. 5 **— de piedra,** coal. 6 **— vegetal,** charcoal.
carbonada *s.f.* 1 coal load. 2 (Am.) stew.
carbonado *s.m.* black diamond.
carbonatar *v.t.* to carbonate.
carbonato *s.m.* QUIM. carbonate.
carboncillo *s.m.* charcoal.
carbonear *v.t.* to convert into charcoal.
carboneo *s.m.* charcoal making.
carbonero, -a *adj.* 1 coal. || *s.m.* y *f.* 2 coal merchant. 3 coal tit.
carbónico, -a *adj.* carbonic.
carbonífero, -a *adj.* carboniferous.
carbonilla *s.m.* 1 fine coal. 2 cinders.
carbonización *s.f.* carbonization.
carbonizar *v.t.* to carbonize.
carborundo *s.m.* carborundum.
carbunclo o **carbunco** *s.m.* carbuncle.
carbúnculo o **carbunclo** *s.m.* ruby.
carburación *s.f.* carburation.
carburador *s.m.* carburettor.
carburante *s.m.* carburant.
carburar *v.t.* 1 to carburet. || *v.i.* 2 to go smoothly.
carca *adj.* 1 Carlist. 2 old-fashioned.
carcaj o **carcax** o **carcaza** *s.c.* 1 quiver. 2 holder.
carcajada *s.f.* loud laugh.
carcamal *s.m.* old fogey.
carcamán *s.m.* MAR. heavy old boat.
carcasa *s.f.* 1 incendiary bomb. 2 chassis.
cárcava *s.f.* 1 ditch. 2 grave.
carcavina *s.f.* 1 ditch. 2 grave.
cárcavo *s.c.* cavity of a water mill wheel.
carcelario, -a *adj.* prison.
carcelera *s.f.* Andalusian prison song.
carcelero, -a *s.m.* y *f.* jailer.
carcinoma *s.m.* carcinoma.
carcoma *s.f.* 1 woodworm. 2 dust. 3 gnawing concern. 4 spendthrift.
carcomer *v.t.* to gnaw away.
carda *s.f.* 1 carding. 2 teasel. 3 reproof.
cardamina *s.f.* pepper cress.
cardar *v.t.* to card.
cardenal *s.m.* 1 cardinal. 2 cardinal bird. 3 bruise.
cardencha *s.f.* teasel.
cardenillo *s.m.* verdigris.
cárdeno, -a *adj.* purple.
cardiáceo, -a *adj.* heart-shaped.
cardiaco, -a *adj.* cardiac.
cardialgia *s.f.* cardialgia.
cardias *s.m.* cardiac orifice.
cardillo *s.m.* golden thistle.
cardinal *adj.* cardinal.
cardiofobia *s.f.* cardiophobia.
cardiografía *s.f.* cardiography.
cardiógrafo, -a *s.m.* y *f.* cardiographer.
cardiograma *s.m.* cardiogram.
cardiología *s.f.* cardiology.
cardiopatía *s.f.* cardiopathy.
carditis *s.f.* MED. carditis.
cardizal *s.c.* thistle field.
cardo *s.c.* 1 thistle. || 2 **— ajonjero,** carline thistle. 3 **— borriqueño,** cotton thistle. 4 **— estrellado,** star thistle.
cardón *s.m.* 1 teasel. 2 carding.
cardoncillo *s.m.* milk thistle.
cardume *s.m.* shoal.
carduzar V. **cardar.**
carear *v.t.* 1 to bring face to face. 2 to compare. || *v.pron.* 3 to come together.
carecer *v.i.* to lack.
careciente *adj.* lacking.
carecimiento *s.m.* lack.
carel *s.m.* top edge (barca).
carena *s.f.* 1 careening. 2 ribbing. 3 submerged hulk.
carenar *v.t.* to careen.
carencia *s.f.* 1 lack. 2 need.
carente *adj.* lacking.
careo *s.m.* confrontation.
carestia *s.f.* 1 scarcity. 2 high cost.
careto, -a *adj.* 1 white-faced (caballo, res vacuna, etc.). || *s.f.* 2 mask.
carey *s.m.* 1 ZOOL. turtle. 2 tortoiseshell. 3 (Am.) polishing cloth.
carga *s.f.* 1 load. 2 weight. 3 cargo. 4 tax. 5 duty. 6 worry. 7 charge (explosivos). 8 refill (bolígrafo, etc.). 9 attack. || 10 **— de un río,** head.
cargadero *s.m.* loading point.
cargado, -a *adj.* 1 loaded. 2 close (tiempo). 3 strong (café, etc.).
cargador, -a *s.m.* y *f.* loader.
cargamento *s.m.* 1 loading. 2 shipment.
cargante *adj.* boring.
cargar *v.t.* 1 to load. 2 to burden. 3 to annoy. 4 to charge. || *v.pron.* 5 to do away with. 6 to become overcast (cielo). 7 to fill oneself up with. 8 to get into trouble. || *v.i.* 9 **— con,** to assume. 10 **— en,** to fall on. 11 **— hacia,** to incline towards. 12 **— sobre,** to lean on. 13 **— contra,** MIL. to attack.
cargazón *s.f.* 1 load. 2 heaviness (cabeza, etc.). 3 mass of heavy clouds.
cargo *s.m.* 1 loading. 2 weight. 3 post. 4 duty. 5 charge. || 6 **hacerse — de algo;** **a)** to take charge of something; **b)** to understand.
cargoso, -a *adj.* annoying.
carguero *s.m.* freighter.
carguío *s.m.* freight.
cariacontecido, -a *adj.* sad.
cariado, -a *adj.* decayed.
cariadura *s.f.* decay.
cariaguileño, -a *adj.* eagle-faced.
cariampollado, -a *adj.* chubby-cheeked.
cariampollar *adj.* chubby-cheeked.
cariar *v.pron.* to decay.
cariátide *s.f.* caryatid.
caribeño, -a *s.m.* y *f.* Caribbean.
caricato *s.m.* 1 comic actor. 2 (Am.) caricature.
caricatura *s.f.* caricature.
caricaturesco, -a *adj.* caricatural.
caricaturista *s.m.* caricaturist.
caricaturizar *v.t.* to caricature.
caricia *s.f.* 1 caress. 2 endearment.
caricioso, -a *adj.* caressing.
caridad *s.f.* 1 charity. 2 alms. || 3 **instituciones de —,** charitable institutions. 4 **vivir de la —,** to live on charity.
caries *s.f.pl.* 1 decay. 2 AGR. blight.
carilucio, -a *adj.* shiny-faced.
carilla *s.f.* 1 page. 2 mask.
carillón *s.m.* carillon.
carimbo *s.m.* (Am.) branding iron.
cariño *s.m.* 1 affection. 2 tenderness.
cariñosamente *adv.* caringly.
cariñoso, -a *adj.* affectionate.
cariocinesis *s.f.* kariokinesis.
cariópside *s.f.* caryopsis.
carisma *s.m.* charisma.
carismático, -a *adj.* charismatic.
cariz *s.m.* look.
carlanca *s.f.* 1 spiked collar. 2 cunning.
carlancón, -a *adj.* crafty.
carlear *v.i.* to pant.
carlinga *s.f.* 1 cabin. 2 MAR. mast step.
carlismo *s.m.* HIST. Carlism.
carlista *adj.* HIST. Carlist.
carlovingio, -a *adj.* HIST. Carlovingian.
carmelina *s.f.* vicuna wool.
carmelita *adj.* Carmelite.
carmelitano, -a *adj.* Carmelite.
carmen *s.m.* 1 villa. 2 carmen (poesía). 3 Carmelite Order.
carmenador o **cardador** *s.m.* carder.
carmesí *adj.* crimson.

carmín *s.m.* 1 carmine. 2 rouge. 3 BOT. dog rose.
carminativo, -a *adj.* carminative.
carmíneo, -a *adj.* carmine-coloured.
carminoso, -a *adj.* carmine-coloured.
carnada *s.f.* 1 bait. 2 lure.
carnadura *s.f.* 1 musculature. 2 healing flesh.
carnal *adj.* carnal.
carnalidad *s.f.* carnality.
carnaval *s.m.* carnival.
carnavalada *s.f.* carnival escapade.
carnavalesco, -a *adj.* carnivalesque.
carnaza *s.f.* 1 bait. 2 inner skin. 3 fatness.
carne *s.f.* 1 flesh. 2 meat. || 3 **— de cañón,** cannon fodder. 4 **— de gallina,** goose flesh. 5 **— de membrillo,** quince jelly. 6 **carnes blancas,** tender meat. 7 **echar carnes,** to get fat. 8 **en — viva,** raw.
carné *s.m.* identity card.
carnear *v.t.* (Am.) to slaughter.
carnecería *s.f.* butcher's shop.
carnerada *s.f.* flock of sheep.
carnero *s.m.* 1 ram. || 2 **— del cabo,** albatross. 3 **— marino,** seal.
carneruno, -a *adj.* sheeplike.
carnestolendas *s.f.pl.* carnival.
carnet *s.m.* identity card.
carnicería *s.f.* butcher's shop.
carnicero *adj.* 1 carnivorous. 2 bloodthirsty. || *s.m.* 3 butcher.
carnificación *s.f.* MED. carnification.
carnívoro, -a *adj.* carnivorous.
carniza *s.f.* 1 meat remains. 2 rotten flesh.
carnosidad *s.f.* obesity.
carnoso, -a *adj.* 1 fleshy. 2 fat.
caro, -a *adj.* dear.
carona *s.f.* 1 cushion. 2 back (caballo).
caroñoso, -a *adj.* mangy (caballo).
carótida *s.f.* carotid.
carotina *s.f.* QUIM. pigment of the carrot.
carozo *s.m.* 1 corncob. 2 (Am.) stone.
carpa *s.f.* 1 carp. 2 tent.
carpanel *adj.* ARCH. basket-handle.
carpanta *s.f.* 1 keen hunger. 2 laziness. 3 (Am.) rowdy crowd.
carpe *s.m.* hornbeam.
carpelar *adj.* carpel.
carpelo *s.m.* carpel.
carpeta *s.f.* 1 portfolio. 2 table cover. 3 (Am.) savoir faire.
carpetazo *s.m.* **dar —,** to shelve.
carpintear *v.t.* to carpenter.
carpintería *s.f.* carpentry.
carpintero, -a *s.m.* y *f.* 1 carpenter. || 2 **— de armar/de obra de afuera,** construction carpenter. 3 **— de blanco,** joiner. 4 **— de prieto,** cartwright. 5 **— de ribera,** shipwright.
carpo *s.m.* carpus.
carraca *s.f.* 1 MAR. carrack. 2 (desp.) old boiler. 3 rattle, ratchet.
carrasca *s.f.* BOT. kermes oak.
carrascal *s.m.* kermes oak grove.
carrasco *s.c.* 1 kermes oak. 2 (Am.) forest.
carraspear *v.i.* to clear one's throat.
carraspeño *adj.* rough.
carraspeo *s.m.* clearing the throat.
carraspera *s.f.* hoarseness.
carrasqueño, -a *adj.* rough.
carrera *s.f.* 1 running. 2 race. 3 career. 4 course of studies. 5 route. 6 row. 7 ladder (media, etc.). 8 parting (pelo). 9 ARCH. girder. 10 stroke (pistón). || 11 **hacer —,** to get on.
carrerilla *s.f.* 1 run up. 2 MUS. scale. || 3 **de —,** straight off.
carrero *s.m.* cart driver.
carreta *s.f.* cart.
carretada *s.f.* 1 cartload. || 2 **a carretadas,** by the ton.
carrete *s.m.* 1 reel. 2 ELEC. coil.
carretear *v.t.* 1 to cart. || *v.pron.* 2 to stoop.
carretera *s.f.* road.
carretilla *s.f.* 1 wheelbarrow. 2 walking frame (niños). 3 firecracker. 4 (Am.) jaw. || 5 **de —,** by heart.
carretón *s.m.* 1 small cart. 2 wheeled box.
carricoche *s.m.* 1 wagon. 2 (desp.) crock.
carriel *s.m.* (Am.) briefcase.
carril *s.m.* 1 lane. 2 rut. 3 rail (ferrocarril).
carrilada *s.f.* track.
carrilera *s.f.* rut.
carrillada *s.f.* pig grease.
carrillera *s.f.* 1 jaw. 2 chin strap.
carrillo *s.m.* 1 small cart. 2 cheek. 3 pulley.
carrilludo, -a *adj.* round-cheeked.
carriola *s.f.* 1 trundle bed. 2 cariole.
carrizal *s.m.* reedbed.
carrizo *s.m.* reed grass.
carro *s.c.* 1 cart. 2 cartload. 3 carriage (máquina de escribir). 4 tank. 5 (Am.) car. || 6 **Carro Mayor,** Great Bear. 7 **Carro Menor,** Little Bear.
carrocería *s.f.* 1 bodywork. 2 coachbuilder's.
carrocero, -a *s.m.* y *f.* coachbuilder.
carrocha *s.f.* eggs (insectos).
carrochar *v.i.* to lay eggs.
carromato *s.m.* cart.
carroño, -a *adj.* rotten.
carroza *s.f.* carriage.
carruaje *s.m.* carriage.
carrujo *s.m.* treetop.
carrusel *s.m.* roundabout.
carta *s.f.* 1 letter. 2 card. 3 map. 4 constitution. 5 charter. || 6 **— abierta,** open letter. 7 **— blanca,** carte blanche. 8 **— credencial,** credentials. 9 **— de marear,** marine chart. 10 **— de naturaleza,** naturalization papers. 11 **— pastoral,** pastoral letter. 12 **a — cabal,** completely. 13 **echar las cartas,** to tell someone's fortune. 14 **tomar cartas en un asunto,** to intervene in an affair.
cartabón *s.m.* set square, drawing triangle.
cartapacio *s.m.* 1 notebook. 2 portfolio.
cartapel *s.m.* useless piece of writing.
cartear *v.i.* 1 to play low (cartas). || *v.pron.* 2 to write to one another.
cartel *s.c.* 1 placard. 2 pasquinade. 3 sardine net. 4 COM. cartel. || 5 **tener —,** to be famous.
cartelera *s.c.* hoarding.
cartera *s.c.* 1 wallet. 2 POL. portfolio. 3 ECON. holdings. 4 pocket flap (coser). 5 handbag.
cartería *s.f.* sorting room.
carterista *s.m.* pickpocket.
cartero *s.m.* postman.
cartesianismo *s.i.* FIL. Cartesianism.
cartesiano, -a *adj.* FIL. Cartesian.
cartilagíneo, -a *adj.* cartilaginous.
cartilaginoso, -a *adj.* cartilaginous.
cartílago *s.m.* cartilage.
cartilla *s.f.* 1 primer. 2 information book. 3 liturgical calendar.
cartografía *s.f.* mapmaking.
cartógrafo, -a *s.m.* y *f.* mapmaker.
cartomancia *s.f.* fortune telling.
cartomántico, -a *s.m.* y *f.* fortune teller.
cartometría *s.f.* cartometry.
cartómetro *s.m.* cartometre.
cartón *s.m.* 1 cardboard. 2 carton. 3 cartoon. || 4 **— piedra,** papier mâché.
cartoné *s.m.* **en —,** in boards.
cartuchera *s.f.* cartridge belt.
cartucho *s.m.* 1 cartridge. 2 roll. 3 cone.
cartuja *s.f.* 1 Carthusian order. 2 Carthusian monastery.
cartujo, -a *adj./s.m.* y *f.* Carthusian.
cartulina *s.f.* pasteboard.
carúncula *s.f.* caruncle.
carvallo *s.m.* oak.
casa *s.f.* 1 house. 2 home. 3 establishment. || 4 **— consistorial,** town hall. 5 **— cuna,** orphanage. 6 **— de Dios/del Señor,** church. 7 **— de expósitos,** foundling hospital. 8 **— de moneda,** mint. 9 **— de socorro,** first-aid building. 10 **— de vecindad,** block of tenements. 11 **— mortuaria,** house of mourning. 12 **— profesa,** convent. 13 **echar la — por la ventana,** to go to great expense.
casabe o **cazabe** *s.m.* GAST. cassava.
casaca *s.f.* smock overall.
casación *s.f.* cessation.
casadero, -a *adj.* marriageable.
casado, -a *p.p.* 1 de **casar.** || *adj.* 2 married.
casal *s.m.* country house.
casamentero, -a *s.m.* y *f.* matchmaker.
casamiento *s.m.* wedding.
casar *s.m.* 1 hamlet. || *v.pron.* 2 to get married. || *v.t.* 3 to marry. 4 to match. || 5 **no casarse con nadie,** to be one's own boss.
casca *s.f.* 1 grape skin. 2 bark.
cascabel *s.m.* 1 tiny bell. || 2 **ser un —,** to be happy-go-lucky.
cascabelear *v.t.* 1 to lead up the garden path. 2 to act recklessly.
cascabillo *s.m.* 1 tiny bell. 2 husk (cereales). 3 acorn up.
cascado, -a *adj.* 1 worn out. 2 cracked (voice). || *s.f.* 3 waterfall.
cascajal *s.m.* gravelly area.
cascajo *s.m.* 1 gravel. 2 crock. 3 copper (moneda).
cascanueces *s.m.* nutcracker.
cascar *v.t.* 1 to crack open. || *v.i.* 2 to chat.
cáscara *s.f.* 1 peel. || *interj.* 2 **¡cáscaras!,** good heavens!
cascarilla *s.f.* cinchona bark.
cascarón *s.m.* 1 eggshell. || 2 **— de nuez,** cockleshell.
cascarrabias *s.m.* y *f.* grouse.
cascarrias *s.f.pl.* mud splashings.

casco *s.m.* 1 skull. 2 helmet. 3 crown (sombrero). 4 hull (barco). 5 bottle. 6 ZOOL. hoof. 7 fragment (vasija). || 8 **ligero de cascos,** muddle-hearded. 9 **— de población,** city.
cascote *s.m.* piece of rubble.
caseína *s.f.* casein.
cáseo, -a o **caseoso, -a** *adj.* cheesy.
caserío *s.m.* country house.
casero, -a *adj.* 1 home. 2 home-loving. 3 homemade. || *s.m.* y *f.* 4 landlord. 5 tenant. 6 (Am.) customer. 7 (Am.) supplier.
casi *adv.* almost.
casilla *s.f.* 1 cabin. 2 compartment (mueble, etc.). 3 pigeonhole. 4 square (ajedrez). || 5 **— postal,** (Am.) box. 6 **sacar a uno de sus casillas,** to get on one's nerves.
casillero *s.m.* filing cabinet.
casimir o **cachemir** o **cachemira** *s.m.* 1 cashmere (tela). 2 Kashmir (estado del norte de la India).
casino *s.m.* casino.
casiterita *s.f.* MIN. cassiterite.
caso *s.m.* 1 case. || 2 **— que/en — de que,** in the event of. 3 **dado el —,** this being so. 4 **en todo —,** at all events. 5 **hacer/venir al — una cosa** to be appropriate. 6 **hacer —,** to pay attention. 7 **hacer — omiso,** to ignore. 8 **— perdido,** hopeless case.
caspa *s.f.* dandruff.
cáspita *interj.* good heavens!
casquería *s.f.* tripe shop.
casquete *s.m.* 1 skullcap. || 2 **— esférico,** spherical segment. 3 **— glaciar,** icecap.
casquillo *s.m.* 1 ferrule. 2 sleeve.
casquivano, -a *adj.* muddle-headed.
cassette *s.f.* 1 cassette. 2 cassette player.
casta *s.f.* caste.
castaña *s.f.* chestnut.
castañar *s.m.* chestnut grove.
castañero, -a *s.m.* y *f.* chestnut vendor.
castañeta *s.f.* 1 castanet. 2 snap (dedos).
castañeteado *s.m.* clicking.
castañetear *v.t.* 1 to play the castanets. || *v.i.* 2 to chatter (dientes). 3 to crack (rodillas).
castaño, -a *adj.* 1 chestnut-coloured. || *s.m.* 2 chestnut tree. || 3 **— de Indias,** horse chestnut tree. 4 **pasar una cosa de — oscuro,** to have gone too far.
castañola *s.f.* pomfret.
castañuela *s.f.* castanet.
castellanizar *v.t.* to Castillianize.
castellano, -a *adj./s.m.* y *f.* Castillian.
casticismo *s.m.* purity.
casticista *s.m.* y *f.* purist.
castidad *s.i.* chastity.
castigador, -a *s.m.* y *f.* punisher.
castigar *v.t.* to punish.
castigo *s.m.* punishment.
Castilla *s.f.* Castille.
castillejo *s.m.* 1 walking frame. 2 scaffolding.
castillo *s.m.* 1 castle. || 2 **hacer castillos de naipes, hacer castillos en el aire,** to build up hopes in vain.
castizo, -a *adj.* 1 pedigree. 2 typical.
casto, -a *adj.* chaste.
castor *s.m.* beaver.
castoreño *adj.* beaver.
castóreo *s.m.* castor.
castra *s.f.* pruning.
castración *s.f.* castration.
castradera *s.f.* extracting blade.
castrar *v.t.* 1 to castrate. 2 to extract honey. || *v.pron.* 3 to dry up (llagas).
castrense *adj.* military.
castro *s.m.* camp.
casual *adj.* unexpected.
casualidad *s.f.* 1 chance. 2 coincidence.
casuario *s.m.* cassowary.
casuísta *s.m.* y *f.* casuist.
casuística *s.i.* casuistry.
casuístico, -a *adj.* casuistical.
casulla *s.f.* chasuble.
cata *s.f.* 1 tasting. 2 sample.
catabolismo *s.m.* BIOL. catabolism.
cataclismo *s.m.* cataclysm.
catacresis *s.f.* LIT. catachresis.
catacumbas *s.f.pl.* catacombs.
catadióptrico, -a *adj.* OPT. catadioptric
catador, -a *s.m.* y *f.* taster.
catadura *s.f.* tasting.
catafalco *s.m.* catafalque.
catalán, -a *adj./s.m.* y *f.* Catalan.
catalanismo *s.m.* Catalanism.
catalejo *s.m.* telescope.
catalepsia *s.f.* catalepsy.
cataléptico, -a *adj.* cataleptic.
catálisis *s.f.* catalysis.
catalizador, -a *s.m.* y *f.* catalyzer.
catalogación *s.f.* cataloguing.
catalogar *v.t.* to catalogue.
catálogo *s.m.* catalogue.
cataplasma *s.f.* poultice.
catapulta *s.f.* catapult.
catapultar *v.t.* to catapult.
catar *v.t.* 1 to taste. 2 to examine. 3 to extract honeycombs.
catarana *s.f.* heron.
catarata *s.f.* 1 waterfall. 2 cataract. || *pl.* 3 torrential rain.
cátaro, a *s.m.* y *f.* cathar.
catarral *adj.* catarrhal.
catarro *s.m.* cold.
catarroso, -a *adj.* 1 prone to catching colds. 2 suffering from catarrh.
catarsis *s.f.* catharsis.
catastral *adj.* cadastral.
catastro *s.m.* cadaster.
catástrofe *s.f.* catastrophe.
catastróficamente *adv.* catastrophically.
catastrófico, -a *adj.* catastrophic.
cataviento *s.m.* burgee.
catavino *s.m.* 1 wineglass. || *m.* y *f.pl.* 2 wine taster.
cate *s.m.* thump.
catear *v.t.* 1 to sample. 2 (Am.) to prospect. 3 to go through (casa). 4 to fail (examen).
catecismo *s.m.* catechism.
catecúmeno, -a *s.m.* y *f.* catechumen.
cátedra *s.f.* 1 professorship. 2 lecture room. || 3 **— de San Pedro,** Chair of Saint Peter. 4 **sentar —,** to hold forth.
catedral *s.f.* cathedral.
catedrático, -a *s.m.* y *f.* professor.
categoremético, -a *adj.* GRAM. meaningful.
categoría *s.f.* category.
categóricamente *adv.* categorically.
categórico, -a *adj.* categorical.
catenaria *s.f.* catenary.
catenular *adj.* chain-like.
catequesis *s.f.* catechesis.
catequismo *s.m.* catechism.
catequista *s.m.* y *f.* catechist.
catequizar *v.t.* to catechize.
caterva *s.f.* crowd.
catéter *s.m.* catheter.
cateto, -a *adj.* 1 boorish. || *s.m.pl.* 2 catheti.
catilinaria *s.f.* scathing attack.
catinga *s.c.* (Am.) stink.
catión *s.c.* cation.
catirrino *adj.* catarrhine.
cátodo *s.c.* 1 cathode. || 2 **— incandescente,** FIS. incandescent cathode.
catódico, -a *adj.* cathodic.
catolicismo *s.m.* catholicism.
católico, -a *adj.* catholic.
catón *s.m.* 1 censor. 2 primer.
catóptrica *s.f.* catoptrics.
catorce *adj.* fourteen.
catorceno, -a *adj.* fourteenth.
catorzavo, -a *adj.* fourteenth (parte).
catre *s.m.* 1 cot. || 2 **— de tijera,** folding bed.
caucáseo, -a o **causiano, -a,** o **caucásico, -a** *adj.* Caucasian (raza blanca).
cauce *s.m.* riverbed.
caución *s.f.* 1 caution. 2 DER. bail.
cauchero, -a *adj.* 1 rubber. || *s.m.* y *f.* 2 rubber worker.
caucho *s.m.* 1 rubber. || 2 **— sintético,** synthetic rubber.
caudal *s.m.* 1 flow (río). 2 fortune. 3 property.
caudalosamente *adv.* copiously.
caudaloso, -a *adj.* copious.
caudillaje *s.m.* leadership.
caudillo *s.m.* leader.
caula *s.f.* (Am.) trick.
cauliforme *adj.* stem-like.
causa *s.f.* cause.
causal *adj.* causal.
causalidad *s.f.* causality.
causante *adj.* 1 causing. || *s.m.* y *f.* 2 originator.
causar *v.t.* to cause.
causear *v.i.* (Am.) to eat.
causticidad *s.f.* causticity.
cáustico, -a *adj.* caustic.
cautela *s.f.* 1 cautiousness. 2 cunning.
cautelar *v.t.* to prevent.
cauteloso, -a *adj.* cautious.
cauterio *s.m.* cautery.
cauterizar *v.t.* to cauterize.
cautivador, -a *adj.* captivating.
cautivar *v.t.* to captivate.
cautiverio *s.m.* captivity.
cautividad *s.f.* captivity.
cautivo, -a *adj.* captive.
cauto, -a *adj.* cautious.
cava *s.f.* 1 wine cellar. 2 digging.
cavador *s.m.* digger.
cavadura *s.f.* digging.
cavar *v.t.* 1 to dig. || *v.i.* 2 to go deep.
cavatina *s.f.* cavatina.
cavazón *s.m.* digging.
caverna *s.f.* 1 cave. 2 cavity.

cavernícola *adj.* cave-dwelling.
cavernosidad *s.f.* cave.
cavernoso, -a *adj.* cavernous.
cavia *s.f.* 1 hole. 2 guinea pig.
caviar *s.m.* caviar.
cavidad *s.f.* cavity.
cavilación *s.f.* rumination.
cavilar *v.t.* to ruminate.
cavilosidad *s.f.* unfounded apprehension.
caviloso, -a *adj.* mistrustful.
caya *s.f.* (Am.) oca.
cayada o **cayado** *s.m.* o *f.* 1 shepherd's hook. 2 bishop's crozier.
cayo *s.m.* key.
cayuco *s.m.* dugout canoe.
caz *s.m.* millrace.
caza *s.f.* 1 hunting. 2 game. 3 AER. fighter. || 4 **— mayor,** big game. 5 **— menor,** small game.
cazadero *s.m.* hunting ground.
cazador, -a *s.m.* y *f.* 1 hunter. 2 MIL. chasseur.
cazar *v.t.* 1 to hunt. 2 to catch. 3 to get.
cazatorpedero *s.m.* MAR., MIL. torpedo destroyer.
cazcalear *v.i.* (fam.) to faff about.
cazcarria *s.f.* mud splashing.
cazo *s.c.* 1 ladle. 2 saucepan. 3 back (cuchillo).
cazolada *s.f.* saucepan contents.
cazolero *s.m.* fusspot.
cazoleta *s.f.* 1 small saucepan. 2 guard (espada). 3 bowl (pipa).
cazón *s.m.* dogfish.
cazuela *s.f.* 1 saucepan. 2 casserole.
cazumbrar *v.t.* to seal.
cazumbre *s.m.* oakum.
cazumbrón *s.m.* cooper.
cazurro, -a *adj.* crafty.
ce *s.m.* 1 c. || 2 **— por be, — por —,** meticulously.
ceba *s.f.* 1 fattening. 2 feeding (horno).
cebada *s.f.* barley.
cebadal *s.m.* barley field.
cebadera *s.f.* 1 barley container. 2 nose bag. 3 MAR. spritsail.
cebadero *s.m.* 1 barley dealer. 2 pack horse. 3 feeding place. 4 falconer. 5 furnace mouth.
cebadilla *s.f.* wall barley.
cebado, -a *adj.* (Am.) man-eating.
cebador *s.m.* gunpowder flask.
cebadura *s.f.* AGR. fattening.
cebar *v.t.* 1 to fatten. 2 to load. 3 to lure (caza).
cebo *s.m.* 1 food. 2 bait (caza). 3 charge (arma de fuego). 4 lure, monkey.
cebolla *s.f.* 1 onion. || 2 **— albarrana,** squill. 3 **— escalonia,** shallot.
cebollar *s.m.* onion patch.
cebolleta *s.f.* chives.
cebollino *s.m.* 1 spring onion. || 2 **mandar a alguien a escardar cebollinos,** to tell someone to get lost.
cebón, -a *adj.* fattened.
cebra *s.f.* 1 zebra. || 2 **paso —,** zebra crossing.
cebrado, -a *adj.* striped.
cebú *s.m.* ZOOL. zebu.
ceca *s.f.* 1 mint. || 2 **de la — a la meca,** from pillar to post.
cecal *adj.* ANAT. blind.
cecear *v.i.* to lisp.
cecina *s.f.* salted dry meat.
cecografía *s.f.* braille.
cecógrafo *s.m.* braille machine.
ceda *s.f.* 1 sow. 2 z.
cedacillo *s.m.* quacking grass.
cedazo *s.m.* 1 sieve. 2 fishing net.
cedente *s.m.* y *f.* transferer.
ceder *v.i.* 1 to give in. || *v.t.* 2 to give up.
cedilla o **zedilla** *s.f.* cedilla.
cedizo, -a *adj.* stale.
cedria *s.f.* cedar resin.
cédride *s.f.* cedar cone.
cedrino, -a *adj.* cedar.
cedro *s.m.* cedar.
cédula *s.f.* 1 document. || 2 **— ante diem,** summons. 3 **— real,** royal decree.
cefalalgia *s.f.* headache.
cefalea *s.f.* migraine.
cefalitis *s.f.* MED. encephalitis.
cefalópodo, -a *adj.* 1 cephalopod. || *s.m.pl.* 2 cephalopods.
cefalorraquídeo *adj.* cephalospinal
cefalotórax *s.m.* cephalothorax.
céfiro *s.m.* 1 breeze. 2 west wind. 3 cotton cloth.
cefo *s.m.* monkey.
cegador, -a *adj.* blinding.
cegajoso, -a o **cegatoso, -a** *adj.* bleary-eyed.
cegar *v.t.* 1 to blind. 2 to block up. || *v.i.* 3 to go blind.
cegarra o **cegato, -a** *adj.* short-sighted.
cegarrita *adj.* weak-eyed.
cegesimal *adj.* C.G.S.
cegrí *s.m.* y *f.* HIST. a member of the Zegris.
ceguedad *s.f.* blindness.
ceguera *s.f.* blindness.
ceja *s.f.* 1 eyebrow. 2 projection. 3 cloud cap. 4 MUS. bridge. || 5 **quemarse las cejas,** to burn the midnight oil. 6 **tener a uno entre — y —,** to hate someone.
cejar *v.i.* 1 to go backwards. 2 to slacken.
cejijunto, -a o **cejudo, -a** *adj.* bushy-eyebrowed.
cejilla *s.f.* MUS. bridge.
cejo *s.m.* 1 river mist. 2 string.
cejuela *s.m.* MUS. capotasto.
celada *s.f.* 1 helmet. 2 ambush. 3 trick.
celador, -a *s.m.* y *f.* 1 guard. 2 inspector.
celaje *s.m.* 1 red sky. 2 cloud mass. 3 skylight. 4 favourable omen.
celandés, -a *adj.* from New Zealand. || *s.m.* y *f.* New Zealander.
celar *v.t.* 1 to see to (obligación). 2 to watch over. 3 to keep a check on. 4 to hide.
celda *s.f.* 1 cell. || 2 **— de castigo,** solitary confinement cell.
celdilla *s.f.* 1 tiny cell. 2 niche.
celebérrimo, -a *adj.* most famous.
celebración *s.f.* celebration.
celebrado, -a *adj.* celebrated.
celebrante *s.m.* celebrant.
celebrar *v.t.* 1 to celebrate. 2 to say mass.
célebre *adj.* 1 famous. 2 funny.
celebridad *s.f.* celebrity.
celemín *s.m.* half a peck (medida).
celeque *adj.* (Am.) tender (fruta).
celeridad *s.f.* speed.
celescopio *s.m.* FIS. coelioscope.
celeste o **celestial** *adj.* celestial.
celestina *s.f.* madam.
celíaco, -a *adj.* coeliac.
celibato *s.m.* 1 celibacy. 2 bachelor.
célibe *adj.* unmarried.
celinda *s.f.* syringe.
celo *s.m.* 1 zeal. 2 fervour. 3 ZOOL. heat. || *pl.* 4 jealousy.
celofán *s.m.* cellophane.
celosamente *adv.* jealously.
celosía *s.f.* blind (tipo de persiana).
celoso, -a *adj.* jealous.
celotipia *s.f.* jealousy.
celsitud *s.f.* 1 grandeur. 2 highness.
celta *adj.* Celtic.
celtibérico, -a o **celtíbero, -a** *adj.* y *s.m.* y *f.* Celtiberian.
celtismo *s.m.* Celtism.
célula *s.f.* 1 cell. || 2 **— fotoeléctrica,** photoelectric cell.
celular *adj.* cellular.
celulitis *s.f.* cellulitis.
celuloide *s.m.* celluloid.
celulosa *s.f.* cellulose.
cellisca *s.f.* sleet storm.
cellisquear *v.i.* to sleet.
cello *s.m.* 1 hoop (cuba). 2 sellotape.
cementación *s.f.* cementation.
cementar *v.t.* to cement.
cementerio *s.m.* cemetery.
cemento *s.m.* 1 cement. || 2 **— armado,** reinforced concrete. 3 **— Portland,** Portland cement.
cementoso, -a *adj.* cement-like.
cena *s.f.* supper.
cenáculo *s.m.* 1 Cenacle. 2 literary circle.
cenadero, -a *s.m.* y *f.* supper room.
cenador *s.m.* arbour.
cenaduría *s.f.* (Am.) cheap restaurant.
cenagal *s.m.* 1 bog. 2 messy business.
cenar *v.i.* 1 to have supper. || *v.t.* 2 to have for supper.
cenceño, -a *adj.* skinny.
cencerrada *s.f.* tin-pan serenade.
cencerrar *v.i.* to jingle.
cencerreo *s.m.* jingling.
cencerro *s.m.* 1 cowbell. || 2 **estar como un —,** to have bats in the belfrey.
cendal *s.m.* 1 sendal. 2 REL. humeral veil. 3 wattle (pluma).
cenefa *s.c.* 1 edging (coser). 2 chasuble stripe. 3 ARCH. ornamental border.
cenestesia *s.f.* coenaesthesis.
cenicero *s.m.* ashtray.
cenicienta *s.f.* Cinderella.
ceniciento, -a *adj.* ash-coloured.
cenit *s.m.* zenith.
cenital *adj.* zenithal.
ceniza *s.f.* 1 ash. || *pl.* 2 ashes. || 3 REL. **tomar la —,** to receive ash.

cenizo, -a *adj.* 1 ash-coloured. || *s.c.* 2 BOT. goosefoot. 3 jinx. 4 oidium (combustión).
cenobio *s.m.* monastery.
cenobita *s.m.* cenobite.
cenotafio *s.m.* cenotaph.
censar *v.t.* (Am.) to take a census of.
censo *s.m.* 1 census. 2 rent charge. || 3 **— electoral,** electoral roll.
censor *s.m.* censor.
censorio, -a *adj.* censorial.
censual *adj.* 1 census. 2 tax.
censualista *s.m.* y *f.* renter.
censura *s.f.* 1 censorship. 2 criticism.
censurable *adj.* censurable.
censurar *v.t.* 1 POL. to censor. 2 to censure.
centauro *s.m.* centaur.
centavo, -a *adj.* 1 hundredth. || *s.m.* 2 cent.
centella *s.c.* 1 flash. 2 spark.
centellar *v.i.* to sparkle.
centellear *v.i.* to sparkle.
centelleo *s.m.* sparkling.
centena o **centenar** *s.m.* o *f.* hundred.
centenario, -a *adj.* 1 centennial. || *s.m.* y *f.* 2 centenary. 3 centenarian (persona).
centenaza *adj.* rye straw.
centeno *s.m.* 1 rye. 2 hundred. || *adj.* 3 hundredth.
centesimal *adj.* centesimal.
centésimo, -a *adj.* 1 hundredth. 2 hundredth (parte).
centímetro *s.m.* 1 centimetre. || 2 **— cuadrado,** square centimetre. 3 **— cúbico,** cubic centimetre.
centinela *s.m.* o *f.* sentinel.
centollo, -a *s.m.* o *f.* crab.
centón *s.m.* 1 patchwork quilt. 2 cento.
central *adj.* 1 central. || *s.c.* 2 headquarters. 3 power station. || 4 **gobierno —,** central government.
centralismo *s.m.* centralism.
centralista *adj.* centralist.
centralización *s.f.* centralization.
centralizar *v.t.* to centralize.
centrar *v.t.* to centre.
céntrico, -a *adj.* central.
centrifugador, -a *adj.* centrifugal.
centrifugar *s.c.* to centrifuge.
centrífugo *s.c.* centrifugal.
centrípeto *adj.* centripetal.
centrismo *s.i.* centralism.
centro *s.c.* 1 centre. 2 (Am.) waistcoat. || 3 **— de gravedad,** centre of gravity.
centroamericano, -a *adj.* 1 Central American. 2 *s.m.* y *f.* Central American.
centrocampista *s.m.* y *f.* midfielder.
centrosoma *s.m.* centrosome.
centuplicar *v.t.* to centuple.
céntuplo, -a *adj.* hundredfold.
centuria *s.f.* century.
centurión *s.m.* centurion.
ceñido, -a *adj.* tight.
ceñidor *s.m.* sash.
ceñir *v.t.* 1 to wrap around. 2 to shorten.
ceño *s.m.* 1 AGR. enclosure. 2 frown. 3 ominous appearance (cielo, mar).
cepa *s.f.* stock.
cepeda o **cepera** *s.f.* heather patch.
cepejón *s.m.* root.
cepellón *s.m.* ball.
cepillar *v.t.* to brush.
cepillo *s.m.* 1 brush. 2 plane (carpintería). 3 collection box (iglesia). || 4 **— bocel,** fluting plane.
cepo *s.m.* 1 lure. 2 collection box. 3 stocks (reos). 4 branch. 5 block (yunque).
ceporro *s.m.* 1 old stock. 2 uncouth individual. || 3 **dormir como un —,** to sleep like a log.
cequí *s.m.* zequin.
cera *s.f.* 1 wax. || 2 **— aleda,** bee glue. 3 **— de los oídos,** earwax.
cerámica *s.f.* ceramics.
cerámico, -a *adj.* ceramic.
ceramista *s.m.* y *f.* ceramist.
cerbatana *s.f.* 1 blowpipe. 2 ear trumpet.
cerbero *s.m.* watchman.
cerca *s.f.* 1 fence. || *adv.* 2 near.
cercado, -a *adj.* fenced-in.
cercamiento *s.f.* fencing-in.
cercar *v.t.* 1 to enclose. 2 to besiege.
cercén *adv.* **cortar a —,** to cut to the root.
cercenadura *s.f.* 1 clipping. 2 reducing.
cercenamiento *s.m.* 1 clipping. 2 reduction.
cercenar *v.t.* 1 to clip. 2 to reduce.
cerceta *s.f.* teal.
cerciorar *v.t.* to ratify.
cercha *s.f.* template.
cerdear *v.i.* 1 to falter (animales). 2 to shirk.
cerda *s.c.* 1 horsehair. 2 bristle. 3 corn.
cerdo, -a *s.m.* y *f.* 1 pig. || 2 **— marino,** porpoise.
cerdoso, -a *adj.* bristly.
cereal *s.m.* cereal.
cerealista *adv.* 1 cereal. || *s.m.* y *f.* 2 grain producer.
cerebelo *s.m.* cerebellum.
cerebral *adj.* cerebral.
cerebro *s.m.* 1 brain. 2 brains. || 3 **— electrónico,** computer.
cerebroespinal *adj.* cerebrospinal.
ceremonia *s.f.* ceremony.
ceremonial *adj.* ceremonial.
ceremoniosamente *adv.* ceremoniously.
ceremonioso, -a *adj.* ceremonious.
céreo, -a *adj.* waxen.
cerero *s.m.* wax chandler.
ceresina *adj.* gum.
cerevisina *s.f.* brewer's yeast.
cereza *s.f.* cherry.
cerezal *s.m.* cherry orchard.
cerezo *s.m.* cherry tree.
cerilla *s.f.* 1 thin candle. 2 match. 3 earwax.
cerillero, -a *s.m.* y *f.* 1 matchbox. 2 matchbox seller.
cerillo *s.m.* (Am.) match.
cerina *s.f.* cork wax.
cerio *s.m.* cerium.
cermeño *s.m.* pear tree.
cerne *s.m.* heart (árbol).
cernedero *s.m.* sifting room.
cernedor *s.m.* sieve.
cerneja *s.f.* fetlock.
cerner *v.t.* 1 to sieve. 2 to observe. || *v.i.* 3 to drizzle. 4 to pollinate (flores). || *v.pron.* 5 to hover (ave). 6 to threaten. 7 to waddle.
cernícalo *s.m.* kestrel.
cernidillo *s.m.* 1 drizzle. 2 waddling (andar).
cernido *s.m.* sifting.
cernidura *s.f.* sifting.
cero *s.m.* 1 zero. || 2 **— absoluto,** absolute zero. 3 **ser un — a la izquierda,** to be a nobody.
cerollo, -a *adj.* greenish (mies).
cerón *s.m.* wax scrapings.
ceroplástica *s.f.* wax modelling.
cerote *s.m.* shoemaker's wax.
cerradero *adj.* 1 shuttable. || *s.m.* 2 lock. 3 purse strings.
cerrado, -a *adj.* 1 closed. 2 incomprehensible. 3 stupid. 4 quiet. 5 thick. 6 cloudy (cielo). || *s.m.* 7 fence. 8 skin (animal).
cerradura *s.f.* lock.
cerraja *s.f.* 1 lock. 2 sow-thistle.
cerrajón *s.m.* big hill.
cerramiento *s.m.* 1 closing. 2 enclosure. 3 partition.
cerrazón *s.m.* darkening (cielo).
cerrejón *s.m.* hillock.
cerrero, -a *adj.* 1 untamed. 2 (Am.) bitter.
cerril *adj.* 1 rough, hilly, uneven. 2 untamed (animal).
cerrillear *v.t.* to mill (monedas).
cerro *s.m.* 1 hill. 2 back (animal). || 3 **irse/salir por los cerros de Ubeda,** to go off at tangents.
cerrojazo *s.m.* abrupt end.
cerrojo *s.m.* bolt.
certamen *s.m.* 1 competition. 2 literary meeting.
certero, -a *adj.* 1 right. 2 well-informed. 3 accurate.
certeza *s.f.* certainty.
certidumbre *s.f.* certainty.
certificación *s.f.* 1 certification. 2 registration (correos).
certificado, -a *adj.* 1 registered. || *s.m.* 2 certificate. 3 registered letter.
certificar *v.t.* 1 to certify. 2 to register.
cerúleo, -a *adj.* sky blue.
cerumen *s.m.* earwax.
cerusa o **cerusita** *s.f.* ceruse.
cerval *adj.* 1 deer. || 2 **tener un miedo —,** to be petrified.
cervantesco, -a *adj.* of Cervantes.
cervantino, -a *adj.* Cervantine.
cervantismo *s.i.* Cervantes studies.
cervantista *s.m.* y *f.* Cervantes specialist.
cervato *s.m.* fawn.
cervecería *s.f.* 1 brewery. 2 bar.
cervecero, -a *s.m.* y *f.* brewer.
cerveza *s.f.* beer.
cervical *adj.* cervical.
cérvido, -a *adj.* cervine.
cervigudo, -a *adj.* 1 thick-necked. 2 pigheaded.
cerviguillo *s.m.* thick nape.
cerviz *s.f.* 1 nape. || 2 **bajar, doblar la —,** to cowtow. 3 **ser duro de —,** to be a rebel.

cervuno, -a *adj.* 1 deer-like. 2 deer-coloured.
cesación *s.f.* cessation.
cesamiento *s.m.* cessation.
cesante *adj.* out of a job.
cesantía *s.f.* 1 dismissal. 2 dismissal compensation.
cesar *v.i.* 1 to cease. 2 to retire.
césar *s.m.* Caesar.
cesáreo, -a *adj.* 1 imperial. 2 Caesarean.
cesarismo *s.m.* Caesarism.
cesarista *s.m.* y *f.* Caesarist.
cese *s.m.* cessation.
cesio *s.m.* cesium.
cesión *s.f.* cession.
cesionario *s.m.* cessionary.
césped *s.m.* lawn.
cesta *s.f.* basket.
cestada *s.f.* basketful.
cestería *s.f.* basketmaker's.
cestero, -a *s.m.* y *f.* basketmaker.
cestodos *s.m.pl.* ZOOL. cestoids.
cestón *s.m.* gabion.
cesura *s.f.* caesura.
cetáceo, -a *adj.* 1 ZOOL. cetacean. || *s.m.* 2 cetacea.
cetaria o **cetarea** *s.f.* fish hatchery.
cetona *s.f.* acetone.
cetrería *s.f.* falconry.
cetrino, -a *adj.* 1 olive-coloured. 2 melancholic. 3 stern.
cetro *s.m.* 1 sceptre. 2 kingdom.
cía *s.f.* hip bone.
ciaboga *s.f.* putting about (embarcación).
cianógeno *s.m.* QUIM. cyanogen.
cianosis *s.f.* MED. cyanosis.
cianuro *s.m.* cyanide.
ciar *v.i.* 1 to back water. 2 to go backwards.
ciática *s.f.* sciatica.
ciático, -a *adj.* sciatic.
cibera *s.f.* fodder.
cibernética *s.f.* cybernetics.
cicatear *v.i.* to be a skinflint.
cicatería *s.f.* meanness.
cicatero, -a *adj.* mean.
cicatriz *s.f.* scar.
cicatrización *s.f.* healing up.
cicatrizar *v.t.* 1 to heal. || *v.pron.* 2 to heal up.
cícero *s.m.* pica.
cicerone *s.m.* y *f.* guide.
ciceroniano, -a *adj.* ciceronian.
ciclamen *s.m.* cyclamen.
ciclamor *s.m.* Judas tree.
cíclico, -a *adj.* cyclic.
ciclista *s.m.* y *f.* cyclist.
ciclo *s.m.* cycle.
cicloide *s.f.* cycloid.
ciclomotor *s.m.* moped.
ciclón *s.m.* cyclone.
ciclónico, -a *adj.* cyclonic.
cíclope o **ciclope** *s.m.* Cyclops.
ciclópeo, -a *adj.* Cyclopean.
cifosis *s.f.* kyphosis.
cifra *s.f.* 1 figure. 2 cipher (clave). 3 abbreviation. 4 monogram.
cifrado, -a *adj.* coded.
cifrar *v.t.* 1 to write in code. 2 to concentrate (en). 3 to summarize.
cigala *s.f.* Norway lobster.
cigarra *s.f.* cicada.
cigarrería *s.f.* (Am.) tobacconist's.
cigarrero, -a *s.m.* y *f.* 1 cigar maker. 2 cigar dealer.
cigarrillo *s.m.* cigarette.
cigarro *s.m.* 1 cigar. 2 cigarette. || 3 **— puro,** cigar.
cigoñal *s.m.* scoop.
cigoñino *s.m.* young stork.
cigoñuela *s.f.* stilt.
cigüeña *s.f.* stork.
cigüeñal *s.m.* crankshaft.
cilantro *s.m.* coriander.
ciliado, -a *adj.* ciliate.
ciliar *adj.* ciliary.
cilicio *s.m.* hair shirt.
cilindrada *s.f.* cylinder capacity.
cilindrar *v.t.* to roll flat.
cilíndrico, -a *adj.* cylindrical.
cilindro *s.m.* cylinder.
cilio *s.m.* ANAT. cilium.
cima *s.f.* 1 summit. 2 culmination. 3 BOT. cyme. || 4 **dar —,** to conclude.
cimacio *s.m.* cymatium.
cimarrón, -a *adj.* (Am.) 1 wild. 2 bitter (mate).
cimarronada *s.f.* (Am.) wild herd.
cimarronear *v.i.* 1 to run away (esclavo). 2 to drink bitter maté.
címbalo *s.m.* cymbal.
cimbel *s.m.* 1 decoy. 2 (fam.) squealer.
cimborrio *s.m.* 1 dome base. 2 dome.
cimbra *s.f.* inner arch curvature.
cimbrado, -a *adj.* curved.
cimbrar *v.t.* 1 to swish (vara). 2 to bend. 3 to hit (con vara, etc.).
cimbrear *v.pron.* to sway.
cimbreño, -a *adj.* flexible.
cimbreo *s.m.* swaying.
cimentación *s.f.* 1 foundation. 2 laying of foundations.
cimentar *v.t.* 1 to lay the foundations of. 2 to found.
cimero, -a *adj.* topmost.
cimiento *s.m.* 1 foundation. 2 origin.
cimitarra *s.f.* scimitar.
cinabrio *s.m.* cinnabar.
cinamomo *s.m.* bead tree.
cinc o **zinc** *s.m.* zinc.
cincel *s.m.* chisel.
cincelado *s.m.* chiselling.
cinceladura *s.f.* chiselling.
cincelar *v.t.* to chisel.
cinco *adj.* 1 five. 2 fifth (fecha).
cincuenta *adj.* 1 fifty. 2 fiftieth.
cincuentavo, -a *adj.* fiftieth.
cincuentena *s.f.* group of fifty.
cincuentenario *s.m.* semicentennial.
cincuenteno, -a *adj.* fiftieth.
cincuentón, -a *adj.* fifty-year old.
cincha *s.f.* strap.
cinchar *v.t.* 1 to girth. 2 to hoop. || *v.i.* (Am.) 3 to work hard.
cinchera *s.f.* girth part (caballería).
cincho *s.m.* 1 sash. 2 hoop (tonel). 3 ARQ. transverse rib.
cine *s.m.* cinema.
cineasta *s.m.* y *f.* 1 film producer. 2 actor.
cinegética *s.f.* hunting.
cinegético, -a *adj.* hunting.
cinemascope o **cinemascopio** *s.m.* cinemascope.
cinemática *s.f.* kinematics.
cinematografía *s.f.* film-making.
cinematográfico, -a *adj.* cinematographic.
cinematografiar *v.t.* to film.
cinematógrafo *s.m.* 1 cine projector. 2 cinema.
cinerama *s.m.* cinerama.
cinerario, -a *adj.* cinerary.
cinética *s.f.* kinetics.
cinético, -a *adj.* kinetic.
cíngaro, -a *adj.* gypsy.
cinglar *v.t.* MET. to puddle. 2 MAR. to scull.
cíngulo *s.m.* cingulum.
cínico, -a *adj.* 1 cynical. || *s.c.* 2 cynic.
cínife *s.m.* mosquito.
cinismo *s.m.* cynicism.
cinquillo *s.m.* 1 card game.
cinta *s.f.* 1 strip (material). 2 ARQ. fillet. 3 MUS. tape. 4 film. 5 ribbon (pelo).
cintarazo *s.m.* sword blow.
cintero, -a *s.m.* y *f.* 1 ribbon maker. 2 ribbon dealer. 3 belt (prenda).
cinto *s.m.* 1 sash. 2 waist (persona).
cintra *s.f.* curvature.
cintura *s.f.* 1 waist. 2 waistband (prenda). || 3 **meter a uno en —,** to keep someone under the thumb, to make someone see reason.
cinturón *s.m.* belt.
ciperáceo, -a *adj.* cyperaceous.
cipo *s.m.* 1 memorial stone. 2 signpost. 3 milestone.
cipote *s.m.* 1 club. 2 (desp.) cretin. 3 (vulg.) prick. 4 milestone. 5 (Am.) lad.
ciprés *s.m.* cypress.
cipresino, -a *adj.* cupressineous.
circense *adj.* circus.
circo *s.m.* circus.
circonio *s.m.* zirconium.
circuición *s.f.* encircling.
circuir *v.t.* to encircle.
circuito *s.m.* 1 circuit. 2 lap (carrera deportiva). || 3 **corto —,** short circuit.
circulación *s.f.* 1 circulation. 2 traffic.
circular *adj.* 1 circular. || *s.c.* 2 circular. || *v.i.* 3 to circulate. 4 to drive (en un vehículo). 5 to run (transporte).
circulatorio, -a *adj.* circulatory.
círculo *s.m.* 1 circle. || 2 **— vicioso,** vicious circle. 3 **— polar,** polar circle.
circuncentro *s.m.* GEOM. circumcentre.
circuncidar *v.t.* 1 to circumcise. 2 to reduce.
circuncisión *s.f.* circumcision.
circunciso, -a *adj.* circumcised.
circundante *adj.* surrounding.
circundar *v.t.* to surround.
circunferencia *s.f.* GEOM. circumference.
circunflejo, -a *adj.* circumflex.
circunlocución *s.f.* circumlocution.
circunloquio *s.m.* circumlocution.
circunnavegación *s.f.* circumnavegation.
circunnavegar *v.t.* to circumnavegate.
circunscribir *v.t.* 1 to circumscribe. 2 to confine.

circunscripción *s.f.* 1 circumscription. 2 division (territorio).
circunscripto, -a *adj.* circumscript.
circunspección *s.f.* circumspection.
circunspecto, -a *adj.* circumspect.
circunstancia *s.f.* 1 circumstance. 2 requisite. || 3 **circunstancias agravantes,** aggravating circumstances. 4 **circunstancias atenuantes,** attenuating circumstances. 5 **circunstancias eximentes,** exonerating circumstances.
circunstancial *adj.* circumstantial.
circunstante *adj.* 1 surrounding. || *s.m.* y *pl.* 2 those present.
circunvalación *s.f.* **carretera de –,** ring road.
circunvalar *v.t.* to go round.
circunvecino, -a *adj.* neighbouring.
circunvolución *s.f.* circumvolution.
cireneo, -a o **cirineo, -a** *adj.* Cyrenaic. || *s.m.* y *f.* someone who helps someone else.
cirial *s.m.* processional candlestick.
cirio *s.m.* 1 candle. || 2 **– pascual,** Easter candle.
cirrípedo o **cirrópodo** *adj.* cirriped.
cirro *s.m.* 1 cirrus. 2 MED. scirrhus.
cirrosis *s.f.* cirrhosis.
cirroso, -a *adj.* cirrus-like.
cirrótico, -a *adj.* cirrhotic.
ciruela *s.f.* plum.
ciruelo *s.m.* 1 plum tree. || *adj.* 2 (desp.) blockhead.
cirugía *s.f.* surgery.
cirujano *s.m.* y *f.* surgeon.
ciscar *v.t.* to dirty.
cisco *s.m.* 1 slack (mineral). 2 commotion.
ciscón, -a *adj.* (Am.) touchy.
cisión *s.f.* incision.
cisma *s.m.* o *f.* 1 split. 2 discord.
cismático, -a *adj.* schismatic.
cisne *s.m.* 1 swan. 2 (Am.) powder puff. || *adj.* 3 brownish (caballo).
císter o **cistel** *s.m.* Cistercian order.
cisterciense *adj./s.m.* y *f.* Cistercian.
cisterna *s.f.* 1 cistern. 2 tank (vehículo).
cisticerco *s.m.* tapeworm larva.
cistitis *s.f.* cystitis.
cisura *s.f.* fissure.
cita *s.f.* 1 appointment. 2 date (chico con chica, etc.). 3 LIT. quotation.
citación *s.f.* summons.
citar *v.t.* 1 to make an appointment with. 2 LIT. to quote. 3 to provoke (toro). 4 DER. to summon.
cítara *s.f.* zither.
citarista *s.m.* y *f.* zither player.
citerior *adj.* near.
citoplasma *s.m.* BIOL. cytoplasm.
citoplasmático, -a *adj.* BIOL. cytoplasmatic.
citrato *s.m.* QUIM. citrate.
cítrico, -a *adj.* citric.
citrón *s.m.* lemon.
ciudad *s.f.* 1 town. 2 city.
ciudadanía *s.f.* citizenship.
ciudadano, -a *s.m.* y *f.* citizen.
ciudadela *s.f.* citadel.
cívico, -a *adj.* 1 civic. 2 civil (modales).
civil *adj.* 1 civil. || *s.m.* 2 civil guard. || 3 **derecho –,** DER. civil law.
civilidad *s.f.* civility.
civilista *s.m.* y *f.* civil law teacher.
civilización *s.f.* civilization.
civilizador, -a *adj.* civilizing.
civilizar *v.t.* to civilize.
civismo *s.m.* 1 national pride. 2 public spirit.
cizalla *s.f.* 1 wire cutters. 2 metal cuttings.
cizaña *s.f.* 1 BOT. darnel. 2 (desp.) fly in the ointment. 3 discord. || **meter –,** to sow dissent, to sow dissent among people.
cizañar *v.t.* to sow discord among.
cizañero, -a *s.m.* y *f.* troublemaker.
clamar *v.i.* to cry out.
clamor *s.m.* 1 clamour. 2 tolling (campana).
clan *s.m.* 1 clan. 2 sect.
clandestino, -a *adj.* 1 clandestine. 2 underground (ley).
claque *s.f.* claque.
clara *s.f.* 1 albumen (huevo). 2 bald patch (cabeza). 3 sunny interval (tiempo). || 4 **a las claras,** openly.
claraboya *s.f.* skylight.
clarear *v.i.* 1 to dawn. 2 to clear (nubes). || *v.t.* 3 to clarify. || *v.pron.* 4 to become clear. 5 (fam.) to show one's hand.
clarecer *v.i.* to dawn.
clareo *s.m.* clearing (de bosque).
clarete *adj.* rosé (vino).
claridad *s.f.* 1 clarity. 2 light. 3 frankness (palabras).
clarificar *v.t.* 1 to light up. 2 (fig.) to clarify.
clarín *s.m.* 1 bugle. 2 bugle prayer (persona).
clarinete *s.m.* 1 clarinet. 2 clarinetist (persona).
clarión *s.m.* chalk.
clarisa *adj.* y *s.f.* REL. Clare.
clarividencia *s.f.* 1 clear-sightedness. 2 clairvoyance (medium).
claro, -a *adj.* 1 bright. 2 clear (idea). 3 clean (sitio). 4 light (color). 5 famous (persona). 6 outspoken (franqueza). 7 intelligent. || *s.m.* 8 interval. 9 window.
claroscuro *s.m.* chiaroscuro.
clase *s.f.* 1 class. 2 classroom (habitación). 3 subject. || 4 **clases pasivas,** pensioners. 5 **clases sociales,** social classes.
clásico, -a *adj.* 1 classical. 2 classic (escritor).
clasificar *v.t.* to classify.
clasismo *s.m.* classism.
claudia *s.f.* greengage.
claudicar *v.i.* 1 to limp. 2 (fig.) to go astray. 3 to give in (de una responsabilidad, etc.).
claustro *s.m.* 1 ARQ. cloister. 2 academic staff (universidad).
claustrofobia *s.f.* claustrophobia.
cláusula *s.f.* clause (documento, oración).
clausura *s.f.* 1 REL. confinement. 2 confined part (convento). 3 closing ceremony (acto).
clausurar *v.t.* 1 to close. 2 to end.
clavado, -a *adj.* 1 exact. 2 most appropriate. 3 studded (clavos). || *s.m.pl.* 4 (Am.) somersault (de un trampolín).
clavar *v.t.* 1 to stick in. 2 (fam.) to pull a fast one on. 3 to nail (clavo). 4 to fix (mirada).
clave *s.f.* 1 key. 2 ARQ. keystone. 3 MUS. clef. || *s.m.* 4 clavichord (instrumento musical).
clavecín *s.m.* clavichord.
clavel *s.m.* 1 carnation. || 2 **– reventón,** large carnation.
clavetear *v.t.* 1 to stud. 2 to finish (asunto).
clavicémbalo *s.m.* harpsichord.
clavicordio *s.m.* clavichord.
clavícula *s.f.* collar bone.
clavija *s.f.* 1 peg. 2 ELEC. plug.
clavijero *s.m.* MUS. pegbox.
claviórgano *s.m.* harmonium.
clavo *s.m.* 1 nail. 2 MED. corn (pie). 3 BOT. clove. 4 MED. pain || 5 **agarrarse a un – ardiendo,** to clutch at straws. 6 **como un –,** spot on. 7 **dar en el –,** to hit the nail on the head.
claxon *s.m.* hooter, horn.
clemencia *s.f.* 1 clemency. 2 DER. reduction of sentence.
clemole *s.m.* (Am.) hot tomato sauce.
clepsidra *s.f.* water clock.
cleptomanía *s.f.* cleptomania.
clerecía *s.f.* clergy.
clergyman *s.m.* REL. dark suit (de cura).
clericalismo *s.m.* clericalism.
clérigo *s.m.* 1 priest. 2 scholar (Edad Media).
clero *s.m.* 1 clergy. || 2 **– regular,** regular priest. 3 **– secular,** secular priest.
cliché *s.m.* 1 negative (foto). 2 stencil (imprenta). 3 LIT. cliché. 4 stereotype.
cliente *s.m.* y *f.* 1 customer. 2 DER. client.
clientela *s.f.* clientèle.
clima *s.m.* climate.
climatérico, -a *adj.* climacteric.
climaterio *s.m.* sexual deterioration.
climatizar *v.t.* to acclimatize.
climatología *s.f.* climatology.
clímax *s.m.* climax.
clínica *s.f.* 1 clinic. 2 clinical training.
clínico, -a *adj.* clinical.
clinómetro *s.m.* TEC. clinometer.
clip *s.m.* 1 paper clip. 2 hair grip (pelo).
clíper *s.m.* MAR. clipper.
clisar *v.t.* to stereotype.
clisé *s.m.* 1 negative (foto). 2 stencil (imprenta). 3 LIT. cliché. 4 stereotype.
clitelo *s.m.* clitellum.
clítoris *s.m.* clitoris.
cloaca *s.f.* 1 sewer. 2 ZOOL. cloaca.
cloque *s.m.* hook.
cloquear *v.i.* to cluck.
cloqueo *s.m.* clucking.
clorato *s.m.* QUIM. chlorate.
clorhídrico, -a *adj.* QUIM. hydrochloric.
cloro *s.m.* QUIM. chlorine.
clorofíceas *s.f.pl.* seaweed.
clorofila *s.f.* chlorophyll.
cloroformo *s.m.* QUIM. chloroform.
clorosis *s.f.* chlorosis.

cloruro *s.c.* QUIM. 1 chloride. || 2 **— de sodio,** common salt.
clown *s.m.* clown.
club *s.m.* club.
clueco, -a *adj.* 1 broody (gallina). 2 (fam.) decrepit (referido a personas mayores).
coacción *s.f.* coercion.
coactivo, -a *adj.* coercive.
coadjutor, -a *s.m.* y *f.* assistant.
coadyuvar *v.t.* to assist.
coagular *v.t.* to coagulate.
coalición *s.f.* coalition.
coartada *s.f.* alibi.
coartar *v.t.* to restrict.
coautor, -a *s.m.* y *f.* co-author.
coaxial *adj.* TEC. coaxial.
coba *s.f.* 1 adulation. 2 (fam.) joke. || 3 **dar —,** to suck up to.
cobalto *s.m.* MIN. cobalt.
cobardía *s.f.* cowardice.
cobaya o **cobayo** *s.m.* guinea pig.
cobertizo *s.m.* shed.
cobertor *s.m.* 1 quilt. 2 blanket.
cobertura *s.f.* 1 covering. 2 COM. guarantee.
cobija *s.f.* 1 over tile (tejado). 2 covert (pluma). 3 covering. || *s.f.pl.* 4 (Am.) bedclothes.
cobijar *v.t.* 1 to cover. 2 to shelter.
cobra *s.f.* 1 cobra. 2 retrieving (caza). 3 team of mares (trilla).
cobrar *v.t.* 1 to gain (dinero). 2 to take. 3 to recover. 4 to retrieve (caza). 5 to pull in (cuerda). 6 to receive (golpe). || *v.pron.* 7 to earn (sueldo).
cobre *s.m.* 1 copper. 2 copper pans (cocina). 3 MUS. brass section. || **batir el —,** to work flat out.
cobrizo, -a *adj.* 1 copper-coloured. 2 copper.
coca *s.c.* BOT. coca.
cocacho *s.m.* (Am.) tap on the head.
cocaína *s.f.* cocaine.
cóccix o **coxis** *s.m.* coccis.
cocear *v.t.* to kick.
cocer *v.t.* 1 to cook. || *v.i.* 2 to boil. 3 to ferment. || *v.pron.* 4 to suffer a lot of pain.
cocido *s.m.* stew.
cociente *s.m.* MAT. quotient.
cocimiento *s.m.* cooking.
cocina *s.f.* 1 kitchen. 2 cooking (el arte).
cocinar *v.t.* 1 to cook. || *v.i.* 2 (fam.)
cocinilla *s.f.* 1 kitchenette. 2 small cooker (aparato).
coco *s.m.* 1 coconut. 2 grub (insecto). 3 coccus (bacteria). 4 (fam.) bogeyman. 5 grimace (expresión).
cocodrilo *s.m.* crocodile.
cocoliche *s.m.* (Am.) Italian immigrant slang.
cocoso, -a *adj.* maggoty.
cocotal *s.m.* coconut plantation.
cocotero *s.m.* coconut palm.
cóctel o **cocktail** *s.m.* 1 cocktail. 2 cocktail party (reunión). || 3 **— molotov,** Molotov cocktail.
cochambre *s.m.* y *f.* a piece of filth.
coche *s.m.* 1 car. || 2 **— de punto,** hired car. 3 coach.
cochera *s.f.* coach depot.
cochero, -a *s.m.* y *f.* coach driver.
cochinilla *s.f.* 1 water slater (crustáceo de agua). 2 wood louse (de madera). 3 cochineal (colorante).
cochino, -a *s.m.* y *f.* 1 pig. 2 (fig. y fam.) dirty person. || *adj.* 3 dirty, filthy, disgusting.
cochiquera *s.f.* pigsty.
cochitril *s.m.* 1 pigsty. 2 (fig.) hovel.
cochura *s.f.* 1 cooking. 2 prepared dough.
coda *s.f.* 1 MUS. coda. 2 joining block (carpintería).
codear *v.i.* 1 to elbow. 2 (Am.) to keep on asking. || *v.pron.* 3 to hobnob.
codeína *s.f.* QUIM. codeine.
codera *s.f.* 1 elbow patch. 2 MAR. rope.
codeso *s.m.* BOT. laburnum.
códice *s.m.* codex.
codicia *s.f.* greed.
codicilo *s.m.* codicil.
codificar *v.t.* to codify.
código *s.m.* 1 code. 2 rules. || 3 **— de señales,** signal code.
codillo *s.m.* 1 ZOOL. elbow. 2 BOT. stump. 3 brace (construcción). 4 stirrup (montar).
codo *s.m.* 1 elbow. 2 TEC. bend. || 3 **alzar, empinar el —,** to drink a lot. 4 **hablar por los codos,** to talk the hind legs off a donkey.
codorniz *s.f.* quail.
coeducación *s.f.* coeducation.
coeficiente *s.m.* 1 coefficient. || 2 **— de inteligencia,** IQ.
coercer *v.t.* to coerce.
coetáneo, -a *adj.* contemporary.
coevo, -a *adj.* coeval.
coexistencia *s.f.* 1 coexistence. || 2 **— pacífica,** peaceful coexistence.
cofia *s.f.* 1 cap. 2 hairnet (pelo). 3 coif (armadura).
cofradía *s.f.* brotherhood.
coger *v.t.* 1 to take hold of. 2 to catch (pelota). 3 to get. 4 to pick up (algo que se ha caído). 4 to catch out (por sorpresa). 5 to hold (capacidad). 6 to cover (extensión). 7 to acquire. || *v.i.* 8 to fit. || 9 **no haber por donde — algo/alguien,** to be untouchable.
cogestión *s.f.* co-partnership.
cogida *s.f.* 1 goring (tauromaquia). 2 AGR. harvest.
cogitabundo, -a *adj.* deep in thought.
cognación *s.f.* 1 blood relationship. 2 relationship.
cognición *s.f.* cognition.
cogollo *s.m.* 1 BOT. shoot. 2 (Am.) sugar cane. 3 (fig.) the cream. 4 heart (lechuga).
cogorza *s.f.* (fam.) booziness, binge.
cogote *s.m.* nape.
cogulla *s.f.* cowl.
cohabitar *v.i.* 1 to live together. 2 to have sex.
cohechar *v.t.* 1 to bribe. 2 AGR. to plough up.
coheredar *v.t.* to inherit jointly.
coherencia *s.f.* 1 coherence. 2 cohesion.
cohesión *s.f.* cohesion.
cohete *s.m.* rocket.
cohibir *v.t.* 1 to inhibit. 2 to restrain.
cohombro *s.m.* 1 cucumber. || 2 **— de mar,** sea cucumber.
cohonestar *v.t.* to give an honest appearance to.
cohorte *s.f.* cohort.
coima *s.c.* 1 concubine. 2 (fam.) rake-off. 3 (Am.) bribe.
coime o **cominero** *s.m.* gambling organizer.
coincidir *v.i.* 1 to agree. 2 to coincide.
coito *s.m.* coitus.
cojear *v.i.* 1 to limp. 2 to wobble (mueble). 3 (fig.) to go astray.
cojín *s.m.* cushion.
cojinete *s.m.* 1 small cushion. 2 chair, rail chair (ferrocarril). 3 bearing (mecánica).
cojitranco, -a *adj.* (desp.) lame.
cok *s.m.* coke.
col *s.f.* 1 BOT. cabbage.
cola *s.f.* 1 ZOOL. tail. 2 end. 3 queue (personas). 4 glue (para pegar). || 5 **tener, traer —,** to have nasty consequences. 6 **— de pescado,** fish glue. 7 **no pegar ni con —,** to have nothing at all to do with.
colaboracionismo *s.m.* (desp.) collaboration.
colaborar *v.i.* to collaborate.
colación *s.f.* 1 collation. 2 light snack (comida).
colactáneo, -a *s.c.* brother (hermano de leche).
colágena *s.f.* QUIM. collagen.
colada *s.f.* 1 wash. 2 washing. 3 bleach (para colar). 4 cattle run (ganado). 5 GEOL. ravine. 6 tapping (altos hornos). 7 lava flow (volcán).
colapso *s.m.* collapse.
colar *v.t.* 1 to strain (líquido). 2 to bleach (ropa). || *v.i.* 3 to be swallowed. || *v.pron.* 4 to slip past (reunión, espectáculo, etc.). 5 to make a mistake. 6 (fam.) to drop a brick (en una conversación).
colateral *adj.* collateral.
colcha *s.f.* bedspread.
colchar *v.t.* to pad.
colchón *s.m.* mattress.
colchoneta *s.f.* 1 cushion. 2 airbed (de aire).
colear *v.i.* 1 to wag the tail. 2 to be still unfinished (asunto). || *v.t.* 3 to grab by the tail (toro).
colección *s.f.* collection.
colecta *s.f.* 1 collection (caridad). 2 REL. collect.
colectividad *s.f.* 1 whole unit (personas). 2 community (pueblo).
colectivismo *s.m.* collectivism.
colector *s.m.* 1 collector (persona). 2 water tank (aguas residuales). || 3 **— de corriente,** current collector.
colega *s.m.*y *f.* colleague.
colegiarse *v.pron.* 1 to become a society. 2 to become a member of a society.
colegiata *s.f.* collegiate church.
colegio *s.m.* 1 school. 2 college (profesional). || 3 **— electoral,** electoral college. 4 **— mayor,** hall of residence.
colegir *v.t.* to deduce.
coleóptero, -a *s.m.* y *f.* beetle.
cólera *s.f.* 1 anger. 2 MED. cholera.

colérico, -a *adj.* choleric.
colerina *s.f.* diarrhoea.
colesterol *s.m.* cholesterol.
coleta *s.f.* 1 pigtail. 2 (fam.) postscript (a una carta). || 3 **cortarse la –,** to retire from bullfighting; (fig.) to cease in an activity.
coletilla *s.f.* postscript.
coleto *s.m.* 1 inner self. 2 body. || 3 **echarse algo al –,** to drink something down. 4 to eat something up.
colgado, -a *adj.* (fam.) out on a limb.
colgar *v.t.* 1 to hang. 2 to attribute (culpa). 3 to drape (adornos). || *v.i.* 4 to hang.
colibrí *s.m.* hummingbird.
cólico *s.m.* colic.
coliflor *s.m.* cauliflower.
coligar *v.t./v.pron.* to bind.
colilla *s.f.* cigarette butt.
colimación *s.f.* OPT. collimation.
colimador *s.m.* collimator.
colina *s.f.* hill.
colindar *v.i.* to be an adjacent.
colino *s.m.* 1 cabbage seed. 2 cabbage patch (área).
colirio *s.m.* eye-drops.
coliseo *s.m.* coliseum.
colisión *s.f.* 1 collision. 2 confrontation (ideas).
colista *s.m.* y *f.* tail-ender.
colitis *s.f.* colitis.
colmado, -a *adj.* 1 full-up. || *s.m.* 2 cheap restaurant. 3 grocer's shop.
colmar *v.t.* 1 to fill to the brim. 2 to satiate (un deseo, etc.).
colmena *s.f.* beehive.
colmillo *s.m.* 1 ANAT. eye tooth. 2 fang (perro). 3 tusk (elefante). || 4 **enseñar los colmillos,** to bear one's teeth.
colmo *adj.* 1 full up. || *s.m.* 2 last drop. 3 culmination. || 4 **ser una cosa el –,** to be the last straw.
colocar *v.t.* y *v.pron.* 1 to place. 2 to find a job for.
colodra *s.f.* 1 wooden bucket. 2 drinking horn.
colodrillo *s.m.* back of the head.
colofón *s.m.* colophon.
coloide *adj.* QUIM. colloidal.
colombiano, -a *adj.* Colombian.
colombino, -a *adj.* of Columbus.
colombofilia *s.f.* pigeon rearing.
colon *s.m.* colon.
colón *s.m.* columbus (moneda).
colonato *s.m.* tenant farming.
colonia *s.f.* 1 colony. 2 cologne (perfumería).
coloniaje *s.m.* colonial period.
colonialismo *s.m.* colonialism.
colonizar *v.t.* to colonize.
colono *s.m.* 1 colonist. 2 AGR. tenant farmer.
coloquio *s.m.* dialogue.
color *s.m.* 1 colour. 2 (fig.) nature. || 3 **sacarle a uno los colores,** to make someone blush. 4 **salirle a uno los colores,** to blush.
colorado, -a *adj.* 1 coloured. 2 red.
colorar *v.t.* to colour.
colorear *v.t.* 1 to colour. 2 (desp.) to camouflage. || *v.i.* 3 to redden.
colorete *s.m.* rouge.
colorido *s.m.* colouring.
colorimetría *s.f.* colourimetry.
colorín *s.m.* 1 linnet (pájaro). 2 gaudy colour.
colorismo *s.m.* floridity (de estilo).
colosal *adj.* colossal.
coloso *s.m.* colossus.
coludir *v.i.* to collude.
columbario *s.m.* HIST. cemetery.
columbino, -a *adj.* of a dove.
columbrar *v.t.* 1 to catch sight of. 2 to guess.
columbrete *s.m.* skerry.
columelar *adj.* canine (diente).
columna *s.f.* 1 column. || 2 **– vertebral,** spinal column. 3 **quinta –,** fifth column.
columnata *s.f.* colonnade.
columnista *s.m.* y *f.* columnist.
columpio *s.m.* 1 swing. 2 seesaw (dos personas).
colla *adj.* 1 Bolivian. || *s.f.* 2 MAR. gang of dockworkers. 3 dancing group (Cataluña).
collado *s.m.* 1 hill. 2 ravine (entre montañas).
collage *s.m.* collage.
collar *s.m.* 1 chain. 2 collar (animales). 3 MECH. ring.
collarino *s.m.* ARQ. ammulet.
collazo *s.m.* 1 farm hand. 2 HIST. vassal.
collera *s.f.* horse collar.
collerón *s.m.* light horse collar.
coma *s.f.* 1 comma (en ortografía, música). 2 MED. coma.
comadre *s.f.* 1 goodmother. 2 MED. midwife. 3 close neighbour.
comadreja *s.f.* weasel.
comadreo *s.m.* gossip.
comadrona *s.f.* midwife.
comanche *adj.* Comanche.
comandancia *s.f.* 1 commandership. 2 commander's jurisdiction (área). 3 commander's office.
comandante *s.m.* commander.
comandar *v.t.* to command.
comandita *s.f.* sleeping partnership.
comando *s.m.* MIL. command.
comarca *s.f.* region.
comarcar *v.i.* to border on.
comatoso, -a *adj.* comatose.
comba *s.f.* 1 bulge. 2 skipping (juego). 3 skipping rope. 4 (Am.) sledge-hammer.
combar *v.t.* y *v.pron.* to bend.
combatir *v.i.* y *v.pron.* 1 to fight. || *v.t.* 2 to attack. 3 to impugn (teoría).
combatividad *s.f.* 1 combativeness. 2 tenacity.
combinación *s.f.* 1 combination. 2 project. 3 slip (prenda de mujer). 4 QUIM. compound.
combinado *s.m.* cocktail.
combinar *v.t.* 1 to combine. 2 to prepare.
comburente *adj.* combustion producing.
combustible *adj.* 1 combustible. || *s.m.* 2 fuel.
combustión *s.f.* combustion.
comedero, -a *adj.* 1 eatable. || *s.m.* 2 AGR. trough.
comedia *s.f.* 1 comedy. || 2 **– de capa y espada,** cloack-and-dagger play. 3 **– de caracteres,** character play. 4 **– de enredo,** comedy of intrigue. 5 **– de figurón,** charicature comedy. 6 (fig.) **hacer la –,** to swing the lead.
comediógrafo, -a *s.m.* y *f.* comedy writer.
comedirse *v.pron.* to show moderation.
comedor *adj.* 1 greedy. || *s.m.* 2 dining room. 3 restaurant.
comején *s.m.* 1 termite. 2 (Am.) anguish.
comelón, -a *adj.* greedy.
comendador, -a *s.m.* y *f.* knight commander.
comendatario, -a *adj.* recommendatory.
comensal *s.m.* y *f.* fellow diner.
comensalismo *s.m.* commensalism.
comentario *s.m.* 1 comment. || *pl.* 2 rumours.
comenzar *v.t.* y *v.i.* to begin.
comer *v.t.* 1 to eat. 2 to corrode (materiales). 3 to consume. 4 to take (ajedrez). || *s.m.* 5 food. || 6 **sin comerlo ni beberlo,** to have no idea why.
comercial *adj.* commercial.
comerciar *v.i.* 1 to trade. 2 to have dealings with (personas).
comercio *s.m.* 1 trade. 2 shop. 3 commerce (de un país).
comestible *adj.* 1 eatable. || *s.m.* 2 food item.
cometa *s.f.* 1 ASTR. comet. 2 kite (juguete).
cometer *v.t.* 1 to commit (crimen). 2 to make (error). 3 to entrust (responsabilidad). 4 to use (un solecismo, etc.).
cometido *s.m.* obligation.
comezón *s.m.* 1 itch. 2 unease (mental).
comicios *s.m.pl.* election.
cómico, -a *adj.* 1 comic. 2 funny. || *s.m.* y *f.* 3 comedian. || 4 **– de la legua,** travelling comedian.
comida *s.f.* 1 food. 2 meal (desayuno, etc.).
comidilla *s.f.* 1 interest. 2 (fig.) main topic of conversation.
comienzo *s.m.* beginning.
comilona *s.f.* (fam.) blow-out.
comilón, -ona *adj.* greedy. || *s.m.* y *f.* 2 greedy person. || *s.f.* 3 abundant meal.
comillas *s.f.pl.* inverted commas.
cominear *v.i.* to behave like a woman (un hombre).
comino *s.m.* 1 cumin seed. || 2 **no valer un –,** (fam.) to be useless.
comisaría *s.f.* 1 MIL. commissariat. 2 police station.
comisario, -a *s.m.* y *f.* 1 commissary. 2 police commissioner.
comisión *s.f.* 1 commission. 2 assignment (tarea). 3 committee (en el parlamento, etc.).
comiso *s.m.* 1 confiscation. 2 confiscated item.
comisorio, -a *adj.* valid for a certain time.
comistrajo *s.m.* (desp.) pigswill.
comisura *s.f.* corner (labios, párpados, etc.).
comité *s.m.* committee.
comitiva *s.f.* retinue.
cómitre *s.m.* 1 HIST. galley slave commander. 2 (desp.) slave-driver.
como *adv.* 1 like: *un hombre como él = a man like him.* 2 as: *como tú bien sabes*

= *as you well know.* **3** since (sentido causal). **4** if (sentido condicional).
cómo *adv.inter.* **1** how? **2** what? **3** why? *¿cómo no te has marchado todavía? = why haven't you gone yet?*
comodín *s.m.* **1** joker (cartas). **2** MEC. utility gadget.
cómoda *s.f.* chest of drawers.
cómodo, -a *adj.* **1** easy to use. **2** comfortable (un sofá, etc.).
comodoro *s.m.* commodore.
comoquiera *adv.* in whatever way.
compacto, -a *adj.* **1** dense. **2** solid (multitud).
compadecer *v.t.* y *v.pron.* **1** to feel sympathy for. || *v.pron.* **2** to square with.
compadraje *s.m.* brotherly affection.
compadrazgo *s.m.* **1** godfather status. **2** favouritism (en la solución de un problema). **3** (Am.) friendship.
compadre *s.m.* fellow parent (nombre).
compaginar *v.t.* **1** to put in order. || *v.pron.* **2** to square with.
compañerismo *s.m.* **1** friendship. **2** solidarity. **3** conviviality.
compañero, -a *s.m.* y *f.* **1** companion. || **2 — de clase,** schoolmate. **3 — de trabajo,** workmate.
compañía *s.f.* **1** company. || **2 — de Jesús,** Company of Jesus.
comparar *v.t.* to compare.
comparativo, -a *adj.* comparative.
comparecer *v.i.* to appear (ante una citación).
comparsa *s.f.* **1** extra (teatro). **2** group of extras. **3** masquerade (fiestas, etc.).
compartimiento *s.m.* **1** sharing. **2** distribution. || **3 — estanco,** watertight compartment. **4** rigid classification.
compartir *v.t.* **1** to divide up. **2** to share.
compás *s.m.* **1** MAT. pair of compasses. **2** MAR. compass. **3** MUS. beat. || **4 — de espera,** lull, short pause.
compasar *v.t.* **1** MUS. to beat time to. **2** MAT. to measure with a pair of compasses.
compasillo *s.m.* MUS. four-four time.
compasión *s.f.* **1** sympathy. **2** pity. || **3 ¡por —!,** for pity's sake!
compatible *adj.* compatible.
compatriota *s.m.* y *f.* compatriot.
compeler *v.t.* to compel.
compendio *s.m.* **1** compendium. || **2 en —,** in brief.
compenetrarse *v.pron.* **1** to share ideas and feelings. **2** QUIM. to fuse.
compensar *v.t.* **1** to compensate (de, for). **2** to make amends for (error).
competencia *s.f.* **1** competition. **2** duty. **3** competence (para una tarea).
competente *adj.* **1** competent. **2** appropriate.
competir *v.i.* **1** to compete (deporte, etc.) **2** (con) rival with.
compilar *v.t.* to compile.
compinche *s.m.* **1** (fam.) mate. **2** accomplice (en un delito).
complacer *v.t.* **1** to please. || *v.pron.* **2** to find pleasure in.
complejo, -a *adj.* **1** complex. || *s.m.* **2** complex. || **3 — de Edipo,** Oedipus complex.
complemento *s.m.* **1** complement.
completar *v.t.* to complete.
completas *s.f.pl.* REL. evensong.
completo, -a *adj.* **1** complete. **2** full (sitio).
complexión *s.f.* constitution (físico).
complexo, -a *adj.* **1** complex. || *s.m.* **2** complex.
complicar *v.t.* **1** to complicate. **2** to mix up (cosas diversas).
cómplice *s.m.* accomplice.
complot *s.m.* conspiracy.
compluvio *s.m.* HIST. rainwater aperture.
componenda *s.f.* **1** (desp.) shady deal. **2** compromise.
componer *v.t.* **1** to compose. **2** to fix (algo roto). **3** to tidy up (algo desordenado). **4** to garnish (comida). **5** to reconcile (una persona). **6** (Am.) to set (huesos dislocados). || *v.pron.* **7** to dress up. || **8 componérselas,** to find a way.
comporta *s.f.* grape basket.
comportable *adj.* bearable.
comportamiento *s.m.* behaviour: *tu comportamiento deja mucho que desear = your behaviour leaves a lot to be desired.*
comportar *v.t.* **1** to put up with. || *v.pron.* **2** to behave.
composición *s.f.* **1** composing. **2** composition (obra musical). || **3 — de lugar,** study of the situation.
compostelano, a *adj.* of Santiago de Compostela.
compostura *s.f.* **1** make-up. **2** overhaul (de un coche). **3** tidying-up (de una habitación). **4** composure (mental). **5** arrangement (asunto).
compota *s.f.* jam.
compotera *s.f.* stewed fruit dish.
compra *s.f.* **1** buying. **2** purchase (cosa comprada). **3** shopping: *hacer la compra = to do the shopping.*
comprador *s.m.* buyer.
comprar *v.t.* **1** to buy. **2** (desp.) to bribe.
comprender *v.t.* **1** to understand. **2** to consist of. || *v.pron.* **3** to be included (un impuesto).
comprensibilidad *s.f.* comprehensibleness.
comprensible *adj.* understandable.
comprensión *s.f.* **1** grasp (facultad de comprender). **2** understanding (emociones).
comprensivo, -a *adj.* **1** comprehensive (que abarca mucho). **2** understanding (persona).
compresa *s.f.* **1** compress. **2** sanitary towel (mujeres).
compresible *adj.* TEC. compressible.
compresión *s.f.* **1** compression. **2** GRAM. synaeresis.
compresivo *adj.* TEC. compressive.
compresor, -a *adj.* **1** compressive. || *s.m.* **2** compressor.
comprimido *s.m.* MED. tablet.
comprimir *v.t.* **1** to compress. || *v.pron.* **2** to control oneself.
comprobación *s.f.* **1** proof (prueba). **2** check (verificación).
comprobar *v.t.* to prove (un hecho).
comprobatorio *adj.* demonstratory.
comprometedor *adj.* compromising: *un documento comprometedor = a compromising document.*
comprometer *v.t.* **1** to compromise (persona). **2** to endanger (por un riesgo). || *v.pron.* **3** to take it upon oneself (tarea). **4** to be consistent (según sus principios).
compromisario, -a *adj.* **1** arbitrating. || *s.m.* **2** representative.
compromiso *s.m.* **1** commitment. **2** difficulty. **3** solution (de un conflicto). **4** POL. delegation. **5** agreement.
compuerta *s.f.* **1** sluice gate (canal). **2** hatch (casa).
compuesto, -a *adj.* **1** composed (persona). **2** composite (flores). || *s.f.pl.* **3** composites. || *s.m.* **4** composite.
compulsa *s.f.* **1** verification (documento). **2** attested copy.
compulsación *s.f.* **1** comparing. **2** DER. attestation.
compulsar *v.t.* **1** to check (documentos). **2** to make attested copies.
compulsión *s.f.* compulsion.
compunción *s.f.* compunction.
compungido, -a *adj.* sad.
computable *adj.* MAT., etc. calculable.
computación *s.f.* calculation.
computadora *s.m.* computer.
computar *v.t.* **1** to calculate. **2** to compute.
comulgante *s.m.* REL. communicant.
comulgar *v.i.* **1** REL. to receive communion. **2** (fig.) to share ideas.
comulgatorio *s.m.* REL. communion rail.
común *adj.* **1** common. **2** ordinary. **3** cheap (en calidad). || *s.m.* **4** community. **5** people in general. **6** toilet (habitación). || **7 en —,** jointly.
comuna *s.f.* **1** commune. **2** (Am.) municipality.
comunal *adj.* **1** common. **2** communal (bienes).
comunero, -a *adj.* **1** popular. **2** HIST. communitarian (Castilla). || *s.m.* **3** joint owner (propiedad).
comunicación *s.f.* **1** communication. **2** contact (entre personas). **3** item of news (telefónicamente). **4** telephone connection. || *pl.* **5** communications. || **6 medios de —,** means of communication.
comunicado *s.m.* communiqué.
comunicar *v.t.* **1** to communicate. **2** to inform. || *v.pron.* **3** to be connected (una habitación con otra, etc.).
comunidad *s.c.* **1** community. || **2 — autónoma,** autonomous region. **3 — de bienes,** profit-making rights. **4 — de vecinos,** neighbours group. **5 de —,** jointly.
comunista *s.m.* y *f.* POL. communist.
comúnmente *adv.* commonly: *ese animal es comúnmente conocido como zorro = that animal is commonly known as a fox.*
comunicabilidad *s.f.* communicableness.
comunicable *adj.* communicable.
comunicante *adj.* **1** communicating. || *s.m.* **2** PER. correspondent (periodismo).
comunicativo *adj.* communicative: *no estás muy comunicativo hoy = you're not very communicative today.*
comunión *s.f.* communion.
comunismo *s.m.* communism.
con *prep.* **1** by means of. **2** with. **3** although: *con ser el último de la clase, sabe*

muchísimo = although he's the bottom of the class, he knows a great deal. || 4 — **que,** as long as: *con que esté aquí mañana, basta = as long as he's here tomorrow, I don't mind.*
conato *s.m.* 1 effort. 2 attempt (algo no consumado).
concatenación *s.f.* 1 concatenation (encadenamiento).
concatenar *v.t.* to string together.
cóncavo, -a *adj.* 1 concave. || *s.m.* y *f.* 2 hollow.
concebible *adj.* conceivable.
concebir *v.t.* 1 to conceive (idea). 2 BIO. to get pregnant.
conceder *v.t.* to concede.
concejal *s.m.* councillor.
concejalía *s.f.* POL. council seat.
concejo *s.m.* 1 town council. 2 council meeting. 3 municipality.
concentración *s.f.* 1 concentration (mental). 2 coming together (agrupación): *la concentración de grandes masas = the coming together of wide masses.*
concentrado *adj.* concentrated.
concentrar *v.t.* to concentrate.
concéntrico, -a *adj.* concentric.
concepción *s.f.* conception.
conceptismo *s.m.* LIT. witty, elaborate style.
conceptista *adj.* witty.
concepto *s.m.* 1 concept. 2 opinion (personal). 3 judgement (en un tribunal, etc.). || 4 **bajo todos los conceptos,** in all respects. 5 **en — de,** as...
conceptual *adj.* conceptual.
conceptuoso *adj.* 1 ingenious. 2 (desp.) affected.
concerniente *adj.* concerning: *en lo concerniente a la vida de Cervantes = as concerning Cervantes' life.*
concernir *v.i.* to concern.
concertar *v.t.* 1 to arrange. 2 to coordinate (esfuerzos). 3 to fix (precio). 4 to tune up (instrumentos musicales). || *v.i.* 5 to agree.
concertina *s.f.* concertina.
concertino *s.m.* first violin.
concertista *s.m.* y *f.* solo performer.
concesión *s.f.* 1 concession. 2 privilege.
concesionario *s.m.* concessionaire.
concesivo, -a *adj.* concessive.
conciencia *s.f.* 1 conscience. 2 consciousness. || 3 **a —,** scrupulously.
concienzudamente *adj.* conscientiously (con mucha atención).
concienzudo, -a *adj.* 1 conscientious. 2 thorough (un trabajo).
concierto *s.m.* 1 agreement. 2 MUS. harmony. 3 concert (espectáculo). || 4 **— económico,** economic pact.
conciliábulo *s.m.* shady get-together.
conciliación *s.f.* 1 conciliation. || 2 **acto de —,** act of reconciliation.
conciliar *adj.* 1 conciliary. || *s.m.* 2 member of a council. || *v.t.* 3 to reconcile. || *v.pron.* 4 to obtain (la amistad de uno).
conciliatorio, -a *adj.* conciliatory.
concilio *s.m.* 1 council (eclesiástico). || 2 **— ecuménico/general,** ecumenical council.
concisión *s.f.* succinctness.
conciso, -a *adj.* concise.
concitar *v.t.* to incite (a una persona contra otra).
conciudadano, -a *s.m.* y *f.* fellow citizen.
cónclave *s.m.* 1 conclave (de cardenales). 2 meeting.
concluir *v.i.* 1 to finish. || *v.t.* 2 to conclude. 3 to decide.
conclusión *s.f.* conclusion (consecuencia). || 2 **en —,** finally.
concluso *adj.* finished.
concluyente *adj.* conclusive.
concluyentemente *adv.* conclusively.
concoide o **concoideo, -a** *adj.* shell-like.
concomerse *v.pron.* 1 to be vexed (por enfado). 2 to mope (por tristeza). 3 to be uneasy. 4 to twitch (los hombros y la espalda).
concomimiento *s.m.* (fam.) fidgeting.
concomitancia *s.f.* accompaniment.
concomitante *adj.* concomitant (circunstancias, etc.).
concomitar *v.t.* to accompany.
concordancia *s.f.* 1 concordance. 2 MUS. harmony. 3 GRAM. agreement. || *s.f.pl.* 4 word index (libro).
concordante *adj.* concordant.
concordar *v.i.* 1 to agree. || *v.t.* 2 to settle.
concordato *s.m.* concordat.
concordatorio *adj.* REL. relating to the concordat.
concorde *adj.* in agreement: *es difícil poner a los dos hermanos concordes = it's hard to make the two brothers see in agreement.*
concordia *s.f.* 1 concord. 2 mutual agreement. 3 double ring (joyería).
concreción *s.i.* 1 concretion. 2 MED. gallstone.
concrecionarse *v.r.* 1 to concrete. 2 MED. to form stones.
concretamente *adv.* specifically: *quiero hablarles de Cervantes, más concretamente del Quijote = I want to talk to you about Cervantes, specifically about Don Quixote.*
concretar *v.t.* 1 to make concrete (planes, etc.). 2 to specify (especificar). || *v.r.* 3 to limit oneself: *me voy a concretar a mencionar un solo nombre = I'm going to limit myself to mentioning only one name.*
concreto, -a *adj.* 1 specific. || *s.m.* 2 (Am.) concrete. || 3 **en —,** to be precise.
concubina *s.f.* concubine.
concubinato *s.m.* 1 concubinage. 2 (fam., desp.) living in sin.
conculcar *v.t.* 1 to trample on. 2 to infringe (ley).
concuñado, -a *s.m.* 1 brother-in-law's brother. || *s.f.* 2 sister-in-law's sister.
concupiscencia *s.f.* 1 desire. 2 sexual appetite.
concupiscente *adj.* 1 greedy (codicioso). 2 lustful (lujurioso).
concurrencia *s.f.* 1 meeting (reunión). 2 concurrence (simultaneidad). 3 COM. competition.
concurrente *adj.* 1 concurrent. 2 COM. competing. || *s.m.* 3 COM. competitor. 4 person present (alguien que asiste a algo).
concurrir *v.i.* 1 to come together. 2 to contribute. 3 to take part in.
concursar *v.t.* 1 DER. to declare insolvent. || *v.i.* 2 to compete. 3 to take a professional exam (examinarse).
concursante *s.m.* 1 participant. 2 examinee (el que se examina).
concurso *s.m.* 1 competition. 2 cooperation. 3 concurrence (sucesos).
concusión *s.f.* 1 MED. concussion. 2 FIN. extortion.
concusionario *adj.* FIN. extortionary.
concha *s.f.* 1 shell. 2 oyster. 3 tortoiseshell. 4 prompter's recess (teatro). 5 GEOG. narrow creek.
conchabar *v.t.* 1 to join. 2 to combine (lana). 3 (Am.) to employ. || *v.pron.* 4 to gang up (contra, on).
conchado *adj.* ZOOL. shelled.
conchudo *adj.* 1 covered with shells. 2 (fig. y fam.) crafty (astuto). 3 (Am.) shameless (sin vergüenza).
condado *s.m.* GEOG. county.
condal *adj.* of a count.
conde *s.m.* count.
condecir *v.i.* 1 to agree. 2 to go with (una cosa con otra).
condecoración *s.f.* 1 MIL. decoration. 2 medal (insignia).
condecorar *v.t.* MIL. to decorate.
condena *s.f.* 1 conviction (criminal). 2 sentence (cárcel).
condenación *s.f.* 1 condemnation. 2 LEG. sentence (condena). 3 (fig.) disapproval (desaprobación).
condenado *adj.* 1 DER. condemned. 2 (desp.) damned. 3 (Am. y fam.) clever. || *s.m.* 4 DER. convicted person.
condenar *v.t.* 1 to condemn. 2 to convict (reo). 3 to disapprove of. 4 REL. to damn. || *v.pron.* 5 to be damned.
condenatorio, -a *adj.* condemnatory.
condensabilidad *s.f.* condensability.
condensable *adj.* condensable.
condensación *s.f.* condensation.
condensador *s.m.* condenser.
condensar *v.t.* 1 to condense. 2 to summarise (texto).
condesa *s.f.* countess.
condescendencia *s.f.* 1 willingness (complacencia). 2 submissiveness (pasividad).
condescender *v.i.* to condescend.
condescendiente *adj.* 1 willing (complaciente). 2 submissive (servicial).
condesil *adj.* of a countess.
condestable *s.m.* HIST. top-ranking officer.
condición *s.f.* 1 condition. 2 status (social).
condicionado, -a *adj.* conditioned.
condicional *adj.* conditional.
condicionante *s.m.* contributing factor.
condicionar *v.t.* 1 to condition. 2 to prepare (disponer).
condigno, -a *adj.* appropriate.
cóndilo *s.m.* MED. condyle.
condimentación *s.f.* seasoning (cocina).
condimentar *v.t.* 1 to season. 2 to add flavour to (dar sabor a).
condimento *s.m.* seasoning.
condiscípulo, -a *s.m.* y *f.* fellow pupil.
condolencia *s.f.* condolence.

condolerse *v.pron.* to feel sorry for.
condonación *s.f.* 1 forgiveness (disculpa). 2 cancellation (deuda).
condonar *v.t.* 1 to condone.
cóndor *s.m.* ORN. condor.
condotiero *s.m.* 1 mercenary leader. 2 mercenary soldier.
conducción *s.f.* 1 driving (vehículo). 2 TEC. pipework.
conducente *adj.* conducive.
conducir *v.t.* 1 to lead. || *v.i.* 2 to drive (en un vehículo). || *v.pron.* 3 to behave.
conducta *s.f.* behaviour.
conductibilidad *s.f.* FIS. conductivity.
conducto *s.m.* 1 conduit (para agua). 2 agent (persona).
conductor, -a *adj.* 1 leading. 2 FIS. conductive. || *s.m.* y *f.* 3 (Am.) conductor (de autobús). 4 driver. || 5 **— eléctrico,** electric cable.
condumio *s.m.* (fam.) grub.
conectador *s.m.* TEC. connecter.
conectar *v.t.* 1 to connect up (máquina). 2 to join.
conectivo, -a *adj.* GRAM. connective.
conejar *s.m.* warren.
conejal *s.m.* rabbit farm.
conejero, -a *adj.* 1 rabbit. || *s.m.* y *f.* 2 rabbit breeder. || *s.f.* 3 rabbit farm. 4 (fam.) hutch.
conejillo *s.m.* 1 small rabbit. || 2 **— de Indias,** guinea-pig.
conejo *s.m.* rabbit.
conejuno *adj.* ZOOL. rabbit-like.
conexión *s.f.* connection.
conexionarse *v.r.* to connect up.
conexo *adj.* connected.
confabulación *s.f.* 1 plot (complot). 2 made-up story (cuento inventado).
confabularse *v.pron.* to conspire.
confección *s.f.* 1 preparation (de un medicamento). 2 making-up (de una prenda de vestir).
confeccionar *v.t.* to make.
confederación *s.f.* confederation.
confederar *v.t.* to league together.
confederativo, -a *adj.* confederative.
conferencia *s.f.* 1 conference. 2 lecture (académica). 3 call (teléfono).
conferenciante *s.m.* y *f.* 1 speaker. 2 lecturer (académico).
conferenciar *v.i.* to be in conference.
conferir *v.t.* 1 to confer (a, on). 2 to compare (documentos).
confesar *v.t.* 1 to confess. 2 to grant absolution (cura). || *v.i.* 3 to make one's confession (en la iglesia).
confesión *s.f.* confession.
confesional *adj.* REL. confessional.
confesionario *s.m.* confessional.
confeso, -a *adj.* 1 confessed. 2 converted (judío). || *s.m.* 3 lay-monk.
confesor *s.m.* confessor.
confeti *s.m.pl.* confetti.
confiadamente *adv.* 1 confidently (con seguridad). 2 immodestly (vanidosamente).
confiado, -a *adj.* 1 confident (seguro). 2 immodest (vanidoso).
confianza *s.f.* 1 trust. 2 confidence (en sí mismo). 3 vanity. 4 familiarity (en el trato con alguien).
confiar *v.t.* 1 to entrust (a, to). || *v.i.* 2 to trust: *confío en ti = I trust you.*
confidencia *s.f.* 1 piece of confidential information. 2 confidence.
confidencial *adj.* confidential.
confidente *s.m.* y *f.* 1 confidant. 2 informer (policía). 3 two-seater settee (mueble). || *adj.* 4 trustworthy.
configuración *s.f.* shape.
configurar *v.t.* to give form to.
confín *s.m.* 1 boundary. 2 horizon. || *adj.* 3 bordering.
confinación *s.f.* restriction.
confinar *v.i.* 1 to border on. || *v.t.* 2 to banish. 3 to lock up.
confirmación *s.f.* REL. confirmation.
confirmando, -a *s.m.* y *f.* REL. confirmee.
confirmar *v.t.* 1 to confirm. || *v.pron.* 2 to gain credence.
confirmatorio, -a *adj.* corroborative.
confiscación *s.f.* confiscation.
confiscar *v.t.* to confiscate.
confitar *v.t.* 1 to preserve (fruta en almíbar). 2 (fig.) to sweeten.
confite *s.m.* sweet.
confitería *s.f.* confectioner's shop.
confitero, -a *s.m.* y *f.* confectioner.
confitura *s.f.* jam.
conflagración *s.f.* 1 conflagration. 2 outbreak (guerra).
conflagrar *v.t.* to burn up.
conflicto *s.m.* 1 conflict. 2 clash (de intereses). 3 impasse. || 4 **— generacional,** generation gap.
confluencia *s.f.* confluence (de dos ríos, etc.).
confluir *v.i.* to join up.
conformación *s.f.* make-up (estructura).
conformar *v.t.* 1 to adjust. || *v.i.* 2 to be in agreement. || *v.pron.* 3 to resign oneself.
conforme *adj.* 1 similar. 2 agreed (opiniones). 3 consistent. || *adv.* 4 in accordance with.
conformidad *s.f.* 1 similarity. 2 tolerance (de ideas). 3 resignation. || 4 **de — con,** in accordance with.
conformista *adj.* 1 conformist. || *s.m.* y *f.* REL. 2 (brit.) conformist. 3 conformer.
confort *s.m.* comfort.
confortable *adj.* 1 comfortable (un sofá). 2 comforting (persona).
confortación *s.f.* comforting (consolación).
confortador *adj.* 1 comforting. || *s.m.* 2 comforter.
confortante *adj.* comforting: *palabras confortantes = conforting words.*
confortar *v.t.* 1 to comfort. 2 to console (a un afligido).
confraternidad *s.f.* camaraderie.
confraternizar *v.i.* to fraternize.
confrontación *s.f.* 1 confronting (de dos personas). 2 checking (comparación de dos cosas).
confrontar *v.t.* 1 to confront. 2 to compare (documentos). || *v.pron.* 3 to face. || *v.i.* 4 to border.
confulgencia *s.f.* effulgence.
confundible *adj.* easily mistakable.
confundir *v.t.* 1 to mix up. 2 to mistake (con, for). 3 to humiliate (al acusado). 4 to confuse (a un enemigo). || *v.pron.* 5 to become indistinct. 6 to make a mistake (en una acción).
confusión *s.f.* 1 confusion. 2 mix-up (falta de claridad). 3 perplexity (desasosiego).
confusionismo *s.m.* confusedness.
confuso, -a *adj.* 1 in a mess (revuelto). 2 garbled (ruido). 3 hazy (imagen). 4 embarrassed (avergonzado). 5 unsure (incierto).
conga *s.f.* conga (baile).
congelación *s.f.* 1 freezing. || 2 **— de créditos,** COM. credit freeze.
congelador *s.m.* freezer.
congelar *v.t.* 1 to freeze. 2 to block (créditos). || *v.pron.* 3 to freeze up.
congénere *adj.* akin.
congeniar *v.i.* to get on well.
congénito, -a *adj.* congenital.
congestión *s.f.* congestion.
congestionar *v.t.* 1 to congest. || *v.pron.* 2 to become congested (una parte del cuerpo).
congestivo, -a *adj.* ANAT. congestive.
conglomeración *s.f.* conglomeration.
conglomerado *s.m.* 1 TEC. conglomerate. 2 COM. conglomeration.
conglomerar *v.t.* 1 to conglomerate. || *v.pron.* 2 to conglomerate.
conglutinación *s.f.* 1 joining (union). 2 adhesion (acción de pegarse).
conglutinar *v.t.* 1 to stick together. || *v.pron.* 2 to gell.
conglutinoso *adj.* adhesive.
congoja *s.f.* grief.
congojoso, -a *adj.* distressful.
congoleño, -a *adj.* Congolese.
congosto *s.m.* mountain pass.
congraciar *v.t.* 1 to win over. || *v.pron.* 2 to ingratiate oneself.
congratulaciones *s.f.pl.* congratulations.
congratularse *v.pron.* to congratulate oneself.
congregación *s.f.* 1 assembly. 2 REL. congregation.
congregante, -a *s.m.* y *f.* congregationalist.
congregar *v.t.* 1 to bring together. || *v.r.* 2 to come together.
congresista *s.m.* y *f.* 1 member (reunión). 2 POL. member of Congress.
congreso *s.m.* 1 congress. 2 assembly. 3 congress hall (edificio).
congrio *s.m.* conger eel.
congruencia o **congruidad** *s.f.* 1 congruence. 2 opportuneness (calidad).
congruente *adj.* 1 appropriate (conveniente). 2 MAT. congruent.
congruo, -a *adj.* 1 oportune. 2 MAT. congruent. || *s.f.* 3 personal stipend (sacerdote).
cónico, -a *adj.* 1 conical. 2 MAT. conic.
conífero, -a *adj.* 1 BOT. coniferous. || *s.f.pl.* 2 conifer.
conirrostro, -a *adj.* coniform-beaked (gorrión, cuervo, etc.).
conjetura *s.f.* conjecture.
conjetural *adj.* given to conjecture.
conjeturar *v.t.* to conjecture.
conjugable *adj.* GRAM. that can be conjugated.

conjuntamente *adv.* 1 jointly. || 2 **— con,** together with.
conjurado, -a *adj.* 1 plotting. 2 averted (alejado).
conjuro *s.m.* 1 incantation (sortilegio). 2 plea (súplica).
conjugación *s.f.* conjugation.
conjugar *v.t.* 1 to bring together. 2 GRAM. to conjugate.
conjunción *s.f.* 1 bringing together. 2 conjunction.
conjuntar *v.t.* 1 to join. 2 to make cohesive.
conjuntivitis *s.f.* conjunctivitis.
conjuntivo, -a *adj.* 1 conjunctive. || *s.f.* 2 ANAT. mucous membrane of the eye.
conjunto, -a *adj.* 1 united. 2 adjoining (una cosa a otra). || *s.m.* 3 group. 4 set (prendas de vestir).
conjura o **conjuración** *s.f.* conspiracy.
conjurar *v.i.* 1 to conspire. || *v.t.* 2 to swear in (en una asociación). 3 to ward off (un mal). 4 to implore (a una persona).
conllevar *v.t.* 1 to stand by. 2 to tolerate (a una persona).
conmemoración *s.f.* commemoration.
conmemorar *v.t.* to commemorate.
conmemorativo *adj.* commemorative.
conmensurable *adj.* 1 having a common measure. 2 MAT. commensurable.
conmensurar *v.t.* to measure by the same unit.
conmigo *pron.* with me.
conminación *s.f.* threat (amenaza).
conminar *v.t.* 1 to threaten. 2 to caution (oficialmente).
conminatorio, -a *adj.* threatening.
conmiseración *s.f.* commiseration.
conmistión *s.f.* 1 mixture. 2 hotchpotch (desorden).
conmisto *adj.* topsy-turvy.
conmoción *s.f.* 1 shaking (tierra). || 2 **— cerebral,** concussion.
conmovedor, -a *adj.* moving (emocionante).
conmover *v.t.* 1 to move (compasión). 2 to disturb. || *v.pron.* 3 to be moved.
conmovible *adj.* prone to showing emotion.
conmutabilidad *s.f.* convertible.
conmutación *s.f.* 1 exchange (reemplazo). 2 DER. commutation.
conmutación *s.f.* 1 exchange. 2 LIT. play on words.
conmutador, -a *adj.* 1 changing. || *s.m.* 2 ELEC. switch. 3 (Am.) telephone exchange (edificio).
conmutar *v.t.* 1 to exchange. 2 DER. to commute.
conmutativa *adj.* y *s.f.* MAT. commutative.
connatural *adj.* inherent (persona o cosa).
connivencia *s.f.* 1 connivance. 2 plotting (intriga).
connotación *s.f.* 1 connotation. 2 distant blood ties (parentesco).
connotar *v.t.* 1 to connote (dos ideas). 2 to relate.
connotativo, -a *adj.* GRAM. connotative.
connubio *s.m.* LIT. marriage.
cono *s.m.* BOT. y MAT. cone.
conocedor, -ora *adj.* 1 knowledgeable. || *s.m.* 2 expert. 3 connoisseur (vinos, etc.). 4 AGR. cattle foreman.
conocer *v.t.* 1 to know. 2 to understand (entender). 3 to recognize (a alguien ya conocido). 4 to have experience in (un oficio). || *v.pron.* 5 to be acquainted (dos personas).
conocido, -a *adj.* 1 well-known. || *s.m.* y *f.* 2 acquaintance.
conocidamente *adv.* clearly.
conocimiento *s.m.* 1 knowing. 2 intelligence. 3 acquaintance (persona). 4 MED. consciousness. || *pl.* 5 knowledge.
conoide *s.m.* GEOM. conoid.
conoideo, -a *adj.* GEOM. conical.
conopeo *s.m.* REL. sanctuary veil.
conque *conj.* and so.
conqué *s.m.* (Am.) money.
conquiliología *s.f.* ZOOL. conchology.
conquiliólogo *s.m.* ZOOL. conchologist.
conquista *s.f.* conquest.
conquistable *adj.* 1 conquerable. 2 (fig.) easily obtainable.
conquistador, -ora *adj.* 1 conquering. || *s.m.* 2 HIST. conqueror.
conquistar *v.t.* 1 to conquer (por fuerza). 2 (fig.) to win. 3 to win over (a una persona).
consabido, -a *adj.* well-known.
consagrar *v.t.* 1 to consecrate (en la comunión religiosa). 2 to confirm (autorizar). || *v.pron.* 3 to devote oneself entirely to.
consanguíneo, -a *adj.* 1 related by blood. || *s.m.* 2 half brother. || *s.f.* 3 half sister.
consanguinidad *s.f.* blood relationship.
consciencia *s.f.* 1 MED. consciousness. 2 (fig.) awareness.
consciente *adj.* 1 conscious. 2 responsible (de sus acciones).
conscientemente *adv.* consciously.
consecución *s.f.* attainment.
consecuencia *s.f.* 1 consequence. || 2 **de —,** important. 3 **con —,** consistently. 4 **sacar la — de que,** to draw the conclusion that.
consecuente *adj.* 1 consequent. 2 consistent: *no eres consecuente contigo mismo = you always contradict yourself.*
consecutivamente *adv.* consecutively.
consecutivo, -a *adj.* consecutive.
conseguir *v.t.* 1 to get. 2 to achieve (una meta).
conseja *s.f.* cock-and-bull story.
consejero, -a *adj.* 1 counselling. || *s.m.* y *f.* 2 POL. councillor. 3 adviser (asesor).
consejo *s.m.* 1 advice (dictamen). 2 council (grupo). || 3 **— de Estado,** Council of State. 4 **— de guerra,** council of war.
consenso *s.m.* 1 approval. 2 POL. consensus.
consentido *adj.* 1 spoiled (mimado). 2 tolerant (marido).
consentimiento *s.m.* consent.
consentir *v.t.* 1 to permit. 2 to tolerate (ceder). 3 to spoil (a un niño). || *v.pron.* 4 to break up (romperse).
conserje *s.m.* y *f.* caretaker (de un edificio).
conserjería *s.f.* 1 post of caretaker (oficio). 2 caretaker's office (habitación).
conserva *s.f.* preserved food.
conservación *s.f.* 1 conservation. 2 preservation (protección).
conservador, -ora *adj./s.m* y *f.* 1 conservative. || 2 **— adjunto,** assistant keeper.
conservaduría *s.f.* 1 keeper's office (de una dependencia pública). 2 curatorship (de un museo).
conservadurismo *s.m.* POL. conservatism.
conservar *v.t.* 1 to conserve. 2 to preserve (comida). || *v.pron.* 3 to last. 4 to be in the best of health (persona).
conservatorio, -a *adj.* 1 preserving. || *s.m.* 2 MUS. conservatory.
conservero, -a *adj.* preserves: *la industria conservera = the preserves industry.*
considerable *adj.* 1 considerable, substancial. 2 large.
considerablemente *adv.* considerably: *los precios han aumentado considerablemente = prices have increased considerably.*
consideración *s.f.* 1 consideration (reflexión). 2 respect (deferencia). || 3 **ser de —,** to be important.
considerado, -a *adj.* 1 considered (estimado). 2 considerate (atento).
considerando *s.m.* DER. explanation.
considerar *v.t.* 1 to consider (reflexionar). 2 to respect (mostrar deferencia). 3 to believe (estimar).
consigna *s.f.* 1 order (a un subordinado). 2 watchword (lema). 3 leftluggage office (en una estación).
consignación *s.f.* COM. consignment.
consignar *v.t.* 1 FIN. to assign. 2 to register (escribir). 3 to consign (una mercancía). 4 to entrust (algo a nombre de uno).
consignatario, -a *s.m.* y *f.* 1 COM. consignee. 2 MAR. shipping agent.
consigo *pron.* 1 with him (hombre). 2 with her (mujer). 3 with you (Vd.). 4 with oneself (uno mismo).
consiguiente *adj.* 1 consequent. || 2 **por —,** as a result.
consiguientemente *adv.* consequently.
consiliario *s.m.* councillor.
consistencia *s.f.* 1 durability. 2 consistency (de un líquido).
consistente *adj.* consistent.
consistir *v.i.* 1 to be composed of. 2 to be based (residir).
consistorial *adj.* 1 REL. consistorial. || 2 **a casa —,** town hall.
consistorio *s.m.* 1 POL. town council. 2 REL. consistory.
consola *s.f.* 1 console-table (mueble). 2 TEC. console panel.
consolador, -a *adj.* consoling.
consolar *v.t.* 1 to console. || *v.pron.* 2 to take comfort.
consolidación *s.f.* consolidation.
consolidar *v.t.* 1 to fortify (una estructura). 2 to consolidate (asegurar). 3 to fund (deuda).
consomé *s.m.* consommé (sopa).
consonancia *s.f.* 1 MUS. consonance. 2 (fig.) harmony.

consonante *adj.* **1** MUS. consonant. **2** GRAM. consonantal. || *s.f.* **3** consonant. **4** rhyming word (poesía).

consonántico, -a *adj.* FON. consonantal.

consonantización *s.f.* consonantization.

consonar *v.i.* **1** MUS. to harmonize. **2** (fig.) to run parallel.

consorcio *s.m.* **1** COM. consortium. **2** union (de amigos).

consorte *s.m.* y *f.* **1** spouse (matrimonio). **2** partner (compañero).

conspicuo, -a *adj.* famous.

conspiración *s.f.* conspiracy.

conspirador, -ora *s.m.* y *f.* POL., etc. conspirator.

conspirar *v.i.* **1** to plot. **2** to conspire.

constancia *s.f.* **1** constancy (perseverancia). **2** proof (prueba). **3** (Am.) written evidence.

constante *adj.* **1** constant. **2** long-lasting (duradero). || *s.f.* **3** MAT. constant.

constantemente *adv.* constantly.

constar *v.i.* **1** to be composed. **2** to be clear (un hecho). **3** to be recorded (en un catálogo). **4** to have correct stress (poesía).

constatación *s.f.* **1** confirmation. **2** substantiation (comprobación).

constatar *v.t.* to confirm (un hecho).

constelación *s.f.* ASTR. constellation.

consternación *s.f.* consternation.

consternar *v.t.* **1** to discourage. || *v.pron.* **2** to be dismayed.

constipado, -a *adj.* **1** suffering from a cold: *estás muy constipado = you've got a bad cold.* || *s.m.* **2** cold.

constiparse *v.pron.* to catch a cold.

constitución *s.f.* **1** composition (de materia). **2** POL. constitution.

constitucional *adj.* constitutional.

constituir *v.t.* **1** to compose. **2** to set up (un negocio). || *v.i.* **3** to count as (implicar).

constitutivo *adj.* **1** elemental. || *s.m.* **2** constituent part.

constituyente *adj.* constituent.

constreñir *v.t.* **1** to force (a una persona). **2** MED. to constrict.

constricción *s.f.* constriction.

construcción *s.f.* ARQ. y GRAM. construction.

constructivo *adj.* constructive: *una crítica constructiva = constructive criticism.*

constructor, -ora *adj.* **1** construction. || *s.m.* y *f.* **2** builder.

construir *v.t.* ARQ. y GRAM. to construct.

consubstanciación *s.f.* REL. consubstantiation.

consubstancial *adj.* REL. consubstantial.

consubstanciarse *v.r.* (Am.) to be consubstantiated.

consuegros, -as *s.m.* y *f.* father/mother in law of one's son/daughter.

consuelo *s.m.* **1** consolation. **2** happiness (alegría).

consuetudinario, -a *adj.* customary.

cónsul *s.m.* POL. e HIST. consul.

consulado *s.m.* **1** consulate: *el consulado británico = the British consulate.* **2** consulship (oficio).

consular *adj.* consular.

consulta *s.f.* **1** consultation (dictamen). **2** MED. consulting room, sugery: *el médico tiene la consulta por la tarde = the doctor's surgery is in the afternoon.* || **3 libro de —,** LIT. reference work.

consultar *v.t.* **1** to consult. **2** to discuss (deliberar).

consultivo, -a *adj.* consultative (comité).

consultor *s.m.* consultant.

consultorio *s.m.* consulting-room (de un médico).

consumación *s.f.* **1** consummation (matrimonio). **2** extinction (fin).

consumado, -a *adj.* **1** consummated (matrimonio). **2** consumate (perfecto).

consumar *v.t.* **1** to accomplish fully. **2** to consummate (matrimonio).

consumición *s.f.* **1** consumption (consumo). **2** drink (bebida): *la consumición está incluida en el precio de la entrada = the price of the drink is included in the ticket.*

consumido, -a *adj.* (fam.) **1** skinny (flaco). **2** scared (tímido).

consumidor, -ora *s.m.* y *f.* consumer.

consumir *v.t.* **1** to consume (mercancías). || *v.r.* **2** to be destroyed (por fuego). **3** to be distressed.

consumo *s.m.* **1** consumption. || *pl.* **2** COM. goods tax.

consunción *s.f.* MED. consumption.

consuno (de) *adv.* with one accord.

consuntivo, -a *adj.* MED. consumptive.

consustancial *adj.* REL. consubstantial.

contabilidad *s.f.* **1** book-keeping. **2** accountancy (profesión). **3** (Am.) accounting department (de una empresa).

contabilizar *v.t.* to register in the accounts.

contable *adj.* **1** countable. || *s.m.* y *f.* **2** book-keeper (oficinista).

contactar *v.i.* to get in touch: *contáctame cuando llegues = get in touch with me when you arrive.*

contacto *s.m.* **1** contact. **2** ELEC. switch.

contado, -a *adj.* **1** scarce (escaso). **2** fixed (determinado). || **3 al —,** cash.

contador, -a *adj.* **1** counter. || *s.m.* **2** COM. book-keeper. **3** meter (del agua). **4** counter (mostrador).

contadero, -a *adj.* countable.

contaduría *s.f.* **1** accountancy (profesión). **2** accountant's office. **3** box office (espectáculo). **4** (Am.) pawnbroker's shop (para empeñar).

contagiar *v.t.* **1** to transmit (enfermedad). || *v.pron.* **2** to become infected.

contagio *s.m.* MED. contagion.

contagioso, -a *adj.* contagious.

container *s.m.* container (para transportar).

contaminación *s.f.* **1** contamination. **2** pollution (medio ambiente).

contaminar *v.t.* **1** to contaminate (infección). **2** to soil (ensuciar). **3** (fig.) to corrupt. || *v.pron.* **4** to become contaminated.

contante *adj.* **1** cash. || **2 — y sonante,** cash down.

contar *v.t.* **1** to count (enumerar). **2** to tell (narrar). **3** to consider (tener cierta opinión de). || **4 — con,** to have. **5** to rely on (poder disponer de).

contemplación *s.f.* **1** contemplation. || *pl.* **2** ceremony, indulgence.

contemplar *v.t.* **1** to contemplate (mirar). **2** to be indulgent with (complacer mucho). || *v.i.* **3** REL. to meditate.

contemplativo, -a *adj.* **1** REL. contemplative. **2** gratifying (complaciente).

contemporaneidad *s.f.* contemporaneity.

contemporáneo, -a *adj.* contemporary.

contemporización *s.f.* playing for time.

contemporizador, -a *adj.* easy to please.

contemporizar *v.i.* to compromize readily.

contención *s.f.* **1** containing. **2** MIL. containment. **3** DER. litigation. **4** struggle (contienda).

contencioso, -a *adj.* **1** contentious (persona). **2** DER. litigious. || **3 — administrativo,** public administration litigation.

contender *v.i.* **1** to contend. **2** MIL. to fight.

contenedor *s.m.* container (para transportar).

contener *v.t.* **1** to contain. **2** to repress (emociones).

contenido, -a *adj.* **1** contained. **2** (fig.) temperate. || *s.m.* **3** content.

contentadizo, -a *adj.* pleased: *bien contentadizo = easily pleased.*

contentamiento *s.m.* contentment.

contentar *v.t.* **1** to satisfy. **2** to make happy (alegrar). || *v.pron.* **3** to be contented.

contento, -a *adj.* **1** content (satisfecho). **2** happy (feliz). || *s.m.* **3** happiness. || **4 estar tan — como unas castañuelas,** (fam.) to be as pleased as Punch. **5 no caber uno de —,** to be over the moon.

contera *s.f.* **1** ferrule (de bastón). **2** (fig.) conclusion. **3** (fam.) pet word (en una conversación). || **4 por —,** to cap it all.

contertulio *s.m.* fellow group member.

contestación *s.f.* **1** reply. **2** argument (disputa).

contestar *v.t.* **1** to answer (a una pregunta, al teléfono). **2** to reply (a una persona). || *v.i.* **3** to confirm (comprobar).

contexto *s.m.* **1** LIT. context. **2** TEC. web.

contextura *s.f.* **1** contexture (estructura). **2** ANAT. constitution.

contienda *s.f.* **1** fight. **2** argument (discusión).

contigo *pron.* with you.

contiguidad *s.f.* nearness.

contiguo, -a *adj.* adjacent.

continencia *s.f.* **1** continence (pasiones). **2** self-denial (sexual). **3** abstinence. **4** chastity (castidad). **5** graceful curtsy in dancing.

continental *adj.* continental.

continente *adj.* **1** continent. || *s.m.* **2** GEOG. continent. **3** container (contenedor). **4** (fig.) bearing (compostura).

contingencia *s.f.* **1** contingency. **2** risk (riesgo).

contingente *adj.* **1** contingent. || *s.m.* **2** contingency. **3** MIL. contingent. **4** COM. quota (contribución proporcional).

continuación *s.f.* continuation.

continuamente *adv.* **1** continuously. **2** always: *me da continuamente la misma contestación = he always gives me the same reply.*

continuar *v.t.* 1 to continue. || *v.i.* 2 to go on. || *v.pron.* 3 to extend.
continuativo, -a *adj.* continuing.
continuidad *s.f.* 1 continuity. || 2 **solución de –,** interruption.
continuismo *s.m.* (Am.) continuism.
continuo, -a *adj.* 1 continuous. 2 continual (ininterrumpido). || 3 **de –,** continually.
contonearse *v.r.* to walk with a waggle.
contorno *s.m.* 1 GEOG. contour. 2 perimeter (cerco).
contorsión *s.f.* ANAT. contortion.
contorsionarse *v.pron.* to writhe about.
contorsionista *s.m.* y *f.* contortionist (circo).
contra *prep.* 1 against. 2 facing (enfrente). || *s.f.* 3 difficulty. || *s.m.* 4 opposing view (concepto opuesto). || 5 **hacer, llevar la –,** to oppose.
contraalmirante *s.m.* MAR. rear admiral.
contraataque *s.m.* 1 MIL. counter-attack. || *pl.* 2 defensive lines.
contrabajo *s.m.* 1 MUS. double pass. 2 double bass player (músico). 3 deep bass (cantor).
contrabandista *s.m.* y *f.* smuggler.
contrabando *s.m.* 1 smuggling (acción). 2 contraband (mercancías ilegales). || 3 **– de armas,** gun-running.
contrabarrera *s.f.* second barrier (plaza de toros).
contracción *s.f.* contraction.
contractibilidad *s.f.* contractibility.
contráctil *adj.* contractile (la fibra de los músculos).
contractual *adj.* contractual.
contradecir *v.t.* 1 to contradict. || *v.pron.* 2 to contradict oneself.
contradicción *s.f.* 1 contradiction. || 2 **en –,** incompatible. 3 **tener espíritu de –,** to argue for the sake of it.
contradictorio, -a *adj.* contradictory.
contraer *v.t.* 1 to contract. 2 to catch (enfermedad). || *v.pron.* 3 to contract (los músculos). 4 to limit oneself (limitarse).
contrafuero *s.m.* DER. regional law infraction.
contrafuerte *s.m.* 1 ARCH. buttress. 2 wing wall (muelle). 3 counter (zapato). 4 GEOG. spur.
contrahecho, -a *adj.* ANAT. deformed.
contrahierba *s.f.* (Am.) antidote (planta).
contrahuella *s.f.* riser.
contraindicación *s.f.* MED. side effects.
contralisio *s.m.* counter trade wind (de la alta atmósfera).
contralmirante *s.m.* MAR. rear admiral.
contralto *s.m.* 1 MUS. counter tenor. || *s.f.* 2 MUS. contralto.
contraluz *s.f.* 1 view facing the light. || 2 **a –,** against the light.
contramaestre *s.m.* 1 TEC. foreman. 2 MAR. boatswain. 3 (Am.) skilled worker.
contramarca *s.f.* (Am.) second branding (ganadería).
contraofensiva *s.f.* MIL. counter-offensive.
contraorden *s.f.* counter-order.
contraparte *s.f.* (Am.) other party (trámites judiciales).
contrapartida *s.f.* 1 COM. correcting entry (contabilidad). 2 (fig.) compensation. || 3 **como – de,** as compensation for.
contrapelo (a) *adv.* (fig.) against the grain.
contrapesar *v.t.* 1 to counterbalance. 2 (fig.) to offset.
contrapeso *s.m.* 1 counterweight (construcción). 2 (fig.) compensation. 3 balancing pole (de un volatinero).
contraponer *v.t.* 1 to compare (una cosa con otra). 2 to set against each other (oponer). || *v.pron.* 3 to be facing (una cosa a otra).
contraposición *s.f.* 1 contrasting. || 2 **en – a,** in contrast with.
contraproducente *adj.* counter-productive.
contrapuerta *s.f.* 1 double door. 2 (Am.) touting (reventa de entradas).
contrapuesto, -a *adj.* opposed.
contrapunto *s.m.* 1 MUS. counterpoint. 2 (Am.) MUS. improvising.
contrariamente *adv.* differently, contrary: *ellos han actuado contrariamente a lo que habían prometido = they have acted contrary to their promise.*
contrariar *v.t.* 1 to oppose. 2 to upset (alterar). 3 to hinder (estorbar).
contrariedad *s.f.* 1 opposition. 2 setback (contratiempo). 3 nuisance (disgusto).
contrario, -a *adj.* 1 opposite. || *s.m.* y *f.* 2 enemy (enemigo). || 3 **al/por el –,** on the contrary. 4 **en –,** against. 5 **llevar la contraria,** to oppose.
contrarreforma *s.f.* REL. Counter-Reformation.
contrarrestar *v.t.* 1 to counter (resistir). 2 to balance (compensar).
contrasentido *s.m.* 1 inexactitude (equivocación). 2 blunder (disparate).
contraseña *s.f.* 1 MIL. password. 2 countersign (firma).
contrastable *adj.* 1 contrastable. 2 resistible (resistible). 3 assayable (metales).
contrastar *v.t.* 1 to resist. 2 to assay (metales preciosos). || *v.i.* 3 to form a contrast.
contraste *s.m.* 1 contrast. 2 assay (metales). 3 check (verificación). 4 weights and measures officer (almotacén).
contrata *s.f.* 1 agreement (para realizar una obra). 2 written agreement.
contratación *s.f.* 1 contracting. 2 COM. dealings.
contratante *s.m.* 1 COM. contractor. 2 LEG. contracting party.
contratar *v.t.* 1 to negotiate for (productos). 2 to contract (trabajador). 3 DEP. to sign up.
contratiempo *s.m.* setback (obstáculo).
contratista *s.m.* y *f.* contractor (de una obra).
contrato *s.m.* contract.
contravenir *v.t.* to contravene (una ley).
contraventana *s.f.* ARCH. window shutter.
contrayente *s.m.* y *f.* contracting party (de un matrimonio).
contribución *s.f.* 1 contribution. 2 FIN. tax. || *s.pl.* 3 taxation. || 4 **– directa,** direct taxation. 5 **– municipal,** rates.
contribuir *v.t.* 1 to pay (impuestos). 2 to contribute (ofrecer dinero).
contribuyente *adj.* 1 contributing. || *s.m.* y *f.* 2 contributor. 3 FIN. taxpayer.
contrición *s.f.* REL. contrition.
contrincante *s.m.* y *f.* rival (competidor).
contristar *v.t.* 1 to make sad. || *v.pron.* 2 to become sad.
contrito, -a *adj.* 1 REL. contrite. 2 sad (triste).
control *s.m.* 1 control. | 2 **– de natalidad,** birth control.
controlar *v.t.* 1 to control. 2 to check (examinar). 3 to keep in check (dominar).
controversia *s.f.* controversy.
controvertible *adj.* 1 debatable (debatible). 2 controversial (polémico).
controvertir *v.i.* 1 to question (disputar). || *v.i.* 2 to argue (discutir).
contubernio *s.m.* 1 conspiracy (conjuración). 2 cohabitation (ilícita). 3 POL. body of conspirators.
contumacia *s.f.* 1 stubbornness. 2 DER. contumacy.
contumaz *adj.* 1 stubborn (terco). 2 MED. infected. || *s.m.* y *f.* 3 rebel.
contundente *adj.* 1 crushing (un golpe). 2 forceful (argumento).
contundir *v.t.* 1 to pound (golpear). 2 to bruise (magullar).
conturbar *v.t.* 1 to trouble. || *v.pron.* 2 to be troubled.
contusión *s.f.* MED. bruise.
contuso, -a *adj.* bruised.
conturbación *s.f.* 1 uneasiness (inquietud). 2 dismay (consternación).
convalecencia *s.f.* MED. convalescence.
convalecer *v.i.* 1 to convalesce. || *v.pron.* 2 to get better.
convaleciente *adj.* convalescent.
convalidación *s.f.* 1 recognition (aceptación). 2 validation (estudios).
convalidar *v.t.* to validate (confirmar).
convección *s.f.* QUIM. convection.
convecino, -a *adj.* 1 neighbouring. || *s.m.* 2 close neighbour.
convencer *v.t.* 1 to convince. || *v.pron.* 2 to be persuaded.
convencimiento *s.m.* 1 persuasion. 2 firm belief (convicción).
convención *s.f.* convention (acuerdo, asamblea y conformidad).
convencional *adj.* 1 conventional. || *s.m.* 2 member of a convention.
convencionalismo *s.m.* conventionalism.
convenible *adj.* 1 easy-going (persona). 2 reasonable (condición).
conveniencia *s.f.* 1 usefulness (utilidad). 2 conformity (de caracteres). 3 agreement (convenio). 4 placing (de un criado). || *s.pl.* 5 COM. property.
conveniente *adj.* 1 useful (provechoso). 2 appropriate (apropiado).
convenientemente *adv.* conveniently.
convenio *s.m.* 1 agreement. || 2 **– colectivo,** collective bargaining agreement (relaciones laborales).
convenir *v.i.* 1 to agree. 2 to suit (ser útil). 3 to be important: *conviene actuar cuanto antes = it is important to act immediately.* 4 to come together (juntarse).

convento *s.m.* **1** monastery (de monjes). **2** convent (de monjas). **3** (Am.) priest's house.
conventual *adj.* **1** REL. conventual. || *s.m.* **2** monk. || *s.f.* **3** nun.
conventualidad *s.f.* REL. conventual existence.
convergencia *s.f.* **1** convergence. **2** (fig.) organized effort. **3** POL. association.
convergente *adj.* convergent.
converger *v.i.* **1** to converge. **2** to concur.
conversable *adj.* easy-going (persona).
conversación *s.f.* **1** conversation. || **2 entablar — con,** to start a conversation with.
conversacional *adj.* conversational (lengua coloquial).
conversar *v.i.* to have a chat.
conversión *s.f.* **1** conversion (en, into). **2** MIL. wheel.
converso, -a *adj.* **1** REL. converted. || *s.m.* y *f.* **2** REL. convert.
convertibilidad *s.f.* ECON. convertibility (dinero).
convertidor *s.m.* MET., ELEC. converter.
convertir *v.t.* **1** to convert. || *v.pron.* **2** to be converted.
convexidad *s.f.* convexness.
convexo, -a *adj.* GEOM. convex.
convicción *s.f.* conviction.
convicto, -a *adj.* **1** DER. convicted. || *s.m.* y *f.* **2** convict (brit.).
convidado, -a *adj.* **1** invited. || *s.m.* y *f.* **2** guest.
convidar *v.t.* **1** to invite (a una persona a beber, comer algo). **2** to be conducive to (incitar). || *v.pron.* **3** to offer one's services.
convincente *adj.* convincing: *una respuesta convincente = a convincing answer.*
convite *s.m.* **1** invitation (a una fiesta). **2** banquet (comida). **3** (Am.) masquerade (mojiganga).
convivencia *s.f.* living together.
convivir *v.i.* to live together (amigablemente).
convocación *s.f.* **1** calling together. **2** convoking (parlamento).
convocar *v.t.* to convoke (a personas o instituciones).
convocatoria *s.f.* **1** summons (a una asamblea, etc.). **2** holding (exámenes).
convoy *s.m.* **1** convoy. **2** train (ferrocarril). **3** cruet stand (vinagreras).
convoyar *v.t.* **1** to escort (escoltar). **2** (Am.) COM. to subsidize. || *v.pron.* **3** (Am.) to plot (confabularse).
convulsión *s.f.* **1** MED. convulsion. **2** tremor (terremoto). **3** POL. disturbance.
convulsionar *v.t.* MED. to cause convulsions.
convulsivo, -a *adj.* MED. convulsive.
convulso, -a *adj.* **1** convulsed (de, with). **2** (fig.) frenzied.
conyugal *adj.* conjugal.
cónyuge *s.m.* y *f.* spouse.
coñac *s.m.* brandy.
cooperación *s.f.* cooperation.
cooperador, -a *adj.* **1** cooperative. || *s.m.* y *f.* **2** cooperator.
cooperar *v.i.* to cooperate (en, in; con, with).
cooperativamente *adv.* cooperatively.
cooperativismo *s.m.* ECON. cooperativism.
cooperativista *s.m.* y *f.* cooperative member.
cooperativo, -a *adj.* cooperative. || *s.f.* **2** cooperative. || **3 — de producción,** worker's cooperative. **4 — de consumo,** cooperative society.
coordinación *s.f.* **1** coordination. **2** ordering (ordenación).
coordenada *s.f.* MAT. coordinate.
coordinado, -a *adj.* **1** coordinated. **2** MIL. combined.
coordinar *v.t.* **1** to coordinate. **2** to combine (esfuerzos).
coordinativo, -a *adj.* coordinating.
copa *s.f.* **1** wine-glass. **2** drink (bebida). **3** top (árbol). **4** crown (sombrero). || *pl.* **5** hearts (naipes).
copal *s.m.* resin (para barniz).
copar *v.t.* **1** MIL. to cut off. **2** (fam.) to romp home (deporte). **3** to stake one's all (apostar).
copear *v.i.* **1** to sell wine. **2** (fam.) to booze.
copec *s.m.* kopeck (moneda rusa).
copela *s.f.* melting pot (crisol).
copelación *s.f.* melting (metales).
copelar *v.t.* to melt down (minerales o metales).
copero *s.m.* **1** drinks cabinet (mueble). **2** HIST. drinks server (persona).
copete *s.m.* **1** quiff (persona). **2** crest (ave). **3** forelock (caballo). **4** head (cerveza). **5** (fig.) haughtiness. **6** (Am.) goshawk. || **7 de alto —,** of aristocratic stock.
copetín *s.m.* (Am.) drink (copita).
copetudo, -a *adj.* **1** crested. **2** (fig.) cocky.
copia *s.f.* **1** copy. **2** abundance (gran cantidad).
copiar *v.t.* **1** to copy (escritos). **2** to imitate (imitar).
copiosamente *adv.* abundantly.
copiosidad *s.f.* abundance.
copioso, -a *adj.* copious.
copista *s.m.* y *f.* copyist.
copla *s.f.* **1** MUS. popular song. **2** LIT. verse. **3** (Am.) TEC. joint (tubería). || *pl.* **4** LIT. verses. || **5 coplas de ciego,** doggerel verse.
coplero *s.m.* **1** popular song writer. **2** (fig.) doggerel poet.
copo *s.m.* **1** snowflake (nieve). **2** ball (algodón). **3** lump (grumo). **4** (fam.) winning hands down (deportes). **5** net (pesca). **6** (Am.) tuft of clouds (nubes).
copón *s.m.* **1** REL. ciborium. **2** (Am.) net (pesca).
copra *s.f.* copra (perfumería).
coproducción *s.f.* joint production (cine).
coprófago, -a *adj.* coprophagous (insectos).
copto, -a *adj.* Coptic (cristiano egipcio).
cópula *s.f.* **1** joining (unión). **2** ARQ. dome. **3** copulation (sexo).
copulativo, -a *adj.* copulative (en especial, verbos y conjunciones).
coque *s.m.* coke (combustible).
coqueta *s.f.* **1** flirt (mujer). **2** dressing table (mueble).
coquetear *v.i.* to flirt (de mujeres).
coqueteo *s.m.* **1** flirtatiousness. **2** flirting (acto).
coquetón, -a *adj.* **1** attractive. || *s.m.* **2** ladykiller (de hombres).
coracero *s.m.* cavalryman (con coraza).
coracha *s.f.* **1** leather bag. || **2 fumar más que una —,** to smoke like a chimney.
coraje *s.m.* **1** courage (valor). **2** anger (ira).
corajina *s.f.* fit of temper.
corajudo, -a *adj.* **1** (fam.) short-tempered. **2** daring (valiente).
coral *s.m.* **1** ZOOL. coral. **2** coral snake (serpiente). || *s.f.* **3** MUS. chorale. || *adj.* **4** MUS. choral.
coralino, -a *adj.* BOT. coral.
corambre *s.f.* **1** skins (conjunto de cueros). **2** wineskin (bota).
coraza *s.f.* **1** breastplate (armadura). **2** ZOOL. shell. **3** MAR. armour-plating.
corazón *s.m.* **1** MED. heart. **2** spirit (ánimo). **3** BOT. core. || **4 buen —,** kindness. **5 mal —,** cruelty. **6 con el — en la mano,** with one's heart on one's sleeve. **7 decirle a uno el — de una cosa,** to feel something in one's bones. **8 encogérsele a uno el —,** to feel one's heart shrink. **9 todo —,** all heart (persona generosa).
corazonada *s.f.* **1** rush of blood (impulso). **2** (fam.) chitterlings (asadura).
corbata *s.f.* **1** tie (prenda de vestir). **2** pendant (bandera).
corbatín *s.m.* bow tie (pajarita).
corbeta *s.f.* MAR. corvette.
corcel *s.m.* charger (caballo).
corcova *s.f.* **1** hump (joroba). **2** (Am.) all night party.
corcovado, -a *adj.* hunchbacked.
corcovar *v.t.* to make curved.
corcoveta *s.m.* y *f.* hunchback.
corcovo *s.m.* **1** prance (salto de algunos animales). **2** (fam.) distorsion.
corchar *v.t.* **1** MAR. to splice. **2** to cork (botellas).
corchea *s.f.* MUS. quaver.
corchete *s.m.* **1** hook (zapato). || *s.m.pl.* **2** square brackets.
corcho *s.m.* cork (árbol y material).
cordada *s.f.* roped group (alpinismo).
cordelería *s.f.* **1** ropemaking (oficio). **2** ropemaker's (tienda). **3** ropes (conjunto de cordeles).
cordelero *s.m.* ropemaker.
cordado, -a *adj.* notochordal (columna vertebral).
cordal *adj.* **1** wisdom (muela). || *s.m.* **2** MUS. tailpiece (ceja). **3** MUS. string fastener (ceja inferior).
cordel *s.m.* **1** cord (cuerda). **2** five steps (medida). **3** cattle track (ganadería trashumante). || **4 a —,** in a straight line.
cordero *s.m.* **1** lamb. **2** (fig.) angel. **3** lambskin (piel). || **4 — de Dios,** Lamb of God (Jesucristo).
cordial *adj.* **1** cordial (afectuoso). **2** MED. tonic. || *s.m.* **3** MED. tonic.
cordialidad *s.f.* **1** friendliness (afabilidad). **2** genuineness (sinceridad).
cordiforme *adj.* heart-shaped.

cordillera *s.f.* 1 mountain range. || 2 (Am.) **por –,** from one to the other.
cordobán *s.m.* goatskin leather (de Córdoba).
cordón *s.m.* 1 string (cuerda pequeña). 2 cordon (p.ej., de policía). 3 (Am.) kerb (acera). || 4 – **umbilical,** umbilical cord.
cordonería *s.f.* 1 stringmaking (oficio). 2 stringmaker's (tienda). 3 strings (conjunto de cordones).
cordoncillo *s.m.* 1 braid (coser). 2 legend (moneda).
cordura *s.f.* 1 sensibleness. || 2 **con –,** sensibly.
corear *v.t.* 1 to sing together (cantar). 2 to cheer (aprobar). 3 to compose choral music (componer).
coreo *s.m.* LIT. trochee.
coreografía *s.f.* choreography (baile).
coreográfico, -a *adj.* choreographic.
coreógrafo, -a *s.m.* y *f.* choreographer (baile).
coriáceo, -a *adj.* leathery.
corifeo *s.m.* 1 HIST. coryphaeus. 2 main character (ópera). 3 POL. leader.
corindón *s.m.* MIN. corundum.
corista *s.m.* y *f.* 1 MUS. member of a choir. || *s.m.* 2 REL. chorister.
corito, -a *adj.* 1 naked (desnudo). 2 shy (tímido). || *s.m.* 3 transporter (industria vinícola).
corladura *s.f.* metal polish (barniz).
corlear *v.t.* TEC. to polish up (objeto plateado).
corma *s.f.* 1 fetters (cepo). 2 (fig.) nuisance.
cornada *s.f.* goring (tauromaquia, etc.).
cornamenta *s.f.* ZOOL. horns.
cornamusa *s.f.* 1 MUS. bagpipe. 2 MAR. mooring device. 3 hunting horn (caza al zorro, etc.).
corneja *s.f.* ORN. rook.
córneo, -a *adj.* 1 horny (de cuerno). || *s.f.* 2 ANAT. cornea.
córner *s.m.* DEP. corner (fútbol).
corneta *s.f.* 1 MUS. cornet. 2 burgee (bandera). || *s.m.* 3 MUS. cornet player.
cornete *s.m.* 1 ZOOL. small horn. || *s.m.pl.* 2 ANAT. nostril walls.
cornetín *s.m.* 1 MUS. tenor horn. 2 MUS. tenor horn player (persona).
corneto *adj.* (Am.) knock-kneed (patizambo).
cornezuelo *s.m.* 1 BOT. ergot. 2 olive (aceituna).
cornijal *s.m.* corner (ángulo).
cornisa *s.f.* 1 eaves (casa). 2 ledge (alpinismo). 3 cornice (arte).
cornisamiento *s.m.* ARQ. entablature.
cornucopia *s.f.* 1 horn of plenty (como símbolo de abundancia). 2 ornamental mirror (espejo).
cornudo, -a *adj.* 1 ZOOL. horned. || *s.m.* 2 cuckold (marido con mujer infiel).
cornúpeta *adj.* 1 butting (que embiste con los cuernos). || *s.m.* (fam.) bull.
coro *s.m.* 1 MUS. choir (cantantes). 2 chorus (canción). 3 ARQ. choir. 4 REL. chant. 5 MET. northwest wind. || 6 **de –,** by heart. 7 **hacer –,** to echo (las palabras de alguien).
corocha *s.f.* 1 frock coat (casaca). 2 ZOOL. beetle larva.
corografía *s.f.* GEOG. toponymy.
coroideo *s.m.* OPT. chorioid.
corola *s.f.* corolla.
corolario *s.m.* corollary (inferencia).
corona *s.f.* 1 crown (de monarca). 2 ASTR. corona. 3 REL. tonsure. 4 garland (de flores). || 5 – **funeraria,** wreath.
coronación *s.f.* 1 coronation (monarca). 2 (fig.) culmination.
coronamiento *s.m.* 1 completion (de una obra). 2 ARQ. top.
coronar *v.t.* 1 to crown (un rey). 2 ARQ. to top. 3 to complete (una obra). 4 to queen (ajedrez, damas). 5 (Am. y fam.) to make a cuckold of (poner los cuernos).
coronaria *s.f.* 1 TEC. second hand wheel (reloj). 2 BOT. carnation.
coronario, -a *adj.* 1 heart-shaped (forma de corazón). 2 ANAT. coronary.
coronel *s.m.* MIL. colonel.
coronilla *s.f.* 1 crown (cabeza). || 2 **andar de –,** to be hard at it. 3 **estar hasta la –,** to be cheesed off.
corpiño *s.m.* 1 bodice. 2 (Am.) bra (sostén).
corporación *s.f.* corporation (asociación; compañía).
corporal *adj.* 1 body. || *s.m.pl.* 2 REL. corporal.
corporativismo *s.m.* corporateness.
corporativo, -a *adj.* corporate.
corpóreo, -a *adj.* 1 corporeal (que tiene cuerpo). 2 body (corporal).
corpulencia *s.f.* largeness (de un cuerpo).
corpus *s.m.* 1 LIT. corpus. || 2 **día del Corpus,** Corpus Christi.
corpuscular *adj.* ANAT. corpuscular.
corpúsculo *s.m.* FIS. corpuscle.
corral *s.m.* 1 pen (animales). 2 open-air theatre. || 3 – **de vacas,** ramshackle house.
correa *s.f.* 1 strap (de cuero). 2 stretch (elasticidad). || *pl.* 3 duster (quitapolvos). || 4 **tener –,** (fam.) to be long-suffering.
correaje *s.m.* 1 strap. 2 TEC. belting system.
correcaminos *s.m.* ORN. roadrunner (tipo de cuclillo).
corrección *s.f.* 1 correction. 2 punishment (reprensión). 3 punishment centre (lugar de castigo). || 4 – **de pruebas,** proof-reading.
correccional *adj.* 1 corrective. || *s.m.* 2 reformatory (prisión).
correctamente *adv.* correctly.
correctivo, -a *adj.* 1 corrective. || *s.m.* 2 punishment (castigo).
correcto, -a *adj.* 1 correct (sin errores). 2 well-mannered (educado).
corrector, -ora *adj.* 1 correcting. || *s.m.* y *f.* 2 proofreader (tipografía).
corredera *s.f.* 1 TEC. track. 2 MAR. log. 3 TEC. sluice valve. 4 upper millstone (de molino). 5 ZOOL. cockroach. || 6 **puerta de –,** sliding door.
corredor, -a *adj.* 1 running. || *s.m.* 2 DEP. runner. 3 corridor (pasillo). 4 COM. agent. 5 MIL. scout.
correduría *s.f.* 1 COM. brokerage. 2 commission (de corredor).
corregidor, -a *adj.* 1 correcting. || *s.m.* 2 HIST. chief magistrate. 3 HIST. mayor (alcalde).
corregir *v.t.* 1 to correct (un trabajo mal hecho). 2 to punish (reprender). || *v.pron.* 3 (fam.) to turn over a new leaf.
correlación *s.f.* MAT., etc. correlation.
corredizo, -a *adj.* 1 sliding (puerta). 2 slip (nudo).
correlacionar *v.t.* to correlate.
correlativamente *adv.* correlatively.
correlativo, -a *adj.* correlative.
correligionario *s.m.* 1 REL. co-religionist. 2 POL. fellow supporter.
correlón, -a *adj.* 1 fast. || *s.m.* 2 (Am.) (fam.) chicken.
correo *s.m.* 1 post. 2 (Am.) mail. 3 HIST. courier (persona). || *pl.* 4 post office (oficina). || 5 **echar al –,** to post. 6 **a vuelta de –,** by return of post. 7 – **aéreo,** airmail. 8 – **certificado,** registered post.
correoso, -a *adj.* tough and flexible (como el cuero).
correr *v.i.* 1 to run. 2 to go (extenderse). 3 to pass (tiempo). 4 to blow (viento). 5 to be payable (devengarse una paga). 6 to be valid (una moneda). || *v.t.* 7 to cover (recorrer). 8 to chase (perseguir, a un animal). 9 to fight (tauromaquia). 10 to draw (cortinas). 11 to shoot (pestillo). 12 to embarrass (avergonzar). || 13 **¡corre!,** hurry up! 14 **¡no corras tanto!,** not so fast! 15 **correrla,** (fam.) to live it up. 16 – **con,** to be responsible for. 17 **a todo –,** at full speed.
correría *s.f.* 1 MIL. raid. 2 (fam.) whirlwind visit.
correspondencia *s.f.* 1 correspondence. 2 contact (enlaces). 3 communication (transporte). 4 reciprocation (armonía). 5 meaning (una palabra en dos idiomas).
corresponder *v.i.* 1 to correspond. 2 to concern (incumbir). 3 to repay (un favor). || *v.pron.* 4 to correspond (cartas).
correspondiente *adj.* 1 corresponding. 2 appropriate (apropiado). 3 respective (respectivo).
corresponsal *s.m.* y *f.* 1 correspondent (periodista). 2 representative (agente).
corresponsalía *s.f.* post of reporter (periódico).
corretaje *s.m.* 1 COM. brokerage. 2 commission (comisión).
corretear *v.i.* 1 (fam.) to roam the streets (errar). 2 to run about (jugando). 3 (Am.) to follow (perseguir). 4 (Am.) to frighten away (ahuyentar).
correve(i)dile *s.m.* y *f.* (fam.) gossiper.
corrida *s.f.* 1 run. 2 bullfight (tauromaquia). 3 (Am.) (fam.) rave-up. || 4 **de –,** straight off.
corrido, -a *adj.* 1 extra (que excede peso o cantidad): *un kilo corrido = a bit over a kilo.* 2 ashamed (avergonzado). 3 experienced (experimentado). 5 ARCH. adjoining. 6 (Am.) complete (acabado). || *s.m.* 7 shed (cobertizo). 8 ballad (romance). 9 (Am.) fugitive (fugitivo).
corriente *adj.* 1 running (agua). 2 usual (normal). 3 present (fecha). || *s.f.* 4 current (agua, electricidad, opinión). || 5

— alterna, ELEC. alternating current. **6 — continua,** ELEC. continuous current. **7 al —,** right on time. **8 estar al —,** to be au fait. **9 — y moliente,** run-of-the-mill.
corrientemente *adv.* **1** normally. **2** easily (fácilmente).
corrillo *s.m.* small group (personas).
corrimiento *s.m.* **1** running (derretimiento). **2** sliding (tierra). **3** (fig.) bashfulness (vergüenza). **4** (Am.) MED. rheumatism.
corro *s.m.* **1** group (personas). **2** ring (círculo). **3** AGR. plot. || **4 formar — aparte,** (fig.) to be on the other side.
corroboración *s.f.* corroboration.
corroborar *v.t.* **1** to corroborate (ratificar). **2** to fortify (fortificar).
corroer *v.t.* **1** to corrode (destruir, un metal). **2** (fig.) to eat away: *le corroe la envidia = he's being eaten away by jealousy.*
corromper *v.t.* **1** to rot (descomponer). **2** (fig.) to corrupt. **3** to seduce (a una mujer). **4** (fam. y fig.) to bother. || *v.i.* **5** to smell bad. || *v.pron.* **6** to go bad.
corrosión *s.f.* **1** corrosion (metales). **2** AGR. erosión.
corrosivo, -a *adj.* corrosive.
corrupción *s.f.* **1** rottenness (putrefacción). **2** (fig.) corruption.
corruptela *s.f.* **1** corruption. **2** corrupt practice (abuso).
corruptible *adj.* **1** corruptible (persona). **2** perishable (fruta, etc.).
corruptibilidad *s.f.* **1** corruptibility (persona). **2** perishableness (alimentos).
corruptor, -ora *adj.* **1** corrupting. || *s.m.* **2** corrupter.
corrusco *s.m.* hard crust (pan).
corsario *s.m.* **1** MAR. privateer. **2** pirate (persona).
corsé *s.m.* **1** corset (prenda de mujer). || **2 — ortopédico,** MED. straitjacket.
corsetería *s.f.* corsetier's (tienda).
corso *s.m.* **1** MAR. privateering. **2** (Am.) cavalcade.
corso, -a *adj/s.m.* y *f.* Corsican.
cortacircuitos *s.m.* ELEC. circuit breaker.
cortadera *s.f.* **1** chisel (para cortar hierro). **2** blade (apicultura).
cortadillo *s.m.* short tumbler (vaso).
cortado, -a *adj.* **1** cut. **2** disjointed (estilo). **3** right (ajustado). **4** (Am.) (fam.) broke. || *s.m.* **5** coffee with a little milk. **6** TEC. cutting.
cortador, -ora *adj.* **1** cutting. || *s.m.* **2** butcher (carnicero). **3** incisor (odontología). **4** TEC. cutter.
cortadura *s.f.* **1** cut (herida). **2** GEOG. narrow path. **3** cutting (periódico). || *pl.* **4** parings (desperdicios).
cortafrío(s) *s.m.* TEC. cold chisel.
cortafuego *s.m.* fire-break.
cortante *adj.* **1** cutting. || *s.m.* **2** butcher's knife.
cortapisa *s.f.pl.* **1** restrictions. || **2 sin cortapisas,** with no limitations.
cortaplumas *s.m.* penknife (navaja pequeña).
cortar *v.t.* **1** to cut. **2** to interrupt (interrumpir). **3** to leave out (suprimir). **4** to cut through (hender). **5** to water down (suavizar un líquido). **6** to go right through (viento frío). || *v.pron.* **7** to be lost for words (no poder hablar por turbación). **8** to become chapped (las manos por el frío). **9** to turn sour (leche). || **10 ¡corta!,** come off it!
corte *s.m.* **1** cut. **2** cutting (acto). **3** cutting edge (filo). **4** tailoring (confección). **5** piece (tela para hacer una prenda). **6** ARQ. section. **7** felling (árboles). **8** ELEC. failure. || *s.f.* **9** court (residencia real). **10** retinue (séquito). **11** AGR. farmyard. || *s.pl.* **12** POL. Spanish parliament. || **13 — celestial,** heaven. **14 hacer la —,** to woo. **15 Corte Suprema,** Supreme Court.
cortejar *v.t.* **1** (form.) to pay court to. **2** to flatter (lisonjear).
cortejo *s.m.* **1** retinue (séquito). **2** (form.) paying court to. **3** flattery.
cortés *adj.* polite.
cortesanía *s.f.* common courtesy.
cortesano, -a *adj.* **1** courtly (de la corte). **2** polite. || *s.m.* y *f.* **3** courtier.
cortesía *s.f.* **1** courtesy. **2** grace (merced). **3** present (regalo). **4** reward (caza).
cortésmente *adv.* politely.
corteza *s.f.* **1** bark (árbol). **2** peel (fruta). **3** rind (queso). **4** crust (pan). **5** (fig. y fam.) coarseness (de una persona).
cortical *adj.* cortical (de la corteza).
cortijero *s.m.* squire.
cortijo *s.m.* farmhouse (Andalucía y Extremadura).
cortina *s.f.* **1** curtain. **2** (fig.) screen. **3** inner wall (caballería). || **4 — de hierro,** iron curtain. **5 correr la —,** (fig.) to lift the veil.
cortinaje *s.m.* curtaining.
cortinal *s.m.* kitchen garden (huerta).
cortisona *s.f.* MED. cortisone.
corto, -a *adj.* **1** short. **2** scanty (escaso). **3** shy (tímido). **4** (fig.) slow (torpe). **5** tongue-tied (falto de palabras). || *s.m.* **6** short film (cine). || *s.f.* **7** felling (árboles). || **8 quedarse —,** to fall short (no calcular bien). **9 — de vista,** short-sighted. **10 — de oído,** hard of hearing. **11 a la corta,** in the short term.
cortocircuito *s.m.* **1** ELEC. short-circuit. || **2 poner en —,** to short-circuit.
cortometraje *s.m.* short film (cine).
coruja *s.f.* **1** owl (lechuza). **2** ace of diamonds (naipes).
corva *s.f.* MED. popliteal space.
corvadura *s.f.* **1** bend (dobladura). **2** curvature (p.ej., de la tierra). **3** wreath (barandilla).
corvar *v.t.* to bend (encorvar).
corvejón *s.m.* **1** hock (caballo). **2** ORN. green cormorant.
corveta *s.f.* courbette (caballería).
corvo, -a *adj.* **1** curved. || *s.m.* **2** hook.
corzo *s.m.* o *f.* ZOOL. roe deer.
corzuelo *s.m.* chaffy corn (trigo).
cosa *s.f.* **1** thing. **2** affair (asunto). **3** fancy (idea). || **4 no ser — del otro jueves,** to be nothing out of the ordinary. **5 como si tal —,** as if nothing special had happened. **6 — de,** about (aproximadamente). **7 las cosas de palacio van despacio,** the mills of God grind slowly.
cosaco *adj.* y *s.m.* **1** Cossack. || **2 beber como un —,** (fig. y fam.) to drink like a fish.
coscón, -a *adj.* y *s.m.* (desp.) clever.
coscorrón *s.m.* **1** bump on the head. **2** (fig.) let-down.
cosecante *s.f.* MAT. cosine.
cosecha *s.f.* **1** AGR. harvest. **2** harvesting (acto). || **3 de su propia —,** (fig.) of one's own invention.
cosechadora *s.f.* AGR. combine-harvester.
cosechar *v.t.* **1** AGR. to harvest (recolectar). **2** to grow (cultivar). **3** (fig.) to glean (información).
cosechero *s.m.* **1** harvester. **2** picker (uvas).
coselete *s.m.* **1** MIL. leather cuirass. **2** ZOOL. thorax (insecto).
coseno *s.m.* MAT. cosine.
coser *v.t.* **1** to sew. **2** to join (unir). || **3 — y cantar,** (fam.) it's a piece of cake.
cosido, -a *adj.* **1** sewn. || *s.m.* **2** embroidery.
cosmético *adj.* y *s.m.* cosmetic.
cósmico, -a *adj.* **1** cosmic. || **2 rayos cósmicos,** cosmic rays.
cosmogonía *s.f.* ASTR. cosmogony.
cosmografía *s.f.* ASTR. cosmography.
cosmología *s.f.* ASTR. cosmology.
cosmonauta *s.m.* o *f.* ASTR. cosmonaut.
cosmopolita *adj./s.m.* y *f.* cosmopolitan.
cosmopolitismo *s.m.* POL. cosmopoliticism.
cosmos *s.m.* cosmos.
coso *s.m.* **1** arena. **2** bullring (tauromaquia). **3** ZOOL. woodworm (carcoma).
cosque *s.m.* (fam.) bump on the head.
cosquillas *s.f.pl.* **1** ticklishness. || **2 buscar a alguien las —,** (fig.) to get someone irritated. **3 hacerle a uno — una cosa,** (fig.) to tickle someone's curiosity.
cosquillear *v.t.* to tickle.
cosquilleo *s.m.* tickling sensation.
cosquilloso, -a *adj.* **1** ticklish. **2** (fig.) oversensitive.
costa *s.f.* **1** FIN. cost. **2** GEOG. coast. || *pl.* **3** DER. costs. || **4 a toda —,** at any price.
costado *s.m.* **1** ANAT. side. **2** MIL. flank. **3** (Am.) platform (ferrocarril). || *pl.* **4** ancestors (genealogía).
costal *adj.* **1** rib. || *s.m.* **2** sack (saco). **3** rammer (herramienta). **4** (Am.) carpet (alfombra).
costalada o **costalazo** *s.f.* o *s.m.* bad fall.
costanera *s.f.* **1** slope. || *pl.* **2** ARQ. rafters.
costanero, -a *adj.* **1** sloping. **2** MAR. coastal.
costar *v.i.* **1** to cost: *how much does this book cost? = ¿cuánto cuesta este libro?* **2** to be difficult: *he finds it difficult to speak Spanish well = le cuesta hablar bien el español.* || **3 — un ojo de la cara,** (fam.) to cost a fortune. **4 cueste lo que cueste,** whatever the cost.
costarricense o **costarriqueño** *adj./s.m.* y *f.* Costa Rican.
coste *s.m.* price (en dinero).
costear *v.t.* **1** to pay for (pagar). **2** MAR. to skirt the coast. **3** (Am.), AGR. to pasture.
costeño, -a *adj.* coastal.
costero, -a *adj.* **1** coastal. || **2** coastal inhabitant (persona). **3** offcut (madera). **4** wall (horno alto). **5** girder (minería).

costilla *s.f.* 1 ANAT. rib. 2 (fig. y fam.) wife. || *pl.* 3 ANAT. back. || 4 — **verdadera,** true rib. 5 — **falsa,** false rib. 6 **medirle a uno las costillas,** (fam.) to give someone a going-over.
costillar *s.m.* ANAT. ribcage.
costo *s.m.* 1 FIN. cost. 2 (Am.) effort (trabajo). 3 (fam.) dope (droga).
costoso, -a *adj.* 1 dear (caro). 2 costly (error).
costra *s.f.* 1 crust. 2 MED. scab.
costumbre *s.f.* 1 custom. || *pl.* 2 way of life. || 3 **como de —,** as usual.
costumbrismo *s.m.* LIT. mores studies.
costumbrista *adj.* 1 LIT. relating to customs. || *s.m.* y *f.* 2 mores writer.
costura *s.f.* 1 sewing. 2 seam (sutura de dos piezas).
costurera *s.f.* dressmaker.
costurero *s.m.* 1 sewing basket. 2 sewing room (cuarto).
cota *s.f.* 1 GEOG. height. 2 MIL. armour.
cotangente *s.f.* MAT. cotangent.
cotarro *s.m.* 1 doss house (albergue). 2 GEOG. ravine slope. || 3 **alborotarse el —,** (fig. y fam.) to be thrown into disorder. 4 **dirigir el —,** to be the boss.
cotejar *v.t.* to compare and contrast.
cotejo *s.m.* comparing and contrasting (textos).
cotense *s.m.* (Am.) hemp cloth.
cotidianamente *adv.* daily.
cotidiano, -a *adj.* daily.
cotiledón *s.m.* BOT. cotyledon.
cotiledóneo *adj.* BOT. of the cotyledon.
cotilla *s.m.* y *f.* (fam.) gossip.
cotillear *v.i.* to gossip.
cotillón *s.m.* 1 country dance. 2 (Am.) party.
cotización *s.f.* 1 FIN. quotation. 2 subscription (cuota). 3 taxation (impuesto). || 4 — **a plazo,** forward price.
cotizante *s.m.* 1 contributor. 2 taxpayer (contribuyente).
cotizar *v.t.* 1 COM. to quote. 2 to price (valorar). || *v.i.* 3 to pay one's dues.
coto *s.m.* 1 game preserve (caza). 2 boundary stone (hito). 3 (fig.) limit (límite). 4 FIN. fixed price. 5 rubber (bridge, etc.).
cotón *s.m.* 1 printed cotton. 2 (Am.) working shirt (prenda de vestir).
cotorra *s.f.* 1 ZOOL. magpie (urraca). 2 parrot (loro). 3 (fam.) gossip.
cotorrear *v.i.* (fam.) to chinwag.
cotorreo *s.m.* (fam.) chit-chat.
cotorrera *s.f.* 1 (fam.) chatterbox (mujer). 2 ZOOL. magpie.
cotufa *s.f.* 1 sweet (golosina). 2 BOT. tiger nut. || *s.pl.* (Am.) popcorn.
coturno *s.m.* 1 HIST. buskin. || 2 **calzar el —,** (fig. y fam.) to put on airs and graces.
covacha *s.f.* 1 small cave. 2 (Am.) greengrocer's (tienda de productos agrícolas). 3 (Am.) lumber room (trastera).
covachuela *s.f.* 1 (fam.) public office (despacho). 2 (desp.) dive.
cow-boy *s.m.* cowboy.
coxal *adj.* ANAT. hip: *hueso coxal = hip bone.*
coy *s.m.* MAR. hammock.
coyol *s.m.* BOT. palm tree.
coyote *s.m.* 1 ZOOL. prairie wolf. 2 (Am.) COM. dealer.
coyunda *s.f.* 1 tether (de animal). 2 bond (matrimonial). 3 (fig.) oppression (dominio).
coyuntura *s.f.* 1 ANAT. joint. 2 (fig.) opportunity. 3 climate (económico).
coyuntural *adj.* 1 contemporary (situación actual). || 2 **medidas coyunturales,** ad hoc measures.
coz *s.f.* 1 kick (de un animal). 2 (fig.) insult.
crac *s.m.* 1 FIN. bankruptcy. 2 (Am.) star (deporte, etc.).
craneal *adj.* ANAT. skull.
cráneo *s.m.* 1 ANAT. skull. 2 (fam.) nut.
crápula *s.f.* 1 debauchery (libertinaje). 2 drunkenness (borrachera). || *s.m.* 3 philanderer. || *adj.* 4 debauched.
crapuloso, -a *adj.* 1 sottish (borracho). 2 (fig.) loose living (libertino).
craquear *v.t.* QUIM. to crack.
craqueo *s.m.* QUIM. cracking.
crasis *s.f.* GRAM. contraction.
crasitud *s.f.* obesity.
craso, -a *adj.* 1 fat. 2 thick (líquido). 3 (fig.) stupid. 4 (Am.) vulgar.
cráter *s.m.* GEOL. crater.
crátera *s.f.* HIST. urn.
creación *s.f.* creation.
creacionismo *s.m.* FIL. creationism.
creador, -a *adj.* 1 creative. || *s.m.* 2 creator.
crear *v.t.* 1 to create. 2 to invent (idear). 3 to found (fundar).
crecer *v.i.* 1 to grow. || *v.pron.* 2 to become bolder (atreverse a más).
creces *s.f.pl.* 1 increase. || 2 **con —,** more than expected.
crecida *s.f.* 1 rise (río). 2 flood (inundación).
crecido, -a *adj.* 1 big, grown: *tienes el pelo muy crecido = your hair has grown a lot.* 2 grown-up (adulto).
creciente *adj.* 1 growing. 2 waxing (luna). || *s.m.* 3 crescent. || *s.f.* 4 crescent moon (luna). || 5 — **del mar,** high tide.
crecimiento *s.m.* 1 growth (físico). 2 increase (cuantitativo).
credencia *s.f.* REL. credence.
credencial *adj.* 1 certifying. || *s.f.* 2 certifying document (para un puesto de trabajo).
credibilidad *s.f.* credibility.
crediticio, -a *adj.* FIN. credit.
crédito *s.m.* 1 reputation (fama). 2 credit (fe, préstamo). || 3 **dar — a una cosa,** to believe something: *no podía dar crédito a mis ojos = I couldn't believe my eyes.*
credo *s.m.* REL., POL. creed.
credulidad *s.f.* credulousness.
crédulo, -a *adj.* unsuspecting.
creederas *s.f.pl.* (fam.) gullibility.
creencia *s.f.* 1 believing (acto). 2 belief (opinión). 3 REL. faith.
creer *v.t.* 1 to believe. 2 consider (juzgar). || 3 **¡ya lo creo!,** you can say that again! 4 **creérselas,** to have a high opinion of oneself.
creíble *adj.* credible.
crema *s.f.* 1 cream (nata). 2 polish (calzado). 3 GRAM. diaeresis. || 4 **la — de la sociedad,** (fig.) the cream of society. 5 — **dentífrica,** tooth paste.
cremación *s.f.* 1 cremation (personas). 2 incineration (cosas).
cremallera *s.f.* 1 MEC. rack. 2 zip fastener (ropa).
crematística *s.f.* ECON. political economy.
crematístico, -a *adj.* ECON. economic.
crematorio, -a *adj.* 1 crematorial. || *s.m.* 2 crematorium.
crencha *s.f.* 1 parting (raya de pelo). 2 parted hair (pelo a cada lado de la raya).
crepe *s.m.* 1 crepe (tela). 2 crepe-soled (zapatos).
crepitación *s.f.* 1 crackling (leña que arde, etc.). 2 MED. cracking (hueso).
crepitante *adj.* 1 crackling. 2 MED. cracking.
crepitar *v.i.* 1 to crackle (leña). 2 to sizzle (salchichas).
crepuscular *adj.* twilight.
crepúsculo *s.m.* twilight, dusk.
creso *s.m.* 1 (fig.) rich person. 2 (Am.) disinfectant.
crespo, -a *adj.* 1 curly (pelo). 2 tortuous (estilo). 3 sullen (hosco).
crespón *s.m.* crape (tela).
cresta *s.f. crest.*
crestería *s.f.* 1 ARQ. crenellations. 2 HIST. battlements.
crestomatia *s.f.* LIT. anthology.
creta *s.f.* GEOL. chalk.
cretáceo, -a *adj.* GEOL. cretaceous.
cretinismo *s.m.* 1 MED. cretinism. 2 (fig.) stupidity.
cretino, -a *adj.* 1 MED. cretinous. || 2 (fam., desp.) thicky.
cretona *s.f.* cretonne (tela).
creyente *adj.* 1 believing. || *s.m.* 2 believer.
cría *s.f.* 1 breeding (acto). 2 young animal. 3 brood (camada).
criada *s.f.* female servant.
criadero *s.m.* 1 BOT. nursery. 2 chicken farm (aves). 3 fish farm (peces). 4 GEOL. lode.
criadilla *s.f.* 1 ANAT. testicle. 2 BOT. potato. 3 small loaf (pan). || 4 — **de tierra,** truffle.
criado, -a *adj.* 1 brought up. || *s.m.* 2 male servant.
criandera *s.f.* (Am.) nursemaid, wetnurse.
crianza *s.f.* 1 breeding (animales). 2 growing (plantas). || 3 **buena —,** good upbringing.
criar *v.t.* 1 to create (crear). 2 to feed (alimentar). 3 to bring up, to rear (educar): *estos son tiempos difíciles para criar hijos = these are difficult times to rear children in.* || *v.pron.* 4 to grow.
criatura *s.f.* 1 child. 2 (fig.) creature.
criba *s.f.* 1 sieve (utensilio). 2 sifting (acto).
cribado, -a *adj.* 1 sifted. || *s.m.* 2 AGR. sifting. 3 TEC. screening.
cribar *v.t.* 1 AGR. to sift. 2 TEC. to screen.
crimen *s.m.* crime.
criminal *adj.* 1 criminal. || *s.m.* 2 criminal.

criminalidad *s.f.* 1 guiltiness. || **2 índice de –,** crime rate.

criminalista *adj./s.m.* y *f.* DER. criminologist.

criminología *s.f.* criminology.

criminoso, -a *adj.* criminal.

crin *s.f.* 1 bristles. || *pl.* 2 mane (caballo).

crío, -a *s.m.* y *f.* child.

criollo, -a *adj.* 1 Creole. 2 (Am.) native. || *s.m.* y *f.* 3 Spanish descendant.

cripta *s.f.* REL. crypt.

criptografía *s.f.* cryptography.

criptograma *s.m.* cryptogram.

críquet *s.m.* DEP. cricket.

crisálida *s.f.* ENT. chrysalis.

crisantemo *s.m.* BOT. chrysanthemum.

crisis *s.f.* 1 crisis. 2 shortage (escasez). || **3 – nerviosa,** nervous breakdown.

crisma *s.m.* 1 Christmas card (tarjeta). || *s.f.* 2 REL. holy oil. 3 (fam.) nut (cabeza).

crisol *s.m.* 1 melting pot. 2 ladle (caldero del hierro crudo).

crispadura *s.f.* 1 twitching (músculos). 2 shivers (nervios).

crispar *v.t.* 1 to contract (músculos). 2 (fig.) to get on one's nerves: *esa voz le crispaba los nervios = that voice used to get on her nerves.*

cristal *s.m.* 1 glass. 2 pane of glass (de una ventana). 3 (fig.) mirror (espejo). 4 (fig.) water (agua). 5 (Am.) glass (copa).

cristalera *s.f.* 1 glassware cabinet (aparador). 2 shop window (vitrina). 3 glass door (puerta).

cristalería *s.f.* 1 glass making (arte). 2 glassware shop (tienda). 3 glassware (vasos).

cristalino, -a *adj.* 1 glass-like. || *s.m.* 2 ANAT. crystalline lens.

cristalización *s.f.* 1 crystallization. || *s.pl.* 2 crystals.

cristalizar *v.i.* to crystallise.

cristalografía *s.f.* crystallography.

cristianamente *adv.* in a Christian way.

cristianar *v.t.* (fam.) to christen.

cristiandad *s.f.* 1 Christendom (territorio). 2 Christianity (fe).

cristaloide *s.m.* QUIM. crystalloid.

cristianismo *s.m.* 1 Christianity. 2 christening (bautizo).

cristianizar *v.t.* to Christianize.

cristiano, -a *adj.* 1 Christian. || *s.m.* 2 Christian. 3 (fam.) Spanish: *¡háblame en cristiano! = speak to me in Spanish!* 4 (fam.) soul: *anoche no se veía un cristiano por la calle = there was not a soul about last night.*

criterio *s.m.* 1 criterion (regla). 2 judgment (juicio). 3 viewpoint (opinión). || **4 cambiar de –,** to change one's mind.

criticar *v.t.* to criticise.

crítica *s.f.* 1 criticism. 2 gossip (murmuración).

crítico, -a *adj.* 1 critical. || *s.m.* 2 critic.

criticón *adj.* 1 hypercritical. || *s.m.* 2 faultfinder.

croar *v.i.* to croak (rana).

croata *adj.* y *s.* Croatian.

crocodiliano, -a *adj.* 1 crocodilian. || *s.m.pl.* 2 ZOOL. crocodilians.

crochet *s.m.* 1 crochet (labor). 2 hook (boxeo).

cromar *v.t.* to cover with chrome.

cromático, -a *adj.* chromatic (color y sonido).

cromatismo *s.m.* FIS. chromatics.

cromo *s.m.* 1 MET. chrome. 2 picture card (estampa). || **3 estar hecho un –,** (fam.) to be dressed up to the nines.

cromosoma *s.m.* ANAT. chromosome.

crónica *s.f.* 1 HIST. chronicle. 2 report (periodismo).

crónico, -a *adj.* 1 MED. chronic. 2 long-lasting (duradero).

cronicón *s.m.* HIST. short chronicle.

cronista *s.m.* y *f.* 1 HIST. chronicler. 2 columnist (periodismo).

cronología *s.f.* chronology.

cronológico, -a *adj.* chronological.

cronometrador *s.m.* 1 DEP. timekeeper. 2 time-and-motion man (trabajo).

cronometrar *v.t.* to time.

cronometría *s.f.* timing.

cronométrico, -a *adj.* chronometric.

cronómetro *s.m.* 1 TEC. chronometer. 2 DEP. stopwatch.

croquet *s.m.* DEP. croquet.

croqueta *s.f.* croquette (cocina).

croquis *s.m.* sketch (diseño).

cross *s.m.* 1 DEP. cross-country running (actividad). 2 DEP. cross-country race (prueba).

crótalo *s.m.* 1 ZOOL. rattlesnake. || *s.pl.* 2 MUS. castanets.

crotorar *v.i.* to screech (cigüeña).

cruce *s.m.* 1 crossing. 2 crossroads (carretera). 3 MAT. intersection. 4 ZOOL. cross.

crucería *s.f.* 1 ARQ. crosswork. || **2 bóveda de –,** cross vault.

crucero *s.m.* 1 transept (iglesia). 2 crossroads (encrucijada). 3 MAR. cruiser (barco). 4 cruise (viaje en barco). 5 crossbearer (procesión). 6 cruising speed (velocidad).

crucial *adj.* crucial.

crucífera *s.f.* BOT. stonecrop.

crucífero *adj.* (poet.) cross-bearing.

crucificar *v.t.* 1 to crucify. 2 (fig.) to mortify.

crucifijo *s.m.* REL. crucifix.

crucifixión *s.f.* crucifixion.

crucigrama *s.m.* crossword puzzle.

crudeza *s.f.* 1 unripeness (fruta). 2 rawness (carne). 3 uncouthness (vulgaridad). 4 harshness (rigor).

crudo, -a *adj.* 1 raw (no cocido). 2 unripe (no maduro). 3 hard (agua). 4 untreated (no elaborado). 5 raw (tiempo frío). 6 (fig.) cruel. 7 coarse (vulgar). || *s.m.* 8 crude (petróleo). 9 sackcloth (tela).

cruel *adj.* cruel.

crueldad *s.f.* cruelty.

cruelmente *adv.* cruelly.

cruento, -a *adj.* (lit.) bloody.

crujía *s.f.* 1 ARQ. corridor. 2 MED. ward. 3 MAR. central gangway. 4 bay (área de carga).

crujido *s.m.* 1 crack (hueso). 2 creak (tabla del suelo). 3 crunch (al comer, p.ej., una manzana). 4 rustle (hojas).

crujiente *adj.* 1 cracking. 2 creaking. 3 crunching. 4 rustling.

crujir *v.i.* 1 to rustle (tela). 2 to grind (dientes). 3 to creak (tablas del suelo). 4 to crackle (leña que arde).

crustáceo *s.m.* ZOOL. crustacean.

cruz *s.f.* 1 cross. 2 (fig.) suffering. 3 tails (moneda). 4 ZOOL. withers. 5 lease rods (tejido). || **6 Cruz Roja,** Red Cross. **7 – gamada,** swastika. **8 hacerse cruces,** (fig.) to be taken aback. **9 por esta –,** by all that is holy. **10 en –,** crossed.

cruzada *s.f.* 1 REL. crusade. 2 (fig.) campaign.

cruzado, -a *adj.* 1 crossed. || *s.m.* 2 HIST. crusader. 3 ZOOL. crossbred. 4 cruzeiro (moneda). || *s.pl.* 5 shading (dibujo).

cruzamiento *s.m.* crossing.

cruzar *v.t.* 1 to cross. 2 to invest (condecorar). 3 AGR. to plough again. || *v.i.* 4 MAR. to cruise. || *v.pron.* 5 to meet (p.ej., dos personas en la calle). 6 to intersect (dos caminos).

cu *s.f.* q (letra).

cuaderna *s.f.* 1 MAR. frame. || *s.pl.* 2 timbers.

cuadernillo *s.m.* 1 section (encuadernación). 2 REL. liturgical calendar. 3 booklet (de sellos, etc.).

cuaderno *s.m.* 1 notebook. || **2 – de bitácora,** MAR. log-book.

cuadra *s.f.* 1 stable (de caballos). 2 MED. ward. 3 (Am.) ARQ. block.

cuadrado, -a *adj.* 1 MAT. square. 2 exact (perfecto). || *s.m.* 3 MAT. square. || 4 raíz cuadrada, MAT. square root.

cuadragésimo, -a *adj.* fortieth.

cuadrangular *adj.* GEOM. quadrangular.

cuadrángulo *adj.* GEOM. quadrangular.

cuadrante *s.m.* 1 GEOM., MAR. quadrante. 2 sundial (solar). 3 face (relojería). 4 dial (contador).

cuadrar *v.t.* 1 MAT. to square. || *v.i.* 2 to tally: *estos números no cuadran = these numbers don't tally.* 3 (fig.) to please: *no me cuadra hacer esto = I don't like doing this.* || *v.pron.* 4 MIL. to stand to attention. 5 to square up (un torero, etc.). 6 (fig. y fam.) to dig one's heels in.

cuadratura *s.f.* MAT. quadrature.

cuadrícula *s.f.* MAT., etc., squares.

cuadriculación *s.f.* criss-crossing.

cuadricular *adj.* 1 divided into squares. 2 chequered (diseño). || *v.t.* 3 to divide into squares.

cuadriga *s.f.* HIST. chariot.

cuadrilátero *adj.* y *s.m.* GEOM. quadrilateral.

cuadrilla *s.f.* 1 group (grupo). 2 gang (banda). 3 MIL. squad. 4 team (tauromaquia). 5 quadrille (baile).

cuadro *s.m.* 1 MAT., etc. square. 2 ART. painting. 3 frame (marco). 4 scene (teatro). 5 LIT. description. 6 chart (datos). 7 staff (personal). 8 POL. cadre. || **9 en –,** square. **10 estar, quedarse en –,** to lose everything.

cuadrúmano, -a *adj.* ZOOL. four-handed.

cuadrúpedo, -a *adj.* ZOOL. four-footed.

cuádruple *adj.* fourfold.

cuadruplicar *v.t.* to quadruple.

cuajada *s.f.* curd cheese (producto lácteo).
cuajaleche *s.m.* bedstraw.
cuajar *s.m.* 1 ZOOL. last stomach (vaca). || *v.i.* 2 to become fixed. 3 to settle (nieve). 4 (fig.) to materialise. || *v.t.* 5 to thicken (espesar). 6 to cover (cubrir). || *v.pron.* 7 to clot (líquido). 8 to fill up with (llenarse). 9 to fall fast asleep (dormirse profundamente).
cuajarón *s.m.* 1 clot (coágulo). 2 (fam.) lazy-bones.
cuajo *s.m.* 1 rennet (fermento). 2 clotting (cuajar). 3 (fig. y fam.) phlegm. 4 (Am. y fam.) idle chitchat (charla ociosa). 5 (Am. y fam.) playtime (recreo). 6 (Am. y fam.) tale (embuste). || 7 **de —,** completely. 8 **coger un —,** to cry one's eyes out.
cual *pron.relat.* 1 which: *el asunto del cual tratamos ayer está resuelto = the subject which we discussed yesterday is settled.* 2 who (personas): *fui a casa del abogado, el cual había salido = I went to the lawyer's house, who was out.* || *adv.* 3 (lit.) like: *él hablaba cual rey = he spoke like a king.* || 4 **—... tal...,** like... like...: *tal el padre, cual el hijo = like father, like son.*
cuál *pron.interrog.* 1 which (one): *¿cuál de las dos casas te gusta más? = which (one) of the two houses do you like best?* || *interj.* 2 (lit.) how!: *¡cuál triste estás hoy! = how sad you are today!*
cualidad *s.f.* 1 quality. 2 FIS. property.
cualitativamente *adv.* qualitatively.
cualitativo, -a *adj.* QUIM. qualitative.
cualquiera *adj.* 1 any: *te lo dirá cualquier médico = any doctor will tell you that.* || *pron.* 2 anybody: *lo puede hacer cualquiera = anybody can do that.* 3 whatever: *cualquiera que sea el resultado, dímelo = tell me whatever the result may be.* || *s.f.* 4 a loose woman.
cuán *adv.* (lit.) how: *¡cuán alegre estuve cuando la vi! = how happy I was when I saw her!*
cuando *adv.* y *conj.* 1 when: *cuando lo vea le diré las buenas noticias = when I see him I shall tell him the good news.* 2 whenever: *cuando fui a verlo él estaba ocupado = whenever I went to see him he was busy.* 3 if: *cuando él te dice que es así, así será = if he tells you that's how it is, it must be so.* 4 even if: *él seguiría trabajando, cuando estuviera rendido = he would heep on working, even if we were shattered.* || 5 **— menos,** at least. 6 **— mucho,** at the most. 7 **de — en —,** from time to time.
cuándo *adv.* y *conj.interrog.* 1 when?: *¿cuándo volverás? = when will you return?* || 2 **¿desde —?,** how long?: *¿desde cuándo trabajas en aquella empresa? = how long have you been working in that firm?* 3 **¿de — acá?,** since when?
cuantía *s.f.* 1 amount (cantidad). 2 value (valor).
cuantioso, -a *adj.* 1 large (grande). 2 plentiful (abundante). 3 considerable (de gran importancia).
cuantitativamente *adv.* quantitatively.
cuantitativo, -a *adj.* QUIM. quantitative.
cuanto, -a *adj.* y *pron.* 1 all: *te diré cuanto quieras saber = I'll tell you all you want to know.* || *s.pl.* 2 all: *cuantos le conocen le toman por un hombre excelente = all who know him consider him an excellent person.* || 3 **en —,** as soon as. 4 **en — a,** as for. 5 **— más,** the more: *cuanto más se aprende, más infeliz se vuelve uno = the more one learns, the more unhappy one becomes.* 6 **por —,** since: *no participarás en el éxito, por cuanto no has colaborado = since you haven't done anything, you won't share in the success.*
cuánto *adv.* 1 how: *¡cuánto me alegro de verte! = hoy happy I am to see you!* || *adj.* 2 what a lot of!: *¡cuánto pan has comido hoy! = what a lot of bread you've eaten today!* || *interrog.* 3 how much?: *¿cuánto has gastado en la comida? = how much have you spent on the meal?* || *s.pl.* 4 how many?: *¿cuántos asistieron a la reunión? = how many attended the meeting?*
cuáquero, -a *s.m.* y *f.* REL. quaker.
cuarcita *s.f.* GEOL. quartzite.
cuarenta *adj.* 1 forty (cardinal). 2 fortieth (ordinal). || 3 **cantarle a uno las —,** (fig. y fam.) to tell someone a few plain truths.
cuarentena *s.f.* 1 forty. 2 MED quarantine. || 3 (fig. y fam.) **ponerle a alguien en —,** to send someone to Coventry.
cuarentón, -a *adj.* in one's forties.
cuaresma *s.f.* REL. Lent.
cuaresmal *adj.* Lenten.
cuarta *s.f.* 1 quarter. 2 span (palmo). 3 run (cartas). 4 (Am.) whip (tralla). 5 (Am.) extra horse (caballería). 6 MAR. point of the compass. 7 MUS. perfect fourth.
cuartana *s.f.* MED. quartan malaria.
cuartear *v.t.* 1 to cut into four. 2 to joint (carne). 3 to zigzag (conduciendo reses). 4 (Am.) to lash (azotar). || *v.i.* 5 to sidestep (tauromaquia). || *v.pron.* 6 to crack (agrietarse). 7 (Am. y fig.) to go back on one's word.
cuartel *s.m.* 1 MIL. barracks. 2 quarter (cuarta parte). 3 quartering (escudo). || 4 **— general,** MIL. headquarters. 5 **de —,** on reduced pay. 6 **no dar —,** (fam.) to beutterly ruthless.
cuartelero, -a *adj.* 1 MIL. of the barracks. || *s.m.* 2 (Am.) waiter (camarero).
cuarteo *s.m.* 1 quartering (dividir). 2 jointing (carne). 3 crack (p.ej., en una pared). 4 side-step (tauromaquia). 5 (Am.) whipping (azoteo).
cuarterón, -a *adj.* 1 of mixed race. || *s.m.* 2 quarter (peso).
cuarteta *s.f.* LIT. quatrain.
cuarteto *s.m.* 1 LIT. quatrain. 2 MUS. quartet.
cuartilla *s.m.* 1 sheet (hoja de papel). 2 quarter (medida).
cuartillo *s.m.* 1 half a litre.
cuarto, -a *adj.* 1 fourth (ordinal). 2 quarter (cuarta parte). || *s.m.* 3 room (habitación). || *s.pl.* 4 money. || 5 **— delantero,** ZOOL. foreleg. 6 **— trasero,** ZOOL. hind leg. 7 **cuatro cuartos,** (fam.) a few coppers. 8 **de tres al —,** two a penny. 9 **echar uno su — a espadas,** (fig. y fam.) to have one's say. 10 **dar un — al pregonero,** (fig. y fam.) to spill the beans. 11 **no tener un —,** (fig. y fam.) to be skint. 12 **en —,** quarto (papel).
cuarzo *s.m.* GEOL. quartz.
cuarzoso, -a *adj.* GEOL. made of quartz.
cuate *adj.* 1 (Am.) twin (gemelo). 2 similar. 3 mate (camarada).
cuaternario, -a *adj.* GEOL. quaternary.
cuatrero, -a *adj.* 1 (Am.) cheating. || *s.m.* 2 rustler (ganadería).
cuatrienio *s.m.* four-year period.
cuatro *adj.* 1 four (cardinal). 2 fourth (ordinal). 3 (fam.) very few: *sólo había cuatro espectadores = there were very few spectators.*
cuatrocientos, -as *adj.* 1 four hundred (cardinal). 2 four-hundredth (ordinal).
cuba *s.f.* 1 barrel. 2 barrelful (contenido). || *s.m.* 3 (Am.) youngest child. || 4 **— libre,** rum and coke (bebida). || 5 **estar como una —,** (fam.) to be legless.
cubero *s.m.* cooper.
cubeta *s.f.* 1 keg (tonel). 2 FOT. wash tank. 3 MED. tray. 4 bulb (barómetro). 5 (Am.) (fam.) top-hat.
cubicación *s.f.* 1 MAT. cubing. 2 GEOM. volume measurement.
cubicar *v.t.* 1 MAT. to cube. 2 GEOM. to measure the volume.
cúbico *adj.* 1 GEOM. cubic. || 2 raíz cúbica, cubed root.
cubículo *s.m.* 1 cubicle (cabina). 2 bedroom (alcoba).
cubierta *s.f.* 1 covering. 2 tyre (automóvil). 3 cover (libro). 4 MAR. deck. 5 ARQ. roof. 6 (fig.) claim. || 7 **a —,** under cover.
cubierto, -a *adj.* 1 covered. || *s.m.* 2 knife, fork and spoon (servicio de mesa). 3 set meal (comida). 4 roof (techumbre). || 5 **estar a —,** to be under cover.
cubil *s.m.* 1 ZOOL. den. 2 stream (cauce).
cubilete *s.m.* 1 dice cup (juegos). 2 mould (cocina). 3 (Am.) top-hat.
cubiletear *v.i.* (fig.) to be up to something (intrigar).
cubilote *s.m.* 1 TEC. melting furnace. 2 concrete bucket (construcción).
cubismo *s.m.* ART. cubism.
cubital *adj.* ANAT. elbow.
cúbito *s.m.* ANAT. ulna.
cubo *s.m.* 1 MAT. cube. 2 bucket (balde). 3 hub (bicicleta). 4 hod (de tejador). 5 drum (de reloj).
cubrecama *s.f.* bedspread.
cubrir *v.t.* 1 to cover. 2 to hide (ocultar). 3 to drown (ahogar). 4 to protect (proteger). 5 to make up for (compensar). 6 ZOOL. to serve. || *v.pron.* 7 to protect oneself: *cubrirse las espaldas = to take measures to protect oneself.* 8 to put one's hat on. 9 to become cloudy (ponerse nublado el cielo).
cucaña *s.f.* 1 slippery pole (juego). 2 (fig. y fam.) cinch.
cucaracha *s.f.* 1 ZOOL. cockroach. 2 loose tobacco (tabaco en polvo). 3 (Am. y fam.) old banger (coche viejo).

cuclillas (en) *adv.* crouching.
cuclillo *s.m.* 1 ZOOL. cuckoo. 2 BOT. ragged robin.
cuco *adj.* 1 neat (bien arreglado). 2 crafty (astuto). || *s.m.* 3 ZOOL. cuckoo. 4 ZOOL. caterpillar.
cucurucho *s.m.* cornet (de helado, etc.).
cuchara *s.f.* 1 spoon. 2 (Am.) trowel (construcción). 3 (Am. y fam.) pickpocket (ratero). || 4 **meter con —,** (fam.) to spoonfeed. 5 **hacer cucharas,** (Am. y fam.) to pout (hacer pucheros).
cucharada *s.f.* 1 spoonful. || 2 (fig. y fam.) meddling.
cucharetear *v.i.* 1 (fam.) to stir (remover). 2 (fig. y fam.) to poke one's nose in.
cucharón *s.m.* ladle (cocina).
cuchichear *v.i.* to whisper.
cuchicheo *s.m.* whispering.
cuchilla *s.f.* 1 cleaver. 2 blade (de arma blanca, etc.). 3 razor-blade (de afeitar). 4 (fig.) sword. 5 (Am.) GEOG. mountain range. 6 (Am.) penknife (cortaplumas).
cuchillada *s.f.* 1 knife-wound. 2 (fig.) street-fight (riña).
cuchillería *s.f.* 1 cutlery making (oficio). 2 cutlery shop (tienda). 3 cutlery (cuchillos, etc.).
cuchillero *s.m.* 1 cutler. 2 (Am.) street-fighter (pendenciero).
cuchillo *s.m.* 1 knife. 2 gore (coser). 3 ARQ. support. 4 ZOOL. bottom fang. || 5 **pasar a —,** to put to the sword.
cuchipanda *s.f.* (fam.) nosh-up.
cuchitril *s.m.* 1 AGR. pigsty. 2 (fig. y fam.) dump.
cuchufleta *s.f.* (fam.) lark.
cuello *s.m.* 1 ANAT. neck. 2 collar (prenda de vestir).
cuenca *s.f.* 1 bowl. 2 ANAT. socket. 3 GEOG. basin. || 4 **— minera,** coalfield.
cuenco *s.m.* 1 bowl. 2 hollow (concavidad).
cuenta *s.f.* 1 calculation (cálculo). 2 bill (restaurante, etc.). 3 COM. account. 4 business (incumbencia): *eso corre de mi cuenta = that's my business.* 5 REL. bead. || 6 **— corriente,** FIN. current account. 7 **caer en la —,** to realise what's going on. 8 **tener en —,** to bear in mind: *ten en cuenta que es un hombre mayor = don't forget that he's an old man.*
cuentacorrentista *s.m.* y *f.* FIN. depositor.
cuentagotas *s.m.* MED. dropper.
cuentakilómetros *s.m.* 1 speedometer (velocidad). 2 milometer (bicicleta).
cuentista *s.m.* 1 storyteller. 2 gossip (chismoso). 3 spoof (fantasioso).
cuento *s.m.* 1 tale. 2 piece of gossip (chisme). 3 lie (falsedad). 4 MAT. calculation. 5 ferrule (contera). 6 ARQ. girder. || 7 **a —,** on purpose. 8 **sin —,** countless. 9 **venir a —,** to be relevant: *lo que dijo no venía a cuento = what he said had nothing to do with it.* 10 **tener mucho —,** (fam.) to make a fuss. 11 **vivir del —,** (fam.) to live by one's wits. 12 **— chino,** (fam.) baloney.
cuerda *s.f.* 1 string. 2 rope (ensambladura más fuerte). 3 spring (relojería). 4 chain gang (presos). 5 MED. tendon. || 6 **cuerdas vocales,** vocal chords. 7 **bajo —,** stealthily, secretly. 8 **bailar en la — floja,** (fig.) to play it cagily.
cuerdo, -a *adj.* 1 sane (persona). 2 prudent (acción).
cuerno *s.m.* 1 ZOOL., MUS. horn. 2 MIL. wing. 3 tip (punta). || *interj.* 4 blimey! || 5 **mandar al — a alguien,** (fam.) to tell someone to get lost. 6 **¡y un —!,** (fam.) no way! 7 **poner los cuernos a alguien,** (fam.) to be unfaithful.
cuero *s.m.* 1 leather. 2 wineskin (odre). || 3 **— cabelludo,** scalp. 4 **en cueros,** naked: *en verano tomo el sol en cueros = in summer I sunbathe naked.* 5 **estar borracho como un —,** (fig. y fam.) to be as drunk as a lord.
cuerpo *s.m.* 1 body: *este vino tiene cuerpo = this wine has body.* 2 QUIM. substance. 3 thickness (grosor): *quiero una tela con más cuerpo = I want a thicker cloth.* 4 volume (libros). 5 MIL. corps. || 6 **— de guardia,** MIL. sentries. 7 **— del delito,** DER. corpus delicti. 8 **— a —,** hand-to-hand (lucha).
cuervo *s.m.* 1 ZOOL. crow. || 2 **— marino,** cormorant.
cuesta *s.f.* 1 hill. || 2 **a cuestas,** on one's shoulders. 3 **ir — abajo,** (fig.) to go downhill. 4 **la — de enero,** (fig.) the after-Christmas lean period.
cuestación *s.f.* charity collection.
cuestión *s.f.* 1 question. 2 argument (riña). || 3 **— batallona,** (fam.) burning question. 4 **— de confianza,** POL. vote of confidence.
cuestionable *adj.* doubtful.
cuestionar *v.t.* 1 to challenge (una opinión). || *v.i.* 2 to have an argument.
cuestionario *s.m.* 1 questionnaire (encuesta). 2 examination paper (examen u oposición).
cuestor *s.m.* 1 HIST. magistrate. 2 charity collector.
cueva *s.f.* 1 cave. 2 wine-cellar (bodega).
cuévano *s.m.* dosser (viticultura).
cuidado *s.m.* 1 care. 2 worry (preocupación). 3 concern: *esto es cuidado mío = that's my concern.* || *interj.* 4 be careful! || 5 **estar de —,** to be seriously ill. 6 **tener — con,** to be careful with. 7 **andarse con —,** to go very carefully. 8 **poner mucho —,** to take great care. 9 **traerle a uno sin —,** (fam.) not to care, to be of no interest to someone: *eso sí que me trae sin cuidado = I just couldn't care less about that!* 10 **de mucho —,** (fam.) really fine; a great deal: *es un atleta de mucho cuidado = he's a really fine athlete.*
cuidador *adj.* 1 caring. || *s.m.* 2 DEP. coach. 3 (Am.) male nurse.
cuidadosamente *adv.* 1 carefully (con atención). 2 apprehensively (con ansiedad).
cuidadoso, -a *adj.* 1 careful (atento). 2 apprehensive (ansioso).
cuidar *v.t.* 1 to take care of. || *v.pron.* 2 to look after oneself: *cuidate mucho = look after yourself.* || 3 **cuidarse de algo,** to worry about something: *ella no se cuida de lo que dicen los vecinos = she doesn't worry about what the neighbours say.* 4 **cuidarse de hacer algo,** to be careful/to make sure to do something: *cuidate de escribirme = make sure you write to me.*
cuita *s.f.* 1 worry (preocupación). 2 grief (aflicción). 3 (Am.) birdlime (excremento de las aves).
cuitado, -a *adj.* 1 troubled (apenado). 2 shy (tímido).
cuitamiento *s.m.* shyness (timidez).
culantrillo *s.m.* BOT. brake.
culata *s.f.* 1 butt (fusil). 2 breech (canon). 3 MEC. cylinder head. 4 ZOOL. hindquarters. 5 (Am.) ARQ. gable end. 6 heel (guadaña). || 7 **salir el tiro por la —,** (fam.) to backfire.
culebra *s.f.* 1 ZOOL. snake. 2 (Am., fig. y fam.) prank. 3 (fig.) disorder. || 4 **saber más que las culebras,** (fig. y fam.) to be a wise owl.
culebrear *v.i.* 1 to twist and turn. 2 (Am. y fig.) to gain time.
culera *s.f.* patch in the seat of one's trousers.
culinaria *s.f.* cuisine (arte).
culinario, -a *adj.* culinary.
culminación *s.f.* culmination.
culminante *adj.* 1 highest. 2 (fig.) paramount. 3 ASTR. culminant.
culminar *v.i.* 1 to culminate. 2 to reach its highest point (estrella).
culo *s.m.* 1 (vulg.) arse, bottom. 2 bottom (de un recipiente, etc.). || 3 **a — pajarero,** (fam.) bare-bottomed. 4 **mueve el —!,** (vulg.) shift your arse!
culpa *s.f.* 1 offence (delito). 2 blame (responsabilidad). || 3 **echarle la — a alguien,** to blame someone.
culpabilidad *s.f.* guilt.
culpable *adj.* 1 to blame: *¿quién es el culpable? = who's to blame?* || *s.m.* y *f.* 2 the guilty one.
cultismo *s.m.* 1 Gongorism (estilo literario). 2 erudite word (palabra culta).
cultivador *s.m.* AGR. farmer.
cultivar *v.t.* 1 AGR., etc., to cultivate. 2 to develop (aptitud).
cultivo *s.m.* 1 AGR. cultivation. 2 crop (producto cultivado). 3 BIO. culture. || 4 **caldo de —,** culture medium. 5 **— intensivo,** intensive farming.
culto, -a *adj.* 1 learned. 2 cultured (que tiene cultura). || *s.m.* 3 adoration. 4 REL. worship. || 5 **rendir — a,** to worship.
cultura *s.f.* 1 culture. 2 civilisation (civilización). || 3 **— física,** physical culture.
cultural *adj.* cultural.
cumbre *s.f.* 1 summit (montaña). 2 POL. summit meeting. 3 (fig.) height, culmination: *ella está en la cumbre de su creatividad = she's at the height of her creative talent.*
cumpleaños *s.m.* birthday.
cumplidamente *adv.* 1 completely (completamente). 2 correctly (formalmente).
cumplido, -a *adj.* 1 finished. 2 long (largo). 3 well-mannered (cortés). || *s.m.* pleasantry, compliment: *me dijo un cumplido = he paid me a compliment.*
cumplidor *adj.* dependable.
cumplimentar *v.t.* 1 to congratulate (felicitar). 2 to carry out (orden).
cumplimiento *s.m.* 1 completion (acto). 2 honouring (responsabilidad). 3 compliment (cumplido).

cumplir *v.t.* 1 to carry out. 2 to turn (edad): *ella ha cumplido los 10 años = she has turned 10.* || *v.i.* 3 to do right, to comply: *hemos cumplido como es debido = we've done exactly the right thing.* 4 to be one's job, to be fitting: *te cumple hacerlo = it's your job to do it.* || *v.pron.* 5 to be up (plazo). 6 to materialise (proyecto, etc.). || 7 **por —,** as a matter of form.

cúmulo *s.m.* 1 accumulation. 2 cumulus (nubes).

cuna *s.f.* 1 cradle (cama). 2 stock (linaje). 3 place of birth (lugar de nacimiento).

cundir *v.i.* 1 to spread (extenderse). 2 to give (dar de sí).

cuneiforme *adj.* 1 wedge-shaped. 2 HIST. cuneiform.

cuneta *s.f.* 1 ditch (foso). 2 gutter (desagüe).

cuña *s.f.* 1 wedge. 2 (Am. y fam.) friend in high places. || 3 **tener cuñas,** to have influence.

cuñada *s.f.* sister-in-law.

cuñado *s.m.* brother-in-law.

cuño *s.m.* 1 coining die (troquel). 2 (fig.) stamp.

cuota *s.f.* quota.

cupé *s.m.* 1 brougham (berlina). 2 coupé (automóvil).

cuplé *s.m.* popular song.

cupletista *s.m.* popular singer.

cupo *s.m.* 1 quota. 2 (Am.) capacity. 3 spare seat (coche).

cupón *s.m.* 1 coupon. 2 COM. dividend.

cúprico, -a *adj.* QUIM. copper.

cúpula *s.f.* 1 ARQ. dome. 2 BOT. involucre. 3 cup (árbol). 4 MAR. turret. 5 POL. party leaders.

cuquería *s.f.* (fam.) scampishness.

cura *s.m.* 1 REL. priest. || *s.f.* 2 MED. cure. 3 remedy (pócima).

curación *s.f.* 1 MED. healing (acto). 2 cure (remedio).

curanderismo *s.m.* quack medicine.

curar *v.t.* to cure, to treat.

curativo, -a *adj.* healing.

curia *s.f.* Curia, papel Curia.

curiosamente *adv.* curiously.

curiosear *v.t.* to glanie at, to look over.

curiosidad *s.f.* 1 curiosity. 2 (desp.) meddling. 3 fastidiousness (limpieza). 4 curio (cosa curiosa).

curioso *adj.* curious, eager.

currante *s.m. f.* worker, labourer.

currar *v.i.* to work.

currículo *s.m.* curriculum.

cursante *s.m. f.* student.

cursar *v.t.* to send, to dispatch.

cursilería *s.f.* 1 bad taste (mal gusto). 2 showiness (ostentación). 3 affectation (amaneramiento).

cursilón *s.m.* 1 (fam.) flash Harry. 2 (fam.) dude.

cursillista *s.m.* y *f.* fellow-student.

cursillo *s.m.* short course.

cursiva *s.f.* italics.

curso *s.m.* course, direction, flow (de río).

cursor *s.m.* sile.

curtido, -a *adj.* 1 tanned (cuero). 2 hardened (piel). 3 (fig.) skilled (experto). || *s.m.* 4 tanning (cuero).

curtidor, -a *s.m.* y *f.* tanner.

curtiduría *s.f.* tannery (fábrica).

curtimiento *s.m.* tanning.

curtir *v.t.* to tan.

curva *s.f.* curve.

curvado, -a *adj.* 1 curved (un arco, etc.). 2 bent (varilla). 3 stooping (persona).

curvar *v.t.* 1 to curve. 2 to bend. 3 to warp (madera).

curvo, -a *adj.* curved.

cúspide *s.f.* 1 cusp. 2 summit, peak.

custodiar *v.t.* 1 to guard. 2 (fig.) to watch over.

custodio, -a *adj.* 1 watchful. || *s.m.* 2 keeper. || 3 **ángel —,** REL. guardian angel.

cúter *s.m.* cutter.

cutícula *s.f.* cuticle.

cutis *s.m.* skin, complexion.

cutre *adj.* mean, stingy (tacaño).

cuyo *adj.* whose, of whom, of which.

cuzgueño *adj.* of Cuzco.

ch, CH *s.f.* ch, Ch (cuarta letra del alfabeto español).
chabacanería *s.f.* **1** vulgar thing, remark. **2** vulgarity, bad taste, tastelessness.
chabacano, -a *adj.* **1** common, plain, cheap, ordinary (persona). **2** vulgar, coarse, uncouth (apariencia). **3** rude, vulgar, crude, in bad taste, shoddy (acción).
chabola *s.f.* shack, shanty; hut, shed.
chacal *s.m.* jackal.
chácara *s.f.* V. **chacra.**
chacina *s.f.* pork sausages.
chacinería *s.f.* porkbutcher's shop.
chacinero, -a *s.m.* y *f.* pork butcher.
chacolí *s.m.* chacolí (vino vasco).
chacolotear *v.i.* to clatter (herradura).
chacota *s.f.* **1** joking, banter, noisy merriment. || **2 echar/tomar a —,** to make fun, to take as a joke. **3 estar de —,** to be in a joking mood.
chacotear *v.i.* **1** to make fun, to mess around, to clown around. || *v.pron.* **2** to make fun of someone, to take something as a joke.
chacoteo *s.m.* messing about, joking, clowning.
chacra *s.f.* (Am.) farm.
chacha *s.f.* (fam.) maid, nursemaid, lass.
cháchara *s.f.* small talk, chatter, idle talk.
chacharear *v.i.* (fam.) to chatter, to chat.
chacharero, -a *adj.* **1** talkative. || *s.m.* y *f.* **2** chatterer.
chafar *v.t.* **1** to flatten, to crush. **2** to crease, to crumple. **3** to cut short, to shut someone up, to take someone down a peg. || *v.pron.* **4** to be crushed.
chaflán *s.m.* **1** bevel, chamfer. **2** cant.
chaflanar *v.t.* to bevel, to chamfer.
chaira *s.f.* **1** steel, sharpener. **2** shoemaker's knife, paring knife.
chal *s.m.* shawl.
chala *s.f.* (Am.) tender leaf of maize, husk, shuck.
chalado, -a *adj.* dotty, crazy, mad, cranky.
chalán *s.m.* **1** (Am.) horse dealer, huckster. **2** sharp dealer, shark. **3** (Am.) horse breaker, broncobuster.
chalana *s.f.* barge, lighter, wherry.
chalanear *v.i.* **1** to be a sharp dealer, to handle cleverly, to bargain shrewdly. || *v.i.* **2** to train, to break, to tame.
chalar *v.t.* **1** (fam.) to drive crazy, to drive round the bend. || *v.pron.* **2** to go off one's rocker, to get a crush on, to go crazy.
chalchihuite *s.m.* sorcery, witchcraft, spell, charm.
chaleco *s.m.* **1** waiscoat, (EE.UU.) vest. || **2 — salvavidas,** life jacket.
chalet o **chalé** *s.m.* chalet, country house, detached house, bungalow.
chalina *s.f.* cravat, floppy bow tie.
chalupa *s.f.* **1** launch, boat, narrow canoe. **2** (Am.) maize cake. **4** madman, crackpot. || *adj.* **5** crazy.
chamaco, -a *s.m.* y *f.* **1** boy, lad, kid. **2** girl, lass.
chamal *s.m.* (Am.) Araucanian cape.
chamarilero, -a o **chamarillero, -a** *s.m.* y *f.* secondhand dealer, junk dealer.
chamarra *s.f.* sheepskin jacket.
chamba *s.f.* **1** (fam.) fluke, lucky break. **2** (Am.) turf, sod; job, occupation; deal.
chambelán *s.m.* chamberlain.
chambergo *s.m.* broad brimmed soft hat.
chambón *adj.* **1** (fam.) lucky, jammy. **2** awkward, clumsy.
chambonada *s.f.* **1** fluke, lucky shot. **2** blunder. **3** awkwardness, clumsiness.
chambra *s.f.* blouse, camisole.
chamiza *s.f.* chamiso (planta usada para techar), brushwood.
chamizo *s.m.* **1** shack, slum, hovel. **2** gambling den. **3** half burnt tree.
chamorro *adj.* y *s.* **1** shave head (persona). **2** beardless (trigo).
champán *s.m.* champagne.
champaña *s.m.* champagne.
champiñón *s.m.* mushroom.
champú *s.m.* shampoo.
chamuchina *s.f.* (Am.) rabble, riffraff, mob.
chamullar *v.t.* (fam.) to speak, to talk; to speak a little, to have a smattering.
chamuscar *v.t.* **1** to scorch/sear/singe. **2** to get cross, to take offence.
chamusquina *s.f.* **1** singeing, smell of burning, scorching. **2** row, quarrel. || **3 esto huele a —,** there's trouble brewing, it smells fishy, it seems doubtful.
chancar *v.t.* **1** (Am.) to crush, to grind, to triturate. **2** to beat, to ill-treat. **3** to bungle, to botch (hacer una chapuza).
chancear *v.i.* **1** to joke, to make jokes, to crack jokes. || *v.pron.* **2** to make fun. || **3 chancearse de,** to make fun of.
chanciller *s.m.* chancellor.
chancillería *s.f.* chancery.
chancla *s.f.* old shoe, slipper.
chancleta *s.f.* **1** old shoe, slipper. **2** (Am.) baby girl. **3** nincompoop.
chancletear *v.i.* to shuffle.
chanclo *s.m.* clog, galosh, overshoe, rubber shoe.
chancro *s.m.* **1** MED. chancre. **2** BOT. canker.
chancha *s.f.* **1** sow. || *s.m.* **2** filthy woman, slovenly woman.
chanchería *s.f.* pork butcher's.
chancho *adj.* **1** (Am.) dirty, filthy. || *s.m.* **2** pig, boar.
chanchullero, -a *adj.* **1** fiddling, crooked. || *s.m.* y *f.* **2** fiddler, crook.
chanchullo *s.m.* **1** wangle, fiddle, crooked deal. || **2 andar en chanchullos,** to be on the fiddle, to be engaged in something shady.
chándal *s.m.* sports clothes.
chanfaina *s.f.* offal stew.
changa *s.f.* (Am.) joke.
changador *s.m.* porter.
chanquete *s.m.* backgammon.
chantaje *s.m.* blackmail.
chantajista *s.m.* y *f.* black mailer.
chantar *v.t.* **1** to thrust, to throw, to chuck. **2** to put on, to dress. || **3 — algo**

a uno, to tell someone something to his face.
chantilly o **chantilli** *s.m.* **1** whipped cream. **2** embroidered lace fabric.
chantre *s.m.* precentor.
chanza *s.f.* joke.
chapa *s.f.* **1** plate, sheet, panel. **2** common sense, prudence. **3** (Am.) lock.
chapado, -a *adj.* **1** veneered, plated: *chapado en oro = gold plated.* || **2 – a la antigua,** old fashioned, of the old school.
chapaleteo *s.m.* **1** lap, lapping. **2** pattering.
chapapote *s.m.* (Am.) bitumen, asphalt.
chapar *v.t.* **1** to plate, to veneer, to tile, to cover. **2** to throw out, to come up with (decir algo desagradable). **3** to study carefully.
chaparral *s.m.* chaparral, thicket.
chaparro, -a *adj./s.m.* y *f.* **1** tubby, plump person, holm oak, holy oak.
chaparrón *s.m.* downpour, cloudburst, shower.
chaparrear *v.i.* to pour in torrents, to pour down.
chapeado, -a *adj.* **1** plated, veneered. **2** (Am.) rich.
chapear *v.t.* **1** to plate, to veneer, to tile. **2** to clatter. || *v.pron.* **3** to become rich.
chapería *s.f.* veneering.
chaperón *s.m.* botch job, shoddy piece of work.
chapeta *s.f.* rosy cheek.
chapetón, -ona *s.m.* y *f.* **1** novice, new in a job. **2** awkward, clumsy, unhandy. **3** Spaniard newly arrived in America.
chapetonada *s.f.* awkwardness, clumsiness, inexperience.
chapín *s.m.* chopine.
chapitel *s.m.* **1** ARQ. spire. **2** ARQ. capital. **3** cap (de brújula).
chapotear *v.t.* **1** to moisten, to dampen, to damp, to wet. || *v.i.* **2** to splash about, to paddle, to dabble.
chapucería *s.f.* **1** botched job, shoddiness. **2** patching up.
chapucero, -a *adj.* **1** careless, shoddy. || *s.m.* y *f.* **2** careless worker, botcher.
chapurrar *v.t.* V. **chapurrear.**
chapurrear *v.t.* **1** to speak a little, to speak a few words, to speak badly, to have a smattering. **2** to mix (licores).
chapuza *s.f.* **1** odd job, botched job, shoddy piece of work. **2** patching up. **3** spare-time job. **4** (Am.) trick, swindle.
chapuzar *v.t.* **1** to duck, to dip, to plunge. || *v.i.* **2** to dive.
chaqué *s.m.* tail coat, morning coat.
chaqueta *s.f.* jacket.
chaquetear *v.i.* **1** to change sides, to be a turncoat, to turn traitor. **2** to back down, to go back on one's word, to rat.
chaquetero, -a *s.m.* y *f.* turncoat.
chaquetilla *s.f.* short jacket, bolero.
chaquetón *s.m.* long jacket, reefer, shooting jacket.
charada *s.f.* charade.
charanga *s.f.* brass band, hullabaloo, merry din.
charca *s.f.* pond, pool.
charco *s.m.* **1** pool, puddle. || **2 pasar el –,** to cross the water, to cross the herring pond.
charçutería *s.f.* pork butcher's.
charla *s.f.* chat, chatter, talk.
charlador, -ora *adj.* **1** talkative, garrulous, gossipy. || *s.m.* y *f.* **2** chatterbox.
charlar *v.i.* **1** to talk, to chat, to chatter, to prattle, to gossip. || **2 – por los codos,** to be a real chatterbox.
charlatán, -ana *adj.* **1** talkative, garrulous, gossipy. || *s.m.* y *f.* **2** chatterbox, gossip. **3** charlatán, hawker, pedlar. **4** trickster, swindler.
charlatanear *v.i.* to chatter, to prattle, to gossip.
charlatanería *s.f.* talkativeness, verbosity, gossip, garrulity, spiel.
charlista *s.m.* y *f.* lecturer.
charlotear *v.i.* to chatter, to prattle.
charloteo *s.m.* chatter, prattle.
charlatanismo *s.m.* charlatanism.
charlestón *s.m.* MUS. carleton.
charlotear *v.i.* to chatter, to prattle.
charnela o **charnela** *s.f.* hinge.
charol *s.m.* **1** patent leather, vanish. || **2 darse –,** to blow one's own trumpet.
charola *s.f.* **1** tray. **2** big eyes.
charolado *adj.* **1** polished, varnished. **2** shiny, bright.
charolar *v.t.* to varnish, to japan.
charquear *v.t.* to jerk, to dry, to cure.
charqui o **charque** *s.m.* jerked meat, dried fruit.
charrada *s.f.* **1** charro dance, Mexican dance. **2** vulgar adornment, gaudy ornament. **3** boorinesh, uncouthness.
charrán *adj.* rascal, villain, rogue, scoundrel.
charranada *s.f.* dirty trick.
charranería *s.f.* dirty trick.
charretera *s.f.* epaulette.
charro, -a *adj.* **1** vulgar, rustic, coarse. **2** gaudy, flashy, showy. || *s.m.* y *f.* **3** peasant (de Salamanca). **4** rustic, boor. **5** Mexican horseman. **6** broad brimmed hat.
chárter V. **vuelo.**
chascar *v.i.* **1** to click, to snap, to crack, to crunch. **2** to swallow.
chascarrillo *s.m.* joke.
chasco *s.m.* **1** disappointment, failure. **2** trick, joke, prank.
chascón *adj.* **1** matted, entangled. **2** slow, clumsy.
chasis *s.m.* **1** MEC. chassis. **2** FOT. plate holder.
chasquear *v.t.* **1** to play a trick, to play a joke, to make a fool of. || *v.i.* **2** to crack, to click, to snap, to crunch. || *v.pron.* **3** to be disappointed, to come to nothing. || **4 – la lengua,** to click one's tongue.
chasquido *s.m.* click, crack, snap, crunch, creak, crackle.
chatarra *s.f.* scrap iron, junk, slag.
chato, -a *adj.* **1** snub, flat: *nariz chata = snub nose.* **2** blunt, flattened. || *s.m.* y *f* **3** snub nosed person. || *s.m.* **4** small glass, glass of wine.
chauvinismo *s.m.* chauvinism.
chauvinista *adj.* **1** chauvinist(ic). || *s.m.* y *f.* **2** chauvinist.
chaval *s.m.* lad, boy, kid.
chavala *s.f.* girl, kid.
chavea *s.m.* (fam.) lad, boy, kid.
chaveta *s.f.* **1** cotter, broad bladed knife. || **2 perder la –,** to go off one's rocker, to go round the bend, to go through the roof.
che *s.f.* **1** name of the letter **ch.** || *interj* **2** hey!, hi!, say!
checa *s.f.* solitary confinement cell.
checo, -a *adj./s.m.* y *f.* **1** Czech, Czechoslovakian. || *s.m.* **2** Czech language.
chécheres *s.m.pl.* bits and pieces, odds and ends, gear, things.
chelín *s.m.* shilling.
chepa *s.f.* hump.
cheposo, -a *s.m.* y *f.* hunchback.
cheque *s.m.* **1** cheque, (EE.UU.) check. || **2 – al portador,** cheque payable to bearer, open cheque. **3 – a la orden,** cheque to order, order cheque. **4 – cruzado,** crossed cheque. **5 – de viaje/viajero,** traveller's cheque.
chequear *v.t.* **1** to check, to compare. **2** to give a checkup.
chequeo *s.m.* **1** check, checking-up, comparisson. **2** MEC. checking, overhauling, servicing. **3** MED. checkup.
chequera *s.f.* chequebook.
chérif *s.m.* (EE.UU.) sheriff.
chévere *adj.* (Am.) **1** nice, smashing, super. **2** benevolent, indulgent, lenient.
cheviot *s.m.* Cheviot.
chibalete *s.m.* composing frame.
chicano, -a *adj./s.m.* y *f.* chicano (sudamericano emigrado a los EE.UU.).
chicarrón *adj.* y *s.m.* sturdy boy, strapping lad.
chicle *s.m.* chewing gum.
chico, -a *adj.* **1** small, little, tiny. || *s.m.* y *f.* **2** boy (m.), girl (f.), young, youngster, lad.
chicote *s.m.* piece of rope, rope end; whip.
chicotear *v.t.* e *i.* to whip, to lash, to fight, to beat up.
chicha *s.f.* **1** meat. **2** chicha, maize liquor. || **3 calma –,** dead calm. **4 no ser ni – ni limonada,** to be neither fish nor fowl. **5 tener pocas chichas,** to be weak, to have no go, to be all skin and bone.
chicharra *s.f.* **1** cicada, harvest bug. **2** heat. **3** (fig.) chatterbox.
chicharrar *v.t.* y *v.pron.* to scortch, overheat, to roast.
chicharro *s.m.* horse mackerel, caranx.
chicharrón *s.m.* **1** crackling, piece of burnt meat. **2** sunburnt person.
chiche *s.m.* (Am.) breast, teat.
chichera *s.f.* (Am.) jail.
chichón *s.m.* bump, lump, swelling.
chichonera *s.f.* helmet (para niños).
chifla *s.f.* hissing, whistling.
chiflado, -a *adj.* **1** daft, barmy, cranky, cracked. **2** crazy person, crank, crackpot.
chifladura *s.f.* **1** craziness, craze, whim, mania. **2** whistle, whistling.

chiflar *v.i.* **1** to hiss, to whistle. **2** to drink, to knock back. **3** to be crazy, to be mad about: *esa chica me chifla = I'm crazy about that girl.*
chiflato *s.m.* whistle.
chifle *s.m.* **1** whistle, bird call. **2** powder horn, powder flask.
chiflido *s.m.* whistle, whistling.
chiflo *s.m.* whistle.
chigre *s.m.* cider shop.
chilaba *s.f.* jellab, jellaba, djellaba.
chile *s.m.* **1** chili, red pepper. **2** lie.
chileno, -a *adj./s.m.* y *f.* Chilean.
chilindrina *s.f.* **1** trifle. **2** joke, story.
chillar *v.i.* **1** to shout, to scream, to shriek, to yell. **2** to get angry, to be annoyed. **3** to howl, to squeal, to squeak, to screech. **4** to protest, to complain.
chillarse *v.i.* **1** to complain, to protest. **2** to get crossed, to take offence.
chillido *s.m.* howl, squeak, squeal, screech, yell, scream, shriek.
chillón, -ona *adj./s.m.* y *f.* **1** loud, shrill, noisy, screaming (persona). **2** shrill, strident, screechy, piercing (sonido). **3** gaudy, loud, lurid (color).
chimenea *s.f.* **1** chimney, smokestack (EE.UU.). **2** hearth, fireplace. **3** funnel (barco); shaft (minería); chimney (montaña). **4** nipple (armas).
chimpancé *s.m.* chimpanzee.
chimpín *adj.* **1** drunk, inebriated. || *s.m.* **2** brandy, liquor.
china *s.f.* V. **chino.**
chinarro *s.m.* stone, large pebble.
chinchar *v.t.* **1** to pester, to bother, to bug, to annoy. **2** to do in, to kill. || *v.pron.* **3** to get on with it, to get crossed, to get upset. **3 ¡chínchate!,** get stuffed, so there!
chinche *s.f.* **1** bug, bedbug. **2** thumbtack. **3** (fig.) nuisance, pest, naughty child.
chincheta *s.f.* drawing pin, thumbtack.
chinchilla *s.f.* chinchilla.
chinchona *s.f.* quinine.
chinchoso *adj.* **1** full of bugs. **2** tiresome, annoying, boring. **3** touchy, irritable.
chiné *adj.* chine (tela).
chinela *s.f.* **1** slipper, mule. **2** clog (chanclo).
chinero *s.m.* china cupboard; dresser.
chinesco *adj.* Chinese.
chingar *v.pron.* to fail, to fail through, to come to nothing.
chino, -a *adj./s.m.* y *f.* **1** Chinese, Chinaman (hombre), Chinese woman (mujer). || *s.m.* **2** stone, pebble. **3** (Am.) half-breed. **4** servant. || **5 cuento –,** tall story. **6 engañar como a un –,** to take someone for a ride. **7 esto es – para mí,** that's Greek to me. **8 tocarle a uno la china,** to fall to someone to do something, to have one's number up. **9 trabajar como un –,** to work like a slave.
chipirón *s.m.* ZOOL. squid.
chipichipi *s.m.* (Am.) continuous drizzle, mist.
chipriota o **chipriote** *adj.* y *s.m.* y *f.* Cypriot.
chiquillo, -a *adj.* **1** stupid, childish. || *s.m.* y *f.* **2** lad, boy (chico), girl (chica), kid.
chiquitura *adj.* small thing, insignificant detail.
chiribita *s.f.* **1** spark. **2** daisy. **3** (pl.) spots before the eyes.
chiribitil *s.m.* attic, garret, small room, slum, den, hole, cubbyhole.
chirigota *s.f.* **1** joke, laughing stock: *hacer de uno una chirigota = to make a laughing stock out of someone.* || **2 estar de –,** to be in a joking mood. **3 tomar algo a –,** to take something as a joke.
chirimbolo *s.m.* **1** thing, thingummy, oddlooking implement. || *pl.* **2** gear, equipment, stuff, odd and ends.
chirimía *s.f.* MUS. chirimia, chirimilla, shwan, hornpipe.
chirimoyo *s.m.* custard apple.
chiripa *s.f.* **1** lucky break, fluke (billar). **2** fluke, stroke of luck, lucky event.
chirla *s.f.* clam.
chirle *adj.* **1** tasteless, insipid, wishy-washy. || **2 agua –,** unsubstantial soup.
chirlo *s.m.* scar, slash, gash.
chirona *s.f.* (argot) jail, nick, prison, clink.
chirote *adj.* (Am.) nice, brave.
chirriar *v.i.* **1** chirp (el grillo), sing, cheep (pájaros). **2** to screech, to squawk; to creak, to squeak (gozne, rueda...); to screech, to squeal (frenos); to sizzle, to crackle (freír). **3** (Am.) to go on a spree, to go drinking.
chirrión *s.m.* (Am.) whip.
chichis *s.m.* drizzle.
chisgarabís *s.m.* meddlar, good-for-nothing, nosey parker, whippersnapper.
chisguete *s.m.* **1** drink, swig. **2** jet, spur, squirt.
chisme *s.m.* **1** gadget, jigger, knick-knack, thingummyjig. **2** piece of gossip, tale (chismorreo). || *pl.* **3** things, stuff, gear, tackle, odds and ends. **4** gossip, tales (habladurías).
chismear *v.i.* to gossip, to tell tales, to spread scandal.
chismería *s.f.* gossip, tittle-tattle, scandal.
chismero, -a *adj.* **1** gossipy, gossiping. || *s.m.* y *f.* **2** gossip, scandalmonger.
chismorrear *v.i.* V. **chismear.**
chismorreo *s.m.* V. **chismería.**
chismoso, -a *adj.* V. **chismero.**
chispa *s.f.* **1** spark. **2** (fig.) sparkle, gleam. **3** drop, sprinkling (lluvia). **4** small diamond. **5** small particule, flake, tiny amount. **5** wit, life, sparkle. **6** drunk, drunkness. **7** flash, thunderbolt. || **8 – eléctrica,** electric spark. **9 echar uno chispas,** to be hopping mad, to spit fire (EE.UU.). **10 tener –,** to be witty /funny, to be lively, to be a live wire. **11 tener una –,** to be tight.
chispazo *s.m.* spark, burn.
chispear *v.i.* **1** to spark, to give off sparks. **2** to drizzle, to spot with rain, to spit. **3** to sparkle, to scintillate. **4** to be brilliant.
chispero *s.m.* **1** bungler, clumsy worker. **2** blacksmith. **3** underworld character from the lower classes of Madrid.
chisporrotear *v.i.* to throw out sparks, to crackle, to spit, to hiss, to splutter.
chisquero *s.m.* tinder lighter.
¡chist! *interj.* ssh!, hush!
chistar *v.i.* **1** to open one's mouth to speak, to say a word: *nadie chistó = nobody said a word.* **2** to attract someone's attention. || **3 sin –,** without a word.
chiste *s.m.* **1** joke, funny story. **2** gibe, taunt, jeer. || **3 caer uno en el –,** to get the joke, to get it. **4 dar uno en el –,** to guess right.
chistera *s.f.* **1** fish basket, angler's basket. **2** top hat, topper.
chistoso, -a *adj.* funny, amusing, jocose, witty.
chistu *s.m.* flute (vasca).
chistulari *s.m.* flute player, flautist (del País Vasco).
chiticallando *adv.* **1** quietly, unobtrusively. **2** on the quiet, on the sly.
chitón *interj.* sh!, hush!
chivar *v.i.* **1** to annoy, to upset, to swindle. || *v.pron.* **2** to get annoyed. **3** to tell, to split. **4** to inform, to squeal.
chivatazo *s.m.* **1** tip-off, telling, informing. || **2 dar el –,** to inform, to give a tip-off, to split, to spill the beans.
chivato, -a *s.m.* y *f.* **1** informer. **2** kid, young goat.
chivo, -a *s.m.* y *f.* **1** kid, goat, billy-goat. || **2 hacer de – expiatorio,** to be the scapegoat. **3 barba de –,** goatee, pointed beard.
choc *s.m.* shock.
chocante *adj.* startling, striking, shocking, offensive, surprising.
chocantería *s.f.* impertinence, coarse joke.
chocar *v.i.* **1** to hit, to run into, to collide with. **2** to clash, to fall out with. **3** to argue. **4** to be surprising, to surprise. **5** to be out of place, not to fit in: *sus modales chocaban con su educación = his manners didn't fit in with his upbringing.* **6** to clink (vasos), to shake (manos): *¡chócala! = put it there!, shake on it!*
chocarrería *s.f.* coarseness, vulgarity, dirty joke, coarse story.
choco *adj.* (Am.) one-eyed.
chocolate *s.m.* chocolate, drinking chocolate.
chocolatera *s.f.* **1** chocolate-pot. **2** old thing, old crock, hulk.
chocolatería *s.f.* chocolate factory, chocolate shop.
chocolatero, -a *adj.* **1** fond of chocolate, chocolate-loving. || *s.m.* y *f.* **2** chocolate maker, chocolate seller, chocolate lover.
chocolatina *s.f.* bar of chocolate.
chochear *v.i.* **1** to dodder, to be in one's dotage, to be senile. **2** to be soft, to go all sentimental.

chochera *s.f.* 1 dotage, senility. 2 doting, favourite. 3 sentimental act.
chochez *s.f.* V. **chochera.**
chocho, -a *adj.* 1 doting, soft, sentimental. 2 doddery, senile. || 3 **estar –,** to dote on, to be soft about/on, to have a crush on.
chófer *s.f.* chauffeur, driver.
cholo *adj.* y *s.* 1 half-breed, mestizo. 2 civilized indian.
cholla o **chola** *s.f.* 1 nut, block, head, brains. 2 wound, sore.
chollo *s.m.* 1 soft job, good number. 2 bargain, snip.
chompa *s.f.* sweater, jumper.
chopera *s.f.* popular groce.
chopo *s.m.* 1 black poplar. 2 MIL. (fam.) gun.
choque *s.m.* 1 impact, jolt, clatter, crash, smash. 2 shock. 3 collision, conflict, clash. 4 blast, shock wave.
chorizo *s.m.* 1 sausage salami. 2 balancing pole. 3 (fam.) thief.
chorlito *s.m.* 1 ZOOL. plover. 2 scatterbrain.
chorrear *v.i.* 1 to flow, to run, to drip. 2 to pour, to drip with. 3 to tick off, to dress down. 4 to give in dribs and drabs.
chorrera *s.f.* 1 spout, channel. 2 mark. 3 frill, jabot, lace adornment. 4 rapids.
chorro *s.m.* 1 jet, spurt, squirt, spout. 2 dribble, trickle. 3 stream, shower, flood. 4 jet, blast. || 5 **a chorros,** in plenty. 6 **– de voz,** a verbal blast, a loud voice. 7 **estar/ser limpia como los chorros del oro,** to be as clean as a whistle. 8 **hablar a chorros,** to gabble, to jabber. 9 **soltar el –,** to burst out laughing, to produce insults. 10 **propulsión a –,** jet propelled.
chotacabras *s.f.* nightjar.
chotear *v.i.* y *pron.* 1 to make fun of, to take the mickey out of. 2 to joke, to take things as a joke. 3 (Am.) to spoil, to pamper.
chotis *s.m.* MUS. shottische.
choto, -a *s.m.* y *f.* 1 kid, young goat, calf. || *s.m.* 2 (Am.) penis. || 3 **estar como una chota,** to be round the bend, to be barmy.
chotuno *adj.* 1 sucking, very young. 2 weakly.
chova *s.f.* ZOOL. crow, rook, chough.
choza *s.f.* hut, shack, shanty.
christmas V. **crisma.**
chubasco *s.m.* 1 shower, downpour, squall. 2 stormcloud. 3 series of troubles or reverses, setback, adversity.
chubascoso *adj.* stormy, squally.
chubasquero *s.m.* oilskin raincoat.
chúcaro *adj.* 1 wild, untamed (animal). 2 shy, unsociable.
chuchada *s.f.* trick, swindle.
chuchería *s.f.* 1 trinket, piece of jewelry. 2 titbit, sweet piece of candy.
chucho *s.m.* 1 dog, hound, mongrel. 2 (Am.) chill, fever, malaria, shiver.
chueco *adj.* 1 bowlegs, bandy legs. 2 ball (de hueso). 3 joke. 4 stump (árbol).
chufa *s.f.* 1 BOT. chufa, earth almond, groundnut. 2 boast, brag. || 3 **dar una –,** to hit. 4 **horchata de –,** orgeat made from chufas.
chufla *s.f.* 1 joke, merry quip. || 2 **tomar algo a –,** to take something as a joke.
chuflar *v.i.* 1 to whistle. || *v.pron.* 2 to make fun of, to make jokes.
chuicas *s.f.pl.* odds and ends.
chulapo, -a *s.m.* y *f.* dandy, elegant person from the lower classes of Madrid.
chulería *s.f.* cheekiness, insolence, showing off, saucy wit.
chuleta *s.f.* 1 chop, cutlet. 2 cheeky person, barefaced individual. 3 slap. 4 crib, trot (EE.UU.) (de estudiantes).
chulo, -a *adj./s.m.* y *f.* 1 cheeky, barefaced, insolent, saucy. 2 flashy, natty, nice, pretty. 3 someone from the lower classes of Madrid. 4 rascally, villanous.
chumbera *s.f.* prickly pear.
chunga *s.f.* joke, fun, banter.
chupa *s.f.* 1 tight fitting waiscoat. || 2 **poner a uno como – de dómine,** to give a tremendous pasting, to call someone all the names under the sun.
chupado, -a *p.p.* de **chupar** *adj.* 1 skinny, gaunt, thin. 2 tight. 3 very easy. 4 drunk.
chupar *v.t.* e *i.* 1 to suck, to absorb, to soak up, to take in, to extract, to sip. 2 (fig.) to milk, to sap, to bleed. 3 to get thin, to lose weight, to waste away. 4 to lick, to moisten. 5 to spend: *se chupó seis años de cárcel = he spent six years in jail.* || 6 **¡chúpate esa!,** put that in your pipe and smoke it.
chupatintas *s.m.* penpusher, scribe.
chupete *s.m.* dummy, teat (biberón), lollipop (caramelo).
chupinazo *s.m.* 1 loud bang, starting signal. 2 hard kick (fútbol).
chupón, -ona *adj.* 1 sucking. 2 parasitic, sponging. || *s.m.* y *f.* 3 sucker. 4 parasite, leech, hanger-on, sponger, swindler. 5 sucking sweet, lollipop (caramelo). 6 dummy, teat. 7 baby's bottle, feeding bottle. 8 BOT. sucker, shoot.
chupóptero, -a *adj./s.m.* y *f.* (fig.) parasite, sponger, leech.
churumbel *s.m.* (fam.) kip, nipper.
churre *s.m.* thick grease, filth, grime.
churrete *s.m.* mark, streak, grease spot, dirty mark.
churretear *v.t.* to spot, to stain.
churriburri *s.m.* 1 turmoil, bustle, confusion, mess, mix-up, hubbub. 2 worthless individual, useless person.
churrigueresco, -a *adj.* 1 ARQ. baroque, Churrigueresque. 2 (fig.) excessively ornate, flowery, flashy, overelaborate, florid.
churro *adj.* y *s.* 1 coarse wooled, coarse. || *s.m.* 2 cruller, fritter. 3 shoddy piece of work, botch, mess. 4 dead loss, flop. 5 fluke.
churruscar *v.t.* y *pron.* to burn.
churrusco *s.m.* piece of burn toast.
chusco, -a *adj.* 1 funny, droll, oddly amusing. 2 ordinary, illmannered (persona). 3 mongrel. || *m.* y *f.* 4 joker, wit. || *s.m.* 5 MIL. ration bread.
chusma *s.f.* 1 rabble, mob, riffraff. 2 gang of galley slaves.
chusmaje *s.m.* rabble, mob, riffraff.
chuspa *s.f.* (Am.) leather bag, pouch.
chusquero *adj.* y *s.m.* MIL. (fam.) ranker.
chuzar *v.t.* to prick, to sting, to hurt.
chuzo *s.m.* 1 pike, spiked stick, pointed stick. 2 metal tipped stick. || 3 **caer/llover chuzos de punta,** to pour down, to rain cats and dogs, to rain pitchforks.
chuzón *adj.* y *s.m.* 1 sharp, cunning, witty. 2 crafty, sly, amusing. 3 stubborn.

d, D *s.f.* d, D (quinta letra del alfabeto español).
dable *adj.* viable, feasible.
dactilar *adj.* 1 digital, finger. || **2 huella –,** fingerprint.
dáctilo *s.m.* dactyl.
dactilografía *s.f.* typing, typewriting.
dactilográfico, -a *adj.* typing.
dactilógrafo, -a *s.m.* y *f.* typist.
dactilología *s.f.* sign language, finger language.
dactiloscopia *s.f.* fingerprint identification.
dadaísmo *s.m.* ART. dadaism.
dádiva *s.f.* 1 present, gift (regalo). 2 donation (donación).
dadivosidad *s.f.* generosity.
dadivoso, -a *adj.* generous, open-hand; liberal (con dinero o parecido).
dado, -a *p.p.* 1 de **dar.** || *s.m.* 2 dice (para jugar). 3 MIL. case-shot, grape-shot (parte que compone la metralla). 4 MEC. block (para soporte). 5 stud (refuerzo de una cadena). || **6 cargar los dados,** to load the dice. **7 correr el –,** to be in luck, to be lucky. **8 –...,** in view of, considering: *dado el estado de las carreteras no saldremos hoy = in view of the state of the roads we won't set out today.* **9 – a,** given to: *mi hijo es muy dado a contestar con mala educación = my son is much given to answering back in a bad manner.* **10 – falso,** false dice, loaded dice. **11 – que,** so long as, given that, granted that: *dado que no quieres, me lo comeré yo = given that you don't want it, I'll eat it.* **12 dar/echar – falso,** to deceive, to trick.
dador, -ora *s.m.* y *f.* 1 giver, donor. 2 bearer (de una carta). 3 drawer (de una letra de cambio).
daga *s.f.* dagger.
daguerrotipia *s.f.* daguerrotypy.
daguerrotipo *s.m.* daguerrotype (imagen o aparato).
dalia *s.f.* BOT. dahlia.
dálmata *adj./s.m.* y *f.* Dalmatian (de Dalmacia y perro).
dalmática *s.f.* dalmatic.
daltoniano, -a *adj.* 1 colour blind, daltonian. || *s.m.* y *f.* 2 sufferer from colour blindness.
daltonismo *s.m.* MED. colour blindness.
dama *s.f.* 1 lady. 2 lady-in-waiting (de cámara). 3 leading lady (actriz principal). 4 Queen (en ajedrez). 5 King (en las damas). 6 lover, mistress (manceba). || *p.l.* 7 draughts (damas). || **8 – cortesana,** courtesan. **9 – de honor,** bridesmaid (en una boda); lady-in-waiting (de una reina). **10 primera –,** POL. first lady. leading lady (teatro). **11 tablero de damas,** draughtboard.
damajuana *s.f.* demijohn.
damascado, -a *adj.* damask.
damasco *s.m.* damask.
damasquinado, -a *adj.* damascene.
damasquinar *v.t.* to damask.
damasquino, -a *adj.* Damascene.
damisela *s.f.* 1 HIST. damsel 2 courtesan. 3 young lady.
damnación *s.f.* damnation.
damnificado, -a *adj.* 1 damned, condemned. 2 injured (herido). **3 los damnificados,** the victims.
damnificar *v.t.* 1 to injure, to harm (herir). 2 to damage (dañar).
dandi *s.m.* dandy.
dandismo *s.m.* dandyism.
danés, -a *adj.* 1 Danish. || *s.m.* y *f.* 2 Dane. || *s.m.* 3 Danish (idioma). || **4 gran –,** Great Dane.
dantesco, -a *adj.* 1 Dantesque. Dantean. 2 horrific, macabre (fig.).
danza *s.f.* 1 dance. 2 shady deal, dubious affair (asunto sucio). 3 row, quarrel (riña). 4 mess (lío). || **5 en –,** full of activity. **6 entrar en –,** to be one's turn (para iniciar una actividad o similar).
danzante *s.m.* 1 dancer. 2 scatterbrain (despistado). 3 meddler, busybody (entrometido). || *adj.* 4 dancing.
danzar *v.t.* 1 to dance. || *v.i.* 2 to dance. 3 to meddle, to butt in (entremeterse).
danzarín, -ina *s.m.* y *f.* dancer.
dañado, -a *adj.* 1 spoiled (podrido). 2 damaged. 3 evil, cruel.
dañar *v.t.* 1 to damage, to spoil, to harm. 2 to injure, to hurt (a una persona). 3 to damage (fruta). 4 to condemn (condenar). || *v.r.* 5 MED. to hurt oneself. 6 to get damaged, to go off (estropearse).
dañino, -a *adj.* 1 harmful, damaging. || **2 animales dañinos,** vermin.
daño *s.m.* 1 harm, injury, hurt. 2 damage. 3 (MED.) problem, trouble. || **4 daños y perjuicios** DER. damages. **5 hacer –,** to hurt, to cause pain. **6 hacerse –,** to hurt oneself. **7 por mi –,** to my cost.
dañoso, -a *adj.* 1 harmful, bad. || **2 – para,** bad for, harmful to.
dar *v.t.* 1 to give: *dame el libro = give me the book.* 2 to hand (dar en la mano). 3 to produce, to bear (algún producto natural). 4 to make, to give (emociones): *me da tristeza saber la noticia = it makes me sad to learn the news.* 5 to cause, to give (enfermedad, reacción, etc.). 6 to show, to put on, to be on (como espectáculo): *dan la película nueva de Spielberg = they are showing Spielberg's new film.* 7 to emit, to give off (olor, sustancia, gas, etc.). 8 to give, to set (ejemplo, modelo, etc.). 9 to deal (cartas). 10 to give, to utter (grito, exclamación, etc.). 11 to give, to deal, to strike (golpe). 12 to strike (las horas del reloj). 13 to give (permiso). || *v.t.* y *v.pron.* 14 to take, to go for (paseo). || *v.i.* 15 to look out (a una parte u orientación). 16 to hit (contra un obstáculo). 17 to feel (dolor, mareo, ataque, etc.): *me ha dado una punzada en el costado = I have felt a jab in my side.* 18 to strike (acertar): *el disparo dio en el mismo blanco = the shot struck in the*

bull's eye. **19** to make (equivocación): *él finalmente dará en un error = in the long run he'll make a mistake.* **20** not to matter: *da igual = it doesn't matter.* **21** to get used, to take a liking to: *los chicos han dado en ensuciarlo todo = the kids have got used to getting everything dirty.* || *v.pron.* **22** to happen, to take place: *it so happens that he's German = se da el caso de que es alemán.* **23** to surrender, to give in. **24** to be found: *este animal sólo se da en esta zona = this animal is only found in this region.* **25** to take to: *darse a la bebida = to take to drink.* || **26 ahí me las den todas,** I don't give a damn. **27 dale,** don't stop, go on (especialmente con vehículos). **28 dale que dale,** without stopping, keeping it up. **29 — a conocer algo,** to let everybody know about something, to inform about something. **30 — a entender algo,** to hint; to explain: *él me dio a entender que no me quería = he hinted that he didn't love me.* **31 — con, a)** to come across, to find (persona o cosa); **b)** to fall; to hit (con una parte del cuerpo): *dio con la cabeza en el suelo = he hit his head on the floor.* **32 — de sí,** to stretch (comida, ropa, etc.). **33 — por bien empleado,** to consider worth the trouble. **34 — por hecho,** to take for granted. **35 — que hablar/decir/pensar,** to give grounds for criticism/suspicion. **36 — que hacer,** to cause trouble. **37 darse bien/mal, a)** to be good/bad at (una asignatura, especialidad, habilidad, etc.); **b)** to come on well/poorly, to grow well/poorly (un fruto, producto, etc.): *en esta región se dan muy bien los tomates = tomatoes grow very well in this region.* **38 dársela a alguien,** to fool somebody. **39 dárselas de,** to pose as, to boast of being, to brag of being. **40 darse por aludido,** to take it personally. **41 darse por vencido,** to surrender. **42 darse uno a conocer, a)** to make oneself known; **b)** to open oneself. **43 — uno en,** to finish up in, to end up in. **44 — uno en blando,** to do something easily. **45 — uno en duro,** to meet resistance. **46 — y tomar,** to discuss. **47 dé donde dé,** without thinking, without stopping to think. **48 donde las dan las toman,** if one sows evil, one will reap it.

OBS. Este verbo tiene una gran riqueza de expresiones que no se pueden incluir en el artículo anterior. Consiste esta riqueza en combinarlo con distintos sustantivos: **49** expresa entonces el significado del sustantivo: *darse prisa = to hurry; dar caza a = to chase.*

dardo *s.m.* **1** dart. **2** (fig.) jibe, barbed remark. **3** dace (pez).

dársena *s.f.* MAR. basin, dock.

darvinismo o **darwinismo** *s.m.* Darwinian.

darvinista o **darwinista** *adj./s.m.* y *f.* Darwinist.

data *s.f.* **1** date (fecha). **2** COM. item. **3** outlet (en un depósito de agua).

datar *v.t.* **1** to date, to place a date on. **2** COM. to credit. || *v.i.* **3** to date. || **4 — de,** to date back to, to date from.

dátil *s.m.* **1** BOT. date. **2** date mussel (molusco).

datilera *s.f.* date palm.

dativo *s.m.* GRAM. dative.

dato *s.m.* **1** fact, datum, item of information. || *pl.* **2** facts, data, information. || **3 datos personales,** personal details.

de *prep.* Indica: **a)** (posesión o pertenencia). **1** *la ventana de la casa = the window of the house.* **2** *el libro de Ana = Ann's book.* **3** *es de ella = it's hers.* **4** *la cama del dormitorio = the bed in the room.* **b)** (procedencia). **1** *son de Londres = they're from London.* **2** *de Madrid a Valladolid hay 180 kms = it's 180 kms from Madrid to Valladolid.* **3** *ir de París a Londres = to go from Paris to London.* **4** *tres de ellos = three of them.* **5** *él tiene un niño de su primera mujer = he's got a child by his first wife.* **6** *de esto se supone que = from this one may suppose.* **7** *la carretera de León = the road to Leon.* **8** *de pueblo en pueblo = from village to village.* **c)** (composición). **1** *un abrigo de pieles = a fur coat.* **2** *un reloj de oro = a gold watch.* **3** *está hecho de madera = it's made of wood.* **d)** (contenido). **1** *un vaso de leche = a glass of milk.* **2** *una botella de vino = a bottle of wine.* **e)** (característica). **1** *el hombre del sombrero = the man with the hat.* **2** *mi ropa de verano = my summer clothes.* **3** *un libro de inglés = an English book.* **4** *una clase de arte = an art class.* **f)** (descripción). **1** *es profesor de profesión = he's a teacher by profession.* **2** *el niño de ojos azules = the boy with blue eyes/the blue-eyed boy.* **3** *con cara de cansancio = with a tired-looking face.* **4** *dos millas de ancho = two miles in width/two miles wide.* **5** *mejor de salud = better in health.* **g)** (tiempo). **1** *a las tres de la noche = three o'clock at night.* **2** *de noche = at night.* **3** *de día = by day, during the day.* **h)** (edad). *una mujer de 40 años = a 40-year old woman/a woman of 40.* **i)** (aposición). **1** *el mes de mayo = the month of May.* **2** *la ciudad de Santander = the city of Santander.* **3** *la pobre de Ana = poor old Ann.* **4** *¿qué hay de comer? = what is there to eat?* **j)** (precio). **1** *una moneda de 100 pesetas = a 100-peseta coin.* **2** *un vino de 50 pesetas = a 50-peseta wine.* **k)** (modo). **1** *vestido de blanco = dressed in white.* **2** *de luto = in mourning.* **3** *de moda = in fashion.* **4** *de mal humor = in a bad mood.* **5** *de regalo = as a present.* **6** *de un salto = with a jump/with a loap/with a bound.* **7** *de un trago = in one gulp.* **8** *morir de hambre = to die of hunger.* **9** *saltar de alegría = to jump for joy.* **10** *trabajar de médico = to work as a Doctor.* **11** *cubierto de hielo = covered in/with ice.* **l)** (uso). **1** *agua de beber = drinking water.* **2** *máquina de coser = sewing machine.* **3** *papel de baño = toilet paper.* **m)** (introduce el agente). **1** *una obra de Picasso = a painting by Picasso.* **2** *odiado de todos = hated by everybody.* **n)** (números). *uno de cada tres = one in every three.* **o)** (condicional). **1** *de haberlo hecho = if I had done it.* **2** *de no ser así = if it were not so.* **p)** (superlativo o comparativo). **1** *la persona más alta de la clase = the tallest person in the class.* **2** *más de 5 = more than 5.* **q)** (partitivo). *dos de ellos = two of them.* **deambular** *v.i.* to saunter, to stroll.

deambulatorio *s.m.* REL. ambulatory.

deán *s.m.* dean.

deanato o **deanazgo** *s.m.* deanery.

debajo *adv.* **1** underneath, below. || **2 — de,** under, underneath, below, beneath. **3 por — de,** under, below.

debate *s.m.* debate, discussion.

debatible *adj.* debatable.

debatir *v.t.* to debate, to discuss.

debe *s.m.* **1** COM. debit side. || **2 — y haber,** debit and credit.

debelación *s.f.* MIL. victory.

debelar *v.t.* MIL. to beat, to defeat.

deber *v.t.* **1** to owe: *me debes mucho dinero = you owe me a lot of money.* || *v.i.* **2** must, to have to (con cierta obligación): *debes estudiar = you must study.* **3** should, ought to: *debía hacerlo ayer = I should have done it yesterday.* **4** must (con sentido de deducción más o menos probable): *he debido perderlo = I must have lost it.* **5** must, ought to (obligación moral): *no deberías fumar = you mustn't smoke.* || *v.pron.* **6** to be due to, to be on account of. || *s.m.* **7** duty, obligation: *cumplir con su deber = to carry out one's duty.* || *s.m.pl.* **8** homework (en el colegio). || **9 — de,** must: *debe de ser rico = he must be rich.*

debidamente *adv.* **1** properly. **2** as it should be done. **3** duly (en debida forma).

debido, -a *adj.* **1** due, correct, proper: *con el debido respeto = with due respect.* || **2 como es —,** as is proper, properly. **3 — a (que),** due to (the fact that).

débil *adj.* **1** weak. **2** feeble, weak (físico). **3** poor (salud). **4** weak, dim (luz). **5** feeble (esfuerzo). **6** weak, faint (grito). **7** weak (carácter). || *s.m.* y *f.* **8** weak person. || **9 — mental,** mentally retarded.

debilidad *s.f.* **1** weakness, feebleness. **2** faintness (sonidos, voces). **3** dimness (luces). || **3 — mental,** mental deficiency. || **4 tener una — por uno,** to have a soft spot for someone.

debilitación *s.f.* debilitation, weakening.

debilitar *v.t.* **1** to weaken, to debilitate. || *v.pron.* **2** to grow/get/become weak. **3** to weaken.

débito *s.m.* **1** debit (debe). **2** debt (deuda).

debut *s.m.* debut.

debutante *s.m.* y *f.* debutante.

debutar *v.i.* to make one's debut.

década *s.f.* **1** decade. **2** series of ten (serie de diez).

decadencia *s.f.* 1 decline, decay, decadence. || 2 **caer en –,** to fall into decline, decay.
decadente *adj.* decadent, dissolute.
decaer *v.i.* 1 to decline, to decay. 2 COM. to fall off. 3 to weaken (fuerzas). 4 to sink, to decline (salud). 5 to lose heart (decaer de ánimo): *no decaigas = don't lose heart.* 6 to drop (el viento).
decaído, -a *adj.* 1 weak (débil). 2 downhearted, depressed (sin ánimos). 3 decayed (en decadencia).
decaimiento *s.m.* 1 weakness (físico). 2 COM. falling-off. 3 decline, decay (decadencia). 4 depression, dejection (sin aliento).
decalvar *v.t.* to crop.
decampar *v.i.* MIL. to decamp, to strike camp.
decanía *s.f.* ecclesiastical lands.
decanato *s.m.* 1 deanship. 2 deanery (despacho).
decano *s.m.* 1 dean (de universidad, etc.). 2 senior member (persona más antigua en una asociación, institución, etc.).
decantación *s.f.* decantation, decanting.
decantar *v.t.* 1 to pour off, to decant (líquidos). 2 to laud, to praise (alabar).
decapitación *s.f.* decapitation, beheading.
decapitar *v.t.* to decapitate, to behead.
decápodo *s.m.* ZOOL. decapod.
decena *s.f.* 1 ten. || *pl.* 2 tens. || 3 **decenas de miles,** tens of thousands. 4 **por decenas,** in tens.
decenal *adj.* decennial.
decencia *s.f.* 1 decency. 2 honesty. 3 cleanness, tidiness. || 4 **faltar a la –,** to offend against decency.
decenio *s.m.* decade.
decentar *v.t.* 1 to start spending, counting (empezar a gastar o contar). 2 to become sore (ulcerarse).
decente *adj.* 1 honest, honorable. 2 decent. 3 reputable, respectable. 4 clean, tidy (limpio).
decentemente *adv.* 1 honestly. 2 decently. 3 respectably. 4 cleanly.
decepción *s.f.* disappointment.
decepcionar *v.t.* to disappoint.
deceso *s.m.* death.
decibel o **decibelio** *s.m.* decibel.
decididamente *adv.* 1 determinedly, resolutely. 2 definitely (realmente).
decidido, -a *adj.* 1 determined, resolute.
decidir *v.t.* 1 to decide. 2 to settle, to decide (un asunto, un problema, una cuestión). || *v.i.* 3 to decide, to choose. || 4 decidir entre dos cosas, to choose between two things. || *v.pron.* 5 to make up one's mind, to decide. || 6 **decidirse a,** to decide to. 7 **decidirse por,** to decide on.
decidor, -ora *adj.* 1 funny, witty (gracioso). || *s.m.* y *f.* 2 wit, witty speaker.
decimal *adj.* 1 decimal. || *s.c.* 2 decimal.
décimo, -a *adj.* 1 tenth. || *s.m.* y *f.* 2 tenth. 2 tenth part (de una lotería). || *s.f.* 4 **décima espinela,** ten-line stanza.
decimoctavo, -a *adj.* eighteenth.
decimocuarto, -a *adj.* fourteenth.
decimonono, -a o **decimonoveno, -a** *adj.* nineteenth.
decimoprimero, -a *adj.* eleventh.
decimoquinto, -a *adj.* fifteenth.
decimosegundo, -a *adj.* twelfth.
decimoséptimo, -a *adj.* seventeenth.
decimosexto, -a *adj.* sixteenth.
decimotercero, -a *adj.* thirteenth.
decimotercio, -a *adj.* thirteenth.
decir *v.t.* y *pron.* 1 to say, to tell: *yo te dije que no podía = I told you I couldn't.* || *v.t.* 2 to tell (una mentira). 3 to say (misa, oración). 4 to say (algo): *say that you don't love him = di que no le quieres.* || *s.m.* 5 saying, phrase: *es un decir = it's just a phrase.* || 6 **a – de todos,** by all accounts. 7 **a – verdad,** to tell you the truth, being completely honest. 8 **como quien no dice nada,** it's no trifle, it's no small matter. 9 **dar que –,** to set tongues wagging. 10 **– bien/mal,** to be right/wrong: *dices bien, es un idiota = you're right, he's stupid.* 11 **– por –,** to talk for the sake of talking, to talk for talking's sake. 12 **– que no/nones,** to say no, to deny. 13 **– que sí,** to say yes, to admit. 14 **– uno para sí,** to say to oneself. 15 **– y hacer,** no sooner said than done, to do very quickly. 16 **¡diga!,** hello! (especialmente en el lenguaje telefónico). 17 **el qué dirán,** the concern for what people will think. 18 **es –,** that is, that is to say. 19 **es mucho –,** that's saying a lot.
decisión *s.f.* 1 decision. 2 DER. judgement. || *s.i.* 3 determination, decision. || 4 **tomar una –,** to make a decision.
decisivamente *adv.* decisively, determinedly.
decisivo, -a *adj.* 1 decisive. || 2 **voto –,** casting vote.
declamación *s.f.* 1 ART. declamation. 2 recital (recital).
declamar *v.t.* e *i.* 1 to declaim. 2 to recite (poesía). 3 to rant (con vehemencia). 4 to speak in public (en público).
declamatorio, -a *adj.* 1 declamatory. 2 ranting (desp.).
declaración *s.f.* 1 declaration. 2 statement (a la prensa). 3 DER. statement, evidence. 4 bid, call (bridge). 5 proposal (de matrimonio). || 6 **– de culpabilidad,** confession of guilt. 7 **– de derechos,** bill of rights. 8 **– de guerra,** declaration of war. 9 **– de renta,** income tax return. 10 **hacer una –,** to make a statement. 11 **prestar –,** to give evidence.
declarado, -a *adj.* declared, open.
declarar *v.t.* 1 to declare, to state: *declaré todo = I declared everything.* 2 to bid (bridge). 3 to declare (guerra). 4 to declare (en aduana). || *v.i.* 6 to declare. 7 DER. to testify, to give evidence. || *v.pron.* 8 to declare oneself. 9 to break out (guerra, fuego, epidemia). 10 to declare one's love (declarar su amor). 11 **declararse culpable,** to plead guilty. 12 **declararse por,** to come out in favour of.
declaratorio, -a *adj.* declaratory.
declinable *adj.* GRAM. declinable.
declinación *s.f.* 1 FIS. declination. 2 GRAM. declension. 3 (fig.) decline, decay. 4 **– magnética,** magnetic variation.
declinar *v.t.* 1 to decline, to turn down. 2 GRAM. to decline. || *v.i.* 3 to decline, to slope down (tierra). 4 to diminish (fiebre, fuerzas). 5 to decay (decaer). 6 GRAM. to decline. 7 (fig.) to fade, to fall off. 8 to draw to an end (el día, una batalla). 9 to get weaker (debilitarse). 10 to sink (el sol).
declive *s.m.* 1 slope, incline (cuesta). 2 decline, decay (decadencia). || 3 **en –,** on a slope, sloping.
decocción *s.f.* decoction.
decoloración *s.f.* fading.
decolorar o **descolorar** *v.t.* 1 to discolour, to fade. || *v.pron.* 2 to fade, to get discoloured.
decomisar *v.t.* to confiscate, to seize.
decomiso *s.m.* confiscation, seizure.
decoración *s.f.* 1 decoration. 2 set, scenery (teatro). || 3 **– de interiores,** interior decorating.
decorado *s.m.* 1 set, scenery (teatro, cine). 2 decoration.
decorador *s.m.* 1 decorator. 2 stage designer (teatro).
decorativo, -a *adj.* 1 decorative, ornamental.
decoro *s.m.* 1 decorum, decency (honra). 2 respect (respeto). 3 dignity (dignidad). 4 modestly, decently (con pudor). 5 purity (pureza).
decorosamente *adv.* 1 decorously. 2 dignifiedly (con dignidad). 3 decently (decentemente).
decoroso, -a *adj.* 1 decorous, decent. 2 respectable (respetable). 3 modest (modesto).
decrecer o **descrecer** *v.i.* 1 to decrease. 2 to go down (agua). 3 to get shorter (días). 4 to diminish (disminuir).
decreciente *adj.* decreasing, diminishing.
decrecimiento *s.m.* 1 decrease. 2 diminution (disminución). 3 subsiding (agua).
decrepitación *s.f.* decrepitation.
decrepitar *v.i.* to decrepitate.
decrépito, -a *adj.* decrepit.
decrepitud *s.f.* decrepitude.
decretar *v.t.* 1 to decree. 2 to order, to ordain (ordenar).
decreto *s.m.* 1 decree, order. 2 decree (del Papa). 3 POL. act. 4 **por –,** by decree. 5 **real –,** DER. royal decree.
decúbito *s.m.* 1 MED. decubitus. || 2 **– lateral,** side position. 3 **– prono,** prone position. 4 **– supino,** supine position.
décuplo, -a *adj.* 1 tenfold, ten times. || *s.m.* y *f.* 2 tenfold.
decurso *s.m.* 1 course. || 2 **en el – del tiempo,** in the course of time.
dechado *s.m.* 1 perfect example (ejemplar). 2 model (modelo). || 3 **un – de perfecciones/virtudes, etc.,** a model of perfection/virtue, etc.
dedal *s.m.* thimble.
dédalo *s.m.* labyrinth.

dedicación *s.f.* 1 dedication. 2 devotion, dedication to (dedicación a). || **3 de — exclusiva,** full-time, on exclusive contract.

dedicar *v.t.* 1 to dedicate. 2 REL. to consecrate. 3 to dedicate (un libro). 4 to devote, to give (tiempo, esfuerzos, dinero, etc.). 5 to inscribe (fotos, libros, etc.). 6 to address (palabras). || *v.pron.* 7 to devote, dedicate oneself. 8 to take up. 9 to spend one's time (pasar el tiempo). || **10 ¿a qué te dedicas?,** what's your job? **11 dedicarse a algo,** to take up something.

dedicatoria *s.f.* inscription, dedication.

dedicatorio, -a *adj.* dedicatory.

dedil *s.m.* fingerstall.

dedo *s.m.* 1 finger (de la mano). 2 toe (del pie). || **3 — anular,** ring finger. **4 — meñique,** little finger. **5 — del corazón,** middle finger. **6 — índice,** index finger, forefinger. **7 — pulgar,** thumb. **8 — gordo del pie,** big toe. **9 comerse los dedos,** to become nervous. **10 contar con los dedos,** to count on one's fingers. **11 chuparse los dedos,** to suck one's fingers. **12 le das un — y se toma hasta el codo,** give him an inch and he takes a mile. **13 estar a dedos de,** to be within an inch of, to be on the point of. **14 hacer dedos,** to practise. **15 meter el — a uno,** to make someone talk. **16 no mover un —,** not to move a finger. **17 poner el — en algo,** to put one's finger on something. **18 poner el — en la llaga,** to touch a sore spot. **19 señalar con el —,** to point. **20 no tener dos dedos de frente,** to be as thick as two short planks.

deducción *s.f.* 1 deduction, inference. 2 COM. deduction.

deducir *v.t.* 1 to deduce, to infer. 2 COM. to deduct. 3 DER. to claim.

deductivo, -a *adj.* deductive.

defecación *s.f.* defecation.

defecar *v.i.* to defecate.

defección *s.f.* defection, desertion.

defectible *adj.* faulty, flawed.

defectivo, -a *adj.* 1 defective, faulty. 2 GRAM. defective.

defecto *s.m.* 1 defect, flaw. 2 ELEC. fault. 3 flaw (de una joya). 4 shortcoming, fault (moral). 5 flaw (argumentos). 6 lack, shortage (carencia). || **7 — físico,** physical defect. **8 — de la palabra,** speech defect. **9 por — de,** for lack of.

defectuosamente *adv.* defectively, faultily.

defectuoso, -a *adj.* defective, faulty.

defender *v.t.* 1 to defend against/from (de contra, de). 2 to protect (proteger). 3 DER. to defend. 4 to uphold, to defend (idea, causa, argumento, etc.). || *v.pron.* 5 to defend oneself. 6 to manage, to get by: *se defiende en inglés = he gets by in English.*

defendible *adj.* defensible.

defendido, -a *adj.* 1 DER. defendant. || *s.m.* y *f.* 2 defendant.

defenestrar *v.t.* to throw out of the window.

defensa *s.f.* 1 defence (deportes, ajedrez, derecho, militar). 2 fender (de un barco). 3 shin guard (para la pierna). 4 protection, shelter. || *pl.* 5 DEP. defenders. 6 MIL. defences.

defensiva *s.f.* 1 defensive. || **2 estar a la —,** to be on the defensive.

defensivo, -a *adj.* defensive.

defensor *s.m.* 1 defender. 2 DER. counsel for the defence. 3 protector, champion (de una causa).

deferencia *s.f.* 1 deference. 2 regard (respeto).

deferente *adj.* deferential.

deferir *v.i.* 1 to defer. || *v.t.* 2 DER. to refer, to transfer.

deficiencia *s.f.* 1 deficiency. 2 lack (falta). 3 faultiness, defectiveness (imperfección). 4 shortcoming (de un equipo, argumento, etc.). 5 defect (defecto). || **6 — mental,** MED. mental deficiency.

deficiente *adj.* 1 deficient, wanting. 2 lacking, insufficient (insuficiente). 3 faulty, defective (defectuoso). 4 weak, poor (alumno, trabajo). || *s.m.* y *f.* **5 — mental,** mentally retarded person, mental deficient.

déficit *s.m.* 1 FIN. deficit. 2 (fig.) shortage, lack, shortfall.

deficitario, -a *adj.* showing a deficit.

definible *adj.* definable.

definición *s.f.* 1 definition. || **2 por —,** by definition.

definido, -a *adj.* 1 definite. || **2 artículo —,** GRAM. definite article. **3 bien —,** well-defined.

definir *v.t.* 1 to define. 2 to explain, to clarify (explicar). 3 to put the final touches to (una obra pictórica).

definitivamente *adv.* 1 finally. 2 for good: *se fue definitivamente = he went for good.*

definitivo, -a *adj.* 1 definitive, final. || **2 en definitiva,** in short, finally.

deflación *s.f.* deflation.

deflagración *s.f.* deflagration.

deflagrador *s.m.* igniter.

deflagrar *v.i.* deflagrate.

defoliación *s.f.* defoliation.

deforestado, -a *adj.* deforested.

deformación *s.f.* 1 deformation. 2 distortion (televisión). 3 TEC. warping.

deformar *v.t.* 1 to deform. 2 to distort (televisión, la cara). 3 MEC. to strain. 4 to warp (madera, puertas, etc.). || *v.pron.* 5 to be deformed (el cuerpo, un miembro, etc.). 6 to become, get deformed. 7 to become, get distorted. 8 to lose one's shape (perder la forma).

deforme o **disforme** *adj.* 1 deformed. 2 misshapen (cosas). 3 distorted (señal, cara, imagen, etc.).

deformidad *s.f.* 1 deformity. 2 (fig.) flaw, shortcoming.

defraudación *s.f.* 1 fraud (fraude). 2 disappointment (decepción). || **3 — fiscal,** tax evasion.

defraudar *v.t.* 1 to defraud. 2 to dash (esperanzas). 3 to disappoint (decepcionar). 4 to deceive (engañar). 5 to evade (impuestos).

defunción *s.f.* 1 demise (fallecimiento). 2 death (muerte).

degeneración *s.f.* 1 degeneration. 2 degeneracy (moral).

degenerado, -a *adj./s.m.* y *f.* degenerate.

degenerar *v.i.* 1 to degenerate. 2 to decay (decaer). || *v.pron.* 3 to become degenerate.

deglución *s.f.* swallowing.

deglutir *v.t.* e *i.* to swallow.

degollación *s.f.* 1 throat slitting. 2 beheading, decapitation (decapitación). 3 massacre, slaughter (masacre). || **4 la — de los Inocentes,** REL. the Massacre of the Innocents.

degolladero *s.m.* 1 ANAT. throat, neck. 2 slaughterhouse (matadero). 3 HIST. scaffold. || **4 llevarse al —,** to expose oneself to great danger.

degollador, -ora *s.m.* y *f.* executioner.

degolladura *s.f.* 1 slit, cut (herida en la garganta). 2 joint (juntura entre ladrillos).

degollar *v.t.* 1 to slit, cut the throat of. 2 to behead, to decapitate (decapitar). 3 to destroy (destruir). 4 to murder (una obra de teatro, etc.). 5 to kill badly (en los toros). 6 MAR. to cut (una vela).

degollina *s.f.* massacre, slaughter.

degradación *s.f.* humiliation, degradation.

degradante *adj.* degrading, humiliating: *una tarea degradante = a humiliating task.*

degradar *v.t.* 1 to degrade, to humiliate. 2 ART. to gradate. 3 MIL. to demote. || *v.pron.* 4 to humiliate, to degrade oneself.

degüello *s.m.* 1 throat slitting, cutting. 2 decapitation, beheading (decapitación). || 3 neck, shaft (de un arma, un dardo, etc.). 4 massacre, slaughter (masacre). || **5 entrar a —,** to put to the sword. **6 tirar a —,** to be after someone's throat. **7 tocar a —,** to give the order to attack (en caballería).

degustación *s.f.* sampling, tasting.

degustar *v.t.* to sample, to taste.

dehesa *s.m.* meadow, pasture.

deidad *s.f.* 1 deity, god. || *s.i.* 2 divinity, deity (divinidad).

deificación *s.f.* deification.

deificar *v.t.* 1 to deify. 2 to praise, to exalt (alabar).

deísmo *s.m.* deism.

deísta *adj.* 1 deistic, deistical. || *s.m.* y *f.* 2 deista.

dejación *s.f.* DER. abandonment, cession.

dejada *s.f.* 1 abandonment, relinquishment. || 2 drop shot (en tenis, squash, etc.).

dejadez *s.f.* 1 laziness (pereza). 2 negligence, carelessness (negligencia).

dejado, -a *adj.* 1 untidy, disorderly (descuidado). 2 careless, negligent (negligente). 3 idle, lazy (perezoso). 4 depressed, dejected (desanimado). || **5 — de la mano de Dios,** (fig.) godforsaken.

dejar *v.t.* 1 to leave, to forget. 2 to give up, to stop (de fumar, trabajar, etc.). 3 to drop off, to drop (depositar). 4 to abandon, to leave (abandonar). 5 to leave (un empleo). 6 to produce, to make (beneficios). 7 to leave out, to omit (omitir). 8 to let, to allow (permitir). 9 to leave alone (no tocar). 10 to wait (esperar). 11 to leave (una herencia). 12 to finish, to stop (terminar una cosa). 13 to lend (prestar). || 14 **— aparte,** to leave aside. 15 **— atrás,** to leave behind. 16 **— caer,** to drop. 17 **— para después,** to leave till later. 18 **dejarlo por imposible,** to give it up as being too difficult. 19 **— mucho que desear,** to leave a lot to be desired. 20 **— las cosas así,** to leave things as they are. 21 **— entrar,** to let in. 22 **— plantado,** to stand up. 23 **¡déjalo!,** stop it! (¡para!), forget it! (¡no te preocupes!). 24 **¡déjame en paz!,** leave me alone! 25 **como dejo dicho,** as I have said. 26 **— en la estacada,** to leave in the lurch. 27 **no — piedra por mover,** to leave no stone unturned. || *v.i.* 28 **— de,** to give up, to stop. 29 **dejó de estudiar,** he gave up studying. 30 **no deja de trabajar,** he doesn't stop working. 31 **no — de,** not to fail to. 32 **no dejes de leerlo,** don't fail to read it. 33 **no puedo — de quererte,** I can't help loving you, I can't stop loving you. || *v.pron.* 34 to allow, let oneself. 35 **no te dejes engañar,** don't let yourself be fooled. 26 to neglect oneself (abandonarse). 37 **dejarse de,** to stop. 38 **¡déjate de bobadas!,** stop fooling around! 39 to forget, to leave (olvidar). 40 **dejarse crecer el pelo,** to let one's hair grow. 41 **dejarse llevar por,** to get carried away with.

deje *s.m.* accent.

dejo *s.m.* 1 end, finish (fin). 2 accent (deje). 3 aftertaste (sabor). 4 carelessness, negligence (dejadez). 5 after-effect (sentimiento después de una acción).

del *art.* 1 of the. 2 from the, V. **de.**

delación *s.f.* 1 accusation. 2 denunciation.

delantal *s.m.* 1 apron. 2 pinafore (con peto).

delante *adv.* 1 in front, ahead. 2 opposite (en frente). || 3 **— de,** in front of, before, ahead of: *delante de mi casa = in front of my house.*

delantera *s.f.* 1 front, front part. 2 front row (de un teatro, cine, etc.). 3 DEP. forward line. 4 (fig.) advantage, lead. || 5 **coger a uno la —,** to get ahead of someone. 6 **llevar la —,** to be in the lead. 7 **sacar la — a uno,** to take a head start on someone. 8 **tomar la —,** to take the lead.

delantero, -a *adj.* 1 front (fila, parte, rueda, etc.). 2 DEP. forward. 3 front, fore (pata). || *s.m.* 4 DEP. forward. 5 front (de prendas). || 6 **— centro,** centre-forward.

delatar *v.t.* 1 to denounce, to accuse. 2 to grass, to betray (soplar). 3 to reveal, to uncover (revelar).

delator *s.m.* 1 informer. 2 (fam.) grass.

delco *s.m.* MEC. distributor.

dele *s.m.* dele.

delectación *s.f.* delight, delectation.

delegación *s.f.* 1 delegation (acción de delegar). || 2 delegation (grupo). 3 COM. branch, local office. || 4 **— de Hacienda,** local tax office.

delegado, -a *s.m.* y *f.* 1 delegate. 2 COM. agent, representative.

delegar *v.t.* to delegate.

deleitable *adj.* delightful, pleasant, enjoyable.

deleitación *s.f.* delight, pleasure, delectation.

deleitar *v.t.* 1 to delight, to charm. || *v.pron.* 2 to delight in, to take pleasure in: *deleitarse en escuchar música = to delight in listening to music.*

deleite *s.m.* delight, pleasure.

deleitoso, -a *adj.* delightful, charming, enjoyable.

deletéreo, -a *adj.* poisonous, deleterious.

deletrear *v.t.* 1 to spell, to spell out. 2 (fig.) to decipher.

deletreo *s.m.* 1 spelling. 2 deciphering (desciframiento).

deleznable *adj.* 1 fragile. 2 slippery (resbaladizo). 3 short, ephemeral (breve). 4 unstable (inestable). 5 weak (débil).

delfín *s.m.* 1 ZOOL. dolphin. 2 HIST. Dauphin.

delgadez *s.f.* 1 thinness (flacura). 2 slimness (esbeltez).

delgado, -a *adj.* 1 thin. 2 slim (esbelto). 3 thin (flaco). 4 poor (tierra). 5 narrow (estrecho). 6 delicate (delicado). 7 clever, sharp (ingenioso). || *s.pl.* 8 flanks (de animales). || 9 **hilar —,** to split hairs.

deliberación *s.f.* deliberation.

deliberadamente *adv.* deliberately, on purpose.

deliberado, -a *adj.* deliberate.

deliberar *v.i.* 1 to deliberate, to ponder. || *v.t.* 2 to debate, to discuss.

deliberativo, -a *adj.* deliberative.

delicadeza *s.f.* 1 delicacy (finura). 2 tactfulness (tacto). 3 sensitivity (sensibilidad). 4 politeness (cortesía). 5 refinement (de modales). 6 scrupulousness (escrupulosidad). 7 frailty, delicacy (de salud). 8 squeamishness (remilgos). || 9 **falta de —,** tactlessness. 10 **tener la — de,** to be kind enough to.

delicado, -a *adj.* 1 delicate. 2 frail, delicate (salud). 3 soft, delicate (color). 4 thin, delicate (material). 5 sensitive (sensible). 5 delicate (situación). 6 refined (gustos). 7 fussy, hard to please (exigente). 8 scrupulous (escrupuloso). 9 squeamish (remilgado). 10 polite (cortés). 11 thoughtful (atento). 12 delicate (rasgos). 13 subtle (sutil). || 14 **hacerse el —,** to be very hard to please.

delicia *s.f.* 1 delight: *su niño es una delicia = their child is a delight.* || 2 **hacer las delicias,** to delight. 3 **no hay — comparable,** there's nothing to beat it.

deliciosamente *adv.* delightfully.

delicioso, -a *adj.* 1 delicious (de sabor). 2 charming, pleasant (encantador). 3 delightful (deleitable).

delictivo, -a *adj.* criminal.

delicuescencia *s.f.* deliquescence.

delicuescente *adj.* deliquescent.

delimitación *s.f.* delimitation.

delimitar *v.t.* to delimit.

delincuencia *s.f.* 1 delinquency. || 2 **— juvenil,** juvenile delinquency.

delincuente *adj./s.m.* y *f.* 1 delinquent, criminal, offender: *joven delincuente = juvenile delinquent.* || 2 *adj.* delinquent, criminal.

delineación *s.f.* delineation.

delineante *s.m.* y *f.* draughtsman.

delinear *v.t.* 1 to delineate, to outline. 2 to draw (dibujar).

delinquir *v.i.* to commit a crime; to break the law.

deliquio *s.m.* faint, fainting fit.

delirante *adj.* delirious.

delirar *v.i.* 1 to be delirious. 2 to talk nonsense (decir disparates). 3 to rant, to rave (desvariar): *está delirando = he's raving.*

delirio *s.m.* 1 MED. delirium. 2 ravings (ilusión). 3 nonsense (disparates). || 4 **con —,** madly: *te amo con delirio = I love you madly.* 5 **tener — por,** (fig.) to be mad about. 6 **delirios de grandeza,** delusions of grandeur.

delírium tremens *s.m.* MED. delirium tremens.

delito *s.m.* crime, offence: *delito político = political crime.*

delta *s.f.* 1 GEOG. delta. 2 delta (letra).

deltoides *adj.* ANAT. 1 deltoid. || 2 *s.m.* deltoid.

demacración *s.f.* emaciation.

demacrarse *v.pron.* to become emaciated, to waste away.

demagogia *s.f.* demagogy.

demagógico, -a *adj.* demagogic, demagogical.

demagogo, -a *s.m.* y *f.* demagogue.

demanda *s.f.* 1 DER. claim, petition. 2 COM. demand. 3 lawsuit, action (acción). 4 search (búsqueda). 5 request, appeal (petición). 6 inquiry (pregunta). || 7 **presentar una —,** to take legal action.

demandado, -a *s.m.* y *f.* DER. defendant.

demandante *s.m.* y *f.* DER. plaintiff.

demandar *v.t.* 1 to desire (desear). 2 to request (pedir). 3 to ask (preguntar). 4 to sue, to take legal action (entablar demanda judicial).

demarcación *s.f.* demarcation.

demarcar *v.t.* to demarcate.

demás *adj.* y *pron.indef.* 1 rest, remaining, other: *los demás deportistas se quedaron en el baile = the other athletes stayed at the dance.* || 2 **los —,** the others, the other people, the people, one's neighbours: *uno debe pensar en los demás = one must think of one's neighbours.* 3 **por —,** uselessly. 4 **por lo —,** as to the rest. 5 **... y —,** ... and so on.

demasía *s.f.* 1 surplus, excess. 2 audacity (atrevimiento). 3 insolence (insolen-

cia). 4 outrage (atropello). || **5 cometer demasías,** to go too far, to go over the top (fam.). **6 en –,** excessively.
demasiado, -a *adj.* 1 too much, excessive: *demasiado dinero = too much money.* || *pl.* 2 too many: *demasiadas plantas = too many plants.* || *adv.* 3 too, too much: *beber demasiado = to drink too much.*
demencia *s.f.* madness, insanity, dementia.
demente *adj.* 1 demented, insane, mad. || *s.m.* y *f.* 2 lunatic, madman.
demérito *s.m.* demerit, disadvantage.
demisión *s.f.* demission.
demiurgo *s.m.* FIL. demiurge.
democracia *s.f.* democracy.
demócrata *s.m.* y *f.* democrat.
democrático, -a *adj.* democratic.
democratización *s.f.* democratization.
democratizar *v.t.* to democratize.
demografía *s.f.* demography.
demográfico, -a *adj.* 1 demographic. || *atr.* 2 population. || **3 explosión demográfica,** population explosion.
demoledor, -a *adj.* 1 demolishing (de un edificio). 2 forceful, powerful (argumento, carácter, etc.). 3 devastating (ataque).
demoler *v.t.* 1 to pull down, to demolish. 2 (fig.) to demolish.
demolición *s.f.* demolition.
demoniaco, -a *adj.* demonic, demoniacal.
demonio *s.m.* 1 REL. devil. 2 evil spirit. || **3 como el –/como todos los demonios,** like the devil, like hell (en muchísimas combinaciones verbales): *corría como todos los demonios = he ran like hell.* **4 ¡–!,** the hell!: *¿qué demonio quieres? = what the hell do you want?* **5 ¡demonios!,** bloody hell!, hang it all! **5 estudiar con el –,** to be full of clever tricks. **6 llevarse a uno el –/los demonios/todos los demonios,** to go absolutely mad, to go up the walls. **7 ser uno un –/ser uno el mismísimo –,** to be full of devilment. **8 tener uno el – en el cuerpo,** to have the devil in one; to be always on the go.
demora *s.f.* delay: *sin demora = without delay.*
demorar *v.t.* 1 to delay. 2 to hold up: *el tren ha sido demorado = the train has been held up.* || *v.i.* 3 to stay on, to linger (detenerse). || *v.pron.* 5 to take a long time, to be a long time (retrasarse).
demoroso, -a *adj.* overdue, late.
demostrable *adj.* demonstrable.
demostración *s.f.* 1 demonstration. 2 show, display: *una demostración de cariño/ira/fuerza = a show of affection/anger/force.*
demostrar *v.t.* 1 to demonstrate (hacer una demostración). 2 to show: *demostrar interés/ignorancia = to show interest /ignorance.* 3 to prove (probar). 4 to prove: *eso demuestra que tiene dinero = that proves that he's got money.*
demostrativo, -a *adj.* 1 demonstrative. || *s.m.* 2 demonstrative.
demótico, -a *adj.* demotic.
demudar *v.t.* 1 to change, to alter (cambiar). 2 to distort (desfigurar). || *v.pron.* 3 to change colour (de color). 4 to change expression (de expresión). 5 to alter, change oneself (alterarse).
denario, -a *adj.* 1 denary. || *s.m.* 2 denarius (moneda).
dendrita *s.f.* MIN. y BOT. dendrite.
denegación *s.f.* 1 refusal (rechazo). 2 denial (negación).
denegar *v.t.* 1 to refuse (negarse). 2 to reject (rechazar). 3 to deny (negar). 4 to turn down, to reject (un recurso).
denegrecer *v.t.* 1 to blacken, to turn black. || *v.pron.* 2 to go black.
denegrido, -a *adj.* blackened.
denegrir *v.t.* 1 to blacken, to turn black. || *v.pron.* 2 to go black.
dengoso, -a *adj.* affected.
dengue *s.m.* 1 affectation (melindre). 2 MED. dengue. || *s.c.* 3 shawl (chal). || **4 hacer dengues,** to act demurely. **5 no me vengas con dengues,** don't be so silly.
denigración *s.f.* denigration.
denigrar *v.t.* 1 to denigrate, to belittle. 2 to insult, to abuse (insultar).
denigrativo, -a *adj.* disparaging
denodadamente *adv.* bravely, daringly.
denodado, -a *adj.* brave, daring.
denominación *s.f.* 1 denomination, name. || 2 denomination, naming (acción).
denominado, -a *adj.* called, named.
denominador *s.m.* 1 MAT. denominator. || **2 – común,** MAT. common denominator. || *adj.* 3 denominative.
denominar *v.t.* to denominate, to name, to call.
denominativo, -a *adj.* denominative.
denostar *v.t.* to insult, to abuse.
denotación *s.f.* denotation.
denotar *v.t.* 1 to denote. 2 to mean (significar). 3 to show, to indicate (indicar).
densidad *s.f.* 1 density. 2 thickness (espesor). || **3 – de población,** population density.
densímetro *s.m.* densimeter.
denso, -a *adj.* 1 dense, compact. 2 thick (humo, líquidos). 3 dry, heavy (libro, discurso, lectura, etc.). 4 dark, black (la noche).
dentado, -a *adj.* 1 toothed (con dientes). 2 cogged, toothed (rueda). 3 perforated (sello). 4 serrated (cuchillo). 5 BOT. dentate.
dentadura *s.f.* 1 teeth, set of teeth. || **2 – postiza,** false teeth.
dental *adj.* 1 dental. || *s.m.* 2 dental. || **3 crema –,** toothpaste. **4 consonante –,** FON. dental consonant.
dentar *v.t.* 1 to furnish with teeth. 2 to furnish with cogs (una rueda). 3 to perforate (un sello). 4 to serrate (un cuchillo). || *v.i.* 5 to cut one's teeth, to teethe (un niño).
dentario, -a *adj.* dental.
dentejón *s.m.* yoke.
dentellada *s.f.* 1 bite, nip (mordisco). 2 toothmark (señal). || **3 a dentelladas,** with one's teeth.
dentellado, -a *adj.* HIST. engrailed.
dentellar *v.i.* to rattle, to chatter: *dentellar de miedo = to rattle with fear.*
dentellear *v.i.* to nibble, to peck.
dentellón *s.m.* 1 ARQ. dentil. 2 large tooth (diente).
dentera *s.f.* 1 setting on edge (dientes). 2 envy (envidia). || **3 darle – a uno,** to set one's teeth on edge.
denticia *s.f.* teething medicine.
dentición *s.f.* 1 teething (acción). 2 ANAT. dentition. **3 estar con la –,** to be teething.
dentífrico *s.m.* 1 toothpaste. || *adj.* 2 tooth.
dentina *s.m.* dentine.
dentista *s.m.* MED. dentist.
dentón, -a *adj.* toothy, buck-toothed: *una persona dentona = a buck-toothed person.*
dentro *adv.* 1 inside, indoors. **2 – de, a)** within, in (en el tiempo): *dentro de unos días = in a few days;* **b)** inside (lugar): *dentro de la casa = inside the house.* **3 – de lo posible,** as far as is possible, as far as one can.
dentudo, -a *adj.* 1 toothy, buck-toothed. || *s.m.* y *f.* 2 toothy o buck-toothed person.
denuedo *s.m.* bravery, daring.
denuesto *s.m.* insult.
denuncia *s.f.* 1 report (informe). 2 denunciation (delación). 3 report (documento). 4 DER. accusation. 5 denunciation (de un tratado).
denunciable *adj.* indictable.
denunciante *s.m.* y *f.* informer, accuser. || 2 *adj.* denouncing.
denunciar *v.t.* 1 to report (un robo, accidente, etc.). 2 to denounce (criticar). 3 to denounce, to report, to inform on (delatar). 4 to make public (promulgar). 5 to indicate (indicar). 6 to accuse, to denounce (acusar): *te denunciaré por muchas razones = I'll denounce you for many reasons.*
denunciatorio, -a *adj.* 1 who denounces. 2 (p.u.) denunciatory.
deontología *s.f.* deontology.
deparar *v.t.* 1 to provide (suministrar). 2 to cause (causar). 3 to give (otorgar). 4 to give (satisfacción).
departamental *adj.* departmental.
departamento *s.m.* 1 department, section. 2 office. 3 district (distrito). 4 compartment (de un tren). 5 compartment (de una caja, un mueble, etc.).
departir *v.i.* to talk, to converse.
depauperar *v.t.* 1 to impoverish, to pauperise. || *v.t.* y *pron.* 2 MED. to weaken, to become weak.
dependencia *s.f.* 1 dependence, reliance. 2 POL. dependency. 3 staff, personnel (empleados). 4 office, branch office (sucursal). 5 section, department (sección). || *pl.* 6 outhouses, outbuildings.
depender *v.i.* 1 to depend (on): *depende de mi estado de salud = it depends on my health.* 2 to be under, to be dependant on (estar subordinado a). || **3 depende de ti,** it's up to you.

dependiente *adj.* 1 dependent, reliant. || *s.m.* y *f.* 2 employee (de un comercio). 3 shop assistant (en una tienda).
depilar *v.t.* 1 to depilate, to shave (piernas, etc.). || *v.r.* 2 to pluck (cejas). 3 to depilate.
deplorar *v.t.* 1 to deplore, to regret something very much.
deponente *adj.* 1 GRAM. deponent. 2 DER. testifying: *la persona deponente = the person testifying.* || *s.m.* y *f.* 3 DER. witness, testifier. 4 GRAM. deponent verb.
deponer *v.t.* 1 DER. to give evidence, to testify. 2 to lay down (las armas). 3 to depose, to overthrow (derrocar). 4 to remove from office (de un cargo). 5 to take down (bajar). || *v.i.* 6 DER. to testify, to give evidence. 7 to defecate (defecar). 8 (Am.) to vomit.
depopulador, -a *adj.* 1 devastating, desolating. || *s.m.* y *f.* 2 pillager, plunderer.
deportar *v.t.* to deport.
deporte *s.m.* 1 sport: *hacer deporte = to practise sport.* || **2 deportes de invierno,** DEP. winter sports. 3 **— de vela,** DEP. sailing. 5 **— de remo,** DEP. rowing.
deposición *s.f.* 1 removal, deposition (acción). 2 deposal (derrocamiento). 3 removal from office (de un cargo). 4 DER. evidence, testimony. 5 defecation (defecación).
depositar *v.t.* 1 to deposit. 2 to store, to store away, to put away (almacenar). 3 to place (poner). 4 to leave (dejar). || *v.pron.* 5 to settle (sedimentarse).
depositaría *s.f.* (form.) depository.
depositario, -a *s.m.* y *f.* 1 trustee, depository. 2 repository (de una confianza, un secreto, etc.). 3 cashier (cajero). 4 treasurer (tesorero).
depósito *s.m.* 1 FIN. deposit. 2 warehouse, store (almacén). 3 tank (para líquidos). 4 MIL. depot. 5 dump (de basuras). 6 sediment, deposit (sedimento). || 7 **— bancario,** FIN. bank deposit. 8 **— de basura,** rubbish dump. 9 **— de cadáveres,** morgue, mortuary. 10 **— de gasolina,** petrol tank. 11 **— de madera,** timber yard. 12 **— de municiones,** ammunition dump. 13 **— de objetos perdidos,** lost-property office.
depravar *v.t.* 1 to deprave, to corrupt. || *v.pron.* 2 to become depraved, corrupted: *se ha depravado en los últimos años = he has become depraved in the last few years.*
deprecar *v.t.* 1 to beg. || *v.i.* 2 to pray.
depreciar *v.t.* 1 to depreciate, to lower the price. || *v.pron.* 2 to depreciate, to lose value.
depredación *s.f.* 1 depredation. 2 pillaging (saqueo).
depresión *s.f.* 1 GEOL. depression, hollow. 2 ECON. slump, depression. 3 MED. depression. || 4 **— atmosférica,** atmospheric depression. 5 **— nerviosa,** nervous breakdown.
deprimir *v.t.* 1 to depress, to flatten. 2 MED. to depress. 3 (fig.) to humiliate. || *v.pron.* 4 to get depressed.
deprisa o **de prisa** *adv.* quickly, fast.
depurar *v.t.* 1 to purify. 2 POL. to purge. 3 to cleanse (la sangre).
derecha *s.f.* 1 right, right-hand side, right side (lado). || **2 a derechas,** rightly, correctly. 3 **a la —,** on the right-hand side, on the right. 4 **a la — de,** on the right of. 5 POL. **la —,** the right; the right wing. 6 **torcer a la —,** to turn/go right.
derechamente *adv.* 1 straight, directly. 2 (fig.) properly, correctly. || 3 **ir — al grano,** to go straight to the point. 4 **portarse —,** to have properly.
derecho, -a *adj.* 1 straight (en dirección). 2 upright, erect (vertical). 3 right (mano). 4 (Am.) honest, straight. 5 fair. || *s.f.* 6 right hand. 7 POL. right. || *s.m.* 8 law (estudio de leyes). 9 justice (concepto general). 10 right (como ley básica y natural): *no tiene derecho a decirte eso = he has no right to tell you that.* 11 claim, title (a algo concreto): *tengo derecho a esas tierras = I have a claim to those lands.* || *s.m.pl.* 12 taxes, duties (impuestos). 13 fee (profesional). || *adv.* 14 straight. || 15 **a derechas,** correctly, in a proper way. 16 **de —,** according to law. 17 **— administrativo,** DER. administrative law. 18 **— canónico,** DER. canon law. 19 **— civil,** V. **civil.** 20 **— común,** DER. civil law. 21 **— consuetudinario,** DER. common law. 22 **— criminal,** DER. criminal law. 23 **— de asilo,** right of asylum. 24 **— de entrada,** COM. import duties. 25 **— de gentes,** DER. international law. 26 **— de pataleo,** (hum.) right to grumble. 27 **— de pernada,** V. **pernada.** 28 **— de regalía,** COM. tax on manufactured tobacco. 29 **— divino,** divine right. 30 **— eclesiástico,** DER. canon law. 31 **— escrito,** DER. statute law, written law. 32 **— internacional,** DER. international law. 33 **— marítimo,** DER. maritime law. 34 **— mercantil,** DER. business law. 35 **— municipal,** DER. municipal law. 36 **— natural,** DER. natural law. 37 **— no escrito,** DER. unwritten law, common law. 38 **— penal,** DER. penal law. 39 **— político,** DER. constitutional law. 40 **— positivo,** DER. statute law, positive law. 41 **— procesal,** DER. prodecural law. 42 **— público,** DER. public law. 43 **derechos reales,** FIN. death duties. 44 **más — que una vela,** as straight as a rod, as straight as a die. 45 **no hay —,** it's not fair. 46 **perder uno de su —,** to yield one's rights, to give in (en algo donde tenía un derecho preferente).
derechura *s.f.* 1 straightness, directness. 2 fairness, justness (justicia). || 3 **en —,** directly, straight.
deriva *s.f.* 1 deviation (desvío del rumbo). 2 drift (sin rumbo). || 3 **a la —,** adrift.
derivación *s.f.* 1 derivation (de palabras). 2 source, origin (origen). 3 deviation (cambio). 4 ELEC. shunt.
derivado, -a *adj.* 1 GRAM. derived, derivative. || *s.m.* y *f.* 2 QUIM. by-product, derivative. 3 derivative (de palabras).
derivar *v.t.* 1 to derive from (de). 2 to divert (desviar). 3 MAT. to calculate. || *v.i.* 4 MAR. to drift. 5 to derive (de palabras). || *v.pron.* 6 to be derived (palabras).
dermatitis *s.f.* MED. dermatitis.
dermatoesqueleto *s.m.* dermoskeleton.
dermatología *s.f.* dermatology.
dermatosis *s.f.* dermatosis.
dermis *s.f.* dermis, cutis.
derogar *v.t.* 1 to abolish, to repeal (una ley). 2 to cancel (un contrato).
derrama *s.f.* distribution, apportionment.
derramado, -a *adj.* wasteful, spendthrift.
derramar *v.t.* 1 to spill (sin querer). 2 to pour, to pour out (echar). 3 to distribute, to share (impuestos). 4 to shed (sangre, lágrimas). 5 to spread (una noticia). || *v.r.* 6 to spill (sin querer). 7 to pour, to pour out (echar). 8 to shed (sangre, lágrimas). 9 to spread (esparcirse). 10 to overflow (rebosar).
derrame *s.m.* 1 spilling (sin querer). 2 pouring (voluntario). 3 shedding (de sangre, lágrimas). 4 overflow (rebosamiento). 5 waste (pérdida). 6 MED. discharge. 7 ARQ. splay. 8 slope (cuestas). || 9 **— sinovial,** water on the knee.
derrapar *v.i.* to skid: *el coche derrapó = the car skidded.*
derredor *s.m.* 1 surroundings. 2 **al — de,** round about; around. 3 **en —,** around.
derrengar *v.t.* 1 to damage one's back (lesionar el espinazo). 2 to twist (torcer). 3 (fig.) to tire out (cansar). || *v.pron.* 4 to damage one's back. 5 to tire oneself out (cansarse).
derretir *v.t.* 1 to melt (hielo, nieve, helado, manteca, etc.). 2 to thaw, to melt (nieve). 3 (fig.) to waste, to squander (derrochar los bienes). 4 to exasperate (exasperar). 5 to melt down (metales). || *v.pron.* 5 to thaw, to melt (nieve). 7 to melt (hielo, nieve, helado, manteca, etc.). 8 to be always falling in love (enamorarse fácilmente). 9 (fam.) to get in a state (sentir impaciencia o inquietud). 10 to burn (consumirse de amor).
derribar *v.t.* 1 to demolish, to knock down (una casa). 2 to batter down (una puerta). 3 to knock down (una persona). 4 to to floor, to lay out (en una lucha). 5 to throw (un caballo). 6 to shoot down (un avión). 7 to shoot (en la caza). 8 to blow down (el viento). 9 POL. to overthrow (derrocar). 10 to remove (a uno de su cargo). || *v.pron.* 11 to fall down (caer). 12 to throw oneself to the ground (tirarse al suelo).
derribo *s.m.* 1 demolition (de una casa). 2 rubble (escombros). 3 demolition site (lugar). 4 POL. overthrow.
derrocadero *s.m.* rocky cliff.
derrocar *v.t.* 1 to demolish, to knock down (un edificio). 2 POL. to overthrow, to topple. 3 to remove (depo-

ner). **4** to throw down, to fling down (despeñar).

derrochar *v.t.* **1** to waste, to squander (dinero, bienes, etc.). || **2 — salud,** to be brimming with good health.

derrota *s.f.* **1** defeat. **2** setback (revés). **3** path (senda). **4** MAR. course (rumbo). **5** disaster, debacle (desastre).

derrotar *v.t.* **1** MIL. to defeat. **2** DEP. to beat, to defeat. **3** to squander (malgastar). **4** MAR. to change course. **5** to destroy (destruir). **6** to ruin (la salud).

derrote *s.m.* butt (de un toro).

derrotero *s.m.* **1** MAR. course (rumbo). **2** sailing instruction. **3** pilot book (libro). **4** (fig.) plan of action, course of action (camino para llegar a un fin).

derrotista *adj.* **1** defeatist. || *s.m.* y *f.* **2** defeatist.

derruir *v.t.* to demolish, to knock down.

derrumbadero *s.m.* **1** cliff, precipice (precipicio). **2** (fig.) danger, hazard.

derrumbar *v.t.* **1** to knock down, to demolish (un edificio). **2** to overturn, to knock over (volcar). **3** to throw down, to fling down (tirar al suelo). || *v.pron.* **4** to collapse, to fall down (un edificio). **5** to cave in, to fall in (el techo). **6** to throw, to fling oneself (tirarse). **7** (fig.) to collapse.

derviche *s.m.* dervish.

desabarrancar *v.t.* **1** to pull someone out of a gully, ravine. **2** (fig.) to get someone out of a tight spot.

desabastecido, -a *adj.* out of supplies.

desabollar *v.t.* to remove the dents from.

desabor *s.m.* tastelessness, insipidness.

desabordarse *v.r.* to cast off.

desabotonar *v.t.* **1** to undo, to unbutton. || *v.i.* **2** BOT. to open out, to blossom. || *v.pron.* **3** to unbutton (desabrocharse). **4** to come undone (sin querer).

desabrido, -a *adj.* **1** tasteless, insipid (soso). **2** tasteless (de mal gusto). **3** unsettled (tiempo). **4** sullen, gruff (persona). **5** bitter (discusión, debate). **6** harsh, sharp (tono).

desabrigado, -a *adj.* **1** uncovered, overcoatless (sin abrigo). **2** (fig.) unprotected, defenceless.

desabrochar *v.t.* **1** to undo, to unfasten. **2** (fig.) to open. || *v.pron.* **3** to undo, to unfasten one's clothes. **4** (fig.) to lay oneself bare, to unburden oneself.

desacatar *v.t.* **1** to be disrespectful to, to show no respect for. **2** to disobey (desobedecer).

desacato *s.m.* DER. **1** disrespect. || **2 — a la autoridad,** DER. contempt of court.

desacertar *v.t.* **1** to get it wrong, to be wrong.

desacomodar *v.t.* **1** to inconvenience. **2** to sack, to fire (despedir de un trabajo). || *v.pron.* **3** to be sacked, to be fired.

desaconsejado, -a *adj.* **1** unwise, ill-advised. **2** imprudent, foolish (imprudente). || *s.m.* y *f.* **3** fool (imprudente).

desaconsejar *v.t.* **1** to dissuade, to warn against.

desacordar *v.t.* **1** MUS. to put out of tune. || *v.pron.* **2** MUS. to get out of tune. **3** to forget something (olvidarse de una cosa).

desacostumbrar *v.t.* **1 — a uno de,** to break someone of the habit of. || *v.pron.* **2** to give up, to break the habit of. || **3 me he desacostumbrado del tabaco,** I've given up smoking, I've broken the habit of smoking.

desacreditar *v.t.* **1** to discredit, to harm the reputation of. **2** to disparage, to denigrate (denigrar). || *v.pron.* **3** to disgrace, to discredit oneself.

desactivar *v.t.* to deactivate.

desacuerdo *s.m.* **1** disagreement, discord. **2** forgetfulness (olvido). || **3 estar en — con,** to be in disagreement with.

desafección *s.f.* disaffection.

desafecto, -a *adj.* **1** disaffected, hostile. || *s.m.* **2** ill will, disaffection.

desafiar *v.t.* **1** to challenge, to dare: *desafiar a uno a hacer algo = to dare someone to do something.* **2** to defy, to face up to (oponer). **3** to compete (competir).

desafinar *v.i.* **1** MUS. to be out of tune. **2** to go out of tune. **3** to play, sing out of tune (tocar, cantar). **4** (fig.) to say something out of turn (decir algo inoportuno).

desaforar *v.t.* **1** to take away one's rights, privileges (privar a uno del fuero o privilegio). **2** to violate the rights of (violar los fueros). || *v.pron.* **3** to act outrageously. **4** to get irritated (irritarse).

desafortunado, -a *adj.* **1** unlucky (sin suerte). **2** unfortunate (desgraciado).

desafuero *s.m.* **1** outrage (abuso). **2** infringement of rights (privación de un fuero). || **3 cometer un —,** to break the law (violar la ley); to commit an outrage (cometer un abuso).

desagraciar *v.t.* to disfigure.

desagradar *v.t.* **1** to displease. **2** to dislike: *me desagrada beber = I dislike drinking.* || *v.i.* **4** to be unpleasant.

desagradecer *v.t.* to be ungrateful for, to show no gratitude for/to (una cosa, una persona).

desagraviar *v.t.* **1** to make amends. **2** to apologize (pedir disculpas). **3** to indemnify (indemnizar).

desagregar *v.t.* to disintegrate.

desaguadero *s.m.* drain.

desaguar *v.t.* **1** to drain, to empty. **2** (fig.) to squander, to waste (derrochar). || *v.i.* **3** to flow into (desembocar en).

desagüe *s.m.* **1** draining, drainage (hecho de desaguar). **2** drain, drainage channel.

desaguisado, -a *adj.* **1** illegal, criminal (contra la ley). **2** disgraceful, outrageous (contra la razón). || *s.i.* **3** insult, offence (injuria). **4** outrage, disgrace (agravio).

desahogar *v.t.* **1** to relieve, to ease (aliviar). **2** to console (consolar). **3** (fig.) to vent (el enfado). || *v.pron.* **4** to relieve one's feelings. **5** to let off steam (físicamente). **6** to relax, to rest (descansar). **7** to rid oneself of a job, debt, problem, etc. (librarse de un trabajo, deuda, problema, etc.). **8** to speak frankly (hablar con franqueza). **9** to confide (confiar).

desahogo *s.m.* **1** relief (alivio). **2** (fig.) outlet (escape). **3** relaxation (descanso). **4** (desp.) cheek, audacity (descaro). **5** freedom (libertad). || **6 vivir en —,** to live comfortably.

desahuciar *v.t.* **1** to kill of all hope (quitar toda esperanza). **2** to give up all hope (declarar sin esperanza para la vida). **3** to evict, to eject (despedir a un inquilino).

desairado, -a *adj.* **1** ungainly, ungraceful (desgarbado). **2** unimpressive, uninspiring (deslucido). **3** unsuccessful (sin éxito).

desairar *v.t.* **1** to offend (ofender). **2** to rebuff, to snub (desdeñar). **3** to disregard, to neglect (desatender).

desajustar *v.t.* **1** to upset the order of, to disorder. **2** to disconnect (desacoplar). || *v.r.* **3** to go wrong, to break down.

desalar *v.t.* **1** to extract the salt from (quitar la sal). **2** to desalinate (el agua de mar). **3** to remove the wings of (quitar las alas). || *v.pron.* **4** to rush, to hurry (con mucha prisa). || **5 — por,** to long to; to yearn to.

desalentar *v.t.* **1** to make breathless. **2** (fig.) to discourage (desanimar). || *v.pron.* **3** to lose heart, to get disheartened.

desalinear *v.t.* **1** to go off line. || *v.pron.* **2** to go out of line.

desaliñar *v.t.* **1** to disorder, to disarrange (desarreglar). **2** to dirty (ensuciar). **3** (fam.) to make a mess.

desalmado, -a *adj.* **1** ruthless (despiadado). **2** cruel, heartless (cruel). **3** evil, wicked (malvado).

desalmar *v.t.* **1** to make uneasy, to disquiet (desasosegar). || *v.pron.* to long (for), to crave (for).

desalojar *v.t.* **1** to eject, to evict (un inquilino). **2** MIL. to dislodge. **3** to abandon, to evacuate (abandonar). **4** to clear (hacer salir a la gente). || *v.pron.* **5** to change house, to move out (mudarse).

desalojo *s.m.* **1** ejection, eviction (expulsión). **2** house moving (cambio de casa). **3** MAR. displacement. **4** MIL. dislodging.

desalquilar *v.t.* **1** to stop renting.

desalumbrado, -a *adj.* **1** dazzling (deslumbrado). **2** disconcerting, worrying (desconcertado).

desamar *v.t.* **1** to stop loving (dejar de amar). **2** to abhor, to detest (aborrecer). **3** to feel hostile (sentir desafecto).

desamarrar *v.t.* **1** MAR. to cast off. **2** to untie (desatar).

desamoblar *v.t.* to clear the furniture from.

desamor *s.m.* **1** indifference, coldness (indiferencia). **2** enmity, dislike (enemistad). **3** lack of love (falta de amor).

desamortizar *v.t.* to sell off.

desamparar *v.t.* **1** to desert, to abandon. **2** to absent oneself, to leave (ausentarse).
desamueblar *v.t.* **1** to clear the furniture from.
desandar *v.t.* **1** to walk back, to go back. || **2 — lo andado o el camino,** to walk back; to retrace one's steps.
desangrar *v.t.* **1** to bleed (sangrar). **2** (fig.) to bleed white. || *v.pron.* **3** to lose blood (perder sangre).
desanimar *v.t.* **1** to discourage. **2** to depress (deprimir). || *v.pron.* **3** to get discouraged, to lose heart (perder las ganas).
desanudar *v.t.* **1** to unknot, to disentangle. **2** (fig.) to sort out, to clear up (aclarar un enredo).
desapacible *adj.* **1** unpleasant, disagreeable. **2** changeable, unsettled (el tiempo).
desapadrinar *v.t.* to disapprove of.
desaparecer *v.i.* **1** to disappear, to vanish. **2** to wear off. || **3 el dolor ha desaparecido,** the pain has worn off. || **4** to hide (esconderse).
desaparejar *v.t.* y *r.* **1** to unhitch, to unharness. **2** MAR. to unrig.
desapasionar *v.t.* **1** to take away the passion. || *v.pron.* **2** to lose interest, to become indifferent: *me he desapasionado del fútbol = I've lost interest in football.*
desapegar *v.t.* **1** to remove (desprender). **2** to unstick (despegar). || *v.pron.* **3** to lose interest in.
desapercibido, -a *adj.* **1** unprepared, unawares (no preparado). **2** unnoticed, unseen (inadvertido). || **3 coger —,** to catch unawares. **4 irse —,** to leave unseen. **5 pasar —,** to go unnoticed.
desaplicar *v.t.* **1** to become lazy. || *v.pron.* **2** to lose interest.
desaprensivo, -a *adj.* **1** unscrupulous. **2** immoral (inmoral). **3** unwise, imprudent (imprudente).
desaprobar *v.t.* **1** to disapprove of, to look down on. **2** to refuse, to reject (rechazar). **3** to be in disagreement (estar en desacuerdo).
desaprovechado, -a *adj.* **1** unfulfilled, unrealised. **2** slow, slack (persona vaga). **3** wasted (oportunidad, tiempo, dinero, etc.).
desapuntar *v.t.* **1** to unsew, to unstitch. **2** to shoot, fire off target (apuntar mal).
desarbolar *v.t.* **1** MAR. to dismast. **2** (fig.) to leave defenceless (dejar indefenso).
desarmar *v.t.* **1** MIL. to disarm. **2** to dismantle, to take apart (desmontar). **3** (fig.) to calm, to appease (templar). **4** MAR. to lay up. || *v.i.* **5** to disarm.
desarme *s.m.* **1** MIL. disarmament. || **2 conferencia de —,** disarmament conerence.
desarraigado, -a *adj.* rootless.
desarraigar *v.t.* **1** to uproot. **2** (fig.) to uproot. || **3 — un pueblo,** to uproot a village. **4** (fig.) to eliminate, to stamp out (criminalidad, la droga, el vicio, etc.). **5** to banish, to expel (desterrar).
desarrapado, -a *adj.* tattered, ragged.
desarreglar *v.t.* **1** to make untidy, to disarrange, to disorder. **2** to spoil (estropear). || *v.pron.* **3** to get disarranged, to get untidy.
desarrendar *v.t.* **1** to unbridle (un caballo). **2** to stop renting (dejar de arrendar).
desarrimar *v.t.* **1** to move, to separate (separar). **2** (fig.) to dissuade (disuadir).
desarrollar *v.t.* **1** to unroll (un mapa, un rollo, etc.). **2** to unfold (desdoblar). **3** to develop (acrecentar). || **4 — la economía,** to develop the economy. **5** to expound, to explain (una teoría, idea, etc.). **6** MAT. to develop, to expand. || *v.pron.* **7** to unroll. **8** to unfold. **9** to develop. **10** to develop: *el país se desarrolla rápidamente = the country's developing quickly.* **11** to take place (tener lugar): *la historia se desarrolla en Londres = the story takes place in London.*
desarrollo *s.m.* **1** development: *el desarrollo de la industria = the development of industry.* **2** MAT. expansión. **3** DEP. course: *durante el desarrollo del partido = during the course of the game.* **4** unrolling (de un papel, mapa, etc.). **5** evolution (evolución). **6** MUS. development. **7** (fig.) unfolding, course, development: *el desarrollo de la crisis = the unfolding of the crisis.*
desarticular *v.t.* **1** to separate, to disconnect (separar). **2** to take apart, to take to pieces (desmontar). **3** (fig.) to break up (un complot, banda, etc.). || *v.t.* y *pron.* **4** to dislocate, to put out of joint (los huesos).
desarzonar *v.t.* to unsaddle, to throw, to unseat.
desasear *v.t.* **1** to soil, to dirty (ensuciar). **2** to mess up, to make untidy (desordenar).
desasentar *v.t.* **1** to remove, to move. || *v.pron.* **2** to stand up.
desasimilación *s.f.* dissimilation.
desasir *v.t.* **1** to release, to loosen (soltar). || *v.pron.* **2** to get rid of something (desprenderse de una cosa). **3** to free oneself of (librarse). **4** to lose interest (desinteresarse).
desasnar *v.t.* **1** to refine, to civilize. **2** (fam.) to polish.
desasosegar *v.t.* **1** to perturb, to make uneasy, to disquiet. || *v.r.* **2** to get perturbed, to become uneasy.
desaspiración *s.f.* disaspiration.
desastrado, -a *adj.* **1** unlucky, unfortunate (desgraciado). **2** dirty (sucio). **3** untidy, scruffy (descuidado). **4** ragged, shabby (harapiento). || *s.m.* **5** wretch, tramp.
desastre *s.m.* **1** disaster. **2** (fam.) disaster, mess: *¡qué desastre! = what a disaster!* **3 un — de película,** a rotten film.
desatar *v.t.* **1** to untie, to undo (nudo, paquete, etc.). **2** to unbutton (desabotonar). **3** to let go (un perro). **4** to unleash (represiones, pasiones, animales). **5** (fig.) to clear up, to sort out (aclarar, resolver). || *v.pron.* **6** to come untied, to come undone. **7** to get loose (animales). **8** to get out of (aprieto, compromiso). || (fig.) **9** to burst (tormenta). **10** to break out (epidemia, motín, rebelión, etc.). **11** to get worked up (calentarse). **12** to get carried away (hablar demasiado). **13** to go too far, to lose one's head (perder los estribos).
desatascar *v.t.* **1** to pull out of the mud (sacar de un atascadero). **2** to unblock, to clear (desobstruir). **3** (fig.) to get someone out of a fix o jam (sacar de un apuro).
desatención *s.f.* **1** inattention. **2** rudeness, discourtesy, disrespect (descortesía).
desatender *v.t.* **1** to ignore, to pay no attention to (no hacer caso). **2** to neglect (obligaciones, órdenes, el jardín, etc.). **3** to offend, to slight (ofender).
desatentar *v.t.* y *pron.* to bewilder, to confuse.
desatinar *v.t.* **1** to bewilder, to confuse. || *v.i.* **2** to talk nonsense (decir desatinos). **3** to do silly things (hacer desatinos).
desatollar *v.t.* y *pron.* to pull out of the mud.
desatornillar *v.t.* y *pron.* to unscrew.
desatracar *v.t.* y *pron.* MAR. to cast off.
desatrampar *v.t.* to unblock a pipe.
desatrancar *v.t.* y *pron.* **1** to unblock, to clear (un conducto). **2** to unbolt, to unbar (una puerta). **3** to clean out (un pozo).
desautorizar *v.t.* **1** to take away someone's authority. **2** to deny (desmentir). **3** to discredit (desacreditar).
desavenencia *s.f.* **1** disagreement, discord (discordia). **2** row, argument (riña).
desavenir *v.t.* y *pron.* to cause a disagreement, to make trouble between.
desaviar *v.t.* y *pron.* **1** to show the wrong way (desviar). **2** to withhold necessities (desproveer).
desayunar *v.i.* y *pron.* **1** to have breakfast. || **2 — con,** to have for breakfast.
desazón *s.m.* **1** tastelessness, insipidness (insipidez). **2** itch, itching (picor). **3** poorness (de la tierra).
desazonar *v.t.* **1** to take the taste away, to make tasteless (quitar el sabor). || *v.t.* y *pron.* **2** to upset, to get upset (disgustar). || *v.pron.* **3** to feel ill (sentirse enfermo).
desbancar *v.t.* **1** to replace, to oust (de un trabajo, posición). **2** to bust the bank, to win the bank (en las cartas). **3** to take away the benches (quitar los bancos).
desbandarse *v.r.* **1** MIL. to disband (dispersarse). **2** to flee in disorder (huir en desorden). **3** to desert (desertar). **4** to keep one's distance, to remain aloof (alejarse de la compañía de otros).
desbarajuste *s.m.* chaos, disorder, mess: *¡qué desbarajuste! = what a mess!*
desbaratar *v.t.* **1** to spoil, to ruin (estropear). **2** to waste, to squander (derrochar). **3** to thwart, to frustrate (los planes, de alguien, un complot, una intriga, etc.). **4** to destroy, to demolish

(una teoría, argumento, etc.). **5** MIL. to rout, to put to flight. **6** to cause chaos. || *v.i.* **7** to talk nonsense, rubbish (disparatar). || *v.pron.* **8** (fam.) to go off the deep end, to get worked up (irritarse).
desbarrancar *v.t.* **1** (Am.) to throw into a chasm (tirar). || *v.pron.* **2** to fall into a chasm (caer).
desbarrar *v.i.* **1** to talk nonsense/rubbish (disparatar). **2** to slip, to slide (deslizarse). **3** to do stupid things, to mess about (hacer disparates).
desbastador *s.m.* **1** TEC. roughing chisel (herramienta para desbastar madera). **2** TEC. roughing mill (laminador).
desbastar *v.t.* **1** TEC. to rough-hew (piedra). **2** to plane (madera). **3** to rough down (metal). || **4** (fig.) to knock the rough edges off, to polish.
desbocado, -a *adj.* **1** broken, chipped (de una herramienta). **2** foul-mouthed (mal hablado). **3** runaway (caballo). **4** with a broken rim (vasija de boca rota). **5** (Am.) overflowing (río).
desbordar *v.t.* **1** to pass, to go beyond (superar). **2** to exceed, to surpass (exceder): *eso desborda mis expectaciones = that surpasses my expectations.* || *v.i.* y *pron.* **3** to flood, to burst its banks, to overflow (ríos): *el río se desbordó = the river burst its banks.* **4** to spill over, to overflow (líquidos). || **5 desbordarse de alegría, a)** to be bursting with happiness; **b)** to get carried away (exaltarse).
desbravar *v.t.* **1** to tame (domesticar). **2** to break in (los caballos). || *v.t.* y *pron.* **3** to get less wild, to become tamer (perder la braveza). || *v.i.* y *pron.* **4** to lose its strength (un licor).
desbridar *v.t.* **1** to unbridle (un caballo). **2** MED. to debride.
desbrozar o **desembrozar** *v.t.* **1** to clear the undergrowth (los matorrales). **2** to weed, to clear the weeds (la hierba). **3** to clear a path, to open the way (eliminar los obstáculos de un camino).
descabalar *v.t.* y *r.* to leave unfinished o incomplete.
descabellado, -a *adj.* **1** (fig.) wild, mad (loco). **2** ridiculous, absurd (absurdo).
descabellar *v.t.* **1** to ruffle (despeinar). **2** to finish off, to kill (with a blow to the neck).
descabezado, -a *adj.* **1** headless. **2** (fig.) wild, crazy (loco).
descabezar *v.t.* **1** to behead, to decapitate (decapitar). **2** to cut the top off, to lop off (cortar la parte superior). **3** to top (flores). **4** (fig.) to begin to get over a problem (empezar a superar una dificultad). || *v.pron.* **5** BOT. to shed the grain.
descachar *v.t.* (Am.) to de-horn (cortar los cuernos).
descalabrar *v.t.* y *pron.* **1** to hit on the head, to injure the head of (herir en la cabeza). || *v.t.* **2** to injure, to hurt (herir). **3** to harm, to damage (perjudicar).
descalcificar *v.t.* **1** MED. to decalcify. || *v.pron.* **2** MED. to become decalcified.
descalificar *v.t.* **1** to disqualify. || *v.t.* y *pron.* **2** to discredit (desacreditar).
descalzar *v.t.* **1** to take off (los zapatos). **2** to remove the chocks (quitar el calzo). **3** to dig under, to undermine (socavar). || *v.pron.* **4** to take off (guantes, zapatos, etc.). **5** to cast a shoe (caballo).
descamar *v.t.* **1** to scale off (pescado). || *v.pron.* **2** MED. to flake off, to scale off (la piel).
descambiar *v.t.* to change again.
descaminar o **desencaminar** *v.t.* **1** to send the wrong way, to misdirect. **2** (fig.) to mislead, to lead astray: *me están descaminando = they're leading me astray.* || *v.pron.* **3** to go the wrong way, to take the wrong road. **6** (fig.) to go astray.
descamisado *adj.* **1** shirtless (sin camisa). **2** (fig.) tattered, ragged (desharrapado). || *s.c.* **3** wretch (un pobre). **4** tramp, down-and-out (desharrapado).
descampado, -a o **escampado, -a** *adj.* **1** open (descubierto). || *s.m.* **2** open ground, open space. || **3 en —**, in the open country, in the wilds.
descansar *v.i.* **1** to rest (parar el trabajo). **2** to sleep, to have a sleep (dormir): *¡que descanses! = sleep tight!* **3** to rest, to lie (muertos): *aquí descansa... = here lies...* **4** to find relief (tener un alivio). **5** to rely on (contar con). **6** AGR. to lie fallow. **7** ARQ. to rest on, to be supported on. || *v.t.* **8** to rest: *descansar la vista = to rest one's eyes.* **9** to lean, to rest (apoyar). **10** to help (ayudar). || *v.pron.* **11** to rest, to have a rest. **12** to sleep (dormir).
descansillo *s.m.* landing (rellano).
descantillar o **descantonar** *v.t.* **1** to embezzle (desfalcar). **2** to deduct (rebajar).
descapotar *v.t.* **1** to take the hood down (coches).
descararse *v.pron.* **1** to be cheeky, to be insolent. || **2 — a hacer algo,** to have the nerve to do something.
descarga *s.f.* **1** unloading. **2** MIL. firing, discharge. || **3 — cerrada,** volley; salvo. **4 — eléctrica,** electrical discharge.
descargadero *s.m.* wharf.
descargar *v.t.* **1** to unload (barco, camión, etc.). **2** MIL. to fire, to shoot. **3** (fig.) to beat, to hit (golpear). **4** to unload/to disarm (arma). **5** to free, to release (de una obligación, una deuda, etc.). **6** ELEC. to discharge. **7** to flatten (una batería). **8** to evacuate (el vientre). **9** to vent (ira, enfado, etc.). **10** to relieve, to release (aliviar). **11** to clear, to acquit (absolver). **12** to unburden (abrir el corazón). || *v.i.* **13** to flow into, to run into (un río). **14** to open, to burst (las nubes). || *v.pron.* **15** to resign (dimitir). **16** to delegate (delegar). **17** ELEC. to discharge. **18** to unburden oneself (abrir el corazón). **19** DER. to clear oneself.
descargo *s.m.* **1** unloading. **2** COM. credit (crédito). **3** receipt, voucher (recibo). **4** release (de una obligación). **5** (fig.) relief (alivio). || **6 en su —**, in his defence.
descariñarse *v.pron.* **1** to lose one's affection/love.
descarnador *s.m.* **1** dental scraper (del dentista). **2** scraper (para pieles, etc.).
descarnar *v.t.* **1** to remove the flesh (quitar la carne del hueso). **2** (fig.) to strip (descubrir). **3** to erode, to wear away (erosionar).
descaro *s.m.* **1** cheek, nerve, impudence: *tuvo el descaro de decir que... = he had the nerve to say that...* || **2 ¡qué —!**, what a cheek!
descarriar *v.t.* **1** to misdirect, to send the wrong way (descaminar). **2** (fig.) to lead astray (apartar del buen camino). **3** to separate from the herd (animales). || *v.pron.* **4** to get lost, to lose one's way (perderse). **5** to go astray (apartarse del buen camino). **6** to get separated from the herd (animales).
descarrilar *v.i.* **1** to go off the rails, to be derailed (tren). || **2** (fig.) to go off the track.
descartar *v.t.* **1** to discard, to put aside (desechar). **2** to reject (rechazar). **3** to rule out (una posibilidad, etc.). **4** to throw away, to discard (cartas). || *v.pron.* **5** to discard, to throw away (cartas). || **6 descartarse de,** to get out of; to excuse oneself (abstenerse de hacer algo).
descasar *v.t.* **1** to dissolve a marriage. **2** (fig.) to disorder, to upset (desordenar). **3** to separate (separar).
descascarillar *v.t.* y *r.* **1** to remove the husk, to husk.
descastado, -a *adj.* **1** unaffectionate, unfeeling, cold (antipático). **2** alienated from one's family (apartado de la familia de uno). **3** ungrateful (ingrato).
descastar *v.r.* **1** to make extinct (exterminar una casta de animales).
descendencia *s.f.* **1** origin, descent (linaje). **2** descendants, offspring (hijos). || **3 morir sin dejar —**, to die without issue.
descender *v.i.* **1** to descend, to go down, to come down (bajar). **2** to drop, to fall, to go down (fiebre, temperatura, etc.). **3** to hang (cortinas). **4** (fig.) **— a,** to stoop to; to lower oneself to. **5** to descend (from); to be descend (from): *descienden de Africa = they descend from Africa.* || *v.t.* **6** to lower, to take down (equipaje, un cuadro, etc.). **7** to go down, to descend (las escaleras, una montaña, una cuesta, etc.): *descender la calle = to go down the street.*
descendimiento *s.m.* **1** descent (una persona). **2** lowering (una cosa). || **3 — de la cruz,** REL. Descent from the Cross.
descentralización *s.f.* descentralization.
descentralizar *v.t.* **1** to descentralize.
descentrar *v.t.* y *pron.* **1** to put off centre. **2** (fig.) to unbalance (desequilibrar).
desceñir *v.t.* to loosen, to unfasten, to undo (desatar).

descerrajar *v.t.* **1** to force open, to break open, to break the lock of. **2** to fire, to shoot (disparar un arma de fuego).
descervigar *v.t.* to break the neck of (desnucar).
descifrar *v.t.* **1** to decipher (lo escrito). **2** to decode (un mensaje). **3** to work out, to figure out (un problema). **4** to solve, to crack (un misterio).
desclavar *v.t.* **1** to unnail, to pull out the nails from (quitar los clavos). **2** to remove (las piedras preciosas).
descocar *v.t.* **1** to pick coconuts (quitar los cocos). **2** to remove the insects from (quitar los insectos). || *v.pron.* **3** to be cheeky (descararse).
descoco *s.m.* cheek, nerve, impudence (descaro).
descolgar *v.t.* **1** to take down (un cuadro). **2** to lower, to let down (algo que cuelga de una cuerda). **3** to pick up, to lift (el teléfono). || *v.pron.* **4** to lower oneself, to let oneself down (por una cuerda, una pared, etc.). **5** to descend, to go down (descender una pendiente). **6** (fig.) to turn up, to pop in (presentarse inesperadamente): *se descolgó después de 2 semanas = he turned up after 2 weeks.* || **7 descolgarse con,** to come out with: *se descolgó con una bobada = he came out with a silly comment.*
descolorar *v.t.* **1** to discolour. **2** to fade (poco a poco). **3** to bleach (dejar blanco). || *v.pron.* **4** to lose colour (perder el color). **5** to become faded (perder el color poco a poco). **6** to be bleached (quedar blanco).
descollar *v.i.* y *pron.* **1** to stand out, to be outstanding: *su libro descuella de entre los demás = his book stands out from the others.* **2** to rise above, to stand out from (un edificio, una montaña, etc.): *la montaña descuella sobre las otras = the mountain rises above the others.*
descombrar *v.t.* **1** to clear, to get rid of (despejar).
descomedido, -a *adj.* **1** excessive, immoderate (excesivo). **2** rude, impolite (descortés). || *s.m.* y *f.* **3** a rude person.
descompasarse *v.pron.* **1** to be rude, to be impolite (faltar al respeto).
descompensar *v.t.* y *pron.* **1** to unbalance, to put off balance (desequilibrar).
descomponer *v.t.* y *pron.* **1** to rot, to decompose (corromperse). **2** QUIM. to break down. **3** to analyse, to break down (un argumento, una teoría, etc.). **4** GRAM. to split up. **5** MEC. to break down, to get out of order. **6** to disarrange, to upset (desorganizar). || *v.t.* **7** to separate into parts, to break down (separar). **8** to spoil, to mess up (estropear). **9** to upset (hacer perder la serenidad). **10** to annoy, to irritate (irritar). **11** to distort (deformar). || *v.pron.* **12** to get angry, to get worked up (irritarse). **13** to get upset (el estómago). **14** to break up (el tiempo). **16** to be distorted (deformarse). || **15 descomponerse con alguien,** to get annoyed with someone.
descompostura *s.f.* **1** breakdown (de un motor). **2** untidiness, slovenliness (descuido). **3** cheekiness, impudence (descaro). **4** disorganization, disorder (desorden). **5** distortion (de la cara). **6** breaking (rotura).
descompuesto, -a *adj.* **1** rotten, decomposed (podrido). **2** MEC. broken, out of order. **3** distorted, twisted (el rostro). **4** chaotic, disorganized (desorganizado). **5** untidy (desordenado). **6** slovenly (desaliñado). **7** annoyed, angry (enfadado). **8** upset (trastornado). **9** impolite, rude (descortés). **10** impudent, cheeky (descarado). || **11 estar –,** (Am.) to be drunk (estar borracho).
descomulgar *v.t.* REL. to excommunicate (excomulgar).
descomunal *adj.* enormous, huge, gigantic.
desconcertar *v.t.* **1** to put out, to upset (perturbar). **2** MED. to dislocate (un hueso). **3** to disorder, to disarrange (desordenar). **4** to surprise (sorprender). **5** to baffle, to confuse (desorientar). || *v.pron.* **6** to be put out, to be upset (turbarse). **7** to be dislocated (un hueso). **8** to be confused, to be baffled (desorientarse). **9** MEC. to break down, to develop a fault. **10** to get angry, to lose one's temper (enfadarse).
desconcierto *s.m.* **1** disorder, chaos (desorden). **2** discord, disagreement (desacuerdo). **3** trouble, disorder (desarreglo). **4** confusion, bewilderment (confusión).
desconchar *v.t.* y *pron.* to peel off, to flake off.
desconectar *v.t.* **1** ELEC. to disconnect. **2** to switch off, to turn off (la luz, la radio, la televisión, etc.). **3** to unplug (desenchufar). || **4 estar desconectado de,** to be out of touch with; to be out of contact with.
desconfianza *s.f.* mistrust, distrust, suspicion, lack of confidence.
descongestionar *v.t.* y *pron.* **1** to clear (la cabeza). **2** to relieve the congestion (de coches, de gente, etc.). || **3** to clear (despejar).
desconocer *v.t.* **1** not to know, to be ignorant of, to be unaware of: *desconozco las razones = I don't know the reasons.* **2** not to remember: *desconozco su cara = I don't remember his face.* **3** to deny (negar). **4** not to recognize (no reconocer). **5** to pretend (disimular). || **6 – a un hijo,** to disown a child.
desconocido, -a *adj.* **1** unknown: *una obra desconocida = an unknown work.* || **3** strange, odd (raro). **4** ungrateful (ingrato). **5** much changed; much altered (muy cambiado). || *s.m.* y *f.* **6** unknown person, stranger. || **7 lo –,** the unknown.
desconsiderar *v.t.* to be inconsiderate towards, to show a lack of consideration for.
desconsolar *v.t.* **1** to distress, to trouble. || *v.pron.* **2** to lose hope (perder la esperanza). **3** to despair (desesperarse).
descontado, -a *adj.* **1 por –,** of course. || **2 dar por –,** to take for granted; to assume.
descontar *v.t.* **1** COM. to deduct, to discount. **2** to take away from (quitar). **3** to assume, to take for granted (dar por cierto). **4** (fig.) to disregard, to discount.
descontento, -a *adj.* **1** unhappy, discontented, dissatisfied. || *s.m.* **2** unhappy o dissatisfied person. || *s.m.* y *f.* **3** displeasure, dissatisfaction. **4** POL. discontent, unrest.
desconveniencia *s.f.* inconvenience, trouble, bother.
desconvenir *v.i.* **1** to disagree, not to agree (personas). **2** not to fit, not to match (cosas). || *v.pron.* **3** to be inconvenient (no convenir).
descorazonar *v.t.* **1** to pull o tear the heart out of (arrancar el corazón). **2** to dishearten, to discourage (desanimar). || *v.pron.* **3** to get disheartened, to lose heart.
descorchador *s.m.* **1** corkscrew (sacacorchos). **2** cork stripper (el que descorcha).
descorchar *v.t.* **1** to uncork (una botella). **2** to remove o strip the bark from (quitar el corcho). **3** (fig.) to force, to break open (abrir con fuerza).
descornar *v.t.* y *pron.* to dehorn (quitar los cuernos).
descorrer *v.t.* **1** to draw back, to open (cortinas). **2** to unbolt (un cerrojo). **3** to drain, to drain away (líquidos).
descortés *adj.* impolite, rude, badmannered.
descortezar *v.t.* **1** to remove o strip the bark from (quitar la corteza). **2** to peel (pelar). **3** to cut the crust off (pan). **4** (fig.) to knock the corners off, to refine (desbastar).
descoser *v.t.* **1** to unsew, to unstitch (las costuras). || *v.pron.* **2** to burst o to come apart at the seams (soltarse las puntadas de las cosas cosidas). || **3 descoserse de risa,** (fig.) to split one's sides laughing.
descosido, -a *adj.* **1** unsewn, unstitched (de una prenda). **2** (fig.) disconnected, disjointed: *un libro descosido = a disjointed book.* **3** indiscreet, talkative (indiscreto). || *s.m.* **4** unstitched seam, open seam (parte de una prenda con la costura suelta). **5 beber como un –,** to drink like a fish. **6 comer como un –,** to eat like a horse. **7 correr como un –,** to run like the devil. **8 estudiar como un –,** to study like mad. **9 gastar como un –,** to spend money like water. **10 hablar como un –,** to talk nineteen to the dozen. **11 reírse como un –,** to laugh one's head off; to split one's sides laughing. **12 soltar tacos como un –,** to swear like a trooper.
descotar *v.t.* **1** to cut out, to cut to fit (escotar). **2** to cut out the neckline. || *v.i.* y *pron.* **3** to pay one's share, to pay one's way (pagar su escote).
descoyuntar *v.t.* y *v.pron.* **1** ANAT. to dislocate, to put out of joint. || **2 desco-**

yuntarse de risa, (fam.) to split one's sides laughing. **3 estar descoyuntado,** to be double-jointed.

descrédito *s.m.* **1** discredit, disrepute. || **2 caer en –,** to fall into disrepute. **3 ir en – de,** to be to the discredit of, to harm the reputation of.

descreído, -a *adj.* **1** unbelieving, disbelieving. || *s.m.* y *f.* **2** doubter, disbeliever.

describir *v.t.* **1** to describe. **2** to trace, to describe (trazar).

descriptivo, -a *adj.* **1** descriptive. || **2 geometría –,** descriptive geometry. **3 música –,** descriptive music.

descuadernar *v.t.* y *pron.* **1** to unbind, to take off the binding.

descuajaringar o **descuajeringar** *v.t.* **1** to take to pieces, to dismount (descomponer). || *v.pron.* **2** to fall to bits (deshacerse). || **3 descuajaringarse de risa,** to split one's sides laughing. **4 estar descuajaringado,** to be worn out.

descuartizar *v.t.* **1** HIST. to quarter. **2** to cut up, to carve up (despedazar algo). **3** (fig.) to pull apart, to tear to pieces.

descubierta *s.f.* **1** MIL. scouting, reconnaissance. || **2 a la –,** openly (abiertamente); in the open (sin protección). **3 ir a la –,** to scout, to reconnoitre.

descubierto, -a *adj.* **1** uncovered, bare (un cuerpo). **2** cloudless, clear (el cielo). **3** open, exposed (expuesto). **4** bare, open (el terreno). **5** MIL. under fire. **6** bare (la cabeza). **7** hatless, bareheaded (sin sombrero). **8** open (un coche). || *s.m.* **9** COM. deficit. **10** shortage (insuficiencia). **11** overdraft (sobregiro). || **12 al –,** in the open. **13 estar en –,** to be overdrawn, to be in the red. **14 quedar al –,** to be obvious, to be manifest.

descubrir *v.t.* **1** to discover: *descubrir un planeta nuevo = to discover a new planet.* **2** to find, to detect (detectar). **3** to uncover (destapar). **4** to take the lid off (una cacerola). **5** to find, to discover (una mina, un tesoro, una tribu, etc.). **6** to unveil (una placa, una estatua, etc.). **7** to strike, to find (petróleo, oro, etc.). **8** to reveal (revelar): *descubrir sus pensamientos = to reveal one's thoughts.* **9** to unearth, to uncover (un fraude, un complot, etc.). **10** to unmask (impostor). **11** to make out, to be able to see (divisar): *se puede descubrir el mar desde aquí = you can make out the sea from here.* **12** to bare (la cabeza, el cuerpo, etc.). **13** MAR. to sight (la tierra). **14** to show, to lay down (en las cartas). **15** to give away, to betray (traicionar): *le descubrieron las huellas = his fingerprints gave him away.* || *v.pron.* **16** to take off one's hat, cap, etc. (quitarse el sombrero, gorra, etc.). **17** to raise one's hat (para saludar). **18** to clear (despejar). **19** to come to light, to be discovered (un secreto, un fraude, un crimen, etc.). **20** to show/to reveal oneself (mostrarse). **21** to confide in someone, to confess to someone (con alguien).

descuello *s.m.* **1** superiority (superioridad). **2** arrogance, disdain (altanería).

descuento *s.m.* **1** discount: *con descuento = at a discount.* **2** reduction, discount (reducción): *hacer un descuento = to give a reduction.* **3** deduction (deducción): *descuento del salario = wage deduction.* || **4 – por el pago al contado,** discount for cash payment.

descuidar *v.t.* **1** to neglect: *descuidar el jardín = to neglect the garden.* **2** to distract (distraer). || *v.i.* **3** not to worry: *¡descuida! = don't worry!* || *v.pron.* **4** to neglect: *se descuidan de su casa = they neglect their house.* **5** to be careless (no prestar atención). **6** not to worry, not to bother (no preocuparse): *se descuida de su apariencia = he doesn't worry about his appearance.* **7** not to be careful, not to be on guard (no tener cuidado): *si te descuidas te cobran demasiado = if you're not on guard, they'll charge you too much.*

descuido *s.m.* **1** carelessness (falta de cuidado). **2** negligence (negligencia). **3** forgetfulness (olvido). **4** inattention, lack of attention (falta de atención): *un momento de descuido = a moment's inattention.* **5** untidiness, slovenliness (de la apariencia). **6** error, mistake (un error). || **7 al –,** casually, nonchalantly. **8 en un –,** (Am.) when least expected. **9 por –,** inadvertently, by an oversight.

descular *v.t.* to break the bottom of.

deschavetado, -a *adj.* (Am.) crazy, daft (chiflado).

desde *prep.* **1** from (espacio): *sólo hay una milla desde aquí al colegio = there's only 1 mile from here to the school.* **2** from, since (tiempo): *desde el año pasado = since last year.* || **3 – hace,** for: *llevo viviendo aquí desde hace 20 años = I've been living here for 20 years.* **4 – que,** since: *te he querido desde que te vi por primera vez = I have loved you since the first time I saw you.*

desdecir *v.t.* **1** to deny, to repudiate (negar). || *v.i.* y *t.* **2** to refute, to deny (desmentir). || *v.i.* **3** not to match, to clash with (no hacer juego). || **5** to be unworthy of, to disappoint: *desdice de su familia = he's unworthy of his family.* **6** to decline, to deteriorate (decaer). || *v.pron.* **7** to retract, to take back what one has said (retractarse). **8** to go back on, to withdraw (renunciar). || **9 desdecirse de una promesa,** to go back on a promise.

desdén *s.m.* disdain, contempt (menosprecio).

desdentado, -a *adj.* **1** toothless. **2** ZOOL. edentate. || *s.pl.* **3** ZOOL. edentata.

desdeñar *v.t.* to disdain, to scorn; to turn one's nosa up at.

desdibujar *v.t.* **1** to blur, to fade (hacer confusa). || *v.pron.* **2** to become blurred, to fade.

desdicha *s.f.* **1** misfortune, mishap: *sufrir una desdicha = to suffer a misfortune.* **2** misfortune, misery (desgracia). **3** poverty, wretchedness (pobreza extrema). || **4 para colmo de desdichas,** on top of everything. **6 para –,** unfortunately.

desdoblar *v.t.* **1** to unwind, to straighten (un alambre, etc.). **2** to unfold, to spread out (un mapa, papel, etc.). **3** QUIM. to break down, to separate.

desdoro *s.m.* **1** dishonour, blemish, blot: *es un desdoro para la familia = it's a blot on the family.*

desear *v.t.* **1** to want (querer): *deseo que vengas = I want you to come.* **2** to desire, to long for (añorar): *deseamos la democracia = we long for democracy.* **3** to wish: *te deseo mucha suerte = I wish you good luck.* **4** to look forward to: *deseo que llegue el fin de semana = I'm looking forward to the weekend.* **5** to like (gustar): *desearía más dinero = I would like more money.* **6** desire (sexualmente). || **7 deja mucho que –,** it leaves a lot to be desired. **18 es de –,** it's to be hoped.

desecar *v.t.* **1** to dry up. **2** QUIM. to desiccate. **3** to drain (drenar). || *v.pron.* **4** to dry up (secarse).

desechar *v.t.* **1** to throw away o out (basura). **2** to get rid of, to scrap (cosas inútiles): *desechar un coche viejo = to get rid of an old car.* **3** to cast off, to discard (ropa vieja). **4** to reject, to turn down (rechazar): *desechar una sugerencia = to reject a suggestion.* **5** to drop, to discard (una idea, un plan, etc.). **6** to turn (una llave). **7** to undervalue, to think little of (menospreciar). **8** to expel, to eject (expeler).

desecho *s.m.* **1** waste, rubbish (basura). **2** residue (resto). **3** offal (de carnicero). **4** castoff (prenda). **5** scrap, junk (de metal). **6** reject (después de elegir lo bueno). **7** contempt, scorn (desprecio). **8** (fig.) dregs, scum: *el desecho de la sociedad = the scum/dregs of society.* || **9 desechos de metal,** scrap metal. **10 desechos radiactivos,** radioactive waste. **11 el hombre es un –,** man is a dead loss.

desembalar *v.t.* to unpack.

desembarazar *v.t.* **1** to evacuate, to clear (evacuar). **2** to clear, to free (un camino, etc.). **3** to empty, to clear (vaciar). || *v.pron.* **4** to get rid of something, to free oneself of: *se desembarazó del coche = he got rid of the car.* **5** (Am.) to give birth (parir).

desembarazo *s.m.* **1** clearing (acción de desembarazar). **2** ease, confidence (desenfado). **3** (Am.) childbirth (parto).

desembarcadero *s.m.* landing stage, quay, pier, wharf.

desembarcar *v.t.* **1** to land, to put ashore (personas). **2** to unload, to disembark (mercancías). || *v.i.* y *pron.* **3** to go ashore, to land, to disembark. **4** (Am.) to get out of (salir de).

desembaular *v.t.* **1** to unpack (deshacer un baúl, maleta, etc.). **2** to take out, to get out (sacar). **3** (fig.) to empty (vaciar). **4** (fig.) to get something off one's chest, to unburden oneself of a problem (desahogarse).

desembocadura *s.f.* **1** outlet, exit (salida). **2** mouth (un río). **3** end, opening (de una calle). **4** outlet (de una cañería).
desembocar *v.i.* **1** to flow into, to run into (un río): *el río desemboca en el Pacífico = the river flows into the Pacific.* **2** to join, to meet (una calle, camino, etc.). **3** (fig.) to end in, to lead to: *desembocó en caos = it ended in chaos.*
desembolsar *v.t.* **1** to pay, to pay out (pagar). **2** (fig.) to lay out, to spend (gastar).
desemboscar *v.r.* **1** to leave the forest (salir del bosque). **2** to escape from an ambush (salir de una emboscada).
desembragar *v.t.* **1** to release o to disengage the clutch (soltar el embrague). **2** MEC. to disconnect, to disengage. || *v.i.* **3** to declutch, to let the clutch out.
desembridar *v.t.* to unbridle.
desembrozar *v.t.* **1** to clear the undergrowth (quitar los matorrales). **2** to weed, to clear the weeds (la hierba). **3** to clear a path, to open the way (eliminar los obstáculos de un camino).
desembuchar *v.t.* **1** to disgorge (los pájaros). **2** (fig.) to let out, to reveal (revelar algo). || *v.i.* **3** (fig.) to let out a secret, to spill the beans (confesar). || **4** **¡desembucha!,** out with it!, spill the beans!
desemejar *v.i.* **1** to be unlike, to be dissimilar, to differ. || *v.t.* **3** to disfigure, to deform (deformar). **4** to change, to alter (cambiar).
desempachar *v.t.* y *r.* **1** to get rid of indigestion (quitar el empacho). || *v.pron.* **2** to become outgoing, to come out of one's shell (adquirir desenvoltura).
desempacho *s.m.* **1** confidence, ease, composure (soltura). **2** (desp.) cheek, impudence (descaro).
desempañar *v.t.* **1** to clean (limpiar lo empañado). || *v.t.* y *v.pron.* **2** to remove o to take off the nappies (quitar los pañales a los niños).
desemparejar *v.t.* y *pron.* **1** to break up a pair (deshacer una pareja). **2** to lose one of a pair (perder uno de una pareja).
desemparentado, -a *adj.* without relatives or relations.
desempeñar *v.t.* **1** to get out of pawn, to redeem (recuperar la cosa empeñada). **2** to hold, to occupy, to fill (un cargo). **3** to perform, to carry out (un deber). **4** to play (un papel en el cine, teatro, etc.). **5** (fig.) to get someone out of a fix o jam (sacar a uno de un apuro). || *v.pron.* **6** to pay off someone's debts, to free someone from debt (librar a uno de sus deudas). **7** to get out of a fix o jam (salir de un apuro).
desempleo *s.m.* unemployment.
desempolvar o **desempolvorar** *v.t.* **1** to dust, to do the dusting (quitar el polvo).
desencadenar *v.t.* **1** to unchain (soltar las cadenas). **2** to unleash (un perro). **3** (fig.) to let loose, to unleash (las pasiones). **4** (fig.) to start, to set off, to spark off: *el gobierno desencadenó una guerra = the government set off a war.* || *v.pron.* **5** to break out (guerra, huelga, etc.). **6** to burst (una tormenta). **7** to rage (pasiones, el viento, el mar, etc.).
desencajar *v.t.* **1** MED. to dislocate (los huesos). **2** MEC. to disconnect, to disengage (desconectar). **3** to unblock, to free (desatascar). || *v.pron.* **4** to become distorted (el rostro). **5** to look crazy o wild (los ojos). **6** to break up, to fall to pieces (deshacerse).
desencallar *v.t.* MAR. to refloat.
desencaminar *v.t.* **1** to send the wrong way, to misdirect. **2** (fig.) to mislead, to lead astry: *me han desencaminado = I've been misled.* || *v.pron.* **3** to go the wrong way, to take the wrong road. **4** (fig.) to go astray.
desencantar *v.t.* **1** to disillusion, to disappoint (decepcionar). || *v.pron.* **2** to become disillusioned, to be disappointed.
desencapotar *v.t.* **1** to uncover, to reveal (descubrir). || *v.pron.* **2** to clear, to clear up (despejarse el cielo). **3** to cheer up, to brighten up (animarse). || *v.t.* y *pron.* **4** (p.u.) to take off one's cloak, to uncloak (quitarse el capote).
desencerrar *v.t.* **1** to unlock, to open (abrir lo encerrado). **2** to get out, to free (sacar del encierro). **3** to uncover, to unmask (descubrir lo oculto).
desenclavar *v.t.* **1** to unnail (desclavar). **2** (fig.) to throw out, to kick out (echar violentamente a uno de un lugar).
desenconar *v.t.* **1** to reduce, to relieve the inflammation. **2** (fig.) to soothe, to ease (moderar el enojo, etc.). || *v.pron.* **3** to calm down, to cool down (suavizarse una cosa).
desencuadernar o **descuadern** *v.t.* **1** to take off the binding, to unbind (un libro). || *v.pron.* **2** to come unbound.
desenfadado, -a *adj.* **1** free-and-easy, carefree (desenvuelto). **2** uncaring, indifferent (sin excesivos respetos humanos).
desenfadar *v.t.* y *pron.* to calm down, to cool down.
desenfado *s.m.* **1** carefree manner, free-and-easy manner (desenvoltura). **2** openness, frankness (franqueza). **3** inhibition, freedom (despreocupación).
desenfilar *v.t.* y *pron.* MIL. to put under cover o to cover from enemy fire (poner a cubierto del fuego enemigo).
desenfrenar *v.t.* **1** to release the brake (quitar el freno). || *v.r.* **2** (fig.) to let oneself go, to go wild (entregarse a los vicios). **3** to run riot, to run wild (la multitud). **4** to burst, to rage (una tormenta). **5** to rage (el viento).
desengañar *v.t.* **1** to open the eyes of, to see the truth, to enlighten: *ya que me han desengañado = now that I've seen the truth.* **2** to disappoint (decepcionar). **3** to disillusion (desilusionar). || *v.pron.* **4** to get disillusioned (desilusionarse). **5** to see the truth (ver la verdad). **6** to realize (caer en la cuenta). **7** to see the light (ver la realidad). **8** **¡desengáñate!,** don't fool yourself!
desenlazar *v.t.* **1** to undo, to unfasten, to untie. **2** (fig.) to solve (un problema). **3** to unravel, to clear up (un asunto, la trama de una obra). || *v.pron.* **4** to come undone (desatarse). **5** to turn out, to end (un libro, una película, etc.).
desenmarañar *v.t.* **1** to unravel, to disentangle (desenredar). **2** to clear up, to clarify (aclarar un enredo).
desenmascarar *v.t.* **1** unmask (quitar la máscara). **2** (fig.) to unmask, to expose: *se desenmascararon sus mentiras = his lies were exposed.*
desenredar *v.t.* **1** to unravel, to disentangle (desenmarañar). **2** (fig.) to straighten out, to put in order (poner en orden). || *v.pron.* **3** (fig.) to get out of a jam/fix (salir de un apuro).
desenredo *s.m.* **1** unravelling, disentanglement (resultado de desenredar). **2** solution (de un problema). **3** denouement, outcome (desenlace). **4** way out (salida de un apuro).
desentenderse *v.pron.* **1** to pretend not to know, to give the impression of ignorance (fingir que no se entiende): *se desentiende del asunto = he pretends not to know about the subject.* **2** not to take part in, to want nothing to do with (no tomar parte en algo): *me desentiendo de esa cosa = I want nothing to do with that.*
desenterrar *v.t.* **1** to disinter, to exhume (un cadáver). **2** (fig.) to dig up, to unearth (una cosa). **2** (fig.) to recall, to recollect (traer a la memoria).
desentonar *v.i.* **1** to be out of tune (voz o instrumento). **2** to sing out of tune (voz). || *v.i.* y *pron.* **3** (fig.) to clash, not to match, not to go with (ropa, colores, etc.). || *v.pron.* **4** to shout, to raise one's voice (levantar la voz).
desentrampar *v.t.* y *pron.* **1** to get out of debt (librar de las deudas). **2** to get out of pawn (desempeñar). **3** (fam.) to get out of the red (salir de los números rojos).
desentrañar *v.t.* **1** to disembowel. **2** (fig.) to work out, to puzzle out (resolver un problema). **3** to get to the bottom of, to unravel (un misterio). || *v.pron.* **4** to do/go without (privarse de algo).
desenvainar *v.t.* **1** to draw, to unsheathe (una espada). **2** to show, to uncover (descubrir lo oculto). **3** to shell (guisantes). **4** to show, to put out (un animal).
desenvoltura *s.f.* **1** grace, ease, naturalness (del cuerpo). **2** fluency, facility (facilidad de palabra). **3** assurance, self-confidence (confianza en sí mismo). **4** cheek, impudence, nerve (desvergüenza). **5** free-and-easy manner, carefreeness (despreocupación).
desenvolver *v.t.* **1** to unwrap (regalo, paquete, etc.). **2** to unroll, to unwind (un rollo, hilo, etc.). **3** to untangle (lana). **4** (fig.) to expound, to set out (una teoría, idea, etc.). **5** to unravel, to clear up

(aclarar). **6** to develop, to expand (un negocio). || *v.pron.* **7** to get out of a fix o jam (salir de una dificultad). **8** to prosper (prosperar). **9** to develop, to grow (desarrollarse). || **10 desenvolverse en la vida,** to look after oneself.

deseo *s.m.* **1** desire, wish: *el deseo de dormir = the desire to sleep.* || **3 buenos deseos,** good intentions. **4 deseos de felicidad,** good wishes. **2 arder en deseos de algo,** to long for; to yearn for. **7 tener – de hacer algo,** to long to do something, to want to do something. **5 es mi mayor –,** it's my dearest wish. **6 según sus deseos,** according to his wishes.

desequilibrado, -a *adj.* **1** unbalanced, off balance. **2** (fig.) unbalanced, disturbed (de la mente).

desequilibrar *v.t.* **1** to unbalance; to throw/knock/put off balance. **2** (fig.) to unbalance (perder el equilibrio mental): *el susto le desequilibró = the shock unbalanced him.* || *v.pron.* **3** to lose one's balance (perder el equilibrio). **4** to become unbalanced, to go mad (volverse loco).

desertar *v.i.* **1** MIL. to desert. **2** to abandon, to leave (de casa, un grupo, etc.). **3** DER. to drop, to give up. || **4 – al enemigo,** to go over to the enemy.

desértico, -a *adj.* **1** desert, desert-like (como un desierto). **2** empty, deserted (vacío). **3** GEOG. desert.

desesperanzar *v.t.* **1** to deprive of hope (quitar la esperanza). || *v.pron.* **2** to lose hope, to despair (quedarse sin esperanza).

desesperar *v.t.* **1** to drive to despair (llevar a uno a la desesperación). **2** (fam.) to drive crazy, to annoy (exasperar). || *v.i.* **3** to give up hope, to despair (perder la esperanza): *desespero de aprobar el examen = I've given up hope of passing the exam.* || *v.pron.* **4** to give up hope, to lose hope, to despair (quedarse sin esperanza). **5** to get impatient, to become impatient (impacientarse). **6** to get exasperated (irritarse).

desestimar *v.t.* **1** to underestimate (menospreciar). **2** to have a low opinion of, to have little respect for (despreciar). **3** to reject (denegar). **4** DER. to turn down, to reject: *me han desestimado la demanda = they have turned down my claim.*

desfachatez *s.f.* impudence, cheek, nerve (descaro): *¡qué desfachatez! = what a nerve!*

desfalcar *v.t.* **1** FIN. to embezzle. **2** to leave incomplete (dejar incompleto).

desfallecer *v.i.* **1** to weaken (perder las fuerzas). **2** to faint (desmayarse). **3** to decline (venir a menos).

desfase *s.m.* **1** unadaptability (inadaptación de una persona o cosa). **2** gap (diferencia).

desfigurar *v.t.* **1** to disfigure (la cara). **2** to deform (el cuerpo). **3** to deface (un edificio, un cuadro, etc.). **4** to distort (la verdad, el significado, los hechos, etc.). **5** to blur (una foto). **6** to alter, to disguise (la voz). || *v.pron.* **7** to change (inmutarse).

desfiladero *s.m.* narrow pass, defile.

desfilar *v.i.* **1** MIL. to march in files, to parade. **2** to file past, to march past: *desfilaron ante el general = they marched past the general.* **3** (fam.) to file out (marcharse).

desflorar *v.t.* **1** to strip off the flower (quitar la flor). **2** to deflower (desvirgar). **3** to tarnish, to mar (quitar el lustre). **4** to touch superficially upon, to brush over (tratar superficialmente un asunto).

desfogar *v.t.* **1** to vent, to let fly: *desfogó su frustración en los demás = he vented his frustration on the others.* || *v.i.* **2** to burst, to break (una tormenta). || *v.pron.* **3** (fam.) to vent one's feelings, to let off steam (manifestar ardientemente una pasión).

desfondar *v.t.* **1** to knock the bottom out of (quitar el fondo). **2** to break the bottom of (romper el fondo). **3** AGR. to plough deeply. || *v.pron.* **4** to wear/tire oneself out (agotarse).

desgaire *s.m.* **1** contemptuous/scornful gesture (ademán de desprecio). **2** carelessness, slovenliness (en el vestir, etc.). **3** affected carelessness, nonchalance (desaliño afectado). || **4 al –,** sloppily, carelessly (con descuido).

desgajar *v.t.* **1** to tear off, to rip off (las ramas). **2** to tear up (despedazar). **3** to tear o tip to pieces (desgarrar). || *v.pron.* **4** to come away from, to break off (desprenderse una cosa de otra). **5** to tear oneself (alejándose de algo).

desgalichado, -a *adj.* clumsy, awkward, ungainly.

desgana *s.f.* **1** lack of appetite (inapetencia). **2** lack of willpower (abulia). **3** unwillingness, reluctance (sin ganas). **4** repugnance, disgust (repugnancia).

desgañitarse *v.r.* **1** to shout o scream one's head off. **2** to go hoarse (enronquecer).

desgarbado, -a *adj.* **1** clumsy, gawky, ungainly. **2** slovenly, careless (en el vestir).

desgarrado, -a *adj.* **1** impudent, cheeky, insolent (descarado). **2** scandalous (escandaloso). **3** reprobate, licentious (libertino).

desgarrar *v.t.* **1** to tear, to rip (rasgar). **2** (fig.) to crush, to shatter (causar mucha pena). **3** to break (el corazón). || *v.r.* **4** to rip, to tear.

desgarro *s.m.* **1** tear, rip (de papel, tela, etc.). **2** tear (de un músculo). || (fig.) **3** boasting, bragging (fanfarronada). **4** cheek, impudence, nerve (desvergüenza).

desgarrón *s.m.* **1** large rip o tear (rotura grande). **2** tear (de un músculo). **3** tatter (jirón).

desgastar *v.t.* **1** to wear away, to wear down (gastar poco a poco). **2** to wear out (la ropa). **3** GEOL. to erode. **4** to fray, to wear (una cuerda, cortina, etc.). **5** to corrode (metal). **6** (fig.) to ruin, to spoil (estropear). || *v.pron.* **7** to tire o to wear oneself out (agotarse). **8** to get weak (debilitarse). **9** to wear out, to get worn (ropa). **10** GEOL. to erode. **11** to wear away (gastarse poco a poco). **12** to corrode (metal).

desglosar *v.t.* **1** to remove, to detach (un escrito de otro). **2** to separate (separar).

desgobernar *v.t.* **1** POL. to misgovern, to misrule. **2** to dislocate (dislocar). **3** to mismanage, to manage badly (llevar un negocio, asunto, etc. mal).

desgoznar o **desengoznar** *v.t.* **1** to unhinge, to take something off its hinges (sacar de los goznes). || *v.pron.* **2** to get upset, to become disturbed (desquiciar).

desgracia *s.f.* **1** misfortune (suceso adverso): *sufrir una desgracia = to have a misfortune.* **2** mishap (contratiempo). **3** bad luck (mala suerte). **4** disgrace, disfavour (pérdida del favoritismo). **5** awkwardness, lack of grace (falta de maña o gracia). || **6 caer en –,** to fall into disgrace. **7 estar en –,** to be unfortunate. **8 no hay que lamentar desgracias personales,** no one was hurt; there were no casualties. **9 para colmo de desgracias,** on top of everything. **10 por –,** unfortunately. **11 ¡qué –!,** what a pity!, what a shame! **12 ser la – de la familia,** to be the disgrace of the family.

desgraciar *v.t.* **1** to ruin, to spoil (estropear). **2** to damage (dañar). || *v.pron.* **3** to be ruined, to be spoilt (estropearse). **4** to be damaged (dañarse). **5** to fall through, to turn out badly (malograrse).

desgranar *v.t.* **1** to remove the grain (sacar el grano). **2** to remove the pips (sacar las pepitas). **3** to thresh (trigo). **4** to shell (guisantes, maíz). || *v.pron.* **5** to shed its grain (maíz, trigo). **6** BOT. to fall. **7** to lose its grapes (uva). **8** to shed its seeds (otras plantas). **9** to come unstrung (cuentas de un collar). || **10 – las cuentas de un rosario,** to tell one's beads.

desgreñar *v.t.* **1** to ruffle, to tousle, to dishevel (despeinar). || *v.pron.* **2** to get ruffled, tousled/dishevelled (despeinarse).

desguarnecer *v.t.* **1** MEC. to strip down, to dismantle (desmontar). **2** to unharness (un caballo). **3** to untrim, to remove the trimmings (quitar los adornos). **4** to strip (instrumentos). **6** MIL. to abandon (abandonar).

desguazar *v.t.* **1** to rough-hew (un madero). **2** to break up, to strip down (deshacer un barco, coche, avión, etc.).

deshacer *v.t.* **1** to undo (en general). **2** to damage (dañar). **3** to spoil (estropear). **4** to destroy (destruir). **5** to undo, to unpick (descoser). **6** to ruin (arruinar). **7** MEC. to take to pieces, to take apart (desmontar). **8** to strip down, to break up (desguazar). **9** to unmake (una cama). **10** to unwrap, to undo (un paquete). **11** to untie, to unfasten, to undo (desatar). **12** to unpack (una maleta). **13** to unknot, to untie (un nudo). **14** to wear down (metal). **15** to melt (derretir). **16** to dissolve (disolver). **17** to put to flight, to rout (un enemigo). **18** to beat, to defeat (ganar). **19** to break, to violate (un tratado). **20** to cancel (un contrato). **21** to wear o tire out (cansar). **22** to right (injusticias, males, etc.). **23** to shatter (una persona): *la noticia le deshizo = the news shattered him.* **24** to divide (dividir). **25** to damage, to harm (la vista). **26** to thwart (una intriga, complot, etc.). || *v.pron.* **27** to come undone o unfastened (cordones, nudo, etc.). || *v.pron.* **28** to come unsewn (descoserse). **29** to come apart, to come to pieces (un objeto). **30** to break (romper). **31** to get spoilt (estropearse). **32** to get damaged (dañarse). **33** to melt (derretirse). **34** to vanish, to disappear (esfumarse). **35** to dissolve (disolver). **36** to break up (desguazar). **37** to be shattered, to go to pieces (una persona): *cuando oyó las noticias se deshizo = when he heard the news, he was shattered.* **38** to get tired, to tire oneself out (cansarse). **39** to do one's utmost (hacer todo lo posible). **40** to get o grow weak (debilitarse). **41** to get o grow impatient (impacientarse). || **42 deshacerse de algo,** to get rid of something, to part with something: *se deshizo del coche = he got rid of the car.* **43 deshacerse de alguien,** to get rid of someone. **44 deshacerse en lágrimas,** to burst into tears. **45 deshacerse en suspiros,** to sigh deeply. **46 deshacerse en cumplidos,** to be full of praise. **47 deshacerse en excusas,** to apologize profusely. **48 deshacerse como el humo,** to vanish into thin air. **49 deshacerse por algo,** to be crazy/mad about something. **50 deshacerse por el arte,** he is crazy about art. **51 deshacerse por hacer algo,** to do one's utmost, to do something, to try one's hardest to do something. **52 deshacerse por encontrar un trabajo,** he's trying his hardest to find a job.

desharrapado, -a *adj.* **1** ragged, tattered. || *s.c.* **2** shabby person, down-and-out.

deshebrar *v.t.* **1** to unthread, to undo (una tela). **2** to tear into strips (dividir en partes muy delgadas).

deshecho, -a *adj.* **1** tired out, worn out (muy cansado). **2** crushed, shattered (por una noticia, etc.). **3** destroyed (destrozado). **4** unsewn (descosido). **5** undone, unfastened (ropa, lazo, nudo). **6** broken (roto). **7** untied (desatado). **8** melted (nieve, hielo). **9** dissolved (disuelto). **10** unmade (una cama). **11** unpacked (una maleta). **12** in pieces, broken up (desmontado). **13** beaten, defeated (vencido). **14** unwrapped (un paquete). **15** ruined, spoilt (estropeado). **16** broken (salud). **17** violent (tormenta). || *s.m.* **18** (Am.) short cut (atajo).

desheredado, -a *adj.* **1** disinherited. **2** (fig.) under-privileged, poor (pobre). || *s.c.* **3** a disinherited person. **4** (fig.) an under-privileged person.

desheredar *v.t.* to disinherit.

deshidratar *v.t.* y *pron.* **1** to dehydrate.

deshielo *s.m.* **1** thaw (nieve, hielo). **2** defrosting (del frigorífico). **3** (fig.) thawing: *el deshielo entre dos países = the thawing between two countries.*

deshilachar *v.t.* **1** to ravel, to fray. || *v.pron.* **2** to become frayed, to get frayed.

deshilar *v.t.* **1** to unravel (sacar hilos). **2** (fig.) to cut into shreds (cortar en partes muy delgadas). || *v.pron.* **3** to get worn, to fray (deshilacharse).

deshilvanado, -a *adj.* **1** disconnected, disjointed (inconexo). **2** incoherent (incoherente). **3** untacked (costura).

deshilvanar *v.t.* to untack, to unstitch.

deshojar *v.t.* **1** to pull o strip the leaves off (quitar las hojas). **2** to pull o strip the petals off (quitar los pétalos). **3** to tear the pages out of (libros). **4** QUIM. to defoliate. || *v.pron.* **5** to lose its leaves (árbol). **6** to lose its petals (una flor).

deshollinador, -a *adj.* **1** who sweeps chimneys (que quita el hollín). || *s.m.* **2** sweep, chimney sweep (persona). **3** chimney sweep's brush (cepillo). **4** brush (escoba).

deshonesto, -a *adj.* **1** dishonest (no honrado). **2** indecent, lewd, obscene (obsceno).

deshonor *s.m.* **1** dishonour, disgrace (pérdida del honor). **2** disgrace (descrédito): *vivir en el deshonor = to live in disgrace.* **3** insult, affront (un insulto, afrenta).

deshonrar *v.t.* **1** to dishonour, to disgrace. **2** to affront (afrontar). **3** to insult (insultar). || *v.pron.* **4** to ruin (a una mujer). **5** (form.) to deflower (desvirgar).

deshora *adv.* awkward moment, inconvenient time (tiempo inoportuno): *a deshora/a deshoras = at an awkward moment/at an inconvenient time.*

deshuesadora *s.f.* stoning machine.

deshuesar o **desosar** *v.t.* **1** to bone (carne). **2** to stone, to pit (fruta).

desiderata *s.pl.* desiderata.

desiderátum *s.m.* desideratum.

desidia *s.f.* **1** negligence, neglect (negligencia). **2** laziness, idleness (gandulería). **3** slovenliness (en el vestir).

desierto, -a *adj.* **1** deserted, empty (vacío). **2** empty, bleak (un paisaje). **3** empty, uninhabited (deshabitado). **4** GEOG. desert. **5** (fig.) deserted: *el pueblo estaba desierto = the village was deserted.* **6** void: *el concurso ha sido declarado desierto = the competition has been declared void.* || *s.m.* **7** desert. || **8 clamar en el —,** to cry in the wilderness.

designar *v.t.* **1** to designate, to name, to appoint (nombrar). **2** to select (seleccionar). **3** to decide upon, to fix, to name (un día, fecha, lugar, etc.): *designar el día de un partido = to fix the day of a game.*

designio *s.m.* **1** plan (plan). **2** project (proyecto). **3** intention (propósito): *con el designio de = with the intention of.*

desigual *adj.* **1** unequal, uneven: *un partido desigual = an uneven game.* **2** different (diferente): *dos chicos desiguales = two different children.* **3** unfair, injust (tratamiento). **4** changeable (el tiempo). **5** unpredictable (carácter). **6** rough, uneven (terreno). **9** uneven, irregular (escritura).

desigualar *v.t.* **1** to make unequal. **2** to make different (una cosa a otra). **3** to make uneven/rough (un terreno). || *v.pron.* **4** to excel, to surpass (aventajarse). **5** to get ahead (adelantarse). **6** to break the equality (deshacer la igualdad).

desigualdad *s.f.* **1** inequality: *la desigualdad entre los sexos = the inequality between the sexes.* **2** unevenness, roughness (de un terreno). **3** changeableness (del tiempo). **4** unpredictability, capriciousness (del carácter). **5** unevenness (de la escritura, estilo). **6** difference (diferencia): *la desigualdad entre dos países = the difference between two countries.* **7** inconsistency (inconsistencia). **8** MAT. inequality.

desinencia *s.f.* GRAM. ending.

desinfectar *v.t.* y *pron.* to disinfect.

desinsectar *v.t.* to fumigate.

desintegración *s.f.* **1** disintegration. || **2 — nuclear,** FIS. nuclear fission. **3 la — del átomo,** the splitting of the atom.

desintegrar *v.t.* y *pron.* **1** to disintegrate. **2** FIS. to split (un átomo). **3** (fig.) to break up: *desintegrar un grupo = to break up a group.*

desinterés *s.m.* **1** disinterestedness. **2** impartiality (imparcialidad). **3** generosity, unselfishness (generosidad).

desistir *v.i.* **1** to desist, to stop. **2** to give up (dejar): *ha desistido de trabajar = he's given up working.* **4** DER. to waive (un derecho).

desjarretar *v.t.* **1** to hamstring (un animal). **2** MED. to get weak, to weaken (debilitar).

deslavar o **deslavazar** *v.t.* **1** to wash gently, to half-wash (lavar ligeramente). **2** to fade (desteñir). **3** to weaken, to get weak (debilitar).

deslavazado, -a *adj.* **1** soft, bland, limp (blando). **2** discoloured, faded (desteñido). **3** wet, limp (persona). **4** colourless, bland (insípido). **5** incoherent, disjointed (un discurso).

desleír o **diluir** *v.t.* y *v.pron.* **1** to dissolve (disolver un sólido). **2** to dilute, to thin (un líquido espeso). **3** (fig.) to dilute. || *v.t.* **4** to be long-winded, to be verbose (hablar con demasiadas palabras).

deslenguar *v.t.* **1** to cut the tongue out/of off. || *v.pron.* **2** to be foul-mouthed (ser mal hablado). **3** to talk too much (hablar demasiado). **4** to speak insolently (hablar con insolencia).

desliar *v.t.* **1** to untie, to undo (desatar). **2** to unwrap, to open (un paquete). ||

v.pron. **3** to come undone o untied (desatarse). **4** to come unwrapped (desenvolverse).
desligar *v.t.* **1** to undo, to unfasten, to untie (desatar). **2** to free, to release (dispensar de una obligación, promesa, etc.). **3** to sort out, to clear up (aclarar un problema, un enredo). **4** to separate, to detach (separar). **5** to extract (extraer). || *v.pron.* **6** to come undone, to come loose (desatarse). **7** to separate, to part company (separarse): *se desligó del grupo = he parted company from the group.* **8** to release o to free oneself: *desligarse de una obligación/promesa = to free oneself from an obligation/promise.*
deslindar *v.t.* **1** to fix, to mark out, to delimit (los límites, las fronteras, etc.). **2** (fig.) to define the limits (definir los límites): *deslindar las actividades de un grupo = to define the limits of the activities of a group.* **3** to spell out, to explain (aclarar una cosa para evitar problemas).
desliz *s.m.* **1** slip (de personas). **2** slide (de cosas). **3** skid (de coches). **4** (fig.) slip, mistake, error (error). **5** lapse, slip (lapsus): *un desliz de lengua = a slip of the tongue.* || **6 cometer un —**, to slip up, to make a mistake.
deslizar *v.t.* **1** to slip: *deslizó la mano en el bolsillo = he slipped his hand into his pocket.* || *v.i.* y *pron.* **2** to slide: *el coche se deslizó por la calle = the car slid along the street.* **3** to slip (resbalar). **4** to slide (patinar). **5** to skid (un coche, moto, etc.). **6** to slip out (un secreto). **7** to slip in, to find its way in (un error, una falta). **8** to slither (una serpiente). **9** to glide (un barco). **10** to glide, to slide (una bailarina). **11** to flow, to run (un líquido). **12** to pass, to slip by (el tiempo). **13** (fig.) to slip off o away (marcharse sin decir nada). **14** to slip up, to make a mistake (caer en una equivocación). **15** to fall into bad ways, to go off the straight and narrow (caer en una flaqueza).
deslomar *v.t.* **1** to break the back of (romper la espalda). **2** (fig.) to tire out, to exhaust (cansar). || *v.r.* **3** (fig.) to break one's back, to work like the devil (trabajar muchísimo).
deslucir *v.t.* **1** to spoil, to ruin (estropear). **2** to damage (dañar). **3** to tarnish (quitar el lustre): *deslucir la reputación = to tarnish the reputation.* **4** to discredit (desacreditar). **5** to dull (quitar brillantez). || *v.pron.* **6** to get dull, to get tarnished (perder el lustre). **7** to do badly, to fail to shine, to fail (fracasar). **8** to discredit oneself (desacreditarse). **9** to be unsuccessful (no tener éxito).
deslumbrar *v.t.* **1** to dazzle, to blind (cegar la vista): *las luces del coche nos deslumbraron = the lights of the car blinded us.* || **2** (fig.) to confuse, to bewilder (confundir). **3** (fig.) to surprise (sorprender).
desmadejar *v.t.* y *pron.* **1** to weaken, to debilitate (debilitar).
desmallar *v.t.* **1** to unravel, to untie (deshacer una malla). **2** to ladder (una media).
desmán *s.m.* **1** ZOOL. desman, muskrat. **2** abuse (abuso). **3** excess (exceso). **4** disgrace (desgracia). **5** outrage (tropelía): *cometer un desmán = to commit an outrage.*
desmandar *v.t.* **1** to annul, to revoke (anular). || *v.pron.* **2** to go too far, to exceed the limits (propasarse). **3** to get out of hand, to get out of control (no someterse a la autoridad): *los niños se están desmandando = the children are getting out of hand.* **4** to misbehave (portarse mal). **6** to be unruly (desobedecer). **6** to rebel (rebelarse). **7** to run away, to bolt (echarse a correr un caballo). **8** to stray (otros animales).
desmanotado, -a *adj.* clumsy, ungainly.
desmantelar *v.t.* **1** to dismantle, to take down (fortificación, estructura, base, etc.). **2** to empty, to strip (una casa). **3** to dismantle, to take to pieces (una máquina). **4** MAR. to unrig (desaparejar). **5** MAR. to unmast (desarbolar).
desmañado, -a *adj.* **1** clumsy, ungainly. || *s.m.* y *f.* **2** ungainly/clumsy person.
desmayar *v.i.* **1** to lose heart, to get discouraged (desanimar). || *v.pron.* **2** to faint, to swoon.
desmayo *s.m.* **1** faint, fainting fit: *sufrir /tener un desmayo = to faint/to have a faint.* **2** BOT. weeping willow (sauce). **3** (fig.) depression, dejection (desánimo). **4** flagging, waning (de la voz). **5** unconsciousness (inconsciencia). **6** limpness, listlessness (del cuerpo).
desmedirse *v.pron.* to go over the top, to go too far.
desmejorar *v.t.* **1** to spoil, to impair (estropear). **2** to deteriorate (deteriorar). **3** to damage (dañar). || *v.i.* y *pron.* **4** to be spoiled, to be impaired (estar estropeado). **5** to deteriorate, to get worse (deteriorarse). **6** MED. to decline, to lose one's health, to get worse: *el equipo se ha desmejorado = the team has got worse.*
desmelenar *v.t.* **1** to ruffle, to dishevel (el pelo). || *v.pron.* **2** to become vain /conceited (crecerse).
desmembrar *v.t.* **1** to dismember. || *v.t.* y *pron.* **2** (fig.) to split up, to break up (dividir): *desmembrar una compañía = to break up a company.* **3** to separate (separar).
desmemoriado, -a *adj.* forgetful, absent-minded.
desmentir *v.t.* **1** to deny, to refute: *desmintió la acusación = he denied the accusation.* **2** to contradict, to refute (contradecir). **3** to refute, to explode (una teoría, sospecha). **4** to go against (proceder uno en desacuerdo con su estado). || *v.i.* **5** to be out of line, to go against the grain (desviarse una cosa de su línea).
desmenuzar *v.t.* **1** to chop up, to cut up (trocear). **2** to chop up (carne). **3** to grate (queso). **4** to crumble (pan). **5** (fig.) to scrutinize, to examine closely (examinar atentamente).
desmerecer *v.i.* **1** to degenerate, to deteriorate (degenerar). **2** to be inferior (ser inferior). **3** to lose in comparison; to compare badly with: *el libro desmerece de los otros = the book compares badly with the others.* **4** to lose value (perder valor). **5** to get worse, to decline (decaer). || *v.t.* **6** to be unworthy of (hacerse indigno de algo).
desmesurar *v.t.* **1** to disarrange, to disorder (desarreglar). || *v.pron.* **2** to go to far, to forget oneself (excederse). **3** (fam.) to go over the top (pasarse).
desmineralización *s.i.* demineralization.
desmirriado, -a o **esmirriado, -a** *adj.* **1** thin, skinny (flaco). **2** weak, feeble (débil).
desmochar *v.t.* **1** to lop, to pollard (un árbol). **2** to cut the top off (cortar la parte superior). **3** to dismantle (desmantelar). **4** to blunt (los cuernos). **5** (fig.) to edit, to cut (un texto, un libro, etc.).
desmonetizar *v.t.* to demonetize.
desmontar *v.t.* **1** to fell, to cut (árboles). **2** to clear of trees (quitar los árboles). **3** to level (allanar). **4** to take off, to remove (quitar): *desmontar una rueda = to remove a wheel.* **5** to take to pieces, to take apart (en piezas). **6** to strip down, to dismantle (desmantelar). **7** ARQ. to demolish, to pull down (demoler). **8** to uncock (un arma de fuego). **9** MAR. to take down (una vela). **10** to throw, to dismount (un caballo al jinete). || *v.t.i.* y *pron.* **11** to dismount (caballo). **12** to get out (un vehículo).
desmonte *s.m.* **1** clearing (de árboles). **2** levelling (de un terreno). **3** dismounting (de un motor, una máquina, etc.). **4** uncocking (de un arma). **5** dismounting (de un caballo). **6** rubble (escombros). **7** (Am.) waste (desechos).
desmoralizar *v.t.* **1** to demoralize. **2** to corrupt (corromper). || *v.pron.* **3** to lose heart, to get demoralized (desanimarse). **4** to rebel (rebelarse).
desmoronar *v.t.* **1** to wear away (deshacerse lentamente). **2** (fig.) to erode. || *v.pron.* **3** to decay (decaer). **4** to crumble, to fall to pieces: *el edificio se está desmoronando = the building is falling to pieces.* **5** to decline, to get worse (venir a menos). **6** (fig.) to crumble, to decline: *el imperio se desmorona = the empire is crumbling.*
desmovilizar *v.t.* to demobilize, (fam.) to demob.
desnarigado, -a *adj.* **1** noseless (sin nariz). **2** stub-nosed, snub-nosed (chato).
desnatar *v.t.* **1** to skim, to take the cream off (quitar la nata). **2** to remove the top of (otros líquidos). **3** (fig.) to take the cream off, to cream off (escoger lo mejor). || **4 leche sin —**, full-cream milk, whole milk.

desnaturalización *s.f.* **1** denaturalization. **2** adulteration (adulteración).
desnaturalizado, -a *adj.* **1** denaturalized (sin nacionalidad). **2** adulterated (adulterado). **3** unnatural (no natural). **4** QUIM. denatured. **5** ungrateful (ingrato). **6** inhuman (inhumano).
desnaturalizar *v.t.* **1** QUIM. to denature. **2** to denaturalize. **3** to pervert, to corrupt (corromper). **4** to misrepresent, to distort (representar mal). **5** to adulterate (adulterar). || *v.pron.* **6** to give up one's nationality.
desnivel *s.m.* **1** height difference (diferencia de altura). **2** slope (talud). **3** unevenness (falta de nivel). **4** (fig.) gap, difference, inequality: *hay un desnivel económico entre los dos países = there is an economic gap between the two countries.*
desnucar *v.t.* **1** to dislocate the neck (descoyuntar la nuca). || *v.pron.* **2** to break one's neck (romperse la nuca).
desnudismo *s.m.* nudism.
desnudo, -a *adj.* **1** naked, nude, bare (cuerpo). **2** bare (un árbol, un brazo, una pared, etc.). **3** bare, barren (un paisaje). **4** ruined (arruinado). || *s.m.* **5** ART. nude. || **6 — de,** without: *desnudo de afecto = without love.*
desnutrición *s.f.* malnutrition, undernourishment.
desobediente *adj.* disobedient.
desocupación *s.f.* **1** unemployment (desempleo). **2** spare time, leisure (tiempo libre). **3** vacation (de una casa). **4** MIL. evacuation.
desocupar *v.t.* **1** to vacate, to leave (una casa). **2** MIL. to evacuate. **3** to empty (vaciar). || *v.pron.* **4** to free oneself, to get out of (librarse de algo).
desodorante *adj.* y *s.m.* deodorant.
desoír *v.t.* **1** to ignore, to disregard, not to pay attention (no hacer caso). **2** not to take notice (despreciar consejos, etc.).
desojarse *v.pron.* to strain one's eyes.
desolar *v.t.* **1** to desolate, to devastate, to lay waste to (devastar). || *v.pron.* **2** to be disconsolate, to be distressed.
desollador *s.m.* **1** skinner (que quita la piel). **2** (fig.) extortioner, swindler.
desollar *v.t.* **1** to skin, to fleece (quitar la piel de un animal). **2** (fig.) to make someone pay through the nose (hacer pagar caro). **3** to criticize, to slate (criticar). **4** to discredit (desacreditar).
desorbitar *v.t.* **1** to leave orbit (satélite). **2** to exaggerate (exagerar). || *v.pron.* **3** to lose one's sense of proportion (una persona). **4** to get out of control (un asunto). **5** to bulge (los ojos).
desorden *s.m.* **1** disorder, confusion. **2** POL. disorder, chaos. **3** excess (exceso en la vida, en general). || *pl.* **4** riots, disorder. || **5 en —,** in a mess.
desorganizar *v.t.* **1** to disorganize, to disrupt. **2** to disband, to dissolve (desordenar una organización).
desorientar *v.t.* **1** to make someone lose his way, to disorientate. **2** (fig.) to confuse someone, to bewilder someone (confundir): *la clase me desorientó = the class confused me.* || *v.pron.* **4** to lose one's way, to get lost (perderse). **5** to get confused, to become bewildered (confundirse).
desorientación *s.f.* disorientation.
desorientador, -a *adj.* disorientating, bewildering.
desovar *v.i.* BIOL. **1** to spawn (peces, anfibios). **2** to lay eggs (insectos).
desove *s.m.* BIOL. **1** spawning (de peces, anfibios). **2** egg-laying (insectos).
desoxidar *v.t.* to deoxidize, (fam.) to derust, to remove the rust from (quitar el óxido).
desoxigenar *v.t.* y *pron.* QUIM. to deoxygenate.
desoxigenación *s.f.* QUIM. deoxigenation.
despabilado *adj.* **1** awake, wide-awake (despierto). **2** (fig.) sharp, smart, bright (listo).
despabilar o **espabilar** *v.t.* **1** to snuff (una vela). **2** to trim (una mecha). **3** (fam.) to wake up (despertar). **4** to wake up, to liven up (avivar el ingenio): *debemos despabilarle = we must liven him up.* **5** to squander (derrochar). **6** (fam.) to pinch, to nick (robar). **7** (fam.) to do in, to do away with (matar). || *v.pron.* **8** to wake up (despertarse). **9** (fig.) to liven up, to look sharp, to get a move on: *¡despabílate! = get a move on!* **10** (Am.) to vanish, to disappear (desaparecer).
despacio *adv.* **1** slowly: *andan despacio = they walk slowly.* **2** (Am.) softly, quietly (silenciosamente).
despachado, -a *adj.* **1** efficient, quick (rápido). **2** (fig.) insolent, rude (insolente). **3** cheeky (descarado). || **4 ir bien — de,** to have bags of, to be well off for.
despachar *v.t.* **1** to settle, to complete, to dispatch (terminar). **2** to deal with, to attend to (atender): *despachar la correspondencia = to deal with the mail.* **3** to serve, to attend (atender en una tienda). **4** to dispatch, to send (cartas, paquetes, etc.). **5** to sell, to issue (vender): *despachar entradas = to issue tickets.* **6** to sack, to fire (despedir). **7** to get rid of, to send packing (deshacerse de alguien): *despaché al mendigo = I sent the beggar packing.* **8** (fam.) to polish off, to put away: *despachamos dos botellas de vino = we put away two bottles of wine.* **9** (fam.) to do in, to kill (matar). || *v.i.* **10** to hurry along, to hurry up (darse prisa). **15** to do business: *no despachamos los domingos = we don't do business on Sundays.* **11** to serve (en una tienda). || *v.pron.* **12** to finish, (fam.) to knock off (terminar): *nos despachamos a las tres = we knock off a three.* **13** to hurry up (darse prisa). || **14 despacharse a gusto,** to speak one's mind, (fam.) not to beat about the bush.
despacho *s.m.* **1** sending, dipatch (envío). **2** settling, dipatch (de un negocio). **3** COM. sale (venta). **4** office (oficina). **5** study, den (en una casa). **6** store, shop (tienda). **7** message (mensaje). **8** MIL. dispatch. || **9 — de billetes,** ticket office.
despachurrar *v.t.* **1** (fam.) to flatten, to crush (en un argumento). || *v.t.* y *pron.* **2** to squash, to flatten (aplastar). **3** to mash (verduras).
despampanante *adj.* amazing, stunning (especialmente con sentido admirativo sobre la belleza física de una mujer).
despanzurrar *v.t.* y *r.* **1** to to disembowel (romper la panza). **2** to crush, to squash (despachurrar). **3** to burst (reventar).
desparpajo *s.m.* **1** self-confidence, naturalness (desenvoltura). **2** nerve, cheek (descaro). **3** (Am.) chaos, disorder (desorden).
desparramado *adj.* **1** scattered (esparcido). **2** (fig.) scattered, spread-out: *un pueblo desparramado = a scattered village.*
desparramamiento *s.m.* **1** scattering (esparcimiento). **2** sprinkling (de líquidos). **3** (fig.) spreading (de una noticia, fama, etc.).
desparramar *v.t.* y *pron.* **1** to spread, to scatter (esparcir). **2** to spread (una noticia). **3** to spill (tirar sin querer): *desparramé el vino por el suelo = I spilled the wine over the floor.* **5** (fig.) to squander, to waste (derrochar). || *v.pron.* **6** (fam.) to have a good time, to enjoy oneself (divertirse).
desparramo *s.f.* dispersion (dispersión).
despavorido, -a *adj.* very scared, terrified (atemorizado).
despavorir *v.i.* y *pron.* to be very scared, to be terrified (atemorizar).
despectivamente *adv.* **1** scornfully, contemptuously. **2** GRAM. pejoratively.
despectivo *adj.* **1** scornful, contemptuous. **2** GRAM. pejorative.
despechar *v.t.* **1** (Am.) to wean (destetar). **2** to anger, to make angry (causar enfado). **3** to drive to despair (causar desesperación).
despecho *s.m.* **1** spite, malice. **2** desperation, despondency (desesperación). **3** (Am.) weaning (destete). || **4 a — de,** in spite of. **5 lo hizo por —,** he did it out of spite.
despechugar *v.t.* **1** to cut the breast off (quitar la pechuga a un ave). || *v.pron.* **2** to bare one's chest (descubrir el pecho).
despedazar *v.t.* **1** to destroy, to smash (destruir). **2** to mistreat (maltratar). **3** to break (el corazón). || *v.pron.* **4** to tear to pieces, to tear apart (hacer pedazos).
despedida *s.f.* **1** good-bye, farewell: *un regalo de despedida = a farewell present.* **2** dismissal, (fam.) sacking, firing (de un trabajo). **3** send-off, farewell (en la estación, aeropuerto, etc.). **4** closing formula (de una carta). **5** LIT. closing couplet, final verse (de un poema).
despedir *v.t.* **1** to say goodbye, to see off: *vamos a despedirle a la estación = we are going to see him off at the station.* **2** to see out (de una habitación, una casa). **3** to dismiss, (fam.) to fire, to sack (echar de un empleo): *me han des-*

pedido = I've been sacked. **4** to send away, to get rid of (librarse). **5** to evict (a un inquilino). **6** to throw, to unseat (a un jinete): *le despidió el caballo = the horse unseated him.* **7** to release, to give out (jugo). **8** to dismiss (una idea, una teoría, una sugerencia). **9** to throw out (echar). **10** to throw, to fling (arrojar). **11** to fire (un arma). **12** to give off, to give out (calor, un olor). || *v.pron.* **13** to say goodbye, to take one's leave: *sin despedirse = without saying goodbye.* **14** (fig.) to say goodbye: *te puedes despedir del dinero = you can say goodbye to the money.* **15** to see off (en la estación, etc.): *me despedí de ella = I saw her off.*

despegado, -a *adj.* **1** unstuck (no pegado). **2** (fig.) cold, detached, indifferent (poco cariñoso).

despegar *v.t.* y *pron.* **1** to unstick, to become unstuck (separar dos cosas pegadas). || *v.i.* **2** to take off (un avión): *el avión despega a las dos = the plane takes off at two.* || *v.pron.* **3** to break away, to lose contact (perder la amistad).

despego *s.m.* **1** separation, detachment (separación). **2** aloofness, coldness, indifference (indiferencia).

despegue *s.m.* **1** takeoff (un avión). **2** launch (un cohete espacial). **3** (fig.) launch. || **4 pista de —,** runway.

despejado, -a *adj.* **1** free, clear, unobstructed (un camino, vista, etc.). **2** clear, cloudless (el cielo). **3** unencumbered, clear (una habitación, plaza, etc.). **4** awake, wide-awake (sin sueño). **5** bright, clever, sharp (listo). **6** self-confident, natural (desenvuelto).

despejar *v.t.* **1** to clear, to free: *la policía despejó la calle = the police cleared the street.* **2** to sort out, to clear up (aclarar): *aclarar un misterio = to clear up a mystery.* **3** DEP. to clear (el balón): *el defensa despejó el balón = the defender cleared the ball.* **4** to explain, to shed light upon (explicar). || *v.i.* y *pron.* **5** to clear, to clear up (el tiempo). **6** to clear (el cielo). || *v.pron.* **7** to liven up, to brighten up (despabilarse). **8** to wake oneself up (despertarse). **9** to enjoy oneself (divertirse). **10** to relax (relajarse). || **11 — la incógnita,** MAT. to find the unknown number.

despeje *s.m.* DEP. clearance.

despejo *s.m.* **1** assurance, self-confidence (confianza en sí mismo). **2** brightness, clearness (claridad).

despeluznante o **espeluznante** *adj.* **1** frightful, dreadful (pavoroso). **2** horrible, terrible (horrible).

despellejar *v.t.* **1** to skin (quitar el pellejo). **2** (fig.) to slate, to flay, to criticize (criticar). **3** to murmur (murmurar). **4** (fig.) to ruin, to fleece (arruinar).

despensa *s.f.* **1** larder, pantry (lugar para la comida). **2** supplies, stock of food (provisiones).

despensero, -a *s.m.* y *f.* **1** steward (hombre). **2** stewardess (mujer). || *s.m.* **3** butler (mayordomo).

despeñadero *s.m.* **1** GEOG. precipice, cliff. **2** (fig.) danger, hazard, risk (riesgo).

despeñar *v.t.* y *pron.* **1** to throw down, to fling down (arrojar de lo alto): *despeñar por un precipicio = to throw over a cliff.* || *v.pron.* **2** to throw oneself into vice, to plunge into vice (en el vicio).

despepitar *v.t.* **1** to remove the pips from (quitar las pepitas). || *v.pron.* **2** to bawl, to shriek (gritar). **3** to act wildly, to forget oneself (actuar con desenfreno). || **4 despepitarse por algo,** to be crazy /mad about something. **5 despepitarse por hacer algo,** to long to do something.

desperdiciar *v.t.* **1** to waste, to squander (malgastar): *desperdiciar el tiempo = to waste time.* **2** to throw away, to waste (una oportunidad): *desperdiciar una sugerencia = to ignore a suggestion.*

desperdicio *s.m.* **1** waste: *desperdicio de dinero o tiempo = waste of money or time.* || *s.pl.* **2** rubbish, scraps (basura): *desperdicios de cocina = kitchen scraps.* || **3 no tener —,** to have no waste (en sentido físico o tangible): *esta carne no tiene desperdicio = this meat has no waste on it.* **4 no tener —,** (fig.) to be excellent, to be faultless: *el libro no tiene desperdicio = the book is faultless.*

desperdigar *v.t.* y *pron.* **1** to scatter, to spread (dispersar): *las casas están desperdigadas por el valle = the houses are spread along the valley.* || **2** to separate (separar).

desperezarse *v.r.* to stretch (estirarse).

desperezo *s.m.* stretch.

desperfecto *s.m.* **1** flaw, imperfection, blemish: *el diamante tiene un desperfecto = the diamond has got a flaw.* **2** damage (daño): *sufrir desperfectos = to suffer slight damage.*

despersonalizar *v.t.* y *pron.* to depersonalize.

despertador *s.m.* **1** alarm clock (reloj). **2** (p.u.) knocker-up (persona). **3** (fig.) warning (aviso).

despertar *v.t.* **1** to wake, to wake up, to awake: *los niños nos despertaron = the children woke us up.* **2** to awake, to arouse (esperanza, deseo, pasión, etc.). **3** to recall, to revive (recordar): *la foto despierta recuerdos = the photo revives memories.* **4** to brighten up, to liven up (despabilar). || *v.i.* y *pron.* **5** to wake, to wake up, to awake: *nos despertamos a las ocho = we wake up at eight.* **6** (fig.) to wake up, to liven up (despabilarse): *despertarse a la realidad = to wake up to reality.*

despestañarse *v.pron.* (Am.) to study eagerly (estudiar con ahínco).

despezar *v.t.* to break up, to split up (descomponer algo en sus piezas distintas).

despiadado, -a *adj.* heartless, cruel, merciless.

despido *s.m.* dismissal, (fam.) sacking, firing (extinción de un contrato de trabajo).

despiece *s.m.* cutting-up, carving-up (de un animal).

despierto, -a *adj.* **1** awake, wide-awake. **2** (fig.) sharp, clever, bright (listo).

despiezar *v.t.* to break up, to split up.

despilfarrado, -a *adj.* **1** spendthrift, wasteful, lavish (con dinero). **2** wasteful (con cosas).

despilfarrador, -a *adj.* 1 V. **despilfarrado.** || *s.m.* y *f.* **2** squanderer, spendthrift (con dinero). **3** waster (con cosas).

despilfarrar *v.t.* y *pron.* to waste, to squander (derrochar).

despilfarro *s.m.* **1** wasting, squandering (resultado de despilfarrar). **2** extravagance, wastefulness (extravagancia).

despintar *v.t.* **1** to take the paint off (quitar la pintura). **2** to alter, to change (cambiar). || *v.i.* **3** to be worse, to be inferior (ser inferior): *este libro no despinta de los otros = this book is not inferior to the others.* || *v.pron.* **4** to fade, to lose colour (desteñir). **5** (fig.) to fade from the memory: *su cara se me ha despintado = his face has faded from my memory.*

despiojar *v.t.* y *pron.* **1** to delouse (quitar los piojos). **2** (fig.) to pull o rescue someone from the gutter (sacar a uno de la miseria).

despioje *s.m.* delousing (de piojos).

despistar *v.t.* **1** to throw off the scent (en la caza): *el zorro les despistó = the fox threw them off the scent.* **2** to shake off, to throw off: *despistar a la policía = to shake off the police.* **3** to mislead, to lead the wrong way (hacer perder la pista): *la señal nos despistó = the sign misled us.* **4** (fig.) to mislead, to confuse (confundir): *la clase me ha despistado = the class has confused me.* || *v.i.* **5** to be misleading: *la película despista = the film is misleading.* || *v.pron.* **6** to lose one's way, to get lost (perderse). **7** to get confused, to get in a muddle (confundirse). **8** to make a mistake (equivocarse).

despiste *s.m.* **1** swerve (viraje). **2** slip, error, mistake (error). **3** (fig.) confusion, mix-up (confusión). **4** absent-mindedness, forgetfulness (distracción): *tengo un despiste fatal = I'm terribly absent-minded.*

desplante *s.m.* **1** bad stance, incorrect position (postura irregular). **2** outspoken comment (dicho descarado). **3** insolent act (hecho descarado). **4** boast (jactancia). || **5 dar un —,** to interrupt someone rudely.

desplazamiento *s.m.* **1** trip, journey (viaje). **2** MAR. y FIS. displacement. **3** GEOL. movement, displacement. || **5** swing, change (de opinión, voto). **6** move, removal (traslado).

desplazar *v.t.* y *pron.* **1** to move, to shift (mover). **2** to move away, to remove (quitar). || *v.t.* **3** FIS. to displace. **4** to transfer, to move (tropas). **5** to replace, to take the place of (sustituir): *los socialistas han desplazado a los liberales = the socialists have replaced the liberals.* || *v.pron.* **6** to travel, to go (viajar): *tengo que desplazarme 10 kms cada día = I have to travel 10 kms every day.* **7** to shift, to swing (votos, opiniones, tendencias).

desplegar *v.t.* **1** to show, to display (mostrar una cualidad): *desplegar entusiasmo = to show enthusiasm.* || *v.t.* y *pron.* **2** to unfold, to open out (lo plegado): *desplegar un mapa = to unfold a map.* **3** to spread, to open (alas). **4** to unfurl (velas, banderas). **5** MIL. to deploy. **6** to open, to open out (una flor).

despliegue *s.m.* **1** unfolding, opening (abertura). **2** MIL. deployment. **3** (fig.) show, display (ostentación).

desplomar o **desaplomar** *v.t.* **1** to put off the vertical (hacer perder la posición vertical). **2** (Am.) to tick off, to scold (regañar). || *v.pron.* **3** to collapse, to crash down, to fall down (caerse): *la casa se desplomó = the house crashed down.* **4** to collapse, to crash to the floor (una persona). **5** to tumble, to crash (precios). **6** to collapse (gobierno). **7** (fam.) to belly-flop, to make a pancake landing (un avión).

desplome *s.m.* **1** drop, fall (caída). **2** ARQ. overhang, projection (saliente). **3** tilting, leaning (acción de inclinar).

desplomo V. **desplome.**

desplumar *v.t.* y *pron.* **1** to pluck (quitar las plumas). **2** (fig.) to fleece, to clean out (dejar sin dinero). || *v.pron.* **3** to moult (perder las plumas).

despoblación *s.f.* depopulation.

despoblado, -a *adj.* **1** uninhabited, deserted (sin habitantes). **2** depopulated (con poca gente). **3** deserted (desierto). **4** (fig.) desolate (desierto). || *s.m.* **5** wilderness, uninhabited place.

despoblar *v.t.* **1** to depopulate. **2** to devastate, to lay waste (devastar). **3** to clear (despojar): *despoblar de árboles = to clear of trees.* || *v.pron.* **4** to become depopulated (quedarse un lugar sin gente).

despojar *v.t.* **1** to strip, to deprive (privar): *despojar a uno de sus derechos = to deprive someone of their rights.* **2** DER. to dispossess. **3** (fig.) to denude, to strip (desnudar). **4** (fam.) to fleece, to clean out (dejar a uno sin dinero). || *v.pron.* **5** to undress, to strip (desnudarse): *despojarse del abrigo = to take off one's overcoat.* **6** BOT. to shed (hojas). **7** to give up, to divest oneself of (privarse voluntariamente de algo): *despojarse de su fortuna = to give up one's fortune.*

despojo *s.m.* **1** despriving, stripping (resultado de despojar). **2** plundeing, despoiling (robo). **3** plunder, spoils, loot (botín). || *pl.* **4** offal (de animales). **5** waste (basura). **6** debris, rubble (escombros). **7** leftovers (de la comida). || **8** **despojos mortales,** mortal remains.

desporrondingarse *v.pron.* **1** to be longwinded, (fam.) to go on and on (explayarse). **2** to confide (confiarse).

desportillar *v.t.* y *pron.* to chip (una vasija, etc.).

desposado, -a *adj.* **1** recently married, newly-wed (recién casado). **2** handcuffed (un preso). || **3** **los desposados,** the newly-weds.

desposar *v.t.* **1** to marry (casar). || *v.pron.* **2** to get engaged (contraer esponsales). **3** to get married (casarse).

desposeer *v.t.* **1** to disposess. **2** to oust, to remove (de un puesto). || *v.pron.* **3** to renounce, to relinquish (renunciar uno a lo que posee).

desposeimiento *s.m.* dispossession.

desposorios *s.m.pl.* **1** engagement, bethrothal (esponsales). **2** wedding (boda). **3** marriage (matrimonio).

déspota *s.m.* y *f.* despot.

despótico, -a *adj.* despotic, tyrannical.

despotismo *s.m.* despotism.

despotizar *v.t.* (Am.) to tyrannise, to terrorise.

despotricar *v.i.* y *r.* to rant, to rave (hablar sin reparo).

despreciable *adj.* **1** despicable, reprehensible, contemptible (persona). **2** insignificant, negligible (cantidades): *una cantidad despreciable = an insignificant amount.* **3** worthless, rubbishy (calidad): *una película despreciable = a worthless film.*

despreciar *v.t.* **1** to scorn, to look down on (tener en poco). **2** to despise (odiar). **3** to belittle, to disparage (menospreciar). **4** to reject (rechazar). **5** to underestimate (subestimar). **6** to ignore (no hacer caso). **7** to snub, to slight (desairar). || *v.pron.* **8** to be beneath oneself (hacer algo).

despreciativamente *adv.* scornfully.

despreciativo, -a *adj.* **1** contemptuous, disdainful: *una mirada despreciativa = a disdainful look.* **3** offensive, derogatory (comentario).

desprecio *s.m.* **1** disdain, contempt, scorn: *me trataron con desprecio = they treated me with contempt.* **2** cynicism (cinismo). **3** affront, slight, rebuff (desaire).

desprender *v.t.* **1** to loosen, to release (soltar). **2** to unfasten (desatar). **3** to take off (quitar). **4** to separate (separar). **5** to give off (un gas, un olor). || *v.pron.* **6** to come off, to become detached (soltarse): *el botón se ha desprendido = the button has come off.* **7** to come off, to be given off (un gas, un olor). **8** to shed (la piel). **9** **desprenderse de algo,** (fig.) to part with something, to get rid of something: *se desprendió del coche = he got rid of the car.* **10** to be implied by, to follow from (deducirse): *se desprende de esto que... = it follows from this that...*

desprendido, -a *adj.* **1** loose, detached (una pieza). **2** generous, unselfish (generoso). **3** disinterested (desinteresado).

desprendimiento *s.m.* **1** detachment, separation (separación). **2** MED. detachment. **3** emission, release (de un gas, etc.). **4** shedding (de la piel). **5** (fig.) unselfishness, generosity (generosidad). **6** impartiality, disinterestedness (desinterés). || **7** **— de tierras,** landslide.

despreocupación *s.f.* **1** impartiality, openmindedness (falta de prejuicios). **2** negligence, carelessness (negligencia). **3** unconcern, lack of worry (falta de preocupación).

despreocupado, -a *adj.* **1** impartial, neutral (imparcial). **2** informal, casual (en el vestir). **3** easy-going, carefree, (fam.) laid-black (libre de preocupaciones). **4** unconcerned, untroubled (sin inquietud). **5** negligent, lax (negligente). **6** indifferent, disinterested (indiferente).

despreocuparse *v.pron.* **1** to give up worrying, to stop worrying (librarse de una preocupación). **2** to want nothing to do, to want no part (desentenderse): *me despreocupo del asunto = I want nothing to do with the business.* || **3** **— de,** to forget (olvidar).

desprestigiar *v.t.* y *pron.* **1** to discredit, to ruin the reputation (quitar el prestigio). **2** to lose prestige, to lose one's reputation (perder el prestigio).

desprestigio *s.m.* **1** loss of prestige (pérdida de prestigio). **2** loss of reputation (pérdida de reputación). **3** discredit (descrédito).

desprevenidamente *adv.* **1** without warning, (fam.) out of the blue (sin avisar). **2** by surprise, off guard (de improviso).

desprevenido, -a *adj.* **1** unprepared, unready, unawares: *coger a alguien desprevenido = to catch someone unawares.*

despropósito *s.m.* nonsense, rubbish, silly remark (disparate): *decir despropósitos = to talk nonsense.*

desprovisto, -a *adj.* **1** without, devoid, lacking. || **2** **— de,** lacking, devoid of, without. **3** **— de méritos,** devoid of merit. **4** **— de forma,** without shape, lacking shape. **5** **estar — de,** to lack, to be devoid of, to be lacking.

después *adv.* **1** afterward(s), later. **2** then, next (en una sucesión de acciones): *todos los días me levanto, me ducho y después desayuno = every day I get up, have a shower and then have breakfast.* || **3** **— de, a)** after (en el tiempo): *después de la clase me fui al cine = after class I went to the cinema;* **b)** next to (en proximidad espacial): *correos está inmediatamente después del restaurante = the post office is just next to the restaurant.* **4** **— de que,** after: *después de que la reunión terminase decidí quedarme a revisar unos cuantos papeles = after the meeting had finished I decided to stay on to check some papers.*

despuntado, -a *adj.* blunt.

despuntar *v.t.* y *pron.* **1** to blunt (gastar la punta). **2** to break the point off (quitar la punta). **3** MAR. to round (pasar un barco por delante de una punta o cabo). || *v.i.* **4** to sprout (las plantas). **5** to bud (las flores). **6** to break (empezar a amanecer). **7** to shine, to show intelligence (manifestar genio). **8** to stand out, to excel (sobresalir): *la niña despunta entre los otros = the girl stands out amongst the others.*

despunte *s.m.* blunting (acción de despuntar).

desquiciamiento *s.m.* **1** upsetting, worrying (perturbación). **2** upset, disturbance (trastorno).

desquiciar *v.t.* y *pron.* **1** to unhinge, to take off its hinges (una puerta). **2** to upset, to trouble (trastornar). **3** to distress, to disturb (perturbar). **4** to unhinge, to unbalance (afectar profundamente): *la muerte de su madre le desquició = his mother's death unbalanced him.*

desquitar *v.t.* y *pron.* **1** to gain/obtain satisfaction (proporcionar(se) satisfacción). **2** to get/gain revenge (vengar(se)). **3** to recover, to get back (recuperar lo perdido).

desquite *s.m.* **1** retaliation, revenge (venganza). **2** DEP. return leg, return match (partido de vuelta). **3** compensation (compensación). || **4 en —,** in retaliation. **5 tomar el —,** to get revenge, (fam.) to get one's own back.

desratización *s.f.* deratting.

desratizar *v.t.* to clear of rats (exterminar las ratas).

desrielar *v.i.* **1** to go off the rails, to be derailed (descarrillar). **2** (fig.) to get off the track.

desriñonar *v.t.* to break the back of (deslomar).

destacable V. **destacado.**

destacadamente *adv.* outstandingly, exceptionally.

destacado, -a *adj.* **1** prominent, distinguished (distinguido). **2** outstanding, exceptional (excepcional): *un alumno destacado = an outstanding student.*

destacamento *s.m.* MIL. detachment.

destacar *v.t.,i.* y *pron.* **1** to make stand out, to bring out (hacer resaltar). **2** to throw into relief (poner de relieve). **3** to emphasize, to point out (recalcar): *me gustaría destacar que... = I would like to point out that...* **4** (fig.) to underline (subrayar). **5** (fig.) to stand out, to be outstanding (sobresalir): *el niño destaca sobre los demás = the child stands out from the rest.* || *v.t.* y *pron.* **6** MIL. to detach, to detail (separar del cuerpo principal unas tropas).

destajo *s.m.* **1** piecework. || **2 a —, a)** eagerly, enthusiastically (con empeño); **b)** by the piece (por una cantidad determinada). **3 hablar a —,** (fam.) to talk nineteen to the dozen. **4 pagar a —,** to pay by the piece (por la pieza). **5 trabajar a —,** to do piecework.

destalonar *v.t.* y *pron.* **1** to wear out the heel (estropear el talón al calzado). || *v.t.* **2** to tear off, to remove (quitar el talón a un documento).

destapadura *s.f.* **1** uncorking (de una botella). **2** opening (acción de abrir). **3** uncovering (acción de descubrir).

destapar *v.t.* **1** to take the top off, to uncover (quitar la tapa). **2** to open, to uncork (una botella). **3** to open, to take the lid off (una caja). **4** to open (abrir). **5** (fig.) to uncover, to reveal (descubrir). || *v.pron.* **6** to start talking (empezar a hablar). **7** to get uncovered (descubrirse). **8 destaparse con alguien,** to open one's heart to someone.

destartalado, -a *adj.* **1** dilapidated, ramshackle (una casa). **2** cluttered, untidy (una habitación). **3** broken-down, rickety (un coche).

destartalar *v.t.* y *pron.* to ruin, to spoil (estropear).

destellar *v.i.* **1** to flash (despedir una luz repentina). **2** to sparkle (los ojos, piedras preciosas, etc.). **3** to twinkle (las estrellas).

destello *s.m.* **1** flash (una luz repentina). **2** sparkle (de los ojos, de una piedra preciosa). **3** twinkling (de las estrellas). **4** (fig.) spark, flash: *un destello de inteligencia = a flash of intelligence.* **6** brilliance (brillo).

destemplado, -a *adj.* **1** harsh, intemperate (irritado). **2** irritable, ill-tempered (carácter). **3** MUS. untuned, out of tune (desafinado). **4** unpleasant, unsettled (tiempo). **5** harsh, gruff (una voz). **6** inharmonious, badly-matched (colores). **7** unwell, off colour (indispuesto).

destemplanza *s.f.* **1** MUS. tunelessness, disonance. **2** unsettledness, inclemency (del tiempo). **3** MED. feverish state. **4** ART. lack of harmony (de un cuadro). **5** lack of moderation (falta de moderación). **6** impatience, irritability (impaciencia).

destemplar *v.t.* **1** MUS. to untune, to put out of tune (desafinar). **2** to untemper (los metales). **3** to disorder, to disturb (desordenar). || *v.t.* y *pron.* **4** MUS. to go out of tune (desafinarse). **5** to lose its temper (perder el temple los metales). || *v.pron.* **6** MED. to get off colour, to become unwell. **7** (fam.) to go too far, to be out of order (descomedirse). **8** to become irregular (el pulso). **9** (Am.) to set one's teeth on edge (sentir dentera).

destemple *s.m.* **1** TEC. untempering, lack of temper (de los metales). **2** MUS. dissonance, lack of harmony.

desteñir *v.t.* y *pron.* **1** to discolour, to fade (decolorar). **2** to run (manchar): *la tela no destiñe = the fabric does not run.*

desternillarse *v.pron.* **1** to break one's cartilage (romperse la ternilla). || **2 — de risa,** to split one's sides laughing, to laugh one's head off.

desterrar *v.t.* **1** to exile, to banish (expulsar de un país). **2** to put aside, to dismiss (apartar de sí): *desterrar un problema = to put aside a problem.* **3** to ban, to prohibit (prohibir). **4** AGR. to remove the soil (quitar la tierra).

destetar *v.t.* y *pron.* to wean (hacer dejar de mamar).

destete *s.m.* weaning.

destiempo *s.m.* **a —,** at the wrong moment, at the wrong time: *lo hizo a destiempo = he did it at the wrong moment.*

destierro *s.m.* **1** exile, banishment (el castigo). **2** place of exile (lugar en que vive el desterrado). **3** (fig.) wilderness, remote place (lugar muy alejado del centro de una población). || **4 vivir en el —,** to live in exile.

destilación *s.f.* distillation.

destiladera *s.f.* **1** still (el aparato). **2** (Am.) filter (filtro). **3** (Am.) distiller (persona).

destilador *s.m.* **1** still (aparato). **2** distiller (persona). **3** filter (filtro).

destilar *v.t.* **1** to distil (alcohol). **2** to purify (quitar las impurezas de un líquido). **3** (fig.) to exude, to ooze: *el poema destila pasiones muy fuertes = the poem exudes strong passions.* || *v.t.* y *pron.* **4** to filter (filtrar). || *v.i.* **5** to drip, to trickle (gotear). **6** to seep, to ooze (rezumar).

destilería *s.f.* **1** distillery. || **2 — de petróleo,** oil refinery.

destinación *s.f.* destination.

destinar *v.t.* **1** to destine: *destinar el dinero a la compra de libros = to destine the money for the buying of books.* **2** to send (enviar): *le han destinado a Italia = they have sent him to Italy.* **3** to appoint, to assign (fijar el puesto donde uno va a trabajar): *me han destinado a Londres = I've been assigned to London.* **4** MIL. to post. **5** to address (cartas): *una carta destinada a Vd. = a letter addressed to you.* **6** MAR. ir destinado a, to be bound for. **7** COM. to put aside, to earmark, to allot: *destinar fondos = to earmark funds.*

destinatario, -a *s.m.* y *f.* **1** addressee (de una carta, un paquete). **2** payee (de un cheque, un giro, etc.).

destino *s.m.* **1** destiny, fate (hado): *un destino triste = a sad fate.* || **2** destination (de un viajero, una carta, etc.). **3** use, utility (uso). **4** job, position (empleo). **5** MIL. posting, station (lugar a que se dirige un militar). || **8 con — a,** going to, bound for: *el tren con destino a Barcelona = the train bound for Barcelona.* **9 dar — a,** (fig.) to find a good use for something. **10 llegar a —,** to arrive at one's destination. **11 salir con — a,** to leave for, to set out for.

destitución *s.f.* dismissal, removal: *la destitución del presidente = the removal of the President.*

destituir *v.t.* to dismiss, to remove, (fam.) to sack, to fire (despedir): *destituir a alguien de su oficio = to remove someone from their post.*

destornillado, -a *adj.* (fam.) crazy, nutty, potty, screwy, dotty (chiflado).

destornillador *s.m.* screwdriver.

destornillamiento *s.m.* unscrewing.

destornillar *v.t.* **1** to unscrew. || *v.pron.* **2** (fig.) to act wildly, to behave madly (actuar sin reflexión). **3** (fam.) to go

round the bend, to go crazy (volverse loco). || 4 **destornillarse de risa,** to split one's sides with laughter.
destornudar *v.i.* (Am.) to sneeze (estornudar).
destrabar *v.t.* y *pron.* 1 to unfetter, to take the shackles off (quitar las trabas). 2 to separate, to detach (separar). 3 to become detached, to come apart (separarse).
destral *s.f.* hatchet.
destreza *s.f.* 1 skill (habilidad). 2 handiness, dexterity (agilidad).
destripamiento *s.m.* 1 disembowelling (de personas, animales). 2 gutting (del pescado).
destripar *v.t.* 1 to disembowel (una persona, un animal). 2 to gut (el pescado). 3 to crush, to flatten (despachurrar). 4 to ruin the end of (un relato, un chiste, etc.): *destripar un cuento = to ruin the end of a story.*
destripaterrones *s.m.* 1 farm labourer, farm worker (jornalero del campo). 2 (fam. y desp.) bumpkin, yokel (gañán).
destronamiento *s.m.* 1 dethronement. 2 (fig.) ousting, overthrow.
destronar *v.t.* 1 to dethrone (deponer al rey). 2 (fig.) to overthrow (derrocar). 3 to take away someone's authority (privar a uno de su autoridad).
destroncamiento *s.m.* 1 felling, chopping down (de un árbol). 2 maiming, mutilation (mutilación). 3 ruination, ruin (arruinamiento). 4 tiredness, exhaustion (cansancio).
destroncar *v.t.* 1 to fell, to chop down (un árbol). 2 to maim, to mutilate (mutilar). 3 to ruin (arruinar). 4 to exhaust, to tire out (cansar). 5 to spoil, to ruin (un plan, un proyecto, etc.). 6 to interrupt (un discurso). 7 (Am.) to uproot (arrancar plantas).
destronque *s.m.* (Am.) uprooting.
destrozar *v.t.* y *pron.* 1 to smash, to break into pieces, to shatter (hacer trozos una cosa). || *v.t.* 2 to ruin, to spoil (estropear). 3 to destroy (destruir). 4 to tear to pieces, to tear up (libros, papel, etc.): *destrozaron el contrato = they tore up the contract.* 5 MIL. to smash, to wipe out (un enemigo, un ejército). 6 to shatter, to destroy (los nervios). 7 to squander, to waste (derrochar): *destrozar una fortuna = to waste a fortune.* 8 to break (romper): *destrozar el corazón de uno = to break someone's heart.* 9 to tire out, to shatter, to exhaust (cansar): *estoy destrozado de tanto estudiar = I'm shattered from so much studying.* 10 to crush (en un debate, discusión, etc.). 11 to destroy, to be a disaster (en una actuación, etc.).
destrozo *s.m.* 1 destruction. 2 MIL. rout, defeat (derrota). || *pl.* 3 damage (daño). 4 debris, rubble (escombros).
destrozón, -ona *adj.* 1 destructive, damaging. 2 hard on one's shoes, clothes, etc. (que estropea mucho el calzado, la ropa, etc.). || *s.m.* y *s.f.* 3 destructive person.
destrucción *s.f.* destruction.
destructivo, -a *adj.* destructive.
destructor, -ora *adj.* 1 destructive. || *s.m.* y *f.* 2 destructive person (persona que destruye). || *s.m.* 3 MAR. destroyer (buque de guerra).
destruir *v.t.* 1 to destroy: *destruir una economía = to destroy an economy.* 2 to demolish, to knock down, to destroy (un edificio, una casa, etc.). 3 to ruin (estropear). 4 to destroy, to wreck (un plan, proyecto, etc.). 5 (fig.) to shatter, to dash (esperanza). 6 (fig.) to crush, to demolish (una teoría, argumento, etc.). || *v.pron.* 7 MAT. to cancel each other out (anularse).
desuello *s.m.* 1 skinning, flaying (hecho de desollar). 2 (fig.) cheek, nerve, impudence (descaro).
desuncir *v.t.* 1 to unyoke (quitar el yugo). || *v.pron.* 2 (fig.) to free oneself, to become independent (independizarse).
desunión *s.f.* 1 disunion, separation (separación). 2 discord, disunity (discordia).
desunir *v.t.* y *pron.* 1 to separate, to detach (separar). 2 to disunite, to foment trouble (provocar discordia).
desusado, -a *adj.* 1 old-fashioned, out of date, antiquated (anticuado): *máquinas desusadas = antiquated machines.* 2 obsolete, disused (caída en desuso): *expresión desusada = obsolete expression.* 3 strange, peculiar (extraño).
desusar *v.t.* (form.) to give up using, to stop using (dejar de usar): *desuso el coche = I've stopped using my car.*
desuso *s.m.* 1 disuse, obsolescence (falta de uso). || 2 **caer en —,** to fall into disuse. 3 **dejar una cosa en —,** to stop using something. 4 **una expresión caída en —,** an obsolete expression.
desvaído, -a *adj.* 1 pale, dull (pálido). 2 blurred, vague (borroso). 3 lanky (larguirucho). 4 characterless, dull (de poca personalidad).
desvalido, -a *adj.* 1 abandoned, destitute (abandonado). || *s.m.* y *f.* 2 needy person, helpless person. || 3 **los desvalidos,** the needy.
desvalijamiento *s.m.* robbery, theft.
desvalijar *v.t.* 1 to rob (robar). 2 to burgle (una casa, tienda). 3 to rifle (un cajón, una maleta).
desvalimiento *s.m.* destitution, penury, neediness.
desván *s.m.* attic, loft.
desvanecedor *s.m.* FOT. mask.
desvanecer *v.t.* y *r.* 1 to fade away (disminuir gradualmente). 2 to vanish, to disappear (desaparecer). 3 to dismiss, to dispel (un recuerdo, una duda, una idea, un temor, etc.). 4 to tone down (colores). 5 to become vain (inducir a vanidad). 6 to blur (los contornos). || *v.pron.* 7 to evaporate (evaporarse). 8 to faint, to swoon (desmayarse).
desvanecido, -a *adj.* 1 MED. faint, dizzy (mareado). 2 vain, proud (vanidoso). 3 superior, smug, self-righteous (presumido).
desvanecimiento *s.m.* 1 MED. faint, dizzy spell (desmayo). 2 RAD. fading. 3 disappearance, vanishing (desaparición). 4 FOT. masking. 5 dispersal, diffusion (de humo, etc.). 6 toning-down (de colores). 7 dismissal, removal (de dudas, problemas, etc.). 8 (fig.) pride, vanity (vanidad). 9 arrogance, conceit (arrogancia).
desvariado, -a *adj.* nonsensical, raving.
desvariar *v.i.* to talk nonsense, to talk rubbish (decir locuras).
desvarío *s.m.* 1 MED. delirium, derangement. 2 caprice, whim (capricho). 3 (fig.) silly comment, foolish remark (tontería). 4 act of madness (una locura): *sería un desvarío hacerlo = it would be an act of madness to do it.* || *pl.* 5 nonsense, ravings.
desvelar *v.t.* 1 to keep awake: *el ruido me ha desvelado = the noise has kept me awake.* || *v.pron.* 2 to stay awake (quedarse despierto). 3 (fig.) to devote oneself, to dedicate oneself (dedicarse). 4 to take great pains, to take great care (esmerarse mucho en algo): *se desvela por hacerlo bien = he takes great pains to do it well.*
desvelo *s.m.* 1 insomnia, sleeplessness (insomnio). 2 attentiveness, vigilance (vigilancia). || *pl.* 3 endeavour, effort (esfuerzo). 4 concern, worry (preocupación).
desvenar *v.t.* 1 to extract the veins from meat (quitar las venas a la carne). 2 MIN. to extract mineral from a vein (extraer el mineral de la vena). 3 to strip (quitar las fibras a las hojas).
desvencijar *v.t.* y *pron.* 1 to loosen (aflojar). 2 to break (romper). 3 to fall apart, to come to pieces (desencajar las partes de una cosa). 4 to ruin, to spoil (estropear). 5 to weaken, to get weaker (debilitar). 6 to exhaust, to tire out (agotar).
desvendar o **desenvendar** *v.t.* y *pron.* to unbandage, to take off a bandage (quitar una venda).
desventaja *s.f.* 1 disadvantage. 2 drawback, snag (desconveniente). 3 handicap: *su falta de altura es una desventaja = his lack of height is a handicap.* || 4 **estar en —,** to be at a disadvantage.
desventajoso, -a *adj.* disadvantageous, detrimental.
desventura *s.f.* bad luck, misfortune (mala suerte).
desventurado, -a *adj.* 1 unlucky, hapless (de mala suerte). 2 ill-fated, ill-omened (de mal agüero). 3 dejected, wretched (desgraciado). 4 shy, timid (tímido). 5 poor (pobre). || *s.m.* y *f.* 6 wretch, poor devil.
desvergonzado, -a *adj.* 1 shameless, barefaced (sinvergüenza). 2 cheeky, impudent (descarado). || *s.m.* y *f.* 3 shameless o barefaced person. 4 cheeky o impudent person.

desvergonzarse *v.pron.* **1** to be insolent, to be impudent (ser impudente). **2** to lose one's scruples, to get into bad ways (perder la vergüenza). || **3 — a decir algo,** (Am.) to have the nerve to say something.

desvergüenza *s.f.* **1** nerve, cheek, impudence (descaro). **2** insolence (insolencia). || **3 es una —,** it's disgraceful. **4 ¡qué —!,** what a cheek! **5 tener la — de,** to have the nerve/cheek to: *tuvo la desvergüenza de llamar = he had the nerve to ring.*

desviación *s.f.* **1** deviation, variation, deflection: *una desviación de sus declaraciones = a deviation from his statements.* **2** PSIQ. deviation (especialmente sexual). **3** POL. deviation. **4** detour, diversion (de carretera). **5** deflection (de un golpe, balón, etc.).

desviacionismo *s.m.* deviationism.

desviar *v.t.* **1** to deviate, to deflect: *desvió el balón = he deflected the ball.* **2** to deflect (un golpe, una flecha, etc.). **3** to divert (agua, un avión, el tráfico, un barco, etc.). **4** to parry (una pregunta, en esgrima). **5** to change (el tema de una conversación). **6** to avert, to look away (los ojos). **7** to alter (alterar). **8** (fig.) to put off, to dissuade (de una acción, un proyecto): *le desviaron de su propósito = they put him off his plan.* || *v.r.* **9** to be deflected, to be deviated: *se desvió el golpe = the blow was deflected.* **10** to change course (avión, barco, etc.). || **11 desviarse del camino,** to leave the road, to turn off the road. **12 desviarse de su rumbo,** MAR. to sail/go off course. **16** (fig.) to wander, to stray. **13 desviarse de un tema,** to wander from the point.

desvío *s.m.* **1** deflection, deviation (desviación). **2** swerve (de un coche). **3** detour, diversion (en una carretera). **4** coldness, indifference, apathy (frialdad).

desvirgar *v.t.* (form.) to deflower (quitar la virginidad a una mujer).

desvirtuar *v.t.* y *pron.* **1** to spoil, to impair (estropear). **2** to adulterate (adulterar). **3** to misrepresent, to distort (tergiversar): *desvirtuar una teoría = to distort a theory.* **4** (fig.) to detract from (quitar valor a): *el último capítulo desvirtúa el libro = the last chapter detracts from the book.* **5** to distort (viciar): *desvirtuar el contenido de un discurso = to distort the contents of a speech.*

desvivirse *v.pron.* **1** to long, to yearn: *desvivirse por hacer algo = to long to do something.* **2** to stay awake (desvelarse). || **3 — por algo/alguien,** to be crazy about something/someone, to do one's utmost for someone.

detall *s.m.* **1 al —,** retail (al por menor). || **2 vender al —,** to retail, to sell retail.

detallado, -a *adj.* detailed.

detallar *v.t.* **1** to detail, to itemize (listas, etc.). **2** to give details, to tell in detail (contar con detalles). **3** COM. to retail, to sell at retail price, to sell retail.

detalle *s.m.* **1** detail: *con todos los detalles = with all the details.* **2** kind gesture, nice thought, sweet thing to do (cosa amable): *¡qué —! = what a kind gesture!* || **3 al —,** COM. retail. **4 tener el — de hacer algo,** to be thoughtful enough to do something. **5 vender al —,** to retail, to sell retail.

detallista *s.m.* y *f.* **1** COM. retailer (comerciante que vende al por menor). **2** perfectionist (persona que tiene en cuenta los detalles). || *adj.* **3** sweet, considerate (cualidad personal).

detección *s.f.* detection.

detectar *v.t.* to detect.

detective *s.m.* y *f.* detective: *detective privado = private detective.*

detector *s.m.* **1** detector. || **2 — de mentiras,** lie detector. **3 — de minas,** mine detector.

detención *s.f.* **1** DER. detention, arrest. **2** holdup, delay (demora). **3** stop, halt (alto). **4** stopping (acción de parar). **5** DEP. stoppage: *hubo una detención de juego de 10 minutos = there was a 10-minute stoppage of play.*

detener *v.t.* **1** to stop (parar): *detener un balón, coche, persona, etc. = to stop a ball, car, person, etc.* **2** to arrest (arrestar). **3** to delay: *me detuvo dos horas = he delayed me for two hours.* **4** to detain, to hold up (retener): *me detuvo la tormenta = the storm held me up.* **5** to hold (la respiración). **6** to keep, to hold up (retrasar): *me detuvieron mucho tiempo = they kept me a long time.* || *v.pron.* **7** to stop (parar). **8** to linger, to hang about: *¡no te detengas! = don't hang about!* **9** to take a long time (estar mucho tiempo): *se detienen mucho en hacerlo = they're taking a long time to do it.*

detenidamente *adv.* **1** carefully, attentively (con cuidado). **2** at length, thoroughly: *estudiar algo detenidamente = to study something thoroughly.*

detenido, -a *adj.* **1** DER. under arrest, arrested (arrestado): *están detenidos = they're under arrest.* **2** timid, shy (tímido). **3** detailed, thorough (minucioso). **4** miserable, wretched (miserable). || *s.m.* y *f.* **5** prisoner (preso).

detenimiento *s.m.* care, attention.

detentación *s.f.* DER. illegal/unlawful possession.

detentador *s.m.* **1** illegal/unlawful possessor (poseedor ilegal). **2** holder, possessor (de un récord).

detentar *v.t.* **1** to hold illegally unlawfully (retener algo sin derecho): *detentar un puesto = to occupy a post unlawfully.* **2** DEP. to hold (un récord).

detergente *s.m.* **1** detergent. || *adj.* **2** detergent.

deteriorar *v.t.* y *pron.* **1** to crack (resquebrajar). **2** to deteriorate (poner viejo o en mal estado). **3** to spoil, to impair (estropear). **4** to damage (dañar). **5** to wear out, to get worn (desgastar).

deterioro *s.m.* **1** deterioration. **2** damage (daño). **3** MEC. wear and tear, wear (con el uso).

determinación *s.f.* **1** determination (decisión): *demostrar determinación = to show determination.* **2** boldness, daring (atrevimiento). **3** fixing, settling (fijación): *la determinación de un acuerdo = the fixing of an agreement.* **4** decision, resolution (elección entre diversas cosas). || **8 faltar —,** to lack determination.

determinado, -a *adj.* **1** determined, resolute (resuelto). **2** decided, determined (decidido). **3** definite, certain (cierto). **4** fixed, set (fijado): *una hora determinada = a set time.* **5** specific, particular (preciso): *tenemos que estudiar un libro determinado = we have to study a specific book.* **6** MAT. determinate. **7** GRAM. definite: *el artículo definido = the definite article.*

determinar *v.t.* **1** to determine: *determinar las razones = to determine the reasons.* **2** to set, to fix (fijar): *determinar el día = to fix the day.* **3** to decide, to make up one's mind: *determinaron comprarlo = they decided to buy it.* **4** to calculate (calcular): *determinar el precio = to calculate the price.* **5** to cause, to give rise to (causar): *ese incidente determinó la guerra = that incident gave rise to the war.* **6** to stipulate (estipular): *las reglas determinan que... = the rules stipulate that...* || *v.pron.* **7** to decide, to make up one's mind (decidir). || **8 determinarse a hacer algo,** to decide to do something.

determinativo, -a *adj.* y *s.m.* GRAM. determinative.

determinismo *s.m.* FIL. determinism.

determinista *adj./s.m.* y *f.* FIL. determinist.

detestable *adj.* detestable, odious, vile.

detestación *s.f.* detestation, hatred, revulsion.

detonación *s.f.* **1** detonation (el acto de detonar). **2** explosion, bang (el resultado de detonar).

detonador *s.m.* detonator.

detonante *adj.* **1** detonating, explosive. **2** (fig.) stunning, devastating. || *s.m.* **3** explosive.

detonar *v.i.* to detonate, to explode, to blow up.

detorsión *s.f.* torn/ripped muscle.

detracción *s.f.* **1** detraction, vilification, (fam.) backbiting. **2** retreat, retraction (retiro).

detractar o **detraer** *v.t.* **1** to defame, to vilify, to denigrate (infamar). **2** (fam.) to knock, to slate (maldecir). **3** to separate (separar). **4** to remove, to take away (quitar).

detractor *s.m.* y *f.* **1** detractor, vilifier, (fam.) knocker. || *adj.* **2** defamatory, disparaging.

detraimiento *s.m.* disgrace, dishonour (deshonra).

detrás *adv.* **1** behind: *hay un enorme lago detrás = there's a huge lake behind.* **2** on the back: *el paquete lleva el precio detrás = the price is on the back of the packet.* **3** at the back: *la gente de detrás de la cola = the people at the back of the queue.* || **5 por —,** behind: *salieron por detrás de un árbol = they came out*

from behind a tree. **6 por — de,** behind. **4 — de,** behind: *le critican detrás de él = they criticize him behind his back.*
detrimento *s.m.* **1** detriment: *en detrimento de = to the detriment of.* **2** damage, harm (daño).
detrito o **detritus** *s.m.* GEOL. detritus.
deuda *s.f.* **1** debt (moral o material): *mi abuelo murió lleno de deudas = my grandfather died full of debts.* || **2 contraer deudas,** to get into debt. **3 — pública,** national debt. **4 perdónanos nuestras deudas,** REL. forgive us our trespasses.
deudo *s.m.* y *f.* relative, relation (pariente).
deudor, -a *s.m.* y *f.* **1** debtor. || *adj.* **2** indebted. || **3 saldo —,** COM. debit balance, adverse balance. **4 ser — de alguien,** to be indebted to someone: *te soy muy deudor = I am enormously indebted to you.*
deuterio *s.m.* QUIM. deuterium.
deuteronómico, -a *adj.* GRAM. deuteronomic.
deutón *s.m.* QUIM. deuteron.
devaluación *s.f.* FIN. devaluation.
devaluar *v.t.* FIN. to devalue.
devanar *v.t.* **1** to wind, to reel (hilo). **2** to spin (arañas, insectos). || *v.pron.* **3 devanarse los sesos,** to rack one's brains.
devanear *v.i.* to talk nonsense, to rave.
devaneo *s.m.* **1** MED. madness, delirium (locura). **2** time-wasting pastime, idle pursuit (pasatiempo vano). **3** flirtation, affair (flirteo). **4** silly comment, nonsense (disparate).
devastación *s.f.* devastation, ruination.
devastador, -a *s.m.* y *f.* **1** devastator, destroyer. || *adj.* **2** devastating.
devastar *v.t.* to devastate, to destroy: *una zona devastada = a devastated area.*
devengar *v.t.* **1** to yield, to earn, to bring in (producir intereses). **2** to earn (ganar dinero).
devengo *s.m.* money to be paid, amount due.
devenir *v.i.* **1** to happen, to occur (suceder). **2** to become (llegar a ser). || *s.m.* **3** change, flux (cambio). **4** movement (movimiento). **4** evolution, development (evolución).
devoción *s.f.* **1** REL. devotion. **2** devoutness, piety (piedad). **3** habit, custom (costumbre): *tener por devoción hacer algo = to be in the habit of doing something.* || *pl.* **4** REL. devotions (oraciones).
devocionario *s.m.* prayer book.
devolución *s.f.* **1** return: *le pedí la devolución de los libros = I asked him for the return of the books.* **2** DEP. return (del balón, golpe, etc.). **3** COM. repayment, refund: *devolución de la entrada = refund of entrance fee.* **4** return (de una cosa a una tienda). **5** DER. devolution. **6** return (de una carta): *devolución al remitente = return to sender.* || **7 no se admiten devoluciones,** goods cannot be returned. **8 sin —,** nonreturnable.
devolver *v.t.* **1** to return, to give back: *devolver un disco = to return a record.* **2** to return, to take back (a una tienda). **3** to send back, to return (una carta). **4** to repay, to pay back (dinero). **5** to throw up, to vomit (vomitar). **6** to return (un favor). **7** to put something back (en su sitio). **8** DEP. to return (un balón, golpe). **9** (fig.) to restore, to give back: *devolver la salud a alguien = to restore someone to health.* || *v.r.* **10** (Am.) to return, to go back (regresar). **11 — el bien por el mal,** to pay back evil with good. **12 — la pelota a uno,** (fig.) to retaliate, (fam.) to give someone tit for tat. **13 — la palabra,** to give someone back the floor (en un debate, etc.).
devorar *v.t.* **1** to devour. || **2 el león devoró su presa,** the lion devoured its prey. || **3** to devour, to eat up, to wolf (comérselo con ganas). **4** (fig.) to devour. || **5 devoran los libros,** they devour books. || **6** (fig.) to consume. || **7 el fuego lo devoró todo,** the fire consumed everything. || **8 la devoran los celos,** she is consumed by jealousy. **9** to destroy (destruir). **10** to squander, to waste (disipar): *devoró su fortuna = he squandered his fortune.*
devoto, -a *adj.* **1** REL. devout, pious (piadoso). **2** devoted. || **3 es muy — de su madre,** he's very devoted to his mother. || **4 tu — amigo,** your devoted friend. || **5** REL. **obra devota,** devotional work. || *s.m.* y *f.* **6** REL. devout o pious person. || **7 los devotos,** the faithful. || **8** (fig.) devotee, fan, aficionado (aficionado). || **9 los devotos del fútbol,** the football fans. || **10** admirer (admirador).
devuelto *p.p.* de **devolver.**
dextrina *s.f.* QUIM. dextrin.
dextrosa *s.f.* QUIM. dextrose.
deyección *s.f.* **1** GEOL. debris. **2** ejecta (materias arrojadas de un volcán). **3** MED. defecation, motion (evacuación de los excrementos). **4** excrement (excrementos).
día *s.m.* **1** day: *estuve aquí tres días = I was here three days.* **2** date (como fecha): *¿qué día es hoy? = what date is it today?* **3** (fig.) day, time (momento de alguna significación): *el día de desenmascarar a los corruptos ya ha llegado = the time has arrived to unmask the corrupted bastards.* **4** day, daylight (en contraste con la noche). || *pl.* **5** (fig.) life, days: *al final de mis días = at the end of my days.* || **6 abrir el —, a)** to dawn; **b)** to clear up (después de que haya habido nubes). **7 a días,** sometimes, from time to time. **8 al —,** up to date. **9 al otro —,** the following day. **10 cerrarse el —,** to get cloudy, to get dull. **11 coger a uno el — en una parte,** to wake up somewhere (un tanto inesperada o accidentalmente). **12 dar a uno el —,** to give someone a bad day: *el bebé nos ha dado el día = the baby has given us an awful day.* **13 dar los buenos días,** to wish somebody good day, to bid somebody good day. **14 de — en —,** day after day, everyday. **15 del —, a)** fresh: *pan del día = fresh bread;* **b)** fashionable (ropa, costumbres, etc.). **16 despertar el —,** to dawn. **17 — astronómico,** 24 hour day. **18 — de año nuevo,** New Year's Day. **19 — del Juicio,** Judgement Day. **20 — de precepto,** REL. holy day of obligation. **21 Día del Señor, a)** Sunday; **b)** Judgement Day; **c)** the Feast of Corpus Christi. **22 — por —,** dayly. **23 — festivo,** holyday. **24 — hábil,** court day, working day. **25 — laborable,** working day. **26 — lectivo,** working day, teaching day, school day. **27 — puente,** working day between two holidays (que se suele tomar de vacaciones). **28 — y noche,** night and day, constantly. **29 el — de mañana,** the future, in the future. **30 el — menos pensado,** one of these days. **31 el otro —,** the other day. **32 en su —,** in due time. **33 entrado en días,** advanced in years. **34 estar al —, a)** to keep up to date; **b)** to be in, to be trendy. **35 hasta otro —,** so long. **36 hoy (en) —,** nowadays, at present. **37 mañana será otro —,** tomorrow it will be another story. **38 no pasar días por uno,** not to get old, not to look old, not to look a day older. **39 no tener más que el — y la noche,** to be utterly poor, to be destitute. **40 oscurecerse el —,** to get cloudy. **41 romper el —,** to dawn. **42 todo el santo —,** all day long, the whole blessed day. **43 vivir al —,** to live from hand to mouth.
diabetes *s.f.* MED. diabetes.
diabético *adj./s.m.* y *f.* diabetic.
diablesco, -a *adj.* diabolical, devilish.
diablo *s.m.* **1** REL. devil, demon. **2** imp, rascal, rogue (especialmente niño). **3** rest (en el billar). || **4 así paga el — a quien le sirve,** that's what one gets for trying to help. **5 como el/un —,** like the devil. **6 darse uno al —,** to go wild, to become very angry. **7 del —,** (fam.) a hell of a: *hace un frío del diablo = it is a hell of a cold day.* **8 — encarnado,** the devil himself (para referirse a una persona sin escrúpulos). **9 ¡diablos!,** ¡hell! **10 haber una de todos los diablos,** there is/etc. a great rumpus, there is/etc. a great uproar. **11 llevarse el — una cosa,** to turn out badly, to fall through. **12 más sabe el — por viejo que por —,** age and experience is what really counts. **13 tener uno el —/los diablos en el cuerpo,** to have an itch.
diablura *s.f.* **1** devilment, devilry, mischief (travesura grande). **2** prank, escapade, practical joke (broma pesada). || **3 hacer diabluras,** to get up to mischief, (fam.) to get up to monkey tricks.
diabólico *adj.* **1** devilish, diabolical, fiendish. **2** intricate, complicated (enrevesado).
diábolo *s.m.* diabolo (juguete).
diaconado *s.m.* REL. deaconate, deaconship.
diaconal *adj.* REL. diaconal.
diaconato *s.m.* REL. deaconate, deaconship.

diaconía *s.f.* REL. deaconry.
diaconisa *s.f.* REL. deaconess.
diácono *s.m.* REL. deacon.
diacrítico, -a *adj.* 1 MED. diagnostic. 2 GRAM. diacritical, diacritic. || **3 signo —,** diacritical o diacritic sign.
diacronía *s.f.* diachronic.
diadema *s.f.* 1 diadem. 2 crown (corona).
diáfano, -a *adj.* 1 diaphanous. 2 (fig.) transparent (transparente).
diafragma *s.m.* ANAT. diaphragm.
diafragmático, -a *adj.* diaphragmatic.
diagnosis *s.f.* MED. diagnosis.
diagnosticar *v.t.* MED. to diagnose.
diagnóstico, -a *adj.* 1 MED. diagnostic. || *s.m.* 2 MED. diagnosis.
diagonal *adj.* 1 diagonal. || *s.m.* y *f.* 2 diagonal. || **3 en —,** diagonally.
diagrama *s.m.* diagram.
dial *s.m.* RAD. dial.
dialectal *adj.* 1 dialectal, dialect: *una palabra dialectal = a dialect word.*
dialectalismo *s.m.* dialectalism.
dialéctica *s.f.* dialectics.
dialéctico, -a *adj.* 1 dialectic, dialectical. || *s.m.* y *f.* 2 dialectician.
dialecto *s.m.* dialect.
diálisis *s.f.* MED. dialysis.
dialogar *v.t.* 1 to compose as a dialogue, to write in dialogue. || *v.i.* 2 to maintain a dialogue, to hold a dialogue. 3 to talk, to converse (conversar).
diálogo *s.m.* dialogue.
dialoguista *s.m.* y *f.* 1 dialogist (persona). 2 dialogue writer (escritor de diálogos).
diamante *s.m.* 1 diamond: *diamante brillante = cut diamond; diamante bruto = uncut o rough diamond.* 2 diamond (en las cartas). || **3 bodas de —,** diamond wedding.
diamantífero, -a *adj.* diamond-bearing (terreno que tiene diamantes).
diamantino, -a *adj.* 1 diamond-like. 2 (fig.) adamantine.
diamantista *s.m.* y *f.* 1 diamond merchant (vendedor). 2 diamond cutter (el que labra diamantes).
diametral *adj.* diametrical, diametric.
diametralmente *adv.* diametrically.
diámetro *s.m.* GEOM. diameter.
diana *s.f.* 1 bull's eye, bull (blanco). 2 MIL. reveille (toque de corneta). || **3 dar en la —,** to hit the bull's eye, to score a bull's eye. **4 tocar —,** to play reveille.
diantre *interj.* oh hell!, oh damn!
diapasón *s.m.* 1 MUS. tuning fork, (p.u.) diapason (instrumento de afinar). 2 MUS. finger board (de un violín). 3 MUS. range, scale, diapason (escala). 4 tone (tono de la voz). || **5 bajar el —,** to lower one's tone of voice. **6 subir el —,** to raise one's tone of voice.
diapositiva *s.f.* FOT. slide, transparency.
diariamente *adv.* daily, every day.
diario *adj.* 1 daily, everyday. || *s.m.* 2 newspaper, paper, daily (periódico). 3 diary (relación histórica). 4 COM. daybook. 5 daily expenses (gastos diarios de una casa). || **6 de/a —,** daily, every day. **7 — de a bordo,** MAR. logbook. **8 — dominical,** PER. Sunday newspaper. **9 — matinal** o **de la mañana,** morning newspaper. **10 — vespertino** o **de la noche,** evening newspaper. **11 para/de —,** everyday. **12 ropa de —,** everyday clothes.
diarismo *s.m.* (Am.) journalism (periodismo).
diarista *s.m.* y *f.* 1 (Am.) reporter, journalist (periodista). 2 diarist (el que escribe un diario).
diarrea *s.f.* MED. diarrhoea.
diáspora *s.f.* diaspora.
diástole *s.f.* 1 MED. diastole. 2 GRAM. diastole.
diatónico, -a *adj.* MUS. diatonic.
diatriba *s.f.* diatribe, invective.
dibujante *s.m.* y *f.* 1 ART. drawer, sketcher. 2 designer (de moda). 3 TEC. draughtsman (de dibujo lineal). 4 cartoonist (de dibujos animados).
dibujar *v.t.* 1 ART. to draw. 2 to design (diseñar). 3 to sketch (bosquejar). 4 (fig.) to describe, to depict (describir). || *v.pron.* 5 to stand out, to loom (destacar): *la montaña se dibuja contra el cielo = the mountain stands out against the sky.* 6 (fig.) to be written, to be evident: *sus problemas se dibujan en su cara = his problems are written in his face.*
dibujo *s.m.* 1 ART. drawing, sketch. 2 sketching, drawing (el arte). 3 TEC. design (diseño). 4 cartoon (en un periódico). 5 pattern, design (de ropa, tela, papel, etc.). 6 description (descripción). **7 — al carbón,** charcoal drawing. **8 — del natural,** drawing from life. **9 — lineal,** draughtsmanship. **10 dibujos animados,** cartoons.
dicción *s.f.* 1 diction (pronunciación). 2 word (palabra). 3 style (estilo). || **4 figuras de —,** figures of speech.
diccionario *s.m.* 1 dictionary. || **2 — de bolsillo,** pocket dictionary.
díceres *s.m.pl.* 1 (Am.) gossip. 2 rumours (rumores).
diciembre *s.m.* December.
dicotomía *s.f.* dichotomy.
dicotómico, -a *adj.* dichotomic.
dictado *s.m.* 1 GRAM. dictation: *hacer un dictado = to give a dictation; escribir al dictado = to take dictation.* 2 title, title of honour (título). || *pl.* 3 dictates: *los dictados de la conciencia = the dictates of conscience.* || **4 al — de alguien,** inspired o influenced by someone.
dictador *s.m.* dictator.
dictadura *s.f.* POL. dictatorship: *dictadura del proletariado = dictatorship of the proletariat.*
dictáfono *s.m.* dictaphone.
dictamen *s.m.* 1 opinion (opinión): *dar un dictamen = to give an opinion.* 2 judgement (juicio). 3 report (informe). 4 advice (consejo). 5 DER. legal opinion. || **6 — médico,** diagnosis.
dictaminar *v.t.* 1 to consider, to regard (considerar): *la policía dictamina el caso cerrado = the police consider the case closed.* 2 DER. to pass (un fallo). || *v.i.* 3 DER. to pass judgement (fallar). 4 to give an opinion, to express an opinion (dar una opinión). 5 to advise, to give advice (aconsejar).
dictar *v.t.* 1 to dictate (una carta, etc.). 2 DER. to pass, to pronounce (una sentencia). 3 to issue, to proclaim (decretos). 4 to legislate, to enact (leyes). 5 to give, to issue (órdenes). 6 to suggest, to advise (aconsejar). 7 (Am.) to give (clases). 8 (Am.) to deliver (conferencia).
dictatorial *adj.* dictatorial.
dicterio *s.m.* insult, abuse.
dicha *s.f.* 1 happiness (felicidad). 2 good luck (buena suerte). || **3 es una — poder...,** it's a pleasure to be able to... **4 hombre de —,** lucky man. **5 para completar nuestra —,** to complete our happiness. **6 por —,** by chance; luckily; fortunately. **7 una —,** a happy event.
dicharachero, -a *adj.* 1 comical, witty, humourous (cómico). || *s.m.* y *f.* 2 comical, witty o humourous person (persona graciosa).
dicharacho *s.m.* 1 witty o humourous remark (dicho gracioso). 2 coarse remark, crude comment (comentario ofensivo).
dicho, -a *p.p.irreg.* 1 de **decir.** || *s.m.* 2 saying, proverb. 3 witty remark. || *s.f.* 4 happiness, joy. 5 good luck; lucky event. || **6 del — al hecho hay mucho trecho,** there's many a slip 'twixt the cup and the lip. **7 — de las gentes,** talk, rumours. **8 — y hecho,** no sooner said than done. **9 lo —,** OK, well that's it. **10 lo —, —,** I meant what I said. **11 por dicha, a)** by chance; **b)** out of sheer luck.
dichoso, -a *adj.* 1 happy, content (feliz): *dichoso con la vida = happy with life.* 2 boring, tedious (aburrido): *¡dichosa película! = what a boring film!* 3 lucky, fortunate (afortunado). 4 wretched, blessed, damned (desventurado): *esa dichosa persona = that blessed person.*
didáctico, -a *adj.* 1 didactic. || *s.f.* 2 didactics.
diecinueve *adj.* 1 nineteen. 2 nineteenth (para la fecha, el siglo, etc.). || *s.m.* 3 nineteen.
diecinueveavo, -a *adj.* nineteenth.
dieciochavo, -a *adj.* y *s.m.* eighteenth.
dieciochesco, -a *adj.* eighteenth century.
dieciocho *adj.* 1 eighteen. 2 eighteenth (para la fecha, el siglo, etc.). || *s.m.* 3 eighteen.
dieciséis *adj.* 1 sixteen. 2 sixteenth (para la fecha, el siglo, etc.). || *s.m.* 3 sixteen.
dieciseisavo, -a *adj.* y *s.m.* sixteenth.
diecho, -a GEOM. *adj.* 1 diechal. || *s.m.* 2 diedron.
diecisiete *adj.* 1 seventeen. 2 seventeenth (para la fecha, el siglo, etc.). || *s.m.* 3 seventeen.
diecisieteavo, -a *adj.* y *s.m.* seventeenth.
diedro, -a GEOM. *adj.* 1 dialectal. || *s.m.* 2 dihedron.
diente *s.m.* 1 tooth. 2 ARQ. toothing. 3 MEC. tooth, cog, prong (cualquier saliente de un mecanismo). || **4 alargár-**

sele a uno los dientes, to have one's teeth set on edge; to long for. **5 a regañadientes,** reluctantly, unwillingly. **6 dar uno — con —,** to have one's teeth chattering (de miedo, frío, etc.). **7 de dientes afuera,** insincerely. **8 — canino /columelar,** eye-tooth (personas); fang (animal); tusk (elefante). **9 — de ajo,** clove of garlic. **10 — de leche,** milk tooth. **11 — de león,** BOT. dandelion. **12 — de perro,** MEC. chisel. **13 — incisivo,** incisor. **14 — molar,** molar. **15 enseñar /mostrar los dientes,** to bare one's teeth (como amenaza). **16 estar a —,** to be very hungry. **17 hablar uno entre dientes,** to mumble, to grumble. **18 hincar uno el —,** to get one's hands on, to get one's teeth into. **19 no llegar a un —/no tener para un —,** to have very little food. **20 pelar el —,** (Am.) **a)** to flatter; **b)** to smile enticingly. **21 rechinar los dientes,** to gnash one's teeth. **22 tener un buen —,** to have a healthy appetite. **23 tomar /traer a uno entre dientes, a)** to run someone down, to speak ill of; **b)** to be hostile to someone.

diéresis *s.f.* **1** MED. diaeresis. **2** GRAM. diaeresis.

diesel *adj.* **1** diesel. || *s.m.* **2** diesel. || **3 motor —,** diesel engine.

diestra *s.f.* right hand.

diestro *s.m.* **1** right (derecho). **2** clever, skilful (hábil): *diestro en jugar = a skilful player.* **3** astute, shrewd (astuto). **4** favourable (favorable). || **5** bullfighter, matador (torero). **6** bridle (correa). **7** halter (rienda). **8** (arc.) swordsman (espada). **9 a — y siniestro,** wildly; left, right and centre: *golpear a diestro y siniestro = to hit out wildly.*

dieta *s.f.* **1** HIST. diet (asamblea). **2** MED. diet: *estar a dieta = to be on a diet.* || *pl.* **3** expense allowance (remuneración de un empleado). **4** emoluments (paga que reciben diputados, jueces, etc.).

dietario *s.m.* account book.

dietética *s.f.* dietetics.

dietético, -a *adj.* **1** dietetic. || *s.m.* y *f.* **2** dietician.

diez *adj.* **1** ten. **2** tenth (para la fecha, el siglo, etc.). || *s.m.* **3** ten. **4** decade (del rosario). **5** ten (en las cartas).

diezmar o **dezmar** *v.t.* **1** to decimate (causar muchas muertes). **2** to pay the tithe (pagar el diezmo). **3** to kill o punish one in ten people (matar o castigar a una persona de cada diez).

diezmo *s.m.* **1** tithe (impuesto). **2** tenth (décimo).

difamación *s.f.* **1** libel, defamation (por escrito). **2** slander, defamation (hablado).

difamador, -ora *s.m.* y *f.* **1** libeller, defamer (por escrito). **2** slanderer, defamer (de palabra). || *adj.* **3** slanderous, defamatory (hablando). **4** libellous, defamatory (escrito).

difamar *v.t.* **1** to libel, to defame (por escrito). **2** to slander, to defame (hablando). **3** (fig.) to malign, to denigrate.

difamatorio, -a *adj.* **1** libellous, defamatory (por escrito). **2** slanderous, defamatory (de palabra).

diferencia *s.f.* **1** difference: *la diferencia entre dos personas = the difference between two people.* || **2 a — de,** unlike; in contrast to: *ella es inteligente a diferencia de su hermano = she is intelligent unlike her brother.* **3 pagar la —,** to pay the difference. **4 partir la —,** to split the difference.

diferenciación *s.f.* differentiation.

diferenciado, -a *adj.* differentiated.

diferencial *adj.* **1** differential. || *s.f.* **2** MAT. differential. || *s.m.* **3** TEC. differential.

diferenciar *v.t.* **1** to differentiate. **2** to distinguish (distinguir): *diferenciar una persona de otra = to distinguish one person from another.* **3** MAT. to differentiate. || *v.i.* **4** to disagree, to differ (no estar de acuerdo): *diferenciamos en las causas de la guerra = we disagree about the causes of the war.* || *v.pron.* **5** to be different, to differ (distinguirse una cosa de otra). **6** to distinguish oneself (distinguirse): *siempre se diferencia en los exámenes = she always distinguishes herself in her exams.* **7** to disagree, to be in disagreement (no estar de acuerdo): *siempre nos diferenciamos = we are always in disagreement.* **8** to be different (ser diferente).

diferente *adj.* **1** different. || *pl.* **2** several, various: *diferentes causas = various causes.* || **3 — a/de,** different to /from.

diferentemente *adv.* differently.

diferir *v.t.* **1** to postpone, to defer (aplazar): *han diferido el partido = the match has been postponed.* || **2** DER. to reserve (un fallo). || *v.i.* **3** to differ, to disagree (no estar de acuerdo).

difícil *adj.* **1** difficult, hard: *difícil de entender = difficult to understand.* **2** difficult (persona): *una persona difícil de conocer = a difficult person to know.* **3** (fig.) odd, peculiar (la cara). **4** unlikely, doubtful (improbable): *es difícil que lleguen a la hora = it's unlikely that they will arrive on time.* **5** embarrassing, awkward (violento).

difícilmente *adv.* hard, with difficulty (con dificultad).

dificultad *s.f.* **1** difficulty: *sin dificultad = without difficulty.* **2** problem, difficulty (problema): *tuvimos unas dificultades en la frontera = we had some problems at the border.* **3** trouble (molestia). **4** obstacle (obstáculo): *crear o poner dificultades = to create obstacles.*

dificultador, -a *adj.* difficult.

dificultar *v.t.* **1** to obstruct, to impede, to hinder (un camino, la circulación de tráfico, etc.). **2** to make difficult (hacer difícil).

dificultoso, -a *adj.* **1** hard, difficult: *una carrera dificultosa = a difficult race.* **2** awkward, troublesome (molesto): *una persona dificultosa = an awkward person.* **3** (fam.) odd, peculiar (la cara). **4** demanding, difficult (exigente).

difracción *s.f.* FIS. diffraction.

difractar *v.t.* FIS. to diffract.

difteria *s.f.* MED. diphtheria.

diftérico, -a *adj.* diphtheric, diphtheritic.

difuminar *v.t.* y *pron.* to fade away, to blur (contornos, formas, etc.).

difundir *v.t.* **1** to spread (extender). **2** to divulge, to spread (divulgar): *difundir las noticias = to spread the news.* **3** to give off, to emit (un gas, olor, etc.). **4** to broadcast, to transmit (la radio). **5** to spread, to disseminate (una doctrina, teoría, etc.). || *v.pron.* **6** to spread (una doctrina, noticia, etc.). **7** to get o become diffused (la luz, etc.).

difunto, -a *adj.* **1** dead, deceased, (fig.) late: *mi difunto abuelo = my late grandfather.* || *s.m.* y *f.* **2** dead o deceased person (persona muerta). **3** corpse, body (cadáver). || **4 Día de los Difuntos,** REL. All Souls' Day. **5 oler a —,** (fam.) to smell dank/fusty (una casa, habitación, etc.).

difusión *s.f.* **1** diffusion (de calor, luz, gas, etc.). **2** spreading, dissemination (de opiniones, noticias, ideas, etc.). **3** RAD. transmission, broadcasting. **4** spreading (de enfermedades, epidemias, etc.). **5** FIS. diffusion.

difuso, -a *adj.* **1** wordy, prolix (estilo, forma de hablar, etc.). **2** diffused (luz). **3** widespread, extensive (extenso).

digerible *adj.* digestible.

digerir *v.t.* **1** to digest (comida). **2** to swallow (tragar). **3** QUIM. to digest, to absorb (absorber). **4** (fig.) to digest, to absorb (una lección, información, etc.). **5** (fam.) to stand, to stick (aguantar): *no le puedo digerir = I can't stand him.* **6** to think over, to ponder (meditar). **7** to simmer (cocer a fuego lento).

digestible *adj.* digestible.

digestión *s.f.* digestion.

digestivo, -a *adj.* y *s.m.* digestive.

digital *adj.* **1** digital. **2** finger. || *s.f.* **3** BOT. foxglove. **4** MED. digitalis (medicina). || **5 huellas digitales,** fingerprints.

dígito *s.m.* MAT. digit.

dignamente *adv.* **1** with dignity (con dignidad). **2** properly, appropriately (como es debido). **3** honourably (honradamente).

dignarse *v.r.* **1** to deign, to condescend: *no se dignaron escribir = they didn't deign to write.* || **2 dígnese llegar pronto,** please be so kind as to arrive early (fórmula de cierta cortesía extremada).

dignatario, -a *s.m.* y *f.* dignatary.

dignidad *s.f.* **1** dignity. **2** honour (honor). **3** self-respect, self-esteem (amor propio): *herir la dignidad de alguien = to hurt someone's self-respect.* || **4** post, office (puesto). **5** rank (rango): *tiene dignidad de presidente = he has the rank of president.*

dignificación *s.f.* dignification.

dignificar *v.t.* y *pron.* to dignify.

digno, -a *adj.* **1** worthy, deserving: *digno de consideración = worthy of considera-*

tion. **2** appropriate, fitting (apropiado): *el digno final = the fitting end.* **3** honourable, upright (honorable): *una persona digna = an honourable person.* **4** decent (decente): *una vivienda digna = a decent home.* **5** dignified (de aspecto). || **6 — de verse/mención/etc.,** worthy of seeing /mention, etc. **7 muy —,** with great dignity.

digresión *s.f.* digression.

dilación *s.f.* delay (retraso).

dilapidación *s.f.* dissipation, squandering.

dilapidar *v.t.* to squander, to dissipate, to waste.

dilatación *s.f.* **1** MED. dilation. **2** FIS. expansion. **3** prolongation, extension (del tiempo). **4** dilation (de la pupila).

dilatado, -a *adj.* **1** MED. dilated (la pupila). **2** FIS. expanded. **3** vast, extensive (extenso). **4** long (largo). **5** (fig.) unlimited (ilimitado): *recursos dilatados = unlimited resources.*

dilatar *v.t.* **1** MED. to dilate. **2** FIS. to expand, to enlarge (ampliar). **3** to spread, to extend (una noticia, la fama, una idea). **4** to defer, to put off, to postpone (posponer): *dilataron su salida = they put off their departure.* **5** to prolong, to draw out (prolongar): *dilató su estancia = he prolonged his stay.* || *v.pron.* **6** MED. to dilate (la pupila, etc.). **7** FIS. to expand. **8** to spread, to stretch (extenderse): *los campos se dilatan hasta las montañas = the fields stretch as far as the mountains.* **9** to draw out, to drag on (alargar): *dilatar un cuento = to draw out a story.* **10** (Am.) to take a long time, to be slow (tardar): *dilatarse en hacer algo = to take a long time to do something.* **11** to be late (llegar tarde): *el tren se ha dilatado mucho = the train has arrived very late.*

dilatorio, -a *adj.* **1** DER. delaying, dilatory. || *s.f.* **2** delay (retraso). || **3 andar con dilatorias,** to delay; to waste time.

dilección *s.f.* fondness, affection.

dilecto, -a *adj.* beloved, cherished.

dilema *s.m.* dilemma.

diletante *s.m.* y *f.* dilettante.

diletantismo *s.m.* dilettantism.

diligencia *s.f.* **1** diligence, attention, care (cuidado). **2** speed, haste (prisa). **3** stagecoach (coche grande de caballos). **4** business (negocio): *hacer diligencias = to do business.* **5** step, measure (trámite). || **6 diligencias judiciales,** DER. judicial proceedings. **7 diligencias previas,** DER. inquiry. **8 hacer una —,** to run an errand.

diligenciar *v.t.* to take the steps necessary to obtain (tramitar un asunto).

diligente *adj.* **1** diligent, conscientious: *un trabajador diligente = a diligent worker.* **2** quick, prompt (rápido).

dilogía *s.f.* ambiguous, double meaning (ambigüedad).

dilucidar *v.t.* **1** to clarify, to elucidate (aclarar). **2** to clear up, to resolve (una duda, misterio, etc.).

dilución *s.f.* dilution.

diluir *v.t.* **1** to dilute (líquidos). **2** to water down, to thin (sopas, salsas, etc.). **3** to dissolve (un sólido). **4** (fig.) to water down. || *v.pron.* **5** to dilute.

diluvial *adj.* **1** diluvial. || *s.m.* **2** diluvium.

diluviano, -a *adj.* diluvian.

diluviar *v.i.* to pour down, to pour with rain, (fam.) to rain cats and dogs (llover a cántaros).

diluvio *s.m.* **1** flood, deluge. **2** (fig.) flood, deluge, avalanche: *un diluvio de quejas = a flood of complaints.* || **3 el Diluvio,** REL. the Flood.

dimanación *s.f.* **1** flowing, running (el agua). **2** (fig.) derivation, origin (origen).

dimanar *v.i.* **1** to spring, to emanate (el agua). || **2 — de,** (fig.) to stem from, to emanate from (proceder una cosa de otra): *los problemas dimanan del mismo sitio = the problems stem from the same place.*

dimensión *s.f.* **1** dimension. **2** size (tamaño). **3** (fig.) standing, stature: *una persona de dimensión mundial = a person of world standing.* || **4 tomar las dimensiones de algo,** to take the measurements of something.

dimensional *adj.* dimensional.

dimes *s.m.pl.* **1 — y diretes,** squabbling, bickering. || **2 andar en — y diretes,** to bicker; to squabble.

diminuendo *adj.* y *s.m.* MUS. diminuendo.

diminuir *v.t.* y *pron.* to diminish, to dwindle (disminuir).

diminutivo, -a *adj.* y *s.m.* diminutive.

diminuto, -a *adj.* **1** minute, tiny, diminutive. **2** defective, imperfect, faulty (defectuoso).

dimisión *s.f.* resignation: *presentar la dimisión = to submit o to hand in one's resignation.*

dimisionario, -a *adj.* recently resigning o outgoing (que acaba de dimitir).

dimisorias *s.f.pl.* REL. dimissory letters.

dimisorio, -a *adj.* recently resigning o outgoing (dimisionario).

dimitir *v.t.* e *i.* to resign.

dimorfismo *s.n.* ZOOL. dimorphism.

dina *s.f.* FIS. dyne (unidad de fuerza).

dinámica *s.f.* FIS. dynamics.

dinámico, -a *adj.* **1** dynamic. **2** (fig.) dynamic (una persona enérgica).

dinamismo *s.m.* dynamism.

dinamita *s.f.* **1** dynamite. || **2 volar con —,** to blow up with dynamite, to dynamite.

dinamitar *v.t.* to dynamite.

dinamitazo *s.m.* explosion, dynamite explosion, blast.

dinamitero, -a *s.m.* y *f.* dynamiter.

dinamo o **dínamo** *s.m.* ELEC. dynamo.

dinamométrico, -a *adj.* dynamoelectric, dynamoelectrical.

dinamómetro *s.m.* dynamometer.

dinastía *s.f.* dynasty.

dinástico, -a *adj.* dynastic, dynastical.

dineral *s.m.* fortune, (fam.) bomb, packet: *cuesta un dineral = it costs a bomb/packet/fortune.*

dinero *s.m.* **1** money. **2** currency, money (moneda de un país). **3** (fig. y fam.) wealth, money (riqueza). **4** fortune (fortuna). || **5 — en tabla** o **— contante y sonante,** cash; ready cash. **6 — de bolsillo,** pocket money. **7 — efectivo,** cash. **8 — en metálico** o **— contante,** cash. **9 — suelto,** change. **10 — de curso legal,** legal tender. **11 — por callar,** hush money. **12 los dineros del sacristán cantando se vienen y cantando se van,** easy come easy go. **13 el — llama al —,** money makes money. || **14 el — lo puede todo,** money is everything. **15 poderoso caballero es don Dinero,** money talks.

dinosaurio *s.m.* dinosaur.

dintel *s.m.* **1** ARQ. lintel. **2** (Am.) threshold (umbral).

diñar *v.t.* **1** (fam.) to give (dar). || **2** (fam.) **diñarla,** to kick the bucket, to snuff it. **3 diñársela a uno,** to cheat/to swindle some one.

diocesano, -a *adj.* y *s.m.* REL. diocesan.

diócesis o **diócesi** *s.f.* REL. diocese.

diodo *s.m.* diode.

dionisíaco, -a o **dionisiaco, -a** *adj.* **1** dionysiac, dionysian. || **2** *s.f.pl.* dionysia.

dios *s.m.* **1** REL. God. **2** god (cualquier deidad pagana). || *pl.* **3** gods. || **4 ¡a Dios!** o **¡adiós!,** good-bye; bye; bye-bye. **5 ¡gracias a —!,** thank God!; thank heavens! **6 a la buena de —,** at random; any old way. **7 armar la de — es Cristo,** to cause an almighty row; to raise hell. **8 clamar a —,** to cry out to heaven. **9 — mediante,** God willing. **10 dar gracias a —,** to thank God, to thank one's lucky stars. **11 estar de — una cosa,** to be inevitable. **12 gozar uno de —,** to be in heaven. **13 irse uno con —,** to leave. **14 llamar — a uno,** to die; to pass away. **15 no servir ni a — ni al diablo,** to be useless; to be a waste of time. **16 ofender uno a —,** to sin (pecar). **17 ponerse uno a bien con —,** to confess (confesarse). **18 recibir uno a —,** to receive Holy Communion. **19 tentar uno a —,** to do o to say dangerous things. **20 venir — a ver a uno,** to have a piece o stroke of luck. **21 — los cría y ellos se juntan,** birds of a feather flock together. **22 dar a — lo que es de — y al César lo que es del César,** render unto Caesar that which is Caesar's and unto God that which is God's. **23 donde — pasó de largo,** a godforsaken place. **24 como — manda,** properly; correctly. **25 — sabe,** God knows. **26 sólo — sabe,** God alone knows. **27 a — rogando y con el mazo dando,** God helps those who help themselves. **28 cuando — quiera,** all in good time. || **29 como — le da a entender,** as best one can. **30 ¡— dirá!,** we shall see; time will tell. **31 — es testigo que...,** God knows that... **32 ¡— te ayude!,** God help you! **33 ¡— te bendiga!,** God bless you! **34 ¡— me libre!,** heaven forbid! **35 — Todopode-**

roso, almighty God. **36 no había ni —,** there wasn't a soul; it was empty. **37 pasar la de — es Cristo,** to go through hell; to have a lousy time. **38 ¡que — me perdone!,** God forgive me! **39 si — quiere,** God willing. **40 ¡válgame —!,** good heavens! **41 ¡vaya con —!,** goodbye; God be with you! **42 ¡vaya por —!,** good lord!; good heavens!; my God! **43 ¡vive —!,** good God! **44 ¡por —!,** for God's sake!, for heaven's sake! **45 ¡— te ampare!,** God protect you! **45 ¡— mío!,** good heavens!, my God! **47 ¡— santo!,** my God!; good God!; good heavens! **48 en el nombre de —,** in the name of God.

diosa *s.f.* **1** goddess. **2** (fig.) goddess (mujer de gran belleza).

dióxido *s.m.* **1** QUIM. dioxide. || **2 — de carbono,** carbon dioxide.

diplodoco *s.m.* diplodocus (fósil).

diploma *s.m.* diploma.

diplomacia *s.f.* diplomacy.

diplomado, -a *adj.* **1** qualified, trained. || *s.m.* y *f.* **2** qualified person. **3** graduate (en la universidad).

diplomática *s.f.* diplomatics.

diplomáticamente *adv.* diplomatically.

diplomático, -a *adj.* **1** diplomatic: *el cuerpo diplomático = the diplomatic corps.* **2** (fig.) diplomatic, sagacious, tactful (sagaz). || *s.m.* **3** diplomat, diplomatist.

diplopía *s.f.* MED. double vision (visión doble).

dipsomanía *s.f.* dipsomania.

dipsómano, -a *adj.* **1** dipsomaniacal, dipsomaniac. || *s.m.* y *f.* **2** dipsomaniac.

díptero, -a *adj.* **1** ARQ. dipteral. **2** ZOOL. dipteran, dipterous. || *s.m.* **3** ZOOL. dipteran. || *pl.* **4** ZOOL. diptera.

díptico *s.m.* diptych.

diptongación *s.f.* GRAM. diphthongization.

diptongar *v.t.* e *i.* GRAM. to diphthongize.

diptongo *s.m.* diphthong.

diputación *s.f.* **1** delegation, deputation (delegación). **2** committee (comité). **3** post of member of parliament (cargo de diputado en Inglaterra). **4** post of member of the Cortes (cargo de diputado en España). **5** town hall (ayuntamiento). || **6 — provincial,** county council.

diputado *s.m.* y *f.* **1** representative, delegate (delegado). **2** POL. member of parliament; (fam.) M.P. (en Inglaterra). **3** POL. member of the Cortes (en España). **4** representative (en Estados Unidos). || **5 — provincial,** county councillor.

diputar *v.t.* **1** to delegate (elegir para un fin). **2** to consider, to think (conceptuar).

dique *s.m.* **1** dike, breakwater, jetty (muro). **2** dike (en Holanda). || **3 — de contención,** dam. **4 — seco,** dry dock. **5 — flotante,** floating dock. **6 hacer** o **entrar en —,** to dock. **7 poner un — a,** to put a check on; to check (contener).

dirección *s.f.* **1** direction, course, way (física): *vamos por la dirección correcta = we're going in the right direction.* **2** COM. running, management (de empresa). **3** guidance, control: *tomó la dirección del proyecto = he took control of the project.* **4** POL. leadership. **5** COM. board of directors (dirección personal colegiada). **6** headship (de institución educativa). **7** address (dirección postal). **8** PER. editorship. **9** MUS. conductorship. **10** MEC. steering (especialmente de un vehículo). **11** office, administrative office.

directa *s.f.* TEC. top gear (coche).

directamente *adv.* **1** directly. **2** immediately (inmediatamente).

directiva *s.f.* **1** board, board of directors (grupo de gente que dirige). || **2** instruction, directive (instrucción): *nos han dado una directiva = they have given us the instructions.*

directivo, -a *adj.* **1** directive. **2** COM. managing, managerial. **2** executive, managerial (clase). **4** administrative, managerial (función). || *s.m.* **5** COM. director, executive. || **6 junta —,** board of directors, board (de cualquier tipo de asociación).

directo, -a *adj.* **1** direct. **2** straight (una línea). **3** GRAM. direct: *una traducción directa = a direct translation.* **4** direct (manera, carácter, acción, vuelo, etc.): *un vuelo directo = a direct flight.* **5** through, non-stop (tren): *un tren directo = a through train.* **6** RAD. y TV. live: *transmitir en directo = to broadcast live.* || *s.m.* **7** straight, straight punch (boxeo). || **8 en —,** live.

director, -ora *adj.* **1** governing, controlling (de una junta, grupo, etc.). **2** master (idea). **3** guiding (principio). **4** directive (V. **directivo**). || *s.m.* y *f.* **5** director (hombre). **6** directress (mujer). **7** COM. manager, director (hombre). **8** COM. directress, manageress (mujer). **9** headmaster (hombre, de un colegio). **10** headmistress (mujer, de un colegio). **11** president (de una compañía, academia, etc.). **12** manager (hombre, de una tienda, hotel). **13** manageress (mujer, de una tienda, hotel). **14** governor (hombre, de una cárcel). **15** governess (mujer, de una cárcel). **16** editor (hombre, de un periódico). **17** editress (mujer, de un periódico). || **18 — de cine,** film director. **19 — de escena,** stage director. **20 — de orquesta,** conductor. **21 — de producción,** director of production.

directorio, -a *adj.* **1** directive, directory. || *s.m.* **2** directory (de normas, reglas, direcciones). **3** directors, board of directors (junta directiva).

directriz *adj./s.f.* y *pl.* **1** MAT. describing, dirigent (línea). **2** guidelines: *el ministro informó sobre las directrices que van a guiar la nueva ley = the minister gave details of the guidelines that will shape the new law.*

dirigente *adj.* **1** directing, ruling: *la clase dirigente = the ruling class.* || *s.m.* y *f.* **2** POL. leader: *el dirigente del partido = the leader of the party.*

dirigible *adj.* **1** AER. dirigible. **2** MAR. navigable. || *s.m.* **3** AER. dirigible (globo).

dirigido, -a *adj.* guided (un misil).

dirigir *v.t.* **1** to direct (en general). **2** to aim, to point (un arma, telescopio, etc.): *dirigió el rifle hacia el policía = he pointed the rifle at the policeman.* || **3** to drive, to steer (un coche). **4** to steer (un barco). **5** to edit (un periódico). **6** to pilot, to fly (un avión). **7** COM. to manage, to run (una empresa, tienda, negocio, etc.). **8** to address (una carta, protesta, comentario, observación, pregunta, etc.): *me dirigieron un comentario = they addressed a remark to me.* **9** to direct (el tráfico). **10** MUS. to conduct (una orquesta). **11** to direct (una mirada). **12** to lead (un partido, expedición, rebelión). **13** to dedicate (dedicar): *dirige todo a ganar dinero = he dedicates everything to making money.* **14** to direct (a un lugar): *me dirigió al hotel = he directed me to the station.* **15** to guide (guiar). **16** to direct (el cine). **17** to produce (el teatro). **18** to supervise, to oversee (una obra, tesis, etc.). **19** to make, to level (una acusación). || *v.pron.* **20** to head for, to make one's way to: *nos dirigimos a las montañas = we are heading for the mountains.* **21** COM. to be managed (un negocio). **22** to write (una carta). **23** to apply (solicitar). **24** to speak, to address: *se dirigió a mí en la tienda = he spoke to me in the shop.* || **32 diríjase a...,** apply to... (en anuncios).

dirigismo *s.m.* management, control: *dirigismo estatal = state control.*

dirimente *adj.* **1** DER. diriment, nullifying (de un contrato, matrimonio). **2** decisive (un argumento, opinión, etc.). || **3** DER. **impedimento —,** diriment impediment.

dirimir *v.t.* **1** to resolve, to settle (resolver): *dirimir un conflicto = to settle a conflict.* **2** to annul, to desolve, to declare void (un matrimonio, contrato, decisión, etc.).

discernible *adj.* discernible.

discernidor, -a *adj.* discerning, judicious.

discernimiento *s.m.* **1** discernment, judiciousness. **2** judgement (juicio). **3** perception (comprensión). **4** discrimination (discriminación).

discernir *v.t.* **1** to discern, to differentiate (distinguir): *discernir el bien del mal = to discern good from evil.* **2** DER. to appoint (encargar el juez a uno la tutela de un menor). **3** (Am.) to award (un premio).

disciplina *s.f.* **1** discipline. **2** subject (asignatura). **3** whip, discipline (azote). || *s.pl.* **4** lashes.

disciplinado, -a *adj.* disciplined.

disciplinal *adj.* disciplinal.

disciplinar *v.t.* **1** to discipline. **2** to instruct, to teach (enseñar). **3** to whip,

(p.u.) to scourge (azotar). 4 MIL. to drill, to train. || *v.pron.* 5 to discipline oneself. 6 to whip oneself (azotarse).
disciplinario, -a *adj.* disciplinary: *castigo disciplinario = disciplinary punishment.*
discípulo *s.m.* y *f.* 1 REL. y FIL. disciple, (fam.) follower. 2 student, pupil (alumno).
disco *s.m.* 1 disk, disc. 2 DEP. discus: *lanzamiento de disco = discus throwing.* 3 dial (del teléfono). 4 MUS. record, disc: *poner un disco = to play a record.* 5 signal (de ferrocarriles). 6 MED. disk, disc. 7 TEC. disk, disc (de los coches, etc.). 8 (fam.) bore, drag (cosa aburrida): *es un disco tener que estudiar = it's a drag to have to study.* 9 boring conversation (conversación monótona). || **10 cambiar el –,** (fam.) to change the record. || **11 nos cantó el – de siempre,** he told us the same old story. || **12 siempre vienes con el mismo –,** you're always going on about the same old thing.
discóbolo *s.m.* discus thrower (atleta que arroja el disco).
díscolo, -a *adj.* disobedient, unruly.
disconforme *adj.* 1 in disagreement, at variance: *estar disconforme con alguien = to disagree with someone.* 2 differing (diferente).
disconformidad *s.f.* 1 disagreement (desacuerdo). 2 difference, nonconformity (falta de conformidad).
discontinuar *v.t.* e *i.* to discontinue, to suspend.
discontinuidad *s.f.* discontinuity, disruption.
discontinuo, -a *adj.* 1 discontinuous (no continuo). 2 interrupted (interrumpido).
discordancia *s.f.* 1 discord (discordia). 2 MUS. dissonance. 3 conflicting, clashing (colores, ropa). 4 difference, disagreement (de opiniones).
discordante *adj.* 1 clashing (colores, ropa). 2 MUS. dissonant. 3 discordant, differing (opiniones, teorías, etc.).
discordar *v.i.* 1 MUS. to be dissonant, to be out of tune. 2 to disagree, to differ, not to agree (no estar de acuerdo). 3 to clash (colores, ropa, opiniones, etc.).
discorde *adj.* 1 MUS. dissonant, discordant (voz, sonido). 2 MUS. out of tune (instrumento). 3 clashing (colores, ropa, opiniones). 4 differing, conflicting (opiniones). || **5 estar discordes,** to disagree; not to be in agreement; not to agree: *están discordes = they're not in agreement/they don't agree.*
discordia *s.f.* discord, disagreement: *reina la discordia = discord reigns.*
discoteca *s.f.* 1 dicothèque, (fam.) disco (salón de baile). 2 record collection (colección de discos). 3 record library (mueble de discos).
discreción *s.f.* 1 discretion, good sense, prudence (prudencia). 2 tact (tacto). 3 wisdom, sagacity (sabiduría). || **4 a –, a)** at one's discretion; **b)** MIL. to stand easy. **5 añadir sal a –,** add salt to one's liking. 6 MIL. **darse, entregarse** o **rendirse a –,** to surrender unconditionally. **7 vino a –,** as much wine as one likes.
discrecional *adj.* 1 discretional, discretionary: *facultades o poderes discrecionales = discretionary powers.* || **2 parada –,** request stop. **3 servicio –,** special service.
discrecionalmente *adv.* at one's discretion.
discrepancia *s.f.* 1 discrepancy: *hay una discrepancia de opiniones = there's a discrepancy of opinions.* || 2 disagreement, difference (desacuerdo).
discrepar *v.i.* to disagree, to differ: *sus ideas discrepan = there ideas differ.*
discreto, -a *adj.* 1 discreet, tactful (lleno de tacto). 2 sagacious, wise (sagaz). 3 shrewd, astute (astuto). 4 prudent (prudente). 5 sensible, sober (al vestir). 6 sober, subdued (color). 7 average, moderate (inteligencia, habilidad). 8 unobtrusive, self-effacing (poco visible). 9 judicious (juicioso). 10 MAT., FIS., MED. discrete. || *s.m.* y *f.* 11 REL. assistant to the superior (persona elegida para asistir al superior). || 12 discreet person (persona discreta). 13 prudent person (persona prudente). 14 wise person (persona sagaz). 15 shrewd o astute person (persona astuta).
discriminación *s.f.* discrimination: *discriminación sexual = sexual discrimination.*
discriminar *v.t.* 1 to discriminate: *discriminar contra = to discriminate against.* 2 to differentiate, to distinguish (diferenciar).
discriminatorio, -a *adj.* discriminatory.
disculpa *s.f.* 1 excuse (excusa): *dar disculpas = to make excuses.* 2 apology (por una ofensa). || **3 pedir disculpas,** to apologize, to offer an apology: *te pido disculpas = I apologize.*
disculpable *adj.* excusable, pardonable.
disculpar *v.t.* 1 to excuse: *sus años lo disculpan = his youth excuses him.* || 2 to forgive, to pardon (perdonar): *discúlpame = forgive me.* || *v.pron.* 3 to apologize, to excuse oneself: *disculparse por haber metido la pata = to apologize for having put one's foot in it.*
discurrir *v.i.* 1 to think, to reflect, to ponder (reflexionar). 2 to wander, to roam (ir de un lado a otro). 3 to pass, to pass by (el tiempo): *han discurrido dos años = two years have passed.* 4 to speak, to converse (hablar). 5 to flow, to run (fluir). 6 to pass, to go (la vida, un mitin, un período, etc.). || *v.t.* 7 to invent, to think up (inventar). 8 to conjecture, to surmise (conjeturar).
discursear *v.i.* to make a speech, to deliver a speech (pronunciar discursos).
discursivo, -a *adj.* thoughtful, pensive, reflective.
discurso *s.m.* 1 speech, address: *pronunciar un discurso = to make o deliver a speech.* 2 reasoning (facultad de discurrir). 3 treatise, dissertation (escrito). 4 course, period (espacio de tiempo): *en el discurso de dos años = in the course of two years.* 5 passage: *en el discurso del tiempo = with the passage of time.*
discusión *s.f.* 1 discussion (hecho y resultado de discutir): *estar en discusión = to be under discussion.* 2 argument (disputa): *tener una discusión = to have an argument.* 3 debate (debate).
discutible *adj.* 1 debatable, arguable: *es discutible si... = it's arguable if...* 2 doubtful, questionable (dudoso): *las posibilidades de ganar son muy discutibles = the chances of winning are very doubtful.*
discutido, -a *adj.* controversial: *una decisión muy discutida = a very controversial decision.*
discutidor *s.m.* y *f.* 1 arguer. || *adj.* 2 argumentative.
discutir *v.t.* 1 to discuss, to debate (examinar una cuestión): *discutir las ventajas y desventajas = to discuss the advantages and disadvantages.* 2 to argue about (argumentar): *discutir la mejor forma de hacer algo = to argue about the best way of doing something.* || *v.i.* 3 to discuss, to talk about, to talk over: *discutir de/sobre el tiempo = to discuss the weather.*
disecación o **disección** *s.f.* 1 MED. dissection. 2 stuffing (el relleno de animales). 3 mounting (de plantas).
disecar *v.t.* 1 MED. to dissect (un cuerpo). 2 to stuff (rellenar un animal). 3 to mount, to preserve (una planta). 4 (fig.) to analyse, to dissect (analizar).
diseminación *s.f.* dissemination, spread: *la diseminación de información = the spread of information.*
diseminar *v.t.* y *pron.* to disseminate, to spread (esparcir).
disensión *s.f.* 1 row, quarrel, argument (riña). 2 dissension (desacuerdo). 3 dissent, disagreement (disentimiento).
disentería *s.f.* MED. dysentery.
disentérico, -a *adj.* MED. dysenteric.
disentimiento *s.m.* disagreement, dissent.
disentir *v.i.* 1 to disagree, not to agree (no estar de acuerdo): *disentimos en todo = we disagree on everything.* 2 to dissent: *disiento de tu opinión = I dissent from your opinion.* || 3 to differ (ser diferente).
diseñador, -ora *s.m.* y *f.* designer.
diseñar *v.t.* 1 to design. 2 to draw (dibujar).
diseño *s.m.* 1 design. 2 drawing, sketch (dibujo).
disertación *s.f.* 1 dissertation (escrito). 2 lecture, discourse, dissertation (discurso).
disertar *v.i.* 1 to lecture, to discourse (hablar). 2 to dissertate, to discourse (escribir).
diserto, -a *adj.* articulate, fluent, eloquent.
disfavor *s.m.* 1 snub, rebuff (desaire). 2 damage, harm (perjuicio).
disforme *adj.* 1 deformed (deformado). 2 disfigured (desfigurado). 3 enormous, huge (enorme). 4 ugly (feo). 5 ill-

proportioned, disproportionate, out of proportion (desproporcionado). **6** formless, shapeless (sin forma).

disfraz *s.m.* **1** disguise. **2** mask (máscara). **3** fancy dress (vestido): *baile de disfraces = fancy dress ball.* **4** simulation (simulación). **5** (fig.) pretext, ploy (pretexto). || **6 ser un –,** (fam.) to be out of place: *el cuadro es un disfraz allí = the picture is out of place there.*

disfrazado, -a *adj.* disguised, dressed up.

disfrazar *v.t.* **1** to disguise. **2** (fig.) to hide, to conceal, to disguise (ocultar): *disfrazar la verdad = to hide the truth.* || *v.pron.* **3** to dress up, to disguise oneself: *disfrazarse de payaso = to dress up as a clown.*

disfrutar *v.t.* **1** to enjoy (gozar): *disfrutar las vacaciones = to enjoy one's holidays.* **2** to own, to possess (poseer). **3** to take advantage of, to make the most of (aprovechar): *¡disfrútalo! = make the most of it!* || *v.i.* **4** to have a good time, to enjoy oneself (pasarlo bien): *disfrutamos mucho ayer = we had a good time yesterday.* || **5 – con algo,** to enjoy something: *disfruto con los discos = I enjoy my records.* **6 – de,** to enjoy: *disfrutan de la presencia de sus nietos = they enjoy the presence of their grandchildren.*

disfrute *s.m.* **1** enjoyment (resultado de disfrutar). **2** possession (posesión). **3** use (uso). **4** advantage (provecho).

disgregación *s.f.* **1** separation (separación). **2** disintegration (desintegración). **3** dispersal, break-up (dispersión).

disgregar *v.t.* y *pron.* **1** to disintegrate, to break up (desintegrar): *el imperio se disgregó = the empire disintegrated.* **2** to separate (separar). **3** to disperse (dispersar).

disgustado, -a *adj.* **1** irritated, annoyed, displeased: *estar disgustado con* o *de alguien = to be annoyed with someone.* **2** disappointed, unhappy (decepcionado): *disgustado con el resultado = disappointed by the result.*

disgustar *v.t.* **1** to annoy, to irritate, to displease (contrariar): *tu actitud me disgusta = your attitude annoys me.* **2** to dislike, not to like (no gustar): *me disgusta tener que hacerlo = I dislike having to do it.* || *v.pron.* **3** to get annoyed, to be displeased, to get angry (enfadarse): *se disgusta si no lo llamo = he gets annoyed if I don't ring him.* **4** to fall out, to get angry with each other (enfadarse dos personas).

disgusto *s.m.* **1** displeasure, annoyance, anger (enfado): *no puedo disimular mi disgusto = I can't hide my displeasure.* **2** misfortune, setback (revés): *hemos sufrido muchos disgustos = we've suffered many setbacks.* **3** grief, sorrow (pena). **4** trouble, problem, bother (problema). **5** quarrel, row, argument (riña): *tener un disgusto con alguien = to have a quarrel with someone.* **6** dispute, altercation (contienda). **7** shock, blow (susto). || **8 a –,** unwillingly, reluctantly, against one's will (de mala gana). **9 estar a –,** to be unhappy, to be upset. **10 llevarse un –,** to be upset, (fam.) to be put out. **11 matar a disgustos a uno,** (fig. y fam.) to make someone's life a misery. **12 tener disgustos con alguien,** to have problems with someone.

disidencia *s.f.* **1** dissidence, disagreement. **2** REL. dissent.

disidente *adj.* **1** dissident. || *s.m.* y *f.* **2** POL. dissident. **3** REL. nonconformist, dissenter.

disidir *v.i.* to dissent.

disimetría *s.f.* dissymmetry.

disimétrico, -a *adj.* dissymmetric, dissymmetrical.

disímil *adj.* different, dissimilar.

disimilación *s.f.* dissimilation.

disimilar *v.t.* y *r.* to dissimilate.

disimilitud *s.f.* dissimilarity, dissimilitude.

disimulación *s.f.* **1** dissimulation, concealment, hiding (ocultación). **2** excusing, forgiving, pardoning (disculpa). **3** cunning (astucia).

disimuladamente *adv.* **1** cunningly, slyly (astutamente). **2** furtively (furtivamente).

disimulado, -a *adj.* **1** concealed, hidden (ocultado). **2** furtive (furtivo). **3** cunning, sly (astuto). **4** dissembling, hypocritical (hipócrita). || **5 hacerse el –,** to pretend o feign ignorance; to act dumb.

disimular *v.t.* **1** to hide, to conceal (esconder). **2** (fig.) to disguise, to hide, to conceal: *disimular sus problemas = to hide one's problems.* **3** to excuse, to forgive, to overlock (perdonar). || *v.i.* **4** to dissemble, to pretend (fingir).

disimulo *s.m.* **1** hiding, concealment (ocultación). **2** dissimulation (disimulación). **3** tolerance, allowance, indulgence (tolerancia). **4** slyness, cunning (astucia).

disipación *s.f.* **1** dissipation. **2** squandering, wasting, dissipation (de recursos, dinero, talento, etc.). **3** dispersion (de las nubes).

disipado, -a *adj.* **1** dissipated. **2** debauched, profligate, dissipated (una persona, una vida, una sociedad). **3** wasteful, extravagant, lavish (derrochador).

disipar *v.t.* **1** to dissipate, to scatter, to disappear (las nubes). **2** to dispel, to remove (una sospecha, duda, temor, etc.). **3** to shatter, to destroy (esperanzas). **4** to waste, to squander, (fam.) to fritter away (dinero, fortuna). **5** to waste (energía). || *v.pron.* **6** to dissipate, to disappear, to scatter (nubes). **7** to vanish (humo). **8** to evaporate (evaporarse). **9** to be removed, to be dispelled (una sospecha, duda, temor). **10** to be wasted, to be squandered, (fam.) to be frittered away (el dinero, una fortuna). **11** to clear up, to blow over (una tormenta).

dislalia *s.f.* disarticulation.

dislate *s.m.* **1** silly thing, stupid thing (tontería). **2** absurdity, foolishness (absurdo). || **3 dislates,** nonsense (disparates).

dislexia *s.f.* PSIC. dislexia.

dislocación *s.f.* **1** MED. dislocation (de los huesos). **2** GEOL. fault, slip (falla). **3** (fig.) dislocation.

dislocar *v.t.* **1** MED. to dislocate (los huesos). **2** to distort, to twist (desfigurar). || *v.pron.* **3** MED. to dislocate, to put out of joint (los huesos).

disloque *s.m.* (fam.) tops, limit.

disminuir o **diminuir** *v.t., i.* y *pron.* **1** to diminish, to reduce (las dimensiones, fuerzas, prestigio, población, etc.). **2** to fall, to drop (la temperatura, precios). **3** to reduce, to decrease (la velocidad). **4** to come down, to lower (el valor). **5** to draw in, to grow shorter (el día). **6** to fail (la memoria). **7** to decline (la salud). **8** to relieve, to ease (el dolor). **9** to come down (la fiebre). **10** to diminish, to dwindle (las posibilidades, el entusiasmo).

disnea *s.f.* MED. dyspnoea.

disociable *adj.* dissociable.

disociación *s.f.* dissociation.

disociar *v.t.* **1** to dissociate, to separate (separar). || *v.pron.* **2** to dissociate oneself.

disoluble *adj.* soluble, dissoluble, dissolvable.

disolución *s.f.* **1** dissolution (del parlamento, un club, una sociedad, un matrimonio, etc.). **2** QUIM. dissolution, solution. **3** COM. liquidation (liquidación). **4** dissoluteness, profligacy, degeneracy (relajación moral y de costumbres).

disoluto, -a *adj.* dissolute, degenerate, dissipated.

disolvente *s.m.* y *adj.* QUIM. solvent, dissolvent.

disolver *v.t.* **1** to dissolve, to melt (pasar un sólido a estado líquido). **2** to dissolve (un parlamento, matrimonio, contrato, sociedad, grupo). **3** to break up (un mitin, disturbio, manifestación, reunión). || *v.pron.* **4** to dissolve, to melt (sólidos). **5** POL. to dissolve (parlamento). **6** to be broken up (manifestación, disturbio, reunión, etc.).

disonancia *s.f.* **1** MUS. dissonance. **2** (fig.) disharmony, dissonance (sin armonía). **3** disagreement, lack of agreement (desacuerdo). || **4 hacer – con,** to be out of harmony with.

disonante *adj.* **1** MUS. discordant, dissonant. **2** (fig.) discordant, (fam.) at odds, incongrous.

disonar *v.i.* **1** MUS. to be out of tune, to be dissonant (desafinar). **2** to look strange, to look funny (parecer mal). **3** to clash, to conflict (no venir bien una cosa con otra). **5** to disagree, not to agree (no estar de acuerdo). **6** (fig.) to lack harmony (faltar armonía). **7** no differ (discrepar).

dísono, -a *adj.* discordant, dissonant.

dispar *adj.* **1** unlike, not like, different (diferente). **2** unequal, uneven (desigual).

disparada *s.f.* 1 (Am.) stampede, flight, rush (fuga). || 2 **a la –,** (fam. y Am.) flat out, at full speed, like a shot (a todo correr). 3 **irse a la –,** to be off like a shot; to leave at full speed.

disparadero *s.m.* 1 trigger (gatillo de un arma). || 2 **poner a uno en el –,** to make someone lose his pacience; to make someone run out of pacience (agotarle la paciencia).

disparador *s.m.* 1 trigger (gatillo de un arma). 2 FOT. shutter release (de una cámara). 3 escapement (de un reloj). || 3 **poner a uno en el –,** to provoke someone; to incite someone (incitarlo); to make someone lose his pacience; to make someone lose his temper (agotarle la paciencia).

disparar *v.t.* 1 to shoot, to fire (un arma). 2 to throw, to fling, to hurl (una piedra). 3 DEP. to shoot (un balón). || *v.pron.* 4 to go off (un arma). 5 to bolt, to run off (un caballo). 6 to shoot off; to rush off (irse de prisa). 7 to lose one's pacience, to lose control (perder la paciencia). 8 (fig.) to talk nonsense o rubbish (decir tonterías); to act stupidly o foolishly (hacer tonterías). 9 **salir disparando,** to shoot off; to leave like a shot.

disparatadamente *adv.* ridiculously, absurdly, foolishly.

disparatado, -a *adj.* ridiculous, absurd, foolish (absurdo).

disparatar *v.i.* 1 to salk nonsense o rubbish (decir disparates). 2 to act foolishly; to do something silly (hacer disparates).

disparate *s.m.* 1 silly comment, foolish remark (comentario tonto): *soltar un disparate = to make a silly comment* o *foolish remark.* 2 absurd thing, foolish act (hecho absurdo): *has hecho un disparate enorme = that was an absurd thing to do.* 3 mistake, blunder, (fam.) bloomer (metedura de pata): *fue un partido de muchos disparates = it was a game full of blunders.* || *pl.* 4 nonsense: *decir disparates = to talk nonsense.* || 5 **¡qué –!,** what nonsense!; how ridiculous! 6 **un –,** a lot, (fam.) a hell of a lot (mucho): *me costó un disparate = it cost me a hell of a lot.*

disparidad *s.f.* disparity.

disparo *s.m.* 1 shot (tiro). 2 DEP. shot (fútbol). 3 firing (acción de disparar). 4 (fig.) silly o foolish thing (disparate). || *pl.* 5 shots, shooting. || 6 **– de aviso,** warning shot.

dispendio *s.m.* 1 waste, squandering (derroche). 2 extravagance (gasto excesivo).

dispendiosamente *adv.* expensively.

dispendioso, -a *adj.* expensive, dear, costly (caro).

dispensa *s.f.* 1 dispensation, exemption. 2 REL. dispensation.

dispensación *s.f.* dispensation, exemption.

dispensar *v.t.* 1 to forgive, to excuse (perdonar una falta): *dispénsame por no venir ayer = forgive me for not coming yesterday.* 2 REL. to dispense. 3 to exempt, to excuse (librar de una obligación). 4 to grant, to give (honores, mercedes). 5 to pay (atención). 6 to give (ayuda). 7 to administer, to dispense (justicia). || *v.pron.* 8 to give (dar).

dispensario *s.m.* MED. dispensary, clinic.

dispepsia *s.f.* MED. dyspepsia.

dispersar *v.t.* y *r.* 1 to disperse, to spread, to scatter (esparcir). 2 to break up (un disturbio, manifestación, etc.). 3 MIL. to rout, to disperse.

dispersión *s.f.* 1 dispersion, dispersal. 2 QUIM. y FIS. dispersion.

disperso, -a *adj.* 1 dispersed, spread out, scattered (esparcido). 2 MIL. separated, scattered.

displicencia *s.f.* 1 lack of enthusiasm, indifference (falta de entusiasmo). 2 bad temper, ill-humour (mal humor). 3 coolness, indifference (frialdad). 4 despair, dejection (desaliento).

displicente *adj.* 1 unpleasant, displeasing (desagradable). 2 bad-tempered, ill-humoured (de mal humor).

disponer *v.t.* 1 to arrange, to order, to put in order (colocar en orden). 2 to get ready, to prepare (preparar). 3 to decide (decidir). 4 to order (mandar). 5 to lay, to set (la mesa). 6 MIL. to form up, to line up (las tropas). 7 DER. to stipulate, to provide: *la ley dispone que... = the law stipulates that...* || *v.i.* 8 to dispose, to sell (vender): *han dispuesto de su casa = they've disposed of* o *sold their house.* 9 to have, to have available, to have at one's disposal: *no dispongo de mucho tiempo = I haven't got a lot of time available.* 10 to have, to own: *disponen de dos cosas = they own o have two houses.* 11 to have the use, to have at one's disposal: *no dispongo del coche hoy = I haven't got the use of my car today.* || 12 **– de dinero,** to have money at hand. || *v.pron.* 13 to get ready, to prepare: *disponerse para salir = to get ready to go out.*

disponibilidad *s.f.* 1 availability. || *pl.* 2 COM. resources, means, assets (recursos).

disponible *adj.* 1 available (utilizable): *tiempo disponible = available time.* 2 COM. at hand, available (dinero): *dinero disponible = money at hand.* 3 free, unengaged, unoccupied (libre). 4 spare, free (tiempo libre). 5 free, vacant (libre): *una plaza disponible = a vacant place.* 6 vacant, unfilled (un puesto de trabajo).

disposición *s.f.* 1 arrangement, disposition (arreglo). 2 disposition, temperament (estado de ánimo, humor). 3 ARQ. layout, plan: *la disposición de la casa = the layout of the house.* 4 DER. order, decree (ley). 5 (fig.) talent, gift, aptitude (don): *tiene disposición para el arte = he has a talent for art.* 6 inclination, bent (propensión). 7 MIL. formation (de las tropas). 8 disposal: *a la disposición de = at the disposal of; a su disposición = at your disposal.* || *pl.* 9 preparations, arrangements (preparativos). 10 steps (medidas): *tomar disposiciones = to take steps.* || 11 **– de ánimo,** state of mind; attitude of mind; frame of mind. 12 **estar** o **hallarse en –,** to be suitable; to be apt (ser apta una persona para algún fin). 13 **estar a la – de alguien,** to be at someone's service; (fam.) to be at someone's beck and call. 14 **poner algo a la – de alguien,** to put something at someone's disposal: *te pongo el coche a tu disposición = my car is at your disposal.* 15 **tener algo a su –,** to have the use of something; to have something at one's disposal. 16 **última –,** last will and testament.

dispositivo *s.m.* 1 mechanism, device (mecanismo). 2 gadget, device (aparato; artificio): *dispositivo de seguridad = safety device.*

dispuesto, -a *p.p.* 1 de **disponer.** || *adj.* 2 ready, prepared (listo): *dispuesto para la batalla = ready for the battle.* 3 disposed, arranged (arreglado): *dispuesto por orden cronológico = arranged in chronological order.* 4 willing, prepared: *estar dispuesto a hacer algo = to be willing* o *prepared to do something.* 5 clever, smart, bright (listo). || 6 **bien –,** handsome (guapo); well-disposed (de carácter). 7 **estar poco – a hacer algo,** to be reluctant o unwilling to do something. 8 **mal –,** ill-disposed (de carácter); MED. ill, sick, indisposed (enfermo).

disputa *s.f.* 1 dispute, quarrel, argument (discusión). 2 controversy, dispute (controversia). || 3 **sin –,** without doubt, undoubtedly, indisputably.

disputable *adj.* disputable, debatable, open to question.

disputar *v.t.* 1 to dispute, to challenge: *disputar una decisión = to challenge a decision.* 2 to defend (defender). 3 to fight for, to contend for (la posesión de algo): *disputar el puesto en un equipo = to fight for one's position in a team.* 4 DEP. to play (jugar). 5 to debate (debatir). || *v.i.* 6 to dispute, to quarrel (discutir). || *v.pron.* 7 to contend for, to fight for, to compete for (la posesión de algo): *se disputan el campeonato = they are contending for the championship.* 8 DEP. to be played (jugarse). 9 to be discussed, to be debated (discutirse).

disquisición *s.f.* 1 disquisition. || *pl.* 2 divergences, digressions, marginal reflections.

distancia *s.f.* 1 distance (de espacio). 2 interval, gap (de tiempo). 3 difference, dissimilarity (desemejanza). 4 coldness, lack of warmth (desafecto entre personas). || 5 **acortar las distancias,** to reduce the distance. 6 **a –,** at a distance; far. 7 **a gran –,** long-distance. 8 **avión de larga –,** long-haul plane. 9 **– focal,** FOT. focal length. 10 **– sobre el suelo,** clearance. 11 **estar a diez millas de –,** to be ten miles away; to be at a distance of ten miles. 12 **guardar las distancias,** to keep one's distance; (fam.) to keep oneself to oneself. **13 mantenerse a –**, to keep one's distance. **14 tener a –**, to keep at a distance.

distanciado, -a *adj.* 1 far apart, not close (muy separados): *estamos muy distanciados = we are not very close.* 2 distant, far away (distante). 3 remote, isolated (aislado). 4 remote (remoto). 5 separated (separado).

distanciar *v.t.* 1 to separate (separar). 2 to place apart, to put apart (apartar). 3 to outstrip, to outdistance (dejar atrás): *el equipo distancia a los demás rivales = the team is outdistancing its other rivals.* 4 to cause a rift between; to open a rift between (causar una ruptura en una relación). || *v.pron.* 5 to become separated (separarse). 6 to leave behind; to get ahead (dejar atrás a un rival). 7 to lose contact; to drift away; to no longer see (perder contacto): *se ha distanciado de su familia = he's lost contact from his family.* 8 to fall out; to quarrel (disgustarse).

distante *adj.* 1 distant, far, far-off (lejos). 2 remote, isolated (aislado). 3 (fig.) distant: *una persona distante = a distant person.*

distar *v.i.* 1 to be away, to be off, to be distant: *el pueblo dista 2 kms = the village is 2 kms away.* 2 (fig.) to be far from; to be a long way off: *dista de la realidad = it's far from the reality; disto mucho de entenderlo = I'm far from understanding it.*

distender *v.t.* y *pron.* 1 to distend, to swell (hinchar). 2 to loosen, to ease, to slacken (aflojar). 3 to stretch (estirar). 4 MED. to pull, to strain (los músculos).

distensible *adj.* stretchable (estirable).

distensión *s.f.* 1 ANAT. distension, swelling (de la piel, cara, etc.). 2 MED. pull, strain (de un músculo): *distensión muscular = strained muscle.* 3 loosening, easing, slackening (aflojamiento).

dístico *s.m.* LIT. (p.u.) distich; (fam.) couplet.

distinción *s.f.* 1 distinction, difference (diferencia): *establecer o hacer una distinción = to make a distinction.* 2 elegance, refinement, distinction (elegancia). 3 honour, distinction (honor): *distinción honorífica = honour.* 4 clarity, lucidity (claridad). 5 deference, respect, esteem (deferencia): *tratar a alguien con distinción = to treat someone with respect.* || **6 a – de**, in contrast to; as opposed to; unlike. **7 de gran –**, highly distinguished. **8 hacer – con alguien**, to show great consideration for someone. **9 sin –**, indistinctly; without distinction. **10 sin – de**, irrespective of.

distingo *s.m.* reservation, qualification (salvedad): *hay que hacer un distingo = one has to make a reservation.*

distinguible *adj.* distinguishable, distinctive

distinguido, -a *adj.* 1 distinguished: *una persona distinguida = a distinguished person.* 2 well-known (bien conocido). 3 elegant, cultivated, distinguished (de carácter, modales, comportamiento). 4 gentlemanly, civilised (caballero). 5 ladylike, refined (una mujer).

distinguir *v.t.* 1 to distinguish: *distinguir entre dos cosas = to distinguish between two things.* 2 to recognize, to tell (reconocer): *no distingo cuál es mi coche = I can't tell which is my car.* 3 to discern, to make out, to distinguish (discernir): *no se puede distinguir la carretera = the road can't be made out.* 4 to honour (otorgar a una persona algo con que se le honra); (fig.) to honour: *nos has distinguido con tu presencia = you have honoured us with your presence.* 5 to prefer, to have a preference for (preferir). 6 to differentiate (diferenciar). 7 to single out, to distinguish (singularizar). || *v.i.* 8 to discriminate, to be discerning (discriminar): *saber distinguir = to be a discerning person; to be a good judge.* || *v.pron.* 9 to be distinguished, to differ (diferenciarse). 10 to stand out, to be noticeable (sobresalir): *se distinguen por su inteligencia = they stand out for their intelligence.* 11 to distinguish oneself: *se distinguió durante la guerra = he distinguished himself during the war.* 12 to be discerned, to be seen (verse): *se distinguen las montañas a lo lejos = the mountains can be seen in the distance.*

distintivo *adj.* 1 characteristic, distinctive (característico): *signo distintivo = distinguishing mark.* || *s.m.* 2 insignia, emblem (insignia). 3 mark (marca). 4 symbol (símbolo). 5 distinguishing mark (signo). 6 characteristic o distinctive feature (aspecto).

distinto *adj.* 1 distinct, clear (claro). 2 different: *prefiero algo distinto = I prefer something different.* || *pl.* 3 several, different, various (varios): *ideas distintas = various ideas.*

distorsión *s.f.* 1 MED. twisting, torsion (torcedura violenta). 2 distortion (aberración óptica, de la radio, etc.).

distracción *s.f.* 1 distraction. 2 amusement, entertainment (entretenimiento): *el pueblo tiene pocas distracciones = the village has few entertainments; la música es mi distracción preferida = music is my favourite amusement.* 3 pastime, hobby, recreation (pasatiempo). 4 type of amusement, form of entertainment (tipo de entretenimiento): *el teatro es una distracción interesante = the theatre is an interesting form of entertainment.* 5 absentmindedness, forgetfulness (descuido): *en una distracción se perdieron = they got lost due to absentmindedness.* 6 dissoluteness, debauchery, dissipation (disipación). || **7 por –**, absent-mindedly, due to forgetfulness (por inadvertencia); as a hobby (como hobby): *escribe por distracción = he writes as a hobby.*

distraer *v.t.* 1 to distract (apartar la atención): *¡no me distraigas! = stop distracting me!* 2 to disturb, to trouble (perturbar la atención). 3 to amuse, to entertain (divertir). 4 to relax (relajar): *la radio me distrae mucho = the radio relaxes me a lot.* 5 to lead astray (llevar a alguien a la vida desordenada). 6 FIN. to embezzle, (fam.) to fiddle (malversar fondos). 7 to take someone's mind off (quitar la preocupación): *distraer a uno de sus problemas = to take someone's mind off his problems.* || *v.i.* 8 to be relaxing, to be entertaining: *la televisión distrae = television is relaxing.* || *v.pron.* 9 to entertain oneself, to amuse oneself (divertirse). 10 to be inattentive, to let one's mind wander (descuidarse): *el niño se distrae mucho = the child is very inattentive.*

distraídamente *adv.* absent-mindedly, forgetfully.

distraído, -a *adj.* 1 absent-minded, forgetful (despistado). 2 entertaining, amusing (divertido): *un libro distraído = an entertaining book.* 3 dissolute, dissipated (disoluto). 4 (desp.) inattentive, vague, dreamy (desatento). 5 casual: *con aire algo distraído = quite casually; in a somewhat causal way.* 6 (Am.) untidy, shabby (andrajoso). || *s.m.* y *f.* 7 absent-minded o forgetful person. || **8 hacerse el –**, to pretend not to be interested; to pretend not to notice.

distribución *s.f.* 1 distribution. 2 delivery (reparto): *distribución de cartas = letter delivery.* 3 MEC. distribution. 4 service, supply (de gas, agua, electricidad, etc.): *distribución de gas = gas supply.* 5 ARQ. layout, plan: *la distribución de una casa = the layout of a house.*

distribuidor, -ora *s.m.* y *f.* 1 distributor (persona). 2 COM. dealer, agent (agente de productos comerciales): *distribuidor de coches = car dealer.* 3 MEC. distributor (de un coche). **distribuir** *v.t.* 1 to distribute (repartir). 2 to deliver (cartas): *distribuir el correo = to deliver the post.* 3 to supply (electricidad, gas, agua). 4 ARQ. to design, to lay out (la distribución de una casa). 5 to allocate, to assign (deberes, trabajo, etc.). 6 to award, to give out (premios). 7 to distribute (cargas, pesos).

distributivo, -a *adj.* distributive.

distrito *s.m.* 1 district. || **2 – electoral,** POL. constituency. **3 – postal,** postal district o area.

distrofia *s.f.* MED. dystrophy: *distrofia muscular = muscular dystrophy.*

disturbar *v.t.* to disturb.

disturbio *s.m.* disturbance, riot.

disuadir *v.t.* 1 to dissuade, to discourage: *disuadir a alguien de fumar = to dissuade from smoking.*

disuasión *s.f.* 1 MIL. dissuasion; deterrent: *disuasión nuclear = nuclear deterrent.*

disuasivo, -a *adj.* 1 dissuasive. 2 MIL. deterrent.

disuelto, -a *adj.* dissolved.

disyunción *s.f.* disjunction.

disyuntiva *s.f.* 1 alternative, choice (alternativa): *no hay otra disyuntiva = there's no other choice o alternative.* 2 dilemma (dilema).

disyuntivo, -a *adj.* disjunctive.
ditirambo *s.m.* dithyramb.
diurético, -a *adj.* y *s.m.* MED. diuretic.
diurno, -a *adj.* 1 daily, (p.u.) diurnal. || *atr.* 2 day.
diuturno, -a *adj.* lasting, enduring (que dura mucho tiempo).
diuturnidad *s.f.* (p.u.) diuturnity.
diva *s.f.* MUS. diva, prima donna.
divagación *s.f.* 1 digression, deviation. || *s.pl.* 2 ramblings, wanderings.
divagador, -a *adj.* rambling, prolix, (fam.) long-winded (prolijo).
divagar *v.i.* 1 to wander, to stray (desviarse del tema). 2 to digress, (fam.) to ramble (hablar sin concierto).
diván *s.m.* divan, couch (sofá sin respaldo).
divergencia *s.f.* divergence.
divergente *adj.* 1 divergent. 2 opposite (opuesto). 3 distinct, different (distinto).
divergir *v.i.* 1 to diverge. 2 to differ, to diverge (opiniones, gustos, etc.). 3 to fork, to turn off, to diverge (carreteras).
diversidad *s.f.* diversity, variety.
diversificación *s.f.* diversification.
diversificar *v.t.* 1 to diversify, to vary, (fam.) to branch out. || *v.pron.* 2 to be diversified. 3 to vary (variar).
diversión *s.f.* 1 pastime, hobby (pasatiempo): *su diversión es coleccionar sellos = his pastime is collecting stamps.* 2 amusement, entertainment (entretenimiento). 3 MIL. diversion (divertimiento estratégico).
divertido, -a *adj.* 1 entertaining (entretenido): *un libro divertido = an entertaining book.* 2 funny, comical, amusing (cómico): *un chiste divertido = a funny joke.* 3 funny, amusing, witty (persona). 4 merry, lively (una fiesta). || **5 ¡estamos divertidos!,** how very funny!; how terribly amusing! (dicho irónicamente).
divertimiento *s.m.* 1 entertainment, amusement. 2 MIL. diversion: *divertimiento estratégico = strategic diversion.*
divertir *v.t.* 1 to amuse, to entertain: *la película nos divirtió mucho = the film entertained us very much.* 2 to distract, to divert (distraer). || *v.pron.* 3 to have a good time (pasárselo bien): *nos divertimos mucho en el campo = we had a good time in the country.* 4 to amuse oneself (distraerse): *divertirse haciendo algo = to have a good time doing something.* 5 to be distracted (la atención).
dividendo *s.m.* COM. dividend.
dividir *v.t.* 1 MAT. to divide: *dividir 50 por 5 = to divide 50 by 5.* 2 to separate, to divide (separar): *el río divide los dos pueblos = the river separates the two villages.* 3 to share, to divide, to share out (repartir): *separar las ganancias = to share the profits.* 4 to divide, to disunite (crear discordia): *divide y vencerás = divide and rule.*
divinamente *adv.* divinely.
divinidad *s.f.* 1 divinity, deity (dios pagano): *divinidad pagana = pagan deity.* 2 god (dios). 3 (fig.) beauty (persona o cosa).
divinizar *v.t.* 1 to deify. 2 (fig.) to venerate, to worship, to exalt.
divino, -a *adj.* 1 divine: *castigo divino = divine punishment.* 2 (fig.) divine, lovely, beautiful, gorgeous (bello).
divisa *s.f.* 1 emblem, badge (insignia). 2 motto (lema de los escudos). || *pl.* 3 FIN. foreign currency o exchange (dinero extranjero): *control de divisas = foreign exchange control.*
divisar *v.t.* to discern, to distinguish, to make out (ver a distancia o confusamente).
divisibilidad *s.f.* divisibility.
divisible *adj.* divisible.
división *s.f.* 1 division. 2 MAT. y MIL. division. 2 POL. division, split (de un partido). 3 GRAM. dash, hyphen (guión). 4 partition, division (de un país). 5 disagreement, difference, division (desacuerdo): *división de opiniones = difference of opinion.*
divisional *adj.* divisional.
divisivo, -a *adj.* divisive.
diviso, -a *adj.* divided.
divisor, -ora *adj.* 1 dividing. ‖ *s.m.* 2 MAT. divisor. 3 factor: *máximo común divisor = highest common factor.*
divisoria *s.f.* 1 GEOL. divide. 2 dividing line (línea que divide).
divisorio, -a *adj.* dividing (que divide).
divo *s.m.* 1 pagan god (dios pagano). || *adj.* 2 divine (divino).
divorciado, -a *adj.* 1 divorced. ‖ *s.m.* y *f.* 2 divorcee.
divorciar *v.t.* 1 to divorce. 2 (fig.) to separate, to divorce (separar). || *v.pron.* 3 to get divorced, to get a divorce: *divorciarse de alguien = to divorce someone.*
divulgación *s.f.* 1 disclosure, divulging (revelación). 2 popularizing (popularización). 3 spreading, propagation (propagación).
divulgador, -ora *adj.* 1 divulging, disclosing. || *s.m.* y *f.* 2 divulger, exposer, revealer.
divulgar *v.t.* 1 to publish (publicar). 2 to spread, to propagate (propagar). 3 to popularize (popularizar). 4 to reveal, to disclose, to divulge (revelar). || *v.pron.* 5 to be revealed, to come out (salir a la luz).
do *s.m.* 1 MUS. do, doh. || **2 — de pecho,** high C. **3 dar el — de pecho,** to strike a high note (dar una de las notas más altas); (fig.) to secure something, to manage to get something (conseguir algo a costa de mucho esfuerzo).
dóberman *adj.* y *s.m.* dobermann (perro).
dobladillar *v.t.* to hem, (fam.) to turn up.
dobladillo *s.m.* 1 hem (remate en los bordes de la ropa). 2 turn-up (de pantalones).
doblado, -a *adj.* 1 doubled, double. 2 double (costura). 3 folded, doubled over (plegado). 4 ANAT. stocky, robust (de cuerpo pequeño y músculos fuertes). 5 uneven, bumpy (terreno desigual). 6 rough (terreno escabroso). 7 sly, (fam.) two-faced (engañoso).
doblaje *s.m.* dubbing (cinema).
doblar *v.t.* 1 to double: *doblar el precio = to double the price.* 2 to fold (papel, tela, periódico, etc.): *doblar un papel en dos = to fold a paper in two.* 3 to bend (un brazo, rodilla, codo, vara, etc.). 4 to turn up (costura). 5 to go round, to turn (una esquina): *doblar la esquina = to turn the corner.* 6 MAR. to round (un cabo). 7 to dub (una película). 8 to overtake (adelantar un coche). 9 to double (en el bridge). 10 to turn down (el pico de una página). 11 to double (en el billar). || **12 te doblo la edad,** I'm twice as old as you. || *v.i.* 13 to turn (a la derecha, a la izquierda). 14 to toll (las campanas): *doblar a muerto = to toll for a death.* 15 to play two roles o parts (representar dos papeles en una obra). 16 (fig.) to submit, to give in (ceder). 17 to collapse, to fall to the ground (caer el toro al morir). || *v.pron.* 18 to double (duplicarse). 19 to bend down (el cuerpo). 20 to fold, to fold up (plegarse). 21 to bend, to give (debido a un peso): *se ha doblado el suelo con los años = the floor has bent with the passing of years.* 22 (fig.) to yield, to submit, to give in (ceder).
doble *adj.* 1 double: *doble sentido = double meaning.* 2 dual (nacionalidad, control, mando): *doble nacionalidad = dual nationality.* 3 thick (grueso): *una manta doble = a thick blanket.* 4 false: *una maleta de doble fondo = a suitcase with a false bottom.* 5 (fig.) hypocritical, two-faced (hipócrita). || *s.m.* 6 double (cantidad): *este año gano el doble = this year I earn double.* 7 fold (pliegue). 8 knell, toll (toque de campanas). 9 double, stand-inn (actor que sustituye a otro). 10 double (en el bridge, billar, dominó). || *pl.* 11 DEP. doubles (tenis): *dobles masculinos = men's doubles.* || **12 —,** a double: *un whisky doble = a double whisky.* **13 el —,** twice as much: *cuesta el doble = it costs twice as much.* **14 el — que,** twice as much as: *bebe el doble que yo = he drinks twice as muchf as me.* **15 la — vista,** double vision. **16 ser el — de alguien,** to be someone's double; to look exactly the same as someone.
doblegar *v.t.* 1 to fold (doblar). 2 to brandish (blandear un arma). 3 to bend (curvar). 4 to twist (torcer). 5 (fig.) to make someone change their mind (hacer cambiar de opinión). 6 to beat, to defeat (vencer). || *v.pron.* 7 (fig.) to give in, to submit, to yield (ceder).
doblemente *adv.* 1 doubly: *doblemente difícil = doubly difficult.* 2 (fig.) two-facedly, falsely, deceitfully (con falsedad).
doblete *adj.* 1 medium-thick (entre doble y sencillo). || *s.m.* 2 GRAM. doublet. 3 doublet (piedra de bisutería).
doblón *s.m.* HIST. doubloon (moneda).

doce *adj.* 1 twelve: *las doce = twelve o'clock.* 2 twelfth (para fechas y siglos). || *s.m.* 3 twelve.
doceavo, -a *adj.* y *s.m.* twelfth.
docena *s.f.* 1 dozen: *una docena de huevos = a dozen eggs.* 2 **a docenas,** by the dozen. 3 **por docenas,** by the dozen; in dozens.
docencia *s.f.* teaching.
docente *adj.* 1 teaching (que enseña): *personal docente = teaching staff.* 2 educational: *centro docente = educational centre.*
dócil *adj.* 1 docile. 2 obedient.
docilidad *s.f.* 1 docility. 2 obedience.
dócilmente *adv.* 1 docilely. 2 obediently.
docto, -a *adj.* 1 wise (sabio). 2 erudite, learned (erudito).
doctor *s.m.* y *f.* MED. doctor: *doctor honoris causa = honourary doctor.*
doctorado *s.m.* doctorate.
doctoral *adj.* 1 doctoral. 2 (fig. y desp.) pedantic, pompous.
doctoralmente *adv.* doctorally.
doctorar *v.t.* 1 to confer a doctor's degree on. || *v.pron.* 2 to obtain o get one's doctorate (obtener el doctorado).
doctrina *s.f.* 1 doctrine: *la doctrina marxista = the Marxist doctrine.* 2 teaching (enseñanza). 3 preaching (predicación). 4 catechism (catecismo).
doctrinal *adj.* doctrinal.
doctrinalmente *adv.* doctrinally.
doctrinar *v.t.* 1 to teach (enseñar). 2 to indoctrinate (adoctrinar).
documentación *s.f.* 1 documentation. 2 papers, documents (de identidad): *documentación del barco = ship's papers; la documentación, por favor = your papers, please.*
documentado, -a *adj.* well-informed, well up (enterado).
documental *adj.* 1 documentary. || *s.m.* 2 TV. documentary.
documentar *v.t.* 1 to document. 2 to inform, to instruct (informar). || *v.pron.* 3 to research, (fam.) to swot up, (fam.) to brush up (instruirse): *me he documentado sobre el tema = I've brushed up on the subject.*
documento *s.m.* 1 document. 2 papers (de identidad): *documento de identidad = identity papers.* 3 **— justificativo,** certificate (certificado).
dodo o **dido** *s.m.* dodo.
dogal *s.m.* 1 halter (para los caballos). 2 noose, hangman's noose o rope (cuerda para ahorcar). || 3 **estar con el — al cuello,** to be in a fix o jam; to be in a tight spot.
dogma *s.m.* dogma.
dogmáticamente *adv.* dogmatically.
dogmático, -a *adj.* 1 dogmatic. || *s.m.* y *f.* 2 dogmatist. || *s.f.* 3 dogmatics (conjunto de dogmas).
dogmatismo *s.m.* dogmatism.
dogmatista *s.m.* y *f.* dogmatist.
dogmatizador, -ora o **dogmatizante** *s.m.* y *f.* dogmatist.
dogmatizar *v.i.* to dogmatize.
dogo *s.m.* bulldog (perro).
dolama *s.f.* ailment, complaint (achaque).
dólar *s.m.* dollar.
dolencia *s.f.* 1 affliction, complaint (achaque). 2 illness (enfermedad). 3 pain, ache (dolor). 4 ills, problems: *la dolencia del país = the problems of the country.*
doler *v.i.* 1 to ache, to hurt: *me duele la pierna = my leg hurts o my leg aches.* 2 to have a pain: *me duele el estómago = I've got a pain in my stomach/I've got stomach ache.* 3 to be sorry, to hurt (ser algo motivo de disgusto): *me duele tener que marchar tan pronto = I'm sorry to have to leave so early.* || *v.pron.* 4 to feel sorry for, to have pity on, to pity (compadecer). 5 to complain (quejarse): *se duelen del trato que reciben = they complain about the treatment they receive.* 6 to regret, to lament (arrepentirse): *dolerse de haber hecho algo = to regret having done something.* 7 to grieve (afligirse). || 8 **ahí me/le duele,** there gou have it; you've put your finger on it.
dolido, -a *adj.* hurt, upset: *estoy muy dolido de lo que me dijiste = I'm very hurt about what you said to me.*
doliente *adj.* 1 painful, aching (que duele). 2 sad (triste). 3 sick, ill (enfermo). || *s.m.* y *f.* 4 MED. ill o sick person (persona enferma). 5 mourner (en un entierro).
dolmen *s.m.* HIST. dolmen.
dolo *s.m.* 1 malice, wickedness (malicia). 2 deceit (engaño). 3 fraud (fraude). 4 trick (trampa).
dolomía o **dolomita** *s.f.* dolomite.
dolor *s.m.* 1 pain: *tener mucho dolor = to be in pain.* 2 ache: *dolor de cabeza = headache.* 3 (fig.) regret, sorrow (arrepentimiento). 4 remorse (remordimiento).
dolorido, -a *adj.* 1 MED. sore, painful, tender: *tengo el brazo dolorido = my arm is sore.* 2 sad, upset (triste). 3 (fig.) grief-stricken, agrieved (afligido).
dolorosa *s.f.* 1 (fam.) bill, damage: *nos trae la dolorosa, por favor = can you bring us the bill, please/what's the damage?* 2 ART. madonna (imagen de la Virgen).
dolorosamente *adv.* 1 MED. painfully. 2 (fig.) painfully, distressingly (afligentemente).
doloroso, -a *adj.* 1 MED. painful: *un tratamiento doloroso = a painful treatment.* 2 (fig.) painful, distressing: *una decisión dolorosa = a painful decision.*
doloso, -a *adj.* DER. fraudulent.
doma *s.f.* 1 taming (de fieras). 2 training (adiestramiento). 3 breaking in (de caballos). 4 (fig.) taming, controlling, dominating (de los instintos, pasiones, etc.).
domador, -a *s.m.* y *f.* 1 tamer (de fieras): *domador de leones = lion tamer.* 2 trainer (que los adiestra). || 3 **— de caballos,** horse-breaker.
domar *v.t.* 1 to tame (fieras). 2 to train (adiestrar). 3 to break in (caballos). 4 (fig.) to dominate, to control, to master (los instintos, pasiones, etc.). 5 to subdue, to bring under control (quitarle la rebeldía a una persona). 6 (fig.) to break in (zapatos, botas, etc.).
domeñable *adj.* 1 tamable. 2 trainable (adiestrable).
domeñar *v.t.* 1 to subdue, to suppress (someter). 2 to tame, to train (domar). 3 to dominate, to master, to control (dominar).
domesticable *adj.* 1 tameable, domesticable (que se puede domar). 2 trainable (que se puede adiestrar).
domesticación *s.f.* 1 domestication. 2 (fam.) house-training (para animales de casa). 3 taming (doma). 4 training (adiestramiento).
domesticado, -a *adj.* tame, pet: *un tigre domesticado = a pet tiger/a tame tiger.*
domésticamente *adv.* domestically.
domesticar *v.t.* 1 to tame, to domesticate: *domesticar un gato = to domesticate a cat.* 2 to train (adiestrar): *domesticar un oso = to train a bear.* 3 (fig.) to domesticate, to house-train.
domesticidad *s.f.* 1 domesticity. 2 captivity (un animal).
doméstico, -a *adj.* 1 domestic: *servicio doméstico = domestic service.* 2 household: *gastos domésticos = expenses.* 3 tame, pet: *un león doméstico = a tame lion.* || *s.m.* y *f.* 3 domestic, servant (criado).
domiciliar *v.t.* to domicile, to house, to home (asignar un domicilio a alguien).
domiciliario, -a *adj.* 1 domiciliary. || *atr.* 2 house: *arresto domiciliario = house arrest.* || *s.m.* y *f.* 3 resident, tenant (ocupante).
domicilio *s.m.* 1 home, residence (p.u.) domicile, (p.u.) abode: *domicilio particular = private residence.* 2 **a —,** DEP. at home: *ganar a domicilio = to win away from home.*
dominación *s.f.* 1 domination. 2 dominance, rule (dominio). 3 MIL. high ground, commanding position (elevación del terreno). 4 DEP. pull-up (en ejercicio gimnástico). 5 REL. dominions, dominations (los ángeles que forman el cuarto coro).
dominador, -a *adj.* 1 dominating, controlling (dominante): *el partido dominador=thedominatingparty.*2domineering (persona).
dominante *adj.* 1 dominating, dominant: *el equipo dominante = the dominant team.* 2 commanding, dominating, dominant (posición, situación, altura). 3 prevailing (viento, opinión): *los vientos dominantes = the prevailing winds.* 4 domineering (despótico): *una persona dominante = a domineering person.* 5 MUS. dominant. || *s.f.* 6 MUS. dominant.
dominar *v.t.* 1 to dominate. 2 to rule, to control (control): *Hitler intentó dominar Europa = Hitler tried to rule Europe.* 3 to control, to contain (un incendio, epi-

demia). **4** to control (las pasiones, instintos, animales, nervios). **5** POL. to suppress, to put down (una rebelión). **6** to recover from, to get over (pesar, pena). **7** to know well, to be fluent in, to have a good knowledge of (un idioma): *domina bien el inglés = he knows English very well.* **8** to dominate, to tower over (edificios altos). **9** to overlook, to dominate (edificios): *la casa domina el valle = the house overlooks the valley.* || *v.i.* **10** to dominate (un edificio, montaña). **11** to stand out (sobresalir). **12** to predominate (predominar). || *v.pron.* **13** to control oneself, to keep oneself under control (controlarse).

dómine *s.m.* **1** latin teacher, latin master (profesor de latín). **2** (desp.) pedant.

domingo *s.m.* **1** sunday. || **2 — de Carnaval,** Shrove Sunday. **3 — de Cuasimodo,** Low Sunday. **4 — de Ramos,** REL. Palm Sunday. **5 — de Pascua** o **de Resurrección,** REL. Easter Sunday. **6 hacer —,** to have o take a day off.

dominguejo *s.m.* (Am.) nobody, nonentity (persona insignificante).

dominical *adj.* **1** Sunday, dominical: *hoja o periódico dominical = Sunday paper o newspaper.*

dominicano, -a *adj.* **1** REL. Dominican. **2** Dominican (de la isla de Santo Domingo). || *s.m.* y *f.* **3** Dominican.

dominico, -a *adj./s.m.* y *f.* REL. Dominican.

dominio *s.m.* **1** dominion, power (poder). **2** control, authority (autoridad): *estoy bajo su dominio = I'm under his authority.* **3** domination (dominación). **4** supremacy, dominance (supremacía): *dominio del mar = sea supremacy.* **5** command, fluency (de un idioma): *tienen un dominio del inglés = they have a command of English.* **6** good knowledge, sound grip (de un tema, asignatura, etc.). **7** dominion (en el Commonwealth). **8** domain (territorio). **9** control (de las pasiones, emociones). **10** DER. ownership (derecho de propiedad). || **11 ser del — público,** to be of common knowledge, to be widely known. **12 — de sí mismo,** self-control.

dominó *s.m.* **1** domino (una ficha). **2** dominoes (el juego).

don *s.m.* **1** Mr.: *Don Miguel García = Mr. Miguel García.* **3** Esquire, Esq. (en un sobre). **4** present, gift (regalo). **5** favour (favor). **6** talent, ability, gift (habilidad, talento): *el don de lenguas = a gift for languages.* **7** wish (deseo, en las cuentas): *el hada le concedió tres dones = the fairy granted o gave him three wishes.* || **8 — de acierto,** gift o knack for getting it right. || **9 — de mando,** leadership qualities. **10 — de gentes,** the gift of getting on with people: *tiene don de gentes = he has the gift of getting on with people.* **11 — de palabra,** (fam.) the gift of the gab: *tiene el don de palabra = he's got the gift of the gab.*

donación *s.f.* **1** donation (bienes dados a una iglesia, etc.). **2** present, gift (regalo). **3** bequest, donation (en un testamento).

donador *s.m.* y *f.* **1** donor (donante). || *adj.* **2** donating.

donaire *s.m.* **1** elegance, grace (elegancia): *escribe con donaire = he writes with elegance.* **2** joke, witticism (chiste). **3** charm (encanto). **4** wit, cleverness (ingenio).

donante *s.m.* **1** donor: *donante de sangre = blood donor.* || *adj.* **2** donating.

donar *v.t.* **1** to donate: *donar sangre = to donate blood.* **2** to give, to grant (dar).

donativo *s.m.* **1** donation. **2** gift, present (regalo). **3** contribution (contribución).

doncel *s.m.* **1** HIST. young nobleman o squire (joven noble). **2** page, pageboy (paje).

doncella *s.f.* **1** HIST. maid, maiden (mujer joven). **2** maid, servant (sirvienta). **3** virgin (virgen).

donde *adv.rel.* **1** where: *fui donde me dijiste = I went where you told me.* || **2 a —,** to where: *fuimos a donde jugaban = we went to where they were playing.* **3 de —,** from: *el país de donde vienen = the country they come from.* **4 en —,** where; in which: *la oficina en donde trabajo = the office where* o *in which I work.* **5 hacia —,** where; to where: *voy hacia donde vive Ana = I'm going to where Ana lives.* **6 hasta —,** as far as: *anduvimos hasta donde el puente = we walked as far as the bridge.* **7 por —, a)** where: *por donde pasa el río = where the river passes;* **b)** through which: *la puerta por donde salí = the door through which I went out.* **8 — no,** otherwise. **9 vayas — vayas,** wherever you go. **10 — quieras,** wherever you want. **11 — sea,** wherever.

dónde *adv.interr.* **1** where?: *¿dónde vives? = where do you live?* || **2 ¿en —?,** where? **3 ¿por —?, a)** where?: *¿por dónde viven? = where do they live?;* **b)** which way? (por qué dirección): *¿por dónde vamos? = which way do we go?;* **c)** why? (por qué). **4 ¿hasta —?,** how far?: *¿hasta dónde tenemos que ir? = how far have we got to go?*

dondequiera, doquiera o **doquier** *adv.* **1** anywhere (en cualquier lugar). **2** everywhere, all over the place (en todas las partes). || **3 — que,** wherever, anywhere: *dondequiera que vayas = wherever you go.*

dondiego *s.m.* **1** BOT. marvel-of-Peru, four o'clock.

donjuán *s.m.* **1** BOT. marvel-of-Peru, four o'clock (dondiego). **2** seducer, womaniser, (fam.) Don Juan, (fam.) Casanova (seductor).

donjuanesco *adj.* donjuanesque.

donjuanismo *s.m.* womanizing, lady-killing, donjuanism.

donosamente *adv.* **1** wittily, amusingly (graciosamente): *escribe donosamente = he writes wittily.* **2** elegantly, gracefully (elegantemente).

donoso, -a *adj.* **1** witty, amusing, funny (divertido): *un comentario donoso = a witty comment.* **2** elegant, graceful (elegante). **3** great, fine (en tono irónico): *¡donosa idea! = that's a great idea!*

donosura *s.f.* **1** humour, wit (gracia). **2** elegance, grace (elegancia).

doña *s.f.* Mrs., (p.u.) madam, (arc.) mistress.

dopar *v.t.* y *r.* to drug, to dope.

doping *s.m.* drugging, doping: *anti-doping = drug test.*

doquier o **doquiera** V. **dondequiera.**

dorado *adj.* **1** golden (de color de oro). **2** TEC. gilt, gilded (con una capa de oro). **3** (fig.) golden: *la edad dorada = the golden age.* || *s.m.* **4** TEC. gilt (capa de oro). **5** TEC. gilding (acción de dorar). **6** dorado (pez).

dorar *v.t.* **1** TEC. to gild (cubrir de oro). **2** to brown (tostar un poco). **3** (fig.) to cloak, to make more palatable, to disguise (disimular lo desagradable): *dorar la píldora = to gild the pill.* || *v.pron.* **4** to turn o go brown (tomar color dorado).

dórico, -a *adj.* ARQ. doric: *orden dórico = doric order.*

dormida *s.f.* **1** sleeping (acción de dormir). **2** (Am.) short sleep, (fam.) nap (siesta).

dormilón, ona *adj.* **1** sleepy, (fam.) sleepy-headed. || *s.m.* y *f.* **2** sleepy-head (persona que duerme demasiado). || *s.f.* **3** earring (pendiente). **4** easy-chair, armchair (sillón).

dormir *v.t.i.* y *pron.* **1** to sleep. || *v.i.* **2** to spend the night, to stay overnight. || *v.pron.* **3** to fall asleep, to go to sleep. **4** to get numb, to go to sleep (un miembro). **5** to neglect one's work, to neglect one's affairs, to neglect one's task: *venga, no te duermas, ponte a trabajar = come on, don't neglect your work, start it again.* || **6 — a pierna suelta,** to sleep soundly. **7 — como un lirón/tronco,** to sleep like a log. **8 — la mona,** to sleep off a hangover. **9 — la siesta,** to have a nap, to have a doze. **10 dormirse en los laureles,** to rest on one's laurels.

dormitar *v.i.* (fam.) to snooze, to doze (estar medio dormido).

dormitorio *s.m.* **1** bedroom (en casa). **2** dormitory (en un colegio, etc.).

dorsal *adj.* **1** back (la parte de atrás). **2** dorsal: *aleta dorsal = dorsal fin.* **3** GRAM. dorsal. || *s.m.* **4** number (el número en la espalda de un atleta): *el atleta con el dorsal número 10 = the athlete wearing the number 10.*

dorso *s.m.* **1** back (espalda o lomo). **2** (fig.) back: *el dorso de la carta = the back of the letter.*

dos *adj.* **1** two: *son las dos = it's two o'clock.* **2** second (segundo): *el dos de junio = the second of June.* || *s.m.* **3** two. || **4 cada — días,** every two days; every other day. **5 cada — por tres,** (fig.) every five minutes: *cambia su coche cada dos por tres = he changes his car every five minutes.* **6 de — en —,** two by two; in

twos. **7 dividir en –,** to divide in o into two. **8 – por – son cuatro,** two times two are four. **9 – veces,** twice. **10 en un – por tres,** (fam.) in a jiffy; (fam.) in a flash; in no time. **11 los –,** both: *han llegado los dos = they've both arrived.*
doscientos *adj.pl.* two hundred: *doscientos mil = two hundred thousand.*
dosel *s.m.* canopy.
dosificar *v.t.* **1** MED. to dose, to measure out (un medicamento). **2** (fig.) to apportion, to measure out.
dosis *s.f.inv.* **1** MED. dose: *en pequeñas dosis = in small doses.* **2** (fig.) dose, dosage, amount (cantidad).
dossier *s.m.* dossier.
dotación *s.f.* **1** endowment (dinero): *dar una dotación = to give an endowment.* **2** MAR. crew (tripulación). **3** staff, personnel (en una oficina, etc.).
dotado, -a *adj.* gifted, talented: *bien dotado = very gifted o talented.*
dotar *v.t.* **1** to give a dowry (dar dote): *sus padres la dotaron con mucho dinero = her parents gave her a lot of money as a dowry.* **2** to endow (aportar dinero para una fundación, etc.). **3** to endow (conceder la naturaleza ciertos dones). **4** to set o fix a salary (fijar un sueldo). **5** to equip (equipar): *dotar un buque = to equip a ship.* **6** to set aside funds for (asignar dinero para premios, etc.). **7** to staff (una oficina, etc.). **8** to man (tripular un barco).
dote *s.f.* **1** dowry (caudal que lleva la mujer al casarse). || *pl.* **2** gift, talent: *tiene dotes para el deporte = he has a gift for sport.*
dovela *s.f.* ARQ. voussoir (cuña de piedra).
dozavo *adj.* y *s.m.* twelfth (doceavo).
dracma *s.f.* drachma (moneda de Grecia).
draconiano, -a *adj.* draconian.
draga *s.f.* **1** dredge (máquina para dragar). **2** dredger (barco).
dragaminas *s.m.* MAR. minesweeper.
dragar *v.t.* **1** to dredge (excavar o limpiar). **2** to sweep (en busca de minas).
drago *s.m.* BOT. dragon tree.
dragón *s.m.* **1** dragon (animal mítico). **2** MIL. dragoon. **3** ZOOL. flying dragon (reptil). **4** BOT. snapdragon (planta). **5** ASTR. dragon (constelación). **6 – marino,** MAR. greater weeven.
dragonear *v.i.* (Am.) to boast, to brag, to show off (alardear).
drama *s.m.* **1** drama. **2** (fig.) drama.
dramática *s.f.* drama, dramatic art.
dramáticamente *adv.* dramatically.
dramático, -a *adj.* dramatic: *una situación dramática = a dramatic situation.*
dramatismo *s.m.* dramatism.
dramatizar *v.t.* to dramatize.
dramaturgia *s.f.* dramatic art.
dramaturgo, -a *s.m.* y *f.* dramatist, playwright.
dramón *s.f.* melodrama.
drástico, -a *adj.* drastic: *medida drástica = drastic measure.*
drenaje *s.m.* AGR. y MED. drainage.
drenar *v.t.* AGR. y MED. to drain, to drain off.
driblar o **driblear** *v.t.* e *i.* DEP. to dribble.
dril *s.m.* drill (tela fuerte).
droga *s.f.* **1** MED. drug. **2** medicine (medicina). **3** (fam.) trick (engaño). **4** (fam.) nuisance, bother, drag (cosa desagradable). **5** (Am.) debt (deuda).
drogadicto, -a *adj./s.m.* y *f.* drug addict.
drogar *v.t.* **1** to drug. **2** DEP. to dope. || *v.pron.* **3** to take drugs.
droguería *s.f.* druggist's, (EE.UU.) drug store.
droguero *s.m.* **1** druggist. **2** (Am.) cheat, swindler (tramposo).
dromedario *s.m.* ZOOL. dromedary.
druida *s.m.* druid.
drupa *s.f.* BOT. drupe.
dual *adj.* **1** dual. || *s.m.* **2** GRAM. dual.
dualidad *s.f.* **1** duality. **2** (Am.) draw (empate).
dubitable *adj.* doubtful, uncertain (dudoso).
dubitación *s.f.* doubt.
dubitativamente *adv.* doubtfully.
dubitativo, -a *adj.* doubtful, dubious.
ducado *s.m.* **1** dukedom (título de duque). **2** duchy (territorio). **3** ducat (moneda antigua).
ducal *adj.* ducal.
dúctil *adj.* **1** MET. soft, malleable, (p.u.) ductile. **2** (fig.) compliant, docile, pliable (dócil).
ductilidad *s.f.* softness, malleability, (p.u.) ductility.
ducha *s.f.* **1** shower: *darse una ducha = to have o take a shower.* **2** MED. douche.
duchar *v.t.* **1** MED. to douche. **2** to give someone a shower (dar una ducha a alguien). **3** to wet, to dowse (mojar). || *v.pron.* **4** to have o to take a shower.
ducho, -a *adj.* experienced, skilful, well versed: *ducho en = skilful at/well versed in/experienced in.*
duda *s.f.* **1** doubt: *sin duda = without doubt.* || **2 entrar en la –,** to begin to have doubts. **3 estar en la –,** to be in doubt. **4 no cabe –,** there is no doubt. **5 no hay –,** there is no doubt. **6 poner algo en –,** to cast doubt on something; to doubt. **7 sacar de dudas a alguien,** to banish o dispel someone's doubts. **8 salir de dudas,** to cast off o shed one's doubts. **9 sin lugar a dudas,** without doubt.
dudar *v.t.* e *i.* **1** to doubt: *no lo dudo = I don't doubt it.* **2** to have doubts, to doubt: *estoy dudando = I'm having doubts.* || **3 – acerca de algo,** to have doubts about something. **4 – de,** to doubt, to question: *no dudo de su habilidad = I don't doubt his ability.* **5 – en,** to hesitate to: *dudo en hacerlo = I hesitate to do it.* **6 – entre dos cosas,** to hesitate between two things. **7 – que,** to doubt whether o if: *dudo que ganemos = I doubt whether we'll win.* **8 – si,** to doubt if: *dudo si llegarán a tiempo = I doubt if they'll arrive on time.*
dudoso, -a *adj.* **1** doubtful, unsure: *la victoria es muy dudosa = the victory is very doubtful.* **2** hesitant, undecided (vacilante). **3** dubious, suspicious (sospechoso). **4** unclear, indecisive (un resultado).
duela *s.f.* stave.
duelo *s.m.* **1** duel (combate entre dos): *batirse en duelo = to fight a duel.* **2** sorrow, grief (dolor). **3** party of mourners (grupo de dolientes). **4** mourning (luto). || **5 sin –,** abundantly: *gastar sin duelo = to spend abundantly/lavishly.*
duende *s.m.* **1** goblin, imp, elf (espíritu travieso). **2** (fig.) imp, mischievous child (niño travieso). || **3 tener –,** to have a magical quality; to have a certain magic.
dueña *s.f.* **1** owner, proprietress (propietaria). **2** landlady (de una pensión, hostal, etc.). **3** owner, mistress (de un animal). **4** mistress, lady: *dueña de la casa = lady of the house.* **5** HIST. lady.
dueño *s.m.* **1** owner, proprietor (propietario). **2** landlord (de un hostal, una pensión, un bar, etc.). **3** head of the household (cabeza de familia). || **4 cambiar de –,** to change hands. **5 hacerse – de,** to take over; to take possession of. **6 ser – de,** to be the owner of; to own. **7 ser – de sí mismo,** to be one's own master (ser libre); to have self-control (dominarse). **8 ser muy – de,** to be free to: *eres muy dueño de venir = you are free to come.*
duermevela *s.m.* (fam.) snooze, nap.
dugongo *s.m.* ZOOL. dugong.
dulce *adj.* **1** sweet: *el postre está muy dulce = the dessert is very sweet.* **2** fresh (agua): *agua fresca = fresh water.* **3** soft (metal). **4** mild, gentle (carácter, clima). **5** soft (sonido, voz, viento). **6** sweet, soft (palabras). || *s.m.* **7** sweet, (EE.UU.) candy (caramelo). || *s.m.pl.* **8** sweets, sweet things (golosinas). || **9 a nadie le amarga un –,** a bit of luck is always welcome. **10 – de almíbar,** preserved fruit.
dulcemente *adv.* **1** sweetly. **2** gently, mildly (de carácter). **3** softly (sonidos, viento, brisa, etc.).
dulcificar *v.t.* **1** to sweeten. **2** (fig.) to soften, to make more gentle (suavizar). || *v.pron.* **3** to turn o become milder (el tiempo o el carácter).
dulía *s.f.* REL. dulia.
dulzaina *s.f.* MUS. dulzaina.
dulzón, -a *adj.* **1** over-sweet, sticky, sickly. **2** (fig.) sickly (persona).
dulzor *s.m.* **1** sweetness, gentleness (del carácter). **2** sweetness (del azúcar, pasteles, etc.).
dulzura *s.f.* **1** sweetness. **2** softness (suavidad). **3** gentleness (bondad). **4** mildness (del clima).
dumping *s.m.* COM. dumping.
duna *s.f.* dune.
dúo *s.m.* MUS. duo, duet.
duodécimo, -a *adj.* twelfth.
duodenal *adj.* MED. duodenal.
duodeno *s.m.* MED. duodenum.

duplicado, -a *adj.* **1** duplicate. **2** double (doblado). || *s.m.* **3** duplicate, copy. **4 por –,** in duplicate.

duplicar *v.t.* **1** to duplicate. **2** to double (multiplicar por dos). **3** DER. to answer (contestar a la réplica). || *v.pron.* **4** to double: *se ha duplicado la contaminación = the pollution has doubled.*

duplicidad *s.f.* duplicity, deceitfulness, (fam.) two-facedness.

duplo *adj.* y *s.m.* double; twice: *diez es el duplo de cinco = ten is double five; ten is twice fice.*

duque *s.m.* duke.

duquesa *s.f.* duchess.

durabilidad *s.f.* durability.

durable *adj.* durable, lasting.

duración *s.f.* **1** duration, length: *la duración de la película es de dos horas = the length of the film is two hours.* **2** life (de una máquina, un coche, un tubo, etc.). || **3 de corta –,** short-lived: *una moda de corta duración = a short-lived fashion.* **4 de larga –,** long-playing (un disco); lenghty (una enfermedad); long (vacaciones). **5 – media de la vida,** average life expectancy.

duradero, -a *adj.* **1** durable, hard-wearing (un vestido, una tela, etc.). **2** lasting (la paz, efectos, etc.).

duramente *adv.* **1** hard: *estudiar duramente = to study hard.* **2** cruelly, harshly (severamente): *en la cárcel le trataron duramente = they treated him harshly in prison.*

durante *prep.* **1** during: *durante el verano = during the summer.* **2** in: *durante la mañana = in the morning.* **3** for: *hemos vivido aquí durante 10 años = we've lived here for 10 years.*

durar *v.i.* **1** to last: *la película duró dos horas = the film lasted two hours.* **2** to stay, to remain (permanecer). **3** to last (ropa): *estos pantalones me han durado mucho tiempo = these trousers have lasted me a long time.* **4** to survive, to last (un recuerdo, efectos, etc.).

durazno *s.m.* BOT. (Am.) **1** peach (el fruto). **2** peach tree (el árbol).

dureza *s.f.* **1** hardness (de metales, de oído, de agua, etc.). **2** toughness (de comida). **3** stale (pan). **4** stiffness (de un cuello, un mecanismo). **5** severity, harshness (severidad). **6** callousness, indifference(insensibilidad).**7**MED.callosity (callosidad).

durmiente *adj.* **1** sleeping: *la bella durmiente del bosque = Sleeping Beauty.* || *s.m.* **2** sleeper (traviesa). **3** sleeper (madero para sostener otros).

duro, -a *adj.* **1** hard: *un trabajo duro = a hard job.* **2** tough (alimentos): *carne dura = tough meat.* **3** stale, old (pan). **4** stiff (un mecanismo, cuello, puerta, articulación, etc.). **5** tough, hard (problema, decisión): *una decisión dura = a tough decision.* **6** tough, harsh, severe (clima). **7** hard (examen, prueba). **8** hardhearted, tough, hard (de carácter). **9** tough, hard (de actitud). **10** tough (un coche, una máquina). **11** hard (agua, luz, sonido): *agua dura = hard water.* **12** hardy, tough, strong (planta, persona de mucho aguante). **13** severe (severo). **14** cruel (cruel). **15** DEP. rough: *juego duro = rough play.* **16** insensitive (insensible). **17** obstinate (obstinado). || **18** hard: *estudiar duro = to study hard.* || *s.m.* **19** five pesetas (cinco pesetas); five-peseta coin (una moneda de cinco pesetas): *estar sin un duro = to be broke o skint.* **20 – de corazón,** hard-hearted. **21 – de roer,** hard to swallow. **22 estar a las duras y a las maduras,** to take the rough with the smooth. **23 hacer algo a duras penas,** to do something with great difficulty. **24 más – que una piedra,** as hard as nails. **25 ser – de mollera,** to be thick o dense (torpe). **26 ser – de oído,** to be hard of hearing. **27 ser – de pelar,** to be a hard nut to crack. **28 tomar las duras con las maduras,** to take the rough with the smooth.

e, E, *s.c.* **1** e, E (sexta letra del alfabeto español). || **2** *conj.* and.
ea! *interj.* come on! (para animar).
ebanista *s.m.* cabinetmaker, joiner.
ebanistería *s.f.* cabinetmaking, joinery.
ébano *s.m.* **1** ebony (madera). **2** ebony (árbol).
ebonita *s.f.* ebonite (caucho endurecido y vulcanizado).
ebriedad *s.f.* drunkenness, intoxication, inebriation.
ebrio, -a *s.m.* y *f.* drunkard, drunk. || **2** *adj.* drunk, inebriated, intoxicated (borracho). **3** (fig.) blind (de ira).
ebullición *s.f.* boiling, ebullition (de un líquido): *punto de ebullición = boiling point.*
ebúrneo, -a *adj.* ivory-like, (lit.) eburnian.
eccehomo *s.m.* **1** REL. ecce homo. **2** (fig.) sorry state.
eccema o **eczema** *s.m.* MED. ecxema.
eclampsia *s.f.* MED. eclampsia.
eclecticismo *s.m.* eclecticism.
ecléctico, -a *adj.* eclectic.
eclesiástico, -a *s.m.* y *f.* **1** REL. clergyman/woman, ecclesiastic (clérico). || **2** *adj.* ecclesiastical, ecclesiastic.
eclipsar *v.t.* **1** ASTR. to eclipse. **2** (fig.) to outshine, to eclipse, to overshadow, to outdo (deslucir).
eclipse *s.m.* **1** ASTR. eclipse. **2** (fam.) eclipse, disappearance.
eclíptica *adj.* ecliptic.
eclosión *s.f.* **1** ZOOL. hatching (de un huevo). **2** BOT. blooming (de una flor). **3** (fig.) appearance (aparición).
eco *s.m.* **1** echo (acústica). **2** distant sound, echo (sonido débil). **3** (fig.) word: *no tenemos eco de él = we haven't had any word from him.*
ecología *s.f.* BIOL. ecology.
ecológico *adj.* ecological.
ecologista *s.m.* y *f.* ecologist.
economato *s.m.* discount store, cash-and-carry.
economía *s.f.* **1** economics (carrera universitaria). **2** economy (de esfuerzo). **3** saving (ahorro): *hice un ahorro de una hora = I made a saving of an hour.* **4** thrift, economy (moderación en los gastos). || **5 hacer economías,** to economize.
económicamente *adv.* economically.
económico, -a *adj.* **1** economic: *Comunidad Económica Europea = European Economic Community.* **2** economic, financial: *crisis económica = financial crisis.* **3** economical: *un coche económico = an economical car.* **4** financial, fiscal: *año económico = fiscal year.*
economista *s.m.* y *f.* economist.
economizar *v.t.* **1** to save, to economize (dinero, tiempo, esfuerzo). || **2** *v.i.* to save, to lay by, to budget: *están economizando para comprarse una casa = they're saving to buy a house.*
ecónomo *s.m.* y *f.* treasurer, burser.
ecosistema *s.m.* ecosystem.
ectoplasma *s.m.* ectoplasm.
ecu *s.m.* ecu (unidad monetaria).
ecuación *s.f.* MAT. equation: *ecuación de segundo grado = quadratic equation.*
ecuador *s.m.* **1** Equator. **2** GEOG. Ecuador (el país). **3** (fam.) halfway point (en un curso de estudios).
ecuatorial *adj.* equatorial.
ecuánime *adj.* **1** impartial, unbiased, unprejudiced, fair (imparcial). **2** composed, calm, cool-headed, collected (equilibrado).
ecuanimidad *s.f.* **1** impartiality, fairness (justicia). **2** composure, (lit.) equanimity (serenidad).
ecuatoriano, -a *adj./s.m.* y *f.* Ecuadorian, Ecuadorean.
ecuestre *adj.* equestrian.
ecuménico, -a *adj.* ecumenical, oecumenical.
ecumenismo *s.m.* ecumenicalism, oecumenicalism, ecumenism, oecumenism.
eczema *s.m.* MED. ecxema.
echado, -a **1** *p.p.* de **echar.** **2** *adj.* lying down, prone, prostrate (tumbado). **3** (fam.) bold, fearless (echado para adelante).
echar *v.t.* e *i.* **1** to throw (arrojar). **2** to give off (un olor, etc.). **3** to put (poner). **4** to pour (agua, etc.). **5** to post (una carta). **6** to add (añadir): *añadir sal = to add salt.* **7** MAR. to cast (redes, anclas, anzuelos). **8** to throw out (a alguien de un sitio). **9** to sack (despedir de un trabajo). **10** BOT. to sprout (hojas y raíces). **11** to grow (pelo). **12** to spread (mantequilla, etc.). **13** to put on, to apply (el freno). **14** to hurl (blasfemias). **15** to play (una partida). **16** to add up (una cuenta). **17** to put to bed (a un niño). || *v.pron.* **18** to throw oneself (arrojarse). **19** to lie down (tumbarse). || **20 – a la calle,** to turn out. **21 – a llorar,** to begin to cry. **22 – a perder,** to spoil; to ruin. **23 – atrás,** to set back. **24 – a volar,** to take wing; to fly away. **25 – barriga,** to get a potbelly; to put on weight. **26 – de menos,** to miss. **27 – los dientes,** to teethe. **28 echarse a perder,** to go bad. **29 echarse atrás,** to throw oneself back (para evitar algo). **30 – una mirada,** to have a look. **31 – una multa,** to impose a fine.
echarpe *s.m.* shawl.
echazón *s.f.* **1** throw (acción). **2** MAR. jettison.
edad *s.f.* **1** age: *a la edad de catorce años = at the age of fourteen.* **2** age (época). || **3 – Media,** Middle Ages. **4 de –,** elderly. **5 mayor –,** to come of age. **6 menor –,** minority, infancy, childhood. **6 ¿qué edad tienes?,** how old are you?
edecán *s.m.* aide-de-camp.
edelweiss *s.m.* BOT. edelweiss.
edema *s.f.* MED. edema, oedema.
edén *s.m.* REL. Eden.
edición *s.f.* edition (de un libro, revista, etc.).
edicto *s.m.* decree, edict.

edificación *s.f.* building, construction.
edificador *s.m.* y *f.* 1 builder, constructor. 2 *adj.* building, constructing.
edificante *adj.* edifying.
edificar *v.t.* to build, to construct.
edificativo, -a *adj.* edifying.
edificatorio, -a *adj.* building, construction.
edificio *s.m.* building, edifice.
edil *s.m.* 1 aedile, edile (magistrado romano). 2 town councillor.
editar *v.t.* to publish.
editor, -ora *s.m.* o *f.* 1 publisher (persona). || 2 *adj.* publishing.
editorial *adj.* 1 publishing, editorial. || *s.m.* 2 leading article, editorial. || 3 *s.f.* publishing house.
edredón *s.m.* eiderdown, duvet.
educación *s.f.* 1 education (enseñanza). 2 upbringing (crianza). 3 manners, politeness (modales).
educado, -a *adj.* 1 educated. || 2 **bien –,** well-mannered, polite. 3 **mal –,** bad-mannered, rude.
educador, -a *s.m.* y *f.* 1 educator, teacher. || *adj.* 2 educating, teaching.
educando, -a *s.m.* y *f.* pupil, student.
educar *v.t.* 1 to educate. 2 to bring up (criar). 3 to train, to educate (el oído, los miembros, etc.).
edulcorante *s.m.* sweetener, sweetening.
edulcorar *v.t.* to sweeten.
efe *s.f.* f. (letra).
efebo *s.m.* ephebe (de gran belleza).
efectismo *s.m.* sensationalism (en el arte y la literatura).
efectista *adj.* sensationalist.
efectivamente *adv.* 1 really, in fact (en realidad). 2 Indeed, of course (por supuesto).
efectividad *s.f.* effectiveness.
efectivo, -a *adj.* 1 effective. 2 real (verdadero). || *s.m.* 3 cash, ready money (dinero efectivo). || 4 **hacer –,** to cash (un cheque). 5 **hacerse –,** to take effect, to come into effect.
efecto *s.m.* 1 effect, result (resultado). 2 effect, impact, impression (impresión). 3 spin (picado): *dar efecto a una pelota = to put a spin on a ball.* 4 ART. trompe-l'oeil. || *pl.* 5 goods (mercancías). 6 effects, belongings (cosas personales). 7 effects, possesions, property (bienes). || 8 **llevar a –,** to carry out. 9 **tener –, a)** to take effect, to come/go into effect/operation (entrar en vigor); **b)** to take place (celebrarse).
efectuar *v.t.* 1 to effect, to carry out, to do (una operación). 2 to make (una visita, un aterrizaje, una detención). || *v.i.* 3 to take place (celebrarse).
efemérides *f.pl.* 1 ASTR. ephemerides. 2 ephemeris (arc.), diary (diario).
efervescencia *s.f.* 1 effervescence. 2 (fig.) excitement, agitation.
efervescente *adj.* 1 effervescent. 2 bubbly (bebidas).
eficacia *s.f.* 1 effectiveness, efficacy (de cosas). 2 efficiency (de personas).
eficaz *adj.* 1 efficient, effective. 2 efficient (de una persona o máquina).
eficazmente *adv.* efficiently.
eficiencia *s.f.* efficiency.
eficiente *adj.* efficient.
efigie *s.f.* effigy, image.
efímero, -a *adj.* ephemeral.
efluvio *s.m.* (lit.) effluvium, exhalation.
efusión *s.f.* 1 effusion. 2 bloodshed (de sangre).
efusivo, -a *adj.* 1 effusive. 2 GEOL. effusive, extrusive.
egipcio, -a *adj./s.m.* y *f.* Egyptian.
egiptología *s.f.* Egyptology.
egiptólogo, -a *s.m.* y *f.* Egyptologist.
égloga *s.f.* eclogue.
egocéntrico, -a *adj.* egocentric, self-centered.
egocentrismo *s.m.* egocentrism, egocentricity, self-centeredness.
egoísmo *s.m.* selfishness, egoism, egotism.
egoísta *adj.* 1 selfish, egoistic, egotistic. || *s.m.* y *f.* 2 egoist, egotist, selfish person.
ególatra *adj.* self-worshipping, self-lauding.
egolatría *s.f.* self-worship.
egregio, -a *adj.* illustrious, eminent.
egresado, -a *s.m.* y *f.* graduate.
egresar *v.i.* (Am.) to pass out (de una academia militar).
egreso *s.m.* (Am.) 1 passing out (de una academia militar). 2 graduation (de la universidad).
¡eh! *interj.* 1 eh!, hey! (para llamar la atención). 2 O.K.?, all right?, understood? (que no vuelva a ocurrir).
eje *s.m.* 1 TEC. axle (de una rueda). 2 shaft (árbol). 3 MAT. y FIS. axis. 4 (fig.) hub, core, crux (de un argumento).
ejecución *s.f.* 1 execution, carrying-out (de un proyecto). 2 execution (de un condenado). 3 MUS. performance, interpretation. || 4 **pelotón de –,** firing squad. 5 **poner en –,** to carry out.
ejecutante *s.m.* y *f.* 1 executant (el que lleva a cabo un plan). 2 MUS. performer.
ejecutar *v.t.* 1 to execute, to carry out (un proyecto). 2 to execute (a un condenado). 3 MUS. to perform, to interpret.
ejecutivo, -a *s.m.* y *f.* y *adj.* executive.
ejecutor, -ora *s.m.* y *f.* 1 executant, executor. 2 executioner (de la justicia).
ejecutoria *s.f.* 1 letters, patent of nobility. 2 writ of execution.
ejemplar *adj.* 1 exemplary: *conducta ejemplar = exemplary behaviour.* || *s.m.* 2 number, issue, copy (de una revista, periódico). 3 specimen, example (de una flor).
ejemplaridad *s.f.* exemplariness.
ejemplarizar o **ejemplificar** *v.t.* to exemplify, to illustrate.
ejemplificación *s.f.* exemplification, illustration.
ejemplo *s.m.* 1 example: *un diccionario sin ejemplos es inútil = a dictionary without examples is useless.* 2 epitome, model: *es un ejemplo de la mala educación = he is the epitome of bad manners.* || 3 **dar –,** to set an example. 4 **por –,** for example. 5 **tomar – de alguien,** to follow someone's example; to take a leaf out of someone's book.
ejercer *v.t.* e *i.* 1 to exert (poder). 2 to exercise (ejercitar). 3 to exercise, to use (la autoridad). 4 to practise: *ejercer la medicina = to practise medicine.*
ejercicio *s.m.* 1 exercise (físico, de un derecho, de latín). 2 exertion (de una influencia/poder). 3 performance (de una función). 4 MIL. training, drill, exercise, practice. || 5 **en –,** practising: *un médico en ejercicio = a practising doctor.*
ejercitación *s.f.* 1 practice (de una profesión). 2. exercise (de la autoridad).
ejercitante *adj.* training.
ejercitar *v.t.* 1 to practise (una profesión). 2 MIL. to drill, to train. || *v.pron.* 3 to train, to practise.
ejército *s.m.* 1 army. || 2 **– del Aire,** The Air Force.
ejido *s.m.* common (de un pueblo).
el *art.def.m.sing.* 1 the: *el libro = the book.* 2 the one: *el de Hong Kong = the one from Hong Kong.* 3 el de usted, yours. 4 his: *le duele el brazo = his arm hurts.*
él *pron.pers.m.sing.* 1 he: *él está aquí = he is here.* 2 him: *cené con él = I had dinner with him.*
elaboración *s.f.* 1 processing (de una materia prima). 2 working (de metal, madera). 3 production, manufacture (de un producto).
elaborar *v.t.* 1 to process (materia prima). 2 to work (metal, madera). 3 to produce, to manufacture (un producto). 4 to prepare, to work out (un proyecto).
elación *s.f.* arrogance, haughtiness.
elasticidad *s.f.* 1 elasticity. 2 stretch (de un material). 3 (fig.) flexibility, elasticity (de un horario).
elástica *s.f.* (Am.) vest.
elástico, -a *adj.* 1 elastic (en general). 2 stretchy, elastic (de materiales). 3 (fig.) flexible, elastic (de un horario, etc.)
ele *s.f.* 1 l (letra).
elección *s.f.* 1 choice, selection: *la elección de un tema = the choice of a subject.* 2 choice, alternative (posibilidad de elegir). 3 election (de un presidente): *presentarse a una elección = to stand for election.*
electivo, -a *adj.* elective.
electo, -a *adj.* 1 elect: *el presidente electo = the president elect.*
elector, -a *adj.* 1 elective. || *s.m.* y *f.* 2 POL. elector, voter.
electorado *s.m.* POL. electorate, electoral body, voters (pl.).
electoral *adj.* POL. electoral: *censo electoral = electoral roll.*
electricidad *s.f.* electricity.
electricista *adj.* 1 electrical: *ingeniero electricista = electrical engineer.* || *s.m.* y *f.* 2 electrician.
eléctrico, -a *adj.* 1 electric, electrical. || *s.m.* 2 electrician (electricista).
electrificación *s.f.* electrification.

electrificar *v.t.* to electrify.
electrizable *adj.* electrifiable.
electrización *s.f.* electrification.
electrizador, -a *adj.* electrifying.
electrizante *adj.* electrifying.
electrizar *v.t.* **1** to electrify, to charge (cargar de electricidad). **2** (fig.) to electrify: *electrizar una audiencia = to electrify an audience.*
electrocutar *v.t.* **1** to electrocute. ‖ *v.pron.* **2** to be electrocuted.
electrodo *s.m.* FIS. electrode.
electrodoméstico *s.m.* household appliance.
electroimán *s.m.* FIS. electromagnet.
electrólisis *s.f.* QUIM. electrolysis.
electrolítico, -a *adj.* QUIM. electrolytic.
electrólito *s.m.* QUIM. electrolyte.
electrolizar *v.t.* to electrolyze.
electrón *s.m.* FIS. electron.
electrónica *s.f.* electronics.
electrónico, -a *adj.* **1** electronic. ‖ **2 microscopio –,** electron microscope.
electroquímica *s.f.* QUIM. electrochemistry.
elefancía *s.f.* MED. elefantiasis.
elefante *s.m.* **1** ZOOL. elephant. ‖ **2** (fig.) **– blanco,** white elephant. **3 – marino,** elephant seal/sea elephant.
elefantiasis *s.f.* MED. elefantiasis.
elegancia *s.f.* elegance, style.
elegante *adj.* **1** elegant, smart, stylish. ‖ *s.m.* **2** man about town; man of fashion. ‖ *s.f.* **3** fashionable woman.
elegía *s.f.* elegy.
elegiaco, -a o **elegíaco, -a** *adj.* elegiac.
elegibilidad *s.f.* eligibility.
elegible *adj.* eligible.
elegido, -a *adj.* **1** chosen. **2** favourite, preferred (predilecto). **3** select, choice (selecto). ‖ *s.m.* y *f.* **4** elected person, the one chosen. ‖ *pl.m.* **5** the elect.
elegir *v.t.* **1** to choose, to select. **2** POL. to elect (por voto).
elemental *adj.* **1** elementary: *eso es elemental = that's elementary.* **2** basic, elementary (nivel). **3** FIS. elemental (de los elementos).
elemento *s.m.* **1** element (parte de una cosa). **2** MEC. part, component (de una máquina). **3** section, unit (muebles). **4** member (de un tribunal, equipo). **5** ingredient (ingrediente). **6** (fig. y fam.) individual, type, character: *es un elemento raro = he's a strange character.* **7** (fig.) factor: *es un elemento a tomar en cuenta = it is a factor to be taken into consideration.* **8** MAT. element. **9** QUIM. y BIOL. element. **10** FIS. cell (de una batería). ‖ *pl.m.* **11** basic principles: *los elementos de la matemática = the basic principles of mathematics.* **12** means (medios). ‖ **13 el líquido –, a)** the sea (mar); **b)** water (agua). **14** (fig.) estar en su elemento, to be in one's element.
elenco *s.m.* **1** catalogue, list. **2** cast (reparto); troupe, company (compañía).
elevación *s.f.* **1** raising, lifting (peso). **2** building, erection (edificio). **3** increase, rise (precio). **4** REL. elevation.
elevado, -a *adj.* **1** high (edificio, precio). **2** high, elevated (categoría, etc.). **3** high, grand (estilo). ‖ **– a,** MAT. (raised) to the power of: *diez elevado a dos es cien = ten (raised) to the power of two is a hundred.*
elevador, -ora *adj.* **1** elevating. ‖ *s.m.* **2** lift, (Am.) elevator (ascensor). **3** ELEC. step-up transformer (transformador).
elevar *v.t.* **1** to raise, to lift (un peso). **2** to build, to put up (un edificio, etc.). **3** to raise, to increase, to put up (precios). **4** to raise (la voz). **5** MAT. to raise to the power of: *elevar a la enésima potencia = to raise to the power of n.* ‖ *v.pron.* to be conceited (envanecerse).
elidir *v.t.* **1** to weaken. **2** GRAM. to elide (suprimir la vocal final de una palabra cuando la siguiente empieza con otra vocal).
eliminación *s.f.* **1** elimination, removal. ‖ **2 – progresiva,** DEP. knock-out.
eliminador, -ora *adj.* eliminating.
eliminar *v.t.* **1** to eliminate, to remove (suprimir). **2** DEP. to eliminate, to knock out. **3** to kill, (fam.) to get rid of (matar).
eliminatorio, -a *adj.* **1** eliminatory: *un examen eliminatorio = an eliminatory exam.* ‖ *s.f.* **2** DEP. heat, qualifying round. ‖ **3 competición –,** DEP. knockout competition.
elipse *s.f.* MAT. elipse.
elipsis *s.f.* GRAM. ellipsis.
elíptico, -a *adj.* eliptic, eliptical.
elisión *s.f.* GRAM. elision (pérdida de una vocal final en contacto con la vocal inicial de la palabra siguiente).
elite o **élite** *s.f.* elite.
elixir o **elíxir** *s.m.* elixir.
elocución *s.f.* elocution.
elocuencia *s.f.* eloquence.
elocuente *adj.* **1** eloquent. **2** telling, significant: *un dato elocuente = a significant fact.*
elocuentemente *adv.* eloquently.
elogiable *adj.* commendable, praiseworthy.
elogiar *v.t.* to praise: *una actuación muy elogiada = a highly praised performance.*
elogio *s.m.* praise, (lit.) eulogy: *está por encima de todo elogio = he is beyond all praise.*
elogioso, -a *adj.* (lit.) eulogistic.
elongación *s.f.* ASTR. y MED. elongation.
elucidar *v.t.* to explain, to elucidate.
eludible *adj.* avoidable, eludible.
eludir *v.t.* to avoid, to evade, to elude: *eludió la pregunta = she avoided the question.*
ella *pron.pers.f.s.* **1** she (sujeto, personas): *ella me miró = she looked at me.* **2** her (con *prep.*, personas): *le miré a ella = I looked at her.* ‖ **3 – misma,** herself. **4 mañana será –,** there will be trouble tomorrow.
elle *s.f.* ll (letra).
ello *pron.pers. neutro.* **1** it: *no tiene fuerzas para ello = he is not strong enough for it.* ‖ **2 ¡a por ello!,** let's go for it! (nosotros); go for it! (tu).
ellos, ellas *pron.pers.pl.* **1** they (sujeto): *ellos vinieron = they came.* **2** them (complemento): *¡díselo a ellos! = tell it to them!* **3 ellos mismos o ellas mismas,** themselves.
emanación *s.f.* emanation.
emanar *v.i.* **1** to emanate from, to come from: *el olor emana de la fábrica = the smell comes from the factory.* **2** to arise from, to result from: *el problema emana de la falta de entendimiento = the problem arises from the lack of understanding.*
emancipación *s.f.* emancipation.
emancipador, -a *adj.* **1** emancipatory. ‖ *s.m.* y *f.* **2** emancipator.
emancipar *v.t.* **1** to emancipate. ‖ *v.pron.* **2** to become emancipated, to free oneself (liberarse).
emasculación *s.f.* to castrate, (fig.) to emasculate.
emascular *v.t.* to castrate, (fig.) to emasculate.
embadurnar *v.t.* **1** to daub (con pintura). **2** to smear (con grasa). **3** to plaster (con barro). ‖ *v.pron.* **4** to daub oneself (con pintura). **5** to smear oneself (con grasa). **6** to plaster oneself (con barro).
embajada *s.f.* **1** embassy. **2** ambassadorship (función del embajador). **3** errand (recado). **4** message (mensaje).
embajador, -a *s.m.* y *f.* ambassador (hombre), ambassadress (mujer).
embalador, -a *s.m.* y *f.* packer, packager.
embalaje *s.m.* **1** packing, packaging. ‖ **2 papel de –,** wrapping paper.
embalar *v.t.* **1** to package, to pack (mercancías, etc.). **2** to wrap up, to parcel up (regalos). **3** MEC. to rev (un motor). ‖ *v.i.* **4** MEC. to race (un motor). ‖ *v.pron.* **5** MEC. to race (un motor). **6** DEP. to sprint (correr). **7** to chatter, (fam.) to gabble (hablar de prisa). **8** to get excited (entusiasmarse).
embaldosado, -a *adj.* **1** tiled. ‖ *s.m.* **2** tiled floor (suelo).
embaldosar *v.t.* to tile (con baldosas).
embalsadero *s.m.* bog, quagmire
embalsamar *v.t.* **1** to embalm (un cadáver). **2** to perfume, to scent (perfumar).
embalsamiento *s.m.* **1** embalming (de un cadáver). **2** perfuming, scenting (perfume).
embalsar *v.t.* **1** to dam up, to dam (agua). **2** MAR. to hoist (izar). ‖ **3** *v.pron.* to be dammed up.
embalse *s.m.* **1** dam (presa). **2** reservoir, dam (lago artificial). **3** collecting (de una cantidad de agua).
embarcarse *v.pron.* **1** MAR. to run aground (encallarse). **2** (Am.) to silt up (cegarse un río o lago). **3** (Am.) TEC. to adhere to the furnace walls (en la fundición de metales, pegarse a las paredes del horno).
embarazada *adj.f.* **1** pregnant: *estar embarazada de tres meses = to be three months pregnant.* ‖ **2 quedarse –,** to get o become pregnant. **3 dejar a una mujer –,** to get a woman pregnant.

embarazar *v.t.* **1** to get a woman pregnant (dejar a una mujer embarazada). **2** to hamper, to hinder (impedir el desenvolvimiento de alguien o alguna cosa). **3** to trouble, to inconvenience (molestar). || *v.pron.* **4** to get embarassed (avergonzarse). **5** to get blocked (obstruirse). **6** to get o become pregnant (quedarse embarazada).

embarazo *s.m.* **1** hindrance (estorbo). **2** obstacle, obstruction (obstáculo). **3** MED. pregnancy.

embarcación *s.f.* **1** boat, craft: *embarcación de pesca = fishing boat.* **2** embarkation (embarco).

embarcadero *s.m.* **1** MAR. landing stage (plataforma). **2** quay, jetty (muelle para viajeros). **3** dock, wharf (muelle para mercancías).

embarcar *v.t.* **1** to embark (pasajeros). **2** to load (mercancías). **3** to involve: *embarcar a alguien en un negocio = to involve someone in business.* || *v.pron.* **4** to embark, to go aboard (un pasajero).

embarco *s.m.* embarkation (de pasajeros).

embargar *v.t.* **1** DER. to seize, to impound, to distrain (retener). **2** to hinder, to hamper (estorbar).

embargo *s.m.* **1** DER. seizure, distraint. **2** MAR. embargo. || **3 sin –,** still, however, (p.u.) none the less.

embarrado, -a *adj.* **1** muddy (un sitio). **2** covered in mud, (fam.) plastered with mud (una persona).

embarrancar *v.i.* **1** MAR. to go o run aground (encallarse). **2** (fig.) to get bogged down. || *v.pron.* **3** MAR. to go/run aground. **4** (fig.) to get stuck, to get bogged down (atascarse).

embarrar *v.t.* **1** to cover/splash with mud (salpicar de barro). || *v.pron.* **2** to get covered in mud (llenarse de barro). **3** to take refuge in the trees (perdices).

embarrilar *v.t.* to barrel, to cask.

embarullar o **embarrullar** *v.t.* **1** to mix up (enredar). **2** to do in a slapdash manner, (fam.) to bodge (chapucear).

embate *s.m.* **1** MAR. dashing, breaking (de olas). **2** (fig.) sudden attack (acometida).

embaucador, -a *adj.* **1** deceiving, deceptive (que engaña). || *s.m.* y *f.* **2** trickster, swindler (timador).

embaucamiento *s.m.* deception, deceit, cheating (engaño).

embaucar *v.t.* to deceive, to cheat (engañar).

embaular *v.tr.* to pack (en un baúl).

embebecer *v.t.* **1** to entertain, to delight (embelesar). || *v.pron.* **2** to be delighted, to be fascinated.

embebecimiento *s.m.* delight, fascination.

embeber *v.t.* **1** to absorb, to soak up (una esponja). **2** to soak, to drench (empapar). **3** to insert (encajar). **4** to contain (contener). || *v.i.* **5** to shrink (encogerse una tela). || *v.pron.* **6** to become absorbed in something: *se embebió en la película = he became absorbed in the film.*

embelecar *v.t.* to deceive, to cheat.

embeleco *s.m.* deceit, deception (engaño).

embelesamiento *s.m.* V. **embebecimiento.**

embelesar *v.t.* V. **embebecer.**

embellecedor, -ora *adj.* **1** beautifying (cosmética). || *s.m.* **2** MEC. hubcap (tapacubos).

embellecer *v.t.* **1** to embellish, to beautify, to adorn. || *v.i.* **2** to improve in looks (de forma natural). || *v.pron.* **3** to beautify oneself (adornarse).

emberrenchinarse o **emberrencharse** *v.pron.* (fam.) to fly off the handle, to fly into a tantrum (enfadarse con demasía).

embestida *s.f.* **1** assault, attack. **2** charge (de un toro).

embestir *v.t.* **1** to assault, to attack. **2** to charge (un toro). | **3 – a uno,** (fig. y fam.) to pester someone for a loan (importunar a uno para pedirle algo).

emblandecer *v.t.* **1** to soften (ablandar). || *v.pron.* **2** to soften up, to relent (enternecerse).

emblema *s.m.* **1** emblem. **2** badge (insignia, chapa).

emblemático, -a *adj.* emblematic.

embobamiento *s.m.* **1** amazement, fascination. **2** stupefaction, bewilderment (estupefacción).

embobar *v.t.* **1** to amaze, to dumbfound (atontar). || *v.pron.* **2** to be stupefied o fascinated (quedarse absorto).

embobecer *v.t.* to go o turn silly.

embocadura *s.m.* **1** GEOG. mouth, entrance (de un río, etc.). **2** taste (de vino). **3** bit (freno de caballo). **4** proscenium arch (boca de escenario de un teatro). **5** MUS. mouthpiece (de un instrumento).

embocar *v.t.* **1** to put in the mouth (meter en la boca). **2** to make someone believe (engañar). **3** to bolt, (fam.) to wolf (engullir). || *v.pron.* **4** to squeeze in (meterse en un sitio estrecho).

embolia *s.f.* MED. clot, embolism (obstrucción de un vaso sanguíneo).

embolismo *s.m.* **1** muddle, mess, confusion (barullo, confusión). **2** trick (embuste).

émbolo *s.m.* MEC. piston.

embolsar *v.t.* **1** to collect, (fam.) to pocket (cobrar). **2** to put into ones pocket, to pocket (meter en el bolsillo).

emboquillado *adj.* tipped, filter-tipped (cigarrillos).

emboquillar *v.t.* **1** to tip, to filter-tip (cigarrillo). **2** MIN. to open up (un túnel, una galería).

emborrachar *v.t.* **1** to get o make someone drunk (emborrachar a alguien). || *v.pron.* **2** to get drunk, (vulg.) to get pissed: *emborracharse con vino = to get drunk on wine.*

emborrascar *v.pron.* to become stormy (el tiempo).

emborronar *v.t.* **1** to scribble (escribir rápido y mal). **2** to scribble on (llenar de garabatos). **3** to blot (hacer un borrón).

emboscada *s.f.* ambush: *tender una emboscada = to lay an ambush.*

emboscar *v.t.* **1** MIL. to place under cover/in ambush. || *v.pron.* **2** MIL. to lie in ambush, to ambush

embotar *v.t.* **1** to blunt, (p.u.) to dull (quitar el filo). **2** (fig.) to dull, to deaden (los sentidos). || *v.pron.* **3** to become blunt (perder el filo).

embotellado, -a *adj.* bottled.

embotellamiento *s.m.* **1** bottling (en botellas). || **2** embotellamiento de coches, traffic jam.

embotellar *v.t.* **1** to bottle (en botellas). **2** MIL. to bottle up (no dejar salir). **3** to immobilize (inmovilizar).

embozar *v.t.* **1** to cover the lower part of one's face. **2** to muzzle (poner el bozal a los animales).

embozo *s.m.* **1** fold, flap (de una capa). **2** (fig.) disguise (disfraz). || **3** (fig.) **quitarse el –,** to take off the mask.

embragar *v.t.* MEC. to engage (el embrague).

embrague *s.m.* MEC. clutch: *embrague hidráulico = hidraulic clutch.*

embravecer *v.t.* **1** to enfuriate, to enrage (enfurecer). || *v.i.* **2** to flourish, to grow well (las plantas). || *v.pron.* **3 a)** to get rough (mar); **b)** to get furious (persona).

embrear *v.t.* **1** to tar, to cover with tar o pitch (untar con brea). || **2 – y emplumar a alguien,** to far and feather someone.

embriagar *v.t.* **1** to get someone drunk, to intoxicate (emborrachar). **2** (fig.) to enrapture, to delight (enajenar). || *v.pron.* **3** to get drunk (emborracharse).

embridar *v.t.* **1** DEP. to bridle (poner la brida). **2** DEP. to make a horse carry its head well (hacer que los caballos muevan con garbo la cabeza).

embriología *s.f.* BIOL. embryology.

embrión *s.m.* **1** BIOL. embryo. **2** (fig.) embryo (principio).

embrollar *v.t.* **1** to muddle, to mix up, to tangle (enmarañar). **2** to confuse, to mix up (confundir). **3** to involve (en un asunto). || *v.pron.* **4** to get mixed up, to get tangled o muddled (enmarañarse). **5** to get confused, to get in a muddle (confundirse). **6** to get involved (en un asunto).

embrollo o **embrolla** *s.m.* o *f.* **1** tangle (de hilo, etc.). **2** muddle, mess, confusion (confusión). **3** trick, lie (embuste).

embromar *v.t.* **1** to make fun of, to tease (burlarse de). **2** to fool, to trick (engañar). **3** (Am.) to annoy (fastidiar). **4** to damage (perjudicar).

embrujar *v.t.* **1** to cast a spell on, to bewitch (una persona). **2** to haunt (un sitio).

embrujo *s.m.* **1** bewitchment (embrujamiento). **2** curse, spell (maleficio). **3** spell, charm (encanto).

embrutecer *v.tr.* to brutalize, to bestialize.
embuchado *s.m.* sausage (embutido).
embuchar *v.t.* **1** to force-feed (un ave). **2** to stuff with sausage meat (para hacer embutidos). **3** to bolt, to gulp down (engullir).
embudo *s.m.* **1** funnel (para trasvasar líquidos). **2** (fig.) trick (engaño). **3** fraud (fraude).
embullo *s.m.* (Am.) bustle, noise, revelry.
embuste *s.m.* **1** trinket (joyas de escaso valor). **2** trick (engaño).
embustero, -a *adj.* **1** deceitful (engañoso). **2** lying (mentiroso). || *s.m.* y *f.* **3** liar (mentiroso).
embutido *s.m.* **1** sausage. **2** stuffing (acción de embutir). **3** TEC. inlay, marquetry (taracea).
embutir *v.t.* **1** to stuff with sausage meat (hacer embutidos). **2** to stuff o cram (meter una cosa en otra y apretar). **3** to bolt, to gulp down, (fam.) to scoff (engullir). **4** TEC. to inlay (taracea). || *v.pron.* **5** (fam.) to stuff oneself with (atiborrarse).
eme *s.f.* m (letra).
emergencia *s.f.* **1** emergency (ocurrencia que sobreviene). **2** emergence (acción de emerger). || **3 salida de –,** emergency exit.
emergente *adj.* **1** (fig.) resulting, resultant, consequent (que resulta). **2** emergente (que emerge).
emerger *v.t.* **1** to emerge (de un líquido). **2** to come into view, to emerge, to appear (aparecer). **3** MAR. to surface (submarino). **4** (fig.) to result.
emérito, -a *adj.* retired, (p.u.) emeritus.
emético, -a *adj.* y *s.m.* MED. emetic (que provoca el vómito).
emétrope *adj.* MED. emmetropic (de vista normal).
emigración *s.f.* **1** emigration. **2** migration (de un pueblo, de aves, etc.).
emigrado, -a *s.m.* y *f.* **1** emigrant. **2** political exile (exiliado).
emigrante *s.m.* emigrant.
emigrar *v.t.* **1** to emigrate. **2** to migrate (de un pueblo, de aves, etc.).
eminencia *s.f.* **1** GEOG. height, eminence. **2** (fig.) eminence, prominence. || **3 su –,** Your Eminence (de Usted); His Eminence (de El).
eminente *adj.* **1** eminent, distinguished, prominent (distinguido). **2** high, lofty (alto).
eminentemente *adv.* eminently.
eminentísimo, -a *adj.* most eminent.
emir *s.m.* emir (príncipe árabe).
emirato *s.m.* emirate.
emisario, -a *s.m.* y *f.* emissary, messenger (mensajero).
emisión *s.f.* **1** emission. **2** RAD. transmission, broadcasting (acción de emitir); broadcast (programa). **3** issue (de monedas, sellos, etc.). || **4 – publicitaria,** commercial o publicity spot. **5 la – de la mañana,** the morning broadcast.
emisor, -a *adj.* **1** issuing: *banco emisor = issuing bank.* **2** RAD. transmitter: *centro emisor = transmitter, broadcasting station.* || *s.m.* **3** RAD. transmitter (aparato). **4** RAD. station (radar). || *s.f.* **5** RAD. transmitter, radio station, broadcasting station. **6** RAD. **emisor receptor,** walkie talkie.
emitir *v.t.* **1** to emit (sonido, luz). **2** to give off (olor). **3** RAD. to broadcast, to transmit: *emitir en onda corta = to broadcast on short wave.* **4** to issue (poner en circulación monedas, sellos, etc.). **5** (fig.) to express, to give (una opinión). || *v.pron.* **6** RAD. to transmit.
emoción *s.f.* **1** emotion (sentimiento). **2** exitement, thrill: *¡qué emoción! = what a thrill/how exciting!*
emocionado, -a *adj.* **1** moved, touched (conmovido). **2** upset (perturbado).
emocional *adj.* emotional.
emocionante *adj.* **1** moving, touching (conmovedor). **2** exciting, thrilling (que entusiasma).
emocionar *v.t.* **1** to move, to touch (conmover): *me emocionó su historia = his story moved me.* **2** to excite, to thrill (entusiasmar): *la velocidad emociona = speed thrills.* **3** to upset (perturbar). || *v.pron.* **4** to be moved, to be touched: *se emocionó por la carta = he was moved by the letter.* **5** to be o get excited (entusiasmarse).
emoliente *adj.* y *s.m.* MED. emollient (para ablandar una dureza o tumor).
emolumento *s.m.* emolument.
emotivo, -a *adj.* **1** emotional (que se emociona con facilidad). **2** emotive (que causa emoción). **3** moving, touching (conmovedor).
empacamiento *s.m.* (Am.) packing (embalaje).
empacar *v.t.* **1** to pack (empaquetar). **2** to bale (paja, algodón, etc.). || *v.pron.* **3** (Am.) to get stubborn o obstinate (obstinarse). **4** to talk, to shy (plantarse un caballo). **5** to get confused (turbarse).
empachar *v.t.* **1** MED. to give indigestion (causar indigestión). **2** to stop up, to clog (atascar). **3** to embarrass (hacer pasar un apuro). || *v.pron.* **4** MED. to have indigestion. **5** (fig.) to get confused /mixed up (turbarse). **6** to be embarrassed (avergonzarse).
empacho *s.m.* **1** MED. indigestion. **2** (fig.) embarrassment, shame (vergüenza). || **3 tener un empacho de,** to have one's fill of.
empachoso, -a *adj.* **1** heavy, indigestable (comida). **2** (fig.) troublesome, annoying (pesado). **3** embarrassing, shameful (vergonzoso).
empadrarse *v.pron.* PSIC. to become excessively attatched to one's father o parents (encariñarse excesivamente con el padre o los padres).
empadronamiento *s.m.* **1** census, register (censo). **2** enrolment (acción de empadronar o empadronarse).
empadronar *v.t.* **1** to take a census of, to register in a census o electoral roll (inscribir en un censo). || **2** *v.pron.* to have one's name registered on the electoral roll o census.
empajar *v.t.* **1** to cover with straw (cubrir con paja). **2** to stuff with straw (rellenar con paja). **3** to mix with straw (el barro). || *v.pron.* **4** to produce a lot of straw and little grain (echar los cereales mucha paja y poco fruto).
empalagoso, -a *adj.* **1** sickeningly sweet (excesivamente dulce la comida). **2** (fig.) sickly, sugary (una película, novela, etc.). **3** cloying, sickening (zalamero).
empalar *v.t.* **1** to impale (atravesar con un palo). || **2** *v.pron.* to become obstinate o persistant (obstinarse).
empalizada *s.f.* MIL. palisade, stockade (estacada).
empalizar *v.t.* **1** MIL. to palisade, to stockade (rodar de empalizadas). **2** to fence (vallar).
empalmar *v.t.* **1** to connect, to join (unir). **2** to butt join, to join (carpintería). **3** TEC. to splice (cuerda, película, cinta magnética, etc.). **4** (fig.) to link up (ideas, planes, etc.). || *v.pron.* **5** to fit (encajar). **6** to link, to connect (caminos, vías de tren, etc.). **7** to connect (trenes, autocares, aviones, etc.). **8 – con,** to follow.
empalme *s.m.* **1** joint, join, connection (conexión). **2** TEC. joint, butt joint (carpintería). **3** TEC. splice (cuerda, película, etc.). **4** junction (ferrocarril). **5** intersección, junction (carreteras). **6** connection (trenes, autocares, aviones, etc.).
empanadilla *s.f.* pasty, turnover (de carne o pescado).
empanado, -a *adj.* **1** covered with breadcrumbs (rebozado con pan rallado). || *s.f.* **2** pastry with savoury filling.
empanar *v.t.* **1** to cover with breadcrumbs (rebozar con pan rallado). **2** to sow the land with wheat (sembrar la tierra con trigo).
empantanar *v.t.* **1** to flood, to swamp (inundar). **2** to fill up a dam (llenar un pantano con agua). **3** to throw something o someone into the dam (meter algo o a uno en el pantano). || *v.pron.* **4** to become flooded (inundarse): *la huerta se empantanó = the field became flooded.* **5** to get o become bogged down: *el coche se empantanó = the car got bogged down.* **6** (fig.) to be held up, to get bogged down: *se empantanó la gestión = the business got bogged down.*
empañar *v.t.* **1** to put a nappy on (ponerle un pañal a un bebé). **2** to steam up, to mist, to cloud up (un cristal). **3** to dull, to tarnish (quitar el brillo). **4** (fig.) to tarnish, to blemish (la reputación). || *v.pron.* **5** to get steamed up, to mist up (un cristal).
empañetar *v.t.* **1** (Am.) to plaster with mud (embarrar). **2** to whitewash (encalar).
empapamiento *s.m.* **1** soaking (remojo para la ropa). **2** soaking, drenching (por la lluvia). **3** absorbtion (absorción).

empapar *v.t.* **1** to soak, to drench (por la lluvia): *la lluvia le empapó = the rain drenched him.* **2** to soak (la ropa): *empapar la ropa sucia = to soak the dirty washing/linen.* **3** to soak up, to absorb (absorber). **4 a)** to mop up (enjugar con una fregona); **b)** to soak up, to mop up (enjugar con un trapo). **5** (fig.) to be drenched/soaked/soaking wet (estar empapado). || *v.pron.* **6** to be soaked: *el pan se empapa en la salsa = the bread is soaked in the sauce.* **7** to be/to get/to become drenched/soaked/soaking wet (por la lluvia): *me empapé esta mañana = I got drenched this morning.* **8** to be absorbed o soaked up: *el agua se empapa en la esponja = the water is absorbed by the sponge.* **9** (fig.) to become imbued o possessed: *se empapó de ideas nuevas = he became possessed with new ideas.* **10** (fig. y fam.) to stuff oneself (empacharse de comida).

empapelado *s.m.* **1** wallpaper (papel para las paredes). **2** wallpapering, papering, paper hanging (colocación de papel en las paredes). **3** lining (de un baúl, etc.).

empapelador, -ora *s.m.* y *f.* paper hanger (que empapela las paredes).

empapelar *v.t.* **1** to wallpaper, to paper (las paredes). **2** to line with paper (baúles, etc.). **3** (fig. y fam.) to have someone up for something (formar causa criminal a uno).

empapuzar *v.t.* to make someone eat too much (hacer comer demasiado a uno).

empaque *s.m.* **1** packing (acción de empaquetar). **2** packing (envoltura de los paquetes). **3** (fam.) presence (aire de una persona). **4** gravity (gravedad). **5** (Am.) cheek, impudence (descaro).

empaquetador, -ora *s.m.* y *f.* packer.

empaquetar *v.t.* **1** to package, to parcel up (embalar). **2** to pack (colocar apretadamente). **3** (fig.) to pack o cram together (a personas).

emparedado, -a *adj.* **1** walled in. **2** imprisoned, confined (prisionero). **3** in reclusion (ermitaño). || *s.m.* y *f.* **4** prisoner (prisionero). **5** recluse (recluso voluntario). **6** hermit (ermitaño).

emparedamiento *s.m.* **1** confinement (de un prisionero). **2** reclusion (de un ermitaño).

emparedar *v.t.* **1** to wall in (encerrar entre dos paredes). **2** to confine, to imprison (emprisionar).

emparejamiento *s.m.* **1** matching (de dos cosas que tienen relación entre sí). **2** levelling (acción de nivelar o nivelarse dos cosas).

emparejar *v.t.* **1** to match (poner dos cosas en pareja). **2** to level, to make level, to bring to the same level (poner una cosa a nivel con otra). **3** to level off, to smooth (alisar). || *v.i.* **4** to draw level, to catch up (alcanzar a otro que iba delante). **5** to match (hacer juego con algo): *la corbata empareja con la camisa = the tie matches the shirt.* || *v.pron.* **6** to match (dos cosas). **7** to draw level, to catch up (ponerse juntos en una carrera, por ejemplo).

emparentar *v.i.* **1** to become related by marriage (contraer parentesco por vía de casamiento). || **2 — con,** to marry into (una familia ilustre).

emparrado *s.m.* **1** trained vine, vine arbour (parra). **2** trellis, trellis-work (armazón que sostiene una parra u otra planta trepadora).

emparrar *v.t.* to train (una planta).

emparrillar *v.t.* **1** to grill (asar en parrillas). **2** ARQ. to reinforce with a metal grating (usar un armazón para fortalecer un cimiento).

empastador *s.m.* **1** paste brush (pincel para pasta). **2** (Am.) bookbinder (encuadernador de libros).

empastar *v.t.* **1** to paste (cubrir de pasta). **2** to bind (encuadernar). **3** to fill, to put a filling in (un diente). || *v.t.* y *v.pron.* **4** to turn into pasture (convertir en prado un terreno). || *v.pron.* **5** to be filled (los dientes). **6** to become covered in/with weeds (llenarse de malas hierbas un terreno).

empaste *s.m.* **1** MED. filling (de un diente). **2** bookbinding (encuadernación de libros). **3** ART. impasto, impasting (unión perfecta de los colores y tintas en la pintura).

empatar *v.i.* **1** to draw, to tie (votos): *los dos candidatos empataron = the two candidates drew.* **2** DEP. to draw: *El Madrid empató con el Barcelona = Madrid drew with Barcelona.* **3** DEP. to equalize: *Barcelona empató en el minuto setenta = Barcelona equalized in the seventieth minute.* **4** DEP. to tie, to have a dead heat (llegar dos a la vez en una carrera). **5** (Am.) to fit (empalmar). || **6 empatados a tres,** three all. **7 estar empatado,** to be tying.

empate *s.m.* **1** draw, tie (en un partido, concurso o elección). **2** dead heat (en una carrera). **3** (Am.) joint (empalme). || **4 el gol del —,** the equalizing goal/the equalizer. **5 — a tres, a)** three all (tanteo); **b)** three all draw (resultado).

empavesar *v.tr.* to deck, to adorn.

empavonar *v.t.* **1** TEC. to blue (dar color azul oscuro a los metales). **2** (Am.) to grease (engrasar).

empecatado *adj.* **1** incorrigible (de extremada travesura). **2** wretched: *ese empecatado señor ha vuelto = that wretched man is back.* **3** unlucky, illfated (a quien salen mal las cosas).

empecinado, -a *adj.* stubborn, obstinate, (fam.) pigheaded (obstinado).

empecinamiento *s.m.* stubbornness, obstinacy, (fam.) pigheadedness.

empecinarse *v.pron.* to be stubborn, to be obstinate (obstinarse).

empedernido, -a *adj.* **1** (fig.) heavy, hardened (fumador, bebedor, apostador). **2** (fig.) hardened, confirmed (criminal). **3** (fig.) callous, unfeeling, insensitive (insensible).

empedrado, -a *adj.* **1** cobbled (con guijarros). **2** paved (con adoquines). **3** pock-marked (la cara). **4** dappled (de las caballerías). || *s.m.* **5** paving (adoquinado). **6** cobbles (enguijarrado).

empedrar *v.t.* **1** to pave (con adoquines). **2** to cobble (con guijarros). **3** (fig.) to fill, to lard (de citas, de errores un libro o un discurso).

empeine *s.m.* **1** instep (de un pie o un zapato). **2** groin (la ingle). **3** MED. impetigo (enfermedad de cutis). **4** BOT. hepatica, liverwort.

empelotarse *v.pron.* **1** to row, to have a row, to squabble (reñir). **2** (fam.) (Am.) to strip, to undress (desnudarse, quedarse en pelotas): *se empelotó = he stripped.* **3** to get confused (enredarse).

empellar o **empeller** *v.t.* to push, (fam.) to shove (empujar).

empellón *s.m.* **1** push, (fam.) shove (empujón). || **2 a empellones,** roughly (violentamente); by force (a la fuerza); in fits and starts (con interrupciones). **3 dar empellones,** to jostle, to shove, to push (en una muchedumbre). **4** (fig. y fam.) **dar un — a algo,** to give something a shove, o push.

empeñado, -a *adj.* **1** insistant, persistant (porfío). **2** heated, bitter (un argumento, discusión). **3** determined (determinado). **4** in debt (endeudado): *empeñado hasta los ojos = up to one's neck in debt.* **5** pawned (en el Monte de Piedad).

empeñar *v.t.* **1** to pawn (en el Monte de Piedad). **2** to leave as security (dejar como fianza). **3** to commit o bind someone to something (obligar a uno a una cosa). **4** to begin, to start (una discusión, una lucha). **5** MIL. to engage in (una batalla). **6** to involve: *le empeñó en una discusión = he involved her in a discussion.* || *v.pron.* **7** to get into debt (endeudarse). **8** to persist, to insist (insistir con tesón en una cosa): *se empeñó en su trabajo = he persisted with/in his work.* **9** to commit/bind oneself to something (obligarse a una cosa). **10** to begin, to start (una discusión, lucha). **11** MIL. to engage (una batalla). **12** to be determined (decidido). **13** to endeavour, to strive, to take pains (esforzarse): *me empeñé en contárselo con todo detalle = I took pains to tell him in detail.* || **14 ¿si te empeñas?,** if you insist?

empeño *s.m.* **1** determination (determinación). **2** eagerness, (p.u.) zeal (afán). **3** pawning (en el Monte de Piedad). **4** pledging (acción de empeñar). **5** insistence, persistence (insistencia): *su empeño aseguró su victoria = his persistence insured his victory.* || **6 tomar o poner — en,** to take pains to. **7 tener — en,** to be determined; to be eager: *tengo empeño en terminarlo hoy = I am determined to finish it today.* **8 casa de —,** pawnshop. **9 en —,** in pawn; pawned.

empeoramiento *s.m.* deterioration, worsening.

empeorar *v.t.* **1** to make worse, to worsen (una situación). **2** to deteriorate (una cosa). || *v.i.* y *v.pron.* **3** to get worse, to worsen (una situación). **4** to deteriorate (una cosa): *la fachada se ha empeorado durante los años = the facade has deteriorated over the years.* **5** MED. to get worse (un enfermo).

empequeñecer *v.t.* **1** to make smaller, to reduce, to diminish (hacer más pequeño). **2** to belittle, to disparage (desprestigiar). **3** (fig.) to make something look small, to dwarf: *el nuevo jugador empequeñece los demás jugadores = the new player dwarfs the other players.* **4** (fig.) to overshadow, to put into the shade: *me empequeñeció con su actuación = he put me into the shade with his performance.*

empequeñecimiento *s.m.* **1** reduction, diminution (disminución). **2** (fig.) belittling, disparagement (desprestigio).

emperador *s.m.* **1** emperor. **2** ZOOL. swordfish (pez espada).

emperatriz *s.f.* empress.

emperchar *v.t.* **1** to put/hang on a coathanger (colgar de una percha). || *v.pron.* **2** to hang (colgarse la caza de una percha). **3** to get dressed up (ponerse elegante).

emperifollar *v.t.* y *v.pron.* **1** to dress up (vestir/se con esmero). **2** to overdress (vestir/se con exceso).

empero *conj.* **1** but (pero). **2** nevertheless, none the less (sin embargo).

emperramiento *s.m.* **1** stubbornness, (fam.) pig-headedness (obstinación). **2** insistence, determination (persistencia). **3** anger, rage (rabia).

emperrarse *v.pron.* **1** to be determined, to insist (estar decidido): *me emperré en hacerlo solo = I was determined to do it myself.* **2** (fam.) to be set (obstinarse): *se emperró en irse andando = he was set on going by foot.* **3** (fam.) to lose one's temper, to get angry (enfadarse).

empezar *v.t.* **1** to start, to begin: *empezó su actuación con un baile = she began her performance with a dance.* **2** to start (iniciar el uso o consumo de algo): *empecé la cerveza pero no la pude terminar = I started the beer but I couldn't finish it.* || *v.i.* **3** to start, to begin: *empecé a estornudar = I started sneezing; empezará por decirnos que no fue él = he will start by telling us that it was not him; todo empezó cuando nos conocimos en el cine = it all began when we met in the cinema.* || **4 al —,** at the beginning. **5 para —,** to start/to begin with. **6 todo es —,** the first step is the hardest.

empicotar *v.t.* to put in the pillory (someter a escarnio público).

empiece *s.m.* (fam.) beginning, start.

empilar *v.t.* to pile up, to pile, to stack (apilar).

empinado, -a *adj.* **1** erect, upright (erguido). **2** steep: *una cuesta empinada = a steep slope.* **3** on tip-toes (de puntillas). **4** on it's hind legs (cuadrúpedo sobre las patas traseras). **5** rearing (caballo). **6** (fig.) haughty, stuck-up (orgulloso).

empinar *v.t.* **1** to stand something up (poner algo vertical). **2** to raise, to lift, to tip up (un vaso o botella para beber). || *v.i.* **3** (fig. y fam.) to drink a lot (beber mucho). || *v.pron.* **4** to stand on tip-toes (ponerse de puntillas). **5** to stand on its hind legs (ponerse un cuadrúpedo sobre las patas traseras). **6** to rear (up) (un caballo). **7** to rise up, to tower (sobresalir un edificio, montaña, etc. de entre otras). **8** (vulg.) to get a hard on (tener una erección). || **9 — el codo,** to drink a lot.

empingorotado, -a *adj.* **1** (fig.) upper-class, high-class, of high social standing (de clase alta). **2** (fam.) stuck-up (engreído).

empingorotar *v.t.* **1** to put something on top of something (levantar una cosa poniéndola sobre otra). || *v.pron.* **2** to go up, to climb (subirse). **3** (fig.) to become haughty, (fam.) to become stuck up (engreírse).

empiñonado *s.m.* pinenut and sugar paste (pasta de piñones y azúcar).

empipada *s.f.* (Am. y fam.) blow-out (comida).

empíreo, -a *adj.* empyreal.

empíricamente *adv.* empirically.

empírico, -a *adj.* **1** empirical, empiric. || **2** *s.m.* y *f.* empiric, empiricist.

empirismo *s.m.* empiricism.

empitonar *v.t.* to gore, to catch with the horns (acornear).

emplastar *v.t.* **1** MED. to put a plaster on somebody (poner un emplasto). **2** to freeze (detener el curso de un negocio). || *v.pron.* **3** to cover oneself with filth (embadurnarse con alguna porquería).

emplaste *s.m.* **1** MED. plaster, (fam.) band-aid (tirita). **2** make-shift arrangement (componenda). **3** (fam.) bodge (chapuza). **4** (Am.) bore, tedious person (aburrido). || **5 estar uno hecho un —,** to be fit for nothing.

emplazamiento *s.m.* **1** DER. summons. **2** MIL. positioning: *emplazamiento de artillería = artillery positioning.* **3** MIL. (gun) emplacement (búnker). **4** site, location: *emplazamiento arqueológico = archaeological site.*

emplazar *v.t.* **1** DER. to summons, to subpoena. **2** MIL. to position. **3** to locate, to situate (colocar).

empleado, -a *s.m.* y *f.* **1** employee. **2** clerk, office worker (oficinista): *empleado bancario = bank clerk.* || **3 — del estado,** civil servant.

empleador, -a *adj.* employing.

emplear *v.t.* **1** to use (una herramienta, una palabra, etc.): *emplea la retórica a menudo = he often uses rethoric.* **2** to employ (a una persona): *este país emplea miles de trabajadores extranjeros = this country employs thousands of foreign workers.* **3** to give a job to, to hire, (p.u.) to engage (conceder un empleo a alguien). **4** to occupy, to spend (tiempo). **5** to invest (invertir dinero). || *v.pron.* **6** to be used (una palabra, una herramienta, etc.): *esa expresión ya no se emplea = that expression is no longer used.* **7** to be employed (una persona). || **8 emplear-se haciendo algo,** to occupy oneself doing something. **9 lo tiene bien empleado,** he deserves it/he had it coming.

empleo *s.m.* **1** job: *tiene un buen empleo = he has got a good job.* **2** employment: *buscar empleo = to look for employment.* **3** use (uso): *el empleo de una expresión = the use of an expression.* **4** use, spending (del tiempo). **5** spending (del dinero). **6** MIL. rank (rango). || **7 sin —,** unemployed, out of a job. **8 solicitan —,** situations wanted. **9 solicitud de —,** application for a job o job application. **10 modo de —,** instructions for use.

emplomar *v.t.* **1** to lead, to cover o line with lead (revestir). **2** to seal with lead (precintar). **3** (Am.) to fill (dientes).

emplumar *v.t.* **1** to feather (una flecha). **2** to tar and feather (castigo). **3** (Am.) to swindle (timar). **4** (Am.) to beat up (darle una paliza a alguien). **5** to fire (despedir de un empleo). || **6** *v.i.* (Am.) to grow feathers. **7** (Am.) to run away, to take to one's heels (huir). || **8** (Am.) **emplumarlas,** to run away (huir).

emplumecerse *v.i.* to grow feathers, to fledge (pájaro).

empobrecedor, -a *adj.* impoverishing.

empobrecer *v.t.* **1** to impoverish. || **2** *v.i.* y *pron.* to become poor o impoverished.

empobrecimiento *s.m.* impoverishment.

empolvar o **empolvorar** o **empolvorizar** *v.t.* **1** to powder (la cara, el pelo). **2** to cover with dust, to make dusty (ensuciar). || *v.pron.* **3** to become covered with/in dust, to become dusty (una mesa, etc.). **4** to powder one's face (la cara).

empolvoramiento *s.m.* **1** covering with dust (acción). **2** layer o accumulation of dust (capa).

empolladura *s.f.* brood of bees.

empollar *v.t.* **1** to incubate, to sit on, to hatch (huevos). **2** to swot up, to mug up (estudiar mucho). || *v.i.* **3** to sit, to brood (la gallina). **4** to breed (insectos). **5** to mug up, to swot up (estudiar mucho).

empollón, -ona *s.m.* y *f.* swot (que estudia mucho).

emponzoñamiento *s.m.* poisoning.

emponzoñar *v.t.* **1** to poison (envenenar). **2** (fig.) to poison, to taint, to corrupt (corromper).

emporcar *v.t.* to soil, to dirty, to foul (llenar de porquería).

emporio *s.m.* **1** emporium, mart, trading centre (centro comercial). **2** (Am.) large department store.

empotrado, -a *adj.* fitted, built-in (alacena).

empotramiento *s.m.* **1** embedding (en cemento). **2** building-in, fitting (de los muebles, etc.).

empotrar *v.t.* **1** to embed (en cemento). **2** to build in, to fit (un mueble, etc.): *armario empotrado = fitted cupboard.*

emprendedor, -a *adj.* enterprising, go-ahead.
emprender *v.t.* **1** to undertake, to take on (un trabajo, una tarea). **2** to start, to set out on, to embark on (un viaje). || **3 — el regreso,** to return, to go back, to begin the homeward journey. **4 — la retirada,** to retreat. **5 — la,** to start, to set out. **6 emprenderla con uno,** (fam.) to have it out with someone, to have a row with someone (reñir con alguien).
empreñar *v.t.* **1** to make pregnant (a una mujer). **2** to impregnate, to mate with, to cover (animales). || *v.pron.* **3** to get /become pregnant.
empresa *s.f.* **1** company, firm (sociedad). **2** enterprise: *empresa privada = private enterprise.* **3** management: *la empresa no se responsabiliza de los daños = the management accepts no responsibility for any damages.* **4** enterprise, undertaking, venture: *el primer viaje a la luna fue una empresa atrevida = the first journey to the moon was a daring venture.* || **5 — particular,** private company. **6 — funeraria,** undertaker's. **7 — de servicios públicos,** public utility company.
empresariado *s.m.* employers (*pl.*).
empresarial *adj.* **1** managerial, management (del empresariado). || *s.m.pl.* **2** business studies (carrera universitaria).
empresario, -a *s.m.* y *f.* **1** employer (que emplea). **2** contractor (contratante). **3** manager (gerente, director). **4** MUS. impresario (de ópera, teatro, etc.). **5** DEP. promoter (de boxeo). || **6** (Am.) **— de transporte,** shipping agent.
emprestar *v.t.* **1** to lend (prestar). **2** to borrow (tomar o pedir prestado).
empréstito *s.m.* **1** loan (préstamo público). || **2 — de guerra,** war loan.
empujada *s.f.* (Am.) push, shove (empujón).
empujar *v.t.* **1** to push, to shove: *¡no empujes! = don't push!* **2** MEC. to drive, to propel, to push: *el motor empuja la hélice = the motor drives the propeller.* **3** TEC. to thrust (de un cohete, etc.). **4** to press, to push (un botón). || **5 ¡empujad!,** push!
empuje *s.m.* **1** push, shove (empujón). **2** MEC. y FIS. thrust. **3** pressure (presión). **4** (fig.) energy, go, drive: *tiene mucho empuje = he has got a lot of drive.*
empujón *s.m.* **1** push, shove: *darle un empujón a alguien = to give someone a push.* || **2 abrirse paso a empujones,** to push one's way through, to get through by shoving. **3 a empujones, a)** roughly, violently (bruscamente); **b)** by force (a la fuerza); **c)** in fits and starts (intermitentemente). **4 trabajar a empujones,** to work intermitently.
empuñadura *s.f.* **1** hilt (de espada, pistola, etc.). **2** grip, handle (de una herramienta). **3** handle (de un paraguas, etc.). **4** start, beginning (de un cuento).
empuñar *v.t.* **1** to grasp, to take (firm) hold of, to clutch (asir). **2** (Am.) to clench (el puño). **3** (Am.) to punch, to hit with one's fist (dar un puñetazo). **4** to land (un empleo). || **5 — las armas,** to take up arms. **6 — el bastón,** to take command.
emú *s.m.* ZOOL. emu.
emulación *s.f.* emulation.
emular *v.t.* to emulate.
émulo, -a *adj.* **1** emulous. || **2** *s.m.* y *f.* emulator, rival.
emulsión *s.f.* QUIM. emulsion.
emulsionar *v.t.* QUIM. to emulsify.
emulsivo, -a *adj.* QUIM. emulsive.
en *prep.* **a)** (lugar) in (dentro de): *está en la bolsa = it is in the bag;* on (sobre): *está en la mesa = it is on the table;* into/in (acción): *no entra en la caja = it won't go into the box;* onto o on: *ponlo en la mesa = put it onto the table;* at: *está en la estación = she is at the station* (esperando el tren); **b)** in (tiempo): *en 1999 = in 1999; en mayo = in May; en el siglo XX = in the 20th. century; en tres años = in three years;* **c)** on: *en aquella ocasión = on that occasion; en el día 15 = on the 15th.* at: *en esa época = at that time; en ese momento = at that moment;* **d)** by (modo): *fuimos en avión = we went by plane; le reconocí en su acento = I recognized him by his accent;* **e)** in: *en voz alta = in a loud voice;* **f)** by (proporción): *reduje mis gastos en un 20% = I reduced my expenses by 20%;* **g)** *convertirse en = to turn into;* **h)** *en cuanto a = with respect to, as regards, regarding;* **i)** *pensar en = to think about/of.*
enagua *s.f.* **1** (Am.) petticoat, underskirt. || *pl.* **2** petticoat, underskirt.
enaguillas *f.pl.* short petticoat.
enajenación o **enajenamiento** *s.f.* **1** DER. alienation, transfer. **2** absentmindedness (distracción). || **3 — mental,** mental dirangement, insanity.
enajar *v.t.* **1** DER. to transfer, to alienate (bienes). **2** (fig.) to drive mad: *su mujer le enajaba = his wife drove him mad.* **3** to carry away, to enrapture (sacar fuera de sí). || *v.pron.* **4** (fig.) to be driven mad (volverse loco). **5** (fig.) to lose one's self control (no poder dominarse). **6** (fig.) to go into ecstasy (extasiarse).
enaltecer *v.t.* **1** to praise, to exalt, to glorify (alabar). **2** to do someone credit (honrar).
enaltecimiento *s.m.* **1** ennoblement (ennoblecimiento). **2** praise, exaltation, glorification (alabanza).
enamoradizo, -a *adj.* of an amorous disposition, who is always falling in love (que se enamora con facilidad).
enamorado, -a *adj.* **1** in love: *está enamorado de ella = he is in love with her.* **2** (Am.) who is always falling in love (enamoradizo). **3** amorous (amoroso). || **4** *s.m.* y *f.* lover (amante): *es un enamorado de la velocidad = he is a lover of speed.*
enamoramiento *s.m.* **1** falling in love (acción de enamorarse). **2** love (amor).
enamoriscarse o **enamoricarse** *v.pron.* **1** to take a fancy to. **2** (Am.) to be just a bit in love with (superficial).
enanismo *s.m.* MED. dwarfism, nanism.
enano, -a *adj./s.m.* y *f.* **1** dwarf. || **2 trabajar como un —,** to work like a Trojan.
enarbolar *v.t.* **1** to hoist, to raise (una bandera). **2** to brandish (una espada, arma, etc.). **3** MAR. to fly: *enarbolar bandera panameña = to fly the Panamanian flag.* || *v.pron.* **4** to get angry (enfadarse una persona). **5** to rear up (empinarse un caballo).
enardecedor, -a *adj.* **1** exciting (emocionante). **2** MED. inflaming (que causa inflamación).
enardecer *v.t.* **1** to fire (una pasión). **2** to fill with enthusiasm (una persona, una discusión, etc.). || *v.pron.* **3** to become excited (entusiasmarse). **4** MED. to become inflamed (inflamarse una parte del cuerpo).
enardecimiento *s.m.* **1** excitement (excitación). **2** MED. inflammation (de una parte del cuerpo).
encabalgamiento *s.m.* **1** TEC. support of crossbeams. **2** MIL. gun-carriage (cureña). **3** (lit.) enjambment.
encabalgar *v.i.* **1** TEC. to rest, to lean (una viga en otra). **2** to mount a horse (subirse a un caballo). || *v.t.* **3** to overlap (traslapar). **4** to provide with horses (proveer de caballos).
encabestrar *v.t.* **1** to put a halter on, to halter (un caballo). **2** DEP. to lead (a bull) with an ox (hacer que un toro siga a los cabestros). **3** to seduce (seducir). || *v.pron.* to get tangled in the halter (enredarse la mano en el cabestro). **5** (Am.) to insist, to be determined (emperrarse).
encabezamiento *s.m.* **1** heading, headline (de un periódico). **2** heading (al principio de una carta). **3** preamble (preámbulo). **4** registration in the census (acción de empadronamiento). **5** census (padrón).
encabezar *v.t.* **1** to head, to lead (una revolución, etc.). **2** to head, to be at the top, to come first (una lista, una liga, etc.). **3** to put a heading (a un documento, etc.). **4** to head, to entitle (un artículo). **5** to register (empadronar). **6** to fortify (un vino con alcohol). **7** TEC. to join (tablones o vigas).
encabezonar *v.pron.* to be stubborn (empeñarse).
encabritarse *v.pron.* **1** to rear (un caballo). **2** to nose up (un avión).
encadenado, -a *adj.* **1** chained (una moto, persona, etc.). || *s.m.* **2** TEC. buttress, pier. **3** dissolve (cine). **4** chain (cadena).
encadenamiento *s.m.* **1** chaining. **2** (fig.) connection, linking, concatenation.
encadenar *v.t.* **1** to chain, to shackle, to fetter (un prisionero). **2** to chain up (una cosa, un perro, etc.). **3** (fig.) to tie down: *su trabajo le encadena = his work ties him down.* **4** to connect, to tie to-

gether (ideas, razonamientos, etc.). **5** to fade in (cine).

encajar *v.t.* **1** to insert, to fit (into): *encajó la llave en la cerradura = he inserted the key into the lock.* **2** to join, to fit together (unir una cosa con otra ajustadamente). **3** to house, to encase (una máquina, etc.). **4** to get in, to put in (comentario en una conversación). **5** to give, to deal: *le encajó un puñetazo = she gave him a punch.* **6** to shoot (disparar). **7** to force someone to listen to something: *le encajó un buen sermón = he forced her to listen to a long sermon.* || *v.i.* **8** to fit (well o properly): *esto no encaja bien = this does'nt fit properly.* **9** (fig.) to fit, to correspond, to square: *esto no encaja con lo que dijo ayer = this does'nt correspond with what you said this morning.* **10** to squeeze in (meterse en un sitio pequeño). **11** (fam.) to gatecrash (colarse en una fiesta).

encaje *s.m.* **1** insertion, fitting (acción de encajar). **2** fitting together (acción de unir). **3** cavity (hueco). **4** groove (ranura). **5** MEC. housing. **6** lace (tejido). **7** inlay, mosaic (taracea).

encajonado, -a *s.m.* **1** cofferdam (dique). **2** mud wall (tapia de barro). || *adj.* **3** hemmed in, boxed in: *una casa encajonada entre rascacielos = a house hemmed in by skyscrapers.*

encajonar *v.t.* **1** to crate, to box, to pack (meter en cajas). **2** to squeeze in (meter en un sitio estrecho). **3** to shutter (construir cimientos en cajones abiertos). || *v.i.* **4** (Am.) to run through a narrow place (un río).

encalar *v.t.* **1** to whitewash. **2** to lime (abonar con cal).

encalado *s.m.* **1** whitewashing (de paredes). **2** whitening (de pieles). **3** liming (abonado con cal).

encalador, -ora *s.m.* y *f.* whitewasher.

encalmar *v.t.* **1** to calm, to pacify (a una persona). || *v.pron.* **2** to calm down (calmarse una persona). **3** to become calm (el tiempo). **4** to drop (el viento).

encalvecer *v.i.* to go o become bald.

encalladero *s.m.* **1** MAR. sandbank (de arena). **2** MAR. reef (de coral).

encallar *v.i.* **1** MAR. to run aground. **2** to founder (un negocio).

encallecer *v.i.* **1** MED. to become callous (la piel). **2** to harden (endurecer). || *v.pron.* **3** to harden (en un vicio o trabajo). **4** to become hardhearted/unfeeling (insensibilizarse).

encamar *v.t.* **1** (Am.) to take to hospital, to hospitalize (hospitalizar). **2** (Am.) to bed down (acostar a los animales). || *v.i.* **3** to take to one's bed (guardar cama). **4** (Am.) to go to bed with someone (acostarse con alguien). **5** to be flattened (el trigo, etc.).

encaminar *v.t.* **1** to show the way, to guide, to put on the right road (poner en camino). **2** to route (una expedición, vehículo, etc.). **3** to direct, to channel (esfuerzos). || *v.pron.* **4** to head, to make one's way (dirigirse): *me encaminé hacia el pueblo = I made my way towards the village.* **5** to be aimed at something (tener como objetivo).

encampanar *v.t.* **1** (Am.) to raise (elevar). **2** (Am.) to leave in the lurch, to leave in a jam (dejar a alguien en la estacada). **3** to send someone to (mandar a alguien a algún sitio). || *v.pron.* **4** (Am.) to boast, to brag (presumir). **5** to fall in love (enamorarse). **6** (Am.) to get into a jam (meterse en un lío). **7** (Am.) to go to a remote spot (ir a un lugar remoto).

encandilar *v.t.* **1** to dazzle (deslumbrar). **2** to bewilder (dejar pasmado). **3** to poke (un fuego). **4** to fire, to stimulate (una emoción). **5** (Am.) to deprive of sleep (no dejar dormir). || *v.pron.* **6** to glitter, to sparkle (los ojos). **7** (Am.) to get scared (tener miedo). **8** (Am.) to get angry (enfadarse).

encanecimiento *s.m.* going grey (el cabello).

encanecer *v.i.* y *v.pron.* **1** to go grey (el cabello). **2** to go grey, to look old (una persona). **3** to go mouldy (ponerse mohoso).

encanijamiento *s.m.* weakening (acción de ponerse enfermizo).

encanijarse *v.r.* **1** to grow/become weak (ponerse enfermizo). **2** to become puny (ponerse flaco).

encantado, -a *adj.* **1** delighted, pleased, charmed: *encantado de conocerle = pleased to meet you, how do you do.* **2** haunted (una casa). **3** bewitched (hechizado). **4** absentminded (distraído). || **5** **yo, encantado,** it's alright with me.

encantador, -a *adj.* **1** charming, delightful: *una película encantadora = a charming film.* **2** bewitching (sonrisa, mirada, etc.). || *s.m.* y *f.* **3** charmer, enchanter (hombre). **4** enchantress (mujer). || **5** **— de serpientes,** snake charmer.

encantamiento *s.m.* **1** spell, curse (maleficio). **2** spell, charm, incantation (invocación mágica). **3** magic: *como por encantamiento = as if by magic.* **4** enchantment, delight (encanto).

encantar *v.t.* **1** to love: *me encanta como haces eso = I love the way you do that.* **2** to delight: *estoy encantado con mi coche nuevo = I'm delighted with my new car.* **3** to bewitch, to cast a spell on (hechizar).

encañado *s.m.* **1** pipe, conduit, tubing (canalización). **2** trellis (para las plantas). **3** drainage pipe o tube (desagüe).

encañar *v.t.* **1** to pipe (agua). **2** to prop up (una planta). **3** to drain (un terreno húmedo). **4** to wind on (hilo, seda).

encañonar *v.t.* **1** to point at, to aim at (con un arma). **2** to pipe (agua). **3** to channel (encauzar). || *v.pron.* **4** to grow feathers, to fledge (aves).

encapillar *v.t.* **1** to hood (un ave). **2** MAR. to rig.

encapotadura *s.m.* **1** clouding over (acción de encapotarse el cielo). **2** to frown (ceña). **3** cloudiness (nubosidad).

encapotar *v.t.* **1** to cloak, to put a cloak on (cubrir con una capa). || *v.pron.* **2** to put a cloak on. **3** to cloud over, to become overcast (ponerse nublado el cielo). **4** to frown (poner el rostro ceñudo).

encapricharse *v.pron.* **1** to set one's mind on: *se ha encaprichado con comprarse un coche = he has set his mind on buying a car.* **2** to become infatuated by, to become mad about (enamorarse). **3** to take a fancy (encariñarse).

encapuchar *v.t.* **1** to hood, to put a hood on. || *v.pron.* **2** to put one's hood on.

encarado, -a *adj.* **1** **bien —,** good-looking, nice-looking. **2** **mal —,** bad looking, nasty-looking.

encaramar *v.t.* **1** to raise, to lift up (levantar). **2** to put high up (colocar muy alto). **3** to praise, to extol (alabar). **4** to promote (elevar a un puesto más alto). **5** (Am.) to embarass (avergonzar). || *v.pron.* **6** to climb (subir). **7** to reach a high position (alcanzar un puesto elevado). **8** (Am.) to get embarassed (avergonzarse). **9** (Am.) to blush (ponerse colorado de vergüenza).

encarar *v.t.* **1** to face (up to), to confront (una dificultad). **2** to aim, to point at (un arma). || *v.pron.* **3** to face (up to), to confront (una dificultad, una persona): *se encaró con el cura = he confronted the priest.* **4** to be faced o confronted with: *nos encaramos con una escalada muy difícil = we are faced with a very difficult climb.*

encarcelación *s.f.* imprisonment, incarceration.

encarcelar *v.t.* **1** to imprison, to put into prison, (p.u.) to incarcerate (meter en la cárcel). **2** TEC. to clamp (madera). **3** to embed in mortar o cement (fijar en yeso o cemento).

encarecer *v.t.* **1** to put the price, to make more expensive (hacer más caro). **2** to recommend, to urge (recomendar). **3** to praise, to extol (alabar). **4** to stress, to emphasize (la importancia de algo). || *v.i.* **5** to go up in price, to get dearer: *las casas han encarecido = houses have gone up in price.*

encarecidamente *adv.* **1** earnestly (seriamente). **2** insistently (insistentemente).

encarecimiento *s.m.* **1** rise in price, price rise/increase (subida de precio). **2** extolling (alabanza). **3** stressing, emphasizing (enfatización). || **4** **con —,** insistently.

encargado, -a *s.m.* y *f.* **1** the one o person in charge: *el encargado de la piscina = the person in charge of the swimming pool.* **2** manager (de un negocio). **3** employee, attendant (empleado). **4** agent, representative (representante). || *adj.* **5** in charge. || **6** **— de la recepción,** receptionist. **7** **— de relaciones públicas,** public relations officer.

encargar *v.t.* **1** to put in charge: *encargar a alguien de la puerta = to put someone in charge of the door.* **2** to entrust: *le encargué la gestión a él = I entrusted him* *with the deal.* **3** to order: *encargó una pizza para dos = he ordered a pizza for two.* **4** to have made: *encargó unos zapatos = he ordered some shoes.* **5** to ask (pedir). || *v.pron.* **6** to take charge of, to take responsability: *se encargó de la seguridad de la casa = he took charge of the security of the house.* **7** to take care of to see about: *se ha encargado de la comida = he has taken care of the meal.* **8** to be in charge of (ser responsable de). **9** to order, to have made (un vestido, etc.). || **10 ¡yo me encargaré de él!** I'll deal with him!, I'll take care of him!

encariñarse *v.pron.* **1** to grow fond, to get attached: *se encariñó con su profesor = he grew attached to his teacher.*

encarnación *s.f.* **1** incarnation. **2** flesh colour (color de carne). || **3 es la — de la bondad,** he's the epitome of kindness, he's kindness personified.

encarnado *adj.* **1** incarnate: *es el diablo encarnado = he's the devil incarnate.* **2** MED. ingrowing (uña). **3** red, blood-red (color). **4** ruddy (complexión). **6** flesh colour (color de carne). || **6 ponerse —,** to blush.

encarnadura *s.f.* MED. wound (herida).

encarnamiento *s.m.* MED. healing, closing up (de una herida).

encarnizado, -a *adj.* **1** bloody, bitter, fierce (una batalla, etc.). **2** MED. red, inflamed (herida, piel, etc.). **3** MED. bloodshot (el ojo).

encarnizamiento *s.m.* bitterness, cruelty, fierceness (en la batalla).

encarnizar *v.t.* **1** to brutalize, to make brutal o fierce: *la lucha encarniza al hombre = fighting brutalizes man.* || *v.pron.* **2** to become fierce o savage (una batalla). **3** to treat cruelly, to be cruel: *se encarnizaron con los rehenes = they treated the hostages cruelly.* **4** to get furious (ponerse furioso). || **5 encarnizarse en la lucha,** to fight bitterly.

encaro *s.m.* **1** stare, staring, gaze (mirada). **2** HIST. blunderbuss (arma). **3** aim (puntería).

encarrilar o **encarrillar** *v.t.* **1** to put back on the rails (un tren descarrilado, etc.). **2** to put on the right road (dar una buena orientación). **3** to direct, to guide (un coche, etc.). **4** to get off to a bad start: *han encarrilado mal el asunto = they have got off to a bad start.*

encarroñar *v.t.* **1** to rot. || *v.pron.* **2** to decay, to rot.

encartar *v.t.* **1** to enroll, to register, to enter (en una lista). **2** to involve, to implicate (implicar). **3** to insert (insertar). **4** DER. to summon (emplazar). **5** to outlaw, to make illegal (ilegalizar). || *v.i.* **6** to fit in, to go: *eso no encarta en mis planes = that doesn't fit in with my plans.* || *v.pron.* **7** si se encarta, should the occasion arise.

encarte *s.m.* **1** lead (naipes). **2** order of the cards (orden de los naipes). **3** TEC. inset, insert (imprenta).

encartonar *v.t.* to cover with cardboard (cubrir con cartón).

encartuchar *v.t.* to roll up into a cone, to make a cone of (enrollar en forma de cucurucho).

encasillado, -a *adj./s.m.* y *f.* **1** type cast (actor) || *s.m.* **2** grid, squares, table. **3** pigeonholes (para cartas).

encasillar *v.t.* **1** to set out in a table, to tabulate (cifras, datos, etc.). **2** to pigeonhole (distribuir en casillas). **3** to classify (clasificar). **4** to typecast (un actor). **5** to designate as a government candidate (en las elecciones para diputados). || *v.pron.* **6** to limit oneself (limitarse).

encasquetar *v.t.* **1** to pull on, to pull down tight (un sombrero). **2** to put into someone's head (persuadir a uno de algo). || *v.pron.* **3** to put on, to pull down tight (el sombrero). **4** to get something into your head: *se le encasquetó la idea de ir a España = he got the idea of going to Spain into his head.*

encasquillar *v.t.* **1** (Am.) to shoe (un caballo). **2** to put a tip on (poner una punta a algo). || *v.pron.* **3** to jam (un arma). **4** (Am.) to lose one's nerve (acobardarse).

encastillado, -a *adj.* **1** fortified (fortificado). **2** obstinate (obstinado). **3** haughty, lofty (soberbio). **4** ARQ. castellated.

encastillar *v.t.* **1** to plie, to pile up (apilar). **2** MIL. to fortify with castles (fortificar con castillos). **3** TEC. to erect scaffolding around something (poner andamios alrededor de algo). || *v.pron.* **4** to take refuge in a castle (refugiarse en un castillo). **5** to stick to one's opinion, to stick to one's guns (emperrarse).

encastrar *v.t.* **1** to embed, to set in. **2** MEC. to mesh, to engage (intentar).

encauzar *v.t.* **1** to channel (encañar). **2** to guide, to direct (una conversación, argumento, etc.).

encauzamiento *s.m.* **1** channelling (de las aguas). **2** guidance, orientation (orientación).

encefalitis *s.m.* MED. encephalitis (inflamación del encéfalo).

encefalalgia *s.f.* MED. cephalalgia, (fam.) headache (dolor de cabeza).

encefálico, -a *adj.* MED. encephalic.

encéfalo *s.m.* MED. encephalon.

encefalograma *s.m.* MED. encephalogram, encephalograph.

encelado, -a *s.m.* y *f.* a jealous person.

encelar *v.t.* **1** to make someone jealous. || *v.pron.* **2** to become jealous. **3** to go on heat (los animales).

encenagado, -a *adj.* **1** muddy (lleno de barro). **2** sited up (un puerto, río, etc.). **3** bogged down, stuck in the mud (atascado). **4** (fig.) sunk, wallowing (en vicio).

encenagarse *v.pron.* **1** to get muddy (llenarse de barro). **2** to get bogged down (atascarse). **3** to become boggy, to become muddy (un terreno). **4** to silt up (un puerto). **5** to wallow, to sink (envilecerse en vicio).

encendedor *s.m.* **1** lighter (mechero). **2** lamplighter (persona).

encender *v.t.* **1** to light (un cigarrillo, vela, fuego, etc.), to ignite (una mezcla combustible, una mecha, etc.). **3** to strike, to light (una cerilla). **4** to set fire to, to set on fire, to set alight (prender fuego a). **5** to switch on, to turn on, to put on (la radio, la luz, etc.). **6** to stir up, to provoke (las pasiones, un conflicto, etc.). **7** to arouse (el entusiasmo). **8** to spark off (una guerra): *la invasión de Kuwait encendió una guerra = the invasion of Kuwait sparked off a war.* **9** (Am.) to beat (golpear). || *v.pron.* **10** to catch fire: *el avión después de estrellarse se encendió = after crashing the plane caught fire.* **11** to light (un cigarro, una vela, etc.): *este mechero no se enciende = this lighter won't light.* **12** to light up (la cara). **13** to blush, to go red (ponerse colorado): *se encendió su cara al oír su nombre = he blushed on hearing his name.* **14** to break out (un conflicto).

encendido, -a *adj.* **1** lit (un cigarro, una vela, etc.). **2** on, switched on (la luz, una radio, etc.). **3** alight, on fire (ardiendo). **4** live (un cable). **5** bright red (rojo). **6** flushed, red (la cara por un esfuerzo, enfermedad). **7** purple (la cara por ira). || *s.m.* **8** MEC. ignition: *encendido electrónico = electronic ignition.* **9** lighting (acción de encender). **10** firing (de un cohete).

encendimiento *s.m.* **1** burning. **2** ardour, passion (pasión). **3** redness (color). **4** blushing (la cara).

encerado, -a *adj.* **1** waxed, polished (el suelo, un mueble). **2** waxy, wax-coloured (de apariencia). || *s.m.* **3** waxing, polishing (del suelo, los muebles, etc.). **4** wax (capa de cera). **5** oilcloth (tela impregnada para proteger contra la humedad). **6** tarpaulin (lona alquitranada). **7** blackboard (pizarra). **8** MED. plaster (tirita). **9** oilskin (prenda).

encerar *v.t.* **1** to wax, to polish (el suelo, los muebles, etc.). **2** to thicken (la argamasa).

encercar *v.t.* (Am.) to encircle (rodear).

encerradero *s.m.* **1** pen, fold (aprisco). **2** bullpen (para los toros).

encerramiento *s.m.* confinement (confinamiento).

encerrar *v.t.* **1** to shut in, to shut up (a alguien): *encerrar un perro = to shut a dog in.* **2** to lock in, to lock up (con llave). **3** to put under lock and key (guardar bajo llave). **4** to include, to contain: *este libro encierra muchas verdades = this book contains a lot of truths.* **5** to contain: *su colección encierra unas obras maestras = her collection contains some master works.* **6** to involve: *el viaje encierra unas subidas muy dificultosas = the journey involves some difficult climbs.* || *v.pron.* **7** to shut oneself in (en casa, en una habitación, etc.). **8** to go into seclusion of retreat (aislamiento). **9** to live in a convent (retirarse a un convento). || **10** encerrarse en una idea, to stick to an idea. **11** encerrarse en sí mismo, to go into one's shell.

encerrona *s.f.* **1** seclusion, retreat (retiro). **2** DEP. private bullfight (corrida de toros particular). **3** ambush (emboscada). **4** trap (trampa).

encestar *v.t.* **1** DEP. to score o make a basket (baloncesto). **2** to put into baskets (meter algo en cestos).

enceste *s.m.* DEP. basket.

encía *s.f.* MED. gum.

encíclica *s.f.* encyclical.

enciclopedia *s.f.* encyclopedia o encyclopaedia.

enciclopédico, -a *adj.* encyclopedic, encyclopaedic, encyclopedical, encyclopaedical.

encierro *s.m.* **1** confinement (personas). **2** shutting in, shutting up (de una casa). **3** DEP. driving of the bulls into the pen before a bullfight (los toros). **4** seclusion (retiro). **5** penning (del ganado vacuno).

encima *adj.* **1** above: *el sospechoso tiene la nariz rota con una cicatriz encima = the suspect has got a broken nose with a scar above.* **2** on top: *un helado con nueces encima = an ice cream with walnuts on top.* **3** overhead, above: *encima los pájaros volaban = overhead the birds were flying.* **4** superficially, hastily: *lo he leído pero muy por encima = I've read it buy very hastily.* **5** imminent: *la tormenta está encima = the storm is imminent.* **6** on one, about one: *no llevo dinero encima = I haven't got any money on me.* **7** besides, in addition: *y muchas más cosas encima = and a lot more things besides.* **8** on top of that, (fam.) to cap it all: *es caro y encima feo = it's expensive and on top of that it's ugly.* || **9 de —,** on top: *mi bolsa es la de encima = my bag is the one on top.* **10 echarse —,** to throw oneself onto o at (atacar): *se echó encima del ladrón = he threw himself onto the thief.* **11 por —,** above (sobre), above, over, overhead: *el avión pasó por encima = the plane passed overhead.* **12 por — de,** above, beyond: *está muy por encima de ese tipo de cosa = he's well above that sort of thing; el problema está por encima de él = the problem is beyond him.* **13 por — de todo,** above all (sobre todo). **14 quitarse de —,** to get rid of (una cosa); to get rid of, to shake off (una persona).

encimar *v.t.* **1** to put on top (poner encima). **2** (Am.) to throw in, to give as a bonus, to put in as an extra (dar encima de lo estipulado, añadir). **3** to add to (en el juego de tresillo). || *v.pron.* **4** to rise (subirse).

encimero, -a *adj.* **1** top: *la ventana encimera = the top window.* || *s.f.* **2** (Am.) leather saddle cover.

encina *s.f.* BOT. holm oak, ilex, evergreen oak.

encinal o **encinar** *s.m.* grove of holm oaks.

encinta *adj.* **1** pregnant. **2** ZOOL. with young. || **3 mujer —,** pregnant woman, expectant mother. **4 dejar a una —,** to get a woman pregnant.

encintado *s.m.* kerb, kerbstone.

encintar *v.t.* **1** to put a ribbon (adornar con cintas). **2** to kerb, to put a kerb on (una acera).

enclaustrar *v.t.* **1** to cloister, to send to a convent. **2** (fig.) to hide away (esconder). || *v.pron.* **3** to shut oneself in (encerrarse).

enclavar *v.t.* **1** to nail (clavar). **2** to situate, to place, to locate (situar). **3** to enclave (un territorio). **4** to transfix (atravesar de parte en parte). **5** to trick (engañar).

enclave *s.m.* **1** POL. enclave. **2** small area, isolated area, (p.u.) enclave (territorio).

enclenque *adj.* **1** weak, sickly (enfermizo). **2** skinny, scrawny (delgaducho).

enclítico, -a *adj.* GRAM. enclitic.

encofrado *s.m.* TEC. **1** shuttering (para el hormigón). **2** timbering (en una mina).

encofrar *v.t.* **1** TEC. to put up shuttering (para el hormigón). **2** to timber, to plank (en las minas).

encoger *v.i.* **1** to shrink. || *v.t.* **2** to shrink (estrechar). **3** MED. to contract (contraer una parte del cuerpo). **4** to intimidate (intimidar). || *v.pron.* **5** to shrink (una prenda). **6** (fig.) to cringe (acobardarse). || **7 encogerse de hombros,** to shrug one's shoulders.

encogido, -a *adj.* **1** shrunken (una tela, una prenda, etc.). **2** shrivelled (una hoja, etc.). **3** shy, timid, bashful (tímido). **4** hunched (el cuerpo). **5** in knots (el estómago): *tenía el estómago encogido = his stomach was in knots.*

encogimiento **1** shrinkage (de una tela, prenda, etc.). **2** hunching (del cuerpo). **3** (fig.) timidness, bashfulness, shyness (timidez). **4** shrug (de los hombros).

encolar *v.t.* **1** to glue, to gum, to paste, to stick (pegar). **2** to size (antes de empapelar o pintar). **3** to clarify (los vinos).

encolerizar *v.t.* **1** to infuriate, to anger (enfadar). || *v.pron.* **2** to get angry, to become infurated (enfadarse).

encomendar *v.t.* **1** to entrust, to commend (confiar): *te encomiendo mi coche = I entrust my car to you.* **2** to commend (a la memoria). || *v.pron.* **3** to commend oneself, to entrust oneself, to put oneself in the hands of somebody: *en sus manos me encomiendo = I put myself in your hands.*

encomendero *s.m.* **1** (Am.) grocer (tendero). **2** (Am.) wholesale meat supplier (vendedor de carne al por mayor).

encomiasta *s.m.* praiser, extoller, eulagist.

encomienda *s.f.* **1** assignment (encargo). **2** HIST. concession, holding (tierras y habitantes concedidos a un conquistador). **3** (Am.) parcel (paquete). || **4** (Am.) **— postal,** postal package.

encomiar *v.t.* to praise, to extol (alabar).

encomio *s.m.* praise, eulogy.

encomiástico, -a *adj.* eulogistic, laudatory.

enconamiento *s.m.* MED. **1** inflammation. **2** infection (infección).

enconar *v.t.* **1** MED. to inflame (inflamar). **2** MED. to infect (infectar). **3** to anger (enfadar). || *v.pron.* **4** MED. to become inflamed (inflamarse). **5** MED. to become infected (infectarse). **6** to get angry (enfadarse).

encono *s.m.* **1** rancour, spitefulness (rencor). **2** ill-feeling, bad blood. **3** fierceness (en una lucha). **4** (Am.) MED. inflammation (inflamación).

encontradizo, -a *adj.* **1** met by chance. || **2 hacerse el —,** to pretend to meet someone by chance, to contrive to apparently meet someone by chance (buscar disimuladamente el encuentro con alguien).

encontrado, -a *adj.* opposing, contrary.

encontrar *v.t.* **1** to find: *lo encontró difícil = she found it difficult.* **2** to meet, to run into, to come across (una persona sin buscarla): *le encontré en el bar = I came across him in the bar.* **3** to come across, to find (una cosa sin buscarlo): *lo encontré en el maletero = I found it in the car boot.* **4** to find, to come across, to encounter (dificultades). **5** to see: *no sé lo que encuentras en él = I don't know what you see in him.* || *v.pron.* **6** to meet, to bump into, to meet each other: *me encontré con ella en el supermercado = I bumped into her in the supermarket.* **7** to be (estar): *se encontraba en la cocina = he was in the kitchen.* **8** to feel, to be: *me encuentro mucho mejor = I feel much better.* **9** to be, to be situated, to stand (estar situado): *la casa se encuentra al lado de correos = the house is next to the post office.* **10** to find oneself: *me encontré sin dinero = I found myself without any money.*

encontrón o **encontronazo** *s.m.* collision, crash, smash.

encopetado, -a *adj.* **1** conceited, haughty, (fig.) high and mighty (presumido). **2** of high social position, upper class (de alto copete). **3** important, prominent (importante).

encopetarse *v.pron.* to get o become conceited.

encorajar *v.t.* **1** to encourage. || *v.pron.* **2** to get angry (enfadarse).

encorajinar *v.t.* **1** to provoke, to make someone angry (provocar). || *v.pron.* **2** to get angry, to lose one's temper (enfadarse).

encorchar *v.t.* **1** to bottle (una botella). **2** to hive (las abejas).

encordadura *s.f.* MUS. strings (cuerdas).

encordar *v.t.* **1** MUS. y DEP. to string (un instrumento, o raqueta). **2** to rope off (aislar un terreno con cuerdas). || *v.pron.* **3** to rope up, to rope oneselves together (alpinismo).

encornado, -a *adj.* **1** horned. || **2 un toro bien —,** a well horned bull.

encornadura *s.f.* 1 horns (de un toro). 2 antlers (de los ciervos, etc.). 3 shape o position of the horns (posición de los cuernos).
encorsetar *v.t.* 1 to corset. || *v.pron.* 2 to put a corset on.
encorvado, -a *adj.* 1 curved, bent (doblado). 2 stooped (por la edad), bent over (agachado). || 3 **hacer la encorvada,** to pretend to be ill.
encorvadura o **encorvamiento** *s.m.* y *f.* 1 bending, curving (acción de doblar). 2 curvature (grado de encorvadura). 3 stoop (de una persona por la edad).
encostrar *v.t.* 1 to put a crust on (un pastel). || *v.pron.* 2 to form a crust (un pastel). 3 MED. to form a scab (una herida).
encovar *v.t.* 1 to put someone o something in a cave (encerrar en una cueva). 2 to hide (ocultar). || *v.pron.* 3 to make someone hide (obligar a uno a ocultarse). 4 to hide in a cave (ocultarse en una cueva).
encrespador *s.m.* curling tongs (para rizar el pelo).
encrespadura *s.f.* curling (acción de rizar el pelo).
encrespar *v.t.* 1 to curl (el pelo). 2 tooste one's hair on end (erizar el pelo). 3 to ruffle (el plumaje). 4 to irritate, to enfuriate (enfurecer). || *v.pron.* 5 to become rough o choppy (el mar). 6 to go curly (el pelo). 7 to stand on end, to bristle (erizarse el pelo), to get angry, to become infuriated (enfadarse).
encorsetado, -a *adj.* conceited, haughty, (fig.) high and mighty (presumido).
encrestarse *v.pron.* to raise it's crest (poner las aves tiesa la cresta).
encrucijada *s.f.* 1 crossroads, junction. 2 (fig.) crossroads: *la encrucijada de la vida = the crossroads of life.*
encuadernación *s.f.* 1 binding: *encuadernación en piel o cuero = leather binding.* 2 bookbinding (el oficio). || 3 **taller de —,** bindery.
encuadernador, -ora *s.m.* o *f.* bookbinder.
encuadernar *v.t.* 1 to bind. || 2 **libro sin —,** an unbound book.
encuadramiento *s.m.* 1 frame, framework (límite). 2 framing (cine). 3 MIL. officering (de tropas).
encuadrar *v.t.* 1 to frame, to put in a frame (poner en un marco). 2 to fit, to insert (encajar). 3 to frame (una imagen en un objetivo, etc.). 4 to incorporate (en un grupo). 5 MIL. to officer.
encubar *v.t.* 1 to vat (el vino). 2 to timber (entibar el interior de un pozo).
encubierta *s.f.* fraud (fraude).
encubridor, -ora *s.m.* o *f.* 1 receiver, (fam.) fence (de artículos robados). 2 DER. accessory after the fact (que encubre un delito o criminal). 3 DER. harbourer (de un delincuente, etc.). || *adj.* 4 hiding, concealing.
encubrimiento *s.m.* 1 cocealment, hiding (ocultación). 2 DER. receiving of stolen goods (de artículos robados). 3 DER. complicity, (p.u.) abetment (acción de auxiliar a un delincuente). 4 DER. harbouring, concealment (ocultación de un delincuente, criminal, etc.).
encubrir *v.t.* 1 to hide, to conceal (ocultar). 2 DER. to receive stolen goods (artículos robados). 3 to harbour (ocultar a un delincuente o criminal).
encuentro *s.m.* 1 meeting, encounter (acto de encontrarse). 2 meeting (dos cosas). 3 DEP. game, match (entre dos equipos). 4 DEP. meeting, fixture: *encuentro deportivo = sports fixture.* 5 MIL. encounter, clash (lucha). 6 (fig.) clash (de ideas diferentes). 7 (fig.) find (hallazgo). 8 collision (de coches, etc.). 9 discovery (descubrimiento). || 10 **ir al — de uno,** to go to meet someone. 11 **salir al — de,** to go to meet (salir a recibirle).
encuesta *s.f.* 1 DER. inquiry, investigation (investigación). 2 poll, opinion poll, survey (opinión pública): *hacer una encuesta = to carry out a survey.* || DER. 3 **— judicial,** post-mortem, coroner's inquest.
encuestador, -ora *s.m.* y *f.* pollster.
encumbrado, -a *adj.* 1 high, lofty, towering (un edificio, etc.). 2 conceited, haughty, (fam.) high and mighty (presumido). 3 eminent, distinguished (eminente). 4 of high social standing, upper o high class (de clase alta).
encumbramiento *s.m.* 1 raising, elevation (elevación). 2 height (altura). 3 praise, extolling (ensalzamiento). 4 exaltation (exaltación).
encumbrar *v.t.* 1 to raise, to elevate (elevar). 2 to elevate, to exalt (a una persona). 3 (fig.) to extol (ensalzar). 4 to climb to the top (subir la cumbre). || *v.pron.* 5 to rise (elevarse). 6 to become conceited (engreírse). 7 to rise, to soar, to tower (un edificio, etc.).
enchapinado, -a *adj.* ARQ. built over vaults (construido sobre bóvedas).
encharcar *v.t.* 1 to flood, to swamp (inundar). 2 to cover with puddles (llenar de charcos). || *v.pron.* 3 to become flooded o swamped (inundarse). 4 to become covered with puddles (llenarse de charcos). 5 to form puddles (formar charcos el agua). 6 (Am.) to get muddy (llenarse uno de barro). 7 (Am.) to get stuck in a puddle (quedarse atascado en un charco). 8 to become bloated (el estómago).
enchilada *s.f.* (Am.) rolled omelette seasoned with chili (comida).
enchilar *v.t.* 1 (Am.) to season with chili (sazonar con chili). 2 (Am.) to annoy (molestar). 3 (Am.) to disappoint (decepcionar). || *v.i.* 4 (Am.) to sting, to burn (escocer, picar). || *v.pron.* 5 (Am.) to become angry (enfadarse).
enchiquerar *v.t.* 1 (Am.) to pen, to corral (encorralar). 2 (fig. y fam.) to put in the nick (encarcelar).
enchironar *v.t.* (fam.) to put in the nick (encarcelar).
enchufar *v.t.* 1 ELEC. to plug in, to connect. 2 to fit together, to couple (acoplar tubos, etc.). 3 COM. to merge (enlazar un negocio con otro). 4 (fig. y fam.) to pull strings (ejercer influencia).
enchufe *s.m.* 1 ELEC. plug (macho). 2 ELEC. socket, point, plug (hembra). 3 TEC. joint, connection (de dos tubos). 4 (fig. y fam.) string pulling (acción de ejercer influencia). || 5 **tener —,** to have friends in the right places, to have contacts.
enchufismo *s.m.* (fig. y fam.) string pulling, use of contacts.
enchufista *s.m.* y *f.* (fig. y fam.) strin puller.
ende *adv.* 1 there. || 2 **por —,** therefore, hence.
endeble *adj.* 1 feeble, weak, frail (una persona, argumento, etc.). 2 puny, scrawny (enclenque). 3 flimsy, fragile (cosa).
endeblez *s.f.* 1 feebleness, weakness (de una persona, argumento, etc.). 2 flimsiness (cosas).
endecasílabo, -a *adj.* 1 GRAM. hendecasyllabic. || *s.m.* 2 GRAM. hendecasyllable.
endecha *s.f.* 1 dirge, lament (lamento). 2 (lit.) quatrain with lines of six or seven syllables (combinación métrica).
endemia *s.f.* MED. endemic disease, endemic.
endémico, -a *adj.* 1 MED. endemic. 2 (fig.) chronic (crónico).
endemoniado, -a *adj.* 1 possessed (of the devil). 2 furious (furioso). 3 mischievous (travieso). 4 diabolical, terrible (terrible). 5 damned, wretched (maldito). 6 devilish, fiendish (endiablado). || *s.m.* y *f.* 7 person possessed (poseído). || 8 **como un —,** like a madman: *correr como un endemoniado = to run like a madman.*
endemoniar *v.t.* 1 to posess with the devil o to possess with an evil spirit. 2 to infuriate, to anger (encolerizar). 3 to provoke (provocar). || *v.pron.* 4 to get angry (enfadarse).
enderezado, -a *adj.* appropriate, suitable (propicio).
enderezamiento *s.m.* 1 straightening (de algo torcido). 2 righting (de una situación).
enderezar *v.t.* 1 to straighten (algo torcido). 2 to put straight (poner derecho). 3 MAR. to right (una embarcación). 4 to stand the right way up, to put back on its wheels (un vehículo, etc.). 5 to put in order, to set to rights, to correct (enmendar). 6 to direct (encaminar). || *v.pron.* 7 MAR. to right itself (una embarcación). 8 to straighten up, to stand up straight (una persona). 9 to straighten out (una cosa). 10 to be directed at (encaminarse). || *v.i.* 11 to head, to make one's way (dirigirse).
endeudarse *v.pron.* 1 to get o run into dept (llenarse de deudas). 2 (fig.) to become indepted (tener que estar agradecido).
endiabladamente *adv.* diabolically, fiendishly.

endiablado, -a *adj.* **1** possessed (poseído). **2** devilish, fiendish, diabolical (diabólico). **3** evil, wicked (malo). **4** miscievous (travieso). **5** diabolical, terrible (terrible): *tiene un aspecto endiablado = it looks diabolical.* **6** furious (furioso). **7** ugly (feo).
endibia *s.f.* BOT. endive.
endilgar *v.t.* **1** to land, to deal (un puñetazo, etc.). **2** to send (mandar), to guide (guiar). **3** to attribute (atribuir). **4** (fam.) to palm off, to lumber someone: *le endilgué el coche a él = I palmed the car off on him.*
endiosamiento *s.m.* **1** vanity (vanidad). **2** conceit (presunción). **3** pride (orgullo).
endiosado, -a *adj.* **1** conceited, stuck-up. **2** deified.
endiosar *v.t.* **1** to deify, to make a god out of (elevar a la divinidad). || *v.pron.* **2** to get o become conceited (engreído). **3** to become proud (orgulloso).
endoblado, -a *adj.* BIOL. a suckling lamb (cordero que se cría mamando de la oveja).
endocardio *s.m.* MED. endocardium.
endocarpio *s.m.* BOT. endocarp.
endocrino, -a *adj.* BIOL. endocrine, endocrinal, endocrinic, endocrinous: *glándula endocrina = endocrine gland.*
endocrinología *s.f.* MED. endocrinology.
endocrinólogo, -a *s.m.* y *f.* endocrinologist.
endodermo *s.m.* BIOL. endiderm.
endogamia *s.f.* endogamy, in breeding.
endogénesis *s.f.* BIOL. endogeny.
endomingarse *v.pron.* to put on one's Sunday best.
endosar *v.t.* **1** COM. to endorse. **2** (fam.) to palm something off on someone, to lumber someone with something (pasar a uno una cosa molesta).
endosfera *s.f.* GEOL. endosphere.
endósmosis o **endosmosis** *s.f.* QUIM. endosmosis.
endoso *s.m.* COM. endorsement.
endosperma *s.f.* BOT. y BIOL. endosperm.
endotelio *s.m.* BIOL. endothelium.
endotérmico, -a *adj.* QUIM. endothermic, endothermal.
endrina *s.f.* BOT. sloe (fruto).
endrino, -a *adj.* **1** blue-black. || *s.m.* **2** BOT. blackthorn, sloe (arbusto).
endulzar *v.t.* **1** to sweeten. **2** (fig.) to sweeten, to soften (a una persona). **3** to alleviate, to soften (el sufrimiento, etc.).
endurecer *v.t.* **1** to harden, to make hard (poner duro). **2** to set, to harden (pegamento, yeso, etc.). **3** (fig.) to harden, to toughen (a una persona): *el boxeo endurece al hombre = boxing hardens a man.* || *v.pron.* **4** to harden to go o get hard (ponerse dura una cosa). **5** to set, to harden (pegamento, yeso, etc.). **6** to become hardened o inured (una persona).
endurecimiento *s.m.* **1** hardening (acción). **2** hardness (estado). **3** setting (de un pegamento, yeso, etc.). **4** toughness (del cuerpo). **5** (fig.) cruelty, hardheartedness (crueldad).
ene *s.f.* n (letra).
eneasílabo *adj.* GRAM. nine syllable.
enebrina *s.f.* BOT. juniper bury.
enebro *s.m.* BOT. juniper (tree).
enema *s.m.* MED. enema.
enemiga *s.f.* **1** ill will (antipatía). **2** enmity, hostility (enemistad).
enemigo, -a *s.m. y f.* **1** enemy, (p.u.) foe. || *adj.* **2** enemy, hostile: *un barco enemigo = an enemy boat.* || **3 al — que huye, puente de plata,** let sleeping does lie. **4 — malo o el Enemigo,** the devil. **5 hacerse enemigos,** to make enemies. **6 pasarse al —,** to go over to the enemy. **7 ser — de,** to dislike.
enemistad *s.f.* enmity.
enemistar *v.t.* **1** to make enemies, to cause a rift, to set a odds: *enemistar a dos personas = to cause a rift between two people.* || *v.pron.* **2** to become enemies (convertirse en enemigos). **3** to fall out (enfadarse).
energético, -a *adj.* **1** TEC. energy. || *s.f.* **2** TEC. energetics. || *pl.m.* **3** fuels.
energía *s.f.* **1** FIS. energy: *energía cinética = kinetic energy.* **2** energy, vitality (de una persona). **3** ELEC. power, current.
enérgicamente *adv.* **1** energetically. **2** vigorously (vigorosamente). **3** forcefully (forzosamente). **4** drastically (drásticamente).
enérgico, -a *adj.* **1** energetic, spirited (carácter). **2** vigorous, strong (ataque). **3** strong (palabras). **4** strenuous (esfuerzo). **5** MED. drastic, powerful (medicina).
energúmeno, -a *s.m.* y *f.* **1** madman (hombre). **2** madwoman (mujer). **3** fanatic (fanático). **4** REL. energumen (poseído del demonio).
enero *s.m.* **1** January (mes): *el dos de enero = the second of January/January the second/January 2nd.*
enervación *s.f.* enervation.
enervante o **enervador, -a** *adj.* enervating.
enésimo, -a *adj.* **1** MAT. Nth, n: *elevar a la enésima potencia = to raise to the Nth power/to raise to the power of n.* **2** (fig.) umpteenth: *es la enésima vez que te lo digo = it's the umpteenth time I've told you.*
enfadadizo, -a *adj.* irritable, crotchety, touchy.
enfadar *v.t.* **1** to annoy, to get on someone's nerves (molestar). **2** to anger, to madden (enojar). || *v.pron.* **3** to get angry, to become irritated, to lose one's temper: *me enfado fácilmente = I lose my temper easily.* || **4 enfadarse con alguien,** to get angry with someone (enojarse): *to fall out with someone (enemistarse).*
enfado *s.m.* **1** anger (enojo). **2** quarrel (riña). **3** annoyance (disgusto).
enfadoso, -a *adj.* **1** irritating, annoying (molesto). **2** unpleasant (desagradable).
enfangar *v.t.* **1** to cover with mud. || *v.pron.* **2** to get muddy, to get covered with/in mud (llenarse de barro). **3** to sink into the mud (hundirse en el barro). **4** (fig.) to dirty one's hands (en asuntos malos). **5** to degrade oneself (deshonrarse). **6** MAR. to stick in the mud. || **7** enfangarse en los vicios, to wallow in vice.
enfardar *v.t.* **1** to package, to parcel up (empaquetar). **2** to bale (hacer fardos).
énfasis *s.m.* emphasis, stress: *poner el énfasis en = to put the emphasis on.*
enfáticamente *adv.* emphatically.
enfático, -a *adj.* emphatic.
enfatizar *v.t.* to emphasize.
enfermar *v.i.* y *pron.* **1** MED. to fall o become ill, to be taken ill (contraer enfermedad). || *v.t.* **2** MED. to make ill, to cause illness. **3** (fig.) to make sick.
enfermedad *s.f.* **1** MED. illness, sickness, disease: *su enfermedad era desconocida = his illness was unknown.* **2** illness, ill health (indisposición): *su enfermedad no le permite trabajar = his illness doesn't let him work.* || **3 ausentarse por —,** to be off o away sick. **4 — contagiosa,** contagious disease.
enfermería *s.f.* **1** MED. sick bary, infirmary (de un colegio, etc.). **2** hospital.
enfermero, -a *s.m.* MED. **1** male nurse (hombre). || *s.f.* **2** nurse (mujer).
enfermizo, -a *adj.* **1** sickly, poorly, unhealthy: *un chico enfermizo = a sickly boy.* **2** morbid: *un sentido del humor enfermizo = a morbid sense of humour.*
enfermoso, -a *adj.* (Am.) V. **enfermizo.**
enfervorizar *v.t.* **1** to encourage (animar). **2** to enthuse: *me enfervorizó con su artículo = he enthused me with his article.*
enfiestar *v.pron.* (Am.) to have a good time, to make merry.
enfilar *v.t.* **1** to line up, to align (colocar en fila). **2** to thread (ensartar). **3** to go straight along o down (una calle). **4** to point, to direct (un arma, etc.). **5** MIL. to rake, to enfilade.
enflaquecimiento *s.m.* **1** loss of weight (pérdida de peso). **2** slimming, losing weight (acción de perder peso). **3** (fig.) weakening.
enflaquecer *v.i.* **1** to lose weight, to get thin (adelgazar). **2** (fig.) to lose heart (desanimarse). || *v.t.* **3** to make thin (adelgazar). **4** (fig.) to weaken (debilitar).
enfocar *v.t.* **1** to focus (una cámara, etc.). **2** to approach, to consider, to look at (un problema, etc.): *se puede enfocar esta cuestión de distintas maneras = you can consider this question in different ways.* **3** to shine: *me enfocó con la linterna = he shone the torch at me.* || *v.i.* y *v.pron.* **4** to focus (una cámara, etc.).
enfoque *s.m.* **1** TEC. focusing (acción de enfocar una cámara, etc.). **2** TEC. focus (resultado obtenido después de enfocar). **3** (fig.) point of view, approach (perspectiva).

enfoscado *s.m.* TEC. pointing (acción de enfoscar un muro).

enfoscar *v.t.* 1 TEC. to point (tapar los agujeros en las paredes). || *v.i.* 2 to look sullen (ponerse hosco). 3 to go o get cloudy, to cloud over (nublarse el cielo). 4 to wrap oneself up (abrigarse). 5 to hide (ocultarse).

enfrascamiento *s.m.* (fig.) absortion.

enfrascar *v.t.* 1 to bottle (embotellar). 2 to put in a jar/flask (meter en un frasco). || *v.i.* 3 to get caught in brambles (enzarzarse). 4 (fig.) to get deeply involved o absorbed in something (en una ocupación).

enfrentar *v.t.* 1 to confront, to face (hacer frente). 2 to put face to face (poner frente a frente). || *v.i.* 3 to face up to, to confront: *se enfrentó con su madre = he confronted his mother.* 4 to face up to, to face (arrostrar): *se enfrentó con su enfermedad = he faced up to his illness.* 5 DEP. to meet, to play against o with: *el Liverpool se enferntará con el Real Madrid el sábado = Liverpool will play against Real Madrid on saturday.* 6 to antagonize (contrariar).

enfrente *adv.* 1 opposite, in front of, facing: *el banco está enfrente* (en contra).

enfriamiento *s.m.* 1 cooling (acción de enfriar). 2 TEC. refrigeration. 3 MED. cold, chill (catarro).

enfriar *v.t.* 1 to cool, to cool down, to chill: *enfriar un líquido = to cool (down) a liquid.* 2 (fig.) to cool down, to take the heat out (una situación). 3 (fig.) to dampen (una pasión, etc.). 4 (Am.) to kill (matar). || *v.i.* 5 to cool, to cool down, to cool off (perder el calor). 6 to go o get cold (ponerse frío). || *v.pron.* 7 to cool, to cool down, to cool off: *déjalo hasta que se enfríe = leave until it cools down.* 8 (fig.) to cool off, to grow cold: *nuestro amor se ha enfriado = our love has grown cold.* 9 MED. to catch a cold (acatarrarse).

enfundar *v.t.* 1 to sheathe (una espada, etc.). 2 to put away, to put in it's case (un violín, unas gafas, etc.). 3 to put in it's holster, to holster (una pistola). 4 to cover (un mueble).

enfurecimiento *s.m.* fury, range, anger.

enfurecer *v.t.* 1 to infuriate, to make angry o mad, to madden. || 2 *v.pron.* to become furious, to lose one's temper, to fly into a rage: *se enfureció con su novio = she lost her temper with her boyfriend.* 3 MAR. to get rough.

enfurruñamiento *s.m.* sulk, (slight) anger.

enfurruñarse *v.pron.* 1 to sulk (enfadarse). 2 to cloud over (nublarse).

engalanar *v.t.* 1 to adorn, to deck: *le engalanaron con flores = they decked him with flowers.* 2 to decorate (decorar). || *v.pron.* 3 to adorn oneself (adornarse). 4 to dress up (en ropa fina).

engallado, -a *adj.* 1 arrogant (presumido). 2 daring (atrevido).

engallarse *v.pron.* 1 to be arrogant, to put on airs and graces (erguirse). 2 to hold it's head high (un caballo).

enganchar *v.t.* 1 to hook (con un gancho). 2 MEC. to hitch (un remolque). 3 MEC. to couple (vagones de tren). 4 to hang (up): *enganchó el sombrero en la percha = he hung his hat on the hanger.* 5 to harness (un caballo). 6 to be habit forming (un vicio, una droga, etc.). 7 TEC. to engage (engranar). 8 MIL. to recruit, to enlist. 9 (fig. y fam.) to catch: *engancharon al ladrón = they caught the thief.* 10 to persuade, to get round (ganar la voluntad de alguien). || *v.pron.* 11 to get caught: *se me ha enganchado la camisa en un clavo = my shirt has got caught on an nail.* 12 (fam.) to get hooked (con el vicio, las drogas, etc.): *se enganchó con la heroína a los catorce años = he got hooked on heroin when he was fourteen.* 13 to get hooked up (en un gancho). 14 MIL. to enlist, to join up, to enrol.

enganche *s.m.* 1 hooking (acción de enganchar con un gancho). 2 hitching (remolque). 3 coupling (vagón de tren). 4 connection (empalme). 5 harnessing (caballo). 6 TEC. engaging (de un engranaje). 7 MIL. recruitment, enlistment, enrolment.

engañabobos *s.m. inv.* 1 (confidence) trickster, swindler (timador). 2 confidence trick, swindle (timo). 3 ZOOL. nightjar (chotacabras).

engañadizo, -a *adj.* gullible, easily taken in.

engañar *v.t.* 1 to deceive, to cheat: *me engañó el tendero = the shopkeeper cheated me.* 2 to trick, to fool: *le engañó al hacerle creer que tuviera diez años menos = he tricked her into thinking that he was ten years younger.* 3 to swindle, to trick, to cheat (timar). 4 to be unfaithful: *su mujer le engaña = his wife is unfaithful to him.* 5 (fam.) to get round (engatusar). 6 DEP. to dummy: *engañó al portero = he dummied the goalkeeper.* || *v.pron.* 7 to deceive oneself: *no te engañes = don't deceive yourself.* 8 to be mistaken, to be wrong (equivocarse). || *v.i.* 9 to be deceptive, to be misleading: *las apariencias engañan = you can't judge by appearances, appearanees are deceptive.*

engañifa *s.f.* 1 (fam.) trick, swindle (timo). 2 fraud (fraude). 3 deceit, deception (engaño).

engaño *s.m.* 1 deceit, deception (acción de engañar). 2 trick, swindle (timo). 3 fraud (fraude). 4 trick, deception (lo que engaña). 5 mistake, misunderstanding (equivocación): *que no haya engaño = let there be no misunderstanding.* 6 DEP. muleta (muleta). 7 (Am.) small gift, token (pequeño regalo).

engañoso, -a *adj.* 1 deceptive: *apariencia engañosa = deceptive appearance.* 2 deceitful, dishonest (una persona). 3 misleading, wrong (información, consejos, etc.).

engarabitarse *v.pron.* 1 to climb (subir). 2 to shin up (subir una cuerda, un palo). 3 to go numb with cold (entumecerse los dedos por el frío). 4 (Am.) to grow weak (debilitarse). 5 (Am.) to get thin (enflaquecerse).

engarce *s.m.* 1 setting, mounting, mount (para las joyas). 2 (fig.) connection, linking (de ideas, etc.). 3 (Am.) row (bronca).

engarzar *v.t.* 1 to set, to mount (joyas). 2 to thread, to string (ensartar cuentas, etc.). 3 to curl (rizar). 4 (Am.) to get caught in brambles (enzarzarse).

engastar *v.t.* to set, to mount (una joya).

engaste *s.m.* 1 setting, mounting (acción de engastar). 2 setting, mount (que sujeta una joya). 3 imperfect pearl (perla imperfecta).

engatusar *v.t.* 1 to get round someone (ganar a alguien con halagos). 2 to trick (engañar).

engendramiento *s.m.* engendering.

engendrar *v.t.* 1 to engender. 2 (fig.) to give rise to, to cause (causar). 3 BIOL. to breed. 4 to produce: *engendrar una reacción química = to produce a chemical reaction.*

engendro *s.m.* 1 BIOL. foetus (feto). 2 runt (criatura deforme). 3 monster, freak (monstruo). 4 deformed child (niño deformado). 5 (fig.) bodge up, botched job (chapuza). 6 brainchild (obra intelectual).

englobado, -a *adj.* 1 emphatic (enfático). 2 wearing a ruff (quienes vestían gola).

englobar *v.t.* 1 to include (incluir). 2 to lump together (poner varias cosas juntas). 3 to put one's arms around (abarcar).

engolfar *v.i.* 1 MAR. to sail out to sea, to lose sight of land. || *v.pron.* 2 MAR. to sail out to sea. 3 (fig.) to become engrossed (dedicarse plenamente). 4 (fig.) to get carried away (dejarse llevar por una pasión).

engolosinar *v.t.* 1 tempt, to entice. || *v.pron.* 2 to grow fond of, to develop a taste for (tomar gusto a una cosa).

engomar *v.pron.* 1 to stick (pegar). 2 to size (los tejidos).

engorda *s.f.* 1 (Am.) fattening up. 2 (Am.) fattened animals (ganado).

engordadero *s.m.* 1 fattening sty (sitio). 2 fattening period (período de tiempo). 3 fattening fodder (pienso para engordar).

engordar *v.t.* 1 to fatten, to make fat (una persona). 2 to fatten up (un animal). || *v.i.* 3 to get fat, to put on weight: *has engordado mucho = you have got very fat.* 4 to be fattening: *el azúcar engorda mucho = sugar is very fattening.*

engorde *s.m.* fattening up (de los animales).

engorro *s.m.* 1 nuisance, bother (molestia). 2 (fam.) snag, difficulty (dificultad).

engorroso, -a *adj.* 1 annoying, bothersome (molesto). 2 cumbersome (difícil de manejar).

engranaje *s.m.* 1 TEC. gear. 2 TEC. cogwheels (ruedas dentadas). 3 TEC. gearing (conjunto de transmisión). 4 TEC. meshing, engaging (acción de engranar). 5 (fig.) connection, linking (enlace).
engranamiento *s.m.* enmeshing, enmeshment.
engranar *v.t.* e *i.* 1 TEC. to mesh, to engage (acción de acoplar la transmisión). || *v.pron.* 2 (Am.) to size up, to get locked (atascarse). 3 (Am.) to get angry (enfadarse).
engrandecer *v.t.* 1 to enlarge, to make bigger (hacer más grande). 2 to praise (alabar). 3 to exaggerate (exagerar).
engrandecimiento *s.m.* 1 enlargement. 2 praise (alabanza). 3 exaggeration (exageración).
engranujarse *v.pron.* 1 MED. to get covered with spots o pimples (llenarse de granos). 2 to become a rogue o rascal (hacerse granuja).
engrasado, -a *adj.* MEC. greasing, lubrication.
engrasar *v.t.* 1 MEC. to grease, to lubricate, to oil. 2 to oil up (un componente eléctrico). 3 to manure (abonar las tierras). 4 to make greasy (manchar con grasa). || *v.pron.* 5 to get covered with o in grease (mancharse con grasa).
engrase *s.m.* 1 MEC. greasing, lubrication (con grasa). 2 MEC. oiling, lubrication (con aceite).
engreimiento *s.m.* arrogance, conceit.
engreír *v.t.* 1 to make arrogant, to make conceited: *su nuevo trabajo le ha engreído = his new job has made him conceited.* 2 (Am.) to spoil, to pamper (mimar). || *v.pron.* 3 to get conceited o arrogant. 4 (Am.) to get spoiled o pampered (con mimos). 5 (Am.) to grow fond of (encariñarse).
engrosamiento *s.m.* 1 fattening (de una persona). 2 swelling (de un río, etc.). 3 increase, enlargement (de una cosa). 4 thickening (espesamiento).
engrosar *v.t.* 1 to enlarge (agrandar). || 2 to increase (aumentar). 3 to swell (un río, etc.). 4 to thicken (espesar). || *v.i.* 5 to get fatter, to put on weight (una persona). 6 to swell (un río). || *v.pron.* 7 to increase (aumentarse). 8 to enlarge (agrandarse).
engrudo *s.m.* (flower and water) paste.
engruesar *v.i.* V. engrosar.
enguijarrado *s.m.* cobbles.
enguijarrar *v.t.* to cobble.
engullir *v.t.* 1 to bolt, to gobble down (comida sólida). 2 to gulp down (un líquido).
engurrio *s.m.* sadness (tristeza).
engurruñar *v.t.* y *v.pron.* 1 to shrink (encoger). 2 to crumple (arrugar). || *v.pron.* 3 (fam.) to become sad, to become gloomy (entristecerse).
enharinar *v.t.* to flour, to sprinkle with flour (cubrir de harina).
enhebrar *v.t.* 1 to thread (una aguja). 2 to string, to thread (ensartar).
enhestar *v.t.* 1 to set upright (poner vertical). 2 to hoist (alzar).
enhiesto, -a *adj.* erect, straight, upright.
enhilar *v.t.* 1 to thread (enhebrar). 2 to put in order, to arrange (poner en orden).
enhorabuena *s.f.* 1 congratulations: *dar la enhorabuena = to congratulate.* || *adv.* 2 thank heavens: *que se vaya enhorabuena = thank heavens he is going.* || 3 **estar de —,** to be very happy. 4 **mi más cordial —,** my very best wishes.
enhoramala *adv.* 1 inopportunely (en un mal momento). || 2 **¡—!,** good riddence!
enigma *s.m.* 1 enigma. 2 mystery, puzzle: *donde consiguió el dinero es un enigma = where he got the money from is a mystery.*
enigmático, -a *adj.* enigmatic, puzzling, mysterious.
enjabonar *v.t.* 1 to soap. 2 (fam. y fig.) to tell someone off (reprender). 3 (Am.) to flatter (adular).
enjaezar *v.t.* 1 to harness.
enjalbegado *s.m.* whitewashing (de una pared).
enjalbegadura *s.f.* whitewashing (de una pared).
enjalbegar *v.t.* 1 to whitewash (una pared). 2 to make up, to paint (maquillar).
enjalma *s.f.* saddle-bag (albarda).
enjambre *s.m.* 1 swarm (de abejas). 2 (fig.) swarm, throng (muchedumbre).
enjaretar *v.t.* 1 to thread through a hem (pasar una cinta por una jareta). 2 to spill out (decir algo con precipitación). 3 to fit in (intercalar). || 4 **— algo a uno,** (Am.) to lumber someone with something.
enjaular *v.t.* 1 to cage, to put in a cage (meter en una jaula). 2 (fam.) to put in prison, to lock up, to put in the slammer (encarcelar).
enjoyar *v.t.* 1 to adorn with jewels (a una cosa). 2 to deck with jewels (a una persona). 3 (fig.) to beautify (embellecer).
enjuagar *v.t.* 1 to rinse (la ropa). 2 to rinse out, to swill out (la boca).
enjuague *s.m.* 1 mouthwash (para enjuagar la boca). 2 rinsing (acción de enjuagar la ropa). 3 rinsing water (líquido). 4 (fig.) plot, scheme (negociación sucia).
enjugar *v.t.* 1 to dry (secar). 2 to mop up (un líquido). 3 to wipe (quitar la humedad). 4 to mop, to wide (el sudor). 5 to wipe out, to cancel (una deuda). || *v.pron.* 6 to get thinner (adelgazar).
enjuiciamiento *s.m.* 1 DER. judgement (acción de juzgar). 2 trial, prosecution (criminal). 3 lawsuit (civil).
enjuiciar *v.t.* 1 DER. to pass judgement, to judge (juzgar). 2 DER. to sue (civil). 3 DER. to try (someter a juicio).
enjundia *s.f.* 1 animal fat o grease. 2 (fig.) substance: *una actuación con mucha enjundia = a performance with a lot of substance.* 3 force, vigour, strength (vigor). 4 character (carácter).
enjundioso, -a *adj.* 1 fat (gordo). 2 substancial, solid, meaty (con mucha sustancia). 3 greasy (grasiento).
enjutar *v.t.* ARQ. to fil up (llenar).
enjuto, -a *adj.* 1 thin (delgado). 2 skinny (flaco). || *s.m.* 3 tinder (palos secos que sirven de yesca).
enlace *s.m.* 1 connection, link, tie-up (relación). 2 marriage (casamiento). 3 QUIM. bond. 4 connection (de trenes, etc.). 5 GRAM. liaison (de dos palabras). 6 meeting, rendez-vous (encuentro). 7 ELEC. linkage. || 8 **— sindical,** shop steward.
enladrillar *v.t.* to pave with bricks.
enlatar *v.t.* to can, to tin (envasar en latas).
enlazar *v.t.* 1 to link, to connect, to relate: *enlazar dos ideas = to connect two ideas.* 2 to tie (together), to bind (atar). 3 (Am.) to lasso (un animal). || *v.i.* 4 to connect (los trenes, etc.). || *v.pron.* 5 to be linked, to link (up) (unirse). 6 to get married, to marry (casarse). 7 to be linked, to be connected, to be related (dos ideas, etc.). 8 to become linked by marriage (dos familias).
enlistonado *s.m.* TEC. laths.
enlobreguecer *v.t.* 1 to darken, to make dark (hacer más oscuro). || *v.pron.* 2 to become/grow dark (anochecer).
enlodar o **enlodazar** *v.t.* 1 to cover in mud, to muddy (cubrir de lodo). 2 to splatter with mud (manchar de lodo). 3 (fig.) to stain, to tarnish (la reputación). || *v.pron.* 4 to get muddy, to get covered with o in mud (mancharse de lodo).
enloquecer *v.pron.* 1 to drive mad, to drive crazy (volver loco): *la música me enloquece = music drives me mad.* 2 to madden, to drive mad (turbar). || *v.pron.* e *i.* 3 to go insane o mad, to go out of one's mind.
enloquecimiento *s.m.* insanity, madness.
enlosado *s.m.* 1 (flagstone) paving (de losas). 2 tiling (de baldosas).
enlozar *v.t.* (Am.) to enamel, to glaze (cubrir con un baño de loza).
enlucido, -a *adj.* 1 plastered (con yeso). 2 whitewashed (blanqueado). 3 polished (las armas). || *s.m.* 3 plaster, coat of plaster (capa de yeso).
enlucir *v.t.* 1 to plaster (una pared). 2 to polish (las armas).
enlutar *v.t.* 1 to dress in mourning (vestirse de luto). 2 to put into mourning (a una persona): *su muerte enlutó a todo el pueblo = her death put the whole village into mourning.* 3 to darken (oscurecer). 4 to make unhappy (entristecer). || *v.pron.* 5 to go into mourning, to dress in mourning (vestirse de luto).
enmadrarse *v.pron.* to become excessively attatched to one's mother (tomar excesivo cariño el hijo por la madre).
enmarañamiento *s.m.* 1 tangle, entanglement (de cosas). 2 (fig.) confusion, muddle (de una situación).
enmarañar *v.t.* 1 to tangle (up), to entangle (enredar). 2 (fig.) to confuse, to make more of a mess, to muddle up (una situación, etc.). || *v.pron.* 3 to get tangled, to get into a tangle, to get entangled (cuerda, etc.). 4 (fig.) to get

muddled, to get confused (una situación, etc.). **5** to darken (ponerse oscuro el cielo); to cloud over (nublarse el cielo).

enmarcar *v.t.* **1** to frame (en un marco). **2** to surround (rodear). **3** (fig.) to provide the setting, to act as a background: *un bosque en Alemania enmarcó la fotografía = a forest in Germany provided the setting for the photograph.*

enmascarado, -a *adj.* **1** masked. || *s.m.* y *f.* **2** a masked person (persona que lleva máscara).

enmascaramiento *s.m.* MIL. camouflage.

enmascarar *v.t.* **1** to mask (poner una máscara). **2** MIL. to camouflage. || *v.pron.* **3** to put on a mask (ponerse una máscara). **4** to masquerade (disfrazarse).

enmendación o **enmendadura** *s.f.* enmendation, correction.

enmendar *v.t.* **1** to correct (corregir). **2** DER. to amend (una ley). **3** to revise (un juicio). **4** to reform (moralmente). **5** to repair (un daño). **6** to rectify (un defecto). **7** to make good, to compensate (una pérdida). **8** MAR. to alter, to change (el rumbo, el fondeadero). || *v.pron.* **9** to mend one's ways, to reform (reformarse).

enmienda *s.f.* **1** correction, amendment: *tuvo que hacer muchas enmiendas en el texto = he had to make a lot of corrections in the text.* **2** DER. amendment: *la quinta enmienda = the fifth amendment.* **3** compensation, indemnity (de un daño). **4** correction, rectification (de un defecto). **5** fertilizer (fertilizante). **6** fertilizing (acción de abonar la tierra). || **7 no tener —,** to be incorrigible. **8 poner —,** to correct. **9 tomar —,** to punish (castigar).

enmohecer *v.t.* **1** to rust (el metal). **2** to make mouldy: *la humedad enmohece las manzanas = the humidity moulds the apples.* || *v.i.* **3** (fig.) to go rusty (embotarse). || *v.pron.* **4** to go o get rusty, to rust (el metal). **5** to go mouldy (el pan, etc.). **6** (fig.) to get rusty (embotarse).

enmohecido, -a *adj.* **1** rusty (metal). **2** mouldy (el pan, etc.).

enmohecimiento *s.m.* **1** rusting (acción de oxidarse un metal). **2** rustiness (estado de oxidación). **3** moulding (acción de enmohecer el pan, etc.). **4** mouldiness (estado).

enmonarse *v.pron.* (Am.) to get drunk (emborracharse).

enmudecer *v.t.* **1** to silence (silenciar). **2** (fig.) to leave speechless (por una emoción fuerte, etc.). || *v.pron.* **3** to be silent, to be quiet, to say nothing (callarse). **4** to lose one's voice (quedar afónico). **5** (fig.) to be dumbfounded, to be speechless (ante una fuerte emoción, etc.).

enmugrecer *v.t.* **1** to cover with filth (cubrir de mugre). || *v.pron.* **2** to get covered in filth (llenarse de mugre).

ennegrecer o **denegrecer** *v.t.* **1** to blacken, to turn black: *el humo le ennegreció la cara = the smoke blackened his face.* **2** *v.i.* y *pron.* to turn black, to go black.

ennegrecimiento *s.m.* blacking, blackening.

ennoblecer *v.t.* **1** to ennoble. **2** (fig.) to give an air of dignity: *su barba le ennobleció = his beard gave him an air of dignity.*

enografía *s.f.* viniculture (la ciencia de los vinos).

enojadizo, -a *adj.* irritable, short tempered, quick tempered.

enojado, -a *adj.* angry, cross (enfadado).

enojar *v.t.* **1** to anger, to make angry (enfadar). **2** to irritate, to annoy (molestar), to offend (ofender). || *v.pron.* **3** to get angry (enfadarse). **4** to get irritated, to get annoyed (molestarse): *me enojo cuando ponen la música muy alta = I get angry when they put the music very loud.* **5** MAR. to get rough (el mar). **6** to get windy (el viento).

enojo *s.m.* **1** anger (ira). **2** annoyance, irritation (fastidio). || **3 de prontos enojos,** quick tempered.

enojón, -ona *adj.* (Am.) V. **enojadizo.**

enología *s.f.* viniculture (la ciencia de los vinos).

enorgullecer *v.t.* **1** to fill with pride, to make proud: *ser reconocida por la calle le enorgullece = being recognized in the street fills her with pride.* || *v.pron.* **2** to be proud: *se enorgullece de sus éxitos = he is proud of his successes.*

enorgullecimiento *s.m.* **1** pride (orgullo). **2** filling with pride (acción).

enorme *adj.* **1** enormous, huge, massive: *un barco enorme = an enormous boat.* **2** (fig.) monstruous, heincus (muy malo).

enormemente *adv.* **1** enormously, vastly: *sus terrenos son enormemente más grandes que antes = his land is vastly bigger than before.* **2** tremendously, extremely: *su obra es enormemente divertida = his play is tremendously funny.*

enormidad *s.f.* **1** enormity, vastness (tamaño). **2** (fig.) heinousness, monstruousness, wickedness (de un pecado).

enqué *s.m.* **1** (Am.) container (contenedor). **2** (Am.) bag (bolsa).

enquiciar *v.t.* **1** to put a door on (una puerta); to put a window in (ventana). **2** (fig.) to put in order (poner en orden).

enquiridión *s.m.* manual (libro manual).

enquistado, -a *adj.* **1** MED. encysted (de forma de quiste). **2** embedded (encajado).

enquistarse *v.pron.* **1** MED. encyst. **2** (fig.) to become embedded (encajarse).

enraizar *v.i.* to take root.

enralecer *v.i.* **1** to become threadbare (tejido). **2** to become thin o sparse (pelo, árboles, etc.).

enramada *s.f.* **1** BOT. arbour, bower. **2** branches (conjunto de ramas). **3** (Am.) cover made of branches (cobertizo hecho de ramas).

enramar *v.t.* **1** to decorate with branches (decorar con ramas). **2** MAR. to fit the frames (a un barco). || *v.i.* **3** BOT. to branch, to grow branches (echar ramas un árbol). || *v.pron.* **4** to hide among the branches (ocultarse).

enrame *s.m.* BOT. branching (acción y efecto de enramar).

enrarecer *v.t.* **1** to rarify (el aire). **2** to make scarce (hacer escaso). || *v.pron.* e *i.* **3** to rarify (el aire). **4** to become scarce (escasear).

enrarecimiento *s.m.* **1** rarefaction. **2** scarcity (escasez).

enrasar *v.t.* **1** to make level o flush (nivelar). **2** to smooth (allanar). **3** to level up (un líquido). || *v.pron.* **4** to be at the same level (estar al mismo nivel).

enrase *s.m.* levelling (acción de enrasar).

enredadera *adj.* **1** climbing: *planta enredadera = climbing plant.* || *s.f.* **2** BOT. bindweed.

enredado, -a *adj.* tangled, tangled up, entangled (cuerda, etc.).

enredador, -a *adj.* **1** mischievous (travieso). **2** trouble-making (que causa riñas). **3** (fig.) gossipy (chismoso). || *s.m.* y *f.* **4** gossip (cotilla). **5** busybody (entrometido).

enredar *v.i.* **1** to tangle (up), to entangle (enmarañar). **2** (fig.) to confuse (una situación, etc.). **3** to involve, to implicate (a alguien en un asunto peligroso, dudoso, etc.). **4** to cause trouble (entre dos personas). **5** to net, to catch in a net (coger con una red). || *v.pron.* **6** to get into a tangle, to get entangled, to get tangled up (enmarañarse). **7** to become muddled o confused (una situación, etc.). **8** MAR. to foul. **9** to get involved, to have an affair: *se enredó con su profesor = he got involved with his teacher.* || *v.i.* **10** to get into mischief (un niño). || **11 — de palabras,** to get into an argument.

enredijo *s.m.* tangle (enredo).

enredista *s.m.* y *f.* (Am.) V. **enredador.**

enredo *s.m.* **1** tangle: *un enredo de hilos = a tangle of threads.* **2** (fig.) confusion, muddle (confusión). **3** love affair (aventura amorosa). **4** jam, difficult situation (situación difícil). **5** mischief (travesura). **6** intrigue (intriga). **7** lie (mentira). **8** plot (sucesos previos al desenlace final en una obra literaria).

enredoso, -a *adj.* **1** complicated (complicado). **2** mischievous (travieso).

enrejado *s.m.* **1** grating, grille (conjunto de rejas). **2** lattice (de una ventana). **3** trellis (en el jardín). **4** bars (en una celda). **5** wire netting o fencing (alambrada). **6** openwork (labor de costura). **7** inmate (preso).

enrejar *v.t.* **1** to put a railing round, to fence (cerrar con rejas). **2** (Am.) to put a halter (poner una soga a un animal). **3** to tie a calf to the legs of a cow (atar un ternero a las patas de una vaca para ordeñarla). **4** to fix a grating to (a una ventana). **5** (Am.) to darn, to patch (reparar ropa). **6** to fit the share to the plough (poner la reja en el arado). **7** to

put in prison, to incarcerate (meter a uno en la cárcel).
enrevesado, -a *adj.* 1 intricate, complicated (revesado). 2 complicated, difficult (difícil).
enrielar *v.t.* 1 TEC. to make into ingots (un metal). 2 (Am.) to lay rails (construir una vía ferroviaria). 3 (Am.) to put on the tracks (encarrilar). 4 (Am.) (fig.) to put on the right track (un negocio). 5 (Am.) to channel, to canalize (encauzar).
enriquecedor, -a *adj.* enrichening.
enriquecer *v.t.* 1 to make rich, to enrich (hacer rico). || *v.pron.* e *i.* 2 to get o become rich. || 3 enriquecerse a costa ajena, to do well at other people's expense.
enriquecimiento *s.m.* enrichment.
enrocar *v.t.* to castle (en ajedrez).
enrojecer *v.t.* 1 to redden, to turn red (poner rojo). 2 to make blush (a una persona). 3 to make red hot (a un metal). || *v.pron.* e *i.* 4 to blush (de vergüenza). 5 to go red with anger (con ira). 6 to become red hot (un metal).
enrojecimiento *s.m.* 1 reddening (de una cosa). 2 blushing (acción de enrojecerse una persona).
enrolar *v.t.* 1 (Am.) to enrol, to sign up, to sign on (reclutar). 2 MIL. to enlist. || *v.pron.* 3 to enrol, to sign on. 4 MIL. to enlist.
enrollamiento *s.m.* 1 rolling up (de papel, etc.). 2 ELEC. coil.
enronquecer *v.t.* 1 to make hoarse: *el viento le enronqueció = the wind made him hoarse.* || *v.pron.* e *i.* 2 to go hoarse: *se enronqueció por el frío = he went hoarse because of the cold.*
enronquecimiento *s.m.* hoarseness.
enroscado, -a *adj.* 1 coiled (enrollado). 2 twisted (torcido). 3 (Am.) angry (enfadado).
enroscadura *s.f.* 1 coiling (acción de enrollar cuerda, cable, etc.). 2 coil (efecto).
enroscamiento *s.m.* (acción de enrollar cuerda, cable, etc.).
enroscar *v.t.* 1 to coil, to wind (enrollar). 2 to screw in (atornillar). || *v.pron.* 3 to coil oneself round, to wind oneself round (una serpiente, etc.).
ensaimada *s.f.* spiral pasty.
ensalada *s.f.* 1 salad. 2 (fig.) mess, mix-up (lío). 3 MUS. medley, (fig.) traffic jam (atasco de coches). 5 clash (mezcla poco armónica de colores). || **6 — de patatas,** potatoe salad. || **7 — rusa,** Russian salad.
ensaladera *s.f.* salad bowl.
ensaladilla *s.f.* 1 diced vegetable salad, Russian salad. 2 (Am.) lampoon, satirical verse (versos satíricos).
ensalmar *v.t.* 1 MED. to set (un hueso). 2 MED. to cure with quack remedies (curar con ensalmos).
ensalmo *s.m.* 1 MED. quack remedy. 2 incantation (conjuro). || **3 por —,** by magic.
ensalzamiento *s.m.* 1 exaltation (engrandecimiento). 2 praise (alabanza).
ensalzar *v.t.* 1 to exalt (enaltecer). 2 to praise (alabar).
ensamblado *s.m.* joint (empalme).
ensamblador *s.m.* y *f.* joiner.
ensambladura *s.f.* 1 joinery (ebanistería). 2 TEC. joint (unión): *ensambladura de inglete = mitre joint.*
ensamblaje *s.m.* 1 TEC. assembly: *planta de ensamblaje = assembly plant.*
ensamblar *v.t.* 1 to join (unir). 2 to assemble (montar).
ensanchador *s.m.* 1 stretcher. || *adj.* 2 widening.
ensanchamiento *s.m.* 1 widening, broadening. 2 expansion, enlargement (de una ciudad).
ensanchar *v.t.* 1 to widen, to broaden (una carretera, etc.). 2 to enlarge, to expand (una ciudad). 3 to widen, to make bigger (un agujero, una apertura, etc.). 4 to stretch (una tela). || *v.pron.* 5 to get wider (hacerse más ancha). 6 to become conceited (engreírse).
ensanche *s.m.* 1 widening, broadening: *el ensanche de la carretera = the widening of the road.* 2 enlargement, expansion (de una ciudad). 3 stretching (de una tela). 4 new suburb o district, new development area (nuevo suburbio).
ensangrentar *v.t.* 1 to stain with blood (manchar). || *v.pron.* 2 to get stained with blood (mancharse). 3 (fig.) to fly into a temper (enfurecerse). 4 (fig.) to become cruel (encruelecerse).
ensañamiento *s.m.* 1 mercilessness, cruelty (crueldad). 2 rage, fury (ira).
ensañar *v.t.* 1 to infuriate, to enrage (enfurecer). || *v.pron.* 2 to delight in tormenting (deleitarse en hacer sufrir al que no puede defenderse). 3 to be merciless (no tener piedad).
ensartar *v.t.* 1 to string (perlas, etc.). 2 to thread (una aguja). 3 to spit, to broach (la carne). 4 to run through (atravesar). 5 (fig.) to reel off: *ensartó una serie de chistes = he reeled off a series of jokes.* || *v.pron.* 6 (Am.) to get into a jam meterse en un embrollo). 7 (Am.) to come out of a deal badly (salir perjudicado).
ensayar *v.t.* 1 to test, to try, to try out (probar). 2 to rehearse (un baile, etc.). 3 TEC. to assay (metal). || *v.i.* 4 to rehearse (un baile, etc.). || *v.pron.* 5 to practise, to rehearse.
ensaye *s.m.* TEC. assay (de metales).
ensayista *s.m.* y *f.* essayist.
ensayo *s.m.* 1 testing, trial (prueba): *el ensayo de una máquina = the testing of a machine.* 2 rehearsal (de un espectáculo): *ensayo general = dress rehearsal.* 3 TEC. assay (metales). 4 (lit.) essay. 5 DEP. try (en el rugby). 6 QUIM. test: *tubo de ensayo = test tube.* || **7 viaje de —,** trial run. **8 vuelo de —,** test flight.
enseguida o **en seguida** *adv.* at once, immediately, straight away.
ensenado, -a *adj.* 1 breast shaped (en forma de seno). || *s.f.* 2 GEOG. inlet, cove, creek (entrada del mar). 3 (Am.) small fenced pasture (pequeño pasto).
enseña *s.f.* standard, ensign.
enseñanza *s.f.* 1 education (educación). 2 teaching: *se dedica a la enseñanza = his job is teaching.* 3 training (instrucción). || **4 — media,** secondary education. **5 — primaria,** primary education. **6 — superior,** higher education. **7 escuela de primera —,** primary school.
enseñar *v.t.* 1 to teach: *enseñar a alguien el inglés = to teach somebody English.* 2 to show: *ahora te enseñaré la cocina = now I'll show you the kitchen.* || **3 — con el dedo,** to point: *me enseñó su coche con el dedo = he pointed at his car.* || *v.pron.* 4 (Am.) to learn (aprender). 5 (Am.) to get used, to get accustomed (acostumbrarse): *no me enseño aquí = I can't get used to it here.*
enseñorear *v.t.* 1 to take control. || *v.pron.* 2 to control oneself (controlarse). 3 to take control of (hacerse dueño de): *se enseñoreó de la situación = he took control of the situation.*
enseres *m.pl.* 1 equipment (*pl.*), goods: *enseres domésticos = household goods.* 2 tools (herramientas). 3 utensils (utensilios).
ensillar *v.t.* to saddle (up), to put a saddle on (un caballo).
ensimismado, -a *adj.* 1 deep in thought (absorto). 2 engrossed: *estaba ensimismado en un libro = he was engrossed in a book.*
ensimismamiento *s.m.* 1 deep thought, pensiveness. 2 (Am.) conceit (envanecimiento).
ensimismarse *v.pron.* 1 to become lost in thought (quedarse abstraído). 2 to become engrossed in something (en la lectura, etc.). 3 (Am.) to become conceited (envanecerse).
ensoberbecer *v.t.* 1 to make proud (causar orgullo). || *v.pron.* 2 to become proud. 3 MAR. to become rough (agitarse el mar).
ensombrecer *v.t.* 1 to cast a shadow (cubrir de sombras): *el edificio ensombrece el parque = the building casts a shadow over the park.* 2 to darken (oscurecer). 3 to darken (oscurecer). 4 to become gloomy o sad (entristecerse).
ensoñación *s.f.* 1 (Am.) fantasy (fantasía). 2 (Am.) dream (sueño).
ensoñador, -a *adj.* 1 dreamy. || *s.m.* y *f.* 2 dreamer (soñador).
ensordecedor, -a *adj.* deafening: *un ruido ensordecedor = a deafening noise.*
ensordecer *v.t.* 1 to deafen: *el avión me ensordeció = the plane deafened me.* 2 to muffle, to deafen (amortiguar un ruido). || *v.pron.* 3 to go deaf, to turn deaf (quedarse sordo). 4 (fig.) to pretend not to hear (fingir no oír).
ensortijamiento *s.m.* 1 curling (del pelo). 2 coiling (de hilo, cable, etc.).
ensortijar *v.t.* 1 to curl, to put curls into (el pelo). 2 to ring, to fix a ring (en la nariz). 3 to coil, to wind (el hilo, cable, etc.). || *v.pron.* 4 to curl (el pelo).
ensuciar *v.t.* 1 to dirty, to make dirty. 2 (fig.) to tarnish (la reputación, etc.). ||

v.pron. **3** to get dirty. **4** to dirty oneself, to soil oneself (un bebé). **5** to tarnish (la reputación, etc.).
ensueño *s.m.* **1** dream (durante el sueño). **2** fantasy, dream (ilusión). **3** (fig.) dream: *un mundo de ensueño = a dream world.* || **4 ni por ensueños,** not likely.
entablado *s.m.* **1** boards (para el baile). **2** wooden floor (suelo). **3** TEC. boarding, planking (conjunto de tablas). **4** floorboards (tablas del suelo).
entablamento *s.m.* ARQ. entablature.
entablar *v.t.* **1** to board up, to plank (asegurar con tablas). **2** MED. to splint, to put into a splint (un brazo, etc.). **3** to set out the pieces (el ajedrez, etc.). **4** to establish, to set up (comunicaciones, etc.). **5** DER. to file, to bring: *entablar un pleito = to file a suit.* **6** to begin (una conversación, etc.). || *v.i.* **7** (Am.) to draw (empatar). **8** (Am.) to boast (presumir). || *v.pron.* **9** (Am.) to settle (el viento). **10** to begin, to start (comenzar). **11** to refuse, to turn (un caballo).
entablillar *v.t.* MED. to splint, to put into a splint (un brazo, etc.).
entalladura *s.f.* **1** ART. sculpture, carving (escultura). **2** ART. engraving (grabado). **3** notch (corte).
entallar *v.t.* **1** ART. to sculpt, to sculpture (la piedra, etc.). **2** ART. to carve (la madera). **3** ART. to engrave (grabar). **4** to notch (hacer un corte). **5** to tap (un árbol para sacar resina). **6** TEC. to mortise o mortice. **7** to cut, to ailor (un traje, etc.). || *v.i.* **8** to fit well: *este traje entalla bien = this suit fits well.*
entarimado *s.m.* **1** bloorboarding (tablas del suelo). || **2 — de hojas quebradas,** parquet floor.
entarimar *v.t.* **1** to board, to plank (con tablas). **2** to parquet (con hojas quebradas).
ente *s.m.* **1** being, entity (ser). **2** (fam.) specimen (sujeto ridículo o extravagante). || **3 — oficial,** official body o entity.
enteco, -a *adj.* weak, sickly, frail.
entejar *v.t.* (Am.) to roof with tiles, to tile (tejar).
entelequia *s.f.* FIL. entelechy.
entendederas *s.f.pl.* **1** (fam.) brains (inteligencia). **2** understanding (entendimiento).
entender *v.t.* **1** to understand (comprender): *no entiendo nada = I don't understand anything.* **2** to believe, to think (creer): *entiendo que sería mejor irnos = I think it would be better if we left.* **3** to mean, to intend: *que entiendes con eso = what do you mean by that.* || *v.i.* **4** to understand, to know about: *tú entiendes de esto = you know about this.* || *v.pron.* **5** to make oneself understood (hacerse entender). **6** to be under stood (comprenderse). **7** to be meant (significar). **8** to get on (llevarse bien): *no se entiende con su primo = he doesn't get on with his cousin.* **9** to agree, to come to an agreement (llegar a un acuerdo): *ya me entenderé con él = I will come to an agreement with him.* **10** to have an affair (mantener relaciones amorosas). || **11 a mi —,** in my opinion. **12 dar a —,** to imply. **13 yo me entiendo,** I know what I'm doing.
entendido, -a *adj.* **1** understood (comprendido). **2** agreed (de acuerdo). **3** well informed, expert (una persona). **4** clever, skilled (hábil). **5** clever, intelligent (inteligente). || *s.m.* y *f.* **6** expert, authority (enterado). || *interj.* **7** all right, O.K. (de acuerdo); understood (comprendido). || **8 bien — que,** on the understanding that. **9 según tenemos —,** as far as we can gather.
entendimiento *s.m.* **1** understanding (comprensión). **2** intelligence, understanding (inteligencia). **3** judgement, understanding (juicio). **4** mid (mente). || **5 de — poco lucido,** of limited understanding; slow to understand.
entenebrecer *v.t.* **1** to darken. || *v.pron.* **2** to darken, to get dark (oscurecer). **3** (fig.) to darken.
entente *s.f.* **1** entente. **2** harmony (armonía).
enterado, -a *adj.* **1** well up, well informed (bien informado): *lo sabe cualquier persona enterada = any well informed person knows.* **2** aware (al tanto). **3** (Am.) arrogant, conceited (engreído). || *s.m.* y *f.* **4** expert, authority (experto). **5** (fam.) know-it-all (sabelotodo). || **6 darse por — de algo,** to be well aware of something. **7 no darse por — de algo,** to pretend not to have heard o understood (hacer el sordo).
enteramente *adv.* completely, entirely, fully.
enterar *v.t.* **1** to inform. **2** (Am.) to pay, to hand over (entregar dinero). **3** (Am.) to make up, to complete (completar una cantidad). || *v.i.* **4** (Am.) to get well, to get better (ponerse mejor). **5** to let the days go by (dejar pasar los días). || *v.pron.* **6** to find out (descubrir). || **7 ¿te enteras?,** do you understand? (¿comprendes?); do you hear? (¿oyes?). **8 ¡entérate!,** listen!
entereza *s.f.* **1** entirety. **2** integrity (integridad). **3** (fig.) firmness (firmeza). **4** impartiality (imparcialidad). **5** determination (determinación).
enteritis *s.f.* MED. enteritis.
enterizo, -a *adj.* **1** in one piece (de una pieza). **2** whole (entero).
enternecedor, -a *adj.* touching, moving (conmovedor).
enternecer *v.t.* **1** to soften (ablandar). **2** to make tender (la carne). **3** (fig.) to touch, to move (conmover). || *v.pron.* **4** to relent (ceder). **5** to be moved o touched (conmoverse).
enternecimiento *s.m.* **1** pity (compasión). **2** tenderness (ternura).
entero, -a *adj.* **1** entire, complete, whole: *vimos la película entera = we saw the whole film.* **2** whole, in one piece (no roto). **3** full, whole: *un saco entero = a whole sack.* **4** MAT. whole, integral. **5** BIO. not castrated (sin castrar). **6** (fig.) firm (firme). **7** upright, honest (honrado). **8** strong, thick (telas). **9** pure, virgin (virgen). **10** (Am.) identical (idéntico). || *s.m.* **11** point (la bolsa): *ha perdido dos enteros = it has lost two points.* **12** MAT. whole number, integer (número). **13** (Am.) payment (pago). **14** (Am.) balance (saldo).
enterradero *s.m.* (Am.) graveyard (cementerio).
enterrador, -ora *s.m.* y *f.* **1** gravedigger. || *s.m.* **2** ZOOL. burying beetle.
enterramiento *s.m.* burial, interment (entierro).
enterrar *v.t.* **1** to bury, to inter (a un cadáver). **2** to bury (una cosa). **3** to outlive (sobrevivir a alguien): *es el más viejo del pueblo pero nos va a enterrar a todos = he is the oldest person in the village but he is going to outlive all of us.* **4** (Am.) to bury, to thrust (un arma blanca): *le enterró el cuchillo = he buried the knife into him.* **5** (fig.) to bury, to forget (olvidar).
entibado *s.m.* MIN. timbering, shoring (apuntalamiento con maderas en las excavaciones).
entibar *v.t.* **1** MIN. to timber, to shore (apuntalar con maderas las excavaciones). **2** to timber (un pozo).
entibiar *v.t.* **1** to cool down (enfriar). **2** to make lukewarm (poner tibio). **3** (fig.) to cool down, to moderate (las pasiones). || *v.pron.* **4** to become lukewarm (ponerse tibio). **5** (fig.) to cool down (una situación, etc.).
entidad *s.f.* **1** FIL. entity. **2** COM. society, firm. **3** organization, body (organización). **4** (fig.) importance, significance: *de poca entidad = of little importance.*
entierro *s.m.* **1** burial, interment (de un cadáver). **2** funeral (ceremonia). **3** grave (sepultura). **4** (Am.) (fam.) buried treasure (tesoro). || **5 santo —,** procession on Good Friday.
entintar *v.t.* **1** to stain with dye (manchar con tinta). **2** to dye (teñir). **3** to ink (aplicar tinta a una imprenta).
entoldar *v.t.* **1** to cover with an awning (cubrir con un toldo). || **2** *v.pron.* to cloud over (nublarse).
entomología *s.f.* entomology.
entomológico, -a *adj.* entomological, entomologic.
entomólogo, -a *s.m.* y *f.* entomologist.
entonación *s.f.* MUS. y GRAM. intonation.
entonar *v.t.* **1** MUS. to intone. **2** to modulate (la voz). **3** to sting in tune (afinar). **4** ART. to tone (una fotografía, etc.). **5** MED. to tone up (un músculo, etc.). || *v.i.* **6** MUS. to intone. || *v.pron.* **7** to be arrogant o conceited (envanecerse).
entonces *adv.* **1** then: *vino y entonces se sentó = he came then he sat down.* **2** at that time, then (en aquel tiempo). **3** so, then (en ese caso). || **4 desde —,** since then. **5 el — director,** the then director. **6 en aquel —,** at that time. **7 fue — que,**

it was then that. **8 pues —,** well then. **9** (Am.) **¡y —!,** (why) of course! (por supuesto).

entonelar *v.t.* to put into barrels, to barrel (en un tonel).

entongado, -a *adj.* (Am.) cross, angry (enfadado).

entongar *v.t.* **1** (Am.) to pile up, to make a pile of (amontonar). **2** (Am.) to stun (atontar). **3** (Am.) to anger (enfadar).

entontecer *v.t.* **1** to make silly. || *v.i.* y *pron.* **2** to get silly.

entontecimiento *s.m.* V. **atontamiento.**

entorchado *s.m.* **1** gold braid (de oro). **2** silver braid (de plata). **3** lace (bordado).

entornar *v.t.* **1** to leave ajar, to half close (puerta, ventana, etc.). **2** to half close (los ojos). || *v.pron.* **3** to lean (inclinar).

entorno *s.m.* V. **contorno.**

entorpecer *v.t.* **1** to make torpid o languid. **2** to hinder, to obstruct (estorbar). **3** to numb (las manos, etc.). **4** to delay (retardar). || *v.pron.* **5** to grow numb (las manos, etc.). **6** to be delayed (retardarse).

entorpecimiento *s.m.* **1** stupefaction (estupefacción). **2** numbing (acción de entorpecer las manos, etc.). **3** numbness (efecto). **4** obstruction (estorbo). **5** delay (retraso).

entrada *s.f.* **1** entrance, way in (donde se entra). **2** access (acceso). **3** entrance (acción de entrar). **4** house, audience (los que asistan a un espectáculo público). **5** ticket (billete). **6** receding hairline (pelo). **7** beginning (de un libro, discurso, año, etc.). **8** takings (dinero acumulado en la puerta de una función). **9** FIN. down payment, deposit (al pagar a plazos). **10** (Am.) attack, assault (asalto). **11** (Am.) beating (paliza). || **12 dar — a,** to lead into (conducir). **13 de —,** straight away. **14 "prohibida la —",** "no entry", "keep out", "no admission".

entrador *s.m.* **1** charming, likeable (simpático). **2** amorously inclined (enamoradizo). **3** spirited (animoso).

entramado *s.m.* **1** trellis (para las plantas trepadoras). **2** half-timbering, wooden framework (de un muro).

entrambos, -as *adj.* both (ambos).

entrampar *v.t.* **1** to trap, to catch, to snare (un animal). **2** (fig.) to trap, to catch out (engañar). **3** to mess up (un negocio). || *v.pron.* **4** to fall/get into debt (contraer deudas).

entraña *s.f.* **1** ANAT. entrails (pl.), insides. **2** core, root, essential part (lo más principal). **3** (fig.) bowels: *las entrañas de la tierra = the bowels of the earth.* || **4 dar hasta las entrañas,** to give one's all. **5 echar las entrañas,** to vomit, (fam.) to chuck one's guts up (vomitar). **6 no tener entrañas,** to be heartless, to lack all feelings.

entrañable *adj.* **1** close, intimate (íntimo). **2** dearly loved, beloved (querido).

entrañar *v.t.* **1** to bury deep (enterrar). **2** to involve (implicar). **3** to entail (acarrear). **4** to carry (contener). || *v.pron.* **5** to become deeply attached (unirse íntimamente).

entrar *v.i.* **1** to go in, to enter: *entra allí = go in there.* **2** to come in: *entre = come in* (pase). **3** to fit (encajar): *la última pieza no encaja = the last piece doesn't fit.* **4** to adopt, to take up (una profesión). **5** to join, to become a member (de una sociedad). **6** to join in (un juego). **7** DEP. to come on (de sustituto). **8** MUS. to come in (empezar a tocar o cantar). **9** to feel (sentir): *me está entrando frío = I'm beginning to feel cold.* **10** to understand (comprender): *no me entra esta lección = I don't understand this lesson.* **11** to fit, to go into (caber). **12** (fig.) to get into, to enter into (malos hábitos, etc.). **13** to invade (invadir). **14** DEP. to charge (los toros). || *v.t.* **15** to put: *entrar la bolsa en la cocina = to put the bag into the kitchen.* **16** to show in (introducir a uno). **17** to smuggle (de contrabando). **18** to invade, to attack (invadir). **19** to take in (costura). || *v.pron.* **20** to get in (a la fuerza). || **21 — ganas de,** to feel like.

entre *prep.* **1** between (entre dos): *entre tú y yo = between the two of us.* **2** among, amongst (entre varias cosas): *entre pinos = among pine trees.* || **3 — pitos y flautas,** what with one thing and another. **4 — rojo y rosa,** halfway between red and pink. **5 — que,** while, whilst. **6 — tanto,** meanwhile, in the meantime. **7 de —,** out of; from among: *salieron de entre la muchedumbre = they came from among the crowd.* **8** between: *lo podemos levantar entre los tres = we can lift it between the three of us.*

entreabrir *v.t.* **1** to half open: *entreabrir los ojos = to half open one's eyes.* **2** to half open, to leave ajar (la puerta). || *v.pron.* **3** to half open, to be ajar.

entreacto *s.m.* interval.

entrecano, -a *adj.* greyish, greying (el cabello).

entrecejo *s.m.* **1** space between the eyebrows (espacio entre las cejas). **2** frown (ceño).

entrecortado, -a *adj.* **1** faltering, broken (la voz). **2** laboured, difficult: *respiración entrecortada = laboured breathing.*

entrecortar *v.t.* **1** to cut into, to partially cut, to cut halfway through. || *v.pron.* **2** to falter (la voz).

entredicho *s.m.* **1** prohibition, ban (prohibición). **2** (Am.) disagreement, split (desacuerdo). **3** (Am.) alarm bell (alarma). **4** REL. interdict. || **5 poner algo en —,** to question something.

entrega *s.f.* **1** delivery: *la entrega de la mercancía será a las cuatro = the delivery of the merchandise will be at four o'clock.* **2** devotion (a una causa). **3** DEP. pass (pase). **4** presentation (de premios, etc.). **5** installment (de una revista, etc.). || **6 por —,** in installments.

entregar *v.t.* **1** to deliver (el periódico, las compras, etc.). **2** to hand over (las llaves, etc.). || *v.pron.* **3** to surrender oneself (a la voluntad de alguien). **4** to abandon oneself (a una pasión, un vicio, etc.). || **5 entregarla,** (fam.) to snuff it; to croak; to kick the bucket.

entrelazar *v.t.* **1** to entwine, to interweave, to interlace.

entremedias *adj.* **1** in between, halfaway. **2** in the meanwhile (mientras tanto). || **3 — de,** between.

entremés *s.m.* **1** short comedy (teatro). **2** side dish (plato ligero). || **3 entremeses,** hors d'oeuvres.

entremeter o **entrometer** *v.t.* to put in, to insert (insertar).

entremetido, -a o **entrometido, -a** *adj.* **1** meddlesome: *es una chica muy entremetida = she is a very meddlesome girl.* || *s.m.* **y** *f.* **2** busybody.

entrenado, -a *adj.* trained.

entrenador, -ora *s.m.* y *f.* DEP. trainer, coach.

entrenamiento *s.m.* DEP. training session.

entrenar *v.t.* **1** DEP. to train, to coach. || *v.pron.* **2** DEP. to train.

entrepaño *s.m.* **1** ARQ. bay (entre columnas o huecos). **2** panel (de puertas). **3** shelf (estante).

entrepiernas *s.f.* **1** crotch, crutch (del cuerpo). || **2 las entrepiernas,** the crotch (del pantalón).

entresacar *v.t.* **1** to pick out, to select (de entre varias). **2** to thin out (las plantas, el pelo, etc.).

entresijo *s.m.* **1** ANAT. mesentery. **2** secret, mystery (misterio). **3** difficulty (dificultad).

entresuelo *s.m.* mezzanine, entresol.

entretanto *adv.* meanwhile, in the meantime (mientras tanto).

entretejer *v.t.* to interweave, to intertwine.

entretela *s.f.* **1** interlining (costura). || **2 entretelas,** heart (corazón).

entretención *s.m.* (Am.) entertainment, amusement (entretenimiento).

entretener *v.t.* **1** to entertain, to amuse (recrear). **2** to distract, to keep occupied: *tú le entretienes y yo le quitaré la cartera = you distract him and I'll take his wallet.* **3** to delay (retrasar). **4** to keep at bay, to hold off (retardar con pretextos): *entretener a los acreedores = to keep one's creditors at bay.* **5** to kill, to stave off (el hambre). **6** MIL. to ward off, to divert (el enemigo). **7** to relieve, to allay (el dolor). || *v.pron.* **8** to pass the time, to amuse oneself: *se entretenía viendo la tele = she passed the time watching the T.V.* **9** to waste one's time (perder el tiempo). || **10 no te entretengas,** don't hang about!

entretenido, -a *adj.* **1** entertaining, amusing (divertido). **2** busy, occupied (ocupado). || *s.f.* **3** mistress, kept woman (amante).

entretenimiento *s.m.* **1** entertainment, amusement. **2** delaying (acción de dar largas).

entretiempo *s.m.* between-season.

entrever *v.t.* 1 to be able to see, to make out (poder ver). 2 to foresee (ver venir una cosa).
entreverado *s.m.* roasted offal (asadurilla).
entreverar *v.t.* to intermingle, to mix.
entrevista *s.m.* interview.
entrevistar *v.t.* 1 to interview. || *v.pron.* 2 to be interviewed. 3 to have a meeting (reunirse).
entristecer *v.t.* 1 to make unhappy, to sadden (contristar). 2 to sadden (dar aspecto de triste). || *v.pron.* 3 to become sad (acción). 4 to be sad, to grieve (estado).
entristecimiento *s.m.* 1 sadness (estado). 2 saddening (acción).
entrometer *v.t.* V. **entremeter.**
entrometido, -a *adj./s.m.* y *f.* V. **entremetido.**
entromparse *v.pron.* to get angry (enfadarse).
entrona *adj.* 1 coquettish, flirtatious. || *s.m.* 2 flirt.
entronar *v.t.* V. **entronizar.**
entroncamiento *s.m.* 1 relationship (parentesco). 2 (Am.) junction (ferrocarril).
entroncar *v.i.* 1 to be related (familias, etc.). 2 to become related by marriage (contraer parentesco). 3 (Am.) to join (empalmar una vía ferroviaria con otra). || *v.t.* 4 to establish a relationship between, to link, to connect (conectar). || *v.pron.* 5 (Am.) to join (empalmar dos vías ferroviarias).
entronque *s.m.* V. **entroncamiento.**
entronización *s.f.* 1 throning, enthroning (acción). 2 enthronement (estado).
entronizar o **entronar** *v.t.* 1 to enthrone, to throne, to put on the throne (colocar en el trono). 2 to exalt, to worship (enaltecer). || *v.pron.* 3 to become conceited, to become arrogant (engreírse).
entuerto *s.m.* 1 wrong (injusticia). 2 injury (daño). || 3 MED. entuertos, afterpains. 4 deshacer entuertos, to right wrongs.
entumecer *v.t.* 1 to numb, to make numb (por el frío). || *v.pron.* 2 to go o become numb: *se me han entumecido los dedos por el frío = my fingers have gone numb with cold.* 3 (fig.) to surge (el mar).
entumecido, -a *adj.* numb (adormecido).
entumecimiento *s.m.* numbness (de los dedos por el frío).
entumido, -a *adj.* (Am.) V. **entumecido.**
entumirse *v.pron.* to go o get numb (adormecerse las manos, etc.).
enturbiamiento *s.m.* cloudiness (en el agua, etc.).
enturbiar *v.t.* 1 to make cloudy, to cloud (el agua, etc.). 2 to disturb (turbar).
entusiasmar *v.t.* 1 to excite, to be crazy o mad about: *me entusiasma su corte de pelo = I'm crazy about his haircut.* || *v.pron.* 2 to be very keen, to love: *me entusiasma con la pintura = I'm very keen on painting.* 3 to get excited o enthusiastic (tener entusiasmo). 4 to be delighted (estar encantado).
entusiasmo *s.m.* 1 enthusiasm. 2 excitement (emoción). 3 inspiration (inspiración).
entusiasta *s.m.* y *f.* 1 enthusiast. || *adj.* 2 enthusiastic: *una afición muy entusiasta = a very enthusiastic following.*
entusiástico, -a *adj.* 1 enthusiastic.
enumeración *s.f.* 1 enumeration. 2 DER. census (censo).
enumerar *v.t.* to enumerate.
enumerativo, -a *adj.* enumerative.
enunciación *s.f.* 1 enunciation. 2 declaration, statement (de los hechos).
enunciado *s.m.* V. **enunciación.**
enunciar *v.t.* 1 to enunciate. 2 to state, to declare (declarar).
enunciativo *adj.* 1 enunciative. 2 GRAM. declarative (oración).
envainar *v.t.* 1 to sheathe, to put in a sheath (meter en la vaina). 2 (Am.) to annoy (enfadar). || *v.i.* 3 (Am.) to succumb (sucumbir). || *v.pron.* 4 (Am.) to get into trouble (meterse en un lío).
envalentonamiento *s.m.* 1 boldness, courage, daring (valor). 2 Dutch courage (valor por emborracharse). 3 encouragement (estímulo).
envalentonar *v.t.* 1 to embolden, to make bold o corageous (dar valor). 2 to encourage (dar valor). || *v.pron.* 2 to get o become brave o corageous, to pluck up courage (armarse de valor). 3 to be encourage: *se envalentonó con los gritos del público = he was encouraged by the shouts of the public.*
envanecer *v.t.* 1 to make conceited (poner vanidoso): *su victoria le envaneció = his victory made him conceited.* || *v.pron.* 2 to be conceited (ponerse vanidoso). 3 to be proud: *se envanece de su nuevo trabajo = he is proud of his new job.*
envanecido, -a *adj.* 1 conceited (presumido). 2 (Am.) superb (soberbio).
envanecimiento *s.m.* 1 conceit (presunción). 2 pride (orgullo). 3 vanity (vanidad).
envaramiento *s.m.* 1 numbness (entumecimiento). 2 stiffness (tiesura).
envarar *v.t.* 1 (Am.) to stake (rodrigar). 2 to make numb, to numb (entumecer). || *v.pron.* 3 to go numb (entumecerse un miembro por el frío). 4 to go stiff (ponerse tieso).
envasado, -a *adj.* 1 tinned, canned (enlatado). 2 bottled (embotellado). 3 in cylinders (gas). 4 packed (empaquetado). || *s.m.* 5 tinning, canning (acción de enlatar). 6 bottling (embotellamiento). 7 packing (en sacos). 8 sacking (en sacos).
envasador *s.m.* 1 tinner, canner (que pone en latas). 2 bottler (en botellas). 3 packer (empaquetador). 4 large funnel (embudo grande).
envasar *v.t.* 1 to can, to tin (enlatar). 2 to bottle (embotellar). 3 to put into a container (poner en un recipiente). 4 to put into sacks (poner en sacos). 5 to pack (empaquetar).
envase *s.m.* 1 canning, tinning (acción de enlatar). 2 bottling (embotellado). 3 container (recipiente). 4 tin, can (lata). 5 box (caja). 6 bottle (botella). 7 sack (saco). 8 packing, packaging (embalaje).
envejecer *v.t.* 1 to make old, to age: *el sol envejece la piel = the sun ages the skin.* 2 (fig.) to make look older (hacer que parezca más viejo). || *v.i.* 3 to get old, to age: *he envejecido mucho = he has got much older.* 4 (fig.) to go out of date (pasar de moda). || *v.pron.* 5 to last (for) a long time (permanecer por mucho tiempo).
envenenamiento *s.m.* 1 poisoning. 2 pollution (contaminación).
envenenar *v.t.* 1 to poison. 2 (fig.) to embitter, to poison (agriar). 3 to pollute (contaminar). || 4 *v.pron.* to poison oneself, to take poison.
enverar *v.i.* to begin to ripen (las frutas).
envergadura *s.f.* 1 expanse, spread, extent (extensión). 2 MAR. beam, breadth (manga). 3 wingspan (de un ave o avión). 4 magnitude, importance (importancia).
envés *s.m.* 1 reverse, back (de una página). 2 wrong side, back (de una tela).
enviado, -a *adj.* 1 sent. || *s.m.* y *f.* 2 representative. 3 envoy (de un gobierno). 4 messenger (mensajero).
enviar *v.t.* 1 to send (mandar).
enviciar *v.t.* 1 to corrupt (corrumpir). || *v.i.* 2 to be addictive, to be habit-forming: *la heroína envicia = heroin is habit-forming.* || *v.pron.* 3 to become corrupted (corromperse). 4 to get o become addicted (a las drogas, etc.).
envidar *v.i.* to bid (en las cartas).
envidia *s.f.* 1 envy, jealousy (celos). || 2 **dar —,** to make jealous. 3 **muerto de —,** green with envy.
envidiable *adj.* enviable.
envidiar *v.t.* 1 to envy, to be envious of.
envidioso, -a *adj.* 1 envious. 2 jealous (celoso). || *s.m.* y *f.* 3 envious man o woman (de envidia). 4 jealous man o woman (de celos).
envido *s.m.* raise (en las cartas).
envilecedor, -a *adj.* degrading, debasing (degradante).
envilecer *v.t.* 1 to degrade, to debase (degradar). || *v.pron.* 2 to degrade oneself.
envilecimiento *s.m.* 1 degradation, debasement.
envío *s.m.* 1 shipment (de mercancías). 2 consignment (remesa). 3 letter (carta). 4 package, parcel (paquete). 5 sending, dispatch (acción de enviar). || 6 **— contra reembolso,** cash-on-delivery.
envite *s.m.* 1 raise (en las cartas). 2 offer (ofrecimiento). 3 push, shove (empujón).
enviudarse *v.pron.* 1 to become a widow, to be widowed (mujer). 2 to become a widower (hombre).
envoltorio *s.m.* 1 wrapping, wrapper (envoltura de un paquete, etc.). 2 mess (lío).

envoltura *s.f.* 1 wrapping, wrapper (de un paquete, etc.). 2 wrapping (acción). 3 cover (cubierta). 4 BOT. envelope. || 5 **envolturas,** swaddling-clothes (pañales).
envolvente *adj.* 1 MIL. encircling, outflanking. 2 surrounding.
envolver *v.t.* 1 to wrap (un regalo). 2 to pack (un paquete). 3 to wrap up (con ropa). 4 to wind (hilo, etc.). 5 to involve, to implicate (mezclar a uno en un asunto). 6 to wrap, to swathe (p.u.) (vestir un niño en pañales, etc.). 7 to stump, to floor (en un argumento, etc.). 8 MIL. to encircle, to surround (rodear). || *v.pron.* 9 to wrap oneself up (abrigarse). 10 to be wrapped (los paquetes, regalos, etc.). 11 (fig.) to get involved, to get mixed up (en un asunto, etc.).
envolvimiento *s.m.* 1 wrapping (de regalos, etc.). 2 winding (de hilos, etc.). 3 MED. coating (de medicamentos). 4 MIL. encircling, surrounding.
envuelto, -a *adj.* 1 wrapped, wrapped (un regalo, etc.). 2 wound (un hilo). 3 (fig.) enveloped, shrouded (en misterio, etc.). 4 involved, mixed up (implicado). || *s.m.* 5 (Am.) tortilla.
enyesado, -a *adj.* 1 plastered. || 2 *s.m.* plastering. 3 plaster cast (escayolado).
enyesar *v.t.* 1 to plaster. 2 MED. to put a plaster (cast) on (poner una escayola).
enyerbarse *v.pron.* 1 to fall madly in love, to fall head over heels in love (enamorarse perdidamente).
enzarzar *v.t.* 1 to cover with brambles (cubrir con zarzas). || *v.pron.* 2 to get caught in brambles. 3 (fig.) to get involved, to get mixed up (enredarse en un asunto).
enzima *s.f.* BIOL. enzyme.
eñe *s.f.* n with tilde (letra).
eoceno *s.m.* y *adj.* GEOL. eocene.
eólico, -a o **eolio, -a** *adj.* aeolian.
epa *s.m.* y *adj.* 1 (Am.) stupid (tonto). || *interj.* 2 hello! (¡hola!). 3 (Am.) come on! (¡ea!).
epiceno, -a *adj.* GRAM. epicene.
epicentro *s.m.* GEOL. epicentre.
épico, -a *adj.* epic.
epicúreo, -a *adj.* y *s.m.* epicurean.
epidemia *s.f.* 1 epidemic. 2 (fig.) plague, epidemic (oleada).
epidémico, -a *adj.* epidemic, epidemical.
epidérmico, -a *adj.* epidermic, epidermal.
epidermis *s.f.* ANAT. epidermis.
epifanía *s.* REL. Epiphany.
epífisis *s.f.* ANAT. epiphysis.
epiglotis *s.f.* ANAT. epiglottis.
epígono *s.m.* epigone.
epígrafe *s.m.* epigraph.
epigrafía *s.f.* epigraphy.
epigráfico, -a *adj.* epigraphic, epigraphical.
epigrafista *s.m.* y *f.* epigraphist.
epigrama *s.m.* epigram.
epigramático, -a *adj.* epigrammatical, epigrammatic.
epigramatista o **epigramista** *s.m.* y *f.* epigrammatist.
epilepsia *s.f.* MED. epilepsy.
epiléptico, -a *adj.* o *s.m.* MED. epileptic.
epilogar *v.t.* 1 to summarize, to sum up (resumir). 3 to round off (terminar).
epílogo *s.m.* 1 epilogue (conclusión). 2 summary (resumen).
episcopado *s.m.* 1 REL. bishopric (oficio). 2 REL. episcopate.
episcopacy (período). 2 REL. bishops, episcopacy (obispos).
episcopal *adj.* REL. episcopal.
episcopalismo *s.m.* REL. episcopalism.
episódico, -a *adj.* episodic, episodical.
episodio *s.m.* episode.
epístola *s.f.* epistle.
epistolar *adj.* epistolary.
epistolario *s.m.* collected letters, collection of letters.
epitafio *s.m.* epitaph.
epitelio *s.m.* ANAT. epithelium.
epíteto *s.m.* epithet.
epítome *s.m.* epitome, summary.
epizootia *s.f.* epizootic.
época *s.f.* 1 epoch, age, era, time. 2 period (periodo). 3 time, season (temporada). || 4 **hacer –,** to make history.
epónimo, -a *adj.* 1 eponymous, eponymic. || *s.m.* 2 eponym.
epopeya *s.f.* 1 epic poem, epopee (poem). 2 (fig.) epic.
equidad *s.f.* 1 equity. 2 fairness, justice (justicia).
equidistancia *s.f.* equidistance.
equidistante *adj.* equidistant.
equidistar *v.i.* MAT. to be equidistant.
équido, -a *adj.* y *s.m.* equine.
equilibrado, -a *adj.* 1 balanced. 2 (fig.) sensible, balanced (una persona).
equilibrar *v.t.* 1 to balance. 2 to counterbalance, to equilibrate (un peso con otro). || *v.pron.* 3 to balance. 4 (fig.) to recover one's balance (mente).
equilibrio *s.m.* 1 balance: *perder el equilibrio = to lose one's balance.* 2 FIS. equilibrium. 3 calmness, composure (compostura). || 4 **mantener el –,** to keep one's balance.
equilibrista *s.m.* y *f.* 1 tightrope walker. 2 acrobat, equilibrist.
equino, -a *adj.* y *s.m.* equine.
equinoccio *s.m.* ASTR. equinox.
equinodermo *s.m.* ZOOL. echinoderm.
equipaje *s.m.* 1 luggage, baggage. 2 MAR. crew (tripulación). || 3 **– de mano,** hand luggage.
equipar *v.t.* 1 to equip (un soldado, etc.). 2 to fit out (con ropa). 3 MAR. to fit out.
equiparar *v.t.* to compare, to put on the same level (comparar).
equipo *s.m.* 1 team (de fútbol, expertos, etc.). 2 equipment, gear, kit: *equipo de montañismo = climbing gear.* 3 instruments (instrumentos). 4 outfit (conjunto de ropa).
equis *s.f.* 1 x (letra). || 2 **estar en la –,** (Am.) to be all skin and bones (estar en los huesos).
equitación *s.f.* horse riding, riding, equitation.
equitativo, -a *adj.* equitable, fair (justo).
equivalencia *s.f.* equivalence.
equivalente *adj.* y *s.m.* equivalent.
equivaler *v.i.* 1 to be equivalent, to be equal, to be the equivalent: *un kilo equivale a 2,2 libras = a kilo is the equivalent of 2,2 pounds.* 2 to mean: *eso equivaldría a una guerra = that would mean war.*
equivocación *s.f.* 1 mistake, error: *existe una equivocación en las cifras = there is a mistake in the figures.* 2 misunderstanding (malentendido). || 3 **por –,** by mistake.
equivocar *v.t.* 1 to get wrong, to mistake. || *v.pron.* 2 to be mistaken, to make a mistake, to mistake: *equivocarse de día = to mistake the day.* 3 to be mistaken (juzgarle a alguien mal).
equívoco, -a *adj.* 1 ambiguous (ambiguo). 2 misleading (engañoso). || *s.m.* 3 ambiguity (ambigüedad). 4 misunderstanding (malentendido).
era *s.f.* 1 era, age. 2 MIN. pithead.
erario *s.m.* 1 treasury. 2 public funds (tesoro público).
erección *s.f.* 1 erection, raising (de un edificio, etc.). 2 (fig.) establishment, foundation (de una institución, etc.). 3 MED. erection (en fisiología).
eréctil *adj.* erectile.
eremita *s.m.* hermit (ermitaño).
eremítico, -a *adj.* hermitical.
ergio *s.m.* FIS. erg.
erguido, -a *adj.* 1 straight, erect (recto). 2 (fig.) proud (orgulloso).
erguir *v.t.* 1 to raise, to lift (levantar). 2 to straighten (desdoblar). || *v.pron.* 3 to stand up straight, to straighten up (ponerse recto). 4 to be conceited (engreírse).
erial *s.m.* uncultivated land (tierra sin cultivar).
erigir *v.t.* 1 to build, to construct (un edificio). 2 to erect (un monumento). 3 (fig.) to establish, to set up (una institución). || *v.pron.* 4 to set oneself up as something.
erizado, -a *adj.* 1 prickly (espinoso). 2 (fig.) thorny (problemas, etc.).
erizarse *v.pron.* 1 to stand on end: *se le erizó el pelo = his hair stood on end.* 2 to bristle (un animal).
erizo *s.m.* 1 ZOOL. hedgehog (mamífero). 2 BOT. burr-burr (envoltura espinosa de la castaña). 3 ZOOL. globefish (pez). || 4 **– de mar,** ZOOL. sea urchin.
ermita *s.f.* hermitage.
ermitaño *s.m.* 1 hermit. 2 ZOOL. hermit crab (cangrejo).
erosión *s.f.* 1 GEOL. erosion. 2 MED. graze (rasguño).
erosionar *v.t.* to erode.
erosivo, -a *adj.* erosive.
erótico, -a *adj.* erotic.
erotismo *s.m.* eroticism, erotism.
errabundo, -a *adj.* wandering, roving.
erradicar *v.t.* to eradicate.
errado, -a *adj.* wrong, mistaken (equivocado).
errante *adj.* 1 wandering, roving. 2 nomadic (nómada). 3 stray (animal).

errar *v.i.* 1 to wander, to rove, to roam (vagar). || *v.t.* 2 to mistake (equivocarse): *errar el camino = equivocarse de camino.* 3 to miss (en el tiro). || *v.pron.* 4 to err, to go astray.
errata *s.f.* erratum.
erre *s.f.* 1 r (letra). || *adv.* 2 **— que —,** stubbornly.
erróneo, -a *adj.* 1 erroneous, mistaken. 2 false (falso).
error *s.m.* 1 mistake, error: *existe un error en las cifras = there is a mistake in the figures.* 2 misunderstanding (malentendido).
eructar o **erutar** *v.i.* to burp, to belch.
eructo o **eruto** *s.m.* belch o burp.
erudición *s.f.* 1 learning, erudition, scholarship. 2 knowledge (conocimiento).
erudito, -a *adj.* 1 scholarly, erudite, knowledgeable. || *s.m.* y *f.* 2 erudite, scholarly person.
erupción *s.f.* 1 eruption (volcánica). 2 MED. rash (de la piel). 3 (fig.) outbreak (de violencia, etc.).
erutar *v.i.* V. **eructar.**
esbeltez *s.f.* slimness, slenderness (delgadez).
esbelto *adj.* slim, slender, (lit.) svelte.
esbirro *s.m.* 1 bailiff (alguacil). 2 henchman.
esbozar *v.t.* 1 to sketch, to outline (dibujar). 2 to rough out, to outline (un proyecto, etc.).
esbozo *s.m.* sketch, outline (dibujo).
escabechar *v.t.* 1 to pickle, to marinade, to pickle, to souse (conservar en vinagre). 2 (fig. y fam.) to do in, to bump off (matar). 3 (fig. y fam.) to plough, to fail (suspender en un examen).
escabeche *s.m.* brine, marinade, pickle (líquido): *sardinas en escabeche = sardines in brine.*
escabechina *s.f.* 1 massacre, slaughter (masacre). || 2 **hacer una escabechina,** to fall a lot of students (suspender a muchos alumnos).
escabel *s.m.* foot stool (para los pies).
escabrosidad *s.f.* 1 roughness, ruggedness (del terreno). 2 toughness, difficulty (de un problema, etc.). 3 harshness (de carácter). 4 crudeness, dirtiness (de un chiste, etc.).
escabroso, -a *adj.* 1 rough, rugged (terreno). 2 uneven (superficie). 3 difficult, tough (un problema, etc.). 4 crude, dirty (un chiste, etc.). 5 harsh (sonido, carácter, etc.).
escabullirse *v.pron.* 1 to slip away, to escape (escapar). || 2 **— por,** to slip through.
escachalandrado, -a *adj.* (Am.) slovenly (dejado de carácter).
escacharrar *v.t.* 1 to break, (fam.) to bust (romper). 2 to ruin (estropear). || *v.pron.* 3 to break, (fam.) to bust (romperse).
escafandra *s.f.* diving suit (traje de buzo).
escala *s.f.* 1 ladder (escalera de mano). 2 scale (proporción). 3 stopover (en un viaje). 4 MUS. scale. 5 MAR. port of call (puerto).
escalador *s.m.* y *f.* 1 DEP. climber (alpinista). 2 burglar (ladrón).
escalafón *s.m.* promotion list (de empleados, soldados, etc.).
escalar *v.t.* 1 to scale (una pared, un acantilado). 2 to climb (una montaña). || *v.i.* 3 to escalate (extenderse una guerra, etc.).
escaldadura *s.f.* 1 scald (quemadura). 2 scalding (acción).
escaldar *v.t.* 1 to scald (quemar). 2 to make red hot (poner a rojo vivo). 3 (fig.) to teach a lesson. || *v.pron.* 4 to scald oneself, to get scalded (quemarse).
escaleno *adj.* y *s.m.* MAT. scalene.
escalera *s.f.* 1 stairs (pl.), staircase (en una casa). 2 ladder (de mano). 3 tailboard (de un carro, etc.). 4 run (en las cartas). || 5 **— de caracol,** spiral staircase.
escalerilla *s.f.* 1 small staircase. 2 sequence of three cards (en las cartas). 3 metal instrument for keeping a horse's mouth open (instrumento veterinario).
escalfar *v.t.* to poach (los huevos).
escalinata *s.f.* flight of stairs.
escalofriante *adj.* bloodcurdling, hair-raising.
escalofrío o **calofrío** *s.m.* 1 MED. chill, feverish chill. || 2 **escalofríos,** shivers.
escalón *s.m.* 1 step, stair (de escalera). 2 rung (de escala). 3 (fig.) step (hacia la promoción, etc.). 4 MIL. echelon.
escalonamiento *s.m.* spreading out.
escalonar *v.t.* 1 to spread out at intervals. 2 to stagger (producción, horas, etc.). 3 MIL. to echelon. 4 to terrace (un terreno).
escalope *s.m.* escalope, veal cutlet.
escalpelo *s.m.* MED. scalpel.
escama *s.f.* 1 BIOL. scale (de un pez). 2 MED. scale, flake (de la piel). 3 BOT. scale. 4 suspicion (sospecha).
escamado, -a *adj.* (Am.) untrusting (desconfiado).
escamar *v.t.* 1 to scale (los peces). 2 (fig.) to make suspicious (hacer sospechar). || *v.pron.* 3 to become suspicious.
escamoso *adj.* 1 scaly (que tiene escamas). 2 flaky (la piel). 3 (fig.) suspicious (sospechoso).
escamotear *v.t.* 1 to make disappear (hacer desaparecer). 2 (fig. y fam.) to pinch, to nick (robar). 3 to skip (eliminar una cosa de forma arbitraria).
escamoteo *s.m.* 1 slight of hand (de un prestidigitador). 2 vanishing, disappearing (desaparición). 3 (fig. y fam.) pinching, nicking (robo). 4 skipping (de una dificultad). 5 TEC. retraction (del tren de aterrizaje).
escampar *v.t.* 1 to clear out. || *v.i.* 2 to clear (el cielo). 3 to stop (la lluvia). 4 (Am.) to shelter from the rain (buscar cobijo).
escanciar *v.t.* 1 to pour (el vino). || *v.i.* 2 to drink wine (beber).
escandalera V. **escándalo.**
escandalizar *v.t.* 1 to scandalize. || *v.i.* 2 (fam.) to make a racket (armar un escándalo). || *v.pron.* 3 to be shocked/scandalized.
escándalo *s.m.* 1 scandal. 2 row, commotion, uproar: *armar un escándalo = to cause an uproar.* 3 DER. disturbance of the peace.
escandaloso, -a *adj.* 1 scandalous, outrageous, shocking (que causa escándalo). 2 rowdy, noisy (que causa mucho ruido). 3 flagrant (flagrante). 4 uproarious (de risa).
escandinavo, -a *adj./s.m.* y *f.* Scandinavian.
escaño *s.m.* 1 bench. 2 POL. seat.
escapada *s.f.* 1 escape, flight (acción de escapar). 2 DEP. breakaway. 3 quick trip (excursión). || 4 **hacer una —,** to slip away; to make a flying visit.
escapar *v.i.* 1 to escape: *el prisionero escapó por la ventana = the prisoner escaped through the window.* 2 to run away, to escape (huir). 3 DEP. to break away. || *v.pron.* 4 to escape, to get out: *se escapará el gato = the cat will get out.* 5 to slip away (irse discretamente). 6 to escape (gas de un cilindro, etc.). 7 DEP. to break away. 8 (fig.) to slip out (una palabra, etc.). || 9 **escaparse de las manos,** to slip out of one's hands.
escaparate *s.m.* 1 shop window (de una tienda). 2 (Am.) cupboard (armario). 3 showcase, display cabinet (vitrina).
escapatoria *s.f.* 1 way out (salida). 2 escape, flight (huida). 3 (fig.) loophole, way out (para eludir). 4 trip (escapada). || 5 **no tener —,** to have no way out.
escape *s.m.* 1 escape (huida). 2 leak, escape (de gas). 3 MEC. exhaust (tubo). 4 TEC. escapement (de un reloj).
escápula *s.f.* ANAT. scapula, shoulder blade.
escapulario *adj.* scapulary.
escaque *s.m.* 1 square (ajedrez). || 2 **escaques,** chess.
escaquearse *v.pron.* to shirt (una responsabilidad, etc.).
escarabajo *s.m.* 1 ZOOL. beetle. 2 stunted person (persona mal formada).
escaramujo *s.m.* 1 BOT. dog-rose (rosal silvestre). 2 hip (fruto).
escaramuza *s.f.* 1 MIL. skirmish. 2 skirmish, (fam.) bundle (pelea de poca importancia).
escarbar *v.t.* 1 to pick, to scratch (las gallinas). 2 to poke (el fuego). 3 to clean one's ears (limpiar los oídos). 4 to clean o pick one's teeth (limpiar los dientes). || 5 **— en un asunto,** to delve into a matter.
escarceo *s.m.* 1 MAR. ripple. 2 nervous movement (de un caballo). || 3 **escarceos amorosos,** flirtation.
escarcha *s.f.* frost.
escarchado, -a *adj.* 1 frost covered, frosty. 2 crystalized (fruta). 3 iced (una tarta). || *s.m.* 4 embroidary (costura).
escarchar *v.t.* 1 to crystallize (fruta). 2 to ice (una tarta). || *v.i.* 3 to become frosty.

escarda *s.f.* 1 weeding, hoeing (acción). 2 weeding hoe.
escardar *v.t.* 1 to weed. 2 (fig.) to weed out (separar lo malo de lo bueno).
escarlata *adj.* 1 scarlet. || *s.f.* 2 scarlet (el color). 3 MED. scarlet fever.
escarlatina *s.f.* MED. scarlet fever.
escarmentar *v.t.* 1 to punish severely (castigar). || *v.i.* 2 to learn one's lesson. || 3 **hacer – a uno,** to teach someone a lesson.
escarmiento *s.m.* 1 lesson (lección). 2 punishment (castigo).
escarnecedor, -a *adj.* 1 jeering, mocking (burlón). 2 shameful (vergonzoso). || *s.m.* 3 mocker, jeerer (burlón).
escarnecer *v.t.* to scoff at, to ridicule, to mock (ridiculizar).
escarnio *s.m.* taunt.
escarola *s.f.* BOT. endive.
escarpa *s.f.* 1 slope. 2 GEOG. y MIL. escarpment, scarp. 3 (Am.) pavement (acera).
escarpado *adj.* steep, sheer.
escarpia *s.f.* hook.
escarpín *s.m.* 1 slipper (zapatilla). 2 outer sock, ankle-warmer (calzado de lana para abrigar).
escasamente *adv.* 1 scarcely, hardly (apenas): *estuvo escasamente dos horas = he was there for scarcely an hour.* 2 only just (por poco).
escasear *v.i.* to be scarce (poco abundante).
escasez *s.f.* 1 shortage, scarcity (de agua, etc.). 2 want, need (necesidad). 3 meanness (tacañería). || 4 **vivir con –,** to live in poverty.
escaso, -a *adj.* 1 scarce (poco abundante). 2 limited (limitado). 3 thin, sparse (cosecha, etc.). 4 slim, slender (posibilidades). 5 only just, hardly, only, barely: *tres horas escasas = barely three hours.* 6 few (pocos). 7 mean, stingy (tacaño). || 8 **andar – de,** to be short of. 9 **ganar por una cabeza –,** to twin by a short head.
escatimar *v.t.* 1 to be stingy, to skimp (ser poco generoso). 2 to be sparing (usar poco): *tendremos que escatimar con el dinero = we'll have to be sparing with the money.* 3 to save (ahorrar).
escatología *s.f.* 1 scatology. 2 FIL. eschatology.
escatológico, -a *adj.* 1 scatological. 2 FIL. eschatological.
escayola *s.f.* 1 MED. plaster. 2 plaster of paris (yeso).
escayolar *v.t.* MED. to put in a plaster (cast).
escena *s.f.* 1 scene (teatro, etc.). 2 stage (escenario). || 3 **– conmovedora,** moving scene. 4 **hacer una –,** to make a scene.
escenario *s.m.* 1 stage (teatro). 2 set (plató). 3 (fig.) scene, setting: *el escenario del crimen = the scene of the crime.*
escénico, -a *adj.* scenic.
escenificar *v.t.* 1 to dramatize, to adapt for the stage. 2 to stage (poner en escena).
escenografía *s.f.* 1 scenography (arte). 2 scenary (decorados).
escenógrafo *s.m.* y *f.* producer.
escepticismo *s.m.* scepticism.
escéptico, -a *adj./s.m.* y *f.* sceptic.
escindible *adj.* 1 divisible. 2 FIS. fissionable.
escindir *v.t.* 1 to split, to divide. 2 FIS. to split (el átomo). || *v.pron.* 3 to split.
escisión *s.f.* 1 splitting (acción). 2 split, division (división). 3 FIS. fission. 4 MED. excision.
esclarecedor, -a *adj.* clarifying.
esclarecer *v.t.* 1 clarify, (fig.) to throw light on (aclarar una cosa). 2 to ennoble (ennoblecer). 3 to make illustrious (ilustrar). || *v.pron.* 4 to get light (amanecer).
esclarecido, -a *adj.* illusorious, distinguished.
esclarecimiento *s.m.* 1 illumination (iluminación). 2 explanation, elucidation, clarification (explicación). 3 ennoblement (ennoblecimiento).
esclavina *s.f.* short cloak, cape, tippet (capa corta).
esclavista *adj.* 1 pro-slavery. || *s.m.* y *f.* 2 slavery supporter.
esclavitud *s.f.* 1 slavery. 2 (fig.) slavery.
esclavizar *v.t.* 1 to enslave. 2 (fig.) to over-work. 3 to dominate (dominar).
esclavo *s.m.* 1 slave. 2 (fig.) slave. || *adj.* 3 enslaved (esclavizado). 4 enslaving, time-consuming: *este trabajo es muy esclavo = this job is vary time-consuming.* 5 devoted (entregado).
esclerosis *s.f.* MED. sclerosis.
esclerótica *adj.* ANAT. sclerotic, sclera.
esclusa *s.f.* 1 lock, sluice (de un canal). 2 floodgate (de una presa). || 3 **– de aire,** airlock.
escoba *s.f.* 1 broom (para barrer). 2 broom-stick (de las brujas). 3 BOT. broom.
escobajo *s.m.* 1 old broom. 2 stalk (de racimo de uvas).
escobilla *s.f.* 1 brush (cepillo). 2 ELEC. brush (del dinamo). 3 BOT. teasle.
escobón *s.m.* 1 large broom (escoba grande). 2 chimney sweeping brush (deshollinador). 3 short broom (de manga corta).
escocedura *s.f.* 1 MED. sore. 2 sting, smarting, soreness (de una herida).
escocer *v.i.* 1 to sting, to smart (picar una herida). || *v.t.* 2 to chafe. || *v.pron.* 3 to get sore (la piel). 4 (fig.) to have one's feelings hurt: *se escoció por lo que oyó = his feelings were hurt by what he heard.*
escocés, -esa *adj.* 1 Scottish, Scots (persona). 2 scotch (whisky, etc.). || 3 *s.m.* Scottish, Scots (lengua). || *s.m.* y *f.* 4 Scotsman, Scot (hombre). 5 Scotswoman, Scot (mujer). || 6 tela escocesa, tartan.
Escocia *s.f.* Scotland.
escoger *v.t.* 1 to choose, to select, to pick (entre varias cosas). 2 to choose (entre dos cosas). 3 POL. to elect. || 4 **a –,** to choose from. 5 **tener donde –,** to have a good choice.
escogido, -a *adj.* 1 chosen, selected. 2 choice (de calidad). 3 MIL. crack: *tropas escogidas = crack troops.*
escolanía *s.f.* 1 choir school (escuela). || *s.m.* 2 choirboys (pl.). 3 choir (coro).
escolapio *s.m.* 1 monk who teaches in a charity school (fraile). 2 charity school pupil (alumno).
escolar *adj.* 1 school, scholastic. || *s.m.* y *f.* 2 schoolboy, pupil (niño); schoolgirl, pupil (niña). || 3 **edad –,** school age. 4 **curso –,** school year.
escolaridad *s.f.* schooling.
escolástico, -a *adj.* 1 scholastic. || *s.m.* y *f.* 2 scholastic.
escoliosis *s.f.* MED. scoliosis.
escolopendra *s.f.* 1 ZOOL. centipede (ciempiés). 2 BOT. scolopendrium, heart's tongue.
escolta *s.f.* 1 escort. || 2 **dar – a,** to escort.
escoltar *v.t.* 1 to escort. 2 MAR. to escort, to convoy.
escollar *v.i.* 1 (Am.) MAR. to hit a reef, to strike a rock (encallarse). 2 (Am.) to fail (malograrse).
escollera *s.f.* MAR. breakwater, jetty.
escollo *s.m.* 1 MAR. reef, rock (arrecife). 2 (fig.) stumbling block (dificultad). 3 danger (peligro).
escombrera *s.f.* 1 rubbish dump o tip. 2 MIN. slag heap.
escombro *s.m.* ZOOL. mackerel (caballa).
escombros *s.m.* 1 debris, rubble (de un edificio). 2 MIN. slag (escoria).
esconder *v.t.* 1 to hide: *escondí el dinero debajo del colchón = I hid the money under the mattress.* || *v.pron.* 2 to hide: *esconderse de uno = to hide from someone.* 3 to hide oneself, to hide: *se escondió en la cocina = he hid in the kitchen.*
escondidas *s.f.* 1 hide-and-seek (el juego). || 2 **hacer algo a –,** to do something secretly.
escondite *s.m.* 1 hiding place. || 2 **jugar al –,** to play hide-and-seek.
escondrijo *s.m.* hiding place (escondite).
escopeta *s.f.* 1 shotgun (de perdigón). || 2 **– de cañones recortados,** sawn-off shotgun. || 3 **– de dos cañones,** double-barrelled shotgun.
escopetazo *s.m.* 1 gunshot (disparo). 2 gunshot wound (herida). 3 (fig.) bad news (malas noticias); (fam.) bombshell.
escopetear *v.t.* 1 to shoot at (disparar contra). 2 (Am.) to get at (aludir de modo ofensivo). || *v.i.* 3 to fire a shotgun (disparar una escopeta). 4 (Am.) to answer irritably (contestar de brusco). || *v.pron.* 5 to shower each other with compliments (lisonjearse). 6 to shower each other with insults (con insultos).
escopeteo *s.m.* 1 volley (de disparos). 2 (fig.) shower (de insultos, etc.).
escopetero *s.m.* gunsmith.
escoplo *s.m.* TEC. chisel (herramienta).

escora *s.f.* 1 MAR. level line (línea del fuerte). 2 MAR. list (inclinación del barco). 3 MAR. stanchion, prop (puntal).
escorarse *v.pron.* (Am.) to get something off one's chest (desahogarse).
escorbuto *s.m.* MED. scurvy.
escoria *s.f.* 1 MAT. slag, dross. 2 (fig.) scum, dregs: *la escoria de la sociedad = the dregs of society.*
escoriación o **excoriación** *s.f.* chaffing (roce de la piel).
escorpión *s.m.* 1 ZOOL. scorpion. 2 ASTR. Scorpio.
escorzo *s.m.* foreshortening.
escotado, -a *adj.* 1 low necked, low cut (blusa, etc.). || *s.m.* 2 (low) neck, (low) neckline (escotadura).
escotadura *s.f.* 1 low neckline (apertura del cuello). 2 large trapdoor (teatro).
escotar *v.t.* 1 to cut out the neckline (para el cuello). 2 to lower the neckline (para desanchar). 3 to cut to fit (ajustar). 4 to divert water (de un río). || *v.pron.* e *i.* 5 to pay one's fair share (pagar su cuota).
escote *s.m.* 1 low neck (line). 2 share, contribution (cuota). || 3 **comprar algo a –,** to club together to buy something. 4 **pagar a –,** to go Dutch.
escotilla *s.f.* MAR. hatch (way).
escozor *s.m.* 1 smart, sting (picor). 2 (fig.) grief, heartache.
escriba *s.m.* scribe.
escribanía *s.f.* 1 writing desk (pupitre). 2 notary's position (oficio). 3 notary's office (oficina).
escribano *s.m.* DER. court clerk. 2 ZOOL. whirligig beetle.
escribiente *s.m.* copyist.
escribir *v.t.* 1 to write. 2 to write, to compose (música). 3 to spell (ortografiar). || *v.i.* 4 to write. || *v.pron.* 5 to be spelt: *no sé como se escribe esta palabra = I don't know how this word is spelt.* || 6 **¿cómo se escribe?,** how do you spell it?
escrito, -a *p.p.* de **escribir.** || *s.m.* 2 writing, works. 3 letter: *le mandé un escrito = I wrote him a letter.* 4 document (documento).
escritor, -ora *s.m.* y *f.* writer.
escritorio *s.m.* 1 writing desk, bureau (mueble). 2 office (oficina).
escritura *s.f.* 1 writing (acción y arte). 2 writing, handwriting (letra). 3 DER. deed. 4 script: *escritura fonética = phonetic script.* || 5 **escrituras,** The Bible.
escriturar *v.t.* DER. to execute by deed, formalize legally.
escroto *s.m.* ANAT. scrotum.
escrúpulo *s.m.* 1 scruple. 2 scrupulousness (escrupulosidad). || 3 **hacer algo con –,** to do something with extreme care. 4 **falta de –,** unscrupulousness.
escrupulosamente *adv.* scrupulously, precisely, exactly.
escrupulosidad *s.f.* scrupulousness.
escrupuloso, -a *adj.* scrupulous.
escrutador, -ora *adj.* 1 scrutinizing, examining. || *s.m.* y *f.* 2 POL. teller, scrutineer.
escrutinio *s.m.* 1 POL. count, counting (de votos). 2 examination, scrutiny (averiguación).
escuadra *s.f.* 1 TECH. carpenter's square (carpintería). 2 MIL. squad. 3 fleet (de barcos).
escuadrilla *s.f.* 1 wing, squadron (de aviones). 2 fleet (de barcos).
escuadrón *s.m.* 1 MIL. squadron, troop. 2 squadron (de aviones).
escuálido, -a *adj.* 1 squalid, sordid (sucio). 2 skinny, thin (flaco).
escualo *s.m.* ZOOL. shark (tiburón).
escucha *s.f.* 1 listening (acción). 2 chaperon (monja). || *s.m.* 3 MIL. scout (centinela). 4 bug (micrófono oculto). 5 listener (radioyente).
escuchar *v.t.* 1 to listen: *escuchar la radio = to listen to the radio.* 2 to hear (oír). || *v.pron.* 3 to like to hear oneself talk (que le gusta escucharse a sí mismo).
escuchimizado, -a *adj.* very thin (muy delgado).
escudar *v.t.* 1 to shield, to protect with a shield. 2 (fig.) to shield, to protect. || *v.pron.* 3 to shield oneself, to protect oneself (protegerse).
escudería *s.f.* 1 stable (de coches de carrera). 2 squiredom.
escudero *s.m.* 1 squire (paje). 2 shield maker (el que fabrica escudos). 3 page (el que servía al señor).
escudilla *s.f.* bowl (recipiente).
escudo *s.m.* 1 shield (para defenderse). 2 escudo (moneda). 3 (fig.) shield, protection. || 4 **– de armas,** coat of arms.
escudriñar *v.t.* to inquire into, to investigate (investigar).
escuela *s.m.* 1 school. 2 training (entrenamiento). || 3 **– de artes y oficios,** technical school. 4 **– de comercio,** business school. 5 **– elemental,** primary school.
escuelero *s.* (Am.) teacher (maestro).
escueto, -a *adj.* plain, unadorned, bare (sin adorno).
esculpir *v.t.* 1 ART. to sculpture. 2 ART. to engrave (grabar).
escultor, -ora *s.m.* y *f.* sculptor (hombre), sculptress (mujer).
escultórico, -a *adj.* sculptural.
escultural *adj.* 1 sculptural. 2 statuesque (figura).
escupidera *s.f.* 1 spittoon, cuspidor (para escupir). 2 chamber pot (orinal).
escupir *v.i.* 1 to spit. 2 to spit out (la comida, etc.). 3 (fig.) to spit, to spit out, to belch out (llamas, etc.).
escupitajo *s.m.* spit, spittle.
escurreplatos *s.m.* dish rack.
escurana *s.f.* darkness (oscuridad).
escurridizo, -a *adj.* 1 slippery. 2 (fig.) slippery: *una persona escurridiza = a slippery person.*
escurrido, -a *adj.* 1 narrow-hipped (estrecho de caderas). 2 (Am.) embarrased (avergonzado).
escurrir *v.t.* 1 to drain. 2 to wring (la ropa). || *v.i.* 3 to drip (gotear). 4 to slip, to slide (resbalar). 5 to be slippery (estar resbaladizo). || *v.pron.* 6 to slip away (escapar). 7 to make a slip (equivocarse).
esdrújulo *s.m.* 1 proparoxytone, accented on the antepenultimate syllable. || *s.m.* 2 proparoxytone (palabra).
ese *s.f.* 1 s (letra). 2 zigzag. || 3 **andar haciendo eses,** to stagger, to zigzag.
ese, -a *adj.* that: *esa casa es preciosa = that house is beautiful.*
ése, ésa *pron.* 1 that one: *me gusta ése = I like that one.* 2 he, she, that one: *ése vino ayer = he came yesterday.* 3 him, her, it: *dáselo a ése = give it to him.*
esencia *s.f.* 1 essence. 2 heart, core (de un problema, etc.). || 3 **en –,** essentially; in essence.
esencial *adj.* 1 essential. 2 chief, main (principal). || *s.m.* 3 essential.
esencialmente *adj.* essentially.
esfera *s.f.* 1 MAT. y GEOG. sphere. 2 dial, face (del reloj). || 3 **– terrestre,** globe.
esférico, -a *adj.* 1 MAT. spherical. || 2 *s.m.* DEP. ball (balón).
esferoide *s.m.* MAT. spheroid.
esfinge *s.f.* 1 sphinx. 2 ZOOL. hawkmoth.
esfínter *s.f.* ANAT. sphincter.
esforzado, -a *adj.* 1 vigorous, energetic (energético). 2 tough (fuerte). 3 courageous, valient (valiente).
esforzar *v.t.* 1 to strengthen (fortalecer). 2 to encourage (animar). || *v.pron.* 3 to make an effort. 4 to do one's best (hacer lo mejor posible).
esfuerzo *s.m.* 1 effort. 2 effort, attempt (intento). 3 TEC. stress. || 4 **sin –,** effortlessly.
esfumar *v.t.* 1 ART. to shade (dar sombra). || *v.pron.* 2 to fade away, to melt away (desaparecer).
esgrima *s.f.* 1 DEP. fencing. 2 MIL. swordsmanship.
esgrimidor *s.m.* 1 DEP. fencer. 2 MIL. swordsman.
esgrimir *v.t.* 1 to wield (una espada). 2 (fig.) to use (un argumento, etc.). || *v.i.* 3 DEP. to fence (practicar la esgrima).
esguince *s.m.* 1 swerve, dodge (acción rápida para evitar un golpe, caída, etc.). 2 MED. sprain, twist (torcedura). 3 frown (gesto de desagrado).
eslabón *s.m.* 1 link. 2 MAR. shackle. || 3 **el – perdido,** the missing link.
eslabonamiento *s.m.* linking (acción).
eslabonar *v.t.* 1 to link together (unir). 2 (fig.) to link, to interlink, to connect (ideas, etc.). || *v.pron.* 3 (fig.) to be linked.
eslálom *s.* DEP. slalom (en el esquí, etc.).
eslogan *s.m.* slogan.
eslora *s.f.* MAR. length: *tiene nueve metros de eslora = she is nine metres in length.*
eslovaco, -a *adj./s.m.* y *f.* Slovak(ian).
esmaltador, -ora *s.m.* y *f.* enameller.
esmaltar *v.t.* 1 TEC. to enamel. 2 to varnish (las uñas). 3 (fig.) to embellish, to adorn (embellecer).

esmerado, -a *adj.* **1** careful (cuidadoso). **2** polished (pulido). **3** elegant (elegante).
esmeradamente *adv.* carefully (cuidadosamente).
esmeralda *s.f.* emerald (piedra).
esmerar *v.t.* **1** to tidy up, to clean up (ordenar un sitio, etc.). || *v.pron.* **2** to take pains (esforzarse).
esmeril *s.m.* emery.
esmero *s.m.* care, carefulness.
esmirriado, -a *adj.* V. **desmirriado, -a.**
esmoquin *s.m.* dinner jacket, smoking jacket.
esnob *s.m.* **1** snob. || *adj.* **2** snobbish (persona). **3** posh (sitio, etc.).
esófago *s.m.* ANAT. oesophagus.
esotérico, -a *adj.* esoteric.
espabilar *v.t.* **1** to snuff (una vela). || *v.i.* **2** (Am.) to blink (parpadear). || *v.pron.* **3** to wake up (despertarse). **4** (fig.) to look lively, to wake up.
espaciador *s.m.* spacer, space bar (en una máquina de escribir).
espacial *adj.* **1** MAT. spatial. **2** space: *programa espacial = space programme.* || **3 nave –,** space ship.
espaciamiento *s.m.* **1** spacing. **2** staggering (escalonamiento).
espaciar *v.t.* **1** to space out. **2** to spread (noticias). **3** to stagger (escalonar). **4** to space (imprenta). || *v.pron.* **5** to spread (divulgarse).
espacio *s.m.* **1** space (entre dos cosas, etc.). **2** room, space (sitio): *no queda espacio en el coche = there isn't any room left in the car.* **3** space, period (de tiempo). || **4 a doble –,** double-spaced. **5 – aéreo,** air space. **6 – publicitario,** advertising spot.
espacioso, -a *adj.* spacious, ample.
espada *adj.* **1** sword. **2** (fig.) sworsman (persona). **3** (fig.) authority (experto). || **4 espadas,** spades (en las cartas). **5 entre la – y la pared,** to be between the devil and the deep blue sea. **6 pez –,** swordfish. **7 primer –,** matador.
espadachín *s.m.* **1** good swordsman (buen esgrimidor). **2** bully (bravucón).
espadaña *s.f.* **1** BOT. bulrush. **2** ARQ. bell gable.
espadón *s.m.* **1** broadsword (espada ancha). **2** MIL. top brass.
espaguetis *s.m.* (pl.) spaghetti.
espalda *s.f.* **1** ANAT. back. **2** DEP. backstroke. || **3 a espaldas de alguien,** behind someone's back. **4 dar de espaldas,** to fall (flat) on one's back. **5 dar la – a uno,** to turn one's back on someone. **6 echarse algo a las espaldas,** to forget about something. **7 echarse una cosa sobre las espaldas,** to take something upon oneself. **8 guardar las espaldas,** to keep something in reserve. **9 hablar a espaldas,** (fam.) to talk behind someone's back. **10 medir las espaldas,** to beat someone up (darle una paliza); to punish (castigar). **11 volver la –,** to turn round (volverse). **12 volver la – a uno,** to turn one's back on someone (sentido propio); to give someone the cold shoulder (sentido figurado).
espaldarazo *s.m.* **1** slap on the back. **2** accolade (de un caballero). **3** (fig.) backking (apoyo).
espaldilla *s.f.* ANAT. shoulder blade.
espantada *s.f.* **1** sudden scare (susto repentino). **2** stampede (de un grupo). **3** running away (huida). **4** bolt (un caballo, etc.). || **5 dar la –,** to run away, to take to one's heels (huir); to bolt (un caballo, etc.); to stampede (un grupo).
espantajo *s.m.* **1** scarecrow (espantapájaros). **2** (fig.) bogeyman (el hombre del saco).
espantapájaros *s.m.* scarecrow.
espantar *v.t.* **1** to scare away, to frighten off (hacer huir). **2** to frighten, to scare (dar miedo). **3** to ward off (sueño, miedo, etc.). **4** to horrify, to disgust (horrorizar). || *v.pron.* **5** to be frightened away, to be scared away (asustarse y huir): *se espantó por el ruido = he was frightened away by the noise.* **6** to be frightened (asustarse).
espanto *s.m.* **1** fright (susto). **2** threat, menace (amenaza). **3** (Am.) ghost (fantasma). || **4 ¡que –!,** how awful!
espantoso, -a *adj.* **1** frightening, terrifying (terrorífico). **2** frightful, dreadful (malísimo).
España *s.f.* **1** Spain. || **2 la – de la pandereta,** the tourist's Spain; typical Spain.
español, -ola *adj.* **1** Spanish. || *s.m.* **2** Spaniard (hombre). **3** Spanish (el idioma). || *s.f.* **4** Spaniard (mujer). || *s.pl.* Spaniards. || **6 a la española,** the Spanish way.
españolado, -a *adj.* **1** Spanish-like. || *s.f.* **2** exaggerated portrait of Spain, typically Spanish idea/manierism.
españolismo *s.m.* **1** love of Spain, love of Spanish things (amor para las cosas españolas). **2** Spanish nature (carácter español). **3** hispanicism (hispanicismo).
españolizar *v.t.* **1** to make Spanish, to hispanicize. || *v.pron.* **2** to adopt Spanish ways.
esparadrapo *s.m.* sticking plaster.
esparcido, -a *adj.* **1** scattered. **2** (fig.) merry, cheerful (alegre). **3** (fig.) widespread (muy difundido).
esparcimiento *s.m.* **1** spreading, scattering (dispersión). **2** relaxation (relajación). **3** amusement, diversion (diversión). **4** (fig.) cheerfulness (alegría).
esparcir *v.t.* **1** to spread, to scatter (dispersar). **2** to sow (sembrar). **3** to amuse (divertir). || **4** *v.pron.* to spread (out), to scatter (desparramarse). **5** to spread (una noticia, etc.). **6** to relax, to take it easy (relajarse). **7** to amuse oneself (recrearse).
espárrago *s.m.* **1** BOT. asparragus. **2** post (poste). **3** peg ladder (escalera).
esparraguera *s.f.* **1** BOT. asparragus plant. **2** asparragus patch (plantación). **3** asparragus dish (plato).
espartero, -a *s.m.* y *f.* esparto worker.
espartería *s.f.* **1** esparto workshop (taller). **2** esparto work (oficio).
espartano, -a *adj.* **1** Spartan. || *s.m.* y *f.* **2** Spartan (de Esparta).
espartizal o **espartal** *s.m.* esparto field.
esparto *s.m.* BOT. esparto (planta).
espasmo *s.m.* **1** spasm. **2** jerk, sudden movement (movimiento repentino).
espasmódico, -a *adj.* spasmodic.
espato *s.m.* **1** GEOL. spar. || **– de Islandia,** Iceland spar.
espátula *s.f.* **1** MED. spatula. **2** ART. palette knife. **3** ZOOL. spoonbill (ave). || **4 estar hecho una –,** to be as thin o skinny as a rake.
espavorido, -a *adj.* V. **despavorido, -a.**
especia *s.f.* spice.
especial *adj.* special.
especialidad *s.f.* **1** speciality, specialty. **2** special branch, special field (estudios, investigación, etc.). || **3 no es de mi –,** it's not my line.
especialista *s.m.* y *adj.* **1** specialist. || **2 médico –,** specialist.
especialización *s.f.* specialization.
especializar *v.t.* y *v.pron.* to specialize.
especie *s.m.* **1** BIOL. species. **2** kind, sort (tipo). **3** matter, affair (asunto). **4** news, piece of news (noticia). || **5 pagar en –,** to pay in kind. **6 especies sacramentales,** REL. species.
especiería o **especería** *adj.* **1** grocer's shop (tienda). **2** spices (especias).
específicamente *adv.* specifically.
especificar *v.t.* **1** to specify. **2** to itemize, to list (detallar).
especificativo, -a *adj.* specifying.
específico *adj.* **1** specific. || *s.m.* **2** MED. specific. **3** MED. patent medicine.
espécimen *s.m.* specimen.
espectacular *adj.* spectacular.
espectacularidad *s.f.* spectacular nature.
espectáculo *s.m.* **1** spectacle, sight (una vista, etc.). **2** entertainment (diversión): *viva el espectáculo = long live entertainment.* **3** show, function, performance (teatro). || **4 dar el –,** to make a scene.
espectador, -ora *s.m.* y *f.* **1** spectator. || **2 los espectadores,** the audience.
espectral *adj.* **1** ghostly. **2** FIS. spectral.
espectro *s.m.* **1** FIS. spectrum. **2** spectre, ghost (fantasma). **3** (fig.) spectre.
espectrografía *s.f.* FIS. spectrography.
espectrógrafo *s.m.* FIS. spectrograph.
espectroscópico, -a *adj.* spectroscopic.
espectroscopio *s.m.* FIS. spectroscope.
especulación *s.f.* speculation.
especulador, -ora *s.m.* y *f.* speculator.
especular *v.i.* **1** COM. to speculate. || *v.t.* **2** to examine, to inspect (inspeccionar). **3** (Am.) to ruffle the hair (desgreñar el pelo).
especulativo, -a *adj.* speculative.
espejismo *s.m.* **1** mirage (fenómeno óptico). **2** (fig.) illusion (ilusión).
espejo *s.m.* **1** mirror, looking glass: *mirarse en el espejo = to look at oneself in the mirror.* **2** (fig.) reflection. || **3 – de cuerpo entero,** full-length mirror. **4 – retrovisor,** rear-view mirror. **5 mírate en este –,** let this be an example to you.
espeleología *s.f.* speleology, potholing.

espeleólogo *s.m.* y *f.* speleologist, potholer.

espeluznante *adj.* 1 (fam.) hair-raising, horrifying: *una experiencia espeluznante = a hair-raising experience.*

espeluznar o **despeluznar** *v.t.* to make someone's hair stand on end: *el mero sonido de su voz me espeluzna = the mere sound of his voice makes my hair stand on end.*

espera *s.f.* 1 wait, period of wait: *una larga espera = a long wait.* 2 waiting: *lo que a mí no me gusta es la espera = what I don't like is the waiting.* 3 DER. stay, respite (plazo). 4 patience (paciencia). || 5 **en — de,** waiting for. 6 **la cosa no tiene —,** the matter is most urgent. 7 **sala de —,** waiting room.

esperanto *s.m.* Esperanto.

esperanza *s.f.* 1 hope (confianza). 2 expectation. 3 faith (fe). || 4 **de esperanzas,** promising. 5 **llenar la — de uno,** to fulfill someone's hopes. 6 **mientras hay vida hay —,** while there is life there is hope. 7 **tener muchas esperanzas,** to have high hopes. 8 **tener pocas esperanzas,** to have little hope. 9 **vivir de esperanzas,** to live on hope.

esperanzar *v.t.* to give hope to.

esperar *v.t.* 1 to wait: *esperar el autobús = to wait far the bus.* 2 to hope (desear): *espero que venga el autobús pronto = I hope the bus comes soon.* 3 to expect: *no esperaba esto = I didn't expect this.* 4 to await, to be in store for: *¡vaya una semana nos espera! = what a week is in store for us!.* || *v.i.* 5 to wait: *esperaré hasta las diez = I'll wait until ten o'clock.* || *v.pron.* 6 to expect: *no se esperaba tanta atención = he didn't expect so much attention.* || 7 **— como agua en mayo,** to be longing for. 8 **espero que sí,** I hope so. 9 **estar esperando familia,** to be expecting a baby. 10 **no esperaba menos de Vd.,** I expected nothing less of you; I hoped for nothing less from you. 11 **se espera que,** it is hoped that.

esperma *s.f.* 1 sperm. 2 (Am.) candle (vela). || 3 **— de ballena,** spermaceti, sperm oil.

espermático, -a *adj.* spermatic.

espermatozoide *s.m.* spermatozoid.

espermatozoo *s.m.* spermatozoon.

esperpento *s.m.* 1 fright, sight (persona o cosa fea). 2 scarecrow (espantapájaros). 3 absurdity, nonsense (disparate).

espesar *v.t.* 1 to thicken: *la harina espesa la salsa = the flour thickens the sauce.* 2 to press together (apretar). || *v.pron.* 3 to thicken, to get thicker (ponerse más espeso). 4 to get thicker o bushier (una planta, árbol, etc.).

espeso, -a *adj.* 1 thick (un líquido). 2 dense (un bosque, etc.). 3 heavy, thick (humo, niebla, etc.).

espesor *s.m.* thickness.

espesura *s.f.* 1 thickness (de un líquido). 2 denseness, thickness (de un bosque, etc.). 3 thicket (matorral). 4 dirtiness (suciedad).

espetar *v.t.* 1 to transfix, to run through (traspasar). 2 to skewer (con una broqueta). 3 (fig.) to rap out (una orden). 4 to read (un sermón, lectura, etc.). *v.pron.* 5 to steady oneself, to settle oneself.

espía *s.m.* y *f.* spy.

espiar *v.t.* 1 to spy. 2 (Am.) to look at, to see, to watch (mirar). 3 to keep watch (acechar). || *v.i.* 4 to spy. 5 MAR. to warp (remolcar).

espiga *s.f.* 1 BOT. ear (de un grano). 2 BOT. spike (de una flor). 3 pin, peg (clavija). 4 tang (de un cuchillo). 5 clapper (de una campana). 6 MIL. fuse (mecha). 7 MAR. masthead.

espigado, -a *adj.* 1 BOT. ripe, gone to seed (maduro). 2 tall, lanky (alto una persona).

espigador, -a *s.m.* y *f.* gleaner.

espigar *v.t.* 1 to glean (en la agricultura). 2 (fig.) to glean (en los libros). 3 TEC. to tenon. || *v.i.* 4 to form ears (el trigo). || *v.pron.* 5 to become very tall (crecer muy alto).

espigón *s.m.* 1 point (punta). 2 MAR. jetty, breakwater (rompeolas). 3 ear of corn (mazorca). 4 peak (cerro).

espina *s.f.* 1 BOT. thorn, prickle. 2 bone (del pescado). 3 ANAT. spine. 4 (fig.) doubt, worry, suspicion. || 5 **me da mala —,** it worries me; I don't like the look of it. 6 **— dorsal,** ANAT. backbone. 7 **tener clavada una — en el corazón,** to have a thorn in one's side. 8 **sacarse uno la —,** to get even.

espinaca *s.f.* spinach.

espinal *adj.* spinal.

espinar *v.t.* 1 to prick (herir). 2 to sping (picar). || *s.m.* 3 thicket. 4 (fig.) difficulty (dificultad).

espinazo *s.* 1 ANAT. spine, backbone. 2 ARQ. keystone. 3 (fig. y fam.) **doblar el —,** to bow down.

espingarda *s.f.* 1 MIL. small canon (cañón pequeño). 2 Arab rifle. 3 tall woman (mujer).

espinilla *s.f.* 1 ANAT. shin. 2 *s.m.* MED. blackhead.

espinillera *s.f.* DEP. shinpad.

espino *s.m.* 1 BOT. hawthorn. || 2 **— negro,** BOT. blackthorn.

espionaje *s.m.* espionage, spying.

espiración *s.f.* breathing out, exhalation.

espiral *adj.* 1 spiral. || *s.f.* 2 hairspring (de un reloj). 3 MAT. spiral.

espirar *v.t.* 1 to breathe out, to exhale. 2 to give off (un olor). || *v.i.* 3 to breathe.

espiritismo *s.m.* spiritualism, spiritism.

espiritoso, -a o **espirituoso, -a** *adj.* 1 spirited (de ánimos). 2 spirituous (vino).

espíritu *s.m.* 1 spirit. 2 mind (mente). 3 intelligence (inteligencia). 4 REL. spirit, soul (alma). 5 spirit, ghost (fantasma). || 6 **— de equipo,** team spirit. 7 **el Espíritu Santo,** REL. the Holy Spirit; the Holy Ghost. 8 **levantar el —,** to raise one's spirits. 9 **levantar el — a alguien,** to raise someone's spirits.

espiritual *adj.* spiritual.

espiritualidad *s.f.* spirituality.

espiritualismo *s.m.* spiritualism, spiritism.

espiritualizar *v.t.* to spiritualize.

espiritualmente *adv.* 1 spiritually. 2 wittily (ingeniosamente).

espita *s.f.* 1 faucet, spigot (grifo de tonel). 2 (fig. y fam.) drunkard (borracho).

espléndidamente *adv.* splendidly, magnificently.

esplendidez *s.f.* 1 splendour. 2 generosity (generosidad).

espléndido *adj.* 1 splendid, magnificent. 2 generous (generoso).

esplendor *s.m.* 1 splendour, magnificence. 2 resplendence, shining (resplandor).

esplendoroso, -a *adj.* 1 splendid, magnificent. 2 resplendent (resplandeciente).

espliego *s.m.* BOT. lavender.

espolear *v.t.* 1 to spur (caballo). 2 (fig.) to spur on, to stimulate (dar ánimos).

espoleta *s.f.* 1 MIL. fuse (mecha). 2 ANAT. wishbone.

espolón *s.m.* 1 ZOOL. spur (de un gallo). 2 ZOOL. fetlock (de un caballo). 3 GEOG. spur (de las montañas). 4 MAR. jetty, breakwater (rompeolas). 5 MED. chilblain (sabañón). || *adj.* 6 (Am.) astute (astuto).

espolvorear *v.t.* 1 to dust, to sprinkle. 2 to dust (quitar el polvo).

espongiarios *s.m.pl.* ZOOL. spongiae.

esponja *s.f.* 1 sponge. 2 (fig. y fam.) sponger (gorrón).

esponjoso *adj.* spongy.

esponsales *s.m.pl.* 1 engagement. || 2 **contraer —,** to get engaged.

espontaneidad *adj.* spontaneity.

espontáneo, -a *adj.* 1 spontaneous. 2 wild, spontaneous (plantas). || *s.m.* 3 DEP. person who tries to join in a bullfight (espontáneo).

espora *s.f.* BOT. spore.

esporádico *adj.* sporadic.

esposa *s.f.* 1 wife, spouse (mujer). || 2 **esposas,** handcuffs.

esposar *v.t.* to handcuff, to put handcuffs on.

esposo *s.m.* husband, spouse (marido).

esprint *s.m.* DEP. sprint.

espuela *s.f.* 1 spur (de jinete). 2 (fig.) spur, incentive (incentivo). 3 (Am.) feminine charm (encanto femenino). 4 one for the road (la última copa). 5 ZOOL. (Am.) spur (del gallo).

espuelear *v.t.* (Am.) to spur (caballo).

espuerta *s.f.* basket (cesta).

espuma *s.f.* 1 foam (en el mar). 2 froth (en las bebidas). 3 foam rubber (para colchones, etc.).

espumadera *s.f.* (Am.) skimmer (utensilio de cocina).

espumante *adj.* sparkling (vinos, etc.).

espumarajo *s.m.* 1 MAR. foam (en el agua). 2 foam, froth (en la boca).

espurio, -a *adj.* bastard.

espútnik *s.m.* Sputnik.

esputo *s.m.* MED. sputum.

esqueje *s.m.* clip, cutting (de una planta).
esquela *s.f.* 1 note, short letter (carta corta). 2 obituary (de un difunto).
esquelético, -a *adj.* skeletal.
esqueleto *s.m.* 1 ANAT. skeleton. 2 (Am.) rough draft (copia sucia). 3 skinny person (persona muy flaca).
esquema *s.m.* 1 outline, sketch (bosquejo). 2 outline, plan, sketch (de un proyecto).
esquemático, -a *adj.* schaematic.
esquí *s.m.* 1 ski. 2 DEP. skiing.
esquiador, -ora *s.m.* y *f.* skier.
esquiar *v.i.* DEP. to ski.
esquife *s.m.* skiff (embarcación).
esquila *s.f.* 1 bell, cowbell (para las vacas). 2 small bell (campanilla). 3 shearing (esquileo).
esquilador, -a *s.m.* y *f.* 1 sheepshearer (persona). || *s.f.* 2 sheepshearer (tijeras).
esquilar *v.t.* to clip, to shear.
esquileo *s.m.* 1 shearing, clipping (acción). 2 shearing time (temporada).
esquilmar *v.t.* 1 to harvest (cosechar). 2 (fig.) to impoverish (empobrecer). 3 to exhaust (la tierra).
esquimal *adj./s.m.* y *f.* Eskimo.
esquina *s.f.* 1 corner: *la tienda de la esquina = the shop on the corner.* || 2 **doblar la –,** to turn the corner; (Am.) to die (morir). 3 **a la vuelta de la –,** just around the corner.
esquinado, -a *adj.* 1 angular (angulado). 2 on the corner (que hace esquina). 3 (fig.) bad-tempered (persona).
esquinar *v.t.* 1 (Am.) to put in the corner (poner en la esquina). 2 to form a corner (formar esquina). 3 to square off (escuadrar un madero). || *v.pron.* 4 to quarrel (enemistar).
esquinazo *s.m.* 1 (fam.) corner. 2 MUS. (Am.) serenade (serenata). || 3 **dar a uno el –,** to dodge someone.
esquirla *s.f.* splinter.
esquirol *s.m.* y *f.* blackleg, strikebreaker.
esquivar *v.t.* 1 to avoid, to evade (evitar). 2 do dodge, to avoid (un golpe, etc.). || *v.pron.* 3 to make oneself scarce (irse). 4 to withdraw (retraerse).
esquivez *s.f.* 1 shyness (timidez). 2 aloofness (frialdad).
esquivo, -a *adj.* unsociable (poco sociable).
esquizofrenia *s.f.* PSIC. schizophrenia.
esquizofrénico, -a *adj.* 1 PSIC. schizophrenic. || *s.m.* y *f.* schizophrenic.
estabilidad *s.f.* stability.
estabilización *s.f.* stabilization.
estabilizador, -ora *adj.* 1 stabilizing. || *s.m.* 2 stabilizer.
estabilizar *v.t.* 1 to stabilize (barco, avión, etc.). || *v.pron.* 2 to become stable.
estable *adj.* 1 stable (barco, avión, etc.). 2 balanced (equilibrado).
establecer *v.t.* 1 to establish, to set up, to found (una fundación, etc.). 2 to take up, to establish (domicilio). 3 to make (investigaciones). 4 to draw up (planes). 5 to set (un record). || *v.pron.* 6 to settle (down), to set up (instalarse). 7 COM. to set up in business (en negocios).
establecimiento *s.m.* 1 establishment, setting up (acción). 2 establishment (local). 3 DER. statute (estatuto).
establo *s.m.* 1 cowshed, stall (para las vacas). 2 (Am.) barn (granero).
estaca *s.f.* 1 stake, post (poste). 2 stick (para apalear). 3 TEC. spike (de hierro). 4 (Am.) spur (espuela).
estacada *s.f.* 1 fence, fencing (valla). 2 palisade, stockade (estocada). 3 MAR. breakwater (rompeolas). || 4 **dejar a uno en la –,** to leave someone in the lurch.
estacar *v.t.* 1 to stake out (los límites). 2 MIL. to palisade, to stockade. 3 to stake (un animal). 4 (Am.) to deceive (engañar). 5 (Am.) to wound (herir). || *v.pron.* 6 (fig.) to freeze to the spot (quedarse inmóvil). 7 (Am.) **estacarse un pie,** to hurt one's foot (hacer daño a un pie). || 8 **quedarse en la –,** to die in battle.
estación *s.f.* 1 station (de trenes, etc.). 2 season (temporada). 3 REL. station: *estaciones del Via Crucis = stations of the Cross.* 4 time (época). 5 resort: *estación veraniega = summer resort.* 6 RAD. station, broadcasting station (emisora).
estacional *adj.* 1 seasonal. 2 ASTR. stationary.
estacionamiento *s.m.* 1 stationing. 2 parking (de un coche).
estacionar *v.t.* 1 to station. 2 to park (un coche). || *v.pron.* 3 to remain stationary (quedarse estacionario). 4 to park (un coche).
estacionario, -a *adj.* 1 stationary, still (inmóvil). 2 COM. slack.
estadio o **estadium** *s.m.* 1 DEP. stadium. 2 stage, phase (período).
estadista *s.m.* 1 POL. Statesman (hombre del estado). || *s.m.* y *f.* 2 MAT. statistician.
estadística *s.f.* 1 statistics (ciencia). 2 statistic (dato).
estadístico, -a *adj.* 1 statistical. || *s.m.* y *f.* 2 statistician.
estado *s.m.* 1 state, condition: *un estado lamentable = a lamentable condition.* 2 status: *estado civil = marital status.* 3 MIL. rank (rango). 4 POL. state, government: *secretos del estado = state secrets.* 5 list (de empleados). 6 statement: *estado de cuenta = bank statement.* || 7 **– de ánimo,** state of mind. 8 **– de cosas,** state of affairs. 9 **– de excepción,** state of emergency. 10 **– de guerra,** state of war. 11 **– de gracia,** REL. state of grace. 12 **– de sitio,** stage of siege. 13 **– mayor,** MIL. staff. 14 **golpe de –,** military coup; coup d'etat. 15 **Ministerio del –,** Foreign Office (en Gran Bretaña); State Department (en Estados Unidos).
estafa *s.f.* 1 swindle, trick (engaño). 2 COM. racket. 3 DER. fraud (fraude).
estafador, -ora *s.m.* y *f.* swindler, trickster (timador).
estafar *v.t.* to swindle, to defraud.
estafeta *s.f.* 1 diplomatic bag (correo diplomático). 2 (sub) post office (oficina de correos).
estafilococo *s.m.* MED. staphylococcus.
estalactita *s.f.* stalactite.
estalagmita *s.f.* stalacmite.
estallar *v.i.* 1 to explode (explotar). 2 to burst (reventar). 3 to shatter (el cristal). 4 to fly off the handle (enfadarse). || 5 **– en llanto,** to burst into tears. 6 **hacer –,** to make something explode.
estallido *s.m.* 1 explosion (de una bomba, etc.). 2 clap (de un trueno). 3 shattering (de cristal). 4 outbreak (de una guerra, etc.). 5 outburst (de aplausos, etc.).
estambre *s.m.* 1 worsted, woolen yarn (tela). 2 BOT. stamen.
estamento *s.m.* POL. state.
estameña *s.f.* serge, worsted (tela).
estampa *s.f.* 1 imprint. 2 footprint (huella de pie). 3 print (de imprenta). 4 plate (en un libro). 5 engraving (grabado). 6 (fig.) look, appearance (aspecto). || 7 **dar a la –,** to print (imprimir); to publish (publicar). 8 **romper la – a uno,** to do someone in (matar). 9 (fam.) **tener – de,** to look like.
estampado, -a *adj.* 1 printed (una tela). 2 engraved (grabado). 3 embossed (cuero). || *s.m.* 4 printing (acción).
estampida *s.f.* stampede.
estampido *s.m.* bang (ruido de una explosión).
estampillado *s.m.* 1 rubber-stamping (con sello de goma). 2 sealing (con precinto).
estampillar *v.t.* 1 to stamp, to put a stamp on (sellar). 2 to rubber-stamp (con sello de goma).
estancamiento *s.m.* 1 damming (de un embalse). 2 stagnation (del agua). 3 standstill (de negociaciones).
estancar *v.t.* 1 MED. to stop the flow of (la sangre). 2 to dam up (un río, etc.). 3 (fig.) to block, to hold up (una transacción, etc.). 4 to bring to a standstill (negociaciones). || *v.pron.* 5 to stagnate, to become stagnant (el agua). 6 to come to a standstill (las negociaciones).
estancia *s.f.* 1 stay: *nuestra estancia en Perú fue muy agradable = our stay in Peru was very nice.* 2 room (habitación). 3 (Am.) ranch, farm (rancho).
estanco *s.m.* 1 tobacconist's (kiosco). 2 (Am.) liquor store (tienda de bebidas alcohólicas). || *adj.* 3 watertight (hermético).
estándar *adj.* y *s.m.* standard.
estandardizar o **estandarizar** *v.t.* to standardize.
estandarte *s.m.* banner, standard.
estanque *s.m.* pool, pond, small lake.
estante *s.m.* 1 shelf. 2 (Am.) prop (apoyo).
estantería *s.f.* shelves (*pl.*), shelving.
estañar *v.t.* 1 to tin. 2 to solder (soldar). 3 (Am.) to wound (herir). 4 to fire (despedir a un empleado).
estaño *s.m.* tin.

estar *v.i.* **1** to be (posición): *mi madre está en la cocina = my mother is in the kitchen.* **2** to be at home: *está la señora de la casa = is the lady of the house at home.* **3** to be, to stay: *estuvo tres días en Sevilla = she stayed for three days in Seville.* **4** to be (con el presente continuo): *estoy viendo la tele = I'm watching T.V.* **5** to keep, to stay: *¡estáte quieto! = keep still!* **6** to cost: *¿a cuánto están las manzanas? = how much do the apples cost?* **7** to be (estado temporal): *estoy cansado = I'm tired.* **8** to be working as: *está de camarero = he is working as a waiter.* **9** to be dressed in: *estamos de etiqueta = we are dressed in formal dress.* **10** to have yet to be: *la cantidad exacta está por medir = the exact quantity is yet to be measured.* **11** to be in the mood for: *no estoy para bromas = I'm not in the mood for jokes.* **12** to be tempted: *estoy por irme a Francia = I'm tempted to go to France.* || **13 está bien,** it's alright. **14 ¿estamos?,** right? (entender); ready? (estar listo). **15 — en grande,** to live like a king. **16 — en todo,** to keep an eye on everything (ocuparse); to think of everything (pensar en todo). **17 — fuera de sí,** to be beside oneself. **18 — hecho,** to have become: *está hecho un idiota = he has become an idiot.* **19 estoy que me subo por las paredes,** I'm going up the wall. **20 ya está,** that's it. **21 ¡ya está bien!,** that's enough!
estatal *adj.* state.
estático, -a *adj.* **1** static. || *s.f.* **2** FIS. statics (la estática).
estatua *s.f.* statue.
estatuario *adj.* **1** statuesque. **2** statuary: *arte estatuario = statuary art.*
estatuir *v.t.* **1** to establish (establecer). **2** to decree (decretar).
estatura *s.f.* height, stature.
estatuto *s.m.* statute.
este *adj.* **1** GEOG. east, easterly (dirección). **2** GEOG. east, eastern (posición): *una provincia del este = an eastern province.* || *s.m.* **3** east.
este y **esta** *dem. adj.m.* y *f. (sing.)* this: *este hombre es mi hermano = this man is my brother.* || *dem. adj. (pl.).* **2 estos y estas,** these: *estas cerillas están húmedas = these matches are wet.*
éste y **ésta** *pron.dem. m.* y *f. (sing.)* **1** this, this one: *éste es mío = this one is mine.* || *pron.dem. m.* y *f. (pl.)* **2 éstos y éstas,** these, these ones: *éstas son mías = these are mine.*
estela *s.f.* **1** MAR. wake, wash. **2** trail (de un avión). **3** trail (de una estrella fugaz). **4** stele (monumento).
estelar *adj.* ASTR. stellar.
estenografía *s.f.* shorthand, stenography.
estenotipia *s.f.* **1** stenotypy (arte). **2** stenotype (máquina).
estentóreo, -a *adj.* stentorean.
estepa *s.f.* **1** steppe (llanura). **2** BOT. Rockrose.
estepario, -a *adj.* steppe.
estera *s.f.* mat, matting.
estercolero *s.m.* dunghill, manure heap.
estéreo *adj.* **1** stereo. || *s.m.* **2** stereo (system).
estereofonía *s.m.* stereophony, stereo.
estereofónico, -a *adj.* stereophonic, stereo.
estereoscopio *s.m.* stereoscope.
estereotipado, -a *adj.* stereotyped.
estereotipar *v.t.* to stereotype.
estereotipo *s.m.* stereotype.
estereotomía *s.f.* stereotomy.
estéril *adj.* **1** sterile, barren (terreno). **2** sterile, infertile (mujer). **3** sterile (hombre). **4** (fig.) vain, futile (un intento, etc.).
esterilidad *s.f.* **1** barrenness, infertility (terreno). **2** sterility, infertility (de una mujer). **3** sterility (de un hombre). **4** (fig.) futility.
esterilización *s.f.* sterilization.
esterilizador, -ora *adj.* **1** sterilizing. || *s.m.* **2** sterilizer (aparato).
esterilizar *v.t.* to sterilize.
esterilla *s.f.* mat for lying down on.
esterlina *adj.* sterling: *libra esterlina = pound sterling.*
esternón *s.m.* ANAT. sternum, breastbone.
estertor *s.m.* death rattle.
esteta *s.m.* y *f.* **1** aesthete. || *s.m.* **2** (fam.) puff (homosexual).
esteticismo *s.m.* aestheticism.
estético, -a *adj.* **1** aesthetic, esthetic. **2** artistic, beautiful (bello).
estetoscopio *s.m.* MED. stethoscope.
estiaje *s.m.* low water.
estibador *s.m.* MAR. stevedore.
estiércol *s.m.* dung, manure: *estiércol de caballo = horse manure.*
estigma *s.m.* **1** BOT., ZOOL. y MED. stigma. **2** (fig.) stigma, disgrace. **3** brand (señal). || **2** REL. estigmas, stigmatas.
estilar *v.t.* **1** DER. to draw up (un documento). **2** to use, to be in the habit of using (acostumbrar, usar). || *v.pron.* e *i.* **3** to be used (emplearse). **4** to be in fashion (estar de moda).
estilete *s.m.* **1** stiletto (puñal). **2** MED. stylet, probe.
estilista *s.m.* y *f.* **1** TEC. stylist, designer (de coches, etc.). **2** stylist (escritor).
estilística *s.f.* stylistics.
estilizar *v.t.* **1** to stylize. **2** TEC. to design, to style.
estilo *s.m.* **1** style, manner (manera). **2** fashion (moda). **3** DEP. stroke (natación). **4** TEC. stylus (para escribir). **5** BOT. style. **6** (fig.) style: *tiene mucho estilo = he's got a lot of style.* **7** type (tipo).
estilográfica *s.f.* fountain pen.
estima *s.f.* **1** esteem, respect: *tener a uno en gran estima = to hold someone in high esteem.* **2** MAR. dead reckoning.
estimable *adj.* **1** estimable, esteemed. **2** considerable (cantidad, etc.).
estimación *s.f.* **1** COM. estimation, valuation. **2** estimate (presupuesto). || **3** DER. **— de una demanda,** admittence of a claim.
estimador, -ora *s.m.* y *f.* valuer, appraiser (tasador).
estimar *v.t.* **1** to esteem, to respect, to hold in esteem (tenerle respeto a alguien). **2** to value (valorar). **3** to consider, to think (considerar). **4** DER. to admit: *estimar una demanda = to admit a claim.* || *v.pron.* **5** to have a high opinion of oneself (uno mismo), to be valued (valorarse).
estimulante *adj.* **1** stimulating. || *s.m.* **2** MED. stimulant.
estimular *v.t.* **1** to stimulate. **2** to encourage, to incite (dar ánimos). **3** to promote, encourage (un negocio).
estímulo *s.m.* **1** stimulus, stimulation. **2** encouragement (ánimo).
estío *s.m.* summer (verano).
estipendiario, -a *adj.* y *s.m.* stipendiary.
estipendio *s.m.* **1** stipend. **2** salary (salario).
estipulación *s.f.* stipulation.
estipular *v.t.* to stipulate.
estirado, -a *adj.* **1** stretched (tela, etc.). **2** (fig.) dressed to kill (acicalado). **3** (fam.) stuck-up (que se da mucha importancia).
estirar *v.t.* **1** to stretch (alargar). **2** to stretch out (el brazo, etc.). **3** (Am.) to kill, to shoot (matar). **4** (Am.) to flog (dar latigazos a alguien). **5** (Am.) to pull (tirar de algo). || *v.pron.* to stretch out (tumbarse).
estirpe *s.f.* stock, lineage (origen de familia).
estival *adj.* summer.
estocada *s.f.* **1** thrust, lunge (con un arma blanca). **2** stab, stab wound (herida).
estofa *s.f.* **1** quilting, quited material. || **2 de baja —,** bad quality.
estofado, -a *adj.* **1** stewed. || *s.m.* **2** stew, hotpot.
estofar *v.t.* to stew.
estoicismo *s.m.* stoicism.
estoico, -a *adj.* **1** stoic, stoical. **2** (fig.) stoic, stoical. || *s.m.* y *f.* **3** stoic.
estola *s.f.* stole.
estolón *s.m.* BOT. stolon, sucker, runner.
estomacal *adj.* y *s.m.* **1** MED. stomachic. || **2 trastorno —,** stomach upset.
estomagar *v.t.* **1** to give indigestion. **2** (fig.) to annoy (irritar).
estómago *s.m.* **1** ANAT. stomach. || **2 dolor de —,** stomach ache. **3 tener el — de piedra,** to have a cast iron stomach.
estomatología *s.f.* MED. stomatology.
estomatólogo, -a *m.* y *f.* MED. stomatologist.
estopa *s.f.* **1** tow (fibra). **2** burlap (tela). **3** MAR. oakum. **4** (Am.) cotton waste.
estoque *s.m.* **1** rapier, sword (espada). **2** BOT. gladiolus. || **3 estar hecho un —,** to be as thin as a rake.
estoquear *v.t.* to stab (a bull) with a sword.
estorbar *v.t.* **1** to hinder, to impede, to get in someone's way (obstaculizar). **2** to bother, to upset (molestar). || *v.i.* **3** to be in the way.
estorbo *s.m.* **1** hindrance. **2** obstacle (obstáculo). **3** obstruction (obstrucción).
estornino *s.m.* ZOOL. starling (pájaro).

estornudar *v.i.* to sneeze.
estornudo *s.m.* sneeze.
estrabismo *s.m.* MED. strabismus, squint.
estrado *s.m.* **1** stage, platform (tarima). **2** MUS. bandstand. || **3** DER. estrados, court rooms.
estrafalario, -a *adj.* **1** odd, outlandish, eccentric (eccéntrico). **2** slovenly (forma de vestir).
estragar *v.t.* **1** to ruin, to devastate (causar estragos). **2** to spoil (estropear). **3** to corrupt (corromper).
estrago *s.m.* **1** ruin, destruction (destrucción). **2** corruption (corrupción). || **3 estragos,** havoc (sing.). **4 hacer estragos en,** to wreak havoc with.
estrambólico, -a *adj.* (Am.) V. **estrambótico, -a.**
estrambote *s.m.* extra verses added to a poem.
estrambótico, -a *adj.* bizarre, weird (raro).
estrangulación *s.f.* strangulation.
estrangulador, -ora *s.m.* y *f.* strangler.
estrangular *v.t.* **1** to strangle (a alguien). **2** MED. to strangulate. **3** TEC. to throttle.
estratega *s.m.* y *f.* MIL. strategist.
estratagema *s.f.* stratagem.
estrategia *s.f.* strategy.
estratégico, -a *adj.* strategic.
estratificar *v.t.* **1** to stratify. || *v.pron.* **2** to stratify, to be stratified.
estrato *s.m.* **1** GEOL. stratum, layer. **2** stratus (nube).
estratosfera *s.f.* stratosphere.
estrechar *v.t.* **1** to narrow (hacer más estrecho). **2** to take in (un vestido, etc.). **3** to hug, to embrace (abrazar). **4** to squeeze (apretar). **5** to shake (la mano). *v.pron.* **6** to narrow, to get narrow (una carretera, etc.). **7** to squeeze together (animarse). **8** to cut down, to reduce spending (reducir los gastos).
estrechez *s.f.* **1** narrowness, tightness. **2** poverty, want, need (pobreza). **3** closeness, intimacy (intimidad). **4** strictness, rigidity (severidad). || **5 — del dinero,** shortage of money. **6 — de miras,** narrow-mindedness.
estrecho, -a *adj.* **1** narrow. **2** tight (apretado). **3** tight, short (dinero). **4** close, intimate (relaciones). **5** strict, severe (severo). **6** mean (tacaño). || *s.m.* **7** GEOG. strait(s): *el Estrecho de Gibraltar = the Straits of Gibraltar.*
estregadura o **estregamiento** *s.m.* o *f.* **1** rubbing (con un trapo). **2** scrubbing (con un cepillo). **3** scouring (con un abrasivo).
estregar *v.t.* **1** to rub (frotar). **2** to scrub (con un cepillo).
estregón *s.m.* hard rubbing.
estrella *s.f.* **1** ASTR. star. **2** asterix (asterisco). **3** MIL. star, pip. **4** star (del cine, etc.). || **5 — fugaz,** shooting star. **6 — de guía,** guiding star. **7 — polar,** pole star. **8 tener (buena) —,** to be lucky. **9 ver las estrellas,** to see stars.
estrellado, -a *adj.* **1** starry (el cielo). **2** star-shaped (con forma de estrella). **3** with a white mark on its forehead (un caballo).
estrellar *v.t.* **1** to smash (romper). **2** to fry (huevos). || *v.pron.* **3** to smash, to shatter (romperse). **4** to crash: *el avión se estrelló en las montañas = the plane crashed in the mountains.* **5** (fig.) to fail (fallar).
estrellón *s.m.* **1** (Am.) crash (choque). **2** big star (estrella grande). **3** star-shaped firework (fuego artificial).
estremecedor, -a *adj.* **1** startling (que asusta). **2** blood-curdling (espeluznante).
estremecer *v.t.* **1** to shake (sacudir). **2** to startle (asustar). **3** to make someone shudder (hacer temblar a alguien). || *v.pron.* **4** to shake, to shudder (vibrar). **5** to tremble (de miedo, etc.). **6** to shake, to tremble (del frío).
estrenar *v.t.* **1** to use for the first time (usar por primera vez). **2** to wear for the first time (ropa). **3** to release, to put on release (una película). || *v.i.* **4** (Am.) to make a down payment (dar dinero de entrada). || *v.pron.* **5** to make one's debut (una persona). **6** to open (teatro). **7** to be shown for the first time (cine).
estreñido, -a *adj.* **1** MED. constipated. **2** (fig.) mean, stingy (tacaño).
estreñimiento *s.m.* MED. constipation.
estreñir *v.t.* **1** MED. to constipate. || *v.pron.* **2** MED. to become constipated.
estrépito *s.m.* **1** noise, racket, row (ruido). || **2 reírse con —,** to laugh uproariously; (fam.) to laugh one's head off.
estrepitosamente *adv.* **1** noisily (ruidosamente). **2** rowdily, boisterously (bulliciosamente).
estrepitoso, -a *adj.* **1** noisy (ruidoso). **2** rowdy, boisterous (persona, etc.).
estreptococo *s.m.* BIOL. streptococcus.
estreptomicina *s.f.* MED. streptomycin (antibiótico).
estría *s.f.* **1** groove. **2** ARQ. flute, fluting. **3** BIOL. striation.
estriar *v.t.* **1** to make a groove. **2** ARQ. to flute. **3** BIOL. to striate.
estribación *s.f.* GEOG. spur.
estribar *v.i.* **1** to be supported, to rest (apoyarse). **2** (fig.) to be based (basarse). **3** to stem: *el problema estriba en la falta de comunicación = the problem stems from the lack of communication.*
estribillo *s.m.* **1** refrain (en poesía). **2** chorus (en una canción).
estribo *s.m.* **1** stirrup (de la montura). **2** running board, footboard (de un coche). **3** TEC. brace, bracket. **4** ARQ. buttress. **5** GEOG. spur. || **6** (Am.) **tomar algo para el —,** to have one for the road (tomar la última copa).
estribor *s.m.* MAR. starboard.
estrichnina *s.f.* MED. strychnine.
estrictamente *adv.* strictly.
estrictez *s.f.* (Am.) strictness (severidad).
estricto, -a *adj.* **1** strict. **2** sever (severo).
estridencia *s.f.* stridency, stridence.
estridente *adj.* **1** strident, raucous. **2** unpleasant-sounding (que suena mal).
estridor *s.m.* **1** stridor, strident sound (ruido estridente). **2** stridency. **3** screech (chillido de un frenazo, etc.).
estrofa *s.f.* verse, stanza.
estrógeno *s.m.* BIOL. oestrogen o estrogen.
estroncio *s.m.* **1** QUIM. strontium: *estroncio 90 = strontium 90.*
estropajo *s.m.* **1** scourer. **2** dirt, rubbish (basura). **2** BOT. loofah.
estropajoso, -a *adj.* **1** tough, leathery (comida, etc.). **2** slovenly (forma de vestir).
estropear *v.t.* **1** to damage, to spoil (una cosa). **2** to spoil, to ruin (una situación, un proyecto, etc.). **3** to hurt to injure (lastimar). || *v.pron.* **4** to break down (una máquina). **5** to get damaged o ruined o spoilt (una cosa). **6** to go bad (la fruta, etc.).
estropicio *s.m.* **1** damage (destrozo). **2** mess (desorden).
estructura *s.f.* **1** structure (social, etc.). **2** frame, framework (armazón).
estructuración *s.f.* structuring, organizing.
estructural *adj.* structural.
estructuralismo *s.m.* structuralism.
estructurar *v.t.* **1** to construct (construir). **2** to organize, to structure (organizar).
estruendo *s.m.* **1** noise, clamour (ruido). **2** crash, clatter (ruido repentino). **3** tumult (tumulto). **4** pomp, ostentation (pompa).
estrujamiento *s.m.* **1** squeezing (de una naranja, etc.). **2** pressing (de la uva).
estrujar *v.t.* **1** to squeeze (una naranja, etc.). **2** to press (la uva). **3** to crush (a una persona). **4** to exploit (explotar). || *v.pron.* **5** to crowd, to throng, to press (atestar).
estrujón *s.m.* **1** squeezing. **2** pressing.
estuario *s.m.* GEOG. estuary.
estucado *s.m.* stucco.
estucar *v.t.* to stucco.
estuco *s.m.* stucco.
estuche *s.m.* **1** box, case, container (para guardar objetos). **2** sheath (para una espada, puñal, etc.). **3** set (conjunto): *estuche de instrumentos = set of instruments.* || **4 — del Rey,** Royal surgeon (cirujano).
estudiado *adj.* **1** student.
estudiante *s.m.* y *f.* student.
estudiantil *adj.* student: *vida estudiantil = student life.*
estudiar *v.t.* e *i.* **1** to study. **2** to read, to study (en la universidad). **3** to consider (un problema).
estudio *s.m.* **1** study. **2** research (investigación). **3** survey, research (encuesta). **4** study (despacho). **5** studio flat (piso). || **6 — del mercado,** market research, marketing.
estudiosamente *adv.* studiously.
estudioso, -a *adj.* **1** studious, hard-working. || *s.m.* y *f.* **2** scholar, specialist.

estufa *s.f.* 1 stove, heater. 2 steam room (en los baños termales). 3 heat cabinet (para disecar, desinfectar, etc.). || 4 **– eléctrica,** electric fire.
estulticia *s.f.* stupidity, foolishness.
estulto, -a *adj.* stupid, foolish.
estupefacción *s.f.* stupefaction.
estupefaciente *adj.* 1 stupefying. 2 narcotic (narcótico). || *s.m.* 3 narcotic, drug. || 4 **tráfico de estupefacientes,** drug-smuggling.
estupefacto, -a *adj.* 1 astonished (atónito). || 2 **me miró –,** she looked at me in amazement.
estupendamente *adv.* 1 stupendously, marvelously, wonderfully. || 2 **estoy estupendamente,** I'm very well (muy bien).
estupendo, -a *adj.* 1 stupendous. 2 marvellous, wonderful, terrific: *una cena estupenda = a marvellous dinner.* || 3 **¡–!,** great!
estupidez *s.f.* 1 stupidity, silliness. 2 stupid thing: *eso es una estupidez = that's a stupid thing to say* (decir); *that's a stupid thing to do* (hacer).
estúpido, -a *adj.* 1 stupid, silly (tonto). || *s.m.* y *f.* 2 a stupid person: *es un estúpido = he's a stupid person.*
estupor *s.m.* 1 MED. stupor. 2 (fig.) astonishment (asombro).
estupro *s.m.* rape.
esturión *s.f.* ZOOL. sturgeon (pez).
esvástica *s.f.* swastica.
etapa *s.f.* 1 stage (de un viaje, etc.). 2 DEP. leg, stage (de una carrera). 3 (fig.) phase, stage (fase). 4 MIL. halt, stop (lugar de parada).
etcétera *s.m.* etcetera.
éter *s.m.* 1 QUIM. ether. 2 (lit.) sky, heavens.
etéreo *adj.* ethereal.
eternamente *adv.* eternally.
eternidad *s.f.* eternity.
eternizar *v.t.* 1 to eternalize, to make eternal. 2 to immortalize (inmortalizar). || *v.pron.* 3 to be endless, to drag on (durar demasiado).
eterno, -a *adj.* 1 eternal. 2 (fig.) endless, everlasting (amor, etc.).
ético, -a *adj.* 1 ethical (moral). 2 MED. consumptive. 3 (Am.) pale (pálido). || *s.m.* 4 moralist (moralista).
etílico, -a *adj.* 1 QUIM. ethylic. || 2 QUIM. alcohol etílico, ethyl alcohol.
etimología *s.f.* etymology.
etimológico, -a *adj.* etymological.
etimologista *s.m.* y *f.* etymologist.
etimologizar *v.i.* to etymologize.
etimólogo, -a *s.m.* y *f.* etymologist.
etíope o **etiope** *adj./s.m.* y *f.* Ethiopian.
etiqueta *s.f.* 1 etiquette, ceremonial, ceremony. 2 label, tag (en una camisa, etc.). || 3 **de –,** formal.
etiquetar *v.t.* to label.
etiquetero, -a *adj.* ceremonious, formal.
étnico, -a *adj.* ethnic.
etnografía *s.f.* ethnography.
etnográfico *adj.* ethnographic, ethnographical.
etnógrafo *s.m.* y *f.* ethnographer.
etnología *s.f.* ethnology.
etnológico, -a *adj.* ethnologic, ethnological.
etnólogo, -a *s.m.* y *f.* ethnologist.
etrusco, -a *adj., s.m.* y *f.* Etruscan.
eucalipto *s.m.* BOT. eucalyptus.
Eucaristía *s.f.* Eucharist.
Eucarístico *adj.* Eucharistic, Eucaristical.
eufemismo *s.m.* euphemism.
eufemístico, -a *adj.* euphemistic.
eufonía *s.f.* euphony.
eufónico, -a *adj.* euphonic, euphonious.
euforia *s.f.* euphoria.
eufórico, -a *adj.* euphoric.
eugenesia *s.f.* eugenics.
eugenésico, -a *adj.* eugenic.
eunuco *s.m.* eunuch.
¡eureka! *interj.* eureka!
Europa *s.f.* Europe.
europeización *s.f.* Europeanization.
europeizante *adj.* (Am.) pro-European (europeísta).
europeizar *v.t.* 1 to Europeanize. || *v.pron.* 2 to become Europeanized.
europeo, -a *adj./s.m.* y *f.* European.
eusquero, -a o **éuscaro, -a** *adj./s.m.* y *f.* Basque.
eutanasia *s.f.* euthanasia, mercy killing.
evacuación *s.f.* 1 evacuation. 2 TEC. exhaust, waste.
evacuante *adj.* y *s.m.* MED. evacuant.
evacuatorio *adj.* 1 MED. evacuant. || *s.m.* 2 public lavatory (retrete público).
evacuar *v.t.* 1 to evacuate: *el ejército tuvo que evacuar a los habitantes = the army had to evacuate the inhabitants.* 2 MED. to evacuate (expeler del cuerpo). 3 MED. to drain (una herida). 4 to carry out, to undertake (una consulta). 5 to transact (una gestión).
evadir *v.t.* 1 to evade, to avoid. 2 to escape, to avoid (un peligro). 3 to shirk (una responsabilidad). || *v.pron.* 4 to escape (fugarse).
evaluación *s.f.* evaluation.
evaluador, -a *s.m.* y *f.* evaluator.
evaluar *v.t.* to evaluate.
evangélico, -a *adj.* evangelic, evangelical.
evangelio *s.m.* 1 REL. Gospel. 2 (fig.) gospel truth (verdad). || 3 **dice como el –,** he speaks the gospel truth. 4 **ser como el –,** to be infallible.
Evangelista *adj.* **San Juan –,** St. John the Evangelist.
evangelista *s.m.* 1 gospeller. 2 evangelist: *los cuatro evangelistas = the four evangelists.* 3 (Am.) public writer, scribe (escriba).
evangelización *adj.* evangelization, evangelizing.
evangelizador, -ora *s.m.* y *f.* evangelist.
evangelizar *v.t.* to evangelize.
evaporación *s.f.* evaporation.
evaporar *v.t.* 1 to evaporate. || *v.pron.* 2 to evaporate. 3 (fig.) to vanish (esfumarse).
evaporizar *v.t.* y *pron.* to vapourize.
evasión *s.f.* 1 escape, flight (huida). 2 (fig.) evasion. || 3 **– fiscal,** tax evasion.
evasivo, -a *adj.* evasive, non-committal.
evento *s.m.* 1 event (acontecimiento). 2 DEP. (Am.) sporting fixture (encuentro).
eventual *adj.* 1 possible (posible). 2 temporary, casual (trabajo). 3 fortuitous (fortuito).
eventualidad *s.f.* eventuality, possibility.
eventualmente *adj.* 1 by chance (por casualidad). 2 possibly (posiblemente).
evidencia *s.f.* 1 DER. evidence, proof (prueba). 2 obviousness. || 3 **poner en –,** to make clear.
evidenciar *v.t.* 1 to prove, to show, to demonstrate (demostrar, probar). || *v.pron.* 2 to be obvious o evident (ser evidente). 3 to stand out (destacar).
evidente *adj.* obvious, clear, evident.
evidentemente *adv.* obviously, clearly, evidently.
evitable *adj.* avoidable, preventable: *el accidente fue evitable = the accident was avoidable.*
evitación *s.f.* prevention, avoidance: *evitación de accidentes = accident prevention.*
evitar *v.t.* 1 to avoid (eludir). 2 to escape, to avoid, to evade (un problema, etc.). 3 to save (ahorrar), to prevent (impedir).
evocación *s.f.* 1 evocation, conjuring up (acción). 2 recollection (descripción).
evocador, -ora *adj.* evocative, evocatory.
evocar *v.t.* 1 to evoke, to conjure up (imágenes, etc.). 2 to call up, to invoke (a los espíritus).
evolución *s.f.* 1 BIOL. evolution. 2 development, evolution (de ideas, etc.). 3 MIL. evolution, manoeuvre (maniobra).
evolucionar *v.i.* 1 BIOL. to evolve. 2 (fig.) to change, to evolve, to develop. 3 MIL. to manoeuvre (maniobrar). 4 to wheel, to circle (un avión).
evolucionismo *s.m.* evolutionism.
evolucionista *adj./s.m.* y *f.* evolutionist.
evolutivo, -a *adj.* evolutionary.
ex abrupto *adv.* abruptly, sharply.
exabrupto *s.m.* 1 (fam.) sharp o abrupt remark. 2 MIL. broadside (andanada).
exacción *s.f.* 1 exaction, extortion (abuso). 2 exaction (de impuestos, etc.).
exacerbación *s.f.* 1 exasperation. 2 MED. exacerbation (de una enfermedad). 3 exacerbation (de sentimientos).
exacerbar *v.t.* 1 to irritate, to provoke (provocar). 2 (fig.) to aggravate, to exacerbate (una enfermedad).
exactamente *adv.* 1 exactly. 2 accurately, precisely (de modo preciso). 3 punctually (puntualmente). 4 correctly (correctamente).
exactitud *s.f.* 1 exactness, accuracy, precision (precisión). 2 punctuality (puntualidad).
exacto, -a *adj.* 1 exact: *el momento exacto = the exact moment.* 2 faithful, exact: *una versión exacta = a faithful version.* 3 accurate (preciso). 4 correct, right, true (verdadero). || *adv.* 5 exactly. || 6 ¡exacto!, exactly!; quite right!
exageración *s.f.* exaggeration.
exagerado, -a *adj.* 1 exaggerated, farfetched (una declaración, etc.). 2 excessive

(excesivo). **3** exorbitant, excessive (precio). || **4 ser un —,** to overdo it; to go too far, to exaggerate.
exagerar *v.t.* **1** to exaggerate. **2** to overdo, to go to far with: *exagera mucho su forma de vestir = he overdoes the way he dresses.* || *v.i.* **3** to overdo things.
exaltación *s.f.* **1** exaltation, elation (alegría). **2** extolling, exalting, praising (alabanza). **3** exaltation, overexcitement (exceso de pasión). **4** exaltation, promotion (promoción).
exaltado, -a *adj.* **1** exalted. **2** over-excited, worked-up (estado de ánimo). **3** exalted, extolled, praised (alabado). || *s.m.* y *f.* **4** hot-head. **5** POL. extremist.
exaltar *v.t.* **1** to exalt. **2** to extol, to praise (alabar). **3** to elevate, to raise (enaltecer). || *v.r.* **4** to be extolled o exalted o praised. **5** to get heated (en un argumento).
examen *s.m.* **1** examenation, exam: *presentarse a un examen = to sit o take an exam.* **2** examination, study (de una situación, etc.). || **3** someter a examen, to examine.
examinando, -a *s.m.* y *f.* examinee, candidate.
examinar *v.t.* **1** to examine. **2** to consider, to study (un problema). || *v.r.* **3** to take o sit an exam (presentarse a un examen).
exangüe *adj.* **1** bloodless (sin sangre). **2** anaemic (anímico). **3** weak (débil).
exánime *adj.* **1** lifeless (sin señales de vida). **2** weak, exhausted (exhausto). || **3 caer —,** to fall in a faint.
exantema *s.m.* MED. exanthema, exanthem (erupción).
exarca *s.m.* exarch.
excarcelar *v.t.* to release from prison (dejar en libertad).
exasperación *s.f.* exasperation.
exasperante *adj.* exasperating.
exasperar *v.t.* **1** to exasperate. || *v.pron.* **2** to be exasperated.
ex cátedra *adj.* y *adv.* ex cathedra.
excavación *s.f.* excavation, digging.
excavadora *s.f.* mechanical digger, (fam.) JCB.
excavar *v.t.* **1** to dig (una zanja, etc.). **2** to excavate, to dig up (el suelo). **3** to excavate (en arqueología). **4** to clear the soil from around the base of plants (quitar la tierra de alrededor de las plantas).
excedencia *s.f.* **1** leave (permiso). **2** sabbatical leave (de profesor). **3** leave pay (sueldo).
excedente *adj.* **1** excess, surplus (sobrante). **2** excessive (excesivo). **3** on leave (un soldado, etc.). || *s.m.* **4** surplus.
exceder *v.t.* **1** to exceed, to surpass. || *v.pron.* **2** to exceed. **3** to go too far: *se excedió ayer con esa chica = she went too far with that girl yesterday.*
excelencia *s.f.* **1** excellence. || **2 por —,** par excellence. **3 su Excelencia,** His Excellence (él); Your Excellence (Vd.).
excelente *adj.* excellent.
excelentísimo, -a *adj.* most excellent.
excelsitud *s.f.* sublimity, sublimeness.
excelso, -a *adj.* sublime.
excentricidad *s.f.* eccentricity.
excéntrico, -a *adj.* **1** ecentric. **2** MAT. eccentric. || *s.m.* y *f.* **3** eccentric.
excepción *s.f.* **1** exception. || **2 — de la regla,** exception to the rule. **3 la — que confirma la regla,** the exception that confirms the rule.
excepcional *adj.* exceptional.
excepcionalmente *adv.* exceptionally.
excepto *prep.* except for, excepting, apart from.
exceptuar *v.t.* **1** to leave out, to exclude (excluir). **2** DER. to exempt. || *v.pron.* **3** to be excluded, to be left out, not to be included.
excesivamente *adv.* excessively, unreasonably.
excesivo, -a *adj.* excessive, unreasonable.
exceso *s.m.* **1** excess. **2** COM. excess, surplus. || **3 — de equipaje,** excess baggage. **4 — de velocidad,** speeding. **5 con —,** too much.
excipiente *s.m.* MED. excipient.
excitabilidad *s.f.* excitability.
excitable *adj.* **1** excitable, easily worked up. **2** temperamental (nervioso).
excitación *s.f.* **1** excitement. || **2 — loca,** hysteria.
excitante *s.m.* **1** exciting. **2** MED. stimulating. || *s.m.* MED. stimulant.
excitar *v.t.* **1** to excite. **2** to arouse, to excite (un sentimiento, etc.). **3** to raise (esperanzas). **4** ELEC. to excite, to energize. || *v.pron.* **5** to get excited, to get worked up.
exclamación *s.f.* exclamación. **2** cry (grito).
exclamar *v.t.* e *i.* to exclaim.
exclamativo *adj.* exclamatory, exclamative.
exclaustración *s.f.* **1** REL. secularization. **2** REL. expulsion (de monjas o frailes).
exclaustrado, -a *s.m.* y *f.* REL. secularized monk (monje); secularized nun (monja).
exclaustrar *v.t.* REL. to secularize.
excluir *v.t.* **1** to exclude, to shut out. **2** to exclude, to rule out (una posibilidad, etc.).
exclusiva *s.f.* **1** COM. sole right (de un producto, etc.). **2** exclusive interview (entrevista). **3** refusal (de un puesto de trabajo).
exclusivamente *adv.* exclusively.
exclusive *adv.* **1** exclusively. || *prep.* **2** not counting.
exclusividad *s.f.* **1** exclusiveness (de moda, etc.). **2** sole right (exclusiva).
exclusivo *adj.* exclusive, sole.
excomulgado *adj.* **1** REL. excommunicated. || *s.m.* **2** REL. excommunicated person.
excomulgar *v.t.* REL. to excommunicate.
excomunión *s.f.* **1** REL. excommunication. **2** REL. excommunication order (orden).
excoriación *s.f.* **1** chafing, rubbing. **2** graze (desolladura).
excrecencia *s.f.* excrescence.
excreción *s.f.* excretion.
excrementar *v.i.* to excrete, to defecate.
excremento *s.m.* excrement.
excretor *adj.* ANAT. excretory.
excursión *s.f.* **1** excursion, outing, trip. **2** MIL. raid. || **2 — campestre,** picnic.
excursionismo *s.m.* **1** going on trips. **2** walking, hiking (a pie).
excursionista *s.m.* y *f.* **1** sightseer (para ver momentos, etc.). **2** hiker, rambler (a pie por el campo).
excusa *s.f.* **1** excuse. **2** apology (disculpa).
excusable *adj.* excusable, pardonable.
excusado, -a *adj.* **1** excused, pardoned (perdonado). **2** exempt (exento). || *s.m.* toilet (retrete).
excusar *v.t.* **1** to excuse, to pardon. **2** to exempt (eximir). **3** to shirk (una responsabilidad). || *v.r.* **4** to excuse oneself. **5** to apologize (disculparse). || **6** excusarse por haber hecho algo, to apologize for having done something.
execrable *adj.* execrable.
execración *s.f.* execration.
execrar *v.t.* **1** to hate, to loathe (odiar). **2** to execrate, to curse (maldecir).
exégesis *s.f.* exegesis.
exegeta *s.m.* exegate.
exegético, -a *adj.* exegetic, exegetical.
exención *s.f.* **1** exemption. **2** immunity (inmunidad).
exento, -a *adj.* **1** exempt. **2** free (libre). **3** clear, unobstructed, open (un lugar). **4** ARQ. free-standing. || **5 — de impuestos,** tax-free.
exequias *s.f.pl.* funeral rights, obsequies.
exfoliación *s.f.* exfoliation.
exfoliador *s.m.* **1** (Am.) tear-off pad, loose-leaf notebook (libreta de taco).
exfoliar *v.t.* to exfoliate.
exhalación *s.f.* **1** exhalation (acción). **2** vapour, fumes (vapor). **3** ASTR. shooting star (estrella fugaz). || **4 como una —,** at top speed.
exhalar *v.t.* **1** to exhale, to breathe out. **2** to emit, to give off (humos, etc.). || *v.pron.* **3** to breathe hard (respirar fuerte). **4** to hurry, to run (apurarse).
exhaustivo, -a *adj.* exhaustive: *pruebas exhaustivas = exhaustive tests.*
exhausto, -a *adj.* exhausted.
exhibición *s.f.* **1** exhibition, show (demostración). **2** presentation, exhibition (presentación).
exhibicionismo *s.m.* exhibitionism.
exhibicionista *s.m.* y *f.* exhibitionist.
exhibir *v.t.* **1** to exhibit, to display, to show. **2** (Am.) to pay in cash (pagar en efectivo). || *v.pron.* **3** to show oneself.
exhortación *s.f.* exhortation.
exhortar *v.t.* to exhort.
exhortativo, -a *adj.* exhortative.
exhortatorio, -a *adj.* exhortatory.
exhorto *s.m.* **1** DER. letters rogatory. **2** REL. charge.
exhumación *s.f.* exhumation.

exhumar *v.t.* 1 to exhume, to dig up, to disinter.
exigencia *s.f.* 1 exigency, demand (demanda). 2 requirement (requisito).
exigente *adj.* 1 demanding, exacting. || 2 **ser — con alguien,** to ask a lot of someone. 3 **ser — en algo,** to be particular about something.
exigible *adj.* 1 demandable, exactable. 2 payable on demand (una deuda).
exigir *v.t.* 1 to exact, to levy (un impuesto, etc.). 2 to demand, to require (requerir). 3 (Am.) to ask for (pedir). 4 (Am.) to beg, to plead with (suplicar). || 5 **— el pago,** to demand payment. 6 **— mucho,** to be demanding.
exigüidad *s.f.* 1 smallness (pequeñez). 2 meagreness, scantiness (de recursos, etc.).
exiguo, -a *adj.* 1 small, tiny (de tamaño). 2 meagre, scanty (de recursos, etc.).
exiliado, -a *adj.* 1 exiled, in exile. || *s.m.* y *f.* 2 exile.
exiliar *v.t.* 1 to exile. || *v.pron.* 2 to go into exile.
exilio *s.m.* exile.
eximio, -a *adj.* 1 choice, select (un producto). 2 distinguished, eminent (una persona).
eximir *v.t.* 1 to exempt. 2 to free (liberar). || *v.pron.* to free oneself (liberarse).
existencia *s.f.* 1 existence. 2 being (ser). 3 life (vida). || 4 **luchar por la —,** to struggle for survival. 5 **quitarse la —,** to commit suicide (suicidarse).
existencial *adj.* existential.
existencialismo *s.m.* existentialism.
existencialista *s.m.* y *f.* existentialist.
existente *adj.* 1 existing. 2 in existence (en existencia). 3 COM. in stock (disponible). || 4 **la situación —,** the present situation.
existir *v.i.* 1 to exist, to be (ser). 2 to still be left: *todavía existe alguno = there are still some left.*
éxito *s.m.* 1 success. 2 hit, success (espectáculo, novela, etc.). || 3 **con —,** successfully. 4 **tener —,** to be successful.
exitoso, -a *adj.* (Am.) successful.
éxodo *s.m.* 1 exodus. 2 depopulation: *el éxodo rural = the depopulation of the countryside.*
exoneración *s.f.* exoneration, freeing.
exonerar *v.t.* 1 to exonerate. 2 to dismiss, (fam.) to sack (despedir de un empleo). || 3 **— a uno de un deber,** to relive someone from a duty. 4 **— el vientre,** to have a movement of the bowels.
exorbitante *adj.* exorbitant.
exorcismo *s.m.* exorcism.
exorcista *s.m.* y *f.* exorcist.
exorcizar *v.t.* to exorcise.
exordio *s.m.* 1 preamble, exordium, introduction (preámbulo). 2 (fig.) beginning (comienzo).
exotérico, -a *adj.* exoteric.
exoticidad *s.f.* exoticism.
exótico, -a *adj.* exotic.
exotismo *s.m.* exoticism.
expandir *v.t.* 1 ANAT. to expand. 2 COM. to expand, to enlarge (un negocio, etc.). 3 to expand, to extend, to spread (extender). || *v.pron.* 4 to expand (crecer). 5 to spread (extenderse una noticia, etc.).
expansión *s.f.* 1 expansion. 2 extension (extensión). 3 enlargement (aumento). 4 spread (de una noticia, etc.). 5 relaxation (relajación). || 6 **la — económica,** economic growth.
expansionarse *v.pron.* 1 to expand. 2 (fig.) to relax (relajarse). || **— con uno,** to open one's heart up to someone.
expansivo, -a *adj.* 1 expansive, expandable (expansible). 2 open, frank (franco).
expatriación *s.f.* 1 expatriation (exilio). 2 emigration (emigración).
expatriarse *v.pron.* 1 to emigrate, to leave one's country (emigrar). 2 POL. to go into exile.
expectación *s.f.* 1 expectation, expectancy, anticipation: *había una gran expectación ante la llegada de los primeros rehenes = the arrival of the first hostages caused great expectation.* 2 excitement (emoción). 3 waiting, wait (espera).
expectante *adj.* 1 expectant. 2 excited (emocionado).
expectativa *s.f.* 1 expectation. 2 hope (esperanza). || **estar a la —,** to wait and see what happens.
expectoración *s.f.* 1 MED. expectoration. 2 sputum (esputo).
expectorante *adj., s.m.* y *f.* MED. expectorant.
expectorar *v.i.* MED. to expectorate.
expedición *s.f.* expedition.
expedientar *v.t.* to make a file (la policía).
expediente *s.m.* 1 expedient. 2 means (medios). 3 DER. action, proceedings. 4 DER. records of a case (documentos de un caso). 5 record, record card (de un estudiante, etc.). || 6 **— policíaco,** police dossier. || 7 **incoar —,** to start proceedings.
expedir *v.t.* 1 COM. to send, to dispatch, to ship (mercancías). 2 DER. to draw up. 3 to issue (un pasaporte, etc.). 4 to deal with (un asunto).
expeditivo, -a *adj.* expeditious.
expedito, -a *adj.* 1 expeditious, speedy, prompt (rápido). 2 clear, free (desbloqueado).
expeler *v.t.* to expel, to eject.
expendedor, -ora *s.m.* y *f.* 1 dealer, retailer (persona). || **— automático,** vending machine. 2 **— de billetes,** ticket clerk.
expendeduría *s.f.* retail shop (tienda).
expender *v.t.* 1 to spend, to expend (money). 2 to pass, to circulate (billetes falsos). 3 to sell, to retail (mercancías al por mayor).
expensas *s.f.pl.* 1 expenses. 2 DER. costs. || 3 **a — de,** at the expenses of.
experiencia *s.f.* 1 experience. 2 QUIM. experiment (experimento).
experimentación *s.f.* 1 testing, experimentation. 2 experiment (experimento).
experimentado, -a *adj.* 1 experienced (una persona). 2 tested (una cosa).
experimental *adj.* experimental.
experimentar *v.t.* 1 TEC. to test, to try out (probar). 2 to experience, to undergo (un cambio). 3 to suffer (una pérdida). 4 to show (un incremento). || *v.pron.* 5 to experiment.
experto, -a *adj./s.m.* y *f.* expert.
expiación *s.f.* expiation, atonement.
expiativo, -a *adj.* expiatory.
expiar *v.t.* 1 to expiate, to atone (un pecado). 2 to serve (una pena).
expiración *s.f.* expiration.
expirar *v.i.* 1 to die, to expire (morir). 2 DER. to expire (un contrato, etc.).
explanación *s.f.* explanation.
explanada *s.f.* esplanade.
explanar *v.t.* 1 TEC. to level, to grade (nivelar). 2 to elucidate, to explain (explicar).
explayar *v.t.* 1 to spread, to extend (extender). || *v.pron.* 2 to be long-winded, to expiate. 3 to open one's heart (confiarse).
expletivo, -a *adj.* expletive.
explicable *adj.* 1 explicable, explainable. 2 justifiable (justificable).
explicación *s.f.* 1 explanation. 2 reason, explanation (razón). 3 excuse (excusa).
explicar *v.t.* 1 to explain. 2 to expound (una teoría, etc.). 3 to lecture on, to teach (un curso, etc.). || *v.pron.* 4 to explain oneself. 5 to understand: *no me lo explico = I can't understand it.* 6 to be explained: *no se explica el cambio = the change can't be explained.*
explicativo, -a *adj.* explanatory, explicative.
explícitamente *adv.* explicitly.
explorable *adj.* explorable.
exploración *s.f.* 1 exploration (de un sitio, etc.). 2 MIN. prospecting (de minas). 3 MIL. reconnaissance, scouting.
explorador, -ora *adj.* 1 exploratory. 2 MIL. scouting. || *s.m.* y *f.* 3 explorer. || *s.m.* 4 TEC. scanner (radar, etc.). 5 MED. probe (sonda).
explorar *v.t.* 1 to explore. 2 MIN. to prospect (minas). 3 MED. to probe (con una sonda). 4 TEC. to scan (con radar, etc.). 5 MIL. to reconnoitre, to scout. 6 (fig.) to explore, to examine.
explosión *s.f.* 1 explosion, blowing up (acción). 2 bursting (de un globo, etc.). 3 explosion, blast: *hubo una gran explosión = there was a big blast.* || 4 **motor de —,** internal combustion engine.
explosionar *v.t.* 1 to explode. || *v.i.* 2 to explode, to blow up.
explosivo, -a *adj./s.m.* y *f.* 1 explosive. || *adj.* y *s.f.* 2 GRAM. plosive.
explotable *adj.* 1 MIN. exploitable (mina). 2 cultivatable, farmable (terreno).
explotación *s.f.* 1 exploitation (de una persona). 2 MIN. working, exploitation (de una mina).

explotador, -ora *adj.* 1 exploiting (que abusa). || *s.m.* y *f.* 2 MIN. worker (de una mina). 3 exploiter (el que abusa).
explotar *v.t.* 1 to exploit (una persona). 2 MIN. to work, to exploit (una mina). 3 to exploit (una situación). 4 MIL. to blow up, to explode (una bomba, puente, etc.). || *v.i.* 5 MIL. to explode (una bomba, etc.).
expoliación *s.f.* despoiling, spoliation.
expoliador, -ora *adj.* 1 despoiling (persona). 2 spoliatory (medida). || *s.m.* y *f.* despoiler, spoliator.
expoliar *v.t.* to despoil, to spoliate (despojar).
exponente *adj.* 1 expounding, exponent (que expone). || *s.m.* 2 MAT. exponent, index. 3 (Am.) model. 4 exponent (representante).
exponer *v.t.* 1 to expound (una teoría). 2 to put forward (una propuesta). 3 to explain (explicar). 4 to show, to exhibit, to put on show (mostrar al público). 5 to expose (al sol, viento, etc.). 6 to expose (una foto). || *v.pron.* 7 to expose oneself. 8 to run the risk (arriesgarse).
exportación *s.f.* 1 export, exportation. 2 export, exported article (artículo). || 3 **comercio de —,** export trade.
exportador, a *adj.* 1 exporting. || *s.m.* y *f.* exporter.
exportar *v.t.* to export.
exposición *s.f.* 1 exposing, exposure (acción). 2 exposure (de una foto). 3 showing (al público). 4 COM. show, fair (feria de muestras). 5 putting forward (de ideas).
expósito, -a *adj.* 1 abandoned. || *s.m.* y *f.* 2 foundling.
exprés *s.m.* (Am.) express train (tren).
expresamente *adv.* 1 expressly. 2 on purpose, deliberately (deliberadamente). 3 clearly, plainly (claramente).
expresar *v.t.* 1 to express. 2 to show, to express (un sentimiento). 3 to convey (comunicar). || *v.pron.* 4 to express oneself: *no se expresa muy bien = she doesn't express herself very well.* 5 to be expressed (cosa, sentimiento, etc.).
expresión *s.f.* 1 expression. || 2 expresions, greetings; regards (recuerdos).
expresionismo *s.m.* expressionism.
expresivamente *adv.* 1 expressively. 2 warmly, affectionately (cariñosamente).
expresividad *s.f.* expressiveness.
expresivo, -a *adj.* 1 expressive. 2 tender, affectionate, warm (cariñoso). 3 significant (significante).
expreso, -a *adj.* 1 expressed (dicho). 2 express (tren). || *s.m.* 3 express (tren).
exprimidera *s.f.* squeezer.
exprimidor *s.m.* squeezer, **— de limones** lemon squeezer.
exprimir *v.t.* 1 to squeeze (fruta), to squeeze out, to press out, to express (zumo). 2 to wring out, to squeeze dry (ropa). || 3 to exploit (a uno).
ex profeso *adv.* on purpose (a propósito).
expropiación *s.f.* 1 expropriation (de terrenos, etc.). 2 commandeering (de un coche, etc.).
expropiar *v.t.* 1 to expropriate (terrenos). 2 to commandeer (un coche, etc.).
expuesto, -a *adj.* 1 on display, on show, on display (un cuadro, etc.). 2 what has been stated: *según lo arriba expuesto = according to what has been stated above.* 3 exposed (al sol, viento, etc.). || 4 **estar — a,** to be exposed to.
expugnar *v.t.* to take by storm.
expulsar *v.t.* 1 to expel (de un colegio, etc.). 2 DEP. to send off. 3 to eject, to throw out (a una persona). 4 MED. to spit out, to bring up.
expulsión *s.f.* 1 expulsion (del colegio, etc.). 2 DEP. sending-off. 3 MED. bringing-up, spitting-out. 4 ejection (de un avión).
expurgación *s.f.* 1 expurgation (de un libro, etc.). 2 (fig.) purging, purgation.
expurgar *v.t.* to expurgate.
exquisitez *s.f.* 1 exquisiteness. 2 excellence (excelencia).
exquisito, -a *adj.* 1 exquisite. 2 delicious (delicioso). 3 excellent (excelente).
extasiarse *v.pron.* to go into raptures o ecstasies.
éxtasis *s.m.* ecstasy, rapture.
extático, -a *adj.* ecstatic, enraptured.
extemporáneo, -a *adj.* 1 unseasonable. 2 ill-timed, unappropriate (inoportuno).
extender *v.t.* 1 to extend. 2 to enlarge, to make bigger (hacer más grande). 3 to prolong (prolongar). 4 to spread (mantequilla, etc.). 5 to extend, to spread (el conocimiento). 6 to draw up (un documento). 7 to make out (un cheque). 8 to issue (un certificado). || *v.pron.* 9 to stretch out (estirarse). 10 to stretch away: *el desierto se extendía delante de él = the desert stretched away before him.* 11 to range: *los precios se extienden entre dos libras y doscientas libras = the prices range from two pounds to two hundred pounds.* 12 to last (durar tiempo). 13 to spread, to extend (costumbres, conocimiento, etc.). 14 to escalate (una guerra). 15 to reach (llegar a).
extensible *adj.* extensible, extendible, extensile.
extensión *s.f.* 1 extension. 2 stretching (estiramiento). 3 spreading (de una noticia, etc.). 4 size (tamaño). 5 expanse, size (de un terreno, etc.). 6 length, duration (de tiempo).
extensivo, -a *adj.* extendable, extendible.
extenso *adj.* 1 extensive, vast (amplio). 2 large, big (grande). 3 widespread (una noticia, etc.). 4 full, extensive (un reportaje, etc.).
extenuar *v.t.* 1 to emaciate, to weaken (debilitar). || *v.r.* 2 to become emaciated, to waste away (quedarse en los huesos).
exterioridad *s.f.* outward o exterior appearance.
exterior *s.m.* 1 exterior, outside (de un edificio, etc.). 2 appearance (apariencia). || *adj.* 3 foreign (extranjero): *noticias exteriores = foreign news.* 4 outer, external, exterior: *la parte exterior = the outer part.* 5 outside: *el servicio exterior = the outside toilet.*
exterioridad *s.f.* outward appearance (aspecto de una persona).
exteriorizar *v.t.* 1 to show, to manifest.
exterminador, -ora *adj.* 1 exterminating. || *s.m.* y *f.* 2 exterminator.
exterminar *v.t.* to exterminate.
exterminio *s.m.* 1 extermination, wiping out. 2 destruction (destrucción).
externamente *adv.* outwardly, externally.
externo, -a *adj.* 1 external: *de uso externo = external use.* 2 outward: *apariencia externa = outward appearance.* 3 outer, external: *la parte externa = the outher part.* || *s.m.* 4 day boy o pupil (alumno).
extinción *s.f.* 1 extinction (de un fuego). 2 extinction, wiping out (de una raza).
extinguir *v.t.* 1 to extinguish, to put out (un fuego, etc.). 2 to wipe out, to obliterate (una raza). 3 to put down, to stop (una rebelión). || *v.pron.* 4 to go out, to die out (un fuego). 5 to go out (una luz). 6 to become extinct, to die out (una raza).
extinto, -a *adj.* extinct.
extintor, -ora *adj.* 1 extinguishing. || *s.m.* 2 fire extinguisher (aparato).
extirpación *s.f.* 1 extirpation, erradication. 2 MED. removal.
extirpar *v.t.* 1 to extirpate, to erradicate, to stamp out. 2 MED. removal: *le extirparon un ojo = they removed an eye.* 3 to fire (despedir a uno).
extorsión *s.f.* extorsion.
extorsionar *v.t.* to extort.
extra *adj.* 1 extra. || *s.m.* 2 extra (en una cuenta, etc.).
extracción *s.f.* extraction.
extractar *v.t.* to summarize (compendiar).
extracto *s.m.* 1 QUIM. extract. 2 (lit.) abstract, summary.
extraer *v.t.* 1 to extract. 2 MAT. to take out, to pull out.
extralimitación *s.f.* abuse.
extralimitarse *v.r.* to go too far, to exceed.
extramuros *adv.* outside the city.
extranjerismo *s.m.* 1 foreign word (palabra). 2 foreign expression (expresión).
extranjero, -a *adj.* 1 foreign. || *s.m.* y *f.* 2 foreigner (persona), foreign country (país). || 3 **ir al —,** to go abroad.
extranjis *adv.* (fam.) secretly (sin que se sepa).
extrañamiento *s.m.* astonishment, surprise (asombro).
extrañar *v.t.* 1 to surprise (sorprender). 2 not to be used to, to find strange: *me extraña su comportamiento = I find his behaviour strange.* 3 (Am.) to miss (echar en falta). || *v.i.* 4 to be strange (ser extraño). 5 to be surprising (ser sorprendente). || 6 **eso me extraña,** I'm

surprised about that. **7 no es de —,** it's not surprising.

extraño, -a *adj.* 1 strange, odd, peculiar (raro). 2 foreign (extranjero). 3 outside (influencias, etc.). || *s.m.* y *f.* 4 stranger.

extraordinariamente *adv.* 1 extraordinarily. 2 extraordinarily well (muy bien).

extraordinario, -a *adj.* 1 extraordinary. 2 unusual (poco usual). || *s.m.* 3 special dish (en un menú, etc.). 4 special (edición, número, etc.). 5 extra pay (pago). 6 special edition (del periódico, etc.).

extraplano *s.m.* DEP. overhang (en alpinismo).

extrapolación *s.f.* MAT. extrapolation.

extrapolar *v.t.* e *i.* to extrapolate.

extravagancia *s.f.* extravagance.

extravagante *adj.* extravagant.

extravertido, -a *adj.* 1 extroverted. || *s.m.* y *f.* 2 extrovert.

extraviar *v.t.* 1 to make lose one's way (hacer perder el camino). 2 to mislead (equivocar). 3 to misplace (perder). || *v.pron.* 4 to get lost (perderse). 5 (fig.) to go astray (llevar mala vida). 6 to wander (la mirada).

extravío *s.m.* 1 misplacing, mislaying, loss (pérdida). 2 losing one's way, getting lost (acción de perderse). 3 mistake (error). 4 misconduct (mala conducta).

extremado, -a *adj.* extreme.

extremar *v.t.* 1 to carry to an extreme, to overdo (precauciones, etc.). || *v.pron.* 2 to take great pains, to do one's utmost.

extremaunción *s.f.* REL. extreme unction.

extremeño, -a *s.m.* y *f.* 1 inhabitant of Extremadura. || *adj.* 2 of o from Extremadura.

extremidad *s.f.* 1 end, tip, extremity (punta). 2 edge, outermost part (borde). || **3 extremidades,** ANAT. extremities.

extremismo *s.m.* extremism.

extremo, -a *adj.* 1 extreme, last (lugar). 2 far, furthest, outer (más alejado). 3 last (dentro de un orden). 4 utmost (precaución, cuidado, etc.). || *s.m.* 5 end (final). 6 highest point (punto más alto). 7 lowest point (punto más bajo). 8 point, matter (asunto). 9 DEP. winger (jugador). || **10 — derecho,** DEP. right-wing. **11 — izquierdo,** DEP. left-wing.

extrínseco *s.f.* extrinsic.

extrovertido, -a V. **extravertido.**

exuberancia *s.f.* 1 exuberance, abundance (abundancia). 2 exuberance (de carácter).

exuberante *adj.* exuberant.

exudación *s.f.* exudation.

exudar *v.t.* e *i.* to exude.

exultación *s.f.* exultation.

exultar *v.i.* to exult.

exvoto *s.m.* REL. ex-voto, votive offering.

eyaculación *s.f.* ejaculation.

eyacular *v.t.* to ejaculate.

eyector *s.m.* TEC. ejector.

f, F, *s.c.* f, F (séptima letra del alfabeto español).
fa *s.m.* **1** MUS. F. **2** fa (en la escala de do).
fabada *s.f.* Asturian dish of haricot beans, pork and bacon.
fábrica *s.f.* **1** factory: *trabajar en una fábrica = to work in a factory.* **2** building (edificio). **3** making, manufacture (fabricación): *la fábrica de coches = car making o manufacture.* **4** mill (de papel, madera, textiles, azúcar). **5** plant (instalación). **6** make (marca). || **7 — de cerveza,** brewery. **8 — de gas,** gasworks. **9 — de harina,** flour mill. **10 — de moneda,** mint. **11 — de montaje,** assembly plant. **12 — de papel,** paper mill. **13 marca de —,** trademark. **14 precio en —,** factory price.
fabricación *s.f.* **1** manufacture, making: *fabricación de televisores = television manufacture.* **2** production (producción): *fabricación en serie = mass production; estar en fabricación = to be in production.* || **3 de fabricación casera,** homemade.
fabricante *s.m.* y *f.* manufacturer, maker: *fabricante de ropa = clothes manufacturer/maker.*
fabricar *v.t.* **1** to manufacture, to make: *fabricar radios = to manufacture radios.* **2** ARQ. to build, to construct (construir). **3** (fig.) to invent, to fabricate (inventar): *fabricar una coartada = to invent an alibi.* **4 — cerveza,** to brew beer.
fabril *adj.* manufacturing.
fábula *s.f.* **1** LIT. fable, tale: *las fábulas de Samaniego = the fables of Samaniego.* **2** rumour (rumor). **3** invention, (fam.) tall tale (narración falsa). **4** mythology (la mitología, en general). **5** laughing stock (hazmerreír): *él es la fábula del pueblo = he's the laughing stock of the village.* || **6 ser una cosa de —,** to be fantastic o marvellous o fabulous.
fabulista *s.m.* LIT. fable writer, writer of fables.
fabulosamente *adv.* fabulously, fantastically.
fabuloso, -a *adj.* **1** fabulous, fantastic: *una memoria fabulosa = a fantastic memory.* **2** fictious, invented (ficticio). **3** (fam.) enormous, fabulous: *un tesoro fabuloso = an enormous/fabulous treasure.* **4** fabled, fabulous (de las fábulas).
faca *s.f.* large knife (cuchillo grande).
facción *s.f.* **1** POL. faction (partido): *una facción política = a political faction.* **2** gang, band (bando). **3** MIL. duty (acto de servicio militar): *estar de facción = to be on duty.* || *pl.* **4** features (rasgos de la cara): *de facciones bonitas = with pretty features.*
faccioso, -a *adj.* **1** factious, rebellious (rebelde): *una persona facciosa = a rebellious person.* || *s.m.* y *f.* **2** a factious o rebellious person, rebel (rebelde). **3** armed rebel (rebelde armado). **4** gang member (que pertenece a un bando).
faceta *s.f.* **1** GEOM. facet (cara o superficie de un poliedro). **2** (fig.) facet, aspect, side: *la faceta desconocida de una persona = the unknown side of a person.*
facial *adj.* facial (que pertenece al rostro).
fácil *adj.* **1** easy: *un trabajo fácil = an easy job; fácil de entender = easy to understand.* **2** simple, easy (sencillo): *un libro fácil = a simple book.* **3** probable, likely (probable): *es fácil que llegue pronto = he's likely to arrive soon.* **4** docile, compliant (dócil). **5** easy, loose (una mujer). **6** easy, fluent (estilo). || *adv.* **6** easily (fácilmente).
facilidad *s.f.* **1** easiness, facility (calidad de fácil): *la facilidad de hacerlo = the easiness of doing it.* **2** ease: *con la mayor facilidad = with the greatest of ease.* **3** straightforwardness, simplicity (sencillez). **4** docility, compliance (docilidad). **5** fluency: *facilidad de palabra = fluency of speech.* **6** gift, talent (talento): *tiene gran facilidad para el inglés = he has a great gift for English.* || *pl.* **7** facilities: *las facilidades para practicar el tenis = the facilities for practising tennis.* || **8 dar facilidades,** to facilitate; to make easier (facilitar); FIN. to give easy terms. **9 facilidades de crédito,** FIN. credit facilities. **10 facilidades de pago,** FIN. easy terms.
facilitar *v.t.* **1** to facilitate, to make easy (hacer fácil). **2** to give, to provide (proporcionar): *el banco nos ha facilitado el dinero = the bank has provided us with the money.* **3** to issue (documentos). **4** to supply (suministrar).
fácilmente *adv.* easily: *aprobó el examen fácilmente = he passed the examination easily.*
facineroso, -a *adj.* **1** criminal. **2** evil, wicked (malvado). || *s.m.* y *f.* **3** criminal. **4** evil o wicked person (persona malvada).
facsímil o **facsímile** *s.m.* facsimile.
factibilidad *s.f.* feasibility.
factible *adj.* feasible, practical.
factor *s.m.* **1** MAT. factor. **2** COM. agent, (p.u.) factor (agente comercial). **3** BIOL. factor. **4** factor, element (elemento): *el factor humano = the human element; el factor determinante = the decisive factor.* **5** luggage clerk, freight clerk (empleado de ferrocarril).
factoría *s.f.* **1** factory (fábrica). **2** agency (oficina del factor). **3** post of agent (empleo del factor). **4** COM. trading post (establecimiento comercial).
factótum *s.m.* factotum.
factura *s.f.* **1** COM. bill (cuenta). **2** invoice (de géneros vendidos): *factura pro forma = pro forma invoice; pasar factura = to send an invoice.* **3** manufacture (hechura). **4** style, imprint: *de buena factura = with good style.*
facturación *s.f.* **1** COM. invoicing (de géneros vendidos). **2 bill** (cuenta). **3** registration (en trenes).

facturar *v.t.* **1** COM. to invoice (de géneros vendidos). **2** to charge (cobrar). **3** to check in; to register (en el aeropuerto o estación).

facultad *s.f.* **1** faculty (potencia física o espiritual): *facultad de hablar = faculty of speech.* **2** power (poder): *tener la facultad de vender = to have the power to sell.* **3** right (derecho). **4** MED. strength (fuerza); resistance (resistencia). **5** faculty, school (en la universidad): *Facultad de Ciencias = Faculty of Science.* **6** permit (permiso). || *pl.* **7** faculties, powers: *facultades mentales = mental faculties.*

facultar *v.t.* **1** to authorize, to empower (autorizar). **2** to give the right (dar derecho): *el título me faculta para enseñar = the title gives me the right to teach.*

facultativo *adj.* **1** optional, non-obligatory (no obligatorio). **2** professional (profesional). **3** MED. medical: *dictamen facultativo = medical report.* || *adj.* **4** faculty (facultad). || *s.m.* **5** MED. doctor (médico); surgeon (cirujano).

facundia *s.f.* **1** eloquence (facilidad en el hablar). **2** verbosity, (fam. y desp.) gift of the gab: *tener facundia = to have the gift of the gab.*

facha *s.f.* **1** (fam.) look, appearance (aspecto): *no me gusta su facha = I don't like his appearance.* **2** sight, disaster, mess: *estar hecho una facha = to look a mess/a sight o disaster.* **3** figure (figura). **4** (fam. y desp.) fascist, right-wing person (fascista). || **5 ponerse en —,** to place o position oneself (colocarse en posición para cierta cosa). **6 tener buena —,** to be good-looking. **7 tener mala —,** to be ugly.

fachada *s.f.* **1** ARQ. façade, front. **2** (fig.) façade, front: *su sinceridad es pura fachada = his sincerity is a façade.* **3** title page (portada de un libro). **4** appearance, look (aspecto exterior de una persona).

fachoso, -a *adj.* odd-looking, absurd, ridiculous (extraño): *tiene un novio fachoso = she's got an odd-looking boyfriend.*

faena *s.f.* **1** job, task (quehacer). **2** work (trabajo): *tengo mucha faena = I've got a lot of work.* **3** dirty trick: *hacer una faena a alguien = to play a dirty trick on someone; ¡qué faena! = what a dirty trick!* **4** ART. series of passes with the cape (los toros). **5** (Am.) overtime (trabajo hecho en horas extraordinarias).

faenar *v.i.* MAR. to fish (pescar).

fagocito *s.m.* BIOL. phagocyte.

fagot *s.m.* **1** MUS. bassoon (instrumento). **2** MUS. bassoonist (músico).

faisán *s.m.* pheasant.

faja *s.f.* **1** sash, cummerbund (tira de tela que se pone alrededor de la cintura). **2** corset, girdle (corsé). **3** wrapper (postal). **4** sash, insignia (insignia). **5** strip (de terreno). **6** band, strip (de tela). **7** MED. bandage (vendaje). **8** ARQ. fascia (moldura). **9** fesse, fess (pieza de los escudos).

fajar *v.t.* y *pron.* **1** to wrap (envolver). **2** to bandage (con una venda). **3** to put a sash on (poner una faja). || *v.t.* **4** to hit, to beat (golpear).

fajín *s.m.* sash.

fajina *s.f.* **1** AGR. pile, rick (almiar). **2** kindling, firewood (leña). **3** bundle of firewood (haz de leña). **4** orchard (huerta). **5** fascine (haz de ramas). **6** MIL. bugle call (toque militar de retirada).

fajo *s.m.* bundle (haz).

falacia *s.f.* **1** deceit, trick (engaño). **2** falacy (reputación falsa). **3** deceitfulness (costumbre de mentir).

falange *s.f.* **1** ANAT. phalange, phalanx. **2** HIST. y MIL. phalanx. || **3 Falange,** POL. partido político español.

falangeta *s.f.* ANAT. third phalanx.

falangina *s.f.* ANAT. second phalanx.

falangista *adj./s.m.* y *f.* Falangist.

falaz *adj.* **1** deceitful (mentiroso). **2** false, misleading (engañoso).

falda *s.f.* **1** skirt (vestido): *minifalda = miniskirt; falda escocesa = kilt.* **2** HIST. skirt (de la armadura). **3** GEOG. slope, hillside (lateral de una montaña); foot, bottom (parte baja de los montes). **4** cover (de una mesa camilla). **5** brisket (carne); flank (parte del animal). **6** ANAT. knees, lap (regazo). || *pl.* **7** girls (chicas); women (mujeres): *ser aficionado a las faldas = to be fond of the girls,* (fam.) *to be a ladies'man.* || **8 estar cosido** o **pegado a las faldas de su madre,** to be tied to one's mother's apron strings.

faldero, -a *adj.* **1** skirt (de la falda). **2** (fam.) ladies' man (aficionado a las mujeres). || **3 perro —,** lapdog.

faldillas *s.f.pl.* coattails.

faldón *s.m.* **1** coattails (faldillas). **2** skirt (falda). || **3 agarrarse a los faldones de uno,** to cling on to someone's coattails.

falibilidad *s.f.* fallibility.

falible *adj.* fallible.

fálico, -a *adj.* phalic.

falo *s.m.* phallus.

falsamente *adv.* falsely.

falsario, -a *adj./s.m.* y *f.* **1** falsifier. **2** forger, counterfeiter (falsificador de dinero, acciones, etc.). **3** liar (mentiroso).

falseador, -ora *adj./s.m.* y *f.* y *f.* **1** falsifier. **2** forger, countfeiter (de dinero). **3** liar (mentiroso). **4** falsifying (que falsea una cosa). **5** forging, counterfeiting (que falsifica dinero, etc.). **6** lying (embustero).

falseamiento *s.m.* falsification.

falsear *v.t.* **1** to falsify (falsificar). **2** to forge, to couterfeit (fabricar dinero falso). **3** TEC. to bevel (un madero, una piedra). || *v.i.* **4** ARQ. to sag (una viga); to buckle, to give way (una pared). **5** MUS. to be out of tune.

falsedad *s.f.* **1** falsity, falseness (cualidad de falso). **2** lie, (p.u.) falsehood: *decir o cometer falsedades = to tell lies.* **3** DER. forgery.

falsete *s.m.* **1** MUS. falsetto. **2** bung, plug (tapón). **3** door (puerta).

falsificación *s.f.* **1** falsification. **2** forging, counterfeiting, forgery (de dinero). **3** forging, forgery (de una firma).

falsificador, -ora *s.m.* y *f.* **1** forger, counterfeiter (de dinero). **2** falsifier (en sentido general).

falsificar *v.t.* **1** to falsify (en sentido general). **2** to forge (una firma). **3** to forge, to counterfeit (dinero). **4** to adulterate (adulterar). **5** to fake, to forge (un cuadro, un sello). **6** to rig, to fiddle (resultados, elecciones).

falsilla *s.f.* lined paper.

falso, -a *adj.* **1** false: *una falsa alarma = a false alarm; falsa modestia = false modesty.* **2** untrue, not true (no verdadero). **3** counterfeit, (fam.) dud (moneda): *una moneda falsa = a dud coin.* **4** fake, immitation (una piedra preciosa). **5** forged, fake (un cuadro, sello). **6** unsound, shaky (opinión, argumento, teoría). **7** MUS. false (una nota). **8** wrong, incorrect (incorrecto). **9** deceitful, false, treacherous (traidor). **10** vicious (caballo). || **11 dar un paso en —,** to trip, to stumble (dar un traspié); to make a mistake (cometer un error). **12 en —,** falsely (falsamente). **13 jurar en —,** to commit perjury. **14 coger a uno en —,** to catch someone in a lie.

falta *s.f.* **1** lack (carencia): *falta de tiempo = lack of time; falta de dinero = lack of money.* **2** shortage (escasez): *falta de agua = water shortage.* **3** need (necesidad). **4** absence (ausencia): *falta de gente = absence of people.* **5** defect, fault (defecto de una cosa). **6** failing, shortcoming (defecto de una persona). **7** lack: *falta de respeto = lack of respect.* **8** mistake, error (error): *falta ortográfica = spelling mistake.* **9** fault (culpa): *es falta suya = it's his fault.* **10** DEP. foul; fault (en el tenis). **11** DER. misdemeanor (infracción de la ley, reglamento, etc.). **12** non-: *falta de pago = non-payment; falta de asistencia = non-attendance.* || **13 a — de,** for lack of: *a falta de agua = for lack of water.* **14 caer en una —,** to make a mistake. **15 echar en —,** to miss: *te he echado en falta = I've missed you.* **16 hacer —,** to be necessary, to need: *no hace falta = it's not necessary; hace falta mucho dinero = we need a lot of money; hace falta llegar pronto = we need to arrive early.* **17 sacar una —,** DEP. to take a free kick. **18 si hace —,** if it's necessary. **19 sin —,** without fail.

faltar *v.t.* **1** to offend, to be rude to (ofender). || *v.i.* **2** to lack, to be lacking: *nos falta tiempo = we're lacking time; me falta dinero = I'm lacking money.* **3** to be missing: *faltan dos personas = two people are missing.* **4** to need (necesitar): *nos falta gasolina = we need petrol.* **5** to miss: *faltar a clase = to mis class.* **6** to fail (un mecanismo, arma). **7** not to go, to stay away (no acudir a un sitio). **8** to die (morir). || **9 falta mucho para el comienzo,** the start is a long way off. **10 faltan diez minutos para las dos,** it's ten to two. **11 faltan dos semanas,** there are

two weeks to go. **12 falta poco para mi cumpleaños,** my birthday is not far off. **13 falta por hacer,** it has yet to be done. **14 — a la verdad,** to lie. **15 — a una promesa,** to break a promise. **16 — al respeto,** to be disrespectful. **17 ¡no faltaba más!,** o **¡sólo faltaba eso!,** that's all we needed!
falto, -a *adj.* **1** lacking, wanting: *falto de escrúpulos = lacking in scruples.* **2** short: *estar falto de ideas = to be short of ideas.*
faltón, -ona *adj.* **1** unreliable, undependable (que falta a sus obligaciones). **2** bad-mannered, ill-mannered (maleducado).
faltriquera *s.f.* **1** apron (delantal). **2** pocket (bolsillo). || **3 rascarse la —,** (fig.) to dig into one's pocket; to pay up.
falla *s.f.* **1** fault, defect (defecto). **2** GEOL. fault. || *pl.* **3** Valencian Carnaval (fiestas de Valencia).
fallar *v.t.* **1** to ruff (naipes). **2** DER. to pronounce sentence o verdict (emitir sentencia o veredicto). || *v.i.* **3** to fail (la memoria, frenos, corazón, etc.). **4** to let down, to disappoint (decepcionar): *me has fallado = you've let me down.* **5** to fail (fracasar): *su intento ha fallado = his attempt has failed.* **6** DEP. to miss (un tiro). **7** to misfire (un arma). **8** to miss (motor).
fallecer *v.i.* to die, (euf.) to pass away.
fallecido, -a *adj.* **1** late. || *s.m.* y *f.* **2** deceased.
fallecimiento *s.m.* death, demise.
fallido, -a *adj.* **1** unsuccessful, vain (sin éxito): *intento fallido = unsuccessful attempt; esperanzas fallidas = vain hopes.* **2** bad (una deuda). **3** bad, unsuccessful, poor (tiro, cosecha): *cosecha fallida = poor harvest.*
fallo *s.m.* **1** DER. sentence, verdict (sentencia). **2** DEP. miss, mistake (de un tiro). **3** MED. failure. **4** MEC. failure: *fallo de los frenos = brake failure.* **5** failure (fracaso). **6** fault, shortcoming (de carácter): *tengo muchos fallos = I've got many faults.* **7** void (naipes): *tener un fallo a corazones = to be void in hearts.*
fama *s.f.* **1** fame, celebrity (celebridad). **2** reputation: *tener buena o mala fama = to have a good o bad reputation.* || **3 correr la —,** to become known, to be revealed (divulgarse). **4 dar fama a,** to make famous. **5 de fama,** famous; well-known: *un escritor de fama = a famous writer.* **6 es —,** it is said, they say. **7 tener mucha —,** to be very famous o well-known.
famélico, -a *adj.* **1** starving, famished (hambriento). **2** very thin, (fam.) skinny (muy delgado).
familia *s.f.* **1** family: *de buena familia = from a good family; familia política: in-laws.* **2** GRAM. family. || **3 cargarse de —,** to have a lot of children. **4 en —,** with one's family. **5 La Sagrada Familia,** the Holy Family. **6 ser como de la —,** to be one of the family. **7 tener mucha —,** to have a big family. **8 venir de —,** to run in the family.
familiar *adj.* **1** family: *los lazos familiares = the family ties.* **2** familiar (conocido): *el libro me es familiar = the book is familiar to me.* **3** natural, informal (natural). **4** colloquial, familiar: *una expresión familiar = a colloquial expression.* || *s.m.* **5** relation, relative (pariente). **6** servant (criado).
familiaridad *s.f.* **1** familiarity. **2** trust (confianza).
familiarizar *v.t.* **1** to familiarize. || *v.pron.* **2** to familiarize oneself, to make oneself familiar; to get to know.
familiarmente *adv.* familiarly.
famoso, -a *adj.* **1** famous: *un escritor famoso = a famous writer.* **2** (fam.) great, superb, fantastic.
fámula *s.f.* servant, maid (criada).
fan *s.m.* y *f.* fan, supporter (hincha, admirador).
fanal *s.m.* **1** lamp, lantern (farol). **2** bell glass (campana de cristal).
fanáticamente *adv.* fanatically.
fanático, -a *adj.* **1** fanatical. || *s.m.* y *f.* **2** fanatic.
fanatismo *s.m.* fanaticism.
fandango *s.m.* **1** MUS. fandango. **2** (fig.) din, racket, uproar (alboroto).
fandanguillo *s.m.* MUS. dance similar to the fandango.
fanega o **hanega** *s.f.* fanega (medida de peso para el grano).
fanfarria *s.f.* **1** MUS. fanfare. **2** boasting, bragging, bluster.
fanfarrón, -ona *adj.* **1** boastful, (fam.) flashy. || *s.m.* y *f.* **2** boaster, show-off.
fanfarronada *s.f.* showing-off, boasting, bragging.
fanfarronear *v.i.* to show off, to boast, to brag.
fanfarronería *s.f.* showing-off, boasting, bragging.
fangal *s.m.* bog, quagmire, mudpit.
fango *s.m.* **1** mud, mire. **2** (fig.) mire, dirt.
fangosidad *s.f.* muddiness.
fangoso, -a *adj.* muddy.
fantasear *v.i.* **1** to dream, to daydream (soñar). **2** to imagine (imaginar).
fantasía *s.f.* **1** fantasy, imagination (facultad). **2** fantasy (producto de la fantasía). **3** LIT. fantasy. **4** MUS. fantasía. **5** whim, caprice (capricho). **6** (fam.) vanity, conceit (presunción). **7 de —,** fancy: *artículos de fantasía = fancy goods.* || *pl.* **8** imitation jewellery (bisutería).
fantasioso, -a *adj.* **1** imaginative, fanciful (fantaseador). **2** conceited, vain (presumido). || *s.m.* y *f.* **3** imaginative o fanciful person (fantaseador). **4** show-off; vain o conceited person (presumido).
fantasma *s.m.* **1** ghost, phantom: *el fantasma de la ópera = the phantom of the opera.* **2** (fam.) show-off (persona presumida). **3** ghost (aparecido).
fantasmagoría *s.f.* phantasmagoria.
fantasmagórico, -a *adj.* phantasmagoric.
fantasmal *adj.* ghostly, phantasmal.
fantasmón, -ona *adj.* vain, conceited (presumido).
fantástico, -a *adj.* **1** fantastic, unreal (perteneciente a la fantasía). **2** fabulous, fantastic, great, tremendous: *un partido fantástico = a fantastic game.* **3** huge, enormous (muy grande).
fantoche *s.m.* **1** puppet, marionette (títere). **2** show-off, braggart (presumido). **3** (fam.) dimwit, dolt, nincompoop (mamarracho).
faquir *s.m.* fakir.
faradio *s.m.* ELEC. farad.
farallón *s.m.* GEOG. outcrop (roca que sobresale).
farándula *s.f.* **1** HIST. troupe of strolling actors (compañía ambulante). **2** acting, theatre (profesión).
farandulero, -a *s.m.* y *f.* strolling actor o player (actor ambulante).
faraón *s.m.* Pharaoh.
faraónico, -a *adj.* Pharaonic.
farda *s.f.* **1** bundle (bulto pequeño). **2** parcel (paquete). **3** TEC. mortise (muesca en un madero).
fardar *v.t.* **1** to supply, to provide (proveer). **2** to outfit, to dress (surtir ropa). || *v.i.* **3** to show off, to boast (presumir). **4** to dress well, to dress up (ir bien vestido).
fardo *s.m.* **1** parcel (paquete). **2** bundle (lío grande, especialmente de ropa).
fardón, -ona *s.m.* y *f.* show off, boaster (presumido).
farfolla *s.f.* AGR. husk (envoltura del maíz, etc.).
farfullar *v.t.* **1** (fam.) to gabble, to jabber (hablar atropelladamente). || *v.i.* **2** (fig.) to botch, to patch (hacer una chapucería).
farfullero, -a *s.m.* y *f.* **1** jabberer, gabbler (persona que habla farfullando). **2** (fam.) botcher, shoddy o careless worker (chapucero). || *adj.* **3** jabbering, gabbling (que habla farfullando). **4** (fam.) slipshod, shoddy, careless (chapucero).
farináceo, -a *adj.* farinaceous, starchy.
faringe *s.f.* ANAT. pharynx.
faríngeo, -a *adj.* ANAT. pharyngal.
faringitis *s.f.* MED. pharyngitis.
farisaico, -a *adj.* **1** pharisaic, pharisaical. **2** (fig.) hypocritical, (fam.) two-faced (hipócrita).
farisaísmo o **fariseísmo** *s.m.* pharisaism, phariseeism.
fariseo *s.m.* **1** pharisee. **2** (fig.) hypocrite, impostor (hipócrita).
farmacéutico, -a *adj.* **1** pharmaceutical. || *s.m.* y *f.* **2** chemist, (EE.UU.) pharmacist.
farmacia *s.f.* **1** chemist's, chemists's shop; (EE.UU.) pharmacy, drugstore (tienda). **2** pharmacy (ciencia).
fármaco *s.m.* MED. medicine (medicamento).
farmacología *s.f.* pharmacology.
farmacopea *s.f.* pharmacopoeia.
faro *s.m.* **1** lighthouse (torre alta en las costas). **2** headlight, headlamp (de los coches). **3** lantern, light (farol). **4** bea-

con (señal luminosa). **5** (fig.) guiding light (guía moral). || **6 — de marcha atrás,** reversing light. || **7 — piloto,** tail o rear light.

farol *s.m.* **1** lantern, lamp (luz). **2** street lamp (en la calle). **3** bluff (en los juegos, cartas). **4** showing off, boasting (presunción). || **5 ¡adelante con los faroles!,** come on! **6 — de viento,** hurricane lamp.

farola *s.f.* **1** street lamp (farol de calle). **2** gas lamp (de gas).

farolear *v.i.* to show off, to boast, to brag (presumir).

farolero, -a *adj.* **1** boastful, vain, (fam.) cocky (presumido). || *s.m.* y *f.* **2** show-off, boaster (presumido). **3** lamp maker (el que hace faroles). **4** lamp lighter (el que enciende o cuida los faroles).

farra *s.f.* (fam.) fling, binge (juerga): *ir de farra = to go on a binge.*

fárrago *s.m.* (fam.) hotchpotch, jumble, farrago.

farragoso, -a *adj.* convoluted, confusing: *un libro farragoso = a convoluted book.*

farruco, -a *adj.* **1** challenging, defiant (desafiante). **2** self-confident, (desp.) cocky (seguro de sí mismo). || *s.m.* y *f.* **3** Galician o Asturian emigrant (Gallego o Asturiano recién salido de su tierra).

farsa *s.f.* **1** farse (comedia teatral). **2** (fig.) farse, sham: *esta ley es una farsa = this law is a farse.*

farsante *s.m.* y *f.* **1** comedian (comediante). **2** (fig.) fraud, sham, fake.

fas o por nefas (por) *adv.* rightly or wrongly; (fam.) by hook or by crook.

fascículo *s.m.* fascicle, part: *el primer fascículo = the first part.*

fascinación *s.f.* fascination.

fascinador, -a *adj.* fascinating.

fascinante *adj.* fascinating.

fascinar *v.t.* to fascinate, to captivate.

fascismo *s.m.* POL. fascism.

fascista *adj.* **1** fascist. || *s.m.* y *f.* **2** fascist.

fase *s.f.* **1** stage, phase: *la primera fase = the first stage; las fases de una enfermedad = the phases of an illness.* **2** ASTR., BIOL., FIS. phase: *las fases de la luna = the phases of the moon.*

fastidiar *v.t.* **1** to bother, to annoy (molestar): *me fastidia tener que estudiar más = it annoys me having to study more; ¡no me fastidies! = stop bothering me!* **2** to spoil o ruin someone's plans (estropear los planes a uno): *el tiempo nos ha fastidiado = the weather has ruined our plans.* **3** to ruin, to spoil (estropear). **4** to harm, to damage (hacer daño). **5** to sicken, to disgust (causar asco). || *v.r.* **6** to put up with: *si las cosas son así, me tengo que fastidiar = if that's the way things are, i'll have to put up with it.* **7** to get bored/fed up (aburrirse). **8** to get angry/annoyed (enfadarse). **9** to be spoilt/ruined (estropearse). **10** to break down, to be damaged (un mecanismo). **11** to hurt oneself (hacerse daño): *me he fastidiado la pierna = I've hurt my leg.* || **12 ¡fastídiate!,** (fam.) get lost! **13 ¡que se fastidie!,** (fam.) too bad for him! **14** (fam.) **¡no fastidies!,** you must be joking!; you're joking.

fastidio *s.m.* **1** bother, nuisance (molestia): *¡qué fastidio! = what a bother!* **2** boredom, (fam.) drag (aburrimiento): *es un fastidio tener que estudiar = it is a drag to have to study.*

fastidioso, -a *adj.* **1** bothersome, annoying, troublesome: *un trabajo fastidioso = a troublesome job.* **2** boring, tedious (aburrido).

fastuosamente *adv.* lavishly, ostentaciously (ostentosamente).

fastuosidad *s.f.* lavishness, ostentaciousness.

fastuoso, -a *adj.* **1** lavish, extremely luxurious (muy lujoso). **2** lavish, ostentacious (amigo del gran lujo).

fatal *adj.* **1** fatal (mortal): *un accidente fatal = a fatal accident.* **2** inevitable, unavoidable (inevitable). **2** (fam.) terrible, lousy, rotten, awful (muy mal): *un partido fatal = a terrible game.* || *adv.* **3** terribly, very badly, awfully: *escribe fatal = he writes terribly.* || **4 estar —,** to feel awful.

fatalidad *s.f.* **1** fate, destiny (destino). **2** bad luck, misfortune (mala suerte).

fatalismo *s.m.* fatalism.

fatalista *adj.* **1** fatalistic. || *s.m.* y *f.* **2** fatalist.

fatalmente *adv.* **1** fatally (mortalmente). **2** inevitably, unavoidably (inevitablemente). **3** unfortunately (desgraciadamente). **4** terribly, very badly, awfully (muy mal).

fatídico, -a *adj.* ominous, fateful: *un día fatídico = a fateful day.*

fatiga *s.f.* **1** tiredness, weariness, fatigue (cansancio). **2** TEC. fatigue: *fatiga del metal = metal fatigue.* **3** laboured breathing (molestia al respirar). **4** shaking, agitation (agitación). || *s.pl.* **5** troubles, hardships, difficulties (dificultades).

fatigar *v.t.* **1** to tire, to weary, (p u.) to fatigue (cansar). || *v.r.* **2** to tire, to get tired, to wear oneself out: *fatigarse nadando = to wear oneself out swimming.*

fatigoso, -a *adj.* **1** tiring, exhausting (que fatiga): *un trabajo fatigoso = a tiring job.* **2** difficult, laboured (la respiración). **3** tiresome, tedious (fastidioso).

fatuidad *s.f.* fatuousness, stupidity, inanity.

fatuo, -a *adj.* **1** fatuous, inane (necio). **2** conceited, vain (presumido).

fauces *s.f.pl.* ANAT. fauces, gullet (parte posterior de la boca de los animales).

fauna *s.f.* fauna.

fauno *s.m.* LIT. faun.

fausto, -a *adj.* **1** happy, cheerful (feliz): *un fausto acontecimiento = a happy event.* || *s.m.* **2** magnificence, splendour (lujo excesivo).

favila *s.f.* cinder (ceniza del fuego).

favor *s.m.* **1** favour: *¿me puedes hacer un favor? = can you do me a favour?* **2** concession (concesión). || **3 a — de,** in favour of: *estar a favor de = to be in favour of.* **4 de —,** free; complimentary: *entrada de favor = free ticket.* **5 estar en — de,** to be in favour of (a beneficio de). **6 hacer el — de,** to be so kind/good as to: *haga el favor de no hablar = please be so kind as not to talk.* **7 pedir un — a alguien,** to ask someone for a favour. **8 por —,** please.

favorable *adj.* **1** favourable (propicio): *un resultado favorable = a favourable result; un viento favorable = a favourable wind.* **2** suitable (apto): *condiciones favorables = suitable conditions.* **3** MED. optimistic (optimista): *diagnóstico favorable = optimistic diagnosis.*

favorablemente *adv.* favourably.

favorecer *v.t.* **1** to favour (beneficiar). **2** to be in favour of: *el tiempo nos favoreció = the weather was in our favour.* **3** to help (ayudar). **4** to enhance (agraciar). **5** to flatter (una foto). **6** to look well on, to suit, to become (ropa): *la falda te favorece = the skirt suits you.*

favorecido, -a *adj.* favoured: *trato de nación más favorecida = most-favoured nation treatment.*

favoritismo *s.m.* favouritism.

favorito, -a *adj.* **1** favourite: *mi libro favorito = my favourite book.* || *s.m.* y *f.* **2** favourite: *el favorito de la carrera = the race favourite.*

faz *s.f.* **1** face (cara): *la faz de la tierra = the face of the earth.* **2** aspect (aspecto). **3** head, obverse (de una moneda).

fe *s.f.* **1** REL. faith: *la fe católica = the Catholic faith; tener fe en = to have faith in.* **2** fidelity, loyalty (fidelidad). **3** certificate (certificado). **4** trust (confianza). **5** promise (promesa). || **6 a — de,** on the word of. **7 buena —,** good faith: *de buena fe = in good faith.* **8 dar —,** to testify; to attest. **9 — de erratas,** list of errata. **10 mala —,** bad faith: *de mala fe = in bad faith.* **11 profesión de —,** profession of faith. **12 tener buena o mala —,** to be honest o dishonest.

fealdad *s.f.* ugliness (calidad de feo).

febrero *s.m.* February.

febril *adj.* **1** MED. feverish. **2** (fig.) feverish, intense (intenso).

fecal *adj.* faecal.

fécula *s.f.* starch.

feculento, -a *adj.* starchy.

fecundación *s.f.* fertilization, (p.u.) fecundation.

fecundante *adj.* fertilizing, (p.u.) fecundating.

fecundar *v.t.* to fertilize, (p.u.) to fecundate.

fecundidad *s.f.* fertility, (p.u.) fecundity.

fecundizar *v.t.* to fertilize, (p.u.) to fecundate.

fecundo, -a *adj.* **1** fertile (fértil). **2** productive (que produce). **3** (fig.) prolific (prolífico). **4** fertile (imaginación). || **5 — en,** full of: *una película fecunda en ideas = a film full of ideas.*

fecha *s.f.* **1** date: *¿cuál es la fecha? = what's the date?* || **2 a estas fechas,** by

now; now. **3 a partir de esta –,** from today; starting today. **4 con – del 20 de mayo,** dated the 20th of May. **5 – tope,** last date; closing date. **6 hasta la –,** so far; to date. **7 para estas fechas,** by this time. **8 sin –,** undated.
fechar *v.t.* to date.
fechoría *s.f.* misdeed, offence.
federación *s.f.* federation: *federación de fútbol = football federation.*
federal *adj.* federal.
federalismo *s.m.* federalism.
federalista *s.m.* y *f.* federalist.
federar *v.t.* y *r.* to federate.
federativo, -a *adj.* federative.
fehaciente *adj.* 1 authentic (auténtico). 2 evident, obvious (evidente).
feldespato *s.m.* MIN. feldspar o felspar.
felicidad *s.f.* 1 happiness. 2 good fortune, happy event (acontecimiento agradable). || 3 **¡felicidades!,** congratulations! **4 te deseo toda clase de felicidades,** I wish you all the happiness in the world.
felicitación *s.f.* congratulation.
felicitar *v.t.* 1 to congratulate: *me felicitó por haber aprobado el examen = he congratulated me on having passed the examination.* || *v.r.* 2 to be pleased/glad.
feligrés *s.m.* y *f.* REL. parishoner.
feligresía *s.f.* REL. 1 parish (parroquia). 2 parishoners (feligreses).
felino, -a *adj.* 1 ZOOL. feline. 2 (fam.) catlike, feline. || *s.m.* 3 feline.
feliz *adj.* 1 happy: *¡feliz cumpleaños! = happy birthday!* 2 clever (acertado). 3 fortunate, lucky (afortunado). 5 favourable (favorable). 6 successful (que tiene éxito): *la operación tuvo un final feliz = the operation had a successful outcome.*
felizmente *adv.* 1 happily: *vivimos felizmente en el campo = we live happily in the country.* 2 fortunately, luckily (afortunadamente). 3 successfully (con éxito).
felón *adj.* 1 treacherous, traitorous (traidor). 2 false, deceitful (falso). || *s.m.* y *f.* 3 traitor, evil person.
felonía *s.f.* treachery, (fam.) double-dealing (traición).
felpa *s.f.* 1 plush (tejido aterciopelado). 2 (fig.) beating, thrashing (paliza). 3 reprimand, (fam.) telling-off (reprimenda).
felpilla *s.f.* chenille.
felpudo *adj.* 1 plushy, velvety. || *s.m.* 2 mat, doormat (esterilla).
femenil *adj.* feminine, womanly.
femenino, -a *adj.* 1 feminine. 2 BOT. y BIOL. female: *sexo femenino = female sex.* || *s.m.* 3 GRAM. feminine.
fementido, -a *adj.* treacherous, false, (fam.) double-dealing.
femineidad *s.f.* femininity.
feminidad *s.f.* femininity.
feminismo *s.m.* feminism.
feminista *s.m.* y *f.* feminist.
femoral *adj.* ANAT. femoral.
fémur *s.m.* ANAT. femur.
fenecer *v.t.* 1 to end, to conclude, to finish (poner fin). || *v.i.* 2 to die (morir). 3 to come to an end, to end, to cease (acabarse).
fenecimiento *s.m.* 1 passing away, death, demise (muerte). 2 end, close, conclusion (fin).
fenicio, -a *adj.* y *s.m.* y *f.* Phoenician.
fénix *s.m.* y *f.* phoenix.
fenol *s.m.* QUIM. phenol.
fenomenal *adj.* 1 phenomenal. 2 (fig.) fantastic, marvellous (magnífico): *una persona fenomenal = a fantastic person.* 3 enormous, huge (enorme).
fenómeno *s.m.* 1 phenomenon: *un fenómeno físico = a physical phenomenon.* 2 freak (persona deforme). || *adj.* 3 (fam.) great, terrific, fantastic: *un hombre fenómeno = a terrific man.*
feo, -a *adj.* 1 ugly: *un hombre feo = an ugly man.* 2 hideous, unsightly (repugnante). 3 awful, lousy, terrible (muy mal): *un partido feo = an awful game; hace un tiempo feo = the weather is lousy.* 4 nasty (una situación, costumbre). 5 not nice: *es muy feo decir tacos = it's not nice to swear.* || *s.m.* 6 insult, slight (insulto).
feracidad *s.f.* fertility.
feraz *adj.* fertile.
féretro *s.m.* coffin (ataúd).
feria *s.f.* 1 fair: *feria de muestras = trade fair.* 2 holiday (fiesta). 3 rest day, day off (día de descanso). 4 carnival (carnaval). 5 week day, working day (día de la semana). 6 (Am.) change (dinero suelto).
ferial *s.m.* 1 fairground (lugar donde está instalada la feria). || *adj.* 2 REL. ferial. 3 fair (de la feria).
feriante *s.m.* y *f.* fair-goer (persona que acude a la feria).
feriar *v.t.* 1 to buy at the fair (comprar en la feria). 2 to trade (comprar o vender en la feria). || *v.i.* 3 to take a holiday, to take time off (guardar fiesta).
ferino, -a *adj.* 1 wild, savage, (p.u.) feral (de fiera). || **2 tos ferina,** MED. whooping cough.
fermentable *adj.* fermentative.
fermentación *s.f.* fermentation.
fermentar *v.t.* e *i.* to ferment.
fermento *s.m.* ferment: (fig.) *fermento revolucionario = revolutionary ferment.*
ferocidad *s.f.* ferocity, fierceness, savageness.
feroz *adj.* 1 fierce, ferocious, savage (un animal). 2 cruel (que obra cruelmente). 3 fierce, savage (una persona). 4 fierce (viento, tormenta, etc.). 5 (fig.) tremendous, enormous (tremendo): *tener un hambre feroz = to have a tremendous appetite.*
férreo, -a *adj.* 1 iron, ferrous (de hierro): *metal no férreo = non-ferrous metal.* 2 (fig.) iron, hard (duro): *disciplina férrea = iron resistance.* 3 railway: *vía férrea = railway.*
ferrería *s.f.* 1 forge (forja). 2 foundry, ironworks (fábrica). 3 blacksmith's workshop (taller).
ferretería *s.f.* 1 ironmonger's, hardware shop (tienda de hierro). 2 hardware, ironmongery (lo que se vende en dicho comercio).
ferretero, -a *s.m.* y *f.* ironmonger.
férrico, -a *adj.* QUIM. ferric, ferrous.
ferrocarril *s.m.* 1 railway, (EE.UU.) railroad. **2 – elevado,** elevated railway. **3 – funicular,** funicular. **4 por –,** by railway.
ferrocarrilero, -a *adj.* (Am.) railway, (EE.UU.) railroad.
ferroso, -a *adj.* QUIM. ferrous.
ferroviario, -a *adj.* 1 railway, (EE.UU.) railroad. || *s.m.* 2 railwayman, railway worker (empleado del ferrocarril).
ferruginoso, -a *adj.* ferruginous.
fértil *adj.* 1 fertile. 2 productive (productivo). 3 (fig.) fertile: *una imaginación fértil = a fertile imagination.* 4 rich (rico).
fertilidad *s.f.* 1 AGR. y fig. 1 fertility. 2 richness (riqueza).
fertilizante *s.m.* fertilizer.
fertilizar *v.t.* to fertilize.
férula *s.f.* 1 MED. splint (tablilla). 2 BOT. ferula o ferule. 3 cane, stick (del profesor). 4 domination, rule (sujección).
férvido, -a *adj.* fervent, passionate, impassioned, fervid.
ferviente *adj.* fervid, fervent.
fervientemente *adv.* fervently, fervidly.
fervor *s.m.* fervour, passion.
fervorosamente *adv.* fervently, passionately.
fervoroso, -a *adj.* fervent, fervid, passionate, ardent.
festejar *v.t.* 1 to wine and dine, to entertain (agasajar a uno). 2 to celebrate (celebrar). 3 to court, to woo (galantear). || *v.r.* 4 to have a good time, to enjoy oneself (divertirse).
festejo *s.m.* 1 entertainment, feast (de un huésped). 2 celebration (celebración). 3 courting, wooing (cortejo). || *s.pl.* 4 festivities, revelries (fiestas).
festín *s.m.* feast, banquet (banquete).
festival *s.m.* festival: *festival de teatro = theatre festival; festival de cine = film festival.*
festividad *s.f.* 1 festivity, revelry, merriment (alegría). 2 REL. feast day, feast (fiesta). 3 ceremony (ceremonia). 4 wit, sharpness, humour (agudeza).
festivo, -a *adj.* 1 festive, jolly, merry (alegre). 2 REL. feast: *día festivo = feast day.* 3 comical, witty (cómico).
festón *s.m.* 1 scallop (bordado). 2 festoon (adorno en forma de guirnaldas).
festoneado *s.m.* festoonery.
festonear o **festonar** *v.t.* to festoon.
fetal *adj.* foetal.
fetiche *s.m.* fetish.
fetichismo *s.m.* fetishism.
fetichista *adj.* 1 fetishist. || *s.m.* y *f.* 2 fetishist.
fetidez *s.f.* stench, smelliness, (p.u.) foetidness.
fétido, -a *adj.* stinking, rank, smelly, (p.u.) foetid.
feto *s.m.* BIOL. foetus.
feudal *adj.* feudal.
feudalismo *s.m.* HIST. feudalism.
feudatario, -a *adj./s.m.* y *f.* feudatatory.

feudo *s.m.* HIST. fief, fued.
fez *s.m.* fez (gorro turco).
fiabilidad *s.f.* reliability, trustworthiness.
fiable *adj.* reliable, trustworthy.
fiado, -a *adj.* 1 loyal, faithful (fiel). 2 trusting (confiado). 3 **al —,** COM. on credit: *comprar al fiado = to buy on credit.*
fiador, -ora *s.m.* y *f.* 1 DER. guarantor, surety (persona). 2 MEC. catch, fastener (cierre). 3 tumbler (del cerrojo). 4 (fam.) bottom (trasero). 5 safety catch (de un arma). || 6 **ser — de uno,** DER. to stand bail for someone.
fiambre *adj.* 1 cold (alimentos fríos). 2 (fig.) old, stale (una noticia, etc.). || *s.m.* 3 cold meat (carne fría). 4 cold food (comida fría). 5 (fam.) stiff, corpse (cadáver): *está fiambre = he's kicked the bucket.*
fiambrera *s.f.* lunch box o basket (para llevar la comida).
fianza *s.f.* 1 deposit (para una casa): *un mes de fianza = a month's deposit.* 2 surety, guarantor (fiador). 3 DER. bail: *libertad bajo fianza = release on bail.* 4 surety, security (garantía).
fiar *v.t.* 1 to guarantee, to vouch for (garantizar). 2 COM. to sell on credit (vender sin cobrar al contado). 3 DER. to stand bail for (pagar fianza). 4 to entrust (confiar una cosa a alguien). || *v.i.* 5 to trust (confiar): *fío en Dios = I trust in God.* || *v.pron.* 6 to trust (poner confianza en alguien): *me fío de ti = I trust you.* || 7 **ser de —,** to be reliable, to be trustworthy.
fiasco *s.m.* fiasco.
fibra *s.f.* 1 fibre: *fibra de vidrio = fibreglass.* 2 (fig.) energy, vigour, verve (vigor). || 3 **fibras artificiales,** man-made fibres.
fibrina *s.f.* BIOL. y QUIM. fibrin.
fibroma *s.* MED. fibroma (tumor).
fíbula *s.f.* fibula.
ficción *s.f.* 1 fiction. 2 (desp.) invention, concoction (cosa inventada). 3 fantasy (fantasía).
ficticio, -a *adj.* 1 fictitious: *dirección ficticia = ficticious address.* 2 false (falso): *simpatía ficticia = false friendliness.*
ficha *s.f.* 1 counter, marker (en ciertos juegos). 2 piece, man (en el ajedrez). 3 chip (en los naipes). 4 index o filing card (de un fichero). 5 COM. token. 6 token (para el teléfono). 7 record: *ficha policíaca = police record.* 8 signing-on (fichaje).
fichaje *s.m.* DEP. signing-on.
fichar *v.i.* 1 DEP. to sign on. 2 to clock in (en una fábrica). || *v.t.* 3 to file, to index (clasificar). 4 to put in the files (por parte de la policía). 5 (fam.) to tape: *te tengo fichado = I've got you taped.* || 6 **tener a alguien fichado,** (fam.) to know somebody's game.
fichero *s.m.* 1 card index (fichas). 2 filing cabinet (mueble). || *pl.* 3 records (de la policía).
fidedigno, -a *adj.* reliable.
fideicomiso *s.m.* DER. trusteeship.
fidelidad *s.f.* 1 loyalty, faithfulness, fidelity. 2 accuracy, exactness (exactitud). || 3 **alta —,** high fidelity.
fideo *s.m.* 1 noodle, vermicelli (pasta). 2 (fam.) rake, skinny person (persona muy delgada): *estar como un fideo = to be as skinny as a rake.*
fiduciario, -a *adj.* 1 fiduciary. || *s.m.* 2 trustee, (p.u.) fiduciary.
fiebre *s.f.* 1 MED. fever: *fiebre amarilla = yellow fever.* 2 (fig.) fever, fevered excitement (excitación grande). || 3 **tener —,** to have a fever.
fiel *adj.* 1 faithful, loyal (leal) 2 exact, accurate (exacto). 3 honest (honrado). || *s.m.pl.* 4 los fieles, the faithful. || *s.m.* 5 pointer, needle (aguja de las balanzas). 6 screw (clavillo de las tijeras).
fielato *s.m.* HIST. tollhouse.
fielmente *adv.* faithfully, loyally.
fieltro *s.m.* felt (género fibroso de lana).
fiera *s.f.* 1 wild animal o beast (animal salvaje). 2 bull (toro). 3 (fig.) beast, devil (persona de carácter violento). || 4 **estar hecho una —,** (fig.) to be furious.
fieramente *adv.* wildly.
fiereza *s.f.* 1 ferocity (ferocidad). 2 cruelty (crueldad). 3 deformity (deformidad).
fiero, -a *adj.* 1 wild (no domesticado). 2 savage (salvaje). 3 ferocious, fierce (feroz). 4 cruel (cruel). 5 horrendous, frightful (horrible). 6 ugly, hideous (muy feo). 7 enormous, huge (muy grande).
fiesta *s.f.* 1 party (en casa). 2 holiday: *el 14 de junio es fiesta = the 14th of June is a holiday.* 3 REL. feast, feast day, holy day. 4 celebration (celebración). 5 ceremony (ceremonia). || *s.pl.* 6 holidays: *las fiestas de Semana Santa = the Easter holidays.* 7 festivities: *las fiestas de Madrid = the festivities in Madrid.* || 8 **aguar la —,** to be a wet blanket o spoilsport. 9 **estar de —,** to be in a good mood. 10 **— de guardar** o **de precepto,** day of obligation. 11 **— fija** o **inmoble,** immovable feast. 12 **— movible,** moveable feast. 13 **— nacional,** public holiday. 14 **— del Trabajo,** Labour Day. 15 **hacer —,** to take a day off. 16 **y como fin de —,** to round it all off.
figura *s.f.* 1 figure (forma exterior de un cuerpo): *tener buena figura = to have a good figure.* 2 shape, form (forma gráfica): *tiene figura de triángulo = it has a triangular shape.* 3 face (cara). 4 aspect (aspecto). 5 figure (personaje célebre): *ella es una gran figura = she's an important figure.* 6 role, character (en el teatro). 7 symbol (símbolo). 8 GRAM. figure: *figura retórica = figure of speech.* 9 MUS. note. 10 piece, man (pieza de ajedrez). 10 ART. figure (escultura, pintura, etc.). || 11 **— central,** central figure. 12 **hacer —,** to cut a figure.
figuración *s.f.* figuration.
figuradamente *adv.* figuratively.
figurado, -a *adj.* figurative.
figurante *s.m.* y *f.* extra, walker-on (en el teatro).
figurar *v.t.* 1 to represent, to depict (representar). 2 to pretend, to feign (fingir). || *v.i.* 3 to figure, to appear: *su nombre no figura en la lista = his name doesn't figure on the list.* || *v.pron.* 4 to imagine, to think (imaginar): *me imagino que sí = I imagine so.* 5 to suppose (suponer).
figurativo, -a *adj.* figurative.
figurín *s.m.* 1 fashion magazine (revista de modas). 2 sketch, drawing (dibujo). 3 (fam.) dandy, popinjay, fop (persona vestida de forma afectada).
figurón *s.m.* 1 huge o enormous figure (figura grande). 2 (fam.) show-off, bighead (presumido).
fijación *s.f.* 1 fixing, setting, fastening (acción de fijar). 2 sticking (de un sello). 3 sticking up, putting up (de carteles). 4 PSIQ. fixation. 5 BOT. fixing.
fijador *adj.* 1 fixative. || *s.m.* 2 FOT. fixative, fixer. 3 ART. fixative. 4 lotion: *fijador para el pelo = hair lotion.*
fijamente *adv.* 1 fixedly (con fijeza). 2 securely, firmly (firmemente). 3 carefully (cuidadosamente). || 4 **mirar —,** to stare.
fijar *v.t.* 1 to stick (pegar). 2 to fix, to fasten (sujetar). 3 to put up, to stick up (carteles). 4 FOT. to fix. 5 to set, to fix (el pelo, el precio, el valor, la fecha, una cita, etc.). 6 to nail (clavar). 7 to determine (determinar). 8 to fix (mirada, ojos, atención). 9 to take up (domicilio). 10 to secure (asegurar). || *v.pron.* 11 to notice: *¿te has fijado en sus ojos? = have you noticed her eyes?* 12 to settle (establecerse). 13 to take notice, to pay attention (prestar atención). 14 to make up one's mind (decidirse). || 15 **¡fíjate!, a)** look! (¡mira!); **b)** just imagine! (es increíble).
fijeza *s.f.* 1 certainty (seguridad): *con fijeza = with certainty.* 2 stability (estabilidad). || 3 **mirar con — a alguien,** to stare at someone.
fijo, -a *adj.* 1 secure, stable, firm (firme). 2 fastened, fixed (sujeto). 3 fixed (precio, ficha, renta). 4 steady, fixed (mirada). 5 permanent (un empleo). 6 stationary (inmóvil). || *adv.* 7 fixedly (fijamente). 8 securely (con seguridad). || 9 **de —,** certainly, for certain. 10 **idea —,** fixed idea.
fila *s.f.* 1 file, line (línea de personas o cosas): *en fila = in file; en fila india = in single file.* 2 row (de asientos): *en primera fila = in the first row.* 3 MIL. rank: *las filas = the ranks.* 4 queue, line (cola). 5 dislike (antipatía). || 6 **cerrar las filas,** to close ranks. 7 **estar en filas,** to be in the army. 8 **ponerse en —, a)** to line up; **b)** to get into line. 9 **romper filas,** to fall out. 10 **romper las filas,** to break ranks.
filamento *s.m.* filament.
filamentoso, -a *adj.* filamentous.
filantropía *s.f.* philanthropy.
filantrópico, -a *adj.* philanthropic.
filántropo, -a *s.m.* y *f.* philanthropist.
filarmonía *s.f.* fond of music.

filarmónico, -a *adj.* MUS. philharmonic.
filatelia *s.f.* philately, (fam.) stamp collecting.
filatélico, -a *adj.* philatelic.
filete *s.m.* **1** steak, fillet (lonja de carne). **2** sirloin (solomillo). **3** fillet (lonja de pescado). **4** TEC. thread (de un tornillo). **5** fillet (moldura). **6** snaffle bit (freno pequeño para caballos). **7** stripe (raya, lista). **8** fillet (de un impreso). **9** (vulg.) lay (mujer para el placer).
filfa *s.f.* lie (mentira).
filiación *s.f.* **1** filiation (lazo de parentesco). **2** dependence (dependencia). **3** personal description (señas personales).
filial *adj.* **1** filial: *amor filial = filial love.* **2** COM. subsidiary. || *s.f.* **3** COM. branch (sucursal). **4** COM. subsidiary (empresa que depende de otra).
filibustero *s.m.* pirate, (p.u.) filibuster (pirata).
filiforme *adj.* filiform.
filigrana *s.f.* **1** filigree (obra). **2** watermark (marca en el papel). **3** delicate thing (cosa delicada).
filípica *s.f.* diatribe, tirade, (p.u.) philippic.
filipino, -a *adj./s.m* y *f.* Philippine, Filipino.
filisteo, -a *adj.* **1** Philistine. || *s.m.* y *f.* **2** Philistine. **3** (fam.) philistine (persona vulgar).
film o **filme** *s.m.* film, picture, (EE.UU.) movie (película).
filmación *s.f.* shooting, filming.
filmar *v.t.* to film, to shoot (rodar).
fílmico, -a *adj.* film.
filmoteca *s.f.* film library, film archive.
filo *s.m.* **1** edge: *el filo del cuchillo = the edge of the knife.* **2** dividing line (línea que divide una cosa en dos mitades). **3** GEOL. ridge. || **4 al — de las dos,** on the stroke of two o'clock. **5 — del viento,** MAR. wind direction. **6 sacar el — a,** to sharpen.
filología *s.f.* **1** philology: *estudio filología inglesa = I'm studying English philology.*
filológico, -a *adj.* philological.
filólogo, -a *s.m.* y *f.* philologist.
filón *s.m.* **1** MIN. vein, seam (vena). **2** (fig.) gold mine (negocio de grandes beneficios).
filosofal *adj.* philosopher's: *piedra filosofal = philosopher's stone.*
filosofar *v.i.* to philosophize.
filosofía *s.f.* **1** philosophy: *filosofía moral = moral phylosophy.* || **2 tomar algo con —,** to take something philosophically.
filosóficamente *adv.* philosophically.
filosófico, -a *adj.* philosophical, philosophic.
filósofo, -a *s.m.* y *f.* philosopher.
filoxera *s.f.* **1** ZOOL. phylloxera (insecto). **2** drunkenness (borrachera).
filtración *s.f.* **1** filtration. **2** (fig.) leak (indiscreción).
filtrar *v.t.* e *i.* **1** to filter. **2** to filter, to strain (café, té, etc.). || *v.pron.* **3** to filter: *filtrarse por = to filter through.* **4** to leak (un secreto). **5** to disappear, (fam.) to fritter away (dinero, bienes).
filtro *s.m.* **1** TEC. filter: *filtro de aceite = oil filter.* **2** strainer (en la cocina): *filtro de café = coffee strainer.* **3** FOT. filter. || **4 cigarrillo con —,** filter-tipped cigarette.
fimosis *s.f.* MED. phimosis.
fin *s.m.* **1** end: *fin de la película = end of the film; el fin del mes = the end of the month.* **2** objective, aim, goal, purpose (finalidad): *el fin de mi trabajo = the aim of my work.* **3** motive (motivo). || **4 a — de,** in order to; so as to: *a fin de llegar pronto = in order to arrive early.* **5 a fines,** at the end: *a fines del año = at the end of the year.* **6 al —,** at last. **7 al — y al cabo,** when all is said and done. **8 dar —,** to end. **9 en fin,** (fig.) well; well then (bueno). **10 — de semana,** weekend. **11 poner — a,** to put an end to. **12 por —, a)** finally (en resumen); **b)** at last! **13 sin —,** endless.
finado, -a *adj.* **1** late, deceased: *mi finado padre = my late father.* || *s.m.* y *f.* **2** deceased (difunto).
final *adj.* **1** last, final (último): *la palabra final = the last word; decisión final = final decision.* **2** GRAM. final. || *s.m.* **3** end: *al final del partido = at the end of the game.* **4** conclusion (conclusión). **5** ending (terminación): *el libro tiene un final triste = the book has a sad ending.* **6** MUS. finale. || *s.f.* **7** DEP. final: *la final de la copa = the cup final.* || **8 al —,** at the end.
finalidad *s.f.* aim, goal, objective (objetivo): *la finalidad de la película = the aim of the film.*
finalista *s.m.* y *f.* finalist.
finalizar *v.t.* **1** to end, to finish, to conclude.
finalmente *adv.* finally.
financiación *s.f.* FIN. financing.
financiar *v.t.* FIN. to finance.
financiero, -a *adj.* **1** financial: *el mundo financiero = the financial world.* || *s.m.* y *f.* **2** financier (persona).
finanzas *s.f.pl.* finance.
finca *s.f.* **1** country house (casa de campo). **2** country estate (terreno en el campo). **2** farm (granja). || **3 — urbana,** town property.
finés, -esa *adj.* **1** Finnic (del pueblo antiguo). **2** Finnish (finlandés). || *s.m.* y *f.* **3** Finn (persona). **4** *s.m.* Finnish (idioma).
fineza *s.f.* **1** courtesy, politeness (cortesía). **2** fineness (finura). **3** kindness, friendliness (muestra de amistad). **4** gift, present (regalo).
fingimiento *s.m.* pretence, feigning.
fingir *v.t.* **1** to pretend: *fingen que están estudiando = they are pretending to study.* **2** to feign (simular). || *v.pron.* **3** to pretend to be: *fingirse amable = to pretend to be friendly; fingirse cansado = to pretend to be tired.*
finiquitar *v.t.* **1** COM. to settle, to close (saldar una cuenta). **2** to end, to finish (terminar).
finiquito *s.m.* COM. settlement, closing (de una cuenta).
finito, -a *adj.* finite (que tiene fin).
finlandés, -esa *adj.* **1** Finnish. || *s.m.* y *f.* **2** Finn. || *s.m.* **3** Finnish (idioma).
fino, -a *adj.* **1** fine, thin (tela, pelo, papel, hilo, etc.). **2** delicate (rasgos). **3** high quality, excellent (de buena calidad). **4** slender, thin, slight (figura). **5** sharp (punta). **6** polite, refined (cortés). **7** shrewd, astute, sharp (astuto). **8** thin (lonja). **9** MIN. pure, refined: *oro fino = pure gold.* **10** sharp, keen (de oído, olfato). || *s.m.* **11** dry sherry (vino de Jerez).
finolis *adj.* affected, mannered (afectado).
finta *s.f.* feint.
finura *s.f.* **1** fineness. **2** delicacy (delicadeza). **3** excellence (excelencia). **4** sharpness, keenness (de oído, olfato). **5** shrewdness, astuteness (agudeza). **6** politeness (cortesía). **7** delicacy, subtlety (sutileza). **8** elegance (elegancia).
finústico, -a *adj.* affected, mannered (finolis).
fiordo o **fiord** *s.m.* GEOG. fjord, fiord.
firma *s.f.* **1** signature (autógrafo). **2** firm, company (empresa). **3** papers, documents (documentos que se pasan a firmar). **4** signing (acción de firmar).
firmamento *s.m.* firmament.
firmante *adj.* **1** signatory. || *s.m.* y *f.* **2** signatory. **3 los abajo firmantes,** the undersigned.
firmar *v.t.* e *i.* to sign: *firmar un documento = to sign a document.*
firme *adj.* **1** secure, firm, stable (seguro). **2** straight, erect (erguido). **3** hard (duro). **4** solid, compact (sólido). **5** fast (colores). **6** COM. steady, firm (un mercado, precios). **7** firm (una oferta, resistencia). **8** resolute, steady (de carácter). || **9** road surface (pavimento de carretera). **10** roadbed, road foundation (cimientos de carretera). **11 de —,** firmly; steadily (con seguridad). **12 ¡firmes!,** MIL. attention! **13 ponerse —,** MIL. to come to attention. **14 tierra —,** terra firma.
firmemente *adv.* **1** firmly, securely (seguramente). **2** resolutely, stead-fastly (resueltamente). **3** strongly (fuertemente).
firmeza *s.f.* **1** firmness (cualidad de firme). **2** stability, steadiness (estabilidad). **3** solidity, compactness (solidez). **4** COM. steadiness. **5** resolution, firmness (resolución).
firulete *s.m.* (Am.) adornment (adorno).
fiscal *adj.* **1** fiscal (relativo al fisco). **2** financial (financiero). **3** *atr.* tax (de los impuestos). || *s.m.* **4** DER. public prosecutor, prosecutor. **5** (fig.) busybody, snooper (fisgón).
fiscalía *s.f.* **1** DER. public prosecutor's job (cargo de fiscal). **2** DER. public prosecutor's office (despacho u oficina del fiscal).
fiscalización *s.f.* inspection (inspección).

fiscalizador, -a *s.m.* y *f.* (fig.) busybody, snooper (fisgón).
fiscalizar *v.t.* **1** to control (controlar). **2** to inspect (inspeccionar). **3** to criticize (criticar). **4** to check, to verify (averiguar).
fisco *s.m.* treasury, exchequer (tesoro público).
fisgar *v.t.* **1** to snoop on, to pry into (curiosear). || *v.pron.* e *i.* **2** to mock, to laugh at, to make fun of (burlarse).
fisgón, -ona *adj.* **1** nosey, snooping. || *s.m.* y *f.* **2** snooper, nosey-parker.
fisgonear *v.t.* to snoop on, to pry into (curiosear).
física *s.f.* FIS. physics: *física nuclear = nuclear physics.*
físico, -a *adj.* **1** physical: *un fenómeno físico = a physical phenomenon.* || *s.m.* **2** ANAT. physique (aspecto exterior). **3** physicist (científico). **4** looks, appearance (aspecto).
fisiocracia *s.f.* ECON. physiocracy.
fisiología *s.f.* physiology.
fisiológicamente *adv.* physiologically.
fisiológico, -a *adj.* physiological.
fisiólogo, -a *s.m.* y *f.* physiologist.
fisión *s.f.* FIS. fission: *fisión nuclear = nuclear fission.*
fisonomía *s.f.* **1** features, face, (p.u.) physiognomy (aspecto de la cara). **2** appearance, aspect (aspecto exterior).
fisonómico, -a *adj.* physiognomical.
fisonomista *s.m.* y *f.* physiognomist.
fístula *s.f.* **1** MED. fistula. **2** MUS. fistula. **3** tube, pipe (conducto).
fisura *s.f.* GEOL. fissure.
fitófago *adj.* plant-eating.
flacidez o **flaccidez** *s.f.* flabbiness, softness, (p.u.) flaccidity.
flácido o **fláccido, -a** *adj.* flabby, soft, flaccid.
flaco, -a *adj.* **1** thin, slim, (fam.) skinny (de pocas carnes). **2** feeble, weak (débil). 3 (fig.) weak-willed, weak (con poca resistencia a las tentaciones): *la carne es flaca = the flesh is weak.* || *s.m.* **4** weakness (debilidad). || **5 punto —,** weak spot.
flacuchento, -a *adj.* (Am.) skinny (flacucho).
flacucho, -a *adj.* (fam.) skinny.
flagelación *s.f.* flagellation, whipping.
flagelado *adj.* **1** flagellate. || *s.m.pl.* **2** ZOOL. flagellatae.
flagelante *adj.* y *s.m.* flagellant.
flagelar *v.t.* **1** to flagellate, to whip. **2** (fig.) to roast, to flay.
flagelo *s.m.* whip, lash (azote).
flagrante *adj.* flagrant: *en flagrante = red-handed/in flagrante.*
flama *s.f.* flame (llama).
flamante *adj.* **1** brilliant, magnificent (brillante). **2** new, brand-new (nuevo): *nuestro flamante jefe = our new boss.*
flamear *v.i.* **1** to blaze, to flame (echar llamas). **2** MAR. to flutter (una bandera). **3** MAR. to flap (una vela). **4** to sterilize (desinfectar algo al fuego).
flamenco, -a *adj.* **1** Flemish (de Flandes). **2** flamenco: *cante flamenco = flamenco singing.* **3** (desp.) flashy, vulgar (chulo). **4** (Am.) thin, slim (delgado). || *s.m.* y *f.* **5** Fleming (persona de Flandes). || *s.m.* **6** Flemish (idioma). **7** flamenco (cante y baile). **8** ZOOL. flamingo (ave).
flamenquismo *s.m.* **1** love of flamenco, fondness for flamenco (afición a lo flamenco). **2** flashiness, cockiness (chulería).
flamígero, -a *adj.* flaming, raging, ablaze.
flan *s.m.* caramel custard, cream caramel (dulce).
flanero o **flanera** *s.m.* o *f.* caramel custard mould.
flanco *s.m.* **1** ANAT. side, flank. **2** MIL. flank.
flanqueado, -a *adj.* flanked.
flanquear *v.t.* **1** MIL. to flank (defender por los lados). **2** to outflank (dominar por el flanco).
flaquear *v.i.* **1** to weaken, to lose strength (perder fuerza). **2** to lose heart (desanimarse). **3** to give in (transigir).
flaqueza *s.f.* **1** thinness (delgadez). **2** weakness (debilidad). **3** frailty, weakness (falta de entereza).
flash *s.m.* FOT. flash.
flato *s.m.* **1** wind, flatulence (acumulación de gases). **2** pride (orgullo). **3** (Am.) melancholy, depression (melancolía).
flatulencia *s.f.* flatulence, wind.
flatulento *adj.* flatulent.
flauta *s.f.* **1** MUS. flute. || **2 estar hecho una —,** to be as thin as a rake. **3 entre pitos y flautas,** what with one thing and another.
flautero *s.m.* flute maker.
flautín *s.m.* MUS. piccolo.
flautista *s.m.* y *f.* MUS. flautist, flute player.
flebitis *s.f.* MED. phlebitis.
fleco *s.m.* **1** fringe (adorno de hilos). **2** frayed edge (borde deshilado).
flecha *s.f.* arrow (arma): *como una flecha = like an arrow.*
flechar *v.t.* **1** to draw (tender la cuerda del arco). **2** to kill with an arrow (matar con flecha). **3** to wound with an arrow (herir con flecha). **4** to fall in love at first sight (enamorar súbitamente).
flechazo *s.m.* **1** arrow shot (golpe de flecha). **2** arrow wound (herida de flecha). **3** (fam.) love at first sight: *fue un flechazo = it was love at first sight.*
fleje *s.m.* metal strip (tira de chapa de acero).
flema *s.f.* **1** MED. phlegm. **2** (fig.) phlegm, calm (calma).
flemático *adj.* phlegmatic, imperturbable, stoical.
flemón *s.m.* MED. gumboil (inflamación en las encías).
flequillo *s.m.* fringe.
fletador *s.m.* charterer.
fletamento *s.m.* chartering.
fletar *v.t.* **1** to charter (alquilar). **2** (Am.) to utter (proferir palabras agresivas). || *v.t.* y *pron.* **3** to embark (embarcar). || *v.pron.* **4** (Am.) to beat it, to take off (marcharse de pronto).
flete *s.m.* **1** hire charge, hiring fee (precio por el alquiler). **2** cargo (carga de un buque). **3** load, freight (carga). **4** (Am.) horse (caballo).
flexibilidad *s.f.* **1** flexibility. **2** (fig.) adaptability, flexibility.
flexible *adj.* **1** flexible. **2** supple, pliable (elástico). **3** soft (sombrero). **4** (fig.) compliant, amenable (fácil de convencer).
flexión *s.f.* **1** flexion. **2** GRAM. inflexion.
flexional *adj.* **1** flexional. **2** GRAM. inflected.
flexo *s.m.* angle-poise lamp (lámpara).
flexor *s.m.* ANAT. flexor.
flirtear *v.i.* to flirt.
flirteo *s.m.* **1** flirting (acción de flirtear). || **2 un —,** a flirtation.
flojear *v.i.* **1** to weaken, to lose strength (flaquear). **2** (fam.) to shirk, to skive (obrar con desgana). **3** to lose interest (perder interés).
flojedad o **flojera** *s.f.* **1** weakness (debilidad). **2** lightness (del viento). **3** looseness (de cables, cuerdas, etc.). **4** laziness, idleness (pereza). **5** limpness, flabbiness (flacidez).
flojo, -a *adj.* **1** loose, slack (cuerda, cable, etc.). **2** loose (tuerca, tornillo, etc.). **3** weak (esfuerzo, intento). **4** limp, soft (de consistencia). **5** weak (vino, café, té, etc.). **6** poor, weak (libro, película, partido, jugador, excusa, estudiante). **7** light (viento). **8** slack (mercado). **9** weak, feeble (débil). **10** lazy, idle (perezoso).
flor *s.f.* **1** BOT. flower. **2** flower, bloom, blossom: *en flor = in bloom/in blossom.* **3** blossom (de árbol frutal). **4** virginity (virginidad). **5** compliment (dicho galante). **6** cream, best part (lo mejor de una cosa). || **7 a — de,** on the surface (en la superficie): **8 a — de piel,** skin-deep. **9 en la — de la vida,** in the prime of life. **10 ir de — en —,** to go o jump from one thing to another. **11 — de harina,** flour. **12 — de la canela,** the tops; the best (cosa muy buena). **13 la — y nata,** (fig.) the cream; the pick: *la flor y nata de la sociedad = the cream of society.*
flora *s.f.* flora.
floración *s.f.* **1** flowering (de una planta). **2** blossoming (de un árbol frutal).
floral *adj.* floral.
florear *v.t.* y *v.pron.* **1** to adorn with flowers (adornar con flores). **2** to compliment (echar flores). **3** to sift (apartar lo mejor de una cosa). **4** to mark (preparar una carta para hacer trampa).
florecer *v.i.* **1** BOT. to flower, to bloom (una planta). **2** BOT. to blossom (un árbol frutal). **3** (fig.) to blossom, to thrive (prosperar). || *v.r.* **4** to go mouldy (ponerse mohoso).
floreciente *adj.* **1** BOT. flowering, blooming. **2** (fig.) blossoming, thriving.
florecimiento *s.m.* **1** BOT. flowering, blooming. **2** (fig.) blossoming, thriving.
florentino, -a *adj./s.m.* y *f.* Florentine.

floreo *s.m.* **1** compliment (piropo). **2** funny comment, witty aside (dicho frívolo). **3** idle talk (conversación de pasatiempo).
florero *s.m.* **1** vase, flower vase (vasija). **2** florist (florista).
floresta *s.f.* **1** glade, grove, beauty spot (terreno frondoso). **2** anthology of poetry (antología poética).
florete *s.m.* DEP. foil (espadín).
floricultor, -ora *s.m.* y *f.* flower-grower.
floricultura *s.f.* flower growing.
florido, -a *adj.* **1** flowery (que tiene flores). **2** (fig.) florid, flowery (estilo ornamental). || **3 lo más —,** the pick; the cream (lo mejor).
florilegio *s.m.* anthology (antología).
florín *s.m.* florin (moneda).
florista *s.m.* y *f.* florist.
floristería *s.f.* florist's, florist's shop.
florón *s.m.* BOT. big flower (flor muy grande).
flota *s.f.* **1** MAR. fleet: *flota pesquera = fishing fleet.* || **2 — aérea,** air fleet. **3** (Am.) crowd (multitud).
flotación *s.f.* flotation.
flotador *s.m.* **1** float. **2** ball-cock (en la cisterna).
flotadura *s.f.* flotation.
flotamiento *s.m.* flotation.
flotante *adj.* **1** floating: *población flotante = floating population.* **2** loose (suelto).
flotar *v.i.* **1** to float. **2** COM. to float (una moneda). **3** to wave, to flutter (una bandera).
flote *s.m.* **1** flotation (flotadura). **2** floating (flotante). || **3 estar a —,** to be afloat. **4 poner a —,** to float, to set afloat (flotar). **5** (fig.) **salir a —,** to get back on one's feet (recuperarse).
flotilla *s.f.* MAR. flotilla.
fluctuación *s.f.* **1** fluctuation: *la fluctuación de la peseta = the fluctuation of the peseta.* **2** (fig.) hesitation, indecision (vacilación).
fluctuante *adj.* fluctuating.
fluctuar *v.i.* **1** to fluctuate. **2** to hesitate, to waver (vacilar). **3** to bob up and down (oscilar un cuerpo sobre aguas agitadas). **4** FIN. to go up and down, to fluctuate (un precio, una moneda, etc.).
fluctuoso, -a *adj.* fluctuating.
fluente *adj.* **1** fluid (fluido). **2** flowing (que fluye).
fluidez *s.f.* **1** fluidity. **2** (fig.) fluency: *hablar francés con fluidez = to speak French with fluency.*
fluido, -a *adj.* **1** fluid. **2** fluent (estilo, lenguaje). || *s.m.* **3** fluid. **4** ELEC. current, power.
fluir *v.i.* **1** to flow, to run (líquidos). **2** (fig.) to flow, to stream (ideas, palabras, proyectos, etc.).
flujo *s.m.* **1** flow (movimiento de líquidos). **2** (fig.) stream, flow: *flujo de insultos = stream of insults.* **3** MAR. rising tide (ascenso de la marea). || **4 — blanco,** MED. leucorrhoea. **5 — de sangre,** MED. flow of blood; haemorrhage.
flúor *s.m.* QUIM. flourine.
fluorescencia *s.f.* fluorescence.
fluorescente *adj.* fluorescent.
fluorhídrico, -a *adj.* QUIM. hydrofluoric.
fluvial *adj.* fluvial, river: *navegación fluvial = river navigation.*
fobia *s.f.* phobia.
foca *s.f.* ZOOL. seal.
focal *adj.* focal.
foco *s.m.* **1** MAT., MED. y FIS. focus. **2** focal point, centre (lugar en que se concentra algo): *el foco del problema = the focal point of the problem.* **3** centre (centro). **4** source (fuente). **5** source, seat (de un incendio). **6** spotlight (en el teatro). **7** floodlight (lámpara muy fuerte). **8** (Am.) light bulb (bombilla). || **9 estar fuera de —,** to be out of focus.
fofo, -a *adj.* **1** soft. **2** spongy (esponjoso). **3** (fam.) plump, fat (gordito).
fogata *s.f.* bonfire (hoguera).
fogón *s.m.* **1** bonfire (hoguera). **2** firebox (de las máquinas de vapor). **3** kitchen range, stove (cocina de carbón). **4** (Am.) fire (fuego).
fogonazo *s.m.* **1** sudden blaze, flash (llamarada momentánea). **2** FOT. flash.
fogonero *s.m.* stoker (de las máquinas de vapor).
fogosidad *s.f.* **1** ardour, eagerness (ardor). **2** enthusiasm, keenness (entusiasmo).
fogoso, -a *adj.* **1** ardent, eager (ardiente). **2** enthusiastic, keen (entusiasta). **3** frisky, fiery (un caballo).
foguear *v.t.* y *pron.* **1** to harden to war (acostumbrar al fuego del combate). **2** to inure, to toughen, to harden (acostumbrar a una cosa desagradable).
fogueo *s.m.* hardening, toughening (acción y efecto de foguear).
foie-gras *s.m.* foie-gras.
foliáceo, -a *adj.* BOT. foliaceous.
foliación *s.f.* BOT. foliation.
foliado, -a *adj.* BOT. foliate.
folio *s.m.* **1** page, sheet, folio (hoja de papel). **2** folio: *edición en folio = folio edition.* **3** (Am.) present, gift (regalo).
folklore *s.m.* folklore.
folklórico, -a *adj.* folk, popular, traditional.
folklorista *s.m.* y *f.* folklorist.
follaje *s.m.* **1** BOT. foliage. **2** horrible adornment (adorno de mal gusto). **3** bombast, verbosity (retórica excesiva).
folletín *s.m.* **1** newspaper serial (novela publicada por partes en los periódicos). **2** melodrama (novela de tema melodramático).
folletinesco, -a *adj.* melodramatic (melodramático).
folletista *s.m.* y *f.* pamphleteer.
folleto *s.m.* brochure, pamphlet.
follisca *s.f.* (Am.) fight, quarrel, row (pendencia).
follón *s.m.* **1** (fam.) row, rumpus, quarrel (alboroto). **2** silent rocket (cohete sin trueno). **3** (vulg.) silent fart (ventosidad sin ruido). **4** coward (cobarde). **5** (fam.) loafer, layabout (vago). **6** show-off, boaster (fanfarrón). **7** chaos (caos). **8** mess (situación enmarañada): *¡qué follón! = what a mess!* || *adj.* **9** lazy (perezoso). **10** cowardly (cobarde). **11** showing off, boasting (fanfarrón). **12** arrogant (arrogante).
fomentar *v.t.* **1** to warm (calentar). **2** to incubate (huevos). **3** MED. to foment. **4** (fig.) to foment, to encourage, to promote (aumentar las actividades de una cosa). **5** to foment, to incite (una rebelión, discordia, odio, etc.).
fomento *s.m.* **1** promotion, encouragement (impulso). **2** warmth, heat (calor). **3** fomentation, incitement (de una rebelión o similar). **4** MED. fomentation. **5** MED. poultice (paño caliente). **6** incubation (de los huevos). || **7 banco de —,** development bank.
fonación *s.f.* phonation.
fonda *s.f.* HIST. inn, tavern (hostelería).
fondeadero *s.m.* MAR. anchorage.
fondeado *adj.* **1** MAR. anchored, at anchor (anclado). **2** (Am.) rich (rico).
fondear *v.t.* **1** to sound, to take soundings (sondear). **2** to examine (examinar). **3** to search (registrar). **4** (fig.) to get to the bottom of (analizar una cuestión hasta el fondo). || *v.t.* y *pron.* **5** MAR. to anchor, to drop anchor (anclar). || *v.pron.* **6** (Am.) to get rich (enriquecerse).
fondo *s.m.* **1** bottom (la parte más baja): *el fondo del pozo = the bottom of the well; fondo falso = false bottom.* **2** end: *el fondo de la calle = the end of the street.* **3** depth (profundidad). **4** bed, floor (lecho de los ríos, mares, estanques, etc.): *el fondo del mar = the sea bed.* **5** background (de un cuadro). **6** DEP. stamina (resistencia). **7** COM. fund: *Fondo Monetario Internacional = International Monetary Fund.* **8** money, resources (dinero): *estar sin fondos = to have no money.* **9** collection (conjunto de libros). **10** bottom (lo que importa en un asunto): *el fondo de la cuestión = the bottom of the question.* **11** MAR. hull (casco de un barco). || **12 a —,** thoroughly: *conocer algo a fondo = to know something thoroughly.* **13 al — de,** at the bottom of. **14 de bajo —,** shallow. **15** en el fondo, at heart; at bottom; deep down: *son buenos en el fondo = at heart they are good.* **16** llegar al fondo, to get to the bottom. **17** MAR. **irse al —,** to sink; to go to the bottom. **18** (fig.) **tener buen —,** to be good-natured.
fonema *s.m.* phoneme.
fonendoscopio *s.m.* MED. stethoscope.
fonética *s.f.* phonetics.
fonético, -a *adj.* phonetic.
foniatra *s.m.* MED. phoniatrician.
foniatría *s.f.* MED. phoniatrics.
fónico, -a *adj.* phonic.
fono *s.m.* (Am.) receiver (auricular del teléfono).
fonográfico, -a *adj.* gramaphonic.
fonógrafo *s.m.* gramaphone (gramófono).
fonología *s.f.* phonology.
fonometría *s.f.* phonometry.
fontana *s.f.* fountain, spring (fuente).

fontanal *s.m.* spring.
fontanela *s.f.* ANAT. fontanel, fontanelle.
fontanería *s.f.* plumbing.
fontanero, -a *s.m.* y *f.* plumber.
foque *s.m.* MAR. jib (vela triangular).
forajido, -a *s.m.* y *f.* 1 bandit, outlaw, desesperado (bandido). || *adj.* 2 outlawed.
foráneo, -a *adj.* 1 foreign (extranjero). 2 odd, strange (raro).
forastero, -a *adj.* 1 strange, odd (raro). 2 foreign, alien (extranjero). || *s.m.* y *f.* 3 stranger (desconocido). 4 foreigner (extranjero). 5 outsider (de fuera).
forcejear o **forcejar** *v.i.* to struggle, to fight (oponer resistencia).
forcejeo o **forcejo** *s.m.* struggle, fight.
fórceps *s.m.* MED. forceps.
forense *adj.* 1 forensic. || *s.m.* 2 MED. pathologist, forensic scientist.
forestal *adj.* forest.
forja *s.f.* 1 forge (fragua). 2 foundry (ferrería). 3 forging (acción de forjar). 4 mortar (argamasa de construir).
forjador *s.m.* forger.
forjar *v.t.* 1 to forge (dar forma a un metal). 2 to construct, to make (construir). 3 (fig.) to invent, to make up (inventar): *forjar una excusa = to make up an excuse.* || *v.r.* 4 to be a self-made man (hacerse a uno mismo).
forma *s.f.* 1 shape (figura): *de forma redonda = round-shaped; la forma de la habitación = the shape of the room.* 2 way, form, means (modo de hacer las cosas): *la forma de llegar = the way of arriving.* 3 mould, form (molde). 4 size (tamaño). 5 structure, form, format (estructura de una obra literaria). || **sagrada —,** REL. host. 7 **estar en —,** DEP. to be in form. 8 **de esta —,** in this way. 9 **de — que,** so that. 10 **de todas formas,** anyway; in any case. 11 **ponerse en —,** to get fit.
formación *s.f.* 1 formation (hecho y resultado de formar). 2 GEOL. formation. 3 MIL. formation. 4 training, education (educación). || 5 **— profesional,** technical training.
formal *adj.* 1 formal (perteneciente a la forma). 2 aware, conscious (consciente). 3 final, definitive (terminante). 4 (fig.) dependable, reliable (persona de fiar). 5 serious (serio): *una persona formal = a serious person.* 6 proper, correct (correcto).
formalidad *s.f.* 1 formality, seriousness (seriedad). 2 formality (acto reglamentario o legal): *es pura formalidad = it's purely a formality.* 3 (fig.) dependability, reliability (fiabilidad).
formalismo *s.m.* formalism.
formalista *s.m.* y *f.* formalist.
formalizar *v.t.* 1 to formalize (dar la última forma). 2 to settle, to fix (concretar). 3 to legalize, to formalize (revestir de fórmulas legales). || *v.pron.* 4 to become o get serious (ponerse serio).
formalmente *adv.* formally.
formar *v.t.* 1 to form (dar forma): *formar una asociación = to form an association.* 2 to make (hacer). 3 to shape, to form (una escultura). 4 to form, to make (un plan). 5 to educate (educar). 6 to bring up (criar). 7 MIL. to form up. 8 DEP. to line up (poner en orden). || 9 estar formado por, to be made up of. || *v.pron.* 10 to develop (irse desarrollando una persona).
formativo, -a *adj.* formative: *los años formativos = the formative years.*
formato *s.m.* 1 format (presentación). 2 size (tamaño).
fórmico *adj.* QUIM. formic: *ácido fórmico = formic acid.*
formidable *adj.* 1 formidable (muy temible): *un equipo formidable = a formidable team.* 2 (fig.) fantastic, magnificent, superb (estupendo). 3 enormous, huge, formidable (muy grande): *una montaña formidable = an enormous mountain.*
formol *s.m.* QUIM. formol.
formón *s.m.* chisel.
fórmula *s.f.* 1 formula (modelo para expresar o realizar una cosa). 2 QUIM. formula. 3 MED. prescription (receta). 4 MAT. formula. || 5 **— química,** QUIM. chemical formula.
formular *v.t.* 1 to formulate: *formular una idea = to formulate an idea.* 2 MED. to prescribe (recetar). 3 to express (expresar). 4 to make (una queja, una petición). 5 to pose, ask (una pregunta): *formular una pregunta = to pose a question.*
formulario *s.m.* 1 formulary (colección de fórmulas). 2 form (impreso).
formulismo *s.m.* 1 formulism. 2 (fam.) red tape (papeleo).
formulista *adj.* formulist.
fornicación *s.f.* (form.) fornication.
fornicador, -ora *s.m.* y *f.* fornicator.
fornicar *v.i.* to fornicate.
fornicario, -a *adj.* 1 fornicating. || *s.m.* y *f.* 2 fornicator.
fornido, -a *adj.* well-built, burly, strapping.
foro *s.m.* 1 DER. lawcourt, court of justice (tribunal). 2 HIST. forum. 3 back, back off the stage (fondo del escenario). 4 legal profession, bar (el ejercicio de la abogacía y magistratura).
forraje *s.m.* 1 forage, fodder (hierba que se da como pasto al ganado). 2 hotchpotch, jumble (mezcla de cosas sin importancia).
forrajear *v.i.* to forage.
forrajero, -a *adj.* fodder.
forrar *v.t.* 1 to line (ropa, cortinas, cajones, etc.). 2 to cover (cubrir). 3 to lag (tubería, depósito). 4 (fig.) **estar forrado,** to be rolling in money (tener mucho dinero). || *v.r.* 5 (fam.) to make a pile (enriquecerse). 6 to stuff oneself (comer mucho).
forro *s.m.* 1 lining (revestimiento interior). 2 cover (cubierta): *forro del sofá = sofa cover.* 3 cover (de un libro). || 4 **ni por el —,** not in the slightest, not in the least: *no me gusta ni por el forro = I don't like it in the slighest.*
fortachón, -a *adj.* well-built, burly, strapping (fornido).
fortalecer *v.t.* 1 to strengthen, to toughen (dar fuerza). 2 MIL. to fortify. || *v.r.* 3 to become stronger (ponerse más fuerte).
fortalecimiento *s.m.* 1 strengthening: *el fortalecimiento de la libra = the strengthening of the pound.* 2 MIL. fortification (fortificación).
fortaleza *s.f.* 1 MIL. fortress (recinto fortificado). 2 strength, force (fuerza). 3 resolution, fortitude (fuerza moral).
fortificación *s.f.* 1 MIL. fortification. 2 strengthening (acción de fortificar).
fortificado *adj.* 1 MIL. fortified. 2 strengthened.
fortificar *v.t.* 1 MIL. to fortify. 2 to strengthen (dar fuerza).
fortín *s.m.* MIL. small fort (fuerte pequeño).
fortuito, -a *adj.* fortuitous (imprevisto).
fortuna *s.f.* 1 fortune, luck (suerte). 2 FIN. fortune, wealth (hacienda). 3 storm (tempestad): *correr fortuna = to weather a storm.* || 4 **por —,** fortunately; luckily. 5 **probar —,** to try one's luck. 6 **tener la — de,** to have the good fortune to.
forúnculo *s.m.* MED. boil, (p.u.) furuncle (divieso).
forzado, -a *adj.* 1 forced (no cómodo o natural): *una risa forzada = a forced laugh.* 2 hard (duro). 3 contrived, strained, false (falso).
forzar *v.t.* 1 to force (emplear fuerza). 2 to break into, to force a way into (entrar por la fuerza). 3 to rape (violar a una mujer). 4 to make, to force (obligar): *me forzaron a hacerlo = they made me do it.*
forzosamente *adv.* 1 inevitably (inevitablemente). 2 necessarily (necesariamente). 3 no choice (sin elección): *tienes que venir forzosamente = you have no choice but to come.*
forzoso, -a *adj.* 1 inevitable (inevitable). 2 obligatory, compulsory (obligatorio). 3 forced (forzado): *aterrizaje forzoso = forced landing.* 4 necessary (necesario). || 5 **es — que,** it's inevitable that.
fosa *s.f.* 1 grave (sepultura): *fosa común = common grave.* 2 ANAT. fossa, cavity (cavidad). 3 hole, pit (hoyo). || 4 **— séptica,** septic tank.
fosal *s.m.* cemetery, graveyard (cementerio).
fosco, -a *adj.* obscure, dark (obscuro).
fosfato *s.m.* QUIM. phosphate.
fosforero, -a *s.m.* y *f.* 1 match seller (vendedor de cerillas). 2 matchbox (caja).
fosforescencia *s.f.* phosphorescence.
fosforescente *adj.* phosphorescent.
fosforescer o **fosforecer** *v.i.* to glow, (p.u.) to phosphoresce.
fosfórico, -a *adj.* QUIM. phosphoric.
fosforita *s.f.* QUIM. phosphorite.
fósforo *s.m.* 1 QUIM. phosphorus. 2 match (cerilla).
fosforoso, -a *adj.* phosphorous.

fósil *s.m.* y *adj.* **1** GEOL. fossil. **2** (fam.) fossil, old fogey (viejo).
fosilización *s.f.* GEOL. fossilization.
fosilizarse *v.r.* GEOL. to fossilize, to become fossilized.
foso *s.m.* **1** hole (hoyo). **2** pit (en el teatro). **3** MIL. moat, (p.u.) fosse (que rodea una fortaleza). **4** DEP. pit, sandpit (de arena).
foto *s.f.* photo, photograph, (fam.) snap (imagen): *sacar o tomar una foto = to take a photo.*
fotocopia *s.f.* photocopy.
fotocopiadora *s.f.* photocopier.
fotocopiar *v.t.* photocopy.
fotoelectricidad *s.f.* FIS. photoelectricity.
fotoeléctrico *adj.* FIS. photoelectric.
fotogénico, -a *adj.* photogenic.
fotograbado *s.m.* photogravure.
fotografía *s.f.* **1** photography (hobby). **2** photo, photograph, (fam.) snap (imagen): *sacar o tomar una fotografía = to take a photo.*
fotografiar *v.t.* to photograph, to take a photo.
fotográfico, -a *adj.* photographic.
fotógrafo, -a *s.m.* y *f.* photographer: *fotógrafo de prensa = newspaper photographer.*
fotólisis *s.f.* photolysis.
fotón *s.m.* FIS. photon.
fotosíntesis *s.f.* photosynthesis.
foxterrier *s.m.* fox terrier.
foxtrot *s.m.* fox-trot.
frac *s.m.* dress coat.
fracasado, -a *adj.* **1** failed, unsuccessful: *una tentativa fracasada = an unsuccessful attempt.* || *s.m.* **2** failure.
fracasar *v.i.* **1** to fail, to be unsuccessful: *el equipo fracasó = the team failed.* **2** to turn out badly, to come to grief (salir mal).
fracaso *s.m.* **1** failure: *la película es un fracaso = the film is a failure.* **2** disaster, debacle (desastre): *la fiesta fue un fracaso = the party was a disaster.* **3 — amoroso,** disappointment in love.
fracción *s.f.* **1** MAT. fraction. **2** fraction, part, fragment (parte). **3** POL. splinter group, break-away group, faction (de un partido). **4** division, breaking-up (acción de fraccionar). || **5 — impropia,** improper fraction. **6 — inversa,** inverse fraction. **7 — propia,** proper fraction.
fraccionamiento *s.m.* **1** division (división). **2** QUIM. fractionation.
fraccionar *v.t.* **1** to divide, to break up, to split up (dividir). **2** QUIM. to fractionate.
fraccionario, -a *adj.* MAT. fractional.
fractura *s.f.* **1** fracture, break (rotura). **2** MED. y GEOL. fracture: *fractura complicada = compound fracture.*
fracturar *v.t.* y *r.* MED. to break, to fracture.
fragancia *s.f.* fragrance.
fragante *adj.* **1** fragrant, sweet-smelling. **2** flagrant (flagrante).
fragata *s.f.* **1** MAR. frigate (embarcación). **2** frigate bird (ave).
frágil *adj.* **1** fragile, delicate (que se rompe con facilidad). **2** frail, fragile (de salud). **3** (fig.) weak, weak-willed (que cae fácilmente en pecado).
fragilidad *s.f.* **1** fragility, fraility (de salud). **2** delicacy, fragility (de cosas). **3** weakness (de carácter).
frágilmente *adv.* **1** fragilely (de salud). **2** delicately (de cosas). **3** weakly (de carácter).
fragmentación *s.f.* fragmentation.
fragmentar *v.t.* to fragment.
fragmentario, -a *adj.* fragmentary.
fragmento *s.m.* **1** fragment, piece (trozo pequeño). **2** passage (de un libro). **3** MUS. fragment, snatch (de una ópera, canción).
fragor *s.m.* **1** din, racket (estrépito). **2** crash (al romperse algo). **3** roar (del viento, un río, una tormenta, etc.).
fragoroso, -a *adj.* deafening, (fam.) ear-splitting.
fragosidad *s.f.* **1** unevnness, roughness (cualidad de fragoso). **2** high ground covered with undergrowth (lugar montañoso lleno de malezas).
fragoso, -a *adj.* **1** noisy (ruidoso). **2** tough, difficult (difícil). **3** rough, uneven (terreno). **4** brambly (con malezas).
fragua *s.f.* forge.
fraguado *s.m.* **1** forging (acción de forjar). **2** hardening (de cemento).
fraguar *v.t.* **1** to forge (forjar). **2** to mould (moldear). **3** to think up (idear). || *v.i.* **4** to harden, to set (endurecerse). **5** to hatch (un complot). **6** to concoct, to make up (mentiras).
fraile *s.m.* REL. friar, monk, brother.
frailecillo *s.m.* puffin (ave).
fraileño, -a, frailero, -a, frailesco, -a o **frailuno, -a** *adj.* (fam.) monkish.
frambuesa *s.f.* BOT. raspberry.
frambueso *s.m.* BOT. raspberry bush.
francachela *s.f.* big feed, feast, (fam.) nosh-up (comilona).
francamente *adv.* **1** frankly, honestly, candidly (con franqueza): *hablar francamente = to speal frankly.* **2** clearly, without doubt (sin duda).
francés, -esa *adj.* **1** French: *a la francesa = in the French way* o *manner.* || **2** (fam.) *marcharse a la francesa = to take French leave.* **3 tortilla francesa,** omelette. || *s.m.* **4** Frenchman (hombre francés). **5** French (idioma). || *s.f.* **6** Frenchwoman.
Francia *s.f.* GEOG. France.
francio *s.m.* QUIM. francium (elemento químico).
franciscano, -a *adj./s.m.* y *f.* REL. Franciscan.
francmasonería *s.f.* freemasonry (masonería).
franco, -a *adj.* **1** frank, sincere, candid (sincero). **2** open (abierto). **3** generous (generoso). **4** liberal (liberal). **5** free: *puerto franco = free port.* **6** Frankish (del pueblo germánico). || *s.m.* **7** Frank (del pueblo germánico). **8** Frankish (idioma). **9** FIN. franc (unidad monetaria).
francotirador, -ora *s.m.* y *f.* **1** MIL. sniper, sharpshooter (soldado). **2** (fig.) sharpshooter (persona que actúa aisladamente).
franela *s.f.* flannel (tela).
franja *s.f.* **1** border, trimming (adorno). **2** fringe (de flecos). **3** strip (de tierra). **4** band, strip (banda).
franqueable *adj.* **1** surmontable (un problema, un obstáculo). **2** crossable, fordable (un río).
franquear *v.t.* **1** to free, to exempt (librar de un pago). **2** to free, to open, to clear (abrir paso). **3** to frank, to pay postage (pagar en sellos). **4** to free, to set free (un esclavo). **5** to grant, to concede (conceder). || *v.pron.* **6** to give way, to give in (acceder a los deseos de otro). **7** to open one's heart (revelar la intimidad a otro).
franqueo *s.m.* **1** postage (cantidad a pagar). **2** stamping, franking (acción de franquear una carta).
franqueza *s.f.* **1** frankness, sincerity, candidness (sinceridad). **2** generosity (generosidad). **3** liberality (libertad).
franquía *s.f.* MAR. searoom.
franquicia *s.f.* exemption: *franquicia postal = exemption from postal charges.*
frasco *s.m.* flask, small bottle (vasija): *frasco de perfume = perfume bottle.*
frase *s.f.* **1** GRAM. sentence (conjunto de palabras): *frase compleja = complex sentence.* **2** expression, phrase (expresión): *frase hecha = set expression.* **3** MUS. phrase.
frasear *v.t.* e *i.* to phrase.
fraseo *s.m.* MUS. phrasing.
fraseología *s.f.* phraseology.
fraseológico, -a *adj.* phraseological.
fraternal *adj.* fraternal, brotherly.
fraternalmente *adv.* fraternally, brotherly.
fraternidad *s.f.* fraternity, brotherhood.
fraternizar *v.i.* to fraternize.
fraterno, -a *adj.* fraternal, brotherly.
fratricida *adj.* **1** fratricidal. || *s.m.* y *f.* **2** fratricide (persona).
fratricidio *s.m.* fratricide.
fraude *s.m.* **1** fraud, swindle. **2** (fig.) cheating, dishonesty.
fraudulento, -a *adj.* fraudulent.
fray *s.m.* REL. brother, friar (apóc. de fraile).
freático, -a *adj.* phreatic.
frecuencia *s.f.* **1** frequency. **2** ELEC. frequency: *alta frecuencia = high frequency.*
frecuentar *v.t.* **1** to frequent (ir a menudo a algún sitio). **2** to repeat, to do repeatedly (hacer algo muchas veces).
frecuente *adj.* **1** frequent. **2** common (corriente).
frecuentemente *adv.* frequently, often.
fregadero *s.m.* sink (de la cocina).
fregado, -a *adj.* **1** stubborn, obstinate (terco). **2** rogue, rascal (mala persona). **3** (Am.) stupid, foolish, silly (majadero). || *s.m.* **4** washing-up (de los platos). **5** washing (del suelo, las ventanas, etc.). **6** mess, mix-up (jaleo). **7** row, quarrel (riña).

fregar *v.t.* 1 to wash-up, to do the washing-up (platos). 2 to mop, to scrub (suelo). 3 to rub (frotar). 4 to scour (con estropajo). || *v.t.* y *pron.* (Am.) to annoy, to bother (molestar).
fregatriz o **fregona** *s.f.* 1 mop (para el suelo). 2 cleaning lady (mujer que friega). 3 (desp.) skivvy (sirvienta).
fregotear *v.t.* to give a quick clean (fregar rápido y mal).
fregoteo *s.m.* quick clean.
freidura *s.f.* frying.
freiduría *s.f.* fish shop.
freimiento *s.m.* frying.
freír *v.t.* y *r.* 1 to fry (cocer con aceite). *v.t.* 2 to annoy, to bother (molestar). 3 to harass, to pester (acosar). || 4 **al — será el reír,** to laugh on the other side of one's face.
fréjol *s.m.* BOT. kidney bean, French bean (judía).
frenar *v.t.* 1 MEC. to brake, to put the brake on. 2 (fig.) to check, to curb, to control (controlar).
frenazo *s.m.* 1 sudden braking 2 **dar un frenazo,** to slam the breaks on.
frenesí *s.m.* frenzy.
frenéticamente *adv.* frenziedly, frantically.
frenético, -a *adj.* frenzied, frantic.
frenillo *s.m.* 1 ANAT. frenum, fraenum. 2 (Am.) skill, ability (tino).
freno *s.m.* 1 MEC. brake (de coche, etc.): *freno de mano = handbrake.* 2 bit (de caballería). 3 (fig.) curb, check (moderación al obrar). || 4 **meter a uno en —,** to check o curb someone.
frente *s.f.* 1 ANAT. forehead, brow (parte superior de la cara). 2 face (cara): *cara a cara = face to face.* 3 front (parte anterior de una cosa). || 4 MIL. front (línea de combate). 5 POL. front: *frente popular = popular front.* 6 GEOG. front (que separa dos zonas de la atmósfera). 7 head (de una moneda). || 8 **al —,** in front (delante); forward (hacia delante). 9 **arrugar la —,** to frown. 10 **con la — levantada,** with one's head held high. 11 **en —,** in front; opposite: *la casa de enfrente = the house opposite.* 12 **— por —,** opposite; in front. 13 **hacer — a,** to stand up to, to face. 14 **ponerse al — de algo,** to take charge of something.
fresa *s.f.* 1 BOT. strawberry (fruto). 2 strawberry plant (planta). 3 TEC. milling cutter (herramienta). 4 drill (de dentista).
fresador, -ora *s.m.* y *f.* miller (persona).
fresadora *s.f.* MEC. milling machine.
fresal *s.m.* strawberry patch.
fresar *v.t.* TEC. to drill.
fresca *s.f.* 1 fresh air, cool air (aire fresco): *tomar la fresca = to get some fresh air.* 2 cool of the day (frescor del día). 3 cheeky remark o comment (dicho descarado).
frescachón, -ona *adj.* ruddy, robust, glowing with health.
frescales *s.m.* y *f.* (fam.) cheeky bugger, cheeky devil (persona desvergonzada).
fresco, -a *adj.* 1 fresh, cool (temperatura): *viento fresco = cool wind.* 2 fresh, new (reciente). 3 cold (agua). 4 cool, cold (bebida). 5 fresh (de buen aspecto). 6 cool (ropa ligera). 7 new-laid (huevos). 8 new, fresh (pan). 9 cool, calm (tranquilo). 10 cheeky, impudent (descarado). || *s.m.* 11 fresh air: *tomar el fresco = to get some fresh air.* 12 ART. fresco. 13 (Am.) drink, cool drink (bebida, bebida fresca). 14 (fam.) cheeky devil, cheeky person (persona descarada). || 15 **al —,** in the fresh o open air.
frescura *s.f.* 1 freshness, coolness (de temperatura, aspecto). 2 freshness (de comida, ropa, cara). 3 coolness, calmness (tranquilidad). 4 (fam.) cheek, nerve: *¡qué cara! = what a cheek!* 5 cheeky remark (dicho descarado).
fresneda *s.f.* BOT. ash grove.
fresno *s.m.* BOT. ash, ash tree.
fresón *s.m.* BOT. large strawberry.
fresquera *s.f.* food safe (armario para guardar frescos los alimentos).
fresquería *s.f.* (Am.) refreshment stall (donde se venden refrescos).
frialdad *s.f.* 1 coldness, coolness (de temperatura). 2 (fig.) coldness, indifference, unconcern (indiferencia). 3 frigidity (frigidez).
fríamente *adv.* coldly, cooly (con frialdad).
fricación *s.f.* V. fricción.
fricativo, -a *adj.* GRAM. fricative.
fricción *s.f.* 1 MEC. friction. 2 rubbing (friega). 3 MED. massage (masaje). 4 (fig.) friction, trouble: *fricción entre dos países = friction between two countries.*
friccionar *v.t.* to rub (frotar).
friega *s.f.* 1 rubbing (fricción). 2 massage (masaje). 3 (Am.) nuisance, annoyance (molestia). 4 (Am.) beating, thrashing (paliza).
frigidez *s.f.* 1 coldness, coolness (frialdad). 2 indifference, unconcern (indiferencia). 3 MED. frigidity (sexual).
frígido, -a *adj.* 1 MED. frigid. 2 (fig.) cold, frigid.
frigorífico *adj.* 1 refrigerating (que produce frío). || *s.m.* 2 refrigerator, (fam.) fridge (doméstico).
frijol, fríjol o **fréjol** *s.m.* BOT, kidney bean, French bean.
frío, -a *adj.* 1 cold: *una noche fría = a cold night.* 2 cold, indifferent, cool (indiferente). 3 impotent, cold (impotente). 4 unfriendly, cold, cool (recibimiento). || 8 **dejar —,** to leave cold. 9 **quedarse uno —,** to be left cold. || *s.m.* 5 cold: *hace frío = it's cold; coger frío = to catch cold; ¡qué frío! = isn't it cold!: tener frío = to be cold.* 6 indifference (indiferencia). 7 coldness (frialdad).
friolera *s.f.* mere nothing, trifle (insignificancia).
friolero *adj.* sensitive to the cold.
frisa *s.f.* 1 (Am.) frieze (de las telas). 2 (Am.) blanket (manta).
friso *s.m.* 1 ARQ. frieze (franja ornamental). 2 wainscot (parte inferior de la pared).
frisón, -ona *adj./s.m.* y *f.* Frisian (de Frisia).
fritada o **fritura** *s.f.* fry, (fam.) fry-up (conjunto de cosas fritas).
frito, -a *adj.* 1 fried: *pescado frito = fried fish; patatas fritas = chips.* || *s.m.* 2 (Am.) daily bread, food (la subsistencia diaria). || 3 (Am.) **estar —,** to be ruined; to be done in (arruinado). 4 (Am.) **ser —,** to be persistent (pertinaz).
frivolidad *s.f.* frivolity.
frívolo, -a *adj.* frivolous.
fronda *s.f.* 1 BOT. frond (hoja). || *s.pl.* 2 BOT. foliage, leaves (follaje).
frondosidad *s.f.* 1 BOT. leafiness (cualidad de frondoso). 2 foliage, leaves (follaje).
frondoso, -a *adj.* BOT. leafy: *un árbol frondoso = a leafy tree.*
frontal *adj.* 1 frontal. 2 REL. frontal (del altar).
frontera *s.f.* 1 border, frontier (entre dos Estados). 2 ARQ. façade.
fronterizo, -a *adj.* 1 atr. border, frontier: *pueblo fronterizo = border village.* 2 opposite, in front, facing (enfrente).
frontis o **frontispicio** *s.m.* 1 ARQ. façade (fachada). 2 face (cara). 3 frontispiece (de un libro). 4 frontispiece (frontón).
frontón *s.m.* 1 DEP. front wall (pared principal). 2 DEP. pelota court (cancha de pelota). 3 ARQ. pediment, fronton (remate triangular).
frotamiento *s.m.* 1 MEC. friction (fricción). 2 rubbing, rub (acción de frotar).
frotar *v.t.* y *r.* 1 to rub: *frotarse las manos = to rub one's hands.* 2 to strike (una cerilla).
fructífero, -a *adj.* 1 BOT. fruit-bearing, fructiferous, productive. 2 (fig.) fruitful: *un negocio fructífero = a fruitful business.*
fructificar *v.i.* 1 BOT. to bear fruit, to give fruit (dar fruto). 2 (fig.) to be fruitful, to produce a profit (ser útil).
fructuoso, -a *adj.* fruitful.
frugal *adj.* frugal: *una vida frugal = a frugal life.*
frugalidad *s.f.* frugality.
fruición *s.f.* delight, pleasure, joy (placer).
fruncido, -a *adj.* 1 frowning (la cara). 2 furrowed (la frente). 3 pleated (ropa). || *s.m.* 4 pleat, tuck (de la ropa, el papel).
fruncir *v.t.* 1 to frown (arrugar la frente). 2 to pleat, to gather (plegar). 3 to purse (los labios). || *v.r.* to feign false modesty, to pretend to be modest (fingir uno modestia).
fruslería *s.f.* trifle, bauble, (fam.) knick-knack (cosilla).
frustración *s.f.* frustration.
frustrar *v.t.* 1 to frustrate, to thwart. 2 to disappoint (decepcionar). || *v.r.* 3 to fail, to flop (fracasar).
fruta *s.f.* 1 fruit: *fruta del tiempo = fresh fruit.* || 2 **— seca,** dried fruit.
frutal *s.m.* 1 fruit tree (árbol). || *adj.* 2 fruit: *árbol frutal = fruit tree.*
frutería *s.f.* fruit shop, (p.u.) fruiterer's.

frutero, -a *s.m.* y *f.* 1 fruiterer, fruit-seller (vendedor). 2 fruit bowl, fruit dish (recipiente). || *adj.* 3 fruit: *plato frutero = fruit bowl o dish.*
fruticultor, -ora *s.m.* y *f.* (Am.) fruit-grower.
fruticultura *s.f.* fruit growing.
fruto *s.m.* 1 BOT. fruit: *dar fruto = to bear o give fruit.* 2 offspring, child (hijo). 3 result (resultado): *el fruto de su trabajo = the result of his work.* 4 benefit, profit (beneficio). || 5 (fig.) **dar –,** to be fruitful (ser provechoso). 6 **frutos secos,** dried fruit. 7 (fig.) **no dar –,** to be fruitless. 8 **sacar – de algo,** to profit from.
fucsia *s.f.* BOT. fuchsia.
fuego *s.m.* 1 fire: *encender un fuego = to light a fire.* 2 fire (incendio, materia en combustión). 3 light (lumbre): *¿tienes fuego? = have you got a light?* 4 passion, fire (pasión). 5 MIL. fire (de un arma). 6 MAR. beacon. 7 home (hogar). || *s.pl.* 8 fireworks (artificiales). || 9 **¡alto el –!,** cease fire! 10 **apagar el –,** MIL. to silence the enemy guns. 11 **atizar el –,** (fam.) to stir up trouble. 12 **echar – por los ojos,** to look daggers. 13 **– graneado,** MIL. heavy fire. 14 **¡–!,** fire! 16 **hacer –,** to shoot; to fire. 16 **hervir a – lento,** to simmer. 17 (fig.) **jugar con –,** to play with fire. 18 **labrar a –,** to brand. 19 **pasar a sangre y –,** to destroy, to devastate. 20 **pegar –,** to set fire; to set on fire. 21 **poner las manos en el –,** to stake one's life. 22 **romper el –,** to open fire.
fuel o **fuel-oil** *s.m.* paraffin, fuel oil.
fuelle *s.m.* 1 bellows (para obtener corrientes de aire). 2 accordion pleat (pliegue). 3 bag (de gaita). 4 folding hood (de coche).
fuente *s.f.* 1 spring (manantial de agua). 2 fountain (construcción): *fuente de beber = drinking fountain.* 3 dish (plato grande). 4 source: *fuente del río = source of a river.* 5 (fig.) source, origin: *la fuente de su riqueza = the source of his wealth.* 6 REL. font (pila bautismal). || 7 **beber en buenas fuentes,** to be well-informed. 8 **de – desconocida,** from an unknown source. 9 **de fuentes informadas,** from a reliable source.
fuera *adv.* 1 outside: *estar fuera en el jardín = to be outside in the garden.* 2 out: *tirar fuera = to throw out; comer fuera = to eat out.* 3 abroad (en el extranjero). 4 out (sin relación): *fuera del contexto = out of context.* || 5 **de –,** outside: *la parte de fuera = the outside part.* 6 **desde –, a)** from abroad (desde el extranjero); **b)** from outside (desde el exterior). 7 **estar –, a)** to be away (de viaje); **b)** to be out (fuera de casa); **c)** DEP. to be out. 8 **¡–!,** get out!; out! 9 DEP. **jugar –,** to play away from home. 10 **por –,** on the outside. || *prep.* 11 fuera de, outside: *fuera de la ciudad = outside the city; fuera de la puerta = outside the door.* 12 out of: *fuera de peligro = out of danger.* || 13 **– de alcance,** out of reach. 14 **– de duda,** beyond doubt. 15 **– de lugar,** out of place. 16 **– de moda,** out of fashion. 17 **– de serie,** out of the ordinary; exceptional.
fuero *s.m.* 1 power (poder): *fuero eclesiástico = eclesiastical power.* 2 municipal charter (ley municipal). 3 privilege (privilegio). 4 arrogance, vanity (presunción). || 5 **a –,** according to the law. 6 **– de la conciencia,** freedom of conscience.
fuerte *adj.* 1 strong: *una mesa fuerte = a strong table.* 2 strong (corriente, viento, voluntad, bebida, olor, creencia, sabor, moneda, etc.). 3 robust, tough, hard (robusto). 4 loud (música, voz, sonido, ruido). 5 great, intense (dolor, calor, frío). 6 grave (crisis). 7 vigorous, strenuous (ejercicio). 8 rough, harduous, difficult (terreno). 9 big, fuerte (comida). 10 strong (palabras). 11 hard, heavy (golpe). 12 intense (intenso). 13 hard (duro): *un examen fuerte = a hard exam.* || 14 MIL. fort, fortress (lugar fortificado). 15 (fig.) strong point, forte (punto fuerte). 16 MUS. forte || *adv.* 17 hard (duro): *jugar* o *trabajar fuerte = to play* o *work hard.* 18 loudly (alto): *cantar* o *hablar fuerte = to sing* o *talk loudly.* 19 heavily (mucho): *fumar* o *beber fuerte = to smoke* o *drink heavily.* 20 **comer –,** to eat a lot. 21 **hacerse –,** to get o become stronger. 22 **¡más –!, a)** speak up! (a un orador); **b)** turn it up! (la música). 23 **pegar –,** to hit hard. 24 **plato –,** main course. 25 **ser – en inglés,** to be very good at/in English.
fuertemente *adv.* 1 strongly (con fuerza). 2 loudly (más alto): *cantar fuertemente = to sing loudly.*
fuerza *s.f.* 1 strength: *la fuerza de la cuerda = the strength of the rope.* 2 force: *utilizar fuerza = to use force.* 3 power (poder): *la fuerza del coche = the power of the car.* 4 resistence (resistencia). 5 FIS. force: *fuerza de gravedad = force of gravity.* 6 ELEC. current, energy, power (corriente). 7 (fig.) force, strength (de carácter, un argumento). 8 violence, force (violencia). || *pl.* 9 MIL. forces: *las fuerzas armadas = the armed forces.* || 10 **a – de,** by force of; by dint of. 11 **a la –,** of necessity. 12 **con todas mis fuerzas,** with all my might. 13 **– de la costumbre,** force of custom. 14 DER. **– mayor,** act of God. 15 **fuerzas aéreas,** Air Force. 16 **por –, a)** by force (con violencia); **b)** of necessity (por necesidad). 17 **recurrir a la –,** to resort to force. 18 **rendirse a la –,** to give in to force. 19 **restar fuerzas,** to weaken. 20 **sacar fuerzas de flaqueza,** to make a big effort. 21 **ser –,** to be necessary: *es fuerza coger el tren = it's necessary to catch the train.* 22 **sin usar –,** without using force. 23 **tener fuerzas para,** to have the strength to.
fuga *s.f.* 1 flight, escape (huida precipitada): *fuga de la cárcel = escape from prison.* 2 escape, leak (de un gas o líquido). 3 MUS. fugue. || 4 **ponerse en –,** to take flight; to flee.
fugacidad *s.f.* fugacity.
fugarse *v.r.* 1 to flee, to escape: *fugarse del país = to flee from the country.* 2 to run away (huir): *fugarse de casa = to run away from home.* 3 to elope (amantes).
fugaz *adj.* 1 fleeting, short-lived, brief (de corta duración). || 2 **estrella –,** shooting star.
fugitivo, -a *s.m.* y *f.* 1 fugitive. || *adj.* 2 fleeting, short-lived, brief (fugaz). 3 fleeting, fugitive (que se fuga).
ful *adj.* useless, worthless (de poco valor).
fulano, -a *s.m.* y *f.* what's his name, so-and-so: *me lo dijo fulano = what's his name told me.*
fulero, -a *adj.* 1 faulty, badly made (defectuoso). 2 shoddy, slapdash (chapucero).
fulgente *adj.* brilliant, dazzling (muy brillante).
fúlgido, -a *adj.* brillant, dazzling (muy brillante).
fulgor *a.m.* brillance, radiance.
fulgurante *adj.* shining, bright, brillant.
fulgurar *v.i.* to shine, to glow (brillar).
fulminación *s.f.* fulmination.
fulminador *s.m.* fulminator.
fulminante *adj.* 1 fulminating (que fulmina): *pólvora fulminante = fulminating powder.* 2 MED. fulminant. 3 (fam.) fantastic, terrific, splendid (un éxito). || *s.m.* 4 cap (cápsula). 5 fuse, detonator (mecha).
fulminar *v.t.* 1 to fulminate, to thunder (arrojar contra alguien). 2 to strike by lightning (dar muerte los rayos). || 3 (fig.) fulminar con la mirada, to look daggers.
fullería *s.f.* cheating, cardsharping (acto del tramposo en las cartas). 2 trick (trampa). 3 astuteness, guile (astucia).
fumadero *s.m.* 1 smoking room. || 2 **– de opio,** smoking den.
fumador, -ora *s.m.* y *f.* 1 smoker. || *adj.* 2 smoking. || 3 **no –,** non-smoker.
fumar *v.i.* y *t.* 1 to smoke. || 2 **– en pipa,** to smoke a pipe. 3 **papel de –,** cigarette paper. 4 **se prohíbe –,** no smoking. || *v.pron.* 5 to spend (gastar). 6 to waste, to squander (derrochar). 7 to miss (faltar a una obligación).
fumarola *s.f.* fumarole.
fumigación *s.f.* fumigation.
fumigador, -ora *adj.* y *s.m.* fumigator.
fumigar *v.t.* to fumigate.
funambulismo *s.m.* tightrope walking.
funámbulo, -a *s.m.* y *f.* tightrope walker.
función *s.f.* 1 function: *la función de la prensa = the function of the press.* 2 duty, function: *las funciones del director = the duties of the director.* 3 MED. function (actividad de un órgano o célula). 4 show, performance (espectáculo). 5 party (fiesta). 6 GRAM. function. 7 MAT. function. || 8 **en – de,** in terms of. 9 **entrar en funciones,** to take up one's duties. 10 **presidente en funciones,** acting president.
funcional *adj.* functional.

funcionamiento *s.m.* **1** functioning (acción de funcionar). **2** MEC. operation, working (de una máquina). **3** performance: *el funcionamiento del coche = the performance of the car.* || **4 entrar en —,** to come into operation. **5 mal —,** malfunction. **6 poner en —,** to put into operation.
funcionar *v.t.* **1** to work, to go, to function: *la radio no funciona = the radio doesn't work.* || **2 "no funciona",** "out of order".
funcionario, -a *s.m.* y *f.* **1** civil servant, official (del estado). || **2 — público,** public official.
funda *s.f.* **1** cover (cubierta). **2** case: *funda de almohada = pillowcase, pillowslip.* **3** case (de gafas, violín). **4** sheath (de espada). || **5 — de pistola,** holster.
fundación *s.f.* foundation.
fundacional *adj.* constituent.
fundador, -ora *s.m.* y *f.* founder.
fundamental *adj.* fundamental.
fundamentalmente *adv.* fundamentally.
fundamentar *v.t.* **1** to found (establecer). **2** to lay the foundations (establecer las bases). || *v.r.* **3** to be based.
fundamento *s.m.* **1** foundation (cimiento de un edificio). **2** seriousness (seriedad). **3** motive, cause (motivo). **4** (fig.) basis, foundation (base). || *pl.* **5** fundamentals (nociones elementales).
fundar *v.t.* **1** to found (empezar a construir). **2** to, build (edificar). **3** to establish, to create (establecer). **4** to base (apoyar con pruebas).
fundición *s.f.* **1** foundry, smelting plant (donde se funde). **2** melting (acción de fundir). **3** smelting (de los metales). || **4 — de acero,** steel foundry. **5 — de hierro,** iron foundry.
fundido *adj.* melted: *queso fundido = melted cheese.*
fundidor *s.m.* founder, smelter.
fundir *v.t.* **1** to cast, to found (metales). **2** to melt (convertir en líquido). || *v.t.* y *r.* **3** to melt (derretir). **4** to merge (unir intereses, ideas, etc.). || *v.r.* **5** (Am.) to ruin oneself (arruinarse).
fúnebre *adj.* **1** *atr.* funeral. **2** (fig.) funereal, mournful (triste).
funeral *s.m.* **1** funeral (ceremonia). **2** funeral (exequias).
funerala (a la) *adv.* with reversed arms.
funeraria *s.f.* undertaker's (empresa).
funerario *adj. atr.* funeral.
funesto, -a *adj.* **1** sad (triste). **2** fatal, ill-fated (desgraciado).
fungible *adj.* fungible.
fungicida *s.f.* **1** fungicide. || *adj.* **2** fungicidal.
funicular *s.m.* y *adj.* funicular.
furcia *s.f.* (desp.) tart, pro, whore (prostituta).
furgón *s.m.* **1** wagon, truck (vehículo largo). **2** van, goods wagon (de tren).
furgoneta *s.f.* van.
furia *s.f.* **1** fury (divinidad romana). **2** fury, rage (enfado violento). **3** frenzy, rage (ataque de locura). **4** fury (de los elementos): *la furia del mar = the fury of the sea.* **5** hurry (prisa): *a la furia = like fury.*
furibundo, -a *adj.* furious (con furia).
furioso, -a *adj.* furious: *ponerse furioso = to get furious.*
furor *s.m.* **1** fury, rage (furia). **2** anger, fury (cólera). **3** (fig.) rage: *hacer furor = to be all the rage.*
furriel *s.m.* quartermaster.
furtivamente *adv.* furtively, slyly.
furúnculo *s.m.* MED. boil.
furtivo, -a *adj.* furtive, sly.
fusa *s.f.* MUS. demisemiquaver.
fuselaje *s.m.* fuselage.
fusible *adj.* **1** fusible. || *s.m.* **2** ELEC. fuse.
fusil *s.m.* rifle, gun.
fusilamiento *s.m.* shooting, execution.
fusilar *v.t.* to shoot, to execute.
fusilazo *s.m.* rifle, gun shot.
fusión *s.f.* **1** fusion, melting (de metales). **2** melting (de líquidos). **3** joining, uniting (unión). **4** merger (de empresas). **5** coming together, joining (de intereses, ideas, etc.). || **6 — nuclear,** nuclear fusion.
fusionar *v.t.* y *pron.* **1** COM. to merge. **2** to fuse (unir).
fusta *s.f.* **1** whip, riding whip (látigo). **2** twigs (leña delgada).
fuste *s.m.* **1** MED. shaft (columna). **2** wood (madera). **3** saddletree (de la silla de montar). **4** substance, essence (consistencia).
fustigación *s.f.* whipping.
fustigar *v.t.* **1** to whip (azotar). **2** (fig.) to censure, to upbraid (censurar con dureza).
fútbol *s.m.* DEP. football, soccer.
futbolista *s.m.* y *f.* footballer, football player.
fútil *adj.* trivial, unimportant (sin importancia).
futilidad *s.f.* triviality, unimportance.
futurista *s.m.* y *f.* **1** futurist. || *adj.* **2** futuristic.
futuro, -a *adj.* **1** future: *los años futuros = the future years.* || *s.m.* **2** future: *en el futuro = in the future.* **3** GRAM. future. **4** (fam.) fiancé (novio). || *s.m.pl.* **5** COM. futures.

g, G *s.c.* g, G (octava letra del alfabeto español).
gabacho, -a *adj.* 1 GEOG. Pyrenean. 2 French (francés). || *s.m.* y *f.* 3 Pyrenean (persona). 4 frenchified Spanish (idioma).
gabán *s.m.* 1 overcoat (abrigo). 2 sleeved cape (capote con mangas). 3 (Am.) sack (saco). 4 (Am.) jacket, coat (chaqueta).
gabardina *s.f.* 1 raincoat, gabardine, (fam.) mac (impermeable). 2 gabardine (tela).
gabarra *s.f.* barge (embarcación).
gabela *s.f.* 1 tax (impuesto). 2 duty, obligation (obligación).
gabinete *s.m.* 1 POL. cabinet (Consejo de ministros). 2 room (sala): *gabinete de lectura = reading room.* 3 study (sala de estudio). 4 laboratory (laboratorio). 5 museum (museo). || **6 — de consulta,** consulting room.
gacela *s.f.* ZOOL. gazelle.
gaceta *s.f.* 1 gazette (publicación). 2 official gazette (del Estado).
gacetilla *s.f.* 1 news in brief (sección de noticias breves). 2 gossip (persona chismosa).
gacha *s.f.* 1 pap, mush (masa muy blanda). 2 (Am.) bowl (cuenco). || *pl.* 3 porridge (comida). 4 flattery (halagos).
gacho, -a *adj.* 1 drooping, floppy (bigote, orejas). 2 bent, bowed (cabeza). 3 down-curved (cuernos). 4 floppy (sombrero).
gachupín *s.m.* 1 Spanish immigrant (español que se establece en América).
gaditano, -a *adj.* 1 of o from Cádiz. || *s.m.* y *f.* 2 inhabitant of Cádiz.
gafas *s.f.pl.* 1 glasses (anteojos): *llevar gafas = to wear glasses.* 2 goggles (de moto, nadar, esquiar). 3 clamp (grapa). || **4 — de sol,** sunglasses.
gafe *s.m.* 1 jinx (que trae mala suerte). 2 disaster (desastre): *soy más gafe... = I'm a complete disaster.* || *adj.* 3 jinxed.
gag *s.m.* gag.
gago, -a *s.m.* y *f.* stutterer, stammerer (tartamudo).
gaguear *v.i.* (Am.) to stutter, to stammer (tartamudear).
gaita *s.f.* 1 MUS. bagpipe (instrumento de viento). 2 nuisance, (fam.) drag (molestia). || *s.m.* y *f.* 3 (Am.) Galician (gallego). 4 (Am.) useless thing (maula). || **5 templar gaitas,** to calm someone down.
gaitero, -a *s.m.* y *f.* 1 MUS. bagpiper, bagpipe player. 2 buffoon, clown (bufo). || *adj.* 3 flashy, showy, gaudy (chillón). 4 clownish (bufo).
gaje *s.m.* 1 salary, wage (sueldo). || 2 **gajes del oficio,** drawbacks; snags.
gajo *s.m.* 1 segment, slice (divisiones de algunos frutos). 2 branch (rama de árbol). 3 prong (de las horcas, bieldos, etc.). 4 bunch (racimo de uvas). 5 lobe (lóbulo).
gala *s.f.* 1 gala (espectáculo musical). 2 best dress, best clothes (vestido): *ir de gala = to be dressed up.* 3 cream (lo más selecto). 4 (Am.) tip (propina). || **5 hacer — de,** to show off; to boast about.
galaico, -a *adj.* Galician (gallego).
galán *s.m.* 1 attractive man (hombre atractivo). 2 suitor (el que corteja a una mujer). 3 leading man, male lead (en el teatro). || 4 BOT. **— de noche,** night jasmine.
galano, -a *adj.* 1 elegant, smart (elegante). 2 pleasant, charming (agradable). 3 beautiful (hermoso). 4 mottled (vaca de varios colores).
galante *adj.* 1 gallant (cortés con las mujeres). 2 flirtatious (que gusta de requiebros).
galanteador *adj.* flattering (aficionado a galantear a las mujeres).
galantear *v.t.* 1 to court, to woo (cortejar). 2 to win the heart of (enamorar). 3 to flatter (requebrar).
galantemente *adv.* gallantly.
galanteo *s.m.* 1 courting, wooing (acción de cortejar). 2 flattery (requiebro). 3 flirting (coqueteo).
galantería *s.f.* 1 gallantry (cualidad de galante). 2 kindness (amabilidad). 3 politeness (cortesía). 4 elegance (elegancia). 5 generosity (generosidad). 6 gallant act (hecho galante).
galanura *s.f.* 1 elegance (elegancia). 2 charm (encanto).
galápago *s.m.* 1 ZOOL. tortoise. 2 AGR. sole (del arado). 3 brick mould (molde de ladrillos). 4 light saddle (silla de montar). 5 TEC. ingot (lingote).
galardón *s.m.* 1 prize (premio). 2 reward (recompensa).
galardonar *v.t.* 1 LIT. to award a prize (dar un premio). 2 to reward, to recompense (recompensar).
galaxia *s.f.* 1 ASTR. galaxy (grupo de estrellas). 2 milky way (Vía Láctea).
galbana *s.f.* laziness, idleness, slackness (pereza).
galbanoso, -a *adj.* lazy, idle (perezoso).
galena *s.f.* MIN. lead sulphide, galena.
galeno *s.m.* doctor (médico).
galeón *s.m.* MAR. galleon.
galeote *s.m.* galley slave (condenado a remar en galeras).
galera *s.f.* 1 MAR. galley (nave). 2 covered wagon (carro). 3 women's prison (cárcel de mujeres). 4 galley (de imprenta). 5 (Am.) top hat (sombrero de copa alta). 6 (Am.) bowler hat (sombrero hongo). || *pl.* 7 galleys: *condenar a galeras = to condemn to the galleys.*
galerada *s.f.* 1 galley proof (prueba de imprenta). 2 galley (composición tipográfica). 3 wagonload (carga de una galera).
galería *s.f.* 1 gallery (de pinturas). 2 gallery (en una casa). 3 gallery (de una mina). 4 passage (paso). 5 gallery, (fam.) gods (en un teatro). 6 pelmet (bastidor para colgar cortinas). 7 (fig.) gallery (gente de gusto vulgar). || **8 — de tiro,**

shooting gallery. **9 — de viento,** wind tunnel.

galés, -esa *adj.* 1 Welsh. || *s.m.* 2 Welsh (idioma). || *s.m.* y *f.* 3 Welshman (hombre). 4 Welshwoman (mujer).

galgo *s.m.* 1 ZOOL. greyhound (perro). || *adj.* 2 fast, quick (rápido): *correr como un galgo = to run like the wind.* 3 (Am.) sweet-toothed (goloso). || **4 ¡échale un —!,** fat chance!

galga *s.f.* boulder (piedra grande).

gálibo *s.m.* TEC. gauge.

galicismo *s.m.* gallicism.

galimatías *s.m.* gibberish, double-Dutch, nonsense (lenguaje confuso).

galio *s.m.* gallium (metal).

galo, -a *adj.* 1 HIST. Gallic. || *s.m.* y *f.* 2 Gaul.

galón *s.m.* 1 gallon (medida inglesa). 2 braid (cinta). 3 MIL. stripe.

galopada *s.f.* gallop.

galopante *adj.* 1 galloping. 2 MED. galloping.

galopar *v.i.* to gallop.

galope *s.m.* 1 gallop. || **2 a —, a)** at a gallop (caballo); **b)** quickly, in a rush (persona). **3 medio —,** canter.

galopín *s.m.* 1 urchin, waif (muchacho sucio y mal vestido). 2 rogue, scoundrel (pícaro). 3 scullion, kitchen boy (pinche).

galvanismo *s.m.* FIS. galvanism.

galvanización *s.f.* FIS. galvanization.

galvanizar *v.t.* FIS. to galvanize.

galvanómetro *s.m.* FIS. galvanometer.

galvanoplastia *s.f.* galvanoplasty.

gallardete *s.m.* pennant.

gallardía *s.f.* 1 elegance, grace (elegancia). 2 bravery, valour (valor). 3 nobleness (nobleza).

gallardo, -a *adj.* 1 elegant, smart (elegante). 2 brave, valient (valiente). 3 excellent, splendid (excelente).

gallear *v.t.* 1 to tread (cubrir el gallo a la gallina). || *v.i.* 2 to raise one's voice (alzar la voz). 3 to stand out, to excel (destacar).

gallegada *s.f.* 1 Galician dance (baile gallego). 2 Galician singing and music (música y cante gallego).

gallego, -a *adj.* 1 Galician. || *s.m.* 2 Galician (idioma). 3 horth-west wind (viento noroeste). || *s.m.* y *f.* 4 Galician (persona).

galleguismo *s.m.* Galician word o expression.

galleta *s.f.* 1 biscuit (bizcocho). 2 slap (bofetada). 3 nuts (carbón). || **4 — de perro,** dog biscuit.

galletero *s.m.* biscuit tin, biscuit barrel (recipiente).

gallina *s.f.* 1 chicken, hen (hembra del gallo). 2 coward, (fam.) chicken (persona cobarde). || **3 acostarse con las gallinas,** to go to bed early. **4 estar como — en corral ajeno,** to be like a fish out of water. **5 — ciega,** blindman's buff (juego). **6 — clueca,** broody hen. **7 — de agua,** coot. **8 — de Guinea,** guinea fowl. **9 — ponedora,** laying hen. **10 matar la — de los huevos de oro,** to kill the goose that lays the golden eggs.

gallináceo, -a *adj.* 1 ZOOL. gallinaceous. || *s.f.* 2 gallinacean.

gallinero, -a *s.m.* y *f.* 1 chicken farmer (el que cría gallinas). 2 poultry dealer (el que vende gallinas). || *s.m.* 3 henhouse, coop (lugar donde se crían gallinas). 4 (fam.) gods (parte alta de un teatro o cine).

gallineta *s.f.* 1 ZOOL. woodcock (chocha). 2 (Am.) guinea fowl (gallina de Guinea).

gallito *s.m.* (fam.) top dog, cock of the walk (el que domina o sobresale el que gallea).

gallo *s.m.* 1 ZOOL. cock, cockerel (ave). 2 John Dory, dory (pez). 3 wrong note, (fam.) squawk (nota desafinada). 4 boss (persona mandona). 5 brave man (hombre valiente). || **6 en menos que canta un —,** in a flash. **7 misa de —,** midnight mass. **8 peso —,** DEP. bantamweight. **9 tener mucho —,** to be cocky.

gama *s.f.* 1 MUS. scale (scala). 2 (fig.) range, scale. 3 ZOOL. doe.

gamada *adj. f.* **cruz —,** swastika.

gamba *s.f.* 1 ZOOL. prawn. 2 (Am.) 100 peso note (billete de cien pesos).

gamberrada *s.f.* senseless act of hooliganism.

gamberrismo *s.m.* hooliganism, loutishness.

gamberro, -a *s.m.* 1 lout, hooligan, yob. || *adj.* 2 loutish, yobbish.

gambeta *s.f.* 1 cross step (paso cruzado). 2 prance (de caballo). 3 DEP. dummy (finta).

gameto *s.m.* BIOL. gamete.

gamma *s.f.* gamma (letra griega).

gamo *s.m.* ZOOL. fallow deer.

gamuza *s.f.* 1 ZOOL. chamois (animal). 2 chamois leather (piel).

gana *s.f.* 1 desire, wish (deseo). 2 inclination (inclinación). 3 will (voluntad). 4 appetite (apetito). || **5 darle a uno la —,** to feel like: *no me da la gana = I don't feel like it.* **6 de buena —,** willingly. **7 de mala —,** reluctantly; unwillingly. **8 quedarse con las ganas,** to go without. **9 tener ganas,** to feel like; to fancy: *tengo ganas de bañarme = I feel like having a swim.*

ganadería *s.f.* 1 cattle breeding (cría de ganado). 2 cattle, livestock (ganado).

ganadero, -a *s.m.* y *f.* 1 cattle breeder (propietario). || *adj.* 2 cattle, livestock (referente a los animales). 3 cattle breeding (cría de ganado).

ganado *s.m.* 1 cattle, livestock (conjunto de animales). || **2 — de cerda,** pigs. **3 — mayor,** horses and cows. **4 — menor,** sheep and goats. **5 — vacuno,** cattle.

ganador, -ora *s.m.* y *F.* 1 winner: *el ganador de la copa = the cup winner.* || *adj.* 2 winning: *el equipo ganador = the winning team.*

ganancia *s.f.* 1 COM. profit (beneficio): *sacar* o *obtener ganancia = to make a profit.* || **2 ganancias y pérdidas,** profit and loss. **3 no te arriendo la ganancia,** I wouldn't like to be in your shoes.

ganancial *adj.* 1 profit. || 2 DER. **bienes gananciales,** acquest; (fam.) common property acquired during a marriage.

ganar *v.t.* 1 to earn, to make (dinero): *ganar un buen sueldo = to earn a good salary.* 2 to win (un partido, premio, apuesta, batalla, etc.). 3 to beat, to defeat (vencer): *les ganamos 3-0 = we beat them 3-0.* 4 MIL. to take, to capture (conquistar). 5 to reach, to make (llegar): *al final llegaron a ganar la orilla = at last they managed to reach the bank.* 6 to win over (captarse la voluntad de alguien). 7 to outstrip (aventajar a alguien). 8 to get, to obtain (obtener). || *v.t.* y *pron.* 9 to win (fama, favor, honra). || *v.i.* 10 to get better, to improve (mejorar): *el enfermo va ganando = the patient is getting better.* || *v.pron.* 11 to earn: *ganarse la vida = to earn one's living.* 12 to deserve (merecer). || **13 — el premio gordo,** to win first prize. **14 — terreno,** to gain ground. **15 — tiempo,** to gain time.

ganchillo *s.m.* 1 crochet needle (aguja de gancho). 2 crochet work (labor de ganchillo). 3 hairpin (horquilla).

gancho *s.m.* 1 hook (para colgar o agarrar). 2 hairpin (horquilla). 3 charm, attractiveness (atractivo). 4 (Am.) go-between (intermediario): **hacer de —,** to play the match-maker. 5 DEP. hook (boxeo). || **6 echar el —,** to hook; to land.

gandul, -a *adj.* 1 lazy, idle (vago). || *s.m.* y *f.* 2 (fam.) lazy-bones, idler.

gandulear *v.i.* to laze about, to lie around.

gandulería *s.f.* laziness, idleness.

ganga *s.f.* 1 COM. bargain (cosa barata). 2 ZOOL. sandgrouse (ave). 3 MIN. gangue (materia inútil de un mineral). || **4 precio de —,** bargain price.

ganglio *s.m.* MED. ganglion.

gangosidad *s.f.* nasality.

gangoso, -a *adj.* nasal (voz).

gangrena o **cangrena** *s.f.* MED. gangrene.

gangrenarse *v.r.* MED. to become o get gangrenous.

gangrenoso, -a *adj.* MED. gangrenous.

gángster *s.m.* gangster.

gangsterismo *s.m.* gangsterism.

ganguear *v.i.* to speak through one's nose.

gangueo *s.m.* nasal accent.

gansa *s.f.* 1 ZOOL. goose (ave). 2 clot, dope, fool (tonta).

gansada *s.f.* 1 daft o silly thing to say (cosa tonta que se dice). 2 daft o silly thing to do (cosa tonta que se hace).

ganso *s.m.* 1 ZOOL. gander (ave). 2 dope, clot, fool (tonto). || **3 hacer el —,** to play the fool. 4 MIL. **paso de —,** goose step.

ganzúa *s.f.* picklock (garfio).

gañán *s.m.* 1 labourer (mozo de labranza). 2 (desp.) big cloud, brute (hombre tosco).

garabatear *v.t.* 1 to scrawl, to scribble (escribir mal). 2 to throw o sling a hook

(tirar un garabato). **3** (fam.) to beat about the bush (hablar con rodeos).
garabateo *s.m.* **1** scrawling, scribbling (acción de escribir mal). **2** beating about the bush (hablando con rodeos).
garabato *s.m.* **1** hook (gancho). **2** scrawl, scribble (letra mal hecha). **3** grace, elegance (garbo).
garaje *s.m.* garage.
garambaina *s.f.* **1** cheap trinket (adorno de mal gusto). **2** scrawl, scribble (garabateo).
garante *adj.* **1** responsible (responsable). || *s.m.* y *f.* **2** guarantor.
garantía *s.f.* **1** guarantee: *garantía de dos años = two-year guarantee.* **2** DER. security (fianza). || **3 bajo –,** under guarantee. **4 certificado de –,** guarantee. **5 garantías constitucionales,** constitutional guarantees.
garantizar *v.t.* **1** to guarantee: *garantizar un coche = to guarantee a car.* **2** to assure, to guarantee (asegurar). **3** DER. to vouch for (avalar).
garañón *s.m.* **1** ZOOL. stud jackass (asno). **2** (Am.) stallion (caballo semental).
garapiña o **garrapiña** *s.f.* **1** frozen lumps of liquid (líquido congelado en grumos). **2** (Am.) iced pineapple drink (refresco de piña).
garapiñado, -a *adj.* frozen (helado).
garapiñar *v.t.* **1** to coat (las almendras). **2** to freeze (helar). **3** to clot (nata). **4** to ice (tartas).
garbancero, -a *adj.* **1** chick-pea (de los garbanzos): *terreno garbancero = chick-pea land.* || *s.m.* y *f.* **2** chick-pea dealer (tratante de garbanzos).
garbanzal *s.m.* chick-pea field (campo).
garbanzo *s.m.* BOT. chick-pea.
garbear *v.i.* **1** to affect elegance (aparentar garbo). **2** to get along, to manage (buscarse la vida). **3** to go for a stroll (pasear). || *v.t.* **4** to rob, (fam.) to pinch (robar).
garbeo *s.m.* walk, stroll (paseo).
garbo *s.m.* **1** grace, elegance (elegancia de movimientos y andares). **2** grace (gracia). **3** liberality, tolerance (liberalidad).
garboso, -a *adj.* **1** graceful, elegant (elegante). **2** graceful (al andar). **3** liberal, tolerant (liberal). **4** generous (generoso).
gardenia *s.f.* BOT. gardenia.
garete *s.m.* MAR. ir/irse al –, to drift, to be adrift.
garfio *s.m.* hook (gancho).
gargajear *v.i.* to spit (escupir).
gargajo *s.m.* spit, phlegm (flema).
garganta *s.f.* **1** ANAT. throat (parte anterior del cuello). **2** throat, gullet (parte interior). **3** GEOG. pass, gorge (paso). **4** ANAT. instep (del pie).
gargantear *v.i.* MUS. to warble, to trill.
gargantilla *s.f.* **1** necklace (collar). **2** bead (cuenta de collar).
gárgaras *s.f.pl.* **1** gargle, gargling: *hacer gárgaras = to gargle.* || **2 mandar a hacer –,** to send to blazes.
gargarismo *s.m.* **1** gargle, gargling (gárgaras). **2** gargle (líquido).
gargarizar *v.i.* to gargle.
gárgol *s.m.* groove.
gárgola *s.f.* ARQ. gargoyle.
garita *s.f.* **1** MIL. sentry box (torrecilla para centinelas). **2** porter's lodge (portería).
garitero *s.m.* **1** gambling-den owner (dueño de un garito). **2** gambler (jugador).
garito *s.m.* **1** gambling-den (casa de juego). **2** winnings (ganancia).
garla *s.f.* chatter.
garlador, -ora *s.m.* y *f.* **1** chatterer. || *adj.* **2** garrulous, talkative.
garlante *adj.* garrulous, talkative.
garlar *v.i.* to chatter, (fam.) to natter.
garlito *s.m.* **1** fish trap (trampa para pescar peces). **2** trap (trampa). **3 caer en el –,** to fall into the trap.
garlopa *s.f.* TEC. jack plane (de carpintería).
garniel *s.m.* (Am.) brief case (maletín).
garra *s.f.* **1** paw (pata del animal). **2** claw (zarpa de ave). **3** (fig.) bite, punch: *tener garra = to have bite.* || *pl.* **3** rags, tatters (harapos). || **4 echarle a uno la –,** to get one's hands on someone.
garrafa *s.f.* decanter, carafe.
garrafal *adj.* **1** terrible, horrendous (muy mal). **2** excessive, enormous (excesivo).
garrafón *s.m.* large carafe, demijohn (damajuana).
garrapata *s.f.* ZOOL. tick (insecto).
garrapatear *v.i.* to scrawl, to scribble.
garrapato *s.m.* **1** scribble, scrawl. || *pl.* **2** scribbling, scrawling.
garrapatoso, -a *adj.* scrawled, scribbled.
garrapiña *s.f.* V. **garapiña.**
garrido, -a *adj.* **1** elegant, smart (elegante). **2** good-looking (guapo).
garrocha *s.f.* **1** pike, lance (vara utilizada por los vaqueros). **2** lance (en las corridas). **3** (Am.) DEP. pole (pértiga).
garrotazo *s.m.* blow with a stick o club.
garrote *s.m.* **1** stick, club (palo fuerte). **2** garrote (para estrangular a los condenados). **3** MED. tourniquet (ligadura fuerte).
garrotear *v.t.* (Am.) to club, to beat (golpear con un palo, etc.).
garrotillo *s.m.* MED. croup.
garrucha *s.f.* pulley (polea).
garrulador, -a *adj.* **1** BOT. twittering, chirping (del ave que canta mucho). **2** talkative, garrulous (muy hablador).
garrulería *s.f.* **1** garrulity, wordiness (exceso de palabras). **2** chatter (charla).
garrulidad *s.f.* garrulousness, talkativeness, (fam.) long-windedness.
gárrulo, -a *adj.* **1** garrulous, talkative (fam.) chatty (persona). **2** twittering, chirping (aves). **3** babbling (agua). **4** sighing (viento).
garúa *s.f.* (Am.) drizzle (llovizna).
garza *s.f.* ZOOL. heron (ave): *garza real = grey heron.*
garzo, -a *adj.* **1** bluish (azulado). **2** blue-eyed (ojos azulados).
gas *s.m.* **1** FIS. y QUIM. gas. || **2 a todo –,** at full speed; flat out. **3 cámara de –,** gas chamber. **4 – butano,** butane. **5 – natural,** natural gas. **6 – tóxico,** poison gas.
gasa *s.f.* **1** gauze (tela). **2** MED. gauze (tejido).
gaseosa *s.f.* lemonade (bebida).
gaseoso, -a *adj.* **1** gaseous. **2** fizzy (espumoso).
gasificación *s.f.* gasification.
gasificar *v.t.* y *r.* to gasify.
gasoducto *s.m.* gas pipeline.
gasógeno *s.m.* gasogene.
gasoil *s.m.* diesel, diesel oil.
gasóleo *s.m.* diesel, diesel oil.
gasolina *s.f.* petrol, (EE.UU.) gas.
gasolinera *s.f.* **1** petrol station, filling station, (EE.UU.) gas station. **2** MAR. motorboat (lancha).
gasómetro *s.m.* gasometer, gasholder.
gastado, -a *adj.* **1** spent (dinero). **2** worn out (ropa, zapatos, neumáticos, metales, telas, etc.). **3** corny, old (chiste). **4** tired, beat, worn out (cansado).
gastador, -a *adj.* **1** spendthrift, extravagant, wasteful. || *s.m.* y *f.* **2** spender, spendthrift. **3** MIL. sapper, pioneer (soldado). **4** prisoner, convict (preso).
gastar *v.t.* **1** to spend (dinero): *gasto mucho en ropa = I spend a lot on clothes.* **2** to spend (tiempo, esfuerzo). **3** to use, to wear (usar): *gasto gafas desde hace dos años = I've been wearing glasses for two years.* **4** to consume, to use up (consumir). **5** to wear out (desgastar). **6** to waste (malgastar): *gastar un día sin hacer nada = to waste a day without doing anything.* **7** to have, to run (un coche). || *v.i.* **8** to spend (dinero). || *v.r.* **9** to wear out (estropearse). **10** to run out (agotarse). **11** to tire oneself out (cansarse). || **12 – bromas,** to play jokes. **13 gastarlas,** to behave.
gasto *s.m.* **1** expense, expenditure (cantidad gastada). **2** spending, expenditure (acción de gastar). **3** MEC. wear (desgaste). **4** flow (de gas, agua, etc.). **5** use, consumption (consumo). || *pl.* **6** COM. expenses, cost, costs: *gastos de reparación = repair costs.* || **7 gastos bancarios,** bank charges. **8 gastos e ingresos,** expenditure and income. **9 gastos generales,** overheads. **10 hacer el –,** to do all the talking. **11 pagar los gastos,** (fam.) to foot the bill.
gástrico, -a *adj.* MED. gastric.
gastritis *s.f.* MED. gastritis.
gastroenteritis *s.f.* MED. gastroenteritis.
gastronomía *s.f.* gastronomy.
gastronómico, -a *adj.* gastronomic.
gastrónomo, -a *s.m.* y *f.* gastronome, gourmet.
gata *s.f.* **1** cat, she-cat (hembra del gato). **2** hill cloud (nube). || **3 a gatas,** on all fours: *andar a gatas = to go on all fours/to crawl.*
gatear *v.i.* **1** to climb (trepar). **2** to go on all fours, to crawl (andar a gatas). || *v.t.* **3** to scratch (arañar). **4** to steal, (fam.) to pinch, to nick (hurtar).

gatera *s.f.* 1 cathole (agujero para el gato). 2 MAR. cathole. 3 (Am.) market woman (mujer que vende en el mercado).
gatillo *s.m.* 1 trigger (de un arma). 2 MED. dental forceps (tenacilla que utiliza el dentista).
gato *s.m.* 1 ZOOL. cat, tomcat. 2 MEC. jack (para levantar coches). 3 bag, money bag (bolsa). 4 thief (ladrón). 5 (fig.) wise owl, fox (hombre astuto). 6 (Am.) open-air market (mercado al aire libre). || 7 **buscarle tres pies al —,** to split hairs. 8 **cuatro gatos,** hardly anybody; hardly a soul. 9 **dar — por liebre,** to sell a pig in a poke. 10 **- escaldado del agua fría huye,** once bitten twice shy. 11 **— montés,** wildcat. 12 **— siamés,** Siamese cat. 13 **hay — encerrado,** there's something fishy; I smell a rat. 14 **llevar el — al agua,** to pull it off; to bring home the bacon.
gatuno, -a *adj.* cat-like, feline.
gatuperio *s.m.* 1 mixture, (fam.) mishmash, hotchpotch (mezcla). 2 mess, quandry, tangle (embrollo). 3 intrigue (intriga).
gaucho *s.m.* 1 gaucho (habitante de la Pampa). 2 (Am.) good rider, good horseman (buen jinete). || *adj.* 3 gaucho (de la Pampa). 4 rough, uncouth (rústico). 5 astute, cunning (astuto).
gausio o **gauss** *s.m.* FIS. gauss (unidad de inducción magnética).
gaveta *s.f.* drawer (cajón).
gavilán *s.m.* 1 ZOOL. sparrowhawk (ave). 2 flourish (rasgo al final de las letras). 3 nib (de las plumas). 4 quillon (de la espada).
gavilla *s.f.* 1 bundle (haz de mieses, etc.). 2 gang, band (reunión de mala gente).
gaviota *s.f.* ZOOL. seagull, gull.
gaya *s.f.* 1 coloured strip (lista de color). 2 winner's insignia (insignia dada al vencedor). || 3 **— ciencia,** ART. art of poetry.
gayo, -a *adj.* cheerful, happy, merry (alegre).
gazapo *s.m.* 1 ZOOL. young rabbit (conejo nuevo). 2 sly fox, wise owl (hombre astuto). 3 lie (mentira). 4 mistake, (fam.) blunder (error). 5 slip, slip of the tongue (lapso).
gazmoñada *s.f.* prudishness, priggishness, prudery (mojigatería).
gazmonería V. **gazmoñada.**
gazmoñero, -a *adj.* 1 prudish, priggish (mojigato). || *s.m.* y *f.* 2 prude, prig (mojigato).
gazmoño, -a V. **gazmoñero.**
gaznápiro, -a *adj.* 1 daft, silly, foolish (bobo). || *s.m.* y *f.* 2 dunce, dolt, dope, twerp (simplón).
gaznate *s.m.* ANAT. gullet, throat (parte superior de la garganta).
gazpacho *s.m.* cold tomato soup, gazpacho.
gazuza *s.f.* hunger (hambre).
ge *s.f.* G (letra).
géiser *s.m.* GEOG. geyser.
gel *s.m.* 1 QUIM. gel. 2 shower soap (jabón de ducha).
gelatina *s.f.* 1 QUIM. gelatine, gelatin. 2 jelly (de los huesos, etc.).
gelatinoso, -a *adj.* gelatinous.
gélido, -a *adj.* frozen, icy (muy frío).
gelignita *s.f.* gelignite.
gema *s.f.* 1 gem (piedra preciosa). 2 BOT. bud (yema o botón).
gemación *s.f.* BOT. gemmation.
gemelo, -a *adj.* 1 twin: *hermanos gemelos = twin brothers; hermanas gemelas = twin sisters.* || *s.m.* y *f.* 2 twin. || *pl.* 3 cufflinks (de la camisa). 4 binoculars, field glasses (prismáticos). 5 AST. Gemini, (fam.) the Twins (Géminis). || 6 **gemelos de teatro,** opera glasses.
gemido *s.m.* 1 moan, groan (de personas). 2 wail (lamento). 3 howl (del viento). 4 whine, howl (de animales).
gemidor, -a *adj.* 1 moaning, groaning (de personas). 2 wailing (que se lamenta). 3 howling (viento). 4 whining, howling (animales).
geminación *s.f.* gemination.
geminado, -a *adj.* geminate.
geminar *v.t.* to geminate.
Géminis *s.m.* ASTR. Gemini, (fam.) the Twins.
gemir *v.i.* 1 to moan, to groan (personas). 2 to wail (con lamentos). 3 to howl (el viento). 4 to whine, to howl (animales).
gen o **gene** *s.m.* BIOL. gene.
gendarme *s.m.* gendarme, policeman (policía francés).
gendarmería *s.f.* gendarmerie, police.
genealogía *s.f.* genealogy.
genealógico, -a *adj.* 1 genealogical 2 **árbol genealógico,** family tree.
genealogista *s.m.* y *f.* genealogist.
generación *s.f.* generation: *generación literaria = literary generation.*
generador, -ora *adj.* 1 generating. || *s.m.* 2 ELEC. generator.
general *adj.* 1 general: *huelga general = general strike.* 2 frequent (frecuente). 3 common (corriente). || *s.m.* 4 MIL. general 5 **general en jefe,** supreme commander. 6 REL. general (superior en una orden religiosa). || 7 **en —,** in general. 8 **por lo —,** generally.
generala *s.f.* 1 MIL. call to arms, general alert (toque de alarma). 2 general's wife (mujer del general).
generalato *s.m.* MIL. generalship.
generalidad *s.f.* 1 generality (vaguedad). 2 majority (el mayor número). 3 community (comunidad). || 4 **la Generalitat,** POL. Catalan autonomous government.
generalísimo *s.m.* MIL. generalissimo, supreme commander.
generalización *s.f.* 1 generalization. 2 MIL. escalation (de un conflicto).
generalizador, -a *adj.* generalizing.
generalizar *v.t.* y *r.* 1 to become widespread o general: *el miedo se ha generalizado = fear has become widespread.* 2 MIL. to escalate (un conflicto). || *v.t.* 3 to generalize.
generalmente *adv.* generally.
generar *v.t.* 1 ELEC. to generate. 2 to engender (engendrar).
generativo, -a *adj.* generative.
generatriz *s.f.* MAT. generatrix.
genérico, -a *adj.* generic.
género *s.m.* 1 type, kind, sort, class (clase, tipo). 2 article (mercancía). 3 ART. y LIT. genre: *género literario = literary genre.* 4 GRAM. gender: *género femenino = feminine gender.* 5 cloth (tela). 6 BIOL. genus. || *pl.* 7 COM. goods, merchandise. || 8 **— chico,** Spanish operetta. 9 **— humano,** human race. 10 **— masculino,** masculine gender. 11 **— neutro,** neutral gender.
generosamente *adv.* generously.
generosidad *s.f.* generosity.
generoso, -a *adj.* 1 generous (desprendido). 2 magnanimous, noble (magnánimo). 3 noble (noble). 4 full-bodied, rich (vino).
genésico, -a *adj.* genetic.
génesis *s.f.* 1 genesis, origen (origin). || *s.m.* 2 Genesis (primer libro de la Biblia).
genética *s.f.* genetics.
genético, -a *adj.* BIOL. genetic.
genial *adj.* 1 inspired, brilliant (con genio creador). 2 funny, witty (gracioso). 3 (fam.) great, marvellous, fantastic (estupendo): *una película genial = a fantastic film.* 4 pleasant, genial (carácter).
genialidad *s.f.* 1 genius (genio). 2 great idea, stroke of genius: *fue una genialidad venir aquí = it was a great idea to come here.* 3 extravagance (acción extravagante). 4 originality (originalidad).
genio *s.m.* 1 character, nature (carácter): *genio triste = sad nature.* 2 genius (inteligencia superior o persona de gran inteligencia). 3 spirit (espíritu): *espíritu del mal = evil spirit.* 4 bad temper (mal humor): *estar de mal genio = to be in a bad temper.* || 5 **mal —,** bad-tempered: *tener mal genio = to be bad-tempered.* 6 **pronto de —,** quick-tempered.
genital *adj.* 1 genital. || *s.m.pl.* 2 genitals, genital organs.
genitivo *s.m.* GRAM. genitive.
genitourinario *adj.* ANAT. genitourinary.
genocidio *s.m.* genocide.
genotipo *s.m.* BIOL. genotype.
gente *s.f.* 1 people (grupo de personas): *hay mucha gente = they are a lot of people.* 2 nation, people (nación). 3 (fam.) folks, relatives, family (familia). || 4 **de — en —,** from generation to generation. 5 **— baja,** lower classes. 6 **— bien,** respectable people. 7 MIL. **¡— de paz!** friend! 8 **— menuda,** children; (fam.) kids. 9 **ser —,** to be somebody, to have social importance.
gentil *adj.* 1 pagan, heathen (pagano). 2 elegant, smart (elegante). 3 charming (encantador). 4 nice, pleasant (agradable). 5 attractive (atractivo). 6 graceful (gracioso). 7 gentile (no judío). || *s.m.* 8 pagan, heathen (pagano). 9 gentile (no judío).
gentileza *s.f.* 1 elegance, poise, gracefulness (gracia). 2 assurance, self-confi-

dence (desenvoltura). **3** politeness, courtesy (cortesía). **4** charm (encanto). **5** show, ostentation (ostentación).

gentilhombre *s.m.* HIST. gentleman.

gentilicio, -a *adj.* **1** national (de una nación). **2** family (de una familia).

gentilmente *adv.* **1** elegantly, gracefully (con elegancia). **2** charmingly (con encanto). **3** politely, courteously (con cortesía).

gentío *s.m.* crowd, throng, (desp.) mob (multitud).

gentuza o **gentualla** *s.f.* rabble, mob, riff-raff (gente despreciable).

genuflexión *s.f.* genuflexion.

genuino, -a *adj.* **1** genuine, true (legítimo). **2** pure (puro). **3** authentic (auténtico).

geocéntrico, -a *adj.* ASTR. geocentric.

geocronología *s.f.* GEOL. geochronology.

geofísica *s.f.* geophysics.

geografía *s.f.* geography.

geográfico, -a *adj.* geographical.

geógrafo, -a *s.m.* y *f.* geographer.

geología *s.f.* geology.

geológico, -a *adj.* geological.

geólogo, -a *s.m.* y *f.* geologist.

geómetra *s.m.* y *f.* geometrician.

geometría *s.f.* geometry: *geometría analítica = analytical geometry; geometría del espacio = solid geometry; geometría descriptiva = descriptive geometry; geometría plana = plane geometry.*

geométricamente *adv.* geometrically.

geométrico, -a *adj.* geometric, geometrically.

geopolítica *s.f.* geopolitics.

geotermia *s.f.* geothermics.

geranio *s.m.* BOT. geranium.

gerencia *s.f.* **1** management (actividad de gerente). **2** manager's office (despacho). **3** managership (cargo).

gerente *s.m.* y *f.* manager, director: *gerente de una fábrica = factory manager.*

geriatra *s.m.* y *f.* MED. geriatrician.

geriatría *s.f.* geriatrics.

gerifalte *s.m.* **1** ZOOL. gerfalcon (ave). **2** thief (ladrón). **3** (fam. y desp.) big shot, big noise (persona importante).

germanesco, -a *adj.* slang (argot).

germanía *s.f.* thieves' slang, underworld slang (argot de los ladrones).

germánico, -a *adj./s.m.* y *f.* Germanic.

germanio *s.m.* QUIM. germanium (elemento).

germanismo *s.m.* Germanism.

germanista *s.m.* y *f.* German scholar.

germanizar *v.t.* e *i.* to germanize.

germano, -a *adj.* **1** German, Germanic. || *s.m.* y *f.* **2** German.

germen *s.m.* **1** BIOL. germ. **2** (fig.) germ, seed (principio).

germinación *s.f.* germination.

germinal *adj.* BIOL. germinal.

germinar *v.i.* BIOL. to germinate.

germinativo, -a *adj.* germinative.

gerontología *s.f.* MED. gerontology.

gerontólogo *s.m.* y *f.* MED. gerontologist.

gerundio *s.m.* GRAM. gerund.

gesta *s.f.* **1** heroic feat o deed, exploit (hazaña). **2** heroic poem, epic poem (poema narrativo).

gestación *s.f.* **1** BIOL. gestation. **2** ground-work, preparation, planning (período de preparación).

gestar *v.t.* BIOL. to gestate.

gestatorio *adj.* gestatorial: *silla gestatoria = gestatorial seat.*

gestero, -a *adj.* gesticulative.

gesticulación *s.f.* **1** gesticulation. **2** grimace (mueca).

gesticular *v.i.* **1** to gesticulate (hacer gestos). **2** to grimace, to pull faces, to make a face (hacer muecas).

gestión *s.f.* **1** measure, step (trámite). **2** negotiation (negociación). **3** COM. management (dirección de una empresa). || *pl.* **4** measures (trámites). || **5 hacer las gestiones,** to take steps (para solucionar algo).

gestionar *v.t.* **1** to negotiate (negociar). **2** to take steps to get, to try to get (hacer gestiones). **3** to manage (dirigir, llevar).

gesto *s.m.* **1** expression, look (expresión de la cara): *un gesto de tristeza = a look of sadness.* **2** gesture (con las manos): *hacer gestos = to make gestures.* **3** grimace, face (mueca). || **4 estar de buen —,** to be in a good mood. **5 estar de mal —,** to be in a bad mood. **6 hacer gestos,** to make o pull faces.

gestor *s.m.* y *f.* **1** manager, director (director). **2** agent (que gestiona). || *adj.* **3** managing.

gestoría *s.f.* agency.

ghetto *s.m.* ghetto.

giba *s.f.* **1** hump (de un cabello). **2** MED. hump, hunch (abultamiento en la espalda o pecho). **3** rise (prominencia de un terreno). **4** (fam.) drag, bore, bother (molestia).

gibar *v.t.* **1** to make a hump (hacer una giba). **2** (fam.) to bother, to annoy (fastidiar).

gibón *s.m.* ZOOL. gibbon.

gibosidad *s.f.* hump, lump (bulto).

giboso, -a *adj.* **1** hunchbacked (jorobado). || *s.m.* y *f.* **2** hunchback.

gibraltareño, -a *adj.* **1** of/from Gibraltar. || *s.m.* y *f.* **2** Gibraltarian.

giganta *s.f.* **1** giantess. **2** BOT. sunflower (girasol).

gigante, -a *adj.* **1** gigantic, giant. || *s.m.* **2** giant.

gigantesco, -a *adj.* gigantic, giant.

gigantismo *s.m.* giantism.

gigantón *s.m.* **1** giant (en festejos). **2** giant (persona).

gimnasia *s.f.* **1** gymnastics, (fam.) gymwork: *hacer gimnasia = to do gym-work.*

gimnasio *s.m.* gymnasium, (fam.) gym.

gimnasta *s.m.* y *f.* gymnast.

gimnástico, -a *adj.* gymnastic.

gimnospermo, -a *adj.* **1** BOT. gymnosperm. || *s.f.pl.* **2** gymnosperms.

gimotear *v.i.* to whimper, to whine.

gimoteo *s.m.* whimpering, whining.

ginebra *s.f.* gin (bebida).

ginebrino, -a adj. of/from Ginebra.

gineceo *s.m.* **1** HIST. gynaeceum, (fam.) women's apartments (habitación para mujeres). **2** harem (harén). **3** BOT. gynaeceum.

ginecología *s.f.* MED. gynaecology.

ginecológico, -a *adj.* MED. gynaecological.

ginecólogo *s.m.* y *f.* MED. gynaecologist.

gingival *adj.* ANAT. gingival.

gingivitis *s.f.* MED. gingivitis.

ginkgo *s.m.* BOT. ginkgo (árbol).

gira *s.f.* **1** trip, outing (excursión). **2** tour (serie de actuaciones).

giralda *s.f.* weather vane, weathercock (veleta).

girar *v.i.* **1** to go round, to rotate (ruedas). **2** to revolve, to rotate (alrededor de un punto o eje). **3** to spin (balón, trompo, etc.). **4** to turn on, to centre on (desenvolverse una conversación en torno a un tema). **5** to swing (una puerta). **6** to turn (desviarse una calle): *girar a la derecha = to turn right.* || *v.i.* y *t.* **7** to send a money order (enviar dinero por giro postal). **8** COM. to draw (enviar una orden de pago).

girasol *s.m.* BOT. sunflower.

giratorio, -a *adj.* **1** revolving, (p.u.) gyratory: *una puerta giratoria = a revolving door.* || **2 puente —,** swing bridge.

giro *s.m.* **1** rotation (revolución). **2** turn (vuelta). **3** turn, turning (hecho y resultado de girar). **4** spin (de un balón, trompo, etc.). **5** COM. draft (letra de cambio). **6** FIS. gyration. **7** (fig.) course, turn (dirección o aspecto que toman ciertas cosas): *sus relaciones han tomado un nuevo giro = their relationship has taken a new turn.* **8** turn of phrase (estructura especial de una frase). || **9 hacer un —,** to turn; to make a turn. **10 — postal,** postal order. || *adj.* **11** (Am.) yellow (gallo).

girondino, -a *adj.* y *s.m.* y *f.* HIST. Girondist.

gitanería *s.f.* **1** band of gipsies (reunión de gitanos). **2** flattery (halago). **3** gipsy-like saying (dicho propio de gitanos). **4** gipsy-like act (hecho propio de gitanos).

gitanismo *s.m.* **1** V. **gitanería. 2** gipsy way of life (manera de vivir de los gitanos). **3** gipsy expression (expresión propia de los gitanos).

gitano *s.m.* y *f.* **1** gipsy. || *adj.* **2** gipsy.

glacial *adj.* **1** glacial (helado). **2** (fig.) icy, indifferent, cold (indiferente).

glaciar *s.m.* **1** GEOL. glacier || *adj.* **2** glacial: *valle glaciar = glacial valley.*

gladiador *s.m.* HIST. gladiator.

gladiolo o **gladíolo** *s.m.* BOT. gladiolus.

glande *s.m.* ANAT. glans penis.

glándula *s.f.* ANAT. gland: *glándula endocrina = endocrine gland; glándula pineal = pineal gland.*

glauco, -a *adj.* pale green, light green (verde claro).

glaucoma *s.f.* MED. glaucoma.

gleba *s.f.* **1** AGR. clod (terrón). || **2 siervo de la —,** HIST. serf.

glicerina *s.f.* QUIM. glycerin, glycerine.

global *adj.* 1 global: *una visión global de la cuestión = a global view of the question.* 2 total, overall (total): *el precio global = the total price.* 3 full, complete (completo): *un estudio global = a complete study.* 4 lump (suma).

globo *s.m.* 1 sphere, globe (cuerpo esférico). 2 globe, earth (mundo). 3 balloon (vejiga elástica). 4 lampshade (de lámpara). || 5 **dar un –,** DEP. to lob (en tenis). 6 **en –,** as a whole. 7 **– aerostático,** balloon. 8 **– cautivo,** captive balloon. 9 **– dirigible,** dirigible. 10 **– ocular,** ANAT. eyeball. 11 **– sonda,** sounding balloon. 10 **– terráqueo,** globe.

globular *adj.* globular, spherical.

glóbulo *s.m.* 1 globule (cuerpo esférico). 2 ANAT. corpuscle (corpúsculo). || 3 **– blanco,** ANAT. white corpuscle. 4 **– rojo,** ANAT. red corpuscle.

gloria *s.f.* 1 glory, fame (fama). 2 REL. heaven, paradise (cielo). 3 pleasure, delight (placer grande). 4 REL. gloria (cántico litúrgico). || 5 **estar en la –,** to be in one's element. 6 **hacer – de una cosa,** to boast about something. 7 **saber a –,** to taste divine o delightful.

gloriado *s.m.* (Am.) hot toddy (especie de ponche).

gloriar *v.t.* 1 to exalt (glorificar). || *v.pron.* 2 to boast, to brag (jactarse). 3 to be happy o glad (alegrarse).

glorieta *s.f.* 1 BOT. bower, arbour (macizo de plantas). 2 small square (plazoleta). 3 roundabout (encrucijada).

glorificación *s.f.* glorification.

glorificar *v.t.* 1 to praise, to extol (alabar). 2 to glorify (dar gloria). || *v.r.* 3 to boast, to brag (jactarse).

glosa *s.f.* 1 annotation, marginal note (comentario de un texto). 2 explanatory note, note (nota explicativa). 3 gloss (composición poética).

glosar *v.t.* 1 to gloss (un texto). 2 to annotate, to comment upon (comentar). 3 to criticize (criticar).

glosario *s.m.* glossary.

glosopeda *s.f.* foot-and-mouth disease (enfermedad del ganado).

glotis *s.f.* ANAT. glottis.

glotón, -a *adj.* 1 greedy, gluttonous. || *s.m.* y *f.* 2 glutton (persona). 3 ZOOL. glutton.

glotonamente *adv.* greedily, gluttonously.

glotonear *v.i.* to eat greedily, to be greedy.

glotonería *s.f.* greediness, gluttony.

glucemia *s.f.* MED. glucemia.

glúcido *s.m.* QUIM. glucide.

glucinio *s.m.* QUIM. glucinium.

glucógeno *s.m.* ANAT. glycogen.

glucosa *s.f.* glucose.

glucósido *s.m.* QUIM. glucoside.

glúteo, -a *adj.* ANAT. gluteus.

gnomo o **nomo** *s.m.* gnome (enano fantástico).

gnosticismo *s.m.* FIL. gnosticism.

gobernación *s.f.* 1 governing, government (acción de gobernar). || 2 **Ministerio de la Gobernación,** POL. Ministry of the Interior. 3 **ministro de la Gobernación,** POL. Minister of the Interior.

gobernador, -a *adj.* 1 governing. || *s.m.* y *f.* 2 governor: *gobernador general = governor-general.*

gobernante, -a *adj.* 1 governing, ruling. || *s.m.* y *f.* 2 governor, ruler.

gobernar *v.i.* y *r.* 1 POL. to govern. 2 to rule (monarca). || *v.t.* y *r.* 3 to direct, to run, to manage (dirigir). 4 to administer (administrar).

gobierno *s.m.* 1 POL. government (Consejo de ministros): *Gobierno central = central government.* 2 direction, control, running (hecho y resultado de gobernar). 3 governership (cargo de gobernador). 4 government house (edificio del gobernador). || 5 **– interino,** caretaker o interin government.

goce *s.m.* 1 enjoyment (disfrute). 2 pleasure, delight (placer).

godo, -a *adj.* 1 Gothic. 2 rich (rico). 3 powerful (poderoso). || *s.m.* y *f.* 3 HIST. Goth. 4 (Am.) Spaniard, (desp.) dago. 5 Spaniard (en las Canarias).

gol *s.m.* DEP. goal (tanto): *marcar un gol = to score a goal.*

gola *s.f.* 1 ANAT. throat (garganta). 2 HIST. y MIL. gorget (pieza de armadura que protegía la garganta). 3 ruff (adorno del cuello). 4 MAR. narrow channel (embocadura estrecha). 5 ARQ. cyma, ogee (moldura).

goleada *s.f.* DEP. (fam.) hatful of goals.

goleador *s.m.* DEP. goal scorer.

golear *v.t.* 1 to score a lot of goals, (fam.) to score a hatful of goals (marcar muchos goles). || *v.i.* 2 to score (marcar un gol).

goleta *s.f.* MAR. schooner (velero).

golf *s.m.* DEP. golf: *campo de golf = golf course; palo de golf = golf club.*

golfo, -a *s.m.* y *f.* 1 rascal. || *s.f.* 2 prostitute, (desp.) whore (prostituta).

golfante *s.m.* rogue, scoundrel (golfo).

golfear *v.i.* 1 to behave like a rogue o scoundrel (cometer acciones de un golfo). 2 to loaf around, to idle around (vagabundear).

golfo *s.m.* 1 GEOG. gulf: *Golfo Pérsico = Persian Gulf.* 2 GEOG. bay (bahía). 3 (fam.) good-for-nothing, rotter, rogue (pillo).

golondrina *s.f.* 1 ZOOL. swallow (ave). 2 swallow fish (pez). || 3 **– de mar,** tern (ave). 4 **una – no hace verano,** one swallow doesn't make a summer.

golondrino *s.m.* 1 ZOOL. baby swallow (cría de la golondrina). 2 swallow fish (pez). 3 deserter (desertor). 4 MED. tumour under the armpit (tumor en el sobaco).

golosina *s.f.* 1 sweet (dulce). 2 titbit (manjar que se come por placer). 3 trifle, bauble (cosa más agradable que útil).

goloso, -a *adj.* 1 sweet-toothed (aficionado a las cosas dulces). 2 tempting, inviting (que excita deseo). 3 greedy (que come mucho). || 4 **ser –,** to have a sweet tooth.

golpazo *s.m.* 1 heavy knock o blow (golpe fuerte). 2 hard bump (choque fuerte).

golpe *s.m.* 1 bump, collision (choque de dos cuerpos). 2 knock, blow (efecto de este choque). 3 punch, hit (de las manos). 4 blow, setback, misfortune (desgracia). 5 beat (latido). 6 (fig.) abundance, crowd (abundancia): *golpe de gente = crowd of people.* 7 surprise, shock (sorpresa). 8 AGR. hole (hoyo). 9 coup (ocurrencia oportuna). 10 gust (de viento). 11 DEP. shot (disparo). 12 DEP. punch, hit (en el boxeo). 13 DEP. stroke, shot (con un palo). || 14 **a – de,** by means of. 15 **a golpes,** intermittently, (fam.) on and off. 16 **dar el –,** to be a hit. 17 **dar –,** to work; (fam.) to get down to it (trabajar). 18 **de – y porrazo,** suddenly (repentinamente). 19 **de un –,** in one go (de una vez). 20 **errar el –,** to make a mistake (equivocarse). 21 **– de Estado,** POL. coup d'état. 22 **– de fortuna,** stroke of luck. 23 **– de gracia,** coup de grace. 24 **– de mar,** enormous wave. 25 **– de pecho,** mea culpa. 26 **– de suerte,** stroke of luck. 27 **– de tos,** fit of coughing. 28 **– franco,** DEP. free kick. 29 **– maestro,** master stroke. 30 **no dar –,** not to do a stroke of work (no trabajar).

golpeador *s.m.* (Am.) door knocker (aldaba).

golpear *v.t.* 1 to knock, to strike, to hit (dar un golpe). 2 to punch, to thump (con el puño). 3 to beat, to pound (con varios golpes). 4 to bang (con golpes fuertes). || *v.i.* 5 MEC. to knock.

golpeo *s.m.* 1 knocking, striking, hitting (en general). 2 banging, knocking (en la puerta). 3 punching, thumping (con los puños). 4 beating (de las olas, viento, lluvia, etc.). 5 knocking (de un motor).

golpetear *v.t.* e *i.* 1 to beat (con golpes repetidos). 2 to tap, to drum (con golpecitos). 3 to rattle (una ventana, un postigo, etc.). 4 (fam.) to pitter-patter (la lluvia).

golpeteo *s.m.* 1 tapping, drumming (con golpecitos). 2 rattling (de una ventana, un postigo, etc.). 3 knocking (de un motor, un coche). 4 pitter-patter (de la lluvia).

golpista *s.m.* 1 insurrectionary, rebel, insurgent. || *adj.* 2 rebellious disloyal, insurrectionary.

goma *s.f.* 1 rubber (caucho). 2 glue, gum (para pegar). 3 rubber band, elastic band (tira elástica para sujetar cosas). 4 condom, (fam.) durex (condón). 5 rubber (de borrar). 6 elastic (en costura).

gomina *s.f.* hair cream.

gomorresina *s.f.* gum resin.

gónada *s.f.* ANAT. gonad.

gonce *s.m.* hinge (gozne).

góndola *s.f.* 1 gondola (barca veneciana). 2 wagon (carro).

gondolero *s.m.* gondolier.

gong o **gongo** *s.m.* gong.

goniómetro *s.m.* goniometer.

gonococo *s.m.* MED. gonoccocus.

gonorrea *s.f.* MED. gonorrhoea.
gorda *s.f.* 1 fat woman (mujer gorda). || 2 **armarse la –,** to be trouble, to be a fuss o rumpus: *se armó una gorda = there was a tremendous rumpus.*
gordiano *adj.* gordian: *nudo gordiano = gordian knot.*
gordiflón, -ona o **gordinflón, -ona** *adj.* flabby, plump, chubby.
gordo *adj.* 1 fat (corpulento). 2 big (grande): *un filete gordo = a big steak.* 3 thick (telas, materiales, etc.). 4 fatty (graso). 5 (fam.) important (importante). 6 (fam.) enormous, huge (enorme). 7 hard (agua). 8 big, first (premio): *el premio gordo = the first prize.* || *s.m.* 9 fat (grasa de la carne). 10 first prize (el premio gordo). 11 fat man (hombre gordo). || 12 **hablar –,** to talk big. 13 **me cae –,** I can't stand him. 14 **pez –,** big shot.
gordura *s.f.* 1 fat (carne o grasa excesiva). 2 fatness, corpulence (cualidad de gordo).
gorgorito *s.m.* warble, trill.
gorgoteo *s.m.* gurgle.
gorigori *s.m.* funeral dirge (canto fúnebre): *cantar el gorigori a alguien = to bury (enterrarlo).*
gorila *s.f.* ZOOL. gorilla.
gorjear *v.i.* 1 MUS. to warble, to trill. 2 to twitter, to chirp (cantar los pájaros). 3 to gurgle (un niño).
gorjeo *s.m.* 1 MUS. warbling, trilling. 2 twittering, chirping (los pájaros). 3 gurgling (los niños).
gorra *s.f.* 1 cap (sombrero sin alas ni visera). 2 peaked cap (con visera). 3 bonnet (de niño). 4 MIL. bearskin. || 5 **de –,** free (gratis).
gorrino, -a *s.m.* y *f.* 1 sucking pig (cerdo de menos de cuatro meses). 2 pig (cerdo). 3 (fam.) pig (persona sucia).
gorrión *s.m.* ZOOL. sparrow (ave).
gorro *s.m.* 1 cap (para abrigar la cabeza). 2 bonnet (de niños). || 3 **estar hasta el –,** to be fed up. 4 **poner el – a alguien,** to ridicule someone (ridiculizarlo).
gorrón, -a *adj.* 1 scrounging, sponging. || *s.m.* y *f.* 2 scrounger, sponger.
gorronear *v.i.* to scrounge, to sponge.
gorronería *s.f.* scrounging, sponging.
gota *s.f.* 1 drop (partícula globular). 2 MED. gout (enfermedad). 3 (fig.) drop, spot (cantidad pequeña): *una gota de whisky = a drop of whisky.* || 4 **cuatro gotas,** a spot of rain (lluvia breve y escasa). 5 **– a –,** drop by drop. 6 **ni –,** nothing (nada).
gotear *v.i.* 1 to drip (caer gota a gota). 2 to spit (empezar a llover). 3 to leak (salirse un líquido). 4 to drip (una vela).
goteo *s.m.* 1 dripping. 2 leaking.
gotera *s.f.* 1 leak, drip (infiltración). 2 crack (grieta). 3 stain (mancha). 4 complaint, ailment (achaque). || *pl.* 5 (Am.) outskirts (alrededores).
gótico, -a *adj.* 1 Gothic. || *s.m.* y *f.* 2 Gothic.
goyesco, -a *adj.* Goyesque, in the style of Goya.
gozar *v.t.* 1 to enjoy: *gozo trabajando = I enjoy working.* || *v.t.* y *v.pron.* 2 to have a good time, to enjoy oneself (pasarlo bien). || *v.i.* 3 to enjoy (sentir placer): *gozan de buena salud = they enjoy good health.*
gozne *s.m.* hinge (bisagra).
gozo *s.m.* 1 pleasure, delight (placer). 2 enjoyment (disfrute). 3 joy, gladness (alegría). || 4 **dar –,** to give pleasure. 5 **mi – en un pozo,** (fam.) that's put a spanner in the works; what rotten luck! 6 **no caber en sí de –,** (fam.) to be over the moon. 7 **ser un –,** to be a delight.
gozoso, -a *adj.* happy, delighted, (fam.) over the moon.
grabación *s.f.* recording (de cintas, discos, etc.): *grabación en directo = live recording.*
grabado *adj.* 1 recorded: *grabado en Londres = recorded in London.* || *s.m.* 2 engraving (en una plancha). 3 picture, illustration (en los libros). 4 recording (grabación). || 5 **– al agua fuerte,** etching. 6 **– en madera,** woodcut.
grabador, -ora *s.m.* y *f.* engraver (persona que se dedica al grabado).
gracia *s.f.* 1 charm, appeal, attractiveness (atractivo). 2 humour, wit (salero). 3 DER. pardon, reprieve (indulto). 4 favour (concesión gratuita): *conceder una gracia = to grant a favour.* 5 grace (don de Dios). 6 grace, elegance (en los movimientos). 7 benevolence, compassion (benevolencia). 8 joke (chiste): *hacer una gracia = to play a joke.* 9 name (nombre propio). || *pl.* 10 thanks: *¡muchas gracias! = many thanks/thanks a lot.* || 11 **caer en –,** to please; (fam.) to hit it off. 12 **dar gracias,** to thank/to give thanks. 13 DER. **derecho de –,** right of pardon. 14 **en – a,** because of/due to (a causa de). 15 **gracias a,** thanks to. 16 **hacer –,** to find funny: *no me hace mucha gracia = I don't find it very funny.* 17 **¡qué –!,** how funny! 18 **tener –,** to be funny: *la película tiene mucha gracia = the film is very funny.*
graciable *adj.* easily granted (que se puede conceder libremente).
grácil *adj.* 1 slender, slim (delgado). 2 small (pequeño). 3 delicate (delicado). 4 subtle (sutil).
gracioso, -a *adj.* 1 funny, amusing (divertido). 2 witty, comical (cómico). 3 charming (encantador). || *s.m.* 4 fool, comic character (en el teatro). 5 **hacerse el –,** (fam.) to play the fool.
grada *s.f.* 1 step (peldaño). 2 row (fila de asientos). 3 platform (tarima). 4 tier (asiento colectivo). 5 MAR. slipway (plano inclinado donde se construyen los barcos). 6 AGR. harrow. || *pl.* 7 flight of steps, steps (escalinata).
gradación *s.f.* 1 gradation (por grados sucesivos). 2 MUS. gradation. 3 climax (figura retórica).
graderío *s.m.* o **gradería** *s.f.* 1 flight of steps (escalinata). 2 DEP. stands, grandstand. 3 row of seats (en el teatro, cine, iglesia, etc.).
gradiente *s.m.* 1 FIS. gradient. 2 (Am.) gradient, slope (pendiente).
grado *s.m.* 1 step (peldaño). 2 degree (de temperaturas y ángulos): *dos grados bajo cero = two degrees below zero.* 3 MIL. rank (rango). 4 GRAM. degree. 5 degree (título universitario). 6 year, form (en el colegio): *del tercer grado = in the third year.* 7 MAT. degree. 8 (fig.) step, stage (fase). 9 degree (parentesco). 10 willingness (voluntad): *de buen grado = willingly; de mal grado = unwillingly.* 11 degree (porcentaje). || 12 **en sumo –,** in the extreme. 13 **por grados,** by degrees/step by step/gradually.
graduado, -a *adj.* 1 graduated (con grados). 2 graduate: *graduado en inglés = English graduate.* || *s.m.* y *f.* 3 graduate (licenciado).
gradual *adj.* gradual.
gradualmente *adv.* gradually.
graduar *v.t.* 1 to graduate (el termómetro, etc.). 2 to regulate, to adjust (ajustar). 3 to measure (medir). 4 to test (la vista). 5 to calibrate (calibrar). 6 MIL. to commision. 7 to confer a degree on (conceder un título universitario). || *v.t.* y *v.pron.* 8 to graduate (obtener un título universitario). 9 MIL. to be commissioned.
grafía *s.f.* GRAM. signs representing the sounds of a word.
gráficamente *adv.* graphically.
gráfico, -a *adj.* 1 graphic: *un informe gráfico = a graphic account.* || 2 **artes gráficas,** graphic arts. || *s.m.* y *f.* 3 MAT. graph. 4 MED. chart. || *s.f.* 5 edge (orla de una moneda).
grafismo V. **grafía.**
grafito *s.m.* QUIM. graphite, black lead.
grafología *s.f.* graphology.
grafólogo *s.m.* graphologist, (fam.) handwriting expert.
gragea *s.f.* MED. sugar-coated pill.
grajo *s.m.* ZOOL. rook, crow (ave).
grama *s.f.* BOT. Bermuda grass.
gramática *s.f.* grammar: *gramática histórica = historical grammar; gramática descriptiva = descriptive grammar; gramática parda = astuteness, acumen, horse sense.*
gramatical *adj.* grammatical.
gramaticalmente *adv.* grammatically.
gramático, -a *adj.* 1 grammatical. || *s.m.* y *f.* 2 grammarian (especialista).
gramíneo, -a o **gramináceo, -a** *adj.* 1 BOT. gramineous. || *s.f.pl.* 2 BOT. gramineae.
gramo *s.m.* gramme, gram.
gramófono *s.m.* gramophone, (fam.) record player.
gramola *s.f.* gramophone, (fam.) record player.
gran *adj.* apócope. de grande.
grana *s.f.* 1 seeding (hecho y resultado de granar). 2 scarlet (color). 3 ZOOL. cochineal (cochinilla). 4 seed (semilla). ||

5 ponerse como la –, to turn o go scarlet, (fam.) to go as red as a beetroot.
granada *s.f.* 1 BOT. pomegranate. 2 MIL. grenade: *granada de mano = hand grenade.* || **3 a prueba de –,** shellproof.
granadero *s.m.* 1 MIL. grenadier. 2 (fam.) tall persona (persona alta).
granadino, -a *adj.* 1 of/from Granada. || *s.m.* y *f.* 2 native of Granada. 3 flamenco song (cante andaluz).
granado *s.m.* BOT. pomegranate tree (árbol).
granar *v.i.* to seed.
granate *s.m.* 1 MIN. garnet (piedra). || *adj.* 2 garnet (color).
grande *adj.* 1 big, large (de tamaño): *un coche grande = a big car.* 2 big, tall (de altura): *un jugador grande = a tall player.* 3 (fig.) great: *una gran mujer = a great woman.* 4 great, high (velocidad, elevación, number): *a gran velocidad = at a great speed.* 5 large, great (cantidad de personas): *una gran cantidad de niños = a large number of children.* || **6 a lo –,** in a big way. **7 en –,** as a whole. **8 – de España,** Spanish grandee. **9 pasarlo en –,** to have a great time; (fam.) to have a whale of a time.
grandemente *adv.* greatly, enormously: *te estoy grandemente agradecido = I'm enormously grateful.*
grandeza *s.f.* 1 size (tamaño). 2 largeness (cualidad de grande). 3 importance, greatness. 4 grandeur, magnificence (esplendor). 5 majesty (majestad). 6 grandees (conjunto de los grandes).
grandilocuencia *s.f.* grandiloquence.
grandilocuente *adj.* grandiloquent.
grandiosidad *s.f.* V. **grandeza.**
grandioso, -a *adj.* 1 magnificent, impressive (magnífico). 2 (desp.) grandiose.
grandullón *adj.* over big, oversized.
graneado *adj.* 1 granulated (reducido a grana). 2 speckled (salpicado de pintas). || **3 fuego –,** heavy fire.
granel *loc. adv.* **a –,** in abundance (en abundancia); loose (sin envase); at random (sin número, orden ni medida).
granero *s.m.* barn, granary.
granítico, -a *adj.* granitic, granite.
granito *s.m.* 1 GEOL. granite (roca). 2 silkworm egg (huevecillo de gusano de seda).
granizada *s.f.* 1 hailstorm (precipitación de granizo). 2 iced drink (bebida helada).
granizar *v.i.* to hail.
granizo *s.m.* hail.
granja *s.f.* 1 farm (terreno y casa). 2 farmhouse (casa). || **3 – colectiva,** collective farm.
granjear *v.t.* 1 to get, to obtain, to acquire (adquirir). || *v.t.* y *r.* 2 to win over (ganar el favor, la simpatía, etc., de una persona).
granjero, -a *s.m.* y *f.* farmer.
grano *s.m.* 1 grain (fruto de los cereales). 2 seed (semilla). 3 bean (semilla pequeña): *grano de café = coffee bean.* 4 particle, grain (partícula): *grano de arena = grain of sand.* 5 MED. spot, pimple (en la piel). 6 grain (peso en farmacias). 7 grain (de la madera, piedra, etc.). || *pl.* 8 AGR. grain, corn. || **9 ir al –,** to get to the point. **10 tomarlo con un – de sal,** to take it with a pinch of salt.
granuja *s.f.* 1 loose grapes (uvas separadas de los racimos). 2 pips, seeds (semillas de la uva y otras frutas). || *s.m.* y *f.* 3 urchin (muchacho vagabundo y pillo). 4 rascal, rogue (pícaro).
granujada *s.f.* band of urchins (grupo de granujas).
granular *adj.* 1 granular. || *v.t.* 2 to granulate.
grao *s.m.* beach (playa).
grapa *s.f.* staple (para sujetar y unir papeles): *coser con grapas = to staple.*
grapadora *s.f.* stapler.
grapar *v.t.* to staple.
grasa *s.f.* 1 lat (sustancia grasa). 2 grease (cosa grasienta). 3 dirt, filth (suciedad). 4 grease (para lubricar).
grasiento, -a *adj.* 1 greasy, oily. 2 (fig.) filthy, dirty (sucio).
graso, -a *adj.* 1 fatty (carne, cuerpos, etc.). 2 greasy (superficies).
gratificación *s.f.* 1 bonus (remuneración distinta del sueldo). 2 reward (recompensa). 3 tip (propina). 4 satisfaction, gratification (satisfacción). 5 incentive (incentivo).
gratificar *v.t.* 1 to gratify, to satisfy (complacer). 2 to tip (dar una propina). 3 to reward, to recompense (recompensar).
gratis *adj.* free, gratis.
gratitud *s.f.* gratitude.
grato *adj.* 1 pleasant, pleasing (agradable): *un resultado muy grato = a very pleasant result.* 2 welcome, gratifying (apreciado): *una noticia grata = a welcome piece of news.* || **3 nos es – informarle...,** we are pleased to inform you...
gratuidad *s.f.* gratuitousness.
gratuitamente *adv.* 1 free, gratis (gratis). 2 gratuitously (sin motivo). 3 effortlessly (sin esfuerzo o sacrificio).
gratuito, -a *adj.* 1 free (sin pagar). 2 gratuitous, arbitrary (arbitrario).
grava *s.f.* gravel (piedra machacada).
gravamen *s.m.* 1 FIN. tax (impuesto). 2 duty, obligation (obligación). 3 burden (carga de responsabilidad).
gravar *v.t.* 1 to burden, to encumber (imponer un gravamen). 2 to tax (imponer un impuesto).
grave *adj.* 1 heavy (que pesa). 2 momentous, very important (de mucha importancia). 3 serious (serio). 4 grave, very ill (muy enfermo). 5 awkward, very difficult (muy difícil). 6 FON. grave: *acento grave = grave accent.* 7 GRAM. paroxytone (palabra que lleva acento en la penúltima sílaba). 8 tiresome, trying (molesto). 9 deep (voz). || *adj.* y *s.m.* 10 MUS. bass (bajo).
gravedad *s.f.* 1 FIS. gravity: *centro de gravedad = centre of gravity.* 2 gravity, seriousness (calidad de grave). 3 seriousness, gravity (seriedad). 4 importance (importancia). || **5 las leyes de la –,** FIS. the laws of gravity.
gravemente *adv.* gravely, seriously: *gravemente enfermo = gravely ill.*
gravidez *s.f.* MED. pregnancy (preñez).
grávido, -a *adj.* 1 heavy, weighty (pesado). 2 pregnant (embarazada).
gravitación *s.f.* FIS. gravitation.
gravitar *v.i.* 1 FIS. to gravitate. 2 to rest on (apoyarse). 3 to weigh down upon (pesar una obligación sobre alguien). 4 to threaten, to hang over (amenazar).
gravoso, -a *adj.* 1 expensive, costly (que ocasiona gastos). 2 onerous, burdensome (oneroso). 3 trying, tedious (molesto).
graznar *v.i.* 1 to squawk (en general). 2 to croak (grajo, cuervo). 3 to quack (pato). 4 to cackle (ganso). 5 to croak (un cantante).
graznido *s.m.* 1 squawk (en general). 2 croak (grajo, cuervo). 3 quack (pato). 4 cackle (ganso). 5 croak (canto destemplado y molesto).
greca *s.f.* fret, border (franja).
greda *s.f.* clay (arcilla).
gregal *adj.* V. **gregario.**
gregario, -a *adj.* 1 gregarious (que vive en rebaños o manadas). 2 (fig.) gregarious (feliz en compañía o grupos). 3 (desp.) sheep-like (sin ideas ni iniciativas propias).
gregarismo *s.m.* gregarious spirit (espíritu gregario).
gregoriano *adj.* Gregorian: *canto gregoriano = Gregorian chant.*
greguería *s.f.* 1 din, racket (alboroto). 2 penetrating o mordant remark (frase intuitiva e ingeniosa sobre la vida corriente).
gremial *adj.* 1 guild (de los gremios). 2 union (de los sindicatos). || *s.m.* y *f.* 3 guildsman (individuo de un gremio). 4 union member (individuo de un sindicato). || *s.m.* 5 REL. gremial (paño).
gremio *s.m.* 1 guild (asociación de personas del mismo oficio). 2 union, trades union (sindicato). 3 (fig.) side, group, team (grupo, equipo).
greña *s.f.* 1 mop of hair (cabellera despeinada). 2 tangle (lo que está enredado). || **3 andar a la –,** to argue; to bicker (armar discusión).
greñudo, -a *adj.* tangled, matted (pelo enredado).
gres *s.m.* GEOL. sandstone (arenisca).
gresca *s.f.* 1 row, din, racket, hubbub, uproar (alboroto). 2 quarrel, row (riña). 3 fight (pelea).
grey *s.f.* 1 herd (rebaño). 2 REL. flock (grupo de fieles).
grial *s.m.* REL. grail (vaso o copa mística): *Santo Grial = Holy Grail.*
griego, -a *adj.* 1 Greek, Grecian. || *s.m.* 2 Greek (lengua) 3 (fig.) **hablar en griego,** to speak double Dutch. || *s.m.* y *f.* 4 Greek (persona).
grieta *s.f.* 1 crack (pequeño). 2 fissure, crevice (grande). 3 MED. chap, crack (en la piel).

grifería *s.f.* plumbing (grifos, tuberías, etc.).
grifo *s.m.* **1** tap (llave del agua). **2** griffin (animal fabuloso). **3** (Am.) drunk (borracho). || *adj.* **4** (Am.) drunk (borracho). **5** stoned, high (intoxicado con marihuana).
grillera *s.f.* **1** cricket hole (agujero donde viven los grillos). **2** cricket rage (jaula de grillos).
grillete *s.m.* fetter, shackle.
grillo *s.m.* **1** ZOOL. cricket. **2** fetter, shackle (grillete). || *pl.* **3** fetter, shackle.
grima *s.f.* **1** horror (horror). **2** displeasure (desagrado).
gringo, -a *adj.* **1** foreign (extranjero). **2** unintelligible, (fam.) gibberish (lenguaje uninteligible). || *s.m.* y *f.* **3** foreigner (extranjero). **4** (Am.) Yankee (norteamericano). || **5** (Am.) **hablar en –,** to speak gibbership.
griñón *s.m.* BOT. nectarine (melocotón pequeño).
gripe *s.f.* MED. flu, influenza: *tener gripe = to have the flu.*
gris *adj.* **1** grey (color). **2** dull, overcast (tiempo). **3** sad (triste). || *s.m.* **4** grey (color). **5** cold wind (viento frío). || **6 – marengo,** dark grey.
grisáceo, -a *adj.* greyish.
grisú *s.m.* firedamp.
gritar *v.i.* **1** to shout, to yell. **2** to scream, to cry (chillar). **3** to boo, to hoot (abuchear). **4** to howl, to shriek (niños).
griterío *s.m.* **1** shouting, screaming. **2** booing, hooting (en el teatro). **3** howling, shrieking (niños).
grito *s.m.* **1** shout, yell (de gritar). **2** scream, cry (chillido). **3** boo, hoot (teatro). **4** cry (de guerra, de los animales). **5** call, cry (de los pájaros). **6** howl, shriek (de los niños). || **7 a gritos,** at the top of one's voice. **8 dar gritos,** to shout. **9 el último –,** the "in" thing; the latest craze. **10 poner el – en el cielo,** to kick up a fuss; (fam.) to scream blue murder.
gritón, -a *adj.* **1** loud-mouthed (que grita mucho). **2** loud-mouthed person.
grosella *s.f.* BOT. currant (fruto): *grosella roja = redcurrant; grosella negra = blackcurrant; grosella espinosa = gooseberry.*
grosellero *s.m.* currant bush (arbusto).
grosería *s.f.* **1** stupidity, crassness (estupidez). **2** rudeness, discourtesy (falta de educación). **3** vulgarity, crudeness (vulgaridad). **4** rude o vulgar thing (cosa grosera).
grosero, -a *adj.* **1** crude, vulgar, rude (basto). **2** rude, discourteous (descortés). **3** stupid, gross (un error).
grosor *s.m.* thickness (grueso de un cuerpo).
grotesco, -a *adj.* **1** ridiculous, absurd (ridículo). **2** grotesque, horrible (horrible o de mal gusto).
grúa *s.f.* **1** crane: *grúa móvil = travelling crane; grúa de puente = overhead crane; grúa de torre = tower crane.* **2** tow-truck (para trasladar coches mal aparcados).
grueso, -a *adj.* **1** thick (espeso): *un libro grueso = a thick book.* **2** fat, stout (gordo). **3** MAR. rough, heavy (con grandes olas). **4** thick (tronco, palo). **5** (fig.) dense, thick (poco inteligente). || *s.m.* **6** thickness (espesor). **7** main part o body (parte principal de un todo). || *s.f.* **8** gross (doce docenas). || **9 en –,** COM. in bulk.
grulla *s.f.* ZOOL. crane (ave).
grullada *s.f.* gang of rogues (cuadrilla de pícaros).
grumete *s.m.* MAR. cabin hoy, ship's boy.
grumo *s.m.* **1** lump, clot (en líquidos). **2** bunch, cluster (grupo de cosas apiñadas). || **3 – de leche,** curd. **4 – de sangre,** blood clot.
grumoso, -a *adj.* **1** clotted (sangre). **2** lumpy (líquidos). **3** curdled (leche).
gruñido *s.m.* **1** grunt (voz del cerdo). **2** growl (de otros animales). **3** (fig.) grunt (persona).
gruñir *v.i.* **1** to grunt (cerdo). **2** to growl (otros animales). **3** (fig.) to grunt (personas). **4** to creak (puerta, ventana, suelo, etc.).
gruñón, -a *adj.* **1** (fam.) grumpy, grumbling. || *s.m.* y *f.* **2** grumbler.
grupa *s.f.* haunch, hindquarters (anca de las caballerías).
grupo *s.m.* **1** group: *grupo parlamentario = parliamentary group.* **2** clump (de árboles). **3** TEC. set, unit (unidad). || **4 – sanguíneo,** blood group.
gruta *s.f.* cave, cavern (cueva).
guacamayo *s.m.* ZOOL. macaw (ave).
guachear *v.i.* (Am.) to be wrong, to make a mistake (errar).
guacho, guajcho o **guascho, -a** *adj.* **1** (Am.) orphaned (huérfano). **2** (Am.) abandoned (abandonado). || *s.m.* y *f.* **3** orphan (huérfano). **4** abandoned child (niño abandonado).
guadaña *s.f.* scythe (herramienta).
guafle *s.m.* (Am.) speaker, loudspeaker (altavoz).
guagua *s.f.* **1** (Am.) bus (autobús). **2** baby (nene). **3** trifle (cosa sin valor).
guajiro, -a *s.m.* y *f.* **1** (Am.) white Cuban peasant (campesino blanco de Cuba). || *s.f.* **2** Cuban peasant song and dance (canto y baile).
gualdo, -a *adj.* yellow (amarillo).
guanche *adj./s.m.* y *f.* Guanche (lengua y habitantes de las Islas Canarias).
guano *s.m.* guano.
guantazo o **guantada** *s.m.* slap (bofetada).
guante *s.m.* **1** glove (prenda): *guante de boxeo = boxing glove; guante de goma = rubber glove.* || **2 arrojar el –,** to challenge; (fam.) to throw down the gauntlet (desafiar). **3 echar el –,** to grab; to seize (coger). **4 – blanco/con – blanco,** diplomatically. **5 poner a uno más blando/más suave que un –,** to make someone as meek as a lamb. **5 recoger el –,** to take up the challenge.
guantelete *s.m.* gauntlet (manopla).
guantero, -a *s.m.* y *f.* **1** glover (que hace o vende guantes). || *s.f.* **2** glove compartment (en un coche).
guantón *s.m.* (Am.) slap (bofetada).
guapamente *adv.* very well (muy bien).
guapetón, -a *adj.* handsome, (fam.) dishy (guapo).
guapo, -a *adj.* **1** handsome, good-looking (hombre). **2** pretty, good-looking (mujer). **3** flashy, ostentatious (ostentoso). **4** brave, bold (valiente). **5** quarrelsome (pendenciero). **6** elegant, smart (elegante). **7** conceited (presumido). || *s.m.* **8** boaster (presumido). **9** bully, tough guy (pendenciero). **10** good-looking chap (hombre guapo).
guaraní *adj./s.m.* y *f.* **1** Guarani (de la población india de Paraguay). || *s.m.* **2** guarani (moneda y lengua).
guarapo *s.m.* **1** (Am.) sugar-cane juice (jugo de la caña de azúcar). **2** sugar-cane liquor (bebida fermentada de la caña de azúcar).
guarda *s.m.* y *f.* **1** guard (en general). **2** keeper (de parque, museo). **3** (Am.) conductor (de autobús). **4** guard (de trenes). || **5** observance (observancia de lo mandado). **6** rib (varilla de abanico). **7** flyleaf (de un libro). **8 ángel de la –,** REL. guardian angel. **9 – nocturno,** night watchman.
guardabarrera *s.m.* y *f.* level-crossing keeper.
guardabarros *s.m.* mudguard, (EE.UU.) fender.
guardabosque *s.m.* y *f.* forester, ranger.
guardacostas *s.m.* coastguard vessel.
guardaespaldas *s.m.* bodyguard.
guardafango *s.m.* (Am.) mudguard, (EE.UU.) fender (guardabarros).
guardafrenos *s.m.* brakeman.
guardagujas *s.m.* switchman.
guardameta *s.m.* DEP. goalkeeper.
guardamonte *s.m.* trigger guard (de las armas de fuego).
guardapolvo *s.m.* dustcoat (prenda).
guardar *v.t.* **1** to keep: *guardar una promesa = to keep a promise; guardar un secreto = to keep a secret.* **2** to observe (una ley, una regla). **3** to look out, to take care (tener cuidado). **4** to keep (conservar). **5** MIL. to guard. **6** to tend, to watch over (un rebaño). **7** to put away: *guardar la ropa = to put away one's clothes.* **8** to protect (proteger). **9** to save: *guardar sitio = to save a place.* **10** REL. to keep (mandamientos). **11** to put by, to lay aside (poner de lado). **12** to save (no gastar). || *v.pron.* **13** to avoid (evitar): *guárdate de no andar por la noche = avoid walking at night.* **14** to look after oneself (cuidarse). || **15 ¡Dios guarde a la Reina!,** God save the Queen. **16 – las distancias,** to keep one's distance. **17 – silencio,** to keep quiet. **18 – su palabra,** to keep one's word.
guardarropa *s.m.* **1** cloakroom (lugar donde se dejan los abrigos, etc.). || *s.m.* y *f.* **2** cloakroom attendant (persona).

guardarropía *s.f.* 1 props (conjunto de trajes y efectos de los actores). 2 wardrobe (lugar en que se guardan).
guardería *s.f.* 1 guard (oficio de guardia). 2 day nursery, crèche (de niños).
guardesa *s.f.* female guard (mujer guarda).
guardia *s.f.* 1 MIL. guard (grupo de soldados). 2 DEP. guard (en boxeo, esgrima, etc.). 3 guard (vigilancia o actitud de defensa). 4 MAR. watch. || *s.m.* y *f.* 5 MIL. guard, guardsman (individuo de ciertos cuerpos armados). 6 policeman (policía). || 7 **estar de —, a)** MIL. to be on guard; **b)** to be on duty (en un hospital, etc.). 8 **— civil,** civil guard. 8 **— marina,** midshipman. 10 **— municipal,** local police. 11 **hacer** o **montar —,** to mount guard. 12 **poner a uno en —,** to put someone on guard. 13 **relevar la —,** to change guard.
guardián, -ana *s.m.* y *f.* 1 guardian, keeper. 2 keeper (de parque, jardín). 3 caretaker (de un edificio). 4 warder (de cárcel).
guardilla *s.f.* attic, garret (buhardilla).
guarecer *v.t.* 1 to protect (proteger). 2 to give shelter to (albergar). || *v.r.* 3 to take refuge (refugiarse).
guarida *s.f.* 1 ZOOL. lair, den (cueva de animales). 2 shelter, refuge (refugio).
guarismo *s.m.* number, figure (cifra).
guarnecer *v.t.* 1 to equip, to provide (poner guarnición). 2 to adorn, to decorate (adornar). 3 to plaster (revestir una pared). 4 MIL. to garrison. 5 to trim (un vestido). 6 to line (los frenos).
guarnición *s.f.* 1 decoration, adornment (adorno). 2 setting (engarce de las piedras preciosas). 3 guard (de las espadas). 4 MIL. garrison. 5 garnish (alimento). 6 provision (provisión). 7 harness (de caballería). 8 lining (de los frenos). 9 plastering (de una pared).
guarrada *s.f.* 1 filth, dirt (suciedad). 2 dirty trick (mala pasada). 3 mess (porquería): *¡qué guarrada! = what a mess!* 4 dirtiness, filthiness (cualidad de sucio). 5 obscenity (obscenidad).
guarrería *s.f.* V. **guarrada.**
guarro, -a *s.m.* y *f.* 1 pig (cerdo). 2 (fam.) pig. || *adj.* 3 dirty, filthy.
guasa *s.f.* (Am.) joke (broma): *con guasa = jokingly.*
guasearse *v.r.* 1 to joke, to tease (bromear). 2 to make fun of, to laugh at (burlarse de).
guasón, -ona *adj.* 1 funny, comical, humorous (cómico). || *s.m.* y *f.* 2 joker, wag (bromista).
guata *s.f.* raw cotton (algodón).
guatemalteco, -a *adj./s.m.* y *f.* Guatemalan.
guateque *s.m.* party (fiesta).
guater *s.m.* (Am.) toilet, loo (wáter).
guayaba *s.f.* 1 BOT. guava (fruto). 2 (Am.) lie, fib (mentira).
guayabal *s.m.* guava grove.
guayabera *s.f.* (Am.) light jacket (chaquetilla ligera).
guayabo, -a *s.m.* 1 BOT. guava tree (árbol). || *s.f.* 2 (Am.) young girl (muchacha joven).
guayaca *s.f.* (Am.) bag (bolsa).
guayar *v.t.* (Am.) to scrape (raspar).
gubernamental *adj.* POL. governamental; loyalist.
gubia *s.f.* TEC. gouge (herramienta).
guedeja *s.f.* 1 long hair (pelo largo). 2 curl (rizo). 3 mane (melena).
gueisa o **geisha** *s.f.* geisha.
guepardo *s.m.* ZOOL. leopard.
güero, -a *adj.* (Am.) blond, fair (rubio).
guerra *s.f.* 1 war (lucha armada). 2 warfare (sistema, teoría): *guerra atómica = atomic warfare.* 3 discord (discordia). 4 opposition (oposición). 5 hostility (hostilidad). 6 conflict, fight (conflicto). || 7 **dar —,** to annoy; to be a nuisance (molestar). 8 **declarar la —,** to declare war. 9 **estar en —,** to be at war. 10 **— abierta,** open warfare. 11 **— bacteriológica,** germ warfare. 12 **— civil,** civil war. 13 **— de nervios,** war of nerves. 14 **— fría,** cold war. 15 **— mundial,** world war. 16 **— nuclear,** nuclear war. 17 **hacer la — a,** to wage war on; to make war on.
guerrear *v.i.* to wage war, to fight.
guerrero, -a *adj.* 1 warring (que pertenece a la guerra). 2 warlike, martial (aficionado a la guerra). 3 (fig.) naughty, troublesome (travieso). || *s.m.* 4 soldier, warrior (soldado). || *s.f.* 5 tunic (uniforme).
guerrilla *s.f.* 1 guerrilla warfare (método de lucha). 2 guerrilla band (grupo). || 3 **— urbana,** urban guerrilla warfare.
guerrillero, -a *s.m.* y *f.* guerrilla, guerrilla fighter.
gueto *s.m.* ghetto (barrio marginado).
guía *s.m.* y *f.* 1 guide (de museo, montaña, ciudad, etc.). || *s.m.* 2 MIL. guide. 3 handlebars (manillar). || *s.f.* 4 guidance, guiding (lo que orienta o dirige). 5 directory: *guía telefónica = telephone directory.* 6 guidebook (libro para turistas). 7 street guide (de calles). 8 railway timetable (horario de trenes). || 9 **— de carga,** waybill.
guiador, -a *adj.* 1 guiding. || *s.m.* y *f.* 2 guide.
guiar *v.t.* 1 to guide: *guiar por las montañas = to guide through the mountains.* 2 to lead, to direct (llevar). 3 to drive (conducir). 4 MAR. to steer. 5 to fly, to pilot (pilotar). 6 BOT. to train (plantas). 7 to advise, to councel (aconsejar). || *v.pron.* 8 to be guided.
guija *s.f.* 1 pebble (piedra pequeña y redonda). 2 BOT. vetch (arbusto).
guijarral *s.m.* stony place (lugar pedregoso).
guijarro *s.m.* V. **guija.**
guillotina *s.f.* 1 guillotine (para decapitar). 2 paper cutter, guillotine (para cortar papel). || 3 **ventana de —,** sash window.
guillotinar *v.t.* to guillotine.
guinda *s.f.* BOT. morello cherry, (fam.) black cherry (fruta).
guindal *s.m.* BOT. morello cherry tree, black cherry tree (árbol).
guindilla *s.f.* 1 red pepper (pimiento pequeño). 2 (fam.) bobby, cop (polizonte). 3 rascal, rogue (pícaro).
guindo *s.m.* V. **guindal.**
guiñapo *s.m.* 1 rag (andrajo o trapo roto). 2 sickly o unhealthy person (persona enfermiza). 3 degenerate, rogue (persona despreciable).
guiñar *v.t.* to wink.
guiño *s.m.* wink.
guiñol *s.m.* puppet show (representación de títeres).
guión *s.m.* 1 standard, (p.u.) guidon (estandarte). 2 leader (lo que va delante y sirve de guía). 3 script (de una película). 4 dash, hyphen (signo de puntuación). 5 scenario (línea argumental de una película).
guionista *s.m.* y *f.* scriptwriter (en el cine).
guirigay *s.m.* 1 nonsense, (fam.) gibberish, double-Dutch (lenguaje incomprensible). 2 hubbub, commotion (griterío).
guirlache *s.m.* almond nougat (turrón de almendras).
guirnalda *s.f.* 1 garland (corona de flores). 2 wreath (de funeral).
guisa *s.f.* 1 way, manner, method (modo): *de tal guisa = in such a way.* 2 will (voluntad).
guisado *s.m.* stew.
guisante *s.m.* BOT. pea (planta y semilla).
guisar *v.t.* 1 to cook (cocinar). 2 to stew (un guisado). 3 to arrange, to order (ordenar).
guiso *s.m.* 1 cooked dish (plato guisado). 2 stew (estofado).
güisqui *s.m.* whisky.
guitarra *s.f.* MUS. guitar.
guitarreo *s.m.* strumming on the guitar.
guitarrero, -a *s.m.* y *f.* 1 guitar maker (que hace guitarras). 2 guitar seller (vendedor). 3 guitar mender (que arregla guitarras).
guitarrillo *s.m.* 1 treble guitar (tiple). 2 small guitar (guitarra pequeña).
guitarrista *s.m.* y *f.* guitarist.
gula *s.f.* gluttony, greed.
guripa *s.m.* 1 MIL. private (soldado raso). 2 (fam.) little devil, little rascal (pilluelo).
gusanera *s.f.* 1 breeding ground for worms (lugar donde se crían los gusanos). 2 rubbish dump (pudridero).
gusano *s.m.* 1 worm. 2 maggot (larva). 3 caterpillar (oruga). 4 earthworm (lombriz). 5 (fig. y fam.) worm (persona despreciable). || 6 **— de seda,** silkworm.
gusanoso, -a *adj.* grub-infested, maggoty.
gusarapo, -a *s.m.* y *f.* bug (bicho).
gustar *v.t.* 1 to taste (sentir el sabor en el paladar). 2 to try, to sample (probar). || *v.i.* 3 to like (agradar): *me gusta leer = I like reading; no me gusta ese hombre = I don't like that man; como te guste = as you wish; ¿qué gustas? = what would you like?* 4 to please, to be pleasing (dar

placer): *el equipo no gustó a la gente = the team didn't please the people.* || **5 — de,** to enjoy; to like (sentir afición): *gusta de pintar = he enjoys painting.*
gustativo, -a *adj.* tasty, (p.u.) gustative.
gustazo *s.m.* great pleasure (gran placer): *darse el gustazo = to treat oneself to.*
gusto *s.m.* **1** taste (sentido). **2** flavour, taste (sabor). **3** pleasure (placer). **4** willpower (voluntad propia). **5** taste (facultad de apreciar lo bello): *tener buen gusto = to have good taste; tener mal gusto = to have bad taste.* **6** whim, caprice (capricho). || **7 a —,** comfortable; at ease: *estar a gusto = to be comfortable.* **8 con —,** with pleasure. **9 dar —,** to be pleasant. **10 despacharse uno a su —,** (fam.) to do what the hell one wants. **11 ¡mucho —!,** pleased to meet you! **12 tomar/coger el —,** to take a liking to.
gustosamente *adv.* with pleasure (con placer).
gustoso, -a *adj.* **1** tasty (sabroso). **2** pleasant, nice (agradable). **3** with pleasure (gustosamente).
gutapercha *s.f.* gutta-percha.
gutural *adj.* guttural, (fam.) throaty.

h, H *s.f.* **1** h, H novena letra del alfabeto español. || **2 — aspirada,** FON. aspirated h.

haba *s.f.* **1** BOT. broad bean. **2** swelling (roncha, en la piel). **3** tumor on horses' palate (tumor en el paladar de los caballos). **4** BOT. bean (semilla, de algunos frutos como el café, coco, etc.). || **5 en todas partes cuecen habas,** it's no different anywhere else, it's the same all over the world. **6 son habas contadas, a)** it's a cinch, it's a certainty; **b)** there's not a lot of it (poca cantidad de algo).

habanero, -a *adj.* **1** of Havana. || *s.m.* y *f.* **2** inhabitant of Havana, native of Havana. || *s.f.* **3** MUS. folk music, folk song from Havana.

habano *s.m.* **1** Havana cigar. || *adj.* **2** brown; ligth tobacco colour (color).

haber *v.imp.* **1** (there) to be: *había mucha gente en el cine = there were many people at the cinema; habrá lluvia mañana = there will be rain tomorrow; si hubiera habido tiempo = if there had been enough time.* **2** to happen; to occur: *¿qué ha habido entre vosotros dos? = what has happened between you two?* || *v.t.* **3** to have: *él hubo necesidad de más dinero = he had need of more money.* || *s.m.* **4** COM. credit (en la contabilidad). || *s.pl.* **5** salary, wages (sueldo). || **6 — de/que,** to be necessary; to have to: *hay que estudiar más = it's necessary to study harder.* **7 haberlo dicho/avisado/puesto antes/etc.,** you should have said it/warned about it/put it on before/etc. (expresando una queja). **8 habérselas con alguien,** to have it out with somebody. **9 no — tal,** not to be true (no ser cierto algo).

OBS. Este verbo tiene una importancia especial como auxiliar al igual que: **10** to have: *hemos trabajado como burros = we have worked very hard; había estado estudiando toda la noche cuando llamó Jim = I had been studying through the night when Jim called; me habría acordado de ti = I would have remembered you.*

habichuela *s.f.* BOT. kidney bean, dwarf French bean, scarlet runner bean.

hábil *adj.* **1** skillful, adroit (con las manos). **2** clever, apt, capable (con el ingenio). || **3 día —,** working day.

habilidad *s.f.* **1** skill, adroitness (con las manos). **2** cleverness, capability (mental).

habilidoso, -a *adj.* skillful, adroit (más bien con las manos); clever, able (ingenioso): *mi hijo es habilidoso con las manos = my son is adroit with his hands.*

habilitación *s.f.* **1** entitlement (derecho). **2** authorization (autorización): *una habilitación especial = a special authorization.*

habilitado, -a *p.p.* **1** de **habilitar.** || *s.m.* **2** paymaster (pagador).

habilitador, -a *adj.* **1** qualifying. || *s.m.* **2** outfitter (de ropa, equipo, etc.).

habilitar *v.t.* **1** to entitle, to legally empower. **2** to finance, to grant the financial means.

hábilmente *adv.* **1** skillfully, adroitly (con las manos). **2** aptly, capably, cleverly (ingeniosamente).

habitabilidad *s.f.* quality of living accomodation.

habitable *adj.* inhabitable, habitable, that can be lived in.

habitación *s.f.* **1** room. **2** bedroom (dormitorio). **3** residence, dwelling (residencia).

habitáculo *s.m.* room; small room.

habitado, -a *adj.* inhabited, lived-in: *un lugar habitado = an inhabited place.*

habitante *s.m.* y *f.* inhabitant, occupant, resident (de una ciudad, casa, residencia, etc.).

habitar *v.t.* e *i.* to inhabit, to dwell, to live: *todo tipo de tribus habitan en esta región = all kinds of tribes live in this region.*

hábitat *s.m.* ECOL. habitat.

hábito *s.m.* **1** habit (personal): *él tiene el hábito de levantarse muy temprano = he has the habit of getting up very early.* **2** custom (social). **3** addiction (adicción, a drogas, alcohol, etc.). **4** REL. habit (vestido religioso). || **5 colgar/ahorcar los hábitos,** REL. to leave the priesthood. **6 tomar el —,** REL. to take Holy Orders; to become a monk (hacerse monje); to take the veil (hacerse monja).

habituación *s.f.* habituation, accustoming.

habitual *adj.* **1** customary, habitual. **2** regular (cliente). **3** hardened (endurecido): *un criminal habitual = a hardened criminal.* || *s.m.* y *f.* **4** habitué (hombre), habituée (mujer).

habitualmente *adv.* usually, habitually, customarily.

habituar *v.t.* **1** to accustom, to habituate; to familiarize: *este método de respiración te habituará a tener más relajación = this method of breathing will accustom you to have more relaxation.* || *v.pron.* **2** to get accustomed, to get used: *acostumbrarse a un nuevo trabajo = to get used to a new job.*

habla *s.m.* **1** speech, faculty of speech. **2** language: *su habla es típicamente australiana = his language is typically Australian.* || **3 estar/ponerse al — con,** to be in contact with/to get in contact with. **4 quedarse sin —,** to be lost for words, to be speechless.

hablada *s.f.* (Am.) **1** boast (fanfarronada). **2** rumour, gossip (habladuría).

habladera *s.f.* (Am.) piece of gossip (habladuría).

hablador, -a *adj.* **1** talkative. **2** (Am.) indiscreet (indiscreto). || *s.m.* y *f.* **3** chatterbox: *es una habladora incorregible = she's an incredible chatterbox.*

habladuría *s.f.* catty remark, catty comment, malicious chatter, gossip.

hablante *adj.* **1** speaking: *máquina hablante = speaking machine.* || *s.m.* y *f.* **2** speaker.

hablar *v.i.* **1** to speak, to talk. **2** to communicate: *tenemos que hablar entre todos = we all have to communicate with each other.* **3** to have one's say: *déjale que hable = let him have his say.* || *v.t.* **4** to speak, to talk (especialmente un idioma): *he speaks ten languages = habla diez idiomas.* || **5 — a tontas y a locas,** to talk through one's hat, to talk without rhyme or reason. **6 — claro,** to speak plainly, to speak bluntly, to speak frankly. **7 — en cristiano,** to speak so that everyone understands. **8 — recio,** to speak in a hard way. **9 — uno consigo mismo,** to talk to oneself.

hablilla *s.f.* tittle-tattle, piece of gossip.

hacedor *s.m.* **1** maker: *el hacedor de reyes = the king maker.* || **2 el Hacedor,** REL. the Creator, the Maker.

hacendado, -a *adj.* **1** landed, property owning. || *s.m.* y *f.* **2** landowner, property owner.

hacendoso, -a *adj.* bustling, hard-working, diligent: *una niña muy hacendosa = a diligent girl.*

hacer *v.t.* **1** to do: *haré algo sobre tu problema = I'll do something about your problem.* **2** to make (fabricar): *hacer una mesa = to make a table.* **3** to make, to oblige, to force, to compel (obligar): *mi madre siempre me hizo estudiar = my mother always made me study.* **4** to pack (la maleta). **5** to make, to make up, to amount to, to equal (en sumas matemáticas): *dos y dos hacen cuatro = two and two make up four.* **6** to inure, to accustom, to condition: *hacer el cuerpo al calor = to accustom the body to the heat.* **7** to assume to be, to suppose to be, to imagine to be: *te hacía en Londres = I supposed you were in London.* **8** to make (someone) look: *ese peinado te hace más joven = that hair style makes you look younger.* **9** to work, to perform (un milagro, una obra de teatro, etc.). **10** to lay (una apuesta). **11** to make, to earn (dinero). **12** to make (la cama, la cena, etc.). **13** to make (el amor). **14** to put into practice (una medida, resolución, etc.). **15** to ask (preguntas). **16** to tie (un nudo, la corbata, etc.). || *v.i.* **17** to act, to behave: *hace como si no me conoce = he acts as if he didn't know me.* **18** to suit, to be suitable: *si te hace, podemos salir ahora = if it suits you, we can go out now.* **19** (Am.) to matter, to be important, to be relevant: *lo que dices no hace al caso = what you're saying is not relevant to the subject.* || *v.pron.* **20** to pretend, to pretend to be: *él se hace el distraído frecuentemente = he often pretends to be abstent-minded.* **21** to become, to turn into: *la nieve se ha hecho agua ya = the snow has already turned into water.* **22** to get used, to become accustomed: *hacerse a la idea = to get used to the idea.* **23** to become, to take up, to go into (algún tipo de profesión): *se hizo bombero = he became a fireman.* **24** to exchange (saludos, insultos, etc.). || *v.imp.* **25** to be (con expresiones sobre el tiempo atmosférico): *hace mal día = it is a horrible day.* **26** ago (con expresiones de tiempo): *hace muchos años = many years ago.* **27** for (con expresiones de tiempo durativo): *hace mucho que no le veo = I have not seen him for a long time.* || *v.t.* e *i.* **28** to evacuate (alguna función corporal): *hacer de vientre = to evacuate one's bowels.* || **29 haberla hecho buena,** to put one's foot into it. **30 — a todo,** to be useful for many things. **31 — bien/mal,** to act rightly, correctly/wrong, in a bad way. **32 — buena una cosa a otra,** to make something good by comparison. **33 — de,** to act as: *hizo de héroe en la obra = he acted as the hero in the play.* **34 — por,** to do one's best to: *haz por estar a la hora = do your best to be on time.* **35 — presente,** to call attention to, to remind of. **36 — que hacemos,** to pretend we are doing something. **37 — una de las suyas,** to do what one pleases, to do one's usual trick, to be up to one's old tricks. **38 hacerse a un lado/** atrás, to move over, to move back. **39 hacerse con algo,** to get hold of something, to take something. **40 hacerse con alguien,** to win somebody over. **41 hacerse de nuevas,** to pretend not to know anything about it. **42 hacerse de rogar,** to let oneself be begged. **43 hacerse duro,** to get very rough.

OBS. Este verbo tiene una enorme cantidad de usos seguido de sustantivo: **44** normalmente con los verbos to make y to do: *hacer ruido = to make a noise; hacer ejercicios físicos = to do work-outs; hacer la casa = to do the housework; hacer una película = to make a film.*

hacia *prep.* **1** towards, in the direction of (lugar): *está caminando hacia la casa = he's walking towards the house.* **2** about, roundabout, approximately (tiempo): *hacia las cinco = about five.* **3** as regards, in relation to (asunto): *la actitud de Byron hacia la muerte era muy extraña = Byron's attitude as regards death was very strange.*

hacienda *s.f.* **1** country estate; farm. **2** (Am.) ranch. **3** fortune, wealth, riches. || **3 Hacienda,** Treasury, Exchequer. **4 Hacienda Pública,** state-owned properties and goods, public treasury.

hacinamiento *s.m.* stacking, piling; crowding, overcrowding.

hacinar *v.t.* y *pron.* to pile, to pile up, to stack.

hacha *s.f.* **1** axe, hatchet, chopper. **2** large wax taper. || **3 ser un —,** to be an ace, to be outstanding.

hachazo *s.m.* **1** axe blow, stroke with an axe. **2** (Am.) gash, open wound.

hache *s.f.* name given to the letter h.

hachís *s.m.* hashish.

hachón *s.m.* large torch (antorcha).

hada *s.f.* fairy, sprite, pixy: *cuento de hadas = fairy tale.*

hado *s.m.* fate, destiny.

hagiografía *s.f.* REL. hagiography.

hagiógrafo, -a *m.* y *f.* hagiographer.

¡hala! *interj.* come on, let's go, hurry up (para apremiar).

halagador, -a *adj.* flattering: *un comentario halagador = a flattering remark.*

halagar *v.t.* **1** to flatter, to praise; (EE.UU.) to sweet-talk. **2** to gratify, to give pleasure (dar placer, a los sentidos, especialmente): *sus palabras me halagan, señor Conde = my dear Count, your words are music to my ears.* **3** to cajole, to wheedle, to coax (con el fin de conseguir algo de alguien).

halago *s.m.* **1** flattery, praise; (EE.UU.) sweet-talk. **2** gratification (de los sentidos, muy especialmente). **3** cajolery (para que alguien haga algo).

halagüeño, -a *adj.* **1** endearing, flattering; attractive. **2** hopeful, promising (prometedor, por ejemplo, las perspectivas para el futuro).

halcón *s.m.* ZOOL. falcon, hawk. **2** (fig.) POL. hawk (en el sentido de querer la guerra como solución política).

halconero *s.m.* HIST. falconer.

hálito *s.m.* **1** breath (de respiración). **2** vapour (vapor). **3** (lit.) gentle breeze (suave viento).

halitosis *s.f.* MED. halitosis, bad breath.

halo *s.m.* **1** ASTR. halo, nimbus. **2** REL. halo. **3** (fig.) halo (gloria o fama que rodea a un personaje importante).

halógeno, -a *adj.* QUIM. halogen.

halterofilia *s.f.* DEP. weight-lifting.

hall *s.m.* hall.

hallar *v.t.* y *pron.* **1** to come across, to encounter, to find, to locate (algo o alguien). || *v.t.* **2** to invent, to discover. **3** to solve, to resolve (cuestión, problema, etc.). **4** to ascertain, to hit upon, to light upon (una idea o solución). || **5 hallárselo todo hecho,** not to have to make any effort at all, to find that everything has been arranged properly, to find that everything is simple and easy. **6 no hallarse uno,** to be uncomfortable, to be discontented, to be annoyed.

hallazgo *s.m.* **1** act of finding, discovery. **2** object found, object encountered, find: *¡qué hallazgo más trascendental! = what an important find!* **3** reward for finding (recompensa, al encontrar algo que se había perdido).

hamaca *s.f.* **1** hammock. **2** (Am.) rocking chair (mecedora).

hambre *s.m.* **1** hunger (de comida). **2** (fig.) hunger, desire, longing (deseo). **3** famine (hambre de un pueblo o similar): *el hambre después de la guerra = the famine after the war.* || **4 — canina,** ravenous hunger. **5 más listo que el —,** very bright, very clever, as sharp as a needle. **6 matar el —,** to stave off hunger, to satisfy one's hunger. **7 morirse de —,** to die of hunger, to starve to death.

hambreado, -a *adj.* (Am.) hungry.

hambriento, -a *adj.* **1** hungry, starving. **2** (fig.) longing, hungry (de conocimiento,

fama, etc.). || *s.m.* y *f.* **3** hungry person, starving person.
hambruna *s.f.* (Am.) famine.
hampa *s.m.* underworld, criminal underworld.
hampón *s.m.* rough, thug, rowdy.
hámster *s.m.* ZOOL. hamster.
hándicap *s.m.* handicap.
hangar *s.m.* AER. hangar.
haragán, -a *adj.* **1** idle, lazy, sluggish. || *s.m.* y *f.* **2** loafer, idler, lounger; (fam.) good-for-nothing.
haraganear *v.i.* to idle, to loaf about, to lounge around, to waste one's time.
haraganería *s.f.* idleness, laziness.
harapiento, -a *adj.* ragged, tattered.
harapo *s.m.* **1** rag, tatter. **2** low-grade alcohol, inferior alcohol.
haraquiri o **harakiri** *s.m.* hara-kiri.
hardware *s.m.* INF. hardware.
harén *s.m.* harem.
harina *s.f.* **1** flour. || **2 estar metido en –**, to be engrossed in something. **3 – fósil,** MIN. kieselguhr, infusorial earth. **4 – lacteada,** malted milk.
harinoso, -a *adj.* floury.
harmonía V. **armonía.**
harpía V. **arpía.**
harpillera o **arpillera** *s.f.* sackcloth.
hartar *v.t.* y *pron.* **1** to fill, to stuff; to gorge. **2** (fig.) to weary, to tire, to bore.
harto, -a *adj.* **1** full, satiated. **2** (fig.) fed up, sick: *estoy harto de la escuela = I am fed up with the school.* || *adv.* **3** very, quite: *harto difícil = quite difficult.*
hartón, -a *adj.* (Am.) greedy (glotón).
hasta *prep.* **1** as far as, up to (en el espacio): *hasta el semáforo = as far as the traffic lights.* **2** until, till (en el tiempo): *no vendrá hasta el jueves = he isn't coming till thursday.* || *conj.* **3** even (incluso).
hastiar *v.t.* **1** to bore, to sicken, to cloy. **2** to disgust (asquear): *estoy hastiado = I'm disgusted.*
hastío *s.m.* **1** boredom, weariness. **2** disgust (asco).
hatajo *s.m.* **1** small herd (ganado bovino o equino); small flock (cabras, ovejas, etc.). **2** (desp.) bunch, pack: *un hatajo de idiotas = a bunch of idiots.*
hatillo *s.m.* small bundle (de pertenencias, especialmente, ropa).
hato *s.m.* **1** herd, flock. **2** (Am.) cattle ranch. || **3 andar uno con el – a cuestas,** to wander about, to roam about. **4 liar el –**, to pack up. **5 revolver el –**, to stir up trouble.
haya *s.f.* **1** BOT. beech tree. **2** beech (madera).
hayedo o **hayal** *s.m.* beech forest.
haz *s.m.* **1** bundle, bunch. **2** beam (de luz). **3** AGR. sheaf, truss (de algún tipo de grano o paja). **4** HIST. haces, fasces (símbolo de algunos movimientos históricos). || **5 – de la tierra,** face of the earth.
hazaña *s.f.* deed, exploit, feat: *¡qué hazaña! = what a feat!*
hazañoso, -a *adj.* heroic, gallant.
hazmerreír *s.m.* laughingstock: *él es el hazmerreír del barrio = he is the laughingstock of the whole district.*
he *adv.* **1** lo, behold. || **2 – aquí,** behold. **3 heme aquí,** here I am.
hebilla *s.f.* buckle, clasp.
hebra *s.f.* **1** thread (hilo de coser). **2** BOT. strand, fibre. **3** grain (de madera). **4** lode, seam, vein (de mineral). || **5 cortar a alguien la – de la vida,** to kill someone. **6 pegar la –**, to talk nineteen to the dozen.
hebraico, -a *adj.* Hebrew.
hebreo, -a *adj.* **1** Jewish. **2** belonging to the Jewish race, belonging to the Jewish religion. || *s.m.* **3** Hebrew (idioma). **4** (desp.) moneylender, extortioner, usurer.
hebroso, -a *adj.* stringy (carne).
hecatombe *s.f.* **1** LIT. hecatomb. **2** (fig.) disaster, slaughter.
hectárea *s.f.* hectare.
hect- o **hecto** *prefijo* hecto- (para medidas).
hechicería *s.f.* **1** witchcraft, sorcery (arte mágica). **2** spell, charm (acción concreta).
hechicero, -a *adj.* **1** enchanting, bewitching. || *s.m.* **2** wizard, sorcerer, bewitcher. **3** witch doctor (en Africa, especialmente); medicine man (de los pieles rojas). || *s.f.* **4** enchantress, witch, sorceress.
hechizar *v.t.* **1** to bewitch, to cast a spell on. **2** (fig.) to charm, to enchant, to fascinate.
hechizo *s.m.* **1** spell, enchantment, charm. || *adj.* **2** (Am.) homemade.
hecho, -a *p.p.* **1** de **hacer.** || *adj.* **2** ripe, mature (maduro, un fruto o similar). **3** done, made: *muy hecha la carne, por favor = the meat well done, please.* **4** to be like, to be: *está hecho un toro = he is as strong as a horse.* || *s.m.* **5** fact: *el hecho es que no ha votado por nosotros = the fact is that he didn't vote for us.* **6** deed, feat (proeza). || **7 a lo – pecho,** it's no use crying over spilt milk; let's make the best of it now, we must make the best of it now. **8 bien –**, well-proportioned (la figura o similar). **9 de esta hecha,** this way. **10 de –**, as a matter of fact, in fact. **11 eso está –, a)** that's as easy as pie (fácil); **b)** that's a deal, agreed (aceptado). **12 – de armas,** MIL. feat of arms. **13 – imponible,** FIN. taxable activity, taxable transaction, activity subject to tax, transaction subject to duty. **14 Hechos de los Apóstoles,** REL. Acts of the Apostles. **15 – y derecho, a)** complete, perfect, the way it should be; **b)** true to God, true (verdadero).
hechura *s.f.* **1** making, creation. **2** creature (criatura, especialmente cuando nos referimos a que Dios nos hizo). **3** build, form, shape (de una persona). **4** cut, style (de un traje o similar). **5** craftsmanship, workmanship (arte). || **6 tener hechuras de,** to be cut out for.
heder *v.i.* **1** to stink, to reek. **2** to annoy, to irritate (irritar).
hediondez *s.f.* stench, stink, reek.
hediondo, -a *adj.* foul-smelling, stinking, smelly.
hedonismo *s.m.* FIL. hedonism.
hedonista *adj.* **1** hedonistic. || *s.m.* y *f.* **2** FIL. hedonist.
hedor *s.m.* stench, stink.
hegemonía *s.f.* hegemony (normalmente política).
hegemónico, -a *adj.* supreme: *poder hegemónico = supreme power.*
hégira o **héjira** *s.f.* REL. hegira.
heladería *s.f.* ice-cream stall; (EE.UU.) ice-cream parlour.
helado, -a *p.p.* **1** de **helar.** || *adj.* **2** very cold: *una habitación helada = a very cold bedroom.* **3** frozen (muy sorprendido): *me quedé helado = I was frozen.* || *s.m.* **4** ice-cream (para comer). || *s.f.* **5** frost (efecto meteorológico).
helador, -a *adj.* freezing: *un tiempo helador = freezing weather.*
heladera *s.f.* (Am.) refrigerator.
helar *v.t.* y *pron.* **1** to freeze: *el agua se hiela a los 0º C. = water freezes at 0 degrees C.* || *v.pron.* **2** to harden, to congeal (endurecerse un líquido, una sustancia, una persona, etc.). **3** BOT. to become frostbitten (plantas, flores, frutas, etc.). || *v.t.* **4** to chill, to ice (una bebida). **5** to amaze; to dumbfound (asombrar). **6** to dispirit, to discourage (desanimar).
helecho BOT. *s.m.* **1** fern. || **2 – arbóreo/arborescente,** tree fern. **3 – común,** bracken. **4 – real,** osmund.
helénico, -a *adj.* **1** Greek, from Greece. **2** FIL. Hellenic.
helenismo *s.m.* FIL. Hellenism.
hélice *s.f.* **1** AER. airscrew, propeller. **2** MAR. propeller, screw. **3** GEOM. spiral, helix.
helicoidal *adj.* GEOM. spiral.
helicóptero *s.m.* AER. helicopter; (EE.UU.) chopper.
helio *s.m.* QUIM. helium.
heliotropismo *s.m.* BIOL. heliotropism.
helipuerto *s.m.* AER. heliport.
helvético, -a *adj./s.m.* y *f.* Swiss.
hematíe *s.m.* FISIOL. red corpuscle.
hematites *s.f.* MIN. hematite.
hematología *s.f.* MED. (EE.UU.) hematology; (brit.) haematology.
hematólogo *s.m.* MED. (EE.UU.) hematologist; (brit.) haematologist.
hematoma *s.m.* bruise, weal.
hembra *s.f.* **1** woman, female. **2** female animal, female. **3** MEC. female; nut (tornillo); socket (enchufe); strike (cerradura).
hembrilla *s.f.* MEC. **1** female, female piece. **2** eyebolt, eyescrew (anilla).
hemeroteca *s.f.* periodicals and newspaper library.
hemiciclo *s.m.* **1** POL. floor of Parliament. **2** GEOM. semicircle. **3** ARQ. hemicycle.
hemiplejía *s.f.* MED. hemiplegia.
hemipléjico, -a *adj.* MED. hemiplegic.
hemisferio *s.m.* hemisphere.
hemistiquio *s.m.* (lit.) hemistich.

hemofilia *s.f.* MED. hemophilia.
hemofílico, -a *adj.* MED. 1 hemophilic. || *s.m.* y *f.* 2 hemophiliac.
hemoglobina *s.f.* FISIOL. hemoglobin.
hemorragia *s.f.* MED. (brit.) haemorrhage; (EE.UU.) hemorrhage; bleeding.
hemorroide *s.m.* MED. (brit.) haemorrhoid; (EE.UU.) hemorrhoid; pile.
henar *s.m.* hayfield, hay meadow.
henchir *v.t.* 1 to fill, to cram, to bloat, to stuff. || *v.pron.* 2 to stuff oneself, to fill oneself (con comida).
hendedura o **hendidura** *s.f.* crack, cleft.
hender (Am. **hendir**) *v.t.* y *pron.* 1 to cleave, to slit, to split. 2 to cut through (atravesar, especialmente por medio del agua). 3 to make one's way through, to elbow one's way through.
hendija *s.f.* (Am.) crack (rendija).
hendir V. **hender.**
heno *s.m.* hay.
hepático, -a *adj.* 1 MED. hepatic. || *s.f.* 2 BOT. liverwort, hepática.
hepatitis *s.f.* MED. hepatitis, inflammation of the liver.
hept- o **hepta-** *prefijo* hepta-.
heptagonal *adj.* GEOM. heptagonal.
heptágono *s.m.* GEOM. heptagon.
heráldico, -a *adj.* 1 heraldic. || *s.f.* 2 heraldry.
heraldo *s.m.* herald.
herbáceo, -a *adj.* BOT. herbaceous, grassy.
herbario, -a *adj.* 1 herbal. || *s.m.* 2 herbalist, botanist.
herbicida *s.m.* weed-killer.
herbívoro, -a *adj.* ZOOL. 1 herbivorous. || *s.m.* 2 herbivore.
herbolario *s.m.* herbalist's shop.
hercúleo, -a *adj.* herculean, immensely strong.
heredable *adj.* inheritable.
heredad *s.f.* country estate, landed property.
heredar *v.t.* 1 to inherit, to fall heir to, to come into. 2 to deed, to institute as heir (instituir como heredero). 3 (fig.) to inherit (características de alguien o similar): *él ha heredado el mal genio de su padre = he has inherited his father's bad humour.*
heredero, -a *adj.* 1 inheriting. || *s.m.* 2 heir. || *s.f.* 3 heiress. || 4 **— forzoso,** heir apparent. 5 **— presunto,** heir presumptive. 6 **— universal,** general heir, residuary legatee. 7 **príncipe —,** crown prince.
hereditario, -a *adj.* hereditary.
hereje *s.m.* y *f.* REL. heretic.
herejía *s.f.* REL. heresy.
herencia *s.f.* 1 inheritance, legacy, estate. 2 BIOL. heredity. 3 heritage, tradition: *es una herencia de muchos siglos = it's a tradition of many centuries.*
herético, -a *adj.* heretical.
herido, -a *p.p.* 1 de **herir.** || *adj.* 2 wounded, injured. 3 (fig.) hurt, offended (ofendido). || *s.m.* 4 MIL. wounded: *los heridos fueron evacuados de la zona = the wounded were evacuated from the area.* || *s.f.* 5 wound, cut (abierta); gash, stab (de arma blanca). 6 (fig.) trauma, afliction, torment, anguish (angustia). || 7 **mal —,** seriously wounded. 8 **respirar por la herida,** to feel very bitterly. 9 **tocar a alguien en la herida,** to touch a sore spot.
herir *v.t.* 1 to wound, to injure. 2 to hurt, to offend (ofender). 3 to fall on, to shine on (caer, los rayos del sol).
hermafrodita *adj.* BIOL. 1 hermaphroditic. || *s.m.* y *f.* 2 hermaphrodite.
hermanable *adj.* fraternal, brotherly.
hermanado, -a *p.p.* 1 de **hermanar.** || *adj.* 2 matching.
hermanamiento *s.m.* matching, twinning: *hermanamiento de ciudades = town twinning.*
hermanar *v.t.* y *pron.* 1 to match, to put together. 2 to pair, to join in pairs (emparejar). 3 to twin (ciudades).
hermanastro, -a *s.m.* 1 stepbrother. || *s.f.* 2 stepsister.
hermandad *s.f.* 1 brotherhood, fraternity. 2 close friendship, intimate friendship (amistad íntima). 3 brotherhood; sisterhood (grupo que se asocia). 4 REL. sodality (cofradía). || 5 **Santa Hermandad,** HIST. rural police.
hermano, -a *s.m.* 1 brother. 2 member of a brotherhood. || *s.f.* 3 sister. 4 member of a sisterhood. 5 REL. nun, sister. || *adj.* 6 MEC. mate, twin (pieza que se corresponde con otra). || 7 **— bastardo,** bastard brother. 8 **— carnal,** blood brother, full brother. 9 **— de leche,** foster brother. 10 **— uterino,** half brother by same mother. 11 **medio —,** half brother.
hermenéutico, -a *adj.* FIL. 1 hermeneutical. || *s.f.* 2 hermeneutics.
herméticamente *adv.* 1 hermetically. 2 (fig.) impenetrably.
hermético, -a *adj.* 1 airtight, watertight (un cierre, por ejemplo). 2 (fig.) impenetrable (especialmente el carácter de alguien).
hermetismo *s.m.* tight secrecy, close secrecy.
hermosamente *adv.* beautifully; handsomely.
hermosear *v.t.* to adorn, to beautify, to decorate, to embellish.
hermoso, -a *adj.* 1 beautiful; handsome; lovely: *una mujer hermosa = a beautiful woman.* 2 fine, splendid (tiempo atmosférico). 3 healthy (sano, especialmente de chicos y chicas pequeños).
hermosura *s.f.* 1 beauty; loveliness. 2 beautiful woman, beauty (mujer bella).
hernia *s.f.* MED. hernia.
herniado, -a *adj.* MED. suffering from a hernia.
herniarse *v.pron.* 1 MED. to rupture. 2 (fig.) to work hard; to make a very serious effort (esforzarse seriamente).
héroe *s.m.* 1 hero. 2 LIT. main character (protagonista de una obra literaria).
heroicamente *adv.* heroically.
heroicidad *s.f.* 1 heroism (calidad). 2 feat, heroic deed (acto concreto de heroísmo).
heroico, -a *adj.* heroic.
heroína *s.f.* 1 heroine. 2 LIT. main female character (de una obra literaria). 3 QUIM. heroin (droga).
heroísmo *s.m.* heroism.
herpe o **herpes** *s.m.* MED. herpes; shingles.
herradura *s.f.* 1 horseshoe. || 2 **mostrar las herraduras,** to kick.
herraje *s.m.* iron fittings, ironwork.
herramienta *s.f.* 1 tool (una concreta). 2 set of tools (juego). 3 (fig.) bull's horns (la cornamenta de un toro). 4 teeth (dentadura).
herrar *v.t.* 1 to shoe. 2 to brand (marcar, especialmente al ganado). 3 to reinforce with ironwork, to bind with ironwork, to trim with metal (reforzar con metal).
herrería *s.f.* 1 forge, smithy. 2 ironworks, foundry (fábrica).
herrero *s.m.* blacksmith.
herrerillo *s.m.* ZOOL. tit (ave).
herrín *s.m.* rust, iron rust.
herrumbre *s.f.* 1 rust. 2 BOT. mildew.
herrumbroso, -a *adj.* rusty.
hertz o **hertzio** *s.m.* FIS. hertz.
hertziano, -a *adj.* FIS. hertzian: *ondas hertzianas = hertzian waves.*
hervidero *s.m.* 1 boiling, bubbling. 2 (fig.) crowd, swarm: *un hervidero de gente = a crowd of people.*
hervir *v.i.* 1 to boil, to bubble. 2 to surge (el mar). 3 to boil, to burn (con pasiones).
hervor *s.m.* 1 boiling, ebullition. 2 (fig.) fervour, ardour (fogosidad). || 3 **— de la sangre,** MED. skin rash.
heter- o **hetero-** *prefijo* hetero-.
heterodoxia *s.f.* heterodoxy.
heterodoxo, -a *adj.* 1 heterodox, unorthodox. || *s.m.* y *f.* 2 heterodox person.
heterogeneidad *s.f.* diversity, variety; heterogeneity.
heterogéneo, -a *adj.* different; heterogeneous.
heterosexual *adj.* o *s.m.* y *f.* heterosexual.
heterosexualidad *s.f.* heterosexuality.
hex- o **hexa-** *prefijo* hexa-.
hexaedro *s.m.* GEOM. hexahedron.
hexagonal *adj.* GEOM. hexagonal, six-sided.
hexágono *s.m.* GEOM. hexagon.
hez *s.f.* 1 sediment. 2 (fig.) scum (cosa despreciable). || *s.pl.* 3 excrement.
hiato *s.m.* FON. hiatus.
hibernación *s.f.* BIOL. hibernation.
hibernar *v.i.* BIOL. to hibernate.
hibridación *s.f.* hybridization.
híbrido, -a *adj.* o *s.m.* y *f.* hybrid.
hidalgo, -a *adj.* 1 noble. || *s.m.* 2 nobleman. || *s.f.* 3 noblewoman.
hidalguía *s.f.* 1 nobility. 2 magnanimity, generosity, gentlemanliness (caballerosidad).
hidatídico, -a *adj.* MED. hydatidinous.
hidr- o **hidro-** *prefijo* hidro-.
hidra *s.f.* 1 ZOOL. poisonous serpent. 2 BOT. freshwater polyp.

hidratación *s.f.* hydration.
hidratante *adj.* moisturizing: *crema hidratante = moisturizing cream.*
hidratar *v.t.* y *pron.* to hydrate.
hidrato *s.m.* QUIM. 1 hydrate. || **2 — de carbono,** carbohydrate.
hidráulico, -a *adj.* 1 hydraulic. || *s.f.* 2 hydraulics.
hidrocarburo *s.m.* QUIM. hydrocarbon.
hidrofobia *s.f.* MED. hydrophobia, rabies.
hidrófobo, -a *adj.* 1 hydrophobic. || *s.m.* y *f.* 2 hydrophobe.
hidrógeno *s.m.* QUIM. hydrogen.
hidrografía *s.f.* GEOG. hydrography.
hidrología *s.f.* 1 hydrology, scientific study of water. || **2 — médica,** scientific study of medicinal waters.
hidrometría *s.f.* hydrometry.
hidropesía *s.f.* MED. hydropsy, dropsy.
hidrosfera *s.f.* GEOL. hydrosphere.
hidrotermal *adj.* hydrothermal.
hiedra o **yedra** *s.f.* BOT. ivy.
hiel *s.f.* 1 FISIOL. bile, gall. 2 (fig.) bitterness (amargura, especialmente por acontecimientos tristes de la vida). || *s.pl.* 3 difficulties; sorrows, troubles (adversidades). || **4 echar la —,** to sweat blood; (fam.) to sweat one's guts out. **5 no tener —,** to be very meek, to be sweet-tempered.
hielo *s.m.* 1 ice. 2 (fig.) coolness, indifference (de carácter). 3 freezing (acción de helar). 4 stupefaction, astonishment. 5 (fig) **romper el hielo,** to break the ice.
hiena *s.f.* ZOOL. hyena.
hieráticamente *adv.* hieratically.
hierático, -a *adj.* 1 REL. hieratic, sacred, sacerdotal. 2 HIST. hieratic, concerning ancient Egyptian writing of hieroglyphics. 3 (fig.) solemn, pompous (solemne).
hieratismo *s.m.* hieratic attitude.
hierba o **yerba** *s.f.* 1 BOT. grass. 2 BOT. herb (especialmente medicinal). 3 (fam.) marihuana, grass. || **4 — artética,** BOT. herb ivy. **5 — belesa,** BOT. lead wort. **6 — bélida,** BOT. buttercup. **7 — callera,** BOT. stonecrop. **8 — cana,** BOT. groundsel. **9 — carmesí,** BOT. pokeweed. **10 — centella,** BOT. cowslip, March marigold. **11 — cinta,** BOT. ribbon grass. **12 — de almizcle,** BOT. musk crowfoot. **13 — de carpintero,** BOT. yarrow. **14 — de la golondrina,** BOT. celandine. **15 del ajo,** BOT. hedge garlic. **16 — de la plata,** BOT. moonwort, iceflower. **17 — de las calenturas,** BOT. goose grass. **18 — de las cucharas,** BOT. scurvy grass, spoon wort. **19 del gato,** BOT. fleabane. **20 — del nácar,** BOT. helmet flower. **21 — de los canarios,** BOT. chick-weed. **22 — de los canónigos,** BOT. lamb's lettuce. **23 — de los gatos,** BOT. common valerian. **24 — de los pordioseros,** BOT. lady's bower. **25 — del pobre,** BOT. hedge-hissop. **26 — de San Alberto/de los cantones,** BOT. hedge mustard. **27 — de San Benito,** BOT. herb bennet. **28 — de San Bonifacio,** BOT. butcher's broom, kneeholly. **29 — de San Cristóbal,** BOT. baneberry. **30 — de San Gerardo,** BOT. goatweed. **31 — de San Guillermo,** BOT. agrimony. **32 ... y otras hierbas,** and other, and so forth and so on.
hierbabuena *s.f.* BOT. mint.
hieroglífico, V. **jeroglífico.**
hierro *s.m.* 1 MET. iron. 2 brand (para marcar animales). 3 iron tip, point (punta de un arma). 4 (fig.) weapon, sword. || **5 — albo,** MET. white-hot iron. **6 — colado/fundido,** MET. cast iron. **7 quien a — mata a — muere,** he who lives by the sword shall die by the sword.
higadillo o **higadilla** *s.m.* o *f.* GAST. liver (de animales pequeños como pollos, aves, etc.).
hígado *s.m.* 1 ANAT. liver. || *s.pl.* 2 (fig.) guts (coraje): *este tipo tiene hígados = this fellow has got guts.*
higiene *s.f.* hygiene.
higiénicamente *adv.* hygienically.
higiénico, -a *adj.* hygienic.
higienizar *v.t.* to make hygienic, to make sanitary.
higo *s.m.* 1 BOT. fig. || **2 de higos a brevas,** once in a blue moon. **3 — chumbo,** BOT. prickly pear. **4 no dársele a uno un —,** (fam.) not to care a fig, not to give a damn.
higrometría *s.f.* FIS. hygrometry.
higroscopia *s.f.* FIS. hygroscopy.
higroscópico, -a *adj.* FIS. hygroscopic.
higuera *s.f.* 1 BOT. fig tree. || **2 estar en la —,** to be at a loss, not to know what to do; to be day-dreaming. **3 caer de la —,** to come back to earth.
higueral *s.m.* BOT. plantation of fig trees.
hijastro, -a *s.m.* o *f.* stepson; stepdaughter.
hijo, -a *s.m.* y *f.* 1 child, offspring: *tengo tres hijos, dos chicos y una chica = I've got three children, two boys and a girl.* || *s.m.* 2 son: *hijo mío = my son.* 3 brain child (algo que alguien ha pensado o imaginado como proyecto): *la nueva fábrica es tu hijo = the new factory is your brain child.* 4 young (de animales). || *s.m.* y *f.* 5 child, son (como forma cariñosa de dirigirse a alguien). 6 native (de un lugar); child (de un tiempo). || *s.f.* 7 daughter. 8 child, daughter (como forma cariñosa). || *s.m.pl.* 9 children, descendants (de uno mismo). || **10 — bastardo/natural,** bastard child, illegitimate child. **11 Hijo de Dios,** REL. Son of God. **12 — de la tierra,** child of unknown parentage. **13 — legítimo,** legitimate child. **14 — sacrílego,** sacrilegous child.
hijodalgo V. **hidalgo.**
hijuela *s.f.* 1 little girl, small daughter. 2 widening piece, widening gore (trozo de tela para ensanchar un vestido). 3 REL. chalice cover. 4 piece of land (tierra como resultado de la división de una herencia). 5 small mattress (colchón pequeño). 6 AGR. small irrigation ditch (pequeño canal). 7 BOT. palm seed (simiente).
hila *s.f.* 1 row, line (hilera). 2 thin gut (hebra). 3 spinning (acción de hilar).
hilacha o **hilacho** *s.f.* o *m.* filament, ravelled thread (especialmente de la ropa).
hilachento, -a *adj.* (Am.) shabby, frayed, tattered (andrajoso).
hilada *s.f.* 1 row, line. 2 ARQ. course (de ladrillos, especialmente).
hilador, -a *s.m.* y *f.* spinner.
hilandería *s.f.* spinning mill.
hilar *v.t.* 1 to spin. 2 BIOL. to spin (los gusanos de seda). 3 to ponder, to consider (discurrir). || **4 — fino/delgado,** to split hairs; to talk very subtly, to discuss using very fine points.
hilarante *adj.* hilarious, uproarious; mirthful.
hilaridad *s.f.* hilarity, mirth.
hilaza *s.f.* 1 yarn, thread. || **2 descubrir la —,** to discover a fault, to show (one's) true colours.
hilera *s.f.* 1 row, line, string: *una hilera de casas independientes = a row of detached houses.* 2 fine thread (hilo). 3 MET. drawplate, wiredrawer (máquina para producir filamentos de metal). 4 ARQ. course, ridgepole (especialmente de ladrillos). 5 MIL. file (en formación militar).
hilo *s.m.* 1 thread, yarn, filament. 2 fine wire (alambre fino). 3 linen (tejido blanco). 4 ZOOL. hilum (en arañas y gusanos de seda). 5 trickle (chorro, de un líquido): *un hilo de sangre = a trickle of blood.* 6 edge (filo, de un cuchillo o similar). || **7 a —,** consecutively, one after another, uninterruptedly. **8 al —,** along the thread. **9 pender/colgar de un —,** to hang by a thread: *la decisión final pende de un hilo = the final decision is hanging by a thread.* **11 por el — se saca el ovillo,** knowing the first details one reaches the final explanation.
hilvanar *v.t.* 1 to stitch; to baste. 2 (fig.) to coordinate, to organize (el pensamiento): *hay que hilvanar todos los argumentos = it's necessary to organize all the different points.*
himen *s.m.* ANAT. hymen, maidenhead.
himeneo *s.m.* (lit.) nuptials.
himno *s.m.* 1 hymn. 2 anthem: *himno nacional = national anthem.*
hincapié *s.m.* 1 planting of one's feet. 2 insistence (insistencia): *hacer hincapié en algo = to insist on something.*
hincar *v.t.* 1 to drive in, to sink, to sink in: *hincar unos clavos en la madera = to drive in a few nails in the wood.* 2 to brace, to plant (una parte del cuerpo como parte de apoyo). || *v.pron.* 3 to kneel, to kneel down (arrodillarse).
hincha *s.m.* y *f.* fan, supporter.
hinchable *adj.* inflatable.
hinchado, -a *p.p.* 1 de **hinchar.** || *adj.* 2 inflated, blown up. 3 MED. swollen. 4 vain (vanidoso). 5 highflown, stilted (estilo de escribir o hablar). || *s.f.* 6 group of supporters, group of fans.
hinchar *v.t.* y *pron.* 1 to swell; to pump up: *hincha el neumático un poquito más = pump up the tyre a little more.* || *v.t.* 2 to inflate, to exaggerate (datos, cifras, etc.). || *v.pron.* 3 MED. to swell. 4 to fill

oneself, to stuff oneself, to bloat oneself (de comida o bebida). **5** to become conceited, to become vain (envanecerse).
hinchazón *s.f.* **1** MED. swelling, lump, bump. **2** (fig.) conceit, vanity (vanidad).
hindú *adj.* o *s.m.* y *f.* REL. Hindu.
hinduismo *s.m.* REL. Hinduism.
hiniesta *s.f.* BOT. broom.
hinojal *s.m.* BOT. fennel bed.
hinojo *s.m.* **1** BOT. fennel. **2** ANAT. knee. || *s.pl.* **2** ANAT. knees. || **3 de hinojos,** on one's knees, kneeling down.
hipar *v.i.* **1** to hiccup, to hiccough. **2** to pant (jadear, los perros). **3** to wear oneself out, to be fagged out (fatigarse). **4** to whimper, to whine (lloriquear). **5** to yearn, to long (codiciar).
hipato, -a *adj.* (Am.) swollen (hinchado).
hipérbaton *s.m.* GRAM. hyperbaton.
hipérbola *s.f.* GEOM. hyperbola.
hipérbole *s.f.* GRAM. hyperbole.
hiperbólicamente *adv.* hyperbolically.
hiperbólico, -a *adj.* hyperbolic, hyperbolical.
hiperclorhidria *s.f.* MED. hyperchlorhydria.
hipertrofia *s.f.* BIOL. hypertrophy.
hipertrófico, -a *adj.* hypertrophic.
hipertrofiarse *v.pron.* to become hypertrophied.
hípico, -a *adj.* horse: *carrera hípica = horse race.*
hipido *s.m.* whimper, whine.
hipnosis *s.f.* MED. hypnosis.
hipnótico, -a *adj.* hypnotic.
hipnotismo *s.m.* hypnotism.
hipnotizador, -a *adj.* **1** hypnotizing. || *s.m.* y *f.* **2** hypnotist, hypnotizer.
hipnotizar *v.t.* to hypnotize.
hipo *s.m.* **1** hiccup, hiccough. **2** (fig.) yearning, longing. || **3 hipo-,** hypo-: *hipotensión = hypotension.*
hipocondría *s.f.* MED. hypochondria.
hipocondríaco, -a *adj.* o *s.m.* y *f.* MEC. hypochondriac.
hipocresía *s.f.* hypocrisy.
hipócrita *adj.* **1** hypocritical. || *s.m.* y *f.* **2** hypocrite.
hipócritamente *adv.* hypocritically.
hipódromo *s.m.* racetrack.
hipófisis *s.f.* ANAT. hypophysis.
hipogeo *s.m.* ARQ. underground chamber.
hipoglucemia *s.f.* MED. hypoglycemia.
hipopótamo *s.m.* ZOOL. hippopotamus.
hipóstasis *s.f.* FIL. hypostasis.
hipostáticamente *adv.* hypostatically.
hipostático, -a *adj.* hypostatic.
hipotálamo *s.m.* ANAT. hypothalamus.
hipoteca *s.f.* FIN. mortgage.
hipotecar *v.t.* **1** FIN. to mortgage. **2** (fig.) to compromise, to place in a dangerous situation: *no quiero hipotecar mi futuro = I don't want to place my future in a dangerous situation.*
hipotecario, -a *adj.* mortgage: *cédula hipotecaria = mortgage certificate.*
hipotenusa *s.f.* GEOM. hypotenuse.
hipótesis *s.f.* FIL. hypothesis.
hipotéticamente *adv.* hypothetically.
hipotético, -a *adj.* hypothetical.
hiriente *adj.* cutting, critical (comentario, indirecta, etc.).
hirsuto, -a *adj.* hairy, shaggy.
hirviente *adj.* boiling, seething.
hisopo *s.m.* **1** REL. aspergill, aspersorium. **2** BOT. hyssop.
hispánico, -a *adj.* Hispanic; Spanish: *el carácter hispánico = the Spanish character.*
hispanidad *s.f.* Spanishness, Spanish world; cultural community of Spanish-speaking nations.
hispanismo *s.m.* interest in Spanish things; study of Spanish culture.
hispanista *s.m.* y *f.* Spanish scholar, Spanish expert.
hispano, -a *adj./s.m.* y *f.* Hispanic.
hispanoamericano, -a *adj.* Latin American, Spanish American.
hispanófilo, -a *adj.* **1** Hispanophilic, admiring of all things Spanish. || *s.m.* y *f.* **2** admirer of all things Spanish.
histeria o **histerismo** *s.f.* o *m.* PSIQ. hysteria.
histérico, -a *adj./s.m.* y *f.* hysterical, histeric.
histología *s.f.* BIOL. histology.
histólogo, -a *s.m.* y *f.* histologist.
historia *s.f.* **1** history (ciencia). **2** story. || *s.pl.* **3** gossip, tale (chismes). || **4 dejarse de historias,** to get to the point, not to beat about the bush. **5 picar en —,** to be a serious matter.
historiado, -a *p.p.* **1** de **historiar.** || *adj.* **2** gaudy (sobrecargado).
historiador, -a *s.m.* y *f.* historian.
historial *s.m.* file, record: *mi historial médico = my medical record.*
historiar *v.t.* to tell the history of, to record, to chronicle.
históricamente *adv.* historically.
histórico, -a *adj.* historic, historical.
historieta *s.f.* **1** short story, anecdote. **2** strip cartoon (de dibujos animados).
histrión *s.m.* clown; actor.
hito *s.m.* **1** boundary marker. **2** bull's eye, target (blanco). || **3 dar en el —,** to hit the nail on the head. **4 mirar de — en —,** to stare, to look fixedly.
hobby *s.m.* hobby, pastime.
hocico *s.m.* **1** muzzle, snout. **2** (fig.) pout (gesto enfadado). **3** kisser, puss (cara). || **4 caer/dar de hocicos,** to fall flat on one's face.
hocicudo, -a *adj.* big-snouted (animal especialmente).
hockey *s.m.* DEP. hockey.
hogaño *adv.* nowadays, these days.
hogar *s.m.* **1** home. **2** hearth, fireplace (del fuego). **3** home life (vida de familia): *el hogar de sus primeros años no fue el mejor = his home life wasn't the best when he was a child.* **4** bonfire (hoguera).
hogareño, -a *adj.* home-loving: *soy muy hogareño = I am very home-loving.*
hogaza *s.f.* **1** large round loaf, large loaf of bread. **2** GAST. coarse bread (pan de salvado).
hoguera *s.f.* bonfire.
hoja *s.f.* **1** BOT. leaf. **2** sheet, leaf (de papel). **3** blade (de arma o similar). **4** BOT. petal (pétalo). **5** sheet, foil (lámina, especialmente de metal). **6** leaf (de ventana); pane (de cristal). || **7 batir —,** to work metal. **8 — de afeitar,** razor blade. **9 — de parra,** fig leaf. **10 — de ruta,** waybill. **11 — de servicios,** record. **12 — de tocino,** side of bacon. **13 — volante,** leaflet. **14 no tener vuelta de —,** to be irremediable; to be unanswerable. **15 volver la —,** to change the subject, to turn the page on a subject.
hojalata *s.f.* MET. tin-plate.
hojalatería *s.f.* **1** tinsmith's shop, tin shop. **2** tinware, tin articles.
hojalatero *s.m.* tinsmith.
hojalda o **hojaldra** *s.f.* (Am.) GAST. puff pastry.
hojaldrado, -a *p.p.* **1** de **hojaldrar.** || *adj.* **2** GAST. flaky; resembling puff pastry.
hojaldrar *v.t.* GAST. to make puff pastry, to cover with puff pastry.
hojaldre *s.m.* GAST. puff pastry.
hojarasca *s.f.* **1** dead leaves, fallen leaves. **2** (fig.) rubbish; nonsense: *lo que dijo era pura hojarasca = what he said was absolute nonsense.* **3** excessive foliage, abundant foliage (frondosidad).
hojear *v.t.* **1** to look through, to leaf through, to skim through, to glance through (especialmente algo para leer). || *v.i.* **2** to flake off, to scale off (formarse en láminas).
hojoso, -a *adj.* leafy.
hojuela *s.f.* **1** GAST. pancake. **2** BOT. small leaf. **3** MET. thin foil. **4** skin of pressed olives (hollejo).
¡hola! *interj.* hello!, hi!.
holanda *s.f.* **1** Dutch linen, holland (textil). || **2 Holland,** Holanda.
holandés, -a *adj.* **1** Dutch. || *s.m.* **2** Dutchman. **3** Dutch (idioma). || *s.f.* **4** Dutchwoman. **5** sheet, leaf (de papel de un tamaño mayor que cuartilla).
holgadamente *adv.* **1** comfortably, easily (con bienestar o facilidad): *viven holgadamente = they live comfortably.* **2** loosely (anchamente, especialmente la ropa). **3** idly (sin hacer nada).
holgado, -a *adj.* **1** comfortable, well-off (especialmente en algo material o monetario). **2** loose (ropa). **3** idle, unoccupied (sin trabajo u ocupación).
holganza *s.f.* **1** rest, leisure; idleness. **2** amusement, enjoyment; pleasure (disfrute).
holgar *v.i.* **1** to rest, to take one's ease. **2** to idle, to loaf, not to work (holgazanear). **3** to be unnecessary: *huelga decir más en este momento = it's unnecessary to add more now.* || *v.pron.* **4** to be happy, to be glad (alegrarse).
holgazán, -a *adj.* **1** lazy, idle. || *s.m.* y *f.* **2** bum, idler, loafer, slacker: *eres un holgazán = you're a loafer.*
holgazanear *v.i.* to bum around, to idle, to loaf around.
holgazanería *s.f.* laziness, idleness, slackness.

holgura *s.f.* 1 looseness (especialmente de ropa). 2 MEC. play, movement (de piezas). 3 comfort, ease (material, financiera, etc.). 4 amusement, enjoyment (diversión).
holocausto *s.m.* 1 REL. burnt offering. 2 (fig.) sacrifice, holocaust: *el holocausto de 1940-45 = the holocaust of 1940-45.*
hológrafo, -a *adj.* DER. 1 holographic. || *s.m.* 2 holograph.
holoturia *s.f.* BOT. sea cucumber.
holladura *s.f.* tramping, treading.
hollar *v.t.* 1 to tramp, to tread. 2 to trample on, to humiliate (humillar).
hollejo *s.m.* skin (uvas); rind (cítricos); peel.
hollín *s.m.* soot.
holliniento, -a o **hollinoso, -a** *adj.* sooty.
hombrada *s.f.* manly deed, brave act; piece of bravado: *¡vaya hombrada que hiciste! = what a manly deed you carried out!*
hombre *s.m.* 1 man. 2 humanity, man, mankind: *el hombre progresa necesariamente = mankind progresses necessarily.* 3 husband, man (marido). 4 adult (adulto). || 5 **gran –,** great men, eminent man. 6 **hacer a alguien un –,** to help somebody greatly, to do somebody a great favour. 7 **– bueno,** DER. arbiter. 8 **– de armas tomar,** man of action, determined man, resolute man. 9 **– de bien,** upright man, honest man. 10 **– de dos caras,** hypocrite, two-faced man. 11 **– de estado,** statesman. 12 **– de letras,** man of letters, scholar. 13 **– de mundo,** man of experience, man of the world. 14 **– de negocios,** businessman. 15 **– de palabra,** honest and worthy man, reliable man, man of his word. 16 **– de pelo en pecho,** real man; bold man. 17 **– de pro,** worthy man. 18 **pobre –,** poor devil, poor wretch. 19 **ser muy –,** to be a real man, to be very manly. 20 **ser otro –,** to be a different man, to be greatly changed.
hombrera *s.f.* 1 shoulder pad (vestido civil). 2 MIL. epaulette.
hombría *s.f.* 1 manliness. || 2 **– de bien,** integrity, honesty.
hombro *s.m.* 1 ANAT. shoulder. || 2 **a hombros,** piggyback, on one's shoulders. 3 **arrimar el –,** to put one's shoulder to the wheel, to lend a helping hand. 4 encogerse de hombros, to shrug, to shrug one's shoulders. 5 **mirar a alguien por encima del –,** to look down on someone.
hombruno, -a *adj.* manly, masculine-looking, mannish (especialmente refiriéndose a una mujer).
homenaje *s.m.* 1 homage, respect, tribute. 2 celebration (para una persona).
homenajeado, -a *p.p.* 1 de **homenajear.** || *s.m.* y *f.* 2 person who receives some sort of tribute.
homenajear *v.t.* 1 to pay homage. 2 (Am.) to treat grandly, to wine and dine (agasajar).
homeopatía *s.f.* MED. homeopathy.
homicida *adj.* 1 homicidal, murderous. || *s.m.* y *f.* 2 homicide, murderer.
homicidio *s.m.* homicide, murder.
homilía *s.f.* REL. sermon, homily.
homínido *s.m.* BIOL. hominid.
homo- *prefijo* homo-.
homofonía *s.f.* FON. homophony.
homófono, -a *adj.* FON. homophonous.
homogeneidad *s.f.* homogeneity.
homogeneización *s.f.* homogenization.
homogeneizar *v.t.* to homogenize.
homogéneo, -a *adj.* homogeneous.
homografía *s.f.* FON. homography.
homógrafo, -a *adj.* FON. homographic.
homologación *s.f.* homologation; confirmation.
homologar *v.t.* 1 DER. to confirm. 2 to sanction, to authorize officially (especialmente por parte de la administración estatal). 3 to standardize (igualar las características de productos).
homología *s.f.* BIOL. homology.
homólogo, -a *adj.* BIOL. homologous.
homonimia *s.f.* GRAM. homonymy.
homónimo, -a *adj.* GRAM. homonymous. || *s.m.* y *f.* 2 homonym.
homosexual *adj./s.m.* y *f.* homosexual.
homosexualidad *s.f.* homosexuality.
hondamente *adv.* deeply, profoundly.
hondo, -a *adj.* 1 deep (físicamente). 2 profoundly, heartflet: *con hondo pesar = with heartfelt regret.* 3 deep, innermost (íntimo). 4 intense (intenso). || *s.m.* 5 bottom (de un objeto). || *s.f.* 6 sling (para tirar piedras).
hondonada *s.f.* ravine, dip, depression.
hondura *s.f.* 1 depth, profundity. || 2 **meterse en honduras,** to get in over one's depth, to be out of one's depth.
hondureño, -a *adj./s.m.* y *f.* Honduran.
honestamente *adv.* 1 honestly, honourably. 2 decently, decorously (decentemente). 3 modestly (modestamente): *debes vestir honestamente = you must dress modestly.*
honestidad *s.f.* 1 uprightness, honesty (honradez). 2 modesty, purity (pudor). 3 decorum, decency (decoro).
honesto, -a *adj.* 1 upright, honest. 2 modest (púdico). 3 decent, decorous (decente).
hongo *s.m.* 1 BOT. mushroom. 2 MED. fungus. 3 bowler, bowler hat (sombrero). 4 BOT. toadstool (cuando es venenoso).
honor *s.m.* 1 honour. 2 virtue, chastity (virtud, especialmente la castidad). 3 good name, prestige (prestigio). 4 dignity, position (dignidad). 5 honesty, decency (honestidad). 6 mark of respect (forma de dirigirse a una persona de gran reputación).
honorabilidad *s.f.* honourableness, honour.
honorable *adj.* honourable.
honorablemente *adv.* honourably.
honorario, -a *adj.* 1 honorary: *cónsul honorario = honorary consul.* || *s.m.pl.* 2 professional fees, fees.
honoríficamente *adv.* honorifically.
honorífico, -a *adj.* honorary, honorific.
honra *s.f.* 1 honour, sense of personal honour, self-esteem, self-respect. 2 good name, reputation, fame (fama). 3 chastity, virtue, purity (castidad). || 4 **a mucha –,** with pride, full of pride; very proud: *tengo a mucha honra ser el primero que le acusó públicamente = I'm very proud to have been the first to accuse him publicly.* 5 **honras fúnebres,** last honours, funeral rites.
honradamente *adv.* honestly, honourably, uprightly.
honradez *s.f.* honesty, integrity, honourableness, uprightness.
honrado, -a *p.p.* 1 de **honrar.** || *adj.* 2 decent, honest: *es un hombre muy honrado = he's a very decent man.*
honrar *v.t.* to honour, to respect.
honrilla *s.f.* concern about what people might say; sense of public shame.
honrosamente *adv.* honourably, with dignity, with integrity.
honroso, -a *adj.* honourable; decent, proper; respectable: *un acuerdo honroso = an honourable agreement.*
hontanar *s.m.* spring, group of springs, area bounding in springs.
hora *s.f.* 1 hour: *estuve dos horas aquí = I was here two hours.* 2 time: *¿qué hora tienes? = what time is it?* 3 hour, end (final de la vida). || 4 **a buenas horas,** too late (demasiado tarde). 5 **a estas horas,** now, at this time. 6 **dar –,** to fix a time, to appoint a time. 7 **dar la –,** to strike: *el reloj dio las doce = the clock struck twelve.*
horadable *adj.* that can be pierced through, that can be bored through.
horadación *s.f.* drilling, boring.
horadar *v.t.* to bore a hole, to drill, to pierce.
horario, -a *adj.* 1 hourly. || *s.m.* 2 timetable, schedule: *horario de clases = timetable of lessons.* 3 clock hand (manecilla del reloj).
horca *s.f.* 1 gallows, gibbet. 2 AGR. hayfork, pitchfork. || 3 **pasar por las horcas caudinas,** to suffer great humiliation.
horcajadas *loc. adv.* **a –,** astride, straddling, astraddle.
horchata *s.f.* orgeat.
horchatería *s.f.* orgeat shop, orgeat stand.
horda *s.f.* 1 HIST. horde (de nómadas). 2 (fig. y desp.) horde, rabble.
horizontal *adj.* 1 horizontal. || *s.f.* 2 horizontal position, horizontal: *tomar una postura horizontal = to take a horizontal position.*
horizontalidad *s.f.* horizontality.
horizontalmente *adv.* horizontally.
horizonte *s.m.* 1 horizon. 2 (fig.) outlook, horizon: *aquí la gente no tiene más horizonte que ir tirando = in this place people's only outlock is to rub along in life.*
horma *s.f.* 1 mould, model, form. 2 last (de zapatos). || 3 **hallar la – del zapato de uno,** to meet one's match, to get what is coming to one, to find just what

one was looking for, to find the very thing.
hormiga *s.f.* 1 ZOOL. ant. || **2 ser una –,** to be a workaholic, to be very hard-working.
hormigón *s.m.* 1 concrete. || **2 – armado,** reinforced concrete. **3 – pretensado,** prestressed concrete.
hormigonera *s.f.* MEC. cement mixer, concrete mixer.
hormiguear *v.i.* 1 to tingle, to itch; to suffer a prickly feeling. 2 to swarm; to abound (bullir): *hombres y animales hormigueando en la noche = people and animals swarming in the night.*
hormigueo *s.m.* 1 tingling; pins and needles: *siento un hormigueo en la pierna = I feel a tingling in my leg.* 2 swarm, throng (bullicio).
hormiguero *s.m.* 1 ZOOL. anthill. 2 (fig.) hub of activity, place swarming with people (lugar transitado o con mucha gente).
hormiguillo *s.m.* itch, itching.
hormona *s.f.* FISIOL. hormone.
hormonal *adj.* FISIOL. hormonal.
hornacina *s.f.* ARQ. vaulted niche.
hornada *s.f.* 1 batch (de pan). 2 (fig.) batch, collection: *¡qué hornada de profesores incompetentes! = what a collection of useless teachers!*
hornazo *s.m.* GAST. bread with hard-boiled eggs.
hornear *v.t.* e *i.* to bake.
hornero, -a *s.m.* y *f.* baker.
hornilla *s.f.* chamber in a kitchen oven.
hornillo *s.m.* 1 stove. 2 MIN. blasthole (cavidad para el explosivo).
horno *s.m.* 1 oven (de cocina). 2 kiln (de cerámica). 3 furnace (de fábrica). || **4 alto –,** TEC. blast furnace. **5 no estar el – para bollos,** not to be ripe the time, to be untimely, to be the wrong moment.
horóscopo *s.m.* horoscope.
horquilla *s.f.* 1 AGR. pitchfork. 2 hairpin, hair clip (para el pelo). 3 fork (de bicicleta). 4 MIL. fork rest (para apoyo).
horrendamente *adv.* horrendously, hideously, horribly.
horrendo, -a *adj.* horrendous, hideous, horrible: *un crimen horrendo = a hideous crime.*
hórreo *s.m.* AGR. raised granary.
horrible *adj.* horrible, dreadful; ghastly.
horriblemente *adv.* horribly, dreadfully: *estaba horriblemente desfigurado = he was horribly disfigured.*
hórrido, -a *adj.* horrid, horrible, hideous.
horripilante *adj.* terrifying, hair-raising, harrowing.
horripilar *v.t.* y *pron.* 1 to horrify, to terrify. 2 to make (someone's) hair stand on end (erizar el cabello).
horrísono, -a *adj.* terrifying (de sonido).
horror *s.m.* 1 horror, terror, fright. || *s.pl.* 2 atrocities. 3 really, very much (enfático coloquial): *me gustas horrores = I really love you.*
horrorizar *v.t.* 1 to horrify, to terrify: *las noticias me han horrorizado = the news has terrified me.* || *v.pron.* 2 to be terrified.
horrorosamente *adv.* terribly, horribly.
horroroso, -a *adj.* horrible, terrible; frightening: *una guerra horrorosa = a horrible war.*
hortaliza *s.f.* BOT. garden produce; vegetable.
hortelano, -a *s.m.* y *f.* 1 market gardener. || *s.m.* 2 ZOOL. ortolan (ave). || *adj.* 3 garden, orchard: *productos hortelanos = orchard produce.*
hortensia *s.f.* BOT. hydrangea.
hortera *s.m.* 1 shop assistant, grocer's boy, counter clerk. || *s.f.* 2 small wooden bowl. || *adj.* 3 (fam. y desp.) cheap, tawdry, vulgar, grotty. 4 (desp.) rough, coarse (típico de pueblo).
horticultor, -a *s.m.* y *f.* AGR. horticulturist.
horticultura *s.f.* AGR. horticulture.
hosco, -a *adj.* 1 crabbed, gloomy, sullen (característica de una persona). 2 dark brown (color).
hospedaje *s.m.* lodging, cost of lodging.
hospedar *v.t.* y *pron.* to board, to lodge, to accommodate: *me hospedé en un hotelito precioso = I lodged at a pretty little hotel.*
hospedería *s.f.* inn, hostel.
hospedero, -a *s.m.* y *f.* innkeeper.
hospiciano, -a *s.m.* y *f.* resident of a poor house, inmate of an orphanage.
hospicio *s.m.* 1 poorhouse. 2 REL. hospice (hospedería). 3 orphanage (orfelinato).
hospital *s.m.* 1 hospital. || **2 – de sangre,** MIL. field hospital, first aid post. **3 – robado,** empty bare house.
hospitalario, -a *adj.* hospitable; inviting.
hospitalicio, -a *adj.* hospitable.
hospitalidad *s.f.* 1 hospitality. 2 entertainment (hospitalidad casera).
hospitalización *s.f.* hospitalization.
hospitalizar *v.t.* to hospitalize; to send to hospital.
hosquedad *s.f.* 1 darkness, gloominess (oscuridad). 2 gruffiness, sullenness (aspereza personal).
hostal *s.m.* hostel, small hotel.
hostelería *s.f.* hotel management, hotel trade (como estudio).
hostelero, -a *s.m.* y *f.* innkeeper.
hostería *s.f.* inn.
hostia *s.f.* 1 REL. sacred host, host, consecrated wafer. 2 (vulg.) belt, punch.
hostigador, -a *adj.* 1 harassing, annoying, scourging. || *s.m.* y *f.* 2 harasser, pest.
hostigamiento *s.m.* 1 whipping, lashing (especialmente de caballos). 2 harassment, pestering, plaguing: *hostigamiento del enemigo = harassment of the enemy.*
hostigar *v.t.* 1 to whip, to lash (especialmente a caballos). 2 to harass, to pester (acosar).
hostil *adj.* hostile: *fuerzas hostiles = hostile forces.*
hostilidad *s.f.* 1 hostility. 2 hostile act (hecho concreto). || *s.pl.* 3 MIL. aggression, attack; warfare. || **4 romper las hostilidades,** MIL. to begin hostilities, to start hostilities.
hotel *s.m.* 1 hotel. 2 detached house (casa unifamiliar).
hotelero, -a *adj.* 1 hotel: *es una zona hotelera = it's an area of hotels.* || *s.m.* y *f.* 2 hotel manager, hotelier, hotel keeper.
hoy *adv.* 1 today. 2 at present, nowadays: *hoy no parece haber mucha educación en la gente joven = nowadays young people don't seem to have very good manners.*
hoya *s.f.* 1 pit, hole. 2 GEOG. valley, vale (valle). 3 grave (sepultura). 4 (Am.) GEOL. river basin, riverbed (cuenca de un río).
hoyo *s.m.* 1 small pit, hole. 2 dent (abolladura). 3 MED. pockmark (en la piel). 4 grave (sepultura). 5 DEP. hole (en el golf).
hoyuelo *s.m.* dimple.
hoz *s.f.* 1 AGR. sickle. 2 GEOL. gorge, narrow pass (desfiladero). || **3 de – y de coz,** recklessly, without thinking, headlong, wildly.
hozar *v.t.* e *i.* to root (típico de los cerdos).
huaca *s.f.* (Am.) burial grounds (sepulturas precolombinas).
hucha *s.f.* 1 piggy bank. 2 savings (dinero ahorrado).
hueco, -a *adj.* 1 hollow (sin nada dentro): *suena a hueco = it sounds hollow.* 2 deep, resounding (voz). 3 vain, conceited (fatuo). 4 blank (sin nada escrito). || *s.m.* 5 space, hollow, interval (en el espacio). 6 ARQ. opening (para ventana, puerta, etc.). 7 gap (que deja alguien): *dejó un hueco difícil de llenar = he left a gap which is very difficult to till.* 8 vacancy (puesto de trabajo libre).
huecograbado *s.m.* photogravure.
huelga *s.f.* 1 strike; (EE.UU.) walkout; (euf.) industrial action. 2 AGR. fallow, rest (de la tierra). || **3 – de brazos caídos,** sitdown strike. **5 ponerse en –,** to go on strike.
huelguista *s.m.* y *f.* striker.
huelguístico, -a *adj.* of a strike, strike.
huella *s.f.* 1 footprint (de piel). 2 trace, sign (señal). 3 ARQ. tread (del escalón). 4 (fig.) footstep: *seguir las huellas de mi padre = to follow in my father's footsteps.* || **5 a la –,** following close. **6 – dactilar,** fingerprint. **7 seguir las huellas de alguien,** to follow the example of; to follow the trails of.
huérfano, -a *adj.* 1 orphaned, fatherless, motherless. 2 (fig.) unprotected, defenceless (desamparado). || *s.m.* y *f.* 3 orphan.
huero, -a *adj.* 1 empty (vacío). 2 infertile (huevo no fecundado).
huerta *s.f.* AGR. orchard, large vegetable garden; kitchen garden.
huertano, -a *adj.* small holder of an orchard.

huerto *s.m.* small orchard; fruit garden.
huesillo *s.m.* (Am.) sun-dried peach (fruta seca).
hueso *s.m.* 1 ANAT. bone. 2 BOT. stone (de algunas frutas). 3 (fig.) drudgery, hard work (trabajo difícil). 3 strict person, stickler (persona inflexible). || 5 **dar con los huesos en tierra,** to land on the ground. 6 **estar en los huesos,** to be nothing but skin and bones. 7 **— de santo,** GAST. roll of marzipan. 8 **la sin —,** (fig.) the tongue. 9 **no dejar a alguien — sano,** to rake someone over the coals; to make catty remarks about someone. 10 **soltar la sin —,** to shoot off one's mouth, to talk far too much. 11 **tener los huesos molidos,** to be knackered, to be dead tired.
huésped *s.m.* y *f.* 1 guest (invitado), host (persona que invita). 2 lodger, boarder, resident (de pago).
hueste *s.f.* MIL. army.
huesudo, -a *adj.* bony.
hueva *s.f.* BIOL. roe.
huevería *s.f.* egg shop.
huevero, -a *s.m.* y *f.* 1 egg dealer, egg seller. || *s.f.* 2 egg cup. 3 BIOL. oviduct (en la anatomía de las aves). 4 egg box.
huevo *s.m.* 1 egg. 2 BIOL. ovum (para unirse al espermatozoide). 3 (vulg.) ball (testículo).
huevón, -a *adj.* (Am.) 1 dim, thick (bobalicón). 2 slow (lento).
huida *s.f.* 1 escape. 2 MEC. leakage (fuga de agua, gas, etc.).
huidizo, -a *adj.* fugitive, illusive, evasive.
huir *v.t., i.* y *pron.* 1 to escape, to run away, to escape, to flee: *huyeron al ver al policía = they ran away when they saw the policeman.* || *v.i.* 2 to slip away (irse, el tiempo).
huiriche *s.m.* (Am.) small boy.
hule *s.m.* 1 oilcloth. 2 (Am.) India rubber. || 3 **haber —,** to be trouble: *va a haber hule = there's going to be trouble.*
hulla *s.f.* MIN. soft coal.
hullero, -a *adj.* of coal, coal: *zona hullera = area of coal.*
humacera *s.f.* cloud of smoke, big cloud of smoke.
humanamente *adv.* humanly; humanely.
humanidad *s.f.* 1 humanity, mankind. 2 humaneness (bondad). 3 tenderness, compassion (compasión). 4 corpulence (corpulencia). || *s.pl.* 5 humanities, art (estudios).
humanismo *s.m.* humanism.
humanista *s.m.* y *f.* humanist.
humanístico, -a *adj.* humanistic.
humanitario, -a *adj.* humanitarian.
humanitarismo *s.m.* humanitarism.
humanización *s.f.* humanization.
humanizar *v.t.* y *pron.* 1 to humanize, to make more human. || *v.pron.* 2 to become more human.
humano, -a *adj.* 1 human. 2 humane (comprensivo).
humarasca *s.f.* (Am.) dense smoke, cloud of smoke.
humareda *s.f.* dense smoke, cloud of smoke.
humeante *adj.* smoking; smoky; steaming: *café humeante = steaming coffee.*
humear *v.i.* 1 to smoke; to steam. 2 (fig.) to smolder (permanecer, por ejemplo, el rencor). || *v.t.* 3 (Am.) to fumigate (fumigar).
humedad *s.f.* 1 dampness, humidity. 2 moisture (líquido en la humedad). 3 FIS. humidity (en medidas atmosféricas).
humedecer *v.t.* 1 to dampen, to moisten. 2 FIS. to humidify. || *v.pron.* 3 to get damp, to get wet. 4 to fill with tears (llenarse los ojos de lágrimas).
húmedo, -a *adj.* 1 humid, damp, moist, wet: *un clima húmedo = a humid climate.* || *s.f.* 2 tongue (lengua).
humeral *adj.* 1 ANAT. humeral. || *s.m.* 2 REL. humeral veil.
húmero *s.m.* ANAT. humerus (hueso).
humildad *s.f.* 1 humility, humbleness; meekness. 2 lowly (baja condición social).
humilde *adj.* 1 humble; meek. 2 lowly (de condición social baja).
humildemente *adv.* humbly, meekly.
humillación *s.f.* humiliation.
humilladero *s.m.* boundary cross.
humillante *adj.* humiliating.
humillar *v.t.* 1 to humiliate, to humble. 2 to bow (una parte del cuerpo, como señal de sumisión). || *v.pron.* 3 to humble oneself. 4 to lower its head (bajar la cabeza, el toro).
humo *s.m.* 1 smoke. 2 vapour, steam (de vapor). 3 fume (malo para la salud). || *s.pl.* 4 airs (de una persona vanidosa). || 5 **bajarle a alguien los humos,** to put someone in his place, to take someone down a peg.
humor *s.m.* 1 humour, mood: *tiene buen humor = he is in a good mood.* 2 FISIOL. humour (líquidos dentro del cuerpo). 3 humour, wit (agudez del ingenio): *un humor mordaz = a penetrating wit.* 4 mood, willingness (disposición a hacer algo): *no tengo humor para ir al cine hoy = I'm not in the mood to go to the cinema today.* || 5 **seguirle a alguien el —,** to humour someone, to go along with someone's mood.
humorada *s.f.* joke.
humorismo *s.m.* humour, wit (especialmente por escrito).
humorista *s.m.* y *f.* humorist, comedian.
humorístico, -a *adj.* funny; humorous.
humus *s.m.* GEOL. humus.
hundible *adj.* sinkable.
hundimiento *s.m.* 1 MAR. sinking. 2 cave-in (derrumbamiento). 3 (fig.) ruin, collapse: *el hundimiento total de la economía = the complete collapse of the economy.*
hundir *v.t.* y *pron.* 1 to sink (especialmente un barco). 2 to ruin (a una persona). || *v.t.* 3 to confuse; to defeat (a una persona, con razones): *le hundí con mis argumentos = I defeated him with my arguments.* || *v.pron.* 4 to collapse, to fall down (especialmente un edificio, puente, etc.). 5 to vanish, to disappear (desaparecer).
húngaro, -a *adj./s.m.* y *f.* Hungarian.
huno *s.m.* HIST. Hun.
hura *s.f.* small hole.
huracán *s.m.* hurricane, tornado, gale.
huracanado, -a *adj.* hurricane-like, hurricane: *viento huracanado = hurricane wind.*
huraco *s.m.* (Am.) 1 hole (agujero). 2 perforation.
hurañamente *adv.* unsociably; shyly.
huraño, -a *adj.* unsociable; shy.
hurgar *v.t.* 1 to poke: *déjate de hurgar en la nariz = stop poking in your nose.* 2 to stir, to incite (incitar).
hurgón *s.m.* 1 poker (atizador). 2 (Am.) prick (pinchazo).
hurguetear *v.t.* (Am.) to finger, to pry into, to rummage among, to shove one's nose into (curiosear).
hurí *s.f.* REL. houri.
hurón *s.m.* 1 ZOOL. ferret. 2 (fig.) unsociable person (persona poco sociable).
¡hurra! *interj.* hurra!.
hurtadillas *loc. adv.* **a —,** secretly, furtively, stealthily, on the sly.
hurtar *v.t.* 1 to steal, to rob, to pilfer, to pinch. 2 to dodge (especialmente el cuerpo, a un golpe o similar). 3 to copy, to plagiarize (plagiar). || *v.pron.* 4 to hide oneself, to hide (ocultarse).
hurto *s.m.* theft; robbery.
húsar *s.m.* MIL. hussar.
husillo *s.m.* 1 MEC. small spindle. 2 drain (tubo de desagüe).
husmear *v.t.* 1 to scent, to smell out. 2 to pry into (indagar): *¿tienes siempre que husmear en mis asuntos? = do you always have to pry into my business?*
huso *s.m.* 1 MEC. spindle. 2 time zone (zona horaria).
¡huy! *interj.* 1 ouch! (dolor). 2 well! (sorpresa). 3 phew! (alivio).

i, I, *s.f.* i, I, décima letra del alfabeto español.
ibérico, -a *adj.* iberian.
íbero, -a o **ibero, -a** *adj.* y *s.m.* y *f.* iberian.
iberoamericano, -a *adj./s.m.* y *f.* Latin-American.
ibídem *adv.* ibidem, in the same place.
iceberg *s.m.* iceberg.
icono *s.m.* ikon, icon.
iconoclasta *adj.* **1** iconoclastic. || *s.m.* y *f.* **2** iconoclast.
iconografía *s.f.* iconography.
iconolatría *s.f.* iconolatry.
ictericia *s.f.* jaundice, icterus.
ictiología *s.f.* ichthyology.
ictiológico, -a *adj.* ichthyologic, ichthyological.
ictiólogo *s.m.* ichthyologist.
ictiosaurio o **ictiosauro** *s.m.* ichthyosaurus, ichthyosaur.
ida V. **ido, -a.**
idea *s.f.* **1** idea. **2** idea, plan, project: *mi idea es irme mañana = my plan is to go tomorrow.* **3** idea, opinion, view: *mis ideas políticas = my political views.* **4** imagination, inventiveness (ingenio).
ideal *adj.* **1** ideal. **2** beautiful, perfect: *an ideal place to live in = un lugar ideal en el que vivir.* || *s.m.* **3** ideal (en la vida, política, etc.).
idealismo *s.m.* idealism.
idealista *adj.* **1** idealistic. || *s.m.* y *f.* **2** idealist.
idealizar *v.t.* to idealize.
idealmente *adv.* ideally.
idear *v.t.* **1** to think up; to plan, to design (un proyecto, una actividad, etc.). **2** to invent (inventar).
ideario *s.m.* ideology (de todo tipo).
ideático, -a *adj.* (Am.) maniatic.
ídem *adv.* idem, ditto, the same.
idénticamente *adv.* identically.
idéntico, -a *adj.* identical; the very same.
identidad *s.f.* **1** identity (de una persona). **2** identity, sameness (igualdad). || **3 carné de —,** V. **carné** y **tarjeta.**
identificable *adj.* identifiable.
identificación *s.f.* identification.
identificar *v.t.* **1** to identify (en general). **2** to recognize (reconocer). || *v.pron.* **3** to be identified (con una ideología, persona, etc.). **4** to show one's identity (mediante un documento o similar): *identifíquese o disparo = show your identity or I'll shoot you.*
ideograma *s.m.* ideogram.
ideología *s.f.* ideology.
ideológicamente *adv.* ideologically.
ideológico, -a *adj.* ideological.
ideólogo, -a *s.m.* y *f.* ideologue.
idílico, -a *adj.* idyllic.
idilio *s.m.* idyll.
idioma *s.m.* language.
idiosincrasia *s.f.* idiosyncrasy.
idiosincrásico, -a *adj.* idiosyncratic.
idiota *adj.* **1** idiotic, stupid, foolish. || *s.m.* y *f.* **2** imbecile, idiot.
idiotez *s.f.* idiocy.
idiotismo *s.m.* **1** ignorance (ignorancia). **2** GRAM. idiom, idiomatic expression.
ido, -a *p.p.* **1** de **ir.** || *adj.* **2** crazy, mentally ill. **3** (fig.) distracted (distraído). **4** (Am.) drunk (borracho). || *s.f.* **5** going: *idas y venidas = comings and goings (venidas e idas).* **6** trail, track (el rastro que deja un animal). **7** DEP. sally (en la esgrima). **8** rashness, hastiness (ímpetu instintivo).
idólatra *s.m.* y *f.* **1** idolater, idolizer. **2** (fig.) fan, lover (amante de algo o alguien). || *adj.* **3** idolazing.
idolatría *s.f.* idolatry.
idolátrico, -a *adj.* idolatrous.
ídolo *s.m.* idol.
idóneamente *adv.* **1** aptly, capably (en cuanto a capacidad mental o similar). **2** suitably (idea de conveniencia): *está situada idóneamente = it is situated very suitably.*
idoneidad *s.f.* **1** aptitude, capacity (capacidad o valía personal). **2** suitability (conveniencia).
idóneo, -a *adj.* **1** apt, capable (con capacidad mental o similar). **2** suitable (conveniente).
ígneo, -a *adj.* igneous.
ignición *s.f.* ignition.
ignominia *s.f.* **1** disgrace, ignominy. **2** disgraceful act, shameful act (acción de gran bajeza moral).
ignominiosamente *adv.* shamefully, disgracefully.
ignominioso, -a *adj.* shameful, disgraceful.
ignorancia *s.f.* **1** ignorance. **2** lack of education; lack of information. || **3 — de derecho,** DER. ignorance of laws. **4 — supina,** guilty ignorance. **5 pretender —,** to feign not to know.
ignoto, -a *adj.* unknown, undiscovered.
igual *adj.* **1** equal. **2** similar, alike (similar). **3** even, level (terreno). **4** uniform, constant, invariable (una cantidad, nivel, etc.). **5** exact (coincidencia de formas o similar). **6** indifferent, the same: *agua o vino, es igual = wine or water, it's the same.* || *adj./s.m.* y *f.* **7** equal, peer (persona): *mis iguales = my peers.* || *s.m.* **8** MAT. sign of equality, equal sign. || **9 al — que,** like, just like. **10 sin —,** unequaled.
iguala *s.f.* **1** equalization. **2** agreement, contract (especialmente de servicios médicos). **3** MEC. level (para uso de albañilería o carpintería).
igualación *s.f.* **1** equalization. **2** smoothing, levelling (lisado de una superficie). **3** MAT. equating.
igualado, -a *p.p.* **1** de **igualar.** || *adj.* **2** of the same level (en intelecto, capacidad física, etc.). **3** DEP. hard-fought (partido). || *s.f.* **4** equalizer (gol que iguala el marcador).
igualador, -a *adj.* **1** equalizing, levelling (desde un punto de vista tanto físico

como social, político, etc.). || *s.m.* y *f.* 2 equalizer, leveller.
igualar *v.t.* 1 to even, to even out, to smooth (allanar, normalmente un terreno). 2 to equalize, to make equal: *la muerte nos iguala a todos = death makes us all equal.* || *v.t.* y *pron.* 3 to become equal, to be equal. 4 to come to an agreement on monthly fees (especialmente en el contexto de los servicios médicos). || *v.i.* 5 DEP. to draw.
igualatorio *s.m.* medical insurance agreement, medical insurance group.
igualdad *s.f.* 1 equality. 2 uniformity; evenness (de terreno o similar). 3 MAT. equality. 4 sameness, equality (semejanza total). || 5 — **de ánimo,** equanimity.
igualitario, -a *adj.* egalitarian.
igualitarismo *s.m.* egalitarianism.
igualmente *adv.* 1 equally. 2 evenly, uniformly (en contexto físico). 3 likewise, also; the same to you (como contestación a un deseo): *happy Christmas!... the same to you = feliz Navidad... igualmente.*
iguana *s.f.* iguana.
ijada o **ijar** *s.f.* 1 flank (de un animal). 2 MED. pain in the side.
ilativo, -a *adj.* illative, inferential.
ilegal *adj.* illegal, unlawful.
ilegalidad *s.f.* illegality, unlawfulness.
ilegalmente *adv.* illegally, unlawfully.
ilegible *adj.* illegible.
ilegítimamente *adv.* illegitimately.
ilegitimar *v.t.* to make illegal.
ilegitimidad *s.f.* illegitimacy.
ilegítimo, -a *adj.* 1 illegitimate. || 2 **hijo** —, illegitimate child.
ileso, -a *adj.* unhurt.
iletrado, -a *adj.* uncultured, illiterate.
ilícitamente *adv.* illicitly.
ilícito, -a *adj.* illicit.
ilicitud *s.m.* illegality.
ilimitado, -a *adj.* unlimited.
iluminación *s.f.* 1 illumination. 2 lighting (alumbrado). 3 (fig.) enlightment (intelectual).
iluminado, -a *p.p.* 1 de **iluminar.** || *adj.* 2 lit, lit up, illuminated. 3 (fig.) enlightened (en cultura). || *s.m.* 4 REL. illuminist.
iluminar *v.t.* 1 to illuminate, to light, to light up. 2 to enlighten (cultural, mental o intelectualmente).
iluminativo, -a *adj.* illuminative.
ilusión *s.f.* 1 illusion, delusion (imaginación fantasiosa). 2 unfounded hope (esperanza sin fundamento). 3 thrill, pleasure: *¡qué ilusión! = what a thrill!.*
ilusionadamente *adv.* hopefully, eagerly.
ilusionado, -a *p.p.* 1 de **ilusionar.** || *adj.* 2 excited, eager: *estoy muy ilusionado con el nuevo empleo = I'm very excited about the new job.*
ilusionar *v.t.* 1 to encourage (someone's) hopes, to build up (someone's) hopes (sin fundamento). 2 (Am.) to deceive. || *v.pron.* 3 to have hopes (sobre algo). 4 to be thrilled, to be excited (estar ilusionado sobre algo).
ilusionista *s.m.* y *f.* magician, conjurer, illusionist.
iluso, -a *adj.* 1 deluded, misted (engañado). 2 dreamer (soñador).
ilusorio, -a *adj.* false, deceptive.
ilustración *s.f.* 1 illustration, explanation. 2 learning: *un hombre de gran ilustración = a man of great learning.* 3 illustration (de un texto).
ilustrado, -a *p.p.* 1 de **ilustrar.** || *adj.* 2 learned, erudite (en conocimiento). 3 illustrated (texto). || *s.m.* y *f.* 4 savant, learned intellectual (persona).
ilustrar *v.t.* 1 to illustrate, elucidate: *te voy a ilustrar sobre el tema = I'm going to illustrate you about the matter.* 2 to illustrate (un texto). 3 to instruct, to enlighten (la inteligencia). || *v.t.* y *pron.* 4 to cultivate oneself.
ilustrativo, -a *adj.* illustrative.
ilustre *adj.* 1 distinguished (distinguido). 2 well-known, famous (famoso).
ilustremente *adv.* illustriously.
ilustrísimo, -a *adj.super.* 1 most illustrious (tratamiento a personajes de importancia). || 2 **su ilustrísima,** REL. Your Eminence (obispo).
imagen *s.f.* 1 image. 2 image, likeness (semejanza). 3 REL. image, statue. 4 mental picure, mental image (la que forma la imaginación). || 5 **quedar para vestir imágenes,** to be an old maid, to become an old maid in the garret.
imaginable *adj.* imaginable, conceivable.
imaginación *s.f.* imagination, fancy.
imaginar *v.t.* y *pron.* 1 to imagine, to suppose. 2 to visualize (imágenes concretas).
imaginario, -a *adj.* 1 imaginary. || *s.f.* 2 barracks guard, barracks duty.
imaginativo, -a *adj.* 1 imaginative, fanciful. || *s.f.* 2 imagination, imaginativeness (facultad de imaginar).
imaginería *s.f.* 1 REL. imagery. 2 ART. carving/painting of sacred images.
imán *s.m.* 1 magnet. 2 (fig.) charm, attraction (atracción). || 3 — **artificial,** magnet.
imanación *s.f.* magnetization.
imanar o **imantar** *v.t.* to magnetize.
imantación *s.f.* magnetization.
imbatibilidad *s.f.* unbeaten record.
imbatible *adj.* unbeatable.
imbatido, -a *adj.* unbeaten.
imbécil *adj./s.m.* y *f.* imbecile, idiot.
imbecilidad *s.f.* stupidity, idiocy.
imberbe *adj.* 1 beardless. 2 (fig.) young and inexpert.
imborrable *adj.* indelible: *recuerdos imborrables = indelible memories.*
imbuir *v.t.* to imbue.
imitable *adj.* worthy of imitation.
imitación *s.f.* imitation.
imitado, -a *p.p.* 1 de **imitar.** || *adj.* 2 artificial; fake (artificial).
imitador, -a *adj.* 1 imitative. || *s.m.* y *f.* 2 imitator.
impaciencia *s.f.* impatience.
impacientar *v.t.* 1 to irritate, to make (someone) lose his patience. || *v.pron.* 2 to lose one's patience, to become irritable.
impaciente *adj./s.m.* y *f.* impatient, restless.
impacientemente *adv.* impatiently, anxiously.
impacto *s.m.* 1 hit (con arma de fuego). 2 impact (choque). 3 repercussion (de una medida, acontecimiento, etc.).
impalpable *adj.* impalpable.
impar *adj.* 1 odd: *número impar = odd number.* 2 (fig.) unique, exceptional.
imparcial *adj.* impartial, neutral, objective.
imparcialidad *s.f.* impartiality, fairness.
imparcialmente *adv.* impartially, neutrally, objectively.
impartir *v.t.* 1 to grant, to give, to concede. || 2 — **la enseñanza,** to teach.
impasibilidad *s.f.* impassibility.
impasible *adj.* unmoved, impassible.
impasiblemente *adv.* in an unmoved manner, impassibly.
impavidez *s.f.* 1 fearlessness, courage. 2 (Am.) impudence, cheek.
impávido, -a *adj.* 1 undaunted (sereno). 2 intrepid, fearless (sin miedo). 3 (Am.) impudent, fresh, cheeky.
impecable *adj.* impeccable, faultness.
impedido, -a *p.p.* 1 de **impedir.** || *adj.* crippled, disabled (minusválido). || *s.m.* y *f.* 3 crippled person, disabled person.
impedimento *s.m.* impediment, obstacle.
impedir *v.t.* 1 to obstruct, to hinder (poner pegas, obstáculos, etc.). 2 to stop, to prevent (parar).
impeler *v.t.* 1 to push, to drive, to propel (empujar). 2 to urge, to stimulate (estimular).
impenetrabilidad *s.f.* impenetrability.
impenetrable *adj.* 1 impenetrable (físicamente). 2 (fig.) obscure, incomprehensible (difícil de entender).
impenitencia *s.f.* impenitence.
impenitente *adj.* impenitent, unrepentant.
impensable *adj.* unthinkable.
impensado, -a *adj.* unexpected, fortuitous, unforeseen: *una oportunidad impensada = an unforeseen chance.*
imperante *adj.* 1 ruling, dominant (dominante). 2 prevailing (en el tiempo).
imperativamente *adv.* urgently, imperatively.
imperativo, -a *adj.* 1 urgent, imperative. 2 GRAM. imperative. || *s.m.* 3 GRAM. imperative.
imperceptible *adj.* imperceptible.
imperceptiblemente *adv.* imperceptibly.
imperdible *s.m.* safety pin.
imperecedero, -a *adj.* imperishable, undying.
imperfección *s.f.* imperfection, fault, flaw, blemish.
imperfectamente *adv.* imperfectly.
imperfecto, -a *adj.* 1 defective (que tiene algún fallo). 2 incomplete, unfinished (incompleto). 3 GRAM. imperfect.
imperial *adj.* imperial.
imperialismo *s.m.* imperialism.

impericia *s.f.* 1 unskil fulness (inhabilidad). 2 inexperience (falta de experiencia).
imperio *s.m.* 1 rule, authority (acción de mandar). 2 POL. empire, dominion. 3 big nation, big power (nación con un gran poder). 4 rule, reign (desde el punto de vista de duración en el tiempo). || **5 valer un –,** to cost a bomb.
imperiosamente *adv.* imperiously.
imperioso, -a *adj.* imperious, lordly (en la actitud de mandar). 2 imperative, overriding (urgente): *necesidad imperiosa = overriding need.*
impermeabilidad *s.f.* impermeability.
impermeabilización *s.f.* waterproofing.
impertérrito, -a *adj.* unshaken, undaunted.
impertinencia *s.f.* impertinence, insolence.
impertinente *adj.* 1 impertinent, insolent (mala educación). 2 irrelevant (no importante). || *s.m.pl.* 3 opera glasses, lorgnette.
impertinentemente *adv.* impertinently, insolently.
imperturbable *adj.* imperturbable.
imperturbablemente *adv.* imperturbably, impassively.
impetrar *v.t.* to beseech, to beg for.
ímpetu *s.m.* 1 impetus, impulse (empuje). 2 violence.
impetuosamente *adv.* impetuously.
impetuoso, -a *adj.* 1 impetuous, impulsive (con empuje). 2 violent.
impiedad *s.f.* 1 impiety (carencia de religión). 2 cruelty (crueldad).
impío, -a *adj.* impious, irreligious.
implacable *adj.* implacable, inexorable.
implantación *s.f.* implantation, introduction.
implantar *v.t.* to implant, to introduce.
implicación *s.f.* implication, consequence.
implícitamente *adv.* implicitly.
implícito, -a *adj.* implicit.
imploración *s.f.* supplication, entreaty.
implorar *v.t.* to implore.
implosión *s.f.* FON. implosion.
implosivo, -a *adj.* FON. implosive.
impoluto, -a *adj.* unpolluted.
imponderable *adj.* 1 imponderable. 2 (fig) invaluable (inapreciable). || *s.m.pl.* 3 imponderables.
imponencia *s.f.* (Am.) grandeur.
imponente *adj.* 1 imposing, impressive. 2 smashing (muy sorprendente). 3 (fam.) peachy, very good looking. || *s.m.* y *f.* 4 COM. depositor (de dineros en banco).
imponer *v.t.* 1 to impose. 2 COM. to deposit. 3 to give, to grant: *le impusieron una medalla = he was given a medal.* || *v.t.* y *pron.* 4 to get familiar (aprender algo). || *v.pron.* 5 to assert oneself, to exact obedience. || *v.i.* 6 to inspire fear, to inspire dread.
imponible *adj.* 1 taxable. || **2 base –,** V. **base. 3 hecho –,** V. **hecho.**
impopular *adj.* unpopular.
impopularidad *s.f.* unpopularity.
importación *s.f.* COM. import, importation; imported goods.
importador, -a *adj.* 1 importing. || *s.m.* y *f.* 2 importer.
importancia *s.f.* 1 importance, significance. 2 relevance, weight (peso específico de una persona en la sociedad). || **3 darse –,** to give oneself airs.
importante *adj.* important, considerable.
importar *v.i.* 1 to matter: *no importa = it doesn't matter.* || *v.t.* 2 COM. to import. 3 to cost, to be worth. 4 to involve, to imply: *esto importa muchos esfuerzos = this involves a lot of effort.*
importe *s.m.* value, cost.
imposibilidad *s.f.* impossibility.
imposibilitado, -a *p.p.* 1 de **imposibilitar.** || *adj.* 2 crippled, disabled.
imposibilitar *v.t.* 1 to make (something) impossible. || *v.pron.* 2 to become disabled, to become crippled.
imposible *adj.* 1 impossible. 2 difficult (especialmente de carácter). || *s.m.pl.* 3 impossible things. || **4 estar/ponerse –,** to be awkward, to become awkward. **5 hacer lo –,** to do one's utmost.
imposición *s.f.* 1 imposition, burden. 2 tax. || **3 – de manos,** REL. laying-on of hands.
impostor, -a *s.m.* y *f.* 1 impostor. 2 slanderer (calumniador).
impotencia *s.f.* 1 powerlessness, impotence. 2 MED. impotence.
impotente *adj.* 1 powerless, impotent: *me vi impotente de parar la carnicería = I realized I was powerless to stop the carnage.* 2 MED. impotent.
impracticable *adj.* 1 impracticable, unfeasible. 2 impassable (carretera o camino).
impracticabilidad *s.f.* impracticability.
imprecación *s.f.* imprecation, curse.
imprecar *v.t.* to curse, to imprecate.
imprecisión *s.f.* lack of precision, vagueness.
impreciso, -a *adj.* imprecise, inexact.
impregnación *s.f.* impregnation.
impregnar *v.t.* to impregnate, to saturate (normalmente con líquidos).
imprenta *s.f.* 1 printing (la habilidad o arte). 2 printing house (taller).
imprescindible *adj.* indispensable, essential.
impresentable *adj.* unpresentable.
impresión *s.f.* 1 print, printing (de cualquier escrito). 2 typeface (tipo concreto de imprenta). 3 edition (edición). 4 INF. printout. 5 impression, mark (visible). 6 shock: *¡vaya impresión que me llevé! = what a shock I had!.* || **7 cambiar impresiones,** to exchange notes. **8 hacer la – de que,** to seem, to look like.
impresionable *adj.* impressionable.
impresionante *adj.* impressive.
impresionar *v.t.* 1 FOT. to expose. || *v.t.* y *pron.* 2 to impress, to affect; to shock (con gran intensidad).
impresionismo *s.m.* impressionism.
impresionista *adj./s.m.* y *f.* ART. impressionist.
impreso, -a *p.p.* 1 de **imprimir.** || *adj.* 2 printed (escrito). || *s.m.* 3 form (normalmente algún formulario).
impresor, -a *s.m.* y *f.* printer.
imprevisible *adj.* 1 unpredictable: *consecuencias imprevisibles = unpredictable consequences.* 2 sudden (súbito).
imprevisión *s.f.* lack of foresight, lack of preparation.
imprevisto, -a *adj.* 1 unforeseen. || *s.m.pl.* 2 incidentals, unexpected events.
imprimátur *s.m.* imprimatur.
imprimir *v.t.* 1 to print. 2 to stamp, to imprint (grabar). 3 to impart, to transmit (una orientación, inclinación, velocidad, etc.).
improbabilidad *s.f.* improbability.
improbable *adj.* improbable, unlikely.
ímprobo, -a *adj.* 1 dishonest, corrupt (como vicio). 2 arduous, laborious, strenuous (como enfático de cualquier tarea negativa): *¡qué ímprobos esfuerzos! = what strenuous efforts!.*
improcedencia *s.f.* 1 inappropiateness, inapplicability. 2 DER. irrelevance, inadmissibility.
improcedente *adj.* 1 inappropiate, inapplicable. 2 DER. irrelevant, inadmissible.
impronta *s.f.* 1 impression (de índole gráfica). 2 (fig.) mark, stamp (especialmente de una persona concreta).
improperio *s.m.* insult, taunt.
impropio, -a *adj.* 1 inappropriate, unsuitable. 2 incorrect.
improvisación *s.f.* 1 improvisation. 2 adlib (en espectáculos de algún tipo).
improvisadamente *adv.* in an improvised manner; unexpectedly.
improvisado, -a *p.p.* 1 de **improvisar.** || *adj.* 2 improvised, impromptu (cualquier dicho o actividad): *un discurso improvisado = an impromptu speech.*
improvisador, -a *adj.* improvising.
improvisar *v.t.* to improvise.
improviso, -a *adj.* 1 unforeseen, unexpected. || **2 de –,** suddenly, unexpectedly.
imprudencia *s.f.* 1 imprudence. || **2 – temeraria,** DER. negligence.
imprudente *adj.* imprudent, indiscreet; rash, unwise.
imprudentemente *adv.* imprudently, indiscreetly; rashly, unwisely.
impúdico, -a *adj.* immodest; shameless.
impudor o **impudicia** *s.m.* o *f.* immodesty; shamelessness.
impuesto, -a *p.p.* 1 de **imponer.** || *s.m.* 2 tax, duty. || *adj.* 3 obligatory. || **4 impuestos directos,** FIN. direct taxation, direct taxes. **5 impuestos indirectos,** FIN. indirect taxation, indirect taxes.
impugnación *s.f.* refutation; challenge.
impugnar *v.t.* to refute; to challenge.
impulsar *v.t.* 1 to push, to drive, to impel. 2 to stimulate (incitar). 3 to improve (alguna actividad): *hemos impulsado el deporte = we have improved sports.*
impulsividad *s.f.* impulsiveness.
impulsivo, -a *adj.* impulsive.

impulso *s.m.* 1 impulse. 2 urge, stimulus (estímulo).
impune *adj.* unpunished.
impunemente *adv.* with impunity.
impunidad *s.f.* impunity.
impureza *s.f.* 1 impurity (en una sustancia o similar). 2 lack of chastity (vicio moral). || *pl.* 3 impure particles.
impuro, -a *adj.* 1 impure (sustancia). 2 lewd, obscene, immoral (vicio).
imputabilidad *s.f.* imputability.
imputable *adj.* imputable, attributable.
imputar *v.t.* to impute, to attribute.
in- *prefijo* 1 in-, im- (con carácter negativo). 2 indica inclusión. 3 movimiento hacia. 4 cierto énfasis en algunos verbos.
inacabable *adj.* endless, interminable.
inaccesibilidad *s.f.* inaccesibility.
inaccesible *adj.* inaccessible.
inaccesiblemente *adv.* inaccessibly.
inacción *s.f.* inaction, inactivity, idleness.
inactividad *s.f.* inactivity.
inactual *adj.* (Am.) out of fashion.
inadaptable *adj.* unadaptable.
inadaptación *s.f.* inadaptation, maladjustment.
inadvertencia *s.f.* 1 carelessness. 2 error, oversight.
inadvertido, -a *adj.* 1 careless (descuidado). 2 unseen, unnoticed (sin ser visto).
inalámbrico, -a *adj.* wireless.
in albis *adv.* 1 in the dark (sin saber). || 2 **dejar/estar/quedarse —**, to be left in the dark; not to know a thing.
inalienable *adj.* inalienable.
inalterable *adj.* immutable.
inamovible *adj.* immovable, fixed.
inanición *s.f.* MED. inanition.
inanimado, -a *adj.* 1 dead, lifeless. 2 inanimate, without a soul (sin alma).
inapelable *adj.* 1 DER. without right to appeal. 2 inevitable: *una derrota inapelable = an inevitable defeat.*
inapetencia *s.f.* lack of appetite.
inapetente *adj.* lacking appetite.
inaplicable *adj.* inapplicable.
inapreciable *adj.* 1 invaluable (que se necesita): *una ayuda inapreciable = an invaluable help.* 2 imperceptible (pequeñísima).
inapropiado, -a *adj.* inappropriate.
inasistencia *s.f.* absence.
inaudito, -a *adj.* 1 unheard-of, unprecedented. 2 monstruous, outrageous (monstruoso).
inauguración *s.f.* inauguration, opening.
inaugurar *v.t.* 1 to inaugurate, to open. 2 to unveil (descubrir, normalmente una estatua o algo visible).
inca *adj./s.m.* y *f.* HIST. inca.
incalculable *adj.* incalculable.
incalificable *adj.* unspeakable, indescribable.
incambiable *adj.* unchangeable.
incandescencia *s.f.* incandescence.
incandescente *adj.* incandescent.
incansable *adj.* untiring, tireless, unflagging (que no decae).
incansablemente *adv.* untiringly, tirelessly, unflaggingly.
incapacidad *s.f.* 1 incompetence (en la profesión o similar). 2 incapacity (física o mental).
incapacitado, -a *p.p.* 1 de **incapacitar.** || *adj.* 2 incapacitated, unfit: *está incapacitado para la vida matrimonial = he's unfit for married life.* 3 (Am.) disabled, crippled.
incapacitar *v.t.* 1 to incapacitate, to render unfit. 2 DER. to disqualify. 3 to handicap, to disable (física o mentalmente, con alguna minusvalía).
incapaz *adj.* 1 incapable, unable: *es incapaz de dar las gracias = he's incapable of thanking anybody.* 2 incompetent, inept (inepto). 3 DER. disqualified.
incardinar *v.t.* to incardinate.
incautación *s.f.* DER. confiscation.
incautarse *v.pron.* to seize, to confiscate.
incauto, -a *adj.* 1 unwary, incautious (descuidado). 2 naive, gullible (ingenuo).
incendiar *v.t.* 1 to set on fire. || *v.pron.* 2 to catch fire.
incendiario, -a *adj./s.m.* y *f.* 1 incendiary. 2 (fig.) revolutionary. 3 pyromaniac (persona que incendia voluntariamente).
incendio *s.m.* 1 fire. 2 (fig.) conflagration (de pasiones o similar).
incensario *s.m.* censer.
incentivar *v.t.* to encourage, to stimulate. 2 to pay extra money, to add a bonus (económicamente).
incentivo *s.m.* 1 incentive (especialmente el económico). 2 stimulation, encouragement.
incertidumbre *s.f.* uncertainty, doubt.
incesantemente *adv.* incessantly, unceasingly, continually.
incesto *s.m.* incest.
incestuoso, -a *adj.* incestuous.
incidencia *s.f.* 1 incidence, occurrence. 2 result; repercussion (repercusión). 3 GEOM. incidence (de los ángulos).
incidentalmente *adv.* incidentally.
incidente *adj.* 1 incident, incidental. || *s.m.* 2 occurrence.
incidir *v.i.* 1 to affect, to influence (afectar). 2 MED. to make an incision (cortando).
incienso *s.m.* incense.
incierto, -a *adj.* 1 uncertain, doubtful (dudoso). 2 unsteady (con movimientos inseguros). 3 false (no verdad).
incinerable *adj.* incinerable.
incineración *s.f.* incineration, cremation.
incinerar *v.t.* to incinerate, to cremate, to burn.
incisión *s.f.* 1 MED. incision, cut. 2 LIT. caesura (de los versos).
incisivo, -a *adj.* 1 cutting, sharp (que corta físicamente). 2 keen (de ironía, pensamiento, etc.). || 3 **diente —**, ANAT. incisor.
inciso *s.m.* 1 interruption. 2 GRAM. pause (pausa).
incitación *s.f.* incitement: *incitación a la rebeldía = incitement to rebellion.*
incitar *v.t.* to instigate, to incite.
incivil *adj.* uncivil, rude.
incivilizado, -a *adj.* unciviliced.
inclemencia *s.f.* 1 severity (especialmente del clima). || 2 **a la —**, exposed to wind and weather.
inclinación *s.f.* 1 bowing (del cuerpo como muestra de respeto o como saludo). 2 inclination, dip, slant (de un objeto, terreno, etc.). 3 inclination (gusto).
inclinar *v.t.* 1 to persuade (persuadir). || *v.t.* y *pron.* 2 to slant, to bow (movimiento físico). || *v.i.* y *pron.* 3 to resemble, to take after (asemejarse). || *v.pron.* 4 to be inclined, to feel inclined; to tend: *me inclino a pensar que está equivocado = I tend to think he's wrong.*
ínclito, -a *adj.* (form.) illustrious.
incluir *v.t.* 1 to include. 2 to enclose, to contain (físicamente dentro).
inclusión *s.f.* inclusion.
inclusivamente *adv.* inclusive, inclusively.
inclusivo, -a *adj.* inclusive.
incluso, -a *p.p.* 1 de **incluir.** || *adj.* 2 enclosed, contained (físicamente dentro). || *s.f.* 3 foundling hospital. || *prep.* y *conj.* 4 even: *incluso ahora después de tantos años, no me cae bien = even now after so many years, I dislike him.* || *adv.* even, inclusively.
incoacción *s.f.* (form.) inception (de un expediente o similar).
incoar *v.t.* 1 to start, to commence. 2 DER. to initiate (un proceso, expediente disciplinario, etc.).
incógnito, -a *adj.* 1 unknown (desconocido). || *s.f.* 2 MAT. unknown quantity. 3 mystery, hidden motive (misterio). || 4 **de —**, incognito.
incoherencia *s.f.* incoherence.
incoherente *adj.* incoherent, disconnected.
incoherentemente *adv.* incoherently, disconnectedly.
incoloro, -a *adj.* colourless.
incólume *adj.* unharmed.
incombustibilidad *s.f.* incombustibility.
incombustible *adj.* incombustible, fireproof.
incómodamente *adv.* uncomfortably, inconveniently.
incomodidad o **incomodo** *s.f.* 1 uncomfortableness (corporal o física). 2 annoyance, anger (enfado). 3 inconvenience, nuisance (fastidio).
incomparable *adj.* incomparable.
incomparablemente *adv.* incomparably.
incompatibilidad *s.f.* incompatibility; conflict.
incompatible *adj.* incompatible.
incompetencia *s.f.* incompetence.
incompetente *adj.* incompetent.
incomprendido, -a *adj.*, misunderstood; not apreciated.
incomprensible *adj.* incomprehensible.
incomprensiblemente *adv.* incomprehensibly.
incomprensión *s.f.* incomprehension, lack of understanding.

incomunicado, -a *p.p.* **1** de **incomunicar.** || *adj.* **2** isolated, cut off. **3** DER. in solitary confinement (un prisionero).
incomunicar *v.t.* **1** to isolate, to cut off. || *v.pron.* **2** to isolate oneself, to shut oneself off, to withdraw from society.
inconcebible *adj.* inconceivable, inimaginable, unthinkable.
inconcluso, -a *adj.* unfinished, incomplete.
incondicional *adj.* **1** unconditional, absolute. || *s.m.* y *f.* **2** follower, stalwart supporter. || **3 rendición —,** unconditional surrender.
inconfesable *adj.* unspeakable: *crimen inconfesable = unspeakable crime.*
inconfeso, -a *adj.* unconfessed.
inconfundible *adj.* unmistakable.
incongruencia *s.f.* incongruousness, incoherence.
incongruente *adj.* incongruous, incoherent.
inconmensurabilidad *s.f.* incommensurability.
inconmesurable *adj.* enormous, immense, vast.
inconmovible *adj.* unyielding, unshakable.
inconsciencia *s.f.* **1** unconsciousness (estado sin conocimiento). **2** thoughtlessness (característica negativa de no pensar adecuadamente).
inconsciente *adj.* **1** unconscious (sin sentido). **2** thoughtless (falta de la virtud de la seriedad).
inconscientemente *adv.* thoughtlessly (sin pensar lo debido).
inconsecuencia *s.f.* inconsistency.
inconsecuente *adj.* inconsistent.
inconsideración *s.f.* thoughtlessness.
inconsiderado, -a *adj.* **1** inconsiderate, thoughtless. **2** rash, hasty, impetuous (irreflexivo).
inconsistencia *s.f.* inconsistency, weakness, flimsiness.
inconsistente *adj.* inconsistent, weak, flimsy.
inconstancia *s.f.* tickleness.
inconstante *adj.* tickle.
incontable *adj.* uncountable, innumerable, countless.
incontenible *adj.* uncontrollable, unstoppable, irrepressible.
incontestable *adj.* unquestionable.
incontinencia *s.f.* incontinence.
incontinente *adj.* incontinent (especialmente en las funciones corporales).
inconveniencia *s.f.* **1** inconvenience, trouble (molestia). **2** disconfort (incomodidad). **3** rude remark, crude remark (comentario grosero). **4** inappropriateness, unsuitability (incompatibilidad).
inconveniente *adj.* **1** inconvenient. || *s.m.* **2** obstacle, difficulty (obstáculo). **3** drawback, disadvantage (perjuicio de una acción o situación).
incordiar *v.t.* to pester, to annoy, to bother.
incordio *s.m.* annoyance, bother.
incorporación *s.f.* **1** inclusion: *la incorporación de un índice ayuda = the inclusion of an index helps.* **2** joining, involvement (inscripción en un grupo, partido, institución, asociación, etc.). **3** sitting up (movimiento corporal).
incorporado, -a *p.p.* **1** de **incorporar.** || *adj.* **2** built-in (en aparatos, casas, etc., con algún añadido): *micrófono incorporado = built-in microphone.*
incorporar *v.t.* **1** to include. || *v.t.* y *pron.* **2** to sit up (adquirir una posición más vertical del cuerpo). || *v.pron.* **3** to join (asociación o similar). **4 incorporarse a filas,** MIL. to join the ranks, to join the army.
incorpóreo, -a *adj.* incorporeal, bodiless.
incorrección *s.f.* **1** incorrectness. **2** unseemliness, impropriety, discourtesy (falta de tacto). **3** mistake (concreta equivocación).
incorrecto, -a *adj.* **1** incorrect, inaccurate. **2** improper, discourteous (en la conducta).
incorregible *adj.* incorrigible.
incorrupción *s.f.* uncorruptness.
incorruptible *adj.* incorruptible.
incorruptibilidad *s.f.* incorruptibility.
incorrupto, -a *adj.* uncorruptness, incorrupt.
incredulidad *s.f.* incredulity, skeptical.
incrédulo, -a *adj.* **1** incredulous. || *s.m.* y *f.* **2** unbeliever (que no cree en Dios).
increíble *adj.* incredible, unbelievable.
increíblemente *adv.* incredibly, unbelievably.
incrementar *v.t.* y *pron.* to increase, to augment.
incremento *s.m.* increase, rise.
increpar *v.t.* to rebuke, to reprimand, to upbraid.
incriminación *s.f.* incrimination.
incriminar *v.t.* to incriminate, to accuse.
incruento, -a *adj.* bloodless.
incrustación *s.f.* **1** encrustation, incrustation. **2** inlaying (de joyas, por ejemplo).
incrustar *v.t.* **1** to inlay (adornos). || *v.t.* y *pron.* **2** to become fixed (una idea). || *v.pron.* **3** to become imbedded (meterse dentro de algo).
incubadora *s.f.* incubator.
incubar *v.t.* to incubate, hatch.
incuestionable V. **indiscutible.**
inculpable *adj.* inculpable, blameless, guiltless.
inculpar *v.t.* to indict, to accuse.
inculto, -a *adj.* uncultured, uncouth; uncultivated.
incultura *s.f.* lack of culture, uncouthness.
incumbencia *s.f.* concern: *no es de mi incumbencia = it's no concern of mine.*
incumbir *v.i.* to be of concern to. V. **incumbencia.**
incumplimiento *s.m.* non-fulfillment, non-completion.
incumplir *v.i.* to fail to keep, to fail to fulfill.
incurable *adj.* incurable.
incurrir *v.i.* **1** to commit an error. **2** to bring on oneself (buscarse un castigo o similar). || **3 — en odio/desprecio/etc.,** to incur the hate of, etc.
incursión *s.f.* MIL. raid, strike, incursion.
indagación *s.f.* investigation, inquiry.
indagar *v.t.* to investigate, to inquire into.
indecencia *s.f.* indecency, obscenity, filth; weetchedness.
indecente *adj.* **1** indecent, obscene. **2** wretched, miserable: *un lugar indecente = a wretched place.*
indecisión *s.f.* indecision, irresolution.
indeciso, -a *adj.* undecided, hesistant.
indeclinable *adj.* **1** unavoidable, obligatory. **2** GRAM. indeclinable.
indefectible *adj.* unfailing.
indefendible *adj.* indefensible.
indefenso, -a *adj.* defenceless.
indefinido, -a *adj.* **1** undefined, indefinite, vague. **2** GRAM. indefinite.
indeleble *adj.* indelible.
indemnidad *s.f.* indemnity.
indemnización *s.f.* indemnization, indemnity, compensation.
indemnizar *v.t.* to indemnify, to compensate (normalmente con dinero).
independencia *s.f.* independence.
independiente *adj.* **1** independent. **2** self-sufficient (autónomo). || *s.m.* y *f.* **3** independent (normalmente en la política). || *adv.* **4** independently.
independientemente *adv.* independently.
independizar *v.t.* y *pron.* to grant independence, to become independent, to become self-sufficient: *quiero independizarme de mis padres = I want to become independent from my parents.*
indeseable *adj.* y *s.m.* y *f.* undesirable; vile.
indestructibilidad *s.f.* indestructibility.
indestructible *adj.* indestructible.
indeterminación *s.f.* indetermination.
indeterminadamente *adv.* indeterminately.
indeterminado, -a *adj.* **1** indeterminate, indefinite. **2** GRAM. indefinite.
indicación *s.f.* **1** indication, sign (visible). **2** suggestion (sugerencia). **3** direction (para llegar a algún sitio). **4** instruction (instrucción). **5** remark, observation (comentario).
indicador, -a *adj.* **1** indicating, indicatory. || *s.m.* y *f.* indicator (especialmente económico).
indicar *v.t.* **1** to indicate, to show. **2** to suggest (sugerir). **3** to give instructions (dar instrucciones).
indicativo, -a *adj.* **1** indicative. || *s.m.* **2** GRAM. indicative.
índice *adj.* y *s.m.* **1** index (dedo). || *s.m.* **2** index, list. **3** rate (coeficiente). **4** REL. index (libros prohibidos). || **5 — cefálico,** BIOL. cephalic index. **6 — de refracción,** FIS. refractive index.
indicio *s.m.* sign, indication.
indiferencia *s.f.* indifference.
indiferente *adj.* indifferent.
indiferentemente *adv.* indifferently.
indígena *adj./s.m.* y *f.* indigenous; native.
indigencia *s.f.* indigence.

indigente *adj./s.m.* y *f.* indigent.
indigestar *v.t.* y *pron.* to cause indigestion; to have indigestion.
indigestible *adj.* indigestible.
indigestión *s.f.* indigestion.
indignación *s.f.* indignation.
indignar *v.t.* y *pron.* to anger, to infuriate.
indignante *adj.* outrageous, infuriating.
indigno, -a *adj.* 1 unworthy: *eres indigno de la confianza que han depositado en ti = you're unworthy of the trust they have placed on you.* 2 contemptible, despicable, mean (despreciable o ruin).
índigo *s.m.* indigo.
indio, -a *adj.* 1 Hindi. 2 Indian (de América del Norte o Sur). || 3 **hacer el —**, to make a fool of oneself, to play the fool.
indirectamente *adv.* indirectly.
indirecto, -a *adj.* indirect.
indisciplina *s.f.* indiscipline.
indisciplinado, -a *adj.* undisciplined.
indiscretion *s.f.* indiscretion.
indiscreto, -a *adj.* indiscreet.
indiscutible *adj.* indisputable, unquestionable.
indiscutiblemente *adv.* indisputably, unquestionably.
indisolubilidad *s.f.* indissolubility.
indispensable *adj.* indispensable, essential.
indisponer *v.t.* 1 to indispose, to upset (hacer caer algo indispuesto). 2 to estrange (enfadar): *lo que dije me indispuso con él = what I said estranged me from him.* || *v.t.* y *pron.* 3 to fall out (enemistarse). || *v.pron.* 4 to fall ill, to become ill.
indisposición *s.f.* 1 indisposition (pequeño malestar corporal). 2 disinclination (pocas ganas de hacer algo).
indispuesto, -a *p.p.* 1 de **indisponer.** || *adj.* 2 slightly ill, unwell.
individual *adj.* 1 individual, single (especialmente tipo de habitación en un hotel). || *s.m.pl.* 2 DEP. singles (en tenis o deportes parecidos).
individualismo *s.m.* individualism.
individualmente *adv.* individually.
individualizar *v.t.* to individualize.
individuo, -a *adj.* 1 individual, undivided. || *s.m.* y *f.* 2 individual (de una especie biológica). 3 member (de una asociación o similar). 4 man, woman, person.
indivisiblemente *adv.* indivisibly.
indiviso, -a *adj.* undivided.
indoctrinar *v.t.* (Am.) to indoctrinate.
indocumentado, -a *adj.* 1 without identification papers, without the identity card. 2 ignoramus. 3 nobody: *es un indocumentado = he's a nobody.*
índole *s.f.* 1 nature, character. 2 sort, kind, type (tipo): *de toda índole = of all kinds.*
indolente *adj.* indolent, lazy, idle.
indoloro, -a *adj.* painless.
indomable *adj.* indomitable, untamable, uncontrollable.
indómito, -a *adj.* 1 untamed (que no está domado). 2 unrully, disobedient (persona que no obedece).
inducción *s.f.* 1 FIL. induction. || 2 **— eléctrica,** ELEC. electrical induction. 3 **— electromagnética,** FIS. electromagnetic induction. 4 **— magnética,** FIS. magnetic induction.
inducido *s.m.* FIS. armature.
inducir *v.t.* 1 to incite, to persuade. 2 FIL. to infer (inducir). 3 ELEC. to induce.
inductivo, -a *adj.* inductive.
indudable *adj.* indubitable, undoubted.
indulgencia *s.f.* 1 indulgence, forbearance. || *pl.* 2 REL. indulgences. || 3 **— plenaria,** REL. plenary indulgence.
indulgente *adj.* lenient.
indultar *v.t.* to pardon.
indulto *s.m.* pardon.
indumentaria *s.f.* clothing, garments, dress, apparel.
industria *s.f.* 1 industry. 2 skill (habilidad). 3 factory, mill (fábrica). || 4 **de —**, on purpose.
industrial *adj.* 1 industrial. || *s.m.* 2 industrialist, manufacturer.
industrialismo *s.m.* industrialism.
industrialista *s.m.* industrialist.
industrialización *s.f.* industrialization.
industrializar *v.t.* to industrialize.
industriosamente *adv.* 1 industriously. 2 skillfully.
inédito, -a *adj.* unpublished.
inefable *adj.* ineffable, inexpressible, indescribable.
ineficacia *s.f.* inefficacy.
ineficaz *adj.* ineffective.
ineludible *adj.* inevitable, inescapable: *deberes ineludibles = inescapable duties.*
inenarrable *adj.* indescribable, inexpressible.
ineptitud *s.f.* ineptitude, incompetence.
inepto, -a *adj.* inept, incompetent.
inequívoco, -a *adj.* unequivoca.
inercia *s.f.* inertia.
inerte *adj.* inert, lifeless.
inesperadamente *adv.* suddenly, unexpectedly.
inesperado, -a *adj.* unexpected, unforeseen.
inestabilidad *s.f.* 1 instability, unsteadiness. 2 unsettled (tiempo atmosférico): *períodos de inestabilidad = spells of unsettled weather.*
inestable *adj.* 1 unstable. 2 unsettled (tiempo).
inestimable *adj.* inestimable, invaluable.
inexacto, -a *adj.* inexact, inaccurate.
inexcusable *adj.* inexcusable.
inexorable *adj.* inexorable.
inexorablemente *adv.* inexorably.
inexperiencia *s.f.* inexperience.
inexperto, -a *adj./s.m.* y *f.* inexpert, inexperienced; inexperienced person.
inexpresivo, -a *adj.* inexpressive; dull: *cara inexpresiva = dull face.*
inexpugnable *adj.* unassailable.
inextinguible *adj.* inextinguishable; eternal, perpetual.
inextricable *adj.* inextricable.
infalibilidad *s.f.* infallibility.
infalible *adj.* infallible (especialmente aplicado al Papa).
infaliblemente *adv.* infallibly.
infamar *v.t.* y *pron.* to defame, to slander.
infame *adj.* 1 infamous. 2 vile, odious (vil). 3 disgusting, horrible (enfatizando la negatividad de algo): *es un sitio infame = it's a disgusting place.*
infamemente *adv.* infamously.
infancia *s.f.* 1 infancy. 2 (fig.) infancy, beginning state (cualquier cosa en su comienzo).
infante, -a *s.m.* y *f.* 1 prince (después del primogénito del rey). 2 MIL. infantry soldier, infantryman. || *s.f.* 3 princess.
infantería *s.f.* MIL. 1 infantry. || 2 **— de línea,** foot infantry. 3 **— de marina,** marines. 4 **— ligera,** light infantry.
infanticida *s.m.* y *f.* infanticide.
infanticidio *s.m.* infanticide.
infantil *adj.* 1 child's, children's: *juegos infantiles = children's games.* 2 innocent (inocente). 3 (desp.) infantile, childish.
infantilismo *s.m.* (desp.) childishness.
infarto *s.m.* MED. heart attack.
infatigable *adj.* untiring.
infección *s.f.* infection.
infeccioso, -a *adj.* infectious.
infectar *v.pron.* 1 to become infected. || *v.t.* 2 to infect, to contaminate (contagiar).
infectado, -a o **infecto, -a** *adj.* infected, contaminated.
infecundidad *s.f.* infecundity, sterility, barrenness.
infecundo, -a *adj.* 1 sterile, infertile (un esfuerzo, plan, etc.). 2 barren, infertile (mujer o tierra).
infeliz *adj.* 1 unfortunate, unhappy. 2 wretched, miserable, sad. 3 simple, kind-hearted (normalmente tiene cierto tono de sorna).
inferior *adj.* 1 lower (en el espacio, más abajo). 2 inferior (en calidad o similar). || *adj.* y *s.m.* subordinate (persona que obedece a otras).
inferioridad *s.f.* inferiority.
inferir *v.t.* 1 to inflict damage (herir). || *v.t.* y *pron.* 2 to infer, to deduce (deducir).
infernal *adj.* infernal.
infestar *v.t.* 1 to overrun (especialmente desde una óptica militar). 2 to infest (invasión de bichos que hacen daños a plantas o similar).
infidelidad *s.f.* 1 infidelity, unfaithfulness. 2 REL. unbelief, disbilief.
infiel *adj.* 1 inaccurate, inexact. 2 unfaithful (especialmente al otro cónyuge). || *s.m.* 3 REL., HIST. infidel.
infielmente *adv.* unfaithfully, disloyally; inaccuratelly.
infiernillo o **infernillo** *s.m.* portable stove.
infierno *s.m.* y *pl.* 1 REL. hell. 2 (fig.) hell, torment (expresando que hace mucho calor, que hay peleas, etc.). || 3 **el quinto —**, the middle of nowhere, the

back of beyond. **4 mandar a alguien al —**, to tell someone to go to hell.
infiltración *s.f.* infiltration.
infiltrar *v.t.* y *pron.* **1** to infiltrate (un líquido). **2** to disseminate, to spread (ideas, teoría, etc.). || *v.pron.* **3** (fig.) to infiltrate, to get into the enemy camp unseen (meterse a escondidas dentro de las filas enemigas): *we don't want anybody to infiltrate our party at this moment = no queremos que nadie se infiltre dentro de nuestro partido en este momento.*
ínfimo, -a *adj.* **1** lowest (más bajo); least (más pequeño). **2** worst, of very low (calidad, hechura, estilo, etc.). **3** vile, despicable, nasty (característica negativa de algo o alguien).
infinidad *s.f.* **1** infinity (concepto especialmente matemático). **2** (fig.) lot, great number, limitless number, big quantity: *una infinidad de problemas = a big quantity of problems.*
infinitamente *adv.* infinitely.
infinitesimal *adj.* infinitesimal.
infinitivo *s.m.* GRAM. infinitive.
infinito, -a *adj.* **1** endless, limitless: *el universo infinito = the limitless universe.* **2** (fig.) boundless, numerous. || *s.m.* **3** MAT. infinity. **4** FIL. infinite. || *adv.* **5** a great deal, a lot, enormously (en gran manera).
inflación *s.f.* **1** ECON. inflation. **2** swelling (hinchazón). **3** vanity, conceit (vanidad).
inflacionario, -a *adj.* ECON. inflationary.
inflacionista *adj.* inflationist, inflationary.
inflador *s.m.* air pump.
inflamable *adj.* inflammable.
inflamación *s.f.* **1** inflammation, ignition, combustion (ignición). **2** MED. inflammation, swelling.
inflamar *v.t.* y *pron.* **1** to ignite (encender con llama). **2** to inflame, to kindle (pasiones o parecido). **3** MED. to cause swelling, to cause inflammation.
inflamatorio, -a *adj.* inflammatory.
inflar *v.t.* y *pron.* **1** to blow up (normalmente con aire). **2** (fig.) to make conceited, to puff up with pride (envanecerse). || *v.t.* **3** to inflate, to exaggerate (cantidades, signos de calidad, etc.).
inflexibilidad *s.f.* **1** inflexibility, rigidity (en opiniones, posturas, etc.). **2** rigidity (en los músculos, movimientos, etc.). **3** severity (de carácter).
inflexible *adj.* **1** rigid (que no se dobla físicamente). **2** inflexible (en posturas ideológicas o similar). **3** strict (estricto).
inflexiblemente *adv.* inflexibly, rigidly; strictly.
inflexión *s.f.* **1** bending, curving (doblar físicamente). **2** inflection, modulation (de la voz). **3** GRAM. inflection. **4** GEOM. inflection (de una curva). **5** (fig.) moment for change, opportunity for change: *hemos llegado a un punto de inflexión en la economía del país = we have reached the right moment for change in the economy of this country.*
infligir *v.t.* to inflict: *murió de una herida de pistola que se infligió él mismo = he died of a self-inflicted gunshot wound.*
influencia *s.f.* influence.
influenciar *v.t.* e *i.* to influence.
influir *v.t.* e *i.* **1** to influence, to have an influence. **2** to have influence, to carry weight (tener importancia una persona, institución, etc.).
influjo *s.m.* **1** influence. **2** MAR. high tide (marea).
influyente *adj.* influential.
información *s.f.* **1** information. **2** PER. news, news report. **3** INF. data. **4** references (información sobre una persona, especialmente con vistas a un empleo).
informador, -a *adj.* **1** informing. || *s.m.* y *f.* **2** informer (especialmente de la policía). **3** PER. newspaperman, pressman.
informal *adj.* **1** informal (lenguaje, proyecto, etc.). || *adj./s.m.* y *f.* **2** unstrustworthy, unreliable (en el que no se puede confiar).
informalidad *s.f.* irresponsibility, unreliability.
informante *adj.* informing.
informar *v.t.* y *pron.* **1** to report, to inform (especialmente desde un punto de vista periodístico). **2** to instruct, to teach (dar instrucciones). || *v.t.* **3** to form (dando forma física). || *v.i.* **4** DER. to plead.
informática *s.f.* INF. data processing; computer science, computing.
informativo, -a *adj.* **1** informative, explanatory, with information. **2** TV. news: *programa informativo = news programme.*
informe *s.m.* **1** report, piece of information (muy especialmente periodístico). **2** DER. plea. || *adj.* **3** shapeless (sin forma definida, visible o no).
infortunado, -a *adj.* unfortunate, unlucky.
infortunio *s.m.* **1** misfortune, mishap, accident. **2** bad luck.
infra- *prefijo* infra-.
infracción *s.f.* DER. infraction, transgression, breach (de leyes).
infractor, -a *s.m.* y *f.* DER. transgressor. || *adj.* **2** transgressing.
infractuoso, -a *adj.* (Am.) sinuous.
infraestructura *s.f.* infrastructure, substructure.
infraganti o **in fraganti** *adv.* red-handed, in the act.
infrahumano, -a *adj.* subhuman.
infranqueable *adj.* insurmountable, insuperable.
infrarrojo, -a *adj.* infrared.
infringir *v.t.* to break, to violate (leyes, pactos, acuerdos, etc.).
infructuosamente *adv.* unfruitfully, unprofitably.
infructuoso, -a *adj.* fruitless, useless.
ínfulas *s.f.pl.* **1** HIST. infulas (cintas en las cabezas de sacerdotes). **2** airs, conceit: *darse ínfulas = to put on airs.*
infundio *s.m.* malicious story, false story; (fam.) fairy tale, fib.
infundir *v.t.* **1** to instill, to put into (un sentimiento): *la historia me infundió pavor = the story put fear into me.* **2** to infuse (normalmente con sentido religioso).
infusión *s.f.* **1** inspiration (de un sentimiento o similar). **2** infusion, brew (especialmente de hierbas medicinales).
infuso, -a *adj.* inborn, innate: *ciencia infusa = innate knowledge.*
ingeniar *v.t.* **1** to devise, to contrive. || *v.t.pron.* **2** to manage, to find a way (para hacer algo difícil). || **3 ingeniárselas para,** to do everything possible in order to, to do one's best to: *tengo que ingeniármelas para que me den permiso = I have to do everything possible in order to get leave.*
ingeniería *s.f.* engineering.
ingeniero, -a *s.m.* y *f.* **1** engineer. || **2 — agrónomo,** agronomist, agricultural expert. **3 — de caminos, canales y puertos,** civil engineer. **4 — de minas,** mining engineer. **5 — eléctrico,** electrical engineer. **6 — electrónico,** electronic ingineer. **7 — forestal/de montes,** forestry expert. **8 — naval,** naval engineer. **9 — químico,** chemical engineer. **10 ingenieros,** MIL. engineering corps.
ingenio *s.m.* **1** talent; creativeness (talento). **2** wit, humour (humor). **3** skill (habilidad manual). **4** device; apparatus (máquina). **5** (Am.) sugar plantation; sugar mill.
ingeniosamente *adv.* cleverly; wittily.
ingeniosidad *s.f.* cleverness, ingenuity, ingeniousness, wittiness.
ingenioso, -a *adj.* clever; witty.
ingente *adj.* huge, enormous.
ingenuamente *adv.* naively, candidly.
ingenuidad *s.f.* candor, ingenuousness.
ingenuo, -a *adj.* naive, candid.
ingerir *v.t.* y *pron.* to ingest, to consume; to swallow.
ingestión *s.f.* ingestion, swallowing.
ingle *s.f.* groin.
inglés, -a *adj.* **1** English (cultura, nacionalidad, etc.). || *s.m.* y *f.* **2** Englishman; Englishwoman. || *s.m.* **3** English (idioma).
ingobernable *adj.* uncontrollable (persona); ungovernable (país, sociedad, etc.).
ingratamente *adv.* ungratefully.
ingratitud *s.f.* ungratefulness, ingratitude.
ingrato, -a *adj.* **1** ungrateful (persona). **2** thankless, unrewarding (tarea, trabajo, etc.). **3** disagreeable, unpleasant (desagradable).
ingravidez *s.f.* weightlessness, lightness.
ingrávido, -a *adj.* weightless, light.
ingrediente *s.m.* ingredient.
ingresar *v.i.* **1** to go in, to enter, to get into: *mi padre tiene que ingresar en el hospital = my father has to get into hospital.* || **2** FIN. to deposit, to put into (dinero en una entidad bancaria).
ingreso *s.m.* **1** entrance, entry (en un sitio). **2** admission (dentro de una asociación o similar). **3** FIN. deposit (ingreso

bancario). || *s.m.pl.* **4** income, revenue (dinero que uno gana).

inhábil *adj.* **1** unskillful (con las manos). **2** unfit, incompetent (por ejemplo para ser juzgado). || **3 día –,** non-working day.

inhabilidad *s.f.* **1** unskillfulness (con las manos). **2** ineptitude, incompetence (incompetente). **3** handicap, disability (minusvalía psíquica o física).

inhabilitación *s.f.* **1** disqualification (castigo): *inhabilitación por dos meses para competir = two-month long disqualification to take part in competitions.* **2** disablement (minusvalía concreta).

inhabilitar *v.t.* **1** to disqualify. || *v.t.* y *pron.* **2** to disable, to render unfit (imposibilitar física o mentalmente).

inhalación *s.f.* inhalation.

inhalador *s.m.* inhaler.

inhalar *v.t.* to inhale (normalmente algún tipo de aerosol medicinal).

inherencia *s.f.* inherence.

inherente *adj.* inherent.

inhibición *s.f.* inhibition.

inhibidor, -a *adj.* restraining, inhibitory.

inhibir *v.t.* **1** to inhibit, to restrain: *su presencia me inhibe = her presence inhibits me.* **2** BIOL. to inhibit (una función corporal). || *v.pron.* **2** to with-draw, to restrain oneself, to stay away, to keep out: *nunca me he inhibido de los problemas sociales = I have never kept out of social problems.*

inhospitalario, -a o **inhóspito, -a** *adj.* **1** inhospitable. **2** uninviting (persona). **3** bleak (lugar, terreno, etc.).

inhospitalidad *s.f.* inhospitality.

inhumación *s.f.* inhumation, burial.

inhumar *v.t.* to bury, to inter.

iniciación *s.f.* **1** beginning, initiation. **2** introduction (introducción, por ejemplo, a un tema de estudio o similar).

inicial *adj.* **1** initial. || *s.f.* **2** initial.

iniciar *v.t.* y *pron.* **1** to begin, to start, to initiate. **2** to introduce; to teach oneself (desde un punto de vista instructivo). || *v.t.* **3** to let (someone) into (contar a alguien un secreto, enseñarle una nueva técnica, etc.).

iniciativa *s.f.* **1** initiative. **2** lead, leadership (capacidad de liderazgo de una persona). **3** POL. initiative. **4** plans, intentions (intención).

inicio *s.m.* beginning, commencement.

inicuo, -a *adj.* iniquitous, wicked.

inigualable *adj.* unsurpassable.

inigualado, -a *adj.* unequaled.

inimaginable *adj.* unimaginable, unconceivable: *un descaro inimaginable = unconceivable cheek.*

inimitable *adj.* inimitable.

ininteligible *adj.* unintelligible.

iniquidad *s.f.* iniquity, wickedness.

injerencia *s.f.* interference, meddling: *injerencia en asuntos de otros = meddling in other people's business.*

injerirse *v.pron.* to meddle (en asuntos que no le conciernen a uno).

injertar *v.t.* **1** AGR. to graft, to implant. **2** MED. to graft (piel u otros elementos corporales). **3** (fig.) to instill (confianza, nuevos bríos, etc. en algunas personas o un lugar).

injerto *s.m.* **1** AGR. grafted tree, graft, grafting. **2** MED. graft (de piel, especialmente).

injuria *s.f.* insult, offense.

injuriante o **injurioso, -a** *adj.* insulting, offensive.

injuriar *v.t.* to insult, to offend; to damage.

injuriosamente *adv.* insultingly, offensively.

injustamente *adv.* unjustly, unfairly.

injusticia *s.f.* injustice, unfairness.

injustificable *adj.* unjustifiable.

injustificado, -a *adj.* unjustified, unwarranted: *insultos injustificados = unwarrented insults.*

injusto, -a *adj.* unjust, unfair.

inmaculado, -a *adj.* **1** immaculate, spotless. || *s.f.* **2** REL. Virgin, Immaculate (la Virgen).

inmancable *adj.* (Am.) unfallible, sureproof.

inmadurez *s.f.* immaturity.

inmarcesible o **inmarchitable** *adj.* unfading (flores).

inmediación *s.f.* **1** immediacy (calidad de lo inmediato en el tiempo). || *s.pl.* **2** outskirts, environs, surroundings.

immediatamente *adv.* immediately.

immediato, -a *adj.* **1** next (en el espacio). **2** immediate, prompt: *una solución inmediata = an immediate solution.*

inmejorable *adj.* excellent, unbeatable.

inmemoriable *adj.* immemorial.

inmemorial *adj.* immemorial.

inmensamente *adv.* immensely.

inmensidad *s.f.* immensity, vastness, hugeness.

inmenso, -a *adj.* immense.

inmerecidamente *adv.* undeservedly.

inmerecido, -a *adj.* undeserved *castigo inmerecido = undeserved punishment.*

inmersión *s.f.* immersion; plunge.

inmerso, -a *adj.* **1** immersed, submerged. **2** (fig.) bogged down (inundado, especialmente de trabajo).

inmigración *s.f.* immigration.

inmigrante *adj.* y *s.m.* y *f.* immigrant.

inmigrar *v.i.* to immigrate.

inmigratorio, -a *adj.* immigrant.

inminencia *s.f.* imminence: *la inminencia de un ataque = the imminence of an attack.*

inminente *adj.* imminent.

inmiscuir *v.t.* **1** to mix (mezclar). || *v.pron.* **2** to meedle, to interfere (en asuntos que no son de uno).

inmobiliario, -a *adj.* **1** real-estate, property: *agencia inmobiliaria = real estate agency.* || *s.f.* **2** building, company; property company.

inmoderadamente *adv.* excessively, immoderately.

inmoderado, -a *adj.* immoderate.

inmodestia *s.f.* immodesty.

inmolación *s.f.* sacrifice, immolation.

inmolar *v.t.* **1** to sacrifice, to immolate. || *v.pron.* **2** to sacrifice oneself, to immolate oneself.

inmoral *adj.* immoral.

inmoralidad *s.f.* immorality.

inmortal *adj.* **1** immortal. **2** (fig.) everlasting, never-ending.

inmortalidad *s.f.* immortality.

inmortalizar *v.t.* to immortalize.

inmovible *adj.* immovable, unfixed.

inmóvil *adj.* motionless.

inmovilidad *s.f.* immobility.

inmovilismo *s.m.* resistance to change (especialmente político-social).

inmovilista *s.m.* y *f.* resistant to change; staunch conservative.

inmovilización *s.f.* immobilization.

inmovilizar *v.t.* **1** to immobilize, to paralize. **2** FIN. to tie up, to lock up (capitales).

inmueble *s.m.* **1** building. || **2 bienes inmuebles,** real estate, landed property.

inmundicia *s.f.* **1** filth, dirt. **2** obscenity, lewdness (impureza moral).

inmundo, -a *adj.* **1** filthy, dirty. **2** obscene, lewd (impuro).

inmune *adj.* **1** MED. immune. **2** exempt (de algo).

inmunidad *s.f.* **1** MED. immunity. **2** POL. immunity. **3** exemption (de alguna obligación).

inmunización *s.f.* immunization.

inmunizar *v.t.* to immunize.

inmunología *s.f.* MED. immunology.

inmutabilidad *s.f.* immutability.

inmutable *adj.* immutable, changeless.

inmutar *v.t.* **1** to change. || *v.pron.* **2** to change countenance, to lose one's composture, to lose one's self-possession: *no se inmutó cuando le despedí = he didn't lose his self-possession when I sacked him.*

innato, -a *adj.* innate.

innovación *s.f.* innovation, new thing, novelty.

innovador, -a *adj.* **1** innovative. || *s.m.* y *f.* **2** innovator.

innovar *v.t.* to innovate.

innumerable *adj.* countless.

inocencia *s.f.* innocence.

inocentada *s.f.* **1** April Fools'joke. **2** blunder (error garrafal). **3** naive remark (dicho ingenuo).

inocente *adj.* **1** innocent. **2** simple, naive (ingenuo). **3** harmless (que no entraña peligro). || *s.m.* y *f.* **3** simple soul, innocent person.

inocentemente *adv.* innocently.

inocentón, -a *adj.* **1** gullible. || *s.m.* y *f.* **2** simpleton, naive person.

inocuidad *s.f.* innocuousness, harmlessness.

inoculable *adj.* inoculable.

inoculación *s.f.* MED. inoculation.

inocular *v.t.* y *pron.* **1** MED. inoculate. **2** to contaminate, to corrupt (con algo negativo).

inodoro, -a *adj.* **1** odourless. || *s.m.* **2** toilet, lavatory.

inofensivo, -a *adj.* inoffensive, harmless.

inolvidable *adj.* unforgettable.

inoperante *adj.* ineffective, unproductive.

inopia *s.f.* 1 poverty, indigence. || **2 estar en la –,** to be dreaming, to be far away; to have no idea.

inopinadamente *adv.* unexpectedly.

inopinado, -a *adj.* unexpected.

inoportunamente *adv.* at the wrong time.

inoportunidad *s.f.* untimeliness.

inoportuno, -a *adj.* ill-timed.

inorgánico, -a *adj.* inorganic.

inoxidable *adj.* rustproof; stainless: *acero inoxidable = stainless steel.*

inquebrantable *adj.* unbreakable, unshakeable, unswerving: *lealtad inquebrantable = unswerving loyalty.*

inquietamente *adv.* restlessly.

inquietante *adj.* disturbing: *un ruido inquietante = a disturbing noise.*

inquietar *v.t.* y *pron.* 1 to disturb, to worry, to trouble. || *v.pron.* 2 to get worried, to get upset: *siempre estás inquietándote por nada = you are always getting worried about nothing.*

inquieto, -a *adj.* restless, worried, anxious.

inquietud *s.f.* restlessness, uneasiness, apprehension.

inquilinato o **inquilinaje** *s.m.* tenancy.

inquilino, -a *s.m.* y *f.* tenant.

inquina *s.f.* animosity, dislike.

inquirir *v.t.* to enquire, to investigate, to probe.

inquisición *s.f.* 1 investigation, inquisition. 2 HIST. Inquisition.

inquisidor, -a *adj.* 1 inquiring, inquisitive. || *s.m.* y *f.* 2 inquirer, investigator. || *s.m.* 3 HIST. Inquisitor.

inquisitivo, -a *adj.* inquisitive.

inquisitorial *adj.* inquisitorial.

inri *s.m.* 1 suffering (algo que hace sufrir). || **2 para más –,** to make matters worse.

insaciable *adj.* insatiable.

insalubre *adj.* unhealthy, insanitary, insalubrious.

insalubridad *s.f.* unhealthiness, insalubrity.

insatisfacción *s.f.* dissatisfaction: *mi insatisfacción con tu trabajo = my dissatisfaction with your work.*

inscribir *v.t.* 1 to inscribe, to engrave. 2 GEOM. to inscribe (dibujar algo dentro de otra cosa). || *v.t.* y *pron.* 3 to enter (para un concurso, curso, asociación, etc.).

inscripción *s.f.* 1 inscription, engraving (algo que está escrito): *una preciosa inscripción sobre una tumba = a beautiful inscription on a tomb.* 2 enrolment (en un cursillo, asociación, etc.).

inscrito, -a *p.p.* 1 de **inscribir.** || *adj.* 2 engraved (grabado). 3 enrolled (para algún cursillo u otra actividad).

insecticida *s.m.* insecticide.

insectívoro, -a *adj.* ZOOL. insectivorous.

insecto *s.m.* insect.

inseguramente *adv.* unsafely; unsteadily.

inseguridad *s.f.* 1 insecurity, unsafeness. 2 unsteadiness (de movimientos corporales). 3 uncertainty (sobre algo).

inseguro, -a *adj.* 1 insecure, unsafe. 2 unsteady (en movimientos). 3 uncertain (inseguridad mental sobre algo): *no estoy seguro de que sea así = I am not certain it is like that.*

inseminación *s.f.* 1 insemination. || **2 artificial –,** MED. artificial insemination.

insensatez *s.f.* 1 senselessness, stupidity, folly. 2 foolish remark (algo dicho absurdamente).

insensato, -a *adj.* 1 senseless, stupid. || *s.m.* y *f.* 2 dolt, fool.

insensibilidad *s.f.* 1 insensitivity, lack of feeling (falta de sentimientos). 2 cruelty (crueldad). 3 insensibility, numbness (en el cuerpo). 4 unconsciousness (inconsciencia).

insensibilizar *v.t.* 1 MED. to desensitize. 2 to make callous, to render insensitive (a una persona ante desgracias o tragedias).

insensible *adj.* 1 insensitive, unfeeling (en sentimientos). 2 cruel (cruel). 3 numb, without any feeling (en el cuerpo). 4 unconscious (inconsciente).

insensiblemente *adv.* 1 insensitively, unfeelingly (con falta de sentimientos). 2 crueltly (cruelmente). 3 numbly (en una parte del cuerpo). 4 unconsciously.

inseparabilidad *s.f.* inseparability.

inseparable *adj.* inseparable.

inseparablemente *adv.* inseparably.

insepulto, -a *adj.* unburied.

inserción *s.f.* insertion.

insertar *v.t.* to insert.

inservible *adj.* useless.

insidia *s.f.* 1 snare, trap. 2 malicious act, malice (malicia).

insidiosamente *adv.* insidiously, treacherously.

insidioso, -a *adj.* insidiously, treacherous.

insigne *adj.* 1 notable, famous. 2 distinguished, illustrious (ilustre).

insignia *s.f.* 1 badge, device, emblem. 2 MAR. pennant. 3 flag, banner (bandera).

insignificancia *s.f.* insignificance.

insignificante *adj.* 1 insignificant. 2 trivial, tiny, petty (pequeño).

insinuación *s.f.* insinuation, suggestion.

insinuante *adj.* 1 insinuating. 2 ingratiating (zalamero).

insinuar *v.t.* 1 to insinuate, to hint at. || *v.pron.* 2 to ingratiate oneself.

insípido, -a *adj.* 1 insipid, tasteless. 2 (fig.) dully, tediously (sin gracia).

insistencia *s.f.* insistence, persistence.

insistente *adj.* insistent, persistent.

insistentemente *adv.* insistently, persistently.

insistir *v.i.* 1 to insist; to stress: *insisto en no hablar de ese tema = I insist on not speaking about that subject.* 2 to persist (permanecer firme).

insobornable *adj.* incorruptible.

insociabilidad *s.f.* unsociability.

insociable *adj.* unsociable.

insolación *s.f.* 1 MED. sunstroke. 2 FIS. insolation.

insolencia *s.f.* 1 insolence, arrogance. 2 insolent remark, insolent action, a rude thing (hecho o dicho muy maleducado).

insolente *adj.* insolent, arrogant, rude, unblushing.

insolentemente *adv.* insolently, arrogantly.

insólito, -a *adj.* unusual, unwonted.

insolubilidad *s.f.* insolubility.

insoluble *adj.* 1 insoluble (que no se disuelve). 2 unsolvable (problema).

insolvencia *s.f.* FIN. insolvency, bankruptcy.

insolvente *adj.* FIN. insolvent, bankrupt.

insomne *adj.* sleepless.

insomnio *s.m.* insomnia, sleeplessness.

insondable *adj.* 1 bottomless (sin fondo). 2 unfathomable, inscrutable, impenetrable.

insonorización *s.f.* soundproofing.

insonorizar *v.t.* to soundproof.

insonoro, -a *adj.* soundless.

insoportable *adj.* unbearable, intolerable (persona, situación, lugar, etc.).

insospechable *adj.* unexpected (algo).

insospechado, -a *adj.* unsuspected.

insostenible *adj.* untenable (especialmente opinión o teoría).

inspección *s.f.* inspection, examination.

inspeccionar *v.t.* 1 to examine, to inspect. 2 to supervise (revisar).

inspector, -a *adj.* 1 inspecting, examining. || *s.m.* y *f.* 2 inspector, supervisor.

inspiración *s.f.* 1 breathing, inhalation. 2 inspiration (de un artista, divina, etc.).

inspiradamente *adv.* inspiringly.

inspirar *v.t.* 1 FISIOL. to inhale, to breathe in. 2 to inspire (ideas, sentimientos, etc.). || *v.pron.* 3 to inspire oneself. || **4 inspirarse en algo,** to get the inspiration from something.

instalación *s.f.* 1 installation. 2 equipment (equipo).

instalador, -a *s.m.* y *f.* fitter (de cualquier cosa).

instalar *v.t.* 1 to install, to fit up. || *v.t.* y *pron.* 2 to set up (negocio); to settle (en una casa nueva).

instancia *s.f.* 1 form (impreso). 2 petition, entreaty. 3 DER. level of court, level of judicial decision. || **4 a – de,** at the request of, upon petition of. **5 de primera –,** primarily. **6 en última –,** as a final resort, in the last analysis.

instantáneamente *adv.* immediately, instantly.

instantáneo, -a *adj.* 1 instant, instantaneous. || *s.f.* 2 FOT. photo, snap, snap shot.

instante *s.m.* 1 instant, moment. 2 (fig.) short time. || **3 a cada –,** all the time, constantly, every single moment. **4 al –,** immediately, at once. **5 por instantes, a)** all the time, incessantly; **b)** just about.

instar *v.t.* 1 to urge, to press (a alguien a hacer algo). || *v.pron.* 2 to be urgent: *insta que se solucione el problema = it is urgent that the problem is solved.*

instauración *s.f.* 1 establishment, setting-up. 2 restoration, renewal (restaurador).

instaurador, -a *adj.* 1 establishing. || *s.m.* y *f.* 2 restorer (restaurador).
instaurar *v.t.* 1 to establish, to set up. 2 to restore (restaurar).
instigación *s.f.* instigation, incitement.
instigador, -a *adj.* 1 instigating. || *s.m.* y *f.* 2 instigator.
instigar *v.t.* to incite, to instigate, to urge: *le instigué a que se drogara = I incited him to take drugs.*
instintivamente *adv.* instinctively.
instintivo, -a *adj.* instinctive.
instinto *s.m.* 1 drive, urge (biológico). 2 instinct: *by instinct = instintivamente.*
institución *s.f.* 1 institution, setting-up, establishment (acción de instituir). 2 institution (organismo). || *s.f.pl.* 2 POL. state, state institutions.
institucional *adj.* institutional.
instituir *v.t.* 1 to establish, to found (algo). 2 to commence, to start (comenzar). 3 to teach (enseñar).
instituto *s.m.* 1 middle school, school (en España). 2 school (de investigación, benéfica, etc.). 3 (Am.) college (de nivel casi universitario). 4 REL. institute (instituto religioso).
institutriz *s.f.* governess.
instrucción *s.f.* 1 instruction, teaching, education (enseñanza). 2 instruction, direction, order (instrucción para hacer algo). 3 MIL. training, drilling (preparación). 4 learning, erudition knowledge (conocimiento): *necesito mejor instrucción = I need better knowledge.* 5 DER. proceedings.
instructivamente *adv.* instructively.
instructivo, -a *adj.* instructive, illuminating, enlightening.
instructor, -a *adj.* 1 instructional, teaching. || *s.m.* y *f.* 2 teacher, master, instructor. 3 DEP. coach, trainer.
instrumentación *s.f.* MUS. instrumentation, arrangement.
instrumental *adj.* 1 MUS. instrumental. 2 DER. documentary. 3 GRAM. instrumental (un caso de declinación).
instrumentar *v.t.* MUS. to orchestrate, to arrange.
instrumentista *s.m.* y *f.* MUS. musician, instrumentalist.
instrumento *s.m.* 1 instrument, implement. 2 tool (herramienta). 3 MUS. instrumento. 4 (fig.) instrument, tool (persona o cosa utilizada): *no quiero ser el instrumento de nadie = I want to be nobody's tool.*
insubordinación *s.f.* insubordination (especialmente militar).
insubordinado, -a *adj.* 1 insubordinate, unruly. || *s.m.* y *f.* 2 rebel (especialmente en el sentido militar).
insubordinar *v.t.* 1 to incite to rebellion. || *v.pron.* 2 to rebel.
insubstancial V. **insustancial.**
insuficiencia *s.f.* 1 insufficiency, inadequacy. 2 shortage (escasez). 3 incompetence, lack of competence (en el estudio).
insuficiente *adj.* 1 insufficient, inadequate. 2 incompetent. || *s.m.* 3 fail, low mark (nota de suspenso).
insufrible *adj.* insufferable, intolerable.
insufriblemente *adv.* insufferably, intolerably.
insularidad *s.f.* insularity.
insulina *s.f.* insulin.
insulsamente *adv.* 1 tastelessly, blandly. 2 (fig.) dully, inanely.
insulsez *s.f.* 1 tastelessness, blandness. 2 (fig.) dullness, inanity (de carácter, comentarios, etc.).
insulso, -a *adj.* 1 tasteless, bland. 2 (fig.) dull, inane: *un espectáculo insulso = an inane spectacle.*
insultante *adj.* insulting, abusive.
insultar *v.t.* to insult, to offend.
insulto *s.m.* insult, offense.
insuperable *adj.* 1 insurmountable, insuperable. 2 unsurpassable (en calidad).
insurgente *adj.* y *s.m.* y *f.* insurgent.
insurrección *s.f.* insurrection, revolt.
insurreccional *adj.* insurrectionary.
insurrecto, -a *adj.* 1 insurrectionary, insurgent. || *s.m.* y *f.* rebel, revolutionary.
insustancial o **insubstancial** *adj.* 1 insubstantial. 2 trite, shallow (trivial). 3 unimportant, unattractive, uninteresting (insulso).
insustituible *adj.* irreplaceable.
intacto, -a *adj.* 1 intact, untouched. 2 whole (entero). 3 pure (puro).
intachable *adj.* irreproachable, faultless.
intangibilidad *s.f.* intangibility.
intangible *adj.* intangible.
integración *s.f.* integration.
integral *adj.* 1 integral. || *s.f.* 2 MAT. integral.
íntegramente *adv.* integrally, wholy: *formado íntegramente por niños de menos de 14 años = wholy formed by children under fourteen.*
integrante *s.m.* y *f.* 1 member (miembro de un grupo). || *adj.* 2 integral.
integrar *v.t.* 1 to make up, to compose: *20 personas integraron el grupo = 20 people made up the group.* 2 MAT. to integrate.
integridad *s.f.* 1 integrity, honesty (virtud). 2 wholeness, completeness (estado entero). 3 (euf.) virginity.
integrismo *s.m.* staunch traditionalism.
íntegro, -a *adj.* 1 upright, honest (honrado). 2 whole, complete, entire.
intelecto *s.m.* intellect, mind.
intelectual *adj.* y *s.m.* y *f.* intellectual.
intelectualidad *s.f.* 1 intellectual character (de algo o alguien). 2 intelligentsia, intellectuals (grupo).
intelectualmente *adv.* intellectually.
inteligencia *s.f.* 1 intelligence, intellect, mind. 2 understanding, knowledge (entendimiento). 3 MIL. intelligence (servicios secretos de un país). || 4 collusion, secret agreement: *actuamos en la inteligencia de que nos ayudarían a salir del país = we acted under the secret agreement that they would help us to get out of the country.*
inteligente *adj.* intelligent, clever, talented.
inteligentemente *adv.* cleverly, intelligently.
inteligibilidad *s.f.* intelligibility.
inteligible *adj.* intelligible.
intemperancia *s.f.* intemperance, excess.
intemperie *s.f.* 1 inclemency, bad weather. || 2 **a la —,** outdoors, exposed to wind and weather, to be out in the open.
intempestivamente *adv.* inopportunely, at the wrong time.
intempestivo, -a *adj.* inopportune, ill-timed.
intención *s.f.* 1 intention, purpose. 2 will, wish (voluntad). || 3 **primera —,** frankness, candor. 4 **segunda —,** underhandedness.
intencionadamente *adv.* intentionally, deliberately.
intencionado, -a *adj.* deliberate: *un fallo intencionado = a deliberate mistake.*
intencional *adj.* intentional, deliberate.
intencionalidad *s.f.* purpose, intention.
intencionalmente *adv.* intentionally.
intendencia *s.f.* MIL. quartermaster corps.
intendente *s.m.* MIL. quartermaster.
intensamente *adv.* intensely, powerfully vividly.
intensidad *s.f.* 1 intensity, strength. 2 vividness, power (de imagen, pensamiento, etc.). || 3 **— eléctrica,** ELEC. electrical strength.
intensificación *s.f.* intensification.
intensificar *v.t.* to intensify.
intensivamente *adv.* intensively.
intensivo, -a *adj.* intensive.
intenso, -a *adj.* 1 intense, strong, powerful. 2 vivid, profound (experiencia, dibujo, etc.). 3 deep (con colores).
intentar *v.t.* to try, to attempt, to mean; to have a go: *déjame intentarlo = let me have a go at it.*
intento *s.m.* 1 intention, purpose. 2 attempt (intento concreto).
intentona *s.f.* 1 rash attempt, wild attempt. 2 POL. rising, putsch (normalmente militar).
inter- *prefijo* inter-.
interacción *s.f.* interaction, interplay.
intercalación *s.f.* intercalation, insertion.
intercalar *v.t.* to intercalate, insert.
intercambiable *adj.* interchangeable.
intercambiar *v.t.* to exchange, to swap.
interceder *v.i.* to intercede.
interceptar *v.t.* 1 to block, to intercept. 2 to cut off (cortar comunicación).
intercesión *s.f.* intercession, mediation.
intercesor, -a *adj.* 1 interceding. || *s.m.* y *f.* 2 intercessor, mediator.
intercomunicación *s.f.* intercommunication.
interconexión *s.f.* interconnection.
intercontinental *adj.* intercontinental.
interdependencia *s.f.* interdependence.
interdicto *s.m.* interdict, prohibition.
interés *s.m.* 1 interest. 2 self-interest, interest (como actitud egoísta). 3 interest, concentration (atención). || *s.m.* o *pl.* 4

FIN. interest. || *s.pl.* 5 interests, concerns (normalmente de un país en el contexto internacional).
interesadamente *adv.* selfishly, self-seekingly.
interesado, -a *p.p.* 1 de **interesar.** || *adj.* 2 interested: *estoy interesado en la política = I am interested in politics.* 3 selfish, self-seeking. 4 biased, prejudiced (parcial). || *s.m.* y *f.* 5 interested party, person concerned. 6 DER. applicant (el que firma un escrito).
interesante *adj.* interesting.
interesar *v.i.* y *pron.* 1 to have an interest, to interest, to appeal: *no me interesa mucho su pintura = his paintings don't appeal much to me.* || *v.t.* 2 to interest, to attract (atraer). 3 to concern, to affect (afectar). 4 MED. to afflict: *la herida interesa el nervio = the wound afflicts the nerve.*
interferencia *s.f.* 1 interference. 2 RAD. interference (fortuita); jamming (intencionada).
interferir *v.i.* 1 to interfere. 2 RAD. to interfere (fortuitamente); to jam (intencionadamente).
ínterin *adv.* 1 meanwhile, meantime. || *s.m.* 2 provisional measure, provisional agreement.
interinamente *adv.* temporarily, provisionally.
interinidad *s.f.* temporary employment.
interino, -a *adj.* 1 temporary, provisional. || *s.m.* y *f.* 2 temporary worker, stand-in.
interior *adj.* 1 interior, inner, internal. 2 innermost (sentimientos o pensamientos). || *adj.* y *s.m.* 3 inside, interior (piso). || *s.m.* 4 inside, interior (parte de dentro de cualquier objeto). 5 (fig.) heart, soul: *en mi interior sabía que no era cierto = in my heart I knew it wasn't true.*
interioridad *s.f.* inner being, inwardness.
interiormente *adv.* inwardly, inside.
interjección *s.f.* interjection.
interlocutor, -a *s.m.* y *f.* speaker: *mi interlocutor = the person I am talking to.*
interludio *s.m.* interlude.
intermediario, -a *adj.* 1 intermediary, mediating. || *s.m.* y *f.* 2 gobetween, intermediary. 3 COM. middleman (de productos). 4 mediator (árbitro en una situación).
intermedio, -a *adj.* 1 half-way, intermediate: *etapa intermedia de un viaje = half-way stage of a journey.* 2 intervening (en el tiempo). || *s.m.* 3 interval (dentro de un espectáculo o similar).
interminable *adj.* interminable, endless.
interminablemente *adv.* interminably, endlessly.
intermisión *s.f.* intermission; interruption.
intermitencia *s.f.* 1 intermittence (en el tiempo). 2 MED. intermission (de síntomas negativos).
intermitente *adj.* 1 intermittent (en el tiempo). || *s.m.* 2 indicator (luz en un vehículo).
internacionalismo *s.m.* internationalism.
internacionalista *s.m.* y *f.* y *adj.* internationalist.
internacionalizar *v.t.* internationalize.
internamente *adv.* internally.
international *adj.* international.
internado, -a *p.p.* 1 de **internar.** || *s.m.* 2 boarding school (tipo de escuela).
internamiento *s.f.* internment (especialmente en hospital).
internar *v.t.* 1 to send inland (enviar tierra adentro). 2 to hospitalize. 3 to confine (privando de libertad). || *v.t.* y *pron.* 4 to advance, to penetrate: *el enemigo se internó en la jungla = the enemy advanced deep into the jungle.*
internista *s.m.* y *f.* MED. internist.
interno, -a *adj.* 1 internal. 2 boarding (interno, de estudiante). 3 MED. on practice (médico). || *s.m.* y *f.* 4 boarder (alumno interno). 5 MED. doctor on practice.
interpelación *s.f.* 1 appeal, plea (ruego). 2 POL. parlamentary question.
interpelante *adj.* 1 interrogating. 2 appealing, pleading (que ruega). || *s.m.* y *f.* 3 POL. questioner (en una interpretación parlamentaria). 4 appealer.
interpelar *v.t.* 1 to plead, to appeal. 2 POL. to question formally, to ask for explanations (dentro del contexto parlamentario).
interpolación *s.f.* interpolation.
interpolar *v.t.* 1 to interpolate. 2 to insert (insertar, especialmente palabras dentro de un texto).
interponer *v.t.* 1 to interpose, to put between, to place between. 2 DER. to lodge, to put in (recurso o apelación). || *v.pron.* 3 to intervene (intervenir). 4 to block, to get in the way of (bloquear el paso, físicamente): *el policía se interpuso y recibió el disparo = the policeman got in the way and received the shot.*
interposición *s.f.* 1 insertion (de una palabra en un texto). 2 DER. lodging (de recurso o similar). 3 blocking of the way (bloqueo del paso, físicamente).
interpretable *adj.* that hasn't got one single interpretation, with more than one possible reading; interpretable.
interpretación *s.f.* 1 interpretation. 2 MUS. performance (actuación). 3 performance (en el teatro, política, etc.).
interpretar *v.t.* 1 to explain, to clarify (explicar el sentido de algo). 2 to translate, to interpret (traducir). 3 to perform (de actor o parecido). 4 MUS. to perform, to sing (actuar, musicalmente, en cualquier aspecto).
interpretativo , -a *adj.* interpretative.
intérprete *s.m.* y *f.* 1 interpreter. 2 MUS. performer, singer (cantante). 3 actor.
interregno *s.m.* 1 HIST. interregnum. 2 (Am.) interval (intervalo).
interrogación *s.f.* 1 question (pregunta). 2 interrogation mark (signo). 3 questioning, interrogation (especialmente policial). || 4 **— retórica,** rhetorical question.
interrogador, -a *adj.* 1 interrogating, questioning. || *s.m.* y *f.* 2 interrogator, questioner.
interrogante *adj.* 1 interrogating, questioning. || *s.f./m.*2 unanswered question (pregunta sin contestar): *mi profesor dejó demasiadas interrogantes en el aire = my teacher left too many unanswered questions in the air.*
interrogar *v.t.* to question, to interrogate; to examine.
interrogativo, -a *adj.* interrogative.
interrogatorio *s.m.* interrogation, examination (especialmente policial o judicial).
interrumpidamente *adv.* with constant interruptions.
interrumpir *v.t.* y *pron.* 1 to stop talking. || *v.t.* 2 to interrupt (hablando). 3 to block (bloquear el paso de algo o alguien).
interrupción *s.f.* 1 interruption (especialmente al hablar). 2 stoppage, hold-up (bloqueo físico).
interruptor *s.m.* ELEC. switch.
intersección *s.f.* 1 intersection. 2 crossing (cruce, normalmente, en una carretera). || 3 **— de dos conjuntos,** MAT. intersection of two conjuncts.
intersticio *s.m.* interstice, gap.
interurbano, -a *adj.* interurban.
intervalo *s.m.* 1 interval (de tiempo o espacio). 2 MUS. interval. 3 gap (hueco).
intervención *s.f.* 1 intervention, participation, contribution. 2 MED. operation. 3 ELECTR. tapping (pinchazo telefónico). 4 COM. auditing (de cuentas). 5 MIL. intervention.
intervencionismo *s.m.* interventionism.
intervencionista *s.m.* y *f.* y *adj.* interventionist.
intervenir *v.i.* 1 to participate, to contribute, to intervene. 2 to mediate, to intercede (mediar o interceder). 3 to have an influence: *en este punto intervienen muchos factores distintos = at this point many different factors have an influence.* || *v.t.* 4 COM. to audit (revisar, especialmente las cuentas). 5 MED. to operate. 6 ELECTR. to tap (pinchar teléfono). 7 DER. to confiscate, to seize.
interventor, -a *adj.* 1 intervening, participating. || *s.m.* y *f.* 2 supervisor, inspector.
interviú *s.f.* PER. interview.
intervocálico, -a *adj.* intervocalic.
intestado, -a *adj.* intestate.
intestinal *adj.* intestinal.
intestino, -a *adj.* 1 internal. 2 domestic, civil (una guerra, conflicto, etc.). || *s.m.* 3 ANAT. intestine. || 4 **— ciego,** ANAT. caecum. 5 **— delgado,** ANAT. small intestine. 6 **— grueso,** ANAT. large intestine. 7 **luchas intestinas,** internal warfare (en todos los sentidos).
intimación *s.f.* 1 hint, intimation. 2 notification, notice (aviso, normalmente de tipo judicial).
íntimamente *adv.* intimately: *este tema está íntimamente relacionado con la fí-*

sica = this subject is intimately connected with physics.

intimar *v.i.* 1 to become intimate, to become friendly: *intimamos el verano pasado = we became friendly last summer.* || *v.t.* 2 to make known; to require, to exhort (exhortar para que se ejecute algo).

intimidación *s.f.* intimidation; warning, serious warning: *disparo de intimidación = warning shot.*

intimidad *s.f.* 1 close relationship, close friendship (amistad). 2 privacy, private life (vida privada). 3 circle of friends, circle of acquaintances (círculo de amistad).

intimidar *v.t.* y *pron.* 1 to intimidate, to overawe. 2 to bully (coaccionar con cierta chulería). 3 to frighten, to scare (asustar): *este hombre me intimida muchísimo = this man scares me no end.*

íntimo, -a *adj.* 1 intimate, close (amigo, relación, trato, etc.). 2 innermost (pensamientos, sentimientos, etc.). 3 essential, fundamental, basic: *la relación íntima de la filosofía con la teología = the essential relationship of philosophy and theology.* 4 private (privado). || *s.m.* y *f.* 5 intimate friend (persona).

intitular *v.t.* y *pron.* to title (un libro o parecido).

intocable *adj.* untouchable; sacrosanct.

intolerable *adj.* intolerable, unbearable.

intolerablemente *adv.* intolerably.

intolerancia *s.f.* 1 intolerance; narrowmindedness. 2 MED. intolerance, rejection (especialmente, hablando de transplantes).

intolerante *adj.* intolerant, narrow-minded.

intoxicación *s.f.* intoxication, poisoning.

intoxicar *v.t.* to intoxicate; to poison.

intra- *prefijo* intra-.

intranquilidad *s.f.* worry, anxiety, uneasiness, restlessness, disquiet.

intranquilizador, -a *adj.* worrying, unsettling.

intranquilizar *v.t.* y *pron.* to worry, to unsettle, to disquiet.

intranquilo, -a *adj.* restless, uneasy, worried.

intranscendencia o **intrascendencia** *s.f.* unimportance, insignificance.

intranscendente o **intrascendente** *adj.* unimportant, insignificant.

intransigencia *s.f.* intransigence.

intransigente *adj.* intransigent.

intransitable *adj.* impassable.

intransitivo, -a *adj.* GRAM. intransitive.

intratable *adj.* rude, unsociable; impossible, difficult (persona).

intravenoso, -a *adj.* intravenous.

intrépidamente *adv.* boldly, dauntlessly, fearlessly.

intrepidez *s.i.* boldness, courage, dauntlessness.

intrépido, -a *adj.* bold, dauntless, fearless, courageous.

intriga *s.f.* 1 plot, scheme (algo malo que se piensa hacer). 2 LIT. plot (argumento). 3 intrigue (complot).

intrigado, -a *p.p.* 1 de **intrigar.** || *adj.* 2 intrigued: *estoy muy intrigado sobre lo que Eva intenta hacer = I'm intrigued about what Eve wants to do.*

intrigante *adj.* intriguing, scheming: *una mujer intrigante = an scheming woman.*

intrigar *v.t.* 1 to intrigue, to interest (causar un interés, en otra persona). || *v.i.* 2 to scheme, to plot (hacer intrigas).

intrincadamente *adv.* intricately; impenetrably.

intrincado, -a *p.p.* 1 de intrincar. || *adj.* 2 complicated, intricate (complicado).

intrincar *v.t.* y *pron.* 1 to complicate, to confuse. || *v.t.* 2 to confuse (a una persona).

intríngulis *s.m.* 1 ultimate reason, ultimate motive (motivo). 2 snag, difficulty (dificultad): *el intríngulis es que no tengo dinero = the snag is that I have no money.* 3 puzzle, mistery (misterio).

intrínsecamente *adv.* intrinsically, inherently.

intrínseco, -a *adj.* intrinsic, inherent.

introducción *s.f.* 1 introduction (a un tema). 2 introduction, preface, prologue (en un libro). 3 MUS. introduction, overture. 4 introduction, insertion (inserción).

introducir *v.t.* y *pron.* 1 to put in, to stick in (poner dentro, físicamente). 2 to introduce (moda, tema, etc.). 3 to help (someone) become acquainted: *él me introdujo en el mundo de los negocios = he helped me to become acquainted with the business world.*

introductor, -a *adj.* 1 introductory. || *s.m.* y *f.* 2 introducer.

introito *s.m.* 1 REL. introit. 2 prologue (en el teatro clásico).

intromisión *s.f.* meddling, intrusion.

introspección *s.f.* introspection.

introspectivo, -a *adj.* introspective.

introversión *s.f.* introversion.

introvertido, -a *adj.* PSIC. introvert.

intrusión *s.f.* 1 DER. trespass (entrada ilegal en un sitio). 2 intrusion.

intrusismo *s.m.* practice of working in professional areas one is not qualified for.

intruso, -a *adj.* 1 intrusive, meddlesome. || *s.m.* y *f.* 2 intruder. 3 DER. trespasser.

intuición *s.f.* intuition.

intuir *v.t.* 1 to know by intuition, to intuit, to sense. 2 to feel (como opinión intuitiva): *intuyo que esto no es verdad = I feel this is not true.*

intuitivamente *adv.* intuitively.

intuitivo, -a *adj.* intuitive.

inundación *s.f.* flooding, flood.

inundar *v.t.* 1 to flood (fenómeno catastrófico con agua). 2 (fig.) to flood, to swamp (con excesivo número de lo que sea).

inusitado, -a *adj.* unusual, uncommon.

inútil *adj.* useless, vain, fruitless: *protestas inútiles = fruitless protests.*

inutilidad *s.f.* uselessness, fruitlessness, ineffectiveness.

inutilización *s.f.* disablement, spoiling (de algún objeto).

inutilizar *v.t.* 1 to ruin, to destroy (algo). 2 to cancel (cancelar). 3 to make (something) unusable (a causa de causas naturales): *la lluvia inutilizó las carreteras = the rain made the roads unusable.*

inútilmente *adv.* uselessly, in vain, to no avail, fruitless.

invadir *v.t.* 1 to invade (especialmente un país extranjero). 2 to overrun (un lugar). 3 (fig.) to come in hords, to swarm (llegar grandes cantidades): *la gente invadía la playa los domingos = people used to come in hords to the beach on Sundays.*

invalidación *s.f.* invalidation, nullification.

inválidamente *adv.* invalidly.

invalidar *v.t.* to invalidate, to nullify: *quiero invalidar el contrato = I want to invalidate the contract.*

inválido, -a *adj.* 1 invalid, null (un contrato, por ejemplo). 2 disabled, invalid (que no se puede mover). || *s.m.* y *f.* 3 invalid, disabled person.

invaluable *adj.* (Am.) invaluable, precious.

invariabilidad *s.f.* invariability.

invariable *adj.* invariable.

invariablemente *adv.* invariably.

invasión *s.f.* invasion.

invasor, -a *adj.* 1 invading. || *s.m.* y *f.* 2 invader.

invectiva *s.f.* invective.

invencible *adj.* invincible.

invenciblemente *adv.* invincibly, insuperably.

invención *s.f.* invention.

inventar *v.t.* 1 to invent, to discover. 2 to imagine, to fabricate, to make up (imaginar): *me inventé la historia = I imagined the story.* 3 to create (artísticamente).

inventariar *v.t.* to inventory, make an inventory of.

inventario *s.m.* inventory.

inventiva *s.f.* inventiveness.

invento *s.m.* 1 invention. 2 creation (creación). 3 fabrication, lie (mentira).

inventor, -a *s.m.* y *f.* inventor.

invernadero *s.m.* 1 greenhouse, hothouse. 2 winter pasture (pasto para invierno). 3 winter quarters (lugar para pasar el invierno).

invernal *adj.* wintry, very cold (tiempo).

invernar *v.i.* 1 BIOL. to hibernate (algunos animales). 2 to winter: *las tropas tuvieron que invernar en Moscú = the troops had to winter in Moscow.*

inverosímil *adj.* improbable, unlikely; unbelievable.

inverosimilitud *s.f.* improbablity, unlikeliness.

inversamente *adv.* inversely, conversely.

inversión *s.f.* 1 inversion (poner al revés). 2 FIN. investment (de dinero).

inversionista *s.m.* y *f.* investor.

inverso, -a *adj.* 1 inverse, inverted, reverse. || 2 **a la inversa,** on the contrary,

conversely, inversely, the other way around.
invertebrado, -a *adj./s.m.* y *f.* ZOOL. invertebrate.
invertido, -a *p.p.* **1** de **invertir.** || *s.m.* **2** homosexual.
investidura *s.f.* **1** investiture. **2** POL. vote of confidence for the election of the Prime Minister (en España).
investigación *s.f.* **1** research (científica). **2** investigation, enquiry (para asuntos sociales, políticos, etc.).
investigador, -a *adj.* **1** research, investigate. || *s.m.* y *f.* **2** research student, researcher. **3** private detective (detective privado).
investigar *v.t.* **1** to research (científicamente). **2** to investigate, to enquire (una situación social o similar).
investir *v.t.* to appoint; to confer.
inveterado, -a *adj.* confirmed, hardened.
inviable *adj.* impossible, non-viable.
invicto, -a *adj.* unconquered, unbeaten.
invidencia *s.f.* sightlessness, blindness.
invidente *s.m.* y *f.* sightless, blind: *los invidentes = the blind.*
invierno *s.m.* winter.
inviolabilidad *s.f.* inviolability, immunity (por ejemplo, parlamentaria).
inviolable *adj.* inviolable.
inviolado, -a *adj.* inviolate.
invisibilidad *s.f.* invisibility.
invisible *adj.* invisible.
invitado, -a *p.p.* **1** de **invitar.** || *adj.* **2** invited. || *s.m.* y *f.* **3** guest: *no puedo, tengo invitados = I can't, I've got guests.*
invitación *s.f.* invitation.
invocación *s.f.* invocation.
invocar *v.t.* **1** to invoke, to call on. **2** to beg for, to implore (pedir).
involución *s.f.* POL. regression, reaction.
involucionista *s.m.* y *f.* POL. reactionary.
involucrar *v.t.* to involve; to meddle: *no quiero involucrarme en tus asuntos = I don't want to meddle in your affairs.*
involuntariamente *adv.* unintentionally.
involuntario, -a *adj.* unintentional, involuntary: *una equivocación involuntaria = an unintentional mistake.*
inyectable *adj.* **1** that can be given in injections. || *s.m.* **2** injection.
inyectar *v.t.* **1** to inject. || *v.pron.* **2** to become red with blood (llenarse de sangre una parte del cuerpo). **3** to get a jab (inyectarse, normalmente droga).
ion *s.m.* ion.
iónico, -a *adj.* ionic.
ionización *s.f.* ionization.
ionosfera *s.f.* ionosphere.
iota *s.f.* iota.
ipso facto *adv.* ipso facto; immediately.
ir *v.i.* y *pron.* **1** to go: *me voy a Madrid mañana = I'm going to Madrid tomorrow.* || **2** to leak, to be spilling, to ooze out (salirse un líquido de un recipiente). || *v.i.* **3** to be good, to be convenient: *esta medicina me va bien = this medicine is good for me.* **4** to get along, to progress, to go: *las clases de guitarra van bien = the guitar classes are going fine.* **5** to work (funcionar): *el coche funciona mal = the car is not working well.* **6** to be: *voy mareado = I am dizzy.* **7** to be dressed: *vas muy bien vestido = you're very well dressed.* **8** to lead, to go (ir, en el juego de las cartas). **9** to be (una diferencia): *del trabajo del año pasado a éste va mucho = there's a big difference between last year's job and this year.* **10** to bet: *¿van dos mil pesetas? = do you want to bet two thousand pesetas?* **11** to be on, to be about, to deal with: *la película iba de un policía que... = the film was about a policeman that...* **12 ¡ahí va!,** dear me!, my God! (expresando gran sorpresa). **13 estar ido, a)** to be mad, to be crazy; **b)** to be far away, to be in an absentminded mood. **14 — adelante,** to get along, to get things done, to improve in general. **15 — demasiado lejos,** to go too far, to go overboard. **16 — descaminado,** to go astray, to go on the wrong path. **17 — detrás de algo** o **alguien,** to be after something/somebody. **18 — lejos,** to go far. **19 — para largo,** to take a long time, to last a long time, to be long. **20 — todos a una,** to go all together, to unite efforts. **21 irse abajo algo,** to be a complete flop, to fall apart, to break into pieces. **22 írsele por alto a uno algo,** not to notice something, to miss something completely. **23 no irle ni venirle a uno nada en algo,** not to have a stake in something, not to mind something at all, not to mind the way something turns up. **24 ¡qué va!,** not at all!, not on your life. **25 ¡vaya!,** well!, what on earth!, bother! (expresando el sentimiento que se quiera imprimir a la voz y el gesto). **26 vaya por Dios,** what a pity, what a shame. **27 váyase lo uno por lo otro,** let's swap, I'll give you this for that. **28 vete a saber,** who knows.
OBS. Este verbo tiene varios usos muy gramaticales: **29** intencionalidad, especialmente futura o con sentido de futuro dentro del pasado: *voy a pegarte un tiro = I'm going to shoot you; iba a comprarlo, pero no pude = I was going to buy it but I couldn't.* **30** expresa que la acción se desarrolla lentamente: *iba oscureciendo cuando llegó el esperado tren = it was already getting dark when the expected train arrived.* **31** con distintas preposiciones el verbo indica comportarse o funcionar en la vida: *va de chulo por la vida = he has a cocky attitude in life.*
ira *s.f.* **1** anger, fury, rage (personal). **2** violence (de los elementos de la naturaleza).
iracundia *s.f.* ire.
iracundo, -a *adj.* irate.
iraní *adj./s.m.* y *f.* Iranian.
iraquí *adj./s.m.* y *f.* Iraqui.
irascibilidad *s.f.* irascibility.
irascible *adj.* irascible.
iris *s.m.* **1** ANAT. iris. **2** rainbow.
irisación *s.f.* iridescence.
irlandés, -esa *adj.* **1** Irish. || *s.m.* **2** Irishman. **3** Irish (idioma). || *s.f.* **4** Irishwoman.
ironía *s.f.* irony.
irónicamente *adv.* ironically.
irónico, -a *adj.* ironical.
ironizar *v.t.* to ridicule.
irr- *prefijo* irr-.
irracional *adj.* **1** irrational, unreasoning. || *s.m.* y *f.* **2** brute.
irracionalidad *s.f.* irrationality, unreasonableness.
irracionalmente *adv.* irrationally.
irradiación *s.f.* irradiation.
irradiar *v.t.* e *i.* to irradiate, radiate.
irrazonable *adj.* unreasonable.
irreal *adj.* unreal.
irrealidad *s.f.* unreality.
irrealista *adj.* unrealistic.
irrealizable *adj.* unworkable.
irrebatible *adj.* irrefutable.
irreconciliable *adj.* incompatible, irreconcilable.
irreconocible *adj.* unrecognizable.
irrecuperable *adj.* irrecoverable, irretrievable: *tiempo irrecuperable = irretrievable time.*
irrecusable *adj.* DER. unimpeachable.
irredimible *adj.* irredeemable.
irreducible o **irreductible** *adj.* irreducible.
irreemplazable *adj.* irreplaceable: *nadie es irreemplazable = nobody is irreplaceable.*
irreflexión *s.f.* thoughtlessness, rashness.
irreflexivamente *adv.* unthinkingly, thoughtlessly.
irreflexivo, -a *adj.* thoughtless: *persona irreflexiva = thoughtless person.*
irrefrenable *adj.* irrepressible.
irrefutable *adj.* irrefutable: *teoría irrefutable = irrefutable theory.*
irregular *adj.* **1** irregular, abnormal. **2** GRAM. irregular. **3** GEOM. irregular.
irregularidad *s.f.* irregularity, abnormality.
irregularmente *adv.* irregulary.
irrelevante *adj.* irrelevant.
irremediable *adj.* irremediable, incurable.
irremediablemente *adv.* irremediably, incurably.
irremisible *adj.* unpardonable.
irreparable *adj.* irreparable.
irreparablemente *adv.* irreparably.
irrepetible *adj.* unique: *una experiencia irrepetible = a unique experience.*
irresistible *adj.* irresistible (especialmente personas muy bellas).
irresoluble *adj.* unsolvable.
irresolución *s.f.* irresolution, hesitation.
irresoluto, -a *adj.* irresolute, hesitant.
irrespetuosamente *adv.* disrespectfully.
irrespetuoso, -a *adj.* disrespectful.
irrespirable *adj.* unbreathable.
irresponsabilidad *s.f.* irresponsibility.
irresponsable *adj.* irresponsible.
irresponsablemente *adj.* irresponsibly.
irreverencia *s.f.* irreverence, disrespect.
irreverente *adj.* irreverent.

irreverentemente *adv.* irreverently.
irrevocable *adj.* irrevocable, irreversible: *dimisión irrevocable = irrevocable resignation.*
irrevocablemente *adv.* irrevocably.
irrigación *s.f.* irrigation.
irrigador *s.m.* sprinkler.
irrigar *v.t.* AGR. to irrigate, to water.
irrisible *adj.* laughable, absurd: *una actitud irrisible = an absurd attitude.*
irrisión *s.f.* **1** derision, ridicule. **2** laughing stock (persona o cosa de la que uno se puede burlar).
irrisoriamente *adv.* ridiculously, absurdly.
irrisorio, -a *adj.* ridiculous, absurd.
irritabilidad *s.f.* irritability.
irritable *adj.* irritable.
irritación *s.f.* irritation (en sentido propio y figurado).
irritante *adj.* **1** irritating: *qué tipo más irritante = what an irritating fellow.* || *s.m.* **2** irritant (sustancia o similar).
irritar *v.t.* y *pron.* **1** to irritate, to get irritated, to get angry. **2** to get an irritation (en la piel).
irrompible *adj.* unbreakable.
irrumpir *v.i.* to burst into, to rush into: *la policía irrumpió en el local = the police burst into the bar.*
irrupción *s.f.* **1** inrush, irruption (normalmente en el sentido atacante). **2** invasion.
isla *s.f.* **1** GEOG. island. **2** (fig.) island: *una isla de paz = an island of peace.*
islam *s.m.* REL. Islam.
islámico, -a *adj.* islamic.
islamismo *s.m.* islamism.
islamizar *v.t.* to Islamize.
islandés, -esa *adj.* **1** Icelandic. || *s.m.* y *f.* **2** Icelander. || *s.m.* **3** Icelandic (idioma).
isleño, -a *s.m.* y *f.* islander.
islote *s.m.* small island, islet.
isobara *s.f.* FIS. isobar.
isotérmico, -a *adj.* isothermal.
isótopo *s.m.* FIS. isotope.
israelí o **israelita** *adj./s.m.* y *f.* Israeli.
istmo *s.m.* GEOG. isthmus.
italianismo *s.m.* italianism.
italianizar *v.t.* to italianize.
italiano, -a *adj./s.m.* y *f* Italian.
itálico, -a *adj.* Italic.
item *s.m.* item, article.
itemizar *v.t.* (Am.) to specify, to itemize (contar todos los elementos en un grupo).
iterar *v.t.* to repeat.
iteración *s.f.* repetition.
itinerante *adj.* itinerant, roving.
itinerario *s.m.* itinerary, route: *hicimos un itinerario precioso = we travelled along a lovely route.*
izar *v.t.* to hoist (especialmente la bandera).
izquierdo, -a *adj.* **1** left: *mi mano izquierda = my left hand.* || *s.f.* **2** left hand: *escribo con la izquierda = I write with my left hand.* || *s.f.pl.* **3** POL. left: *las izquierdas han caído en Europa del Este = the left has fallen an Eastern Europe.* || **4 ser un cero a la izquierda,** V. **cero.**
izquierdismo *s.m.* POL. left wing, leftism.
izquierdista *s.m.* y *f.* POL. leftist, left-winger. || *adj.* **2** leftist, leftwing.
izquierdoso, -a *adj.* POL. leftish.

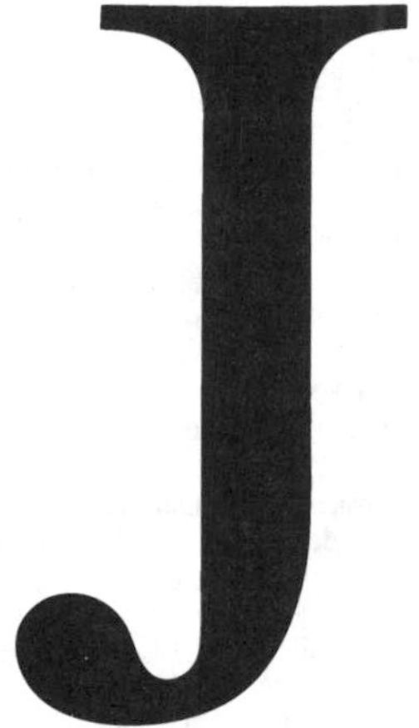

j, J *s.f.* j, J (undécima letra del alfabeto español).
jabalí *s.m.* ZOOL. wild boar.
jabalina *s.f.* **1** ZOOL. wild sow. **2** DEP. javelin.
jabato *s.m.* **1** young wild boar. || **2 ser un —,** to be very brave; to be a boastful young man.
jabón *s.m.* **1** soap: *una pastilla de jabón = a bar of soap.* || **2 dar a uno un —,** to rake someone over the coals; to tell someone off. **3 dar — a uno,** to flatter somebody, to soft-soap somebody.
jabonadura *s.f.* soaping, leathering.
jabonar *v.t.* **1** to wash with soap. **2** to leather (la barba).
jaboncillo *s.m.* **1** toilet soap (fino y aromatizado). **2** French chalk, soapstone (que utilizan los sastres para marcar la tela). **3** BOT. soapberry tree.
jabonería *s.f.* soap factory.
jabonero, -a *adj.* **1** off-white, dull yellowish white (color de toro). || *s.m.* y *f.* **2** soapmaker. || *s.f.* **3** soapdish. **4** BOT. soapwort.
jabonoso, -a *adj.* soapy: *agua jabonosa = soapy water.*
jaca *s.f.* small horse; mare.
jacal *s.m.* (Am.) hut, shed.
jacarandoso, -a *adj.* (fam.) merry, lively (con gran alegría de vivir).
jacinto *s.m.* **1** BOT. hyacinth (planta o flor). || **2 — de Compostela,** MIN. jacinth, zircon. **3 — occidental,** MIN. topaz.
jaco *s.m.* **1** short-sleeved coat of mail (un tipo de cota de malla). **2** (desp.) hack, nag (caballo ruin).
jacobeo, -a *adj.* REL. of St. James.
jacobinismo *s.m.* POL. radicalism (por el extremismo de los jacobinos).
jacobino, -a *adj.* HIST. Jacobin, radical (de la Revolución Francesa).
jactancia *s.f.* arrogance, boasting.
jactanciosamente *adv.* boastfully, full of bragging.
jactancioso, -a *adj.* boastful, bragging.
jactarse *v.pron.* to boast, to brag.
jaculatoria *s.f.* REL. aspiration.
jade *s.m.* MIN. jade.
jadeante *adj.* breathless, panting, short of breath.
jadear *v.i.* to pant.
jadeo *s.m.* panting, difficult breathing.
jaez *s.m.* **1** harness (arreos). **2** (desp.) ilk, sort, kind: *no me gustan las personas de ese jaez = I don't like people of that kind.*
jaguar o **yaguar** *s.m.* ZOOL. jaguar.
jalar *v.t.* **1** (fam.) devour, gulp down. **2** (Am.) to pull, to haul. || **3 mandarse a —,** (Am.) to go away, to leave (sin decírselo a nadie).
jalbegar V. **enjalbegar.**
jalea *s.f.* jelly.
jalear *v.t.* **1** to urge un (a los perros en la caza). **2** to encourage, to cheer on.
jaleo *s.m.* **1** clapping and cheering. **2** MUS. Andalusian dance. **3** (fig.) binge, spree (alboroto).
jalifa *s.m.* HIST. Moroccan governor.
jalón *s.m.* **1** stake, range pole (para medidas topográficas). **2** (fig.) milestone (hito). **3** (Am.) pull, tug (tirón).
jalonar *v.t.* to mark out, to mark with range poles.
jamar *v.tr.* (fam.) to eat, to eat up (lenguaje gitano).
jamás *adv.* never; ever.
jamba *s.f.* ARQ. jamb (de puerta).
jamelgo *s.m.* (desp.) nag, jade.
jamón *s.m.* **1** GAST. ham. **2** (fig. y fam.) leg, thigh.
jamuga o **jamugas** *s.f.* sidesaddle.
jangada *s.f.* **1** raft (balsa). **2** (fam.) dirty trick. **3** (fam.) silly remark.
jangadero *s.m.* (Am.) raftman.
jansenismo *s.m.* REL. Jansenism.
japonés, -esa *adj.* **1** Japanese. || *s.m.* y *f.* **2** Japanese.
jaque *s.m.* **1** check (en el ajedrez). || **2 — mate,** checkmate (ajedrez). **3 tener a uno en —,** to keep somebody in check, to hold someone at bay.
jaquear *v.t.* to check (en el ajedrez).
jaqueca *s.f.* **1** MED. migraine, migraine headache. || **2 dar —,** to bother, to pester; to bore, to death.
jara V. **jaro, -a.**
jarabe *s.m.* **1** syrup, sweet drink. **2** MED. mixture, syrup.
jaramugo *s.m.* ZOOL. small fish, young fish (pez joven).
jarana *s.f.* (Am.) spree, binge.
jaranear *v.i.* (Am.) to go on a binge, to have a high old time.
jaranero, -a *adj.* (Am.) fun-loving, merry.
jarcia *s.f.* MAR. **1** rigging, ropes. **2** fishing tackle.
jarcha *s.f.* LIT. old couplet.
jardín *s.m.* **1** garden. || **2 — botánico,** botanical garden. **3 — de infancia,** kindergarten, nursery school.
jardinera *s.f.* **1** woman gardener. **2** flower stand (donde se ponen flores). **3** open carriage (para transporte).
jardinería *s.f.* gardening.
jardinero *s.f.* gardener.
jareta *s.f.* hem, casing (en la costura).
jaretón *s.m.* wide hem.
jaripeo *s.m.* (Am.) rodeo.
jaro, -a *adj.* **1** carroty, red-haired. || *s.f.* **2** BOT. rockrose. **3** dart, arrow, spear (lanza o similar).
jarra *s.m.* **1** jug, pitcher. || **2 en —/en jarras,** arms akimbo, hands on hips.
jarrete *s.m.* **1** ANAT. back of the knee. **2** hock (de animales).
jarretera *s.f.* **1** garter. **2** (brit.) military order (Order of the Garter).
jarro *s.m.* pitcher, jug.
jarrón *s.m.* vase.
jaspe *s.m.* MIN. **1** jasper. **2** veined marble.
jaspeado, -a *adj.* marbled, speckled.
jaspear *v.t.* to marble, to speckle.
jato, -a *s.m.* y *f.* calf.

jauja *s.f.* utopia, eldorado, the promised land.
jaula *s.f.* 1 cage (para animales). 2 crate (embalaje). 3 MIN. cage.
jauría *s.f.* pack (of hounds).
jazmín *s.m.* BOT. jasmine.
jazz *s.m.* MUS. jazz.
jebe *s.m.* (Am.) rubber, elastic rubber, elastic.
jedentina *s.f.* (Am.) foul smell, stink.
jeep o **yip** *s.m.* jeep.
jefa *s.f.* female boss.
jefatura *s.f.* 1 leadership. 2 headquarters, central office (oficina central).
jefe *s.m.* 1 boss, chief. 2 leader (general): *el jefe de la oposición = the leader of the opposition party.* 3 MIL. commanding officer. 4 (fam.) sir: *oiga jefe = hey, sir.*
jenízaro *s.m.* HIST. janissary.
jeque *s.m.* sheik (árabe).
jerarca *s.m.* hierarch, high official.
jerarquía *s.f.* hierarchy.
jerárquicamente *adv.* according to rank, according to the hierarchy.
jerárquico, -a *adj.* hierarchical.
jerarquizar *v.t.* to rank.
jeremiada *s.f.* jeremiad, lamentation.
jeremías *s.m.* (fig.) complainer, born complainer.
jerez *s.m.* sherry.
jerga *s.f.* GRAM. slang, jargon.
jergón *s.m.* straw mattress.
jerigonza *s.f.* 1 gibberish; slang. 2 (fam.) piece of folly, foolish action.
jeringa o **jeringuilla** *s.f.* 1 syringe. 2 (Am.) bother; annoyance, nuisance.
jeringar *v.t.* (fam.) to pester, to annoy.
jeringazo *s.m.* injection, squirt.
jeroglífico, -a *adj.* 1 hieroglyphic. || *s.m.* 2 crossword puzzle. 3 HIST. hieroglyph. 4 (fig.) puzzle (problema difícil).
jersey *s.m.* jersey.
jesuita *s.m.* REL. Jesuit.
jesuítico, -a *adj.* jesuitic.
jet *s.m.* y *f.* 1 jet (avión a reacción). 2 (fig.) de mucho postín, jet.
jeta *s.f.* 1 snout (de animales). 2 (fig.) cheek.
jíbaro, -a *adj.* y *s.m.* y *f.* 1 jivaroan (tribu). 2 (Am.) rural, rustic.
jibia *s.f.* ZOOL. cuttlefish (molusco).
jibión *s.m.* ZOOL. cuttlebone (molusco).
jícara *s.f.* 1 cup (especialmente para el chocolate). 2 (Am.) gourd (tipo de taza).
jilguero *s.m.* ZOOL. linnet (ave).
jineta *s.f.* 1 ZOOL. genet. 2 (Am.) horsewoman.
jinete *s.m.* 1 horseman, rider. 2 MIL. cavalryman.
jipijapa *s.f.* straw hat, Panama hat.
jira *s.f.* 1 strip, shred (de ropa). 2 outing, excursion, picnic.
jirafa *s.f.* ZOOL. giraffe.
jirón *s.m.* 1 shred, tafter (de ropa). 2 facing (de costura). 3 (fig.) small bits (trozos pequeños, de muy distintas materias). 4 pennant (como estandarte).
jiu-jitsu *s.m.* yiu-yitsu (estilo de lucha japonesa).
job *s.m.* (fig.) saintly man, patient man.
jockey *s.m.* jockey.
jocosamente *adv.* amusingly, humorously.
jocosidad *s.f.* humor.
jocoso, -a *adj.* humorous, amusing.
jocundidad *s.f.* cheerfulness.
jocundo, -a *adj.* cheerful, jocund.
joder *v.t.* (vulg.) to fuck, to screw.
jofaina *s.f.* washbasin.
jolgorio u **holgorio** *s.m.* merriment, fun.
jondo V. **cante.**
jónico, -a *adj.* ART. Ionic.
jordano, -a *adj./s.m.* y *f.* Jordanian.
jornada *s.f.* 1 day's journey, journey. 2 day's work: *jornada laboral = working day.* 3 MIL. expedition. 4 act (en el teatro clásico español). || 5 **— intensiva,** full working schedule.
jornal *s.m.* 1 wage. 2 day's wage.
jornalero, -a *s.m.* y *f.* AGR. day labourer.
joroba *s.f.* 1 ANAT. hump, hunchback. 2 nuisance, bother. 3 (Am.) impertinence.
jorobado, -a *p.p.* 1 de **jorobar.** || *adj.* 2 hunchbacked. 3 (fam.) not too well, exhausted. || *s.m.* y *f.* 4 hunchback.
jorobar *v.t.* to bother, to pest.
joropo *s.m.* MUS. popular dance in some parts of South America.
jota *s.f.* 1 name of the letter "j". || 2 **no entender/saber ni —,** not to understand a word.
joven *adj.* 1 young. || *s.m.* y *f.* 2 young woman, young man.
jovial *adj.* merry, cheerful, jolly.
jovialidad *s.f.* merriment, cheerfulness.
jovialmente *adv.* merrily, cheerfully.
joya *s.f.* 1 jewel. 2 (fig.) gem, treasure (persona de gran valía).
joyería *s.f.* 1 jewelry trade, jewelry business. 2 jewelry shop (tienda). 3 jewels: *un tipo de joyería preciosa = a beautiful type of jewels.*
joyero *s.m.* 1 jeweller (persona). 2 jewel case, jewelry box (objeto).
juanete *s.m.* 1 ANAT. bunion. 2 MAR. topgallant (tipo de vela).
juanillo *s.m.* (Am.) bribe (soborno).
jubilación *s.f.* 1 retirement. 2 retirement pension (dinero). 3 (form.) joy, jubilation.
jubilado, -a *adj.* 1 retired. || *s.m.* y *f.* 2 old-age pensioner.
jubilar *v.t.* y *pron.* 1 to retire. || *v.t.* 2 (fig.) to put aside, to discard (un objeto innecesario o que funciona mal). || *adj.* 3 (form.) of a jubilee.
jubileo *s.m.* jubilee.
júbilo *s.m.* (form.) jubilation, joy.
jubilosamente *adv.* joyfully, jubilantly.
jubiloso, -a *adj.* joyful, jubilant.
jubón *s.m.* HIST. doublet, jerkin (prenda de vestir antigua).
júcaro, -a *adj.* (Am.) roguish, knavish, naughty.
judaico, -a *adj.* Jewish.
judaismo *s.m.* REL. Judaism.
judaizante *adj.* Judaizing.
judaizar *v.t.* to Judaize.
judas *s.m.* (fig.) traitor.
judería *s.f.* Jewish quarter, Jewish ghetto.
judía V. **judío, -a.**
judiada *s.f.* (desp.) cruel thing; extortion.
judicatura *s.f.* DER. judicature.
judicial *adj.* juridical.
judicialmente *adv.* according to the law; juridically.
judío, -a *adj.* 1 Jewish. || *s.f.* 2 BOT. bean. || *s.m.* 3 (fig.) miser (avaro).
judión *s.m.* BOT. large variety of French bean.
judo *s.m.* DEP. judo.
juego *s.m.* 1 game, play, playing (en general). 2 sport (como deporte). 3 DEP. juego (en tenis). 4 gambling (de apostar). 5 hand (en las cartas). 6 set (de objetos): *un juego de café = a coffee set.* 7 play, movement (en las articulaciones o en un objeto). 8 (fig.) game, scheme (intenciones normalmente deshonestas): *no me gusta su juego = I don't like his game.* || 9 **dar — (una cosa),** to offer many possibilities (de uso, comentario, crítica, etc.): *este hombre va a dar juego para la empresa = this man is going to offer many possibilities for the firm.* 10 **entrar en —,** to come into play: *mucho dinero entrará en juego = a lot of money will come into play.* 11 **estar en —,** to be at work; to be at stake: *muchos intereses están en juego = many interests are at stake.* 12 **hacer el — a alguien,** to play into somebody's hands. 13 **hacer —,** to match (ropa o similar). 14 **— de azar,** game of chance. 15 **— de manos,** conjuring trick. 16 **— de niños,** (fig.) child's play. 17 **— de palabras,** play on words. 18 **juegos forales,** poetry competition.
juerga *s.f.* fun, spree, binge.
juerguearse *v.pron.* 1 to have plenty of fun. 2 to make fun (of) (de algo o alguien).
juerguista *s.m.* y *f.* o *adj.* reveller, funloving.
jueves *s.m.* Thursday.
juez *s.m.* 1 DER. judge. 2 REL. Judge (el libro de los Jueces).
jueza *s.f.* DER. female judge.
jugada *s.f.* 1 move, play (acción o movimiento). 2 dirty trick (mala pasada).
jugador, -a *s.m.* y *f.* 1 DEP. player. 2 gambler (de cartas, dados, etc.).
jugar *v.i.* y *t.* 1 to play (deportes). 2 to play, to cavort (entretenerse o divertirse). || *v.i.* 3 to make a move, to make a play (un movimiento concreto). 4 to gamble (dinero o parecido). 5 not to be serious, to play: *estás jugando con fuego = you are playing with fire.* || *v.t.* 6 to wield, to handle (un dado o carta concreta). || *v.pron.* 7 to risk (arriesgar): *jugarse la vida = to risk one's life.* || 8 **— con alguien,** to toy with someone (haciendo lo que uno quiere). 9 **— limpio/sucio,** to play fair/dirty, to play the game/to indulge in dirty play. 10 **jugársela a alguien, a)** to be unfaithful to somebody (engañar): *su mujer se la ha jugado = his wife has been unfaithful to him;* **b)** to deceive somebody, to trick somebody.

J K L

jugarreta *s.f.* dirty trick.
juglar *s.m.* HIST. minstrel, troubadour.
juglaresco, -a *adj.* of minstrels.
juglaría o **juglería** *s.f.* HIST. minstrelsy.
jugo *s.m.* **1** juice, fluid, sap (secreción de animales o plantas). **2** (fig.) substance, essence: *hay que sacar el jugo de estas conferencias = we must get all the substance from these lectures.* || **3 — gástrico,** FISIOL. gastric juice. **4 — pancreático,** FISIOL. pancreatic juice.
jugosidad *s.f.* **1** juiciness. **2** (fig.) essence, substance.
jugoso, -a *adj.* **1** juicy. **2** (fig.) essential, substantial.
juguete *s.m.* **1** toy. **2** (fig.) plaything, toy: *él es el juguete de Mary = he is a Mary's plaything.*
juguetear *v.i.* to toy.
jugueteo *s.m.* playing, romping.
juguetería *s.f.* **1** toy business, toy trade. **2** toy shop.
juguetón, -ona *adj.* playful; frolicsome.
juicio *s.m.* **1** DER. trial. **2** judgement, discernment (inteligencia). **3** sanity, sound mind (sanidad mental). **4** opinion, judgement (opinión). **5** sense, common sense (sentido común). || **6 estar uno en su (sano) —,** to be of sound mind, to be in one's right mind. **7 estar uno fuera de —,** to be out of one's mind. **8 perder el —,** to lose one's mind.
juiciosamente *adv.* wisely, judiciously.
juicioso, -a *adj.* wise, judicious.
julepe *s.m.* **1** MED. syrup. **2** card game. **3** tongue lashing, telling-off, dressing-down. **4** (Am.) scare, fright.
julepear *v.t.* (Am.) to scare, to terrify.
julio *s.m.* July.
juma o **jumera** *s.f.* (Am.) drunken state, drunkenness.
jumarse *v.pron.* (Am.) to get drunk, to get stoned.
jumental o **jumentil** *adj.* pertaining to a donkey.
jumento *s.m.* ass, donkey.
jumo, -a *adj.* (Am.) drunk, stoned.
juncal *adj.* slim, gallant, good-looking.
junco *s.m.* **1** BOT. rush, reed. **2** MAR. junk.
juncoso, -a *adj.* rushy, reedy.
jungla *s.f.* jungle.
junio *s.m.* June.
junior *s.m.* **1** DEP. junior (deportista entre 17 y 21 años). **2** REL. novice. **3** junior (hijo).
junípero *s.m.* BOT. juniper.
junquera *s.f.* BOT. rush, bulrush.
junquillo *s.m.* **1** BOT. jonquil. **2** raftan (bastón).
juntamente *adv.* jointly, together.
juntar *v.t.* y *pron.* **1** to join (unir). **2** to gather, to collect (reunir). || *v.pron.* **3** to live together (sin casarse).
junto, -a *adj.* **1** near, close. || *s.f.* **2** board (comité). **3** meeting, session. **4** union, junction (unión). **5** MIL. junta. **6** MEC. joint, coupling (juntura).
juntura *s.f.* MEC. joint, coupling, junction.
jura *s.f.* **1** oath, pledge. **2** swearing in (ceremonia).
juraco *s.m.* (Am.) hole.
jurado *p.p.* **1** de **jurar.** || *s.m.* **2** DER. jury. || *adj.* **3** under oath.
juramentar *v.t.* to put under oath.
juramento *s.m.* **1** oath. **2** swearword, curse.
jurar *v.t.* **1** to swear, to take an oath. **2** to pledge (prometer). || *v.i.* **3** to swear, to curse. || **4 jurársela a alguien,** to have it in for someone, to swear to get even with someone.
jurel *s.m.* ZOOL. mackerel (pez).
jurídicamente *adv.* legally.
jurídico, -a *adj.* legal, juridical.
jurisconsulto *s.m.* legal expert.
jurisdicción *s.f.* **1** jurisdiction, authority. **2** district, area (zona).
jurisdiccional *adj.* jurisdictional.
jurispericia *s.f.* jurisprudence.
jurisperito o **jurisprudente** *s.m.* legal expert.
jurisprudencia *s.f.* DER. case law.
jurista *s.m.* y *f.* lawyer.
justamente *adv.* **1** just, exactly, precisely: *justamente ahora = just now.* **2** fairly, justly (en justicia).
justicia *s.f.* **1** DER. justice. **2** fairness (virtud moral). **3** law (ley). **4** justice, retribution (castigo).
justiciable *adj.* DER. actionable (que puede ser llevado ante la justicia).
justicialismo *s.m.* POL. political belief in Argentina.
justiciero, -a *adj.* strict, severe.
justificable *adj.* justifiable.
justificación *s.f.* **1** justification. **2** proof, evidence. **3** alignment (de tipografía). **4** REL. salvation.
justificadamente *adv.* justifiably.
justificado, -a *p.p.* **1** de **justificar.** || *adj.* **2** justified.
justificador, -a *adj.* justifying.
justificante *s.m.* receipt, voucher.
justificar *v.t.* **1** to justify. **2** to explain: *esto justifica su comportamiento = this explains his behaviour.* **3** REL. to make holy, to free from sin. **4** to align (en imprenta). || *v.t.* y *pron.* **5** to be proved innocent.
justificativo, -a *adj.* justifying.
justillo *s.m.* jerkin (prenda interior de mujer).
justipreciar *v.t.* to appraise, to estimate.
justiprecio *s.m.* appraisal, estimate.
justo, -a *adj.* **1** fair, just, right. **2** exact, precise, correct: *el precio justo = the exact price.* **3** tight, tight-fitting (sobre todo ropa). **4** righteous, upright (virtuoso). || *s.m.* y *f.* **5** just man; just woman. || *adv.* **6** justly, fairly (con justicia). **7** sparingly (con falta de dinero). **8** exactly, precisely.
juvenil *adj.* young, youthful.
juventud *s.f.* **1** youth, early life: *fui un magnífico deportista en mi juventud = I was a very good athlete in my early life.* **2** young people, youth: *la juventud = the young people.* **3** youthfulness (calidad).
juzgado, -a *p.p.* **1** de **juzgar.** || *s.m.* **2** court, tribunal.
juzgador, -a o **juzgante** *adj.* **1** judging. || *s.m.* y *f.* **2** judge.
juzgar *v.t.* **1** DER. to judge, to pass judgement on. **2** to consider, to believe: *juzgo que estás equivocado = I believe you are wrong.* **3** to assess.

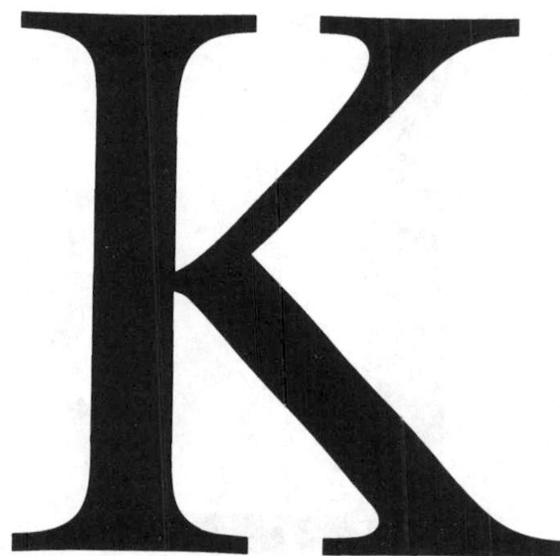

k, K *s.f.* 1 k, K (duodécima letra del alfabeto español). || abreviatura. 2 k (vitamina). 3 (grado Kelvin).
kaki *adj.* 1 khaki. 2 date plum.
kayac *s.m.* kayak (pequeña canoa).
kilate o **quilate** *s.m.* carat.
kilo *s.m.* kilo.
kilogramo *s.m.* kilogramme, (EE.UU.) kilogram.
kilolitro *s.m.* kilolitre, (EE.UU.) kiloliter.
kilometraje *s.m.* distance in kilometres.
kilométrico *adj.* 1 kilometric. 2 (fig.) very long: *un anuncio kilométrico = a very long advertisement.* || **3 billete –,** runabout ticket. **4 punto –,** kilometric point.
kilómetro *s.m.* kilometre, (EE.UU.) kilometer.
kilowatio *s.m.* 1 kilowatt 2 **kilowatios-hora,** kilowatt hour.
kiosco o **quiosco** *s.m.* 1 kiosk, stall (en la calle). 2 summerhouse (en el jardín). 3 bandsand (para los músicos). 4 news stand (de periódicos).
kiwi o **kivi** *s.m.* BOT. kiwy.
klínex *s.m.* tissue (marca registrada).
k.o. *s.m.* DEP. knock out (boxeo).
kodak *s.f.* camera (marca registrada).
kumis *s.m.* GAST. kumis (bebida fermentada).

l, L *s.f.* **1** l, L (décimotercera letra del alfabeto español). || **2 L,** 50 (número romano).

la *art. f.sing.* **1** the: *la mesa = the table.* || *pron.pers. 3.ª pers. f.sing.* o *d.* **2** her (persona), it (cosa). **3** you (usted): *la vi a usted ayer = I saw you yesterday.* || **3 la de(l), a)** *la de él = his; la de María = Mary's;* **b)** *la del sombrero verde = the one in the green hat;* **c)** the quantity, the amount of, the number of: *¡la de gente que había! = there were lots of people!* **4 la que,** the one who.

laberíntico, -a *adj.* labyrinthic, labyrinthical, labyrinthine, labyrinthian; rambling: *una casa laberíntica = a rambling house; divagaciones = rambling talk.*

laberinto *s.m.* **1** labyrinth, maze. **2** (fig.) tangle, maze. **3** ANAT. labyrinth.

labia *s.f.* **1** fluency, glibness; persuasive verbosity, winning eloquence. || **2 tener mucha labia,** to have the gift of the gab.

labiado, -a *adj.* BOT. labiate.

labial *adj., s.f.* labial.

labializar *v.t.* to labialize.

lábil *adj.* **1** labile. **2** weak, feeble.

labilidad *s.f.* lability, instability, proneness to lapse.

labio *s.m.* **1** ANAT. lip. **2** lip, edge, rim. || *pl.* **3** (pl.) mouth. **4** BOT., ZOOL. labrum, labium, lip. || **3 estar pendiente-/colgado de los labios de alguien,** to hang on to someone's every word. **4 – leporino,** harelip. **5 morderse los labios,** to bite one's lip. **6 no morderse los labios,** to pull no punches, to speak one's mind, to be outspoken.

labiodental *adj., s.f.* GRAM. labiodental.

labiosear *v.t.* (Am.) to flatter, to blarney.

labioso, -a *adj.* **1** talkative, glib. **2** flattering, persuasive.

labor *s.f.* **1** job, labour, work, piece of work, task, toil. **2** AGR. farm work, farming, tillage, tilling, ploughing, (EE.UU.) plowing. **3** MIN. works, workings, excavations. **4** knitting, sewing, needlework, embroidery, crochet, lacework. **5** manufactured tobacco. **6** thousand tiles or bricks. || **7 sus labores,** housewife.

laborable *adj.* **1** AGR. arable, tillable, workable. **2** working day.

laboral *adj.* labour.

laboralista *adj./s.m.* y *f.* left-wing lawyer.

laborar *v.t.* e *i.* to work, to till, to plough.

laboratorio *s.m.* **1** laboratory. || **2 – de idiomas,** language laboratory.

laboreo *s.m.* **1** AGR. tilling, ploughing, (EE.UU.) plowing, cultivation, working. **2** MIN. exploitation, working.

laboriosidad *s.f.* industry, laboriousness.

laborioso, -a *adj.* **1** laborious, hard-working, industrious, painstaking. **2** laborious, difficult, tough, arduous.

laborismo *s.m.* Labour Party, Labour Movement, worker's movement.

laborista *adj.* **1** labour: *partido laborista = Labour Party.* || *s.m.* y *f.* **2** Labour Party member/supporter.

labrado, -a *adj.* **1** worked; wrought (metal); ploughed, (EE.UU.) plowed (tierra); cut, carved, (madera, piedra); embroidered, patterned (tela). || *s.m.* **2** working, cutting, carving, ploughing, embroidery. || *s.m.pl.* **3** cultivated fields.

labrador, -a *adj.* **1** farming. || *s.m.* y *f.* **2** peasant, farmer, ploughman.

labrantío, -a *adj.* **1** arable, tillable. || *s.m.* **2** arable, tillable land.

labranza *s.f.* **1** farming, cultivation, work. **2** farmland, farm. || **3 aperos de –,** farming tools, implements.

labrar *v.t.* **1** to work, to plough, (EE.UU.) to plow, to till, to cultivate. **2** to work (metals); to cut, to carve (madera, piedra); to embroider (tela). **3** (fig.) to work, to forge, to cause, to bring about: *labrarse la propia ruina = to cause one's own ruin.* **4** to make, to build, to forge: *labrarse un porvenir = to build one's future.*

labriego, -a *s.m.* y *f.* peasant, farm labourer, farm worker, farmhand, farmer.

laca *s.f.* **1** lac, gum lac, lacqueur, lacqueur shellac, japan. **2** hair spray, nail varnish or polish. **3** lake (dye, pigment).

lacayo *s.m.* **1** lackey, lacquey, footman, groom. **2** (fig.) lackey, flunkey, toady.

lacear *v.t.* **1** to beribbon, to trim, to adorn with bows. **2** to drive (game) into range, to snare. **3** to lasso.

laceración *s.f.* laceration.

lacerado, -a *adj.* **1** unhappy, unlucky. **2** lacerated, wounded. || *s.m.* **3** leper.

lacerante *adj.* harrowing, heartrending, sharp, wounding.

lacerar *v.t.* **1** to lacerate, to damage, to harm, to tear. **2** (fig.) to damage, to spoil, to mangle, to injure (reputación).

laceria *s.f.* **1** misery, poverty, want, wretchedness. **2** distress, toil, trouble.

lacería *s.f.* **1** bows, ornamental bows. **2** ARQ. ornament imitating bows, interlacing arches.

lacio, -a *adj.* **1** whitered, faded. **2** lank, straight (pelo). **3** flaccid, flabby, limp, weak, languid, strengthless.

lacón *s.m.* shoulder of pork.

lacónico, -a *adj.* laconic, terse.

laconismo *s.m.* laconism, terseness.

lacra *s.f.* **1** MED. mark, trace, scar. **2** (Am.) sore ulcer, scab. **3** (fig.) blot, blemish, scourge, blight. **4** defect, flaw, fault.

lacrar *v.t.* **1** to strike (con enfermedad), to contaminate, to infect. **2** to injure, to harm, to cause damage to. **3** to seal.

lacre *s.m.* sealing wax.

lacrimal *adj.* **1** ANAT. lachrymal, lacrimal. || **2 conducto –,** tear duct.

lacrimógeno, -a *adj.* **1** lachrymogenic, tear producing. **2** tear-jerker, sentimental, tearful. || **3 gas –,** tear gas.

lacrimoso, -a *adj.* lachrymose, tearful.

lactación *s.f.* lactation, nursing.

lactancia *s.f.* lactation, nursing, suckling.

lactante *adj.* nursing, suckling (madre, niño).

lactar *v.t.* e *i.* to nurse, to suckle, to feed on milk, to breast feed.
lacteado, -a *adj.* mixed with milk.
lácteo, -a *adj.* 1 milky, lacteous, lacteal: *productos lácteos = milk/dairy products.* || **2 Vía Láctea,** Milky Way.
lactosa *s.f.* lactose, milk sugar.
lacustre *adj.* lake, lacustrine.
lacha *s.f.* 1 anchovy. 2 shame: *tener lacha = to be/feel ashamed.*
lacho *s.m.* (Am.) lover.
ladear *v.t., i.* y *pron.* 1 to lean, to tilt, to slant, to tip, to incline: *el cuadro está ladeado = the picture is lopsided.* 2 AER. to bank. 3 to go off the straight and narrow. 4 to bend, to swerve. 5 to avoid, to get round (una dificultad), to get round the skirt of a mountain. 6 (Am.) to fall in love.
ladera *s.f.* slope, side, hillside, mountainside.
ladero, -a *adj.* side, lateral.
ladilla *s.f.* crab louse.
ladino, -a *adj.* 1 Spanish language. 2 multilingual, poliglot. 3 cunning, wily, shrewd.
lado *s.m.* 1 side, edge, flank. 2 end (deporte), faction (política). 3 favour, protection, connections. || **4 al —,** near, nearby, at hand. **5 cada cosa por su —,** in a mess. **6 dar de — a alguien,** to cold-shoulder, to desert, to disregard. **7 mirar de medio —,** to look down on, to look at out of the corner of one's eye, to look askance. **8 estar/ponerse del — de alguien,** to be on someone's side, to side with, to take sides with. **9 ir cada uno por su —,** each goes his own way. **10 por un —,** on the one hand. **11 ver el — bueno de las cosas,** to look on the bright side.
ladrador, -ora *adj.* barking.
ladrar *v.i.* 1 to bark, to yap. 2 (fig.) to growl, to bark.
ladrido *s.m.* 1 bark, yap. 2 backbitting, slander.
ladrillado *s.m.* brick floor, tile floor.
ladrillar *v.t.* 1 to brick, to pave with bricks. || *s.m.* 2 brickworks, brickyard.
ladrillazo *s.m.* blow with a brick.
ladrillo *s.m.* 1 brick, tile. 2 block. 3 check (cloth).
ladrón, -ona *adj.* 1 thieving, thievish, light-fingered. || *s.m.* y *f.* 2 thief, robber, burglar. 3 ELEC. multiple socket. || **4 cueva de ladrones,** den of thieves. **5 — cuatrero,** horse thief, cattle thief. **6 — de corazones,** ladykiller.
lagar *s.m.* 1 wine, apple, olive press. 2 press house.
lagarta *s.f.* 1 ZOOL. female lizard, gipsy moth. 2 (fig.) sly minx, tart.
lagartija *s.f.* ZOOL. (small) lizard.
lagarto *s.m.* 1 ZOOL. lizard, (Am.) alligator. 2 ANAT. biceps. 3 sly fellow, crafty, fellow. || **4 — de Indias,** alligator.
lagartón, -ona *adj.* 1 (Am.) sly, wily, crafty, greedy. || *s.m.* 2 sly devil. || *s.f.* 3 sly minx.
lago *s.m.* lake.
lagotería *s.f.* cajolery, flattery, adulation.
lágrima *s.f.* 1 tear. 2 drop, drop of sap. || **3 deshacerse en lágrimas/llorar a — viva,** to burst into tears, to sob one's heart out, to cry one's eyes out, to shed bitter tears. **4 lágrimas de cocodrilo,** crocodile tears. **5 ser el paño de lágrimas de alguien,** to give someone a shoulder to cry on.
lagrimal *adj.* 1 lachrymal. | *s.m.* 2 ANAT. corner of the eye.
lagrimar *v.i.* to weep, to cry.
lagrimear *v.i.* to shed tears, to blubber, to be tearful; to water, to fill with tears.
laguna *s.f.* 1 small lake, tarn (montaña), lagoon (atolón), pool. 2 gap, lacuna. 3 gap, blank, hiatus, break.
lagunajo *s.m.* pool, puddle.
laicismo *s.m.* laicism.
laico, -a *adj.* 1 lay, secular, laical. || *s.m.* 2 layman.
laísmo *s.m.* use of **la/las** as indirect object instead of **le/les.**
laja *s.f.* flat stone, stone slab, flagstone.
lama *s.f.* 1 mud, slime, slit, ooze. 2 (Am.) moss, duckweed. 3 goldor silver tissue. 4 blind strip. || *s.m.* 5 REL. lama.
lamaísmo *s.m.* REL. lamaism.
lamaísta *adj./s.m.* y *f.* lamaist.
lambada *s.f.* lambada.
lambarero *s.m.* 1 flatterer. 2 wanderer, rover.
lambeculo *s.m.* (Am.) creep, toady.
lambeojos *s.m.* (Am.) creep, toady.
lambeplatos *s.m.* (Am.) 1 bootlicker, poor wretch. 2 beggar.
lamber *v.t.* to lick.
lambeta *s.m.* (Am.) creep, toady.
lamentable *adj.* regrettable, pitiful.
lamentablemente *adv.* regrettably.
lamentación *s.f.* lamentation, sorrow.
lamentar *v.t.* y *pron.* 1 to be sorry about, to regret, to lament, to bemoan, to mourn, to grieve. 2 to lament, to complain about; to bewail, to mourn over.
lamento *s.m.* 1 lament, lamentation. 2 wail, moan.
lamer *v.t.* 1 to lick, to lap (against). 2 touch lightly.
lametada *s.f.* lick, lap.
lametazo V. **lametada.**
lametón V. **lametada.**
lamia *s.f.* 1 lamia (monstruo fabuloso con cuerpo de mujer), witch, she-demon. 2 ZOOL. lamia (especie de tiburones).
lamido, a *adj.* 1 very thin, pale, scrawny. 2 licked, scrubbed. 3 dandified, prim, spick-and-span, affected.
lámina *s.f.* 1 sheet, plate, lamina. 2 illustration, picture, engraving. 3 ANAT., BOT. lamina. 4 (fig.) appearance.
laminable *adj.* rollable.
laminación *s.f.* 1 rolling, splitting, lamination. || **2 tren de —,** rolling mill.
laminado, -a *adj.* 1 laminated. 2 TEC. sheet, rolled.
laminador *s.m.* 1 rolling mill. 2 roller, rolling mill operator.
laminar *adj.* 1 laminar. || *v.t.* 2 to laminate, to roll, to split.
lampa *s.f.* (Am.) spade, hoe.
lampadario *s.m.* candelabra, candlestick.
lámpara *s.f.* 1 lamp, light, bulb. 2 valve, tube. || **3 — de mineros/de seguridad,** miner's/safety lamp. **4 — de pie,** standard lamp.
lamparería *s.f.* lamp works, lamp shop.
lamparero *s.m.* lampmaker, lamplighter.
lamparilla *s.f.* 1 BOT. aspen, nightlight. 2 small lamp.
lamparón *s.m.* 1 large lamp. 2 MED. scrofula. 3 grease stain.
lampiño, -a *adj.* hairless, beardless, clean-shaven.
lampista *s.m.* lamp maker, tinsmith.
lamprea *s.f.* 1 BOT. lamprey. 2 MED. sore, ulcer.
lamprear *v.t.* 1 to cook with wine spices and honey. 2 to whip.
lampreazo *s.m.* lash, crack of a whip.
lana *s.f.* 1 wool, fleece. 2 woollen cloth. || *pl.* 3 hair, mop. || **4 ir por — y salir-/volver trasquilado,** to go for wool and come home shorn, to get nothing for one's pains, to be disappointed in one's hopes.
lanada *s.f.* cleaning rod (para limpiar el alma de las piezas de artillería).
lanado *adj.* BOT. lanate.
lanar *adj.* wool-bearing: *ganado lanar = sheep.*
lance *s.m.* 1 throw, cast, catch. 2 event, episode, chance, incident. 3 critical moment, difficult moment. 4 move, movement, piece of play, stroke. 5 row, quarrel. 6 pass with the cape (tauromaquia). || **7 de —,** secondhand. **8 — de honor,** challenge, duel, affair of honour.
lanceolado *adj.* BOT. lanceolate, lanceolar.
lancería *s.f.* 1 set of spears. 2 troop of lancers.
lancero *s.m.* 1 MIL. lancer. || *pl.* 2 MUS. lancers.
lancha *s.f.* 1 flat stone, stone slab; partridge trap. 2 boat, pinnace; motor launch, motorboat; barge: *lancha cañonera = gunboat.*
lanchaje *s.m.* MAR. lighterage.
landa *s.f.* moor, moorland, heathland, waste land.
landó *s.m.* landau.
lanero, -a *adj.* 1 wool. || *s.m.* 2 wool dealer; wool warehouse.
langosta *s.f.* 1 ZOOL. locust (insecto); lobster (crustáceo). 2 (fig.) scourge.
langostino *s.m.* ZOOL. prawn.
lánguidamente *adv.* languidly, weakly, listlessly.
languidecer *v.i.* to languish.
languidez *s.f.* languour, lassitude; listlessness.
lánguido, -a *adj.* languid, weak, listless.
lanilla *s.f.* nap, thin flannel cloth.
lanolina *s.f.* lanoline.
lanosidad *s.f.* down.
lanoso, -a *adj.* V. **lanudo.**
lanudo, -a *adj.* 1 woolly, fleece, downy, furry. 2 (Am.) rustic, uncouth
lanuginoso, -a *adj.* lanuginous, downy.
lanza *s.f.* 1 lance, spear. 2 shaft (carreta), nozzle (manguera). 3 MIL. lancer. || **4 a punta de —,** rigorously, meticulously, accurately. **5 correr lanzas,** to joust. **6 estar con la — en ristre,** to be ready for action, to be all set to go, to have one's lance at the ready. **7 romper**

lanzas por alguien/por algo, to fight for, to defend.
lanzada *s.f.* **1** lance thrust, spear thrust. **2** lance wound, spear wound.
lanzadera *s.f.* shuttle (telar).
lanzamiento *s.m.* **1** throw, throwing, fling, flinging, hurl, hurling. **2** MIL. firing (misil, proyectil); launching (barco, sonda, campaña), release. **3** jump, drop (paracaidistas). **4** DEP. put, pitch, ball, throw.
lanzar *v.t.* y *pron.* **1** to throw; to hurl, to fling (con violencia). **2** to fire, to launch (proyectil, satélite,etc.). **3** DEP. to throw, to bowl, to pitch, to put. **3** to release (dejar libre). **4** DER. to dispossess. **5** (fig.) to launch (un producto). **6** to utter, to hurl, to heave (grito, insulto, maldición). **7** to cast, to give (mirada). **8** to make (acusación), to throw down /out (desafío). **9 to throw up.** || *v.pron.* **10** to rush, to throw/fling/hurl oneself, to hurtle, to jump, to dive. **11** to launch oneself into, to embark upon, to dash off (in pursuit of someone).
laña *s.f.* **1** clamp. **2** BOT. green coconut.
lañador *s.m.* clamper.
lañar *v.t.* **1** to clamp. **2** to clean (pescado).
lapa *s.f.* **1** ZOOL. limpet. **2** vegetal film. **3** (fam.) hanger-on. || **4 pegarse como una –,** to stick like glue/a leech.
lapachar *s.m.* marsh, swamp, bog.
lapicero *s.m.* propelling pencil, pencil holder.
lápida *s.f.* memorial tablet, commemorative stone; tombstone, gravestone.
lapidación *s.f.* stoning, lapidation.
lapidar *v.t.* **1** to stone, to stone to death, to lapidate. **2** (Am.) to cut (gemas).
lapidario, -a *adj.* y *s.m.* lapidary.
lapislázuli *s.m.* GEOL. lapis lazuli.
lápiz *s.m.* **1** pencil, crayon (de color): *escribir a/con lápiz = to write in pencil.* **2** GEOL. blacklead, graphite. || **3 – de labios,** lipstick. **4 – de plomo,** graphite pencil. **5 – rojo,** red ochre.
lapo *s.m.* **1** lash, blow, swig; slap. **2** (fam.) spit. **3** (Am.) simple soul, mug.
lapso *s.m.* **1** lapse, space (tiempo). **2** slip, lapse, lapsus.
lapsus *s.m.* **1** slip, lapse. || **2 – cálami,** slip of the pen. **3 – linguae,** slip of the tongue.
lar *s.m.* **1** lar (divinidad protectora del hogar). **2** hearth. **3** home.
lardo *s.m.* lard, animal fat.
largamente *adv.* at length, for a long time; generously.
largar *v.t.* **1** to let go, to let loose, to release; to loosen, to slacken. **3** to unfurl (bandera, vela), to launch (bote, barco). **4** to fetch, to give (un golpe). || *v.pron.* **5** to clear off, to beat it, to push off. **6** to put to sea, to set sail.
largo, -a *adj.* **1** long, lengthy. **2** prolonged. **3** GRAM. long (vocal, sílaba). **4** liberal, generous. **5** full, good: *tardó un rato largo = he took a good while.* || *s.m.* **6** length. **7** MUS. largo. || *s.f.* **8** lengthening piece (pieza de la horma para alargar el zapato). **9** longest billiard cue. || *adv.* **10** far, at lentgh, abundantly. || **11 a la larga,** in the long run, in the end. **12 a lo –,** lengthwise, lengthways. **13 a lo – y a lo ancho,** to and fro, up and down; all over. **14 dar largas,** to put off (un asunto), to delay. **15 hablar – y tendido,** to talk something over. **16 ¡–!/¡– de ahí!/¡– de aquí!,** clear off!
largometraje *s.m.* film, movie, motion picture.
larguero *s.m.* **1** main beam, chief support jamb; slide (cama); bolster (travesaño). **2** DEP. crossbar, goal post.
largueza *s.f.* generosity.
larguirucho, -a *adj.* (fam.) lanky, gangling.
largura *s.f.* length.
laringe *s.f.* ANAT. larynx.
laringitis *s.f.* MED. laryngitis.
laringología *s.f.* MED. laryngology.
laringólogo *s.m.* MED. laryngologist.
larva *s.f.* MIT., ZOOL. larva, *(pl.)* larvae.
larvado, -a *adj.* MED. larvate, larval.
las *art. def. f.pl.* **1** the. || *pron.pers. f.pl.* **2** them. **3** you (ustedes): *las vi a ustedes ayer = I saw you yesterday.* || **4 las de (los), a)** *las de él = his; las de María = Mary's;* **b)** *las de los sombreros verdes = the ones/those in the green hats.* **5 – que,** the ones who, those who.
lasca *s.f.* chip (de piedra).
lascivamente *adv.* lasciviously, lewdly, lustfully, playfully, wantonly.
lascivia *s.f.* lasciviousness, lechery, lewdness, lust, lustfulness; playfulness.
lascivo, -a *adj.* lascivious, lewd, lustful; playful, wanton.
láser *s.m.* TEC. laser, laser beam.
lasitud *s.f.* lastitude, weariness.
laso, -a *adj.* tired, weary, weak.
lástima *s.f.* **1** compassion, sympathy. **2** pity, shame. **3** complaint, lamentation, tale of woe. || **4 dar –,** to be pitiful.
lastimar *v.t.* **1** to hurt, to injure; to wound, to bruise. **2** to offend, to distress. || *v.pron.* **3** to hurt oneself, to injure oneself. **4** to pity, to feel sorry for, to sympathize with. **5** to complain about.
lastimero *adj.* **1** harmful, injurious. **2** plaintive, doleful.
lastimosamente *adv.* pitifully, pathetically.
lastimoso, -a *adj.* pitiful, pitious, lamentable.
lastra *s.f.* flat stone, stone slab, flagstone.
lastrar *v.t.* to ballast, to weigh down.
lastre *s.m.* **1** ballast. **2** (fig.) ballast, dead weight.
lata *s.f.* **1** tin, can, tinplate. **2** lath. **3** drag, nuisance, bore, bind; pest.
latente *adj.* latent, alive, intense, vigorous.
lateral *adj.* **1** side, lateral. **2** FON. lateral. || *s.m.* **3** wings, side of the stage.
lateralmente *adv.* laterally, sideways.
látex *s.m.* BOT. latex.
latido *s.m.* **1** beat, beating, throbbing. **2** yelp, yelping (ladrido).
latifundio *s.m.* latifundium, large state.
latifundismo *s.m.* latifundium system.
latifundista *s.m.* y *f.* owner of a large state.
latigazo *s.m.* **1** lash, crack of a whip. **2** (fam.) drink, swig.
látigo *s.m.* **1** whip, riding whip. **2** correa. **3** whip (carrusel de feria).
latiguear *v.i.* to crack one's whip, to whip, to lash, to thrash
latiguera *s.f.* strap.
latiguillo *s.m.* **1** small whip. **2** BOT. runner. **3** overacting, hamming. **4** platitude, empty phrase.
latín *s.m.* **1** Latin. || **2 bajo –,** Low Latin. **3 – clásico,** Classical Latin. **4 – vulgar,** Vulgar Latin. **5 saber –,** to be pretty sharp, to be nobody's fool, there are no fies on someone. **6 echarle a uno los latines,** to marry, get married.
latina V. **latino.**
latinajo *s.m.* **1** latinism, latin word or phrase. **2** dog latin.
latinidad *s.f.* latinity, latin countries.
latinismo *s.m.* latinism.
latinizar *v.t.* e *i.* to latinize.
latino, -a *adj./s.m.* y *f.* **1** Latin. || *s.m.* **2** MAR. lateen.
latinoamericano, -a *adj./s.m.* y *f.* Latin-American.
latir *v.i.* **1** to beat (corazón), to throb (herida). **2** to yelp (ladrar).
latitud *s.f.* latitude.
lato *s.f.* **1** width, breath, area. **2** GEOG. latitude. **3** (fig.) latitude, freedom.
latón *s.m.* brass.
latonería *s.f.* brassworks, brass shop.
latonero *s.m.* brassworker, brazier.
latría *s.f.* REL. latria.
latrocinio *s.m.* robbery, theft.
laúd *s.m.* **1** MUS. lute. **2** MAR. catboat.
laudable *adj.* laudable, praiseworthy.
láudano *s.m.* MED. laudanum.
laude *s.f.* **1** engraved tombstone. **2** *(pl.)* REL. lauds.
laudo *s.m.* DER. award, decision, finding.
laureado, -a *adj.* **1** honoured, distinguished, famous. || *s.m.* **2** laureate.
laurear *v.t.* **1** to crown with laurels. **2** to honour, to reward.
laurel *s.m.* **1** BOT. laurel. **2** (fig.) laurels, honour, reward. || **3 dormirse en los laureles,** to rest on one's laurels.
lauro *s.m.* **1** laurel. **2** laurels, glory, fame.
lava *s.f.* **1** GEOL. lava. **2** MIN. washing.
lavabo *s.m.* **1** washbasin, washstand. **2** washroom, toilet, lavatory. **3** REL. lavabo.
lavadero *s.m.* **1** washing place, laundry, wash house. **2** gold-bearing sands, place where gold-bearing sands are panned.
lavado *s.m.* **1** wash, washing. **2** ART. wash.
lavador *adj.* **1** washing. || *s.m.* **2** washer.
lavadora *s.f.* washing machine.
lavaje *s.m.* washing (de lana).
lavajo *s.m.* pool, pond.
lavanda *s.f.* **1** BOT. lavender. || **2 agua de –,** lavender water.
lavandería *s.f.* laundry, launderette, laundromat (EE.UU.).
lavándula *s.f.* lavender.
lavar *v.t.* y *pron.* **1** to wash, to clean. **2** to wipe away, to wipe out. **3** to paint in

water colour. || **4 lavarse las manos,** to wash one's hands of that.
lavativa *s.f.* 1 enema. 2 nuisance, bind, bother, bore.
lavatorio *s.m.* 1 washing. 2 (Am.) washbasin, washstand, lavatory, washroom. 3 MED. lotion. 4 REL. Maundy (ceremonia), lavabo (misa).
lavazas *s.f.pl.* dishwater, dirty water, slops.
lavotear *v.t.* 1 to wash quickly and badly. || *v.pron.* 2 to have a quick wash.
lavoteo *s.m.* quick wash, cat-lick.
laxante *adj.* y *s.m.* laxative.
laxar *v.t.* to loosen, to ease, to slacken, to relax.
laxo, -a *adj.* slack, loose, lax.
lay *s.m.* lay (poema).
laya *s.f.* 1 AGR. spade. 2 quality, sort, kind.
lazada *s.f.* bow, knot.
lazador *s.m.* lassoer, poacher, dogcatcher.
lazar *v.t.* to lasso, to rope.
lazareto *s.m.* lazaretto, lazaret.
lazarillo *s.m.* blindman's guide.
lazarino, -a *adj./s.m.* y *f.* leprous, leper.
lázaro *s.m.* ragged, beggar.
lazo *s.m.* 1 bow, knot, loop, lasso. 2 bond, link, tie. 3 ARQ. interlaced design. 4 figure (danza). 5 slipknot. 6 snare, trap. 7 shoelace. || **8 caer en el –,** to fall into the trap. **9 echar el –,** to catch, to capture. **10 tender un –,** to set a trap.
lazulita *s.f.* lazulite, lapis lazuli.
le *pron.pers. 3.ª pers.* (to) him, (to) her, (to) you (usted), (to) it (cosas): *no le vi a usted ayer = I didn't see you yesterday.*
leal *adj./s.m.* y *f.* loyal, faithful, trustworthy.
lealmente *adv.* loyally, faithfully.
lealtad *s.f.* loyalty, fidelity, trustworthiness.
lebrada *s.f.* hare stew.
lebrato *s.m.* leveret.
lebrel *adj.* y *s.m.* greyhound.
lebrero, -a *adj.* 1 harehunting. || *s.m.* 2 greyhound.
lebrillo *s.m.* earthenware pot.
lección *s.f.* 1 lesson, lecture, class. 2 reading. 3 warning, example. 4 REL. lesson, lection, reading. 5 chapter of a textbook. || **6 dar una – a alguien,** to teach someone a lesson. **7 repasarle a uno la –,** to tell off, to scold.
lectivo, -a *adj.* school: *día lectivo = school day.*
lector *s.m.* y *f.* 1 reader, assistant, conversation assistant. 2 lecturer (universidad). 3 REL. lector.
lectorado *s.m.* 1 assistantship. 2 REL. lectorate.
lectoría *s.f.* assistantship (universidad).
lectura *s.f.* 1 reading. 2 reading matter. 3 lecture. 4 culture, knowledge. 5 TEC. pica. || **6 una persona de mucha =,** a well-read person.
lecha *s.f.* milt, roe.
lechada *s.f.* 1 whitewash. 2 paste, grout, pulp. 3 milky liquid.
lechal *adj.* 1 sucking. 2 BOT. lactiferous, milky. || *s.m.* 3 milk, milky juice, milky sap (plantas). 4 suckling (cordero).
lechar *adj.* 1 V. **lechal.** || *v.t.* 2 (Am.) to milk, to produce milk for, to give suck to. 3 to whitewash.
lechazo *s.m.* young lamb.
leche *s.f.* 1 milk. 2 milky sap, milky juice. 3 rubber, rubber tree. 4 (vulg.) spunk, semen. 5 good luck. || **6 café con –,** white coffee. 7 **¡leche!,** hell! **8 tener mala –,** to be vindictive/nasty, to be a nasty piece of work.
lechecillas *s.f.pl.* 1 sweetbread. 2 offal.
lechera *s.f.* 1 milkmaid, dairymaid, milk seller. 2 milk can, milk churn, milk jug, milk pot. 3 milk cow, milch cow.
lechería *s.f.* 1 dairy, creamery. 2 milking parlour. 3 meanness.
lechero, -a *adj.* 1 milk, dairy. 2 (Am.) lucky. 3 (fig., fam., Am.) mean, stingy, greedy, grasping, tightfisted. || *s.m.* 3 milkman, dairyman.
lechigada *s.f.* 1 litter (animales), brood (aves). 2 gang.
lecho *s.m.* 1 bed, couch. 2 bed, bottom, floor (río). 3 GEOL. layer, stratum. 4 ARQ. base. 5 AGR. bedding.
lechón *s.m.* 1 sucking pig, piglet. 2 hog, swine. 3 filthy person.
lechoso, -a *adj.* 1 milky. 2 (Am.) lucky.
lechuga *s.f.* 1 lettuce. 2 ruff, frill, flounce. 3 pleat, flute, crimp. 4 rotter, cad, heel. 5 banknote. || **6 más fresco que una –,** to be as cool as a cucumber.
lechuguilla *s.f.* 1 wild lettuce. 2 ruff, frill, flounce.
lechuguino *s.m.* 1 young lettuce. 2 plot of small lettuce (plantío). 3 (fig. y fam.) toff, dude (EE.UU.) dandy, beau.
lechuza *s.f.* 1 ZOOL. owl. 2 (fig. y fam.) hag.
leer *v.t.* e *i.* 1 to read. 2 to teach, to lecture. || **3 – en los ojos/la mirada,** to read in someone's eyes. **4 – entre líneas,** to read between lines.
lega V. **lego.**
legación *s.f.* legation.
legado *s.m.* 1 legacy. 2 legate. 3 (fig.) legacy, bequest.
legajar *v.t.* (Am.) to file.
legajo *s.m.* 1 bundle of papers. 2 dossier, file.
legal *adj.* 1 legal, lawful. 2 scrupulous, honest, fair. 3 trustworthy, truthfull.
legalidad *s.f.* legality, lawfulness.
legalista *adj.* 1 legalistic. || *s.m.* 2 legalist.
legalizable *adj.* legalizable.
legalización *s.f.* 1 legalization. 2 authentication.
legalizar *v.t.* to legalize, to authenticate.
légamo *s.m.* 1 slime, mud, ooze. 2 loam, clay.
legaña *s.f.* sleep, rheum.
legar *v.t.* 1 to bequeath, to legate, to leave to. 2 to delegate.
legatario *s.m.* y *f.* DER. legatee, heir.
legendario, -a *adj.* 1 legendary. || *s.m.* 2 collection of legends, book of legends.
legibilidad *adj.* legibility.
legible *adj.* legible.
legión *s.f.* 1 legion. || **2 – extranjera,** Foreign Legion.
legionario, -a *adj.* y *s.m.* legionary.
legislación *s.f.* legislation.
legislativo, -a *adj.* 1 legislative. || *s.m.* 2 legislator.
legislatura *s.f.* legislatura.
legista *s.m.* legist, law student.
legítima V. **legítimo.**
legitimar *v.t.* 1 to legitimate, to legitimize, to legalize. || *v.pron.* 2 to establish one's identity, to establish one's own title.
legitimario, -a *adj.* legitimate, entitled.
legitimidad *s.f.* legitimacy, justice, authenticity.
legitimismo *s.m.* legitimism.
legitimista *adj.* y *s.* legitimist.
legítimo, -a *adj.* 1 legitimate, rightful, just. 2 authentic, genuine, real. 3 pure, right.
lego, -a *adj.* 1 lay, laic, secular. 2 ignorant, uninformed. || *s.m.* 3 layman. 4 REL. laybrother. || **5 ser – en la materia,** to know nothing about the subject.
legrar *v.t.* MED. to scrape, to curette.
legua *s.f.* 1 league. || **2 a la –,** far away, a mile away. **3 – cuadrada,** square league. **3 se ve a la –,** you can see/tell it a mile away, it stands out a mile.
leguleyo *s.m.* pettifogging lawyer.
legumbre *s.f.* BOT. legume, pot, vegetable.
leguminoso, -a *adj.* 1 leguminous. || *s.m.* y *f.* 2 pulse, leguminous plant.
leíble *adj.* legible.
leído, -a *p.p.* 1 de **leer.** || *adj.* 2 well-read (instruido). 3 read: *una obra muy leída = a widely read book.* || *s.f.* 4 reading.
leísmo *s.m.* the use of the pronoun **le** as direct object.
leitmotiv *s.m.* leitmotiv, leitmotif.
lejanía *s.f.* distance, remoteness, remote place.
lejano, -a *adj.* distant, remote, far off: *Lejano Oriente = Far East.*
lejía *s.f.* bleach, lye.
lejos *adv.* 1 far, far away. || *s.m.* 2 distant view, appearance from a distance: *este cuadro tiene buen lejos = this picture looks good from a distance.* 3 similarity: *esta casa tiene un lejos con la tuya = this house looks like yours from a distance.* || **4 a lo –/desde –/de –,** in the distance, from afar, from a distance, from a long way off. **5 – de,** far from: *estoy lejos de creer que... = I'm far from believing that...* **6 para no ir más –,** to take an obvious example.
lelo, -a *adj.* 1 silly, stupid, simple. || *s.m.* y *f.* 2 simpleton, fool.
lema *s.m.* 1 theme, subject. 2 epigraph. 3 assumed name (concurso). 4 motto (heráldica). 5 slogan. 6 MAT. lemma.
lémur *s.m.* 1 ZOOL. lemur. || *pl.* **2 lemures, phantoms, ghosts.**
lencería *s.f.* linen, drapery, lingerie; underwear.
lendrera *s.f.* toothcomb.
lengua *s.f.* 1 tongue. 2 language, tongue. 3 clapper, tongue (badajo). 4 neck, spit (de tierra). || **5 con la – fuera,** puffing and panting. **6 irse de la –,** to blab, to talk too much, to spill the beans, to let the cat out of the bag. **7 – de estro-**

pajo, slammerer, mumbler, stutterer. **8 — de fuego,** tongue of fire. **9 — de víbora,** poisonous tongue. **10 — madre,** parent tongue. **11 — materna,** mother tongue. **12 — muerta,** dead language. **13 — viva,** modern language, living language. **14 lenguas hermanas,** related languages, sister tongues. **15 malas lenguas,** evil tongue. **16 morderse la —,** to hold one's tongue. **17 no tener pelos en la —,** not to mince one's words. **18 sacar la —,** to stick out/to put out one's tongue. **19 tener mucha —/tener la — suelta,** to be outspoken. **20 tirar de la —,** to make someone talk. **21 trabarse la —,** to get tongue-tied.
lenguado *s.m.* sole.
lenguaje *s.m.* 1 speech. 2 language. 3 idiom. 4 stile.
lenguarada *s.f.* lick.
lenguaraz *adj.* 1 garrulous, talkative. 2 polyglot, multilingual. 3 slanderous.
lengüeta *s.f.* 1 ANAT. epiglottis. 2 MUS. reed. 3 pointer, needle (balanza). 4 flap, tab, tongue. 5 barb, bit. 6 paper cutter. 7 (Am.) chatterbox, gossip.
lengüetada *s.f.* lick.
lengüicorto *adj.* timid, shy, quiet.
lengüilargo *adj.* 1 talkative. 2 foul-mouthed.
lengüón, -ona *adj.* 1 talkative, gossipy, gossiping, garrulous, outspoken. || *s.m.* 2 chatterbox, gossip, talebearer.
lenitivo, -a *adj.* 1 shoothing, lenitive. || *s.m.* 2 MED. lenitive, palliative.
lenocinio *s.m.* 1 pimping, procuring, pandering. || **2 casa de —,** brothel.
lente *s.m.* y *f.* 1 lens, magnifying glass. || *m.pl.* 2 glasses, spectacles. || **3 lentes de contacto/lentilla,** contact lenses.
lenteja *s.f.* 1 BOT. lentil. 2 bob, disk of a pendulum.
lentejuela *s.f.* sequin, spangle.
lenticular *adj.* 1 lenticular. || *s.m.* 2 ANAT. lenticular ossicle.
lentilla V. **lente.**
lentitud *s.f.* slowness, sluggishness.
lento, -a *adj.* 1 slow. 2 sluggish. 3 viscous, viscid.
leña *s.f.* 1 firewood, sticks, kindling. 2 rough play, thrashing.
leñador, -ora *s.m.* y *f.* woodcutter.
leñero, -a *s.m.* y *f.* 1 wood seller. 2 woodshed.
leño *s.m.* 1 log, firewood, timber. 2 vessel. 3 (fig. y fam.) blockhead, thickhead.
leñoso, -a *adj.* ligneous.
leo *s.m.* ASTR. Leo.
león *s.m.* 1 ZOOL. lion. || **2 — marino,** sea lion.
leonado, -a *adj.* fulvous, tawny.
leonera *s.f.* 1 lion's cage, lion's den. 2 gambling den. || **3 es/parece una —,** it is a mess, it is shockingly dirty.
leonino, -a *adj.* 1 leonine. || **2 contrato —,** one-sided contract.
leontina *s.f.* watch chain.
leopardo *s.m.* y *f.* ZOOL. leopard.
leotardo *s.m.* 1 leotard. || *pl.* **2 tights.**
Lepe *n.pr.* **saber más que — (Lepijo y su hijo),** to be pretty smart, to be nobody's fool, to have no flies on one.
lepidóptero, -a *adj./s.m.* y *f.* ZOOL. lepidopterous, lepidopteran.
leporino, -a *adj.* 1 leporine. || **2 labio —,** harelip.
lepra *s.f.* MED. leprosy.
leprosería *s.f.* lazaretto, leprosarium, leper colony.
leproso, -a *adj./s.m.* y *f.* leprous, leper.
lerdo. -a *adj.* 1 dull, heavy, slow, dim. 2 sluggish, clumsy, lumbering, slow witted. || *s.m.* 3 dullard, sluggard.
les *pron.pers.* *3.ª pers. m.* (to) them, you (ustedes).
lesbianismo *s.m.* lesbianism.
lesbiano, -a *adj.* y *s.f.* lesbian.
lesión *s.f.* 1 injury, wound, lesion. 2 damage. || *pl.* 3 DER. assault and battery.
lesivo, -a *adj.* injurious, harmful, damaging.
lesna *s.f.* V. **lezna.**
leso, -a *adj.* 1 injured, hurt, offended, wronged. 2 disturbed, warped. 3 (Am.) simple, stupid. || **4 crimen de lesa majestad,** high treason, lese majesty.
letal *adj.* lethal, deadly.
letanía *s.f.* 1 REL. litany. 2 REL. supplicatory procession. 3 (fam.) string, long list, tedious, recitation, rigmarole.
letárgico, -a *adj.* lethargic.
letargo *s.m.* 1 MED. lethargy. 2 drowsiness.
letificar *v.t.* to make happy, to cheer up, to give life.
letón, -ona *adj.* 1 Latvian, Lettish. || *s.m.* y *f.* 2 Latvian, Left.
letra *s.f.* 1 letter. 2 sound. 3 handwriting, writing. 4 character, letter. 5 meaning, literal meaning. 6 LIT. rondeau. 8 lyrics, words (en una canción). 9 letter, bill, draft. || **10 al pie de la —,** to the letter. **11 hombre de letras,** man of letters. **12 — bastardilla,** italic letters, italics. **13 — cursiva,** cursive writing. **14 — de cambio,** bill of exchange, draft. **15 — negrita,** bold type, bold-face. **16 — redonda,** round hand. **17 — versal,** capital letters. **18 — versalita,** small capital letter. **19 letra por letra,** word for word. **20 letras divinas/sagradas,** The Bible, The Scriptures. **21 letras humanas,** humanities. **22 primeras letras,** the three R's, elementary education.
letrado, -a *adj.* 1 lettered, learned. 2 pedantic. || *s.m.* y *f.* 3 lawyer.
letrero *s.m.* sign, notice, placard, poster, label, inscription.
letrilla *s.f.* LIT. rondeau.
letrina *s.f.* 1 latrine, privy. 2 sewer, sump, filthy place.
leucemia *s.f.* MED. leucaemia, leukaemia.
leucocito *s.m.* BIOL. leucocyte.
leucoma *s.m.* MED. leucoma.
leva *s.f.* 1 MAR. weighing anchor. 2 MIL. levy. 3 TEC. lever, cam: *árbol de levas = camshaft.* 4 trick, swindle, ruse.
levadizo, -a *adj.* **puente —,** drawbridge.
levadura *adj.* 1 leaven (pan), yeast (cerveza). 2 seed.
levantamiento *s.m.* 1 raising, lifting, elevation. 2 rising, insurrection, revolt. 3 erection, construction. 4 TEC. hoisting, lifting. 5 GEOL. upheaval. 6 drawing up.
levantar *v.t.* 1 to raise, put up, to set. 2 to lift, to lift up, to pick up. 3 to throw up. 4 to erect, to raise, to construct. 5 to draw up (plano, acta). 6 to weigh (ancla). 7 MIL. to levy, to recruit. 8 DEP. to rear (caballo), to flush out (caza). || *v.pron.* 9 to get up. 10 to stand up, to rise, to come up. 11 to break out (escándalo) || **12 — cabeza,** to get better. **13 — la casa,** to move house. **14 levantarse en armas,** to rise up in arms. **15 se me levantó el estómago,** my stomach turned.
levante *s.m.* 1 East Orient. 2 East wind, levanter.
levantino, -a *adj.* Levantine, of the eastern coast of Spain.
levantisco, -a *adj.* turbulent, restless.
levar *v.t.* 1 MAR. to weigh (el ancla). || *v.i.* 2 to set sail, to weigh anchor.
leve *adj.* 1 light. 2 slight, trivial, unimportant, small.
leviatán *s.m.* Leviathan.
levita *s.m.* 1 Levite. 2 frock, coat.
levitación *s.f.* levitation.
levítico, -a *adj.* 1 levitical. 2 clerical.
lexema *s.m.* GRAM. lexeme.
léxico *adj.* 1 lexical. || *s.m.* 2 lexicon, dictionary, vocabulary, word list.
lexicografía *s.f.* lexicography.
lexicográfico, -a *adj.* lexicographic, lexicographical.
lexicógrafo, -a *s.m.* y *f.* lexicographer.
lexicología *s.f.* lexicology.
lexicológico, -a *adj.* lexicologic, lexicological.
lexicólogo, -a *s.m.* y *f.* lexicologist.
lexicón *s.m.* lexicon, dictionary, vocabulary.
ley *s.f.* 1 law. 2 bill, act. 3 rule, regulations, law. 4 measure, quality. 5 loyalty, devotion. 6 legal standard of fineness, sterling, purity. 7 religion. 8 liking. || **9 — del embudo,** one law for oneself and one for everyone else. **10 — marcial,** martial law. **11 — sálica,** Salic law.
leyenda *s.f.* 1 legend. 2 legend, inscription, key.
lezna *s.f.* awl.
lía *s.f.* plaited esparto grass.
liana *s.f.* BOT. liana.
liar *v.t.* 1 to tie, to bind. 2 to wrap, to roll (cigarrillo). 3 to coax, to take in, to mix up, to involve. 4 to muddle up, to complicate. || *v.pron.* 5 to wrap oneself up. 6 to get confused, to become complicated. 7 to become lovers. || **8 liarse la manta a la cabeza,** V. **manta.**
libación *s.f.* libation.
libanés, -esa *adj./s.m.* y *f.* Lebanese.
libar *v.t.* 1 to suck. 2 to sip, to taste.
libelo *s.m.* 1 lampoon, satire. 2 DER. libel, petition.
libélula *s.f.* ZOOL. dragonfly, libellula.
líber *s.m.* BOT. inner bark.
liberación *s.f.* 1 liberation, release, freeing. 2 remission, exemption. 3 receipt.
liberal *adj.* 1 liberal, generous, lavish. || *s.m.* 2 liberal. || **3 artes liberales,** liberal arts. **4 Partido —,** Liberal Party.
liberalismo *s.m.* liberalism.

liberar *v.t.* 1 to liberate, to free. 2 to release, to exempt.
libertad *s.f.* 1 liberty, freedom. 2 ease, freedom, familiarity. || *pl.* 3 liberties. || 4 **— de comercio,** free trade. 5 **— de conciencia,** freedom of conscience. 6 **— de pensamiento,** freedom of thinking. 7 **— provisional,** bail, parole. 8 **tomarse la —,** to take the liberty of. 9 **tomarse libertades,** to take liberties.
libertado, -a *p.p.* 1 de **libertar.** || *adj.* 2 free. 3 daring, bold.
libertar *v.t.* 1 to liberate, to free, to set free. 2 to exempt, to release from. 3 to emancipate. 4 to save, to deliver from.
libertario, -a *adj.* libertarian.
libertinaje *s.m.* libertinism, licentiousness.
libertino, -a *adj.* libertine, profligate.
liberto, -a *adj.* 1 emancipated. || *s.m.* y *f.* 2 freedman/woman.
libídine *s.f.* lewdness, libido.
libidinoso, -a *adj.* libidinous, lewd, lustful.
libido *s.f.* libido.
libio, -a *adj./s.m.* y *f.* libyan.
libra *s.m.* 1 pound (peso). 2 pound sterling (moneda). 3 (Am.) leave of top quality tobacco. 4 ASTR. Libra. || 5 **— carnicera,** kilogramme.
librado, -a *p.p.* 1 de **librar.** || *s.m.* y *f.* 2 drawee. || 3 **salir bien/mal —,** to fare well/badly, to succeed, to fail.
librador, -ora *s.m.* y *f.* drawer.
librancista *s.m.* bearer.
libranza *s.f.* 1 order of payment. 2 draft, bill of exchange.
librar *v.t., v.pron.* 1 to save, to recue. 2 to free, to liberate, to deliver. 3 to relieve, to exempt. 4 to join in, to engage (batalla). 5 to draw (letra). 6 to pronounce, to pass (sentencia); to issue, to promulgate (ley). 7 to give birth. 8 to have one's day off. 9 to avoid, to escape, to get out. 10 to get rid of.
libre *adj.* 1 free. 2 open: *al aire libre = in the open air.* 3 free, clear, vacant. 4 bold, outspoken; licentious. 5 independent, unattached. 6 DEP. freestyle.
librea *s.f.* livery, coat.
librecambismo *s.m.* free trade.
librecambista *adj/s.m.* y *f.* free-trade; free-trader.
librepensador, -ora *s.m.* y *f.* freethinker.
librepensamiento *s.m.* freethinking.
librería *s.f.* 1 library. 2 bookshop. 3 bookcase, bookshelf. 4 book trade.
libresco, -a *adj.* 1 bookish. 2 acquired from books, book learning.
libreta *s.f.* 1 notebook. 2 savings book, account book, bank book, pass book. 3 memorandum, agenda. 4 one-pound loaf (pan).
libreto *s.m.* MUS. libretto.
librillo *s.m.* 1 small book, booklette. 2 packet of cigarette paper. 3 ZOOL. third stomach (rumiantes), omasum.
libro *s.m.* 1 book. 2 volume. 3 ZOOL. third stomach, omasum. 4 record book, register. 5 notebook. 6 libretto. || 7 **colgar los libros,** to put away one's books. 8 **explicarse como un — abierto,** to speak very well and clearly. 9 **— blanco/amarillo/rojo...,** white/yellow/red paper. 10 **— canónico,** sacred book. 11 **— de caballerías,** book of knight errantry. 12 **— de caja,** cashbook. 13 **— de texto,** textbook. 14 **llevar los libros,** to keep the books.
licencia *s.f.* 1 permission, leave, licence. 2 licence, permit. || 3 **— absoluta,** discharge. 4 **— poética,** licence.
licenciado, -a *p.p.* 1 de **licenciar.** || *adj.* 2 graduated. 3 discharged, dismissed. 4 priggish. || *s.m.* y *f.* 5 graduate, bachelor. 6 lawyer. 7 discharged soldier.
licenciar *v.t.* 1 to dismisse, to confer a bachelor's degree. 2 to licence, to give permission, to authorize. 3 to discharge, to demobilize. || *v.pron.* 4 to graduate.
licenciatura *s.f.* 1 bachelor's degree. 2 degree course, university degree. 3 graduation. || 4 **— de ciencias/derecho...,** bachelor's degree in science/law.
licencioso, -a *adj.* licentious, dissolute.
liceo *s.m.* 1 literary society. 2 Lyceum (gimnasio ateniense donde funcionaba la escuela aristotélica). 3 grammar school, high school, secondary school.
licitar *v.t.* to bid for, to tender for.
lícito, -a *adj.* lawful, legal, allowed.
licor *s.m.* liquid, liqueur.
licorera *s.f.* cocktail cabinet.
licoroso, -a *adj.* aromatic.
licuante *ger.* 1 de **licuar.** || *adj.* 2 liquefying. 3 TEC. liquating.
licuar *v.t.* y *pron.* 1 to liquify. 2 to liquate.
licurgo, -a *adj.* 1 inteligent, witty, sharp. || *s.m.* 2 legislator.
lid *s.f.* 1 fight, combat, dispute, controversy. || 2 **en buena —,** in fair fight, by fair means, fairly. 2 **persona avezada en estas lides,** an old hand, someone who knows how to handle these matters.
liderato *s.m.* leadership.
líder *s.m.* y *f.* 1 leader. 2 DEP. league leader, top club.
lidia *s.f.* 1 fight, battle. 2 bullfight.
lidiador *s.m.* 1 bullfighter. 2 fighter, arguer.
lidiar *v.t.* 1 to bullfight (torear). 2 to fight against/for, to put up with, to combat, to contend with. 3 to deal with.
liebre *s.f.* 1 hare. 2 (fig.) coward, mouse. || 3 **donde/cuando menos se espera salta la —,** things always happen when you least expect them. 4 **levantar la —,** to blow the gaff, to let the cat ouf of the bag.
lied *s.m.* MUS. lied.
liendre *s.f.* nit.
lienzo *s.m.* 1 linen, canvas. 2 fabric, material, cloth. 3 painting, picture. 4 stretch (de muro, pared), wall, face, front, section. 5 handkerchief. 6 (Am.) corral, pen.
liga *s.f.* 1 band, suspender, garter. 2 league (confederación, de fútbol). 3 alloy, mixture. 4 birdlime (sustancia pegajosa). 5 mistletoe (muérdago).
ligada *s.f.* V. **ligadura.**
ligado *s.m.* 1 bond, slur, tie. 2 MUS. ligature.
ligadura *s.f.* 1 MED. ligature. 2 MAR. lashing. 3 bond, tie.
ligamento *s.m.* 1 ANAT. ligament. 2 bond, tie. 3 weave.
ligamentoso, -a *adj.* ligamentous.
ligamiento *s.m.* 1 bond, tie. 2 tying, attaching. 3 harmony.
ligar *v.t.* y *pron.* 1 tie, bind, to fasten. 2 to join, to unite, to slur (notas de música) to band together. 3 alloy, to mix. 4 to thicken (salsa). || *v.i.* 5 to mix, to blend. 6 to combine, to go well together. 7 to pick up a girl, to flirt with someone.
ligazón *s.f.* 1 bond, tie, union. 2 MAR. rib, beam, futtock.
ligereza *s.f.* 1 lightness, agility, swiftness. 2 flippancy, inconstancy, fickleness.
ligero, -a || adj. 1 light, light-weight thin. 2 swift, quick, rapid. 3 agile, quick, nimble. 4 unimportant, slight. 5 superficial, flippant, frivolous. 6 weak (bebida). || *adv.* 7 fast, rapidly, quickly, lightly, swiftly.
lignito *s.m.* lignite.
ligón *s.m.* hoe.
liguero *adj.* 1 league: *campeonato liguero = league championship.* || *s.m.* 2 suspender belt, garter belt (EE.UU.).
lija *s.f.* 1 ZOOL. dogfish. 2 sandpaper.
lijar *v.t.* to sandpaper.
lila *s.f.* 1 BOT. lilac. 2 lilac (color). 3 (fig.) fool, twit, simpleton.
liliáceo, -a *adj.* 1 liliaceous. || *s.f.pl.* 2 liliaceae.
liliputiense *adj./s.m.* y *f.* Lilliputian.
lima *s.f.* 1 file, filling. 2 BOT. lime. 3 ARQ. rafter, hip.
limaco *s.m.* slug.
limar *v.t.* 1 to file, to file down. 2 to polish.
limatón *s.m.* crossbeam, roofbeam.
limbo *s.m.* 1 limbo. 2 limb, hem, edge. || 3 **estar en el —,** to be in the clouds.
limero *s.m.* y *f.* lime seller, lime tree.
limitar *v.t.* 1 to limit, to restrict, to cut down, to reduce. || *v.i.* 2 to border on, to be adjacent to, to be bounded by. || *v.pron.* 3 to limit oneself, to restrict oneself.
límite *s.m.* 1 limit, end, ceiling. || *pl.* 2 **boundaries, borders.**
limítrofe *adj.* bordering, neighbouring.
limo *s.m.* mud, slime.
limón *s.m.* 1 lemon, lemon tree. 2 MEC. shaft. || 3 **estrujar a uno como un —,** to bleed someone white/dry.
limonada *s.f.* lemonade, lemon juice, lemon squash.
limonado *adj.* lemon, lemon-yellow.
limonar *s.m.* lemon grove.
limoncillo *s.m.* BOT. lime, small lemon.
limonero *s.m.* 1 lemon tree 2 lemon dealer. 3 shaft horse.
limosna *s.f.* 1 alms. || 2 **vivir de —,** to live on charity.
limosnear *v.i.* to beg.
limosnero, -a *adj.* 1 charitable, alms giving, beggarly. || *s.m.* 2 almoner. 3 beggar.
limpia *s.f.* 1 cleaning, cleansing. 2 clean up. || *s.m.* 3 bootblack (limpiabotas).
limpiadera *s.f.* 1 brush. 2 ploughstuff.

limpiar *v.t./i.* y *pron.* **1** to clean, to cleanse. **2** to wipe, to wipe off. **3** to weep (chimenea). **4** to shine, to polish (zapatos). **5** to pinch, to nick, to clean out. **6** (fig.) to purify, to clear up (despejar), to mop up. **7** to prune (podar).
límpido, -a *adj.* limpid, crystal-clear.
limpieza *s.f.* **1** cleanness, cleanliness, cleaning. **2** clearing. **3** fair-play, skill. **4** purity, chastity, honesty, integrity. || **5 — de sangre,** purity of blood.
limpio, -a *adj.* **1** clean, tidy, neat. **2** pure. **3** free, clear. **4** fair, clean. **5** (fam.) broke, penniless. || *adv.* **6** fairly. || **7 en —,** net, clear. **8 — de polvo y paja,** V. **polvo. 9 sacar en —,** to get something out of.
linaje *s.m.* **1** leanage, family, line. **2** genre, kind, category. **3** nobility. || **4 — humano,** the human race, mankind. **5 de otro —,** of another kind.
linaza *s.f.* linseed, flax seed.
lince *s.m.* **1** ZOOL. lynx wild cat. **2** (fig.) sharp eyed person, observant, crafty.
linchar *v.t.* to lynch.
lindar *v.i.* **1** to border, to adjoin, to be adjacent. **2** to extend to, to be bounded by. **3** ARQ. to be about on.
linde *s.m.* y *f.* boundary, limit, edge.
lindero *adj.* bordering, adjoining, adjacent.
lindeza *s.f.* **1** beauty, niceness. *pl* **2** (fam., fig.) insults, improprieties.
lindo, -a *adj.* **1** pretty, lovely, nice, charming. **2** (euf.) fine: *¡lindo amigo! = fine friend you are!* || *s.m.* **3** coxcomb, dandy. || **4 de lo —,** a lot, a great deal.
línea *s.f.* **1** line (en todos los sentidos). **2** line, cable. **3** line, leanage, family. || **2 decir/leer/haber algo entre líneas,** to say/to read something between the lines. **3 en líneas generales,** in broad outline, approximately, roughly. **4 en primera —,** front line. **5 en toda la —,** all along the line. **6 en su —,** of its kind. **7 guardar la —,** to keep/watch one's figure. **8 — poligonal,** polygonal line. **9 vencer/ganar/triunfar en toda la —,** to beat/defeat/triumph all along the line.
linear *adj.* **1** linear. || *v.t.* **2** to draw lines, to sketch, to outline.
linfa *s.f.* ANAT. lymph.
linfático, -a *adj.* lymphatic.
linfatismo *s.m.* MED. lymphatism.
linfocito *s.m.* ANAT. lymphocyte.
lingote *s.m.* **1** ingot. **2** pig (fundición), slug (imprenta). **3** gold bar, gold bullion.
lingual *adj.* lingual.
lingüista *s.m.* y *f.* linguist.
lingüística *s.f.* linguistics.
lingüístico, -a *adj.* linguistic.
linimento *s.m.* liniment.
linio *s.m.* line of trees, or plants.
lino *s.m.* **1** flax, linen. **2** flax seed, linseed.
linóleo *s.m.* linoleum, lino.
linotipia *s.f.* linotype.
linotipista *s.m.* y *f.* linotypist, linotyper.
lintel *s.m.* ARQ. linel.
linterna *s.f.* **1** lantern, lamp. **2** torch, spotlight, flashlight. **3** ARQ. lantern. || **4 — mágica,** magic, dark lantern.
linternón *s.m.* **1** large lantern. **2** MAR. poop lantern.
liño *s.m.* V. **linio.**
lío *s.m.* **1** bundle, parcel. **2** (fig.) muddle, mess, problem, trouble. **3** mess, clutter. **4** affair. **5** tale. || **6 hacerse un —,** to get into a muddle. **7 meterse en un —,** to get into trouble, to get into a jam.
lipoideo *adj.* lipoid.
lipotimia *s.f.* faint, fainting.
liquen *s.m.* BOT. lichen.
liquidar *v.t.* y *v.pron.* **1** to liquefy. **2** to settle, to pay off, to clear. **3** to liquidate, to sell off, to wind up. **4** to resolve, to clear up, to end. **5** to murder, to kill off.
líquido, -a *adj., s.* **1** liquid, fluid. **2** net profit. **3** GRAM. liquid. || **4 — imponible,** taxable income.
lira *s.f.* **1** MUS. lyre. **2** lire (moneda italiana). **3** LIT. stanza. **4** ZOOL. lyrebird. **5** ASTR. Lyra.
lírico, -a *adj.* **1** lyric, lyrical; musical. **2** (EE.UU.) fantastic, utopian. **3** dreamy (persona). || *s.f.* **4** LIT. lyrical poetry. **5** dreamer.
lirio *s.m.* **1** BOT. iris. || **2 — blanco,** white lily. **3 — de agua,** calla lily. **4 — de los valles,** lily of the valley.
lirismo *s.m.* **1** lyricism. **2** (fig.) effusiveness, gush, lyrical feeling.
lirón *s.m.* **1** ZOOL. dormouse. **2** (fig. y fam.) sleepyhead. || **3 dormir como un —,** to sleep like a log, to sleep soundly.
lirondo, -a *adj.* V. **mondo.**
lis *s.f.* **1** BOT. lily, iris. **2** fleur de lis (heráldica).
lisa *s.f.* V. **liso.**
lisiado, -a *adj.* **1** disabled, cripple. **2** wounded ex-serviceman. **3** dead tired.
lisiar *v.t.* **1** to disable, to cripple, to maim. **2** to injure, to hurt.
liso, -a *adj.* **1** flat. **2** smooth, even. **3** plain (tela), straight (pelo). **4** (Am.) shameless, brazen. || *s.m.* **5** MIN. smooth face of a rock. || **6 lisa y llanamente,** purely and simply. **7 — y llano,** plain, simple.
lisol *s.m.* lysol.
lisonja *s.f.* **1** flattery. **2** lozenge (heráldica).
lisonjeador, -ora *s.m.* y *f.* flatterer.
lisonjear *v.t.* **1** to fatter. **2** to delight, to please.
lisonjeramente *adv.* flatteringly, gratifyingly.
lista *s.f.* **1** band, stripe. **2** list, roll, register roll. **3** catalogue. || **4 — de espera,** waiting list. **5 — de correos,** poste restante. **6 pasar —,** to take/to call the register. **7 tela a listas,** striped material.
listar *v.t.* **1** to list. **2** to stripe.
listear *v.t.* to stripe.
listero *adj.* rolltaker, timekeeper, wages clerk.
listín *s.m.* **1** short list. **2** telephone directory/book.
listo, -a *adj.* **1** clever, alert, shrewd, cunning. **2** ready, prepared. || **3 ¡estamos listos!,** we're in a fine fix. **4 pasarse de —,** to be too clever by half.
listón *adj.* **1** bull with a white stripe down its back. || *s.m.* **2** lath, stripe. **3** listel, fillet. **4** ribbon. **5** DEP. bar (para saltar), pole (con pértiga).
lisura *s.f.* **1** smoothness, evenness, calmness. **2** straightness. **3** frankness, sincerity, naivety. **4** (Am.) shamelessness, brazenness.
litera *s.f.* **1** berth (barco), bunk bed, bunks. **2** litter.
literal *adj.* literal.
literalmente *adv.* literally, to the letter.
literario, -a *adj.* literary.
literatura *s.f.* **1** literature. **2** (fig.) culture.
lítico, -a *adj.* lithic.
litigar *v.t.* **1** DER. to ligitate, to go to law. **2** to contend, to dispute, to argue.
litigio *s.m.* **1** lawsuit, litigation. **2** dispute. || **3 en —,** in dispute, at sake.
litio *s.m.* lithium.
litografía *s.f.* **1** lithography. **2** lithograph.
litografiar *v.t.* to litograph.
litología *s.f.* litology.
litoral *adj.* **1** littoral, coastal. || *s.m.* **2** littoral, coast.
litosfera *s.f.* GEOL. lithosphere.
lítote *s.f.* litotes.
litri *adj.* dandified, snob, affected person.
litro *s.m.* litre.
lituano, -a *adj./s.m.* y *f.* Lithuanian.
liturgia *s.f.* REL. liturgy.
litúrgico, -a *adj.* liturgical.
liviano, -a *adj.* **1** light, slight. **2** inconstant, frivolous, fickle, trivial. **3** loose, lewd. || *s.m.* **4** (*pl.*) lungs, lights. **5** leading donkey.
lividecer *v.i.* to become livid.
lividez *s.f.* lividity, lividness.
lívido *adj.* **1** livid, pale, pallid. **2** black and blue.
living *s.m.* living room.
livor *s.m.* **1** livid colour. **2** (fig.) malignity, hatred, envy.
liza *s.f.* **1** lists, combat, contest. **2** ZOOL. mullet. **3** hemp rope. || **4 entrar en —,** to enter the lists.
lizo *s.m.* **1** heddle, headdle, leash. **2** warp, thread.
lo *art. det. n.* **1** the: *lo peor = the worst part, lo bueno del caso = the good thing, lo suyo = his.* || *pron.pers. 3.ª pers. m.* **2** him, you (usted), it, that. || **3 a —, a)** in the: *a lo ruso = in the Russian style;* **b)** like: *a lo loco = like a madman;* **c) a lo sumo,** at the most. **4 así lo creo,** I think so. **5 lo + adj.,** how + adj.: *¡lo fuertes que eran! = how strong they were!* **6 lo de, a)** the affair of the business about; **b)** *— inf., the idea of.* **lo que,** what: *lo que digo = what I say.* **7 lo que es eso,** as for that. **8 por —,** because of. **9 todo — + adj.** as + *adj.* + as: *todo lo divertido que hubiera podido = as funny as it could have been.*
loa *s.f.* **1** praise. **2** prologue. **3** playlet. **4** elegy, eulogy.
loable *adj.* laudable, praiseworthy.
loar *v.t.* to praise.
loba *s.f.* **1** she-wolf. **2** ridge. **3** soutane, cassock.

lobagante *s.m.* ZOOL. lobster (bogavante).
lobanillo *s.m.* 1 cyst, wen. 2 BOT. gall.
lobera *s.f.* wolf's lair.
lobero, -a *adj.* 1 wolf, wolfish. || *s.m.* 2 wolf hunter.
lobezno *s.m.* wolf cub.
lobo *adj.* 1 (Am.) shrewd, cunning, shy. || *s.m.* 2 wolf. 3 loach (pez). 4 iron for climbing walls. 5 (Am.) fox, coyote. || 6 **el — feroz,** the big bad wolf. 7 **estar como boca de —,** to be pitch-dark. 8 **— cerval, a)** lynx; **b)** shark, profiteer. 9 **— de mar,** old salt, sea dog. 10 **meterse en la boca del —,** to put one's head into the lion's mouth. 11 **ser un — con piel de cordero,** to be a wolf in sheep's clothing. 12 **ser lobos de la misma camada,** to be birds of a feather, to be tarred with the same brush.
lóbrego, -a *adj.* 1 gloomy, dark, murky. 2 gloomy, sad.
lóbulo *s.m.* lobe, lobule.
lobuno *adj.* wolf, wolfish, wolflike.
locación *s.f.* lease.
local *adj.* 1 local. || *s.m.* 2 place, site, scene, rooms. 3 premises, headquarters. || 4 **en el —,** on the spot, on the premises. 5 **equipo —,** home team.
localidad *s.f.* 1 locallity, location, place. 2 seat, ticket. || 3 **no hay localidades,** house full, sold out. 4 **reserva de localidades,** booking, advanced booking.
localizar *v.t.* y *pron.* 1 to find, to locate. 2 to situate, to track down, to localize. 3 to place, to site: *aquí se va a localizar el bloque de pisos = the block of flats is to be sited here.* 4 to spot, to localize.
locatis *s.m.* y *f.* *(fam.)* madcap, nutcase.
locativo, -a *adj.* 1 renting, lettin, leasing. 2 GRAM. locative.
locaut V. **lock-out.**
locero *s.m.* potter (alfarero).
loción *s.f.* lotion, wash.
lock-out *s.m.* lock-out.
loco, -a *adj.* 1 mad, crazy, insane. 2 fantastic, ridiculous: *precios locos = fantastic prices.* 3 huge, tremendous: *prisa loca = tremendous rush.* 4 MEC. free, loose. || *s.m.* y *f.* 5 madman, madwoman, lunatic. || 6 **a lo —,** wildly, lightly, helter skelter. 7 **a tontas y a locas,** without rhyme or reason. 8 **cada — con su tema,** everyone has his hobbyhorse. 9 **estar — por,** to be mad about. 10 **— de atar/más — que una cabra,** as mad as a hatter, as mad as a March hare. 11 **tener una suerte loca,** to be ever so lucky, to be fantastically lucky.
locomoción *s.f.* locomotion.
locomotora *adj.* 1 locomotor, locomotive. || *s.f.* 2 engine.
locomotriz *adj.* y *s.f.* locomotor.
locuacidad *s.f.* loquacity, talkativeness.
locuaz *adj.* loquatious, talkative, voluble.
locución *s.f.* 1 phrase, expression, turn of phrase, locution. 2 GRAM. phrase.
locuelo, -a *adj./s.m.* y *f.* madcap, daft.
locura *s.f.* 1 madness, insanity, lunacy. 2 act of madness, crazy thing. 3 mad passion, wild enthusiasm. || *pl.* 4 folly. || 5 **con —,** madly. 6 **hacer locuras,** to do foolish things. 7 **¡qué —!,** it's madness! 8 **querer con —,** to be crazy about.
locutor, -ora *s.m.* y *f.* announcer, commentator, presenter, newscaster, newsreader.
locutorio *s.m.* 1 locutory, parlour, visiting room. 2 booth, telephone box.
lodo *s.m.* 1 mud, mire, sludge.
loess *s.m.* GEOL. loess, löss.
logarítmico, -a *adj.* logarithmic.
logaritmo *s.m.* 1 MAT. logarithm. || 2 **tabla de logaritmos,** logarithm table.
logia *s.f.* lodge.
lógicamente *adv.* logically.
lógico, -a *adj.* 1 logical. || *s.m.* 2 logician. || *s.f.* 3 logic. || 4 **como es —,** naturally, of course. 5 **es — que...,** it is natural that, it stands to reason that.
logomaquia *s.f.* logomachy.
lograr *v.t.* 1 to get, to obtain, to attain. 2 to twin, to achieve, to gain. 3 to succed in, to manage to. 4 to satisfy, to fulfill, to realize. || *v.pron.* 5 to be successful, to turn out well/successfully. || 6 **¡no lo lograrán!,** they won't get away with it.
logrero, -a *s.m.* y *f.* 1 moneylender, profiteer, usurer. 2 sponger, parasite.
logro *s.m.* 1 achievement, accomplishment. 2 realization, satisfaction, fulfilment. 3 winning, success. 4 gain, profit, usury.
loísmo *s.m.* use of **lo** instead of **le** as indirect object of the personal pronoun.
loma *s.f.* 1 hillock, low ridge, rise, long little hill. 2 eminence, slope. || 2 **en la — del diablo,** (Am.) at the back of beyond.
lombarda *s.f.* 1 red cabbage. 2 lombard (cañón).
lombardo, -a *adj./s.m.* y *f.* Lombard.
lombriguera *s.f.* earthworm hole.
lombriz *s.f.* 1 earthworm. || 2 **— solitaria,** tapeworm.
lomera *s.f.* 1 backband. 2 ridge.
lomillo *s.m.* cross-stich.
lomo *s.m.* 1 ANAT. back. 2 loin (carne). 3 AGR. balk, ridge. 4 spine, back (libro). 5 shoulder (montaña), gradient.
lona *s.f.* 1 sailcloth, canvas. 2 bigtop (circo). 3 (Am.) sackcloth.
loncha *s.f.* 1 slice. 2 slab (piedra).
lonchería *s.f.* restaurant.
londri *s.f.* (Am.) launderette, laundry.
longanimidad *s.f.* forbearance, magnanimity, longanimity.
longaniza *s.f.* 1 sausage. || 2 **atar los perros con —,** money does not grow on trees. 3 **hay más días que longanizas,** there's all the time in the world.
longevidad *s.f.* longevity.
longevo, -a *adj.* long-lived, longevous.
longitud *s.f.* 1 length. 2 GEOG. longitude.
lonja *s.f.* 1 slice, rasher. 2 commodity exchange, market exchange. 3 wool warehouse. 4 grocer's shop. 5 ARQ. porch, raised porch, vestibule. 6 leather strap, tip of a whiplash.
lonjear *v.t.* 1 to cut into strips. 2 (Am.) to whip. 3 to store, to warehouse.
lontananza *s.f.* 1 ART. background. || 2 **en —,** in the distance, far away, far off.
loor *s.m.* praise.
loquear *v.i.* 1 to act like a fool, to play the fool, to talk nonesense. 2 to make merry, to have a high old time, to frolic.
loquera *s.f.* 1 padded cell. 2 madhouse, lunatic asylum.
loquero, -a *s.m.* y *f.* 1 lunatic asylum nurse. 2 (Am.) confusion, pandemonium.
lord *s.m.* 1 Lord. || 2 **Cámara de los lores,** House of Lords.
loriga *s.f.* 1 lorica, suit of armour, coat of mail. 2 horse armour. 3 TEC. band.
loro *adj.* 1 dark brown. || *s.m.* 2 ZOOL. parrot. 3 cherry laurel. 4 (fam.) hag.
lorza *s.f.* tuck.
los *art. det. m.pl.* 1 the: *los Brown = the Browns.* || *pron.pers. m.pl.* 2 them. || 3 **— que,** those which/who, the ones: *los que estábais aquí = those of you who were here.* 4 **— de, a)** *los de mi madre = those of my mother;* **b)** *los de María = Mary's.*
losa *s.f.* 1 stone slab, paving stone, flagstone, tile. 2 grave stone, tombstone.
losar *v.t.* to tile, to pave, to flag.
lote *s.m.* 1 share, portion. 2 lot, tombola prize. 3 (Am.) clot, idiot.
lotería *s.f.* 1 lotery. || 2 **tocarle a uno la —,** to strike it lucky.
lotero, -a *s.m.* y *f.* lottery-ticket seller.
lotificar *v.t.* (Am.) to divide into lots.
loto *s.m.* BOT. lotus.
loza *s.f.* 1 earthenware, pottery. 2 crockery. || 3 **fregar/hacer la —,** to wash up, to do the washing. 4 **— fina,** china.
lozanamente *adv.* 1 luxuriantly, profusely, in a lively way, vigorously, rankly, in a sprightly way. 3 haughtily, proudly.
lozanear *v.i.* to flourish, to do well, to be full of life.
lozanía *s.f.* 1 luxuriance, lushness. 2 freshness. 3 vigour, robustness. 4 liveliness, sprightliness. 5 haughtiness, pride.
lozano, -a *adj.* 1 BOT. luxuriant, fresh, rank, profuse, lush. 2 vigorous, lively, sprightly, lusty. 3 haughty, proud.
lubigante *s.m.* ZOOL. lobster.
lubina *s.f.* ZOOL. bass.
lubricación *s.f.* lubrication.
lubricante *adj.* 1 lubricant, lubricating. || *s.m.* 2 lubricant.
lubricar *v.t.* to lubricate.
lubricativo, -a *adj.* lubricant.
lubricidad *s.f.* 1 lubricity, lewdness, lasciviousness. 2 slipperiness, lubricity.
lúbrico, -a *adj.* 1 lubricous, lewd, lascivious. 2 slippery, lubricous.
lubrificante V. **lubricante.**
lubrificar V. **lubricar.**
lucerna *s.f.* 1 chandelier, skylight. 2 glowworm.
lucero *s.m.* 1 bright star, evening/morning star, Venus. 2 window shutter. 3 lustre, brilliance. 4 star (lunar en la frente de algunos cuadrúpedos).
lucidez *s.f.* 1 lucidity, clarity. 2 (Am.) brilliance.
lucido, -a *p.p.* 1 de **lucir.** || *adj.* 2 brilliant, successful, sumptuous, magnificent, elegant. 3 generous, splendid. 4

bonny. || **5 estamos –,** we're in a fine mess!
lúcido, -a *adj.* lucid, clear.
luciérnaga *s.f.* ZOOL. glowworm.
lucifer *s.m.* 1 Lucifer. 2 demon. 3 Venus.
luciferino, -a *adj.* satanic.
lucífero, -a *adj.* 1 luciferous. || *s.m.* 2 lucifer. 3 Venus.
lucio, -a *adj.* 1 shining, bright, glossy. || *s.m.* 2 luce, pike.
lucir *v.i.* 1 to shine, to give off light. 2 to glitter, to sparkle, to gleam. 3 (fig.) to shine (sobresalir). 4 to look nice. 5 to be of benefit, to turn out to advantage, to do good. || *v.i.* 6 to iluminate, to light up. 7 to show off, to cut a dash, to make a show of, to display, to sport. 8 to plaster (enlucir). || *v.pron.* 9 to dress up, to drese elegantly, to deck oneself out. 10 to come out brilliantly/with flying colours, to shine, to excel, to be brilliant, to be a success, to distinguish oneself. 11 to make a fool of oneself, to make a mess of things. || **12 lucirse en un examen,** to pass with flying colours. **13 ¡si que nos hemos lucido!,** we've really gone and don it now, that a mess we've made!
lucrar *v.t.* 1 to gain, to obtain, to win. || *v.pron.* 2 to profit, to enrich oneself, to do well out of a deal, to feather one's nest.
lucrativo, -a *adj.* 1 lucrative, profitable, remunerative, profitmaking. || **2 institución no lucrativa,** non-profit making institution.
lucro *s.m.* gain, profit, benefit.
luctuosamente *adv.* sorrowfully, mournfully, sadly.
luctuoso, -a *adj.* sorrowful, sad mournful, tragic.
lucubración *s.f.* lucubration.
lucubrar *v.t.* to lucubrate.
lúcuma *s.f.* 1 BOT. (Am.) a pear shaped fruit. 2 (fam.) head.
lúcumo *s.m.* Peruvian fruit tree.
lucha *s.f.* 1 fight, battle, conflict, war. 2 struggle, strife. 3 (fig.) dispute, contest, contention. 4 DEP. wrestling. || **5 – de clases,** class struggle. **6 – de la cuerda,** tug-of-war. **7 – por la existencia,** struggle for survival.
ludibrio *s.m.* 1 shame, derision, mockery. 2 contempt, scorn, laughingstock.
lúdicro, -a *adj.* ludicrous, sportive, jocular.
luego *adv.* 1 then, afterwards. 2 then, next. 3 later, later on. 4 soon, at once, straightaway. || *conj.* 5 therefore. 6 (Am.) sometimes, at times. 7 near, close by. || **8 desde –,** of course, naturally. **9 hasta –,** see you later, so long (EE.UU.). **10 – que,** as soon as.
luengo, -a *adj.* long.
lugar *s.m.* 1 place, spot. 2 room. 3 village, locality. 4 part, passage. 5 position, post, office. 6 time, moment. 7 cause, reason, motive. || **8 dar – a,** to give rise to, to provoke. **9 dejar en mal –,** to let someone down. **10 en – de,** instead of. **11 en último –,** finally, last of all, lastly. **12 fuera de –,** out of place. **13 hacer –,** to make room. **14 – común,** commonplace, topic. **15 – de predición,** den of iniquity. **16 poner las cosas en su –,** to put things straight. **17 sin – a dudas,** without any doubt. **18 tener –,** to take place. **19 yo en tu –,** if I were you.
lugareño, -a *s.m.* y *f.* villager, countryman.
lugarteniente *s.m.* deputy, lieutenant.
lugre *s.m.* MAR. lugger.
lúgubre *adj.* lugubrious, dismal.
luis *s.m.* louis (moneda).
lujo *s.m.* 1 luxury, sumptuousness, lavishness. 2 profusion, wealth, abundance. || **3 con – de,** with great abundance of. **4 no poder permitirse el –,** to be unable to afford the luxury of. **5 vivir con todo –,** to live in the lap of luxury.
lujosamente *adv.* luxuriously, sumptuously, lavishly.
lujoso, -a *adj.* luxurious, sumptuous, lavish.
lujuria *s.f.* 1 lust, lechery, lust, lewdness. 2 profusion, abundance.
lulú *s.m.* Pomeranian (perro).
lumbago *s.m.* MED. lumbago.
lumbar *adj.* ANAT. lumbar.
lumbre *s.f.* 1 fire. 2 glow, light. 3 luminary. 4 brilliance, brightness, radiance. 5 tinder box, sparks. 6 ARQ. light. 7 toe (de herradura). || **8 al amor de la –,** by the fire. **9 ¿tienes –?,** have you got a light? **9 ser la – de los ojos de alguien,** to be the apple of someone's eyes.
lumbrera *s.f.* 1 luminary, light, skylight. 2 MEC. vent port. 3 authority.
luminar *s.m.* luminary.
luminaria *s.f.* 1 light, lantern. 2 altar light.
luminiscencia *s.f.* luminiscence.
luminoso, -a *adj.* 1 luminous, bright. 2 brilliant, crystal-clear.
luminotecnia *s.f.* lighting, illuminating engineering.
luminotécnico, -a *s.m.* y *f.* lighting/illuminating engineer.
lumpen-proletariado *s.m.* lumpen-proletariat.
luna *s.f.* 1 moon. 2 moonlight. 3 mirror glass. 4 window pane. || **5 a la – de Valencia,** in the lurch. **6 armario de –,** wardrove with a mirror. **7 estar en la –,** to be miles away. **8 – creciente,** waxing moon, crescent moon, first quarter. **9 – de miel,** honey moon. **10 – llena,** full moon. **11 – menguante,** waning moon, last quarter. **12 – nueva,** new moon. **13 media –, a)** half-moon; **b)** Crescent, Turkish Empire; **c)** demilune; **d)** butcher's curved knife. **14 pedir la –,** to ask the earth. **15 vivir en la –,** to have one's head in the clouds.
lunar *adj.* 1 lunar. || *s.m.* 2 mole, spot, stain. 3 flaw, blemish, blot.
lunático, -a *adj.* lunatic, whimsical.
lunes *s.m.* Monday.
luneta *s.f.* 1 lens, glass. 2 half-moon shape, crescent-shaped object. 3 stall, orchestra seat. 4 rear window.
lúnula *s.f.* 1 MAT. lunule, lunula, lune. 2 half-moon lunule.
lupa *s.f.* magnifying glass.
lupanar *s.m.* brothel.
lúpulo *s.m.* BOT. hop.
lusitanismo o **lusismo** *s.m.* Portuguese saying.
lusitano, -a *adj./s.m.* y *f.* lusitanian.
lustrabotas *s.m.* bootblack.
lustrador *s.m.* 1 polisher. 2 bootblack.
lustrar *v.t.* to polish, to shine, to lustrate.
lustre *adj.* 1 lustre, shine, gloss, polish. 2 sheen, gloss (telas). 3 splendour, distinction, glory. 4 shoe polish. || **5 dar – a,** to put a shine on. **6 para su mayor –,** to his greater glory.
lustro *s.m.* 1 lustre, lustrum, period of five years. 2 hanging lamp, chandelier.
luteína *s.f.* BOT. lutein.
luteranismo *s.m.* luteranism.
luto *s.m.* 1 mourning. 2 grief, sorrow. || **3 llevar – por,** to be in mourning of.
lutoso, -a *adj.* sorrowful, sad, mournful.
lutria *s.f.* otter (nutria).
lux *s.m.* FIS. lux.
luxación *s.f.* MED. luxation, dislocation.
luz *s.f.* 1 light, daylight, daytime, day; sparkle. 2 light, lamp, lightning, electricity, electric current. 3 electricity bill. 4 ARQ. light, window, opening, aperture; span, space. 5 (fig.) light, luminary, guiding light. 6 news, information. 7 culture, enlightenment, intelligence. || **8 a la – de,** in the light of. **9 año de –,** light year. **10 a primera –,** at day break, at first light. **11 arrojar/echar – sobre,** to shed/to throw/to cast light on. **12 a todas luces,** obviously, evidently, clearly. **13 claro como la – del día,** as clear as daylight. **14 dar a –,** to give birth, to publish. **15 de pocas luces/corto de luces,** dim, stupid. **16 entre dos luces,** at day break; at dusk, in the twilight. **17 gusano de –,** glowworm. **18 la – de sus ojos,** the apple of his eyes. **19 luces de carretera,** full beam. **20 luces de cruce,** dipped headlights. **21 – intermitente,** indicator, flasher, winker. **22 sacar a la –,** to bring out, to publish. **23 tener pocas luces,** to be dim-witted, not to be very bright. **24 traje de luces,** bullfighter's costume. **25 ver la –,** to see the light of day, to draw one's first breath.

ll, LL *s.f.* ll, LL decimocuarta letra del alfabeto español (no existe en el alfabeto inglés).

llaga *s.f.* 1 MED. sore, ulcer; wound. 2 (fig.) wound; affliction.

llagar *v.t.* to wound, to injure.

llama *s.f.* 1 flame. 2 blaze (llamarada). 3 (fig.) passion. 4 ZOOL. llama. || **5 en llamas,** burning, in flames.

llamada *s.f.* 1 call: *llamada telefónica = telephone call.* 2 call, appeal (llamamiento). 3 knock, ring (a la puerta). 4 ring (de teléfono). 5 gesture, signal (ademán de llamada). 6 FILOL. reference mark (en un texto). 7 MIL. call; fall-in.

llamado, -a *adj.* 1 so-called: *un llamado liberal = a so-called liberal.* || *s.m.* 2 (Am.) call, calling.

llamador, -a *s.m.* y *f.* 1 caller. 2 knocker (a la puerta). || *s.m.* 3 door bell (timbre). 4 doorknocker (aldaba).

llamamiento *s.m.* 1 call, calling. 2 appeal, summons (a las masas). 3 calling together, convocation.

llamar *v.t.* 1 to call. 2 to call, to call up, to ring up (por teléfono). 3 to summon (convocar). 4 to call, to ask for (a alguien para que acuda). 5 to invoke, to call upon (invocar). 6 to name (poner de nombre; denominar). 7 to appeal (hacer un llamamiento). 8 to beckon (por medio de señales). 9 to attract (la atención, etc.). || *v.i.* 10 to knock, to ring. || *v.pron.* 11 to be called. 12 (Am.) to break one's promise. || **13 ¿cómo te llamas?,** what is your name? **14 — a filas,** MIL. to call up. **15 — a la puerta,** to knock at the door. **16 mandar —,** to send for. **17 ¿quién llama?,** who is it?

llamarada *s.f.* 1 sudden flame, flare-up. 2 (fig.) flushing, flush (en la cara). 3 (fig.) outburst (arrebato).

llamativo, -a *adj.* 1 gaudy, loud, flashy, showy: *una camisa llamativa = a loud shirt.* 2 striking, attractive.

llameante *adj.* flaming, blazing.

llamear *v.i.* 1 to flame, to blaze. 2 to flare, to flare up.

llanada V. **llanura.**

llanamente *adv.* 1 simply. 2 clearly. 3 frankly, sincerely.

llanero, -a *s.m.* y *f.* (Am.) plainsman (hombre); plainswoman (mujer); plaindweller.

llaneza *s.f.* 1 simplicity; plainness; sincerity. 2 informality.

llano, -a *adj.* 1 even, smooth, level, flat: *paisaje llano = flat countryside.* 2 frank, straightforward. 3 (fig.) simple, natural (personas, modales). 4 informal. 5 common: *pueblo llano = common people.* 6 GRAM. paroxytone. || *s.m.* 7 plain, flatland, level ground. || *s.f.* 8 TEC. mason's trowel. 9 plain (llanura).

llanta *s.f.* 1 rim (de automóvil, bicicleta, etc.). 2 hoop (de carro). 3 flat piece of iron. 4 (Am.) tyre, tyre casing. 5 (Am.) large sunshade (utilizada en los mercados). 6 BOT. type of cabbage.

llantén *s.m.* BOT. plantain.

llantera V. **llantina.**

llantina *s.f.* (fam.) blubber.

llanto *s.m.* 1 crying, weeping. 2 (fig.) tears, flood of tears. 3 (fig.) lamentation.

llanura *s.f.* 1 evenness, flatness. 2 plain, extensive plain; prairie, flatlands.

llar (p.u.) *s.m.* 1 hearth (hogar, fogón). || **2 llares,** pothook.

llave *s.f.* 1 key. 2 tap, faucet, cock (grifo). 3 ELEC. key, switch (interruptor). 4 (fig.) key (clave). 5 DEP. lock, hold (lucha). 6 MUS. stop (de órgano); key (de instrumentos de viento). 7 MUS. clef (clave). 8 brace (en imprenta). 9 TEC. spanner. || **10 bajo siete llaves,** under lock and key. **11 cerrar con —,** to lock. **12 echar la —,** to lock up. **13 — de contacto,** MEC. ignition key. **14 — inglesa,** monkey-wrench, adjustable spanner. **15 — maestra,** master key, skeleton key.

llavero, -a *s.m.* y *f.* 1 keeper of the keys. 2 key maker. || *s.m.* 3 key ring. 4 turnkey (en una cárcel).

llegada *s.f.* arrival; coming.

llegar *v.i.* 1 to arrive (a un destino). 2 to come: *la paz llegará = peace will come.* 3 to reach; to attain: *no llegará a los ochenta = he will not reach eighty.* 4 [— *inf.*] to manage to, to succeed in: *llegó a hacerlo = he succeeded in doing it.* 5 to come to, to reach (a una conclusión, a un acuerdo). 6 to reach: *esta escalera no llegará = this ladder won't reach.* 7 to anount to (ascender a una cantidad). 8 to be enough, to suffice (bastar). 9 to last (durar). 10 to get to (conseguir). 11 to have time to: *llegarás a aburrirte = you will have time to get bored.* || *v.t.* 12 to bring up, to draw up (acercar). || *v.pron.* 13 to come near to, to approach, to go to (acercarse a). 14 to go round (ir a casa de): *me llegaré a casa de Juan = I'll go round to John's.* || **15 — a las manos,** to come to blows. **16 — a saber,** to find out. **17 — a ser,** to become.

llenar *v.t.* 1 to fill: *llenó mi vaso = he filled my glass.* 2 to stuff: *llenó el pote de alubias = she stuffed the pot with beans.* 3 (fig.) to fill: *me llenó de ira = it filed me with rage.* 4 to occupy, to take up (un espacio). 5 to fulfil (cumplir). 6 (fig.) to shower, to overwhelm; to load (colmar). 7 to please, to satisfy (satisfacer). 8 to fill in (rellenar). 9 to pervade (impregnar). || *v.pron.* 10 to get crowded (un sitio). 11 to fill up, to overeat, to stuff oneself (hartarse, atiborrarse). 12 [**— de**] to get filled with, to get covered with.

lleno, -a *adj.* 1 full: *el vaso está lleno = the glass is full.* 2 crowded (de gente). 3 replete, complete. 4 full, full up (un cine, etc.). 5 full, pregnant. 6 full up (atiborrado). 7 plump (regordete). 8 covered (cubierto). || *s.m.* **9** full house, sell out (en teatro). **10** ASTR. full moon. **11** fullness, abundance. || *s.f.* **12** spate (crecida de un río).

llevadero, -a *adj.* tolerable, bearable.

llevar *v.t.* **1** to take: *llévala a casa = take her home.* **2** to carry (transportar). **3** to wear (llevar puesto). **4** to bear (soportar). **5** to charge (cobrar). **6** FIN. to keep (libros, contabilidad). **7** to lead: *esta discusión no os llevará a ninguna parte = this discussion won't lead you anywhere.* **8** to lead: *lleva una vida de perros = he leads a dog's life.* **9** to carry off (un premio). **10** to run, to manage (un negocio, etc.). **11** to have: *esta blusa no lleva botones = this blouse doesn't have buttons.* **12** to take (tiempo): *me llevará dos horas = it will take me two hours.* **13** to bear (un nombre). **14** to take care of (hacerse cargo de). **15** MAT. to carry (un número). || *v.pron.* **16** to take away, to carry away. **17** to be fashionable (estar de moda). || *v.i.* **18** to go, to lead (conducir). || **19 dejarse — por,** to be carried away with; to be influenced by. **20 — a cabo,** to carry out. **21 — adelante algo,** to go ahead with, to carry out. **22 — la delantera,** to lead. **23 llevarse bien,** to get along (well), to get on. **24 llevarse las de perder,** to look like losing, to be in a bad way. **25 llevarse lo mejor,** to get the best part of. **26 llevarse mal,** not to get along, to be on bad terms. **27 — ventaja,** to be ahead. **28 — y traer,** to go around gossiping.

lloradera V. **llorera.**

lloraduelos *s.m.* y *f.* (fig.) sniveller.

llorar *v.i.* **1** to cry, to weep. **2** to water (los ojos). **3** to lament: *llorar a un amigo = to lament for a friend.* **4** (fig.) to drip (gotear). || *v.t.* **5** to weep, to cry. **6** to mourn, to lament: *llora la muerte de su hijo = she laments the death of her son.* **7** to bewail (lamentar).

llorera *s.f.* (fam.) blubbering, crying.

llorica *s.m.* y *f.* (fam.) whining; crybaby.

lloriquear *v.i.* to whimper, to whine, to snivel.

lloriqueo *s.m.* whimper, whining.

llorón, -ona *adj.* **1** wheeping, snivelling. **2** whining. || *s.m.* **3** weeper; crybaby. || *s.f.* **4** weeper; hired mourner (plañidera). || **5 sauce —,** BOT. weeping willow.

lloroso, -a *adj.* tearful; weeping; sad.

llorosamente *adv.* tearfully.

llover *v.imp.* **1** to rain: *¿llueve? = is it raining?* **2** (fig.) to shower. || **3 como quien oye —,** (fig.) quite unmoved. **4 — a cántaros,** to pour, to rain cats and dogs. **5 llueva o truene,** (fig.) rain or shine. **6 nunca llueve a gusto de todos,** (fig.) you can't please everybody.

llovizna *s.f.* drizzle.

lloviznar *v.imp.* to drizzle.

lluvia *s.f.* **1** rain: *bajo la lluvia = in the rain.* **2** rainfall (cantidad de lluvia). **3** rainwater (agua de lluvia). **4** (fig.) shower (de golpes, piedras, regalos, etc.). **5** (fig.) hail (de balas, flechas, etc.). **6** (fig.) mass, heap (montón, gran cantidad). || **7 — ligera,** shower. **8 — menuda,** drizzle. **9 — radioactiva,** fallout.

lluvioso, -a *adj.* wet, rainy: *un día lluvioso = a rainy day.*

m, M *s.f.* m, M (décimoquinta letra del alfabeto español)
macabro, -a *adj.* 1 macabre. 2 (fig.) sadistic (sádico). 3 sordid (sórdido).
macaco, -a *adj.* 1 (Am.) ugly, grotesque (feo). || *s.m.* 2 ZOOL. macaque (mono).
macana *s.f.* 1 club (palo pesado y corto). 2 pole-axe (arma). 3 bother, nuisance, (fam.) drag (engorro). 4 joke (broma). 5 (Am.) blunder, error (error). 6 (Am.) bad job, (fam.) botch (chapucería).
macanada *s.f.* 1 nonsense, ridiculousness (tonterías). 2 stupidity, idiocy, folly (estupidez).
macanazo *s.m.* 1 blow with a club (golpe dado con una macana). 2 (Am.) nonsense, ridiculousness (disparate).
macaneador, -a *adj.* 1 (Am.) deceitful, tricky (charlatán). 2 lying (que miente). || *s.m.* y *f.* 3 charlatan, trickster (charlatán). 4 liar (mentiroso).
macanudo, -a *adj.* 1 (Am.) terrific, fantastic, great (estupendo). 2 admirable (admirable). 3 surprising (sorprendente).
macarrón *s.m.* 1 macaroon (mostachón). 2 MAR. bulwark. 3 ELEC. plastic insulation (tubo de plástico). || *pl.* 3 macaroni (pasta).
macarrónico, -a *adj.* macaronic.
macarronismo *s.m.* macaronic style (estilo).
macedonia *s.f.* 1 fruit salad (de frutas). 2 vegetable salad (de verduras).
mecedónico, -a o **macedonio, -a** *adj./s.m.* y *f.* Macedonian.
maceración o **maceramiento** *s.f.* y *m.* maceration.
macerar *v.t.* 1 to soften, to macerate (ablandar). || *v.t.* y *pron.* 2 to mortify oneself (mortificar el cuerpo).
macero *s.m.* mace-bearer (portador de una maza).
maceta *s.f.* 1 flowerpot (para flores). 2 mallet (mazo corto).
macetero *s.m.* flowerpot stand (soporte de macetas).
macetón *s.m.* tub (para flores).
macilento, -a *adj.* emaciated, gaunt (demacrado).
macillo *s.m.* MUS. hammer (que golpea las cuerdas del piano).
macizamente *adv.* 1 massively. 2 solidly.
macizo, -a *adj.* 1 compact, solid (compacto). 2 massive (masivo). || *s.m.* 3 solid, mass (masa). 4 GEOG. massif (grupo de montañas). 5 group (de edificios). 6 BOT. bed, plot (conjunto de plantas). 7 stretch (pared).
macro *prefijo* macro.
macrobiótica, -o *s.f.* y *m.* macrobiotics.
macrocefalia *s.f.* MED. macrocephaly.
macrocéfalo, -a *adj.* MED. macrocephalic.
macrocosmo *s.m.* macrocosm.
macrodáctilo, -a *adj.* macrodactyl.
macrofotografía *s.f.* macrophotography.
macroscópico, -a *adj.* macroscopic.
macrosmático, -a *adj.* macrosmatic.
macuco, -a *adj.* 1 (Am.) cunning, crafty (taimado). 2 (Am.) astute, clever (astuto).
mácula *s.f.* 1 stain (mancha). 2 trick (engaño). || 3 ASTR. **— solar,** sunspot.
maculatura *s.f.* faulty sheet (pliego inservible).
macuto *s.m.* rucksack, haversack (mochila).
machacador, -a *adj.* 1 crushing (que machaca). 2 grinding (que muele).
machacadora *s.f.* MEC. crushing machine, crusher.
machacante *s.m.* MIL. sergeant's orderly.
machacar *v.t.* 1 to crush, to mash (aplastar). 2 to grind (moler). 3 to smash, to crush (un enemigo). 4 to cut, to slice (precios, presupuesto). 5 to crush, to flatten (en un debate). || *v.i.* 6 to persist, to go on (porfiar insistentemente): *machacar en negar algo = to persist in denying something.* 7 to swot (estudiar mucho).
machacón, -a *adj.* 1 tiring, tiresome (fastidioso). || *s.m.* y *f.* 2 nuisance, bore (pesado).
machaconería o **machaquería** *s.f.* tediousness, tiresomeness (de machacón).
machamartillo, a —, *loc.adv.* with conviction (con convicción); consistently (con consistencia); firmly (firmemente).
machado, -a *adj.* (Am.) drunk (borracho).
machar *v.t.* 1 V. **machacar.** || *v.pron.* 2 to get drunk (emborracharse).
machete *s.m.* 1 machete (arma blanca). 2 board rubber (borrador).
machetero *s.m.* 1 path opener (que despeja los pasos). 2 cane cutter (que corta cañas). 3 (Am.) guerrilla, guerrilla fighter (guerrillero).
machificar *v.t.* (Am.) to trick, to take in (burlar).
machimbarse *v.pron.* to live together, to cohabit (amancebarse).
machismo *s.m.* sexism, machismo.
macho *s.m.* 1 BIOL. male (animal del sexo masculino). 2 ZOOL. mule (mulo). 3 MEC. pin, peg (clavija). 4 ELEC. plug (de un enchufe). 5 ARQ. buttress (machón). 6 sledgehammer (mazo grande de hierro). 7 square anvil (yunque cuadrado). 8 anvil block (banco de yunque). 9 (fam.) tough guy, bully-boy (hombre fuerte). || *adj.* 10 BIOL. male: *ratón macho = male rat.* 11 (fig.) tough, strong (fuerte): *es muy macho = he's a real tough guy.* 12 TEC. male. 13 (fam.) stupid, thick (tonto).
machón *s.m.* ARQ. buttress (pilar).
machona *s.f.* (Am.) mannish woman (marimacho).
machote *adj.* 1 manly, tough (muy hombre). || *s.m.* 2 tough guy, he-man (muy hombre). 3 mallet (mazo).
machuelo *s.m.* BIOL. germ (germen).
madama *s.f.* brothel keeper.

madeja *s.f.* 1 hank (de madera). 2 mop of hair (mata de pelo). 3 loafer, (fam.) bummer (persona perezosa). 4 hotchpotch, jumble (mezcla).
madera *s.f.* 1 wood: *una madera = a piece of wood.* 2 timber (para construir). 3 (fig.) nature, character, stuff (disposición). 4 horn (materia del casco de las caballerías). 5 DEP. wood (palo de golf). || 6 **de –,** wooden. 7 **– de deriva,** driftwood. 8 **– dura,** hardwood. 9 **tener –,** to have it in one. 10 **tocar –,** to touch wood.
maderable *adj.* timber-yielding.
maderada *s.f.* raft.
maderaje o **maderamen** *s.m.* 1 carpentry, woodwork (carpintería). 2 wood, timber (madera).
maderero, -a *adj.* 1 wood. || *s.m.* y *f.* 2 timber merchant (el que comercia con la madera). 3 (fig.) dope, clot, oaf (persona inepta).
madrastra *s.f.* 1 stepmother (madre nueva). 2 cruel mother (mala madre).
madraza *s.f.* indulgent mother.
madre *s.f.* 1 mother: *Madre de Dios = Mother of God.* 2 REL. mother: *madre superiora = mother superior.* 3 ANAT. womb (matriz). 4 (fig.) origin (origen de una cosa). 5 bed (cauce de un río). 6 dregs (heces del vino, etc.). 7 main irrigation ditch (acequia principal). 8 main sewer (alcantarilla maestra). 9 **día de la –,** Mother's Day. 10 **– adoptiva,** foster mother. 11 **buque –,** mother ship. 12 **– de leche,** wet nurse. 13 **¡– mía!,** my God! 14 **– política,** mother-in-law. 15 **sacar de – a uno,** to madden someone. 16 **salirse de –, a)** to overflow (río); **b)** to go over the top; to go over the limit (exceder los límites).
madreña *s.f.* clog, wooden shoe (almadreña).
madreperla *s.f.* 1 mother-of-pearl 2 pearl oyster (ostra)
madrépora *s.f.* ZOOL. white coral, madrepore (pólipo).
madrepórico *adj.* ZOOL. madreporic.
madrero, -a *adj.* 1 mother's boy (chico). 2 mother's girl (chica).
madreselva *s.f.* BOT. honey suckle.
madrigal *s.m.* LIT. y MUS. madrigal.
madrigalesco, -a *adj.* 1 MUS. madrigalian. 2 (fig.) sweet, tender (tierno).
madrigalista *s.m.* y *f.* madrigalist.
madriguera *s.f.* 1 ZOOL. den, burrow (cuevecilla). 2 (fig.) den (refugio de personas de mal vivir).
madrina *s.f.* 1 bridesmaid (de boda). 2 godmother (de un niño). 3 protectress (protectora). 4 post (poste). 5 AGR. leading mare (yegua). 6 strap, brace (atadura). 7 (Am.) tame herd (ganado manso).
madrinazgo *s.m.* role of godmother (papel de madrina).
madroñal *s.m.* strawberry bush patch (sitio poblado de madroños).
madroñera *s.f.* 1 BOT. strawberry bush (madroño). 2 strawberry tree patch (madroñal).
madroño *s.m.* 1 BOT. strawberry bush (arbusto). 2 strawberry (fruta). 3 round, tassel (borlita).
madrugada *s.f.* 1 early morning (primeras horas del día). 2 daybreak, dawn (alba). || 3 **despertarse de –,** to wake early.
madrugador, -a *adj.* 1 early rising. || *s.m.* y *f.* 2 early riser, (fam.) early bird.
madrugar *v.i.* 1 to get up early, (fam.) to get up with the lark (levantarse temprano). 2 to jump the gun (anticiparse). || 3 **a quien madruga, Dios le ayuda,** the early bird catches the worm.
madrugón, -ona, *adj.* 1 getting-up early, early rising. || *s.m.* 2 very early riser. || 3 **pegarse un –,** (fam.) to get up at the crack of dawn.
maduración *s.f.* ripening, maturing.
maduradero *s.m.* favourable site for ripening fruit (lugar).
madurador, -a *adj.* ripening.
maduramente *adv.* maturely.
madurar *v.t., i.* y *r.* 1 AGR. to ripen (fruta). || *v.t.* 2 to think over, to ponder (considerar detenidamente). || *v.i.* 3 to mature (desarrollarse física y espiritualmente). || *v.i.* y *r.* 4 MED. to soften (reblanderse).
madurativo, -a *adj.* maturative (que puede madurar).
madurez *s.f.* 1 ripeness (de frutos). 2 maturity (de personas).
maduro, -a *adj.* 1 ripe (frutos): *poco maduro = unripe.* 2 mature (personas): *poco maduro = immature.* || 3 **edad madura,** middle age.
maese *s.m.* (arc.) master (maestro).
maestra *s.f.* 1 teacher, schoolmistress (de colegio): *maestra de inglés = English teacher.* 2 queen bee (abeja maestra). 3 ARQ. guide line (listón).
maestradamente *adv.* (arc.) masterly.
maestranza *s.f.* 1 MIL. arsenal (conjunto de talleres). 2 arsenal workers (conjunto de operarios). 3 (Am.) machine shop (cualquier conjunto de talleres).
maestrazgo *s.m.* 1 HIST. office of grand master (dignidad del maestre). 2 territory under the grand master's control (territorio).
maestre *s.m.* HIST. grand master.
maestresala *s.m.* head servant (criado principal).
maestría *s.f.* 1 mastery, skill (competencia en un asunto). 2 master's degree (título de maestro).
maestro, -a *adj.* 1 master: *esta pintura es una obra maestra = this painting is a master piece; golpe maestro = master stroke.* 2 main, principal (principal): *la puerta maestra = the main door.* 3 trained: *tigre maestro = trained tiger.* || *s.m.* 4 teacher, schoolmaster (profesor). 5 master (de un arte): *es un maestro del balón = he's a master of the ball.* 6 master (de alto grado en su oficio): *maestro albañil = master mason.* 7 MUS. maestro. || 8 **– de ceremonias,** master of ceremonies. 9 **– de cocina,** chef. 10 **– de obras,** master builder.
mafia *s.f.* mafia.
mafioso, -a *s.m.* y *f.* mafioso, member of the Mafia.
magancería *s.f.* trick, fraud (embuste).
magancés, -esa *adj.* treacherous (traidor).
magdalena *s.f.* 1 grieving o sorrowful woman (mujer apenada). 2 sponge cake (bollo pequeño). || 3 **llorar como una –,** to cry one's eyes out.
magia *s.f.* 1 magic: *magia negra = black magic; magia blanca = white magic.* 2 (fig.) magic, charm.
magiar *adj.* 1 Magyar. || *s.m.* y *f.* 2 Magyar.
mágicamente *adv.* magically.
mágico, -a *adj.* 1 magic, magical: *varita mágica = magic wand.* 2 (fig.) magic, fantastic (estupendo). || *s.m.* y *f.* 3 magician (mago).
magisterial *adj.* magisterial.
magisterio *s.m.* 1 teaching (enseñanza). 2 teachers, teaching staff (conjunto de maestros). 3 (fig.) pompousness, pedantry, affected solemnity (en la manera de hablar)
magistrado, -a *s.m.* y *f.* magistrate, judge.
magistral *adj.* magistral.
magistralmente *adv.* magistrally.
magistratura *s.f.* magistracy (dignidad y cargo de magistrado).
magma *s.m.* GEOL. magma.
magnánimamente *adv.* magnanimously.
magnanimidad *s.f.* magnanimity.
magnánimo, -a *adj.* magnanimous.
magnate *s.m.* magnate, tycoon.
magnesia *s.f.* QUIM. magnesia.
magnesiano, -a *adj.* QUIM. magnesian.
magnésico, -a *adj.* QUIM. magnesic.
magnesio *s.m.* QUIM. magnesium.
magnético, -a *adj.* magnetic: *campo magnético = magnetic field; polo magnético = magnetic pole.*
magnetismo *s.m.* 1 magnetism. 2 magnetics (ciencia).
magnetizable *adj.* magnetizable.
magnetización *s.f.* magnetization.
magnetizador, -a *s.m.* y *f.* magnetiser.
magnetizar *v.t.* 1 to magnetize. 2 to hypnotize (hipnotizar). 3 (fig.) to fascinate, to captivate, to spellbind (fascinar).
magneto *s.m.* ELEC. magneto (generador de electricidad).
magnetofónico, -a *adj.* magnetic.
magnetófono o **magnetofono** *s.m.* tape recorder.
magnicidio *s.m.* assassination (de un personaje importante).
magnificador, -ora *adj.* magnifying. || *s.m.* y *f.* magnifier.
magníficamente *adj.* magnificently, wonderfully.
magnificar *v.t.* 1 to praise, to extol (alabar). 2 to exalt (ensalzar).
magníficat *s.m.* magnificat (cántico).
magnificencia *s.f.* 1 magnificence, splendour (esplendor). 2 generosity (generosidad).
magnificente *adj.* magnificent.

magnífico, -a *adj.* magnificent, marvellous, wonderful.
magnitud *s.f.* 1 magnitude. 2 importance (importancia). 3 size (tamaño).
magno, -a *adj.* 1 great (grande). 2 illustrious (ilustre). || 3 **carta magna,** magna carta.
magnolia *s.f.* BOT. magnolia.
magnoliáceo, -a *adj.* y *s.f.pl.* BOT. magnoliaceae.
mago, -a *s.m.* y *f.* 1 magician, wizard. || 2 **los Reyes Magos,** the Three Wise Men.
magra *s.f.* slice of ham (loncha de jamón).
magro, -a *adj.* 1 thin, (fam.) skinny (flaco). 2 lean (carne). || *s.m.* 3 lean pork (carne de cerdo sin grasa).
magrura o **magrez** *s.f.* 1 thinness (de personas). 2 leanness (de carne).
maguarse *v.pron.* (Am.) to be sad (entristecerse).
magulladura *s.f.,* **magullamiento** *s.m.* o **magullón** *s.m.* bruise (contusión).
magullar *v.t.* y *pron.* to bruise.
mahometano, -a *adj.* y *s.m.* y *f.* Mahommedan.
mahometismo *s.m.* Mahommedanism.
mahometista *adj.* y *s.m.* y *f.* Mahommedan.
maicena *s.f.* cornflour.
maicero, -a *adj.* 1 maize. || *s.m.* y *f.* 2 maize dealer (vendedor de maíz).
maitines *s.m.pl.* REL. matins.
maíz *s.m.* BOT. maize, (EE.UU.) corn.
maizal *s.m.* maiz field.
maja *s.f.* 1 pestle (mano del mortero). 2 (Am. y fam.) lazybones (persona holgazana).
majada *s.f.* 1 fold (redil). 2 dung, manure (estiércol).
majadal *s.m.* 1 fold (majada). 2 sheep pasture (lugar de pasto).
majaderear *v.t.* (Am.) to annoy, to be a nuisance (molestar).
majadería *s.f.* 1 stupidity, foolishness (idiotez). 2 silly o stupid thing (dicho o hecho inoportuno).
majadero, -a *adj.* 1 silly, foolish (torpe). || *s.m.* y *f.* 2 fool, idiot, clot (bobo). || *s.m.* 3 bobbin (palito para hacer encajes). 4 pestle (mazo).
majara o **majareta** *adj.* (fam.) 1 crazy, mad, round the bend (chiflado). || *s.m.* y *f.* 2 madman, lunatic (loco).
majestad *s.f.* 1 majesty: *Vuestra Majestad = Your Majesty.* 2 stateliness (grandeza).
majestuosamente *adv.* majestically.
majestuosidad *s.f.* majesty.
majestuoso, -a *adj.* majestic.
majeza *s.f.* 1 smartness, elegance (elegancia). 2 niceness (simpatía). 3 bragging, boasting (bravuconería).
majo, -a *adj.* 1 nice, friendly (simpático). 2 smart, fashionable (bien vestido). 3 attractive (atractivo). 4 flashy, cocky (que afecta desenvoltura). 5 pretty, beautiful (guapo).
majolar *s.m.* hawthorn grove (lugar poblado de majuelos).
majorca *s.f.* corn, cob (mazorca).
majuela *s.f.* 1 BOT. hawthorn berry (fruto del majuelo). 2 lace (para atar los zapatos).
mal *adj.* 1 apócope de malo: *mal olor = bad smell.* || *adv.* 2 badly: *tocar mal = to play badly; salir mal = to turn out badly.* 3 bad: *huele mal = it smells bad.* 4 ill, sick (enfermo): *estoy mal = I'm sick.* 5 wrongly, badly (incorrectamente): *lo haces mal = you're doing it wrongly.* || *s.m.* 6 evil, wrong: *hay que luchar contra el mal = one must fight against evil; el bien y el mal = good and evil.* 7 harm, hurt, damage (daño): *no te quiero hacer mal = I don't want to do you any harm.* 8 illness, disease (enfermedad). 9 reverse, misfortune (desgracia). || 10 **andar — de dinero,** to be short of money. 11 **caer en el —,** to fall into bad ways. 12 **decir — de uno,** to speak ill of someone. 13 **encontrarse —,** to feel bad. 14 **llevar a — una cosa,** to be offended by something. 15 **— de la tierra,** homesickness. 16 **— de mar,** seasickness. 17 **— de ojo,** the evil eye. 18 **— menor,** lesser evil. 19 **¡menos —!,** thank God for that! 20 **no hay — que por bien no venga,** every cloud has a silver lining. 21 **parar en —,** to come to a bad end. 22 **si — no recuerdo,** if I'm not mistaken. 23 **tomar algo a —,** to take something badly.
malabares *adj.* 1 malabar. 2 **hacer juegos malabares,** to juggle.
malabarismo *s.m.* juggling.
malabarista *s.m.* y *f.* juggler.
malaconsejado, -a *adj.* ill-advised, badly advised.
malacostumbrado, -a *adj.* 1 bad-mannered, ill-mannered (que tiene mala costumbre). 2 pampered, spoiled (mimado).
málaga *s.m.* Malaga wine (vino de Málaga).
malagana *s.f.* faint (desmayo).
malagueño, -a *adj.* 1 of/from Málaga. || *s.m.* y *f.* 2 native o inhabitant of Málaga.
malamente *adv.* badly: *juegan malamente = they play badly.*
malandante *adj.* unlucky, hapless (desgraciado).
malandanza *s.f.* bad luck, misfortune (infortunio).
malandrín, -ina *adj.* 1 evil (malvado). || *s.m.* y *f.* 2 wicked/evil person (malvado).
malaquita *s.f.* MIN. malachite.
malaria *s.f.* MED. malaria.
malasangre *adj.* 1 perverse, wicked, evil (avieso). || *s.m.* y *f.* 2 evil person.
malasombra *s.m.* y *f.* clumsy/awkward person (persona patosa).
malaventura o **malaventuranza** *s.f.* misfortune, bad luck (desgracia).
malaventurado, -a *adj.* unfortunate (desgraciado).
malayo, -a *adj.* y *s.m.* y *f.* Malayan, Malay.
malbaratador, -a *s.m.* y *f.* squanderer, spendthrift (derrochador).
malbaratar *v.t.* 1 to squander, to waste (derrochar). 2 COM. to sell at a loss (malvender).
malbarato *s.m.* 1 squandering, wasting (acción de derrochar). 2 COM. selling at a loss (acción de malvender).
malcriadez o **malcriadeza** *s.f.* bad upbringing.
malcriado, -a *adj.* bad-mannered, rude.
malcriar *v.t.* to bring up badly.
maldad *s.f.* 1 badness, evil (calidad de malo). 2 bad thing, evil thing (acción mala).
maldecir *v.t.* 1 to curse (echar maldiciones). 2 to abhor, to detest (aborrecer). || 3 to swear (blasfemar). 4 to criticize, (fam.) to knock (criticar). 5 to complain (quejarse).
maldiciente *adj.* 1 critical (que critica). 2 knocking, bitching (que calumnia). 3 abusive, offensive (que blasfema). || *s.m.* y *f.* 4 knocker, backbiter (que difama). 5 complainer, moaner (que se queja).
maldición *s.f.* 1 curse: *bajo una maldición = under a curse.* 2 curse, oath (blasfemia). || 3 **¡—!,** damn it!; curse it!
maldispuesto, -a *adj.* 1 MED. indisposed, ill (indispuesto). 2 ill-disposed, unwilling (sin disposición para una cosa).
maldito, -a *adj.* 1 accursed, damned (que ha recibido una maldición). 2 (fam.) damned, bloody, lousy (malo, adverso): *ese maldito hombre = that damned man; maldito lo que me importa = I don't give a damn; ese maldito sol me está quemando = that bloody sun is burning me.* 3 evil, wicked (malvado). || *s.m.* 4 devil (diablo). || 5 **¡maldita sea!,** damn it!
maleabilidad *s.f.* malleability.
maleable *adj.* malleable.
maleante *adj.* 1 malignant, evil (maligno). 2 corrupting (que corrompe). || *s.m.* y *f.* 3 tramp, vagrant (vagabundo). 4 evil o bad person (persona mala).
maleamiento *s.m.* corrupting.
malear *v.t.* y *pron.* 1 to corrupt, to pervert (corromper). 2 to spoil, to deteriorate (deteriorar).
malecón *s.m.* 1 dike (dique). 2 breakwater (rompeolas).
maledicencia *s.f.* slander (acción de difamar).
maleducado, -a *adj.* 1 bad-mannered, ignorant. || *s.m.* y *f.* 2 bad-mannered person.
maleducar *v.t.* to bring up badly (educar mal).
maleficencia *s.f.* harm, (p.u.) maleficence.
maleficiar *v.t.* 1 to hurt, to cause damage (causar daño). 2 to bewitch, to cast a spell on (hechizar).
maleficio *s.m.* 1 hurt, damage (daño). 2 witchcraft, sorcery (hechizo).
maléfico, -a *adj.* 1 evil, harmful (dañino). || *s.m.* y *f.* 2 sorcerer (hechicero).
malencarado, -a *adj.* ugly, grotesque.

malentender *v.t.* to misunderstand.
malentendido *s.m.* misunderstanding.
malestar *s.m.* 1 MED. sickness, discomfort. 2 (fig.) unease, unrest.
maleta *s.f.* 1 suitcase, case: *hacer la maleta = to pack (one's case).* || *s.m.* y *f.* 2 inept o ham-fisted person (persona que desarrolla con torpeza un trabajo).
maletero *s.m.* 1 boot (del coche). 2 suitcase maker (que hace maletas). 3 porter (el que transporta equipajes).
maletilla *s.m.* novice bullfighter (aprendiz de torero).
maletín *s.m.* attaché case, briefcase.
malevolencia *s.f.* malevolence, malice, spite: *por malevolencia = out of spite.*
malévolo, -a *adj.* malevolent, spiteful.
maleza *s.f.* 1 undergrowth (espesura de vegetación, etc.). 2 weeds (abundancia de hierbas inútiles). 3 (Am.) complaint, ailment (achaque).
malformación *s.f.* deformity, malformation.
malgastador, -ora *s.m.* y *f.* 1 spendthrift. || *adj.* 2 wasteful, spendthrift.
malgastar *v.t.* 1 to waste, to squander (dinero, talento, recursos). 2 to waste (tiempo). 3 to ruin (la salud).
malhablado, -a *adj.* 1 rude, foulmouthed. || *s.m.* y *f.* 2 rude o foulmouthed person.
malhadado, -a *adj.* unfortunate, ill-fated.
malhechor, -a *adj.* 1 wicked, evil. || *s.m.* y *f.* 2 criminal, wrongdoer.
malherir *v.t.* to injure seriously.
malhumorado, -a *adj.* angry, bad-tempered.
malhumorar *v.t.* y *pron.* to annoy, to anger.
malicia *s.f.* 1 evil, badness (maldad). 2 malice, spite (malevolencia). 3 slyness, cunning, guile (astucia). 4 viciousness (de los animales). 5 nautiness, mischief (de los niños).
maliciar *v.t.* y *pron.* 1 to mistrust, to distrust (sospechar con malicia). 2 to corrupt, to pervert (malear).
maliciosamente *adv.* maliciously, spitefully.
malicioso, -a *adj.* 1 malicious, spiteful (que tiene malicia). 2 cunning, sly (astuto). 3 vicious (animales). 4 naughty, mischievous (niños).
malignamente *adv.* malignantly.
malignidad *s.f.* 1 MED. malignancy. 2 malice, spite (malicia).
maligno, -a *adj.* 1 MED. malignant. 2 evil, malignant, malicious (persona). 3 evil, bad (malo).
malintencionado, -a *adj.* 1 ill-intentioned, malicious. || *s.m.* y *f.* 2 ill-intentioned o malicious person.
malmandado, -a *adj.* 1 disobedient, defiant. || *s.m.* y *f.* 2 disobedient/defiant person.
malmeter *v.t.* 1 to squander, to waste (derrochar). 2 to drive apart, to divide (malquistar). 3 to entice, to incite (tentar a uno a cometer malas acciones).
malmirado, -a *adj.* disliked, unpopular.
malo, -a *adj.* 1 bad (no bueno): *una película mala = a bad film; un disco malo = a bad record.* 2 evil, bad (malvado). 3 harmful, bad (dañino). 4 naughty, bad (travieso). 5 ill, sick (enfermo): *estar malo = to be ill.* 6 useless, no good (inútil): *soy malo para el inglés = I'm useless at English.* 7 bad, unpleasant (olor, sabor). || *s.m.* 8 el Malo, the Devil (el diablo); the bad guy (en una película, etc.). || 9 **andar a malas,** to be on bad terms. 10 **estar de malas,** to be in a bad mood (de mal humor); to be on bad terms (estar enemistados). 11 **mala jugada,** dirty trick. 12 **por las malas,** by force. 13 **sentirse —,** to feel unwell.
malograr *v.t.* y *pron.* 1 to waste (echar a perder una cosa). || *v.pron.* 2 to fail (no conseguirse una cosa). 3 to fall short, to disappoint (no alcanzar el desarrollo apetecido).
maloliente *adj.* stinking, smelly, reeking.
malparado, -a *adj.* 1 damaged, (fam.) in a sorry state. 2 **salir malparado,** to come off badly.
malparar *v.t.* 1 to damage, to spoil (estropear). 2 to hurt, to harm (dañar). 3 to ill-treat, to maltreat (maltratar).
malparida *s.f.* woman who has had a miscarriage.
malparir *v.i.* MED. to have a miscarriage, to miscarry.
malparto *s.m.* MED. miscarriage.
malquerencia *s.f.* 1 malice, spite, malevolence (malevolencia). 2 dislike (antipatía).
malquerer *v.t.* 1 to show malice, to be spiteful (tener malevolencia a alguien). 2 to dislike (tener antipatía a alguien).
malqueriente *adj.* 1 spiteful, malevolent (malicioso). 2 unfriendly (antipático).
malquistar *v.t.* y *pron.* to fall out.
malquisto, -a *adj.* disliked, unpopular.
malsano, -a *adj.* 1 unhealthy (nocivo a la salud). 2 sickly (enfermizo).
malsonante *adj.* 1 off/ill-sounding (que suena mal). 2 rude, offensive (grosero).
malta *s.m.* malt (generalmente cebada germinada y tostada).
maltés, -a *adj.* y *s.m.* y *f.* Maltese.
maltosa *s.f.* QUIM. maltose.
maltraer *v.t.* 1 to insult (insultar). 2 to ill-treat (maltratar). || 3 **llevar o tener a uno a —, a)** to annoy (molestar); **b)** to ill-treat (maltratar); **c)** to irritate (irritar).
maltratar *v.t.* 1 to maltreat, to ill-treat (dar un mal trato). 2 to damage (causar daños).
maltrato o **maltratamiento** *s.m.* ill-treatment, maltreatment.
maltrecho, -a *adj.* injured, battered.
maltusianismo *s.m.* Malthusianism.
maltusiano, -a *adj.* y *s.m.* y *f.* Malthusian.
malva *s.f.* 1 BOT. mallow. || 2 **— real** o **loca,** hollyhock. 3 **ser como una —,** not to say boo to a goose: *es como una malva = he wouldn't say boo to a goose.*
malvadamente *adv.* maliciously, spitefully.
malvado, -a *adj.* 1 evil, wicked. || *s.m.* y *f.* 2 evil o wicked person.
malvarrosa *s.f.* BOT. hollyhock.
malvasía *s.f.* 1 malvasia (uva). 2 malmsey (vino).
malvender *v.t.* to undersell, to sell at a loss.
malversación *s.f.* embezzlement, (fam.) fiddling, (p.u.) malversation.
malversador, -a *adj.* 1 embezzling, (fam.) fiddling. || *s.m.* y *f.* 2 embezzler (fam.) fiddler.
malversar *v.t.* to embezzle, (fam.) to fiddle.
malvís *s.m.* ZOOL. song thrush, mavis (ave).
malvivir *v.i.* to live badly.
malla *s.f.* 1 mesh (de una red). 2 HIST. chain mail (armadura). 3 net, mesh (red de hilo). || *pl.* 4 DEP. net (portería). 5 tights (medias).
mama *s.f.* 1 ANAT. breast (pecho). 2 mammary gland, mamma (teta). 3 mum, mummy, mommy, mom (madre).
mamá *s.f.* (fam.) mum, mummy, mommy, mom (madre).
mamada *s.f.* 1 suck, sucking (acción de mamar). 2 mouthful (cantidad de leche que traga una criatura cada vez que mama). 3 (Am.) binge, drinking spree (borrachera).
mamado, -a *adj.* 1 drunk, plastered (borracho).
mamador, -a *adj.* sucking.
mamagrande *s.f.* (Am.) grandmother (abuela).
mamar *v.t.* 1 to suck (chupar). 2 to eat (comer). 3 (fig.) to absorb, to soak up (adquirir conocimientos, etc.). || *v.pron.* 4 (Am.) to get drunk, (fam.) to get plastered (emborracharse).
mamarrachada *s.f.* 1 buffoonery, clowning (acción ridícula). 2 gang of clowns (reunión de mamarrachos).
mamarracho *s.m.* 1 buffoon, clown (figura ridícula). 2 (fam.) idiot, nincompoop, dolt (hombre despreciable).
mamá-señora *s.f.* (Am.) grandmother (abuela).
mameluco *s.m.* 1 clot, dolt, dope (hombre necio). 2 HIST. mameluke (soldado egipcio).
mamerto, -a *adj.* silly, stupid (bobo).
mamífero *s.m.* 1 ZOOL. mammal. || *adj.* 2 ZOOL. mammalian.
mamila *s.f.* 1 udder, teat (teta de los animales). 2 nipple (tetilla del hombre).
mamilar *adj.* ANAT. mammillary.
mamola *s.f.* chuck under the chin.
mamón, -a *adj.* 1 suckling, unweaned (que aún mama). || *s.m.* y *f.* 2 baby, unweaned baby (que aún mama). || *s.m.* 3 BOT. sucker, shoot (chupón).
mamotreto *s.m.* 1 large book, tome (libro voluminoso). 2 notebook (bloc).
mampara *s.f.* frame (armazón).
mamporro *s.m.* whack, clout, blow (golpe).
mampostear *v.t.* ARQ. to make of rubble.
mampostería *s.f.* rubblework.

mampostero *s.m.* stonemason.
mampuesto *s.m.* **1** rough stone (piedra sin labrar). **2** parapet (parapeto). **3** (Am.) rest, stand (objeto que apoya un arma de fuego).
mamut *s.m.* ZOOL. mammoth.
maná *s.m.* manna.
manada *s.f.* **1** ZOOL. herd, flock (rebaño). **2** pack (de lobos, perros). **3** pride (de leones). **4** (fam.) crowd, mob. **5** handful (porción que se puede coger con una mano).
manager *s.m.* manager.
manante *adj.* flowing, running (que mana).
manantial *s.m.* **1** spring, source (donde manan las aguas). **2** source, birth (origen de una cosa). || *adj.* **3** flowing, running (que mana).
manar *v.i.* **1** to flow, to run (salir un líquido). **2** to flourish, to abound (abundar).
manaza *s.f.* **1** big hand. || **2 ser un manazas,** to be clumsy.
mancamiento *s.m.* maiming, crippling (acción de mancar).
mancar *v.t.* y *pron.* to cripple, to maim.
manceba *s.f.* concubine (concubina).
mancebía *s.f.* **1** brothel. **2** youth (mocedad).
mancebo *s.m.* **1** youth, young man (hombre joven). **2** single man, bachelor (hombre soltero). **3** clerk (empleado de poca categoría).
mancilla *s.f.* **1** stain. || **2** REL. **sin mancilla**, immaculate.
mancillar *v.t.* **1** to sully, to stain (dañar la reputación). **2** to tarnish (deslucir).
manco, -a *adj.* **1** one-armed (de un solo brazo). **2** one-handed (de una mano). **3** faulty, defective (defectuoso). || *s.m.* y *f.* **4** one-armed person (persona con un solo brazo). **5** one-handed person (persona con una sola mano). || **6 no ser alguien —,** to be useful.
mancomún (de) *adv.* by common agreement; jointly.
mancomunadamente *adv.* by common agreement; jointly.
mancomunar *v.t.* **1** to unite, to join (personas). **2** to join (esfuerzos). **3** to pool (recursos). **4** to combine (interés). **5** DER. to make jointly responsible. || *v.pron.* **6** to unite, to combine, to join.
mancomunidad *s.f.* **1** POL. commonwealth (de países, provincias, etc.). **2** association (asociación). **3** pool (de recursos). **4** joining (de esfuerzos). **5** DER. joint responsibility.
mancha *s.f.* **1** stain, spot (huella de suciedad). **2** stain, blemish (cosa inmoral o deshonrosa). **3** ZOOL. spot, mark (de los animales). **4** ZOOL. speckle (de los pájaros). **5** spot (en la ropa, tela, etc.). **6** ART. sketch, rough draft (boceto). **7** AGR. patch (terreno de mejor calidad). **8** spot (mácula del sol). **9** smudge, blot (de tinta). **10** MED. spot, mark.
manchadizo, -a *adj.* dirty (sucio).
manchado, -a *adj.* **1** stained, dirty (con huellas de suciedad). **2** speckled (los pájaros). **3** spotted (animales). **4** spotty (piel de persona). **5** smudged, smudgy (papel). **6** blemished, stained (reputación, etc.).
manchar *v.t.* **1** to stain, to dirty (ensuciar). **2** to spot, to mark (poner una mancha). **3** (fig.) to stain, to blemish (la honra, reputación, etc.). **4** to smudge (papel). || *v.pron.* **5** to get dirty (ensuciarse). **6** to stain oneself (con manchas). **7** (fig.) to tarnish one's reputation (la reputación).
manchón *s.m.* **1** large stain (mancha grande). **2** patch of dense vegetation (zona de plantas muy espesas). **3** area of pastureland (zona que se deja por un año para pasto).
manda *s.f.* legacy, bequest (legado).
mandado, -a *s.m.* y *f.* **1** (desp.) lackey, tool, minion (que se limita a cumplir órdenes): *yo no soy más que un mandado = I'm just a minion.* **2** commission (comisión). **3** command, order (orden).
mandamás *s.m.* y *f.* leader, boss, chief (persona que tiene mando).
mandamiento *s.m.* **1** REL. commandment. **2** command, order (orden). **3** DER. writ, mandate (mandato). **4** warrant: *mandamiento de entrada y registro = search warrant.* || **5 — de venir,** summons.
mandanga *s.f.* **1** nuisance, (fam.) drag (cosa molesta). **2** composure, cool (flema).
mandar *v.t.* **1** to order (obligar a hacer una cosa): *me mandaron venir = they ordered me to come.* **2** to send (enviar): *mandar una carta = to send a letter.* **3** to order, to ask for (encargar). **4** to rule, to govern (gobernar). **5** to bequeath, to leave (legar un testamento). **6** MIL. to command, to lead: *mandar un ejército = to lead an army.* || **7 — hacer algo,** to have something done: *mandar arreglar un reloj = to have a watch repaired.* **8 — por algo,** to send for something.
mandarín *s.m.* mandarin.
mandarina *s.f.* **1** BOT. mandarin, tangerine (naranja). **2** Mandarin (idioma).
mandarino o **mandarinero** *s.m.* BOT. mandarin tree (árbol).
mandatario, -a *s.m.* y *f.* **1** agent (persona a quien se encomienda una gestión). **2** president (presidente).
mandato *s.m.* **1** order (orden). **2** POL. mandate, term of office (tiempo durante el que se manda). **3** DER. power of attorney (contrato por el que una persona confía una gestión a otra). **4** REL. maundy (ceremonia). || **5** DER. **— judicial,** writ, summons.
mandíbula *s.f.* **1** ANAT. jaw, (p.u.) mandible. || **2 reír a — batiente,** to laugh one's head off.
mandil *s.m.* **1** apron (delantal). **2** fishing net (red de pesca).
mandioca *s.f.* BOT. manioc, cassava (arbusto).
mando *s.m.* **1** command, control (poder de mandar): *alto mando = high command; tener el mando = to have control/to be in control.* **2** DEP. lead: *tomar el mando = to take the lead.* **3** MEC. control: *mando a distancia = remote control.* **4** POL. term of office (mandato). || *pl.* **5** MEC. controls (de televisión, radio, coche, etc.). **6** leaders, leadership (los líderes). || **7 estar al —,** to be in command. **8 ejercer el —,** to be in command. **9 palanca de —,** control lever. **10 tomar el —,** to take command.
mandoble *s.m.* **1** slash (cuchillada). **2** broadsword (espada grande). **3** severe ticking-off (amonestación severa).
mandolina *s.f.* MUS. mandolin, mandoline.
mandón, -a *adj.* **1** bossy, over-bearing. || *s.m.* y *f.* **2** bossy/over-bearing person. **3** (Am.) starter (de carreras de caballos).
mandrágora *s.f.* BOT. mandrake (planta).
mandria *adj.* **1** cowardly (cobarde). **2** useless (inútil). || *s.m.* y *f.* **3** coward (cobarde). **4** useless person (persona inútil).
mandril *s.m.* **1** ZOOL. mandril (mono). **2** TEC. mandrel. **3** rod (vástago).
manducar *v.t.* to eat, (fam.) to scoff (comer).
manearse *v.pron.* (Am.) to trip over (tropezarse).
manecilla *s.f.* **1** hand (aguja de reloj, etc.). **2** clasp (broche de un libro).
manejable *adj.* **1** manageable. **2** easy to use, handy (fácil de usar).
manejar *v.t.* **1** to handle (usar una cosa con las manos): *manejar una herramienta = to handle a tool.* **2** to use (usar). **3** to operate, to run (una máquina). **4** to handle (un caballo). **5** to run (una casa, hotel). **6** to manage (personas): *maneja bien a los niños = she manages the children very well.* **7** to rule, to govern (gobernar). **8** to handle (dinero, acciones, etc.). **9** to administer (administrar). **10** to direct, to run (dirigir). **11** (Am.) to drive (conducir). || *v.pron.* **12** MED. to get about (moverse bien). **13** to behave (comportarse).
manejo *s.m.* **1** handling (de personas, recursos, dinero, herramientas, caballos, armas, etc.). **2** running (de una casa). **3** running, operating (de una máquina). **4** running, administrating (un negocio, departamento, administración, etc.). **5** intrigue (intriga). **6** (Am.) driving (de coche).
manera *s.f.* **1** way, manner, method (forma de ser o realizar una cosa): *su manera de escribir = his way of writing.* **2** type, kind (clase): *otra manera de trabajo = another type of work.* || *pl.* **3** manners (modales). || **4 a la — de,** in the manner of; in the fashion of. **5 a mi —,** in my own way. **6 de buenas o malas maneras,** politely o impolitely. **7 de esta —,** in this way; like this. **8 de otra —,** otherwise. **9 de mala —,** badly. **10 de — que,** so that. **11 ¡de ninguna —!,** no way! **12 de tal — que...,** in such a way that... **13 de todas maneras,** anyway; at any rate. **14 en cierta —,** up to a point. **15 — de obrar,** way of going about things. **16**

— **de ver,** way of looking at things; point of view. **17 no hay —,** it's impossible; there's no way. **18 sobre —,** exceedingly.
manflora *s.m.* (Am.) effeminate man, (desp.) pansy (afeminado).
manga *s.f.* **1** sleeve (del vestido): *manga de camisa = shirtsleeve.* **2** hose (tubo largo y flexible). **3** MAR. beam (anchura de un barco). **4** strainer, filter (filtro). **5** net (red). **6** DEP. game (partido). **7** (Am.) funnel, entrance (que da acceso a un corral, etc.). **8** (Am.) crowd (multitud). || **9 de — corta,** short-sleeved. **10 de — larga,** long-sleeved. **11 en mangas de camisa,** in shirt sleeves. **12 — de agua,** water-spout. **13 — de viento,** whirlwind. **14 ser de — ancha** o **tener — ancha,** to be overindulgent.
manganeso *s.m.* QUIM. manganese.
mangante *adj.* **1** thieving (que roba). **2** sponging, scrounging (pedigüeño). || *s.m.* y *f.* **3** thief (ladrón). **4** (fam.) sponger, scrounger (pedigüeño).
mangar *v.t.* **1** (fam.) to pinch, to swipe, to nick (robar). **2** to beg, to scrounge (mendigar). **3** to ask for (pedir).
mangazo *s.m.* (Am.) punch (puñetazo).
mango *s.m.* **1** handle (parte por donde se cogen algunos utensilios). **2** BOT. mango (árbol y fruta).
mangoneador, -ora *s.m.* y *f.* **1** meddler, interferer (que se entremete). **2** bossy type (mandón).
mangonear *v.i.* **1** to meddle, to interfere (mezclarse uno en un asunto). **2** to wander, to roam (vagabundear). **3** to organize, to manage (manejar).
mangoneo *s.m.* meddling, interfering (acción de mangonear).
mangonero, -a *adj.* **1** interfering, meddlesome (aficionado a mangonear). **2** bossy (mandón). || *s.m.* y *f.* **3** meddler, interfering type (que se entremete). **4** bossy type (mandón).
mangosta *s.f.* ZOOL. mongoose.
manguera *s.f.* **1** hose (manga de riego). **2** ventilation shaft (tubo de ventilación). || **3 — de incendios,** fire hose.
mangueta *s.f.* **1** MED. enema (vejiga para lavativas). **2** U-pipe (de los retretes). **3** lever (palanca).
manguito *s.m.* **1** muff (tubo de piel). **2** oversleeve (media manga). **3** ring (anillo que refuerza los tubos). **4** TEC. coupling, sleeve (tubo que empalma dos piezas).
maní *s.m.* (Am.) peanut (cacahuete).
manía *s.f.* **1** mania, obsession (obsesión mental). **2** mania (afición exagerada): *la manía del fútbol = football mania.* **3** craze, fad, mania (capricho): *la manía del inglés = the craze for English.* **4** fashion (moda): *la manía de los pendientes = the fasion for earrings.* || **5 — de grandezas,** megalomanía. **6 tener la — de hacer algo,** to have the habit of doing something. **7 tener manías,** to be odd: *ella tiene sus manías = she's a little odd.* **8 tener — a uno,** to dislike someone; not to stand someone: *le tengo manía = I can't stand him.*
maníaco, -a o **maniático, -a** *adj.* **1** maniacal, crazy (loco). **2** obsessive (obsesivo). **3** odd, peculiar, eccentric (excéntrico). **4** stubborn, obstinate (obstinado). || *s.m.* y *f.* **5** maniac (loco). **6** strange person (persona rara). **7** eccentric (excéntrico).
maniatar *v.t.* to tie the hands of (atar las manos).
manicomio *s.m.* mental hospital.
manicorto, -a *adj.* **1** tight, mean (poco generoso). || *s.m.* y *f.* **2** skinflint, pennypincher, meanie.
manicura *s.f.* manicure.
manicuro *s.m.* y *f.* manicurist (persona).
manida *s.f.* den, lair (guarida).
manido, -a *adj.* **1** off (comida pasada). **2** stale (pan). **3** high (carne). **4** stale, trite (un tema, asunto). **5** common, vulgar (vulgar).
manierismo *s.m.* ART. mannerism.
manierista *adj.* **1** manieristic. || *s.m.* y *f.* **2** mannerist.
manifestación *s.f.* **1** manifestation, show: *manifestación de amor = show of love.* **2** POL. demonstration (reunión masiva). **3** declaration, statement (declaración).
manifestante *s.m.* y *f.* POL. demonstrator.
manifestar *v.t.* **1** to manifest, to show (emociones, opiniones, etc.): *manifestaron su enojo = they showed their anger.* **2** to declare, to state (declarar): *el primer ministro manifestó lo que iban a hacer = the Prime Minister stated what they were going to do.* **3** to make known (dar a conocer). || *v.pron.* **4** POL. to demonstrate (hacer una manifestación). **5** to show, to be manifest (poner al descubierto). || **6 manifestarse en,** to be shown by.
manifestativo, -a *adj.* manifest, evident.
manifiestamente *adv.* manifestly, evidently.
manifiesto, -a *adj.* **1** obvious, clear, manifest, evident (evidente). || *s.m.* **2** manifesto (escrito político o literario). **3** MAR. manifest. || **4 poner de —,** to make clear, to show, to reveal.
manilla *s.f.* **1** bracelet (pulsera). **2** handle (asidero para puertas, etc.). **3** hand (de un reloj).
manillar *s.m.* handlebars (de una bicicleta o moto).
maniobra *s.f.* **1** handling (con las manos). **2** control, managing (de un negocio, asunto, etc.). **3** manoeuvring (conjunto de operaciones). **4** shunting (de ferrocarriles). **5** MIL. manoeuvre. **6** (fig.) manoeuvre, move (estratagema). **7** MAR. handling (de un barco). || *pl.* **8** MIL. manoeuvres. || **9 hacer maniobras,** to manoeuvre.
maniobrable *adj.* manoeuvrable.
maniobrar *v.t.* **1** to operate, to handle (máquinas). **2** to manoeuvre, to handle (un barco). **3** to drive (transportes). **4** to shunt (ferrocarril). **5** (fig.) to manoeuvre (mover).
maniobrero, -a *adj.* MIL. manoeuvring.
maniobrista *adj.* **1** skilled o good at manoeuvring. || *s.m.* y *f.* **2** good manoeuvrer.
manipulación *s.f.* manipulation.
manipulador, -a *adj.* **1** manipulating. || *s.m.* y *f.* **2** manipulator.
manipulante *adj.* **1** manipulating. || *s.m.* y *f.* **2** manipulator.
manipular *v.t.* **1** to manipulate, to handle (manejar objetos). **2** (fig.) to manipulate (controlar).
manipuleo *s.m.* manipulation.
maniqueísmo *s.m.* FIL. Manicheism.
maniqueo, -a *adj./s.m.* y *f.* FIS. Manichean.
maniquí *s.m.* **1** dummy, mannequin (figura o armazón de forma humana). || *s.m.* y *f.* **2** model (modelo). **3** pawn, puppet (persona de voluntad débil).
manirroto, -a *adj.* extravagant, lavish (pródigo).
manisero, -a *s.m.* y *f.* (Am.) peanut seller (vendedor de cacahuetes).
manisuelto, -a *s.m.* y *f.* **1** (Am.) spendthrift, squanderer (derrochador). || *adj.* **2** spendthrift, wasteful (derrochador).
manitas *s.m.* y *f.* handyman, skilled person (hábil con las manos).
manito, -a *s.m.* y *f.* (Am.) mate, pal (amigo).
manivela *s.f.* MEC. crank.
manjar *s.m.* **1** food (cualquier comestible). **2** tasty dish (alimento exquisito). || **3 — blanco,** blancmange. **4 — espiritual,** food for the spirit.
mano *s.f.* **1** ANAT. hand: *la mano izquierda = the left hand.* **2** ZOOL. front foot, forefoot (pie delantero). **3** foot (de pájaro). **4** trunk (del elefante). **5** hand (de reloj). **6** coat (capa de pintura). **7** hand (en las cartas). **8** DEP. hands, handball: *¡mano! = hands!* **9** side (lado): *a mano derecha = on the right hand side.* **10** pestle (de almirez). **11** quire (conjunto de veinticinco pliegos de papel). **12** starter, lead (jugador que empieza la partida). **13** game (partida). **14** worker, hand (gente para trabajar). **15** hand (ayuda): *¿me echas una mano? = can you give me a hand?* **16** flair, gift (habilidad): *tienes buena mano para dibujar = you've got a gift for drawing.* **17** MUS. scale (escala). || **18 abrir la —,** to ease off (adoptar una actitud menos rigurosa). **19 a —, a)** by hand (no con máquinas); **b)** nearby (cerca). **20 a manos llenas,** liberally. **21 caerse de las manos,** to become boring. **22 cerrar la —,** to tighten one's belt. **23 coger a alguien con las manos en la masa,** to catch someone red-handed. **24 dar la —,** to shake hands. **25 de primera —,** brand-new. **26 de segunda —,** second hand. **27 echar — de,** to make use of. **28 estar dejado de la — de Dios,** to be unfortunate. **29 hecho a —,** made by hand. **30 írsele la — a alguien,** to go over the top. **31** (fig.) **lavarse las manos,** to wash one's hands of something. **32 llegar a las manos,** to come to blows (terminar pegándose). **33**

llevar entre manos, to be working on something. **34 — a —,** together. **35 — blanda,** with kid gloves. **36 — derecha,** right-hand man. **37 — dura** o **fuerte,** iron hand. **38 — de obra,** labour. **39 — de santo,** sure-fire remedy. **40 ¡manos a la obra!,** everybody to work! **41 ¡manos quietas!,** hands off! **42 meter — a alguien,** to start an investigation into someone. **43** (fam.) **meter — a una/uno,** to touch up (a alguien). **44 pedir la — de una mujer,** to ask for the hand of a woman. **45 poner algo en las manos de alguien,** to place in the hands of someone. **46 tener buena —,** to be good at. **47 tener mucha mano,** to be in charge. **48 untar la — a uno,** to grease someone's palm.

manojear *v.t.* (Am.) to bundle tobacco leaves (poner en manojos las hojas de tabaco).

manojo *s.m.* **1** bunch: *manojo de llaves = bunch of keys.* **2** bundle (haz). **3** (fig.) handful (puñado). **4** (fam.) group, brunch (grupo).

manolo, -a *s.m.* y *f.* archetypal Madrilenian.

manómetro *s.m.* FIS. pressure gauge, manometer.

manopla *s.f.* **1** HIST. gauntlet (de armadura). **2** whip (látigo). **3** mitten (guante sin separaciones para los dedos). **4** flannel, washing mitten (para lavarse). **5** (Am.) knuckleduster (puño de hierro).

manoseador, -a *s.m.* y *f.* person fond of touching things.

manosear *v.t.* to to uch, to handle, to finger (tocar).

manoseo *s.m.* touching, handling, fingering.

manotada *s.f.*, **manotazo** s.m. o **manotón** *s.m.* slap, smack (golpe con la mano).

manotear *v.i.* to gesticulate.

manoteo *s.m.* gesticulation.

mansalva, a mansalva, *loc. adv.* without risk (sin riesgo); with certainty (con seguridad).

mansamente o **mansito** *adv.* **1** gently (de personas). **2** tamely (de animales). **3** mildly (del tiempo). **4** calmly (del mar).

mansedumbre *s.f.* **1** gentleness, meekness (de personas). **2** tameness (de animales). **3** mildness (del tiempo). **4** calmness (del mar).

mansejón, -a *adj.* very tame (de animales, muy manso).

mansión *s.f.* **1** mansion (casa grande). **2** stay (estancia).

manso, -a *adj.* **1** gentle, mild (personas). **2** tame (animales). **3** mild (clima). **4** calm (mar, agua). || *s.m.* **5** bellwether (res que guía el rebaño). **6** country house (casa de campo).

mansurrón, -a *adj.* (desp.) docile, dopey (despectivo de manso).

manta *s.f.* **1** blanket (de la cama): *manta eléctrica = electric blanket.* **2** beating, hiding (paliza). **3** manta (pez). **4** poncho (abrigo suelto). || **5 liarse la — a la cabeza,** to go the whole hog. **6 — de viaje,** travelling rug. **7 tirar de la —,** to let the cat out of the bag.

manteador, -ora *adj.* **1** tossing. || *s.m.* y *f.* **2** tosser.

manteamiento o **manteo** *s.m.* tossing.

mantear *v.t.* to toss in a blanket.

manteca *s.f.* **1** fat, animal fat, grease (grasa). **2** lard (manteca de cerdo). **3** butter (de la leche). || **4 — de cacahuete,** peanut butter. **5 — de cacao,** cocoa butter. **6 — vegetal,** vegetable butter.

mantecada *s.f.* **1** butter roll (bollo). **2** slice of bread and butter (rebanada de pan con mantequilla).

mantecado *s.m.* **1** roll, bun (rollo). **2** ice cream (helado).

mantecoso, -a *adj.* **1** greasy, fatty (con mucha manteca). **2** buttery (de sabor a manteca).

mantel *s.m.* **1** tablecloth (para cubrir la mesa). **2** REL. altar cloth (que cubre la mesa del altar).

mantelería *s.f.* table linen.

mantenedor, -a *s.m.* y *f.* **1** chairman, presenter (de concursos, certamen). **2** president (presidente). **3** juryman (miembro de un jurado).

mantenencia *s.f.* maintenence.

mantener *v.t.* y *pron.* **1** to maintain, to keep (conservar en su ser o estado): *este termo mantiene el agua caliente = this thermos flask keeps the water warm.* **2** to hold (sujetar): *mantén la puerta abierta = hold the door open.* **3** to feed, to support (alimentar): *con su sueldo mantiene a toda la familia = on his salary he supports all the family.* || *v.t.* **4** to maintain (defender una idea): *mantengo que... = I maintain that...* **5** to maintain (defender un derecho propio). **6** to hold, to maintain (realizar durante cierto tiempo una acción): *mantener una conversación = to hold a conversation.* **7** to sustain (sostener). **8** to present (dirigir un torneo, certamen, etc.). **9** to keep (la ley, la paz): *mantener la paz = to keep the peace.* **10** FIN. to support, to maintain. **11** to keep up, to maintain (costumbres, disciplina, relaciones, etc.). || *v.pron.* **12** to stay, to remain (proseguir en una actitud o postura). || **13 — a distancia,** to keep at a distance. **14 mantenerse en sus trece,** to dig one's heels in; to stick to one's guns.

mantenimiento *s.m.* **1** maintenance, holding (acción de mantener ideas, actitudes, posiciones): *el mantenimiento de la ley = the maintenance of law.* **2** sustenance (alimento). **3** upkeep, maintenance (conservación): *el mantenimiento de una casa = the upkeep of a house.* **4** provisioning (provisión de víveres).

manteo *s.m.* **1** tossing (acción de mantear). **2** REL. long cloak (capa larga). || *pl.* **3** skirt (faldillas de mesa camilla).

mantequería *s.f.* dairy.

mantequera *s.f.* **1** churn, butter churn (máquina). **2** butter dish (recipiente).

mantequero, -a *s.m.* y *f.* **1** dairyman (hombre); dairymaid (mujer). || *adj.* **2** butter.

mantequilla *s.f.* butter.

mantequillero, -a *s.m.* y *f.* butter dish (recipiente).

mantilla *s.f.* **1** mantilla. **2** shawl (para niños). || **3 estar en mantillas,** to be very green, to be very naive.

mantillo *s.m.* **1** humus, mould (capa de materias orgánicas). **2** manure (abono).

mantis *s.f.* ZOOL. mantis: *mantis religiosa = praying mantis.*

manto *s.m.* **1** cloak (capa). **2** large mantilla (mantilla grande). **3** ZOOL. mantle (de los moluscos). **4** (fig.) cover, cloak, mantle (lo que encubre una cosa).

mantón *s.m.* **1** shawl. || **2 — de Manila,** embroidered silk shawl.

manuable *adj.* manageable, easy to use, handy.

manual *adj.* **1** manual (que se hace con las manos): *trabajo manual = manual labour.* **2** manageable, easy to use (manuable). || *s.m.* **3** handbook, manual (libro que resume una materia).

manualmente *adv.* manually, by hand.

manubrio, -a *s.m.* y *f.* **1** MEC. crank (manivela). **2** handle (mango).

manufactura *s.f.* **1** manufacture (fabricación). **2** factory (fábrica).

manufacturar *v.t.* to manufacture.

manumisión *s.f.* DER. manumission.

manumitir *v.t.* DER. to set free, (p.u.) to manumit, to emancipate.

manuscribir *v.t.* to write by hand.

manuscrito, -a *adj.* y *s.m.* manuscript.

manutención *s.f.* **1** feeding (acción de dar de comer). **2** food (comida). **3** maintenance, upkeep (conservación).

manzana *s.f.* **1** apple (fruto). **2** block (grupo de casas). **3** knob (bola de adorno). **4** pommel (pomo de la espada). **5** (Am.) Adam's apple (nuez de la garganta).

manzanal *s.m.* apple orchard.

manzanar *s.m.* apple orchard.

manzanilla *s.m.* **1** BOT. camomile (hierba). **2** camomile tea (infusión). **3** manzanilla (vino). **4** small olive (aceituna pequeña). **5** knob (adorno esférico). **6** point of the chin (extremo inferior de la barbilla).

manzanillo *s.m.* BOT. olive tree (árbol).

manzano *s.m.* BOT. apple tree (árbol).

maña *s.f.* **1** skill, ability (destreza). **2** astuteness, craftiness, craft (astucia). || *pl.* **3** whims, caprices (caprichos). || **4 malas mañas,** bad habits. **5 tener —,** to have the knack.

mañana *s.f.* **1** morning: *por la mañana = in the morning.* || *s.m.* **2** future (tiempo futuro). || *adv.* **3** tomorrow: *mañana por la mañana = tomorrow morning.* **4** later, some other time (en un tiempo futuro). || **5 a la —,** in the morning. **6 a partir de —,** starting tomorrow. **7 de —,** in the morning. **8 de la — a la noche,** from morning to night. **9 hasta —,** see you tomorrow. **10 muy de —,** very early in the morning. **11 pasado —,** the day after tomorrow.

mañanear *v.i.* to get up early.

mañanero, -a *s.m.* y *f.* 1 early riser. || *adj.* 2 early-rising.
mañanita *s.f.* 1 bed jacket (especie de chal). 2 early morning (principio de la mañana). 3 (Am.) Mexican song (canción de Méjico).
mañosamente *adv.* 1 skilfully, artfully (con habilidad). 2 cunningly, craftily (con astucia).
mañoso, -a *adj.* 1 skilful, clever (hábil). 2 cunning, sly (astuto). 3 (Am.) lazy, idle (perezoso).
maorí *adj./s.m.* y *f.* Maori.
mapa *s.m.* 1 map: *mapa del mundo = world map.* || 2 **desaparecer del –,** to vanish from the face of the earth. 3 **– meteorológico,** weather map.
mapache *s.m.* ZOOL. racoon.
mapamundi *s.m.* 1 world map. 2 (fam.) bottom, (vulg.) arse, bum (culo).
maqueta *s.f.* 1 model (modelo reducido). 2 dummy (montaje de una futura publicación).
maquetista *s.m.* y *f.* model maker.
maquiavélico, -a *adj.* Machiavellian.
maquiavelismo *s.m.* Machiavellianism.
maquillador, -a *s.m.* y *f.* make-up artist.
maquillaje *s.m.* 1 make-up (producto). 2 making-up (acción).
maquillar *v.t.* y *pron.* to make up, to put on make-up.
máquina *s.f.* 1 machine: *sala de máquinas = machine room.* 2 locomotive, engine (locomotora). 3 organism (organismo). 4 stage machinery (tramoya). 5 (fam.) car (coche). 6 (fam.) bicycle, bike (bicicleta). 7 camera (de fotos). || 8 **a toda –,** full speed. 9 **escribir a –,** to type. 10 **escrito a –,** typewritten. 11 **– de afeitar,** razor. 12 **– de coser,** sewing machine. 13 **– de discos,** juke box. 14 **– de escribir,** typewriter. 15 **– de vapor,** steam engine. 16 **– fotográfica,** camera. 17 **– herramienta,** machine tool. 18 **– registradora,** cash register. 19 **– tragaperras,** slot machine; fruit machine; one-armed bandit.
maquinación *s.f.* machination, plotting.
maquinador, -a *s.m.* y *f.* plotter, schemer.
maquinal *adj.* mechanical.
maquinalmente *adv.* mechanically.
maquinar *v.t.* to machinate, to plot (tramar).
maquinaria *s.f.* 1 machinery (conjunto de máquinas). 2 mechanism, works (conjunto de piezas que componen una máquina). 3 machine-making (construcción de máquinas).
maquinismo *s.m.* mechanization.
maquinista *s.m.* y *f.* 1 machine worker, machinist. 2 engine driver (de trenes).
mar *s.m.* o *f.* 1 sea (masa de agua): *mar Caspio = Caspian Sea.* 2 swell (marejada). 3 tide (marea). 4 loads, stacks, lots (abundancia de una cosa): *la mar de trabajo = loads of work.* || 5 **alta –,** high seas. 6 **caer al –,** to fall overboard. 7 **de alta –,** seagoing. 8 **estar hecho un – de lágrimas,** to cry one's eyes out. 9 **hablar de la –,** to daydream. 10 **la – de bien,** terrific. 11 **la – de guapa,** gorgeous; smashing. 12 **llover a mares,** to rain cats and dogs. 13 **– adentro,** offshore. 14 **– de fondo,** groundswell. 15 **– de sangre,** sea of blood. 16 **– gruesa,** rough sea. 17 **– llena,** high tide. 18 **– picado,** choppy sea. 19 **por –,** by sea.
marabú *s.m.* ZOOL. marabou (ave).
maraca *s.f.* 1 MUS. maraca. || *adj.* 2 (Am.) awkward, clumsy (torpe).
maraña *s.f.* 1 BOT. thicket, undergrowth (espesura de arbustos). 2 mess, tangle, jumble (enredo).
marasmo *s.m.* 1 MED. wasting, (p.u.) marasmus. 2 paralysis (parálisis).
maratón *s.m.* y *f.* marathon.
maravedí *s.m.* maravedi (antigua moneda española).
maravilla *s.f.* 1 marvel, wonder (que causa admiración). 2 admiration (admiración). 3 BOT. marigold (planta). || 4 **hacer maravillas,** to do/to make wonders. 5 **las siete maravillas del mundo,** the seven wonders of the world. 6 **¡qué –!,** wonderful; marvellous.
maravillar *v.t.* 1 to astonish, to amaze (sorprender). || *v.pron.* 2 to marvel, to wonder: *me maravillo con su ignorancia = I marvel at her ignorance.*
maravillosamente *adv.* marvellously, wonderfully.
maravilloso, -a *adj.* marvellous, wonderful.
marbete *s.m.* 1 label, tag (etiqueta). 2 shore (orilla). 3 border (borde).
marca *s.f.* 1 mark (señal hecha para distinguir). 2 DEP. record: *mejorar su marca = to improve one's record.* 3 make (de coches). 4 COM. brand, make (de productos). 5 footprint (huella de pies, zapatos, etc.). 6 trademark (marca registrada). 7 MAR. marker, buoy. 8 frontier area (distrito fronterizo). 9 mark, scar (cicatriz). 10 watermark (de papel). 11 brand (hecho con hierro caliente). || 12 **de –,** outstanding. 13 **– de agua,** watermark. 14 **– de ley,** hallmark.
marcadamente *adv.* markedly.
marcado, -a *adj.* 1 marked (en sentido general). 2 marked, pronounced: *con acento marcado = with a marked accent.*
marcador, -ora *adj.* 1 marking (que marca). || *s.m.* 2 DEP. scoreboard (tablero que señala el resultado). || *s.m.* y *f.* 3 feeder (de imprenta).
marcaje *s.m.* DEP. marking.
marcar *v.t.* 1 to mark (hacer una marca): *marcar un papel = to mark a paper.* 2 to indicate (indicar). 3 to distinguish (distinguir). 4 to dial (el teléfono). 5 to brand (el ganado). 6 DEP. to score (meter un gol, tanto, etc.). 7 to show, to register (el termómetro, barómetro, etc.). 8 to mark out (delimitar). 9 to mark, to price (poner el precio). 10 to bid (en los naipes). 11 to feed (en la imprenta). 12 to mark (en la música). 13 DEP. to mark (vigilar al jugador contrario). 14 to assign (destinar). 15 to stamp (sellar). 16 to set (el pelo). || 17 MIL. **– el paso,** to mark time. 18 **– las cartas,** to mark the cards.
marcial *adj.* 1 martial: *ley marcial = martial law.* 2 military (porte, disciplina).
marcialidad *s.f.* military bearing.
marciano, -a *adj./s.m.* y *f.* Martian.
marco *s.m.* 1 mark (moneda alemana). 2 frame (armazón). 3 setting (conjunto de circunstancias y ambiente físico): *el jardín ofrecía un marco muy bonito = the garden offered a beautiful setting.* 4 DEP. goal-posts.
marcha *s.f.* 1 marcha (acción de marchar): *marcha del hambre = hunger march.* 2 speed (grado de velocidad): *a toda marcha = at full speed.* 3 MEC. gear: *primera marcha = first gear.* 4 running, progress (desarrollo de un asunto o negocio). 5 MUS. march (pieza musical). 6 DEP. walk. 7 (fig.) course, trend (paso): *la marcha de la guerra = the curse of the war.* || 8 **abrir la –,** to be at the head. 9 **cerrar la –,** to bring up the rear. 10 **¡en –!,** let's go! 11 **estar en –, a)** MEC. to be working; **b)** (fig.) to be on the move. 12 **poner en –,** to start up. 13 (fam.) **tener –,** to be lively (una ciudad); to be full of life (persona).
marchamo *s.m.* 1 stamp (señal de los aduaneros). 2 (fig.) stamp, mark.
marchante, -a *s.m.* y *f.* 1 commercial traveller (viajante comercial). 2 (Am.) customer, client (cliente).
marchantía *s.f.* (Am.) customers, clients (clientela).
marchar *v.i.* 1 to go, to travel (ir de un lugar a otro). 2 to work, to run, to go (moverse ciertos mecanismos): *el coche marcha bien = the car is working well.* 3 MIL. to march. 4 to go (irse realizando algo): *las cosas no marchan bien = things are not going well.* || *v.pron.* 5 to leave, to go (partir de un lugar): *nos marchamos a las dos = we left at two.*
marchitable *adj.* short-lived.
marchitamiento *s.m.* whitering, shrivelling.
marchitar *v.t.* y *pron.* to wither, to shrivel (las flores).
marchitez *s.f.* withered o shrivelled state.
marchito, -a *adj.* withered, shrivelled.
marchoso, -a *adj.* 1 lively, swinging (sitio). 2 full of life (persona).
marea *s.f.* 1 MAR. tide: *marea alta = high tide.* 2 sea breeze (viento suave marítimo). 3 dew (rocío). 4 dirt, filth (inmundicia). || 5 **– creciente,** rising tide. 6 **– viva,** spring tide.
mareado, -a *adj.* 1 sick, ill (enfermo). 2 seasick (malo, en el mar). 3 dizzy (aturdido). 4 drunk (borracho).
mareaje *s.m.* 1 course (rumbo). 2 seamanship (arte de marear). 3 navigation (arte de navegar).
mareamiento *s.m.* V. **mareo.**
mareante *adj.* 1 sailing (navegante). 2 sickening (que marea). 3 (fam.) head-spinning (persona que marea con su pesadez, charla, etc.). || *s.m.* 4 navegator (comerciante por mar).

marear *v.t.* **1** to sail (navegar). **2** to captain (gobernar un barco). **3** MED. to make someone feel sick: *me marea el olor = the smell makes me feel sick.* **4** MED. to make someone seasick (en el mar). **5** to make someone dizzy (aturdir): *las alturas me marean = heights make me dizzy.* **6** (fig.) to annoy, to bother (molestar). || *v.pron.* **7** MED. to get seasick (en un barco). **8** MED. to feel sick (sentirse malo). **9** to feel dizzy (estar aturdido).
marejada *s.f.* **1** MAR. heavy swell, rough sea (movimiento muy agitado). **2** groundswell of unrest (señales de descontento de un grupo).
maremagno o **maremagnum** *s.m.* **1** noisy crowd (de personas). **2** jumble, mess (de cosas).
maremoto *s.m.* tidal wave.
marengo *adj.* dark grey (gris oscuro).
mareo *s.m.* **1** sickness, nausea (náusea). **2** seasickness (en un barco). **3** dizziness, giddiness (aturdimiento). **4** nuisance, annoyance (molestia).
marfil *s.m.* ivory.
marfileño, -a *adj.* ivory-like (de aspecto de marfil).
marga *s.f.* MIN. marl, loam.
margarina *s.f.* margarine.
margarita *s.f.* **1** BOT. daisy (planta). **2** pearl (perla). **3** ZOOL. winkle (caracol pequeño).
margen *s.m.* **1** border, edge (extremidad). **2** side, bank (orilla). **3** margin (de una hoja): *al margen = in the margin.* **4** opportunity, occasion (oportunidad). **5** COM. margin, profit margin (beneficio económico sobrante). **6** verge, side (de una carretera). || **7 dar — para,** to give an opportunity for. **8 dejar algo al —,** to leave something to one side. **9 mantenerse al —,** to keep out of the way. **10 — de beneficio,** profit margin. **11 — de error,** margin of error. **12 — de seguridad,** safety margin.
marginado, -a *adj.* **1** on the outside. || *s.m.* y *f.* **2** outcast.
marginal *adj.* marginal.
marginar *v.t.* **1** to make notes in the margin (anotar en el margen). **2** to leave a margin (dejar margen). || *v.t.* y *pron.* **3** to exclude (excluir).
mariachi o **mariache** *s.m.* **1** MUS. (Am.) mariachi (música mexicana). **2** mariachi orchestra (orquesta). **3** mariachi player (músico).
marianista *adj./s.m.* y *f.* REL. marianist.
mariano, -a *adj.* REL. marian.
marica *s.m.* **1** (fam.) puff, pansy (hombre afeminado). **2** gay, homosexual (homosexual). || *s.f.* **3** ZOOL. magpie (urraca).
maricón, -a *s.m.* y *f.* (fam. y desp.) puff, queer.
mariconada o **mariconería** *s.f.* **1** (fam.) dirty trick (mala pasada). **2** stupidity (estupidez).
maridaje *s.m.* **1** married life (unión conyugal). **2** (fig.) marriage, harmony (armonía).
maridar *v.i.* **1** to marry (contraer matrimonio). || *v.t.* **2** to join, to unite (unir).
marido *s.m.* husband.
marihuana o **marijuana** *s.f.* marijuana, (fam.) grass.
marimacho *s.m.* mannish woman.
marimandona *s.f.* bossy woman, harridan, (fam.) battle-axe.
marimba *s.f.* **1** MUS. drum (tambor). **2** (Am.) marimba, xylophone (xilófono). **3** kettledrum (tímpano).
marimorena *s.f.* (fam.) rumpus, row (alboroto).
marina *s.f.* **1** coast, coastal region (costa). **2** navy (conjunto de barcos). **3** navigation (arte de navegar). **4** seascape, seapiece (cuadro). || **5 — mercante,** merchant navy.
marinaje *s.m.* seamanship (arte de marear).
marinar *v.t.* **1** to marinate, to marinade (preparar el pescado). **2** MAR. to man (tripular).
marinear *v.i.* to work on a boat.
marinera *s.f.* V. **marinero.**
marinería *s.f.* **1** seamanship (arte de marear). **2** sailoring (ejercicio de marinero). **3** crew (tripulación).
marinero, -a *adj.* **1** sea, marine (relativo a la marina): *pez marino = sea fish.* **2** seaworthy: *barco marinero = seaworthy ship.* || *s.m.* y *f.* **3** sailor, seaman, mariner (persona que trabaja en un barco). || *s.f.* **4** sailor blouse (blusa de marinero).
marinesco, -a *adj.* seaman-like, sailor-fashion.
marino, -a *adj.* **1** sea, marine (relativo al mar): *fauna marina = marine life.* || *s.m.* **2** sailor, seaman.
marioneta *s.f.* **1** puppet, marionette (muñeco). **2** puppet show (representación teatral).
mariposa *s.f.* **1** butterfly (insecto). **2** DEP. butterfly stroke. **3** TEC. wing nut (tuerca con alas). || **4 — nocturna,** moth.
mariposeador, -ora *adj.* **1** capricious, unpredictable, fickle (caprichoso). **2** flitatious (galanteador). || *s.m.* y *f.* **3** fickle person (persona caprichosa). **4** flirt (galanteador).
mariposear *v.i.* **1** to be fickle (cambiar con frecuencia de gustos). **2** to be inconsistent (tener inconsistencia con las personas). **3** to flirt (galantear).
mariposón *s.m.* flirt, tease (hombre que galantea).
mariquita *s.f.* ZOOL. ladybird (insecto). || *s.m.* **2** (desp.) puff, queer (maricón).
marisabidilla *s.f.* know-all.
mariscal *s.m.* MIL. marshall.
mariscala *s.f.* marshall's wife.
mariscalato o **mariscalía** *s.m.* y *f.* MIL. marshallship.
mariscador, -ora *s.m.* y *f.* shellfisherman (hombre); shellfishwoman (mujer).
mariscar *v.t.* to fish for shellfish.
marisco *s.m.* shellfish, seafood.
marisma *s.f.* mud flats.
marismeño, -a *adj.* marsh.
marisquería *s.f.* seafood restaurant/bar.
marisquero, -a *s.m.* y *f.* shellfisherman (hombre); shellfisherwoman (mujer).
marista *adj.* y *s.m.* REL. marist.
marital *adj.* marital.
marítimo, -a *adj.* **1** maritime, sea, marine (perteneciente al mar). || **2 pueblo marítimo,** seaside village.
maritornes *s.f.* slut, trollop.
marjoleto o **marzoleto** *s.m.* BOT. hawthorn.
marketing *s.m.* marketing.
marmita *s.f.* pot, pan (olla).
mármol *s.m.* GEOL. marble.
marmoleño, -a *adj.* marmoreal.
marmolería *s.f.* **1** marble workshop (taller). **2** marblework (obras de mármol).
marmolista *s.m.* marble cutter.
marmóreo, -a *adj.* marmoreal.
marmota *s.f.* **1** ZOOL. marmot. **2** (fig.) sleepyhead (persona dormilona).
maroma *s.f.* **1** rope (cuerda). **2** (Am.) acrobatic performance (función de acrobacia). **3** volte-face, about-turn (pirueta política).
maronita *adj./s.m.* y *f.* REL. maronite.
marqués, -a *s.m.* y *f.* marquis, marquess.
marquesado *s.m.* marquisate.
marquesina *s.f.* canopy.
marquetería *s.f.* marquetry, inlaid work.
marra *s.f.* **1** stone hammer (almádena). **2** lack (falta). || *adv.* **3** at some other time (en otro tiempo).
marrajo, -a *adj.* **1** dangerous (toro). **2** false (falso). || *s.m.* **3** ZOOL. shark (tiburón).
marrana *s.f.* ZOOL. sow (hembra del cerdo).
marranada *s.f.* **1** filth, dirt (suciedad). **2** dirty trick, rotten trick, lousy act (cochinada).
marranchón, -ona *s.m.* y *f.* pig, hog (cerdo).
marrano *s.m.* **1** pig, hog (puerco). **2** (fig.) pig (persona sucia). **3** pig, swine (persona grosera). || *adj.* **4** filthy, dirty (sucio).
marras, de marras *loc. adv. same old thing; same old story.*
marrasquino *s.m.* maraschino (bebida).
marrillo *s.m.* stick, club.
marro *s.m.* **1** dodge, faint (movimiento del cuerpo). **2** lack, absense (falta).
marrón *adj.* **1** brown, maroon (color). || *s.m.* **2** brown, maroon.
marroquí *adj.* **1** Moroccan. || *s.m.* y *f.* **2** Moroccan (persona). || *s.m.* **3** Morocco leather (cuero).
marroquinería *s.f.* **1** leather goods industry (industria). **2** leather working (arte de trabajar el cuero).
marrubio *s.m.* BOT. horehound.
marrullería o **marulla** *s.f.* low-down o nasty trick (engaño solapado).
marrullero, -a *adj.* **1** nasty, despicable (ruin). || *s.m.* y *f.* **2** nasty person.
marsopa o **marsopla** *s.f.* ZOOL. porpoise.
marsupial *adj.* y *s.m.* marsupial.
marta *s.f.* ZOOL. marten.
martellina *s.f.* sledgehammer.
martes *s.m.* Tuesday (día): *martes de carnaval = Shrove Tuesday.*

martillador *s.m.* hammersmith.
martillazo *s.m.* 1 hammer blow (golpe). || 2 **a martillazos,** by hammering.
martillear o **martillar** *v.t.* 1 to hammer (golpear con martillo). 2 to torment, to bother (atormentar).
martilleo *s.m.* hammering.
martillo *s.m.* 1 hammer (herramienta). 2 MUS. tuning hammer. 3 ANAT. hammer, malleus (huesecillo del oído medio). 4 DEP. hammer. || 5 hammer (de despertador). || 6 **a macha —,** thoroughly.
martín *s.m.* 1 ZOOL. martin (ave). || 2 **—, pescador,** kingfisher.
martinete *s.m.* 1 MUS. hammer (del piano). 2 drop hammer (mazo pesado). 3 ZOOL. heron (ave).
martingala *s.f.* 1 trick (treta). 2 cunning (astucia).
mártir *s.m.* y *f.* martyr.
martirio *s.m.* martyrdom.
martirizador, -ora *adj.* 1 martyring. || *s.m.* y *f.* 2 torturer, tormentor.
martirizar *v.t.* 1 to martyr. 2 (fig.) to torture, to kill: *esta ropa me martiriza = these clothes are killing me.*
martirologio *s.m.* martyrology.
marxismo *s.m.* POL. Marxism.
marxista *adj./s.m.* y *f.* Marxist.
marzo *s.m.* March.
marzoleta *s.f.* BOT. hawthorn berry.
marzoleto *s.m.* BOT. hawthorn.
mas *conj.* 1 but (pero). || *s.m.* 2 farm (granja).
más *adv.* 1 more: *no quiero más = I don't want any more; gano más dinero que el año pasado = I earn more money than last year.* 2 (en frases comparativas): *ella es más alta que él = she's taller than him; somos más inteligentes que ellos = we're more intelligent than them.* 3 (en frases superlativas): *él es el más rico = he's the richest; ella es la chica más guapa = she's the most beautiful girl.* 4 MAT. plus, and: *tres más seis son nueve = three and six are nine.* 5 more than, over: *tengo más de cuarenta discos = I've got over forty records.* 6 more than (más que): *gano más que tú = I earn more than you.* 7 no other: *no tengo más remedio que hacerlo = I have no other choice but to do it.* 8 past, after (tiempo): *son más de las diez = it's after ten.* 9 more, another (otro): *un día más = another day; one more day.* 10 so (tan): *estoy más cansado = I'm so tired.* || *s.m.* 11 MAT. plus (signo aritmético de adición). || *pl.* 12 *este trabajo tiene sus más y sus menos = this job has its good and bad points.* || *adj.* 13 better (mejor): *sois más equipo que nosotros = you're a better team than we are.* || *comp.* 14 (sin traducir): *¡qué día más bueno! = what a beautiful day!; ¡qué tío más estúpido! = what a stupid bloke!* || 15 **a lo —,** at the most. 16 **a — y mejor,** a lot; a great deal. 17 **de —,** spare, extra (que sobra): *hay dos sillas de más = there are two extra chairs.* 18 **estar de —,** not to be needed: *estamos de más = we are not needed.* 19 **— bien,** on the contrary (por el contrario). 20 **— o menos,** more or less. 21 **nada —,** nothing else. 22 **no —,** only. 23 **por — que,** however much; no matter how much. 24 **sin — ni —,** without further ado.
masa *s.f.* 1 FIS. mass: *unidad de masa = unit of mass.* 2 dough (harina y agua). 3 (fig.) mass, heap, pile (cosas apiñadas): *una masa de hojas = a mass of leaves.* 4 ARQ. mortar, plaster (argamasa). || *pl.* 5 masses (gente indiferenciada). || 6 **en —,** en masse. 7 **— encefálica,** brain. 8 **producción en —,** mass production.
masacrar *v.t.* to massacre.
masacre *s.f.* massacre.
masada *s.f.* farm (granja).
masaje *s.m.* 1 massage. || 2 **dar — a,** to massage.
masajista *s.m.* y *f.* 1 masseur. || *s.f.* 2 masseuse.
mascador, -a *adj.* chewing.
mascar *v.t.* 1 to chew, (p.u.) to masticate. 2 (fam.) to mumble, to mutter (hablar entre dientes).
máscara *s.f.* 1 mask (para cubrir el rostro). 2 disguise, mask (disfraz). 3 pretence, sham (disimulo). || *s.m.* y *f.* 4 masked figure (persona enmascarada). || *s.f.pl.* 5 masquerade, masked ball (mascarada).
mascarilla *s.f.* 1 mask (máscara). 2 plaster cast (de la cara). 3 death mask (de un muerto). 4 face mask (de crema).
mascarón *s.m.* 1 ARQ. mascaron (adorno en forma de cara deforme). || 2 **— de proa,** figurehead.
mascota *s.f.* mascot.
masculinidad *s.f.* masculinity, manliness.
masculinizar *v.t.* GRAM. to make masculine.
masculino, -a *s.m.* 1 GRAM. masculine. || *adj.* 2 BIOL. male (dotado de órganos para fecundar). 3 masculine, manly (relativo a los hombres). 4 GRAM. masculine: *un sustantivo masculino = a masculine noun.*
mascullar *v.t.* to mumble, to mutter (hablar bajo o poco claro).
masía o **masería** *s.f.* farm (granja).
masilla *s.f.* putty.
masivamente *adv.* massively.
masivo, -a *adj.* massive (dosis, ataque, etc.).
masón, -ona *adj./s.m.* y *f.* mason, freemason.
masonería *s.f.* masonry, freemasonry.
masónico, -a *adj.* masonic: *logia masónica = masonic lodge.*
masoquismo *s.m.* masochism.
masoquista *s.m.* y *f.* 1 masochist. || *adj.* 2 masochistic.
masticación *s.f.* chewing, mastication.
masticador, -a *adj.* 1 chewing. || *s.m.* 2 masticator.
masticar *v.t.* 1 to chew, to masticate. 2 (fig.) to chew over, to think over (reflexionar).
masticatorio *adj.* masticatory.
mástil *s.m.* 1 MAR. mast (para sujetar las velas). 2 pole, post (palo). 3 MUS. neck (de un instrumento de cuerda). 4 BOT. stem (tallo). 5 quill (nervio central de la pluma de un ave). || 6 **— de tienda,** tent pole.
mastín *s.m.* 1 mastiff (perro). || 2 **— danés,** Great Dane.
mastitis *s.f.* MED. mastitis.
mastodonte *s.m.* mastodon.
mastoides *adj.* y *s.m.* MED. mastoid.
mastuerzo *s.m.* 1 BOT. cress (planta). 2 dope, dolt, clot (necio).
masturbación *s.f.* masturbation.
masturbarse *v.r.* to masturbate.
mata *s.f.* 1 BOT. bush, shrub (arbusto). 2 plantation (terreno de la misma especie de árboles). 3 tuft, clump (parte arrancada de una planta). || *pl.* 4 scrub (matorral). || 5 **— de pelo,** tuft of hair.
mataburros *s.m.* (Am.) dictionary (diccionario).
matacán *s.m.* ARQ. machicolation.
matacandelas *s.m.* snuffer.
matadero *s.m.* slaughterhouse, abattoir.
matador, -a *adj.* 1 killing (que mata). 2 absurd, ridiculous (absurdo). || *s.m.* 3 matador, bullfighter (torero). 4 killer (asesino).
matadura *s.f.* sore (llaga en el cuerpo de un animal).
matamoros *adj.* 1 swaggering, arrogant. || *s.m.* 2 braggart, boaster.
matamoscas *s.f.* 1 fly swat (utensilio). 2 fly paper (papel). 3 fly spray (vaporizador).
matanza *s.f.* 1 slaughter, massacre (masacre). 2 killing (acción de matar). 3 slaughtering season (época de matar los cerdos). 4 pork products (productos de cerdo).
matar *v.t.* to kill (quitar la vida). 2 to slaughter, to kill (animales). 3 (fig.) to kill, to destroy (ocasionar algún trastorno). 4 to file, to smooth (una arista). 5 to tone down (un color). 6 to kill (tiempo). 7 to stave off, to stay (el hambre). 8 to put out (el fuego). || *v.pron.* 9 to kill oneself, to commit suicide (suicidarse). 10 to be killed (ser matado). 11 (fig.) to kill oneself, to tire oneself out (afanarse con mucho empeño). || 12 **estar a — con uno,** to be at daggers with someone. 13 **matarlas callando,** to be a sly devil. 14 **— dos pájaros de un tiro,** to kill two birds with one stone.
matarife *s.m.* butcher, slaughterman (matador de reses).
matarratas *s.m.* 1 rat killer (para matar ratas). 2 (fam.) hootch, rotgut (bebida fuerte, de mala calidad).
matasanos *s.m.* (fam. y desp.) quack, saw-bones (médico).
matasellos *s.m.* 1 postmark (señal). 2 canceller (máquina).
matasiete *s.m.* bully, braggart (bravucón).
matasuegras *s.m.* paper serpent.
matazón *s.m.* (Am.) slaughter, massacre (matanza).
match *s.m.* DEP. match.
mate *s.m.* 1 mate (en el ajedrez). 2 BOT. maté (planta). 3 (Am.) maté, Paragua-

yan tea (infusión). 4 maté (yerba mate). || *adj.* 5 dull (sin brillo). || **6 jaque —,** checkmate.

matemáticamente *adv.* mathematically.

matemático, -a *adj.* 1 mathematical. || *s.m.* y *f.* 2 mathematician. || *s.f.pl.* 3 mathematics (ciencia).

materia *s.f.* 1 FIS. y MED. matter. 2 material, stuff (material). 3 matter, subject (tema, asunto o contenido de un libro, etc.). 4 subject (asignatura). || **5 en — de,** on the subject of. **6 entrar en —,** (fam.) to get down to brass tacks. **7 índice de materias,** table of contents. **8 — gris,** grey matter. **9 — prima,** raw material.

material *s.m.* 1 material: *material de construcción = building material.* 2 FIS. material (materia). 3 equipment, materials (equipo): *material escolar = teaching materials; material deportivo = sports equipment.* || *adj.* 4 material (relativo a la materia). 5 physical (físico y corpóreo). 6 materialistic (que prefiere lo físico a lo espiritual).

materialidad *s.f.* substance, material nature.

materialismo *s.m.* materialism.

materialista *adj.* 1 materialistic, materialist. || *s.m.* y *f.* 2 materialist.

materialización *s.f.* materialization.

materializar *v.t.* y *pron.* to materialize.

materialmente *adv.* 1 materially. 2 physically (físicamente). 3 totally, completely (completamente).

maternal *adj.* maternal.

maternidad *s.f.* 1 maternity, motherhood (condición de madre). 2 maternity hospital (hospital).

materno, -a *adj.* 1 motherly, maternal (maternal). 2 mother (idioma).

matidez *s.f.* dullness.

matinal *adj.* morning.

matiz *s.m.* 1 shade, tint (gradación de color). 2 (fig.) shade, nuance (de sentido, palabra, obra).

matizar *v.t.* 1 to blend, to harmonize (combinar armónicamente). 2 to vary (variar). 3 to sharpen, to focus (dar mayor nitidez). 4 to tinge, to tint (colores).

matojo *s.m.* small bush, shrub (mata pequeña).

matón, -a *s.m.* y *f.* boaster, braggart (matamoros).

matorral *s.m.* 1 scrubland (terreno de matas). 2 thicket (conjunto de matas y maleza).

matraca *s.f.* 1 rattle (instrumento rotatorio). 2 (fam.) drag, nuisance, pest (insistencia molesta): *dar la matraca = to pester.*

matraqueo *s.m.* 1 rattle (acción de matraquear). 2 pestering (acción de dar la matraca).

matraz *s.m.* QUIM. flask (vasija).

matrerear *v.i.* (Am.) to wander, to roam (vagabundear).

matrero, -a *s.m.* y *f.* (Am.) bandit, brigand (bandolero).

matriarcado *s.m.* matriarchy.

matriarcal *adj.* matriarchal.

matricaria *s.f.* BOT. feverfew (planta).

matricida *s.m.* y *f.* 1 matricide (persona). || *adj.* 2 matricidal.

matricidio *s.m.* matricide.

matrícula *s.f.* 1 registration, enrolment (inscripción en una lista). 2 registration o enrolment documents (documentos). 3 roll (conjunto de personas inscritas). 4 register, roll, list (lista). 5 licence plate, registration number (de un coche).

matriculación *s.f.* 1 enrolment, matriculation (en un colegio, etc.). 2 registration (de un coche).

matriculado, -a *adj.* 1 registered (coche, etc.). 2 enrolled, registered (un alumno).

matricular *v.t.* y *pron.* 1 to enrol, to register, to matriculate (en un colegio, etc.). || *v.t.* 2 to register (un coche, barco, etc.).

matrimonial *adj.* 1 marital, matrimonial. 2 married: *vida matrimonial = married life.* **3 capitulaciones matrimoniales,** marriage settlement.

matrimonialmente *adv.* maritally.

matrimoniar *v.i.* to get married.

matrimonio *s.m.* 1 marriage, matrimony (unión legal). 2 married couple (mujer y marido). || **3 cama de —,** double bed. **4 — civil,** civil marriage. **5 — por la iglesia,** church marriage.

matriz *s.f.* 1 ANAT. womb, uterus. 2 TEC. die, mould (molde). 3 MAT. matrix. 4 nut (tuerca). 5 stub (de un talonario). || *adj.* 6 principal, first (principal).

matrona *s.f.* 1 MED. midwife (partera). 2 matron (en la cárcel). 3 matriarch (madre de noble familia romana). 4 stout woman (mujer robusta).

matronal *adj.* matronly.

matusalén *s.m.* Methuselah.

matute *s.m.* 1 smuggling, trafficking (introducción ilegal de productos). 2 contraband (contrabando). 3 fraud, swindle (timo).

matutear *v.i.* to smuggle.

matutero, -a *s.m.* y *f.* smuggler, trafficker.

matutino, -a *adj.* morning, morning time.

maula *s.m.* y *f.* 1 inept person, (fam.) ne'er-do-well (persona inepta). || *s.f.* 2 dead loss (persona o cosa sin valor ni estima). 3 remnant, scrap (retal). 4 dirty trick (engaño solapado).

maulería *s.f.* 1 second-hand goods shop (tienda de retales). 2 slyness, trickery (hábito de engañar).

maulero *s.m.* cheat, shark, con man (timador).

maullador, -a *adj.* miaowing.

maullar *v.i.* to miaow.

maullido o **maído** *s.m.* miaow.

maúllo *s.m.* miaow.

máuser *s.m.* MIL. mauser (arma).

mausoleo o **mauseolo** *s.m.* mausoleum.

maxilar *adj.* 1 ANAT. maxillary. || *s.m.* 2 jawbone, jaw.

máxima *s.f.* 1 maxim. 2 adage (adagio).

máximamente o **máxime** *adv.* 1 above all (sobre todo). 2 principally (principalmente).

máximo, -a *s.m.* 1 maximum: *al máximo = to the maximum.* || **2 como —,** at most. || *adj.* 3 maximum, highest: *el punto máximo = the highest point.*

máximum *s.m.* 1 maximum (máximo). || **2 al —,** completely.

maya *adj.* 1 Mayan (de la antigua civilización). || *s.m.* y *f.* 2 Mayan, Maya. 3 BOT. daisy (planta).

mayal *s.m.* flail (para desgranar el centeno).

mayear *v.t.* to be May weather.

mayestático, -a *adj.* 1 majestic. || **2 plural —,** royal "we".

mayéutica, -o *s.f.* y *m.* maieutics.

mayo *s.m.* 1 May (mes). 2 maypole (palo).

mayonesa *s.f.* mayonnaise.

mayor *adj.* 1 bigger, larger (comparativo de grande). 2 elder, older (comparativo de viejo): *mi hermana mayor = my elder sister.* 3 biggest, largest (superlativo de grande). 4 oldest, eldest (superlativo de viejo). 5 greater (superior): *su hambre es mayor = his hunger is greater.* 6 greatest (superlativo): *tiene la mayor cantidad de discos = she has the greatest number of records.* 7 elderly (anciano): *un hombre mayor = an elderly man.* 8 adult, grown-up (adulto). 9 main, high (calles). 10 main (plazas): *la plaza mayor = the main square.* 11 MUS. major. 12 high (misa). 13 main (mástil). || *s.m.* 14 adult, grown-up (adulto). 15 boss, chief (jefe). || *pl.* 16 adults, grown-ups (adultos). 17 ancestors, forefathers (ascendientes). || **18 al por —,** wholesale. **19 hacerse —,** to grow up. **20 ser — de edad,** to be of age.

mayoral *s.m.* 1 farm foreman (capataz de labores agrícolas). 2 HIST. coachnan (el que guiaba un carruaje). 3 rent collector (recaudador de rentas).

mayorazgo *s.m.* 1 primogeniture (primogenitura). 2 heir (heredero). 3 eldest son (primogénito). 4 DER. entailed estate (bienes).

mayordomía *s.f.* butlership (cargo de mayordomo).

mayordomo *s.m.* 1 butler (criado principal). || *s.m.* 2 REL. churchwarden.

mayoría *s.f.* 1 majority, most: *la mayoría de la gente = the majority of the people;* most of the people. 2 POL. majority: *ganar por una mayoría = to win by a majority.* || **3 en su —,** in the main. **4 — absoluta,** absolute majority. **5 — simple,** simple majority. **6 — de edad,** adult age.

mayorista *s.m.* y *f.* COM. wholesaler.

mayoritario, -a *adj.* majority: *gobierno mayoritario = majority government.*

mayormente *adv.* 1 especially (especialmente). 2 mainly (principalmente).

mayúscula *s.f.* capital (letra mayúscula).

mayúsculo, -a *adj.* 1 capital (letra). 2 enormous, huge (muy grande): *una sorpresa mayúscula = an enormous surprise.*

maza *s.f.* 1 HIST. mace (arma). 2 TEC. pounder (para machacar). 3 bore, nui-

sance (persona pesada). **4** MUS. drumstick. **5** butt (de los tacos de billar). **6** HIST. mace (insignia).
mazacote *s.m.* **1** concrete (hormigón). **2** mess, eyesore (obra de arte tosca). **3** drag, bore (hombre molesto). **4** stodgy food (manjar indigesto).
mazada *s.f.* mace blow (golpe de maza).
mazamorrero *s.m.* (Am.) plotter (intrigante).
mazapán *s.m.* marzipan (dulce).
mazazo *s.m.* mace blow.
mazmorra *s.f.* dungeon.
mazo *s.m.* **1** mallet (martillo de madera). **2** TEC. pounder (maza para machacar). **3** drag, nuisance (hombre pesado). **4** bunch (grupo de cosas).
mazorca *s.f.* **1** ear, cob (espiga del maíz). **2** spindle (husada). **3** cacao (fruto del cacao).
mazurca *s.f.* mazurka (danza polaca).
me *pron. personal* **1** (acusativo) me: *¡dime! = tell me!* **2** (dativo) me, to me: *me han escrito = they've written to me; me han dicho = they've told me.* **3** (reflexivo) myself: *me voy a matar = I'm going to kill myself.* **4** for me (para mí): *me lo compraron = they bought it for me.*
meada *s.f.* (vulg.) piss.
meadero *s.m.* (fam.) bog, (vulg.) shit house (urinario).
mear *v.t.* **1** (vulg.) to piss on. || *v.i.* **2** (vulg.) to piss. || *v.pron.* **3** to piss oneself.
meandro *s.m.* **1** meander (de un río). **2** ARQ. meander (adorno).
mecánica *s.f.* FIS. **1** mechanics (ciencia). **2** mechanism (mecanismo). **3** (fig.) mechanics.
mecánicamente *adv.* mechanically.
mecanicismo *s.m.* mechanicalism.
mecánico, -a *s.m.* y *f.* **1** mechanic (persona). || *adj.* **2** mechanical (perteneciente a la mecánica). **3** machine-made (hecho con máquina).
mecanismo *s.m.* **1** mechanism, works (estructura interna de un artefacto). **2** (fig.) machinery: *el mecanismo del estado = the machinery of state.*
mecanización *s.f.* mechanization.
mecanizado, -a *adj.* mechanized.
mecanizar *v.t.* to mechanize.
mecano *s.m.* meccano (juego).
mecanografía *s.f.* typing, typewriting.
mecanografiar *v.t.* to type.
mecanográfico, -a *adj.* typing.
mecanógrafo, -a *s.m.* y *f.* typist.
mecate *s.m.* **1** (Am.) cord, string (cordel). **2** rough type (basto). **3** ignoramus (inculto).
mecedero *s.m.* stirrer (para mecer el líquido).
mecenas *s.m.* y *f.* patron.
mecenazgo *s.m.* patronage.
mecer *v.t.* **1** to stir (agitar líquidos o mezclas). || *v.t.* y *pron.* **2** to rock (a un niño). **3** to sway, to move to and fro (balancear). **4** to swing (columpiar).
mecha *s.f.* **1** wick (cuerda combustible). **2** MIL. fuse (de bombas). **3** slice of bacon (lonja de tocino). **4** bundle (conjunto de hebras). **5** (Am.) joke (broma). || **6 aguantar –,** to grin and bear it. **7 a toda –,** like greased lightning.
mechas *s.pl.* (Am.) mops of hair (greñas de cabello).
mechazo *s.m.* lighter fuel (combustible).
mechero *s.m.* **1** lighter (encendedor). **2** wick holder (tubito donde se mete la mecha). **3** candle holder (donde se mete la vela).
mechón *s.m.* **1** tuft, wisp (porción de pelos). **2** bundle (de hilos).
medalla *s.f.* **1** medal: *medalla de oro = gold medal.* **2** medallion, pendant (medallón).
medallón *s.m.* **1** medallion (medalla grande). **2** locket (cajita redonda). **3** ARQ. medallion (bajorrelieve).
media *s.f.* **1** stocking (prenda). **2** MAT. mean. **3** DEP. half-back line. **4** average (promedio). || **5 hacer –,** to knit.
mediación *s.f.* mediation.
mediado, -a *adj.* **1** half full (medio lleno): *la botella está mediada = the bottle is half full.* **2** half done (medio hecho). **3** half complete (medio completo). **4** halfway through (hacia la mitad): *llevo mediado el libro = I'm halfway through the book.* || **5 a mediados de,** in the middle of; mid-; halfway through: *a mediados de año = in the middle of the year; a mediados de mayo = mid-May.*
mediador, -ora *s.m.* y *f.* mediator.
medial *adj.* medial.
mediana *s.f.* MAT. median.
medianamente *adv.* moderately, reasonably.
medianería *s.f.* party wall (pared común).
medianero, -a *adj.* **1** dividing (en medio de dos cosas). **2** party, dividing (pared). **3** boundary (para vallas). **4** mediating (que intercede). || *s.m.* y *f.* **5** mediator (que intercede por alguien). **6** neighbour (vecino).
medianía o **medianidad** *s.f.* **1** average person, mediocrity (mediocridad). **2** average means, modest means (posición económica). **3** average (término medio). **4** average social position (posición social).
mediano, -a *adj.* **1** average, normal, medium (de calidad intermedia). **2** mediocre, below average (de poca calidad): *vino mediano = mediocre wine.*
medianoche *s.f.* midnight.
mediante *prep.* **1** by means of, via, using (por medio de): *lo hicieron mediante la fuerza = they did it by means of force.* **2** thanks to (gracias a). || **3 Dios –,** God willing.
mediar *v.i.* **1** to be halfway, to be in the middle (llegar a la mitad). **2** to mediate (interceder). **3** to be between (estar en medio de varias cosas). **4** to pass, to go by (transcurrir un tiempo entre dos hechos).
mediatamente *adv.* indirectly.
mediatización *s.f.* mediatization.
mediatizar *v.t.* **1** to mediatize. **2** to hinder (coartar).
mediato, -a *adj.* mediate.
mediatriz *s.f.* MAT. bisector.
médica *s.f.* MED. woman doctor, doctor.
medicable *adj.* MED. treatable.
medicación *s.f.* treatment, medication.
medicamento *s.m.* medicine, drug.
medicamentoso, -a *adj.* medicinal.
medicar *v.t.* to medicate.
medicastro, -a *s.m.* y *f.* (desp.) quack.
medicina *s.f.* medicine (medicina y medicamento): *medicina forense = forensic medicine.*
medicinal *adj.* medicinal.
medicinalmente *adv.* medicinally.
medicinar *v.t.* **1** to treat. || *v.pron.* **2** to take medicine.
medición *s.f.* measurement.
médico, -a *adj.* **1** medical: *examen médico = medical check-up.* || *s.m.* **2** doctor, physician, practitioner: *médico de cabecera = family doctor; médico general = general practitioner;* (fam.) G.P.
medicucho *s.m.* (desp.) quack.
medida *s.f.* **1** measurement (dimensión). **2** measuring, measurement (hecho y resultado de medir). **3** measure (lo que sirve para medir). **4** size (de ropa, zapatos, etc.). **5** measure (cosa medida). **6** measure, step (disposición): *medida preventiva = preventive measure.* **7** prudence, restraint (prudencia). || **8 a la – de,** in proportion to. **9 a –,** according to. **10 en gran –,** to a great extent. **11 hasta cierta –,** up to a point. **12 pesos y medidas,** weights and measures. **13 tomar medidas,** to take steps o measures.
medidor, -a *adj.* **1** measuring. || *s.m.* **2** measure (aparato). **3** (Am.) gauge, meter (contador).
mediero *s.m.* y *f.* **1** hosier (vendedor). **2** stocking maker (fabricante).
medieval o **medioeval** *adj.* medieval.
medievalismo *s.m.* medievalism.
medievalista *s.m.* y *f.* medievalist.
medievo o **medioevo** *s.m.* Middle Ages.
medio, -a *adj.* **1** half (mitad): *media hora = half an hour.* **2** middle (entre dos extremos): *clase media = middle class.* **3** average, typical (típico): *el hombre medio = the average man.* **4** MAT. mean, average: *altura media = average height.* || *adv.* **5** half: *medio lleno = half full; medio muerto = half dead.* || *s.m.* **6** middle, centre (centro): *en medio de la ciudad = in the middle of the city.* **7** half (mitad). **8** step, means (acción conveniente para conseguir un fin). **9** environment (ambiente). **10** circle (ambiente social). **11** medium (medium). **12** DEP. halfback. || *pl.* **13** money (dinero). **14** means, resources (recursos). || **15 a medias,** half: *ir a medias = to go halves.* **16 de – a –,** totally. **17 de por –,** in the middle. **18 edad media,** Middle Ages. **19 en –,** in the middle. **20 justo –,** happy medium. **21 media aritmética,** arithmetical mean. **22 – ambiente,** environment. **23 poner tierra por –,** to beat it. **24 por – de,** through the middle of. **25**

quitarse de en –, to get out of the way. **26 solución a medias,** partial solution.
mediocre *adj.* mediocre.
mediocremente *adv.* poorly.
mediocridad *s.f.* mediocrity.
mediodía *s.m.* **1** midday: *a mediodía = at midday.* **2** south (sur).
mediopevo *s.m.* V. **medievo.**
medir *v.t.* **1** to measure: *medir por kilómetros = to measure in kilometers.* **2** to judge, to gauge (apreciar el valor): *medir la inteligencia de alguien = to judge the intelligence of someone.* **3** to weigh up (un plan, posibilidad, consecuencias, etc.). **4** to scan (versos). **5** to weigh (palabras): *hay que medir las palabras = one has to weigh one's words.* || *v.r.* **6** to act with moderation, to act with restraint (moderarse).
meditabundo, -a *adj.* pensive, reflexive, thoughtful.
meditación *s.f.* meditation.
meditador, -a *adj.* meditative.
meditar *v.t.* to meditate, to think over, to ponder.
mediterráneo *s.m.* y *adj.* Mediterranean.
médium *s.m.* y *f.* medium.
medra *s.f.* **1** increase (aumento). **2** improvement (mejora). **3** affluence, prosperity (prosperidad).
medrana *s.f.* fear (miedo).
medrar *v.i.* **1** to improve, to get better (mejorar). **2** to grow (crecer). || **3 ¡medrados estamos!,** what a fine mess!
medro *s.m.* V. **medra.**
medrosamente *adv.* **1** itmidly (tímidamente). **2** fearfully (miedosamente).
medroso, -a *s.m.* y *f.* **1** coward (cobarde). || *adj.* **2** cowardly (cobarde). **3** timid (tímido). **4** afraid (miedoso). **5** frightening (que da miedo).
médula o **medula** *s.f.* **1** ANAT. marrow (de los huesos). **2** BOT. pith (de algunos tallos). **3** (fig.) pith, essence (de una consideración). || **4 – espinal,** spinal chord.
medular *adj.* medullary.
meduloso, -a *adj.* **1** MED. marrowy. **2** BOT. pithy.
medusa *s.f.* ZOOL. jellyfish.
mefistofélico, -a *adj.* (p.u.) Mephistophelian, (fam.) diabolical, devilish.
megacéfalo, -a *adj.* megacephalic.
megaciclo *s.m.* megacycle.
megáfono *s.m.* megaphone.
megalítico, -a *adj.* megalithic.
megalito *s.m.* megalith.
megalocéfalo, -a *adj.* megalocephalic.
megalomanía *s.f.* megalomania.
megalómano, -a *s.m.* y *f.* megalomaniac.
megaterio *s.m.* megathere (fósil).
megatón *s.m.* megaton.
mejicanismo o **mexicanismo** *s.m.* Mexicanism.
mejicano, -a o **mexicano, -a** *adj./s.m.* y *f.* Mexican.
mejido, -a *adj.* beaten.
mejilla *s.f.* ANAT. cheek.
mejillón *s.m.* ZOOL. mussel.
mejor *adj.* **1** (comparativo) better: *juegan mejor que yo = they play better than me.* **2** (superlativo) best: *el mejor libro = the best book.* || *adv.* **3** better (comparativo de bien): *escucha mejor tu hermano que tú = your brother listens better than you.* **4** best (superlativo de bien): *el disco mejor grabado = the best recorded record.* || **5 a lo –,** perhaps, maybe. **6 lo –,** the best part; the best thing. **7 – dicho,** or rather. **8 tanto –,** all the better.
mejora *s.f.* **1** MED. improvement (progreso). **2** improvement (en general): *la mejora de la economía = the improvement of the economy.* **3** increase (aumento).
mejorable *adv.* improvable.
mejoramiento *s.m.* improvement.
mejorana *s.f.* BOT. marjoram.
mejorar *v.t.* to improve, to make better: *mejorar la casa = to improve the house.* **2** to increase (aumentar). **3** MED. to make better. **4** DEP. to break, to better (batir). || *v.r.* y *pron.* **5** MED. to get better: *¡qué te mejores! = I hope you get better!* **6** to clear up, to improve (el tiempo).
mejoría *s.f.* improvement.
mejunje o **menjunje** *s.m.* **1** brew, concoction (mezcla desagradable). **2** botch (chapucería). **3** swindle, robbery (chanchullo).
melado, -a *adj.* **1** honey-coloured (de color de miel). || *s.m.* **2** sugar cane juice (zumo de caña). || *s.f.* **3** slice of bread and honey (pan con miel).
melancolía *s.f.* **1** MED. melancholy. **2** sadness, melancholy (tristeza).
melancólicamente *adv.* melancholically, sadly.
melancólico, -a *adj.* melancholic, gloomy.
melanina *s.f.* melanism (pigmento).
melanosis *s.f.* melanosis.
melar *v.t.* e *i.* **1** to produce honey (elaborar la miel las abejas). || *adj.* honey-tasting (que sabe a miel).
melaza *s.f.* molasses, treacle.
melena *s.f.* **1** long hair (pelo largo). **2** mane (crin del león).
melenudo, -a *adj.* long-haired.
melifluo, -a *adj.* mellifluous, sweet.
melifluamente *adv.* mellifluously, sweetly.
melifluencia o **melifluidad** *s.f.* sweetness, mellifluousness.
melindre *s.m.* **1** affected mannerisms, affectation (delicadeza afectada). **2** sweet bun o cake (manjar con miel y harina). **3** marzipan (mazapán).
melindrería *s.f.* V. **melindre.**
melindrero, -a o **melindroso, -a** *adj.* **1** affected, mannered (afectado). **2** fussy, finicky (remilgado).
melindrosamente *adv.* **1** affectedly (afectadamente). **2** fussily, finickly (remilgadamente).
melocotón *s.m.* **1** peach (fruto). **2** peach tree (árbol).
melocotonar *s.m.* peach orchard.
melocotonero *s.m.* peach tree (árbol).
melodía *s.f.* MUS. melody, tune.
melódico, -a *adj.* melodic.
melodiosamente *adv.* melodiously, tunefully.
melodioso, -a *adj.* melodious, tuneful.
melodrama *s.m.* melodrama.
melodramáticamente *adv.* melodramatically.
melodramático, -a *adj.* melodramatic.
melomanía *s.f.* melomania.
melómano, -a *s.m.* y *f.* **1** melomaniac. || *adj.* **2** melomane.
melón *s.m.* **1** BOT. melon. **2** (fam.) nut, loaf (cabeza). || **3 – de agua,** water melon (sandía).
melonar *s.m.* melon patch.
melonero, -a *s.m.* y *f.* **1** melon seller (vendedor). **2** melon grower (cultivador).
meloncillo *s.m.* ZOOL. mongoose.
melopea o **melopeya** *s.f.* **1** MUS. melopoeia. **2** (fam.) drunkenness (borrachera).
melosidad *s.f.* sweetness.
meloso, -a *adj.* **1** sweet, honied (con propiedades de la miel). **2** sweet (dulce). **3** soft (blando).
mella *s.f.* **1** dent, notch (deterioro en la superficie de metales, dientes, etc.). **2** harm, damage (daño). **3** gap (hueco). || **4 hacer –,** to impress; to make an impression (impresionar).
mellado, -a *adj.* **1** dented, nothed (de metales). **2** chipped (cerámica). **3** gap-toothed (con huecos en la dentadura).
melladura *s.f.* V. **mella.**
mellar *v.t.* **1** to chip (cerámica). **2** to nick, to notch (metales). **3** (fig.) to damage, to harm (dañar).
mellizo, -a *adj./s.m.* y *f.* twin.
memada *s.f.* foolish o stupid thing (cosa tonta).
membrana *s.f.* **1** MED. membrane. **2** ZOOL. web, membrane (de los pies).
membranoso, -a *adj.* membranous.
membrete *s.m.* **1** resume, precis (resumen). **2** note (nota). **3** letterhead (inscripción impresa).
membrillero *s.m.* BOT. quince tree (árbol).
membrillo *s.m.* **1** BOT. quince (fruto). **2** quince tree (árbol).
membrudamente *adv.* robustly.
membrudo, -a *adj.* robust, burly.
memento *s.m.* REL. memento.
memez *s.f.* foolishness, stupidity.
memo, -a *adj.* **1** foolish, silly. || *s.m.* y *f.* **2** dope, clot.
memorable *adj.* memorable, unforgettable.
memorándum o **memorando** *s.m.* **1** POL. memorandum. **2** notebook (agenda de notas). **3** (Am.) bank slip (resguardo bancario).
memorar *v.t.* to remember, to recall.
memorativo *s.m.* commemorative.
memoria *s.f.* **1** memory (facultad de recordar): *mala memoria = bad memory.* **2** essay, paper (exposición de estudio). **3** memory (recuerdo). **4** report, account (informe): *memoria anual = annual report.* **5** memorandum (memorándum).

|| *pl.* **6** memoirs (narración autobiográfica). || **7 de –,** by heart. **8 en – de,** in memory of. **9 falta de –,** forgetfulness. **10 refrescar la –,** to refresh one's memory.

memorial *s.m.* **1** petition, memorial (petición). **2** memorandum (libro).

memorión, -ona *s.m.* **1** long memory (memoria grande). || *adj.* **2** having a long memory (que tiene muy buena memoria).

memorista *adj.* **1** having a long memory (que tiene muy buena memoria). || *s.m.* y *f.* **2** person with a long memory (persona con buena memoria).

memorístico, -a *adj.* done from memory.

mena *s.f.* **1** MIN. ore. **2** MAR. thickness (grueso de una cuerda).

ménade *s.f.* **1** maenad (bacante). **2** (fam.) dragon (mujer encolerizada).

menaje *s.m.* **1** furniture (conjunto de muebles). **2** kitchen equipment (de cocina). || **3 sección de –,** household goods department.

menarquía *s.f.* MED. first period.

mención *s.f.* mention: *mención honorífica = honourable mention.*

mencionar *v.t.* **1** to mention, to comment (comentar). **2** to name (nombrar). || **3 sin – ...,** not to mention...

menda *s.m.* y *f.* yours truly.

mendacidad *s.f.* mendacity.

mendaz *adj.* **1** mendacious, lying. || *s.m.* y *f.* **2** liar.

mendeliano, -a *adj.* BIOL. Mendelian.

mendelismo *s.m.* BIOL. Mendelism.

mendicante *adj./s.m.* y *f.* mendicant.

mendicidad *s.f.* **1** begging, (p.u.) mendicity (acción de mendigar). **2** beggary, (p.u.) mendicity (condición).

mendigante *s.m.* y *f.* beggar.

mendigar *v.t.* **1** to beg (pedir limosna). **2** to beg for (suplicar algo).

mendigo, -a *s.m.* y *f.* beggar.

mendrugo *s.m.* **1** crust (pedazo de pan duro). **2** dope, dolt, clot (tonto).

menear *v.t.* y *pron.* **1** to move, to sway (mover a uno y otro lado). **2** to wag (el rabo). **3** to shake (la cabeza). **4** to sway, to waggle (la cadera). || *v.t.* **5** to stir (remover un asunto). || *v.pron.* **6** (fam.) to get a move on (obrar con rapidez).

meneo *s.m.* **1** movement (movimiento). **2** shake (de la cabeza, mano, etc.). **3** wag (del rabo). **4** sway, waggle (de cadera). **5** stir (de un líquido). **6** beating, thrashing (paliza).

menester *s.m.* **1** necessity, need (necesidad). || *pl.* **2** occupation, job (trabajo). **3** tools, gear (materiales).

menesteroso, -a *adj.* **1** needy (necesitado). **2** poor (pobre).

menestra *s.f.* **1** mixed vegetable dish (guiso de verduras). || *pl.* **2** dried vegetables (legumbres secas).

menestral, -la *s.m.* y *f.* **1** artisan (artesano). **2** manual worker (obrero manual).

mengano, -a *s.m.* y *f.* **1** what's-her-name (mujer). **2** what's-his-name (hombre).

mengua *s.f.* **1** shrinkage (de ropa). **2** lack, shortage (falta). **3** scarcity (escasez). **4** disgrace, discredit (descrédito). **5** decrease (disminución).

menguadamente *adv.* **1** decreasingly (decrecientemente). **2** disgracefully (desgraciadamente). **3** stupidly (tontamente).

menguado, -a *adj.* **1** cowardly (cobarde). **2** stupid, foolish (tonto). **3** foul, despicable (ruin). || *s.m.* y *f.* **4** coward (cobarde). **5** dope, fool, idiot (tonto). **6** wretch, despicable person (desgraciado). || *s.m.* decreased stitch (punto).

menguamiento *s.m.* V. **mengua.**

menguante *adj.* **1** shrunk (de ropa). **2** waning (la luna). **3** ebb (marea). **4** decreasing, diminishing (decreciente). || *s.f.* **5** ebb tide (descenso del mar). **6** fall, falling (de los ríos). **7** decay, decline (decadencia). || **2 cuarto –,** last quarter (cuarta fase de la luna).

menguar *v.i.* y *t.* **1** to shrink (ropa). **2** to decrease, to diminish (disminuir). **3** to go down (la marea). **4** to wane (la luna). **5** to fall (ríos). || *v.t.* **6** to decrease (hacer menguados en las prendas de punto).

menhir *s.m.* GEOL. menhir.

meninge *s.f.* ANAT. meninx.

meníngeo, -a *adj.* meningeal.

meningitis *s.f.* MED. meningitis.

meningococo *s.m.* MED. meningococcus.

menino *s.m.* y *f.* **1** page (paje). **2** maid (doncella).

menisco *s.m.* ANAT. y FIS. meniscus.

menjunje *s.m.* V. **mejunje.**

menopausia *s.f.* ANAT. menopause.

menor *adj.* **1** smaller (más pequeño): *el número de coches en este país es menor que en otros = the number of cars in this country is smaller than in others.* **2** smallest (superlativo): *la menor provincia = the smallest province.* **3** lesser (mínimo): *es un peligro menor = it's a lesser danger.* **4** least (superlativo): *no tiene la menor importancia = it hasn't the least importance.* **5** younger (de menos años): *mi padre es menor que mi madre = my father is younger than my mother.* **6** youngest (superlativo): *mi primo menor = my youngest cousin.* || *s.m.* **7** young person, minor, youngster (menor de edad). || **8** COM. **al por –,** retail. **9 – de edad,** under age. **10 por –,** minutely (minuciosamente).

menos *adv.* **1** less, fewer: *menos tiempo = less time; menos coches = fewer cars.* **2** less of a: *es menos equipo = it's less of a team.* **3** least (superlativo de poco): *soy el menos puntual de todos = I'm the least punctual of all.* || *prep.* **4** except, less (excepto): *todos vamos menos ellos = everybody is going except them.* || *s.m.* **5** MAT. minus (signo). || *conj.* **6 a – que,** unless. || **7 al –** o **por lo –,** at least. **8 cada vez –,** less and less. **9 echar de –,** to miss. **10 lo –,** at least. **11 – mal,** thank goodness; what a relief. **12 nada –,** none less. **13 ni mucho –,** far from it. **14 poco –,** a little less. **15 venir a –,** to go downhill.

menoscabar *v.t.* **1** to reduce, to lessen (disminuir). **2** to damage, to harm (dañar). **3** to spoil (estropear). **4** to discredit (desacreditar).

menoscabo *s.m.* **1** reduction, lessening (merma). **2** damage, harm (daño). **3** discredit (descrédito).

menospreciable *adj.* contemptible.

menospreciablemente *adv.* contemptibly.

menospreciar *v.t.* **1** to show contempt, to scorn (despreciar). **2** to shun, to slight (ignorar). **3** to undervalue, to underestimate (atribuir poca importancia): *menospreciar el riesgo = to underestimate the risk.*

menospreciativo, -a *adj.* contemptuous, disdainful.

menosprecio *s.m.* **1** contempt, disdain (desdén). **2** underestimation, undervaluation (subestimación). **3** disrespect, impertinence (impertinencia).

mensaje *s.m.* message.

mensajería *s.f.* **1** public transport (carruaje público). || *pl.* **2** MAR. sea transport, boats (buques). **3** transport company (empresa).

mensajero, -a *adj.* **1** messenger. || *s.m.* y *f.* **2** messenger.

menstruación *s.f.* menstruation.

menstrual *adj.* menstrual.

menstrualmente *adv.* menstrually.

menstruante *adj.* menstruating.

menstruar *v.i.* to menstruate.

menstruo *s.m.* **1** menses (sangre). **2** menstruation (función de evacuar la sangre).

mensual *adj.* **1** monthly (cada mes). **2** a month: *gano 500 dólares mensuales = I earn 500 dolars a month.*

mensualidad *s.f.* monthly wages o salary (sueldo de un mes).

mensualmente *adv.* monthly, every month.

ménsula *s.f.* **1** bracket (soporte). **2** ARQ. corbel (repisa).

mensura *s.f.* (Am.) measurement (medida).

mensurabilidad *s.f.* measurability.

mensurable *adj.* measurable.

mensurar *v.t.* to measure.

menta *s.f.* BOT. mint (hierbabuena).

mentado, -a *adj.* famous (famoso).

mental *adj.* mental: *trabajo mental = mental effort.*

mentalidad *s.f.* mentality, mind.

mentalmente *adv.* mentally.

mentar *v.t.* to mention, to comment (mencionar).

mentas *s.f.pl.* (Am.) fame (fama).

mente *s.f.* **1** mind: *mente subconsciente = subconscious mind.* **2** intelligence, intellect (inteligencia). **3** understanding (entendimiento). || **4 irse de la –,** to slip one's mind. **5 venir a la –,** to cross one's mind.

mentecatez *s.f.* stupidity, foolishness.

mentecato, -a *adj.* **1** stupid, foolish, silly (bobo). || *s.m.* y *f.* **2** idiot, fool.

mentidero *s.m.* (fam.) gossip shop (lugar de murmuraciones).

mentido, -a *adj.* illusory, deceptive (ilusorio).
mentir *v.i.* **1** to lie, to tell lies (decir mentiras). **2** (fig.) to lie, to deceive, to be deceptive (engañar): *las apariencias mienten = appearances are deceptive.* || **3 ¡miento!,** I tell a lie!
mentira *s.f.* **1** lie, fib: *decir mentiras = to tell lies.* **2** invention, story (algo inventado). **3** error (errata). || **4 parece —,** it seems incredible. **5 una — como un piano,** a whopping lie.
mentirijillas o **mentirillas (de)** *adv.* jokingly, in fun.
mentirosamente *adv.* lyingly, falsely.
mentiroso, -a *adj.* **1** untruthful, lying (que miente). **2** full of errors (un texto). || *s.m.* y *f.* **3** liar.
mentís *s.m.* **1** denial (réplica a una mentira). **2 dar el —,** to refute, to deny.
mentol *s.m.* menthol.
mentolado, -a *adj.* mentholated.
mentón *s.m.* ANAT. chin (barbilla).
mentor *s.m.* mentor.
menú *s.m.* menu.
menudamente *adv.* detailed, in minute detail (detallada).
menudear *v.t.* **1** to repeat frequently (repetir muchas veces). || *v.i.* **2** to rain down, to come think and fast (producirse algo reiteradamente). **3** to tell in great detail (narrar detalladamente).
menudencia *s.f.* **1** small thing, trifle (chuchería). **2** minuteness, meticulousness (minuciosidad).
menudeo *s.m.* **1** repetition (acción de menudear). **2** COM. retail trade.
menudillo *s.m.* **1** fetlock (articulación). || *pl.* **2** giblets (entrañas y sangre de las aves).
menudo, -a *adj.* **1** small, tiny (pequeño). **2** petty, unimportant (de poca importancia). **3** scrupulous, meticulous (minucioso). || *s.m.pl.* **4** offal (entrañas, etc. de los animales). || **5 a —,** often. **6 — rollo,** what a fine mess. **7 — libro,** what a book. **8 por —,** in great detail.
meñique *adj.* **1** tiny, minute, little (muy pequeño): *dedo meñique = little finger.* || *s.m.* **2** little finger (dedo pequeño).
meollo *s.m.* **1** core, essence (parte interior de una cosa). **2** encephalon (encéfalo). **3** marrow (médula). **4** judgement (juicio). **5** content, gist (contenido).
meón, -ona *adj.* **1** (vulgar) who is constantly pissing. || *s.m.* y *f.* **2** (vulg.) piss artist.
mequetrefe *s.m.* buffoon, clown, good-for-nothing.
meramente *adv.* merely, solely.
merca *s.f.* (Am.) shopping (compra).
mercachifle *s.m.* pedlar, hawker (vendedor de poca categoría).
mercader *s.m.* y *f.* trader, dealer.
mercadería o **mercaduría** *s.f.* **1** article, commodity. || *pl.* **2** goods.
mercado *s.m.* **1** market (comercio público). || **2 Mercado Común,** Common Market. **3 — libre,** free market. **4 — mundial,** world market. **5 — de valores,** stock market.
mercancía *s.f.* **1** commodity, article (cosa que se comercia). || *pl.* **2** goods, merchandise. || **3 mercancías** o **tren mercancías,** goods train.
mercante *s.m.* **1** MAR. merchant ship. || *adj.* **2** merchant (que compra). **3** mercantile (mercantil).
mercantil *adj.* mercantile, commercial.
mercantilismo *s.m.* mercantilism.
mercantilista *adj.* y *s.m.* y *f.* mercantilist.
mercantilizar *v.t.* to commercialize.
mercar *v.t.* to buy (comprar).
merced *s.f.* **1** favour (favor). **2** reward (recompensa). **3** benefit (beneficio). **4** grace (gracia). || **5 a — de,** at the mercy of. **6 — a,** thanks to. **7 tenga la — de,** please be so good as to.
mercedario, -a *adj.*/*s.m.* y *f.* Mercedarian.
mercenario, -a *adj.* **1** MIL. mercenary (soldado). **2** (fig.) mercenary, greedy (avaricioso). **3** salaried (asalariado). || *s.m.* y *f.* **4** MIL. mercenary. **5** day labourer (jornalero).
mercería *s.f.* **1** haberdasher's (tienda). **2** haberdashery (comercio).
mercero, -a *s.m.* y *f.* haberdasher.
mercurial *adj.* mercurial.
mercúrico, -a *adj.* QUIM. mercuric.
mercurio *s.m.* QUIM. mercury.
merecedor, -a *adj.* **1** deserving, worthy. || **2 — de confianza,** worthy of trust; trustworthy. **3 ser — de,** to deserve.
merecer *v.t.* **1** to deserve, to merit: *merecer una recompensa = to merit a reward.* **2** to deserve, to be worth (tener un determinado valor): *no merece ni una peseta = it isn't worth even a peseta.* || **3 — la pena,** to be worth the trouble. **4 — mucho,** to be deserving.
merecidamente *adv.* deservedly, worthily.
merecido, -a *adj.* **1** well deserved: *una victoria merecida = a well deserved victory.* || *s.m.* **2** due, just deserts (castigo que merece alguien).
merecimiento *s.m.* emerit, worth (mérito).
merendar *v.i.* **1** to have tea (comer la merienda). || *v.pron.* **2** to take over (apropiarse por completo de algo).
merendero *s.m.* picnic site (en el campo).
merendola o **merendona** *s.f.* **1** picnic (merienda campestre). **2** feast, binge (merienda abundante).
merengado, -a *adj.* beaten.
merengar *v.t.* to whip, to beat (batir).
merengue *s.m.* **1** meringue (dulce). **2** (Am.) disorder (desorden). **3** (Am.) trouble, mess (lío).
meretriz *s.f.* prostitute (ramera).
meridiano, -a *adj.* **1** meridian. **2** bright, brilliant (luminoso). || *s.m.* **3** ASTR. y GEOG. meridian.
meridional *adj.* **1** meridional, southern. || *s.m.* y *f.* **2** meridional, southerner
merino, -a *s.m.* y *adj.* merino (oveja).
mérito *s.m.* **1** merit: *partido de poco mérito = game of little merit.* **2** worth, value (valor): *pintura de poco mérito = painting of little value.* || **3 de —,** worthy. **4 hacer — de,** to mention.
meritoriamente *adv.* worthily.
meritorio, -a *adj.* **1** worthy, deserving (persona). **2** meritorius (cosa).
merluza *s.f.* **1** hake (pez). **2** drunkenness (borrachera): *pillar o coger una merluza = to get drunk;* (fam.) to get paralytic (emborracharse).
merma *s.f.* **1** loss (pérdida). **2** decrease (disminución).
mermar *v.t.* **1** to take away, to reduce (quitar una parte de algo). || *v.i.* y *pron.* **2** to lessen, to decrease (disminuir).
mermelada *s.f.* **1** jam: *mermelada de zarzamora = blackberry jam.* **2** marmalade: *mermelada de naranjas amargas = orange marmalade.*
mero, -a *adj.* **1** mere (simple): *un mero examen = a mere examination.* **2** pure, complete (puro): *un mero accidente = a pure accident.* || *s.m.* **3** grouper (pez).
merodeador, -a *adj.* **1** MIL. marauding. **2** prowling (con malas intenciones). || *s.m.* y *f.* **3** MIL. marauder **4** prowler (de malas intenciones).
merodear *v.i.* **1** MIL. to maraud. **2** to prowl (con malas intenciones).
merodeo *s.m.* **1** MIL. marauding. **2** prowling (con malas intenciones).
mes *s.m.* **1** month: *el mes de junio = the month of June.* **2** month's pay o wages o salary (sueldo de un mes). **3** MED. menses (período de menstruación). || **4 el — pasado,** last month. **5 el — que viene,** next month. **6 — lunar,** lunar month.
mesa *s.f.* **1** table (mueble). **2** counter (mostrador). **3** desk, writing desk (escritorio). **4** desk (pupitre). **5** board (conjunto de personas que ocupan una mesa de dirección, etc.). **6** food, table (comida). **7** GEOG. plateau, meseta. **8** table (de las piedras). **9** ARQ. landing (descansillo). || **10 levantarse de la —,** to leave the table. **11 — de noche,** bedside table. **12 — redonda,** round table. **13 poner la —,** to lay the table. **14 sentarse a la —,** to sit down at the table. **15 quitar, alzar** o **levantar la —,** to clear the table.
mesar *v.t.* y *pron.* to pull out, to tear out.
mescolanza *s.f.* **1** mixture (mezcla). **2** (fam.) jumble, mess (baturrillo).
mesenterio *s.m.* MED. mesentery.
mesera *s.f.* (Am.) waitress (camarera).
mesero *s.m.* (Am.) waiter (camarero).
meseta *s.f.* **1** GEOG. plateau, meseta, tableland. **2** landing (rellano).
mesiánico, -a *adj.* messianic.
mesianismo *s.m.* messianism.
mesías *s.m.* Messiah.
mesilla *s.f.* **1** bedside table (de la cama). **2** small table (mesa pequeña). **3** landing (rellano).
mesnada *s.f.* y *pl.* **1** band, gang (conjunto de hombres armados). **2** (fig.) crowd, (desp.) mob (agrupación de personas).
mesocarpio *s.m.* BOT. mesocarp.

mesolítico, -a *adj./s.m.* y *f.* mesolithic.
mesón *s.m.* 1 HIST. inn, tavern (posada). 2 restaurant. 3 FIS. meson.
mesonero, -a *s.m.* y *f.* 1 HIST. innkeeper. 2 restaurant owner (dueño).
mesotórax *s.m.* ANAT. mesothorax.
mesotron *s.m.* FIS. mesotron.
mesta *s.f.* 1 mesta (sin traducir). || *pl.* 2 confluence (confluencia).
mester *s.m.* 1 trade (oficio). || 2 **— de clerecía,** clerical verse. 3 **— de juglaría,** minstrel verse.
mestizaje *s.m.* crossbreeding.
mestizar *v.t.* to crossbreed.
mestizo, -a *s.m.* y *f.* 1 half-caste, half-breed (persona). 2 hybrid (flor, vegetal). 3 mongrel (perro). 4 crossbreed (animal). || *adj.* 5 half-caste o half-breed (persona). 6 hybrid (flor, vegetal). 7 mongrel (perro). 8 crossbred (animal).
mesura *s.f.* 1 moderation, control (moderación). 2 correctness, decorum (corrección). 3 dignity, gravity (dignidad). 4 respect (respeto).
mesuradamente *adv.* with moderation.
mesurado, -a *adj.* 1 moderate (moderado). 2 calm, composed (sereno).
mesurar *v.t.* 1 to moderate (moderar). 2 to consider, to think over, to ponder (considerar). 3 (Am.) to measure (medir). || *v.pron.* 4 to restrain oneself (contenerse).
meta *s.f.* 1 DEP. finishing line, finish (término señalado en una carrera). 2 goal, objective, aim (fin de una acción). || *s.m.* 3 DEP. goalkeeper (portero).
metabólico, -a *adj.* BIOL. metabolic.
metabolismo *s.m.* BIOL. metabolism.
metacarpiano, -a *adj.* ANAT. metacarpal.
metacarpo *s.m.* ANAT. metacarpus.
metafísicamente *adv.* metaphysically.
metafísico, -a *adj.* 1 metaphysical. || *s.m.* y *f.* 2 metaphysician. || *s.f.* 3 metaphysics.
metáfora *s.f.* metaphor.
metafóricamente *adv.* metaphorically.
metafórico, -a *adj.* metaphoric, metaphorical.
metaforismo *s.m.* metaphorism.
metaforizar *v.t.* to metaphorize, to say metaphorically.
metal *s.m.* 1 metal. 2 brass (latón). 3 timbre (timbre de la voz). || *pl.* 3 MUS. brass (instrumentos de latón). || 4 **el vil —,** filthy lucre. 5 **— precioso,** precious metal.
metálico, -a *adj.* 1 metallic. || *s.m.* 2 cash (dinero en efectivo). || 3 **en —,** in cash.
metalista *s.m.* y *f.* metalworker.
metalización *s.f.* metallization.
metalizar *v.t.* y *pron.* 1 to metallize. || *v.pron.* 2 to become obsessed with money (interesarse demasiado por el dinero).
metaloide *s.m.* QUIM. metalloid.
metalurgia *s.f.* metallurgy.
metalúrgico, -a *adj.* 1 metallurgic, metallurgical. || *s.m.* 2 metallurgist.
metalurgista *s.m.* metallurgist.
metamorfismo *s.m.* GEOL. metamorphism.
metamorfosear *v.t.* 1 to metamorphose, to transform. || *v.pron.* 2 to change, to be metamorphosed.
metamorfosis *s.f.* metamorphosis, transformation.
metano *s.m.* QUIM. methane.
metástasis *s.f.* MED. metastasis.
metatarso *s.m.* ANAT. metatarsus.
metátesis *s.f.* GRAM. metathesis.
metedura *s.f.* 1 placing, putting (acción de meter). || 2 **— de pata,** bloomer; (fam.) clanger; faux pas.
metempsicosis o **metempsícosis** *s.f.* metempsychosis.
meteórico, -a *adj.* meteoric.
meteorismo *s.m.* MED. meteorism.
meteorito *s.m.* meteorite.
meteorizar *v.t.* 1 MED. to produce meteorism. || *v.pron.* 2 to get meteorism.
meteoro o **metéoro** *s.m.* meteor.
meteorología *s.f.* meteorology.
meteorológico, -a *adj.* meteorological, (*atr.*) weather.
meteorologista o **meteorólogo, -a** *s.m.* y *f.* meteorologist.
meter *v.t.* 1 to put, to place (poner): *meter algo en un cajón = to put something in a drawer.* 2 to insert, to introduce, to put (insertar): *meter una moneda en una máquina = to insert a coin in a machine.* 3 DEP. to score (marcar). 4 DEP. to pot (billar). 5 DEP. to hole (golf). 6 to smuggle in (contrabando). 7 to give (dar): *le metió una bofetada = he gave him a smack.* 8 to take up (acortar una prenda). 9 to put something into someone's head (hacer creer a uno una cosa): *¿quién te ha metido esas ideas? = who has put those ideas into your head?* 10 to get mixed up, to involve (enredar): *no me metas en ese asunto = don't involve me in that business.* 11 to make, to cause (causar): *meter ruido = to make a noise.* 12 to bet, to wager (apostar). 13 FIN. to invest (invertir). 14 to put in (ingresar). || *v.pron.* 15 to meddle, (fam.) to poke one's nose in (participar en algo sin derecho): *no te metas en asuntos míos = don't poke your nose in my business.* 16 to become (dedicarse a un asunto o profesión): *se ha metido de pintor = he's become a painter.* 17 to get into, to go into (introducirse): *meterse en un coche = to get into a car.* 18 to enter (entrar). || 19 **a todo —,** at full speed. 20 **estar metido en algo,** to be involved in something. 21 **— la pata,** to put one's foot in it. 22 **— mano,** to touch up. 23 **— prisa,** to hurry up. 24 **meterse con alguien,** to annoy; to bother.
meticulosamente *adv.* meticulously, thoroughly.
meticulosidad *s.f.* meticulousness, thoroughness.
meticuloso, -a *adj.* meticulous, thorough.
metido, -a *adj.* 1 full (lleno). 2 abundant (abundante). 3 (Am.) meddling, interfering (entrometido). 4 (Am.) tipsy, merry (achispado). || *s.m.* 5 hem (tela que se mete en las costuras de una prenda). 6 (Am.) meddlesome person (entrometido). || 7 **estar muy — en algo,** to be deeply involved in something. 8 **— en años,** advanced in years, (fam.) getting on. 9 **— en carnes,** plump.
metílico, -a *adj.* QUIM. methylic.
metilo *s.m.* QUIM. methyl.
metimiento *s.m.* 1 putting, placing (acción de meter). 2 favour (favor).
metódicamente *adv.* methodically.
metódico, -a *adj.* Methodical.
metodismo *s.m.* REL. Methodism.
metodista *adj./s.m.* y *f.* REL. methodist.
método *s.m.* method.
metodología *s.f.* methodology.
metomentodo *s.m.* meddler, interferer.
metonimia *s.f.* metonymy.
metonímico *adj.* metonymical.
metraje *s.m.* length: *largo metraje = full-length film; corto metraje = short film.*
metralla *s.f.* MIL. shrapnel.
metrallazo *s.m.* burst of shrapnel.
metralleta *s.f.* MIL. submachine gun.
métrica *s.f.* ART. metrics.
métricamente *adv.* metrically.
métrico, -a *adj.* 1 metric, metrical. 2 cinta métrica, tape measure.
metrificación *s.f.* metrification.
metrificar *v.t.* e *i.* to versify.
metro *s.m.* 1 metre (medida). 2 metre (verso). 3 tape measure (cinta). 4 underground, tube (ferrocarril). || 5 **— cuadrado,** square metre. 6 **— cúbico,** cubic metre.
metrónomo *s.m.* MUS. metronome.
metrópoli *s.f.* 1 metropolis (ciudad). 2 mother country (nación).
metropolitano, -a *adj.* 1 metropolitan. || *s.m.* 2 underground, tube (ferrocarril). 3 REL. metropolitan.
mexicano, -a *adj./s.m.* y *f.* Mexican.
mezcla *s.f.* 1 mixing (acción de mezclar). 2 mixture (resultado). 3 mortar (argamasa). 4 (fig.) combination, mixture, blend (combinación).
mezclable *adj.* mixable.
mezcladamente *adv.* mixed up.
mezclador, -a *s.m.* y *f.* mixer.
mezcladura o **mezclamiento** *s.m.* y *f.* mixture.
mezclar *v.t.* y *pron.* 1 to mix (juntar cosas): *mezclar agua y harina = to mix water and flour.* 2 to involve, to mix up (meter a alguien en un asunto): *no me mezcles en la discusión = don't involve me in the discussion.* 3 to combine, to mix (combinar). || *v.pron.* 4 to get mixed up, to mix (meterse entre otras personas): *no te mezcles con esa pandilla = don't get mixed up with that gang.* 5 to meddle, to interfere (entremeterse). || *v.t.* 6 to mix up (desordenar).
mezcolanza o **mescolanza** *s.f.* mess, jumble (mezcla desordenada).
mezquino, -a *adj.* 1 mean, tight (tacaño). 2 poor (pobre). 3 worthless (de poca valía).
mezquita *s.f.* REL. mosque.
mezzo-soprano *s.f.* MUS. mezzo-soprano.

mi, mis *adj.pos.* my: *mi casa = my house; mis discos = my records.*
mi *s.m.* MUS. E, me (nota).
mí *pron.pers.* 1 me: *para mí = for me.* || 2 **a — me toca,** it's my turn. 3 **por — mismo,** by myself; on my own.
miaja *s.f.* 1 crumb (migaja). 2 (fig.) bit, tiny bit (cacho).
miasma *s.m.* miasma.
miasmático, -a *adj.* miasmatic.
mica *s.f.* 1 MIN. mica. 2 female long-tailed monkey (hembra del mico).
micada *s.f.* (Am.) affectation (afectación).
micción *s.f.* (p.u.) micturition.
mico *s.m.* ZOOL. long-tailed monkey.
micología *s.f.* mycology.
micólogo, -a *s.m.* y *f.* mycologist.
micosis *s.f.* MED. mycosis.
micra *s.f.* micron.
micro *pref.* micro, mini.
microbiano, -a *adj.* microbic, microbial.
microbio *s.m.* microbe.
microbiología *s.f.* microbiology.
microbiológico, -a *adj.* microbiological.
microbiólogo, -a *s.m.* y *f.* microbiologist.
microbús *s.m.* minibus.
microcefalia *s.f.* microcephaly.
microcéfalo, -a *adj.* microcephalic.
microcopia *s.f.* microcopy.
microclima *s.f.* microclimate.
microcosmo *s.m.* microcosm.
microfilm o **microfilme** *s.m.* microfilm.
microfilmar *v.t.* to microfilm.
microfísica *s.f.* microphysics.
micrófito *s.m.* microbe.
micrófono *s.m.* microphone, (fam.) mike.
microfotografía *s.f.* microphotography.
micrografía *s.f.* micrography.
micrográfico, -a *adj.* micrographic.
micrógrafo, -a *s.m.* y *f.* micrographist.
microlentilla *s.f.* contact lense.
micrométrico, -a *adj.* micrometric.
micrómetro *s.m.* micrometer.
micrómnibus *s.m.* minibus.
micrón *s.m.* micron.
microonda *s.f.* microwave.
microscópico, -a *adj.* microscopic.
microscopia *s.f.* microscopy.
microscopio *s.m.* 1 microscope. 2 **— electrónico,** electron microscope. 3 **— solar,** solar microscope.
microsurco *s.m.* microgroove.
mieditis *s.f.* fear, (fam.) jitters (miedo).
miedo *s.m.* 1 fear (temor). 2 distrust, mistrust (recelo). || 3 **dar —,** to be frightening. 4 **dar — a alguien,** to scare someone. 5 **de —, a)** fantastic, great (estupendo); **b)** terrible, awful (terrible). 6 **— cerval,** enormous fear. 7 **morirse de —,** to be frightened to death. 8 **por — de,** for fear of. 9 **tener —,** to be afraid.
miel *s.f.* 1 honey (sustancia dulce). || 2 **hacerse de —,** to be over kind. 3 **luna de —,** honeymoon. 4 **— sobre hojuelas,** all the better.
mielga *s.f.* 1 BOT. alfalfa. 2 pithfork (horca para levantar las mieses).
mielgo, -a *adj.* twin (mellizo).
mielina *s.f.* ANAT. myeline.
mielitis *s.f.* MED. myelitis.
miembro *s.m.* 1 ANAT. limb, member (extremidad del cuerpo). 2 member, penis (miembro viril). || *s.m.* y *f.* 3 member (persona que pertenece a una comunidad). 4 MAT. member. || 5 **hacerse —,** to become a member.
miente *s.f.* 1 thought (pensamiento). || 2 **caer en mientes,** to realize; to come in mind. 3 **parar mientes,** to reflect; to consider. 4 **traer, venirle a uno a las mientes,** to recall; to remember.
mientras *adv.* y *conj.* 1 while: *mientras yo estudio ella lee = while I study she reads.* 2 as long as: *mientras vivamos aquí = as long we live here.* || 3 **— más,** the more. 4 **— menos,** the less. 5 **— que,** whereas: *yo estudiaba mientras que tú dormías = I was studying whereas you were sleeping.* 6 **— tanto,** meanwhile.
miércoles *s.m.* Wednesday (día): *miércoles de ceniza = Ash Wednesday.*
mierda *s.f.* 1 (vulg.) shit, crap (excremento). 2 filth, dirt, (fam.) shit (suciedad). 3 (fig.) shit, crap: *el libro es una mierda = the book is crap.* || 4 **¡vete a la —!,** go to hell!
mies *s.f.* y *pl.* 1 corn, wheat (plantas cereales). 2 harvest time (época de la siega). || *pl.* 3 cornfields (los sembrados).
miga *s.f.* 1 crumb (trocito de pan). 2 (fig.) bit, crumb (trocito). 3 problem, snag (dificultad). || *pl.* 4 fried breadcrumbs (plato de pan frito). || 5 **hacer buenas migas con uno,** to get on well with someone. 6 **hacer malas migas con uno,** to get on badly with someone.
migaja o **miaja** *s.f.* 1 crumb (trocito de pan). 2 (fig.) bit, crumb (porción pequeña de una cosa). || *pl.* 3 scraps, leftovers (restos).
migar *v.t.* to crumble.
migración *s.f.* migration.
migraña *s.f.* MED. migraine.
migrar *v.i.* to migrate.
migratorio, -a *adj.* migratory.
mihrab *s.m.* mihrab.
mijo *s.m.* BOT. millet.
mil *adj.* 1 thousand: *dos mil personas = two thousand people.* 2 thousandth (milésimo). || *s.m.* 3 thousand (número).
milagrería *s.f.* 1 story of miracles (narración de milagros). 2 belief in miracles (tendencia a creer en milagros).
milagrero, -a *adj.* 1 who believes in miracles (que cree en milagros). 2 who invents miracles (que inventa milagros).
milagro *s.m.* 1 miracle. 2 wonder, marvel, miracle (suceso maravilloso). || 3 **de —,** by a miracle. 4 hacer milagros, to work wonders.
milagrosamente *adv.* miraculously.
milagroso, -a *adj.* 1 miraculous. 2 (fig.) wonderful, miraculous.
milano *s.m.* 1 kite (ave). 2 flying gurnard (pez). 3 villain (villano).
mildeu o **mildiu** *s.m.* mildew (enfermedad de la vid).
milenario, -a *adj.* 1 millenial. || *s.m.* 2 millennium.
milenio *s.m.* milennium.
milésimo, -a *adj.* 1 thousandth. || *s.m.* 2 thousandth.
milhojas *s.f.* 1 BOT. yarrow. || *s.m.* 2 flaky pastry (pastel).
mili *s.f.* 1 MIL. military service (servicio militar). || 2 **hacer la —,** to do military service.
miliamperio *s.m.* ELEC. miliampere.
milibar *s.m.* FIS. millibar.
milicia *s.f.* 1 military service (servicio militar). 2 military, soldiery (profesión). 3 militia (tropa de gente). || 4 **milicias universitarias,** cadet corps.
miliciano, -a *s.m.* y *f.* 1 militiaman, conscript (que sirve en la milicia). 2 (Am.) revolutionary soldier (soldado revolucionario).
miligramo *s.m.* milligramme.
mililitro *s.m.* millilitre.
milimétrico, -a *adj.* millimetric.
milímetro *s.m.* millimetre.
milimicra *s.f.* milimicron.
militante *adj./s.m.* y *f.* militant.
militar *adj.* 1 military: *academia militar = military academy; gobierno militar = military government.* || *v.i.* 2 to serve in the army (servir en la milicia). 3 to belong, to be a member (pertenecer a un partido). 4 to fight (luchar). 5 to defend (defender). || 6 **— contra,** to militate against.
militarismo *s.m.* militarism.
militarista *adj.* 1 militaristic. || *s.m.* y *f.* 2 militarist.
militarización *s.f.* militarization.
militarizar *v.t.* to militarize.
miloca *s.f.* owl (ave).
milonga *s.f.* 1 (Am.) popular song (canción). 2 popular dance (baile).
milord *s.m.* lord (noble inglés).
milla *s.f.* mile (medida): *milla marina = nautical mile.*
millar *s.m.* 1 thousand: *un millar de personas = a thousand people.* || 2 **a millares,** by the thousand; in thousands.
millo *s.m.* BOT. millet.
millón *s.m.* 1 million: *un millón de libras = a million pounds.* || 2 **a millones,** in millions; by the million.
millonada *s.f.* 1 about a million. 2 an enormous amount (gran cantidad).
millionario, -a *s.m.* y *f.* millionaire.
millonésimo, -a *adj./s.m.* y *f.* millionth.
mimado, -a *adj.* spoiled, pampered.
mimador, -a *s.m.* y *f.* 1 mimer. || *adj.* 2 miming.
mimar *v.t.* 1 to spoil, to pamper (a los niños). 2 to mime (expresar con mimos). 3 to bring up badly, to indulge (malcriar).
mimbre o **vimbre** *s.m.* o *f.* 1 osier, willow (arbusto). 2 wicker (materia).
mimbrear *v.i.* y *pron.* to sway.
mimesis *s.f.* mimicry.
mimético, -a *adj.* mimetic.
mimetismo *s.m.* mimicry.
mímico, -a *adj.* 1 mimic. || *s.f.* 2 mimicry.
mimo *s.m.* 1 caress, cuddle (demostración afectuosa). 2 spoiling (con los ni-

ños). 3 mime (representación teatral). 4 mime, mime artist (persona). || **5 hacer mimos a uno,** to make a fuss over someone.
mimosa *s.f.* BOT. mimosa (flor).
mimosamente *adv.* affectionately.
mina *s.f.* 1 mine (instalación subterránea): *mina de oro = gold mine.* 2 shaft, tunnel (galería subterránea). 3 MIL. mine (artefacto explosivo). 4 lead (grafito de los lápices). 5 (fig.) mine: *mina de información = mine of information.*
minar *v.t.* 1 MIN. to mine (abrir galerías). 2 MIL. to mine. || *v.t.* y *pron.* 3 to wear away, to undermine (desgastar).
minarete *s.m.* minaret.
mineral *s.m.* 1 GEOL. mineral. 2 MIN. ore: *mineral de hierro = iron ore.* || *adj.* 3 mineral: *agua mineral = mineral water.*
mineralización *s.f.* mineralization.
mineralizador, -a *adj.* mineralizing.
mineralizar *v.t.* to mineralize.
mineralogía *s.f.* mineralogy.
mineralógico, -a *adj.* mineralogical.
mineralogista *s.m.* y *f.* mineralogist.
minería *s.f.* 1 mining (actividad minera). 2 mines (grupo de minas). 3 miners (personal de una mina).
minero, -a *adj.* 1 mining. || *s.m.* y *f.* 2 miner (obrero): *minero de oro = goldminer.* 3 mineowner (dueño de una mina).
mingitorio *s.m.* MED. urinal.
miniatura *s.f.* 1 miniatura (pintura). || *adj.* 2 miniature. || **3 en –,** in miniature.
miniaturista *s.m.* y *f.* miniaturist.
miniaturizar *v.t.* to miniaturize.
minifalda *s.f.* miniskirt.
minifundio *s.m.* smallholding, (p.u.) minifundio.
minimizar *v.t.* to minimize.
mínimo, -a *adj.* 1 smallest, least (*super.* de pequeño): *cantidad mínima = smallest amount.* 2 minute, very small (muy pequeño). 3 minimum (más bajo): *temperatura mínima = minimum temperature.* 4 minute (minucioso). || *s.m.* 5 minimum: *trabajar un mínimo de diez horas = to work a minimum of ten hours.* || **6 como –,** at the very least. **7 sin el más – esfuerzo,** without the slightest effort.
mínimum *s.m.* minimum.
minino, -a *s.m.* y *f.* cat, (fam.) pussy (gato).
miniar *v.t.* to pain miniatures (pintar miniaturas).
minio *s.m.* MIN. minium, red lead.
ministerial *adj.* ministerial.
ministerialmente *adv.* ministerially.
ministerio *s.m.* ministry: *Ministerio de Educación = Ministry of Education.*
ministra *s.f.* minister, woman minister.
ministrar *v.t.* e *i.* to minister.
ministro *s.m.* minister: *primer ministro = prime minister; ministro sin cartera = minister without portfolio.*
minoración *s.f.* reduction, lessenning.
minorar *v.t.* to reduce, to lessen.
minoría *s.f.* minority: *minoría de edad = minority.*
minorista *adj.* 1 retail (al por menor). || *s.m.* 2 retailer.
minoritario, -a *adj.* minority.
minotauro *s.m.* minotaur.
minucia *s.f.* 1 trifle, trinket (cosa de poco valor). 2 uninteresting thing, bore (cosa de escaso interés).
minuciosamente *adv.* meticulously, thoroughly.
minuciosidad *s.f.* metiulousness, thoroughness.
minucioso, -a *adj.* meticulous, thorough.
minué *s.m.* MUS. minuet.
minuendo *s.m.* MAT. minuend.
minúsculo, -a *adj.* 1 minuscule, tiny, minute (pequeño). 2 worthless (de poco valor). 3 small (letras). || *s.f.* 4 small letter (letra pequeña).
minuta *s.f.* 1 minute, note (anotación). 2 rough draft, draft (borrador de un escrito). 3 menu (menú). 4 bill (cuenta).
minutar *v.t.* to draft.
minutero *s.m.* minute hand.
minuto *s.m.* 1 minute: *el minuto diez = the tenth minute.* 2 MAT. minute.
mío, -a *adj.* y *pron.pos.* 1 mine: *el coche es mío = the car is mine.* 2 my: *la casa es mía = my house.* 3 of mine: *una novia mía = a girlfriend of mine.* || **4 amigo –,** my friend. **5 ¡Dios –!,** my God!
miocardio *s.m.* ANAT. myocardium.
miocarditis *s.f.* MED. myocarditis.
miope *adj.* 1 short-sighted, myopic. || *s.m.* y *f.* 2 shortsighted person.
miopía *s.f.* MED. shortsightedness, myopia.
mira *s.f.* 1 sight (para dirigir la vista a un objeto). 2 aim, intention (intención). 3 look-out post, watchtower (torre de vigilancia). 4 levelling rod (para medidas topográficas). 5 mason's rule (reglón). || **6 a la –,** on the look-out. **7 con miras a algo,** with a view to something. **8 de miras estrechas,** narrow-minded.
mirada *s.f.* 1 look, (modo de mirar): *una mirada cariñosa = a loving look.* 2 look (acción de mirar). 3 glance (vistazo): *echar una mirada = to have a glance.* 4 look, expression (expresión): *una mirada triste = a sad look.* || **5 apartar la –,** to look away. **6 levantar la –,** to look up. **7 – fija,** stare.
mirado, -a *adj.* 1 thoughtful, prudent (prudente). 2 thought of: *bien mirado = well thought of; mal mirado = badly thought of.* 3 careful (cuidadoso).
mirador *s.m.* 1 view point, vantage point (para contemplar un panorama). 2 ARQ. enclosed balcony (balcón cerrado).
miramiento *s.m.* 1 looking, look (acción de mirar). 2 consideration (acción de considerar). 3 respect (respeto). 4 care, caution (precaución). 5 timidity (timidez).
mirar *v.t.* e *i.* 1 to look at: *miraban una escultura = they were looking at a sculpture.* 2 to watch: *mirar los coches = to watch the cars.* 3 to think about, to think carefully about (pensar): *mira bien lo que haces = think about what you're doing.* 4 to think highly of (apreciar): *no te miran bien = they don't think very highly of you.* 5 to look in (buscar): *mira en el libro a ver si está = look in the book to see if it's there.* 6 to keep an eye on, to watch (vigilar). 7 to mind, to watch (cuidar): *mira por donde vas = look where you're going.* 8 to face, to look on to (estar enfrente): *el balcón mira al jardín = the balcony looks on to the garden.* || *v.pron.* 9 to look at oneself: *mírate en el espejo = look at yourself in the mirror.* 10 to look at each another (uno a otro): *se estaban mirando = they were looking at each other.* || **11 bien mirando, mirándolo bien o si bien se mira,** all in all. **12 ¡mira!, a)** look! (que expresa admiración o extrañeza); **b)** look out! (para avisar). **13 – bien a alguien,** to like. **14 – mal a alguien,** to dislike. **15 – por alguien,** to take care of someone. **16 – por algo,** to take care of something.
mirasol *s.m.* BOT. sunflower.
miríada *s.f.* myriad: *una miríada de insectos = a myriad of insects.*
miriámetro *s.m.* myriametre.
mirilla *s.f.* 1 spyhole, peephole (abertura en las puertas). 2 sight (para dirigir visuales).
mirlo *s.m.* blackbird (ave).
mirón, -a *adj.* 1 inquisitive, (desp.) nosey. || *s.m.* y *f.* 2 nosey-parker.
mirra *s.f.* BOT. myrrh.
misa *s.f.* 1 REL. mass: *decir misa = to say mass.* || **2 cantar –,** to sing mass. **3 como en –,** in dead silence. **4 – de campaña,** outdoor mass. **5 – de gallo,** midnight mass. **6 – mayor,** high mass. **7 no saber uno de la – la media,** not to have the faintest idea. **8 oir –,** to go to mass.
misal *s.m.* REL. missal.
misantropía *s.f.* misanthropy.
misantrópico, -a *adj.* misanthropic.
misántropo, -a *s.m.* y *f.* misanthrope.
miscelánea *s.f.* 1 miscellany, mixture (mezcla). 2 miscellany (obra).
misceláneo, -a *adj.* miscellaneous.
miserable *adj.* 1 mean, miserly (tacaño). 2 miserable, paltry (cantidad, sueldo, etc.). 3 wretched, poor (pobre). 4 wretched, contemptible (desgraciado). 5 perverse (perverso). || *s.m.* y *f.* 6 wretch, rotter.
miserere *s.m.* miserere.
miserablemente *adv.* miserably, wretchedly.
miseria *s.f.* 1 wretchedness, poverty (pobreza grande). 2 misfortune, misery (desgracia). 3 meanness, tightness (mezquindad). 4 pittance, a tiny amount (cosa escasa).
misericordia *s.f.* compassion, mercy, pity.
misericordiosamente *adv.* compassionately, mercifully.
misericordioso, -a *adj.* compassionate, merciful.
mísero, -a *adj.* V. **miserable.**

misil o **mísil** *s.m.* MIL. missile.
misión *s.f.* 1 mission. 2 REL. mission.
misional *adj.* missionary.
misionero, -a *adj./s.m.* y *f.* REL. missionary.
misiva *s.f.* missive (carta o papel).
mismamente *adv.* just, exactly.
mismo, -a *adj.* 1 same: *el mismo día = the same day.* 2 (con el pron. pers.) -self: *ella misma = herself; ellos mismos = themselves.* 3 itself: *en el coche mismo = in the car itself.* 4 very (enfático): *en ese mismo mes = in that very month.* || *adv.* 5 right (por ejemplo): *ahí mismo = right here.* 6 only (solo): *hoy mismo = only today.* || *conj.* 7 **lo — que,** just as: *lo mismo que son españoles yo soy inglés = just as they are Spanish I'm English.* || 8 **ahora —,** right now. 9 **del — modo,** in the same way. 10 **lo —,** the same: *es lo mismo = it's all the same.* 11 **lo — da,** it's makes no difference. 12 **por lo —,** that is why.
misógamo, -a *s.m.* y *f.* misogamist.
misoginia *s.f.* misogyny.
misógino, -a *s.m.* y *f.* misogynist.
misterio *s.m.* 1 mystery. 2 secret, mystery (secreto). 3 HIST. mystery play (representación dramática).
misteriosamente *adv.* mysteriously.
misterioso, -a *adj.* mysterious.
místico, -a *s.m* y *f.* mysticism.
místicamente *adv.* mystically.
misticismo *s.m.* mysticism.
mistificación *s.f.* 1 falsification, perversion (falsificación). 2 hoax, trick (trampa).
mistificador, -ora *s.m.* y *f.* trickster, hoaxer.
mistificar o **mixtificar** *v.t.* 1 to trick, to deceive (engañar). 2 to falsify, to alter (falsificar).
mistral *s.m.* mistral (viento).
mistura o **mistión** *s.f.* mixture (mixtura).
misturar *v.t.* to mix (mixturar).
mitad *s.f.* 1 half: *la mitad del pastel = half of the cake.* 2 middle (medio centro): *en la mitad del día = in the middle of the day.* || 3 **en — de,** in the middle of. 4 **hacia la —,** towards the middle; halfway through. 5 **— y —,** half and half. 6 **partir por la —,** to cut in half.
mítico, -a *adj.* mythical.
mitificar *v.t.* y *pron.* to mythicize.
mitigación *s.f.* mitigation.
mitigante *adj.* mitigating.
mitigar *v.t.* y *pron.* to mitigate, to attenuate, to diminish.
mitigativo, -a o **mitigatorio, -a** *adj.* mitigatory.
mítin *s.m.* meeting.
mito *s.m.* myth.
mitología *s.f.* mythology.
mitológico, -a *adj.* mythological.
mitologista o **mitólogo, -a** *s.m.* y *f.* mythologist.
mitomanía *s.f.* mythomania.
mitómano, -a *adj.* y *s.* mythomaniac.
mitón *s.m.* mitt (guante).
mitosis *s.f.* BIOL. mitosis.
mitra *s.f.* REL. mitre (gorro).
mitrado, -a *s.m.* 1 prelate (prelado). || *adj.* 2 mitred.
miura *s.m.* fighting bull from Miura.
mixomatosis *s.f.* myxomatosis.
mixto, -a *adj.* 1 mixed (mezclado). || 2 **tren —,** passenger and freight train. || *s.m.* 3 match (cerilla).
mixtión o **mixtura** *s.f.* mixture (mezcla).
mixtura o **mistura** *s.f.* (Am.) confetti (confeti).
mízcalo *s.m.* milk mushroom (níscalo).
mnemotecnia o **nemotecnia** *s.f.* mnemonics.
mnemotécnico, -a *adj.* mnemonic.
mobiliario *adj.* 1 furniture. || *s.m.* 2 furniture (muebles).
moblar *v.t.* to furnish (amueblar).
moca *s.m.* mocha coffee (café).
mocasín *s.m.* moccasin (zapato).
mocedad *s.f.* 1 youth (juventud). 2 lark, prank (travesura). 3 fiddle, fraud (diversión deshonesta).
moceril o **mocil** *adj.* youthful, juvenile.
mocerío, -a *s.m.* y *f.* youngsters, young people.
mocetón, -a *s.m.* y *f.* burly o brawny youth.
moción *s.f.* 1 motion, movement (impulso). 2 inspiration (inspiración). 3 motion (proposición): *moción de censura = motion of censure.*
mocito, -a *adj.* 1 very youthful. || *s.m.* y *f.* 2 youngster, young person.
moco *s.m.* 1 mucus, (fam. y vulg.) snot (líquido que sale de la nariz). 2 lump (grumo). 3 TEC. hot slag (escoria del hierro candente). 4 candle drippings (cera derretida de la vela). || 5 **llorar a — tendido,** to cry one's eyes out. 6 **no es — de pavo,** (fam.) it's not chicken feed.
mocoso, -a *adj.* 1 (fam. y vulg.) snotty (que tiene mocos). 2 naughty, cheeky (atrevido). 3 paltry, (fam.) two-bit (insignificante). 4 (Am.) immature, childish (joven). || *s.m.* 5 little devil, brat.
mochales *adj.* potty, round the bend, cracked (chiflado).
mochar *v.t.* 1 (fam.) to nut, to head-butt, to butt (dar golpes con la cabeza). 2 to cut (cortar).
mochila *s.f.* 1 rucksack, haversack (saco). 2 gamebag (del cazador). 3 MIL. pack (de un soldado). 4 supplies, provisions (víveres).
mocho, -a *adj.* 1 blunt (sin punta). 2 truncated (truncado). 3 shorn (pelado). 4 stubby (remate grueso y sin punta). 5 (Am.) spot (grano). || *s.f.* 6 (fam.) nut, bonce (cabeza humana).
mochuelo *s.m.* ZOOL. little owl (ave).
moda *s.f.* 1 fashion (costumbre pasajera): *estar de moda = to be in fashion.* || 2 **a la —,** fashionable; in fashion. 3 **fuera de —,** out of fashion. 4 **pasado de —,** old-fashioned. 5 **ponerse de —,** to become fashionable.
modal *adj.* 1 GRAM. modal. || *s.m.pl.* 2 manners: *buenos modales = good manners; malos modales = bad manners.*
modalidad *s.f.* 1 way, manner (modo de ser algo). 2 kind, class, form (clase): *una nueva modalidad literaria = a new literary form.*
modelado *s.m.* modelling.
modelador, -ora *s.m.* y *f.* modeller.
modelar *v.t.* 1 to model (hacer figuras). 2 to fashion, to shape (dar forma). 3 to model (copiar un modelo).
modelista *s.m.* y *f.* modeller.
modelo *s.m.* y *f.* 1 model (objeto de imitación). 2 model (muestra). 3 model, fashion model (maniquí). 4 model (persona que posa). || *adj.* 5 model: *un colegio modelo = a model school.*
moderación *s.f.* moderation: *con moderación = with moderation.*
moderadamente *adv.* moderately.
moderado, -a *adj.* moderate.
moderador, -a *adj.* 1 moderating. || *s.m.* y *f.* 2 moderator (que dirige un debate, asamblea, etc.). || *s.m.* 3 FIS. moderator.
moderar *v.t.* y *pron.* 1 to moderate (templar). 2 to reduce, to moderate (velocidad). 3 to control (controlar).
moderativo, -a *adj.* moderating.
modernamente *adv.* 1 recently (recientemente). 2 nowadays, in modern times (hoy en día).
modernidad *s.f.* modernity.
modernismo *s.m.* modernism.
modernista *adj.* y *s.* modernist.
modernización *s.f.* modernization.
modernizador, -a *s.m.* y *f.* modernizer.
modernizar *v.t.* 1 to modernize. || *v.pron.* 2 to get up to date, to update.
moderno, -a *adj.* modern, up-to-date.
modestamente *adv.* modestly.
modestia *s.f.* modesty.
modesto, -a *adj.* 1 modest. || *s.m.* y *f.* 2 modest person.
módicamente *adv.* moderately.
módico, -a *adj.* 1 moderate, fair (moderado). 2 limited (limitado).
modificable *adj.* modifiable.
modificación *s.f.* modification.
modificador, -ora *s.m.* y *f.* 1 modifier. || *adj.* 2 modifying.
modificar *v.t.* y *pron.* 1 to modify, to change (cambiar). || *v.t.* 2 GRAM. to modify.
modificativo, -a *adj.* modifying.
modificatorio, -a *adj.* modifying.
modismo *s.m.* idiom, saying.
modistería *s.f.* dressmaking (actividad de las modistas).
modista *s.f.* 1 dressmaker (que hace vestidos). 2 dress shop owener (dueña de tienda).
modisto *s.m.* fashion designer (diseñador).
modo *s.m.* 1 way, manner (forma de ser o hacerse una cosa): *modo de pensar = way of thinking.* 2 GRAM. mood. 3 MUS. mode. || *pl.* 4 manners (modales). || 5 **a** o **al — de,** like. 6 **buenos modos,** good manners. 7 **malos modos,** bad manners. 8 **— adverbial,** adverbial phrase. 9 **— de empleo,** instructions for use.
modorrar *v.t.* to get drowsy o sleepy (amodorrarse).

modorro, -a *adj.* 1 sleepy, drowsy. 2 awkward, clumsy (torpe). 3 ignorant (ignorante). || *s.m.* 4 clumsy person (torpe). 5 ignorant person (persona ignorante). || *s.f.* 6 heavy sleep (sueño pesado).
modosidad *s.f.* 1 good behaviour (buena conducta). 2 good manners (buenos modales).
modoso, -a *adj.* 1 well-behaved (de buena conducta). 2 well-mannered (de buenos modales).
modulación *s.f.* modulation.
modulador, -a *adj.* 1 modulating. || *s.m.* y *f.* 2 modulator.
modular *v.t.* to modulate.
módulo *s.m.* 1 MAT. modulus. 2 ARQ. module. 3 MUS. modulation.
mofa *s.f.* 1 ridicule, mockery. || **2 hacer — de,** to ridicule; to mock.
mofador, -a *adj.* 1 ridiculing, mocking. || *s.m.* 2 mocker, taunter.
mofarse *v.pron.* to ridicule, to mock.
mofeta *s.f.* ZOOL. skunk.
moflete *s.m.* chubby cheek.
mofletudo, -a *adj.* chubby-cheeked.
mogol, -a *adj./s.m.* y *f.* mongolian, mongol.
mogólico, -a *adj.* mongolic.
mogollón *s.m.* crowd (multitud): *mogollón de gente = enormous crowd.*
mohecerse *v.pron.* to get mouldy.
mohiento, -a o **mohoso, -a** *adj.* mouldy.
mohín *s.m.* gesture (gesto).
mohína *s.f.* 1 sadness (tristeza). 2 displeasure, annoyance (disgusto). 3 quarrel, row (reyerta).
mohíno, -a *adj.* sad (triste)..
moho *s.m.* 1 BOT. mould, mildew. 2 rust (de capa de óxido).
moisés *s.m.* cradle, Moses basket (cuna).
mojada *s.f.* 1 weeting, soaking (acción de mojar). 2 stab (herida).
mojado, -a *adj.* wet, soaked.
mojama *s.f.* dried and salted tuna (atún salado y seco).
mojadura *s.f.* wetting, soaking.
mojar *v.t.* 1 to wet, to soak (humedecer). 2 to dip, (fam.) to dunk (en el café, etc.). 3 to dip (una pluma). 4 (Am.) to bribe (sobornar). || *v.i.* y *pron.* 5 to get involved (intervenir). || *v.pron.* 6 to get wet o soaked (humedecerse).
moje o **mojo** *s.m.* broth (caldo).
mojicón, -ona *s.m.* y *f.* 1 sponge cake (especie de bizcocho). 2 punch (puñetazo).
mojigatería *s.f.* prudishness, priggishness.
mojigato, -a *adj.* 1 prudish, priggish. || *s.m.* y *f.* 2 prude, prig.
mojón *s.m.* 1 boundary marker, landmark (señal para fijar límites). 2 signpost (señal que sirve de guía). 3 pile, heap (montón). 4 (fam.) turd (porción de excremento humano).
molar *adj.* 1 molar. || *s.m.* 2 molar (diente).
molde *s.m.* 1 mould (objeto hueco). 2 form (para imprimir). 3 (fig.) model (modelo). || **4 pan de —,** sliced dread.
moldeable *adj.* 1 mouldable. 2 pliable, pliant (persona).
moldeado *s.m.* moulding.
moldeador, -ora *s.m.* y *f.* 1 moulder. || *adj.* 2 moulding.
moldear *v.t.* 1 to mould, to shape (hacer molde). 2 to cast (de yeso). 3 (fig.) to shape, to mould.
moldura *s.f.* moulding.
mole *adj.* 1 smooth (suave). 2 soft (blando). || *s.f.* 3 mass, bulk (cosa de gran tamaño). || *s.m.* 4 (Am.) chili stew (guisado de carne y chiles).
molécula *s.f.* FIS. molecule: *molécula gramo = gram molecule.*
molecular *adj.* FIS. molecular.
moledor, -a *adj.* 1 grinding (que muele). 2 boring, tedious (aburrido). || *s.m.* y *f.* 3 bore (persona). 4 TEC. grinder, crusher (aparato).
moledura *s.f.* 1 grinding (acción de moler). 2 tiredness, weariness (cansancio).
moler *v.t.* 1 to grind, to crush (hacer polvo). 2 to mistreat, to maltreat (maltratar). 3 to mill, to grind (trigo). || *v.t.* y *pron.* 4 to tire (cansar).
molestador, -a *adj.* 1 annoying, bothersome. || *s.m.* y *f.* 2 bore.
molestamente *adv.* annoyingly.
molestar *v.t.* 1 to annoy, to irritate (irritar). 2 to bother, to pester (incomodar): *no me molestes = stop bothering me.* 3 to hurt (hacer daño). 4 to mind (importar): *¿te molesta que ponga la radio? = do you mind if I put on the radio?* 5 to get on one's nerves (poner nervioso): *me molesta ese hombre = that man gets on my nerves.* 6 to disturb (incordiar). || *v.i.* 7 to get in the way, to be a nuisance (fastidiar): *no te quiero molestar = I don't want to get in your way.* || *v.pron.* 8 to worry (preocuparse): *no te molestes por mí = don't worry about me.* || 9 molestarse en, to bother to: *se molestó en comprármelo = he bothered to buy me it.*
molestia *s.f.* 1 nuisance, bother (perturbación del bienestar). 2 anger (enfado). 3 MED. discomfort (sensación dolorosa). 4 nuisance (fastidio). || **5 es una —,** it's a nuisance. **6 ¡qué —!,** what a nuisance! **7 tomarse la — de,** to take the trouble to: *se tomaron la molestia de llamar = they took the trouble to call.*
molesto, -a *adj.* 1 annoying, bothersome (fastidioso). 2 boring, tedious (aburrido). 3 nasty, unpleasant (olor, sabor, tarea). 4 trying, tiresome (pesado). 5 inconvenient (inconveniente). 6 uncomfortable (incómodo). 7 annoying, irritating (irritante). 8 angry, irked (enfado).
molicie *s.f.* 1 softness (blandura). 2 soft living, easy living (gusto por la comodidad).
molienda *s.f.* 1 grinding, crushing (acción de moler). 2 milling (acción de moler trigo). 3 quantity ground (cantidad que se muele de una vez). 4 grinding period (temporada de moler). 5 mill (molino). 6 tiredness (cansancio). 7 nuisance, drag (cosa molesta).
molimiento *s.m.* 1 grinding (moledura). 2 extreme tiredness (cansancio muy intenso).
molinero, -a *s.m.* y *f.* miller.
molinete *s.m.* 1 fan (ventilador). 2 windmill (juguete).
molinillo *s.m.* 1 hand mill (para moler). || **2 — de café,** coffee mill.
molino *s.m.* 1 mill (máquina). 2 mill (edificio). || **3 — de agua,** water mill. **4 — de viento,** windmill.
molondro o **molondrón** *s.m.* 1 (fam.) lazybones (perezoso). 2 blow (golpe).
molusco *s.m.* mollusc.
molla *s.f.* 1 lean meat (parte magra de la carne de los animales). 2 (fam.) flab (de las personas).
mollar *adj.* 1 soft (blando). 2 fragile (frágil). 3 cushy, plum (de gran ventaja y poco esfuerzo). 4 dopey, docile (dócil). 5 frank, candid, open (cándido).
molledo o **mollero** *s.m.* 1 fleshy o soft part (parte carnosa de un miembro). 2 crumb (miga del pan).
molleja *s.f.* 1 gizzard. || *pl.* 2 sweetbreads.
mollera *s.f.* 1 ANAT. crown (parte superior del cráneo). 2 intelligence, (fam.) brains (inteligencia). 3 fontanel (fontanela). || **4 cerrado de —,** thick; dense. **5 ser uno duro de —, a)** to be as thick as a brick (tener poca inteligencia); **b)** to be stubborn (ser obstinado).
momentáneamente *adv.* momentarily.
momentáneo, -a *adj.* momentary.
momento *s.m.* 1 moment (espacio mínimo de tiempo): *dentro de un momento = in a moment.* 2 occasion, moment (ocasión). 3 MEC. momentum. 4 (fig.) importance (importancia): *de poco momento = of little importance.* || **5 a cada —,** all the time. **6 al —,** at once. **7 de** o **por el —,** at the moment. **8 de un — a otro,** at any moment. **9 en este —,** at this moment. **10 por momentos,** little by little; progressively. **11 ¡un —!,** just a moment!; just a second!
momia *s.f.* mummy.
momificación *s.f.* mummification.
momio, -a *adj.* 1 lean (sin grasa). || *s.m.* 2 bonus, extra (prima). 3 bargain (ganga). 4 skinny person (persona muy delgada).
mona *s.f.* 1 ZOOL. female monkey (hembra del mono). 2 drunkenness (borrachera). 3 old maid (juego de naipes). 4 leg guard (refuerzos que usan los picadores). 5 silk worm (gusano de seda). 6 (fam.) ape (persona muy fea). || **7 coger una —,** to get drunk. **8 corrido como una —,** ashamed. **9 dormir la —,** to sleep it off.
monacal *adj.* monastic.
monacato *s.m.* 1 monasticism, monastic life (estado de monje). 2 monastic institution (institución monástica).
monada *s.f.* 1 cute o sweet thing (cosa bonita). 2 cute o sweet person (persona bonita). 3 silliness, foolishness (acción tonta). || **4 ¡qué —!,** how cute! **5 ser una —,** to be lovely.

mónada *s.f.* monad.
monadismo *s.m.* monadism.
monadista *s.m.* y *f.* monadist.
monaguillo o **monago** *s.m.* REL. altar boy.
monarca *s.m.* monarch, ruler.
monarquía *s.f.* monarchy.
monárquicamente *adv.* monarchically.
monárquico, -a *adj.* **1** monarchic, monarchical. || *s.m.* y *f.* **2** monarchist.
monarquismo *s.m.* monarchism.
monasterio *s.m.* monastery.
monásticamente *adv.* monastically.
monástico, -a *adj.* monastic.
monda *s.f.* **1** pruning, trimming (acción de mondar). **2** cleaning (acción de limpiar). || *pl.* **3** peel, peelings (desperdicios de verduras). || **4 es la —, a)** it's tremendous; it's great (tremendo); **b)** it's the limit (es el colmo).
mondadientes *s.m.* toothpick.
mondadura *s.f.* V. **monda.**
mondar *v.t.* y *pron.* **1** to peel (quitar la piel). **2** to shell (quitar la cáscara). **3** (Am.) to whip (azotar). || *v.t.* **4** to clean (limpiar). **5** to trim, to prune (podar). **6** to cut (cortar). **7** to pare (privar de lo superfluo).
mondarajas *s.pl.* peelings, peel (mondas).
mondo, -a *adj.* **1** clean (limpio). **2** pure (puro). **3** unadulterated, plain (sin mezcla). || **4 — y lirondo,** pure and simple; plain. **5 sueldo —,** bare salary.
moneda *s.f.* **1** coin (pieza metálica). **2** currency (moneda de un país): *la moneda francesa = the French currency.* || **3 — dura,** hard currency. **4 — falsa,** dud coin. **5 — suelta,** loose change. **6 pagar en** o **con la misma —,** to get one's own back.
monedero *s.m.* **1** purse (bolsita). **2** minter (fabricante de moneda).
monería *s.f.* V. **monada.**
monetario, -a *adj.* **1** monetary, financial. || *s.m.* **2** coin collection (colección de monedas).
mongol, -a o **mogol, -a** *adj.* **1** Mongolian (persona). **2** Mongolic (idioma). || *s.m.* y *f.* **3** Mongol (persona). **4** Mongol (idioma).
mongólico, -a *adj.* y *s.m.* y *f.* **1** V. **mongol. 2** MED. mongol, mongolian.
mongolismo *s.m.* MED. mongolism.
monigote *s.m.* **1** REL. lay brother (lego). **2** rag doll (muñeco). **3** ridiculous figure (figura ridícula). **4** dope, clown (persona ignorante). **5** daub, bad drawing (dibujo mal hecho).
monín o **monino, -a** *adj.* V. **mono.**
monis *s.m.* **1** money, (fam.) bread (dinero). || *s.f.* **2** bauble, trinket (cosa pequeña y pulida).
monitor, -a *s.m.* **1** monitor (televisor). || *s.m.* y *f.* **2** monitor (persona).
monja *s.f.* **1** REL. nun, sister. || *pl.* **2** sparks (chispas).
monje *s.m.* REL. monk.
monjil *adj.* **1** nun's (de monjas). **2** prim, priggish (mojigato). || *s.m.* **3** nun's habit (vestido de monja).
mono, -a *adj.* **1** pretty, attractive (bonito): *¡qué tía más mona! = what a pretty chick!* **2** sweet (dulce). **3** nice, friendly (simpático). **4** cute (lindo, guapo). || *s.m.* **5** ZOOL. monkey, ape (animal). **6** overalls (traje de faena). **7** terrible drawing (dibujo tosco). **8** ugly devil (hombre feo).
monobásico, -a *adj.* QUIM. monobasic.
monocameral *adj.* POL. single chamber.
monoceronte o **monocerote** *s.m.* unicorn (unicornio).
monociclo *s.m.* monocycle.
monocorde *adj.* MUS. single-stringed.
monocromo, -a *adj.* y *s.m.* monochrome.
monóculo *s.m.* monocle.
monocultivo *s.m.* monoculture, single-crop farming.
monofásico, -a *adj.* singlephase.
monofisismo *s.m.* monophysitism.
monofisista *s.m.* y *f.* monophysite.
monogamia *s.f.* monogamy.
monógamo, -a *adj.* monogamous.
monogenismo *s.m.* monogenism.
monografía *s.f.* monograph.
monográfico, -a *adj.* monographic.
monograma *s.m.* monogram.
monolítico, -a *adj.* monolithic.
monolito *s.m.* monolith.
monólogo *s.m.* monologue.
monomanía *s.f.* monomania, obsession.
monomaníaco, -a o **monomaniaco, -a** *adj.* **1** monomaniacal. || *s.m.* y *f.* **2** monomaniac.
monomaniático, -a *adj./s.m* y *f.* V. **monomaniaco.**
monomio *s.m.* monomial.
monoplano *s.m.* monoplane.
monopolio *s.m.* monopoly.
monopolista *s.m.* y *f.* monopolist.
monopolización *s.f.* monopolization.
monopolizador, -ora *s.m.* y *f.* **1** monopolizer. || *adj.* **2** monopolistic.
monopolizar *v.t.* to monopolize.
monorail *s.m.* monorail.
monorrimo, -a *adj.* single rhyming.
monorrítmico, -a *adj.* monorhythmical.
monosilábico, -a *adj.* monosyllabic.
monosílabo, -a *s.m.* || *adj.* **1** monosyllabic. **2** monosyllable.
monoteísmo *s.m.* monotheism.
monoteísta *adj.* **1** montheistic. || *s.m.* y *f.* **2** monotheist.
monotipia *s.f.* monotype.
monótonamente *adv.* monotonously.
monotonía *s.f.* monotony.
monótono, -a *adj.* monotonous.
monovalente *adj.* y *s.m.* monovalent.
monóxido *s.m.* QUIM. monoxide.
monseñor *s.m.* REL. monsignor.
monserga *s.f.* **1** untimely speech (discurso inoportuno). **2** jibberish, nonsense (lenguaje embrollado).
monstruo *s.m.* **1** monster. || **2** great, fantastic, tremendous (tremendo). **3** monstruous (demasiado grande).
monstruosamente *adv.* monstrously.
monstruosidad *s.f.* monstrosity.
monstruoso, -a *adj.* monstrous.
monta *s.f.* **1** mount (hecho y resultado de montar). **2** value, worth (valor de una cosa). **3** mating (cópula entre animales). **4** MAT. total, sum.
montacargas *s.m.* goods lift.
montado, -a *adj.* **1** MIL. mounted (soldado, etc.). **2** saddled (caballo). **3** TEC. set (joyas, etc.). **4** staged (obra de teatro).
montadura *s.f.* **1** mounting. **2** harnass (del caballo). **3** mount, setting (de joyas, etc.).
montaje *s.m.* **1** MEC. assembly, mounting (hecho y resultado de montar). **2** editing, cutting (de una película). **3** staging (en el teatro).
montante *s.m.* **1** window over a door (ventana sobre una puerta). **2** post (poste). **3** mullion (de una ventana). **4** leg (pie de una máquina). **5** sum, total (cuantía).
montaña *s.f.* **1** GEOL. mountain. **2** mountains, mountainous area (territorio cubierto de montes). || **3 cadena de montañas,** chain o range of mountains. **4 — rusa,** roller coaster.
montañero, -a *adj.* **1** mountain. || *s.m.* y *f.* **2** mountaineer, climber.
montañés, -a *adj.* **1** mountain, highland. || *s.m.* y *f.* **2** highlander.
montañismo *s.m.* mountaineering, climbing.
montañoso, -a *adj.* mountainous.
montar *v.t.* y *pron.* **1** to mount, to get on (subir encima). || *v.i., t.* y *pron.* **2** to ridge (cabalgar): *montar a caballo = to ride a horse.* || *v.i.* **3** to be of importance (ser de importancia). **4** to amount to (importar una cantidad). || *v.t.* **5** to assemble (una máquina). **6** to make (un vestido). **7** to set up (un negocio). **8** MIL. to cock (poner en disposición de disparar). **9** to whip, to beat (nata, huevos). **10** to mount (película, obra de teatro). **11** to cover, to mate with (cubrir el macho a la hembra). **12** MIL. to mount (un ataque). **13** MIL. to mount (guardia). **14** to mount (una joya). **15** to lift (subir).
montaraz *adj.* **1** mountain (de los montes). **2** rural, rustic (agreste). **3** wild, untamed (indomable). || *s.m.* **4** gamekeeper (guarda de fincas).
monte *s.m.* **1** mountain (montaña). **2** woodland, forest (bosque). **3** snag, difficulty, obstacle (dificultad). || **4 — alto,** forest. **5 — bajo,** scrubland. **6 — de piedad,** pawnshop. **7 — de venus,** pubis.
montepío *s.m.* charitable fund.
montera *s.f.* **1** bullfighter's hat (gorra del torero). **2** skylight (techumbre de cristales).
montero *s.m.* **1** hunter (cazador). **2** beater (que ojea la caza).
montés o **montesino, -a** *adj.* wild: *gato montés = wildcat.*
montículo *s.m.* mound, hillock.
monto *s.m.* total, amount.
montón *s.m.* **1** pile, heap. **2** (fig.) loads, piles, heaps, stacks (mucho): *un montón de trabajo = loads of work.* **3** many,

good many (muchos): *un montón de siglos = a good many years.* || **4 a montones,** lots. **5 ser del –,** to be just one of the crowd.

montonero *s.m.* (Am.) guerilla (guerrillero).

montura *s.f.* **1** mount (cabalgadura). **2** mounting, setting (montaje). **3** frame (de gafas). **4** harness (de caballo). **5** saddle (silla de montar).

monumental *adj.* **1** monumental (relativo al monumento). **2** enormous (muy grande). **3** tremendous, fantastic (estupendo). **4** horrible, awful (malo).

monumento *s.m.* **1** monument (edificio). **2** memorial (obra en recuerdo de algo o alguien). **3** historical document (documento histórico). **4** historical object (objeto histórico).

monzón *s.m.* monsoon.

moña *s.f.* **1** ribbon, bow (lazo). **2** bullfighter's ribbon (lazo de torero). **3** anger (enfado). **4** doll (muñeca). **5** drunkenness (borrachera).

moño *s.m.* **1** bun (de pelo). **2** bow (lazo de cintas). **3** crest (penacho de ave). || **4 ponérsele a uno algo en el –,** to dig one's heels in.

moquero *s.m.* handkerchief.

moqueta *s.f.* moquette.

moquillo *s.m.* distemper.

mor *adv.* **por mor de,** considering; in consideration of.

mora *s.f.* **1** BOT. blackberry. **2** delay (retraso).

morada *s.f.* **1** dwelling, abode (casa o habitación). **2** stay (estancia).

morado, -a *adj.* **1** purple (color). || **2 pasarlas moradas,** to have a lousy time. **3 ponerse –,** to stuff oneself.

morador, -ora *s.m.* y *f.* dweller, resident, inhabitant.

moral *adj.* **1** moral: *aspecto moral = moral aspect.* || *s.f.* **2** morality, morals (ciencia). **3** morale (ánimo). **4** conduct (conducta). || *s.m.* **5** BOT. mulberry tree (árbol).

moraleja *s.f.* moral.

moralidad *s.f.* morality, morals.

moralismo *s.m.* moralism.

moralista *s.m.* y *f.* **1** moralist. || *adj.* **2** moralistic.

moralización *s.f.* moralization.

moralizador, -a *adj.* **1** moralizing. || *s.m.* y *f.* **2** moralist.

moralizar *v.t.* to moralize.

moralmente *adv.* morally.

morapio *s.m.* red wine (vino tinto).

morar *v.i.* to inhabit, to dwell.

morbidez *s.f.* softness.

mórbido, -a *adj.* **1** morbid (que padece enfermedad). **2** soft (blando).

morbilidad *s.f.* morbility.

morbo *s.m.* sickness, illness (enfermedad).

morbosidad *s.f.* morbidity, morbidness.

morboso, -a *adj.* **1** sickly (enfermizo). **2** morbid (que se deleita en sentimientos desagradables). **3** sadistic (sádico). **4** morbific (que causa enfermedad).

morcilla *s.f.* **1** black pudding (embutido). **2** ad lib (texto inventado).

morcillero, -a *s.m.* y *f.* ad-libber (actor).

morcillo, -a *adj.* black with red hairs (caballo).

mordacidad *s.f.* mordacity, bite.

mordaz *adj.* **1** corrosive (corrosivo). **2** mordant, biting (con maldad).

mordaza *s.f.* gag (contra la boca).

mordazmente *adv.* mordantly, bitingly.

mordedor, -a *adj.* **1** fierce, ferocious (con propensión a morder). **2** sharp, backbiting (maldiciente).

mordedura *s.f.* bite.

morder *v.t.* y *pron.* **1** to bite (clavar los dientes): *me ha mordido un perro = a dog has bitten me.* || *v.t.* **2** to eat away, to eat into (desgastar). **3** to gossip about (murmurar). **4** to criticize, to knock (criticar). || **5 morderse las uñas,** to bite one's nails.

mordido, -a *adj.* **1** bitten. **2** scarce (escaso). || **3** bite (en la pesca).

mordiente *adj.* **1** corrosive (que corroe). **2** mordant, aggressive (agresivo). || *s.m.* **3** mordant (cosa corrosiva). **4** (fig.) bite (garra).

mordisco *s.m.* **1** biting (acción de morder). **2** bite (herida). **3** nibble, bite (pedazo).

mordisquear *v.t.* to nibble.

morena *s.f.* **1** moray (pez). **2** negress (negra).

moreno, -a *adj.* **1** brown (color). **2** dark (persona). **3** tanned (por el sol). || *s.m.* y *f.* **4** negro (persona). || **5 ponerse –,** to get a suntan.

morera *s.f.* mulberry tree (árbol).

morería *s.f.* **1** Moorish quarter (barrio). **2** Moorish territory (tierras).

morfema *s.m.* morpheme.

morfina *s.f.* morphine.

morfinomanía *s.f.* morphine addiction.

morfinómano, -a *adj.* **1** addicted to morphine. || *s.m.* y *f.* **2** morphine addict.

morfología *s.f.* morphology.

morfológico, -a *adj.* morphological.

morganático, -a *adj.* morganatic.

moribundo, -a *adj.* **1** moribund. || *s.m.* y *f.* **2** moribund person.

morillo *s.m.* firedog.

morir *v.i.* y *pron.* **1** to die (dejar de vivir): *morir de infarto = to die of a heart attack.* **2** to die down (fuego). **3** to end (terminar). || *v.t.* **4** to kill (matar): *le he muerto = I've killed him.* || **5 – de frío,** to die of cold. **6 morirse de hambre,** to die of hunger. **7 morirse de risa,** to die laughing. **8 morirse por hacer algo,** to be dying to do something.

morisco, -a *adj.* **1** Moorish. || *s.m.* y *f.* **2** Morisco.

morisma *s.f.* sect o group of Moors (secta o grupo de moros).

morisquete *s.f.* (Am.) grimace (mueca).

mormón, -ona *s.m.* y *f.* Mormon.

mormónico, -a *adj.* Mormon.

mormonismo *s.m.* Mormonism.

moro, -a *adj.* **1** Moorish. || *s.m.* y *f.* **2** Moor (del norte de Africa). || **3 hay moros en la costa,** the coast isn't clear.

morondo o **moroncho** *adj.* bald, bare (pelado).

morosamente *adv.* slowly.

morosidad *s.f.* **1** slowness (lentitud). **2** lateness (tardanza).

moroso, -a *adj.* **1** slow, dilatory (lento). **2** late (que tarda). || **3** slow payer (que retrasa el pago de una deuda).

morral *s.m.* **1** rucksack (mochila). **2** nosebag (talego).

morralla *s.f.* **1** small fry (boliche). **2** rubbish (cosas inútiles).

morrena *s.f.* GEOL. moraine.

morrillo *s.m.* **1** fleshy part of the neck (parte carnosa del cogote). **2** pebble (china rodada).

morriña *s.f.* melancholy, depression.

morrión *s.m.* **1** HIST. morion (casco de bordes levantados). **2** helmet, shako (gorro militar).

morro *s.m.* **1** snout (hocico abultado). **2** (fam.) lips (labios). **3** hill, hillock (montico). **4** nose (de un avión). **5** estar de morros, to be angry. **6 tener mucho –,** to have a lot of cheek.

morrocotudo, -a *adj.* **1** imperative (de gran importancia). **2** very difficult (de gran dificultad). **3** tremendous, terrific (tremendo).

morrón *s.m.* **1** blow (golpe). **2** fall (caída).

morsa *s.f.* ZOOL. walrus.

morse *s.m.* morse.

mortadela *s.f.* mortadella.

mortaja *s.f.* **1** shroud (vestidura de un cadáver). **2** mortice (muesca). **3** (Am.) cigarette paper (papel de fumar).

mortal *adj.* **1** mortal (que produce la muerte). **2** mortal (que ha de morir). **3** fatal, mortal (herida). **4** deadly (golpe). **5** deadly, dreadful (fatigoso): *un trabajo mortal = a dreadful job.* || *s.m.* **6** mortal (hombre). || **7 restos mortales,** mortal remains.

mortalidad *s.f.* mortality.

mortalmente *adv.* mortally.

mortandad *s.f.* heavy loss of life (gran número de muertes).

mortecino, -a *adj.* **1** weak (débil). **2** fading (que se está apagando).

mortero *s.m.* **1** MIL. mortar. **2** mortar (argamasa).

mortífero, -a *adj.* fatal, lethal.

mortificación *s.f.* mortification.

mortificante *adj.* mortifying.

mortificar *v.t.* y *pron.* **1** to mortify (castigar). **2** to bother, to annoy (molestar).

mortuorio, -a *adj.* death, mortuary.

mosaico. -a *adj.* **1** Mosaic, of Moses (relativo a Moisés). || *s.m.* **2** Mosaic.

mosca *s.f.* **1** fly (insecto). **2** tuft of hair (pelo). **3** money, (fam.) bread (dinero). **4** pest, drag (cosa o persona molesta). || **5 – muerta,** hypocrite. **6 peso –,** flyweight. **7 por si las moscas,** just in case. **8 soltar** o **aflojar la –,** to cough up. **9 tener** o **estar con la – detrás de la oreja,** to smell a rat.

moscada *adj.f.* **nuez —,** nutmeg.
moscarda *s.f.* meat fly, bluebottle.
moscardón *s.m.* 1 ZOOL. blowfly (moscón). 2 botfly (mosca grande). 3 (fig.) pest, drag (persona inoportuna).
moscatel *s.m.* 1 muscatel (uva). 2 muscatel (vino).
moscón *s.m.* 1 ZOOL. bluebottle (mosca azul). 2 meatfly (mosca de la carne). 3 BOT. maple (arce). 4 (fam.) pest, drag (persona inoportuna).
moscovita *adj./s.m.* y *f.* Muscovite.
mosén *s.m.* Sir (título).
mosquear *v.t.* 1 to shoo away (ahuyentar las moscas). || *v.pron.* 2 to get annoyed (enojarse).
mosqueo *s.m.* 1 shooing (de moscas). 2 annoyance, bother (enojo).
mosquetazo *s.m.* musket shot (disparo).
mosquete *s.m.* musket.
mosquetero *s.m.* HIST. musketeer.
mosquetón *s.m.* musketoon (carabina corta).
mosquitero o **mosquitera** *s.m.* o *f.* mosquito net.
mosquito, -a *s.m.* y *f.* mosquito.
mostacho *s.m.* moustache.
mostaza *s.f.* mustard.
mosto *s.m.* grape juice, (p.u.) must.
mostrable *adj.* demonstrable.
mostrador, -ora *adj.* 1 showing (que muestra). || *s.m.* 2 counter (de tienda). 3 bar (de un bar).
mostrar *v.t.* 1 to show (poner a la vista). 2 to indicate, to show (indicar). 3 to demonstrate (demostrar). 4 to explain (explicar). 5 to show, to point out. || *v.pron.* 6 to appear, to show up (aparecer).
mostrenco, -a *adj.* 1 ownerless (sin dueño). 2 stray (animal). 3 fat (gordo). 4 heavy (pesado). 5 clumst, awkward (torpe).
mota *s.f.* 1 speck, spot (mancha pequeña). 2 flaw, fault (defecto). 3 burl (en el paño). 4 hillock (montículo). 5 dot (pinta de color distinto al fondo). 6 not a hint, nothing (nada): *no hacía ni una mota de viento = there wasn't a hint of wind.*
mote *s.m.* 1 HIST. motto, device (lema) 2 nickname (apodo). 3 (Am.) boiled maíz (maíz cocido).
motear *v.t.* to speck, to dot.
motejar *v.t.* 1 to call, to label (llamar). 2 to accuse (acusar).
motel *s.m.* motel.
motete *s.m.* MUS. motet.
motilón, -a *adj.* 1 bald, hairless (pelón). 2 lay brother (lego).
motín *s.m.* 1 riot (en una cárcel, la calle, etc.). 2 mutiny (de tropas).
motivación *s.f.* motivation.
motivador, -a *adj.* motivating.
motivar *v.t.* 1 to motivate, to cause (causar). 2 to explain (explicar).
motivo *s.m.* 1 motive, cause, reason (causa, razón): *motivo oculto = ulterior motive.* 2 grounds: *motivos de divorcio = grounds for divorce.* 3 MUS. motif. 4 motif (elemento ornamental). || **5 con este —,** for this reason. **6 con — de,** on the occasion of. **7 dar — a,** to give rise to. **8 sin —,** without a motive.
moto *s.f.* motorbike.
motocarro *s.m.* three-wheeler.
motocicleta *s.f.* motorbike.
motociclismo *s.m.* motorcycling.
motociclista *s.m.* y *f.* motorcyclist.
motociclo *s.m.* motorcycle.
motocultivo *s.m.* mechanized agriculture.
motonave *s.m.* motorboat.
motopropulsión *s.f.* motor propulsion.
motor *adj.* 1 motive. || *s.m.* 2 motor, engine (máquina): *motor de arranque = starting motor.* || **3 — de explosión,** internal combustion engine. **4 — de reacción,** jet engine.
motorismo *s.m.* motorcycling.
motorista *s.m.* y *f.* motorcyclist.
motorización *s.f.* motorization.
motorizar *v.t.* y *pron.* to motorize.
motovelero *s.m.* motor sailer.
motriz *adj.* motive, driving.
motu propio *adv.* voluntarily.
movedizo, -a *adj.* 1 moving, movable (que se mueve fácilmente). 2 shifting (sand). 3 shaky, unsteady (inseguro). 4 inconsistent (persona). 5 unsettled (situación). || **6 arenas movedizas,** quicksand.
movedor, -a *adj.* 1 moving. || *s.m.* y *f.* 2 mover.
mover *v.t.* y *pron.* 1 to move: *mover la silla = to move the chair.* 2 to shake (agitar). 3 to wag (el rabo). 4 to shake, to nod (la cabeza). 5 to move (ajedrez). 6 to drive, to power (impulsar). 7 to persuade (persuadir). 8 to excite, to stir (excitar). 9 to cause (causar): *van a terminar moviendo una guerra = they're going to end up causing a war.* 10 to rise (el viento). || *v.i.* 11 to bud (empezar a brotar). || *v.pron.* 12 to get a move on (darse prisa): *¡muévete! = get a move on!* || **13 — cielo y tierra,** to move heaven and earth.
movible *adj.* movable, mobile.
movido, -a *adj.* 1 blurred (fotografía). 2 active, restless (activo). 3 lively (animado). || **4 — de** o **por,** moved by: *movido por compasión = moved by pity.*
moviente *adj.* movable.
móvil *adj.* 1 mobile, movable (movible). || *s.m.* 2 cause, motive (causa). 3 FIS. moving body (cuerpo en movimiento). 4 mobile (objeto con hilos).
movilidad *s.f.* mobility.
movilización *s.f.* mobilization.
movilizar *v.t.* to mobilize.
movimiento *s.m.* 1 movement: *movimiento de las hojas = movement of the leaves.* 2 FIS. y MAT. motion. 3 MUS. tempo (velocidad). 4 traffic (de coches). 5 movement (entradas y salidas de barcos, trenes, dinero, aviones, etc.). 6 action (de un libro). 7 GEOL. tremor. 8 MIL. movement. 9 POL., ART. y MUS. movement. 10 fit (de risa, celos). | **11 poner en —,** to set in motion.
moza *s.f.* 1 girl (chica). 2 servant (criada). 3 single girl (soltera). || **4 buena —,** pretty girl.
mozalbete *s.m.* lad, kid.
mozo, -a *adj.* 1 young (joven). 2 single (soltero). || *s.m.* 3 youth, lad (joven). 4 single man (soltero). 5 servant (criado). 6 porter (en la estación). 7 conscript (soldado). || **8 — de estoques,** sword by. **9 buen —,** handsome lad.
mucosidad *s.f.* mucus.
mucoso, -a *adj.* mucous.
muchacha *s.f.* 1 girl (chica). 2 servant, maid (criada).
muchachería *s.f.* 1 kids (chicos y chicas). 2 gang of kids (panda de chicos). 3 prank (broma).
muchachil *adj.* 1 boyish (de chico). 2 girlish (de chica).
muchedumbre *s.f.* crowd, mass.
mucho, -a *adj.* o *pron. indef.* 1 a lot of, much (singular): *mucho trabajo = a lot of work.* 2 a lot of, many (plural): *muchas personas = a lot of people.* || *adv.* 3 a lot, much: *gano mucho más = I earn much more; juego mucho al golf = I play golf a lot.* 4 very: *me alegro mucho = I'm very glad.* || **5 como —,** at the most. **6 con —,** by far. **7 muchas gracias,** thank you very much. **8 — más,** much more. **9 — menos,** much less. **10 — peor,** much worse. **11 ni con —,** not nearly. **12 ni — menos,** by no means; far from it. **13 por — que,** however much. **14 tener en — a uno,** to think a lot of someone.
muda *s.f.* 1 change of clothing (ropa de cambio). 2 moult (de los animales). 3 slough (de las serpientes). 4 breaking (cambio de voz).
mudable o **mutable** *adj.* 1 changeable.
mudamente *adv.* silently.
mudanza *s.f.* 1 change (cambio). 2 move (cambio de domicilio). 3 figure (de un baile). 4 changing (acción de mudar). || **5 camión de mudanzas,** removal van. **6 estar de —,** to be moving.
mudar *v.t.* 1 to change (cambiar). 2 to alter (alterar). 3 to moult (un animal). 4 to break (la voz). 5 to move (mover). || *v.t.* y *pron.* 6 to move (trasladar). || *v.pron.* 7 to change clothes (cambiarse de ropa). 8 to move house (cambiar de casa).
mudéjar *adj./s.m.* y *f.* Mudejar.
mudez *s.f.* dumbness.
mudo, -a *adj.* 1 MED. dumb (que no puede hablar). 2 silent, mute (callado). 3 GRAM. silent (letra). 4 silent (película). || *s.m.* y *f.* 5 dumb person.
mueblaje *s.m.* furniture.
mueblar *v.t.* to furnish.
mueble *adj.* 1 movable. || *s.m.* 2 piece of furniture. || *pl.* 3 furniture. || **4 con muebles,** furnished. **5 sin muebles,** unfurnished.
mueca *s.f.* 1 grimace, face. || **2 hacer muecas,** to pull faces.
muecín *s.m.* REL. muezzin.
muela *s.f.* 1 ANAT. tooth, molar (diente). 2 grindstone (de afilar). 3 millstone (de moler). 4 mound, hilock (cerro). 5 BOT.

vetch (almorta). || **6 dolor de muelas,** toothache. **7 — del juicio,** wisdom tooth.
muelle *adj.* 1 soft (blando). 2 voluptuous (voluptuoso). 3 smooth (suave). 4 luxurious (lujoso). || *s.m.* 5 quay, wharf (para barcos). 6 loading bay (para trenes). 7 spring (pieza elástica).
muellemente *adv.* 1 softly (blandamente). 2 comfortably (cómodamente).
muérdago *s.m.* mistletoe.
muerdo *s.m.* 1 bite (hecho y resultado de morder). 2 bite (mordisco).
muerte *s.f.* 1 death (terminación de la vida): *muerte natural = natural death.* 2 murder (homicidio). 3 destruction, ruin (destrucción, ruina). || **4 a —,** to the death. **5 de mala —,** useless, rotten (de poco valor). **6 — violenta,** violent death. **7 odiar a —,** to despise.
muerto, -a *adj.* 1 dead (sin vida). 2 killed (matado). 3 dull, (sin brillo). 4 dead (agotado). 5 dead (idioma). || *s.m.* y *f.* 6 dead person (persona muerta). 7 body, corpse (cadáver). || **8 echarle a uno el —,** to put the blame on someone. **9 horas muertas,** dead hours. **10 más — que vivo,** half-dead. **11 — de cansancio,** dead tired. **12 nacido —,** stillborn.
muesca *s.f.* 1 notch (corte). 2 earmark (del ganado).
muestra *s.f.* 1 model (modelo). 2 sample (pequeña cantidad de una mercancía). 3 proof (prueba). 4 example (ejemplo). 5 sign (señal). 6 show (manifestación). 7 sign (rótulo de una tienda).
muestrario *s.m.* collection of samples.
muestreo *s.m.* sampling.
mugido *s.m.* 1 moo (de vaca). 2 bellow (del toro). 3 howl (del viento).
mugiente *adj.* 1 mooing (de vaca). 2 bellowing (del toro). 3 howling (del viento).
mugir *v.i.* 1 to moo (vaca). 2 to bellow (toro). 3 to howl (viento).
mugre *s.f.* filth, dirt.
mugriento, -a *adj.* filthy, dirty.
mujer *s.f.* 1 woman (de sexo femenino). 2 wife (esposa). || **3 — pública** o **de mala vida,** prostitute. **4 tomar —,** to get married.
mujerero, -a o **mujeriego, -a** *adj.* 1 feminine, womanly (relativo a la mujer). 2 lecherous (lujurioso).
mujeril *adj.* 1 feminine, womanly (relativo a la mujer). 2 effeminate (afeminado).
mujerilmente *adv.* 1 feminely. 2 effeminately.
mujerío *s.m.* group of women.
mujik *s.m.* moujik (campesino ruso).
mula *s.f.* ZOOL. mule, she-mule (hembra del mulo).
mulada *s.f.* drove of mules.
muladar *s.m.* manure heap, dungheap (estercolero).
mular *adj.* mule.
mulatero o **mulero** *s.m.* muleteer.
mulato, -a *adj.* 1 mulatto. || *s.m.* y *f.* 2 mulatto.
muleta *s.f.* 1 crutch (bastón para andar). 2 muleta (del torero).
muletada *s.f.* drove of mules.
muletear *v.t.* to use the muleta.
muletilla *s.f.* 1 muleta (del torero). 2 cross-handled cane (bastón de puño atravesado). 3 cliché, padding (frase o palabra repetida).
muletillero, -a *adj.* padder.
muleto, -a *s.m.* y *f.* young mule.
mulo *s.m.* ZOOL. mule.
multa *s.f.* 1 fine (sanción). 2 parking ticket (por aparcar mal).
multar *v.t.* to fine.
multicelular *adj.* multicellular.
multicolor *adj.* multicoloured.
multicopiar *v.t.* to duplicate.
multicopista *s.m.* y *f.* duplicator.
multiforme *adj.* multiform.
multilátero o **multilateral** *adj.* multilateral.
multimillonario, -a *adj./s.m.* y *f.* multimillionaire.
multinacional *adj.* y *s.f.* multinational.
multípara, -o *adj.* 1 multiparous. || *s.f.* 2 multipara.
múltiple *adj.* 1 multiple. || *s.m.pl.* 2 numerous, many.
multiplicable *adj.* multipliable.
multiplicación *s.f.* multiplication.
multiplicador, -a *adj.* 1 multiplying. || *s.m.* 2 multiplier.
multiplicando *adj.* y *s.m.* MAT. multiplicand.
multiplicar *v.t.* 1 MAT. to multiply. || *v.pron.* 2 to multiply. 3 to increase (aumentar). || **4 tabla de multiplicar,** multiplication table.
multiplicativo, -a *adj.* multiplicative.
multiplicidad *s.f.* multiplicity.
múltiplo *adj.* y *s.m.* MAT. multiple.
multisecular *adj.* centuries-old.
multitud *s.f.* 1 multitude (gran número): *una multitud de deudas = a multitude of debts.* 2 crowd, multitude (de gente).
multitudinario *adj.* multitudinous.
mullido *s.m.* 1 stuffing, padding (para rellenar). 2 bedding (para el ganado).
mullir *v.t.* 1 to soften (hacer menos duro). 2 to hoe (plantas).
mundanal *adj.* worldly, of the world.
mundanalidad *s.f.* worldliness.
mundanamente *adv.* worldly.
mundanear *v.i.* to be worldly.
mundanería *s.f.* worldliness.
mundano, -a o **mundanal** *adj.* 1 worldly, of the world (relativo al mundo). 2 hedonistic, pleasure-loving (aficionado a placeres y lujos).
mundial *adj.* 1 world (guerra, marca, etc.): *récord mundial = world record.* 2 worldwide, universal (universal): *una empresa mundial = a worldwide company.*
mundo *s.m.* 1 world (la tierra). 2 people (todos los hombres). 3 world (parte de la sociedad): *el mundo del deporte = the world of sport.* 4 REL. world. 5 society (sociedad). || **6 de —,** of the world. **7 echar al —,** to bring into the world. **8 el otro —,** the other world. **9 hundirse el —,** to be the end of the world. **10 medio —,** lots of people. **11 ponerse el — por montera,** not to care what the world thinks. **12 tener —,** to be a man of the world. **13 todo el —,** everybody. **14 venir al —,** to come into the world. **15 ver —,** to see the world.
mundología *s.f.* worldliness.
munición *s.f.* 1 MIL. ammunition. || *pl.* 2 MIL. munitions, stores.
municionamiento *s.m.* MIL. stores, supplies.
municionar *v.t.* to supply with munitions.
municipal *adj.* 1 municipal. || *s.m.* 2 policeman (policía).
municipalidad *s.f.* municipality.
municipalización *s.f.* municipalization.
municipalizar *v.t.* to municipalize.
munificencia *s.f.* munificence.
munificiente *adj.* munificent.
munífico, -a *adj.* munificent.
muñeca *s.f.* 1 ANAT. wrist (articulación). 2 doll (juguete). 3 dummy (maniquí). 4 cleaning rag (lío de trapo). 5 (fam.) bimbo (joven frívola o de poco juicio).
muñeco *s.m.* 1 doll (juguete). 2 (fig.) puppet (hombre fácil de manejar). 3 sissy (hombre afeminado).
muñequera *s.f.* wristband.
muñón *s.m.* 1 ANAT. stump. 2 MEC. trunnion.
mural *adj.* 1 mural. || *s.m.* 2 mural.
muralla *s.f.* wall: *la gran muralla = the great wall.*
murallón *s.m.* rampart.
murar *v.t.* to wall.
murciélago *s.m.* ZOOL. bat.
murga *s.f.* 1 group of buskers. || **2 dar —,** to annoy; to bother.
murmullar *v.t.* to mumble, to mutter.
murmullo *s.m.* murmur, mutter, mumble.
murmuración *s.f.* gossip.
murmurador, -a *adj.* 1 gossiping. || *s.m.* y *f.* 2 gossip.
murmurante *adj.* 1 murmuring. 2 gossiping (maldiciente).
murmurar *v.i.* 1 to gossip (cotillear). 2 (fam.) to knock (hablar mal de alguien). 3 to criticize (criticar). 4 to murmur (hacer un ruido suave) *v.t.* e *i.* 5 to mumble, to mutter (hablar entre dientes).
muro *s.m.* wall.
murria *s.f.* homesickness.
murrio, -a *adj.* sad, depressed (triste).
musa *s.f.* 1 Muse (deidad). 2 muse (inspiración). || *pl.* 3 the Muses.
musaraña *s.f.* 1 ZOOL. shrew. || **2 mirar a/pensar en las musarañas,** to have one's head in the clouds.
muscular *adj.* muscular.
musculatura *s.f.* musculature, muscles.
músculo *s.m.* muscle.
musculoso, -a *adj.* muscular.
muselina *s.f.* muslin.
museo *s.m.* museum.
musgaño *s.m.* ZOOL. shrew.
musgo *s.m.* BOT. moss.

música *s.f.* 1 music. 2 band, group (compañía de músicos). || 3 **— celestial,** hot air. 4 **— de cámara,** chamber music. 5 **— de fondo,** back-ground music.
musical *adj.* musical.
musicalidad *s.f.* musicality.
musicalmente *adv.* musically.
músico, -a *adj.* 1 musical. || *s.m.* y *f.* 2 musician.
musicología *s.f.* musicology.
musitar *v.t.* to mumble, to mutter.
muslo *s.m.* 1 ANAT. thigh. || 2 **— de pollo,** chicken leg.
mustiamente *adv.* sadly.
mustiarse *v.pron.* to wither.
mustio, -a *adj.* 1 sad, depressed (triste). 2 withered (marchito).
musulmán, -ana *adj./s.m.* y *f.* REL. Moslem, Muslim.
mutabilidad *s.f.* mutability.
mutable *adj.* mutable.
mutación *s.f.* mutation.
mutante *adj./s.m.* y *f.* mutant.
mutilación *s.f.* mutilation.
mutilado, -a *adj.* 1 crippled, disabled. || 2 *s.m.* y *f.* crippled person.
mutilar *v.t.* y *pron.* 1 to mutilate (cortar un miembro). || *v.t.* 2 to cut, to mutilate (quitar parte de una cosa).
mutis *s.m.* 1 exit (acto de retirarse). || 2 **hacer —, a)** to keep quiet (callar); **b)** to exit (retirarse de la escena).
mutismo *s.m.* silence.
mutual *adj.* 1 mutual. || *s.f.* 2 mutual benefit society (mutualidad).
mutualidad o **mutua** *s.f.* mutual benefit society (asociación).
mutualismo *s.m.* mutualism.
mutualista *adj.* 1 mutualistic. || *s.m.* y *f.* 2 mutualist.
mutuamente *adv.* mutually.
mutuo, -a *adj.* mutual, reciprocal.
muy *adv.* 1 very: *muy borracho = very drunk; muy bueno = very good.* 2 widely, much: *muy escuchado = widely listened to.* || 3 **es — hombre,** he's a real man. 4 **— conocido,** very well-known. 5 **— mujer,** real woman.

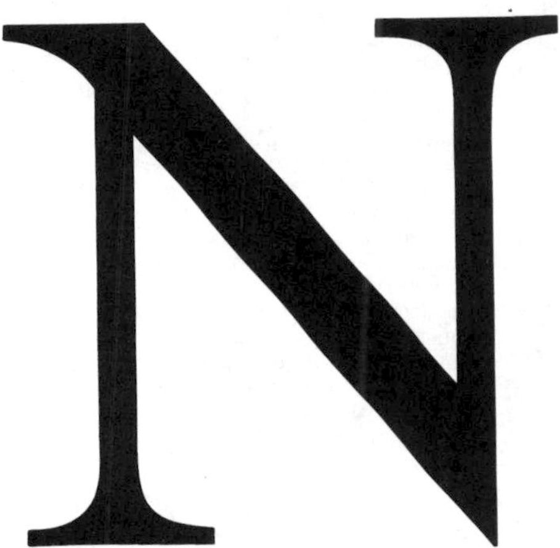

n, N *s.f.* 1 n, N (decimosexta letra del alfabeto español). 2 MAT. número indeterminado.
OBS. Con mayúscula tiene los siguientes significados: **N** es el símbolo del nitrógeno y del newton. 3 **N.** es la abreviatura de norte.
nabo *s.m.* 1 BOT. turnip. 2 ARQ. newel.
nácar *s.m.* mother-of-pearl.
nacarado, -a *adj.* pearly. 2 (lit.) nacreous.
nacer *v.i.* 1 to be born (venir al mundo): *nació en Londres = he was born in London.* 2 (fig.) to spring, to stem; to originate (una idea, etc.). 3 BOT. to bud, to sprout. 4 to sprout, to grow (pelo, plumas, alas, etc., a un animal). 5 to rise (un astro, un río): *el río nace en las montañas = the river rises in the mountains.* || 6 **— de pie,** to be born lucky. 7 **— para,** to be a born: *nació para escritor = he is a born writer.* 8 **volver a —,** to have a narrow escape.
nacido, -a *adj.* 1 born. || *s.m.* 2 human being. || 3 **bien —,** well-bred. 4 **mal —,** ill-bred; vile.
naciente *adj.* 1 rising (el sol). 2 (form.) nascent. 3 budding (incipiente, que comienza). || *s.m.* 4 orient, east.
nacimiento *s.m.* 1 birth. 2 source (de un río). 3 (fig.) origin, beginning. 4 REL. nativity scene.
nación *s.f.* 1 nation (población de una nación): *el presidente hablará a la nación = the President will speak to the nation.* 2 nation, country (territorio).
nacional *adj.* 1 national: *himno nacional = national anthem.* 2 domestic (opuesto a extranjero): *información nacional = domestic news.* || *s.m.* 3 national (conciudadano); citizen. || 4 **carretera —, a)** (brit.) arterial road; **b)** (EE.UU.) arterial highway.
nacionalidad *s.f.* nationality.
nacionalismo *s.m.* POL. nationalism.
nacionalista *adj./s.m.* y *f.* 1 POL. nationalist. || *adj.* 2 POL. nationalistic.
nacionalización *s.f.* 1 POL. nationalization. 2 naturalization (de un extranjero).
nacionalizar *v.t.* 1 POL. nationalize (una empresa, una industria, etc.). 2 naturalize (a un extranjero).
nacionalmente *adv.* nationally.
nacionalsindicalismo *s.m.* POL. National Syndicalism.
nacionalsocialismo *s.m.* POL. National Socialism.
nacionalsocialista *adj./s.m.* y *f.* POL. National Socialist.
nada *s.f.* 1 nothingness (la nada, el no ser). || *pron.ind.* 2 nothing, not... anything: *no dijo nada = he said nothing; he didn't say anything.* || *adv.* 3 not at all: *no me gusta nada = I don't like her at all.* || *interj.* 4 no! || 5 **a cada —,** (Am.) constantly. 6 **ahí va es —,** just fancy! 7 **casi —,** next to nothing. 8 **como si —,** as though it were nothing at all. 9 **de —,** you are welcome, don't mention it. 10 **— de —,** nothing at all. 11 **— menos que,** no / nothing less than. 12 **— más,** that's all. 13 **no tener — que ver con,** to have nothing to do with. 14 **no vale —,** it's worthless. 15 **por menos de —,** at the slightest thing. 16 **por —,** for nothing. 17 **por — del mundo,** for all the tea in China. 18 **quedarse en —,** to come to nothing. 19 **una cosa de —,** just a little.
nadador, -a *adj.* 1 swimming. || *s.m.* y *f.* 2 swimmer.
nadar *v.i.* 1 to swim: *¿sabes nadar? = can you swim?* 2 to float. 3 (fig.) to rattle about (en una ropa demasiado ancha). 4 (fig. y fam.) to be rolling (en dinero). 5 (fig.) to wallow (en la abundancia). || 6 **— a braza,** DEP. to swim breaststroke. 7 **— a crawl,** DEP. to do the crawl.
nadería *s.f.* mere trifle, worthless thing.
nadie *pron.ind.* 1 nobody, no one, not... anybody: *no hay nadie aquí = there is nobody here / there isn't anybody here.* || *s.m.* 2 nonentity, insignificant person. || 3 **ser un don —,** to be a nobody.
nado *adv.* forma parte de la expresión "a nado": *cruzar a nado = to swim across.*
nafta *s.f.* 1 naphta. 2 (Am.) petrol.
naftalina *s.f.* naphtaline.
nagual *s.m.* (Am.) 1 wizard. 2 lie, trick.
nailon V. **nilon.**
naipe *s.m.* 1 playing card. || 2 **naipes,** cards.
nalga *s.f.* ANAT. buttock. || 2 **nalgas,** buttocks, rump, bottom.
nalgado, -a *adj.* 1 big-bottomed. || *s.f.* 2 GAST. ham. 3 spank.
nana *s.f.* 1 lullaby. 2 grandma, granny. 3 (Am.) child's nurse (ama de cría). 4 (Am.) hurt, injury (pupa de niño).
nanay *interj.* (fam.) no!; out of the question!
nanaya *s.f.* (Am.) 1 grandma, granny. 2 lullaby.
nao *s.f.* MAR. vessel, ship.
napalm *s.m.* MIL. napalm.
napias *s.m.* (fam.) conk, nozzle.
naranja *s.f.* 1 BOT. orange: *zumo de naranja = orange juice.* || *adj.* 2 orange (color). || 3 **media —,** (fig.) better half. 4 **— mandarina,** BOT. tangerine. 5 **¡naranjas! / ¡naranjas de la china!,** no!, nonsense!
naranjado, -a *adj.* 1 orange, orangish (color). || *s.f.* 2 orangeade.
naranjal *s.m.* BOT. orange grove.
naranjero, -a *adj.* 1 orange (relativo a la naranja). || *s.m.* y *f.* 2 orange grover (que cultiva naranjas). 3 orange seller (que vende naranjas). || 4 **trabuco —,** MIL. blunderbuss.
naranjo *s.m.* BOT. orange tree.
narciso *s.m.* 1 BOT. narcissus; daffodil. 2 (fig.) dandy, narcissist.
narcisismo *s.m.* narcissism.
narcisista *s.m.* y *f.* 1 narcissist. || *adj.* 2 narcissistic.

narcosis *s.f.* MED. narcosis.
narcótico *adj.* y *s.m.* MED. narcotic.
narcotizante *adj.* y *s.m.* MED. narcotic.
narcotizar *v.t.* 1 MED. to narcotize. 2 to dope, to drug with narcotics.
nardo *s.m.* BOT. nard.
narguile *s.m.* hookah (pipa oriental).
narigón, -ona *adj.* 1 long-nosed. || *s.m.* 2 long nose, big nose. || *s.m.* y *f.* 3 long-nosed person.
narigudo, -a *adj.* big-nosed, long-nosed.
nariz *s.f.* 1 nose: *nariz aguileña = Roman nose.* 2 nostril (ventanilla de la nariz). 3 (fig.) smell, sense of smell. 4 (fig.) perspicacity, discernment. 5 TEC. neck (cuello de una retorta). || **6 dar a alguien en las narices,** to show somebody what for. **7 dar en la –,** to have a feeling. **8 darle a uno con la puerta en las narices,** to slam the door in someone's face. **9 darse de narices con,** to bump into. **10 dejar a alguien con un palmo de narices,** to let somebody down. **11 de narices,** (fam.) huge. **12 estar delante de las narices,** (fam.) to be right under one's nose. **13 estar hasta las narices,** (fam.) to be completely fed up. **14 hinchársele a uno las narices,** (fam.) to get very cross, to flare up. **15 meter las narices en algo,** to poke/stick one's nose into something. **16 narices, a)** nostrils; **b)** (fam.) nonsense!, rot! **17 no ver más allá de sus narices,** (fam.) not to be able to see further than the end of one's nose. **18 por narices,** (fam.) under compulsion. **19 ¡qué narices!,** (fam.) my hind foot! **20 romper las narices a alguien,** (fig. y fam.) to smash someone's face in. **21 romperse/darse de narices,** (fam.) to fall flat on one's face. **22 sonarse la –,** to blow one's nose.
narizón, -ona *adj.* (fam.) long-nosed.
narizota *s.f.* 1 (fam.) nozzle, conk. || *s.m.* 2 (fam.) long-nosed man. || **3 narizotas,** (fam.) long-nosed person.
narizudo, -a *adj.* (Am.) big-nosed, long-nosed.
narrable *adj.* narratable.
narración *s.f.* 1 narration, narrating. 2 account, story (relato). 3 LIT. narrative (arte de narrar).
narrador, -a *s.m.* y *f.* 1 narrator, narrater. 2 teller.
narrar *v.t.* to narrate, to tell, to relate, to recount.
narrativo, -a *adj.* 1 narrative. || *s.f.* 2 LIT. narrative (género literario).
narria *s.f.* trolley (carrito para arrastrar pesos).
narval *s.m.* ZOOL. narwhal.
nasa *s.f.* 1 creel; fish trap (para pescado). 2 bin (para pan, etc.). 3 basket.
nasal *adj.* y *s.f.* nasal: *fosas nasales = nasal cavities.*
nasalidad *s.f.* nasality.
nasalización *s.f.* 1 FON. nasalization. 2 nasal intonation.
nasalizar *v.t.* to nasalize.
nata *s.f.* 1 cream: *pastel de nata = cream cake.* 2 (fig.) cream, best part. 3 scum; skin (en la leche). 4 (Am.) scum, slag (gente despreciable). || **5 la flor y –,** (fig.) the pick, the cream. **6 – montada,** GAST. whipped cream.
natación *s.f.* 1 DEP. swimming.
natal *adj.* 1 natal (del nacimiento). 2 native: *mi tierra natal = my native land.* 3 home: *ciudad natal = home town.*
natalicio *s.m.* y *adj.* (form.) birthday.
natalidad *s.f.* 1 birth rate, natality. || **2 índice de –,** birth rate, natality rate.
natatorio *adj.* natatorial, natatory, swimming.
natillas *s.f.* y *pl.* GAST. custard.
natividad *s.f.* 1 nativity. 2 Christmas.
nativo, -a *adj.* 1 native (natal): *país nativo = native country.* 2 native (habitante): *un español nativo = a native Spaniard.* 3 indigenous, native: *costumbres nativas = native customs.* 4 MIN. native: *oro nativo = native gold.* 5 innate, natural. || *s.m.* y *f.* 6 native (natural): *los nativos de un país = the natives of a country.* 7 (fam.) native teacher.
nato, -a *adj.* 1 born, natural: *es un escritor nato = he is a born writer.* || 2 (form.) *p.p.* de **nacer.**
natura *s.f.* 1 (form.) nature. || **2 contra –,** unnatural.
natural *adj.* 1 natural: *muerte natural = natural death.* 2 simple unaffected, natural: *una chica muy natural = a very natural girl.* 3 fresh (fruta, agua). 4 MUS. natural. || *s.m.* y *f.* 5 natural, inhabitant: *soy natural de Francia = I am a natural of France.* 6 disposition, nature (índole, carácter). || **7 al –, a)** natural, in its own juice (conservas); **b)** true-to-life, realistic (una descripción); **c)** just as it comes, with nothing added (bebidas); **d)** according to nature; **e)** without affectation. **8 ciencias naturales,** natural sciences. **9 del –,** from nature, from life. **10 de tamaño –,** life-sized. **11 hijo –,** natural child.
naturaleza *s.f.* 1 nature. 2 disposition (temperamento). 3 nationality. 4 naturalización. || **5 Madre Naturaleza,** Mother Nature. **6 – muerta,** ART. still life. **7 por –,** by nature.
naturalidad *s.f.* 1 naturalness. 2 simplicity. || **3 con la mayor –, a)** as if nothing had happened, quite calmly; **b)** in an ordinary tone; in a natural voice; **c)** simply, straightforwardly.
naturalismo *s.m.* ART. naturalism.
naturalista *adj.* 1 ART. naturalistic. || *s.m.* y *f.* 2 BIOL. naturalist.
naturalización *s.f.* naturalization.
naturalizar *v.t.* 1 to naturalize. 2 BOT. to acclimatize. || *v.pron.* 3 to become naturalized.
naturalmente *adv.* 1 naturally. 2 of course.
naturismo *s.m.* 1 ECOL. naturism. 2 nudism.
naturista *adj.* 1 ECOL. naturistic. || *s.m.* y *f.* 2 ECOL. naturist. 3 nudist.
naufragar *v.i.* 1 MAR. to sink, to be wrecked (un barro). 2 to be shipwrecked (una persona). 3 (fig.) to fail (un proyecto, una empresa, un negocio).
naufragio *s.m.* 1 MAR. shipwreck, wreck. 2 (fig.) failure, ruin, disaster (de un proyecto, de una empresa, de un negocio).
náufrago, -a *adj.* 1 shipwrecked. || *s.m.* y *f.* 2 castaway; shipwrecked person.
náusea *s.f.* nausea. 2 sick feeling, sickness. 3 (fig.) repugnance, disgust (asco). || **4 dar náuseas,** to nauseate, to sicken. **5 tener náuseas,** to feel sick, to fell nauseated, to be sick to one's stomach.
nauseabundo, -a *adj.* nauseating, sickening.
nauseado, -a *adj.* (Am.) sick to one's stomach.
nauta *s.m.* LIT. mariner, seaman.
náutico, -a *adj.* MAR. 1 nautical. || *s.f.* 2 navigation, seamanship (ciencia, arte). || **3 club –,** yatch club. **4 deporte –,** aquatic sport.
navaja *s.f.* 1 jacknife, pocketknife, penknife. 2 razor (de afeitar). 3 (EE.UU.) straightrazor (de afeitar). 4 ZOOL. tusk (colmillo de jabalí). 5 ZOOL. sting (aguijón de insecto). 6 ZOOL. razor clam, razor shell (molusco). 7 (fig.) sharp tongue. || **8 – barbera,** cut-throat. **9 – de muelle,** clasp knife.
navajada V. **navajazo.**
navajazo *s.m.* 1 stab. 2 slash, gash. 3 stab wound, razor wound.
navajero *s.m.* 1 razor case. 2 quarrelsome (pendenciero que utiliza una navaja).
naval *adj.* MAR. naval: *fuerzas navales = naval forces.*
nave *s.f.* 1 MAR. ship, boat, vessel. 2 ARQ. nave. 3 TEC. shed (industrial). || **4 – espacial,** ASTRON. spacecraft, spaceship. **5 – lateral,** ARQ. aisle.
navecilla *s.f.* REL. censer (naveta para incienso).
navegable *adj.* MAR. navigable: *un río navegable = a navigable river.*
navegación *s.f.* 1 MAR. navigation: *navegación fluvial = river navigation.* 2 sea voyage (viaje en barco). 3 shipping: *es peligroso para la navegación = it is dangerous for shipping.* 4 seamanship (arte de la navegación). || **5 – aérea,** AER. aviation. **6 – a vela/de recreo,** yachting. **7 – de altura,** ocean navigation.
navegador, -ora V. **navegante.**
navegante *s.m.* MAR. 1 navigator. || 2 *adj.* navigating.
navegar *v.t.* e *i.* MAR. to sail, to navigate.
naveta *s.f.* 1 REL. censer. 2 drawer. 3 small vessel. 4 ARQ. prehistoric tomb (en la isla de Menorca).
navidad *s.f.* 1 Christmas (fiesta). 2 REL. Nativity. || **3 árbol de –,** Christmas tree. **4 en –/por –,** at Christmas, at Christmas time. **5 feliz –,** Merry Christmas. **6 Navidades,** Christmas season.
navideño, -a *adj.* Christmas: *tarjeta navideña = Christmas card.*
naviero, -a *adj.* 1 MAR. 1 shipping: *compañía naviera = shipping company.* || *s.m.* 2 shipowner.

navío *s.m.* MAR. 1 ship, vessel. || **2 capitán de –,** sea captain. **3 – de guerra,** warship. **4 – de línea,** ship of the line.
náyade *s.f.* naiad.
nazareno, -a *adj.* y *s.m.* REL. 1 nazarene. 2 penitent (en las procesiones de Semana Santa). 3 (Am.) spur (que utilizan los gauchos).
nazi *adj./s.m.* y *f.* POL. nazi.
nazismo *s.m.* POL. nazism.
neblina *s.f.* 1 haze. 2 light fog, mist (calina).
nebulosamente *adv.* 1 nebulously. 2 (fig.) vaguely.
nebulosidad *s.f.* 1 nebulosity, mistiness. 2 (fig.) vagueness.
nebuloso, -a *adj.* 1 cloudy (el cielo). 2 foggy, misty (atmósfera). 3 (fig.) vague, obscure. 4 gloomy (oscuro). 5 ASTR. nebular, nebulous. || *s.f.* 6 ASTR. nebula.
necedad *s.f.* 1 foolishness, stupidity, nonsense: *no digas necedades = don't talk nonsense.* 2 ignorance.
necesariamente *adv.* 1 necessarily. 2 inevitably. 3 really.
necesario, -a *adj.* 1 necessary: *requisito necesario = necessary requirement.* 2 needful: *haz lo necesario = do the needful.* 3 inevitable. || **5 lo estrictamente –,** the bare necessities. **6 no es – decir que,** no need to say that. **7 si es –,** if necessary, in case of necessity.
neceser *s.m.* 1 toilet case, dressing case, vanity case (de tocador). 2 holdall. 3 sewing kit (de costura). 4 week-end case (de fin de semana).
necesidad *s.f.* 1 necessity. 2 need (for): *necesidad de reformas = need for reforms.* 3 poverty, want, need. 4 difficult situation, emergency. 5 hunger. || **6 artículo de primera –,** basic necessities. **7 de/por –,** of necessity, necessarily. **8 de primera –,** basic, absolutely essential. **9 en caso de –,** in case of need. **10 hacer sus necesidades,** (fam.) to relieve oneself, to go to stool. **11 necesidades, a)** needs: *no tiene suficiente dinero para satisfacer sus necesidades = she hasn't got enough money to satisfy her needs;* **b)** hardships (apuros, dificultades); **c)** (fam.) needs, bodily needs. **12 no hay – de,** there is not need to. **13 por –,** out of necessity. **14 satisfacer las necesidades de,** to supply the needs of. **15 tener – de,** to need, to have need of, to stand in need of.
necesitado, -a *adj.* 1 in need of: *están necesitados de amor = they are in need of love.* 2 needy, necessitous (pobre). || *s.m.* 3 a needy person. || **4 estar – de dinero,** to be short of money. **5 los necesitados,** the needy.
necesitar *v.t.* 1 to need, to want, to be in need of: *eso es lo que necesito = that's what I need.* 2 to require, to necessitate. 3 to need to, to have to, must (ser preciso): *necesito descansar = I need to rest.* || *v.pron.* 4 to be wanted, to be needed: *"se necesita asistenta" = "au-pair wanted".*
neciamente *adv.* foolishly; stupidly.
necio, -a *adj.* 1 foolish. 2 ignorant, silly, stupid. 3 (Am.) touchy. 4 (Am.) stubborn, peevish. || *s.m.* y *f.* 5 idiot, fool.
necrología *s.f.* 1 necrology. 2 obituary, obituary notice, obituary column (en la prensa).
necrológico, -a *adj.* 1 necrological, obituary. || **2 nota –,** obituary notice.
néctar *s.m.* nectar.
nectáreo, -a *adj.* nectareous, nectarous.
nectarina *s.f.* BOT. nectarine.
nectario *s.m.* BOT. nectary.
neerlandés, -a *adj.* 1 Dutch, Netherlands (holandés). || *s.m.* y *f.* 2 Netherlander, Dutchman, Dutchwoman. || *s.m.* 3 Dutch, Netherlandish (idioma).
nefando, -a *adj.* 1 hateful; abominable. 2 wicked, detestable. 3 heinous (un crimen).
nefario, -a *adj.* wicked, detestable, nefarious.
nefasto, -a *adj.* 1 ominous, sad. 2 unlucky, ill-fated. 3 funest. 4 inauspicious.
nefato *adj.* (Am.) stupid, dim.
nefrítico *adj.* MED. nephritic.
nefritis *s.f.* MED. nephritis.
negable *adj.* deniable.
negación *s.f.* 1 negation, denial, refusal. 2 GRAM. negative (partícula negativa); negation. || **3 ser la – de,** to be anything but: *es la negación del arte = it is anything but art.*
negado, -a *adj.* 1 inapt, incapable, incompetent. 2 dull, clumsy. || *s.m.* y *f.* 3 (fam.) nonentity. || **4 – para,** useless at, unfitted for.
negador, -a *adj.* 1 denying. || *s.m.* y *f.* 2 denier.
negar *v.t.* 1 to deny: *no lo niego = I don't deny it.* 2 to refuse (rehusar). 3 to withhold (negarse a conceder). 4 to disown, to disclaim (una responsabilidad, una relación). 5 to refuse, to deny (un permiso). || *v.pron.* 6 to refuse to: *se negó a darme la mano = she refused to shake hands with me.* 7 to decline (rechazar). || **8 – el saludo a alguien,** to cut someone.
negativamente *adv.* 1 negatively. || **2 contestar –,** to answer in the negative.
negativo, -a *s.f.* 1 refusal, negative: *una negativa rotunda = a flat refusal.* 2 denial (de un hecho). || *adj.* 3 negative: *crítica negativa = negative criticism.* 4 MAT. minus: *un número negativo = a minus number.* || *s.m.* 5 FOT. negative.
negligencia *s.f.* 1 negligence, carelessness, slackness. 2 neglect (desidia, dejadez).
negligente *adj.* 1 negligent, neglectful. 2 careless, slack: *un trabajador negligente = a slack worker.*
negligentemente *adv.* negligently, neglectfully, carelessly.
negociable *adj.* COM. negotiable.
negociación *s.f.* 1 COM. negotiation, deal, business transaction. 2 FIN. clearance (de un talón). || **3 en –,** under negotiation. **4 entrar en/entablar negociaciones,** to enter into negotiations.
negociado *s.m.* 1 department, office. 2 business, affair. 3 (Am.) **a)** dirty business, illegal transaction; **b)** shop.
negociador, -a *s.m.* y *f.* 1 negotiator. || *adj.* 2 negotiating.
negociante *s.m.* y *f.* 1 COM. trader, merchant, dealer. || 2 FIN. businessman.
negociar *v.t.* 1 to negotiate (gestionar): *negociar una venta = to negotiate a sale.* || *v.t.* e *i.* 2 to trade, to negotiate; to deal (comerciar). 3 to negotiate (un tratado, una letra). 4 to transact.
negocio *s.m.* 1 business, business deal. 2 COM. transaction, deal. 3 affair, business (asunto). 4 FIN. business: *traspasará su negocio = he will transfer his business.* 5 (fig.) bargain (una buena transacción). 6 COM. trade; business: *el negocio del espectáculo = the show business.* 7 (Am.) store, shop. 8 (Am.) fact (caso): *el negocio es que... = the fact is that...* 9 (Am.) matter (asunto, cuestión). || **10 de negocios,** on business. **11 hombre de negocios,** businessman. **12 – redondo,** profitable business. **13 negocios,** business. **14 – sucio,** dirty business. **15 poner un –,** to start/set up a business.
negrada *s.f.* (Am.) negroes (grupo de negros).
negrear *v.i.* 1 to become black, to turn black. 2 to look black, to appear black. 3 to blacken.
negrero, -a *s.m.* y *f.* 1 slave trader. 2 (fig.) tyrant. || *adj.* 3 slave trading; black slave. 4 (Am.) cruel boss.
negrillo, -a *adj.* 1 blackish. || *s.m.* 2 BOT. elm. || *s.f.* 3 boldface (negrita).
negrito, -a *s.f.* 1 boldface (tipo de letra). || *s.m.* 2 piccaninny. 3 gollywog (muñeco).
negro, -a *adj.* 1 black: *ojos negros = black eyes.* 2 negro; dark, black. 3 dark (pelo, ojos, etc.). 4 (euf.) coloured (de raza negra). 5 (fig.) black: *tengo un futuro muy negro = I have a black future.* 6 (fig.) sad, gloomy (estado de ánimo). 7 (fig.) awful: *una suerte negra = an awful luck.* 8 (fam.) furious. || *s.m.* y *f.* 9 negro (hombre); negress (mujer). 10 (Am.) dear, darling, honey. 11 (desp.) nigger. || *s.m.* 12 black (color). 13 black tobacco. || *s.f.* 14 MUS. crochet. 15 (fig.) bad luck. || **16 cerveza –,** brown ale, stout. **17 cinturón –,** DEP. black belt. **18 el Continente Negro,** the Dark Continent. **19 magia –,** black art, black magic. **20 – como el azabache,** jet-black. **21 – como un tizón,** as black as coal/pitch/ink. **22 peste –,** black death. **23 ponerse –, a)** to get mad, to get cross; **b)** to get a suntan; **c)** to look bad: *la cosa se pone negra = it looks bad.* **24 tener la –,** (fig.) to have bad luck. **25 trabajar como un –,** to work like a nigger. **26 verlo todo –,** to be pessimistic. **27 verse –,** to be in a jam, to have a tough time.
negroide *adj.* negroid.
negrura *s.f.* blackness.
negruzco, -a *adj.* blackish.
nemotecnia *s.f.* TEC. mnemonics, mnemotechny.

nemotécnico, -a *adj.* TEC. mnemotechnic.

nene, -a *s.m.* y *f.* 1 baby. 2 darling (apelativo cariñoso).

nenúfar *s.m.* BOT. water lily, white water lily; nenuphar.

neo *prefijo* 1 neo-; neo. || *s.m.* 2 QUIM. neon.

neocatolicismo *s.m.* REL. neo-Catholicism.

neocatólico, -a *adj.* REL. neo-Catholic.

neocelandés, -esa *adj.* 1 of/from New Zealand. || *s.m.* y *f.* 2 New Zealander.

neoclasicismo *s.m.* ART. neoclassicism.

neoclásico, -a *adj.* ART. 1 neoclassical. || *s.m.* y *f.* 2 neoclassicist.

neófito, -a *s.m.* y *f.* 1 REL. neophyte, novice. 2 (fig.) beginner.

neológico *adj.* FILOL. neological.

neologismo *s.m.* FILOL. neologism.

neologista V. **neólogo.**

neólogo, -a *s.m.* y *f.* FILOL. neologist.

neón *s.m.* QUIM. neon.

neonazi *adj./s.m.* y *f.* POL. neonazi.

nepotismo *s.m.* POL. nepotism.

nervadura (también **nervatura**) *s.f.* 1 ARQ. nervure, ribs, nerve. 2 BOT. ribs, nervation, vein. 3 ZOOL. vein, nerve (en las alas de los insectos).

nérveo, -a *adj.* nerveal.

nerviación V. **nervadura.**

nervio *s.m.* 1 ANAT. nerve. 2 (fig.) strength, energy, vigour. 3 rib (en el lomo de un libro). 4 BOT. nerve (filamento de una hoja). 5 ARQ. rib (nervadura). 6 GAST. sinew (de la carne). 7 MUS. string. || **8 ataque de nervios,** hysterics, fit of nerves. **9 crisparle a uno los nervios,** to get on someone's nerves. **10 guerra de nervios,** war of nerves. **11 nervios,** (fam.) nervousness (nerviosismo). **12 nervios de acero,** (fig.) nerves of steel. **13 ser un manojo de nervios,** (fig.) to be a bundle of nerves. **14 tener los nervios de punta,** (fig.) to have one's nerves on edge, to be on edge.

nerviosamente *adv.* nervously.

nerviosidad *s.f.* 1 nerviness, nervosity. 2 flexibility, vigour.

nerviosismo *s.m.* 1 nerves, nervousness. 2 restlessness, impatience. 3 irritability, agitation.

nervioso, -a *adj.* 1 nervous: *una enfermedad nerviosa = a nervous disease.* 2 ANAT. sinewy (nervudo). 3 nerve: *célula nerviosa = nerve cell.* 4 nervy (de temperamento nervioso). 5 nervous, excited, restless. 6 (fig.) energetic, vigourous. 7 BOT. nerved. || **8 estar muy –,** to be in a state of nerves. **9 no te pongas –,** take it easy. **10 ponerse –,** to lose one's nerve, to get excited, to get worked up.

nervudo, -a *adj.* 1 sinewy (manos, cuerpo). 2 strong, powerful.

netamente *adv.* 1 clearly, distinctly. 2 purely, genuinely.

neto, -a *adj.* 1 FIN. net (precio, peso, beneficio, etc.). 2 pure, genuine. 3 simple, pure (verdad). 4 bare (sueldo). 5 neat, clear.

neumático, -a *adj.* 1 pneumatic. || *s.m.* 2 tyre, rubber tyre, pneumatic tyre. 3 (EE.UU.) tire. || **4 – de repuesto,** spare tyre. **5 – sin cámara,** tubeless tyre.

neumonía *s.f.* MED. pneumonia.

neumotórax *s.m.* MED. pneumothorax.

neuralgia *s.f.* MED. neuralgia.

neurálgico, -a *adj.* MED. neuralgic.

neurastenia *s.f.* 1 MED. neurasthenia. 2 nervous prostration. 3 excitability.

neurasténico, -a *adj.* 1 MED. neurasthenic. 2 excitable. 3 neurotic.

neuritis *s.f.* MED. neuritis.

neurocirugía *s.f.* MED. neurosurgery.

neurología *s.f.* MED. neurology.

neurólogo, -a *s.m.* y *f.* MED. neurologist, nerve specialist.

neurona *s.f.* ANAT. neuron, neurona, nerve cell.

neurópata *s.m.* y *f.* MED. neuropath.

neuropatía *s.f.* MED. neuropathy.

neurosis *s.f.* 1 MED. neurosis. || **2 – de guerra,** PSIQ. shell shock.

neurótico, -a *adj.* y *s.m.* y *f.* MED. neurotic.

neurovegetativo, -a *adj.* ANAT. neurovegetative.

neutral *adj./s.m.* y *f.* neutral: *su país permaneció neutral = his country remained neutral.*

neutralidad *s.f.* neutrality.

neutralismo *s.m.* POL. neutralism.

neutralista *adj.* y *s.m.* y *f.* POL. neutralist.

neutralización *s.f.* neutralization.

neutralizador, -ora V. **neutralizante.**

neutralizante *adj.* 1 neutralizing. || *s.m.* y *f.* 2 neutralizer.

neutralizar *v.t.* 1 to neutralize. 2 to counteract (contrarrestar).

neutro, -a *adj.* 1 neutral. 2 GRAM. neuter (género). 3 BIOL. sexless, neuter. || *s.m.* 4 GRAM. neuter. || **5 verbo –,** GRAM. intransitive verb.

neutrón *s.m.* FIS. neutron.

nevado, -a *adj.* 1 snow-covered; covered with snow. 2 (fig.) snowy, white as snow, snow-white. || *s.m.* 2 (Am.) snow-capped mountain. || *s.f.* 3 snowfall.

nevar *v.i.* 1 to snow. || *v.t.* 2 to cover with snow; to make snow-white.

nevera *s.f.* 1 refrigerator, icebox; ice house. 2 (fam.) fridge. 3 (fig.) icebox (habitación muy fría). 4 (Am.) ice-cream vendor.

nevero *s.m.* GEOL. 1 snowfield. 2 perpetual snow.

nevisca *s.f.* light snowfall; sleet.

nexo *s.m.* 1 nexus, link, connection. 2 bond, tie.

ni *conj.* 1 nor, neither: *no lo conozco ni ella tampoco = I don't know him nor does she.* 2 or: *sin padres ni amigos = without parents or friends.* 3 not even (ni siquiera): *no quedó ni un pastel = there was not even one cake left.* 4 not one, not a single: *ni un pariente = not a single relative.* || **5 – ... –, a)** neither... nor: *no está ni gorda ni delgada = she is neither fat nor thin;* **b)** either... or: *no quiero ni café ni té = I don't want either coffee or tea.* **6 – que... (como si),** anyone would think... **7 – que,** not even if...: *ni que fueses el presidente = not even if you were the president.* **8 – siquiera,** not even. **9 – tampoco,** neither: *él no fue ni ella tampoco = he didn't go and neither did she.*

nicotina *s.f.* QUIM. nicotine.

nicotinismo *s.m.* MED. nicotinism.

nicotismo V. **nicotinismo.**

nicho *s.m.* 1 niche. 2 recess, hollow (en una pared).

nidada *s.f.* 1 brood, hatch, covey (de pollos). 2 clutch, sitting (de huevos). 3 nestful of eggs.

nidal *s.m.* 1 nest, nest box (ponedero de aves domésticas). 2 (fig.) hiding place. 3 (fig. y fam.) hangout.

nido *s.m.* 1 nest (de aves). 2 (fig.) nest, abode (morada, hogar). 3 (fig.) hiding place. 4 (fig.) nest, haunt (guarida): *nido de criminales = nest of criminals.* || **5 – de abeja,** smocking (labor). **6 – de amor,** love nest. **7 patearle el – a alguien,** (Am.) to upset someone's applecart.

niebla *s.f.* 1 fog, mist. 2 (fig.) confusion, fog. 3 fogginess. || **4 envolver en –,** to fog. **5 hay –,** it is foggy. **6 inmovilizado por la –,** fogbound. **7 – espesa,** fogbank.

nieto, -a *s.m.* y *f.* 1 grandchild. || *s.m.* 2 grandson. || *s.f.* 3 granddaughter.

nieve *s.f.* 1 snow. 2 (Am.) sherbet, ice-cream. 3 (vulg.) cocaine. | **4 a punto de –,** GAST. stiff. **5 copo de –,** snowflake. **6 nieves,** snows, snowfall.

nigromancia *s.f.* 1 necromancy. 2 (fam.) black magic.

nigromante *s.m.* 1 necromancer. 2 (fam.) magician.

nigromántico, -a *adj.* 1 necromantic. || *s.m.* y *f.* necromancer.

nigua *s.f.* ZOOL. chigoe.

nihilismo *s.m.* FIL. nihilism.

nihilista *s.m.* y *f.* FIL. 1 nihilist. || *adj.* nihilistic.

niki V. **niqui.**

nilón *s.m.* nylon.

nimbar *v.t.* to halo (rodear con un halo).

nimbo *s.m.* 1 REL. halo (aureola). 2 nimbus (nube). 3 ASTR. halo.

nimiamente *adv.* 1 trivially. 2 fussily. 3 excessively.

nimiedad *s.f.* 1 triviality. 2 prolixity. 3 small-mindedness. 4 excessive detail, meticulousness. 5 smallness.

nimio, -a *adj.* 1 insignificant, petty, trivial. 2 meticulous, detailed. 3 small-minded, stingy, miserly (mezquino). 4 (Am.) very small.

ninfa *s.f.* 1 nymph. 2 (fig.) prostitute.

ninfómana *adj.* y *s.f.* PSIC. nymphomaniac.

ninfomanía *s.f.* PSIC. nymphomania.

ningún V. **ninguno.**

ninguno, -a *adj.* 1 no: *ninguna mujer = no woman.* || *pron.* 2 no one, nobody: *ninguno lo sabe = no one knows.* 3 none: *ninguno de ellos lo pudo hacer = none of them could do it.* 4 [con negación] either (ninguno de los dos): *no vi a ninguno = didn't see either of them.* **5** neither (ninguno de los dos): *ninguno de los padres = neither of the parents.* || **6 de — manera,** not at all, by no means. **7 — parte,** nowhere.

OBS. **Ningún** es el apócope de **ninguno** como *adj.* y se utiliza delante de los s.m.: *ningún hombre = no man.*

niñería *s.f.* **1** childishness, childish act. **2** child's play. **3** (fig.) trifle, triviality (nadería, insignificancia). **4** gewgaw (chuchería, pequeñez).

niñero, -a *adj.* **1** fond of children. || *s.f.* **2** nanny, nursemaid. **3** (Am.) child's nurse.

niñez *s.f.* childhood.

niño, -a *adj.* **1** (fig.) young, small: *es todavía muy niña = she is still very small.* **2** (desp.) childlike, childish (infantil): *no seas niña = don't be childish.* **3** (fig.) inmature. || *s.m.* **4** boy, little boy, child. **5** baby: *va a tener un niño = she is going to have a baby.* **6** infant: *el niño Jesús = the infant Jesus.* **7** (Am.) master (tratamiento respetuoso). **8** (fam.) dear. || *s.f.* **9** girl, little girl, child. **10** (Am.) lady, mistress, miss (tratamiento respetuoso). **11** (fam.) dear. **12** ANAT. pupil. || **13 desde —,** from childhood. **14 la niña de mis/tus/etc. ojos,** (fig.) the apple of my-/your/etc. eye; my/your/etc. pride. **15 — de pecho,** small baby, babe-in-arms. **16 — expósito,** foundling. **17 — mimado,** pet, blue-eyed boy, white-haired boy. **18 — prodigio,** child prodigy.

nipón, -ona *adj./s.m.* y *f.* Japanese.

níquel *s.m.* **1** nickel (metal). **2** (Am.) money. **3** (Am.) small coin, nickel.

niquelado, -a *adj.* **1** nickel-plated. || *s.m.* **2** nickel plate.

niquelar *v.t.* to nickel-plate.

niqui *s.m.* T-shirt.

nirvana *s.m.* REL. nirvana.

níscalo *s.m.* GAST. milk mushroom.

níspero *s.m.* **1** BOT. medlar (árbol, fruto). **2** (Am.) sapodilla (árbol). || **3 — de Japón,** loquat.

nitidez *s.f.* **1** clarity, clearness; brightness. **2** sharpness: *la nitidez de una foto = the sharpness of a photograph.* **3** (fig.) unblemished nature.

nítido, -a *adj.* **1** clear, sharp, well-defined: *un contorno nítido = a clear outline.* **2** bright, shining. **3** (fig.) unblemished.

nitrato *s.m.* **1** QUIM. nitrate. || **2 — de Chile,** Chile saltpetre.

nitrificación *s.f.* QUIM. nitrification.

nitrificar *v.t.* QUIM. to nitrify.

nitro *s.m.* QUIM. nitre, saltpetre.

nitrógeno *s.m.* QUIM. nitrogen.

nitroglicerine *s.f.* QUIM. nitroglycerine.

nivel *s.m.* **1** level: *nivel del mar = sea level.* **2** height (altura). **3** (fig.) standard: *nivel de vida = standard of living.* **4** (fig.) level: *a nivel local = at a local level.* **5** TEC. level (instrumento). || **6 al mismo —,** dead level. **7 al — de,** level with; on a level with. **8 estar al mismo — que,** to be level with. **9 paso a —,** level-crossing, (EE.UU.) railroad crossing.

nivelación *s.f.* levelling.

nivelador, -ora *adj.* **1** levelling. || *s.m.* y *f.* **2** leveller. || *s.f.* **3** TEC. bulldozer (máquina).

nivelar *v.t.* **1** to level: *estos tractores nivelaron más de 500 acres de terreno = these tractors levelled more than 500 acres of land.* **2** to grade (una carretera, una vía férrea). **3** to even (un terreno). **4** (fig.) to balance, to adjust (un presupuesto). || *v.pron.* **5** to level off, to level out, to become balanced.

níveo, -a *adj.* (lit.) snowy, niveous.

no *adv.* **1** no: *no, gracias = no, thanks.* **2** not: *no vendrán = they will not come.* **3** (p.u.) nay. || *s.m.* **4** no: *un no categórico = a definite no.* **5** non (en compuestos): *no conformismo = nonconformity.* || **6 ¡a que —!** (desafío) I bet you can't; I bet you don't. **7 ¡cómo —!,** of course! **8 creo que —,** I don't think so. **9 decir que —,** to say no. **10 — bien,** (enseguida que, apenas) as soon as; no sooner: *no bien salí de la habitación cuando sonó el teléfono = I had no sooner left the room than the phone rang.* **11 — más,** (Am.) only. **12 — obstante,** notwithstanding. **13 — sea que,** lest. **14 todavía —,** not yet.

nobiliario, -a *adj.* **1** nobiliary. || **2 título —,** title of nobility.

noble *adj.* **1** noble: *noble linaje = noble descent.* **2** honest, noble (persona, carácter). **3** generous. || *s.m.* y *f.* **4** HIST. noble; nobleman (hombre); noblewoman (mujer). || **5 los nobles,** HIST. the nobility.

noblemente *adv.* **1** nobly. **2** honestly.

nobleza *s.f.* **1** nobility, nobleness, honesty. **2** HIST. aristocracy, nobility. || **3 — obliga,** noblesse oblige.

noblote *adj.* (fam.) noble, goodnatured, open-hearted.

noción *s.f.* **1** notion, idea. || **2 nociones,** rudiments, smattering, slight knowledge (conocimientos elementales): *tenía nociones de alemán = he had a smattering of German.*

nocividad *s.f.* harmfulness, noxiousness.

nocivo, -a *adj.* harmful, pernicious, injurious, noxious.

noctambulismo *s.m.* noctambulism.

noctámbulo, -a *adj.* **1** noctambulant, night-wandering. || *s.m.* y *f.* **2** night-wanderer, noctambule.

nocturnidad *s.f.* DER. condition of nocturnal, nocturnal character (de un delito).

nocturno, -a *adj.* **1** nocturnal. **2** night: *vuelo nocturno = night flight.* **3** nightly. **4** evening: *una clase nocturna = an evening class.* || *s.m.* **5** MUS. nocturne.

noche *s.f.* **1** night: *pasé una mala noche = I had a bad night.* **2** evening. **3** (fig.) dark, darkness (oscuridad). **4** night-time. || **5 al caer la —,** at dark, at nightfall. **6 altas horas de la —,** small hours. **7 ayer —,** last night. **8 buenas noches,** good night. **9 de la — a la mañana,** overnight. **10 de —,** at night, by night. **11 esta —,** tonight. **12 hacer —,** to spend the night. **13 hacerse de —,** to grow dark. **14 — vieja,** New Year's Eve. **15 pasar la — en vela,** to have a sleepless night. **16 por la —,** at night. **17 traje de —,** evening dress.

nochebuena *s.f.* Christmas Eve.

nochecita *s.f.* (Am.) nightfall.

nochero, -a *adj.* (Am.) **1** night-wanderer. || *s.m.* **2** night watchman. **3** bedside table.

nodo *s.m.* **1** MED. node. **2** newsreel (noticiario documental).

nodriza *s.f.* **1** child's nurse, wet-nurse. **2** nanny. **3** TEC. vacuum tank.

nódulo *s.m.* nodule, node.

nogal *s.m.* BOT. walnut (árbol, madera).

nogalina *s.f.* walnut stain.

nómada *adj.* ANTR. **1** nomadic. || *s.m.* y *f.* **2** nomad.

nomadismo *s.m.* ANTR. nomadism.

nombrado, -a *adj.* **1** (fig.) famous, well-known: *un médico muy nombrado = a very famous doctor.* **2** aforementioned (mencionado anteriormente).

nombramiento *s.m.* **1** nomination, appointment, naming (designación). **2** MIL. commission (de un oficial).

nombrar *v.t.* **1** to appoint, to nominate (designar para un cargo). **2** to mention, to name. **3** MIL. to commission (a un oficial).

nombre *s.m.* **1** name: *me gusta tu nombre = I like your name.* **2** (fig.) fame, reputation, name. **3** GRAM. noun: *nombre propio = proper noun.* || **4 buen —,** good reputation. **5 de —,** by name. **6 — artístico,** stage name, nom de plume. **7 — de pila,** Christian name. **8 — y apellidos,** full name. **9 no tener — (una acción),** (fig.) to be unspeakable. **10 poner — a,** to name, to call. **11 sin —,** nameless.

nomenclatura *s.f.* nomenclature.

nomeolvides *s.f.* BOT. forget-me-not.

nómina *s.f.* FIN. payroll. **2** list of names. || **3 estar en —,** to be on the staff.

nominación *s.f.* **1** nomination. **2** appointment.

nominal *adj.* **1** nominal, titular (sólo de nombre). **2** FIN. nominal. **3** GRAM. nominal, substantival. || **4 valor —,** FIN. face value.

nominalismo *s.m.* FIL. nominalism.

nominalista *s.m.* y *f.* FIL. **1** nominalist. || *adj.* **2** nominalist, nominalistic.

nominalmente *adv.* nominally; in name.

nominar V. **nombrar.**

nominativo *adj.* y *s.m.* GRAM. nominative (caso). || **2** FIN. nominative, nominal.

nominilla *s.f.* FIN. pay warrant.

non *adj.* y *s.m.* **1** (p.u.) uneven, odd (número). || *s.m.* **2** uneven number. || **3 estar/quedar de nones,** (fig.) to be left alone, to be left out. **4 decir que nones,** to say no; to refuse point blank. **5 nones,** (fam.) no (negación).

nonagenario, -a *adj./s.m.* y *f.* nonagenarian.

nonagésimo, -a *adj./s.m.* y *f.* ninetieth.

nonato, -a *adj.* 1 unborn. 2 MED. not naturally born, born by Caesarian section.
noningentésimo, -a *adj./s.m.* y *f.* nine-hundredth.
nonio *s.m.* TEC. vernier.
nopal *s.m.* BOT. prickly pear, nopal.
noquear *v.t.* DEP. to knock out (en boxeo o lucha).
norabuena V. **enhorabuena.**
noramala V. **enhoramala.**
nordeste V. **noreste.**
nórdico, -a *adj.* 1 Northern, Northerly (del Norte). 2 Nordic; Norse. || *adj./s.m.* y *f.* 3 Nordic (de los países nórdicos). || *s.m.* y *f.* 4 Northerner. 5 HIST. Norseman. || *s.m.* 6 Norse (idioma).
noreste *adj.* 1 north-east, north-eastern. 2 north-easterly (dirección). || *s.m.* 3 north-east.
noria *s.f.* 1 water wheel, chain-pump. 2 draw wheel, big wheel (recreo de feria).
norma *s.f.* 1 norm, standard. 2 pattern, model. 3 rule, regulation. 4 ARQ. square.
normal *adj.* 1 normal. 2 standard: *tamaño normal = standard size.* || *adj.* y *s.f.* 3 MAT. normal, perpendicular line. || 4 **escuela —,** Teacher's Training College.
normalidad *s.f.* 1 normality. 2 (fig.) calm. || 3 **volver a la —,** to return to normal.
normalista *s.m.* y *f.* normal-school student.
normalización *s.f.* normalization.
normalizar *v.t.* 1 to normalize, to make normal. 2 TEC. to standardize (tipificar). || *v.pron.* 3 to return to normal, to become normal, to settle down.
normalmente *adv.* normally, usually.
normativo, -a *adj.* 1 normative. 2 standard. || *s.f.* 3 set of rules, regulations.
noroeste *adj.* 1 northwest, northwestern. 2 north-westerly (dirección). || *s.m.* 3 northwest. 4 north-west wind.
norte *s.m.* 1 North. 2 north wind, northerly wind. 3 (fig.) aim (objetivo). 4 North Pole. 5 (fig.) guide (orientación). 6 (Am. y fam.) United States of America. || *adj.* 7 North, northern. 8 northerly (dirección).
norteamericano, -a *adj./s.m.* y *f.* North American, American (de los Estados Unidos).
norteño, -a *adj.* 1 northern. || *s.m.* y *f.* 2 northerner.
nos *pron.pers.* 1 us: *dinos lo que viste = tell us what you saw.* 2 (to) us: *danos el libro = give us the book; give the book to us.* 3 ourselves: *podemos lavarnos = we can wash ourselves.* 4 each other; one another: *no nos hablamos = we don't speak to each other.* 5 we (en el plural mayestático).
nosotros, -as *pron.pers.* 1 [como *suj.*] we. 2 [como *o.*] us: *ven con nosotros = come with us.* 3 [como *r.*] ourselves: *estamos hablando de nosotros = we are speaking of ourselves.*
nostalgia *s.f.* nostalgia; homesickness.
nostálgico, -a *adj.* nostalgic.

nota *s.f.* 1 note, annotation. 2 mark, grade (calificación académica). 3 fame, renown. 4 COM. account. 5 remark (observación). 6 (fig.) touch, note: *una nota de elegancia = a touch of elegance.* 7 column (de sociedad). 8 MUS. note. || 9 **dar la —,** (fig.) to make oneself conspicous. 10 **— a pie de página,** LIT. foot note. 11 **tomar — de,** to take note of.
notable *adj.* notable, noteworthy: *un éxito notable = a notable success.* 2 noticeable (sensible): *una diferencia notable = a noticeable difference.* 3 remarkable (excelente). 4 outstanding (destacado). || *s.m.* 5 merit; good mark (en un examen). 6 worthy, notable (persona principal).
notablemente *adv.* 1 notably. 2 remarkably. 3 outstandingly.
notación *s.f.* 1 MAT. notation. 2 note.
notar *v.t.* 1 to notice, to note, to observe. 2 to mark, to indicate. 3 to write down, to note down (apuntar). 4 (fig.) to criticize. || *v.pron.* 5 to write down, to note down (apuntar). 4 (fig.) to criticize. || *v.pron.* 5 to feel, to perceive. 6 to show: *la mancha no se nota = the stain does not show.* || 7 **hacerse —,** to stand out, to catch the eye.
notaría *s.f.* 1 notary's office. 2 profession of notary, notarial profession.
notariado, -a *adj.* notarized (certificado por notario).
notarial *adj.* notarial.
notario *s.m.* 1 notary, notary public; commissioner for oaths.
noticia *s.f.* 1 news: *buena noticia = good news.* 2 piece of news, news item; report. 3 information. || 4 **dar una — a alguien,** to break the news to somebody. 5 **las malas noticias llegan las primeras,** no news is good news. 6 **no tener —,** to have no idea. 7 **noticias, a)** RAD. y TV. news; **b)** tidings; **c)** advice (notificación). 8 **noticias de última hora,** late news. 9 **tener — de algo,** to be informed of. 10 **tener — de alguien,** to hear from somebody. 11 **últimas noticias,** latest news.
noticiario *s.m.* 1 RAD. y TV. news sheet, news bulletin, newscast. 2 newsreel (cine).
noticiero, -a *s.m.* y *f.* 1 reporter (periodista). 2 newspaper. || *adj.* 3 news-giving. 4 news.
notición *s.m.* (fam.) big news.
notificación *s.f.* 1 notification. 2 notice; official notice.
notificar *v.t.* 1 to notify, to inform. 2 to announce, to intimate. 3 COM. to advise.
notoriamente *adv.* obviously, evidently, plainly; glaringly.
notoriedad *s.f.* 1 notoriety, fame, renown. 2 (fig.) notoriety, ill repute. || 3 **de —,** well-known.
notorio, -a *adj.* 1 well known, notorious. 2 obvious, evident. 3 glaring, manifest.
novatada *s.f.* 1 hazing (broma a un novato). 2 beginner's blunder, beginner's mistake. || 3 **dar una — a,** to haze. 4 **pagar la —,** to make a beginner's blunder.
novato, -a *s.m.* y *f.* 1 novice, beginner, tyro. 2 freshman, fresher (un estudiante). || *adj.* 3 new.
novecientos, -as *adj.num.pl.* nine hundred.
novedad *s.f.* 1 novelty, newness. 2 change, new feature. 3 latest news; latest fashion; latest event. || **novedades,** latest fashions (moda). 5 **sin —, a)** as usual; well; **b)** all quiet, without incident.
novedoso, -a *adj.* novel, new.
novel *adj.* 1 new, inexperienced; green. || *s.m.* 2 beginner.
novela *s.f.* 1 LIT. novel. 2 fiction (género novelístico). 3 (fig.) lie, story (cuento, mentira). || 4 **— por entregas,** serial. 5 **— romántica,** romance. 6 **— rosa,** novelette, sentimental novel.
novelar *v.t.* 1 to novelize. 2 to make a novel out of. || *v.i.* 3 to write novels. 4 (fig.) to tell lies.
novelesco, -a *adj.* 1 LIT. novelistic, fictional. 2 (fig.) fantastic. 3 romantic, sentimental.
novelista *s.m.* y *f.* LIT. novelist.
novelístico, -a *adj.* 1 novelistic. || *s.f.* 2 LIT. fiction, novel.
novelón *s.m.* (fam.) three-decker novel.
noveno, -a *adj.num.* ninth.
noventa *adj.num.* ninety.
noviazgo *s.m.* 1 engagement, courtship. 2 bethrothal (esponsales).
noviciado *s.m.* 1 REL. novitiate. 2 (fig.) apprernticeship (aprendizaje).
novicio, -a *s.m.* y *f.* 1 REL. novice. 2 (fig.) apprentice, beginner. || *adj.* 3 (fig.) inexperienced, new.
noviembre *s.m.* November.
noviero *adj.* (Am.) always falling in love (enamoradizo).
novilunio *s.m.* new moon.
novillada *s.f.* 1 bullfight using young bulls. 2 herd of young bulls.
novillero *s.m.* 1 novice bullfighter. herdsman (que cuida novillos). 3 stable for young bulls. 4 (fam.) truant.
novillo, -a *s.m.* y *f.* 1 ZOOL. young bull. || 2 **hacer novillos,** to play truant.
novio, -a *s.m.* 1 boyfriend (sin compromiso). 2 fiancé (formal). 3 bridegroom, groom (el día de la boda) || *s.f.* 4 girl friend (sin compromiso). 5 fiancée (formal). 6 bride (el día de la boda). || 7 **los novios,** the newly weds; bride and bridegroom. 8 **ser novios formales,** to be engaged. 9 **traje de —,** wedding dress. 10 **viaje de novios,** honeymoon.
novísimo, -a *adj.super.* 1 newest; latest. 2 REL. each of the end of one's life (muerte, juicio, infierno y gloria).
nubarrón *s.m.* large storm cloud.
nube *s.f.* 1 cloud. 2 OPT. film, spot (mancha en la córnea). 3 (fig.) crowd, swarm (de personas). 4 (fig.) cloud (de polvo, humo, etc.). || 5 **estar en las nubes,** (fig.) to be daydreaming, to be up in the clouds. 6 **estar por las nubes,** (fig.) to be sky-high (precios). 7 **— de verano,**

(fig.) passing annoyance, passing cloud. **8 poner por las nubes,** (fig.) to praise to the skies.
núbil *adj.* marriageable, nubile.
nublado, -a *adj.* 1 cloudy, overcast. || *s.m.* 2 storm cloud. 3 (fig.) imminent danger, threat.
nublar *v.t.* 1 to cloud. 2 to darken, to obscure. 3 (fig.) to disturb (turbar). 4 (fig.) to mar, to destroy (estropear). || *v.pron.* 5 to grow cloudy, to cloud over. 6 (fig.) to cloud over (la vista, etc.).
nublo, -a *adj.* (Am.) cloudy.
nubloso, -a *adj.* 1 cloudy, overcast. 2 (fig.) gloomy.
nubosidad *s.f.* cloudiness.
nuboso, -a *adj.* cloudy.
nuca *s.f.* ANAT. nape.
nuclear *adj.* nuclear: *central nuclear = nuclear station.*
nucleico, -a *adj.* nucleic: *ácido nucleico = nucleic acid.*
núcleo *s.m.* 1 nucleus. 2 (fig.) kernel, nucleus. 3 TEC. core. 4 (fig.) central point. 5 BOT. stone (de las frutas).
nudillo *s.m.* 1 ANAT. knuckle. 2 TEC. plug (taco de madera).
nudismo *s.m.* nudism.
nudo *s.m.* 1 knot. 2 LIT. crisis, turning point. 3 function (de ferrocarriles). 4 MAR. knot (unidad de velocidad). 5 BOT. node, joint. 6 centre (de comunicaciones). 7 (fig.) link, bond, tie (vínculo). 8 (fig.) hitch (dificultad, pega). 9 tangle, knot (en el pelo). 10 BOT. gnarl (en la madera). 11 (fig.) lump: *tengo un nudo en la garganta = I have a lump in my throat.* || **12 — ciego,** hard knot. **13 — corredizo,** noose, slipknot.
nudoso, -a *adj.* 1 knotted, knotty. 2 gnarled.
nuera *s.f.* daughter-in-law.
nuestro, -a *adj.pos.* 1 our: *nuestro amigo = our friend.* 2 of ours: *un amigo nuestro = a friend of ours.* || *pron.pers.* 3 ours: *este coche es nuestro = this car is ours.* || **4 los nuestros,** ours, our people, our friends, our family, etc.
nueve *adj.num.* 1 nine. 2 ninth (en fechas). || **3 las —,** nine o'clock.
nuevamente *adv.* again, anew.
nuevo, -a *adj.* 1 new: *un coche nuevo = a new car.* 2 fresh: *empezar una vida nueva = to start a fresh life.* 3 newly arrived. 4 unused (sin emplear, sin usar). || **5 año —,** New Year. **6 de —,** again, anew. **7 ¿qué hay de —?,** what's new?
nuez *s.f.* 1 BOT. walnut (fruto del nogal). 2 nut (fruto seco). 3 MUS. nut (de violín). 4 ANAT. Adam's apple (de la garganta). || **5 — moscada,** GAST. nutmeg.
nulamente *adv.* in vain.
nulidad *s.f.* 1 DER. nullity. 2 incompetence. 3 nonentity. || **4 ser una —,** (fam.) to be a dead loss.
nulo, -a *adj.* 1 DER. null, void (inválido). 2 useless (persona). 3 misère (en juegos de naipes). 4 DEP. tied, drawn. || **5 — y sin valor,** DER. null and void.
numen *s.m.* 1 REL. numen, divinity. 2 artistic inspiration.
numerable *adj.* numerable.
numeración *s.f.* 1 numeration. 2 numbering (de páginas, etc.). 3 numerals: *numeración romana = Roman numerals.* 4 numbers.
numerador, -a *s.m.* 1 MAT. numerador. || *s.m.* y *f.* 2 TEC. numbering machine.
numeral *adj.* numeral.
numerar *v.t.* 1 to number. 2 to count; to calculate; to enumerate.
numerario, -a *adj./s.m.* y *f.* cash, hard cash (dinero efectivo).
numérico, -a *adj.* numerical.
número *s.m.* 1 number. 2 numeral, figure. 3 number, edition, issue (de una publicación). 4 ART. act, number, sketch; item. 5 size (de zapatos, etc.). 6 GRAM. number. 7 quantity. || **8 en números redondos,** in round figures/numbers. **9 — atrasado,** back number (de una publicación). **10 — extraordinario,** special edition. **11 — uno,** (fig.) the best, the number one. **12 sin —,** (fig.) numberless.
numerosamente *adv.* numerously.
numeroso, -a *adj.* 1 numerous. || **2 familia —,** large family.
numismático, -a *adj.* 1 numismatic. || *s.m.* y *f.* 2 numismatist. || *s.f.* 3 numismatics (ciencia).
nunca *adv.* 1 never: *no vinieron nunca = they never came.* 2 ever: *mejor que nunca = better than ever.* || **3 casi —,** hardly ever. **hasta —,** farewell for ever. **5 más que —,** more than ever. **6 — jamás,** never, never again. **7 — más,** nevermore.
nunciatura *s.f.* REL. nunciature.
nuncio *s.m.* 1 REL. nuncio, Papal envoy. 2 messenger. 3 (fig.) herald, harbinger.
nupcial *adj.* nuptial, wedding: *marcha nupcial = wedding march.*
nupcias *s.f. pl.* 1 nuptials, marriage, wedding. || **2 casarse en segundas —,** to remarry.
nutria *s.f.* ZOOL. otter.
nutrición *s.f.* nutrition.
nutrido, -a *adj.* 1 fed, nourished: *bien nutrido = well-nourished.* 2 (fig.) full, abundant. 3 (fig.) large: *una nutrida concurrencia = a large attendance.*
nutrimento *s.m.* 1 nourishment, food. 2 nutrition.
nutrir *v.t.* 1 to feed, to nourish. 2 (fig.) to fill, to increase. 3 (fig.) to encourage, to support.
nutritivo, -a *adj.* 1 nutritious, nourishing. 2 nutritional: *valor nutritivo = nutritional value.*
nylon V. **nilón.**

ñ, Ñ *s.f.* ñ, Ñ, decimoséptima letra del alfabeto español (no existe en el alfabeto inglés).
ñame *s.m.* BOT. yam, sweet potato.
ñandú *s.m.* ZOOL. nandu, rhea, American ostrich.
ñandutí *s.m.* (Am.) nanduti (labor).
ñapa V. **llapa.**
ñapango,-a *adj.* (Am.) mulatto; halfbreed.
ñato,-a *adj.* (Am.) **1** snub-nosed, flatnosed. **2** (fig.) ugly; deformed. **3** insignificant.
ñeque *adj.* (Am.) **1** strong, vigourous. **2** clever. || *s.m.* **3** strength; vigour. **4** courage.
ñoñería *s.f.* **1** insipidness, insipidity. **2** silly remark. **3** (Am.) dotage, senility (chochez).
ñoñez V. **ñoñería.**
ñoño,-a *adj.* **1** insipid; spineless; whining. **2** silly, feebleminded. **3** (Am.) old, decrepit, senile. **4** old-fashioned. || *s.m.* y *f.* **5** (fam.) drip.
ñu *s.m.* ZOOL. gnu.
ñudo V. **nudo.**
ñudoso,-a V. **nudoso, -a.**
ñufla *s.f.* (Am.) piece of junk.

...

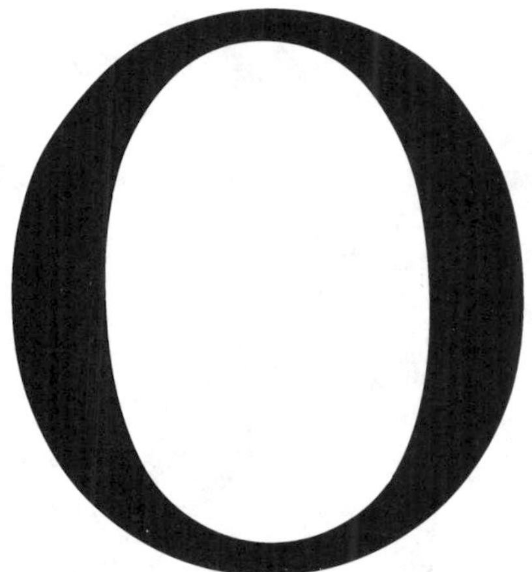

o, O *s.f.* 1 o, O (decimaoctava letra del alfabeto español) || *conj.* 2 or; — ... —, either... or.
oasis *s.m.* oasis.
obcecación *s.f.* stubbornness; blindness (mental).
obcecado, -a *p.p.* 1 de **obcecar.** || *adj.* 2 stubborn; blind (mentalmente).
obcecadamente *adv.* stubbornly; blindly.
obcecar *v.t.* 1 (fig.) to blind. 2 to disturb the mind (por la pasión, especialmente). || *v.r.* 3 to persist obstinately.
obedecer *v.t.* 1 to obey. || 2 — **a,** MED. to respond to: *su enfermedad no obedece al tratamiento = his illness is not responding to treatment.* 3 — **a,** to be due to: *estos fallos obedecen a tu falta de interés = these failures are due to your lack of interest.*
obediencia *s.f.* 1 obedience, docility. || 2 — **ciega,** blind obedience.
obediente *adj.* obedient, docile.
obedientemente *adv.* obediently.
obelisco *s.m.* 1 ARQ. obelisk. 2 BOT. type of Mexican plant.
obertura *s.f.* MUS. overture.
obesidad *s.f.* obesity.
obeso, -a *adj.* obese.
óbice *s.m.* obstacle, impediment.
obispado *s.m.* REL. bishopric.
obispo *s.m.* REL. 1 bishop. || 2 — **auxiliar,** assistant bishop. 3 — **sufragáneo,** suffragan bishop.
óbito *s.m.* (lit.) decease, demise, (euf.) loss.
objeción *s.f.* 1 objection. || 2 — **de conciencia,** conscientious objection. 3 — **denegada,** DER. objection overruled.
objetable *adj.* objectionable.
objetar *v.t.* 1 to object (to), to protest (against). 2 to contradict, to oppose.
objetivamente *adv.* objectively.
objetividad *s.f.* objectivity.
objetivo, -a *adj.* 1 objective. 2 unbiassed, impartial. || *s.m.* 3 objective, aim, goal (finalidad en la vida, trabajo, etc.). 4 FOT. lens.
objeto *s.m.* 1 object. 2 topic, subject matter (del que hablar). 3 object, aim, end (finalidad, objetivo). 4 FIL. object. 5 GRAM. object.
objetor, -ora *s.m.* y *f.* 1 objector. || 2 — **de conciencia,** conscientious objector.
oblación *s.f.* oblation, offering.
oblato *s.m.* REL. oblate (miembro de algunos institutos religiosos).
oblea *s.f.* 1 REL. wafer. 2 (Am.) stamp. 3 (vulg.) smack, blow.
oblicuamente *adv.* obliquely.
oblicuidad *s.f.* 1 obliquity. 2 GEOM. oblique angle.
oblicuo, -a *adj.* 1 GEOM. oblique. 2 slanting (tejado o alguna otra superficie).
obligación *s.f.* 1 obligation, duty. 2 FIN. bond.
obligacionista *s.m.* FIN. bondholder.
obligado, -a *adj.* 1 obligatory, compulsory. 2 (form.) obliged: *le estoy muy obligado por lo que ha hecho conmigo = I am very obliged to him for what he has done for me.*
obligar *v.t.* 1 to oblige, to compel. 2 to force, to stretch: *estos zapatos sólo se ponen obligándolos = these shoes need stretching to get them on.* || *v.r.* to bind oneself to (a hacer algo).
obligatorio, -a *adj.* 1 obligatory, compulsory. 2 DER. binding.
obligatoriedad *s.f.* obligatory nature; DER. legally binding.
obliteración *s.f.* MED. obliteration, staunching.
obliterar *v.t.* 1 MED. to obliterate, to staunch. 2 (Am.) to destroy, to obliterate.
oblongo, -a *adj.* GEOM. oblong.
obnubilación *s.f.* V. **ofuscación.**
obnubilar *v.t.* V. **ofuscar.**
oboe *s.m.* 1 MUS. oboe. 2 oboeist.
óbolo *s.m.* 1 (fig.) mite, small contribution. 2 HIST. obolus.
obra *s.f.* 1 work: *obra de arte = work of art.* 2 building site. 3 (Am.) brickworks. || *pl.* 4 LIT. works: *estas son las obras completas de Antonio Machado = these are the complete works of Antonio Machado.* 5 ARQ. repairs: *cerrado por obras = closed for repairs.* || 6 **obras benéficas,** good works.
obrada *s.f.* AGR. a day's work.
obrar *v.i.* 1 to act, to behave: *él obra con buena intención = he acts with the best of intentions.* || 2 — **en poder,** to be in someone's hands: *esos datos obran en poder del abogado = that information is in the lawyer's hands.*
obrepción *s.f.* DER. obreption.
obrerismo *s.m.* workers' movement.
obrero, -a *adj.* 1 working-class. || *s.m.* y *f.* 2 worker. 3 manual worker, working man.
obscenidad *s.f.* obscenity.
obsceno, -a *adj.* obscene (especialmente en temas sexuales).
obscurantismo *s.m.* obscurantism.
obscurecer V. **oscurecer.**
obscuro V. **oscuro.**
obsecración *s.f.* (form.) plea, entreaty.
obsecuente *adj.* (form.) obedient, humble.
obsequiar *v.t.* 1 to present with, to give (regalo o similar). 2 to regale, to lavish attentions on (prestar una atención especial a alguien por ser su aniversario, cumpleaños, etc.).
obsequio *s.m.* 1 gift. 2 (form.) kindness, courtesy, deference. || 3 **en — de,** in honour of.
obsequioso,-a *adj.* 1 helpful, attentive. 2 (Am.) fond of giving presents.
observación *s.f.* 1 observation (visual). 2 remark (de palabra). 3 MED. observation: *ella está en observación = she's under observation.*

observador, -a *adj.* 1 observant. || *s.m.* y *f.* 2 observer (del cumplimiento de un acuerdo internacional, de algún fenómeno natural, etc.).
observancia *s.f.* observance.
observar *v.t.* 1 to observe, to watch, to notice, to see. 2 to obey, observe (una ley o similar).
observatorio *s.m.* observatory.
obsesión *s.f.* PSIQ. obsession.
obsesivo, -a *adj.* obsessive (psicológicamente).
obseso, -a *adj.* obsessed (psicológicamente).
obsidiana *s.f.* QUIM. obsidian.
obsoleto, -a *adj.* obsolete.
obstaculizar *v.t.* to obstruct, to hinder, to stand in the way of, to hold up.
obstáculo *s.m.* obstacle.
obstante, no —, *loc. adv.* 1 however, nevertheless. 2 *prep.* in spite of: *no obstante su amabilidad, la reunión salió fatal = in spite of his kindness, the meeting was a flop.*
obstar *v.i.* 1 to hinder. 2 *v.imp.* to prevent: *eso no obsta para que Vd. no se marche en seguida = that should not prevent you from leaving straightaway.*
obstetra *s.m.* y *s.f.* MED. obstetrician.
obstetricia *s.f.* MED. obstetrics.
obstétrico, -a *adj.* MED. obstetric.
obstinación *s.f.* stubbornness, (form.) obstinacy.
obstinadamente *adv.* obstinately.
obstinado, -a *p.p.* 1 de **obstinarse.** || *adj.* 2 stubborn, obstinate, headstrong.
obstinarse *v.pron.* 1 to be obstinate, to insist. 2 to dig one's heels in.
obstrucción *s.f.* obstruction (física o figurativamente).
obstruccionismo *s.m.* obstructionism; POL. filibustering (la obstrucción del camino legal parlamentario por un miembro del Parlamento).
obstruccionista *adj.* 1 obstructive. || *s.m.* y *f.* 2 obstructionist.
obstruir *v.t.* 1 to obstruct (el paso o similar). 2 to hinder, to impede (la realización de algo). || *v.pron.* 3 to clog up (cañería).
obtención *s.f.* obtaining; achievement (logro de algo).
obtener *v.t.* 1 obtain. 2 to achieve.
obturador *s.m.* 1 FOT. shutter. 2 MEC. choke.
obturar *v.t.* to plug (a hole), to stop up.
obtuso *adj.* 1 blunt: *la cuchilla está obtusa = the razor is blunt.* 2 obtuse.
obús *s.m.* 1 MIL. shell. 2 MIL. howitzer.
obviar *v.t.* to obviate.
obvio, -a *adj.* obvious.
oca *s.f.* 1 ZOOL. goose. 2 (Am.) BOT. root vegetable.
ocasión *s.f.* 1 occasion. 2 opportunity, chance. 3 cause, reason. 4 COM. bargain. 5 (Am.) bargain. || 6 **de —,** second hand. 7 **precio de —,** bargain price.
ocasional *adj.* 1 chance, fortuitous. 2 occasional.
ocasionalmente *adv.* by chance, fortuitously.
ocasionar *v.t.* to cause, to bring about.
ocaso *s.m.* 1 sunset. 2 GEOG. west. 3 ASTR. setting. 4 (fig.) decline, end: *el ocaso de las ideologías políticas = the decline of political ideologies*
occidental *adj.* 1 western. || *s.m.* y *f.* 2 Westerner.
occidente *s.m.* west.
occipital *adj.* ANAT. occipital.
occipucio *s.m.* ANAT. occiput.
océano *s.m.* 1 GEOG. ocean. || 2 **— Atlántico,** Atlantic Ocean. 3 **— Pacífico,** Pacific Ocean. || 4 **— Indico,** Indian Ocean.
oceanografía *s.f.* oceanography.
ocelote *s.m.* ZOOL. ocelot.
ocio *s.m.* 1 leisure, idleness. 2 pastime, hobby.
ociosamente *adv.* 1 idly (con vaguería). 2 uselessly, pointlessly (sin ningún sentido).
ocioso, -a *adj.* 1 at leisure, idle. 2 pointless, useless: *no hagas observaciones ociosas = don't make pointless comments.*
oclusión *s.f.* FON. occlusion.
oclusivo *adj.* FON. plosive.
ocote *s.m.* (Am.) BOT. ocote pine.
ocre *s.m.* 1 ochre. || *adj.* 2 ochre (color).
octaedro *s.m.* GEOM. octahedron.
octágono *s.m.* GEOM. 1 octagon. || *adj.* 2 octagonal.
octano *s.m.* octane.
octava *s.f.* MUS. octave.
octavilla *s.f.* 1 political pamphlet. 2 small piece of paper.
octavo, -a *adj. num.* 1 eighth. || *s.m.* 2 eighth. 3 **octavos de final,** DEP. quarterfinals. 4 **libro en —,** octavo.
octogenario, -a *adj.* octogenarian. || *s.m.* y *s.f.* octagenarian.
octógono V. **octágono.**
octosílabo, -a *adj.* 1 octosyllabic. || *s.m.* 2 octosyllable.
octubre *s.m.* October.
ocular *adj.* 1 ocular; eye: *testigo ocular = eyewitness.* || *s.m.* 2 eyepiece (objeto).
oculista *s.m.* y *f.* oculist.
ocultación *s.f.* concealment (de algo).
ocultador, -a *adj.* 1 hiding (que oculta). || *s.m.* y *f.* 2 hider, concealer.
ocultar *v.t.* y *pron.* 1 to hide, to conceal; to hide (oneself). || *v.t.* 2 to mask, to screen (encubrir, normalmente una acción negativa). || 3 **ocultarse a uno la razón (de),** to be a mystery to one.
ocultismo *s.m.* occultism.
oculto, -a *adj.* 1 hidden, concealed. 2 secret, mysterious.
ocupación *s.f.* 1 occupation, job. 2 DER. squatting. || 3 **— militar,** MIL. military occupation.
ocupado, -a *adj.* occupied.
ocupante *s.m.* y *f.* occupant.
ocupar *v.t.* 1 to occupy, to fill. 2 to keep (someone) busy. 3 to use (una cosa o similar). || 4 **ocuparse, ocuparse con /ocuparse de,** to deal with, to take care of: *vete, yo me ocuparé de él = go, I'll deal with him.* 5 **¡ocúpate de lo tuyo!,** mind your own business!
ocurrencia *s.f.* 1 occurrence, incident. 2 bright idea.
ocurrente *adj.* witty, bright, amusing (cualidad personal positiva).
ocurrir *v.i.* 1 to happen, to occur. 2 to come to mind (una idea inesperada).
ochava *s.f.* eighth.
ochavo *s.m.* 1 wothless coin. || 2 **no tener un —,** to be destitute, not to have any money. 3 **no valer un —,** to be worthless, not to be worth anything.
ochenta *num.card.* 1 eighty. || *num.ord.* 2 eightieth. || *s.m.* 3 eighty.
ocho *num.card.* 1 eight. || *num.ord.* 2 eighth: *el ocho de enero.* || *s.m.* 3 eight.
ochocientos, -as *num.card.* 1 eight hundred. 2 *num.ord.* eight hundredth. || *s.m.* 3 eight hundred.
oda *s.f.* LIT. ode.
odalisca *s.f.* (form.) odalisque, concubine.
odiar *v.t.* 1 to hate. 2 (Am.) to annoy, to irk, to bother.
odio *s.m.* 1 hate, hatred. 2 (Am.) annoyance, boredom.
odiosamente *adv.* 1 hatefully. 2 irritatingly.
odioso, -a *adj.* 1 hateful. 2 (Am.) irksome, irritating.
odisea *s.f.* odyssey (viaje o acontecimiento).
odontología *s.f.* MED. dentistry, dental surgery.
odontólogo, -a *s.m.* y *f.* MED. dentist, dental surgeon.
odorífero, -a *adj.* sweet-smelling, aromatic.
odre *s.m.* 1 (lit.) wineskin. 2 sot, toper (persona borracha).
oeste *s.m.* 1 west. 2 west wind. || *adj.* 3 westerly, western.
ofender *v.t.* 1 to offend. 2 to insult. || *v.pron.* y *tr.* 3 to take offence: *me ofendieron tus palabras = I took offence [illegible] your words.*
ofendido, -a *p.p.* 1 de **ofender.** || *adj.* 2 insulted, hurt. || 3 **darse por —,** to take offense, to take exception.
ofensa *s.f.* offence, slight.
ofensivo, -a *adj.* 1 offensive. || *s.f.* 2 MIL. offensive. 3 disgusting (color, por ejemplo).
ofensor, -a *s.m.* y *f.* offender.
oferente *s.m.* (form.) REL. priest, celebrant (especialmente cuando dice misa).
oferta *s.f.* 1 offer. 2 sale price, special offer. 3 ECON. supply: *la oferta y la demanda = supply and demand.* || 4 **estar en —,** to be on offer.
ofertorio *s.m.* REL. offertory.
offset *s.m.* offset (sistema de impresión).
oficial *adj.* 1 official. || *s.m.* 2 official, officer. 3 MIL. officer (up to the rank of captain). 4 craftsman (en una rama de la artesanía o manualidad).
oficiala *s.f.* clerk, skilled woman worker.
oficialía *s.f.* 1 clerical worker status. 2 craft training (artesanía).

oficialidad *s.f.* MIL. officer corps, officers.
oficialismo *s.m.* (Am.) POL. the party of government.
oficialmente *adv.* officially.
oficiante *s.m.* REL. officiant, celebrant.
oficiar *v.i.* **1** REL. to officiate. || *v.t.* **2** to inform officially.
oficina *s.f.* **1** office. **2** laboratory (de una farmacia). **3** (Am.) nitrate works. || **4 — de colocación,** employment agency. **5 — de información,** information bureau. **6 — de objetos perdidos,** lost property.
oficinesco, -a *adj.* office, (desp.) bureaucratic.
oficio *s.m.* **1** profession, occupation, trade. **2** official letter. **3** MEC. function. **4** REL. service. || **5 de —,** officially. **6 Santo Oficio,** HIST. Holy Office, Inquisition. **7 tener —,** to be skilled, to be an expert.
oficiosamente *adv.* **1** unofficially (de una noticia o acto no oficial). **2** obligingly, kindly (de una manera exagerada). **3** diligently.
oficioso, -a *adj.* **1** unofficial. **2** diligent. **3** kind, obliging (exageradamente).
ofrecer *v.t.* **1** to offer. **2** REL. to offer up. || *v.pron.* **3** to volunteer. **4** to occur to: *si algo se os ofrece, se lo decís a los organizadores = if something occurs to you, tell the organizers.* **5** (form.) to happen.
ofrecimiento *s.m.* offering, offer (de cualquier tipo).
ofrenda *s.f.* offering (normalmente de carácter religioso).
oftalmia *s.f.* MED. ophthalmia.
oftalmología *s.f.* MED. ophthalmology.
oftalmológico, -a *adj.* MED. ophthalmological.
oftalmólogo, -a *s.m.* y *s.f.* MED. ophthalmologist.
ofuscación o **ofuscamiento** *s.f.* dazzled state, blindness (pasional); confusion mental).
ofuscar *v.t.* **1** to dazzle. **2** to darken. **3** to bewilder, to confuse. **4** (fig.) to blind: *se ofuscó de cólera = he got blinded by anger.*
ogro *s.m.* **1** ogre (personaje de los cuentos). **2** (fam.) ugly fellow.
oh *interj.* oh! (expresando pena, sorpresa y muchos otros sentimientos).
ohmio *s.m.* FIS. ohm.
oída *s.f.* **1** hearing. || **2 de oídas,** hearsay.
oído *s.m.* **1** (sense of) hearing. **2** ANAT. ear. **3** MUS. ear. || **4 abrir los oídos,** to listen carefully. **5 aplicar el —,** to listen very carefully, to pay a lot of attention. **6 cerrar los oídos,** to turn a deaf ear. **7 dar oídos,** to listen favourably, to listen willingly. **8 de —,** by ear. **9 entrar por un — y salir por el otro,** to go in one ear and out the other. **10 llegar a oídos,** to come to one's ears. **11 regalar el —,** to flatter, to praise no end. **12 taparse los oídos,** to stop up one's ears. **13 tener buen —,** to have a good ear (especialmente para la música).
oír *v.t.* e *i.* **1** to hear, to listen (to). || **2 lo oyó como quien oye llover,** he took no notice.
ojal *s.m.* buttonhole.
ojalá *interj.* if only...; would that..., I wish...: *ojalá no hiciera tanto calor = I wish it wasn't so hot.*
ojeada *s.m.* **1** glance, look. || **2 echar una — (a),** to have a look (at).
ojear *v.t.* **1** to eye, to stare at. **2** to cast the evil eye on. **3** to beat (asustar la caza).
ojén *s.m.* anisette.
ojeo *s.m.* beating for game (en la caza).
ojera *s.f.* **1** MED. eyebath. || *pl.* **2** rings under the eyes, (fam.) bags under the eyes.
ojeroso, -a *adj.* haggard, with bags under the eyes.
ojeriza *s.f.* **1** spite, grudge. || **2 tener — a,** to have a grudge against.
ojete *s.m.* **1** eyelet. **2** anus. **3** (Am. y vulg.) arsehole.
ojiva *s.f.* ARQ. ogive.
ojival *adj.* ARQ. ogival.
ojo *s.m.* **1** eye. **2** ARQ. bull's eye window. **3** (fig. y fam.) care, attention. **4** ARQ. arch of a bridge. || **5 a —,** approximately. **6 a — de buen cubero,** at a rough guess. **7 a ojos cerrados,** blindly. **8 a ojos vistas,** openly, before one's eyes. **9 con los ojos cerrados,** easily. **10 clavar los ojos (en),** to stare (at). **11 costarle a uno un — de la cara,** (fam.) to cost (someone) an arm and a leg. **12 en un abrir y cerrar de ojos,** in the twinkling of an eye. **13 mirar con buenos ojos,** to look favourably upon. **14 mirar con malos ojos,** to look unfavourably upon. **15 ¡mucho —!,** watch it! **16 no pegar —,** not to get a wink of sleep. **17 poner los ojos,** to choose. **18 tener entre ojos,** to detest.
ojota *s.f.* (Am.) **1** sandal. **2** tanned llama leather.
okapi *s.m.* ZOOL. okapi.
ola *s.f.* **1** wave. **2** (fig.) wave, spell: *ola de calor = heat wave; ola de frío = cold spell.* **3** trend, fashion, style (de vestido, música, modos de comportamiento, etc.).
olé *interj.* hooray!; bravo!
oleada *s.f.* **1** large wave. **2** (fig.) surge, wave: *una oleada de gente = a great surge of people.*
oleaginoso, -a *adj.* oily, oleaginous.
oleaje *s.m.* swell, surf.
oleícola *adj.* oil; olive-oil.
óleo *s.m.* **1** REL. oil. **2** ART. oil, oil painting. **3** (Am.) (fig.) baptism.
oleoducto *s.m.* pipeline.
oleoso, -a *adj.* oily.
oler *v.t.* e *i.* **1** to smell. || *v.t.* **2** to sniff out, to uncover (algo negativo o secreto).
olfatear *v.t.* **1** to sniff. **2** (fig.) to pry.
olfato *s.m.* **1** sense of smell. **2** (fam.) nose, instinct (for something): *José tiene olfato para los negocios = José has a nose for business.*
oligarca *s.m.* oligarch.
oligarquía *s.f.* POL. oligarchy.
oligárquico, -a *adj.* oligarchic.
oligofrenia *s.f.* PSIQ. mental deficiency.
olimpiada *s.f.* **1** DEP. olimpiada (de alguna actividad). **2** Olympiad.
olímpicamente *adv.* arrogantly, without paying any attention to anybody.
olímpico, -a *adj.* **1** Olympic. **2** Olympian.
oliscar *v.t.* **1** to sniff carefully. **2** (fig.) to look into.
olisquear V. **oliscar.**
oliva *s.f.* **1** BOT. olive tree. **2** olive. **3** olive wood. || *adj.* **4** olive.
olivar *s.m.* **1** olive grove. || *v.t.* **2** to prune (ramas inferiores).
olivarda *s.f.* **1** ZOOL. green goshawk. **2** BOT. elecampane.
olivicultura *s.f.* AGR. olive cultivation.
olivo *s.m.* **1** BOT. olive tree. **2** olive wood.
olmeda *s.f.* elm grove.
olmedo V. **olmeda.**
olmo *s.m.* BOT. elm.
ológrafo *s.m.* **1** DER. holograph. **2** autograph. || *adj.* **3** DER. holographic.
olor *s.m.* smell.
oloroso, -a *adj.* sweet-smelling, fragrant.
olvidadizo, -a *adj.* **1** forgetful. **2** ungrateful.
olvidar *v.t.* to forget.
olvido *s.m.* **1** oblivion. **2** carelessness, oversight. || **3 caer en el —,** to fall into oblivion. **4 echar en —,** to forget completely. **5 enterrar en el —,** to cast into oblivion. **6 rescatar del —,** to save from oblivion.
olla *s.f.* **1** stewpot. **2** stew. || **3 — común,** (Am.) canteen. **4 — de presión,** pressure cooker. **5 — podrida,** Spanish stew, pot pourri, hotchpotch.
ombligo *s.m.* **1** ANAT. umbilical cord. **2** ANAT. umbilicus, navel. **3** (fig.) centre (del mundo, de la atención). || **4 encogérsele a uno el —,** (fam.) to get cold feet.
omega *s.f.* omega.
ominosamente *adv.* (form.) ominously; fightfully.
ominoso, -a *adj.* awful, frightful; (form.) ominous.
omisión *s.f.* **1** omission. **2** neglect (más o menos culpable).
omiso, hacer caso — (de), *loc. adv.* to ignore.
omitir *v.t.* **1** to omit. **2** to forget (hacer algo).
ómnibus *s.m.* (Am.) (municipal) bus.
omnibús *s.m.* (Am.) bus.
omnipotencia *s.f.* omnipotence (normalmente atribuida a Dios).
omnipotente *adj.* omnipotent.
omnipotentemente *adv.* omnipotently.
omnisciencia *s.f.* omniscience.
omnisciente *adj.* omniscient, all-knowing (suele atribuirse a Dios).
omóplato *s.m.* shoulder blade.
onagro *s.m.* ZOOL. wild ass, onager.
onanismo *s.m.* masturbation, onanism.
once *num.card.* **1** eleven. || *num.ord.* **2** eleventh: *el once de noviembre.* || **3 a)**

las —, eleven o'clock; **b)** (fam.) elevenses; **c)** (Am.) tea, afternoon snack.

onceavo, -a *adj.* eleventh.

onceno, -a *adj.* eleventh.

oncología *s.f.* MED. oncology.

onda *s.f.* **1** wave. || **2 estar en la —,** to be on the ball; to be in. **3 — corta,** short wave. **4 — expansiva,** shock wave, blast. **5 — larga,** long wave. **6 — luminosa,** light wave. **7 — sonora,** sound wave.

ondeante *adj.* waving, swaying.

ondear *v.i.* **1** to be wavy, to undulate. **2** to wave, to flutter: *ondea la bandera = the flag is fluttering.* || *v.t.* **3** to wave. **4** to scallop: *ella ondeó el borde del mantel = she scalloped the edge of the tablecloth.* || **5 — a media asta,** to fly at half mast.

ondulación *s.f.* **1** ripple (de las olas). **2** wave (en el pelo). **3** wavy motion, winding (movimiento físico de los objetos).

ondulado, -a *p.p.* **1** de **ondular.** || *adj.* **2** wavy (pelo). **3** rolling (terreno). **4** corrugated (superficie).

ondular *v.i.* **1** to undulate, to sway. **2** to be wavy (el pelo).

ondulatorio, -a *adj.* undulatory, wavy.

oneroso, -a *adj.* **1** onerous, burdensome. **2** costly (de dinero).

ónice *s.m.* onyx.

ónique V. **ónice.**

ónix V. **ónice.**

onírico, -a *adj.* dreamlike, (form.) oneiric.

onomástico, -a *adj.* **1** onomastic, name. **2** relative to one's saint's day: *hoy es la fiesta onomástica de mi hermano = today is my brother's saint's day.* || *s.m.* **3** one's saint's day. || *s.f.* **4** onomastics.

onomatopeya *s.f.* GRAM. onomatopoeia.

ontogénesis *s.f.* BIOL. ontogenesis.

ontogenia *s.f.* BIOL. ontogeny.

ontología *s.f.* FIS. ontology.

ontológico, -a *adj.* FIL. ontological.

onza *s.f.* **1** ounce (medida de peso). **2** square of chocolate. **3** HIST. Spanish coin. **4** (Am.) ZOOL. ounce, snow leopard.

oosfera *s.f.* BOT. oosphere.

opacidad *s.f.* opacity, opaqueness.

opaco, -a *adj.* **1** opaque. **2** dull, lifeless (una materia o persona).

opalino, -a *adj.* opal.

ópalo *s.m.* MIN. opal.

opción *s.f.* **1** option, choice. **2** right: *opción a ayuda familiar = right to family allowance.* **3** COM. option (a comprar, por ejemplo). **4** chance, likelihoud: *el joven atleta no tenía opción real a la victoria = the young athlete didn't have a real chance of winning.*

opcional *adj.* optional.

ópera *s.f.* MUS. opera.

operación *s.f.* **1** MED. operation. **2** FIN. transaction. **3** (Am.) mining operation. **4** COM. management. **5** operation, functioning.

operador, -ora *s.m.* y *f.* **1** operator. **2** MED. surgeon. **3** film cameraman. **4** projectionist. **5** *s.m.* MAT. operator.

operar *v.t.* **1** to operate. || *v.i.* **2** to operate.

operario, -a *s.m.* y *f.* operative.

operativo, -a *adj.* **1** operative. || *s.m.* **2** (Am.) operation.

opereta *s.f.* MUS. operetta.

opimo, -a *adj.* (form.) plentiful, rich, abundant.

opinable *adj.* debatable.

opinar *v.i.* to think, to be of the opinion.

opinión *s.f.* **1** opinion, view. || **2 — pública,** public opinion.

opio *s.m.* opium.

opíparamente *adv.* sumptuously (especialmente en comidas).

opíparo, -a *adj.* sumptuous (comida).

oponer *v.t.* **1** to oppose. || *v.r.* **2** to be opposed, to be in opposition, to be against, to object: *me opongo al uso de fertilizantes químicos = I am against the use of chemical fertilizers.*

oporto *s.m.* port wine.

oportunidad *s.f.* **1** opportunity, chance. || *pl.* **2** COM. bargains.

oportunismo *s.m.* opportunism.

oportuno, -a *adj.* **1** opportune, timely. **2** suitable, appropriate.

oportunamente *adv.* **1** opportunely. **2** suitably, appropriately.

oposición *s.f.* **1** opposition. || *pl.* **2** (public) competitive examinations.

opresión *s.f.* **1** oppression (normalmente política). **2** MED. tightness (especialmente alrededor del pecho).

opresivamente *adv.* oppresively.

opresivo, -a *adj.* oppressive (ideología, ambiente climatológico, etc.).

opresor, -ora *s.m.* y *f.* **1** oppresor, tyrant. || *adj.* **2** tyrannical, oppressive.

oprimir *v.t.* **1** to oppress (a una nación, por ejemplo). **2** to be too fight (la ropa).

oprobio *s.m.* opprobrium, ignominy.

oprobiosamente *adv.* shamefully, ignominiously.

oprobioso, -a *adj.* shameful, ignominious.

optar *v.i.* **1 — por,** to opt for, to choose. **2 — a,** to aspire to.

optativo, -a *adj.* optional: *asignatura optativa = optional subject.*

óptica *s.f.* optics.

óptico *s.m.* optician.

óptico, -a *adj.* optical.

óptimamente *adv.* optimally, perfectly.

optimismo *s.m.* optimism.

optimista *adj.* **1** optimistic. || *s.m.* y *f.* **2** optimist.

óptimo, -a *adj.* optimal, optimum, best.

opuesto, -a *adj.* **1** opposite, opposing. **2** contrary (en ideas, actitudes, etc.).

opulencia *s.f.* oppulence, affluence.

opulentamente *adv.* affluently (especialmente en medios naturales).

opulento, -a *adj.* oppulent, affluent.

opúsculo *s.m.* short work, minor work.

oquedad *s.f.* **1** hollow. **2** (fig.) void (espiritual, de valores, etc.).

oquedal *s.m.* cultivated woodland.

oración *s.f.* **1** speech, oration. **2** prayer. **3** GRAM. clause, sentence. **4** (Am.) magic charm, incantation.

oráculo *s.m.* **1** oracle. **2** (fig.) prophet, person who foresees the future (normalmente tiene cierto sentido humorístico).

orador, -ora *s.m.* y *f.* **1** orator, public speaker. **2** prayer (persona que reza). || *s.m.* **3** preacher.

oral *adj.* oral.

oralmente *adv.* orally, verbally.

orangután *s.m.* ZOOL. orang-utan.

orante *adj.* in a praying position (especialmente en cuadros).

oratoria *s.f.* oratory, art of speaking in public.

oratorio, -a *adj.* oratorical.

oratorio, -a *s.m.* **1** REL. oratory. **2** REL. Congregation of the Oratory. **3** MUS. oratorio. || *s.f.* **4** oratory, eloquence.

orar *v.i.* **1** to make a speech. **2** to pray.

orate *s.m.* y *f.* lunatic.

orbe *s.m.* **1** orb. **2** (fig.) world.

órbita *s.f.* **1** orbit. **2** ANAT. eye-socket.

orbital *adj.* orbital.

orca *s.f.* killer whale.

órdago *s.m.* **1** bid or bet in the card game mus. || **2 de —,** (fam.) fabulous, terrific.

orden *s.m.* **1** order: *pon esos libros en orden = tidy those books.* **2** order: *conviene que haya orden en la clase = it's better to have order in the class.* **3** ARQ. order: *orden corintio.* || *s.f.* **4** order, command. || **5 a la —, a sus órdenes,** MIL. yes sir! **6 consignar órdenes,** MIL. to command, to order. **7 de primer —,** first-rate, of great importance. **8 en —,** in its place, in order, tidy. **9 en — a,** in order to, in order that (con sentido de finalidad). **10 — de batalla,** MIL. in battle order. **11 órdenes mayores,** REL. major orders. **12 órdenes menores,** REL. minor orders. **13 — público,** law and order. **— religiosa,** REL. religious order.

ordenación *s.f.* **1** ordering. **2** arrangement. **3** REL. ordination. **4** command.

ordenado, -a *adj.* **1** tidy, orderly. **2** REL. ordained. || *s.m.* **3** ordained priest.

ordenador *s.m.* **1** INF. computer. || **2 — personal,** personal computer.

ordenancista *adj.* **1** strict. || *s.m.* y *f.* **2** martinet, disciplinarian.

ordenando *s.m.* REL. ordinand.

ordenanza *s.f.* **1** ordinance. **2** rules. || *s.m.* **3** MIL. batman, orderly. **4** COM. messenger.

ordenar *v.t.* **1** to put in order, to arrange. **2** to marshal: *deberíamos ordenar nuestros esfuerzos para lograr el contrato = we ought to marshal our efforts to win the contract.* **3** to command. **4** REL. to ordain. || *v.r.* **5** REL. to be ordained.

ordeñar *v.t.* to milk.

ordinal *adj.* **1** ordinal. || *s.m.* **2** ordinal.

ordinariamente *adv.* ordinarily, in the ordinary course of events.

ordinariez *s.f.* vulgarity, coarseness.

ordinario, -a *adj.* 1 ordinary, common. 2 (desp.) vulgar, coarse. || 3 **de —,** usually, frequently.

orear *v.t.* 1 to air. || *v.r.* 2 to air, to be aired.

orégano *s.m.* BOT. marjoram.

oreja *s.f.* 1 ear. || 2 **aguzar las orejas,** to prick up one's ears. 3 **bajar las orejas,** to submit. 4 **calentar las orejas,** (fam.) to tell someone off, to box someone's ears. 5 **mojar la —,** to provoke (someone). 6 **ver las orejas al lobo,** to foresee a danger.

orejera *s.f.* earflap, ear muff.

orejeta *s.f.* TEC. lug.

orejón *s.m.* 1 dried peach. 2 (Am.) goitre. 3 (Am.) herdsman, plainsman. 4 (Am.) cuckold. 5 HIST. Inca nobleman.

orejón, -ona *adj.* (Am.) 1 coarse. 2 absent-minded. 3 big-eared.

orejudo, -a *adj.* big-eared.

orfanato *s.m.* orphanage.

orfandad *s.f.* 1 orphanhood. 2 orphan's pension. 3 (fig.) neglect.

orfebre *s.m.* y *f.* goldsmith, silversmith.

orfelinato *s.m.* orphanage.

orfeón *s.m.* MUS. choral society.

organdi *s.m.* organdie.

orgánico, -a *adj.* 1 organic. 2 harmonic. || *s.f.* 3 organic chemistry. || 4 **ley —,** DER. constitutional law.

organigrama *s.m.* organization chart, management structure.

organillo *s.m.* MUS. barrel organ.

organismo *s.m.* 1 organism. 2 organization, body.

organista *s.m.* y *f.* MUS. organist.

organización *s.f.* 1 organization (de cualquier tipo). 2 order, arrangement (del tiempo, trabajo, etc.).

organizado, -a *p.p.* 1 de **organizar.** || *adj.* 2 organized, structured (una empresa, trabajo, estructura administrativa). 3 well-organized (persona).

organizador, -a *s.m.* y *f.* organizer.

organizar *v.t.* 1 to organize. || *v.pron.* 2 to organize oneself, to get organized.

órgano *s.m.* 1 ANAT. organ. 2 MUS. organ.

orgasmo *s.m.* orgasm.

orgía *s.f.* orgy.

orgiástico, -a *adj.* orgiastic.

orgullo *s.m.* pride.

orgullosamente *adv.* proudly.

orgulloso, -a *adj.* proud.

orientación *s.f.* 1 orientation, bearing. 2 direction. || 3 **— profesional,** vocational guidance.

orientador, -ora *adj.* 1 guiding. || *s.m.* y *f.* 2 orientator (de significado psicológico o parecido).

oriental *adj.* 1 eastern, oriental. 2 (Am.) Uruguayan.

orientalismo *s.m.* orientalism.

orientalista *s.m.* y *f.* orientalist.

orientar *v.t.* 1 to orientate, to position. 2 to inform. 3 to point, to guide. || *v.pron.* 4 to get one's bearings, to find one's way.

oriente *s.m.* 1 east. 2 **el Oriente,** the Orient. 3 east wind. 4 sheen (de perlas).

orificio *s.m.* orifice, vent.

origen *s.m.* 1 origin. 2 (fig.) reason, cause: *el origen del problema = the cause of the problem.* || 3 **dar — a,** to give rise to.

original *adj.* 1 original. 2 unusual, novel. || *s.m.* 3 original (no la copia).

originalidad *s.f.* 1 originality. 2 oddness.

originalmente *adv.* originally.

originar *v.t.* y *pron.* to give rise to, to cause, to start; to be started (problemas, tendencias, actitudes, etc.): *con esa forma de actuar se originan los problemas = with that behaviour problems are caused.*

originario, -a *adj.* 1 original. 2 originating.

orilla *s.f.* 1 edge. 2 bank (of river). 3 shore (of lake, sea). 4 (Am.) pavement, sidewalk. 5 cool breeze. || *pl.* 6 (Am.) the outskirts, (desp.) slums.

orillar *v.t.* to get round (problemas).

orín *s.m.* 1 rust. 2 urine.

orina *s.f.* urine.

orinal *s.m.* chamberpot.

orinar *v.i.* to urinate.

oriundo, -a *adj.* native.

orla *s.f.* 1 border, fringe. 2 graduate class photograph.

ornamento *s.m.* 1 ornament. 2 virtue, good qualities. 3 decoration.

ornar *v.t.* to adorn.

ornato *s.m.* adornment.

ornitología *s.f.* ornithology.

ornitorrinco *s.m.* ZOOL. duck-billed platypus.

oro *s.m.* 1 gold. 2 gold piece. 3 (fig.) wealth. || 4 **— batido,** gold leaf. 5 **— molido,** rolled gold. 6 **como — en paño,** something worth treasuring. 7 **de —,** first class. 8 **hacerse uno de —,** to make a fortune. 9 **oros son triunfos,** money talks. 10 **ponerle a uno de — y azul,** to give someone a dressing down.

orogénesis *s.f.* GEOL. orogenesis.

orogenia *s.f.* GEOL. orogeny.

orografía *s.f.* GEOG. orography.

orondo, -a *adj.* 1 rounded, potbellied. 2 vain, proud. 3 smug. 4 (Am.) calm, serene.

oropel *s.m.* tinsel.

oropéndola *s.f.* ZOOL. golden oriole.

orquesta *s.f.* MUS. 1 orchestra. 2 orchestra pit.

orquestación *s.f.* MUS. orchestration.

orquestar *v.t.* MUS. orchestrate.

orquídeo, -a *adj.* orchidaceous.

orquídea *s.f.* BOT. orchid, orchis.

orquitis *s.f.* MED. orchitis.

ortiga *s.f.* BOT. nettle.

orto *s.m.* 1 ASTR. rising (of a star). 2 (Am. y vulg.) arse, arsehole.

ortocentro *s.m.* (brit.) orthocentre, (EE.UU.) orthocenter.

ortodoxia *s.f.* orthodoxy.

ortodoxo, -a *adj.* orthodox.

ortografía *s.f.* spelling, orthography.

ortográfico, -a *adj.* spelling (error); orthography.

ortopedia *s.f.* (brit.) orthopaedics, (EE.UU.) orthopedics.

ortosa *s.f.* GEOL. orthoclase.

oruga *s.f.* 1 BIOL. caterpillar. 2 BOT. rocket. 3 MEC. caterpillar (vehículo).

orujo *s.m.* 1 skin of the grape. 2 grape and olive waste after pressing.

orza *s.f.* 1 earthenware jar. 2 MAR. luff, luffing.

orzuelo *s.m.* 1 MED. stye. 2 partidge snare.

os *pron. pl.* 1 [o.d.] you: *¿puedo ayudaros? = may I help you?* 2 [o.indirecto] you: *os envío dos cartas = he sent two letters.*

OBS Cuando en español se usa con carácter recíproco o reflexivo debe traducirse por "yourselves": *lavaros = wash yourselves.*

osa *s.f.* 1 ZOOL. she-bear. || 2 **— Mayor,** ASTR. Great Bear, Ursa Major. 3 **— Menor,** ASTR. Little Bear, Ursa Minor.

osadamente *adv.* daringly, boldly.

osadía *s.f.* boldness, daring.

osado, -a *p.p.* 1 de **osar.** || *adj.* 2 daring, bold (atrevido).

osamenta *s.f.* 1 skeleton. 2 bones.

osar *v.i.* to dare.

osario *s.m.* charnel house, ossuary.

óscar *s.m.* oscar.

oscilación *s.f.* 1 oscillation. 2 hesitation, wavering.

oscilante *adj.* 1 oscillating. 2 hesitating, wavering.

oscilar *v.i.* 1 oscillate, swing. 2 fluctuate. 3 hesitate, vacillate, waver.

ósculo *s.m.* kiss.

oscuramente *adv.* 1 darkly (sin luz). 2 (fig.) obscurely (difícil de entender). 3 uncertainly, dangerously.

oscurantismo *s.m.* V. **obscurantismo.**

oscuridad *s.f.* 1 darkness. 2 obscurity.

oscurecer *v.i.* 1 to grow dark. || *v.pron.* 2 to get dark, to grow dark. || *v.t.* 3 to darken, to blacken. 4 to cloud, to obscure.

oscuro, -a *adj.* 1 dark. 2 (fig.) obscure. 3 (fig.) confused. 4 uncertain, dangerous.

óseo, -a *adj.* 1 bony. 2 (form.) osseus.

osera *s.f.* bear's lair.

osezno *s.m.* bear cub.

osificación *s.f.* MED. ossification.

osificarse *v.r.* to ossify.

ósmosis *s.f.* osmosis.

oso *s.m.* 1 bear. || 2 **hacer uno el —, a)** to act the goat; **b)** to woo in public. 3 **— blanco,** polar bear. 4 **— hormiguero,** anteater. 5 **— marino,** elephant seal. 6 **— pardo,** brown bear.

osteítis *s.f.* osteitis.

ostensible *adj.* 1 obvious, evident. || 2 **hacer algo —,** (Am.) to express something.

ostensiblemente *adv.* ostensibly, clearly, patently.

ostentación *s.f.* 1 ostentation. 2 vanity. 3 display, pomp.

ostentar *v.t.* 1 to show. 2 to display, to show off. 3 to hold (office).

ostentosamente *adv.* ostentatiously, sumptuously.

ostentoso, -a *adj.* ostentatious, sumptuous.

ostra *s.f.* oyster.
ostracismo *s.m.* ostracism.
ostrogodo, -a *adj.* 1 HIST. Ostrogothic. || *s.m.* y *f.* Ostrogoth.
otear *v.t.* 1 to look down on, to espy. 2 to scrutinise.
otero *s.m.* hillock, knoll.
otitis *s.f.* MED. otitis.
otomán *s.m.* ottoman (corded fabric).
otomano, -a *adj.* 1 HIST. Ottoman. || *s.f.* 2 ottoman, couch.
otoño *s.m.* (brit.) autumn, (EE.UU.) fall.
otoñal *adj.* autumnal, autumn, (EE.UU.) fall.
otorgamiento *s.m.* granting, awarding.
otorgar *v.t.* 1 to grant, to authorize, to allow. 2 to swear (before a notary). || 3 **quien calla otorga,** silence grants consent.
otorrinolaringólogo, -a *s.m.* y *f.* ear, nose and throat specialist.
otro, -a *adj.* 1 other. 2 another. || *pron.* 3 another, another one. || 4 *pron.pl.* others. || 5 **— vez,** again.
ovación *s.f.* ovation.
ovacionar *v.t.* to cheer.
oval *adj.* oval.
ovario *s.m.* ANAT. ovary.
oveja *s.f.* 1 sheep. 2 ewe.
ovejería *s.f.* (Am.) sheep farm.
ovejuno, -a *adj.* sheep.
oviducto *s.m.* ANAT. oviducts, Fallopian tubes.
ovillo *s.m.* 1 ball (of wool, etc.). 2 tangle. || 3 **hacerse un —, a)** to curl up into a ball; **b)** to get in a tangle.
ovino, -a *adj.* 1 sheep. || *s.m.* 2 sheep.
ovio V. **obvio.**
ovíparo, -a *adj.* oviparous.
ovni *s.m.* UFO, unidentified flying object.
ovoide *adj.* ovoid, egg-shaped.
ovoideo, -a V. **ovoide.**
óvolo *s.m.* ARQ. ovolo, quarter round, thumb.
ovulación *s.f.* BIOL. ovulation.
óvulo *s.m.* BIOL. ovule.
oxidar *v.t.* 1 to rust. 2 QUIM. to oxidize. || *v.r.* 3 to rust, to go rusty.
óxido *s.m.* 1 QUIM. oxide. 2 rust. || 3 **— de carbono,** QUIM. carbon monoxide.
oxigenación *s.f.* QUIM. oxygenation.
oxigenar *v.t.* 1 oxigenate. || *v.r.* 2 to become oxygenated. 3 (fig.) to get some fresh air.
oxígeno *s.m.* oxygen.
oxítono, -a *adj.* stressed on the last syllable.
oxiuro *s.m.* MED. oxyurus, pinworm.
oyente *s.m.* y *s.f.* 1 listener, hearer. 2 unofficial student.
ozono *s.m.* QUIM. ozone.

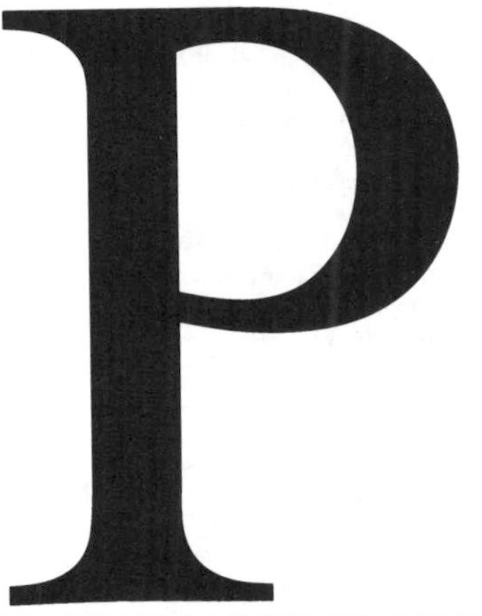

p, P *s.f.* p, P (decimonovena letra del alfabeto español).

pabellón *s.m.* **1** pavilion. **2** MIL. officers' quarters, billets. **3** national flag (bandera). **4** bell tent (tienda). **5** canopy (dosel). || **6 — de la oreja,** ANAT. outer ear.

pabilo o **pábilo** *s.m.* **1** wick. **2** snuff (de vela).

pábulo *s.m.* **1** food, sustenance. || **2 dar — (a),** (fig.) to fuel; to give encouragement (to).

paca *s.f.* **1** bale. **2** (Am.) ZOOL. spotted cavy.

pacato, -a *adj.* **1** shy, retiring (tímido). **2** easily shocked, prudish (modesto).

pacay *s.m.* (Am.) **1** pacay tree. **2** pacay fruit.

pacaya *s.f.* (Am.) **1** BOT. pacaya shrub. **2** sorrow, grief (dolor).

pacer *v.i.* **1** to graze. || *v.t.* **2** to feed (ganado). **3** to eat away.

paciencia *s.f.* **1** patience. **2** small roll; almond cake (bollo).

pacienciososo, -a *adj.* (Am.) long-suffering.

paciente *adj.* **1** patient (cualidad personal). || *s.m.* y *f.* MED. patient.

pacientemente *adv.* patiently.

pacificación *s.f.* pacification (de un país, situación o similar).

pacificador, -a *s.m.* y *f.* **1** peacemaker (fundamentalmente en el sentido internacional). || *adj.* **2** pacifying.

pacíficamente *adv.* peaceably.

pacificar *v.t.* **1** MIL. to pacify. **2** to appease (apaciguar). || *v.pron.* **3** to calm down.

pacífico, -a *adj.* peaceable, pacific.

pacifismo *s.m.* pacificism.

pacifista *s.m.* y *f.* POL. pacifist.

paco, -a *adj.* (Am.) reddish, reddish-brown (de color).

pacotilla *s.f.* **1** goods carried by seamen free of freight charges. || **2 hacer su —,** to make a nice little profit. **3 ser de —, a)** to be shoddily made; **b)** to be jerry-built (edificio).

pactar *v.t.* to agree (contrato).

pacto *s.m.* **1** pact (político, económico, sindical, etc.). **2** agreement (acuerdo).

pachá *s.m.* **1** pasha. || **2 vivir como un —,** to live like a king.

pachamanca *s.f.* (Am.) **1** barbecue. **2** rumpus, mess, muddle (desorden).

pachamanquearse *v.pron.* (Am.) to make the most of (something).

pachocha *s.f.* (Am.) sluggishness, laziness.

pachón, -ona *adj.* **1** (Am.) hairy, shaggy (peludo). **2** (Am.) woolly (lanudo). || *s.m.* **3** placid individual. **4** (Am.) cape (capote). || **5 perro —,** beagle.

pachorra *s.f.* sluggishness.

pachucho, -a *adj.* **1** overripe (fruta). **2** drooping (flojo). **3** poorly; (fig.) under the weather (enfermo).

padecer *v.t.* **1** to suffer (from). **2** to endure (aguantar). || *v.i.* **3** to suffer from, to suffer with: *padece de los ojos = he suffers with his eyes.* || **4 — un error,** to be mistaken, to be wrong.

padecimiento *s.m.* suffering.

padilla *s.f.* **1** skillet (cazuela). **2** bread oven (horno).

padrastro *s.m.* **1** stepfather. **2** (fig.) cruel father. **3** hangnail (en los dedos).

padrazo *s.m.* indulgent father, loving father.

padre *s.m.* **1** father. **2** ZOOL. sire. **3** REL. father, priest. || *pl.* **4** parents. **5** forefathers. || **6 — espiritual,** REL. confessor. **7 — Eterno,** REL. God the Father. **8 — nuestro,** REL. Lord's Prayer. **9 — Santo,** REL. Holy Father, Pope. **10 padres políticos,** in-laws. || **11 ser el — de la criatura,** to be the author, to be the creator (de un proyecto, idea, etc.).

padrear *v.i.* **1** to behave or look like one's father. **2** to breed (from the male).

padrino *s.m.* **1** REL. godfather. **2** sponsor (que patrocina). **3** best man (bodas). **4** second (duelo). **6** patron (mecenas). || *pl.* **7** godparents.

padrón *s.m.* **1** local census. **2** electoral roll. **3** TEC. pattern. **4** inscribed column. **5** (fig.) mark of ignominy.

paella *s.f.* GAST. paella.

paga *s.f.* **1** salary, pay, wages. **2** repayment (gratitud). **3** payment (expiación).

pagadero, -a *adj.* payable (un cheque, por ejemplo).

pagaduría *s.f.* cashier's office.

paganismo *s.m.* REL. paganism.

paganizar *v.t.* y *r.* to paganize.

pagano, -a *adj.* **1** heathen, pagan. || *s.m.* y *s.f.* **2** pagan. **3** (fig.) the person who ends up paying; (EE.UU.) fall guy.

pagar *v.t.* **1** to pay. **2** to pay off (crimen). **3** to repay (deuda). || *v.pron.* **4** to take a liking to something. **5** to show off, boast (fanfarronear).

pagaré *s.m.* I.O.U., promissory note.

pagel *s.m.* ZOOL. red sea bream (tipo de pez).

página *s.f.* page.

paginación *s.f.* pagination.

paginar *v.t.* to paginate.

pago *s.m.* **1** payment. **2** prize, reward (premio). || *adj.* **3** paid. || *s.m.* **4** agricultural district, field. **5** (Am.) region. || **6 en estos pagos,** in this neck of the woods, in these parts.

pagoda *s.f.* ARQ. pagoda.

paidología *s.f.* (brit.) paedology, (EE.UU.) pedology.

paila *s.f.* large frying pan.

pailebot *s.m.* MAR. pilot's boat.

paipai *s.m.* palm fan (típico de Filipinas).

país *s.m.* **1** country, nation. **2** ART. landscape. **3** fan paper, back of fan (abanico).

paisaje *s.m.* **1** countryside. **2** ART. landscape.

paisajista *adj.* 1 landscape. || *s.m.* y *f.* 2 landscape painter.
paisajístico, -a *adj.* scenic.
paisano, -a *adj.* 1 of the same country. || *s.m.* y *s.f.* 2 MIL. civilian (civil). 3 peasant (campesino). 4 (Am.) foreigner. || *s.f.* 5 name of a dance.
paja *s.f.* 1 straw. 2 blade of grass. 3 trifling matter: *por un quítame allá esas pajas = for a trifling reason.* 4 (fig.) padding, waffle. 5 (vulg.) wank (masturbación). 6 (Am.) tap, stopcock (grifo). || 7 **no dormirse en esas pajas,** to keep alert.
pajar *s.m.* 1 straw loft. 2 straw rick.
pajarear *v.i.* 1 to shoot or catch birds. 2 to loaf about (gandulear).
pájara *s.f.* 1 ZOOL. hen bird. 2 sly woman.
pajarero, -a *adj.* 1 fun-loving. 2 garish, gaudy (colores). 3 (Am.) nervous, highly-strung, spirited (nervioso). || *s.m.* 4 bird snarer, bird fancier, bird dealer. || *s.f.* 5 aviary, birdcage.
pajarita *s.f.* 1 paper bird. 2 bowtie (para vestir elegantemente). 3 BOT. toadflax, snapdragon. || 4 **cuello de –,** wing collar.
pájaro *s.m.* 1 bird. 2 (fam.) slippery customer, wily individual (hombre astuto). || 3 **más vale – en mano que ciento volando,** a bird in the hand is worth two in the bush. 4 **matar dos pájaros de un tiro,** to kill two birds with one stone. 5 **– diablo,** ZOOL. cormorant. 6 **– gordo,** (fam.) fat cat, big shot.
pajarraco *s.m.* 1 big, ugly bird. 2 (fam.) shifty character (hombre de honestidad dudosa).
paje *s.m.* 1 page, page-boy. 2 cabin-boy (de un barco).
pajizo *adj.* 1 straw (de paja). 2 straw-coloured (color).
pajolero, -a *adj.* (fam.) damned, irritating.
pajuato, -a o **pajúo, -a** *adj.* (Am.) daft, silly, stupid.
pala *s.f.* 1 spade, shovel (herramienta). 2 blade of an oar (remo). 3 flat part of the teeth. 4 skill (destreza). 5 upper (de un zapato). 8 DEP. bat.
palabra *s.f.* 1 word. 2 power of speech. 3 eloquence. 4 promise. 5 right to speak (en parlamento, etc.). || 6 **beberle a uno las palabras,** to hang on someone's every word. 7 **coger la – a uno,** to take someone at his word. 8 **comerse las palabras,** to mumble. 9 **correr la –,** to pass the word on. 10 **dirigir la – a uno,** to address someone. 11 **estar pendiente de las palabras,** to be hanging on (someone's) words. 12 **faltar a la –,** to break one's word. 13 **medir las palabras,** to choose one's words carefully. 14 **no tener uno más que palabras,** to be all talk. 15 **– de Dios,** REL. Word of God. 16 **– de rey,** word of honour. 17 **palabras mayores,** insults, abuse. 18 **quitar la – de la boca,** to take the words out of someone's mouth. 19 **tener palabras con alguien,** to have words with someone.
palabreo *s.m.* bandying words; (fam.) hot air.
palabrería o (Am.) **palabrerío** *s.f.* o *m.* idle chatter.
palabrero, -a *adj.* 1 garrulous. 2 (fam.) all talk.
palabrota *s.f.* swear word, obscenity.
palacete *s.m.* small palace.
palacial *adj.* (Am. y fig.) palatial, luxurious.
palaciego, -a *adj.* 1 palace, court. || *s.m.* courtier.
palacio *s.m.* 1 palace. 2 (fig.) mansion.
palada *s.f.* 1 spadeful, shovelful. 2 stroke (de un remo).
paladar *s.m.* ANAT. palate.
paladear *v.t.* to taste, to savour.
paladín *s.m.* 1 paladin. 2 (fig.) champion (de una causa, etc.).
paladino, -a *adj.* 1 public, open. || *s.m.* 2 paladin.
paladio *s.m.* MET. palladium.
paladión *s.m.* palladium, talisman.
palafrén *s.m.* palfrey.
palafrenero *s.m.* HIST. groom.
palamenta *s.f.* set of oars.
palanca *s.f.* 1 lever. 2 (fam.) influence, pull. || 3 **hacer –,** to act as a lever.
palangana *s.f.* 1 washbasin. || *s.m.* y *s.f.* 2 (Am.) intruder (intruso). 3 (Am.) (fam.) windbag (charlatán), braggart (jactancioso).
palanganear *v.i.* (Am.) to brag, (fam.) to show off.
palanganero *s.m.* (arc.) washstand.
palangre *s.m.* MAR. trot line, paternoster line (para pescar).
palanqueta *s.f.* 1 crowbar, jemmy (pie de cabra). 2 grappling iron. 3 (Am.) weight(s).
palanquín *s.m.* 1 porter. 2 palanquin.
palatal *adj.* ANAT. 1 palatal. 2 FON. palatal.
palatalización *s.f.* FON. palatalization.
palatinado *s.m.* 1 palatine prince. 2 palatinate.
palatino, -a *adj.* 1 ANAT. palatine. 2 palatine.
palco *s.m.* 1 box (teatro, toros). 2 row of seats. || 3 **– de platea,** (brit.) ground floor box; (EE.UU.) parquet box. 4 **– escénico,** stage.
palear *v.t.* 1 to shovel, to dig. 2 AGR. to winnow. 3 (Am.) to pole. 4 (Am.) AGR. to thresh. || *v.i.* to paddle (canoa).
palenque *s.m.* 1 fence, palisade (valla). 2 arena, enclosure (recinto). 3 (Am.) tethering post.
paleo- *prefijo* palaeo-.
paleoantropología *s.f.* palaeoanthropology.
paleofítico, -a *adj.* palaeophitic.
paleografía *s.f.* palaeography.
paleolítico, -a *adj.* HIST. 1 palaeolithic. || *s.m.* 2 Palaeolithic.
paleología *s.f.* palaeology.
paleontología *s.f.* 1 palaeontology. || 2 **– lingüística,** linguistic palaeontology.
palestino, -a *adj.* 1 Palestinian. || *s.m.* y *f.* 2 Palestinian.
palestra *s.f.* 1 palaestra. 2 (fig.) lists. 3 wrestling (lucha). || 4 **salir a la –,** (fig.) to take the floor.
paletilla *s.f.* shoulder blade.
paleto, -a *adj.* 1 (desp.) rustic. || *s.m.* y *s.f.* 2 (desp.) country bumpkin. || *s.f.* 3 ART. palette. 4 palette knife. 5 trowel (de albañil). 6 turbine blade (de turbina). 7 fan blade (de ventilador). 8 propeller (hélice). 9 ANAT. shoulder blade. 10 (Am.) lollipop (pirulí).
paletó *s.m.* paletot, heavy overcoat.
palia *s.f.* 1 altar cloth. 2 curtain in front of the tabernacle.
paliar *v.t.* 1 to conceal, (fig.) to cloak. 2 to alleviate, to mitigate (aliviar).
paliativo, -a *adj.* 1 palliative. || 2 **sin paliativos,** without excuses.
pálidamente *adv.* 1 palely. 2 wanly (indicando probable debilidad o enfermedad).
palidecer *v.i.* 1 to turn pale, to turn white (el rostro normalmente). 2 to grow dim (la fuerza de una luz).
palidez *s.f.* 1 paleness, whiteness. 2 wanness (a causa de debilidad o enfermedad).
pálido, -a *adj.* 1 pale. 2 wan: *está tan pálido desde su enfermedad = he's so wan since he got sick.*
paliducho, -a *adj.* palish, pale, sickly.
palier *s.m.* MEC. bearing.
palillo *s.m.* 1 toothpick. 2 MUS. drumstick. 3 lacemaker's bobbins. || *s.pl.* 4 castanets. 5 pins (en el billar). 6 chopsticks (chinos).
palimpsesto *s.m.* HIST. palimpsest.
palíndromo o **palíndrome** *s.m.* palindrome (figura literaria).
palingenesia *s.f.* (form.) palingenesis.
palinodia *s.f.* 1 recantation. || 2 **cantar la –,** to recant in public; to retract.
palio *s.m.* 1 HIST. pallium. 2 REL. pallium, mantle. 3 REL. baldachin. 4 prize (premio). 5 ZOOL. pallium, mantle.
palique *s.m.* chatter, chitchat, small talk.
palisandro *s.m.* BOT. rosewood.
palitroque o **palitoque** *s.m.* 1 stick (palo). || *pl.* 2 banderillas. 3 (Am.) bowling, skittles. 4 (Am.) bowling alley.
paliza *s.f.* 1 beating, thrashing. || 2 **ser un palizas,** to be a bore.
palizada *s.f.* 1 palisade. 2 embankment. 3 stockade, enclosure.
palma *s.f.* 1 BOT. palm. 2 palm leaf. 3 (fig.) palm, glory. 4 ANAT. palm. 5 sole (casco). || 6 *pl.* clapping (aplausos). || 7 **andar en palmas,** to be the toast of the town. 8 **llevarse la –,** to triumph.
palmada *s.f.* 1 slap (bofetada). 2 clap (palmas). || *pl.* 3 clapping.
palmado, -a *adj.* 1 BOT. palmate (hoja). 2 ZOOL. webbed (dedo de animal).
palmar *s.m.* 1 palm grove. 2 fuller's thistle (para cardar). || *adj.* 3 BOT. palm. 4 self-evident (obvio). || *v.i.* 5 (fam.) to snuff it, to kick the bucket.
palmarés *s.m.* 1 record (historial). 2 honours list.
palmario, -a *adj.* V. **palmar 4.**
palmatoria *s.f.* candleholder.

palmeado, -a *adj.* 1 palm-shaped. 2 BOT. palmate. 3 ZOOL. webbed.
pálmer *s.m.* micrometer.
palmero, -a *adj.* 1 of La Palma. || *s.m.* y *s.f.* 2 native of La Palma. || *s.f.* 3 BOT. palm, palm tree. || *s.m.* 4 person who looks after palm trees.
palmito *s.m.* 1 BOT. dwarf palm. 2 (fam.) a woman's face.
palmo *s.m.* 1 21 centimetres. 2 span (de la mano). || **3 dejar a uno con un — de narices,** to leave someone crestfallen. **4 — a —,** inch by inch.
palmotear *v.t.* 1 to slap (someone) on the back. || *v.i.* 2 to clap.
palmoteo *s.m.* clapping, applause.
palo *s.m.* 1 stick. 2 pole, post. 3 DEP. goalpost. 4 blow (golpe). 5 ascender, descender (imprenta). 6 suit (naipes): *tienes que seguir el palo = you have to follow suit.* 7 mast (mástil). || **8 — de ciego,** wild swipe. **9 — macho,** mainmast. **10 — dulce,** liquorice root.
paloduz *s.m.* liquorice root.
paloma *s.f.* 1 ZOOL. dove, pigeon. 2 POL. dove (en el sentido de querer la paz internacional, no la guerra). || **3 — mensajera,** carrier pigeon. **4 — duende,** domestic pigeon. **5 - torcaz,** wood-pigeon.
palomar *s.m.* pigeon loft.
palometa *s.f.* 1 pomfret. 2 MEC. pillow block.
palomilla *s.f.* 1 ZOOL. moth. 2 ZOOL. small butterfly. 3 TEC. wall bracket. 4 TEC. subframe (coche). 5 MEC. wing nut (tuerca). 6 MEC. rack, stand (soporte). 7 (Am.) rabble, riffraff (gentuza).
palomina *s.f.* pigeon droppings.
palomita *s.f.* 1 popcorn. 2 anisette and water (bebida).
palomo *s.m.* cock pigeon.
palote *s.m.* 1 piece of stick. 2 drumstick. 3 penstroke, downstroke (de letra).
palotear *v.i.* 1 to bang sticks together. 2 to squabble (discutir).
paloteo *s.m.* squabbling.
palpable *adj.* 1 obvious. 2 palpable, tangible.
palpablemente *adv.* patently, clearly.
palpar *v.t.* 1 to touch, to feel (tocar). 2 to fondle (acariciar). 3 to grope (andar a tientas). 4 MED. to palpate.
palpitante *adj.* 1 palpitating. 2 throbbing: *un corazón palpitante = a throbbing heart.*
palpitar *v.i.* 1 to palpitate (corazón). 2 to throb (nerviosidad). 3 to flutter, to quiver (temblar): *palpitaban las hojas muertas por la suave brisa = the dead leaves quivered in the soft breeze.*
pálpito *s.m.* 1 excitement, thrill (emoción). 2 (Am.) hunch, feeling (presentimiento).
palpo *s.m.* ZOOL. palp, palpus, feeler.
palta *s.f.* (Am.) avocado pear.
paltó *s.m.* (Am.) jacket.
palúdico, -a *adj.* MED. malarial.
paludismo *s.m.* 1 swamp fever. 2 malaria.
palurdo, -a *adj.* 1 (desp.) rustic, uncouth. || *s.m.* y *s.f.* (desp.) bumpkin, yokel.
palustre *adj.* marsh.
pallador *s.m.* V. **payador.**
pallar *s.m.* (Am.) haricot bean.
pamela *s.f.* picture hat.
pamema *s.f.* humbug (cosa sin importancia).
pampa *s.f.* (Am.) GEOG. pampa.
pámpana *s.f.* 1 BOT. vine leaf. || **2 tocar la —,** (fam.) to wallop.
pámpano *s.m.* BOT. vine shoot.
pamplina *s.f.* 1 BOT. chickweed. 2 trivialty (banalidad): *eso son pamplinas = those are mere trivialities.*
pamporcino *s.m.* BOT. cyclamen.
pan *s.m.* 1 bread. 2 loaf (hogaza). 3 BOT. wheat. 4 Pan (mitología). 5 gold leaf, silver leaf (imprenta). || **6 coger a uno el — bajo el brazo,** to win someone over. **7 con su — que se lo coma,** that's his problem, not mine; that's his funeral. **8 ganarse el —,** to earn a living. **9 el — de cada día,** a common occurrence. **10 — ázimo** o **cenceño,** unleavened bread. **11 — de flor,** white bread. **12 — de boda,** newlyweds' presents. **13 — de munición,** dry bread. **14 — eucarístico,** REL. host. **15 — perdido,** wastrel, good-for-nothing. **16 venderse como — bendito,** to sell like hot cakes.
pana *s.f.* 1 corduroy, velveteen. 2 (Am.) liver, (fig.) guts. 3 (Am.) breakdown: *el carro ha tenido una pana = the car's broken down.*
panacea *s.f.* 1 panacea. || **2 — universal,** HIST. universal panacea.
panaché *s.m.* mixed vegetables.
panadera *s.f.* 1 baker; baker's wife. 2 spanking (paliza).
panadería *s.f.* bakery, baker's shop.
panadero *s.m.* baker.
panadizo *s.m.* 1 MED. whitlow. 2 pallid individual.
panal *s.m.* 1 honeycomb (de colmena). 2 spongy sugar cake (dulce).
panamericanismo *s.m.* Panamericanism.
panamericano, -a *adj.* Panamerican.
pancarta *s.m.* 1 placard, banner (cartel). 2 parchment, manuscript (pergamino).
panceta *s.f.* spiced bacon.
pancista *adj.* 1 unprincipled. || *s.m.* y *f.* 2 self-seeker, opportunist.
páncreas *s.m.* ANAT. pancreas.
pancho *s.m.* 1 sea bream spawn. 2 (fam.) belly. || *adj.* 3 quiet.
panda *s.f.* 1 gang. 2 (desp.) bunch. 3 ZOOL. panda.
pandear *v.pron.* to warp, to sag, to bow, to bulge (paredes, vigas, etc.).
pandectas *s.m.* (form.) 1 pandects. 2 summary, digest.
pandemia *s.f.* pandemic.
pandereta *s.f.* tambourine.
panderete *s.m.* partition wall made with bricks laid on edge.
pandero *s.m.* 1 MUS. tambourine. 2 prattler (charlatán). 3 kite (cometa).
pandilla *s.f.* V. **panda.**
pando, -a *adj.* 1 warped, sagging, bowed. 2 slow moving (lento). 3 (Am.) round-shouldered. || *s.m.* 4 GEOG. flat-bottomed valley.
pandorga *s.f.* 1 kite (cometa). 2 fat lazy woman. 3 drum (tambor).
panegírico, -a (form.) *adj.* panegyrical. || *s.m.* panegyric.
panel *s.m.* 1 panel (de madera). 2 panel (jurado). || **3 — de instrumentos,** dashboard.
panera *s.f.* 1 granary. 2 bread bin. 3 bread basket (cestillo).
pánfilo, -a *adj.* 1 slow-witted (lerdo). 2 gullible (inocente). || *s.m.* y *s.f.* 3 fool, (fam.) mug (ingenuo).
panfletario, -a *adj.* 1 (Am.) violent, of fiery style. 2 bad, poor quality (estilo).
panfletista *s.m.* y *f.* pamphleteer (normalmente con la idea de que escribe satíricamente).
panfleto *s.m.* 1 pamphlet (folleto). 2 (Am.) lampoon. 3 tract, pamphlet (con insultos, sátira, etc.).
pangolín *s.m.* ZOOL. pangolin.
paniaguado *s.m.* 1 servant. 2 POL. henchman, protégé.
pánico *s.m.* panic.
panículo *s.m.* ANAT. membrane.
paniego, -a *adj.* 1 fond of bread, bread-loving. 2 wheat growing (tierra). || *s.m.* 3 charcoal bag.
panificar *v.t.* 1 to plough wheatfields (arar). 2 to make bread.
panislamismo *s.m.* Panislamism.
panizo *s.m.* 1 BOT. millet. 2 BOT. maize.
panoja *s.f.* 1 BOT. panicle, corncob, ear of wheat, ear of millet. 2 BOT. bunch (colgajo).
panoli *adj.* simple, daft.
panoplia *s.f.* 1 panoply. 2 collection of arms. 3 study of ancient weapons.
panorama *s.m.* 1 panorama, view. 2 POL. scene: *el panorama es desesperante = the panorama is depressing.*
panorámico, -a *adj.* panoramic: *vista panorámica = panoramic view.*
pantagruélico, -a *adj.* Pantagruellian.
pantalón *s.m.* 1 (brit.) trousers, (EE.UU.) pants. || **2 llevar una mujer los pantalones,** a woman wears the trousers (en casa). **3 — vaquero,** jeans.
pantalla *s.f.* 1 lampshade. 2 screen: *hay que ajustar la pantalla de la televisión = the television screen needs adjusting.* 3 blind: *sirve de pantalla al jefe = he's a blind for the boss.* 4 someone blocking the light, view, etc. 5 (Am.) bodyguard.
pantano *s.m.* 1 swamp, marsh (marisma). 2 reservoir (embalse). 3 difficulty, (fam.) tight spot (apuro).
pantanoso, -a *adj.* 1 marshy, swampy (tierra). 2 (fig.) difficult, fraught with difficulties (problema).
panteísmo *s.m.* FIL. pantheism.
panteísta *adj.* 1 FIL. pantheistic. || *s.m.* y *f.* 2 pantheist.
panteón *s.m.* 1 pantheon. 2 (Am.) cemetery.
pantera *s.f.* ZOOL. panther.
pantógrafo *s.m.* pantograph.

pantomima *s.f.* pantomime, dumb show.
pantorra o **pantorrilla** *s.f.* ANAT. calf.
pantufla o **pantuflo** *s.f.* slipper.
panza *s.f.* 1 ANAT. paunch, belly. 2 bulge (saliente). 3 ZOOL. rumen. || 4 **— de burra, a)** overcast sky; **b)** (arc.) degree certificate.
panzada *s.f.* 1 bellyful. 2 slog (brega). 3 belly flop (al tirarse al agua).
pañal *s.m.* 1 (brit.) nappy, (EE.UU.) diaper. 2 shirt tail. 3 infancy (niñez). || 4 **estar uno en pañales,** to be wet behind the ears; to be in the early stages: *el proyecto está en pañales = the project is in the early stages.*
paño *s.m.* 1 woollen cloth. 2 cloth, material (tela). 3 wall hanging (lienzo). || *pl.* 4 clothes. || 5 **al —,** offstage. 6 **haber — que cortar, a)** to have a lot to do; **b)** to have a lot to talk about. 7 **— berbí,** coarse woven cloth. 8 **— burriel,** cloth made from undyed wool. 9 **paños calientes,** half measures. 10 **— de lágrimas,** (fig.) a shoulder to cry on. 11 **— de lampazo,** tapestry depicting plants. 12 **— pardillo,** rustic cloth. 13 **paños menores,** underclothes. 14 **poner el — al púlpito,** (fig.) to get on a soapbox.
pañoleta *s.f.* fichu.
pañolón *s.m.* shawl.
pañuelo *s.m.* 1 handkerchief. || 2 **— de cabeza,** headscarf.
papa *s.m.* 1 REL. pope. || *s.f.* 2 (Am.) potato (patata). || *s.f.* 3 V. **paparrucha.** || *s.f.pl.* 4 soaps (comida como de papilla).
papá *s.m.* (fam.) dad, daddy.
papapa *s.f.* 1 double chin. 2 ZOOL. dewlap.
papado *s.m.* REL. papacy.
papagayo *s.m.* 1 ZOOL. parrot. 2 wrasse, peacock fish (pez). 3 BOT. caladium. 4 (Am.) bedpan (silleta). 5 (Am.) large kite (cometa).
papalina *s.f.* 1 cap with earflaps. 2 sun bonnet. 3 (fam.) binge, drunken spree (borrachera).
papamóvil *s.m.* popemobile.
papamoscas *s.m.* 1 ZOOL. flycatcher. 2 (fam.) simpleton (papanatas).
papanatas *s.m.* simpleton; (fam.) wally (necio).
papapa *s.f.* (Am.) stupidity.
paparrucha *s.f.* 1 hoax. 2 lie (mentira). 3 (fig.) potboiler, piece of hack writing. 4 nonsense, (fam.) rubbish: *estás diciendo paparruchas = you're talking rubbish.*
paparruchada *s.f.* (Am.) nonsense, (fig.) rubbish (desatino).
paparulo *s.m.* (Am. y fam.) sucker, mug (ingenuo).
papaverina *s.f.* QUIM. papaverine.
papel *s.m.* 1 paper. 2 letter (carta). 3 document. 4 role, part (rol). 5 character (de un drama, etc.). || 6 **hacer un buen papel, a)** to be lucky; **b)** to make a good impression. 7 **— carbón,** carbon paper. 8 **— continuo,** fanfold paper. 9 **— cuché,** glossy paper. 10 **— de estraza,** brown paper, wrapping paper. 11 **— de barba,** untrimmed paper. 12 **— moneda,** paper money. 13 **— volante,** memo paper. 14 **ser un — mojado,** to be worthless. 15 **tener buenos papeles, a)** to have the right background; **b)** to have the right backing; to be right.
papeleo *s.m.* 1 bureaucratic procedure. 2 (fam.) red tape: *hay demasiado papeleo en esta nación = there is too much red tape in this country.*
papelero, -a *adj.* 1 showy, boastful. 2 paper. 3 paper-selling. || *s.m.* y *s.f.* 4 poseur, (fam.) con man. 5 stationer. || *s.f.* 6 waste paper basket.
papelería *s.f.* stationer's, stationer's shop.
papelada *s.f.* (Am.) 1 farce (farsa). 2 pretence, charade (simulación).
papeleta *s.f.* 1 (Am.) visiting card. 2 (fig.) tough one, touchy problem: *¡qué papeleta! = what a tough one!*
papelón *s.m.* 1 laughing stock. || 2 **hacer un —,** to do something ridiculous.
papera *s.f.* 1 MED. goitre. || *pl.* 2 MED. mumps.
papiamento *s.m.* Papiamento (criollo hablando en Curaçao).
papila *s.f.* ANAT. papilla.
papiloma *s.m.* MED. papilloma.
papilla *s.f.* 1 baby food. 2 guile, (fig.) soft soap (astucia). || 3 **echar la —,** to be sick.
papiro *s.m.* papyrus.
papisa *s.f.* female pope.
papista *adj.* 1 papist. || *s.m.* y *s.f.* 2 papist. || 3 **ser más — que el papa,** (fig.) to be more catholic than the pope.
papo *s.m.* 1 ZOOL. dewlap. 2 MED. goitre. 3 ZOOL. crop (aves). || **hablar de —,** to boast.
paquebote o **paquebot** *s.m.* packet boat.
paquete *s.m.* 1 packet, parcel, package. 2 (fam.) dandy (majo). || *adj.* 3 (Am.) chic, elegant. || 4 **— integrado,** INF. integrated package.
paquetear *v.i.* (Am.) to give oneself airs, (fam.) to swank.
paquidermo *s.m.* ZOOL. pachyderm.
paquistaní *adj.* 1 Pakistani. || *s.m.* y *s.* Pakistani.
par *adj.* 1 equal, similar. 2 even (números). || *s.m.* 3 pair, couple. 4 peer (noble). 5 DEP. par. || 6 **a la —,** FIN. at par. 7 **a pares,** in twos. 8 **de — en —,** wide open. 9 **ir a la —,** to go halves. 10 **sin —,** peerless, unique.
para *prep.* 1 for (finalidad): *una pala para cavar = a spade for digging with.* 2 for (destino): *estas flores son para tu madre = these flowers are for your mother.* 3 for, by (tiempo): *se lo tendremos preparado para mañana = we'll have it ready for you by tomorrow.* 4 for (adecuación): *pesa demasiado para mí = it's too heavy for me.* || 5 **— colmo,** to cap it all. 6 **— que,** *conj.,* so that, in order that: *te lo digo para que aprendas = I'm telling you so that you learn.*
parabién *s.m.* congratulations.
parábola *s.f.* 1 parable (literaria, alegórica, etc.). 2 GEOM. parabola.
parabrisas *s.m.* (brit.) windscreen, (EE.UU.) windshield.
paracaídas *s.m.* parachute.
paracaidismo *s.m.* parachute jumping.
paracaidista *s.m.* y *f.* 1 parachutist. 2 MIL. paratrooper.
paracleto o **paráclito** *s.m.* REL. Paraclete.
parachoques *s.m.* (brit.) bumper, (EE.UU.) fender.
parada *s.f.* stop; pause, break.
paradero *s.m.* 1 whereabouts, location. 2 end. 3 (Am.) railway station. 4 (Am.) bus stop. || 5 **ignorar el — de algo** o **alguien,** not to know where to locate something or someone.
paradigma *s.m.* 1 model. 2 GRAM. paradigm.
paradigmático, -a *adj.* exemplary, paradigmatic.
paradisiaco, -a o **paradisíaco, -a** *adj.* heavenly, blissful.
parado, -a *pp.* 1 de **parar.** || *adj.* 2 shy (tímido). 3 at a standstill, motionless (inmóvil). 4 out of work, unemployed (desempleado). 5 standing (en pie). || *s.f.* 6 stop. 7 (bus) stop. 8 halt, pause (pausa). 9 MIL. parade. 10 staging post (posta). 11 enclosure, cattle pen (corral). 12 bet (envite). || 13 **— en firme,** dead stop (de un caballo). 14 **salir bien —,** to come out of it well.
paradoja *s.f.* paradox.
paradójicamente *adv.* paradoxically.
paradójico, -a *adj.* paradoxical.
parador, -a *adj.* 1 stopping. || *s.m.* 2 inn. 3 state-owned hotel.
paraestatal *adj.* semi-official.
parafernales *adj.pl.* **bienes —,** DER. paraphernalia.
parafina *s.f.* 1 paraffin wax. 2 (Am.) paraffin.
parafrasear *v.t.* to paraphrase.
paráfrasis *s.f.* 1 paraphrase. 2 free verse translation.
paragoge *s.f.* paragoge, paragogue.
paragolpes *s.m.* (Am.) (brit.) bumper, (EE.UU.) fender (parachoques).
parágrafo *s.m.* 1 section of text. 2 paragraph.
paraguas *s.m.* umbrella.
paraguayo, -a *adj.* 1 Paraguayan. || *s.m.* y *f.* Paraguayan.
paragüero *s.m.* 1 umbrella maker, umbrella seller. 2 umbrella stand.
parahúso *s.m.* drill, awl.
paraíso *s.m.* 1 REL. paradise. 2 gallery, (fam.) gods (teatro). || 3 **— terrenal,** Earthly paradise, Garden of Eden. 4 **— de los bobos,** fools' paradise.
paraje *s.m.* faraway place, isolated spot: *¡qué paraje tan desolado! = what a bleak isolated spot!*
paral *s.m.* 1 prop. 2 shore (puntal). 3 chock, putlog (náutico).
paralelamente *adv.* 1 comparably (idea de comparación). 2 at the same time.
paralelepípedo *s.m.* GEOM. parallelepiped.
paralelismo *s.m.* parallelism.

paralelo, -a *adj.* 1 parallel. || *s.m.* 2 parallel of latitude. || *s.f.* 3 MIL. trench. || *s.f.pl.* 4 DEP. parallel bars.

paralelogramo *s.m.* GEOM. parallelogram.

parálisis *s.f.* MED. paralysis.

paralítico, -a *adj.* 1 paralytic; paralyzed: *tengo una hija paralítica = I've got a daughter who is paralyzed.* || *s.m.* y *f.* 2 paralytic.

paralización *s.f.* 1 MED. paralysis. 2 ECON. stagnation. 3 stoppage, suspension (de unas obras, proyecto, etc.).

paralizador, -a o **paralizante** *adj.* 1 MED. paralyzing. 2 (fig.) stunning, shocking.

paralizar *v.t.* y *pron.* 1 to paralyse. 2 to be paralysed, to become paralysed: *el miedo me paralizó = fear paralysed me.*

paralogismo *s.m.* FIL. paralogism.

paramecio *s.m.* BIOL. paramecium.

paramento *s.m.* 1 ornament. 2 adornment. 3 ARQ. face (de una pared, un sillar). || 4 **paramentos sacerdotales,** priest's liturgical vestments.

paramera *s.f.* GEOG. high moorland.

parámetro *s.m.* parameter.

paramnesia *s.f.* MED. paramnesia.

páramo *s.m.* 1 GEOG. moor. 2 bleak plateau (altiplanicie). 3 (Am.) high grassland. 4 wilderness. 5 (Am.) drizzle (llovizna).

parangón *s.m.* 1 comparison, parallel. || 2 **no tener —,** to be matchless. 3 **sin —,** matchless.

parangonar *v.t.* 1 compare. 2 justify (alinear letras desiguales).

paraninfo *s.m.* 1 main hall (universidades). 2 (p.u.) paranymph, best man (de una boda).

paranoia *s.f.* MED. paranoia.

paranoico, -a *adj.* PSIQ. paranoic.

paranomasia *s.f.* V. **paronomasia.**

parapetar *v.t.* y *r.* to fortify (oneself), to protect (oneself).

parapeto *s.m.* parapet.

paraplejía *s.f.* MED. paraplegia.

parapsicología *s.f.* PSIC. parapsychology.

parar *s.m.* 1 pairs (naipes). || *v.t.* 2 to stop, to halt. 3 to point (perro de caza). || *v.i.* y *v.pron.* 4 to stop, to come to a halt. || *v.i.* 5 to stop, to cease: *no para de hablar = he doesn't stop talking.* 6 to stop, to stay, to lodge: *los viajantes suelen parar en el hostal de la plaza = the travelling salesmen usually stay at the hotel in the square.* 7 to become, to end up: *¡mira en qué ha venido a parar! = look where he's ended up!* || *v.pron.* 8 (Am.) to stand up (levantarse). 9 (Am.) to become, wealthy (enriquecerse). || 10 **sin —,** at once: *lo hice sin parar = I did it at once.*

pararrayos *s.m.* lightning conductor.

parasceve *s.f.* 1 preparation. 2 REL. Good Friday.

parasimpático *adj.* y *s.m.* FISIOL. parasympathetic.

parasíntesis *s.f.* GRAM. parasynthesis.

parasitismo *s.m.* MED. parasitism.

parásito, -a o **parasito, -a** *adj.* 1 parasitic. || *s.m.* 2 parasite: *un parásito social = a social parasite.*

parasol *s.m.* parasol, sunshade.

parata *s.f.* AGR. terrace.

paratifoidea *s.f.* MED. paratyphoid.

parcamente *adv.* frugally (en comidas), moderately (en comidas y otras materias).

parcas *s.f.pl.* Fates, Parcae.

parcela *s.f.* 1 plot of land. 2 smallholding. 3 part (partícula).

parcelación *s.f.* division into plots, division into lots (especialmente tierra para usos agrícolas).

parcelar *v.t.* to divide into plots, to divide into lots (especialmente parcelas cultivadas).

parcelario, -a *adj.* divided into plots (especialmente tierra de cultivo).

parcial *adj.* 1 partial. 2 incomplete (inacabado). 3 biased (prejuzgado). 4 partisan (partidista): *una opinión parcial = a partisan view.*

parco, -a *adj.* 1 parsimonious. 2 frugal. || *s.f.pl.* 3 Fates (figura mitológica). 4 death.

parchar *v.t.* (Am.) to patch (ropa).

parche *s.m.* 1 MED. sticking plaster. 2 patch. 3 drumhead (piel de tambor). 4 drum (tambor). 5 botch (chapuza). || 6 **pegar un — a alguien,** (fam.) to con somebody.

parchís *s.m.* lotto.

pardal *adj.* 1 rustic. 2 brown, dun (color). || *s.m.* 3 wily rouge. 4 ZOOL. sparrow.

pardela *s.f.* ZOOL. small seagull.

¡pardiez! *interj.* by Jove!

pardillo *adj.* 1 rustic. || *s.m.* 2 coarse brown cloth (paño). 3 ZOOL. linnet. 4 beginner, novice: *eres un pardillo, después de todo = you're a beginner, after all.*

pardo, -a *adj.* 1 dun, tawny. || *s.m.* 2 mulatto. || 3 **oso —,** ZOOL. brown bear.

pardusco, -a o **parduzco, -a** *adj.* greyish, brownish.

pareado, -a *adj.* 1 semi-detached (casa). || *s.m.* 2 LIT. couplet.

parear *v.t.* 1 to match. 2 to form pairs. 3 to compare. 4 ZOOL. to mate.

parecer *s.m.* 1 opinion. 2 looks (aspecto). || *v.i.* 3 to seem, to appear. 4 to look: *pareces muy cansado hoy = you look very tired today.* || *v.imp.* 5 to believe, to think: *me parece que ha llegado = I think he's come.* || *v.r.* 6 to resemble each other, to look alike. || 7 **— a,** to resemble; to look like. 8 **— bien** o **mal,** to look good or bad, to think it's right/not to think it's right: *me parece mal que le hayas engañado = I don't think it's right your deceiving him.*

parecido, -a *adj.* 1 similar, alike, like. || *s.m.* 2 similarity. || 3 **bien —,** good-looking.

pared *s.f.* 1 wall. || 2 **arrimarse uno a las paredes,** (fam.) to be sozzled. 3 **entre cuatro paredes,** lonely. 4 **las paredes oyen,** walls have ears. 5 **hasta la — de enfrente,** resolutely. 6 **— maestra,** load-bearing wall. 7 **pegado a la —,** ashamed. 8 **subirse por las paredes,** (fam.) to go up the wall.

paredaño, -a *adj.* next door, adjoining.

paredón *s.m.* 1 wall left standing. || 2 **¡asesinos al —!,** murderers up against the wall! 3 **llevar al —,** to put up against a wall and shoot.

parejero, -a *adj.* 1 cocky, conceited. || *s.m.* y *s.f.* 2 (Am.) racehorse.

parejo, -a *adj.* 1 similar, alike, equal. 2 flat. || *s.f.* 3 couple. 4 partner. || 5 **correr parejas** o **correr a las parejas, a)** to keep pace with; **b)** to be on a level with. 6 **por —,** on a par.

paremia *s.f.* 1 proverb, wise saw (refrán). 2 fable (fábula).

parénquima *s.m.* BIOL. parenchyma.

parentela *s.f.* 1 relations. 2 blood relationship.

parentesco *s.m.* 1 relationship. 2 relations.

paréntesis *s.m.* 1 parenthesis. 2 bracket. 3 interruption: *un paréntesis en mi vida = an interruption in my life.* || 4 **entre —,** incidental. 5 **hacer un —,** to pause for a moment: *hagamos un paréntesis para tomar un bocadillo = let's pause for a moment to have a sandwich.*

paria *s.m.* y *s.f.* pariah.

parias *s.f.pl.* 1 BIOL. placenta. 2 HIST. princely tribute.

parida *s.f.* (vulg.) stupid remark; bullshit.

paridad *s.f.* 1 parity, equality: *paridad monetaria = monetary parity.* 2 comparison.

paridera *adj.* 1 child-bearing, fertile. || *s.f.* 2 place where livestock drop their young. 3 giving birth (parto).

pariente, -a *adj.* 1 related. 2 similar. || *s.m.* y *s.f.* 3 relation, relative, kin. || 4 **la parienta,** (fam.) the wife, the missus.

parietal *adj.* 1 wall. 2 ANAT. parietal. || *s.m.* ANAT. parietal: parietal bone.

parihuela(s) *s.f.* stretcher.

paripé *s.m.* (fam.) **hacer el —,** to show off; to kid oneself.

parir *v.t.* 1 to give birth (to), to bear. 2 to drop (animales). 3 to foal (yeguas); to calve (vacas); to farrow (cerdas); to lamb (ovejas). 4 to lay eggs. 5 (fig.) to reveal. || 6 **— a medias,** to produce as a joint effort.

parisiense o **parisino, -a** *adj.* 1 Parisian. || *s.m.* y *f.* 2 Parisian.

paritario, -a *adj.* joint (de las reuniones u organismos donde los obreros y empresarios u otros dos grupos están proporcionalmente representados).

paritorio *s.m.* 1 MED. antenatal room. 2 (Am.) childbirth.

parking *s.m.* (brit.) car park; (EE.UU.) parking lot.

parkinson *s.m.* MED. Parkinson's disease.

parlamentar *v.i.* 1 to parley, to negotiate a treaty. 2 to converse.

parlamentario, -a *adj.* 1 parliamentary. || *s.m.* y *f.* 2 member of Parliament.

parlamentarismo *s.m.* POL. parliamentarianism.
parlamento *s.m.* 1 POL. Parliament. 2 Houses of Parliament. 3 speech (discurso). 4 parley (con enemigos).
parlanchín, -ina *adj.* 1 loose talking, loose-tongued. || *s.m.* y *s.f.* 2 loose talker, (fam.) big mouth.
parlante *adj.* 1 talking, speaking. || *s.m.* 2 (Am.) loudspeaker.
parlar *v.i.* 1 to chatter, to prattle. 2 to gossip (cotillear).
parlero, -a *adj.* 1 garrulous. 2 gossipy (cotilla). 3 talking, singing (pájaro). 4 expressive, musical. || *s.m.* y *s.f.* 5 gossip. 6 chatterbox (charlatán).
parlotear *v.i.* to prattle, to blather.
parloteo *s.m.* prattle, chatter.
parmesano, -a *adj.* parmesan (queso).
Parnaso *s.m.* 1 Parnassus. 2 LIT. anthology of poetry.
parné *s.m.* (fam.) dough; cash, money.
paro *s.m.* 1 unemployment (desempleo). 2 knocking-off time (final de jornada). 3 lockout. 5 (Am.) strike (huelga). 6 ZOOL. tit.
parodia *s.f.* 1 LIT. parody. 2 travesty.
parodiar *v.t.* to parody.
paronimia *s.f.* GRAM. paronym.
parónimo, -a *adj.* paronymic.
paronomasia *s.f.* FON. paronomasia.
parótida *s.f.* 1 ANAT. parotid; parotid gland. 2 MED. parotitis.
paroxismo *s.m.* paroxysm.
paroxítono, -a *adj.* GRAM. paroxytone.
parpadear *v.i.* 1 to flutter the eyelids (repetidamente). 2 to blink (puede ser solamente una vez). 3 to twinkle (estrellas). 4 to flicker (luz).
parpadeo *s.m.* blinking, flickering (de luces u ojos).
párpado *s.m.* eyelid.
parque *s.m.* 1 park. 2 MIL. depot. 3 stock, total (vehículos). || 4 **— zoológico,** zoo.
parqué *s.m.* parquet.
parquear *v.t.* e *i.* (Am.) to park.
parquedad *s.f.* 1 frugality, moderation. 2 parsimony.
parqueo *s.m.* (Am.) car park.
parra *s.f.* 1 BOT. climbing vine. || 2 **subirse a la —,** (fam.) to go up the wall. 3 (fam.) to go over the top.
parrafada *s.f.* 1 long chat. || 2 **echar una —,** to have a long chat.
párrafo *s.m.* 1 paragraph. 2 paragraph marker.
parral *s.m.* 1 BOT. vine arbour. 2 BOT. vineyard.
parranda *s.f.* 1 spree, binge, party. 2 group of revellers.
parricida *s.m.* y *f.* parricide (persona).
parrilla *s.f.* 1 gridiron, grating. 2 grill. || **a la —,** grilled; barbecued.
párroco *adj.* 1 parish. || *s.m.* 2 parish priest.
parroquia *s.f.* 1 REL. parish church (iglesia). 2 REL. congregation (feligreses). 3 REL. parish (zona). 4 customers, clientela: *este bar tiene una buena parroquia = this pub has good customers.*
parroquial *adj.* REL. parochial, of the parish.
parroquiano, -a *adj.* 1 REL. parochial, pertaining to the parish. || *s.m.* y *f.* 2 REL. parishioner. 3 customer, client.
parsimonia *s.f.* 1 thrift. 2 prudence. 3 unhurried attitude (sin prisa).
parsimonioso, -a *adj.* slow, unhurried.
parte *s.f.* 1 part. 2 portion. 3 share. 4 contender (contendiente). 5 COM. party. || *s.m.* 6 bulletin. 7 DER. litigant. || *s.f.pl.* 8 genitals. || 9 **de — a —,** absolutely. 10 **de — de,** on behalf of, in the name of. 11 **echar a mala —,** to look disappovingly upon. 12 **echar uno por otra —,** to go off in a different direction. 13 **hacer uno de su —,** to do one's best. 14 **llevar uno la mejor —,** to get the best of it. 15 **nombrar partes,** to name names. 16 **— alicuanta,** MAT. aliquant part. 17 **— alicuota,** MAT. aliquot part. 18 **— de la oración,** GRAM. part of speech. 19 **— homogénea,** homogeneous part. 20 **— integrante,** integrant part. 21 **por la mayor —,** in the main. 22 **por — de:** *es primo por parte de madre = he's my cousin on my mother's side.*
parteluz *s.m.* ARQ. mullion.
partenaire *s.m.* y *s.f.* partner.
partenogénesis *s.f.* REL. parthenogenesis, virgin birth.
partera *s.f.* MED. midwife.
parterre *s.m.* 1 public garden (jardín). 2 flowerbed (maceta). 3 stalls (teatro).
partición *s.f.* POL. partition.
participación *s.f.* 1 participation. 2 news (novedad). 3 part of a lottery ticket.
participar *v.t.* 1 to announce, to inform. || *v.i.* 2 to take part, to participate.
participio *s.m.* 1 GRAM. participle. || 2 **— presente** o **activo,** present participle. 3 **— pasado** o **pasivo,** past participle.
partícula *s.f.* 1 particle. 2 GRAM. particle. || 3 **partículas alfa,** FIS. alpha particles. 4 **partículas beta,** FIS. beta particles.
particular *adj.* 1 particular, special. 2 peculiar: *el canguro es particular de Australia = the kangaroo is peculiar to Australia.* 3 private: *una casa particular.* 4 peculiar, odd, strange (extraño). || *s.m.* 5 member of the public, private individual. 6 matter, subject (asunto).
particularismo *s.m.* particularism, self-interest.
particularizar *v.t.* 1 to detail, to specify. 2 to favour. || *v.pron.* 3 to stand out.
particularmente *adv.* 1 particularly, specially. 2 privately.
partida *s.f.* 1 departure (salida). 2 certificate: *me hacen falta sus partidas de nacimiento y matrimonio = I need his birth and marriage certificates.* 3 COM. entry (contabilidad). 4 COM. consignment, batch (lote). 5 armed band. 6 game (naipes, etc.). || 7 **— doble,** COM. double entry (contabilidad). 8 **por — doble,** doubly; for two reasons.
partidario, -a *adj.* 1 partisan, partial. || *s.m.* y *f.* 2 supporter, follower.
partidismo *s.m.* 1 partisanship, party line. 2 bias (prejuicio): *tu partidismo es evidente = your bias is evident.*
partido, -a *p.p.* 1 de **partir.** || *adj.* 2 split, divided. 3 cracked (agrietado). 4 departed (salido). 5 party (heráldico). || *s.m.* 6 POL. party. 7 side (bando). 8 match, game (contienda). 9 district (distrito). || 10 **sacar —,** to benefit. 11 **ser buen —,** (fig.) to be a good catch. 12 **ser mal —,** to be not worth bothering with. 13 **tomar —, a)** to take sides; **b)** to change over to the other side.
partir *v.t.* 1 to divide, to split, to break in two. 2 to share out (repartir). 3 to crack (nueces, etc.). || *v.i.* 4 to leave, to depart. || 5 **a — de,** starting from. 6 **— a uno,** to demoralise someone.
partisano, -a *adj.* 1 partisan. || *s.m.* y *f.* MIL. partisan.
partitivo, -a *adj.* GRAM. partitive.
partitura *s.f.* MUS. score.
parto *s.m.* 1 childbirth, delivery. 2 (fig.) brainchild. || 3 **el — de los montes,** anticlimax. 4 **venir el — derecho,** (fig.) to turn out hunky dory.
parturienta *s.f.* MED. parturient, woman in labour, woman who has just given birth.
parva *s.f.* 1 light breakfast. 2 AGR. corn ready for threshing. 3 AGR. threshed corn.
parvedad *s.f.* 1 smallness. 2 light morning snack (en días de vigilia).
parvo, -a *adj.* small, little.
parvulario *s.m.* nursery school.
párvulo *adj.* 1 little, tiny. 2 naive, innocent (ingenuo). || *s.m.* 3 infant.
pasa *s.f.* raisin.
pasable *adj.* passable, fair, so-so: *la película es pasable = the film is passable.*
pasablemente *adv.* passably, fairly.
pasacalle *s.m.* passacaglia.
pasadero, -a *adj.* 1 passable. 2 fair, acceptable. || *s.f.* 3 footbridge (puente). 4 stepping stone (piedra).
pasadizo *s.m.* 1 corridor (pasillo). 2 alleyway (pasaje).
pasado, -a *p.p.* 1 de **pasar.** || *s.m.* 2 past. 3 GRAM. past. || *pl.* 4 ancestors. || *s.f.* 5 passing, passage. 6 coat: *le he dado dos pasadas de pintura = I've given it two coats of paint.* 7 (Am.) shame, embarrassment (vergüenza). || 8 **dar pasada,** to allow. 9 **de pasada, a)** incidentally; **b)** passing through. 10 **mala pasada,** dirty trick, bed turn.
pasador, -a *adj.* 1 smyggling. || *s.m.* 2 bolt, latch (pestillo). 3 tie clip, tie pin (sujetacorbatas); slide (pelo). 4 strainer (coladera). 5 colander (colador). 6 MEC. pin; split pin (chaveta). 7 MEC. filter (filtro). 8 smuggler (contrabandista).
pasaje *s.m.* 1 passage, crossing (travesía). 2 toll (peaje). 3 alley (callejuela). 4 fare (tarifa). 5 passengers (pasajeros). 6 LIT. passage. 7 passageway (pasillo). 8 (Am.) ticket (billete).
pasajero, -a *adj.* 1 busy: *es una calle muy pasajera = it's a very busy street.* 2 fleeting, transient (efímero). || 3 **pájaro**

—, bird of passage. || *s.m.* y *f.* 4 passenger.
pasamano(s) *s.m.* 1 banister(s). 2 handrail. 3 braid (galones).
pasamontañas *s.m.* balaclava.
pasante *adj.* 1 passing. || *s.m.* 2 teaching assistant. 3 DER. articled clerk.
pasaporte *s.m.* 1 passport. || **2 dar — a uno,** (fig. y fam.) to give someone the push, to dismiss.
pasar *v.t.* 1 to pass: *¿quieres pasarme una servilleta? = do you mind passing me a serviette?* 2 to cross (atravesar). 3 to overtake, to pass (adelantar). 4 to pass on (transferir). 5 to pass through. 6 to strain (colar). 7 to sift, to sieve (cerner). 8 to swallow (tragar). 9 to pass: *he pasado el examen = I've passed the exam.* 10 to overlook: *ella pasa todas sus faltas = she overlooks all his mistakes.* 11 to miss out, to skip: *voy a pasar las próximas diez páginas = I'm going to skip the next ten pages.* 12 to spend (tiempo): *pasé cinco años en Inglaterra = I spent five years in England.* 13 to endure, suffer: *los pobres pasan mucha hambre = the poor suffer considerable hunger.* 14 to subsist. || *v.i.* 15 to happen (suceder). 16 to go in (to), to come in (to), to enter. 17 DEP. to pass. || *v.pron.* 18 (fig.) to overstep the mark, to go too far. 19 to go bad, to go off, to go rotten (pudrirse). 20 to change sides. 21 to forget: *se me pasó avisarte = I forgot to tell you.* || **22 — a mejor vida,** (euf.) to pass away. **23 — de largo,** to pass by. **24 — de, a)** to exceed: *pasas de los 100 kms. por hora = you are exceeding 100 kms. per hour;* **b)** to be not interested in: *él pasa de todo = he's not interested in anything.* **25 pasarse de listo,** to be too clever by half.
pasarela *s.f.* 1 footbridge (puente). 2 gangway (de un barco).
pasatiempo *s.m.* pastime, hobby.
pascal *s.m.* FIS. pascal.
pascana *s.f.* (Am.) roadside inn.
pascua *s.f.* 1 REL. Passover. 2 REL. Easter. 3 REL. Christmas. 4 REL. Epiphany. 5 Christmas holidays. || **6 dar** o **felicitar las Pascuas, a)** to wish (someone) a happy Christmas; **b)** to wish (someone) a happy Easter. **7 de Pascuas a Ramos,** once in a blue moon; once a flood. **8 estar uno como unas pascuas,** to be as happy as a dog with two tails. **9 — florida,** Easter. **10 — de Pentecostés,** Whitsuntide. **11 santas pascuas,** that's that: *tú te conformas con lo que te den, y santas pascuas = you'll make do with what you're given and that's that.*
pascual *adj.* REL. paschal.
pascuilla *s.f.* REL. Low Sunday.
pase *s.m.* 1 pass: 2 safeconduct (salvoconducto). 3 DEP. pass.
paseante *s.m.* y *f.* stroller, promenader.
pasear *v.i.* 1 to stroll, to walk (andar). 2 to go for a ride (a caballo, en bicicleta, en moto). 3 to go for a drive (en coche). || *v.t.* 4 to take for a walk. 5 to parade. || **6 — la imaginación,** to let one's imagination roam. **7 — la mirada por,** to run one's eyes over.
paseíllo *s.m.* opening parade (de toreros).
paseo *s.m.* 1 walk, stroll (caminata). 2 ride (a caballo, en bicicleta, en moto). 3 drive (en coche). 4 throughfare, promenade (calle). 5 walking distance. || **6 ¡a —!,** (fam.) hop it!, scram! **7 dar un —, a)** to go for a stroll, to go for a walk; **b)** to go for a ride; **c)** to go for a drive.
pasible *adj.* LIT. able to suffer.
pasiflora *s.f.* BOT. passionflower.
pasillo *s.m.* 1 passage, corridor. 2 short play (saeta).
pasión *s.f.* 1 passion. 2 enthusiasm. 3 REL. Passion, Passion of Christ.
pasional *adj.* passional (emociones fuertes).
pasionaria *s.f.* BOT. passion flower.
pasivamente *adv.* passively.
pasividad *s.f.* passivity.
pasivo, -a *adj.* 1 passive. 2 state (pensión). || *s.m.* 3 FIN. liabilities, debts. || **4 voz —,** V. **voz. 5 participio —,** V. **participio.**
pasmado, -a *p.p.* 1 de **pasmar.** || *adj.* 2 stonished, stunned. 3 (fam.) dopey. || **4 dejar a alguien —,** to amaze somebody. **5 quedar —,** to stand open-mouthed, to stand gaping.
pasmar *v.t.* 1 to freeze, to chill (enfriar). 2 to amaze (asombrar). 3 to stun (aturdir). || *v.r.* 4 MED. to be frozen, to catch a chill. 5 to be dumbfounded (aturdirse). 6 MED. to get lockjaw (tétanos). 7 to fade (desleírse), to tarnish (deslustrarse).
pasmarota o **pasmarotada** *s.f.* 1 feigned display of shocked surprise. 2 overreaction.
pasmarote *s.m.* (fam.) drip, twit.
pasmo *s.m.* 1 MED. chill (enfriamiento). 2 MED. lockjaw, tetanus. 3 wonder, astonishment (asombro). 4 source of wonder.
pasmosamente *adv.* amazingly, astonishingly.
pasmoso, -a *adj.* amazing, astonishing.
paso, -a *adj.* 1 dried (fruta). || *s.f.* y *adj.* 2 raisin.
paso *s.m.* 1 step, stride (zancada). 2 pace (ritmo). 3 rung, step (peldaño). 4 passing (pasada). 5 passage, way through. 6 move, measure (medida). 7 footprint (huella). 8 progress, rate. 9 REL. stage in the Passion of Christ. 10 REL. portable or mobile tableau (en una procesión religiosa). 11 short play, sketch (saeta). 12 strait(s) (estrecho). 13 passage, migration (of birds). 14 MEC. pitch. || **15 a cada —,** at every turn, all the time. **16 acortar los pasos a alguien,** (fig.) to hinder someone's progress. **17 a dos pasos,** close by. **18 a ese —,** at that rate. **19 al — que,** at the rate that, at the tempo that. **20 andar en malos pasos,** (fig.) to stray from the straight and narrow. **21 contar los pasos,** (fig.) to tread warily. **22 de —, a)** passing through; **b)** by the way. **23 hacer el —,** to look foolish. **24 — a nivel,** level crossing. **25 — de comedia, a)** excerpt of a play, etc.; **b)** comical incident. **26 — geométrico,** geometric pace. **27 salir uno al —, a)** to face up to; **b)** to forestall. **28 salir uno del —,** to get out of an awkward situation.
pasodoble *s.m.* pasodoble.
pasparse *v.pron.* MED. to chap, to crack.
pasquín *s.m.* lampoon, poster.
pasquinada *s.f.* lampoon, scurrilous article.
pasta *s.f.* 1 dough, paste. 2 MET. molten metal. 3 pulp (de madera). 4 papier mâché. 5 binding, hardback (encuadernación). 6 biscuit, sponge (bizcocho). || **7 buena —,** (fig.) good sort. **8 media —,** half-binding.
pastadero *adj.* 1 grazing ground. 2 pasture.
pastar *v.i.* to graze: *había ovejas pastando = there were sheep grazing.*
pastel *s.m.* 1 cake. 2 BOT. woad. 3 ART. pastel. 4 ART. pastel drawing. 5 (fig.) mess, bodge (chapuza). 6 (fig.) dumpy person (persona gorda). || **7 se le descubrió el —,** (fig.) he was rumbled.
pastelear *v.i.* 1 (fig.) to play for time, (fig.) to stall, (fam.) to flannel.
pastelería *s.f.* 1 confectionery (productos). 2 confectioner's cake, shop.
pastelero, -a *s.m.* y *f.* confectioner.
pasterizar o **pasteurizar** *v.t.* to pasteurise.
pastiche *s.m.* pastiche.
pastilla *s.f.* 1 MED. tablet, lozenge. 2 bar (jabón, chocolate), square (chocolate). || **3 a toda —,** at full speed, like the wind, like a flash. **4 gastar uno pastillas de boca,** to make empty promises.
pastizal *s.m.* pasture.
pasto *s.m.* 1 grass, fodder. 2 pasture land, meadow (prado). 3 grazing. 4 feed (pienso). || **5 a —/a todo —,** in abundance, galore. **6 de —,** ordinary, everyday. **7 — espiritual,** spiritual sustenance. **8 — de las llamas/del fuego,** fuel to the flames.
pastor, -a *s.m.* 1 shepherd. 2 priest. || *s.f.* 3 shepherdess. || **3 El Buen —,** REL. The Good Shepherd. **4 — sumo** o **universal,** REL. the Pope.
pastoral *adj.* 1 LIT. pastoral. 2 REL. pastoral. || **3 carta —,** pastoral letter.
pastorear *v.t.* to shepherd.
pastorela *s.f.* 1 MUS. pastourelle, pastorale. 2 LIT. pastoral.
pastoreo *s.m.* shepherding.
pastoril *adj.* 1 pastoral. 2 LIT. pastoral.
pastosidad *s.f.* 1 doughiness (de una sustancia). 2 mellowness (de voz).
pastoso, -a *adj.* 1 doughy, pasty. 2 rich, mellow: *voz pastosa = mellow voice.* 3 thick (pintura). 4 (Am.) grassy.
pastura *s.f.* 1 pasture. 2 fodder, feed.
pata *s.f.* 1 ZOOL. foot, leg, paw. 2 foot, leg (muebles). 3 ZOOL. duck (ánade). 4 ANAT. (fam.) leg, foot. || **5 a — chula,** cripple. **6 a cuatro patas,** on all fours. **7 a la — coja,** hopping. **8 a la — la llana,** simply. **9 a —,** on foot. **10 estirar la —,** (fam.) to snuff it. **11 enseñar la —,** (fam.) to give the game away. **12 meter la —,**

(fam.) to put one's foot in it. **13 patas arriba, a)** upside down; **b)** (fam.) cock-eyed. **14 poner a uno de — en la calle,** (fam.) to give someone the boot. **15 tener uno mala —, a)** to be unlucky; **b)** to be clumsy. **16 (El) patas,** (fam.) Old Nick.

pataco, -a *adj.* **1** peasant, uncouth (inculto). || *s.m.* y *f.* **2** (desp.) peasant, bumpkin. || *s.f.* **3** HIST. old silver coin. || *s.m.* **4** HIST. ten cents coin.

patacón *s.m.* **1** HIST. old coin. **2** peso (moneda). **3** HIST. ten cents coin. **4** (Am.) slice of fried banana. **5** (Am.) bruise (magulladura).

patache *s.m.* **1** tender. **2** MAR. trading vessel (mercante).

patada *s.f.* **1** kick (puntapié). **2** stamp (pisotón). **3** footprint (huella). **4** step, stride (paso). || **5 a patadas, a)** (fam.) galore (a montones); **b)** roughly (maltratar).

patagio *s.m.* patagium.

patalear *v.i.* **1** to throw a tantrum (rabieta). **2** to kick one's legs in the air: *el bebé está pataleando en la camita = the baby's kicking his legs in the air in the cot.*

pataleo *s.m.* **1** kicking, stamping. || **2 derecho al —,** right to make a fuss, right to protest (aunque no sirva de nada a la larga).

pataleta *s.f.* **1** tantrum (rabieta). **2** MED. fit.

patán *adj.* **1** rustic. **2** loutish (grosero). **3** uncouth (zafio). || *s.m.* **4** country bumpkin (cateto). **5** lout (gamberro). **6** boor.

patarata *s.f.* **1** inanity (idiotez). **2** (fam.) smarminess. **3** affectation.

patata *s.f.* **1** potato. **2** chip (frita). **3** crisp (frita).

patatero, -a *adj.* **1** fond of potatoes. || *s.m.* y *f.* **2** potato seller. **3** potato buyer. || *s.m.* **4** MIL. officer who has come up through the ranks.

patatús *s.m.* **1** dizzy spell (síncope). **2** slight mishap (percance).

paté *s.m.* paté.

patear *v.t.* **1** to kick. **2** (fig.) to trample on (pisotear), to abuse. **3** to boo, to jeer. || *v.t.* y *v.i.* to chase around: *he estado durante toda la mañana pateando y no he encontrado a Ignacio = I've been chasing around all morning and I haven't found Ignacio.* || *v.i.* **5** to stamp (patalear).

patena *s.f.* **1** a large medal. **2** REL. paten. || **3 limpio como una —,** (fig.) clean as a whistle.

patentar *v.t.* **1** to patent. **2** to register patents.

patente *adj.* **1** patent, obvious, evident. || *s.f.* **2** DER. licence. **3** DER. warrant. **4** COM. patent. || **5 — de corso, a)** letter of marque; **b)** (fig.) free hand. **6 — de navegación,** ship's certificate of registration.

patentemente *adv.* patently, obviously.

patentizar *v.t.* to make clear, to demonstrate.

pateo *s.m.* stamping, kicking.

paternal *adj.* fatherly, paternal.

paternalismo *s.m.* paternalism.

paternalista *adj.* **1** paternalistic, (desp.) patronizing. || *s.m.* **2** paternalist.

paternalmente *adv.* paternally.

paternidad *s.f.* **1** paternity, fatherhood. **2** authorship (autoría).

paterno, -a *adj.* paternal, fatherly.

pateta *s.m.* (fam.) Old Nick.

patéticamente *adv.* pathetically.

patético, -a *adj.* **1** pathetic, touching. **2** moving (conmovedor).

patibulario, -a *adj.* **1** gallows. **2** sinister, horrifying.

patíbulo *s.m.* scaffold, gallows.

patidifuso, -a *adj.* flabbergasted, nonplussed, dumbfounded: *le dejé patidifuso con la noticia = I had him dumbfounded with the news.*

patilla *s.f.* **1** side whisker, sideburn (pelo). **2** arm (de gafas). **3** scar (de arma de fuego). **4** (Am.) bench. || *s.m.pl.* (fam.) Old Nick.

patín *s.m.* **1** skate. **2** runner (de trineo). **3** scooter (patinete). **4** ZOOL. goosander.

pátina *s.f.* patina.

patinador, -a *s.m.* y *f.* skater.

patinaje *s.m.* **1** skating. || **2 — artístico,** figure skating.

patinar *v.i.* **1** to skate. **2** to skid (coche, etc.). **3** (fig.) to slip up, to make a blunder (equivocarse).

patinazo *s.m.* **1** skid (de un vehículo). **2** (fig.) blunder (metedura de pata).

patinete *s.m.* scooter.

patio *s.m.* **1** ARQ. patio, courtyard. **2** quad, playground (de recreo). **3** stalls (de teatro).

patitieso, -a *adj.* **1** stiff-legged. **2** flabbergasted (patidifuso). **3** (fig.) stuck up, snooty (engreído).

patizambo, -a *adj.* knock-kneed.

pato *s.m.* **1** duck, drake. || *adj.* **2** (fig.) wet, boring (pesado). || **3 estar hecho un —,** to be sopping wet. **4 pagar el —, a)** (fig.) to carry the can (cargar con el muerto); **b)** to foot the bill (pagar). **5 — de flojel,** ZOOL. eider.

patochada *s.f.* **1** nonsense, (fig.) rubbish (tonterías). **2** (fam.) cock-up (equivocación).

patógeno, -a *adj.* MED. pathogenic.

patología *s.f.* FISIOL. pathology.

patológico, -a *adj.* **1** MED. pathological. **2** (fig.) incredible, exaggerated: *miedo patológico al agua = exaggerated fear of water.*

patoso, -a *adj.* **1** tiresome (pesado). **2** clumsy (torpe).

patraña *s.f.* hoax, misrepresentation: *eso es una patraña = that's a gross misrepresentation.*

patria *s.f.* **1** homeland, native country. **2** mother country, fatherland. || **3 — chica, a)** home town; **b)** home region. **4 — celestial,** heaven.

patriarca *s.m.* **1** patriarch. || **2 vivir como un —,** to live a life of ease.

patriarcado *s.m.* patriarchy.

patriarcal *adj.* patriarchal.

patricio, -a *adj.* **1** patrician, noble. || *s.m.* **2** patrician, aristocrat.

patrimonio *s.m.* **1** patrimony, heritage. **2** DER. inheritance. **3** wealth (caudal). **4** FIN. assets. || **5 — real,** crown land. **6 — nacional,** national heritage.

patrio, -a *adj.* **1** native, home. **2** paternal.

patriota *adj.* patriot.

patriotero, -a *adj.* jingoistic, chauvinistic.

patriótico, -a *adj.* patriotic.

patrióticamente *adv.* patriotically.

patriotismo *s.m.* patriotism.

patrístico, -a *adj.* **1** REL. patristic. || *s.f.* **2** patristics.

patrocinador, -a *adj.* **1** sponsoring. || *s.m.* y *f.* **2** sponsor, backer (de un acontecimiento cultural, deportivo, etc.).

patrocinar *v.t.* to sponsor (artes, cultura, deportes, etc.).

patrocinio *s.m.* **1** patronage, sponsorship. || **2 — de Nuestra Señora,** REL. Feast of Our Lady. **3 — de San José,** Feast of St. Joseph.

patrología *s.f.* REL. patristics.

patrón *s.m.* **1** patron (que patrocina). **2** landlord (de pensión, etc.). **3** master (amo). **4** skipper (de un barco). **5** pattern, template (plantilla). **6** ECON. standard: *patrón oro = gold standart.* **7** BOT. stock, host. **8** boss, employer (patrono).

patrona *s.f.* **1** patroness (que patrocina). **2** landlady (de pensión, etc.). **3** owner, employer (dueña).

patronal *adj.* **1** managerial, employer's, employer: *organización patronal = employer's organization.* || **2 cierre —,** lockout. **3 la —,** the employers.

patronato *s.m.* **1** patronage, sponsorship. **2** COM. employers' organization. **3** board of trustees, management board (junta). **4** trust. || **5 — real,** royal patronage.

patronazgo *s.m.* patronage.

patronímico *adj.* y *s.m.* patronymic.

patrono *s.m.* V. **patrón.**

patrulla *s.f.* **1** patrol. **2** group, band.

patrullar *v.t.* e *i.* to patrol.

patulea *s.f.* **1** mob (gentuza). **2** (fam.) bunch of kids.

patuleco, -a *adj.* bandy, bandy-legged.

paúl *adj.* y *s.m.* **1** REL. Vincentian. || *s.m.* **2** marsh, swamp (pantano).

paular *s.m.* **1** swamp, bog. **2** marshy ground.

paulatinamente *adv.* slowly, gradually.

paulatino, -a *adj.* slow, gradual: *una paulatina mejoría = a gradual improvement.*

pauperismo *s.m.* pauperism.

paupérrimo, -a *adj.* poverty-stricken.

pausa *s.f.* **1** pause. **2** interval, break. **3** MUS. rest.

pausadamente *adv.* unhurriedly, slowly, deliberated.

pausado, -a *adj.* slow, deliberate.

pauta *s.f.* **1** rule (regla). **2** writing guide (línea). **3** model, example: *esta persona nos da la pauta = this person is a model for us.*

pautado, -a *adj.* 1 ruled. || **2 papel —,** music paper.
pava *s.f.* 1 ZOOL. turkey hen. 2 (Am.) kettle. 3 (fig.) drab woman. || **4 pelar la —,** to serenade, to court, (fig.) to bill and coo.
pavada *s.f.* 1 flock of turkeys. 2 children's game. 3 (Am.) silliness (necedad).
pavana *s.f.* MUS. pavan.
pavero, -a *adj.* 1 funny, amusing. || *s.m.* y *f.* 2 turkey farmer, turkey dealer. 3 (Am.) practical joker. || *s.f.* 4 pan for cooking turkeys.
pavés *s.m.* 1 HIST. long shield. || **2 levantar a uno sobre el —,** to give someone an accolade, to appoint someone as leader.
pavesa *s.f.* 1 spark. || **2 estar hecho una —,** to be very weak.
pavía *s.f.* BOT. clingstone peach.
pávido, -a *adj.* terrified, (fig.) petrified.
pavimentación *s.f.* paving (especialmente de calles).
pavimentar *v.t.* to pave, to tile (suelos).
pavimento *s.m.* 1 flooring (solería). 2 paving (losas). 3 surfacing (firme).
pavo *adj.* 1 (fig.) wet, gormless. 2 (Am.) stupid, idiotic. || *s.m.* 2 (fam.) drip, prat. 3 ZOOL. turkey. || **4 — real,** peacock. **5 comer el —,** (fam.) to be a wallflower. **6 subírsele a uno el —,** to blush like a schoolgirl.
pavonar *v.t.* 1 TEC. to blue, to bronze. 2 (Am.) to coat with quicksilver.
pavonear *v.i.* y *pron.* to strut, to show off.
pavor *s.m.* terror, dread, horror.
pavorido, -a *adj.* terrified.
pavorosamente *adv.* frightfully, terrifyingly.
pavoroso, -a *adj.* frightful, terrifying.
paya *s.f.* (Am.) gaucho folksong improvised in competition with someone else.
payador *s.m.* (Am.) gaucho minstrel.
payaso *s.m.* 1 clown. 2 (fig.) buffoon.
payé *s.m.* 1 (Am.) sorcerer, wizard (brujo). 2 sorcery, wizardry (brujería).
payés, -esa *s.m.* y *f.* peasant farmer from Catalonia or the Balearics.
payo, -a *adj./s.m.* y *s.f.* 1 peasant. 2 rustic. 3 non-gipsy (uso gitano).
payucano, -a *s.m.* y *f.* peasant.
paz *s.f.* 1 peace. 2 peacefulness. || **3 descansar en —,** to rest in peace. **4 estar** o **quedar en —, a)** to be at peace; **b)** to be quits. **5 hacer las paces,** to make it up, to make peace. **6 — octaviana,** Octavian peace.
pazguato, -a *adj.* 1 easily impressed. 2 simple, stupid. || *s.m.* y *f.* 3 fool, nitwit.
pazo *s.m.* country seat in Galicia; manor house.
pazpuerco, -a *adj.* filthy.
pche o **pchs** *interj.* bah!
pe *s.f.* 1 name of the letter p. || **2 de — a pa,** from A to Z, from beginning to end.
peaje *s.m.* toll: *autopista de peaje = toll road.*
peana *s.f.* 1 ARQ. plinth, pedestal. 2 REL. platform. 3 window sill (alféizar). 4 piste (esgrima).
peatón *s.m.* 1 pedestrian. 2 village postman (cartero).
pebete *s.m.* 1 joss stick (incienso). 2 touch paper, fuse (mecha). 3 stench (hedor). 4 (Am.) youngster, kid (niño).
pebetero *s.m.* 1 incense burner.
peca *s.f.* freckle.
pecado *s.m.* 1 REL. sin. 2 guilt, shame (vergüenza). || **3 — capital,** mortal sin. **4 — habitual,** habitual sin. **5 — mortal,** deadly sin. **6 — nefando,** sodomy. **7 — original,** original sin. **8 — venial,** venial sin.
pecaminoso, -a *adj.* REL. sinful.
pecar *v.i.* 1 REL. to sin. 2 (fig.) to be at fault. 3 (fig.) to go astray. 4 to do wrong. || **5 — de,** to be too..., to be over...: *peca de confiado = he's too trusting.*
pecblenda o **pechblenda** *s.f.* MIN. pitchblende.
peccata minuta *s.pl.* peccadillo.
pececillo *s.m.* 1 little fish, small fry. || **2 — de plata,** silver fish.
peceño, -a *adj.* 1 fishy (olor). 2 fish-coloured.
pecera *s.f.* 1 aquarium, fishtank (normalmente rectangular). 2 fishbowl (redonda).
pecina *s.f.* slime, silt.
peciolo o **pecíolo** *s.m.* BOT. petiole.
pécora *s.f.* 1 head of sheep, etc. || **2 mala —, a)** loose woman, (fam.) slag, tart (golfa); **b)** harpy (arpía).
pecorear *v.t.* 1 to steal sheep, etc.; to rustle (cattle). || *v.i.* 2 to go on the rampage (especialmente soldados).
pecoso, -a *adj.* freckled.
peculiaridad *s.f.* peculiarity, characteristic.
peculiarmente *adv.* peculiarly, typically.
péctico, -a *adj.* pectic, pectinous.
pectina *s.f.* QUIM. pectin.
pectoral *adj.* 1 ANAT. pectoral. || *s.m.* 2 REL. pectoral cross.
pecuario, -a *adj.* livestock.
peculiar *adj.* peculiar, characteristic, typical.
peculio *s.m.* 1 HIST. peculium. 2 own personal money.
pecunia *s.f.* cash; (fam.) dough.
pechar *v.t.* 1 (Am.) to shove, to push (empujar). 2 to knock down (atropellar). 3 to pay (impuesto). 4 to take on (responsabilidad): *tienes que pechar con lo que has hecho = you have to take on responsibility for what you've done.* 5 (Am. y fam.) to touch someone for money, to scrounge.
pechera *s.f.* 1 dicky. 2 jabot. 3 shirt-front. 4 breast collar (caballo). 5 ANAT. breast, chest.
pechicatería *s.f.* (Am.) meanness, miserliness, (fam.) stinginess.
pechicato, -a *adj.* (Am.) mean, miserly, (fam.) stingy.
pechiches *s.m.pl.* (Am.) pampering, coddling.
pechichoso, -a *adj.* (Am.) finicky, prudish.
pechina *s.f.* 1 REL. pilgrim's shell. 2 ARQ. pendentive.
pecho *s.m.* 1 ANAT. chest. 2 LIT. breast. 3 bosom, breast, bust (de mujer). 4 (fig.) heart (corazón). 5 (fig.) courage (valentía). || **6 abierto de —,** open-chested. **7 a — descubierto, a)** defenceless, unarmed; **b)** openly. **8 criar a uno a los pechos,** to take someone under one's wing. **9 dar el —,** to breastfeed, to suckle. **10 estar de pechos sobre algo,** to be leaning over something. **11 echar el — al agua,** (fam.) to get stuck into something. **12 echarse uno a pechos una cosa,** to work at something. **13 meter entre — y espalda,** (fam.) to tuck away, to eat. **14 no caber a uno una cosa en el —,** (fig.) to be bursting with something: *no le cabía el orgullo en el pecho = he was bursting with pride.* **15 tomarse algo muy a —,** to take something very much to heart.
pechuga *s.f.* 1 ZOOL. breast. 2 ANAT. (hum.) breast, bosom. 3 GEOG. slope.
pechugón, -ona *adj.* 1 big-breasted, busty. 2 (Am.) cynical, (fig.) hardfaced (descarado). || *s.m.* 3 punch in the chest. 4 great effort (esfuerzo).
pedagogía *s.f.* (brit.) paedagogy, (EE.UU.) pedagogy.
pedagógicamente *adv.* pedagogically.
pedagógico, -a *adj.* pedagogic, pedagogical.
pedagogo, -a *s.m.* y *f.* pedagogue; educator.
pedal *s.m.* 1 pedal. 2 MUS. pedal.
pedáneo *adj.* **juez —,** Justice of the Peace.
pedante *adj.* 1 pedantic. || *s.m.* y *f.* 2 pedant.
pedantería *s.f.* pedantry.
pedazo *s.m.* 1 piece, bit, lump. || **2 a pedazos,** in pieces, in bits. **3 caerse a pedazos,** (fam.) to be knackered, to be dead beat. **4 — de alcornoque/de animal/de bruto,** idiot. **5 — de alma/de las entrañas,** the apple of one's eye. **6 ser un — de pan,** to be kindness itself.
pederasta *s.m.* pederast.
pedernal *s.m.* 1 MIN. silex. 2 flint (especialmente en las armas de fuego).
pedestal *s.m.* 1 pedestal. 2 plinth, base (peana). 3 basis (base). 4 podium (podio).
pedestre *adj.* 1 (fig.) pedestrian. 2 foot: *una carrera pedestre = a footrace.* 3 common, vulgar (ordinario).
pediatra *s.m.* y *f.* MED. pediatrician.
pediatría *s.f.* MED. paediatrics.
pedicuro, -a *s.m.* y *f.* chiropodist.
pedidera *s.f.* (Am.) request, demand.
pedido *s.m.* 1 COM. order. 2 tax (impuesto). 3 request, petition (petición).
pedigüeño, -a *adj.* demanding, persistent. || *s.m.* y *f.* (fig.) pest, nuisance.
pediluvio *s.m.* foot bath.
pedir *v.t.* 1 to ask for, to request. 2 to beg (mendigar). 3 to ask (precio), to price. 4 COM. to order. 5 DER. to sue, to

file a claim against. **6** (fig.) to want, to need: *esas paredes piden una moqueta verde = those walls need a green carpet.*
pedo *s.m.* **1** fart. || **2 agarrarse un —,** (Am. y fam.) to get plastered (emborracharse).
pedología *s.f.* pedology.
pedrada *s.f.* **1** stone throw. **2** hit (con una piedra). **3** (fig.) snide comment.
pedrea *s.f.* **1** fight with stones. **2** hailstorm (granizada). **3** consolation prizes in a lottery.
pedregal *s.m.* stony outcrop, rocky ground.
pedregoso, -a *adj.* stony, rocky.
pedrera *s.f.* stone quarry.
pedrería *s.f.* jewels, gemstones, precious stone.
pedrero *s.m.* **1** quarryman. **2** cannon (cañón). **3** HIST. slinger (hondero).
pedriscal *s.m.* V. **pedregal.**
pedrisco o **pedrisca** *s.m.* hailstones, hailstorm.
pedrusco *s.m.* lump of stone.
pedúnculo *s.m.* **1** BOT. peduncle, stalk. **2** BIOL. peduncle.
pega *s.f.* **1** sticking, gluing. **2** prank (travesura). **3** hoax (burla). **4** snag, problem (dificultad). **5** pitch, varnish (barniz). **6** (Am.) work, job (trabajo). **7** ZOOL. magpie. || **8 de —,** false, fake.
pegadizo, -a *adj.* **1** sticky (pegajoso). **2** scrounging (gorrón). **3** MUS. catchy, easy to remember.
pegajosidad *s.f.* stickiness, clamminess.
pegajoso, -a *adj.* **1** sticky. **2** MED. contagious, catching. **3** (fig.) smarmy, cloying (obsequioso). **4** annoying (molesto). **5** too free with one's hands (sobón).
pegamento *s.m.* glue, gum.
pegar *v.t.* **1** to stick, to glue. **2** MED. to infect with, to pass on. || **3** to hit: *no pegues al niño = don't hit the child.* || *v.pron.* **4** to be close together. **5** to match, to look right: *este cuadro no pega en esa pared = this picture doesn't look right on that wall.* || *v.i.* y *pron.* **6** to burn, to stick (quemarse). **7** to hang around, to follow (seguir). || **8 — fuego,** to set alight. **9 — un golpe,** to hit. **10 — un grito,** to yell, to cry out. **11 — un tiro,** to fire a shot. **12 — un salto,** to jump. **13 — un susto,** to frighten. **14 pegársele a uno,** to dupe someone, (fig.) to take someone for a ride.
pegatina *s.f.* sticker.
pego *s.m.* **1** trick, deception. || **2 dar el —,** (fam.) to fool, to con.
pegoste *s.m.* **1** (Am.) sticking plaster (esparadrapo). **2** scrounger (gorrón).
pegote *s.m.* **1** patch (parche). **2** plaster (esparadrapo). **3** (fam.) scrounger (gorrón). **4** bragging (jactancia): *siempre se da pegotes = he's always bragging.*
pegotear *v.i.* **1** (fam.) to scrounge, to sponge.
peinado, -a *p.p.* **1** de **peinar.** || *adj.* **2** combed, groomed. || *s.m.* **3** hair style, hairdo. || *s.f.* **4** combing.
peinador, -a *s.m.* y *s.f.* **1** hairdresser. **2** peignoir. **3** (Am.) dressing table (tocador).
peinar *v.t.* **1** to comb, to groom. **2** to brush (against) (rozar). **3** to cut (piedras, etc.). **4** (Am.) to flatter (adular). || *v.pron.* **5** to comb one's hair, to do one's hair. || **5 no — una mujer para uno,** not to be a woman for one, not to be a woman destined for one.
peine *s.m.* **1** comb. **2** card (para lana). **3** MIL. cartridge clip.
peineta *s.f.* back comb, ornamental comb.
peje *s.m.* **1** ZOOL. fish. **2** (fam.) crafty individual. || **3 — ángel,** ZOOL. angel fish. **4 — araña,** ZOOL. weever, stingfish.
pejesapo *s.m.* ZOOL. angler fish, monkfish, (EE.UU.) goosefish.
pejiguera *s.f.* *(fam.)* nuisance.
pela *s.m.* **1** (Am.) beating, thrashing (azotaina). **2** (fam.) pela (dinero español, peseta).
pelada *s.f.* (Am.) mistake.
peladilla *s.f.* **1** sugared almond (dulce). **2** pebble (guijarro).
pelado, -a *p.p.* **1** de **pelar.** || *adj.* **2** hairless, bald. **3** (fam.) broke (sin dinero). **4** bare: *el tronco del árbol está pelado = the tree trunk is bare.* **5** peeled (mondado). **6** round (cifras). **7** (fig.) bare: *le dan el sueldo pelado = he only gets the bare salary.* **8** barren: *es un terreno pelado = it's barren ground.* || *s.m.* y *f.* **9** (Am.) pauper, (fam.) nobody (pelagatos).
pelagatos *s.m.* (fam.) nobody, poor devil.
pelagianismo *s.m.* Pelagianism.
pelágico, -a *adj.* pelagic.
pelagra *s.f.* MED. pellagra.
pelaje *s.m.* **1** ZOOL. coat, fur. **2** (fig.) look, appearance. || **3 de ese —,** (fig.) of that ilk.
pelambre *s.m.* **1** ZOOL. coat, hair, fur. **2** mop of hair (melena).
pelambrera *s.f.* **1** thick hair (melena, vello).
pelandrún *adj.* **1** (Am.) idle, lazy. || *s.m.* **2** (Am.) loafer, idler.
pelandusca *s.f.* whore, slut.
pelar *v.t.* **1** to pluck (desplumar). **2** to shear (trasquilar). **3** to cut hair (cortar el pelo). **4** to peel (mondar). **5** (fig.) to fleece. **6** (fig.) to clean out: *no puedo jugar más, me has pelado = I can't play any more, you've cleaned me out.* **7** (Am.) to speak ill of, to slander (desacreditar). || *v.pron.* **8** to have a haircut. **9** to go bald (quedarse calvo). **10** (Am.) to flee, to run away (fugarse). || **11 duro de —,** (fam.) a tough nut to crack.
pelargonio *s.m.* BOT. pelargonium.
peldaño *s.m.* **1** step. **2** rung (of a ladder).
pelear *v.i.* **1** to fight, to brawl. **2** to battle. **3** to quarrel (reñir). **4** to struggle (luchar). **5** to fall out: *han peleado = they've fallen out.*
pelechar *v.i.* **1** to moult. **2** (Am.) to prosper (enriquecerse).
pelele *s.m.* **1** rag doll, puppet (muñeco). **2** rompers (de bebé). **3** (fig.) puppet, tool: *es el pelele de Alfonso Batalla = he's Alfonso Batalla's tool.*
peleón *adj.* **1** quarrelsome. **2** rough (vino). || *s.m.* **3** troublemaker. **4** (fam.) plonk (vino).
peleona *s.f.* quarrel.
peletería *s.f.* **1** furriery. **2** furrier's.
peletero, -a *s.m.* y *f.* furrier.
peliagudo, -a *adj.* **1** tricky, thorny: *es un problema peliagudo = it's a tricky problem.* **2** clever, skilful (hábil).
pelicano o **pelícano** *s.m.* ZOOL. pelican.
película *s.f.* **1** photographic film. **2** film, (EE.UU.) movie. **3** film, thin covering (lámina). **4** BOT. pellicle.
peligro *s.m.* **1** risk (riesgo). **2** danger, peril.
peligrosamente *adv.* dangerously, riskily.
peligrosidad *s.f.* riskiness.
peligroso, -a *adj.* **1** risky (arriesgado). **2** dangerous, perilous.
pelillo *s.m.* **1** slight annoyance. || **2 echar pelillos a la mar,** to let bygones be bygones.
pelirrojo, -a *adj.* red-haired, ginger.
pelma *s.m.* V. **pelmazo.**
pelmazo *s.m.* bore, nuisance.
pelo *s.m.* **1** hair. **2** (head of) hair. **3** down. **4** pile, nap (de telas). **5** flaw (en joyas). **6** trifle (bagatela). || **7 a —, a)** bareheaded; **b)** barebacked (montar). **8 a contrapelo,** (fig.) against the grain. **9 de — en pecho,** brave, tough. **10 echar pelos a la mar,** to make it up (with someone). **11 estar hasta los pelos,** (fam.) to be fed up. **12 no tener pelos en la lengua,** to speak one's mind, not to mince one's words. **13 lucirle el — a uno,** (fig.) to come unstuck. **14 — de la dehesa,** rustic manners. **15 pelos y señales,** chapter and verse, with all the details. **16 ponérsele a uno los pelos de punta,** to make someone's hair stand on end. **17 relucirle a uno el —,** to look good. **18 tomar el —,** (fig.) to pull (someone's) leg.
pelón, -ona *adj.* **1** with a crew cut (al rape). **2** bald (calvo). **3** poor (pobre). || *s.m.* **4** (fam.) baldy. || *s.f.* **5** MED. alopecia.
pelona *s.f.* (Am.) death.
pelota *s.f.* **1** ball. **2** ball game. **3** DEP. pelota. || **4 — de viento,** inflatable ball. **5 estar la — en el tejado,** the outcome to be uncertain. **6 no tocar —,** to miss the point. **7 rechazar, volver la —,** (fig.) to put the ball in the other person's court. **8 sacar uno pelotas de una alcuza,** to be clever. **9 en pelotas,** to be stark naked. **10 dejar a uno en —,** (fig.) to strip someone naked. **12 hacer la —,** to flatter, to toady.
pelotari *s.m.* DEP. pelota player.
pelotazo *s.m.* **1** blow with the ball. **2** jar, booze, drink.
pelotear *v.t.* **1** FIN. to audit, to check accounts. || *v.i.* **2** DEP. to kick a ball about. **3** to quarrel, to argue (discutir).
pelotera *s.f.* squabble, quarrel.

pelotilla *s.f.* 1 pellet. 2 (fam.) creep, toady.
pelotón *s.m.* 1 big ball. 2 MIL. platoon. 3 crowd (multitud). 4 DEP. bunch (de ciclistas).
pelotudo, -a *adj.* (Am. y fam.) slack, sloppy (negligente).
peluca *s.f.* 1 wig. 2 long hair (melenas).
peluche *s.m.* plush.
peludo *s.m.* (Am.) drunkenness: *se agarró un peludo = he got sloshed.*
peluquería *s.f.* 1 hairdresser's (salon), barber's. 2 hairdressing.
peluquero, -a *s.m.* y *s.f.* 1 hairdresser (hombres y mujeres), barber (hombres). || *s.f.* 2 hairdresser. 3 hairdresser's wife, barber's wife.
peluquín *s.m.* 1 toupée. 2 HIST. periwig, peruke. || **3 ni hablar del –,** not a word about that, mum's the word.
pelusa *s.f.* 1 down (vello). 2 fluff (lanilla). 3 petty jealousy (celos).
pelvis *s.f.* ANAT. pelvis.
pella *s.f.* 1 lump, block. 2 BOT. head of caulifower, etc. 3 MET. pig. 4 lump of lard (tocino). 5 debt (deuda). 6 theft (estafa).
pelleja *s.f.* 1 skin. 2 ZOOL. hide.
pellejería *s.f.* 1 tannery. 2 tanning (acto). 3 skins (pieles). || **4 hacer pellejerías,** (Am.) to make trouble.
pellejero *s.m.* y *s.f.* 1 tanner. 2 leather dealer.
pellejo *s.m.* 1 skin. 2 wineskin (odre). 3 drunk (borracho). || **4 dejar** o **perder el –,** to lose one's life. **5 estar en el – de otro,** (fig.) to be in somebody else's shoes. **6 mudar de –,** to change one's habits. **7 no caber en el –, a)** to be fat; **b)** to be bursting with pride. **8 salvar el –,** to save one's skin.
pellica *s.f.* fur blanket, coat.
pellico *s.m.* sheepskin jacket.
pelliza *s.f.* 1 pelisse. 2 MIL. dolman jacket.
pellizcar *v.t.* 1 to pinch. 2 to take a pinch.
pellizco *s.m.* 1 pinch. 2 (fig.) pinch, small bit.
pello *s.m.* sheepskin jacket.
pena *s.f.* 1 DER. penalty, punishment. 2 grief, sorrow (tristeza). 3 pain, distress (congoja). || *pl.* 4 hardships. || **5 a duras penas,** with great difficulty. **6 sin/ni – ni gloria:** a non event. **7 – capital,** capital punishment. **8 – de daño,** Damnation. **9 – grave,** DER. stiff sentence. **10 – leve,** DER. light sentence. **11 valer la –,** to be worth the trouble, to be worth it.
penacho *s.m.* 1 ZOOL. crest, tuft. 2 MIL. plume. 3 (fig.) arrogance, vanity.
penal *adj.* 1 penal. || *s.m.* 2 (brit.) prison, (EE.UU.) penitentiary.
penalidad *s.f.* 1 suffering, hardship. 2 DER. punishment, penalty.
penalista *s.m.* y *s.f.* DER. specialist in criminal law.
penalización *s.f.* penalty, penalization.
penalizar *v.t.* to penalize.
penalty *s.m.* DEP. penalty.
penar *v.t.* 1 to suffer (sufrir). 2 to punish (castigar). || *v.i.* 3 to die suffering. || *v.pron.* 4 to grieve, to mourn. || **5 – por algo,** to long for.
penates *s.m.pl.* HIST. penates.
penca *s.f.* 1 BOT. fleshy leaf. 2 lash (látigo). 3 (Am.) BOT. palm leaf (palmera), leaf of prickly pear (chumbera). || **4 agarrar una –,** (Am.) to get drunk.
penco *s.m.* ZOOL. (desp.) nag.
pendejo *s.m.* 1 (fam.) prat, berk. 2 ANAT. pubic hair. || **3 ser un –,** (Am.) **a)** to be clever, smart; **b)** (desp.) to be a smartarse.
pendejada *s.f.* 1 (Am.) foolishness, act of stupidity (tontería). 2 cowardice (cobardía).
pendencia *s.f.* 1 brawl, fight. 2 DER. case in progress.
pendenciero, -a *adj.* 1 quarrelsome. || *s.m.* y *f.* 2 troublemaker.
pender *v.i.* 1 to hang, to hang down (colgar). 2 to depend (depender). 3 to be pending (estar pendiente).
pendiente *adj.* 1 hanging (colgante). 2 pending, unsettled (sin resolver). || *s.m.* 3 earring. || *s.f.* 4 slope. 5 gradient. || **6 estar – de,** to hang on; to hang by: *todo está pendiente de un hilo = everything hangs by a thread.*
péndola *s.f.* 1 pendulum clock. 2 ARQ. queen post. 3 suspension cable (de un puente, etc.).
pendón *s.m.* 1 banner, standard (bandera). 2 (desp.) swine, rat. || *pl.* 3 reins. || **4 seguir el – de uno,** (fig.) enlist under someone's standard.
pendonear *v.i.* to roam the streets.
péndulo, -a *adj.* 1 hanging, hanging down. || *s.m.* 2 pendulum. || **3 – de compensación,** compound pendulum.
pene *s.m.* ANAT. penis.
penetración *s.f.* 1 penetration (física). 2 insight, intelligence (perspicacia).
penetrante *adj.* 1 penetrating, piercing (físicamente). || 2 (fig.) penetrating, keen, clear-sighted (mirada, capacidad mental, etc.).
penetrar *v.t.* 1 to penetrate, to pierce. 2 to be penetrating, to be piercing. 3 to become aware of, to grasp (comprender). || *v.i.* 4 to enter, to go in (to).
penicilina *s.f.* penicillin.
península *s.f.* GEOG. peninsula.
peninsular *adj.* 1 GEOG. peninsular. || *s.m.* y *f.* 2 inhabitant of a peninsula.
penique *s.m.* penny.
penitencia *s.f.* 1 REL. penitence (confesión). 2 penance (castigo).
penitencial *adj.* 1 penitential. || *s.m.* REL. penitential.
penitenciaría *s.f.* 1 REL. penitentiary. 2 prison (cárcel).
penitenciario, -a *adj.* 1 REL. penitentiary. 2 prison, penitentiary. || *s.m.* 3 REL. penitentiary.
penitente *adj.* REL. 1 penitent. || *s.m.* y *f.* 2 penitent.
penosamente *adv.* 1 sorrowfully, grievously, painfully (relativo al dolor). 2 laboriously, arduously (movimiento o similar).
penoso, -a *adj.* 1 arduous, laborious. 2 distressing, heart-breaking (triste).
pensado, -a *p.p.* 1 de **pensar.** || *adj.* 2 planned, prepared, devised. || **3 bien –, a)** well devised (plan, proyecto, etc.); **b)** evilminded (persona). **4 mal –, a)** badly devised (plan o similar); **b)** well-intentioned.
pensador, -ora *adj.* 1 thinking. || *s.m.* 2 philosopher. || *s.m.* y *f.* 3 thinker. 4 intellectual.
pensamiento *s.m.* 1 thought. 2 mind (mente). 3 idea. 4 BOT. pansy. || **5 beber a uno los pensamientos,** to read someone's thoughts. **6 como el –,** in a flash.
pensar *v.i.* 1 to think, to ponder. || *v.t.* 2 to think, to think about, to think over, (fig.) to weigh up. 3 to intend: *pienso ir mañana a Zamora = I'm intending to go to Zamora tomorrow.* || **4 pensándolo bien,** on reflection. **5 sin –,** without stopping to think.
pensativamente *adv.* thoughtfully, pensively.
pensativo, -a *adj.* thoughtful, pensive.
penseque *s.m.* slip, lapsus.
pensil *adj.* 1 hanging. || *s.m.* 2 beautiful garden.
pensión *s.f.* 1 FIN. pension. 2 bursary, fellowship (beca). 3 guest house, boarding house (hostal). 4 board (comida). 5 (Am.) anxiety, remorse (remordimiento).
pensionado, -a *adj.* on a pension. || *s.m.* y *f.* pensioner. || *s.m.* boarding school.
pensionista *s.m.* y *f.* 1 pensioner. 2 lodger, boarder (huésped). 3 boarding school pupil, boarder (interno). || **4 medio –,** day pupil.
pentágono, -a *adj.* 1 pentagonal. || 2 *s.m.* GEOM. pentagon. 3 MIL. Pentagon.
pentecostés *s.m.* 1 Whitsun, Whitsuntide. 2 Pentecost.
penúltimo, -a *adj.* 1 penultimate. || *s.m.* y *f.* 2 penultimate.
penumbra *s.f.* penumbra.
penuria *s.f.* penury.
peña *s.f.* 1 GEOG. crag. 2 group (de amigos). 3 DEP. supporters' club, fanclub.
peñasco *s.m.* 1 GEOG. large rock. 2 ZOOL. murex. 3 ANAT. petrosal bone.
peñón *s.m.* rock, large crag.
peón *s.m.* 1 unskilled worker. 2 MIL. foot soldier, infantryman. 3 pawn (ajedrez). 4 (spinning) top (peonza). 5 LIT. foot of four syllables.
peonada *s.f.* 1 day's labour (jornada). 2 land measure of about three thousand square metres.
peonaje *s.m.* 1 gang of labourers. 2 MIL. squad of infantrymen.
peonía *s.f.* 1 V. **peonada.** 2 BOT. peony.
peonza *s.f.* 1 (spinning) top. 2 (fam.) little fidget (persona).
peor *adj.* 1 (*comp.*) worse; (*super.*) worst. || *adv.* 2 (*comp.*) worse; (*super.*) worst. || **3 tanto –,** so much the worse.

Pepa *s.f.* 1 Josie. || 2 **¡Viva la –!**, (hum.) **a)** hooray!; **b)** (fam.) and to hell with everybody else!
pepazo *s.m.* (Am.) lie, (fam.) whopper (mentira).
pepe *s.m.* (Am.) drunkenness.
pepinillo *s.m.* 1 BOT. gherkin. 2 MIL. shell.
pepino *s.m.* 1 BOT. cucumber. 2 (Am.) carnival figure. || 3 **importar un –**, not to care two hoots. 4 **no dársele a uno un – por una cosa**, not to give a fig for something.
pepita *s.f.* 1 BOT. seed, pip. 2 MIN. nugget. 3 pip (enfermedad de gallinas).
pepitoria *s.f.* 1 GAST. fricassée. 2 jumble, tangle (desorden).
pepona *s.f.* large cardboard doll.
pepónide *s.f.* BOT. pepo.
pepsina *s.f.* BIOL. pepsin.
péptico, -a *adj.* BIOL. peptic.
peptona *s.f.* BIOL. peptone.
pequeñez *s.f.* 1 littleness, smallness. 2 triviality, insignificance (insignificancia). 3 meanness (mezquindad). 4 infancy (niñez).
pequeño, -a *adj.* 1 small (chico). 2 young (joven). 3 unimportant (poco importante). 3 short (breve). 4 humble (humilde).
pequinés, -esa *adj.* ZOOL. 1 Pekinese (tipo de perro). || *s.m.* y *s.f.* 2 Pekinese.
pera *s.f.* 1 pear. || *adj.* 2 vain, conceited. || *s.m.* 3 (fam.) bighead. || 4 **partir peras con uno,** to be extremely friendly with someone. 5 **pedir peras al olmo,** to ask for the moon. 6 **poner a uno las peras a cuarto,** to clamp down on someone, to make someone toe the line.
peral *s.m.* BOT. pear tree.
peralte *s.m.* 1 ARQ. superelevation. 2 embankment, bank.
perborato *s.m.* QUIM. 1 perborate. || 2 **– sódico,** sodium perborate.
perca *s.f.* ZOOL. perch (tipo de pez).
percal *s.m.* 1 percale, calico. 2 (fam.) dough (dinero).
percance *s.m.* setback, mishap: *fue un percance desafortunado = it was an unfortunate setback.*
percatar *v.i.* y *pron.* to realise, to notice: *no me percaté de que nos seguían = I didn't realize that we were being followed.*
percebe *s.m.* ZOOL. goose barnacle.
percepción *s.f.* 1 perception. 2 feeling (sensación). 3 idea. 4 receipt (recibo).
perceptible *adj.* noticeable, perceptible, visible.
perceptiblemente *adv.* noticeably, perceptibly, visibly.
perceptividad *s.f.* perceptivity.
perceptor, -a *s.m.* y *f.* collector, receiver (de una ayuda económica, nómina o tema similar monetario).
percibir *v.t.* 1 to receive, to collect (recibir). 2 to perceive, to sense (sentir). 3 to notice (conocer).
percusio, -a *adj.* (Am.) insignificant, trivial.
percusión *s.f.* percussion.
percusor *s.m.* 1 TEC. hammer, firing pin. 2 striker, hitter.
percutir *v.t.* to strike, to hit.
percutor *s.m.* V. **percusor.**
percha *s.f.* 1 hanger, coat hanger. 2 hatstand, clothes rack (mueble). 3 carding (lana). 4 perch (pájaros). 5 rack (para la caza). || 6 **tener uno buena –**, to have a good figure, to have a fine physique.
perchero *s.m.* 1 clothes rack, hatstand. 2 coat hanger (percha).
percherón *s.m.* ZOOL. percheron (tipo de caballo).
perdedor, -a *adj.* 1 losing: *el equipo perdedor = the losing team.* || *s.m.* y *f.* 2 loser.
perder *v.t.* 1 to lose. 2 to waste (malgastar). 3 to miss: *perdió el tren = he missed the train.* 4 to ruin (arruinar). 5 to spoil, to damage (estropear). || *v.i.* 6 to lose. 7 to fade, to discolour (desteñirse). || *v.pron.* 8 to lose one's way, to go astray. 9 to go to rack and ruin (arruinarse). 10 to founder (irse a pique). 11 (fig.) to be crazy (about). 12 to get lost (despistarse).
perdición *s.f.* undoing (especialmente en sentido moral o religioso).
pérdida *s.f.* 1 loss. 2 waste (desperdicio). 3 wastage, leakage (goteo).
perdidamente *adv.* passionately, hopelessly (manera de estar enamorado).
perdido, -a *adj.* 1 stray. 2 lost. 3 (Am.) vicious, hardened (vicioso). || *s.m.* y *s.f.* 4 wastrel, libertine. 5 (Am. y brit.) tramp, (EE.UU.) bum, hobo (vagabundo). || 6 **estar –, a)** to be in a desperate plight; **b)** to be filthy.
perdigón *s.m.* 1 ZOOL. young partridge (perdiz). 2 (lead) shot, pellet.
perdiguero, -a *adj.* 1 partridge-hunting. || *s.m.* 2 ZOOL. setter (perro).
perdiz *s.f.* ZOOL. partridge.
perdón *s.m.* 1 DER. pardon. 2 forgiveness. 3 mercy (indulto). || 4 **con –**, if you don't mind.
perdonable *adj.* forgivable.
perdonar *v.t.* 1 to forgive. 2 DER. to pardon. 3 to excuse (disculpar). || 4 **no – esfuerzo** o **ocasión,** not to miss an opportunity, to spare no effort.
perdonavidas *s.m.* bully, braggart.
perdulario, -a *adj.* 1 negligent, slovenly (negligente). 2 dissolute. 3 forgetful, careless (olvidadizo). || *s.m.* y *f.* 4 slovenly person. 5 rake (perdis). 6 absent-minded individual (despistado).
perdurable *adj.* lasting.
perdurablemente *adv.* lastingly.
perdurar *v.i.* to last a long time, to endure: *han perdurado muchas costumbres = many customs have lasted a long time.*
perecedero, -a *adj.* perishable (productos).
perecer *v.i.* to perish, to die.
peregrinación *s.f.* pilgrimage.
peregrinamente *adv.* oddly, strangely.
peregrinar *v.i.* 1 REL. to go on a pilgrimage. 2 to travel far afield.
peregrino, -a *adj.* 1 REL. of pilgimage. 2 wandering, travelling (errante). 3 odd, outlandish (extraño): *una idea peregrina = an outlandish idea.* 4 outstanding (excelente).
perejil *s.m.* BOT. parsley.
perendengue *s.m.* trinket, cheap earring.
perengano, -a *s.m.* y *f.* so-and-so.
perenne *adj.* perennial, everlasting.
perennemente *adv.* everlastingly, constantly.
perennifolio, -a *adj.* evergreen.
perentoriamente *adv.* peremptorily.
perentorio, -a *adj.* 1 peremptory. 2 urgent, pressing (apremiante): *un asunto perentorio = an urgent matter.*
pereza *s.f.* 1 laziness. 2 idleness. 3 sloth. || 4 **sacudir la –**, to shake off one's laziness.
perezosamente *adv.* lazily, idly.
perezoso, -a *adj.* 1 lazy, sluggish, slothful. || *s.m.* 2 ZOOL. sloth.
perfección *s.f.* 1 perfection. || 2 **a la –**, to perfection.
perfeccionador, -ora *adj.* perfecting.
perfeccionamiento *s.m.* improvement (de una persona, obra, institución, etc.).
perfeccionar *v.t.* 1 to perfect, to improve. 2 to complete (terminar).
perfeccionista *s.m.* y *f.* perfectionist.
perfectible *adj.* perfectible.
perfectivo, -a *adj.* 1 perfective. 2 GRAM. perfective.
perfecto, -a *adj.* 1 perfect. 2 finished, complete. 3 GRAM. perfect.
pérfidamente *adv.* perfidiously, treacherously.
perfidia *s.f.* perfidy, treachery.
pérfido, -a *adj.* perfidious, treacherous.
perfil *s.m.* 1 profile. 2 edging (franja). 3 outline, silhouette (contorno). || *pl.* 4 finishing touches. || 5 **de –**, in profile, side on.
perfilado, -a *adj.* 1 in profile (de lado). 2 outlined. 3 thin faced (en el rostro).
perfilar *v.t.* 1 to profile. 2 (fig.) to round off, to put the finishing touches to (rematar). || *v.pron.* 3 to titivate (acicalarse). 4 to turn sideways, to show one's profile. 5 to take shape, to look likely: *se perfilaba como el ganador pero tuvo que abandonar la competición = he was looking a likely winner but he had to drop out of the competition.* 6 (Am.) to slim (adelgazar).
perforación *s.f.* perforation.
perforador, -a o **perforante** *adj.* piercing.
perforar *v.t.* to perforate, to pierce, to drill.
perfumador, -a *adj.* 1 perfuming, *s.m.* y *f.* 2 perfumer. || *s.m.* 3 perfume jar, incense burner.
perfume *s.m.* 1 perfume, scent. 2 fragrance.
perfumería *s.f.* 1 perfumery (tienda). 2 perfumery (arte).
pergamino *s.m.* 1 parchment. || 2 **en –**, bound in parchment.
pergeñar *v.t.* 1 (fig.) to knock together, to fix up. 2 to rough out, to sketch out (esbozar).

pergeño o **pergenio** *s.m.* appearance, look.
pérgola *s.f.* 1 pergola (emparrado). 2 roof garden.
perica *s.f.* (Am. y fam.) drunkenness: *agarró una perica = he got drunk.*
pericia *s.f.* expertise, skill.
pericial *adj.* expert.
pericialmente *adv.* expertly.
periclitar *v.i.* 1 to be in danger. 2 to decline, to decay (caducar).
perico *s.m.* 1 ZOOL. parakeet. 2 chamber pot (orinal). 3 (Am.) compliment (piropo). 4 (Am. y fam.) windbag (charlatán). || 5 **— de los palotes,** (fam.) any Tom, Dick or Harry. 6 **— entre ellas,** lady's man.
pericón *s.m.* (Am.) popular Argentinian dance.
periferia *s.f.* 1 periphery. 2 contour (contorno). 3 outskirts (afueras).
periférico, -a *adj.* 1 peripheral, marginal (de temática distinta). 2 on the outskirts (físicamente separado del centro de la ciudad). || *s.m.pl.* 3 INF. peripherals.
perifollo *s.m.* 1 BOT. chervil. 2 frills, fripperies.
perífrasis o **perífrasi** *s.f.* GRAM. periphrasis.
perifrástico, -a *adj.* periphrastic.
perigeo *s.m.* ASTR. perigee.
perihelio *s.m.* ASTR. perihelion.
perilla *s.f.* 1 pear-shaped ornament (adorno). 2 goatee beard, Vandyke (barba). || 3 **de perillas,** to a tee, perfectly: *eso me viene de perillas = that suits me to a tee.*
perillán, -ana *s.m.* o *s.f.* rascal.
perímetro *s.m.* GEOM. perimeter.
perindola *s.f.* V. **perinola.**
perineo *s.m.* ANAT. perineum.
perinola *s.f.* teetotum.
periódicamente *adv.* periodically.
periodicidad *s.f.* frequency, periodicity, recurrence.
periódico *adj.* 1 periodic, periodical. 2 MAT. recurring. || *s.m.* 3 newspaper. || 4 **sistema —,** QUIM. periodic system.
periodismo *s.m.* journalism.
periodista *s.m.* y *f.* 1 journalist, pressman. 2 newspaper publisher.
periodístico, -a *adj.* journalistic.
período o **periodo** *s.m.* 1 period (tiempo). 2 MED. period. 3 MAT. period. 4 GRAM. sentence.
periostio *s.m.* ANAT. periosteum.
peripatético, -a *adj.* 1 FIL. Aristotelian. 2 ridiculous (de opiniones). || *s.m.* y *f.* 2 FIL. Aristotelian.
peripecia *s.f.* 1 vicissitude, incident. 2 twist in the plot of a story.
periplo *s.m.* 1 circumnavigation. 2 HIST. periplus. 3 long tour or voyage.
peripuesto, -a *adj.* dandified, spruced up.
periquete *s.m.* 1 (fam.) jiffy. || 2 **en un —,** in a jiffy.
periquito *s.m.* ZOOL. parakeet.
periscopio *s.m.* periscope.
peristáltico, -a *adj.* FISIOL. peristaltic.
peritación *s.f.* 1 expert opinion. 2 expert's report (informe). 3 specialist's fee (honorario).
peritaje *s.m.* specialist professional training.
perito, -a *adj.* 1 expert, specialist. || 2 *s.m.* y *f.* expert, specialist. 3 technical qualification (título).
peritoneo *s.m.* ANAT. peritoneum.
peritonitis *s.f.* MED. peritonitis.
perjudicar *v.t.* to harm, to damage: *no quise perjudicarte = I didn't want to harm you.*
perjudicial *adj.* harmful, damaging, detrimental.
perjudicialmente *adv.* harmfully, damagingly, detrimentally.
perjuicio *s.m.* 1 harm, damage (daño). 2 wrong (agravio). || 3 **sin — de,** even though, without prejudice to.
perjurar *v.i.* y *pron.* 1 DER. to perjure oneself, to commit perjury. || *v.i.* 2 to curse, to swear.
perjurio *s.m.* DER. perjury.
perjuro, -a *s.m.* y *f.* perjurer (especialmente en un contexto judicial).
perla *s.f.* 1 pearl. 2 (fig.) pearl. || 3 **venir de perlas,** to suit down to the ground.
perlesía *s.f.* MED. 1 paralysis. 2 palsy.
perlongar *v.i.* MAR. to sail inshore, to coast (barcos).
permanecer *v.i.* to stay, to remain.
permanencia *s.f.* 1 permanence. 2 stay (estancia). 3 payment for teachers' administrative duties.
permanente *adj.* 1 permanent. || *s.f.* 2 permanent wave, perm (estilo de pelo).
permanentemente *adv.* permanently, constantly.
permanganato *s.m.* 1 QUIM. permanganate. || 2 **— potásico,** potassium permanganate.
permeabilidad *s.f.* permeability.
permeable *adj.* 1 permeable. 2 pervious, impressionable (persona).
permisible *adj.* permissible.
permisión *s.f.* 1 permission. 2 MIL. leave.
permisivo, -a *adj.* permissive (en asuntos morales).
permiso *s.m.* 1 permission. 2 MIL. leave. 3 licence (carnet).
permitir *v.t.* 1 to permit, to allow. 2 to tolerate. 3 to turn a blind eye (hacer la vista gorda). || *v.r.* 4 to be allowed. 5 to be tolerated.
permuta *s.f.* exchange (especialmente referido a dos puestos de trabajo).
permutar *v.t.* 1 to exchange. 2 to switch (empleos). 3 to swap (trocar).
pernada *s.f.* 1 kick. || 2 **derecho de —,** HIST. droit de seigneur, ius primae noctis.
pernera *s.f.* trouser leg.
perniciosamente *adv.* harmfully, perniciously.
pernicioso, -a *adj.* pernicious (normalmente en temas de salud).
pernil *s.m.* 1 ham, haunch. 2 trouser leg.
pernio *s.m.* hinge.
perno *s.m.* MEC. bolt.
pernoctar *v.i.* to spend the night, to stay overnight.
pero *conj.* 1 but: *quiero comer pero no hay nada = I want to eat but there's nothing.* || *s.m.* 2 problem, fault, objection. 3 (Am.) pear tree (peral).
perogrullada *s.f.* platitude.
perogrullesco, -a *adj.* platitudinous, trite.
perol *s.m.* 1 pot. 2 (Am.) tack, stud (tachuela). 3 (Am.) cauldron (caldera). 4 (Am.) frying pan (sartén).
perola *s.f.* large pot.
peroné *s.m.* ANAT. fibula.
perorar *v.i.* 1 to give a speech. 2 (hum.) to spout.
perorata *s.f.* long-winded speech.
peróxido *s.m.* QUIM. peroxide.
perpendicular *adj.* 1 perpendicular. 2 at right angles. || *s.f.* 3 perpendicular, vertical.
perpendicularmente *adv.* perpendicularly.
perpetrar *v.t.* to perpetrate.
perpetuación *s.f.* perpetuation.
perpetuamente *adv.* perpetually, everlastingly.
perpetuar *v.t.* perpetuate.
perpetuidad *s.f.* 1 perpetuity. || 2 **a —,** for ever. 3 **condena a —,** DER. life sentence.
perpetuo, -a *adj.* 1 perpetual, everlasting. 2 for life. || 3 *s.f.* BOT. everlasting, immortelle. || 4 **cadena —,** DER. life sentence.
perplejidad *s.f.* 1 perplexity, bafflement. 2 confusion, dilemma.
perra *s.f.* 1 ZOOL. bitch. 2 tantrum (rabieta). 3 small coin (moneda). 4 drunkenness (borrachera). || *pl.* 5 perras, (fig.) dough (dinero).
perrada *s.f.* 1 pack of dogs (perros). 2 dirty trick (mala pasada).
perrera *s.f.* 1 kennel. 2 dog's home, dog pound.
perrería *s.f.* 1 pack of dogs (perrada). 2 dirty trick (mala pasada).
perrero *s.m.* 1 dog-catcher. 2 dog lover (aficionado).
perro, -a *adj.* 1 vile, dreadful. 2 (fam.) lousy, rotten. || *s.m.* y *f.* 3 ZOOL. dog. || 4 **atar los perros con longaniza,** to be extravagant. 5 **como perros y gatos,** like cat and dog. 6 **morir como un —,** to die forgotten. 7 **— alano,** mastiff. 8 **— dogo,** bulldog. 9 **— galgo,** greyhound. 10 **— mastín,** mastiff. 11 **— marino,** dogfish. 12 **— setter,** setter.
persa *adj.* 1 Persian. || *s.m.* y *s.f.* 2 Persian.
persecución *s.f.* chase, hunt (tras algo o alguien).
perseguir *v.t.* 1 to pursue (seguir). 2 to chase (cazar). 3 to strive after (luchar por). 4 to persecute, to hound (acosar): *no me persigas así = don't hound me.*
perseverancia *s.f.* perseverance.
perseverante *adj.* persevering.
perseverantemente *adv.* perseveringly.
perseverar *v.i.* 1 to persevere. 2 to persist.

persiano, -a *adj.* 1 Persian. || *s.f.* venetian blind.
pérsico, -a *adj.* 1 Persian: *el golfo pérsico = the Persian Gulf.* || *s.m.* 2 peach tree. 3 peach (fruta).
persignarse *v.r.* to cross oneself.
persistencia *s.f.* persistence.
persistente *ajd.* persistent.
persistentemente *adv.* persistently.
persistir *v.i.* to persist.
persona *s.f.* 1 person. || **2 de — a —,** person to person, face to face. **3 en —,** in person, personally: *este asunto lo resolveré en persona = I'll sort this matter out personally.* **4 tercera —, a)** third party; **b)** GRAM. third person.
personaje *s.m.* 1 personage (importante). 2 character.
personal *adj.* 1 personal. || *s.m.* 2 personnel, staff.
personalmente *adv.* personally, in person.
personalidad *s.f.* 1 personality. 2 DER. legal status, legal entity.
personalizar *v.t.* 1 personalise. 2 GRAM. to make personal.
personarse *v.r.* 1 to appear in person. 2 to report (to) (acudir). 3 DER. to appear.
personificación *s.f.* personification, embodiment: *la personificación del mal = the embodiment of evil.*
personificar *v.t.* 1 to personify, to embody. 2 to allude to (en un discurso).
perspectiva *s.f.* 1 ART. perspective. 2 point of view (punto de vista). 3 ART. view. || *pl.* 4 prospects. || **5 — aérea,** aerial view. **6 — lineal,** linear perspective.
perspicacia *s.f.* sagacity, shrewdness.
perspicaz *adj.* 1 keen-sighted, sharp-eyed. 2 (fig.) shrewd, perceptive.
perspicuo, -a *adj.* 1 clear (claro). 2 perspicuous (inteligible).
persuadir *v.t.* 1 to persuade. || *v.pron.* 2 to become convinced.
persuasión *s.f.* 1 persuasion (acto concreto). 2 conviction (de ideas).
persuasivo, -a *adj.* persuasive, convincing.
pertenecer *v.i.* to belong.
perteneciente *adj.* 1 member (de una organización o similar). 2 pertaining, belonging: *perteneciente al consejo económico = belonging to the economic council.*
pertenencia *s.f.* 1 ownership. 2 possession, estate (propiedad). 3 outbuilding (dependencia).
pértiga *s.f.* pole.
pertinaz *adj.* 1 pertinacious, obstinate (terco). 2 persistent: *lluvia pertinaz = persistent rain.*
pertinencia *s.f.* pertinence, relevance (de un tema, asunto, punto, etc.).
pertinente *adj.* 1 pertinent. 2 relevant, opportune.
pertinentemente *adv.* appropiately.
pertrechar *v.t.* to equip (normalmente con sentido militar).
pertrechos *s.m.pl.* 1 MIL. stores, munitions. 2 equipment, tackle, gear (equipo).
perturbación *s.f.* 1 disturbance (del orden público, disciplina, etc.). 2 PSIQ. mental disorder.
perturbado, -a *p.p.* 1 de **turbar.** || *adj.* 2 PSIQ. mentally unbalanced.
perturbador, -a *adj.* 1 disturbing, upsetting (noticia o similar). || *s.m.* y *f.* 2 disturber (del orden establecido, organización, etc.).
perturbar *v.t.* 1 to disturb (alterar). 2 to upset, to unsettle (trastornar). 3 MED. to perturb.
pertuza *s.f.* rabble, riffraff.
peruétano, -a *adj.* annoying, tedious.
perulero, -a *adj./s.m.* y *f.* HIST. emigrant returned from Peru having made his fortune.
perversamente *adv.* perversely.
perversidad *s.f.* perversity, wickedness.
perversión *s.f.* perversion; corruption.
perverso, -a *adj.* perverse.
pervertido, -a *p.p.* 1 de **pervertir.** || *adj.* 2 perverted. || *s.m.* y *f.* 3 pervert (normalmente con sentido sexual).
pervertir *v.t.* 1 to pervert. 2 to corrupt (corromper). 3 to distort (texto).
pervivencia *s.f.* 1 survival (salvaguarda de la vida). 2 persistence (de un fenómeno, costumbre, etc.).
pervivir *v.i.* 1 to survive. 2 to subsist.
pesa *s.f.* 1 weight. 2 DEP. shot. || *pl.* 3 DEP. barbell, dumbell.
pesacartas *s.m.* 1 letter-weighing scales. 2 fine balance.
pesadamente *adv.* 1 heavily (físicamente). 2 slowly, moving with difficulty. 3 boringly (sin interés o atractivo).
pesadez *s.f.* 1 heaviness. 2 obstinacy, (fam.) pigheadedness (terquedad). 3 (fig.) bind, tedium (faena). 4 sluggishness (pereza).
pesadilla *s.f.* 1 nightmare. 2 bugbear (obsesión).
pesado, -a *adj.* 1 heavy. 2 overweight (obeso). 3 tedious, annoying (molesto). 4 sluggish, slow (lento). 5 deep (sueño). 6 sultry, muggy (tiempo). || *s.f.* 7 weighing.
pesadumbre *s.f.* 1 bother, irritation (molestia). 2 sorrow, grief (tristeza). 3 displeasure, disagreement (disgusto).
pésame *s.m.* 1 condolences. 2 expression of sympathy. || **3 dar el —,** to express one's condolences.
pesar *v.i.* 1 to weigh, to be heavy. 2 (fig.) to carry weight. 3 to cause distress, to cause regret (acongojar). || *v.t.* 4 to weigh. 5 to weigh up. || *s.m.* 6 sorrow, grief (tristeza). 7 regret (arrepentimiento). || **8 a — de,** in spite of, despite.
pesaroso, -a *adj.* sad, sorrowful; regretful.
pesca *s.f.* 1 fishing, angling (acto) 2 catch (peces). || **3 — de altura,** deep-sea fishing. **4 — de bajura,** inshore fishing.
pescadería *s.f.* fish shop.
pescadero, -a *s.m.* y *f.* fishmonger.
pescadilla *s.f.* ZOOL. whiting.
pescado *s.m.* 1 fish. || **2 ahumársele a uno el —,** to make someone angry, to make someone see red.
pescante *s.m.* 1 coachman's seat, driver's seat. 2 hoist (tramoya).
pescar *v.t.* 1 to fish. 2 to catch (coger). 3 (fig.) to land: *ha pescado un puesto en Sevilla = he's landed a job in Seville.* 4 to catch out.
pescocear *v.t.* 1 (Am.) to grab by the scruff of the neck. 2 to slap (abofetear).
pescozón *s.m.* smack round the neck.
pescuezo *s.m.* 1 ZOOL. neck. 2 ANAT. scruff of the neck.
pesebre *s.m.* 1 manger, crib. 2 stall (cuadra).
pesebrera *s.f.* (Am.) Nativity scene, crib.
peseta *s.f.* peseta.
pesetero, -a *adj.* 1 (fam.) money-grubbing (avaro). 2 (fam.) penny-pinching (tacaño). 3 (Am.) scrounging, sponging (gorrón).
pésimamente *adv.* wretchedly, hopelessly, very badly.
pesimista *adj.* 1 pessimistic. || *s.m.* y *f.* 2 pessimist.
pesimismo *s.m.* pessimism.
pésimo, -a *adj.* very bad, dreadful.
peso *s.m.* 1 FIS. gravity. 2 weight. 3 weightiness. 4 scales (balanza). 5 (Am.) peso (moneda). || **6 — atómico,** atomic weight. **7 — bruto,** gross weight. **8 — corrido,** slightly over the weight. **9 — específico,** specific weight. **10 — gallo,** DEP. bantamweight. **11 — ligero,** DEP. lightweight. **12 — molecular,** molecular weight. **13 — neto,** net weight. **14 — pesado,** DEP. heavyweight. **15 caerse una cosa por su propio —,** to be obvious. **16 tomar una cosa a —,** to weigh something up.
pespuntar *v.t.* to backstitch.
pespunte *s.m.* backstitch.
pesquero, -a *adj.* 1 fishing.
pesquis *s.m.* insight, (fam.) nous.
pesquisa *s.f.* inquiry.
pestaña *s.f.* 1 ANAT. eyelash. 2 ANAT. fringe. 3 edging (franja). 4 MEC. flange.
pestañear *v.i.* 1 to blink, to wink. 2 to flutter one's eyelashes. 3 to show signs of life. || **4 sin —, a)** without batting an eyelid; **b)** without turning a hair.
peste *s.f.* 1 MED. plague. 2 stench (hedor). 3 pestilence, evil (mal). 4 plague (de ratas, etc.). || 5 *pl.* curses, threats.
pestífero, -a *adj.* 1 pestiferous. 2 foul-smelling (hediondo).
pestilencia *s.f.* 1 pestilence, plague. 2 stench, reek (hediondez).
pestilente *adj.* stinking, foul.
pestillo *s.m.* 1 bolt (ventana, puerta, etc.). 2 latch.
pestiño *s.m.* honey-coated pancake.
pesuña *s.f.* V. **pezuña.**
pesuño *s.m.* ZOOL. digit (of a cloven hoof).
petaca *s.f.* 1 tobacco pouch. 2 cigarette case (pitillera). 3 (Am.) leather chest, suitcase.

petacón, -a *adj.* chubby, tubby.
pétalo *s.m.* BOT. petal.
petanca *s.f.* boules, French bowls.
petardo *s.m.* 1 firecracker, squib. 2 (fig.) bore (pesado). 3 (fam.) ugly old bag (mujer fea). 4 swindle, fraud (timo). 5 MIL. petard. || 6 **pegar un –,** to defraud, (fam.) to rip off.
petate *s.m.* 1 bedroll. 2 (Am.) palm matting (para dormir). 3 (fam.) runt, poor devil. || 4 **liar el –, a)** to pack up and go (marcharse); **b)** (fam.) to turn up one's toes (morir).
petenera *s.f.* 1 Andalusian popular song. || 2 **salir por peteneras,** to go off at a tangent, to come up with a stupid remark.
petición *s.f.* 1 request, demand. 2 petition, plea (favor). 3 DER. plea. || 4 **– de principio,** begging the question.
peticionario, -a *s.m.* y *f.* petitioner; applicant.
petimetre *s.m.* dandy, fop, (EE.UU.) dude.
petirrojo *s.m.* ZOOL. robin, redbreast.
petiso, -a *adj.* (Am.) short, stumpy. || *s.m.* small horse, pony.
petitorio, -a *adj.* 1 petitionary. 2 **mesa –,** stall (en cuestaciones benéficas). || *s.m.* y *s.f.* 3 petitionary. || *s.m.* 4 medicine catalogue. || *s.f.* 5 request, plea.
peto *s.m.* 1 bib, bodice. 2 MIL. breastplate. 3 peen (de herramienta).
petrel *s.m.* petrel.
pétreo, -a *adj.* 1 stone, of stone. 2 stony, rocky.
petrificación *s.f.* GEOL. petrification.
petrificar *v.t.* 1 to petrify. 2 (fig.) to turn to stone, (fig.) to root to the spot. || *v.r.* 3 to petrify, to become petrified.
petrodólar *s.m.* petrodollar.
petrogénesis *s.f.* GEOL. petrogenesis.
petrografía *s.f.* GEOL. petrography.
petrolear *v.t.* to spray with oil.
petróleo *s.m.* QUIM. 1 oil, petroleum. 2 (Am.) paraffin.
petrolero, -a *adj.* 1 petroleum: *intereses petroleros = petroleum interests.* || *s.m.* y *f.* 2 MAR. oil tanker, petrol tanker.
petrolífero, -a *adj.* oil-bearing (roca, zona, mar, etc.).
petrología *s.f.* petrology.
petroquímica *s.f.* petrochemistry.
petulancia *s.f.* 1 insolence, effrontery. 2 arrogance, vanity, smugness.
petulante *adj.* vain.
petulantemente *adv.* vainly.
petunia *s.f.* BOT. petunia.
peyorativo, -a *adj.* pejorative, deprecatory.
pez *s.m.* 1 fish. 2 ASTR. Piscis Austrinus. || *s.f.* 3 pitch, tar. || 4 **estar uno – en una materia,** to be a dunce at something. 5 **estar uno como el – en el agua,** to be in one's element, (fig.) to be at home.
pezón *s.m.* 1 BOT. stem, stalk. 2 ANAT. nipple. 3 knob, extremity.
pezuña *s.f.* ZOOL. hoof.
pi *s.f.* 1 pi (letra griega). 2 MAT. pi.
piadosamente *adv.* 1 piously, devoutly (especialmente en asuntos religiosos). 2 (fig.) kind-heartedly, compassionately (que es objeto de compasión).
piadoso, -a *adj.* 1 pious, devout (pío). 2 pitiful. 3 compassionate, sympathetic (compasivo).
piafar *v.i.* ZOOL. to paw the ground.
piamáter *s.f.* ANAT. pia mater.
pianista *s.m.* y *f.* MUS. pianist, piano player.
piano *s.m.* 1 MUS. piano. || *adv.* 2 piano.
pianola *s.f.* pianola.
piar *v.i.* 1 ZOOL. to chirp, to cheep. 2 (fig.) to cry for, to be longing for.
piara *s.f.* herd.
piastra *s.f.* piastre.
pibe, -a *s.m.* y *s.f.* (Am.) child, (fam.) kid.
pibería *s.f.* (Am.) crowd of youngsters, (fam.) bunch of kids.
pica *s.f.* 1 MIL. pike. 2 goad, lance (garrocha). 3 measurement of depth equal to just over two fathoms. 4 ZOOL. magpie. 5 (Am.) pique, resentment. || 6 **poner una – en Flandes,** (fig.) to pull off something difficult.
picacera *s.f.* (Am.) pique, resentment.
picacho *s.m.* GEOG. peak.
picadero *s.m.* 1 riding school. 2 ring for taming wild horses.
picadillo *s.m.* 1 minced meat, mincemeat. 2 saussage meat.
picado, -a *adj.* 1 minced. 2 pitted, perforated. 3 sour (vino). 4 piqued. 5 (Am.) tipsy. || *s.m.* 6 AER. nosedive. 7 mince. 8 MUS. pizzicato. || *s.f.* 9 ZOOL. peck, pecking. 10 bite, sting (picadura). 11 MED. decayed, bad: *tengo una muela picada = I've got a bad tooth.*
picador *s.m.* 1 picador. 2 horse breaker, horse trainer. 3 MIN. face worker.
picadura *s.f.* 1 (insect) bite, sting. 2 prick (pinchazo). 3 cut tobacco. 4 MED. tooth decay, caries.
picaflor *s.m.* (Am.) ZOOL. hummingbird.
picajoso, -a *adj.* touchy, testy.
picamaderos *s.m.* ZOOL. woodpecker.
picanear *v.t.* (Am.) to spur on, to goad, to provoke (provocar).
picante *adj.* 1 spicy, peppery, hot: *la comida está picante = the food is hot.* 2 saucy, risqué, racy, piquant: *suele decir cosas picantes = he comes out with some risqué remarks.* || *s.m.* 3 hot taste, piquancy.
picapedrero *s.m.* quarryman, stonecutter.
picapica *s.f.* itching powder.
picapleitos *s.m.* 1 litigious individual. 2 (desp.) lawyer. 3 (fam.) charlatan.
picaporte *s.m.* 1 doorknocker (aldaba). 2 latch (pestillo). 3 latchkey (llave). 4 door handle, window catch (manivela).
picar *v.t.* 1 to peck (de un ave). 2 to bite, to sting (de un insecto). 3 to prick (pinchar). 4 to mince. 5 to peck at, to nibble. 6 to punch (billetes). 7 to chip at (con pico). 8 to goad, to lance (a un toro). 9 to spur, to dig one's spurs in (caballo). || *v.t.* y *v.i.* 10 to bite, to take the bait: *hoy los peces están picando = today the fish are biting.* 11 MED. to itch. 12 to nibble (comida). || *v.i.* 13 (fig.) to be caught out, to take the bait. 14 to burn: *el sol pica mucho en agosto = the sun burns in August.* || *v.r.* 15 to go off, to turn sour (vino). 16 to get choppy (el mar): *cuando se pica el mar, yo me mareo en seguida = when the sea gets choppy, I get seasick.* 17 to take offence (ofenderse). || 18 **– uno muy alto,** (fig.) to aim high.
picardía *s.f.* 1 naughtiness, mischief (travesura). 2 villainy (maldad). 3 craftiness (astucia). 4 dirty trick (mala pasada). || *s.pl.* 5 insults, naughty things. || *s.m.pl.* 6 baby-doll nightie.
picaresco, -a *adj.* 1 roguish. 2 LIT. picaresque. || *s.f.* 3 LIT. picaresque. 4 picaresque way of life.
pícaro, -a *adj.* 1 villainous, sly, naughty. || *s.m.* y *s.f.* 2 rogue, villain. 3 scamp, tyke (pilluelo). 4 anti-hero of picaresque novels.
picatoste *s.m.* fried bread.
picaza *s.f.* ZOOL. magpie.
picazón *s.f.* 1 MED. itch (comezón), stinging sensation (ardor). 2 discomfort (molestia). 3 irritation, pique (disgusto).
pick-up *s.m.* record player.
picnic *s.m.* picnic.
pícnico, -a *adj.* squat.
pico *s.f.* 1 ZOOL. beak, bill. 2 point, corner: *el pico del pañuelo = the corner of the handkerchief.* 3 pick (herramienta). 4 GEOG. peak. 5 (hum.) mouth, (fam.) gob, trap. || 6 **y –, a)** and a bit, just after: *son las nueve y pico = it's just after nine o'clock;* **b)** odd: *vinieron cincuenta y pico personas = fifty-odd people came.* 7 **– de oro,** (fig.) gift of the gab. 8 **hincar el –,** (fam.) to snuff it. 9 **perderse por el –,** (fam.) to shoot one's mouth off. 10 **tener mucho –,** (fam.) to be a bigmouth.
picón, -ona *adj.* 1 with protruding front teeth, (fam.) buck-toothed. || *s.m.* 2 small coal (carbón). 3 kidding (broma). 4 ZOOL. stickleback.
picor *s.m.* 1 MED. itch, itchiness, prickling. 2 hot taste, burning sensation. 3 MED. rash.
picoreto, -a *adj.* (Am.) talkative, gossipy.
picota *s.f.* 1 HIST. pike, pikestaff (for displaying the heads of criminals). 2 HIST. pillory. 3 ARQ. spire, point. 4 GEOG. peak. || 5 **poner en la –,** (fig.) to pillory, to expose to public ridicule.
picotazo *s.m.* 1 peck (de un ave). 2 bite, sting (de un insecto, etc.).
picotear *v.t.* 1 to peck, to peck at. 2 (fam.) to gossip, to prattle (parlotear).
picotijera *s.m.* ZOOL. shearwater, skimmer.
picotón *s.m.* 1 (Am.) peck (de un ave). 2 bite, sting (de un insecto, etc.).
pícrico *adj.* QUIM. picric.
pictografía *s.f.* 1 pictography. 2 pictograph.

pictográfico, -a *adj.* pictographic.
pictórico, -a *adj.* pictorial.
picudo, -a *adj.* 1 pointed (puntiagudo). 2 long-nosed, long-billed (aves). 3 with a spout, with a lip (para verter).
picharse *v.r.* (Am.) 1 to be scared, to flinch (acobardarse). 2 to die, to snuff it (morirse).
piche *s.m.* (Am.) fear, cowardice.
pichel *s.m.* tankard, jug.
pichicata *s.f.* (Am.) hard drugs.
pichicatero, -a *adj.* (Am.) 1 drug-taking, drug-dealing. || *s.m.* y *f.* 2 drug-pusher (camello), junkie (drogadicto).
pichicato, -a *adj.* (Am.) mean (mezquino), (fig.) tight-fisted.
pichincha *s.f.* (Am.) bargain.
picholear *v.i.* (Am. y fam.) to screw, to bonk (fornicar).
pichón, -a *adj.* 1 (fam.) darling. 2 (Am.) unwary, gullible (incauto). 3 (Am.) inexperienced (inexperto). || *s.m.* 2 ZOOL. young pigeon.
pichonear *v.t.* (Am.) to dupe, (fam.) to con (engañar).
pichuncho *s.m.* (Am.) drink made from hard liquor and vermouth.
pie *s.m.* 1 ANAT. foot. 2 ZOOL. foot, paw. 3 base, stand (peana). 4 pretext. 5 MAT. foot. 6 LIT. foot. 7 foot, bottom (página). 8 caption (título). 9 (Am.) down payment. || **10 a cuatro pies,** on all fours. **11 al —, a)** at the foot; **b)** beside. **12 al — de la letra,** literally, word for word. **13 a —,** on foot. **14 de — o de pies** o **en —,** standing, upright. **15 a — enjuto,** running no risks. **16 a — firme,** steadfastly. **17 a — juntillas,** (fig.) firmly, absolutely. **18 asentar el —,** to proceed with caution. **19 buscar uno tres pies al gato,** to quibble, to make life unnecessarily difficult. **20 caer de pies,** (fig.) to fall on one's feet. **21 con pies de plomo,** carefully. **22 dar —,** to give cause, to give a pretext. **23 en — de guerra,** on a war footing. **24 meter el —,** to gain a foothold. **25 no caber de pies,** to scarcely have room to breathe. **26 no dar — con bola,** to do nothing right. **27 perder el —, a)** to be out of one's depth; **b)** to slip. **28 — de imprenta,** publisher's imprint. **29 — forzado,** LIT. forced rhyme. **30 — quebrado,** LIT. verse which is a mixture of short and long lines. **31 sacar los pies del plato,** to overstep the mark. **32 volver pies atrás,** to turn back, to retract.
piedad *s.f.* 1 REL. piety, piousness. 2 filial respect (respeto). 3 pity (compasión). 3 ART. Pietà.
piedemonte *s.m.* GEOL. piedmont deposit.
piedra *s.f.* 1 stone, flint. 2 MED. stone. 3 large hailstone (granizo). 4 millstone (de molino). || **5 hasta las — (lo saben, etc.),** the whole world (knows, etc.). **6 no dejar — por mover,** (fig.) to leave no stone unturned. **7 — angular,** cornerstone. **8 — de escándalo,** source of scandal. **9 — de toque,** touchstone. **10 — filosofal,** philosopher's stone. **11 — preciosa,** precious stone. **12 — imán,** lodestone. **13 — pómez,** pumice stone. **14 señalar con — blanca,** to be a red letter day. **15 — miliaria** o **miliar,** milestone.
piel *s.f.* 1 ANAT. skin. 2 leather, skin. 3 BOT. peel, skin. || **4 dar uno la —, a)** (fig.) to give one's right arm (for); **b)** to die (for). **5 — de Rusia,** Russian leather. **6 — roja,** redskin. **7 ser uno de la — del diablo,** (fig.) to be a little devil, to be an imp.
piélago *s.m.* 1 LIT. sea, deep. 2 high seas. 3 (fig.) sea, abundance.
pielitis *s.f.* MED. pyelitis.
pienso *s.m.* fodder, feed.
pierna *s.f.* 1 ANAT. leg. 2 ZOOL. haunch, drumstick (de un ave). 3 downstroke (de letra). || **4 dormir a — suelta,** to sleep like a top, to sleep like a baby.
pietismo *s.m.* REL. pietism.
pieza *s.f.* 1 piece, part. 2 item (artículo). 3 piece, roll (de tela). 4 room (habitación). 5 coin (moneda). 6 specimen (de caza). 7 LIT. play, piece of music. 8 patch, repair (remiendo). || **9 quedarse de una —,** to be taken aback, to be dumbfounded.
piezoelectricidad *s.f.* FIS. piezoelectricity.
piezómetro *s.m.* FIS. piezometer.
pífano *s.m.* 1 fife. 2 fife player.
pifia *s.f.* 1 (fam.) bloomer (error). 2 (Am.) mockery.
pifiar *v.t.* 1 DEP. to miscue. 2 (fig.) to botch, to mess up (estropear). 3 (Am.) to fail (fracasar).
pigmentación *s.f.* pigmentation.
pigmentar *v.t.* to pigment.
pigmento *s.m.* pigment.
pigmeo, -a *adj.* 1 pygmy. || *s.m.* y *s.f.* 2 pygmy.
pijama *s.m.* (brit.) pyjamas, (EE.UU.) pajamas.
pijotero, -a *adj.* 1 stingy, mean (mezquino). 2 tiresome, irritating (latoso).
pila *s.f.* 1 basin, sink. 2 ELEC. battery. 3 pile, heap. 4 ARQ. pile, bridge support. || **5 — bautismal,** REL. font. **6 — atómica,** FIS. atomic pile. **7 sacar de —,** to be a godparent.
pilar *s.m.* 1 pillar. 2 pier, pilaster (pilastra). 3 milestone (mojón).
pilastra *s.f.* ARQ. pilaster.
pilatuna *s.f.* (Am.) dirty trick.
pilcate *s.m.* (Am.) youngster, little boy.
píldora *s.f.* 1 pill. 2 (fig.) bad news, bitter pill. || **3 dorar la —,** to sweeten the pill. **4 tragarse uno la —,** (fig.) to fall for it.
pileta *s.f.* 1 small basin. 2 stoup (para agua bendita). 3 kitchen sink (fregadero). 4 (Am.) pond, swimming pool (piscina).
pilón *s.m.* 1 basin (de una fuente). 2 mortar (mortero). 3 sugarloaf. 4 steelyard weight (romana). 5 counterpoise (de un molino). 6 (Am.) tip (propina).
pilongo, -a *adj.* 1 baptised in the same font. 2 thin, scrawny (flacucho). 3 dried (disecado). || *s.f.* 4 dried chestnut.
píloro *s.m.* ANAT. pylorus.
piloso, -a *adj.* BIOL. pilose.
pilotaje *s.m.* 1 pilotage, piloting. 2 pilotage (derechos).
pilotar *v.t.* 1 to pilot: *está pilotando un avión = he's piloting a plane.* 2 to steer: *está pilotando un barco = he's steering a ship.* 3 to drive: *está pilotando un coche de carreras = he's driving a racing car.*
pilote *s.m.* ARQ. pile, stake.
pilotear *v.t.* (Am.) to help.
piloto *s.m.* 1 pilot (de un avión). 2 pilot, helm (de un barco). 3 first mate (de un barco), navigator. 4 driver (de un coche). || **5 — de altura,** high-sea pilot.
piltra *s.f.* (argot) bed, pit, sack.
piltrafa *s.f.* 1 gristly meat (carne). 2 rag, tatter (harapo). || *pl.* 3 scraps, remnants (restos): *sólo han quedado piltrafas = there are only scraps left.*
pillaje *s.m.* 1 plunder. 2 pillage, looting.
pillar *v.t.* 1 to catch (atrapar), (fam.) to grab. 2 MIL. to plunder, to loot. 3 to catch out (sorprender). 4 to knock down, to run over: *le pilló un coche = a car ran over him.* || **5 pillarle a uno de camino,** to be on one's way. **6 pillarle a uno lejos,** to be out of one's way.
pillastre *s.m.* scoundrel, rogue.
pillería *s.f.* (fam.) prank.
pillo, -a *adj.* 1 rascally, roguish, impish (niño). 2 sly, crafty (taimado). || *s.m.* 3 rogue, scoundrel, scamp (niño). 4 villain.
pimentero *s.m.* 1 BOT. pepper plant. 2 pepper pot.
pimentón *s.m.* paprika.
pimienta *s.f.* 1 pepper. || **2 comer uno —,** to get angry, (fam.) to get worked up.
pimiento *s.m.* 1 BOT. pimiento plant. 2 pimiento, green pepper, red pepper.
pimpinela *s.f.* BOT. pimpernel.
pimplar *v.t.* 1 to tipple. || *v.pron.* 2 (fam.) to booze.
pimpollo *s.m.* y *f.* 1 BOT. shoot. 2 BOT. rosebud. 3 good-looking child, pretty young woman.
pinacoteca *s.f.* art gallery, picture gallery.
pináculo *s.m.* 1 ARQ. spire, top. 2 (fig.) pinnacle, acme. 3 GEOG. pinnacle.
pinar *s.m.* pinewood.
pincel *s.m.* paintbrush.
pincelada *s.f.* 1 ART. brushstroke. 2 (fig.) broad outline. || **3 dar la última —,** to give the finishing touch.
pincelar *v.t.* 1 to paint. 2 to portray.
pinchadiscos *s.m.* y *f.* disc jockey.
pinchar *v.t.* 1 to prick. 2 to puncture, to pierce (perforar). 3 to annoy, to tease (incordiar). 4 TEC. (fam.) to bug. 5 (fam.) to give (someone) a jab. || **6 no — ni cortar,** (fam.) to cut no ice, to carry no weight.
pinchazo *s.m.* 1 puncture (en una rueda). 2 prick, jab (de una aguja o similar).
pinche *s.m.* kitchen-boy.
pincho *s.m.* 1 point (punta). 2 snack. || **3 — moruno,** GAST. shish kebab.
pindonga *s.f.* gadabout (mujer).
pineal *adj.* 1 ANAT. pineal. 2 BOT. pineal.

pinga *s.f.* pole (slung across the shoulders for carrying things).
pingajo *s.m.* tatter, rag.
pingar *v.i.* **1** to ooze, to drip (gotear). **2** to leap about, to jump (brincar). **3** to hang down (colgar).
pingo *s.m.* **1** tatter, rag. **2** shabby dress. **3** (Am.) horse.
ping-pong *s.m.* DEP. ping-pong, table tennis.
pingüe *adj.* **1** fat, greasy, fatty. **2** (fig.) abundant, juicy, fat: *pingües beneficios = fat profits.*
pingüino *s.m.* ZOOL. penguin.
pinito *s.m.* **1** child's first step. || **2 hacer pinitos, a)** to toddle; **b)** (fig.) to be just getting going (una empresa, etc.).
pino *s.m.* **1** BOT. pine, pine tree. || **2 — albar,** Scots pine. **3 — carrasco,** Aleppo pine. **4 — negral,** larch, Corsican pine. **5 — piñonero,** umbrella pine, stone pine. **6 — rodeno,** cluster pine. **7 — tea,** pitch pine. **8 ser un — de oro,** to look handsome/beautiful. **9 hacer el —,** to stand on one's head.
pinocha *s.f.* BOT. pine needle.
pinrel *s.m.* foot, (fam.) trotter.
pinta *s.f.* **1** ZOOL. mark, marking, spot. **2** GEOL. mark. **2** polka dot (lunar). **3** look, appearance (aspecto). **4** pint (medida). || **5 ser uno un —,** to be a scoundrel.
pintado, -a *p.p.* **1** de **pintar.** || *adj.* **2** colourful, multi-coloured, dappled. || *s.f.* **3** ZOOL. Guinea fowl. **4** painted slogan, graffito. || **5 el más —,** the slickest, the cleverest. **6 venir como —** o **que ni —,** to suit perfectly, to suit down to the ground.
pintamonas *s.m.* dauber.
pintar *v.t.* **1** to paint. **2** to depict, to portray (retratar). **3** (fig.) to describe. **4** (fam.) to be important, to carry weight: *yo no pinto nada aquí = I'm not important here.* || **5 — bien** o **mal una cosa,** something to turn out well or badly. **6 pintarla,** to put on airs. **7 pintarse uno solo para hacer una cosa,** (fam.) to be a dab hand at doing something.
pintarrajar o **pintarrajear** *v.t.* **1** to daub, to bedaub.
pintear *v.i.* to drizzle, to spit with rain.
pintiparado, -a *adj.* **1** identical. **2** just right.
pinto, -a *adj.* pinto, dappled.
pintor, -a *s.m.* y *s.f.* **1** painter, artist. || **2 — de brocha gorda,** painter and decorator.
pintoresco, -a *adj.* picturesque, colourful.
pintura *s.f.* **1** ART. painting. **2** picture, paintig (cuadro). **3** paint (material). **4** (fig.) portrayal, description. || **5 — al fresco,** fresco. **6 — al óleo,** oil painting. **7 — al pastel,** pastel. **8 — al temple,** tempera.
pinturero, -a *adj.* **1** conceited, flashy, showily dressed. || *s.m.* y *f.* **2** dandy, flashy dresser, show-off.
pinza *s.f.* **1** TEC. pincers. **2** tweezers (bruselas). **3** tongs (tenazas). **4** clothes peg. **5** MED. forceps. **6** ZOOL. claw, pincer.
pinzón *s.m.* ZOOL. finch, chaffinch.
piña *s.f.* **1** BOT. pine cone (de pino). **2** BOT. pineapple (ananás). **3** cluster, group (grupo). **4** (Am.) punch, (fam.) thump (bofetada).
piñata *s.f.* **1** container of sweets suspended from the ceiling and smashed with sticks by blindfold revellers. **2** masked ball, masquerade. **3** (Am.) brawl (pelea).
piñón *s.m.* **1** BOT. pine seed. **2** pine nut. **3** MEC. pinion, sprocket.
pío, -a *adj.* **1** REL. pious. **2** charitable. **3** piebald (de varios colores). || *s.m.* **4** ZOOL. chirping, cheeping. || **5 no decir ni —,** not to say a word, (fam.) not to say boo to a goose.
piocha *s.f.* pickaxe.
piojillo *s.m.* bird louse.
piojo *s.m.* **1** louse. || **2 — resucitado,** (fam.) upstart.
piojoso, -a *adj.* **1** lice-ridden, lousy. **2** stingy (mezquino), (fig.) tight-fisted.
piola *s.f.* twine.
piolet *s.m.* ice axe.
piolín *s.m.* (Am.) cord, twine.
pionero, -a *s.m.* y *s.f.* pioneer.
piorrea *s.f.* MED. (brit.) pyorrhoea, (EE.UU.) pyorrhea.
pipa *s.f.* **1** pipe (para fumar). **2** cask (tonel). **3** BOT. pip, seed (de girasol). **4** (Am. y fam.) belly (barriga).
pipe *s.m.* (Am.) friendly form of address.
pipermín *s.m.* peppermint, creme de menthe (licor).
pipeta *s.f.* pipette.
pipiolo, -a *s.m.* y *f.* **1** novice (novato). **2** newcomer (recién llegado). **3** (Am.) youngster, little boy (chiquillo); young girl (chiquilla). **4** (Am.) gullible type (inocente).
pipón, -ona *adj.* **1** (Am.) potbellied, paunchy. || *s.m.* **2** (Am.) belly, gut.
pique *s.m.* **1** pique, resentment (resentimiento). **2** grudge (rencor). **3** rivalry (rivalidad). || **4 irse a —, a)** to founder, to sink (hundirse); **b)** to fail (fracasar).
piqué *s.m.* piqué.
piqueta *s.f.* pickaxe.
piquetazo *s.m.* **1** (Am.) peck (de un ave). **2** (Am.) bite, sting (de un insecto, etc.).
piquete *s.m.* **1** MIL. squad. **2** fence post (jalón). **3** small hole (agujero). **4** MIL. picket, detail. || **5 — de autodefensa,** steward at demonstrations. **6 — de huelga,** strike picket.
pira *s.f.* **1** pyre. **2** bonfire (fogata). || **3 irse de —,** to play truant, to cut class.
piragua *s.f.* **1** pirogue. **2** canoe.
piragüista *s.m.* y *f.* canoeist.
pirámide *s.f.* pyramid.
piraña *s.f.* ZOOL. piranha.
pirarse *v.pron.* **1** to run away (fugarse). **2** to clear off, to leave (marcharse).
pirata *s.m.* **1** pirate. **2** (fig.) brute, hard-hearted person.
piratería *s.f.* piracy.
piratona *s.f.* (Am.) arbitrariness.
pirca *s.f.* (Am.) dry-stone wall.
pirenaico, -a *adj.* GEOG. Pyrenean.
pirético, -a *adj.* MED. pyretic.
pirexia *s.f.* MED. pyrexia.
pírico, -a *adj.* pertaining to fire or fireworks.
pirindola *s.f.* spinning top.
pirita *s.f.* **1** MIN. pyrites. || **2 — arsenical** o **cobriza,** arsenical or copper pyrites. **3 — magnética,** magnetic pyrites.
pirograbado *s.m.* **1** pyrogravure. **2** pyrography.
pirolusita *s.f.* MIN. pyrolusite.
piromancia o **piromancía** *s.f.* pyromancy.
pirómano, -a *adj.* **1** pyromaniacal, fireraising. || *s.m.* y *s.f.* **2** pyromaniac, arsonist.
piropo *s.m.* **1** garnet (joya). **2** flattering remark, compliment (cumplido).
pirotecnia *s.f.* pyrotechnics.
pirotécnico, -a *adj.* pyrotechnic; fireworks.
piroxeno o **piroxena** *s.m.* o *f.* pyroxene.
pirrarse *v.r.* to be crazy about, (fam.) to be potty about.
pirriquio *s.m.* LIT. pyrrhic.
pirueta *s.f.* pirouette.
pirulí *s.m.* lollipop.
pisada *s.f.* **1** footprint (huella). **2** footstep (paso). **3** footfall (sonido).
pisapapeles *s.m.* paperweight.
pisar *v.t.* **1** to tread on, to stand on, to step on. **2** to tread (apretar con el pie). **3** MUS. to pluck (cuerdas), to strike (teclas). **4** (fig.) to trample (pisotear). **5** to disregard (infringir). **6** (fig.) to get in first, to beat someone to something. || **8 no — en un sitio,** not to set foot in the place. **9 — huevos** o **andar pisando huevos,** to tread carefully. **10 — los talones,** to be on someone's heels. **11 — el terreno de otro,** to beat someone to it.
pisaverde *s.m.* dandy, (EE.UU.) dude.
piscicultura *s.f.* fish farming.
piscicultor, -ora *s.m.* y *f.* expert in fishbreeding.
piscifactoría *s.f.* fish farm, fish hatchery.
pisciforme *adj.* pisciform, fish-shaped.
piscina *s.f.* **1** DEP. swimming pool. **2** fishpond, fishtank (estanque).
Piscis *s.m.* ASTR. Pisces.
pisco, -a *adj.* **1** (Am.) conceited, (fam.) cocky. || *s.m.* **2** pisco brandy.
piscolabis *s.m.* light snack.
piso *s.m.* **1** ground, flooring (suelo). **2** sole (suela). **3** GEOL. layer, stratum. **4** floor, storey (planta). **5** flat (apartamento).
pisón *s.m.* **1** ram, beetle (herramienta). **2** (Am.) stamp on the foot (pisotón).
pisotón *s.m.* stamp (en el suelo o en el pie de una persona).
pista *s.f.* **1** trail, track (huella). **2** DEP. track, course; court (cancha). **3** runway, airstrip (de aterrizaje). **4** clue (indicio). **5** (Am. y fam.) dough (dinero). || **6 seguir la —,** to track, to follow the trail.
pistilo *s.m.* BOT. pistil.
pisto *s.m.* **1** gravy (jugo). **2** dish of fried vegetables. **3** hotchpotch (mezcla). **4** (Am.) elegance, style (garbo). **5** (Am. y

fam.) dough (dinero). || **6 darse —,** to give oneself airs, (fam.) to show off.
pistola *s.f.* 1 pistol (arma). 2 TEC. spray gun.
pistolera *s.f.* holster.
pistolero *s.m.* gunman, gangster.
pistoletazo *s.m.* 1 pistol shot, gun shot. || **2 — de salida,** DEP. starting signal.
pistón *s.m.* 1 piston (émbolo). 2 percussion cap (de un arma). 3 MUS. valve. 4 (Am.) corn tortilla. 5 (Am.) MUS. cornet.
pistonudo, -a *adj.* (fam.) terrific, great: *es un tipo pistonudo = he's a terrific fellow.*
pita *s.f.* 1 BOT. agave. 2 pita fibre. 3 hissing, booing.
pitagórico, -a *adj.* 1 Pythagorean. || *s.m.* y *f.* 2 Pythagorean. || **3 tabla —,** MAT. Pythagorean table.
pitanza *s.f.* 1 daily ration. 2 dole (para los pobres). 3 daily bread. 4 price (precio).
pitar *v.i.* 1 to whistle, to blow a whistle. 2 (fam.) to go well (funcionar). 3 (Am.) to smoke (fumar). || **4 salir pitando,** to zoom off.
pitecantropo o **pitecántropo** *s.m.* ZOOL. pithecanthropus.
pitera *s.f.* 1 BOT. agave plant. 2 hole (ropa).
pitido *s.m.* whistling, whistle (sonido del pito), hooting.
pitillera *s.f.* 1 cigarette case (petaca). 2 cigarette maker.
pitillo *s.m.* cigarette, (brit. y fam.) fag.
pitiminí *s.m.* BOT. fairy rose bush.
pito *s.m.* 1 whistle (silbato). 2 cigarette, (brit. y fam.) fag (cigarrillo). 3 (Am.) pipe (pipa). 4 (Am.) kind of sweet. || **5 cuando pitos, flautas,** when it's not one thing, it's another. **6 entre pitos y flautas,** what with one thing and another. **7 no darse un — de una cosa,** not to care two hoots about something. **8 no valer un — una cosa,** not to be worth a light. **9 por pitos o por flautas,** for one reason or another. **10 — real,** ZOOL. woodpecker.
pitón *s.m.* 1 ZOOL. python. 2 ZOOL. budding horn. 3 spout (de botijo, etc.). 4 marble (canica).
pitonisa *s.f.* 1 pythoness (sacerdotisa de Apolo). 2 sorceress (hechicera).
pitorrearse *v.r.* to make fun (of), (fam.) to take the mickey (out of).
pitorreo *s.m.* teasing; mockery, jeering.
pitorro *s.m.* spout (de un botijo).
pitpit *s.m.* ZOOL. pitpit.
pituita *s.f.* FISIOL. phlegm (flema), mucus (moco).
pituitario, -a *adj.* 1 ANAT. pituitary.
pituso, -a *adj.* 1 cute, tiny. || *s.m.* y *f.* 2 tot.
piular *v.i.* to chirp, to cheep, to chirrup.
pivote *s.m.* 1 TEC. pivot. 2 DEP. pivot.
pizarra *s.f.* 1 GEOL. slate. 2 blackboard (encerado).
pizarrín *s.m.* slate pencil.
pizca *s.f.* 1 pinch: *una pizca de sal = a pinch of salt.* 2 (fig.) spot, jot, scrap: *no tiene pizca de verdad = there's not a scrap of truth in it.* 3 the least bit: *no me hace ni pizca de gracia = I'm not in the least bit amused.*
pizcar *v.t.* 1 to pinch, to tweak. 2 to take a pinch.
pizpireta *s.f.* (fam.) bright spark, (fam.) bundle of fun.
placa *s.f.* 1 badge (insignia). 2 plate (lámina). 3 plaque (conmemorativa). 4 numberplate (matrícula). 5 plate (fotográfica).
placable *adj.* placable.
pláceme *s.m.* 1 congratulations, felicitations. || **2 dar el —,** to congratulate.
placenta *s.f.* 1 ANAT. placenta. 2 BOT. placenta.
placenteramente *adv.* with pleasure, joyfully.
placentero, -a *adj.* pleasing, agreeable.
placer *v.t.* 1 to please. || *s.m.* 2 pleasure (gusto). 3 contentment (del ánimo). 4 enjoyment (diversión). 5 pleasure, will (voluntad). 6 GEOL. placer. 7 sandbank. 8 (Am.) oyster bed (ostras perleras). || **9 a —,** at one's pleasure, as one likes.
plácet *s.m.* 1 approval. 2 placet (del gobierno).
plácidamente *adv.* placidly.
plácido, -a *adj.* 1 placid, tranquil. 2 pleasing (grato): *una tarde plácida = a pleasing afternoon.*
plafón *s.m.* ARQ. soffit.
plaga *s.f.* 1 MED. plague. 2 AGR. pest, blight. 3 (fig.) scourge.
plagado, -a *adj.* 1 full, crawling. || **2 — de,** crawling with, infested with.
plagiar *v.t.* to plagiarise.
plagio *s.m.* copying.
plan *s.m.* 1 plan (proyecto). 2 (Am.) GEOG. plateau.
planctón *s.m.* plankton.
plancha *s.f.* 1 sheet, plate (lámina). 2 iron (útil). 3 ironing (acto). 4 blunder (equivocación). 5 DEP. horizontal dive. 6 TEC. plate.
planchado, -a *p.p.* 1 de **planchar.** || *adj.* 2 ironed (ropa). 3 speechless (sin saber qué decir).
planchar *v.t.* 1 to iron. || *v.i.* 2 to iron, to do the ironing.
planchazo *s.m.* blunder, gaffe.
planeador *s.m.* glider.
planeadora *s.f.* 1 V. **acepilladora.** 2 MAR. fast boat (con varios fuerabordas).
planear *v.t.* 1 to draw a plan (trazar). 2 to plan (forjar planes). || *v.i.* 3 AER. to glide.
planeo *s.m.* gliding.
planeta *s.m.* planet: *los planetas giran alrededor del sol = the planets revolve around the sun.*
planetario *s.m.* planetarium.
planicie *s.f.* 1 GEOG. plain. 2 level ground (terreno nivelado).
planificación *s.f.* planning.
planificador, -a *adj.* 1 planning, well-organized. || *s.m.* y *f.* 2 planner.
planificar *v.t.* to plan.
planimetría *s.f.* 1 survey. 2 surveying, planimetry (arte de medir).
planisferio *s.m.* GEOM. planisphere.
plano, -a *adj.* 1 flat, level (llano), smooth (liso). || *s.m.* 2 MAT. plane. 3 (fig.) plane: *habla en un plano más elevado = he talks on a higher plane.* 4 plan (mapa). || *s.f.* 5 float (de albañil). 6 page (hoja). || **7 cerrar la plana,** to bring (something) to an end. **8 de —,** outright: *lo rechacé de plano = I rejected it outright.* **9 en primer —,** in the foreground. **10 plana mayor,** MIL. staff. **11 — coordenado,** coordinate. **12 — de nivel,** datum level. **13 — inclinado,** inclined plane.
planta *s.f.* 1 ANAT. sole of the foot. 2 ARQ. ground plan. 3 ARQ. floor, storey. 4 BOT. plant. || **5 — baja,** ground floor. **6 tener buena —,** to look good, to be attractive.
plantación *s.f.* AGR. plantation (de cultivo).
plantar *v.t.* 1 AGR. to plant (plantas o terreno). 2 to put in (poste). 3 to pitch (tienda). 4 to throw out: *lo plantaron en la calle = they threw him (out) into the street.* 5 to finish with, to leave (someone) stranded: *los que eran mis amigos me han plantado = my friends have left me stranded.* || *v.r.* 6 to stand firm, (fam.) to dig one's heels in (mantenerse en sus trece). 7 to reach, to turn up: *se plantó en Zamora en menos de dos horas = he reached Zamora in less than two hours.* 8 to plant oneself: *el matón se plantó delante de la puerta = the gangster planted himself in front of the door.* || *adj.* 9 ANAT. plantar: *sufría de verrugas plantares = he suffered from plantar warts.*
plante *s.m.* 1 stoppage, strike (huelga). 2 stand (postura). 3 expression of defiance (desafío).
planteamiento *s.m.* 1 outlining (de problema, asunto, etc.). 2 approach (enfoque).
plantear *v.t.* 1 to plan, to set out (planificar). 2 to establish, to set up (establecer). 3 to pose, to raise: *esto plantea una serie de problemas = this raises a number of problems.*
plantel *s.m.* 1 nursery, seedbed (criadero). 2 (fig.) nursery, training centre. 3 DEP. squad.
plantificar *v.t.* 1 to establish, to institute. || *v.r.* 2 to install oneself, to plant oneself: *la chica se plantó en el salón sin más ni más = the girl planted herself in the living-room without any more ado.*
plantígrado, -a *adj.* 1 ZOOL. plantigrade. || *s.m.* y *f.* 2 plantigrade.
plantilla *s.f.* 1 insole (zapato), sole (calcetín). 2 TEC. model, pattern, template. 3 staff, payroll (nómina). 4 DEP. squad, team.
plantío, -a *adj.* 1 cultivable, cultivated. || *s.m.* 2 planting (acción). 3 plot, patch, field (campo sembrado).
plantón *s.m.* 1 guard, watchman (vigilante). 2 MIL. sentry (centinela). 3 MIL. soldier punished with extra guard duty (castigo). 4 tedious wait (espera). 5 BOT.

seedling. **6** (Am.) MIL. standing facing a wall (castigo).

plañidero, -a *adj.* **1** plaintive, mournful. || *s.f.* **2** paid mourner.

plañido *s.m.* wail, lament.

plañir *v.i.* (p.u.) to wail, to lament, to moan.

plaqueta *s.f.* **1** BIOL. blood platelet. **2** ceramic tile (azulejo).

plasma *s.m.* **1** BIOL. plasma (sangre). **2** BIOL. protoplasm.

plasmar *v.t.* **1** to shape, to give form to (formar). **2** to mould (moldear).

plasta *s.f.* lump, soft mass.

plaste *s.m.* size, sizing.

plasticidad *s.f.* plasticity.

plástico, -a *adj.* **1** plastic. **2** ductile (dúctil). **3** evocative, expressive (expresivo). || *s.m.* **4** plastic. || *s.f.* **5** plastic art.

plata *s.f.* **1** QUIM. silver. **2** (Am. y fam.) money. || **3 como la —,** clean as a whistle. **4 hablar en —,** to speak frankly, to put it buntly.

plataforma *s.f.* **1** platform, stage (tablado). **2** open goods wagon, (EE.UU.) flatcar (ferrocarril). **3** platform (de autobús, etc.). **4** POL. (fig.) platform. || **5 — continental,** GEOL. continental shelf.

platanal o **platanar** *s.m.* AGR. banana plantation.

plátano *s.m.* BOT. **1** banana tree (árbol). **2** banana (fruta). **3** plane tree.

platea *s.f.* orchestra stalls (teatro).

plateado, -a *p.p.* **1** de **platear.** || *adj.* **2** silvery-plated, silvery.

platear *v.t.* **1** to silver. **2** TEC. to silver-plate.

plateresco, -a *adj.* ARQ. plateresque.

platería *s.f.* silverware shop.

platero, -a *s.m.* y *s.f.* **1** silversmith (orfebre). **2** jeweller (joyero).

plática *s.f.* **1** chat, talk (conversación). **2** REL. sermon.

platicar *v.i.* (Am.) to talk, to chat.

platija *s.f.* ZOOL. plaice (tipo de pez).

platillo *s.m.* **1** saucer (de taza). **2** MUS. cymbal. **3** kitty (juegos de naipes). || **4 — volante,** flying saucer.

platina *s.f.* **1** stage, slide (de microscopio). **2** deck (tocadiscos). **3** platen (impresora). **4** QUIM. platinum.

platino *s.m.* MIN. platinum.

plato *s.m.* **1** plate (vasija plana). **2** dish, course (comida). **3** (fig.) daily fare. || **4 comer en un mismo —,** to be very close friends, (fam.) to be as thick as thieves. **5 nada entre dos platos,** a storm in a teacup, a lot of fuss about nothing. **6 él no ha roto un — nunca,** (fig.) butter wouldn't melt in his mouth. **7 — compuesto,** mixed dish. **8 — sopero,** soup dish.

plató *s.m.* film set.

platónicamente *adv.* platonically.

platónico, -a *adj.* FIL. **1** Platonic. || *s.m.* y *f.* **2** Platonist.

platudo, -a *adj.* (Am.) wealthy, (fam.) loaded (adinerado).

plausibilidad *s.f.* plausibility.

plausible *adj.* **1** praiseworthy, laudable (loable). **2** plausible, acceptable (admisible).

plausiblemente *adv.* plausibly.

playa *s.f.* **1** beach (orilla). **2** seaside, seaside resort (punto de veraneo).

playero, -a *adj.* **1** beach. || *s.f.pl.* **2** popular Andalusian songs. **3** beech shoes, sandals (calzado).

plaza *s.f.* **1** square, town square. **2** market place (mercado). **3** MIL. stronghold (fuerte). **4** post, position (empleo). **5** open space (espacio). **6** COM. town, centre. **7** seat. || **8 — de toros,** bullring. **9 sentar —, a)** MIL. to join up, to enlist; **b)** (fig.) to be successful. **10 sacar —,** to fill a post, to get a job.

plazo *s.m.* **1** period (tiempo). **2** time limit, expiry date (vencimiento). **3** instalment: *estoy pagándolo a plazos = I'm paying for it in instalments.* || **4 a largo —,** COM. **a)** long-term (préstamo); **b)** long-dated (valores). **5 a corto —,** COM. **a)** short-term (préstamo); **b)** short-dated (valores).

plazoleta *s.f.* small square.

plazuela *s.f.* small square.

pleamar *s.f.* high tide, high water, flood tide.

plebe *s.f.* **1** HIST. plebs, plebeians. **2** common people, masses (masas). **3** (desp.) plebs, rabble, riff-raff.

plebeyo, -a *adj.* **1** HIST. plebeian. **2** (desp.) common, vulgar, coarse. || *s.m.* y *s.f.* **3** (desp.) plebeian, commoner.

plebiscito *s.m.* POL. plebiscite.

plectro *s.m.* **1** MUS. plectrum (púa). **2** inspiration (musa).

plegable *adj.* collapsible.

plegamiento *s.m.* **1** folding. **2** GEOL. folding.

plegar *v.t.* **1** to fold (hacer un pliegue). **2** to bend (doblar). **3** to pleat (costura). || *v.pron.* **4** to bend (doblarse), to crease (arrugarse). **5** (fig.) to give way, to yield (ceder).

plegaria *s.f.* REL. **1** prayer (oración). **2** angelus bell.

pleistoceno, -a *adj.* GEOL. **1** Pleistocene. || *s.m.* **2** Pleistocene.

pleita *s.f.* plaited length of esparto grass.

pleitear *v.t.* **1** DER. to engage in litigation. **2** (fig.) to break off relations (romper las relaciones). **3** (Am.) (fig.) to argue (discutir).

pleitesía *s.f.* homage, tribute (homenaje).

pleitista *adj.* **1** DER. litigious. **2** (fig.) quarrelsome. || *s.m.* y *f.* **3** DER. litigious person. **4** (fig.) troublemaker.

pleito *s.m.* **1** DER. lawsuit, case. **2** DER. action: *voy a entablar un pleito contra mi socio = I am going to bring an action against my partner.* **3** (fig.) dispute (disputa). **4** (Am.) quarrel (discusión). **5** (Am.) brawl (pendencia). || **6 poner — a uno,** to sue someone, to take someone to court. **7 tener mal —,** (fig.) not to have a leg to stand on, to be wrong.

plenamente *adv.* fully, completely.

plenario, -a *adj.* plenary: *sesión plenaria = plenary session.*

plenilunio *s.m.* full moon.

plenipotencia *s.f.* unlimited powers.

plenipotenciario, -a *adj.* **1** plenipotentiary. || *s.m.* y *f.* **2** plenipotentiary.

plenitud *s.f.* **1** plenitude, fullness. **2** (fig.) height: *en la plenitud de sus poderes = at the height of his powers.* **3** (fig.) prime: *ha alcanzado su plenitud = he's in his prime.* || **4 — de los tiempos,** the fullness of time.

pleno, -a *adj.* **1** full. || *s.m.* **2** plenary meeting (junta). **3** completely correct forecast (quinielas). **4** win (ruleta). || **5 en — día,** in broad daylight.

pleonasmo *s.m.* GRAM. pleonasm: *"el pequeño chico diminuto" es un pleonasmo = "the wee little boy" is a pleonasm.*

plesiosauro *s.m.* ZOOL. plesiosaur (animal ya extinto).

pletina *s.f.* iron plate.

plétora *s.f.* plethora, abundance (demasía).

pletórico, -a *adj.* **1** plethoric; full of energy. || **2 — de,** brimming with (algo positivo): *pletórico de energía = brimming with energy.*

pleura *s.f.* ANAT. pleura.

pleuritis o **pleuresía** *s.f.* MED. pleurisy.

plexiglás *s.m.* perspex, plexiglass.

plexo *s.m.* ANAT. **1** plexus. || **2 — sacro,** sacral plexus. **3 — solar,** solar plexus.

pléyade *s.f.* **1** pleiad (grupo). || *pl.* **2** ASTR. Pleiades.

plica *s.f.* **1** sealed envelope. **2** DER. escrow.

pliego *s.m.* **1** sheet (folio). **2** signature (medida de papel). **3** sealed letter (carta sellada). || **4 — de condiciones,** specifications. **5 — de cargos,** DER. list of accusations. **6 — de descargo,** DER. evidence in favour of the defendant, answers to the charges.

pliegue *s.m.* **1** fold (doblez). **2** crease (arruga). **3** pleat (plisado), tuck (alforza).

plinto *s.m.* **1** plinth. **2** DEP. horse, vaulting horse (gimnasio).

plioceno, -a *adj.* GEOL. **1** Pliocene, Pleiocene. || *s.m.* **2** GEOL. Pliocene, Pleiocene.

plisado, -a *p.p.* **1** de **plisar.** || *adj.* **2** pleated (especialmente faldas).

plisar *v.t.* to pleat.

plomada *s.f.* **1** ARQ. plumb line. **2** lead, sounding line (sonda). **3** cat o'nine tails (látigo). **4** sinker, weight (pesca).

plomar *v.t.* to seal with lead.

plomizo, -a *adj.* gray, lead-coloured (especialmente el cielo).

plomo *s.m.* **1** QUIM. lead. **2** ARQ. plumb line. **3** (Am.) bullet, shot. **4** fuse (fusible). **5** (fig. y fam.) pest, drag, bore, nuisance (pelmazo). || **6 — de obra,** argentiferous lead, silver-bearing lead. **7 — blanco,** lead carbonate. **8 — dulce, 9 a —,** vertically, plumb, true.

pluma *s.f.* **1** ZOOL. feather. **2** ZOOL. plumage (conjunto de plumas). **3** pen (estilográfica, etc.), quill (de ave). **4** (fig.)

writer (escritor). **5** style (estilo). || **6 al correr de la –,** letting one's pen run on. **7 escribir a vuela de –,** to write quickly, to write freely. **8 vivir uno de su –,** to write for a living.

plumaje *s.m.* plumage, feathers (de aves).

plumario *s.m.* (Am.) journalist.

plumazo *s.m.* **1** stroke of the pen (para tachar). **2** feather bed, feather mattress (colchón). || **3 de un –, a)** with one stroke of the pen; **b)** without more ado.

plúmbeo, -a *adj.* **1** leaden, heavy as lead. **2** (fig.) boring, tiresome.

plumear *v.t.* **1** ART. to hatch in. **2** (Am.) to write, to pen.

plumero *s.m.* **1** feather duster (para quitar polvo). **2** penholder (portaplumas). **3** plume (penacho). || **4 vérsele a uno el –,** (fig.) to see through someone, to see what someone's thinking.

plumífero, -a *adj.* **1** feathered, plumed (con plumas). || *s.m.* y *f.* **2** (fam.) hack journalist (periodista), penpusher (chupatintas).

plumilla *s.f.* nib, pen nib.

plumín *s.m.* fountain pen nib.

plumón *s.m.* **1** ZOOL. down. **2** eiderdown (edredón).

plural *adj.* **1** GRAM. plural. || *s.m.* **2** GRAM. plural.

pluralidad *s.f.* **1** GRAM. plurality. **2** collection (conjunto). **3** mass (multitud). || **4 a – de votos,** by a majority of votes.

pluralismo *s.m.* pluralism (especialmente político).

pluriempleado, -a *adj.* (fam.) moonlighter.

pluriempleo *s.m.* (fam.) moonlighting.

plus *s.m.* **1** bonus. || **2 – de peligrosidad,** danger money.

pluscuamperfecto *s.m.* GRAM. pluperfect.

plusmarquista *s.m.* y *f.* DEP. record holder.

plusvalía *s.f.* **1** gain in value, appreciation (aumento de valor). **2** windfall profit (beneficio abusivo del capital sobrante).

plúteo *s.m.* shelf, bookshelf.

plutocracia *s.f.* plutocracy.

plutócrata *s.m.* y *f.* plutocrat.

plutonio *s.m.* QUIM. plutonium.

pluvial *adj.* **1** rain, pluvial. || **2 capa –,** REL. pluvial, cope.

pluviómetro o **pluvímetro** *s.m.* rain gauge.

pluvioso, -a *adj.* rainy, wet (del clima).

población *s.f.* **1** population (habitantes). **2** town (poblado). || **3 densidad de –,** population density.

poblacho *s.m.* (desp.) dump, hole.

poblada *s.f.* uprising (insurrección).

poblado *s.m.* **1** town (ciudad). **2** village (pueblo). **3** built-up area (zona urbana).

poblador, -a *s.m.* y *f.* HIST. settler.

poblar *v.t.* **1** to populate, to inhabit (habitar). **2** to settle, to colonise (colonizar). **3** to stock (plantas/animales). **4** to plant (plantar). || *v.pron.* **5** to become populated. **6** to fill up (llenarse), to stock (plantarse). **7** to breed, to multiply (multiplicarse).

pobre *adj.* **1** poor (indigente/desafortunado). || *s.m.* y *f.* **2** poor person, pauper (indigente). **3** (fig.) poor devil, poor wretch. || **4 el – de Juan,** poor old John. **5 – de solemnidad,** utterly poor, destitute.

pobremente *adv.* poorly.

pobrete *adj.* **1** poor, unfortunate. **2** (fam.) tight-fisted (tacaño). || *s.m.* y *f.* **3** poor thing (persona), (fam.) poor devil (desgraciado). **4** (fam.) cheapskate (tacaño).

pobretería *s.f.* **1** poor people (gente pobre). **2** penury (miseria). **3** avarice, (fam.) tight-fistedness (tacañería).

pobreza *s.f.* **1** poverty, penury (de medios). **2** scantiness (demasiado poco). **3** barenness (de la tierra).

procero *s.m.* well-digger.

pocilga *s.f.* **1** pigsty. **2** (fig.) pigsty: *esta habitación es una pocilga = this room is a pigsty.*

pocillo *s.m.* **1** sump (vasija empotrada). **2** (Am.) cup (taza).

pócima o **poción** *s.f.* **1** MED. potion. **2** (fig.) concoction, brew (brebaje).

poco, -a *adj.sing.* **1** not much: *tiene poco sentido común = he's not got much common sense.* **2** little: *hay poca diferencia = there's little difference.* **3** small: *de poco interés = of small interest.* || *adj.pl.* **4** not many: *he visto pocos elefantes hasta ahora = I haven't seen many elephants so far.* **5** few: *pocos ingleses llevan bombín = few Englishmen wear a bowler hat.* || *s.m.* y *f.* *(sing.)* **6** little: *¿quieres vino? Sí, un poco = would you like some wine? Yes, a little.* || *s.m.* y *f.pl.* **7** few, not many. || *adv.* **8** little, not much: *come poco = he eats little* o *he doesn't eat much.* **9** not very: *es poco inteligente = he's not very intelligent.* **10** a little: *es un poco diferente = it's a little different.* || **11 a –,** shortly, shortly after, presently. **12 – a –,** little by little, gradually. **13 – más o menos,** (fam.) near enough, about (aproximadamente). **14 por –,** nearly, almost. **15 tener en –,** to despise, to hold in contempt.

pocho, -a *adj.* **1** faded, discoloured (descolorido). **2** pale, (fam.) under the weather (pálido). **3** overripe, soft (fruta).

poda *s.f.* pruning.

podagra *s.f.* MED. podagra, gout.

podar *v.t.* to prune.

podenco, -a *adj.* **1** hunting (de caza). || *s.m.* y *f.* **2** hound.

poder *s.m.* **1** power, authority (dominio). **2** possession (posesión). **3** capacity (capacidad). **4** power, strength (fuerza). **5** power, ability (facultad). **6** DER. power. || *pl.* **7** powers, power. || *v.i.* **8** can, to be able: *no puedo hacerlo = I can't do it/I'm not able to do it.* **9** may: *puedo no venir = I may not come.* **10** to cope, to manage: *¿tú puedes con ese trabajo? = can you cope with/manage that work?* || *v.imp.* **11** may, might: *puede que no venga = he may/might not come.* || **12 hacer un –,** to make an effort. **13 hasta más no –,** to the limit, as much as possible, to the utmost. **14 no – más,** to be all in (agotado), (fig.) to be at the end of one's tether. **15 no – menos,** not to be able to help: *no puedo menos de fumar = I can't help smoking.* **16 – ejecutivo,** executive power. **17 – judicial,** judicial power. **18 – legislativo,** legislative power.

poderdante *s.m.* y *s.f.* DER. principal.

poderhabiente *s.m.* y *s.f.* **1** DER. (brit.) proxy, (EE.UU.) attorney. **2** agent (que representa).

poderío *s.m.* **1** power (dominio). **2** wealth (bienes). **3** might (fuerza).

poderosamente *adv.* powerfully, mightily.

poderoso, -a *adj.* powerful, mighty.

podíatra o **podiatra** *s.m.* MED. chiropodist.

podio o **pódium** *s.m.* **1** podium. **2** (Am.) rostrum.

podólogo *s.m.* MED. chiropodist.

podre *s.f.* pus.

podredumbre *s.f.* **1** putrefaction. **2** MED. pus, rot. **3** (fig.) corruption.

podridero *s.m.* compost heap, midden.

podrido, -a *p.p.* **1** de **pudrir.** || *adj.* **2** rotten. || **3 estar – de dinero,** to be filthy rich.

podrir V. **pudrir.**

poema *s.m.* **1** poem. || **2 – épico,** LIT. epic poem. **3 – sinfónico,** symphonic poem. **4 ser un –,** to be out of the ordinary, to be really something.

poesía *s.f.* **1** poetry (género). **2** poem (poema).

poeta *s.m.* poet.

poetastro *s.m.* poetaster.

poéticamente *adv.* poetically.

poético, -a *adj.* **1** poetic. || *s.f.* **2** poetics, theory of poetry.

poetisa *s.f.* poetess.

póker *s.m.* poker (naipes).

polaco, -a *adj.* **1** Polish. || *s.m.* y *f.* **2** Pole. || *s.m.* **3** Polish (idioma).

polaina *s.f.* **1** gaiter, legging (media calza). **2** (Am.) annoyance, irritation (contrariedad).

polar *adj.* GEOG. **1** polar. || **2 estrella –,** Pole Star.

polaridad *s.f.* FIS. polarity.

polarización *s.f.* **1** FIS. polarization. **2** (fig.) exclusive attention (a algo o alguien).

polarizar *v.t.* **1** FIS. to polarize. **2** (fig.) to concentrate on (concentrar). || *v.pron.* **3** to polarize. **4** to concentrate (concentrarse).

polca *s.f.* MUS. polka.

polea *s.f.* **1** pulley. || **2 – combinada, 3 – móvil,** block and tackle.

poleame *s.m.* set of pulleys.

polémico, -a *adj.* **1** polemical. **2** controversial. || *s.f.* **3** polemic, controversy.

polemizar *v.i.* to get involved in an argument (normalmente teórico o ideológico).

polen *s.m.* BOT. pollen.

poleo *s.m.* 1 BOT. pennyroyal. 2 (fig.) swagger, cockiness.
poliandria *s.f.* 1 ANTR. polyandry. 2 BOT. polyandry.
poliarquía *s.f.* polyarchy.
pólice *s.m.* ANAT. pollex.
policía *s.f.* 1 police (cuerpo), police woman (agente). || *s.m.* 3 policeman (agente).
policíaco, -a o **policiaco, a** *adj.* 1 police (*atr.*). 2 detective (*atr.*): *me gusta leer novelas policíacas = I like reading detective stories.*
policial *adj.* police: *intensa actividad policial = intense police activity.*
polícromo, -a *adj.* polychrome.
polichinela o **pulchinela** *s.m.* Punch, Punchinello.
poliedro *adj.* 1 GEOM. polyhedral. || *s.m.* 2 MAT. polyhedron. || 3 **— regular,** GEOM. regular polyhedron.
polifacético, -a *adj.* 1 versatile. 2 multifaceted, many sided.
polifonía *s.f.* 1 MUS. polyphony. 2 FON. polyphony.
polifónico, -a *adj.* polyphonic.
poligamia *s.f.* polygamy.
polígamo, -a *adj.* 1 polygamous. || *s.m.* y *f.* 2 polygamist.
poligenismo *s.m.* polygenesis.
políglota o **poliglota** *adj.* 1 polyglot. || *s.m.* y *f.* polyglot.
poligonáceo, -a *adj.* 1 BOT. polygonaceous. || *s.f.pl.* 2 BOT. polygonaceae.
polígono, -a *adj.* 1 MAT. polygonal. || *s.m.* 2 MAT. polygon. || 3 **— industrial,** industrial estate.
polígrafo, -a *s.m.* y *f.*polygraph.
polilla *s.f.* 1 clothes moth (insecto). 2 clothes moth larva (gusano).
polímero *s.m.* QUIM. polymer.
polimerización *s.* QUIM. polymerization.
polimetría *s.f.* diversity of metre in a single poem.
polimorfismo *s.m.* (form.) polymorphism.
polimorfo, -a *adj.* 1 polymorphous, polymorphic. 2 LIT. free (poesía).
polinización *s.f.* BOT. pollination.
polinomio *s.m.* 1 MAT. polynomial.
poliomielitis *s.f.* MED. poliomyelitis, infantile paralysis.
polipasto o **polispasto** *s.m.* hoisting tackle.
pólipo *s.m.* 1 ZOOL. polyp, polypus. 2 MED. polyp, polypus.
polisacáridos *s.m.pl.* QUIM. polysaccharides.
polisemia *s.f.* GRAM. polysemy.
polisón *s.m.* bustle.
polistilo *adj.* 1 ARQ. polystyle. 2 BOT. polystylous.
politeísmo *s.m.* REL. polytheism.
políticamente *adv.* politically.
politicastro *s.m.* (desp.) petty politician.
político, -a *adj.* 1 POL. political: *es líder de un partido político = he's the leader of a political party.* 2 politic (sagaz): *no sería político plantear ese problema ahora = it wouldn't be politic to raise that problem now.* || *s.m.* y *f.* 3 POL. politician (persona). || *s.f.* 4 POL. politics: *la política es el arte de lo posible = politics is the art of the possible.* 5 policy (programa): *la política exterior de su gobierno es un desastre = their government's foreign policy is a disaster.* 6 courtesy, politeness (cortesía). 7 tact (habilidad). || 8 **padre —,** father-in-law. 9 **hermana política,** sister-in-law. 10 **hermano —,** brother-in-law.
politiquear *v.i.* to dabble in politics, to play at politics.
politiquería *s.f.* shady political dealings, political manoeuvring.
póliza *s.f.* 1 stamp duty (impuesto). 2 certificate (certificado). 3 policy (seguros). 4 contract (contrato).
polizón *s.m.* 1 stowaway (pasajero clandestino). 2 (brit.) tramp, (EE.UU.) bum (vago). 3 police informer (confidente de la policía). 4 (fam.) grass (soplón).
polizonte *s.m.* (desp.) copper, flatfoot.
polo *s.m.* 1 GEOG. pole. 2 FIS. pole. 3 popular Andalusian tune. 4 ice-lolly (helado). 5 polo neck sweater, tee shirt (camiseta). 6 DEP. polo. || 7 **— ártico,** GEOG. North Pole. 8 **— antártico,** GEOG. South Pole. 9 **— magnético,** FIS. magnetic pole.
polonés, -a *adj.* 1 Polish. || *s.m.* y *f.* 2 Pole (nativo). || *s.f.* 3 MUS. polonaise: *las polonesas de Chopin son de las más famosas = Chopin's polonaises are among the most well-known.*
polonio *s.m.* MIN. polonium.
poltrón, -ona *adj.* 1 lazy, idle. || *s.m.* y *f.* 2 idler, loafer (haragán). || *s.f.* 3 easy chair (silla).
poltronería *s.f.* indolence, laziness.
polución *s.f.* 1 pollution: *los fosfatos son una de las múltiples causas de la polución de los ríos = phosphates are one of the many causes of river pollution.* || 2 **— nocturna,** nocturnal emission, (fam.) wet dream.
poluto, -a *adj.* stained, soiled (manchado).
polvareda *s.f.* 1 dust cloud, cloud of dust. 2 (fig.) fuss, storm (revuelo): *la corrupción política aprobó una polvareda = the political corruption created a fuss.*
polvera *s.f.* powder compact.
polvero *s.m.* (Am.) dust cloud.
polvillo *s.m.* (Am.) blight (hongos).
polvo *s.m.* 1 dust. 2 QUIM. powder. 3 pinch (pizca). || 4 **polvos de la madre Celestina,** magic panacea. 5 **echar un —,** (vulg.) to have a shag, to have a screw. 6 **estar hecho —,** (fam.) to be shattered, (vulg.) to be knackered. 7 **hacerle a uno —,** to crush someone, to annihilate someone. 8 **morder el —,** (fam.) to bite the dust. 9 **limpio de — y paja,** (fam.) in the clear. 10 **sacudirle a uno el —,** to give someone a thrashing.
polvoriento, -a *adj.* dusty.
pólvora *s.f.* 1 gunpowder. || 2 **gastar la — en salvas,** to waste time and energy. 3 **ser como la —,** to have a fiery temper, (fam.) to have a short fuse. 4 **tirar con — ajena,** to spend somebody else's money.
polverar *v.t.* to powder, to dust (empolvar).
polvorín *s.m.* 1 MIL. munitions dump. 2 gunpowder keg, powder keg (barril). 3 very fine gunpowder (pólvora fina).
polvorón *s.m.* 1 dry Spanish sweet of a floury consistency. 2 (Am.) cake.
polvoroso, -a *adj.* 1 (p.u.) dusty. || 2 **poner los pies en —,** (fam.) to beat it.
polla *s.f.* 1 pullet, young hen (gallina). 2 (fig.) young girl, (fam.) chick (chica). 3 (vulg.) prick (pene). || 3 **— de agua,** moorhen, marsh hen.
pollero, -a *s.m.* y *f.* 1 chicken farmer, poultry seller. || *s.m.* 2 chicken-run (criadero), poultry shop (tienda). || *s.f.* 3 henhouse (criadero). 4 baby walker (aparato). 5 (Am.) skirt (falda).
pollino, -a *adj.* 1 obstinate (terco). 2 stupid (tonto). || *s.m.* y *f.* 2 ZOOL. donkey, ass. 3 (fig.) ass, dunce.
pollo *s.m.* 1 ZOOL. chick, young bird. 2 lad, youngster (chaval), young man (joven). 3 spit (esputo).
poma *s.f.* 1 BOT. apple.
pomada *s.f.* 1 MED. ointment. 2 cream, pomade (crema).
pomar *s.m.* 1 apple orchard (manzanar). 2 orchard (frutales).
pomarrosa *s.f.* BOT. 1 jambo (fruto). 2 jambo, rose apple (árbol).
pomelo *s.m.* BOT. grapefruit.
pómez *s.f.* GEOL. pumice.
pomo *s.m.* 1 BOT. pome. 2 perfume bottle (frasco). 3 pommel (de espada). 4 knob (picaporte).
pompa *s.f.* 1 pomp (fausto). 2 bubble (burbuja). 3 TEC. pump (bomba). || 4 **pompas fúnebres, a)** funeral procession (ceremonia); **b)** Undertaker's Funeral Director's (empresa).
pompón *s.m.* 1 crest (del morrión). 2 tassle (borla).
pomposamente *adv.* pompously, self-importantly.
pomposo, -a *adj.* 1 splendid, magnificent (majestuoso). 2 (desp.) pompous, bombastic (rimbombante): *tiene un estilo a la vez alambicado y pomposo = they have a style that is both refined and pompous.*
pómulo *s.m.* ANAT. cheekbone.
ponchada *s.f.* 1 (Am.) vast amount, (fam.) pile, (fam.) heap (cantidad). 2 (Am.) puncture (pinchazo).
ponche *s.m.* punch (bebida).
ponchera *s.f.* 1 punch bowl. 2 (Am.) washbasin (jofaina).
poncho *s.m.* 1 (Am.) poncho (manta). 2 cape (capa).
ponderación *s.f.* 1 consideration, deliberation (de pensamiento). 2 balance, equilibrium (objetividad).
ponderadamente *adv.* judiciously, cautiously; calmly.
ponderado, -a *p.p.* 1 de **ponderar.** || *adj.* 2 prudent, cautious; calm.
ponderal *adj.* pertaining to weight.

ponderar *v.t.* 1 to weigh up, to ponder over, to deliberate upon (considerar). 2 to speak highly of, to praise warmly (elogiar). 3 to balance (contrapesar). 4 to weight (estadísticas).

ponderativo, -a *adj.* 1 thoughtful, reflective (pensativo). 2 eulogistic, effusive, (fam.) gushing (efusivo).

ponderoso, -a *adj.* 1 ponderous, tedious (pesado). 2 steady, earnest, circumspect, serious (serio).

ponedero, -a *adj.* 1 egg-laying. || *s.m.* 2 nest box, nesting box.

ponencia *s.f.* report; paper.

ponente *adj.* 1 reporting. || *s.m.* y *s.f.* 2 rapporteur (conferencia). 3 speaker (conferenciante).

poner *v.t.* 1 to put, to place (colocar). 2 to set: *han puesto un examen difícil = a difficult exam has been set; voy a poner la mesa = I'm going to set the table.* 3 to put on, to turn on, to switch on (encender): *¿quieres poner la radio? = do you mind turning the radio on?* 4 to suppose (suponer). 5 to lay: *esta gallina pone seis huevos por día = this hen lays six eggs a day; hazme el favor de poner la mesa = please lay the table for me.* 6 to bet, to wager (apostar). 7 to expose (exponer). 8 FIN. to put up, to invest: *yo pongo el dinero = I'm putting up the money.* 9 to put on, to show (película, etc.): *ponen una película genial en el cine = they're showing a brilliant film at the cinema.* || *v.r.* 10 to put oneself, to stand: *ella se ponía delante del piano = she used to stand in front of the piano.* 11 to put on (ropa). 12 to reach, to arrive (in), to get (to): *decía que se podía poner en Madrid en veinte minutos = he used to say he could get to Madrid in twenty minutes.* 13 to set (sol, etc.). || 14 **ponerse a,** to begin to. 15 **no ponérsele a uno nada por delante,** to press on regardless. 16 **— por encima,** to prefer. 17 **ponerse al corriente,** to find out. 18 **ponerse uno bien,** to get better, to recover. 19 **— en claro,** to make clear. 20 **— a mal,** to cause a rift: *ella le puso a mal con su suegra = she caused a rift between him and his mother-in-law.*

poney *s.m.* ZOOL. pony.

poniente *s.m.* 1 GEOG. West. 2 West wind (viento).

póntico, -a *adj.* 1 HIST. Pontic. 2 GEOG. Pontic.

pontificado *s.m.* papacy, pontificate.

pontifical *adj.* 1 REL. pontifical. || *s.m.* 2 REL. pontifical (libro). 3 REL. tithe (diezmo). || 4 **de —,** in pontifical dress.

pontificar *v.i.* to pontificate, to pontify.

pontífice *s.m.* 1 REL. pontiff. 2 HIST. Pontifex.

pontificio, -a *adj.* papal.

ponto *s.m.* (lit.) deep, ocean, sea.

pontón *s.m.* 1 lighter (barco). 2 pontoon (puente). 3 float (de hidroavión).

pontonero *s.m.* MIL. pontonier.

ponzoña *s.f.* 1 poison (veneno). 2 (fig.) poison.

ponzoñoso, -a *adj.* poisonous, venomous (real y figurativamente).

pop *adj.* pop: *a ella le encanta la música pop = she loves pop music.*

popa *s.f.* 1 stern. || 2 **ir viento en —,** (fig.) to go swimmingly, to go like a dream, to prosper. 3 **viento en —,** following wind.

pope *s.m.* pope (sacerdote ruso).

popelín o **popelina** *s.f.* poplin.

populachería *s.f.* cheap popularity.

populachero, -a *adj.* vulgar, cheap.

populacho *s.m.* (desp.) populace, masses, plebs.

popular *adj.* 1 popular: *es popular por ser tan simpático = he's popular because he's so nice.* 2 folk, of the people (costumbres, etc.).

popularidad *s.f.* popularity.

popularización *s.f.* popularization.

popularizar *v.t.* 1 to make popular, to popularize. || *v.pron.* 2 to become popular.

popularmente *adv.* commonly (comúnmente).

populoso, -a *adj.* populous.

popurrí o **potpurrí** *s.m.* MUS. potpourri, medley.

poquedad *s.f.* 1 paucity, meagreness. 2 (fig.) timidity. 3 trifle (nimiedad).

póquer *s.m.* poker (naipes).

por *prep.* 1 for, for the sake of (a favor de): *murió por la patria = he died for his country.* 2 for (a cambio de): *le di un millón de pesetas por su coche = I gave him a million pesetas for his car.* 3 for, because of (a causa de): *cierran las tiendas por ser fiesta = they're shutting the shops because of the holiday.* 4 as: *esto podemos darlo por sabido = this can be taken as read.* 5 in, around (tiempo): *ocurrió por mayo = it happened around May; vendré por la tarde = I'll come in the afternoon.* 6 through: *el Duero pasa por Zamora = the Douro flows through Zamora.* 7 by: *la novela fue escrita por Galdós = the novel was written by Galdós.* 8 MAT. times: *3 por 7 son 21 = 3 times 7 is 21.* 9 **ir —,** to fetch.

porcelana *s.f.* 1 china, porcelain (materia). 2 china, chinaware (loza fina). 3 bluish-white (color). 4 jewel enamel (esmalte).

porcentaje *s.m.* percentage.

porcentual *adj.* percentage: *incremento porcentual = percentage increase.*

porcino, -a *adj.* 1 porcine, pig. || *s.m.* 2 porker, piglet (lechón).

porción *s.f.* 1 portion, share, part (parte). 2 crowd, number (personas). 3 sum, amount (cuota). 4 helping (ración).

porciúncula *s.f.* REL. Franciscan jubilee.

porcuno, -a *adj.* porcine, pig.

porche *s.m.* 1 porch (pórtico). 2 arcade (soportal).

pordiosear *v.i.* to beg around, to go begging.

pordiosero, -a *adj.* 1 begging, mendicant. || *s.m.* y *f.* 2 beggar.

porfía *s.f.* 1 persistence (persistencia). 2 obstinacy (testarudez). || 3 **a —,** in competition.

porfiadamente *adv.* stubbornly, obstinately.

porfiado, -a *adj.* stubborn, obstinate.

porfiar *v.i.* 1 to argue stubbornly, to wrangle (disputar). 2 to persist (persistir). 3 to vie (competir).

pórfido *s.m.* GEOL. porphyry.

pormenor *s.m.* 1 detail. 2 minor point.

pormenorizar *v.t.* 1 to detail, to give a detailed account of. || *v.i.* 2 to go into detail: *no se ha pormenorizado todo = they haven't gone into all the details.*

pornografía *s.f.* pornography.

pornográfico, -a *adj.* pornographic.

poro *s.m.* 1 ANAT. pore. 2 (Am.) maté gourd. 3 (Am.) BOT. leek.

porosidad *s.f.* porosity, porousness.

poroso, -a *adj.* porous.

poroto *s.m.* (Am.) BOT. bean (frijol).

porque *conj.* 1 because (causa): *estoy cansado porque he trabajado mucho = I'm tired because I have worked hard.* 2 so that (finalidad): *sal y espérame a la puerta porque vea si has llorado = go and wait for me by the door so that I can see if you've been crying.*

porqué *s.m.* 1 reason, cause (motivo). 2 FIN. amount, portion.

porquería *s.f.* 1 filth, dirt (suciedad). 2 nastiness (comportamiento vil). 3 dirty trick, mean action (acción vil). 4 obscenity (grosería). 5 (fig.) rubbish: *su traducción era una porquería = his translation was rubbish.*

porqueriza *s.f.* pigsty.

porquerizo *s.m.* swineherd, pigman.

porra *s.f.* 1 club, cudgel (cachiporra). 2 truncheon (de policía). 3 (fig.) bore, nuisance, pest (pelmazo). 4 TEC. sledgehammer (martillo). 5 thick fritter (churro). || *interj.* 6 **mandar a la —,** to send (someone) packing, to kick (someone) out. 7 **¡Porras!** Damn it! 8 **¡Vete a la —!,** scram!

porrada *s.f.* 1 blow, thump, (fam.) wallop (golpe). 2 (fam.) codswallop, twaddle, (fig.) rubbish (necedad). 4 (fam.) load(s), (fam.) heap(s) (montón).

porrazo *s.m.* 1 blow, thump, (fam.) wallop (golpe). 2 knock, bump (caída).

porrería *s.f.* 1 nonsense, stupidity (necedad). 2 slowness, sluggishness (pesadez).

porrillo *loc.* **a —,** *adv.* galore, (fam.) by the cartload.

porro *s.m.* (fam.) joint, smoke (de droga).

porrón *s.m.* 1 earthenware jug (botijo). 2 glass wine jar with a spout.

portaaviones *s.m.inv.* MIL. aircraft carrier.

portabandera *s.f.* 1 flag holder (cosa). 2 standard bearer (abanderado).

portada *s.f.* 1 ARQ. front, frontispiece, facade (fachada). 2 PER. front page (periódico). 3 PER. front cover (revista). 4 title page (libro).

portadilla *s.f.* half-title, bastard title (libro).
portador, -a *s.m.* y *f.* **1** carrier, bearer. **2** MED. carrier (de una enfermedad).
portaequipajes *s.m.inv.* **1** (brit.) boot, (EE.UU.) trunk (de un coche). **2** luggage rack (rejilla). **3** roof rack (baca).
portaestandarte *s.m.* standard bearer (abanderado).
portafolio *s.m.* **1** (Am.) briefcase (cartera). **2** folder, file (carpeta).
portafusil *s.m.* MIL. sling.
portal *s.m.* **1** ARQ. entrance, entrance hall (zaguán). **2** arcade (soportal). **3** city gate (puerta de ciudad). **4** crib (belén).
portalada *s.f.* ARQ. imposing entrance.
portalámparas *s.m.inv.* light socket, lamp holder.
portalibros *s.m.inv.* book straps.
portalón *s.m.* **1** ARQ. imposing entrance, monumental door. **2** gangway (barco).
portallaves *s.m.inv.* keyring.
portamonedas *s.m.inv.* purse.
portante *adj.* **1** ambling. || *s.m.* **2** amble. || **3 tomar el –,** to leave, (fam.) to make oneself scarce, (fam.) to beat it.
portaobjetos *s.m.inv.* slide (de microscopio).
portaplumas *s.m.inv.* penholder.
portar *v.t.* to carry, to bear.
portarse *v.pron.* **1** to behave. || **2 – mal,** to misbehave, to behave badly.
portátil *adj.* portable.
portaviandas *s.m.inv.* lunchbox.
portavoz *s.m.* y *f.* **1** spokesperson, spokesman (persona). || *s.m.* megaphone, loudhailer. **2** (desp.) mouthpiece (periódico).
portazgo *s.m.* (arc.) toll (antiguo impuesto local).
portazo *s.m.* **1** bang, slam (de una puerta): *dio un portazo = he slammed the door (shut).* || **2 dar un – a uno,** (fig.) to slam the door in somebody's face.
porte *s.m.* **1** COM. carriage, transport (acción). **2** COM. carriage charges, transport costs (gastos). **3** behaviour, conduct (conducta). **4** bearing (compostura). **5** nobility (nobleza de sangre). **6** capacity (capacidad).
porteador, -a *s.m.* y *f.* porter.
portento *s.m.* marvel, wonder, prodigy.
porteño, -a *adj.* **1** of Puerto de Santa María (Cádiz), from Puerto de Santa María (Cádiz). **2** (Am.) of Buenos Aires (Argentina), from Buenos Aires (Argentina). **3** (Am.) of Valparaíso (Chile), from Valparaíso (Chile). || *s.m.* y *f.* **4** native of Puerto de Santa María (Cádiz). **5** (Am.) native of Buenos Aires (Argentina). **6** (Am.) native of Valparaíso (Chile).
portería *s.f.* **1** porter's lodge, caretaker's office (conserjería). **2** porter's job (empleo). **3** DEP. goal (meta).
portero, -a *s.m.* y *f.* **1** hall porter (hotel), caretaker (pisos), doorkeeper, doorman, commissionaire (delante de la puerta). **2** DEP. goalkeeper.
portezuela *s.f.* door (de coche).
pórtico *s.m.* **1** ARQ. portico, porch. **2** arcade (galería).
portilla *s.f.* **1** gate (de campo). **2** porthole (de buque).
portillo *s.m.* **1** opening, gap (abertura). **2** wicket gate, postern (postigo). **3** GEOG. pass (puerto). **4** chip (desportilladura), dent (abolladura).
portuario, -a *adj.* port, harbour.
portugués, -esa *adj.* **1** Portuguese. || *s.m.* y *f.* **2** Portuguese.
portulano *s.m.* portulan, portolano (planos de puertos).
porvenir *s.m.* **1** future. || **2 de –,** promising.
pos *prep.* en – de, after, in pursuit of: *ir en pos de la felicidad = in pursuit of happiness.*
pos(t) *prefijo* post.
posada *s.f.* **1** shelter, lodging (hospedaje). **2** inn (mesón). **3** guest house (pensión). || **4 – franca,** free board and lodging.
posadero, -a *s.m.* **1** innkeeper (de mesón), landlord (de pensión). **2** easy chair (silla). || *s.f.* **3** innkeeper (mesón), landlady (de pensión). || *s.f.pl.* **4** behind, backside (nalgas).
posar *v.i.* **1** to rest (reposar). **2** to pose, to sit (para pintor, etc.). || *v.i.* y *pron.* **3** to alight, to settle (pájaros, insectos), to perch (pájaros). **4** to lodge (hospedar). **5** to put down, to land (aterrizar). || *v.pron.* **6** to settle (poso, polvo). || *v.t.* **7** to put down, to lay down (depositar): *posé el vaso en la estantería superior = I put down the glass on the top shelf.*
pose *s.f.* **1** pose, airs, affectation (afectación). **2** pose (de modelo).
poseedor, -a *s.m.* y *f.* **1** owner, possesor (de una propiedad u objeto). **2** DEP. holder (de un récord).
poseer *v.t.* **1** to possess, to own, to have (tener). **2** to enjoy (cualidades). **3** to hold (récord). || *v.pron.* **4** to keep oneself under control.
poseído, -a *p.p.* **1** de **poseer.** || *adj.* **1** overcome, crazed (enloquecido). **2** possessed (poseso). || *s.m.* y *f.* **3** one possessed. || **4 estar – uno, a)** to be overcome (de enojo, etc.); **b)** to be full of oneself (presumido).
posesión *s.f.* **1** possession, ownership (hecho de poseer). **2** possession (cosa). **3** possession (por espíritu). **4** property (finca). || *pl.* **5** POL. colony, possessions. || **6 dar – a uno,** to hand over to someone.
posesivo, -a *adj.* **1** possessive. || *s.m.* **2** possessive.
poseso, -a *p.p.irr.* **1** de **posser.** || *adj.* **2** possessed (por espíritu). || *s.m.* y *f.* **3** one possessed, someone possessed.
posibilidad *s.f.* **1** possibility; chance. || **2 vivir por encima de sus posibilidades,** to live above one's means.
posibilitar *v.t.* to make possible.
posible *adj.* **1** possible. || *s.m.pl.* **2** means, resources (recursos). || **3 hacer todo lo –,** to do everything in one's power.
posiblemente *adv.* possibly, probably.
posición *s.f.* **1** position, place (sitio). **2** social position, status (categoría). **3** MIL. position. **4** positioning, placing (acción de poner).
posicional *adj.* **1** positional. **2** DEP. positional (tipo de fuera de juego).
positivista *s.m.* y *f.* **1** FIL. positivist. || *adj.* **2** (fig.) optimistic.
positivo, -a *adj.* **1** positive. **2** practical. **3** GRAM. positive.
positivismo *s.m.* **1** realism (realismo). **2** materialism. **3** FIL. positivism.
positrón *s.m.* FIS. positron.
poso *s.m.* **1** sediment, lees (vino, etc.), dregs (de café, vino, etc.), grounds (de café). **2** repose (quietud).
posología *s.f.* **1** dosage (dosis). **2** MED. posology.
pososo, -a *adj.* **1** (Am.) porous, permeable (poroso). **2** absorbent.
posponer *v.t.* **1** to postpone, to put off (aplazar). **2** to value less, to downgrade (valorar menos).
pospuesto, -a *adj.* postponed.
posta *s.f.* **1** relief horses, relay team (caballos). **2** staging post (lugar). **3** stage (distancia). **4** slug, pellet (perdigón). **5** stake (naipes). **6** slice (tajada). || **7 a –,** on purpose, deliberately.
postal *adj.* **1** postal. || *s.f.* **2** postcard.
poste *s.m.* **1** post, pole. **2** DEP. post, goalpost, upright. || **3 ser uno un –, a)** to be dense; **b)** to be as deaf as a post.
postema *s.f.* MED. abscess.
postergar *v.t.* **1** to put off, to postpone (aplazar). **2** to pass over (a un empleado). **3** to disregard, to leave on one side (posponer injustamente).
posteridad *s.f.* posterity.
posterior *adj.* **1** later (tiempo). **2** rear, back (trasero). **3** FON. back.
posteriori *loc.* **a posteriori,** *adv.* a posteriori.
postergación *s.f.* **1** passing over, ignoring (el hecho de rechazar a alguien). **2** delayig, postponement.
posteriormente *adv.* later, at a later time, subsequently, afterwards.
postigo *s.m.* **1** secret door (puerta falsa). **2** wicket (en otra puerta mayor). **3** postern (portillo). **4** shutter (contraventana).
postilla *s.f.* **1** MED. scab. **2** note, comment (nota).
postillón *s.m.* postillion.
postín *s.m.* **1** (desp.) airs and graces, side (presunción). **2** elegance, stylishness, chic (elegancia). || **3 darse –,** to put on airs, to give oneself airs, (fam.) to show off, (fam.) to swank (presumir).
postizo, -a *adj.* **1** false, artificial: *dentadura postiza = false teeth.* || *s.m.* **2** hairpiece, toupée (peluca). || *s.f.* **3** MUS. castanet.
postor *s.m.* bidder: *vendido al mejor postor = sold to the highest bidder.*
postración *s.f.* prostration, exhaustion.
postrar *v.t.* **1** to prostrate, to humble (humillar). **2** to overthrow, to overcome

(derribar). 3 MED. to weaken (debilitar). || *v.pron.* 4 to exhaust oneself, to be overcome (debilitarse). 5 to kneel down (arrodillarse).

postre *adj.* 1 last. || *s.m.* 2 dessert, sweet (plato). || 3 **a la –,** finally, in the end.

postremo, -a *adj.* final, ultimate, last: *las palabras postremas de Nelson fueron "Bésame, Hardy" = Nelson's last words were "Kiss me, Hardy".*

postrero, -a *adj.* 1 last, ultimate (último). 2 rear, hindmost (detrás). || *s.m.* y *f.* 3 last one, (fam.) tail-ender.

postrimerías *s.f.pl.* 1 end (de la vida). 2 dying moments, closing stages (final). 3 REL. death. || 3 **en las – del siglo,** at the close of the century.

postulación *s.f.* REL. postulation.

postulado, -a *p.p.* 1 de **postular.** || *s.m.* 2 postulate, proposition.

postulante, -a *adj.* 1 postulating. || *s.m.* y *f.* 2 REL. postulant.

postular *v.t.* 1 postulate (proponer). 2 to request (pedir), to claim (pretender). 3 to collect for charity (dinero).

póstumo, -a *adj.* posthumous.

postura *s.f.* 1 position, attitude, posture (del cuerpo). 2 (fig.) attitude, posture (actitud). 3 bid (subasta). 4 bet, stake (juego). 5 laying (huevos). 6 transplanting (plantar). 7 seedling (plantón).

potabilidad *s.f.* potability.

potable *adj.* 1 drinkable. 2 (fam.) acceptable, passable (aceptable). || 3 **agua –,** drinking water.

potaje *s.m.* 1 broth (caldo). 2 vegetable stew (olla). 3 dish of dried vegetables (legumbres). 3 (fig.) jumble, mishmash (mezcla).

potasa *s.f.* QUIM. potash.

potásico, -a *adj.* QUIM. potassic.

potasio *s.m.* QUIM. potassium.

pote *s.m.* 1 earthenware pot (de barro). 2 pan (de hierro). 3 stew (Galicia, Asturias). || 4 **darse –,** (fam.) to show off, (fam.) to swank.

potencia *s.f.* 1 power, capability (capacidad). 2 power, strength (fuerza). 3 potency (virilidad). 4 power (nación): *las grandes potencias = the Great Powers.* 5 MAT. power. 6 FIS. power. || 7 **en –,** potential, in the making: *un campeón en potencia = a champion in the making.* 8 **– al freno,** brake horsepower.

potencial *adj.* 1 potential. 2 GRAM. conditional. || *s.m.* 3 potentiality. 4 ELEC. potential energy.

potencialidad *s.f.* potential.

potencialmente *adv.* potentially.

potenciar *v.t.* 1 to promote (promover). 2 to boost, to reinforce (reforzar): *tenemos que potenciar los cursos de verano = we have to boost the summer courses.*

potenciómetro *s.m.* ELEC. potentiometer.

potentado, -a *s.m.* y *f.* potentate.

potente *adj.* 1 potent (sexualmente). 2 powerful (con fuerza).

potentemente *adv.* powerfully, mightily.

poterna *s.f.* postern.

potestad *s.f.* 1 power (poder). 2 authority (autoridad), jurisdiction (jurisdicción). || 3 **patria –,** paternal authority.

potestativo, -a *adj.* DER. facultative, optional, not compulsory.

potingue *s.m.* (fam.) concoction, brew.

potosí *s.m.* 1 immense wealth. || 2 **valer una cosa un –,** (something) to be worth a fortune. 3 **valer una persona un –,** (someone) to be worth their weight in gold.

potpurrí *s.m.* V. **popurrí.**

potra *s.f.* 1 ZOOL. filly. 2 MED. (fam.) rupture (hernia). 3 **tener –,** tener suerte.

potranca *s.f.* ZOOL. young filly.

potrero *s.m.* 1 herdsman (persona). 2 paddock (prado), pasture (pastizal).

potril *adj.* 1 horse-grazing, grazing. || *s.m.* 2 pasture for colts, paddock.

potro *s.m.* 1 ZOOL. colt. 2 HIST. rack (tormento). 3 shoeing frame (herrero). 4 DEP. vaulting horse (de madera). 5 (fam.) drag, bind, bore (molestia).

poyata *s.f.* 1 kitchen dresser (vasar). 2 ledge, shelf (repisa).

poyo *s.m.* stone bench.

poza *s.f.* 1 large puddle, pool (charca). 2 deepest part (del río).

pozal *s.m.* 1 pail, bucket (cubo). 2 large jar (tinaja).

pozo *s.m.* 1 well (agua, petróleo). 2 MIN. pit (excavación). 3 mine shaft (mina). 4 deepest part (del río). 5 (fig.) fount, source, mine: *es un pozo de sabiduría = he's the fount of all wisdom.* || 6 **– artesiano,** artesian well.

práctica *s.f.* 1 practice (ejercicio). 2 experience, knowledge (pericia). 3 custom (costumbre). 4 method (modo particular). 5 skill (destreza). || *pl.* 6 practical training (formación). 7 practicals (clases). || 8 **en la –,** in practice. 9 **la – hace maestro,** practice makes perfect.

practicable *adj.* 1 feasible (que se puede hacer). 2 usable (carretera).

prácticamente *adv.* practically.

practicante *adj.* 1 (brit.) practising, (EE.UU.) practicing. || *s.m.* y *f.* 2 practitioner. 3 medical assistant (ayudante médico). 4 nurse (enfermero). 5 assistant chemist (farmacéutico).

practicar *v.t.* 1 (brit.) to practise, (EE.UU.) to practice. 2 to make a practice of (hacer habitualmente). 3 DEP. to play, to go in for, to do: *¿practicas deporte? = do you go in for sport?/do you do much in the way of sport?* || *v.i.* y *pron.* 4 to undergo practical training.

práctico, -a *adj.* 1 practical, handy (útil). 2 skilled, expert (perito). 3 sensible, practical: *esos zapatos son muy prácticos = those are very sensible shoes.* || *s.m.* 4 coastal pilot (marino).

practicón, -ona *adj.* expert, skilled, adept.

pradera *s.f.* 1 meadow (prado). 2 (EE.UU.) prairie (prado extenso). 3 grasslands (pastos).

pradería *s.f.* meadowlands, grasslands.

prado *s.m.* meadow, pasture land.

pragmático, -a *adj.* 1 pragmatic. || *s.m.* y *f.* 2 pragmatist. || *s.f.* 3 DER. pragmatic sanction.

pragmatismo *s.m.* 1 FIL. pragmatism. 2 pragmatism, realism (en un sentido vital y práctico).

pragmatista *s.m.* y *f.* pragmatist.

praseodimio *s.m.* QUIM. praseodymium.

praviana *s.f.* popular Asturian song.

pravo, -a *adj.* perverse, depraved.

preámbulo *s.m.* 1 preamble, introduction (prefacio). 2 (desp. y fam.) waffle, (fig.) beating about the bush (rodeos).

prebenda *s.f.* 1 REL. prebend. 2 REL. benefice, living. 3 sinecure, (fam.) cushy job (chollo). 4 (fam.) perk (gaje).

preboste *s.m.* provost.

precariamente *adv.* precariously.

precario, -a *adj.* precarious, uncertain, (fam.) shaky.

precaución *s.f.* 1 precaution (acto), preventive measure (medida). 2 foresight, wariness (cautela).

precaver *v.t.* 1 to guard against, to try to prevent (prevenir). 2 to forestall (anticipar). || *v.pron.* 3 to be forewarned, to be on one's guard.

precavidamente *adv.* warily, guardedly.

precavido, -a *adj.* wary, guarded.

precedente *adj.* 1 preceding, previous, former. || *s.m.* 2 precedent.

preceder *v.t.* 1 to precede, to go before. 2 (fig.) to take precedence over.

preceptivamente *adv.* compulsorily, mandatorily.

preceptivo, -a *adj.* 1 mandatory, compulsory. || *s.f.* 2 precepts, rules. || 3 **preceptiva literaria,** list of literary rules.

precepto *s.m.* 1 precept. 2 rule, order (regla).

preceptor, -a *s.m.* y *f.* 1 teacher, private tutor. || *s.f.* 2 governess.

preceptuar *v.t.* 1 to establish, to lay down. 2 to act as a tutor for.

preces *s.f.pl.* 1 supplications (ruegos). 2 prayers (oraciones).

preciado, -a *adj.* precious, valued.

preciar *v.t.* 1 to value. || *v.pron.* 2 to be conceited (presumir), to boast (vanagloriarse).

precinta *s.f.* 1 customs seal (aduana). 2 corner reinforcement (cajones). 3 (brit.) parcelling, (EE.UU.) parceling (náutico).

precintado, -a *p.p.* 1 de **precintar.** || *adj.* 2 sealed.

precintar *v.t.* 1 COM. to seal. 2 DER. to seal off. 3 to reinforce, to parcel (cuerda).

precinto *s.m.* 1 sealing (acto). 2 COM. seal. 3 DER. seal: *colocación de precinto = sealing off.*

precio *s.m.* 1 price, cost (costo), value (valor). 2 (fig.) worth.

preciosamente *adv.* beautifully, exquisitely, charmingly.

preciosidad *s.f.* beauty (cosa o persona).

precioso, -a *adj.* 1 precious, valuable (de valor). 2 lovely, delightful (hermoso): *fue una puesta de sol preciosa = it was a lovely sunset.*

preciosismo *s.m.* preciosity.
preciosura *s.f.* 1 (Am.) preciousness, value (valor). 2 (Am.) precious object, beautiful thing (algo precioso). 3 (desp. y Am.) preciosity.
precipicio *s.m.* 1 GEOG. precipice, cliff. 2 (fig.) downfall, ruin.
precipitación *s.f.* 1 haste (prisa), rashness (imprudencia). 2 GEOG. precipitation, rainfall (lluvia), snowfall (nieve). 3 QUIM. precipitation.
precipitadamente *adv.* hastily, rashly.
precipitado, -a *adj.* 1 hasty, hurried (veloz). 2 impulsive, rash, reckless precipitate (imprudente). || *s.m.* 3 QUIM. precipitate.
precipitar *v.t.* 1 to hurl down, to throw down (arrojar). 2 to hasten (apresurar), to accelerate, to speed up (acelerar). 3 to endanger (exponer a peligro). 4 QUIM. to precipitate. || *v.pron.* 5 to hurl oneself down, to throw oneself down (arrojarse). 6 to hasten, to rush (apresurarse). 7 to pounce (presa).
precisamente *adv.* precisely.
precisar *v.t.* 1 to specify, to determine exactly (delimitar). 2 to compel, to force (obligar). 3 to need, to require (necesitar). || *v.i.* 4 to be necessary, to be essential (ser necesario): *se precisa más dinero = more money is necessary.*
precisión *s.f.* 1 precision, accuracy (exactitud). 2 necessity, need (necesidad).
preciso, -a *adj.* 1 exact, accurate; precise (cantidad o tiempo). 2 necessary, essential.
preclaramente *adv.* illustriously.
preclaro, -a *adj.* (lit.) illustrious, celebrated.
precocidad *s.f.* precociousness, precocity.
preconización *s.f.* commendation, recommendation.
preconizador, -a *adj.* 1 laudatory. || *s.m.* y *f.* 2 commender.
preconizar *v.t.* 1 to praise, to eulogise (elogiar). 2 to recommend (recomendar), to propose (proponer), to advocate (abogar por).
precoz *adj.* 1 BOT. early. 2 precocious (avanzado).
precursor, -a *adj.* 1 precursory, precursive. || *s.m.* y *f.* 2 precursor, forerunner.
predecesor, -a *s.m.* y *f.* predecessor.
predecir *v.t.* to predict, to foretell, to forecast.
predefinir *v.t.* to predetermine.
predestinación *s.f.* REL. predestination.
predestinar *v.t.* 1 to predestine. 2 REL. to predestine.
predeterminar *v.t.* to predetermine.
prédica *s.f.* 1 REL. sermon. 2 harangue (perorata).
predicable *s.m.* 1 LOG. predicable. 2 GRAM. predicable.
predicado *s.m.* 1 LOG. predicate. 2 GRAM. predicate. || 3 **— nominal,** noun predicate. 4 **— verbal,** verb predicate.
predicamento *s.m.* 1 standing, prestige (prestigio). 2 LOG. predicament.
predicar *v.t.* 1 REL. to preach. 2 (desp.) to sermonize. 3 to flatter (elogiar con exceso). 4 to rebuke (increpar). || *v.i.* 5 REL. to preach.
predicativo, -a *adj.* GRAM. predicative.
predicción *s.f.* 1 prediction, forecast. 2 forecast (tiempo).
predilección *s.f.* 1 predilection. || 2 **predilecciones y aversiones,** likes and dislikes.
predilecto, -a *adj.* (brit.) favourite, (EE.UU.) favorite.
predio *s.m.* estate, property.
predisponer *v.t.* 1 to predispose. 2 (desp.) to prejudice (against).
predisposición *s.f.* 1 predisposition, inclination (para una habilidad o similar). 2 prejudice, bias (contra una persona).
predispuesto, -a *p.p.* 1 de **predisponer.** || *adj.* 2 inclined, with a tendency (a una enfermedad, habilidad o similar). 3 prejudiced, biased (contra una persona).
predominante *adj.* predominant, prevailing.
predominar *v.t.* 1 to predominate over, to dominate. 2 (fig.) to overlook (dar a). || *v.i.* 3 to prevail (prevalecer), to predominate (dominar).
predominio *s.m.* predominance, prevalence.
predorsal *adj.* 1 ZOOL. predorsal. 2 FON. front: *una vocal predorsal = a front vowel.*
predorso *s.m.* FON. front of the tongue.
preeminencia *s.f.* preeminence, supremacy.
preeminente *adj.* pre-eminent, superior.
preexistencia *s.f.* pre-existence.
preexistente *adj.* pre-existent.
preexistir *v.i.* to pre-exist.
prefabricación *s.f.* prefabrication.
prefabricar *v.t.* to prefabricate.
prefacio *s.m.* 1 preface, foreword (preámbulo). 2 REL. preface.
prefecto *s.m.* prefect.
prefectura *s.f.* prefecture (en Francia y en algunas órdenes religiosas).
preferencia *s.f.* preference.
preferente *adj.* 1 preferential (en general). 2 DER. preferent, having priority.
preferentemente *adv.* preferentially.
preferible *adj.* preferable.
preferiblemente *adv.* preferably.
preferir *v.t.* to prefer, 'd rather: *prefiero quedarme = I'd rather stay.*
prefijación *s.f.* GRAM. prefixation.
prefijar *v.t.* 1 to prearrange, to arrange beforehand. 2 GRAM. to prefix.
prefijo *s.m.* GRAM. prefix.
prefulgente *adj.* (p.u.) gleaming, glittering.
pregón *s.m.* 1 public announcement, proclamation (aviso público). 2 street cry (de vendedor). 3 speech opening a ceremony, etc.: *pregón de la Semana Santa.*
pregonar *v.t.* proclaim, announce.
pregonero, -a *adj.* 1 proclaiming. || *s.m.* 2 town crier.
pregunta *s.f.* 1 question. || 2 **andar, estar** o **quedar uno a la cuarta —,** (fam.) to be broke, (fam.) to be skint. 3 **hacer una —,** to ask a question. 4 **— capciosa,** catch question.
preguntar *v.t.* 1 to ask. 2 to question, to interrogate (interrogar). || *v.i.* 3 to ask, to enquire. || *v.pron.* 4 to wonder. || 5 **— por uno,** to ask for someone, to ask after someone, to enquire about someone.
preguntón, -ona *adj.* 1 (fam.) nosey, inquisitive. || *s.m.* y *f.* 2 inquisitive person, (fam.) nosey parker.
prehistoria *s.f.* HIST. prehistory.
prehistórico, -a *adj.* HIST. prehistoric.
prejuicio *s.m.* 1 prejudice, bias (parcialidad). 2 prejudgment (acción).
prejuzgar *v.t.* to prejudge.
prelación *s.f.* precedence, preference, priority.
prelado *s.m.* REL. prelate.
prelatura *s.f.* REL. prelature.
preliminar *adj.* 1 preliminary. || *s.m.* 2 preliminary.
preliminarmente *adv.* preliminarily.
preludio *s.m.* 1 (fig.) prelude (preámbulo). 2 MUS. prelude (composición). 3 MUS. tuning up (ensayo).
prematuramente *adv.* prematurely.
prematuro, -a *adj.* premature: *un bebé prematuro = a premature baby.*
premeditación *s.f.* 1 premeditation. 2 DER. premeditation.
premeditadamente *adv.* deliberately, with full awareness.
premeditar *v.t.* to premeditate.
premiación *s.f.* awards ceremony, prize-giving.
premiado, -a *p.p.* 1 de **premiar.** || *adj.* 2 prize-winning (billete, cupón, novela, etc.).
premiar *v.t.* to give a prize to, to give an award to.
premio *s.m.* 1 reward, recompense (recompensa). 2 COM. premium. 3 prize (lotería, etc.), award (literario). || 4 **— gordo,** first prize, top prize.
premiosamente *adv.* awkwardly, clumsily.
premiosidad *s.f.* awkwardness, clumsiness.
premioso, -a *adj.* 1 tight (ajustado). 2 urgent (urgente). 3 burdensome (gravoso). 4 clumsy, awkward (movimientos). 5 tongue-tied. 6 (desp.) stilted, awkward (estilo).
premisa *s.f.* LOG. premise, premiss.
premonición *s.f.* 1 premonition. 2 foreboding (advertencia).
premonitorio, -a *adj.* 1 MED. premonitory. 2 indicative, warning.
premura *s.f.* urgency, haste.
prenda *s.f.* 1 pledge, security (garantía). 2 darling (persona). 3 garment, article of clothing (ropa). 4 bed linen (cama). || *pl.* 5 talents, qualities, gifts (cualidades). 6 household articles (enseres). 7 forfeits (juego). || 8 **no soltar —,** (fig.) to give nothing away, to be noncommittal.
prendar *v.t.* 1 to give a guarantee, to pledge. 2 to captivate (encantar), to win over (ganar la voluntad). || *v.pron.* 3 to

be captivated, (fig.) to be spellbound (encantado). **4** (lit.) to fall in love (enamorarse).

prendedor *s.m.* clasp, brooch, fastener.

prender *v.t.* **1** to grasp, to seize (agarrar). **2** to arrest, to detain (detener). **3** to imprison (aprisionar). **4** to fasten (enganchar). **5** to set (fuego): *acaban de prender fuego a la casa = they've just set fire to the house.* || *v.i.* **6** to take root (echar raíces). **7** to take, to catch (fuego). **8** (Am. y fam.) to con, to catch (engañar).

prendido, -a *p.p.* **1** de **prender.** || *s.m.* **2** clip, brooch.

prendimiento *s.m.* capture, seizure.

prensa *s.f.* **1** MEC. press. **2** printing press (imprenta). **3** press (publicaciones). || **4 — hidráulica,** hydraulic press.

prensar *v.t.* to press.

prensil *adj.* prehensile.

prensor, -a *adj.* **1** gripping. **2** ZOOL. zygodactyl, zygodactylous. || *s.f.* **3** ZOOL. zygodactyl.

prenuncio *s.m.* prediction (predicción), portent (presagio).

preñado, -a *adj.* **1** pregnant (embarazada). **2** bulging, sagging (abombado). **3** full (lleno), charged (cargado). || *s.m.* **4** pregnancy (embarazo). **5** pregnancy (tiempo que dura). **6** foetus, fetus (feto).

preñar *v.t.* to make pregnant.

preñez *s.f.* pregnancy (embarazo).

preocupación *s.f.* preocupation, worry, concern.

preocupadamente *adv.* worriedly.

preocupado, -a *p.p.* **1** de **preocupar.** || *adj.* **2** worried, concerned.

preocupar *v.t.* **1** to worry, to cause concern, to preoccupy (inquietar). **2** to previously occupy (ocupar previamente). || *v.pron.* **3** to worry, to be worried, to be concerned (inquietarse), to care (importar).

prepalatal *adj.* FON. prepalatal.

preparación *s.f.* **1** preparation (estado de estar preparado). **2** training, culture (en temas científicos o culturales). **3** MED. preparation (farmacéutica). **4** preparedness (militar, física, mental, etc.).

preparado, -a *p.p.* **1** de **preparar.** || *adj.* **2** prepared, ready (listo). **3** DEP. trained. **4** able (capacitado). **5** ready cooked (comida). || *s.m.* **6** preparation (medicamento).

preparar *v.t.* **1** to prepare. **2** DEP. to train, to coach. **3** TEC. to process.

preparativo, -a *adj.* **1** preparatory. || *s.m.* **2** preparation.

preparatorio, -a *adj.* preparatory.

preponderancia *s.f.* preponderance.

preponderante *adj.* preponderant, prevailing.

preponderar *v.i.* to preponderate, to predominate, to prevail.

preposición *s.f.* GRAM. preposition.

preposicional *adj.* GRAM. prepositional.

prepósito *s.m.* **1** chairman (de una junta). **2** REL. provost.

preposterar *v.t.* to reverse, to upset.

prepotencia *s.f.* **1** power, superiority. **2** (desp.) arrogance.

prepotente *adj.* overbearing, haughty.

prepucio *s.m.* ANAT. foreskin, prepuce.

prerrogativa *s.f.* prerogative, privilege.

prerromance *adj.* **1** Vulgar Latin. **2** pre-Romance.

presagiar *v.t.* to predict, to foretell.

presagio *s.m.* **1** portent, omen (agüero). **2** foreboding, premonition (premonición).

presbicia *s.f.* MED. presbyopia, long sightedness.

presbiteriano, -a *adj.* REL. **1** Presbyterian. || *s.m.* y *f.* **2** Presbyterian.

presbiterio *s.m.* REL. presbytery.

presbítero *s.m.* **1** REL. presbyter (del presbiterianismo). **2** REL. priest (catolicismo).

prescindible *adj.* dispensable.

prescindir *v.t.* **1** to disregard, to omit, (lit.) to eschew (omitir). **2** to do without (no contar con). **3** to get rid (of), to dispense (with) (deshacerse de).

prescribir *v.t.* **1** to prescribe (ordenar). **2** DER. to prescribe. || *v.i.* **3** DER to prescribe.

prescripción *s.f.* **1** prescription. **2** DER. legal principle.

prescriptivo, -a *adj.* prescriptive.

prescrito, -a *p.p.* **1** de **prescribir.** || *adj.* **2** prescribed.

presea *s.f.* (lit.) jeweal, precious thing.

presecretaría *s.f.* (Am.) **1** undersecretaryship (cargo). **2** undersecretary's office (oficina).

preselección *s.f.* **1** preselection. **2** DEP. seeding. **3** shortlisting (acción de elegir candidatos), shortlist (candidatos elegidos).

preseleccionar *v.t.* **1** to short list (personas para un trabajo, beca, premio, etc.). **2** DEP. to seed.

presencia *s.f.* **1** presence (asistencia). **2** presence, bearing (porte). **3** (desp.) pomp, ostentation (boato). || **4 — de ánimo,** presence of mind.

presencial *adj.* **testigo —,** eyewitness.

presenciar *v.t.* **1** to be present at (asistir). **2** to witness, to see (ver).

presentable *adj.* presentable.

presentación *s.f.* **1** introduction (de personas). **2** presentation (de un tema, libro, etc.).

presentador, -a *s.m.* y *f.* TV. host, hostess (de un programa).

presentar *v.t.* **1** to present. **2** to offer: *María presenta sus disculpas = Maria offers her excuses.* **3** to put forward, to submit (proponer). **4** to introduce, to present: *me presentó a sus padres = I was introduced to his parents; le presentaron a la Reina = he was presented to the Queen.* || *pron.* **5** to present oneself/itself, to turn up (aparecer). **6** to volunteer, to put oneself forward (ofrecerse). **7** to report, to appear (comparecer): *tiene que presentarse ante el juez mañana = he has to appear before the judge tomorrow.*

presente *adj.* **1** present (asistente). **2** present (corriente). **3** GRAM. present. || *s.m.* **4** GRAM. present, present tense. **5** present, gift (regalo). || **6 mejorando lo —,** present company excepted. **7 ¡—!,** present!, here!

presentimiento *s.m.* premonition, foreboding.

presentir *v.t.* to have a presentiment, to have a premonition of.

preservar *v.t.* to preserve, to protect.

preservación *s.f.* preservation, conservation.

preservante *s.f.* QUIM. preservative.

preservativo, -a *adj.* **1** preservative. || *s.m.* **2** contraceptive, condom.

presidencia *s.f.* **1** presidency (de estado, club), chairmanship (de empresa, junta). **2** president's office, chairman's office. || **3 ocupar la —,** to take the chair, to preside (reuniones).

presidencial *adj.* presidential.

presidencialismo *s.m.* POL. presidential system.

presidente, -a *s.m.* y *f.* **1** POL. President (jefe del Estado). **2** POL. Prime Minister (en España). **3** POL. Speaker (parlamento). **4** chairman (empresa, junta), chairperson (comités).

presidiario, -a *s.m.* y *f.* convict.

presidio *s.m.* **1** prison (cárcel). **2** convicts (presos). **3** hard labour (trabajos forzados). **4** POL. praesidium. **5** MIL. garrison, fortress.

presidir *v.t.* **1** to preside at, to preside over (gobierno, reuniones). **2** to chair (reuniones). **3** (fig.) to prevail in, to dominate (predominar). || *v.i.* **4** to preside, to take the chair.

presilla *s.f.* **1** loop. **2** buttonhole stitch.

presión *s.f.* **1** pressure. **2** FIS. pressure. || **3 grupos de —,** pressure groups. **4 — atmosférica,** atmospheric pressure. **5 — arterial,** blood pressure. **6 — osmótica,** osmotic pressure. **7 — sanguínea,** blood pressure.

presionar *v.t.* **1** to press (haciendo fuerza física). **2** (fig.) to put pressure on (una persona, no físicamente). || **3 — por /para,** to press for: *presioné para que mi hijo fuera admitido = I pressed for my child to be admitted.*

preso, -a *p.p.irr.* **1** de **prender.** || *adj.* **2** under arrest, imprisoned. || *s.m.* y *f.* **3** prisoner. || *s.f.* **4** seizure, capture (acción de prender). **5** catch, prize, haul (cosa(s) apresadas). **6** MIL. spoils. **7** ZOOL. prey, quarry. **8** ditch, irrigation channel (acequia). **9** (brit.) millrace, (EE.UU.) flume (de molinos, etc.). || *s.f.pl.* **10** fangs (colmillos), claws, talons (garras).

prestación *s.f.* **1** contribution (aportación). **2** service. || *pl.* **3** performance: *este coche tiene fabulosas prestaciones = this car has a fantastic performance.* || **4 — personal,** compulsory community work (castigo).

prestamista *s.m.* y *f.* moneylender, pawnbroker.

préstamo *s.m.* 1 FIN. loan. 2 lending (dar). 3 borrowing (pedir). 4 loan word (lingüística).
prestancia *s.f.* 1 excellence. 2 distinction, elegance, dignity (estilo).
prestar *v.t.* 1 to lend, to loan. 2 (fig.) to lend, to give: *nos prestó su ayuda = he gave us his help.* || *v.pron.* 3 to lend oneself/itself.
prestatario, -a *s.m.* y *f.* borrower.
preste *s.m.* REL. (arc.) priest.
presteza *s.f.* promptness, alacrity.
prestidigitación *s.f.* juggling; sleight of hand.
prestidigitador, -ora *s.m.* y *f.* conjuror, magician.
prestigiador, -ora *adj.* fascinating.
prestigiar *v.t.* to give prestige to.
prestigio *s.m.* 1 prestige (renombre). 2 trick (truco), spell (ensalmo). 3 sleight of hand (artimaña).
prestigioso, -a *adj.* prestigious; renowned.
presto, -a *adj.* 1 prompt, quick (diligente). 2 ready, prepared (listo). 3 MUS. presto. || *adv.* 4 promptly, quickly, (fam.) at the double.
presumible *adj.* probable: *parece presumible que habrá problemas = it seems probable there will be problems.*
presumiblemente *adv.* probably; presumably.
presumido, -a *p.p.* 1 de **presumir.** || *adj.* 2 conceited, vain.
presumir *v.t.* 1 to give oneself airs, to be conceited, (fam.) to show off, (fam.) to kid oneself. || *v.t.* 2 to presume, to assume, to suppose: *presumo que os conocéis = I assume that you know each other.*
presunción *s.f.* 1 supposition, presumption (suposición). 2 conceit (algo de lo que presumir un poco vanamente).
presuntamente *adv.* supposedly, presumably.
presunto, -a *adj.* 1 presumed, supposed (supuesto). 2 (desp.) so-called. 3 DER. alleged. || 4 **heredero —,** heir presumptive.
presuntuosamente *adv.* conceitedly, vainly.
presuntuoso, -a *adj.* 1 presumptuous, conceited (engreído). 2 pretentious.
presuponer *v.t.* 1 to presuppose. 2 FIN. to cost, to work out a budget for.
presuposición *s.f.* presupposition.
presupuestar *v.t.* to budget for; to reckon up.
presupuestario, -a *adj.* budgetary.
presupuesto, -a *p.p.irr.* 1 de **presuponer.** || *s.m.* 2 reason, motive (pretexto). 3 assumption (suposición). 4 FIN. budget. 5 estimate (obras). || 6 **— del Estado,** state budget. 7 **— nacional,** national budget.
presura *s.f.* 1 difficulty, (fam.) jam (apuro). 2 haste, urgency (prisa). 3 persistence (porfía).
presurosamente *adv.* quickly; hastily.
presuroso, -a *adj.* quick; hastly.
pretender *v.t.* 1 to try for, to seek (aspirar). 2 to try, to attempt, to endeavour (procurar). 3 to apply, to hope, (desp.) to purport: *pretende ser lexicógrafo = he hopes to become/he purports to be a lexicographer.* 4 to court, to woo (cortejar).
pretendiente *s.m.* y *f.* 1 suitor (de carácter amoroso). 2 pretender (al trono). 3 claimant, candidate (a un puesto de trabajo, responsabilidad o similar).
pretensión *s.f.* 1 claim (exigencia). || *pl.* 2 aim(s), objective(s) (deseos). 3 pretension(s) (vanidad).
preterición *s.f.* 1 preterition (en retórica). 2 omission.
preterir *v.t.* 1 to leave out, to pass over. 2 (p.us.) to pretermit.
pretérito, -a *adj.* 1 past. 2 GRAM. past. || *s.m.* 3 past, past tense. || 4 **— imperfecto,** GRAM. imperfect. 5 **— perfecto,** GRAM. perfect.
preternatural *adj.* preternatural.
pretextar *v.t.* to give as a pretext, to use as an excuse.
pretexto *s.m.* excuse, pretext.
pretil *s.m.* 1 parapet (muro pequeño). 2 guardrail (baranda).
pretina *s.f.* 1 belt (correa). 2 waistband (cintura). 3 waist (forma). 4 girdle (lo que ciñe).
pretónico, -a *adj.* FON. pretonic.
pretor *s.m.* HIST. praetor.
pretoriano, -a *adj.* 1 HIST. praetorian. || 2 **guardia —,** praetorian guard.
pretorio, -a *adj.* HIST. praetorian.
prevalecer *v.i.* 1 prevail (sobresalir). 2 to prevail, to triumph (triunfar). 3 (fig.) to thrive (prosperar). 4 BOT. to take root.
prevaler *v.i.* 1 to prevail (prevalecer). || *v.pron.* 2 to avail oneself: *se ha prevalido de la oferta = he has availed himself of the offer.* 3 (desp.) to make the most (of), to cash in (on): *ella se ha prevalido de su generosidad = she has cashed in on his generosity/she has made the most of his generosity.*
prevaricación *s.f.* DER. prevarication, perversion of the course of justice.
prevaricador, -a *s.m.* y *f.* person who fails in his/her duties.
prevaricar *v.i.* 1 to betray one's trust (faltar a su deber). 2 to perjure oneself, to prevaricate (cometer perjurio). 3 (fig.) to rave, to talk nonsense (desvariar).
prevención *s.f.* 1 readiness, preparedness (preparación). 2 preparation (preparativo). 3 prevention (impedir). 4 precaution (precaución). 5 provision. 6 prejudice (prejuicio). 7 police station (comisaría). 8 MIL. guardroom, guardhouse. || 9 **de —,** to be on the safe side, just in case.
prevenidamente *adv.* cautiously; with preparation.
prevenido, -a *p.p.* 1 de **prevenir.** || *adj.* 2 prepared, ready (ante algún acontecimiento). 3 stocked (con alguna cosa necesaria probablemente). || 4 **hombre — vale por dos,** forwewarned is forearmed.
prevenir *v.t.* 1 to prepare, to get ready (preparar). 2 to foresee (anticipar). 3 to prejudice (predisponer). 4 to prevent, to forestall (impedir). || *v.pron.* 5 to get ready (prepararse). 6 to take precautions.
preventivamente *adv.* preventively.
preventivo, -a *adj.* 1 MED. preventive (en contra de la enfermedad). 2 DER. preventive (preso). 3 precautionary (cualquier medida).
preventorio *s.m.* MED. preventorium.
prever *v.t.* 1 to foresee. 2 to forecast (pronosticar). 3 to plan, to have in mind: *tenemos prevista la fiesta para el jueves = we have the party planned for Thursday/we have Thursday in mind for the party.*
previamente *adv.* previously.
previo, -a *adj.* 1 previous, prior (anterior). 2 preliminary (preliminar).
previsible *adj.* predictable, foreseeable.
previsiblemente *adv.* predictably, foreseeably.
previsión *s.f.* 1 foresight (de lo que va a ocurrir). 2 caution (cuidado). 3 forecast (del tiempo, de la política, de la Bolsa, etc.). || 4 **en — de,** as a precaution against; in anticipation of: *llevaré el paraguas en previsión de que llueva = I'll take the umbrella as a precaution against rain.*
previsor, -a *adj.* prudent, wise.
prez *s.m.* (brit.) honour, (EE.UU.) honor, glory.
prieto, -a *adj.* 1 firm: *de prietas carnes = with a firm body.* 2 tight, compressed (apretado). 3 very dark, blackish (color). 4 mean, (fam.) tight-fisted (tacaño).
primacía *s.f.* 1 primacy, (superioridad), priority (prioridad). 2 REL. primacy.
primado *s.m.* REL. primate.
primario, -a *adj.* 1 primary: *enseñanza primaria = primary education.* 2 elementary, rudimentary (elemental). 3 GEOL. primary.
primate *s.m.* 1 important figure, outstanding person (prócer). 2 ZOOL. primate. || *pl.* 3 ZOOL. primates.
primavera *s.f.* 1 spring, springtime (estación). 2 (fig.) springtime, prime. 3 BOT. primrose. 4 ZOOL. blue tit (pájaro).
primazgo *s.m.* 1 cousinhood, cousinship (parentesco). 2 primacy (primacía).
primer *adj.* V. **primero, -a.**
primerizo, -a *adj.* 1 inexperienced, (fig.) green. 2 MED. primiparous. || *s.m.* y *f.* 3 novice, beginner. || *s.f.* 4 MED. primipara.
primero, -a *adj.* [**primer** delante de *s.m.*] 1 first. 2 former (anterior). 3 primary: *primera enseñanza = primary education.* 4 (fig.) best (mejor). 5 (fig.) leading, principal (más importante). 6 prime: *las primeras necesidades = prime necessities; el primer ministro = the prime minister.* 7 (fig.) basic, fundamental (básico). || *adv.* 8 first, firstly (primeramente). 9 sooner, rather (antes): *¡primero morir! = I/we would rather die!* || 10 **la primera página,** PER. the front page. 11 **los pri-**

meros años del siglo XX, the early years of the twentieth century.

primicia *s.f.pl.* 1 first fruits. || *s.f.* 2 PER. scoop (noticia bomba).

primigenio, -a *adj.* primitive, original.

primitivamente *adv.* 1 originally (en un principio). 2 in a primitive manner, primitively (de manera primitiva).

primitivismo *s.m.* primitivism.

primitivo, -a *adj.* 1 early (temprano): *una versión primitiva = an early version.* 2 original: *el texto primitivo apareció en Santo Domingo = the original text turned up in Santo Domingo.* 2 primitive (lingüística). 3 primitive, uncivilised. 4 ART. primitive.

primo, -a *adj.* 1 MAT. prime. 2 raw (materia). || *s.m.* y *f.* 3 cousin (pariente). 4 simpleton (ingenuo). 5 (fam.) mug, sucker (engañado). || *s.f.* 6 MIL. first quarter of the night. 7 REL. prime. 8 MUS. first string. 9 bonus (plus). 10 insurance premium (seguros).

primogénito, -a *adj.* 1 first-born, eldest. || 2 first-born, eldest.

primogenitura *s.f.* primogeniture; DER. birthright (que conlleva el derecho preferente a la herencia).

primor *s.m.* 1 skill, care (destreza). 2 thing of beauty, fine work (obra). 3 beauty, exquisiteness (belleza), delicacy, daintiness (delicadeza).

primordial *adj.* 1 prime, primary (primero). 2 basic, fundamental (básico).

primorosamente *adv.* 1 beautifully, exquisitely. 2 very skillfully (con maña).

primoroso, -a *adj.* 1 delicate, exquisite, dainty (exquisito). 2 (brit.) skilful, (EE.UU.) skillful, (diestro).

princesa *s.f.* princess.

principado *s.m.* 1 princedom (título). 2 principality (territorio). 3 primacy (primacía).

principal *adj.* 1 principal, main, chief (más importante). 2 illustrious (noble). 3 essential (fundamental). 4 first, main (planta). 5 GRAM. main. || *s.m.* 6 principal, head (jefe). 7 FIN. principal, capital.

principalidad *s.f.* superiority, pre-eminence.

principalmente *adv.* chiefly, mainly, principally.

príncipe *adj.* 1 first, original: *edición príncipe = first edition.* || *s.m.* 2 prince. || 3 **el — azul,** Prince Charming. 4 **el — heredero,** Crown Prince.

principesco, -a *adj.* princely.

principiante *s.m.* y *f.* beginner, novice (en cualquier tema).

principiar *v.t.* e *i.* to begin, to start, to commence.

principio *s.m.* 1 beginning, start (comienzo). 2 (fig.) source (fuente). 3 origin (origen). 4 FIL. principle. 5 principle (moral). 6 entrée (plato). || 7 **a los principios** o **al —,** at first, in the beginning. 8 **en —,** in principle. 9 **por —,** on principle.

pringado, -a *s.m.* y *f.* 1 (hum.) fall guy, victim. || 2 *s.f.* bread dipped in pork dripping.

pringar o **empringar** *v.t.* 1 to dip in fat (mojar). 2 to stain with fat, to splash with grease (manchar). 3 to baste (asado). 4 (fam.) to wound (herir); (fam.) to make someone bleed (hacer sangre). 5 (fam.) to slander (infamar). 6 (fam.) to get someone mixed up (in), to involve someone (in): *a su hermano le pringaron en un asunto de tráfico de influencias = his brother was involved in a case of trade in influences.* || *v.i.* 7 (fam.) to be involved (in), to be mixed up (in) (involucrarse). || *v.pron.* 8 to get greasy, to get stained with fat, to splash oneself with fat (mancharse). 6 (fig.) to make money dishonestly, (fam.) to be on the make (forrarse). 7 (fig.) to be put upon, to be the unlucky one, (fam.) to be the fall guy (fastidiarse).

pringoso, -a *adj.* greasy, grease-stained.

pringue *s.m.* y *f.* 1 dripping, fat (grasa animal). 2 filth, grime (mugre), grease stain, grease spot (mancha).

prior *s.m.* REL. prior.

priorato o **priorazgo** *s.m.* REL. priory.

priori, a priori, *loc.adv.* LOG. a priori.

prioridad *s.f.* 1 priority (anterioridad). 2 seniority (antigüedad).

prisa *s.f.* 1 speed (rapidez). 2 haste, urgency (premura). || 3 **darse —,** to hurry up, (fam.) to get a move on. 4 **de — o deprisa,** quickly, in a hurry. 5 **de — y corriendo,** at top speed. 6 **meter uno —,** to rush someone, to hurry someone up. 7 **tener —,** to be in a hurry.

prisión *s.f.* 1 arrest, capture (acción). 2 prison, gaol, jail (cárcel). 3 (fig.) bond (moral). 4 imprisonment (privación de libertad). || *pl.* 5 shackles, irons, fetters (grillos).

prisionero, -a *s.m.* y *s.f.* 1 prisoner of war. 2 (fig.) prisoner: *es prisionero de sus pasiones = he is a prisoner of his passions.* 3 captive, kidnap victim (secuestrado).

prisma *s.m.* 1 MAT. prism. 2 (fig.) point of view, perspective. || 3 **— óptico,** prism.

prismático, -a *adj.* 1 MAT. prismatic. || *s.m.pl.* 2 binoculars, field glasses.

prístino, -a *adj.* 1 pristine, original (original). 2 pristine, pure, untarnished (puro).

privación *s.f.* 1 want, privation (de cosas necesarias). 2 lack (falta de libertad o de otro derecho). || *pl.* 3 hardships (especialmente materiales).

privadamente *adv.* privately.

privado, -a *p.p.* 1 de **privar.** || *adj.* 2 confidential (confidencial). 3 personal, private (particular). 4 senseless, unconscious (desmayado). || *s.m.* 5 POL. (brit.) favourite, (EE.UU.) favorite. 6 privy (retrete). || *s.f.* 7 animal dropping (excremento).

privanza *s.f.* (brit.) favour, (EE.UU.) favor (para con una persona).

privar *v.t.* 1 to deprive (desposeer). 2 to forbid (prohibir). || *v.i.* 3 POL. to be in favour (disfrutar privanza). 4 to be popular (tener aprobación). 5 to be in fashion, (fam.) to be all the rage (estar de moda). || *v.r.* 6 to go without, to do without, to deprive oneself.

privativamente *adv.* exclusively.

privativo, -a *adj.* 1 exclusive, restricted, peculiar (propio): *esta cualidad es privativa de los políticos = this quality is exclusive to politicians.* 2 GRAM. privative.

privilegiadamente *adv.* in a privileged way.

privilegiado, -a *p.p.* 1 de **privilegiar.** || *adj.* 2 privileged (por su fortuna o similar). 3 exceptionally good (capacidad mental o similar). || *s.m.* y *f.* 4 (the) privileged.

privilegiar *v.t.* to favour.

privilegio *s.m.* privilege.

pro *s.m.* y *f.* 1 profit, advantage (provecho). || 2 **el — y el contra,** the pros and the cons. 3 **en —,** in favour. 4 **hombre de —,** honest man.

proa *s.f.* 1 prow, bow, bows (de barco). 2 nose (de avión). || 3 **mascarón de —,** figurehead.

probado, -a *p.p.* 1 de **probar.** || *adj.* 2 proven, proved, tried and tested (confirmado). 3 experienced (baqueteado).

probabilidad *s.f.* 1 probability, likelihood. 2 chance, prospect: *no hay probabilidades de que venga = there are no chances that he will come.*

probable *adj.* 1 probable, likely (puede ocurrir). 2 provable (capaz de probarse).

probablemente *adv.* probably.

probador, -a *adj.* 1 testing, test. || *s.m.* y *f.* 2 tester (cheque), taster (catavinos). || *s.m.* 3 fitting room, changing room (de una tienda).

probar *v.t.* 1 to prove, to demonstrate (demostrar). 2 to test (aparatos, etc.). 3 to try, to try on (ropa). 4 to taste, to sample (comida, etc.). || *v.i.* 5 to try (intentar).

probatorio, -a *adj.* convincing.

probeta *s.f.* 1 QUIM. graduated test-tube, test-tube. 2 FIS. pressure gauge. 3 MIL. eprouvette (de la pólvora).

probidad *s.f.* integrity, rectitude.

problema *s.m.* 1 problem, difficulty (dificultad). 2 MAT. problem.

problemáticamente *adv.* problematically.

problemático, -a *adj.* 1 problematic, problematical. || *s.f.* 2 problems, set of problems.

probo, -a *adj.* honest, upright, honourable.

proboscidio, -a *adj.* 1 ZOOL. proboscidean, proboscidian. || *s.m.* 2 ZOOL. proboscidean, proboscidian. || *pl.* 3 ZOOL. Proboscidea, proboscideans.

procacidad *s.f.* indecency, obscenity.

procaz *adj.* 1 insolent, impudent (insolente). 2 disgusting, indecent, obscene (desvergonzado): *una película procaz = an obscene film.*

procedencia *s.f.* 1 origin, source (origen). 2 properness, seemliness (moralidad). 3 DER. soundness. 4 port of origin (barco). 5 point of departure (tren, etc.).
procedente *adj.* 1 proper, justified (como es debido). || 2 — **de,** coming from, originating in.
proceder *s.m.* 1 (brit.) behaviour, (EE.UU.) behavior, conduct. || *v.i.* 2 to come from, to originate in (tener como origen). 3 to behave, to act (actuar). 4 to proceed, to go ahead (seguir adelante). 5 to proceed (comenzar). 6 to be fitting, to be right (ser apropiado). 7 DER. to be admissible. || 8 **táchese lo que no proceda,** cross out what does not apply.
procedimiento *s.m.* 1 procedure (general). 2 process, method (concreto). 3 DER. proceedings.
procela *s.f.* (lit.) squall, storm.
proceloso, -a *adj.* (lit.) stormy, tempestuous: *aguas procelosas.*
prócer *adj.* 1 eminent, worthy. || *s.m.* 2 eminent man, distinguished figure.
procesado, -a *p.p.* 1 de **procesar.** || *adj.* 2 DER. procedural (del proceso). 3 DER. accused (acusado). || *s.m.* y *f.* 4 DER. accused, defendant (acusado). 5 TEC. processing.
procesador *s.m.* — **de textos,** INF. word processor.
procesal *adj.* DER. 1 procedural. || 2 **derecho —,** procedural law.
procesamiento *s.m.* 1 DER. indictment. 2 processing (método de transformación de alguna materia). || 3 — **de textos,** INF. word processing.
procesar *v.t.* 1 DER. to prosecute, to try, to bring to trial (meter en proceso). 2 DER. to sentence (dictar resolución). 3 TEC. to process.
procesión *s.f.* 1 procession. || 2 **la — va por dentro,** (fig.) still waters run deep, there's more to this than meets the eye.
proclama *s.f.* 1 POL. manifiesto. 2 announcement, declaration.
proclamación *s.f.* proclamation.
proclamar *v.t.* 1 proclaim (notificar). 2 acclaim (aclamar). || *v.r.* 3 to proclaim oneself.
proclítico, -a *adj.* GRAM. proclitic.
proclive *adj.* inclined, disposed.
proclividad *s.f.* inclination, propensity.
procónsul *s.m.* HIST. proconsul.
procreación *s.f.* procreation.
procreador, -ora *s.m.* y *f.* begetter.
procrear *v.t.* to procreate.
procura *s.f.* 1 DER. power of attorney (procuración). 2 office of lawyer or procurator. 3 search (busca). 4 (Am.) getting.
procurador, -a *adj.* 1 procuring, obtaining. || *s.m.* y *f.* 2 DER. proxy, procuratory (procuración). 3 DER. lawyer, (brit.) solicitor, (EE.UU.) attorney (abogado). 4 HIST. procurator.
procurar *v.t.* 1 to try, to endeavour (intentar). 2 to obtain, to secure (obtener). 3 to yield, to produce, to give (proporcionar). || *v.r.* 4 to secure for oneself, to obtain for oneself.
prodigalidad *s.f.* lavishness.
pródigamente *adv.* lavishly.
prodigar *v.t.* 1 to squander, to waste (malgastar). 2 to lavish, to give generously (colmar). || *v.r.* to do one's utmost to please/to help, to be unstinting (in), (fig.) to go out of one's way: *se prodiga con sus esfuerzos = he is unstinting in his efforts/he does his utmost to help/he goes out of his way to be helpful.*
prodigio *s.m.* 1 prodigy, marvel. || 2 **niño —,** child prodigy.
prodigiosamente *adv.* marvellously, wonderfully.
prodigioso, -a *adj.* marvellous, wonderful.
pródigo, -a *adj.* 1 (desp.) prodigal, wasteful (despilfarrador). 2 rich, productive (productivo). 3 lavish, generous (generoso). || *s.m.* y *f.* 4 spendthrift, wastrel.
producción *s.f.* 1 production (proceso). 2 production, yield, output (rendimiento). || 3 — **en cadena,** mass production.
producir *v.t.* 1 to produce (en general). 2 AGR. to give, to bear, to produce, to yield. 3 FIN. to yield, to produce, to bear. 4 to cause, to bring about (ocasionar). 5 to make, to manufacture, to produce (fabricar). || *v.pron.* 6 to be produced, to be manufactured (fabricarse). 7 to happen, to take place (ocurrir). 8 to come about: *se produjo un cambio repentino.*
productividad *s.f.* productivity.
productivo, -a *adj.* productive.
productivamente *adv.* productively.
producto *s.m.* 1 product (en general). 2 FIN. profit, yield. 3 MAT. product. || *pl.* 4 products (en general). 5 AGR. produce. || 6 — **interior bruto,** ECON. Gross Domestic Product. 7 **productos alimenticios,** foodstuffs. 8 **productos básicos,** commodities. 9 **productos de consumo,** consumer goods.
productor, -a *adj.* 1 producing (que produce). 2 productive (productivo). 3 producer: *nación productora = producer nation.* || *s.m.* y *f.* 4 producer (en general). 5 worker (obrero). 6 producer (cine).
proel *adj.* 1 bow. || *s.m.* 2 bowman (marino).
proemio *s.m.* preface, introduction.
proeza *s.f.* 1 heroic deed, exploit, feat (hazaña). 2 prowess (valentía).
profanación *s.f.* desecration (de algo santo o importante).
profanador, -a *s.m.* y *f.* defiler.
profanamente *adv.* irreverently.
profanar *v.t.* to defile, to desecrate.
profano, -a *adj.* 1 profane, secular, worldly (mundanal). 2 profane, irreverent (impío). 3 indecent, immodest (inmodesto). 4 licentious, immoral (libertino). 5 ignorant, uninitiated (indocto). || *s.m.* y *f.* 6 ignoramus, layman: *soy profano en informática = I'm an ignoramus when it comes to computers.* || *s.m.* 6 libertine, rake. || *s.f.* 7 hussy, (desp.) trollop.
profase *s.f.* BOT. prophase.
profecía *s.f.* prophecy.
proferir *v.t.* 1 to utter. || 2 — **insultos,** to hurl insults, to hurl abuse. 3 — **un suspiro,** to heave a sigh.
profesar *v.t.* 1 (brit.) to practise, (EE.UU.) to practice (ejercer). 2 to profess, to declare (declarar). 3 to feel, to have (sentir). 4 to profess (doctrina). || *v.i.* 5 REL. to profess vows, to take vows.
profesión *s.f.* 1 profession, declaration (acto). 2 profession, career (empleo). || 4 — **liberal,** liberal profession. 3 **hacer — de,** to profess.
profesional *adj.* 1 professional. || *s.m.* y *f.* 2 professional.
profesionalidad *s.f.* professionalism.
profesionalismo *s.m.* professionalism.
profesionalizar *v.t.* to make more professionally-orientated: *tenemos que profesionalizar estos puestos consultivos = we have to make these advisory posts more professionally-orientated.*
profesionalmente *adv.* professionally.
profeso, -a *adj.* REL. 1 professed. || *s.m.* 2 professed monk. || *s.f.* 3 professed nun.
profesor, -a *s.m.* y *f.* 1 teacher (instituto), (brit.) lecturer, (EE.UU.) professor (Universidad). || *s.m.* 2 master, schoolmaster (instituto). || *s.f.* 3 mistress, schoolmistress (instituto).
profesorado *s.m.* 1 post of teacher (instituto), (brit.) post of lecturer, (EE.UU.) professorship (Universidad). 2 teaching profession (profesión). 3 staff, teaching staff, (EE.UU.) faculty.
profeta *s.m.* prophet.
proféticamente *adv.* prophetically.
profético, -a *adj.* prophetic.
profetisa *s.f.* prophetess.
profetizar *v.t.* to prophesy.
proficiente *adj.* proficient.
profiláctico, -a *adj.* MED. 1 preventive, prophylactic. || *s.m.* 2 condom.
profilaxis *s.f.* MED. prophylaxis.
prófugo, -a *adj.* 1 fugitive. 2 MIL. deserting. || *s.m.* y *f.* 3 fugitive. 4 deserter.
profundamente *adv.* 1 deeply (hondamente). 2 deeply, profoundly (en pensamiento, sentimientos, etc.). 3 soundly (manera de dormir).
profundizar *v.t.* 1 to deepen, to make deeper (excavar). 2 to study in depth, to go into in detail (estudiar).
profundo, -a *adj.* 1 deep (hondo). 2 (fig.) profound (erudito). 3 heartfelt, profound (intenso): *expresaba una profunda tristeza = he expressed a heartfelt-/profound sorrow.* 4 low: *hizo una inclinación profunda = he bowed low.* || 5 **poco —,** shallow.
profusamente *adv.* profusely, lavishly, extravagantly.
profusión *s.f.* profusion, abundance.
profuso, -a *adj.* profuse, lavish, extravagant.
progenie *s.f.* 1 lineage, line, family (linaje). 2 offspring, progeny (hijos).

progenitor, -a *s.m.* y *f.* 1 progenitor. || *s.m.pl.* 2 ancestors (antepasados). 3 (hum.) parents (padres).

prognatismo *s.m.* ANAT. prognathism.

programa *s.m.* 1 (brit.) programme, (EE.UU.) program (en general). 2 INF. program. 3 (Am.) love affair. || 4 **— de aplicación,** INF. application program. 5 **— de estudios,** syllabus. 6 **— de televisión,** television programme.

programación *s.f.* 1 TV. programme planning, timetable of programmes. 2 INF. programming. 3 planning of work (en escuelas, empresas, etc.).

programador, -a *s.m.* y *f.* 1 INF. programmer. || *adj.* 2 programming.

programar *v.t.* 1 to plan, to arrange (actividades o similar). 2 INF. to programme.

progre *s.m.* y *f.* (fam.) trendy.

progresar *v.i.* to make progress.

progresión *s.f.* 1 progression. || 2 **— aritmética,** arithmetic progression. 3 **— geométrica,** geometric progression.

progresismo *s.m.* advocation of progress, progressive outlook (talante progresista).

progresista *adj.* 1 progressive. || *s.m.* y *f.* 2 progressive.

progresivamente *adv.* progressively, gradually.

progresivo, -a *adj.* 1 progressive. 2 GRAM. progressive, continuous.

progreso *s.m.* 1 progress, advance. || 2 **hacer progresos,** to make progress.

prohibición *s.f.* prohibition, ban.

prohibicionista *s.m.* y *f.* HIST. prohibitionist (partidario de la prohibición del alcohol en los Estados Unidos en los años 20).

prohibir *v.t.* 1 to ban, to prohibit, to forbid: *se ha prohibido la venta de alcohol en los partidos de fútbol = the sale of alcohol has been banned at football matches.* || 2 **se prohíbe fumar,** no smoking.

prohibitivo, -a *adj.* prohibitive: *los precios son prohibitivos.*

prohijar *v.t.* 1 to adopt: *acaban de prohijar a un crío chino = they've just adopted a Chinese baby.* 2 (fig.) to take up, to adopt: *¡vaya causa que ha prohijado ella! = what a cause she has taken up!*

prohombre *s.m.* great man, outstanding figure.

prójima *s.f.* 1 (fam.) tart, loose woman (de mala fama). || 2 (fam.) **la —,** the old woman, the missus (la parienta).

prójimo *s.m.* 1 fellow man, neighbour: *amarás al prójimo como a ti mismo = love thy neighbour as thyself.* 2 (fam.) chap, bloke (tío).

prole *s.f.* 1 progeny, offspring. 2 (desp.) brood, brats.

prolegómeno *s.m.* 1 prolegomenon. || *pl.* 2 prolegomena.

prolepsis *s.f.* prolepsis.

proletariado *s.m.* POL. proletariat.

proletario, -a *adj.* 1 proletarian. || *s.m.* y *f.* 2 proletarian.

proletarización *s.f.* POL. proletarianization.

proletarizar *v.t.* to proletarianize.

proliferación *s.f.* proliferation.

proliferante *adj.* 1 abundant (abundante). 2 multiplying, proliferating (que cada vez hay más).

proliferar *v.i.* to proliferate, to multiply: *no deben proliferar las armas nucleares = atomic weapons must not proliferate.*

prolífico, -a *adj.* 1 prolific. 2 (desp.) long-winded, interminable.

prolijamente *adv.* extensively, with an excess of detail.

prolijo, -a *adj.* 1 prolix, extensive (largo). 2 thorough, exhaustive (esmerado). 3 (desp.) long-winded, tedious (cargante).

prologar *v.t.* to write an introduction to, to write a preface to.

prólogo *s.m.* 1 prologue, preface, introduction. 2 (fig.) prelude.

prologuista *s.m.* y *f.* writer of introductions, writer of prefaces.

prolongable *adj.* extendible.

prolongación *s.f.* 1 prolongation, extension. 2 lenghtening, extension.

prolongadamente *adv.* at great length, lengthily.

prolongado, -a *p.p.* 1 de **prolongar.** || *adj.* 2 lengthy.

prolongamiento V. **prolongación.**

prolongar *v.t.* 1 to prolong, to extend (alargar). 2 to prolong, (desp.) to drag out (durar más de lo normal). || *v.r.* 3 to extend, to go on (extenderse). 4 to go on longer, (desp.) to drag on (durar demasiado).

promecio *s.m.* QUIM. promethium.

promediar *v.t.* 1 to divide equally, to divide in two. || *v.i.* 2 to mediate (de intermediario). 3 to be halfway through, to be in the middle of (tiempo): *promediaba el mes de agosto = it was halfway through August.*

promedio *s.m.* 1 middle, mid-point (mitad). 2 average (media).

promesa *s.f.* 1 promise (voluntad). 2 pledge (ofrecimiento solemne). || 3 **faltar a su —,** to break one's promise.

promesero, -a *s.m.* y *f.* (Am.) pilgrim.

prometedor, -ora *adj.* promising.

prometer *v.t.* 1 to promise (ofrecer). 2 to pledge (comprometer). || *v.i.* 3 to be promising, to show promise: *promete mucho = he shows a lot of promise/he is very promising.* || *v.r.* 4 to expect, to promise oneself. 5 to get engaged (novios). || 6 **prometérselas uno muy felices,** to have high hopes.

prometido, -a *p.p.* 1 de **prometer.** || *adj.* 2 promised. || *s.m.* 3 fiancé (novio). 4 promise, commitment (promesa). || *s.f.* fiancée (novia).

prominencia *s.f.* 1 protuberance (elevación). 2 bulge, swelling (hinchazón). 3 rise (terreno). 4 hillock (montículo). 5 (fig.) prominence.

prominente *adj.* 1 prominent, distinguished (importante). 2 protuberant, that sticks out, that juts out (físicamente).

promiscuamente *adv.* promiscuously.

promiscuidad *s.f.* promiscuity.

promiscuo, -a *adj.* 1 mixed, mixed up, in disorder (mezclado). 2 ambiguous (ambiguo). 3 promiscuous (sexualmente).

promisión *s.f.* **Tierra de —,** the Promised Land.

promisorio, -a *adj.* promissory.

promoción *s.f.* 1 promotion, preferment (ascenso). 2 DEP. promotion. 3 year, class, intake: *somos de la misma promoción = we were in the same year (at University)/we were in the same intake.* 4 COM. promotion: *ella se dedica a la promoción de ventas = she is involved in sales promotion.* || 5 **partido de —,** DEP. play-off (for promotion).

promocionar *v.t.* 1 COM. to promote. 2 to give rapid promotion to (facilitar el camino). || *v.pron.* 3 to better oneself (mejorarse). 4 to put oneself forward, to push oneself forward (ofrecerse).

promontorio *s.m.* 1 GEOG. hill, rise (elevación). 2 GEOG. promontory, headland (uqe se adentra en el mar). 3 ANAT. promontory.

promover *v.t.* 1 to promote, to further, to foster (activar). 2 to promote (ascender).

promulgación *s.f.* promulgation.

promulgar *v.t.* 1 to proclaim, to make public (publicar). 2 to enact, to pass, to promulgate (leyes).

pronaos *s.m.* ARQ. pronaos.

prono, -a *adj.* 1 (fig.) prone (inclinado). 2 prone (de bruces).

pronombre *s.m.* GRAM. pronoun.

pronominal *adj.* GRAM. pronominal.

pronosticar *v.t.* 1 to forecast, to foretell, to predict (predecir). 2 MED. to give a prognosis of.

pronóstico *s.m.* 1 forecast, prediction (del tiempo, del futuro, etc.). 2 MED. prognosis. || 3 **de — leve,** MED. slight. 4 **de — reservado,** of unknown gravity.

prontamente *adv.* promptly, quickly.

prontitud *s.f.* promptness, quickness.

pronto, -a *adj.* 1 prompt, rapid, quick (rápido). 2 ready, prepared (listo). || *s.m.* 3 impulse, urge (impulso). || *adv.* 4 promptly, at once, quickly (rápido). 5 soon (dentro de poco). || 6 **al —,** at first. 7 **de —, a)** on the spur of the moment (sin reflexión); **b)** suddenly, all of a sudden (de repente). 8 **por lo —** o **por de —,** for the time being, for the present.

prontuario *s.m.* 1 summary (resumen). 2 handbook, compendium (compendio).

pronunciable *adj.* utterable.

pronunciación *s.f.* pronunciation.

pronunciado, -a *p.p.* 1 de **pronunciar.** || *adj.* 2 pronounced (marcado). 3 sharp, tight (curva). 4 noticeable (rasgo).

pronunciamiento *s.m.* POL. pronunciamiento, revolt, insurrection.

pronunciar *v.t.* 1 to pronounce, to utter (emitir sonidos). 2 to deliver (discurso). 3 DER. to pronounce (sentencia). || *v.pron.* 4 POL. to rise up in rebellion. 5

to pronounce oneself, to declare oneself (declararse).
propaganda *s.f.* 1 POL. propaganda. 2 COM. advertising, publicity.
propagandista *s.m.* y *f.* propagandist.
propagandístico, -a *adj.atr.* propaganda.
propagar *v.t.* 1 BIOL. to propagate. 2 (fig.) to propagate, to disseminate, to spread. || *v.pron.* 3 BIOL. to propagate. 4 to be disseminated, to spread.
propalar *v.t.* to divulge, to reveal.
propano *s.m.* QUIM. propane.
proparoxítono, -a *adj.* proparoxytone.
propasar *v.t.* 1 to overstep, to go beyond. || *v.pron.* 2 to go too far, to overstep the mark, to take liberties.
propedéutico, -a *adj.* 1 pertaining to preparatory studies. || *s.f.* 2 preparatory studies.
propender *v.i.* to be inclined, to tend: *propenden a las artes = they tend towards the arts/they are inclined towards the arts.*
propensión *s.f.* inclination, propensity.
propenso, -a *adj.* inclined, prone: *soy propenso a deprimirme demasiado fácilmente = I'm inclined to get depressed too easily.*
propiamente *adv.* 1 properly, correctly. || 2 **— dicho,** in the strict sense: *el té, propiamente dicho, no es tan fuerte como el café = tea in the strict sense is not as strong as coffee.*
propiciación *s.f.* atonement (normalmente con sentido mágico o religioso).
propiciamente *adv.* favourably.
propiciar *v.t.* to propitiate, to appease, to placate.
propiciatorio, -a *adj.* 1 propitiatory. || 2 **víctima propiciatoria,** scapegoat.
propicio, -a *adj.* propitious, (brit.) favourable, (EE.UU.) favorable.
propiedad *s.f.* 1 ownership (derecho). 2 property (cosa). 3 property (edificio), estate (finca). 4 QUIM. property. 5 quality (atributo). 6 accuracy, correctness (lenguaje). || 7 **— literaria,** copyright. 8 **tener una plaza en —,** to have security of tenure, to have tenure.
propietario, -a *adj.* 1 proprietary. || *s.m.* 2 owner, proprietor (dueño). 3 landowner (terrateniente). || *s.f.* 4 owner, proprietress.
propileo *s.m.* ARQ. propylaeum.
propina *s.f.* 1 tip, gratuity. || 2 **de —, a)** as a tip (gratificación); **b)** in addition, as an extra.
propinar *v.t.* 1 to give, to deal (golpe): *ella le propinó un golpe = she dealt him a blow/she hit him.* 2 to administer, to give (medicamento).
propincuo, -a *adj.* near, close.
propio, -a *adj.* 1 own: *viven en su propia casa = they live in their own house.* 2 peculiar, characteristic, typical: *esos árboles son propios de la región = those trees are peculiar to/characteristic of the region.* 3 suitable, correct (conveniente). 4 natural. 5 selfsame, very, very own (mismo): *pronunció las propias palabras del Rey = he uttered the very words of the King/he uttered the King's very (own) words.* 6 proper, true: *el sentido propio de la palabra es "asustado" = the proper meaning of the word is "frightened".* 7 GRAM. proper: *nombre propio = proper noun.*
proponente *s.m.* y *f.* proposer.
proponer *v.t.* 1 to propose, to suggest, to put forward (presentar un plan, etc.). 2 to nominate, to propose, to put forward, to put up: *le propusieron como candidato = they put him forward as a candidate.* 3 to move, to propose (reunión, debate). 4 MAT. to make a proposition. || *v.pron.* 5 to propose, to plan, to mean, to intend: *me propongo desplazarme a Madrid mañana = I propose/plan/mean/intend to go to Madrid tomorrow.*
proporción *s.f.* 1 proportion (en general). 2 MAT. ratio: *en una proporción de 7 a 3 = in a ratio of 7 to 3.* || *pl.* 3 size, dimensions: *una navaja de enormes proporciones = a knife of enormous size.* || 4 **estar fuera de —,** to be out of proportion. 5 **guardar bien las proporciones con,** to keep in proportion to, to be in proportion to.
proporcionado, -a *p.p.* 1 de **proporcionar.** || *adj.* 2 well-proportioned (de cuerpo). 3 proportionate (que guarda relación): *the punishment is not proportionate to the crime = el castigo no guarda proporción con el delito.*
proporcional *adj.* proportional.
proporcionalmente *adv.* proportionally.
proporcionalidad *s.f.* proportionality.
proporcionar *v.t.* 1 to provide, to furnish, to supply (proveer). 2 to proportion, to adjust (adaptar).
proposición *s.f.* 1 proposition, proposal (propuesta). 2 GRAM. clause. 3 MAT. proposition. 4 LOG. proposition. || 5 **— de ley,** POL. draft legislation.
propósito *s.m.* 1 intention (intención). 2 aim, objective, purpose (objeto). 3 subject matter (tema). || 4 **a —, a)** at the right moment, opportunely (oportunamente); **b)** by the way, incidentally (de paso); **c)** on purpose, intentionally, deliberately (adrede). 5 **de —,** on purpose, intentionally, deliberately (adrede). 6 **fuera de —,** beside the point, irrelevant(ly).
propuesto, -a *p.p.irr.* 1 de **proponer.** || *s.f.* 2 proposal, proposition (proposición). 3 offer (ofrecimiento). 4 COM. tender.
propugnación *s.f.* advocacy.
propugnar *v.t.* 1 to advocate, to defend (amparar): *propugna la derogación de la ley de extranjería = he advocates the repeal of the law on aliens.* 2 to propose, to suggest (proponer).
propulsar *v.t.* 1 to reject, to refute (repulsar). 2 MEC. to propel, to drive. 3 (fig.) to encourage (animar).
propulsión *s.f.* 1 propulsion. || 2 **— a chorro,** jet propulsion.
propulsor, -a *adj.* 1 driving, propellent: *fuerza propulsora = propellent force.* || *s.m.* y *f.* 2 propellent.
prorrata *s.f.* quota, share, (EE.UU.) prorate.
prórroga *s.f.* 1 postponement. 2 DEP. extra time. 3 MIL. deferment. 4 COM. extension. 5 DER. stay of execution.
prorrogar *v.t.* 1 to prolong, to extend: *se prorrogó el partido porque los equipos estaban empatados a dos = the match was prolonged as there was a 2-2 draw.* 2 to adjourn (levantar la sesión). 3 to postpone, defer (aplazar). 4 MIL. to defer. 5 DER. to grant a stay of execution. 6 DER. to defer judgment.
prorratear *v.t.* to distribute proportionally.
prorrateo *s.m.* 1 apportionment, pro rata distribution. || 2 **a —,** pro rata.
prorrogable *adj.* that can be extended, that can be deferred.
prorrumpir *v.i.* 1 to shoot forth, to erupt (salir con fuerza). 2 to burst out: *ella prorrumpió en lágrimas = she burst into tears/she burst out crying.*
prosa *s.f.* 1 prose. 2 (fig.) prosaicness, prosaic nature (lenguaje). 3 verbiage, (fam.) hot air (exceso de palabras). 4 prosaic, humdrum aspects: *estas miserias constituyen la prosa de la vida = these hardships represent the humdrum aspects of life.*
prosador, -a *s.m.* y *f.* 1 prose writer (prosista). 2 (fam.) windbag, prattler, babbler (hablador malicioso).
prosaicamente *adv.* 1 prosaically. 2 monotonously, tediously.
prosaico, -a *adj.* 1 prosaic. 2 monotonous, tedious.
prosaísmo *s.m.* 1 prosaic nature. 2 (fig.) monotony, dreariness (tedio).
prosapia *s.f.* 1 ancestry, lineage.
proscenio *s.m.* proscenium.
proscribir *v.t.* 1 to proscribe, to banish (desterrar). 2 to proscribe, to prohibit, to ban, to outlaw (prohibir).
proscripción *s.f.* DER. proscription.
proscripto, -a V. **proscrito, -a.**
proscrito, -a *p.p.* 1 de **proscribir.** DER. || *adj.* 2 proscribed; exiled. || *s.m.* y *f.* 3 proscript, outlaw.
prosecretaría *s.f.* 1 (Am.) undersecretaryship (cargo). 2 (Am.) undersecretary's office (oficina).
prosecución *s.f.* 1 pursuit, pursuance (acción de proseguir). 2 continuation (persecución).
proselitismo *s.m.* proselytism.
proselitista *adj.* 1 proselytizing. || *s.m.* y *f.* 2 proselytizer.
prosélito *s.m.* 1 catholic convent. 2 proselyte.
prosificar *v.t.* to put into prose, to turn into prose.
prosimio *adj.* 1 ZOOL. prosimian. || *s.m.* 2 ZOOL. Prosimii.
prosista *s.m.* y *f.* prose writer.
prosodia *s.f.* GRAM. prosody.
prosódico, -a *adj.* prosodic (para la poesía); FON. orthoepic (acento).

prosopografía *s.f.* description of the external features of a person or an animal.

prosopopeya *s.f.* 1 LIT. prosopopoeia, personification. 2 (fig.) pomposity.

prospección *s.f.* 1 exploration (exploración). 2 MIN. prospecting.

prospectivo, -a *adj.* (Am.) prospective.

prospecto *s.m.* 1 prospectus. 2 explanatory leaflet (instrucciones).

prósperamente *adv.* prosperously, successfully.

prosperar *v.i.* 1 to prosper, to thrive (en medios materiales). 2 to be successful, to get through (idea, proyecto, propuesta, etc.).

prosperidad *s.f.* 1 success (éxito). 2 prosperity (bienestar).

próspero, -a *adj.* 1 prosperous, thriving, flourishing (propicio). 2 prosperous, wealthy, affluent (acaudalado).

próstata *s.f.* ANAT. prostate, prostate gland.

prosternación *s.f.* exhaustion (de salud corporal); dejection (de salud mental).

prosternarse *v.r.* to prostrate oneself.

prostíbulo *s.m.* brothel, whorehouse.

prostitución *s.f.* prostitution.

prostituir *v.t.* 1 to prostitute (persona). 2 (fig.) to prostitute. || *v.pron.* 3 to prostitute oneself, to take up prostitution.

prostituto, -a *s.m.* y *f.* prostitute.

protactinio *s.m.* QUIM. protactinium.

protagonismo *s.m.* leadership (liderazgo), leading role (papel).

protagonista *s.m.* 1 protagonist, main character, leading man, hero (papel). 2 protagonist (no literario). || *s.f.* 3 protagonist, main character, leading lady, heroine (papel).

protagonizar *v.t.* 1 to play a leading role in (película, obra de teatro, etc.). 2 to be involved in (una acción llamativa): *mi amigo ha protagonizado un incidente diplomático = my friend has been involved in a diplomatic incident.*

prótasis *s.f.* 1 GRAM. protasis. 2 LIT. protasis.

protección *s.f.* 1 protection (general). 2 shield (física). 3 shelter (contra el mal tiempo).

proteccionismo *s.m.* protectionism.

proteccionista *adj.* ECON. protectionist.

protector, -ora *adj.* 1 protecting. || *s.m.* y *f.* 2 protector; patron (de las artes y cultura).

protectorado *s.m.* POL. protectorate.

protectoría *s.f.* protectorship.

proteger *v.t.* 1 to protect, to shield (defender). 2 to treat as a protegé, to be a patron to (patrocinar). || *v.pron.* to protect oneself, to shield oneself.

protegido, -a *p.p.* 1 de **proteger.** || *adj.* 2 sheltered (de los elementos). || *s.m.* 3 protégé. || *s.f.* 4 protégée.

proteína *s.f.* QUIM. protein.

protervia *s.f.* 1 perversity (perversidad). 2 wickedness (maldad).

prótesis *s.f.* 1 MED. prosthesis. 2 GRAM. prosthesis, prothesis.

protesta *s.f.* protest.

protestante *adj.* REL. 1 Protestant. || *s.m.* y *f.* 2 Protestant.

protestantismo *s.m.* REL. Protestantism.

protestar *v.t.* 1 to protest. 2 to profess (fe). 2 COM. to protest, to give notice of protest (una letra, etc.). 3 FIN. to refer to drawer, to return, (fam.) to bounce (cheque): *el banco me ha protestado un cheque = the bank has returned/bounced one of my cheques.* || *v.i.* 4 to protest: *protesta siempre contra la injusticia = he always protests against injustice.* 5 to grumble, (fam.) to gripe (refunfuñar).

protesto *s.m.* 1 protestation. 2 COM. protest (letra), referral (cheque).

protocolario, -a *adj.* formal, required by protocol.

protocolo *s.m.* 1 POL. protocol. 2 (fig.) social etiquette. 3 formalities (ceremonia). 4 MED. medical record.

protón *s.m.* FIS. proton.

protónico, -a o **pretónico, -a** *adj.* FON. pretonic.

protoplasma *s.m.* BIOL. protoplasm.

prototipo *s.m.* 1 prototype (arquetipo). 2 BIOL. prototype.

protozoo o **protozoario, -a** *adj.* 1 ZOOL. protozoan, protozoon, protozoic. || *s.m.* y *f.* 2 ZOOL. protozoan, protozoon. *pl.* 3 ZOOL. Protozoa.

protráctil *adj.* protractile: *músculo protráctil.*

protuberancia *s.f.* protuberance, bulge.

protuberante *adj.* protuberant, jutting, bulging.

provecto, -a *adj.* 1 advanced in years, experienced (adelantado). 2 aged, elderly (viejo).

provecho *s.m.* 1 benefit, profit, advantage (ventaja). 2 FIN. profit. 3 progress (adelanto). || 4 **¡buen —!,** enjoy your meal! (cortesía). 5 **de —, a)** profitable (negocio); **b)** useful (persona/cosa).

provechosamente *adv.* beneficially, profitably.

provechoso, -a *adj.* beneficial (para la salud); profitable (económicamente).

proveedor, -ora *s.m.* y *f.* supplier.

proveer *v.t.* 1 to provide, to supply, to furnish (suministrar). 2 to get ready (disponer). 3 to appoint (empleo). || *v.pron.* 4 to provide oneself with: *antes de la excursión nos proveímos de lo necesario = before the excursion we provided ourselves with everything necessary.*

proveniente *adj.* coming, originating, issuing: *alguien proveniente del norte = somebody coming from the north.*

provenir *v.i.* to come (from), to originate (from/in): *mi padre proviene de una de las mejores familias del país = my father comes from one of the best families in the land.*

provenzal *adj.* 1 Provençal. || *s.m.* y *f.* 2 Provençal (habitante). || *s.m.* 3 Provençal (lengua).

proverbial *adj.* proverbial.

proverbialmente *adv.* (form.) proverbially.

proverbio *s.m.* 1 proverbio. || *pl.* 2 Proverbs (de la Biblia).

providencia *s.f.* 1 providence: *Divina Providencia = Divine Providence.* 2 foresight, forethought (prevención). 3 step, measure: *hay que tomarse providencias para asegurar que semejante cosa no pase otra vez = measures/steps must be taken to ensure that such a thing doesn't happen again.* 4 DER. ruling.

providencial *adj.* providential.

providencialmente *adv.* providentially.

providente *adj.* 1 provident, prudent, farsighted.

provincia *s.f.* province.

provincial *adv.* provincial.

provincialismo *s.m.* 1 (desp.) provincialism. 2 dialect word (lenguaje).

provinciano, -a *adj.* too provincial (con matiz derogativo).

provisión *s.f.* 1 provision (acción). 2 provision, supply (suministro). 3 measure, precautionary measure: *hagamos provisiones para que no ocurra = let's take measures so that it doesn't happen.*

provisional *adj.* provisional, acting (interino).

provisionalmente *adv.* provisionally, temporarily.

provisor, -a *s.m.* y *f.* 1 supplier, purveyor (abastecedor). 2 REL. vicar general.

provisoriamente *adv.* (Am.) provisionally.

provisorio, -a *adj.* (Am.) provisional.

provisto, -a *p.p.* 1 de **proveer.** || 2 **— de,** supplied with, armed with.

provocación *s.f.* provocation.

provocador, -ora *adj.* 1 provoking, provocative. || *s.m.* y *f.* 2 provoker.

provocante o **provocativo, -a** *adj.* provocative (especialmente en temas sexuales).

provocar *v.t.* 1 to provoke (incitar). 2 to provoke, to rouse, to stir up (irritar). 3 to bring about, to cause (facilitar). 4 to arouse, to stimulate (sexualmente). 5 to induce nausea (vomitar). 6 (Am.) to feel like, to appeal to, to fancy (apetecer): *no me provoca la idea de ir solo = I don't fancy the idea of going on my own.* || 7 **— un fuego,** to start a fire deliberately.

proxeneta *s.m.* 1 pimp, procurer, (vulg.) ponce. || *s.f.* 2 procuress.

proxenetismo *s.m.* pimping, procuring.

próximamente *adv.* shortly, very soon.

proximidad *s.f.* 1 nearness, closeness (física). 2 proximity (temporal).

próximo, -a *adj.* 1 near, close (cercano). 2 next (que viene).

proyección *s.f.* 1 projection (acción). 2 FOT. projection. 3 showing (film). 4 projection (representación). 5 PSIC. projection.

proyectar *v.t.* 1 to throw, to hurl, to fling (lanzar). 2 to plan, to design (idear un plan). 3 to cast (sombra, luz). 4 to show, to screen, to project (film). 5 MAT. to project. 6 to direct, to squirt (líquido).

proyectil *s.m.* 1 projectile. 2 MIL. missile: *proyectil balístico intercontinental = intercontinental balistic missile.* 3 MIL. shell (de cañón).

proyectista *s.m.* y *f.* 1 ARQ. planner, designer. 2 projectionist (en el cine).
proyecto *s.m.* 1 TEC. plan, project. 2 (fig.) plan, scheme. 3 draft estimate (presupuesto). || 4 — **de ley,** POL. bill.
proyector, -a *adj.* 1 projecting. || *s.m.* 2 FOT. projector. 3 MIL. searchlight. 4 spotlight (foco). 5 condenser (óptico).
prudencia *s.f.* 1 prudence, caution (cautela). 2 discretion (cordura), wisdom (juicio). 3 moderation (moderación).
prudencial *adj.* 1 prudential, judicious. 2 rough, approximate (cálculos numéricos o similar).
prudencialmente *adv.* prudentially.
prudenciarse *v.r.* 1 (Am.) to be cautious. 2 to hold back, to control oneself (moderarse).
prudente *adj.* wise, prudent, sensible.
prudentemente *adv.* wisely, prudently, sensibly.
prueba *s.f.* 1 proof (en general). 2 proof, sign (testimonio). 3 test (ensayo). 4 TEC. test, trial. 5 DEP. event, race. 6 proof (imprenta). 7 FOT. proof. 8 DER. proof, evidence. || 9 **a — de bala,** bulletproof. 10 **a — de bombas,** bombproof. 11 **a — de niños,** childproof.
pruebista *s.m.* y *f.* 1 (Am.) magician, conjuror (ilusionista). 2 (Am.) juggler (malabarista). 3 (Am.) acrobat (acróbata), tightrope walker (funámbulo).
prurito *s.m.* 1 (fig.) urge, itch, need. 2 MED. pruritis, itch.
psicastenia o **sicastenia** *s.f.* MED. psychasthenia.
psicoanálisis o **sicoanálisis** *s.f.* psychoanalysis.
psicología o **sicología** *s.f.* 1 psichology. || 2 — **social,** social psychology.
psicológico, -a o **sicológico, -a** *adj.* psychological.
psicológicamente o **sicológicamente** *adv.* psychologically.
psicólogo, -a o **sicólogo, -a** *s.m.* y *f.* psychologist.
psicópata o **sicópata** *s.m.* y *f.* PSIQ. psychopath.
psicopatía o **sicopatía** *s.f.* psychopathy.
psicosis o **sicosis** *s.f.* psychosis.
psicoterapia o **sicoterapia** *s.f.* psychotherapy.
psique o **psiquis** *s.f.* psyche.
psiquiatra o **siquiatra** *s.m.* y *f.* psychiatrist, therapist.
psiquiatría o **siquiatría** *s.f.* psychiatry.
psíquico, -a o **síquico, -a** *adj.* psychic.
pterigio *s.m.* ZOOL. pterygium.
púa *s.f.* 1 sharp point, barb (punta). 2 tooth (peine). 3 MUS. plectrum (plectro). 4 ZOOL. spine, quill, prickle. 5 BOT. cutting, graft.
pubertad *s.f.* puberty.
pubis *s.m.* 1 ANAT. pubes (parte inferior del vientre). 2 ANAT. pubis (hueso).
publicación *s.f.* 1 publication: *listo para publicación = ready for publication.* 2 book, writing (de cualquier tipo).
públicamente *adv.* openly.
publicar *v.t.* 1 to publicize, to make public (anunciar). 2 to divulge, to reveal (revelar). 3 to publish (editar).
publicidad *s.f.* 1 publicity. 2 advertising (en anuncios).
publicista *s.m.* y *f.* 1 publicist. 2 journalist (periodista). 3 (Am.) publicity agent (agente de publicidad).
publicitario, -a *adj.* advertising: *campaña publicitaria = advertising campaign.*
público, -a *adj.* 1 public. 2 (desp.) of ill repute. || *s.m.* 3 public (pueblo). 4 audience (de una función). || 5 **casa pública,** house of ill repute, brothel. 6 **dar al —,** to publish. 7 **en —,** in public. 8 **mujer pública,** prostitute. 9 **sacar al —, a)** to publish; **b)** to publicize.
pucherazo *s.m.* 1 blow with a pot (golpe). 2 (fam.) electoral fiddle, election rigging (trampa electoral). 3 (fam.) coup d'état (golpe de estado).
puchero *s.m.* 1 cooking-pot (vasija). 2 stew (olla). 3 (fig.) daily bread. 4 pout. || 5 **hacer pucheros,** to pout, to sulk, to screw up one's face.
pudibundo, -a *adj.* 1 bashful, demure (tímido). 2 coy, exaggeratedly modest (vergonzoso).
púdico, -a *adj.* chaste, modest, demure.
pudiente *adj.* 1 rich, wealthy, well-off (rico). 4 powerful man (poderoso). || *s.f.* 5 wealthy woman (rica). 6 powerful woman (poderosa).
pudor *s.m.* 1 modesty, demureness (recato). 2 bashfulness (timidez). 3 chastity, inocence, virtue (castidad). 4 sense of shame (vergüenza).
pudoroso, -a *adj.* modest.
pudridero *s.m.* 1 rubbish dump, compost heap (vertedero). 2 temporary vault (para cadáveres).
pudrir o **podrir** *v.t.* 1 to rot, to decompose (descomponer). 2 to annoy, to irritate, to aggravate (irritar). || *v.i.* 3 (fig.) to be dead and buried. || *v.pron.* 4 to rot, to decay (descomponerse).
pueblerino, -a *adj.* 1 provincial, small-town: *mentalidad pueblerina = small-town mentality.* || *s.m.* y *f.* 2 country person, provincial.
pueblo *s.m.* 1 POL. people, nation (nación). 2 masses, common people (plebe). 3 village (aldea). 4 country town (poblado).
puente *s.m.* 1 bridge. 2 bridge (barco). 3 deck (cubierta). 4 bridge (dientes). 5 MUS. bridge. || 6 **hacer de —,** to act as intermediary. 7 **hacer —,** to take extra time off between two public holidays. 8 **— aéreo, a)** shuttle service (servicio comercial); **b)** airlift (para abastecer). 9 **— colgante,** suspension bridge. 10 **— levadizo,** drawbridge.
puercamente *adv.* filthily; disgustingly.
puerco, -a *adj.* 1 filthy, foul. || *s.m.* 2 ZOOL. pig (raza), ZOOL. hog (macho). || *s.f.* 3 ZOOL. sow (cerda). 4 slut, slattern (puta). || 5 **— espín,** ZOOL. porcupine.
puericultor, -a *s.m.* y *f.* expert in child care.
puericultura *s.f.* (brit.) paediatrics, (EE.UU.) pediatrics, puericulture.
pueril *adj.* 1 childish, child *(atr.)* (relativo al niño). 2 (desp.) puerile, childish, infantile.
puerilidad *s.f.* childishness.
puerilmente *adv.* childishly.
puerperio *s.m.* MED. puerperium.
puerqueza *s.f.* 1 (Am.) filthy thing. 2 (Am.) dirty trick.
puerro *s.m.* BOT. leek: *el puerro es el emblema nacional del País de Gales = the leek is the national emblem of Wales.*
puerta *s.f.* 1 doorway (por ejemplo, de una casa). 2 gateway (por ejemplo de un jardín). 3 door (de habitación, etc.) 4 gate (verja, portal, etc.) 5 (fig.) gateway. 6 INF. port. 7 DEP. goal. || 8 **abrir la —,** (fig.) to open the door (to). 9 **a — cerrada,** behind closed doors. 10 **cerrársele a uno todas las puertas,** (fig.) to close off every avenue to someone. 11 **dar a uno con la — en la cara, en las narices, en los hocicos** o **en los ojos,** (fig.) to slam the door in someone's face. 12 **de — en —,** begging from door to door. 13 **— excusada,** private door, side door. 14 **— falsa,** concealed door. 15 **— franca, a)** free passage; b) free of consumer tax, duty free. 16 **tomar uno la —,** to leave, (fig.) to pack up and go.
puerto *s.m.* 1 port, harbour (para barcos). 2 GEOG. pass (paso). 3 (fig.) haven, refuge. 4 weir (presa en un río). 5 (fig.) shelter. || 6 **— de escala,** port of call. 7 **— franco,** free port.
pues *conj.* 1 since, for: *que lo cuente él, pues lo ha visto = let him tell you about it since he saw it.* || *adv.* 2 well, well then (bueno): *¿no quieres venir con nosotros? pues no te quejes si te quedas solo = don't you want to come with us? Well, don't complain if you end up on your own.* 3 then: *¿no vienes conmigo, pues? = aren't you coming with me, then?* 4 um, er, well (vacilando): *pues... me parece que no = um/er/well... I don't think so.*
puesto, -a *p.p.irreg.* 1 de **poner.** || *adj.* 2 on, wearing (ropa): *con el abrigo puesto = with his coat on/wearing a coat.* 3 dressed (persona): *María está bien puesta = Mary is well dressed.* 4 laid, set (mesa). || *s.m.* 5 place (sitio). 6 market stall, stand (mercadillo). 7 small shop (tienda). 8 post (empleo). 9 MIL. post. || *s.f.* 10 laying, setting (mesa). 11 laying (huevos). 13 bet, stake (naipes). 14 setting (astro). || 15 **puesta en marcha, a)** starter (motor); **b)** starting (acción). 16 **puesta del sol,** sunset. 17 **— que,** since, as.
puf *interj.* 1 ugh! || *s.m.* 2 pouf (mueble).
pufo *s.m.* swindle, (fam.) con.
púgil *s.m.* 1 DEP. pugilist, boxer. 2 HIST. pugilist.
pugilismo *s.m.* DEP. boxing.
pugilístico, -a *adj.* DEP. boxing: *combate pugilístico = boxing match.*

pugna *s.f.* conflict, fight, struggle.
pugnar *v.i.* 1 to fight, to struggle (luchar). 2 (fig.) to insist.
puja *s.f.* 1 bid (en subastas). 2 (fig.) effort (para conseguir algo).
pujador, -a *s.m.* y *f.* bidder.
pujante *adj.* forceful, vigorous; powerful: *¡qué forma de negociar más pujante! = what a vigorous style of negotiation!*
pujanza *s.f.* strength, (brit.) vigour, (EE.UU.) vigor.
pujar *v.t.* 1 to bid, to bid up (subasta). 2 to strain, to strive (hacer fuerza). || *v.i.* 3 to struggle for words, to grope for words (dificultad de palabra). 4 to pout, to be on the verge of tears (hacer pucheros). 5 to dither, to hesitate (vacilar).
pujo *s.m.* 1 MED. tenesmus, straining. 2 urge, yearning (deseo). 3 aspiration. 4 irresistible urge (de llorar o reír).
pulcritud *s.f.* neatness, tidiness; exquisiteness.
pulcro, -a *adj.* 1 neat, smart, tidy (limpio). 2 immaculately turned out (bien puesto). 3 upright, utterly scrupulous (honrado).
pulga *s.f.* 1 ZOOL. flea. || 2 **tener malas pulgas,** to be touchy, to be bad tempered.
pulgada *s.f.* inch.
pulgar *s.m.* 1 ANAT. thumb. 2 BOT. shoot, bud.
pulgón *s.m.* ZOOL. plant louse.
pulidamente *adv.* neatly, tidily.
pulido, -a *p.p.* 1 de **pulir.** || *adj.* 2 polished, smooth (bello). 3 neat, smart, refined (pulcro).
pulir *v.t.* 2 to polish, to shine (sacar brillo). 2 to smooth (alisar). 3 to adorn (adornar). 4 (fig.) to polish, to polish up, to touch up (perfeccionar). 5 to refine, to polish up (educar). 5 (fam.) to nick, (fam.) to pinch (robar). 6 to sell off, (fam.) to flog (vender). 7 (fam.) to blow (derrochar).
pulmón *s.m.* 1 ANAT. lung. || 2 **— de acero,** MED. iron lung.
pulmonar *adj.* ANAT. pulmonary, lung.
pulmonía *s.f.* MED. pneumonia.
pulpa *s.f.* 1 pulp: *papel hecho de pulpa de madera = paper made from wood pulp.* 2 BOT. pulp, flesh.
pulpejo *s.m.* 1 ANAT. soft flesh. 2 ZOOL. soft part of horse's hoof.
púlpito *s.m.* pulpit.
pulpo *s.m.* ZOOL. octopus.
pulposo, -a *adj.* pulpy, fleshy.
pulque *s.m.* pulque.
pulsación *s.f.* 1 BIOL. pulsation, beat. 2 touch, tap (en máquina de escribir).
pulsador *s.m.* button, push-button.
pulsar *v.t.* 1 MUS. to play. 2 to push, to press (botón, etc.). 3 to strike, to hit, to press, to touch (tecla). 4 MED. to take somebody's pulse. 5 (fig.) to sound out (sondear). || *v.i.* 6 to throb, to beat.
pulsera *s.f.* 1 bracelet, bangle (brazalete). 2 DEP. wristlet, sweatband. || 3 **reloj de —,** wristwatch.
pulso *s.m.* 1 FISIOL. pulse. 2 ANAT. wrist (muñeca). 3 strength of wrist (fuerza). 4 steadiness of hand, sureness of touch (firmeza). 5 (fig.) prudence, good sense (prudencia). || 6 **a —,** (fig.) by one's own efforts, by sheer hard work. 7 **echar un —,** to arm wrestle, to Indian wrestle. 8 **tomar el —, a)** to take somebody's pulse; **b)** (fig.) to test opinion.
pulular *v.i.* 1 BOT. to pululate, to bud, to shoot. 2 to pululate, to teem with (abundar): *pululan las mariquitas este verano = it's teeming with ladybirds this summer.* 2 to swarm, to teem with (moverse mucho): *pululan los turistas en la Costa del Sol = the Costa del Sol is swarming/teeming with tourists.*
pulverización *s.f.* atomization, spraying.
pulverizador *s.m.* spray, spray-gun.
pulverizar *v.t.* 1 to pulverize, to powder (reducir a polvo). 2 to spray, to sprinkle (líquido). 3 (fig.) to smash, to tear to pieces, to pulverize. || *v.pron.* 4 to pulverize, to be reduced to powder, to be reduced to dust.
pulverulento, -a *adj.* 1 pulverulent, powdered, powdery (en forma de polvo). 2 dusty (polvoriento).
pulla *s.f.* 1 obscene comment (palabrota). 2 taunt, jibe (mofa). 3 (fam.) dig, cutting remark, snide comment (expresión hiriente).
pull-over *s.m.* pullover, jumper.
puma *s.f.* ZOOL. puma, cougar, mountain lion.
puna *s.f.* 1 GEOG. high Andean plateau, puna. 2 GEOG. bleak steppe. 3 mountain sickness (enfermedad). 4 cold mountain wind (viento).
punción *s.f.* 1 MED. puncture. 2 sharp pain (dolor).
punchar *v.t.* (Am.) to punch (picar).
pundonor *s.m.* 1 dignity, self-respect (amor propio). 2 honour (honra).
pundonorosamente *adv.* honourably.
pundonoroso, -a *adj.* honourable.
punga *s.f.* 1 (Am.) thieving, (fam.) nicking (acción). || *s.m.* y *f.* 2 (Am.) pickpocket, petty thief.
pungente *adj.* stinging.
pungir *v.t.* 1 to prick, to pierce (punzar). 2 to sting (picar). 3 (fig.) to wound, to hurt, to cause anguish to (herir el ánimo).
punible *adj.* punishable.
punición *s.f.* punishment.
púnico, -a *adj.* HIST. punic, Carthaginian.
punitivo, -a *adj.* (form.) punitive.
punta *s.f.* 1 point (extremo agudo). 2 tip, end: *lo tengo en la punta de la lengua = it's on the tip of my tongue.* 3 small nail, tack (clavo). 4 GEOG. point. 5 horn (cuerno). 6 (brit.) cigarette end, stub, (EE.UU.) butt, (colilla). 7 small bunch (ganado). 8 pointing, point (perro de caza). 9 BOT. tobacco leaf. 10 touch, hint, suggestion, bit: *tu hermano tiene sus puntas de cantante = your brother has the touch of a singer about him/there's the suggestion/hint of a singer in your brother.* || *pl.* 11 point lace (encaje). || 12 **de — en blanco,** dressed up to the nines, in best bib and tucker. 13 **sacar — a una cosa, a)** to sharpen; **b)** (fig.) to read more into something than is there.
puntada *s.f.* 1 pinhole, needle hole (agujero). 2 stitch (de coser). 3 (fig.) dig, insinuation (indirecta). 4 sharp pain (dolor).
puntal *s.m.* 1 ARQ. prop, shore (madero). 2 GEOG. elevation. 3 (fig.) support (apoyo). 4 depth of hold (nave). 5 (Am.) snack, refreshment.
puntapié *s.m.* kick.
punteado *p.p.* 1 de **puntear.** || *s.m.* 2 dotted line, dotted, covered with dots (tipográfico). 3 MUS. pizzicato.
puntear *v.t.* 1 to dot, to mark with dots. 2 ART. to stipple. 3 to stitch, to sew (coser). 4 MUS. to pluck. 5 (Am.) to brand, to label, to call (tildar).
punteo *s.m.* MUS. plucking.
puntera *s.f.* 1 toecap (calzado). 2 toecap repair (remiendo). 3 kick, toe punt (puntapié).
puntería *s.f.* 1 aiming, aim (acción). 2 markmanship (destreza).
puntero, -a *adj.* 1 leading (primero). 2 latest (último). || *s.m.* 3 pointer (vara). 4 chisel (cincel). 5 (Am.) hand (manilla). 6 punch (punzón).
puntiagudo, -a *adj.* pointed, sharp.
puntilla *s.f.* 1 fine lace, lace trimming (encaje). 2 short dagger (tauromaquia). || 3 **dar la —,** (fig.) to finish off, to give the coup de grace, to put out of (its) misery. 4 **de puntillas,** on tiptoe.
puntillo *s.m.* 1 punctilio. 2 (desp.) touchiness, exaggerated sense of honour. 3 MUS. dot.
puntilloso, -a *adj.* 1 punctilious. 2 (desp.) touchy, over sensitive.
punto *s.m.* 1 dot. 2 (brit.) full stop, (EE.UU.) period (puntuación). 3 place, spot, point (lugar). 4 MUS. pitch. 5 DEP. point. 6 spot, pip (naipes). 7 mark, point (calificación). 8 tip, point (pluma). 9 stitch (puntada). 10 knitting (labor de tejido). 11 moment, point (instante). 12 point, subject matter, question (asunto). 13 hole (agujero). 14 point (imprenta). 15 sight (de fusil). 16 point (punto principal): *el punto que quiero hacer... = the point I wish to make...* 17 point, purpose (finalidad). 18 dignity, honour (pundonor). 19 MED. stitch. 20 INF. pixel. || 21 **al —,** at once. 22 **a —, a)** ready; **b)** on time. 23 **dar en el —,** (fig.) to hit the nail on the head. 24 **de todo —,** absolutely, completely. 25 **en —,** exactly, on the dot. 26 **estar a o en — de,** to be on the point of, to be about to. 27 **estar en su —,** to be just right, to be done to a turn. 28 **hasta cierto —,** to a certain extent, up to a point. 29 **poner en su —,** to bring up to scratch, to knock into shape. 30 **poner los puntos sobre las íes,** to dot the i's and cross the t's. 31 **¡— en boca!,** not a word to anyone! 32 **— por —,** point by point. 33 **— cardinal,** cardinal point. 34

— **céntrico,** central point. **35 — de apoyo,** fulcrum. **36 — de ebullición,** boiling point. **37 — de partida,** starting point. **38 — de penalty,** penalty spot. **39 — de taxis,** taxi rank. **40 — de verano,** holiday resort. **41 — de vista,** point of view. **42 — muerto, a)** MEC. dead centre; **b)** neutral (cambios); **c)** (fig.) deadlock. **31 — y coma,** semicolon.
puntuación *s.f.* **1** punctuation (tipográfica). **2** DEP. score, scoring. **3** marks (escolares).
puntualizar *v.t.* **1** to fix in one's mind (recordar). **2** to describe in detail, to specify, to detail (referir con detalle). **3** to perfect, (fig.) to polish (perfeccionar). **4** to arrange, to fix (precisar).
puntualmente *adv.* punctually.
puntuar *v.t.* **1** GRAM. to punctuate. **2** (brit.) to mark, (EE.UU.) to grade (corregir). || *v.i.* **3** DEP. to score, to count, to keep the score.
puntudo, -a *adj.* **1** (Am.) sharp, pointed (puntiagudo). **2** (Am.) (fig.) faultfinding (crítico).
punzada *s.f.* stab (normalmente de dolor).
punzante *adj.* sharp: *objeto punzante = sharp object.*
punzar *v.t.* **1** to prick, to pierce, to puncture (pinchar). **2** TEC. to punch. || **3** to give twinges, to give stabbing pains (dolor). **4** (fig.) to have pangs, to have twinges: *a ella le punzan remordimientos = she is having pangs/twinges of conscience/remorse.*
punzón *s.m.* **1** needle (aguja). **2** TEC. awl, bradawl, punch (puntero). **3** TEC. burin (grabar).
puñado *s.m.* **1** fistful, handful. || **2 a puñados,** by the handful, galore.
puñal *s.m.* dagger.
puñalada *s.f.* stab wound, stab.
puñeta *s.f.* **1** (Am.) (vulg.) wank. || **2 ¡vete a hacer puñetas!** (vulg.) sod off.
puñetazo *s.m.* punch.
puño *s.m.* **1** ANAT. fist. **2** fistful (puñado). **3** handle, grip (mango de herramienta). **4** hilt (mango de espada). **5** grasp (agarro). **6** punch (puñetazo). **7** cuff (ropa). || **8 meter en un — a uno,** to have someone in the palm of one's hand. **9 ser como un —, a)** (fig.) to be tight-fisted; **b)** to be on the short side (retaco).
pupa *s.f.* **1** MED. pimple, pustule (grano). **2** MED. cold sore (en los labios). **3** scab (postilla). **4** hurt, sore, bump (lenguaje de niños). **5** ZOOL. pupa, chrysalis.
pupilaje *s.m.* **1** DER. pupillage, ward(ship). **2** boarding house, guesthouse (pensión). **3** board (precio de la pensión).
pupilo, -a *s.m.* y *f.* **1** DER. ward. **2** inmate (orfelinato). **3** boarder, paying guest (huésped). || *s.f.* **4** ANAT. pupil.
pupitre *s.m.* desk.
puquío *s.m.* GEOG. (Am.) spring, fountain.
puramente *adv.* **1** purely, chastely (moralmente). **2** purely, simply.
puré *s.m.* **1** purée. || **2 — de patatas,** mashed potatoes.
pureza *s.f.* **1** purity (calidad). **2** innocence (inocencia). **3** virginity. **4** (fig.) purity.
purga *s.f.* **1** MED. purgative, cathartic. **2** POL. purge. **3** MEC. draining, bleeding (acción). **4** MEC. drain valve (válvula).
purgación *s.f.* MED. purging.
purgante *adj.* (form.) purgative.
purgar *v.t.* **1** to purge, to cleanse (limpiar). **2** POL. to purge. **3** REL. to purge, to expiate. **4** MED. to purge. **5** MEC. to drain, to bleed. || *v.r.* **6** MED. to take a purgative. **7** REL. to purge oneself. **8** (fig.) to purge oneself.
purgatorio *s.m.* **1** REL. purgatorio. **2** (fig.) purgatory.
purificación *s.f.* purification, cleansing.
purificador, -a o **purificante** *adj.* purifying.
purificar *v.t.* **1** to purify, to cleanse (limpiar). **2** TEC. to purify, to refine. **3** (fig.) to purify, to purge.
purismo *s.m.* purism.
purista *s.m.* y *f.* purist (especialmente en temas del idioma).
puritanismo *s.m.* HIST. puritanism.
puritano, -a *adj.* **1** puritanical (postura). **2** REL. Puritan. || *s.m.* y *f.* Puritan.
puro, -a *adj.* **1** pure (sin mezcla). **2** pure, unsullied, chaste (casto). **3** pure, sheer (simple). **4** correct, refined (lenguaje). || *s.m.* **5** cigar. || **6 a — de** o **de — de,** by means of, by dint of.
púrpura *s.f.* **1** ZOOL. purpura. **2** purple (color). **3** purple (ropa).
purpurado *s.m.* REL. cardinal.
purpurino, -a *adj.* **1** purple. || *s.f.* **2** QUIM. purpurin. **3** metallic paint (pintura).
purulencia *s.f.* MED. purulence.
purulento, -a *adj.* MED. purulent.
pus *s.m.* MED. pus.
pusilánime *adj.* pusillanimus, fainthearted.
pusilanimidad *s.f.* pusillanimity, faintheartedness.
pústula *s.f.* MED. pustule.
putativo, -a *adj.* putative.
putear *v.i.* (Am.) to go whoring.
putrefacción *s.f.* **1** putrefaction, rotting, decay. || **2 — fungoide,** dry rot. **3 sujeto a —,** perishable.
putrefacto, -a *adj.* putrid, rotten, decayed.
pútrido, -a *adj.* putrid, rotten, rancid.
puya *s.f.* **1** steel point, goad. **2** point of picador's goad (tauromaquia).
puyar *v.t.* (Am.) (fig.) to needle, to annoy, to upset (molestar).
puyazo *s.m.* **1** jab with a goad (en los toros). **2** (fig.) cruel hint, dig.
puzzle *s.m.* **1** puzzle. **2** (Am.) jigsaw puzzle (rompecabezas). **3** (Am.) riddle (acertijo).

q, Q *s.f.* q, Q (vigésima letra del alfabeto español).
que *pron.rel.* **1** *suj.* (con personas) who, that; (con objetos) that, which. || **2** *o.d.* (con personas) whom, that; (con cosas) which, that. || *conj.* **3** that: *siento que no venga = I am sorry that he's not coming.* **4** and: *te dije medio kilo, que no tres cuartos = I told you half a kilo and not three quarters.* **5** whether: *que le guste, que no le guste, llegaré tarde = whether he likes it or not, I shall get there late.* **6** because: *vendrá disculpándose, que yo le conozco = he'll arrive with some excuse, because I know what he's like.* || *comp.* **7** than: *es más alto que yo = he's taller than me.* || **8 el —, la —,** the one who; the one that; who; that. **9 los —, las —,** the ones who; the ones that; who; that.
qué *pron.interr.* **1** what?: *¿qué pasa? = what's the matter?* || *adj.interr.* **2** what?: *¿qué clase de libro quieres? = what sort of book do you want?* || *interj.* **3** what! *¡qué lío! = what a mess!* || **4 y —?,** so what?
quebracho *s.m.* **1** BOT. quebracho. **2** (EE.UU.) break-ax.
quebrada *s.f.* **1** GEOG. gorge. **2** GEOG. pass. **3** (Am.) stream.
quebradero *s.m.* **— de cabeza,** (fig.) headache.
quebrado *s.m.* **1** MAT. fraction. **2** FIN. bankruptcy.
quebrado, -a *adj.* **1** rough, bumpy: *terreno quebrado* = rough ground. **2** weakened. **3** washed out, faded. **4** MED. ruptured. || **5 línea —,** zigzag line. **6 pie —,** V. **pie.**
quebraja *s.f.* crack, fissure.
quebrantadura *o* **quebrantamiento** *s.f.* o *m.* **1** cracking, act of breaking. **2** DER. violation (de alguna ley). **3** MED. weak state, exhausted state.
quebrantahuesos *s.m.* **1** ZOOL. lammergeier, bearded vulture. **2** bore, (fig. y fam.) pain in the neck. **3** children's game.
quebrantar *v.t.* **1** to break, to damage, to shatter. **2** to infringe, to break: *quebrantó la ley = he broke the law.* **3** to tone down. **4** to weary. **5** to persuade. || *v.t.* y *pron.* **6** to crack, to split. || *v.pron.* **7** to weaken, to ail.
quebranto *s.m.* **1** FIN. heavy loss (económico). **2** MED. exhaustion. **3** (fig.) sorrow, great affliction.
quebrar *v.t.* **1** to break, to crack. **2** to interrupt. || *v.t.* y *r.* **3** to bend, to twist. **4** to become sallow. || *v.i.* **5** to yield, to give in. **6** to go bankrupt. || *v.r.* **7** to get broken. **8** MED. to be ruptured.
quechemarin *s.m.* MAR. ketch.
quechua *adj.* *(Am.)* **1** Quechua. || *s.m.* y *f.* **2** Quechua.
quedada *s.f.* joke, hoax.
quedamente *adv.* softly, quietly, in a soft voice.
quedar *v.i.* y *pron.* **1** to stay, to remain. || *v.i.* **2** to be left: *quedan dos manzanas = there are two apples left.* **3** to meet (a una hora convenida): *he quedado con él a las tres = we're meeting at three o'clock.* || *v.r.* **4** to be: *todos quedan invitados = everyone is invited.* **5 — con,** to retain, to keep. || **6 quedarse uno en albis/en blanco,** to be mystified. **8 — en algo,** to agree on something.
quedo, -a *adj.* **1** quiet. || *adv.* **2** softly: *él habló quedo = he spoke softly.* **3** silently. || *s.f.* **4** curfew. || **6 toque de queda,** curfew, curfew bell.
quehacer *s.m.* task, chore.
queja *s.f.* complaint, grumble.
quejar *v.t.* **1** to distress, to worry. || *v.pron.* **2** to complain. **3** to protest. **4** DER. to file a complaint, to bring a complaint.
quejica *adj.* moaning, complaining.
quejido *s.m.* sigh, moan, groan.
quejigo *s.m.* BOT. **1** gall-oak. **2** oak sapling.
quejosamente *adv.* complainingly, grumblingly.
quejoso, -a *adj.* **1** complaining. **2** whining.
quejumbroso, -a *adj.* grumbling, complaining.
quema *s.f.* **1** burning. **2** fire, combustion. **3** waste tip. **4** burning off (vegetation). || **5 huir de la —,** flee from danger, avoid a commitment.
quemado, -a *p.p.* **1** de **quemar.** || *adj.* **2** burnt, scorched (físicamente). **3** burnt out (persona exhausta física y anímicamente). **4** sunburnt (por el sol).
quemador *s.m.* MEC. burner.
quemadura *s.f.* **1** burn. **2** scald. **3** BOT. withering. **4** sunburn (por el sol).
quemar *v.t.* **1** to burn. **2** to scorch. **3** to overheat. **4** to distil wine. **5** to sell off cheap. **6** to waste (one's life). **7** to annoy. || *v.r.* **8** to burn oneself. || *v.pron.* **9** (fam.) to be roasting. **10** to be passionate (about). **11** (fig.) to be getting warm. **12** to get depressed, to become dejected.
quemarropa, a —, at point-blank range, point-blank.
quemazón *s.f.* **1** burn. **2** intense heat. **3** MED. itch, stinging sensation.
quena *s.f.* (Am.) Indian flute.
quepis *s.m.* kepi (tipo de sombrero).
queratina *s.f.* QUIM. keratin.
querella *s.f.* **1** dispute. **2** complaint. **3.** DER. charge, accusation.
querellante *s.m.* y *f.* DER. plaintiff.
querellarse *v.i.* DER. to bring an action, to bring suit, to file a complaint.
querencia *s.f.* **1** affection, liking. **2** ZOOL. haunt, territory. **3** ZOOL. lair. **4** personal inclination. **5** bull's territory in bull-ring.
querer *s.m.* **1** love, affection. || *v.t.* **2** to love. **3** to want, to desire. **4** to need, to require: *esta tierra quiere abono = this land needs fertiliser.* || *v.imp.* **5** to try, to be about to: *quiere nevar = it's trying to snow.* **6 como quiera que,** given that, as-

suming that; *como quiera que sabes el camino, no necesitas que te acompañe = given that you know the way, you don't need me to go with you.* **7 sin –,** unwittingly, by mistake.
querido, -a *adj.* 1 dear, beloved. || *s.m.* y *f.* 2 lover.
quermes *s.m.* 1 kermes, cochineal insect. 2 cochineal.
quermés *s.f.* kermis, kirmess.
queroseno *s.m.* kerosene, paraffin.
querube *s.m.* V. **querubín.**
querubín *s.m.* cherub.
quesero, -a *adj.* 1 cheese. || *s.m.* y *f.* 2 cheesemaker, cheese seller. 3 cheese board, cheese dish.
queso *s.m.* 1 cheese. || *pl.* 2 (fam.) feet.
quetzal *s.m.* ZOOL. quetzal (ave americana).
quevedos *s.m.pl.* prince-nez.
quia! *interj.* come off it!
quiasmo *s.m.* chiasmus.
quibutz *s.m.* kibbutz.
quicio *s.m.* 1 pivot hole, eye of door hinge. 2 door jamb. 3 (Am.) front steps. || **4 estar fuera de –, a)** (fig.) to be out of control, to be furious **b)** to be out of order, out of kilter. **5 sacar de –,** to exasperate, (fam.) to drive (someone) round the bend.
quichua V. **quechua.**
quid *s.m.* nub, crux (de un asunto).
quiebra *s.f.* 1 COM. bankruptcy. 2 crack, split. 3 damage, harm.
quiebro *s.m.* 1 dodge, swerve. 2 MUS. grace note.
quien *pron.rel.suj.* 1 who, the one who. || 2 *pron.rel. o.d.* whom. || *pron.ind.suj.* 3 whoever, whosoever. || *pron.ind. o.d.* 4 whomever, whomsoever.
quién *pron.interr.* 1 who? 2 if only!, who wouldn't?: *¡quién pudiera irse contigo! = if only I could go with you!/who wouldn't like to go with you!* || **3 de –?,** whose?
quienquiera *pron.ind.* whoever.
quietismo *s.m.* 1 peace and quiet, calm. 2 REL. quietism.
quieto, -a *adj.* 1 still, motionless. 2 calm. || **3 ¡estate –!,** keep still!
quietud *s.f.* 1 stillness. 2 quietude.
quif *s.m.* kif, kef, marijuana.
quijada *s.f.* jawbone.
quijotada *s.f.* quixotic act.
quijote *s.m.* 1 HIST. cuisse, thigh-armour. 2 quixotic person, idealistic dreamer. 3 prickly individual.
quijotesco, -a *adj.* quixotic.
quilate *s.m.* carat.
quilo *s.m.* 1 V. **kilo.** 2 ANAT. chyle. 3 BOT. Chilean species of polygonaceous shrub.
quilla *s.f.* 1 MAR. keel. 2 ANAT. carina. 3 (Am.) cushion.
quimera *s.f.* 1 chimera. 2 hallucination. 3 quarrel.
quimérico, -a *adj.* fanciful.
químico, -a *adj.* 1 chemical. || *s.m.* y *f.* 2 chemist. || *s.f.* 3 chemistry. || **4 química orgánica,** organic chemistry. **5 química inorgánica,** inorganic chemistry.
quimioterapia *s.f.* MED. chemotherapy.
quimo *s.m.* FISIOL. chyme.
quimono *s.m.* kimono.
quina *s.f.* 1 cinchona bark. 2 quinine.
quinario, -a *adj.* 1 quinary. || *s.m.* 2 REL. quinaries.
quincalla *s.f.* ironmongery.
quincallería *s.f.* (brit.) ironmonger's, (EE.UU.) hardware store.
quince *num.card.* 1 fifteen. || *num.ord.* 2 fifteenth.
quincena *s.f.* (brit.) fortnight.
quinceno, -a *adj.* fifteenth.
quincuagésimo, -a *num.ord.* fiftieth.
quingentésimo, -a *num.ord.* five hundredth.
quiniela *s.f.* pools coupon.
quinielista *adj./s.m.* y *f.* punter (apostador).
quinientos, -ass *num.ord.* 1 five hundredth. || *num.card.* 2 five hundred.
quinina *s.f.* quinine.
quino *s.m.* 1 cinchona tree. 2 quinine.
quinqué *s.m.* oil lamp.
quinquenal *adj.* five-year.
quinquenio *s.m.* quinquennium.
quinqui *s.m.* bandit, crook.
quinta *s.f.* 1 country house. 2 (Am.) small estate. 3 MIL. draft, call-up. 4 (fam.) age: *somos de la misma quinta = we're about the same age.* 5 MUS. fifth.
quintaesencia *s.f.* quintessence.
quintal *s.m.* 1 quintal. || **2 – métrico,** hundred kilograms.
quintería *s.f.* farmhouse.
quinteto *s.m.* quintet, quintette.
quintilla *s.f.* LIT. five line stanza.
quinto, -a *num.ord.* 1 fifth. || *s.m.* 2 fifth.
quíntuple *adj* y *s.m.* V. **quíntuplo.**
quíntuplo, -a *adj.* 1 quintuple, fivefold. || *s.m.* 2 quintuple.
quiñón *s.m.* AGR. cultivated common land.
quiosco *s.m.* kiosk.
quirófano *s.m.* MED. operating theatre.
quiromancia *s.f.* palmistry, chiromancy.
quiromántico, -a *adj.* chiromantic.
quirquincho *s.m.* ZOOL. South American mammal similar to the armadillo.
quirúrgico, -a *adj.* surgical.
quisicosa *s.f.* puzzle, enigma.
quisque *s.m.* **cada –; todo –,** (fam.) every man-Jack.
quisquilla *s.f.* ZOOL. shrimp.
quisquilloso, -a *adj.* 1 touchy, peevish. 2 finicky.
quiste *s.m.* MED. cyst.
quitamanchas *s.m.* 1 stain remover. 2 dry cleaner. 3 dry-cleaner's.
quitanieves *s.m.* snowplough.
quitar *v.t.* 1 to remove. 2 to take off. 3 to take down. 4 to take away. 5 to steal. 6 to stop, to prevent. || *v.pron.* 7 to withdraw, to get out of the way. || **8 de quita y pon,** removable, detachable. **9 quitarse de encima a alguien/algo,** to get rid of someone or something. **10 – de la cabeza,** to change (somebody's) mind.
quitasol *s.m.* sunshade.
quite *s.m.* 1 removal. 2 enticing the bull away from a bullfighter who is in trouble. 3 DEP. parry. 4 DEP. (Am.) tackle.
quitina *s.f.* QUIM. chitin.
quizá *adv.* perhaps, maybe: *quizás venga pronto = perhaps he'll come soon.*
quizás *adv.* V. **quizá.**
quórum *s.m.* quorum.

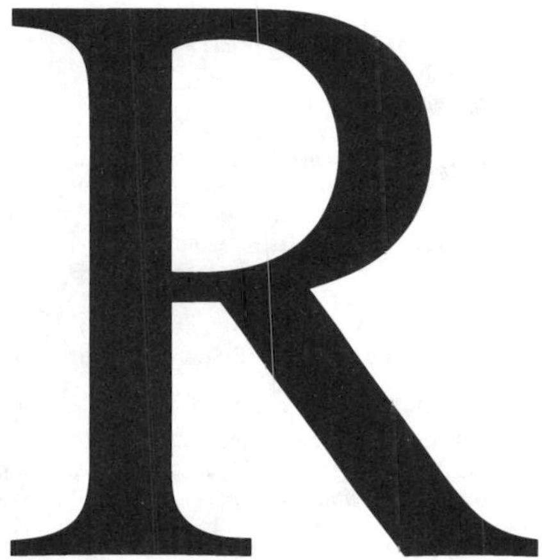

r, R *s.f.* (vigésima primera letra del alfabeto español).
rabadilla *s.f.* 1 ANAT. coccyx. 2 ZOOL. parson's nose.
rabanillo *s.m.* 1 BOT. wild radish. 2 (fig.) aloofness (desdén). 3 (fig. y fam.) longing for (deseo).
rábano *s.m.* 1 BOT. radish. || **2 tomar el – por las hojas,** (fam.) to get hold of the wrong end of the stick. **3 importar un – algo a alguien,** (fam.) not to care/not to give a damn about something: *todo eso me importa un rábano = I couldn't give a damn about that.*
rabel *s.m.* 1 MUS. lute. 2 (fam.) bottom (trasero).
rabí o **rabino** *s.m.* REL. rabbi.
rabia *s.f.* 1 MED. rabies. 2 anger, rage (ira).
rabiar *v.i.* 1 MED. to suffer from rabies. 2 (fig.) to suffer a lot. 3 (fig.) to be dying to: *rabio por irme de vacaciones = I'm dying to go on holiday.* 4 (fig.) to be impatient to. 5 to be far too much: *esta guindilla pica que rabia = this chili burns like mad.* || **6 a –,** an awful lot.
rabieta *s.f.* (fam.) tantrum.
rabillo *s.m.* 1 BOT. stalk. 2 ZOOL. small tail. 3 tip (punta). 4 corner (ángulo). || **5 mirar con el – del ojo,** to look out of the corner of one's eye.
rabo *s.m.* 1 ZOOL. tail. 2 (Am. y fig.) dirty old man (viejo verde). || **3 faltar aún el – por desollar,** to be only part of the way through a piece of work. **4 irse con el – entre las piernas,** to go off with one's tail between one's legs. **5 mirar a uno con el – del ojo,** to look askance at someone.
rabón, -ona *adj.* 1 ZOOL. short-tailed (de rabo corto), tailless (sin rabo). 2 (Am.) broken (cuchillo).
raboso, -a *adj.* frayed (con los rabos deshilachados).
racial *adj.* race, racial: *discriminación racial = racial discrimination.*
racimo *s.m.* 1 BOT. raceme. 2 bunch (flores). 3 (fig.) gang (personas).
racimoso, -a *adj.* BOT. with plenty of racemes.
raciocinar *v.i.* to reason.
raciocinación *s.f.* reasoning.
raciocinio *s.m.* 1 reasoning (acto). 2 reason (juicio).
ración *s.f.* 1 helping (comida). 2 MAT. ratio. || *pl.* 3 MIL. rations.
racional *adj.* 1 rational (razonable). || *s.m.* 2 REL. rational.
racionalidad *s.f.* rationality.
racionalismo *s.m.* FIL. rationalism: *racionalismo cartesiano = Cartesian rationalism.*
racionalista *adj./s.m.* y *f.* rationalist.
racionalización *s.f.* rationalization: (organización eficaz del trabajo) *la racionalización del trabajo = labour rationalization.*
racionalizar *v.pron.* 1 to rationalize (organizar según cálculos). 2 COM. to revamp (una fábrica).
racionalmente *adv.* rationally, prudently (prudentemente).
racionar *v.t.* 1 to ration (limitar). 2 MIL. to supply with rations.
racismo *s.m.* racism, racialism.
racista *adj.* 1 racialist. || *s.m.* y *f.* 2 racist.
racha *s.f.* 1 gust (viento), squall (borrasca). 2 (fig.) fortune: *buena racha = piece of good fortune; mala racha = piece of ill fortune.*
racheado, -a *adj.* gusty, squally (viento).
rada *s.f.* MAR. bay (bahía), anchorage (fondeadero).
radar o **rádar** *s.m.* radar.
radiación *s.f.* 1 FIS. radiation. 2 broadcasting (emisión por radio).
radiactividad *s.f.* radioactivity.
radiactivo, -a *adj.* radioactive.
radiado, -a *adj.* 1 broadcast, went out (emitido por radio): *el programa fue radiado a las doce = the programme went out at twelve.* 2 BOT. radiate. || *s.m.pl.* 3 ZOOL. radiata.
radiador *s.m.* TEC. radiator.
radiante *adj.* 1 radiant, glowing (resplandeciente). 2 (fig.) beaming: *mi hermana estaba radiante = my sister's face was beaming.*
radiar *v.t.* 1 FIS. to radiate. 2 MED. to treat with X-rays. 3 to broadcast (emitir por radio).
radical *adj.* 1 radical (fundamental). 2 total (completo). || *s.m.* y *f.* 3 POL. radical. || *s.m.* 4. GRAM. root. 5 MAT. square-root sign.
radicalismo *s.m.* 1 POL. radicalism. 2 (fig.) dogmatic behaviour.
radicalizar *v.t.* 1 to radicalize. || *v.pron.* 2 to become radical.
radicalmente *adv.* radically.
radicar *v.i.* 1 to take root (arraigar). 2 to be, to lie, be situated: *el problema radica en que no tenemos suficiente dinero = the problem is that we haven't got enough money.* || *v.pron.* 3 to settle down (establecerse).
radio *s.m.* 1 GEOM. radius. 2 QUIM. radium. 3 spoke (de rueda de bicicleta). || *s.f.* 4 radio (aparato).
radiodifusión *s.f.* broadcasting (emisión por radio).
radioelectricidad *s.f.* FIS. radioelectricity.
radioeléctrico, -a *adj.* FIS. radioelectric.
radiofonía *s.f.* radiophonics.
radiografía *s.f.* 1 radiography. 2 X-ray (foto).
radiográfico, a *adj.* radiographic.
radiología *s.f.* radiology.
radiológico, -a *adj.* radiological.
radiólogo, -a *s.m.* y *f.* radiologist.
radioscopia *s.f.* radioscopy.
radiotecnia *s.f.* radio engineering.
radiotécnico, -a *s.m.* y *f.* radio engineer.
radiotelefonía *s.f.* radiotelephony.
radiotelefonista *s.m.* y *f.* radiotelephonist.
radiotelegrafía *s.f.* radiotelegraphy.

radioterapia *s.f.* radiotherapy.
raedura *s.f.* 1 scraping. 2 MED. scratch. || *pl.* 3 parings.
raer *v.t.* 1 to scrape. 2 to skim (rasar). 3 (fig.) to eradicate (extirpar). 4 MED. to graze.
ráfaga *s.f.* 1 squall, gust (viento). 2 burst (disparos). 3 flash (relámpago). 4 (Am. y fig.) fortune (racha).
rafia *s.f.* 1 BOT. Raphia palm. 2 raffia (material).
raglán o **ranglán** *adj.* raglan (diseño de prenda de vestir).
raíble *adj.* liable to fray (material).
raído, -a *adj.* 1 tatty (paño). 2 shabby (persona o prenda de vestir). 3 (fig.) cheeky (descarado).
raigambre *s.f.* 1 BOT. root-system. 2 (fig.) rootedness, stability (estabilidad): *mi tía tiene raigambre conservadora = my aunt is a long-established conservative.*
raíl *s.m.* rail (riel).
raíz *s.f.* 1 root. || 2 COM. **bienes raíces,** real state. 3 **a — de,** right after. 4 **de —,** completely: *tenemos que cortar de raíz estas injusticias = we must get rid of these injustices.* 5 **echar raíces,** (fig.) to settle down, take root. 6 MAT. **— cuadrada,** square root. 7 MAT. **— cúbica,** cube root.
raja *s.f.* 1 slit (hendedura). 2 piece (fruta). 3 wedge (leño). 4 (vulg.) fanny (órgano sexual de la mujer).
rajá *s.m.* rajah.
rajable *adj.* easy to cut: *esta madera es rajable = this wood is easy to cut.*
rajado, -a *adj.* 1 split, cut. || *s.m.* 2 (fam.) chicken (cobarde).
rajar *v.t.* 1 to slice (dividir en rajas). 2 to split (hender). 3 (fam.) to knife, to stab (apuñalar). || *v.i.* 4 (fam.) to gab (hablar mucho). 5 (fam.) to shoot one's mouth off (jactarse). || *v.pron.* 6 (fam.) to turn chicken (acobardarse). 7 (Am.) to get it wrong (equivocarse). 8 (Am.) to blow money (gastar mucho). 9 (Am.) to run off (huir).
rajatabla (a) *adv.* to the letter, rigorously: *cumplimos nuestras instrucciones a rajatabla = we carried out our instructions to the letter.*
ralea *s.f.* 1 class, kind (clase). 2 (desp.) **de baja —,** no good, evil, wicket, wretchet.
ralentí *s.m.* 1 slow motion (cine). 2 MEC. **al —,** ticking over: *el coche estaba al ralentí = the car was just ticking over.*
ralo, -a *adj.* 1 thin, spaced out, gappy: *pelo ralo = thin on top; dientes ralos = gappy teeth.* 2 (Am. y fig.) brittle (insubstancial). 3 rarefied (aire).
rallador *s.m.* grater (utensilio).
rallar *v.t.* 1 to grate (desmenuzar). 2 (fam.) to get on one's nerves: *esos ruidos continuos me rallan = those constant noises get on my nerves.*
rally *s.m.* rally (de coches).
rama *s.f.* 1 branch. 2 COM. department. 3 side (ligamento textil). || 4 **andarse por las ramas,** to beat about the bush. 5 **en —,** raw (materia no manufacturada), unbound (libro no encuadernado). 6 **poner una cosa en la última —,** to put in mothballs.
ramadán *s.m.* Ramadan.
ramal *s.m.* 1 strand (cabo de soga). 2 halter (de caballo). 3 branch: *ramal de una vía férrea = branch line.* 4 distributing pipe (fontanería).
ramalazo *s.m.* 1 lash (azote). 2 weal (verdugón). 3 (fig.) acute pain (dolor agudo). 4 (fig.) ordeal (pesar).
rambla *s.f.* 1 avenue (avenida). 2 riverbed (lecho fluvial). 3 (Am.) wharf (muelle).
ramera *s.f.* whore (puta).
ramería *s.f.* the game (prostitución).
ramificación *s.f.* 1 BOT. branching. 2 ramification (subdivisión).
ramificarse *v.pron.* 1 BOT. to branch out. 2 to ramify (subdividirse).
ramillete *s.m.* 1 posy, buquet (flores). 2 table decoration (adorno de mesa). 3 (fig.) choice selection (colección de cosas excelentes).
ramaje *s.m.* BOT. branches.
rameado, -a *adj.* floral (decoración de papel pintado).
ramo *s.m.* 1 BOT. branch. 2 bunch (flores). 3 COM. department. 4 (fig.) touch: *mi tío tiene un ramo de gota = my uncle has a touch of gout.*
ramonear *v.t.* 1 to prune (árboles). || *v.i.* 2 to graze (comer los animales).
rampa *s.f.* 1 ramp. 2 (Am.) sedan chair (andas). || 3 **— de lanzamiento,** launching pad.
rampante *adj.* rampant (blasón).
ramplón, -ona *adj.* 1 uncouth, coarse (tosco). || *s.m.* 2 stud (de herradura).
ramplonería *s.f.* uncouthness, coarseness.
rana *s.f.* 1 ZOOL. frog. || 2 (fam.) **cuando las ranas críen pelo,** when pigs can fly. 3 **salir —,** (fam.) to fail to deliver: *prometía mucho de joven, pero salió rana = he was very promising when he was young, but in later life failed to deliver.*
rancidez o **ranciedad** *s.f.* 1 rancidness (sebo). 2 mellowness (madurez). 3 (fig.) oldness (antigüedad).
rancio, -a *adj.* 1 rancid (de mal sabor). 2 mellow (de sabor maduro). 3 (fig.) old-school.
ranchera *s.f.* (Am.) popular Mexican song.
ranchero, -a *s.m.* y *f.* 1 (Am.) ranch owner (jefe de rancho). 2 army cook (cocinero del ejército). || *adj.* 3 (Am.) rustic (rudo).
rancho *s.m.* 1 communal meal (comida hecha para mucha gente). 2 (Am.) AGR. ranch (granja). 3 (Am.) country shack (cobertizo de campo). 4 MAR. crew's berths (alojamiento de tripulación). 5 MAR. gang of sailors (grupo de marineros). || 6 (fam.) **hacer —,** to make space. 7 **hacer — aparte,** to go one's own way (alejarse de los demás).
rango *s.m.* 1 rank, hierarchy (jerarquía). 2 prominence. 3 **de rango,** prestigious. 4 (Am.) pomp, magnificence (rumbo). 5 (Am. y fam.) old nag (rocín).
ranura *s.f.* slot, aperture.
rapador *s.m.* (fam.) barber (barbero).
rapamiento *s.m.* 1 cut (pelo). 2 shave (afeitado).
rapapolvo *s.m.* 1 (fam.) dressing-down, telling-off (reprensión dura). || 2 **echar un — a alguien,** to give someone a good dressing-down.
rapar *v.t.* 1 to crop, to cut hair very short. 2 to shave (afeitar). 3 (fam.) to nick, to swipe (robar): *alguien me ha rapado la cartera = someone's swiped my wallet.*
rapacería *s.f.* piece of tomfoolery (muchachada).
rapacidad *s.f.* greed, avarice (codicia).
rapaz *adj.* 1 greedy, avaricious (codicioso). 2 light-fingered (ladrón). 3 ZOOL. predatory. || *s.f.pl.* 4 ZOOL. birds of prey. || *s.m.* 5 young lad (chiquillo).
rapaza *s.f.* young lass (chiquilla).
rape *s.m.* 1 crop (corte de pelo muy corto). 2 fast shave (afeitado descuidado). 3 ZOOL. angler fish. || 4 **pelar al — a alguien,** to give someone a skinhead cut. 5 **dar un — a alguien,** (fig.) to give someone a dressing-down (echar una bronca).
rapé *s.m.* snuff (tabaco en polvo).
rápel o **ráppel** *s.m.* 1 COM. price discount. 2 DEP. absailing: (forma de bajar en alpinismo) *descendimos por la pared de la roca en rápel = we absailed down the rock face*
rápidamente *adv.* quickly, fast.
rapidez *s.f.* speed, quickness.
rápido, -a *adj.* 1 fast, quick, speedy: *era un tren rápido = it was a fast train.* || *s.m.pl.* 2 GEOG. rapids. || 3 **¡—!,** (fam.) make it snappy!
rapiña *s.f.* 1 robbery with violence, looting (saqueo). 2 greed (avidez). || 3 ZOOL. **ave de —,** bird of prey.
raposo, -a *adj.* 1 cunning, sly (taimado). || *s.m.* 2 ZOOL. fox (zorro). || *s.f.* 3 ZOOL. vixen (zorra).
rapsoda *s.m.* HIST. wandering minstrel (poeta).
rapsodia *s.f.* MUS. rhapsody.
raptar *v.t.* to abduct, kidnap (secuestrar).
rapto *s.m.* 1 abduction, kidnapping (secuestro). 2 (fig.) rush of blood (impulso). 3 (fig.) rapture, enchantment (embelesamiento).
raptor, -ora *s.m.* y *f.* abductor, kidnapper (secuestrador).
raqueta *s.f.* 1 DEP. racquet. 2 island (cambio de dirección en una carretera). 3 snowshoe (zapato para andar por la nieve). 4 croupier's rake (juego).
raquítico, -a *adj.* 1 MED. rachitic. 2 (fig.) meagre, wanting (insuficiente).
raquitis *s.f.* o **raquitismo** *s.m.* MED. rickets.
raramente *adv.* 1 seldom, hardly ever (rara vez). 2 strangely (de forma rara).

rareza *s.f.* 1 peculiarity, idiosyncrasy (manía). 2 rareness, scarcity (escasez). 3 rarity (objeto raro).
raro, -a *adj.* 1 strange, odd (extraño). 2 rare, scarce (poco común). 3 eccentric, cranky (extravagante). 4 remarkable, impressive (notable).
ras *s.m.* 1 evenness. || 2 **a — de,** flush with. 3 **— con —,** dead even.
rasa *s.f.* 1 run (tela). 2 GEOG. clearing (claro).
rasante *adj.* 1 low. || *s.f.* 2 incline, slope (cuesta en una carretera). || 3 **cambio de —,** top of the hill. 4 **tiro —,** ground-level shot. 5 **vuelo —,** low-level flight.
rasar *v.t.* 1 to graze, brush (rozar). 2 AGR. to strickle. || *v.pron.* 3 to clear up (despejarse el cielo).
rascacielos *s.m.* skyscraper.
rascar *v.t.* 1 to scratch, scrape (raer). 2 MUS. to scrape (tocar mal). || *v.pron.* 3 (Am.) to get drunk (emborracharse).
rascador *s.m.* 1 scraper (herramienta). 2 hairpin (alfiler de mujer).
rascadura *s.f.* scratching, scraping.
rasero *s.m.* 1 AGR. strickle. || *s.f.* 2 spatula (cocina). || 3 **medir por el mismo —,** (fig.) to treat in exactly the same way.
rasgado, -a *adj.* 1 wide: *ella tiene unos ojos muy rasgados = her eyes are very wide.* 2 (fam.) down-to-earth (desenvuelto).
rasgadura *s.f.* rip, tear (desgarro).
rasgar *v.t.* 1 to rip, to tear (desgarrar). 2 MUS. to strum (tocar la guitarra). 3 to write with flourishes (escribir con rasgos). || 4 (fig.) **rasgarse las vestiduras,** to kick up a fuss.
rasgo *s.m.* 1 flourish, stroke (adorno hecho con la pluma). 2 trait, feature (característica). 3 splendid gesture (acción notable). || *pl.* 4 features (facciones).
rasgón *s.m.* rip, tear (desgarradura).
rasgueado *s.m.* MUS. strumming (guitarra).
rasguear *v.t.* 1 MUS. to strum. || *v.i.* 2 to write with flourishes.
rasguño o **rascuño** *s.m.* 1 scratch (arañazo). 2 ART. rough sketch (tanteo).
rasilla *s.f.* 1 fine wool cloth (tela). 2 ARQ. thin brick (ladrillo).
raso, -a *adj.* 1 flat, smooth (liso). 2 low, ground level (casi tocando el suelo). 3 clear, cloudless (cielo despejado). 4 ordinary. 5 **soldado raso,** private. 6 backless (de silla sin respaldo). || *s.m.* 7 satin (satén). 8 open country. || 9 **al —,** in the open air.
raspa *s.f.* 1 BOT. beard. 2 fishbone (pez). 3 stem (racimo). 4 (Am.) mean trick (burla). 5 (Am. y fam.) telling-off (reprimenda).
raspado, -a *adj.* 1 scraped. || *s.m.* 2 scraping. 3 water-ice (bebida).
raspador *s.m.* 1 scraper (de albañil, etc.). 2 rasp (de carpintero). 3 MED. scoop.
raspadura *s.f.* 1 scraping. 2 (Am.) unrefined sugar (panela). 3 (fam.) crop (corte de pelo al rape). || *pl.* 4 shavings (madera), filings (metal), scrapings (en general).
raspante *adj.* rough, coarse: *bebimos un vino muy raspante = we drank a very rough wine.*
raspar *v.t.* 1 to scrape, scratch (rallar ligeramente). 2 to scrub out (borrar). 3 to leave a sharp taste, to take the skin off the month: *este vino raspa = this wine takes the skin off the month.* 4 (fam.) to nick (robar). 5 (Am.) to tell off (reprender). 6 (Am.) to kill (matar). || *v.i.* 7 (Am.) to go away (largarse).
raspón o **rasponazo** *s.m.* MED. abrasion, graze.
rastra *s.f.* 1 trail, track (huella). 2 AGR. harrow (grada). 3 cart (carro de arrastre). 4 object dragged along (objeto arrastrado). 5 string (ristra). 6 (Am.) belt buckle (adorno de cinturón). 7 (fig.) unfortunate consequence (consecuencia desagradable). || 8 **a la —,** o **a rastras,** (fig.) reluctantly (a la fuerza). 9 **andar a rastras,** (fig.) to go through a bad patch.
rastrear *v.t.* 1 to track down (buscar y encontrar). 2 to trail (seguir). 3 AGR. to harrow, to rake (utilizar el rastro). 4 to trawl (pesca). 5 to comb (explorar una zona). 6 to sell meat at the market (al por mayor). 7 (fig.) to suss out (averiguar). || *v.i.* 8 to fly low (avión).
rastreador, -a *s.m.* 1 trawler (barco de pesca). || *s.m.* y *f.* 2 searcher (persona). || 3 **— de minas,** minesweeper.
rastreo *s.m.* 1 trawling (pesca). 2 combing (exploración). 3 dredging (dragado). 4 AER. tracking.
rastrero, -a *adj.* 1 dragging, crawling. 2 BOT. creeping. 3 (fig.) ingratiating, bootlicking (servil). 4 tracking. 5 **perro —,** retriever, tracker. || *s.m.* y *f.* 6 wholesale market worker (trabajador del rastro).
rastrillo *s.m.* 1 rake (instrumento de jardinería). 2 TEC. flax comb. 3 MIL., HIST. portcullis. 4 ward (cerradura). 5 (Am.) COM. deal.
rastro *s.m.* 1 track, trail (huella). 2 AGR. rake (rastrillo), harrow (grada). 3 (fig.) sign, trace. 4 abattoir, slaughterhouse (matadero). || 5 **el Rastro,** fleamarket in Madrid.
rastrojera *s.f.* 1 AGR. field of stubble. 2 stubble season (temporada).
rastrojo *s.m.* 1 stubble. 2 ploughed field (tierra labrada). 3 (Am.) shrub forest (bosque de arbustos).
rasura *s.f.* 1 scraping, shaving (afeitar). 2 flatness (llanura). || *pl.* 3 parings (raspaduras).
rasurar *v.t.* 1 to shave (afeitar). 2 to scrape, to scratch (raspar).
rata *s.f.* 1 ZOOL. rat. || *s.m.* 2 pickpocket (ladrón). || 3 **más pobre que una —,** (fig.) as poor as a church mouse. 4 **— común,** common rat. 5 **— de agua,** water vole. 6 **— de montaña,** marmot.
ratear *v.t.* 1 to pilfer, to thieve, to steal (robar con maña). 2 to distribute (repartir). || *v.i.* 3 to creep, to crawl (arrastrarse).
rateramente *adv.* in a thieving manner.
ratería *s.f.* 1 pilfering, petty larceny (robo). 2 deviousness, unscrupulousness (deshonestidad).
ratero, -a *adj.* 1 pilfering, thieving. 2 beneath contempt (bajo). || *s.m.* y *f.* 3 petty crook, pickpocket (ladrón).
raticida *s.m.* rat poison
ratificación *s.f.* 1 ratification (confirmación). 2 approval (aprobación).
ratificar *v.t.* 1 to ratify, to confirm. 2 to approve.
rato *s.m.* 1 while, short time, spell (breve período): *espérame un rato = wait just a little while for me.* || 2 **a ratos,** from time to time. 3 **(Am.) hasta cada —,** see you later. 4 **pasar el —,** to kill time. 5 **ratos perdidos,** free time. 6 **tener para —,** to have a long way to go. 7 **un —,** (fam.) tons: *él sabe un rato de geografía = he knows tons about geography.*
ratón *s.m.* 1 ZOOL. mouse. || 2 **— de biblioteca,** (fig.) bookworm.
ratona *s.f.* ZOOL. she-mouse.
ratonero, a *adj.* 1 mouser: *tenemos un perro ratonero = we've got a mouser.* 2 (fam.) tuneless (música mala). || *s.f.* 3 mousetrap (trampa). 4 mousehole (agujero). || 5 **caer en la ratonera,** (fig.) to fall into the trap.
ratonesco, -a o **ratonil** *adj.* fit for mice. 2 **música ratonil,** tuneless music.
raudal *s.m.* 1 torrent (torrente). 2 (fig.) surfeit, spate (abundancia). || 3 **a raudales,** in floods.
raudamente *adv.* precipitately, at high speed.
raudo, -a *adj.* precipitate, high-speed, rash.
ravioles *s.m.pl.* GAST. ravioli.
raya *s.f.* 1 stripe, line (trazo). 2 GEOG. limit, boundary (límite). 3 (fig.) end, limit: *vas a tener que poner raya a tus excesos = you must put an end to your excesses.* 4 parting (pelo). 5 crease (pantalón). 6 dash (guión largo). 7 ZOOL. skate, ray. 8 (Am.) day's wages. 9 (Am.) hopscotch (juego). 10 (argot) dose (cocaína). || 11 **a —,** in check. 12 **hacer —,** (fig.) to steal the show. 13 **pasarse de la —,** to go too far. 14 **poner a —,** to restrain, to keep back.
rayado, -a *adj.* 1 striped, lined (con rayas). || *s.m.* 2 drawing ruled lines (acción de rayar). 3 stripes, ruled lines (conjunto de rayas).
rayano, -a *adj.* 1 bordering (lindante). 2 next to, close to (cercano).
rayar *v.t.* 1 to rule, line (hacer rayas). 2 to cross out, to erase (borrar). 3 to underline (subrayar). 4 (Am.) to pay wages (pagar). 5 (Am.) to spur (caballo). || *v.i.* 6 to border on, to be near (lindar). 7 (fig.) to be similar (asemejarse). 8 (fig.) to stand apart (sobresalir). 9 to break (alba, día): *rayaba el alba cuando salimos = dawn was breaking as we left.*
rayo *s.m.* 1 beam, ray (luz). 2 flash of lightning (relámpago). 3 spoke (radio de bicicleta). 4 (fig. y fam.) whizz-kid (genio). 5 (fig.) thunderbolt (bomba). 6 (fig.) setback, bane (desgracia impre-

vista). || **7 echar rayos** (fig.) to explode (enfadarse). **8 rayos gamma,** ELEC. gamma rays. **9 rayos X,** MED. X-rays.
rayón *s.m.* rayon (material).
raza *s.f.* 1 breed, species (animal). 2 race (humana). 3 crack, splitting (hendedura). 4 run, ladder (rasa). || **5 — humana,** human race. **6 de —,** ZOOL. thoroughbred (caballo), pedigree (perro).
razón *s.f.* 1 FIL. reasoning, reason. 2 reason (argumento). 3 cause, motive (motivo). 4 right: *tienes toda la razón del mundo = you're absolutely right.* || **5 a — de,** at the rate of. **6 en — de,** as concerns. **7 perder la —,** to go mad. **8 poner en —,** to reconcile. **9 — de pie de banco,** a load of nonsense. **10 — de estado,** reasons of state. **11 — social,** COM. firm name.
razonable *adj.* 1 reasonable, acceptable (aceptable). || **2 precio —,** fair price.
razonablemente *adv.* reasonably, acceptably.
razonadamente *adv.* by reasoning.
razonado, -a *adj.* logical, systematic (según razonamiento).
razonador, -ora *s.m.* y *f.*thinker, reasoner (persona que discurre).
razonamiento *s.m.* reasoning, deduction.
razonar *v.i.* 1 to reason, to put forward an argument (exponer razones). 2 to discourse, to talk (hablar).
razzia *s.f.* 1 MIL. foray, attack (correría). 2 raid (policía).
re *s.m.* MUS. D.
rea *s.f.* DER. female accused.
reacción *s.f.* 1 reaction. || **2 motor de —,** TEC. jet engine. **3 — en cadena,** chain reaction.
reaccionar *v.i.* 1 to react. 2 to respond: *¿cómo está reaccionando el paciente al tratamiento? = how is the patient responding to the treatment?* 3 to be oneself again (sobreponerse).
reaccionario, -a *adj./s.m.* y *f.* reactionary.
reacio, -a *adj.* 1 obstinate, stubborn (terco). 2 opposed, unwilling (opuesto).
reactivación *s.f.* reactivation.
reactivar *v.t.* to reactivate.
reactivo, -a *adj.* 1 reactive. || *s.m.* 2 QUIM. reagent.
reactor *s.m.* 1 FIS. reactor. 2 AER. jet. || **3 — nuclear,** nuclear reactor.
real *adj.* 1 real, genuine (auténtico). 2 royal (del rey): *la familia real = the royal family.* 3 (fig.) great, splendid (muy bueno). || *s.m.* 4 MIL. camp (campamento). 5 fairground (feria). 6 HIST. (fig.) Spanish coin: *no tengo ni un real = I haven't a penny.* || **7 asentar los reales,** to settle down in a place.
realce *s.m.* 1 TEC. embossed work (adorno). 2 (fig.) splendour (esplendor), grandeur (grandeza). || **3 dar — a una cosa,** to highlight something.
realengo, -a *adj.* 1 HIST. of the king (tierras). 2 (Am.) ownerless (animal sin dueño). 3 (Am.) bone-idle, lazy (holgazán).
realeza *s.f.* royalty.
realidad *s.f.* 1 reality. 2 the facts, truth (verdad). || **3 en —,** in fact.
realismo *s.m.* 1 realism. 2 royalism (tendencia monárquica).
realista *adj.* 1 realistic. || *s.m.* y *f.* 2 realist.
realizable *adj.* 1 feasible, possible (posible). 2 FIN. realizable.
realización *s.f.* 1 fulfilment, completion (cumplimiento). 2 FIN. realization. || **3 — de beneficios,** FIN. profit-taking.
realizador, -ora *s.m.* y *f.* director (televisión, cine).
realizar *v.t.* 1 to carry out, to fulfil, to complete (cumplir). 2 FIN. to realize. 3 (Am.) to sell off (liquidar mercancías). || *v.pron.* 4 to be achieved, to take place, to come true: *se realizó su sueño = his dream came true.*
realzar *v.t.* 1 (fig.) to enhance, to highlight (hacer resaltar). 2 TEC. to raise, to emboss.
reanudación *s.f.* resumption, renewal.
reanudar *v.t.* 1 to renew (una cosa caducada). 2 to resume (una cosa que había sido interrumpida).
rearme *s.m.* MIL. rearmament.
reasegurar *v.t.* FIN. to reinsure.
reaseguro *s.m.* FIN. reinsurance.
reasumir *v.t.* 1 to resume (resumir). 2 (form.) to reassume.
reasunción *s.f.* 1 resumption. 2 (form.) reassumption.
reata *s.f.* 1 rope (para unir caballerías). 2 team (caballerías). 3 (Am.) flower-border (jardinería). 4 (Am.) cotton strip (cinta de algodón). || **5 de —,** in a line, (fig.) like sheep.
reavivar *v.t.* to revive, to get going (alentar).
rebaja *s.f.* 1 reduction (abaratamiento). || *pl.* 2 COM. sales: *todas las tiendas están de rebajas = the sales are on in all the shops.*
rebajado, -a *adj.* 1 reduced, down in price (precio). || *s.m.* 2 MIL. soldier exempted from duty.
rebajamiento *s.m.* 1 reduction, lowering. 2 (fig.) humiliation.
rebajar *v.t.* 1 to lower, to bring down (precios). 2 to reduce, to lessen (disminuir). 3 (fig.) to humble, to bring down a peg or two (humillar). || *v.pron.* 4 MIL. to gain exemption. 5 to abase oneself (abatirse), to condescend to: *se rebajó a pedirme perdón = he condescended to tell me he was sorry.*
rebaje *s.m.* 1 MIL. exemption. || **2 — de rancho,** MIL. food expenses.
rebanada *s.f.* 1 slice (pan, jamón, etc.). 2 (Am.) bolt (pestillo).
rebanar o **rebanear** *v.t.* to slice (pan, etc.).
rebañadera *s.f.* hooked pole (instrumento de hierro con garfios).
rebañar *v.t.* 1 to polish off (apurar comida). 2 to rake in, to scrape together (recoger fondos). 3 to scrape up (recoger residuos).
rebaño *s.m.* 1 flock (ovejas). 2 herd (ganado). 3 (fig.) flock.
rebasar *v.t.* 1 to go past (pasar), to overtake (adelantar). 2 to get round, to avoid (peligro). 3 to exceed (límite de tiempo).
rebatible *adj.* refutable (argumento).
rebatimiento *s.m.* refutal, refutation.
rebatiña *s.f.* 1 mad rush, scramble. || **2 andar a la —,** to make a mad desh (luchar por apoderarse de algo).
rebatir *v.t.* 1 to beat off, to fend off (ataque). 2 to refute, to reject (argumento). 3 to knock off, to reduce (precio). 4 to strengthen, to redouble (reforzar).
rebato *s.m.* 1 alarm-bell (llamamiento). 2 (fig.) alarm, panic. 3 MIL. lightning attack.
rebeca *s.f.* cardigan (prenda de vestir).
rebeco *s.m.* ZOOL. chamois.
rebelarse *v.pron.* 1 MIL. to rise up, to rebel. 2 (fig.) to resist, to challenge, to rebel.
rebelde *adj.* 1 rebellious, rebel: *el comandante rebelde = the rebel commander.* || *s.m.* y *f.* 2 rebel. 3 DER. defaulter. || **4 enfermedad —,** MED. chronic illness (enfermedad que resiste a todos los remedios).
rebeldía *s.f.* 1 disobedience, rebelliousness. 2 DER. default.
rebelión *s.f.* 1 rebellion, revolt. 2 MIL. uprising.
rebobinar *v.t.* to rewind (casete, película).
rebojo *s.m.* piece of bread (pan).
reborde *s.m.* fringe, border (orla).
rebordear *v.t.* to put a border on (tela, etc.).
rebosadero *s.m.* 1 overflow pipe (fontanería). 2 spillway (construcción hidráulica). 3 (Am.) GEOL. deposit.
rebosamiento *s.m.* 1 overflowing (líquido). 2 (fig.) abundance (abundancia).
rebosante *adj.* (fig.) overflowing, brimming (con, with).
rebosar *v.i.* 1 to overflow, spill over. 2 (fig.) to be brimming with: *mi hermana rebosa de salud = my sister is brimming with health.* 3 (fig.) to abound. **4 — de riquezas,** to be rolling in money.
rebotación *s.f.* 1 bouncing (pelota). 2 (Am.) annoyance, irritation (bilis).
rebotar *v.i.* 1 to bounce, to rebound (botar una pelota). || *v.t.* 2 to clench (clavo). 3 to reject, to refuse (rechazar). 4 (fam.) to get in to one's hair (irritar). 5 (Am.) to churn up, to make muddy (enturbiar el agua).
rebote *s.m.* 1 rebound (baloncesto), bounce. || **2 de —,** (fig.) on the rebound, in a roundabout way.
rebozar *v.t.* 1 to cover in batter (cocina). 2 to cover up one's face (cubrir el rostro).
rebozo *s.m.* 1 muffling (cubriendo el rostro). 2 (fig.) pretence, bluff (simulación). || **3 sin —,** (fig.) honestly, openly.
rebujar *v.t.* 1 to jumble together (coger desordenadamente). 2 to wrap up (cubrir bien con ropa).

rebujo *s.m.* 1 shawl (embozo). 2 untidy parcel (envoltorio desordenado).
rebullicio *s.m.* commotion, turmoil (alboroto).
rebullir *v.i.* o *v.pron.* 1 to start moving (empezar a moverse). 2 to start boiling (empezar a bullir). 3 (fig.) to show signs of life. || *v.t.* 4 (Am.) to shake, to stir.
rebusca *s.f.* 1 search (busca). 2 AGR. gleaning. 3 (fig.) dregs, left-overs (desecho). 4 (Am.) black-market trading (comercio ilegal).
rebuscado, -a *adj.* 1 pretentious, affected (persona). 2 recherché (palabra).
rebuscador, -ora *s.m.* y *f.* searcher (persona).
rebuscamiento *s.m.* 1 searching, inspection (registro). 2 pretentiousness, affectation (afectación).
rebuscar *v.t.* 1 to search painstakingly for (buscar minuciosamente). 2 AGR. to glean. || *v.pron.* 3 (Am.) to seek employment (buscar empleo).
rebuznar *v.i.* to bray (hacer ruido el asno).
rebuzno *s.m.* braying (voz del asno).
recabar *v.t.* 1 to manage to get (conseguir obtener). 2 to ask for (pedir).
recadero, -a *s.m.* y *f.* 1 messenger (mensajero). 2 errand boy (mozo).
recado *s.m.* 1 message (mensaje). 2 present, gift (regalo). 3 groceries (la compra diaria). 4 equipment, tackle (conjunto de útiles). 5 caution, carefulness (precaución). 6 (Am.) riding accoutrements (montura).
recaer *v.i.* 1 to fall again. 2 MED. to undergo a relapse. 3 to recidivate, to backslide (volver a cometer un acto criminal).
recaída *s.f.* 1 MED. relapse. 2 recidivism (reincidencia criminal).
recalar *v.t.* 1 to soak (impregnar en líquido). || *v.i.* 2 MAR. to pull into port (llegar a un puerto), to catch sight of land (reconocer tierra). 3 to swin under water (buscar). 4 (Am.) to reach (alcanzar).
recalcadamente *adv.* 1 very tightly (apretadamente). 2 insistently (con mucha insistencia).
recalcar *v.t.* 1 to press down tightly (apretar mucho). 2 to fill up, to pack in (llenar). 3 (fig.) to emphasize, to put great stress, to use forcefully (palabras): *mi jefe recalcó mucho sus palabras = my boss put great stress on each word.* || *v.i.* 4 MAR. to heel over (inclinarse). || *v.pron.* 5 MED. to dislocate (hueso), to sprain (tobillo).
recalcitrante *adj.* 1 stubborn, obstinate (terco). 2 POL. recalcitrant.
recalcitrar *v.i.* 1 to take backward steps (retroceder). 2 (fig.) to listen to nobody, to be defiant (resistir).
recamado *s.m.* embroidery work (bordado).
recamar *v.t.* to embroider (bordar).
recámara *s.f.* 1 side room (cuarto pequeño). 2 (Am.) bedroom (dormitorio). 3 explosives chamber (minería). 4 cartridge chamber (arma de fuego). || 5 **tener mucha —,** (fig.) to tread warily, to leave nothing to chance.
recambiar *v.t.* 1 to change again. 2 to exchange (pieza de repuesto). 3 COM. to make a revised draft of.
recambio *s.m.* 1 second change. 2 spare part (pieza de repuesto). 3 refill (cartucho de bolígrafo). || 4 **piezas de —,** spares.
recapacitar *v.t.* to ponder, to think over (meditar en).
recapitulación *s.f.* summing up, recapitulation.
recapitular *v.t.* 1 to recapitulate (repetir). 2 to sum up (resumir).
recapitulativo, -a *adj.* recapitulative.
recargado, -a *adj.* 1 reloaded (cargado de nuevo). 2 overloaded (sobrecargado). 3 added (gravamen). 4 (fig.) excessive, overdone (exagerado).
recargar *v.t.* 1 to reload (volver a cargar). 2 to overload (sobrecargar). 3 to overburden (abrumar). 4 (fig.) to lay it on thick (adornar excesivamente). 5 DER. to up, to increase (aumentar la sentencia). 6 FIN. to make an extra charge (gravar más).
recargo *s.m.* 1 extra load, extra burden (nueva carga). 2 DER. fresh charge (nuevo cargo). 3 FIN. extra charge (gravamen adicional). 4 MED. rise in temperature. 5 MIL. period of extra duties.
recatadamente *adv.* 1 modestly unpretentiously (modestamente). 2 carefully, prudently (prudentemente).
recatado, -a *adj.* 1 modest, unpretentious. 2 careful, prudent.
recatar *v.t.* 1 to hide (esconder). || *v.pron.* 2 to take one's time, to delay (vacilar). 3 to act with discretion (actuar discretamente).
recato *s.m.* 1 discretion, wariness, prudence (circunspección). 2 modesty, unpretentiousness (modestia).
recauchutar *v.t.* TEC. to retread, to remould (neumáticos).
recaudación *s.f.* 1 collecting. 2 FIN. levy, levying (impuestos). 3 FIN. tax office (oficina). 4 FIN. receipts, takings (cantidad).
recaudador, -ora *s.m.* y *f.* FIN. tax collector.
recaudamiento *s.m.* 1 collecting. 2 FIN. levying.
recaudar *v.t.* 1 to collect, levy (impuestos). 2 to take, to obtain (dinero). 3 to get back, to recover (deuda). 4 to safeguard (asegurar).
recaudo *s.m.* 1 FIN. collecting, levying. 2 safeguarding, care (protección). 3 precaution (precaución). 4 (Am.) assorted vegetables (legumbres surtidas). 5 (Am.) spices (especias). || 6 **a buen —,** (fig.) in good hands, in safekeeping.
recelar *v.t.* 1 to fear, to suspect. || *v.pron.* 2 to distrust (desconfiar de).
recelo *s.m.* 1 fear, suspicion (sospecha). 2 distrust (desconfianza).
receloso, -a *adj.* 1 suspicious, sceptical (incrédulo). 2 distrustful.
recensión *s.f.* 1 review (obra literaria), report (descripción). 2 LIT. critical revision.
recensor *s.m.* reviewer, commentator.
recepción *s.f.* 1 receiving. 2 admission, admitting (admisión). 3 reception (reunión). 4 reception desk (hotel).
receptáculo *s.m.* 1 recipient, container. 2 BOT. receptacle.
receptar *v.t.* 1 to receive (cosas robadas). 2 to conceal, hide (ocultar a un delincuente).
receptividad *s.f.* 1 receptiveness (capacidad para recibir). 2 proneness (aptitud para contraer enfermedades).
receptivo, -a *adj.* receptive, sensitive (sensible).
receptor, -a *adj.* 1 receiving. || *s.m.* 2 TEC. receiver, set (televisión). 3 DER. receiver.
recesión *s.f.* 1 regression (retroceso). 2 ECON. recession, slump.
receso *s.m.* 1 break, separation (separación). 2 pause (descanso). 3 (Am.) recess (suspensión de actividades formales). || 4 **estar en —,** to have a break in the proceedings. 5 **— económico,** lull in the economy.
receta *s.f.* 1 recipe (cocina). 2 MED. prescription.
recetar *v.t.* 1 MED. to prescribe. 2 (Am.) to deliver (golpe).
recetario *s.m.* 1 MED. prescription list, formulary. 2 list of ingredients (formulario).
recibidor, -a *adj.* 1 receiving. || *s.m.* y *f.* 2 receiver (persona). || *s.m.* 3 visits room (sala de visitas). 4 entrance hall (vestíbulo).
recibimiento *s.m.* 1 reception (recepción). 2 welcome (acogida): *me dieron un recibimiento caluroso = they gave me a warm welcome.* 3 entrance hall (vestíbulo). 4 main room (sala principal).
recibir *v.t.* 1 to receive. 2 to accept, to admit (admitir): *su propuesta no fue recibida = her proposal wasn't accepted.* 3 to welcome (dar la bienvenida, acoger). 4 MIL. to await (esperar un ataque). 5 to face without moving (tauromaquia). 6 to apply plaster to (asegurar con yeso). || *v.i.* 7 to entertain, to have guests: *en mi casa recibimos todos los fines de semana = in my house we have guests every weekend.* || *v.pron.* 8 to graduate (Universidad), to qualify (tomar el título profesional): *mi hermana acaba de ser recibida de dentista = my sister is now a qualified dentist.*
recibo *s.m.* 1 reception, receiving (recibimiento). 2 COM. receipt. || 3 **estar de —,** to be dressed to receive visitors.
reciclaje *s.m.* 1 recycling (materiales). 2 modification (tecnología).
recién *adv.* newly, only just: *son recién casados = they're newly-weds.*
reciente *adj.* 1 recent (acontecimiento). 2 fresh, just made: *pan reciente = freshly-baked bread.* || *s.m.* 3 yeast (levadura).

recientemente *adv.* recently, not very long ago.
recial *s.m.* rapids (río).
reciamente *adv.* **1** strongly, forcefully (con fuerza). **2** loudly (voz).
reciedumbre *s.f.* **1** strength, vigour (fuerza). **2** loudness (ruido). **3** hardness, inflexibility (dureza).
recinto *s.m.* enclosed area, enclosure.
recio, -a *adj.* **1** strong, vigorous (constitución). **2** hard, severe (duro). **3** bad, foul (tiempo desapacible). **4** quick, fast, speedy (veloz). **5** loud (voz): *mi tío habla muy recio = my uncle's got a loud voice.* **6** bulky, thick (abultado).
recipiente *adj.* **1** receiving. || *s.m.* **2** recipient, receptacle (vaso).
reciprocación *s.f.* reciprocation.
recíprocamente *adv.* reciprocally, in a reciprocal manner.
reciprocar *v.t.* to reciprocate, to respond.
reciprocidad *s.f.* mutual relation, reciprocity.
recíproco, -a *adj.* **1** reciprocal, mutual. **2** GRAM. reflexive. || **3 a la recíproca,** vice versa.
recitación *s.f.* recitation, reciting.
recitado *s.m.* **1** recitation. **2** MUS. recitative, recitativo.
recitador, -ora *s.m.* y *f.* declaimer, recitationist (persona).
recital *s.m.* **1** LIT. reading (poesía). **2** MUS. recital.
recitar *v.t.* to recite, to read aloud (leer en voz alta).
recitativo, -a *adj.* MUS. recitative.
reclamación *s.f.* **1** demand, claim (exigencia): *reclamación salarial = wage claim.* **2** complaint, grievance (queja): *libro de reclamaciones = complaints book; ¡oiga! quiero formular una reclamación = excuse me! I with to lodge a complaint.*
reclamante *s.m.* y *f.* **1** claimant (persona que pide). **2** person complaining (persona que formula una queja).
reclamar *v.t.* **1** to demand, to claim (pedir con insistencia). **2** to beg for (implorar). **3** to lure (caza). **4** DER. to file a claim against. || *v.i.* **5** to lodge a complaint, to protest (quejarse). **6** (poet.) to resound, to echo. || *v.pron.* ZOOL. to call to one another.
reclamo *s.m.* **1** ZOOL. lure (caza). **2** bird-call (caza). **3** call (llamada). **4** DER. claim. **5** COM. publicity, advertising. **6** (fig.) enticement, temptation. **7** LIT. catchword.
reclinación *s.f.* reclining, leaning.
reclinar *v.t.* **1** to recline, to rest on (apoyar). || *v.pron.* **2** to lean back, to recline (apoyarse, descansar).
reclinatorio *s.m.* **1** reclining seat (asiento para reclinarse). **2** REL. priedieu (mueble para orar).
recluir *v.t.* **1** to lock up, to put behind bars (cárcel). || *v.pron.* **2** to lock oneself away, to shut oneself up.
reclusión *s.f.* **1** withdrawal, retirement (acto de recluirse). **2** confinement, imprisonment (encarcelamiento). **3** prison, jail (cárcel).
recluso, -a *s.m.* y *f.* **1** prisoner (preso). **2** recluse (solitario).
reclusorio *s.m.* prison, jail, place of confinement (cárcel).
recluta *s.f.* **1** recruitment, recruiting (acto). || *s.m.* **2** recruit (persona).
reclutamiento *s.m.* **1** recruiting (acto). **2** soldiers recruited (soldados).
reclutar *v.t.* **1** MIL. to recruit. **2** to sign up, to contract (trabajo). **3** (Am.) to corral, to round up (ganado).
recobrar *v.t.* **1** to recover, to regain (recuperar). || *v.pron.* **2** MED. to get better, recover. **3** to be oneself again (volver en sí). **4** to get one's own back (desquitarse): *me he recobrado de aquella mala jugada = I got my own back for that dirty trick.*
recobro *s.m.* **1** recovery, regaining. **2** MED. recovery, convalescence.
recocer *v.t.* **1** to cook a second time (cocina). **2** to anneal (metal). || *v.r.* **3** (fig.) to suffer torment, to agonize (atormentarse).
recocido, -a *adj.* **1** recooked, overcooked (cocido demasiado). || *s.m.* **2** annealing (metal).
recochinearse *v.pron.* (fam.) to have a good laugh (regodearse).
recochineo *s.m.* **1** (fam.) monkeying around. **2** (desp.) unholy joy.
recodo *s.m.* turn, bend (de un río o una calle).
recogedor *s.m.* **1** dustman (basurero). **2** dustpan (pala). **3** AGR. harvester (persona). **4** AGR. rake (herramienta).
recoger *v.t.* **1** to pick up. **2** AGR. to pick, to harvest (cosechar). **3** to collect (hacer colección). **4** to rake in, to net (dinero). **5** to bring together (juntar personas). **6** to take up (reducir una prenda de vestir), to take in (estrechar). **7** to take in (dar asilo a). **8** to call in, to seize (retirar de la circulación): *todos los ejemplares de aquel libro fueron recogidos = all the copies of that book were seized.* || *v.pron.* **9** to retire (a la cama), to go home (ir a casa). **10** to be lost in thought (abstraerse).
recogidamente *adv.* in a sheltered manner.
recogido, -a *adj.* **1** apart, separate (apartado). **2** sheltered, secluded (fuera de la civilización). || *s.f.* **3** collecting, AGR. harvesting. **4** collection (correo).
recogimiento *s.m.* **1** collecting, AGR. harvesting. **2** privacy, solitude (soledad). **3** REL. piety, devotion.
recolección *s.f.* **1** AGR. harvest. **2** LIT. summary. **3** FIN. netting, receipt. **4** REL. place of seclusion, retreat.
recolectar *v.t.* **1** to gather together (recoger). **2** AGR. to harvest.
recolector, -ora *s.m.* y *f.* **1** collector. **2** AGR. picker (uvas), harvester.
recoleto, -a *adj.* **1** retiring, unassuming (modesto). || *s.m.* **2** REL. conventual.
recomendable *adj.* **1** recommendable (cosa). **2** fine, commendable (persona).
recomendablemente *adv.* recommendably.
recomendación *s.f.* **1** recommendation, piece of advice. **2** reference, testimonial: *el catedrático mandó una carta de recomendación = the professor sent off a reference.* **3** praise (alabanza).
recomendado, -a *adj.* **1** recommended. **2** (Am.) registered (correos). || *s.m.* y *f.* **3** recommended person, person given a reference.
recomendante *s.m.* y *f.* referee, person giving a reference.
recomendatorio, -a *adj.* recommendatory.
recomendar *v.t.* **1** to recommend (hablar en favor de). **2** to advise, to suggest: *te recomiendo que veas esa película = I recommend you to see that film.* **3** to consign (confiar). **4** (Am.) to register (correo). **5** (desp.) to buy favours (enchufar).
recompensa *s.f.* **1** compensation (compensación). **2** reward (premio).
recompensable *adj.* worthy of recompense (que merece recompensa).
recompensar *v.t.* **1** to compensate for. **2** to reward, to provide recompense: *sus esfuerzos fueron bien compensados = her efforts were amply rewarded.*
reconcentración *s.f.* **1** concentration, bringing together (acto de reunir).
reconcentrar *v.t.* **1** to concentrate, to bring together. **2** (fig.) to conceal (sentimiento): *ella intentó reconcentrar su enfado = she tried to conceal her annoyance.* || *v.pron.* **3** to be deep in thought (abstraerse).
reconciliable *adj.* reconcilable.
reconciliación *s.f.* reconciliation, reconcilement.
reconciliador, -ora *adj.* **1** reconciliatory. || *s.m.* y *f.* **2** reconciler.
reconciliar *v.t.* **1** to reconcile, to bring back together (armonizar). || *v.pron.* **2** to become reconciled, to be friends again. **3** REL. to make a confession.
reconditez *s.f.* (fam.) brain-twister (cosa bien escondida).
recóndito, -a *adj.* hidden, obscure, profound.
reconfortante *adj.* **1** comforting, soothing. || *s.m.* **2** (Am.) MED. tonic.
reconfortar *v.t.* **1** to comfort, to cheer up: *me reconfortó pensar que ya no dependía de nadie = it cheered me up to think I no longer depended on anybody.* || *v.pron.* to gain strength.
reconocer *v.t.* **1** to recognize (recordar a alguien). **2** to acknowledge, to accept (aceptar): *Israel no reconoce la legitimidad de Palestina = Israel doesn't accept Palestine's legitimacy.* **3** MED. to examine. **4** to confess, to admit (confesar): *él no quiere reconocer su complicidad = he won't admit to being involved.* **5** to agree that, to recognize as: *ella reconoce a la niña por suya = she recognizes the little girl as her own.* || *v.pron.* **6** to be plain, to be quite clear: *ya se reconoce*

que él es el culpable = it's quite clear that he's the guilty one.

reconocible *adj.* recognizable, acknowledgeable.

reconocidamente *adv.* gratefully, with thanks.

reconocido, -a *adj.* 1 recognized, acknowledged. 2 grateful (agradecido).

reconocimiento *s.m.* 1 acknowledgement, recognition: *su reconocimiento como presidente = his recognition as president.* 2 identification (documento). 3 confession, admission (confesión). 4 MED. check-up. 5 gratitude, thanks (agradecimiento). 6 AER. reconnaissance.

reconstitución *s.f.* reconstitution, reshaping.

reconstituir *v.t.* 1 to reconstitute, to reconstruct (constituir de nuevo). 2 MED. to restore.

reconstituyente *adj.* 1 reconstituent. || *s.m.* 2 MED. restorative.

reconstrucción *s.f.* reconstruction, remodelling.

reconstructivo, -a *adj.* reconstructive.

reconstruir *v.t.* 1 to reconstruct, to remodel (construir de nuevo). 2 POL. to reshuffle (reorganizar el gabinete).

reconvención *s.f.* 1 reproof, reprimand (reproche). 2 DER. counter-claim.

reconvenir *v.t.* 1 to reprove, to reprimand (reprender). 2 DER. to counterclaim. 3 to remonstrate with (intentar persuadir).

reconversión *s.f.* reconversion, remodification.

reconvertir *v.t.* to reconvert, to remodify.

recopilación *s.f.* 1 collection, compilation (escritos). 2 LIT. summary.

recopilador, -ora *s.m.* y *f.* compiler (de escritos).

recopilar *v.t.* 1 to compile, to collect (escritos). 2 LIT. to summarize. 3 LEG. to codify.

récord *s.m.* DEP. record: *Aouita ha vuelto a batir el récord mundial = Aouita has once again broken the world record.*

recordable *adj.* 1 rememberable (que se puede recordar). 2 memorable (digno de ser recordado): *una canción recordable = a memorable song.*

recordar *v.t.* 1 to remember: *recuerdo que aquel año hizo mucho calor = I remember that year being very hot.* 2 to remind: *recuérdale que me llame por teléfono = remind him to phone me.* 3 to remind of: *aquella chica me recuerda a mi prima = that girl reminds me of my cousin.* || *v.pron.* 4 (Am.) to wake up (despertarse). 5 (Am.) to come round (volver en sí).

recordativo, -a *adj.* 1 remindful. || *s.m.* 2 reminder (advertencia).

recordatorio *s.m.* 1 reminder (recordativo). 2 memorandum (nota).

recorrer *v.t.* 1 to cross, to go through (cruzar un territorio). 2 to go over, to look through (documento). 3 to fix, to mend (reparar). 4 to bring down (tipografía).

recorrido, -a *adj.* 1 crossed, travelled. || *s.m.* 2 route, journey (trayecto). 3 (fam.) beating (paliza). 4 description of an illustration (tipografía).

recortado, -a *adj.* 1 cut off. 2 irregular, uneven (borde de una cosa). || *s.m.* 3 cutting (recorte). || 4 **escopeta recortada**, sawn-off shotgun.

recortar *v.t.* 1 to cut off. 2 to make paper cut-outs (hacer figuras). 3 ART. to draw in relief. || *v.pron.* 4 to stand out (perfilarse).

recorte *s.m.* 1 cutting out. 2 newspaper cutting (periódico). 3 feign (tauromaquia). || *pl.* 4 clippings, trimmings (residuos).

recostar *v.t.* 1 to rest, to lean on. || *v.pron.* 2 to recline, to lie back (reclinar).

recoveco *s.m.* 1 turn, corner (curva de una calle). 2 (fig.) ruse, trick (ardid). 3 (Am.) elaborate decoration (adorno complicado). || *pl.* 4 nooks and crannies (rinconcitos de la casa). 5 (fig.) twists and turns (complejidades) complicated: *la historia no carece de recovecos = it's quite a complicated story.*

recreación *s.f.* 1 entertainment, relaxation. 2 playtime (escuela).

recrear *v.t.* 1 to recreate (crear de nuevo). 2 to entertain (divertir). || *v.pron.* 3 to have a good time.

recreativo, -a *adj.* entertaining, recreational (que divierte).

recrecer *v.t.* 1 to make bigger (aumentar). || *v.i.* 2 to happen again (ocurrir de nuevo). || *v.pron.* 3 to buck up (reanimarse).

recreo *s.m.* 1 entertainment (recreación). 2 playtime (escuela).

recría *s.f.* fattening up (acto de cebar animales).

recriar *v.t.* to fatten up (cebar animales).

recriminación *s.f.* recrimination, reproach (reproche).

recriminador, -ora *adj.* 1 recriminating. || *s.m.* y *f.* 2 denouncer (persona).

recriminar *v.t.* 1 to recriminate. 2 DER. to countercharge.

recriminatorio, -a *adj.* recriminatory, reproachful (acusador).

recrudecer *v.i.* to get worse, to take a turn for the worse (empeorar).

recrudecimiento *s.m.* 1 worsening (empeoramiento). 2 fresh outbreak, renewal: *ha habido un recrudecimiento de hostilidades = there has been a renewal of violence.*

recrudescente *adj.* recrudescent, deteriorating.

rectal *adj.* ANAT. rectal.

rectangular *adj.* rectangular: *coordenadas rectangulares = rectangular coordinates.*

rectángulo, -a *adj.* 1 rectangular, right-angled (triángulo). || *s.m.* 2 MAT. rectangle, oblong figure (oblongo).

rectificador, -a *adj.* 1 rectifying. || *s.m.* 2 ELEC. rectifier (de corriente).

rectificar *v.t.* 1 to rectify, to put right (enmendar). 2 to flatten out, to straighten (carretera). 3 to distil (purificar líquidos). 4 MEC. to coat, to face (revestir).

rectificativo, -a *adj.* amendatory, corrective (que enmienda).

rectilíneo, -a *adj.* GEOM. rectilinear, made up of straight lines.

rectitud *s.f.* 1 straightness (línea recta). 2 (fig.) rectitude.

recto, -a *adj.* 1 straight (línea). 2 (fig.) upright, honest (justo). 3 FILOL. basic, proper (sentido de una palabra). || *s.m.* 4 ANAT. rectum. || *s.f.* 5 GEOM. straight line (línea).

rector, -a *adj.* 1 ruling. || *s.m.* y *f.* 2 superior, head (jefe). 3 rector (universidad). 4 REL. parish priest.

rectorado *s.m.* 1 rectorship (oficio). 2 rector's office (oficina).

rectoral *adj.* 1 of the rector. || *s.f.* 2 parish priest's house (casa).

recua *s.f.* 1 ZOOL. pack, team (acémilas). 2 (fig. y fam.) herd, bunch.

recuadrar *v.t.* MAT. to divide into squares.

recuadro *s.m.* 1 box (formulario). 2 inset (libro).

recuento *s.m.* 1 recount (electoral). 2 registration, enumeration (lista).

recuerdo *s.m.* 1 memory, remembrance (memoria). 2 keepsake, souvenir (regalo). 3 commemoration (conmemoración). || *pl.* 4 regards.

reculada *s.f.* 1 backward movement (retroceso). 2 kick (fusil). 3 (fig.) cold feet (acobardarse).

recular *v.i.* 1 to go back, to go backwards (retroceder). 2 to kick (fusil). 3 (fig.) to get cold feet (acobardarse). 4 MIL. to beat a retreat.

reculones, a *adv.* backwards: *andar a reculones = to go backwards.*

recuperable *adj.* recuperable, retrievable.

recuperación *s.f.* 1 recovery, recuperation. 2 repeat (examen).

recuperar *v.t.* 1 to get back, to recover (recobrar). 2 to repeat (examen). 3 to reclaim (tierras, bosques). || *v.pron.* 4 to get better, to recover.

recurrente *adj.* 1 recurrent. || *s.m.* 2 DER. claimant.

recurrir *v.i.* 1 to look to, to ask for help (al médico, etc.). 2 to make use of (valerse de). 3 DER. to appeal.

recurso *s.m.* 1 recourse (acción de recurrir). 2 means (medio). 3 DER. appeal. || *pl.* 4 resources (medios de subsistencia), natural resources (de un país). || 5 **como último —**, as a last resort.

recusación *s.f.* DER. objection, appeal.

recusar *v.t.* 1 to reject (rechazar). 2 DER. to object to, to challenge.

rechazar *v.t.* 1 to reject, to turn down (oferta). 2 to beat off, to parry (ataque). 3 to refuse (proposición).

rechazo *s.m.* 1 rebound (rebote). 2 MED. rejection. || 3 **de —,** as a result.
rechifla *s.f.* 1 whistling (silbido). 2 (fig.) ridicule.
rechiflar *v.t.* 1 to go on whistling (silbar con insistencia). 2 to hiss (sisear). 3 (fig.) to jeer at, to poke fun at (burlarse de).
rechinante *adj.* 1 creaking (puerta). 2 grinding (dientes). 3 scraping (tiza en la pizarra). 4 screeching (frenos).
rechinar *v.i.* 1 to creak (puerta, tabla). 2 to grind, to gnash (dientes). 3 to scrape, scratch (tiza). 4 to screech (frenos).
rechistar *v.i.* 1 to make a sound, to utter a word (hablar). 2 to answer (responder). 3 to protest (protestar).
rechoncho, -a *adj.* (fam.) short and stocky.
rechupete, de — *loc.adv.* (fam.) smashing, just right, craking good: *tuvimos una cena de rechupete = we had a cracking good supper.*
red *s.f.* 1 net (caza, pesca). 2 TEC. network (infraestructura). 3 (fig.) trap, device (ardid): *has vuelto a caer en la red = you've fallen into the trap again.* 4 hairnet (redecilla para el pelo). 5 mesh (malla).
redada *s.f.* 1 cast (lance de red). 2 swoop, raid (policía). 3 (fig.) netful, haul, load: *cogieron una buena red de conspiradores = they caught a load of plotters.*
redil *s.m.* 1 sheepfold. || 2 **volver al —,** (fig.) to mend one's ways.
redacción *s.f.* 1 LIT. composition, essay. 2 writing (acto de escribir). 3 editorial staff (periódico). 4 newspaper office (oficina).
redactar *v.t.* 1 to write, to compose. 2 to edit (periódico).
redactor, -ora *s.m.* y *f.* 1 writer, journalist (periodista). 2 editor (director).
rededor *s.m.* 1 surroundings (contorno). || 2 **al —/en —,** around.
redención *s.f.* 1 ransom (rescate). 2 REL. redemtpion.
redicho, -a *adj.* (fam.) pedantic, donnish (que habla afectadamente).
redimir *v.t.* 1 to redeem, to buy back (volver a obtener por dinero). 2 HIST. to buy the freedom of (esclavitud). || *v.pron.* 3 to free oneself from (librarse): *se ha redimido de esa obligación = she has freed herself from that obligation.*
redentor, -a *adj.* 1 redeeming. || *s.m.* 2 REL. redeemer.
rédito *s.m.* 1 FIN. return, interest.
redivivo, a *adj.* resuscitated (aparecido).
redoblado, -a *adj.* 1 short and squat (rechoncho). 2 increased, redoubled (esfuerzo). 3 MUS. double-quick (paso).
redoblante *s.m.* 1 MUS. long-sided drum. || *s.m.* y *f.* 2 drummer (persona).
redoble *s.m.* 1 redoubling, increase (acto de redoblar). 2 MUS. drumroll.
redoblar *v.t.* 1 to redouble, to increase (aumentar). 2 to bend over (clavo). 3 to repeat (repetir). || *v.i.* 4 MUS. to play a drumroll.
redoma *s.f.* 1 narrow-necked round bottle (vasija). 2 (Am.) goldfish bowl (pecera). 3 (Am.) safety island (circulación).
redomado, -a *adj.* perfect (*atr.*): *es un hipócrita redomado = he's a perfect hypocrite.*
redonda *s.f.* 1 MUS. semibreve. 2 GEOG. región (comarca). 3 meadow (dehesa). || 4 **a la —,** round about: *en muchísimas millas a la redonda = for miles and miles round about.*
redondamente *adv.* 1 around (en torno). 2 (fig.) categorically.
redondeado, -a *adj.* round, rounded (de forma redonda).
redondear *v.t.* 1 to make round, to make curved (tornear). 2 MAT. to round up. || *v.pron.* 3 to clear oneself of debts (librarse de deudas). 4 to become rich (adquirir cierta fortuna).
redondel *s.m.* 1 (fam.) circle. 2 arena, bullring (tauromaquia).
redondez *s.f.* roundness, curvature (de la tierra).
redondilla *s.f.* LIT. quatrain.
redondo, -a *adj.* 1 round, circular (esférico). 2 (fig.) straightforward (sin rodeo). 3 (Am.) separate, external, adjacent: *una tienda redonda = an adjacent shop.* 4 successful, very well: *la cosa me salió redonda = it went very well for me.* || *s.m.* 5 round figure (cosa circular). || 6 **caer —,** (fam.) to fall like a dead weight. 7 **en —,** round about. 8 **mesa redonda,** round table. 9 **número —,** round number. 10 **negocio —,** successful business. 11 **virar en —,** to turn right round.
redrojo o **redruejo** *s.m.* 1 BOT. late fruit (fruto tardío). 2 vine stubble (racimo). 3 (fig. y fam.) puny lad (muchacho enclenque).
reducción *s.f.* 1 reduction (disminución). 2 subjecting (rebeldes). 3 MAT. conversion. 4 MED. setting (huesos).
reducido, -a *adj.* 1 reduced. 2 restricted (limited). 3 small (número).
reducir *v.t.* 1 to reduce, to shorten (disminuir). 2 to restrict (limitar). 3 to subject, to subdue (enemigos). 4 MAT. to convert, to transform. 5 MED. to set (huesos). 6 to summarize, to resume (resumir). 7 QUIM. to concentrate (una disolución). || *v.pron.* 8 FIN. to make economies (moderarse en el modo de vivir). 9 to be reduced to, to come down to, to be, after all: *la rebelión se redujo a una pequeña escaramuza = the uprising was, after all, a mere skirmish.* || 10 **— a común denominador,** to reduce to a common denominator.
reducto *s.m.* MIL. redoubt.
redundancia *s.f.* 1 surfeit, superabundance (abundancia excesiva). 2 GRAM. redundancy, pleonasm.
redundante *adj.* 1 superfluous, profuse (profuso). 2 GRAM. redundant.
redundar *v.i.* 1 to overflow (rebosar). 2 to be reflected, to be avantatje of: *la acción redundó en mi beneficio = the action was to my advantage.*
reduplicación *s.f.* 1 reduplication, reduplicating. 2 re-echo, repetition (repetición).
reduplicar *v.t.* 1 GRAM. to reduplicate. 2 to re-echo, to repeat (repetir).
reeducación *s.f.* 1 re-education (acción de educar de nuevo). 2 rehabilitation de enfermos, delincuentes).
reeducar *v.t.* 1 to re-educate (académico). 2 to rehabilitate (trabajo).
reembolsar *v.t.* y *v.pron.* FIN. to be repaid, to be reimbursed.
reembolso *s.m.* 1 repayment, reimbursement. || 2 **a/contra —,** cash on delivery.
reemplazar *v.t.* 1 to replace (cosa). 2 to stand in for (persona).
reemplazo *s.m.* 1 replacement (cosa). 2 substitution (persona). 3 MIL. annual reserve. || 4 **de —,** MIL. out of the reserve.
reencarnación *s.f.* reincarnation.
reencarnar *v.i.* to be reincarnated.
reengendrar *v.t.* to regenerate spiritually.
refajo *s.m.* underskirt, slip (ropa femenina).
refectorio *s.m.* refectory (en comunidades religiosas y colegios).
referencia *s.f.* 1 reference (alusión). 2 report, account (informe). || 3 **con — a,** with reference to. 4 **— múltiple,** LIT. cross-reference.
referéndum *s.m.* POL. referendum.
referente, a *adj.* referring to, relating to.
referir *v.t.* 1 to tell, to relate (contar). 2 to refer, to relate to (relacionar): *aquel tema se refería a mi trabajo = that matter related to my work.* 3 (Am.) to throw in somebody's face: *él me lo refirió en cara = he threw it in my face.* || *v.pron.* 4 to refer to: *no me estaba refiriendo a eso = I wasn't referring to that.* || 5 **por lo que se refiere a,** as regards, as for.
refilón, de *adv.* 1 aslant, obliquely: *ella me miró de refilón = she took a quick glance at me.* 2 (fig.) quite by chance (de pasada).
refinado, -a *adj.* 1 refined (purificado). 2 (fig.) distinguished (distinguido). 3 (fig.) bright, clever (astuto). || *s.m.* 4 TEC. refining. 5 refined spirit (aguardiente).
refinación *s.f.* TEC. refining.
refinamiento *s.m.* 1 extreme care, refinement (esmero). 2 cruelty (crueldad). || 3 **— por pasos,** stepwise refinement (informática).
refinar *v.t.* 1 TEC. to refine. 2 to polish, to perfect (perfeccionar). || *v.pron.* 3 to become refined, to learn social etiquette (educarse).
refinería *s.f.* TEC. refinery: *refinería de petróleo = oil refinery.*
refino, -a *adj.* 1 very fine, refined. || *s.m.* 2 TEC. refining (depuración). 3 (Am.) refined spirit (aguardiente).
reflector, -a *adj.* 1 reflecting. || *s.m.* 2 TEC. reflector. 3 spotlight (luz).
reflejar *v.t.* 1 to reflect. || *v.pron.* 2 (fig.) to be reflected, to be seen.
reflejo *s.m.* 1 reflection (imagen). 2 reflex (movimiento). 3 GRAM. reflexive. 4 streak, rinse (pelo).

reflexión *s.f.* 1 reflection. || 2 **hacer reflexiones,** to meditate.
reflexionar *v.i.* 1 to reflect, to think (pensar). || *v.pron.* 2 to think over.
reflexivo, -a *adj.* 1 reflective, contemplative (que obra con reflexión). 2 reflecting (que reflecta). 3 GRAM. reflexive.
refluir *v.i.* 1 to flow back (líquido). 2 (fig.) to turn out (resultar).
reflujo *s.m.* 1 ebb (descenso de marea). 2 (fig.) backward step (retroceso).
refocilar *v.t.* 1 to amuse, to cheer up (alegrar). || *v.i.* 2 (Am.) to lighten (relampaguear). || *v.pron.* 3 to have a fabulous time (pasarlo muy bien).
refocilo *s.m.* 1 enjoyment, delight. 2 (Am.) lightning (relámpago).
reforma *s.f.* 1 reform, modification. 2 REL. e HIST. Reformation.
reformación *s.f.* reformation, modification.
reformado, -a *adj.* 1 reformed, modified. 2 REL. protestant.
reformador, -a *adj.* 1 reforming. || *s.m.* 2 reformer.
reformar *v.t.* 1 to reform. 2 ARQ. to restore, to repair. || *v.pron.* 3 (fig.) to mend one's ways, to show moderation (moderarse).
reformatorio *s.m.* reformatory, borstal: *le mandaron al reformatorio de menores = he was sent to borstal.*
reformista *adj.* 1 reforming. || *s.m.* y *f.* reformist.
reforzado, -a *adj.* reinforced, strengthened.
reforzar *v.t.* 1 to reinforce (hacer más fuerte). 2 (fig.) to bolster up, to encourage (animar). 3 to intensify, to increase (aumentar).
refracción *s.f.* FIS. refraction.
refractar *v.t.* FIS. to refract (reflejar).
refractario, -a *adj.* 1 heat-resistant: *una cazuela refractaria = a heat-resistant cooking-pot.* 2 (fig.) insubordinate, rebellious (rebelde).
refracto, -a *adj.* FIS. refracted.
refrán *s.m.* LIT. saying, proverb.
refranero *s.m.* LIT. anthology of proverbs.
refregar *v.t.* 1 to scrub, to rub (frotar). 2 (Am. y fam.) to be nasty, to dig the knife in: *se lo refregó en cara = he really dug the knife in.*
refrenable *adj.* containable, repressible.
refrenamiento *s.m.* 1 (fig.) curbing, restraining. 2 holding back (caballo).
refrenar *v.t.* 1 (fig.) to curb, to restrain. 2 to hold back (caballo).
refrendación *s.f.* 1 endorsement, ratification. 2 stamping (pasaporte).
refrendar *v.t.* 1 to endorse, to ratify (ratificar). 2 to stamp (pasaporte), to approve (aprobar). 3 (fig.) to do a second time (repetir).
refrendario *s.m.* endorser, countersignatory.
refrendo *s.m.* 1 endorsing, ratification. 2 approval, rubber-stamping.
refrescante *adj.* 1 cooling (temperatura). 2 refreshing (bebida).
refrescar *v.t.* 1 to cool, to refresh. 2 to repeat, to renew (renovar una acción). || *v.i.* 3 to be cooler (temperatura). 4 to get some fresh air (tomar el fresco). 5 to have a cool drink (beber un refresco). 6 (Am.) to have an evening snack (merendar). || *v.pron.* 7 to feel cooler (persona).
refresco *s.m.* 1 cool drink (bebida). || *pl.* 2 refreshments. || 3 **de –,** once more (de nuevo).
refriega *s.f.* fight, scrap (pelea).
refrigeración *s.f.* 1 refrigeration. 2 MEC. cooling. || 3 **– con agua corriente,** coolant system (energía nuclear).
refrigerador, -a *adj.* 1 cooling. || *s.m.* 2 refrigerator. 3 TEC. cooling system.
refrigerante *adj.* 1 cooling. || *s.m.* 2 QUIM. condenser.
refrigerar *v.t.* 1 to refrigerate, to cool (enfriar). 2 to air-condition (climatizar). 3 (fig.) to restore energy (reparar las fuerzas).
refrigerio *s.m.* 1 refreshment, relief (alivio). 2 snack (piscolabis).
refuerzo *s.m.* 1 strengthener, reinforcement (cosa que refuerza). 2 TEC. strut, prop. 3 (fig.) support, aid (auxilio). || *pl.* 4 MIL. reinforcements. 5 MAR. structure.
refugiado, -a *s.m.* y *f.* refugee.
refugiar *v.t.* 1 to give refuge (acoger). || *v.pron.* 2 to take refuge.
refugio *s.m.* 1 shelter, place of refuge (asilo). 2 hut (en el campo). 3 MIL. underground shelter. || 4 **– antiaéreo,** MIL. air-raid shelter.
refulgencia *s.f.* brightness, brilliance, shining (resplandor).
refulgente *adj.* brilliant, shining.
refulgir *v.i.* to shine, burn, be brilliant.
refundición *s.f.* 1 LIT. adaptation, revision. 2 TEC. recasting.
refundidor *s.m.* LIT. adapter, reviser.
refundir *v.t.* 1 LIT. to adapt, to revise. 2 TEC. to recast. 3 to comprise, to include (comprender). || *v.pron.* 4 (Am.) to get lost, to get mislaid (perderse).
refunfuñador, -a *adj.* grumbling, grumpy.
refunfuñar *v.i.* 1 to grumble, to moan (rezongar). 2 to growl (gruñir).
refunfuño *s.m.* 1 grumble, moan, complaint (queja). 2 growl, grunt (gruñido).
refunfuñón, -ona *adj.* 1 grumbling, moaning. 2 growling, grunting. || *s.m.* y *f.* 3 grumbler, moaner, grouser.
refutable *adj.* refutable: *una opinión refutable = a refutable opinion.*
refutación *s.f.* 1 refuting (acción de refutar). 2 refutation (argumento).
refutar *v.t.* to refute, to disprove (contradecir).
regadera *s.f.* 1 BOT. watering can. 2 AGR. irrigation ditch. || 3 **estar como una –,** (fam.) to be as nutty as a fruitcake.
regadío, -a *adj.* 1 AGR. irrigation. || *s.m.* 2 irrigated land.
regalado, -a *adj.* 1 free, given away (gratis). 2 delicate (delicado). 3 pleasant, gratifying (ameno). 4 comfortable (cómodo).
regalar *v.t.* 1 to give away (una cosa no querida). 2 to give a present (de cumpleaños, etc.). 3 to treat, to regale: *regalamos a nuestros abuelos con una fiesta = we treated our grandparents to a party.* || *v.pron.* 4 to give oneself a special treat.
regalía *s.f.* 1 royal privilege (privilegio real). 2 (fig.) fringe benefit, perk (sobresueldo). 3 (Am.) present, gift (regalo). || 4 **tabaco de –,** good quality tobacco.
regalismo *s.m.* POL. regalism.
regalista *s.m.* y *f.* POL. regalist.
regaliz *s.f.* liquorice.
regalo *s.m.* 1 present, gift (obsequio). 2 (fig.) delight, pleasure (placer). 3 titbit, treat (comida delicada). 4 (fig.) gracious living, contentment (comodidad).
regañadientes, a *loc.adv.* reluctantly, in spite of oneself (de mala gana).
regañar *v.i.* 1 to snarl (perro). 2 to moan, to bellyache (quejarse). 3 to argue (discutir). || *v.t.* 4 to tell off, to scold (reñir).
regañina *s.f.* telling off, scolding (reprensión).
regaño *s.m.* snarl, scowl (ceño). 2 (fam.) ticking off (reprensión): *le di un buen regaño = I gave him a really good ticking off.* 3 (fig.) split crust (parte del pan que revienta al cocerse).
regañón *adj.* moaning, grumbling: *¡vaya un tipo más regañón! = what a moaner!*
regar *v.t.* 1 to water (plantas). 2 to hose down (calle). 3 to spray (rociar): *regué las rosas con insecticida = I sprayed the roses with insecticide.* 4 to wash against: *el mar riega una costa preciosa = the sea washes against a beautiful coastline.* 5 to wash down (beber con la comida): *regamos el lechazo con un buen tinto = we washed down the lamb with a fine red wine.* 6 to spill (derramar). 7 AGR. to sow (sembrar). || *v.pron.* 8 (Am. y fam.) to take a shower. 9 (Am.) to scatter in all directions (dispersarse). || *v.i.* 10 (Am.) to jape, to banter (bromear).
regata *s.f.* 1 MAR. regatta, boat-race. 2 AGR. small irrigation ditch. 3 (Am.) haggling, bargaining (regateo).
regate *s.m.* 1 dodging movement. 2 DEP. piece of dribbling. 3 (fig. y fam.) pretext, chicanery.
regatear *v.t.* 1 COM. to haggle over, to bargain over. 2 to sell retail (vender al por menor). 3 (fam.) to deny, to refuse to admit (negar). || *v.i.* 4 to dodge (dar una finta con el cuerpo). 5 DEP. to dribble. 6 MAR. to take part in a regatta, to race.
regateador *s.m.* DEP. dribbler.
regateo *s.m.* 1 COM. haggling, bargaining. 2 DEP. dribbling.
regato *s.m.* GEOG. pool.
regazo *s.m.* 1 lap. 2 (fig.) bosom (seno).
regencia *s.f.* 1 governing, ruling (acto de gobernar). 2 POL. regency.
regeneración *s.f.* 1 regeneration. 2 (fig.) renewal (renovación).

regenerador *adj.* 1 regenerative. || *s.m.* 2 TEC. regenerator.
regentar *v.t.* 1 to hold temporarily (puesto). 2 (fig.) to shove around, to domineer (dominar).
regente *s.m.* 1 POL. regent. 2 master, foreman (trabajo). 3 REL. principal. 4 (Am.) mayor, governor.
regicida *s.m.* y *f.* regicide (persona).
regicidio *s.m.* regicide (acción de matar al rey).
regidor, -ora *adj.* 1 ruling. || *s.m.* 2 POL. councillor, alderman.
régimen *s.m.* 1 POL. régime. 2 diet (alimenticio): *mi hermana está a régimen = my sister's on a diet.* 3 set of rules (reglamentos). 4 GRAM. government. 5 MEC. optimal performance.
regimiento *s.m.* 1 ruling, governing. 2 MIL. regiment. 3 POL. councillors.
regio, -a *adj.* 1 royal (real). 2 (fig.) splendid, magnificent.
región *s.f.* 1 GEOG. region, part. 2 area (estudios). 3 ANAT. tract.
regional *adj.* regional.
regionalismo *s.m.* regionalism.
regionalista *adj./s.m.* y *f.* regionalist.
regir *v.t.* 1 to rule, to control. 2 GRAM. to govern. 3 to run, to be in charge of (establecimiento). || *v.i.* 4 to be in operation: *esa ley rige todavía = that law is still in force.* 5 MEC. to function, to work.
registrador, -ora *s.m.* 1 registrar (persona). 2 register (aparato). || *adj.* 3 recording. || 4 **caja registradora,** COM. till.
registrar *v.t.* 1 to examine, to inspect (examinar). 2 to register, to note down (anotar). 3 MUS. to record (grabar). || *v.pron.* 4 to put one's name down, to register (matricularse). 5 to take place (tener lugar).
registro *s.m.* 1 registration (acción). 2 register (libro). 3 registry office (oficina). 4 register entry (asiento). 5 check, search (búsqueda). 6 manhole (abertura del alcantarillado). 7 MUS. coupler. 8 recording (cine). 9 bookmark (recordatorio). || 10 **— civil,** civil register. 11 **— mercantil,** mercantile register. 12 **— de la propiedad,** property register.
regla *s.f.* 1 rule, ruler (instrumento). 2 rule, regulation (reglamento). 3 precept, canon (norma). 4 (fig.) moderation, self-discipline (moderación). 5 MED. period. || 6 **en —,** in order. 7 **salir de —,** to go too far, to exceed the limit.
reglaje *s.m.* 1 MEC. adjustment, overhaul (mantenimiento). 2 amendment, correction (puntería).
reglamentación *s.f.* 1 regulation (acto). 2 rules (reglas).
reglamentar *v.t.* to regulate.
reglamentario, -a *adj.* 1 appropriate, proper (apropiado). 2 statutory, stipulated, mandatorio (estatuario): *es reglamentario = it is stipulated.*
reglamento *s.m.* rule, regulation.
reglar *v.t.* 1 to rule, to regulate (reglamentar). 2 to rule (papel). || *v.r.* 3 to be ruled, to adhere.
regocijadamente *adv.* merrily, joyfully.
regocijado, -a *adj.* merry, joyful.
regocijar *v.t.* 1 to cheer up, to gladen. || *v.pron.* 2 to be pleased, to cheer up.
regocijo *s.m.* 1 joy, gladness (alegría). || *pl.* 2 festivities.
regodearse *v.pron.* 1 to be delighted (deleitarse). 2 (fam.) to have a good laugh. 3 (Am.) to be touchy, to be hard to please (ser exigente).
regodeo *s.m.* 1 delight, joy (deleite). 2 bawdiness (lo verde). 3 (desp.) unholy delight.
regojo o **rebojo** *s.m.* piece of bread (pan).
regoldar *v.i.* (vulg.) to belch (eructar).
regordete, -a *adj.* chubby, plump.
regresar *v.i.* to go back, to return.
regresión *s.f.* 1 regression. 2 (fig.) decline, deterioration.
regresivo, -a *adj.* regressive, backward.
regüeldo *s.m.* (vulg.) belch.
reguero *s.m.* 1 AGR. irrigation ditch. 2 steady flow, trickle (sangre). 3 trail (humo), mark, stain (vestigio).
regulación *s.f.* 1 regulation, controlling. 2 MEC. adjustment.
regulador, -a *adj.* 1 regulating. || *s.m.* 2 MEC. regulator. 3 control (radio).
regular *adj.* 1 regular, normal. 2 average (mediano). 3 (desp.) so-so, neither good nor bad: *tenemos un profesor regular = our teacher is neither good nor bad.* || *v.t.* 4 to regulate, put right (ajustar). 5 to govern, control (reglar). || 6 **por lo —,** regularly.
regularidad *s.f.* regularity, order.
regularizar *v.t.* 1 to regularize. 2 to synchronize (sincronizar).
regularmente *adv.* regularly, frequently.
régulo *s.m.* 1 POL. petty ruler. 2 ZOOL. goldcrest. 3 basilisk (basilisco). 4 QUIM. prime constituent.
regurgitación *s.f.* regurgitation.
regurgitar *v.i.* to regurgitate.
rehabilitación *s.f.* 1 rehabilitation (persona). 2 (fig.) restoration.
rehabilitar *v.t.* 1 MED. to rehabilitate. 2 to restore (restablecer).
rehacer *v.t.* 1 to remake, to make again (crear de nuevo). 2 to redo, to do again (repetir). 3 to refurbish, to reconstitute (reponer). || *v.pron.* 4 to be strengthened, to gain strength (fortificarse). 5 (fig.) to keep calm.
rehala *s.f.* ZOOL. combined flock (ovejas), combined herd (vacas).
rehecho, -a *adj.* 1 remade. 2 stocky (rechoncho).
rehén *s.m.* y *f.* hostage.
rehogar *v.t.* to sauté (cocina).
rehuir *v.t.* 1 to escape, to avoid (evitar). || *v.i.* 2 to run off again (caza mayor). || *v.pron.* 3 to distance oneself (apartarse).
rehusar *v.t.* 1 to reject (rechazar). 2 to refuse: *ella rehusó acompañarme = she refused to go with me.*
reina *s.f.* 1 queen. 2 ZOOL. female, queen. || 3 **— de la belleza,** beauty queen. 4 **— mora,** hopscotch (juego de niños).
reinado *s.m.* reign: *bajo el reinado de Carlos III = in the reign of Charles III.*
reinar *v.i.* 1 POL. to rule. 2 to predominate, to take precedence (predominar).
reincidencia *s.f.* 1 relapse, backsliding.
reincidente *s.m.* y *f.* 1 backslider. 2 recidivist (criminal).
reincidir *v.i.* 1 to relapse, to backslide. 2 to recidivate (delincuente).
reineta *s.f.* BOT. russet apple.
reino *s.m.* 1 kingdom: *el reino animal = the animal kingdom.*
reintegración *s.f.* 1 reintegration, reinstatement (rehabilitación). 2 FIN. return, repayment (restitución).
reintegrar *v.t.* 1 FIN. to repay, to reimburse. 2 to reintegrate, to reinstate (persona en algo). 3 to attach a tax stamp (documentos). || *v.pron.* 4 to get back, to be reimbursed (recobrarse).
reintegro *s.m.* 1 FIN. reimbursement, repayment. 2 withdrawal (cuenta bancaria). 3 money back (lotería nacional).
reír *v.i.* 1 to laugh. 2 (fig.) be to cheerful, to beam, to smile. || *v.t.* 3 to laugh at: *nadie le ríe sus bromas pesadas = nobody laughs at his silly tricks.* || *v.pron.* 4 to laugh: *¡no te rías de mí! = don't laugh at me!* 5 (fig. y fam.) to come apart, to split (ropa que empieza a rajarse): *su vieja falda ya se ríe = her old skirt is coming apart.*
reiteración *s.f.* reiteration, repetition.
reiteradamente *adv.* repeatedly, over and over again.
reiterar *v.t.* to reiterate, to repeat.
reiterativo, -a *adj.* reiterative, repetitive.
reivindicable *adj.* claimable, recoverable.
reivindicación *s.f.* 1 claim: *reivindicación salarial = wage claim.* 2 complaint, grievance (queja). 3 DER. recovery. 4 vindication (justificación).
reivindicar *v.t.* 1 to claim (reclamar). 2 to recover, to restore (restorar). 3 to claim responsibility for: *ETA reivindicó el crimen = ETA claimed responsibility for the crime.* || *v.pron.* 4 to clear oneself.
reivindicatorio, -a *adj.* vindicatory.
reja *s.f.* 1 AGR. ploughshare. 2 bars (ventana). 3 (Am. y fam.) clink, nick (cárcel). 4 (fig.) ploughing (labor con arado).
rejilla *s.f.* 1 ARQ. grille, grating. 2 wicker (mueble). 3 brazier (brasero). 4 luggage rack (ferrocarril). 5 lattice (parrilla).
rejo *s.m.* 1 metal tip (punta). 2 (fig.) strength, vigour. 3 BOT. radicle. 4 ZOOL. sting (aguijón). 5 whip (látigo). 6 herd of cows (vacas lecheras). 7 (Am.) coarse leather (cuero crudo). 8 (Am.) milking (acción de ordeñar).
rejón *s.m.* 1 pike, pointed bar. 2 lance (tauromaquia).
rejonazo *s.m.* blow with a lance.
rejoneador *s.m.* mounted bullfighter (tauromaquia).
rejonear *v.t.* to spike, to lance (tauromaquia).

rejoneo *s.m.* spiking, lancing (tauromaquia).
rejuvenecedor, -a *adj.* rejuvenating.
rejuvenecer *v.t.* 1 to make young again. || *v.i.* 2 to grow young again.
rejuvenecimiento *s.m.* rejuvenation.
relación *s.f.* 1 relation. 2 list (lista). 3 MAT. ratio. 4 relationship (trato). 5 report (informe). 6 story (narración). || *pl.* 7 relations, courtship (noviazgo). || 8 — **bancaria,** banking relationship. 9 **relaciones públicas,** public relations.
relacionar *v.t.* 1 to relate, to connect (poner en relación). || *v.pron.* to have contacts, to be related. 3 (fig.) to hobnob: *ese hombre intenta relacionarse con gente rica = that man tries hobnobbing with the rich.*
relajar *v.t.* 1 to relax, to loosen (aflojar). 2 (fig.) to weaken (debilitar). || *v.pron.* 3 to relax, to take things easy. 4 (fig.) to become lax (moralmente). 5 MED. to be weak. 6 (fig.) to turn corrupt (viciarse).
relajación *s.f.* 1 relaxation (sosiego). 2 slackening (aflojamiento). 3 MED. hernia. 4 (fig.) slackness, negligence.
relajante *adj.* 1 relaxing. 2 (Am. y fam.) sickly (comida empalagosa). || *s.m.* 3 MED. laxative.
relajo *s.m.* (Am.) 1 derision, ridicule (escarnio). 2 pandemonium (desorden). 3 indecency, bad taste (indecencia). 4 filthy act (acto inmoral).
relamer *v.t.* 1 to lick time and time again. || *v.pron.* 2 to lick one's lips (labios). 3 (fig.) to make up one's face (maquillarse). 4 (fig.) to shoot one's mouth off (gloriarse).
relamido, -a *adj.* 1 priggish, conceited (afectado). 2 (Am. y fam.) brazen (descarado). 3 (fam.) dressed up to the nines (vestido pulcramente).
relampagueante *adj.* flashing.
relampaguear *v.i.* 1 to flash, to lighten (tormenta). 2 (fig.) to sparkle, to twinkle: *dos ojos que relampagueaban = a pair of sparkling eyes.*
relampagueo *s.m.* 1 flashing. 2 sparkling, twinkling.
relámpago *s.m.* 1 flash of lightning (tormenta). 2 (fig.) flash: *ocurrió como un relámpago = it happened in a flash.* || 3 **guerra** —, MIL. blitzkrieg. 4 **viaje** —, lightning trip.
relatar *v.t.* to relate, to tell.
relativamente *adv.* 1 relatively. 2 in relation to (respecto de).
relatividad *s.f.* 1 relativeness. 2 FIS. relativity.
relativismo *s.m.* FIL. relativism.
relativista *adj.* 1 relativistic. || *s.m.* y *f.* 2 relativist.
relativo, -a *adj.* y *s.m.* relative.
relator, -ora *s.m.* y *f.* 1 narrator, teller. 2 DER. reporter.
relé *s.m.* ELEC. relay.
relegación *s.f.* 1 relegation, relegating. 2 HIST. expulsion (destierro).
relegar *v.t.* 1 to relegate. 2 to expel, to banish, to exile (desterrar).
relente *s.m.* 1 night humidity (humedad nocturna). 2 (fig. y fam.) brazenness, sauciness (descaro).
relevante *adj.* 1 relevant, pertinent. 2 outstanding (sobresaliente).
relevancia *s.f.* relevance, pertinence.
relevar *v.t.* 1 to relieve, to substitute (de un cargo). 2 to absolve, to acquit (de una pena). 3 TEC. to emboss. 4 ART. to paint in relief. || *v.pron.* 5 to take over from one another (hacer algo alternativamente).
relicario *s.m.* 1 trinket-box. 2 (Am.) locket (medallón).
relieve *s.m.* 1 ART. relief. 2 GEOG. contours. 3 three dimensions (cine): *un film en relieve = a three-dimensional film.* 4 (fig.) importance, prestige. || *pl.* 5 leftovers (comida). || 6 **bajo** —, bas-relief.
religión *s.f.* 1 religion: *la religión católica = the Catholic religion.* 2 piety, religiousness (piedad). || 3 **entrar en** —, to enter a holy order. 4 — **reformada,** Protestantism.
religiosamente *adv.* 1 religiously. 2 punctiliously (con exactitud).
religiosidad *s.f.* 1 religiousness 2 punctiliousness (exactitud).
religioso, -a *adj.* 1 religious. 2 punctilious. || *s.m.* y *f.* 3 man/woman of the Church.
relinchador, -a *adj.* always whinnying, always neighing (caballo).
relinchar *v.i.* to whinney, to neigh (hacer ruido el caballo).
relincho *s.m.* whinnying, neighing.
reliquia *s.f.* 1 relic. 2 (Am.) offering (ofrenda). || *pl.* 3 relics, remains (residuos). 4 MED. (fig.) aftereffects.
reloj *s.m.* 1 clock (de pared). 2 wristwatch (de pulsera). 3 timer (de aparato). 4 clock, meter (contador). || 5 — **de agua,** water-clock. 6 — **de arena,** sandglass. 7 — **de caja,** grandfather clock. 8 — **de cuarzo,** quartz watch. 9 — **despertador,** alarm clock. 10 — **joya,** bracelet watch. 11 — **de laboratorio,** lab timer. 12 — **de sol,** sundial. 13 **contra** —, against the clock. 14 **estar como un** —, to be as regular as clockwork. 15 **ser como un** —, to be punctilious.
relojería *s.f.* 1 watchmaking, clockmaking (oficio). 2 watchmaker's (tienda). 3 clockwork: *mecanismo de relojería = clockwork device.* || 4 **bomba de** —, time bomb.
relojero, -a *s.m.* y *f.* watchmaker, clockmaker.
relucir *v.i.* 1 to shine (brillar). 2 (fig.) to be brilliant, to be outstanding (destacar). || 3 **sacar a** —, to go on about (citar).
reluctancia *s.f.* ELEC. reluctance.
reluctante *adj.* stubborn, reluctant (reacio).
relumbrante *adj.* shining, resplendent, brilliant.
relumbrar *v.i.* to shine, to be brilliant (resplandecer).
relumbro o **relumbrón** *s.m.* 1 flash, sparkle (chispazo). 2 tinsel (oropel). || 3 **de** —, tinselly, gaudily (con ostentación).
rellano *s.m.* 1 landing (escalera). 2 GEOG. plateau.
rellenar *v.t.* 1 to fill up. 2 to stuff (comida). || *v.pron.* 3 to gorge oneself, to stuff oneself (comer mucho).
relleno, -a *adj.* 1 stuffed. || *s.m.* 2 stuffing, filling (comida). 3 padding (cosa). 4 centre (caramelo). 5 (fig.) wadding, dead wood.
remachado *adj.* 1 reserved (callado). 2 sullen, surly (cazurro).
remachar *v.t.* 1 to bang in (clavo). 2 (fig.) to drive home (argumento). 3 (fig.) to tie up, to make good (contrato). || *v.pron.* 4 (Am.) to say nothing.
remache *s.m.* 1 TEC. rivetting, clinching. 2 rivet (pasador). 3 (Am. y fig.) tenacity, drive (tenacidad).
remanente *adj.* 1 remaining. || *s.m.* 2 remnant, remainder (residuo). 3 FIN. carryover. 4 COM. surplus.
remangar *v.t.* 1 to turn up (levantar las mangas o la ropa). || *v.pron.* 2 to make up one's mind (decidirse).
remansarse *v.pron.* 1 to become stagnant (estancarse). 2 to form a pool (rebalsarse).
remanso *s.m.* 1 pond, pool of still water. 2 (fig.) peaceful spot (lugar tranquilo). 3 (fig.) leisureliness, steady pace (lentitud).
remador *s.m.* DEP. rower, oarsman.
remar *v.i.* 1 DEP. to row. 2 (fig.) to strive, to battle on.
rematadamente *adv.* completely, entirely.
rematado, -a *adj.* 1 MED. desperate, past cure. 2 complete, utter.
rematador *s.m.* 1 DEP. goal scorer, opportunist (fútbol): *es un rematador nato = he's a born opportunist.* 2 (Am.) COM. auctioneer (subastador).
rematar *v.t.* 1 to finish off, to conclude (terminar). 2 to finish off (matar). 3 DEP. to shoot for goal. 4 (Am.) to sell at auction (vender en subasta). 5 to fasten the last stitch (costura). 6 (Am.) to pull up (caballo). || *v.i.* 7 to finish, to end. 8 (fig.) to pass away, to perish (fenecer). || *v.pron.* 9 to be destroyed, to be lost for ever (destruirse).
remate *s.m.* 1 finishing off, end (fin). 2 killing off (acto de matar). 3 ARQ. pinnacle. 4 selling-off (subasta). 5 DEP. shot at goal. 6 tip (punta). 7 (Am.) edging (borde de paño). || 8 **de** —, completely, absolutely, out-and-out: *es un loco de remate = he's absolutely crazy.* 9 **loco de** —, raving lunating. 10 **por** —, finally, as a final touch. 11 **poner** — **a,** to round off. 12 **venta de** —, FIN. breakout sale.
remedar *v.t.* 1 to imitate, to copy (copiar). 2 (desp.) to ape, to mimic.
remediable *adj.* that can be remedied: *es un problema fácilmente remediable = it's a problem that can be easily remedied.*
remediar *v.t.* 1 to remedy, to put right (corregir). 2 to meet (socorrer una necesidad). 3 to help, to save (persona). 4

to avoid, to impede: *no pude remediarlo = I couldn't help it.*
remedio *s.m.* 1 remedy, solution. 2 MED. cure. 3 panacea, relief (alivio). 4 DER. recourse. || 5 **no hay —,** there's nothing to be done. 6 **no hay más — que,** the only thing to do is to (*inf.*). 7 **no tener para un —,** to be in a hopeless situation. 8 **no tener —,** to have no alternative: *no tenemos más remedio que dejarlo = we have no alternative but to forget it.* 9 **¿qué remedio tengo?,** what else can I do?
remedo *s.m.* poor imitation, rough copy.
remembranza *s.f.* memory, recollection (memoria).
remembrar *v.t.* to remember (recordar).
rememoración *s.f.* remembrance, recollection.
rememorar *v.t.* to remember, recall.
remendón *s.m.* cobbler (zapatero).
remero, -a *s.m.* 1 DEP. rower, oarsman. || *s.f.* 2 ORN. wing feather.
remesa *s.f.* 1 FIN. remittance (dinero). 2 COM. consignment (mercancía). || 3 **— documentaria,** bill batch.
remendar *v.t.* 1 to mend, to repair (reparar). 2 to patch up (poner parches). 3 (fig.) to correct.
remiendo *s.m.* 1 patch (parche). 2 (fig.) correction. 3 ZOOL. spot. 4 MIL. decoration. 5 small-scale publication (imprenta).
remilgado, -a *adj.* 1 very prim and proper (muy delicado). 2 (desp.) hypercritical, pernickety. 3 squeamish (susceptible).
remilgo *s.m.* 1 fastidiousness (suma delicadeza). 2 hypercriticism (intolerancia). 3 squeamishness (susceptibilidad). || 4 **hacer remilgos a,** to consider beneath one: *ella siempre hace remilgos a fregar = she always thinks that washing-up is beneath her.*
reminiscencia *s.f.* 1 faint recollection (recuerdo de algo casi olvidado). 2 reminiscence (acción de recordar).
remirado, -a *adj.* 1 circumspect, cautious (prudente). 2 (desp.) particular.
remirar *v.t.* 1 to look over a second time (mirar de nuevo). 2 to look hard at (mirar con atención). || *v.pron.* 3 to be very painstaking (esmero).
remisamente *adv.* 1 reluctantly (con desgana). 2 sluggishly (lentamente).
remisible *adj.* remissible, pardonable.
remisión *s.f.* 1 COM. consignment. 2 remittance (correo). 3 DER. remission. 4 REL. forgiveness. 5 LIT. reference. 6 postponement, adjournment (aplazamiento).
remiso, -a *adj.* 1 irresolute (irresoluto). 2 sluggish, slow, lazy (perezoso).
remitente *adj.* 1 remittent: *fiebre remitente = remittent fever.* || *s.m.* y *f.* 2 sender (carta).
remitir *v.t.* 1 to send (enviar). 2 DER. to remit. 3 to put off, to postpone (aplazar). 4 REL. to pardon, to forgive. 5 LIT. to refer. || *v.i.* 6 to lessen, to abate (disminuir): *la tormenta remitió por fin = the storm finally abated.* || *v.pron.* 7 to stick by, to stand by (atenerse a): *me remito a lo que dijo Unamuno = I stand by the words of Unamuno.*
remo *s.m.* 1 DEP. oar. 2 rowing (práctica deportiva). 3 ANAT. limb. 4 ZOOL. wing. 5 (fig.) hard slog (trabajo duro). || 6 **andar al —,** (fig. y fam.) to slog away.
remoción *s.f.* 1 shift, removal (cambio). 2 sacking, firing (despido).
remojar *v.t.* 1 to soak, to steep. 2 to dip (pan). 3 (fig.) to invite friends for a celebratory drink (convidar). 4 (Am.) to buy over (sobornar).
remojo *s.m.* 1 soaking, steeping: *he puesto los garbanzos al remojo = I've put the chickpeas to soak.* 2 (Am.) present (regalo). 3 (Am.) bribe (soborno).
remojón *s.m.* 1 soaking, dipping. 2 sop (comida). || 3 **pegarse un —,** (fam.) to go for a dip (nadar).
remolacha *s.f.* 1 beet: *remolacha azucarera = sugar beet.* 2 beetroot (para ensalada).
remolachero *s.m.* beet grower, beet producer.
remolcador *s.m.* 1 MAR. tug. 2 breakdown van (furgoneta).
remolcar *v.t.* 1 to tow (vehículo, barco, etc.) 2 (fig.) to win over (convencer).
remolino *s.m.* 1 whirlpool (de río). 2 whirlwind (de viento). 3 sandstorm (de arena). 4 ringlet (pelo). 5 riot (disturbio). 6 (fig.) swarm, throng (muchedumbre). 7 (fig.) fidget (persona inquieta).
remolinear *v.t.* 1 to swirl (agitar). || *v.i.* 2 to eddy (formar remolinos).
remolón, -ona *adj.* 1 idle, lazy (perezoso). 2 lethargic, indifferent (indolente). || *s.m.* 3 ZOOL. upper tusk (jabalí).
remolonear *v.i.* (fam.) to be idle, to shirk (rehuir).
remolque *s.m.* 1 towing, tow: *llevar a remolque = to tow.* 2 towrope (cabo para remolcar). 3 trailer (caravana).
remontar *v.t.* 1 to put to flight (caza). 2 to mend, to repair (botas). 3 (fig.) to elevate, to raise up (elevar). 4 to stuff, to pack (silla de montar). 5 to remount (montar de nuevo un caballo). 6 DEP. to pull back (un gol). || *v.pron.* 7 to fly high (vuelo). 8 to go back: *vamos a remontarnos hasta el alba de la civilización = we're going to go right back to the drawn of civilization.*
remonte *s.m.* 1 remount (caballería). 2 DEP. ski lift. 3 flying (cometa).
rémora *s.f.* 1 ZOOL. remora, sucking-fish. 2 (fig. y fam.) spanner in the works, fly in the ointment (obstáculo).
remorder *v.t.* 1 to bite again. 2 (fig.) to trouble, to concern (inquietar). || *v.pron.* 3 to suffer deep down.
remordimiento *s.m.* 1 remorse. || 2 **tener remordimientos**, to suffer remorse, to suffer pangs of regret.
remotamente *adv.* 1 remotely: *ya no es ni remotamente lo que era = he's not even remotely like he used to be.* 2 vaguely: *recuerdo remotamente su cara = I vaguely remember her face.*
remoto, -a *adj.* 1 remote, far off, distant. 2 most unlikely (inverosímil).
remover *v.t.* 1 to shift, to remove (cambiar). 2 to stir (líquido). 3 to trouble, to disturb (alterar). 4 to fire, to sack, to dismiss (despedir del trabajo). || *v.pron.* 5 to become agitated.
remozar *v.t.* 1 to rejuvenate (persona). 2 to renovate (edificio). 3 to revamp (organización). 4 to do up (habitación). || *v.pron.* 5 to be rejuvenated, to look years younger.
remunerable *adj.* remunerable, paid.
remuneración *s.f.* 1 remuneration, pay (sueldo). 2 compensation (recompensa).
remunerador, -a *adj.* remunerative, profitable.
remuneratorio, -a *adj.* remuneratory.
renacentista *adj.* of the Rennaissance.
renacer *v.i.* 1 to be born again. 2 (fig.) to regain strength (fuerza).
renacimiento *s.m.* 1 rebirth. 2 HIST. Rennaissance.
renacuajo *s.m.* 1 ZOOL. tadpole. 2 (fig. y desp.) pip-squeak, shrimp.
renal *adj.* MED. of the kidney.
rencilla *s.f.* 1 quarrel (riña). || 2 **tener —,** to bear a grudge.
rencilloso, -a *adj.* cantankerous, quarrelsome.
renco, -a *adj.* 1 lame, disabled. || *s.m.* y *f.* 2 disabled person.
rencor *s.m.* 1 resentment, soreness. || 2 **guardar —,** to have a grudge, let it rankle: *siempre me había guardado rencor = he had always borne me a grudge.*
rencorosamente *adv.* 1 resentfully, bitterly.
rencoroso, -a *adj.* resentful, bitter.
rendición *s.f.* 1 MIL. surrender. 2 FIN. interest (rendimiento).
rendidamente *adv.* 1 resignedly, obediently. 2 tiredly (cansadamente).
rendido, -a *adj.* 1 resigned, unresisting. 2 tired (cansado). 3 adulatory, obsequious (obsequioso).
rendija *s.f.* 1 crack, cleft (hendedura). 2 (fig.) rift (escisión).
rendimiento *s.m.* 1 MEC. performance, output. 2 FIN. return, yield. 3 tiredness, weariness (fatiga). 4 submission, obsequiousness (sumisión excesiva): *ella le trata con rendimiento = she's very submissive in his company.* || 5 **ley de los rendimientos decrecientes,** FIN. law of diminishing returns.
rendir *v.t.* 1 to yield, to produce (dar). 2 to give back, to return (restituir). 3 MIL. to cause to surrender. 4 to tire out (cansar mucho). 5 to bring back, to vomit (vomitar). || *v.i.* 6 COM. to give a good return, to be profitable: *es un negocio que rinde bien = it's a very profitable business.* || *v.pron.* 7 MIL. to surrender. 8 to yield (ceder). 9 to tire oneself out (cansarse mucho). || 10 **¡me rindo!,** I give up!

renegado *s.m.* 1 **turncoat.** 2 REL. apostate. || *adj.* 3 renegade (traidor). 4 short-tempered, testy (malhumorado).
renegar *v.t.* 1 to flatly deny (negar). 2 to detest, to abhor (aborrecer). || *v.i.* 3 REL. to abandon one's faith. 4 to blaspheme (blasfemar). 5 (fam.) to use swear words (jurar). 6 (fam.) to kick up a fuss (enojarse).
renegón, -ona *adj.* obstreperous, cantankerous (que reniega mucho).
renegrido, -a *adj.* blackish, inky.
renglón *s.m.* 1 line of writing (línea). 2 COM. income, source of income (renta). || 3 **a — seguido,** immediately afterwards. 4 **leer entre renglones,** (fig.) to read between the lines.
rengo, -a *adj.* 1 lame. || 2 **hacer la de —,** (fam.) to swing the lead.
renguear *v.i.* (Am.) 1 to limp. 2 (fam.) to sniff after (perseguir).
reniego *s.m.* 1 swear word, curse (juramento). 2 REL. blasphemy.
reno *s.m.* ZOOL. reindeer.
renombrado, -a *adj.* renowned, famous: *una obra muy renombrada = a most famous work.*
renombre *s.m.* 1 renown, prestige. 2 surname, family name (apellido).
renovable *adj.* renewable.
renovación *s.f.* 1 renewal (contrato). 2 ARQ. renovation, restoration. 3 revamping (industria). 4 POL. reorganization.
renovador, -a *adj.* 1 renovating. || *s.m.* 2 renovator.
renovar *v.t.* 1 to renew. 2 ARQ. to renovate, to restore. 3 POL. to reorganize. 4 to repeat, to reiterate (repetir).
renquear *v.i.* 1 to limp (cojear). 2 (fam.) to hobble along (ir tirando).
renquera *s.f.* (Am.) lameness (cojera).
renta *s.f.* 1 income (ingresos). 2 rent (alquiler). 3 public debt (deuda pública). || 4 **— fija,** fixed interest securities. 5 **— fiscal,** taxable income. 6 **— per capita,** per capita income. 7 **— variable,** equity securities. 8 **— vitalicia,** annuity.
rentabilidad *s.f.* 1 profitability. || 2 **tasa de —,** rate of return.
rentable *adj.* profitable: *sería poco rentable = it wouldn't be too economic.*
rentar *v.t.* 1 to give a return (rendir). 2 (Am.) to rent out (alquilar).
rentero, -a *adj.* 1 tributary (tributario). || *s.m.* y *f.* 2 AGR. tenant farmer.
rentista *s.m.* y *f.* COM. 1 rentier (accionista). 2 tax expert (entendido de materias fiscales).
renuencia *s.f.* disinclination, unwillingness.
renuente *adj.* unwilling, disinclined, reluctant.
renuevo *s.m.* 1 renewal, renovation (renovación). 2 BOT. sprout, shoot.
renuncia *s.f.* 1 renunciation (abandono). 2 resignation (dimisión).
renunciable *adj.* able to be renounced.
renunciar *v.t.* 1 to renounce, give up (abandonar). 2 to reject (rechazar). 3 to leave off. 4 POL. to abdicate: *el rey renunció al trono = the king abdicated.* 5 not to follow suit (cartas).
renuncio *s.m.* 1 revocation, recall (cartas). 2 (fam.) tall story.
reñidamente *adv.* in a hard-fought manner.
reñido, -a *adj.* 1 angry, to be at loggerheads (con alguien): *están muy reñidos = they're at loggerheads.* 2 DEP. hard-fought.
reñir *v.i.* 1 to argue, to quarrel (disputar). 2 to fight (pelear). 3 to fall out: *he reñido con mi novia = I've fallen out with my girlfriend.* || *v.t.* 4 to tell off, to reprimand (reprender). 5 to wage (batalla).
reo, -a *s.m.* y *f.* 1 guilty person (culpable). 2 DER. defendant, accused. 3 (Am. y fam.) hobo, good-for-nothing. || 4 **— de Estado,** person charged with a crime against the State.
reojo, mirar de —, *loc.* to look askance, to look out of the corner of one's eye: *me miró de reojo = he looked at me out of the corner of his eye.*
reóstato o **reostato** *s.m.* ELEC. rheostat.
repanchigarse o **repantigarse** *v.pron.* to settle down comfortably (sentarse).
reparable *adj.* repairable, that can be repaired.
reparado, -a *adj.* 1 repaired, fixed, mended. 2 made amends for (rectificado). 3 cross-eyed (bizco).
reparar *v.t.* 1 to repair, to fix, to mend. 2 to make amends for (ofensa). 3 to restore (fuerzas). 4 to observe, to notice: *no has reparado en sus defectos = you haven't noticed her faults.* 5 to parry, to counter (evitar un golpe). 6 (Am.) to imitate, to take off (remedar). || *v.pron.* 7 to show restraint (contenerse). 8 (Am.) to rear up (caballo).
reparo *s.m.* 1 ARQ. restoration. 2 TEC. repair. 3 MED. tonic. 4 criticism (crítica): *no pusieron ningún reparo a mi idea = they didn't raise any objection to my plan.* 5 reservation, misgiving (escrúpulo): *ella no tuvo reparos en decirles la verdad = she had no misgivings about telling them the truth.* 6 (Am.) rearing up (caballo).
repartición *s.f.* 1 dividing up, sharing out. 2 (Am.) POL. branch of government administration. 3 (Am.) AGR. reallocation of land.
repartidor *s.m.* 1 COM. deliveryman. 2 distributor.
repartimiento *s.m.* distribution, division.
repartir *v.t.* 1 to divide up (partir). 2 to share out (distribuir). 3 (fam.) to deal out, to dish out: *repartió unas cuantas bofetadas = he dished out some knuckle.*
reparto *s.m.* 1 sharing out (repartimiento). 2 distribution (distribución). 3 casting (teatro). 4 delivery (correo). || 5 **— de mercado,** COM. market sharing. 6 FIN. **— de utilidades,** profit sharing.
repasar *v.t.* 1 to revise (apuntes), to reread (texto). 2 to skim through (leer muy por encima). 3 to go over again (volver a explicar). 4 to mend, to sew (remendar). 5 MEC. to overhaul. 6 to go along again (calle).
repaso *s.m.* 1 revision, rereading. 2 MEC. overhaul. 3 (fam.) dressing-down (reprimenda): *le dieron un buen repaso = they gave him a real dressing-down.*
repatriación *s.f.* repatriation.
repatriado, -a *adj.* 1 repatriated. || *s.m.* y *f.* 2 repatriate.
repatriar *v.t.* 1 to repatriate. 2 to deport (criminales). || *v.pron.* 3 to return to one's own country.
repecho *s.m.* 1 steep little climb (cuesta corta). 2 (Am.) hut (refugio).
repelencia *s.f.* (Am.) repugnance, loathing.
repelente *adj.* 1 repellent, off-putting (que produce repulsión). 2 (Am. y fam.) saucy, cheeky (impertinente). || *s.m.* 3 insect repellent.
repeler *v.t.* 1 to reject, to throw out (rechazar). 2 to repel, to disgust (repugnar). 3 to drive back (enemigo).
repelo *s.m.* 1 knot (madera). 2 hair out of place (pelo). 3 scuff (tela). 4 (fig. y fam.) squabble (riña sin importancia). 5 (fig.) bad blood (odio). 6 (Am.) old rag (harapo). || 7 **— de frío,** hot and cold shiver.
repelón *s.m.* 1 tug (pelo). 2 caught thread (media). 3 pinch (porción). 4 short gallop (caballo). 5 (Am. y fam.) dressing-down (regaño). || *pl.* 6 TEC. sparks (chispas). || 7 **de —,** slightly.
repelús o **repeluzno** *s.m.* hot and cold shiver: *me dio repelús = it sent the shivers right down my spine.*
repente *s.m.* 1 (fam.) quick jerk (movimiento rápido). 2 (fig.) sudden reaction (impulso). || 3 **de —,** all of a sudden.
repentinamente *adv.* suddenly, all of a sudden.
repentino, -a *adj.* sudden, unexpected (inesperado).
repentizar *v.i.* 1 MUS. to play without rehearsal. 2 to speak straight off the cuff, to improvise (hablar improvisando).
repercusión *s.f.* 1 repercussion (consecuencia). 2 reverberation (sonido).
repercutir *v.i.* 1 to have repercussions: *tus acciones repercutirán en su decisión = your actions will have repercussions of their decision.* 2 to bounce off (objeto). 3 to reverberate (sonido). 4 (Am. y fam.) to pong (oler mal). || *v.t.* 5 MED. to reject.
repertorio *s.m.* 1 repertoire (teatro): *compañía de repertorio = repertory company.* 2 LIT. index (lista).
repetición *s.f.* 1 repetition. 2 MUS. repeat. 3 MEC. repeater. 4 DER. action of recovery.
repetidamente *adv.* repeatedly, time and time again.
repetidor *s.m.* TEC. 1 repeater (telegrafía). 2 booster (radio, televisión).
repetir *v.t.* 1 to repeat. 2 DER. to claim, to demand (reclamar). || *v.i.* 3 to repeat: *el ajo repite mucho = garlic repeats on you.* || *v.pron.* 4 to recur, to keep coming up: *son palabras que se repiten*

mucho = they're words that keep coming up.

repicar *v.t.* **1** to chop up fine (cocina). || *v.i.* **2** to peel (campanas). || *v.pron.* **3** to show off (presumir). || **4 — gordo,** (fam.) to celebrate in style.

repintar *v.t.* **1** to repaint. || *v.pron.* **2** to use loads of make-up (pintarse mucho). **3** to be imprinted (imprenta).

repipi *adj.* (fam.) stuck-up (engreído). **2** pseudo-refined, affected (afectado). **3** precocious (precoz), little horror: *es un niño repipi = he's a little horror.*

repique *s.m.* **1** peal, pealing (campanas). **2** (fam.) squabble (riña). **3** (Am. y fam.) threat, insult (insulto).

repiquete *s.m.* **1** MUS. pleasant peal of bells. **2** MIL. clash. **3** (Am.) spite, revengefulness. || *pl.* **4** (Am.) chirping (gorjeos).

repiquetear *v.t.* **1** to ring with gusto (campanas). **2** to beat in a lively manner (tambor). || *v.i.* **3** MUS. to peal out merrily (campanas). **4** to rattle (máquina). || *v.pron.* **5** (fig. y fam.) to indulge in mud-slinging.

repiqueteo *s.m.* **1** MUS. pealing (campanas). **2** lively beating (tambor). **3** clattering (máquina).

repisa *s.f.* **1** ARQ. ledge, corbel (ménsula). **2** shelf (anaquel).

replantear *v.t.* **1** to raise again (asunto). **2** to retrace (proyecto).

replanteo *s.m.* **1** reopening (cuestión). **2** retracing (proyecto).

replegar *v.t.* **1** to fold over (doblar). || *v.pron.* **2** MIL. to beat an orderly retreat, to fall back (retenerse en orden).

repleto, -a *adj.* crammed full, full up.

réplica *s.f.* **1** reply, answer (respuesta). **2** ART. replica. **3** COM. clone. || *pl.* **4** (fam.) lip. || **5 derecho de —,** DER. right of reply.

replicar *v.i.* **1** to contend, argue (argüir). **2** to answer (contestar). **3** (desp.) to answer back, to give backchat.

replicón, -ona *adj.* (fam.) brassy, cheeky.

repoblación *s.f.* **1** repopulating, repopulation (gente). **2** restocking (objetos). || **3 — forestal,** reafforestation.

repoblar *v.t.* **1** to repopulate (gente). **2** to restock (río). **3** to reafforest.

repollo *s.m.* BOT. cabbage.

reponer *v.t.* **1** to put back (volver a poner). **2** to replace (reemplazar). **3** to put on a second time (obra de teatro). || *v.pron.* **4** MED. to get better: *ya me he repuesto de la operación = I've now recovered from the operation.* **5** to regain one's composture (serenarse).

reportación *s.f.* calmness, restraint (moderación).

reportaje *s.m.* **1** newspaper report (periódico). **2** news item (televisión).

reportar *v.t.* **1** to restrain, to hold back (reprimir). **2** to obtain, to achieve (conseguir). **3** to bring: *su elección le ha reportado mucho dinero = her election has made her rich.* **4** (Am.) to report. || *v.i.* **5** to show for an appointment (ir a una cita). || *v.pron.* **6** to show restraint (moderarse).

reporte *s.m.* **1** news report (noticia). **2** piece of gossip (chisme).

reportero, -a *s.m.* y *f.* newspaper reporter.

reposadamente *adv.* restfully, calmly.

reposado, -a *adj.* **1** calm, leisurely (pacífico). **2** quiet, peaceful (tranquilo).

reposar *v.i.* **1** to rest (descansar). **2** to sleep (dormir). **3** to be at rest (estar enterrado). || *v.pron.* **4** to settle (líquido). || **5 — la comida,** to digest one's food unhurriedly.

reposición *s.f.* **1** replacement. **2** MED. recovery. **3** re-showing (teatro).

reposo *s.m.* **1** rest (descanso). **2 dejar en —,** to leave something to stand: *hay que dejar el vino en reposo = the wine should be left to stand.*

repostar *v.t.* **1** to restock (comida). || *v.i.* **2** to fill up with petrol (gasolina). || *v.pron.* **3** to stock up.

repostería *s.f.* **1** confectionery business (oficio). **2** confectioner's (tienda). **3** pantry, larder (despensa).

repostero, -a *s.m.* y *f.* **1** confectioner (persona). **2** HIST. embroidered cloth (tapiz).

reprender *v.t.* to tell off, to reprimand, to be angry: *el profesor le reprendió su mal comportamiento = the teacher was angry at his bad behaviour.*

reprensible *adj.* blameworthy, reprehensible.

reprensión *s.f.* reprehension, censure.

represa *s.f.* **1** MAR. recapture. **2** dam (presa). **3** temporary halt (parada).

represalia *s.f.* reprisal: *tomaron justas represalias = they took fair reprisals.*

representación *s.f.* **1** representation. **2** performance (teatro). **3** body of representatives (representantes). **4** (fig.) distinction, eminence (importancia). || **5 — proporcional,** POL. proportional representation.

representante *s.m.* y *f.* **1** representative, rep: *ella es nuestra representante comercial = she's our sales rep.* **2** actor (actor). **3** actress (actriz).

representar *v.t.* **1** to represent. **2** to put on (obra de teatro). **3** to symbolize (simbolizar). **4** to inform (informar). **5** (fig.) to seem (edad): *representa más años de los que en realidad tiene = he seems older than he really is.*

representativo, -a *adj.* representative.

represión *s.f.* repression, restraint.

reprimenda *s.f.* rebuke, reproof, reprimand.

represivo, -a *adj.* repressive: *acción represiva = repressive action.*

represor, -ora *s.m.* y *f.* repressor.

reprimir *v.t.* **1** to check, to curb (contener). **2** to repress, to put down: *las autoridades reprimieron la rebelión = the authorities put down the rebellion.* **3** to stifle (bostezo).

reprobable *adj.* unpraisworthy, blameworthy.

reprobación *s.f.* reprobation, censure: *esto merece la reprobación de todos = this deserves universal condemnation.*

reprobar *v.t.* to reprove, to condemn, to censure.

reprobatorio, -a *adj.* disapproving, reproachful.

réprobo *s.m.* REL. reprobate.

reprochable *adj.* reproachable, censurable.

reprochar *v.t.* **1** to reproach, to censure: *le han reprochado sus acciones = they have reproached her for her actions.* || *v.pron.* **2** to reproach oneself.

reproche *s.m.* reproach, censure: *siempre le han dirigido reproches = he has always been the object of reproach.*

reproducción *s.f.* reproduction.

reproducir *v.t.* **1** to reproduce. || *v.pron.* **2** to breed. **3** to recur (síntomas).

reproductor, -a *adj.* **1** reproductive. || *s.m.* **2** ZOOL. inseminator.

reptación *s.f.* crawling, creeping.

reptante *adj.* crawling, creeping.

reptar *v.i.* to creep, to crawl, to slither: *la culebra iba reptando por la hierba = the snake slithered along through the grass.*

reptil *adj.* **1** reptilian. || *s.m.* **2** ZOOL. reptile. **3** (fig.) slimy person.

república *s.f.* republic: *la República Francesa = the Republic of France.*

repudiar *v.t.* **1** DER. to repudiate. **2** to renounce (herencia).

repudio *s.m.* **1** repudiation. **2** renouncing.

repuesto, -a *adj.* **1** restored to health (bien de salud). || *s.m.* **2** stock (víveres). **3** buffet table (mesa para comida). || **4 pieza de —,** MEC. spare part, spare.

repugnancia *s.f.* **1** repugnance, disgust (asco). **2** unwillingness (desgana), despite oneself: *lo hizo con repugnancia = he did it despite himself.*

repugnante *adj.* repugnant, disgusting.

repugnar *v.t.* **1** to disgust, to sicken. **2** to contradict (contradecir). || *v.i.* **3** to be sickening (ser asqueroso). || *v.pron.* **4** to be in opposition (contradecirse).

repujado *s.m.* TEC. metalwork.

repujar *v.t.* TEC. to emboss metal: *una bandeja bien repujada = a nicely worked tray.*

repulido, -a *adj.* **1** polished (pulido). **2** (fig.) classy, swanky (afectado).

repulir *v.t.* **1** to repolish. || *v.pron.* **2** (fig.) classy, swanky (afectado).

repulir *v.t.* **1** to repolish. || *v.pron.* **2** to get dressed up (persona).

repulsa *s.f.* **1** rebuff, snub (rechazo). **2** rebuke (reprimenda). **3** MIL. check, reverse: *el ejército sufrió una repulsa = the army was checked.*

repulsar *v.t.* **1** to reject, to rebuff (rechazar). **2** (fig.) to condemn, to rebuke (censurar). **3** MIL. to check.

repulsión *s.f.* **1** rebuff (repulsa). **2** repulsion, repulsiveness (asco).

repulsivo, -a *adj.* repulsive, disgusting.

reputación *s.f.* reputation: *él tiene mala reputación = he has a bad reputation.*

reputar *v.t.* **1** to repute, to regard (estimar). **2** to esteem highly (apreciar).
requebrar *v.t.* **1** to break again. **2** to pay compliments, to flatter (a una mujer). **3** (fig.) to praise, to worship (adular).
requemar *v.t.* **1** to burn again. **2** to burn (comida). || *v.pron.* **3** to dry up (plantas). **4** to be burning (lengua). **5** to get burnt (sol). **6** (fig.) to be seething with indignation.
requemazón *s.f.* **1** hotness (comida picante). **2** burnt taste (mal sabor).
requerimiento *s.m.* **1** request (petición). **2** DER. summons. **3** demand (demanda).
requerir *v.t.* **1** DER. to summon. **2** to require (necesitar). **3** to request: *le han requerido para que no lo vuelva a hacer = they have requested him not to do it again.* **4** to say nice things (a una mujer).
requesón *s.m.* **1** curd (cuajada). **2** cream cheese (queso blando).
requeté *s.m.* POL., HIST. Carlist soldier.
réquiem *s.m.* **1** REL. requiem mass. **2** MUS. requiem.
requisa *s.f.* **1** inspection (inspección). **2** MIL. requisition.
requisición *s.f.* **1** MIL. requisition. **2** (Am.) confiscation (embargo). **3** (Am.) perquisition (registro).
requisito *s.m.* requisite, requirement: *ella tiene los requisitos para ser la nueva secretaria = she has the necessary requirements for being the new secretary.*
requisitorio, -a *adj.* **1** requisitory. || *s.f.* **2** DER. formal dispatch.
res *s.f.* AGR. head of cattle.
resabiado, -a *adj.* (fam.) crafty, not born yesterday.
resabiarse *v.r.* **1** to acquire bad habits (coger vicios). **2** to get angry (enfadarse). **3** to take an evil delight (in).
resabio *s.m.* **1** aftertaste (sabor desagradable). **2** bad habit. **3** wild nature (caballo). || **4 tener resabios de,** (fig.) to suggest.
resaca *s.f.* **1** (fam.) hangover (por beber). **2** backward movement (olas). **3** (Am. y fam.) going-over, beating-up (paliza). **4** (Am.) good-quality liquor (bebida). **5** (Am.) slime, mud (limo).
resaltar *v.i.* **1** to stand out (sobresalir). **2** to rebound (rebotar). **3** to jut out: *nuestro balcón resalta mucho = our balcony juts out a lot.* || **4 hacer –,** ART. to throw into relief.
resalte o **resalto** *s.m.* **1** ARQ. salient, projection. **2** rebound (rebote).
resarcir *v.t.* **1** FIN. to indemnify, to compensate (for).
resarcimiento *s.m.* FIN. indemnification, compensation.
resbaladero, -a *adj.* **1** slippery (resbaladizo). || *s.m.* **2** slide (corredera). **3** slippery area (lugar resbaladizo).
resbaladizo, -a *adj.* slippery.
resbaladura *s.f.* skid-mark (señal de resbalar).
resbalar *v.i.* **1** to slip (caerse). **2** to slide (deslizarse). **3** to skid (coche). **4** (fig.) to slip up. || **5 me resbala,** (fam.) I couldn't care less.
resbalón *s.m.* **1** to slip, slide. || **2 dar un –,** (fig.) to slip up.
rescatar *v.t.* **1** to ransom, to recover (a una persona). **2** to rescue (de peligro). **3** (fig.) to redeem (redimir). **4** to recuperate (dinero). || *v.i.* **5** to hawk from village to village (viajar vendiendo).
rescate *s.m.* **1** recovery, recapture (liberación). **2** ransom (dinero). || **3 – de terreno,** land reclamation.
rescindir *v.t.* to cancel (contrato).
rescisión *s.f.* DER. rescission, cancellation.
rescoldo *s.m.* **1** ember (brasa). || **2 avivar el –,** (fig.) to revive the dying embers.
rescripto *s.m.* REL. rescript.
resecar *v.t.* **1** to dry completely (secar). **2** to scorch, to parch (quemar). **3** MED. to remove (órgano).
resección *s.f.* MED. resection.
reseco, -a *adj.* **1** very dry. **2** (fig.) thin, lean (flaco). || *s.m.* **3** dry part.
resentido, -a *adj.* resentful, sore, smarting.
resentimiento *s.m.* resentment, vindictiveness (rencor).
resentirse *v.pron.* **1** to begin to weaken (flojear). **2** to suffer from: *él todavía se resiente de su accidente = he's still suffering from his accident.* **3** (fig.) to feel bitter about (enojarse).
reseña *s.f.* **1** description, outline (resumen). **2** LIT. review. **3** MIL. review.
reseñar *v.t.* **1** to describe. **2** to report on (acontecimiento). **3** MIL. to review. **4** LIT. to review.
reserva *s.f.* **1** reserve (provisión). **2** aloofness, reticence (cualidad). **3** MIL. reserve. **4** booking (plaza). **5** reservation (territorio). || *s.m.* **6** DEP. reserve, substitute. || *s.f.pl.* **7** reservations (salvedades). || **8 – de cambio,** allowance for exchange losses. **9 – de espacios,** space booking. **10 reservas bancarias,** bank reserves. **11 reservas exteriores,** foreign reserves.
reservado, -a *adj.* **1** reserved, circumspect (circunspecto). || *s.m.* **2** private room. **3** (Am.) out of bounds field (prado cerrado).
reservar *v.t.* **1** to reserve. **2** to book (plaza). **3** to conceal, to hush up (callar). || *v.pron.* **4** to save oneself: *ese corredor se está reservando para la final = that runner is saving himself for the final.* **5** to be on one's guard (de, against).
reservista *s.m.* y *f.* MIL. reservist.
reservón, -ona *adj.* **1** extremely reserved, extremely wary. **2** very tame (toro).
resfriado, -a *adj.* **1** (Am.) indiscreet, tactless. || *s.m.* **2** MED. cold: *mi hermana ha cogido un resfriado = my sister has caught a cold.*
resfriamiento *s.m.* MED. cold.
resfriar *v.t.* **1** to chill. **2** (fig.) to dampen. || *v.pron.* **3** to catch a cold. || *v.i.* **4** to begin to get cold (tiempo): *está resfriando = it's getting cold.*
resguardar *v.t.* **1** to defend, to protect (proteger). || *v.pron.* **2** to safeguard/protect oneself: *los esquimales se resguardaban de la ventisca = the eskimos protected themselves from the blizzard.*
resguardo *s.m.* **1** defence, protection (protección). **2** guard (guardia). **3** receipt (recibo). **4** voucher (cupón). **5** ticket (consigna).
residencia *s.f.* **1** residence. **2** DER. inquiry. || **3 – para ancianos,** old folk's home. **4 – sanitaria,** hospital.
residencial *adj.* **1** residential. || *s.f.* **2** housing estate (barrio).
residente *adj./s.m.* y *f.* resident.
residir *v.i.* **1** to reside, to live, to stay (permanecer). **2** (fig.) to reside/consist: *el mayor problema reside en que no tenemos armas = the main problem consists in our not posessing weapons.*
residual *adj.* residual, residuary.
residuo *s.m.* **1** remainder (lo que queda). **2** waste (basura). **3** FIN. residue. **4** QUIM. residuum. || **5 residuos nucleares,** nuclear waste.
resignación *s.f.* **1** relinquishing (abandono). **2** resignation (sumisión).
resignadamente *adv.* resignedly, with resignation.
resignarse *v.r.* to resign oneself: *me he resignado a que nunca seré rico = I've resigned myself to the fact that I'll never be rich.*
resina *s.f.* resin: *resina sintética = synthetic resin.*
resinar *v.t.* to extract resin.
resinoso, -a *adj.* resinous: *aspecto resinoso = resinous appearance.*
resistencia *s.f.* **1** resistance. **2** endurance (aguante). **3** DEP. stamina. **4** (fig.) opposition. || **5 – eléctrica,** electrical resistence. **6 – pasiva,** passive resistance.
resistente *adj.* **1** resistant. **2** BOT. hardy. || *s.m.* y *f.* **3** POL. member of the Resistance.
resistible *adj.* resistible.
resistir *v.t.* **1** to resist. **2** to tolerate, to endure (tolerar). || *v.i.* **3** to fight: *resistieron hasta el final = they fought right to the end.* **4** to keep going, to last out: *no creo que el televisor resista mucho más = I think the television can't last out much longer.* || *v.pron.* **5** to have difficulty. **6 resistirse a aceptar/creer algo,** to find hard to belive something.
resma *s.f.* ream (cantidad de papel).
resol *s.m.* sun's glare: *es difícil soportar el resol = it's hard to stand the glare of the sun.*
resolano *s.m.* sunny spot, spot for sunbathing (lugar para tomar el sol).
resolución *s.f.* **1** solution (problema). **2** resolution (decisión). **3** (fig.) initiative (iniciativa). **4** DER. ruling, legal opinion. **5** (Am.) end (término).
resoluto, -a *adj.* **1** resolute, determined (decidido). **2** brief (abreviado).
resolutorio, -a *adj.* providing a solution.

resolver *v.t.* 1 to solve (problema). 2 QUIM. to dissolve. 3 to break down, to analyse (materiales). || *v.i.* 4 to decide, to determine: *hemos resuelto ofrecerle el puesto de trabajo = we've decided to offer you the job.* || *v.pron.* 5 to decide, to resolve (decidir): *resuélvetelo tú mismo = decide it for yourself.* 6 to end in (acabar siendo). 7 MED. to vanish.

resollar *v.i.* 1 to breathe heavily (aspirar). 2 (fig. y fam.) to show signs of life (dar señales de vida).

resonador, -a *adj.* 1 resounding. || *s.m.* 2 ELEC. resonator.

resonancia *s.f.* 1 resonance (prolongación). 2 echo (repercusión). 3 (fig.) far-reaching effects, importance.

resonante *adj.* 1 resounding, resonant (sonido). 2 (fig.) thorough, resounding, decisive: *fue una victoria resonante = it was a resounding victory.*

resonar *v.i.* 1 to resound, to echo (repercutir el sonido). 2 (fig.) to be neard about everywhere: *su triunfo ha resonado = her triumph is common knowledge.*

resoplar *v.i.* to puff and blow (respirar fuertemente).

resoplido *s.m.* heavy breathing, panting (jadeo).

resorte *s.m.* 1 MEC. spring (muelle). 2 (fig.) means (medio). 3 (Am.) rubber band (gomita). 4 (Am.) responsibility, concern (incumbencia).

respaldar *v.t.* 1 to support, to back (apoyar). 2 to endorse (escrito). 3 to guarantee, to ensure. || *v.pron.* 4 to lean back. || *s.m.* 5 chair back (respaldo).

respaldo *s.m.* 1 chair back. 2 back (documento). 3 endorsement (firma). 4 support, backing (apoyo). 5 (fig.) guarantee, protection (garantía).

respectar *v.i.* 1 to deal with, to concern. 2 **por lo que respecta**, as for.

respectivamente o **respective** *adv.* respectively.

respectivo, -a *adj.* respective: *sus respectivos maridos = their respective husbands.*

respecto *s.m.* 1 respect. || 2 **al —**, with regard to this matter. 3 **con — a** o **— de**, with regard to, as for.

respetabilidad *s.f.* respectability.

respetable *adj.* 1 respectable. || *s.m.* 2 (fam.) the audience (espectadores).

respetar *v.t.* 1 to respect, to show respect for (honrar). || *v.i.* 2 to concern (corresponder). || 3 **hacerse —**, to command respect.

respetuosamente *adv.* respectfully.

respetuoso, -a *adj.* respectful: *un joven respetuoso = a respectful young man.*

respingar *v.i.* 1 to jib (caballo). 2 (fig. y fam.) to drag one's feet. || *v.pron.* 3 to ride up (levantarse): *este suéter se me respinga = this sweater rides up on me.*

respingo *s.m.* 1 jib. 2 (fig. y fam.) gesture of discontent (mueca). 3 (Am.) part of skirt that rides up.

respingón, -ona *adj.* 1 jibbing (caballo). 2 snub-nosed (nariz).

respiración *s.f.* 1 breathing, respiration. 2 ventilation (ventilación). || 3 **quedarse sin —**, to be left breathless.

respiradero *s.m.* 1 vent (abertura). 2 ARQ. dormer window (lumbrera). 3 air-hole (cañería). 4 (fig.) break (descanso). 5 (fam.) ANAT. lungs.

respirador, -a *adj.* 1 respiratory. || *s.m.* 2 MED. respirator. 3 DEP. snorkel.

respirar *v.i.* 1 ANAT. to breathe. 2 (fig. y fam.) to make a murmur, to open one's month (hablar): *ella no ha respirado en toda la semana = she hasn't opened her mouth once this week.* 3 (fig. y fam.) to have a breather (descansar): *¡déjala respirar! = let her have a breather!* || *v.t.* 4 to inhale (gas). 5 (fig.) to give off (despedir olor). || 6 **— confianza,** (fig.) to ooze confidence.

respiratorio, -a *adj.* respiratory.

respiro *s.m.* 1 ANAT. breathing. 2 (fam.) breather (descanso). 3 (fig.) relief (alivio). 4 (fig.) COM. breathing space (prórroga).

resplandecer *v.i.* 1 to shine, to glow. 2 (fig.) to shine, to be outstanding.

resplandeciente *adj.* 1 shining, glowing. 2 (fig.) radiant (radiante).

resplandor *s.m.* 1 shine, glow (brillo). 2 (fig.) brilliance, splendour (esplendor). 3 (Am.) diadem (corona).

responder *v.t.* 1 to answer, to reply to (carta, llamamiento). || *v.i.* 2 to answer, to reply. 3 to respond: *la paciente está respondiendo bien al tratamiento = the patient is responding well to the treatment.* 4 to answer back (ser respondón). 5 to be responsible: *la empresa no responde de los posibles daños = the firm is not responsible for possible damages.* 6 to guarantee, to recommend: *yo respondo por mi amiga = I can guarantee my friend is alright.* 7 (fig.) to function well, to be fine: *este coche responde = this is a fine car.*

respondón, -ona *adj.* (fam.) saucy, insolent, cheeky: *ese chaval es muy respondón = that lad is an insolent.*

responsabilidad *s.f.* 1 responsibility. || 2 **— civil,** civil liability.

responsable *adj.* 1 responsible. 2 answerable: *todos somos responsables ante la ley de nuestras acciones = we are all answerable before the law for our actions.* || 3 **hacerse — de algo,** to claim responsibility for something: *me hago responsable de la derrota = I claim responsibility for the defeat.*

responsabilizar *v.t.* 1 to make responsible, to put in charge (encargar). || *v.pron.* 2 to hold oneself responsible.

responsar *v.i.* REL. to say responses.

responso *s.m.* 1 REL. response. 2 (Am.) rebuke, telling-off (regaño).

respuesta *s.f.* answer, reply.

resquebradura o **resquebrajadura** *s.f.* split, crack.

resquebradizo *adj.* brittle, easily breakable.

resquebrajar *v.t.* to break, to crack.

resquebrar *v.i.* to start to crack/chip: *la pintura está resquebrando = the paintwork is starting to chip.*

resquemar *v.t.* 1 to burn (comida). 2 (fig.) to pique, nettle (picar).

resquemor *s.m.* 1 stinging, burning (escozor). 2 (fig.) pique (resentimiento).

resquicio *s.m.* 1 fault, chink (hendedura). 2 (fig.) opportune occasion. 3 (Am.) bit, scrap (pizca).

resta *s.f.* 1 MAT. subtraction. 2 reminder.

restablecer *v.t.* 1 to re-establish. || *v.pron.* 2 MED. to get better.

restablecimiento *s.m.* 1 re-establishment. 2 MED. recovery, recuperation.

restallar *v.i.* 1 to crack (látigo). 2 to crackle (madera que arde).

restante *adj.* 1 remaining, left over. || *s.m.* 2 remainder.

restañadura *s.f.* MED. stanching (sangre).

restañar *v.t.* 1 MED. to stanch. 2 TEC. to re-tin.

restaño *s.m.* 1 MED. stanching. 2 backwater, pool (remanso).

restar *v.t.* 1 to take away (quitar). 2 MAT. to deduct. 3 DEP. to return (tenis). || *v.i.* 4 to remain, to be left: *lo único que me resta es olvidarlo = the only thing left for me to do is to forget it.*

restauración *s.f.* ART., etc. restoration.

restaurador *s.m.* 1 ART. restoration. 2 reviver (tradiciones).

restaurante *s.m.* restaurant.

restaurar *v.t.* 1 ART. to restore: *el cuadro ha sido restaurado = the painting has been restored.* 2 to recover (recobrar).

restaurativo, -a *adj.* y *s.m.* restorative.

restitución *s.f.* return, giving back.

restituir *v.t.* 1 to return (devolver). 2 to restore (restablecer). || *v.pron.* 3 to return, to go back: *se ha restituido a la empresa = he has gone back to the company.*

resto *s.m.* 1 remainder, rest (residuo). 2 DEP. return, return of service (tenis). 3 MAT. remainder. || *pl.* 4 left-overs (comida). 5 remains: *restos mortales = dead body.* || 6 **echar el —**, (fig.) to try one's very best.

restregar *v.t.* to scrub hard (fregar): *restregué el suelo = I scrubbed the floor.*

restregón *s.m.* scrubbing, scouring (perol).

restricción *s.f.* 1 restriction, limitation. || 2 **— salarial,** wage restraint. 3 **sin restricciones**, liberally, freely.

restrictivo, -a *adj.* restrictive, limiting.

restringir *v.t.* 1 to restrict, to limit (limitar). 2 to constrict (apretar).

resucitar *v.t.* 1 to revive, to bring back to life. 2 (fig.) to give fresh life to. || *v.i.* 3 to be resurrected (Jesucristo).

resuelto, -a *adj.* 1 determined, resolute. 2 assiduous (diligente).

resuello *s.m.* 1 breathing (respiración). 2 breath (aliento).

resulta *s.f.* 1 result, consequence. 2 vacancy (vacante). || 3 **de resultas,** as a result, as a consequence.

resultado *s.m.* **1** result. **2** upshot, outcome (desenlace).

resultante *adj.* **1** resultant. || *s.f.* MEC. resultant.

resultar *v.i.* **1** to turn out, prove: *resultó ser muy caro = it turned out to be very dear.* **2** to turn out well (salir bien). **3** to be born, to be originated/created (originarse): *de la pluma de Dickens resultaron muchas obras = many works were created from the pen of Dickens.* **4** (fam.) to please (agradar).

resumen *s.m.* **1** summary, résumé. || **2 en —,** to sum up.

resumidero *s.m.* (Am.) **1** sewer (cloaca). **2** sink (fregadero). **3** quagmire (cenegal). **4** TEC. sump.

resumir *v.t.* **1** to sum up. **2** to bridge (abreviar). || *v.pron.* **3** to be epitomized (convertirse): *esto se resume en sus acciones = this is epitomized in her actions.*

resurgimiento *s.m.* revival, resurgence.

resurgir *v.i.* **1** to reappear. **2** to be resurrected (resucitarse).

resurrección *s.f.* resurrection.

retablo *s.m.* REL. altar-piece.

retaco **1** short shotgun (escopeta). **2** short cue (billar). **3** (fam.) stocky little fellow (hombrecito rechoncho).

retaguardia *s.f.* **1** MIL. rearguard. || **2 a —,** in the rear.

retahíla *s.f.* **1** long line, string. **2** (fig.) barrage, shower (injurias).

retal *s.m.* remnant, left-over piece.

retama *s.f.* BOT. broom.

retamal o **retamar** *s.m.* BOT. area covered in broom.

retar *v.t.* **1** to challenge (desafiar). **2** (fam.) to take to task (reprender). **3** (Am. y fam.) to slang (denostar).

retardación *s.f.* **1** delay (retraso). **2** MEC. slowing down.

retardar *v.t.* **1** to delay, to make late (retrasar). || *v.pron.* **2** to slow down.

retardo *s.m.* **1** delay (retraso). **2** slowing down (retardación).

retazo *s.m.* **1** remnant, piece (tela). **2** (fig.) literary fragment. **3** (Am. y fam.) scrap, worthless bit (piltrafa).

retel *s.m.* crab net (pesca).

retén *s.m.* **1** stock, store, reserve (reserva). **2** control (policía). **3** MIL. reinforcements. || **4 estar de —,** to be on call.

retención *s.f.* **1** retaining, keeping back. **2** MED. retention. **3** FIN. withholding, stoppage: *mis retenciones anuales suman más de cincuenta mil pesetas = my yearly stoppages total more than two hundred and fifty pounds.*

retener *v.t.* **1** to keep back, to retain (conservar). **2** FIN. to withhold. **3** to retain (en la memoria). || *v.pron.* **4** to show restraint (moderarse).

retentivo, -a *adj.* retentive, retaining.

reticencia *s.f.* **1** insinuation, suggestion: *hablar con reticencias = to insinuate.* **2** reticence, incommunicativeness (taciturnidad).

reticente *adj.* **1** insinuating, suggestive (sugestivo). **2** reticent (callado).

retícula *s.f.* FIS. retina.

retintín *s.m.* **1** jingle, tinkle (tilín). **2** (fig.) sardonic tone (sarcasmo).

retinto, -a *adj.* dark chestnut (color).

retiradamente *adv.* in isolation, quietly.

retirado, -a *adj.* **1** far-off, distant (apartado). || *s.m.* **2** MIL. retired soldier. || *s.f.* **3** MIL. retreat: *emprender la retirada = to retreat.* **4** retreat, refuge (refugio).

retirar *v.t.* **1** to take away, to remove (apartar). **2** to withdraw (tropas, embajadores). || *v.pron.* **3** to retire, to go away (apartarse). **4** to retire (jubilarse), to stop working: *mi tío se ha retirado = my uncle has stopped working.*

retiro *s.m.* **1** retirement (jubilación). **2** FIN. withdrawal (dinero). **3** seclusion, privacy (aislamiento). **4** secluded place (lugar). **5** MIL. retirement pension. **6** REL. retreat.

reto *s.m.* **1** challenge: *acepto el reto = I accept the challenge.* **2** threat (amenaza). **3** (Am.) telling-off, dressing-down (regaño).

retocar *v.t.* **1** to touch over and over again (tocar repetidamente). **2** to touch up (cuadro). **3** to give a last coat of paint to (pintura).

retoñar *v.i.* **1** BOT. to sprout. **2** (fig.) to reoccur (reproducirse).

retoño *s.m.* **1** BOT. sprout, shoot. **2** (fig.) stripling (niño).

retoque *s.m.* **1** touching up, retouching (perfeccionamiento). **2** last coat of paint (pintura). **3** MED. symptom.

retorcimiento *s.m.* **1** twisting. **2** (fig.) complicated nature. **3** (fig.) artfulness, subtlety (astucia).

retorcido, -a *adj.* **1** twisted. **2** (fig.) devious, scheming (de malas intenciones). **3** (fig.) complicated (estilo).

retorcer *v.t.* **1** to twist. **2** (fig.) to distort, to twist (argument). || *v.pron.* **3** to get twisted || **4 retorcerse de dolor,** to double up in pain.

retoricismo *s.m.* (desp.) verbosity.

retórico, -a *adj.* **1** rhetorical. **2** (desp.) long-winded, verbose. || *s.f.* **2** rhetoric. **4** (desp.) verbosity, long-windedness.

retornar *v.t.* **1** to return, to replace (devolver). || *v.i.* to return, to go back.

retorno *s.m.* **1** return. **2** FIN. rebate. **3** exchange (cambio).

retorsión *s.f.* **1** twisting. **2** (fig.) payment in kind.

retortero *s.m.* **1** turn. || **2 andar al —,** (fam.) to run around like a scalded cat. **3 traer a uno al —,** (fam.) to keep someone continually on the go: *mi jefe me trae siempre al retortero = my boss keeps me continually on the go.*

retortijar *v.t.* to twist repeatedly.

retortijón *s.m.* **1** sharp twist. **2** MED. painful cramp: *tengo unos retortijones de tripas horribles = I've got terrible stomach cramps.*

retostado, -a *adj.* very dark (color).

retostar *v.t.* **1** to toast a lot (tostar mucho). **2** to burn (quemar).

retozar *v.i.* **1** to skip about, to leap about (brincar). **2** to get up to mischief: *los niños de su edad siempre están retozando = children of his age are always getting up to mischief.* || *v.pron.* **3** (fig.) to get worked up.

retozo *s.m.* **1** skip, spring, frolic. || **2 — de la risa,** the giggles.

retozón, -ona *adj.* playful, frisky (cordero).

retractación *s.f.* retraction, revocation.

retractar *v.t.* **1** to retract, to take back (palabras). || **2 me retracto,** I take back what I've said.

retráctil *adj.* retractable.

retraer *v.t.* **1** to bring back (retirar). || *v.pron.* **2** to withdraw, to retreat (retirarse). **3** to take refuge, to take shelter (ampararse). **4** to live in seclusion (vivir aisladamente). **5** to be temporarily absent (ausentarse).

retraído, -a *adj.* **1** retiring, reserved. **2** (fig.) diffident, shy (tímido).

retranca *s.f.* **1** wide strap (caballería). **2** (Am.) brake. **3** ZOOL. female greyhound.

retrancar *v.t.* **1** (Am.) to stop, to brake. || *v.pron.* **2** (Am.) to come to a halt.

retransmisión *s.f.* retransmission.

retransmitir *v.t.* **1** to transmit a second time. **2** to retransmit.

retrasar *v.t.* **1** to delay, to put back (retardar). || *v.i.* **2** to fall back, to decline (ir a menos). **3** to put back (reloj). || *v.pron.* **4** to be late: *el tren se ha retrasado = the train is going to arrive late.* **5** to be slow (reloj).

retraso *s.m.* **1** delay (demora). **2** tardiness, lateness (tardanza). || **3 — mental,** MED. mental deficiency.

retratar *v.t.* **1** to paint someone's portrait. **2** to photograph (fotografiar). **3** (fig.) to depict, to evoke (representar).

retratista *s.m.* y *s.f.* **1** ART. portrait painter. **2** photographer (fotógrafo).

retrato *s.m.* **1** ART. portrait. **2** description, portrayal (descripción). **3** (fig.) resemblance, similarity (semejanza).

retreta *s.f.* **1** MIL. retreat. **2** (Am.) MUS. open-air concert. **3** (Am.) string, long line (retahíla).

retrete *s.m.* lavatory, toilet.

retribución *s.f.* **1** FIN. compensation, remuneration. **2** TEC. compensation.

retribuir *v.t.* **1** to pay (pagar). **2** to compensate (compensar). **3** to return (favor).

retribuyente *adj.* retributive.

retroacción *s.f.* **1** regression (regresión). **2** TEC. feedback.

retroactividad *s.f.* retroactivity.

retroactivo, -a *adj.* retroactive: *efecto retroactivo = retroactive effect.*

retroceder *v.i.* **1** to move backwards. **2** (fig.) to give way (cejar). **3** MIL. to retreat. **4** to recede (nivel).

retroceso *s.m.* **1** moving back. **2** COM. recession. **3** MED. fresh outbreak. **4** kick (arma de fuego). **5** backspin (billar).

retrógrado, -a *adj.* **1** retrograde. || *s.m.* y *f.* **2** POL. reactionary.

retropropulsión *s.f.* AER. jet propulsion.

retrospección *s.f.* retrospection, reminiscence.

retrospectivo, -a *adj.* retrospective, backward.

retrotraer *v.t.* DER. to claim to be earlier.

retrovisor *s.m.* rear-view mirror (coche).

retruécano *s.m.* GRAM. play on words, pun.

retumbante *adj.* **1** resonant, sonorous. **2** (fig.) pompous, bombastic (ampuloso): *nos dirigió unas palabras retumbantes = he spoke to us bombastically.*

retumbar *v.i.* **1** to resound, to echo (reverberar). **2** to boom, to thunder (trueno).

retumbo *s.m.* **1** resounding, echoing. **2** booming, thunder.

reuma o **reúma** *s.m.* y *f.* MED. rheumatism.

reumático, -a *adj.* **1** MED. rheumatic. || *s.m.* **2** person suffering from rheumatism.

reumatismo *s.m.* MED. rheumatism.

reunión *s.f.* **1** meeting, gathering (asamblea). **2** party (fiesta). || **3 — cumbre,** POL. summit meeting. **4 — de evaluación,** appraisal interview.

reunir *v.t.* **1** to bring together, to join (juntar). **2** to collect, to pool (recursos). **3** to save (ahorrar). || *v.pron.* **4** to meet, to come together (juntarse). **5** to unite, to join forces (unirse).

revacunar *v.t.* MED. to vaccinate again.

reválida *s.f.* **1** confirmation, ratification. **2** resit (examen).

revalidar *v.t.* **1** to ratify, confirm (aprobar). || *v.pron.* **2** to sit an exam.

revalorización *s.f.* FIN. revaluation.

revalorizar *v.t.* FIN. to revalue, to reassess.

revancha *s.f.* **1** revenge. **2** DEP. return match. || **3 tomar —,** to take revenge.

revanchismo *s.m.* revanchism.

revanchista *s.m.* y *f.* revanchist.

revelación *s.f.* revelation, discovery: *una revelación importante = an important discovery.*

revelado, -a *adj.* **1** revealed. **2** developed (fotos). || *s.m.* **3** developing (fotos).

revelador, -a *adj.* **1** revealing. || *s.m.* **2** developer (fotos).

revelar *v.t.* **1** to reveal, to disclose. **2** to develop (fotos). **3** to tell on, to detray (delatar): *reveló a sus amigos = he told on his friends.*

revendedor, -ora *s.m.* y *f.* **1** retailer (vendedor al por menor). **2** (desp.) speculator. **3** tout (vendedor de entradas).

reventa *s.f.* **1** resale. **2** (desp.) speculation. **3** touting (entradas).

reventazón *s.f.* **1** bursting. **2** blow-out (neumático). **3** (Am.) GEOG. low mountain range. **4** MED. wind. **5** (Am.) spring (manantial).

reventar *v.i.* **1** to burst, to explode (estallar). **2** to break (olas). **3** (fig.) to be bursting: *ella reventaba de impaciencia = she was bursting with impatience; yo reventaba por decírtelo = I was bursting to tell you.* || *v.t.* **4** to smash to pieces (romper con violencia): *él reventó su reloj = he smashed his watch to pieces.* **5** (fig.) to gall (molestar): *me revienta verte siempre dormido en el trabajo = it galls me to see you always asleep at work.* **6** (fig.) to be damaging to, to destroy: *la enfermedad de su hijo le ha reventado = her son's illness has destroyed her.* || *v.pron.* **7** (fam.) to croak, to snuff it, to peg out, to kick the bucket (morir): *el pobre por fin se reventó = the poor boy finally kicked the bucket.*

reventón *s.m.* **1** bursting, exploding. **2** blow-out (neumático). **3** sharp climb (subida fuerte). **4** (fig.) fix, hole (apuro). **5** (fig.) muscle, elbow-grease (esfuerzo). **6** (fig.) grind, toil (trabajo).**7** (Am.) TEC. ore outcropping. **8** (Am. y fig.) explosion. **9** (Am.) push (empujón).

reverberación *s.f.* reverberation.

reverberar *v.i.* **1** to be reflected (luz). **2** to reverberate (sonido).

reverencia *s.f.* **1** reverence, veneration. **2** bow (inclinación del cuerpo del hombre). **3** curtsy (mujer). **4** REL. Reverence.

reverencial *adj.* reverential.

reverenciar *v.t.* to revere, venerate.

reverendo, -a *adj.* **1** worthy of veneration. **2** (fam.) overcareful (muy circunspecto). || *s.m.* **3** REL. reverend.

reversible *adj.* reversible: *una chaqueta reversible = a reversible jacket.*

reverso *s.m.* **1** reverse. **2** tails (moneda). || **3 el — de la moneda,** (fig.) the other side of the coin.

reverter *v.i.* to overflow (rebosar).

revertir *v.i.* **1** to revert. **2** to come to be (redundar).

revés *s.m.* **1** back, reverse (reverso). **2** slap (golpe). **3** DEP. backhand. **4** (fig.) blow, bad patch (desgracia). **5** MIL. defeat. || **6 al —,** the other way round; inside-out (chaqueta), upside-down (plato), vice versa (vice versa). **7 de —,** from left to right.

revesado, -a *adj.* **1** complicated, obtuse: *palabras muy revesadas = very obtuse words.* **2** (fig.) irrepressible, restive (travieso).

revestimiento *s.m.* **1** surface (calzada). **2** QUIM. casing. **3** layer (suelo). **4** TEC. coating. **5** panelling (madera).

revestir *v.t.* **1** TEC. to coat, to cover. **2** to disguise, to envelope. **3** to contain, possess. || *v.pron.* **4** (fig.) to give oneself airs (engreírse). **5** to arm oneself: *se revistió de paciencia = he armed himself with patience.* **6** (fig.) to enthuse over (apasionarse).

revirado, -a *adj.* (Am.) **1** uncontrollable (revoltoso). **2** hard to please, grumpy (malhumorado). **3** (fam.) barmy, loony (loco).

revisada *s.f.* (Am.) **1** inspection, check. **2** MEC. overhaul.

revisión *s.f.* **1** check, inspection. **2** review, reconsideration (reexaminación). **3** MEC. overhaul. || **4 — limitada,** FIN. limited review.

revisar *v.t.* **1** to check, inspect (inspeccionar). **2** to review, reconsider (reexaminar). **3** MEC. to overhaul. **4** LIT. to revise. **5** MIL. to review.

revisionismo *s.m.* POL. revisionism.

revisionista *s.m.* y *f.* revisionist.

revisor *s.m.* **1** conductor (autobús). **2** ticket collector (tren). || **3 — de cuentas,** FIN. auditor.

revista *s.f.* **1** LIT. magazine. **2** inspection, examination (examen). **3** MIL. review. **4** revue (teatro). **5** column, section (periódico). || **6 pasar —,** MIL. to inspect, review.

revistero *s.m.* **1** LIT. columnist, critic. **2** magazine stand (mueble).

revivificar *v.t.* to restore, revive (reavivar).

revivir *v.i.* **1** to revive, to come back to life (volver a la vida). **2** (fig.) to reappear/resurface (resurgir): *revivieron las viejas discrepancias = the old discrepancies resurfaced.*

revocable *adj.* retractable, revocable.

revocación *s.f.* **1** revocation, cancelling, repeal.

revocar *v.t.* **1** to cancel, to revoke (una orden). **2** to disencourage, to dissuade (disuadir): *logramos revocarle de sus intenciones = we managed to dissuade him from his plans.* **3** to blow back (humo). **4** ARQ. to whitewash (piintura), to plaster (yeso).

revocatorio, -a *adj.* revocatory.

revoco *s.m.* **1** revoking, annulment. **2** ARQ. plastering.

revolcadero *s.m.* ZOOL. mud-hole.

revolcar *v.t.* **1** to bring down, to knock to the ground (derribar). **2** (fig. y fam.) to tear to bits (dejar vencido y humillado). || *v.pron.* **3** to roll about, to wallow: *los elefantes se revolcaban en el agua = the elephants wallowed about in the water.* **4** (fig.) to stand firm (empeñarse).

revolcón *s.m.* **1** (fam.) tumble, cropper (acto de revolcar). **2** (fam.) flunk (suspenso). **3** FIN. slump. || **4 dar un — a alguien,** to wipe the floor with someone (en un debate).

revolotear *v.i.* **1** to flutter (mariposa). **2** to blow about (volar dando vueltas). || *v.t.* **3** to hurl upwards (arrojar al aire).

revoloteo *s.m.* **1** fluttering. **2** blowing about, circling.

revoltijo o **revoltillo** *s.m.* **1** hotchpotch (mescolanza). **2** (fig.) mix-up, mess (confusión). **3** (Am.) bunch, bundle (fardo).

revoltoso, -a *adj.* **1** uncontrollable, unstable (rebelde). **2** rough, turbulent (agua). **3** mischievous, naughty (travieso). || *s.m.* **4** POL. trouble-maker, agent provocateur.

revolución *s.f.* **1** revolution. || **2 la — francesa,** the French Revolution. **3 la — industrial,** the Industrial Revolution.

revolucionar *v.t.* **1** to revolutionize. **2** MEC. to make something turn faster, to increase the revolutions: *revolucionar un* *motor = to increase the revolutions in the engine.*

revolucionario, -a *adj.* revolutionary. || *s.m.* y *f.* **2** revolutionary (persona).

revolvedor *s.m.* TEC. shaker.

revolver *v.t.* **1** to shake (agitar). **2** to turn upside down (poner al revés). **3** to stir (líquido). **4** to muddle, to mess up (desordenar). **5** to turn over in one's head (discurrir). **6** to infect, to excite (pasiones). **7** to go through, to rummage through (registrar): *alguien ha revuelto mis documentos = someone's been going through my documents.* **8** to cover, to wrap up (envolver). **9** to turn round (a un caballo). || *v.pron.* **10** to face, to turn on: *se revolvieron contra el enemigo = they turned on the enemy.* **11** to retrace one's footsteps (andar lo andado). **12** to turn cloudy (ponerse borrascoso el tiempo). **13** to get churned up (líquido). **14** to fidget (moverse uno sentado). **15** to writhe (con dolor): *el soldado se revolvía en el suelo = the soldier was writhing about on the floor.*

revólver *s.m.* revolver.

revotarse *v.pron.* POL. to vote differently from in past elections.

revuelco *s.m.* **1** tumble, cropper, fall. **2** ZOOL. wallowing.

revuelo *s.m.* **1** ZOOL. second flight. **2** fluttering (revoloteo). **3** (fig.) ferment, stir. || **4 armar —,** to cause a rumpus.

revuelto, -a *adj.* **1** topsy-turvy, upside-down (en desorden). **2** wayward, ungovernable (revoltoso). **3** mischievous, naughty (travieso). **4** restless, on edge (inquieto). **5** (fig.) involved, complicated (enrevesado). **6** cloudy (líquido). **7** unsettled (tiempo). || *s.f.* **8** POL. riot, disturbance. **9** argument, quarrel (riña). **10** turn, bend (camino). **11** (fig.) change of opinion (cambio de parecer).

revulsión *s.f.* MED. revulsion.

revulsivo *s.m.* **1** MED. revulsive. **2** (fig.) short, sharp shock.

rey *s.m.* **1** king. || *pl.* **2** king and queen. || **3 los Reyes Católicos,** the Catholic Monarchs. **4 los Reyes Magos,** the Three Wise Men. **5 ni — ni roque,** not a single soul. **6 servir al —,** to be a soldier.

reyerta *s.f.* **1** argument, quarrel (riña). **2** set-to, fight (pelea).

rezado *s.m.* REL. prayer.

rezagar *v.t.* **1** to leave behind (dejar atrás). **2** to put off, to leave until later (atrasar). || *v.pron.* **3** to fall behind.

rezar *v.i.* **1** REL. to pray, to say prayers. **2** (fam.) to say, to read: *el texto reza como sigue = the text reads as follows.* **3** (fam.) to grumble, to grouch (gruñir). **4** (fam.) to be concerned with: *esa cuestión no reza contigo = that matter doesn't concern you.* || *v.t.* **5** REL. to say (oraciones). **6** to ask for, to plead for (pedir).

rezongar *v.i.* **1** to grumble, to complain (quejarse). **2** (Am.) to tick off (regañar): *el jefe le rezongó = the boss gave him a ticking-off.*

rezongón, -ona *adj.* grumbling, grumpy, sullen.

rezumadero *s.m.* **1** leak, hole (vasija). **2** seepage (lo rezumado).

rezumar *v.i.* **1** to ooze, to seep. **2** (fig.) to exude, to ooze, to be full of: *a ella le rezuma la seguridad en sí misma = she oozes self-confidence.*

rhesus *s.m.* ZOOL. rhesus monkey.

ría *s.f.* GEOG. estuary: *la ría de Bilbao = the Bilbao estuary.*

riachuelo o **riacho** *s.m.* stream, rivulet.

riada *s.f.* **1** flood, great flow (río). **2** (fig.) crowd (multitud).

riba o **ribazo** *s.m.* y *f.* GEOG. hill, steep bank (colina).

ribera *s.f.* **1** riverside (río). **2** shore, coast (mar). **3** AGR. flat, irrigated area.

ribereño, -a *adj.* **1** riverside (cerca del río). **2** coastal (cerca del mar).

riberiego, -a *adj.* ZOOL. non-migrating (ganado lanar).

ribero *s.m.* safeguard, bulwark (presa).

ribete *s.m.* **1** trimming, border (prenda de vestir). **2** (fig.) frills, embellishments (adornos). || *pl.* **3** signs.

ribetear *v.t.* to border, to trim (confección de vestidos, etc.).

ricacho, -a o **ricachón, -ona** *s.m.* y *f.* (fam.) nouveau riche.

ricamente *adv.* **1** richly. **2** (fam.) a treat, fabulously: *todo marchó tan ricamente = everything went off a treat.*

ricino *s.m.* BOT. castor-oil plant.

rico, -a *adj.* **1** rich, wealthy, well-off (adinerado). **2** delicious, very tasty, scrumptions (sabor): *esta tarta está riquísima = this cake is scrumptious.* **3** AGR. rich, fertile (tierra). **4** superb, brilliant (magnífico). **5** (fam.) bonny, sweet: *es una niña muy rica = she's a bonny little girl.* || *s.m.* y *f.* **6** rich man, rich person. **7** (fam.) mate, pal: *¡oye, rico! = listen, pal!* || **8 nuevo —,** nouveau riche.

rictus *s.m.* rictus, gape, smile (contracción de los labios): *un rictus sardónico = a sardonic smile.*

ricura *s.f.* **1** tastiness (lo sabroso). **2** (fam.) tasty thing, smashing: *¡que ricura de chica! = what a smashing girl!*

ridículamente *adv.* ridiculously, ludicrously.

ridiculez *s.f.* folly, absurdity.

ridiculizar *v.t.* to ridicule, to make a mockery of: *la película ridiculiza la Iglesia = the film ridicules the Church.*

riego *s.m.* **1** AGR. irrigation. **2** watering (plantas). || **3 — sanguíneo,** ANAT. blood flow.

riel *s.m.* **1** rod (barra). **2** rail (ferrocarril).

rielar *v.i.* (poét.) to shimmer, to glimmer (estrellas).

rienda *s.f.* **1** reins (caballería). **2** (fig.) self-control, moderation (moderación). || *pl.* **3 llevar las riendas,** to be in charge/control. || **4 aflojar las riendas,** to let up, to ease up. **5 a — suelta,** with free rein. **6 dar — suelta,** to give free rein to. **7 empuñar las riendas de algo,** to be in charge of something. **8 tirar de las riendas,** to keep a firm hold on.

riesgo *s.m.* **1** risk (contingencia). **2** danger (peligro). || **3 correr el —,** to run the risk. **4 — bancario,** FIN. credit exposure. **5 — de cambio,** FIN. foreign exchange risk. **6 — vivo,** FIN. exposure. **7 seguro a todo —,** full-cover insurance.

rifa *s.f.* **1** raffle (sorteo). **2** quarrel, dispute (riña).

rifar *v.t.* **1** to raffle (sortear). || *v.i.* **2** to quarrel, have an argument (reñir). || *v.pron.* **3** to tear (vela de barco). **4** (fig. y fam.) to be a hit: *mi hermana se rifa entre los chicos del colegio = my sister is a big hit with the boys at school.*

rifle *s.m.* rifle, gun.

riflero *s.m.* (Am.) **1** MIL. armed soldier. **2** (fam.) good shot (buen tirador).

rigidez *s.f.* **1** stiffness, rigidity: *la rigidez de las botas = the stiffness of the boots.* **2** (fig.) strictness, rigor: *la rigidez del profesor = the teacher's strictness.*

rígido, -a *adj.* **1** rigid, stiff (cosa). **2** (fig.) strict, stern (persona). **3** expressionless, impassive (mirada).

rigodón *s.m.* MUS., HIST. rigadoon.

rigor *s.m.* **1** strictness, severity (dureza). **2** toughness, hardness (aspereza). **3** exactitude, precision (exactitud). **4** (Am.) great quantity, oceans: *hay un rigor de libros = there are oceans of books.* || **5 en —,** in fact. **6 ser de —,** to be absolutely necessary. **7 ser el — de las desdichas,** to be down in the dumps.

rigorismo *s.m.* strictness, severity.

rigoroso, -a o **riguroso, -a** *adj.* **1** strict, severe (severo). **2** tough, hard (áspero). **3** exact, precise (exacto). **4** cruel, merciless (cruel).

rigurosidad *s.f.* severity, rigour.

rija *s.f.* **1** MED. fistula under the eye. **2** fight, quarrel (riña).

rilar *v.i.* **1** to be scared, to tremble (temblar). || *v.pron.* **2** (fam.) to chicken out, to get cold feet (acobardarse).

rima *s.f.* **1** rhyme. || **2 — asonante,** LIT. vowel-rhyme. **3 — consonante,** LIT. consonance.

rimar *v.i.* LIT. **1** to rhyme. || *v.t.* **2** to make rhyme.

rimbombancia *s.f.* **1** resonance, echo (resonancia). **2** (fig.) fustian, high-sounding language (ampulosidad). **3** (fig.) show, ostentation (ostentación).

rimbombante *adj.* **1** resonant, echoing (resonante). **2** (fig.) bombastic, high sounding (ampuloso). **3** (fig.) showy, ostentatious (ostentoso).

rimbombar *v.i.* to resound, to echo: *un sonido que rimbomba = a booming sound.*

rímel o **rímmel** *s.m.* eye shadow (maquillaje).

rincón *s.m.* **1** corner (ángulo). **2** cranny (escondrijo). **3** (fig.) retreat, private quarters (retiro). **4** lumber room (trastero). **5** (Am.) confined area.

rinconada *s.f.* corner (casas, calles, etc.).

rinconera *s.f.* **1** corner section (mueble). **2** ARQ. wall section.

ringorrango *s.m.* **1** LIT. flourish. **2** (fam.) frill, knick-knack.

rinitis *s.f.* MED. rhinitis.
rinoceronte *s.m.* ZOOL. rhinoceros.
riña *s.f.* 1 dispute, quarrel, argument (discusión). 2 fight, set-to (pelea).
riñón *s.m.* 1 ANAT. kidney. 2 (fig.) heart (centro). 3 small chunk (mineral). || 4 **costar una cosa un –,** to cost a packet.
río *s.m.* 1 river. 2 (fig.) torrent (gran abundancia). || 3 **a – revuelto, ganancia de pescadores,** adverse times are kind to some. 4 **cuando el – suena, agua lleva,** there's no smoke without fire. 5 **– abajo,** downstream. 6 **– arriba,** upstream.
ripio *s.m.* 1 waste, remains (residuo). 2 LIT. meaningless word. 3 (Am.) rubble (cascote). || 4 **no perder –,** not to miss a trick.
riqueza *s.f.* 1 wealth, riches: *la riqueza de la reina es incalculable = the queen's wealth is incalculable.* 2 richness (fecundidad): *la riqueza de sus ideas = the richness of his ideas.* || 3 **efecto –,** FIN. wealth effect. 4 **vivir en la –,** to live in luxury.
risa *s.f.* 1 laugh: *mi tía reprimió una risa = my aunt stifled a laugh.* 2 laughter: *la risa es lo mejor del hombre = laughter is the best thing in man.* || 3 **– sardónica,** sardonic smile, sneer. 4 **morirse de –,** to crack up, laugh one's head off: *me moría de risa = I laughed my head off.* 5 **tomar a –,** to take something as a joke, not to take something seriously. 6 **¡vaya –!,** what a laugh!
riscal *s.m.* craggy terrain.
risco *s.m.* 1 crag, scar. || *pl.* 2 rough terrain.
risible *adj.* laughable, ridiculous, ludicrous: *un plan risible = a ludicrous plan.*
risotada *s.f.* loud laugh, horse laugh: *solté una risotada = I laughed out loud.*
ristra *s.f.* 1 string: *una ristra de ajos = a string of garlic.* 2 (fig.) long line.
ristre *s.m.* HIST. lance rest (armadura).
risueño, -a *adj.* 1 smiling (cara). 2 (fig.) pleasant-looking, charming: *un riachuelo risueño = a charming little brook.* 3 (fig.) favourable (propicio).
rítmico, -a *adj.* MUS. rhythmic, rhythmical.
ritmo *s.m.* 1 MUS. rhythm. 2 (fig.) rate: *el ritmo de aumento = the rate of increase.* 3 DEP. pace: *los corredores aumentaron el ritmo = the runners stepped up the pace.* || 4 **trabajar a – lento,** to go slow.
rito *s.m.* 1 REL. rite. 2 ceremony (ceremonia).
ritual *adj.* 1 ritual. || *s.m.* 2 REL. ritual. || 3 **ser de –,** to be normal.
ritualidad *s.f.* protocol.
ritualismo *s.m.* ritualism.
rival *adj.* 1 rival. || *s.m.* y *f.* 2 rival, competitor.
rivalizar *v.i.* to compete, to vie, to rival: *los boxeadores rivalizan en preparación física = the boxers rival each other in physical fitness.*
rivera *s.f.* stream, rivulet.
rizado *s.m.* curling, perm: *mi hermana ha pedido un rizado del pelo = my sister has asked for a perm.*
rizar *v.t.* 1 to curl. || *v.pron.* 2 to ripple (agua). || 3 **– el rizo,** (fig.) to split hairs: *estás rizando el rizo = you're splitting hairs.*
rizo, -a *adj.* 1 curly. || *s.m.* 2 curl (pelo). 3 AER. loop. || 4 **rizar el –,** AER. to loop the loop.
robalo, róbalo o **lobarro** *s.m.* ZOOL. sea bass.
robar *v.t.* 1 to steal: *me han robado la cartera = someone's stolen my wallet.* 2 to rob: *robar un banco = to rob a bank.* 3 to burgle (casa). 4 to cheat (timar). 5 to abduct, to kidnap (secuestrar). 6 to take (cartas). 7 (fig.) to capture: *aquella mujer le ha robado el corazón = that woman has captured his heart.*
roble *s.m.* 1 oak tree (árbol). 2 oak (madera). 3 (fig.) strong and healthy person, as hard as nails: *mi amigo es un roble = my friend is as hard as nails.*
robledal o **robledo** *s.m.* oak grove.
roblón *s.m.* 1 TEC. rivet. 2 ARQ. coping tile.
roborar *v.t.* 1 to strengthen, to bolster (dar fuerza). 2 (fig.) to corroborate, to confirm (corroborar).
robot *s.m.* 1 MEC. robot. 2 (fig.) pawn, puppet.
robustecer *v.t.* 1 to fortify, to make robust. || *v.pron.* 2 to increase in strength.
robustez *s.f.* strength, robustness, toughness.
robusto, -a *adj.* robust, vigorous, tough.
roca *s.f.* 1 rock. || 2 **ser como una –,** to be as hard as a rock.
rocalla *s.f.* 1 pebbles, rock chippings (piedrecillas). 2 large bead (abalorio).
rocambolesco, -a *adj.* 1 fortuitous (casual). 2 odd (extraño). 3 flamboyant, baroque, extravagant (estilo).
roce *s.m.* 1 rubbing, rub. 2 (fig.) familiarity, regular dealings, contacts: *tengo roces con el alcalde = I often have contacts with the mayor.* 3 (fig.) brush (hostilidad): *siempre ha habido roces entre las dos familias = there have always been brushes between the two families.*
rociado, -a *adj.* 1 sprinkled, sprayed. || *s.f.* 2 spraying, sprinkling. 3 AGR. spray. 4 (fig.) shower: *una rociada de flechas = a shower of arrows.* 5 (fig.) stern dressing-down (reprensión fuerte).
rociar *v.i.* 1 to fall (rocío). || *v.t.* 2 to spray, sprinkle (esparcir).
rocín *s.m.* 1 ZOOL. (desp.) nag. 2 carthorse (caballo de trabajo). 3 (fam.) slob, lout, uncouth individual (persona).
rocinante *s.m.* (fig.) rickety old nag.
rocío *s.m.* 1 dew (por la mañana). 2 fine drizzle (llovizna). 3 (fig.) light shower, touch.
rococó *adj.* y *s.m.* ARQ. rococo.
rodaballo *s.m.* ZOOL. turbot.
rodado, -a *adj.* 1 on wheels (vehículos). 2 lying on the ground (mineral). || *s.m.* 3 underskirt (prenda de vestir). 4 (Am.) vehicle. || *s.f.* 5 wheel mark (marca de rueda en el suelo). || 6 **salir –,** to go sweetly.
rodaja *s.f.* 1 slice (melón, etc.). 2 small wheel (ruedecilla).
rodaje *s.m.* 1 TEC. set of wheels (conjunto de ruedas). 2 shooting (película). 3 running-in (coche). 4 taxying (avión): *pista de rodaje = taxi-way.* || 5 **poner en –,** to start up, set going.
rodamiento *s.m.* MEC. bearing: *rodamiento de bolas = ball bearing.*
rodapié *s.m.* ARQ. skirting board.
rodante *adj.* 1 rolling: *material rodante = rolling stock.* || *s.m.* 2 (fam.) old banger, old crock (coche).
rodar *v.i.* 1 to roll. 2 to go on wheels (coche). 3 to tumble down (caer dando vueltas). 4 (fig.) to rove around (vagar). 5 to film (cine). 6 to be still in existence (existir aún). || *v.t.* 7 to roll (objeto). 8 to run in (coche). 9 to film (película). 10 (Am.) to fell (derribar).
rodear *v.t.* 1 to surround, encircle (cercar). 2 (Am.) AGR. to round up (ganado). || *v.i.* 3 to go round (andar alrededor). 4 to make a detour (en coche). 5 (fig.) to digress, to ramble (hablar).
rodeo *s.m.* 1 long way round (camino más largo). 2 (fig.) safe distance (escape). 3 (Am.) AGR. roundup. 4 (Am.) rodeo (espectáculo). 5 (fig.) evasive words (circunlocución). || 6 **andar con rodeos,** to beat about the bush. 7 **dejarse de rodeos,** to get to the point.
rodero, -a *adj.* 1 of a wheel. || *s.f.* 2 cart track (camino para carros). 3 rut, track (rodada).
rodete *s.m.* 1 bun (de pelo). 2 pad (almohadilla). 3 ward (cerradura).
rodilla *s.f.* 1 ANAT. knee. 2 rough cloth (paño). || 3 **de rodillas,** kneeling. 4 **doblar la –,** (fig.) to kowtow (humillarse): *no hace falta que dobles la rodilla ante mí = you don't have to kowtow to me.*
rodillazo *s.m.* blow with the knee: *le dio un buen rodillazo = he kneed him hard.*
rodillera *s.f.* 1 DEP. kneepad. 2 patch on the knee of the trousers (remiendo). 3 baggy knee part of the trousers (bolsa).
rodillo *s.m.* 1 roller (herramienta). 2 rolling pin (cocina). 3 platen (máquina de escribir). 4 mangle (exprimidor). || 5 **– de vapor,** steamroller.
rododendro *s.m.* BOT. rhododendron.
roedor *s.m.* ZOOL. rodent: *el ratón es un roedor = the mouse is a rodent.*
roedura *s.f.* gnawing (acto).
roer *v.t.* 1 to gnaw, gnaw at: *la rata roe la madera = the rat gnaws wood.* 2 to pick at (hueso). 3 to nibble at (mordiscar): *el hámster roía el queso = the hamster nibbled at the cheese.* 4 (fig.) to torment, nag: *le está royendo la preocupación = she's being nagged by worry.*
rogante *adj.* pleading: *unas palabras rogantes = a few pleading words.*
rogar *v.t.* 1 to beg for, plead for (cosa). 2 to beg, plead with (persona): *te ruego que me ayudes = I beg you to help me.* || *v.i.* 3 to beg, plead. 4 REL. to pray. || 5 **se ruega no pisar el césped,** please

keep off the grass. **6 se ruega silencio,** silence please.

rogativas *s.f.pl.* REL. rogations.

roído, -a *adj.* **1** gnawed, gnawed through. **2** (fig. y fam.) stingy (mezquino).

rojete *s.m.* rouge (maquillaje).

rojez *s.f.* redness.

rojizo, -a *adj.* reddish, ruddy: *una tez rojiza = a ruddy complexion.*

rojo, -a *adj.* **1** red. **2** POL. red, communist. || *s.m.* **3** red. **4** POL. red, communist. || **5 al — vivo,** red-hot, electric: *la tensión está al rojo vivo = the tension is electric.* **6 ponerse —,** to blush, go red.

rol *s.m.* **1** roll, list, catalogue (lista). **2** role (teatro). **3** MAR. muster-book.

rollizo, -a *adj.* **1** round (cosa). **2** chubby, plump (persona). || *s.m.* **3** roundwood, round timber (madero).

rollo *s.m.* **1** roll (cilindro): *un rollo de papel pintado = a roll of wall-paper.* **2** roll of film (película fotográfica). **3** (fam.) bore, bind, drag: *¡qué rollo! = what a drag!; la película fue un rollo = the film bored me stiff; ¡qué rollo de tío! = what a pain that guy is!* **4** (fam.) the scene, the action: *esa chica tiene un buen rollo = that girl's got a nice little scene going.*

romana *s.f.* steelyard (aparato para pesar).

romance *adj.* **1** LIT. Romance: *el francés es una lengua romance = French is a Romance language.* || *s.m.* **2** Spanish. **3** LIT. romance novel. **4** MUS. ballad. || **5 hablar en —,** (fig.) to speak in simple terms.

romancear *v.t.* **1** to translate into Spanish. **2** (Am. y fam.) to chat up (galantear). || *v.i.* **3** (Am.) to indulge in idle chatter (charlar).

romancero *s.m.* **1** MUS. ballad singer. **2** LIT. ballad anthology.

romanear *v.t.* to weigh with a steelyard.

románico, -a *adj.* **1** ARQ. Romanic. **2** LIT. Romance.

romanista *s.m.* y *f.* **1** Roman Law specialist (profesor). **2** student of Romance languages (filólogo).

romanística *s.f.* FILOL. study of Romance languages.

romanizar *v.t.* **1** to Romanize. || *v.pron.* **2** to become Romanized.

romano *adj.* **1** Roman. || *s.m.* **2** (fam.) copper, bluebottle (policía).

romanticismo *s.m.* romanticism.

romántico, -a *adj.* romantic.

romantizar *v.i.* to romanticize, fantasize.

romanza *s.f.* MUS. ballad.

rombo *s.m.* **1** GEOM. rhombus. **2** ZOOL. turbot (rodaballo).

romboedro *s.m.* GEOM. rhombohedron.

romboide *s.m.* GEOM. rhomboid.

romería *s.f.* **1** REL. pilgrimage. **2** trip into the country (viaje al campo). **3** country feast (feria en el campo). **4** throng (multitud de gente).

romeral *s.m.* BOT. patch of rosemary.

romero *s.m.* **1** pilgrim (peregrino). **2** BOT. rosemary.

romo, -a *adj.* **1** blunt (lapicero). **2** snub-nosed (chato). **3** (fig.) dim, obtuse.

romper *v.t.* **1** to break (plato, etc.). **2** to tear (papel). **3** to wear out (ropa). **4** AGR. to plough (campo). **5** (fig.) to interrupt: *romper el silencio = to break the silence.* **6** MIL. to open: *romper el fuego = to open fire.* || *v.i.* **7** to start, to begin: *está rompiendo el día = day is breaking.* **8** to burst out **9 — a llorar =** burst into tears. **10** (fig.) to break out (brotar). **11** to finish with, break with: *mi hermano ha roto con su novia = my brother has broken with his girlfriend.* || **12 de rompe y rasga,** couldn't-care-less, hot-headed, risk-taking.

rompible *adj.* breakable.

rompiente *s.m.* MAR. reef, shoal.

ron *s.m.* rum.

roncar *v.i.* **1** to snore. **2** to bellow (gamo). **3** (fig.) to threaten (amenazar).

roncero, -a *adj.* **1** slow, lazy (lento). **2** grumbling, grousing (gruñón). **3** unctuous, soapy (adulador). **4** MAR. slow, leisurely (embarcación).

ronco, -a *adj.* **1** hoarse (persona): *mi padre está ronco hoy = today my father is hoarse.* **2** croaky, husky (voz). **3** raucous, guttural (sonido).

roncha *s.f.* **1** ZOOL. boil (bulto). **2** bruise (cardenal). || **3 hacer —,** (Am.) to create an impression. **4 levantar —,** (Am.) to hurt a great deal.

ronda *s.f.* **1** night check, night patrol (vigilancia). **2** patrol, group of guards (vigilantes). **3** MUS. group of serenaders. **4** round (bebida). **5** DEP. round (golf). **6** HIST. surrounding road. **7** hand (cartas). **8** (Am.) ring-a-ring-a-roses (juego de niños). || **9 canción de —,** MUS. round.

rondalla *s.f.* **1** MUS. band of street players. **2** old wives' tale (cuento).

rondar *v.i.* **1** to go on a night patrol (ir vigilando). **2** MUS. to go serenading. **3** to walk the streets (pasear). || *v.t.* **4** to go round: *las golondrinas rondaban la torre = the swallows flew round the tower.* **5** (fig.) to plague, badger (acosar). **6** MED. to produce warning signs (enfermedad).

rondó *s.m.* MUS. rondo.

rondón, de — *loc.adv.* quite unexpectedly, suddenly: *entró en la casa de rondón = he suddenly burst into the house.*

ronquera *s.f.* MED. hoarseness, rough voice.

ronquido *s.m.* **1** snoring, snore. **2** (fig.) gruff sound, raspy sound.

ronronear *v.i.* **1** ZOOL. to purr (gato). **2** MEC. to hum, to purr (motor).

ronroneo *s.m.* purr, purring.

ronzal *s.m.* ZOOL. halter (caballería).

ronzar *v.i.* **1** to munch, to champ, to scrunch (comer ruidosamente). || *v.t.* **2** MAR. to lever, to move with levers (mover con palancas).

roña *s.f.* **1** scab (oveja). **2** mange (perro). **3** layer of filth, grime (mugre). **4** rust (metal). **5** BOT. mould. **6** (fig.) tight-fistedness (tacañería). || *s.m.* y *f.* **7** tight-fisted person, miser.

roñería *s.f.* (fam.) tight-fistedness, meanness.

roñica *s.m.* y *f.* (fam.) miserly devil, skinflint.

roñoso, -a *adj.* **1** scabby (oveja). **2** mangy (perro). **3** (fig.) stingy, mean.

ropa *s.f.* **1** clothes. || **2 — blanca,** underwear. **3 — de cama,** bed linen. **4 a quemarropa,** at point-blake range. **5 guardar la —,** to act with caution. **6 nadar y guardar la —,** to have one's cake and eat it. **7 tentarse la —,** to weigh the pros and cons.

ropaje *s.m.* **1** clothes. **2** evening dress, formal dress (vestidura de gala). **3** REL. vestments. **4** (fig.) drapery (colgaduras).

ropero *s.m.* **1** wardrobe (mueble). **2** outfitter (persona).

roquedal o **roqueda** *s.m.* y *f.* rocky area.

roquedo *s.m.* **1** boulder (piedra). **2** crag (risco).

roquero *s.m.* rocker, teddy boy.

rosa *s.f.* **1** BOT. rose. **2** ANAT. spot. **3** MUS. sound hole. || **4 — de los vientos,** compass card. **5 agua de rosas,** rose-water. **6 estar como una —,** to be in the pink. **7 verlo todo de color de —,** to see everything through rose-coloured spectacles. || *adj.* **8** pink.

rosáceo, -a *adj.* **1** pink, rosy (color). **2** BOT. rosaceous.

rosal *s.m.* **1** BOT. rosebush, rosetree. || **2 — arbusto,** bush rose. **3 — silvestre,** dog rose. **4 — trepador,** rambling rose. **5 — de tallo alto,** standard rose tree.

rosaleda o **rosalera** *s.f.* BOT. rosegarden.

rosario *s.m.* **1** REL. rosary. **2** (fig.) stream, series (retahíla). **3** ANAT. backbone. **4** TEC. waterwheel.

rosbif *s.m.* roast beef.

rosca *s.f.* **1** screw thread (tornillo). **2** screw base (bombilla). **3** schnecke (pan). **4** pad (rodete). || **5 comerse una —,** (fam.) to score (ligar). **6 hacer la — a uno,** (fam.) to lick someone's boots. **7 pasarse de —,** to have a crossed thread (tornillo); (fig.) to go over the top.

rosco *s.m.* **1** round loaf (pan). **2** rubber ring (natación). **3** (Am.) COM. intermediary, middleman. **4** (fam.) nought (cero).

roscón *s.m.* large round loaf (pan).

roséola *s.f.* MED. German measles.

roseta *s.f.* **1** BOT. miniature rose. [illegible] ANAT. red spot. **3** DEP. rosette. **4** nozzl[illegible] *roseta de la ducha = shower nozzle.* [illegible] (Am.) rowel (espuela). **6** TEC. copper crust (costra). || *pl.* **7** popcorn (maíz tostado).

rosetón *s.m.* **1** ARQ. rose window. **2** DEP. rosette.

roso, -a *adj.* red (rojo).

rosquete *s.m.* pretzel (confitería).

rosquilla *s.f.* **1** pretzel (rosquete). **2** ZOOL. grub. **3** circle, ring (humo).

rostro *s.m.* **1** ANAT. face. **2** ZOOL. beak. **3** MAR., HIST. stem. || **4 tener —,** (fam.) to be saucy.

rotación *s.f.* **1** rotation: *la rotación de la Tierra = the rotation of the Earth.* || **2 — de cultivos,** AGR. crop rotation.

rotar *v.i.* 1 to roll (rodar). 2 to work a rota system (trabajo).

rotativo, -a *adj.* 1 revolving. || *s.m.* 2 newspaper (periódico). || *s.f.* 3 TEC. rotary letterpress press (tipografía).

roto, -a *adj.* 1 broken. 2 torn (papel, tela). 3 smashed (ventana). 4 (fig.) dissolute, debauched (licencioso). 5 ruined, destroyed (vida). || *s.m.* 6 torn bit (vestido). 7 (Am.) pauper (pobre). 8 (Am. y fam.) dude (petimetre). 9 (Am.) half-caste (mestizo). || **10 nunca falta un — para un descosido,** you can always find someone worse-off than yourself.

rotonda *s.f.* 1 round building (edificio circular). 2 circular square (plaza circular). 3 rondhouse (ferrocarril). 4 (Am.) roundabout (tráfico).

rotor *s.m.* MEC. rotor.

rótula *s.f.* 1 ANAT. kneecap. 2 MEC. ball-joint.

rotular *adj.* 1 ANAT. of the kneecap. || *v.t.* 2 to label (poner rótulos).

rótulo *s.m.* 1 sign (letrero). 2 title, heading (título). 3 label (etiqueta).

rotundamente *adv.* categorically, emphatically.

rotundidad *s.f.* 1 rotundity, roundness (lo redondo). 2 plain speaking, frankness: *habló con rotundidad = she spoke frankly.*

rotundo, -a *adj.* 1 rotund, round (redondo). 2 (fig.) decisive, flat, categorical (terminante): *me dio una rotunda negativa = he gave me a flat denial.*

rotura *s.f.* 1 break, breaking. 2 crack, split (hendedura).

roturar *v.t.* AGR. to plough the first time.

roturador *s.m.* MEC. rotavator.

roulotte o **rulot** *s.f.* (Am.) caravan, trailer.

roza *s.f.* 1 AGR. field burning. 2 hole, hollow (agujero en la pared).

rozagante *adj.* 1 dressy, showy (vestido). 2 (fig.) haughty (ufano).

rozamiento *s.m.* 1 rubbing. 2 MEC. friction.

rozar *v.t.* 1 to graze, rub, scrape (tocar). 2 AGR. to clear (limpiar). 3 to graze, feed on (comer hierba los animales). || *v.i.* 4 to brush past (pasar). || *v.pron.* 5 to be in close contact (con, with). 6 to trip up (tropezar). 7 to get tongue-tied (trabarse la lengua).

roznar *v.i.* 1 to champ (ronzar). 2 to bray (asno).

rúa *s.f.* 1 (fam.) street. 2 (Am.) open poncho (vestido).

rubéola *s.f.* MED. German measles.

rubí *s.m.* ruby.

rubia *s.f.* 1 blonde: *la rubia de la cafetería = the blonde from the café.* 2 (fam.) estate car (furgoneta). 3 (fam.) FIN. peseta: *no tengo ni una rubia = I haven't got a penny.*

rubiales *s.m.* y *f.* (fam.) blondy.

rubicón *s.m.* 1 Rubicon. || **2 pasar el —,** (fig.) to cross the Rubicon.

rubicundo, -a *adj.* 1 reddish (pelo). 2 ruddy (cara).

rubio, -a *adj.* 1 fair, blonde (pelo). || **2 tabaco —,** Virginian tobacco.

rublo *s.m.* FIN. rouble.

rubor *s.m.* 1 bright red (color). 2 blushing, blush (color de cara). 3 (fig.) bashfulness (vergüenza).

ruborizarse *v.pron.* to blush, flush, go red (cara).

ruborosamente *adv.* bashfully, with bashfulness.

ruboroso, -a *adj.* 1 blushing. || **2 ser —,** to blush very easily.

rúbrica *s.f.* 1 rubric. 2 red sign, red mark (marca roja). 3 flourish (rasgo de la firma). 4 signature (firma). 5 title, heading (título). || **6 ser de —,** to be according to an established rule.

rubricar *v.t.* 1 to sign (firmar). 2 to sign with a flourish (firmar con rasgo). 3 (fig.) to testify to (dar testimonio a).

rucio, -a *adj.* 1 light brown (pardo claro). 2 (fam.) grey-haired (entrecano).

ruda *s.f.* 1 BOT. rue. || **2 ser más conocido que la —,** (fam.) to be a household name.

rudimentario, -a *adj.* rudimentary.

rudimento *s.m.* 1 rudiment. || *pl.* 2 rudiments (ciencia o arte).

rudamente *adv.* 1 (desp.) roughly, uncouthly. 2 basically, plainly (llano).

rudeza *s.f.* 1 (desp.) coarseness, vulgarity. 2 matter-of-factness (simplicidad). 3 slowness, dullness, stupidity (estupidez).

rudo, -a *adj.* 1 (desp.) coarse, uncouth. 2 matter-of-fact (sencillo). 3 simple, dull, stupid (estúpido). 4 rough (áspero). 5 MEC. stiff (pieza).

rueca *s.f.* MEC. distaff, spinning machine.

rueda *s.f.* 1 wheel. 2 tyre (neumático). 3 slice (rodaja). 4 circle (personas). 5 ZOOL. sunfish (pez). || **6 — hidráulica,** waterwheel. **7 — de la fortuna,** wheel of fortune. **8 — motriz,** drive wheel. **9 — de prensa,** press conference. **10 — de recambio,** spare wheel. **11 — volante,** band wheel. **12 comulgar con ruedas de molino,** (fig.) to take everything in. **13 hacer la — a uno,** (fig.) to suck up to someone.

ruedo *s.m.* 1 turn (revolución). 2 circumference (circunferencia). 3 arena (tauromaquia). 4 round mat (esterilla). 5 (Am.) luck at cards (suerte).

ruego *s.m.* plea, request (petición).

rufián *s.m.* 1 pimp (chulo). 2 (desp.) hoodlum, ruffian.

rufianada *s.f.* (Am.) practical joke, cheap trick (burla).

rugby *s.m.* DEP. rugby.

rugir *v.i.* 1 to roar (león). 2 to howl, boom, rage (tormenta).

rugoso, -a *adj.* 1 bumpy, uneven (desigual). 2 rough (áspero).

ruibarbo *s.m.* BOT. rhubarb.

ruido *s.m.* 1 noise. 2 din, racket (alboroto). || **3 meter —,** (fig.) to cause a rumpus. **4 quitarse de ruidos,** not to get involved. **5 ser más el — que las nueces,** much ado about nothing.

ruidoso, -a *adj.* 1 noisy. 2 (fig.) in the news.

ruin *adj.* 1 stingy, mean, worthless (despreciable). 2 small, pathetic (pequeño). 3 nasty, vicious (malo).

ruina *s.f.* 1 ruin. 2 (fig.) downfall, destruction. || *pl.* 3 ARQ. ruins. || **4 estar hecho una —,** to have gone to the dogs (persona).

ruinoso, -a *adj.* 1 ARQ. ruinous, dilapidated. 2 FIN. calamitous, disastrous.

ruiseñor *s.m.* ZOOL. nightingale.

ruleta *s.f.* roulette.

rulo *s.m.* 1 roller (rodillo). 2 hair-curler (pelo). 3 (Am.) AGR. unirrigated land (secano). 4 (Am.) curl (bucle).

rumano, -a *adj./s.m.* y *f.* Rumanian.

rumba *s.f.* 1 MUS. rumba. 2 (Am.) party (fiesta).

rumbón, -ona *adj.* 1 (fam.) big-hearted, open-handed (generoso). 2 (fam.) out of this world, hunky-dory (magnífico).

rumiante *adj.* y *s.m.* ZOOL. ruminant.

rumiar *v.t.* 1 to chew again (masticar de nuevo). 2 (fig.) to chew over (asunto): *estoy rumiando esa idea = I'm chewing that idea over.* || *v.i.* 3 ZOOL. to chew the cud (ganado). 4 (fig.) to moan, complain (renegar).

rumor *s.m.* 1 rumour (noticia). 2 buzz (voces). 3 muffled sound (ruido sordo). 4 murmuring (agua).

rumorearse *v.pron.* to be rumoured: *se rumorea que ya no le quieres = they say you no longer love him.*

rumoroso, -a *adj.* 1 rumorous (que causa rumores). 2 murmuring (agua).

runrún *s.m.* 1 buzz (voces). 2 purr (motor). 3 whirr (máquina). 4 murmur (rumor). 5 (Am.) ZOOL. hummingbird (pájaro mosca).

runrunearse *v.pron.* to be rumoured (rumorearse).

rupestre *adj.* 1 rock **2 pinturas rupestres,** cave paintings.

rupia *s.f.* FIN. 1 rupee. 2 (fam.) peseta.

ruptura *s.f.* 1 break, rupture (hecho de romperse). 2 breaking-off (relaciones). || **3 — de contrato,** breach of contract. **4 — de existencias,** inventory break.

rural *adj.* 1 rural. 2 (Am.) peasant-like, rustic (rústico).

ruso *adj./s.m.* y *f.* Russian.

rústicamente *adv.* crudely, coarsely.

rusticidad *s.f.* 1 rural nature. 2 (desp.) coarseness, uncouthness, crudity.

rústico *adj.* 1 rustic, rural. 2 (desp.) coarse, uncouth, crude.

ruta *s.f.* 1 route, itinerary (itinerario). 2 road, way (camino). 3 (fig.) method of procedure. 4 COM. sales route.

rutilar *v.i.* to sparkle, to glitter: *el diamante rutilaba = the diamond sparkled.*

rutilante *adj.* sparkling, glittering: *una copa rutilante = a sparkling glass.*

rutina *s.f.* 1 routine: *forma parte de mi rutina diaria = it forms part of my daily routine.* || **2 por —,** as a matter of routine.

rutinario *adj.* 1 routine, customary, habitual. 2 (desp.) unimaginative, stereotyped: *ese hombre lleva una vida tan rutinaria = that man leads such a stereotyped existence.*

S, s *s.f.* S, s (vigésimo segunda letra del alfabeto español).

sa *s.m.* shah.

sábado *s.m.* **1** Saturday; Sabbath (judío). **2 Sábado Santo de Gloria,** Easter Saturday.

sabana *s.f.* Savannah, savanna, open grasslands.

sábana *s.f.* **1** sheet. **2** altar cloth (del altar). **3** (fig.) sheet; layer. **4 estirarse más de lo que dan de sí las sábanas,** to bite off more than one can chew. **5 pegársele a uno las sábanas,** to get up late.

sabandija *s.f.* **1** insect, bug, pest. || *s.m.* y *f.* **2** louse, insect (persona). || **3 sabandijas,** vermin.

sabanear *v.t.* (Am.) **1** to catch; to pursue. **2** to flatter, cajole. || *v.i.* **3** to travel over the savannah; to round up cattle (en un llano).

sabanero, -a *adj.* (Am.) **1** of/from the plains; savannah. || *s.m.* y *f.* **2** plainsman, lowlander. **3** bully.

sabanilla *s.f.* **1** small cloth (del altar). **2** light bedspread, counterpane. **3** cradle sheet; small sheet.

sabañón *s.m.* **1** chilblain. || **2 comer como un —,** to eat without restraint, devour.

sabático *adj.* **1** sabbatical. || **2 año —,** sabbatical year/sabbatical leave.

sabatino, -a *adj.* Saturday: *Saturday leave = permiso sabatino.*

sabedor, -a *adj.* **1** aware, informed. || **2 es — de ello,** he knows about it.

sabelotodo *s.m.* y *f.* know-all, smartyboots, clever dick, (Am.) know-it-all.

saber *s.m.* **1** knowledge, learning: *según mi leal saber y entender = to the best of my knowledge.* || *v.t.* **2** to know: *lo sé = I know.* **3 — de,** to know about, be aware of, know of: *¿sabes algo de ellos? = have you heard from them?; sin saberlo ellos = without their knowledge; hacer saber algo a uno = to inform someone of something.* **4** to find out, learn, hear: *cuando supo el resultado = when he heard the result.* **5** to know how to, can: *¿sabes conducir? = can you drive?* || *v.i.* **6 — a,** to taste of, taste like; (fig.) to smack of. || *v.r.* **7** to be known: *se sabe que... = it is known that..., we know that...; no se sabe = nobody knows.* **8 a —,** namely; **a — dónde lo guarda,** I can't think where he keeps it. **9 no — dónde meterse,** to be overcome with shame. **10 no — por dónde se anda,** not to know how to act, to act incorrectly. **11 — ir a un sitio,** to know one's way to a place. **12 — andar por un sitio,** to know one's way about a place. **13 el señor no sé cuantos,** Mr. so-and-so. **14 ¡quién sabe!,** who knows! **15 ¡yo qué sé!,** how should I know! **16 que sepamos,** as far as we know. **17 un no sé qué,** a certain some-
thing, a je ne sais quoi. **18 ¿tú qué sabes?,** what do you know about it? **19 vete a —,** your guess is as good as mine, goodness only knows. **20 ¡haberlo sabido!,** if only I'd known!

sabia *s.f.* learned woman; scholar, expert.

sabiamente *adv.* **1** wisely, sensibly. **2** learnedly, knowledgably, expertly.

sabidillo, -a *adj./s.m.* y *f.* know-all, clever-dick, smart aleck.

sabiduría *s.f.* **1** wisdom. **2** knowledge, learning.

sabiendas, 1 a —, knowingly; wittingly, consciously, deliberately. **2 a — de que...,** knowing full well that...

sabihondez o **sabiondez** *s.f.* pedantry, affectation of knowledge.

sabihondo, -a o **sabiondo, -a** *adj.* know-all.

sabina *s.f.* BOT. savin.

sabio, -a *adj.* **1** learned (persona), knowledgeable; wise, sensible, prudent. **2** sane (persona). **3** trained (animal). || *s.m.* y *f.* **4** learned man, wise man, sage; scholar, expert.

sablazo *s.m.* **1** strike o slash with a sabre. **2** sabre wound. **3** (fam.) sponging, cadging. || **4 dar un — a uno,** (fam.) to scrounge money off someone, touch someone for a loan.

sable *s.m.* **1** sabre, cutlass, (EE.UU.) saber. **2** sable (heráldica).

sablear *v.i.* (fam.) to sponge, cadge, scrounge, live by sponging; to ask for money (pedir un préstamo).

sablista *s.m.* y *f.* (fam.) sponger, cadger, scrounger.

sabor *s.m.* **1** taste, flavour, (EE.UU.) flavor. **2** (fig.) flavour: *con sabor romántico = with a romantic flavour.* **3 con — a pescado,** fish flavoured. **4 sin —,** tasteless. **5** (fig.) *dejarle a uno mal sabor de boca = to leave a nasty taste in one's mouth.* **6** (fig.) *sabor local = local colour.*

saborear *v.t.* **1** to flavour, give flavour to. **2** to savour, relish, taste. **3** (fig.) to enjoy, relish: *saboreó su momento de triunfo = he relished his moment of triumph.*

sabotaje *s.m.* sabotage.

saboteador *s.m.* saboteur.

sabotear *v.t.* to sabotage.

sabresura *s.f.* (Am.) **1** delight, pleasure. **2** gentleness, mildness.

sabroso, -a *adj.* **1** tasty, delicious, pleasant, rich. **2** (fig.) meaty, full of substance (un libro o similar producto intelectual).

sabueso *s.m.* **1** hound, blood hound (perro). **2** detective, sleuth (persona).

saburra *s.f.* fur (en la lengua).

saca *s.f.* **1** sack, big bag (costal), mail bag (de correos). **2** withdrawal, taking out, removal. **3** COM. exportation. **4** DER. authorized copy of a bill of sale.

sacabalas *s.m.inv.* bullet-extractor, worm.

sacabocados *s.m. inv.* punch.

sacabuche *s.m.* **1** MUS. sackbut. **2** sackbut player. **3** kind of rustic drum.

sacacorchos *s.m.inv.* corkscrew.
sacadineros *s.m.* y *f.inv.* **1** sponger, scrounger. **2** swindler.
sacadura *s.f.* **1** sloping cut, cut on the bias. **2** (Am.) removal, taking out.
sacamuelas *s.m.inv.* **1** charlatan. **2** dentist.
sacapotras *s.m.inv.* bad surgeon.
sacapuntas *s.m.inv.* pencil sharpener.
sacar *v.t.* **1** to take out, pull out, bring out; draw, get out (pistola); to extract, remove, (dinero del banco) withdraw. **2** to make, get (dinero): *vamos a sacar mucho dinero de este negocio = we're going to make a lot of money from this business.* **3** to bring out (inventar): *acaban de sacar una nueva gama de productos = they've just brought out a new range of products.* **4** to make (copia): *saca dos copias de esta hoja = make two copies of this page.* **5** to let out (costura): *sácale un centímetro en la cintura = let the waist out one centimetre.* **6** to get out, remove (mancha), get off. **7** FOT. to take: *sácame una foto aquí = take a photo of me here.* **8** to mention, bring up: *no saques el tema del coche = don't bring up the subject of the car.* **9** to win, get (premio, elecciones). **10** to get, buy (comprar): *saca las entradas tú = you get the tickets.* **11** to stick out, thrust out (parte del cuerpo): *me sacó la lengua = he stuck his tongue out at me.* **12** to reach, obtain, (respuesta, solución) get; to draw, come to, reach (conclusión). || *v.t.* e *i.* **13** to serve (tenis); (fútbol) to kick off, throw in. **14 — adelante** to bring up (niño); to carry on (negocio). **15 — en limpio** o **en claro,** to come to a conclusion. **16 me saca diez años,** he's ten year older than me. **17 — faltas,** to find faults. **18 — a bailar a alguien,** to ask someone to dance. **19 — a la luz,** to publish, bring to light. **20 — al perro a pasear,** to take the dog (out) for a walk. **21 — a uno de quicio, — a uno de sí, — a uno de sus casillas,** to infuriate someone, drive someone mad, make someone see red.
sacarina *s.f.* saccharine, saccarin.
sacaromicetos *s.m.pl.* saccharomyces.
sacarosa *s.f.* QUIM. saccharose, sucrose.
sacatrapos *s.m.inv.* **1** wormer (armas). **2** person who worms secrets out of someone.
sacerdocio *s.m.* priesthood.
sacerdotal *adj.* priestly.
sacerdote *s.m.* **1** priest. **2 — obrero,** worker priest. **3 sumo —,** high priest.
sacerdotisa *s.f.* priestess.
saciable *adj.* satiable.
saciar *v.t.* **1** to satiate, satisfy. **2** to quench (one's thirst). || *v.r.* **3** to satiate oneself; **— con** o **de,** to be satisfied o satiated with.
saciedad *s.f.* **1** satiation, satiety. || **2 comer hasta la —,** to eat one's fill. **3 repetir algo hasta la —,** to repeat something over and over again.
saco *s.m.* **1** sack, bag. **2** bagful, sackful, sack, bag (medida). **3** coarse dress (ropa); Roman sagum. **4** (Am.) jacket. **5** loose-fitting overcoat. **6** pillage, sack (saqueo). **7** ANAT. sac. || **8 caer en — roto,** to fall upon deaf ears. **9** MIL. **entrar a —,** to plunder, sack, loot. **10 no echar algo en — roto,** to take care not to forget something. **11 — de dormir,** sleeping-bag. **12 — de huesos,** bag of bones.
sacón, -a *adj.* (Am.) talebearing.
saconería *s.f.* (Am.) flattery.
sacramental *adj.* **1** sacramental. **2** ritualistic.
sacramentar *v.t.* **1** to consecrate (hostia). **2** to administer the last sacraments to.
sacramento *s.m.* REL. **1** sacrament. **2 recibir los sacramentos,** to receive the last sacraments. **2 el Santísimo Sacramento,** the Blessed Sacrament. **3 recibir los sacramentos,** to receive the last sacraments. **4 últimos sacramentos,** last rites.
sacratísimo, -a *adj.* most sacred.
sacrificar *v.t.* **1** to sacrifice. **2** to slaughter (res); to put to sleep, put down (animal domesticado). || *v.r.* **3** to sacrifice oneself, suffer.
sacrificio *s.m.* **1** sacrifice, offering. **2** slaughter (res); putting down (animal domesticado). **3 — del altar,** REL. sacrifice of the mass. **4 — de la misa,** REL. sacrifice of the mass.
sacrilegio *s.m.* sacrilege.
sacrílego, -a *adj.* sacrilegious.
sacristán *s.m.* **1** sacristan, verger, sexton. **2 ser gran —,** to be very cunning, astute.
sacristía *s.f.* sacristy, vestry.
sacro, -a *adj.* **1** sacred, holy: *música sacra = sacred music.* **2** ANAT. sacral. || *s.m.* **3** ANAT. sacrum.
sacrosanto, -a *adj.* sacrosanct, most holy.
sacudida *s.f.* **1** shake, jerk, jolt. **2** shock, tremor (terremoto). **3** blast (bomba). **4** toss, jerk (cabeza). || **5 — eléctrica,** electric shock.
sacudido, -a *adj.* **1** shaken. **2** (fig.) harsh, unpleasant. **3** (fig.) determined, daring.
sacudir *v.t.* **1** to shake, to jerk, to jolt. **2** to beat (alfombra). **3** to toss, to jerk, to shake (cabeza). **4** to wag (rabo). **5** to brush off (ahuyentar). **6** (fam.) to beat up. **7** to spank, to beat, to thrash (castigo). || *v.r.* **8** to shake (oneself). **9** to shake off, to get rid of.
sacudidor, -a *adj.* **1** shaking, beating. || *s.m.* **2** shaker, beater.
sacudidura *s.f.* shaking, dusting.
sacudimiento *s.m.* **1** shaking, shake, shock, jerk, jolt. **2** shaking off.
sacudón *s.m.* (Am.) shake, jolt, jerk.
sachar *v.t.* to weed.
sacho *s.m.* hoe.
sádico, -a *adj.* **1** sadistic. || *s.m.* **2** sadist.
sadismo *s.m.* sadism.
sadista *s.m.* y *f.* sadist.
saeta *s.f.* **1** arrow, dart. **2** religious song sung in Holy Week processions. **3** hand (reloj). **4** magnetic needle (brújula). **5** vine shoot o bud.
saetera *s.f.* **1** MIL. loophole. **2** narrow window.
saetín *s.m.* **1** tack (clavo). **2** millcourse, millrace (molino).
safari *s.m.* safari: *están de safari = they're on safari.*
safena *adj.* **1** ANAT. saphenous. || *s.f.* **2** ANAT. saphena.
sáfico, -a *adj.* y *s.m.* y *f.* LIT. sapphic.
saga *s.f.* **1** saga (leyenda). **2** witch (bruja).
sagacidad *s.f.* astuteness, shrewdness; sagacity, cleverness.
sagaz *adj.* astute, shrewd; sagacious, clever.
sagita *s.f.* sagitta, segment.
sagital *adj.* sagittal, arrow-shaped.
sagitaria *s.f.* BOT. sagittaria.
sagitario *s.m.* **1** ASTR. Sagitarius. **2** archer.
sagrado, -a *adj.* **1** holy, sacred, consecrated. **2** venerable. || *s.m.* **3** asylum, sanctuary, safe place.
sagrario *s.m.* **1** shrine, sanctuary. **2** Tabernacle.
sahumar *v.t.* to perfume with incense.
sahumerio *s.m.* aromatic smoke.
saín *s.m.* **1** animal fat, grease; fish oil. **2** grease, dirt (en la ropa).
sainar *v.t.* to fatten.
sainete *s.m.* **1** ART. one-act farce. **2** sauce, seasoning (cocina). **3** titbit, delicacy (comida).
sainetear *v.i.* to act a farce.
sainetero *s.m.* farce writer.
sainetesco, -a *adj.* farcial, burlesque.
saja o **sajadura** *s.f.* incision, cut.
sajar *v.t.* MED. to cut open, make an incision in; to lance (un absceso).
sajón *adj.* y *s.m.* Saxon.
sal *s.f.* **1** salt: *una pizca de sal = a pinch of salt.* **2** wit, wittiness; charm, winning manners: *tienen mucha sal = they're very charming/they're great fun.* **3 — gorda,** cooking salt. **4 — de la higuera,** Epsom Salts. **5 — marina,** sea salt. **6 — de frutas,** fruit salts. **7 — y pimienta,** (fig.) wit. **7 echar — a,** to salt.
sala *s.f.* **1** living room, sitting room, lounge. **2** large room, room. **3** court (tribunal): *sala de apelación = court of appeal.* **4 — de conferencias,** lecture theatre, conference hall. **5 — de espera,** waiting room. **6 — de exposición,** showroom. **7 — de fiestas,** dance hall, ballroom. **8 — de máquinas,** engine room.
salacot *s.m.* pith helmet, topi.
saladar *s.m.* salt marsh.
saladero *s.m.* salting tub.
saladillo, -a *adj.* unsalted and fresh.
salado, -a *adj.* **1** salty, salted, briny, salt: *agua salada = salt water.* **2** witty, amusing, funny. **3** (Am.) unfortunate, unlucky, hapless (infortunado). **4** (Am.) dear, expensive (caro).
salamanca *s.f.* (Am.) natural cave.
salamandra *s.f.* **1** ZOOL. salamander. **2** salamander stove.
salamanquesa *s.f.* lizard, gecko.
salar *v.t.* **1** to salt, season with salt. **2** to salt, cure. **3** (Am.) to spoil, ruin (estro-

pear); to bring bad luck to (traer mala suerte). **4** (Am.) to dishonour (deshonrar), (EE.UU.) dishonor.
salarial *adj.* wage, salary.
salariar *v.t.* to pay a wage to.
salario *s.m.* **1** salary, wages, wage, pay. || **2 — a destajo,** piece rate. **3 — base,** basic wage.
salazón *s.f.* **1** salting, seasoning. **2** salted meat o fish. **3** salting industry.
salce *s.m.* willow.
salcochar *v.t.* GAST. to boil in salt water.
salchicha *s.f.* sausage, pork sausage.
salchichería *s.f.* pork butcher's (shop).
salchichero *s.m.* pork butcher.
salchichón *s.m.* salami, large pork sausage.
saldar *v.t.* **1** to liquidate, settle, pay, pay off. **2** to sell off (en una tienda). **3** (fig.) to settle (diferencias).
saldo *s.m.* COM. **1** balance: *saldo acreedor = credit balance; saldo deudor = debit balance.* **2** payment, settlement (deuda). **3** clearance sale. **4** remnant, left-over.
saledizo, -a *adj.* **1** jutting, projecting. || *s.m.* y *f.* **2** ARQ. projection, corbel, overhang.
salero *s.m.* **1** saltcellar. **2** wit, charm.
salicina *s.f.* QUIM. salicin.
sálico, -a *adj.* salic: *ley sálica = Salic Law.*
salida *s.f.* **1** departure, leaving. **2** exit, way out. **3** (fig.) excuse (pretexto), way out, loophole. **4** ASTR. rising, rise: *la salida del sol = sunrise.* **5** opening (de trabajo). **6** way out, solution (de un problema). **7** result (resultado). **8** MIL. sally, sortie. **9** lead (cartas). **10** COM. outlet, sale, market. **11** TEC. outlet, vent. **12 calle sin —,** cul-de-sac. **13 — de artistas,** stage door. **14 — de tono,** improper remark.
salidizo *s.m.* ARQ. projection, corbel, overhang.
salido, -a *adj.* **1** projecting, prominent, bulging. **2** ZOOL. on heat.
saliente *adj.* **1** projecting, prominent, bulging. **2** rising (sol). **3** outgoing, retiring (persona que deja sus funciones). **4** (fig.) salient; outstanding. || *s.m.* **5** ARQ. projection.
salificable *adj.* salifiable.
salificar *v.t.* QUIM. to salify.
salina *s.f.* **1** salt mine. **2** saltworks.
salinero, -a *adj.* salt.
salinidad *s.f.* salinity.
salino, -a *adj.* saline.
salir *v.i.* **1** to leave, to come out, to go out. **2 — de,** to depart from, to leave from, to sail from (tren, barco). **3** to get out (librarse), to escape: *no pude salir del cuarto de baño porque la puerta estaba bloqueada = I couldn't get out of the bathroom because the door was stuck.* **4** to appear: *la noticia salió en la prensa al día siguiente = the news appeared in the press the next day.* **5** to come out (flores). **6** to rise to come out (sol, luna, estrellas): *no salió el sol en todo el día = the sun didn't come out all day.* **7** to be published (periódico). **8** (moda) to come in: *sale una moda nueva cada mes = a new fashion comes in every month.* **9** to start, to make the first move (juegos), to lead (cartas). **10** to come up (lotería). **11** to cease to be (cesar): *salió de alcalde = he ceased to be mayor.* **12** to be elected, win (elección): *¿quién ha salido presidente? = who's been elected president?* **13** to come up with, to come out with: *mira con qué nos ha salido ahora = just look what he's come out with now.* **14** to turn out: *salió la niña muy inteligente = the girl turned out (to be) very intelligent.* **15** to go, to turn out: *el examen me salió muy bien = my exam went very well; salió que su abuelo había sido espía = it turned out that his grandfather had been a spy.* **16** to come up, to present itself, to arise (oportunidad). **17** to be able to think of: *nunca le sale mi nombre = he can never think of my name.* **18** to go out with, to date (novios, amigos, etc.). **19** to come out, in, to lead to (desembocar): *esta calle sale a una plaza = this street leads to a square.* **20** to come out, to come off (mancha). **21** to enter, to come on (teatro). **22** to cost: *nos ha salido el piso por dos millones de pesetas = the flat has cost us two million pesetas.* **23 — a,** to look like, take after (parecerse): *este niño sale a su padre = this boy takes after his father.* || *v.pron.* **24** to boil over (líquidos); to overflow; to leak out. **25** to leak: *esta cazuela se sale = this saucepan leaks.* **26 salirse con la suya,** to get o have one's own way. **27 salirse de tono,** to make improper remarks. **28 salirse de sus casillas,** to lose one's temper, get angry. **29 al niño le está saliendo un diente,** the baby is cutting a tooth. **30 me ha salido un grano en la nariz,** I've got a pimple on my nose. **31 — a la mar,** to put to sea. **32 — de la costumbre,** to break with custom. **33 salga lo que salga,** come what may. **34 — pitando,** to shoot off, be off like a shot. **35 — a luz,** to be published. **36 — de dudas,** to shed one's doubts. **37 — mal,** to miscarry, go badly: *me salió mal el proyecto = my plan miscarried.*
salitrado, -a *adj.* impregnated with saltpetre.
salitral *adj.* saltpetrous, nitrous.
salitre *s.m.* saltpetre, nitre.
salitrería *s.f.* saltpetre works, nitrate fields.
salitrero *s.m.* saltpetre dealer.
saliva *s.f.* **1** saliva. || **2 gastar —,** (fig.) to waste one's breath. **3 tragar —,** (fig.) to swallow hard, hold one's peace.
salivajo *s.m.* spit, spittle.
salival *adj.* salivary.
salivar *v.i.* **1** to salivate. **2** (Am.) to spit.
salivazo *s.m.* spit, spittle.
salivera *s.f.* spittoon.
salivoso, -a *adj.* salivous.
salmear *v.i.* to sing psalms.
salmista *s.m.* psalmist, psalm singer.
salmo *s.m.* psalm.
salmodia *s.f.* **1** psalmody. **2** (fam.) drone, monotonous singing.
salmodiar *v.i.* **1** to sing psalms. **2** (fam.) to drone, sing monotonously.
salmón *s.m.* ZOOL. salmon.
salmonado, -a *adj.* **1** salmon-like. || **2 trucha salmonada,** salmon trout.
salmonera *s.f.* salmon net.
salmonete *s.m.* ZOOL. red mullet.
salmorejo *s.m.* rabbit sauce.
salmuera *s.f.* brine, pickle.
salobre *adj.* brackish, salty, briny.
salobreño, -a *adj.* brackish, salty, briny.
salobridad *s.f.* brackishness, saltiness.
saloma *s.f.* working song; sea shanty.
salomónico, -a *adj.* **1** salomonic. || **2** ARQ. **columna salomónica,** wreathed column.
salón *s.m.* **1** sitting room, lounge; drawing room. **2** hall: *salón de actos = assembly hall.* **3** salon, coterie, circle (político, literario, etc...). **4** show, exhibition: *salón del automóvil = motor show.* **5** common room (de un colegio). **6 — de baile,** dance hall, ballroom. **7 — de belleza,** beauty parlour. **8 — de demostraciones,** showroom. **9 — de fiestas,** dance hall. **10 — de peluquería,** hair dressing salon. **11 — de pinturas,** art gallery. **12 — de té,** tearoom.
saloncillo *s.m.* private room, special room; rest room.
salpicadero *s.m.* dashboard, fascia (form.).
salpicado, -a *adj.* **1 — de,** splashed with; sprinkled with; dotted with. **2** (Am.) spotted, dappled, mottled (animales).
salpicadura *s.f.* **1** splashing, spattering (acción). **2** splash, spatter (un líquido).
salpicar *v.t.* **1 — de,** to splash with, spatter with. **2** to sprinkle (with). **3** to scatter (with), strew (about). **4** (fig.) to sprinkle, intersperse (with): *un discurso salpicado de anglicismos = a speech sprinkled with anglicisms.*
salpicón *s.m.* **1** salmagundi (guiso). **2** splash, spatter (salpicadura). **3** (Am.) cold fruit juice drink.
salpimentar *v.t.* **1** to season, to add salt and pepper to. **2** (fig.) to season, to improve.
salpresar *v.t.* to salt, to preserve with salt.
salpullido *s.m.* MED. **1** rash, eruption. **2** swelling (from a bite), fleabite (de una pulga).
salsa *s.f.* **1** sauce: *salsa de tomate = tomato sauce, ketchup;* gravy (con carne); dressing (con ensalada). **2** (fam.) sauce, zest. **3** (fig.) spice, appetizer: *la salsa de la vida = the spice of life.* **4 cocerse en su —,** to stew in one's own juice. **5 trabar una —,** GAST. to thicken a sauce.
salsera *s.f.* sauceboat, gravy boat.
salsifí *s.m.* BOT. salsify.
saltabancos *s.m.inv.* mountebank, quack.
saltacharquillos *s.m.inv.* person with a mincing walk.
saltadizo, -a *adj.* fragile.

saltador, -a *adj.* 1 jumping. || *s.m.* y *f.* 2 jumper, leaper, hopper. 3 skipping rope. || 4 **— de pértiga,** DEP. pole vaulter.
saltamontes *s.m.inv.* grasshopper.
saltadura *s.f.* chip.
saltante *adj.* (Am.) outstanding.
saltaparedes *s.m.inv.* wild youth.
saltar *v.i.* 1 to jump, to leap. 2 to skip, to hop (de un pie). 3 to fidget. 4 to bounce (botar). 5 to burst, to explode (estallar). 6 to come off, to come away, to come loose (desprenderse); to pop out (un tapón); to come off (un botón); to peal off (pintura); to fly off (trozos de madera). 7 to break, to crack, to snap (romperse). 8 to jump (about), to skip (about): *siempre salta de un tema a otro = he's always skipping about from one subject to another.* 9 to blow up, to explode (enfadarse). || *v.t.* 10 to jump (over), to leap (over); to vault (over): *saltó el charco = he jumped over the puddle.* 11 to blow up (hacer estallar). 12 to knock out (dientes). || *v.r.* 13 to skip, to jump, to miss (out), to leave out: *me he saltado la clase de inglés = I've skipped the English class; te has saltado un nombre en la lista = you've missed out a name on the list.* 14 to well up (lágrimas): *se me saltaron las lágrimas = tears welled up in my eyes.* 15 to break (reglas): *se salta todas las reglas = he breaks all the rules.* 16 **— a la vista,** to be very obvious. 17 **— a la comba,** to skip. 18 **— con pértiga,** to pole vault. 19 **saltarse la tapa de los sesos,** to blow one's brain out. 20 **— a la mente,** to spring to mind, leap to one's mind. 21 **— de alegría,** to jump for joy. 22 **estar a la que salta,** to be on the look out for mistakes. 23 **hacer —,** to blow up. 24 **hacer — las lágrimas a uno,** to bring tears to one's eyes.
saltarín, -a *adj.* 1 restless. || *s.m.* y *f.* 2 dancer.
saltarina *s.f.* dancer.
salteado, -a *adj.* GAST. sauté.
salteador *s.m.* highwayman; holdup man.
salteamiento *s.m.* hold-up, robbery (highway).
saltear *v.t.* 1 to hold up, rob. 2 to take by surprise. 3 to assault. 4 to do something in fits and starts. 5 to sauté.
salteo *s.m.* hold-up, (highway) robbery.
salterio *s.m.* 1 Book of Psalms. 2 psalter. 3 MUS. psaltery. 4 rosary.
saltimbanqui *s.m.* acrobat, juggler, circus artist; puppeteer.
salto *s.m.* 1 jump, leap, bound, spring, vault. 2 precipice, cliff, chasm. 3 omission, gap, skip, hiatus. 4 sudden change. 5 GEOG. waterfall, cascade; TEC. chute. 6 **— de agua,** waterfall, cascade. 7 **— de altura,** high jump. 8 **— de cama,** negligé, (EE.UU.) negligee. 9 **— de longitud,** long jump. 10 **— de pértiga,** pole vault. 11 **a saltos,** in leaps and bounds. 12 **a — de mata,** headlong, haphazardly. 13 **de un —,** at one bound, with one jump.
saltón, -ona *adj.* 1 bulging (ojos); protruding (dientes). 2 hopping, leaping. 3 (Am.) undercooked.
salubre *adj.* healthy, salubrious.
salubridad *s.f.* healthiness, salubrity.
salud *s.f.* 1 health. 2 welfare, wellbeing. 3 state of grace. 4 salvation. || *interj.* 5 (fam.) greetings; good health!, cheers! (bebiendo). || 6 **curarse en —,** to take precautions. 7 **rebosar —,** to be brimming with health.
saludable *adj.* 1 healthy, salutary. 2 (fig.) salutary, beneficial.
saludar *v.t.* 1 to greet. 2 to say hello to, to acknowledge. 3 MIL. to salute. 4 (fig.) to hail, to welcome. 5 **ir a — a alguien,** to drop in to see someone, to go and say hello to someone. 6 **le saluda atentamente,** yours faithfully (en una carta). 7 **saluda de mi parte a,** give my regards to.
saludo *s.m.* greeting; bow.
salvabarros *s.m.* mudguard.
salva *s.f.* 1 MIL. salvo, volley; salute. || 2 **— de aplausos,** volley of applause.
salvación *s.f.* 1 salvation, deliverance, rescue. 2 REL. salvation: *salvación eterna = eternal salvation.* 3 **Ejército de Salvación,** Salvation Army.
salvada *s.f.* (Am.) salvation.
salvado *s.m.* bran.
salvaguardar *v.t.* to safeguard.
salvaguardia *s.m.* 1 guardian. || *s.f.* 2 safe-conduct; (fig.) safeguard.
salvajada *s.f.* savage act, brutal deed, savagery; atrocity.
salvaje *adj.* 1 wild (plantas, animales); wild uncultivated (tierra). 2 savage (feroz). 3 savage (personas). || *s.m.* y *f.* 4 savage. 5 (fig.) savage, boor.
salvajina *s.f.* 1 group of wild beasts o animals. 2 meat o skins of wild beasts.
salvajismo *s.m.* savagery.
salvamanteles *s.m.inv.* table-mat.
salvamento *s.m.* 1 rescue, saving. 2 REL. salvation. 3 salvage. 4 refuge, haven. || 5 **bote de —,** lifeboat. 6 **operaciones de —,** rescue operations.
salvar *v.t.* 1 to save, rescue; to salvage (un barco). 2 REL. to save (el alma). 3 to cross, to get round, to negotiate (un obstáculo); to clear, to jump across (un arroyo); to overcome (una dificultad). 4 to cover, to do (distancia). 5 to exclude, to except. || *v.r.* 6 to save oneself, to escape; to survive. 7 REL. to be saved, to save one's soul. 8 **salvarse por los pelos,** to escape by the skin of one's teeth. 9 **¡sálvese el que pueda!,** every man for himself!
salvavidas *s.m.* 1 life preserver; life belt; life boat; life buoy. || *adj.atr.* 2 life-saving. 3 **bote —,** lifeboat. 4 **chaleco —,** life jacket.
salve *interj.* 1 hail! || *s.f.* 2 REL. Hail Mary (oración).
salvedad *s.f.* 1 reservation, qualification. 2 exception. 3 condition, proviso.
salvia *s.f.* BOT. sage.
salvo, -a *adj.* 1 safe. || *adv.* y *prep.* 2 except (for), save. || 3 **a —,** safe and sound, out of danger. 4 **a — de,** safe from. 5 **dejar la reputación de uno a —,** to keep someone's reputation safe. 6 **poner a —,** to put in a safe place. 7 **ponerse a —,** to reach safety. 8 **— que,** unless.
salvoconducto *s.m.* safe-conduct.
samario *s.m.* samarium.
samba *s.f.* samba.
sambenito *s.m.* 1 (EE.UU.) disgrace, dishonour. 2 HIST. scapular (que se ponía a los penitentes de la Inquisición). 3 placard in a church with names of penitents. || 4 **colgar el — a uno,** to pin the blame on someone: *le han colgado ese sambenito = they have given him a bad name.* 5 **quedar con el — toda la vida,** to be branded for life.
samblaje *s.m.* joinery.
san *adj.* Saint, (escrito) St.
sanable *adj.* curable.
sanalotodo *s.m.* cure-all, general remedy, panacea.
sanar *v.t.* 1 to cure, to heal. || *v.i.* 2 to recover, to get well (una persona); to heal (una herida).
sanatorio *s.m.* 1 sanatorium. 2 nursing home, clinic. 3 hospital, clinic: *sanatorio psiquiátrico = psychiatric clinic.*
sanción *s.f.* 1 sanction. 2 ratification.
sancionable *adj.* sanctionable, punishable.
sancionar *v.t.* 1 to sanction. 2 to ratify.
sanco *s.m.* 1 gruel. 2 thick mud.
sancochar *v.t.* to parboil.
sancocho *s.m.* 1 half-cooked food. 2 (Am.) stew of meat, yucca and banana.
sanctasanctórum *s.m.* 1 sanctuary, holy of holies. 2 (fig.) sanctum.
sandalia *s.f.* sandal.
sándalo *s.m.* BOT. sandal, sandalwood.
sandez *s.f.* 1 nonsense (palabra): *deja de decir sandeces = stop talking nonsense.* 2 silly thing, stupid thing (acto). 3 silliness (cualidad personal).
sandia *s.f.* fool.
sandía *s.f.* BOT. watermelon.
sandio, -a *adj.* 1 silly, stupid, foolish, nonsensical. || *s.m.* y *f.* 2 fool.
sandunga *s.f.* 1 (Am.) party, celebration. 2 (fam.) charm; wit.
sandwich *s.m.* sandwich.
saneado, -a *adj.* sound.
saneamiento *s.m.* 1 drainage, draining (de un terreno). 2 ECON. stabilization (de una moneda). 3 (fig.) remedy. 4 guarantee, insurance, security. 4 compensation, reparation, indemnification. 5 **artículos de —,** bathroom ware.
sanear *v.t.* 1 to drain (un terreno); to remove the damp (from) (una casa). 2 to put right, to remedy, to repair. 3 to compensate, to indemnify. 4 to guarantee, to insure. 5 ECON. to stabilize (moneda).
sanedrín *s.m.* HIST. Sanhedrin.
sangradera *s.f.* 1 MED. lancet. 2 MED. basin, (para realizar una sangría). 3 AGR. irrigation channel. 4 AGR. sluice.
sangrador *s.m.* bloodletter.

sangradura *s.f.* 1 ANAT. inner part of the elbow. 2 MED. cut made into a vein; bleeding, bloodletting. 3 AGR. outlet, drainage channel.

sangrante *adj.* 1 bleeding. 2 (fig.) flagrant.

sangrar *v.t.* 1 MED. to bleed. 2 AGR. to draw resin from, to tap (un árbol). 3 to indent (imprenta). 4 (fig.) to bleed dry; to filch. 5 TEC. to tap. || *v.i.* 6 to bleed. || *v.r.* 7 to be bled. **8 está sangrando,** it's still fresh. **9 estoy sangrando por la nariz,** my nose is bleeding.

sangre *s.f.* 1 blood. 2 (fig.) blood: *sangre azul = blue blood.* **3 — de horchata,** unemotional, impassive, unmoved. **4 — fría,** coolness, sangfroid. **5 a — fría,** in cold blood. **6 a — y fuego,** mercilessly. **7 a — caliente,** in the heat of the moment. **8 pura —,** thoroughbred. **9 alterársele, encendérsele o quemársele a uno la —,** to exasperate someone. **10 no llegó la — al río,** it wasn't too disastrous. **11 lo llevan en la —,** it runs in their blood. **12 — ligera,** (Am.) kind (person).

sangría *s.f.* 1 MED. bleeding, bloodletting. 2 ANAT. inner part of the elbow. 3 tap (árbol). 4 (fig.) outflow, drain. 5 sangría (bebida).

sangrientamente *adv.* bloodily.

sangriento, -a *adj.* 1 bleeding. 2 blood-red. 3 bloody, blood-stained. 4 (fig.) bloody: *una batalla sangrienta = a bloody battle.*

sanguijuela *s.f.* 1 ZOOL. leech, bloodsucker. 2 (fig.) leech, sponger (persona).

sanguinaria *s.f.* 1 bloodstone. 2 BOT. bloodroot.

sanguinario, -a *adj.* bloodthirsty, callous.

sanguíneo, -a *adj.* 1 ANAT. blood: *grupo sanguíneo = blood group.* 2 (temperamento) sanguineous.

sanguinolento, -a *adj.* 1 bleeding, bloody, blood-stained. 2 (fig.) blood-red. **3 ojos sanguinolentos,** bloodshot eyes.

sanguinoso, -a *adj.* bloody, sanguinary.

sanidad *s.f.* 1 health, healthiness. 2 public health, sanitation: *sanidad pública = public health.* **3 Ministerio de —,** Ministery of Health. **4 inspector de —,** sanitary inspector.

sanitario, -a *adj.* 1 sanitary, health. **2 aparato —,** bathroom fixture.

sano, -a *adj.* 1 healthy, fit. 2 healthy (comida), wholesome; good (fruta). 3 (fig.) sound, healthy. 4 whole, intact (objeto). **5 — y salvo,** safe and sound. **6 cortar por lo —,** to go straight to the root of the problem.

sánscrito, -a *adj.* y *s.m.* Sanskrit.

sanseacabó *loc.* (fam.) y —, and that's the end of it.

sansón *s.m.* tremendously strong person.

santa *s.f.* saint.

santabárbara *s.f.* MAR. magazine.

santafereño, -a *s.m.* y *f.* inhabitant of Santa Fe de Bogotá (Colombia).

santafesino, -a *s.m.* y *f.* inhabitant of Santa Fe (Argentina).

santero, -a *adj.* 1 excessively devoted to Saints' images. || *s.m.* y *f.* 2 sanctuary caretaker. 3 alms-beggar.

santiamén *s.m.* 1 instant. **2 en un —,** in an instant, in a jiffy.

santidad *s.f.* REL. 1 saintliness, holiness, sanctity. || **2 Su Santidad,** His Holiness (para dirigirse o hablar del Papa).

santificar *v.t.* 1 to sanctify, hallow: *santificado sea Tu nombre = hallowed be Thy name.* 2 to consecrate (un lugar). 3 to keep, observe (una fiesta).

santiguar *v.t.* 1 to make the sign of the cross over, to bless. 2 (Am.) to heal. 3 (fam.) to slap. || *v.r.* 4 to cross oneself, to make the sign of the cross.

santísimo, -a *adj.super.* most holy.

santo, -a *adj.* 1 holy, sacred. 2 consecrated, holy (tierra lugar). 3 saintly, holy (persona). || *s.m.* y *f.* 4 saint. 5 image of a saint. 6 saint's day, name day. **7 Semana Santa,** Holy Week. **8 jueves —,** Maundy Thursday. **9 viernes —,** Good Friday. **10 — oficio,** Inquisition. **11 todo el — día,** all day long. **12 ¡y Santas Pascuas!,** and that's that! **13 ¿a — de qué...?,** why on earth...? **14 — y seña,** password. **15 desnudar a un — para vestir a otro,** to rob Peter to pay Paul. **16 llegar y besar el —,** to be a piece of cake. **17 el día de Todos los Santos,** All Saints'Day.

santón *s.m.* 1 mohammedan hermit, dervish. 2 false saint.

santoral *s.m.* collection of life stories of the Saints.

santuario *s.m.* 1 sanctuary, shrine. 2 (Am.) hidden treasure.

santulario, -a *adj.* 1 (Am.) sanctimonious. 2 (Am.) hypocritical.

santurrón, -a *adj.* 1 sanctimonious. 2 hypocritical. || *s.m.* y *f.* 3 sanctimonious person. 4 hypocrite.

santurronería *s.f.* 1 sanctimoniousness. 2 hypocrisy.

saña *s.f.* 1 anger, rage, fury. 2 cruelty.

sañudo, -a *adj.* furious, enraged, angry.

sapaneco, -a *adj.* (Am.) chubby, plump; stocky.

sapidez *s.f.* taste.

sápido, -a *adj.* tasty, savoury, high-flavoured.

sapiencia *s.f.* 1 widsom. 2 knowledge.

sapiente *adj.* wise.

sapo *s.m.* 1 ZOOL. toad. 2 (fig.) bug, creature. || *adj.* 3 (Am.) sly, cunning; telltale. **4 echar sapos y culebras,** to rant and rave, swear black and blue.

saponáceo, -a *adj.* soapy.

saponaria *s.f.* BOT. common soapwort.

saponificar *v.t.* to saponify.

saporífero, -a *adj.* saporific.

saque *s.m.* 1 DEP. serve, service (tenis); kick-off (fútbol); line-out (rugby). 2 DEP. server (tenis: persona). 3 DEP. service line (raya). || **4 tener buen —,** to be a big eater, to eat heartily.

saqueador, -a *adj.* 1 sacking, looting, pillaging, plundering. || *s.m.* y *f.* 2 sacker, looter, pillager, plunderer.

saquear *v.t.* to sack, to loot, to pillage, to plunder.

saqueo *s.m.* sacking, looting, pillaging, plundering.

saquería *s.f.* manufacture of sacks.

saquero *s.m.* sackmaker.

saquete *s.m.* cartridge bag.

saragüete *s.m.* family dance, soirée.

sarampión *s.m.* MED. measles.

sarao *s.m.* family dance, soirée, evening party.

sarape *s.m.* blanket, shawl, serape.

sarasa *s.m.* effeminate man; (fam.) sissy, queer, fairy.

sarcasmo *s.m.* sarcasm.

sarcástico, -a *adj.* sarcastic.

sarcófago *s.m.* tomb, sarcophagus.

sarcoma *s.m.* MED. sarcoma.

sarda *s.f.* horse mackeral.

sardina *s.f.* 1 ZOOL. sardine. **2 estar como sardinas en banasta,** to be (packed) like sardines. **3 — arenque,** pilchard.

sardinal *s.m.* sardine net.

sardinero, -a *adj.* sardine (*atr.*).

sardo, -a *adj.* y *s.m.* y *f.* Sardinian.

sardonia *s.f.* BOT. crowfoot.

sardónico, -a *adj.* sardonic, ironical, insincere.

sarga *s.f.* serge, twill.

sargazo *s.m.* gulf-weed.

sargenta *s.f.* 1 (fam.) dragon, mannish woman. 2 sergeant's wife. 3 sergeant's halberd.

sargento *s.m.* 1 MIL. sergeant. 2 (fam.) tyrant. **3 — mayor,** sergeant major.

sargentona *s.f.* (fam.) dragon, bossy woman, mannish woman.

sarmentoso, -a *adj.* 1 full of vine shoots; climbing. 2 (fig.) gnarled, bony.

sarmiento *s.m.* vine shoot, runner.

sarna *s.f.* 1 MED. itch, scabies. 2 ZOOL. mange.

sarnoso, -a *adj.* MED. itchy, scabby. 2 ZOOL. mangy. 3 (Am.) contemptible, despicable. 4 (Am.) mean.

sarpullido *s.m.* rash, eruption.

sarracénico, -a *adj.* Saracenic.

sarraceno, -a *s.m.* y *f.* 1 Saracen. || *adj.* 2 Saracen.

sarracina *s.f.* (form.) fight, scuffle, brawl.

sarro *s.m.* 1 deposit, incrustation. 2 tartar (dientes); fur, coating (lengua), scale, fur (caldera). 4 BOT. rust, mildew.

sarroso, -a *adj.* 1 incrusted. 2 tartarous, covered with tartar (dientes), furry, coated (lengua). 3 scaly, furry (caldera). 4 BOT. rusted, mildewed, blighted.

sarta *s.f.* 1 string, line, row, series: *sarta de perlas = string of pearls.* 2 (fig.) string: *una sarta de mentiras = a string of lies.*

sartén *s.f.* 1 frying pan. || **2 tener la — por el mango,** to rule the roost, to have the whip hand.

sartenada *s.f.* panful (frying), frying pan.

sartenazo *s.m.* blow with a frying pan.

sartorio *s.m.* y *adj.* ANAT. sartorious.

sastra *s.f.* woman tailor, tailoress.

sastre *s.m.* 1 tailor. **2 — de teatro,** costumier. **3 hecho por —,** tailor-made.

sastrería *s.f.* 1 tailoring, tailor's trade. 2 tailor's (shop).

satán o **satanás** *s.m.* satan.

satélite *s.m.* 1 ASTR. satellite: *un satélite artificial = an artificial satellite.* 2 (fig.) satellite, hanger-on (persona).
satén *s.m.* sateen.
satín *s.m.* satin.
satinado, -a *adj.* 1 satiny, shiny, glossy: *papel satinado = glossy paper.* || *s.m.* y *f.* 2 gloss, shine.
satinador *s.m.* glazer, burnisher.
satinar *v.t.* to gloss, burnish, glaze, satinize.
sátira *s.f.* satire.
satírico, -a *adj.* 1 satirical. || *s.m.* y *f.* 2 satirist.
satirizante *adj.* satirizing.
satirizar *v.t.* to satirize.
sátiro *s.m.* satyr.
satisfacción *s.f.* 1 satisfaction. 2 satisfaction, redress: *pidió satisfacción de la ofensa = he demanded an apology for the offence.* 3 satisfying, sating (apetito). 4 **a — de,** to the satisfaction of. 5 **— de sí mismo,** self satisfaction.
satisfacer *v.t.* 1 to satisfy. 2 to pay (una deuda, etc.). 3 to compensate. 4 to meet, satisfy (una demanda). 5 COM. to honour, (EE.UU.) honor. 6 **— a uno de una ofensa,** to give someone satisfaction for an offence. 7 to solve, explain (una duda). || *v.r.* 8 to satisfy oneself. 9 to avenge oneself.
satisfactorio, -a *adj.* satisfactory.
satisfecho, -a *adj.* 1 satisfied, content. 2 self-satisfied, smug, complacent. 3 **darse por —,** to be satisfied/content (with). 4 **dejar — a,** to satisfy.
sátrapa *s.m.* 1 HIST. satrap. 2 sly o cunning governor.
saturación *s.f.* saturation, permeation.
saturar *v.t.* to saturate, permeate.
saturnal *adj.* 1 saturnalian. || *s.f.* 2 saturnalia.
sauce *s.m.* 1 BOT. willow. 2 BOT. **— llorón,** weeping willow.
sauceda o **saucedal** *s.m.* **saucera** *s.f.* willow plantation.
saúco *s.m.* BOT. elder.
saurio, -a *adj.* y *s.m.* y *f.* ZOOL. saurian.
sauzal *s.m.* willow plantation.
savia *s.f.* 1 BOT. sap. 2 (fig.) vitality, sap. 3 (fig.) *nueva savia = new blood.*
saxofón o **saxófono** *s.m.* MUS. saxophone, sax.
saya *s.f.* 1 skirt. 2 underskirt, petticoat. 3 (Am.) woman.
sayal *s.m.* sackcloth, serge.
sayo *s.m.* 1 cassock, cloak. 2 smock, tunic. 3 **decir para su —,** to say to oneself, laugh in one's sleeve. 4 **hacer de su capa un —,** to do what one likes with one's own things.
sayón *s.m.* 1 long, flared skirt. 2 executioner. 3 henchman, ugly-looking customer.
sazón *s.f.* 1 maturity, ripeness. 2 opportunity, chance, time, moment. 3 seasoning. 4 **a la —,** then, at that time. 5 **en —,** in season, ripe, ready (to eat) (fruta); (fig.) opportunely.
sazonado, -a *adj.* 1 ripe (fruta). 2 **— de,** seasoned with. 3 tasty. 4 (fig.) witty.
sazonar *v.t.* 1 to season, flavour, (EE.UU.) flavor. 2 to ripen, mature. 3 (fig.) to add spice to.
scherzo *s.m.* MUS. scherzo.
se *pron.pers.r.* 1 oneself, yourself, yourselves, himself, herself, itself, themselves: *cuídese = look after yourself.* 2 each other, one another: *se cuidan siempre = they always take care of each other; se aman = they love each other.* 3 **se ha roto el brazo,** he's broken his arm; *se compró un pastel = he bought himself a cake.* 4 (uso impersonal) *se sabe que = it is known that; se dice que = is is said that.* 5 (uso pasivo) *la casa se vendió ayer = the house was sold yesterday; se siembra el trigo en octubre = the corn is sown in October.* 6 one, you, they, we, people: *no se habla con la boca llena = you shouldn't speak with your mouth full; nunca se sabe = one never knows, you never know.* 7 to him, to her, to it, to you, to them: *se lo daré = I'll give it to him,* (o *to her, to you, to them*). 8 for him, for her, for it, for you, for them: *se lo haré = I'll do it for him* (o *for her, for you, for them*). 9 from him, from her, from it, from them: *se los arrancó = he snatched them from him.*
OBS. Algunos verbos pueden ser o no ser reflexivos en inglés: *se lavan = they wash* o *they wash themselves.*
sebáceo, -a *adj.* sebaceous.
sebo *s.m.* 1 suet (para cocinar); tallow (para velas); grease, fat (grasa). 2 fat (de una persona). 3 filth, grime, grease (suciedad). 4 ANAT. sebum.
seboso, -a *adj.* 1 fatty, greasy; suety; tallowy. 2 filthy, grimy.
seborrea *s.f.* MED. seborrhea.
seca *s.f.* 1 AGR. drought; dry season. 2 MAR. sandbank. 3 MED. swollen gland. || 4 **a secas,** alone, just, simply.
secadero *s.m.* 1 drying floor, drying shed. 2 (Am.) dry land.
secador *s.m.* 1 dryer, drier: *secador de pelo = hair-drier; secador centrífugo = spin-drier.* 2 (Am.) towel.
secamiento *s.m.* drying.
secano *s.m.* 1 dry land, unirrigated land, dry region: *cultivo de secano = crop not requiring irrigation.* 2 MAR. sandbank. 3 anything very dry. || 4 **de —,** (fam.) childless.
secante *adj.* 1 drying. 2 MAT. secant. || *s.m.* 3 blotter. || *s.f.* 4 MAT. secant. || 5 **papel —,** blotting-paper, blotter.
secar *v.t.* 1 to dry, to dry up. 2 to wipe dry (superficie). 3 to dry, to wipe away (lágrimas). 4 to blot (tinta). 5 to wipe up (líquido). 6 to wither, to dry up (planta). || *v.r.* 7 to dry, to dry up, to dry off. 8 to wither, to dry up, to wilt (planta). 9 to run dry, to dry up (río). 10 to dry oneself, to get dry (persona). 11 (fig.) to waste away (persona). 12 to be very thirsty. 13 to become hard-hearted. 14 to heal up (herida).
sección *s.f.* 1 section, cutting. 2 department; division, branch. 3 MAT. section. 4 MIL. section, platoon. 5 **— transversal,** cross section.
seccionar *v.t.* to section, divide into sections, divide up.
secesión *s.f.* secession.
secesionista *adj.* y *s.m.* y *f.* secessionist.
seco, -a *adj.* 1 dry. 2 dried up, withered (planta). 3 dry (río, pozo). 4 dried (flores, fruta). 5 dead (árbol, hojas). 6 blunt, cold, hard (carácter). 7 dry, plain, flat (estilo). 8 plain (explicación). 9 brusque, curt (respuesta). 10 sharp (golpe); dull. 11 hacking, dry (tos). 12 dry (vino). 13 skinny, wizened, thin (persona). 14 (fig.) parched, thirsty (sed). 15 **dejar a uno —,** to bump someone off, kill someone stone-dead; to leave someone speechless. 16 **en —,** high and dry; dry: *limpieza en seco = dry cleaning;* suddenly, sharply: *parar en seco = to stop dead; frenar en seco = to brake sharply.* 17 **parar a uno en seco,** to cut someone short.
secoya, secuoya o **sequoia** *s.f.* BOT. sequoia, redwood.
secreción *s.f.* secretion.
secreta *s.f.* 1 secret police. 2 secret investigation, private examination.
secretar *v.t.* to secrete.
secretaría *s.f.* 1 secretary's office. 2 secretaryship. 3 secretariat. 4 (Am.) ministry, department.
secretariado, *s.m.* 1 secretariat. 2 secretaryship. 3 (Am.) profession of secretary. 4 (Am.) secretarial course.
secretaria *s.f.* secretary: *secretaria particular = private secretary.*
secretario *s.m.* 1 secretary. 2 (Am.) POL. minister, secretary. 3 **— Municipal** o **de Ayuntamiento,** town clerk. 4 **— general,** POL. secretary general. 5 **secretario de Estado,** POL. Secretary of State.
secretear *v.i.* 1 to whisper. 2 to talk confidentially.
secreteo *s.m.* whispering.
secreter *s.m.* writing desk.
secreto, -a *adj.* 1 secret, hidden. 2 confidential, secret, classified. 3 secretive (persona). || *s.m.* 4 secret: *nunca reveló el secreto = he never told anyone the secret.* 5 secrecy: *lo hice con mucho secreto = I did it in great secrecy.* 6 combination (de una cerradura). 7 **en —,** in secrecy, secretly, in secret. 8 **— a voces,** open secret. 9 **bajo — de confesión,** under the seal of the confessional. 10 **— de fabricación,** trade secret. 11 **hacer — de algo,** to be secretive about something.
secta *s.f.* sect.
sectario, -a *adj.* 1 sectarian. || *s.m.* y *f.* 2 sectarian, member of a sect.
sectarismo *s.m.* sectarianism.
sector *s.m.* 1 MAT. sector. 2 COM. sector: *el sector público = the public sector.* 3 area; section.
secuaz *s.m.* 1 follower, supporter, partisan. 2 (desp.) henchman, hireling. || *adj.* 3 following, attendant.
secuela *s.f.* 1 consequence, sequel, result. 2 trace, sign.
secuencia *s.f.* sequence.

secuestración *s.f.* 1 sequestration. 2 kidnapping.
secuestrador *s.m.* 1 kidnapper (de personas). 2 hijacker (de aviones).
secuestrar *v.t.* 1 to kidnap, abduct (persona). 2 to hijack (avión). 3 DER. to sieze, confiscate (bienes).
secuestro *s.m.* 1 kidnapping, abduction (de personas). 2 hijacking (de aviones). 3 DER. seizure, confiscation (de bienes).
secular *adj.* 1 century-old, age-old, ancient: *una costumbre secular = an age-old custom.* 2 REL. secular, lay. 3 secular (del siglo).
secularización *s.f.* secularization.
secularizar *v.t.* to secularize.
secundar *v.t.* to second, to support, to help.
secundario, -a *adj.* 1 secondary. 2 minor, secondary, of little importance.
secundinas *s.f.pl.* afterbirth.
secuoya *s.f.* ZOOL. sequoia.
sed *s.f.* 1 thirst, thirstiness; *tenemos sed = we're thirsty.* 2 AGR. drought. 3 (fig.) thirst, hunger, lust: *la sed de venganza = the thirst for revenge; tienen sed de venganza = they thirst for revenge.* 4 **apagar la —,** to quench one's thirst. 5 **dar —,** to make thirsty. 6 **morirse de —,** to be dying of thirst.
seda *s.f.* 1 silk: *seda floja = floss silk.* 2 ZOOL. bristle. 3 **como una —,** easily, smoothly, as smooth as silk. 4 **de —,** silk: *un vestido de seda = a silk dress;* silky, wilken (como la seda). 5 **gusano de —,** silkworm. 6 **— artificial,** artificial silk.
sedal *s.m.* fishing line.
sedante *adj.* y *s.m.* sedative.
sedar *v.t.* (form.) to calm (down), quieten, appease.
sedativo, -a *adj.* sedative.
sede *s.f.* 1 REL. see. 2 seat (de un gobierno). 3 headquarters, central office (de una empresa, etc.). 4 **Santa Sede,** Holy See. 5 **— social,** head office, central office.
sedentario, -a *adj.* sedentary.
sedente *adj.* sitting, seated.
sedeña *s.f.* flaxen tow.
sedeño, -a *adj.* 1 silk, silky, silken. 2 bristly.
sedería *s.f.* 1 silk shop. 2 silk goods, silk stuff, silks. 3 silk trade. 4 silk manufacture, silk raising, sericulture.
sedición *s.f.* sedition.
sedicioso, -a *adj.* 1 seditious, factious, mutinous. || *s.m.* y *f.* 2 rebel. 3 troublemaker. 4 mutineer.
sediento *adj.* 1 thirsty. 2 (fig.) thirsty, eager: *sediento de sangre = blood thirsty.*
sedimentación *s.f.* sedimentation.
sedimentar *v.t.* 1 to deposit, to settle. 2 (fig.) to settle, to calm, to quieten. || *v.r.* 3 to settle. 4 (fig.) to calm down, to settle down.
sedimentario, -a *adj.* sedimentary.
sedimento *s.m.* sediment, deposit.
sedoso, -a *adj.* silky, silken.
seducción *s.f.* 1 seduction (acto). 2 seductiveness, charm, allure, fascination (cualidad).
seducir *v.t.* 1 to seduce (a una mujer). 2 (fig.) to seduce, to tempt, to lead on. 3 (fig.) to charm, to attract, to captivate, to fascinate: *ella seduce a todo el mundo con su sonrisa = she charms everyone with her smile.*
seductivo, -a *adj.* 1 seductive. 2 (fig.) seductive, tempting. 3 (fig.) charming, captivating.
seductor, -ora *adj.* 1 seductive. 2 (fig.) seductive, tempting. 3 (fig.) charming, captivating. || *s.m.* y *f.* 4 seducer.
sefardí o **sefardita** *adj.* 1 Sephardic. || *s.m.* y *f.* 2 Sephardi.
segable *adj.* ready to be reaped.
segadera *s.f.* 1 sickle. 2 scythe.
segadero, -a *adj.* ready for reaping.
segador *s.m.* harvester, reaper.
segar *v.t.* 1 to reap, to cut, to harvest (mies). 2 to mow, to cut (hierbas). 3 to cut off (objeto). 4 (fig.) to cut down, to mow down. 5 (fig.) to ruin, to destroy.
segazón *s.m.* reaping, harvest.
seglar *adj.* 1 secular, lay. || *s.m.* y *f.* 2 layman.
segmentación *s.f.* segmentation.
segmentar *v.t.* to segment.
segmento *s.m.* 1 MAT., ZOOL. segment. 2 TEC. ring: *segmento de émbolo = piston ring.*
segregación *s.f.* 1 segregation, separation. 2 BIOL. secretion. 3 **— racial,** POL. racial segregation, apartheid.
segregacionismo *s.m.* segregationism.
segregacionista *adj./s.m.* y *f.* segregationist.
segregar *v.t.* 1 to segregate, separate. 2 BIOL. to secrete.
segregativo, -a *adj.* segregative.
segueta *s.f.* fretsaw.
seguida *s.f.* 1 following, continuation. 2 **de —,** (form.) continuously, uninterruptedly, without a break. 3 **en —,** immediately, (form.) forthwith, at once, straight away.
seguidamente *adv.* 1 continuously, successively, without a break. 2 straight away, next.
seguidilla *s.f.* LIT. four o seven line stanza.
seguido, -a *adj.* 1 continuous. 2 straight, direct. 3 consecutive, successive. 4 in a row, running, in succession: *ha llegado tarde cuatro días seguidos = he's been late four days running.* || *adv.* 5 straight (on): *vaya todo seguido = go straight on/go straight ahead.* 6 behind, after.
seguidor, -a *adj.* 1 following. || *s.m.* y *f.* 2 follower. 3 DEP. fan, supporter, follower.
seguimiento *s.m.* 1 chase, pursuit. 2 continuation. || 3 **estación de —,** tracking station. 4 **ir en — de,** to go in pursuit of.
seguir *v.t.* 1 to follow. 2 to chase, to pursue. 3 to continue, to carry on. 4 to follow (un consejo), to take. 5 to track (un satélite). 6 to court (a una mujer). 7 to take do, to follow (un cursillo). 8 to hound, chase, to pursue (un animal). 9 to follow (las huellas). 10 to follow, to pursue (una carrera). 11 **— su camino,** to continue on one's way. || *v.i.* 12 to follow, to come next, to come after. 13 to follow on, to continue: *el programa sigue mañana = the programme follows on tomorrow.* 14 to continue, to carry on, to go on: *sigamos = let's go on.* 15 to be still: *¿sigues en la fábrica? = are you still at the factory.* || *v.r.* 16 to follow. 17 to follow, to ensue, to happen in consequence: *de esto se sigue que... = it follows that...* 18 to issue, to spring. 19 **— adelante,** to go straight on, to continue straight ahead. 20 **sigue sin saber el resultado,** he still doesn't know the result; *sigo sin entender = I still don't understand.* 21 **— haciendo algo,** to carry on o go on o continue doing something: *sigue trabajando = go on working.* 22 **seguir de pie,** to remain o stay standing. 23 **como sigue,** as follows. 24 **— en sus trece,** to stick to one's guns. 25 **sigue,** please turn over (en una carta o documento).
según *prep.* 1 according to, depending on: *vendré o no según el trabajo que tenga = I'll come depending on the amount of work I've got.* 2 according to, in accordance with, in line with: *según el protocolo de Montreal = in accordance with the Montreal Protocol.* 3 according to: *según el profesor... = according to the teacher...* || *adv.* 4 as: *podemos hablar según seguimos andando = we can talk as we go on walking.* 5 it depends, it all depends: *lo compraré o no, según = I might or might not buy it, it all depends.* || *conj.* 6 depending on, according to: *según estén las cosas = depending on how things stand.* 7 **— que...,** depending on whether...: *según digan que sí o que no = depending on whether they say yes or no.*
segunda *s.f.* 1 MUS. second. 2 (fig.) double o veiled meaning: *siempre hablaba con segundas = he always spoke with double meanings.* 3 **viajar en —,** to travel (in) second class.
segundar *v.t.* 1 to repeat, do again. || *v.i.* 2 to be/come second.
segundero *adj.* 1 AGR. referring to the second crop of the same plant in one year. || *s.m.* 2 second hand (of a watch).
segundo *adj.* 1 second. || *s.m.* 2 second. 3 **en — lugar,** in the second place. 4 **en un —,** immediately, at once. 5 **sin —,** second to none.
segundón, -ona *s.m.* y *f.* 1 second son. 2 younger son.
segur *s.f.* 1 axe. 2 sickle.
seguramente *adv.* 1 for certain, for sure, certainly. 2 surely. 3 probably. 4 safely, securely.
seguridad *s.f.* 1 safety, security: *medidas de seguridad = security measures.* 2 safeness, safety. 3 certainty. 4 DER. surety, security. 5 sureness, firmness. 6 reliability. 7 **— en carretera,** road safety. 8 —

social, social security. **9 con –,** securely, for certain. **10 cinturón de –,** safety belt. **11 en la – de que,** with the certainty that, knowing that. **12 en la – de hacer algo,** being sure of doing something. **13 en –,** in a safe place, in safety, safe. **14 para mayor –,** to be on the safe side. **15 – en sí mismo,** self confidence. **16 tenga la – de que...,** rest assured that...

seguro, -a *adj.* **1** secure, safe: *un lugar seguro = a safe place.* **2** certain, sure: *estoy seguro de lo que digo = I'm sure of what I'm saying.* **3** firm, solid. **4** reliable, trustworthy. **5** definite, firm (una fecha). **6** stable, steady. **7** securely fastened. **8** (Am.) honest. || *s.m.* **9** insurance: *seguro contra incendios = fire insurance.* **10** safety catch (en armas). **11** safety device. **12** tumbler, catch (en cerraduras). **13** TEC. catch, pawl, ratchet. || *adv.* **14** for sure, for certain. || **15 – a todo riesgo,** fully comprehensive insurance. **16 – contra terceros,** third party insurance. **17 a buen –,** surely. **18 de –,** without a doubt. **19 en –,** in a safe place. **20 ir sobre –,** to be on safe ground.

seis *adj.* **1** six. **2** six o'clock (hora). || *s.m.* **3** (fecha) sixth: *el seis de mayo = the sixth of May, May the sixth,* (EE.UU.) *May sixth.*

seiscientos, -as *adj.* y *s.m.* six hundred.

seísmo o **sismo** *s.m.* earthquake, tremor.

selacio *s.m.* ZOOL. selachian.

selección *s.f.* selection.

seleccionado, -a *adj.* DEP. selected.

seleccionador, -a *s.m.* y *f.* DEP. selector.

seleccionar *v.t.* to select, pick.

selectas *s.f.pl.* analects.

selectividad *s.f.* **1** selectivity. || **2 examen de –,** university entrance exam.

selectivo, -a *adj.* selective.

selecto, -a *adj.* **1** selected (obras literarias). **2** (fig.) select, fine, choice. **3** select, exclusive. **4** the best: *es de lo más selecto = it's of the very best.*

selector *s.m.* selector.

selenio *s.m.* QUIM. selenium.

selenita *s.m.* y *f.* **1** moon dweller, inhabitant of the moon. || *s.f.* **2** selenite.

selenografía *s.f.* ASTR. selenography.

seltz *s.m.* seltzer: *agua de seltz = seltzer water.*

selva *s.f.* **1** jungle, forest, woods. **2** (fig.) jungle: *la ley de la selva = the law of the jungle.* **3 la – amazónica,** GEOG. the Amazon Rain Forest.

selvático, -a *adj.* **1** woodland, forest. **2** BOT. wild.

selvoso, -a *adj.* wooded, forested.

sellador, -ora *s.m.* y *f.* sealer.

selladura *s.f.* sealing; stamping.

sellar *v.t.* **1** to seal; to stamp. **2** to hallmark (joyas). **3** (fig.) to seal: *sellar los labios = to seal one's lips.*

sello *s.m.* **1** rubber stamp (de goma). **2** stamp, seal, mark (señal). **3** stamp (de correos). **4** (fig.) stamp, mark, hallmark. **5** MED. capsule. **6 – de correos,** postage stamp. **7 – aéreo,** airmail stamp. **8 poner el – a un documento,** to stamp a document.

semáforo *s.m.* **1** traffic light. **2** MAR. semaphore. **3** signal (de ferrocarril).

semana *s.f.* **1** week. **2 – inglesa,** five-and-a-half-day working week. **3 entre –,** during the week, mid-week || *atr.* **4 días entre –,** weekdays. **5 fin de –,** weekend. **6 – laboral,** working week.

semanal *adj.* weekly.

semanalmente *adv.* every week, weekly.

semanario, -a *adj.* **1** weekly. || *s.m.* **2** weekly (revista, publicación, etc.).

semántica *s.f.* semantics.

semántico, -a *adj.* semantic.

semblante *s.m.* **1** countenance, face, features. **2** look, appearance, expression. || **3 componer el –,** to regain one's composure. **4** mudar de –, to change colour. **5 tener buen –,** to look well.

semblanza *s.f.* biographical sketch.

sembradera *s.f.* sowing machine.

sembradío, -a *adj.* **1** cultivatable. || *s.m.* **2** arable land.

sembrado *s.m.* sown field/ground.

sembrador *adj.* **1** sowing, seeding. || *s.m.* **2** sower.

sembradora *s.f.* **1** MEC. seed drill. **2** sower (persona).

sembradura *s.f.* sowing, seeding.

sembrar *v.t.* **1** to sow, to seed (un terreno): *un campo sembrado de trigo = a field sown with corn.* **2** to sow (semillas). **3** (fig.) to sow, to spread: *sembrar cizaña entre... = to sow discord among...* **4** to spread (noticias). **5** (fig.) to scatter, to strew, to sprinkle. || **6 quien siembra recoge,** one reaps what one has sown.

sembrío *s.m.* (Am.) sown field.

semejante *adj.* **1** similar, alike, the same. **2** similar, such: *nunca he visto semejante caso = I've never seen such a case.* **3** MAT. similar. **4 – a,** like. **5** (Am.) huge, enormous. || *s.m.* **6** fellowman, fellow creature. **7** likeness, resemblance, equal.

semejanza *s.f.* **1** similarity. **2** resemblance, likeness, similarity. || **3 a – de,** like, after, as. **4 – de familia,** family likeness. **5 tener – con,** to bear a resemblance to, look like.

semejar *v.i.* **1** to resemble, be like, look like. || *v.r.* **2** to be alike, be similar, resemble each other. || **3 semejarse a,** to resemble, look like.

semejas *s.f.pl.* (Am.) similarity, resemblance.

semen *s.m.* semen.

semental *adj.* **1** seminal, germinal. **2** breeding, stud (animal). || *s.m.* **3** sire, stud animal, stallion.

sementar *v.t.* to sow.

sementera *s.f.* **1** sowing, seeding. **2** sown land. **3** sowing season, seedtime. **4** seed bed, seed plot. **5 una – de,** (fig.) a breeding ground for, a hotbed of.

semestral *adj.* half-yearly, biannual.

semestralmente *adv.* half-yearly, biannually.

semestre *s.m.* **1** period of six months. **2** (EE.UU.) semester (en la universidad). **3** COM. half-yearly payment.

semibreve *s.f.* MUS. semibreve, (EE.UU.) whole note.

semicilindro *s.m.* semicylinder, half cylinder.

semicircular *adj.* semicircular.

semicírculo *s.m.* semicircle.

semiconsciente *adj.* half-conscious, semiconscious.

semicorchea *s.f.* MUS. semiquaver.

semicultismo *s.m.* semilearned word, half-learned word.

semidifunto *adj.* half-dead, almost dead.

semidiós *s.m.* demigod.

semidormido *adj.* half-asleep.

semiesfera *s.f.* hemisphere.

semiesférico *adj.* hemispherical.

semifinal *s.f.* semifinal.

semifinalista *adj.* **1** semifinal. || *s.m.* y *f.* **2** semifinalist.

semilla *s.f.* **1** BOT. seed. **2** (fig.) cause, origin, source. **3** (Am.) baby, child.

semillero *s.m.* **1** nursery, seedbed. || **2 un – de,** (fig.) a hotbed of, a breeding ground for.

semimedio *s.m.* DEP. welterweight.

seminal *adj.* seminal.

seminario *s.m.* **1** REL. seminary. **2** seminar (de investigación).

seminarista *s.m.* seminarist.

seminífero, -a *adj.* ANAT. seminiferous.

semiología *s.f.* semiology, semeiology.

semiotica *s.f.* semiotics.

semipesado, -a *adj.* y *s.m.* DEP. light heavyweight.

semita *adj.* **1** semitic. || *s.m.* y *f.* **2** Semite.

semítico, -a *adj.* semitic.

semitismo *s.m.* semitism.

semitista *s.m.* y *f.* semitist.

semivocal *s.f.* semivowel.

sémola *s.f.* semolina.

sempiterno, -a *adj.* eternal, everlasting.

senado *s.m.* **1** senate. **2** (fig.) assembly, gathering.

senadoconsulto *s.m.* senatorial decree.

senador, -ora *s.m.* y *f.* POL. senator.

senaduría *s.f.* senatorship.

senario, -a *adj.* **1** senary. || *s.m.* **2** senarius.

senatorial o **senatorio, -a** *adj.* senatorial.

sencillez *s.f.* **1** simplicity, plainness: *siempre se expresaba con mucha sencillez = he always expressed himself with great simplicity.* **2** naturalness, unaffectedness, simplicity.

sencillo *adj.* **1** simple, plain. **2** easy, simple. **3** unaffected, natural, unsophisticated, unadorned. **4** harmless, guileless, simple. **5** naïve, ingenuous, gullible. **6** single (billete de tren, etc.). || *s.m.* **7** (Am.) small change, loose change.

senda *s.f.* path, footpath, track.

sendos *adj.pl.* each, both (of them): *llegaron su padre y su hermano en sendos coches = his father and his brother arrived each by car; llevaban sendos trajes = they each wore a suit, they were both wearing suits.*

senectitud *s.f.* old age.

senil *adj.* senile.

senilidad *s.f.* senility.
sénior *adj.* y *s.m.* y *f.* senior.
seno *s.m.* 1 bosom, breast. 2 lap (regazo). 3 womb. 4 cavity, hollow, hole. 5 (fig.) bosom. 6 ANAT. sinus: *seno frontal = frontal sinus.* 7 GEOG. gulf, bay, inlet. 8 MAR. trough. 9 MAT. sine.
sensación *s.f.* 1 feeling, sensation (del sentido). 2 sensation (gran noticia). 3 emotion.
sensacional *adj.* sensational.
sensacionalismo *s.m.* sensationalism.
sensacionalista *adj.* sensationalist.
sensatez *s.f.* 1 sensibleness, good sense, sense. 2 wisdom, sense.
sensato, -a *adj.* sensible, wise.
sensibilidad *s.f.* 1 sensitivity, sensitiveness, feeling. 2 sensibility.
sensibilización *s.f.* FOT. sensitization.
sensibilizar *v.t.* FOT. to sensitize.
sensible *adj.* 1 sensitive. 2 perceptible, sensible, appreciable, noticeable. 3 sentient, feeling: *un ser sensible = a sentient being.* 4 grievous, lamentable, regrettable. 5 sensitive, emotional, impressionable. 6 FOT. sensitive. || 7 **— de,** capable of. 8 **ser — de,** (form.) to be conscious of.
sensiblemente *adj.* appreciably, perceptively, noticeably.
sensiblería *s.f.* 1 sentimentality, sentimentalism. 2 (fam.) sloppiness, mushiness.
sensiblero *adj.* 1 sentimental. 2 (fam.) sloppy, mushy.
sensitiva *s.f.* BOT. mimosa.
sensitivo, -a *adj.* 1 sentient. 2 sense (*atr.*): *órgano sensitivo = sense organ.* 3 sensitive.
sensorio, -a *adj.* 1 sensorial, sensory. || *s.m.* 2 sensorium.
sensorial *adj.* sensorial.
sensual *adj.* 1 sensual. 2 sensuous. 3 (Am.) attractive.
sensualidad *s.f.* 1 sensuality. 2 sensuousness.
sensualismo *s.m.* sensualism.
sensualista *adj.* 1 sensualistic. || *s.m.* y *f.* sensualist.
sentada *s.f.* 1 sitting. 2 sit-in. 3 sit-down strike. || 4 **de una —,** in one go.
sentado, -a *adj.* 1 sitting, seated: *está sentado = he's sitting (down).* 2 judicious, sedate. 3 BOT. sessile. 4 settled, established. 5 (persona) steady, sensible, prudent. 6 **dar algo por —,** to take something for granted. 7 **dejar — que...,** to make it clear that...
sentar *v.t.* 1 (a una persona) to sit, seat. 2 to set, place (un objeto). || *v.t.* e *i.* 3 to suit, become: *ese color te sienta bien = that colour suits you.* 4 to fit: *el pantalón te sienta bien = the trousers fit you well.* 5 to agree with (comida): *me sienta mal el pepino = cucumber disagrees (o doesn't agree) with me.* 6 (fig.) to go down, like, appreciate: *le sentó mal lo que dije = he didn't appreciate what I said, what I said didn't go down too well with him.* || *v.pron.* 7 to sit, sit down. 8 to settle, become steady. || 9 **— la cabeza,** to calm down. 10 **— las bases de,** to lay the foundations of. 11 **— por escrito,** to put down in writing.
sentencia *s.f.* 1 DER. sentence. 2 decision, ruling. 3 maxim, saying, axiom. || 4 **dictar —,** to pass sentence. 5 **— de muerte,** death sentence. 6 **— firme,** final judgement.
sentenciar *v.t.* 1 DER. to sentence. 2 to judge. 3 (Am.) **— a uno,** to swear vengeance against. || *v.i.* 4 to give one's opinion.
sentencioso, -a *adj.* sententious.
sentido, -a *adj.* 1 deeply felt, regrettable. 2 sincere, deeply felt, deep: *mi más sentido pésame = my deepest sympathy, my sincere condolences.* 3 (fig.) sensitive, touchy, easily hurt. 4 (Am.) with sharp hearing. || *s.m.* 5 sense: *el sentido del olfato = the sense of smell.* 6 (fig.) sense, discernment. 7 meaning, sense: *la expresión tiene dos sentidos = the expression has two meanings.* 8 feeling: *tiene sentido de la pintura = he has a feeling for painting.* 9 (Am.) ear. 10 direction, way: *una calle de sentido único = a one-way street; en sentido contrario = in the opposite direction.* 11 **con los cinco sentidos,** for all one's worth. 12 **poner los cinco sentidos en algo,** to give one's full attention to something. 13 **costar un —,** to cost the earth, cost a fortune. 14 **perder el —,** to lose consciousness, faint. 15 **— común,** common sense. 16 **sin —,** unconscious, senseless; meaningless. 17 **tener —,** to make sense. 18 **recobrar —,** to regain consciousness.
sentimental *adj.* 1 sentimental. 2 **aventura —,** love affair.
sentimentalismo *s.m.* sentimentalism, sentimentality.
sentimentero, -a *adj.* (Am.) mushy, sloppy.
sentimiento *s.m.* 1 feeling, sentiment. 2 regret, sorrow, grief. 3 sense: *un sentimiento de responsabilidad = a sense of responsibility.* 4 **le acompaño en el —,** my deepest sympathy. 5 **herir los sentimientos de uno,** to hurt someone's feelings.
sentina *s.f.* 1 MAR. bilge. 2 (fig.) sewer, den of iniquity.
sentir *v.t.* 1 to feel. 2 to hear. 3 to perceive, to sense. 4 to feel, to sense, to have the feeling (that). 5 to have a feeling for (la música, poesía, etc.). 6 to be o feel sorry, to regret: *lo siento = I'm sorry.* 7 to suffer, to feel the effect of (una enfermedad). || *v.pron.* 8 to feel. 9 (Am.) to get angry. || *s.m.* 10 feeling. 11 opinion, judgment: *a mi sentir = in my opinion.* 12 **dar que —,** to give cause for regret. 13 **sentirse como en su casa,** to feel at home.
seña *s.f.* 1 sign, signal. 2 (fig.) sign, token. 3 MIL. password. 4 mark. || *s.f.pl.* 5 address. 6 **señas mortales,** unmistakable signs. 8 **santo y —,** password. 9 **hablar por señas,** to talk in sign language. 10 **dar señas de,** to show signs of. 11 **hacer una — a alguien para que...,** to signal to someone to... 12 **por las señas,** so it seems.
señal *s.f.* 1 signal. 2 sign, indication. 3 mark. 4 scar, mark (cicatriz). 5 MED. symptom. 6 trace, vestige. 7 COM. deposit, token payment. 8 (por teléfono) dialling tone, tone: *señal de ocupado = engaged tone/*(EE.UU.) *busy signal.* 9 **en — de,** as a token of, as a sign of. 10 **dar señales de,** to show signs of. 11 **hacer la — de la cruz,** to make the sign of the cross. 12 **señales de tráfico,** traffic o road signs. 13 **sin dejar —,** without a trace.
señaladamente *adv.* 1 especially, expressly. 2 clearly, distinctly.
señalado, -a *adj.* 1 distinct, clear. 2 exceptional. 3 appointed. 4 noticeable, marked. 5 marked, scarred. 6 famous, distinguished.
señalar *v.t.* 1 to mark. 2 to point to, to show. 3 to point out, to call someone's attention to. 4 to mark, to denote. 5 to set, to fix. 6 to scar, to mark. 7 to appoint, to designate. || *v.pron.* 8 to stand out, to distinguish oneself.
señalización *s.f.* 1 signposting. 2 road signs.
señalizar *v.t.* to signpost.
señero *adj.* 1 unique, unequalled. 2 (fig.) outstanding.
señor *adj.* 1 distinguished, noble. 2 (fig.) some, fine, really big: *nos sirvieron una señora trucha = they served us a really big trout; ¡eso es un señor tomate! = that's some tomato!* || *s.m.* 3 man, gentleman. 4 Mr.: *el señor Sánchez = Mr. Sánchez.* 5 Sir: *buenos días, señor = good morning, Sir.* 6 owner, master: *el señor de la casa = the master of the household.* 7 lord, noble. 8 REL. *Nuestro Señor = The Lord/Our Lord.* || 9 **estimado —/muy — mío,** Dear Sir. 10 **¡sí —!,** yes, indeed! it certainly is (does, etc.).
señora *s.f.* 1 lady, woman. 2 Mrs.: *la señora de Anaya = Mrs. Anaya.* 3 Madam: *buenos días señora = good morning Madam.* 4 wife. 5 REL. **Nuestra Señora,** Our Lady, the Virgin Mary. 6 **muy — mía** o **estimada —,** Dear Madam. 7 **¡Señores y Señoras!,** Ladies and Gentlemen!
señorear *v.t.* 1 to rule, to domineer. 2 (pasiones) to control, to master. || *v.r.* 3 to control oneself. 4 to seize (control) of.
señoría *s.f.* 1 lordship, ladyship. 2 rule, sway, dominion. 3 government of a particular state. 4 senate. 5 **Su Señoría,** your o his lordship, your o her ladyship; my lord, my lady.
señorial *adj.* 1 lordly. 2 aristocratic, stately: *una casa señorial = a stately home.* 3 elegant. 4 gentlemanly.
señorío *s.m.* 1 dominion, rule, sway. 2 manor, estate, domain. 3 nobility. 4 dignity, lordliness, majesty. 5 distinguished people, (fam.) toffs. 6 (de las pasiones) control, mastery.
señorita *s.f.* 1 young lady. 2 Miss: *la señorita Hernández = Miss Hernández.* 3 (Am.) school teacher.

señoritingo, -a *s.m.* y *f.* rich little daddy's boy or girl.
señorito *s.m.* 1 young gentleman. 2 master (of the house). 3 (desp.) playboy. 4 (fam.) toff, dandy, nob.
señorón, -ona *adj.* 1 distinguished, lordly. || *s.m.* 2 (fam.) big shot.
señuelo *s.m.* 1 lure. 2 (fig.) bait, trap. 3 (Am.) leading steer.
seo *s.f.* cathedral.
sépalo *s.m.* BOT. sepal.
separable *adj.* 1 separable. 2 TEC. detachable, removable.
separación *s.f.* 1 separation. 2 TEC. removal. 3 gap, space. || 4 **— matrimonial,** legal separation. 5 **— racial,** racial segregation.
separadamente *adv.* separately.
separado, -a *adj.* 1 separated: *estoy separado de mi mujer = I'm separated from my wife.* 2 separate: *duermen en camas separadas = they sleep in separate beds.* 3 TEC. detached. 4 **por —,** separately.
separar *v.t.* 1 to separate. 2 to move away, to remove, to take away: *separa la planta de la ventana = move the plant away from the window.* 3 to put aside, to keep: *separé un pastel para ti = I put a cake aside for you.* 4 TEC. to detach, to remove. 5 to separate, to pull apart: *si no los hubiéramos separado se habrían matado = if we hadn't pulled them apart they would have killed each other.* 6 (a una persona de su puesto) to dismiss, to remove. 7 to keep away: *mi trabajo me separa de mi casa durante meses enteros = my job keeps me away from home for months at a time.* || *v.pron.* 8 to separate, to part company. 9 to leave: *se separó de su marido el año pasado = she left her husband last year.* 10 to cut oneself off: *se ha separado de todos sus amigos = he's cut himself off from all his friends.* 11 to come away: *el papel se está separando de la pared = the paper is coming away from the wall.* 12 DER. to withdraw. 13 POL. to secede.
separata *s.f.* offprint.
separatismo *s.m.* separatism.
separatista *adj.* y *s.m.* y *f.* separatist.
sepelio *s.m.* (form.) burial, interment.
sepia *s.f.* 1 sepia. 2 ZOOL. cuttlefish.
septenario, -a *adj.* 1 septenary. || *s.m.* 2 septenaries.
septentrion *s.m.* 1 ASTR. Great Bear. 2 North.
septentrional *adj.* northern, north.
septicemia *s.f.* MED. septicaemia.
septiembre o **setiembre** *s.m.* September.
séptimo, -a *adj./s.m.* y *f.* 1 seventh. 2 the seventh: *Enrique VII = Henry the seventh.* || *s.f.* 3 MUS. seventh. 4 **la séptima parte,** one seventh.
septingentésimo, -a *adj.* seven hundredth.
septuagenario, -a *adj.* 1 septuagenarian, seventy-year-old. || *s.m.* y *f.* 2 person in his seventies, seventy-tear-old.
septuagésimo, -a *adj.* seventieth.
septuplicar *v.t.* to septuple, multiply by seven.
séptuplo *adj.* sevenfold.
sepulcral *adj.* 1 sepulchral. 2 (fig.) deathly, sepulchral, gloomy. || 3 **lápida —,** gravestone, tombstone.
sepulcro *s.m.* 1 tomb, grave, sepulchre, (EE.UU.) sepulcher. || 2 **el Santo Sepulcro,** the Holy Sepulchre. 3 **— blanqueado,** whited sepulchre.
sepultador *s.m.* gravedigger.
sepultar *v.t.* 1 to bury, entomb. 2 (en una mina) to trap. 3 (fig.) to hide, conceal, bury: *sepultado en sus pensamientos = buried in thought.*
sepulto, -a *adj.* buried.
sepultura *s.f.* 1 burial (el acto). 2 tomb, grave. || 3 **dar — a,** to bury. 4 **recibir —,** to be buried.
sepulturero *s.m.* gravedigger.
sequedad *s.f.* 1 dryness. 2 (fig.) abruptness, curtness, bluntness.
sequedal o **sequeral** *s.m.* dry land.
sequía *s.f.* 1 drought, dry season. 2 (Am.) thirst.
séquito *s.m.* 1 entourage, retinue. 2 POL. adherents. 3 aftermath, train (de acontecimientos).
ser *s.m.* 1 being: *un ser humano = a human being.* 2 existence, life: *dar el ser = to give life, bring into the world.* 3 essence. 4 **en lo más íntimo de mi ser,** in my innermost being, deep down inside, in my heart of hearts. 5 **un — vivo,** a living creature. || *v.i.* 6 to be: *ser o no ser = to be or not to be.* 7 to be, to happen: *¿qué ha sido? = what was it?/what happened?* 8 to be, to belong: *el coche es de Juan = the car is Juan's, the car belongs to Juan.* 9 to be, to make: *tres y dos son cinco = three and two makes five.* 10 to be, to cost: *¿cuánto es el kilo de manzanas? = how much is a kilo of apples?* 11 to be, to come: *soy de Salamanca = I'm from Salamanca.* 12 **como debe —,** as it should be. 13 **¿cómo es que...?,** how come...? how is it that...? 14 **con —,** in spite of being. 15 **érase que se era,** once upon a time. 16 **es más,** what's more. 17 **por si fuera poco,** to top it all. 18 **puede —,** perhaps. 19 **¿quién es?,** who's speaking?, who is it?
sera *s.f.* pannier, basket.
seráficamente *adv.* angelically, like an angel.
seráfico, -a *adj.* angelic, seraphic.
serafín *s.m.* 1 REL. seraph. 2 (fam.) angel.
serenar *v.t.* 1 to calm (el mar). 2 (fig.) to calm down, to pacify. 3 to clarify, settle (un líquido). || *v.i.* 4 (Am.) to drizzle. || *v.pron.* 5 to calm down, to calm oneself. 6 to grow calm (el mar). 7 to settle, to clear (un líquido).
serenata *s.f.* MUS. serenade.
serenera *s.f.* cape, wrap.
serenísimo, -a *adj.* serene: *Su Alteza Serenísima = His Serene Highness.*
sereno, -a *adj.* 1 calm, serene, tranquil (persona). 2 tine, settled (el tiempo); clear, cloudless (el cielo). 3 peaceful, quiet, calm (un ambiente). 4 (fam.) sober. || *s.m.* 5 night watchman. 6 night dew, cool night air. || 7 **al —,** in the open air: *dormir al sereno = to sleep out in the open.*
serial *s.m.* serial.
seriar *v.t.* to arrange in series.
serie *s.f.* 1 series. 2 MAT. series. 3 (fig.) string, series, succession. || 4 **artículos fuera de —,** oddments, remnants. 5 **en —,** mass-produced. 6 **fuera de —,** out of the ordinary, special.
seriedad *s.f.* 1 seriousness. 2 gravity, solemnity. 3 staidness. 4 reliability, dependability, trustworthiness. 5 honesty, straightness. 6 sense of propriety. 7 gravity, seriousness (de una enfermedad, crisis, etc.). || 8 **falta de —,** frivolity, irresponsibility.
sérif, chérif o **shérif** *s.m.* sheriff.
serigrafía *s.f.* serigraphy, silk screen process.
serio, -a *adj.* 1 serious. 2 grave, solemn. 3 staid. 4 reliable, dependable, trustworthy. 5 honest. 6 proper. 7 grave, serious (de una crisis, etc.). 8 **hablar en —,** to speak seriously, be serious. 9 **ponerse —,** to look serious, become serious. 10 **poco —,** frivolous, irresponsible, unreliable. 11 **tomar en —,** to take seriously. 12 **mantenerse —,** to keep a straight face.
sermón *s.m.* sermon.
sermoneador, -a *adj.* 1 fault-finding. || *s.m.* 2 fault-finder. 3 sermonizer.
sermonear *v.t.* (fam.) 1 to lecture. 2 to preach. || *v.i.* 3 to sermonize.
sermoneo *s.m.* sermon, lecture.
serosidad *s.f.* serosity.
seroso, -a *adj.* serous.
serpenteante *adj.* 1 winding, twisting. 2 meandering, winding (río).
serpentear *v.i.* 1 ZOOL. to slither, to wriggle. 2 (fig.) to wind, to twist and turn (un camino). 3 (fig.) to meander, to wind (un río).
serpenteo *s.m.* 1 slithering, wriggling. 2 winding, twisting. 3 meandering, winding (un río).
serpentín *s.m.* 1 coil. 2 worm.
serpentino, -a *adj.* 1 snaky. 2 serpentine. 3 winding, meandering.
serpiente *s.f.* 1 ZOOL. snake, serpent. 2 (fig.) snake, snake in the grass (una persona). || 3 **— boa,** ZOOL. boa constrictor. 4 **— cascabel,** ZOOL. rattlesnake. 5 **— de mar,** sea serpent. 6 **— de anteojo,** ZOOL. cobra. 7 **— pitón,** ZOOL. python. 8 **— de vidrio,** slow worm.
serpollo *s.m.* shoot.
serrado, -a *adj.* 1 serrated. 2 jagged, uneven.
serraduras *s.f.pl.* sawdust.
serrallo *s.m.* harem, seraglio.
serranía *s.f.* mountains, mountain range, mountainous country.
serranilla *s.f.* LIT. lyric composition.
serrano, -a *adj.* 1 mountain, highland. || *s.m.* 2 highlander. || 3 **jamón —,** cured ham.
serrar *v.t.* to saw.
serrería *s.f.* sawmill.
serreta *s.f.* small saw.
serrín o **aserrín** *s.m.* sawdust.

serruchar *v.t.* (Am.) to saw.
serrucho *s.m.* 1 handsaw, saw. 2 (Am.) whore.
servible *adj.* serviceable, usable.
servicial *adj.* helpful, obliging.
servicio *s.m.* 1 service. 2 servants; domestic help. 3 service, set (juego): *un servicio de mesa = a dinner service.* 4 service charge, service. 5 serve, service (en el tenis). 6 REL. service. || *s.m.pl.* 7 toilet, lavatory; (EE.UU.) rest room. || 9 **hacer un flaco — a uno,** to play a dirty trick on someone. 10 **poner en —,** to put into operation. 11 **prestar —,** to serve. 12 **— a domicilio,** home delivery service. 13 **— de información,** MIL. intelligence service.
servidor *s.m.* 1 servant. 2 your humble servant. || *interj.* 3 present! (en clase). || 4 **— de usted,** at your service. 5 **su seguro —,** yours faithfully, your humble servant (en una carta, al final).
servidumbre *s.f.* 1 servants, staff. 2 servitude. 3 DER. obligation. || 4 **— de la gleba,** HIST. serfdom. 5 **— de paso,** right of way.
servil *adj.* 1 servile. 2 menial (un trabajo). 3 abject, base. 4 slavish (imitación o similar).
servilismo *s.m.* 1 servility. 2 submissiveness. 3 (fig.) subservience.
servilleta *s.f.* serviette, napkin.
servilletero *s.m.* serviette ring, napkin ring.
serviola *s.f.* MAR. cathead.
servir *v.t.* 1 to serve: *servir a la patria = to serve one's country.* 2 to serve, to wait on (en un restaurante). 3 to be of service, to help: *¿en qué le puedo servir? = what can I do for you?* 4 to tend, to man, to mind (una máquina). 5 to serve (en el tenis). 6 REL. to serve. 7 to serve up (comida); to pour (out) (bebida): *¿sirvo yo las patatas? = shall I serve out the potatoes?* || *v.i.* 8 (en el ejército) to serve; to do one's military service (servicio militar). 9 to be in service (doméstico). 10 to serve, wait (en un restaurante). 11 to serve, be useful: *eso no sirve para nada = that's useless/that's of no use at all/that's no good.* 12 to follow suit (en un juego de naipes). || *v.pron.* 13 to help/serve oneself: *sírvete albóndigas = help yourself to meat balls.* 14 to be kind enough: *sírvase decirme sus señas = would you be kind enough to tell me your address.* || 15 **para servirle,** at your service. 16 **— de,** to serve as, to act as: *la bandeja puede servir de mesa = the tray can serve as a table.* 17 **— para,** to be good at: *yo no sirvo para enseñar = I'm no good at teaching.* 18 **servirse de algo, to use something,** make use of something: *algunos se sirven de su cargo para conseguir lo que quieren = some people use their position to get what they want.*
servofreno *s.m.* servo brakes.
servomotor *s.m.* servomotor.
sésamo *s.m.* 1 BOT. sesame. || 2 **¡ábrete —!,** open sesame!
sesear *v.i.* to pronounce c (before e or i) and z as s.
sesenta *adj.* 1 sixty. 2 sixtieth. || *s.m.* 3 sixty.
sesentón, -ona *adj.* 1 in one's sixties, sixty-year-old. || *s.m.* 2 sixty-year-old (person), man in his sixties. || *s.f.* 3 woman in her sixties.
seseo *s.m.* pronunciation of c (before e and i) and z as s.
sesera *s.f.* 1 ANAT. brainpan. 2 (fam.) grey matter, brains.
sesgadamente *adv.* on the bias, on a slant.
sesgado *adj.* 1 slanted, slanting. 2 cut on the bias (en costura).
sesgadura *s.f.* cut on the bias.
sesgar *v.t.* 1 to cut on the bias, cut on a slant (en costura). 2 TEC. to bevel. 3 to slant, slope; to put askew, skew.
sesgo, -a *adj.* 1 cut o placed askew. 2 slanting, slanted. || *s.m.* 3 bias (en costura). 4 slant, slope. 5 TEC. bevel. 6 (fig.) turn, direction. 7 **al —,** on the bias. 8 (fam.) dodge, subterfuge.
sesión *s.f.* 1 session, sitting, meeting. 2 performance, show (del teatro). 3 showing (delcine): *sesión continua = continuous showing.* || 4 **abrir la —,** to open the meeting. 5 **en — pública,** in public meeting. 6 **levantar la —,** to adjourn-/close the meeting. 7 **— de espiritismo,** séance.
sesionar *v.i.* (Am.) to meet.
seso *s.m.* 1 ANAT. brain. 2 (fig.) brains, grey matter, intelligence. || *s.m.pl.* 3 brains (en cocina). 4 **calentarse o devanarse los sesos,** to rack one's brains. 5 **perder el —,** to lose one's head, go off one's head. 6 **tener sorbido el — a uno,** to be crazy about something: *el proyecto le tiene sorbido el seso = he's crazy about the plan.*
sestear *v.i.* 1 to take a nap, to have a siesta. 2 to rest in the shade (el ganado).
sesteo *s.m.* (Am.) nap, siesta.
sesudo, -a *adj.* 1 wise, sensible. 2 brainy. 3 (Am.) stubborn.
seta *s.f.* BOT. mushroom (wild).
setecientos, -as *adj.* y *s.m.* seven hundred.
setenta *adj.* 1 seventy. 2 seventieth. || *s.m.* 3 seventy.
setentón, -ona *adj.* 1 seventy-year-old, in one's seventies. || *s.m.* 2 seventy-year-old, man in his seventies. || *s.f.* 3 woman in her seventies.
setiembre *s.m.* September.
seto *s.m.* 1 hedge. 2 fence.
seudónimo *adj.* 1 pseudonymous. || *s.m.* 2 pseudonym, pen name: *escribe con seudónimo = he writes under a pen name.*
seudópodo *s.m.* ZOOL. pseudopod.
severidad *s.f.* 1 severity, strictness. 2 sternness, grimness (de expresión).
severo, -a *adj.* 1 severe, harsh. 2 (un padre o profesor) strict. 3 (una expresión) stern, grim, harsh. 4 (un invierno) harsh, hard, bleak; bitter (el frío).
sevicia *s.f.* cruelty, brutality.
sexagenario, -a *adj.* 1 sexagenarian, sixty-year-old. || *s.m.* 2 sexagenarian, man in his sixties. || *s.f.* woman in her sixties.
sexagésimo *adj.* sixtieth.
sexo *s.m.* 1 sex. || 2 **el bello —,** the fair sex. 3 **el — débil,** the weaker sex. 4 **el — fuerte,** the stronger sex.
sextante *s.m.* sextant.
sexteto *s.m.* sextet, sextette.
sexto, -a *adj.* y *s.m.* sixth; the sixth.
sextuplicar *v.t.* 1 to sextuple, to multiply by six. || *v.pron.* 2 to sextuple, to increase sixfold.
séxtuplo, -a *adj.* sixfold.
sexuado, -a *adj.* BIOL. sexed.
sexual *adj.* 1 sexual: *relaciones sexuales = sexual relations.* 2 sex: *vida sexual = sex life; órganos sexuales = sex organs.*
sexualidad *s.f.* sexuality.
sexualmente *adv.* sexually.
sexy *s.m.* sex appeal.
sha V. **sa.**
shérif V. **sérif.**
shock V. **choc.**
short *s.m.* shorts.
show *s.m.* show.
si *conj.* 1 if: *si te vas, me moriré = if you go, I'll die.* 2 whether: *dime si me quieres o no = tell me whether you love me or not.* 3 but (con sorpresa): *si no te has lavado! = ¡but you haven't washed!*
sí *adv.* 1 yes. || *s.m.* 2 aye. || 3 **dar el —,** to agree, to consent.
siamés, -esa *adj./s.m.* y *f.* 1 Thai. 2 siamese twin.
sibarita *adj.* 1 sybaritic. || *s.m.* y *f.* 2 sybarite.
sibaritismo *s.m.* sybaritism, love of luxury.
sibila *s.f.* sibyl, prophetess.
sibilante *adj.* 1 sibilant (sonido). || *s.f.* 2 FON. sibilant.
sibilino, -a *adj.* 1 mysterious. 2 that can be interpreted in different ways.
sic *adv.* sic (normalmente entre paréntesis).
sicario *s.m.* hired assassin.
sico- V. **psico.**
sicoanálisis V. **psicoanálisis.**
sicofanta o **sicofante** *s.m.* slanderer.
sicología V. **psicología.**
sicomoro *s.m.* BOT. sycamore.
sicopatía V. **psicopatía.**
sicosis V. **psicosis.**
sicoterapia V. **psicoterapia.**
sidecar *s.m.* sidecar.
sideral *adj.* ASTR. astral, sidereal.
siderurgia *s.f.* iron and steel industry.
siderúrgico, -a *adj.* iron and steel: *industria siderúrgica = iron and steel industry.*
sidra *s.f.* cider.
sidrería *s.f.* cider shop.
siega *s.f.* AGR. 1 harvesting, reaping (acción). 2 harvest time (tiempo). 3 crop, harvest (cantidad segada).
siembra *s.f.* AGR. 1 sowing (acción). 2 sowing time. 3 sowd land, sown land.

siempre *adv.* 1 always, all the time. || 2 **desde —,** always: *lo he sabido desde siempre = I've always known that.* 3 **— que, a)** as long as; **b)** every time; whenever: *siempre que te veo llevas el mismo vestido = every time I see you you're wearing the same dress.* 4 **— y cuando,** as long as.
siempreviva *s.f.* BOT. everlasting flower.
sien *s.f.* ANAT. temple.
siena *s.m.* sienna (color).
sierpe *s.f.* 1 serpent. 2 (fig.) fierce person; ugly-looking person. 3 anything that wriggles. 4 BOT. sprout, shoot (vástago que aparece en raíces leñosas).
sierra *s.f.* 1 MEC. saw. 2 GEOG. mountain range, sierra.
siervo, -a *s.m.* y *f.* 1 slave (esclavo). 2 (fig.) servant (uno se llama así a sí mismo por humildad). || 3 **— de la gleba,** HIST. serf.
siesta *s.f.* nap, afternoon nap.
siete *s.m.* 1 seven. 2 tear (roto). || *adj.* 3 seventh.
sietemesino, -a *adj.* y *s.m.* y *f.* premature; premature baby (prematuro).
sífilis *s.f.* MED. v.d., syphilis.
sifilítico, -a *adj.* MED. syphilitic.
sifón *s.m.* 1 MEC. U-bend, trap (en un sistema de tuberías). 2 siphon, syphon, syphon bottle (botella). 3 soda water (agua). 4 BIOL. feeler (extremidad de algunos moluscos).
sigilar *v.t.* 1 to conceal, to keep secret (mantener secreto). 2 to seal, to stamp (sellar).
sigilo *s.m.* 1 secrecy; stealth (secreto). 2 discretion, prudence. 3 stamp, seal (sello).
sigilosamente *adv.* 1 secretly, stealthily (con secreto). 2 prudently, discreetly (con discreción).
sigiloso, -a *adj.* 1 secret, stealthy (secreto). 2 prudent, discreet (discreto).
sigla *s.f.* acronym; abbreviation.
siglo *s.m.* 1 century. 2 (fig.) ages, a long time: *te he esperado un siglo = I have been waiting for you for ages.* 3 secular life, wordly matters (la vida de este mundo). || 4 **por los siglos de los siglos,** for ever and ever, eternally.
signar *v.t.* 1 to sign (firmar). 2 to mark. || *v.t.* y *pron.* 3 REL. to cross oneself, to make the sign of the cross.
signatorio, -a *adj.* y *s.m.* y *f.* signatory.
signatura *s.f.* catalogue number (de un libro en biblioteca).
significación *s.f.* 1 signification, meaning (significado). 2 importance, significance (importancia).
significado, -a *p.p.* 1 de **significar.** || *adj.* 2 significant, important (importante). || *s.m.* 3 signification, meaning. 4 FILOL. signification.
significante *s.m.* FILOL. significant.
significar *v.t.* 1 to mean: *¿qué significa esta palabra? = what does this word mean?* 2 to express: *quiero significarle mis respetos = I want to express my respect towards you.* || *v.i.* 3 to have importance, to mean: *esto no significa nada = this has no importance.* || *v.pron.* 4 to become famous, to become well-known (hacerse famoso o conocido).
significativo, -a *adj.* significant.
signo *s.m.* 1 symbol, sign, mark: *signo de los tiempos = sign of the times.* 2 MAT. sign. 3 sign (del Zodíaco). 4 FILOL. symbol, sign. 5 REL. sign of the cross. 6 fate (destino).
siguiente *adj.* following, next: *el día siguiente = the following day.*
sílaba *s.f.* syllable.
silabario *s.m.* spelling book (libro para aprender ortografía).
silabear o **silabar** *v.i.* to speak slowly, to speak making each syllable.
silabeo *s.m.* slow way of speaking.
silábico, -a *adj.* syllabic.
silba *s.f.* hissing, booing.
silbante V. **sibilante.**
silbar *v.i.* 1 to whistle. || *v.t.* e *i.* 2 to hiss, to jeer (burlándose).
silbato *s.m.* whistle.
silbido *s.m.* 1 whistling, whistle. 2 hiss, hissing (de la serpiente). 3 whizzing (especialmente de una bala).
silenciador *s.m.* 1 silencer (de pistola). 2 MEC. silencer (de automóvil).
silenciar *v.t.* 1 to silence, to make silent. 2 to keep silent (no mencionar).
silencio *s.m.* 1 silence. 2 silence, quietness. 3 MUS. rest. || 4 **pasar en — una cosa,** to keep mum about something, to keep silent about something.
silenciosamente *adv.* silently, quietly.
silencioso, -a *adj.* silent, quiet.
silex *s.m.* MIN. flint, silex.
sílfide *s.f.* sylph.
silicato *s.m.* QUIM. silicate.
sílice *s.f.* QUIM. silica.
silicio *s.m.* QUIM. silicon.
silicosis *s.f.* MED. silicosis.
silo *s.m.* 1 AGR. silo. 2 MIL. silo (especialmente para armas atómicas).
silogismo *s.m.* LOG. syllogism.
silogístico, -a *adj.* LOG. syllogistic.
silueta *s.f.* 1 silhouette, form. 2 outline drawing (seguir los contornos de un dibujo).
silvestre *adj.* 1 wild. 2 rustic, rural.
silvicultura *s.f.* forestry.
silla *s.f.* 1 chair, seat. 2 saddle (de montar a caballo). 3 see (sede). || 4 **— curul,** curule chair. 5 **— de manos,** sedan chair. 6 **— de tijera,** folding chair. 7 **— eléctrica,** electric chair. 8 **— gestatoria,** gestatorial chair.
sillar *s.m.* ARQ. ashlar, block of stone.
sillería *s.f.* 1 set of chairs. 2 chairmaker's workshop. 3 ashlars, building stones (para la construcción). 4 ARQ. masonry (estilo de construcción).
silleta *s.f.* (Am.) stool.
silletín *s.m.* stool for the feet (para descansar los pies).
sillín *s.m.* 1 seat, saddle (de bicicleta o similar). 2 sidesaddle (para montar a caballo).
sillón *s.m.* armchair.
sima *s.f.* chasm, abyss; deep fissure.
simbiosis *s.f.* BIOL. symbiosis.
simbólicamente *adv.* symbolically.
simbólico, -a *adj.* symbolic.
simbolismo *s.m.* symbolism.
simbolista *s.m.* y *f.* symbolist.
simbolización *s.f.* symbolization.
simbolizar *v.t.* 1 to symbolize (en general). 2 to tipify (tipificar). 3 to represent, to stand for: *este carácter simboliza larga vida = this character stands for long life.*
símbolo *s.m.* 1 symbol. 2 QUIM. symbol. || 3 **— de la fe/de los apóstoles,** REL. Apostle's Creed.
simetría *s.f.* symmetry.
simétrico, -a *adj.* symmetric, symmetrical.
simiente *s.f.* seed.
simiesco, -a *adj.* simian, apish.
símil *adj.* 1 similar. || *s.m.* 2 comparison; LIT. simile.
similar *adj.* similar, alike.
similitud *s.f.* similarity, similitude.
simio, -a *s.m.* y *f.* ZOOL. ape, monkey.
simonía *s.f.* HIST. simony.
simpatía *s.f.* 1 liking, affection: *siento mucha simpatía por él = I feel a lot of affection towards him.* 2 charm (cualidad): *tiene mucha simpatía = he has a lot of charm.* 3 MED. sympathy.
simpáticamente *adv.* congenially.
simpático, -a *adj.* 1 likeable, congenial, charming. 2 FISIOL. sympathetic. || 3 **gran —,** ANAT. sympathetic nervous system.
simpatizante o **simpatizador, -a** *adj.* 1 supporting. || *s.m.* y *f.* 2 supporter.
simpatizar *v.i.* to get along together.
simple *adj.* 1 easy, not complicated (fácil). 2 plain, simple, natural (sencillo). 3 plain, unadorned (sin adornos). 4 single (no doble). 5 not important. || *s.m.* 6 a little bit foolish, a little bit gone in the head. || 7 **oración —,** GRAM. simple clause.
simplemente *adv.* plainly, simply.
simpleza *s.f.* nonsense.
simplicidad *s.f.* simplicity.
simplificar *v.t.* to simplify (una operación, trámite, etc.).
simplista *adj.* simplistic.
simplón *s.m.* simpleton.
simposio o **symposium** *s.m.* symposium.
simulación *s.f.* simulation, pretense.
simulacro *s.m.* 1 image (fantasía). 2 practice, drill: *simulacro de incendio = fire-drill.* 3 mock, game (especialmente militar).
simuladamente *adv.* in a feigned way.
simulado, -a *adj.* simulated, feigned.
simular *v.t.* to feign (fingir).
simultáneamente *adv.* simultaneously.
simultanear *v.t.* to do simultaneously.
simultaneidad *s.f.* simultaneity.
simultáneo, -a *adj.* simultaneous.
simún *s.m.* simoon (viento desértico).
sin *prep.* 1 without: *sin amor y sin dinero = without love or money.* 2 excluding: *sin contar el gasto = excluding the cost.*
sinagoga *s.f.* REL. synagogue.
sinalefa *s.f.* GRAM. elision.
sinceramente *adv.* sincerely.

sincerarse *v.pron.* to tell the truth.
sinceridad *s.f.* sincerity.
sincero, -a *adj.* sincere, truthful.
síncopa *s.f.* 1 GRAM. syncope. 2 MUS. syncopation.
sincopado, -a *p.p.* 1 de **sincopar.** || *adj.* 2 MUS. syncopated.
sincopar *v.t.* MUS. syncopate.
síncope *s.m.* MED. attack (normalmente del corazón).
sincrético, -a *adj.* syncretic.
sincretismo *s.m.* FIL. syncretism.
sincronía *s.f.* FILOL. synchrony.
sincrónicamente *adv.* synchronically.
sincrónico, -a *adj.* synchronic.
sincronismo *s.m.* synchronism.
sincronización *s.f.* synchronization.
sincronizar *v.t.* 1 to synchronize. 2 RAD. to tune in.
sindicado, -a *p.p.* 1 de **sindicar.** || *adj.* 2 unionized.
sindical *adj.* of the trade unions.
sindicalismo *s.m.* trade union movement.
sindicalista *s.m.* y *f.* unionist.
sindicar *v.t.* y *pron.* to unionize; to join a union.
sindicato *s.m.* trade union.
síndico *s.m.* DER. trustee.
síndrome *s.m.* syndrome.
sinecura *s.f.* sinecure.
sinfín *s.m.* endless number, endless quantity: *un sinfín de cartas = an endless number of letters.*
sinfonía *s.f.* 1 MUS. symphony. 2 (fig.) symphony: *una sinfonía de colores = a simphony of colour.*
sinfónico, -a *adj.* MUS. symphonic.
singladura *s.f.* MAR. day's run.
singular *adj.* 1 single, singular. 2 unique, exceptional (único). || *s.m.* 3 GRAM. singular. || **4 en –,** in particular, especially.
singularidad *s.f.* 1 uniqueness. 2 singularity.
singularizar *v.t.* 1 to make stand out (resaltar). 2 GRAM. to make singular. || *v.pron.* 3 to stand out, to distinguish oneself.
singularmente *adv.* singularly; especially.
siniestrado, -a *adj.* damaged; injured.
siniestramente *adv.* sinisterly, wickedly.
siniestro, -a *adj.* 1 left-handed. 2 sinister, wickedly. 3 fateful, unlucky (funesto). || *s.m.* 4 accident (de muchos tipos). || *s.f.* 5 left hand.
sinnúmero *s.m.* countless number, endless number.
sino *s.m.* 1 fate (destino). || *conj.* 2 but: *no es español sino inglés = he's not Spanish but English.*
sínodo *s.m.* REL. synod.
sinónimo, -a *adj.* 1 synonymous. || *s.m.* 2 GRAM. synonym.
sinopsis *s.f.* synopsis.
sinóptico, -a *adj.* 1 synoptical. || **2 cuadro –,** chart.
sinrazón *s.f.* absurdity.
sinsabor *s.m.* displeasure, sorrow: *los sinsabores de la vida = the sorrows of life.*
sintáctico, -a *adj.* syntactic.
sintagma *s.m.* GRAM. syntagma.
sintaxis *s.f.* GRAM. syntax.
síntesis *s.f.* synthesis.
sintéticamente *adv.* synthetically.
sintético, -a *adj.* synthetical.
sintetizador *s.m.* MUS. synthesizer.
sintetizar *v.t.* to synthesize.
sintoísmo *s.m.* REL. Shintoism.
síntoma *s.m.* symptom.
sintomático, -a *adj.* symptomatic.
sinfonía *s.f.* 1 RAD. tuning. 2 MUS. musical theme.
sintonización *s.f.* RAD. tuning.
sintonizador *s.m.* RAD. tuner, tuning knob.
sintonizar *v.t.* RAD. to tune in.
sinuosidad *s.f.* sinuosity.
sinuoso, -a *adj.* winding, sinuous.
sinusitis *s.f.* MED. sinusitis.
sinvergonzonería *s.f.* shamelessness, brazenness.
sinvergüenza *s.m.* y *f.* 1 shameless person. || *adj.* 2 shameless.
sionismo *s.m.* POL. Zionism.
sionista *s.m.* y *f.* POL. Zionist.
siquiatra o **siquíatra** V. **psiquiatra.**
siquiatría V. **psiquiatría.**
síquico, -a V. **psíquico, -a.**
siquiera o **siquier** *conj.* 1 although, if only. || *adv.* 2 at least: *siquiera un beso = at least a kiss.* || **3 ni –,** not even.
sirena *s.f.* 1 siren, foghorn (alarma). 2 mermaid (mujer).
sirimiri *s.m.* drizzle.
siringa *s.f.* 1 BOT. rubber tree. 2 MUS. shepherd's flute.
sirio, -a *adj./s.m.* y *f.* Syrian.
siroco *s.m.* sirocco (viento).
sirviente, -a *s.m.* y *f.* 1 servant. || *adj.* 2 serving.
sisa *s.f.* 1 petty theft (especialmente de las criadas a sus amas). 2 dart, tapering seam, armhole (en costura).
sisar *v.t.* to pilfer, to steal small a quantity.
sisear *v.t.* e *i.* to hiss, to boo (como sonido silbante o como sonido reprobatorio).
siseo *s.m.* hissing sound, hissing, booing, V. **sisear.**
sísmico, -a *adj.* seismic.
sismo V. **seísmo.**
sismógrafo *s.m.* seismograph.
sismología *s.f.* seismology.
sisón *s.c.* ZOOL. little bustard (ave).
sistema *s.m.* 1 system (general). 2 BIOL. systema (nervioso, respiratorio, etc.). 3 way, system, method (de hacer una cosa concreta). || **4 hacer algo por –,** to do something systematically, to do something as a rule. **5 – de montañas/montañoso,** GEOG. mountain range. **6 – periódico,** QUIM. periodic system.
sistemáticamente *adv.* systematically, methodically.
sistemático, -a *adj.* systematic, methodic.
sistematización *s.f.* systematization.
sistematizar *v.t.* to systematize.
sístole *s.f.* FISIOL. sistole.
sitiador, -a *adj.* 1 besieging. || *s.m.* y *f.* besieger.
sitiar *v.t.* MIL. to besiege.
sitio *s.m.* 1 place, spot. 2 MIL. siege. || **3 dejar a alguien en el –,** to kill somebody on the spot. **4 quedarse uno en el –,** to die instantly, to die on the spot.
sito, -a *adj.* situated: *edificio sito en la calle principal = building situated on the high street.*
situación *s.f.* 1 situation, circumstances (de una persona). 2 location, site (físico).
situado, -a *p.p.* 1 de **situar.** || *adj.* situated. 3 with a (good/bad/etc.) position in life: *mi hermano está bien situado, gana mucho dinero = my brother has a good position in life, he earns a lot of money.*
situar *v.t.* y *pron.* to place; to put.
sketch *s.m.* sketch (teatral).
slip *s.m.* underpants.
slogan V. **eslogan.**
smoking V. **esmoquin.**
snob *adj.* 1 snobbish. || *s.m.* y *f.* 2 snob.
snobismo o **esnobismo** *s.m.* snobbism.
so *prep.* 1 under: *so pretexto de estudiar = under pretense of studying.* || *s.m.* 2 you: *so bruto = you brute.* || *interj.* 3 whoa (para parar caballos).
soba *s.f.* 1 kneading. 2 thrashing, beating, walloping.
sobaco *s.m.* ANAT. armpit.
sobado, -a *p.p.* 1 de **sobar.** || *adj.* 2 kneaded. 3 worn, rumpled, crumpled (gastado). || *s.m.* short (tipo de bizcocho).
sobaquera *s.f.* 1 armhole. 2 armhole reinforcement. 3 underarm mark, underarm smell. 4 shoulder holster (para armas).
sobaquillo, de/a – *loc.adv.* **a)** way of sticking "banderillas" into the bull; **b)** way of throwing something under one's arm.
sobar *v.t.* 1 to knead, to bull (ablandar). 2 to thrash, to beat. 3 (fam.) to fondle, to paw (especialmente a una mujer). 4 to bother, to pest.
soberanía *s.f.* sovereignty.
soberano, -a *adj.* 1 sovereign, supreme. || *s.m.* y *f.* 2 sovereign, monarch. || *s.m.* 3 sovereign (moneda).
soberbiamente *adv.* 1 superbly (positivamente). 2 arrogantly, haughtily (negativamente).
soberbio, -a *adj.* 1 superb (magnífico). 2 proud, vain. || *s.f.* 3 pride. 4 magnificence, grandeur. 5 anger, fury (furia).
sobón, -ona *adj.* 1 mushy, overly fond (tocón). 2 fawning, flattering (halagador). || *s.m.* y *f.* 3 mushy person. 4 flatterer.
sobornable *adj.* bribable.
sobornador, -ora *adj.* 1 bribing. || *s.m.* y *f.* 2 briber.
sobra *s.f.* 1 excess, surplus. || *s.pl.* 2 leftovers (de la comida). 3 remnants (de cualquier cosa). || **4 de –,** superfluous, more than enough.
sobradamente *adv.* only too well, amply, more than enough.

sobradillo *s.m.* ARQ. sloping roof over a balcony.
sobrado, -a *p.p.* 1 de **sobrar.** || *adj.* 2 plenty of; more than enough: *tiene sobrada energía = he has more than enough energy.* || *s.m.* 3 attic, garret. || *adv.* only too well, more than enough.
sobrante *adj.* 1 remaining. || *s.m.* 2 excess, surplus.
sobrar *v.i.* 1 to be left over, to remain (quedar). 2 to be unnecessary: *sobran tus sarcasmos = your sarcasm is unnecessary.*
sobrasada *s.f.* type of sausage.
sobre *s.m.* 1 envelope. || *prep.* 2 on (encima). 3 about (acerca de): *está hablando sobre China = he is talking about China.* 4 approximately, about: *sobre las once llegaremos = we'll arrive at 11 approximately.* 5 over: *estamos volando sobre Londres = we're flying over London.* 6 above: *sobre el nivel del mar = above sea level.* 7 upon, on top of, after: *insulto sobre insulto = one insult on top of another.* 8 to, towards: *nos dirigimos sobre el enemigo = we went towards the enemy.* || 9 **sobre-,** super, over (en compuestos): *sobrecama = bedspread.*
sobreabundancia *s.f.* superabundance.
sobreabundante *adj.* superabundant.
sobreabundar *v.i.* to be superabundant, to abound.
sobrealimentación *s.f.* overfeeding.
sobrealimentar *v.t.* overfeed.
sobreasada, V. **sobrasada.**
sobrecarga *s.f.* overload.
sobrecargar *v.t.* to overload, to overburden.
sobrecargo *s.m.* 1 MAR. purser. 2 AER. steward.
sobrecogedor, -a *adj.* frightening.
sobrecoger *v.t.* y *pron.* to frighten, to startle.
sobrecogimiento *s.m.* fight.
sobrecubierta *s.f.* 1 cover, outer cover. 2 dust jacket, jacket (de un libro).
sobreentender o **sobrentender** *v.t.* to understand.
sobreesdrújulo, -a o **sobresdrújulo, -a** *adj.* accented on the syllable preceding the antepenult.
sobreestimar o **sobrestimar** *v.t.* to overvalue, to overstimate.
sobreexcitar o **sobrexcitar** *v.t.* to overexcite.
sobrehumano, -a *adj.* superhuman.
sobrellenar *v.t.* to overfill.
sobrellevar *v.t.* 1 to put up with, to bear (dificultades). 2 to help carry (a otra persona).
sobremanera *adv.* exceedingly.
sobremesa *s.f.* 1 table cover. 2 after-meal conversation. || 3 **de —,** immediately after dinner.
sobrenadar *v.t.* to float.
sobrenatural *adj.* supernatural.
sobrenaturalizar *v.t.* to give a religious touch (a la vida de uno).
sobrenaturalmente *adv.* supernaturally.
sobrenombre *s.m.* nickname.
sobrepaga *s.f.* bonus.
sobrepasar *v.t.* 1 overtake. || *v.t.* y *pron.* 2 to surpass, to exceed.
sobrepelliz *s.f.* REL. surplice.
sobreponer *v.t.* 1 to place on top. || *v.pron.* 2 to control oneself; to pull through: *debes sobreponerte a la muerte de tu padre = you must pull through your father's death.*
sobreproducción *s.f.* overproduction.
sobrero *s.m.* extra bull, spare bull (para las corridas).
sobresaliente *adj.* 1 outstanding, extraordinary. 2 projecting, overhanging. || *s.f.* 3 highest mark; first class.
sobresalir *v.i.* 1 to overhang, to jut out (físicamente). 2 to be outstanding, to excel.
sobresaltar *v.t.* y *pron.* to startle.
sobresalto *s.m.* startle.
sobrescrito *s.m.* address.
sobreseer *v.t.* e *i.* DER. to stay (una causa).
sobreseimiento *s.m.* DER. stay.
sobresante *s.m.* supervisor.
sobresueldo *s.m.* extra pay.
sobretodo *s.m.* overcoat.
sobrevenida *s.f.* unexpected occurrence.
sobrevenir *v.i.* 1 to happen unexpectedly. 2 to follow, to ensue (seguir).
sobreviviente *adj.* 1 surviving. || *s.m.* y *f.* 2 survivor.
sobrevivir *v.i.* to survive.
sobriamente *adv.* soberly.
sobriedad *s.f.* sobriety, moderation.
sobrio, -a *adj.* 1 sober (en la bebida). 2 moderate (en costumbres).
sobrina *s.f.* niece.
sobrino *s.m.* nephew.
socaire *s.m.* side protected by the wind.
socapa *s.f.* 1 pretext. || 2 **a —,** surreptitiously.
socarrón, -a *adj.* 1 ironic. || *s.m.* y *f.* 2 ironic person.
socarronería *s.f.* irony.
socavar *v.t.* to excavate, to dig.
socavón *s.m.* 1 cave-in. 2 gallery, tunnel.
sociabilidad *s.f.* sociability.
sociable *adj.* sociable.
social *adj.* social.
socialismo *s.m.* socialism.
socialista *adj./s.m.* y *f.* socialist.
socialización *s.f.* socialization.
socializar *v.t.* to socialize.
sociedad *s.f.* 1 society. 2 society, association. 3 COM. firm, company. || 4 **buena —,** high society. 5 **— anónima,** COM. stock company. 6 **— conyugal,** DER. joint property by husband and wife. 7 **— limited,** COM. limited-liability company.
sociología *s.f.* sociology.
sociológico, -a *adj.* sociological.
sociólogo, -a *s.m.* y *f.* sociologist.
socorrer *v.t.* to help, to aid.
socorrido, -a *p.p.* 1 de **socorrer.** || *adj.* 2 helpful. 3 trite, hackneyed: *frase muy socorrida = hackneyed sentence.*
socorrismo *s.m.* life-saving.
socorrista *s.m.* y *f.* lifeguard, life-saver.
socorro *s.m.* 1 help, aid. 2 MIL. reinforcement. || *interj.* 3 help.
soda *s.f.* 1 QUIM. soda. 2 soda water.
sódico, -a *adj.* QUIM. sodium.
sodio *s.m.* QUIM. sodium.
sodomía *s.f.* sodomy.
sodomita *adj.* 1 sodomitical. || *s.m.* y *f.* 2 sodomite.
soez *adj.* (desp.) rude, obscene, crude, vulgar.
sofá *s.m.* sofa.
sofisma *s.m.* FIL. sophism.
sofista FIL. *adj.* 1 sophistic. || 2 *s.m.* y *f.* sophist.
sofisticación *s.f.* sophistication.
sofisticado, -a *adj.* sophisticated.
sofisticar *v.t.* to falsify; to adulterate.
soflama *s.f.* 1 harangue. 2 blush (por vergüenza). 3 glow, flicker (del fuego).
sofocación *s.f.* suffocation.
sofocante o **sofocador, -a** *adj.* suffocating.
sofocar *v.t.* 1 to suffocate, smother (matando). 2 to suppress, to put down (una rebelión, por ejemplo). || *v.t.* y *pron.* 3 to blush (ruborizar). || *v.pron.* 4 to chocke (por el cansancio, disgusto, etc.). 5 to get angry: *no te sofoques = don't get angry.*
sofoco *s.m.* 1 suffocation (asfixia). 2 chocking sensation (sensación de ahogo). 3 embarrassment (vergüenza): *qué sofoco he pasado = how very embarrassing.*
sofocón *s.m.* 1 annoyance, vexation (disgusto). 2 chocking fit (de cansancio).
sofoquina *s.f.* 1 mortification, vexation. 2 stifling heat.
sofrito *s.m.* GAST. lightly fried dish.
sofronizar *v.t.* to hypnotize.
soga *s.f.* 1 rope. || 2 **con la — al cuello,** with the knife at one's throat, in a real fix.
soja *s.f.* 1 BOT. soya, soybean. 2 GAST. soybean (en salsa normalmente).
sojuzgador, -a *adj.* 1 subduing, subjugating. || *s.m.* y *f.* 2 subduer, subjugator.
sojuzgar *v.t.* to subdue, to subjugate.
sol *s.m.* 1 ASTR. sun. 2 sun, sunshine (luz). 3 sun, sunny (al sol). 4 (fig.) gem, treasure (persona dispuesta a ayudar de verdad). || 5 **arrimarse al — que más calienta,** to know on which side one's bread is buttered on, to climb on the bandwagon. 6 **de — a —,** the whole day long, from sunrise to sunset. 7 **no dejar ni a — ni a sombra,** to give no peace, to pester continually. 8 **tomar el —,** to take the sun.
solador *s.m.* floorer (un trabajo manual).
solamente *adv.* 1 only, just. || 2 **— que,** provided that.
solana *s.f.* sunny place.
solano *s.m.* 1 BOT. nightshade. 2 east wind.
solapa *s.f.* 1 flap (de sobre de carta). 2 lapel (de chaqueta). 3 (fig.) pretext.
solapadamente *adv.* slyly, in an underhand way.
solapado, -a *p.p.* 1 de **solapar.** || 2 *adj.* sly, underhanded: *un ataque solapado = a sly attack.*

solapar *v.t.* 1 to put lapels on (chaqueta). 2 (fig.) to conceal (disimular).
solar *s.m.* 1 building site. 2 ancestral home (casa solariega). 3 lineage. || *adj.* 4 solar: *energía solar = solar energy.* || *v.t.* 5 to sole (calzado). 6 to pave (pavimentar).
solariego, -a *adj.* ancestral (familia).
solario o **solarium** *s.m.* solarium.
solaz *s.m.* relaxation, recreation.
soldadesco, -a *adj.* 1 soldierly. || *s.f.* 2 (desp.) rowdy gang of soldiers.
soldado, -a *p.p.* 1 de **soldar.** || *s.m.* 2 soldier. || *s.f.* 3 MIL. service pay.
soldador *s.m.* solderer, welder.
soldadura *s.f.* 1 soldering, welding. 2 soldered joint (juntura).
soldar *v.t.* y *pron.* 1 to solder, to weld. 2 to knit (huesos). || *v.t.* 3 to repair, to mend.
solear *v.t.* y *pron.* to expose to the sun.
solecismo *s.m.* GRAM. solecism.
soledad *s.f.* 1 loneliness, solitude. 2 grieving, mourning (sentimiento). 3 lonely place (lugar solitario).
solemne *adj.* solemn, grave.
solemnemente *adv.* solemnly, gravely.
solemnidad *s.f.* solemnity.
soler *v.i.* to be in the habit of: *suelo levantarme temprano = I usually get up early.*
OBS. Esta palabra tiene distintas posibles traducciones ya que en inglés sólo se da en tiempo de pasado. Para los otros tiempos del español se utilizan paráfrasis.
solera *s.f.* 1 ARQ. crossbeam (viga de soporte). 2 tradition: *una familia de gran solera = a family of great tradition.* 3 lower millstone (de un molino). 4 lees, mother (del vino).
soleta *s.f.* 1 patch (de una media). || 2 **tomar –,** to beat it.
solfa *s.f.* 1 MUS. musical notation. 2 beating, thrashing. || 3 **estar en –,** to be written illegibly. 4 **poner algo en –, a)** to ridicule; **b)** to tidy up (poner en orden).
solfear *v.t.* 1 MUS. to sol-fa. 2 to beat, to thrash. 3 to reprimand, to tell of (reprender).
solfeo *s.m.* MUS. theory of music.
solicitación *s.f.* request.
solicitante o **solicitador, -a** *adj.* 1 requesting. || *s.m.* y *f.* 2 petitioner.
solícitamente *adv.* diligently, carefully.
solicitar *v.t.* 1 to petition, to request. 2 to apply for (gestionando algún documento). 3 to court, to woo (a una mujer).
solícito, -a *adj.* diligent, careful.
solicitud *s.f.* 1 care, diligence. 2 application form.
sólidamente *adv.* solidly.
solidariamente *adv.* in an attitude of solidarity.
solidaridad *s.f.* solidarity.
solidario, -a *adj.* 1 mutually binding, jointly shared. 2 common.
solidarizarse *v.pron.* 1 to make common cause. 2 to become jointly responsible (responsabilizarse en común).
solideo *s.m.* REL. skullcap.
solidez *s.f.* 1 solidity, strength. 2 soundness (estado de salud de una empresa o similar).
solidificación *s.f.* solidification.
solidificar *v.t.* y *pron.* to solidify.
soliloquio *s.m.* monologue.
solio *s.m.* canopied throne.
solipsismo *s.m.* FIL. solipsism.
solista *s.m.* y *f.* MUS. soloist.
solitario, -a *adj.* 1 lonely (sitio o persona). || *s.m.* 2 ZOOL. hermit crab. 3 solitaire (juego de cartas). || *s.f.* 4 ZOOL. tapeworm (enfermedad).
soliviantar *v.t.* y *pron.* to rouse, to irritate.
solo, -a *adj.* 1 on one's own, alone, by oneself: *estoy solo = I am on my own.* 2 isolated (aislado física o anímicamente). 3 unique (único). || *s.m.* 4 MUS. solo. || 5 **a solas,** alone, by oneself, on one's own.
sólo *adv.* only: *sólo soy un pobre hombre = I am only a poor man.*
solomillo *s.m.* sirloin.
solsticio *s.m.* ASTR. 1 solstice. || 2 **– de invierno/hiemal,** winter solstice. 3 **– de verano/estío/vernal,** summer solstice.
soltar *v.t.* y *pron.* 1 to free, to let loose, to loosen, to untie. 2 to let go of: *suelta al niño o grito = let go of the child or I'll cry for help.* || *v.t.* 3 to blurt out, to let out (palabras). || *v.pron.* 4 to loosen up, to lose one's timidity (perder la timidez). 5 to become proficient: *quiero soltarme en inglés = I want to become proficient in English.* || 6 **soltarse a,** to start to: *el pequeño se soltó a hablar cuando sólo tenía medio año = the baby started to talk when he was only six months old.*
soltería *s.f.* bachelorhood.
soltero, -a *adj.* 1 single. || *s.m.* y *f.* 2 bachelor (hombre); unmarried woman (mujer).
solterón, -ona *s.m.* y *f.* 1 confirmed bachelor (hombre); spinster (mujer). || *adj.* 2 old and unmarried.
soltura *s.f.* 1 loosening (soltar). 2 confidence, assurance (en el trato social o similar). 3 nimbleness (física). 4 fluency (en los idiomas).
solubilidad *s.f.* solubility.
soluble *adj.* 1 soluble (un producto). 2 that can be resolved, solvable (un problema o similar).
solución *s.f.* 1 dissolution, solution (disolver, especialmente en un líquido). 2 answer, solution (a un problema). 3 ending, denouement (desenlace). || 4 **– de continuidad,** interruption, break in continuity.
solucionar *v.t.* y *pron.* to solve, to resolve.
solvencia *s.f.* solvency; dependability (económica).
solventar *v.t.* y *pron.* 1 to settle (deudas). 2 to solve (cualquier problema).
solvente *adj.* 1 trustworthy; free of debt (en situaciones financieras, especialmente). || *s.m.* 2 QUIM. solvent.
sollozante *adj.* sobbing.
sollozar *v.i.* to sob.
sollozo *s.m.* sob: *ella no pudo contener un sollozo = she couldn't hold back a sob.*
somanta *s.f.* beating (paliza).
somatén *s.m.* HIST. civilian militia.
somático, -a *adj.* physical, corporeal; of the body, body.
sombra *s.f.* 1 shadow (figura movible causada por el sol, luz, etc.). 2 shadow, darkness (oscuridad). 3 shade (lugar protegido del sol). 4 ghost (espectro). 5 stain, blot (mancha, especialmente sobre la honestidad de alguien o una actividad). 6 (fig.) shadow, trace (apariencia): *ni sombra de duda = without a shadow of a doubt.* 7 place in the shade (en una plaza de toros). || 8 **a la –,** (fig. y fam.) in jail. 9 **hacer –,** to overshadow; to put in shade (a alguien): *no quiere que nadie le haga sombra = he doesn't want anybody to overshadow him.* 10 **ni por –,** not at bit, no way. 11 **no ser alguien ni – de lo que era,** not to be a shadow of one's former self. 12 **ser la – de uno,** to follow someone everywhere. 13 **sombras chinescas,** shadow play. 14 **tener buena/mala –,** to be lucky/unlucky; to be pleasant/unpleasant.
sombrajo o **sombraje** *s.m.* sunshade, shelter from the sun.
sombrear *v.t.* to shade, to shade in (especialmente una pintura).
sombrerazo *s.m.* tip of the hat.
sombrerería *s.f.* hatter's shop, hat shop.
sombrerero, -a *s.m.* y *f.* milliner (para señoras); hatter, hat maker.
sombrerete *s.m.* 1 small hat. 2 hood (de chimenea, especialmente).
sombrerillo *s.m.* BOT. cap (de los hongos).
sombrero *s.m.* 1 hat. || 2 **– calañés,** low-crowned black velvet hat with a rolled-up brim (típico en Andalucía). 3 **– cordobés,** wide-brimmed hat with a tall crown. 4 **– chambergo,** jaunty fedora. 5 **– de copa,** top hat. 6 **– de pelo,** (Am.) top hat. 7 **– de tres picos,** three-cornered hat. 8 **– hongo,** bowler.
sombrilla *s.f.* parasol.
sombrío, -a *adj.* 1 shaded (con sombra). 2 somber, gloomy (triste). || *s.f.* 3 place with shade.
someramente *adv.* superficially; briefly.
somero, -a *adj.* 1 shallow (poco profundo). 2 superficial; brief.
someter *v.t.* y *pron.* 1 to subdue, to put down (sujetar). 2 to put under the control of (controlar). || *v.t.* 3 to submit, to present (un plan o similar a la consideración de otros).
sometimiento *s.m.* 1 subjection (al poder de otro). 2 submission, presentation (a la consideración de otros).
somier *s.m.* spring mattres.
somnambulismo o **sonambulismo** *s.m.* sleepwalking.

somnámbulo, -a o **sonámbulo, -a** *adj.* **1** sleepwalking. || *s.m.* y *f.* **2** sleepwalker.

somnífero, -a *s.m. adj.* **1** sleep-inducing. || **2** QUIM. sleeping-pill.

somnolencia o **soñolencia** *s.f.* sleepiness.

somnoliento, -a o **soñoliento, -a** *adj.* sleepy.

somorgujo o **somormujo** *s.m.* ZOOL. grebe (ave).

son *s.m.* **1** sound; tune. || **2 ¿a qué —?/¿a — de qué?,** why, why on earth? for what reason? **3 bailar a cualquier —,** to adapt to any circumstances. **4 en — de,** as, like; fashion: *en son de guerra = in a warlike fashion.* **5 sin —,** without any logic, without any reason. **6 sin ton ni —,** without rhyme or reason.

sonado, -a *p.p.* **1** de **sonar.** || *adj.* **2** famous, well-known. **3** talked-about (divulgado). **4** touched (un poco ido en la cabeza, especialmente los boxeadores). || **5 hacer una sonada,** to cause a major scandal.

sonaja *s.f.* **1** metal disk. || *s.pl.* **2** MUS. tambourine.

sonajero *s.m.* o **sonajera** o *s.f.* rattle.

sonar *v.i.* **1** to sound, to ring (muchos objetos); to strike (reloj). **2** to be sounded, to be pronounced: *esta letra no suena en español = this letter is not pronounced in Spanish.* **3** to sound like: *esto me suena a cuento = this sounds like a hoax to me.* **4** to be mentioned, to be drought up (un tema, un nombre, una obra de arte, etc.). || *v.t.* **5** to sound, to cause a sound. || *v.t.* y *pron.* **6** to blow (one's nose). || *v.pron.* **7** to ring a bell: *su cara me suena = her face rings a bell.* || *v.imp.* y *pron.* **8** to be rumoured. || *s.m.* **9** MEC. sonar. || **10 como suena,** literally.

sonata *s.f.* MUS. sonata.

sonda *s.f.* **1** sounding, fathoming (acción). **2** MAR. sounding line, sounding lead. **3** MEC. drill (para excavar). **4** MED. probe.

sondable *adj.* soundable, fathomable.

sondear o **sondar** *v.t.* **1** to sound, to fathom (queriendo saber la profundidad). **2** MED. to probe. **3** to explore, to inquire into; to sound out (a una persona).

sondeo *s.m.* **1** MAR. sounding, fathoming. **2** MED. probing. **3** poll, survey (estadístico): *hacer un sondeo = to carry out a survey.*

sonetista *s.m.* y *f.* LIT. sonneteer, writer of sonnets.

soneto *s.m.* LIT. sonnet.

sonido *s.m.* **1** sound, noise (físico). **2** FON. sound.

sonoramente *adv.* sonorously.

sonoridad *s.f.* sonority.

sonorización *s.f.* FON. voicing.

sonorizar *v.t.* y *pron.* **1** to record the sound track of (una película). **2** FON. to voice. **3** to install sound equipment (en una sala, discoteca, etc.).

sonoro, -a *adj.* **1** sound, with sound. **2** resonant, sonorous. **3** FON. voiced.

sonreír *v.i.* y *pron.* **1** to smile. **2** (fig.) to smile on: *la fortuna le sonríe = good luck smiles on him.*

sonriente *adj.* smiling.

sonrisa *s.m.* smile.

sonrojar *v.t.* y *pron.* to blush, to turn pink.

sonrojo *s.m.* blush.

sonrosado, -a *adj.* pink, pinkish.

sonrosar *v.t.* y *pron.* to turn pink.

sonrosear *v.t.* y *pron.* **1** to turn pink. || *v.pron.* **2** to blush (sonrojar).

sonsacar *v.t.* **1** to worm out of; to get by cunning (información o similar). **2** to wheedle, to coax (sacar).

sonso, -a V. **zonzo, -a.**

sonsonete *s.m.* **1** tapping (sonido rítmico). **2** (desp.) rattle, jangling. **3** mocking tone (burlador). **4** monotonous tone, sing-song (al hablar una persona).

soñador, -a *adj.* **1** dreamy. || *s.m.* y *f.* **2** dreamer.

soñar *v.t.* e *i.* **1** to dream. **2** (fig.) to dream, to daydream. || *v.i.* **3** to have a strong desire for, to wish for (desear). || **4 ni soñarlo,** not on your life, don't even dream it, don't let it go through your mind.

soñolencia V. **somnolencia.**

soñoliento, -a V. **somnoliento.**

sopa *s.f.* **1** soup. **2** sop (de pan). **3** soup distributed free in convents. || *s.pl.* **4** slices of bread dipped into soup. || **5 comer la — boba/andar a la — boba,** to live off someone else, to sponge off someone else. **6 dar sopas con honda,** to excel, to be streets ahead of (alguien). **7 hecho una —,** soaking wet. **8 — juliana,** GAST. julienne soup.

sopapear *v.t.* to slap.

sopapo *s.m.* slapping.

sopero, -a *adj.* **1** soup: *plato sopero = soup dish.* **2** that likes soups a lot (persona). || *s.f.* **3** soup tureen.

sopetón *s.m.* **1** slap (sopapo). || **2 de —,** suddenly, unexpectedly.

sopicaldo *s.m.* thin soup.

soplado, -a *p.p.* **1** de **soplar.** || *adj.* **2** neat (limpio y ordenado). **3** drunk, stoned. **4** stuck-up, conceited (engreído).

soplamocos *s.m.* slap on the face.

soplar *v.t.* e *i.* **1** to blow (con la boca u otro objeto, como un fuelle). || *v.i.* **2** to blow (el viento). || *v.t.* **3** to blow up (normalmente un globo). **4** to swipe, to pinch (quitar): *me han soplado todo el dinero = they pinched all my money.* **5** to split on, to squeal (traicionar). **6** to prompt; to whisper (algo que uno no sabe y otro le dice). || *v.pron.* **7** to become conceited, to become full of himself (engreírse). **8** to gulp down (comida o bebida). || **9 ¡sopla!,** I'm blowed!

soplete *s.m.* **1** MEC. blowpipe. **2** MUS. air tube (de una gaita).

soplido *s.m.* blast, puff.

soplo *s.m.* **1** blowing. **2** gust (de viento). **3** second, instant (tiempo muy breve): *en un soplo = in a second.* **4** tip-off (información). **5** MED. murmur (en el corazón). **6** tales, denunciation, accusation: *dio el soplo al dire = he told tales to the headmaster.*

soplón, -ona *adj.* **1** informing, squealing. || *s.m.* y *f.* **2** informer, squealer, stool pidgeon.

soponcio *s.m.* faint, swoon.

sopor *s.m.* sleepiness, drowsiness.

soporífero, -a *adj.* boring; sleep-inducing.

soportable *adj.* bearable: *apenas soportable = harly bearable.*

soportal *s.m.* ARQ. **1** porch (delante de una casa). **2** arcade (a todo lo largo de un edificio).

soportar *v.t.* **1** to support, to hold up. **2** to bear, to stand, to endure (a alguien o alguna situación).

soporte *s.m.* **1** support (físico). **2** pillar (columna).

soprano *s.f.* MUS. soprano.

sor *s.f.* REL. sister, nun.

sorber *v.t.* **1** to suck, to sip (beber). **2** to absorb. **3** to swallow (atraer). || **4 — el seso,** to be crazy about: *María me sorbe el seso = I am crazy about María.*

sorbete *s.m.* **1** sherbet. **2** (Am.) drinking straw (pajita).

sorbible *adj.* that can be sipped.

sorbo *s.m.* **1** sip. **2** sipping (acción).

sordera *s.f.* deafness.

sórdidamente *adv.* sordidly.

sordidez *s.f.* **1** squalor (de un lugar). **2** meanness, vileness, miserliness (de una persona).

sórdido, -a *adj.* **1** dirty, squalid (sucio). **2** sordid, vile, mean, miserly.

sordina *s.f.* **1** MUS. damper, muffler. || **2 con —,** surreptitiously, on the quiet.

sordo, -a *adj.* **1** deaf. **2** silent, noiseless (casi silencioso). **3** muffed, dull (de poco sonido). **4** FON. voiceless. **5** (fig.) deaf, indifferent: *sordo a mis ruegos = indifferent to my begging.* || *s.m.* y *f.* **6** deaf person. || **7 a lo —/a sordas,** silently, noiselessly.

sordomudez *s.f.* deaf-mutism.

sordomudo, -a *adj.* **1** deaf-mute, deaf and dumb. || *s.m.* y *f.* **2** deafmute.

sorna *s.f.* sarcasm.

soroche *s.m.* (Am.) mountain sickness.

sorprendente *adj.* surprising, amazing.

sorprendentemente *adv.* surprisingly, amazingly.

sorprender *v.t.* **1** to surprise, to take by surprise (a alguien). **2** to discover, to find out: *les sorprendieron juntos = they were found together.* || *v.t.* y *pron.* **3** to amaze, to be amazed, to be surprised: *me sorprendió su actitud = I was amazed by his attitude.*

sorpresa *s.f.* surprise: *¡vaya sorpresa! = ¡what a surprise!*

sorpresivamente *adv.* surprisingly.

sorpresivo, -a *adj.* (Am.) sudden, unexpected.

sorteable *adj.* avoidable.

sorteamiento *s.m.* drawing lots.

sortear *v.t.* **1** to draw lots for, to decide by lot. **2** to avoid, to dodge (evitar físicamente).

sorteo *s.m.* 1 drawing, draw. 2 avoiding, dodging, V. **sortear.**
sortija *s.f.* 1 ring. 2 curt, ringlet (en el pelo).
sortilegio *s.m.* 1 sorcery, witchcraft (arte). 2 spell, charm (acto concreto).
sos o **s.o.s.** *s.m.* s.o.s.
sosa V. **soso, -a.**
sosaina *adj.* 1 dull. || *s.m.* y *f.* 2 dull person.
sosamente *adv.* tastelessly, insipidly.
sosegadamente *adv.* calmly, quietly.
sosegado, -a *p.p.* 1 de **sosegar.** || *adj.* 2 calm, quiet.
sosegador, -a *adj.* calming, quieting.
sosegar *v.t.* y *pron.* 1 to calm down, to cool down; to reassure. || *v.pron.* e *i.* 2 to calm down.
sosera o **sosería** *s.f.* insipidness, dullness.
sosiego *s.m.* calmness, peacefulness.
soslayar *v.t.* 1 to put sideways (problema). 2 to dodge, to sidestep.
soslayo *s.m.* 1 slant. || 2 **mirar de —,** to look out of the corner of one's eye; to look askance.
soso, -a *adj.* 1 tasteless, insipid. 2 unsalted (sin sal). 3 dull, uninteresting (persona). || *s.f.* 4 QUIM. soda.
sospecha *s.f.* suspicion.
sospechable *adj.* suspicious, suspect.
sospechar *v.t.* 1 to suspect. || *v.i.* 2 to be suspicious.
sospechosamente *adv.* suspiciously.
sospechoso, -a *adj.* 1 suspicious, suspect: *comportamiento sospechoso = suspect behaviour.* 2 distrustful (desconfiado). || *s.m.* y *f.* 3 suspect.
sostén *s.m.* 1 support, prop, stand (físico). 2 sustenance (económico). 3 brassiere, bra (prenda de mujer).
sostenedor, -a *adj.* supporting.
sostener *v.t.* y *pron.* 1 to support, to hold up. || *v.t.* 2 to maintain, to uphold (opinión). 3 to sustain (dar sustento); to maintain (financieramente). 4 to tolerate.
sostenido, -a *p.p.* 1 de **sostener.** || *adj.* 2 supported (físicamente). 3 sustained (esfuerzo o similar). || *s.m.* 4 MUS. sharp.
sostenimiento *s.m.* 1 support (físico). 2 maintenance (económico, alimentario, etc.).
sota *s.f.* 1 jack (en cartas). || 2 **sota-,** under (en palabras compuestas).
sotabanco *s.m.* attic, garret.
sotabarba *s.f.* beard growing under the chin.
sotana *s.f.* REL. soutane, cassock.
sotavento *s.m.* MAR. leeward, lee.
soterramiento *s.m.* burial.
soterrar *v.t.* 1 to bury. 2 to conceal, to hide away (ocultar).
sotileza V. **sutileza.**
soto *s.m.* 1 thicket. || 2 **soto-,** under (en palabras compuestas).
soviet *s.m.* POL. 1 Soviet. || 2 **Soviet Supremo,** Central Soviet.
soviético, -a *adj.* 1 soviet. || *s.m.* y *f.* 2 citizen of the Soviet Union.
spaghetti *s.m.* GAST. espagueti.
speaker *s.m.* speaker.
speech *s.m.* speech.
sport *s.m.* 1 sport. || *adj.* 2 sportive.
spot *s.m.* spot (de publicidad).
sprint *s.m.* sprint.
sprintar *v.i.* to sprint.
stádium *s.m.* stadium.
stand *s.m.* stand.
standard *s.m.* 1 standard, model. || *adj.* 2 standard.
standarizar o **standardizar** *v.t.* y *pron.* to standardize.
statu quo *s.m.* statu quo.
status *s.m.* status, standing.
stock *s.m.* stock.
stop *s.m.* stop.
stress *s.m.* stress.
su *adj.* 1 his, her, its: *su hermano está en Austria = his brother is in Austria.* || 2 **su-,** under, below (en palabras compuestas).
suave *adj.* 1 soft, smooth (al toque). 2 gentle, mild (de carácter). 3 soft, sweet (grato a los sentidos). 4 easy, slow (lento).
suavemente *adv.* 1 softly, smoothly (al tacto). 2 gently, mindly (conducta). 3 softly, sweetly (gratamente). 4 easily, slowly (lentamente).
suavidad *s.f.* 1 softness, smoothness (al tacto). 2 softness, sweetness (dulzura). 3 gentleness, mildness (de carácter). 4 easiness, slowness (lentitud).
suavización *s.f.* softening, smoothing.
suavizador, -a *adj.* 1 softening, smoothing. || *s.m.* 2 razor strop (para afilar la navaja de afeitar).
suavizante *s.m.* softening cream.
suavizar *v.t.* y *pron.* 1 to soften (físicamente). 2 to ease. 3 to tone down (el tono de la voz o parecido).
sub- *prefijo* sub-.
subalterno, -a *adj./m.s.* y *f.* subordinate.
subarrendador, -a *s.m.* y *f.* subtenant.
subarrendamiento o **subarriendo** *s.m.* underlease, sublease.
subarrendar *v.t.* to sublease, to underlease.
subasta *s.f.* auction.
subastar *v.t.* to auction.
subconsciencia o **subconsciente** *s.f.* subconscious.
subcutáneo, -a *adj.* subcutaneous.
subdesarrollado, -a *adj.* underdeveloped.
subdesarrollo *s.m.* underdevelopment.
subdirección *s.f.* assistant directorship.
subdirector, -a *s.m.* y *f.* assistant director, assistant, manager.
súbdito, -a *adj.* 1 subject. || *s.m.* y *f.* citizen.
subdividir *v.t.* y *pron.* to subdivide.
subdivisión *s.f.* subdivision.
subestimar *v.t.* y *pron.* to underestimate.
subgénero *s.m.* BIOL. subgenus.
subibaja o **sube y baja** *s.m.* (Am.) seesaw.
subido, -a *p.p.* 1 de **subir.** || *adj.* 2 high (precio). 3 intense, deep (color, olor, etc.). || *s.f.* 4 increase: *subida de precios = price increase.* 5 ascent, climb (ascensión).
subinspección *s.f.* post of assistant inspector, post of assistant supervisor.
subinspector, -a *s.m.* y *f.* assistant inspector, assistant supervisor.
subintendente *s.m.* assistant superintendent.
subir *v.t., i.* y *pron.* 1 to go up, to come up, to climb. 2 to increase, to raise (elevar). 3 to carry up, to take up (trasladar arriba). || *v.t.* e *i.* 4 to increase to go up (precio). || *v.i.* 5 to go up, to rise (algo): *el nivel del agua está subiendo = the water level is rising.* 6 to move up, to be promoted. 7 to amount to (una cantidad, especialmente de dinero).
súbitamente *adv.* suddenly, all of a sudden.
súbito, -a *adj.* 1 sudden, unexpected. 2 hasty (forma de actuar demasiado deprisa de una persona).
subjefe, -a *s.m.* y *f.* assistant chief.
subjetivamente *adv.* subjectively.
subjetividad *s.f.* subjectivity.
subjetivismo *s.m.* subjectivism.
subjetivo, -a *adj.* subjective.
subjuntivo, -a *adj.* GRAM. 1 subjunctive. || *s.m.* 2 subjunctive.
sublevación o **sublevamiento** *s.f.* uprising, revolt; MIL. mutiny.
sublevar *v.t.* y *pron.* 1 to incite to rebellion; to rebel (contra alguien o algo). || *v.t.* 2 (fig.) to irritate, to annoy no end: *ese tipo de conducta me subleva = that kind of behaviour annoys me no end.*
sublimación *s.f.* sublimation.
sublimar *v.t.* 1 PSIQ. to sublimate. 2 to exalt (enaltecer). 3 QUIM. to sublimate (pasar de estado físico a gaseoso).
sublime *adj.* sublime, lofty, grand.
sublimemente *adv.* sublimely, loftily, grandly.
subliminal *adj.* PSIC. subliminal.
submarinismo *s.m.* DEP. diving, scuba diving; underwater exploration.
submarinista *s.m.* y *f.* driver, underwater diver.
submarino, -a *adj.* 1 underwater. || *s.m.* 2 MIL. submarine.
subnormal *adj.* 1 subnormal. || *s.m.* y *f.* 2 subnormal person.
suboficial *s.m.* y *f.* MIL. non-commissioned officer, warrant officer.
suborden *s.m.* BIOL. suborder.
subordinación *s.f.* subordination.
subordinadamente *adv.* secondarily; subordinately.
subordinado, -a *p.p.* 1 de **subordinar.** || *adj.* 2 subordinate, secondary. || *s.m.* y *f.* subordinate (especialmente referido al soldado en la milicia).
subordinante *adj.* GRAM. subordinating.
subordinar *v.t.* y *pron.* to subordinate.
subrayable *adj.* worth emphasizing.
subrayado, -a *p.p.* 1 de **subrayar.** || *adj.* 2 underlined: *las frases subrayadas = the underlined sentences.* || *s.m.* 3 underlining.
subrayar *v.t.* 1 to underline (una palabra, frase, etc.). 2 to emphasize: *debo*

subrayar mi desacuerdo = I must emphasize my disagreement.
subrepticiamente *adv.* surreptitiously.
subrepticio, -a *adj.* surreptitious.
subrogación *s.f.* DER. subrogation.
subrogar *v.t.* y *pron.* DER. to subrogate.
subsanable *adj.* repairable, rectifiable.
subsanar *v.t.* **1** to excuse (excusar, normalmente una falta). **2** to repair, to correct, to rectify.
subscribir o **suscribir** *v.t.* **1** to sign (carta, documento, etc.). **2** to endorse, to subscribe to (una postura, opinión, etc.) || *v.pron.* **3** COM. to underwrite (comprometerse a un pago, un envío, etc.). || *v.t.* y *pron.* **4** to subscribe (a una revista, periódico o similar).
subscripción o **suscripción** *s.f.* subscription (a periódico o similar).
subscriptor, -a o **suscriptor, -a** *s.m.* y *f.* subscriber.
subscrito, -a o **suscrito, -a** *p.p.* **1** de **subscribir** o **suscribir.** || *adj.* **2** subscribed (a una publicación). **3** DER. undersigned.
subsecretaría *s.f.* undersecretaryship; undersecretary's office.
subsecretario, -a *s.m.* y *f.* **1** assistant secretary (en una oficina). **2** POL. undersecretary.
subsecuente o **subsiguiente** *adj.* following, subsequent.
subseguir *v.i.* y *pron.* to follow.
subsidiariamente *adv.* **1** subsidiarily. **2** DER. ancillarily.
subsidiario, -a *adj.* **1** subsidiary (que ayuda). **2** DER. ancillary.
subsidio *s.m.* subsidy, benefit, compensation.
subsistencia *s.f.* **1** subsistence (el hecho de sobrevivir). **2** sustenance (alimento para sobrevivir).
subsistente *adj.* subsistent, lasting, enduring (que dura).
subsistir *v.i.* **1** to survive, to live. **2** to endure, to last (durar).
substancia o **sustancia** *s.f.* **1** substance (física). **2** FIL. substance. **3** substance, essence (de un escrito, discurso, opinión, etc.). **4** judgement, sense (sensatez). **5** value, importance (valor o importancia de una obra de arte o similar). || **6 en –,** in brief, briefly; in essence. **7 – blanca,** ANAT. white matter. **8 – gris,** ANAT. grey matter.
substanciación *s.f.* **1** DER. substantiation. **2** condensation.
substancial o **sustancial** *adj.* **1** FIL. substantial. **2** substantial (sustancioso). **3** essential, fundamental, basic.
substancialmente *adv.* substantially, essentially; basically.
substanciar o **sustanciar** *v.t.* **1** to abridge, to condense. **2** DER. to substantiate.
substancioso, -a o **sustancioso, -a** *adj.* **1** substantial, nourishing. **2** substantial, important.
substantivar *v.t.* GRAM. to make a noun, to turn into a noun.
substantivo, -a o **sustantivo, -a** *adj.* **1** substantive. || *s.m.* **2** GRAM. noun.
substitución *s.f.* substitution; replacement.
substituible *adj.* replaceable.
substituir o **sustituir** *v.t.* y *pron.* to substitute, to replace.
substitutivo, -a *adj.* substitute.
substituto, -a o **sustituto, -a** *s.m.* y *f.* substitute, replacement (persona).
substracción *s.f.* **1** removal (acto de quitar). **2** deduction. **3** theft (robo). **4** MAT. subtraction.
substraer o **sustraer** *v.t.* **1** to remove, to take away (quitar). **2** to steal (robar). **3** MAT. to subtract. || *v.pron.* **4** to elude (responsabilidad, obligación, etc.).
substrato o **sustrato** *s.m.* **1** GEOL. substratum. **2** FIL. substance, essence. **3** FILOL. underlying language.
subsuelo *s.m.* GEOL. subsoil.
subteniente *s.m.* MIL. second lieutenant.
subterfugio *s.m.* pretext, subterfuge.
subterráneamente *adv.* subterraneanly.
subterráneo, -a *adj.* **1** underground: *pasadizos subterráneos = underground passages.* || *s.m.* **2** underground place; (Am.) subway.
subtitular *v.t.* to subtitle.
subtítulo *s.m.* subtitle.
suburbano, -a *adj.* **1** suburban. || *s.m.* **2** suburban train.
suburbio *s.m.* **1** suburb, outer district. **2** slum (barrio pobre).
subvención *s.f.* subsidy, grant (normalmente estatal).
subvencionar *v.t.* to subsidize, to aid.
subvenir *v.i.* **1** to provide (ayudar materialmente).
subversión *s.f.* subversion; revolution.
subversivo, -a *adj.* subversive (en sentido político o social).
subvertir *v.t.* **1** to subvert (política o socialmente). **2** to upset (perturbar).
subyacente *adj.* underlying.
subyacer *v.i.* to underlie.
subyugación *s.f.* subjugation.
subyugador, -ora *adj.* **1** subjugating, dominating: *los poderes subyugadores = the subjugating powers.* **2** captivating, enchanting (persona ,etc.). || *s.m.* y *f.* **3** subjugator (dominador). **4** captivator, charmer.
subyugar *v.t.* y *pron.* **1** to subjugate, to oppress, to dominate. **2** to captivate, to charm.
succión *s.f.* suction.
succionar *v.t.* to suck.
sucedáneo, -a *adj.* **1** subsitute. || *s.m.* **2** substitute.
suceder *v.i.* **1** to follow, to succeed: *a esto sucedió la guerra = the war followed after this.* **2** to inherit (normalmente el trono o poder parecido). || *v.pron.* **3** to happen: *sucedió en primavera = it happened in the spring.*
sucedido *p.p.* **1** de **suceder.** || *s.m.* **2** happening, event.
sucesión *s.f.* **1** succession. **2** inheritance (herencia). **3** (form.) issue (descendencia).
sucesivamente *adv.* successively.
sucesivo, -a *adj.* successively, consecutive.
suceso *s.m.* **1** event, happening, ocurrence. **2** course, lapse (de tiempo).
sucesor, -a *adj.* **1** succeeding. || *s.m.* y *f.* **2** successor; heir.
suciamente *adv.* **1** dirtily, filthily. **2** (fig.) vilely, basely (con vileza).
suciedad *s.f.* **1** dirt, filth. **2** (fig.) vileness, baseness (vileza).
sucintamente *adv.* succinctly, concisely.
sucinto, -a *adj.* **1** succinct, concise. **2** brief, scanty (corto o escaso en una prenda de vestir, etc.).
sucio, -a *adj.* **1** dirty, filthy. **2** (fig.) vile, base. **3** shady, dishonest (acción o actividad). **4** blurred, smudged (en los colores). || *adv.* **5** dirtily, unfairly (especialmente en el juego).
suculentamente *adv.* succulently.
suculento, -a *adj.* succulent.
sucumbir *v.i.* **1** to die, to perish (morir). **2** to yield, to succumb (ceder). **3** DER. to lose a suit (perder un pleito).
sucursal *s.f.* branch office (de banco, empresa, etc.).
sudadera *s.f.* (Am.) sweatshirt.
Sudáfrica *s.f.* South Africa.
sudafricano, -a *adj./s.m.* y *f.* South African.
Sudamérica *s.f.* South America.
sudamericano, -a *adj./s.m.* y *f.* South American.
sudar *v.t.* e *i.* **1** to sweat, to perspire (el cuerpo). **2** to ooze, to exude (emitir, normalmente humedad). || *v.i.* **3** to work hard. || *v.t.* **4** to sweat for (esforzarse por conseguir algo).
sudario *s.m.* shroud.
sudor *s.m.* **1** sweat, perspiration (del cuerpo). **2** moisture (humedad). **3** swear, toil (esfuerzo).
sudoroso, -a *adj.* sweaty.
sueco, -a *adj./s.m.* y *f.* **1** Swedish. || **2 hacerse el –,** to pretend not to hear, to pretend not to understand.
suegro, -a *s.m./f.* father-in-law; mother-in-law.
suela *s.f.* **1** sole (del zapato). **2** tanned leather (cuero). **3** leather tip (del taco de billar). || **4 media –,** half sole.
suelazo *s.m.* (Am.) bump, fall.
sueldo *s.m.* **1** salary, wages, pay. || **2 a –,** on a salary.
suelo *s.m.* **1** floor (dentro de casa). **2** ground (fuera de casa). **3** AGR. soil: *buen suelo = good soil.* **4** territory, land.
sueltamente *adv.* **1** agilely, nimbly. **2** impudently (impúdicamente).
suelto, -a *p.p.* **1** de **soltar.** || *adj.* **2** loose (físicamente). **3** nimble, agile. **4** untied (desatado). **5** easy, flowing (estilo de escribir, hablar, etc.). **6** odd, unmatched: *un calcetín suelto = an unmatched sock.* **7** loose (dinero en calderilla). **8** blank (verso sin rima). || *s.m.* **9** insert (suelto de periódico). || *s.f.* **10** release (de animales especialmente).
sueñera *s.f.* (Am.) sleep; sleepy state.
sueño *s.m.* **1** sleep (de dormir). **2** dream (de soñar). **3** dream, wish. || **4 conciliar**

el —, to sleep, to fall asleep. **5 descabezar un —,** to take a short nap. **6 echar un —,** to take a nap. **7 ni por —,** not even in one's dreams. **8 — dorado,** life's dream. **9 — eterno,** (euf.) eternal rest. **10 — pesado,** heavy sleep.

suero *s.m.* MED. serum.

suerte *s.f.* **1** luck. **2** fate, lot (destino). **3** condition, circumstances: *la suerte del pueblo = the condition of the people.* **4** stage (de una corrida de toros). **5** kind, sort: *toda suerte de mentiras = all kinds of lies.* **6** way, manner: *de esta suerte = in this way.* || **7 de — que,** in such a way that, so that, in a way that. **8 echar a suertes,** to cast lots, to draw lots.

suertudo, -a *adj.* (Am.) lucky.

sueter *s.m.* sweater.

suficiencia *s.f.* **1** sufficiency. **2** competence, ability. **3** self-importance (superioridad pedante).

suficiente *adj.* **1** sufficient, enough. **2** smug, pedantic (pedante).

suficientemente *adv.* sufficiently, enough.

sufijo *s.m.* GRAM. suffix.

sufragar *v.t.* **1** to aid, to support. || *v.t.* y *pron.* **2** to pay. || *v.i.* **3** (Am.) to vote (votar).

sufragio *s.m.* **1** assistance, aid. **2** REL. service for the redemption of souls from Purgatory. **3** vote (voto). || **4 — universal,** universal suffrage.

sufragismo *s.m.* POL. women's suffrage.

sufragista *s.f.* POL. suffragette.

sufrible *adj.* endurable, bearable.

sufrido, -a *p.p.* **1** de **sufrir.** || *adj.* **2** patient, long-suffering.

sufridor, -a *adj.* suffering.

sufrimiento *s.m.* **1** suffering. **2** endurance, tolerance.

sufrir *v.t.* y *pron.* **1** to suffer. **2** to bear, to endure (aguantar): *no puedo sufrir su comportamiento = I can't bear his behaviour.* || *v.t.* **3** to undergo, to experience (experimentar). **4** to carry, to hold up (aguantar, un peso o parecido).

sugerencia *s.f.* suggestion.

sugerente o **sugeridor, -a** *adj.* suggestive.

sugerir *v.t.* to suggest.

sugestión *s.f.* **1** suggestion. **2** autosuggestion (mental). **3** fascination.

sugestionable *adj.* impressionable.

sugestionar *v.t.* **1** to influence (influenciar). **2** to hypnotize.

sugestivo, -a *adj.* **1** appealing (que atrae). **2** suggestive.

suicida *adj.* **1** suicidal. || *s.m.* y *f.* **2** suicide (persona).

suicidarse *v.pron.* to commit suicide.

suicidio *s.m.* suicide.

suite *s.f.* **1** MUS. suite. **2** suite (en un hotel).

suizo, -a *adj./s.m.* y *f.* Swiss.

sujeción *s.f.* **1** subjection (poder). **2** fastening (atado físico concreto).

sujetador *s.m.* bra.

sujetapapeles *s.m.* paper clip.

sujetar *v.t.* y *pron.* **1** to dominate (con poder). || *v.t.* **2** to fasten (físicamente).

sujeto, -a *p.p.* **1** de **sujetar.** || *adj.* **2** subject, liable (a castigo o parecido). || *s.m.* **3** GRAM. subject. **4** fellow, individual. || **5 — pasivo,** tax-payer.

sulfamida *s.f.* QUIM. sulphonamide.

sulfato *s.m.* QUIM. sulfate.

sulfúrico, -a *adj.* QUIM. sulfuric.

sultán *s.m.* sultan.

suma V. **sumo, -a.**

sumamente *adv.* extremely, highly: *sumamente interesante = highly interesting.*

sumando *s.m.* MAT. addend.

sumar *v.t.* **1** to add (añadir). || *v.t.* y *pron.* **2** MAT. to add. || *v.pron.* **3** to join (participar en algo): *nos sumamos a la fiesta = we joined the party.* **4** to adhere (adherirse, especialmente a una doctrina, teoría, etc.).

sumariamente *adv.* without any delay.

sumario, -a *adj.* DER. summary.

sumarísimo *adj.* DER. swift.

sumergible *adj.* **1** submergible. || *s.m.* **2** MAR. submarine.

sumergir *v.t.* y *pron.* **1** to submerge, to immerse. **2** to overwhelm (sumir).

sumersión *s.f.* immersion.

sumidero *s.m.* drain, sewer.

suministrable *adj.* that can be supplied.

suministración *s.f.* supplying, providing.

suministrar *v.t.* y *pron.* to supply, to furnish.

suministro *s.m.* supply.

sumir *v.t.* y *pron.* **1** to sink (hundir). || *v.pron.* **2** to immerse oneself: *se ha sumido en una profunda depresión = he has immersed himself in a profound depression.*

sumisamente *adv.* submissively, obediently.

sumisión *s.f.* **1** submission. **2** obedience, compliance (obediencia).

sumiso, -a *adj.* **1** submissive. **2** obedient, compliant. V. **sumisión.**

sumo, -a *adj.* **1** supreme, enormous, great: *suma descortesía = supreme lack of politeness.* || *s.f.* **2** sum, collection (de cosas). **3** MAT. addition. || **4 a lo —,** at most. **5 con suma rapidez,** as quick as possible. **6 en suma,** in short.

suntuario, -a *adj.* (form.) sumptuary.

suntuosamente *adv.* sumptuously.

suntuosidad *s.f.* sumptuousness.

suntuoso, -a *adj.* sumptuous.

supeditación *s.f.* subjection, subordination.

supeditar *v.t.* y *pron.* **1** to subject, to subordinate. || *v.t.* **2** to overpower (dominar).

super- *prefijo* super-.

superabundancia *s.f.* superabundance.

superabundante *adj.* superabundant.

superabundantemente *adv.* superabundantly.

superabundar *v.i.* to be very plentiful.

superávit *s.m.* COM. surplus, benefit.

superchería *s.f.* deceit.

supereminente *adj.* pre-eminent.

superestimar *v.t.* to overestimate.

superestructura *s.f.* superstructure (especialmente política).

superficial *adj.* **1** superficial (de la superficie). **2** shallow (no profundo). **3** (desp.) superficial, frivolous.

superficialidad *s.f.* superficiality.

1 de **surtir.** || *adj.* **2** assorted (galletas u otros productos). **3** supplied, provided: *estamos bien surtidos de todo = we are well supplied with everything.* || *s.m.* **4** assortment, selection.

superficialidad *s.f.* superficiality.

superficialmente *adv.* superficially.

superficie *s.f.* **1** surface (por ejemplo, del agua). **2** GEOM. area.

superfluamente *adv.* needlessly.

superfluo, -a *adj.* needless, unnecessary.

superintendencia *s.f.* superintendence.

superintendente *s.m.* y *f.* supervisor, overseer.

superior *adj.* **1** top, higher: *parte superior = top part.* **2** GEOG. upper. **3** magnificent, of great quality (de gran calidad). || *s.f.* **4** REL. superior.

superioridad *s.f.* **1** higher authority (en una institución, organización, etc.). **2** superiority (mejor que otro).

superiormente *adv.* magnificently.

superlativo, -a *adj.* **1** excellent. || *s.m.* **2** GRAM. superlative.

supermercado *s.m.* supermarket.

superponer *v.t.* y *pron.* superimpose, to place above.

superposición *s.f.* superposing.

superproducción *s.f.* **1** ECON. overproduction. **2** big-budget film.

supersónico, -a *adj.* supersonic.

superstición *s.f.* superstition.

supersticiosamente *adv.* superstitiously.

supersticioso, -a *adj.* superstitious.

supervisar *v.t.* supervise.

supervisión *s.f.* supervision.

supervisor, -a *adj.* **1** supervising. || *s.m.* y *f.* supervisor.

supino, -a *adj.* **1** face-up (posición del cuerpo). **2** crass, excessive: *supina ignorancia = crass ignorance.*

suplantar *v.t.* to impersonate, to take the place of (otra persona).

suplementario, -a *adj.* supplementary.

suplemento *s.m.* **1** PER. supplement. **2** extra charge (cobro extra).

suplencia *s.f.* substitution, replacement.

suplente *adj.* **1** substitute. || *s.m.* y *f.* **2** DEP. reserve, player. **3** substitute, replacement (en cualquier trabajo o puesto).

supletorio, -a *adj.* **1** supplementary. || *s.m.* **2** extension (teléfono).

súplica *s.f.* plea; petition.

suplicación *s.f.* **1** plea; petition. **2** DER. appeal (apelación).

suplicante *adj.* **1** entreating, pleading. || *s.m.* y *f.* **2** supplicant, petitioner.

suplicar *v.t.* **1** to plead, to implore. **2** to beg: *te suplico que seas más considerado = I beg you to be more considerate.* **3** DER. to appeal (apelar).

suplicatorio o **suplicatoria** *s.m.* o *f.* DER. letters rogatory.

suplicio *s.m.* torture.

suplir *v.t.* **1** to make up; to supplement. **2** to replace, to substitute (reemplazar). **3** to infer (entender leyendo entre líneas). **4** to conceal (esconder, especialmente defectos en otras personas).

suponer *v.t.* **1** to suppose, to assume: *supongo que estás cansado = I suppose you are tired.* **2** to imply, to mean; to involve: *esto supone un gran gasto = this involves an enormous expenditure.*

suposición *s.f.* **1** supposition, assumption. **2** guess (adivinanza).

supositorio *s.m.* MED. suppository.

supra- *prefijo* supra-: *intereses supranacionales = supranational interests.*

supremacía *s.f.* supremacy.

supremo, -a *adj.* **1** supreme. || **2 Tribunal Supremo,** DER. Supreme Court.

supresión *s.f.* **1** suppression, elimination. **2** omission (omisión, especialmente de algo en un escrito, discurso, etc.).

suprimir *v.t.* y *pron.* **1** to suppress, to eliminate. **2** to leave out (omitir).

supuesto, -a *p.p.* **1** de **suponer.** || *adj.* **2** assumed, false: *nombre supuesto = assumed name.* || *s.m.* **3** hypothesis. || **4 por —,** certainly, of course. **5 — que,** granted that, since, inasmuch as.

supuración *s.f.* suppuration.

supurante *adj.* suppurating, festering.

supurar *v.i.* suppurate.

suramericano V. **sudamericano.**

surcar *v.t.* **1** to plow (hacer surcos). **2** to groove (hacer líneas paralelas). **3** MAR. to cut through, to ply (los mares).

surco *s.m.* **1** furrow (en la tierra). **2** groove (hendedura). **3** wrinkle (arruga, normalmente en la cara). || **4 echarse al —,** to lie down on the job.

sureste V. **sudeste.**

surgir *v.i.* **1** to spurt, to shoot out. **2** to emerge, to appear, to rise: *una nueva situación ha surgido en Europa = in Europa a new situation has emerged.*

surmenaje *s.m.* mental fatigue.

suroeste V. **sudoeste.**

surrealismo *s.m.* ART. surrealism.

surrealista *s.m.* y *f.* ART. surrealist.

sursuncorda *s.m.* **1** (fam.) great guy. || **2 ser el —,** to be number one.

surtido, -a *p.p.* **1** de **surtir.** || *adj.* **2** assorted (galletas u otros productos). **3** supplied, provided: *estamos bien surtidos de todo = we are well supplied with everything.* || *s.m.* **4** assortment, selection.

surtidor, -a *adj.* **1** providing, supplying. || *s.m.* **2** supplier. **3** jet (chorro, normalmente de agua). **4** pump (normalmente de gasolina).

surtir *v.t.* y *pron.* **1** to supply (suministrar). || *v.i.* **2** to spout (arrojar un líquido). || **3 — efecto,** to have the desired effect.

sus- *prefijo* under, sub. (en este diccionario aparece mayormente **sub**).

susceptibilidad *s.f.* susceptibility.

susceptible *adj.* **1** susceptible (característica personal). **2** (desp.) touchy (quisquilloso). **3** capable, open: *susceptible de mejora = open to improvement.*

suscitar *v.t.* y *pron.* **1** to provoke. **2** to originate: *se han suscitado problemas = some problems have originated.*

sus V. **subs.**

susodicho, -a *adj.* aforesaid, abovementioned.

suspender *v.t.* **1** to hang; to suspend (físicamente). **2** to stop, to suspend (pagos, a una persona por un descuido, etc.). **3** to fail (un examen). **4** to astonish, to amaze (asombrar). || *v.t.* y *pron.* **5** to call off, to postpone (posponer).

suspense *s.m.* suspense.

suspensión *s.f.* **1** suspension, hanging (acción física). **2** stoppage, suspension, interruption (de una publicación, acto público, etc.). **3** DER. adjournment. **4** MEC. suspension (sistema de vehículos). **5** QUIM. suspension. **6** MUS. suspension. || **7 — de pagos,** COM. suspension of payments.

suspensivo *adj.* **puntos suspensivos,** dots.

suspenso, -a *p.p.* **1** de **suspender.** || *adj.* **2** hanging, hung, suspending (de manera física). **3** astonished; baffled, bewildered (sorprendido). **4** failed (examen). || *s.m.* **5** failing mark (en examen).

suspicacia *s.f.* suspicion, distrust.

suspicaz *adj.* suspicious, distrustful.

suspicazmente *adv.* suspiciously, distrustfully.

suspirado, -a *p.p.* **1** de **suspirar.** || *adj.* **2** longed for, desired (especialmente una persona a la que se desea tener cerca).

suspirar *v.i.* **1** to sigh. || **2 — por una cosa,** to long for something, to desire something very much.

suspiro *s.m.* sigh.

sustentación o **sustentamiento** *s.m.* o *f.* **1** support (físico). **2** holding (de una opinión o parecido). **3** sustenance, nourishment (alimento).

sustentador, -a *adj.* supporting, sustaining (que sustenta).

sustentar *v.t.* y *pron.* **1** to maintain, to uphold (opinión). **2** to sustain, to nourish (con alimento). **3** to support (el peso físico).

sustento *s.m.* sustenance, food (alimento).

susto *s.m.* **1** scare, fright. **2** dread, deep worry (preocupación).

susurrador, -a *adj.* **1** whispering, murmuring; rustling (hojas de árboles, plantas, etc.). || **2** *s.m.* y *f.* whisperer.

susurrante *adj.* whispering, murmuring; rustling (hojas, plantas, etc.).

susurrar *v.i.* **1** to whisper, to murmur. **2** to murmur (el agua); to rustle (hojas, plantas, etc.). || *v.i.* y *pron.* **3** to be rumoured (noticias o similar).

susurro *s.m.* **1** whisper, murmur. **2** murmur (agua); rustling (de hojas, plantas o similar).

sutil *adj.* **1** fine, delicate (delgado o fino). **2** subtle. **3** clever, sharp (de pensamiento).

sutileza o **sutilidad** *s.f.* **1** fineness, delicateness (finura física). **2** subtlety (tanto un dicho sutil como la calidad en sí). **3** cleverness, sharpness (de inteligencia).

sutilmente *adv.* **1** subtly: *lo dijo sutilmente = he said it very subtly.* **2** finely, delicately (en el aspecto de fineza física).

sutura *s.f.* **1** MED. suture, stitch. **2** ANAT. suture (entre algunos huesos).

suturar *v.t.* MED. to suture, to stitch, to stitch up.

suyo, -a *adj.pos.* **1** his (de él); her (de ella); its (de ello); their (de ellos o ellas); yours (de usted o ustedes): *el coche suyo es bastante bueno = their car is quite good.* **2 muy suyo,** just like, very typical of: *lo que dijo es muy suyo = what he said is just like him.* **3 muy suyo,** very reserved, very independent sort: *este chico es muy suyo = this boy is very independent.* || *pron.pos.* **4** his (de él): hers (de ella); its (de ello); theirs (de ellos o ellas); yours (de usted o ustedes): *mi casa es cara pero la suya es todavía más = my house is expensive but his is yet more expensive.* || **5 de —, a)** in itself, per se; **b)** naturally, inherently; intrinsically. **6 hacer de las suyas,** to be up to one's tricks, to get up to one's old tricks. **7 los suyos,** one's people, one's family. **8 salirse con la suya,** to get one's way.

symposium V. **simposio.**

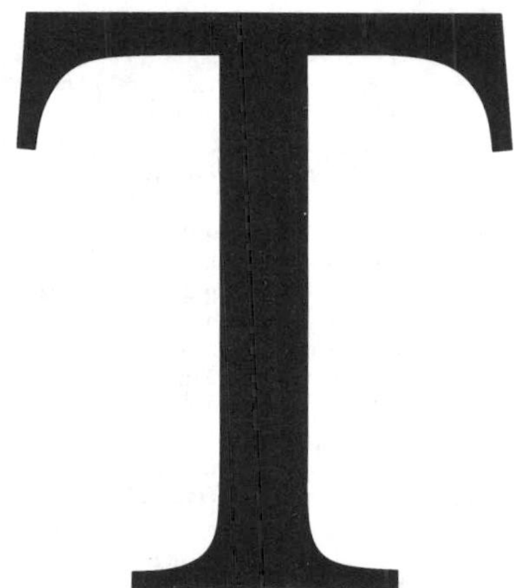

t, T *s.f.* t, T (vigésima tercera letra del alfabeto español).
taba *s.f.* ANAT. astragulus; anklebone. || *s.f.pl.* knucklebones, (EE.UU.) jackstones.
tabacal *s.m.* tobacco plantation, tobacco field.
tabacalero, -a *adj.* tobacco. || *s.m.* tobacconist, tobacco grower, tobacco merchant. || *s.f.* (Am.) cigarette factory.
tabaco *s.m.* **1** tobacco. **2** cigarettes. || **3 — de hebra,** long cut tobacco. **4 — de mascar,** chewing tobacco. **5 — en polvo,** snuff. **6 — negro,** black or dark tobacco. **7 — rubio,** Virginian tobacco.
tabacón *s.m.* (Am. y fam.) marijuana, grass, dope.
tabalear *v.t.* to rock to and fro. || *v.i.* to drum one's fingers.
tabaleo *s.m.* **1** rocking. **2** drumming of one's fingers.
tabanco *s.m.* **1** market stall, stand, booth. **2** (Am.) loft (desván).
tábano *s.m.* horsefly, gadfly.
tabaquera *s.f.* **1** snuff box. **2** tobacco box, jar, pouch. **3** cigarette case.
tabaquería *s.f.* **1** tobacconist's. **2** (Am.) cigar factory.
tabaquismo *s.m.* addiction to tobacco, nicotism.
tabardillo *s.m.* **1** MED. typhoid fever. **2** sunstroke. **3** (fam.) pain in the neck.
tabardo *s.m.* tabard.
tabarra *s.f.* **1** (fam.) nuisance, bore, pain in the neck. **2 dar la —,** to be a nuisance, a bore, to be a pain in the neck, to get on someone's nerves.
tabasco *s.m.* tabasco sauce.
taberna *s.f.* **1** bar, pub, tavern. **2** (Am.) gambling joint. **3** (Am.) small grocery shop (ultramarinos).
tabernáculo *s.m.* REL. tabernacle.
tabernario, -a *adj.* (fam.) rude, coarse, vulgar language.
tabernero *s.m.* **1** landlord, publican, licensee. **2** barman, bartender.
tabicar *v.t.* **1** to partition off. **2** to wall up, brick up. **3** to stop up (nariz).
tabique *s.m.* **1** thin wall, partition. **2** (Am.) brick (ladrillo). **3 — nasal,** ANAT. nasal bone.
tabla *s.f.* **1** plank, board (de madera). **2** slab (de piedra, mármol). **3** pleat, box-pleat (costura). **4** index, table of contents. **5** table, list. **6** scale (de salarios). **7** ART. panel. **8** AGR. strip of land between two rows of trees. **9** garden bed, patch, plot. **10** butcher's block. || *f.pl.* **11** stage: *pisar las tablas = to go on stage.* **12** barrier, fence (en la plaza de toros). **13** DEP. tie, draw: *hacer tablas = to tie, draw.* **14 a rajatabla,** exactly, strictly, at all costs, without fail. **15 estar en las tablas,** (Am.) to be broke, destitute. **16 hacer — rasa de algo,** to sweep aside, to disregard completely. || **17 — a vela,** windsurfing board. **18 — de dibujo,** drawing board. **19 — de planchar,** ironing board. **20 — de salvación,** (fig.) last hope. **21 salvarse, escaparse por —,** to have a near escape, a close shave.
tablado *s.m.* **1** platform. **2** stage. **3** floorboards.
tablaje *s.m.* **1** planks, boards. **2** gaming-house.
tablajería *s.f.* **1** gaming, gambling. **2** butcher's shop.
tablao *s.m.* flamenco show.
tablazón *s.f.* **1** planking. **2** MAR. deck planks.
tablar *v.t.* **1** to saw (en tablas). **2** to divide into plots (jardín). **3** to level (nivelar suelo). **4** to pleat (tela). **5** to hammer iron into plates, to laminate.
tablero *s.m.* **1** board, panel. **2** blackboard, (EE.UU.) chalkboard. **3** notice board, (EE.UU.) bulletin board. **4** DEP. board (de ajedrez, damas, etc.). **5** shop counter. **6** gambling house. **7** planking (de un puente). **8** ELEC. switchboard. **9 — de instrumentos,** instrument panel (avión), dashboard (automóvil). **10 — contador,** abacus. **11** garden plots, beds.
tableta *s.f.* **1** small board, block (madera). **2** writing pad. **3** MED. tablet. **4** bar (de chocolate).
tabletear *v.i.* to rattle or clatter boards.
tableteo *s.m.* rattle, rattling, clatter.
tablilla *s.m.* **1** small board, slab. **2** notice board, (EE.UU.) bulletin board. **3** MED. splint. **4** (Am.) bar (de chocolate).
tablista *s.m.* y *f.* surfer, windsurfer.
tabloide *s.m.* PER. tabloid.
tablón *s.m.* **1** plank, thick board. **2** notice board, (EE.UU.) bulletin board. **3 coger un —,** (fam.) to get drunk, to get tight.
tabú *s.m.* taboo.
tabuco *s.m.* hovel.
tabulación *s.f.* tabbing.
tabulador *s.m.* tabulator.
tabular *adj.* tabular. || *v.t.* to tabulate, tab.
taburete *s.m.* stool.
taca *s.f.* **1** stain. **2** small pantry, cupboard. **3** QUIM. plates of a crucible.
tacañamente *adv.* in a miserly way.
tacañear *v.i.* to be miserly/stingy/mean.
tacañería *s.f.* **1** miserliness, stinginess, meanness. **2** cunning, craftiness.
tacaño, -a *adj.* **1** miserly, stingy, mean. **2** cunning, crafty.
tacita *s.f.* **1** small cup. **2 — de plata,** (fig.) very neat and tidy.
tácitamente *adv.* tacitly.
tácito, -a *adj.* silent, tacit, implied, inferred: *aprobación tácita = silent approval.*
taciturnidad *s.f.* **1** taciturnity. **2** moodiness, sullenness.
taciturno, -a *adj.* **1** taciturn, silent. **2** moody, melancholy, sull.
taco *s.m.* **1** plug, stopper. **2** peg (de madera). **3** wedge (cuña). **4** wad: *taco de billetes = a wad of notes.* **5** book (of tickets). **6** stub (parte que queda de un billete). **7** pad: *taco de papel = pad of notepaper.* **8** cue (billar). **9** piece, snack,

bite (trocito): *taco de jamón = piece of ham.* **10** stud (de una bota). **11** swear word: *soltar un taco = to swear/curse.* **12** desk calendar. **13** (Am.) rolled tortilla. **14** (Am.) heel (de zapato). **15** MIL. ramrod. || **16 — de salida,** DEP. starting block.

tacómetro *s.m.* tachometer.

tacón *s.m.* heel: *tacones altos = high heels.*

taconear *v.i.* **1** to stamp with one's heels. **2** MIL. to click one's heels. **3** (fig.) to strut.

tácticamente *adv.* tactically.

táctico, -a *adj.* **1** tactical. || *s.m.* **2** tactician. || *s.f.* **3** tactic. **4** MIL. tactics.

táctil *adj.* tactile.

tacto *s.m.* **1** touch, feel. **2** tact. || **3 falta de —,** tactless. **4 tener —,** to be tactful.

tacha *s.f.* **1** defect, fault, flaw, blemish. **2** TEC. large tack, stud. || **3 sin —,** flawless, faultless, unblemished, perfect.

tachadura *s.f.* crossing out, correction, erasure.

tachar *v.t.* **1** to cross out, erase, rub out. **2** (fig.) to find fault with, to accuse.

tachón *s.m.* **1** crossing-out, erasure. **2** ornamental stud.

tachonado, -a *adj.* adorned, studded: *tachonado de estrellas = star-studded.*

tachuela *s.f.* **1** tack, stud. **2** (Am.) drawing pin (chincheta).

tafetán *s.m.* **1** taffeta. || *s.pl.* **2** flags, colours, ensign, standard. **3** frills. || **4 — de heridas/inglés,** sticking plaster.

tafilete *s.m.* morroco leather.

tagalo, -a *adj./s.m.* y *f.* Tagalog.

tagarnina *s.f.* **1** BOT. golden thistle. **2** cheap cigar. **3** (Am. y fam.) drunkenness. || **4 agarrar una —,** to get tight, plastered.

tahalí *s.m.* swordbelt, baldric.

tahona *s.f.* **1** flour mill (molino). **2** bakery, bakehouse (panadería).

tahúr, -a *adj.* y *s.* gambler, cardsharper.

taifa *s.f.* **1** party, faction. **2** (fam.) gang of thieves.

taimado, -a *adj.* sly, crafty, cunning.

tajada *s.f.* **1** slice, sliver, piece, chunk: *tajada de carne = slice of meat.* **2** cut, slash. || **3 agarrar una —,** (fam.) to get drunk, plastered. **4 llevarse la mejor —,** to get the lion's share. **5 sacar uno —,** (fig.) to get one's share, to get a rake-off.

tajadera *s.f.* **1** chopper. **2** cold chisel, gouge.

tajamar *s.m.* **1** MAR. stem, cutwater. **2** (Am.) dike, seawall, dam.

tajante *adj.* **1** cutting, sharp. **2** (fig.) emphatic, categorical, sharp: *una respuesta tajante = a categorical reply.*

tajar *v.t.* to cut, chop, slice.

tajo *s.m.* **1** cut, incision. **2** GEOG. steep cliff, gorge. **3** (fam.) job: *vamos al tajo = let's get on with the job.* **4** place of work. **5** small three-legged stool. **6** chopping block.

tal *adj./adv.* **1** such a, such: *tal cosa = such a thing; tales cosas = such things.* **2** such, so great, so large: *su interés es tal = his interest is so great.* **3** a certain: *un tal Sr. Pérez = a certain Mr. Pérez.* || *pron.* **4** such a one, someone: *tal habrá que lo piense = there'll be someone who thinks so.* **5** such a thing, something: *no haré tal = I'll do no such thing.* || **6 con — de/con — de que/con — que,** provided that, as long as. **7 fulano de —,** Mr. So-and-so. **8 — como/— cual,** just as, the way: *está tal como me lo dijo = it's just as he told me; sigue tal cual = he's just the same.* **9 — para cual,** two of a kind. **10 — vez,** perhaps. **11 ¿qué —?,** how's things? **12 ¿qué — es?,** what's it like? **13 ¿qué tal estás?,** how are you?

taladrar *v.t.* **1** to drill, bore, pierce, perforate. || **2 — un ruido que taladra los oídos,** (fig.) an ear-splitting noise.

taladro *s.m.* **1** drill, bore, auger, gimlet. **2** drill hole.

tálamo *s.m.* (form.) **1** nuptial, marriage bed. **2** nuptial, bride chamber.

talante *s.m.* **1** humour, mood, temper, disposition: *estar de buen talante = to be in a good mood.* **2** will. **3** appearance, look.

talar *adj.* **1** full-length (vestido). || *v.t.* **2** to fell, to cut down trees. **3** to prune. **4** to destroy, to devastate, to lay waste.

talco *s.m.* **1** MIN. talc, talcum: *polvos de talco = talcum powder.* **2** tinsel.

talega *s.f.* **1** sack, bag. **2** bagful, sackful.

talegazo *s.m.* heavy fall, bump.

talego *s.m.* **1** long bag, sack. **2** (fam.) clumsy, fat person. **3** money. || **4 no tengo —,** I'm broke.

taleguilla *s.f.* bullfighter's breeches.

talento *s.m.* **1** talent, gift: *tener talento para la música = to have a gift for music.* **2** understanding, intellect. **3** talent (moneda).

talentoso, -a *adj.* talented, gifted.

Talgo *s.m.* Talgo (abrev. Tren Articulado Ligero Goicoechea-Oriol) high speed inter-city train.

talio *s.m.* QUIM. thallium.

talión *s.m.* talion, retaliation.

talismán *s.m.* talisman, amulet, lucky charm.

Talmud *s.m.* REL. Talmud.

talo *s.m.* BOT. thallus.

talófitas *s.f.pl.* BOT. thallophytes.

talón *s.m.* **1** heel. **2** flange, rim (de un neumático). **3** FIN. cheque, (EE.UU.) check. **4** FIN. voucher, receipt, stub, counterfoil. || **5 apretar uno los talones,** to take to one's heels. **6 pisar los talones a uno,** to be on someone's heels. **7 Talón de Aquiles,** Achilles' heel.

talonario *s.m.* **1** receipt book, book of counterfoils. **2** FIN. cheque book (EE.UU.) check book.

talud *s.m.* **1** slope, bank. **2** ARQ. talus.

talla *s.f.* **1** wood carving. **2** engraving (metal). **3** cutting (piedras preciosas). **4** height, stature. **5** size (de ropa). **6** tally, measuring rod. **7** ransom, reward (para el rescate de un criminal). **8** (Am.) fib, lie (mentira). **9** (Am.) gossip (charla). || **10 dar la —,** (fig.) to be up to standard.

tallado, -a *adj.* **1** carved, sculptured (madera). **2** engraved (metal). **3** cut (piedras preciosas). || *s.m.* **4** carving. **5** engraving. **6** cutting.

tallador *s.m.* **1** carver. **2** engraver. **3** (Am.) card dealer.

talladura *s.f.* engraving.

tallar *v.t.* **1** to carve, to shape (madera). **2** to sculpt (piedra, mármol). **3** to engrave (metal). **4** to cut (joyas). **5** MIL. to measure the height of (medir). **6** to deal (naipes). || *v.i.* **7** (Am.) to chat, to gossip.

tallarín *s.m.* noodle.

talle *s.m.* **1** waist (cintura). **2** figura (de mujer): *de talle esbelto = slim-figured.* **3** build, physique (de hombre). **4** (fig.) appearance, look, shape, outline. **5** (Am.) bodice.

taller *s.m.* **1** workshop, shop: *taller de reparaciones = repair shop.* **2** ART. studio. **3** factory mill.

tallista *s.m.* wood carver, sculptor, engraver.

tallo *s.m.* **1** BOT. stem, stalk. **2** BOT. shoot, sprout (renuevo). **3** (Am.) cabbage (col). || *s.m.pl.* **4** (Am.) greens, vegetables.

talludo, -a *adj.* **1** BOT. tall, long-stemmed. **2** tall, lanky (personas). **3** (fig.) grown-up. **4** (Am.) tough, leathery (fruta).

tamal *s.m.* **1** (Am.) tamale. **2** package, bundle, pile. **3** (Am. y fam.) intrigue, trick, hoax.

tamaño, -a *adj.* **1** so big a, such a big (grande). **2** so small a, such a small (pequeño). || *s.m.* **2** size: *¿de qué tamaño es? = what size is it?* || **3 de — natural,** life-size.

tamarindo *s.m.* BOT. tamarind.

tambaleante *adj.* **1** staggering, swaying, reeling, tottering wobbly. **2** (fig.) shaky, unstable: *negocio tambaleante = shaky business.*

tambalearse *v.pron.* **1** to stagger, to sway, to reel, to totter, to wobble (de personas). **2** to wobble (de muebles). **3** (fig.) to be shaky, to unstable.

tambaleo *s.m.* **1** staggering, swaying, reeling, tottering (de personas). **2** wobbliness (de muebles).

también *adv.* **1** also, too, as well, likewise: *es médico también = he's also a doctor/he's a doctor too/he's a doctor as well.* **2** too, so: *yo también = me too... so (do) I.*

tambor *s.m.* **1** drum. **2** drummer (persona). **3** ARQ. tambour. **4** ANAT. eardrum, tympanum. **5** embroidery frame. **6** MAR. capstan-drum, paddle-box. **7** cylinder (de un revólver).

tamboril *s.m.* MUS. small drum, tabor.

tamborilear *v.t.* **1** (fig.) to praise, to extol. || *v.i.* **2** to beat (tamboril), to play a drum. **3** (fig.) to drum one's fingers. **4** (fig.) to patter, to drum (lluvia).

tamborileo *s.m.* drumming, beating.

tamborilero *s.m.* drummer.

tamiz *s.m.* **1** sieve, sifter. || **2 pasar por el —,** to sieve, sift.

tamizar *v.t.* to sieve, sift.
tamo *s.m.* 1 fluff, down, dust. 2 AGR. chaff.
tampoco *adv.* neither, not either, nor: *tampoco come pan = he doesn't eat bread either/neither does he eat bread; él no juega y yo tampoco = he doesn't play and nor do I.*
tampón *s.m.* 1 ink-pad. 2 MED. tampon. 3 TEC. plug.
tam-tam *s.m.* MUS. tom-tom.
tan *adv.* 1 so: *es tan bueno = he is so good.* 2 such: *una casa tan grande = such a big house.* 3 What...!: *¡qué chica tan guapa! = what a pretty girl!* 4 **es — ... que,** so... that: *está tan débil que no puede andar = he's so weak that he can't walk.* 5 **— ... como,** as... as: *tan alto como su padre = as tall as his father.* 6 **— siquiera,** not even: *no tiene tan siquiera un vestido = she hasn't even got a dress.*
tanates *s.m.pl.* (Am. y fig.) bits and pieces, odds and ends, gear.
tanda *s.f.* 1 group. 2 batch: *tanda de huevos = batch of eggs.* 3 series. 4 layer (de ladrillos). 5 shower of blows (golpes). 6 turn (turno). 7 shift (grupo de obreros, turno de trabajo): *tanda de noche = night shift.* 8 game (billar), innings (béisbol). 9 (Am.) performance, show.
tándem *s.m.* 1 tandem. 2 carriage with two horses. 3 (fig.) jointly, together.
tangente *adj.* y *s.f.* 1 tangent. || 2 **salir por la —,** (fig.) to go off, to fly off at a tangent (hacer una digresión), to avoid, dodge the issue (esquivar una pregunta).
tangible *adj.* tangible, (fig.) concrete.
tango *s.m.* MUS. tango.
tanino *s.m.* QUIM. tannin.
tanque *s.m.* 1 tank (depósito). 2 MIL. tank. 3 tanker (barco). 4 water reservoir, pool. || 5 **buque —,** tanker. 6 **— de,** (fam.) big glass of, pint of: *un tanque de cerveza = a pint of beer.*
tantalio *s.m.* QUIM. tantalum.
tanteador *s.m.* 1 scoreboard. 2 scorer (goleador).
tantear *v.t.* 1 to size up, to guage, to take the measure of (medir). 2 to work out roughly, to guess, to calculate (calcular aproximadamente). 3 to consider carefully, to weigh up. 4 (fig.) to sound out, to try out, to test (una persona). 5 ART. to sketch, outline. 6 (Am.) to lie in wait for (acechar). 7 (Am.) to swindle (estafar). || *v.i.* 8 DEP. to keep score. 9 to grope, to feel one's way (ir a tientas). || 10 **— el terreno,** to see how the land lies.
tanteo *s.m.* 1 sizing up. 2 rough estimate, approximate calculation. 3 weighing up, careful consideration. 4 test, trial. 5 DEP. score. 6 ART. outline, sketch.
tanto *adj.* 1 so much, so many: *tanta agua = so much water; tantas peras = so many pears.* 2 so much, as much: *tengo tanto dinero como tú = I've got as much money as you.* 3 **— tiempo,** such a long time. 4 so: *siento tanta alegría = I feel so happy.* || *s.m.* 1 DEP. point, goal. 2 FIN. a certain amount, a percentage. 3 **al —,** up to date, in the know. 4 **estar al —,** (fam.) to be on the look out, to keep an eye on. 5 **otro —,** as much again. 6 **no es para —,** there's no need to make such a fuss. 7 **las tantas,** late, in the small hours. 8 **y tantos,** odd: **30 y tantos,** 30 odd. || *adv.* 1 so much, so often, so long. 2 **cuanto más ... — más,** the more... the more. 3 **en —, entre —, mientras —,** in the meantime, meanwhile. 4 **ni — ni tan poco,** neither one extreme nor the other. 5 **— mejor,** all the better, so much the better. 6 **¡y —!,** and how! 7 **por lo —,** so, therefore. 8 **un —,** rather, somewhat: *un tanto cansado = rather tired.* || *conj.* **con — que, en — que,** provided that, while.
tañer *v.t.* 1 to play a musical instrument. 2 to toll (campanas).
tapa *s.f.* 1 lid, cover, top. 2 MEC. head (de cilindro). 3 heel plate (zapato). 4 apperitive, snack taken with a drink. 5 **saltar la — de los sesos,** (fig.) to blow one's brains out.
tapacubos *s.m.* MEC. hubcap.
tapadera *s.f.* 1 lid, cover. 2 (fig.) cover, front (encubridor).
tapado, -a *adj.* 1 covered, wrapped (envuelto). 2 (Am.) all the same colour (de un animal). || *s.m.* (Am.) 3 coat (para mujeres o niños). 4 candidate for the Mexican Presidency (cuyo nombre no se ha revelado).
tapadura *s.f.* 1 covering. 2 plugging, stopping-up.
tapar *v.t.* 1 to cover, to cover up. 2 to put the lid on (recipiente). 3 to put the top on, to stopper, to cork (botella). 4 to plug, to stop, to stop up (agujero). 5 (fig.) to conceal, to hide: *las nubes tapan el sol = the clouds hide the sun.* 6 (Am.) to fill (diente).
taparrabo *s.m.* 1 swimming trunks. 2 loincloth (de salvaje).
tapete *s.m.* 1 table runner, table cover (de mesa) rug (alfombra). 2 **poner sobre el —,** (fig.) to be under consideration. 3 **— verde,** card table.
tapia *s.f.* 1 adobe or mud wall. 2 garden wall. 3 **más sordo que una —,** as deaf as a post.
tapial *s.m.* (Am.) mud wall.
tapiar *v.t.* 1 to wall in, to enclose. 2 (fig.) to block up, to stop up.
tapicería *s.f.* 1 ART. tapestry making. 2 tapestry (tapiz). 3 upholstery (coches). 4 upholsterer's (tienda).
tapicero, -a *s.m.* y *f.* tapistry maker, upholsterer.
tapioca *s.f.* tapioca.
tapir *s.m.* ZOOL. tapir.
tapiz *s.m.* tapestry.
tapizar *v.t.* 1 to hang with tapestries (pared). 2 to carpet (suelo). 3 to upholster (coches, muebles).
tapón *s.m.* 1 stopper, cap, top, cork (botella). 2 plug, wad. 3 bung (tonel). 4 MED. tampon. 5 (Am.) ELEC. fuse. 6 (fig.) a shorty, a chubby person. 6 (fig.) hindrance, obstacle (estorbo).
taponar *v.t.* 1 to stopper, to put the top on, to put the cap on, to cork (una botella). 2 to plug up, to stop up, to block. 3 **— los oídos,** to stop up one's ears.
taponazo *s.m.* 1 pop. 2 (fam.) shot (fútbol).
tapujo *s.m.* 1 muffler (para la cara). 2 (fig.) deceit, subterfuge. || 3 **venirle a uno con tapujos,** to beat about the bush; to behave dishonestly.
taquear *v.t.* (Am.) to fill to the top, to pack tight.
taquicardia *s.f.* MED. tachycardia.
taquigrafía *s.f.* shorthand, stenography.
taquigrafiar *v.t.* to take down in shorthand.
taquigráfico, -a *adj.* 1 shorthand, stenographic. || 2 *acta taquigráfica = verbatim report.*
taquígrafo, -a *s.m.* y *f.* shorthand writer, stenographer, verbatim reporter (de una conferencia).
taquilla *s.f.* 1 booking office, ticket office, ticket window (estaciones, etc.). 2 box-office. 3 filing cabinet (archivador), locker. 4 takings (recaudación), DEP. gate money. 5 (Am.) bar, liquor store. 6 (Am.) tack (clavo).
taquillaje *s.m.* takings, box-office receipts.
taquillero, -a *adj.* 1 box-office draw: *el actor más taquillero = the biggest box-office draw.* || *s.m.* y *f.* 2 person in charge of the box-office or ticket office.
taquímetro *s.m.* speedometer, tachymeter, tacheometer.
tara *s.f.* 1 defect. 2 COM. tare. 3 tally stick.
taracea *s.f.* marquetry, inlaid work.
tarado, -a *adj.* 1 defective, damaged (mercancías). 2 crippled, maimed (persons). 3 (fam.) cretinous, idiotic. || *s.m.* y *f.* 4 (fam.) cretin, idiot.
tarambana *adj.* 1 (fam.) mad, wild. || *s.m.* y *f.* 2 madcap, crackpot.
taranta *s.f.* 1 (Am.) madness, sudden impulse (locura). 2 drunkenness (embriaguez). 3 giddiness (mareo).
tarantela *s.f.* MUS. tarantella.
tarántula *s.f.* ZOOL. tarantula.
tararear *v.t.* to hum.
tarareo *s.m.* humming.
tarasca *s.f.* 1 monster. 2 (fam.) old hag (de una mujer).
tarascada *s.f.* 1 bite, snap. 2 tart, rude reply.
tarascar *v.t.* to bite, to snap at.
tarascón *s.m.* bite, nip.
tardanza *s.f.* 1 delay, linger. 2 slowness.
tardar *v.i.* 1 to delay. 2 to take: *tardar seis horas = to take six hours; no tarde en llegar = don't take long/don't be long.*
tarde *s.f.* 1 afternoon, evening. || *adv.* 2 late. || 3 **más vale — que nunca,** better late than never. 4 **— o temprano,** sooner or later. 5 **de — en —,** from time to time.
tardío, -a *adj.* 1 late, overdue, belated, tardy. 2 slow: *tardío en decidirse = slow to decide.* 3 late (fruta).

tardo, -a *adj.* slow, sluggish, lazy, dull.
tarea *s.f.* 1 job, task, chore. || 2 **— de colegio,** homework.
tarifa *s.f.* 1 tariff, rate, fare: *tarifa turística = tourist rate.* 2 price list.
tarifar *v.t.* to price, to fix a price.
tarima *s.f.* 1 platform, dais. 2 foot stool. 3 bench. 4 stand (soporte).
tarja *s.f.* 1 tally, tally stick (medida). 2 shield, buckler (escudo).
tarjar *v.t.* 1 to keep tally. 2 (Am.) to cross out (tachar).
tarjeta *s.f.* 1 card. || 2 **— de crédito,** FIN. credit card. 3 **— de embarque,** boarding pass. 4 **— de identidad,** identity card. 5 **— de visita,** visiting card, (EE.UU.) calling card. 6 **— postal,** postcard.
tarlatana *s.f.* tarlatan, transparent mulin.
tarquín *s.m.* mud, slime, ooze.
tarro *s.m.* jar.
tarso *s.m.* ANAT. tarsus.
tarta *s.f.* 1 cake, tart. || 2 **— de cumpleaños,** birthday cake. 3 **— de manzana,** apple tart.
tartajear *v.i.* to stammer, to stutter.
tartajeo *s.m.* stammering, stuttering.
tartamudear *v.i.* to stammer, to stutter.
tartamudeo *s.m.* stuttering, stammering.
tartamudo, -a *adj.* 1 stuttering, stammering. || *s.m.* y *f.* 2 stuterer, stammerer.
tartana *s.f.* light carriage, trap.
tártaro, -a *adj.* y *s.* 1 Tartar. || *s.m.* 2 QUIM. tartar. 3 (lit.) Tartarus, hell.
tartera *s.f.* 1 lunch box (fiambrera). 2 cake tin, baking pan.
tarugo *s.m.* 1 imbecil, blockhead, dolt, idiot. 2 (Am.) fright, scare (susto). 3 chunk, peg, plug (madera). 4 wooden paving block (adoquín).
tarumba *adj.* 1 (fam.) confused. || 2 **volver — a uno,** to drive one mad.
tas *s.m.* small anvil (de platero).
tasa *s.f.* 1 appraisal, valuation, estimate. 2 tax: *tasa de importación = import tax.* 3 measure, standard, norm. 4 rate: *tasa de natalidad = birth rate; tasa de interés = interest rate.* || 5 **— de cambio,** ECON. exchange rate.
tasación *s.f.* valuation, assessment, appraisal.
tasadamente *adv.* sparingly, with moderation.
tasador, -a *adj.* 1 appraising. || *s.m.* y *f.* valuer, (EE.UU.) appraiser.
tasca *s.f.* 1 bar, tavern. || 2 **ir de tascas,** to go on a pub crawl, (EE.UU.) to go barhopping.
tascar *v.t.* 1 to beat flax (lino). 2 to graze, browse, munch (hierba). || 3 **— el freno,** to bite the bit.
tata *s.f.* 1 (Am.) dad, daddy. 2 (fam.) sister. 2 nursemaid, nanny (niñera).
tatarabuela *s.f.* great-great-grandmother.
tatarabuelo *s.m.* 1 great-great-grandfather. || *s.pl.* 2 great-great-grandparents.
tataranieta *s.f.* great-great-granddaughter.
tataranieto *s.m.* 1 great-great-grandson. || *s.pl.* 2 great-great-grandchildren.
¡tate! *interj.* 1 look out! be careful! watch your step! 2 so that's it, oh, I see.
tatuaje *s.m.* 1 tatoo. 2 tatooing.
tatuar *v.t.* to tatoo.
tauca *s.f.* (Am.) heap, pile.
taumaturgo *s.m.* miracle worker, thaumaturge.
taurino, -a *adj.* 1 bull-fighting. || 2 **fiesta —,** bullfight.
Tauro *s.m.* Taurus.
tauromaquia *s.f.* art of bullfighting.
tautología *s.f.* LIT. tautology.
tautológico, -a *adj.* LIT. tautological.
taxativamente *adv.* limitedly, specifically, precisely.
taxativo, -a *adj.* limited, restricted, precise, specific.
taxi *s.m.* taxi, cab, taxi-cab.
taxidermia *s.f.* taxidermy.
taxidermista *s.m.* y *f.* taxidermist.
taxímetro *s.m.* taximeter.
taxista *s.m.* y *f.* taxidriver, cabby.
taxonomía *s.f.* taxonomy.
taza *s.f.* 1 cup. 2 cupful. 3 bowl (lavabo). 4 (Am.) basin (palangana).
tazarse *v.pron.* to fray.
tazón *s.m.* bowl, basin (cuenco), large cup.
te *pron.* 1 you: *te llamaré = I'll call you; te lo mandé = I sent it to you.* 2 REL. thee (Dios). || *pron.r.* 3 yourself: *diviértete = enjoy yourself.* 4 REL. thyself (Dios).
té *s.m.* 1 tea. || 2 **— con leche,** white tea.
tea *s.f.* 1 torch, firebrand. || 2 **coger una —,** (fam.) to get plastered.
teatral *adj.* 1 theatre, drama: *temporada teatral = theatre season; grupo teatral = drama group.* || 2 **obra —,** dramatic work, play. 3 (fig.) theatrical, melodramatic, histrionic.
teatro *s.m.* 1 theatre, (EE.UU.) theater edificio. 2 theatre, acting, stage (profesión): *dejar el teatro = to give up the stage.* 3 LIT. drama, plays, dramatic work. || 4 **hacer —,** (fig.) to exaggerate, to be dramatic.
tebeo *s.m.* comic, comic book.
teca *s.f.* 1 teak. 2 ANAT. Theca.
tecla *s.f.* 1 key, spacer (de instrumento musical, máquina de escribir, etc.): *tecla de borrado = delete key; tecla de cambio = shift key; tecla de cursor = cursor key; tecla de desplazamiento = scroll key; tecla de retroceso = back spacer; tecla de tabulación = tab key.* || 2 **dar en la —,** (fig.) to strike the right note, to get the hang of s'thg. 3 **no le queda ninguna — por tocar,** there's nothing else left for him to try.
teclado *s.m.* keyboard, keys (instrumento musical, máquina de escribir, etc.).
teclear *v.i.* 1 to finger the keyboard, to play (the piano). 2 to type (escribir a máquina). 3 (fig.) to drum one's fingers. 4 (Am.) to be weak, ill, to go badly.
técnica *s.f.* technique, method, craft, skill.
técnicamente *adv.* technically.
tecnicidad *s.f.* technicality.
tecnicismo *s.m.* technical term.
técnico, -a *adj.* 1 technical. || *s.m.* y *f.* 2 technician, expert, especialist.
tecnicolor *s.m.* technicolor.
tecnocracia *s.f.* technocracy.
tecnócrata *s.m.* y *f.* technocrat.
tecnocrático, -a *adj.* technocratic.
tecnología *s.f.* technology.
tecnológico, -a *adj.* technological.
tecnólogo, -a *s.m.* y *f.* technologist.
tecolote (Am.) *adj.* 1 reddish-brown (color). || *s.m.* 2 ZOOL. owl.
tectónico, -a *adj.* tectonic.
techado *s.m.* roof, covering.
techar *v.t.* to roof, to cover with a roof.
techo *s.m.* 1 ceiling (interior). 2 roof (exterior): *techo corredizo = sunroof, sliding roof; techo de paja = thatched roof.* 3 (fig.) limit, ceiling.
techumbre *s.f.* roof, roofing.
tedéum *s.m.* REL. Te Deum.
tedio *s.m.* (fam.) boredom, tedium, lack of interest.
tedioso, -a *adj.* (form.) tedious, boring, wearisome.
tegumento *s.m.* tegument.
teísmo *s.m.* theism.
teísta *adj.* 1 theistic. || *s.m.* y *f.* 2 theist.
teja *s.f.* 1 tile. || 2 **de tejas abajo,** in this world. 3 **de tejas arriba,** in heaven. 4 **pagar a toca —,** (fam.) to pay cash.
tejado *s.m.* 1 roof, tiled roof. 2 **hasta el —,** (fig.) full, packed.
tejar *v.t.* to tile.
tejemaneje *s.m.* (fam.) 1 to-do, fuss, bustle. 2 trickery, intrigue. || 3 **se trae un —,** he's up to something.
tejedor, -a *adj.* 1 (Am.) scheming, intriguing. || *s.m.* y *f.* 2 weaver. 3 (Am.) intriguer, schemer, meddler.
tejedura *s.f.* 1 weaving (acción de tejer). 2 texture, weave.
tejer *v.t.* 1 to weave, to knit (hacer punto). 2 to spin: *la araña teje su tela = the spider spins its web.*
tejido *s.m.* 1 material, fabric: *tejido de punto = knitted fabric.* 2 weave, texture. 3 ANAT. tissue. || *s.m.pl.* 4 textile: *fábrica de tejidos = textile mill.*
tejo *s.m.* 1 disk (plancha metálica). 2 quoits (juego). 3 hopscotch (rayuela). 4 BOT. yew (árbol). || 5 **tirar/echar los tejos a alguien,** (fam.) to make advances (entre mujer y hombre).
tejón *s.m.* ZOOL. badger.
tejuelo *s.m.* book label.
tela *s.f.* 1 material, cloth, fabric, stuff: *tela de saco = sackcloth.* 2 ANAT. membrane, film, skin. 3 ART. canvas (lienzo), painting (cuadro). 4 (fam.) dough (dinero). 5 **— metálica,** wire netting. 6 **— de araña,** spider's web, cobweb. 7 (fig.) matter: *hay tela que cortar = there's lots to be done; estar en tela de juicio = to be in doubt; un asunto de mucha tela = a complicated matter.*
telar *s.m.* 1 loom, frame. || *s.m.pl.* 2 textile mill. 3 gridiron, flies (en un teatro).
telaraña *s.f.* web, spider's web, cobweb.
tele *s.f.* (fam.) telly, T.V.

telecomunicación *s.f.* telecommunication.
telediario *s.m.* television news bulletin.
teledifusión *s.f.* television broadcast.
teledirigido, -a *adj.* remote controlled.
teleférico *s.m.* 1 cable car, cable railway. 2 skilift.
telefilm *s.m.* telefilm.
telefonazo *s.m.* (fam.) 1 ring, call. || 2 **dar un — a alguien,** to ring someone up.
telefonear *v.t.* e *i.* to telephone, to phone, to call, to ring.
telefonema *s.m.* telephoned telegram.
telefonía *s.f.* telephony.
telefónicamente *adv.* by telephone.
telefónico, -a *adj.* telephone, telephonic: *cabina telefónica = telephone box; compañía telefónica = telephone company.*
telefonista *s.m.* y *f.* telephone operator, telephonist.
teléfono *s.m.* 1 telephone, phone. || 2 **está hablando por —,** he's on the phone. 3 **llamar por —,** to call, to phone, to telephone, to ring up.
telefoto *s.f.* telephotograph, telephoto.
telegrafía *s.f.* telegraphy.
telegrafiar *v.t.* e *i.* to telegraph, to wire, to send a wire.
telegráficamente *adv.* by telegraph, by telegram.
telegráfico, -a *adj.* telegraphic.
telegrafista *s.m.* y *f.* telegrapher, telegraphist, operator.
telégrafo *s.m.* 1 telegraph. || 2 **— óptico,** semaphore.
telegrama *s.m.* telegram, wire: *poner un telegrama = to send a telegram/to wire.*
teleimpresor *s.m.* teleprinter, teletype.
telele *s.m.* (fam.) fainting fit, turn.
telemando *s.m.* remote control.
telemática *s.f.* telematics, data transmission.
telemedir *v.t.* INF. to telemeter.
telemetro *s.m.* rangefinder, telemeter.
telenovela *s.f.* TV. television serial.
teleobjetivo *s.m.* FOT. telephoto lens, zoom lens.
teleología *s.f.* FIL. teleology.
teleósteo *adj.* y *s.m.* ZOOL. teleost.
telepatía *s.f.* telepathy.
telepático, -a *adj.* telepathic.
telera *s.f.* 1 plough pin (arado). 2 transom, crosspiece (carro). 3 jaw, cheek (prensa). 4 MIL. transom of a gun carriage. 5 MAR. rack block.
telescópico, -a *adj.* telescopic.
telescopio *s.m.* telescope.
telesilla *s.m.* chair lift, ski lift.
telespectador, -ora *s.m.* y *f.* televiewer.
telesquí *s.m.* ski lift.
teletipo *s.m.* teletype, teleprinter, teletypewriter.
televidente *s.m.* y *f.* viewer, televiewer.
televisar *v.t.* to televise.
televisión *s.f.* television, T.V.: *televisión por cable = cable television; ver la tele = to watch television.*
televisivo, -a *adj.* 1 television: *serie televisiva = television series/television serial.* 2 telegenic (de una persona).
televisor *s.m.* television set, T.V. set.
télex *s.m.* telex.
telón *s.m.* 1 curtain: *telón de boca = house curtain.* || 2 **— de acero,** POL. iron curtain. 3 **— de fondo,** back drop. 4 **— metálico,** safety curtain.
telúrico, -a *adj.* telluric, of the earth, (fig.) earthy.
telurio *s.m.* QUIM. tellurium.
tema *s.m.* 1 topic, subject, theme, issue: *el tema del debate = the subject of the debate; tema de actualidad = current issue.* 2 MUS. theme, motif. 3 GRAM. stem. 4 **pasar del —,** to dodge the issue, **cada loco con su —,** everyone has his own hobbyhorse, **tener — por un rato,** to have plenty to talk about. || *s.f.* 1 fixed idea, mania, obsession: *tener tema = to be stubborn.* 2 grudge, ill will: *tener tema a uno = to have a grudge againsts' one.*
temario *s.m.* 1 programme, set of themes, group of subjects. 2 agenda, subjects to discuss (de una reunión).
temática *s.f.* theme, subjects, topics.
temático, -a *adj.* 1 thematic. 2 GRAM. stem.
tembladera *s.f.* shaking fit, trembling fit.
tembladeral *s.m.* (Am.) quagmire.
temblar *v.i.* 1 to tremble, to shake, to shudder, to quiver: *temblar de miedo = to shake with fright; temblar como un azogado = to shake like a leaf.* 2 to shiver: *temblar de frío = to shiver with cold.* || 3 **— por la vida,** to fear for one's life.
tembleque *s.m.* shaking fit.
temblequear *v.i.* 1 to shake, to tremble, to quiver. 2 (fig.) to pretend to tremble.
temblor *s.m.* 1 trembling, shaking, shuddering, shivering, shivers. || 2 **— de tierra,** earthquake.
tembloroso, -a *adj.* 1 shaking, trembling, quivering. 2 tremulous (de voz).
temedero, -a *adj.* dread, redoubtable.
temer *v.t.* 1 to be afraid, to fear, to dread: *temer la oscuridad = to be afraid of the dark; temer a Dios = to fear God.* || *v.i.* 2 to be afraid, to fear for: *no temas = don't be afraid; temo por su vida = I fear for his life.* || *v.r.* 3 to be afraid: *me temo que es imposible = I'm afraid it's impossible.*
temerario, -a *adj.* rash, reckless, hasty, temerarious.
temeridad *s.f.* temerity, recklessness, rashness, hastiness, folly.
temerosamente *adv.* fearfully, timidly.
temeroso, -a *adj.* 1 fearful, frightful (cosa). 2 fearful, frightened, temerous (persona). || 3 **— de Dios,** God-fearing.
temible *adj.* fearsome, fearful, frightful, dreadful.
temor *s.m.* 1 fear, dread (miedo). 2 apprehension, mistrust (recelo).
témpano *s.m.* 1 floe, iceberg. 2 MUS. small drum, kettledrum. 3 MUS. drumhead. 4 ARQ. tympan. || 5 **quedarse como un —,** to be chilled to the bone.
temperamento *s.m.* 1 temperament, nature, disposition: *tener temperamento = to be temperamental.* 2 (Am.) climate, wather.
temperante *adj.* 1 calming, sedative. 2 (Am.) teetotal, abstemious. || *s.m.* y *f.* 3 teetotaller, abstainer.
temperar *v.t.* 1 to moderate, to mitigate, to calm, to relieve. 2 MUS. to temper. || *v.i.* 3 (Am.) to have a change of air, to spend the summer.
temperature *s.f.* 1 temperature. 2 MED. temperature, fever.
tempestad *s.f.* 1 storm, tempest. || 2 **— de arena,** sandstorm. 3 **— de insultos,** a storm of insults. 4 **una — en un vaso de agua,** a storm in a teacup.
tempestivo, -a *adj.* seasonable, opportune, timely.
tempestuoso, -a *adj.* tempestuous, turbulent, stormy.
templado, -a *adj.* 1 restrained, moderate (en comer o beber). 2 warm, lukewarm (de temperatura). 3 temperate, mild (de clima o tiempo). 4 MUS. tuned, in tune. 5 (fig.) brave, courageous (valiente). 6 **nervios bien templados,** (fig.) nerves of steel.
templanza *s.f.* 1 temperance, moderation, restraint. 2 MET. mildness.
templar *v.t.* 1 to moderate, to restrain, to temper. 2 to warm up (agua fría), to cool down (agua caliente). 3 MUS. to tune, to temper. 4 MEC. to adjust. 5 to temper (acero). 6 to knock down, to beat (pegar, golpear). || *v.i.* 7 to warm up (del tiempo). || *v.r.* 8 to be moderate, to control oneself. 9 (fam.) to get drunk (emborracharse). 10 (fig. y Am.) to fall in love.
templario *s.m.* REL. Templar, Knight Templar.
temple *s.m.* 1 temper (de vidrio, metal). 2 MUS. tuning. 3 weather. 4 mood, humour: *estar de buen temple = to be in a good mood.* 5 ART. tempera. 6 **pintar al —,** to distemper.
templo *s.m.* 1 temple, church, chapel, shrine, sanctuary. 2 **como un —,** (fam.) huge, enormous. 3 **es una verdad como un —,** it is the plain truth.
temporada *s.f.* 1 season: *temporada alta = high season; fuera de temporada = off season; en plena temporada = at the height of the season.* 2 spell, period, time: *temporada de exámenes = examination period; pasar una temporada = to spend some time.* 3 **por temporada,** on and off.
temporal *adj.* 1 temporary, provisional. || *s.m.* 2 storm, tempest, spell of rough weather. 3 **capear el —,** to weather the storm, to ride out the storm. 4 **poder —,** REL. temporal power.
temporalidad *s.f.* temporality.
temporalmente *adv.* temporally, provisionally.
temporero *adj.* 1 seasonal, temporary, casual. || *s.m.* 2 temporary worker, seasonal worker.
temporizar *v.i.* 1 to temporize. 2 to pass the time, to kill time (matar el tiempo).
tempranal *adj.* early (fruta y hortalizas).
tempranamente *adv.* prematurely, early.

tempranear *v.i.* 1 (Am.) to get up early. 2 (Am.) to sow early.
tempranero, -a *adj.* 1 (Am.) early-rising. 2 AGR. early.
temprano, -a *adj.* 1 early. || *adv.* 2 early.
tenacidad *s.f.* tenacity, stubbornness, perseverance.
tenaz *adj.* 1 tenacious, stubborn, resistant. 2 persistant (dolor). 3 hard to remove (mancha). 4 ingrained (suciedad).
tenazas *s.f.pl.* 1 pliers, pincers. 2 tongs (para el fuego). 3 MED. forceps. 4 TEC. jaws. 5 claws, pincers (crustáceos).
tenazmente *adv.* tenaciously, stubbornly.
tendal *s.m.* 1 awning. 2 canvas used to catch olives (para recoger aceitunas). 3 (Am.) heap, disorder.
tendedero *s.m.* 1 drying place. 2 clothes line.
tendencia *s.f.* tendency, inclination, trend: *tendencia imperante = dominant trend; tendencia política = political tendency; tendencia de zurdo = to have a tendency towards left-handedness.*
tendencioso, -a *adj.* tendentious, (EE.UU.) tendencious.
tender *v.t.* 1 to stretch, to spreat out, to lay out. 2 to hang out (ropa). 3 to build (puente). 4 to draw (arco). 5 to lay (cable). 6 (Am.) to set (la mesa o la cama). || *v.i.* 7 to tend towards, to have a tendency towards. || *v.pron.* to lie down, to stretch out.
tenderete *s.m.* 1 stall, market booth. 2 display (de mercancías). 3 clothes line (para la ropa).
tendero, -a *s.m.* y *f.* shopkeeper.
tendido, -a *adj.* 1 lying down. 2 spread out, laid out. 3 hung out (ropa). || *s.m.* 1 ARQ. coat of plaster. 2 front rows of seats (plaza de toros). 3 laying (de cable o vía). 4 (Am.) bedclothes (ropa de cama). 5 (Am.) long tether, rope (cuerda). 6 (Am.) stall, booth (puesto de mercado). || *p.p.* 7 de **tender.**
tendón *s.m.* ANAT. tendon, sinew.
tenebrosidad *s.f.* 1 darkness, gloom. 2 (fig.) dimness, blackness, obscurity, shadiness.
tenebroso, -a *adj.* dark, gloomy, dim, dismal. 2 (fig.) sinister, shady, obscure.
tenedor *s.m.* 1 fork. 2 COM. holder, bearer: *tenedor de acciones = shareholder.* || 3 **— de libros,** bookkeeper.
teneduría *s.f.* bookkeeping.
tenencia *s.f.* 1 tenancy, occupancy (de casa). 2 tenure (de puesto). 3 possession: *tenencia ilícita de armas = illicit possession of arms.* 4 deputyship: *tenencia de alcaldía = post of deputy mayor.*
tener *v.t.* 1 to have, to have got: *tiene dolor de cabeza = he has a headache; no tengo dinero = I haven't got any money.* 2 to have, to own, to possess: *tienen una casa en el campo = they own a house in the country.* 3 to have, to hold: *lo tiene en la mano = he is holding it in his hand; ¡ten! = here you are!/catch!/take it!* 4 to hold, to contain: *la caja tiene galletas = the box contains biscuits.* 5 to be: *tiene dos años = he is two years old; tiene hambre = he is hungry; tiene frío = he is cold; tienes razón = you are right; ¡ten cuidado! = be careful!* 6 to be, to measure: *tiene un metro de largo = it is one meter long.* 7 to keep, to maintain: *tener al día = to keep up to date; tener al corriente = to keep informed.* 8 **— a mano,** to have on hand. 9 **— por,** to consider: *le tengo por listo = I consider him clever.* 10 **— que,** to have, to must: *tengo que irme = I have to go, I must go.* 11 **— puesto,** to wear, to have on. 12 **— ganas,** to want to, to feel like: *tengo ganas de cantar = I feel like singing.* 13 **— en pie,** to stand up. 14 **— por,** to consider oneself: *se tiene por listo = he considers himself clever.* 15 **¿qué tiene?,** what's the matter?, what's wrong?.
tenia *s.f.* ZOOL. tapeworm, taenia.
tenida *s.f.* (Am.) meeting (reunión).
teniente *s.m.* 1 MIL. lieutenant. 2 deputy: *teniente de alcalde = deputy mayor.*
tenis *s.m.* 1 tennis. || 2 **— de mesa,** table tennis, ping pong.
tenista *s.m.* y *f.* tennis player.
tenístico, -a *adj.* tennis.
tenor *s.m.* 1 MUS. tenor. 2 (fig.) meaning, sense, purport, condition, tenor. || 3 **a —,** likewise, in the same fashion, in accordance with.
tenorio *s.m.* ladykiller, Don Juan.
tensar *v.t.* 1 to tauten (cable). 2 to draw (arco).
tensión *s.m.* 1 tension, tautness. 2 MEC. stress, strain. 3 ELEC. tension, voltage. 4 MED. pressure (sangre): *tener la tensión alta = to have high blood pressure.* 5 MED. strain, nervous tension, stress (estrés). 6 (fig.) tenseness: *la tensión de la situación política = the tenseness of the political situation.*
tenso, -a *adj.* 1 tense, taut, tight. 2 (fig.) tense, strained: *relaciones tensas = strained relations.*
tensor, -a *adj.* tensible, tightening. || *s.m.* 1 tensor, tightener. 2 TEC. turnbuckle, guy, strut. 3 MED. tensor, stiffener (cuello), chest-expander.
tentación *s.f.* temptation: *ceder a la tentación = to yield to temptation; vencer la tentación = to overcome the temptation.*
tentacular *adj.* tentacular.
tentáculo *s.m.* tentacle, feeler.
tentador, -a *adj.* 1 tempting, enciting. || *s.m.* 2 tempter. || *s.f.* 3 temptress.
tentar *v.t.* 1 to touch, to feel (tocar). 2 to attempt, to try (intentar). 3 to try, to test, to try out (probar). 4 to tempt, to entice: *le tentó con un helado = he tempted him with an icecream.* 5 MED. to probe.
tentativa *s.f.* attempt, try: *tentativa de asesinato = attempted murder.*
tentativo, -a *adj.* tentative: *es una cosa tentativa = it's a tentative thing.*
tentemozo *s.m.* prop, support.
tentempié *s.m.* bite to eat, snack.
tentetieso *s.m.* tumbler, roly-poly.
tenue *adj.* 1 thin, tenuous, insubstantial, slight. 2 light (neblina). 3 subdued, faint, weak (sonido, luz). 4 simple, natural (estilo). 5 insignificant.
tenuidad *s.f.* 1 thinness, fineness, tenuousness, tenuity. 2 thinness (niebla). 3 weakness, faintness (sonido, luz). 4 simplicity (estilo). 5 trifle, triviality.
teñible *adj.* dyeable.
teñido, -a *adj.* 1 dyed. 2 dyed, tinted (pelo). 3 (fig.) tinged. || *s.m.* 1 dyeing (acción). 2 dye (color).
teñir *v.t.* 1 to dye. 2 ART. to tone down. 3 (fig.) to tinge, to colour. 4 to stain (marchar).
teocracia *s.f.* theocracy.
teocrático, -a *adj.* theocratic.
teodicea *s.f.* theodicy.
teodolito *s.m.* theodolite.
teologal *adj.* theological, theologic.
teología *s.f.* REL. theology.
teológico, -a *adj.* theological, theologic.
teólogo *adj.* theologian.
teorema *s.m.* MAT. theorem.
teorético, -a *adj.* (Am.) theoretic, theoretical.
teoría *s.f.* theory: *en teoría = in theory/theoretically.*
teórica *s.f.* theoretics, theory.
teóricamente *adv.* theoretically.
teórico, -a *adj.* theoretic, theoretical. || *s.m.* y *f.* theoretician.
teorizante *s.m.* y *f.* 1 theoretician, theorist. 2 (desp.) theorizer.
teorizar *v.i.* to theorise.
teosofía *s.f.* theosophy.
teosófico, -a *adj.* theosophical.
teósofo, -a *s.m.* y *f.* theosophist.
tepe *s.m.* turf, sod.
tequila *s.f.* tequila.
TER *s.m.* intercity high speed train (abr. de tren español rápido).
terapeuta *s.m.* y *f.* therapist.
terapéutica *s.f.* therapeutics, therapy.
terapéutico, -a *adj.* therapeutic, therapeutical.
terapia *s.f.* therapy: *terapia laboral = occupational therapy.*
terbio *s.m.* QUIM. terbium.
tercamente *adv.* obstinately, stubbornly.
tercelete *adj.* ARQ. tierceron.
tercer *adj.* third: *el tercer piso = the third floor; tercer mundo = Third World.*
tercero, -a *adj.* 1 third: *una tercera parte = a third.* || *s.m.* 2 third person, third party. 3 mediator, arbitrator, go-between. 4 (desp.) pimp, pander, procurer.
terceto *s.m.* 1 LIT. tercet, triplet (estrofa). 2 MUS. trio.
terciar *v.t.* 1 to divide into three parts. 2 to slant, to slope, to place crosswise or diagonally. 3 to wear across one's chest (una prenda). 4 (Am.) to water down (vino, etc.). || *v.i.* to arbitrate, to mediate: *tercer entre dos rivales = to mediate between two rivals.* || *v.pron.* to occur, to arise, to present itself: *si se tercia = if it so happens/should the occasion arise.*
terciario, -a *adj.* tertiary.

tercio, -a *adj.* 1 third. || *s.m.* y *f.* 1 third. 2 MIL. infantry regiment (hace muchos años). 3 MIL. legion: *tercio extranjero = foreign legion.* 4 MIL. division (de la Guardia Civil). 5 stage, part of a bullfight: *tercio de varas = opening stage.* 6 (Am.) pack, bale. || 7 **hacer buen —,** to do a good turn. 8 **— de libre disposición,** DER. disposable portion of an estate.
terciopelo *s.m.* velvet.
terco, -a *adj.* 1 obstinately, stubborn: *terco como una mula = as stubborn as a mule.* 2 hard, tough, hard to work (material).
terebenteno *s.m.* QUIM. terebenthene.
tergiversable *adj.* twisted, distorted.
tergiversación *s.f.* distortion, twisting, misrepresentation.
tergiversador, -a *adj.* 1 distorting. || *s.m.* y *f.* 2 person who distorts the facts.
tergiversar *v.t.* to distort, to twist, to misrepresent. || *v.i.* to prevaricate, (fam.) to chop and change.
termal *adj.* thermal.
termas *s.f.pl.* hot baths, hot springs.
termes *s.m.* ZOOL. termite.
térmico, -a *adj.* thermal, thermic, heat.
terminación *s.f.* 1 end, ending, conclusion, termination. 2 completion: *la terminación de los planes = the completion of the plans.* 3 TEC. finish (acabado). 4 GRAM. ending.
terminador, -a *s.m.* y *f.* finisher.
terminal *adj.* 1 final, ultimate, terminal. 2 BOT., ELEC. terminal. || *s.f.* 1 terminal (aérea). 2 (Am.) terminus (ferrovial).
terminante *adj.* 1 terminating, ending. 2 final, decisive, definitive (resultados). 3 categorical, conclusive: *respuesta terminante = categorical answer.* 4 strict (prohibición).
terminantemente *adv.* finally, decisively, definitively, categorically, conclusively, strictly: *queda terminante prohibido = it is strictly forbidden.*
terminar *v.t.* 1 to finish, to end, to conclude, to complete. || *v.i.* 2 to finish, to end. 3 to have just: *termino de llegar = I have just arrived.* 4 to end up: *terminar por hacer algo = to end up doing something; terminaron mal = they ended up on bad terms; este chico terminará mal = this boy will end up badly/he'll come to no good.* || *v.pron.* 5 to come to an end, to draw to a close (de una reunión). 6 to run out: *se ha terminado el pan = the bread has run out.*
terminativo, -a *adj.* terminative.
término *s.m.* 1 end, finish, conclusion: *poner término a = to finish off/to put an end to/to conclude.* 2 terminus (de una línea de transporte). 3 boundary, limit. 4 period, term, time (plazo). 5 POL. district, area. 6 GRAM. term: *en términos sencillos = in simple terms; en términos generales = terminally speaking; en otros términos = in other words; según los términos del contrato = according to the terms of the contract.* 7 point (argumento): *invertir los términos = to stand an argument on its head.* 8 compromise, middle way: *no hay término medio = there is no compromise.* || 9 **en primer —,** in first, place, firstly. 10 **en último —,** lastly, in the last analysis, as a last resort. 11 **— medio,** average.
terminología *s.f.* terminology.
termita *s.f.* termite *s.m.* ZOOL. termite.
termo *s.m.* 1 thermos flask. 2 water heater (calentador).
termodinámica *adj.* thermodynamic. || *s.f.* thermodynamics.
termoelectricidad *s.f.* thermoelectricity.
termómetro *s.m.* thermometer.
termométrico, -a *adj.* thermometric, thermometrical.
termosifón *s.m.* 1 boiler, water heater. 2 FIS. thermosiphon.
termostato *s.m.* thermostat.
terna *s.f.* 1 list of three candidates for a post, short list. 2 pair of threes (en los dados). 3 set of dice.
ternario *adj.* ternary.
ternera *s.f.* 1 heifer calf. 2 veal (carne).
ternero *s.m.* calf, bull calf.
terneza *s.f.* 1 tenderness. || *s.f.pl.* 2 tender words, endearments, sweet nothings.
ternila *s.f.* gristle, cartilage.
ternilloso, -a *adj.* gristly, cartilaginous.
terno *s.m.* 1 set of three. 2 three piece suit (traje). 3 (Am.) set of jewellry (necklace, earrings, brooch). 4 oath, swearword, curse (palabrota).
ternura *s.f.* tenderness, fondness, affection.
terquedad *s.f.* stubbornness, obstinacy, inflexibility.
terracota *s.f.* terracotta.
terrado *s.m.* flat roof, terrace.
terraja *s.f.* 1 die-stock, screw-plate (para tornillos). 2 modelling board (para molduras).
terraplén *s.m.* 1 embankment (de la vía, carretera). 2 MIL. rampart, mound, earthwork. 3 slope, gradient. 4 AGR. terrace.
terraplenar *v.t.* 1 to level off. 2 to bank up. 3 AGR. to terrace.
terráqueo, -a *adj.* terraqueous: *globo terráqueo = globe/earth.*
terrateniente *s.m.* landowner, landholder.
terraza *s.f.* 1 terrace. 2 flat roof (azotea). 3 balcony. 4 pavement café. 5 AGR. terrace, terracing. 6 two-handled glazed jar.
terrazo *s.m.* terrazzo.
terremoto *s.m.* earthquake.
terrenal *adj.* worldly, earthly, mundane.
terreno, -a *adj.* terrestrial, earthly, worldly. || *s.m.* 1 ground, land, terrain. 2 AGR. soil, land, earth: *terreno arenoso = sandy soil.* 3 plot, piece of land, lot, site: *comprar un terreno = to buy a piece of land; terrenos para la construcción = building lots.* 4 DEP. field, ground, pitch. 5 (fig.) field, sphere: *en el terreno de la política = in the political field.* || 6 **ganar/perder —,** to gain/to lose ground. 7 **ceder —,** to give way. 8 **preparar el —,** to prepare, to pave the way. 9 **reconocer el —,** MIL. to reconnoitre. 10 **sobre el —,** on the spot, as we go along. 11 **tantear el —,** to see how the land lies. 12 **un coche todo —,** jeep, four-wheel drive.
térreo, -a *adj.* 1 earthy, earthen. 2 earth-coloured.
terrestre *adj.* 1 terrestrial, earthly. 2 ground, land: *fuerzas terrestres = ground troops.*
terrible *adj.* terrible, awful, dreadful.
terriblemente *adv.* terribly, dreadfully, awfully.
terrícola *adj.* 1 terricolous. || *s.m.* y *f.* 2 earth dweller, earthling.
territorial *adj.* territorial.
territorio *s.m.* 1 territory. 2 (Am.) region, district.
terrón *s.m.* 1 clod (de tierra). 2 lump (de azúcar). 3 AGR. field, patch.
terror *s.m.* terror.
terrorífico, -a *adj.* terrifying, frightening.
terrorismo *s.m.* terrorism.
terrorista *adj./s.m.* y *f.* terrorist.
terrosidad *s.f.* earthiness.
terroso, -a *adj.* 1 earthy. 2 brown, earth-coloured.
terruño *s.m.* 1 plot, piece of land. 2 lump, clod. 3 (fig.) country, land, native land.
terso, -a *adj.* 1 clear. 2 smooth: *piel tersa = smooth skin.* 3 polished, shining, glossy. 4 (fig.) flowing, smooth, polished, easy (estilo).
tersura *s.f.* 1 smoothness, glossiness, polish, shine. 2 (fig.) smoothness, polish (estilo).
tertulia *s.f.* 1 social gathering, get-together. 2 group, circle, set: *tertulia literaria = literary circle.* 3 **estar de —,** to get together, to sit around, talking. 4 (Am.) gallery, boxes (teatro).
tesela *s.f.* tessala, mosaic piece.
tesina *s.f.* project, minor thesis, dissertation (for a first degree).
tesis *s.f.* 1 thesis: *tesis doctoral = doctoral thesis.* 2 theory, idea: *tenemos la misma tesis = we hold the same idea.*
tesitura *s.f.* 1 mood, attitude, frame of mind. 2 situation, circumstances. 3 MUS. tessitura.
teso, -a *adj.* tight, taut.
tesón *s.m.* firmness, inflexibility, tenacity, persistance: *oponer con tesón = to oppose firmly.*
tesonería *s.f.* stubbornness, obstinacy, perseverance, tenacity.
tesonero, -a *adj.* tenacious, persistant, persevering.
tesorería *s.f.* 1 treasury, treasurer's office. 2 treasurership.
tesorero, -a *s.m.* y *f.* treasurer.
tesoro *s.m.* 1 treasure: *tesoro escondido = buried treasure.* 2 POL. treasury, exchequer. 3 LIT. thesaurus. 4 (fig.) treasure, gem, jewel: *la chica es un tesoro = the girl is a real treasure.* 5 (fam.) dear, darling.
test *s.m.* test.
testa *s.f.* 1 head (cabeza): *testa coronada = crowned head.* 2 front (frente). 3 (fig.) brains, gumption.

testador *s.m.* testate, testator.
testadora *s.f.* testate, testatrix.
testamentaría *s.f.* 1 testamentary execution, execution of a will. 2 estate, inheritance. 3 meeting of executors.
testamentario, -a *adj.* 1 testamentary. || *s.m.* 2 executor. || *s.f.* 3 executrix.
testamento *s.m.* 1 will, testament: *hacer testamento = to make one's will; testamento auténtico = legal will; testamento cerrado = sealed will.* || 2 **Antiguo –,** REL. Old Testament. 3 **Nuevo –,** REL. New Testament.
testar *v.i.* to make a will or testament.
testarada *s.f.* bump, bang on the head: *darse una testarada = to bump one's head.*
testarazo *s.m.* 1 bump on the head. 2 butt, header (dar un golpe con la cabeza).
testarudez *s.f.* stubbornness, pigheadedness.
testarudo, -a *adj.* stubborn, pigheaded.
testera *s.f.* front, face, front part, forehead (de un animal).
testículo *s.m.* ANAT. testicle.
testificación *s.f.* testification, testimony.
testificar *v.t.* 1 to testify. || *v.i.* 2 to testify, to give evidence, to attest.
testigo *s.m.* y *f.* 1 witness: *testigo de cargo = witness for the prosecution; testigo de la defensa = witness for the defense; testigo presencial = eye witness.* 2 DEP. baton, stick. 3 proof, evidence, witness (de algo). || 4 **luz de –,** pilot light.
testimonial *adj.* testimonial.
testimoniar *v.t.* to be evidence of, to be proof of, to bear witness to, to testify to.
testimonio *s.m.* 1 testimony, evidence, attestation, affidavit: *falso testimonio = false evidence/perjury/slander.* 2 mark, token (de amistad).
testuz *s.m.* 1 forehead (frente). 2 nape (nuca del toro).
teta *s.f.* 1 teat, nipple (pezón). 2 breast (fig.) tit, boob. 3 udder, teat (de animal). || 4 **dar la –,** to breast-feed. 5 **niño de –,** babe-in-arms.
tétano *s.m.* MED. tetanus.
tetera *s.f.* 1 teapot, tea urn. 2 (Am.) feeding bottle.
tetero *s.m.* (Am.) feeding bottle, baby's bottle.
tetilla *s.f.* 1 nipple (de mamíferos). 2 teat (de biberón).
tetina *s.f.* teat (de biberón).
tetón *adj.* 1 (Am.) stupid, thick (fam.). || *s.m.* 2 bubble, swelling (neumático).
tetraca *s.m.* HIST. Tetrarch.
tetraedro *s.m.* GEOM. tetrahedron.
tetrágono *s.m.* GEOM. tetragon.
tetralogía *s.f.* tetralogy.
tetrápodo *adj.* y *s.m.* ZOOL. tetrapod.
tétrico *adj.* 1 sullen, gloomy, dismal. 2 dim, wan (luz).
teutón, -ona *adj.* 1 teutonic. || *s.m.* y *f.* 2 teuton.
teutónico, -a *adj.* teutonic.
textil *adj.* 1 textile, fibrous: *industria textil = textile industry.* || *s.m.* 2 textile.
texto *s.m.* text: *libro de texto = textbook.*
textual *adj.* 1 textual. 2 (fig.) exact, literal: *palabras textuales = exact words.*
textualmente *adv.* 1 textually. 2 (fig.) literally, exactly: *dijo textualmente = his exact words were.*
textura *s.f.* 1 texture. 2 weaving (acción de tejer). 3 structure (de un mineral).
tez *s.f.* complexion, skin, colouring.
ti *pron.* 1 you: *es para ti = it is for you.* 2 yourself: *hazlo para ti = do it for yourself.* 3 REL. thee, thyself.
tía *s.f.* 1 aunt: *vivo con mi tía = I live with my aunt.* 2 (fam.) bird, gal, dame doll. 3 (desp.) whore (puta), old bag (bruja). 4 **cuéntaselo a tu –,** (fam.) tell it to the marines.
tialina *s.f.* BIOL. ptyalin.
tialismo *s.m.* MED. ptyalism.
tiara *s.f.* tiara, diadem.
tibetano, -a *adj./s.m.* y *f.* Tibetan.
tibia *s.f.* ANAT. tibia, shinbone.
tibiamente *adv.* tepidly, lukewarmly, unenthusiastically.
tibieza *s.f.* 1 tepidity, tepidness, lukewarmness. 2 (fig.) lack of enthusiasm, coolness.
tibio, -a *adj.* 1 lukewarm, tepid. 2 (fig.) lukewarm, unenthusiastic, cool. 3 (Am.) cross, angry.
tiburón *s.m.* 1 ZOOL. shark. 2 (fig.) shark, go-getter.
tic *s.m.* 1 tic, twitch. 2 (fig.) habit, mannerism.
tichela *s.f.* (Am.) vessel for collecting rubber.
ticket *s.m.* ticket.
tictac *s.m.* 1 ticktock, tick (de reloj). 2 tapping (de máquina de escribir). 3 beating (de corazón). || 4 **hacer –,** to tick, to tap, to beat.
tiempo *s.m.* 1 time: *no tengo tiempo = I haven't got time.* 2 time, period, age, epoch, era, days: *en tiempo de los Romanos = in Roman times.* 3 age: *son del mismo tiempo = they are the same age.* 4 weather: *¿qué tiempo hace? = what is the weather like?* 5 DEP. half: *primer tiempo = first half.* 6 MUS. movement. 7 GRAM. tense. 8 MEC. stroke: *motor de 2 tiempos = a two stroke engine.* 9 season: *fuera de tiempo = out of season.* 10 **a –,** in time, on time. 11 **a su debido –,** in due course. 12 **al mismo –,** at the same time. 13 **al poco –,** soon after. 14 **con el –,** in time, in the course of time, eventually. 15 **¿cuánto –?,** how long? 16 **de algún – a esta parte,** for some time now. 17 **de – en –,** from time to time. 18 **desde hace –,** for a long time. 19 **en los buenos tiempos,** in the good old days. 20 **estar a – de,** to still have time to. 21 **ganar –,** to save time. 22 **hacer –,** to kill time, to while away the time. 23 **más –,** longer. 24 **perder el –,** to waste time. 25 **tomarlo con –,** to take one's time.
tienda *s.f.* 1 shop, store: *tienda de comestibles = grocery, grocer's store; ir de tiendas = to go shopping.* 2 tent (tienda de campaña): *tienda de oxígeno = oxigen tent.* 3 MAR. awning.
tienta *s.f.* 1 MED. probe. 2 cleverness, astuteness. || 3 **a tientas,** gropingly, blindly: *andar a tientas = to grope one's way along.*
tiento *s.m.* 1 touch, feel, feeling: *por el tiento = by touch.* 2 (fig.) tact, care, wariness, circumspection, prudence. 3 steady-handedness, sureness of hand. 4 blind person's stick. 5 blow, punch (puñetazo). 6 swig (trago). 7 ZOOL. feeler, tentacle. 8 MUS. preliminary notes in tuning up.
tiernamente *adv.* tenderly.
tierno, -a *adj.* 1 tender, soft. 2 loving, affectionate, sensitive. 3 (fig.) young. 4 (Am.) green, unripe (frutos).
tierra *s.f.* 1 earth, world (planeta). 2 land: *tierra firme = dry land.* 3 soil, earth, ground. 4 country: *tierra native = native country/homeland.* || 5 **dar en – con,** to drop, to throw on the ground, to knock over. 6 **echar a –,** to pull down, demolish. 7 **echar por –,** (fig.) to ruin, to wreck, to destroy. 8 **poner – por medio,** to make o's scarce, to get out quick. 9 **por –,** overland. 10 **tocar –,** AER. to land, to touch down. 11 **tomar –,** AER. to land, to touch down. 12 **– de nadie,** noman's land. 13 **venirse a –,** to collapse, to crumble, to fall through.
tierral *s.m.* (Am.) cloud of dust.
tieso, -a *adj.* 1 stiff, rigid. 2 erect, straight, upright. 3 fit (sano). 4 taut, tense. 5 (fig.) proud, arrogant, conceited, stuck-up (presumido): *tieso de cogote = haughty.* 6 (fig.) stiff, starchy (de manera). 7 (fig.) stubborn, unbending, rigid (de actitud). 8 (fam.) stiff, dead (muerto). 9 **estar –,** to be stony broke. 10 **estar más – que un ajo,** to be as stiff as a board. 11 **poner las orejas tiesas,** to prick up its ears. 12 **tenérselas tiesas con alguien,** to stand up to someone. 13 **quedarse –,** to be frozen stiff.
tiesto *s.m.* 1 flowerpot. 2 shard, postherd, piece of pottery or earthenware. 3 (Am.) bowl, pot, vessel.
tifoideo, -a *adj.* typhoid.
tifón *s.m.* 1 typhoon, waterspout. 2 (Am.) outcrop of ore.
tifus *s.m.* typhus.
tigre *s.m.* 1 tiger. 2 (Am.) jaguar.
tigresa *s.f.* ZOOL. tigress.
tijera *s.f.* 1 scissors. 2 sawbuck, sawhorse (para aserrar). || *s.f.pl.* 3 scissors. 4 shears, clippers. 5 secateurs. 6 backbiter, gossip (persona).
tijereta *s.f.* 1 small scissors. 2 BOT. tendril. 3 ZOOL. earwig.
tijeretada *s.m.* 1 snip, small cut. 2 (Am.) gossip (chismes).
tijeretear *v.t.* 1 to snip, to snick, to cut. || *v.i.* 2 (Am.) to gossip, to backbite, to meddle.
tila *s.f.* 1 lime tree, linden tree. 2 lime blossom, linden blossom (flor). 3 lime-

blossom tea, linden-blossom tea (infusión).
tildar *v.t.* 1 to put an accent on, to put a tilde over. 2 (fig.) to label, brand, stigmatise.
tilde *s.m.* 1 tilde, accent. 2 (fig.) fault, flaw, blemish. || 3 **poner —,** (fig.) to criticise.
tilín *s.m.* 1 ting-a-ling, tinkle. || 2 **en un —,** (fam. y Am.) in a flash. 3 **hacer —,** to become a favourite, to be well liked.
tilo *s.m.* BOT. linden tree, lime tree.
tilingo, -a *adj.* irresponsible.
timador, -ora *s.m.* y *f.* swindler, cheat, trickster.
timar *v.t.* 1 to swindle, to cheat, to trick. 2 to make eyes at s'one. || *v.pron.* 3 (fam.) to make eyes at each other. 4 to play s'body along, to lead s'one on (engatusar).
timba *s.f.* 1 (fam.) hand (of cards). 2 (fam.) gambling den.
timbal *s.m.* 1 MUS. small drum, kettledrum. 2 meat pie.
timbalero *s.m.* kettledrummer.
timbrado, -a *adj.* 1 stamped. || 2 **papel —,** letterhead stationery, stamped paper.
timbrador *s.m.* stamper, rubber-stamp, stamping machine.
timbrar *v.t.* to stamp, to seal.
timbrazo *s.m.* loud ring: *dar un timbrazo = to ring loudly.*
timbre *s.m.* 1 stamp, seal. 2 COM. fiscal stamp. 3 bell. 4 MUS. timbre. 5 (fig.) mark, honour. 6 (Am.) description.
tímidamente *adv.* shyly, timidly, bashfully.
timidez *s.f.* shyness, timidity, bashfulness.
tímido, -a *adj.* shy, timid, bashful.
timo *s.m.* swindle, confidence trick: *dar un timo = to swindle, to hoax.*
timón *s.m.* 1 rudder, helm. 2 pole (de carro). 3 beam (de arado). 4 (Am.) steering wheel (volante). || 5 **empuñar el —,** to take charge, to take the helm.
timonear *v.t.* 1 (Am.) to direct, to manage. 2 (Am.) to drive. || *v.i.* 3 to steer, to be at the helm.
timonel *s.m.* 1 MAR. steersman, helmsman. 2 cox.
timonera *s.f.* 1 MAR. wheelhouse. 2 ZOOL. tail feather, rectrix.
timorato, -a *adj.* 1 feeble-spirited, timorous. 2 REL. Godfearing. 3 (desp.) pious.
tímpano *s.m.* 1 MUS. small drum, kettledrum. 2 ANAT. tympanum, eardrum. 3 ARQ. tympanum. || *s.m.pl.* MUS. tympani.
tina *s.f.* 1 vat, tub. 2 bathtub.
tinaja *s.f.* large earthen jar.
tinglado *s.m.* 1 shed. 2 raised floor, platform. 3 (fig.) intrigue, plot, trick: *armar un tinglado = to lay a plot.* 4 mess-up, muddle: *¡menudo tinglado! = what a fuss!* 5 ZOOL. sea turtle.
tinieblas *s.f.pl.* 1 darkness, shadows, obscurity. 2 hell. 3 (fig.) ignorance, confusion: *estar en tinieblas = to be in the dark.*
tino *s.m.* 1 skill, dexterity. 2 feel, touch: *a tino = by touch/gropingly.* 3 judgment, tact, common sense, moderation. 4 good aim, good marksmanship. || 5 **sacar de — a uno,** to make s'one mad.
tinta *s.f.* 1 ink: *tinta china = Indian ink; con tinta = in ink.* 2 dye. 3 ART. colour, shade, hue. || 4 **de buena —,** on good authority, straight from the horse's mouth. 5 **medias tintas,** half measures.
tinte *s.m.* 1 dye. 2 dyeing process. 3 (fam.) dry cleaner's. 4 (fig.) shade, colouring overtone. 5 veneer, gloss (barniz).
tintero *s.m.* inkwell, inkstand, inkpot.
tintinear *v.i.* 1 to tinkle, to jingle. 2 to clink (vasos).
tintineo *s.m.* 1 tinkle, tinkling, jingle, jingling, ting-a-ling. 2 clink, clinking (vasos).
tinto, -a *adj.* 1 dyed. 2 stained. 3 red (vino). 4 (Am.) black (café). 5 (fig.) tinged. || *s.m.* 6 red wine. 7 (Am.) black coffee.
tintorería *s.f.* 1 dyeing (proceso), dyer's, dyeworks. 2 drycleaning (limpieza en seco), dry cleaner's.
tiña *s.f.* 1 MED. ringworm. 2 ZOOL. honeycomb moth. 3 (fig.) poverty, meanness.
tiñoso, -a *adj.* 1 MED. scabby. 2 (fig.) poor, wretched, mean.
tío *s.m.* 1 uncle: *tío-abuelo = great-uncle.* 2 (fam.) fellow, bloke, chap, guy: *un tío formidable = a fantastic fellow.* || *s.m.* y *f.pl.* uncles and aunts.
tiovivo *s.m.* roundabout, merry-go-round, (EE.UU.) carousel.
tipear *v.t.* (Am.) to type.
tipejo *s.m.* (fam.) wretch, blighter, heel.
típico, -a *adj.* 1 typical, characteristic. 2 traditional, picturesque, full of local colour.
tipificación *s.f.* 1 classification. 2 standardisation.
tipificar *v.t.* 1 to typify. 2 to standardise.
tiple *s.m.* MUS. soprano, treble.
tipo *s.m.* 1 type, kind, class, norm, model. 2 COM. rate: *tipo de cambio = exchange rate.* 3 figure, shape, build, physique: *tiene un tipo bonito = she has a nice figure.* 4 type (imprenta). 5 (fam.) chap, fellow, guy. || 6 (fig.) *jugarse el tipo = to risk one's neck.*
tipografía *s.f.* 1 typography, printing. 2 printing works, printing press (imprenta).
tipográfico, -a *adj.* typographic, typographical, printing.
tipógrafo, -a *s.m.* y *f.* typographer, printer.
tiquear *v.t.* (Am.) to punch.
tíquet *s.m.* ticket.
tiquismiquis *s.m.* 1 silly scruples, silly objections, fussy details. 2 bowing and scraping, affectations. 3 bickering squabbles (riñas).
tira *s.f.* 1 strip, band. 2 comic strip, strip cartoon. || *s.m.* 3 (Am. y fam.) cop. || 4 **la — de,** lots of, masses of. 5 **— y afloja,** give and take, touch and go.
tirabuzón *s.m.* 1 ringlet, curl. 2 DEP. twist, spin.
tirachinas *s.m.* catapult.
tirada *s.f.* 1 throw, shot. 2 distance, stretch. 3 series, edition, offprint (imprenta). || 4 **de una —,** at one go.
tirado, -a *adj.* 1 (fam.) dead easy, a cinch. 2 dirt cheap.
tirador *s.m.* 1 marksman, shot, shooter. 2 archer (de arco). 3 handle, knob (de una puerta). 4 catapult, slingshot (EE.UU.). 5 TEC. drawplate. 6 (Am.) wide gaucho belt. || *s.m.pl.* (Am.) braces, suspenders (EE.UU.).
tirafondo *s.m.* screw, bolt.
tiraje *s.m.* 1 printing, print run. 2 (Am.) chimney flue.
tiralíneas *s.m.* drawing pen.
tiranía *s.f.* tyranny.
tiranicidio *s.m.* tyrannicide.
tiránico, -a *adj.* tyrannic, despotic.
tiranizar *v.t.* to tyrannise, to domineer.
tirano, -a *adj.* 1 tyrannic, tyrannical, despotic. || *s.m.* 2 tyrant, despot.
tirante *adj.* 1 tight, taut, tense. 2 (fig.) strained, tense (relaciones). || *s.m.* 3 ARQ. tie, tie beam, crosspiece. 4 TEC. brace, stay, strut. 5 trace, harness (de caballos). 6 strap (de vestido). || *s.m.pl.* 7 braces, suspenders (EE.UU.).
tirar *v.t.* 1 to throw, to sling, to hurl, to cast, to toss. 2 to drop (caer), to spill (líquido). 3 to knock over (volcar). 4 to pull down, to knock down (derribar). 5 to pull. 6 to stretch, to draw (estirar). 7 to throw away, to throw out, to discard, (fam.) to chuck out. 8 to waste, to squander: *tirar la casa por la ventana = spare no expense.* 9 to print, to run off (imprimir). 10 to fire, to shoot (disparar). || *v.i.* 1 to fire, to shoot (con arma). 2 to pull, to tug (de una cuerda). 3 to pull out, to take out (sacar). 4 to draw, to attract (imán), to appeal to. 5 to draw (chimenea) to turn, to go: *tira a la derecha = turn right; tira adelante = go straight on.* 6 to tent towards: *tira a verde = it's greenish.* 7 DEP. to shoot: *tirar al gol = shoot for goal,* to go, to play, to have one's turn. 8 to throw, to hurl oneself, to jump, to rush at, to dive (al agua). 9 to lie down. 10 to spend (tiempo). || 11 **dejar tirado,** to abandon, to leave behind. 12 **ir tirando,** to get along, to get by, to manage. || 13 **tirarse a una,** (vulg.) to screw, to have, to lay.
tirilla *s.f.* 1 strip, band. 2 neckband.
tirita *s.f.* sticking plaster, bandaid.
tiritar *v.i.* to shiver, to shake, to tremble.
tiritera *s.f.* shivers, shivering, shaking, trembling.
tiro *s.m.* 1 throw (lanzamiento). 2 shot (disparo). 3 report, discharge, sound of a shot (ruido). 4 impact, hit, bullet mark (huella). 5 shooting, firing (acción). 6 range: *a tiro = within range; campo de tiro = shooting range.* 7 flight (escalera). 8 draught, (EE.UU.) draft (chimenea). 9 rope, cord, strap (cuerda). 10 DEP. shot,

kick, throw. **11** team (de animales). || **12 de tiros largos,** all dressed up, dressed to kill. **13 sentar como un –,** to take badly, to come as a blow. **14 – al plato/– de pichón,** clay-pigeon shooting. **15 – con arco,** archery. **16 – de gracia,** death blow. **17 pegarse un –,** to shoot oneself. **18 por donde van los tiros,** the way the wind blows. **19 (le) salió el – por la culata,** it backfired.

tiroides *adj.* y *s.m.* ANAT. thyroid.

tirón *s.m.* **1** tug, pull, jerk, snatch: *dar un tirón = to tug at, to pull at.* **2** bag snatching (de bolso). || **3 de un –,** at a stretch, in one go, all at once, straight through.

tironear *v.t.* (Am.) to drag.

tirotear *v.t.* to snipe at, to shoot at, to fire at. || *v.r.* to shoot at each other, to exchange shots.

tirria *s.f.* dislike, antipathy: *tener tirria = to have a grudge against, to have it in for; tomar tirria a = to take a dislike to.*

tisana *s.f.* infusion, tisane.

tisis *s.f.* MED. phthisis, tuberculosis, consumption.

tisú *s.m.* **1** tissue. **2** lamé (tela).

titánico, -a *adj.* titanic, colossal, huge.

titanio *s.m.* QUIM. titanium.

títere *s.m.* **1** puppet, marionette. || *s.m.pl.* **2** puppet show. || **3 no dejar – con cabeza,** (fig.) to turn everything upside down.

titiritero *s.m.* **1** puppeteer. **2** acrobat. **3** juggler.

tití *s.m.* ZOOL. titi.

titilar *v.i.* **1** to quiver, to tremble. **3** to flicker, to twinkle (luz).

tititar *v.i.* to tremble, to shiver, to shake.

tito *s.m.* (fam.) uncle.

titubeante *adj.* **1** shaky, unsteady, unstable, tottering. **2** stammering, faltering. **3** (fig.) hesitant, vacillating.

titubear *v.i.* **1** to stagger, to totter, to be unsteady, to be unstable. **2** to stammer, to falter. **3** (fig.) to be hesitant, to falter, to waver.

titubeo *s.m.* **1** staggering, tottering, unsteadiness, instability. **2** stammering. **3** (fig.) hesitancy, faltering.

titulado, -a *adj.* **1** entitled, titled, called. **2** qualified, with a degree.

titular *adj.* **1** titular: *profesor titular = titular professor.* **2** DEP. reigning, defending (campeón). || *s.m.* y *f.* **3** holder (de pasaporte, record). **4** REL. incumbent. || *s.m.pl.* **5** headlines. || *v.t.* **6** to title, to entitle, to call. **7** QUIM. to titrate. || *v.i.* **8** to be titled, to be called. || *v.pron.* **9** to graduate (universidad).

título *s.m.* **1** title. **2** degree: *título de licenciado = bachelor's degree,* qualification, diploma. **3** COM. bond: *título al portador = bearer bond.* **4** DER. title: *título de propiedad = title deed.* **5** DER. heading (de texto legal). **6** QUIM. titre. **7** headline (periódico). **8** (fig.) right, quality: *¿con qué título? = by what right?* **9 a – de,** (fig.) by way of, in capacity of.

tiza *s.f.* chalk.

tizna *s.f.* grime, soot, stain.

tiznar *v.t.* **1** to blacken, to smudge, to soil. **2** (fig.) to blacken, to stain: *manchar la reputación de alguien = to blacken someone's reputation.* || *v.pron.* **3** to blacken, to get dirty. **4** (Am.) to get drunk (emborracharse).

tizne *s.m.* y *f.* **1** soot (hollín). **2** grime, dirt, smut. **3** (fig.) stain.

tizón *s.m.* **1** brand, firebrand, half-burnt stick. **2** stain.

tizona *s.f.* (fam.) sword.

toa *s.f.* (Am.) towrope, rope.

toalla *s.f.* towel.

toallero *s.m.* towel rack.

tobillera *s.f.* ankle strap, ankle support.

tobillo *s.m.* ankle.

tobogán *s.m.* **1** slide, chute (para mercancías). **2** toboggan (trineo, especialmente para la nieve). **3** slide (en juegos de niños).

toca *s.f.* **1** REL. wimple (de monjas). **2** hat (sombrero de señoras con el ala corta). || *pl.* **3** (arc.) compensation given to a widow of a deceased employee.

tocadiscos *s.m.* ELEC. record-player.

tocado, -a *p.p.* **1** de **tocar.** || *adj.* **2** touched, crazy, mad (loco). **3** dressed (con sombrero): *ella iba tocada de un precioso sombrero = she was dressed in a beautiful hat.* || *s.m.* **4** hairdo, hair style (estilo de peinado).

tocador *s.m.* **1** MUS. player. **2** dressing table.

tocante, -a *adj.* concerning, with reference to.

tocar *v.t.* **1** to touch, to feel (palpando): *toqué su frente y estaba ardiendo = I felt his forehead and it was burning.* **2** to play (un instrumento musical). **3** (fig.) to touch, to affect (de una manera sentimental): *este año Dios le ha tocado el corazón y ha regalado mucho dinero = this year God touched his heart and he gave away a lot of money.* **4** to handle (cosas, especialmente en las tiendas). **5** to sound, to ring, to toll (objetos que despiden sonidos). || *v.t.* y *pron.* **6** to touch on, to allude to (aludir, a un tema o asunto en la conversación): *era el momento de tocar el asunto del dinero = it was the right time to allude to the money matter.* **7** to be next (de situación): *nuestras casas se tocan = our houses are next to each other.* **8** to cover one's head (especialmente con toga). **9** to hit, to strike (tropezar muy ligeramente). **10** to comb and dress (arreglarse el pelo). || *v.i.* **11** to be one's turn: *todavía no me toca = it's not my turn yet.* **12** to be the right time: *ahora toca irse a la cama = now it is the right time to go to bed.* **13** to win (ganar): *me tocaron muchos millones en la lotería = I won many millions in the lottery.* || **14 – a uno de cerca,** to hit home (la desgracia).

tocata *s.f.* MUS. toccata.

tocayo, -a *s.m.* y *f.* namesake.

tocino *s.m.* GAST. **1** bacon, salt pork. || **2 – entreverado,** streaky bacon. **3 –/tocinillo de cielo,** a type of custard cake.

tocología *s.f.* tocology, obstetrics.

tocólogo, -a *s.m.* y *f.* tocologist, obstetrician.

todavía *adv.* **1** still (afirmativa); yet (negativa): *todavía estoy cansado = I'm still tired; no tengo hambre todavía = I'm not hungry yet.* **2** even: *¡y todavía se enfada porque se lo digo! = he even got angry because I told him!*

todo, -a *adj.* **1** all: *todos los tanques usan gasolina = all the tanks use gasoline.* **2** every, each: *todo hombre tiene derecho a la libertad = each man has a right to freedom.* **3** entire, whole (entero): *toda la mañana = the whole morning.* || *pron.pl.* **4** everybody, everyone, all: *todos vinieron = everybody came.* || *s.m.* **5** everything: *eres mi vida, mi amor, mi todo = you're my life, my love, my everything.* || **6 ante –,** first of all, in the first place. **7 así y –,** in spite of everything, in spite of all. **8 con –,** however, still. **9 del –,** completely, absolutely. **10 en – y por –,** completely, thoroughly. **11 sobre –,** above all, above everything else. **12 y –,** even, and all (con énfasis): *vino a verme al hospital y todo = he came to see me at the hospital and all.*

todopoderoso, -a *adj.* **1** all-powerful. || *s.m.* **2** REL. God.

toga *s.f.* toga, gown.

toldilla *s.f.* poop deck.

toldo *s.m.* awning, oap.

tolerable *adj.* tolerable.

tolerablemente *adv.* tolerably.

tolerado, -a *p.p.* **1** de **tolerar.** || *adj.* **2** permissible (especialmente al hablar de las películas y quién tiene la suficiente edad para verlas).

tolerancia *s.f.* **1** tolerancia: *tolerancia y respeto = tolerance and respect.* **2** MEC. tolerance (en ciertas medidas).

tolerante *adj.* tolerant.

tolerar *v.t.* **1** to bear, to endure: *él no tolera el dolor = he doesn't endure pain.* **2** to allow, to permit, to give permission: *no tolero ese tipo de comportamiento = I don't allow that kind of behaviour.* **3** to keep down (mantener comida en el estómago). **4** MEC. tolerate (ciertos pesos, medidas, etc.).

tolva *s.f.* hopper, chute.

toma *s.f.* **1** taking (acción de tomar): *the taking of somebody's life = el tomar la vida de alguien.* **2** capture, seizure (captura). **3** intake (ingestión de comida o bebida). **4** tap, outlet (toma de agua). **5** ELEC. plug, connection.

tomado, -a *adj.* (Am.) drunk (borracho).

tomadura *s.f.* **1** taking. || **2 – de pelo,** practical joke, pulling of the leg.

tomar *v.t.* y *pron.* **1** to take: *tomar el autobús = to take the bus.* **2** to take, to eat, to drink: *toma unas copas = take a few drinks.* || *v.t.* **3** to take, to hold, to seize (agarrar). **4** to take (una decisión). **5** to take, to buy (adquirir). **6** to take, to consider: *no te lo tomes seriamente =*

don't take it seriously. **7** to take (una dirección): *take the first turning on the right = toma la primera bocacalle a la derecha.* **8** to take on, to hire (empleados). **9** to take, to mistake: *te tomé por mi hermano = I mistook you for my brother.* **10** to take, to adopt (medidas). **11** to take, to have (lecciones). || **12 tomarla con alguien,** to pick on someone, to have a grudge against someone. **13 – las de Villadiego,** V. **Villadiego.**
tomatal *s.m.* AGR. tomato field.
tomate *s.m.* **1** BOT. tomato. **2** tear, hole (agujero, en la ropa). **3** mess, fuss (alboroto).
tomatera *s.f.* tomato plant.
tomatero *s.m.* AGR. tomato grower.
tomavistas *s.m.pl.* cinecamera, film camera.
tómbola *s.f.* tombola.
tomillo *s.m.* BOT. thyme.
tomismo *s.m.* thomism.
tomo *s.m.* **1** volume, book. **2** (fig.) importance. || **3 de – y lomo,** weighty, important.
ton *s.m.* **1** apócope de tono. **2 sin – ni son,** without rhyme or reason.
tonada *s.f.* MUS. tune, melody.
tonal *adj.* tonal.
tonalidad *s.f.* MUS. tonalidad.
tonel *s.m.* barrel, keg, cask.
tonelada *s.f.* ton (medida).
tonelaje *s.m.* tonnage: *de gran tonelaje = of tremendous tonnage.*
tongo *s.m.* fixing (especialmente en combates de boxeo, lucha, etc.).
tónico, -a *adj.* **1** tonic: *agua tónica = tonic water.* **2** FON. tonic, accented, stressed. || *s.f.* **3** MUS. keynote. **4** (fig.) trend, tendency: *la tónica estos días es no hacer nada = the trend these days is not to do anything.*
tonificación *s.f.* invigorating.
tonificador, -a *adj.* invigorating.
tonificante *adj.* invigorating.
tonificar *v.t.* to invigorate, to tone up.
tonillo *s.m.* **1** singsong, monotone (de una persona). **2** accent, sound, brogue (acento local). **3** mocking undertone (de sarcasmo).
tono *s.m.* **1** tone, level (de voz). **2** MUS. pitch, key. **3** shade, hue (de color). **4** tone (muscular). **5** tone (social): *buen tono social = good social tone.* || **6 bajar uno el –,** to hold one's tongue. **7 darse –,** to give oneself airs. **8 de buen/mal –,** of good/bad breeding, elegant/vulgar. **9 estar/ponerse a –,** to behave oneself, to toe the line. **10 fuera de –,** out of tune, inoportune. **11 salida de –,** impertinence.
tonsura *s.f.* REL. tonsure.
tontaina *s.m.* y *f.* fool, dimwit.
tontamente *adv.* foolishly, stupidly.
tontear *v.i.* **1** to fool around. **2** to flirt (flirtear).
tontería *s.f.* **1** foolishness, silliness. **2** trivialities (trivialidades). **3** stupid remark (como algo dicho).
tonto, -a *adj.* **1** foolish, silly. **2** naive (ingenuo). || **3 a tontas y a locas,** any which way, haphazardly. **4 hacer el –,** to fool around, to mess around. **5 hacerse el –,** to play the fool, to act the fool. **6 ponerse –, a)** to get stupid, to get vain; **b)** to get very stubborn. **7 – de capirote,** total fool.
topacio *s.m.* topaz.
topar *v.t., i.* y *pron.* to run into, to bump into: *me topé con él en la calle = I bumped into him on the street.*
tope *s.m.* **1** MEC. stop, catch (en cualquier mecanismo). **2** buffer (parachoques de ferrocarriles). **3** butt, end (extremidad de un objeto). **4** limit, maximum: *he alcanzado el tope de mi salario = I have reached the maximum of my salary.* || *adj.inv.* **5** top, maximum (máximo). || **6 hasta los topes,** up to the brim, full up.
tópico, -a *adj.* **1** MED. for external application (especialmente cremas). || *s.m.* **2** commonplace, platitude. **3** (Am.) topic, subject (para hablar).
topetón *s.m.* butt, bump.
topo *s.m.* ZOOL. mole.
topografía *s.f.* topography.
topográfico, -a *adj.* topographic.
topógrafo *s.m.* topographer, surveyor.
toponimia *s.f.* toponymy.
topónimo *s.m.* place-name.
toque *s.m.* **1** louch. **2** ART. touch, dab (en pintura). **3** QUIM. test (prueba). **4** warning: *tendré que darle otro toque mañana = I'll have to give him another warning tomorrow.* **5** peal (de campana). || **6 dar un –,** to sound out (a una persona para saber sus intenciones).
toquetear *v.t.* to finger repeatedly, to touch repeatedly.
toquilla *s.f.* knitted shawl.
torbellino *s.m.* **1** whirlwind. **2** (fig.) restless person: *ella es un torbellino = she is a very restless person.*
torcedura *s.f.* MED. sprain.
torcer *v.t.* **1** to twist. **2** to distort (malinterpretar). || *v.t.* y *pron.* **3** to bend (torcerse físicamente). **4** to go astray, to go wrong: *las cosas se han torcido = things have gone astray.* **5** to corrupt, to pervert (pervertirse, una persona). || *v.pron.* **6** MED. to sprain (torcerse una extremidad). || *v.i.* **7** to turn (un camino, calle, etc.).
torcido, -a *p.p.* **1** de **torcer.** || *adj.* **2** twisted, crooked (torcido físicamente). **3** crooked, shady (torcido de carácter).
tordo *s.m.* ZOOL. thrush (ave).
tormenta *s.f.* **1** storm, tempest. **2** trouble, misfortune (desgracia). **3** (fig.) turmoil (de pasiones): *una tormenta de pasiones = a turmoil of passions.*
toreo *s.m.* bullfighting.
torero, -a *s.m.* y *f.* bullfighter.
toril *s.m.* bullpen.
torio *s.m.* thorium.
tormento *s.m.* **1** torment, torture (física). **2** torment, anguish (mental).
torna *s.f.* **1** turning. || **2 volver las tornas,** to change one's luck, to turn the tables.
tornado *s.m.* tornado, hurricane.
tornar *v.t.* **1** to return (devolver). || *v.t.* y *pron.* **2** to change into, to turn: *el cielo se tornó blanco = the sky turned white.* || *v.pron.* **3** to return (regresar).
tornasol *s.m.* BOT. sunflower.
tornasolado, -a *adj.* iridescent.
torneo *s.m.* **1** HIST. tournament. **2** DEP. championship (campeonato).
tornillo *s.m.* **1** screw. || **2 apretar a alguien los tornillos,** to put the screws to someone. **3 faltarle a uno un –,** to have a screw loose. **4 – sin fin,** MEC. worm gear.
torniquete *s.m.* MED. tourniquet.
torno *s.m.* **1** winch, windlass. **2** MEC. lathe. || **3 en – a,** around, about: *hay dudas en torno al crimen de Valladolid = there are some doubts about the crime in Valladolid.*
toro *s.c.* **1** ZOOL. bull. || *s.pl.* **2** bullfighting, bullfights. || **3 coger el – por los cuernos,** to take the bull by the horns. **4 estar hecho un –,** to as strong as a horse. **5 ver los toros desde la barrera,** to sit on the fence (sin comprometerse).
toronja *s.f.* BOT. grapefruit.
toronjil o **toronjina** *s.m.* balm.
toronjo *s.m.* BOT. grapefruit tree.
torpe *adj.* **1** clumsy, awkward (desmañado con las manos). **2** dull-witted, stupid (de inteligencia).
torpedear *v.t.* MIL. to torpedo.
torpedero *s.m.* torpedo boat.
torpedo *s.m.* **1** MIL. torpedo. **2** ZOOL. torpedo fish.
torpemente *adv.* **1** clumsily, awkwardly (con las manos). **2** stupidly, slowly (mentalmente).
torpeza *s.f.* **1** clumsiness, awkwardness (manual). **2** stupidity, slowness (mental). **3** blunder (de carácter social o similar): *vaya torpeza la mía, pensar que ella estaba viuda = what a blunder it was to think she was a widow.*
tórpido, -a *adj.* torpid, sluggish.
torpor *s.m.* torpor.
torrado, -a *p.p.* **1** de **torrar.** || *s.m.* **2** toasted chickpea.
torrar *v.t.* to boast, roast.
torre *s.f.* **1** tower. **2** belfry (campanario). **3** rook, castle (en el ajedrez). **4** block of flats, high-rise building. || **5 – del homenaje,** keep, donjon.
torrencial *adj.* torrential.
torrente *s.m.* **1** torrent. **2** FISIOL. bloodstream (de la sangre). **3** (fig.) flood, rush, onrush (de luz, de personas, etc.).
torrentera *s.f.* gully.
torreón *s.m.* fortified tower.
tórrido, -a *adj.* torrid.
torso *s.m.* ART. torso.
torta *s.f.* **1** GAST. cake. **2** slap (golpe).
tortazo *s.m.* slap.
tortícolis *s.f.* MED. torticollis.
tortilla *s.f.* **1** GAST. omelette. || **2 volverse la –,** to turn the tables.
tórtola *s.f.* ZOOL. turtledove.
tórtolo, -a *adj.* (Am.) silly, to change completely (una situación social, política, intrapersonal, etc.).

tortuga *s.f.* 1 ZOOL. turtle, tortoise. 2 (fig.) slow person (persona lenta en algo).
tortuosidad *s.f.* 1 tortuousness (físicamente con curvas pronunciadas). 2 deviousness (torcido de carácter).
tortuosamente *adv.* 1 windingly, tortuously (físicamente). 2 deviously (característica personal negativa).
tortuoso, -a *adj.* 1 winding, tortuous (con curvas). 2 devious (torcido de carácter).
tortura *s.f.* 1 torture. 2 (fig.) torture, suffering (sufrimiento agudo).
torturar *v.t.* to torture.
torvamente *adv.* grimly, fiercely (especialmente de la mirada).
torvo, -a *adj.* grim, fierce.
torzal *s.m.* cord, twist.
tos *s.f.* 1 cough. || 2 — **ferina,** MED. whooping cough.
toscamente *adv.* coarsely, rudely.
tosco, -a *adj.* coarse, crude.
tosquedad *s.f.* coarseness, crudeness, roughness.
tostado, -a *p.p.* 1 de **tostar.** || *adj.* 2 toasted, roasted. 3 tanned, suntanned (por el sol). || *s.f.* 4 toast: *una tostada = a piece of toast.*
tostador, -a *adj.* 1 toasting, roasting. || *s.m.* y *f.* 2 toaster (utensilio y personas).
tostón *s.m.* 1 GAST. roast suckling pig. 2 bore, nuisance (persona o cosa aburrida).
total *adj.* 1 total, complete, whole: *una revisión total = a complete revision.* || *s.m.* 2 total, sum: *el total asciende a 5.000 pesetas = the sum amounts to 5.000 pesetas.* || *adv.* 3 in short, all in all: *total, nos fuimos al día siguiente = in short, we left the following day.*
totalidad *s.f.* whole, entirely, totality, all: *la totalidad de la plantilla se puso en huelga = all the workers went on strike.*
totalitario, -a *adj.* y *s.m.* y *f.* totalitarian.
totalitarismo *s.m.* POL. totalitarianism.
totalizador, -a *adj.* totalizer.
totalizar *v.t.* to totalize.
totalmente *adv.* totally, wholly.
tótem *s.m.* totem.
totémico, -a *adj.* totemic.
totemismo *s.m.* totemism.
toxemia *s.f.* MED. toxaemia.
toxicidad *s.f.* toxicity.
tóxico, -a *adj.* toxic.
toxicomanía *s.f.* drug addiction.
toxicómano, -a *adj.* 1 addicted to drugs. || *s.m.* y *f.* 2 drug addict.
toxina *s.f.* toxin.
tozudez *s.f.* obstinacy, stubbornness.
tozudo, -a *adj.* obstinate, stubborn.
traba *s.f.* 1 tie, bond. 2 hobble (para los caballos). 3 (fig.) obstacle, hindrance: *no me pongas trabas para irme al extranjero = don't put obstacles in front of me so that I can't go abroad.*
trabado, -a *p.p.* 1 de **trabar.** || *adj.* 2 joined, linked (unido físicamente). 3 (fig.) coherent, well-constructed (discurso, escrito, etc.). 4 (fig.) strong (fuerte).
trabajado, -a *p.p.* 1 de **trabajar.** || *adj.* 2 worn out (agotada, una persona). 3 elaborate, carefully worked, ornate (cualquier objeto que requiere mucho trabajo en su forma de ser presentado).
trabajador, -a *adj.* 1 hard-working, diligent, industrious. || *s.m.* y *f.* 2 worker.
trabajar *v.t.* 1 to work: *tengo que trabajar la madera = I have to work wood.* 2 AGR. to till, to work: *trabajar la tierra = to till the land.* 3 to deal in: *no trabajamos este tipo de producto = we don't deal in this kind of thing.* || *v.i.* 4 to work: *hay que trabajar mucho = one must work a lot.*
trabajo *s.m.* 1 work, employment. 2 job (trabajo concreto): *here my job consists of watching over these children = aquí mi trabajo consiste en cuidar de estos niños.* 3 effort; trouble: *cuesta trabajo = it takes an effort.* 4 labour (trabajo desde el punto de vista del esfuerzo que conlleva, especialmente cuando es manual o castigo): *trabajos forzados = hard labour.* 5 harship (penalidad). 6 report, composition, task (trabajo intelectual): *un trabajo sobre la influencia del ambiente en las hormigas = a report about the influence of the environment on ants.* || 7 — **en cadena,** V. **cadena.**
trabajosamente *adv.* laboriously, painfully.
trabalenguas *s.m.* tongue twister.
trabajoso, -a *adj.* laborious.
trabar *v.t.* 1 to link, to join, to unite (físicamente). 2 to start up (conversación); to join, to engage in (batalla); to strick up (amistad). 3 to hinder, to obstruct (impedir). || *v.t.* e *i.* 4 to lay hold of, to hold, to seize (agarrar). || *v.pron.* 5 to come to blows (pegarse). 6 (Am.) to stammer (tartamudear).
trabazón *s.f.* 1 bond, union (física). 2 relation, connection (conexión, entre dos o más cosas).
trabucar *v.t.* y *pron.* 1 to upset (el orden de algo). 2 to mix up, to confuse (confundir algo). 3 to get all mixed up (hablar de manera confusa): *me trabuqué al verla otra vez = I got all mixed up when I saw her again.*
trabuco *s.m.* MIL. blunderbuss.
traca *s.f.* string of firecrackers.
tracción *s.f.* 1 traction, haulage (acción). 2 MEC. drive: *tracción delantera = front-wheel drive.*
tracto *s.m.* 1 lapse, interval (de tiempo). 2 REL. tract.
tractor *s.m.* tractor.
tractorista *s.m.* y *f.* tractor driver.
tradicional *adj.* traditional.
tradicionalismo *s.m.* traditionalism.
tradicionalista *adj./s.m.* y *f.* traditionalist.
tradicionalmente *adv.* traditionally.
traducible *adj.* translatable.
traducir *v.t.* e *i.* 1 to translate (escrito). 2 to interpret (hablado).
traductor, -a *s.m.* y *f.* translator.
traer *v.t.* 1 to bring, to get: *trae los vasos de la cocina = bring the glasses from the kitchen.* 2 to wear: *traía un abrigo nuevo = she was wearing a new dress.* 3 to bring about, to cause: *tu comportamiento te traerá dificultades = your behaviour will cause difficulties.* 4 to carry (un artículo de la prensa): *el periódico no lo traía = the newspaper didn't carry that story.* 5 to bring forward, to bring into play, to adduce (aducir casos, ejemplos, etc.). || *v.pron.* 6 to plan: *¿qué te traes en la cabecita? = what are you planning in your mind?* || 7 — **a alguien mal,** to pester somebody, not to leave somebody alone. 8 — **entre manos,** to be up to: *esos dos se traen algo entre manos = those two are up to something.*
tráfago *s.m.* 1 bustle, hustle (ajetreo). 2 traffic; movement (tráfico).
traficante *s.m.* trader, dealer.
traficar *v.t.* to trade, to deal with/in: *me he dedicado a traficar en pieles = I have taken up trading in furs.*
tráfico *s.m.* 1 trading, dealing (comerciar). 2 traffic (de vehículos). 3 (Am.) transit, passage (tránsito).
tragaderas *s.f.pl.* 1 gullibility (credulidad). 2 throat (garganta).
tragaldabas *s.m.* y *f.* gluttonous.
tragaluz *s.m.* skylight.
tragaperras *s.m.* slot machine.
tragar *v.t.* 1 to swallow. 2 (fig.) to eat a lot. 3 to swallow up, to eat up (hacer desaparecer): *la nieve se tragó a los perros = the dogs were swallowed up by the snow.* || *v.t.* y *pron.* 4 to use up, to eat up (algo en exceso): *ese vehículo traga mucha gasolina = this car uses up a lot of petrol.* 5 to absorb (especialmente líquidos): *este tipo de tierra traga mucha agua = this kind of soil absorbs a lot of water.* 6 (fig.) to swallow (creer algo inverosímil): *se tragó el cuento = he swallowed the story.* 7 to endure (dificultades, tragedias, amarguras, etc.). || 8 **no — a algo o alguien,** not to stomach something/someone, not to stand something/someone; to feel a strong dislike towards something/someone.
tragedia *s.f.* tragedy.
trágicamente *adv.* tragically.
trágico, -a *adj.* 1 tragic. 2 LIT. tragic (del teatro). || *s.m.* y *f.* 3 tragedian.
tragicomedia *s.f.* tragicomedy.
tragicómico, -a *adj.* tragicomic.
trago *s.m.* 1 swig, gulp. 2 (fig.) drink, shot: *vamos a tomar un trago = let's go and have a drink.* 3 bad time, problem, fix: *vaya trago que nos hiciste pasar = what a bad time we had because of you.* || 4 **pasar un mal —,** to have a very rough time.
tragón, -a *adj.* 1 greedy, glutonous. || *s.m.* y *f.* 2 greedy person.
traguearse *v.pron.* (Am.) to get drunk.
traición *s.f.* 1 treason, treachery (especialmente contra la patria de uno). 2 disloyalty (hacia una persona). || 3 **alta —,** high treason. 4 **a —,** treacherously.
traicionar *v.t.* 1 to betray. 2 to give away (sentimientos o ideas que uno quería

tener ocultos): *te ha traicionado tu sonrisa = your smile gave you away.*
traicionero, -a *adj.* treacherous.
traído, -a *p.p.* 1 de **traer.** || *adj.* 2 worn-out, threadbare (para ropa muy usada).
traidor, -a *s.m.* y *f.* 1 traitor: betrayer. || *adj.* 2 treacherous.
traílla *s.f.* leash (para perros).
traína *s.f.* MAR. dragnet.
trainera *s.f.* 1 MAR. small fishing boat (especialmente para la sardina). 2 DEP. big rowing boat.
traje *s.m.* 1 suit. 2 costume (de una región, de un espectáculo, etc.). || **3 – de ceremonia/etiqueta,** full dress, evening dress. **4 – de luces,** bullfighter's costume.
trajeado, -a *p.p.* 1 de **trajear.** || **2 bien-/mal –,** to be well rigged out, to be well dressed up/to be shabbily dressed.
trajear *v.t.* y *pron.* to dress, to clothe.
trajín *s.m.* hustle and bustle.
trajinar *v.t.* 1 to transport, to carry. || *v.i.* 2 to bustle around, to come and go: *siempre andas trajinando por la casa = you're always bustling around the house.*
tralla *s.f.* cord, whipcord.
trallazo *s.m.* lash, crack of the whip.
trama *s.f.* 1 plot (de una novela). 2 scheme, plot, intrigue (intriga). 3 MEC. woof (de tejidos). 4 FOT. screen.
tramar *v.t.* 1 to plot, to scheme, to intrigue. 2 TEC. to weave (tejidos). || *v.pron.* 3 to be afoot, to be hatching up: *algo se está tramando, lo sé = something is afoot, I know.*
trámite *s.m.* 1 procedure, transaction (especialmente burocrático). || **2 de –,** without any complication, easily done, easily managed (hablando de gestiones, normalmente burocráticas).
tramo *s.m.* 1 section, stretch (de terreno). 2 flight (de escalera). 3 span (de un puente o similar).
tramontana *s.f.* north wind.
tramoya *s.f.* stage machinery (en un teatro).
tramoyista *s.m.* y *f.* stagehand.
trampa *s.f.* 1 trap, snare (física). 2 trick (broma o similar). 3 hatch (escotilla). 4 bad debt: *tenemos que vivir a base de trampas = we are forced to live with bad debts.* || **5 coger en una –,** to catch red-handed, to catch out.
trampear *v.i.* to live from hand to mouth, to live with great economic difficulties.
trampero, -a *s.m.* y *f.* frapper.
trampilla *s.f.* trap door.
trampolín *s.m.* 1 DEP. trampoline. 2 diving-board (para saltar al agua). 3 (fig.) springboard (cosa o persona que nos sirve para alcanzar algo).
tramposo, -a *adj.* 1 cheating, tricking. || *s.m.* y *f.* 2 cheat, swindler. 3 cardsharp (tramposo en el juego de cartas).
tranca *s.f.* 1 cudgel, club. 2 crossbar (para sujetar puertas y ventanas). 3 (fam.) drinking spree. || **4 a trancas y barrancas,** with great difficulty, through fire and water.
trancazo *s.m.* 1 blow with a club, blow with a cudgel. 2 (fig.) bad cold (resfriado fuerte).
trance *s.m.* 1 tight spot, difficulty: *he pasado por muchos trances en la vida = I have gone through many difficulties in my life.* 2 moment, time (especialmente cuando es muy importante para la vida de uno). 3 trance (en el espiritismo). || **4 a todo –,** at all costs. **5 estar en –,** to be in a trance. **6 estar en – de,** to be on the point of: *está en trance de muerte = he is on the point of death.*
tranquilidad *s.f.* 1 stillness, calmness, peacefulness (especialmente de un paisaje, sitio, etc.). 2 lack of worry, freedom from anxiety (persona).
tranquilizante *adj.* 1 tranquilizing; reassuring. || *s.m.* 2 MED. tranquillizer.
tranquilizar *v.t.* y *pron.* 1 to quieten, to calm. 2 to reassure, to relieve, to set at ease (especialmente cuando había posibilidad de problemas): *lo que dices me tranquiliza = what you're saying reassures me.*
tranquilo, -a *adj.* 1 still (sin movimiento). 2 quiet, peaceful (persona). 3 free of worry, free of anxiety.
tranquillo *s.m.* 1 (fam.) knack. **2 coger el –,** (fam.) to get the knack, to get the hang.
trans- *prefijo* trans- (en este diccionario se dará en muchos casos la variable posible de este sufijo que es **tras**).
transacción *s.f.* 1 COM. transaction. 2 agreement (acuerdo).
transaccional *adj.* DER. transitory (se refiere especialmente a enmiendas que con el transcurso del tiempo no tendrán aplicación).
transatlántico, -a o **trasatlántico, -a** *adj.* 1 transatlantic. || *s.m.* 2 MAR. ocean liner.
transar *v.i.* (Am.) to compromise, to give in.
transbordador, -a o **trasbordador, -a** *adj.* 1 transferring. || *s.m.* 2 MAR. ferry.
transbordar o **trasbordar** *v.t.* to transfer; to change (autobús o ferrocarril).
transbordo o **trasbordo** *s.m.* transfer; change (de ferrocarril, autobús, etc.).
transcendencia o **trascendencia** *s.f.* transcendence; importance.
transcendental o **trascendental** *adj.* transcendental.
transcendentalismo o **trascendentalismo** *s.m.* FIL. transcendentalism.
transcendente o **trascendente** *adj.* transcendent.
transcender o **trascender** *v.i.* 1 to stink a mile off. 2 to transpire (irse conociendo una noticia importante): *ha transcendido que el rey está gravemente enfermo = it has transpired that the king is seriously ill.* 3 FIL. to transcend.
transcontinental o **trascontinental** *adj.* transcontinental.
transcribir o **trascribir** *v.t.* to transcribe.
transcripción o **trascripción** *s.f.* transcription.
transcriptor o **trascriptor** *s.m.* transcriber.
transculturización o **trasculturización** *s.f.* cross-cultural influence.
transcurrir *v.i.* to pass (el tiempo): *transcurrieron diez años = ten years passed.*
transcurso *s.m.* passing; course (de tiempo).
transeúnte *adj.* 1 passing, transient, transitory. || *s.m.* y *f.* 2 passer-by (por la calle). 3 non-resident (normalmente extranjeros).
transexual *adj./s.m.* y *f.* transexual.
transferencia o **trasferencia** *s.f.* 1 transfer, transference (de un puesto de trabajo, responsabilidad, institución, etc.). 2 FIN. transfer, order (de dinero): *transferencia bancaria = banker's order.*
transferible o **trasferible** *adj.* transferable.
transferir o **trasferir** *v.t.* 1 to transfer (trasladar). 2 to postpone (posponer).
transfiguración o **trasfiguración** *v.t.* y *pron.* to transfigure.
transfigurar o **trasfigurar** *v.t.* y *pron.* to transfigure.
transformable o **trasformable** *adj.* transformable, convertible.
transformación o **trasformación** *s.f.* transformation.
transformador, -a o **trasformador, -a** *adj.* 1 transforming. || *s.m.* 2 ELEC. transformer.
transformante o **trasformante** *adj.* transforming.
transformismo o **trasformismo** *s.m.* transformism.
transformar o **trasformar** *v.t.* y *pron.* to transform. 2 DEP. to convert (un tanto).
transfusión o **trasfusión** *s.f.* transfusion.
transgredir o **trasgredir** *v.t.* to transgress.
transgresión o **trasgresión** *s.f.* transgression, violation (de leyes).
transgresor, -a o **trasgresor, -a** *adj.* 1 transgressing, violating. || *s.m.* y *f.* 2 transgressor, violator.
transición *s.f.* transition: *la transición española a la democracia = the Spanish transition into democracy.*
transicional *adj.* transitional.
transido, -a *adj.* torn, wracked (por el dolor, especialmente).
transigencia *s.f.* compromise, accommodating attitude, spirit of compromise: *tu transigencia es excesiva = your spirit of compromise is too much.*
transigente *adj.* compromising, accommodating, tolerant.
transigir *v.t.* e *i.* to compromise, to give in.
transistor *s.m.* ELEC. transistor.
transitable *adj.* passable.
transitar *v.i.* to walk along the street, to pass; to travel: *mucha gente transitaba por la plaza = many people were walking around the square.*
transitivamente *adv.* transitively.
transitivo, -a *adj.* transitive.
tránsito *s.m.* 1 transit, passage. 2 (euf.) REL. passing, death. 3 stop, stopping place (lugar de descanso). 4 traffic, busy traffic (tráfico importante rodado).

transitoriamente *adv.* transitorily, temporarily.
transitorio, -a *adj.* transitory, temporary.
transitoriedad *s.f.* transitoriness, temporariness.
translación o **traslación** *s.f.* 1 movement. 2 ASTR. translation (de los planetas alrededor del Sol).
transliteración o **trasliteración** *s.f.* transliteration.
translucidez o **traslucidez** *s.f.* translucence, translucency.
translúcido, -a o **traslúcido, -a** *adj.* translucent.
transmigración o **trasmigración** *s.f.* transmigration.
transmigrar o **trasmigrar** *v.intr.* to transmigrate.
transmisible o **trasmisible** *adj.* transmissible.
transmisión o **trasmisión** *s.f.* 1 TV. broadcasting (emisión). 2 ELEC. transmission. 3 MEC. transmission (de marchas en vehículos).
transmisor, -ora o **trasmisor, -ora** *adj.* 1 transmitting. || *s.m.* 2 ELEC. transmitter.
transmitir o **trasmitir** *v.t.* y *pron.* 1 to transmit, to communicate. || *v.t.* 2 TV. to broadcast (emitir). 3 MED. to infect (una enfermedad). 4 DER. to transfer (derechos, bienes, etc.).
transmutable o **trasmutable** *adj.* transmutable.
transmutación o **trasmutación** *s.f.* transmutation.
transmutar o **trasmutar** *v.t.* y *pron.* to change, to turn into (en otra cosa distinta).
transnacional *adj.* transnational (especialmente empresas multinacionales).
transparencia o **trasparencia** *s.f.* 1 transparence (calidad de transparente). 2 FOT. slide (diapositiva).
transparentarse o **trasparentarse** *v.pron.* 1 to show through (especialmente vestidos). 2 to be transparent (ser transparente). 3 (fig.) to be obvious (verse claramente, un sentimiento o parecido).
transparente o **trasparente** *adj.* 1 transparent, filmy, see-through (vestidos, especialmente). 2 (fig.) transparent, clear (en sus sentimientos o similar).
transpirable o **traspirable** *adj.* transpirable.
transpiración o **traspiración** *s.f.* 1 perspiration (del cuerpo). 2 BOT. transpiration (en plantas).
transpirar o **traspirar** *v.i.* y *pron.* to perspire (sudar).
transportable o **trasportable** *adj.* easily transported.
transportación o **trasportación** *s.f.* transportation.
transportador, -a o **trasportador, -a** *adj.* 1 transporting. || *s.m.* y *f.* 2 transporter. 3 MEC. conveyor: *cinta transportadora = conveyor belt.*
transportar o **trasportar** *v.t.* 1 to transport, to haul. || *v.pron.* 2 (fig.) to fall into ecstasy (caer en éxtasis).
transporte o **trasporte** *s.m.* 1 transport (de todas las clases). 2 COM. freight: *gastos de transporte = freight costs.* 3 MAR. transport ship (barco). 4 (fig.) rapture, ecstasy (éxtasis).
transportista o **trasportista** *s.m.* 1 AER. carrier. 2 distributor (con camión propio).
transposición o **trasposición** *s.f.* transposition.
transubstanciación *s.f.* REL. transubstantiation.
transvasar o **trasvasar** *v.t.* y *pron.* 1 to divert (en ríos). 2 to decant; to transfer (entre utensilios).
transvase o **trasvase** *s.m.* 1 diversion (de ríos). 2 decanting, pouring (de líquidos entre utensilios).
transversal o **trasversal** *adj.* 1 GEOM. transversal. 2 cross, oblique, transverse (calle).
transversalmente o **trasversalmente** *adv.* transversally.
transverso, -a o **trasverso, -a** *adj.* 1 transverse. || *s.m.* 2 ANAT. transverse muscle (músculo).
tranvía *s.m.* tram, tramcar, tramway; (EE.UU.) streetcar.
trapacear *v.i.* to cheat, to act in a shady way.
trapacería *s.f.* cheating, swindle.
trapacero, -a *adj.* 1 cheating, swindling. || *s.m.* y *f.* 2 cheater.
trapatiesta *s.f.* racket, uproar, shindy.
trapecio *s.m.* 1 trapeze (circense). 2 GEOM. trapezoid. 3 ANAT. trapezius (músculo). 4 ANAT. trapezium (hueso).
trapecista *s.m.* y *f.* trapeze artist.
trapense *adj.* y *s.m.* REL. Trappist (monje).
trapezoidal *adj.* GEOM. trapezoidal.
trapichear *v.i.* 1 to hawk, to scrape a living buying and selling. 2 to plot, to scheme (andar en intrigas mezquinas).
trapicheo *s.m.* 1 hawking. 2 plotting, scheming.
trapisonda *s.f.* (fam.) 1 row, commotion, shindy (alboroto). 2 monkey business, shady affair (asunto un tanto deshonesto o ilegal).
trapisondista *s.m.* y *f.* 1 schemer, plotter (intrigante). 2 trouble-maker (que arma follones).
trapo *s.m.* 1 rag, tatter (jirón). 2 cloth (para limpiar). 3 MAR. sails. 4 muleta (para los toros). || **5 a todo —, a)** MAR. under full sail; **b)** at full throttle (con mucha actividad). **6 poner a alguien como un —, a)** to rake someone over the coals (a base de insultos, etc.); **b)** to wipe the floor with someone (desacreditando). **7 soltar el —,** to burst out crying/to burst out laughing.
tráquea *s.f.* ANAT. trachea, windpipe.
traqueal *adj.* tracheal.
traqueotomía *s.f.* MED. tracheotomy.
traquetear *v.i.* 1 to clatter, to rattle. || *v.t.* 2 to shake (causar el traqueteo).
traqueteo *s.m.* 1 bang, crack (sonido). 2 rattling, jolting (movimiento).
tras *prep.* 1 after: *día tras día = day after day.* 2 behind: *iban tras de los caballos = they were walking behind the horses.* 3 in pursuit of, in search of: *ir tras el éxito no es lo importante para mí = to go in search of success is not the important thing for me.* 4 in addition to, besides: *tras ser tonto no tiene un duro = besides being foolish he hasn't got a penny.* || *s.m.* 5 backside (trasero). || 6 **tras-,** trans- (en este diccionario se encuentran dos posibilidades: **trans** y **tras,** de las cuales se ha elegido la primera para referencia).
trasegar *v.t.* 1 to untidy, to jumble, to mix up. 2 to guzzle (beber mucho).
trasero, -a *adj.* 1 back: *parte trasera de la casa = back side of the house.* || *s.m.* 2 (euf.) backside, bottom (trasero). || *s.f.* 3 back part, rear (de un objeto o vehículo).
trasfondo *s.m.* background.
trashumante *adj.* AGR. migrating, transhumant (rebaños).
trashumar *v.i.* AGR. to make seasonal migrations (de rebaños).
trasiego *s.m.* 1 bustle, hustle (movimiento). 2 guzzling (de bebida).
trasladar *v.t.* y *pron.* 1 to move, to shift (de un lado a otro). || *v.t.* 2 to transfer (a un empleado). 3 to copy, to transcribe (copiar). 4 to postpone, to delay; to change (fechas). 5 to translate (traducir).
traslado *s.m.* 1 move, removal (de enseres y muebles). 2 transfer (de un puesto de trabajo). 3 copy, transcript (copia). 4 DER. communication, notification.
trasluz *s.m.* 1 reflected light. || **2 al —,** against the light.
trasmano, (a) *adv.* out of reach; remote: *ese lugar me pilla a trasmano = that place is a bit out of reach.*
trasmundo *s.m.* the other world, the hereafter.
trasnochado, -a *p.p.* 1 de **trasnochar.** || *adj.* 2 out of fashion, obsolete; ancient (pasado de moda). 3 wan, haggard (persona); stale (cosa). || *s.f.* 4 sleepless night, night watch.
trasnochador, -a *s.m.* y *f.* night owl.
trasnochar *v.i.* to stay up all night, to spend a sleepless night.
trasnocharse *v.i.* (Am.) to stay up all night, to spend a sleepless night.
traspapelar *v.t.* y *pron.* to misplace, to mislay.
traspasar *v.t.* 1 to cross, to go across (pasar a otra parte). 2 COM. to transfer, to sell (negocio). || *v.t.* y *pron.* 3 to pierce (con un arma puntiaguda o por el dolor): *me traspasó el alma como una espada de dolor = a sharp pain pierced my soul.*
traspaso *s.m.* 1 COM. transfer, sale. 2 grief, anguish (la aflicción).
traspié *s.m.* 1 slip, stumble. || **2 dar un —,** to slip; to stumble; (fig.) to make a mistake.

trasplantar *v.t.* 1 to transplant (vegetales, órganos, etc.). || *v.pron.* 2 to uproot oneself, to emigrate (emigrar).
trasponer *v.t.* y *pron.* 1 to move, to shift (cambiar de sitio). || *v.pron.* 2 to set (ponerse, el sol u otro planeta). 3 to disappear from sight (perderse de vista). 4 to doze off, to nod off (quedarse ligeramente dormido).
traspunte *s.m.* y *f.* callboy, prompter.
trasquilador, -a *s.m.* y *f.* shearer (de ovejas).
trasquiladura *s.f.* shearing, clipping.
trasquilar *v.t.* y *pron.* 1 to clip, to crop (el pelo). 2 to shear (ovejas). 3 to cut down, to curtail (menoscabar algo).
trastada *s.f.* 1 prank (típica de chicos). 2 senseless act, stupid act: *fue una trastada = it was a stupid act.*
trastazo *s.m.* whack, blow.
traste *s.m.* 1 MUS. fret. || 2 **dar al — con algo,** to spoil something, to ruin something.
trastear *v.i.* 1 to move things around, to rummage around. 2 to play around, to mess around (jugueteando). || *v.t.* 3 MUS. to strum (rasguear un instrumento de cuerda). 4 to tease (juguetear con un toro). 5 to manipulate (cosa o persona).
trastero, -a *adj.* 1 junk. || *s.m.* 2 junk room, storage room.
trastienda *s.f.* stock room.
trasto *s.m.* 1 old piece of furniture. 2 piece of junk, piece of lumber (objeto). 3 good-for-nothing, dead loss (persona). || *s.pl.* 4 tools (de una especialidad). || 5 **tirarse los trastos a la cabeza,** to have a good fight, to have a blazing row: *la pareja de al lado siempre se está tirando los trastos a la cabeza = the couple beside us are always having blazing rows.*
trastrocar o **trastocar** *v.t.* y *pron.* to upset, to disturb (algo que está en orden).
trastornado, -a *p.p.* 1 de **trastornar.** || *adj.* 2 mad, crazy: *está un poco trastornado = he's a bit mad.*
trastornador, -a *adj.* 1 upsetting, disturbing. || *s.m.* y *f.* 2 disturber.
trastornar *v.t.* 1 to upset, to overturn (dar la vuelta físicamente a un objeto): *trastornar las mesas = to overturn the tables.* 2 to disturb, to disrupt (perturbar). 3 to drive mad (volver loco): *la noticia me ha trastornado = the piece of news has driven me mad.* || *v.pron.* 4 to go mad (volverse loco).
trastorno *s.m.* 1 disturbance, upheaval, confusion. 2 MED. upset, disturbance (de tipo mental).
trasunto *s.m.* copy, imitation, transcription.
trata *s.f.* 1 slave trade. || 2 **— de blancas,** white slave trade.
tratable *adj.* sociable, friendly.
tratadista *s.m.* y *f.* LIT. essayist.
tratado, -a *p.p.* 1 de **tratar.** || *s.m.* 2 treatise (libro). 3 POL. treaty, pact.
tratamiento *s.m.* 1 MED. treatment. 2 form of address (forma de dirigirse a alguien). 3 TEC. processing (de materiales).
tratante *s.m.* y *f.* dealer, trader.
tratar *v.t.* 1 to handle, to use (objeto): *tratar bien los muebles = to handle the furniture with care.* 2 to treat (a personas): *trátele bien = treat him well.* 3 to address (dirigirse a alguien): *nunca le trataré de usted = I'll never address you as "usted".* 4 to take care of (cuidado): *el doctor que me trata es muy bueno = the doctor that takes care of me is very good.* || *v.t.* e *i.* 5 to be, to deal (de distintos asuntos, en forma de libros, películas, etc.): *el libro trata de las Matemáticas = the book deals with Mathematics.* || *v.t., i.* y *pron.* 6 to have contacts, to have to do: *yo con él no me trato = I don't have anything to do with him.* || *v.i.* 7 **— de,** to try: *trato de ser amable = I'm trying to be nice.* 8 to deal, to trade (comerciar): *trato en pieles = I deal in furs.* || *v.imp.* 9 to be (el tema, la cuestión, etc.): *en el juego se trata de meter la pelota por el agujero = in the game it is a question of getting the ball through the hole.*
trato *s.m.* 1 treatment. 2 form of address (forma de llamar a alguien). 3 relationship, dealings (tratos). 4 deal, agreement (acuerdo). || 5 **cerrar/hacer un —** to do a deal, to strike an agreement. 6 **— de gentes,** social charm.
trauma *s.m.* trauma.
traumático, -a *adj.* traumatic.
traumatismo *s.m.* traumatism.
traumatizante *adj.* traumatic, causing a dangerous trauma.
traumatizar *v.t.* to traumatize.
traumatología *s.f.* MED. traumatology.
traumatólogo, -a *s.m.* y *f.* MED. traumatologist.
través *s.m.* 1 slant, incline (ligera inclinación). 2 missfortune, adversity (desgracia). || 3 **a —, a)** across, through: *a través de la jungla = through the jungle;* **b)** across (de un sitio a otro): *a través de la habitación = across the room;* **c)** through, by means of: *a través del estudio = by means of study.* 4 **de —,** crosswise, crossways.
travesaño *s.m.* 1 ARQ. crossbeam. 2 DEP. crossbar. 3 bolster (de la cama).
travesía *s.f.* 1 MAR. crossing, voyage. 2 crossroad, cross street (calle transversal).
travestí o **travestido** *s.m.* transvestite.
travesura *s.f.* 1 prank, mischief. 2 wit (ingenio).
travieso, -a *adj.* 1 mischievous, naughty. 2 transverse (que atraviesa). 3 lively (vivo). || *s.f.* 4 crosstie (los maderos de la vía del tren).
trayecto *s.m.* 1 distance, stretch, section (zona). 2 route, way (camino).
trayectoria *s.f.* 1 path (por ejemplo, de una bala). 2 line, development, evolution (de un partido, persona, movimiento, etc.): *la trayectoria del partido es muy limpia = the development of the party has been very honourable.*
traza *s.f.* 1 design. 2 plan. 3 appearance, looks: *esto tiene trazas de no acabar nunca = this has all the the looks of never finishing.* 4 GEOM. trace.
trazo *s.f.* 1 line. 2 stroke (de las letras). 3 sketch, outline (idea general).
trébol *s.m.* 1 BOT. clover. 2 ARQ. trefoil (como adorno). 3 club (palo de la baraja).
trece *num.card.* 1 thirteen. 2 thirteenth (con fechas). || *s.m.* 3 thirteen (como signo). || 4 **mantenerse/seguir en sus trece,** to stick to one's guns.
trecho *s.m.* 1 stretch (de un camino). || 2 **de — en —,** at intervals, every now and then.
tregua *s.f.* 1 truce (especialmente militar). 2 (fig.) rest, respite (descanso): *sin tregua = without respite.*
treinta *num.card.* 1 thirty. 2 thirtieth (con fechas). || *s.m.* 3 thirty (como conjunto de signos).
treintavo, -a *adj.num.ord.* thirtieth.
treintena *s.f.* 1 thirty. 2 thirtieth part (parte).
tremebundo, -a *adj.* dreadful, terrible, frightening.
tremendo, -a *adj.* 1 tremendous, gigantic, huge (enorme). 2 terrible, horrible (que asusta). 3 tremendous, imposing, awesome (digno de respeto). || 4 **por la tremenda,** with a big fuss.
trementina *s.f.* QUIM. turpentine.
tremolar *v.t.* e *i.* to wave.
tremolante *adj.* waving.
tremolina *s.f.* 1 rustling, howling (del viento). 2 row, fuss (alboroto).
tren *s.m.* 1 train. 2 gear, equipment (equipo). || 3 **a todo —,** in style. 4 **— de vida,** way of life.
trémulamente *adv.* tremulously.
trémulo, -a *adj.* tremulous, flickering.
trena *s.f.* (argot) clink.
trenca *s.f.* duffle coat.
trenza *s.f.* braid, plait.
trenzado *p.p.* 1 de **trenzar.** || *s.m.* 2 braid, plait (del pelo). 3 ARQ. entrechat.
trenzar *v.t.* to braid, to plait.
trepa *s.f.* 1 climbing, climb. || *s.m.* y f 2 (argot) social climber.
trepador, -a *adj.* 1 climbing (especialmente plantas).
trepanar *v.t.* to trepan.
trepanación *s.f.* trepanation.
trepar *v.t.* e *i.* 1 to climb, to clamber up. 2 to climb (plantas).
trepidación *s.f.* vibration, trembling, shaking, trepidation.
trepidante *adj.* 1 shaking, vibrating. 2 (fig.) extreme, shaterring, smashing (ritmo de vida).
trepidar *v.i.* 1 to shake, to vibrate. 2 (Am.) to hesitate, to doubt (dudar).
tres *adj.num.card.* 1 three. 2 third (con fechas). || *s.m.* 3 three (como signo). || 4 **como — y dos son cinco,** with absolute certainty, as sure as I am standing here. 5 **ni a la de —,** not by a long shot, on no account.

trescientos *adj.num.card.* 1 three hundred. || *s.m.* 2 three hundred (como grupo de signos).
tresillo *s.m.* 1 three pieces suite (mueble). 2 card game for three people. 3 MUS. triplet.
treta *s.f.* 1 trick, ruse: *utilizaremos una treta que confundirá al enemigo = we'll use a ruse that will deceive the enemy.* 2 DEP. feint (en la esgrima).
tri- *prefijo* tri-.
tríada *s.f.* triad.
triangular *adj.* 1 triangular. || *v.t.* 2 to triangulate.
triangularmente *adv.* triangularly.
triángulo *s.m.* 1 GEOM. triangle. 2 MUS. triangle. || GEOM. 3. **— equilátero,** equilateral triangle. 4 **— escaleno,** scalene triangle. 5 **— esférico,** spherical triangle. 6 **— isósceles,** isosceles triangle. 7 **— rectángulo,** right triangle.
triásico, -a *adj.* y *s.m.* triassic.
tribal o **tribual** *adj.* tribal.
tribu *s.f.* tribe.
tribulación *s.f.* tribulation.
tribuna *s.f.* 1 rostrum, platform (para hablar desde aquí). 2 grand-stand, gallery (en lugares de espectáculo). 3 (fig.) political oratory (oratoria política).
tribunal *s.m.* DER. 1 court, court of justice, tribunal. 2 board of examiners (tribunal de oposiciones). || 3 **Tribunal Constitucional,** Constitutional Tribunal. 4 **Tribunal de Cuentas,** Audit Court, Accounts Tribunal. 5 **Tribunal de Dios,** God's own court. 6 **Tribunal de la Rota,** Rote Tribunal. 7 **Tribunal Supremo,** Supreme Court, High Court. 8 **Tribunal Tutelar de menores,** juvenile court.
tribuno *s.m.* 1 HIST. tribune. 2 (fig.) orator.
tributable *adj.* taxable: *ingresos tributables = taxable income.*
tributación *s.f.* 1 payment of taxes (pago). 2 tax system (sistema). 3 tax, taxes (desde un punto de vista abstracto): *la tributación es alta en este país = in this country taxes are high.*
tributar *v.t.* 1 to pay taxes. 2 (fig.) to pay, to show, to give (respeto o similar): *todos le tributamos el respeto que se merecía = we all paid him the respect he deserved.*
tributario, -a *adj.* 1 tax: *derecho tributario = tax law.* || *s.m.* 2 GEOG. tributary (río afluente).
tributo *s.m.* 1 tax. 2 tribute, respect (respeto). 3 recognition (de algo logrado): *le damos esta medalla como tributo a sus esfuerzos = we are awarding you this medal as a sign of recognition of all your work.*
tríceps *adj.* y *s.m.* ANAT. triceps (músculo).
triciclo *s.m.* tricycle.
tricot *s.m.* tricot.
tricotosa *s.f.* knitting machine.
tridente *adj.* y *s.m.* trident.
trienal *adj.* triennial.
trienio *s.m.* triennium.
triforio *s.m.* triforium.
trifulca *s.f.* scuffle, rumpus.
trifurcación *s.f.* trifurcation.
trifurcado, -a *adj.* trifurcate.
trifurcarse *v.pron.* to divide into three.
trigal *s.m.* AGR. wheat field.
trigémino *s.m.* ANAT. trigeminal nerve.
trigésimo, -a *adj.num.ord.* thirtieth.
triglifo *s.m.* ARQ. triglyph.
trigo *s.m.* 1 BOT. wheat. || 2 **no ser — limpio,** to be dishonest, not to be completely aboveboard.
trigonometría *s.f.* MAT. trigonometry.
trigueño, -a *adj.* dark blond (color).
triguero, -a *adj.* of wheat.
trilingüe *adj.* trilingual.
trilogía *s.f.* trilogy.
trilla *s.f.* AGR. threshing.
trillado, -a *p.p.* 1 de **trillar.** || *adj.* 2 beaten, worn-out (muy común y conocido).
trilladora *s.f.* AGR. threshing machine.
trilladura *s.g.* threshing.
trillar *v.t.* 1 AGR. to thresh. 2 to use frequently, to use a lot; to wear out with frequent use.
trillizo, -a *s.m.* y *f.* triplet.
trillo *s.m.* AGR. thresher.
trillón *s.m.* trillion.
trimestral *adj.* quarterly: *una revista trimestral = a quarterly review.*
trimestralmente *adv.* every term, every three months.
trimestre *s.m.* term (especialmente en el mundo educativo).
trinar *v.i.* 1 to trill (especialmente los pájaros). 2 to go wild, to get mad (enfadarse mucho): *está que trina = he has gone wild.*
trinca *s.f.* trio, triad.
trincar *v.t.* 1 MAR. to tie, to lash (atar). 2 to break up (partir en trozos). 3 to put away, to gulp down (comida o bebida). 4 to hold down (sujetar fuertemente).
trinchador *s.m.* carving knife.
trinchar *v.t.* to carve.
trinchera *s.f.* 1 MIL. trench. 2 cutting (del ferrocarril).
trineo *s.m.* sleigh, sledge, sled.
trinidad *s.f.* 1 REL. Trinity. 2 trio, set of three.
trinitario, -a *adj.* 1 REL. of the Trinity. || *s.f.* 2 BOT. wild pansy.
trinitrotolueno *s.m.* QUIM. trinitrotoluene.
trino, -a *adj.* 1 REL. triune. || *s.m.* 2 trill (de los pájaros).
trinquete *s.m.* 1 MAR. foremast (palo). 2 MAR. foresail (vela). 3 MEC. pawl, ratchet (mecanismo).
trío *s.m.* trio.
tripa *s.f.* 1 bowel (intestino). 2 (fam.) tummy (estómago). || *pl.* 3 guts (dentro del cuerpo). 4 innards, insides (de cosas o personas). || 5 **hacer de tripas corazón,** to pluck up one's courage, to screw up one's courage. 6 **revolvérsele a uno las tripas,** to turn one's stomach, to make somebody's stomach turn.
tripartito, -a *adj.* tripartite.
triple *adj.* 1 triple. || *adj.* y *s.m.* 2 triple, three times: *el triple de lo que gano = three times what I earn.*
triplicación *s.f.* triplication.
triplicado, -a *p.p.* 1 de **triplicar.** || *s.m.* 2 triplicate: *por triplicado = triplicate.*
triplicar *v.t.* to triplicate.
triplicidad *s.f.* triplicity.
triplo, -a *adj.* y *s.m.* triple, treble.
trípode *s.m.* tripod.
tríptico *s.m.* triptych.
triptongo *s.m.* FON. triphthong.
tripudo, -a *adj.* pot-bellied.
tripulación *s.f.* crew.
tripulante *s.m.* y *f.* crew member.
tripular *v.t.* 1 to man (proveer de tripulantes). 2 to be a member of the crew.
triquina *s.f.* MED. trichina.
triquinosis *s.f.* trichinosis.
triquiñuela *s.f.* trick, dodge.
triquitraque *s.m.* 1 clickety-clack (sonido acompasado). 2 firecracker (cohete).
trirreme *s.m.* trireme.
tris *s.m.* 1 jiffy, trice (período cortísimo de tiempo). || 2 **en un —,** very close, within an inch.
trisca *s.f.* crack, crunch (ruido onomatopéyico).
triscar *v.i.* 1 to trisk (retozar). 2 to trample (pisotear).
trisección *s.f.* GEOM. trisection.
triste *adj.* 1 sad, melancholy. 2 sad, sorrowful (noticias, por ejemplo). 3 dismal, miserable (vida).
tristemente *adv.* 1 sadly. 2 sadly, sorrowfully. 3 dismally, miserably. V. **triste.**
tristeza *s.f.* 1 sadness. 2 sadness, sorrow (que causa tristeza). 3 gloom (que deprime).
tristón, -a *adj.* a little sad.
tritón *s.m.* ZOOL. newt.
trituración *s.f.* crushing, grinding.
triturar *v.t.* 1 to crush, to grind. 2 to chew well (comida). 3 to beat up (a una persona): *te voy a triturar = I'm going to beat you up.*
triunfador, -a *adj.* 1 victorious. || *s.m.* y *f.* 2 winner: *este chico nació triunfador = this boy was born a winner.*
triunfal *adj.* triumphal, triumphant.
triunfalmente *adv.* triumphantly.
triunfar *v.i.* to triumph, to win (en la guerra, el deporte, la vida, etc.).
triunfo *s.m.* 1 triumph, victory, success. 2 trump (en las cartas).
triunvirato *s.m.* triumvirate.
trivial *adj.* 1 trivial, unimportant: *asunto trivial = unimportant matter.* 2 trite, common (mediocre).
trivialidad *s.f.* 1 triviality (característica). 2 trite remark (dicho concreto).
trivialmente *adv.* trivially, tritely.
triza *s.f.* 1 small piece, shred. || 2 **hacer trizas,** to tear into pieces, to pull to pieces (material o figurativamente).
trocable *adj.* exchangeable.
trocar *v.t.* y *pron.* 1 to exchange, to change, to swap, to barter. 2 to mix up, to confuse (el orden o parecido).
trocear *v.t.* to divide into pieces.

trocha *s.f.* path, train (en la jungla).
trochemoche, a —/a troche y moche, pell-mell, helter-skelter, in a mess.
trofeo *s.m.* **1** trophy. **2** spoils of war (botín). **3** (fig.) victory, success, triumph.
troglodita *s.m.* y *f.* **1** cave-dweller, troglodyte. **2** (fig.) gluton (glotón).
troica *s.f.* troika.
troje o **troj** *s.f.* granary, barn.
trola *s.f.* (fam.) lie.
trolebús *s.m.* trolley bus.
trolero, -a *s.m.* y *f.* (fam.) liar.
tromba *s.f.* whirlwind, waterspout (especialmente de agua).
trombo *s.m.* thrombus.
tromboflebitis *s.f.* MED. thrombophlebitis.
trombón *s.m.* MUS. trombone.
trombosis *s.f.* MED. thrombosis.
trompa *s.f.* **1** MUS. horn. **2** ZOOL. trunk (de elefante). **3** drunken spree (borrachera). **4** ANAT. tube. **5** snout (de algunos animales). **6** whirlwind (tormenta). || **7 — de Eustaquio,** ANAT. Eustachian tube.
trompazo *s.m.* bump, crash.
trompeta *s.f.* **1** MUS. trumpet, bugle. **2** (Am.) rogue, rascal (charlatán).
trompetazo *s.m.* trumpet blast, bugle blast.
trompeteo *s.m.* trumpet playing.
trompetilla *s.f.* ear trumpet (para los sordos).
trompezón *s.m.* (Am.) stumple, trip.
trompicón *s.m.* stumble, trip.
tronado, -a *p.p.* **1** de **tronar.** || *adj.* **2** mad, crazy, potty (loco).
tronar *v.i.* **1** to thunder (con truenos). **2** (fig.) to make a lot of noise: *el piano estaba tronando = the piano was making a lot of noise.*
tronco *s.m.* **1** BOT. trunk (de un árbol). **2** ANAT. trunk. **3** team of horses (caballos). **4** lineage (tronco genealógico). **5** blockhead. **6** GEOM. frustum. || **7 dormir como un —,** to sleep like a log. **8 estar como un —,** to be deep asleep.
tronchar *v.t.* y *pron.* to break off (ramaje especialmente).
tronera *s.f.* ARQ. small window.
trono *s.m.* **1** throne. || *pl.* **2** REL. thrones (ángeles).
tropa *s.f.* **1** MIL. troop, army. **2** (fig.) crowd.
tropel *s.m.* **1** bustle, confusion. **2** jumble (de cosas desordenadas): *un tropel de vasos y platos = a jumble of glasses and plates.* || **3 en —,** in a disorderly way; in a mad rush.
tropelía *s.f.* **1** rush, confusion. **2** outrage, abuse (atropello).
tropezar *v.i.* **1** to stumble, to trip: *cuidado, no tropieces = take care, don't stumble.* **2** to slip up (cometer un error). || *v.pron.* **3** to bump into, to run into (con alguien).
tropezón *s.m.* **1** stumble, trip. **2** slip, mistake (error). **3** GAST. small piece of meat added to a stew.
tropical *adj.* tropical.
trópico *s.m.* GEOG. **1** tropic. || **2 Trópico de Cáncer,** Tropic of Cancer. **3 Trópico de Capricornio,** Tropic of Capricorn.
tropiezo *s.m.* **1** obstacle, stumbling block. **2** stumble, trip (hecho concreto). **3** slip, mistake. **4** downfall (como pecado).
tropismo *s.m.* BIOL. tropism.
tropo *s.m.* trope.
troposfera *s.f.* troposphere.
troquel *s.m.* MEC. die.
troquelar *v.t.* to coin, to mint.
troqueo *s.m.* trochee.
trotacalles *s.m.* (fam.) y *f.* gaddabout.
trotamundos *s.m.* y *f.* globetrotter.
trotar *v.i.* to trot.
trote *s.m.* **1** trot, quick pace. **2** difficult chore (tarea ardua). || **3 al —,** trotting, quickly. **4 para todo —,** for everyday wear, for everyday use.
trotskista *adj./s.m.* y *f.* trotskyite.
trovador *s.m.* HIST. troubadour.
troyano, -a *adj./s.m.* y *f.* trojan.
trozo *s.m.* piece, chunk: *un trozo de pan = a chunk of bread.*
trucaje *s.m.* trick photography.
trucar *v.i.* to rig, to fix: *hemos trucado el resultado de las carreras = we have rigged the result of the races.*
truco *s.m.* **1** trick (de manos). **2** deception (engaño). **3** knack (el truco que hace que algo se solucione): *sabe el truco de cómo hacerlo = he has the knack of doing it.*
truculencia *s.f.* truculence, cruelty.
truculento, -a *adj.* truculent, cruel
trucha *s.f.* ZOOL. trout.
trueno *s.m.* **1** thunder. **2** bang, explosion (normalmente de un arma). **3** reckless youngster (joven alborotador).
trueque *s.m.* barter, exchange.
trufa *s.f.* BOT. truffle.
truhán, -a *s.m.* y *f.* scoundrel, crook.
truhanería *s.f.* roguishness, buffoonery.
truhanesco, -a *adj.* roguish, buffoonish.
truísmo *s.m.* truism.
truncadamente *adv.* truncatedly, incompletely.
truncado, -a *p.p.* **1** de **truncar.** || *adj.* **2** truncated, shortened.
truncamiento *s.m.* truncation, mutilation, cutting.
trust *s.m.* trust.
tse-tsé *s.f.* ZOOL. tsetse.
tu *adj.pos.* **1** your: *tu radio no tiene pilas = your radio has no batteries.*
tú *pron.pers.* **1** you: *fuiste tú quien lo estropeó = it was you who broke it.* || **2 hablar/tratar de — a — a alguien,** to be on friendly terms with someone.
tuba *s.f.* MUS. tuba.
tuberculina *s.f.* tuberculin.
tubérculo *s.m.* BOT. tuber.
tuberculosis *s.f.* MED. tuberculosis.
tuberculoso, -a *adj.* MED. **1** tubercular. || *s.m.* y *f.* **2** tuberculosis sufferer.
tubería *s.f.* plumbing, pipes.
tubo *s.m.* **1** tube, pipe. **2** ANAT. tract, canal (de personas y animales). || **3 — de ensayo,** test tube. **4 — intestinal,** ANAT. intestine.
tubular *adj.* tubular.
tucán *s.m.* ZOOL. toucan (ave).
tuerca *s.f.* MEC. wing nut.
tuerto, -a *adj.* **1** one-eyed. || *s.m.* y *f.* **2** one-eyed person.
tueste *s.m.* toasting (con frutos secos y café especialmente).
tuétano *s.m.* **1** ANAT. marrow. **2** (fig.) essence, core (esencia de algo). || **3 hasta los tuétanos,** through and through.
tufo *s.m.* stink, stench.
tugurio *s.m.* hovel, shack: *¡vaya tugurio! = what a shack!.*
tul *s.m.* tulle.
tulipán *s.m.* BOT. tulip.
tullido, -a *adj.* crippled, disabled.
tullir *v.t.* to cripple, to maim.
tumba *s.f.* tomb, grave.
tumbar *v.t.* **1** to knock down, to knock over: *me tumbó de un puñetazo = he knocked me down with a blow.* **2** to make (someone) dizzy. | *v.pron.* **3** to lie down.
tumbo *s.m.* **1** tumbe, fall. **2** jolt (golpe violento).
tumbona *s.f.* deck chair, sling chair.
tumefacción *s.f.* tumefaction, swelling.
tumefacto, -a *adj.* tumid.
tumescencia *s.f.* MED. tumescence.
tumescentee *adj.* MED. tumescent.
tumor *s.m.* MED. tumour.
tumulto *s.m.* commotion, riot.
tumultuario, -a *adj.* tumultuary.
tumultuosamente *adv.* tumultuously.
tumultuoso, -a *adj.* tumultuous.
tuna V. **tuno, -a.**
tunantada *s.f.* dirty trick.
tunanta *s.f.* hussy.
tunante *s.m.* rascal, crook.
tunantería *s.f.* **1** dirty trick (acción concreta). **2** roguishness (cualidad).
tunda *s.f.* whipping, beating.
tundra *s.f.* tundra.
tunecino, -a *adj./s.m.* y *f.* Tunisian.
túnel *s.m.* tunnel.
tungsteno *s.m.* tungsten.
túnica *s.f.* tunic, robe, gown.
tuno, -a *adj.* **1** rascally. || *s.m.* **2** player in a group of student mistrels. || *s.f.* **3** band of student minstrels. **4** idleness (holgazanería).
tuntún (al o **al buen)** *adv.* trusting to luck, without due calculation.
tupé *s.m.* lock of hair on the forehead.
tupir *v.t.* y *pron.* to block, to stop up.
turba *s.f.* MIN. peat, turf.
turbante *s.m.* turban.
turbación *s.f.* upset, disturbance; confusion: *la turbación de ella me sorprendió = her confusion surprised me.*
turbadamente *adv.* worriedly, confusedly.
turbador, -a *adj.* disturbing, upsetting, confusing.
turbamulta *s.f.* mob, rabble.
turbar *v.t.* y *pron.* **1** to upset, to disturb. **2** to bewilder, to confuse (poner nervioso). **3** to stir up (el agua o cualquier otra cosa).

turbiamente *adv.* **1** muddily (con barro). **2** shadily, suspiciously (con sospechas). **3** turbulently (agitadamente).
turbiedad *s.f.* muddiness.
turbina *s.f.* ELEC. turbine.
turbio, -a *adj.* **1** muddy (barroso). **2** shady, suspicious (sospechoso). **3** troubled, turbulent (especialmente un período de tiempo). **4** blurred (la visión).
turbulencia *s.f.* turbulence.
turbulento, -a *adj.* turbulent.
turco, -a *adj./m.* y *f.* **1** Turkish. || *s.m.* **2** Turkish (idioma). || **3 cama turca,** V. **cama.**
turgencia *s.f.* turgescence.
turgente *adj.* turgent.
turismo *s.m.* tourism.
turista *s.m.* y *f.* tourist.
turístico, -a *adj.* tourist.
turnar *v.i.* y *pron.* to take turns: *tenemos que turnarnos en el cuidado del niño = we have to take turns at looking after the baby.*
turno *s.m.* turn; shift: *el turno de la noche = the night shift.*
turquesa *s.f.* MIN. turquoise.
turrón *s.m.* GAST. Christmas nougat.
turulato, -a *adj.* (fam.) dazed, stunned.
tute *s.m.* **1** card game. **2** hard work, laborious chore: *¡qué tute me he pegado! = what a lot of hard work I have done!.* || **3 darse un –,** to make a special effort, to work extra hard.
tutear *v.t.* to address (a alguien) with familiar terms.
tuteo *s.m.* familiar address.
tutela *s.f.* guardianship, tutelage; protection: *bajo la tutela de mis padres = under the protection of my parents.*
tutelar *adj.* tutelary; protective.
tutiplén, a –, *loc.adv.* in abundance, abundantly.
tutor, -a *s.m.* y *f.* **1** tutor (en la enseñanza). **2** guardian, protector.
tutoría *s.f.* **1** tutor's job. **2** guardianship.
tuyo, -a *pron.pos.* yours: *is this book yours? = ¿es tuyo este libro?*

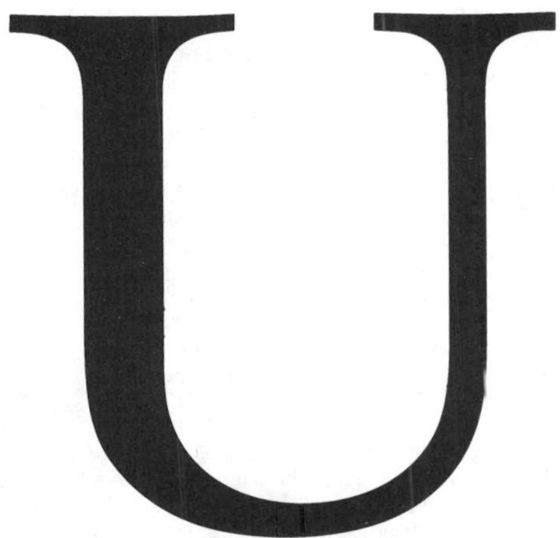

u, U *s.f.* 1 u, U (vigésimocuarta letra del alfabeto español). || *conj.* 2 or (ante palabras que empiezan por "o" u "ho").
ubérrimo *adj.* 1 very fertile, very productive. 2 abundant, teeming, luxuriant.
ubicación *s.f.* position, location; placing.
ubicar *v.t.* 1 to place, to locate. || *v.i.* 2 to be located, to be situated, to lie. || *v.pron.* 3 to be situated. 4 (Am.) to get a job (colocarse).
ubicuidad *s.f.* ubiquity.
ubre *s.f.* udder.
ufanamente *adv.* proudly; boastfully.
ufanarse *v.pron.* 1 to pride oneself, to be conceited. 2 (desp.) to boast (jactarse). 3 [– con/de] to pride oneself on, to boast of; to glory in.
ufanía *s.f.* 1 pride. 2 (desp.) conceit, vanity.
ufano, -a *adj.* 1 proud. 2 self-satisfied. 3 cheerful, gay. 4 (desp.) conceited, vain.
ujier *s.m.* 1 usher; doorman, janitor; attendant.
úlcera *s.f.* MED. ulcer; sore.
ulceración *s.f.* MED. ulceration.
ulcerante *adj.* MED. ulcerative.
ulcerar *v.t.* y *v.pron.* MED. to ulcerate.
ulceroso, -a *adj.* MED. ulcerous, full of sores.
ulterior *adj.* 1 ulterior. 2 following. 3 further, farther (referido a lugar). 4 subsequent, later (posterior).
ulteriormente *adv.* subsequently, later.
ultimación *s.f.* conclusion.
últimamente *adv.* 1 finally, lastly (por último). 2 lately (recientemente).
ultimar *v.t.* 1 to finish, to end, to complete; to put an end to. 2 to conclude (un trato, un acuerdo). 3 to finalize (los preparativos, los detalles). 4 (Am.) to kill (rematar).
ultimátum *s.m.* ultimatum.
último, -a *adj.* 1 last: *la última vez = the last time.* 2 latest, latter (más reciente): *las últimas noticias = the latest news.* 3 latter (de dos). 4 furthest (más lejano). 5 top: *último piso = top floor.* 6 final: *último capítulo = final chapter.* 7 bottom: *último dólar = bottom dolar.* 8 (fig.) best, superior (calidad). 9 back: *última fila = back row.* 10 lowest (posición). || *s.m.* y *f.* 11 last: *¿quién es el último? = who is the last?* || **12 a la última,** up to date. **13 a últimos de (mes, etc.),** towards the end of, in the latter part of. **14 en – caso,** as a last resort. **15 estar en las últimas; a)** to be near one's end, to be on one's last legs; **b)** to be down to one's last penny. **16 por última vez,** for the last time. **17 por –,** lastly, finally.
ultra *prep.* 1 besides. || *adj./s.m.* y *f.* 2 ultra (extremista).
ultra- *prefijo* ultra-: *ultramoderno = ultramodern.*
ultrajador V. **ultrajante.**
ultrajante *adj.* 1 outrageous. 2 offensive, injurious; insulting.
ultrajar *v.t.* 1 to outrage. 2 to offend; to insult.
ultraje *s.m.* 1 outrage. 2 insult, offence.
ultramar *s.m.* 1 place/country across the sea. || **2 de –,** from across the sea. **3 en –,** overseas. **4 países de –,** overseas countries.
ultramarino, -a *adj.* 1 overseas. || **2 ultramarinos, a)** groceries (productos); **b)** grocer's (tienda).
ultranza, a ultranza *loc.adv.* 1 to the death. 2 (fig.) regardless, at any price (a toda costa). 3 out-and-out, extreme: *un ecologista a ultranza = an out-and-out ecologist.*
ultratumba *s.f.* beyond the grave.
ultravioleta *adj.* ultraviolet.
ulular *v.i.* 1 to hoot, to screech (el búho, la lechuza). 2 to howl (el viento, los animales).
ululato *s.m.* 1 hoot, screech (del búho, de la lechuza). 2 howl (del viento, de un animal).
umbilical *adj.* ANAT. umbilical.
umbral *s.m.* 1 threshold (de una puerta). 2 (fig.) threshold, beginning.
umbrío, -a *adj.* shady, shadowy, umbrageous.
un, -a *art.ind.* 1 a, an: *un coche = a car; un huevo = an egg.* || *adj.num.* 2 one: *un perro = one dog.*
OBS. **Un** es la forma apocopada de **uno** delante de *s.m.* o de un *s.f.* que empiece por "a" o "ha" tónicas: *un hacha = an axe.*
unánime *adj.* unanimous.
unánimemente *adv.* unanimously.
unanimidad *s.f.* 1 unanimity, complete accord. || **2 por –,** unanimously.
unción *s.f.* 1 unction, anointing (acción de ungir). 2 REL. unction, religious fervour. 3 REL. Extreme Unction. || **4 – de enfermos,** REL. Extreme Unction.
uncir *v.t.* to yoke.
undécimo, -a *adj./s.m.* y *f.* eleventh.
undulación V. **ondulación.**
undulante V. **ondulante.**
undular V. **ondular.**
ungido, -a *adj.* y *s.m.* anointed
ungir *v.t.* 1 to anoint, to apply ointment to. 2 REL. to anoint; to consecrate.
ungüento *s.m.* unguent, salve, ointment.
únicamente *adv.* only; simply; solely.
unicidad *s.f.* unicity, uniqueness.
único, -a *adj.* 1 sole, only, single: *hijo único = only child; el único superviviente = the sole survivor.* 2 alone: *¿es la única en hablar así? = is she alone in speaking so?* 3 (fig.) unique; singular, rare, unusual.
unicornio *s.m.* unicorn.
unidad *s.f.* 1 MAT. unit, unity: *unidades métricas = metric units.* 2 LIT. unity: *unidad de tiempo = unity of time.* 3 (fig.) unity, oneness: *no había unidad en sus planes = there was no unity about their plans.* 4 MIL. unit. || **5 coste por –,** COM. unit cost. **6 – móvil,** TV. mobile unit.
unido, -a *adj.* 1 joined. 2 (fig.) united. || **3 mantenerse –,** to keep together.

unificación *s.f.* unification.
unificador, -a *adj.* 1 unifying. || *s.m.* y *f.* 2 unifier.
unificar *v.t.* to unify; to unite.
uniformar *v.t.* 1 to furnish with uniforms, to provide a uniform for. 2 to make uniform. 3 to standardize (métodos).
uniforme *adj.* 1 uniform; regular, steady; even: *velocidad uniforme = uniform velocity.* 2 level: *un tono uniforme = a level tone.* || *s.m.* 3 uniform: *uniforme del colegio = school uniform.* || 4 **— de gala,** MIL. full-dress uniform. 5 **— militar,** MIL. regimentals.
uniformemente *adv.* uniformly; regularly.
uniformidad *s.f.* 1 uniformity; regularity; evenness.
unigénito *adj.* 1 only (hijo). 2 REL. only begotten (el hijo de Dios).
unilateral *adj.* unilateral, one-sided: *una decisión unilateral = a one-sided decision.*
unión *s.f.* 1 union, uniting; unity. 2 POL. union (confederación). 3 union, marriage (casamiento). 4 MEC. union, joint.
unipersonal *adj.* 1 individual (de una sola persona). 2 GRAM. unipersonal (verbo).
unir *v.t.* 1 to unite, to join: *juntemos las mesas = let's join the tables.* 2 to unite (por matrimonio). 3 to merge, to bring together (intereses, etc.). 4 to attach, to connect (vincular). 5 to mix (mezclar). 6 to pool (aunar). 7 to link, to link up (enlazar). || *v.pron.* 8 to unite, to join together; to merge, to become united. 9 to wed, to marry.
unísono, -a *adj.* 1 unisonous; in harmony. || 2 **al —,** (fig.) in unison.
unitario, -a *adj.* 1 unitary. || *adj./s.m.* y *f.* 2 REL. unitarian.
unitarismo *s.m.* REL. unitarianism.
universal *adj.* 1 universal: *sufragio universal = universal suffrage.* 2 world: *historia universal = world history.* || 3 **de fama —,** world-famous, known all over the world.
universalidad *s.f.* universality.
universalmente *adv.* universally; all over the world.
universidad *s.f.* university.
universitario, -a *adj.* 1 university: *estudios universitarios = university education.* || *s.m.* y *f.* 2 academic; student (estudiante universitario); lecturer (profesor universitario). 3 (EE.UU.) collegiate.
universo *s.m.* 1 universe; world. || *adj.* 2 universal.
unívoco, -a *adj.* univocal.
uno, -a *adj.num.* 1 one: *una mesa = one table.* || *pron.ind.* 2 one: *¿tienes uno? = have you one?* 3 you, one: *uno nunca sabe = one never knows.* 4 somebody: *una que dice que te conoce = somebody who says knows you.* || *s.m.* 5 one (la unidad): *el número uno = the number one.* 6 first: *el día uno de enero = the first of January.* || *s.f.* 7 one: *la una = one o'clock.* || 8 **a —,** al together, of one accord. 9 **cada —,** each one, everyone. 10 **lo — por lo otro,** it comes to the same thing. 11 **una de las tuyas, suyas,** etc. (fam.) trick, prank. 12 **— a —,** one by one. 13 **— mismo,** oneself. 14 **unos/unas, a)** some, a few: *hace unos meses = some months ago;* **b)** some (aproximadamente): *unas cinco horas = some five hours.* 15 **unos cuantos,** a few, some.
untadura *s.f.* 1 smearing, greasing, oiling (acción de untar). 2 ointment (untura).
untar *v.t.* 1 to anoint, to rub, to smear (con ungüento). 2 (fig.) to bribe (sobornar). 3 to spread (mantequilla, etc.). || *v.pron.* 4 to smear oneself. 5 (fam.) to practise embezzlement. || 6 **— la mano a,** (fig.) to grease the hand of, to anoint the palm of (sobornar).
untuosidad *s.f.* unctuousness, untuosity, greasiness, oiliness.
untuoso, -a *adj.* unctuous, greasy, oily; sticky.
untura V. **untadura.**
uña *s.f.* 1 nail; fingernail (de la mano); toenail (del pie). 2 ZOOL. claw (garra, pezuña). 3 ZOOL. hoof (de caballo). 4 ZOOL. sting (de alacrán). 5 hook (de una herramienta). 6 MAR. fluke, bill (punta de ancla). 7 MEC. pallet. || 8 **a — de caballo,** (fig.) at full speed, at full gallop. 9 **estar de uñas,** to be at daggers drawn. 10 **largas uñas,** (Am. y fig.) thief. 11 **ser — y carne,** to be inseparable friends, to be hand and glove.
uñada *s.f.* nailmark; nail scratch.
uñarada V. **uñada.**
uñero *s.m.* 1 MED. whitlow. 2 ingrowing nail. || 3 **uñeros,** thumb index (en un libro).
uralita *s.f.* ARQ. fibrocement.
uranio, -a *s.m.* 1 QUIM. uranium. || *adj.* 2 ASTR. uranic.
urbanamente *adv.* urbanely, politely.
urbanidad *s.f.* urbanity, politeness, good manners.
urbanismo *s.m.* ARQ. urbanism, town-planning.
urbanístico, -a *adj.* 1 urban. 2 ARQ. town-planning.
urbanización *s.f.* 1 urbanization. 2 ARQ. development (de una ciudad). 3 new residential area; housing state.
urbanizar *v.t.* 1 to urbanize. 2 ARQ. to develop (un terreno). || *v.pron.* y *v.t.* 3 to civilize (personas).
urbano, -a *adj.* 1 urban: *población urbana = urban population.* 2 urbane, polite.
urbe *s.f.* large city, metropolis.
urdimbre *s.f.* 1 warp (de una tela). 2 (fig.) plot, scheme.
urdir *v.t.* 1 to warp. 2 (fig.) to plot (una conspiración, etc.). 3 (fig.) to invent.
urea *s.f.* FISIOL. urea.
uremia *s.f.* MED. uremia.
uréter *s.m.* ANAT. ureter.
uretra *s.f.* ANAT. urethra.
urgencia *s.f.* 1 urgency. 2 pressing need. 3 haste, rush (prisa). 4 MED. emergency.
urgente *adj.* 1 urgent, pressing. 2 rush: *un trabajo urgente = a rush job.* 3 express: *una carta urgente = an express letter.* || 4 **correo —,** express.
urgentemente *adv.* urgently.
urgir *v.i.* 1 to urge, to press (apremiar). 2 to be pressing, to be urgent.
úrico, -a *adj.* FISIOL. uric.
urinario, -a *adj.* 1 urinary. || *s.m.* 2 urinal (servicio público).
urna *s.f.* 1 urn. 2 glass case (de cristal). 3 POL. ballot box (electoral). 4 casket (para cenizas de los muertos). || 5 **acudir a las urnas,** POL. to go to the polls.
urogallo *s.m.* ZOOL. capercaillie.
urología *s.f.* MED. urology.
urólogo, -a *s.m.* y *f.* MED. urologist.
urraca *s.f.* ZOOL. magpie.
urticaria *s.f.* MED. hives, nettle rash, urticaria.
uruguayo, -a *adj.* y *s.m.* y *f.* Uruguayan.
usado, -a *adj.* 1 used (utilizado). 2 worn, worn out (gastado). 3 second-hand (ropa). 4 (p.u.) accustomed, skilled. || 5 *p.p.* de **usar.**
usanza *s.f.* 1 usage, custom. || 2 **a la antigua —,** in the old style.
usar *v.t.* 1 to use (utilizar). 2 to wear (llevar puesto). || *v.i.* 3 to make use of (hacer uso de). 4 (p.u.) to be accustomed, to use to. || *v.pron.* 5 to be used. 6 to be in use, to be in fashion (ropa). 7 to wear out (gastarse).
usía *pron.* (arc.) your lordship (vuestra señoría).
uso *s.m.* 1 use (empleo, manejo): *uso personal = personal use.* 2 usage, custom: *al uso de la época = according to the custom of the period.* 3 wear: *uso diario = everyday wear.* 4 practice, habit (costumbre). 5 enjoyment, use (usufructo). 6 DER. usage. || 7 **con el —,** with wear. 8 **en buen —,** in good condition. 9 **hacer — de la palabra,** to speak. 10 **lengua de —,** colloquial language. 11 **— de razón,** discernment. 12 **— externo,** MED. external application, external use.
usted *pron.pers.* you.
usual *adj.* 1 usual; customy, habitual. 2 ordinary, common.
usualmente *adv.* usually; ordinarily.
usuario, -a *s.m.* y *f.* user.
usufructo *s.m.* DER. usufruct.
usufructuario, -a *adj./s.m.* y *f.* usufructuary.
usura *s.f.* 1 usury. 2 profiteering (ganancia excesiva).
usurario, -a *adj.* 1 usurer; loanshark. 2 (fig.) profiter (aprovechado).
usurpación *s.f.* 1 usurpation. 2 encroachment (apropiación).
usurpador, -a *adj.* 1 usurping. || *s.m.* y *f.* 2 usurper.
usurpar *v.t.* 1 to usurp: *usurpar el poder = to usurp power.* 2 (fig.) to encroach (derechos ajenos).
utensilio *s.m.* 1 utensil (especialmente de cocina). 2 tool, implement: *utensilios de jardinería = gardening tools.* 3 material (artículo): *utensilios de escritorio = office materials.*

uterino, -a *adj.* ANAT. uterine.
útero *s.m.* ANAT. uterus, womb.
útil *adj.* **1** useful, profitable, helpful, handy. **2** usable (utilizable). **3** MIL. fit (apto, capacitado). || *s.m.* **4** utensil. || **5 día —,** weekday, working day. **6 útiles,** set of tools; instruments; implements.
utilidad *s.f.* **1** usefulness, utility. **2** profit, benefit. || **3 utilidades,** FIN. profits.
utilitario, -a *adj.* **1** utilitarian. **2** utility: *coches utilitarios = utility vehicles.* || *s.m.* **3** utility car.
utilizable *adj.* **1** useable, utilizable, usable. **2** fit for use, ready for use. **3** serviceable, available.
utilización *s.f.* use, utilization.
utilizar *v.t.* **1** to use, to utilize, to make use of. **2** TEC. to harness (energía, recursos naturales, etc.).
útilmente *adv.* usefully.
utillaje *s.m.* set of tools, instruments.
utopía *s.f.* utopia.
utópico, -a *adj.* utopian.
uva *s.f.* **1** BOT. grape. || **2 mala —,** (vulg.) bad mood. **3 — pasa,** raisin.
uve *s.f.* **1** name of the letter v. || **2 escote en —,** V-neck.
úvula *s.f.* ANAT. uvula.
uvular *adj.* ANAT. uvular.

v, V *s.f. v, V* (vigésimoquinta letra del alfabeto español).
vaca *s.f.* **1** cow. **2** cowhide (piel). **3** GAST. beef. || **4 – marina,** ZOOL. sea-cow, manatee. **5 vacas gordas, a)** period of prosperity; **b)** (fam.) boom.
vacación *s.f.* **1** vacation, holiday. || *pl.* **2** holidays. || **3 estar de vacaciones,** to be on holiday(s). **4 tomarse vacaciones,** to take a day off, to take on holiday(s).
vacante *adj.* **1** empty (lugares y espacios). **2** unfilled || *s.f.* **3** vacant, post: *cubrir una vacante = to fill a post.*
vacar *v.i.* **1** to become vacant. **2** to fall vacant. **3** to remain unfilled.
vaciar *v.t.* **1** to empty (out): *vaciar los bolsillos = to empty out one's pockets.* **2** to drain, to pour (líquidos). **3** to grind, to sharpen (cuchillos y herramientas): *voy a afilar este cuchillo = I'm going to have this knife sharpened.*
vaciedad *s.f.* (fig.) silliness, piece of nonsense (tontería).
vacilar *v.i.* **1** to be unsteady, to wobble. **2** to totter, to stumble (para personas). **3** to falter (referente al habla). **4** to flicker (una llama). **5** (fig.) to hesitate, to vacillate: *vacilar entre dos opciones = to hesitate between two posibilities.*
vacío, -a *adj.* **1** empty. **2** unfilled. **3** (fig.) vain, frivolous. || *s.m.* **4** FIS. vacuum. **5** vacant place; hollow (sin nada que ocupe un espacio). || **6 caer en el –,** to fall flat, to be ineffective. **7 de –,** empty. **8 hacer a uno el –,** to pretend that someone does not exist. **9 marcharse de –,** to go away empty-handed.
vacuno, -a *adj.* **1** bovine. **2** cattle (ganado). || *s.f.* **4** vaccine. **5** (Am.) vaccination.
vacunar *v.i.* **1** to vaccinate. **2** (fig.) to immunize: *estoy vacunado contra los pesados = I am immunized against bores.*
vacuo, -a *adj.* **1** empty. **2** vacant. **3** (fig.) frivolous, superficial, vacuous. || **4** *s.m.* hollow (objeto desprovisto de materia). **5** gap (espacio material).
vadear *v.t.* **1** to ford (un río). **2** to wade across, to wade through: *cruzar un río vadeando = to wade across a river.*
vademecum *s.m.* **1** textbook. **2** satchel, case (cartera). **3** memorandum, agenda.
vado *s.m.* **1** ford. **2** (fig.) wayout.
vadeable *adj.* **1** fordable, which can be forded. **2** (fig.) not insuperable, not imposible.
vagabundo, -a *adj.* **1** wandering. **2** (desp.) vagrant, vagabond. || *s.m.* y *f.* **3** (EE.UU.) bum. **4** wanderer. **5** (desp.) tramp.
vagabundear *v.i.* **1** to wander, to roam (sin rumbo). **2** to iddle (ociosamente).
vagamente *adv.* **1** vaguely, not clearly. **2** in a lazy manner (con pereza).
vagancia *s.f.* **1** idleness. **2** laziness (por gusto). **3** DER. vagrancy.
vagar *v.i.* **1** to idle, to loiter. **2** to laze about (por pereza). **3** to wander (sin dirección).
vagido *s.m.* **1** wail (llanto del recién nacido). **2** cry (llanto del niño).
vagina *s.f.* ANAT. vagina.
vaginal *adj.* vaginal.
vaginismo *s.m.* MED. vaginism.
vago, -a *adj.* **1** ART. blurred. **2** ill-defined (en sus formas). **3** indeterminate (plan). **4** indistinct. **5** lazy (perezoso). || *s.m.* y *f.* **6** down-and-out (persona). **7** vagrant. **8** tramp. **9** (desp.) slaker. **10** (fam.) dead loss. || *s.m.* **11** ANAT. vagus (nervio neumogástrico).
vagón *s.m.* **1** coach, carriage (para pasajeros). **2** truck, wagon, van (mercancías). || **3 – cisterna,** tanker, tank wagon. **4 – de ganado,** cattle truck. **5 – directo,** through carriage. **6 – de mercancías,** goods van; (EE.UU.) freight car. **7 – de pintura,** first-class carriage. **8 – de segunda,** second-class carriage. **9 – restaurante,** dining car.
vagoneta *s.f.* light truck.
vaguear V. **vagar.**
vaguedad *s.f.* **1** vagueness (contenido). **2** indistinctness (imagen). **3** indeterminacy (incierto, dudoso). || **4 hablar sin vaguedades,** to talk in a down-to-earth way, to speak with precision. **5 una –,** vague remark, woolly idea.
vaguada *s.f.* **1** water course, stream bed. **2** lowest part of a valley (parte más honda de un valle).
vaharada *s.f.* **1** puff (humo). **2** gust of breath (aliento). **3** whiff (soplo). **4** reek (mal olor).
vahído *s.m.* **1** dizzy spell, dizziness (mareo). **2** vertigo.
vaho *s.m.* **1** breath (aliento). **2** vapour, steam: *las ventanas están empañadas = the windows are steamed up.* || *pl.* **3** MED. inhalation. **4** fumes (emanaciones).
vaina *s.f.* **1** seath (funda). **2** scabbard (de espada). **3** case (de herramientas). **4** BOT. pod, husk, shell: *cáscara de avellana = nutshell.* **5** (Am.) nuisance, troublesome thing. **6** (fam.) fluke, piece of luck. **7** (Am. y vulg.) screw. **8** (Am.) thing, knick-knack. || *adj.* (Am.) **9** annoying. || *s.m.* y *f.* **10** good for nothing.
vainica *s.f.* hemstitch (tipo de punto en costura).
vainilla *s.f.* vainilla.
vaivén *s.m.* **1** swinging (oscilación de un péndulo). **2** swaying (balanceo). **3** rocking (mecedora, tren). **4** to-and-fro movement (de acá para allá). **5** lurch (movimiento brusco y repentino). **6** seesaw (columpio). **7** (fig.) change of fortune.
vajilla *s.f.* **1** crockery. **2** china. **3** dishes: *una vajilla = a set of dishes.*
val *s.m.* valley.
OBS. Se usa en composición de palabras: *Valdecaballeros.*
vale *s.m.* **1** receipt (recibo). **2** promisory note. **3** (Am. y fam.) mate. **4** warrant (garantía).

valedor *s.m.* 1 protector. 2 sponsor (patrocinador). 3 supporter (defensor).
valencia *s.f.* 1 QUIM. valency. 2 GEOG. Valencia.
valenciano, -a *m.* y *s.f.* 1 Valencian. 2 Valencian (dialecto catalán). || 3 *adj.* Valencian, from Valencia.
valentía *s.f.* 1 bravery, courage. 2 boldness (atrevimiento). || 3 resoluteness. 4 (desp.) boastfulness. || 5 **un acto de —,** an act of courage.
valentón *s.m.* 1 braggart (fanfarrón). 2 bluster, bully (bravucón). 3 (desp.) boastful.
valentonada *s.f.* 1 brag, piece of bluster. 2 boast (con chulería). 3 arrogant act.
valer *v.t.* 1 to be worth, to cost: *esta casa vale un montón = this house is worth a good deal.* 2 to help, to aid: *no le valió que su padre fuera el jefe = the fact that his father was the boss didn't help him.* 3 to result: *esta táctica les valió la derrota = this move resulted in their defeat.* 4 to earn: *su comportamiento le valió una paliza = his behaviour earned him a beating.* 5 to cause, to win, to get, to give: *mi ensayo me valió un premio = my composition won me a prize.* || *v.i.* 6 to be useful, to be of use: *esto no me vale = this is not useful to me.* 7 to be worth (persona): *él vale mucho = he's worth a lot.* || *v.pron.* 8 to make use of: *me serví de mi carnet de policía para entrar = I made use of my police card to go in.* || *s.m.* 9 worth, value (valor).
valerosamente *adv.* bravely, valiantly, courageously.
valerosidad *s.f.* courage, valiance, bravery.
valeroso, -a *adj.* brave, valiant, courageous.
valía *s.f.* 1 worth. 2 value. 3 merit (personas). || *adj.* 4 worthy. 5 valuable. 6 estimable (personas): *este hombre es de gran valía = this man is very estimable.*
válido, -a *adj.* 1 valid: *válido hasta junio = valid until june; válido para cocinar = valid for cooking.* 2 useful (útil). 3 MED. fit, robust, strong. 4 apt (apropiado); suitable (adecuado).
válido, -a *s.m.* y *f.* favourite (real).
valiente *s.m.* y *f.* 1 brave man. 2 hero. 3 gallant man. 4 (desp.) braggart. || *adj.* 5 brave. 6 valiant. 7 bold. 8 (desp.) boastful; blustering. 9 (fig.) excellent, noble, strong. 10 (fig. y fam.) fine: *¡valiente amigo! = a fine friend you are!* || 11 (fig. y fam.) **¡— hombre!,** some man!
valija *s.f.* 1 case. 2 valise (portamantas). 3 satchel (cartera). 4 mail bag (correos). || 5 **— diplomática,** diplomatic bag.
valimiento *s.f.* 1 value. 2 benefit. 3 POL. favour protection, status of the royal favourite.
valor *s.m.* 1 value. 2 worth. 3 price. 4 importance. 5 meaning: *el valor de las palabras = the meaning of words.* 6 bravery, courage, nerve: *tuvo el valor de hacerlo = he had the nerve to do it.* 9 FIN. securities (títulos); bonds (obligaciones); stock (capital). 10 credit: *no doy valor a sus palabras = I do not give credit to his words.* || 11 **armarse de —,** to gather up one's courage. 12 **¡qué —!,** of all the cheek! (qué caradura), what a nerve! 13 **quitar — a,** to minimize the importance of. 14 **por — de,** to the value of. 15 **tener más — que un torero,** do not to be afraid of anything. 16 **— adquisitivo,** purchasing power. 17 **— alimenticio,** food value, nutritional value. 18 **— nominal,** nominal value, par value, (acciones). 19 **valores en cartera,** holdings, investments, port-folio. 20 **valores fiduciarios,** banknotes. 21 **valores inmuebles,** real state.
valorar *v.t.* 1 to value. 2 to price. 3 to assess: *valoraron la casa en 5000 libras = they assessed the house at 5000.* 4 to estimate (calcular el valor). 5 to rate (en escala numérica). 6 QUIM. to titrate.
valorizar *V.* **valorar.**
vals *s.m.* waltz.
valuar *v.tr.* 1 (fig.) to price. 2 to assess (tasar). 3 to rate (valuar en escala).
válvula *s.f.* 1 MEC. valve. 2 ANAT. valve (de las venas). || 3 **— de admisión,** inlet valve. 4 **— de escape,** exhaust valve. 5 **— de mariposa,** butterfly valve. 6 **— de purga,** vent. 7 **— de seguridad,** safety valve.
valla *s.f.* 1 fence (cerca). 2 palisade (empalizada). 3 MIL. barricade, stockade (barricada). 4 (fig.) obstacle, hindrance (estorbo); barrier, limit. 5 DEP. hurdle: *100 metros vallas = 100 metres hurdles.* 6 (Am.) cockpit (para peleas de gallos). || 7 **saltarse las vallas,** to disregard the social conventions, to do away with social niceties. 8 **romper las vallas,** to burst through the barriers of convention. 9 **— para nieves,** snow fence. 10 **— publicitaria,** advertisement fence.
valladar *s.m.* 1 (fig.) defence. 2 barrier.
vallado, -a *s.m.* y *f.* 1 fence (cerca). 2 defensive wall.
vallar *v.t.* 1 to fence. 2 to put a fence round. 3 to enclose.
valle *s.m.* 1 vale, valley, dale. || 2 **— de lágrimas,** valley of tears.
vampiresa *s.f.* vamp (mujer fatal).
vampiro *s.m.* 1 ZOOL. vampire. 2 (fig.) exploiter. 3 blood sucker, vampire (espíritu maligno).
vanagloria *s.f.* vainglory.
vanagloriarse *v.i.* 1 to boast. 2 to be arrogant. || 3 **— de,** to boast of.
vándalo, -a *s.m.* y *f.* HIST. vandal. 2 (fig.) vandal, brute.
vandálico, -a *adj.* 1 vandalic. 2 (fig.) outish, destructive.
vandalismo *s.m.* vandalism.
vanguardia *s.f.* 1 MIL. vanguard: *soldados de vanguardia = soldiers of the vanguard.* 2 ART. avant-garde. 3 van: *estar en la vanguardia = to be in the van of progress.* 4 fore front: *ir a la vanguardia del progreso = to go at the fore front of progress.*
vanguardismo *s.m.* 1 ultramodern manner. 2 revolutionary style. 3 new tendency. 4 far out tendencies.
vanidad *s.f.* 1 vanity. 2 futity (inutilidad). 3 (fig.) ilusion. || 4 **hacer algo por pura —,** to do something out of sheer vanity. 5 **alargar la — de uno,** to play up someone's vanity.
vanidoso, -a *s.m.* y *f.* 1 vain person. || 2 *adj.* vain. 3 conceited (presumido). 4 smug.
vano, -a *adj.* 1 vain. 2 useless: *esfuerzos vanos = useless efforts.* 3 groundless, unfounded. 4 frivolous. || 5 **en —,** in vain. 6 **promesas vanas,** empty promises.
vapor *s.m.* 1 vapour (de agua), (EE.UU.) vapor. 2 steam (vaho). 3 MAR. steamer, steamship (barco). 4 mist. 5 fumes. || 6 **a todo —,** at full steam. 7 **caldera de —,** steam boiler. 8 **los vapores del vino,** vapour of fumes given off by wine. 4 **máquina de —,** steam engine. 10 **patatas al —,** steamed potatoes. 11 **— de ruedas,** paddle steamer. 12 **vapores,** MED. vapours, hysteria.
vapora *s.f.* 1 steam launch. 2 (Am.) steam engine.
vaporización *s.f.* vaporization.
vaporizador, -ora *s.m.* y *f.* 1 vaporizer. 2 (fam.) spray.
vaporoso, -a *adj.* 1 vaporous, steamy, misty (atmosférico). 2 steaming (procedente de agua en ebullición). 3 light (tela). 4 airy (estilo). 5 sheer (transparente).
vapulear *v.t.* 1 to beat (personas, alfombras). 2 to thrash, to give a thrashing: *vapulear a alguien = to give someone a thrashing.* 3 (fig.) to slate (criticar).
vapuleo *s.m.* 1 beating, hiding. 2 thrashing.
vaguería *s.f.* 1 cowshed (lugar). 2 dairy (donde se vende leche y derivados). 3 herd of caws (manada de ganado vacuno).
vaquerizo, -a *adj.* 1 cattle (ganado). 2 cow. 3 cattle enclosure (corral).
vaquero *s.m.* 1 cattle. 2 cowboy (profesión). 3 cowhand (pastor). 4 (Am.) milkman, truant, rawhide whip. || *pl.* 5 jeans.
vara *s.f.* 1 stick (pequeño). 2 pole (poste). 3 rod (caña). 4 MEC. rod. 5 BOT. branch, twig (rama desprovista de hojas). 6 main stalk (tallo). 7 MAT. yard (0,836 m.). 8 pike, lance (tauromaquia): *poner varas = to wound with lance.* 9 MUS. slide (de trombón). || 10 **poner varas al toro,** to wound the bull with the lance. 11 **— de medir,** yardstick. 12 **— de San José,** goldenrod. 13 **— mágica,** magic wand.
varal *s.m.* 1 long pole (poste). 2 stout stick. 3 frame work of poles (vara donde se encajan los travesaños de los costados de los carros). 4 shaft (carruajes). 5 ART. batten. 6 (fam.) thin person, bean pole.
varapalo *s.m.* 1 long pole. 2 blow with a stick (golpe con un palo). 3 beating (pa-

liza). 4 dissapointment (pesadumbre). 5 blow (contratiempo).

varar *v.t.* 1 MAR. to launch (botar). 2 to beach (poner en seco). 3 to run aground (encallar). 4 to drop anchor (anclar).

varadero *s.m.* 1 MAR. skid. 2 MAR. dry dock (muelle seco).

varadura *s.f.* 1 runing aground (encalladura). 2 beaching.

varea *s.f.* beating (árboles).

vareador, -a *s.m.* y *f.* beater (de árboles).

vareo *s.m.* 1 knocking down (de nueces). 2 measuring in "varas" (medición por varas).

varetazo *s.m.* sideways butts (tauromaquia).

variabilidad *s.f.* variability.

variable *adj.* 1 variable. 2 changeable (inestable). || s.f. 3 MAT. variable.

variación *s.f.* 1 MUS. variation. 2 change.

variado, -a *adj.* 1 varied. 2 mixed (mezclado). 3 assorted (surtido).

variante *adj.* variant.

variar *v.t.* 1 to vary: *variar el menú = to vary the menu.* 2 to change round (de posición). 3 MAT. to vary. 4 to differ (ser diferente). || 5 **v.i.** to change: *el viento ha variado = the wind has changed.* 6 to vary: *sus respuestas varían = his answers vary.* || 7 **por no variar,** as usual. 8 **— de opinión,** to change one's mind.

varice V. **variz.**

varicoso, -a *adj.* 1 varicose. 2 suffering from varicose vains.

variedad *s.f.* 1 ART. variety show. 2 BIOL. variety. 3 variation. || 4 **en la — está el buen gusto,** variety is the spice of life.

varilla *s.f.* 1 stick. 2 BOT. twing. 3 wand. 4 switch. 5 MEC. road. 6 MEC. bar. 7 link. 8 spoke (de rueda). 9 stay (de corset). 10 rib (de paraguas). 11 ANAT. jawbone. 12 (Am.) small vares, trinkets.

vario *adj.* 1 varied. 2 variegated (color). 3 motted (multicolor). 4 *s.pl.* varying, variable, changeable. 5 (fig.) fickle (voluble). || 6 **varios,** several, some, a number of.

variopinto, -a *adj.* colourful; of all kinds, of all colours.

varón *s.m.* 1 man. 2 male (masculino). 3 adult male (adulto). 4 (fig.) worthy man. 5 (Am.) bean, timber. || 6 **esclarecidos varones,** great men. 7 **¡santo —!,** saint.

varonía *s.f.* 1 male issue. 2 male descent.

vasallaje *s.m.* 1 vassalage. 2 subjetion. 3 servitude. || 4 **rendir —,** to pay homage.

vasallo *s.m.* 1 vassal. 2 subject (súbdito).

vasco, -a *s.m.* y *f.* 1 Basque (nativo y lengua). || 2 **País Vasco,** Basque Country.

vascongado, -a V. **vasco.**

vascular *adj.* vascular.

vaselina *s.f.* 1 vaseline. 2 petroleum jelly.

vasija *s.f.* 1 vessel. 2 container. 3 recipient. 4 urn.

vaso *s.m.* 1 glass. 2 tumbler (vaso alto). 3 glassful (medida). 4 ANAT. vessel, tube, duct. 5 MEC. grease cup. || 6 **ahogarse en un — de agua,** to get worked up about nothing. 7 MED. **— capilar,** capillary. 8 FIS. **vasos comunicantes,** comunicanting vessels. 9 **— sanguíneo,** ANAT. blood vessel.

vástago *s.m.* 1 BOT. shoot. 2 BOT. sprout (brote). 3 BOT. bud (yema). 4 MEC. rod, stem. 5 (fam.) scion, offspring. 6 (Am.) trunk of the banana tree. || 7 **— de émbolo,** piston rod. 8 **— de perforación,** drill stem.

vasto, -a *adj.* 1 vast. 2 huge, immense, large: *un vasto territorio = a vast land.*

vate *s.m.* 1 poet, bard. 2 prophet.

Vaticano *s.m.* Vatican.

vaticinar *v.t.* 1 to prophes. 2 to foretell.

vatio *s.m.* 1 watt (unidad). 2 watage (potencia en vatios).

vaudeville *s.m.* 1 commedy. 2 vaudeville (espectáculo de variedades).

vecinal *adj.* 1 neighbouring. 2 adjacent.

vecindad *s.f.* 1 neighbourhood. 2 vicinity. 3 residents. 4 nearness (cercanías). 5 tenement (casa de la vecindad).

vecindario *s.m.* 1 neighbourhood. 2 local comunity. 3 residents. 4 population (población). 5 inhabitants.

vecino, -a *s.m.* y *f.* 1 neighbour. 2 resident. 3 inhabitant: *un pueblo de 300 vecinos = a village of 300 inhabitants.* || *adj.* 4 neighbouring. 5 adjacent. 6 adjoining: *territorio de vecinos = adjoining states.* 7 nearby. || 8 **como cualquier hijo de —,** as anyone, every mother son. 9 **en el pueblo —,** in the next village. 10 **es mi —,** he lives next door. 11 **una vecina de la calle...,** a resident in... street.

vector *s.m.* vector.

veda *s.f.* 1 close season. 2 (EE.UU.) closed season. 3 prohibition. 4 Veda (libro sagrado de la India). || 5 **levantamiento de la —,** opening of the season.

vedado, -a *s.m.* y *f.* 1 preserve. || 2 **cazar en —,** to poach, to hunt illegally.

vedar *v.t.* 1 to prohibit. 2 to forbid. 3 to ban (proscribir). 4 to veto.

vega *s.f.* 1 fertile plain. 2 rich low land area. 3 water meadow (prado). 4 (Am.) tobacco plantation. 5 GEOG. stretch of alluvial soil.

vegetación *s.f.* 1 vegetation. 2 growth. || MED. **vegetaciones,** adenoids.

vegetal *adj.* y *s.m.* 1 vegetal. 2 plant. 3 vegetable. || 4 **reino —,** the vegetable kingdom.

vegetar *v.i.* 1 to grow. 2 to vegetable (plantas y personas).

vegetarianismo *s.m.* vegetarianism.

vegetariano, -a *adj./s.m.* y *f.* vegetarian.

vegetativo, -a *adj.* vegetative.

vehemencia *s.f.* 1 vehemence, passion; (fig.) impetuosity. 2 violence.

vehemente *adj.* 1 vehement, pasionate (apasionado); impetuous. 2 violent.

vehículo *s.m.* 1 vehicle. 2 (fig.) transmiter (transmisor). 3 **— espacial,** spacecraft.

veinte *num.* 1 twenty: *veinte personas = twenty people; siglo XX = twentieth century.* || 2 **los años —,** the twenties. 3 **unos —,** some twenty, about twenty.

veinteavo *adj.* twentieth.

vejación V. **vejamen.**

vejamen *s.m.* 1 satire. 2 vexation. 3 humiliation. 4 satirical composition. 5 taunt (mofa).

vejatorio *adj.* 1 humiliating (condiciones de vida). 2 hurtful. 3 offensive, vexatious.

vejestorio *s.m.* 1 old chap. 2 (fam.) old boy, old crock.

vejez *s.f.* old age. 2 (fig.) peevishness. 3 (fam.) grumpiness. || 4 **los males de la —,** the ills of old age. 5 **se hizo famoso en la —,** he became famous in his old age.

vejiga *s.f.* 1 ANAT. bladder. 2 blister. || 3 **— de la bilis,** gall bladder. 4 **— natatoria,** air bladder.

vela *s.f.* 1 MAR. sail. 2 candle 3 vigil. 4 watch (de un difunto). 5 night work (trabajo nocturno). || 6 **aguantar la —,** (Am.) to face the music. 7 **a toda —,** under full sail. 8 **barco de —,** sailing boat. 9 **encender una — a Dios y otra al diablo,** to run with the hare and hunt with the hounds. 10 **estar a dos velas,** to be broke. 11 **izar velas,** to set sails. 12 **no tener — en un entierro,** to have no say in the matter. 13 **pasar la noche en —,** to have a sleepless night, not to get a wink of sleep all night. 14 **¿quién te dio — en este entierro?,** who asked you to poke your nose in? 15 **recoger velas,** to back down. 16 **ser más derecho que una —,** to be as straight as a die. 17 **— mayor,** MAR. main sail. 18 **velas** (fam.) mucus, snots (en la nariz).

velado, -a *adj.* 1 veiled (cubierto con velo). 2 FOT. blurred, fogged. 3 muffled voice (voz). || 4 **ojos velados por las lágrimas,** eyes veiled by tears. 5 **velada alusión,** veiled referenced. || *s.f.* 6 evening party. 7 social gathering. || 8 **pasar una buena velada,** to spend a pleasant evening. 9 **velada musical,** musical evening.

velador, -a *s.m.* y *f.* 1 watchman (vigilante), caretaker. || *s.m.* 2 HIST. sentinel. 3 candelestick (candelero). 4 pedestal table, night table (mueble). 5 (Am.) lampshade, night light. 6 (Am.) bedside table.

velamen o **velaje** *s.m.* 1 MAR. sails. 2 canvas (toldo). 3 ANAT. velamen.

velar *v.t.* 1 to watch, to keep watch over. 2 to sit up with, to stay by the side of (gente enferma). 3 (Am.) to look covetuosly at. 4 (fig.) to veil, to hide (disimular). 5 FOT. to blur, to fog. 6 ART. to glaze. || *v.i.* 7 to state awake (no dormir). 8 to stay up (no acostarse); to keep watch over (vigilar). 10 REL. to keep vigil. 11 (fig.) to watch over, to look after. 12 to work late. || *adj.* 13 ANAT. velar. || 14 **no hay quien vele por sus intereses,** there's no one to watch over her interest. 15 **— a un cadáver,** to stand vigil over a corpse. 16 **— armas,** to carry out the vigil of arms. 17 **— por la**

observancia de la ley, to make sure that the laws are observed. **18 — por la salud de uno,** to watch over one's health, to look after one's health. **19 — porque se haga algo,** to see to it, to ensure that something is done.

velarización *s.f.* making a sound velar.

velatorio *s.m.* funeral wake.

veleidad *s.f.* **1** capriciousness; whim (antojo). **2** umpredictability. **3** fickleness (versatilidad).

velero *adj.* **1** sailing; sailing ship (grande), sailing boat (pequeño). **2** swift-sailing. || *s.m.* **3** MAR. sailboat. **4** AER. glider. **5** sailmaker (constructor). || *s.m.* y *f.* **6** chandler (fabricante de velas de cera).

veleta *s.f.* **1** weather vane, weather cock. **2** float (de caña de pescar). **3** (fig. y fam.) fickle person, inconstant person.

velo *s.m.* **1** veil, light covering. **2** (fig.) shroud, film. **3** FOT. fog, veiling. **4** ANAT. velum. || **5 correr un tupido — sobre algo,** to draw a veil over something, to hush something up. **6 tomar el —,** to become a nun, to take the veil. **7 — de novia,** bridge's veil. **8 — de paladar,** soft palate.

velocidad *s.f.* **1** speed, velocity. **2** gear (marcha de un coche): *tiene 5 velocidades = it has got five gears.* **3** rate (de trabajo): *velocidad de trabajo = rate of work.* || **4 a gran —,** at high speed. **5 ¿a qué — ibas?,** what speed were you doing? **6 confundir la — con el tocino,** not to know one's left hand from one's right. **7 de alta —,** high speed. **8 disminuir la —,** to slow down. **9 exceder el límite de —,** to exceed the speed limit. **10 meter la segunda —,** to change into the second gear. **11 primera —,** low gear. **12 segunda —,** second gear. **13 — de crucero,** cruising speed. **14 — limitada,** speed limit. **15 — punta,** top speed, maximum speed.

velódromo *s.m.* **1** cycle track. **2** (EE.UU.) velodrome.

velomotor *s.m.* **1** moped, small motorcycle. **2** (autocycle).

velorio *s.m.* **1** party, celebration. **2** (Am.) dull party, flat affair. **3** wake, vigil (velatorio). **4** REL. taking off the veil (de una monja).

veloz *adj.* **1** fast (automóviles). **2** quick (referente al modo de actuar). **3** swift (repentino).

vello *s.m.* **1** ANAT. down, fuzz (pelusa). **2** bloom (en la fruta). **3** nap (en la ropa).

vellocino *s.m.* **1** fleece. || **2 — de oro,** golden fleece.

vellosidad *s.f.* **1** downiness. **2** flufflines (que tiene mucha pelusa), fuzziness. **3** hairiness.

velloso *adj.* hairy, fuzzy, fluffy.

vena *s.f.* **1** ANAT. vein. **2** MIN. seam, lode. **3** grain (en piedra). **4** BOT. vein, rib. **5** GEOG. underground stream. **6** (fig.) mood, disposition: *coger a uno en vena = to catch someone in the right mood.* **7** (fig.) talent, promise: *tiene vena de escritor = he shows a talent for writing.* || **8 darle a uno la —** (de o por + infinitivo), the mood has taken him (for + ger.). **9 estar en — para** (+ infinitivo), to be in the mood (for + ger.). **10** (fig. y fam.) **trabajar con venas,** to work in fits and starts. **11** ANAT. **— porta,** portal vein. **12 — de loco,** a streak of madness. **13** ANAT. **— cava,** vena cava.

venablo *s.m.* **1** javelin (jabalina). **2** dart (dardo). **3 echar venablos por la boca,** to burst out angrily, to roar with anger.

venado *s.m.* **1** deer (dual), stag (macho), doe (hembra). **2** GAST. venisson. **3** (Am.) deersking (cornudo). **4** (Am.) whore. || **5** (Am.) **correr el —,** to play truant.

venal *adj.* **1** venal: *funcionario venal = venal official.* **2** ANAT. venous. **3** (desp.) corrupt.

venalidad *s.f.* venality, corruptness.

vencejo *s.m.* **1** ZOOL. swift. **2** AGR. strow plait, string (para atar gavillas).

vencedor, -a *adj.* **1** victorious. **2** winning, successful (triunfador). || *s.m.* y *f.* **3** winner. **4** victor, conqueror.

vencer *v.t.* **1** to defeat (al enemigo). **2** to conquer (conquistar). **3** (lit.) vanguish. **4** DEP. to beat. **5** to over come (dificultades), to surmount (obstáculos). **6** to master, to control (pasiones). **7** to out do (exceder): *vencer a uno en algo = to out do someone in something.* || *v.i.* **8** to win (ganar). **9** to triumph. **10** to fall due (una factura): *la factura vence mañana = the bill falls due tomorrow.* **11** (fig.) to succeed (tener éxito). **12** to expire (un plazo). || **13 dejarse —,** to give in, to yield. **14 divide y vencerás,** divide and conquer. **15 le venció el sueño,** sleep came over him. **16 no dejarse —,** not to give in, not to let yourself be beaten. **17 ¡venceremos!,** we shall win, we shall overcome. **18 — una cima,** to conquer a summit. **19 — una distancia,** to cover a distance.

vencido, -a *adj.* **1** beaten. **2** defeated (derrotado). **3** losing (que pierde). **4** due (un pagaré). **5** falling due (deuda). **6** expired (plazo). **7** DEP. loser. **8** conquered, vanquished (personas). || **9 ¡ay de los vencidos!,** woe betide the conquered! **10 darse por —,** to admit defeat. **11 los vencidos,** the conquered, the vanquished. **12 pagar por meses vencidos,** to pay the month in arrears.

vencimiento *s.m.* **1** falling due (de una deuda). **2** breaking, snapping (por un peso). **3** overcoming, surmounting (de un obstáculo). **4** maturity (de una deuda). **5** expiration (de un período de tiempo).

venda *s.f.* **1** bandage (de gasa). **2** band, fillet (de cabeza). || **3 caérsele a uno la — de los ojos,** to get someone's eyes opened. **4 quitar a uno la — de los ojos,** to open someone's eyes.

vendaje *s.m.* **1** dressing. **2** bandaging. || **3 — provisional,** first-aid bandage.

vendar *v.t.* **1** to bandage (una herida). **2** to cover, to put a vandage over (los ojos). **3** (fig.) to blind, to hoodwink. || **4 tener los ojos vendados,** to go away blindfolded, to go around with one's eyed closed. **5 — los ojos a alguien,** to blindfold someone.

vendaval *s.m.* **1** gale, strong wind. **2** hurricane (huracán). **3** (fig.) storm.

vendedor, -a *s.m.* y *f.* **1** seller. **2** salesman (en una tienda). **3** shop asistant (dependiente). **4** (EE.UU.) vendor, pedler.

vender *v.t.* **1** to sell: *vendió su casa vieja = he sold his old house.* **2** to market (comercializar): *están empezando a vender un producto nuevo = they are marketing a new product.* **3** (fig.) to betray (traicionar): *vender a un amigo = to betray a friend.* || **4 no se vende,** not for sale. **5 se vende,** for sale. **6 se vende piso,** flat for sale. **7 se vende al contado,** to sell for cash. **8 — al por mayor,** to sell wholesale, to wholesale. **9 — al por menor,** to retail. **10 — a plazos,** to sell on credit. **11 — cara la vida,** to sell one's life dearly. **12 — caro,** to sell at high price. **13 — de contrabando,** to sell illegally. **14 — en pública subasta,** to auction. **15 — por las casas,** to sell from door to door. **16 — salud,** to be glowing with health.

vendible *adj.* saleable, markettable.

vendimia *s.f.* **1** grape harvest, wine harvest. **2** vintage (recolección): *la vendimia de 1973 = the 1973 vintage.* **3** (fig.) big profit, killing.

vendimiar *v.t.* **1** to harvest (cosechar). **2** to pick, to gather (uvas). **3** (fig. y vulg.) to bump off (cargarse a): *se vendimió al jefe = he bumped his boss off.*

veneno *s.m.* **1** poison (químico o vegetal): *el cianuro es un veneno potente = cyanide is a powerful poison.* **2** venom (procedente de animal). **3** (fig.) venom: *tus palabras destilan veneno = your words are full of venom.*

venenoso, -a *adj.* **1** polsonous: *hay setas venenosas = there are some poisonous mushrooms.* **2** venomous: *hay ciertas serpientes venenosas = there are venomous snakes.* **3** (fig.) venomous: *sus palabras eran venenosas = his words were venomous.*

venerable *adj.* venerable.

veneración *s.m.* **1** veneration. **2** worship (adoración).

venerar *v.t.* **1** to venerate. **2** to revere (reverenciar). **3** to worship (adorar).

venéreo, -a *adj.* MED. veneral.

venero *s.m.* **1** spring (arroyo). **2** MIN. seam, vein (yacimiento). **3** (fig.) source (origen, fuente). **4** mine: *venero de información = mine of information.*

venezolano, -a *adj./s.m.* y *f.* Venezuelan.

vengador, -a *adj.* avenging, avenger.

venganza *s.f.* **1** vengeance, revenge. **2** retaliation (devolver el mal que le han hecho a uno).

vengar *v.t.* **1** to avenge. || *v.pron.* **2** to retaliate (devolver el mal que le han hecho a uno). **3** to revenge (desqui-

tarse). || **4 vengarse de alguien por una afrenta,** to take revenge on someone for an insult.
vengativo, -a *adj.* **1** vindictive (espíritu). **2** retaliatory (acto).
venia *s.f.* **1** pardon, forgiveness (perdón). **2** permission. **3** greeting (saludo). || **4 casarse sin la — de los padres,** to marry without the consent of one's parents.
venial *adj.* venial: *pecado venial = venial sin.*
venialidad *s.f.* veniality.
venida *s.f.* **1** coming: *idas y venidas = comings and goings.* **2** arrival (llegada): *la venida del otoño = the arrival of autumn.* **3** return (regreso).
venidero, -a *adj.* **1** coming. **2** future: *el siglo venidero = the future century.* || **3 en lo —,** in (the) future. **4 generaciones venideras,** coming generations.
venir *v.i.* **1** to come: *mi hermano va a venir = my brother is coming.* **2** to arrive (llegar): *viene mañana = she's arriving tomorrow.* || *v.pron.* **3** to come back (volverse). **4** to come upon (venirse encima una situación). **5** to ferment (el vino). || **6 ¿a qué viene eso?,** what's the point of that? **7 como te venga en gana,** as you like, just as you wish. **8 de ahí viene que,** so it is that. **9 eso no viene a cuento,** that has nothing to do with it, there is no sense in it. **10 estar a verlas —,** to wait and see what happens. **11 este vino viene de Francia,** this wine comes from France. **12 hacer — a uno,** to summon someone, to send for me. **14 no le va ni le viene,** it has nothing to do with him, it is none of his business. **15 no me vengas con historias,** don't come telling tales to me. **16 tu foto viene en el periódico,** your photo is in the newspaper. **17 ¡ven acá!,** come here! **18 ¡venga!,** come along! **19 ¡venga lo que venga!,** come what may! **20 venga o no venga a cuento,** with no rhyme or reason. **21 vengo cansado,** I'm tired. **22 — bien,** to be convenient, to be fit. **24 — bien a alguien,** to suit someone. **25 — bien algo,** to come in handy. **16 — hecho polvo,** to come worn out. **27 venirle a uno en ganas de,** (inf.) to feel like (ger.). **28 venirse abajo,** to fall down, to collapse. **29 ver — a uno,** (fig.) to see someone coming. **30 viene a ser lo mismo,** it comes to the same thing.
venoso, -a *adj.* **1** venous (sangre). **2** BOT. veined (hojas). **3** BOT. ribbed (nervudo).
venta *s.f.* **1** COM. sale, selling, marketing: *la venta del pescado = the selling of fish.* **2** country inn (posada). **3** (fam.) small shop, stall. **4 estar en —,** to be on sale. **5 poner algo a la —,** to put something on sale. **6 precio de —,** selling price. **7 precio de — al público,** retail price. **8 — a domicilio,** door to door selling. **9 — al contado,** cash sale. **10 — al por mayor,** wholesale. **11 — al por menor,** retail. **12 — a plazos,** hire purchase. **13 — por balance,** stocktaking sale. **14 — pública,** public sale.
ventaja *s.f.* **1** advantage: *tiene la ventaja de ser listo = he has the advantage of being intelligent.* **2** benefit: *ventajas sociales = social benefits.* **3** profit (provecho). **4** odds (apuestas). **5** DEP. vantage (tenis). **6** DEP. headstart (en una carrera). || **7 dejar buena —,** to bring in a good profit. **8 llevar la —,** to have the advantage over, to be ahead of. **9 sacar — de,** to derive profit from.
ventajista *adj.* **1** unscrupulous. **2** self-seeking, grasping (buscador). **3** sly, treacherous (aprovechado).
ventajoso, -a *adj.* **1** advantageous. **2** FIN. profitable bussiness.
ventana *s.f.* **1** window. **2** ANAT. nasal cavity, nostril. **3** (Am.) florest clear glade. || **4 tirar la casa por la —,** to spare not expense, to go overboard; **b)** (fam.) to lash out. **5 — de guillotina,** sash window.
ventanaje *s.m.* windows.
ventanal *s.m.* large window.
ventanilla *s.f.* **1** window (trenes, coches, aviones). **2** porthole (barcos). **3** ANAT. nostril.
ventano *s.m.* **1** wicket. **2** small window. **3** peephole (mirilla). **4** ventilator (de un sótano).
ventarrón, -ona *s.m.* y *f.* **1** gale, strong wind. **2** blast (ráfaga).
ventear *v.t.* **1** to air to sniff (respirar). **2** to air, to air out (una habitación, ropa). **3** to put out to dry. **4** (fig.) to snoop (investigar). **5** (fig.) to smell (sospechar). || *v.pron.* **6** to split (agrietarse), to crack, to split (los ladrillos al caerse). **7** to get too dry (resecarse). **8** to spoil. **9** ANAT. to break wind (ventosear). **10** (Am.) to be out doors a great deal, to spend a long time away from home.
ventero, -a *s.m.* y *f.* innkeeper.
ventilación *s.f.* **1** ventilation. **2** draught (corriente de aire). || **3 sin —,** unventilated. **4 — pulmonar,** pulmonary ventilation.
ventilador, -a *s.m.* y *f.* **1** ventilator. **2** fan (abanico). **3** window fan (en una ventana).
ventilar *v.t.* **1** to ventilate (una habitación). **2** to air, to put out to air, to dry in the air (ropa). **3** (fig.) to air (hacer público). **4** (fig.) to discuss a matter, to clear up (ventilar un problema). || *v.pron.* **5** to get some air, to take a breather.
ventisca *s.f.* snowstorm, blizzard.
ventisquear *v.imp.* **1** to blow a blizzard: *va a ventisquear = a blizzard is going to blow.* || *v.pron.* **2** to drift (acumularse la nieve).
ventisquero *s.m.* **1** glacier (helero). **2** snowdrift (nieve acumulada). **3** snowstorm, blizzard.
ventolera *s.f.* **1** gust of wind, blast (ráfaga). **2** windmill (juguete). **3** (fig.) vanity, arrogance. **4** wild idea: *le dio la ventolera de irse = he had the wild idea of going away.*
ventorrillo *s.m.* **1** roadhouse (merendero). **2** small inn (venta pequeña). **3** (Am.) small shop.
ventosear *v.i.* to break wind.
ventosidad *s.f.* wind, flatulence.
ventoso, -a *adj.* **1** windy (atmosférico). **2** ANAT. windy, flatulent.
ventrículo *s.m.* **1** ventricle. || **2 — derecho,** right ventricle. **3 — izquierdo,** left ventricle.
ventrílocuo, -a *s.m.* y *f.* **1** ventriloquist. || **2** *adj.* ventriloquistic.
venturoso, -a *adj.* **1** happy (feliz). **2** fortunate, lucky.
venturosamente *adv.* fortunately.
venus *s.f.* **1** venus. || **2** ANAT. **monte de —,** mound of venus.
ver *v.t.* **1** to see: *no la vi = I didn't see her.* **2** to look at: *estoy viendo un O.V.N.I. = I'm looking at an U.F.O.* **3** to watch (la televisión): *está viendo la televisión = he is watching the television.* **4** (fig.) understand: *¿ves lo que te quiero decir? = do you understand what I mean?* **5** (fig.) find: *te veo muy cansado = I find you very tired.* || *v.pron.* **6** to find oneself, to be: *me veo calvo = I find myself bald; me veo arruinado = I'm broke.* **7** to meet (encontrarse): *¿dónde nos vemos? = where shall we meet?* **8** to look (parecer): *se te ve bien = you look well.* || **9 a mi modo de —,** in my view. **10 a —,** lets see. **11 ¡a — que pasa!,** lets see what happens! just you dare! (atrévete). **12 de buen —,** good looking, of agreeable appearance. **13 dejarse —,** to show up, to show one's face. **14 eso está por —,** that remains to be seen. **15 verlas venir,** to cath on quickly. **16 ¡habráse visto!,** what a cheek! **17 hasta más —,** see you later. **18 ¡hay que —!,** you should see, it's amazing! **19 mirar a — si alguien puede hacer algo,** to see if someone can do something. **20 mire a —,** have a look. **21 no poder — a una persona,** not to be able to bear the sight of someone: *no puedo verlo = I can't bear the sight of him.* **22 no tener nada que —,** to have nothing to do with. **23 no — más allá de sus narices,** V. **nariz. 24 no — ni jota,** to be as blind as a bat. **25 ¡para que veas!,** so there! **26 por lo visto,** apparently. **27 tener que — con,** to concern with, to have to do with. **28 tener un hambre que no se ve,** to be ever so hungry. **29 vamos a —,** we'll see. **30 verás,** you'll see. **31 — de,** to try to (infinitivo.), to see about (*ger.*). **32 — es creer,** seeing is believing. **33 — y callar,** it is better to keep one's mounth shut.
vera *s.f.* edge, side.
veracidad *s.f.* truthfulness, veracity.
veraneante *adj./s.m.* y *f.* **1** holiday maker. **2** (EE.UU.) summer vacationist.
veranear *v.i.* **1** to spend one's summer holidays: *¿dónde veraneas? = where do you spend your summer holidays?* **2** to holiday: *ellos veranean en el sur = they are holidaying in the south.* || **3 ser un buen sitio para —,** to be a nice place for a summer holiday.

veraneo *s.m.* **1** summer holidays. **2** (EE.UU.) summer vacation. || **3 ir de –,** to go on summer holidays. **4 lugar de –,** summer ressort.
veraniego, -a *adj.* **1** summer: *vestido veraniego = summerdress.* **2** (fig.) slight, trivial.
veranillo *s.m.* **1** dry spell in the wet season. **2** spell of good weather. || **3 – de san Juan,** warm spell in june. **4 – de san Martín,** indian summer.
verano *s.m.* **1** summer. **2** (Am.) dry season.
veras *s.f.pl.* truth.
veraz *adj.* **1** truthful, veracious. **2** realiable (de fiar).
verbal *adj.* verbal, oral.
verbalismo *s.m.* verbalism.
verbalista *adj.* **1** verbalistic. || **2** *s.m.* y *f.* verbalist.
verbalmente *adv.* verbally, orally.
verbena *s.f.* **1** BOT. verbena. **2** open air celebration, fair (fiesta). **3** open air dance (baile la víspera de una fiesta).
verbigracia *adv.* for example, for instance, e.g. (abreviatura de exempli gratia).
verbo *s.m.* **1** verb. **2** LIT. language, style: *de verbo sobrio = moderate in style.* || **3 – auxiliar,** auxiliary verb. **4 – transitivo,** transitive verb.
verborrea *s.f.* **1** verbosity. **2** wordiness (palabrería). **3** (vulg.) verbal diarrhoea. || **4 tener mucha –,** to be verbose.
verbosidad *s.f.* verbosity, wordiness (palabrería).
verboso, -a *adj.* verbose, wordy.
verdad *s.f.* **1** truth: *es la pura verdad = it is the plain truth.* **2** reliability (veracidad). || **3 a decir –,** to tell the truth. **4 bien es – que,** it is of course true that. **5 decir cuatro verdades a uno,** to tell someone a few home truth. **6 de –,** really. **7 de – de la buena,** honest to God, honestly. **8 en – os digo,** verily I say into you. **9 hora de la –,** moment of truth. **10 jurar decir la –, toda la – y nada más que la –,** to swear to tell the truth, the whole truth and nothing but the truth. **11 las verdades amargan,** the truth hurts. **12 la – al desnudo,** the naked truth. **13 ¿no es –?,** isn't that so? **14 ser una – como un puño,** to be as plain as a pikestaff. **15 sólo la – ofende,** nothing hurts like the truth.
verdaderamente *adv.* **1** truly, really. **2** indeed (ciertamente).
verdadero, -a *adj.* **1** true: *verdadero = it is true.* **2** real, genuine (auténtico). **3** veracious (veraz).
verde *adj.* **1** green (color): *un toldo verde = a green canvas.* **2** unripe (fruta). **3** unseasoned (leña). **4** premature (planes). **5** dirty, blue (chistes, vocabulario). **6 estar – de envidia,** to be green with envy. **7 poner a uno –,** to call someone all the names under the sun, to run someone down.
verdear *v.i.* **1** to look green (aspecto). **2** to turn green, to grow green: *los árboles empiezan a verdear = the trees are growing green.* **3** AGR. to graze (pastar). **4** (Am.) to drink mate.
verdecer *v.i.* **1** to turn green, to grow green (plantas). **2** to go green (personas).
verdemar *adj.* **1** sea-green. || *s.m.* **2** sea-green.
verdolaga *s.f.* pursulance (planta).
verdor *s.m.* **1** greenish (color). **2** BOT. verdure, lushness. **3** (fig.) youthful vigour (juventud). **4** (fig.) lustiness (lasciva).
verdoso, -a *adj.* greenish.
verdugo, -a *s.m.* y *f.* **1** executioner, hangman (ejecutor de la ley). **2** (fig.) cruel master, tyrant, tormentor. **3** BOT. twig, shoot, sprout (vástago). **4** whip (látigo). **5** torment, scourge (tormento).
verduguillo *s.m.* **1** weal-like swelling (especie de roncha en las hojas). **2** small razor (navaja). **3** sword for accomplishing the "descabello" (tauromaquia).
verdulería *s.f.* **1** greengrocer's (tienda). **2** coarseness (grosería).
verdulero, -a *s.m.* y *f.* greengrocer. **2** (fig. y vulg.) fishwife: *habla como una verdulera = she speaks like a fishwife.*
verdura *s.f.* **1** verdure, greenery. **2** greeness (color). **3** GAST. vegetables, greens. **4** cabbage (col). **5** (fig.) scabrous matter.
verdusco, -a *adj.* dark green, dirty green.
vereda *s.f.* **1** lane, path. **2** (EE.UU.) sidewalk, pavement. **3** (Am.) village, settlement (asentamiento).
veredicto *s.m.* veredict.
verga *s.f.* **1** rod, stick (palo). **2** MAR. yard, spar. **3** ANAT. (vulg.) prick.
vergonzante *adj.* **1** shamefaced. **2** full of shame.
vergonzosamente *adv.* **1** bashfully, shyly. **2** modestly. **3** shamefully, disgracefully.
vergonzoso, -a *adj.* **1** bashful, shy, timid (persona). **2** shameful, disgraceful, shocking (materia). || **3 es – que...,** it is disgraceful that...
vergüenza *s.f.* **1** shame: *es una vergüenza = it is a shame.* **2** embarrashment (bochorno). **3** blasfulness, shyness, timidity (timidez). **4** (fig.) disgrace: *eres una vergüenza = you are a disgrace.* **5** modesty (pudor). || **6 caérsele a uno la cara de –,** to blush with shame, to die of shame. **7 eres la – de la familia,** you are a disgrace to your family. **8 ¿no te da –?,** aren't you shamed? **9 sinvergüenza,** shameless. **10 vergüenzas,** private parts.
vericueto *s.m.* roughpath, rough track, rugged path.
verídico, -a *adj.* true, truthful.
verificación *s.m.* **1** check, checkup, inspection, testing (de una máquina). **2** verification (de un resultado). **3** carrying out, fulfilment (ejecución).
verificador, -a *adj.* **1** checking, inspecting. **2** verifying (de un resultado).
verificar *v.t.* **1** to check, to inspect (máquinas, materiales). **2** to test, to verify (resultados). **3** to carry out, to perform (realizar). **4** to take place: *se verificó un atentado = an assault took place.* **5** to come true (una predicción).
verismo *s.m.* **1** realism, truthfulness. **2** factual nature.
verja *s.f.* **1** grating, grille (de puerta, de ventana). **2** railing(s) (cerca).
vermicida *s.m.* o **vermífugo, -a** *s.m.* y *f.* vermicide, vermifuge.
vermut *s.m.* **1** vermouth. **2** (Am.) martinee (de teatro o cine).
vernáculo, -a *adj.* **1** vernacular. || **2 lengua vernácula,** vernacular language.
verónica *s.f.* **1** BOT. speedwell. **2** pass with the cape (tauromaquia).
verosímil *adj.* **1** likely, probable (probable). **2** credible (cuento, relato).
verraco o **varraco** *s.m.* **1** boar, hog (cerdo). **2** (Am.) ram, wild boar. || **3 gritar como un –,** to squeal like a pig.
verruga *s.f.* **1** MED. y BOT. wart. **2** (fam.) bore, pest, nuisance. **3** (fam.) defect, stain (carácter).
verrugoso, -a *adj.* warty, covered in warts.
versado, -a *adj.* **1** versed in. **2** coversant with. **3** skilled in, expert in. || *s.f.* **4** long tedious poem.
versalita *adj.* y *s.f.* small capitals.
versar *v.i.* **1** to turn, to go round (girar). **2** (Am.) to versify, to improvise verses. **3** (Am.) to chat, to talk. || **4 – sobre,** to deal with, to be about, to turn on.
versátil *adj.* **1** ANAT. versatile, mobile, loose, easily turned. **2** (desp.) changeable, flickle (inconstante).
versículo *s.m.* **1** versicle. **2** verse (de la Biblia).
versificación *s.f.* versification.
versificador, -a *s.m.* y *f.* versifier.
versificar *v.t.* **1** to versify, to put into a verse. || *v.i.* **2** to versify, to write verse.
versión *s.f.* **1** version (interpretación). **2** translation (traducción).
verso *s.m.* **1** verse: *verso blanco = blank verse.* **2** line: *un poema de diez versos = a poem of ten lines.* || **3 echar –,** (Am.) to talk just for talking a sake, to talk nonsense. **4 teatro en –,** verse drama.
vértebra *s.f.* ANAT. vertebra.
vertebrado, -a *adj.* ZOOL. vertebrate.
vertebral *adj.* **1** vertebral. || **2 columna –,** spine, spinal column.
vertedero *s.m.* **1** drain (desagüe). **2** spillway (sumidero). **3** rubbish dump, rubbish tip (de basuras). **4** (Am.) hillside, cliff, slope.
vertedor, -a *adj.* **1** pouring. || *s.m.* y *f.* **2** overflow (desagùe). **3** drain (para aguas residuales). **4** MAR. bailer, scoop (achicador). **5** small shovel (en tiendas).
verter *v.t.* **1** to pour (voluntariamente). **2** to spill (involuntariamente): *verter la sal trae mala suerte = spilling salt draws in bad luck.* **3** to empty (out) (vaciar). **4** to shed (sangre, lágrimas). **5** to dump (basuras). **6** FILOL. to translate into. || *v.i.* **7** to flow (río). **8** to slope, to fall (una vertiente).
vertical *adj.* **1** vertical: *posición vertical = vertical position,* upright. || **2** *s.f.* vertical.

verticalidad *s.f.* 1 verticality. 2 vertical position. 3 vertical direction.
verticalmente *adv.* vertically.
vértice *s.m.* 1 MAT. vertex. 2 GEOM. apex (ápice). 3 ANAT. crown of the head (cornilla).
vertiente *adj.* 1 pouring, flowing: *aguas vertientes = flowing waters.* || *s.f.* 2 slope (de una montaña o tejado). 3 (fig.) aspect, variant. 4 (fam.) spring, fountain.
vertiginosamente *adv.* 1 vertiginously, guiddily, dizzily. 2 (fig.) excesively, very rapidly: *los precios han subido vertiginosamente = prices are rising very rapidly.*
vertiginosidad *s.f.* vertiginousness.
vertiginoso, -a *adj.* 1 vertiginous, giddy, dizzy. 2 (fig.) speed dizzy, very rapid, excessive.
vértigo *s.m.* 1 MED. vertigo, giddiness, dizziness (mareo). 2 (fig.) a fit of madness, sudden frenzy (arrebato). || 3 **velocidad de –,** giddy speed.
vesánico, -a *adj.* 1 MED. insane, raging, furious. || *s.m.* y *f.* 2 madman, madwoman, insane person.
vesícula *s.f.* 1 vesicle. 2 blister (ampolla). 3 – **biliar,** gall-bladder.
vesicular *adj.* vesicular.
vespertino, -a *adj.* vespertine, evening.
vestal *adj.* y *s.f.* vestal (virgen o sacerdotisa de vesta).
vestíbulo *s.m.* 1 hall (de una casa). 2 lobby (edificio público). 3 foyer.
vestido, -a *p.p.* de **vestir.** 1 dressed. || *adj.* 2 dressed, wearing: *vestido de azul = dressed in blue,* wearing blue. || *s.m.* 3 dress (de mujer). 4 garment, cloth. 5 suit (traje).
vestidura *s.f.* 1 clothing, apparell. 2 REL. vestment: *vestiduras sacerdotales = priestly vestments.* || 3 **rasgarse las vestiduras,** to make a great to-do.
vestigio *s.m.* 1 vestige (restos). 2 trace (huellas). || 4 **vestigios,** remains.
vestimenta *s.f.* 1 clothing. 2 (desp.) gear. 3 REL. vestemts.
vestir *v.t.* 1 to clothe, to dress (personas): *va siempre muy bien vestida = she is always very well dressed.* 2 to wear: *viste traje oscuro = he is wearing a dark suit.* 3 to drape (superficies, estatuas). 4 (fig.) to adorn, to emelish: *vestir un poema = to emelish a poem.* || *v.r.* 5 to get dressed, to put on one's clothes: *se está vistiendo = he's getting dressed.* 6 (fig.) to cover itself, to become covered in. || 7 **el mismo que viste y calza,** the very same. 8 **los campos se visten de verde,** the fields are turning green. 9 **vestirse de tiros largos,** to put on one's sunday best. 10 **vísteme despacio que tengo prisa,** more haste less speed.
vestuario *s.m.* 1 wardrove, clothes. 2 MIL. uniform. 3 dressing room (habitación). 4 costumes (cine, teatro). 5 cloakroom (ropero en edificio público). 6 changing room (deportes).
veta *s.f.* 1 MIN. lode, seam. 2 grain (en madera). 3 streak, stripe (piedra, carne). 4 vein (de oro).
vetar *v.t.* to veto, to put a veto on.
veteado, -a *adj.* 1 veined, grained. 2 stripped (con rayas). || *s.m.* 3 vening, graining, maring.
vetear *v.t.* 1 to grain (madera, piedra). 2 to streak (con rayas). 3 (Am.) to flog, to beat.
veteranía *s.f.* 1 long experience. 2 seniority (antigüedad). 3 status of being a veteran.
veterano, -a *adj.* 1 veteran: *una maestra veterana = a veteran teacher.*
veterinario, -a *s.m.* y *f.* 1 veterinary surgeon. 2 (fam.) vet. 3 (EE.UU.) veterinarian. || *s.f.* 4 veterinary science.
veto *s.m.* veto.
vetustez *s.m.* 1 great age, ancientness, antiquity. 2 (fig.) venerable nature.
vetusto, -a *adj.* 1 very old, ancient. 2 (fig.) venerable.
vez *s.f.* 1 time: *una vez al día = once a day.* 2 turn (turno): *su vez, señora = your turn, madam; perder la vez = to miss one's turn.* 3 occasion, instance. || 4 **acabemos de una –,** let's get it over. 5 **a la –,** at the same time. 6 **alguna –,** sometimes, ever: *¿has comido pato alguna vez? = have you ever eaten duck?* 7 **cada – más,** more and more. 8 **cada – menos, a)** (+ *adj.*) less and less; **b)** (+ s.) fewer and fewer. 9 **cada – que,** every time, whenever: *cada vez que te veo estás comiendo = whenever I see you, you are eating.* 10 **ceder la –,** to give up one's turn. 11 **contadas veces,** seldom, rarely. 12 **demasiadas veces,** too often. 13 **de una sola –,** in one go. 14 **de una – para siempre,** once and for all. 15 **de – en cuando,** from time to time. 16 **dos veces,** twice. 17 **en – de,** instead of. 18 **érase una –,** once upon a time. 19 **la mayoría de las veces,** most times, usually. 20 **miles de veces,** thousand of times, lots of times. 21 **otras veces,** other times. 22 **por enésima –,** for the umpteenth time. 23 **tal –,** perhaps. 24 **una – al año no hace daño,** once in a while hurts no one. 25 **una y otra –,** time and time again. 26 **varias veces,** several times.
vía *s.f.* 1 road, route, track (pista). 2 (fig.) way, means (medio, modo de). 3 railway, rail (trenes). 4 MAR. route. 5 lane (de carreteras o autopistas). 6 QUIM. process: *vía húmeda = wet process.* 7 ANAT. tract, passage, tube: *vías respiratorias = breathing tract.* 8 procedure (jurídico). || 9 *prep.* vía: *Madrid-Roma vía París = Madrid-Rome via Paris.* || 10 **cuaderna –,** verse with four alexandrines. 11 **de – única,** single track. 12 **en vías de,** in the process of (+ *ger.*). 13 **un país en vías de desarrollo,** a developing country. 14 – **aérea,** airmail (correos), by air. 15 – **láctea,** milky way. 16 **¡– libre!,** make way!, clear the way! 17 – **romana,** Roman road. 18 – **sumarísima,** summary proceeding (jurisprudencia).
viabilidad *s.f.* viability, feasibility.
viable *adj.* viable, feasible.
viaducto *s.m.* viaduct.
viajante *s.m.* 1 comercial traveller, salesman. || *adj.* 2 travelling. 3 (EE.UU.) traveling.
viajar *v.i.* 1 to travel, to journe: *viajar por Francia = to travel through France.* 2 to tour (hacer turismo): *está viajando por Canadá = she is touring Canada.*
viaje *s.m.* 1 journey, tour. 2 trip (excursión). 3 travel. 4 (fig.) punch (puñetazo). 5 butt (tauromaquia). 6 voyage (viaje marítimo largo). 7 load (carga): *viaje de leña = wood load.* || 8 **¡buen –!,** bon voyage!, have a good journey! 9 **estar de –,** to be away. 10 **para este – no se necesitan alforjas,** a fat lot of good that is. 11 – **de ida y vuelta,** round trip, journey there and back. 13 – **de novios,** honey-moon. 14 – **de recreo,** pleasure trip.
viajero, -a *s.m.* y *f.* 1 traveller, passenger (pasajero). || *adj.* 2 travelling. 3 ZOOL. migratory.
vial *adj.* 1 road (de la carretera). 2 traffic (de la circulación).
vianda *s.f.* 1 food (alimento). 2 (EE.UU.) dinner pail. 3 (Am.) lunch tin.
viandante *s.m.* y *f.* 1 traveller, wayfarer (viajero). 2 passerby (transeúnte).
viático *s.m.* 1 REL. viaticum. 2 HIST. food for a journey. 3 travel allowance (dietas).
víbora *s.f.* 1 snake, viper. 2 (Am.) money belt.
viborezno *s.m.* small viper.
vibración *s.f.* 1 vibration. 2 ANAT. throbbing.
vibrador *s.m.* 1 vibrator. || *adj.* 2 vibrating.
vibrante *adj.* vibrant, vibrating.
vibrar *v.t.* e *i.* 1 to vibrate, to shake, to rattle (traquetear). 2 ANAT. to throb, to pulsate, to beat.
vibratorio, -a *adj.* vibratory.
vicarial *adj.* vicarial.
vicariato *s.m.* vicariate.
vicario, -a *s.m.* 1 curate, vicar. || *s.f.* 2 vicarage (residencia), vicariate. 3 deputy, to the mother superior (monjas).
vice *prefijo* vice.
viceversa *adv.* vice versa.
viciar *v.t.* 1 to corrupt, pervet, subvert (costumbres). 2 to nullify, to invalidate (ley). 3 to falsify (falsificar). 4 to contaminate, to pollute (la atmósfera). 5 to spoil (estropear). 6 to adulterate (una sustancia). 7 to bend, to warp, to put out of place (objetos, prendas). 8 to distort (el sentido de algo). || *v.pron.* 9 to become spoil (estropearse). 10 to take to vice, to get depraved, to become corrupted (viciarse). 11 to go out of shape (cualquier objeto). 12 to become polluted (el aire).
vicio *s.m.* 1 vice, viciousness, depravity. 2 bad habit. 3 fault. 4 BOT. rankness, lushness. 5 warp, twist, bend (superficie, objeto). || 6 **no poder quitarse el –,** not to be able to get oneself out of the habit. 7 **por –,** out of sheer habit, for no reason at all. 8 **quejarse de –,** to complain for no reason at all.

viciosamente *adv.* **1** viciously, disolutely, wrongly. **2** BOT. luxurianty.
vicioso, -a *adj.* **1** vicious (persona, animal). **2** faultly, defective (objetos). **3** spoiled (niño mimado). **4** adict, fiend (adicto).
vicisitud *s.f.* **1** vicissitude. **2** accident. **3** suddent change (cambio repentino).
víctima *s.f.* **1** victim: *es una víctima = he's a victim.* **2** (fig.) prey: *es víctima de una depresión = he is a prey to depression.* **3** casualty (en accidente): *no hubo víctimas en el accidente = there were no casualties in the accident.*
victoria *s.f.* **1** victory. **2** win, triumph. ‖ **3 cantar —,** to proclaim a victory. **4 — pírrica,** pyrrhic victory. **5 — rotunda,** overwhelming victory.
victoriosamente *adv.* victoriously.
victorioso, -a *adv.* victorious.
vid *s.f.* vine, grapevine.
vida *s.f.* **1** life. **2** lifetime (duración de). **3** living: *ganarse la vida = to earn one's living.* ‖ **4 dar — a,** to give birth to. **5 de por —,** for life, for the rest of one's life. **6 en mi —** (negativo), never in my life. **7 entre la — y la muerte,** at death's door. **8 esto es —,** this is living. **9 la otra —,** the next life, the life to come. **10 meterse en vidas ajenas,** to interfere in other people's affairs. **11 mujer de — alegre,** prostitute. **12 ¡por mi —!,** upon my soul! **13 ¿qué es de tu —?,** what's the news? **14 ¡qué — esta!,** what a life! **15 un amigo de toda la —,** a lifelong friend. **16 ¡— perra!,** dog's life! **17 — privada,** private life. **18 — y milagros de uno,** full details about someones.
vidente *s.m.* y *f.* **1** seer, prophet. **2** clairvoyant (clarividente).
vidorra *s.f.* gay life, easy life.
vidriado, -a *adj.* **1** glazed. ‖ *s.m.* **2** glaze, glazing. **3** glazed earthenware (de cerámica).
vidriar *v.t.* **1** to glaze. ‖ *v.pron.* **2** to become glazed. **3** to glaze over (los ojos).
vidriera *s.f.* **1** glass door, glass partition (puertas). **2** stained-glass window (ventanas). **3** (Am.) shopwindow. **4** (EE.UU.) show window.
vidriería *s.f.* **1** glassworks (taller). **2** glass shop (tienda).
vidriero *s.m.* **1** glassworker (obrero). **2** glassmaker (fabricante). **3** glazier (fabricante o colocador de cristales).
vidrio *s.m.* **1** glass (cristal). **2** stained glass (coloreado). ‖ **3 fibra de —,** glass fibre. **4 pagar los vidrios rotos,** to carry the can. **5 — laminado,** splinterproof glass.
vidrioso, -a *adj.* **1** glasy, glazed: *ojos vidriosos = glazy eyes.* **2** brittle (frágil). **3** slippery (superficie). **4** touchy, sensitive (persona).
viejo, -a *s.m.* y *f.* **1** old age. **2** s.m. old man. **3** *s.f.* old lady, old woman. **4** (Am.) craker, squib. ‖ *adj.* **5** old. ‖ **6** *s.m.* **cuento de viejas,** old-wive's tale. **7 hacer la cuenta de la vieja,** to count on one's fingers. **8 hacerse —,** to grow old. **9 no llegar a —,** not to make old bones. **10 ser más — que Matusalén,** to be as old as Methuselah.
viento *s.m.* **1** wind: *vientos alisios = trade winds.* **2** breeze (brisa). **3** ANAT. flatulence. **4** scent (caza). **5** (fig.) vanity, conceit. **6** guy rope (de tienda de campaña). **7** (Am.) strings of a kite. **8** (Am.) rheumatism. ‖ **9 beber los vientos por uno,** to be crazy about someone. **10 contra — y marea,** at all cost, regardless of all the difficulties. **11 echar a uno con — fresco,** to chuck someone out. **12 hacer un — de mil demonios,** to blow a gale. **13 ir — en popa,** to go esplendily, to go extremely well. **14 libre como el —,** free as the wind. **15 publicar algo a los cuatro vientos,** to shout something from the roof tops. **16 ¡vete con — fresco!,** to go blazes and good riddance! **17 — huracanado,** hurricane wind, violent wind.
vientre *s.m.* **1** ANAT. abdomen. **2** (fam.) belly. **3** ANAT. womb (seno materno). **4** (fig.) bowels (intestino). ‖ **5 descargar el —, hacer de —,** to have a bowel movement. **6 echar —,** to get a pot belly. **7 el fruto de tu —,** the fruit of thy womb. **8 — flojo,** looseness of the bowels.
viernes *s.m.* **1** Friday. ‖ **2 comer de —,** to abstain from eating meat. **3 Viernes Santo,** good Friday.
viga *s.f.* **1** timber (de madera). **2** beam (construcción): *viga principal = main beam.* **3** girder (metálica).
vigencia *s.f.* **1** validity, aplicability. ‖ **2 entrar en —,** to come into force. **3 estar en —,** to be in force. **4 tener —,** to be valid.
vigente *adj.* valid, in force: *la ley vigente = the law in force.*
vigésimo, -a *adj./s.m.* y *f.* twentieth.
vigía *s.m.* **1** look out, watchman. **2** MAR. watch. **3** MIL. watchtower. **4** GEOG. reef, rock.
vigilancia *s.f.* **1** vigilance, watchfulness. **2** surveillance (acción de vigilar).
vigilante *s.m.* **1** watchman. **2** guard (de seguridad). **3** (Am.) policeman. **4** supervisor (colegio, trabajo). **5** warder (prisión). **6** shopwalker (tiendas). **7** night watchman (nocturno). ‖ *adj.* **8** vigilant, watchful, alert.
vigilar *v.t.* **1** to watch (over). **2** to look after (cuidar). **3** to supervise (un trabajo). **4** to keep an eye on: *vigila esta máquina = keep an eye on this machine.* **5** to guard (presos). ‖ *v.i.* **6** to be vigilant, to be watchful. **7** to keep watch.
vigilia *s.f.* **1** vigil (el que no duerme), wakefulness. **2** eve (víspera). ‖ **3 día de —,** day of abstinence. **4 pasar la noche de —,** to stay awake all night.
vigor *s.m.* **1** vigour, energy. **2** force: *entrar en vigor = to come into force.* **3** strength (fortaleza). **4** vitality.
vigorizador, -a *adj.* invigorating, fortifying, revitalizing.
vigorizar *v.t.* **1** to invigorate, to strengthen, to stimulate. ‖ *v.pron.* **2** to be invigorated, to be fortified.
vigorosidad *s.f.* vigour, strength.
vigoroso, -a *adj.* vigorous, strong, tough.
vigueta *s.f.* **1** small beam (de madera). **2** small girder (metálica). **3** joint (junta).
vihuela *s.f.* MUS. an early kind of guitar.
vil *adj.* **1** low, villanous (personas). **2** vile, rotten (acto). **3** unjust, shabby, mean (tratamiento).
vileza *s.f.* **1** low character. **2** vileness. **3** vile deed (acto). **4** shabbiness, meaness.
vilipendiar *v.t.* **1** to vilify, to vilipend. **2** to despise, to scorn (despreciar). **3** to abuse.
vilipendio *s.m.* **1** scorn, contempt (desprecio). **2** abuse, humillation (insulto).
vilo *adv.* **1** in the air, suspended (en el aire). **2** (fig.) on tenterhooks (intranquilo). ‖ **3 mantener algo en —,** to keep something up. **4 quedar en —,** to be left in the air.
vilorta *s.f.* **1** wooden ring (aro de madera). **2** washer (arandela).
villa *s.f.* **1** villa (casa). **2** small town (pueblo). **3** POL. borough (condado), municipality.
villadiego, (tomar las de) to beat it quick, to take to one's heels.
villanaje *s.m.* **1** humble status (humilde). **2** peasant condition, peasantry (campesinos). **3** HIST. villeinage (condición).
villanamente *adv.* basely.
villancico *s.m.* christmas carol.
villanería *s.f.* villainy, villeinage.
villanesco, -a *adj.* peasant, village, rustic.
villanía *s.f.* **1** humble birth, lowly status (condición), villainy, baseness (cualidad).
villano, -a *adj.* **1** peasant, rustic. **2** (fig.) coarse. ‖ *s.m.* y *f.* **3** villain. **4** low individual. **5** (desp.) rotter.
villorrio *s.m.* one-horse town, dump (poblacho).
vinagre *s.m.* y *f.* vinegar.
vinagrero, -a *adj.* **1** vinegar, pertaining to vinegar. ‖ *s.m.* y *f.* **2** vinegar maker (fabricante). **3** vinegar seller (vendedor). ‖ *s.f.* **4** vinegar bottle. **5** (Am.) heartburn, acidity.
vinagreta *s.f.* vinagrette (salsa).
vinagroso, -a *adj.* **1** vinegary, tart. **2** (fig.) bad-tempered, sour.
vinajera *s.f.* REL. altar cruet.
vinatero, -a *adj.* **1** wine: *industria vinatera = wine trade.* ‖ *s.m.* y *f.* **2** wine merchant. **3** vintner (viniculfor).
vinaza *s.f.* nasty wine, wine from the dregs.
vinculación *s.f.* **1** linking (acción). **2** bond, link (lazos). **3** entailment (jurisprudencia).
vincular *v.t.* **1** to link, to tie, to bind. **2** to relate, to connect (relacionar). **3** to entail (jurídicamente). ‖ *v.pron.* **4** to link oneself to.
vínculo *s.m.* **1** link, bond, tie. **2** entail (jurídico).
vindicación *s.f.* vengeance, revenge, vindication.
vindicador, -a *adj.* avenging, revenging, vindicatory.

vindicar *v.t.* 1 to avenge, to revenge, to vindicate. 2 to claim, to vindicate (jurídicamente).
vindicativo, -a *adj.* vindictive, vindicatory.
vindicatorio, -a *adj.* vindicatory.
vínico *adj.* wine, pertaining to wine.
vinícola *adj.* wine-producing, wine-growing.
vinicultor, -a *s.m.* y *f.* wine-producer, winer grower.
vinicultura *s.f.* wine-growing, wine-producing.
vino *s.m.* 1 wine: *vino añejo = mellow wine; vino de la tierra = rough wine.* || 2 **ahogar las penas en —,** to drown one's sorrows. 3 **bautizar el —,** to water the wine. 4 **— a granel,** wine from the barrel. 5 **— añejo,** vintage wine. 6 **— blanco,** white wine. 7 **— de honor,** special wine. 8 **— espumoso,** sparkling wine. 9 **— tinto,** red wine.
vinoso, -a *adj.* vinous, vinaceous, winecoloured.
viña *s.f.* 1 vineyard. 2 (Am.) rubbish dump.
viñador *s.m.* viticulturist, vine grower.
viñedo *s.m.* vineyard.
viñeta *s.f.* 1 vignette (imprenta). 2 emblem, badge.
viola *s.f.* viola.
violáceo, -a *adj.* 1 violaceous, violet. || *s.f.pl.* 2 BOT. violaceae.
violación *s.f.* 1 violation, rape. 2 (fig.) offence. 3 infringement (de la ley).
violado, -a *adj./s.m.* y *f.* violet.
violador, -a *adj.* 1 rapist (personas). 2 violator (ley).
violar *v.t.* 1 to rape, to ravish (a una persona). 2 to infringe, break.
violencia *s.f.* 1 violence, force. 2 assault (atentado). 3 rape (violación sexual). 4 embarrassment (situación).
violentamente *adv.* violently, furiously, wildly.
violentar *v.t.* 1 to force (forzar). 2 to break into (una casa). 3 to outrage, to violate (un principio). 4 to distort (el sentido de algo).
violento, -a *adj.* 1 violent, furious, wild. 2 DEP. rough. 3 akward, unnatural (posición). 4 embarrassing (situación).
violeta *s.f.* 1 violet. || *adj.* 2 violet.
violín *s.m.* 1 violin. 2 (Am.) bad breath. || 3 (Am., fig. y fam.) **embolsarse el —,** to come back with one's tail between one's legs.
violinista *s.m.* y *f.* violinist.
violonchelista *s.m.* y *f.* cellist.
violonchelo *s.m.* cello.
viperino, -a *adj.* 1 (fig.) viperish. 2 viperine (animal).
viraje *s.m.* 1 bend (curva). 2 turn (el coche). 3 swerve (bruscamente). 4 FOT. toning. 5 change of direction.
virar *v.t.* 1 MAR. to put about, to turn. 2 FOT. to tone. 3 (Am.) to turn upside down, to turn over, to whip. || *v.i.* 4 to change direction. 5 MAR. to tack. 6 to turn, to swerve (un vehículo). 7 (fig.) to change one's views (cambiar de opinión). || 8 **— a babor,** to turn to port. 9 **— en redondo,** to switch round completely.
virgen *s.f.* 1 virgin. 2 guide (en lagares). || 3 *adj.* virgin. || 4 **la santísima —,** the blessed Virgin Mary. 4 **ser un viva la —,** to be a happy-go-lucky.
virginal *adj.* maidenly, virginal.
virginidad *s.f.* virginity.
viril *adj.* virile, manly.
virilidad *s.f.* 1 virility, manliness. 2 manhood (hombría).
virreinato *s.m.* viceroyalty.
virrey *s.m.* viceroy.
virtual *adj.* 1 virtual. 2 strength, potential. 3 future, posible. 4 apparent.
virtualidad *s.f.* 1 virtuality. 2 potentiality.
virtualmente *adv.* virtually.
virtud *s.f.* 1 virtue. 2 ability (habilidad): *tiene la virtud de convencerme = she has the ability of convincing me.* 3 power, efficacy: *esta planta tiene virtudes medicinales = this plant is effective against certain diseases.*
virtuosamente *adv.* virtuously.
virtuosismo *s.m.* virtuosity.
virtuoso, -a *adj.* 1 virtuous (relativo a la virtud). 2 skilled (con habilidad). || *s.m.* virtuoso.
viruela *s.f.* 1 small pox. 2 pockmark (marcas). || 3 picado de viruelas, pockmarked.
virulencia *s.f.* virulence.
virus *s.m.pl.* 1 virus. 2 (fig.) poison, venom.
viruta *s.f.* 1 shaving (de madera, metales). 2 (fig.) bill (factura).
visado *s.m.* 1 visa (de un pasaporte). 2 permit (permiso).
visaje *s.m.* 1 face (rostro). 2 grimace (gesto).
visar *v.t.* to visa. 2 to pass, to approve, to endorse (confirmar).
vísceras *s.f.pl.* 1 viscera, entrails. 2 (fig.) guts, bowels.
viscosa *s.f.* viscose.
viscosidad *s.f.* viscosity, stickiness (pegajosidad).
viscoso, -a *adj.* 1 viscous, sticky. 2 thick (líquido).
visera *s.f.* 1 MIL. visor. 2 peak (de una gorra). 3 eyeshade (en hokey). 4 (Am.) blinkers (para caballos).
visibilidad *s.f.* 1 visibility: *visibilidad de tres metros = visibility under three metres.* || 2 **curva con poca —,** blind bend.
visible *adj.* 1 visible. 2 (fig.) clear, plain, evident.
visiblemente *adv.* 1 visibly. 2 (fig.) evidently, clearly.
visigodo, -a *adj.* 1 Visigotic. 2 *s.m.* y *f.* Visigoth.
visillo *s.m.* small curtain.
visión *s.f.* 1 ANAT. vision. 2 sight (vista): *perdió la visión = he lost his sight.* 3 view: *visión de conjunto = overall view.* 4 (desp.) fright: *iba echa una visión = she looked a real fright.*
visionario, -a *adj.* 1 visionary. 2 (fig.) deluded. || *s.m.* y *f.* 3 visionary.
visita *s.f.* 1 visit: *hacer una visita = to pay a visit.* 2 call: *visita de cumplido = courtesy call.* 3 visitor, caller (persona). || 4 **devolver una —,** to return a visit. 5 **— de médico,** short call. 6 **— de pésame,** visit of condolence. 7 **tarjeta de —,** visiting card.
visitador, -a *adj.* 1 fond of visiting. || *s.m.* y *f.* 2 visitor, inspector. || *s.f.* 3 (Am.) syringe, enema.
visitante *adj.* 1 visiting. || *s.m.* y *f.* 2 visitor.
visitar *v.t.* 1 to visit, to call on, to go and see. 2 to inspect (oficialmente). || *v.pron.* 3 to visit each other.
vislumbrar *v.t.* 1 to glimpse, to catch a glimpse of. 2 (fig.) to see some light possibility of (una solución).
viso *s.m.* 1 shimmer, sheen (destellos, coloreados). 2 appearance, aspect (aspecto). 3 gleam (metal). 4 GEOG. viewpoint. 5 undersleep (especie de forro de un vestido transparente). || 6 **ser una persona de visos,** to have some standing. 7 **tener visos de verdad,** to have the appearance of truth.
visón *s.m.* mink.
visor *s.m.* 1 MIL. bombsight. 2 FOT. viewfinder.
víspera *s.f.* 1 day before. 2 eve (de alguna fiesta). || *pl.* 3 vesper (oficio religioso). || 4 **en vísperas de,** on the eve of.
vista *s.f.* 1 sight. 2 vision (capacidad). 3 view (perspectiva): *vista panorámica = panoramic view.* 4 visible (a la vista). 5 glance, look (vistazo). 6 hearing, trial (jurídica). || 7 **aguzar la —,** to look more carefully. 8 **apartar la —,** to look away. 9 **a primera —,** at first sight. 10 **a simple —,** at a glance. 11 **a treinta días —,** thirty days after sight. 12 **conocer a uno de —,** to know someone by sight. 13 **con vistas al mar,** overlooking the sea. 14 **en — de,** in view of. 15 **hacer la — gorda,** to turn a blind eye. 16 **perder algo de —,** to lose sight of something. 17 (fig.) **tener mucha —,** to be farsighted. 18 **— de pájaro,** bird's-eye view.
vistazo *s.m.* look, glance: *echar un vistazo = to have a look.*
visto, -a *p.p.* 1 de ver. || *adj.* 2 in view of: *visto lo ocurrido = in view of what happened.* 3 approval (visto bueno). || 4 **estar bien —,** to be well looked on. 5 **estar mal —,** to be thought improper. 6 **estar muy —,** to be very commonly worn; to be old hat. 7 **está — que,** it is clear that. 8 **por lo —,** evidently, apparently. 9 **— que...,** since..., seeing that...
vistosamente *adv.* showily, attractively, colourfully.
vistosidad *s.f.* colourfulness.
vistoso, -a *adj.* colourful, showy, flashy (llamativo).
visual *adj.* 1 visual: *campo visual = visual field.* || *s.f.* 2 line of sight, look, glance.
vital *adj.* 1 life, living: *espacio vital = living space.* 2 vital: *órgano vital = vital organ.* 3 (fig.) essential (importancia).

vitalicio, -a *adj.* 1 life: *cargo vitalicio = post held for life.* || *s.m.* 2 life annuity.
vitalidad *s.f.* vitality.
vitalizar *v.t.* to vitalize, to revitalize.
vitamina *s.f.* vitamin.
vitaminado, -a *adj.* vitaminized, vitamin-enriched.
vitaminar *v.t.* to vitaminize, to add vitamins to.
vitela *s.f.* bellum.
vitícola *adj.* vinegrowing, vine.
viticultor, -a *s.m.* y *f.* vinegrower, viticulturist.
viticultura *s.f.* vinegrowing, viticulture.
vitola *s.f.* 1 cigar band. 2 looks, appearance (traza, facha). 3 calibrator (para armas).
vitorear *v.t.* to acclaim, to applaud, to cheer.
vitrina *s.f.* 1 glass, showcase. 2 (Am.) shop window.
vitualla *s.f.* victuals, provisions.
vituperable *adj.* reprehensible, blameworthy.
vituperar *v.t.* to vituperate, to censure, to condemn.
viudedad *s.f.* 1 windowhood (masculino). 2 windowerhood (femenino).
viudo, -a *adj.* 1 windowed. || *s.m.* 2 window. || *s.f.* 3 windower.
vivacidad *s.f.* 1 vivacity. 2 liveliness (alegría). 3 sharpeness (inteligencia).
vivaracho, -a *adj.* 1 janunty (garboso). 2 lively (alegre), vivacious.
vivaz *adj.* 1 long-lived, lasting (duradero). 2 quick-witted (ingenio). 3 vigorous. 4 lively, vivacious (lleno de vida).
víveres *s.pl.* 1 provisions. 2 MIL. stores, supplies.
vivero *s.m.* 1 tree nursery (árboles). 2 fish pond (peces). 3 fish-hatch (donde se crían). 4 vivarium (animales).
viveza *s.f.* 1 vividness, liveliness. 2 sharpness, brightness.
vivido, -a *adj.* vivid, graphic.
vividor, -a *adj.* 1 (desp.) unscrupulous, opportunist. 2 shrewd, capable. 3 living, alive.
vivienda *s.f.* 1 accomodation, housing. 2 habitat, dwelling (habitáculo). 3 (EE.UU.) tenement.
viviente *adj.* living: *los vivientes = the living.*
vivíparo, -a *adj.* viviparous.
vivir *v.t.* 1 to live through, to experience, to go through: *he vivido momentos terribles = I ve gone through terrible moments.* || 2 *v.i.* to live. 3 to live on (vivir de). || 4 **alegría de —,** joy of living. 5 **de mal —,** dissolute, delinquent. 6 **ir viviendo,** to get along. 7 **no dejar — a uno,** not to leave someone in peace. 8 **no — del miedo que se tiene,** to be scared to death. 9 **¿quién vive?,** who goes there? 10 **saber —,** to enjoy life to the full. 11 **tener con que —,** to have enough to live on. 12 **¡viva!,** hurrah! 13 **¡viva España!,** up with Spain! 14 **¡vivan los novios!,** three cheers for the bride and the groom. 15 **— para ver,** to live and learn.
vivo, -a *adj.* 1 living: *seres vivos = living beings.* 2 alive: *¡estoy vivo! = I'm alive!* 3 vivid, graphic (descripción, color, memoria). 4 (fig.) sharp, clever (persona). 5 (Am.) naughty. 6 vivacious (lleno de vida). 7 quick tempered: *tiene el genio vivo = he is quick tempered.* 8 (Am.) crafty, unscrupulous. || *s.m.* 9 living: *los vivos y los muertos = the living and the dead.* 10 trimming, border (en costura). 11 vivos: *donación entre vivos = gift inter vivos* (jurídico). || 12 **a fuerza viva,** by main force. 13 **ser el — retrato de...,** to be the spitting image of someone. 14 **seto —,** hedgerow. 15 **transmitir en —,** to broadcast something live. 16 **vender algo —,** to sell something alive.
vizconde *s.m.* viscount. || **vizcondesa** *s.f.* viscountess.
vocablo *s.m.* 1 word, vocable. | 2 **jugar al —,** to make a pun.
vocabulario *s.m.* vocabulary.
vocación *s.f.* vocation, calling: *errar la vocación = to miss one's vocation.*
vocacional *adj.* vocational.
vocal *s.f.* 1 vowel. || *s.m.* 2 comitee member, director. || *adj.* 3 vocal.
vocálico *adj.* vocalic, vowel.
vocalizar *v.t.* e *i.* 1 to vocalize. || *v.i.* MUS. to hum.
vocativo *s.m.* vocativo (declinación latina).
vocear *v.i.* 1 to shout, to yell, to bawl. || *v.t.* 2 to cry, to shout out (un vendedor). 3 to acclaim, to hail (aclamar).
voceo *s.m.* shouting, jelling, bawling.
vocería *s.f.* 1 uproar, clamour. 2 (fam.) hullabaloo.
vocero *s.m.* spokesman (portavoz).
vociferación *s.f.* vociferation.
vociferador, -a *adj.* loud-mouthed.
vociferar *v.i.* y *t.* to vociferate, to shout, to scream (gritar).
vocinglero, -a *adj.* 1 loud-mouthed, loquacious. 2 garrulous.
vodka *s.m.* o *f.* vodka.
voladizo, -a *adj.* 1 ARQ. projecting. || 2 projection.
volado, -a *adj.* 1 superior, raised (en impresión). 2 (Am.) protuberant, big. 3 (Am.) in love (enamorado). || *adv.* 4 (Am.) hastily (de prisa).
volador, -a *adj.* 1 flying. 2 (fig.) swift, fleeting. || *s.m.* 3 rocket. 4 flying fish (calamar).
voladura *s.f.* 1 blowing up, demolition. 2 blast (cantera).
volandas *adv.* in the air, through the air.
volante *adj.* 1 flying. 2 (fig.) unsettled, itinerant. 3 DEP. wing half, half back (medio volante). || *s.m.* 4 steering, wheel (coches). 5 MED. card. 6 TEC. flywheel. 7 (Am.) two wheeled carriage.
volar *v.i.* 1 to fly: *los pájaros vuelan = birds can fly.* 2 to fly off, to fly away. 3 (fig.) to pass swiftly: *el tiempo vuela = time passes swiftly.* 4 to spread rapidly (noticias). 5 to rush, to scorch (coches), to go like wind. 6 (fig.) disappear, vanish: *mi dinero ha volado = my money has vanished.* 7 (Am.) to bluff (juego). || *v.t.* 8 to fly: *volar una cometa = to fly a kite.* 9 to blow up, to demolish (edificios). 10 to blast (una cantera). 11 to rouse, to put to fly (caza). 12 (Am. y fig.) to pinch. 13 (Am.) to swindle, to flirt with (coquetear).
volátil *adj.* 1 volatile. 2 (fig.) changeable, inconstant.
volatilidad *s.f.* 1 volatility. 2 (fig.) inconstancy, fickleness.
volatilizar *v.t.* 1 to volatilize, to vaporize. 2 (fig.) to spirit away. || *v.r.* 3 to volatilize. 4 to vanish into thin air.
volcán *s.m.* 1 volcano. 2 (Am.) breakdown (colapso). 3 (Am.) avalanche.
volcánico, -a *adj.* volcanic.
volcar *v.t.* 1 to upset, to overturn (contenido). 2 to empty out, to pour out (deliberadamente). 3 to overturn (un coche). || *v.i.* 4 to overturn (un coche). 5 to capsize (un barco). || *v.pron.* 6 to be upset, to tip over (contenido). 7 to fall over (un vaso botella). 8 (fig.) to do one's utmost, to be excessively kind.
volear *v.t.* 1 to volley (pelota). 2 to scatter (semillas). 3 to broadcast (sembrar).
voleo, -a *s.m.* y *f.* 1 volley. 2 lob (tenis, fútbol). || *s.m.* 3 hard slap (bofetón). 4 high kick (baile). 5 random: *a voleo = at random.* 6 haphazardly (arbitrariamente).
volframio *s.m.* QUIM. wolfram.
volición *s.f.* volition.
volquete *s.m.* 1 tipcart (carro). 2 tip-up (camión). 3 (EE.UU.) chump truck.
voltaje *s.m.* voltage.
voltear *v.t.* 1 to swing. 2 to turn, to turn over (dar la vuelta). 3 to toss (una moneda). 4 to turn upside down (revólver). 5 to spill (derramar).
voltereta *s.f.* 1 somersault. 2 handspring (apoyando las manos).
voltímetro *s.m.* voltemer.
voltio *s.m.* volt.
volubilidad *s.f.* flickeness, changeableness, umpredictability.
voluble *adj.* 1 changeable, inconstant. 2 BOT. twining.
volumen *s.m.* 1 volume (capacidad). 2 size (tamaño). 3 bulk (grande). 4 (fig.) important, sizeable. 5 volume (libro).
voluminoso, -a *adj.* 1 voluminous. 2 bulky: *tomo voluminoso = bulky volume.*
voluntad *s.f.* 1 will. 2 volition. 3 wish, desaire (deseo). 4 intention: *buena voluntad = good intention.* 5 will power (fuerza de voluntad). 6 fondness, affection. || 7 **buena —,** goodwill. 8 **con poca —,** reluctantly. 9 **ganar la — de alguien,** to win someone over. 10 **hacer su santa —,** to do exactly as one pleases. 11 **¡hágase tu —!,** thy will be done! (oración). 12 **no tener — para,** not to have the willpower to. 13 **por — propia,** of one's own volition.
voluntariamente *adv.* voluntarily.
voluntario, -a *adj.* voluntary, willful.
voluntarioso, -a *adj.* 1 (desp.) headstrong. 2 dedicated, well-intentioned.
voluptuosidad *s.f.* 1 voluptuousness. 2 (desp.) sensuality.

voluptuoso, -a *adj.* 1 voluptuous. 2 (desp.) sensual.
voluta *s.f.* 1 ARQ. scroll. 2 spiral, column (humo, similar).
volver *v.t.* 1 to turn, to turn over. 2 to turn upside down (boca abajo). 3 to turn inside on (de dentro hacia fuera). 4 (fig.) to turn (convertir). 5 drive: *me vuelves loco = you drive me mad.* || *v.i.* 6 to go back, to return (regresar). 7 to revert (a un hábito). || *v.pron.* 8 to turn: *se volvió a mí = he turned to me.* 9 to turn round (darse la vuelta). 10 to turn over (una página). 11 to become, to go (convertirse, volverse): *se volvió loco = he went mad.* 12 to turn sour (agriarse).
vomitar *v.t.* 1 to vomit, to bring up, to throw up. 2 to spit: *vomitar sangre = to spit blood.* 3 to belch (llamas). 4 to spew (lava). || *v.i.* 5 to vomit, to be sick.
vómito *s.m.* 1 vomiting (acción). 2 vomit (resultado).
vomitona *s.f.* 1 bad sick turn. 2 to throw up (echar una).
voracidad *s.f.* voracity, voraciousness.
voraz *adj.* 1 voracious, greedy. 2 raging (llamas).
vosotros *pron.pers.pl.* 1 you. || *pron.r.pl.* 2 yourselves.
votación *s.f.* 1 voting (acción), vote. 2 ballot (de desempate).
votante *adj.* 1 voting. || *s.m.* y *f.* 2 voter.
votar *v.t.* 1 to vote. 2 (fig.) to curse, to swear (blasfemar).
voto *s.m.* 1 vote. 2 vow (promesa). 3 (vulg.) swearword, curse, oath. || 4 **derecho a –,** right to vote. 5 **no tener ni voz ni –,** to have no say in the matter. 6 **por mayoría de votos,** by a majority vote. 7 **– de censura,** vote of censure. 8 **– de confianza,** confidence vote. 9 **votos emitidos,** votes cast. 10 **votos indecisos,** floating votes.
voz *s.f.* 1 voice. 2 word (palabra). 3 MUS. tone, sound, note. 4 shout, yell (alta). 5 call (cartas). 6 (fig.) rumour. 7 MIL. order, command. || 8 **a – en grito,** at the top of one's voice. 9 **llevar la – cantante,** to rule roost. 10 **pedir a voces,** to cry out.
vozarrón, -ona *s.m.* y *f.* loud voice, powerful voice.
vuelco *s.m.* 1 overturn. 2 upset. 3 (fig.) collapse, ruin.
vuelo *s.m.* 1 flight (aparato). 2 wing, flight feathers (aves). 3 loose part, fright (costura). 4 ARQ. projection. 5 BOT. timber, woodland. 6 (fig.) ambitious. 7 gliding (vuelo planeado).
vuelta *s.f.* 1 walk, stroll (paseo). 2 turn (giro). 3 ASTR. revolution. 4 return (retorno). 5 bend, turn (recodo). 6 turn up (de un pantalón). 7 row (de un collar). 8 DEP. lap. 9 ARQ. vault. 10 (fig.) change (cambio). 11 round (elecciones). 12 reverse (el otro lado). 13 strip, facing (costura). 14 (fam.) beating.
vulcanizar *v.t.* to vulcanize.
vulgar *adj.* 1 common, general, ordinary. 2 (desp.) vulgar.
vulgaridad *s.f.* 1 triviality, banality. 2 ordinariness. || 3 **decir vulgaridades,** bad language.
vulgarismo *s.m.* vulgarism (expresión popular).
vulgarizar *v.t.* 1 to vulgarize (hacer vulgar). 2 to popularize (popularizar). 3 (fig.) to extend (difundir).
vulgo *s.m.* 1 common people. 2 masses. 3 vulgus (pueblo).
vulnerable *adj.* vulnerable.
vulnerar *v.t.* 1 to injure, to wound (herir). 2 to violate (ley, tratado).
vulva *s.f.* ANAT. vulva.

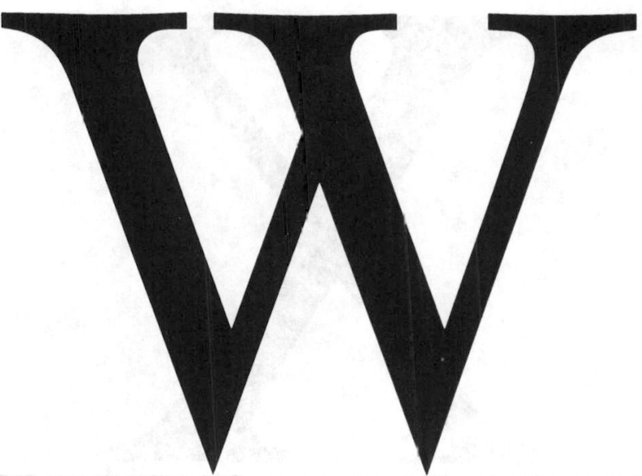

w, W *s.f.* **1** w, W (vigésimotercera letra del alfabeto español). || *abreviatura* **2** watio. **3** voltio.

wagneriano, -a *adj./s.m.* y *f.* wagnerian (amante o relativo a la música de Wagner).

wahabita *adj.* wahhabi, wahabi (seguidores de Mohamed Abdul Mahab, reformador islamita).

walkiria *s.f.* Walkyrie (divinidad escandinava).

walki-talki *s.m.* walkie-talkie.

wáter *s.m.* **1** lavatory, toilet. **2** water closet (taza).

welter *s.m.* welterweight (boxeo).

watio *s.m.* watt.

western *s.m.* western (género cinematográfico).

whisky o **güisky** *s.m.* whisky.

winchester *s.m.* winchester (fusil).

wolframio *s.m.* MIN. wolfram.

x, X *s.f.* **1** x, X (vigesimoséptima letra del alfabeto español). || **2 rayos X,** MED. X rays.
OBS. el signo **x** representa una incógnita: *un número x de cosas = x number of things.*
xantofila *s.f.* BOT. xanthophyll.
xenón *s.m.* QUIM. xenon.
xenofobia *s.f.* xenophobia.
xenófobo, -a *adj.* **1** xenophobic. || *s.m.* y *f.* **2** xenophobe.
xerocopia *s.f.* xerox.
xerocopiar *v.t.* to xerox.
xerófilo, -a *adj.* BIOL. xerophilous.
xerografía *s.f.* xerography, xerox copy.
xerografiar *v.t.* to xerox.
xilófono *s.m.* MUS. xylophone.
xilografía *s.f.* ART. **1** xylography, wood engraving. **2** xylograph.
xilográfico, -a *adj.* ART. xylographic, xylographical.
xilógrafo, -a *s.m.* y *f.* ART. xylographer, wood engraver.

y, Y *s.f.* 1 y, Y (vigésimoctava letra del alfabeto español). || *conj.* 2 and: *en blanco y negro = in black and white.*
ya *adv.* 1 already: *ya lo acabaron = they have already finished it.* 2 now: *ya son las tres = it's three o'clock now.* 3 soon, presently. 4 finally (por fin). || **5 — lo creo,** of course; I should say so. **6 — no,** no longer, not any more. **7 — que,** since, as (puesto que). **8 — se ve,** that's obvious. **9 — veremos,** well see. **10 ¡— voy!,** I'm coming!
yaacabó *s.m.* ZOOL. insectivorous bird.
yacaré *s.m.* ZOOL. (Am.) alligator.
yacente *adj.* 1 lying (tendido, echado). 2 recumbent (estatua).
yacer *v.i.* 1 to lie (en la tumba). 2 to be lying down (estar echado). 3 to lie, to be situated (en un lugar). || **4 aquí yace,** there lies (en una tumba).
yacija *s.f.* 1 makeshift bed. 2 grave, tomb.
yacimiento *s.m.* 1 GEOL. bed (de un mineral). || **2 — de petróleo,** oil field.
yaguar V. **jaguar.**
yak *s.m.* ZOOL. yak.
yámbico, -a *adj.* LIT. iambic.
yambo *s.m.* 1 LIT. iamb, iambic, iambus. 2 BOT. jambo.
yanki *adj./s.m.* y *f.* (fam.) yankee, North American.
yantar *v.i.* (arc.) 1 to eat. || *s.m.* 2 food, meal (manjar).
yarabí *s.m.* (Am.) Indian song.
yarará *s.f.* ZOOL. (Am.) poisonous snake.
yarda *s.f.* yard.
yate *s.m.* MAR. yatch.
yayo, -a *s.m.* y *f.* (fam.) grandpa (abuelito); grandma (abuelita).
yedra *s.f.* BOT. ivy.
yegua *s.f.* 1 ZOOL. mare. 2 (Am.) butt (colilla de cigarro). || **3 — de cría,** ZOOL. stud mare.
yeguada *s.f.* 1 herd of mares. || 2 (Am.) act of folly (disparate).
yeguar *s.m.* herd of mares.
yelmo *s.m.* helmet.
yema *s.f.* yolk (de huevo). 2 BOT. bud, shoot (brote). 3 (fig.) the cream, the best part. 4 GAST. sweet made of egg yolk. 5 fingertip (de los dedos).
yerba V. **hierba.**
yermo, -a *adj.* 1 uninhabited, desert, waste. 2 sterile, uncultivated. || *s.m.* 3 desert, wilderness; wasteland.
yerno *s.m.* son-in-law.
yerro *s.m.* fault, error, mistake.
yerto, -a *adj.* stiff, rigid (tieso, rígido).
yesal *s.m.* gypsum pit.
yesar V. **yesal.**
yesca *s.f.* 1 tinder. 2 (fig.) fuel, incentive (de pasión). || **3 estar hecho una —,** (Am.) to be very angry. **4 yescas,** tinder gox.
yesería *s.f.* gypsum kiln.
yesero, -a *adj.* 1 plaster. || *s.m.* 2 plasterer. || *s.f.* 3 gypsum pit (yesal).
yeso *s.m.* 1 GEOL. gypsum. 2 plaster (para paredes, etc.). 3 MED. cast, plaster (para miembros rotos, etc.). 4 chalk (polvo). 5 plaster cast (escultura). || **6 — mate,** plaster of Paris.
yesoso, -a *adj.* 1 gypseous. 2 chalky.
yip V. **jeep.**
yo *pron.pers.* 1 I. || **2 el —,** FIL. the self, the I, the ego. **3 soy —,** (fam.) it's me.
yod *s.f.* FILOL. yod.
yodado, -a *adj.* iodized.
yodo *s.m.* QUIM. iodine.
yoduro *s.m.* QUIM. iodide.
yoga *s.m.* FIL. yoga.
yogui *s.m.* FIL. yogi.
yogur *s.m.* GAST. yogurt, yoghurt, yoghourt.
yola *s.f.* MAR. yawl; sailing-boat.
yóquei (también **yoqui**) *s.m.* DEP. jockey.
yoyó *s.m.* yo-yo.
yuca *s.f.* BOT. yucca.
yudo (también **judo**) *s.m.* DEP. judo.
yudoca *s.m.* DEP. judoka.
yugada *s.f.* 1 AGR. yoke of land. 2 yoke of oxen (yunta de bueyes).
yugo *s.m.* 1 yoke (de animales, de campana). 2 marriage tie (en una ceremonia nupcial). 3 (fig.) bondage, slavery. 4 MAR. transom.
yugoeslavo, -a (también **yugoslavo, -a**) *adj./s.m.* y *f.* Jugoslavian, Yugoslavian, Yugoslav, Jugoslav.
yugular *adj.* y *s.f.* 1 ANAT. jugular. || *v.t.* 2 (fig.) to nip in the bud.
yunque *s.m.* 1 anvil. 2 ANAT. incus, anvil. 3 (fig.) tireless worker.
yunta *s.f.* 1 yoke of oxen. 2 AGR. yoke of land (yugada). 3 pair, couple (de animales de tiro).
yute *s.m.* jute (textil).
yuxtaponer *v.t.* y *pron.* to juxtapose.
yuxtaposición *s.f.* juxtaposition.
yuxtapuesto, -a *adj.* juxtaposed.
yuyo *s.m.* (Am.) 1 weed, wild grass. || **2 volverse —,** to faint.

z, Z *s.f.* z, Z, (vigesimonovena letra del alfabeto español).
zabordar *v.i.* MAR. to run aground, to be stranded.
zacatal *s.m.* pasture.
zacate *s.m.* fodder, hay.
zacatear *v.t.* **1** to beat. || *v.i.* **2** to graze.
zacatín *s.m.* clothing quarter of a town.
zafacoca *s.f.* (Am.) row, squabble quarrel.
zafado *adj.* **1** (Am.) brazen, shameless, cheeky, impudent. **2** dislocated (hueso).
zafadura *s.f.* dislocation, sprain.
zafaduría *s.f.* effrontery, shamelessness, cheek, insolence.
zafar *v.t.* **1** (superficie, etc.) to clear, to free. **2** to undo, to untie, to unfasten. **3** to decorate. || *v.i.* **4** (Am.) to leave, to go away. || *v.r.* **5** to escape, to run away, to slip away. **6** (fig.) to get away, to shake off: *zafarse de una persona = to shake someone off.* **7** (fig.) to evade, to get out (of): *zafarse de una situación delicada = to get out of a delicate situation.* **8** (Am.) to be dislocated (hueso).
zafarrancho *s.m.* **1** MAR. clearing for action. **2** (fam.) quarrel, row. **3** (fig.) havoc, muddle, mess. || **4 armar un –,** to cause havoc, to kick up a rumpus, to make a terrible mess: *el ataque del enemigo armó un zafarrancho = the enemy attack wrought havoc.* **5 – de combate,** call to action stations.
zafio *adj.* coarse, rude, uncouth.
zafiro *s.m.* sapphire.
zafo *adj.* **1** MAR. free and clear, unobstructed. **2** unharmed, undamaged, unscathed: *salir zafo de = to come unscathed out of.* **3** (Am.) free, disentangled. || *prep.* **4** (Am.) except (for).
zafón *s.m.* slip, mistake, error.
zafra *s.f.* **1** oil jar, oil container. **2** (Am.) AGR. sugar harves, sugar making.
zaga *s.f.* **1** rear. || **2 a la –, a –, en –,** at the rear, in the rear. **3 no irle a la – de nadie,** to be second to none. **4 no irle a uno a la –,** to be every bit as good as someone. **5 no quedarse a la –,** not to be outdone.
zagal *s.m.* **1** boy, lad, youth. **2** shepherd boy.
zagala *s.f.* **1** girl, lass. **2** shepherdess.
zaguán *s.m.* hall, entrance, hallway, vestibule.
zaguero *adj.* **1** rear, back, trailing. **2** (fig.) slow, laggard, lagging behind. **3** overloaded in the rear. || *s.m.* **4** DEP. back, full-back (en fútbol).
zahareño *adj.* wild, disdainful, unsociable.
zaheridor *adj.* **1** upbraiding. **2** scoffing, mocking.
zaherimiento *s.m.* sarcastic criticism; mortification; reprimand, upbraiding, reproach; mockery.
zaherir *v.t.* to criticise sharply/sarcastically, to attack; to wound, to shame, to hurt someone's feelings; to upbraid, to reproach: *zaherir a uno con algo = to reproach someone for something.*
zahína *s.f.* sorghum.
zahinar *s.m.* sorghum field.
zahón *s.m.* (generalmente *pl.*) breeches, chaps.
zahondar *v.t.* **1** to deepen, to dig. || *v.i.* **2** to sink into the ground (los pies).
zahorí *s.m.* **1** seer, soothsayer, clairvoyant. **2** water diviner. **3** (fig.) highly perceptive person, mind reader, very observant person.
zahúrda *s.f.* **1** (EE.UU.) pigsty, pigpen. **2** (fig.) hovel, pigsty.
zahorra *s.f.* (fam.) din, commotion, hullabaloo.
zaida *s.f.* type of heron.
zaino *adj.* **1** false, treacherous, deceitful. || **2 un caballo –,** a chestnut horse. **3 un toro –,** a pure black bull.
zalamerear *v.i.* to flatter, to cajole, to wheedle.
zalamería *s.f.* flattery, cajoling, wheedling, coaxing by flattery.
zalamero, -a *adj.* **1** flattering, cajoling, wheedling; suave. || *s.m.* y *f.* **2** flatterer, wheedler; suave person; cajoler.
zalema *s.f.* **1** deep bow, salaam. **2** coaxing by flattery. || *pl.* **3** (desp.) bowing and scraping, flattering courtesies.
zalenquear *v.i.* to limp, to hobble.
zamarra *s.f.* **1** sheepskin jacket. **2** sheepskin.
zamarrear *v.t.* **1** to shake, to worry (perro). **2** (fam.) to knock about, to push about, to shove around. **3** (fam.) to sit on, to squash.
zamarreo *s.m.* **1** shaking, shake, dragging about. **2** (fam.) rough treatment.
zamarrilla *s.f.* BOT. mountain germander.
zamarro *s.m.* **1** sheepskin jacket. **2** sheepskin. **3** stupid person, yokel. || *pl.* **4** (Am.) riding breeches, chaps.
zamba *s.f.* **1** samba. **2** knock-kneed woman.
zambo *adj.* **1** knock-kneed. **2** half-breed, mulatto. || *s.m.* **3** knock-kneed man. **4** ZOOL. spider monkey.
zambomba *s.f.* type of drum.
zambombazo *s.m.* **1** explosion, bang. **2** punch, blow, thump (al cuerpo).
zambra *s.f.* **1** gypsy dance. **2** noise, commotion, uproar, rumpus.
zambucar *v.t.* **1** to hide away. **2** to jumble up.
zambuco *s.m.* hiding, concealing.
zambullida *s.f.* dive, plunge; dip; ducking: *darse una zambullida = to dive into the water.*
zambullidor, -ora *s.m.* y *f.* diver.
zambullidura *s.f.* dive, plunge.
zambullimiento *s.m.* dive, plunge.
zambullir *v.t.* **1** to dip, to plunge give a ducking. || *v.r.* **2** to dive, to plunge, to take a dive. **3** to get involved. **4** to hide.
zampabollos *s.m.* y *f.* **1** glutton, greedy pig. **2** stupid person, clot, nitwit.
zampar *v.t.* **1** to gobble, to wolf down (comida). **2** to put away hurriedly. **3** to

hurl, to throw, to dash. **4** to deal (un golpe). || *v.r.* **5 zamparse en,** to dart into, to whip into, to shoot into.
zampón *adj.* greedy.
zampoña *s.f.* **1** panpipe, rustic flute. **2** stupid remark.
zampullín *s.m.* grebe.
zanahoria *s.f.* **1** carrot. || *s.m.* **2** (Am.) errand boy. **3** (Am.) halfwit; clumsy person.
zanca *s.f.* **1** leg. **2** shank. **3** ARQ. string-piece (de una escalera); leg (de un andamio). **4 por zancas o por barrancas,** by hook or by crook.
zancada *s.f.* **1** stride: *a grandes zancadas = with long strides.* **2** (fig.) **en dos zancadas,** in a couple of ticks, quickly.
zancadilla *s.f.* **1** trip. **2** ruse, trick. **3** booby trap, snare. || **4 echar la — a uno,** to trip someone up.
zancadillear *v.t.* **1** to trip up, to make (someone) trip (físicamente). **2** (fig.) to lay a trap for.
zancajo *s.m.* **1** heel. **2** leg bone.
zancajoso *adj.* **1** bandy-legged. **2** big-heeled. **3** with a hole in the heel of one's stocks (tights, etc.).
zancarrón *s.m.* **1** leg bone. **2** old bag of bones. **3** poor teacher.
zanco *s.m.* **1** stilt. || **2 estar en zancos,** to be well up, to be in a good position.
zancudo *adj.* **1** long-legged, lanky. **2** ZOOL. wading: *ave zancuda = wading bird/wader.* || *s.m.* **3** long-legged person (bird, etc.). **4** (Am.) mosquito.
zanganear *v.t.* **1** to idle, to loaf, to fool around, to waste one's time. **2** to make stupid comments.
zanganería *s.f.* **1** (fam.) fooling around. **2** idleness.
zángano *s.m.* **1** ZOOL. drone. **2** (fig.) lazy bones, idler, slacker, drone. **3** boor.
zangolotear *v.t.* **1** to fiddle with, keep playing with; to shake. || *v.i.* y *r.* **2** to rattle, shake (puerta, ventana, etc.). **3** to fidget; to fuss around (persona).
zangoloteo *s.m.* fiddling; shaking, jiggling; fidgeting; rattling.
zangolotino *adj.* **niño —,** older boy with a childish appearance; (desp.) weedy youth; (desp.) overgrown baby.
zanja *s.f.* **1** ditch; drainage channel; trench; pit; grave. **2** (Am.) gully, water-course.
zanjar *v.t.* **1** to settle, to clear up; to conclude. **2** to excavate; to dig trenches in.
zanquear *v.t.* **1** (Am.) to hunt for. || *v.i.* **2** to waddle, to walk awkwardly about; to stride along, to walk fast; (fig.) to rush about, to bustle about.
zapa *s.f.* **1** spade. **2** MIL. trench, sap: *caminar a la zapa = to advance by trench.*
zapador *s.m.* sapper.
zapapico *s.m.* pick, pickaxe.
zapata *s.f.* **1** half boot. **2** MEC., MAR. (de un freno) shoe.
zapatazo *s.m.* **1** blow with a shoe; thud; bump; bang. **2** MAR. violent flapping of a sail. || **3 tratar a uno a zapatazos,** to treat someone uncivilly.
zapateado *s.m.* tap-dance.
zapateador, -ora *s.m.* y *f.* tap-dancer.
zapatear *v.t.* **1** to tap with one's foot. **2** to kick, to prod with one's foot. **3** to ill-treat, to treat roughly. || *v.i.* **4** (baile) to stamp one's feet, to tap one's feet. || *v.r.* **5** (fam.) to get rid of, to polish off. || **6 saber zapatearlas,** (fam.) to know how to look after oneself.
zapateo *s.m.* **1** tapping, stamping with the feet (baile). **2** tap-dance.
zapatería *s.f.* **1** shoe shop, (EE.UU.) shoe store. **2** shoe factory, footwear factory. **3** shoemaking.
zapatero *adj.* **1** hard, undercooked, underdone: *zanahorias zapateras = undercooked carrots.* **2** tough: *filete zapatero = tough steak.* || *s.m.* **3** shoemaker. **4** shoe seller, shoe dealer. || **5 ¡— a tus zapatos!,** mind your own business. **6 — remendón,** cobbler.
zapateta *s.f.* jump with a slap on one's shoe (at the same time).
zapatiesta *s.f.* quarrel, disturbance, (fam.) rumpus: *armar una zapatiesta = to kick up a rumpus.*
zapatilla *s.f.* **1** slipper. **2** pump, plimsoll. **3** shoe: *zapatilla de baile = dancing shoe; zapatilla de deporte = sports shoe, training shoe.* **4** MEC. washer, gasket.
zapato *s.m.* **1** shoe: *zapatos de tacón = high-heeled shoes.* **2 estar como tres en un —,** to be packed in like sardines. **3 meter a uno en un —,** to bring someone to heel. **4 saber dónde aprieta el —,** to know where the shoe pinches, know where one's weakness lies.
zapear *v.t.* (Am.) to spy on, watch.
zaporro *s.m.* (Am.) dwarf, runt.
zapote *s.m.* **1** BOT. sapodilla. **2** sapodilla plum, naseberry, sapota (tipo de fruta).
zaque *s.m.* **1** small wineskin. **2** boozer, tippler, old soak.
zar *s.m.* czar, tzar, tsar.
zarabanda *s.f.* **1** MUS. sarabande. **2** (fig.) whirl, turmoil, confused movement, rush.
zaragata *s.f.* **1** rumpus, row, squabble, set-to. **2** bustle, turmoil, (fam.) hullabaloo. || **3 zaragatas,** (Am.) cajolery, wheedling.
zaragatero, -a *adj.* **1** rowdy, noisy. **2** quarrelsome, trouble making. || *s.m.* y *f.* **3** rowdy person, hooligan, trouble maker.
zaragüelles *s.m.pl.* **1** wide legged overalls. **2** large breeches.
zaranda *s.f.* **1** sieve. **2** (Am.) cruet.
zarandajas *s.f.pl.* (fam.) odds and ends, trifles.
zarandar *v.t.* **1** to sieve, sift. **2** (fam.) to shake vigorously. **3** (fam.) to jostle, shove. **4** to push, swing. || *v.r.* **5** to strut, swagger.
zarazas *s.f.pl.* poison (for killing animals).
zarazo, -a *adj.* (Am.) underripe (fruit).
zarcillo *s.m.* **1** earring. **2** BOT. runner, tendril.
zarco, -a *adj.* light blue (ojos).
zarevitz *s.m.* czarevitch, tzarevitch.
zarina *s.f.* czarina, tzarina.
zarpa *s.f.* **1** claw, paw. **2** mud splash.
zarpada *s.f.* clawing, blow with a paw, lash with a claw.
zarpar *v.i.* MAR. to put to sea, set sail, weigh anchor.
zarpazo *s.m.* blow with a paw, clawing, lash with a claw.
zarpear *v.i.* spatter, splash with mud.
zarposo, -a *adj.* spattered, splashed with mud.
zarrapastroso, -a *adj.* (fam.) dirty, ragged, shabby.
zarza *s.f.* BOT. blackberry bush, bramble.
zarzal *s.m.* bramble patch, brier patch.
zarzamora *s.f.* BOT. blackberry.
zarzaparrilla *s.f.* sarsaparilla.
zarzuela *s.f.* MUS. light opera, musical comedy, operetta (Spanish).
zarzuelista *s.m.f.* composer, lyricist (of zarzuela).
zas *interj.* bang!, crash!, whack!
zascandil *s.m.* **1** scatterbrain. **2** meddler, busybody.
zascandilear *v.i.* **1** to idle, waste time. **2** to meddle, snoop, pry.
zazoso, -a *adj.* lisping.
zeda *s.f.* name of the letter z.
zedilla *s.f.* cedilla.
zenit *s.m.* zenith.
zepelín *s.m.* Zeppelin.
zeta *s.f.* name of the letter z.
zigzag *s.m.* zigzag.
zigzaguear *v.i.* to zigzag.
zinc *s.m.* zinc.
zíngaro, -a *adj.*/s.m. y *f.* gypsy (húngaro).
zipizape *s.m.* (fam.) row, rumpus, scuffle, set-to.
zócalo *s.m.* **1** ARQ. socle (edificio), plinth (pedestal). **2** skirting board, (EE.UU.) baseboard. **3** (Am.) town square, walk, boulevard. **4** GEOL. insular shelf.
zocato, -a *adj.* **1** left-handed. **2** overripe (fruit, vegetables). || *s.m.* left-handed person, left-hander.
zoco, -a *adj.* **1** left-handed. **2** one-armed, maimed, limbless. || *s.m.* **3** left-handed person, left-hander. **2 —,** fcol. **4** (Am.) punch. || *s.m.* **5** Morrocan market square.
Zodiaco *s.m.* Zodiac.
zollenco, -a *adj.* (Am.) big, tough.
zona *s.f.* **1** zone, area, belt. **2 — catastrófica,** disaster area. **3 — edificada,** built-up area. **4 — fronteriza,** border area. **5 — verde,** green belt. || *s.m.* **6** MED. shingles.
zoncería *s.f.* silliness, stupidity, dullness.
zonzo, -a *adj.* **1** silly, stupid, inane. || *s.m.* y *f.* **2** idiot, dunce, booby, bore.
zoo *s.m.* zoo.
zoófito *s.m.* zoophyte.
zoología *s.f.* zoology.
zoológico *adj.* zoological.
zoólogo, -a *s.m.* y *f.* zoologist.
zopenco, -a *adj.* **1** dull, stupid. || *s.m.* y *f.* **2** (fam.) dunce, blockhead, clot, nitwit.

zopo, -a *adj.* deformed, crippled, maimed (de manos o pies).
zoquete *s.m.* **1** small block, chunk of wood. **2** piece of stale bread. **3** (fam.) dunce, blockhead. **4** (fam.) smack, punch. **5** tubby man.
zorcico *s.m.* Basque folksong and dance.
zorongo *s.m.* **1** Andalusian folksong and dance. **2** kerchief, head scarf (Aragón y Navarra). **3** flat wide bun, chignon.
zorra *s.f.* **1** vixen. **2** (desp.) whore, tart. || **3 no tengo ni — idea,** (vulg.) I haven't got a clue. **4 toda la — noche,** (vulg.) all bloody night.
zorrera *s.f.* **1** foxhole. **2** smoky room. **3** drowsiness, lethargy.
zorrería *s.f.* **1** foxiness, craftiness, cunning, knavery. **2** dirty, sly trick.
zorro *s.m.* **1** fox. **2** (fig.) cunning, sly, astute person; knave. || *pl.* duster (made from strips of cloth).
zorruno, -a *adj.* foxy, fox-like.
zorzal *s.m.* **1** ZOOL. thrush. **2** shrewd, cunning fellow, old fox.
zote *adj.* **1** dull, dim, stupid. || *s.m.* **2** dimwit, dunce.
zozobra *s.f.* **1** MAR. capsizing, sinking. **2** worry, anxiety, uneasiness, anguish. || **3 vivir en una perpetua —,** to live in constant anxiety.
zozobrar *v.i.* **1** MAR. to capsize, overturn, founder, sink. **2** to worry, fret, be anxious, be uneasy. **3** (fig.) to fail, to come to naught, to be ruined (en negocios).
zozobroso, -a *adj.* worried, anxious, uneasy, anguished.
zueco *s.m.* clog, wooden shoe.
zulaque *s.m.* **1** packing stuff. **2** MAR. oakum.
zulo *s.m.* cache.
zulú *adj.*/s.m. y *f.* Zulu.
zulla *s.f.* **1** BOT. French honeysuckle. **2** human excrement.
zullarse *v.r.* **1** to dirty oneself. **2** (fam.) to break wind.
zumaque *s.m.* **1** BOT. sumach tree. **2** (fam.) wine.
zumaya *s.f.* ZOOL. owl, barn owl, goatsucker, nightjar.
zumba *s.f.* **1** (fam.) banter, teasing, raillery. || **2 hacer — a,** to rag, tease. **3** beating.
zumbador *s.m.* **1** buzzer. **2** (Am.) ZOOL. humming bird.
zumbar *v.t.* **1** to tease, rag, to make fun of. **2** to smack, to slap, to hit, to cuff. **3** (Am.) to throw, to toss, (fam.) to chuck. || *v.i.* **4** to buzz, hum, to drone (insectos). **5** to ring: *me zumban los oídos = my ears are ringing.* **6 salir zumbando,** to shoot off, to streak off. **7 zumbarle a uno,** to give someone a beating, to give someone a thrashing.
zumbel *s.m.* cord for spinning tops.
zumbido *s.m.* **1** buzzing, humming, drone (insects). **2** ringing (ears). **3** punch, slap.
zumbón, -ona *adj.* **1** waggish, teasing, bantering. || *s.m.* **2** wag, joker, jester, tease.
zumiento, -a *adj.* juicy, succulent.
zumo *s.m.* **1** juice. **2** profit, gain.
zumoso, -a *adj.* juicy.
zuncho *s.m.* metal band, hoop.
zurcido *s.m.* **1** darning, mending. **2** darn, patch.
zurcidor, -ora *s.m.* y *f.* darner, mender.
zurcir *v.t.* **1** to darn, mend, patch. **2** (fig.) to join together. **3** (fig.) *¡anda que te zurzan! = go jump in the lake!/go to hell!*
zurdear *v.t.* (Am.) to do things with the left hand.
zurdo, -a *adj.* **1** left-handed. || *s.m.* **2** the left hand. **3** left-handed person, left-hander, (fam.) south-paw.
zurdería *s.f.* left-handedness.
zureo *s.m.* coo, billing and cooing.
zurra *s.f.* **1** tanning (de cuero). **2** (fig.) hiding, flogging beating. **3** (fam.) brawl, scuffle.
zurrador *s.m.* tanner.
zurrar *v.t.* **1** to tan (cuero). **2** (fam.) to tan, to give a hiding, to lay into, to wallop, to flog. **3** to criticize. **4** (fam.) to give a tongue lashing. **4** (fam.) to beat, to be frightened, (fam.) to plaster (en una discusión). || *v.r.* to be frightened, to be scared stiff.
zurriago *s.m.* whip, lash.
zurribanda *s.f.* **1** flogging, whipping. **2** noisy scuffle, fight, roughouse.
zurriburri *s.m.* **1** (fam.) worthless individual, ragamuffin, scamp. **2** gang, riffraff, rabble. **3** turmoil, confusion, mix-up, mess.
zurrón *s.m.* provision bag, game-bag.
zutano, -a *s.* so-and-so, a Mr. So-and-So, what's-his-name.

Spanish Grammar

Gramática española

The Article

	Singular		Plural	
	masc.	fem.	masc.	fem.
definite article	**el** caballo the horse	**la** casa the house	**los** caballos the horses	**las** casas the houses
indefinite article	**un** caballo a horse	**una** casa a house	**unos** caballos (some) horses	**unas** casas (some) houses

The article **el** combines with the prepositions **de** and **a** to form **al** and **del**:

Voy al teatro. I'm going to the theater.
Vengo del cine. I'm coming from the cinema.

The definite articles **el** or **la** precede **señor** and **señora: el señor Gómez** (Mr. Gómez). They are omitted in forms of address: **Buenas tardes, señora Martínez** (Good evening, Mrs. Martínez).

The words **otro** and **medio** do not take an article. **Quisiera otro vaso de vino** (I would like another glass of wine). **Quisiera medio kilo de pan** (I would like half a kilo of bread).

THE NOUN

All nouns ending in **-ción** and **-dad** as well as most nouns ending in **-a** are feminine. Most nouns ending in **-o** are masculine. Exceptions: **la mano** the hand; **la radio** the radio; **la foto** the photo; **el mapa** the map, and others.

Plurals are formed by adding **-s**. Plurals of words ending in consonants are usually formed by adding **-es**.

	Singular	Plural
masc.	**el** libro the book **el** tren the train	**los** libros the books **los** trenes the trains
fem.	**la** cama the bed **la** pared the wall	**las** camas the beds **las** paredes the walls

Words ending in **-s** in the singular do not change in the plural: **el paraguas** the umbrella, **los paraguas** the umbrellas.

Masculine and feminine designations for the professions are usually distinguished by the article: **el dentista** the (male) dentist, **la dentista** the (female) dentist. Feminine nouns with a stressed **a** at the beginning of the word take the masculine article **el** in the singular: **el agua** the water, **las aguas** the waters.

ADJECTIVES AND ADVERBS

Adjectives

Adjectives agree in number and gender with their nouns.

Most masculine adjectives end in **-o** and take the **-a** ending when used with a feminine noun: **pequeño – pequeña** small. When an adjective ends in **-án, – ón** or **-or** or refers to a nationality, the **-a** is added to that ending: **español – española** Spanish. For other adjectives ending in consonants, the masculine and feminine forms are the same: **difícil** difficult, **feliz** happy.

The plural is formed by adding **-s**; when the word ends in a consonant, **-es** is added.

	Singular	Plural
masc.	**el** caballo pequeño the small horse	**los** caball**os** pequeñ**os** the small horses
fem.	**la** cama pequeña the small bed	**las** cam**as** pequeñ**as** the small beds

Usually, adjectives follow the nouns they modify; **el restaurante francés** the French restaurant, **la ciudad española** the Spanish city.

Note: **Bueno** good and **malo** bad become **buen** and **mal** before a masculine singular noun: **un buen/mal restaurante** a good/bad restaurant. **Grande** big becomes **gran** before a singular noun: **una gran ciudad** a big city.

Adverbs

Adverbs are formed by adding **-mente** to the feminine form of the adjective: **rápido** → **rápida** → **rápidamente** quickly; **claro** → **clara** → **claramente** clearly.

Sale rápidamente del metro. He leaves the subway quickly.

Other adverbs are not derived from adjectives: **ahora** now, **aquí** here, **allí** there, **poco** a little, **bastante** enough.

Comparatives and Superlatives

The comparatives of adjectives and adverbs are formed by **más**; the superlatives are formed by **más** and the definite article:

bonito pretty	→ **más bonito** prettier	→ **el más bonito** the prettiest
caro expensive	→ **más caro** more expensive	→ **el más caro** most expensive

Este bolso es más bonito que el otro.
This bag is prettier than the other one.

Esta bicicleta es la más cara.
This bicycle is the most expensive.

Note: In the case of adverbs use **lo: lo más rápidamente posible** as quickly as possible.

The English "very" is expressed in Spanish by the suffix **-ísimo** for masculine adjectives and **-ísima** for feminina adjectives:

caro expensive → **carísimo** very expensive
grande big → **grandísimo** very big

In addition, the word **muy** very can also be used: **muy grande** very big.

The most important irregular comparatives and superlatives are:

bueno good → **mejor** better → **el mejor** the best
malo bad → **peor** worse → **el peor** the worst
grande big → **mayor** bigger, older → **el mayor** the biggest, the oldest
pequeño small → **menor** smaller, younger → **el menor** the smallest, the youngest

PRONOUNS

Personal Pronouns

	Subject		Direct Object		Indirect Object	
Sing.	**yo**	I	**me**	me	**me**	to me
	tú	you	**te**	you	**te**	to you
	él	he	**lo, le***	him, it	**le**	to him, to her
	ella	she	**la**	her, it		to you, to it
	usted	you	**le, la, lo**	you		
Plural	**nosotros**	we	**nos**	us	**nos**	to us
	vosotros	you	**os**	you	**os**	to you
	ellos	they (*m.*)	**los, les***	them	**les**	to them, to you
	ellas	they (*f.*)	**las**	them (*f.*)		
	ustedes	you	**los, les*, las**	you		

* In some regions you will hear **lo** and in others **le** but you will be understood with both forms.

When you speak to one person, use **usted** you (singular) and when you speak to two or more people use **ustedes** you (plural).

The subject pronouns are used for emphasis; the ending of the verbs indicate the person you are talking to or about.

Reflexive Pronouns

Singular	Plural
me myself	**nos** ourselves
te yourself	**os** yourselves
se himself, herself, yourself, itself	**se** themselves, yourselves

The reflexive pronoun may serve as either the direct or the indirect object of a verb. The reflexive **se** form is often used to express the English passive: **En España se cena más tarde que en Estados Unidos.** In Spain, dinner is eaten later than in the United States.

Possessive Pronouns

Singular				Plural			
masc.		fem.		masc.		fem.	
mi			my	**mis**			my
tu			your	**tus**			your
su			his, her, its	**sus**			their
nuestro	our	**nuestra**	our	**nuestros**	our	**nuestras**	our
vuestro	your	**vuestra**	your	**vuestros**	your	**vuestras**	your
su			their, your	**sus**			their, your

In the first and second persons of the singular and plural, the possessive adjectives agree with their nouns: **nuestro hermano** our brother; **nuestra hermana** our sister.

For the other persons, the form of the personal pronoun does not change: **mi casa** my house; **mi pueblo** my village.

Demonstratives

	este this (near me) masc.	 fem.	ese that (near you) masc.	 fem.	aquel that (over there) masc.	 fem.
Singular	**este**	**esta**	**ese**	**esa**	**aquel**	**aquella**
Plural	**estos**	**estas**	**esas**	**esas**	**aquellos**	**aquellas**

The neuter demonstratives **estos, eso,** and **aquello** refer to a whole idea rather than to a specific noun: **Esto es lo que quiero.** That (in general) is what I want; **¡Eso es!** That's it!

Demonstrative pronouns are formed by placing a written accent on the stressed vowel of the demonstrative adjective. Thus, when **este, ese** and **aquel** are used without a noun, they are accented on the first **e**: **Quisiera comprar este libro**, I would like to buy this book; **¿Cuál, éste?** Which one? This one?

Placement of Pronouns

Object pronouns are placed before the entire verb form. The indirect object pronouns stand before the direct pronouns: **Me lo compro** I'll buy it.

When the verb is a present participle or an infinitive, the direct and indirect object pronouns may be placed either before the verb or attached to the end of the verb: **Quiero comprármelo** I want to buy it.

VERBS

Present Tense

Spanish has three regular conjugations ending in **-ar, -er** and **-ir.**

	viajar to travel	**comer** to eat	**vivir** to live
yo	**viajo**	**como**	**vivo**
tú	**viajas**	**comes**	**vives**
él, ella, usted	**viaja**	**come**	**vive**
nosotros, nosotras	**viajamos**	**comemos**	**vivimos**
vosotros, vosotras	**viajáis**	**coméis**	**vivís**
ellos, ellas, ustedes	**viajan**	**comen**	**viven**

In addition, some Spanish verbs are irregular:

1. Radical Changing Verbs

Some verbs change the vowel of the root form in the singular and in the 3rd person of the plural:

e → ie **entender** to understand	**o → ue** **contar** to tell	**u → ue** **jugar** to play	**e → i** **pedir** to ask
entiendo	**cuento**	**juego**	**pido**
entiendes	**cuentas**	**juegas**	**pides**
entiende	**cuenta**	**juega**	**pide**
entendemos	**contamos**	**jugamos**	**pedimos**
entendéis	**contáis**	**jugáis**	**pedís**
entienden	**cuentan**	**juegan**	**piden**

2. Consonant Changing Verbs

Verbs ending in **-ecer, -ocer** or **-ucir** change the **c** to **zc** in the 1st person singular: **conocer** to know **(yo) conozco, (tú) conoces, (él) conoce** etc.

Some verbs add a **g** in the first person singular: **hacer** to make **(yo) hago, (tú) haces, (él) hace** etc.

3. Verbs with Two Changes

tener to have	**decir** to say	**venir** to come	**oír** to hear
tengo	**digo**	**vengo**	**oigo**
tienes	**dices**	**vienes**	**oyes**
tiene	**dice**	**viene**	**oye**
tenemos	**decimos**	**venimos**	**oímos**
tenéis	**decís**	**venís**	**oís**
tienen	**dicen**	**vienen**	**oyen**

4. Other Irregular Verbs

Some important verbs have an irregular 1st person singular:

dar to give → **(yo) doy**
saber to know → **(yo) sé**
ver to see → **(yo) veo**

5. **Ser, estar** and **ir**

ser to be	**estar** to be	**ir** to go
soy	**estoy**	**voy**
eres	**estás**	**vas**
es	**está**	**va**
somos	**estamos**	**vamos**
sois	**estáis**	**vais**
son	**están**	**van**

On the difference between **ser** and **estar** see below.

Past Tenses

The most important past tenses are the preterite, the imperfect and the present perfect.

The preterite is used with **ayer** yesterday, **el otro día** the other day, **la semana pasada** last week, **el año pasado** last year etc. The preterite records events as completed units in the past: **Anoche fuimos al cine** Last night we went to the movies.

The imperfect relives an action or state as it was taking place in the past. **El hotel era muy barato y teníamos el mar cerca** The hotel was very cheap and the ocean was nearby.

The perfect is used with **hoy** today, **esta mañana** this morning etc.

	Preterite	
viajar to travel	**comer** to eat	**vivir** to live
viajé	**comí**	**viví**
viajaste	**comiste**	**viviste**
viajó	**comió**	**vivió**
viajamos	**comimos**	**vivimos**
viajasteis	**comisteis**	**vivisteis**
viajaron	**comieron**	**vivieron**

The following verbs have irregular forms:

ser to be	**estar** to be	**hacer** to make
fui	**estuve**	**hice**
fuiste	**estuviste**	**hiciste**
fue	**estuvo**	**hizo**
fuimos	**estuvimos**	**hicimos**
fuisteis	**estuvisteis**	**hicisteis**
fueron	**estuvieron**	**hicieron**

The following verbs have the same endings as **estar:**

decir → **dije** I said
tener → **tuve** I had
poder → **pude** I could
venir → **vine** I came
querer → **quise** I wanted

Perfect

It is formed by the present indicative of **haber** plus the past participle of the main verb. The participle is formed by adding **-ado** (for **-ar** verbs) and **-ido** (for **-er** and **-ir** verbs) to the root. Its use corresponds to the present perfect in English: **Lo he oído muchas veces** I have heard it many times.

The present tense of **haber** is: **he, has, ha, hemos, habéis, han.**

viajar → **he viajado** I have traveled
comer → **he comido** I have eaten
vivir → **he vivido** I have lived

Some irregular participles of important verbs are:

abrir → **abierto** opened
escribir → **escrito** written
decir → **dicho** said
hacer → **hecho** made
poner → **puesto** put
ver → **visto** seen
volver → **vuelto** returned

Imperfect

viajar to travel	**comer** to eat	**vivir** to live
viajaba	**comía**	**vivía**
viajabas	**comías**	**vivías**
viajaba	**comía**	**vivía**
viajábamos	**comíamos**	**vivíamos**
viajabais	**comíais**	**vivíais**
viajaban	**comían**	**vivían**

Almost all verbs are regular in the imperfect tense, with the exception of **ser** and **ir:**

ser to be	**ir** to go
era	**iba**
eras	**ibas**
era	**iba**
éramos	**íbamos**
erais	**ibais**
eran	**iban**

The Future Tense

The future is formed by adding an ending to the infinitive of the verb. The endings for all three conjugations are: **-é, -ás, -á, -emos, -éis, án,** therefore: **viajaré** I will travel, **viajarás** you will travel **etc.**

A few irregular verbs change their roots in the future:

tener → **tendré** I will have
hacer → **haré** I will make
poder → **podré** I will be able to
querer → **querré** I will like
venir → **vendré** I will come

The endings are the same as for the regular verbs.

The future can also be conveyed by the present tense of **ir** + **a** + verb, equivalent to the English "going to": **Voy a comprar pan** I am going to buy bread.

The Conditional

The conditional is often used as a polite form: **¿Podría ayudarme?** Could you help me?

It is formed like the future with infinitive + ending. The endings for all three conjugations are: **-ía, -ías, -ía, -íamos, -íais, -ían**; therefore: **viajaría** I would travel, **viajarías** you would travel, etc.

The root changes of some irregular verbs are the same as in the future.

Ser and Estar

Ser refers to

Origin	**Soy español.** I am Spanish.
Profession	**Es mecánico.** He is a mechanic.
Relationship	**Es mi padre.** He is my father.
Time and Day	**Son las cuatro.** It is four o'clock.
	Hoy es martes. Today is Tuesday.
Essential Qualities	**Juana es alta.** Juana is tall.
Possession	**Éste es mi libro.** This is my book.
Material	**El pantalón es de algodón.** The pants are cotton.

Estar refers to

Location	**Madrid está en España.** Madrid is in Spain.
Temporary Conditions	**Está enfadada.** She is angry.
	Estoy enfermo. I am sick.

NEGATION

no, not: **no**
Ésta no es mi maleta. This is not my suitcase.
nothing, not at all, anything (in negative sentence): **nada**
No entiendo nada. I don't understand anything.

nobody, anybody (in negative sentence): **nadie**
No he visto a nadie. I have not seen anybody.
Nadie sabe dónde está mi maleta. Nobody knows where my suitcase is.
never: **nunca**
No va nunca a comprar. He/She never goes shopping.

INTERROGATIVES

When?	**¿cuándo?**	**¿Cuándo se van del hotel?** When are they leaving the hotel?
Why?	**¿por qué?**	**¿Por qué no va usted en taxi?** Why don't you take a taxi?
What?	**¿qué?**	**¿Qué dices?** What are you saying?
Which?	**¿cuál?**	**¿Cuál es el camino más corto?** Which is the shortest route?
Whose?	**¿de quién?**	**¿De quién es el coche rojo?** Whose car is the red one?
Who?	**¿quién?**	**¿Quién es ese hombre?** Who is that man?
How?	**¿cómo?**	**¿Cómo está Ud.?** How are you?
Where?	**¿dónde?**	**¿Dónde está mi abrigo?** Where is my coat?
Where? (direction)	**¿a dónde?**	**¿A dónde vas?** Where are you going?
How many?	**¿cuántos?**	**¿Cuántos hijos tiene Ud.?** How many children do you have?
How much?	**¿cuánto?**	**¿Cuánto tiempo nos queda?** How much time do we have?

Alphabetical List of the Spanish Irregular Verbs

Lista alfabética de los verbos irregulares españoles

Infinitive	Present Indicative 1st person sg.	Present Indicative 1st person pl.	Present Subjunctive	Preterite	Past Participle
acentuar	acentúo	acentuamos	acentúe	acentué	acentuado
agorar	agüero	agoramos	agüere	agoré	agorado
andar	ando	andamos	ande	anduve	andado
caber	quepo	cabemos	quepa	cupe	cabido
caer	caigo	caemos	caiga	caí	caído
coger	cojo	cogemos	coja	cogí	cogido
concluir	concluyo	concluimos	concluya	concluí	concluido
conducir	conduzco	conducimos	conduzca	conduje	conducido
contar	cuento	contamos	cuente	conté	contado
creer	creo	creemos	crea	creí	creído
cruzar	cruzo	cruzamos	cruce	crucé	cruzado
dar	doy	damos	dé	di	dado
decir	digo	decimos	diga	dije	dicho
delinquir	delinco	delinquimos	delinca	delinquí	delinquido
dirigir	dirijo	dirigimos	dirija	dirigí	dirigido
distinguir	distingo	distinguimos	distinga	distinguí	distinguido
dormir	duermo	dormimos	duerma	dormí	dormido
erguir	irgo, yergo	erguimos	irga, yerga	erguí	erguido
errar	yerro	erramos	yerre	erré	errado
esparcir	esparzo	esparcimos	esparza	esparcí	esparcido
estar	estoy	estamos	esté	estuve	estado
evacuar	evacuo	evacuamos	evacue	evacué	evacuado
fraguar	fraguo	fraguamos	fragüe	fragüé	fraguado

Infinitive	Present Indicative 1st person sg.	Present Indicative 1st person pl.	Present Subjunctive	Preterite	Past Participle
gruñir	gruño	gruñimos	gruña	gruñí	gruñido
haber	he	hemos	haya	hube	habido
hacer	hago	hacemos	haga	hice	hecho
ir	voy	vamos	vaya	fui	ido
jugar	juego	jugamos	juege	jugué	jugado
lucir	luzco	lucimos	luzca	lucí	lucido
medir	mido	medimos	mida	medí	medido
merecer	merezco	merecemos	merezca	merecí	merecido
mover	muevo	movemos	mueva	moví	movido
oír	oigo	oímos	oiga	oí	oído
oler	huelo	olemos	huela	olí	olido
pagar	pago	pagamos	pague	pagué	pagado
pensar	pienso	pensamos	piense	pensé	pensado
perder	pierdo	perdemos	pierda	perdí	perdido
poder	puedo	podemos	pueda	pude	podido
poner	pongo	ponemos	ponga	puse	puesto
querer	quiero	queremos	quiera	quise	querido
reír	río	reímos	ría	reí	reído
saber	sé	sabemos	sepa	supe	sabido
salir	salgo	salimos	salga	salí	salido
sentir	siento	sentimos	sienta	sentí	sentido
ser	soy	somos	sea	fui	sido
tañer	taño	tañemos	taña	tañí	tañido
tener	tengo	tenemos	tenga	tuve	tenido
tocar	toco	tocamos	toque	toqué	tocado
traer	traigo	traemos	traiga	traje	traído
valer	valgo	valemos	valga	valí	valido
variar	varío	variamos	varíe	varié	variado
vencer	venzo	vencemos	venza	vencí	vencido
venir	vengo	venimos	venga	vine	venido
ver	veo	vemos	vea	vi	visto

Spanish Abbreviations

Abreviaturas españolas

Each entry contains an expansion of the Spanish abbreviation, and wherever possible the equivalent English abbreviation with its expansion in parentheses.

A

a *área.*
(a) *alias* alias.
ab.[1] *abril* Apr. (April).
a.c. *año corriente* current year, present year.
A. (de) C. *año de Cristo* A.D. (Anno Domini).
a/c *al cuidado* c/o (care of).
acr. *acreedor* creditor.
adj. *adjunto* Enc. (enclosure, enclosed).
adm(ón). *administración* admin. (administration).
a/f. *a favor* in favor.
afmo. *afectísimo*: *suyo* ~ yours truly.
ag. *agosto* Aug. (August).
a. (de) J.C. *antes de Jesucristo* B.C. (before Christ).
AI *Amnistía Internacional* AI (Amnesty International).
Al.º *Alonso* personal name.
ALALC *Asociación Latinoamericana de Libre Comercio* LAFTA (Latin American Free Trade Association).
amp. *amperios* amp. (ampères).
Ant.º *Antonio* personal name.
ap. *thea. aparte* aside.
apdo. *apartado* (*de correos*) P.O.B. (Post Office Box).
Apto. *apartamento* apt. (apartment).
art., art.º *artículo* art. (article).
arz. *arzobispo* abp. (archbishop).
A.T. *Antiguo Testamento* O.T. (Old Testament).
atmo. *atentísimo*: *suyo* ~ yours truly.
atta. *atenta.*
atte. *atentamente.*
a/v. *a vista* at sight.
Av., Av.[da] *Avenida*, Av., Ave. (Avenue).

B

B. *eccl. beato* blessed.
B.A. *Buenos Aires capital of Argentina.*
BIC *Brigada de Investigación Criminal* CID, FBI.
Bº *banco* bk. (bank).
Bón. *batallón* Battn, Bn. (battalion).

C

c. *capítulo* ch. (chapter).
C. *compañía* Co. (company).
c/ *Calle* Street.
c[3] *centímetro cúbico* c.c. (cubic centimeter).
c.ª *compañía* Co. (company).
c.a. *corriente alterna* A.C. (alternating current).
C.A.E. *cóbrese al entregar* C.O.D. (cash on delivery).
cap. *capítulo* ch. (chapter).
Cap.[n] *Capitán* Capt. (Captain).
cap.º *capítulo* ch. (chapter).
c.c. *centímetro cúbico* c.c. (cubic centimeter).
c.c. *corriente continua* D.C. (direct current).
c/c *cuenta corriente* C/A (current account).
C.D. *Club Deportivo* S.C. (Sports Club).
c/d 1. *con descuento* with discount. **2.** *en casa de* c/o (care of).
C. de J. *Compañía de Jesús* S.J. (Society of Jesus).
CE *Comunidad Europea* EC (European Community).
C.F. *Club de Fútbol* F.C. (Football Club).
cg. *centigramo* centigram.
ch. *cheque* chq. (cheque).
Cía *compañía* Co. (company).
c.i.f. *costo, seguro y flete* c.i.f. (cost, insurance, freight).
cl. *centilitro* centiliter.
cm. *centímetro* cm. (centimeter).
cm[2] *centímetro cuadrado* sq. cm. (square centimeter).
cm[3] *centímetro cúbico* c.c. (cubic centimeter).
Cnel *Coronel* Col. (Colonel).
CNT *Confederación Nacional de Trabajo* (*de Trabajadores*) workers' union.
COI *Comité Olímpico Internacional* IOC (International Olympic Committee).
col., col.ª *columna* col. (column).
comp. *compárese* cf. (confer).
comp.ª *compañía* Co. (company).
corrte. *corriente, de los corrientes* inst. (instant).
C.P. *contestación pagada* R.P. (reply paid).
CPA *Caja Postal de Ahorros* Post Office Savings Bank.
CRI *Cruz Roja Internacional* IRC (Int'l Red Cross).
cs. *céntimos*; *centavos* cents.
c.s.f. *costo, seguro, flete* c.i.f. (cost, insurance, freight).
cta, c.[ta] *cuenta* A/C (account).
cte *corriente, de los corrientes* inst. (instant).
cts. *céntimos*; *centavos* cents.
c/u *cada uno* ea. (each).
c.v. *caballo(s) de vapor* HP (horsepower).

D

D. *debe* debit side.
D. *Don* Esq. (Esquire) (*Sr.D., en el sobre delante del nombre de pila*; *Esq., en el sobre después del apellido*).
Da. *Doña title of courtesy to ladies*; *no equivalent.*
dcho., dcha. *derecho, derecha* right.
d. (de) J.C. *después de Jesucristo* A.D. (Anno Domini).
Del. *Delegación* district office.

Dest. *destinatario* addressee.
D.F. *México*: *Distrito Federal* Federal District.
dg. *decigramo* decigram.
Dg. *decagramo* decagram.
D.G.T. *Dirección General del Turismo state tourist organization.*
dho. *dicho* aforesaid.
dic.[e] *diciembre* Dec. (December).
dl. *decilitro* deciliter.
Dl. *decalitro* decaliter.
dm. *decímetro* decimeter.
d.[na] *docena* doz. (dozen).
do. *descuento* dis., dist (discount).
doc. *docena* doz. (dozen).
dom.[o] *domingo* Sun. (Sunday).
d/p. *días plazo* day's time.
Dpto. *Departamento* dept. (department).
Dr. *Doctor* Dr (doctor).
dro., dra. *derecho*, *derecha* right.
d.[to] *descuento* dis., dist (discount).
dup.[do] *duplicado* duplicate.
d/v. *días vista* d.s., d/s. (days after sight).

E

E *este* E. (East[ern]).
ed. *edición* ed. (edition).
EE.UU. *Estados Unidos* U.S., U.S.A. (United States [of Americal]).
ej. *ejemplo* ex. (example).
E.M. *Estado Mayor* staff.
Encia. *Eminencia* Eminence.
en.[o] *enero* Jan. (January).
E.P.D. *en paz descanse* R.I.P. (requiescat in pace).
ES *Ejército de Salvación* S.A. (Salvation Army).
esq. *esquina* corner.
etc. *etcétera* etc. (et caetera, etcetera).
EU *Estados Unidos* US (United States).
Exc. *Excelencia* Excellency.

F

f. *femenino* f., fem. (feminine).
fa *factura* bill, account.
f.a.b. *franco a bordo* f.o.b. (free on board).
f.c. *ferrocarril* Rly. (railway).
feb.[o] *febrero* Feb. (February).
Fern.[do] *Fernando personal name.*
fha. *fecha* d. (date).
FMI *Fondo Monetario Internacional* I.M.F. (International Monetary Fund).
f.[o]**, fol.** *folio* fo., fol. (folio).
Fr. *Fray* Fr. (Friar).
Fran.[co] *Francisco personal name.*

G

g. *gramo(s)* gr(s). (gram[s], *British* gramme[s]).
g/ *giro* draft, money order.
gde. *guarde*: *que Dios guarde* whom God protect.
Genl *General* Gen. (General).
G.[o] *Gonzalo personal name.*
gob.[no] *gobierno* Govt. (Government).
g.p. *giro postal* p.o. money order.
Gral, gral. *General* Gen. (General).
grs *gramos* grs. (grams).

H

h. *habitantes* pop. (population).
h. *hacia* c. (circa).
H. *haber* Cr. (credit).
hect. *hectárea* hectare.
Hg. *hectogramo* hectogram.
Hl. *hectolitro* hectoliter.
Hnos. *Hermanos* Bros. (Brothers).
H.P. (*inglés* = horse-power) *caballos*, *caballaje* H.P. (horse-power).

I

ib., ibid. *ibídem* ibid. (ibidem).
igl.[a] *iglesia* church.
Il. *ilustre courtesy title.*
Ilmo. *ilustrísmo courtesy title.*
Imp. *Imprenta* printers, printing works.
I.N.I. *Instituto Nacional de Industria state industrial council.*
IVA *Impuesto sobre el valor agregado* (*o añadido*) VAT (value-added tax).
izdo., izda. *izquierdo*, *izquierda* left.

J

J.C. *Jesucristo* Jesus Christ.
JJ.OO. *Juegos Olímpicos* Olympic Games.
juev. *jueves* Thurs. (Thursday).

K

K *Kilobyte* Kilobyte.
k/c *kilociclos* k/c. (kilocycles).
Kg. *kilogramo* kg. (kilogram).
Kl. *kilolitro* kiloliter.
Km. *kilómetro* km. (kilometer).
Km./h. *kilómetros por hora* kilometers per hour.
kv. *kilovatio* kw. (kilowatt).

L

l. ⚖ *ley* law.
l. *libro* bk. (book).
l. *litro* l. (liter).
lbs. *libras* lbs. (pounds).
lib. *libra* lb. (pound).
lib., lib.[o] *libro* bk. (book).
Lic. en Fil. y Let. *Licenciado en Filosofía y Letras* B.A. (Bachelor of Arts).
lun. *lunes* Mon. (Monday).

M

m. *minuto* m. (minute).
m. *metro* m. (meter).
m. *masculino* m., masc. (masculine).
m. *muerto*, *murió* d. (died).
m^2 *metro cuadrado* sq. m. (square meter).
m^3 *metro cúbico* cu. m. (cubic meter).
M. *Madrid capital of Spain.*
Ma. *María personal name.*
mart. *martes* Tues. (Tuesday).
M.C. *Mercado Común* C.M. (Common Market).
Md. *Madrid capital of Spain.*
M.F. *modulación de frecuencia* F.M. (frequency modulation).
mg *miligramo* mg. (milligram).
miérc. *miércoles* Weds. (Wednesday).
mm *milímetro* mm. (millimeter).
MMS *manuscritos* MSS (manuscripts).
m/n *moneda nacional* local currency.
Mons. *Monseñor* Mgr. (Monsignor).
MS *manuscrito* Ms (manuscript).

N

n. *nacido, nació* b. (born).
N *norte* N. (North[ern]).
nal. *nacional* national.
Na. Sra. *Nuestra Señora* Our Lady, The Virgin.
N.B. *nótese bien* N.B. (nota bene).
NE *noreste* N.E. (North East[ern]).
NNE *nornordeste* NNE (north-northeast).
NNO *nornordoeste* NNW (north-northwest).
NN.UU. *Naciones Unidas* U.N. (United Nations).
n.º *número* No. (number).
NO *noroeste* N.W. (North West[ern]).
nov.[e] *noviembre* Nov. (November).
nro., nra. *nuestro, nuestra* our.
N.S. *Nuestro Señor* Our Lord.
N.T. *Nuevo Testamento* N.T. (New Testament).
ntro., ntra. *nuestro, nuestra* our.
N.U. *Naciones Unidas* U.N. (United Nations).
Núm. *número* No. (number).

O

O *oeste* W. (West[ern]).
O.A.A. *Organización de Agricultura y Alimentación* F.A.O. (Food and Agriculture Organization).
O.A.C.I. *Organización de Aviación Civil Internacional* I.C.A.O. (International Civil Aviation Organization).
ob., obpo. *obispo* Bp. (bishop).
obr. cit. *obra citada* op. cit. (opere citato).
OCDE *Organización de Cooperación y Desarrollo Económico* O.E.C.D. (Organization for Economic Cooperation and Development).
oct.[e] *octubre* Oct. (October).
OEA *Organización de los Estados Americanos* O.A.S. (Organization of American States).
OIT *Organización Internacional de Trabajo* ILO (International Labor Organization).
OLP *Organización para la Liberación de Palestina* P.L.O. (Palestine Liberation Organization).
OMS *Organización Mundial de la Salud* W.H.O. (World Health Organization).
ONU *Organización de las Naciones Unidas* UNO (United Nations Organization).
O.P. *Orden de Predicadores* O.S.D. (Order of St. Dominic).
O.P. *Obras Públicas* P.W.D. (Public Works Department).
OPEP *Organización de Países Exportadores de Petróleo* OPEC (Organization of Petroleum-Exporting Countries).
O.S.B. *Orden de San Benito* O.S.B. (Order of St. Benedict).
OTAN *Organización del Tratado del Atlántico Norte* NATO (North Atlantic Treaty Organization).
OTASE *Organización del Tratado del Sudeste Asiático* (or *del Asia Sudeste*) SEATO (South East Asia Treaty Organization).
OVNI *u* **ovni** *objeto volante no identificado* UFO (unidentified flying object).

P

P. *papa* pope.
P. *padre* Fr. (Father).
P% *por cien(to)* %, p.c. (per cent).
pág. *página* p. (page).
págs. *páginas* pp. (pages).
p.c. *por cien(to)* %, p.c. (per cent).
PC *Partido Comunista* C.P. (Communist Party).
P.D. *posdata* P.S. (postscript).
PDC *Partido Demócrata Cristiano* Christian Democratic Union.
pdo. *pasado* ult. (ultimo).
Pe. *Padre* Fr. (Father).
PED *Procesamiento Electrónico de Datos* E.D.P. (electronic data processing).
p. ej. *por ejemplo* e.g. (exempli gratia, for example).
pmo. *próximo* prox. (proximo).
PNB *producto nacional bruto* G.N.P. (gross national product).
P.º *Paseo* Avenue.
p.º n.º *peso neto* nt. wt. (net weight).
p.o. *por orden* per pro(c)., p.p. (per procurationem, by proxy).
p.p. *por poder* per pro(c)., p.p. (per procurationem, by proxy).
P.P. *porte pagado* C.P. (carriage paid).
p.pdo. *(el mes) próximo pasado* ult. (ultimo).
pral. *principal* first.
pr. fr. *próximo futuro* prox. (proximo).
PRI *Partido Revolucionario Institucional* Mexican political party.
Prof. *Profesor* Prof. (Professor).
prov. *provincia* province.
PS *Partido Socialista* Socialist Party.
ps. *pesos* pesos.
P.S. *postscriptum* (*posdata*) P.S. (postscript).
ptas. *pesetas* pesetas.
P.V.P. *precio de venta al público* retail price.
pzs *piezas* pcs. (pieces).

Q

q.D.g. *que Dios guarde* whom God protect (*used after mention of king*).
q.e.p.d. *que en paz descanse* R.I.P. (requiescat in pace).
q.e.s.m. *que estrecha su mano courtesy formula.*
qts. *quilates* carats.
quil. *quilates* carats.

R

R. *Real* Royal.
R. *Reverendo* Rev. (Reverend).
R.A.C.E. *Real Automóvil Club de España equivalent to British A.A. and R.A.C.*
Rdo *Reverendo* Rev. (Reverend).
RENFE *Red Nacional de Ferrocarriles Españoles Spanish railway company.*
R.O. *real orden* royal decree.
r.p.m. *revoluciones por minuto* r.p.m. (revolutions per minute).
rúst. *en rústica* paper-backed.

S

s/ *su* yr. (your).
S. *San(to), Santa* St. (Saint).
S *sur S.* (South[ern]).
s.a. *sin año* s.a. (sine anno).
S.A. *Su Alteza* H.H. (His [*or* Her] Highness).
S.A. ✝ *Sociedad Anónima* Inc. (Incorporated); Ltd. (Limited).
sáb. *sábado* Sat. (Saturday).
Sdo. *saldo* bal. (balance).
SE *sudeste* S.E. (South East[ern]).
seg. *segundo* sec (second).
sept.[e] *septiembre* Sept. (September).
s.e.u.o. *salvo error u omisión* E. & O.E. (errors and omissions excepted).
s.f. *sin fecha* n.d. (no date).
sgte. *siguiente* f. (following).
SIDA *síndrome de inmunidad deficiente adquirida* AIDS (aquired immune-deficiency syndrome).

igs. (*y*) *siguientes* et seq. (et sequentia), ff. (following).
S.I.M. *Servicio de Información Militar* M.I. (Military Intelligence).
s.l.ni f. *sin lugar ni fecha* n.p. or d. (no place or date).
S.M. *Su Majestad* H.M. (His [*or* Her] Majesty).
s/n. *sin número* not numbered.
SO *suroeste* S.W. (South West[ern]).
Sr. *Señor* Mr (Mister).
Sra. *Señora* Mrs (mistress).
S.R.C. *se ruega contestación* R.S.V.P. (répondez s'il vous plaît).
Sres. *Señores* Messrs (Messieurs).
Srio. *Secretario* Sec. (Secretary).
S.R.M. *Su Real Majestad* H.M. (His [*or* Her] Majesty).
Srta. *Señorita* Miss.
SS *Seguridad Social British* N.I. (National Insurance); *Am.* (Social Security).
SS. *Su Santidad* His Holiness.
SS *Santos* SS (Saints).
SSE *sudsudeste* SSE (south-southeast).
SSO *sudsudoeste* SSW (south-southwest).
s.s.s. *su seguro servidor* yours truly.

T

t. *tomo(s)* vol(s). (volume[s]).
TAE *tasa anual efectiva* APR (annual percentage rate).
Tel. *teléfono* Tel. (Telephone).
Tente. *Teniente* Lieut. (Lieutenant).
TLC *Tratado de Libre Comercio* FTA (Free Trade Act).
Tlf. *teléfono* Tel. (Telephone).
T.R.B. *toneladas registradas brutas* G.R.T. (gross register tonnage).
Tte *Teniente* Lieut. (Lieutenant).
TV *televisión* T.V. (television).

U

UCE *Unidad de Cuenta Europea* ECU (European Currency Unit).
Ud. *usted* you.
Uds. *ustedes you.*
UE *Unión Europea* EU (European Union)
U.E.P. *Unión Europea de Pagos* E.P.U. (European Payments Union).
UPA *Unión Panamericana* PAU (Pan-American Union).
U.P.U. *Unión Postal Universal* U.P.U. (Universal Postal Union).
UVI *Unidad de vigilancia intensiva* ICU (intensive care unit).

V

v. *voltio* v. (volt).
v. *véase* see.
V. *usted you.*
V.ºB.º *visto bueno* approval, OK.
Vd. *usted* you.
Vda de *viuda de* widow of.
Vds. *ustedes* you.
verso *versículo* v. (verse).
v.g., v.gr. *verbigracia* viz. (videlicet).
vid. *vide* see.
vier. *viernes* Fri. (Friday).
V.M. *Vuestra Majestad* Your Majesty.
v(t)ro., v(t)ra. *vuestro*, *vuestra* yr. (your).

W

w. *watio* w. (watt).

X

Xpo. *Cristo* Christ.

Spanish Proper Names

Nombres propios españoles

A

Abrahán Abraham.
Adán Adam.
Adén Aden.
Adolfo Adolf, Adolphus.
Adriano Hadrian.
Adriático *m* Adriatic.
Afganistán *m* Afghanistan.
Africa *f* Africa; ~ *del Norte* North Africa.
Agustín Augustine.
Albania *f* Albania.
Alberto Albert.
Alejandría Alexandria.
Alejandro Alexander; ~ *Magno* Alexander the Great.
Alemania *f* Germany.
Alfredo Alfred.
Alicia Alice.
Alpes *m/pl.* Alps.
Amalia Amelia.
Amazonas *m* Amazon.
América *f* America; ~ *Central* Central America; ~ *del Norte* North America; ~ *del Sur* South America; ~ *Latina* Latin America.
Ana Ann(e).
Andalucía *f* Andalusia.
Andes *m/pl.* Andes.
Andrés Andrew.
Angola *f* Angola.
Aníbal Hannibal.
Antártida *f* Antarctic.
Antillas *f/pl.* West Indies, Antilles; *Grandes* ~ Greater Antilles; *Pequeñas* ~ Lesser Antilles.
Antonio Anthony.
Apeninos *m/pl.* Apennines.
Arabia *f* Arabia; ~ *Saudita o Saudí* Saudi-Arabia.
Aragón *m* Aragon.
Arcadia *f* Arcady.
Ardenas *m/pl.* Ardennes.
Argelia *f* Algeria.
Argentina *f* Argentina.
Armenia *f* Armenia.
Arquímedes Archimedes.
Arturo Arthur.
Artús: *el* **Rey** ~ King Arthur.
Asia *f* Asia, ~ *Menor* Asia Minor.
Asiria *f* Assyria.
Asunción *Capital of Paraguay.*
Atenas Athens.
Atila Attila.
Atlántico *m* Atlantic.
Augusto Augustus.
Australia *f* Australia.
Austria *f* Austria.
Azerbaiyán *m* Azerbaijan.
Azores *m/pl.* Azores.

B

Bahamas *f/pl.* Bahamas.
Balcanes *m/pl.* Balkans.
Baleares f/pl. Balearic Isles.
Báltico *m* Baltic.
Bangladesh *m* Bangladesh.
Barcelona *f City in Catalonia.*
Bartolomé Bartholomew.
Baviera *f* Bavaria.
Beatriz Beatrice.
Bélgica *f* Belgium.
Belgrado Belgrade.
Belice *m* Belize.
Benedicto Benedict.
Bengala *f* Bengal.
Benito Benedict.
Benjamín Benjamin.
Bernardo Bernhard.
Bética *f* Andalusia.
Bielorusia *f* Belarus.
Birmania *f* Burma.
Bizancio Byzantium.
Bizkaia *f* Biscay, *Basque province.*
Bogotá *Capital of Columbia.*
Bolivia *f* Bolivia.
Bósforo *m* Bosphorus.
Brasil *m* Brazil.
Brasilia *f Capital of Brasil.*
Brígida Bridget.
Bruto Brutus.
Buda Buddha.
Buenos Aires *Capital of Argentina.*
Bulgaria *f* Bulgaria.
Burundi *m* Burundi.
Bután *m* Bhutan.

C

Cabo *m* **de Buena Esperanza** Cape of Good Hope.
Cabo *m* **de Hornos** Cape Horn.
Cabo *m* **Cañaveral** Cape Canaveral.
Cabo: (Ciudad *f* **de) El** ~ Cape Town.
Cachemira *f* Kashmir.
Cádiz Cadiz.
Caín Cain; F *pasar las de* ~ have a terrible time.
Cairo: El ~ Cairo.
Camboya *f* Cambodia.
Camerún *m* Cameroons.
Canadá *m* Canada.
Canal *m* **de la Mancha** English Channel.
Canal *m* **de Panamá** Panama Canal.
Canal *m* **de Suez** Suez Canal.
Canarias *f/pl.* Canaries.
Cantórbery Canterbury.
Caracas *Capital of Venezuela.*
Caribe *m* Caribbean (Sea).
Carlitos Charlie.
Carlomagno Charlemagne.
Carlos Charles.
Carlota Charlotte.
Cárpatos *m/pl.* Carpathians.
Casa Blanca: *la* ~ the White House.
Casandra Cassandra.
Castilla *f* Castile.
Catalina Catherine, Catharine; Katherine; Kathleen.
Cataluña *f* Catalonia.
Cáucaso *m* Caucasus.
Cecilia Cecily.
Cerdeña *f* Sardinia.
Clemente Clement.
Colombia *f* Colombia.
Colón Columbus.
Concha, Conchita pet names for *Concepción.*
Congo *m* the Congo.
Constanza Constance.
Córcega *f* Corsica.
Córdoba Cordova.
Corea *f* Korea; ~ *del Norte* North Korea; ~ *del Sur* South Korea.
Cornualles *m* Cornwall.
Coruña: La ~ Corunna.
Costa *f* **de Marfil** Ivory Coast.
Costa Rica *f* Costa Rica.
Creta *f* Crete.
Cristo Christ.
Cristóbal Christopher.
Croacia *f* Croatia.
Cuba *f* Cuba.

Ch

Chad *m* Chad.
Chechenia *f* Chechnya.
Chile *m* Chile.

China *f* China.
Chipre *f* Cyprus.

D

Dalmacia *f* Dalmatia.
Danubio *m* Danube.
Dardanelos *m/pl.* Dardanelles.
Darío Darius.
David David.
Diego James.
Dinamarca *f* Denmark.
Dorotea Dorothy.
Dublín Dublin.

E

Ecuador *m* Ecuador.
Edimburgo Edinburgh.
Eduardo Edward.
Egeo (Mar) *m* Aegean Sea.
Egipto *m* Egypt.
Elena Helen.
Emilia Emily.
Emilio Emil(e).
Eneas Aeneas.
Enrique Henry, Harry.
Erasmo Erasmus.
Ernesto Ernest.
Escandinavia *f* Scandinavia.
Escocia *f* Scotland.
Eslovenia *f* Slovenia.
España *f* Spain.
Estados *m/pl.* **Unidos (de América)** United States (of America).
Esteban Stephen.
Estocolmo Stockholm.
Estonia *f* Estonia.
Etiopía *f* Etiopia.
Euclides Euclid.
Eugenio Eugene.
Eurípedes Euripedes.
Europa *f* Europe.
Euskadi *m* Basque Country.
Eva Eve.
Extremadura *f* Estremadura.

F

Federico Frederick.
Felipe Philip.
Fernando Ferdinand.
Filadelfia Philadelphia.
Filipinas *f/pl.* Philippines.
Finlandia *f* Finland.
Flandes *m* Flanders.
Florencia Florence.
Francia *f* France.
Francisca Frances.
Francisco Francis.

G

Gabón *m* Gaboon.
Gales *m* Wales.
Geofredo Geoffrey.
Gertrudis Gertrude.
Ghana *f* Ghana.
Gibraltar *m* Gibraltar; *Estrecho de* ~ Straits of Gibraltar; *Peñón de* ~ Rock of Gibraltar.
Gil Giles.
Ginebra Geneva; (*p.*) Guinevere.
Godofredo Godfrey.
Golfo *m* **Pérsico** Persian Gulf.
Golfo *m* **de Vizcaya** Bay of Biscay.
Gran Bretaña *f* Great Britain.
Granada Granada; Grenada.
Gran Cañón *m* Grand Canyon.
Grecia *f* Greece.
Gregorio Gregory.
Groenlandia *f* Greenland.
Guadalupe *f* Guadeloupe.
Gualterio Walter.
Guatemala *f* Guatemala.
Guayana *f* **(Francesa)** (French) Guiana.
Guayaquil *Capital of Ecuador.*
Guido Guy.
Guillermo William.
Guinea *f* Guinea; ~ *Ecuatorial* Equatorial Guinea.
Gustavo Gustave.
Guyana *f* Guyana.

H

Habana: La ~ Havana.
Haití *m* Haiti.
Hawai *m* Hawaii.
Hébridas *f/pl.* Hebrides.
Helena Helen.
Himalaya *m* the Himalayas.
Hispanoamérica *f* Spanish America.
Holanda *f* Holland.
Honduras *f* Honduras.
Horacio Horace.
Hugo Hugh, Hugo.
Hungría *f* Hungary.

I

Iberia *f* Iberia.
Ignacio Ignatius.
India: *la* ~ India.
Indias *f/pl.* Indies; ~ *Occidentales* West Indies.
Indonesia *f* Indonesia.
Inés Agnes.
Inglaterra *f* England.
Irak *m* Irak, Iraq.
Irán *m* Iran.
Irlanda *f* Ireland; ~ *del Norte* Northern Ireland.
Isabel Isabel, Elizabeth.
Isabelita Bess(ie), Bessy, Betty.
Iseo Isolde.
Islandia *f* Iceland.
Islas *f/pl.*: ~ *Bahamas* Bahamas; ~ *Baleares* Balearic Isles; ~ *Bermudas* Bermuda; ~ *Británicas* British Isles; ~ *de Cabo Verde* Cape Verde Islands; ~ *Canarias* Canary Isles; ~ *Hawai* Hawaii; ~ *Normandas* Channel Isles; ~ *de Sotavento* Leeward Isles.
Isolda Isolde.
Israel *m* Israel.
Italia *f* Italy.

J

Jacob Jacob.
Jacobo (*reyes de Escocia e Inglaterra*) James.
Jaime James.
Jamaica *f* Jamaica.
Japón *m* Japan.
Jehová Jehovah.
Jerónimo Jerome.
Jesús Jesus
Joaquín *m* Joachim.
Job Job.
Jordán m Jordan (*river*).
Jordania *f* Jordan (*country*).
Jorge George.
José Joseph.
Josefina Josephine.
Juan John.
Juana Jane; Joan; ~ *de Arco* Joan of Arc.
Juanito Jack; Johnny.
Julieta Juliet.
Julio Julius.

K

Kenia *f* Kenya.
Kuwait *m* Kuwait.

L

Laos *m* Laos.
La Paz *Capital of Bolivia.*
Laponia *f* Lapland.
Leandro Leander.
Leonor Eleanor.
Letonia *f* Latvia.
Levante *m* Levant; *South-east part* (*or coasts*) *of Spain.*
Líbano *m* Lebanon.
Liberia *f* Liberia.
Libia *f* Libya.
Lima *Capital of Peru.*
Lisboa Lisbon.
Lituania *f* Lithuania.
Loira *m* Loire.
Lola, Lolita *pet names for Dolores.*
Londres London.
Lorenzo Laurence.
Lucas Luke.
Luis Louis.
Luxemburgo *m* Luxembourg.
Lyón Lyons.

M

Madera *f* Madeira.
Madrid *m* Madrid.
Magallanes *m* Magellan; *Estrecho de* ~ Magellan Straits.
Magdalena *f* Magdalen.
Mahoma Mahomet.
Málaga Malaga.
Malawi *m* Malawi.
Malaisia *f* Malaysia.
Malí *m* Mali.
Mallorca *f* Majorca.
Malvinas *f/pl.* Falkland Isles.
Managua *Capital of Nicaragua.*
Manolo *pet name for Manuel.*
Manuel Emmanuel.
Mar *m*: ~ *Adriático* Adriatic Sea; ~ *Báltico* Baltic Sea; ~ *Caribe* Caribbean (Sea), ~ *Caspio* Caspian Sea; ~ *de las Indias* Indian Ocean; ~ *Mediterráneo* Mediterranean Sea; ~ *Muerto* Dead Sea; ~ *Negro* Black Sea; ~ *del Norte* North Sea; ~ *Rojo* Red Sea.

Marcos Mark.
Margarita Margaret.
María Mary.
Marruecos *m* Morocco.
Martín Martin.
Martinica *f* Martinique.
Mateo Matthew.
Matilde Mat(h)ilda.
Mauricio Mauritius; (*p.*) Maurice.
Mauritania *f* Mauretania.
Meca: La ~ Mecca.
Mediterráneo *m* Mediterranean.
Méjico *m* Mexico.
Menorca *f* Minorca.
Mesías Messiah.
México *m* Mexico.
Miguel Michael.
Milán Milan.
Misisipí *m* Mississippi.
Misurí *m* Missouri.
Moisés Moses.
Montevideo *Capital of Uruguay.*
Moscú Moscow.
Mosela *m* Moselle.
Montañas *f/pl.* **Rocosas** Rocky Mountains.
Montes *m/pl.* **Apalaches** Appalachian Mountains.
Mozambique *f* Mozambique.

N

Navarra *f* Navarre.
Nepal *m* Nepal.
Niágara Niagara.
Nicaragua *f* Nicaragua.
Nicolás Nicholas.
Níger *m* Niger.
Nigeria *f* Nigeria.
Nilo *m* Nile.
Noé Noah.
Noruega *f* Norway.
Nueva Escocia *f* Nova Scotia.
Nueva Gales *f* **del Sur** New South Wales.
Nueva Guinea *f* New Guinea.
Nueva York New York.
Nueva Zelanda *f* New Zealand.

O

Océano *m*: ~ *Atlántico* Atlantic Ocean; ~ *glacial Antártico* Southern Ocean; ~ *glacial Artico* Arctic Ocean; ~ *Indico* Indian Ocean; ~ *Pacífico* Pacific Ocean.
Octavio Octavian.
Oliverio Oliver.
Orcadas *f/pl.* Orkney Islands.
Oriente *m* East; *Extremo* ~ Far East; ~ *Medio* Middle East; *Próximo* ~ Near East.

P

Pablo Paul.
Paca *pet name for Francisca* Frances.
Pacífico *m* Pacific.
Paco *pet name for Francisco* Frank.
País *m* **Vasco** Basque Country.
Países *m/pl.* **Bajos** Netherlands.
Pakistán *m* Pakistan.
Palestina *f* Palestine.
Panamá *m* Panama.
Paquita *pet name for Francisca* Frances.
Paquito *pet name for Francisco* Frank.
Paraguay *m* Paraguay.
París Paris.
Patricio Patrick.
Pedro Peter.
Península *f* **Ibérica** Iberian Peninsula.
Pensilvania *f* Pennsylvania.
Pepa *pet name for Josefa.*
Pepe *pet name for José* Joe.
Pepita *pet name for Josefa*
Perú *m* Peru.
Pirineos *m/pl.* Pyrenees.
Polinesia *f* Polynesia.
Polonia *f* Poland.
Portugal *m* Portugal.
Puerto Rico *m* Puerto Rico.

Q

Quito *Capital of Ecuador.*

R

Rafael Raphael.
Raimundo, Ramón Raymond.
Raquel Rachel.
Rebeca Rebecca.
Reginaldo, Reinaldos Reginald.
Reino *m* **Unido** United Kingdom.
República *f* **Centroafricana** Central African Republic.
República *f* **Checa** Czech Republic.
República *f* **Dominicana** Dominican Republic.
República *f* **Malgache** Republic of Madagascar.
República *f* **Popular de China** People's Republic of China.
República *f* **Sudafricana** Republic of South Africa.
Ricardo Richard.
Rin *m* Rhine.
Roberto Robert.
Ródano *m* Rhône.
Rodas *f* Rhodes.
Rodesia *f* Rhodesia.
Rodrigo Roderick.
Roldán, Rolando Roland.
Roma Rome.
Rosa Rose.
Ruanda *f* Rwanda.
Rumania *f* Rumania.
Rusia *f* Russia.

S

Sáhara *m* Sahara.
Salvador: El ~ El Salvador.
Samuel Samuel.
San José *Capital of Costa Rica*
San Juan *Capital of Puerto Rico.*
San Salvador *Capital of El Salvador.*
Santiago Saint James; *capital of Chile.*
Santo Domingo *Capital of the Dominican Republic.*
Satanás Satan.
Saturno Saturn.
Saúl Saul.
Sena *m* Seine.
Senegal *m* Senegal.
Serbia *f* Serbia.
Sevilla Seville.
Siberia *f* Siberia.
Sibila Sibyl.
Sicilia *f* Sicily.
Sierra Leona *f* Sierra Leone.
Singapur Singapore.
Sión *m* Zion.
Siria *f* Syria.
Somalia *f* Somalia.
Sri Lanka *m* Sri Lanka.
Sudán *m* Sudan.
Suecia *f* Sweden.
Suiza *f* Switzerland.
Surinam *n* Surinam.

T

Tailandia *f* Thailand.
Tajo *m* Tagus.
Támesis *m* Thames.
Tanzania *f* Tanzania.
Tegucigalpa *Capital of Hunduras.*
Tejas *m* Texas.
Terencio Terence.
Teresa Theresa.
Terranova *f* Newfoundland.
Tesalia *f* Thessaly.
Tíber *m* Tiber.
Tibet *m* Tibet.
Ticiano Titian.
Tierra *f* **Santa** Holy Land.
Timoteo Timothy.
Togo *m* Togo.
Toledo Toledo.
Tomás Thomas.
Trinidad *f* **y Tobago** *m* Trinidad and Tobago.
Tunicia *f* Tunisia.
Turquía *f* Turkey.

U

Ucrania *f* Ukraine.
Uganda *m* Uganda.
Unión *f* **de Emiratos Arabes** United Arab Emirates.
Unión *f* **de India** Union of India.
Uruguay *m* Uruguay.
Utopia *f* Utopia.

V

Vascongadas *f/pl.* Basque Provinces.
Vaticano *m* Vatican.
Venezuela *f* Venezuela.
Vicente Vincent.
Vietnam *o* **Viet Nam** *m* Viet Nam.
Vizcaya *f* Biscay.

Y

Yemen *m* Yemen.

Z

Zaire *m* Zaïre.
Zambia *f* Zambia.
Zaragoza Saragossa.
Zimbabue *m* Zimbabwe.

Numerals — Numerales

Cardinal Numbers — Números cardinales

0 cero *nought*
1 uno, una *one*
2 dos *two*
3 tres *three*
4 cuatro *four*
5 cinco *five*
6 seis *six*
7 siete *seven*
8 ocho *eight*
9 nueve *nine*
10 diez *ten*
11 once *eleven*
12 doce *twelve*
13 trece *thirteen*
14 catorce *fourteen*
15 quince *fifteen*
16 dieciséis *sixteen*
17 diecisiete *seventeen*
18 dieciocho *eighteen*
19 diecinueve *nineteen*
20 veinte *twenty*
21 veintiuno *twenty-one*
22 veintidós *twenty-two*
30 treinta *thirty*
31 treinta y uno *thirty-one*
40 cuarenta *forty*
50 cincuenta *fifty*
60 sesenta *sixty*
70 setenta *seventy*
80 ochenta *eighty*
90 noventa *ninety*
100 cien(to) *a (one) hundred*
101 ciento uno *a hundred and one*
110 ciento diez *a hundred and ten*
200 doscientos, -as *two hundred*
300 trescientos, -as *three hundred*
400 cuatrocientos, -as *four hundred*
500 quinientos, -as *five hundred*
600 seiscientos, -as *six hundred*
700 setecientos, -as *seven hundred*
800 ochocientos, -as *eight hundred*
900 novecientos, -as *nine hundred*
1000 mil *a thousand*
1959 mil novecientos cincuenta y nueve *nineteen hundred and fifty-nine*
2000 dos mil *two thousand*
1.000.000 un millón (de) *a (one) million*
2.000.000 dos millones (de) *two million*

Ordinal Numbers — Números ordinales

(The ordinal numbers in Spanish agree with the noun in number and gender, *primero -a -os -as etc.*)

1 primero *first*
2 segundo *second*
3 tercero *third*
4 cuarto *forth*
5 quinto *fifth*
6 sexto *sixth*
7 séptimo *seventh*
8 octavo *eighth*
9 noveno, nono *ninth*
10 décimo *tenth*
11 undécimo *eleventh*
12 duodécimo *twelfth*
13 decimotercero, decimotercio *thirteenth*
14 decimocuarto *fourteenth*
15 decimoquinto *fifteenth*
16 decimosexto *sixteenth*
17 decimoséptimo *seventeenth*
18 decimoctavo *eighteenth*
19 decimonoveno, decimonono *nineteenth*
20 vigésimo *twentieth*
21 vigésimo prim(er)o *twenty-first*
22 vigésimo segundo *twenty-second*
30 trigésimo *thirtieth*
31 trigésimo prim(er)o *thirty-first*
40 cuadragésimo *fortieth*
50 quincuagésimo *fiftieth*
60 sexagésimo *sixtieth*
70 septuagésimo *seventieth*
80 octogésimo *eightieth*
90 nonagésimo *ninetieth*
100 centésimo *hundredth*
101 centésimo primero *hundred and first*
110 centésimo décimo *hundred and tenth*
200 ducentésimo *two hundredth*
300 tricentésimo *three hundredth*
400 cuadringentésimo *four hundredth*
500 quingentésimo *five hundredth*
600 sexcentésimo *six hundredth*
700 septingentésimo *seven hundredth*
800 octingentésimo *eight hundredth*

900 noningentésimo *nine hundredth*
1000 milésimo *thousandth*
2000 dos milésimo *two thousandth*
1.000.000 millonésimo *millionth*
2.000.000 dos millonésimo *tw… millionth*

En inglés, los números ordinales suelen abreviarse **1**st., **2**nd., **3**rd., **4**th., **5**th., etc.; in Spanish, the ordinal numbers may be written **1°**, **2°** etc.

Fractions and other Numerals — Números quebrados y otros

$^1/_2$ medio, media *one* (*a*) *half*; **1** $^1/_2$ uno y medio *one and a half*; **2** $^1/_2$ dos y medio *two and a hafl*; $^1/_2$ hora *half an hour*; **1** $^1/_2$ kilómetros *a kilometer and a half*

$^1/_3$ un tercio, la tercera parte *one* (*a*) *third*; $^2/_3$ dos tercios, las dos terceras partes *two thirds*

$^1/_4$ un cuarto, la cuarta parte *one* (*a*) *quarter*; $^3/_4$ tres cuartos, las tres cuartas partes *three quarters*; $^1/_4$ hora *a quarter of an hour*; **1** $^1/_4$ horas *an hour and a quarter*

$^1/_5$ un quinto *one* (*a*) *fifth*; **3** $^4/_5$ tres y cuatro quintos *three and four fifths*

$^1/_{11}$ un onzavo *one* (*an*) *eleventh*;
$^5/_{12}$ cinco dozavos *five twelfths*;
$^{75}/_{100}$ setenta y cinco centésimos *seventy-five hundredths*

$^1/_{1000}$ un milésimo *one* (*a*) *thousandth*

simple *single*
doble, duplo *double*
triple *treble*, *triple*, *threefold*
cuádruplo *fourfold*
quíntuplo *fivefold etc.*

una vez *once*
dos veces *twice*
tres veces *three times etc.*
siete veces más grande *seven times as big*;
doce veces más *twelve times more*

en primer lugar *firstly*
en segundo lugar *secondly etc.*

7 + 8 = 15 siete y (*or* más) ocho son quince *seven and eight are fifteen*

10 − 3 = 7 diez menos tres resta siete, de tres a diez van siete *three from ten leaves seven*

2 × 3 = 6 dos por tres son seis *two times three are six*

20 ÷ 4 = 5 veinte dividido por cuatro es cinco *twenty divided by four is five*

Spanish Weights and Measures

Pesos y medidas españoles

Metric system — Sistema métrico

(The various ancient measures still in use are listed and defined in the main part of the dictionary)

Multiples and fractions formed with the following prefixes are not listed separately:

deca- **10** times; *hecto-* **100** times; *kilo-* **1000** times;
deci- one tenth, *centi-* one hundredth; *milli-* one thousandth

1. Linear measures — Medidas de longitud

1 centímetro (centimeter) = **10** milímetros (millimeters) = **0.3937** inches
1 metro (meter) = **100** centímetros (centimeters) = **39.37** inches *or* **1.094** yards
1 kilómetro (kilometer) = **1000** metros (meters) = **0.6214** mile (almost exactly five-eighths of a mile)

2. Square measures — Medidas cuadradas

1 centímetro cuadrado (square centimeter) = **0.155** square inch
1 metro cuadrado (square meter) = **10.764** square feet
1 kilómetro cuadrado (square kilometer) = **247.1** acres *or* **0.3861** square mile
1 área (are) = **100** metros cuadrados (square meters) = **119.6** square yards
1 hectárea (hectare) = **100** áreas (ares) = **2.471** acres

3. Cubic measures — Medidas de cubicación

1 centímetro cúbico (cubic centimeter) = **0.061** cubic inch
1 metro cúbico (cubic meter) = **35.31** cubic feet *or* **1.308** cubic yards

4. Measure of capacity — Medidas de capacidad

1 litro (liter) = **1000** centímetros cúbicos (cubic centimeters) = **1.76** pints *or* **0.22** gallon

5. Weights — Pesos

1 gramo (gram, *British* gramme) = **0.0352** ounce
1 kilo(gramo) (kilogram, *British* kilogramme) = **2.2045** pounds
1 quintal métrico = **100** kilogramos (kilograms) = **220.45** pounds
1 tonelada = **1000** kilogramos (kilograms) = **0.9842** ton

Second Part

English-Spanish

Contents

Materias

How to use this dictionary

Cómo usar este diccionario

Para que el lector de esta pequeña introducción vea con claridad la estructura de la obra, y se haga una idea del material que puede encontrar en su interior, haremos a continuación un análisis detallado de los datos que en ella aparecen y que esperamos que sean de gran utilidad para quienes la consulten.

To assist the reader of this short introduction in understanding the structure of the dictionary and in forming an idea of its contents, we provide below a detailed analysis of the information which appears with each entry in the hope that this will facilitate the consultation of this work.

Para ello hemos elegido el artículo de **make** como amplio ejemplo de las características de este diccionario en su sección inglés-español (completaremos con otros textos las explicaciones de los detalles que no aparecen en él).

We have selected the entry **make** to exemplify the characteristics of this dictionary in the English-Spanish section (examples not covered here will be completed with other explanations).

En primer lugar, e inmediatamente después de la entrada, se consigna la transcripción fonética correspondiente, indicando incluso, cuando se da el caso, la diferencia de pronunciación entre el inglés británico y el americano:

Immediately after the headword in bold face is the corresponding phonetic transcription which also indicates the differences, if any, between British and American pronunciation:

make | meɪk |
bowdlerization | ˌbaʊdləraɪ'zeɪʃn |, (EE.UU.) | ˌbaʊdlərɪ'zeɪʃn |

En todos los artículos ponemos la categoría gramatical a que corresponde cada acepción y cuando, como en este caso, una entrada tiene varias categorías, los grupos de acepciones de cada una de ellas van separados por doble barra:

The grammatical category for each headword follows and, in this case, in which the word belongs to various categories, the different definitions of each one are separated by two parallel lines:

make ... *v.t.* **1** hacer, fabricar, ... **2** hacer, preparar, ... || *s.i.* **33** comportarse, ... || **38** marca, ...

Llamamos también la atención, con anotaciones entre corchetes, sobre las irregularidades gramaticales y el tipo de construcción correcto, cuando consideramos que puede ofrecer dificultad o cuando un tipo determinado de construcción implica un significado o un uso específico:

When irregular grammatical constructions offer difficulties or when a specific form indicates a change of meaning or a specific use, these are placed in brackets along with the correct grammatical construction:

make ... 3 [to- + s.] hacer (un esfuerzo, un descubrimiento, un comentario). **10** [to — + o. + adj.] poner, hacer, volver; *it makes me crazy* = *me vuelve loco.*

En cuanto a las correspondencias, cuando nos ha parecido necesario damos, entre paréntesis, aclaraciones que ayuden al consultante a solucionar las dudas que puedan surgirle a la hora de decidir en qué casos es apropiado o no el uso de determinado término:

In some cases, when necessary, definitions are expanded by explanations in parenthesis to assist the user in selecting the appropriate term:

make ... 1 hacer, fabricar, manufacturar, construir, elaborar, confeccionar, crear (un objeto, un vestido, etc.). **2** hacer, preparar, enderezar (una comida, una bebida). **3** ... hacer (un esfuerzo, un descubrimiento, un comentario). **4** traer, proporcionar (problemas).

Cuando es un caso muy específico, difícil de precisar fuera de contexto, hemos dado un ejemplo que ayude a concretar:

In some specific cases in which translations are difficult to understand out of context, concrete examples are provided:

make ... 34 disponerse a, empezar a: *he made as if to talk = se disponía a hablar ...*

Por otro lado, incluye este diccionario gran cantidad de locuciones y frases hechas con sus correspondientes traducciones:

In addition, the dictionary includes a large number of idioms and phrases with their corresponding translations:

make ... || **57 to – a day/evening/night of it,** pasar un día/tarde/noche fantásticos, de maravilla ...

Para situar al consultante en los contextos sociales en que suelen usarse las distintas palabras, cuando se trata de términos cuyo uso no es general hemos anotado entre paréntesis los registros correspondientes, tanto en los casos relativos al ámbito cultural como en aquellos en que la diferencia se da entre el inglés americano y el inglés británico:

To assist the user in recognizing the specific contexts in which certain terms are generally used, especially in the case of terms less widely used, the corresponding semantic or cultural register is noted in parenthesis as well as the differences, if any, between British and American English:

make ... 15 (fam.) llegar a, ... **26** (lit. y arc.) estar a punto de, ... **31** (fam. y vul.) seducir, llevar al huerto, ... **50 to make something over, ...** (EE.UU.) rehacer, ... **56 to – with,** (EE.UU.) y argot) traer, ... **61 to – one's way**, (form.) progresar, avanzar, ...
gas ... 3 (EE.UU. y fam.) gasolina ... **7** (brit. y fam.) cháchara, cotorreo, palique.
gear ... 15 (brit.) **– lever,** (EE.UU.) **– shift,** palanca de cambios (de velocidades).
gallon ... galón (medida; brit. = 4,5 l.; EE.UU. = 3,7 l.).

Así mismo, incluimos la anotación correspondiente cuando un vocablo o una acepción son propios de determinado ámbito profesional o técnico:

When a word forms part of the vocabulary of a specific professional or technical field, this is indicated by an appropriate label:

make ... 32 MAR. avistar (tierra), llegar a puerto, ...
garbage ... 3 INF. información inservible, incorrecta.
garnishment ... 1 DER. embargo, ejecución de una deuda ...
garrison ... 1 ... MIL. guarnición, destacamento.

Además de todas las especificaciones expuestas hasta aquí, y para evitar en lo posible errores de traducción, hemos procurado poner en primer lugar las acepciones más usuales y por otro lado, incluir, como entrada, formas irregulares de verbos:

In addition to the references indicated above and in order to avoid translation errors, the most common translation of a headword is placed first and verb entries include their irregular forms.

made ... *pret. y p.p.* V. **make**

Abbreviations used in this dictionary

Abreviaturas usadas en este diccionario

AER. *aeronáutica* aeronautics
adj. *adjetivo* adjective
adv. *adverbio* adverb
AGR. *agricultura* agriculture
Am. *América Latina* Latin America
ANAT. *anatomía* anatomy
ANTR. *antropología* anthropology
arc. *arcaísmo* archaism
ARQ. *arquitectura* architecture
ART. *bellas artes* fine arts
art. *artículo* article
ASTR. *astronomía* astronomy
ASTRON. *astronáutica* astronautics
atr. *atributo*, *atributivo* attributive
BIOL. *biología* biology
BIOQ. *bioquímica* biochemistry
BOT. *botánica* botany
brit. *inglés británico* British English
c. *contable* countable
card. *cardinal* cardinal
COM. *comercio* commerce
comp. *comparativo* comparative
conj. *conjunción* conjunction
contr. *contracción* contraction
cuant. *cuantificador* quantifier
def. *definido* definite
DEP. *deportes* sport
DER. *derecho* law
DER. MAR. *derecho marítimo* maritime law
desp. *despectivo* deregatory
ECOL. *ecología* ecology
ECON. *economía* economy
EE.UU. *americanismo* American English
ELEC. *electricidad* electricity
ELECTR. *electrónica* electronics
euf. *eufemismo* euphemism
f. *género femenino* feminine gender
fam. *familiar* (*lenguaje*) informal language
fig. *figuradamente/figurado* figurative
FIL. *filosofía* philosophy
FILOL. *filología* philology
FON. *fonética* phonetics
form. *formal* (*nivel de lengua*) formal language
FOT. *fotografía* photography
GAST. *gastronomía* gastronomy
GEOG. *geografía* geography
GEOL. *geología* geology
GEOM. *geometría* geometry
ger. *gerundio* gerund
GRAM. *gramática* grammar
HIST *historia* history
hum. *humorístico* humorous
i. *intransitivo* intransitive
imp. *impersonal* impersonal
ind. *indefinido* indefinite
indic. *indicativo* indicative
INF. *informática* computer science
int. *intensificador* intensifier
interj. *interjección* interjection
interr. *interrogativo* interrogative
inv. *invariable* invariable
irr. *irregular* irregular
juv. *juvenil* (*lenguaje*) juvenile language
LIT. *literatura* literature
lit. *literario* literary
LOG. *lógica* logic
m. *masculino* masculine
MAR. *marina/marítimo* marine/maritime
MAT. *matemáticas* mathematics
MEC. *mecánica* mechanics
MED. *medicina* medicine
MET. *metalurgia* metallurgy
MIL. *militar* military
MIN. *minería* mining
MUS. *música* music
n.c. *nombre contable* countable noun
num. *numeral* numeral
o.d. *objeto directo* direct object
OPT. *óptica* optics
ord. *ordinal* ordinal
pers. *personal* personal
pl. *plural* plural
POL. *política* politics
pos. *posesivo* possessive
p.p. *participio pasado* past participle
prep. *preposición* preposition
pres. *presente* present
pred. *predicativo* predicative
pret. *pretérito* preterite

pron.	*pronombre/pronominal* pronoun/pronominal
pron. rel.	*pronombre relativo* relative pronoun
PSIC.	*psicología* psychology
PSIQ.	*psiquiatría* psychiatry
p.u.	*poco usado* little used
QUIM.	*química* chemistry
r.	*reflexivo* reflexive
RAD.	*radio* radio
REL.	*religión* religion
rel.	*relativo* relative
RET.	*retórica* rhetoric
s.	*sustantivo* noun
s.c.	*sustantivo contable* countable noun
s.i.	*sustantivo incontable* uncountable noun
sing.	*singular* singular
suj.	*sujeto* subject
super.	*superlativo* superlative
t.	*transitivo* transitive
TEC.	*tecnología, tecnicismo* technology
TV	*televisión* television
v.	*verbo* verb
v. i.	*verbo intransitivo* intransitive verb
v.pron.	*verbo pronominal* pronominal verb
v.t.	*verbo transitivo* transitive verb
vulg.	*vulgarismo/vulgar* vulgarism/vulgar
ZOOL.	*zoología* zoology

English Phonetics

La fonética inglesa

VOCALES Y DIPTONGOS

Símbolo:	*Sonido que representa*:	*Ejemplo*:	
[i]	sonido largo como la *i* en *misma*	beet	[bit]
[ɪ]	sonido breve, abierto como la *i* en *afirmar*	bit	[bɪt]
[eɪ]	como *ei* en *seis*	bait	[beɪt]
[e]	sonido breve, bastante abierto, como la *e* en *perro*	bet	[bet]
[æ]	sonido intermedio entre la *a* en *caso* y la *e* en *perro*	bat	[bæt]
[ʌ]	sonido intermedio entre la *o* y la *e*, parecido al de la *o* en la palabra francesa *homme*	but	[bʌt]
[ə]	sonido intermedio entre la *e* y la *o*, parecido al de la *e* en el artículo definido francés *le*	irk ago	[əːk] [əgəʊ]
[ər]	versión corta del sonido norteamericano [ɜr] en sílabas átonas	pepper	[ˈpɛpər, B -ə]
[u]	sonido de la *u* en *sumo*, prolongado	boot	[but]
[ʊ]	sonido de la *u* en *burro*, acortado	book	[bʊk]
[əʊ]	sonido de la *o* en *bola* seguido de la *u* en *burro*	boat	[bəʊt]
[ɔ]	sonido de la *o* en *por*, prolongado	bought	[bɔːt]
[ɑ]	sonido de la *a* en *bajo*, prolongado	balm	[bɑːm]
[aɪ]	como *ai* en *baile*	bite	[baɪt]
[aʊ]	como *au* en *causa*	bout	[baʊt]
[ɔɪ]	como *oi* en *roy*	boil	[bɔɪl]
[ɪə]	como *ia* en *tía*	beer	[bɪə]
[eə]	como *ea* en *fea*	bare	[beə]
[ʊə]	como *uo* en *búho*	boor	[bʊə]
[eɪə]	como *eie* en *reyes*	payer	[peɪər, B -ə]
[aɪə]	como *aie* en *aire*	buyer	[baɪər, B -ə]
[ɔɪə]	como *oie* en *oye*	employer	[ɪmplɔɪər, B -ə]
[aʊə]	como *aue* en *fraude*	bower	[baʊər, B -ə]
[əʊə]	como *ó-u-e* en *incólume*	blower	[bləʊər, B -ə]

CONSONANTES

Símbolo:	*Sonido que representa*:	*Ejemplo*:	
[b]	como la *b* en *mambo* (aspirada)	be	[biː]
[k]	como la *c* en *caso* (aspirada)	cold	[kəʊld]
[d]	como la *d* en *conde* (aspirada)	deed	[diːd]
[f]	como la *f* en el español	fee	[fiː]
[g]	como la *g* en *goma* (aspirada)	game	[geɪm]
[h]	como la *j* en *jerga*, pero mucho más suave	heed	[hiːd]
[l]	como la *l* en el español	leaf	[liːf]
[m]	como la *m* en el español	me	[miː]
[n]	como la *n* en *nota*	need	[niːd]
[p]	como la *p* en *pan* (aspirada)	pea	[piː]
[r]	(la *r* norteamericana es un sonido semivocal que se articula elevando la lengua hacia la bóveda palatina) (la *r* británica, prevocálica o intervocálica, es un sonido fricativo parecido a la *r* en *perro*)	around	[ə'raʊnd]
[s]	como la *s* en el español	see	[siː]
[t]	como la *t* en *tos* (aspirada)	tea	[tiː]
[v]	*v* fuerte y definida	veal	[viːl]
[w]	como *hu* en *huevo*	wine	[waɪn]
[z]	como la *s* en *mismo*, pero más sonora y vibrada	zeal	[ziːl]
[ð]	como la d en *nada*	then	[ðen]
[θ]	como la *c* en *dice* y la *z* en *zapato* en la pronunciación del Sur de España	theme	[θiːm]
[ʒ]	como la *ll* en *llegar* y la *y* en *ayer* en la pronunciación argentina	measure	[meʒər, B -ə]
[dʒ]	como al sonido anterior, pero mucho más fuerte y con un vestigio de *ch*	jeep	[dʒiːp]
[ʃ]	sonido parecido al que hacemos al callar a alguien, como la *ch* en la palabra francesa *chez*	sheet	[ʃiːt]
[tʃ]	como la *ch* en *hucha*	chest	[tʃest]
[j]	como la *y* en *yo* y la *i* en *ionosfera*	yield	[jiːld]
[hw]	como *ju* en *jungla*, pero mucho más suave	wheel	[hwiːl]
[ŋ]	como la *n* en *vengo*	sing	[siŋ]

Normas de ortografía en el inglés británico

Existen ciertas diferencias entre el inglés escrito en Gran Bretaña (British English, BE) y el inglés escrito en Estados Unidos (American English, AE). Son las principales:

1. **El guión** con que se escriben en BE muchas palabras compuestas se suprime a menudo en AE, p.ej. heeltap, soapbox, shinbone.
2. La **u** que se escribe en BE en las palabras que terminan en **-our** (p.ej. col*our*, hum*our*) se suprime en AE: col*or*, hum*or*.
3. Muchas palabras que en BE terminan en **-re** (p.ej. cent*re*, met*re*, theat*re*) se escriben en AE **-er**, p.ej. cent*er*, met*er*, theat*er* (pero no massacre).
4. En muchos casos, las palabras que en BE tienen **ll** en posición media se escriben en AE con una **l**, p.ej. counci*l*or, trave*l*ed. Sin embargo, hay palabras que en BE se escriben con una **l** que en AE se escriben con **ll**, p.ej. enro*ll*(s), ski*ll*ful, insta*ll*ment.
5. En ciertos casos, las palabras que en BE terminan en **-ence** (p.ej. def*ence*, off*ence*) se escriben en AE con **-ense**: def*ense*, off*ense*.
6. Ciertas vocales finales, que no tienen valor en la pronunciación, se escriben en BE (p.ej. catalog*ue*, dialog*ue*, prolog*ue*, programm*me*) pero no en AE: catalog, dialog, prolog, program.
7. Se ha extendido más en AE que en BE la costumbre de escribir **e** en lugar de **ae** y **oe**, p.ej. an(a)*e*mia, an(a)*e*sthesia, (o)*e*sophagus.
8. Algunas consonantes que en BE suelen escribirse dobles (p.ej. wa*gg*on) se escriben en AE sencillas, p.ej. wa*g*on, kidna*p*ed, worshi*p*ed.
9. En AE se suprime a veces la **u** del grupo **ou** que tiene BE, p.ej. m*o*(*u*)ld, sm*o*(*u*)lder, y se escribe en AE pl*ow* en lugar del BE pl*ough*.
10. En AE suele suprimirse la **e** muda en las palabras como abridg(*e*)ment, acknowledg(*e*)ment.
11. Hay otras palabras que se escriben de distinto modo en BE y AE, p.ej. BE cosy = AE *cozy*, BE moustache = AE *mustache*, BE sceptical = AE *skeptical*, BE grey = AE *gray*.

La pronunciación del inglés británico

Entre la pronunciación del inglés en Gran Bretaña (British English, BE) y la del inglés en Estados Unidos (American English, AE) existen múltiples diferencias que es imposible tratar aquí en forma adecuada. Señalamos únicamente las diferencias más notables:

1. **Intonación.** El AE se habla en un tono más monótono que el BE.
2. **Ritmo.** Las palabras que tienen dos sílabas o más después del acento principal [''] llevan en AE un acento secundario que no tienen en BE, p.ej. *dictionary* [AE ''dikʃə'neri = BE 'dikʃənri].
3. La **r** escrita en posición final después de una vocal o entre vocal y consonante es normalmente muda en BE, pero se pronuncia claramente en AE, p.ej. *car* [AE kɑːr = BE kɑː], *care* [AE ker = BE keə], *border* [AE 'bɔːrdər = BE 'bɔːdə].
4. Una de las peculiaridades más notables del AE es la **nasalización** de las vocales antes y después de las consonantes nasales [m, n, ŋ].
5. La **a** [BE ɑː] se pronuncia en AE como [æ] en palabras del tipo *pass* [AE pæs = BE pɑːs], *answer* [AE 'ænsər = BE 'ɑːnsə], *dance* [AE dæns = BE dɑːns], *laugh* [AE læf = BE lɑːf].
6. La sílaba final **-ile** (BE generalmente [-ail]) se pronuncia a menudo en AE como [-əl] o bien [-il], p.ej. *missile* [AE 'mis(ə)l, 'misil = BE 'misail].

a, A | eɪ | *s.c.* **1** a (primera letra del abecedario). || *s.c.* e *i.* **2** MUS. La (sexta nota en la escala de Do). **3** sobresaliente (nota académica máxima). || **4 A1,** (fam.) excelente, de primera clase. **5 from A to B,** de un lugar a otro, de un sitio a otro (hipotéticamente): *you have to have a car to be able to go from A to B = tienes que tener un coche para poder ir de un sitio a otro.* **6 from A to Z,** de cabo a rabo, de principio a fin, de pe a pa.
a | eɪ | pronunciación relajada | ə | (ante vocal o h muda **an**) *art. ind.* **1** un, una, uno: *a car, a house, an aeroplane.* **2** un, una, uno (sentido general): *a bird can fly = todos los pájaros saben volar.* OBS: Esta palabra tiene los siguientes otros sentidos y usos: **3** un, una (delante de una cantidad numérica): *a hundred = cien, a quarter = un cuarto.* **4** cada, por, al, a la (indicando frecuencia o distribución): *I work five days a week = trabajo cinco días por semana.* **5** se pone delante de profesiones: *he is a doctor = él es médico.* **6** con algunos sustantivos tiene el sentido de bueno, magnífico, largo en valor, tiempo o cantidad: *that's an idea = ésa es una buena idea.* **7** un, una (con expresiones de tiempo significando una ocasión particular): *the party will be on a Saturday = la fiesta se celebrará un sábado.* **8** un tal (con nombres propios): *Mr Williams? A Mr Brown for you = Señor Williams, un tal señor Brown le busca.* **9** un, una (hablando de un miembro de una familia): *Jim is a typical Bartlet = Jim es un Bartlet típico.* **10** un, una (con nombres de pintores, escultores, etc.): *I bought a Dalí recently = recientemente adquirí un Dalí.*
Finalmente, esta letra sirve como prefijo negativo en sustantivos, adjetivos y adverbios: **11** *asexual = asexual...* y como prefijo que indica un estado: **12** *asleep = dormido.*
aback | ə'bæk | V. **take.**
abacus | 'æbəkəs | *s.c.* **1** ábaco (instrumento para contar): *Chinese children learn to count with an abacus = los niños chinos aprenden a contar con un ábaco.* **2** ARQ. ábaco.
abaft | ə'bɑːft | MAR. *adv.* **1** a popa, en popa, hacia popa. || *prep.* **2** a popa de.
abandon | ə'bændən | *v.t.* **1** abandonar, dejar; desamparar (a alguien). **2** abandonar, desistir de (un plan, un proyecto, etc.) || *v.r.* **3 [to – to]** abandonarse a, entregarse a; dejarse llevar por: *she abandoned herself to grief = se dejó llevar por la pena.* || *s.i.* **4** abandono; despreocupación: *all his student years he lived with total abandon = todos sus años de estudiante vivió con total despreocupación.* || **5 to – ship,** MAR. abandonar el barco.
abandoned | ə'bændənd | *adj.* **1** abandonado; desierto. **2** descuidado, desenfadado; espontáneo: *in an abandoned manner = de una manera descuidada.* **3** (fig.) libertino, vicioso.
abandonment | ə'bændənmənt | *s.i.* **1** abandono; desamparo. **2** cesación, suspensión (de un proyecto, plan, etc.).
abase | ə'beɪs | *v.r.* humillarse, rebajarse, degradarse; envilecerse: *don't abase yourself in that way = no te rebajes de esa manera.*
abasement | ə'beɪsmənt | *s.i.* humillación, degradación; envilecimiento.
abashed | ə'bæʃt | *adj.* avergonzado; desconcertado, confuso, corrido.
abate | ə'beɪt | *v.i.* (form.) mitigar(se), disminuir(se), ceder, menguar(se).
abatement | ə'beɪtmənt | *s.i.* (form.) disminución, mitigación.
abattoir | 'æbətwɑr | *s.c.* matadero.
abbess | 'æbɪs | *s.c.* abadesa.
abbey | 'æbɪ | *s.c.* abadía, monasterio, convento.
abbot | 'æbət | *s.c.* abad.
abbreviate | ə'briːvɪeɪt | *v.t.* **1** abreviar, acortar, resumir. **2** reducir a siglas, poner en siglas.
abbreviated | ə'briːvɪeɪtɪd | *adj.* abreviado, acortado, resumido.
abbreviation | əˌbriːvɪ'eɪʃn | *s.c.* **1** abreviatura, abreviación. **2** resumen, condensación.
ABC | ˌeɪbiː'siː | *s.i.* **1** alfabeto, abecedario. **2** abecé, rudimentos (de un tema, de una asignatura, etc.).
abdicate | 'æbdɪkeɪt | *v.t.* e *i.* **1** abdicar, renunciar (al trono). || *v.t.* **2** eludir, rechazar, rehuir (responsabilidades, obligaciones, derechos, etc.).
abdication | ˌæbdɪ'keɪʃn | *s.c.* e *i.* **1** abdicación, renuncia (al trono). **2** rechazo, huida (de responsabilidades, obligaciones, derechos, etc.).
abdomen | 'æbdəmen | *s.c.* ANAT. abdomen.
abdominal | æb'dɒmɪnl | *adj.* abdominal.
abdominally | æb'dɒmɪnəlɪ | *adv.* abdominalmente.
abduct | æb'dʌkt | *v.t.* secuestrar, raptar.
abduction | æb'dʌkʃn | *s.c.* e *i.* secuestro, rapto.
abductor | æb'dʌktər | *s.c.* **1** raptor, secuestrador. **2** ANAT. abductor (músculo).
abeam | ə'biːm | *adv.* MAR. por el través, al través (en ángulo recto con la quilla).
abed | ə'bed | *adj.* (arc.) en cama, encamado.
aberrant | ə'berənt | *adj.* aberrante, anormal.
aberration | ˌæbe'reɪʃn | *s.c.* e *i.* PSIC. aberración, anormalidad.
abet | ə'bet | *v.t.* **1** instigar, incitar (al mal). || **2 to aid and –,** DER. ser cómplice de, encubrir: *to aid and abet the enemy = ayudar y encubrir al enemigo.*
abettor | ə'betər | *s.c.* DER. instigador (de un delito).
abeyance | ə'beɪəns | DER. *s.i.* **1** suspensión. || **2 in –,** en suspenso, en espera: *it will be in abeyance for a year = eso estará en suspenso un año.*
abhor | əb'hɔːr | *v.t.* aborrecer, abominar, detestar.
abhorrence | əb'hɒrəns | *s.i.* aborrecimiento, aversión, odio.
abhorrent | əb'hɒrənt | *adj.* aborrecible, abominable, detestable.
abide | ə'baɪd | [*v.irr.* en la correspondencia. **3** y su *pret.* y *p.p.* es **abode**] *v.t.* **1** soportar, aguantar; tolerar. || *v.i.* **2** aguantar (el paso del tiempo); permanecer, durar. **3** (arc.) morar, habitar. || **4 to – by,** respetar, acatar, atenerse a (una ley).

abiding | ə'baɪdɪŋ | *adj.* duradero, perdurable; permanente.
ability | ə'bɪlɪtɪ | *s.c.* e *i.* **1** capacidad; facultad: *a great ability to speak languages = una gran capacidad para hablar idiomas.* **2** talento, dotes, aptitudes (naturales de inteligencia): *a man of great ability = un hombre de gran talento.* || **3 to the best of one's –/abilities,** como mejor uno pueda, lo mejor que uno pueda: *to the best of my ability = lo mejor que yo pueda.*
abject | 'æbdʒekt | *adj.* **1** abyecto; vergonzante: *abject poverty = pobreza vergonzante.* **2** (desp.) despreciable, vil, rastrero: *an abject apology = una excusa despreciable.*
abjectly | 'æbdʒektlɪ | *adv.* vergonzantemente; abyectamente.
abjuration | ˌæbdʒʊə'reɪʃn | *s.c.* e *i.* (form.) renuncia, abjuración.
abjure | əb'dʒʊər | *v.t.* (form.) renunciar, abjurar (de una creencia, fe, modo de vida, etc.): *he abjured his own faith = abjuró de su propia fe.*
ablative | 'æblətɪv | *s.c.* GRAM. ablativo. || *adj.* del ablativo.
ablaze | ə'bleɪz | *adj.* y *adv.* **1** en llamas, ardiendo. **2** (fig.) brillante, radiante (con colores muy vivos). **3** excitado, emocionado.
able | 'eɪbl | *adj.* **1** capaz (de hacer algo). **2** competente; valioso: *an able student = un estudiante competente.* || **3 to be – to,** poder, ser capaz de.
OBS. Esta última expresión se usa en sustitución de **can** en los tiempos que éste no tiene.
able-bodied | ˌeɪbl'bɒdɪd | *adj.* sano, fuerte, robusto.
ablutions | ə'bluːʃnz | *s. pl.* (form. o hum.) ablución, lavado.
ably | 'eɪblɪ | *adv.* capazmente, competentemente; hábilmente.
abnegation | ˌæbnɪ'geɪʃn | *s.i.* (form.) abnegación, sacrificio.
abnormal | æb'nɔːml | *adj.* anormal; deforme: *an abnormal child.*
abnormality | ˌæbnɒː'mælɪtɪ | *s.c.* e *i.* anormalidad; deformidad.
abnormally | æb'nɔːməlɪ | *adv.* excepcionalmente, de manera anormal.
aboard | ə'bɔːd | *prep.* **1** a bordo de: *aboard a ship = a bordo de un barco.* || *adv.* **2** a bordo.
abode | ə'bəʊd | *pret.* y *p.p.* **1** de **abide.** || *s.c.* **2** (arc.) morada; domicilio. || **3 to make/take up one's –,** fijar la residencia de uno. **4 no fixed –/address,** sin dirección conocida, sin vivienda fija. **5 right of –,** (form.) DER. derecho de residencia/estancia (en un país extranjero).
abolish | ə'bɒlɪʃ | *v.t.* abolir, revocar, suprimir: *to abolish a privilege.*
abolition | ˌæbə'lɪʃn | *s.i.* abolición, supresión, revocación; erradicación.
abolitionist | ˌæbə'lɪʃənɪst | *s.c.* abolicionista.
A-bomb | 'eɪbɒm | *s.c.* bomba atómica.
abominable | ə'bɒmɪnəbl | *adj.* **1** abominable, execrable; pésimo. || **2 the – snowman,** al abominable hombre de las nieves, el yeti.
abominably | ə'bɒmɪnəblɪ | *adv.* abominablemente, execrablemente; pésimamente.
abominate | ə'bɒmɪneɪt | *v.t.* abominar, aborrecer, detestar.
abomination | əbɒmɪ'neɪʃn | *s.c.* **1** (p.u.) abominación. || *s.i.* **2** odio, aborrecimiento: *my abomination of insects = mi odio hacia los insectos.*
aboriginal | ˌæbə'rɪdʒənl | *adj.* **1** primitivo, originario, indígena: *aboriginal population = población indígena.* **2** aboriginal (referido a la población nativa australiana). || *s.c.* **3** aborigen (de Australia).
Aborigine | ˌæbə'rɪdʒɪnɪ | *s.c.* aborigen (de Australia).
abort | ə'bɔːt | *v.t.* e *i.* **1** MED. abortar, causar un aborto (voluntariamente). **2** (fig.) malograr(se), frustrar(se), hacer fracasar (un plan, proyecto, etc.).
aborted | ə'bɔːtɪd | *adj.* BIOL. atrofiado (árbol, órgano, etc.).
abortion | ə'bɔːʃn | *s.c.* aborto (deseado): *to have an abortion = abortar.*
abortionist | ə'bɔːʃənɪst | *s.c.* abortista.
abortive | ə'bɔːtɪv | *adj.* infructuoso, frustrado, malogrado: *an abortive try = un intento frustrado.*
abound | ə'baʊnd | *v.i.* **1** abundar, haber muchos: *difficulties abound = hay muchos problemas.* **2 [to – with/in]** estar lleno/repleto/rebosante de: *the countryside abounds with wild flowers = el campo está lleno de flores silvestres.*
about | ə'baʊt | *prep.* **1** acerca de, sobre, de, alrededor de: *a book about terrorism; my feelings about her = mis sentimientos acerca de ella.* || *adv.* **2** aproximadamente, alrededor de (con cantidades, horas, etc.). || **3 to be – to,** [+ *inf.*] estar a punto de. **4 that's – it/all,** eso es todo más o menos (al acabar una conversación, trabajo, actividad, etc.). **5 what are you –?,** (fam.) ¿A qué te dedicas? **6 while one is – it,** de paso, aprovechando eso: *clean the kitchen and while you're about it defrost the fridge = limpia la cocina y de paso descongela la nevera.*
OBS: Esta palabra tiene además los siguientes usos preposicionales: **7** definiendo instituciones o actividades: *democracy is about letting people live their lives freely = la democracia significa realmente dejar que la gente viva su vida con libertad.* **8** señalando características de personas, instituciones o cosas: *what I hate about the boss is his voice = lo que detesto del jefe es su voz.* **9** señalando la posición alrededor de algo: *I put my arms about the frightened child = puse mis brazos en torno al niño asustado.*
Y el siguiente uso adjetival: **10** la posición física cercana y disponible de algo o alguien: *is there any water about? = ¿hay algo de agua por aquí?*
Finalmente, esta palabra añadida a un verbo matiza el verbo de las maneras siguientes: **11** en muchas direcciones (al mismo tiempo o sucesivamente): *the group was wandering about the park = el grupo vagabundeaba de aquí para allá en el parque.* **12** sin lugar fijo (implicando que la acción expresada además no tiene finalidad determinada): *people were lying about the beach = la gente estaba tumbada por la playa.*
about-face | əˌbaʊt'feɪs | V. **about-turn.**
about-turn | əˌbaʊt'tən | *s.c.* **1** giro de 180° (expresando un total cambio de opinión): *I'm used to about-turns in politics = estoy acostumbrado a giros de 180° en la política.* **2** MIL. media vuelta.
above | ə'bʌv | *prep.* **1** sobre, encima de, por encima de (directamente sobre la vertical o a un lado): *the sky above us = el cielo sobre nosotros; above sea level = sobre el nivel del mar.* || *adv.* **2** encima, por encima, de encima. || *adj.* **3** de arriba; anterior (con referencia a algo escrito antes): *the above chapter = el capítulo anterior.* || **4 – all,** sobre todo. **5 to get – oneself,** darse importancia, creerse mejor que todos los demás.
OBS: Esta palabra tiene otras matizaciones preposicionales que se expresan a continuación: **6** sobre, por encima de (con cifras): *10% above the usual price = 10% por encima del precio normal.* **7** por encima de (algún fenómeno acústico): *above the noise/music = por encima del ruido/de la música.* **8** por encima de; antes de (con referencia a palabras o textos): *the word is a few entries above = el término está unas cuantas entradas más arriba.* **9** por encima de; mejor que (comparando personas en su clase, oposición, concurso, etc.): *that girl is above anybody else in Mathematics = esa chica es la mejor en Matemáticas.* **10** por encima de; más que (en autoridad, importancia, valor, etc.): *I value honesty above anything else = yo valoro la honradez más que cualquier otra cosa.* **11** por encima de, más allá de, fuera de (crítica, sospecha, etc.): *the monarchy should be above criticism = la monarquía debería estar por encima de toda crítica.* **12** indica demasiada dificultad: *nuclear physics was quite above me = la física nuclear era con mucho demasiado difícil para mí.*
Los matices adverbiales son los mismos expresados en los números anteriores siguientes: **6, 8, 9** y **10.**
aboveboard | ə'bʌvbɔːd | *adj.* legítimo, legal; sin engaño: *the deal is aboveboard = el acuerdo es legal.*
above-mentioned | ə'bʌvmenʃnd | *adj.* citado anteriormente.
abracadabra | ˌəbrəkə'dæbrə | *interj.* abracadabra (especialmente utilizada por los magos).
abrade | ə'breɪd | *v.t.* desgastar (especialmente mediante rozamiento).
abrasion | ə'breɪʒn | *s.c.* **1** MED. abrasión, raspadura (en el cuerpo). **2** GEOL. erosión.
abrasive | ə'breɪsɪv | *adj.* **1** hosco, desconsiderado. **2** abrasivo, raspante (sustancia, líquido). || *s.c.* **3** QUIM. abrasivo.
abreast | ə'brest | *adv.* **1** lado a lado, juntos; de frente: *to walk abreast = caminar juntos.* || **2 – of,** a la altura de (en superficie); parejo con; en línea con: *the car came abreast of the policeman = el coche llegó a la altura del policía.* **3 to be/keep – of,** estar al día de/en; mantenerse informado de.
abridge | ə'brɪdʒ | *v.t.* resumir, abreviar, acortar (normalmente libros, artículos, documentos, etc.).

abridged | ə'brɪdʒt | *adj.* resumido, abreviado, acortado.
abridgement | ə'brɪdʒmənt | *s.c.* resumen, compendio.
abroad | ə'brɔːd | *adv.* **1** al extranjero, en el extranjero: *to be abroad = estar en el extranjero; to go abroad = ir al extranjero.* **2** extendido, propagado (rumor, noticia, etc.). || **3 to be a ... abroad,** correr: *there's a rumour abroad = corre el rumor.*
abrogate | 'æbrəgeɪt | *v.t.* (form.) anular, revocar, abrogar (ley, regla, rol tradicional, etc.).
abrogation | ˌæbrə'geɪʃn | *s.i.* (form.) anulación, revocación, abrogación, abolición.
abrupt | ə'brʌpt | *adj.* **1** brusco, repentino, abrupto: *an abrupt stop.* **2** (desp.) áspero, desabrido: *abrupt behaviour = comportamiento desabrido.*
abruptly | ə'brʌptlɪ | *adv.* **1** bruscamente, repentinamente. **2** (desp.) ásperamente, desabridamente.
abruptness | ə'brʌptnɪs | *s.i.* **1** brusquedad. **2** (desp.) aspereza, desabrimiento.
abscess | 'æbsɪs | *s.c.* MED. absceso.
abscond | əb'skɒnd | *v.i.* **1** fugarse, huir; desaparecer (especialmente con algo robado). **2 [to – (from)]** escaparse, fugarse, huir (de la cárcel, reformatorio, etc.).
abseil | 'æbseɪl | *v.i.* DEP. deslizarse montaña abajo (utilizando la técnica del rápel).
absence | 'æbsəns | *s.i.* e *c.* **1** ausencia, falta (de una persona o cosa). || **2 – of mind,** distracción. **3 in the – of,** en ausencia de.
absent | 'æbsənt | *adj.* **1 [– (from)]** ausente (de clase, del trabajo, etc.). **2 [– (from)]** ausente (de una institución, sistema, situación, etc.). **3** distraído, abstraído. || | əb'sent | *v.r.* **4** ausentarse, faltar, no acudir.
absentee | ˌæbsən'tiː | *s.c.* **1** absentista. || **2 – ballot,** (EE.UU.) POL. voto por correspondencia. **3 – landlord,** HIST. propietario absentista.
absenteeism | ˌæbsən'tiːɪzəm | *s.i.* absentismo, ausentismo.
absentia | əb'sentɪə | **in –,** (form.) en ausencia.
absently | 'æbsəntlɪ | *adv.* distraídamente, abstraídamente.
absent-minded | ˌæbsənt'maɪndɪd | *adj.* distraído, ensimismado, despistado.
absent-mindedly | ˌæbsənt'maɪndɪdlɪ | *adv.* distraídamente, ensimismadamente.
absent-mindedness | ˌæbsənt'maɪndɪdnɪs | *s.i.* distracción, ensimismamiento.
absinthe | 'æbsɪnθ | (también **absinth**) *s.i.* ajenjo.
absolute | 'æbsəluːt | *adj.* **1** completo, total (enfatizando un sustantivo): *an absolute fool = un tonto de remate.* **2** absoluto (poder, autoridad, etc.). **3** FIL. universal, absoluto (válido siempre): *an absolute truth = una verdad absoluta.* || *s.c.* **4** dogma, absoluto. || **5 – majority,** POL. mayoría absoluta. **6 – zero,** FIS. cero absoluto (temperatura por debajo de -276°C.).
absolutely | 'æbsəluːtlɪ | *adv.* **1** completamente, totalmente, absolutamente (como énfasis): *you're absolutely right = estás completamente en lo cierto.* || **2 –:** ciertamente, seguro, claro que sí. **3 – not,** claro que no, seguro que no, no. **4 I –** lo niego rotundamente.
absolution | ˌæbsə'luːʃn | *s.i.* REL. absolución.
absolutism | 'æbsəluːtɪzəm | *s.i.* POL. absolutismo.
absolutist | 'æbsəluːtɪst | *s.c.* POL. absolutista.
absolve | əb'zɒlv | *v.t.* **1 [to – (from/ of)]** absolver, exculpar, exonerar, eximir: *to be absolved of a crime = ser absuelto de un crimen.* **2** REL. absolver, perdonar.
absorb | əb'zɔːb | *v.t.* **1** absorber (líquido, gas, calor, energía, etc.). **2** reducir, amortiguar (un golpe). **3** (fig.) encajar; aguantar (un cambio o similar). **4** absorber, captar, comprender. **5** interesar; atraer (la atención). **6 to be absorbed into,** ser absorbido dentro de (un estamento o grupo mayor).
absorbed | əb'zɔːbd | *adj.* **[– (in)]** absorto.
absorbent | əb'zɔːbənt | *adj.* absorbente (de líquidos o similar).
absorber | əb'sɔːbə | V. **shock absorber.**
absorbing | əb'zɔːbɪŋ | *adj.* interesante, atrayente.
absorption | əb'szɔːpʃn | *s.i.* **1** fascinación (en algún tema): *my absorption with philosophy.* **2** absorción (de líquidos, grupos, impactos, etc.).
abstain | əb'steɪn | *v.i.* **1 [to – (from)]** abstenerse, privarse. **2** POL. abstenerse (en votaciones).
abstainer | əb'steɪnər | *s.c.* abstemio.
abstemious | əb'stiːmɪəs | *adj.* abstemio; frugal.
abstemiously | əb'stiːmɪəslɪ | *adv.* frugalmente; sin probar bebida.
abstemiousness | əb'stiːmɪəsnɪs | *s.i.* frugalidad; estado abstemio.
abstention | əb'stenʃn | *s.c.* e *i.* POL. abstención (en votaciones). || *s.i.* **2 [– (from)]** privación, abstención.
abstinence | 'æbstɪnəns | *s.i.* **1** abstinencia; continencia. **2** REL. abstinencia.
abstinent | 'æbstɪnənt | *adj.* continente; abstinente.
abstract | 'æbstrækt | *adj.* **1** abstracto; teórico. **2** FIL. abstracto. **3** ART. abstracto. || *s.c.* **4** resumen, extracto. **5** FIL. idea abstracta. **6** ART. cuadro abstracto. || | əb'strækt | *v.t.* **7** resumir, extractar. **8** (form. y hum.) sustraer, robar. || *v.r.* **9** (form.) retirarse; abstraerse, ensimismarse (de una actividad, trabajo, etc.). || **10 – noun,** GRAM. nombre abstracto. **11 in the –,** en abstracto; en general.
abstracted | æb'stræktɪd | *adj.* abstraído, absorto, distraído.
abstractedly | æb'stræktɪdlɪ | *adv.* abstraídamente, distraídamente.
abstraction | æb'strækʃn | *s.c.* **1** FIL. abstracción. || *s.i.* **2** ensimismamiento, abstracción; distracción. **3** MIN. extracción (de minerales).
abstruse | æb'struːs | *adj.* abstruso, oscuro, difícil de entender.
abstrusely | æb'struːslɪ | *adv.* abstrusamente, oscuramente.
abstruseness | æb'struːsnɪs | *s.i.* incomprensibilidad, ininteligibilidad.
absurd | əb'sɜːd | *adj.* absurdo, disparatado; ridículo.
absurdity | əb'sɜːdɪtɪ | *s.c.* e *i.* absurdo, ridiculez, disparate.
absurdly | əb'sɜːdlɪ | *adv.* **1** absurdamente, disparatadamente; ridículamente. **2** ridículamente, extremadamente (como énfasis): *an absurdly low salary = un salario ridículamente bajo.*
abundance | ə'bʌndəns | *s.i.* **1 [– (of)]** abundancia, riqueza. || **2 an – of,** una gran cantidad de. **3 in –,** en abundancia.
abundant | ə'bʌndənt | *adj.* abundante, copioso.
abundantly | ə'bʌndəntlɪ | *adv.* **1** abundantemente, copiosamente. **2** rotundamente, claramente (enfatizando una verdad que parece incuestionable): *abundantly clear = rotundamente claro.*
abuse | ə'bjuːs | *s.i.* **1** improperios, insultos. **2 [– (of)]** maltrato, abuso: *abuse of children = maltrato de niños.* || *s.i.* y *c.* **3 [– (of)]** abuso, mal uso (de poder, posición, droga, etc.). || | ə'bjuːz | *v.t.* **4** abusar de, hacer mal uso de (posición, poder, etc.). **5** insultar, injuriar, denostar. **6** maltratar (con violencia física y crueldad).
abusive | ə'bjuːsɪv | *adj.* insultante, ofensivo, injurioso: *abusive behaviour = comportamiento injurioso.*
abusively | ə'bjuːsɪvlɪ | *adv.* insultantemente, ofensivamente, injuriosamente.
abut | ə'bʌt | *v.i.* (form.) **[to – on]** lindar con, estar contiguo a.
abutment | ə'bʌtmənt | *s.c.* TEC. empalme (de construcciones).
abysmal | ə'bɪzməl | *adj.* abismal, insondable; fatal, total (enfatizando algo negativo).
abysmally | ə'bɪzməlɪ | *adv.* totalmente, fatalmente; abismalmente.
abyss | ə'bɪs | *s.c.* (lit.) **1** GEOL. sima, abismo. **2** (fig.) infierno; precipicio (como situación muy peligrosa). **3** abismo; separación (entre dos cosas).
acacia | ə'keɪʃə | *s.c.* acacia.
academic | ˌækə'demɪk | *adj.* **1** académico, escolar. **2** intelectual, erudito, cultivado. **3** teórico, especulativo, bizantino. || *s.c.* **4** profesor universitario, investigador superior. || **5 – freedom,** libertad de cátedra.
academically | ˌækə'demɪklɪ | *adv.* académicamente, escolarmente
academician | əˌkædə'mɪʃn | *s.c.* académico.
academy | ə'kædəmɪ | *s.c.* academia, instituto especializado, colegio (normalmente dedicado a una única especialidad).
accede | æk'siːd | *v.i.* (form.) **[to – (to)]** acceder, consentir.
accelerando | ækˌselə'rændəʊ | MUS. *adj.* y *adv.* acelerando.
accelerate | æk'seləreɪt | *v.i.* **1** acelerar, incrementar la velocidad. **2** (fig.) incrementar, aumentar, acelerarse. || *v.t.* **3** acelerar (un nombramiento, un proceso, etc.).
acceleration | əkˌselə'reɪʃn | *s.i.* **1** FIS. aceleración. **2** (fig.) aumento, incremento, aceleración. || *s.i.* y *c.* **3** aceleración, aumento de velocidad (de un vehículo).
accelerator | ək'seləreɪtər | *s.c.* acelerador.
accent | 'æksənt | *s.c.* **1** FON. acento. **2** GRAM. acento, tilde (gráfico). **3** énfasis: *the accent is on participation = el énfasis está en la participación.* || | æk'sent | *v.t.* **4** acentuar, enfatizar.

accented | æk'sentɪd | *adj.* acentuado, con acento (de un país o región).
accentuate | ək'sentʃʊeɪt | *v.t.* acentuar, aumentar, intensificar (la desigualdad, las diferencias, etc.).
accept | ək'sept | *v.t.* aceptar, admitir; aprobar (infinidad de matices).
acceptability | əkˌseptə'bɪlɪtɪ | *s.i.* aceptabilidad.
acceptable | ək'septəbl | *adj.* aceptable, admisible; adecuado.
acceptably | ək'septəblɪ | *adv.* aceptablemente.
acceptance | ək'septəns | *s.i.* **1** aceptación, admisión, conformidad. || *s.i.* y *c.* **2** aceptación, adopción, inclusión (dentro de un grupo social, institución, trabajo). **3** aprobación, aceptación (de ideas, creencias políticas, etc.). || *s.c.* **4** COM. aceptación (de una letra, pago, etc.).
accepted | ək'septɪd | *adj.* aceptado, reconocido.
acceptor | ək'septər | *s.c.* FIS. aceptador (tipo de átomo o molécula).
access | 'ækses | *s.i.* **1** **[– to]** entrada, acceso a. **2** **[– (to)]** derecho, derecho de acceso, acceso. || *v.t.* **3** INF. acceder (a la información almacenada). || **4 – road,** (EE.UU.) vía de acceso (a una autopista, autovía, etc.). **5 – time,** INF. tiempo de acceso (a la información).
accessibility | ækˌsesɪ'bɪlɪtɪ | *s.i.* accesibilidad, asequibilidad.
accessible | æk'sesəbl | *adj.* **1** accesible (físicamente). **2** **[– to]** disponible para, asequible para.
accesion | æk'seʃn | *s.i.* **[– (to/of)]** POL. ascenso (a trono, poder, etc.).
accesory | æk'sesərɪ | *s.c.* **1** accesorio, complemento. **2** **[– (to)]** DER. cómplice. || **3 – after the fact,** DER. encubridor, copartícipe.
accident | 'æksɪdənt | *s.c.* **1** accidente, descuido, infortunio. **2 accidents will happen,** siempre habrá accidentes. **3 by –,** accidentalmente, fortuitamente, por casualidad.
accidental | ˌæksɪ'dentl | *adj.* **1** accidental, fortuito. || *s.i.* **2** **[(the) –]** (lo) accidental.
accidentally | ˌæksɪ'dentəlɪ | *adv.* accidentalmente, casualmente, fortuitamente.
accident-prone | 'æksɪdəntprəʊn | *adj.* tendente a sufrir accidentes.
acclaim | ə'kleɪm | *v.t.* **1** aclamar, vitorear, alabar. || *s.i.* **2** aclamación, aprobación, alabanza.
acclamation | ˌæklə'meɪʃn | *s.i.* aclamación, aplauso.
acclimatization | əˌklaɪmətaɪ'zeɪʃn | *s.i.* aclimatización.
acclimatize | ə'klaɪmətaɪz | (también **acclimatise**) *v.i.* y *r.* **[to – (to)]** aclimatizarse, adaptarse (a).
accolade | 'ækəleɪd | *s.c.* (form.) alabanza, encomio.
accommodate | ə'kɒmədeɪt | *v.t.* **1** alojar, hospedar, albergar (cosas o personas). **2** complacer, hacer un favor a. || *v.i. r.* **3** **[to – (to)]** acomodarse, ajustarse, hacerse (a un cambio, una situación, una institución, etc.).
accommodating | ə'kɒmədeɪtɪŋ | *adj.* complaciente, servicial.
accommodation | əˌkɒmə'deɪʃn | *s.i.* **1** alojamiento, hospedaje. || **2 – address,** señas transitorias, dirección momentánea. **3 – ladder,** MAR. escala de portalón.
accompaniment | ə'kʌmpənɪmənt | *s.i.* **1** MUS. acompañamiento. || *s.c.* **2** **[– (to/of)]** complemento, acompañamiento: *his death was the accompaniment to the other tragedies of his life = su muerte fue el complemento de las otras tragedias de su vida.*
accompanist | ə'kʌmpənɪst | *s.c.* MUS. acompañante, acompañamiento (una persona).
accompany | ə'kʌmpənɪ | *v.t.* **1** MUS. acompañar. **2** ir con, acompañar. **3** (fig.) acompañar, venir con (ocurrencia simultánea): *pain accompanies this illness = el dolor acompaña a esta enfermedad.*
accomplice | ə'kʌmplɪs | *s.c.* cómplice.
accomplish | ə'kʌmplɪʃ | *v.t.* lograr, llevar a cabo, realizar.
accomplished | ə'kʌmplɪʃt | *adj.* experto, consumado, perfecto: *an accomplished singer = un cantante consumado.*
accomplishment | ə'kʌmplɪʃmənt | *s.c.* **1** logro, realización. || *s.i.* **2** habilidad, capacidad, talento. **3** finalización, conclusión, terminación (con éxito). || **4 accomplishments,** talentos, dotes.
accord | ə'kɔːd | *v.t.* **1** conceder, otorgar. || *v.i.* **2** (form.) **[to – with]** concordar con, armonizar con. || *s.i.* **3** acuerdo, armonía: *in perfect accord.* || *s.c.* **4** acuerdo, convenio (político, sindical, asociativo, etc.) || **5 in – with,** de acuerdo con, en armonía con. **6 of one's own –,** por propia iniciativa. **7 with one –,** de común acuerdo.
accordance | ə'kɔːdəns | *prep.* **in – with,** de acuerdo con, según.
accordingly | ə'kɔːdɪŋlɪ | *adv.* **1** consecuentemente, como consecuencia, en consecuencia. **2** adecuadamente, apropiadamente, en justicia.
according to | ə'kɔːdɪŋ tuː | *prep.* según, de acuerdo con, con arreglo a.
accordion | ə'kɔːdɪən | *s.c.* MUS. acordeón.
accost | ə'kɒst | *v.t.* abordar, dirigirse a (molestando).
account | ə'kaʊnt | *s.c.* **1** relato, narración; informe (detallado). **2** cuenta (bancaria): *current account = cuenta corriente.* || **3 to – for,** explicar, aclarar, responder de; justificar: *how do you account for this loss? = ¿cómo explicas esta pérdida?* **4 accounts,** contabilidad, cuentas. **5 to be accounted,** *[adj.]* (form.) ser considerado. **6 to bring/call to –,** pedir cuentas. **7 by/according to one's own –,** según la versión de uno. **8 from/by all accounts,** a decir de todos, según todos. **9 to give a good – of oneself,** causar buena impresión. **10 of little/ small –,** de poca importancia. **11 of no –,** sin ninguna importancia. **12 on –,** a cuenta. **13 on – of,** a causa de, por razón de. **14 on no –,** de ninguna manera, de ningún modo. **15 on one's –,** para beneficio de uno. **16 on this/that –,** por esta/esa razón. **17 to take into –/to take – of,** tomar en consideración. **18 to turn/put to good –,** aprovechar, sacar provecho de.
accountability | əˌkaʊntə'bɪlɪtɪ | *s.i.* responsabilidad.
accountable | ə'kaʊntəbl | *adj.* **[– (for/ to)] responsable.**
accountancy | ə'kaʊntənsɪ | *s.i.* contabilidad en el mundo anglosajón, estudios que conllevan cierto nivel de economía de empresas y derecho fiscal.
accountant | ə'kaʊntənt | *s.c.* contable.
accoutrements | ə'kuːtrəmənts | *s.pl.* **1** (form. y hum.) equipaje, equipo, pertrechos. *2* MIL. pertrechos.
accredit | ə'kredɪt | *v.t.* **1** acreditar, autorizar, dar credenciales (a un embajador, emisario, institución, etc.). **2** **[to – to/with]** atribuir: *he is accredited with many supernatural gifts = se le atribuyen muchos dones sobrenaturales.*
accreditation | əˌkredɪ'teɪʃn | *s.i.* acreditación, autorización.
accredited | ə'kredɪtɪd | *adj.* **1** acreditado (diplomático). **2** autorizada (opinión, teoría, etc.). **3** de calidad acreditada.
accretion | ə'kriːʃn | *s.c.* e *i.* (form.) aumento, adición, acrecentamiento, aditamento (capa sobre capa).
accrue | ə'kruː | *v.t.* e *i.* **1** ECON. acumular(se), aumentar(se) (intereses, dinero, propiedades, etc.). **2** (lit.) coleccionar; acumular(se) (poco a poco durante mucho tiempo).
accumulate | ə'kjuːmjʊleɪt | *v.t.* e *i.* acumular(se), amontonar(se).
accumulation | əˌkjuːmjʊ'leɪʃn | *s.c.* **1** montón, gran cantidad. || *s.i.* **2** acumulación, acopio.
accumulative | ə'kjuːmjʊlətɪv | *adj.* **1** acumulativo. **2** (desp.) acumulador, acaparador, codicioso.
accumulator | ə'kjuːmjʊleɪtər | *s.c.* **1** ELEC. acumulador. **2** INF. acumulador.
accuracy | 'ækjʊrəsɪ | *s.i.* **1** precisión, exactitud, corrección. **2** veracidad, verdad, exactitud.
accurate | 'ækjʊrɪt | *adj.* preciso, correcto, exacto; acertado.
accurately | 'ækjʊrɪtlɪ | *adv.* exactamente, fielmente, acertadamente, con precisión.
accursed | ə'kɜːsd | *adj.* (form.) maldito, deleznable (personas o cosas).
accusation | ˌækjuː'zeɪʃn | *s.c.* **1** **[– (of/ against)]** acusación, inculpación; imputación. || *s.i.* **2** denuncia, acusación; hostilidad.
accusative | ə'kjuːzətɪv | *adj.* **1** GRAM. acusativo. || *s.c.* **2** GRAM. acusativo.
accusatory | ə'kjuːzətərɪ | *adj.* acusatorio.
accuse | ə'kjuːz | *v.t.* **1** acusar, culpar. || **2 to stand accused of,** estar/ser acusado de.
accused | ə'kjuːzd | *s. sing.* DER. acusado.
accuser | ə'kjuːzər | *s.c.* acusador.
accusing | ə'kjuːzɪŋ | *adj.* acusador, acusatorio: *an accusing look = una mirada acusadora.*
accusingly | ə'kjuːzɪŋlɪ | *adv.* con reproche, en tono acusatorio.
accustom | ə'kʌstəm | *v.t.* y *r.* **[to – (to)]** habituar(se), acostumbrar(se).
accustomed | ə'kʌstəmd | *adj.* **1** **[– (to)]** acostumbrado, habituado. **2** habitual, usual. || **3 to be – to,** estar acostumbrado a, estar habituado a. **4 to get – to,** acostumbrarse a, habituarse a.
ace | eɪs | *s.c.* **1** as (en el juego de las cartas). **2** DEP. tanto directo de saque (en el tenis). || *adj.* **3** (fam.) excelente, sobresaliente: *an ace player = un jugador excelente.* || **4 to be/come within an –**

of, estar a un paso de, estar a punto de. **5 to have an – up one's sleeve,** guardar una carta en la bocamanga. **6 to hold all the aces,** llevar las de ganar.
acerbic | ə'sɜːbɪk | *adj.* acerbo, cruel (una observación o similar).
acerbity | ə'sɜːbɪtɪ | *s.i.* (form.) acritud, aspereza (en el hablar o en el comportamiento).
acetate | 'æsɪteɪt | *s.i.* QUIM. acetato (un tipo de tejido).
acetone | 'æsɪtəʊn | *s.i.* QUIM. acetona.
acetylene | ə'setɪliːn | *s.i.* QUIM. acetileno.
ache | eɪk | *v.i.* **1** doler: *my leg aches = me duele la pierna.* **2** (fig.) **[to – (for)]** ansiar, anhelar. || *s.c.* **3** dolor. **4** (fig.) anhelo, ansia, deseo.
achieve | ə'tʃiːv | *v.t.* **1** lograr, conseguir, realizar. || *v.i.* **2 [to – (in)]** tener éxito.
achievement | ə'tʃiːvmənt | *s.c.* e *i.* **1** logro, realización.
Achilles heel | əˌkɪliːz'hiːl | V. **heel.**
Achilles tendon | əˌkɪliːz'tendən | V. **tendon.**
achy | 'eɪkɪ | *adj.* (fam.) dolorido.
acid | 'æsɪd | *s.c.* e *i.* **1** ácido. || *s.i.* **2** (fam.) LSD (droga alucinógena). || *adj.* **3** ácido: *acid soil = suelo ácido.* **4** agrio. **5** mordaz, burlón (humor, comentario, etc.). || **6 acetic –,** QUIM. ácido acético. **7 an – test,** prueba de fuego, puesta a prueba: *the contract is an acid test of his real intention = el contrato es la puesta a prueba de su intención real.*
acidic | ə'sɪdɪk | *adj.* ácido.
acidity | ə'sɪdɪtɪ | *s.i.* **1** acidez. **2** burla, mordacidad.
acidly | 'æsɪdlɪ | *adv.* ásperamente, mordazmente, burlonamente.
acknowledge | ək'nɒlɪdʒ | *v.t.* **1** reconocer, admitir, aceptar. **2 [to – + o. + (with)]** saludar (con un gesto, sonrisa, etc.). **3** agradecer, apreciar (un favor, un detalle, etc.). **4** acusar recibo de, confirmar. || **5 to be acknowledged (as):** ser admirado, ser reconocido (como).
acknowledged | ək'nɒlɪdʒt | *adj.* reconocido, admirado.
acknowledgement | ək'nɒlɪdʒmənt | *s.c.* e *i.* **1** reconocimiento, admisión. **2** saludo (gesto, sonrisa). **3** agradecimiento, apreciación. **4 [– (of)]** acuse de recibo, confirmación (de). || **5 acknowledgements, agradecimientos, menciones (en un libro por parte del autor a las personas que le ayudaron).**
acme | 'ækmɪ | *s.i.* (form.) apogeo, cenit.
acne | 'æknɪ | *s.i.* MED. acné, espinillas, barrillo.
acolyte | 'ækəlaɪt | *s.c.* **1** REL. monaguillo, acólito. **2** (lit.) discípulo, seguidor.
aconite | 'ækənaɪt | *s.c.* e *i.* BOT. acónito, napelo.
acorn | 'eɪkɔːn | *s.c.* bellota.
acoustic | ə'kuːstɪk | *adj.* acústico.
acoustically | ə'kuːstɪkəlɪ | *adv.* acústicamente.
acoustics | ə'kuːstɪks | *s.i.* **1** FIS. acústica. || *s.pl.* **2** acústica (condiciones del sonido en un determinado lugar).
acquaint | ə'kweɪnt | *v.t.* **1 [to – + *o.* + with]** (form.) informar de, dar detalles de. || *v.r.* **2 [to – with]** familiarizarse con, informarse. || **3 to be acquainted with,** conocer superficialmente a. **4 to get/become acquainted with,** entablar una amistad con, iniciar unas relaciones amistosas con.
acquaintance | ə'kweɪntəns | *s.c.* **1** conocido (no amigo íntimo). || *s.i.* **2** relación, trato (superficial). **3 [– (with)]** conocimiento (de un tema, asignatura, etc.): *my acquaintance with music.* || **4 a nodding/passing –,** una relación/amistad muy superficial. **5 to make someone's –,** entablar una cierta amistad, conocer. **6 of one's –,** que uno conoce ligeramente: *a man of my acquaintance.* **7 on further/closer –,** cuando uno profundiza más, cuando uno conoce mejor (a alguna persona o un tema).
acquiesce | ˌækwɪ'es | *v.i.* **[to – (to/in)]** consentir, asentir, acceder.
acquiescence | ˌækwɪ'esns | *s.i.* consentimiento, asentimiento, conformidad.
acquiescent | ˌækwɪ'esnt | *adj.* condescendiente, acomodaticio.
acquire | ə'kwaɪər | *v.t.* **1** adquirir, obtener, recibir. **2** aprender, adquirir (hábito, habilidad, destreza, etc.).
acquired | ə'kwaɪəd | *adj.* **1** adquirido, recibido, heredado. **2** aprendido, adquirido. || **3 an – taste,** una cosa a la que uno se puede hacer después de esfuerzos y que acaba por gustar.
acquisition | ˌækwɪ'zɪʃn | *s.c.* e *i.* **1** adquisición, compra. || *s.i.* **2** aprendizaje, adquisición: *acquisition of languages = aprendizaje de idiomas.*
acquisitive | ə'kwɪzɪtɪv | *adj.* (desp.) codicioso, acaparador.
acquisitively | ə'kwɪzɪtɪvlɪ | *adv.* (desp.) codiciosamente, acaparadoramente.
acquisitiveness | ə'kwɪzɪtɪvnɪs | *s.i.* (desp.) codicia.
acquit | ə'kwɪt | *v.t.* **1** DER. absolver, exculpar. || *v.r.* **2** (form.) comportarse, desempeñar su papel.
acquittal | ə'kwɪtl | *s.i.* y *c.* DER. absolución, exculpación.
acre | eɪkər | *s.c.* **1** acre (medida de superficie). || **2 acres,** (fam.) montones, grandes cantidades.
acreage | 'eɪkərɪdʒ | *s.i.* superficie, área (medida en acres).
acrid | 'ækrɪd | *adj.* **1** (desp.) acre, punzante (olor o sabor). **2** desabrido, corrosivo, agrio (comentario, palabra, etc.).
acridity | ə'krɪdɪtɪ | *s.i.* acrimonia, acritud.
acrimonious | ˌækrɪ'məʊnɪəs | *adj.* (form.) cáustico, mordaz.
acrimoniously | ækrɪ'məʊnɪəslɪ | *adv.* (form.) cáusticamente, mordazmente.
acrimony | 'ækrɪmənɪ | *s.i.* (form.) aspereza, acrimonia, acritud.
acrobat | 'ækrəbæt | *s.c.* acróbata.
acrobatic | ˌækrə'bætɪk | *adj.* acrobático; ágil.
acrobatically | ˌækrə'bætɪklɪ | *adv.* acrobáticamente; ágilmente.
acrobatics | ˌækrə'bætɪks | *s.i.* acrobacia.
acronym | 'ækrənɪm | *s.c.* sigla.
across | ə'krɒs | *prep.* **1** a través de, por, de un lado a otro (en una superficie). **2** al otro lado de: *my house is across the street = mi casa está al otro lado de la calle.* || *adv.* **3** de ancho: *the eye of that creature can measure 34 cms. across = el ojo de esa criatura puede medir 34 cm de ancho.* **4 – from,** en frente de.
OBS. Esta preposición matiza significados con verbos de la siguiente manera: **5** indica acercamiento a través de una superficie: *she came across to talk to me = se acercó a hablarme.* **6** señala un movimiento por encima de un objeto cruzándolo o quedándose cruzado por encima: *he leant across the dead body to take the gun = se inclinó por encima del cadáver para coger el arma.* **7** expresa la escritura de un lado a otro de una superficie: *the words were writen across the wall = las palabras estaban escritas de un lado a otro de la pared.* **8** indica por toda una superficie, en toda su extensión: *my father gave many talks across Spain last summer = mi padre dio muchas charlas por toda España el verano pasado.* **9** señala que algo afecta a todos los implicados, sin excepción: *the issues at stake cut across party lines = los temas en candelero afectaron por igual a todos los partidos.* **10** matiza miradas, llamadas, gritos, expresando el recorrido de las mismas hacia la persona receptora: *he shouted across the room = gritó de un lado a otro de la habitación.* **11** con partes del cuerpo indica la extensión de un golpe o dolor: *to hit across the face = abofetear en la cara; I have a pain across my back = tengo un dolor en la espalda.*
acrostic | ə'krɒstɪk | *s.c.* LIT. acróstico (poema o escrito en el que las primeras, intermedias o últimas letras forman una palabra o frase).
acrylic | ə'krɪlɪk | *adj.* QUIM. acrílico (tejido o pintura).
acrylics | ə'krɪlɪks | *s. pl.* QUIM. pintura acrílica.
act | ækt | *v.t.* **1** representar, hacer el papel de: *I acted Hamlet.* **2** (fig.) hacer de, representar, hacer el papel de (no en el teatro): *Peter acted the host beautifully = Peter hizo de anfitrión maravillosamente.* || *v.i.* **3** actuar, hacer algo (con un propósito): *act quickly = actúe rápidamente.* **4** funcionar, tener un resultado, servir (una medicina, una medida de fuerza, etc.). **5 [to – for/on behalf of]** DER. representar a (un cliente). **6 [to – on/upon]** actuar de acuerdo con, hacer caso de, seguir (un consejo, instrucción, etc.). **7** comportarse, conducirse, actuar (de una manera u otra). **8 [to – like/as]** actuar de, servir de, hacer de: *to act as an interpreter.* || *s.c.* **9** acto, acción. **10** acto (en una obra de teatro o en un espectáculo). || *s.sing.* **11** fingimiento, teatro. || **12 Act,** POL. ley, decreto (gubernamental). **13 – of God,** catástrofe; caso de fuerza mayor. **14 Act of Parliament,** POL. ley. **15 to – one's age,** comportarse de acuerdo con su edad. **16 to – out, a)** expresar, sacar a la luz (mediante la conducta): *he acts out his sorrow by singing songs = él expresa su pena cantando canciones.* **b)** representar (un hecho real teatralmente). **17 to –/play the fool,** hacer el tonto, hacer el payaso. **18 to –/play the goat,** (fam.) hacer el bobo. **19 to – up,** (fam.) **a)** ir

mal, funcionar mal, dar problemas: *the TV is acting up,* **b)** comportarse mal (especialmente los niños). **20 balancing –,** equilibrio, juego equilibrista (de alguien que no desea comprometerse). **21 to be acting,** estar fingiendo. **22 to catch/nab someone in the –,** coger/cazar a alguien in fraganti. **23 disappearing –,** desaparición por arte de magia. **24 to get/muscle in on the –,** (fam.) aprovecharse de algo, chupar del bote. **25 to get one's – together,** (fam.) arreglárselas, organizarse debidamente. **26 in the – of,** justo en el momento de. **27 juggling –,** habilidad (para salir de una situación comprometida).

acting | 'æktɪŋ | *s.i.* **1** profesión de actor; capacidad/habilidad dramática. || *adj.* **2** en funciones, interino: *the acting President = el presidente en funciones.*

action | 'ækʃn | *s.c.* **1** acción, hecho, acto: *a man of action.* **2** DER. demanda. **3** movimiento (de una parte del cuerpo). || *s.sing.* **4** funcionamiento (de una máquina). || *s.c.* e *i.* **5** MIL. batalla, lucha, acción de guerra. || *s.i.* **6** acción, movimiento (de una parte del cuerpo). **7** efecto; proceso (una sustancia química). **8** acción (de una novela, el mundo de los negocios, etc.). || **9 – replay, TV repetición. 10 to be in –,** MIL. estar en alguna batalla/guerra. **11 to go into –, a)** MIL. entrar en batalla. **b)** entrar en funcionamiento, lanzarse a trabajar (una persona). **12 in –,** en funcionamiento. **13 out of –,** inutilizado, sin posibilidad de acción alguna. **14 to put/bring/call into –,** poner en práctica, implementar. **15 to see –,** MIL. tomar parte en una batalla, participar en la guerra. **16 to take –,** tomar medidas. **17 to take no –,** no hacer nada.

actionable | 'ækʃnəbl | *adj.* DER. demandable; de juzgado.

activate | 'æktɪveɪt | *v.t.* activar, poner en marcha/funcionamiento (máquinas).

activation | ˌæktɪ'veɪʃn | *s.i.* activación.

active | 'æktɪv | *adj.* **1** activo, enérgico, energético. **2** vivo, fuerte (como énfasis): *an active discussion.* **4** QUIM. activo (en productos, sustancias, etc.). **5** GRAM. activa (voz). **6** ELECTR. activo (capaz de emitir señales de amplificación). || **7 – service,** MIL. servicio activo.

actively | 'æktɪvlɪ | *adv.* **1** activamente, vigorosamente, enérgicamente. **2** totalmente, radicalmente.

activeness | 'æktɪvnɪs | *s.i.* vigor, energía.

activist | 'æktɪvɪst | *s.c.* activista (normalmente hablando de política o ideología).

activity | æk'tɪvɪtɪ | *s.i.* **1** actividad; diligencia. || *s.c.* **2** actividad, ocupación (no profesional, sino de ocio). || **3 activities,** actividades (de asociaciones, grupos, etc.).

actor | 'æktər | *s.c.* **1** actor (profesional). **2** (fig.) actor (persona que finge).

actress | 'æktrɪs | *s.c.* **1** actriz (profesional). **2** (fig.) actriz (persona que finge).

actual | 'æktʃuəl | *adj.* **1** real, verdadero; objetivo. **2** mismo, en sí mismo: *the actual performance only starts at 6 = la actuación en sí no empieza hasta las 6.*

actuality | ˌæktʃu'ælɪtɪ | *s.i.* **1** realidad, objetividad. || **2 in –,** realmente, en realidad (como contraste o contraposición).

actually | 'æktʃuəlɪ | *adv.* **1** realmente, verdaderamente, en realidad.

OBS: Este adverbio tiene, además, las siguientes matizaciones: **2** además, y lo que es más (añadiendo detalles sobre algo). **3** además, ni más ni menos que, fíjate (señalando un ligero énfasis). **4** de hecho (introduciendo un comentario o añadiendo información contrastiva). **5** a propósito, en realidad (diciendo algo totalmente nuevo en la conversación). **6** de hecho, en realidad (la persona que está hablando se interrumpe). **7** en realidad (corrigiendo el comentario de otra persona).

actuary | 'æktʃuərɪ | *s.c.* actuario (de seguros).

actuate | 'æktʃueɪt | *v.t.* TEC. activar, accionar.

acuity | ə'kjuːɪtɪ | *s.i.* (form.) agudeza (de pensamiento, vista, oído, etc.).

acumen | 'ækjumen | *s.i.* perspicacia; buen sentido (financiero, político, etc.).

acupunture | 'ækjupʌŋktʃər | *s.i.* acupuntura.

acupunturist | 'ækjupʌŋktʃərɪst | *s.c.* experto en acupuntura.

acute | ə'kjuːt | *adj.* **1** agudo; extremo (dolor, sentimiento, etc.). **2** perspicaz, sagaz: *an acute observer.* **3** penetrante; fuerte (con referencia a los sentidos). **4** GEOM. agudo (ángulo). **5** FON. agudo (acento).

acutely | ə'kjuːtlɪ | *adv.* **1** intensamente, fuertemente. **2** dolorosamente; extremadamente. **3** perspicazmente, sagazmente.

acuteness | ə'kjuːtnɪs | *s.i.* intensidad, fuerza.

ad | æd | *s.c.* (fam.) anuncio.

AD | ˌeɪ'diː | *adv.* antes de Cristo.

adage | 'ædɪdʒ | *s.c.* (p.u.) adagio.

adagio | ə'daːdʒɪəu | *adj.* y *adv.* MUS. adagio.

Adam | 'ædəm | **1 Adam's apple,** ANAT. nuez (de la garganta). **2 not to know somebody from –,** no conocer en absoluto a nadie.

adamant | 'ædəmənt | *adj.* inflexible, firme; obstinado.

adamantly | 'ædəməntlɪ | *adv.* inflexiblemente, firmemente; obstinadamente.

adapt | ə'dæpt | *v.t.* **1** adaptar; refundir. **2 [to – + *o.* + (to)]** acomodar, adaptar. || *v.i.* y *r.* **3 [to – (to)]** adaptarse, acomodarse.

adaptability | əˌdæptə'bɪlɪtɪ | *s.i.* adaptabilidad; flexibilidad.

adaptable | ə'dæptəbl | *adj.* flexible.

adaptation | ˌædæp'teɪʃn | *s.c.* **1 [– (of)]** adaptación, versión. || *s.i.* **2** adaptación, acomodación.

adapted | ə'dæptɪd | *adj.* adecuado, adaptado.

adaptor | ə'dæptəːr | *s.c.* adaptador.

add | æd | *v.t.* **1** añadir, agregar. **2** añadir (como comentario). **3** MAT. sumar. || *v.i.* **4 [to – to]** sumarse a, añadirse a, unirse a: *his stupidity adds to our problems = su estupidez se suma a nuestros problemas.* || **5 added to this/– to this/if you –,** además de, encima. **6 to – in,** incluir; contabilizar. **7 to – insult to injury,** añadir insulto al daño; para más inri; cebarse. **8 to – on, a)** añadir, juntar. **b)** adjuntar, añadir. **9 to – on to,** aumentar, engrandecer; añadir. **10 to – up, a)** calcular el total, sumar todo, ascender a. **b)** tener sentido, ser lógico; querer decir por lógica: *yes, it adds up = sí, tiene sentido.* **11 to – up to,** resultar en, querer decir: *it all adds up to one thing: I don't love you = todo esto quiere decir una cosa: no te quiero.*

added | 'ædɪd | *adj.* añadido, adicional.

addendum | ə'dendəm | [*pl.* **addenda**] *s.c.* apéndice.

adder | 'ædəːr | *s.c.* ZOOL. víbora.

addict | 'ædɪkt | *s.c.* **1** adicto (a las drogas). **2** (fig.) amante, fanático, adicto.

addicted | ə'dɪktɪd | *adj.* **1 [– (to)]** adicto. **2** (fig.) **[– (to)]** amante, fanático.

addiction | ə'dɪkʃn | *s.i.* **1 [– (to)]** adicción, drogodependencia. || *s.c.* e *i.* **2** (fig.) **[– (to)]** afición.

addictive | ə'dɪktɪv | *adj.* **1** causante de drogodependencia. **2** (fig.) apasionante, muy interesante.

addition | ə'dɪʃn | *s.c.* **1** adición, suplemento. || *s.i.* **2** añadido, adición extra. **3** MAT. suma. || **4 in – to,** además de.

additional | ə'dɪʃənl | *adj.* adicional.

additionally | ə'dɪʃənəlɪ | *adv.* **1** adicionalmente, por añadidura. **2** además.

additive | 'ædɪtɪv | *s.c.* QUIM. aditivo.

addle | 'ædl | *v.t.* **1** confundir, desconcertar. **2 to be addled,** estar confuso, estar desconcertado.

addled | 'ædld | *adj.* podrido (sólo huevos).

address | ə'dres | *s.c.* **1** dirección, señas. **2** discurso, conferencia; locución. || *v.t.* **3** dirigirse a, dirigir la palabra a. **4 [to – as]** llamar: *you must address him as sir = debes llamarle señor.* **5** dirigir (a) (una carta, etc.). **6** acometer (una tarea, un problema). || *v.r.* **7 [to – (to)]** dedicarse, atender (un problema, tarea, para solucionarlo).

address-book | ə'dresbuk | *s.c.* agenda (de direcciones).

addressee | ˌædre'siː | *s.c.* destinatario.

adduce | ə'djuːs | *v.t.* (form.) aducir, citar.

adenoidal | ˌædɪ'nɔɪdl | *adj.* MED. nasal (de la voz).

adenoids | 'ædɪnɔɪdz | *s. pl.* ANAT. adenoides, vegetaciones.

adept | 'ædept | *adj.* **1 [– (at/in)]** experto, versado (en). || *s.c.* **2** experto.

adequacy | 'ædɪkwəsɪ | *s.i.* suficiencia (en cantidad y cualidad).

adequate | 'ædɪkwɪt | *adj.* adecuado, suficiente.

adequately | 'ædɪkwɪtlɪ | *adv.* adecuadamente, suficientemente.

adhere | əd'hɪər | *v.i.* **1 [to – to]** pegarse a, adherirse a. **2 [to – to]** apoyar; mantener (una ley, creencia, opinión): *I adhere to the new law = apoyo la nueva ley.*

adherence | əd'hɪərəns | *s.i.* **[– to]** observancia de, fidelidad a.

adherent | əd'hɪərənt | *s.c.* seguidor, discípulo, fiel.

adhesion | əd'hiːʒn | *s.i.* adherencia (física).

adhesive | əd'hiːsɪv | *s.i.* **1** pegamento, adhesivo. || *adj.* **2** adhesivo.

ad hoc | ˌæd'hɒk | *adj.* **1** ad hoc, con un objetivo concreto único: *an ad hoc committee.* || *adv.* **2** temporalmente, provisionalmente.
adieu | ə'djuː | *interj.* (lit. y arc.) adiós.
ad infinitum | ˌædˌɪnfɪ'naɪtəm | *adv.* sin límite, sin fin.
adipose | 'ædɪpəʊs | *adj.* ANAT. adiposo.
adiposity | ˌædɪ'pɒsɪtɪ | *s.i.* adiposidad.
adjacent | ə'dʒeɪsnt | *adj.* adyacente, contiguo.
adjectival | ˌædʒek'taɪvl | *adj.* GRAM. adjetival.
adjective | 'ædʒɪktɪv | *s.c.* GRAM. adjetivo.
adjoin | ə'dʒɔɪn | *v.t.* estar contiguo a, lindar con.
adjoining | ə'dʒɔɪnɪŋ | *adj.* contiguo, adyacente.
adjourn | ə'dʒəːn | *v.t.* **1** aplazar, diferir (reunión, encuesta, etc.). **2** DER. levantar (la sesión). || **3** aplazarse, diferirse. **4** DER. levantarse (la sesión). **5 [to – to]** (form.) trasladarse, pasar (a): *let's adjourn to the salon for coffee = pasemos al salón a tomar el café.*
adjournment | ə'dʒəːnmənt | *s.c.* **1** aplazamiento, suspensión temporal (de una reunión o similar). *2* DER. aplazamiento (de juicio).
adjudge | ə'dʒʌdz | *v.t.* (form.) DER. juzgar, decretar, fallar (sobre una persona).
adjudicate | ə'dʒuːdɪkeɪt | *v.t.* **1** DER. fallar, decidir. **2** declarar (ganador). || *v.i.* **3 [to – (on)]** DER. fallar, decidir (judicialmente).
adjudication | ə'dʒuːdɪ'keɪʃn | *s.i.* **1** DER. fallo, sentencia. **2** adjudicación (de plazas en una competición).
adjudicator | ə'dʒuːdɪ'keɪtər | *s.c.* árbitro, juez.
adjunct | 'ædʒʌŋkt | *s.c.* **1** accesorio; apéndice.
2 GRAM. adjunto (concepto nuevo para definir un elemento adverbial, preposicional, etc., de una oración).
adjuration | ˌædʒʊə'reɪʃn | *s.c.* e *i.* (form.) juramento solemne.
adjure | ə'dʒʊər | *v.t.* (form.) conjurar; implorar.
adjust | ə'dʒʌst | *v.t.* **1** modificar, cambiar; ajustar (para que sea mejor). **2** ajustar, regular (objetos). || *v.i.* **3 [to – (to)]** adaptarse, ajustarse, regularse (a una situación, trabajo, ingenio). || *v.r.* **4 [to – (to)]** adaptarse.
adjustable | ə'dʒʌstəbl | *adj.* regulable, graduable.
adjusted | ə'dʒʌstɪd | *adj.* equilibrado (de salud mental).
adjustment | ə'dʒʌstmənt | *s.c.* e *i.* **1 [– (to/in)]** ajuste, adaptación (de un objeto o actuación). **2 [– (from/to)]** ajuste, acomodación (a una persona).
adjutant | 'ædʒətənt | *s.c.* MIL. ayudante, asistente.
ad-lib | ˌæd'lɪb | *v.t.* e *i.* **1** improvisar, añadir de cosecha propia (en teatro, discurso, etc.). || *s.c.* **2** improvisación, adición extraoficial. || *adj.* **3** improvisado. || *adv.* **4** improvisadamente.
adman | 'ædmæn | [pl. **admen**] *s.c.* (fam.) publicista.
admass | 'ædmaes | *s.c.* parte de la población que está considerada como fácilmente influible por los medios actuales de publicidad o de propaganda comercial, conjunto de consumidores con poco sentido crítico.
admin | 'ædmɪn | *s.i.* (fam.) administración.
administer | əd'mɪnɪstər | *v.t.* **1** administrar; dirigir, llevar. **2** organizar, administrar (una oposición, un examen, la justicia, etc.). **3** (form.) dar, atizar (una patada, bofetada, etc.). **4** (form.) dar, suministrar (una medicina).
administration | ədˌmɪnɪ'streɪʃn | *s.i.* **1** administración, dirección, organización (de empresa, universidad, institución, etc.). **2 the Administration,** el Gobierno, la Administración (de un país, pero especialmente de los Estados Unidos).
administrative | əd'mɪnɪstrətɪv | *adj.* administrativo.
administratively | əd'mɪnɪstrətɪvlɪ | *adv.* administrativamente.
administrator | əd'mɪnɪstreɪtər | *s.c.* administrador.
admirable | 'ædmərəbl | *adj.* admirable.
admirably | 'ædmərəblɪ | *adv.* admirablemente.
admiral | 'ædmərəl | *s.c.* MIL. almirante.
Admiralty | 'ædmərəltɪ | *s. sing.* MIL. Almirantazgo, Ministerio de Marina.
admiration | ˌædmə'reɪʃn | *s.i.* **[– (for/of)]** admiración.
admire | əd'maɪər | *v.t.* **1** admirar (a una persona, una acción, etc.). **2** admirar, apreciar (los rasgos de algo o alguien con la vista).
admirer | əd'maɪərər | *s.c.* **1 [– (of)]** admirador: *an admirer of art.* **2** cortejador, pretendiente (de una mujer).
admiring | əd'maɪərɪŋ | *adj.* admirador, de admiración.
admiringly | əd'maɪərɪŋlɪ | *adv.* apreciativamente, con admiración.
admissibility | ədˌmɪsə'bɪlɪtɪ | *s.i.* admisibilidad.
admissible | əd'mɪsəbl | *adj.* admisible, aceptable.
admissibly | əd'mɪsəblɪ | *adv.* admisiblemente, aceptablemente.
admission | əd'mɪʃn | *s.c.* e *i.* **1** admisión, recepción. **2** reconocimiento, admisión (de culpa, error, etc.). || *s.i.* **3 [– (to/of)]** admision, ingreso. || **4 –/– fee,** precio de entrada, matrícula. **5 by one's own –,** por admisión propia.
admit | əd'mɪt | *v.t.* **1** admitir, aceptar, reconocer. **2 [to – (to)]** admitir, dejar entrar. **3 [to – +** *o.* **+ (to/into)]** entrar, ingresar (en una organización, un hospital, etc.). **4** (form.) acomodar, tener capacidad para (hablando de un teatro, cine, etc.). || *v.i.* **5** (form.) **[to – of]** permitir, admitir: *the novel admits of only one interpretation = la novela sólo permite una interpretación.* || **to – defeat,** reconocer la derrota, reconocer el fracaso.
admittance | əd'mɪtns | *s.i.* admisión, acceso, entrada.
admittedly | əd'mɪtɪdlɪ | *adv.* justo es reconocerlo, es cierto (normalmente entre comas).
admonish | əd'mɒnɪʃ | *v.t.* (form.) amonestar, reprender.
admonition | ˌædmə'nɪʃn | *s.c.* e *i.* (form.) amonestación.
ad nauseam | ˌæd'nɔːsɪæm | *adv.* interminablemente, sempiternamente (como expresión de queja).
ado | ə'duː | **without further –/without more –,** *adv.* inmediatamente, sin más tardar.
adobe | ə'dəʊbɪ | *s.i.* adobe.
adolescence | ˌædə'lesns | *s.i.* adolescencia.
adolescent | ˌædə'lesnt | *adj.* **1** adolescente. **2** inmaduro, juvenil (con cierto sentido negativo). || *s.c.* **3** adolescente.
adopt | ə'dɒpt | *v.t.* **1** adoptar (un bebé). **2** adoptar, asumir (una actitud, un método de actuación, etc.). **3** fingir, simular (un acento, un gesto, un tono, etc.). **4** adquirir (una nacionalidad o nombre nuevos). **5 [to – +** *o.* **+ as]** elegir de, seleccionar de (en la política): *they adopted him as their candidate = lo eligieron como candidato.*
adopted | ə'dɒptɪd | *adj.* adoptivo (familia o país).
adoption | ə'dɒpʃn | *s.c.* e *i.* **1** adopción (de bebés). || *s.i.* **2 [– of]** adopción de, asunción de, determinación de. **3** elección, selección.
adorable | ə'dɔːrəbl | *adj.* adorable, precioso, encantador.
adorably | ə'dɔːrəblɪ | *adv.* adorablemente, encantadoramente.
adoration | ˌædə'reɪʃn | *s.i.* adoración.
adore | ə'dɔːr | *v.t.* **1** adorar, reverenciar. **2** (fam.) encantar, chiflar.
adoring | ə'dɔːrɪŋ | *adj.* devoto: *an adorying husband = un marido devoto.*
adoringly | ə'dɔːrɪŋlɪ | *adv.* con adoración, con devoción absoluta.
adorn | ə'dɔːn | (lit.) *v.t.* **1** ornamentar, adornar. **2** embellecer; dar prestancia a: *her presence adorned our dining-table = su presencia embelleció nuestra mesa.*
adornment | ə'dɔːnmənt | *s.c.* **1** ornamento, adorno. || *s.i.* **2** decoración.
adrenalin | ə'drenəlɪn | *s.i.* QUIM. adrenalina.
adrift | ə'drɪft | *adj.* **1** MAR. a la deriva. **2** (fig.) desorientado, a la deriva (en la vida personal). || **3 to be –,** ser un fracaso, ir mal (un proyecto, plan, etc.). **4 to go –,** irse al garete; fracasar totalmente (un proyecto, plan, etc.).
adroit | ə'drɔɪt | *adj.* hábil, mañoso; listo (en el comportamiento, no con las manos).
adroitly | ə'drɔɪtlɪ | *adv.* hábilmente, mañosamente.
adroitness | ə'drɔɪtnɪs | *s.i.* habilidad, maña; astucia.
adulation | ˌædjʊ'leɪʃn | *s.i.* adulación.
adult | 'ædʌlt | *s.c.* **1** adulto, persona mayor. || *adj.* **2** adulto, mayor. **3** desarrollado, crecido (hablando de personas o animales físicamente).
adulterate | ə'dʌltəreɪt | *v.t.* diluir; aguar, rebajar (calidad de comida o bebida): *adulterated wine = vino aguado.*
adulteration | əˌdʌltə'reɪʃn | *s.i.* adulteración, disminución (de la calidad de un producto).
adulterer | ə'dʌltərər | *s.c.* adúltero.
adulteress | ə'dʌltərɪs | *s.c.* adúltera.
adultery | ə'dʌltərɪ | *s.c.* e *i.* adulterio.
adulthood | 'ædʌlthʊd | *s.i.* madurez, edad adulta.
adumbrate | 'ædʌmbreɪt | *v.t.* (form.) bosquejar, esbozar.
adumbration | ˌædʌm'breɪʃn | *s.c.* y *i.* (form.) bosquejo, esbozo.

advance | əd'vaːns | *v.i.* **1** avanzar, adelantarse. **2** avanzar, mejorar, progresar. **3** (form.) pasar, transcurrir, avanzar (en el tiempo). **4** (form.) aumentar, incrementar (el precio o valor de algo). || *v.t.* **5** (form.) apoyar; promover (una causa, un interés, etc.). **6** adelantar (una reunión, una conferencia, etc.). **7** (form.) sugerir, proponer, avanzar (una idea, una teoría, etc., de manera hipotética). **8** avanzar, dar hacia adelante (en un aparato). **9** anticipar, adelantar (dinero). || *s.c.* e *i.* **10** avance, progreso (físico y científico). || *s.i.* **11** comienzo, llegada: *the advance of old age has made him clumsy = el comienzo de la vejez le ha hecho torpe.* || *s.c.* **12** adelanto (de dinero); cantidad a cuenta. || *adj.* **13** por adelantado, previo: *advance booking = reserva previa.* **14** de reconocimiento, de avanzadilla: *an advance party = una patrulla de reconocimiento.* || **15 advances,** acercamiento (para mejorar las relaciones); sugerencias, indirectas (para el comienzo de una relación amorosa). **16 in – (of), a)** más avanzado; mejor (que) (en calidad). **b)** por adelantado; antes (que).

advanced | əd'vaːnst | *adj.* **1** adelantado, avanzado, aventajado (hablando de estudiantes, estudios o países). **2** moderno, progresista, avanzado (ideas, libros, etc.). **3** maduro, mayor, de edad. **4** tardío, avanzado (un día, estación, año, etc.). || **5 – credit,** (EE.UU.) crédito por adelantado (cuando una Universidad reconoce estudios en otra).

advancement | əd'vaːnsmənt | *s.i.* **1** ascenso, mejora (profesional o social). **2** promoción, fomento (de un ideal).

advantage | əd'vaːntɪdʒ | *s.c.* **1** ventaja; mejora. || *s.i.* **2** provecho; ventaja. **3** DEP. ventaja (en tenis). || **4 to be to one's –,** ser interés de uno. **5 to give one the – over,** dar a uno ventaja sobre. **6 to have the – over,** gozar de ventaja sobre. **7 to take – of,** aprovecharse de; usar inteligentemente. **8 to good –/to the best –,** favorablemente, con luz favorable; para lucimiento. **9 to turn something to one's –,** dar la vuelta a algo para propio provecho.

advantaged | əd'vaːntɪdʒt | *adj.* privilegiado (social o económicamente).

advantageous | ˌædvən'teɪdʒəs | *adj.* ventajoso, favorable.

advantageously | ˌædvən'teɪdʒəslɪ | *adv.* ventajosamente, favorablemente.

advent | 'ædvənt | *s. sing.* **1** (form.) llegada, advenimiento, aparición: *the advent of new technologies = la llegada de nuevas tecnologías.* || **2 the Advent:** REL. el Adviento.

adventitious | ˌædven'tɪʃəs | *adj.* (form.) accidental, inesperado, no planeado.

adventure | əd'ventʃər | *s.c.* e *i.* **1** aventura. || **2 – playground,** parque infantil (con puentes y otros elementos un poco peligrosos).

adventurer | əd'ventʃərər | *s.c.* **1** aventurero. **2** (desp.) estafador; bandido.

adventurous | əd'ventʃərəs | *adj.* **1** arriesgado, atrevido, intrépido. **2** aventurero.

adventurously | əd'ventʃərəslɪ | *adv.* arriesgadamente, atrevidamente, intrépidamente.

adverb | 'ædvəːb | *s.c.* GRAM. adverbio.

adverbial | æd'vəːbɪəl | *adj.* GRAM. adverbial.

adversary | 'ædvəsərɪ | *s.c.* oponente, adversario, contrario.

adverse | 'ædvəːs | *adj.* adverso, desfavorable, contrario.

adversely | 'ædvəːslɪ | *adv.* desfavorablemente; negativamente.

adversity | ədvəːsɪtɪ | *s.c.* e *i.* adversidad, infortunio.

advert | 'ædvəːt | *s.c.* (fam.) anuncio.

advertise | 'ædvətaɪz | *v.t.* **1** anunciar, divulgar, propagar. **2** publicar, notificar, avisar, anunciar. **3** descubrir, anunciar, proclamar (una característica de los gestos, la voz, etc. de una persona): *the glow in his eyes advertises the hate in him = el brillo de sus ojos descubre el odio que tiene dentro de él.*

advertisement | əd'vəːtɪsmənt | *s.c.* **1** anuncio. **2 [– for]** (fig.) modelo de, definición de: *you are an advertisement for happiness = eres la definición de la felicidad.*

advertiser | 'ædvətaɪzər | *s.c.* anunciante (persona o empresa).

advertising | 'ædvətaɪzɪŋ | *s.i.* publicidad: *an advertising agency.*

advice | əd'vaɪs | *s.i.* **1** consejo. **2** notificación, aviso: *a letter of advice = una carta de aviso.* **3 to lake (legal) –,** DER. recabar consejo de un abogado.

advisability | ədˌvaɪzə'bɪlɪtɪ | *s.i.* conveniencia.

advisable | əd'vaɪzəbl | *adj.* aconsejable; prudente.

advise | əd'vaɪz | *v.t.* **1** aconsejar, asesorar. **2** (form.) informar; avisar. || *v.i.* **3** aconsejar: *I advise that... = aconsejo que...*

advisedly | əd'vaɪzɪdlɪ | *adv.* deliberadamente.

adviser | əd'vaɪzər | *s.c.* asesor, consejero.

advisory | əd'vaɪzərɪ | *adj.* asesor, consultativo.

advocacy | 'ædvəkəsɪ | *s.i.* **[– (of)]** defensa, apoyo: *their advocacy of nationalization is ridiculous = su defensa de la nacionalización es ridícula.*

advocate | 'ædvəkeɪt | *v.t.* **1** recomendar; abogar por. || | 'ædvəkət | *s.c.* **2** DER. abogado defensor, letrado. **3** (fig.) defensor (de un grupo, plan, método, etc.). || **4 devil's –,** V. **devil.**

adze | ædz | *s.c.* MEC. azuela (instrumento para cortar madera).

aegis | 'iːdʒɪs | **under the – of/under one's aegis,** (form.) bajo la tutela de; patrocinado por.

aeon | 'iːən | (también **eon**) *s.c.* HIST. eón.

aerate | 'eəreɪt | *v.t.* QUIM. oxigenar, gasear (sustancias líquidas).

aerial | 'eərɪəl | *s.c.* **1** RAD. antena. || *adj.* **2** aéreo.

aerobatics | ˌeərə'bætɪks | *s. pl.* acrobacia aérea.

aerobic | eə'rəubɪk | *adj.* **1** BIOQ. aeróbico (que utiliza oxígeno). **2** DEP. aeróbico.

aerobics | eə'rəubɪks | *s.i.* DEP. aerobic.

aerodrome | 'eərədrəum | *s.c.* (brit.) aeródromo, aeropuerto (de aviones pequeños).

aerodynamic | ˌeərəudaɪ'næmɪk | *adj.* aerodinámico.

aerodynamics | ˌeərəudaɪ'næmɪks | *s.i.* FIS. aerodinámica.

aeronautical | ˌeərə'nɔːtɪkl | *adj.* aeronáutico.

aeronautics | ˌeərə'nɔːtɪks | *s.i.* aeronáutica.

aeroplane | 'eərəpleɪn | *s.c.* avión.

aerosol | 'eərəsɒl | *s.c.* aerosol.

aerospace | 'eərəuspeɪs | *adj.* aeroespacial.

aesthete | 'iːsθiːt | (EE.UU. **esthete**) *s.c.* esteta.

aesthetic | iːs'θetɪk | (EE.UU. **esthetic**) *adj.* estético.

aesthetically | iːs'θetɪklɪ | (EE.UU. esthetically) *adv.* estéticamente.

aesthetics | iːs'θetɪks | (EE.UU. **esthetics**) *s.i.* FIL. estética.

aether | 'iːθər | V. **ether.**

afar | ə'faː | *adv.* **1** (arc. y lit.) lejos. || **2 from –,** desde lejos, de lejos, a cierta distancia.

affability | ˌæfə'bɪlɪtɪ | *s.i.* (lit.) afabilidad, cordialidad, amabilidad.

affable | 'æfəbl | *adj.* (lit.) afable, cordial, amable.

affably | 'æfəblɪ | *adv.* (lit.) afablemente, cordialmente, amablemente.

affair | ə'feər | *s.c.* **1** asunto, caso, negocio. **2** aventura amorosa, asunto. **3** (fam.) cosa, objeto: *his car is a gorgeous affair = su coche es una cosa espectacular.* || **4 affairs, a)** (lit.) asuntos, temas (de un país, institución, organismo, etc.): *Foreign Affairs = Asuntos Exteriores.* **b)** asuntos; cosas (personales).

affect | ə'fekt | *v.t.* **1** afectar; influir. **2** afectar, emocionar, conmover. **3** (lit.) fingir, aparentar: *she affected to laugh = ella fingió reír.* **4** (lit. y desp.) lucir, pavonearse (ropa o estilo de vestir).

affectation | ˌæfek'teɪʃn | *s.c.* e *i.* (desp.) afectación, melindre.

affected | ə'fektɪd | *adj.* (desp.) amanerado; artificial.

affectedly | ə'fektɪdlɪ | *adv.* (desp.) amaneradamente; artificialmente.

affecting | ə'fektɪŋ | *adj.* (lit.) conmovedor, emocionante.

affection | ə'fekʃn | *s.i.* **1** afecto, cariño. || **2 affections,** (lit.) atenciones; amor, cariño (entre hombre y mujer).

affectionate | ə'fekʃənɪt | *adj.* cariñoso, afectuoso.

affectionately | ə'fekʃənɪtlɪ | *adv.* cariñosamente, afectuosamente.

affidavit | ˌæfɪ'deɪvɪt | *s.c.* DER. declaración jurada.

affiliate | ə'fɪlɪeɪt | *v.i.* y *r.* (form.) **1 [to – to/with]** afiliarse a, asociarse con. || | ə'fɪlɪət | *s.c.* **2** afiliado, socio (sólo organizaciones, no personas).

affiliated | ə'fɪlɪeɪtɪd | *adj.* (form.) afiliado, asociado.

affiliation | əˌfɪlɪ'eɪʃn | *s.c.* e *i.* (form.) **1 [– (with/for)]** afinidad; atracción. **2** similaridad, semejanza.

affirm | ə'fəːm | *v.t.* (form.) **1** afirmar, aseverar. **2** apoyar, sostener (ideas, acciones, derechos, etc.). **3** confirmar, ratificar (una creencia o impresión).

affirmation | ˌæfə'meɪʃn | (lit.) *s.i.* **1** afirmación, aserto. **2** apoyo, sustentación. || *s.c.* **3** DER. promesa (de decir la verdad en un juicio).

affirmative | ə'fɜːmətɪv | *adj.* **1** afirmativo. || *s.c.* **2** afirmativa. || **3 in the –,** afirmativamente. **4 – action,** POL. acción afirmativa (de ayuda a minorías discriminadas a conseguir trabajo mediante cuotas).

affirmatively | ə'fɜːmətɪvlɪ | *adv.* afirmativamente.

affix | æ'fɪks | *v.t.* **1** (form.) **[to – (to)]** pegar, adherir, fijar. || | 'æfɪks | *s.c.* **2** GRAM. prefijo, sufijo.

afflict | ə'flɪkt | *v.t.* afligir, aquejar, atribular: *a strange disease afflicted him = una extraña enfermedad le afligió.*

affliction | ə'flɪkʃn | *s.c.* e *i.* aflicción, congoja, tribulación.

affluence | 'æfluəns | *s.i.* (form.) opulencia.

affluent | 'æfluənt | *adj.* opulento; rico.

afford | ə'fɔːd | *v.t.* **1** [+ *inf.*] arriesgarse a, permitirse el lujo de (comprar algo o acometer una acción imprudente). **2** adquirir, comprar (porque hay medios suficientes): *I can afford a new house now = puedo adquirir ya una casa nueva.* **3** disponer de (tiempo, energías, etc.). **4** (form.) proporcionar, conceder (protección, apoyo, etc.). **5** (form.) ofrecer, proporcionar, dar (un sentimiento, oportunidad, etc.): *it will afford your father great satisfaction to see you now = le dará a tu padre una gran satisfacción verte ahora.*

afforestation | æ'fɒrɪ'steɪʃn | *s.i.* AGR. repoblación forestal, forestación.

affray | ə'freɪ | *s.c.* (form.) reyerta, disputa, pendencia.

affront | ə'frʌnt | *s.c.* **1** afrenta, ultraje, agravio. || *v.t.* **2** afrentar, ofender.

Afghan | 'æfgæn | *s.c.* **1** afgano. **2** ZOOL. afgano (perro de raza afgana). || *adj.* **3** afgano (nacionalidad, idioma, etc.).

Afghanistan | æf'gænɪstaːn | *s. sing.* Afganistán.

aficionado | ə'fɪsjə'naːdəu | *s.c.* entusiasta (de algún pasatiempo).

afield | ə'fiːld | **far –,** lejos, a mucha distancia.

afire | ə'faɪəːr | *adj.* y *adv.* (lit.) **1** en llamas, ardiendo. **2** (fig.) **[– with]** rebosante de, lleno de (sentimientos encendidos).

aflame | ə'fleɪm | *adj.* y *adv.* (lit.) **1** ardiente, enrojecido (por los sentimientos o por los rayos del sol): *aflame with excitement = enrojecido de excitación.* **2** en llamas, llameante.

afloat | ə'fləut | *adj.* y *adv.* **1** a flote, flotando: *the burning ship was still afloat = el barco ardiendo todavía estaba a flote.* **2** (fig.) en el mar. **3** solvente (económicamente). || *adj.* **4** flotante, flotando (en el aire). || **5 to set –,** poner en marcha (proyecto, empresa, etc.).

afoot | ə'fut | *adj.* en ciernes, en preparación.

aforementioned | əˌfɔː'menʃənd | *adj.* (form.) anteriormente mencionado, susodicho.

aforesaid | ə'fɔː'sed | *adj.* (form.) anteriormente mencionado.

afraid | ə'freɪd | *adj.* **1 [– (of)]** temeroso, asustado. || **to be – of/to,** tener miedo de, temer. || **3 I'm afraid (not)/I'm afraid to say,** me temo (que no), desgraciadamente: *she's leaving you, I'm afraid to say = te deja, me temo.*

afresh | ə'freʃ | *adv.* de nuevo, nuevamente.

Africa | 'æfrɪkə | *s.sing.* Africa.

African | 'æfrɪkən | *adj.* **1** africano. || *s.c.* **2** africano.

Afrikaans | ˌæfrɪ'kaːns | *s.i.* **1** afrikaans (variedad del holandés hablado en Sudáfrica). || *adj.* **2** afrikaans; sudafricano (de la parte procedente de Holanda).

Afrikaner | ˌæfrɪ'kaːnəːr | *s.c.* **1** afrikaner (sudafricano blanco descendiente de holandeses). || *adj.* **2** afrikaner; sudafricano (de la parte procedente de Holanda).

Afro | 'æfrəu | *s.c.* **1** afro, estilo afro (peinado). || **2 afro-,** afro (en compuestos).

aft | ɑːft | *adv.* popa (en barcos y aviones).

after | ɑːftər | *prep.* **1** después de, tras: *after the film, we left = tras la película nos fuimos.* || *adv.* **2** después, posteriormente. || *conj.* **3** después que, después de que: *after we left we went home = después de que nos fuéramos nos dirigimos a casa.* || *pret.* **4** post: *after-sales service = servicio postventa.* || **5 day – day/week – week/etc.,** día tras día/semana tras semana/etc. **6 afters,** (fam.) postre. **7 – you,** después de Vd, después de ti. **8 one – another,** uno tras otro, una tras otra. **9 one – the other,** consecutivamente, una después de la otra.

OBS: Esta palabra tiene además las siguientes matizaciones cuando sigue a un verbo: **10** tras. detrás, en persecución (verbos de movimiento): *he ran after her = corrió tras ella.* **11** (lit.) señalando una inspiración o parecido con otra cosa: *this novel is after Charles Dickens = esta novela está escrita en el estilo de Charles Dickens.* **12** indicando la igualdad de nombres propios: *I was named after my grandfather = me llamaron como mi abuelo.* **13** denotando interés amoroso en alguien: *Peter has been after Mary for a long time = Peter lleva tras Mary mucho tiempo.* **14** (EE.UU.) en las horas del reloj: *it was ten after seven = eran las siete y diez.* **15** a por (algo en poder de otra persona): *that fellow is after my teaching post = ese tipo va a por mi puesto de profesor.* **16** detrás o más allá de un punto en el espacio: *Newport is just after Trund = Newport queda justo después de Trund.* **17** indica que la mirada o la voz siguen a una persona que está a cierta distancia o alejándose: *they looked after him as he descended the stairs = miraron tras él según descendía la escalera.* **18** significa persecución: *the police are after him = la policía va tras él.* **19** señala la idea de limpiar algo que otro ha ensuciado: *my mother spent her life cleaning up after us.* **20** posterior grado o importancia: *I'm the third after him in the Department = soy el tercero detrás de él en el Departamento.*

afterbirth | 'ɑːftəbɜːʃ | *s.i.* MED. secundinas, placenta (expulsada tras el parto).

aftercare | 'aːftəkeər | *s.i.* convalecencia; postoperatorio.

after-damp | 'ɑːftədæmp | *s.i.* MIN. moteta, gas moteta (que aparece después de una explosión de grisú).

aftereffect | 'aːftəɪfekt | *s.c.* consecuencia; efecto posterior.

afterglow | 'ɑːftəgləu | *s.sing.* resplandor crepuscular.

after-image | 'aːftəɪmɪdʒ | *s.c.* PSIC. imagen consecutiva, imagen accidental.

afterlife | 'ɑːftəlaɪf | *s.i.* vida después de la muerte.

aftermath | 'ɑːftəmæːθ | *s.i.* secuela, corolario.

afternoon | ˌɑːftə'nuːn | *s.c.* e *i.* **1** tarde (entre el mediodía y la llegada de la oscuridad aproximadamente). || **2 – tea,** (lit.) té de la tarde (comida muy ligera con té). **3 in the –,** por la tarde.

aftershave | 'ɑːftəʃeɪv | *s.i.* loción para después del afeitado.

aftertaste | 'ɑːftəteɪst | *s.sing.* dejo, postgusto.

afterthought | 'ɑːftəθɔːt | *s.sing.* ocurrencia, idea tardía, idea repentina.

afterward | 'ɑːftəwədz | (*brit.* **afterwards**) *adv.* después, luego.

again | ə'gen | *adv.* **1** otra vez, de nuevo, nuevamente. **2** repita; dímelo otra vez: *What's your name again? = ¿Cómo se llama Vd, repita?* **3** sin embargo, no obstante (introduciendo un punto que contradice lo anterior). **4** una vez más, nuevamente (como enfático): *again you are saying the same thing = una vez más, estás diciendo lo mismo.* || **5 – and –/time and –,** una y otra vez, repetidamente. **6 as much –,** otro tanto. **7 as many –,** otros tantos. **8 then –,** no obstante, sin embargo, a pesar de todo. **9 there –,** no obstante, sin embargo, a pesar de todo.

against | ə'genst | *prep.* **1** contra, en contra de: *I leant against the wall = me apoyé contra la pared.* || *adv.* **2** en contra: *for or against? = ¿a favor o en contra?* || **3 as –,** en contraste con: *we got 5.000 pounds as against 3.000 for Liam = nosotros sacamos 5.000 libras en contraste con 3.000 de Liam.* **4 to have something – someone,** tener algo contra alguien; tenerle inquina a alguien.

OBS: Esta preposición matiza verbos de las siguientes maneras: **5** contraste de colores: *his white face stood out against her tan = su cara pálida sobresalía contra su tez morena.* **6** en contra de algo legal: *it's against the Constitution = está en contra de la Constitución.* **7** anticipación de un peligro, precaución: *precautions against fire = precauciones contra incendios.* **8** en oposición de una acción: *we warned her against marrying him = le advertimos que no se casara con él.* **9** en contra de ideas, creencias, modas, etc.: *against my deepest beliefs = en oposición a mis creencias más profundas.* **10** comparación: *the punt has fallen against the sterling = la libra irlandesa ha caído en relación con la libra inglesa.* **11** relación de contraste: *we have to measure resistance against bulk = tenemos que medir la resistencia en relación con el volumen.* **12** oposición deportiva: *we will play against Arsenal = jugaremos contra el Arsenal.*

agape | ə'geɪp | *adj.* boquiabierto.
agate | 'ægət | *s.c.* e *i.* MIN. ágata.
age | eɪdʒ | *s.c.* e. *i.* **1** edad: *age: 19 years old = edad: 19 años.* || *s.c.* **2** época, era. || *s.i.* **3** vejez, ancianidad. **4** envejecimiento, paso del tiempo. || *v.i.* **5** envejecer; hacerse muy mayor (cosas o personas). || **6 – of consent,** DER. mayoría de edad (para casarse legalmente). **7 an –/ages,** (fam.) muchísimo tiempo, un siglo, años y años. **8 to be/act one's –,** comportarse de acuerdo con la edad de uno (en oposición a una conducta infantiloide e inapropiada). **9 to come of –,** hacerse mayor de edad, adquirir madurez, asentarse con madurez. **10 to feel one's –,** sentirse de acuerdo con la edad real de uno (consciente del paso del tiempo). **11 of –,** DER. maduro, mayor (mayoría de edad legal). **12 of an –,** (p.u.) de la misma edad (refiriéndose a dos cosas o personas). **13 over –,** demasiado mayor (para un trabajo o similar). **14 under –,** menor, sin la edad suficiente.
aged | eɪdʒt | *adj.* **1** de edad: *John Peters, aged 50, killed his wife last night = John Peters, de 50 años de edad, mató a su mujer la noche pasada.* **2** anciano, envejecido. || **3 the aged,** los viejos, los ancianos; la tercera edad.
age-group | 'eɪdʒgruːp | *s.c.* grupo de personas de igual edad.
ageing | 'eɪdʒɪŋ | (también **aging**) *adj.* **1** que está envejeciendo. || *s.i.* **2** envejecimiento.
ageism | 'eɪdʒɪzəm | *s.i.* discriminación contra personas mayores.
ageless | 'eɪdʒlɪs | *adj.* siempre joven, perenne.
age-limit | 'eɪdʒlɪmɪt | *s.c.* límite de edad.
agelong | 'eɪdʒlɒŋ | *adj.* de siempre, eterno: *the agelong fight against illness = la lucha de siempre contra la enfermedad.*
agency | 'eɪdʒənsɪ | *s.c.* **1** agencia (de noticias, de viajes, etc.). **2** POL. agencia (de la administración de USA). || **3 through/by the – of,** por medio de, por mediación de.
agenda | ə'dʒendə | *s.c.* orden del día; programa.
agent | 'eɪdʒənt | *s.c.* **1** representante, agente, delegado (de empresa, de arte, etc.). **2** espía, agente. **3** instrumento, medio, agente: *an agent of progress = un instrumento de progreso.* **4** QUIM. agente. || **5 – provocateur,** infiltrado, agente provocador.
age-old | ˌeɪdʒ'əʊld | *adj.* muy antiguo, muy viejo, secular.
agglomerate | ə'glɒməreɪt | *v.t.* **1** aglomerar, amontonar (en gran cantidad). || | ə'glɑmərət | *adj.* **2** amontonado. || *s.i.* **3** GEOL. roca fundida (especialmente volcánica).
agglomeration | əˌglɒmə'reɪʃn | *s.c.* amontonamiento, acumulación.
agglutinate | ə'gluːtɪneɪt | *v.t.* e *i.* **1** aglutinar(se), pegar(se) (con pegamento). **2** FILOL. aglutinarse (los idiomas).
agglutination | əˌgluːtɪ'neɪʃn | *s.i.* **1** aglutinación, pegamiento. **2** FILOL. aglutinación.
agglutinative | ə'gluːtɪnətɪv | *adj.* **1** aglutinante, adhesivo. **2** FILOL. aglutinante.
aggrandize | ə'grændaɪz | *v.t.* (form.) engrandecer, exaltar (a una persona, institución, país, etc.).
aggrandizement | ə'grændɪzmənt | (también **aggrandisement**) *s.i.* (form.) engrandecimiento, exaltación.
aggravate | 'ægrəveɪt | *v.t.* **1** agravar, exacerbar. **2** exasperar, irritar, sacar de quicio.
aggravating | 'ægrəveɪtɪŋ | *adj.* exasperante, irritante, molesto.
aggravation | ˌægrə'veɪʃn | *s.i.* irritación, exasperación.
aggregate | 'ægrɪgɪt | *s.c.* **1** total; conjunto: *an aggregate of 12 years = un total de 12 años.* || *adj.* **2** total, global; general. || | 'ægrɪgeɪt | *v.t.* **3** sumar, juntar, englobar. || **4 in (the) –,** en total, en su conjunto; todo incluido.
aggression | ə'greʃn | *s.i.* **1** agresividad; competitividad. **2** hostilidad, agresión.
aggressive | ə'gresɪv | *adj.* agresivo, hostil; despiadado.
aggressively | ə'gresɪvlɪ | *adv.* agresivamente, hostilmente.
aggressiveness | ə'gresɪvnɪs | *s.i.* beligerancia, agresividad, acometividad.
aggressor | ə'gresər | *s.c.* agresor.
aggrieved | ə'griːvd | *adj.* ofendido; humillado.
aggro | 'ægrəʊ | *s.i.* (fam.) **1** conducta violenta, conducta agresiva. **2** molestia, follón.
aghast | ə'gɑːst | *adj.* **[– at]** horrorizado por/de.
agile | 'ædʒaɪl | *adj.* ágil, ligero, expedito.
agilely | 'ædʒaɪllɪ | *adv.* ágilmente, ligeramente, expeditamente.
agility | ə'dʒɪlɪtɪ | *s.i.* agilidad, ligereza.
agin | ə'gɪn | *prep.* contra (forma escocesa).
aging | 'eɪdʒɪŋ | V. **ageing.**
agitate | 'ædʒɪteɪt | *v.t.* **1** agitar, sacudir (con fuerza). **2** inquietar, perturbar. || *v.i.* **3 [to – for/against]** hacer propaganda a favor de/en contra de, hacer campaña a favor de/en contra de.
agitated | 'ædʒɪteɪtɪd | *adj.* conmocionado, perturbado.
agitatedly | 'ædʒɪteɪtɪdlɪ | *adv.* conmocionadamente, perturbadamente.
agitation | ˌædʒɪ'teɪʃn | *s.i.* **1** inquietud, perturbación. **2** POL. agitación (de matiz político o social), campaña.
agitator |'ædʒɪteɪtər | *s.c.* POL. agitador.
aglow | ə'gləʊ | *adj.* (lit.) **1 [– with]** encendido de, fulgurante por. **2** (fig.) **[– with]** radiante de.
agnostic | æg'nɒstɪk | *s.c.* **1** agnóstico. || *adj.* **2** agnóstico. **3** (lit.) escéptico; indeciso.
agnosticism | æg'nɒstɪsɪzəm | *s.i.* agnosticismo.
ago | ə'gəʊ | *adv.* hace (se coloca detrás de la expresión de tiempo): *five minutes ago = hace cinco minutos.*
agog | ə'gɒg | *adj.* **[– with]** ansioso de, anhelante por.
agonize | 'ægənaɪz | (también **agonise**) *v.i.* **[– over/about]** angustiarse por/sobre, atormentarse por/sobre.
agonized | 'ægənaɪzd | (también **agonised**) *adj.* angustiado, atormentado.
agonizing | 'ægənaɪzɪŋ | (también **agonising**) *adj.* **1** atormentador, angustioso. **2** (fig.) doloroso (decisión o elección).
agonizingly | 'ægənaɪzɪŋlɪ | *adv.* **1** atormentadamente, angustiosamente. **2** dolorosamente.
agony | 'ægənɪ | *s.i.c.* **1** angustia, aflicción, agonía. || **2 – aunt,** (fam. y brit.) escritora que contesta las cartas de consultas sentimentales en un periódico o revista. **3 – column,** sección de consultas sentimentales y personales en la prensa. **4 to pile on the –,** (fam. y brit.) ser un llorica, comportarse como un llorica.
agoraphobia | ˌægərə'fəʊbɪə | *s.i.* MED. agorafobia (fobia a los lugares abiertos y a salir de casa).
agoraphobic | ˌægərə'fəʊbɪk | *adj.* MED. agorafóbico, que tiene agorafobia.
agrarian | ə'greərɪən | *adj.* agrario.
agree | ə'griː | *v.i.* **1 [to – with/on]** estar de acuerdo con/sobre. **2** [+ *inf.*] consentir en, estar de acuerdo en. **3** (fam.) **[to – with]** ir bien a, sentar bien a. **4 [to – with/on]** coincidir con/en, concordar con/en (cifras, versiones de acontecimientos, etc.). || **5 to be agreed on/that,** estar de acuerdo en/acordar que: *are we agreed? Good! = ¿estamos de acuerdo? ¡Estupendo!*
agreeable | ə'griːəbl | *adj.* **1** agradable, ameno. **[– to]** de acuerdo en: *is your brother agreeable to doing the job? = ¿está de acuerdo tu hermano en hacer el trabajo?*
agreeably | ə'griːəblɪ | *adv.* agradablemente, amenamente.
agreement | ə'griːmənt | *s.c.* **1** acuerdo; contrato, pacto, convenio. || *s.i.* **2 [– on/about]** concordancia en, conformidad sobre. **3** consentimiento; acuerdo. || **4 in –:** de acuerdo: *they were in agreement = estaban de acuerdo.*
agricultural | ˌægrɪ'kʌltʃərəl | *adj.* agrícola, agrario.
agriculturalist | ˌægrɪ'kʌltʃəralɪst | *s.c.* experto agrícola, agrónomo.
agriculture | 'ægrɪkʌltʃər | *s.i.* agricultura.
agronomist | ə'grɒnəmɪst | *s.c.* ingeniero agrónomo, técnico agrónomo.
agronomy | ə'grɒnəmɪ | *s.i.* agronomía.
aground | ə'graʊnd | *adv.* **1** encallado, varado. || **2 to run/go –,** encallar, embarrancar.
ah | ɑː | *interj.* ¡ah! (expresa sorpresa, duda, admiración y un gran número de posibles sentimientos y sensaciones).
aha | ɑː'hɑː | *interj.* ¡ajá! (expresa comprensión, satisfacción, triunfo, interés y algunas otras reacciones).
ahead | ə'hed | *adj.* **1** adelantado, avanzado (en un concurso, competición o similar). || *adv.* **2 [– of]** por delante de, delante de (en el espacio). **3** hacia delante. **4** (fig.) en el futuro; con antelación: *you must think ahead and invest now = debes pensar en el futuro e invertir ahora.* **5 [– of]** antes que: *he arrived ahead of me = llegó antes que yo.* **6 [– of]** delante de (en orden de espera). **7 [– of]** delante de, por delante de (en el trabajo, en calidad, etc.). || **8 to go –,** seguir, continuar, proseguir. **9 to move/go –,** progresar, avanzar (con éxito). **10 on –,** anticipadamente, por adelantado.
ahem | ə'həm | *interj.* ejém.
ahoy | ə'hɔɪ | *interj.* MAR. ¡ah!; ¡a la vista!: *ship ahoy! = ¡ah del barco!*

aid | eɪd | *s.i.* **1** ayuda, auxilio, socorro: *medical aid.* || *s.c.* **2** instrumento auxiliar, complemento auxiliar: *audiovisual aids.* || *v.t.* **3** ayudar, auxiliar, socorrer. **4** (fig.) facilitar, hacer posible. || **5 to go to the aid of/to come to one's aid,** ir/acudir en ayuda de. **6 in – of,** en pro de, a beneficio de. **7 what's this/that... in – of?,** (fam.) ¿a qué viene esto/eso...?, ¿de qué sirve esto/eso...? **8 with the – of,** mediante los servicios de, con la ayuda de.
aide | eɪd | *s.c.* consejero (en el Gobierno); asistente (en el Ejército).
aide-de-camp | ˌeɪddə'kɒm | *s.c.* MIL. ayudante de campo, edecán.
AIDS | eɪdz | **(Acquired Inmune Deficiency Sindrome)** *s.i.* SIDA, Síndrome de Inmunodeficiencia Adquirida.
ail | 'eɪl | *v.i.* **1** (p.u.) doler; sufrir. || *v.t.* **2** afligir, aquejar: *too many strikes ail the car industry = demasiadas huelgas aquejan a la industria automovilística.* || **3 what ails you/him...?,** ¿qué te/le... pasa?
aileron | 'eɪlərɒn | *s.c.* AER. alerón.
ailing | 'eɪlɪŋ | *adj.* **1** enfermizo, achacoso. **2** (fig.) enfermo, enfermizo, que va mal: *an ailing economy.*
ailment | 'eɪlmənt | *s.c.* achaque, dolencia.
aim | eɪm | *s.c.* **1** objetivo, fin, finalidad, propósito. || *s.i.* **2** puntería (con armas). || *v.t.* **[to – at]** apuntar a. **4 [to – at]** dirigir (acciones, palabras, golpes, etc.) a. || *v.i.* **5 [to – at/for]** aspirar a, ambicionar; pretender. || **6 to be aimed at,** estar dirigida a (una actividad o similar). **7 to take – at,** apuntar a.
aimless | 'eɪmlɪs | *adj.* sin voluntad, sin objetivo; pasivo: *an aimless life = una vida sin un objetivo.*
aimlessly | 'eɪmlɪslɪ | *adv.* sin rumbo fijo; al tuntún.
aimlessness | 'eɪmlɪsnɪs | *s.i.* indeterminación, falta de objetivo en la vida.
ain't | eɪnt | *contrac.* (fam.) de **isn't, am not, aren't, hasn't** y **haven't.**
air | eər | *s.i.* **1** aire. **2** (fig.) aire, aspecto, apariencia: *a nostalgic air = un aspecto nostálgico.* || *s.c.* **3** MUS. melodía, tonada. || *v.t.* **4** ventilar, orear. **5** divulgar, airear; revelar (opiniones, conocimientos, etc.). || *v.i.* **6** ventilarse, orearse, airearse. || *adj.* **7** aéreo: *an air attack.* || **8 – base,** MIL. base aérea. **9 – brake,** freno aerodinámico. **10 a change of –,** un cambio de ambiente, un cambio de aires. **11 – pocket,** turbulencia; bache (en un avión). **12 airs,** vanidad, engreimiento: *what airs she has! = ¡qué engreimiento tiene!* **13 airs and graces,** melindres; afectación. **14 – terminal,** terminal aérea (en un aeropuerto). **15 to be walking/floating on –,** estar/sentirse extremadamente feliz, estar en el cielo. **16 by –,** en avión. **17 to clear the –,** aclarar las cosas. **18 to give oneself airs,** dárselas, dárselas de importante. **19 in the –,** en el ambiente: *there are war forebodings in the air = hay presagios de guerra en el ambiente.* **20 into thin –,** sin dejar rastro. **21 off the –,** RAD. apagado, sin emitir. **22 on the –,** RAD. emitiendo, transmitiendo. **23 out of thin –,** de improviso, sin saber de dónde, por arte de magia: *the lost money turned up out of thin air = el dinero extraviado apareció de improviso.* **24 to take the –,** (p.u.) tomar el aire. **25 to take to the –,** elevarse por los aires, comenzar a volar. **26 up in the –/in the –,** incierto, inseguro.
airbed | 'eəbed | *s.c.* colchón neumático.
air-bladder | 'eəblædər | *s.c.* ANAT. ZOOL. vejiga natatoria (en peces), vejiga del aire (en pájaros).
airborne | 'eəbɔːn | *adj.* **1** MIL. aerotransportado. **2** volando, en el aire.
airbrick | 'eə'brɪk | *s.c.* ladrillo agujereado.
air-brush | 'eəbrʌʃ | *s.c.* espray de pintura, aerosol de pintura (para las típicas pintadas en las paredes).
airbus | 'eəbʌs | *s.c.* aerobús.
air-conditioned | 'eəkəndɪʃnd | *adj.* con aire acondicionado.
air-conditioner | 'eəkəndɪʃənər | *s.c.* aparato de aire acondicionado.
air-conditioning | 'eəkəndɪʃənɪŋ | *s.i.* aire acondicionado, sistema de aire acondicionado.
air-cooled | ˌeə'kuːld | *adj.* MEC. refrigerado por aire, enfriado por aire.
aircraft | 'eəkrɑːft | *s.c.* **1** aeronave (cualquier aparato volador). || **2 – carrier,** portaaviones.
aircraftman | 'eəkrɑːftmən | (*pl.* **aircraftmen**) *s.c.* (brit.) MIL. soldado de las Fuerzas Aéreas.
aircraftwoman | 'eəkrɑːftwʊmən | (*pl.* **aircraftwomen**) *s.c.* (brit.) MIL. mujer soldado de las Fuerzas Aéreas.
aircrew | 'eəkruː | *s.c.* tripulación (de un avión).
air-cushion | 'eəkʊʃn | *s.c.* MEC. cojín neumático.
airfield | 'eəfiːld | *s.c.* aeródromo, campo de aviación (más pequeño que un aeropuerto).
airforce | 'eəfɔːs | *s.c.* Fuerzas Aéreas, Ejército del Aire.
airgun | 'eəgʌn | *s.c.* escopeta/pistola de aire comprimido.
air-hostess | 'eəhɒstɪs | *s.c.* azafata (de avión).
airily | 'eərɪlɪ | *adv.* frívolamente, con ligereza.
airing | 'eərɪŋ | *s.i.* **1** ventilación. **2** (fig.) divulgación (de ideas, opiniones, etc.). || **3 – cupboard;** armario para secado de la ropa.
airlane | 'eəleɪn | *s.c.* pasillo aéreo.
airless | 'eəlɪs | *adj.* sofocante, sin ventilación, no ventilado.
airletter | 'eəletər | *s.c.* aerograma.
airlift | 'eəlɪft | *s.c.* **1** MIL. puente aéreo (en situación de guerra o urgencia). || *v.t.* **2** aerotransportar (como puente aéreo).
airline | 'eəlaɪn | *s.c.* aerolínea, compañía aérea.
airliner | 'eəlaɪnər | *s.c.* avión (de gran tamaño).
airlock | 'eəlɒk | *s.c.* **1** MEC. antecámara de compresión. **2** burbuja de aire.
airmail | 'eəmeɪ | *s.i.* correo aéreo.
airman | 'eəmən | (pl. **airmen**) *s.c.* MIL. aviador.
air mattress | 'eəmætrɪs | V. **airbed.**
airplane | 'eəpleɪn | *s.c.* (EE.UU.) avión.
airport | 'eəpɔːt | *s.c.* aeropuerto.
air-raid | 'eəreɪd | *s.c.* MIL. ataque aéreo.
air-rifle | 'eəraɪfl | *s.c.* escopeta de aire comprimido.
air-sea rescue | ˌeəsiː'reskjuː | *s.i.* servicio de salvamento aéreo y marítimo.
airship | 'eəʃɪp | *s.c.* dirigible, aeronave.
airsick | 'eəsɪk | *adj.* mareado, con mal de altura.
airspace | 'eəspeɪs | *s.i.* espacio aéreo.
airspeed | 'eəspiːd | *s.i.c.* velocidad de vuelo.
airstrike | 'eəstraɪk | V. **air-raid.**
airstrip | 'eəstrɪp | *s.c.* pista de aterrizaje.
air terminal | 'eatɜːiminl | *s.c.* terminal.
airtight | 'eətaɪt | *adj.* **1** hermético, herméticamente cerrado. **2** (fig.) perfecto, libre de error (una teoría, argumento, etc.).
airtime | 'eətaɪm | *s.i.* RAD. tiempo de emisión (de un programa).
air-to-air | ˌeətuː'eər | *adj.* aire-aire: *air-to-air (*misiles*).*
air-traffic control | eətræfɪkkəntrəul | *s.i.* **1** control del tráfico aéreo. **2** personal del control de tráfico aéreo.
airwaves | 'eəweɪvz | *s.c.* (sólo pl.) **1** RAD. ondas radiofónicas. || **2 on the –,** V. **air 22.**
airway | 'eəweɪ | *s.c.* V. **airlane.**
airwoman | 'eəwʊmən | *s.c.* (*pl.* **airwomen**) MIL. aviadora.
airworthiness | 'eəwɜɘɪnɪs | *s.i.* seguridad para el vuelo: *I don't believe in that plane's airworthiness = no creo en la seguridad para el vuelo de ese avión.*
airworthy | 'eəwəːɘɪ | *adj* en condiciones de volar, seguro para el vuelo.
airy | 'eərɪ | *adj.* **1** bien ventilado; fresco. **2** frívolo, ligero (de actitud y comportamiento). **3** insustancial; vacío; imaginario (teorías, promesas, etc.).
airy-fairy | ˌeərɪ'feərɪ | *adj.* vacuo; nebuloso (palabras, ideas, etc.).
aisle | aɪl | *s.c.* **1** ARQ. nave. **2** pasillo; pasillo central; pasillo lateral. || **3 to walk down the –/to lead someone down the –,** (fam.) casarse. **4 rolling in the aisles,** (fam.) partiéndose de risa, muertos de risa.
aitch | eɪtʃ | *s.c.* **1** hache (letra del alfabeto). || **2 to drop one's aitches,** no pronunciar las haches (rasgo generalmente considerado como indicio de clase social baja).
ajar | ə'dʒɑːr | *adj.* entreabierta, entornada (puerta o similar).
akimbo | ə'kɪmbəʊ | **(with) arms akimbo,** con los brazos en jarras.
akin | ə'kɪn | *adj.* **[to]** semejante a, parecido a, análogo a.
alabaster | 'æləbɑːstər | *s.i.* alabastro.
à la carte | ˌæːlæː'kɑːt | *adj.* y *adv.* a la carta (en un restaurante).
alacrity | ə'lækrɪtɪ | *s.i.* presteza, rapidez.
à la mode | ˌɑːlɑː'məud | *adj.* y *adv.* (lit. o p.u.) a la moda.
alarm | ə'lɑːm | *s.i.* **1** alarma; sobresalto. || *s.c.* **2** alarma (en una casa, edificio, etc.). **3** despertador, reloj despertador. || *v.t.* **4** alarmar; asustar. || **5 in –,** alarmado, sobresaltado. **6 to sound/ raise the –,** dar la alarma.
alarm-clock | ə'lɑːmklɒk | *s.c.* reloj despertador, despertador.
alarmed | ə'lɑːmd | *adj.* alarmado; asustado.
alarming | ə'lɑːmɪŋ | *adj.* alarmante; inquietante.

alarmingly | ə'lɑːmɪŋlɪ | *adv.* alarmantemente; inquietantemente.
alarmist | ə'lɑːmɪst | *s.c.* **1** alarmista. || *adj.* **2** alarmista.
alas | ə'læs | *adv.* **1** (lit. y p.u.) desgraciadamente, tristemente. || *interj.* **2** (arc.) ¡oh dioses!, ¡oh destino!
Albania | æl'benɪə | *s.c.* Albania.
Albanian | æl'benɪən | *adj.* albanés. || *s.c.* albanés. || *s.i.* albanés (idioma).
albatross | 'ælbətrɒs | *s.c.* ZOOL. albatros. **2** obstáculo; carga: *she's always been an albatross round the family's neck = ella siempre ha sido una carga para la marcha de la familia.*
albeit | ˌɔl'biːɪt | *conj.* (form.) si bien; aunque: *he continues to travel, albeit seldom, to Ireland = él continúa viajando, si bien con poca frecuencia, a Irlanda.*
albino | æl'biːnəʊ | *s.c.* **1** albino. || *adj.* **2** albino.
album | 'ælbəm | *s.c.* **1** L.P., álbum (musical). **2** álbum (de diversos tipos).
albumen | 'ælbjʊmɪn | *s.i.c.* GAST. clara de huevo.
albumin | ælbjʊmɪn | *s.i.* QUIM. albúmina.
alchemist | 'ælkɪmɪst | *s.c.* alquimista.
alchemy | 'ælkɪmɪ | *s.i.* **1** alquimia. **2** (lit.) poder de persuasión, poder de atracción: *his alchemy is obvious on the stage = su poder de atracción es patente sobre el escenario.*
alcohol | 'ælkəhɒl | *s.i.* **1** alcohol. **2** (fig.) bebida alcohólica.
alcoholic | ˌælkə'hɒlɪk | *adj.* **1** alcohólico. || *s.c.* **2** alcohólico.
alcoholism | ˌælkə'hɒlɪzəm | *s.i.* alcoholismo.
alcove | 'ælkəʊv | *s.c.* ARQ. nicho, hueco, rincón ovalado (en una habitación).
alder | 'ɔːldər | *s.c.* BOT. aliso (tipo de árbol).
alderman | 'ɔːldəmən | *s.c.* POL. concejal (de un municipio).
ale | eɪl | *s.i.* **1** (p.u.) cerveza (cualquier tipo). **2** cerveza amarga (un tipo concreto).
ale-house | 'eɪlhaʊs | *s.c.* taberna, bodega.
alert | ə'ləːt | *adj.* **1** prevenido, alerta. **2** **[– to]** despierto ante, consciente de. || *s.c.* **3** MIL. alerta: *general alert.* || *v.t.* **4** alertar, poner sobre aviso. **5** **[– to]** avisar de, alertar sobre. || **6 on the –,** alerta, sobre aviso.
alertly | ə'ləːtlɪ | *adv.* prevenidamente, con prevención.
alertness | ə'ləːtnɪs | *s.i.* estado de alerta.
A-level | 'eɪlevl | *s.c.* nivel A (examen al final de la enseñanza secundaria en Inglaterra, Gales y Norte de Irlanda).
alfalfa | æl'fælfə | *s.i.* alfalfa.
alfresco | æl'freskəʊ | *adj.adv.* al aire libre.
algae | 'ældʒiː | *s.i.* MAR. alga.
algebra | 'ældʒɪbrə | *s.i.* MAT. álgebra.
algebraic | ˌældʒɪ'breɪk | *adj.* MAT. algebraico.
Algeria | æl'dʒɪərɪə | *s.c.* Argelia.
Algerian | æl'dʒɪərɪən | *adj.* **1** argelino. || *s.c.* **2** argelino.
ALGOL | 'ælgɒl | *s.i.* INF. lenguaje Algol (siglas inglesas de "algorithmic oriented language").
algorithm | 'ælgərɪðəm | *s.c.* INF. conjunto de instrucciones (en un programa de ordenador).
alias | 'eɪlɪæs | *s.c.* **1** apodo, pseudónimo. || *prep.* **2** alias: *Jim Hawkins, alias Jaws, was arrested = Jim Hawkins, alias el Mandíbulas, fue arrestado.*
alibi | 'ælɪbaɪ | *s.c.* **1** DER. coartada. **2** (fam.) excusa, cuento.
alien | 'eɪlɪən | *adj.* **1** extranjero, forastero, extraño. **2** alienígena. **3** **[to]** extraño a, inusitado para: *hate is something alien to him = el odio es algo extraño a él.* || *s.c.* **4** extranjero, forastero, extraño. **5** alienígena.
alienate | 'eɪlɪəneɪt | *v.t.* **1** alienar; antagonizar. **2** DER. enajenar. || **3 to be alienated from,** apartarse de, alejarse de, aislarse de.
alienated | 'eɪlɪəneɪtɪd | *adj.* alienado, separado, aislado.
alienation | ˌeɪlɪə'neɪʃn | *s.i.* **1** alienación. **2** DER. enajenación (de propiedades).
alight | ə'laɪt | *adj.* **1** encendido (que está ardiendo). **2** **[– with]** (fig.) brillante de, iluminado con. **3** (fig.) excitado, emocionado (la cara, el gesto, etc.). || *v.i.* **4** posarse (pájaros, insectos, etc.). **5** **[to – from]** bajarse de, descender de.
align | ə'laɪn | *v.t.* **1** **[to – with/on]** alinear con/en, poner en línea con/sobre, colocar paralelamente a. || *v.i.* **2** **[to – with/against]** aliarse con/contra.
alignment | ə'laɪnmənt | *s.c.* **1** alianza; alineamiento (internacional, político, etc.). || *s.i.* **2** colocación (en un mecanismo). || **3 out of –,** descolocado.
alike | ə'laɪk | *adj.* **1** igual; parecido. || *adv.* **2** de la misma manera, igualmente, igual. **3** por igual.
alimentary | ˌælɪ'mentərɪ | *adj.* **1** alimenticio. || **2 – canal,** ANAT. conducto digestivo, tubo digestivo.
alimony | 'ælɪmənɪ | *s.i.* DER. pensión (de un separado o divorciado a su mujer).
alive | ə'laɪv | *adj.* **1** vivo (no muerto). **2** vital, animado: *he's very much alive = él es muy vital.* **3** activo, vivo, en funcionamiento (institución, organización, actividad, etc.). **4** **[– with]** lleno de, pululante con: *the night was alive with sounds = la noche estaba llena de sonidos.* **5** **[– to]** consciente de; atento a, sensible a (una situación, problema, etc.). || **6 – and kicking,** vivito y coleando. **7 – and well,** vivo y con buena salud. **8 to bring a story/account –,** dar vida a una historia/narración. **9 to come –, a)** hacerse realidad, cobrar vida (una historia, descripción, carácter novelesco, etc.). **b)** animarse.
alkali | 'ælkəlaɪ | *s.i.* QUIM. álcali.
alkaline | 'ælkəlaɪn | *adj.* QUIM. alcalino.
all | ɔːl | *adj.ind.* **1** todo, toda, todos, todas: *all the boys.* || *adv.* **2** completamente, todo: *he was all smiles = él era todo sonrisas.* **3** DEP. empate: *three all.* **4** por todo, todo, totalmente (delante de preposiciones para mayor énfasis): *he travelled all over Europe = viajó por toda Europa.* **5** principalmente, todo: *all muscles = todo músculos.* || *pron.* **6** todo, toda, todos, todas: *all quiet = todo tranquilo.* **7** **[– of]** todos: *stand up, all of you! = ¡levantaos, todos vosotros!* **8** todos (como énfasis): *they all knew = todos ellos lo sabían.* **9** todo lo que: *all I know is that I love you = todo lo que sé es que te quiero.* || **10 above –/above – else,** sobre todo. **11 after –,** después de todo. **12 –:** todo (como prefijo en compuestos): *all-Ireland football championship = el campeonato de fútbol de toda Irlanda.* **13 – but, a)** todos menos: *all but Mary.* **b)** casi: *he all but died = casi murió.* **14 – clear, a)** señal de que ha pasado el peligro. **b)** (fig.) permiso: *the children got the all clear from their parents = los chicos lograron el permiso de sus padres.* **15 – in, a)** (fam.) exhausto, agotado. **b)** todo incluido. **16 – in –,** con todo; en conjunto: *all in all; I disagree = con todo, yo estoy en desacuerdo.* **17 – of,** ni más ni menos que: *the car cost all of six thousand pounds = el coche costó 6.000 libras ni más ni menos.* **18 – that,** [con negativa] tan: *he is not all that intelligent = no es tan inteligente.* **19 – the better,** tanto mejor, incluso mejor. **20 – the more,** incluso más. **21 – very well/– very fine... but,** todo está muy bien... pero (expresa celos, envidia, desacuerdo, etc.). **22 and –, a)** y todo eso, y todo lo demás (acortando una lista de referencias similares). **b)** y todo, y todos (enfático): *he ate the whole chicken, heart and all = se comió todo el pollo, con el corazón y todo.* **c)** (fam. y Brit.) sí señor, claro que sí, ciertamente. **23 at –,** en absoluto (como enfático en negativas). **24 to be –,** ser lo más importante, ser lo más vital: *under the ferocious attack speed was all = ante el feroz ataque la velocidad era lo más vital.* **25 for –, a)** a pesar de: *for all his strength he wasn't able to lift it = a pesar de su fuerza no pudo levantarlo.* **b)** por lo que, en lo que: *for all I care he can go to hell = se puede ir a hacer puñetas en lo que a mí respecta.* **26 to give one's –,** dar todo lo que uno lleva dentro. **27 in –,** en total. **28 of –,** de todo, de todos (con superlativos). **29 of – the cheek/of – the luck...,** ¡qué cara/qué suerte! etc. **30 of – things/people/places,** entre todas las cosas/personas/sitios: *he went to live to Aberdeen of all places = entre todos los sitios donde vivir se fue a Aberdeen.* **31 one and –,** todos y cada uno. **32 that's –,** eso es todo. **33 that's – I want/it was – I needed,** lo que me faltaba.
Allah | 'ælə | *s.sing.* Alá (Dios del Islam).
allay | ə'leɪ | *v.t.* apaciguar, calmar (nervios, temor, etc.).
all-comers | 'ɔːlkʌməz | *s.pl.* participantes.
allegation | ˌæle'geɪʃn | *s.c.* alegación, alegato.
allege | ə'ledʒ | *v.t.* alegar; afirmar.
alleged | ə'ledʒd | *adj.* supuesto: *the alleged criminal = el supuesto criminal.*
allegedly | ə'ledʒɪdlɪ | *adv.* supuestamente.
allegiance | ə'liːdʒəns | *s.c.li.* **[– to]** lealtad a, fidelidad a.
allegorical | ˌælɪ'gɒːrɪkl | *adj.* LIT. alegórico.
allegorically | ˌælɪ'gɒːrəklɪ | *adv.* LIT. alegóricamente.

allegory ǀ ˌælɪgərɪ ǀ *s.c.li.* LIT. alegoría.
allegretto ǀ ˌælɪ'gretəʊ ǀ MUS. *adj.* y *adv.* 1 allegretto. ǁ *s.c.* 2 allegretto.
allegro ǀ ə'legrəʊ ǀ MUS. *adj.* y *adv.* 1 allegro. ǁ *s.c.* 2 allegro.
alleluia ǀ ˌælɪ'luːjə ǀ V. **hallelujah.**
all-embracing ǀ 'ɔːlɪmbreɪsɪŋ ǀ *adj.* global, que lo abarca todo.
allergic ǀ ə'lɜːdʒɪk ǀ *adj.* 1 **[– to]** MED. alérgico a. ǁ 2 **to be – to,** (fam.) aborrecer, repatear: *I'm allergic to swaggerers = me repatean los fanfarrones.*
allergy ǀ 'ælədʒɪ ǀ *s.c. e i.* 1 MED. alergia. 2 (fam.) aversión, repugnancia, antipatía.
alleviate ǀ ə'liːvɪeɪt ǀ *v.t.* aliviar, mitigar; disminuir.
alleviation ǀ əˌliːvɪ'eɪʃn ǀ *s.i.* alivio; disminución.
alley ǀ 'ælɪ ǀ *s.c.* 1 callejón. 2 paseo (flanqueado por árboles o setos). ǁ 3 **– cat,** gato callejero.
alleyway ǀ 'ælɪweɪ ǀ *s.c.* callejón.
alliance ǀ ə'laɪəns ǀ *s.c.* 1 alianza (entre países, partidos, etc.). 2 relación; amistad (entre personas). ǁ 3 **in – with,** aliado con, en conjunción con.
allied ǀ æ'laɪd ǀ *adj.* 1 aliado. 2 relacionado; conexo: *during the war the explosives and allied industries were brought under state control = durante la guerra las industrias de explosivos y las relacionadas con ellas quedaron bajo control estatal.* ǁ 3 **the Allied,** los Aliados (las naciones que lucharon juntas en la II Guerra Mundial contra alemanes y japoneses).
alligator ǀ 'ælɪgeɪtər ǀ *s.c.* 1 caimán. ǁ *s.i.* 2 piel de caimán.
alliteration ǀ əˌlɪtə'reɪʃn ǀ *s.c.* LIT. aliteración.
alliterative ǀ ə'lɪtrətɪv ǀ *adj.* LIT. aliterativo, aliterado.
alliteratively ǀ ə'lɪtrətɪvlɪ ǀ *adv.* LIT. a modo de aliteración, de manera aliterativa.
allocate ǀ 'æləkeɪt ǀ *v.t.* asignar; distribuir.
allocation ǀ ˌælə'keɪʃn ǀ *s.c.* 1 asignación. ǁ *s.i.* 2 **[– of]** reparto de.
allot ǀ ə'lɒt ǀ *v.t.* **[to – to]** asignar a, adjudicar a.
alloted ǀ ə'lɒtɪd ǀ *adj.* asignado, adjudicado.
allotment ǀ ə'lɒtmənt ǀ *s.i.* 1 porción; cupo. ǁ *s.c.* 2 (brit.) huertos (que se alquilan en las ciudades).
all-out ǀ 'ɔːlaʊt ǀ *adj.* total, completo, masivo (en acciones agresivas o violentas): *an all-out attack = ataque masivo.*
allow ǀ ə'laʊ ǀ *v.t.* 1 permitir, dejar. 2 reconocer, admitir. ǁ *v.r.* 3 permitirse, darse. ǁ 4 **to – for,** tener en cuenta, tomar en consideración, calcular: *allow for five minutes to give time for the taxi to come = calcula cinco minutos para dar tiempo a que llegue el taxi.* 5 **– me,** permíteme, permítame (como ofrecimiento educado).
allowable ǀ ə'laʊəbl ǀ *adj.* 1 FIN. deducible. 2 admisible, permisible.
allowance ǀ ə'laʊəns ǀ *s.c.* 1 FIN. subsidio; subvención, ayuda: *a maternity allowance = ayuda a la maternidad.* 2 paga, dinero de bolsillo (de los padres a los hijos). ǁ 3 **to make allowances for somebody,** ser comprensivo con alguien, ser indulgente con. 4 **to make allowances for something,** tener en cuenta algo.
alloy ǀ 'ælɔɪ ǀ *s.i.* MET. 1 aleación (de metales). ǁ ǀ ə'lɔɪ ǀ *v.t.* 2 MET. hacer aleación de (metales).
all-powerful ǀ 'ɔːlpaʊəfl ǀ *adj.* omnipotente, todopoderoso.
all-purpose ǀ ˌɔːl'pɜːpəs ǀ *adj.* multiuso, con muchos usos.
all-rounder ǀ ˌɔːl'raʊndər ǀ *s.c.* (brit.) persona muy completa (en el deporte, estudio, etc.): *he knows everything, he's an all-rounder = él sabe todo, es muy completo.*
allspice ǀ 'ɔːlspaɪs ǀ *s.i.* GAST. pimienta inglesa.
all-star ǀ 'ɔːlstɑːr ǀ *adj.* cuajado/lleno de grandes figuras/de estrellas (una película, equipo de algún deporte): *an all-star team = un equipo lleno de estrellas.*
all-time ǀ 'ɔːltaɪm ǀ *adj.* de todos los tiempos, como nunca: *housing prices are at an all-time high = los precios de las viviendas están altos como nunca.*
allude ǀ ə'luːd ǀ *v.i.* **[to – to]** (form.) aludir a, referirse a.
allure ǀ ə'lʊəː ǀ *s.c.* 1 fascinación, encanto; seducción. ǁ *v.t.* 2 (form.) fascinar, encantar.
allurement ǀ ə'lʊəmənt ǀ V. **allure 1.**
alluring ǀ ə'lʊərɪŋ ǀ *adj.* fascinante, encantador, atrayente.
allusion ǀ ə'luːʒn ǀ *s.c.li.* **[– to]** alusión a, referencia a.
allusive ǀ ə'luːsɪv ǀ *adj.* alusivo: *allusive expression.*
alluvial ǀ ə'luːvɪəl ǀ *adj.* GEOG. aluvial.
ally ǀ æ'laɪ ǀ *s.c.* 1 aliado. ǁ *v.r.* 2 **[– with]** aliarse con, alinearse con, ponerse al lado de.
alma mater ǀ ˌælmə'mɑːtər ǀ *s.sing.* (lit.) alma mater, universidad (donde uno ha estudiado).
almanac ǀ 'ɔːlmənæk ǀ (también **almanack**) *s.c.* 1 (p.u.) almanaque, anuario (sobre un único tema). 2 calendario (con detalles sobre astronomía y astrología).
almighty ǀ ɔːl'maɪtɪ ǀ *adj.* 1 todopoderoso, omnipotente (de Dios). 2 (fig.) todopoderoso, omnipotente: *the almighty Communist Party = el todopoderoso Partido Comunista.* 3 enorme, gran; terrible (problema, error, etc.). ǁ 4 **God/Christ Almighty,** Dios mío. 5 **the Almighty,** el Todopoderoso.
almond ǀ 'ɑːmənd ǀ *s.c.* 1 almendra. 2 almendro. ǁ 3 **– paste,** mazapán.
almond-eyed ǀ ˌɑːmənd'aɪd ǀ *adj.* de ojos almendrados.
almoner ǀ 'ɑːmənər ǀ *s.c.* 1 limosnero. 2 (brit.) asistente social de hospital.
almost ǀ 'ɔːlməʊst ǀ *adv.* casi.
alms ǀ ɑːmz ǀ *s.pl.* (p.u.) limosna.
almshouse ǀ 'ɑːmzhaʊs ǀ *s.c.* asilo de pobres, casa de beneficencia.
aloe ǀ 'æləʊ ǀ *s.i.* BOT. áloe.
aloft ǀ ə'lɒft ǀ *adv.* en alto, en lo alto, en el aire: *he looked at the whole town aloft = miró la ciudad entera en lo alto.*
alone ǀ ə'ləʊn ǀ *adj.* 1 solo: *I'm alone = estoy solo.* 2 solitario, solo: *they felt so alone they called = se sentían tan solos que vinieron a vernos.* 3 único: *she is not alone in her dislike of Tom = ella no es la única a la que no le gusta Tom.* 4 por sí mismo (un hecho, evidencia, etc.): *the letter alone saved her = la carta por sí misma le salvó.* ǁ *adv.* 5 sólo: *he acted alone = actuó solo.* ǁ 6 **to go it –,** (fam.) actuar por su cuenta (uno solo sin nadie).
along ǀ ə'lɒŋ ǀ *prep.* 1 a lo largo de, por (con o sin movimiento): *I went along the long street = fui por la larga calle.* ǁ 2 **all –,** todo el tiempo, durante todo el tiempo. 3 **– with,** junto con; al mismo tiempo que.
OBS: Esta palabra matiza verbos de las siguientes maneras: 4 señalando la situación a lo largo de una línea imaginaria a intervalos: *there were flowers along the canal = había flores a lo largo del canal a intervalos.* 5 indicando en una calle o pasillo un punto concreto: *half way along the street = a medio camino de la calle.* 6 expresando la situación: junto o contra una superficie vertical: *the armchair was along the wall = el sillón estaba junto a la pared.* 7 llevando consigo: *carry the suitcase along = llévate la maleta.* 8 señalando el sitio donde está una persona: *the bus will be along at 8 o'clock = el autobús llegará aquí a las 8 en punto.* 9 indica cierta continuidad: *the soldiers were marching along = los soldados iban marchando hacia delante.*
alongside ǀ ə'lɑŋsaɪd ǀ *prep./adv.* 1 al lado, al lado de, junto a: *the police car came alongside ours = el coche de policía se acercó al lado del nuestro.* 2 junto con: *men were working alongside women = los hombres trabajaban junto con las mujeres.*
aloof ǀ ə'luːf ǀ *adj.* 1 alejado, apartado; reservado. ǁ 2 **to stand/keep – from,** mantenerse al margen de, estar al margen de.
aloofness ǀ ə'luːfnɪs ǀ *s.i.* distanciamiento; reserva, retraimiento.
aloud ǀ ə'laʊd ǀ *adv.* en voz alta.
alpaca ǀ æl'pækə ǀ *s.i.* alpaca.
alpenstock ǀ 'ælpɪnstɒk ǀ *s.c.* piolet, bastón de alpinista, bastón de montañero.
alpha ǀ 'ælfə ǀ *s.c.i.* 1 alfa (letra griega). ǁ 2 **Alpha and Omega,** el principio y el fin, el alfa y omega. 3 **– particle,** FIS. partícula alfa. 4 **– radiation,** FIS. radiación alfa. 5 **– ray,** rayo alfa.
alphabet ǀ 'ælfəbet ǀ *s.c.* alfabeto, abecedario.
alphabetical ǀ ˌælfə'betɪkl ǀ *adj.* alfabético.
alphabetically ǀ ˌælfə'betɪklɪ ǀ *adv.* alfabéticamente, en orden alfabético.
alpine ǀ 'ælpaɪn ǀ *adj.* 1 alpino; montañoso. ǁ *s.c.* 2 flor alpina.
already ǀ ɔːl'redɪ ǀ *adv.* ya.
alright ǀ ɔːl'raɪt ǀ (también **all right**) *adj.* 1 bien (de salud). 2 no mal, bien; aceptable (en estos sentidos tiene una amplia gama según la entonación). ǁ *adv.* 3 bien, satisfactoriamente. 4 ciertamente, sin duda: *you'll pass all right = aprobarás sin duda.* 5 vale, de acuerdo, bien. ǁ 6 **– by one,** bien en lo que a uno concierne.
Alsatian ǀ æl'seɪʃn ǀ *s.c.* ZOOL. perro lobo.
also ǀ 'ɔːlsəʊ ǀ *adv.* también, además.
also-ran ǀ 'ɔːlsəʊræn ǀ *s.c.* (fam.) perdedor; fracasado.

altar | 'ɔːltər | *s.c.* 1 altar, ara. || 2 **– boy,** REL. monaguillo. 3 **on the – of,** en aras de, en el altar de.
altar-piece | 'ɔːltəpiːs | *s.c.* REL. retablo, esculturas del altar.
alter | 'ɒːltər | *v.t.li.* 1 alterar(se), cambiar(se), modificar(se). 2 **– ego, a)** alter ego, otro yo. **b)** amigo íntimo.
alterable | 'ɒːltərəbl | *adj.* mudable, cambiable.
altered | 'ɒːltəd | *adj.* alterado.
alteration | ˌɒːltə'reɪʃn | *s.c.* e *i.* cambio, modificación, alteración.
altercation | ˌɒːltə'rkeɪʃn | *s.c.* (form.) altercado.
alternate | 'ɒːltəneɪt | *v.i.* y *t.* 1 alternar(se), tornar(se). || | ɔːl'tɜːnət | *adj.* 2 alterno. 3 alternativo. || 4 **– angles,** GEOM. ángulos alternos.
alternately | 'ɒːl'tɜːnətlɪ | *adv.* alternativamente; uno tras otro.
alternating | 'ɒːltəneɪtɪŋ | *adj.* 1 alternante. 2 **– current,** ELEC. corriente alterna.
alternation | ˌɒːltə'neɪʃn | *s.i.* y *c.* turno, alternancia: *alternation of power = alternancia de poder.*
alternative | ɒːl'tɜːnətɪv | *adj.* 1 alternativo. 2 no convencional, heterodoxo, alternativo (referido a formas de vida y uso de energía más naturales). || *s.c.* 3 alternativa. || 4 **the –,** POL. la alternativa (movimiento político que apoya un programa descrito en la correspondencia **2**).
alternatively | ɒːl'tɜːnətɪvlɪ | *adv.* en otro caso; alternativamente, como alternativa.
alternator | 'ɒːltə'neɪtər | *s.c.* ELEC. alternador.
although | ɔːl'ðəʊ | *conj.* aunque.
altimeter | 'æltɪmiːtər | *s.c.* AER. altímetro.
altitude | 'æltɪtjuːd | *s.i.* y *c.* altitud.
alto | 'æltəʊ | *s.c.* MUS. 1 contralto (hombre o mujer). || *s.i.* 2 contralto. || *adj.* 3 contralto.
altogether | ˌɔːltə'geðər | *adv.* 1 completamente, enteramente. 2 en conjunto: *his house is very attractive altogether = su casa es muy atractiva en conjunto.* 3 en total. || 4 **in the –,** (fam.) en cueros.
altruism | 'æltruːɪzəm | *s.i.* altruismo.
altruist | 'æltruːɪst | *s.c.* altruista.
altruistic | ˌæltruː'ɪstɪk | *adj.* altruista.
altruistically | ˌæltruː'ɪstɪklɪ | *adv.* de manera altruista.
alum | 'æləm | *s.i.* QUIM. alumbre.
aluminium | ˌælju'mɪnɪəm | *s.i.* MET. aluminio.
alumna | ə'lʌmnə | (*pl.* **alumnae**) *s.c.* (EE.UU.) alumna (ya licenciada de la Universidad).
alumnus | ə'lʌmnəs | (*pl.* **alumni**) *s.c.* (EE.UU.) alumno (ya licenciado de la Universidad).
alveolar | ˌæl'vɪələr | FON. *adj.* 1 alveolar. || *s.c.* 2 alveolar.
always | 'ɔːlweɪz | *adv.* 1 siempre. || 2 **as –,** como siempre, como es normal.
am | æm | pronunciación relajada | əm | 1.;sa persona sing. del verbo ser/estar.
a.m. | ˌeɪ'm | *adv.* a.m. (desde las 12 de la noche hasta las 12 del mediodía).
amalgam | ə'mælgəm | *s.c.* amalgama, mezcla.
amalgamate | ə'mælgəmeɪt | *v.i.* unirse; federarse, confederarse.
amalgamated | ə'mælgəmeɪtɪd | *adj.* 1 federado, confederado. || 2 **Amalgamated,** Federado, Confederado (aparece en el título de muchas asociaciones, sindicatos, empresas, etc.).
amalgamation | əˌmælgə'meɪʃn | *s.i.* y *c.* fusión, unión.
amanuensis | əˌmænju'ensɪs | *s.c.* (lit.) 1 amanuense. 2 (fig.) secretario.
amass | ə'mæs | *v.t.* amasar, acumular, reunir.
amateur | 'æmətər | *s.c.* 1 amateur. || *adj.* 2 principiante.
amateurish | 'æmətərɪʃ | *adj.* (desp.) chapucero, de aficionado.
amateurishly | 'æmətərɪʃlɪ | *adv.* de manera no profesional.
amateurism | 'æmətərɪzəm | *s.i.* deporte/práctica no profesional.
amatory | 'æmətərɪ | *adj.* (lit.) amoroso, amatorio.
amaze | ə'meɪz | *v.t.* asombrar, dejar estupefacto.
amazed | ə'meɪzd | *adj.* asombrado, estupefacto.
amazement | ə'meɪzmənt | *s.i.* asombro, estupefacción.
amazing | ə'meɪzɪŋ | *adj.* asombroso.
amazingly | ə'meɪzɪŋllɪ | *adv.* asombrosamente.
ambassador | æm'bæsədər | *s.c.* embajador.
ambassador-at-large | æm'bæsədətlɑːdʒ | *s.c.* (EE.UU.) enviado especial, embajador especial.
ambassadorial | æmˌbæsə'dɔːrɪəl | *adj.* del embajador, de embajada.
ambassadress | æm'bæsədrɪs | *s.c.* 1 embajadora. 2 embajadora (mujer del embajador).
amber | 'æmbər | *adj.* 1 ámbar (color). || *s.i.* 2 ámbar (sustancia y color).
ambergris | 'æmbəgriːs | *s.i.* ámbar gris.
ambidextrous | ˌæmbɪ'dekstrəs | *adj.* ambidiestro.
ambience | 'æmbɪəns | (también **ambiance**) *s.c.* (lit.) ambiente.
ambient | 'æmbɪənt | *adj.* (lit.) ambiente: *ambient temperature.*
ambiguity | ˌæmbɪ'gjuːɪtɪ | *s.c.* e *i.* ambigüedad.
ambiguous | ˌæm'bɪgjuəs | *adj.* ambiguo.
ambiguously | ˌæm'bɪgjuəslɪ | *adv.* ambiguamente.
ambit | 'æmbɪt | *s.i.* (form.) ámbito.
ambition | æm'bɪʃn | *s.c.* 1 ambición; sueño. || *s.i.* 2 (a veces desp.) ambición. || 3 **ambitions,** ambición, ambiciones, aspiraciones: *political ambitions.*
ambitious | æm'biʃəs | *adj.* 1 (a veces desp.) ambicioso. 2 aventurado, ambicioso (plan, programa, etc.).
ambitiously | æm'bɪʃəslɪ | *adv.* (a veces desp.) ambiciosamente.
ambivalence | æm'bɪvələns | *s.i.* 1 ambivalencia; indecisión. 2 ambivalencia, ambigüedad.
ambivalent | æm'bɪvələnt | *adj.* ambivalente, indeciso.
ambivalently | æm'bɪvələntlɪ | *adv.* ambiguamente, de forma ambivalente.
amble | 'æmbl | *v.i.* 1 deambular. || *s.sing.* 2 paso relajado.
ambrosia | æm'brəuzɪə | *s.i.* 1 LIT. ambrosía. 2 (fig.) delicia (de comer).
ambulance | 'æmbjuləns | *s.c.* ambulancia.
ambulanceman | 'æmbjulənsmən | *s.c.* conductor de ambulancia.
ambush | 'æmbuʃ | *v.t.* MIL. 1 emboscar. || *s.c.* 2 emboscada. || 3 **in –,** emboscado.
ameba | ˌəmɪ'bə | V. **amoeba.**
amelioration | əˌmiːlɪə'reɪʃn | *s.i.* (lit.) mejora.
ameliorate | ə'miːlɪəreɪt | *v.t.* (lit.) mejorar.
amen | ɑːmen | o | eɪ'men | *interj.* 1 REL. amén, así sea. 2 (fig.) sí, de acuerdo.
amenable | ə'miːnəbl | *adj.* **[– to]** dispuesto a, a favor de: *amenable to the plan = a favor del plan.*
amend | ə'mend | *v.t.* 1 enmendar, reformar, modificar. || 2 **to make amends (for),** expiar (por), dar satisfacción (por).
amendment | ə'mendmənt | *s.c.* 1 DER. enmienda (de una ley, Constitución, etc.). 2 modificación, reforma (de un texto o similar). || *s.i.* 3 enmienda, rectificación (del comportamiento, leyes, etc.).
amenity | ə'miːnɪtɪ | *s.c.* comodidad, disposición adecuada (en una tienda, edificio, etc.).
America | ə'merɪkə | *s.c.* América (referido a Estados Unidos).
American | ə'merɪkən | *adj.* 1 americano. || *s.c.* 2 americano. || 3 **– football,** DEP. rugby americano. 4 **– Indian,** indio americano.
Americanism | ə'merɪkənɪzəm | *s.c.* americanismo.
Americanize | ə'merɪkənaɪiz | (también **Americanise**) *v.t.* americanizar.
Amerindian | ˌæmə'rɪndɪən | *s.c.* indio americano.
amethyst | 'æmɪθɪst | *adj.* 1 púrpura, violeta (color). || *s.c.* 2 amatista.
amiability | ˌeɪmɪə'bɪlɪtɪ | *s.i.* cordialidad.
amiable | 'eɪmɪəbl | *adj.* cordial.
amiably | 'eɪmɪəblɪ | *adv.* cordialmente.
amicable | 'æmɪkəbl | *adj.* amistoso.
amicably | 'æmɪkəblɪ | *adv.* amistosamente.
amicability | ˌæmɪkə'bɪlɪtɪ | *s.i.* cordialidad, amistad.
amid | ə'mɪd | (también **amidst**) *prep.* 1 entre, en medio de, rodeado de. 2 durante, en el curso de.
amidships | ə'mɪdʃɪps | *adv.* MAR. en medio del barco.
amino acid | ə'miːnəʊ'æsɪd | *s.i.* QUIM. aminoácido.
amiss | ə'mɪs | *adj.* 1 horrible; errado, impropio. || 2 **to take something –,** tomar algo a mal. 3 **to go/come –,** ir mal, surgir un problema.
amity | 'æmɪtɪ | *s.i.* (lit.) amistad; buenas relaciones.
ammeter | 'æmɪtər | *s.c.* ELEC. amperímetro.
ammo | 'æməʊ | *s.i.* (fam.) MIL. munición.
ammonia | ə'məunɪə | *s.i.* QUIM. amoníaco.
ammonite | 'æmənaɪt | *s.c.* HIST. molusco fósil, amonites.
ammunition | ˌæmju'nɪʃn | *s.i.* 1 MIL. munición. 2 (fig.) información de índo-

le sensible (que se puede utilizar en contra de alguien).
amnesia | æm'niːzɪə | *s.i.* MED. amnesia.
amnesty | 'æmnɪstɪ | *s.c.* amnistía, indulto.
amoeba | ə'miːbə | (también **ameba** en EE.UU.; pl. **amoebas** o **amoebae**) *s.c.* BIOL. ameba.
amok | ə'mɒk | (también **amuck**) **to run amok,** volverse frenético (con violencia y descontrol).
among | ə'mʌŋ | (también **amongst**) *prep.* **1** entre, en medio de (más de dos unidades). || **2 to keep something – themselves/yourselves, etc.,** guardar un secreto entre ellos/vosotros, etc.
amoral | ˌeɪ'mɒrəl | *adj.* (desp.) amoral.
amorality | ˌeɪ'mɒrələtɪ | *s.i.* (desp.) amoralidad.
amorous | 'æmərəs | *adj.* (lit.) amoroso.
amorously | 'æmərəslɪ | *adv.* amorosamente.
amorousness | 'æmərəsnɪs | *s.i.* naturaleza amorosa (de una persona).
amorphous | ə'mɔːfəs | *adj.* amorfo, informe.
amortization | əˌmɔːtɪ'zeɪʃn | *s.i.* FIN. amortización, finalización del pago de una deuda.
amortize | ə'mɔːtaiz | *v.t.* FIN. amortizar, terminar el pago de una deuda.
amount | ə'maʊnt | *s.c.* **1 [– of]** cantidad de: *one million is an enormous amount.* || *v.i.* **2 [to –]** ascender a, totalizar. **3 [to – to]** equivaler, significar, ser igual a (dicho de ideas, sentimientos, palabras). **4 [to – to]** valer, servir de: *his peace efforts amount to a great deal = sus esfuerzos por la paz valen muchísimo.* || **5 an/the – of,** una/la cantidad de: *a great amount of work = una gran cantidad de trabajo.* **6 any – of,** cualquier cantidad de, cualquier número de; todo tipo de.
amour | ə'mʊər | *s.c.* (lit. y p.u.) amor, amor secreto.
amp | æmp | *s.c.* (fam.) **1** ELEC. amperio. **2** ELECTR. amplificador.
amperage | 'æmpərɪdʒ | *s.i.* ELEC. amperaje.
ampère | 'æmpeər | *s.c.* ELEC. amperio.
ampersand | 'æmpəsænd | *s.c.* el signo & (utilizado con el sentido de "y").
amphetamine | æm'fetəmiːn | *s.c.* MED. anfetamina.
amphibian | æm'fɪbɪən | *s.c.* **1** ZOOL. anfibio, animal anfibio. || *adj.* **2** anfibio.
amphibious | æm'fɪbɪəs | *adj.* **1** ZOOL. anfibio. **2** MIL. anfibio (fuerzas, tanques, etc.).
amphitheatre | 'æmfɪθɪətər | (en EE.UU. **amphitheater**) *s.c.* **1** ART. anfiteatro. **2** GEOL. anfiteatro.
ample | 'æmpl | *adj.* **1** amplio. **2** adecuado, suficiente: *ample supplies of food = suministros suficientes de alimentos.*
amplification | ˌæmplɪfɪ'keɪʃn | *s.i.* y *c.* amplificación, ampliación (de cualquier cosa).
amplified | 'æmplɪfaɪd | *adj.* amplificado.
amplifier | 'æmplɪfaɪər | *s.c.* amplificador
amplify | 'æmplɪfaɪ | *v.t.* **1** amplificar (sonido, música, etc.). **2** ampliar, amplificar (un texto, una idea, etc.). **3** aumentar, ampliar (la capacidad, fuerza, importancia, etc., de alguna cosa).
amplitude | 'æmplɪtjuːd | *s.i.* (form.) amplitud, extensión.
amply | 'æmplɪ | *adv.* adecuadamente, suficientemente.
ampoule | 'æmpuːl | (también EE.UU. **ampule**) *s.c.* ampolla (inyección).
amputate | 'æmpjʊteɪt | *v.t.* MED. amputar.
amputation | ˌæmpjʊ'teɪʃn | *s.c.* e *i.* MED. amputación.
amuck V. **amok.**
amulet | 'æmjʊlɪt | *s.c.* amuleto, talismán.
amuse | ə'mjuːz | *v.t.* **1** divertir, distraer, entretener. || *v.r.* **2** divertirse, distraerse, entretenerse: *amuse yourselves = divertíos.*
amused | ə'mjuːzd | *adj.* **1** divertido, gracioso: *an amused look = un aspecto gracioso.* || **2 to be – at/by,** *divertirse con/por.* **3 to keep oneself –,** entretenerse, pasar el tiempo.
amusedly | ə'mjuːzɪdlɪ | *adv.* divertidamente, jocosamente.
amusement | ə'mjuːzmənt | *s.c.* **1** diversión, entretenimiento, pasatiempo. || *s.i.* **2** regocijo, diversión, entretenimiento. || **3 – arcade,** sala de juegos (electrónicos y similares). **4 – park,** parque de atracciones, feria. **5 amusements,** juegos (electrónicos, tragaperras y de feria en general).
amusing | ə'mjuːzɪŋ | *adj.* divertido, gracioso, entretenido.
amusingly | ə'mjuːzɪŋlɪ | *adv.* divertidamente, graciosamente, entretenidamente.
an | ən | V. **a.**
anaconda | ˌænə'kɒndə | *s.c.* ZOOL. anaconda.
anachronism | ə'nækrənɪzəm | *s.c.* anacronismo.
anachronistic | ə'nækrə'nɪstɪk | *adj.* anacrónico.
anaemia | ə'niːmɪə | (también **anemia**) *s.i.* MED. anemia.
anaemic | ə'niːmɪk | (también **anemic**) *adj.* **1** MED. anémico. **2** debilucho; anémico, pálido.
anaesthesia | ˌænɪs'θiːzɪə | (también **anesthesia**) *s.i.* MED. anestesia.
anaesthetic | ˌænɪs'θetɪk | (también **anesthetic**) *s.c.* **1** MED. anestésico. || *adj.* **2** anestésico.
anaesthetist | æ'niːsθɪtɪst | (también **anesthetist**) *s.c.* MED. anestesista.
anaesthetize | æ'niːsθɪtaɪz | (también **anesthetise/anesthetize**) *v.t.* MED. anestesiar.
anagram | 'ænəgræm | *s.c.* anagrama.
anal | 'eɪnl | *adj.* ANAT. anal.
analgesic | ˌænæl'dʒiːsɪk | *s.c.* **1** MED. analgésico. || *adj.* **2** analgésico.
analogous | ə'næləgəs | *adj.* **[– to]** análogo, semejante.
analogously | ə'næləgəslɪ | *adv.* de manera análoga.
analogue | 'ænəlɒg | (también **analog**) *s.c.* **1** copia (algo o alguien exactamente igual que alguna otra cosa o persona). || *adj.* **2** tradicional, de manillas (sólo de relojes). **3** FIS. análogo (indicando que el mecanismo mide la información usando energía variable). || **4 – computer,** INF. ordenador no digital, analógico.
analogy | ə'nælədʒɪ | *s.c.* **1** analogía, semejanza. || **2 by –,** por analogía.
analyse | 'ænəlaɪz | (EE.UU. **analyze**) *v.t.* **1** analizar, estudiar (cualquier cosa). **2** QUIM. analizar (sangre, comida, etc.). **3** MED. psicoanalizar.
analysis | ə'næləsɪs | *s.c.* **1** análisis, examen, estudio. || *s.i.* **2** MED. psicoanálisis. || *s.c.* e *i.* **3** QUIM. análisis (de gran número de cosas). **4 in the last –/in the final –,** en último término, a fin de cuentas.
analyst | 'ænəlɪst | *s.c.* **1** experto, analista: *a political analyst.* **2** MED. psicoanalista.
analytic | ˌænə'lɪtɪk | (o **analytical**) *adj.* analítico.
analytically | ˌænə'lɪtɪklɪ | *adv.* analíticamente.
anapaest | ˌænəpiːst | (EE.UU. **anapest**) *s.c.* LIT. anapesto (pie métrico).
anapaestic | 'ænəpestɪk | (EE.UU. **anapestic**) *adj.* LIT. anapéstico.
anaphora | ə'næfərə | *s.i.* LIT. anáfora.
anaphoric | ˌænə'fɒrɪk | *adj.* LIT. anafórico.
anarchic | ə'nɑːkɪk | *adj.* (desp.) anárquico.
anarchism | 'ænəkɪzəm | *s.i.* POL. anarquismo.
anarchist | 'ænəkɪst | *s.c.* **1** POL. anarquista. **2** (desp.) anarquista (que no respeta leyes, etc.). || *adj.* **3** anarquista: *the anarchist creed = el credo anarquista.*
anarchistic | ˌænə'kɪstɪk | *adj.* anárquico.
anarchy | 'ænəkɪ | *s.i.* **1** POL. anarquía. **2** (desp.) desgobierno.
anathema | ə'næθɪmə | *s.i.* **[– to]** anatema.
anatomical | ˌænə'tɒmɪkl | *adj.* anatómico.
anatomically | ˌænə'tɒmɪklɪ | *adv.* anatómicamente.
anatomist | ə'nætəmɪst | *s.c.* experto en anatomía.
anatomy | ə'nætəmɪ | *s.i.* **1** MED. anatomía. || *s.c.* **2** estructura anatómica (de una persona o animal). **3** (hum.) cuerpo, anatomía. **4 [– of]** estudio de, análisis de.
ancestor | 'ænsɪstər | *s.c.* **1** predecesor, antepasado. || **2 ancestors,** antepasados: *my ancestors.*
ancestral | æn'sestrəl | *adj.* ancestral.
ancestry | 'ænsɪstrɪ | *s.c.* e *i.* abolengo, linaje, raza.
anchor | 'æŋkər | *s.c.* **1** MAR. ancla. **2** (fig.) soporte: *the anchor of marriage.* || *v.t.* **3** anclar, ancorar (barcos, etc.). **4** (fig.) sujetar, fijar (un objeto). || *v.i.* **5** echar el ancla. || **6 at –,** anclado. **7 to be anchored,** estar enraizado, estar asentado: *I was always anchored to my hometown = siempre estuve enraizado en mi ciudad.* **8 to drop/cast –,** MAR. echar el ancla. **9 to weigh/up –,** MAR. levar anclas.
anchorage | 'æŋkərɪdʒ | *s.c.* MAR. fondeadero.
anchorite | 'æŋkəraɪt | *s.c.* REL. anacoreta.
anchor-man | 'æŋkəmæn | *s.c.* TV. presentador.
anchovy | 'æntʃəvɪ | *s.c.* ZOOL. anchoa.
ancient | 'eɪnʃənt | *adj.* **1** antiguo, vetusto. **2** viejísimo. **3** antiguo, clásico. ||

4 – history, a) historia antigua (del período clásico de Grecia y Roma). **b)** (fam.) en tiempos de Maricastaña. **5 the ancients,** la antigüedad, los clásicos.
ancillary | æn'sɪlərɪ | *adj.* **1** auxiliar (describe el trabajo de porteros, limpiadoras, cocineros, etc.). **2 [– to]** complementario de, auxiliar: *his shopwork is ancillary to the big automobile industry = su taller es auxiliar de la gran industria del automóvil.*
and | ænd | pronunciación relajada | əndd̩ən | *conj.* **1** y (en múltiples usos). || **2 – so forth,** y así sucesivamente.
OBS: Esta conjunción tiene dos matizaciones que pueden no traducirse: **3** TV. enlazando un tema ya mencionado con una noticia concreta sobre él: *basketball, and the league is very exciting at the moment = baloncesto, pues la liga está muy emocionante en este momento.* **4** con números compuestos: *three thousand and forty = tres mil cuarenta.*
andante | æn'dæntɪ | *s.c.* MUS. **1** andante. || *adv.* en andante. || *adj.* **3** de andante.
andiron | 'ændaɪən | *s.c.* morillo (los hierros donde descansa la madera en una chimenea).
androgynous | æn'drɒdʒɪnəs | *adj.* (lit.) andrógino.
anecdotal | ˌænɪk'dəutl | *adj.* anecdótico.
anecdote | 'ænɪkdəut | *s.c.* anécdota.
anemia V. **anaemia.**
anemic V. **anaemic.**
anemometer | ˌænɪ'mɒmɪtər | *s.c.* FIS. anemómetro.
anemone | ə'nemənɪ | *s.c.* BOT. anémona.
anesthesiologist | ænəsθiʒɪɒlədʒɪst | (también **anaesthesiologist**) *s.c.* (EE.UU.) anestesista.
anew | ə'njuː | *adv.* **1** (lit.) nuevamente, otra vez. **2** de manera diferente.
angel | 'eɪndʒl | *s.c.* **1** REL. ángel. **2** (fig.) ángel (persona buena, dulce, etc.). **3** cariño, amor. **4 – cake,** GAST. bizcocho. **4 to be on the side of the angels,** actuar correctamente, hacer lo que es debido.
angeltish | 'eɪngltɪʃ | *s.c.* ZOOL. angelote (un tipo de pez).
angelic | æn'dʒelɪk | *adj.* **1** REL. angelical. **2** (fig.) buenísimo, angelical.
angelica | æn'dʒelɪkə | *s.i.* BOT. angélica.
angelus | 'ændʒɪləs | *s. sing.* REL. ángelus.
anger | 'æŋgər | *s.i.* **1** cólera, ira. || *v.t.* **2** enfurecer, encolerizar. || **3 more in sorrow than in –,** más con pena que con ira.
angina | æn'dʒaɪnə | *s.i.* MED. **1** angina. || **2 – pectoris,** angina de pecho.
angle | 'æŋgl | *s.c.* **1** ángulo. **2** esquina, codo, ángulo. **3** punto de vista, ángulo. || *v.t.* **4** poner en ángulo, colocar en ángulo. **5 [– to/towards]** dirigir hacia (una actividad, idea, etc.): *the talks were angled to more parental involvement = las charlas estaban dirigidas hacia una mayor participación de los padres.* || *v.i.* **6** doblarse en ángulo. **7 [to – for]** buscar indirectamente: *angle for information.* || **8 at an –,** en ángulo.
angler | 'æŋglər | *s.c.* DEP. pescador.
Anglican | 'æŋglɪkən | *s.c.* REL. **1** anglicano (la iglesia inglesa). || *adj.* **2** anglicano.
Anglicanism | 'æŋglɪkənɪzəm | *s.i.* REL. anglicanismo.
anglicize | 'æŋglɪsaɪz | (también **anglicise**) *v.t.* hacer inglés, hacer británico, anglicanizar.
angling | 'æŋglɪŋ | *s.i.* pescar (con caña).
Anglo- | 'æŋgləu | *pref.* anglo: *Anglo-Portuguese.*
Anglo-American | ˌæ'gləuə'merɪkən | *adj.* angloamericano.
Anglo-Catholic | ˌæŋgləu'kæθlɪk | *adj.* REL. anglocatólico (sección de los anglicanos que no quiere llamarse Protestante).
Anglo-French | ˌæŋgləu'frenʃ | *adj.* anglofrancés.
Anglo-Indian | ˌæŋgləu'ɪndɪən | *adj.* angloindio.
Anglophile | 'æŋgləufaɪl | *adj.* anglófilo.
Anglophobe | 'æŋgləufəub | *adj.* anglófobo.
Anglophobia | ˌæŋgləu'fəubjə | *s.i.* anglofobia.
Anglo-Saxon | ˌæŋgləu'sæksn | *s.c.* **1** anglosajón (idioma). **2** HIST. anglosajón. **3** anglosajón (descendiente). || *adj.* **4** HIST. anglosajón. **5** anglosajón (de influencia inglesa).
Angola | æŋ'gəulə | *s.sing.* Angola.
Angolan | æŋ'gəulən | *adj.* **1** angoleño. || *s.c.* **2** angoleño.
angora | æŋ'gɔːrə | *s.c.* **1** ZOOL. gato de angora, cabra de angora. || *s.i.* **2** angora (tela).
angrily | 'æŋgrɪlɪ | *adv.* coléricamente, con gran enfado.
angry | 'æŋgrɪ | *adj.* **1** colérico, lleno de ira. **2** inflamado, de mal aspecto (herida). **3** (lit.) amenazador (cielo, mar, nubes).
angst | æŋst | *s.i.* (lit.) angustia, ansiedad.
anguish | 'æŋgwɪʃ | *s.i.* angustia, aflicción.
anguished | 'æŋgwɪʃt | *adj.* atormentado, angustiado.
angular | 'æŋgjulər | *adj.* angular.
angularity | ˌæŋgu'lærɪtɪ | *s.c.* e *i.* angulosidad, angularidad.
aniline | 'ænɪliːn | *s.i.* QUIM. anilina.
animadversion | ˌænɪmædvɜːʃn | *s.c.* e *i.* animadversión; censura.
animal | 'ænɪməl | *s.c.* **1** animal. **2** (fig.) bruto, animal. **3** tipo, clase: *Spanish socialism is exactly the same political animal as European socialism = el socialismo español es exactamente del mismo tipo político que el socialismo europeo.* || *adj.* **4** instintivo, animal; carnal. || **5 – husbandry,** AGR. ganadería. **6 – spirits,** exuberancia vital.
animate | 'ænɪmɪt | *v.t.* **1** avivar, animar. || | 'ænɪmət | *adj.* **2** animado.
animated | 'ænɪmeɪtɪd | *adj.* **1** animado, entusiasmado. **2** VT. animado: *animated cartoons = dibujos animados.*
animatedly | 'ænɪmeɪtɪdlɪ | *adv.* animadamente, vivamente, excitadamente.
animation | ˌænɪ'meɪʃn | *s.i.* **1** animación, entusiasmo. **2** VT. animación (de dibujos para películas).
animator | 'ænɪmeɪtər | *s.c.* VT. animador, dibujante (para películas).
animism | 'ænɪmɪzəm | *s.i.* REL. animismo.
animosity | ˌænɪ'mɒsɪtɪ | *s.i.* y *c.* hostilidad, aversión.
animus | 'ænɪməs | *s.i.* rencor, animosidad.
anise | 'ænɪs | *s.i.* BOT. anís, planta de anís.
aniseed | 'ænɪsiːd | *s.i.* anís, semilla de anís.
ankle | 'æŋkl | *s.c.* **1** ANAT. tobillo. || *adj.* **2** hasta el tobillo.
annals | 'ænəlz | *s.pl.* anales.
annex | ə'neks | (también **annexe**) *v.t.* **1** POL. anexionar (trozo de país, nación). **2** apoderarse de, quedarse ilegalmente con. || *s.c.* **3** edificio anexo, ala anexa, pabellón anexo.
annexation | ˌænek'seɪʃn | *s.i.* POL. anexión.
annihilate | ə'naɪəleɪt | *v.t.* **1** aniquilar, exterminar. **2** ganar por completo (en elecciones, discusiones, etc.).
annihilation | əˌnaɪə'leɪʃn | *s.i.* exterminio, aniquilamiento.
anniversary | ˌænɪ'vɜːsərɪ | *s.c.* aniversario.
Anno Domini | 'ænəudɒmɪnaɪ | V. **A.D.**
annotate | 'ænəteɪt | *v.t.* anotar, poner anotaciones.
annotation | ˌænə'teɪʃn | *s.c.* e *i.* anotación.
announce | ə'nauns | *v.t.* **1 [— to]** anunciar a (expresando aviso o similar). **2** anunciar, proclamar (por los altavoces o por un maestro de ceremonias). **3** avisar de, indicar (un letrero, un aviso, una señal, etc.). **4** (lit.) pregonar, anunciar (la llegada o advenimiento de algún acontecimiento).
announcement | ə'naunsmənt | *s.c.* **1** declaración (oficial o similar). **2** anuncio, aviso. || *s.i.* **3 [– of]** anuncio de, declaración de: *the announcement of my marriage = el anuncio de mi matrimonio.*
announcer | ə'naunsər | *s.c.* **1** TV. locutor, presentador. **2** persona que da avisos por los altavoces.
annoy | ə'nɔɪ | *v.t.* **1** molestar, incomodar, irritar. **2** molestar, acosar (un hombre a una mujer de mala manera).
annoyance | ə'nɔɪəns | *s.c.* e *i.* molestia, irritación, fastidio.
annoyed | ə'nɔɪd | *adj.* molesto, irritado, incomodado.
annoying | ə'nɔɪɪŋ | *adj.* irritante, fastidioso, molesto.
annoyingly | ə'nɔɪɪŋlɪ | *adv.* de manera irritante/molesta, fastidiosamente.
annual | 'ænjuəl | *adj.* **1** anual. || *s.c.* **2** anuario. **3** BOT. planta anual.
annually | 'ænjuəlɪ | *adv.* anualmente.
annuity | ə'njuːɪtɪ | *s.c.* anualidad, pensión anual (mediante una aseguradora).
annul | ə'nʌl | *v.t.* DER. anular, invalidar (matrimonio, contrato, etc.).
annular | 'ænjulər | *adj.* **1** anular. || **2 – eclipse,** FIS. eclipse anular.
annulment | ə'nʌlmənt | *s.c.* e *i.* DER. anulación, invalidación.
Annunciation | əˌnʌnsɪ'eɪʃn | *s.sing.* REL. Anunciación.

anode | 'ænəud | *s.c.* ELECTR. ánodo.
anodyne | 'ænədaɪn | *adj.* **1** anodino. || *s.c.* **2** paliativo, anodino.
anoint | ə'nɔɪnt | *v.t.* ungir; untar.
anointment | ə'nɔɪntmənt | *s.i.* unción.
anomalous | ə'nɒmələs | *adj.* (form.) anómalo, irregular.
anomalously | ə'nɒmələslɪ | *adv.* anómalamente, de manera anómala.
anomaly | ə'nɒməlɪ | *s.c.* (form.) anomalía, irregularidad.
anomie | 'ænəmɪ | *s.i.* FIL. anomia (ausencia de valores éticos).
anon | ə'nɒn | *adv.* (arc. y fam.) prontamente.
anonymity | ˌænə'nɪmɪtɪ | *s.i.* anonimato.
anonymous | ə'nɒnɪməs | *adj.* anónimo, del montón.
anonymously | ə'nɒnɪməslɪ | *adv.* anónimamente.
anorak | 'ænəræk | *s.c.* anorak.
anorexia | ˌænə'reksɪə | *s.i.* PSIQ. anorexia.
anorexic | ˌænə'reksɪk | *adj.* PSIQ. anoréxico.
another | ə'nʌðər | *pron.* **1** otro, otra. || *adj.* **2** otro, otra. **3** otro, otra (como, igual): *he's another Dalí = él es otro Dalí.* **4** otro, otra, otros, otras (sólo con cantidades numéricas de distancias, tiempos, etc.): *I need another 3 hundred pounds = necesito otras trescientas libras.* || **5 one –,** el uno al otro (dentro de un grupo). **6 one... after –,** un... detrás de otro, una... detrás de otra. **7 or –,** u otro, u otra: *one thing or another = una cosa u otra.*
answer | ɑːnsər | *v.t.* **1** contestar, responder. **2** abrir (la puerta), contestar, coger (el teléfono). **3** satisfacer (una necesidad o propósito). **4** responder a (una acusación, ataque, etc.). **5 [to** optativo**]** responder a, cuadrar con (una descripción, característica, etc.). || *v.i.* **6** contestar, responder. || *s.c.* **7** respuesta, contestación. **8 [– to]** respuesta a, solución de (una pregunta de examen, un ataque, etc.). || **9 to – back,** (fam.) responder malamente, contestar con mala educación. **10 to – for, a)** pagar: *you'll answer for the consequences = pagarás las consecuencias.* **b)** hacerse responsable de, responder por (alguien: sus buenas cualidades, etc.). **11 to have a lot to – for,** tener la mayor parte de la culpa (de algo), tener mucho de que dar cuenta. **12 in – (to),** en contestación (a), en respuesta (a).
answerable | 'ɑːnsərəbl | *adj.* **1 [– for]** responsable de. **2 [– to]** responsable ante (obligado a dar cuentas a alguien): *she's answerable to the head nurse = ella está obligada a dar cuentas a la enfermera jefe.*
answering | 'ɑːnsərɪŋ | *adj.* **1** de respuesta: *answering laughs = risas de respuesta.* || **2 – machine,** contestador automático.
ant | ænt | *s.c.* ZOOL. hormiga.
antacid | ænt'æsɪd | *s.i.* QUIM. antiácido.
antagonism | æn'tægənɪizəm | *s.i.* **[– towards]** antagonismo hacia, hostilidad hacia.
antagonist | æn'tægənɪst | *s.c.* antagonista, rival, contrario.
antagonistic | ænˌtægə'nɪstɪk | *adj.* **[– to/towards]** hostil hacia, antagónico a.
antagonistically | ænˌtægə'nɪstɪklɪ | *adv.* hostilmente, antagónicamente.
antagonize | æn'tægənaɪz | (también **antagonise**) *v.t.* enemistarse con, provocar a.
Antarctic | æn'tɑːktɪk | *s.c.* **1** Antártida. || **2 the – Circle,** GEOG. El Círculo Polar Antártico.
ante | 'æntɪ | V. **up/raise.**
ant-eater | 'æntiːtər | *s.c.* ZOOL. oso hormiguero.
antecedence | ˌæntɪ'siːdəns | *s.c.* (form.) prioridad.
antecedent | ˌæntɪ'siːdnt | *s.c.* **1 [– of/to]** antecedente de. || **2 antecedents,** orígenes, antecedentes (familia).
antechamber | 'æntɪtʃeɪmbər | *s.c.* vestíbulo, antesala.
antedate | ˌæntɪ'deɪt | *v.t.* (lit.) preceder, anteceder (sólo en el tiempo).
antediluvian | ˌæntɪdɪ'luːvɪən | *adj.* (lit. y hum.) antediluviano.
antelope | 'æntɪləup | *s.c.* ZOOL. antílope.
antenatal | ˌæntɪ'neɪtl | *adj.* MED. **1** prenatal. || *s.c.* **2** consulta prenatal.
antenna | æn'tenə | (*pl.* **antennae** o **antennas**) *s.c.* **1** ANAT. ZOOL. antena. **2** (EE.UU.) RAD. antena.
anterior | æn'tɪərɪər | *adj.* (lit.) anterior, delantero (en el espacio y tiempo).
anteroom | 'æntɪrum | *s.c.* antesala, antecámara.
anthem | 'ænθəm | *s.c.* MUS. REL. himno.
anther | 'ænθər | *s.c.* BOT. antera (parte de la flor).
ant-hill | 'ænthɪl | *s.c.* hormiguero (en forma de pequeño montículo).
anthologist | æn'θɒlədʒɪst | *s.c.* LIT. antólogo.
anthology | æn'θɒlədʒɪ | *s.c.* antología.
anthracite | 'ænθrəsaɪt | *s.i.* MIN. QUIM. antracita.
anthrax | 'ænθræks | *s.i.* MED. ZOOL. ántrax (enfermedad de animales).
anthropoid | 'ænθrəpɔɪd | *adj.* **1** antropoide. || **2 anthropoids,** ZOOL. antropoideos.
anthropological | ˌænθrəpə'lɒdʒɪkl | *adj.* antropológico.
anthropologist | ˌænθrə'pɒlədʒɪst | *s.c.* antropólogo.
anthropology | ˌænθrə'pɒlədʒɪ | *s.i.* antropología.
anthropomorphic | ˌænθrəpə'mɔːfɪk | *adj.* antropomórfico.
anthropomorphism | ˌænθrəpə'mɔːfɪzəm | *s.i.* antropomorfismo.
anti- | 'æntɪ | *pref.* anti: *anticapitalist.*
anti-aircraft | ˌæntɪ'eəkrɑːft | *adj.* MIL. antiaéreo.
antibiotic | ˌæntɪbaɪ'ɒtɪk | *s.c.* QUIM. antibiótico.
antibody | ˌæntɪbɒdɪ | *s.c.* QUIM. anticuerpo.
anticipate | æn'tɪsɪpeɪt | *v.t.* **1** prever. **2** esperar con anticipación, esperar con ilusión. **3** adelantar (en una historia o narración): *don't anticipate the end = no adelantes el final.* **4** anticipar (cualquier cosa).
anticipation | ænˌtɪsɪ'peɪʃn | *s.i.* **1** expectación, anticipación. **2** ilusión.
anticipatory | ænˌtɪsɪ'peɪtərɪ | *adj.* (lit.) expectante.
anticlimactic | ˌæntɪklaɪ'mæktɪk | *adj.* decepcionante.
anticlimax | ˌæntɪ'klaɪmæks | *s.c.* e *i.* desilusión, decepción.
anticlockwise | ˌæntɪ'klɒkwaɪz | *adj./adv.* (brit.) en dirección contraria a las manecillas del reloj (describiendo movimiento).
antics | 'æantiks | *s.pl.* **1** travesuras, payasadas. **2** (desp.) bufonadas, bobadas.
anticyclone | ˌæntɪ'saikləun | *s.c.* anticiclón.
antidote | 'æntɪdəut | *s.c.* **1** QUIM. antídoto. **2 [– to]** (fig.) remedio contra, cura para, antídoto contra: *an antidote to laziness = un remedio contra la pereza.*
antifreeze | 'æntɪfriːz | *s.i.* anticongelante.
antigen | 'æntɪdʒən | *s.c.* QUIM. antígeno.
antihero | 'æntɪhɪərəu | *s.c.* antihéroe.
antihistamine | ˌæntɪ'hɪstəmiːn | *s.c.* QUIM. antihistamínico.
antiknock | ˌæntɪ'nɒk | *s.i.* QUIM. combustible antidetonante.
antilogarithm | ˌæntɪ'lɒgərɪðəm | (también **antilog**) *s.c.* MAT. antilogaritmo.
antimacassar | ˌæntɪməkæsər | *s.c.* antimacasar, funda protectora (de muebles).
antimatter | 'æntɪmætər | *s.i.* FIS. antimateria.
antimony | 'æntɪmənɪ | *s.i.* MET. antimonio.
antipathetic | ˌæntɪpə'θetɪk | *adj.* **[– to]** opuesto a; hostil a.
antipathy | æn'tɪpəθɪ | *s.i.* **[– to/towards]** antipatía hacia.
anti-personnel | ˌæntɪˌpɜːsə'nel | *adj.* MIL. antipersonal, contra personas (no cosas).
antiperspirant | ˌæntɪ'pɜːspərənt | *s.c.* e *i.* desodorante.
Antipodes | æn'tɪpədiːz | *s.pl.* (hum.) antípodas.
antiquarian | ˌæntɪ'kweərɪən | *adj.* **1** de cosas antiguas, de antiguallas. || *s.c.* **2** anticuario.
antiquary | 'æntɪkwərɪ | *s.c.* anticuario.
antiquated | 'æntɪkweɪtɪd | *adj.* **1** anticuado, pasado de moda. **2** (fam.) antediluviano, carroza.
antique | æn'tiːk | *s.c.* **1** objeto, antiguo, antigüedad. || *adj.* **2** antiguo, de objetos antiguos. || **3 – shop,** tienda de antigüedades.
antiquity | æn'tɪkwɪtɪ | *s.c.* **1** antigüedad (objeto o edificio de arte antiguo). || *s.i.* **2** antigüedad (época). **3 [– of]** antigüedad de (edad): *the antiquity of these churches = la antigüedad de estas iglesias.*
anti-Semite | ˌæntɪ'siːmaɪt | *s.c.* antisemita, antijudío.
anti-Semitic | ˌæntɪsɪ'mɪtɪk | *adj.* antisemítico.
anti-Semitism | ˌæntɪ'semɪtɪzəm | *s.i.* antisemitismo.
antiseptic | ˌæntɪ'septɪk | *adj.* **1** antiséptico. **2** (desp.) aséptico. || *s.c.* e *i.* **3** antiséptico.
anti-social | ˌæntɪ'səuʃl | *adj.* **1** (desp.) antisocial. **2** no social, individual.
anti-tank | ˌæntɪ'tæŋk | *adj.* MIL. antitanque.
antithesis | æn'tɪθɪsɪs | (*pl.* **antitheses**) (form.) *s.c.* **1 [– of]** opuesto a, antítesis de. || *s.i.* **2** FIL. antítesis.

antithetical | ˌæntɪ'θetɪkl | *adj.* **[– to]** (form.) opuesto a, incompatible con; antitético.
antithetically | ˌæntɪ'θetɪklɪ | *adv.* (lit.) antitéticamente.
antitoxin | ˌæntɪ'tɒksɪn | *s.c.* QUIM. antitoxina.
antitrust | ˌæntɪ'trʌst | *adj.* antitrust (prevención contra monopolios).
antler | 'æntlər | *s.c.* asta, cornamenta (de ciervo).
antonym | 'æntənɪm | *s.c.* GRAM. antónimo.
antonymous | æn'tɒnəməs | *adj.* GRAM. antónimo.
anus | 'eɪnəs | *s.c.* ANAT. ano.
anvil | 'ænvɪl | *s.c.* MET. yunque.
anxiety | æŋ'zaɪətɪ | *s.i.* **1 [– about/over]** ansiedad de, ansia por. **2** anhelo, ansia. || *s.c.* **3** preocupación grave, angustia.
anxious | 'æŋkʃəs | *adj.* **1 [– about]** muy preocupado sobre, inquieto por. **2 [— to** *inf.***]** ansioso por, deseoso de. **3** preocupante, inquietante.
anxiously | 'æŋkʃəslɪ | *adv.* preocupadamente, ansiosamente, angustiosamente.
anxiousness | 'æŋkʃəsnɪs | *s.i.* ansiedad, grave preocupación.
any | 'enɪ | *adj.* **1** [con *neg.*] ningún, ninguna, ningunos, ningunas, nada de. **2** [con *interr.*] algún, alguna, algunos, algunas, algo de. **3** cualquier: *any child knows that = cualquier niño sabe eso.* **4** [con *neg.*] gran, mucho: *there wasn't any great interest in it = no había mucho interés en ello.* || *pron.* **5** alguno, alguna; cualquier. **6** nada, nadie: *there was a lot of milk but now there isn't any = había muchísima leche pero ahora no hay nada.* **7 [– of]** alguno de, alguna de, alguien de; cualquiera de. || *adv.* **8** [enfatizando *comp. neg.*] de ningún modo, de ninguna manera: *after all you won't be any the richer = después de todo no serás más rico de ningún modo.* **9** (EE.UU. y fam.) en absoluto: *I didn't like that any = no me gusta eso en absoluto.* || **10 not just –;** no cualquier, no cualquiera: *she's not just any actress = ella no es una actriz cualquiera.*
anybody | 'enɪbɒdɪ | V. **anyone.**
anyhow | 'enɪhəʊ | *adv.* **1** todos los sentidos de **anyway. 2** (fam.) de cualquier modo, de cualquier manera: *don't leave your room anyhow = no dejes tu habitación de cualquier modo.* || *adj.* **3** (fam.) desordenado, de cualquier manera.
anyone | 'enɪwʌn | (también anybody) *pron. ind.* **1** [con *neg.* e *interr.*] nadie; alguien. **2** cualquiera. **3** alguien (importante, influyente, etc.): *here nobody is anybody = aquí nadie es alguien importante.*
anyplace | 'enɪpleɪs | *adv.* (EE.UU.) en cualquier sitio, en cualquier lado.
anything | 'enɪθɪŋ | *pron. ind.* **1** [con *neg.* e *interr.*] algo, alguna cosa; nada, ninguna cosa. **2** cualquier cosa. **3** cualquier (cantidad, tiempo, etc.): *the house costs anything between 5 and 8 million = la casa cuesta cualquier cantidad entre 5 y 8 millones.* || **4 – but,** y en absoluto, nada: *he's anything but nice = no es agradable en absoluto.* **5 – like/near,** [con *neg.*] ni de lejos: *he hasn't anything near the level of Spanish necessary = no tiene ni de lejos el nivel de español necesario.* **6 as... as –,** (fam.) tan... como nadie/nada en el mundo. **7 for –,** por nada en el mundo. **8 like –,** (fam.) a más no poder (como énfasis de cualquier acción). **9 not just –,** (fam.) no cualquier cosa en absoluto: *the party is not just anything, it is a very special event for him = la fiesta no es cualquier cosa en absoluto, es un acontecimiento especial para él.* **10 or –,** (fam.) o alguna otra cosa, o cualquier otra cosa: *have you got whisky or anything? = ¿tienes whisky o cualquier otra cosa?*
anyway | 'enɪweɪ | (o también **anyhow**) *adv.* **1** en cualquier caso, de cualquier forma, en todo caso.
OBS: Se usa con las siguientes matizaciones: **2** terminando una conversación: *anyway, I must go = pues bien, me tengo que ir.* **3** acelerando o saltándose puntos de un relato o similar: *I went to London on the train. Everything happened to me, but, anyway, I arrived safely = fui a Londres en tren. Me ocurrió de todo, pero, después de todo, llegué bien.* **4** cambiando de conversación: *it was a fantastic film. Anyway, the other day I saw John = fue una película fascinante. Bueno, pues el otro día vi a John.* **5** queriendo una contestación o comentario real en profundidad: *what are you crying for anyway? = ¿por qué lloras realmente?* **6** corrigiendo algo dicho anteriormente: *I loved her, o so I though anyway = yo la quería o por lo menos eso pensaba.*
anywhere | 'enɪweər | *adv.* **1** [con *neg.* e *interr.*] en ningún sitio, a ningún sitio, en algún sitio. **2** en cualquier caso. **3** en todo (como énfasis): *that's the biggest building anywhere in the region = ese es el edificio más grande de toda la región.* **4 [– from/between]** en algún punto desde/entre: *he must be anywhere between Dallas and Denver = debe estar en algún punto entre Dallas y Denver.* || **5 to get/go –,** llegar/ir a alguna parte, lograr algo. **6 miles from –,** (fam.) en el quinto pino.
aorta | eɪ'ɔːtə | *s.c.* ANAT. aorta, vena aorta.
apace | ə'peɪs | *adv.* (lit.) presto, con presteza.
apart | ə'pɑːt | *adv.* **1 [– from]** separado de, separadamente de, a un lado de. **2** de intervalo: *the exams took place two days apart = los exámenes tuvieron lugar con dos días de intervalo.* **3** aparte, a un lado: *joking apart, he's a very helpful chap = bromas aparte, es un tipo muy servicial.* || *adj.* **4** separado, alejado, aparte. || **5 – from,** aparte de, con la excepción de. **6 to tell –,** distinguir (una cosa de otra).
OBS: Esta partícula matiza el significado de muchos verbos de las siguientes maneras: **7** alejamiento gradual en costumbres, sentimientos, etc.: *before they divorced they had already grown completely apart = antes de que se divorciaran ya se habían alejado completamente el uno del otro.* **8** desmenuzamiento, rotura, hacerse añicos (una cosa) : *the toy fell apart after a few weeks = el juguete se hizo añicos después de unas cuantas semanas.* **9** separación: *pull the boys apart, don't lef them fight like that = separa a los chicos, no les dejes que se peleen así.* **10** fracaso, daño a algo: *the party fell apart after the election defeat = el partido quedó destrozado después de la derrota de la elección.*
apartheid | ə'pɑːteɪt | *s.i.* POL. apartheid (un tipo de racismo).
apartment | ə'pɒːtmənt | *s.c.* **1** (EE.UU.) apartamento, piso. **2** estancia (de un rey o presidente). || **4 – house,** (EE.UU.) bloque de pisos, edificio de apartamentos. **3 – block,** (brit.) edificio de apartamentos, bloque de pisos.
apathetic | ˌæpə'θetɪk | *adj.* apático, indiferente; impasible.
apathetically | ˌæpə'θetɪklɪ | *adv.* apáticamente, indiferentemente; impasiblemente.
apathy | 'æpəθɪ | *s.i.* apatía, indiferencia, desinterés.
ape | eɪp | *s.c.* **1** ZOOL. mono (antropoide). **2** (desp.) torpón, bruto; estúpido. || *v.t.* **3** imitar, copiar (gestos, forma de hablar).
aperient | ə'pɪərɪənt | MED. *s.c.* e *i.* **1** laxativo. || *adj.* **2** laxativo.
aperitif | ə'perətɪf | *s.c.* aperitivo (bebida).
aperture | 'æpətʃər | *s.c.* **1** (lit.) abertura, orificio. **2** FOT. abertura de diafragma.
apex | 'eɪpeks | *s.c.* **1 [– of]** vértice de, punta de. **2** (fig.) **[– of]** cúspide de (una organización, institución, etc.).
aphasia | æ'feɪzɪə | *s.i.* MED. afasia.
aphasic | ə'feɪzɪk | *adj.* MED. afásico.
aphid | 'eɪfɪd | *s.c.* ZOOL. pulgón.
aphorism | 'æfərɪzəm | *s.c.* FILOL. aforismo.
aphoristic | ˌæfə'rɪstɪk | *adj.* LIT. aforístico.
aphrodisiac | ˌæfrə'dɪzɪæk | *s.c.* **1** afrodisíaco. || *adj.* **2** afrodisíaco.
apiarist | 'eɪpɪərɪst | *s.c.* apicultor.
apiary | 'eɪpɪərɪ | *s.c.* colmenar.
apiece | ə'piːs | *adv.* cada uno, por cada uno, a cada uno.
apish | 'eɪpɪʃ | *adj.* **1** (desp.) simiesco, como un mono. **2** bobo, necio.
aplomb | ə'plɒm | *s.i.* aplomo.
apocalypse | ə'pɒkəlɪps | *s.i.* **1** catástrofe, destrucción total. || **2 Apocalypse,** Apocalipsis.
apocalyptic | əˌpɒkə'lɪptɪk | *adj.* **1** apocalíptico, catastrófico. **2** profético.
apocalyptically | əˌpɒke'lɪptɪklɪ | *adv.* apocalípticamente, catastróficamente.
apocryphal | ə'pɒkrɪfəl | *adj.* apócrifo; supuesto.
apogee | 'æpədʒiː | *s.sing.* **1** FIS. apogeo (astronómico). **2** (fig.) apogeo, punto culminante.
apolitical | ˌeɪpə'lɪtɪkl | *adj.* apolítico.
apologetic | əˌpɒlə'dʒetɪk | *adj.* apologético.
apologetically | əˌpɒlə'dʒetɪklɪ | *adv.* apologéticamente.
apologia | ˌæpə'ləudʒɪə | *s.c.* **[– for]** (lit.) apología de, defensa de.
apologist | ə'pɒlədʒɪst | *s.c.* (lit.) apologista, defensor.
apologize | ə'pɒlədʒaɪz | (también **apologise**) *v.i.* **[to – for/to]** pedir perdón por/a, disculparse por/ante.

apology | ə'pɒlədʒɪ | *s.c.* e *i.* **1 [– for/to]** disculpa por/ante, excusa por/a. || *s.c.* **2 [– for]** (desp.) substituto malo de, asco de, birria de: *that's an apology for a ball, it's made of plastic = esa es una birria de balón, es de plástico.* **3** (lit.) apología, defensa.
apophthegm | 'æpəθem | (también **apothegm**) *s.c.* apotegma, sentencia breve e ingeniosa.
apoplexy | 'æpəpleksɪ | *s.i.* MED. (p.u.) apoplejía.
apostasy | ə'pɒstəsɪ | *s.i.* y *c.* (lit.) apostasía (de religión, ideas, etc.).
apostate | ə'pɒsteɪt | (lit.) *s.c.* **1** apóstata. || *adj.* **2** apóstata.
a posteriori | ˌeɪˌpɑsterɪ'ɔːrəɪ | *adj./adv.* FIL. a posteriori.
apostle | ə'pɒsl | *s.c.* **1** REL. apóstol. **2** (fig.) apóstol, campeón.
apostolic | ˌæpə'stɒlɪk | *adj.* **1** REL. apostólico. || **2 – succession,** sucesión apostólica.
apostrophe | ə'pɒstrəfɪ | *s.c.* GRAM. apóstrofe.
apothecary | ə'pɒθəkərɪ | *s.c.* (arc.) boticario.
apotheosis | əˌpɒθɪ'əʊsɪs | (*pl.* **apotheoses**) *s.c.* **1** divinización, deificación. **2 [– of]** (lit.) apoteosis de: *she's the apotheosis of generosity = ella es la apoteosis de la generosidad.*
appal | ə'pɔːl | (EE.UU. **appall**) *v.t.* asombrar, pasmar, consternar.
appalled | ə'pɔːld | *adj.* **[– at/by]** asombrado por/de, pasmado por/de.
appalling | ə'pɔːlɪŋ | *adj.* **1** asombroso, increíble. **2** horrible (como énfasis): *I had an appalling time = lo pasé fatal.*
appallingly | ə'pɔːlɪŋlɪ | *adv.* **1** asombrosamente, increíblemente. **2** horriblemente (como énfasis).
apparatus | ˌæpə'reɪtəs | *s.c.* **1** aparato, mecanismo, ingenio. **2** (desp.) aparato (del estado, de un partido, etc.). || *s.i.* **3** equipamiento, maquinaria.
apparel | ə'pærəl | *s.i.* (lit.) ropaje.
apparent | ə'pærənt | *adj.* **1** aparente. **2 [– to]** manifiesto a, patente para.
apparently | ə'pærəntlɪ | *adv.* **1** al parecer, aparentemente, por lo visto. **2** en apariencia.
apparition | ˌæpə'rɪʃn | *s.c.* aparición.
appeal | ə'piːl | *v.i.* **1 [to —]** agradar, atraer, llamar la atención, interesar. **2 [to – to]** apelar a, recurrir a (alguien con autoridad). **3 [to – to/against]** DER. apelar a favor de/en contra de. **4 [to – to]** hacer un llamamiento a, apelar a (sentido de la justicia, del honor, de la razón, etc.). **5 [to – for]** solicitar; suplicar. || *s.c.* **6 [to – for]** súplica, ruego: *an appeal for money = una petición suplicante de dinero.* **7 [to – to/against]** solicitud de, petición de. || *s.c.* e *i.* **8** DER. apelación. || *s.i.* **9** encanto, atractivo (de un lugar, de una persona, etc.). || **10 on –,** DER. mediante apelación. **11 without –,** inapelable.
appealing | ə'piːlɪŋ | *adj.* **1** atrayente, encantador. **3** suplicante, implorante.
appealingly | ə'piːlɪŋlɪ | *adv.* **1** atractivamente, encantadoramente. **2** de manera suplicante.
appear | ə'pɪər | *v.i.* **1** aparecer; manifestarse, materializarse. **2 [to – in/on]** aparecer en, salir en (un libro, una revista, una película, etc.). **3** DER. comparecer. **4** parecer, tener pinta de estar: *he appears tired = parece cansado.* **5 [— inf./that]** parecer: *she appears to be afraid = parece tener miedo.* **6** publicarse, aparecer, salir (libros y cosas en general).
appearance | ə'pɪərəns | *s.c.* **1 [— of]** aparición de, llegada de. **2** DER. comparecencia. || *s.i.* **3 [– of]** irrupción de, llegada de (algo nuevo o distinto). **4** apariencia (física). || **5 appearances,** apariencias: *you shouldn't judge by appearances = no deberías juzgar por las apariencias.* **6 contrary to all appearances/against all appearances,** en contra de todas las apariencias, contra lo que parece. **7 to have the – of/to have all the appearances of,** parecer enteramente. **8 to keep up appearances,** salvar las apariencias. **9 to make an –,** aparecer (en televisión, etc.). **10 to put in an –,** hacer acto de presencia. **11 to all appearances/by all appearances,** a todas luces.
appease | ə'piːi | *v.t.* **1** apaciguar, calmar. **2** (lit.) aplacar (el hambre, la ira, etc.).
appeasement | ə'piːzmənt | *s.i.* apaciguamiento, pacificación.
appellant | ə'pelənt | *s.c.* DER. apelante.
appellation | ˌæpə'leɪʃn | *s.c.* (form.) denominación, título (nombre).
append | ə'pend | *v.t.* (form.) poner como anexo, añadir.
appendage | ə'pendɪdʒ | *s.c.* (form.) **1** anexo; dependencia. **2** ZOOL. apéndice (en el cuerpo de animales).
appendectomy | ˌæpen'dektəmɪ | *s.c.* MED. apendicectomía.
appendicitis | əˌpendɪ'saɪtɪs | *s.i.* MED. apendicitis.
appendix | ə'pendɪks | (*pl.* **apendices**) *s.c.* **1** ANAT. apéndice. **2** (fig.) anexo, apéndice (en un libro o similar).
appertain | ˌæpə'teɪn | *v.i.* **[— to]** (lit.) tener que ver con; pertenecer a, corresponder a.
appetite | 'æpɪtaɪt | *s.i.* y *c.* **1** apetito (de comer). || *s.c.* **2** (fig.) deseo, apetito: *sexual appetite.*
appetizer | 'æpɪtaɪzər | (también **appetiser**) *s.c.* aperitivo, tapa.
appetizing | 'æpɪtaɪzɪŋ | *adj.* apetitoso, apetecible; tentador.
appetizingly | 'æpɪtaɪɪŋlɪ | *adv.* apetitosamente, apeteciblemente.
applaud | ə'plɔːd | *v.t.* e *i.* **1** aplaudir; alabar. || **2 to be applauded,** ser aplaudido, ser alabado.
applause | ə'plɔːz | *s.i.* **1** aplauso. **2** (fig.) alabanza, encomio, aplauso.
apple | 'æpl | *s.c.* e *i.* **1** manzana. || **2 the apple of one's eye,** la niña de los ojos (el más amado).
applecart | 'æplkɑːt | **to upset the –/to upset someone's –,** dar al traste con algún plan/dar al traste con los planes de alguien.
applejack | 'æpldʒæk | *s.i.* (EE.UU.) aguardiente de manzana.
apple-pie | ˌæpl'paɪ | *s.c.* e *i.* **1** pastel de manzana. || **2 in – order,** en orden impecable, en perfecto orden.
appliance | ə'plaɪəns | *s.c.* **1** aparato, artefacto, dispositivo (especialmente de electricidad o gas). **2** TEC. bomba de incendios.
applicability | ˌæplɪkə'bɪlɪtɪ | *s.i.* pertinencia; campo de aplicación.
applicable | 'æplɪkəbl | *adj.* **[– to]** aplicable a, pertinente a.
applicant | 'æplɪkənt | *s.c.* **[– for]** solicitante de.
application | ˌæplɪ'keɪʃn | *s.c.* **1** solicitud (verbal o escrita). || *s.c.* e *i.* **2 [– of]** utilización de, aplicación de (una ley, un conocimiento, etc.). **3 [– of]** aplicación de, uso de (un material, una pintura, etc.). || *s.i.* **4** aplicación, dedicación, esmero. **5** petición, acto de petición: *you'll get it on application = lo recibirás en el acto de petición.*
applied | ə'plaɪd | *adj.* aplicado (teoría que tiene aplicación): *applied linguistics.*
apply | ə'plaɪ | *v.t.* **1** aplicar, poner en práctica, emplear (una idea, sistema, mecanismo, etc.). **2** poner, aplicar (medicina en una herida, una pintura, etc.). || *v.r.* **3 [— to]** dedicarse a, concentrar los esfuerzos en. || *v.i.* **4** ser relevante, estar en vigor. **5 [— for]** solicitar.
appoint | ə'pɔɪnt | *v.t.* **1** nombrar, designar. **2** fijar, señalar (sitio u hora).
appointed | ə'pɔɪntɪd | *adj.* **1** fijado, señalado (sitio u hora). || **2 well –/badly –,** (u otros adj. positivos o negativos) (lit.) bien/mal amueblado.
appointee | ə'pɔɪn'tiː | *s.c.* nombrado, designado (las personas).
appointment | ə'pɔɪntmənt | *s.c.* **1** persona nombrada/designada. **2** puesto (que se cubre mediante nombramiento). **3 [– with]** cita con. || *s.c.* e *i.* **4** nombramiento, designación. || **5 by –,** mediante cita previa.
apportion | ə'pɔːʃn | *v.t.* **[to – between/among]** distribuir entre, repartir entre.
apposite | 'æpəzɪt | *adj.* (lit.) oportuno, adecuado, a propósito.
appositely | 'æpəzɪtlɪ | *adv.* (lit.) oportunamente, adecuadamente.
appositeness | 'æpəzɪtnɪs | *s.i.* (lit.) oportunidad, tiempo adecuado.
apposition | ˌæpə'ziʃn | *s.i.* **1** GRAM. aposición. || **2 in – to,** GRAM. en yuxtaposición con.
appraisal | ə'preɪzl | *s.c.* e *i.* evaluación, valoración (de situaciones, cosas y personas).
appraise | ə'preɪz | *v.t.* evaluar, hacer una valoración de.
appraising | ə'preɪzɪŋ | *adj.* evaluador, valorador.
appreciable | ə'priːʃəbl | *adj.* considerable, notable (de una cantidad o similar).
appreciably | ə'priːʃəblɪ | *adv.* considerablemente, notablemente.
appreciate | ə'priːʃɪeɪt | *v.t.* **1** apreciar, estimar, valorar (como bueno). **2** entender, comprender (los detalles de una situación, problema, etc.). **3** agradecer. || *v.i.* **4** revalorizarse, aumentar de valor.
appreciation | əˌpriːʃɪ'eɪʃn | *s.i.* **1** valoración, apreciación; elogio. **2** gratitud, agradecimiento. **3** comprensión, entendimiento; reconocimiento. || *s.c.* **4** estimación, crítica (de alguna obra de arte). || *s.c.* e *i.* **5** revaloración (de acciones, joyas, etc.).
appreciative | ə'priːʃətɪv | *adj.* **1** favorable, elogioso: *an appreciative review*

= *una crítica elogiosa.* **2** agradecido, reconocido.
appreciatively | ə'pri:ʃətɪvlɪ | *adv.* **1** favorablemente, elogiosamente. **2** reconocidamente, agradecidamente.
apprehend | ˌæprɪ'hend | *v.t.* (lit.) **1** apresar, detener, prender. **2** comprender, captar en su totalidad.
apprehension | ˌæprɪ'henʃn | *s.i.* y *c.* **1** recelo, aprehensión, temor. || *s.i.* **2** (lit.) comprensión. **3** (lit.) captura, detención, aprehensión.
apprehensive | ˌæprɪ'hensɪv | *adj.* **[– about]** aprensivo acerca de, temeroso de.
apprehensively | ˌæprɪ'hensɪvlɪ | *adv.* con aprensión.
apprentice | ə'prentɪs | *s.c.* **1** aprendiz; principiante. || *v.t.* **2 [to – to]** poner de aprendiz con: *his father apprenticed him to me = su padre me lo puso de aprendiz conmigo.*
apprenticeship | ə'prentɪʃɪp | *s.i.* y *c.* **1** aprendizaje, período de aprendiz. || **2 to serve one's –,** hacer el período de aprendizaje.
apprise | ə'praɪz | *v.t.* **[to – of]** (lit.) informar de.
appro | 'æprəʊ | **on appro,** (fam. y brit.) a prueba.
approach | ə'prəʊtʃ | *v.t.* **1** aproximarse a, acercarse a (un lugar o una fecha). **2** abordar a, entablar conversación con (alguna persona). **3** enfocar, encarar (una situación, problema, etc.). **4** aproximarse, acercarse (a una cifra, cantidad, estado, etc.). || *v.i.* **5** acercarse, aproximarse. || *s.c.* **6** aproximación, acercamiento. **7 [– to]** vía de acceso a. **8** propuesta, proposición. **9 [– to]** enfoque de, planteamiento de. || *s.i.* **10** llegada, aproximación (de algún acontecimiento).
approachability | əˌprəʊtʃə'bɪlɪtɪ | *s.i.* accesibilidad: *being a Minister his approachability amazes me = siendo Ministro me sorprende muchísimo su accesibilidad.*
approachable | ə'prəʊtʃəbl | *adj.* **1** tratable, accesible (una persona). **2 [— by/from]** accesible por/desde (un lugar).
approaching | ə'prəʊtʃɪŋ | *prep.* próximo a, cercano a: *that's a figure approaching the million mark = esa era una cifra cercana al millón.*
approbation | ˌæprə'beɪʃn | *s.i.* (lit.) aprobación, asentimiento, beneplácito.
appropriate | ə'prəʊprɪɪt | *adj.* **1** apropiado, adecuado. || | ə'prəʊprɪeɪt | *v.t.* **2** (lit.) apropiarse de, adueñarse de (algo no propio). **3 [— for]** asignar para, consignar para, destinar a (hablando de cantidades de dinero).
appropriately | ə'prəʊprɪɪtlɪ | *adv.* apropiadamente, adecuadamente.
appropriation | ə'prəʊprɪ'eɪʃn | *s.i.* y *c.* (lit.) **1** consignación, asignación (de dinero).
approval | ə'pru:vl | *s.i.* **1** aprobación, aceptación. **2** visto bueno. **3** admiración; favor: *he looked at his son with approval = miró a su hijo con admiración.* || **4 on –,** a prueba, provisionalmente.
approve | ə'pru:v | *v.i.* **1 [to – of]** aprobar, dar la aprobación a, consentir. || *v.t.* **2** ratificar, sancionar. **3** dar el visto bueno a (un proyecto, un plan, una iniciativa, etc.).
approved | ə'pru:vd | *adj.* **1** aprobado, autorizado, sancionado (personas, planes, etc.)|| **2 – school,** (arc.) reformatorio.
approving | ə'pru:vɪŋ | *adj.* favorable, a favor.
approvingly | ə'pru:vɪŋlɪ | *adv.* favorablemente, con aprobación.
approximate | ə'prɒksɪmɪt | *adj.* **1** aproximado, aproximativo. || | ə'prɒksɪmeɪt | *v.t.* e *i.* **2 [to – to]** aproximar(se) a, acercar(se) a (una cifra o a algo o alguien en semejanza).
approximately | ə'prɒksɪmetlɪ | *adv.* aproximadamente.
approximation | əˌprɒksɪ'meɪʃn | *s.c.* **[– to/of]** aproximación a (en cifras o en semejanza).
appurtenances | ə'pɜ:tɪnənsɪz | *s.pl.* (lit.) accesorios.
apricot | 'eɪprɪkɒt | *s.c.* BOT. albaricoque (la fruta y el árbol).
April | 'eɪprəl | *s.i.* **1** Abril. || **2 – Fool's Day,** Día de los Inocentes (el primero de Abril en la cultura anglosajona).
a priori | ˌeɪpraɪ'ɔ:raɪ | *adj./adv.* FIL. a priori.
apron | 'eɪprən | *s.c.* **1** delantal, mandil. **2** AER. pista de estacionamiento. || **3 tied to his mother's – strings/tied to his wife's – strings,** cosido a las faldas de su mamá/cosido a las faldas de su mujer, dominado por su madre/dominado por su esposa.
apropos | ˌæprə'pəʊ | *prep.* **1** a propósito de, tocante a. || *adv.* **2** (lit.) a propósito. || *adj.* **3** (lit.) pertinente, oportuno.
apse | æps | *s.c.* ARQ. ábside.
apt | æpt | *adj.* **1 [— to** *inf.***]** propenso a. **2 [– at]** habilidoso en, capaz de. **3** apropiado, adecuado (palabras, comportamiento, etc.).
aptitude | 'æptɪtju:d | *s.c.* **1 [– for]** aptitud para, talento para. || **2 – test,** prueba de aptitud (para una cosa concreta).
aptly | 'æptlɪ | *adv.* apropiadamente, adecuadamente (dicho o hecho).
aptness | 'æptnɪs | *s.i.* aptitud (de palabras, comportamiento, etc.).
aqualung | 'ækwəlʌŋ | *s.c.* botella de aire comprimido (para el submarinismo).
aquamarine | ˌækwəmə'ri:n | *s.c.* e *i.* **1** MIN. aguamarina. || **2** aguamarina (color).
aquaplane | 'ækwəpleɪn | *s.c.* DEP. hidropatín.
aquarium | ə'kweərɪəm | (pl. **aquaria** o **aquariums**) *s.c.* **1** pecera. **2** acuario.
aquatic | ə'kwætɪk | *adj.* acuático.
aquatint | 'ækwətɪnt | *s.i.* ART. aguatinta (tipo de pintura).
aqueduct | 'ækwɪdʌkt | *s.c.* acueducto.
aqueous | 'eɪkwɪəs | *adj.* acuoso.
aquiline | 'ækwɪlaɪn | *adj.* aquilino, aguileño.
Arab | 'ærəb | *s.c.* **1** árabe. || *adj.* **2** árabe.
arabesque | ˌærə'besk | *s.c.* figura del ballet.
Arabian | ə'reɪbɪən | *adj.* de Arabia, arábigo.
Arabic | 'ærəbɪk | *adj.* **1** árabe, arábigo (cultura, tradiciones, lengua, literatura, etc.). || *s.i.* **2** árabe (idioma). || **3 arabic numerals/figures,** números arábigos.
Arabist | 'ærəbɪst | *s.c.* arabista, experto en temas arábigos.
arable | 'ærəbl | *adj.* **1** arable, cultivable. **2** agrícola (no dedicado a la ganadería). || *s.i.* **3** tierra cultivable.
arachnid | ə'ræknɪd | *adj.* ZOOL. arácnido.
arbiter | 'ɑ:bɪtər | *s.c.* **1** (lit.) DER. árbitro. **2 [– of]** (fig.) árbitro de, artífice de.
arbitrarily | 'ɑ:bɪtrərɪlɪ | *adv.* arbitrariamente.
arbitrariness | 'ɑ:bɪtrərɪnɪs | *s.i.* arbitrariedad.
arbitrary | 'ɑ:bɪtrərɪ | *adj.* **1** arbitrario, caprichoso. **2** (desp.) arbitrario.
arbitrate | 'ɑ:bɪtreɪt | *v.t.* arbitrar (disputa, conflicto, etc.).
arbitration | ˌɑ:bɪ'treɪʃn | *s.i.* **1** arbitraje (de disputas). || **2 to go to –,** recurrir al arbitraje.
arbitrator | 'ɑ:bɪtreɪtər | *s.c.* árbitro (de disputas).
arboreal | ɑ:'bɔ:rɪəl | *adj.* arbóreo, arborícola (de animales que viven en los árboles).
arboretum | ˌɑ:bə'ri:təm | *s.c.* AGR. vivero.
arbour | 'ɑ:bər | (*brit.* **arbour**) *s.c.* cenador, pérgola.
arc | ɑ:k | *s.c.* **1** GEOM. arco. **2** arco, semicircunferencia. || *v.i.* **3** hacer una circunferencia, formar un arco. **4** ELEC. formar un arco voltaico.
arcade | ɑ:'keɪd | *s.c.* **1** soportales. **2** galería (de tiendas). || **3 shopping –,** centro comercial.
arcane | ɑ:'keɪn | *adj.* (lit.) **1** arcano, misterioso. || *s.c.* (sólo sing.) **2** arcano.
arch | ɑ:tʃ | *s.c.* **1** ARQ. arco. **2** (fig.) curva (en el cuerpo o en una figura). **3** ANAT. empeine. || *v.t. e i.* **4** arquear(se), curvar(se). || *adj.* **5** pícaro, socarrón. **6** soberbio, orgulloso (tono de voz). || **7 arch-;** archi- (como prefijo).
archaeological | ˌɑ:kɪə'lɒdʒɪkl | (también archeological) *adj.* arqueológico.
archaeologist | ˌɑ:kɪ'ɒlədʒɪst | (también **archeologist**) *s.c.* arqueólogo.
archaeology | ˌɑ:kɪ'ɒlədʒɪ | (también **archeology**) *s.i.* arqueología.
archaic | ɑ:'keɪɪk | *adj.* **1** (hum. y desp.) anticuado, pasado de moda. **2** (lit.) arcaico. **3** FILOL. arcaico (sólo encontrado en literatura antigua).
archaism | 'ɑ:keɪɪzəm | *s.c.* e *i.* arcaísmo.
archangel | 'ɑ:keɪndʒl | *s.c.* REL. arcángel.
archbishop | ˌɑ:tʃ'bɪʃəp | *s.c.* REL. arzobispo.
archdeacon | ˌɑ:tʃ'di:kən | *s.c.* REL. arcediano (especialmente en la iglesia anglicana).
archdiocese | ˌɑ:tʃ'daɪəsɪs | *s.c.* REL. archidiócesis.
arch-duke | ˌɑ:tʃ'dju:k | *s.c.* archiduque.
arch-duchess | ˌɑ:tʃ'dʌtʃɪs | *s.c.* archiduquesa.
arched | ɑ:tʃt | *adj.* arqueado, curvado.
arch-enemy | ˌɑ:tʃ'enəmɪ | *s.c.* **1** enemigo principal. || **2 the Archenemy,** REL. Satanás, el Enemigo.
archer | 'ɑ:tʃər | *s.c.* arquero.
archery | 'ɑ:tʃərɪ | *s.i.* DEP. tiro con arco.
archetypal | 'ɑ:kɪtaɪpl | *adj.* (lit.) arquetípico.
archetypally | 'ɑ:kɪtaɪpəlɪ | *adv.* (lit.) arquetípicamente.

archetype | 'ɑːkɪtaɪp | *s.c.* **[– of]** arquetipo de, prototipo de.
archipelago | ˌɑːkɪ'pelɪgəʊ | *s.c.* GEOG. archipiélago.
architect | 'ɑːkɪtekt | *s.c.* **1** arquitecto. **2** (fig.) artífice, arquitecto: *he was the architect of peace = él fue el artífice de la paz.*
architectural | ˌɑːkɪ'tektʃərəl | *adj.* arquitectónico.
architecturally | ˌɑːkɪ'tektʃərəlɪ | *adv.* arquitectónicamente.
architecture | 'ɑːkɪtektʃər | *s.i.* **1** arquitectura. **2** (fig.) estructura: *the architecture of neutrons = la estructura de los neutrones.*
archive | 'ɑːkaɪv | *s.c.* **1** archivo (lugar donde se guardan documentos históricos, etc.). || **2 archives,** archivos.
archivist | 'ɑːkɪvɪst | *s.c.* archivero.
archly | 'ɑːtʃlɪ | *adv.* **1** picaronamente, socarronamente. **2** orgullosamente, soberbiamente (tono de voz).
archway | 'ɑːtʃweɪ | *s.c.* pasaje abovedado.
arctic | 'ɑːktɪk | *adj.* **1** polar, digno del Artico (expresando mucho frío). **2** para el Artico (hablando de ropa). || **3 the Arctic,** GEOG. el Artico. **4 the Arctic Circle,** GEOG. el Círculo Polar Artico.
ardent | 'ɑːdənt | *adj.* **1** apasionado, fervoroso, entusiasta (sobre algún tema). **2** ardiente, vehemente (sentimientos).
ardently | 'ɑːdntlɪ | *adv.* **1** apasionadamente, fervorosamente, entusiásticamente. **2** ardientemente, vehementemente.
ardour | 'ɑːdər | (*brit.* **ardour**) *s.i.* **1** pasión, fervor (sentimiento). **2 [– for]** vehemencia a favor de, ardor hacia (interés, entusiasmo): *his ardour for justice = su vehemencia a favor de la justicia.*
arduous | 'ɑːdjʊəs | *adj.* arduo, trabajoso.
arduously | 'ɑːdjʊəslɪ | *adv.* arduamente, trabajosamente.
are | ɑr | pronunciación relajada | ə | (2. persona *sing.* y *pl.*) V. **be.**
area | 'eərɪə | *s.c.* **1** área, zona. **2** trozo (distinto del resto en una superficie). **3** MAT. área (medida de superficie). **4** campo, especialidad (de estudio). **5** área, terreno (de la vida, de la experiencia, etc.). || **5 – code,** (EE.UU.) prefijo telefónico de zona.
arena | ə'riːnə | *s.c.* **1** pista, ruedo, arena (de un espectáculo). **2** foro: *the political arena = el foro político.*
aren't | ɑːnt | pronunciación relajada | ənt | *contr.* de **are** y **not,** y en interrogativas también de **am** y **not.**
Argentina | ˌɑːdʒən'tiːnə | *s.sing.* Argentina.
Argentinian | ˌɑːdʒən'tɪnɪən | *s.c.* **1** argentino. || *adj.* **2** argentino.
argon | 'ɑːgɒn | *s.i.* QUIM. argón.
argot | 'ɑːgəʊ | *s.c.* (lit.) jerga, argot.
arguable | 'ɑːgjʊəbl | *adj.* **1** discutible, disputable. **2** posible, probable: *it is arguable that the Prime Minister will resign = es posible que el Primer Ministro dimita.*
arguably | 'ɑːgjʊəblɪ | *adv.* posiblemente, probablemente.
argue | 'ɑːgjuː | *v.t.* **1** sostener, afirmar (ideas, opiniones, etc.). **2** discutir, debatir (un punto). || *v.i.* **3 [to – for/against]** argumentar a favor de/en contra de, razonar a favor de/en contra de. **4 [to – with]** discutir con, pelearse con (verbalmente). || **5 to – into,** convencer de, persuadir de. **6 to – out,** discutir hasta llegar a una decisión, discutir de cabo a rabo: *we argued out all the possibilities = discutimos de cabo a rabo todas las posibilidades.* **7 to – out of,** disuadir de: *I argued him out of the idea = le disuadí de la idea.* **8 to – the toss,** andar en dimes y diretes.
argument | 'ɑːgjʊmənt | *s.c.* **1 [– for/against]** razonamiento a favor de/en contra de, argumento a favor de/en contra de. **2** discusión, pelea (verbal). || *s.i.* **3** discusión, disputa: *don't accept it without argument = no lo aceptes sin discusión.*
argumentation | ˌɑːgjumen'teɪʃn | *s.i.* (form.) argumentación, raciocinio.
argumentative | ˌɑːgjʊ'mentətɪv | *adj.* (desp.) pendenciero (en peleas verbales), discutidor.
argy-bargy | ˌɑːdɪ'bɑːdʒɪ | *s.i.* (fam.) dimes y diretes, discusión futil.
aria | 'ɑːrɪə | *s.c.* MUS. aria.
arid | 'ærid | *adj.* **1** árido, poco fértil. **2** (fig.) árido, sin ideas (en escritos, en la vida, etc.).
aridity | ə'rɪdɪtɪ | *s.i.* **1** aridez. **2** (fig.) aridez, falta de ideas (en el arte o en la vida, etc.).
aridly | 'ærɪdlɪ | *adv.* áridamente.
aridness | 'ærɪdnɪs | *s.c.* aridez, estado de aridez.
aright | ə'raɪt | *adv.* **1** (p.u.) correctamente, bien. || **2 to put/set –,** corregir, rectificar, solucionar.
arise | ə'raɪz | *v.i.* **1** surgir, presentarse, producirse (una situación, problema, etc.). **2** aparecer, surgir, darse: *new beings will arise in the future = nuevos seres aparecerán en el futuro.* **3** elevarse, levantarse, surgir (olor, sabor, ruido, sonido, etc.): *a mist arose = se levantó una neblina.* **4 [to – from/out of]** ser resultado de, surgir como resultado de: *that arises from your lack of courage = eso es el resultado de tu falta de coraje.* **5** rebelarse, levantarse (como grupo reivindicativo): *workers arose at different times = los trabajadores se rebelaron en momentos distintos.* **6** (lit. y p.u.) levantarse (de la cama), ponerse en pie. **7** (lit.) aparecer, surgir (un objeto a cierta distancia): *the castle arose in the middle of the hills = el castillo surgió en medio de las colinas.*
aristocracy | ˌærɪs'tɒkrəsɪ | *s.c.* aristocracia.
aristocrat | 'ærɪstəkræt | *s.c.* aristócrata.
aristocratic | ˌærɪstə'krætɪk | *adj.* aristocrático.
aristocratically | ˌærɪstə'krætɪklɪ | *adv.* aristocráticamente.
arithmetic | ə'rɪθmətɪk | *s.i.* **1** aritmética. **2** cálculo, cálculos: *your arithmetic is completely wrong = tus cálculos están completamente equivocados.* || | ˌærɪʃ'metɪk | *adj.* **3 aritmético.**
arithmetical | ˌærɪʃə'metɪkl | *adj.* **1** aritmético, matemático. || **2 – progression,** progresión aritmética.
arithmetically | ə'rɪθmətɪklɪ | *adv.* aritméticamente, matemáticamente.
arithmetician | əˌrɪθmə'tɪʃn | *s.c.* especialista en aritmética, experto en aritmética.
ark | ɑːk | *s.c.* **1** REL. arca. || **2 out of the –,** (fam. y hum.) salido de los tiempos de Maricastaña. **3 the Ark of Covenant,** REL. el Arca de la Alianza.
arm | ɑːm | *s.c.* **1** ANAT. brazo. **2** manga (de vestimenta). **3** brazo (de asientos). **4** brazo, lengua (de mar, agua, tierra). **5** ala, brazo (de una organización): *the political arm of organization = el brazo político de la organización.* **6** (fig.) autoridad, poder, mano: *the long arm of the law = el largo brazo de la ley.* **7** MEC. brazo, polea, brazo mecánico. || *v.t.* **8** armar, dar un arma a. **9** (fig.) armar, proveer de (información, autoridad, etc.). || **10 – in –,** del brazo. **11 arms, a)** armas, armamento. **b)** escudo de armas (heráldica). **12 arms race,** carrera armamentista. **13 as long as one's –,** muy largo. **14 at arm's length,** a prudente distancia. **15 at arm's reach:** al alcance de la mano. **16 to be the – of,** ser el brazo derecho de. **17 to give one's right – for,** dar el brazo derecho por. **18 to keep someone at arm's length,** mantener a alguien a prudente distancia (para que no se tome confianzas). **19 to lay down one's arms,** (p.u.) rendirse, entregar las armas. **20 to present arms,** MIL. presentar armas. **21 to push into someone's arms,** obligar a caer bajo la influencia de alguien, empujar dentro del área de influencia de alguien: *I was pushed into Mary's arms by my mother = me vi obligado a caer bajo la influencia de Mary debido a mi madre.* **22 to rise up in arms,** alzarse en armas. **23 to take up arms,** tomar las armas. **24 to twist someone's –,** (fam.) presionar a alguien (para que haga lo que quieres). **25 under arms,** MIL. en situación de guerra, armados. **26 up in arms,** muy enfadado (poniendo el grito en el cielo). **27 with open arms,** con los brazos abiertos.
armada | ɑː'mɑːdə | *s.c.* **1** MIL. Armada. || **2 the Armada,** HIST. la Armada Invencible.
armadillo | ˌɑːmə'dɪləʊ | *s.c.* ZOOL. armadillo.
armament | 'ɑːməmənt | *s.i.* **1** MIL. potencia ofensiva, preparación bélica. || **2 armaments,** MIL. armamento, armas.
armature | 'ɑːmətʃər | *s.c.* MEC. armadura (de una dinamo).
armband | 'ɑːmbænd | *s.c.* brazalete.
armchair | 'ɑːmtʃeər | *s.c* **1** sillón, butaca. || *adj.* **2** (desp.) teórico, de sillón.
armed | ɑːmd | *adj.* **1** armado, con armas. **2 [– with]** (fig.) dotado de, provisto de. || **3 -armed:** de brazos (como sufijo): *strong-armed soldiers = soldados de brazos fuertes.* **4 – forces,** Fuerzas Armadas, Ejército. **5 – robbery,** DER. robo a mano armada. **6 – to the teeth,** armado hasta los dientes.
armful | 'ɑːmful | *s.c.* montón (que se puede llevar en los brazos).
armhole | 'ɑːmhəʊl | *s.c.* sisa, sobaquera.
armistice | 'ɑːmɪstɪs | *s.c.* e *i.* **1** POL. armisticio. || **2 Armistice Day,** HIST. Día del Armisticio (que marca el final de la I Guerra Mundial).

armour | 'ɑːmər | (EE.UU. **armor**) *s.i.* **1** armadura. **2** blindaje, coraza. **3** MIL. vehículos blindados: *send the armour = envía los vehículos blindados.* **4** (fig.) defensa, protección, escudo: *my armour against her hate is your love = mi defensa contra su odio es tu amor.*
armoured | 'ɑːməd | (EE.UU. **armored**) *adj.* **1** MIL. blindado. **2** ZOOL. con coraza (animales que tienen una piel fuerte especial).
armourer | 'ɑːmərər | (EE.UU. **armorer**) *s.c.* MIL. armero.
armour-plated | 'ɑːməpleɪtɪd | EE.UU. **armor-plated**) *adj.* blindado (especialmente coches).
armoury | 'ɑːmərɪ | (EE.UU. **armory**) *s.c.* **1** MIL. armería, depósito de armas. **2** MIL. arsenal (de todo un país). **3** (fig.) arsenal, colección (de cualquier cosa).
armpit | 'ɑːmpɪt | *s.c.* ANAT. axila, sobaco.
army | 'ɑːmɪ | *s.c.* **1** MIL. ejército. **2 [– of]** (fig.) ejército de, montón de: *an army of advisers = un montón de consejeros.*
aroma | ə'rəumə | *s.c.* aroma, fragancia.
aromatic | ˌærə'mætɪk | *adj.* aromático.
arose | ə'rəuz | V. **arise.**
around | ə'raund | (también **round**) **1** V. **round.** || **2 to be –,** estar por ahí: *I'm going to the pub to see who is around = voy al bar a ver quién hay por ahí.* **3 to have been –,** (fam.) ser una persona que ha viajado, ha experimentado otros lugares, que sabe de la vida en general y en profundidad: *It's obvious that he's been around = es obvio que tiene experiencia de la vida.*
arousal | ə'rauzəl | *s.i.* **1** excitación, excitación sexual. **2 [– of]** despertar de (sentimientos, intereses, etc.): *the arousal of hate = el despertar del odio.*
arouse | ə'rauz | *v.t.* **1** despertar (interés, atención, etc.). **2** incitar, provocar, despertar (sentimientos). **3** excitar (sexualmente). **4** despertar (del sueño).
arpeggio | ɑː'pedʒɪəu | *s.c.* MUS. arpegio.
arraign | ə'reɪn | *v.t.* DER. citar, emplazar (ante un tribunal para contestar a una acusación).
arraignment | ə'reɪnmənt | *s.c.* e *i.* DER. emplazamiento, citación.
arrange | ə'reɪndʒ | *v.t.* **1** organizar, ordenar, planificar. **2** cuidar los detalles de, tomar medidas: *arrange everything, please = por favor, cuida todos los detalles.* **3** disponer, colocar (un objeto para mayor belleza). **4** MUS. arreglar. || *v.i.* **5** disponer, ordenar, fijar: *I arranged that my son should go too = dispuse que mi hijo se fuera también.* || **6 arranged marriage,** boda concertada (de antemano y sin el consentimiento de los implicados).
arrangement | ə'reɪndʒmənt | *s.c.* **1** plan, organización; acuerdo. **2** disposición, colocación. **3** MUS. arreglo. || **4 arrangements,** planificación, planes. **5 to make arrengements,** hacer preparativos.
arrant | 'ærənt | *adj.* (desp.) redomado, notorio: *an arrant idiot.*
array | ə'reɪ | *v.r.* **1 [to – in]** (lit.) ataviarse con, engalanarse con (vestidos). || *v.t.* **2** (lit.) ataviar, engalanar, adornar. **3** (lit.) MIL. poner en orden de batalla, formar en orden de batalla. || *s.c.* **4 [– of]** conjunto de, serie de, colección de: *an array of new possibilities = un conjunto de posibilidades nuevas.* || **5 a battle –/a military –,** MIL. una disposición de batalla/una formación de batalla. **6 to be arrayed,** (lit.) estar colocado, estar dispuesto (a la vista de la gente de modo correcto).
arrears | ə'rɪəz | *s.c.* (sólo *pl.*) **1** atrasos, deudas. || **2 in –, a)** endeudado, atrasado en sus pagos. **b)** a mes, semana, etc. vencido (forma de recibir el sueldo).
arrest | ə'rest | *v.t.* **1** arrestar, detener. **2** cautivar; atraer (la atención). **3** atajar, detener (haciendo su progresión más lenta): *don't arrest the child's growth = no detengas el crecimiento del niño.* || *s.c.* e *i.* **4** arresto, detención. || **5 to make an –,** llevar a cabo una detención, hacer un arresto. **6 under –,** bajo arresto. **7 under house –,** bajo arresto domiciliario.
arresting | ə'restɪŋ | *adj.* atrayente, cautivador, llamativo.
arrival | ə'raɪvl | *s.i.* **1** llegada (de un tren, de un acontecimiento, etc.). **2** nacimiento, llegada (de un bebé). || *s.c.* **3** recién llegado: *that fellow is the new arrival = ese tipo es el (nuevo) recién llegado.* **4** (hum.) bebé.
arrive | ə'raɪv | *v.i.* **1** llegar. **2 [to – at]** llegar a, alcanzar (una conclusión, idea, etc.). **3** aparecer, llegar: *new inventions arrived = aparecieron nuevos inventos.* **4** nacer (un bebé). **5** (fam.) tener éxito, alcanzar el éxito: *thanks to her film director friend, she has arrived = gracias a su amigo director de cine, ella ha alcanzado el éxito.*
arrogance | 'ærəgəns | *s.i.* (desp.) arrogancia, altivez.
arrogant | 'ærəgənt | *adj.* (desp.) arrogante, altivo.
arrogantly | 'ærəgəntlɪ | *adv.* con arrogancia, altivamente.
arrogate | 'ærəgeɪt | *v.r.* **[to – to]** (desp. y lit.) arrogarse, atribuirse (funciones no merecidas).
arrow | 'ærəu | *s.c.* **1** flecha (como arma o como señal).
arrowhead | 'ærəuhed | *s.c.* punta de flecha.
arrowroot | 'ærəuruːt | *s.i.* arrurruz.
arse | ɑːs | *s.c.* (fam. y vulgar). **1** culo. || **2 to – about/around,** hacer el tonto. **3 to get off one's –,** darse prisa, moverse, ponerse a ello. **4 to move/shift one's –,** echarse a un lado, dejar sitio.
arsehole | 'ɑːshəul | *s.c.* (fam. y tabú) **1** ano. **2** imbécil, idiota, gilipollas.
arse-licker | 'ɑːslɪkər | *s.c.* (fam. y vulg.) lameculos, pelota.
arsenal | 'ɑːsɪnl | *s.c.* **1** MIL. arsenal. **2** (fig.) arsenal, caudal (de ideas, etc.).
arsenic | 'ɑːsnɪk | *s.i.* QUIM. arsénico.
arson | 'ɑːsn | *s.i.* DER. incendio premeditado.
art | ɑːt | *s.i.* **1** arte. **2** dibujo, pintura: *my child is very good at art = mi hijo es muy bueno en dibujo.* **3** (fig.) arte, habilidad: *the art of listening = el arte de escuchar.* **4** astucia, maña, arte: *all your art will be useless = toda tu astucia será inútil.* || *s.c.* **5** arte (cine, pintura, etc.). || **6 arts,** letras, humanidades. **7 arts and crafts,** trabajos manuales. **8 to get something down to a fine –,** hacer algo a la perfección, bordar algo. **9 the arts,** las artes.
artefact | 'ɑːtɪfækt | (también **artifact**) *s.c.* artefacto, objeto.
arterial | ɑː'tɪərɪəl | *adj.* **1** ANAT. arterial. **2** principal (carretera nacional, ferrocarril).
arteriosclerosis | ɑːˌtɪərɪəusklə'rəusɪs | *s.i.* MED. arteriosclerosis.
artery | 'ɑtərɪ | *s.c.* **1** ANAT. arteria. **2** carretera principal, línea principal de ferrocarril.
artesian well | ɑːˌtiːzɪən'wel | *s.c.* pozo artesiano.
artful | 'ɑːtfl | *adj.* **1** astuto, taimado, ladino. **2** ingenioso, habilidoso (en su expresión artística).
artfully | 'ɑːtfəlɪ | *adv.* **1** astutamente, taimadamente, ladinamente. **2** ingeniosamente, habilidosamente (en el arte).
arthritic | ɑː'θrɪtɪk | *adj.* **1** MED. con artritis, artrítico, de artritis. || *s.c.* **2** artrítico, reumático.
arthritis | ɑː'θraɪtɪs | *s.i.* MED. artritis.
artichoke | 'ɑːtɪtʃəuk | *s.c.* BOT. **1** alcachofa. || **2 Jerusalem –,** pataca.
article | 'ɑːtɪkl | *s.c.* **1** PER. artículo. **2** artículo, cosa, objeto. **3** DER. artículo, cláusula. **4** GRAM. artículo. || **5 – of faith,** artículo de fe, creencia básica. **6 articles,** DER. acuerdo de prácticas de abogacía.
articled | 'ɑːtɪkld | *adj.* de prácticas profesionales.
articulate | ɑː'tɪkjulɪt | *adj.* **1** articulado, claro, inteligible. || | ɑː'tɪkjuleɪt | *v.t.* **2** (lit.) expresar, articular (ideas, opiniones, etc.).
articulated | ɑː'tɪkjuleɪtɪd | *adj.* articulado (de vehículos).
articulately | ɑː'tɪkjulɪtlɪ | *adv.* articuladamente, inteligiblemente.
articulateness | ɑː'tɪkjulətnɪs | *s.i.* claridad (de expresión o de pensamiento).
articulation | ɑːˌtɪkju'leɪʃn | *s.i.* **1** (lit.) articulación, expresión (de ideas, sentimientos, etc.). || *s.c.* e *i.* **2** FON. articulación.
artifice | 'ɑːtɪfɪs | *s.c.* e *i.* (lit.) artificio, ardid, estratagema.
artificer | ɑːtɪfɪsər | *s.c.* MIL. artificiero.
artificial | ɑː'tɪfɪʃl | *adj.* **1** artificial (de situaciones, objetos, materiales, etc.). **2** (desp.) artificial, artificioso, afectado. **3** postizo, artificial (partes del cuerpo). || **4 – insemination,** MED. inseminación artificial. **5 – intelligence,** INFO. inteligencia artificial. **6 – light,** luz artificial. **7 – respiration,** respiración artificial.
artificiality | ˌɑːtɪfɪʃɪ'ælɪtɪ | *s.i.* **1** artificialidad (de gran número de cosas). **2** (desp.) afectación, artificialidad.
artificially | ɑː'tɪfɪʃəlɪ | *adv.* artificialmente.
artillery | ɑː'tɪlərɪ | *s.i.* MIL. **1** artillería. || **2 the Artillery,** la Artillería.
artisan | ˌɑːtɪ'zæn | *s.c.* artesano.
artist | 'ɑːtɪst | *s.c.* **1** artista (de todo género). **2** (fig.) artista (en cualquier profesión o empeño).
artiste | ɑː'tiːst | *s.c.* artista (sólo en el canto, el baile y el circo).
artistic | ɑː'tɪstɪk | *adj.* artístico.
artistically | ɑː'tɪstɪklɪ | *adv.* artísticamente.
artistry | 'ɑːtɪstrɪ | *s.i.* **1** saber hacer artístico. **2** (fig.) habilidad, toque.
artless | 'ɑːtlɪs | *adj.* sencillo, natural.

artlessly | 'ɑːtlɪslɪ | *adv.* sencillamente, con naturalidad.
artlessness | 'ɑːtlɪsnɪs | *s.i.* sencillez, naturalidad.
artwork | 'ɑːtwəːk | *s.i.* ilustraciones (acompañando a un texto).
arty | 'ɑːtɪ | *adj.* (desp.) ostentoso, repipi, pseudoartístico.
arty-crafty | ˌɑːtɪ'krɑːftɪ | *adj.* (desp.) artificialmente artístico.
as | æz | pronunciación relajada | əi | *conj.* **1** como, porque, ya que: *as I'm tired, I'll go to bed = como estoy cansado, me voy a la cama.* **2** cuando, al mismo tiempo que, en el momento en que: *he was shot as he was walking out of the house = le dispararon en el momento en que salía de la casa.* **3** de la misma manera que, como, igual que: *do as I do = haz como yo.* **4** [detrás de *adj.*] aunque: *tired as she was, she left the child sleep on the only bed available = aunque estaba cansada, dejó dormir al chico en la única cama disponible.* **5** en la medida en que: *his speech only highlighted unemployment as measured by the Government Statistical Office = su discurso sólo resaltó el paro en la medida en que estaba cuantificado por el Instituto de Estadística.* || *adv.* **6** [en *comp.*] tan; como: *he's as strong as a horse = es tan fuerte como un caballo.* **7** hasta, incluso (como énfasis): *he earns as much as 5.000 dollars a month = gana hasta 5.000 dólares al mes.* || *prep.* **8** como, de (con profesiones, estadios vitales y diversas situaciones): *he worked as a teacher for 15 years = trabajó de profesor durante 15 años.* || **9 – against,** comparado con, contrastado con. **10 – ever,** como siempre. **11 – follows,** como sigue: *the text is as follows = el texto es como sigue.* **12 – for/to,** en cuanto a, en lo que concierne a: *as for your petition I have no good news at all = en lo que concierne a su petición no tengo en absoluto buenas noticias.* **13 – from/– of,** a partir de, desde, (con expresión de tiempo). **14 – if/– though,** como si. **15 – I see it/– I understand it,** en mi opinión, tal como lo veo. **16 – it is/– it turns out/– things stand,** tal como está la situación, tal como están las cosas, tal como está todo. **17 – it were,** por decirlo así. **18 – opposed to,** en contraposición con, en contra de: *it's necessary to have specialists as opposed general workers = es necesario tener especialistas en lugar de trabajadores no especializados.* **19 – regards,** en lo que respecta a, en lo tocante a. **20 – such,** per se, en sí mismo, por sí mismo: *I'm not interested in literature as such, but as a reflection of our society = yo no estoy interesado en la literatura por sí misma, sino como reflejo de nuestra sociedad.* **21 – to,** (brit.) sobre, acerca de. **22 — well,** también. **23 – yet,** hasta ahora, aún. **24 – you wish/– you like,** como quieras, como desees, como gustes. **25 it isn't – if/it isn't – though,** no es el caso que, no es precisamente como si (o en otros tiempos como el pasado, etc.).
asbestos | æz'bestəs | *s.i.* asbesto.
asbestosis | ˌæzbes'təusɪs | *s.i.* MED. asbestosis.
ascend | ə'send | (lit.) *v.i.* **1** ascender, elevarse. **2 [to – to]** llevar a (subiendo): *those steps ascend to the tower = esos escalones llevan a la torre.* || *v.t.* **3** subir (una escalera, una montaña, etc.). || **to – the throne,** subir al trono.
ascendancy | ə'sendənsɪ | (también **ascendency**) *s.i.* (lit.) **[– over]** dominio sobre, predominio sobre.
ascendant | ə'sendənt | (también **ascendent**) *adj.* **1** (lit.) predominante: *the ascendant class.* || **2 in the –,** ganando en fuerza, adquiriendo influencia.
ascending | ə'sendɪŋ | *adj.* ascendiente, hacia arriba: *in ascending order = en orden ascendiente.*
ascension | ə'senʃn | *s.i.* **1** ascensión. || **2 the Ascension,** REL. la Ascensión.
ascent | ə'sent | *s.c.* **1** ascenso, ascensión, subida. **2** cuesta, pendiente. || *s.i.* **3** (lit.) ascenso, progreso (de una persona en la sociedad).
ascertain | ˌæsə'teɪn | *v.t.* (form.) averiguar, determinar, cerciorarse de.
ascertainable | ˌæsə'teɪnəbl | *adj.* (form.) determinable, de posible averiguación, indagable.
ascertainment | ˌæsə'teɪnmənt | *s.i.* (form.) indagación, averiguación, comprovación.
ascetic | ə'setɪk | *adj.* **1** ascético. || *s.c.* **2** asceta.
ascetically | ə'setɪklɪ | *adv.* ascéticamente.
asceticism | ə'setɪsɪzəm | *s.i.* asceticismo.
ascorbic acid | əˌskɔːbɪk'æsɪd | *s.i.* QUIM. ácido ascórbico.
ascribable | ə'skraɪbəbl | *adj.* atribuible, imputable: *his success is ascribable to good luck = su éxito es imputable a la buena suerte.*
ascribe | ə'skraɪb | *v.t.* atribuir, imputar (un suceso, una virtud, una obra de arte, etc.).
ascription | ə'skrɪpʃn | *s.c.* e *i.* (form.) atribución, adscripción.
asepsis | ˌeɪ'sepsɪs | *s.i.* MED. asepsia.
aseptic | ˌeɪ'septɪk | *adj.* MED. aséptico, libre de gérmenes.
asexual | ˌeɪ'sekʃuəl | *adj.* asexual.
asexuality | eɪˌsekʃu'ælətɪ | *s.i.* asexualidad.
ash | æʃ | *s.i.* **1** ceniza. **2** madera de fresno. || *s.c.* **3** BOT. fresno. || **4 ashes,** cenizas (de cigarrillos, madera, personas quemadas, etc.). **5 – Wednesday,** REL. Miércoles de Ceniza.
ashamed | ə'ʃeɪmd | *adj.* **1 [– of]** avergonzado de. || **2 to be – to,** [+ *inf.*] tener vergüenza de, darle a uno vergüenza.
ashcan | 'æʃkæn | *s.c.* (EE.UU.) cubo de basura.
ashen | 'æʃn | *adj.* ceniciento (color de la cara), horriblemente pálido.
ashore | ə'ʃɔː | *adv.* MAR. **1** a tierra, a la costa. || **2 to go –,** ir a tierra, desembarcar.
ashpan | 'æʃpæn | *s.c.* cajón para la ceniza (debajo de un fuego de chimenea o similar).
ashtray | 'æʃtreɪ | *s.c.* cenicero.
ashy | 'æʃɪ | *adj.* de ceniza, con ceniza, parecido a la ceniza.
Asia | 'eɪʃə | *s.c.* GEOG. Asia.
Asian | 'eɪʃn | *adj.* **1** asiático. || *s.c.* **2** asiático.
Asiatic | ˌeɪsɪ'ætɪk | *adj.* asiático.
aside | ə'saɪd | *adv.* **1** a un lado: *move aside = échate a un lado.* **2** aparte; excluyendo, dejando aparte, dejando a un lado: *her drinking problem aside, she is a great actress and a very beautiful woman = dejando a un lado su problema con el alcohol, es una actriz estupenda y una mujer guapísima.* || *s.c.* **3** indirecta intencionada: *oh! it's so hot in here. She said in a loud and clear aside = ¡oh, hace tanto calor aquí dentro! Dijo con una indirecta claramente intencionada y en voz alta.* **4** digresión. || **5 – from,** (EE.UU.) aparte de, fuera de. OBS: Esta partícula matiza el significado de los verbos de las siguientes maneras: **6** expresando separación física mantenida: *I held the curtains aside to see who was coming = mantuve las cortinas separadas para ver quién venía.* **7** señalando rechazo, descarte, etc. de una idea, sugerencia, saludo o similar: *I was never able to sweep all her doubts aside as to my intentions = nunca pude despejar todas sus dudas en cuanto a mis intenciones.*
asinine | 'æsɪnaɪn | *adj.* (lit.) estúpido, necio.
ask | ɑːsk | *v.t.* **1** preguntar. **2** [someone + *inf.*] pedir: *I asked him to come = le pedí que viniera.* **3 [to – in/out]** invitar a entrar/a salir: *I've asked her out fifty times and she's always rejected me = la he invitado a salir cincuenta veces y siempre me ha rechazado.* **4** pedir, solicitar (una opinión, un permiso, etc.). || *v.i.* **5** preguntar, formular una pregunta. || **6 as** (*adj.*) **as one could – for,** lo/él/la/los/las más o mejores (superlativo del adjetivo) que uno podría desear: *they are as good teachers as he could ask for = ellos son los mejores profesores que él podría desear.* **7 to – after, a)** preguntar por (queriendo ver a una persona). **b)** pedir (una cosa). **8 to – for it/to – for trouble,** (fam.) provocar líos, buscarse problemas voluntariamente, meterse en follones queriéndolo. **9 for the asking,** gratis, con sólo pedirlo. **10 I – you!,** (fam.) ¡será posible!: *cars being allowed to park on the pavements, I ask you! = ¡que a los coches se les permita aparcar en las aceras, será posible!* **11 if you – me,** si quieres saber mi opinión, si se me pregunta.
askance | ə'skɑns | *adv.* **1** de reojo, oblicuamente. || **2 to look – at,** mirar sospechosa o despectivamente a.
askew | ə'skjuː | *adj.* y *adv.* torcido, torcidamente.
asking price | 'ɑːskɪŋ praɪs | *s.c.* precio inicial.
aslant | ə'slɑːnt | *adv.* **1** oblicuamente, sesgadamente. || *prep.* **2** al través de (en forma oblicua): *the sword had been placed aslant the window sill = la espada había sido colocada a través del alféizar de la ventana.*
asleep | ə'sliːp | *adj.* **1** dormido. **2** (fam.) adormecido, ido, sin atender. **3** (fig.) dormido (una parte del cuerpo). || **4 to fall –,** dormirse. **5 fast –/sound –,** profundamente dormido.
asp | æsp | *s.c.* ZOOL. áspid (una clase de serpiente).
asparagus | ə'spærəgəs | *s.i.* BOT. espárrago.

aspect | 'æspekt | *s.c.* **1** aspecto, faceta. **2** apariencia, aspecto general. **3** (lit.) aspecto, apariencia (referido al rostro). **4** (lit.) orientación (de una casa). **5** (lit.) orientación, posición (para contemplar un paisaje o un lugar especial). || *s.i.* **6** GRAM. aspecto (de los verbos).

aspectual | æ'spektʃuəl | *adj.* GRAM. aspectual.

aspen | 'æspən | *s.c.* BOT. álamo temblón.

asperity | æ'sperɪtɪ | *s.i.* (lit.) aspereza; severidad (en el tono de voz).

aspersion | ə'spɜːʃn | *s.c.* **1** calumnia, injuria. || **2 to cast aspersions on,** (lit.) injuriar, calumniar; arrojar serias dudas sobre.

asphalt | 'æsfælt | *s.i.* **1** asfalto. || *v.t.* **2** asfaltar.

asphyxia | æs'fɪksɪə | *s.i.* MED. asfixia.

asphyxiate | æs'fɪksɪeɪt | *v.t.* e *i.* asfixiar(se), sofocar(se).

asphyxiating | æsˌfɪksɪ'eɪtɪŋ | *adj.* asfixiante.

asphyxiation | æsˌfɪksɪ'eɪʃn | *s.i.* asfixia.

aspic | 'æspɪk | *s.i.* GAST. gelatina de caldo.

aspidistra | ˌæspɪ'dɪstrə | *s.i.* BOT. aspidistra.

aspirant | æ'spɪrənt | *s.c.* **[– to]** aspirante a, candidato a.

aspirate | 'æspərɪt | *s.c.* **1** FON. aspirada. || | 'æspəreɪt | *v.t.* **2** FON. aspirar.

aspiration | ˌæspə'reɪʃn | *s.c.* e *i.* **1 [– to]** aspiración a, anhelo de, deseo de. || *s.c.* **2** REL. jaculatoria. || *s.i.* **3** FON. aspiración.

aspire | ə'spaɪər | *v.i.* **[to – to]** aspirar a, ambicionar.

aspirin | 'æsprɪn | *s.c.* e *i.* QUIM. aspirina.

aspiring | ə'spaɪərɪŋ | *adj.* ambicioso, aspirante al éxito.

ass | æs | *s.c.* **1** ZOOL. asno, burro. **2** (fam.) tonto, bobo. **3** (fam. y EE.UU.) culo, trasero. || *s.i.* **4** (desp., fam. y EE.UU.) coño. || **5 to make an – of oneself,** (fam.) hacer el tonto, hacer el ridículo.

assail | ə'seɪl | *v.t.* (lit.) **1** agredir, acometer, atacar (violentamente o como crítica). **2** asaltar (dudas, temores, problemas, etc.). **3** Abrumar (con preguntas).

assailant | ə'seɪlənt | *s.c.* (lit.) agresor, asaltante.

assassin | ə'sæsɪn | *s.c.* asesino.

assassinate | ə'sæsɪneɪt | *v.t.* asesinar, matar alerosamente.

assassination | əˌsæsɪ'neɪʃn | *s.c.* e *i.* asesinato.

assault | ə'sɔːlt | *s.c.* **1** MIL. asalto, ataque. **2** (fig.) ataque (a creencias, actitudes sociales, etc.). || *s.c.* e *i.* **3** agresión (personal). || *v.t.* **4** agredir, atacar. || **5 – and battery,** DER. asalto y agresión. **6 – course,** MIL. carrera de obstáculos (con todo tipo de dificultades típicas militares). **7 – craft,** MIL. lancha de asalto.

assaulter | ašɔːltər | *s.c.* asaltante, agresor.

assay | ə'seɪ | *v.t.* **1** TEC. ensayar (comprobar la pureza de una sustancia o metal). || *s.c.* **2** ensayo (comprobación de la pureza de un metal). || **3 to make an –,** llevar a cabo un ensayo (sobre un metal).

assemblage | ə'semblɪdʒ | *s.c.* e *i.* (lit.) **1** agrupamiento, conjunción, conjunto. **2** TEC. empalme.

assemble | ə'sembl | *v.i.* **1** reunirse, juntarse (para algún propósito). || *v.i.* **2** montar, ensamblar, empalmar.

assembled | ə'semblɪ | *adj.* reunido, congregado: *the assembled deputies cheered = los diputados congregados dieron vivas.*

assembly | ə'semblɪ | *s.c.* **1** asamblea, reunión. **2** POL. parlamento (regional o nacional). **3** MEC. montaje. || *s.c.* e *i.* **4** reunión general, asamblea (de todos los profesores y alumnos de una escuela a primera hora de la mañana). || *s.i.* **5** reunión: *right of assembly = derecho de reunión.* **6** MEC. montaje, ensamblaje.

assembly-line | ə'semblɪ laɪn | *s.c.* línea de montaje.

assent | ə'sent | *s.i.* **1** asentimiento, consentimiento, aquiescencia. || *v.i.* **2 [to – to]** asentir a, consentir en. || **3 to receive Royal Assent/to be given Royal Assent,** POL. sancionar oficialmente, ratificar oficialmente (las leyes emanadas del Parlamento por parte del Rey o la Reina).

assert | ə'sɜːt | *v.t.* **1** declarar, afirmar, aseverar. **2** hacer valer, sostener (derecho, autoridad, etc.). || *v.r.* **3** imponerse, infundir respeto.

assertion | ə'sɜːʃn | *s.i.* y *c.* **1** declaración, afirmación, aseveración. **2** afirmación (de derechos, autoridad, etc.).

assertive | ə'sɜːtɪv | *adj.* enérgico, agresivo, lanzado.

assertively | ə'sɜːtɪvlɪ | *adv.* enérgicamente, agresivamente.

assertiveness | ə'sɜːtɪvnɪs | *s.i.* agresividad, energía.

assess | ə'ses | *v.t.* **1** valorar, enjuiciar, juzgar (una situación, a una persona, un objeto). **2** tasar, calcular, estimar (cantidades).

assessment | ə'sesmənt | *s.c.* e *i.* **1** valoración, juicio (de una situación o similar). **2** tasación, cálculo (cantidades).

assessor | ə'sesər | *s.c.* **1** asesor (fiscal u otros tipos). **2** DER. tasador.

asset | 'æset | *s.c.* **1** punto fuerte, ventaja. || **2 assets,** bienes, posesiones.

asset-stripping | 'æsetstrɪpɪŋ | *s.i.* COM. liquidación de bienes (compra de una empresa con dificultades y venta progresiva de su capital inmobiliario).

asseverate | ə'sevəreɪt | *v.t.* (form.) aseverar, afirmar firmemente.

asseveration | əˌsevə'reɪʃn | *s.c.* e *i.* (form.) aseveración, afirmación firme.

assiduity | ˌæsɪ'djuːɪtɪ | *s.i.* (form.) perseverancia, asiduidad.

assiduous | ə'sɪdjuəs | *adj.* diligente, perseverante, asiduo.

assiduously | ə'sɪdjuəslɪ | *adv.* diligentemente, con perseverancia, asiduamente.

assign | ə'saɪn | *v.t.* **1** asignar, distribuir (tareas, trabajos, etc.). **2** repartir, dar: *they assigned the big desk to the head office = dieron la mesa grande a la oficina principal.* **3** destinar (a un puesto de trabajo o militar). **4** señalar, atribuir, asignar (un rol, un nombre, un día etc.): *let's assign a day for the big meeting = señalemos un día para la gran reunión.*

assignable | ə'saɪnəbl | *adj.* asignable, atribuible.

assignation | ˌæsɪg'neɪʃn | *s.c.* (lit.) encuentro, cita (especialmente amorosa).

assignment | ə'saɪnmənt | *s.c.* **1** cometido, misión. **2** trabajo, tarea (académica). || *s.i.* **3** nombramiento, destino.

assimilate | ə'sɪməleɪt | *v.t.* **1** asimilar, comprender. || *v.i.* **2** integrarse (en un grupo mayor). || **3 to be assimilated into,** ser integrado en: *we should try and help immigrants be assimilated into our society = debemos intentar ayudar a los emigrantes a que se integren en nuestra sociedad.*

assimilation | əˌsɪmɪ'leɪʃn | *s.i.* **1** asimilación, comprensión. **2** integración, asimilación (en un grupo).

assist | ə'sɪst | *v.t.* **1** ayudar, socorrer, auxiliar, prestar ayuda. || *v.i.* **2 [to – in /with]** ayudar en/con, prestar ayuda en /con: *the new nurse will assist with the blind children = la nueva enfermera ayudará a (cuidará) los niños ciegos.*

assistance | ə'sɪstəns | *s.i.* **1** ayuda, auxilio, asistencia. || **2 to be of assistance,** ayudar, servir de ayuda: *can I be of any assistance? = ¿puedo servirle de ayuda?*

assistant | ə'sɪstənt | *s.c.* **1** ayudante, secretario personal. **2** dependiente (en una tienda). || *adj.* **3** ayudante, auxiliar, sub-: *assistant manager.*

assizes | ə'saɪzɪz | *s.pl.* DER. sesión de un tribunal de ámbito provincial (en el sistema jurídico de Inglaterra y Gales).

associate | ə'səuʃɪɪt | *v.t.* **1 [to – with]** asociar con, relacionar con. || *v.r.* **2 [with]** asociarse con, relacionarse con, tratar con. || *v.i.* **3 [to – with]** (desp.) juntarse con, asociarse con, mezclarse con. || | ə'səuʃɪet | *adj.* **4** adjunto, asociado (no de pleno derecho). || **5 associates,** colegas, socios. **6 to be associated with,** estar asociado, relacionado con, estar unido a: *this problem is associated with the new engine = este problema está relacionado con el nuevo motor.*

associated | əˌsəu'ʃɪe'ɪtɪd | *adj.* **1** asociado, conexo, relacionado. || **2 Associated,** COM. afiliado, asociado.

association | əˌsəusɪ'eɪʃn | *s.c.* **1** asociación. **2** conexión, asociación (de ideas, memorias, etc.). || *s.i.* **3** asociación, participación, relación: *his association with the left is clear = su relación con la izquierda está clara.* || **4 in – with,** en colaboración con.

assonance | 'æsənəns | *s.i.* LIT. asonancia (en la rima).

assorted | ə'sɔːtɪd | *adj.* **1** surtido, variado. || **2 well/badly/... –,** emparejado: *they are a well assorted couple = son un matrimonio bien emparejado.*

assortment | ə'sɔːtmənt | *s.c.* **[– of]** surtido de, variedad de.

assuage | æ'sweɪdʒ | *v.t.* (lit.) **1** calmar, aliviar, mitigar. **2** satisfacer (un deseo, una necesidad, etc.).

assume | ə'sjuːm | *v.t.* **1** asumir, suponer. **2** asumir, tomar (responsabilidad, poder, autoridad, etc.). **3** adoptar, asumir (apariencia, expresión facial, comportamiento, etc.) || **4 assumed name,** seudónimo. **5 assuming that,** suponiendo que, dado que. **6 let's –,** supongamos, imaginemos (hipotéticamente).

assumption | ə'sʌmpʃn | *s.c.* **1** noción, suposición, idea. || *s.i.* **2 [– of]** asunción de (poder, responsabilidades, etc.). || **3 the Assumption,** REL. la Asunción.
assurance | ə'ʃʊəːrəns | *s.c.* e *i.* **1** promesa, afirmación enfática, garantía. || *s.i.* **2** seguridad, confianza. **3** seguro (como actividad de empresa).
assure | ə'ʃʊər | *v.t.* **1** asegurar, garantizar. || *v.r.* **2 [to – of]** asegurarse, hacerse con (un dinero, un futuro, etc.). || **3 to be assured of,** estar seguro de, asegurarse de. **4 I can – you/I – you,** te lo aseguro; créeme. **5 to rest assured,** estar totalmente seguro; convencerse de.
assured | ə'ʃʊəːd | *adj.* **1** seguro, confiado; sereno. **2** seguro, hecho: *her University degree is assured = su licenciatura universitaria está hecha.* || **the –,** el asegurado, los asegurados (en compañía de seguros).
assuredly | ə'ʃʊəːrɪdlɪ | *adv.* seguramente, ciertamente, con toda seguridad.
aster | 'æstər | *s.c.* BOT. áster.
asterisk | 'æstərɪsk | *s.c.* **1** asterisco. || **2 to be asterisked,** estar marcado con un asterisco.
astern | ə'stəːn | *adj.* **1** a popa, en la popa. || *adv.* **2** de popa, hacia atrás.
asteroid | 'æstərɔɪd | *s.c.* asteroide.
asthma | 'æsmə | *s.i.* MED. asma.
asthmatic | æs'mætɪk | *adj.* **1** asmático. || *s.c.* **2** asmático (persona con asma).
astigmatism | æ'stɪgmətɪzəm | *s.i.* MED. astigmatismo.
astigmatic | ˌæstɪg'mætɪk | *adj.* que tiene astigmatismo.
astir | ə'stər | *adj.* y *adv.* **1** en movimiento, en actividad. **2** (arc.) levantado, fuera de la cama.
astonish | ə'stɒnɪʃ | *v.t.* asombrar, pasmar, sorprender en gran manera.
astonished | ə'stɒnɪʃt | *adj.* asombrado, pasmado, muy sorprendido.
astonishing | ə'stɒnɪʃɪŋ | *adj.* asombroso, sorprendente.
astonishingly | ə'stɒnɪʃɪŋlɪ | *adv.* asombrosamente, sorprendentemente.
astonishment | ə'stɒnɪʃmənt | *s.i.* asombro, gran sorpresa, pasmo.
astound | ə'staʊnd | V. **astonish.**
astounded | ə'staʊndɪd | V. **astonished.**
astounding | ə'staʊndɪŋ | V. **astonishing.**
astoundingly | ə'staʊndɪŋlɪ | V. **astonishingly.**
astrakhan | ˌæstrə'kæn | *s.i.* astracán.
astral | 'æstrəl | *adj.* (lit.) astral.
astray | ə'streɪ | *adv.* **1** (p.u.) por mal camino, en el error. || **2 to go –,** extraviarse, perderse (un objeto). **3 to lead someone –, a)** despistar a alguien, engañar a alguien. **b)** llevar a alguien por mal camino, descarriar.
astride | ə'straɪd | *prep.* a horcajadas sobre: *astride a horse.*
astringency | ə'strɪndʒənsɪ | *s.i.* **1** MED. astringencia. **2** (fig.) severidad.
astringent | ə'strɪndʒənt | *adj.* **1** MED. astringente. **2** (fig.) severo, adusto. || *s.c.* e *i.* **3** MED. astringente.
astrologer | æ'strɑlədʒər | *s.c.* astrólogo.
astrological | ˌæstrə'lɒdʒɪkl | *adj.* astrológico.
astrology | ə'strɒlədʒɪ | *s.i.* astrología.
astronaut | 'æstrənɔːt | *s.c.* astronauta.
astronomer | ə'strɒnəmər | *s.c.* astrónomo.
astronomical | ˌæstrə'nɒmɪkl | *adj.* **1** de la astronomía. **2** (fig.) astronómico, gigantesco (especialmente con cantidades).
astronomically | ˌæstrə'nɒmɪkəlɪ | *adv.* astronómicamente, enormemente.
astronomy | ə'strɒnəmɪ | *s.i.* astronomía.
astrophysics | ˌæstrəʊ'fɪzɪks | *s.i.* astrofísica.
astute | ə'stjuːt | *adj.* astuto, sagaz.
astutely | ə'stjuːtlɪ | *adv.* astutamente, sagazmente.
astuteness | ə'stjuːtnɪs | *s.i.* astucia.
asunder | ə'sʌndər | *adv.* (lit.) en trozos, en pedazos, en dos trozos.
asylum | ə'saɪləm | *s.c.* **1** manicomio, asilo (para enfermos mentales). || *s.i.* **2** asilo, amparo, protección.
asymmetrical | ˌeɪsɪ'metrɪkl | (también **asymmetric**) *adj.* asimétrico.
asymmetry | eɪ'sɪmətrɪ | *s.i.* asimetría.
at | æt | pronunciación relajada | ət | *prep.* **1** en (un sitio más bien pequeño y concreto): *I was standing at the bus-stop = yo estaba de pie en la parada del autobús.* **2** a, en (con un tiempo puntual): *I got up at 9 o'clock = me levanté a las 9 en punto.* || **3 where it is –,** (fam.) lo mejor del mundo: *this school is where it is at = esta escuela es la mejor del mundo.*
OBS. Esta preposición tiene los siguientes matices: **4** asistiendo a algún acontecimiento: *we were at the race = estuvimos en la carrera.* **5** expresando la razón o causa de una emoción: *we were delighted at your success = nos encantó tu éxito.* **6** señalando el lugar de trabajo o estudio: *I work at that hospital = trabajo en ese hospital.* **7** indicando capacidad o falta de capacidad en algo: *my sister is very good at music = mi hermana es muy buena en música.* **8** durante alguna comida del día: *Mr. Williams is still at breakfast, sir = el Señor Williams está todavía desayunando, señor.* **9** como suposición, cálculo, etc.: *he's thirty at a guess = adivino que tiene 30 años.* **10** expresando el movimiento de los ojos y de los gestos del cuerpo: *he gazed at the trees on the hill = contempló los árboles sobre la colina.* **11** significando que se ha ganado en algo (calidad, virtud, técnica, etc.): *Spanish fiction is at its most prolific = la novela española está en su momento más prolífico.* **12** como dirección de un ataque o violencia: *the dog ran at me = el perro corrió hacia mí con intención de atacarme.* **13** indicando una acción no totalmente voluntaria, casi desganada: *the baby was fiddling at the television = el bebé estaba manoseando la televisión como jugueteando.* **14** posicionamiento en relación con otro objeto o persona: *he wore his hat at an angle = llevaba el sombrero inclinado en ángulo.* **15** señalando cómo se lleva a cabo una acción: *he did it at his own risk = lo hizo con riesgo para sí mismo.* **16** con edades: *he died at 75 = murió a los 75 años.* **17** expresando un estado o situación: *the escaped lion was still at large = el león escapado estaba todavía en libertad.* **18** con frecuencias, relaciones de cantidades, precios o similar: *our book is prized at 10 dollars = nuestro libro tiene un precio de 10 dólares.* **19** velocidad: *the car was going at 100 miles per hour = el coche iba a 100 millas la hora.* **20** indicando que lo que ocurre es resultado de una orden, invitación o similar de otra persona: *OK I'll do it at your word = de acuerdo, lo haré porque tú lo dices.* **21** finalidad: *she's always at me to repair the fence = siempre está encima de mí para que repare la valla.* **22** volumen de sonido: *the television is at full blast = la televisión está atronando.*
atavism | 'ætəvɪɪzəm | *s.i.* (form.) atavismo.
atavistic | ˌætə'vɪstɪk | *adj.* (form.) atávico; primitivo.
ate | et | V. **eat.**
atheism | 'eɪθɪɪzəm | *s.i.* REL. ateísmo.
atheist | 'eɪθɪɪst | *s.c.* REL. ateo.
atheistic | ˌeɪθɪ'ɪstɪk | *adj.* REL. ateo.
athlete | 'æθliːt | *s.c.* **1** DEP. atleta. || **2 – foot,** (fam.) pie de atleta (enfermedad de hongos).
athletic | æθ'letɪk | *adj.* **1** DEP. de atletismo. **2** atlético, robusto.
athletics | æθ'letɪks | *s.i.* DEP. atletismo.
athwart | ə'θwɔːt | MAR. *adv.* **1** contra, en contra, en oposición. | *prep.* **2** a través de, en ángulo (oblicuo): *athwart the harbour = a través del puerto.*
atlas | 'ætləs | *s.c.* GEOG. atlas.
atmosphere | 'ætməsfɪər | *s.c.* **1** FIS. atmósfera. || *s.i.* **2** atmósfera (de una ciudad, lugar, etc.). **3** ambiente: *a very good atmosphere.*
atmospheric | ˌætməs'ferɪk | *adj.* **1** atmosférico. || **2 – pressure,** FIS. presión atmosférica.
atoll | 'ætɒl | *s.c.* GEOG. atolón.
atom | 'ætəm | *s.c.* **1** FIS. átomo. **2** (fig.) átomo, pizca: *not an atom of common sense = ni una pizca de sentido común.* || **3 – bomb,** bomba atómica.
atomic | ə'tɒmɪk | FIS. *adj.* **1** atómico, del átomo. || **2 – bomb,** bomba atómica. **3 – energy,** energía atómica. **4 – number,** número atómico. **5 – pile,** pila atómica. **6 – weight,** peso atómico.
atomize | 'ætəmaɪz | (también **atomise**). *v.t.* **1** destrozar mediante bomba atómica, destruir totalmente por artefacto nuclear. **2** (lit.) fragmentar, atomizar (una sociedad, comunidad, etc.).
atomizer | 'ætəmaɪzər | (también **atomiser**) *s.c.* aerosol, atomizador.
atonal | æɪ'təʊnl | *adj.* MUS. atonal.
atonality | ˌæɪtəʊ'nælɪtɪ | *s.i.* MUS. atonalidad.
atone | ə'təʊn | *v.i.* **[for – for]** (lit.) expiar por.
atonement | ə'təʊnmənt | *s.i.* **[– for]** (lit.) expiación por.
atop | ə'tɒp | *prep.* (EE.UU.) encima de.
atrocious | ə'trəʊʃəs | *adj.* atroz, fatal, infame.
atrociously | ə'trəʊʃəslɪ | *adv.* atrozmente, fatalmente, infamemente.
atrociousness | ə'trfəʊəsnɪs | *s.i.* atrocidad.
atrocity | ə'trɒsɪtɪ | *s.c.* e *i.* atrocidad, crueldad, salvajismo.

atrophy | 'ætrəfɪ | (lit.) *v.i.* **1** atrofiarse. || *s.c.* **2** atrofia. || **3 to be atrophied,** quedar atrofiado, estar atrofiado.

attach | ə'tætʃ | *v.t.* **[to – to]** pegar a, unir a, juntar a. **2** dar, conceder (importancia, interés o similar). || *v.i.* **3 [to – to]** (lit.) corresponder a, pertenecer a (cuando se asocia a una persona con algo): *a lot of blame is attached to him = gran parte de la culpa le corresponde a él.* || **4 to be attached to,** formar parte de, ser parte de (una organización, institución, etc.).

attaché | ə'tæʃeɪ | *s.c.* **1** POL. agregado (de embajada): *military attaché.* || **2 – case,** maletín, cartera.

attached | ə'tætʃt | *adj.* **[– to]** apegado a (una persona); celoso de (una tradición, etc.).

attachment | ə'tætʃmənt | *s.c.* **1 [– to]** apego a, cariño a. **2** accesorio, complemento (de una máquina para hacer distintas funciones). **3** unión; atadura (en un objeto o similar). || *s.i.* **4 [– to]** adhesión a, unión con. || **5 on –,** en destino transitorio: *he was sent there on attachment before the real thing came up = fue enviado allí en destino transitorio antes de que saliera el destino definitivo.*

attack | ə'tæk | *v.t.* **1** atacar, asaltar, agredir. **2** (fig.) criticar; condenar. **3** abordar, acometer (un problema, una dificultad, etc.). **4** atacar, intentar destruir (expresa el efecto de una enfermedad, un producto químico nocivo o similar). || *v.i.* **5** DEP. atacar, lanzarse al ataque. || *s.c.* **6 [– on]** ataque a, agresión a, asalto a. **7 [– of]** ataque de (enfermedad): *an attack of arthritis.* || *s.c.* e *i.* **8 [– on]** MIL. ataque a, asalto a. **9 [– on]** crítica a, condena a. || *s.i.* **10** DEP. ataque: *that team is best in attack = ese equipo es mejor en el ataque.*

attacker | ə'tækər | *s.c.* asaltante, agresor.

attain | ə'teɪn | *v.t.* **1** lograr, conseguir, obtener: *Senegal attained its independence in the sixties = Senegal consiguió su independencia en los años sesenta.* **2** llegar hasta, alcanzar (un estadio dentro de un desarrollo natural): *he attained maturity early in his life = llegó a la madurez pronto en su vida.*

attainable | ə'teɪnəbl | *adj.* alcanzable, realizable.

attainment | ə'teɪnmənt | (lit.) *s.c.* **1** talento, dotes. || *s.i.* **2** consecución, logro.

attar | 'ætər | *s.i.* esencia (de rosas).

attempt | ə'tempt | *v.t.* **1 [— *inf.*] intentar, procurar, probar. 2** intentar hacer, emprender: *after my sickness I didn't attempt any writing at all = después de mi enfermedad no intenté hacer ningún trabajo literario en absoluto.* || *s.c.* **3** intento, prueba, tentativa. || **4 an – on someone's life,** tentativa de matar a alguien, tentativa de asesinato sobre alguien.

attempted | ə'temptɪd | *adj.* DER. frustrado: *attempted murder = asesinato frustrado.*

attend | ə'tend | *v.t.* **1** asistir a (una clase, conferencia, etc.). **2** (lit.) atender, cuidar (a enfermos). **3** (lit.) acompañar: *the jealousy attends her success = la envidia acompaña a su éxito.*|| *v.i.* **4 [to – to]** atender, intentar resolver, ocuparse de (un problema o similar). **5 [to – to]** (lit.) atender, servir (en una tienda). **6 [to – to]** (lit.) prestar atención a.

attendance | ə'tendəns | *s.c.* e *i.* **1 [— at]** asistencia a: *attendance at Mass = asistencia a Misa.* || *s.i.* **2 [– at]** concurrencia a, presencia en. **3 [– on]** (lit.) asistencia a (enfermos o similar). || **4 in –,** (lit.) presente, concurrente, asistente.

attendant | ə'tendənt | *s.c.* **1** ayudante, dependiente (en cualquier tipo de tienda o servicio). || *adj.* **2** acompañante. **3** (lit.) concurrente: *the attendant dangers of inflation = los peligros concurrentes de la inflación.*

attender | ə'tendər | *s.c.* asistente (a una clase, conferencia, etc.).

attention | ə'tenʃn | *s.i.* **1** atención, concentración. **2** atención, interés. **3** atención, cuidado (médico, mecánico, etc.). || **4 –!,** MIL. ¡firmes! **5 attentions,** atenciones (mostrando cariño). **6 to attract/ catch one's –,** llamar la atención de uno. **7 to bring/come to one's –,** hacérsele presente a uno. **8 to pay – [to],** prestar atención (a), atender (a). **9 to pay little/no – [to],** hacer poco/ningún caso (a). **10 to stand to/at –,** MIL. estar firmes, estar en posición de firmes.

attentive | ə'tentɪv | *adj.* **1** atento, interesado, concentrado. **2** solícito, atento, cortés.

attentively | ə'tentɪvlɪ | *adv.* **1** con atención, con interés, concentradamente. **2** solícitamente, atentamente.

attenuate | ə'tenjʊeɪt | *v.t.* (lit.) atenuar, debilitar.

attenuated | ə'tenjʊeɪtɪd | *adj.* (lit.) estilizado (objeto).

attenuating | ə'tenjʊeɪtɪŋ | *adj.* DER. atenuante: *attenuating circumstances.*

attenuation | əˌtenjʊ'eɪʃn | *s.i.* (form.) atenuación, debilitamiento.

attest | ə'test | (form.) *v.t.* **1** atestiguar, dar fe de. || *v.i.* **2 [— to]** atestiguar, testificar.

attestation | ˌæte'steɪʃn | *s.c.* (form.) testimonio, declaración.

attested | ə'testɪd | *adj.* (brit.) certificado (como libre de enfermedad).

attic | 'ætɪk | *s.c.* ARQ. ático.

attire | ə'taɪər | *s.i.* (lit.) vestimenta, ropaje (normalmente en grandes ocasiones).

attired | ə'taɪəd | *adj.* **[– in]** (lit.) vestido con, ataviado con.

attitude | 'ætɪtjuːd | *s.c.* **1** actitud, disposición. **3** actitud, modo de tratar (a una persona). **3** postura (física).

attorney | ə'təːnɪ | *s.c.* **1** (EE.UU.) DER. abogado. || **2 Attorney General,** Fiscal General del Estado.

attract | ə'trækt | *v.t.* **[to – to]** atraer a. **2** interesar, atraer. **3** recibir, atraer (publicidad, apoyo). **4** FIS. atraer (un imán).

attracted | ə'træktɪd | *adj.* **[– to]** atraído por, interesado por: *I'm attracted to her = estoy interesado por ella.*

attraction | ə'trækʃn | *s.i.* **1** atracción (por el otro sexo). **2** atractivo, atracción (general). || *s.c.* **3** atracción (general). || **4 attractions,** atractivos, encantos (de un lugar, persona, etc.).

attractive | ə'træktɪv | *adj.* **1** atrayen-te, sugestivo, interesante (plan, paga y muchas cosas más). **2** guapo, atractivo.

attractively | ə'træktɪvlɪ | *adv.* con atractivo, de manera atrayente.

attractiveness | ə'træktɪvnɪs | *s.i.* **1** cualidad atractiva, cualidad atrayente. **2** de buen ver, atractivo.

attributable | ə'trɪbjʊtəbl | *adj.* **[– to]** atribuible a, imputable a.

attribute | 'ætrɪbjuːt | *s.c.* **1** atributo, característica, propiedad. || | ə'trɪbjuːt | *v.t.* **2** atribuir, imputar, achacar (cualquier cosa, hecho o palabra a alguien).

attribution | ˌætrɪ'bjuːʃn | *s.i.* atribución, imputación: *the attribution of these paintings to Dalí is completely false = la atribución de estas pinturas a Dalí es completamente falsa.*

attributive | ə'trɪbjʊtɪv | *adj.* GRAM. atributivo.

attributively | ə'trɪbjʊtɪvlɪ | *adv.* GRAM. de manera atributiva.

attrition | ə'trɪʃn | *s.i.* (lit.) MIL. desgaste, agotamiento: *a war of attrition = una guerra de desgaste.*

attuned | ə'tjuːnd | *adj.* **1 [– to]** en armonía con; en la misma onda que: *I am not attuned to the problems of the immigrants = no estoy en la misma onda (que los problemas) de los emigrantes.* **2 [– to]** sensibilizado con, sensible a (hablando del oído): *I'm attuned to this kind of music = me siento sensibilizado con este tipo de música.*

atypical | ˌeɪ'tɪpɪkl | *adj.* atípico.

atypically | ˌeɪ'tɪpɪklɪ | *adv.* atípicamente.

aubergine | 'əʊbəʒiːn | *s.c.* (brit.) berenjena.

auburn | 'ɔːbən | *adj.* castaño rojizo (color del pelo).

auction | 'ɔːkʃn | *s.c.* **1** subasta, licitación. || *v.t.* **2** subastar, vender mediante subasta. || **3 to – off,** librarse mediante subasta de, desembarazarse mediante subasta de: *the Browns didn't want their old inherited furniture and auctioned it off = los Brown no querían los viejos muebles heredados y se libraron de ellos mediante subasta.*

auctioneer | ˌɔːkʃə'nɪər | *s.c.* subastador.

audacious | ɔː'deɪʃəs | *adj.* audaz, osado, intrépido (tiene matiz positivo).

audaciously | ɔː'deɪʃəslɪ | *adv.* audazmente, osadamente, intrépidamente.

audacity | ɔː'dæsətɪ | *s.i.* audacia, atrevimiento, osadía.

audibility | ˌɔːdə'bɪlɪtɪ | *s.i.* audibilidad.

audible | 'ɔːdɪbl | *adj.* audible, perceptible (por el oído).

audibly | 'ɔːdəblɪ | *adv.* audiblemente, perceptiblemente.

audience | 'ɔːdɪəns | *s.c.* **1** público, asistentes, telespectadores, lectores: *this novelist has an audience of 5 million people = este novelista tiene 5 millones de lectores.* **2** audiencia: *a private audience = una audiencia privada.*

audio | 'ɔːdɪəʊ | *adj.* audio: *audio tapes = cintas de audio (cintas para magnetófono).*

audiotypist | 'ɔːdɪəʊtaɪpɪst | *s.c.* mecanógrafo (que transcribe cintas).

audiovisual | ˌɔːdɪəʊ'vɪʒʊəl | *adj.* audiovisual.

audit | ˌɔːdɪt | *s.c.* **1** auditoría. || *v.t.* **2** llevar a cabo una auditoría, hacer una auditoría.

audition | ɔː'dɪʃn | *s.c.* **1** audición; prueba artística (actores y músicos). || *v.t.* **2** hacer una audición, hacer una prueba. || *v.i.* **3 [to – for]** hacer una prueba para, tomar parte en una audición para.
auditor | 'ɔːdɪtər | *s.c.* ECON. auditor, censor/interventor de cuentas.
auditorium | ˌɔːdɪ'tɔːrɪəm | (*pl.* **auditoriums** o **auditoria**) *s.c.* **1** auditorio (donde se sienta la audiencia). **2** (EE.UU.) sala de conciertos.
auditory | 'ɔːdɪtrɪ | *adj.* (lit.) auditorio, auditivo.
au fait | ˌəʊ'feɪ | *adj.* **[– with]** al tanto de, conocedor de: *I'm not au fait with the technics of it = no estoy al tanto de las técnicas del tema.*
au fond | ˌəʊ'fn | *adv.* en el fondo (tomado del francés).
auger | 'ɔːgər | *s.c.* MEC. taladro, berbiquí (de carpintería).
aught | ɔːt | *pron.* (arc.) algo, nada.
augment | ɔːg'ment | *v.t.* (lit.) aumentar, incrementar.
augmentation | ˌɔːgmen'teɪʃn | *s.c.* e *i.* (form.) aumento, incremento.
augur | 'ɔːgər | *v.i.* **[to – for]** (lit.) pronosticar, augurar, ser un augurio para: *this does not augur well for the immediate future = esto no es un buen augurio para el futuro inmediato.*
augury | 'ɔːgjʊrɪ | *s.c.* (lit.) augurio, presagio.
august | ɔː'gʌst | *adj.* **1** (lit.) augusto, majestuoso. || | 'ɔːgəst | **2 August,** Agosto.
auk | ɔːk | *s.c.* ZOOL. alca (un tipo de pájaro).
aunt | ɑːnt | *s.c.* tía (relación de parentesco).
auntie | 'ɑːntɪ | (también **aunty**) *s.c.* (fam.) tita.
au pair | ˌəʊ'peə | *s.c.* au pair (chica que ayuda en una familia, pero no como una criada).
aura | 'ɔːrə | *s.c.* aura; aire.
aural | 'ɔːrə | *adj.* auditivo, auricular.
aureola | ɔː'rɪələ | (también **aureole**) *s.c.* aureola.
au revoir | ˌəʊrə'vwɑːr | *adv.* (lit.) adiós.
auricle | 'ɔːrɪkl | *s.c.* ANAT. aurícula.
auricular | ɔː'rɪkjʊlər | *adj.* auricular: *auricular appendix = apéndice auricular.*
auriferous | ɔː'rɪfərəs | *adj.* MIN. aurífero.
aurora borealis | ɔːˌrɔːrəbɔːrɪ'eɪlɪs | *s.i.* FIS. aurora boreal.
auspices | 'ɔːspɪsɪz | **under the – of,** bajo los auspicios de.
auspicious | ɔː'spɪʃəs | *adj.* (lit.) prometedor, propicio.
Aussie | 'ɒɪɪ | *adj.* (fam.) australiano.
austere | ɑ'stɪər | *adj.* **1** austero; sin adornos. **2** adusto, severo, estricto.
austerely | ɒ'stɪəlɪ | *adv.* austeramente.
austerity | ɒ'sterɪtɪ | (lit.) *s.i.* **1** austeridad. || **2 austerities,** privaciones; dificultades materiales.
Australasia | ˌɒstrə'leɪʃə | *s.i.* GEOG. Australasia.
Australasian | ˌɒstrə'leɪʃn | *adj.* GEOG. de Australasia.
Australia | ɒ'streɪlɪə | *s.i.* GEOG. Australia.
Australian | ɒ'streɪlɪən | *adj.* **1** australiano. || *s.c.* **2** australiano. || **3 – English,** inglés australiano.
Austria | 'ɒstrɪə | *s.i.* GEOG. Austria.
Austrian | 'ɒstrɪən | *adj.* **1** austríaco. || *s.c.* **2** austríaco.
autarchy | ɔː'tɑːkɪ | (lit.) *s.i.* **1** autarquía (sistema). || *s.c.* **2** autarquía (país autárquico).
authentic | ɔː'θentɪk | *adj.* auténtico, verdadero, real.
authentically | ɔː'θentɪklɪ | *adv.* auténticamente, verdaderamente, realmente.
authenticate | ɔː'θentɪkeɪt | *v.t.* (lit.) autentificar, compulsar; confirmar.
authentication | ɔːˌθentɪ'keɪʃn | *s.i.* (lit.) autentificación, compulsa; confirmación.
authenticity | ˌɔːθen'tɪsɪtɪ | *s.i.* autenticidad, veracidad.
author | 'ɔːθər | *s.c.* **1** autor (de un libro), escritor. **2** (lit.) autor, creador, inventor (de un plan, proyecto, etc.). || *v.t.* **3** (lit.) escribir, crear, idear: *James authored a book about energy = James escribió un libro sobre la energía.*
authoress | 'ɔːθərɪs | *s.c.* autora, escritora.
authoritarian | ɔːˌθɒrɪ'teərɪən | *adj.* **1** autoritario. || *s.c.* **2** autoritario.
authoritarianism | ɔːˌθɒrɪ'teərɪənɪzəm | *s.i.* (lit.) POL. autoritarismo.
authoritative | ɔː'θɒrətətɪv | *adj.* **1** autoritario; dominante. **2** experto, ver–sado; erudito: *an authoritative book on biology = un libro erudito sobre biología.*
authoritatively | ɔː'θɒrɪtətɪvlɪ | *adv.* autoritariamente, perentoriamente.
authority | ɔː'θɒrɪtɪ | *s.i.* **1** autoridad; poder. **2** autorización, permiso (oficial). || *s.c.* **3 [– on]** autoridad en, experto en (una materia, especialidad, etc.). **4** organismo (estatal), dirección (de un organigrama gubernamental): *local authority = autoridad local (Ayuntamiento).* || **5 authorities,** autoridades (de un país). **6 to have it on good –,** saber de buena tinta, saber de fuentes de información fiables.
authorization | ˌɔːθərai'zeɪʃn | (también **authorisation**) *s.c.* e *i.* autorización.
authorize | 'ɔːθəraɪz | (también **authorise**) *v.t.* **1** autorizar, permitir. || **2 to be authorized, [— *inf.*] estar autorizado, autorizársele a uno.**
authorship | 'ɔːθəʃɪp | *s.i.* autoría (de obra de arte).
authorship | 'ɔːθəʃɪp | *s.i.* **1** autoría (de libros, artículos, etc.). **2** profesión literaria, actividad profesional literaria: *it's a great risk to depend solely on authorship for a living = significa un gran riesgo depender únicamente de la profesión literaria para ganarse la vida.*
autism | 'ɔːtɪzəm | *s.i.* PSIQ. autismo.
autistic | ɔː'tɪstɪk | *adj.* PSIQ. autista.
auto | 'ɔːtəʊ | *s.c.* (EE.UU. y fam.) coche, auto.
autobiographical | ˌɔːtəbaɪə'græfɪkl | *adj.* autobiográfico.
autobiography | ˌɔːtəbaɪ'ɒgrəfɪ | *s.c.* e *i.* LIT. autobiografía.
autocracy | ɔː'tɒkrəsɪ | *s.i.* **1** POL. autocracia, dictadura. **2** (fig.) dictadura, autoritarismo (en una empresa, colegio, etc.). || *s.c.* **3** POL. autocracia, dictadura (hablando de un país).
autocrat | 'ɔːtəkræt | *s.c.* **1** POL. dictador, autócrata. **2** (fig.) déspota, dictador (en una empresa o similar).
autocratic | ˌɔːtə'krætɪk | *adj.* dictatorial, despótico, autocrático.
autocratically | ˌɔːtə'krætɪklɪ | *adv.* dictatorialmente, despóticamente, autocráticamente.
autocross | 'ɔːtəʊkrɒs | *s.i.* DEP. rally.
autocue | 'ɔːtəʊkjuː | *s.c.* TV. letrero recordatorio, apuntador visual (ingenio donde se ven las palabras que el presentador puede leer mirando a la cámara).
autograph | 'ɔːtəgrɑːf | *s.c.* **1** autógrafo. || *v.t.* **2** dedicar (un libro, foto, etc.).
automat | 'ɔːtəmæt | *s.c.* **1** máquina automática (donde comprar comida). **2** restaurante lleno de máquinas automáticas.
automate | 'ɔːtəmeɪt | *v.t.* automatizar.
automation | ˌɔːtə'meɪʃn | *s.i.* automatización.
automatic | ˌɔːtə'mætɪk | *adj.* **1** automático. **2** mecánico, inconsciente, automático (sin pensar): *breathing is a completely automatic action = el respirar es una acción totalmente inconsciente.* **3** inmediato, automático, inevitable: *what you have done means automatic punishment = lo que has hecho significa un castigo inmediato.* || *s.c.* **4** automática (pistola). **5** coche automático. **6** lavadora automática. || **7 – pilot,** AER. piloto automático. **8 to be on – pilot,** actuar inconscientemente; ir con el piloto automático (por las muchas veces que se ha realizado la misma acción).
automatically | ˌɔːtə'mætɪklɪ | *adv.* **1** automáticamente. **2** inconscientemente, mecánicamente, automáticamente. **3** inmediatamente, inevitablemente, automáticamente.
automaton | ɔː'tɒmətən | (*pl.* **automatons** o **automata**) *s.c.* **1** autómata. **2** robot.
automobile | 'ɔːtəməbiːl | *s.c.* (EE.UU.) coche, automóvil.
autonomous | ɔː'tɒnəməs | *adj.* **1** autónomo (región, organismo, etc.). **2** (lit.) independiente, autónomo (una persona).
autonomy | ɔː'tɒnəmɪ | *s.i.* **1** autonomía (de una región, organismo, etc.). **2** (lit.) independencia, autonomía (de una persona).
autopsy | ɔː'tɒpsɪ | *s.c.* **1** MED. autopsia. **2** (lit.) disección, estudio detallado (de un tema).
autosuggestion | ˌɔːtəʊsə'dʒeɪstʃən | *s.c.* e *i.* PSIQ. autosugestión.
autumn | 'ɔːtəm | *s.i.* y *c.* otoño.
autumnal | ɔː'tʌmnəl | *adj.* otoñal.
auxiliary | ɔːg'zɪlɪərɪ | *s.c.* **1** ayudante, auxiliar (normalmente en contextos hospitalarios y militares). **2** GRAM. auxiliar (verbo). || *adj.* **3** auxiliar, de apoyo: *auxiliary troops = tropas de apoyo.* **4** secundario, auxiliar (en equipos, maquinaria, etc.). || **5 – verb,** GRAM. verbo auxiliar.
avail | ə'veɪl | *v.r.* **1 [to – of]** (lit.) aprovecharse de, valerse de, aprovechar: *avail yourself of this wonderful oppor-*

tunity = aprovecha esta maravillosa oportunidad. || **2 of no –/to little –, etc.,** en vano, inútilmente, de poco provecho.
availability | ə,veɪlə'bɪlɪtɪ | *s.i.* disponibilidad, asequibilidad: *availability of information is important in a free society = la asequibilidad de la información es importante en una sociedad libre.*
available | ə'veɪləbl | *adj.* **1** disponible, asequible: *all the information is available = toda la información está disponible.* **2** libre, a mano: *we still have five rooms available = todavía tenemos cinco habitaciones libres.* **3** libre, sin compromiso (de tiempo): *I'm not available tomorrow = no estoy libre mañana.* **4** (fig.) libre (sin novia).
avalanche | 'ævəlɑːnʃ | *s.c.* **1** avalancha, alud. **2** (fig.) montón, avalancha: *an avalanche of holiday-makers = una avalancha de personas de vacaciones.*
avant-garde | ,ævɒŋ'gɑːd | *adj.* **1** vanguardista, progresista. || **2 the –,** la progresía, los progresistas; los vanguardistas.
avarice | 'ævərɪs | *s.i.* avaricia, codicia.
avaricious | ,ævə'rɪʃəs | *adj.* (desp.) avaricioso, codicioso.
avariciously | ,ævə'rɪʃəslɪ | *adv.* (desp.) avariciosamente, codiciosamente.
avenge | ə'vendʒ | *v.t.* vengar: *he avenged the death of his father = él vengó la muerte de su padre.*
avenue | 'ævənjuː | *s.c.* **1** avenida; vía (con árboles a ambos lados). **2** medio, ruta (para alcanzar un objetivo): *we explored every avenue before taking the decision = investigamos todos los medios posibles antes de tomar la decisión.* || **3 Avenue,** Avenida (con un nombre de calle).
aver | ə'vər | *v.t.* (lit.) declarar, afirmar.
average | 'ævərɪdʒ | *s.c.* **1** promedio, término medio, media. || *adj.* **2** medio, de término medio. **3** mediano, medio, normal; aceptable. || *v.t.* **4** producir por término medio, fabricar por término medio: *he averages about 100 pages a day = produce por término medio unas 100 páginas al día.* || **5 to – out,** calcular el término medio, resultar por término medio: *when you average it out, it means 5.000 dollars per person = cuando calculas su término medio, significa 5.000 dólares por persona.* **6 on –/on an –,** por término medio, como media. **7 the law of averages,** la ley del término medio, la ley estadística: *if there are some many in your family, the law of averages states that a least one will have blue eyes = si sois tantos de familia, la ley del término medio dice que por lo menos uno tendrá los ojos azules.*
averagely | 'ævərɪdʒlɪ | *adv.* medianamente; normalmente: *an averagely clever child = un muchacho medianamente listo.*
averse | ə'vəːs | *adj.* **[– to]** contrario a, opuesto a: *I'm averse to drink = soy contrario a la bebida.*
aversion | ə'vəːʃn | *s.c.* **1** aversión, repugnancia, antipatía. **2** ojeriza, manía (cosa o persona aborrecida): *in food cabbage is my only aversion = mi única manía en comidas es (contra) el repollo.*
avert | ə'vəːt | *v.t.* **1** impedir: *revenge is to be averted = la venganza debe ser impedida.* **2** apartar (ojos, mirada, etc.).
aviary | 'eɪvɪərɪ | *s.c.* aviario.
aviation | ,eɪvɪ'eɪʃn | *s.i.* aviación.
aviator | 'eɪvɪeɪtər | *s.c.* (p.u.) aviador.
avid | 'ævɪd | *adj.* **[– for] ávido de, ansioso por:** *avid for attention.*
avidity | ə'vɪdɪtɪ | *s.i.* (form.) avidez (de conseguir algo).
avidly | 'ævɪdlɪ | *adv.* ávidamente, ansiosamente.
avocado | ,ævə'kɑːdəʊ | *s.c.* e *i.* BOT. **1** aguacate. || **2 – pear,** aguacate.
avocet | 'ævəset | *s.c.* ZOOL. avoceta (ave zancuda).
avoid | ə'vɔɪd | *v.t.* **1** evitar, eludir (a alguien, una responsabilidad, etc.). **2 [– *ger.*] evitar, abstenerse de.** || **3 to – like the plague,** evitar como si fuera la peste.
avoidable | ə'vɔɪdəbl | *adj.* evitable, eludible.
avoidance | ə'vɔɪdəns | *s.i.* exclusión, evitación (acto de evitar): *the avoidance of a subject = la evitación de un tema.*
avow | ə'vaʊ | *v.t.* (lit.) declarar, confesar, reconocer.
avowal | ə'vaʊəl | *s.c.* e *i.* (lit.) declaración, confesión: *an avowal of love.*
avowed | ə'vaʊd | *adj.* (lit.) declarado; reconocido: *he's an avowed leftist = él es un izquierdista declarado.*
avowedly | ə'vaʊɪdlɪ | *adv.* abiertamente, por confesión propia.
avuncular | ə'vʌŋkjʊlər | *adj.* (p.u.) afable; paternal.
await | ə'weɪt | *v.t.* (lit.) esperar, aguardar.
awake | ə'weɪk | *adj.* **1** despierto. **2 [– to]** alerta ante; consciente de: *I'm awake to the risks = soy consciente de los riesgos.* || *v.* [*pret.* **awoke** y *p.p.* **awoken**] *t.* e *i.* **3** (lit.) despertar(se). || **4 wide –,** totalmente despierto.
awaken | ə'weɪkən | (lit.) *v.t.* **1** despertar. **2 [to – to]** despertar a, alertar ante (una situación). **3** (fig.) despertar (una emoción, un deseo, etc.). || *v.i.* **4** despertarse. **5 [to – to]** despertarse a, alertarse ante (una situación).
awakening | ə'weɪknɪŋ | (lit.) *s.c.* **1** despertar, surgimiento (de emociones o similar). **2** comienzo, despertar: *the awakening of modern times = el comienzo de los tiempos modernos.* || **3 rude –,** sorpresa desagradable.
award | ə'wɔːd | *v.t.* **1** conceder, otorgar (como recompensa). **2** dar, adjudicar (beca, dinero, etc.). **3** DER. conceder (como decisión judicial): *the judge awarded him 1.000 pounds' compensation = el juez le concedió una compensación de 1.000 libras.* || *s.c.* **4** premio; honor. **5** beca, ayuda. **6** DER. adjudicación, laudo (fruto de decisión judicial).
aware | ə'weər | *adj.* **1 [– of]** consciente de, al tanto de, enterado de: *I'm not aware of the situation = no estoy al tanto de la situación.* **2** concienciado, atento: *he is politically aware = está concienciado políticamente.* || **3 to be – of/to become – of,** caer en la cuenta de, darse cuenta de: *I was suddenly aware of Jenny standing at the door = de repente me di cuenta de que Jenny estaba de pie junto a la puerta.*
awareness | ə'weənɪs | *s.i.* **1** conciencia, concienciación: *political awareness.* **2 [– of]** conocimiento de: *his awareness of the problems of education = su conocimiento de los problemas de la educación.*
awash | ə'wɒʃ | *adj.* **1** inundado, lleno de agua. **2 [– with]** (fig.) rebosante de, lleno de: *the nation is awash with gold = la nación está llena de oro.*
away | ə'weɪ | *adv.* **1** fuera (del lugar habitual de residencia o trabajo): *John is away in London = John está fuera, en Londres.* **2 [– from]** a... de distancia de, a... de camino de: *the village is 5 miles away = el pueblo está a 5 millas de distancia. The school is half an hour away from here = la escuela está a media hora de camino de aquí.* || *adj.* **3** DEP. fuera (no en casa, hablando de partidos): *an away match = un partido fuera.*
OBS. Esta partícula matiza el significado de los verbos precedentes de la siguiente manera: **4** alejamiento gradual: *he drove away = se alejó en su coche.* **5** colocación en un lugar seguro: *put it away = guárdalo en sitio seguro.* **6** desaparición lenta: *the sound of the music died away = el sonido de la música se apagó gradualmente.* **7** desgaste: *the sides of the armchairs were worn away = los lados de los sillones estaban desgastados.* **8** disminución de cantidades: *the number of illegales dropped away = el número de ilegales disminuyó.* **9** cambio: *the party has moved away to the left = el partido se ha deslizado a la izquierda.* **10** repetición continua: *She was smiling away = no cesaba de sonreír.* **11** desviación de mirada, gesto o movimiento: *don't look away from me = no desvíes tu mirada de mí.* **12** extensión hacia el horizonte: *the hills rolled away towards the sea = las colinas se extendían hacia el mar.* **13** acción en el futuro: *the meeting is only a month away = sólo queda un mes para el encuentro.* **14** desposesión de algo (voluntaria o involuntaria): *I took away the dangerous toy from the child = le quité al niño el juguete peligroso.*
awe | ɔː | *s.i.* **1** temor, respeto. || *v.t.* **2** imponer respeto, dejar atemorizado, impresionar. || **3 to be in – of/to stand in – of,** tener un temor reverencial a.
awed | ɔːd | *adj.* impresionado, atemorizado.
awe-inspiring | 'ɔːɪnspaɪərɪŋ | *adj.* impresionante, imponente.
awesome | 'ɔːsəm | *adj.* impresionante, imponente.
awesomely | 'ɔːsəmlɪ | *adv.* impresionantemente, imponentemente.
awe-struck | 'ɔːstrʌk | (también **awe-stricken**) *adj.* (lit.) impresionado, atemorizado.
awful | 'ɔːfl | *adj.* **1** fatal, horrible, mal: *awful weather = tiempo fatal.* **2** mal, enfermo. **3** (lit.) temible. || **4 an – lot,** muchísimo.
awfully | 'ɔːflɪ | *adv.* muy, terriblemente: *I'm awfully busy = estoy muy ocupado.*

awhile | ə'waɪl | *adv.* **1** un rato, un corto espacio de tiempo. || **2 for –,** durante un rato.

awkward | 'ɔːkwəd | *adj.* **1** torpe, desmañado (de movimiento, posición, etc.). **2** incómodo; nervioso: *he feels awkward at social parties = se siente incómodo en reuniones sociales.* **3** difícil (con quien vivir, tratar, trabajar, etc.). **4** complicado, problemático (de uso): *this machine is very awkward = esta máquina es muy complicada.* **5** embarazoso, espinoso, inconveniente: *an awkward time = un tiempo inconveniente.* || **6 to make things –,** poner las cosas difíciles. **7 the – age,** la edad del pavo, la edad difícil (de los adolescentes).

awkwardly | 'ɔːkwədlɪ | *adv.* **1** torpemente, desmañadamente. **2** incómodamente, nerviosamente.

awkwardness | 'ɔkwədnɪs | *s.i.* **1** torpeza (en movimientos o similar). **2** tensión, incomodidad. **3** inconveniencia (de una situación, tiempo, etc.).

awl | ɔːl | *s.c.* MEC. lezna, punzón.

awning | 'ɔːnɪŋ | *s.c.* toldo, marquesina.

awoke | ə'wəʊk | V. **awake.**

awoken | ə'wəʊkn | V. **awake.**

awry | ə'raɪ | *adj.* **1** torcido (posición de algo). **2** (fig.) mal, torcido. | **3 to go –,** salir mal (un plan, proyecto, etc.).

axe | æks | *s.c.* **1** hacha. **2** corte, recorte (de un presupuesto). || *v.t.* **3** recortar, reducir (un programa, plan, etc. por falta de dinero). || **4 to have an – to grind,** actuar de manera interesada.

axiom | 'æksɪəm | *s.c.* axioma.

axiomatic | 'æksɪə'mætɪk | *adj.* (lit.) axiomático, incontrovertible.

axis | 'æksɪs | (pl. **axes**) *s.c.* **1** GEOM. eje. **2** MAT. coordenada.

axle | 'æksl | *s.c.* eje, árbol (de unión de dos ruedas).

ayatollah | ˌaɪə'tɒlə | *s.c.* REL. ayatollah (en la religión musulmana, un sacerdote).

aye | aɪ | (también **ay**) *adv.* **1** MIL. sí. || *s.c.* e *i.* **2** POL. sí (en votaciones).

azalea | ə'zeɪlɪə | *s.c.* BOT. azalea.

azimuth | 'æzɪməθ | *s.c.* FIS. azimut.

azure | 'æʒər | *adj.* (lit.) **1** azul, azul celeste. || *s.i.* **2** azul, azul celeste.

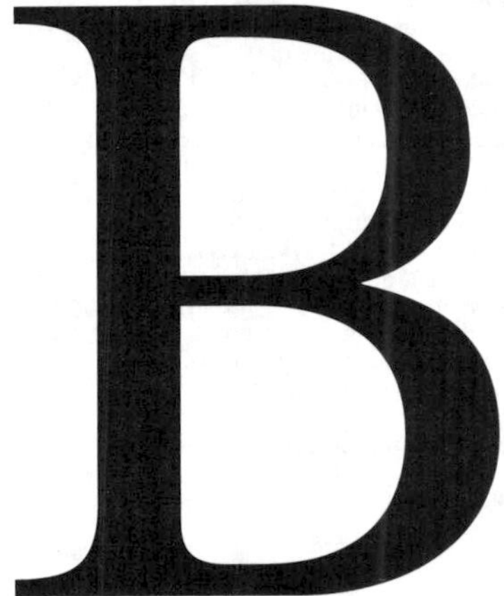

b, B | bi: | *s.c.* **1** segunda letra del abecedario. || *s.c.* e *i.* **2** MUS. si (nota musical). **3** notable (nota académica). **4 – and –,** (brit.) cama y desayuno (casas particulares o pequeñas pensiones que sólo ofrecen esos dos servicios).

OBS. Puede utilizarse también como sigla de **born, book** y otras palabras.

babble | 'bæbl | *v.i.* **1** balbucir, balbucear. **2** hacer ba, parlotear (los bebés de manera incomprensible). **3** (lit.) susurrar, murmurar (el agua de un arroyo o similar). || *v.t.* **4** decir balbuceando, barbotar. || *s.c.* **5** balbuceo, parloteo. **6** (lit.) susurro, murmullo (de un arroyo o similar).

babe | beɪb | *s.c.* **1** (fam. y EE.UU.) cariño, querida; nena (dirigiéndose a mujeres). **2** (p.u.) bebé, pequeñín. || **3 a – in arms,** como un bebé, como un niño de pecho (no experimentado): *he was a babe in arms = era como un niño de pecho.*

babel | 'beɪbl | *s.sing.* **[– of]** caos de, algarabía de; ruido incomprensible: *the party was just a babel of voices and noises = la fiesta fue sólo un caos de voces y ruidos.*

baboon | bə'bu:n | *s.c.* ZOOL. mandril, babuino.

baby | 'beɪbɪ | *s.c.* **1** bebé, recién nacido. **2** (desp.) infantil, pueril: *you are a baby! = ¡eres infantil!* **3** (fam. y EE.UU.) cariño, lucero, amor. || *adj.* **4** pequeño, de bebé, para bebés: *a baby boy = un chico pequeño.* || **5 – buggy,** (EE.UU.) cochecito, sillita (para bebés). **6 to be left holding the –,** (fam.) quedarse sólo con una responsabilidad; cargarle a uno con el mochuelo. **7 to be one's –,** (fam.) ser el proyecto de uno, ser cosa de uno: *the new petrol station was your baby, not mine = la nueva estación de servicio fue cosa tuya, no mía.* **8 to throw/fling the – out with the bathwater,** (fam.) tirar todo por la borda (lo bueno y lo malo).

babyhood | 'beɪbɪhud | *s.i.* infancia (hasta los tres años aproximadamente).

babyish | 'beɪbɪɪʃ | *adj.* de bebé, infantil.

baby-minder | 'beɪbɪmaɪndər | *s.c.* chica/mujer que cuida a un niño (normalmente en su propia casa): *I have an excellent baby-minder = tengo una chica excelente para cuidar al niño.*

baby-sit | 'beɪbɪsɪt | *v.i.* cuidar niños (sólo unas horas normalmente esporádicas): *I got some money baby-sitting for my sister = me gané algún dinero cuidando los niños de mi hermana.*

baby-sitter | 'beɪbɪsɪtər | *s.c.* niñera, chica canguro.

baby-sitting | 'beɪbɪsɪtɪŋ | *s.i.* cuidado de niños: *I love baby-sitting = me gusta cuidar niños.*

baby-talk | 'beɪbɪtɔ:k | *s.i.* balbuceo infantil, habla infantil, modo de hablar típico de los niños.

bacchanal | 'bækənl | *s.c.* (lit.) bacanal.

bacchanalian | ˌbækə'neɪlɪən | *adj.* (lit.) orgiástico, bacanal, báquico.

bachelor | 'bætʃələr | *s.c.* **1** soltero. || **2 bachelor's degree,** licenciatura de primer grado. **3 Bachelor of Arts,** Licenciado en Letras. **4 Bachelor of Science,** Licenciado en Ciencias.

back | bæk | *s.c.* **1** ANAT. espalda. **2** lomo (de animal). **3** respaldo, reverso, dorso, parte de atrás (de cualquier objeto o lugar). **4** DEP. defensa, zaguero. || *adj.* **5** posterior, de atrás, trasero. **6** secundario; apartado (carretera, calle, camino, etc.). || *v.t.* **7** dar marcha atrás (a un vehículo). **8** apoyar, dar su apoyo a: *I'll never back him for that important post = nunca le daré mi apoyo para ese puesto importante.* **9** empujar hacia atrás, hacer retroceder: *he backed her towards the bedroom = la hizo retroceder hacia el dormitorio.* **10** apostar por (un caballo, un galgo, etc.). **11** MUS. acompañar. **12 [to – with]** revestir con (un material). || *v.i.* **13** ir marcha atrás, retroceder (vehículos). **14 [to – onto]** dar a (por la parte de atrás de una casa o similar): *my garden backs onto the golf course = mi jardín da al campo de golf.* **15** MAR. virar (el viento). || *adv.* **16** hacia atrás, detrás, atrás: *I looked back = miré detrás.* **17** de regreso, de vuelta: *he came back from London = él llegó de regreso de Londres.* || **18 – and forth,** de atrás a delante; de allí para allá. **19 to – away,** retroceder, dar pasos hacia atrás (normalmente nervioso o asustado ante algo): *he saw the strange creature and backed away = vio la extraña criatura y retrocedió.* **20 – copy,** ejemplar atrasado. **21 to – down,** desdecirse, ceder, echarse atrás (en una protesta, exigencia, etc.). **22 – issue,** ejemplar atrasado. **23 – number,** número atrasado. **24 to – off,** retirarse; abandonar (dejando a alguien o algo solos): *he was willing for a time but in the end he backed off = estuvo dispuesto durante bastante tiempo pero al final se retiró.* **25 to – out,** echarse para atrás, salirse (de una decisión, acuerdo, etc.). **26 – passage,** (euf.) culo; ojete. **27 – pay,** atrasos (dinero). **28 – street, a)** callejuela, calle poco transitada. **b)** ilegal, no oficial. **29 – to front,** al revés (cuando la parte de atrás está delante). **30 to – up, a)** respaldar; confirmar (una historia, una protesta, etc.). **b)** secundar, apoyar (con dinero). **c)** retroceder, ir hacia atrás (en coche o a pie). **31 to be on one's –,** estar postrado (enfermo). **32 behind someone's –,** a espaldas de alguien, sin que alguien lo sepa. **33 to break one's –,** matarse a trabajar; esforzarse sin medida: *I broke my back to get a new car = me maté a trabajar para comprar un coche nuevo.* **34 to break the — of,** hacer la parte más difícil de. **35 to get off one's –,** (fam.) dejar a uno en paz, dejar de fastidiar a uno. **36 to have one's – to the wall,** estar acorralado, estar entre la espada y la pared. **37 to live off the backs of,** gorronear, vivir a expensas de. **38 out the –/round the –,** (fam.) atrás, a la vuelta. **39 to put one's – into,** esforzarse al máximo en/con; arrimar el hombro. **40 to put someone's – up,** (fam.) sacar de quicio a alguien. **41 to scratch someone's – if they scratch one's,** (fam.) hacerse un favor mutuo. **42 to see the – of someone,** de que alguien se vaya: *I'm very happy to see the back of the boss = estoy muy con-*

tento de que el jefe se vaya. **43 to turn one's –,** dar la espalda, volver la espalda. **44 to turn one's – back on,** no hacer caso a, abandonar a; desdeñar.
OBS. Esta partícula detrás de verbos añade las siguientes matizaciones: **45** posición alejada de otro punto especial: *keep those children back from the door = mantén a esos niños alejados de la puerta.* **46** respuesta o reacción similar a un estímulo mediante el mismo medio por el que ha venido ese estímulo: *I'll phone you back in a few minutes = te llamaré yo a ti dentro de unos minutos.* **47** posición retraída, normalmente para no tapar algo: *hold back the curtains, I want to see the scenery = no dejes que las cortinas tapen el paisaje que quiero ver.* **48** posición del cuerpo recostada, relajada: *sit back and enjoy the music = recuéstate y disfruta de la música.* **49** regreso al tema que ocupaba la conversación: *come back to the point we are discussing = vuelve al tema que estamos tratando.* **50** regreso a una situación anterior: *this takes us back to the beginning = esto nos devuelve al principio.* **51** regreso al pasado en pensamiento: *I cast back my mind to those times = vuelvo con mi mente a aquellos tiempos.* **52** recuperación de algo: *I got the money back after a long time = recuperé el dinero después de mucho tiempo.* **53** devolución de algo: *put it back = ponlo donde estaba.* **54** señalización del tiempo transcurrido: *a few months back he was deeply in love = hace unos cuantos años estaba profundamente enamorado.* **55** señalización del tiempo a que se remonta algo: *this goes back to the times when the business was just starting = esto se remonta a los tiempos en que el negocio estaba empezando.*

backache | 'bækeɪk | *s.i.* dolor de espalda.

backbench | ˌbæk'bentʃ | *s.c.* POL. escaño de políticos poco conocidos y que no tienen puestos oficiales (esta palabra quiere decir "banco de atrás").

backbencher | ˌbæk'bentʃər | *s.c.* POL. parlamentario poco conocido y sin puesto oficial alguno: *he's been a backbencher all his political life = lleva toda su vida política de parlamentario poco conocido y sin responsabilidad oficial.*

backbiting | 'bækbaɪtɪŋ | *s.i.* calumnia, murmuración.

backbone | 'bækbəun | *s.c.* **1** ANAT. columna vertebral, espinazo. **2** (fig.) base, punto fundamental, columna (de una organización, sistema, etc.). || *s.i.* **3** determinación, firmeza (para llevar a cabo ideales o similar).

backbreaking | 'bækbreɪkɪŋ | *adj.* agotador, matador.

backchat | 'bæktʃæt | *s.i.* (fam. y brit.) descaro (en respuestas a alguien en autoridad).

backcloth | 'bækklɵ | *s.c.* **1** (brit.) ART. telón de fondo (en un escenario). **2** (fig.) telón de fondo (de acontecimientos).

back-comb | 'bækkəum | *v.t.* peinar (el pelo) de detrás hacia delante.

backdate | 'bækdeɪt | *v.t.* conceder efectos retroactivos: *we backdated the pay rise = concedimos efectos retroactivos al aumento de sueldo.*

backdoor | 'bækdɔːr | *adj.* (desp.) clandestino; deshonesto.

backdrop | 'bækdrp | *s.c.* **1** (EE.UU.) telón de fondo. **2** fondo (de un paisaje, lugar, cuadro, etc.).

-backed | bækt | *suf.* indica de qué está recubierto o cómo es la parte de atrás de un objeto: *a hard-backed chair = una silla de respaldo duro.*

backer | 'bækər | *s.c.* partidario; patrocinador (que da dinero).

backfire | 'bækfaɪər | *v.i.* **1** salir el tiro por la culata, tener un efecto contrario al deseado. **2** MEC. petardear, hacer explosiones (un motor).

backgammon | ˌbæk'gæmən || 'bækgæmən | *s.i.* juego de chaquete.

background | 'bækgraund | *s.c.* **1** historial, antecedentes (de la vida de una persona). **2** ART. fondo, trasfondo (de un cuadro o imagen). || *s.sing.* **3** marco (de una situación): *the political background at the present moment = el marco político en la actualidad.* || *adj.* **4** de fondo: *background music = música de fondo.* **5** básico, fundamental (para el entendimiento de algo): *background information = información básica.* || **6 in the –,** en segundo término, en segundo plano.

backhand | 'bækhænd | *s.c.* DEP. **1** revés. **2** la mano mala; lado contrario al de su mano buena: *I tried to serve to his backhand = intenté servir a su mano mala.*

backhanded | ˌbæk'hændɪd | *adj.* **1** con el revés de la mano. **2** indirecto, irónico: *that was a backhanded remark = eso fue una observación irónica.*

backhander | 'bækhændər | *s.c.* **1** (fam.) astilla; pequeño soborno. **2** indirecta.

backing | 'bækɪŋ | *s.i.* **1** apoyo (moral o monetario). **2** MUS. acompañamiento. || *s.c.* e *i.* **3** revestimiento, forro.

backlash | 'bæklæʃ | *s.sing.* reacción violenta, contragolpe: *it was a backlash against the government = fue una reacción violenta contra el gobierno.*

backless | 'bæklɪs | *adj.* sin espalda (un vestido).

backlog | 'bæklɒg | *s.c.* acumulación, amontonamiento (de trabajo, de pedidos, etc.).

backpack | 'bækpæk | *s.c.* (EE.UU.) mochila, macuto.

back-pedal | ˌbæk'pedl | *v.i.* recoger velas (desdecirse en palabras o actos de lo que uno primero decía o hacía).

backroom | ˌbæk'ruːm | *s.c.* **1** cuarto interior, cuarto de la parte de atrás. || **2 – boy,** persona que trabaja en la sombra.

back-seat | ˌbæk'siːt | *s.c.* **1** asiento de atrás, asiento trasero. || **2 – driver,** pasagero que molesta al conductor con sus advertencias. **3 to take a –,** tomar una posición secundaria; mantenerse en la sombra: *his wife took a back seat after he got the prize = su mujer se mantuvo en la sombra después de que él consiguiera el premio.*

backside | 'bæksaɪd | *s.c.* **1** (fam.) trasero, culo. || **2 to sit on one's –,** (desp.) no hacer nada, hacer el vago: *don't sit on your backside all day = no hagas el vago todo el día.*

backsliding | 'bækslaɪdɪŋ | *s.i.* vuelta a las andadas, reincidencia.

backstage | 'bæksteɪdʒ | *s.i.* **1** bambalinas, detrás del telón; camerinos. **2** (fig.) entre bastidores; secretamente. || *adj.* **3** de detrás del telón. **4** secreto, confidencial: *backstage talks = conversaciones confidenciales.*

backstroke | 'bækstrəuk | *s.i.* DEP. espalda (especialidad de natación).

backtrack | 'bæktræk | *v.i.* **1** retroceder, volver sobre los pasos de uno. **2** desdecirse, tragarse las palabras.

backup | 'bækʌp | *s.i.* **1** soporte, apoyo: *a backup teacher = un profesor de apoyo.* **2** sustituto, sustitución: *to use it as backup = utilizarlo como sustituto.*

backward | 'bækwəd | *adj.* **1** hacia atrás, atrás, de atrás. **2** (desp.) subdesarrollado, atrasado (país, región, etc.). **3** atrasado; torpe (en estudios).

backward-looking | ˌbækwəd'lukɪŋ | *adj.* (desp.) retrógrado.

backwards | 'bækwədz | (también EE.UU. **backward**) *adv.* **1** atrás, hacia atrás. **2** hacia atrás, hacia el pasado (en el tiempo): *when I look backwards, I realize I made mistakes = cuando miro hacia atrás me doy cuenta que cometí equivocaciones.* **3** al revés: *you do everything backwards = haces todo al revés.* || **4 – and forwards,** hacia delante y atrás, de aquí para allá. **5 to know something –,** saber algo al dedillo.

backwash | 'bækwɑʃ | *s.i.* **1** contracorriente; oleaje (causado por un bote). **2** consecuencias, secuelas.

backwater | 'bækwɔːtər | *s.c.* (desp.) lugar alejado, lugar apartado, lugar atrasado.

backwoods | 'bækwudz | *s.pl.* lugar remoto; quinto pino.

backyard | ˌbækjɑːd | *s.c.* **1** (brit.) patio posterior, patio trasero. **2** (EE.UU.) jardín posterior, jardín trasero.

bacon | 'beɪkən | *s.i.* **1** bacon, panceta. || **2 to bring home the –,** (fam.) **a)** traer los garbanzos a casa; ser el proveedor de la familia. **b)** conseguirlo, lograrlo. **3 to save one's –,** (fam. y brit.) salvar el pellejo.

bacteria | bæk'tɪərɪə | (**bacterium** *sing.*) *s.pl.* BIOL. bacteria.

bacterial | bæk'tɪərɪəl | *adj.* BIOL. bacteriano.

bacteriological | bækˌtɪərɪə'ldʒɪkl | *adj.* bacteriológico.

bacteriologist | bækˌtɪərɪ'ldʒɪst | *s.c.* bacteriólogo.

bacteriology | bækˌtɪərɪ'lədʒɪ | *s.i.* bacteriología.

bacterium | bæk'tɪərɪəm | *sing.* de **bacteria.**

bad | bæd | (comp. **worse,** super. **worst**) *adj.* **1** malo, desagradable, fatal: *bad weather = tiempo desagradable.* **2** grave, serio (herida, accidente, error, etc.). **3** fuerte (catarro, dolor, enfermedad, etc.). **4** malo, vicioso (del comportamiento y carácter). **5** inapropiado, feo (palabras, forma de hablar). **6** podrido (comida). **7** inútil, malo (parte del cuerpo): *I can't do that with my bad arm = no puedo hacer eso con el brazo malo.* **8** travieso (chico o chica). **9 [– at]** torpe en, malo en (una asignatura o similar). || **10 a – buy,** una mala compra, una compra en el peor momento (del mercado). **11 a – lot/sort/type, etc.,** un tipo/sujeto/elemento malo, etc. **12 a – name,** mala reputación. **13 a – turn,** una faena (en sentido negativo). **14 – blood,** malos sentimientos; mala disposición, animosidad. **15 – breath,** mal aliento. **16 – cheque,** COM. cheque sin fondos; cheque erróneo (por algún defecto de forma). **17 – debt,** COM. deuda irrecuperable (deuda que hay que dar por perdida). **18 – feeling,** resentimiento. **19 – form,** de mala educación. **20 – luck,** mala suerte. **21 – news,** (fam.) algo malo, alguien malo; mala persona: *he's bad news = es mala persona.* **22 – taste,** mal gusto, de mal gusto. **23 to feel – about,** sentirse culpable sobre; sentir tristeza sobre. **24 to go –,** pudrirse (comida). **25 to go from – to worse,** ir de mal en peor, ir de guatemala a guatepeor. **26 not –,** regular, aceptable, bien (con una entonación no convencida del todo). **27 to take the – with the good,** aceptar lo bueno y lo malo. **28 too –/it's too –/that's too –,** (fam.) **a)** lástima. **b)** mala suerte; desgraciadamente así están las cosas (con dureza o impaciencia).

baddy | 'bædɪ | *s.c.* (fam.) malo (en las películas, libros, etc.).

bade | beɪd | V. **bid.**

badge | bædʒ | *s.c.* **1** insignia, placa, chapa. **2** (fig.) distintivo, señal, símbolo: *a badge of wealthiness = un distintivo de riqueza.*

badger | 'bædʒər | *s.c.* **1** ZOOL. tejón. || *v.t.* **2** acosar, importunar (verbalmente): *I badgered him until he gave in = le importuné hasta que se rindió.*

badinage | 'bædɪnɑːʒ | (EE.UU.) | ˌbædən'ɑːʒ | *s.i.* (lit.) chanza.

badly | 'bædlɪ | *adv.* **1** mal. **2** seriamente, gravemente (hablando de heridas o similar). **3** mal, pobremente, de mala calidad. **4** muchísimo (con la idea de necesitar o desear). **5** mal, desfavorablemente. || **6 – off,** sin blanca, sin un duro. **7 – off for,** muy necesitado de, con falta de: *we're badly off for space = estamos muy necesitados de espacio.*

badminton | 'bædmɪntən | *s.i.* DEP. badminton.

baffle | 'bæfl | *v.t.* desconcertar, confundir.

bafflement | 'bæflmənt | *s.i.* desconcierto, confusión.

baffling | 'bæflɪŋ | *adj.* desconcertante.

bag | bæg | *s.c.* **1** bolsa (de papel, plástico, etc.). **2** bolso (de señora). **3** (fig.) bolsa (contenido): *he ate a bag of crisps = se comió una bolsa de patatas fritas.* || *v.t.* **4** (fam. y brit.) reservar (una cosa que todos quieren). **5** capturar, cazar (en una cacería). || **6 a – of bones,** (desp. y fam.) flacucho, en los huesos. **7 a – of tricks,** todos los medios propios (para hacer algo). **8 old/stupid –,** (desp.) mujer fea, antipática, desagradable. **9 – and baggage,** (fam.) con todo lo de uno (normalmente cuando se le echa a alguien de algún sitio). **10 bags,** ojeras. **11 bags of,** (brit. y fam.) montones de. **12 to – up,** meter en bolsas, ensacar. **13 in the –,** (fam.) en el bolso. **14 to pack one's bags,** hacer las maletas (para irse de un lugar).

bagatelle | ˌbægə'tel | *s.c.* (lit.) bagatela, fruslería.

baggage | 'bægɪdʒ | *s.i.* (EE.UU.) equipaje.

baggy | 'bægɪ | *adj.* holgado, que está demasiado ancho por el uso.

bagpipes | 'bægpaɪps | *s.pl.* MUS. gaita.

bah | bɑː | *interj.* (p.u.) ¡bah! (expresa desprecio, desencanto o irritación).

Bahamas | bə'hɑːməz | (EE.UU.) | bə'heɪməz | *s.i.* Bahamas.

Bahamian | bə'heɪmɪən | *adj.* **1** de las Bahamas. || *s.c.* **2** habitante de las Bahamas.

Bahrain | bɑː'reɪn | *s.i.* Bahrain.

Bahraini | bɑː'reɪnɪ | *adj.* **1** de Bahrain. || *s.c.* **2** habitante de Bahrain.

bail | beɪl | (a veces **bale**) *s.c.* **1** DER. fianza. **2** DER. libertad bajo fianza. || *v.t.* e *i.* **3** MAR. achicar (el agua en un barco). || **4 to – out, a)** DER. sacar bajo fianza; pagar la fianza. **b)** sacar de apuros (económicos). **5 to – out (of),** AER. saltar en paracaídas (de) (un avión en peligro). **6 bails,** DEP. estacas (siempre dos en el críquet). **7 to jump –,** DER. desaparecer; escaparse (estando bajo fianza). **8 to stand/go – (for),** DER. salir fiador (de), pagar la fianza (a).

bailiff | 'beɪlɪf | *s.c.* **1** (brit.) DER. alguacil (persona que ejecuta una decisión de embargo). **2** (EE.UU.) DER. corchete (administrativo de un tribunal). **3** (brit.) administrador (de propiedades).

bairn | beən | *s.c.* chaval, chico (en Escocia y el Norte de Inglaterra).

bait | beɪt | *s.i.* **1** DEP. cebo, carnada (pesca). **2** (fig.) añagaza, cebo. || *v.t.* **3 [to – (with)]** poner un cebo, cebar. **4** (fig.) picar, hacer rabiar. **5** azuzar, atacar (a osos o tejones con perros). || **6 to rise to the –/to take the –,** tragar el anzuelo, picar (reaccionar como otro esperaba).

baize | beɪz | *s.i.* bayeta (tejido normalmente verde recubriendo mesas de billar).

bake | beɪk | *v.t.* **1** cocer, hornear, cocer al horno. || *v.i.* **2** cocerse, hacerse al horno. **3** endurecerse (normalmente la tierra por el sol).

baked | beɪkt | *adj.* **1** cocido, hecho al horno. || **2 – beans,** judías cocidas (normalmente enlatadas).

baker | 'beɪkər | *s.c.* **1** panadero, tahonero. || **2 the –/the baker's,** la panadería. **3 baker's dozen,** (p.u.) trece, docena del fraile.

bakery | 'beɪkərɪ | *s.c.* panadería, tahona.

baking | 'beɪkɪŋ | *s.i.* **1** GAST. cocción, horneado. || *adj.* **2** ardiente, calurosísimo: *today it's baking hot = hoy es un día calurosísimo.* **3 – powder,** QUIM. levadura. **4 – soda,** QUIM. bicarbonato sódico.

bakelite | 'beɪkəlaɪt | *s.i.* baquelita (marca registrada de un tipo de plástico).

baksheesh | bæk'ʃiːʃ | | 'bækʃiːʃ | *s.i.* propina (en los países árabes).

balaclava | ˌbælə'klɑːvə | *s.c.* **1** pasamontañas (gorro). || **2 – helmet,** pasamontañas.

balalaika | ˌbælə'laɪkə | *s.c.* MUS. balalaica (instrumento ruso como un laúd).

balance | 'bæləns | *s.i.* **1** equilibrio (de una persona, entre naciones, etc.). **2** equilibrio, armonía (entre varias partes). || *v.t.* **3** sopesar (una cosa en comparación con otra). **4** equilibrar (un presupuesto). || *v.i.* **5** equilibrarse (hablando de cuentas o presupuestos). **6** compensarse: *his youth is balanced by his maturity = su juventud está compensada por su madurez.* || *v.r.* **7** equilibrarse, balancearse. || *s.c.* **8** balanza. **9** COM. balance. **10** (fig.) balanza, peso (a favor de alguien en algún tipo de competición): *the balance is tipping in the Englishman's favour = la balanza se está inclinando del lado del inglés.* **11** COM. resto, residuo, balance final. || **12 – of payments,** ECON. balanza de pagos. **13 to – out,** igualarse; equilibrarse (una cantidad con otra o similar). **14 – sheet,** COM. balance general. **15 to hold the –,** tener la llave de la solución; tener un peso específico decisivo. **16 in the –,** sin decidir; pendiente de un hilo. **17 off –, a)** desequilibrado, a punto de caerse. **b)** (fig.) lelo, aturdido. **18 on —,** pensándolo mejor, pensándolo con cuidado. **19 to strike a –,** lograr un equilibrio adecuado.

balanced | 'bælənst | *adj.* **1** equilibrado, medido, mesurado (opinión, persona, etc.). **2** compensado, equilibrado, simétrico (algo cuyas partes están adecuadamente unidas). **3** COM. equilibrado, ajustado (cuentas, economía, etc.).

balancing act | 'bælənsɪŋ ækt | V. **act.**

balcony | 'bælkənɪ | *s.c.* **1** ARQ. balcón. **2** galería, paraíso, arriba (en cine o teatro).

bald | bɔːld | *adj.* **1** calvo, sin un pelo. **2** sin dibujo (en las ruedas de coches). **3** desnudo, descubierto (una superficie que debería estar más protegida). **4** franco, directo. || **5 – eagle,** ZOOL. águila calva (de USA). **6 to go –,** quedarse calvo.

balderdash | 'bɔːldədæʃ | *s.i.* (p.u.) tonterías, bobadas.

bald-headed | 'bɔːldhedɪd | *adj.* calvo.

balding | 'bɔːldɪŋ | *adj.* que se está quedando calvo: *a balding man.*

baldly | 'bɔːldlɪ | *adv.* francamente, sin pelos en la lengua.

baldness | 'bɔːldnɪs | *s.i.* calvicie.

bale | beɪl | *s.c.* **1** bala, fardo. || *v.t.* **2** embalar, hacer fardos (normalmente de paja o similar).

baleful | 'beɪlful | *adj.* (lit.) pernicioso, malsano.

balefully | 'beɪlfəlɪ | *adv.* perniciosamente, malsanamente.

balk | bɔːk | (también **baulk**) *v.i.* **1 [to – at]** resistirse a; oponerse a. **2 [to – at]** detenerse ante, plantarse ante (caballos o algún otro animal). || **3 to be balked of,** (lit.) impedir, no dejar conseguir: *he was balked of his prey = no le dejaron conseguir su presa.*

ball | bɔːl | *s.c.* **1** pelota, balón. **2** (fig.) pelota, bola (cualquier cosa con esa forma). **3** DEP. pelota, balón (en la habilidad o falta de ella para jugarla): *it was a magnificent ball = fue un balón magnífico.* **4** (fam.) pelota, huevo (manera maleducada de referirse al testículo). **5** gran baile, fiesta por todo lo alto. || *v.t.* e *i.* **6** hacer(se) una bola, hacer(se) una pelota. || **7 a – game,** (EE.UU.) partido de béisbol. **8 a whole new – game/a completely different – game, etc.,** (fam.) una cosa totalmente distinta, un tema totalmente distinto. **9 balls,** (fam.) **a)** pelotas, agallas, huevos (vulg.). **b)** una mierda, vaya estupidez (vulg.). **10 to have a –,** (fam.) pasarlo de fábula. **11 on the –,** al tanto, enterado, muy despierto. **12 to play –,** (fam.) cooperar con gusto. **13 to start/set/keep the – rolling,** no dejar decaer el tema una vez comenzado. **14 the – is in someone's court,** le toca a alguien dar el siguiente paso, es el turno de alguien para tomar la siguiente medida. **15 the – of one's thumb/foot,** la parte del pulgar/pie donde se unen los dedos a la mano o al pie.

ballad | 'bæləd | *s.c.* MUS. **1** balada. **2** balada (canción lenta de la música moderna).

ballast | 'bæləst | *s.i.* **1** MAR. lastre. **2** grava, gravilla, balasto (en carreteras y líneas de ferrocarril).

ball-bearing | ˌbɔːl'beərɪŋ | *s.c.* MEC. cojinete de bolas, rodamiento.

ballcock | 'bɔːlkɑk | *s.c.* MEC. llave de flotador, llave de bola (fontanería).

ballerina | ˌbælə'riːnə | *s.c.* ART. bailarina.

ballet | 'bæleɪ | *s.i.* **1** ART. ballet. || *s.c.* **2** ART. grupo de ballet. **3** MUS. pieza musical para ballet, ballet. || **4 – dancer,** ART. bailarín.

ballistic | bə'lɪstɪk | *adj.* **1** balístico. || **2 – missile,** MIL. misil balístico.

ballistics | bə'lɪstɪks | *s.i.* balística.

balloon | bə'luːn | *s.c.* **1** globo (para niños). **2** globo aerostático. **3** nube de viñeta (donde están las palabras que dicen los dibujos). || *v.i.* **4** inflarse (a la manera de un globo). **5** (fig.) aumentar a toda velocidad, subir/crecer vertiginosamente. || **6 the – went up,** estalló la noticia; el globo explotó (algo que debía ser secreto y ya no lo es).

ballot | 'bælət | *s.c.* **1** votación (secreta). **2** papeleta (para votar). || *v.t.* **3** decidir mediante votación, solicitar una opinión mediante votación: *the union will ballot its members = el sindicato solicitará a sus miembros una opinión mediante votación.* || **4 – paper,** papeleta (de voto). **5 by –,** mediante votación secreta.

ballot-box | 'bælətbks | *s.c.* **1** urna (para votar). || **2** *s.sing.* (fig.) las urnas; el sistema democrático.

ballpoint | 'bɔːlpɔɪnt | *s.c.* **1** bolígrafo. || **2 – pen,** bolígrafo.

ballroom | 'bɔːlruːm | | bɔːlrʊm | *s.c.* **1** salón de baile. || **2 – dancing,** baile de salón.

ballsup | 'bɔːlzʌp | (EE.UU. **ball-up**) *s.c.* (fam.) follón; estropicio.

balls up *v.t.* hacer una chapuza de: *don't balls up this job, please = no hagas una chapuza de este trabajo.*

ball-up | 'bɔːlʌp | V. **ballsup.**

ballyhoo | ˌbælɪ'huː | (EE.UU.) | 'bælɪhuː | *s.sing.* (fam. y p.u.) bombo, alharaca: *I don't understand all the ballyhoo about it = no comprendo todo el bombo que se le ha dado.*

balm | bɑːm | (también **balsam**) *s.c.* e *i.* **1** bálsamo. || *s.i.* **2** (fig.) consuelo, bálsamo.

balmy | bɑːmɪ | *adj.* suave; excelente (hablando del tiempo atmosférico).

baloney | bə'ləʊnɪ | *s.i.* (fam. y EE.UU.) tontería, bobada.

balsa | 'bɔːlsə | BOT. *s.i.* **1** madera de balsa. || *s.c.* **2** balsa (árbol).

balsam | 'bɔːlsəm V. **balm.**

balustrade | ˌbælə'streɪd | *s.c.* ARQ. balustrada, baranda.

bamboo | bæm'buː | *s.c.* e *i.* BOT. bambú.

bamboozle | bæm'buːzl | *v.t.* **[to – (into)]** (fam.) embaucar, engañar.

ban | bæn | *v.t.* **1** prohibir, proscribir. **2 [to – + *o.d.* + from]** prohibir; inhabilitar para: *he was banned from driving = le prohibieron conducir.* || *s.c.* **3 [– (on)]** prohibición, proscripción.

banal | bə'nɑːl | (EE.UU.) | 'beɪnl | *adj.* banal, trivial, insignificante.

banality | bə'nælɪtɪ | *s.c.* e *i.* trivialidad, banalidad.

banana | bə'nɑːnə | (EE.UU.) | bə'nænə | *s.c.* e *i.* **1** BOT. plátano. || **2 bananas,** loco, chiflado. **3 – republic,** POL. (desp.) república bananera. **4 – skin,** (fam.) POL. metedura de pata. **5 – split,** GAST. postre hecho con plátanos. **6 to go bananas,** (fam.) **a)** ponerse negro, ponerse malo (de enfado). **b)** comportarse chifladamente, hacer el loco.

band | bænd | *s.c.* **1** MUS. grupo, conjunto, banda, orquesta. **2** grupo, banda (de personas). **3** franja, tira (de cualquier tejido). **4** RAD. banda (de frecuencias). **5** anillo (de un cigarro). **6** MEC. abrazadera, aro, fleje. **7** haz (de luz). **8** muñequera; brazalete (en el deporte o como señal de algo). **9** zona alargada (de tierra). **10** banda (de color distinto al que le rodea). || **11 to – together,** juntarse; asociarse: *let's band together against them = juntémonos contra ellos.* **12 to be banded with,** estar marcado en franjas con, estar adornado en franjas con: *the house is banded with beautiful marble = la casa está adornada con franjas de mármol.*

bandage | 'bændɪdʒ | MED. *s.c.* **1** venda, vendaje. || *v.t.* **2** vendar. || **3 to – up,** vendar prietamente/muy bien; proteger completamente mediante un vendaje.

bandaged | 'bændɪdʒt | *adj.* vendado.

bandanna | bæn'dænə | (también **bandana**) *s.c.* pañuelo grande (normalmente de colores).

-banded | 'bændɪd | *sufijo* a... bandas, con... franjas (se combina con números y colores principalmente): *a two-banded hat = un sombrero con dos franjas.*

bandit | 'bændɪt | *s.c.* bandido, bandolero.

bandmaster | 'bændmɑːstər | *s.c.* MUS. director de una banda.

bandsman | 'bændzmən | [*pl.* **bandsmen**] *s.c.* **1** MUS. músico (en una orquesta). **2** MIL. MUS. miembro de una banda militar.

bandsmen | 'bændzmən | *pl.irreg.* de **bandsman.**

bandstand | 'bændstænd | *s.c.* MUS. estrado para orquesta, quiosco de música.

bandwagon | 'bændwægən | *s.c.* **1** (arc.) carro de la banda (especialmente en circos). || **2 to jump/climb on the –,** unirse a los ganadores, adherirse a los ganadores.

bandy | 'bændɪ | *adj.* **1** patizambo, estevado. || *v.t.* **2** intercambiar (palabras, insultos, etc.). || **3 to – about,** esgrimir (palabras, nombres, expresiones). **4 to – words with,** discutir con, pelearse con (verbalmente).

bandy-legged | 'bændɪlegd | *adj.* patizambo, estevado.

bane | beɪn | *s.sing.* **1 [the – of]** ruina; plaga, azote: *he's the bane of gamblers = es el azote de los jugadores.* || **2 the – of one's life,** la ruina de la vida de uno.

bang | bæŋ | *v.i.* **1** chocar, golpear (haciendo un ruido similar a "bang"). **2** detonar (con ruido parecido a un disparo). || *v.t.* **3** colocar, poner (con un ruido): *he banged the cup on the shelf = colocó con un golpe fuerte la taza en la estantería.* **4** golpear, chocar (una parte del cuerpo de manera accidental). **5** dar un portazo (sólo con una puerta). **6** (fam. y muy fuerte) tirarse, follarse (a una mujer). || *s.c.* **7** golpe; impacto. **8** detonación, gran ruido, fuerte sonido: *with a bang = con un fuerte ruido.* || *adv.* **9** (fam.) justo, exactamente (en una oposición): *the house is bang in the middle = la casa está exactamente en medio.* || **10 to – about,** (fam.) maltratar, dar golpes descuidadamente. **11 to – around/about,** (fam.) andar a golpes por, dar golpes por (un sitio): *she didn't stop banging around in the kitchen the whole night = no paró de dar golpes por la cocina toda la noche.* **12 to – away,** no cesar de golpear. **13 – goes,** (vulg.) al carajo con, a la mierda con (indicando fracaso): *bang goes our trip abroad if you fall sick = al carajo con nuestro viaje al extranjero si caes enferma.* **14 to – one's head against a brick wall,** darse cabezadas contra la pared sin ningún resultado. **15 to – out,** (fam.) dar la murga (cantando o tocando un instrumento). **16 to go –,** explotar, estallar. **17 with a –,** (fam.) con gran éxito, con mucho ímpetu.

banger | 'bæŋər | *s.c.* (fam. y brit.) **1** salchicha. **2** cacharro (coche viejo). **3** petardo.

Bangladesh | ˌbæŋglə'deʃ | *s.sing.* Bangladesh.

Bangladeshi | ˌbæŋglə'deʃɪ | *adj.* **1** de Bangladesh. || *s.c.* **2** habitante de Bangladesh.

bangle | 'bæŋgl | *s.c.* pulsera, brazalete, esclava.

bang-on | ˌbæŋ'ɒn | *adj.* (fam. y brit.) correcto, perfecto.

banish | 'bænɪʃ | *v.t.* **1 [to – (from)]** desterrar, exiliar. **2 [to – (from)]** disipar;

rechazar (pensamientos): *banish it from your thoughts, I'll never love anybody else = quítatelo de la cabeza, nunca querré a otra persona.*
banishment | 'bænɪʃmənt | *s.i.* exilio, destierro.
banister | 'bænɪstər | (también **bannister**) *s.c.* ARQ. pasamano.
banjo | 'bændʒəu | *s.c.* MUS. banjo.
bank | bæŋk | *s.c.* **1** FIN. banco. **2** orilla (de un río o lago). **3** talud, terraplén. **4** montículo: *the village is on a bank = el pueblo está sobre un montículo.* **5** montón (longitudinal y elevado de tierra). **6** banca (en los juegos). **7** INF. banco (de datos). **8** MED. banco (de sangre o similar). **9** ELEC. grupo, fila (de transformadores), batería (de lámparas). **10** MEC. fila, hilera (de instrumentos). **11** banco (de niebla). || *v.t.* **12** meter en el banco (dinero). **13** hacer un montón, amontonar (formando como un terraplén): *the soldiers banked the snow for self-protection = los soldados amontonaron la nieve formando un terraplén para su protección.* || *v.i.* **14 [to – with]** tener una cuenta bancaria con. **15** AER. inclinarse, ladearse (normalmente para cambiar de dirección). || **16 a – of keys,** un teclado (de órgano o máquina de escribir). **17 – account,** FIN. cuenta bancaria. **18 – holiday,** día no laboral en que están cerrados los bancos y el comercio en general. **19 – loan,** FIN. préstamo bancario. **20 – manager,** FIN. director bancario, director de banco. **21 to – on,** contar con; confiar en: *you mustn't bank on fidelity these days = no debes confiar en la fidelidad en estos tiempos. 22 – statement,* FIN. extracto bancario, estado de cuentas (donde se da la lista de las entradas y salidas de una cuenta). **23 to – up, a)** amontonar, apilar (formando un montón en forma de terraplén). **b)** alimentar (un fuego poniendo gran cantidad de combustible). **24 to be banked,** estar limitado, estar bordeado (por montones de tierra que formen terraplén). **25 to break the –,** V. **break.**
bank-balance | 'bæŋkbæləns | *s.c.* FIN. activo bancario, estado de una cuenta.
banker | 'bæŋkər | *s.c.* **1** FIN. banquero. **2** (fig.) banquero, encargado de la banca (en un juego). || **3 banker's card,** FIN. tarjeta bancaria. **4 banker's order,** FIN. orden bancaria (para pagar recibos).
banking | 'bæŋkɪŋ | *s.i.* FIN. **1** banca. || **2 – house,** (lit. y p.u.) banco.
banknote | 'bæŋknəut | *s.c.* FIN. billete de banco.
bank-rate | 'bæŋkreɪt | *s.sing.* FIN. tipo de interés bancario; tipo de descuento bancario.
bankroll | 'bæŋkrəul | (EE.UU.) *v.t.* **1** financiar, apoyar financieramente. || *s.c.* **2** fondos financieros.
bankrupt | 'bæŋkrʌpt | *adj.* **1** FIN. sin dinero, sin fondos, insolvente. **2** (fig.) con deficiencias, deficiente: *we live in a politically bankrupt society = vivimos en una sociedad políticamente deficiente.* || *s.c.* **3** FIN. insolvente (la persona). || *v.t.* **4** hacer caer en bancarrota, causar una bancarrota. || **5 to go –,** entrar en bancarrota, caer en la bancarrota; declararse en quiebra.
bankruptcy | 'bæŋkrəpsɪ | *s.i.* **1** bancarrota, quiebra, insolvencia. **2** (fig.) quiebra, insolvencia, deficiencia. || *s.c.* **3** bancarrota, fracaso financiero.
banner | 'bænər | *s.c.* **1** estandarte, cartel (de tejido). **2** pancarta (en manifestaciones). **3** (fig.) bandera; nombre: *he always fought under the banner of communism = siempre luchó bajo la bandera del comunismo.* || **4 – head-line,** PER. titular a toda plana, titular a toda página.
banning | 'bænɪŋ | *s.i.* prohibición.
banns | bænz | *s.pl.* **[the –]** REL. amonestaciones (antes de casarse).
banquet | 'bæŋkwɪt | *s.c.* banquete.
banshee | bæn'ʃiː | (EE.UU.) | 'bænʃiː | *s.c.* espíritu (en el folklore irlandés, que anuncia con sus gritos una muerte próxima).
bantam | 'bæntəm | *s.c.* ZOOL. gallo de Bantam (enano).
banter | 'bæntər | *s.i.* **1** chanza, guasa; burlas (bienintencionadas): *there was some banter about Jim's new job = hubo algunas burlas sobre el trabajo nuevo de Jim.* || *v.i.* **2 [to – (with/about)]** bromear, tomar el pelo (sin sentido negativo).
Bantu | ˌbæn'tuː | *adj.* bantú (cultura, idioma, etc.).
banyan | 'bænɪən | *s.c.* BOT. baniano, higuera de Bengala (árbol frutal).
baptise V. **baptize.**
baptism | 'bæptɪzəm | *s.c.* e *i.* REL. bautismo.
Baptist | 'bæptɪst | *s.c.* REL. baptista (persona que cree fundamental que el bautismo tenga lugar en edad consciente y responsable).
baptize | bæp'taɪz | (también **baptise**) *v.t.* REL. bautizar.
bar | bɑːr | *s.c.* **1** (brit.) bar (habitación dentro de un pub donde las bebidas cuestan un poco menos). **2** (EE.UU.) bar (todo el local). **3** barra (de un local). **4** bar (dentro de otro edificio o lugar): *the hotel bar.* **5** barra (de metal). **6** ELEC. elemento; resistencia (la parte de una estufa que se pone roja). **7 [a – of]** lingote (de metales), pastilla (de jabón), tableta (de chocolate). **8** prohibición: *there was a bar on alcohol = había prohibición de bebidas alcohólicas.* **9** MUS. compás. **10** establecimiento; salón (con distintas especialidades): *a wine bar = un bar especializado en vinos; a tea bar = un salón de té.* || *v.t.* **11** obstruir, atrancar (una puerta). **12** poner rejas: *to bar the windows = poner rejas a las ventanas.* **13** prohibir: *to bar all sorts of firearms = prohibir todo tipo de armas de fuego.* **14 [to – *o.d* from]** impedir, impedir la entrada en; prohibir la entrada en: *I barred him from the house = le impedí la entrada en la casa.* || *prep.* **15** (lit.) salvo, menos, con la excepción de. || **16 – mitzvah,** REL. ceremonia judía en que se concede la mayoría de edad a un muchacho de trece años. **17 – none,** sin excepción. **18 bars,** rejas. **19 to – someone's way/path,** obstruir el camino de alguien, bloquear el paso de alguien. **20 behind bars,** (euf. y fam.) tras las rejas, en la cárcel. **21 no holds barred,** sin reglas, sin tener en cuenta ninguna regla. **22 the Bar** DER. la abogacía.
barb | bɑːb | *s.c.* **1** púa, lengüeta (de una flecha). **2** pincho, espino (de un alambre). **3** (fig.) indirecta, dardo verbal.
Barbadian | bɑː'beɪdɪən | *adj.* **1** de Barbados. || *s.c.* **2** habitante de Barbados.
Barbados | bɑː'beɪdɒs | *s.pl.* Barbados.
barbarian | bɑː'beərɪən | *s.c.* **1** HIST. bárbaro. **2** (desp.) salvaje, bestia, bárbaro.
barbaric | bɑː'bærɪk | *adj.* salvaje, brutal.
barbarism | 'bɑːbərɪzəm | *s.i.* barbarie.
barbarity | bɑː'bærɪtɪ | *s.c.* e *i.* barbaridad.
barbarous | 'bɑːbərəs | *adj.* (desp.) brutal, bárbaro.
barbarously | 'bɑːbərəslɪ | *adv.* (desp.) brutalmente, vandálicamente.
barbecue | 'bɑːbɪkjuː | *s.c.* **1** barbacoa (el objeto, la comida, la fiesta). || *v.t.* **2** hacer en barbacoa. || **3 – sauce,** salsa de barbacoa.
barbed | bɑːbd | *adj.* **1** con púas, con lengüetas. **2** (fig.) mordaz, con segundas. || **3 – wire,** alambre de espino.
barber | 'bɑːbər | *s.c.* **1** peluquero, barbero. || *v.t.* **2** cortar finamente, recortar cuidadosamente. || **3 barber's pole,** percha de barbero (a rayas rojas y blancas en espiral). **4 the barber's,** la peluquería.
barbershop | 'bɑːbəʃɒp | *s.i.* MUS. estilo de canción a cuatro voces.
barbiturate | bɑː'bɪtjurɪt | *s.c.* MED. barbitúrico.
bard | bɑːd | *s.c.* (lit. y p.u.) poeta, bardo.
bare | beər | *adj.* **1** desnudo: *bare feet = pies desnudos.* **2** descubierta (cabeza). **3** desnudo, desolado (paisaje o similar). **4** vacío (habitación, alacena, etc.). **5** sin hojas (árbol). **6** descubierto, desnudo (suelo, superficie, etc.). **7** mero, nada más que (con cantidades): *a bare five pounds = nada más que cinco libras.* || *v.t.* **8** descubrir, desnudar: *bare your arm = descúbrase el brazo.* || **9 to – one's head,** descubrirse la cabeza (normalmente como signo de respeto). **10 to – one's soul,** abrir el corazón (revelando detalles muy íntimos o similar). **11 to lay –, a)** desnudar completamente, exhibir. **b)** revelar, descubrir (algo importante o secreto). **12 the – bones,** los detalles indispensables, la información más indispensable. **13 the – facts/the barest details,** los hechos básicos, los detalles fundamentales. **14 the – minimum/the barest essentials,** lo mínimo, lo esencial. **15 with one's – hands,** sólo con las manos de uno, con las propias manos.
bareback | 'beəbæk | *adv./adj.* sin silla (montando a caballo).
barefaced | 'beəfeɪst | *adj.* (desp.) desvergonzado, descarado.
barefoot | 'beəfut | (también **barefooted**) *adj./adv.* descalzo, con los pies desnudos.

bareheaded | ˌbeə'hedɪd | *adj.* con la cabeza descubierta, sin sombrero, sin nada en la cabeza.
barely | 'beəlɪ | *adv.* apenas: *he could barely talk = apenas podía hablar.*
bareness | 'beənɪs | *s.i.* desnudez (de un paisaje o similar).
bargain | 'bɑːgɪn | *s.c.* **1** trato, pacto. **2** ganga. || *v.i.* **3 [to – (for/with)]** negociar, pactar. **4** regatear. || **5 to – for,** prever, anticipar: *I hadn't bargained for such hard opposition = no había previsto una oposición tan dura.* **6 to drive a hard –, regatear hasta lo indecible. 7 into the –,** además, encima de todo, por añadidura: *he was a teacher and a very good one into the bargain = era profesor y además muy bueno.* **8 to strike/make a —,** cerrar un trato.
bargaining | 'bɑːgɪnɪŋ | *s.i.* forcejeo (de una negociación).
barge | bɑːdʒ | *s.c.* **1** barcaza, gabarra. || *v.i.* (fam. y desp.) **2 [to – into]** darse de bruces contra, darse contra (una persona). **3 [to – (through/into)]** irrumpir; moverse intempestivamente. || **4 to – in/into,** interrumpir (una conversación). **5 to – one's way through,** abrirse camino por medio de, abrirse camino a empellones entre (gente). **6 I wouldn't touch something/someone with a – pole,** no tocaría algo/alguien ni de lejos.
bargee | bɑː'dʒiː | *s.c.* gabarrero, piloto de barcaza.
baritone | 'bærɪtəun | *s.c.* MUS. barítono.
barium | 'beərɪəm | *s.i.* MIN. bario.
bark | bɑːk | *v.i.* **1** ladrar. **2** (fig.) gritar, (una orden, un aviso, etc.). **3** sonar como un ladrido (armas de fuego, altavoces y similar). || *v.t.* **4** escupir (humo, llamas, etc.): *his old gun barked smoke after the first shot = su vieja carabina escupía humo después del primer disparo.* || *s.c.* **5** ladrido. **6** (fig.) sonido como un ladrido (de armas, aparatos de alta fidelidad, etc.). || *s.i.* **7** BOT. corteza (de un árbol). || **8 to – up the wrong tree,** (fam.) equivocarse de cabo a rabo. **9 someone's – is worse than his/her bite,** (fam.) perro ladrador poco mordedor.
barking | 'bɑːkɪŋ | *s.i.* ladridos.
barley | 'bɑːlɪ | *s.i.* **1** BOT. cebada. || **2 – water,** bebida de cebada, hordiate. **3 – wine,** vino de cebada (tipo de cerveza fuerte y de sabor dulce).
barley-sugar | 'bɑːlɪʃugər | *s.i.* azúcar cande, alfeñique.
barmaid | 'bɑːmeɪd | *s.c.* camarera (en un pub o similar).
barman | 'bɑːmən | [*pl.irreg.* **barmen**] *s.c.* camarero (en un pub o similar).
barmen | 'bɑːmən V. **barman.**
barmy | 'bɑːmɪ | *adj.* (fam. y brit.) chiflado, lelo.
barn | bɑːn | *s.c.* **1** granero, pajar. **2** (EE.UU.) establo, cuadra. **3** (EE.UU.) cochera (de autobuses, furgonetas de una empresa o similar). || **4 – dance,** baile popular rural (que se hace en un granero).
barnacle | 'bɑːnəkl | *s.c.* ZOOL. percebe.
barnstorming | 'bɑːnstɔːmɪŋ | *s.i.* (EE.UU.) **1** viaje de pueblo en pueblo con algún espectáculo. **2** POL. visita de pueblo en pueblo haciendo campaña.
barnyard | 'bɑːnjɑːd | *s.c.* corral, patio de granja.
barometer | bə'rmɪtər | *s.c.* **1** FIS. barómetro. **2** (fig.) indicador, barómetro (de una situación).
baron | 'bærən | *s.c.* **1** barón (título nobiliario). **2** (fig.) magnate, potentado, barón: *the press barons = los magnates de la prensa.* || **3 Baron,** barón (con un nombre).
baroness | 'bærənɪs | | ˌbærə'nes | *s.c.* **1** baronesa (título nobiliario). || **2 Baroness,** baronesa (con un nombre).
baronet | 'bærənɪt | *s.c.* baronet (título nobiliario en Gran Bretaña).
baronetcy | 'bærənɪtsɪ | *s.c.* rango de baronet.
baronial | bə'rəunɪəl | *adj.* baronial.
barony | 'bærənɪ | *s.c.* baronía.
baroque | bə'rk | (EE.UU.) | bə'rəuk | *adj.* **1** ART. barroco. **2** (fig. y desp.) barroco, recargado. || *s.i.* **3** ART. barroco (estilo artístico).
barque | bɑːk | *s.c.* (lit. y p.u.) barca, barco.
barrack | 'bærək | *v.t.* e *i.* abuchear, lanzar improperios.
barracking | 'bærəkɪŋ | *s.i.* abucheos, improperios.
barracks | 'bærəks | *s.pl.* **1** MIL. cuartel. **2** barracones.
barracuda | ˌbærə'kuːdə | *s.c.* ZOOL. barracuda.
barrage | 'bærɑːʒ | *s.c.* **1** MIL. andanada, descarga; cortina de fuego. **2** (fig.) andanada, descarga (de preguntas, quejas, críticas, etc.). **3** presa, barrera (de un río). || **4 – balloon.** MIL. globo de barrera.
barred | bɑːd | *adj.* enrejado, con rejas: *a barred window = una ventana enrejada.*
barrel | 'bærəl | *s.c.* **1** barril, tonel. **2** cañón (de un arma de fuego). **3** barril (medida para el petróleo de 159 litros). **4** MEC. cilindro, tambor. || **5 to have someone over a –,** (fam.) tener a alguien con el agua al cuello, tener a alguien bajo el poder de uno. **6 to scrape the –/to scrape the bottom of the –,** (fam.) utilizar los últimos recursos (en personas o cosas).
barrel-organ | 'bærəlɔːgən | *s.c.* MUS. organillo.
barren | 'bærən | *adj.* **1** estéril, yermo (terreno o planta); árido. **2** improductivo, inútil (discusión o similar). **3** (lit.) estéril (mujer sin hijos).
barricade | ˌbærɪ'keɪd | *s.c.* **1** barricada, obstáculo. || *v.t.* **2** bloquear, poner barricadas en, colocar obstáculos en. || *v.r.* **3** atrincherarse, hacerse fuerte.
barrier | 'bærɪər | *s.c.* **1** barrera, valla. **2** (fig.) barrera, impedimento, obstáculo: *the language barrier = el obstáculo del idioma.* **3 [– to]** obstáculo para, impedimento para: *a barrier to communication = un obstáculo para la comunicación.*
barring | 'bɑːrɪŋ | *prep.* con la excepción de, a no ser por, menos, salvo: *barring unexpected incidents, there will not be any more problems = salvo incidentes inesperados, no habrá más problemas.*
barrister | 'bærɪstər | *s.c.* (brit.) abogado (para tribunales superiores).
bar-room | 'bɑːruːm | *s.c.* (EE.UU.) bar.
barrow | 'bærəu | *s.c.* **1** carretilla (de mano). **2** carretón (para ventas ambulantes). **3** HIST. túmulo.
bartender | 'bɑːtendər | *s.c.* (EE.UU.) camarero.
barter | 'bɑːtər | *v.t.* e *i.* **1** intercambiar mercancías (sin mediar dinero), hacer trueques, cambalachear. || *s.i.* **2** trueque, cambalacheo, intercambio de mercancías.
basalt | 'bæsɔːlt | (EE.UU.) | 'beɪsɔːlt | | bə'sɔːlt | *s.i.* GEOL. basalto.
base | beɪs | *s.c.* **1 [the – of]** parte inferior, parte baja, base: *at the base of a mountain = en la parte inferior de una montaña.* **2** ARQ. basa. **3** QUIM. base. **4** GEOM. base. **5** DEP. base (béisbol). **6** POL. base: *power base = base de poder.* **7** MAT. base (de cálculo). **8** fondo (con pinturas): *I'd choose a blue base = yo elegiría un fondo azul.* **9** GAST. base, sustancia principal (a la que se pueden añadir diversos ingredientes). **10** base (en el trabajo): *my base is London although I spend most of my time in the North = mi base es Londres aunque paso la mayor parte del tiempo en el Norte.* **11** base, referencia (en cálculos, precios, etc.): *base price = precio de referencia.* **12 [– for]** fundamento de, apoyo para (sentido físico): *use this as a base for the big box = usa esto como base para la caja grande.* **13 [– for]** base de, fundamento de (sentido intangible): *the basis for his belief is his sad childhood = el fundamento de su creencia es su triste infancia.* || *s.c.* e *i.* **14** MIL. base. **15** DEP. base, campamento base (montañismo). || *v.t.* **16 [to – (on)]** basar, fundamentar: *he based his novel on his experiences abroad = basó su novela en sus experiencias en el extranjero.* || *v.r.* **17** basarse, estacionarse (en un sitio). || *adj.* **18** vil, ruin. || **19 -based, a)** con base en: *a Madrid-based firm = una empresa con base en Madrid.* **b)** basado en: *export-based economies = economías basadas en la exportación.* **20 – metal,** MET. metal base (no preciado como el oro, plata, etc.). **21 – rate,** FIN. tipo de interés básico. **22 to be based,** estar basado, tener la oficina central: *we are based in Boston = nuestra oficina central está en Boston.* **23 to get to first –,** (fam. y EE.UU.) salvar el primer obstáculo, dar el primer paso (en un proyecto, plan o similar). **24 off –,** (fam. y EE.UU.) despistado, equivocado; desmarcado: *I caught you a bit off base = te cogí un poco despistado.*
baseball | 'beɪsbɔːl | *s.i.* DEP. béisbol.
baseless | 'beɪslɪs | *adj.* sin base, sin fundamento, infundado.
baseline | 'beɪslaɪn | *s.c.* **1** DEP. línea de fondo, línea de saque (en tenis, badminton y algún otro deporte similar). **2** punto de referencia, referencia (en un cálculo imaginario dentro de una posible escala).

basement | 'beɪsmənt | *s.c.* 1 sótano. 2 ARQ. basamento.
bases | 'beɪsi:z | *pl.* de **basis.**
bash | bæʃ | *v.t.* 1 golpear, atizar, vapulear (con fuerza). 2 golpearse (una parte del cuerpo), darse con (un objeto). 3 (fig.) criticar, vapulear (especialmente grupos, no individuos). || *v.i.* 4 **[to – at]** golpear, atizar, vapulear (con fuerza). 5 **[to – into]** darse contra, darse un encontronazo con/contra (fuertemente). || *s.c.* 6 golpe, porrazo. || **7 to – on (with),** continuar, aguantar, ir tirando (con) (dificultosamente y sin entusiasmo). **8 to – up,** dar una paliza, aporrear, destrozar. **9 to have a – at/to give it a –,** (fam.) probar, llevar a cabo una tentativa, intentar: *tomorrow I'll have a bash at the machine = mañana probaré la máquina.*
bashful | 'bæʃfl | *adj.* tímido, vergonzoso.
bashfully | 'bæʃfəlɪ | *adv.* tímidamente, vergonzosamente.
bashfulness | 'bæʃflnɪs | *s.i.* timidez, cortedad, vergüenza.
bashing | 'bæʃɪŋ | *s.c.* e *i.* 1 paliza, aporreo. || **2 -bashing, a)** crítica: *party-bashing = crítica de los partidos.* **b)** uso enérgico: *bible-bashing = uso enérgico de la Biblia.*
basic | 'beɪsɪk | *adj.* 1 básico, fundamental, esencial. 2 **[– (to)]** vital, esencial, necesario. 3 básico, elemental (de nivel sencillo). 4 primitivo, sencillo, rudimentario: *the small village has basic facilities = el pueblecito tiene servicios rudimentarios.* 5 QUIM. de base, alcalino. 6 GEOL. básico. || **7 BASIC, (beginner's Allpurpose Symbolic Instruction Code)** INF. BASIC lenguaje informático **8 Basic English,** FILOL. inglés básico (método de comunicación en inglés con un vocabulario de 850 palabras). **9 – slag,** AGR. fertilizante fosfatado.
basically | 'beɪsɪklɪ | *adv.* 1 básicamente, fundamentalmente, en esencia, esencialmente. 2 (fam.) realmente, en el fondo (señalando la importancia de lo que se quiere expresar): *the revolution was, basically, violent = la revolución fue, en el fondo, violenta.*
basics | 'beɪsɪks | *s.pl.* 1 temas fundamentales, cosas esenciales, fundamentos. 2 **[the – of]** los rudimentos de, los puntos básicos de (una asignatura, trabajo, actividad, etc.). 3 **[the –]** la manutención imprescindible, la comida imprescindible, las cosas necesarias para el sustento.
basil | 'bæzl | *s.i.* BOT. albahaca.
basilica | bə'zɪlɪkə | *s.c.* ARQ. basílica.
basilisk | 'bæzɪlɪsk | *s.c.* 1 ZOOL. basilisco, lagarto americano. 2 basilisco (reptil mítico).
basin | 'beɪsn | *s.c.* 1 cuenco, tazón grande (para comida). 2 palangana, jofaina. 3 dique, dársena (para barcos). 4 lavabo. 5 GEOG. cuenca (de un río, lago o mar). 6 GEOL. depresión, hoya, hondón.
basinful | 'beɪsnful | *s.c.* cuenco, tazón, palangana (entendido como su contenido): *a few basinfuls of water = unos cuantos cuencos de agua.*
basis | 'beɪsɪs | *[pl.* **bases**] *s.c.* 1 **[– (for/of/on)]** fundamento, base: *the basis of society = el fundamento de la sociedad.* 2 punto de partida: *there is no basis for further negotiations = no existe punto de partida alguno para más negociaciones.* || **3 on a... –,** con un sistema...; a..., por...: *on a weekly basis = por semana... this is done on a compulsory basis = esto se hace con un sistema obligatorio.* **4 on the – of,** en base a, con base en.
bask | bɑ:sk | (EE.UU.) | bæsk | *v.i.* 1 **[to – in]** tomar (el sol), solearse; disfrutar del sol: *the whole village was basking in the sunshine = todo el pueblo estaba tomando el sol.* 2 **[to – in]** (fig.) complacerse en; disfrutar de (favores, prestigio, etc.).
basket | 'bɑ:skɪt | (EE.UU.) | 'bæskɪt | *s.c.* 1 cesto, canasta. 2 **[– (of)]** cesto, canasta (expresando su contenido). 3 **[the –]** DEP. la canasta. 4 **[– of]** (fig.) conjunto de, paquete de (medidas económicas o similar). || **5 – case,** (EE.UU.) caso para el manicomio, tipo loco. **6 to put all one's eggs in one –,** V. **egg.**
basketball | 'bɑ:skɪtbɔ:l | (EE.UU.) | 'bæskɪtbɔ:l | *s.i.* DEP. baloncesto.
basketful | 'bɑ:skɪtful | (EE.UU.) | 'bæskɪtful | *s.c.* canasta, cesta. V. **basket 2.**
basketry | 'bɑ:skɪtrɪ | (EE.UU.) | 'bæskɪtrɪ | V. **basketwork.**
basketweave | 'bɑ:skɪtwi:v | (EE.UU.) | 'bæskɪtwi:v | *s.i.* tejido de esterilla (patrón en el corte y confección).
basketwork | 'bɑ:skɪtwɔ:k | (EE.UU.) | 'bæskɪtwɔ:k | *s.i.* 1 cestería, cestos. 2 labor de cestería, estilo de cestería.
bas-relief | ˌbæsrɪ'li:f | | 'bɑ:rɪli:f | ARQ. *s.i.* 1 bajo relieve, estilo de bajo relieve. || *s.c.* 2 bajo relieve (un ejemplo concreto de esta técnica).
bass | bæs | *[pl.* **bass** o **basses**] *s.c.* ZOOL. róbalo, perca (pez).
bass | beɪs | MUS. *s.c.* 1 bajo (cantante). 2 bajo (guitarra o violón). **3 — baritone,** barítono bajo. || *s.sing.* 4 **[the –]** los bajos, los graves (en un aparato de música, altavoces, sintonizadores, etc.). || *adj.* 5 bajo, grave.
basset | 'bæsɪt | (también **basset-hound** | 'bæsɪthaund) *s.c.* ZOOL. perro basset.
bassinet | ˌbæsɪ'net | *s.c.* cuna de mimbre.
bassoon | bə'su:n | *s.c.* MUS. fagot.
bast | bæst | *s.i.* estera, esterilla (para hacer cuerdas, alfombrillas, etc.).
bastard | 'bɑ:stəd | (EE.UU.) | 'bæstəd | *s.c.* 1 bastardo, ilegítimo. 2 (desp.) hijo de puta, bastardo. 3 (fam.) briboncillo, granujilla. 4 (fam.) lata, engorro: *this problem is a bastard = este problema es un engorro.* || *adj.* 5 bastardo, ilegítimo.
bastardization | ˌbɑ:stədɪ'zeɪʃn | (también **bastardisation**) *s.i.* degeneración, degradación, envilecimiento (del idioma, costumbres, etc.).
bastardize | 'bɑ:stədaɪz | (EE.UU.) | 'bæstədaɪz | (también **bastardise**) *v.t.* degradar, degenerar (el idioma, las costumbres, etc.).
bastardy | 'bɑ:stədɪ | (EE.UU.) | 'bæstədɪ | *s.i.* DER. bastardía.
baste | beɪst | *v.t.* 1 GAST. lardear, pringar. || *v.t.* e *i.* 2 hilvanar (como parte de la costura).
bastinado | ˌbæstɪ'nɑ:dəu | | ˌbæstɪ'neɪdəu | *s.c.* 1 paliza (normalmente mediante un bastón en las plantas de los pies). || *v.t.* 2 golpear con bastón (normalmente en las plantas de los pies).
bastion | 'bæstɪən | *s.c.* 1 ARQ. baluarte. 2 MIL. fuerte (especialmente situado cerca del enemigo). 3 **[– (of)]** (fig.) bastión, baluarte: *they believe they are the bastion of freedom = ellos creen ser el baluarte de la libertad.*
bat | bæt | *s.c.* 1 ZOOL. murciélago. 2 DEP. bate (de béisbol o similar). || *v.i.* 3 DEP. batear, golpear con el bate. || **4 at a... bat,** (fam.) a... velocidad: *he walked at a terrific bat = él caminaba a gran velocidad.* **5 bats,** (fam.) como una chota. **6 blind as a –,** V. **blind. 7 to have bats in the/one's belfry,** (fam.) estar como una chota; tener pájaros en la cabeza. **8 like a – out of hell,** (fam.) como si le llevaran los demonios. **9 not to – an eyelid,** no pestañear, no inmutarse, no mostrar sorpresa. **10 off one's own –,** por propia iniciativa, sin que nadie se lo diga. **11 right off the –,** (fam.) sin demora alguna, al instante.
batch | bætʃ | *s.c.* 1 hornada (de pan, pasteles, etc.). 2 **[– (of)]** grupo, montón, serie, tanda (de cosas o personas iguales): *a batch of letters = un montón de cartas.* 3 INF. lote, conjunto, colección. || **4 – processing,** INF. procesamiento por lotes.
bated | 'beɪtɪd | **with – breath,** con la respiración contenida; ansiosamente.
bath | bɑ:θ | (EE.UU.) | bæθ | *s.c.* 1 baño, bañera. 2 baño, lavado completo (en un producto químico, aceite, etc.). || *s.sing.* 3 baño: *I love a bath when I'm tired = un baño cuando estoy cansado es algo que me encanta.* || *v.t.* 4 bañar (a un niño o enfermo). || *v.i.* 5 (brit.) darse un baño, bañarse (en la bañera). || **6 – chair,** silla de ruedas (especialmente la utilizada en balnearios). **7 baths,** (brit.) piscina cubierta. **8 to have/ take a –,** darse un baño, tomar un baño. **9 in the –,** en el baño, bañándose. **10 to run a –,** llenar el baño. **11 swimming —,** piscina cubierta.
bathe | beɪð | *v.i.* 1 **[to – (in)]** bañarse (en río, lago o mar). 2 (EE.UU.) bañarse (en la bañera). || *v.t.* 3 bañar, lavar (una herida). 4 **[to – *o.* (in/with)]** inundar, cubrir (de luz, brillo o similar): *they were bathed in sunlight = fueron inundados por la luz del sol.* 5 [normalmente pasiva] inundar (con un sentimiento o emoción): *bathed in love = inundado por el amor.* || *s.sing.* 6 baño, chapuzón. || **7 to be bathed in sweat,** estar bañado en sudor. **8 to go bathing,** irse a bañar (al río, lago o mar).
bather | 'beɪðər | *s.c.* bañista (persona que se baña).
bathing | 'beɪðɪŋ | *s.i.* 1 bañarse (actividad): *I love bathing = me encanta bañarme.* || **2 – beauty,** joven guapa en bañador (típico de concursos de belleza).

bathing-cap | 'beɪðɪŋkæp | *s.c.* gorro de baño.
bathing-costume | 'beɪðɪŋkstju:m | (EE.UU.) | 'beɪðɪŋkɑstu:m | *s.c.* (brit.) traje de baño (de mujer).
bathing-suit | 'beɪðɪŋsu:t | V. **bathing costume.**
bathing-trunks | 'beɪðɪŋtrʌŋks | *s.pl.* (brit.) bañador (de hombre).
bathmat | 'bɑ:θmæt | *s.c.* alfombrilla de baño.
bath-oil | 'bɑ:θɔɪl | *s.i.* aceite perfumado de baño.
bathos | 'beɪθɑs | *s.i.* LIT. trivialidad, anticlímax forzado (en una novela o similar).
bathrobe | 'bɑ:θrəʊb | *s.c.* **1** albornoz. **2** (EE.UU.) bata.
bathroom | 'bɑ:θru:m | *s.c.* **1** baño, cuarto de baño. **2** (EE.UU.) servicio: *can I go to the bathroom? = ¿puedo ir al servicio?* **3** (euf.) servicio, excusado. OBS. En Inglaterra, normalmente el baño contiene un lavabo y la bañera; el retrete suele estar aparte.
bath-salts | 'bɑ:θsɔ:lts | *s.pl.* sales de baño.
bath-towel | 'bɑ:θtaʊəl | *s.c.* toalla de baño.
bathtub | 'bɑ:θtʌb | *s.c.* (p.u.) bañera.
bathwater | 'bɑ:θwɔ:tər | *s.sing.* **1** agua (con la que uno llena el baño). || **2 to throw out the baby with the —,** V. **baby.**
bathysphere | 'bæθɪsfɪər | *s.c.* MAR. batisfera (esfera para observar la vida marítima a grandes profundidades).
batik | bə'tɪk | | 'bætɪk | *s.i.* **1** batik, método de batik (para teñir en colores). || *s.c.* **2** batik, pieza de tejido batik.
batiste | bæ'ti:st | | bə'ti:st | *s.i.* batista (un tipo de tejido).
batman | 'bætmən | [*pl.* **batmen**] *s.c.* (brit.) MIL. ordenanza, asistente.
batmen | 'bætmən | *pl.* de **batman.**
baton | 'bætn | | 'bætən | (EE.UU.) | bə'tɑn | *s.c.* **1** MUS. batuta. **2** DEP. testigo, posta (para relevos). **3** porra (de policía). **4** MIL. vara, bastón de mando. || **5 – charge,** carga policial con porras.
batsman | 'bætsmən | [*pl.* **batsmen**] *s.c.* DEP. bateador (en críquet).
batsmen | 'bætsmən | *pl.* de **batsman.**
battalion | bə'tælɪən | *s.c.* MIL. batallón.
batten | 'bætn | *s.c.* **1** tabla, listón. || **2 to – down,** clavar tablas en, asegurar con tablas (una ventana ante una tormenta o similar). **3 to – down the hatches,** MAR. asegurar las escotillas. **4 to – on/upon,** vivir a costa de, chupar de.
batter | 'bætər | *v.t.* **1** maltratar, causar malos tratos (especialmente a niños y mujeres, por parte de padres y maridos). **2** golpear, aporrear (un objeto repetidamente). **3** batir, golpear (cuando es causado por la lluvia o el mar). || *s.c.* **4** DEP. bateador (en béisbol). || *v.i.* **5 [to – (at/on)]** golpear, aporrear (sobre un objeto repetidamente). || *s.i.* **6** GAST. pasta (para rebozar). || **7 to – down,** derribar, echar abajo (a base de muchos golpes).
battered | 'bætəd | *adj.* **1** estropeado, destrozado; abollado (vehículos). **2** objeto de malos tratos, maltratado. V. **batter 1.**
battering | 'bætərɪŋ | *s.c.* **1** paliza, apaleamiento. **2** (fig.) paliza, crítica demoledora. || **3 – ram,** ariete (para derribar un gran portón).
battery | 'bætərɪ | *s.c.* **1** batería, pila (de linterna, coche, etc.). **2 [– (of)]** MIL. batería. **3 [– of]** serie de, conjunto de (cosas, personas, etc.): *a battery of tests = un conjunto de pruebas.* || *adj.* **4** en batería (posicionalmente). || **5 – farm,** AGR. granja factoría, granja con métodos sistemáticos de producción. **6 – farming,** AGR. sistema de gran factoría. **7 to recharge one's batteries,** (fam.) recargar las baterías de uno, renovar las fuerzas de uno.
battle | 'bætl | *s.c.* e *i.* **1** batalla, combate. **2 [– (against/between/for)]** (fig.) batalla, lucha, conflicto. || *v.i.* **3** batallar, combatir. || **4 – of wits,** guerra de ingenio, guerra de inteligencia. **5 to do – with,** pelear contra, luchar con, combatir contra. **6 to fight a losing –,** participar en una batalla perdida, librar un combate perdido. **7 to give –,** (p.u.) dar batalla. **8 half the –,** la mitad del problema resuelto, la mitad del tema solucionado: *get her to go to a doctor, that's half the battle = consigue que ella vaya al médico, esa es la mitad del problema resuelto.* **9 in –,** MIL. en combate: *he was killed in battle = murió en combate.*
battle-axe | 'bætlæks | *s.c.* **1** hacha de guerra. **2** (fam. y desp.) mujer dominante, arpía.
battle-cruiser | 'bætlkru:zər | *s.c.* MAR. crucero de combate.
battle-cry | 'bætlkraɪ | *s.c.* **1** grito de guerra. **2** (fig.) lema atrayente, eslogan.
battledress | 'bætldres | *s.i.* MIL. traje de campaña.
battlefield | 'bætlfi:ld | *s.c.* campo de batalla.
battleground | 'bætlgraʊnd | *s.c.* **1** campo de batalla. **2** (fig.) punto contencioso, tema de discrepancia: *the big bang theory is still a battleground = la teoría del gran estallido es un tema de discrepancia todavía.*
battlements | 'bætlmənts | *s.pl.* almenas.
battleship | 'bætlʃɪp | *s.c.* barco de guerra.
batty | 'bætɪ | *adj.* (fam.) como una regadera.
bauble | 'bɔ:bl | *s.c.* (desp.) bisutería.
baulk | bɔ:k | V. **balk.**
bauxite | 'bɔ:ksaɪt | *s.i.* MIN. bauxita.
bawdily | 'bɔ:dɪlɪ | *adv.* obscenamente, indecentemente.
bawdiness | 'bɔ:dɪnɪs | *s.i.* obscenidad, indecencia.
bawdy | 'bɔ:dɪ | *adj.* obsceno, indecente, verde.
bawl | bɔ:l | *v.i.* **1** berrear, llorar a gritos. || *v.t.* e *i.* **2** decir a gritos, berrear. || **3 to – out, a)** pegar gritos, gritar desaforadamente. **b)** (fam.) regañar, cantar las cuarenta.
bay | beɪ | *s.c.* **1** GEOG. bahía, ensenada, rada. **2** ZOOL. bayo, caballo bayo. **3** BOT. laurel. **4** compartimento, zona: *bomb bay = compartimento de bombas.* **5** esquina, mirador (dentro de una habitación). || *v.i.* **6** ladrar, aullar (típico de perros y lobos). || **7 at –,** acorralado, rodeado. **8 to – at the moon,** ladrar a la luna. **9 – window,** ARQ. ventana saliente (algo parecido al mirador). **10 to bring to –,** acorralar, rodear. **11 to keep/hold at –,** mantener a raya.
bay-leaf | 'beɪli:f | [*pl.* **bay-leaves**] *s.c.* hoja de laurel.
bay-leaves | 'beɪli:vz | *pl.* de **bay-leaf.**
bayonet | 'beɪənɪt | *s.c.* **1** bayoneta. || *v.t.* **2** clavar la bayoneta.
bay-tree | 'beɪtri: | *s.c.* BOT. árbol de laurel.
bayou | 'baɪu: | *s.c.* GEOG. brazo pantanoso de un río, típico de ciertas zonas del sur de los Estados Unidos.
bazaar | bə'zɑ:r | *s.c.* **1** bazar (zona de tiendas). **2** tómbola con fines caritativos.
bazooka | bə'zu:kə | *s.c.* MIL. bazoka, lanzacohetes portátil.
BBC | ˌbi:bi:'si: | *s.sing.* **1 [the –]** la BBC (siglas de **British Broadcasting Corporation**). || **2 on –,** en la BBC, por la BBC.
B.C. | ˌbi:'si: | *s.i.* HIST. antes de Cristo.
be | bɪ | (forma fuerte | bi:) *v.* [*pret.* **was** y **were,** *p.p.* **been**] *i.* **1** ser: *I'm John Smith = soy John Smith.* **2 [to – *adj./adv.*]** ser, estar: *she's very happy = ella es muy feliz.* **3 [to – profesión]** ser, trabajar de: *my brother is a teacher = mi hermano es profesor.* **4** hacer (fenómenos atmosféricos): *it's windy and cold = hace viento y frío.* **5** ser (para expresar la hora): *it is 12 o'clock = son las 12 en punto.* **6** estar (con un lugar): *I'm in the bedroom = estoy en el dormitorio.* **7** FIL. existir: *I think, therefore I am = pienso, luego existo.* **8 [to – of]** ser de, estar hecho de: *there were of real cotton = estaban hechos de algodón auténtico.* **9 [there –]** haber: *there were many difficulties = hubo muchas dificultades.* **10** ser, costar: *the meal was 20 pounds = la comida costó 20 libras.* **11** tener (con medidas de altura, densidad, distancia, edad, etc.): *I am 20 = tengo 20 años.* **12** ser, comportarse: *don't be stupid = no seas estúpido.* || **13 as... as can/could –,** lo más... del mundo, tan... como uno se pueda imaginar: *I feel as contented as can be = me siento tan satisfecho como uno se pueda imaginar.* **14 to – fair/frank/etc.,** siendo justos/sinceros, a fuer de justos/sinceros, etc. **15 to – in for,** (fam.) ir a por, andar detrás de: *most of them are in for money = la mayor parte de ellos andan detrás del dinero.* **16 to – on to,** (fam.) **a)** ir detrás de; estar cerca de la solución de: *I think Jim is on to something = me parece que Jim va detrás de algo.* **b)** sospechar de, tener sospechas sobre: *remember that I am on to you = recuerda que sospecho de ti.*
OBS. Este verbo tiene las siguientes importantes funciones auxiliares en el inglés: **17 [to – *inf.*]** indica los siguientes matices: **a)** obligación de llevar a cabo algo previsto: *I am to see the doctor tomorrow = tengo que ver al médico mañana.* **b)** tiene la idea de futuro dentro del pasado: *marrying her was to be*

his biggest mistake = el casarse con ella sería su mayor equivocación. **18** sirve de auxiliar de todos los tiempos de la forma continua, con la traducción de "estar": *I was crossing the street when I saw her = estaba cruzando la calle cuando la vi.* **19** también sirve de auxiliar para la voz pasiva, con la traducción de "ser": *I was deceived = fui engañado.* **20** como prefijo indica que uno está cubierto de algo: *bejewelled = enjoyado.*

beach | biːtʃ | *s.c.* **1** playa. || *v.t.* e *i.* **2** varar(se), poner(se) en seco, arrastrar(se) dentro de una playa. || **3 – ball,** balón de playa. **4 – buggy,** coche de carreras en playas.

beachcomber | ˈbiːtʃkəumər | *s.c.* raquero; vagabundo de playa.

beachhead | ˈbiːtʃhed | *s.c.* MIL. cabeza de puente.

beachwear | ˈbiːtʃweər | *s.i.* ropa de playa, vestimenta de playa.

beacon | ˈbiːkən | *s.c.* **1** luz de aviso, fanal, baliza de señalización. **2** faro. **3** torre de aviso, fuego de aviso (especialmente sobre un altozano para avisar de la llegada del enemigo). || **4 Belisha –,** luz ámbar intermitente (junto a los pasos cebra).

bead | biːd | *s.c.* **1** cuenta, abalorio, bolita (en un collar, rosario o similar). **2** burbuja, gota (de sudor). || **3 beads, a)** REL. rosario. **b)** collares. **4 to draw a – on,** apuntar cuidadosamente a.

beaded | ˈbiːdɪd | *adj.* **1 [– (with)]** adornado (con cosas como cuentas, bolitas o similar). **2 [– (with)]** lleno de gotas (de sudor).

beading | ˈbiːdɪŋ | *s.c.* e *i.* ARQ. moldura, reborde.

beadle | ˈbiːdl | *s.c.* (brit.) bedel (en universidad); alguacil (en tribunales).

beady | ˈbiːdɪ | *adj.* pequeños, diminutos (ojos).

beagle | ˈbiːgl | *s.c.* pachón, sabueso pequeño.

beagling | ˈbiːglɪŋ | *s.i.* caza con sabuesos.

beak | biːk | *s.c.* **1** pico (de pájaro). **2** (fig. y fam.) narizota. **3 [the –]** (p.u., brit. y fam.) el jefazo, el jerifalte (especialmente un juez o director de escuela).

beaked | biːkt | *adj.* con la nariz como un pico.

beaker | ˈbiːkər | *s.c.* **1** jarra (con pico). **2** QUIM. cubeta, vaso de laboratorio.

be-all and end-ball | ˌbɪɔːlənd'endɔːl | *s.sing.* **[the –]** el único objeto, el solo objetivo.

beam | biːm | *s.c.* **1** rayo (de sol, luz, etc.). **2** sonrisa, sonrisa amplia (de satisfacción, felicidad, etc.). **3** ELEC. rayo, haz (de partículas eléctricas). **4** ARQ. viga, travesaño. || *s.sing.* **5 [the –]** DEP. la barra fija. || *v.i.* **6 [to – (at)]** sonreír, sonreír ampliamente. **7** irradiar, emitir haces de luz. || *v.t.* **8** RAD. emitir, dirigir (la emisión). **9** expresar mediante una sonrisa (la buena disposición, el agradecimiento, etc.). || **10 broad in the –,** ancha de caderas. **11 off –/off the –,** (fam.) despistado, equivocado; descaminado. **12 on the –,** (fam.) en la pista correcta, por buen camino.

beam-ends | biːm'endz | **on one's –, a)** MAR. escorado (un barco). **b)** (fam.) sin un duro.

bean | biːn | *s.c.* **1** (normalmente *pl.*) judía, frijol, haba. **2** grano (de café o similar). || **3 full of beans,** (fam.) lleno de vida, lleno de energía: *the baby is full of beans again after his illness = el bebé está lleno de energía otra vez después de su enfermedad.* **4 not to be worth a –,** (fam.) no valer un higo, no valer una mísera peseta. **5 not to have a –,** (fam.) no tener ni una perra, no tener un duro. **6 to spill the beans,** (fam.) revelar el secreto involuntariamente; contar el secreto.

beanfeast | ˈbiːnfiːst | (también **beano**) *s.c.* (brit., fam. y p.u.) fiesta por todo lo alto.

beano | ˈbiːnəu | V. **beanfeast.**

beanpole | ˈbiːnpəul | *s.c. (fam.)* larguirucho.

beanshoot | ˈbiːnʃuːt | V. **beansprout.**

beansprout | ˈbiːnspraut | (también **beanshoot**) *s.c.* (generalmente *pl.*) GAST. brote tierno de soja (plato típico de la cocina china).

bear | beər | *v.* [*pret.* **bore,** *p.p.* **borne**] *t.* **1** llevar, portar (una señal, una etiqueta, etc.). **2** aguantar, soportar (un peso físico). **3** dar a luz, dar (a un marido hijos): *she bore him a beautiful daughter = ella le dio una hija preciosa.* **4** (form.) transportar, acarrear, llevar. **5** producir, dar (fruto tangible): *this tree bears fruit in spring = este árbol da fruta en la primavera.* **6** aguantar, soportar (una situación). **7** (form.) llevar, traer (algo a alguien). **8** (form. y lit.) llevar, empujar, traer, transportar (un objeto por el viento, el aire o el mar): *the wind bore the sound of steps = el viento llevó el sonido de pasos.* **9** (form.) tener, llevar, ostentar (un título, nombre o similar). **10** aguantar, permitir (examen o inspección cuidadosas): *the new project doesn't bear close examination = el nuevo proyecto no resiste un examen atento.* **11 [to – (of)]** llevar, tener, poseer: *the murder bore all the marks of the terrorists = el asesinato tenía todas las características de los terroristas.* **12** tener, soportar (la responsabilidad de algo). **13** tener (parecido), guardar (relación): *the lecture bore no relation to the interests of the audience = la conferencia no guardaba relación con los intereses de los oyentes.* **14** (lit.) abrigar, profesar, guardar (sentimientos). **15** (lit.) llevar, mantener (una parte del cuerpo de una manera u otra): *he bears his head low, always brooding = mantiene la cabeza gacha, siempre meditando.* || *i.* **16** escorarse, dirigirse suavemente (a derecha o izquierda). || *r.* **17** (lit.) conducirse, tener una postura corporal: *she bears herself beautifully = tiene un porte bellísimo.* || *s.c.* **18** oso. **19** FIN. tendencia a la baja, bajista (en la bolsa): *we'll have a bear market for years = tendremos un mercado bajista durante años.* || **20 to – a grudge,** guardar rencor. **21 to – comparison,** V. **comparison. 22 to – down (on), a)** aproximarse amenazadoramente (sobre), echarse encima amenazadoramente (sobre). **b)** apoyarse fuertemente (sobre), cargar el peso fuertemente (sobre). **23 to – on/upon,** (form.) afectar, tener relación con, atañer (como pura conexión): *your difficult situation doesn't bear on his new job at all = tu situación difícil no tiene relación en absoluto con su nuevo empleo.* **24 to – out,** confirmar, probar, corroborar, sostener: *the facts bear out my theory = los hechos confirman mi teoría.* **25 to – something in mind,** V. **mind. 26 to – the brunt of,** V. **brunt. 27 to – up, a)** sostenerse, tenerse en pie (una idea, teoría, resultado concreto, etc.). **b)** poner buena cara (a las dificultades), aguantar sonriendo. **28 to – with,** soportar pacientemente, aguantar con benignidad: *bear with me, I am too fired to explain it coherently = sopórtame pacientemente, estoy demasiado cansado como para explicarlo con coherencia.* **29 to – witnes,** V. **witness. 30 to bring pressure/influence to –,** aplicar presión/influencias (para conseguir los fines que se quieren). **31 can't/couldn't –,** no poder soportar, aguantar (algo o alguien). **32 to grin and – it,** V. **grin. 33 like a – with a sore head,** (fam.) irritable, de mal carácter.

bearable | ˈbeərəbl | *adj.* tolerable, soportable, aguantable.

beard | bɪəd | *s.c.* **1** barba. || **2 a goat's –,** una barba de chivo, una perilla de chivo. || *v.t.* **3** desafiar, retar. **4 to – the lion in his den,** entrar en la boca del lobo, meterse en la boca del lobo (para enfrentarse a él o concertar un acuerdo con él).

bearded | ˈbɪədɪd | *adj.* con barba, barbado.

beardless | ˈbɪədlɪs | *adj.* barbilampiño, imberbe.

bearer | ˈbeərər | *s.c.* **1** portador (de un objeto). **2** FIN. portador (de un cheque o documento). **3** (arc.) criado, mozo (en la India y otras colonias). **4** portador, poseedor (de un título o similar).

bear-hug | ˈbeəhʌg | *s.c.* abrazo fuerte, abrazo de oso.

bearing | ˈbeərɪŋ | *s.sing.* **1** porte, aspecto, presencia: *her bearing was impressive = su porte era impresionante.* || *s.c.* **2** posición, situación, orientación (geográfica). **3** (generalmente *pl.*) MEC. cojinete, soporte, asiento. || *s.i.* **4 [– (on)]** relación, conexión: *what you're saying has no bearing on the matter = lo que estás diciendo no tiene conexión con el asunto.* || **5 –bearing,** portador (en compuestos con sustantivos): *nitrogen-bearing = portador de nitrógeno.* **6 bearings,** aspectos, características (de una situación). **7 beyond (all) –/past all –,** absolutamente inaguantable, que no se puede seguir aguantando. **8 to get/find/take one's bearings,** encontrar el rumbo de uno, dar con la posición exacta de uno, lograr saber la situación de uno, orientarse. **9 to lose one's bearings,** perder el rumbo, desorientarse.

bearish | ˈbeərɪʃ | *adj.* **1** hosco, malhumorado, rudo, áspero. **2** FIN. bajista, de tendencia a la baja (en la Bolsa).

bearksin | 'beəskɪn | *s.c.* **1** piel de oso (como adorno o alfombra). **2** gorro de plumero, morrión (típicos de soldados vestidos a la antigua usanza en el Reino Unido).

beast | biːst | *s.c.* **1** (lit.) bestia, animal salvaje. **2** (fig. y fam.) bruto, animal, bestia (de una persona). **3** (lit.) hombre bruto, hombre bestial (especialmente en el aspecto sexual). || *s.sing.* **4 [the – in]** la bestia que hay en, lo peor que hay en (la naturaleza humana): *the beast in me = la bestia que hay en mí.* **5** (fam.) engorro: *fixing the toilet is a beast of a job = reparar el retrete es un trabajo lleno de engorro.* || **6 – of burden,** bestia de carga (burro, buey, etc.). **7 – of prey,** animal de rapiña, predador.

beastly | 'biːstlɪ | (fam.) *adj.* **1** desagradable, horrible, asqueroso. **2** deleznable, detestable (una persona). || *adv.* **3** (brit.) horriblemente, terriblemente (como enfático de algo negativo).

beat | biːt | *v.* [*pret.* **beat,** *p.p.* **beaten**] *t.* **1** golpear repetidamente, dar una paliza, aporrear sin cesar, azotar ininterrumpidamente. **2** DEP. ganar, vencer, derrotar. **3** GAST. batir. **4** MUS. tocar, golpear (un instrumento de percusión). **5** adelantarse a (un acontecimiento en el tiempo): *we must beat the traffic today and leave early for Paris = debemos adelantarnos al tráfico hoy y salir temprano para París.* **6** (fam.) ser mejor que, ganar (en calidad u otra característica): *reading beats any other hobby I can think of = la lectura es mejor que cualquier otro entretenimiento que se me pueda ocurrir.* **7 [to – + *o.* + (through)]** abrirse (paso o camino). **8** batir (para la caza). **9** batir, agitar (alas). **10** ganar, vencer (en una competición o a un sistema de organización): *we have got to beat the system = tenemos que ganar al sistema.* **11** sobrepasar (una marca anterior), batir (un récord). **12 [to – + *o.* + (for)]** ganar (a alguien en una virtud o a algo en una característica positiva): *you can't beat the Spaniards for generosity = no se puede ganar a los españoles en generosidad.* || *i.* **13** agitarse, moverse (alas). **14** batir (en la caza). **15** latir (el corazón). **16 [to – (against/at/on)]** golpear, dar: *the rain was beating on the window-pane = la lluvia golpeaba en el cristal de la ventana.* || *s.c.* **17** latido (del corazón). **18** movimiento (de las alas), aleteo. **19** MUS. golpe de compás, tiempo de compás. **20** ronda (de un policía o similar). || *s.sing.* **21** MUS. ritmo: *keep to the beat of this song = mantén el ritmo de esta canción.* **22** golpeteo, martilleo (de un objeto contra otro o algo de ese estilo). **23 [– (of)]** MUS. golpe, redoble (de tambor). || *adj.* **24** (fam.) para el arrastre, exhausto, tirado. **25** rebelde, beat (típico de la década de los 50 y 60): *the beat generation = la generación rebelde.* || **26 a rod/stick to – someone with,** un argumento irrefutable con el que derrotar a alguien. **27 to – about the bush,** V. **bush. 28 to – a retreat,** V. **retreat. 29 to – down, a)** estar achicharrado, achicharrar (el sol): *the sun was beating down at midday = el sol achicharraba al mediodía.* **b)** caer a cántaros, caer como un diluvio (lluvia). **c)** hacer bajar (el precio de algo): *he wanted 1.000 but I beat him down to 500 = él quería 1.000 pero le hice bajar a 500.* **30 – it,** (fam.) lárgate, vete por ahí, márchate, desaparece. **31 to – out, a)** extinguir, apagar (un fuego a base de aporrearlo con mantas o algo parecido). **b)** MUS. aporrear, redoblar (tambores con gran estruendo). **32 to – one's breast,** darse golpes de pecho (como muestra de arrepentimiento). **33 to – someone at his own game,** ganar a alguien en su propio juego, vencer a alguien en su propio campo. **34 to – someone black and blue,** moler a golpes, dar una paliza solemne. **35 to – someone hollow,** dar a alguien una tunda, vencer a alguien facilísimamente. **36 to – someone to it,** ganar por la mano a alguien, llegar antes que alguien (a alguna actividad). **37 to – the hell/shit/etc. out of somebody,** (fam. y vulg.) dar una paliza de muerte a alguien, destrozar a alguien de una paliza. **38 to – the rap,** (EE.UU. y vulg.) quedar absuelto, librarse de una buena. **39 to – time,** llevar el ritmo. **40 to – to death,** matar a golpes. **41 to – up,** dar una paliza, moler a golpes, atizar una buena tunda. **42 can you – that/it?,** (fam.) ¡a que es el mayor cara dura? ¡a que no puedes imaginarte mayor cara? (expresando sorpresa) **43 if you can't – them, join them,** si no puedes vencerlos, únete a ellos. **44 it beats me/what beats me is,** (fam.) me deja con la boca abierta/ lo verdaderamente alucinante es. **45 on the –,** de ronda (especialmente la policía). **46 out/off one's –,** (fam.) fuera de lo regular, desconocido, fuera de lo acostumbrado. **47 two hearts that – as one,** V. **heart.**

beaten | 'biːtn | *p.p.* **1** de **beat.** || *adj.* **2** MET. batido, amartillado (una pieza metálica). || **3 off the – track,** V. **track.**

beaten-up | 'biːtnʌp | *adj.* medio destrozado, abollado (vehículo), en condiciones bastante malas (cualquier objeto).

beater | 'biːtər | *s.c.* **1** batidor (en la caza). **2** batidora (en la cocina). || **3 -beater,** para batir, de batir, batidora: *an egg-beater.*

beatific | bɪə'tɪfɪk | *adj.* (lit.) beatífico, felicísimo.

beatifically | bɪə'tɪfɪklɪ | *adv.* (lit.) beatíficamente, felicísimamente.

beatification | bɪˌætɪfɪk'eɪʃn | *s.i.* REL. beatificación.

beatify | bɪ'ætɪfaɪ | *v.t.* REL. beatificar.

beating | 'biːtɪŋ | *s.c.* **1** paliza, zurra, tunda. || *s.sing.* **2** derrota (normalmente deportiva). || **3 – up,** paliza fuerte, zurra de espanto. **4 to take a –,** sufrir una clara derrota, salir derrotado. **5 to take some –,** (fam.) ser imposible de superarlo, ser muy difícil de mejorar: *his latest novel will take some beating = su última novela será muy difícil de mejorar.*

beatitude | bɪ'ætɪtjuːd | (EE.UU.) | bɪ'ætɪtuːd | *s.i.* **1** (form.) bienaventuranza, beatitud. || **2 the Beatitudes,** REL. las Bienaventuranzas.

beatnik | 'biːtnɪk | *s.c.* (p.u.) rebelde, joven rebelde, beatnik (persona inconformista de los años 50 y 60).

beat-up | ˌbiːt'ʌp | *adj.* (fam.) escacharrado, en mala condición, semidestrozado (cualquier objeto).

beau | bəu | [*pl.* **beaus** o **beaux**] *s.c.* **1** (p.u.) admirador, enamorado, pretendiente. || **2 – geste,** gesto noble. **3 – monde,** gran mundo, mundo de la elegancia.

beaut | bjuːt | *s.c.* (fam.) buenísimo, insuperable, magnífico, genial (cualquier objeto o acción): *that goal was a beaut = ese gol fue magnífico.*

beauteous | 'bjuːtɪəs | *adj.* (lit.) bello, hermoso.

beautician | bjuː'tɪʃn | *s.c.* esteticien, experta en tratamientos de belleza.

beautification | ˌbjuːtɪfɪ'keɪʃn | *s.i.* embellecimiento.

beautiful | 'bjuːtɪfl | *adj.* **1** hermoso, bello, atractivo, precioso (ante el sentido de la vista). **2** exquisito, bueno, precioso (en muchísimos contextos, como la comida, las artes, la vida, etc.): *that was a beautiful meal = fue una comida exquisita.* **3** magnífico, insuperable, excelente (cualquier acción, como el deporte, la música, etc.): *she is a beautiful swimmer = ella es una excelente nadadora.* **4** maravilloso, único (experiencia vital): *living with you for so many years has been a beautiful experience = vivir contigo tantos años ha sido una experiencia única.*

beautifully | 'bjuːtɪfəlɪ | *adv.* **1** hermosamente, bellamente, atractivamente, preciosamente. **2** exquisitamente, bien. **3** magníficamente, insuperablemente, excelentemente.

beautify | 'bjuːtɪfaɪ | *v.t.* embellecer, mejorar el aspecto de.

beauty | 'bjuːtɪ | *s.i.* **1** belleza, beldad, hermosura (cualidad). || *s.c.* **2** mujer bella, belleza, de gran belleza, beldad. **3** (fig. y fam.) maravilla (objeto): *my car is a beauty = mi coche es una maravilla.* **4** (generalmente *pl.*) maravilla, belleza (de algo): *the beauties of nature = la belleza de la naturaleza.* || *adj.* **5** de belleza, estética: *beauty creams = cremas de belleza.* || **6 – contest,** concurso de belleza. **7 – parlour,** salón de belleza. **8 – queen,** reina de un concurso de belleza. **9 – salon,** salón de belleza. **10 – sleep,** (hum.) primer sueño (que se dice que ayuda a mantener la juventud). **11 – spot, a)** lunar postizo (especialmente usado en siglos anteriores). **b)** lugar de gran belleza natural. **12 the – (of),** el atractivo (de), lo mejor (de): *the beauty of the whole project is that it seeks to improve the workers' lives = el atractivo de todo el proyecto es que busca mejorar la vida de los obreros.*

beaux | bəuz | V. **beau.**

beaver | 'biːvər | *s.c.* **1** ZOOL. castor. || *s.i.* **2** castor (la piel). || **3 to – away,** (brit. y fam.) trabajar sin parar, estar ocupado al máximo. **4 eager –,** (fam.) hormiguita (trabajadora), tipo trabajador, sujeto muy trabajador.

bebop | 'biːbɒp | [también **bop**] *s.i.* MUS. (tipo de música de jazz).

becalmed | bɪ'kɑːmd | *adj.* MAR. estático, inmóvil (un barco, por falta de viento).

became | bɪ'keɪm | *pret.* de **become.**
because | bɪ'kɑz | (EE.UU.) | bɪ'kɔːz | *conj.* **1** porque, como, ya que: *I drove him home because he couldn't walk = le llevé a casa en mi coche porque él no podía caminar.* || **2 – of,** a causa de, por: *because of his ignorance = a causa de su ignorancia.* **3 just –,** (fam.) sólo por, únicamente por: *just because you spent ten years abroad you are not a genius = sólo por haber pasado diez años en el extranjero no eres un genio.*
OBS. esta palabra suele ser la contestación a la pregunta **why,** manteniendo el significado **1** de arriba: *why did you go? because I wanted to = ¿por qué te fuiste? porque quise.*
beck | bek | *s.c.* **1** arroyo, riachuelo (en el dialecto del norte de Inglaterra). || **2 at someone's – and call,** estar a la entera y total disposición de alguien, estar al servicio en cuerpo y alma de alguien.
beckon | 'bekən | *v.t.* **1 [to – +** *o.* **(+** *inf./prep.***)]** hacer señas, llamar por señas: *he beckoned them to follow = les hizo señas de que le siguieran; he beckoned me out of the house = me hizo señas para que saliera de la casa.* || *v.i.* **2 [to – (to)]** hacer señas, llamar por señas. **3 [to – (to)]** (fig.) atraer, llamar poderosamente, atraer con fuerza: *New York beckoned to us = Nueva York nos atraía con fuerza.*
become | bɪ'kʌm | *v.* [*pret.* **became,** *p.p.* **became**] *i.* **1** llegar a ser; convertirse en, hacerse: *what do you want to become when you're older? = ¿qué quieres (llegar a) ser cuando te hagas mayor?; the situation became awkward = la situación se hizo embarazosa.* || *t.* **2** (form.) convenir, sentar bien, caer bien: *mourning becomes Electra = el luto le sienta bien a Electra.* || **3 what has/will – of,** qué ha sido/será de, qué ha pasado/pasará con: *I wonder what has become of old Jimmy = me pregunto qué ha sido del viejo Jimmy.*
OBS. Este verbo tiene un uso muy extendido en conexión con adjetivos y adverbios, indicando cambio de estado, apariencia, tiempo atmosférico, etc., con la traducción como verbalización del adjetivo o adverbio o hacerse, convertirse, ponerse: *the day is becoming colder = el día se está poniendo más frío; she became sad = ella se entristeció.*
becoming | bɪ'kʌmɪŋ | *adj.* (form.) **1** decoroso, adecuado, que sienta bien (comportamiento o lenguaje). **2** precioso, atractivo, favorecedor (ropa, estilo de peinado, etc.).
becomingly | bɪ'kʌmɪŋlɪ | *adv.* (form.) **1** decorosamente, adecuadamente (en el comportamiento o lenguaje). **2** preciosamente, atractivamente, favorecedoramente (de ropa, estilo de peinado, etc.).
becquerel | 'bekərel | *s.c.* FIS. (unidad de medida de la radioactividad).
bed | bed | *s.c.* **1** cama, lecho. **2** (fig.) cama, sitio (en un hospital, residencia, etc.). **3** GEOL. lecho, cauce (de un río, lago, etc.). **4** GEOL. estrado, capa: *a bed of hard rock = una capa de roca dura.* **5** base (de una construcción), firme (de carretera). **6** cuadro, macizo (de flores, plantas, etc.). || *v.t.* **7** (fam.) llevar a la cama (para tener contacto sexual). || **8 a – of roses,** V. **rose. 9 – and board,** cama y comida, techo y sustento. **10 – and breakfast,** cama y desayuno, habitación y desayuno. **11 to – down, a)** meter en la cama, acostar (a niños, por ejemplo). **b)** acomodarse a pasar la noche (normalmente en un sitio transitorio poco cómodo). **c)** asentarse, quedarse fijo (parte de algún objeto). **12 to – out,** AGR. pasar del semillero a la tierra, trasladar del semillero a la tierra natural, plantar en tierra natural (procedente de un semillero). **13 to get out of – on the wrong side,** levantarse de la cama con el pie izquierdo. **14 to go to –,** irse a la cama, acostarse. **15 to go to – with,** acostarse con, irse a la cama con (expresando que van a tener relaciones sexuales). **16 in –,** acostado, en la cama. **17 in – with,** acostado con, en la cama con (realizando el acto sexual). **18 to make the –,** hacer la cama. **19 one makes one's – so one must lie on it,** a lo hecho, pecho, hacer frente a las consecuencias ocasionadas por uno mismo. **20 to take to one's –,** caer en cama, quedar en cama (a causa de una enfermedad o similar). **21 to wet one's –,** V. **wet.**
bedaub | bɪ'dɔːb | *v.t.* **[to – (with)]** embadurnar.
bed-bath | 'bedbɑːθ | *s.c.* lavado de un enfermo, lavado en la cama.
bedbug | 'bedbʌg | *s.c.* ZOOL. chinche.
bedchamber | 'bedtʃeɪmbər | *s.c.* (form. y arc.) alcoba, dormitorio.
bedclothes | 'bedkləuðz | *s.pl.* ropa de cama.
-bedded | 'bedɪd | *sufijo* de... camas: *double-bedded rooms = habitaciones de dos camas.*
bedding | 'bedɪŋ | *s.i.* **1** ropa de cama. || **2 – plant,** planta de semillero (que cuando florece se traslada a un semillero).
bedeck | bɪ'dek | *v.t.* **[to – (with)]** adornar, embellecer.
bedevil | bɪ'devl | *v.t.* confundir, acosar, desesperar: *this problem has bedevilled us for ages = este problema nos ha desesperado durante muchísimo tiempo.*
bedfellow | 'bedfeləu | *s.c.* **1** compañero de cama, compañero íntimo (del otro sexo). **2** (fig.) compañero, asociado, aliado: *during the war conservatives and socialists became strange bedfellows = durante la guerra los conservadores y los socialistas se convirtieron en aliados extraños.*
bedhead | 'bedhed | *s.c.* cabecera (de una cama).
bedlam | 'bedləm | *s.i.* follón, escándalo (de ruido).
bed-linen | 'bedlɪnɪn | *s.i.* ropa de cama blanca.
Bedouin | 'beduɪn | [*pl.* **Bedouin** o **Bedouins**] *s.c.* beduino, nómada.
bedpan | 'bedpæn | *s.c.* orinal, bacín.
bedpost | 'bedpəust | *s.c.* **1** pilar de la cama, poste de la cama. || **2 between you and me and the –,** muy confidencialmente, con mucha discreción.
bedraggled | bɪ'drægld | *adj.* sucio, ensuciado; mojado, enlodado.
bedridden | 'bedrɪdn | *adj.* postrado en la cama (por enfermedad o vejez).
bedrock | 'bedrɑk | *s.i.* **1** GEOL. capa de piedra dura, capa de roca base. **2** (fig.) principio fundamental, fundamento, base: *family is the bedrock of society = la familia es la base de la sociedad.*
bedroll | 'bedrəul | *s.c.* petate (para dormir en cualquier sitio).
bedroom | 'bedruːm | *s.c.* **1** dormitorio, habitación (de dormir). || **2 -bedroomed,** de... dormitorios: *a four-bedroomed house = una casa de cuatro dormitorios.* **3 the – scene/rituals/etc.,** (euf.) el mundo del sexo, el mundo de la cama (en sentido sexual).
bedside | 'bedsaɪd | *s.sing.* **1** lado de la cama: *the dog was lying by his bedside = el perro estaba tumbado al lado de su cama.* **2** (fig.) cabecera, cabecera de la cama (de un enfermo). || **3 – manner,** forma de comportarse con un enfermo, manera de tratar a un enfermo (por parte de un médico).
bedsit | 'bedsɪt | V. **bedsitter.**
bedsitter | ˌbed'sɪtər | [también **bedsit**] (brit.) apartamento, estudio (con una sola habitación).
bed-sitting-room | ˌbed'sɪtɪŋruːm | V. **bedsitter.**
bedsore | 'bedsɔː | *s.c.* MED. úlcera (por prolongada estancia en cama).
bedspread | 'bedspred | *s.c.* colcha, sobrecama.
bedstead | 'bedsted | *s.c.* armadura de cama.
bedtime | 'bedtaɪm | *s.i.* hora de acostarse, hora de irse a la cama.
bed-wetting | 'bedwetɪŋ | *s.i.* PSIC. mojar la cama por la noche, micción nocturna, enuresis.
bee | biː | *s.c.* **1** ZOOL. abeja. **2** (EE.UU.) reunión, tertulia. || **3 busy –,** (fam.) trabajador nato, persona ocupadísima. **4 to have a – in one's bonnet,** dar vueltas a una cosa; tener una idea demasiado fija. **5 the bee's knees,** (fam.) lo más fetén (persona o cosa).
Beeb | biːb | *s.sing.* **[the –]** (fam.) la BBC.
beech | biːtʃ | BOT. *s.c.* e *i.* **1** haya. || *s.i.* **2** madera de haya. || **3 – tree,** haya.
beef | biːf | *s.i.* **1** carne de vacuno, carne de ternera. **2** (fam.) fuerza, músculo. || [*pl.* **beeves**] *s.c.* **3** ganado para matanza, ganado para el matadero. [*pl.* **beefs**] **4** (fam.) quejas, lloriqueos. || *v.i.* **5 [to – (about)]** (fam.) quejarse, llorar. || **6 – cattle,** ganado de engorde. **7 to – up,** reforzar; mejorar; dar más relieve: *we must beef up security = tenemos que reforzar el sistema de seguridad.*
beefburger | 'biːfbəːgər | *s.c.* hamburguesa.
beefeater | 'biːfiːtər | *s.c.* HIST. alabardero (de la Torre de Londres).
beefiness | 'biːfɪnɪs | *s.i.* corpulencia, robustez.
beefsteak | 'biːfsteɪk | V. **steak.**
beef-tea | biːf'tiː | *s.i.* GAST. caldo de carne, consomé de carne, caldo concentrado de carne.
beefy | 'biːfɪ | *adj.* (fam.) corpulento, robusto, musculoso.
beehive | 'biːhaɪv | *s.c.* colmena (de abejas).

bee-keeper | 'biːkiːpər | *s.c.* apicultor.

bee-keeping | 'biːkiːpɪŋ | *s.i.* apicultura.

beeline | 'biːˌlaɪn | **to make a – for,** (fam.) ir pitando para, perder el culo por llegar a.

been | biːn | *p.p.* **1** de **be.** || **2 to have –,** haber pasado (por la casa de uno, especialmente el cartero, lechero, etc.). **3 to have – and,** (fam.) ir y, atreverse a (expresando sorpresa o disgusto ante una acción): *he has been and hit him in the face = él va y le golpea en la cara.* **4 to have – to,** haber estado en, haber ido a, haber visitado (un país): *have you ever been to his restaurant? = ¿has estado alguna vez en su restaurante?*

beep | biːp | *s.c.* **1** pip (sonido de aparatos diversos eléctricos). || *v.t.* e *i.* **2** emitir un pip, hacer emitir un pip.

beer | bɪər | *s.c.* e *i.* **1** cerveza. || **2 – and skittles,** diversión; color de rosa (la vida, por ejemplo). **3 – belly,** (fam.) panza, michelín (causado por beber mucha cerveza).

beer-mat | 'bɪəmæt | *s.c.* posavasos.

beery | 'bɪərɪ | *adj.* que huele a cerveza, que sabe a cerveza.

beeswax | 'biːzwæks | *s.i.* cera de abejas.

beet | biːt | *s.i.* remolacha.

beetle | 'biːtl | *s.c.* **1** escarabajo. **2** mazo, martillo de mazo. || *v.i.* **3** (fam.) darse prisa, apresurarse, dirigirse apresuradamente. || **4 death-watch –,** escarabajo de la madera.

beetle-browed | ˌbiːtl'braʊd | *adj.* de cejas pobladas.

beetling | 'biːtlɪŋ | *adj.* sobresalido, que sobresale (un acantilado, un tejado, etc.).

beetroot | 'biːtruːt | *s.c.* e *i.* **1** raíz de remolacha. || *adj.* **2** rojo, atomatado, como un tomate (de vergüenza, cólera, etc.).

beeves | biːvz | V. **beef 3.**

befall | bɪ'fɔːl | *v.* [*pret.* **befell,** *p.p.* **befallen**] *t.* (form. y lit.) ocurrir, suceder, acontecer, sobrevenir.

befit | bɪ'fɪt | *v.t.* (form.) ser propio de, convenir: *he treated her as befitted a Prime Minister = él la trató como era propio de un Primer Ministro.*

befitting | bɪ'fɪtɪŋ | *adj.* (form.) digno, conveniente, adecuado.

befittingly | bɪ'fɪtɪnlɪ | *adv.* (form.) dignamente, convenientemente, adecuadamente.

befog | bɪ'fɒg | [*ger.* **befogging,** *pret.* y *p.p.* **befogged**] *v.t.* confundir, oscurecer (en el pensamiento).

before | bɪ'fɔːr | *conj.* **1** antes de que, antes que, antes de: *before I got married I finished college = antes de que me casara acabé la carrera.* || *prep.* **2** antes de: *before the traffic lights = antes de los semáforos.* **3** ante (un comité, juez, etc.): *he was brought before the headmaster = le trajeron ante el director.* **4** delante de (físicamente): *before the wall = delante de la pared.* **5** ante (con sentido de peligro o similar): *the man stood back before the horrible beast = el hombre retrocedió ante la horrible bestia.* **6** (form.) antes que, con preferencia a: *I love my parents before my wife = amo a mis padres antes que a mi mujer.* **7 [– + *pron.*]** ante, por delante de: *we've got the whole day before us = tenemos todo el día ante nosotros; I have quite a lot of problems before me = tengo bastantes problemas ante mí.* **8** antes de (en el tiempo): *before the war = antes de la guerra.* || *adj.* **9** [*s.* –] anterior: *the night before = la noche anterior.* || *adv.* **10** anteriormente. || **11 – long,** V. **long. 12 – one's time,** V. **time. 13 – one's very eyes,** V. **eye.**

beforehand | bɪ'fɔːhænd | *adv.* anteriormente, con anterioridad, de antemano.

befriend | bɪ'frend | *v.t.* actuar como un amigo con, hacerse amigo de, tratar como un amigo a, amparar.

befuddle | bɪ'fʌdl | *v.t.* aturdir, confundir (mentalmente).

befuddled | bɪ'fʌdld | *adj.* aturdido, confundido (mentalmente).

beg | beg | [*ger.* **begging,** *pret.* y *p.p.* **begged**] *v.t.* **1** pedir, mendigar (comida, cobijo, dinero, etc.). **2 [to – + *pron.* (+ *inf.*)]** implorar, suplicar: *I beg you to understand = te suplico que entiendas.* || *v.i.* **3 [to – (for)]** pedir, mendigar. **4 [to – (for)]** implorar, suplicar. **5** levantar las patas delanteras sentándose (movimiento de los perros, especialmente para pedir algo). || **6 to – leave,** (form.) solicitar permiso. **7 to – off,** excusarse (de hacer algo prometido). **8 to – someone's pardon,** V. **pardon. 9 to – the question,** V. **question. 10 to – to differ,** sentir estar en desacuerdo, no complacerse en opinar lo contrario. **11 to go begging,** no aparecer nadie que lo quiera, no tener nadie que lo desee: *I'll drink that coffee, it's going begging = me beberé ese café, no aparece nadie que lo quiera.*

began | bɪ'gæn | V. **begin.**

beget | bɪ'get | *v.* [*pret.* **begot,** *p.p.* **begotten**] *t.* **1** (form.) causar, generar, provocar: *laziness begets boredom = la pereza provoca el aburrimiento.* **2** (lit.) engendrar (hijos por parte de un padre).

beggar | 'begər | *s.c.* **1** mendigo, indigente. **2** (fam.) diablillo, tío: *he's a wealthy old beggar = es un tío viejo y acaudalado.* || *v.t.* **3** (form.) pauperizar, empobrecer. || **4 to – description,** ser imposible describirlo, desafiar la descripción correcta. **5 beggars can't be choosers,** a caballo regalado no le mires el diente.

beggarly | 'begəlɪ | *adj.* mísero, miserable, mezquino (una cantidad).

beggary | 'begərɪ | *s.i.* mendicidad, pobreza absoluta.

begin | bɪ'gɪn | *v.* [*pret.* **began,** *p.p.* **begun**] *t.* **1** empezar, comenzar, iniciar: *I began my studies in 1970 = yo comencé mis estudios en 1970.* **2** encabezar, iniciar (un libro, un documento, etc.). **3 [to – + *o.* + by]** empezar (algo mediante una cierta acción): *he began his speech by pointing out the main points he was going to develop = comenzó su discurso señalando los puntos principales que iba a desarrollar.* || *i.* **4 [to – + *inf./ger.*]** empezar, comenzar: *he started to run = él comenzó a correr.* **5** iniciarse, empezar: *winter began early = el invierno se inició pronto.* **6 [to – (by)]** comenzar, empezar (un discurso o similar). **7 [to – as]** empezar de, ser en un principio: *the building began as the village school = el edificio fue en un principio la escuela del pueblo.* **8** empezar, comenzar (un espacio físico): *Spain begins beyond that mountain = España comienza más allá de esa montaña.* **9** [con *neg.*] ni siquiera, con mucho, en absoluto: *after a long explanation he didn't begin to understand half of it = después de una larga explicación ni siquiera entendió la mitad.* **10 [to – with]** empezar con, comenzar con (una letra o signo). || **11 to – with,** en principio, primeramente, inicialmente. **12 charity begins at home,** V. **charity.**

beginner | bɪ'gɪnər | *s.c.* **1** principiante, novato, aprendiz. || **2 beginner's –,** suerte de principiante (típicamente accidental).

beginning | bɪ'gɪnɪŋ | *s.c.* **1 [(the) – (of)]** comienzo, inicio, principio (la primera parte en el tiempo). || *s.sing.* **2 [the – of]** el inicio de, el comienzo de (en su primerísimo momento). || **3 the – of the end,** el comienzo del fin.

begone | bɪ'gɒn | (EE.UU.) | bɪ'gɔːn | *interj.* (arc.) ¡fuera!

begonia | bɪ'gəʊnɪə | *s.c.* BOT. begonia.

begot | bɪ'gɒt | (arc.) | bɪ'gæt) V. **beget.**

begotten | bɪ'gɒtn | V. **beget.**

begrudge | bɪ'grʌdʒ | *v.t.* **1** tener envidia de, resentir (el que otros tengan o alcancen cosas agradables). **2** dar de mala gana (dinero o similar).

begrudgingly | bɪ'grʌdʒɪŋlɪ | *adv.* de mala gana, a regañadientes.

beguile | bɪ'gaɪl | *v.t.* **1 [to – *o.* + (with/into)]** seducir, encantar, encandilar (para que hagan cosas estúpidas). **2** (arc.) encantar: *we were beguiled by her voice = su voz nos encantó.* **3** entretener (para pasar el tiempo).

beguilement | bɪ'gaɪlmənt | *s.i.* encantamiento, seducción, encandilamiento.

beguiling | bɪ'gaɪlɪŋ | *adj.* seductor, encantador.

beguilingly | bɪ'gaɪlɪŋlɪ | *adv.* seductoramente, encantadoramente.

begum | 'beɪgəm | *s.c.* begum (dama musulmana de gran categoría).

begun | bɪ'gʌn | V. **begin.**

behalf | bɪ'hɑːf | (EE.UU.) | bɪ'hæf | **on – of/on someone's –,** en nombre de, de parte de, por encargo de.

behave | bɪ'heɪv | *v.i.* **1** comportarse, conducirse, portarse. **2** portarse bien. **3** MEC. funcionar: *this chemical product behaves in a strange way = este producto químico funciona de una manera extraña.* || *v.r.* **4** portarse bien, comportarse como es debido. || **5 – behaved,** de conducta (en compuestos): *a well-behaved child = un chico de buena conducta.*

behavior | bɪ'heɪvjər | (*brit.* **behaviour**) *s.i.* **1 [– (of)]** comportamiento, conducta. **2** (fig.) funcionamiento, reacción (de productos químicos, etc.). || **3 animal –,** conducta animal. **4 to be on one's best –,** comportarse lo mejor posible, portarse como es debido.

behavioral | bɪ'heɪvjərəl | (*brit.* **behavioural**) *adj.* **1** PSIC. conductista. || **2 – science,** ciencia conductista, ciencia del estudio del comportamiento humano.
behaviorism | bɪ'heɪvjərɪzəm | (*brit.* behaviourism) *s.i.* PSIC. conductismo.
behaviorist | bɪ'heɪvjərɪst | (*brit.* **behaviourist**) *s.c.* PSIC. conductista, seguidor del conductismo.
behead | bɪ'hed | *v.t.* cortar la cabeza de, decapitar.
beheld | bɪ'held | V. **behold.**
behest | bɪ'hest | **at someone's –,** (form.) por orden de, a instancias de, por mandato de.
behind | bɪ'haɪnd | *prep.* **1** detrás de, tras (en el espacio): *I'm sitting behind her = estoy sentado detrás de ella.* **2** detrás de, tras (escondido): *the stood behind the door = se quedó de pie detrás de la puerta.* **3** detrás de, siguiendo: *I walked behind the porter = caminé siguiendo al mozo.* **4** retrasado con respecto a, por detrás de (en cuanto a conocimientos): *as he started school late, he is behind the others = como empezó tarde la escuela está retrasado con respecto a los otros.* **5** detrás de, tras (como causa de una situación): *the real reasons behind his resignation are unknown = las causas reales de su dimisión son desconocidas.* **6** detrás de, bajo (apariencias): *behind her stand-offish manner there lies a warm and affectionate person = bajo su forma distante de tratarte hay una persona cariñosa y con sentimientos.* **7** apoyando, en apoyo de: *I have the whole party behind me = tengo a todo el partido apoyándome.* **8** detrás de (como artífice de un proyecto, plan, etc.): *the man behind the export drive is the new managing director = el hombre detrás del impulso a la exportación es el nuevo director gerente.* || *adv.* **9** detrás, atrás (en el espacio). **10** atrasado (reloj). **11 [– (in/with)]** atrasado (en pagos de cualquier clase). || *s.c.* **12** (fam. y euf.) trasero, culo. || **13 – the scenes,** V. **scene. 14 – the times,** V. **time. 15 close/not far –,** inmediatamente, sin más tardar, inmediatamente después. **16 – someone's back,** V. **back. 17 to leave –,** olvidarse, dejarse olvidado. **18 linger/stay –,** quedarse rezagado; retrasarse (en el espacio).
behindhand | bɪ'haɪndhænd | *adv.* atrasado, retrasado (en pagos, trabajo, consejo, etc.).
beheld | bɪ'held | *pret.* y *p.p.* de **behold.**
behold | bɪ'həʊld | (lit. o p.u.) *v.t.* [*irreg. pret.* y *p.p.* **beheld**] **1** contemplar, mirar. || **2 –!,** ¡he aquí!, ¡contemplad! **3 lo and –,** V. **lo.**
beholden | bɪ'həʊldən | *adj.* **[– (to)]** (form. o p.u.) agradecido.
beholder | bɪ'həʊldər | *s.c.* espectador, observador (el que mira).
behoove | bɪ'hu:v | V. **behove.**
behove | bɪ'həʊv | (EE.UU. **behoove**) *v.t.* **[it –]** (form. o p.u.) es menester: *it behoves you to take care of her = es menester que la cuides.*
beige | beɪʒ | *adj.* **1** beige (color). || *s.i.* **2** beige (color).
being | 'bi:ɪŋ | *ger.* **1** de **be.** || *s.c.* **2** ser, persona: *a human being.* **3** ser, criatura (cualquier cosa viva). || *s.i.* **4** FIL. ser, naturaleza. || *conj.* **5** como, porque; al ser, siendo: *being English, he didn't understand us = al ser inglés, no nos comprendía.* || **6 to bring something into –,** engendrar, procrear, crear. **7 to come into –,** empezar su vida, empezar su existencia, ser creado. **8 for the time –,** V. **time. 9 in –,** en existencia, existente. **10 all things – equal,** V. **equal. 11 the Supreme Being,** REL. el Ser Supremo.
bejeweled | bɪ'dʒu:əld | (*brit.* **bejewelled**) *adj.* enjoyado, adornado con joyas.
belabor | bɪ'leɪbər | (*brit.* **belabour**) *v.t.* **1** (arc.) apalear, golpear. **2** elaborar (un tema, idea, etc.).
belated | bɪ'leɪtɪd | *adj.* tardío, retrasado, (Am.) demorado.
belatedly | bɪ'leɪtɪdlɪ | *adv.* tardíamente, con retraso, (Am.) demoradamente.
belay | bɪ'leɪ | DEP. *v.i.* **1** amarrar, fijar un agarradero (en escalada de montañas). || *s.c.* **2** agarradero.
belch | beltʃ | *v.i.* **1** eructar, regoldar. **2** (fig.) eructar, hacer un ruido (parecido a un eructo). || *v.t.* **3** (fig.) emitir, arrojar, vomitar (humo, fuego, etc.). || *s.c.* **4** eructo. || **5 to – out,** emitir, arrojar, vomitar (humo, fuego, etc.).
beleaguered | bɪ'li:gəd | *adj.* (form.) **1** MIL. sitiado, cercado. **2** (fig.) molestado, importunado (por personas); acosado (por problemas o similar).
belfry | 'belfrɪ | *s.c.* **1** campanario. || **2 to have bats in the –,** V. **bat.**
Belgian | 'beldʒən | *adj.* **1** belga (costumbres, tradiciones, cultura, etc.). || *s.c.* **2** belga (ciudadano).
Belgium | 'beldʒəm | *s.sing.* Bélgica.
belie | bɪ'laɪ | [*ger.* **belying**] *v.t.* (form.) **1** representar mal, representar falsamente; contradecir: *his physical fitness belies his age = su buena forma física contradice su edad.* **2** desmentir (una teoría); defraudar (esperanzas o similar).
belief | bɪ'li:f | *s.c.* e *i.* **1 [– (in)]** creencia (filosófica, ética, etc.). || *s.c.* **2** convicción firme, opinión segura. **3** REL. creencia, fe. || **4 beyond –,** increíble, sorprendente hasta un grado máximo. **5 contrary to popular –,** en contra de la opinión extendida, en contra de lo que todo el mundo cree. **6 in the – that,** en la creencia de que, en la convicción de que. **7 to the best of one's –,** según el leal saber y entender de uno.
believable | bɪ'li:vəbl | *adj.* creíble, digno de crédito.
believably | bɪ'li:vəblɪ | *adv.* creíblemente.
believe | bɪ'li:v | *v.t.* **1** creer: *I believe you = te creo.* **2** tener el convencimiento de que, confiar que; considerar, creer: *we believed him gone forever = le creímos ido para siempre; I believe that the President is right = tengo el convencimiento de que el Presidente tiene razón.* || **3 [to – (in)]** REL. creer (en Dios). **4 [to – in]** creer en (una teoría), confiar en (una persona), tener fe (en algo o alguien). || **5 – it or not,** lo puedes creer o no, sorprendente pero es cierto. **6 – me/– me you,** créeme, no miento. **7 to give somebody to –,** V. **give. 8 I –,** creo, opino, me parece. **9 to make –,** fingir. **10 not to – one's ears/eyes,** no creer en lo que uno oye/ve. **11 seeing is believing,** ver es creer. **12 would you – it?,** increíblemente (expresando gran sorpresa).
believer | bɪ'li:vər | *s.c.* **1** REL. creyente. **2** (fig.) creyente, partidario (de una teoría, persona, etc.).
belittle | bɪ'lɪtl | *v.t.* menospreciar, despreciar (no considerando importante).
belittlement | bɪ'lɪtlmənt | *s.i.* (form.) menosprecio.
belittling | bɪ'lɪtlɪŋ | *adj.* humillante, que indica desprecio/menosprecio.
Belize | be'li:z | *s.sing.* Belice.
Belizean | be'li:zɪən | *s.c.* **1** habitante de Belize. || *adj.* **2** de Belize.
bell | bel | *s.c.* **1** campana (de un campanario). **2** timbre (de la puerta, bicicleta, etc.). **3** cencerro (en animales). **4** cascabel (en un collar o similar). **5** (normalmente *sing.*) campana, timbre (como sonido). || **6 –, book and candle,** (form.) REL. por completo (como fórmula de condenación anatemática). **7 – pepper,** pimiento dulce. **8 clear as a –,** con un sonido nítido. **9 to give someone a –,** (fam.) dar a alguien un telefonazo. **10 to ring a –,** (fam.) sonar, sonar familiar, sonar conocido. **11 sound as a –,** en perfecto estado de salud. **12 with bells on,** (fam.) hecho un dandi, en plan guapetón.
belladonna | ˌbelə'dɒnə | *s.i.* BOT. belladona.
bell-bottomed | 'belbɒtəmd | *adj.* acampanado (de pantalones).
bell-bottoms | 'belbɒtəmz | *s.pl.* pantalones acampanados.
bell-boy | 'belbɔɪ | (también **bell-hop**) *s.c.* (EE.UU.) botones (de hotel).
bell-buoy | 'belbɔɪ | *s.c.* MAR. boya sonora.
belle | bel | *s.c.* (p.u.) belleza, mujer bella, bella: *the typical Southern belle = la típica belleza sureña.*
bell-hop | 'belhɒp | V. **bell-boy.**
belles-lettres | ˌbel'letrə | *s.pl.* (form.) estudios de letras, bellas letras (literatura).
bellicose | 'belɪkəʊs | *adj.* (lit.) belicoso, agresivo.
bellicosity | ˌbelɪ'kɒsɪtɪ | *s.i.* (lit.) belicosidad, agresividad.
belligerence | bɪ'lɪdʒərəns | (también **belligerency**) *s.i.* beligerancia, hostilidad.
belligerency | bɪ'lɪdʒərənsɪ | V. **belligerence.**
belligerent | bɪ'lɪdʒərənt | *adj.* **1** beligerante, hostil, agresivo. **2** POL. beligerante (de un país en guerra). || *s.c.* **3** POL. país en guerra, país beligerante.
bellow | 'beləʊ | *v.i.* **1** rugir, bramar (toros o animales parecidos). **2** (fig.) rugir, vociferar. || *v.t.* **3** decir con un rugido, lanzar con un rugido: *the sergeant bellowed the orders = el sargento dio las órdenes con un rugido.* || *s.c.* **4** rugido (de toro o similar). **5** (fig.) rugido (de voz).
bellows | 'beləʊz | *s.pl.* **[– *v.sing./pl.*] 1** fuelle (para avivar el fuego). **2** MUS. fuelle, barquín (de un acordeón).

bell-pull | 'belpʊl | *s.c.* cordón del timbre, cordón para llamar.
bell-push | 'belpʊʃ | *s.c.* timbre (de tocar presionando).
bell-ringer | 'belrɪŋgər | *s.c.* campanero.
bell-ringing | 'belrɪŋɪŋ | *s.i.* sonido de campanas.
bell-tent | 'beltent | *s.c.* tienda de campaña (en forma de campana).
belly | 'belɪ | *s.c.* **1** (brit. y fam.) barriga, barriguita, tripa. **2** abdomen, vientre. **3** abdomen, tripa, panza (de un animal). **4** (fig.) panza (de un objeto, vehículo, etc.). || **5 -bellied,** de barriga, de abdomen (en compuestos): *a big-bellied fellow = un tipo con una barriga grandota.* **6 to – out,** MAR. hincharse, inflarse (velas).
bellyache | 'belɪeɪk | (fam.) *s.c.* e *i.* **1** dolor de barriga, dolor de tripas. || *v.i.* **2** quejarse, lamentarse, estar en plan llorón.
belly-band | 'belɪbænd | *s.c.* cincha.
belly-button | 'belɪbʌtn | *s.c.* (fam.) ombligo.
belly-dance | 'belɪdɑːns | *s.c.* baile árabe (de movimientos sensuales).
belly-dancer | 'belɪdɑːnsər | *s.c.* bailarina árabe. V. **belly-dance.**
belly-flop | 'belɪflɒp | (fam.) *s.c.* **1** panzazo, panzada (al tirarse al agua). || **2 to do a –,** darse un panzazo, darse una panzada (sobre el agua).
bellyful | 'belɪfʊl | **to have a – (of),** (fam.) darse una comilona (a base de), atiborrarse (a base de).
belly-laugh | 'belɪlɑːf | *s.c.* (fam.) risotada, carcajada.
belong | bɪ'lɒŋ | (EE.UU. | bɪ'lɔːŋ | *v.i.* **1 [to – to]** pertenecer a, ser de: *that car belongs to me = ese coche es mío.* **2 [to – to]** ser miembro de (una asociación, grupo, familia, etc.). **3 [to – to]** corresponderse con, ser parte de: *these keys belong to another set = estas llaves son parte de otro juego.* **4** ser de, estar en su ambiente (un sitio en un sentido espiritual): *I realize I don't belong here = me doy cuenta de que no soy de aquí.* **5** ir bien (en el sentido de ser el sitio que corresponde): *these books don't belong on this shelf = estos libros no van bien en esta estantería.* || **6 a sense of belonging,** una sensación de pertenecer a un ambiente, un sentimiento de estar en el sitio de uno.
belongings | bɪ'lɒŋɪŋz | (EE.UU.) | bɪ'lɔːŋgɪŋz | *s.pl.* pertenencias, efectos personales (que no están fijos, como una casa o la tierra).
beloved | bɪ'lʌvd | | bɪ'lʌvɪd | *adj.* **1** amado, querido. || *s.c.* **2** (p.u.) amado, persona amada.
below | bɪ'ləʊ | *prep.* **1** debajo de, por debajo de: *they live below us = ellos viven debajo de nosotros.* **2** debajo de, por debajo de (en un río). **3** menos de, por debajo de (con cantidades). || *adv.* **4** debajo, abajo. **5** más adelante (en un escrito). **6** MAR. bajo cubierta, abajo. **7** (arc.) en el infierno. || **8 – ground/ – the ground,** bajo el suelo, por debajo del suelo.
belt | belt | *s.c.* **1** cinturón, cinto. **2** DEP. cinturón (negro, marrón, etc. en karate). **3** (fig.) cinturón, franja (con una característica especial): *this is the Bible belt = ésta es la franja de la Biblia.* **4** (fam.) golpetón, golpazo, tortazo. **5** MEC. correa (de un ventilador u otra maquinaria). || *v.t.* **6** poner cinto, poner cinturón (a una prenda de vestir). **7** (fam.) golpear, atizar (un fuerte golpe). || *v.i.* **8** (fam.) ir a toda velocidad, marchar a gran velocidad: *he belted after a bus = él fue a toda velocidad tras un autobús.* || **9 at one's –,** en el cinturón de uno, en el cinto de uno; sujeto en el cinturón de uno. **10 below the –,** DEP. debajo del cinto, bajo (golpe). **11 – line,** (EE.UU.) trayecto de circunvalación, línea de circunvalación (en autobuses o trenes). **12 to – out,** (fam.) chillar, vocear; cantar a gritos. **13 to – up,** (vulg.) cerrar la boca, callarse. **14 to hit below the –,** (fam.) dar un golpe bajo, asestar golpes bajos; criticar furibundamente. **15 to tighten one's –,** apretarse el cinturón de uno (como medida ahorradora). **16 under one's –,** en poder de uno, casi logrado, casi conseguido: *he's got everything under his belt = ha conseguido casi todo.*
belting | 'beltɪŋ | *s.c.* (fam.) paliza, zurra.
beluga | bəluːgə | *s.c.* ZOOL. beluga (un tipo de ballena).
bemoan | bɪ'məʊn | *v.t.* (form.) lamentar, llorar por.
bemused | bɪ'mjuzd | *adj.* estupefacto, desconcertado.
ben | ben | *s.c.* cima de montaña (en Escocia).
bench | bentʃ | *s.c.* **1** banco (para sentarse). **2** banco de trabajo. **3** (normalmente *sing.*) estrado (de un tribunal). || *s.sing.* **4 [the –]** la magistratura; el tribunal. || *s.pl.* **5** (brit.) POL. escaños: *the Conservative benches.* || **6 – seat,** asiento corrido, asiento a todo lo ancho (especialmente en un vehículo). **7 to serve/sit on the –,** ser nombrado para la judicatura.
benchmark | bentʃmɑːk | *s.c.* **1** cota de referencia (en topografía). **2** punto de referencia: *my benchmark in life is my neighbour = mi punto de referencia en la vida es mi prójimo.*
bend | bend | *v.* [*pret.* y *p.p. irreg.* **bent**] *t.* **1** inclinar, doblar (una parte del cuerpo). **2** doblar, curvar (normalmente un objeto). **3** doblegar, hacer cambiar (de opinión, modo de actuación, etc.). **4** torcer, curvar, cambiar de dirección. || *v.i.* **5** inclinarse, doblarse (parte del cuerpo). **6** doblarse, curvarse (normalmente un objeto). **7 [to – to]** doblegarse ante (en opiniones o similar). **8** torcerse, curvarse, cambiarse de dirección. || *s.c.* **9** curva, vuelta, recodo (de carretera, río, tubería, etc.). **10** ejercicio de doblar (partes del cuerpo). || **11 to – over backwards,** hacer todo lo posible humanamente, batirse el cobre (por alguna persona). **12 to – the rules,** sortear las leyes, manipular la interpretación de las leyes (en favor de uno). **13 to drive/ send one round the –,** volver a uno loco. **14 to go round the –,** volverse loco. **15 round the –,** loco. **16 the bends,** MAR. parálisis de buceador (al regresar demasiado rápido a la superficie).
bended | 'bendɪd | **on – knee,** (form.) arrodillado, en posición genuflecta.
bender | 'bendər | *s.c.* (fam.) borrachera, juerga alcohólica.
bendy | 'bendɪ | *adj.* **1** llena de curvas (especialmente una carretera). **2** flexible, que se puede doblar fácilmente.
beneath | bɪ'niːθ | (form.) *prep.* **1** bajo, debajo de, por debajo de: *beneath the waves = por debajo de las olas.* **2** bajo, debajo de (en categoría). **3** indigno de: *what you did to her was beneath you = lo que le hiciste fue indigno de ti.* || **4** debajo, abajo. || **5 – contempt,** V. **contempt.**
OBS. A veces esta palabra, cuando va seguida de una parte del cuerpo o un objeto, no se traduce: *he couldn't stand straight beneath his legs = no podía sostenerse derecho.*
Benedictine | ˌbenɪ'dɪktɪn | *s.i.* **1** benedictine (licor). || *adj.* **2** REL. benedictino. || *s.c.* **3** monje benedictino.
benediction | ˌbenɪ'dɪkʃn | *s.c.* e *i.* REL. bendición.
benefaction | ˌbenɪ'fækʃn | (form.) *s.c.* **1** acto caritativo. || *s.i.* **2** beneficencia; merced.
benefactor | 'benɪfæktər | *s.c.* bienhechor, benefactor (especialmente de obras benéficas).
benefactress | 'benɪfæktrɪs | *s.c.* bienhechora, benefactora. V. **benefactor.**
benefice | 'benɪfɪs | *s.i.* REL. beneficio (puesto eclesial que asegura un cierto ingreso).
beneficed | 'benɪfɪst | *adj.* REL. con beneficio. V. **benefice.**
beneficence | bɪ'nefɪsns | *s.i.* (form.) beneficencia.
beneficent | bɪ'nefɪsnt | *adj.* (form.) benéfico.
beneficial | ˌbenɪ'fɪʃl | *adj.* **[– (to)]** beneficioso, provechoso.
beneficially | ˌbenɪ'fɪʃəlɪ | *adv.* beneficiosamente, provechosamente.
beneficiary | ˌbenɪ'fɪʃerɪ | (EE.UU.) | ˌbenɪ'fɪʃɪerɪ | *s.c.* **1** beneficiario (de un proceso, actividad, etc.): *the European bankers were the main beneficiaries of the Spanish discovery = los banqueros europeos fueron los beneficiarios principales del descubrimiento español.* **2** DER. beneficiario, heredero beneficiario.
benefit | 'benɪfɪt | *s.c.* **1** beneficio, provecho; ventaja: *becoming an American citizen has brought you a lot of benefits = el ser un ciudadano americano te ha traído muchas ventajas.* || *s.c.* e *i.* **2** subsidio (de algún tipo de los existentes en la Seguridad Social): *unemployment benefit = subsidio de desempleo.* || *s.sing.* **3 [the – of]** el beneficio de, la ventaja de: *I was born with the benefit of being rich = nací con la ventaja de ser rico.* || *s.i.* **4 [– (to)]** provecho, ventaja: *this will be of benefit to you = esto será de provecho para ti.* || *adj.* **5** de caridad (función, espectáculo, etc.). || *v.t.* (EE.UU. *ger.* **benefitting,** *pret.* y *p.p.* **benefitted**) **6** beneficiar, aprovechar. || *v.i.* **7 [to – from/by]** beneficiarse de/por. || **8 for the – of,** para beneficio de, para provecho de, para ventaja de. **9 to give**

someone the – of the doubt, conceder a alguien el beneficio de la duda, no juzgar a alguien por adelantado.
benevolence | bɪ'nevələns | *s.i.* benevolencia.
benevolent | bɪ'nevələnt | *adj.* **1** benigno, benévolo (virtud personal). **2** caritativo (organización, institución, etc.). || **3 – fund,** fondo de ayuda (a alguien necesitado).
benevolently | bɪ'nevələntlɪ | *adv.* benignamente, benévolamente.
Bengal | beŋ'gɔːl | *s.sing.* Bengala.
Bengali | beŋ'gɔːlɪ | *adj.* **1** de Bengala, bengalí. || *s.c.* **2** bengalí (habitante). || *s.i.* **3** bengalí (idioma).
benighted | bɪ'naɪtɪd | *adj.* (lit.) ignorante.
benign | bɪ'naɪn | *adj.* **1** benigno, afable. **2** MED. benigno. **3** suave, benigno (clima).
benignly | bɪ'naɪnlɪ | *adv.* benignamente, afablemente.
bent | bent | *pret.* y *p.p.* **1** de **bend.** || *adj.* **2** inclinado, doblado (posición de persona u objeto). **3** torcido, curvado. **4** abollado (objetos metálicos). **5 [– on/upon]** decidido firmemente a, resuelto a, empeñado en. **6** (fam.) corrupto, comprado: *a bent referee = un árbitro comprado.* **7** (vulg. y desp.) sarasa, maricón. || *s.sing.* **8 [a – (for)]** tendencia, propensión; afición: *he's got a bent for chess = él tiene afición al ajedrez.* || **9 – doubtle, V. double.**
benumbed | bɪ'nʌmd | *adj.* (form.) aterido, entumecido.
benzene | 'benziːn | *s.i.* QUIM. benceno.
benzine | 'benziːn | *s.i.* QUIM. bencina.
benzocaine | 'benzəːkeɪn | *s.i.* QUIM. benzocaína.
bequeath | bɪ'kwiːð | *v.t.* (form.) **1** legar, dejar en herencia. **2** (fig.) dejar, pasar a generaciones siguientes (especialmente una situación determinada, una teoría, etc.).
bequest | bɪ'kwest | *s.c.* (form.) legado, herencia.
berate | bɪ'reɪt | *v.t.* (form.) censurar, reprender.
bereave | bɪ'riːv | *v.t.* **[to – *o.* (of)]** (form.) privar.
bereaved | bɪ'riːvd | (form.) *adj.* **1** desconsolado, desolado (por la muerte de un familiar). || **2 the –,** los deudos.
bereavement | bɪ'riːvmənt | *s.i.* **1** luto, duelo, desolación (por la muerte de un ser querido). || *s.c.* **2** pérdida, muerte (de un familiar).
bereft | bɪ'reft | (form.) *adj.* **1 [– of]** privado de: *bereft of happiness = privado de felicidad.* **2** desolado (como sentimiento).
beret | 'bereɪ | (EE.UU.) | bə'reɪ | *s.c.* boina, gorra (del estilo de boina).
beriberi | ˌberɪ'berɪ | *s.i.* MED. beriberi (enfermedad tropical).
berk | bəːk | *s.c.* (vulg., brit. y desp.) agilipollado.
berry | 'berɪ | *s.c.* **1** BOT. baya, fruta pequeña (como moras, fresas, etc.). || **2 brown as a –,** V. **brown.**
berserk | bə'səːk | | bə'zɜːk | *adj.* **1** loco, furioso. || **2 to go –,** volverse loco.
berth | bəːθ | *s.c.* **1** litera, cama (en transporte ferroviario, marítimo, etc.). **2** atracadero. || *v.t.* e *i.* **3** MAR. amarrar, echar amarras, atracar. || **4 to give somet-hing a wide –,** evitar, no acercarse a, mantenerse apartado de (un sitio).
beryl | 'berəl | *s.i.* MIN. berilo.
beryllium | bə'rɪljəm | *s.i.* QUIM. berilio.
beseech | bɪ'siːtʃ | *v.t.* [*pret.* y *p.p.* **beseeched** o **besought**] (lit.) implorar, suplicar.
beseeching | bɪ'siːtʃɪŋ | *adj.* (form.) implorante, suplicante.
beseechingly | bɪ'siːtʃɪŋlɪ | *adv.* (form.) en actitud implorante, de manera suplicante.
beset | bɪ'set | *v.t.* [*pret.* y *p.p.* **beset**] (form.) **1 [to – + *o.* (with/by)] acosar, asediar (problemas, dudas, etc.). 2** [**to** + *o.* + **(with/by)**] atacar, molestar, hostigar (a personas).
beside | bɪ'saɪd | *prep.* **1** al lado de, junto a. **2** al lado de, en comparación con: *you're a mite beside him = eres un microbio a su lado.* **3** junto a, al lado de, en cooperación con: *he worked beside him for years = trabajó junto a él durante años.* || **4 – oneself with,** fuera de sí con (un sentimiento). **5 – the point,** V. **point.**
besides | bɪ'saɪdz | *prep.* **1** además de; aparte de: *he speaks English besides German = habla inglés además de alemán.* **2** [*neg.* –] con la excepción de, menos: *she doesn't love anybody besides her mother = no quiere a nadie más que (excepto) a su madre.* || *adv.* **2** además; por otro lado.
besiege | bɪ'siːdʒ | *v.t.* **1** asediar, sitiar (normalmente en sentido militar). **2 [to + *o.* + (by/with)] abrumar (con problemas, peticiones, favores, etc.).**
besmear | bɪ'smɪər | *v.t.* (form.) ensuciar, manchar (especialmente con sustancia barrosa, grasienta, etc.).
besmirch | bɪ'sməːtʃ | *v.t.* (lit.) mancillar, deshonrar; ensuciar (reputación o similar).
besom | 'biːzəm | *s.c.* escoba (hecha con ramas finas).
besotted | bɪ'sɑtɪd | *adj.* entontecido (especialmente por enamoramiento).
besought | bɪ'sɔːt | *pret.* y *p.p.* de **beseech.**
bespeak | bɪ'spiːk | *v.t.* [*pret.* **bespoke,** *p.p.* **bespoken**] (form. o p.u.) revelar, denotar: *his manner bespoke the Englishman in him = su forma de comportarse denotaba el inglés que llevaba dentro.*
bespectacled | bɪ'spektɪkld | *adj.* (form.) con gafas, que lleva gafas.
bespoke | bɪ'spəuk | *pret.* **1** de **bespeak.** || *adj.* **2** a medida, hecho a medida (especialmente ropa). **3** INF. a medida, para solucionar una problemática particular.
bespoken | bɪ'spəukən | *p.p.* de **bespeak.**
best | best | *super.* **1** de **good** y **well.** || *adj.* **2** mejor, de más calidad, de mejor calidad: *that's the best film = ésa es la mejor película.* **3** [– *inf.*] lo más prudente, más prudente: *I thought it best not to go out in the storm = pensé que sería más prudente no salir con la tormenta.* || *adv.* **4** mejor, de más calidad, con más calidad: *the best written book = el libro mejor escrito.* **5** de la mejor manera, del mejor modo: *I hope this functions best now = espero que esto funcione de la mejor manera ahora.* **6** más, mejor (con verbos que indiquen gustar, sentar, complacer, etc.): *which subject do you like best? = ¿qué asignatura te gusta más?* || *s.sing.* **7 [the –]** lo mejor, lo más conveniente, lo más adecuado: *the best is to go abroad when you are older = lo mejor es ir al extranjero cuando eres mayor.* **8** lo mejor, lo más ventajoso, lo más a su favor (de alguien): *the best you can say about him is that he is young = lo más ventajoso que se puede decir de él es que es joven.* **9** [*adj.pos.* –] mejor ropa: *they went out in their best = salieron con su mejor ropa.* || **10 all the –,** que vaya todo bien (como despedida). **11 as – one can/could/etc.,** de la mejor manera posible. **12 at –,** a lo más, en el mejor de los casos, puestos a decir lo mejor. **13 at the – of times,** V. **time. 14 best-,** mejor, más (en compuestos): *the best-dressed women in America = las mujeres mejor vestidas de América.* **15 – man,** padrino (en una boda). **16 – of luck,** V. **luck. 17 – seller,** "best-seller" (libro con gran éxito de venta). **17 to be the – thing since sliced bread,** V. **bread. 18 to do one's –,** V. **do. 19 for the –,** con la mejor intención, con el mejor propósito. **20 had –,** (fam.) será mejor que, sería mejor que: *you'd best shut up = sería mejor que cerraras la boquita.* **21 to hope for the –,** V. **hope. 22 to know –,** V. **know. 23 to make the – of,** hacerlo lo mejor que uno pueda en (una mala situación), sacar el mayor provecho posible de (algo no muy bueno), salir de un mal negocio lo mejor posible. **24 to make the – of a bad job,** V. **job. 25 six of the –,** una buena tunda, unos palmetazos (castigo disciplinar escolar). **26 the – of both worlds,** V. **world. 27 the – part of,** V. **part. 27 to the – of one's ability,** V. **ability. 28 to the – of one's knowledge,** V. **knowledge. 29 to the – of someone's belief,** V. **belief.**
bestial | 'bestɪəl | (EE.UU.) | bestʃəl | *adj.* (form. o lit.) bestial, brutal.
bestiality | ˌbestɪ'ælətɪ | (EE.UU.) | ˌbestʃɪ'ælətɪ | *s.i.* **1** (form. o lit.) depravación. **2** PSIQ. bestialismo (contacto sexual con animales).
bestially | 'bestɪəlɪ | (EE.UU.) | 'bestʃəlɪ | *adv.* (form. o lit.) bestialmente, brutalmente.
bestiary | 'bestɪərɪ | (EE.UU.) | 'bestɪerɪ | *s.c.* LIT. bestiario.
bestir | bɪ'stəːr | *v.r.* (form.) rebullirse, moverse.
bestow | bɪ'stəu | *v.t.* **[to – *o.* + (on)]** otorgar.
bestowal | bɪ'stəuəl | *s.i.* otorgamiento.
bestrew | bɪ'struː | *v.t.* [*pret.* **bestrewed,** *p.p.* **bestrewn**] esparcir, desparramar.
bestrewn | bɪ'struːn | *p.p.* de **bestrew.**
bestride | bɪ'straɪd | *v.i.* [*pret.* **bestrode,** *p.p.* **bestridden**] (form.) sentarse a horcajadas sobre.

bestridden | bɪ'strɪdn | *p.p.* de **bestride.**
bestrode | bɪ'strəʊd | *pret.* de **bestride.**
best-selling | ˌbest'selɪŋ | *adj.* exitoso, que vende mucho.
bet | bet | *v.* [*pret.* y *p.p. irreg.* **bet** o **betted**] *t.* **1** **[to – + o. + (on)]** apostar: *I bet five pounds on a horse = aposté cinco libras a un caballo.* || *i.* **2** hacer apuestas, jugar. || *s.c.* **3** **[– (on)]** apuesta. || **4 a good –/one's best –,** una adecuada manera de resolver un asunto/la mejor propuesta de uno. **5 a safe –/a good –,** una suposición probable; una cosa segura. **6 do you want a –/to –?,** ¿quieres apostar?, ¿apuestas algo? **7 to hedge one's bets,** apostar a los dos caballos, no comprometerse en una sola dirección. **8 I –,** (fam.) seguro, claro, claro que sí, ya lo creo. **9 I –/I'll –,** (fam.) y un jamón. **10 I –/I'll –/I'm willing to –/my – is,** seguro que, a que. **11 I wouldn't – on/don't – on,** yo no pondría la mano en el fuego por. **12 you –,** por supuesto, no faltaría más.
beta | 'biːtə | (EE.UU.) | 'beɪtə | *s.c.* e *i.* **1** beta (letra del alfabeto griego). **2** notable (nota académica). || *s.c.* **3** FIS. partícula beta. || **4 – ray,** FIS. rayo beta.
betel | 'biːtl | *s.i.* BOT. nuez de betel, nuez de areca.
bête noire | ˌbeɪt'nwɑː | *s.c.* bestia negra, persona detestable.
betide | bɪ'taɪd | **woe –,** (form.) Dios socorra, el Cielo ayude (ante una equivocación): *woe betide the student who makes a mistake here = Dios socorra al estudiante que cometa un error en este sitio.*
betoken | bɪ'təʊkən | *v.t.* (form. o p.u.) indicar, demostrar.
betray | bɪ'treɪ | *v.t.* **1** traicionar, engañar. **2** revelar (secreto). **3** defraudar (esperanzas), violar (principios). **4** delatar, descubrir (un sentimiento que se quiere ocultar): *his nervous behaviour betrayed him = su comportamiento nervioso le delató.*
betrayal | bɪ'treɪəl | *s.c.* **1** **[– (of)]** traición, engaño. || *s.i.* **2** traición, defraudación.
betrayer | bɪ'treɪər | *s.c.* traidor, delator.
betrothal | bɪ'trəʊðl | *s.c.* **[– (of/to)]** (arc.) compromiso matrimonial.
betrothed | bɪ'treʊðd | (arc.) *adj.* **1** prometido (para matrimonio). || **2 the –,** los prometidos.
better | 'betər | *comp.* **1** de **good** y **well.** || *adj.* **2** mejor, de mejor calidad: *he's a better man than his father = es un hombre mejor que su padre; I feel better = me siento mejor; you look better = tienes mejor aspecto.* **3** **[– for/*inf.*]** mejor, más conveniente, más adecuado: *it's better to go now = es más conveniente irnos ahora.* **4** **[– at]** mejor en (de calidad intelectual, manual, etc.): *I am better at music = yo soy mejor en música.* || *adv.* **5** mejor, más adecuadamente, en mayor grado: *this is better written = esto está mejor escrito.* || *v.t.* **6** mejorar (la categoría, posición, estamento, etc.), superar (una cifra, un resultado, etc.). || *v.r.* **7** subir de categoría, subir en la escala social, subir de categoría social: *we want to better ourselves = queremos mejorar de categoría social.* || **8 to be all the – for,** venir bien, sentar bien, caer bien: *we'll be all the better for these holidays = nos vendrán bien estas vacaciones.* **9 to be – off, a)** estar mucho mejor, ser más conveniente, venir mejor, sentar mejor: *you'll be better off going to bed = estarás mucho mejor acostándote.* **b)** tener más dinero, estar mejor acomodado, disponer de medios materiales. **10 – half,** V. **half. 11 – nature,** V. **nature. 12 betters,** superiores: *pay attention to your betters = haz caso a tus superiores.* **13 – the devil you know,** V. **devil. 14 discretion is the – part of valour,** V. **discretion. 15 for – or worse,** para bien o para mal, en la fortuna como en la desventura. **16 for the –,** hacia mejor, con mejora. **17 to get the – of,** vencer, ganar: *she got the better of me at the debate = me ganó en el debate.* **18 had –,** será mejor, sería mejor, lo mejor es que: *we'd better get started = será mejor que nos pongamos en camino.* **19 to know –,** V. **know. 20 so much the –/all the –,** tanto mejor, mejor así. **20 that's –,** así está mejor, mucho mejor así. **21 the – part of,** V. **part. 22 the – to,** para... mejor: *the better to see you = para verte mejor.* **23 the sooner the –/the more the –,** mientras antes sea mejor, cuanto antes mejor. **24 to think – of,** V. **think.**
better | 'betər | *s.c.* apostante.
betterment | 'betəmənt | *s.i.* (form.) mejora, mejoramiento.
betting | 'betɪŋ | *s.i.* **1** apuesta, apuestas. || *s.sing.* **2** probabilidad: *what is the betting she'll be hungry in a few minutes? = ¿cuál es la probabilidad de que tenga hambre dentro de pocos minutos?*
betting-shop | 'betɪŋʃɒp | *s.c.* despacho de apuestas.
between | bɪ'twiːn | *prep.* **1** entre (dos cosas o personas): *sitting between two policemen = sentado entre dos policías.* **2** entre (varias cosas): *he walked between the corpses = caminó entre los cadáveres.* **3** entre (compartido): *we drank the whole bottle between Jim and me = nos bebimos la botella entera entre Jim y yo.* || *adv.* **4** en medio, de por medio, por el medio: *there was room so she sat between = había sitio, por lo que se sentó en medio.* || **5 – the devil and the deep blue sea,** V. **devil. 6 – you and me,** entre tú y yo (confidencialmente). **7 in –,** en medio, en medio de: *I wanted to look but she was standing in between = quería mirar pero ella estaba de pie en medio.*
betwixt | bɪ'twɪkst | **– and between,** entre una cosa y otra, entre una posición y otra.
bevel | 'bevl | *s.c.* **1** bisel. **2** escuadra. || *v.t.* **3** biselar.
bevelled | 'bevld | *adj.* biselado.
beverage | 'bevərɪdʒ | *s.c.* (form.) bebida.
bevy | 'bevɪ | *s.c.* (desp.) montón, montonazo.
bewail | bɪ'weɪl | *v.t.* (form.) lamentar, llorar.
beware | bɪ'weər | *v.i.* **[to – (of)]** tener cuidado (porque hay peligro).
bewhiskered | bɪ'wɪskəd | *adj.* (lit. o hum.) barbado.
bewilder | bɪ'wɪldər | *v.t.* desconcertar, azorar, dejar perplejo.
bewildered | bɪ'wɪldəd | *adj.* **[– (at/by /about)]** desconcertado, azorado, aturullado.
bewildering | bɪ'wɪldərɪŋ | *adj.* desconcertante.
bewilderment | bɪ'wɪldəmənt | *s.i.* desconcierto, perplejidad.
bewitch | bɪ'wɪtʃ | *v.t.* **1** hechizar, embrujar. **2** (fig.) encantar, fascinar.
bewitched | bɪ'wɪtʃt | *adj.* **1** hechizado, embrujado. **2** (fig.) encantado, fascinado.
bewitching | bɪ'wɪtʃɪŋ | *adj.* fascinante, encantador.
bewitchingly | bɪ'wɪtʃɪŋlɪ | *adv.* fascinantemente, encantadoramente.
beyond | bɪ'jɒnd | *prep.* **1** más allá de: *beyond the mountains = más allá de las montañas.* **2** fuera de (la responsabilidad, cuidado, etc. de alguien): *doing that is beyond my duty = el hacer eso está fuera de mi obligación.* **3** fuera de, más allá de (posibilidades económicas). **4** [– + *pron.*] imposible de entender, muy por encima de: *Mathematics is beyond me = las Matemáticas son imposibles de entender para mí.* **5** después de, más tarde de: *beyond that age = después de esa época.* || *adv.* **6** más allá, más lejos. || **7 – a joke,** V. **joke. 8 – belief,** increíble. **9 – one's wildest dreams,** V. **dream. 10 – someone's means,** V. **mean. 11 – the pale,** V. **pale. 12 the back of –,** V. **back.**
Bhutan | buː'tɑːn | *s.sing.* Bután.
Bhutanese | ˌbuːtɑː'niːz [*pl.* **Bhutanese**] *s.c.* **1** butanés (ciudadano). || *adj.* **2** butanés (costumbres, tradiciones, etc.).
Bhutani | buː'tɑːnɪ | V. **Bhutanese.**
bi- | baɪ | *prefijo* bi (indica dos): *bilingualism = bilingüismo.*
biannual | baɪ'ænjʊəl | *adj.* bianual.
bias | 'baɪəs | *s.c.* e *i.* **1** prejuicio. **2** parcialidad, sesgo. **3** inclinación, tendencia: *I have no scientific bias in my character = no tengo ninguna inclinación hacia la ciencia en mi carácter.* || *v.t.* **4** influenciar, predisponer: *my parents biassed me against her opinion = mis padres me predispusieron contra la opinión de ella.*
biased | baɪəst | (también **biassed**) *adj.* **1** parcial, sesgado. **2** **[– (towards)]** sesgado (hacia unos estudios o especialización).
bib | bɪb | *s.c.* **1** babero. **2** peto, pechera (de ropa). || **3 to be in one's best – and tucker,** (fam.) ir de punta en blanco; vestir lo mejor que uno tiene.
bible | 'baɪbl | *s.c.* **1** REL. biblia, ejemplar de la biblia. **2** (fig.) biblia, manual principal. || **3 the Bible,** REL. la Biblia.
bible-bashing | 'baɪblbæʃɪŋ | (también **bible-punching**) *adj.* REL. agresivo en la predicación evangélica (típico de grupos protestantes).
bible-punching | 'baɪblpʌntʃɪŋ | V. **bible-bashing.**
biblical | 'bɪblɪkl | *adj.* REL. bíblico.
bibliographer | ˌbɪblɪ'ɒgrəfər | *s.c.* bibliógrafo.
bibliographical | ˌbɪblɪə'græfɪkl | *adj.* bibliográfico.

bibliography | ˌbɪblɪ'ɒgrəfɪ | *s.c.* e *i.* bibliografía.
bibliophile | 'bɪblɪəfaɪl | *s.c.* bibliófilo.
bibulous | 'bɪbjʊləs | *adj.* (hum.) borrachín.
bicameral | ˌbaɪ'kæmərəl | *adj.* POL. bicameral.
bicarb | ˌbaɪ'kɑːb | *s.i.* (fam.) bicarbonato.
bicarbonate of soda | ˌbaɪ'kɑːbənɪtəv səʊdə | *s.i.* QUIM. bicarbonato sódico.
bicentenary | ˌbaɪsen'tiːnərɪ | (EE.UU.) | ˌbaɪ'sentənerɪ | *s.c.* bicentenario.
bicentennial | ˌbaɪsen'tenɪəl | *adj.* bicentenario.
biceps | 'baɪseps | [*pl.* **biceps**] *s.c.* ANAT. bíceps (músculo).
bicker | 'bɪkər | *v.i.* reñir, pelearse (sobre algo sin importancia).
bickering | 'bɪkərɪŋ | *s.i.* riña, pelea. V. **bicker.**
bicycle | 'baɪsɪkl | *s.c.* **1** bicicleta. || *v.i.* **2** ir en bicicleta, montar en bicicleta.
bicycle-clip | 'baɪsɪklklɪp | *s.c.* pinza para montar en bicicleta (para que los bajos de los pantalones no se ensucien).
bicyclist | 'baɪsɪklɪst | *s.c.* ciclista.
bid | bɪd | *v.* [*pret.irreg.* **bid** o **bade,** *p.p.* **bid** o **bidden**] *t.* **1 [to – +** *o.* **+ (for)]** ofertar, licitar. **2** (form.) dar, decir (un saludo). **3 [to –** + *o.* + *inf.*] (form.) solicitar, pedir. || *i.* **[to – for]** licitar a favor de, licitar por (algún objeto, contrato, etc.). || *s.c.* **4 [– (for)]** oferta, licitación. **5** [– + *inf.*] intento, tentativa: *he made a bid to control the party = hizo una tentativa de controlar el partido.*
bidden | 'bɪdn | *p.p.* de **bid.**
bidder | 'bɪdər | *s.c.* **1** postor, licitador. || **2 the highest –,** el mejor postor.
bidding | 'bɪdɪŋ | *s.sing.* **1** licitación, oferta. || **2 at someone's –,** (form.) al servicio de alguien, obedeciendo a alguien, en actitud de servicio hacia alguien. **3 to do someone's –,** (form.) hacer lo que alguien dice, hacer lo que otro manda.
bide | baɪd | *v.i.* **1** (p.u.) esperar, aguardar. || **2 to – one's time,** esperar la ocasión de uno, aguardar el momento oportuno de uno.
bidet | 'biːdeɪ | (EE.UU.) | biː'deɪ | *s.c.* bidé.
biennial | baɪ'enɪəl | *adj.* **1** bienal, bianual. || *s.c.* **2** BOT. planta bienal.
biennially | baɪ'enɪəlɪ | *adv.* cada dos años.
bier | bɪər | *s.c.* andas funerarias.
biff | bɪf | (fam.) *v.t.* **1** arrear un tortazo, atizar un mamporro. || *s.c.* **2** mamporro, tortazo, sopapo.
bifocal | ˌbaɪ'fəʊkl | *adj.* bifocal.
bifocals | ˌbaɪ'fəʊkls | *s.pl.* lentes bifocales, gafas bifocales.
bifurcate | 'baɪfəkeɪt | *v.i.* (form.) bifurcarse, dividirse en dos.
bifurcation | ˌbaɪfə'keɪʃn | *s.c.* (form.) bifurcación.
big | bɪg | [*comp.* **bigger,** *super.* **biggest**] *adj.* **1** grande, gran (físicamente, un objeto o una persona). **2** importante, influyente (persona): *a big bureaucrat.* **3** (a veces desp.) grandioso, rimbombante (idea, proyecto, etc.). **4** generoso, magnánimo (corazón). **5** (fam.) mayor (especialmente hermano o hermana). **6** mayúscula: *written with a big A = escrito con una A mayúscula.* **7** (fam. y EE.UU.) pegando fuerte: *war films are big this season = las películas de guerra están pegando fuerte esta temporada.* **8** trascendental, importante (problema, desafío, etc.). **9** (desp.) monumental, enorme: *he's a big fool = es un tonto monumental.* || *adv.* (fam.) **10** jactanciosamente, con enorme chulería: *he's always acting big = siempre está comportándose jactanciosamente.* **11** con gran éxito, con mucho éxito. || **12 – bang,** FIS. gran explosión, big bang (hipótesis sobre la formación del Universo). **13 – bang theory,** FIS. teoría de la gran explosión, teoría del big bang. **14 – brother, a)** hermano mayor. **b)** (fig.) hermano mayor (fuerte estructura estatal, fuerte personalidad dictatorial, etc.). **15 – business, a)** gran empresa, gran mundo empresarial. **b)** negocio fuerte, buen negocio: *I never thought pop music would become such a big business = nunca pensé que la música moderna se convertiría en un negocio tan bueno.* **16 – cat,** (fam.) felino (un tigre, leopardo, pantera, etc.). **17 – cheese,** (vulg. y desp.) pájaro de cuenta (poderoso). **18 – city,** gran ciudad (en el sentido de la atracción que ejerce). **19 – deal,** V. **deal. 20 — dipper,** (brit.) montaña rusa. **21 Big Dipper,** (EE.UU.) ASTR. Osa Mayor. **22 – fish,** (fam.) pez gordo. **23 – game,** caza mayor. **24 – hand,** manilla larga (del reloj). **25 – head,** (fam. y desp.) sabelotodo. **26 – money,** dinero en gran escala. **27 – mouth,** (fam. y desp.) soplón, chismoso. **28 – name,** nombre conocido por todos; persona de gran relevancia. **29 – noise,** (fam.) tipo de fuste, tipo de gran influencia (dentro de una empresa, institución, etc.). **30 – shot,** (fam.) tipo de importancia, pez gordo, personaje importante. **31 – time,** (fam.) momento de gran trascendencia, período de gran influencia: *this is big time for me now = éste es un momento de gran trascendencia para mí.* **32 – toe,** dedo gordo (del pie). **33 – top,** carpa central (de un circo). **34 – wheel,** noria (en ferias). **35 – with child,** embarazada, encinta. **36 in a – way,** de una manera decidida; a lo grande: *I'm going to get into the building trade in a big way = me voy a meter en la construcción a lo grande.* **37 to make it –,** (fam.) tener un gran éxito. **38 to talk –,** (fam.) chulearse, fanfarronear. **39 to think –,** pensar a lo grande; no andarse con chiquitas en los planes. **40 that's – of you,** (fam.) eso es muy detallista por tu parte (sarcásticamente). **41 too – for one's boots,** V. **boot.**
bigamist | 'bɪgəmɪst | *s.c.* bígamo.
bigamous | 'bɪgəməs | *adj.* bígamo.
bigamously | 'bɪgəməslɪ | *adv.* de forma bígama.
bigamy | 'bɪgəmɪ | *s.i.* bigamia.
biggish | 'bɪgɪʃ | *adj.* **1** grandote, tirando a grande. **2** de cierta consideración, de cierta importancia: *a biggish salary = un buen sueldo.*
big-headed | 'bɪghedɪd | *adj.* (fam. y desp.) sabelotodo; vanidoso.
big-hearted | 'bɪghɑːtɪd | *adj.* generoso, magnánimo, de gran corazón.
bight | baɪt | *s.c.* **1** GEOG. ensenada, cala. **2** vuelta, lazo (en una cuerda).
bigness | bɪgnɪs | *s.i.* **1** enormidad (física). **2** importancia (de una persona, proyecto, etc.).
bigot | 'bɪgət | *s.c.* (desp.) fanático, sectario, intolerante.
bigoted | 'bɪgətɪd | *adj.* (desp.) lleno de prejuicios; fanático, intolerante.
bigotry | 'bɪgətrɪ | *s.i.* (desp.) sectarismo, intolerancia, fanatismo.
bigwig | 'bɪgwɪg | *s.c.* (fam.) VIP, tipo importante.
bijou | 'biːʒuː | [*pl.* **bijoux** (misma pronunciación)] *s.c.* **1** joya. || *adj.* **2** chic, mono.
bijoux V. **bijou.**
bike | baɪk | (fam.) *s.c.* **1** bici; moto. || *v.i.* **2** ir en bicicleta, ir por ahí en bici, ir en moto. || **3 on your –,** (brit.) lárgate, pírate.
bikini | bɪ'kiːnɪ | *s.c.* **1** bikini. || **2 – pants,** bragas ajustadas, bragas muy pequeñas.
bilabial | ˌbaɪ'leɪbɪəl | FON. *s.c.* **1** bilabial. || *adj.* **2** bilabial.
bilateral | ˌbaɪ'lætərəl | *adj.* bilateral: *bilateral treaty = tratado bilateral.*
bilateralism | ˌbaɪ'lætərəlɪzəm | *s.i.* POL. reciprocidad (en acuerdos internacionales o similar).
bilaterally | ˌbaɪ'lætərəlɪ | *adv.* bilateralmente, recíprocamente.
bilberry | 'bɪlbrɪ | (EE.UU.) | 'bɪlberɪ | *s.c.* arándano.
bile | baɪl | *s.i.* FISIOL. bilis. **2** (fig.) mal genio. || **3 – duct,** ANAT. conducto biliar.
bilge | bɪldʒ | *s.c.* **1** MAR. sentina. || *s.i.* **2** agua sucia (que se acumula en la sentina). **3** (fig. y fam.) sandez, bobada. || **4 – water,** agua sucia, agua de sentina.
bilingual | ˌbaɪ'lɪŋgwəl | *adj.* bilingüe (persona, sociedad, diccionario, etc.). || *s.c.* **2** bilingüe (persona).
bilingually | ˌbaɪ'lɪŋgwəlɪ | *adv.* desde el punto de vista bilingüe.
bilious | 'bɪlɪəs | *adj.* **1** pálido, con mala cara, de mal semblante. **2** como de bilis (color). **3** (fig.) con mal genio, de mal genio, de mal humor. || **4 to feel –,** sentirse a punto de vomitar, sentir ganas de vomitar.
biliousness | 'bɪlɪəsnɪs | *s.i.* **1** biliosidad. **2** (fig.) mal humor, mal genio.
bilk | bɪlk | *v.t.* estafar, no pagar, evitar el pago de (dinero).
bill | bɪl | *s.c.* **1** cuenta (de restaurante u hotel); factura (de compras); recibo (de luz, teléfono, etc.). **2** (EE.UU.) billete (de dinero). **3** DER. proyecto de ley parlamentaria. **4** cartel, letrero (para pegar en paredes). **5** pico (de pájaros). || *s.sing.* **6 [the –]** el elenco (en espectáculos). **7** programa (en espectáculos). || *v.t.* **8** enviar la factura a, pasar la cuenta a. **9** anunciar, promocionar, poner en cartelera (en espectáculos, congresos, etc.). || **10 to – and coo,** (fam.) arrullarse, besarse y susurrarse (típico de amantes). **11 -billed,** de pico... (en compuestos hablan-

do del tipo de pico de pájaros): *a blue-billed bird = un pájaro de pico azul.* **12 – of exchange,** FIN. letra de cambio. **13 – of fare,** (p.u.) carta (menú). **14 – of health,** buen informe sobre la salud, patente de buena salud. **15 – of lading,** COM. MAR. conocimiento de embarque (lista de artículos de cargo). **16 – of rights,** DER. POL. declaración de derechos fundamentales. **17 – of sale,** DER. contrato de compraventa. **18 to fill/fit the –,** (fam.) satisfacer todos los requisitos, cumplir los requisitos. **19 to foot the –,** V. **foot.**

billabong | 'bɪləbɒŋ | *s.c.* GEOL. arroyo seco, brazo de río seco (en Australia).

billboard | 'bɪlbɔːd | *s.c.* cartelera, valla para anuncios.

billet | 'bɪlɪt | MIL. *v.t.* **1** alojar (especialmente a soldados en casas privadas). || *s.c.* **2** alojamiento, alojamiento para soldados.

billet-doux | bɪleɪ'duː | [*pl.* **billets-doux** (se pronuncia igual)] *s.c.* (lit. o hum.) carta de amor, carta amorosa.

billfold | 'bɪlfəʊld | (brit. **wallet**) *s.c.* (EE.UU.) billetera, cartera.

bill-hook | 'bɪlhʊk | *s.c.* podadera (instrumento).

billiards | 'bɪlɪədz | *s.i.* **1** [– *v.sing.*] billar (juego). || **2 billiard-,** de billar (en compuestos): *billard-table = mesa de billar.*

billing | 'bɪlɪŋ | *s.i.* publicidad (de un espectáculo concreto).

billion | 'bɪlɪən | *num.card.* **1** (brit.) billón; (EE.UU.) cien mil millones. || **2 by the –,** en cantidades ingentes. **3 billions (of),** cantidades ingentes (de); billones (de).

billionaire | 'bɪlɪəneə | *s.c.* **1** billonario. || *adj.* **2** billonario.

billow | 'bɪləʊ | *v.i.* **1** ondular, agitarse (banderas, velas, etc., al viento). **2** levantarse, alzarse (polvo, humo, etc.). || *s.c.* **3** (arc.) ola (de mar). **4** oleada, ola (de humo, polvo, etc.).

billowy | 'bɪləʊɪ | *adj.* ondulante (como el movimiento de las olas).

bill-poster | 'bɪlpəʊstər | (también **bill-sticker**) *s.c.* cartelero (persona).

bill-sticker | 'bɪlstɪkər | V. **bill-poster.**

billy | 'bɪlɪ | *s.c.* **1** bote, lata (especial para cocinar a cielo abierto). || **2 – can,** bote, lata. V. **billy 1. 3 – goat,** ZOOL. macho cabrío.

billy-oh | 'bɪlɪəʊ | (también **billy-o**) **like –,** (p.u., fam. y brit.) con todas las fuerzas.

biltong | 'bɪltɒŋ | *s.i.* cecina, tasajo (especialmente en Africa del Sur).

bimonthly | ˌbaɪ'mʌnθlɪ | *adj.* bimensual.

bin | bɪn | *s.c.* **1** cubo (normalmente de basura). **2** recipiente, cajón (del pan, harina, etc.).

binary | 'baɪnərɪ | *adj.* **1** MAT. binario. || **2 – digit,** MAT. dígito binario. **3 – notation/– system,** INF. sistema binario. **4 – star,** ASTR. estrella binaria.

bind | baɪnd | *v.t.* [*pret.* y *p.p. irreg.* **bound**] **1** atar, liar, amarrar. **2** (fig.) ligar, unir, vincular (a personas): *the gratitude that binds me to you = la gratitud que me une a ti.* **3** GAST. aglutinar, hacer compacto (una masa o mezcla). **4** recoger, sujetar (el pelo). **5** obligar, comprometer (moral o legalmente): *the contract binds you = el contrato te obliga.* **6** encuadernar (un libro). **7 [to – + *o.* + (with)]** ribetear (ropa). **8** estreñir (comida). || *s.sing.* **9 [a –]** (fam.) un apuro, un aprieto; molestia inaguantable. || **10 to be bound (to),** estar asociado (con), estar relacionado íntimamente (con): *political power is bound to economic power = el poder político está relacionado íntimamente con el poder económico.* **11 to – over,** DER. obligar bajo amenaza legal, obligar (por un juez a hacer algo durante un cierto tiempo).

binder | 'baɪndər | *s.c.* **1** archivador, carpeta. **2** aglutinante (sustancia como el cemento). **3** encuadernador (persona). **4** cordel, cuerda para atar.

bindery | 'baɪndərɪ | *s.i.* taller de encuadernación.

binding | 'baɪndɪŋ | *adj.* **1** obligatorio, que compromete. **2** astringente. || *s.c.* e *i.* **3** encuadernación. **4** ribete, tira (para ropa).

bindweed | 'baɪndwiːd | *s.c.* e *i.* BOT. correhuela, convólvulo.

bine | baɪn | *s.c.* BOT. tallo trepador, vástago.

binge | bɪndʒ | (fam.) *s.sing.* **1** ventolera (de hacer algo repentinamente): *a shopping binge = una ventolera por hacer compras.* || **2 to go on a –,** irse de parranda, irse de juerga (especialmente bebiendo alcohol).

bingo | 'bɪŋgəʊ | *s.i.* **1** bingo (como juego): *a bingo hall = una sala de bingo.* || **2 –!,** (fam.) ¡acerté!, ¡me salió bien!, ¡bingo!

binnacle | 'bɪnəkl | *s.c.* MAR. bitácora (caja donde se guarda el compás).

binoculars | bɪ'nɒkjʊləz | *s.pl.* gemelos, prismáticos.

binomial | baɪ'nəʊmɪəl | *s.c.* MAT. binomio.

bio- | baɪəʊ | *prefijo* bio: *biorhythm.*

biochemical | ˌbaɪəʊ'kemɪkl | *adj.* bioquímico.

biochemist | ˌbaɪəʊ'kemɪst | *s.c.* bioquímico, experto en bioquímica.

biochemistry | ˌbaɪəʊ'kemɪstrɪ | *s.i.* bioquímica.

biodegradable | ˌbaɪəʊdɪ'greɪdəbl | *adj.* biodegradable.

biographer | baɪ'ɒgrəfər | *s.c.* biógrafo.

biographical | ˌbaɪə'græfɪkl | *adj.* biográfico.

biography | baɪ'ɒgrəfɪ | *s.i.* **1** LIT. biografía. || *s.c.* **2** biografía (libro).

biological | ˌbaɪə'lɒdʒɪkl | *adj.* **1** biológico, de las ciencias naturales. **2** natural (padre o madre). **3** biológico, bioquímico; bacteriológico: *biological weapons = armas bacteriológicas.* || **4 – control,** AGR. control de plagas por métodos naturales. **5 – warfare** (también **germ warfare**), MIL. guerra bacteriológica, guerra biológica.

biologically | ˌbaɪə'lɒdʒɪklɪ | *adv.* biológicamente.

biologist | baɪ'ɒlədʒɪst | *s.c.* biólogo.

biology | baɪ'ɒlədʒɪ | *s.i.* **1** biología. || *s.sing.* **2** biología, comportamiento biológico, mecanismo biológico (de un organismo).

bionic | baɪ'ɒnɪk | *adj.* (fam.) biónico (con partes del cuerpo electrónicas): *the bionic woman = la mujer biónica.*

biophysicist | ˌbaɪə'fɪzɪsɪst | *s.c.* biofísico.

biophysics | ˌbaɪə'fɪzɪks | *s.i.* biofísica.

biopsy | 'baɪɒpsɪ | *s.c.* MED. biopsia.

biosphere | 'baɪəsfɪər | *s.sing.* ASTR. bioesfera.

biosynthesis | ˌbaɪə'sɪnθɪsɪs | *s.i.* BIOQ. biosíntesis.

biotechnology | ˌbaɪəʊtek'nɒlədʒɪ | *s.i.* BIOL. biotecnología.

bipartisan | ˌbaɪpɑːtɪ'zæn | (EE.UU.) | ˌbaɪ'pɑːrtɪzn | *adj.* POL. bipartidario, de dos partidos.

bipartite | ˌbaɪ'pɑːtaɪt | *adj.* POL. bipartito (tratado o similar).

biped | 'baɪped | *s.c.* bípedo.

biplane | 'baɪpleɪn | *s.c.* AER. biplano.

birch | bəːtʃ | *s.c.* e *i.* **1** BOT. abedul. || *s.c.* **2** vara de abedul (para dar azotes).

bird | bəːd | *s.c.* **1** pájaro, ave. **2** (fam.) chica, moza, muchacha. **3** (fam.) tipo, bicho: *he's an odd bird = es un bicho raro.* || **4 a – in the hand is worth two in the bush,** más vale pájaro en mano que ciento volando. **5 – of paradise,** ZOOL. ave del paraíso. **6 – of passage, a)** ZOOL. ave migratoria. **b)** (fig.) ave de paso (persona). **7 – of prey,** ZOOL. ave de rapiña, ave de presa. **8 – santuary,** parque natural para pájaros. **9 bird's eye view,** vista de pájaro. **10 to kill two birds with one stone,** matar dos pájaros de un tiro. **11 the — has flown,** el pájaro ha volado (se ha escapado la persona requerida). **12 the birds and the bees,** (euf.) las florecitas y los animalitos (comparación para enseñar a los niños la reproducción sexual).

bird-bath | 'bəːdbɑːθ | *s.c.* alberquilla (colocada para el baño de pájaros en el jardín).

birdbrained | 'bəːdbreɪnd *adj.* (fam. y desp.) de cabeza de chorlito.

birdcage | 'bəːdkeɪdʒ | *s.c.* jaula.

birdie | 'bəːdɪ | *s.c.* **1** pajarito. **2** DEP. birdie (golpe de golf).

birdlike | 'bəːdlaɪk | *adj.* de pájaro, como un pájaro, similar a un pájaro.

birdlime | 'bəːdlaɪm | *s.i.* liga, ajonje (sustancia para cazar pájaros).

birdseed | 'bəːdsiːd | *s.i.* alpiste.

bird-song | 'bəːdsɒŋ | *s.i.* reclamo musical de pájaro.

bird-table | 'bəːdteɪbl | *s.c.* mesita para el alpiste de los pájaros.

bird-watcher | 'bəːdwɒtʃər | *s.c.* observador de pájaros.

bird-watching | 'bəːdwɒtʃɪŋ | *s.i.* observación de pájaros en libertad (un hobby con muchos seguidores en el Reino Unido).

biretta | bɪ'retə | *s.c.* REL. birreta, birrete.

Biro | 'baɪərəʊ | *s.c.* bolígrafo (marca registrada).

birth | bəːθ | *s.c.* e *i.* **1** nacimiento, alumbramiento. || *s.i.* **2** cuna, linaje, ascendencia: *of noble birth = de noble cuna.* || *s.sing.* **3 [(the) – (of)]** (fig.) comienzo, origen, nacimiento. || **4 – cer-**

tificate, partida de nacimiento. **5 by –,** de nacimiento. **6 to give – (to),** MED. alumbrar, dar a luz. **7 to give – to,** dar lugar a, causar, ocasionar, dar origen a: *his decision gave birth to a lot of resentment = su decisión dio lugar a mucho resentimiento.* **8 of one's –,** del nacimiento de uno, del origen de uno: *the city of my birth = la ciudad de mi origen.*

birth-control | 'bɜːθkəntrəl | *s.i.* control de nacimientos, control de la natalidad.

birthday | 'bɜːθdeɪ | *s.c.* **1** cumpleaños. || **2 in one's – suit,** (fam. y hum.) en el traje de Adán, en porretas.

birthmark | 'bɜːθmɑːk | *s.c.* marca de nacimiento, mancha de nacimiento.

birthplace | 'bɜːθpleɪs | *s.c.* **1** lugar de nacimiento. **2 [– (of)]** (fig.) lugar de origen (de algún hecho histórico o importante).

birth-rate | 'bɜːθreɪt | *s.c.* GEOG. índice de natalidad.

birthright | 'bɜːθraɪt | *s.c.* e *i.* derecho básico (por haber nacido como ser humano).

biscuit | 'bɪskɪt | *s.c.* **1** (brit.) galleta. **2** (EE.UU.) bizcocho. || *s.i.* **3** marrón claro. || **4 to take the –,** (fam.) ser el colmo, ser la pera.

bisect | baɪ'sekt | *v.t.* **1** dividir en dos. **2** GEOM. bisecar.

bisection | baɪ'sekʃn | *s.c.* e *i.* **1** división en dos. **2** GEOM. bisección.

bisexual | ˌbaɪ'sekʃuəl | *adj.* **1** bisexual. **2** BIOL. hermafrodita. || *s.c.* **3** bisexual, persona bisexual.

bisexuality | ˌbaɪsekʃu'æləti | *s.i.* bisexualidad; hermafroditismo.

bishop | 'bɪʃəp | *s.c.* **1** REL. obispo. **2** alfil (en ajedrez).

bishopric | 'bɪʃəprɪk | *s.c.* REL. obispado.

bismuth | 'bɪzməθ | *s.i.* QUIM. bismuto.

bison | 'baɪsn | *[pl.* **bison**] *s.c.* ZOOL. búfalo, bisonte.

bistro | 'biːstrəu | *s.c.* casa de comidas, restaurante pequeño.

bit | bɪt | *pret.irreg.* **1** de **bite.** || *s.c.* **2** (fam.) trocito, pedazo, pedacito: *bits of cardboard on the floor = trocitos de cartón sobre el suelo.* **3** (fam.) zona, parte, espacio pequeño: *this bit of Spain is beautiful = esta zona de España es preciosa.* **4** (fam.) pequeña parte, pequeña muestra (de un conjunto de cosas): *that bit of writing is not bad at all = esa pequeña muestra escrita no está nada mal.* **5** (fam.) parte, trozo, escena (de película, libro, etc.): *I enjoyed the bit about the teacher = me gustó mucho la escena del profesor.* **6** INF. bit. **7** freno (de un caballo). **8** (arc.) moneda (peniques). || *s.sing.* **9** (fam.) rollo: *I don't like the heavy metal bit = no me gusta el rollo de la música heavy.* || *s.pl.* **10** (EE.UU.) 12 centavos y medio. || **11 a –,** (fam.) **a)** un poco, un poquito, una pizca, una pizquita. **b)** bastante, un poco (con entonación que expresa mucho): *I've been waiting for a long time, you are a bit late, eh? = llevo esperando mucho tiempo, llegas un poco tarde, ¿no?* **12 a – much/a – steep/a – strong/etc.,** demasiado: *he talks a bit too much = habla demasiado.* **13 a – of a,** bastante fuerte, considerable; importante: *we are in a bit of a mess = estamos en un follón considerable.* **14 a – of all right,** (fam.) estupendo, fenomenal. **15 – by –,** poquito a poquito, muy cuidadosamente, muy gradualmente. **16 – part,** papel pequeño, papel sin importancia (en el cine, teatro, etc.). **17 bits and pieces,** (fam.) **a)** cachivaches, cosas sueltas. **b)** pequeñas posesiones. **c)** trozos, partes sueltas (de una teoría, ideología, etc.). **18 to do one's –,** hacer la aportación de uno, poner el granito de arena de uno. **19 every – as,** igual de, justo tan: *I am every bit as good as you = yo soy igual de bueno que tú.* **20 for a –,** durante un ratito, durante un corto espacio de tiempo. **21 for quite a –,** durante bastante tiempo, durante bastante rato. **22 to get/take the – between one's teeth,** fajarse, disponerse (para acometer un trabajo). **23 not a –,** en absoluto, en nada. **24 not a – of it,** (fam.) de ninguna manera, nada de nada; todo lo contrario: *I thought he was a bit stupid, but not a bit of it = creía que él era un poquito tonto, pero todo lo contrario.* **25 quite a –/a —,** bastante; mucho: *I've got quite a bit of trouble now = tengo bastantes problemas ahora.* **26 to bits, a)** en trocitos (romperse o similar). **b)** (fam.) la mar de, hasta un grado tremendo, muy: *I am frightened to bits = estoy la mar de asustado.*

bitch | bɪtʃ | *s.c.* **1** (desp. y vulg.) bruja, perra (mujer despreciable). **2** ZOOL. perra, loba, zorra. || *v.i.* **3 [to – (about)]** (fam. y desp.) quejarse, lloriquear, estar en plan quejica. || *s.sing.* **4** (fam.) fastidio: *this job is a bitch = este trabajo es un fastidio.* || **5 son of a –,** (desp. y vulg.) hijo de puta.

bitchiness | 'bɪtʃɪnɪs | *s.i.* malicia, rencor.

bitchy | 'bɪtʃɪ | *adj.* malicioso, rencoroso.

bite | baɪt | *v.* [*pret.* **bit,** *p.p.* **bitten**] *t.* **1** morder. **2** morder, picar (animales). || *i.* **3** morder: *this dog never bites = este perro nunca muerde.* **4** picar (los peces). **5** agarrarse (una superficie contra otra). **6** hacer mella, escocer (una medida de fuerza, una ley, etc.): *the strike hasn't bitten yet = la huelga no ha hecho mella todavía.* || *s.c.* **7** mordisco, dentellada. **8** mordedura, picadura (de animales). **9 [– (of/out of)]** mordisco (trozo de alimento). **10** picada (de pez). || *s.sing.* **11** (fam.) un poco de comida, un bocado: *I haven't had a bite for two days = no he probado bocado durante dos días.* **12** fuerza cortante (del viento, del frío, etc.). || *s.i.* **13** picante, sabor picante, sabor fuerte. || **14 to be bitten (by),** estar llamativamente interesado (en/por), ser atraído poderosamente (por): *I was bitten by painting = estaba atraído poderosamente por la pintura.* **15 to – back,** reprimir un deseo de decir algo; morderse los labios (para no decir algo). **16 to – into,** corroer; cortar gradualmente: *the acid bit into the metal box = el ácido corroyó la caja metálica.* **17 to – off more than one can chew,** abarcar más de lo que uno puede. **18 to – someone's head off,** V. **head. 19 to – the bullet,** hacer de tripas corazón; soportar con decisión, apretar los dientes aguantando (una dificultad). **20 to – the dust,** V. **dust. 21 to – the hand that feeds one,** V. **hand. 22 once bitten, twice shy,** el gato escaldado del agua fría huye. **23 someone's bark is worse than their –,** V. **bark. 24 something/someone won't –,** no muerde. **25 what's biting you/him/etc.?,** (fam.) ¿qué te/le/etc. está reconcomiendo?, ¿qué te/le/etc. está preocupando tanto?

biting | 'baɪtɪŋ | *adj.* **1** cortante (frío, viento, etc.). **2** mordaz, sarcástico (modo de expresarse de alguien).

bitten | 'bɪtn | *p.p.* de **bite.**

bitter | 'bɪtər | *adj.* **1** amargo (de sabor). **2** amargado, resentido (persona). **3** encarnizado, implacable (pelea, guerra, etc.). **4** cortante, desapacible (frío y viento). **5** duro, doloroso (experiencia, desilusión, etc.): *It was a bitter result = fue un resultado doloroso.* || *s.i.* **6** cerveza amarga. || **7 – lemon,** tónica de limón (bebida). **8 bitters,** biter (bebida). **9 to the – end,** hasta el final, hasta no poder más.

bitterly | 'bɪtəlɪ | *adv.* **1** desesperadamente, fieramente, implacablemente (lucha). **2** muy (con emociones fuertes): *I was bitterly angry = yo estaba muy enfadado.* **3** amargamente (sabor). **4** resentidamente, amargadamente. || **5 – cold,** frío penetrante, frío insoportable.

bitterness | 'bɪtənɪs | *s.i.* **1** resentimiento, amargura (en una persona). **2** (lo) amargo, sabor amargo. **3** dureza, severidad (de un clima, viento, etc.). **4** severidad, crueldad (de una batalla, acto, experiencia, etc.).

bittern | 'bɪtən | *s.c.* ZOOL. avetoro (un tipo de ave de marisma).

bitter-sweet | ˌbɪtə'swiːt | *adj.* **1** agridulce. **2** (fig.) agridulce, bueno y malo a la vez, positivo y negativo a la vez.

bitty | 'bɪtɪ | *adj.* (fam.) fragmentado, a trozos (inconexos); desigual, irregular (especialmente de escritos, discursos, conferencias, etc.).

bitumen | 'bɪtjumɪn | (EE.UU.) | bə'tuːmən | *s.i.* alquitrán (especialmente en carreteras).

bituminous | bɪ'tjuːmɪnəs | (EE.UU.) | bɪ'tuːmɪnəs | *adj.* bituminoso.

bivouac | 'bɪvuæk | *s.c.* **1** vivac, campamento (especialmente de soldados o escaladores). || [*ger.* **bivouacking,** *pret.* **bivouacked**] *v.i.* **2** acampar. V. **bivouac 1.**

bizarre | bɪ'zɑːr | *adj.* extraño, grotesco, extravagante (cosas y personas).

blab | blæb | [*ger.* **blabbing,** *pret.* **blabbed**] *v.i.* **[to – (about/to)]** (fam.) soltar un secreto, chismear (sobre cosas que deberían quedar en secreto).

blabber | 'blæbər | *v.i.* (fam. y desp.) cotorrear, parlotear.

blabbermouth | 'blæbəmauθ | *s.c.* (fam. y desp.) chismoso.

black | blæk | *adj.* **1** negro (color de cosas o personas). **2** solo (café o té). **3** negro, desesperado (situación, posición, etc.). **4** negro (humor). **5** negra (magia). **6** (lit.) perverso, malvado, siniestro. **7** negro (de suciedad). **8** sombrío, lúgubre: *a black pool = un estanque lúgubre.* **9** melancólico, tristón (paisaje, día, estado de ánimo, etc.): *a black day = un día tristón.* **10** oscuro (de color). **11** prohibido para un sindicalista (en caso de huelga): *if you are a true trade unionist you can't handle black goods now = si eres un sindicalista genuino no puedes llevar mercancías prohibidas a los sindicalistas.* || *s.c.* **12** negro (persona). || *s.i.* **13** negro, (lo) oscuro. || *v.t.* **14** boicotear, no tratar con. V. **black 11. 15** poner morado, amoratar (un ojo). **16** embetunar, dar betún (a zapatos). || **17 as – as ink/pitch,** tan negro como el carbón. **18 as – as thunder,** negro de ira, negro de cólera. **19 Black,** negro (persona). **20 – Africa,** GEOG. POL. Africa negra (al sur del Sahara). **21 – and blue,** totalmente amoratado, lleno de cardenales (por una paliza). **22 – and white,** blanco y negro (especialmente televisor o película). **23 – art,** magia negra. **24 – belt, a)** DEP. cinturón negro (en artes marciales). **b)** (fig.) cinturón negro (parte donde viven personas de color). **25 – box,** AER. caja negra. **26 – comedy,** comedia de humor negro. **27 – economy,** ECON. economía negra, economía sumergida. **28 – eye,** ojo morado, ojo amoratado (por un golpe). **29 Black Friar,** REL. dominico. **30 – hole,** ASTR. agujero negro. **31 – ice,** hielo (de carretera que no se puede ver). **32 Black Maria,** (fam.) furgón de policía (para transporte de prisioneros). **33 – mark,** punto negro, punto negativo; mala nota: *I'll give you a black mark for what you've done = te pondré una mala nota por lo que has hecho.* **34 – market,** ECON. mercado negro. **35 – marketeer,** ECON. estraperlista, tratante del mercado negro. **36 – mass,** REL. misa negra, misa satánica. **37 Black Muslim,** (EE.UU.) musulmán del grupo de Musulmanes negros. **38 to – out, a)** perder el sentido, desmayarse. **b)** dejar totalmente oscuro, apagar completamente las luces. **c)** ocultar, esconder (algo escrito con pintura o similar). **d)** censurar, bloquear (un programa de televisión o radio). **39 – pepper,** pimienta negra. **40 Black Power,** (EE.UU.) POL. movimiento para el poder de los negros. **41 – pudding,** morcilla. **42 – sheep,** oveja negra (persona). **43 – spot, a)** punto negro (de tráfico peligroso). **b)** (fig.) punto negro (lugar con algún tipo de problema). **44 – tie,** de etiqueta. **45 – widow,** ZOOL. viuda negra (araña). **46 in – and white, a)** por escrito. **b)** en términos absolutos de bueno y malo, en términos absolutos de blanco y negro. **47 in the –,** FIN. con superávit (en una cuenta). **48 not as – as something is painted,** no tan negro como algo se pinta, no tan mal como se dice. **49 the Black Country,** GEOG. la zona industrial de Gran Bretaña. **50 the Black Death,** HIST. la peste negra (la peste de la época medieval).

blackball | 'blækbɔːl | *v.t.* excluir, rechazar (especialmente a una persona que quiere hacerse de un club, asociación, etc.).

black-beetle | ˌblæk'biːtl | *s.c.* ZOOL. escarabajo negro.

blackberry | 'blækbrɪ | | 'blækberɪ | *s.c.* **1** BOT. zarza. **2** zarzamora, mora.

blackberrying | 'blækberɪŋ | *s.i.* recolección de moras, recolección de zarzamoras.

blackbird | 'blækbəːd | *s.c.* ZOOL. mirlo (ave).

blackboard | 'blækbɔːd | (EE.UU. **chalkboard**) *s.c.* pizarra, encerado.

blackcurrant | ˌblækkʌrənt | *s.c.* **1** BOT. grosella negra (matorral). **2** grosella negra (fruto).

blacken | 'blækən | *v.t.* **1** ennegrecer, pintar de negro. **2** (fig.) desacreditar, difamar (a personas o grupos).

blackguard | 'blækgɑːd | *s.c.* (arc.) tunante, bribón, desalmado.

blackhead | 'blækhed | *s.c.* espinilla (en la piel).

blacking | 'blækɪŋ | *s.i.* betún negro, betún abrillantador (para calzado).

blackish | 'blækɪs | *adj.* negruzco, tirando a negro.

blackjack | 'blækdʒæk | *s.c.* **1** (EE.UU.) cachiporra. **2** veintiuna (juego de cartas). V. **pontoon.**

blackleg | 'blækleg | *s.c.* (brit. y desp.) esquirol.

blacklist | 'blæklɪst | *s.c.* **1** lista negra (donde se apuntan nombres de personas que serán represaliadas). || *v.t.* **2** poner en la lista negra, incluir en la lista negra.

blackmail | 'blækmeɪl | *s.i.* **1** chantaje, extorsión. || *v.t.* **2** chantajear.

blackmailer | 'blækmeɪlər | *s.c.* chantajista.

blackness | 'blæknɪs | *s.i.* **1** oscuridad. **2** negritud (como raza).

blackout | 'blækaut | *s.c.* **1** apagón, corte de electricidad, corte de luz. **2** MIL. velo negro; luces apagadas. **3** PER. censura, supresión (de noticias o similar). **4** luces fuera (en el teatro). **5** desmayo.

blackshirt | 'blækʃəːt | *s.c.* POL. camisa negra (fascista).

blacksmith | 'blæksmɪθ | *s.c.* herrero.

blackthorn | 'blækθɔːn | *s.c.* BOT. endrino.

bladder | 'blædər | *s.c.* **1** ANAT. vejiga. **2** cámara (en balones de fútbol, baloncesto, etc.).

blade | bleɪd | *s.c.* **1** hoja, cuchilla (de espada u objeto cortante). **2** pala (de remo), aspa (de molino, hélice, etc.). **3** brizna (de hierba). **4** (arc.) espada, espadachín.

blah | blɑː | *s.i.* (fam.) bla, bla, bla (cháchara aburrida, repetitiva, etc.).

blame | bleɪm | *v.t.* **1 [to – *o.* + (for)]** culpar, echar la culpa, reprochar. || *s.i.* **2** culpa. **3** censura, crítica. || **4 to be to – (for),** tener la culpa (de), ser responsable (de). **5 to lay the –,** V. **lay.**

blameless | 'bleɪmlɪs | *adj.* libre de culpa, inocente, intachable.

blamelessly | 'bleɪmlɪslɪ | *adv.* inocentemente, intachablemente.

blameworthy | 'bleɪmwəːðɪ | *adj.* censurable, culpable.

blanch | blɑːntʃ | (EE.UU.) | blæntʃ | *v.t.* e *i.* **1** palidecer. || *v.t.* **2** GAST. escaldar; blanquear.

blanched | blɑːntʃt | (EE.UU.) | blæntʃt | *adj.* pálido, demacrado.

bland | blænd | *adj.* **1** insípido, insulso, imperturbable (persona). **2** (desp.) insípido (de sabor). **3** (desp.) aburrido (música, libro, etc.).

blandly | 'blændlɪ | *adv.* **1** insípidamente, imperturbablemente. **2** (desp.) insípidamente (sabor). **3** (desp.) aburridamente, sin interés.

blandness | 'blændnɪs *s.i.* **1** imperturbabilidad. **2** (desp.) falta de sabor. **3** (desp.) falta de fuerza, carencia de atractivo (especialmente en el arte).

blandishments | 'blændɪʃmənts | *s.pl.* (form.) lisonjas, zalamerías, halagos.

blank | blæŋk | *adj.* **1** en blanco, sin nada (papel, cintas vírgenes, etc.). **2** liso (pared), libre, vacío (cielo). **3** sin expresión (rostro). **4** total, absoluto (rechazo, negativa, etc.). || *s.c.* **5** espacio en blanco (en papel). **6** MIL. cartucho de fogueo. || *s.sing.* **7 [a –]** un vacío total (de pensamiento): *my mind is a blank = mi cabeza es un vacío total.* || **8 – cartridge,** MIL. cartucho de fogueo. **9 – cheque,** cheque en blanco. **10 – verse,** LIT. verso libre. **11 to draw a –,** (fam.) no sacar nada en claro, no obtener resultado alguno. **12 to give someone a – cheque,** dar a alguien carta blanca. **13 to go –,** no saber qué decir, no saber qué responder; quedarse en blanco (la mente).

blanket | 'blæŋkɪt | *s.c.* **1** manta (cama). **2** (fig.) capa, manto (de nieve, niebla, etc.). **3** (fig.) sensación sofocante, sensación opresora (de desesperación o similar). || *adj.* **4** general, comprehensivo, que abarca a todo/todos: *a blanket agreement = un acuerdo comprehensivo.* || *v.t.* **5** cubrir por completo, tapar totalmente. || **6 – stitch,** punto de manta (para protección de los bordes).

blankly | 'blæŋklɪ | *adv.* **1** inexpresivamente (rostro). **2** totalmente, absolutamente (rechazar, negar, etc.).

blankness | 'blæŋknɪs | *s.i.* **1** inexpresividad (rostro). **2** (lo) absoluto, (lo) radical (de una negativa o similar).

blare | bleər | *v.i.* **1** sonar con gran estruendo, atronar, pegar fuertes pitidos. || *s.sing.* **2** estruendo, fragor, ruido fuerte. || **3 to – out,** sonar atronadoramente, lanzar un estruendo infernal.

blarney | 'blɑːnɪ | *s.i.* (fam.) labia.

blasé | 'blɑːzeɪ | (EE.UU.) | blɑː'zeɪ | *adj.* indiferente, hastiado.

blaspheme | blæs'fiːm | *v.i.* REL. blasfemar.

blasphemer | blæs'fiːmər | *s.c.* REL. blasfemo.

blasphemous | 'blæsfəməs | *adj.* REL. blasfemo.

blasphemously | 'blæsfɪməslɪ | *adv.* REL. de modo blasfemo.

blasphemy | 'blæsfəmɪ | *s.i.* REL. blasfemia.

blast | blɑːst | (EE.UU.) | blæst | *s.c.* **1** explosión, estallido. **2** ráfaga (de viento). **3** FIS. onda expansiva (de una bomba). **4** trompetazo, toque de trompeta. || *v.t.* **5** destrozar, hacer añicos (mediante bomba). **6** abrir paso, abrir camino (mediante bombas). **7** (fig.) abrirse paso a tiros, abrirse paso a bombazos. **8** emitir un estruendo ensordecedor. **9** (fig. y fam.) criticar despiadadamente. || *v.i.* **10** hacer explosión, explotar. **11** hacer un ruido fuerte, sonar atronadoramente. _ **blast!** *interj.* (vulg.) **12** ¡mierda!, ¡me cago en la mar! || **13 at full –/full –, a)** atronadoramente, ensordecedoramente. **b)** a toda máquina, a todo vapor. **14 to – away, a)** disparar sin parar. **b)** sonar estruendosamente, hacer un sonido atronador. **15 – furnace,** MET. alto horno. **16 – it!,** ¡maldita sea! **17 to – off,** despegar (cohete espacial). **18 to – out,** emitir con sonido fuerte.

blasted | 'blɑːstɪd | *adj.* (fam.) maldito, condenado: *blasted car! = ¡maldito coche!*

blasting | 'blɑːstɪŋ | *s.i.* voladura (mediante explosivo).

blast-off | 'blɑːstɒf | *s.i.* despegue (de cohetes espaciales).

blatancy | 'bleɪtnsɪ | *s.i.* evidencia, (lo) flagrante.

blatant | 'bleɪtnt | *adj.* patente, evidente, flagrante.

blatantly | 'bleɪtntlɪ | *adv.* patentemente, evidentemente, flagrantemente.

blaze | bleɪz | *v.i.* **1** arder, llamear, lanzar llamas (con gran esplendor). **2 [to – (with)]** (fig.) llamear, brillar, resplandecer: *the countryside blazed with colour = el campo brillaba con todo tipo de colores.* **3 [to – (with)]** (fig. y lit.) arder (ojos o emoción). **4** disparar, escupir fuego (sin parar). || *v.t.* **5** PER. anunciar con grandes titulares, proclamar a grandes titulares. || *s.c.* **6** estallido, llamarada (de sol, color, etc.). **7** PER. fuego, incendio. || *s.sing.* **8 [(a) – of]** alarde de; resplandor de: *a blaze of colour = un alarde de color.* || **9 to be blazed abroad,** (p.u.) ser anunciado con bombo y platillo. **10 to – a trail,** abrir caminos nuevos (en zonas salvajes, experimentos, alguna ciencia, etc.). **11 to blaze away, a)** disparar sin parar, hacer fuego repetidamente. **b)** arder con gran brillo, resplandecer con gran atractivo. **12 to – up, a)** avivarse repentinamente, coger fuerza inesperada (un fuego). **b)** (fig.) ponerse hecho un basilisco, montar en cólera. **13 go to blazes!,** (vulg.) ¡vete a la mierda! **14 like blazes,** (fam.) como un rayo; como si te fuera la vida en ello. **15 the blazes,** (fam.) porras, narices: *where the blazes is my shirt? = ¿dónde narices está mi camisa?*

blazer | 'bleɪzər | *s.c.* chaqueta de sport, chaqueta deportiva (que llevan normalmente miembros de una misma escuela, asociación, etc.).

blazing | 'bleɪzɪŋ | *adj.* **1** ardiente, abrasador (calor). **2** brillante, deslumbrante. **3** (fig.) violento, airado (discusión o similar).

blazon | 'bleɪzn | *v.t.* (form.) blasonar, exhibir, hacer obstención (de unas palabras en algún sitio).

bleach | bliːtʃ | *s.i.* **1** lejía. || *v.t.* e *i.* **2** blanquear, quitar el color. **3** teñir de rubio (cabello).

bleachers | 'bliːtʃəz | *s.pl.* (EE.UU.) gradas descubiertas (estadio).

bleaching-powder | 'bliːtʃɪŋpaʊdər | *s.c.* e *i.* lejía.

bleak | bliːk | *adj.* **1** desolado, yermo (lugar). **2** sombrío, triste (situación, perspectiva, etc.). **3** desapacible (tiempo). 4 frío, triste (persona).

bleakly | 'bliːklɪ | *adv.* **1** sombríamente, tristemente (situación). **2** desapaciblemente (tiempo). **3** fríamente, tristemente (manera de saludar, comportarse, etc.).

bleakness | 'bliːknɪs | *s.i.* **1** desolación (de un lugar). **2** (lo) desapacible (tiempo). **3** frialdad, tristeza, hosquedad (en las maneras de comportarse).

blearily | 'blɪərɪlɪ | *adv.* con mirada cansina, con mirada cansada.

bleary | 'blɪərɪ | *adj.* cansado, agotado, enrojecido (ojos, a causa de falta de sueño o fenómeno parecido).

bleary-eyed | ˌblɪərɪ'aɪd | *adj.* con los ojos enrojecidos.

bleat | bliːt | *v.i.* **1** balar (oveja). || *v.t.* e *i.* **2** (fig.) gemir, decir con gemidos, decir entre gemidos. || *s.c.* **3** balido (oveja). **4** (fig.) balido, gemido, grito plañidero.

bled | bled | *pret.* y *p.p.* de **bleed.**

bleed | bliːd | *v.i.* **1** sangrar, echar sangre. **2** descolorarse, desteñirse (a causa del lavado). || *v.t.* **3** sangrar (líquidos o gases de radiadores o similar). **4** MED. sacar sangre, sangrar (especialmente con sanguijuelas en el pasado). **5** (fam. y fig.) sacar el dinero a, chupar la sangre a. || **6 to – for,** derramar la sangre por (una causa, la patria, etc.). **7 to – someone dry/white,** arrancar el último céntimo a alguien, dejar a alguien sin un céntimo. **8 to – to death,** morir desangrado.

bleeder | 'bliːdər | *s.c.* (vulg.) cabrón, gilipollas (en sentido ofensivo o de lástima): *you poor bleeder = pobre cabrón.*

bleeding | 'bliːdɪŋ | *s.i.* **1** hemorragia. || *adj.* **2** (brit. y vulg.) jodido; condenado: *the bleeding taxes! = ¡los jodidos impuestos!*

bleep | bliːp | *s.c.* **1** sonido agudo, pitido. || *v.i.* **2** emitir un sonido agudo, dar un pitido. || *v.t.* **3** llamar mediante chivato, llamar con un buscapersonas (típico en médicos y otros profesionales).

bleeper | 'bliːpər | *s.c.* ELEC. buscapersonas, chivato buscapersonas.

blemish | 'blemɪʃ | *s.c.* **1** defecto, mancha, tacha (en la apariencia de personas especialmente). || *v.t.* **2** manchar (apariencia personal); estropear un poco (fruta). **3** mancillar, empañar (reputación o similar).

blemished | 'blemɪʃt | *adj.* estropeado, con algún defecto (especialmente fruta).

blench | blentʃ | *v.i.* **[to – (at)]** acobardarse, retroceder con miedo.

blend | blend | *v.t.* **1** mezclar (sustancias, convirtiéndolas en una). **2** combinar, armonizar (colores, sonidos, estilos, etc.). || *v.i.* **3** mezclarse (varias sustancias en una). **4 [to – (with)]** combinar(se), armonizar(se): *the colours blended beautifully = los colores se combinaban bellísimamente.* || *s.c.* **5** mezcla (sustancias, especialmente café, té y whisky). || *s.sing.* **6 [– of]** combinación de: *a blend of beauty and intelligence = una combinación de belleza e inteligencia.* || **7 to – in/into,** entremezclarse, desaparecer entre (haciéndose parte del objeto en el que desaparece): *the lizard blended into the undergrowth = el lagarto desapareció en la maleza.*

blended | 'blendɪd | *adj.* mezclado (tabaco, café, té, whisky, etc.).

blender | 'blendər | *s.c.* ELECTR. licuadora.

bless | bles | *v.t.* [*pret.* y *p.p.* **blessed** o **blest**] **1** REL. bendecir. **2 [to – + *o.* + (for)]** agradecer profusamente, bendecir (a alguien en agradecimiento). **3 [to – + *o.* + (with)]** bendecir (con alguna virtud, gracia, etc.). **4** (normalmente pasiva) aprobar, dar la bendición a (un plan o similar). || **5 – my soul,** (p.u.) válgame Dios. **6 – you, a)** Jesús (al estornudar). **b)** Dios te lo agradezca. **7 God –,** adiós, Dios te guarde, Dios quede contigo. **8 God – you/him/etc.,** Dios te/le/etc. bendiga, Dios te lo agradezca/Dios se lo agradezca/etc. (como agradecimiento, muestra de lástima, alivio, etc.): *he talked to the boss on my behalf, God bless him = habló con el jefe por mí, Dios se lo agradezca.*

blessed | 'blesɪd | [a veces **blest** detrás de *s.*] *adj.* **1** REL. bendito, santo: *the Blessed Virgin = la Virgen Bendita.* **2** REL. bienaventurado (de las bienaventuranzas). **3** dichoso, feliz (situación): *days of blessed peace = días de paz dichosa.* **4** (fam. y euf.) bendito (queriendo señalar enfado o similar): *the blessed neighbour again! = ¡el bendito vecino otra vez!* || **5 – with,** bendecido con, afortunado con la posesión de, dotado de: *he was blessed with an incredible intelligence = estaba dotado de una inteligencia increíble.*

blessedly | 'blesɪdlɪ | *adv.* dichosamente, felizmente.

blessedness | 'blesɪdnɪs | *s.i.* **1** REL. beatitud, santidad. **2** dicha, felicidad.

blessing | 'blesɪŋ | *s.c.* **1** [normalmente *sing.*] REL. bendición (en la iglesia, antes de comer, etc.). **2** (fig.) bendición, dicha, gran alegría: *his success in the examinations is a blessing = su éxito en los exámenes constituye una gran alegría.* **3** (fig.) aprobación, visto bueno, bendición: *she got married with her father's blessing = ella se casó con la aprobación de su padre.* || **4 a – in disguise,** V. **disguise. 5 a mixed –,** una cosa con pros y contras. **6 to count one's blessings,** darse cuenta de lo afortunado que uno es, estar agradecido (porque uno tiene una buena situación en la vida).

blest | blest | *pret.* y *p.p.* de **bless.**

blether | 'bleðər | *v.i.* **[to – (about)]** (fam.) decir bobadas, decir chorradas.

blew | bluː | *pret.* de **blow.**

blight | blaɪt | *s.i.* **1** AGR. plaga, enfermedad. || *s.c.* **2** (fig.) plaga, ruina, decadencia: *drugs are a modern blight = las drogas son una plaga moderna.* || *v.t.* **3** arruinar, destrozar (a la manera de una plaga).

blighter | 'blaɪtər | *s.c.* (fam.) diablo: *poor blighter = pobre diablo.*

blimey | 'blaɪmɪ | *interj.* (fam. y brit.) mecachis, caramba.

blind | blaɪnd | *adj.* **1** ciego, invidente. **2 [– (with)]** cegado (por el humo, lágrimas, emoción, etc.). **3 [– (to)]** ciego, insensible, sin capacidad de razonamiento. **4** ciego (en la creencia): *blind faith = fe ciega.* **5** ARQ. sin vanos, ciega (pared sin aperturas como puertas o ventanas). **6** cerrada, cegada (ventana). || *s.c.* **7** persiana. **8** (fig.) pantalla, cortina de humo, pretexto, subterfugio. || *v.t.* **9** cegar, dejar ciego. **10** deslumbrar, cegar momentáneamente. **11 [to – + *o.* + (to)]** cegar, ofuscar (la razón). **12 [to – + *o.* + (with)]** (fig.) confundir, deslumbrar (con datos, lenguaje rimbombante, etc.). || *adv.* **13** a ciegas (conducción, caminar, etc.). || **14 as – as a bat,** tan ciego como un topo, más ciego que un murciélago. **15 – alley, a)** callejón sin salida. **b)** (fig.) callejón sin salida, situación sin solución. **16 – date,** (fam.) encuentro/cita de dos personas desconocidas mutuamente (mujer y hombre). **17 – drunk,** (fam.) con una melopea impresionante, bebido como un cosaco, borracho como una cuba. **18 – man's bluff,** gallina ciega (juego). **19 – spot, a)** ANAT. punto ciego (en la retina). **b)** punto negro, sitio de conducción peligrosa. **c)** punto débil (en una persona): *I have a blind spot about this subject = tengo un punto débil en este tema.* **20 love is –,** el amor es ciego. **21 not to take a – bit of notice,** (fam.) no prestar la más mínima atención, no hacer caso alguno, hacer caso omiso. **22 to swear –,** (fam.) jurar sobre la Biblia, jurar por todos los santos. **23 the –,** los ciegos. **24 the – leading the –,** tan ciego el uno como el otro, un ciego ayudando a otro ciego. **25 to turn a – eye (to),** hacer la vista gorda (ante).

blinder | 'blaɪndər | *s.c.* (brit. y vulg.) **1** orgía, borrachera. **2** virguería (especialmente en el deporte).

blinders | 'blaɪndəz | V. **blinkers.**

blindfold | 'blaɪndfəuld | *s.c.* **1** venda (para no ver). || *v.t.* **2** vendar (los ojos). || *adv.* **3** con los ojos vendados.

blindfolded | 'blaɪndfəuldɪd | *adj.* vendados (ojos).

blinding | 'blaɪndɪŋ | *adj.* **1** deslumbrante, cegador (luz). **2** llamativo, notable (indicando sorpresa grande): *blinding stupidity = notable estupidez.*

blindingly | 'blaɪndɪŋlɪ | *adv.* **1** cegadoramente, deslumbradoramente (luz). **2** llamativamente, notablemente. V. **blinding 2.**

blindly | 'blaɪndlɪ | *adv.* **1** ciegamente, sin ver. **2** (fig.) ciegamente, sin base real, sin datos objetivos.

blindness | 'blaɪndnɪs | *s.i.* **1** ceguera, invidencia. **2 [– (to)]** irracionalidad, insensatez. **3** ceguera mental, ceguedad intelectual.

blink | blɪŋk | *v.i.* **1** parpadear, pestañear. **2** brillar intermitentemente. || *v.t.* **3** abrir y cerrar (los ojos). || *s.c.* **4** parpadeo, pestañeo. **5** destello, brillo intermitente. || **6 a – of an eye/eyelid,** un instante, un segundo; un abrir y cerrar de ojos. **7 on the –,** (fam.) estropeado, escacharrado (objeto).

blinkered | 'blɪŋkəd | *adj.* (brit.) **1** con anteojeras (caballo). **2** (fig. y desp.) cerrado (de mente), de mentalidad estrecha.

blinkers | 'blɪŋkəz | (EE.UU. **blinders**) *s.pl.* (brit.) **1** anteojeras (de caballo). **2** (fig.) cerrazón mental.

blinking | 'blɪŋkɪŋ | *adj.* (fam. y vulg.) asqueroso, mierda de: *blinking watch! = ¡reloj de mierda!*

blip | blɪp | *s.c.* **1** punto de luz (en un radar indicando la presencia de algo). **2** cresta, punto de subida (en cualquier aparato con pantalla).

bliss | blɪs | *s.i.* dicha, ventura, felicidad.

blissful | 'blɪsfl | *adj.* **1** dichoso, venturoso, feliz. **2** feliz (ignorancia o similar).

blissfully | 'blɪsfəlɪ | *adv.* **1** dichosamente, venturosamente, felizmente. **2** felizmente (en su ignorancia, desconocimiento, etc.).

blister | 'blɪstər | *s.c.* **1** ampolla. **2** (fig.) burbuja, ampolla (en una superficie). || *v.t.* e *i.* **3** salir ampollas, ampollar, levantar ampollas. **4** salir burbujas, levantarse burbujas (en una superficie).

blistered | 'blɪstəd | *adj.* con ampollas, lleno de ampollas.

blistering | 'blɪstərɪŋ | *adj.* **1** abrasador (calor). **2** feroz, que levanta ampollas (palabras).

blisteringly | 'blɪstərɪŋlɪ | *adv.* **1** abrasadoramente (calor). **2** ferozmente, severamente (crítica verbal).

blithe | blaɪð | *adj.* **1** jovial, alegre, animado. **2** (p.u.) despreocupado, descuidado.

blithely | 'blaɪðlɪ | *adv.* **1** jovialmente, alegremente, animadamente. **2** (p.u.) despreocupadamente, descuidadamente.

blithering | 'blɪðərɪŋ | *adj.* (fam.) de capirote, del culo: *blithering fool = tonto de capirote.*

blitz | blɪts | *s.c.* **1** MIL. ataque sorpresa, ataque relámpago. **2 [– (on)]** (fam.) acometida, ataque de actividad (para llevar a cabo algo). || *v.t.* **3** bombardear (una ciudad). || **4 the Blitz,** HIST. el ataque aéreo sobre Inglaterra (durante la Segunda Guerra Mundial).

blitzing | 'blɪtsɪŋ | *s.i.* MIL. bombardeo aéreo.

blitzkrieg | 'blɪtskriːg | *s.c.* MIL. guerra relámpago.

blizzard | 'blɪzəd | *s.c.* ventisca; tempestad de nieve.

bloated | 'bləutɪd | *adj.* **1** hinchado, inflado (con líquido o gas). **2** harto, hasta arriba (de comer).

bloater | 'bləutər | *s.c.* arenque ahumado.

blob | blɒb | *s.c.* **1** masa informe. **2** mancha (objeto o persona visto a distancia).

bloc | blɒk | *s.c.* **1** POL. bloque (grupo de naciones). || **2 en –,** en bloque, en masa.

block | blɒk | *s.c.* **1 [– (of)]** bloque, edificio (de pisos, apartamentos, etc.). **2** manzana, (Am.) cuadra. **3** témpano (de hielo). **4** bloque (de madera, piedra, etc.). **5** tapón, obstáculo (que bloquea una tubería o similar). **6** fajo (de billetes o similar). **7** bloqueo mental, colapso mental. || *v.t.* **8** obstruir, bloquear, obstaculizar. **9** obstruir, bloquear (la vista). **10** bloquear (acuerdo o similar). || **11 a chip off the old –,** V. **chip.** **12 – and tackle,** MEC. aparejo de poleas. **13 – capitals/letters,** letras mayúsculas. **14 to – in, a)** encajonar (coche). **b)** ART. esbozar en negro (dentro de una figura). **15 to – off,** tapar completamente, bloquear por completo. **16 to – out, a)** obstaculizar (la publicación de información). **b)** impedir el paso (del sol, luz, etc.). **17 to – up,** bloquearse por completo (conducto o parecido). **18 – vote,** POL. voto proporcional, voto representativo de calidad (un voto que representa a un grupo de gente). **19 to knock someone's – off,** (fam.) pegarle una tunda a alguien, dar a alguien un mamporro en la cabeza. **20 to lay/put one's head on the –,** arriesgar el cuello, arriesgar la cabeza.

blockade | blɒkeɪd | *s.c.* **1** bloqueo, asedio (normalmente militar). || *v.t.* **2** bloquear, asediar (normalmente mediante la marina). || **3 to break/run a –,** atravesar/romper un asedio. **4 to lift /raise a –,** levantar/finalizar un asedio.

blockage | 'blɒkɪdʒ | *s.c.* e *i.* obstrucción, atrancamiento (normalmente de líquido en tuberías o parecido).

blockbuster | 'blɒkbʌstər | *s.c.* (fam.) **1** MIL. bomba de demolición. **2** exitazo (de novela, película, etc.). **3** (EE.UU.) agente de la propiedad que asusta a propietarios para que vendan sus casas rápido y barato.

blockbusting | 'blɒkbʌstɪŋ | *s.i.* actividad inmobiliaria. V. **blockbuster 3.**

blockhead | 'blɒkhed | *s.c.* (fam.) cabeza de chorlito.

blockhouse | 'blɒkhaus | *s.c.* MIL. **1** búnker. **2** (EE.UU.) fuerte.

bloke | bləuk | *s.c.* (brit. y fam.) tipo, tío.

blonde | blɒnd | (también **blond**) *adj.* **1** rubia. || *s.c.* **2** rubia, mujer rubia.

blood | blʌd | *s.i.* **1** sangre. **2** (fig.) sangre, origen, ascendencia: *oriental blood = ascendencia oriental.* || **3 bad –,** mala intención, malos sentimientos. **4 to be after someone's –,** ir a degüello contra alguien, ir a por el cuello de alguien. **5 to be in someone's –,** estar en la naturaleza de alguien, llevarlo en la sangre. **6 – and thunder,** (fam.) de acción violenta (películas y novelas). **7 – bank,** MED. banco de sangre, banco de plasma. **8 – cell,** FISIOL. glóbulo rojo. **9 – count,** MED. recuento de glóbulos rojos en la sangre. **10 – group,** grupo sanguíneo. **11 – is thicker than water,** los lazos de la sangre son muy fuertes (por encima de muchas otras lealtades a amigos, ideologías, etc.). **12 – money,** dinero ensangrentado (de haber matado a alguien). **13 – relation,** familiar de la misma sangre, familiar consanguíneo. **14 – test,** MED. análisis de sangre. **15 – transfusion,** MED. transfusión de sangre. **16 – type,** tipo de sangre, grupo sanguíneo. **17 to get – from a stone,** sacar agua de las piedras (casi imposible). **18 to give/donate –,** donar sangre. **19 to have someone's – on one's hands,** tener la sangre de alguien en las manos de uno (ser responsable de la muerte de alguien). **20 in cold –,** a sangre fría. **21 to make one's – boil,** quemarle a uno la sangre, sacar a uno de quicio. **22 to make one's – freeze/run cold,** helársele a uno la sangre. **23 new/fresh/young –,** nuevas ideas, nuevo impulso (en una empresa o similar). **24 one's blood is up,** uno está hecho un basilisco, uno se encoleriza. **25 one's own flesh and –,** V. **flesh. 26 to sweat –,** sudar sangre; trabajar como un negro.

bloodbath | 'blʌdbɑːθ | *s.c.* carnicería, matanza (de hombres o animales).

blood-brother | 'blʌdbrʌðər | *s.c.* hermano de sangre (no de familia).

blood-curdling | 'blʌdkəːdlɪŋ | *adj.* que hiela la sangre, espeluznante.

blood-donor | 'blʌddənər | *s.c.* donante de sangre.

blood-heat | 'blʌdhiːt | *s.i.* FISIOL. temperatura de la sangre normal.

bloodhound | 'blʌdhaund | *s.c.* sabueso.

bloodless | 'blʌdlɪs | *adj.* **1** sin derramamiento de sangre (una revolución política, por ejemplo). **2** pálido, anémico. **3** (fig.) sin fuerza, sin entusiasmo.

blood-letting | 'blʌdletɪŋ | *s.i.* **1** MED. flebotomía, sangría. **2** (fam.) derramamiento de sangre. **3** (fig.) lucha encarnizada, lucha sin cuartel (dentro de una asociación, familia, etc.).

bloodlust | 'blʌdlʌst | *s.i.* deseo de matar, deseo de asesinar.

blood-poisoning | 'blʌdpɔɪznɪŋ | *s.i.* MED. envenenamiento de la sangre.

blood-pressure | 'blʌdpreʃər | *s.i.* FISIOL. presión sanguínea, tensión arterial.

blood-red | ˌblʌd'red | *adj.* rojo como la sangre.

bloodshed | 'blʌdʃed | *s.i.* derramamiento de sangre.

bloodshot | 'blʌdʃɒt | *adj.* inyectados de sangre, fuertemente enrojecidos (ojos).

bloodsport | 'blʌdspɔːt | *s.c.* deporte con derramamiento de sangre (caza, toros, etc.).

bloodstained | 'blʌdsteɪnd | *adj.* ensangrentado, manchado de sangre.

bloodstock | 'blʌdstɒk | *s.i.* caballos de raza.

bloodstream | 'blʌdstriːm | *s.sing.* corriente sanguínea, flujo sanguíneo.

bloodsucker | 'blʌdsʌkər | *s.c.* **1** ZOOL. sanguijuela. **2** (fig.) chupasangre, sanguijuela (persona que se aprovecha).

bloodthirstily | 'blʌdθəːstɪlɪ | *adv.* sanguinariamente, cruelmente.

bloodthirstiness | 'blʌdθəːstɪnɪs | *s.i.* crueldad, sed de sangre.

bloodthirsty | 'blʌdθəːstɪ | *adj.* sanguinario, cruel.

blood-vessel | 'blʌdvesl | *s.c.* ANAT. vaso sanguíneo.

bloodily | 'blʌdɪlɪ | *adv.* **1** violentamente, cruelmente, sanguinariamente. **2** de manera sanguinolente.

bloodiness | 'blʌdɪnɪs | *s.i.* **1** crueldad, violencia. **2** sanguinolencia.

bloody | 'blʌdɪ | *adj.* **1** cruel, violento, cruento (guerra o lucha). **2** sanguinolento, lleno de sangre. **3** (arc.) puñetero, desagradable (con alguien). || *v.t.* **4** ensangrentar. || *adj.* y *adv.* **5** (brit. y vulg.) jodido, maldito, asqueroso; muy: *that's not bloody funny = eso no es muy divertido.* || **6 bloodied but unbowed,** vencido pero no derrotado, ensangrentado pero no humillado. **7 – mary,** combinado de vodka y jugo de tomate.

bloody-minded | ˌblʌdɪ'maɪndɪd | *adj.* (desp.) malintencionado, perverso.

bloody-mindedness | ˌblʌdɪ'maɪndɪdnɪs | *s.i.* (desp.) mala intención, perversidad.

bloom | bluːm | *v.i.* **1** florecer. **2** (fig.) florecer; ser evidente, salir a la luz (para admiración de todos): *the children's health was blooming = la salud de los niños era evidente.* || *s.c.* **3** BOT. florecimiento, floración. || *s.sing.* **4** lozanía, frescor: *the bloom of youth = la lozanía de la juventud.* || *s.i.* **5** BOT. vello, pelusa. || **6 in –/in full –,** en flor, en plena floración, lleno de flores. **7 to take the – off something,** quitar la alegría a algo, quitar la frescura a algo (un matrimonio, amistad, etc.).

bloomer | 'bluːmər | *s.c.* (brit., fam. y p.u.) metedura de pata.

bloomers | 'bluːməz | *s.pl.* pololos.

blooming | 'bluːmɪŋ | *adj.* **1** lozano, fresco: *she was a beautiful blooming girl = era una chica preciosa y lozana.* **2** (brit., fam. y euf.) asqueroso, maldito.

blooper | 'bluːpər | *s.c.* (EE.UU. y fam.) metedura de pata, gazapo.

blossom | 'blɒsəm | *v.i.* **1** florecer. **2 [to – (into)]** (fig.) convertirse, desarrollarse (para admiración de otros): *she blossomed into a lovely girl = ella se convirtió en una chica preciosa.* || *s.c.* e *i.* **3** floración, florecimiento. || **4 in –/in full –,** en flor, en plena floración, lleno de flores.

blot | blɒt | *s.c.* **1** borrón, mancha (especialmente de tinta). || *s.sing.* **2 [– on]** mancha en, borrón sobre (reputación de alguien). **3 [– on]** borrón en, punto negro en (paisaje, obra de arte, etc.). || *v.t.* **4** secar (normalmente con papel secante). || **5 to – one's copybook,** V. **copybook. 6 to – out, a)** ocultar, no dejar ver. **b)** suprimir, borrar (pensamientos o recuerdos). **7 to – up,** absorber (un líquido, dejando una superficie totalmente seca).

blotch | blɒtʃ | *s.c.* mancha, roncha (en la piel especialmente).

blotched | blɒtʃt | (también **blotchy**) *adj.* manchado, con ronchas.

blotchy | 'blɒtʃɪ | V. **blotched.**

blotter | 'blɒtər | *s.c.* hoja de papel secante.

blotting-paper | 'blɒtɪŋpeɪpər | *s.i.* papel secante.

blotto | 'blɒtəʊ | *adj.* (fam.) mamado (borracho).

blouse | blauz | (EE.UU.) | blaus | *s.c.* blusa.

blow | bləʊ | *v.* [*pret.* **blew,** *p.p.* **blown**] *i.* **1** soplar (el viento). **2** soplar (con la boca). **3** volar, flotar (en el viento): *the shirts were blowing in the wind = las camisas flotaban en el viento.* **4** sonar (un instrumento de soplar): *the whistle blew = el pito sonó.* **5** explotar (neumático). **6** ELEC. saltar (fusible). || *t.* **7** soplar, traer (el viento): *the wind blew this piece of paper here = el viento trajo este trozo de papel hasta aquí.* **8** echar, soplar (con la boca). **9** hacer (burbujas o similar). **10** sonarse (la nariz). **11 [to – (*prep.*)]** hacer (mediante una explosión): *the bomb blew a huge hole = la bomba hizo un enorme hoyo.* **12** hacer resonar, tocar (instrumento o similar). **13** hacer estallar (neumático). **14** ELEC. hacer saltar (fusible). **15 [to – + *o.* + (on)]** (fam.) malgastar (dinero). **16** (fam.) estropear, echar a perder (una oportunidad). **17** (fam.) revelar (secreto). || *s.c.* **18** golpe, tortazo, porrazo. **19** resoplido (al sonarse la nariz). **20 [– (to)]** (fig.) golpe, desilusión, contratiempo. **21 [– for/ against]** empujón a/contra, impulso a/contra: *a blow for equality = un impulso a la igualdad.* || **22 – ...,** (vulg.) **a)** a la mierda con: *blow the expense, I've passed = a la mierda con el gasto, he aprobado.* **b)** mierda. **23 to – hot and cold,** V. **hot. 24 – me/– me down/I'll be blowed,** (fam. y p.u.) vaya, pues sí, caramba. **25 to – one's own trumpet,** V. **trumpet. 26 to – one's top,** V. **top. 27 to – out, a)** apagar(se). **b)** terminarse (tormenta). **28 to – over, a)** apagarse, terminarse (problema). **b)** disminuir su fuerza (tormenta). **29 to – someone's mind,** (fam.) impresionar, dejar lelo (un libro, idea, etc.). **30 to – the cobwebs away,** V. **cobweb. 31 to – the whistle on something,** V. **whistle. 32 to – up, a)** destrozar totalmente (mediante explosión). **b)** (fam.) estallar de cólera, estallar de ira. **c)** inflar (globo, balón, etc.). **d)** FOT. ampliar (foto). **e)** formarse, presentarse, acercarse (tormenta). **33 to – up in someone's face,** V. **face. 34 to come to blows,** liarse a golpes, agarrarse a puñetazos. **35 to soften/cushion the –,** amortiguar el golpe; disminuir la pena.

blow-by-blow | 'bleubaɪbləʊ | *adj.* detallada (narración).

blow-dry | 'bləʊdraɪ | *v.t.* **1** secar (el pelo con secador). || *s.sing.* **2** secado (con secador).

blower | 'bləʊər | *s.c.* (brit. y fam.) aparato de teléfono, teléfono.

blowhole | 'bləʊhəʊl | *s.c.* **1** respiradero (en un túnel). **2** agujero en el hielo (para facilitar la respiración de mamíferos acuáticos). **3** ANAT. ZOOL. espiráculo (en los cetáceos).

blowing-up | ˌbləʊɪŋ'ʌp | *s.c.* regañina: *I got a blowing up for being late = me dieron una regañina por llegar tarde.*

blowlamp | 'bləʊlæmp | (EE.UU. **blowtorch**) *s.c.* soplete, lámpara de soldar.

blown | bləʊn | *p.p.* de **blow.**

blow-out | 'bləʊaʊt | *s.c.* **1** pinchazo, reventón (neumático). **2** (fam.) comilona, festín. **3** ELEC. fallo (en un fusible). **4** escape (en un pozo de petróleo).

blowpipe | 'bləʊpaɪp | *s.c.* **1** cerbatana. **2** caña de vidriero.

blowsy | 'blauzɪ | (también **blowzy**) *adj.* desaliñado (se dice, especialmente, de la persona gorda y colorada).

blowtorch | 'bləʊtɔːtʃ | V. **blowlamp.**

blow-up | 'bləʊʌp | *s.c.* FOT. ampliación.

blowy | 'bləʊɪ | *adj.* (fam.) con viento.

blubber | 'blʌbər | *s.i.* **1** grasa de cetáceo. || *v.i.* **2** llorar a lágrima viva, lloriquear como un niño.
bludgeon | 'blʌdʒən | *s.c.* **1** cachiporra, porra. || *v.t.* **2** aporrear, golpear con una porra. **3 [to – + *o.* + (into)]** intimidar, obligar mediante intimidación: *the bully bludgeoned the girl into getting into his car = el matón intimidó a la chica para que subiera a su coche.*
blue | bluː | *adj.* **1** azul. **2** (EE.UU., fam. y p.u.) triste, melancólico. **3** verde (obsceno). **4 [– (with)]** helado (de frío). || *s.i.* **5** azul. || *v.t.* **6 [to – + *o.* + (on)]** (fam. y brit.) tirar, malgastar (dinero). **7 a bolt from the –,** V. **bolt. 8 – blood,** sangre azul, sangre aristocrática. **9 – chip,** COM. acción de una empresa sólida. **10 – pencil,** (fig.) correcciones, alteraciones (en un original escrito). **11 – riband/ribband,** cinta azul (como condecoración). **12 – ribbon,** V. **blue 11. 13 – tit,** ZOOL. herrerillo (ave). **14 once in a – moon,** V. **moon. 15 out of the –,** sin saber de dónde ha salido, sin saber porqué (tan de repente). **16 to scream – murder,** V. **murder. 17 the blues, a)** (fam.) depresión **b)** MUS. blues. **18 till I/you/he/etc. am/are/is – in the face,** (fam.) hasta que estoy/estás/etc. harto de repetir lo mismo sin parar.
bluebell | 'bluːbel | *s.c.* BOT. campánula, campanilla.
blueberry | 'bluːbrɪ | (EE.UU.) | 'bluːberɪ | *s.c.* BOT. arándano.
blue-black | 'bluːblæk | *adj.* azul negruzco, negro azulado.
blue-blooded | ˌbluː'blʌdɪd | *adj.* de sangre aristocrática.
bluebottle | 'bluːbɒtl | *s.c.* ZOOL. moscarda, mosca azul.
blue-collar | ˌbluː'kɒlər | *adj.* de obrero, de obreros; laboral: *blue-collar workers = trabajadores manuales.*
blue-eyed | 'bluːaɪd | *adj.* **1** de ojos azules. || **2 – boy,** (brit. y fam.) niño guapo, niño preferido.
blueprint | 'bluːprɪnt | *s.c.* **1 [– (for/of)]** ARQ. diseño, proyecto. **2 [– (for/of)]** anteproyecto, borrador (de una idea o similar).
bluestocking | 'bluːstɒkɪŋ | *s.c.* (desp. y p.u.) marisabidilla, mujer pretenciosa sabionda.
bluff | blʌf | *s.c.* **1** engaño, farol (exagerado). **2** GEOG. risco, farallón, escarpadura. || *s.i.* **3** farolada. || *v.t.* e *i.* **4** engañar, farolear, tirarse faroles. || *adj.* **5** brusco: *I don't like his bluff manner = no me gustan sus modos bruscos.* || **6 to – it out,** salir de una situación mediante faroles. **7 to call someone's –,** desenmascarar a alguien como farsante; coger a alguien en un farol.
bluffness | 'blʌfnɪs | *s.i.* brusquedad.
bluish | 'bluːɪʃ | *adj.* azulado.
blunder | 'blʌndər | *s.c.* **1** metedura de pata, gazapo. || *v.i.* **2** meter la pata. **3** pasar por error, pasar por equivocación (a/por un lugar).
blunderbuss | 'blʌndəbʌs | *s.c.* MIL. trabuco.
blunderer | 'blʌndərər | *s.c.* metedor de gazapos.
blundering | 'blʌndərɪŋ | *adj.* torpe, torpón (de movimiento y palabra).
blunt | blʌnt | *adj.* **1** romo, poco afilado, desafilado. **2** franco, sincero; brusco. || *v.t.* **3** mellar, desafilar. **4** (fig.) embotar (los sentimientos, mente, etc.).
bluntly | 'blʌntlɪ | *adv.* francamente, sinceramente; bruscamente.
bluntness | 'blʌntnɪs | *s.i.* **1** franqueza, sinceridad; brusquedad. **2** falta de filo, falta de punta.
blur | bləːr | *v.t.* e *i.* **1** empañar(se), nublar(se), velar(se). **2** (fig.) oscurecer(se), nublar(se) (el pensamiento). || *s.c.* **3** borrón, manchón. || *s.sing.* **4** borrosidad, nebulosidad (mental).
blurb | bləːb | *s.sing.* **[the –]** la propaganda.
blurred | bləːd | *adj.* **1** nublado, velado, empañado. **2** (fig.) oscurecido, nublado (el pensamiento).
blurry | 'bləːrɪ | *adj.* poco definido, borroso.
blurt | bləːt | **to – out, a)** dejar escapar, soltar sin darse cuenta. **b)** confesar, descubrir (algo oculto).
blush | blʌʃ | *v.i.* **1** sonrojarse, ponerse colorado, enrojecer. || *s.c.* **2** sonrojo, rubor. || **3 to spare someone's blushes,** callar algo para no poner colorado a alguien, ahorrarle a alguien rubor.
blusher | 'blʌʃər | *s.c.* e *i.* colorete.
blushingly | 'blʌʃɪŋlɪ | *adv.* de manera que produce sonrojo.
bluster | 'blʌstər | *v.i.* **1** bramar (viento). **2** vociferar, gritar amenazadoramente. || *s.i.* **3** bravata, fanfarronada (verbal). **4** ráfaga, bramido (del viento).
blustery | 'blʌstərɪ | *adj.* borrascoso, tempestuoso (tiempo).
boa | 'bəʊə | *s.c.* ZOOL. boa.
boar | bɔːr | [*pl.* **boar** o **boars**] *s.c.* ZOOL. **1** verraco. **2** jabato, jabalí.
board | bɔːd | *s.c.* **1** tablero, tabla (para todo tipo de usos). **2** tarima (del suelo). **3** tablón (de anuncios). **4** COM. consejo de dirección, consejo. **5** ELEC. tablero (con mandos). || *s.i.* **6** comida, pensión (comida). || *v.t.* **7** subirse a, embarcarse en (tren, avión, etc.). || *v.i.* **8** subir, embarcar. **9 [to – with]** hospedarse con. || **10 above –,** V. **above. 11 across the –,** a todos los niveles. **12 – and lodging,** cama y comida, pensión completa. **13 to – out,** enviar a vivir fuera de casa: *the children were boarded out = los niños fueron enviados a vivir fuera de casa.* **14 boards,** tablas (de teatro). **15 to be on the boards,** (fig.) ser actor o actriz. **16 to – up,** tapar con tablas. **17 to go by the –,** echarse a perder, frustrarse (un proyecto, plan, etc.). **18 on –,** a bordo, embarcado (en tren, avión, etc.). **19 to sweep the –,** llevarse todos los premios. **20 to take on –,** (fam.) aceptar, comenzar a entender; entrar en el rollo de. **21 to take something on –,** aceptar la responsabilidad (de una tarea, trabajo, obra, etc.).
OBS. Esta palabra, que puede ser el segundo elemento de un compuesto, aparece frecuentemente sin la primera parte, cuando se sabe de qué se está hablando: *the board = la pizarra (blackboard)... the board = el trampolín (diving board).*
boarder | 'bɔːdər | *s.c.* **1** huésped (en una pensión). **2** alumno interno.
board-game | 'bɔːdgeɪm | *s.c.* juego de tablero (ajedrez, damas, etc.).
boarding | 'bɔːdɪŋ | *s.i.* **1** entarimado, juego de tablas (para una valla, una estantería, etc.). || *adj* **2** de internado: *boarding fees = precio de matrícula de internado.* || **3 – card,** tarjeta de embarque.
boarding-house | 'bɔːdɪŋhaʊs | *s.c.* pensión, casa de huéspedes.
boarding-school | 'bɔːdɪŋskuːl | *s.c.* escuela con internado, internado.
boardroom | 'bɔːdruːm | *s.c.* **1** sala de juntas, sala de reuniones. || *s.sing.* **2 [the –]** (fig.) la dirección, la jefatura (de una empresa o similar).
boardwalk | 'bɔːdwɔːk | *s.c.* (EE.UU.) paseo marítimo con tablas de madera.
boast | bəʊst | *v.i.* **1 [to – (that/of/about)]** jactarse, chulearse, alardear: *he boasted about his new car = se jactó de su coche nuevo.* || *v.t.* **2** ostentar, jactarse de tener, ufanarse de poder mostrar: *it's nothig to boast of = no hay nada de que jactarse.* || *s.c.* **3** jactancia, alarde.
boastful | 'bəʊstful | *adj.* (desp.) jactancioso.
boastfully | 'bəʊstfulɪ | *adv.* (desp.) jactanciosamente.
boastfulness | 'bəʊstfulnɪs | *s.i.* (desp.) jactancia.
boat | bəʊt | *s.c.* **1** bote, barca (siempre pequeño). **2** (fam.) barco (grande). **3** salsera (plato profundo). || *v.i.* **4** ir en barca, navegar (como pasatiempo). || **5 – people,** refugiados que huyen en barca (especialmente asiáticos). **6 – race,** DEP. carrera de barcas, competición de remo. **7 to burn one's boats,** (fam.) quemar las naves de uno, quedarse sin salida posible. **8 in the same –,** (fam.) en el mismo fregado, en la misma tesitura. **9 to miss the –,** (fam.) perder la oportunidad, perder la ocasión, no aprovechar la ocasión. **10 to push the – out,** (fam.) organizar la fiesta por todo lo grande. **11 to rock the –,** (fam.) menearlo, agitar las aguas (una situación de calma preciada).
boater | 'bəʊtər | *s.c.* sombrero de paja.
boat-hook | 'bəʊthuk | *s.c.* MAR. bichero.
boathouse | 'bəʊthaʊs | *s.c.* cobertizo para barcas.
boatman | 'bəʊtmən | [*pl.irreg.* **boatmen**] *s.c.* barquero.
boatmen | 'bəʊtmən | *pl.* de **boatman.**
boatswain | 'bəʊsn | *s.c.* MAR. contramaestre.
boat-train | 'bəʊttreɪn | *s.c.* tren de enlace con puerto.
bob | bɒb | [*ger.* **bobbing,** *pret.* y *p.p.* **bobbed**] *v.i.* **1** balancearse (hacia arriba y abajo). **2 [to – *prep.*]** moverse, balancearse, ir balanceándose (dentro, fuera, arriba, abajo, etc.). **3** hacer una reverencia. || *v.t.* **4** mover (la cabeza arriba o abajo). **5** dirigir, hacer (una reverencia). **6** cortar muy corto (el pelo, sólo en mujeres). || *s.c.* **7** gesto rápido, inclinación rápida (de la cabeza). **8** estilo de corte corto (de pelo, especialmente en mujeres). **9** reverencia. **10** [*pl.* **bob**] (p.u. y fam.) chelín. || **11 bits and bobs,** (fam.)

cachivaches. **12 bob's your uncle,** (fam.) ya está, ahí lo tienes: *where's the library?, turn right and bob's your uncle = ¿dónde está la biblioteca?, tuerza a la derecha y ya está.*
bobbed | bɒbd | *adj.* cortado corto (el pelo, especialmente de una mujer).
bobbin | 'bɒbɪn | *s.c.* bobina, carrete.
bobble | 'bɒbl | *s.c.* pompón (de decoración).
bobby | 'bɒbɪ | *s.c.* **1** (fam. y brit.) poli. || **2 – pin,** (EE.UU.) horquilla, pasador.
bobsled | 'bɒbsled | V. **bobsleigh.**
bobsleigh | 'bɒbsleɪ | (también **bobsled**) *s.c.* trineo.
bobtail | 'bɒbteɪl | *s.c.* cola recortada.
bod | bɒd | *s.c.* (fam. y brit.) tío, tipo, gachó.
bode | bəʊd | **to – well/ill/no good,** ser de buen/mal agüero, presagiar buenas /malas noticias.
bodge | bɒdʒ | (brit. y fam.) *v.i.* **1** hacer una chapuza. || *s.c.* **2** chapuza.
bodice | 'bɒdɪs | *s.c.* corpiño, corsé.
bodily | 'bɒdɪlɪ | *adv.* **1** físicamente, corporalmente. **2** en un solo cuerpo, en un solo bloque; sin desmontar. || *adj.* **3** corporal, del cuerpo.
bodkin | 'bɒdkɪn | *s.c.* punzón; pasador.
body | 'bɒdɪ | *s.c.* **1** cuerpo. **2** torso, tronco (del cuerpo). **3** cadáver, cuerpo muerto. **4** colectivo, grupo, organización: *different official bodies = distintas organizaciones estatales.* **5** chasis, casco (de un barco), carrocería (de un vehículo), cuerpo (de un mecanismo). **6** **[– of]** comunidad de, conjunto de (gente con algo en común). **7** cantidad (de datos, información, etc.). **8** (form.) extensión (de agua principalmente). **9** FIS. cuerpo sólido. || *s.i.* **10** fuerza, cuerpo (en un licor o vino). || *s.sing.* **11** **[the – of]** la parte principal de, el bloque principal de, el segmento principal de (un edificio, libro, obra, etc.). || **12 – and soul,** en cuerpo y alma, con todo el alma, con todo el corazón. **13 – clock,** BIOL. reloj biológico. **14 – odour,** olor corporal (normalmente desagradable). **15 – politic,** (form.) POL. el conjunto de los ciudadanos, el conjunto del Estado. **16 in a –,** como un solo hombre, todos juntos. **17 to keep – and soul together,** V. **soul. 18 over my dead –,** V. **dead.**
body-blow | 'bɒdɪbləʊ | *s.c.* **1** DEP. golpe al cuerpo (en boxeo). **2** (fig.) mazazo, golpe fuerte (espiritual o mental): *his failure was a body-blow to his parents = su fracaso fue un mazazo para sus padres.*
body-builder | 'bɒdɪbɪldər | *s.c.* culturista.
body-building | 'bɒdɪbɪldɪŋ | *s.i.* culturismo.
bodyguard | 'bɒdɪgɑːd | *s.c.* guardaespaldas.
body-language | 'bɒdɪlæŋgwɪdʒ | *s.i.* lenguaje corporal, expresión corporal.
body-snatcher | 'bɒdɪsnætʃər | *s.c.* ladrón de cadáveres (para su posterior venta para prácticas de anatomía).
body-stocking | 'bɒdɪstɒkɪŋ | *s.c.* malla (para ballet, gimnasia, etc.).
bodywork | 'bɒdɪwɜːk | *s.i.* MEC. carrocería (de un vehículo).
Boer | bɔː | *s.c.* HIST. descendiente de colonos holandeses en Suráfrica, bóer.
boffin | 'bɑfɪn | *s.c.* (brit. y fam.) científico, investigador.
bog | bɒg | *s.c.* **1** GEOL. pantano, zona de pantanos, marisma, ciénaga. **2** (brit. y fam.), retrete. || **3 to – down, a)** atorarse, atascarse, hundirse (en nieve, barro, etc.). **b)** (fig.) atascarse, empantanarse (en una tarea).
bogey | 'bəʊgɪ | (también **bogie** o **bogy**) *s.c.* **1** pesadilla, preocupación constante. **2** (brit.) DEP. media (de golpes en golf). **3** (fam.) moco. **4** coco, sacamantecas (para asustar a los niños).
bogeyman | 'bəʊgɪmæn | V. **bogey 4.**
boggle | 'bɒgl | *v.i.* **1** **[to – (at)]** intimidarse, sobrecogerse (mentalmente ante algo difícil). **2** **[to – (at)]** vacilar, dudar (ante algo que no se entiende bien). || *v.t.* **3** intimidar, sobrecoger (la mente).
boggy | 'bɒgɪ | *adj.* pantanoso, cenagoso.
bogie V. **bogey.**
bogus | 'bəʊgəs | *adj.* falso, fraudulento (especialmente cuando se quiere hacer pasar por bueno).
bogy V. **bogey.**
bohemian | bəʊ'hiːmɪən | *adj.* **1** bohemio. || *s.c.* **2** bohemio.
boil | bɔɪl | *v.i.* **1** hervir. **2** GAST. hervir, cocer. **3** **[to – with]** hervir de/con (alguna emoción fuerte). **4** **[to – with]** bullir con (actividad). || *v.t.* **5** hervir. **6** GAST. hervir, cocer. **7** hervir, lavar en agua hirviente (ropa). || *s.c.* **8** MED. furúnculo, divieso. || **9 to – away,** hervir hasta hacer desaparecer. **10 to – down, a)** reducir hirviendo, hervir para que disminuya (líquido). **b)** (fig.) condensar (información o similar). **11 to – down to,** (fam.) resumirse en, reducirse a: *it all boils down to lack of money = todo se resume en falta de dinero.* **12 to – dry,** hervir hasta que se quede seco, dejar seco a base de hervir. **13 to – over, a)** salirse, rebosar (líquido). **b)** (fig.) descontrolarse, estallar (una situación peligrosa, un conflicto, etc.). **14 to – up,** hervir (para que suba un líquido). **15 to bring something to the –,** hervir algo, subir algo a punto de cocción. **16 to come to the –,** llegar al punto de cocción. **17 to make someone's blood –,** V. **blood. 18 on the –,** hirviendo, en el punto de cocción.
boiled | bɔɪld | *adj.* hervido.
boiler | 'bɔɪlər| *s.c.* **1** caldera. **2** cazo.
boiler-suit | 'bɔɪləsuːt | *s.c.* (brit.) mono de trabajo, mono.
boiling | 'bɔɪlɪŋ | *adj.* **1** hirviendo, sofocante (calor). **2** hirviendo, que hierve. || **3 – hot,** un calor sofocante. **4 – point, a)** punto de ebullición, punto de cocción. **b)** (fig.) punto álgido, momento de crisis (de emociones fuertes).
boisterous | 'bɔɪstərəs | *adj.* travieso, bullicioso, tumultuoso.
boisterously | 'bɔɪstərəslɪ | *adv.* con travesuras, bulliciosamente, tumultuosamente.
boisterousness | 'bɔɪstərəsnɪs | *s.i.* tumulto, bullicio.
bold | bəʊld | *adj.* **1** atrevido, osado. **2** descarado, lanzado. **3** vívido, fuerte (color). **4** negrita (en tipografía). **5** marcado, pronunciado (trazo). || **6 as – as brass,** (fam.) más osado que nadie, más atrevido que nadie. **7 If I may be so –,** (form.) si me permites ser atrevido.
boldly | 'bəʊldlɪ | *adv.* **1** atrevidamente, osadamente. **2** descaradamente. **3** vívidamente, fuertemente (color). **4** pronunciadamente, con trazo muy marcado (al escribir, dibujar, etc.).
boldness | 'bəʊldnɪs | *s.i.* **1** atrevimiento, osadía. **2** descaro. **3** fortaleza, fuerza (color). **4** (lo) marcado, (lo) pronunciado (de un trazo).
bole | bəʊl | *s.c.* tronco (de un árbol).
bolero | bə'leərəʊ | *s.c.* **1** chaquetilla corta, bolero. **2** MUS. bolero.
Bolivia | bə'lɪvɪə | *s.sing.* Bolivia.
Bolivian | bə'lɪvɪən | *adj.* **1** boliviano. || *s.c.* **2** boliviano.
bollard | 'bɒləːd | *s.c.* **1** MAR. bolardo. **2** baliza de aviso (en el centro de las carreteras). **3** tachuela (para hacer bajar la velocidad).
bollocks | 'bɑləks | (brit. y vulg.) *s.pl.* **1** cojones, cataplines. || *interj.* **2** y un cojón, y una mierda (en desacuerdo). **3** cojones, qué cojones.
Bolshevik | 'bɑlʃəvɪk | HIST. *s.c.* **1** bolchevique. || *adj.* **2** bolchevique.
Bolshevism | 'bɑlʃəvɪzəm | *s.i.* POL. bolchevismo.
bolshy | 'bɑlʃɪ | (también **bolshie**) *adj.* (brit. y fam.) rebelde, inconformista; molestón.
bolster | 'bəʊlstər| *v.t.* **1** apoyar, reforzar, reanimar (la confianza, seguridad, etc. de alguien). || *s.c.* **2** cabezal, almohada dura. || **3 to – up,** apoyar con fuerza, apoyar con decisión (una causa, empresa, etc.).
bolt | bəʊlt | *s.c.* **1** MEC. tornillo, perno. **2** pasador, cerrojo (en puertas o ventanas). **3** saeta, flecha de ballesta. **4** rollo (de tejido). **5** relámpago. || *v.t.* **6** sujetar con tornillo, asegurar con tornillo. **7** echar el cerrojo (a puerta o ventana). **8** engullir, tragar (comida). || *v.i.* **9** **[to – to/on/onto]** sujetar con un tornillo a, asegurar con tornillo en. **10** desbocarse (caballo). **11** escaparse a toda velocidad, marcharse rápidamente. **12** AGR. crecer bruscamente sin florecer. || **13 a – from the blue,** caído del cielo, lo más inesperado/inesperadamente. **14 to – down,** engullir, tragar sin masticar. **15 – upright,** totalmente tieso, completamente derecho, derecho como un palo. **16 to make a – for/to make a – for it,** precipitarse hacia, dar un salto brusco hacia, saltar bruscamente hacia. **17 nuts and bolts,** V. **nut. 18 to shoot one's –,** echar el resto, agotársele a uno el ingenio. **19 to shut the stable door after the horse has bolted,** V. **stable.**
bolt-hole | 'bəʊlthəʊl | *s.c.* (brit.) refugio, escondrijo.
bomb | bɒm | *s.c.* **1** MIL. bomba. || *s.sing.* **2** **[the –]** la bomba (atómica). **3** **[a –]** (brit. y fam.) un ojo de la cara, un riñón. || *v.t.* **4** MIL. bombardear. || *v.i.* **5** **[to – along]** (fam.) ir a toda velocidad, ir a toda pastilla. || **6 to – out,** devastar, destrozar totalmente. **7 to go like a –,** (fam.) ir a toda velocidad, ir a todo meter. **8 to go like a –/to go down a –,** (brit. y fam.) salir a pedir de boca, resultar un éxito fabuloso.

bombard | bɒm'bɑːd | *v.t.* **1** MIL. bombardear. **2** **[to – (with)]** (fig.) abrumar, acosar, bombardear (con preguntas, ataques personales, etc.).
bombardier | ˌbɒmbə'dɪər | *s.c.* MIL. **1** (brit.) cabo artillero. **2** (EE.UU.) AER. bombardero, miembro de la tripulación de un bombardero.
bombardment | bɒm'bɑːdmənt | *s.c.* e *i.* **1** MIL. bombardeo. **2** **[– (of)]** (fig.) acoso, ataque (de preguntas, crítica, etc.).
bombastic | bɒm'bæstɪk | *adj.* pomposo, grandilocuente, rimbombante (forma de hablar).
bombastically | bɒm'bæstɪklɪ | *adv.* pomposamente, grandilocuentemente, rimbombantemente; ampulosamente (hablando).
bomb-bay | 'bɒmbeɪ | *s.c.* MIL. compartimento de bombas (en avión).
bomb-disposal | 'bɒmdɪspəʊzl | MIL. *s.i.* **1** desactivación de bombas (sin explotar). || **2 – squad/team/unit,** unidad de desactivación de bombas.
bomber | 'bɒmər | *s.c.* **1** AER. MIL. bombardero, avión de bombardeo. || **2 –,** cazadora, cazadora de vuelo.
bombing | 'bɒmɪŋ | *s.c.* e *i.* bombardeo, explosión de bombas, colocación de bombas (por ejemplo en actos terroristas).
bomb-proof | 'bɒmpruːf | *adj.* a prueba de bombas.
bombshell | 'bɒmʃel | *s.c.* (normalmente *sing.*) (fam.) bombazo, bomba; sorpresa.
bombsite | 'bɒmsaɪt | *s.c.* zona arrasada por una bomba, lugar donde explotó una bomba.
bona fide | ˌbəʊnə'faɪdɪ | *adj.* y *adv.* verdadero, auténtico, genuino, de buena fe.
bona fides | ˌbəʊnə'faɪdɪz | *s.pl.* DER. buena fe, buena intención.
bonanza | bə'nænzə | *s.c.* **1** bonanza, período bueno, boom. **2** (EE.UU.) bonanza, riqueza (conseguida en una mina, pozo petrolífero, etc.).
bon-bon | 'bɒnbɒn | *s.c.* bombón.
bond | bɒnd | *s.c.* **1** **[– (between/of)]** lazo, vínculo, unión (de amistad, ideología compartida, matrimonio, etc.). **2** COM. bono, obligación, título (de renta fija). **3** DER. compromiso, garantía (escrita). || *s.pl.* **4** (fig.) lazos, compromisos: *ideological bonds = compromisos ideológicos.* **5** (lit.) cadenas, ataduras. || *v.t.* e *i.* **6** pegar(se), adherir(se), unir(se) (con pegamento). || **7 someone's word is their –/someone's word is a good as his –,** la palabra de alguien es de absoluta confianza, la palabra de alguien vale tanto como un contrato por escrito.
bondage | 'bɒndɪdʒ | *s.i.* (form.) esclavitud, servidumbre.
bone | bəʊn | *s.c.* y *i.* **1** hueso. **2** espina (pez). || *s.c.* **3** ballena (en la ropa para que no se arrugue). || *v.t.* **4** quitar los huesos, deshuesar; quitar las espinas (al pescado). || *adj.* **5** de hueso: *a bone handle = un mango de hueso.* **6 a bag of bones/all skin and –,** (desp. y fam.) en los huesos, chupado, más flaco que la pata de un jilguero. **7 – china,** porcelana fina, porcelana china. **8 -boned,** de huesos, de configuración ósea (en compuestos): *a small-boned girl = una chica de huesos pequeños.* **9 – idle,** (desp.) redomadamente vago, gandul. **10 – meal,** AGR. harina de huesos (fertilizante). **11 – of contention,** (fig.) manzana de la discordia; tema de desavenencia. **12 close to the –/near the –,** (fam.) **a)** certero, verdadero (aunque escuece). **b)** atrevido, rayano en lo indecente (en temas escabrosos). **13 to feel/know something in one's bones,** tener el presentimiento de algo; estar convencido de algo intuitivamente. **14 to have a – to pick with someone,** (fam.) tener una cuenta pendiente con alguien, tener que arreglar las cuentas a alguien. **15 to make no bones (about),** no andarse con rodeos (sobre). **16 the bare bones,** datos básicos, datos fundamentales: *give me the bare bones of the story = dame los datos básicos de la historia.* **17 to work one's fingers to the –,** trabajar como un negro, dejarse las uñas trabajando.
bone-dry | ˌbəʊn'draɪ | *adj.* totalmente seco, completamente seco.
boner | 'bəʊnər | *s.c.* (EE.UU. y fam.) desatino; patochada, metedura de pata.
bonehead | 'bəʊnhed | *s.c.* (desp. y fam.) imbécil, mentecato, idiota.
boneshaker | 'bəʊnʃeɪkər | *s.c.* (fam. y p.u.) armatoste (vehículo).
bonfire | 'bɒnfaɪər | *s.c.* **1** hoguera, fogata, quema (de hojarasca otoñal). || **2 – night,** (brit.) noche de las hogueras (5 de Noviembre cuando es tradicional quemar la hojarasca del otoño acumulada en los jardines).
bongo | 'bɒŋgəʊ | [*pl.* **bongos** o **bongoes**] *s.c.* MUS. bongo (tambor que se toca con las manos).
bonhomie | 'bɒnɒmɪ | *s.i.* afabilidad, camaradería.
bonkers | 'bɒŋkəz | *adj.* (fam.) chalado.
bonnet | 'bɒnɪt | *s.c.* **1** (brit.) capó (de coche). **2** gorrito (de bebé); cofia (de mujer). || **3 to have a bee in one's –,** V. **bee.**
bonny | 'bɒnɪ | *adj.* bonito, (Am.) lindo (usado en Escocia y Norte).
bonsai | 'bɒnsaɪ | [*pl.* **bonsai** o **bonsais**] *s.c.* BOT. bonsai.
bonus | 'bəʊnəs | *s.c.* **1** prima, cantidad extra, gratificación. **2** COM. dividendo extra. **3** (fig.) beneficio añadido, punto extra a favor, ventaja inesperada.
bony | 'bəʊnɪ | *adj.* **1** huesudo, flaco. **2** lleno de huesos (carne); lleno de espinas (pescado). **3** de hueso, con hueso, parecido a un hueso.
boo | buː | *v.t.* e *i.* **1** abuchear. || *s.c.* **2** abucheo. || *interj.* **3** bú (para asustar). || **4 not to say – to a goose,** (fam.) no decir ni pío, no decir ni tus ni mus (de timidez).
boob | buːb | (fam.) *s.c.* **1** [normalmente *pl.*] (vulg.) teta. **2** (p.u.) bobalicón. **3** (brit.) patochada, metedura de pata, gazapo. || *v.i.* **4** (brit.) meter la pata.
booby | 'buːbɪ | *s.c.* **1** (fam. y p.u.) bobalicón, atontado. || **2 – prize,** premio de consolación (al último).
booby-trap | 'buːbɪtræp | *s.c.* **1** MIL. trampa-bomba. **2** (fig.) trampa de broma. || *v.t.* **3** poner una trampa explosiva.
boodle | 'buːdl | *s.i.* (EE.UU. y fam.) dinero sucio, dinero de soborno.
boogie | 'buːgɪ | (EE.UU.) | 'bʊgɪ | *v.i.* (fam.) MUS. bailar al son de música moderna.
boohoo | ˌbuː'huː | *v.i.* (fam.) berrear (como lloran los niños).
book | bʊk | *s.c.* **1** libro, tomo, volumen. **2** libro (parte de una obra más grande). **3** libro, libreta (para colecciones de sellos, monedas, etc.). || *s.pl.* **4** COM. libro de contabilidad, libro de asientos (en una empresa). || *s.sing.* **5** ART. libreto (de opera). || *v.t.* **6** (brit.) reservar (hotel, entrada a espectáculo, etc.). **7** **[to – +** *o.* **+ (for)]** (fam.) multar, poner una multa. **8** **[to – +** *o.* **+ (for)]** DEP. sacar tarjeta. || **9 to be a closed – to,** ser un misterio para, ser un tema del que uno no sabe nada. **10 to be in someone's bad/black books,** estar a mal con alguien. **11 to be in someone's good books,** estar a bien con alguien, estar a partir un piñón con alguien. **12 – club,** club de lectura, círculo de lectura. **13 booked up/fully booked up/fully booked, a)** lleno hasta arriba, hasta arriba (hotel, cine, etc.). **b)** tener otros compromisos apalabrados, estar ocupado con otros compromisos (un cantante, conferenciante, etc.). **14 to – in/into, a)** reservar (en hotel o similar). **b)** inscribirse; tomar habitación (en hotel o similar). **15 – token,** cheque para compra de libros. **16 to bring someone to –,** pedir cuentas a alguien, llamar a alguien a capítulo. **17 to go by the –,** actuar según las reglas, proceder según el reglamento. **18 in my –,** según mi opinión, según mi modo de ver. **19 to keep a –,** tener las apuestas abiertas, aceptar apuestas. **20 to open/start a –,** apostar, entrar en apuestas. **21 to take a leaf out of someone's –,** V. **leaf. 22 to throw the – at,** echar la culpa severamente, reprender con toda severidad.
bookable | 'bʊkəbl | *adj.* abierto a reservas, reservable.
bookbinder | 'bʊkbaɪndər | *s.c.* encuadernador.
bookbinding | 'bʊkbaɪndɪŋ | *s.i.* encuadernación.
bookcase | 'bʊkkeɪs | *s.c.* librería, estantería (para libros).
bookend | 'bʊkend | *s.c.* (normalmente *pl.*) sujetalibros, apoyalibros.
bookie | 'bʊkɪ | *s.c.* (fam.) corredor de apuestas.
booking | 'bʊkɪŋ | *s.c.* **1** reserva (hotel, teatro, etc.); contratación por adelantado (artistas). || **2 – clerk,** taquillero, encargado de la taquilla. **3 – office,** taquilla (teatro o similar); despacho de billetes.
bookish | 'bʊkɪʃ | *adj.* empollón; pedante.
bookkeeper | 'bʊkkiːpər | *s.c.* contable.
bookkeeping | 'bʊkkiːpɪŋ | *s.i.* contabilidad.

book-learning | 'bʊklɜːnɪŋ | *s.i.* (fam.) estudio de libros, libros, erudición académica (no práctica).
booklet | 'bʊklɪt | *s.c.* folleto.
bookmaker | 'bʊkmeɪkər | *s.c.* corredor de apuestas.
bookmaking | 'bʊkmeɪkɪŋ | *s.i.* apuestas.
bookmark | 'bʊkmɑːk | *s.c.* señal de lectura, señal de libro (para saber en qué página se ha dejado la lectura).
book-plate | 'bʊkpleɪt | *s.c.* etiqueta para señalar el nombre, etiqueta para escribir el nombre (señalando quién es el dueño de un libro).
bookseller | 'bʊkselər | *s.c.* librero, vendedor de libros.
bookshelf | 'bʊkʃelf | [*pl.* **bookshelves**] **1** estantería para libros. **2** librería. V. **bookcase.**
bookshop | 'bʊkʃɑp | (EE.UU. **bookstore**) *s.c.* librería.
bookstall | 'bʊkstɔːl | *s.c.* puesto de libros, caseta de libros; quiosco.
bookstore | 'bʊkstɔː | V. **bookshop.**
bookworm | 'bʊkwɜːm | *s.c.* **1** ZOOL. polilla (de libros). **2** (fig.) ratón de biblioteca (persona).
boom | buːm | *s.c.* **1** (normalmente *sing.*) boom, auge, prosperidad súbita. **2** estampido, trueno, ruido profundo, ruido que retumba. **3** MAR. botavara, botalón. **4** ELECTR. jirafa, brazo (de micrófono). || *v.i.* **5** prosperar muchísimo, desarrollarse con una rápida prosperidad. **6** retumbar, sonar con ruido profundo. || *v.t.* **7** hacer retumbar. **8** decir con voz fuerte. || **9 to – out,** decir con una voz tronante, decir con voz profunda.
boomerang | 'buːməræŋ | *s.c.* **1** bumerang. || *v.i.* **2** ser contraproducente; salir al revés de lo deseado (plan).
booming | buːmɪŋ | *adj.* tronante, profundo (sonido, voz, etc.).
boom-town | 'buːmtaʊn | *s.c.* ciudad de repentina prosperidad.
boon | buːn | *s.c.* **1 [– (to)]** bendición, dicha. || **2 – companion,** (lit.) compañero del alma, compañero de aventuras.
boor | bʊər | | bɔː | *s.c.* bruto, bestia.
boorish | 'bʊərɪʃ | | bɔːrɪʃ | *adj.* patán, grosero.
boorishly | 'bʊərɪʃlɪ | | bɔːrɪʃlɪ | *adv.* groseramente, con cierta brutalidad.
boorishness | 'bʊərɪʃnɪs | | bɔːrɪʃnɪs | *s.i.* grosería.
boost | buːst | *v.t.* **1** elevar, aumentar (la producción, el rendimiento, etc.). **2** (fig.) dar un empujón, elevar (la moral, el ánimo, etc.). **3** dar el espaldarazo, apoyar (algo o a alguien): *we have to boost our new leader = tenemos que apoyar a nuestro nuevo líder.* || *s.c.* **4** elevación, aumento (de la producción, rendimiento, etc.). **5** empujón, elevación (de la moral, ánimo, etc.). **6** espaldarazo, apoyo (a algo o alguien).
booster | 'buːstər | *s.c.* **1** MED. inyección de refuerzo, inyección supletoria. **2** ELEC. elevador de potencia; elevador de voltaje. **3** (fig.) inyección de moral. || **4 – rocket,** AER. cohete acelerador.
boot | buːt | *s.c.* **1** bota, botín. **2** (brit.) portaequipajes, maletín (de un coche). || *s.sing.* **3 [a –]** (fam.) patada, patadón. || *v.t.* **4** (fam.) dar una patada, dar un patadón. || **5 to – out,** (fam.) echar, poner en la calle, dar la patada (de un empleo, asociación, lugar, etc.). **6 to die with one's boots on,** morir con las botas puestas. **7 to get the –/to be given the –,** (fam.) ser despedido, ser echado (de un trabajo). **8 to get too big for one's boots,** (fam.) tener demasiados humos, darse demasiados humos. **9 to lick someone's boots,** (desp.) hacer la pelota a alguien. **10 to put the – in,** (fam.) **a)** cebarse, abusar (cuando alguien está mal de forma o similar). **b)** cebarse a patadas. **11 the – is on the other foot,** ha dado la vuelta la tortilla, los poderes han dado un vuelco. **12 to –,** (lit. o p.u.) por añadidura, además.
bootee | buː'tiː | *s.c.* botín (de bebé).
booth | buːð | (EE.UU.) | buːθ | *s.c.* **1** cabina (de teléfono, votación, etc.). **2** puesto, barraca (normalmente en una feria).
bootlace | 'buːtleɪs | *s.c.* cordón.
bootleg | 'buːtleg | [*ger.* **bootlegging,** *pret.* y *p.p.* **bootlegged**] *v.i.* **1** hacer contrabando de alcohol. || *adj.* **2** de contrabando.
bootlegger | 'buːtlegər | *s.c.* contrabandista de alcohol.
bootstraps | 'buːtstræps | **to pull oneself up by one's –,** lograr algo con el propio esfuerzo, hacer algo sin la ayuda de nadie.
booty | 'buːtɪ | *s.i.* botín (especialmente de los soldados vencedores).
booze | buːz | (fam.) *s.i.* **1** jarabe, bebida alcohólica, licor. || *v.i.* **2** beber, atiborrarse de alcohol. || **3 on the –,** de jarana, de juerga, de borrachera.
booze-up | 'buːzʌp | *s.c.* (fam.) juerga (con consumo de alcohol).
boozy | 'buːzɪ | *adj.* (fam.) de borrachera, de borracho.
bop | bɑp | [*ger.* **bopping,** *pret.* y *p.p.* **bopped**] (fam.) *v.i.* **1** menear el esqueleto. || *s.c.* **2** baile. **3** puñetazo, meneo (golpe). || *v.t.* **4** golpear, dar un meneo.
borage | 'bɑrɪdʒ | (EE.UU.) | 'bɔːrɪdʒ | *s.i.* BOT. borraja.
borax | 'bɔːræks | *s.i.* QUIM. bórax.
bordello | bɔː'deləʊ | *s.c.* (lit.) burdel.
border | 'bɔːdər | *s.c.* **1** frontera (entre países). **2** orla, franja, ribete (de un objeto). **3** borde, margen (del césped). **4** límite, orilla (de tierra, agua, etc.). || *v.t.* **5** limitar con, tener frontera común con. **6** bordear, estar situado a ambos lados de: *trees bordered the long path = algunos árboles bordeaban el largo sendero.* || *v.i.* **7 [to – on]** limitar con, tener frontera común con. || **8 to – on,** (fig.) rayar en; acercarse a: *his attitude borders on madness = su actitud raya en la locura.* **9 the Border,** GEOG. la frontera (entre Inglaterra y Escocia).
borderland | 'bɔːdəlænd | *s.sing.* **1 [– (between)]** zona fronteriza. **2 [– (between)]** (fig.) estado intermedio, zona intermedia (entre realidad y fantasía o parecido).
borderline | 'bɔːdəlaɪn | *s.sing.* **1 [– (between/of)]** línea divisoria, línea limítrofe. || *adj.* **2** limítrofe: *a borderline case = un caso limítrofe.*
bore | bɔː | *pret.irreg.* **1** de **bear.** || *v.t.* **2 [to – + *o.* + (with)]** aburrir, hartar. || *v.t.* e *i.* **3** taladrar, perforar. || *v.i.* **4 [to – into]** (fig.) taladrar, perforar (con la mirada). || *s.c.* **5** pesado, aburrido, pelmazo. **6** MAR. oleada de marea (especialmente en estuarios). || *s.sing.* **7 [a –]** una lata, una pesadez. || **8 -bore,** de calibre (en compuestos): *a 38 bore gun = un arma de fuego del calibre 38.* **9 to – somebody stiff/to tears/to death,** (fam.) matar de aburrimiento.
bored | bɔːd | *adj.* **[– (with)]** aburrido, harto.
boredom | bɔːdəm | *s.i.* aburrimiento, tedio.
borehole | 'bɔːhəʊl | *s.c.* perforación (especialmente de pozos).
boric | 'bɔːrɪk | QUIM. *adj.* **1** bórico. || **3 – acid,** ácido bórico.
boring | 'bɔːrɪŋ | *adj.* **1** aburrido, que hace aburrir. **2** sin interés, pedestre.
born | bɔːn | *adj.* **1** de nacimiento, innato, nato: *a born runner = un corredor nato.* || **2 to be –, a)** nacer, venir al mundo: *he was born blind = nació ciego.* **b)** poner a uno el nombre de (al nacer): *I was born Thomas = me pusieron el nombre de Tomás.* **3 to be – of, a)** nacer de, ser hijo de, ser descendiente de. **b)** nacer en circunstancias de, ser hijo de (una situación): *he was born of hatred = él fue hijo del odio.* **4 to be – to,** (form.) tener (descendencia): *yesterday a baby girl was born to the Nortons = ayer los Norton tuvieron una niña.* **5 -born,** nacido en (para compuestos): *my France-born son = mi hijo, nacido en Francia.* **6 – of,** resultado de, venido de, causado por: *born of jealousy = causado por los celos.* **7 – with a silver spoon in one's mouth,** V. **spoon. 8 I wasn't – yesterday,** (fam.) no nací ayer. **9 I wish I had never been –,** ojalá no hubiera nacido nunca, ojalá no estuviera vivo.
borne | bɔːn | *p.p.* **1** de **bear.** || **2 -borne,** transportado en, transportado por (en compuestos): *air-borne goods = mercancías aerotransportadas.* **3 it is – in upon/on,** (fam.) uno se ha dado cuenta, uno ha caído en la cuenta: *it is borne in on my son that he has to help the family = mi hijo se ha dado cuenta de que tiene que ayudar a la familia.*
borough | 'bʌrə | (EE.UU.) | 'bʌrəʊ | *s.c.* **1** (brit.) POL. municipio, distrito municipal (con autogobierno). **2** (brit.) distrito municipal de Londres. **3** (EE.UU.) municipio (en algunos Estados y la ciudad de Nueva York).
borrow | 'bɒrəʊ | *v.t.* **1 [to – + *o.* + (from/off)]** tomar prestado, coger prestado. **2** sacar (libro de la biblioteca). **3** agenciar, sacar (un préstamo bancario). **4** coger, tomar prestado, apropiarse (una palabra de otro idioma, una idea de otra persona, etc.). || *v.i.* **5** tomar a préstamo, agenciarse un préstamo bancario. || **6 to live/exist on borrowed time,** vivir un tiempo prestado, estar aún vivo de milagro.
borrower | 'bɒrəʊər | *s.c.* prestatario, persona que toma algo prestado.

borrowing | 'bɒrəuɪŋ | *s.c.* **1** FILOL. préstamo, palabra tomada de otro idioma. || *s.i.* **2** adopción de préstamos financieros.
borstal | 'bɔːstl | *s.c.* reformatorio.
bortsch | bɔːtʃ | *s.i.* GAST. borsch (sopa rusa de remolacha).
bosh | bɒʃ | *interj.* (fam. y p.u.) qué necedad.
bosom | 'buzəm | (form. o lit.) *s.c.* **1** pecho, seno (de mujer). **2** pecho (entendido como la parte delantera del tronco). **3** (fig.) corazón, interior: *in your bosom = en tu interior.* || *s.sing.* **4 [the – of]** la parte delantera de, la pechera de (una prenda de vestir de mujer). **5 [the – of]** el seno de (una institución, la Iglesia, etc.) || **6 – friend,** amigo íntimo, entrañable, amigo del alma. **7 to take someone to one's –,** coger afecto a alguien.
bosomy | 'buzəmɪ | *adj.* de pechos grandes, de pecho voluminoso.
boss | bɒs | *s.c.* **1** jefe, capataz, patrón. **2** (fam.) mandamás, jefazo. **3** almohadilla (techo), protuberancia, tachón. || *v.t.* **4 [to – (about/around)]** (desp.) mangonear, estar en plan mandón hacia (alguien): *my mother bosses us about = mi madre nos mangonea.* || **5 to be one's own –,** trabajar de manera independiente, ser autónomo en el trabajo, no depender de nadie en el trabajo.
boss-eyed | 'bɒsaɪd | *adj.* (fam.) bizco.
bossily | 'bɒsɪlɪ | *adv.* de manera mandona, de modo mandón.
bossiness | 'bɒsɪnɪs | *s.i.* manera de ser mandón, modo de ser mandón.
bosun (también **bo'sun**) V. **boatswain.**
botanic | bə'tænɪk | V. **botanical.**
botanical | bə'tænɪkl | (también **botanic**) *adj.* **1** botánico. || **2 – gardens,** jardín botánico.
botanist | 'bɒtənɪst | *s.c.* experto en botánica, botánico.
botany | 'bɒtənɪ | *s.i.* botánica.
botch | bɒtʃ | (fam.) *v.t.* **1** hacer algo chapuceramente. || *s.c.* **2** chapuza, chapucería. || **3 to – up,** chapucear al máximo, hacer una chapuza redonda.
botcher | 'bɒtʃər | *s.c.* (fam.) chapucero.
botch-up | 'bɒtʃʌp | *s.c.* (fam.) chapuza completa, chapucería.
both | bəuθ | *adj.* **1** los dos, ambos: *both countries are guilty = ambos países son culpables.* || *pron.* **2 [– (of)]** ambos, los dos, dos: *you both stand up = vosotros dos poneros en pie; both of my brothers are doctors = mis dos hermanos son médicos.* || **3 – ... and ...,** tanto... como...; *both John and Mary have many difficulties = tanto Juan como María tienen muchas dificultades.* **4 to have/want things – ways,** V. **way.**
bother | 'bɒðər | *v.i.* **1 [to – (*inf./ger.*with/about)]** molestarse, fastidiarse: *I don't usually bother to cook for myself = normalmente no me molesto en cocinar para mí sólo.* **2 [to – about]** preocuparse por, inquietarse por: *don't bother about what he says = no te inquietes por lo que dice él.* **3 [to – about]** hacer caso de, prestar atención a, importar, molestar (para su aprobación o no): *do they bother about shorts in this place? = ¿les molesta que se lleven pantalones cortos en este sitio?* || *v.t.* **4** molestar, fastidiar: *don't bother me = no me molestes.* **5** preocupar, inquietar. **6** hacer caso de, prestar atención a, importar, molestar (para su aprobación o no). || *s.i.* **7** molestia, fastidio. **8** (fam.) problemas, dificultades. || *s.sing.* **9** (fam.) pelma, pelmazo, latoso. || **10 –,** (brit. y fam.) a la porra con, al carajo con: *let's go in and bother the cost = vamos a entrar y a la porra con lo que cueste.* **11 –!/– it!,** (brit. y p.u.) ¡porras!, ¡pardiez!, ¡mecachis! (expresando disgusto). **12 to – oneself/to – one's head (about),** (fam.) molestarse innecesariamente (con), preocuparse innecesariamente (de): *you needn't bother your head about the report, I'll do it = no tienes por qué molestarte por el informe, lo haré yo.* **13 to go to the –/to go to all the – (of),** ir hasta el extremo (de), llegar (a) (indicando una enorme molestia). **14 it's no –,** no es ninguna molestia, no significa ninguna molestia (ofreciendo ayuda). **15 I/you/etc. can't be bothered (to),** no me/te/etc. apetece molestarme (en), no me/te/etc. parece necesaria la molestia (de).
botheration | ˌbɒðə'reɪʃn | *interj.* (brit. y p.u.) porras, mecachis.
bothered | 'bɒðəd | *adj.* **1** molesto, incómodo. **2** indiferente, neutro: *I am not bothered about politics = soy indiferente en política.* || **3 hot and –,** V. **hot.**
bothersome | 'bɒðəsəm | *adj.* (fam. y p.u.) molesto, irritante, cargante.
bottle | 'bɒtl | *s.c.* **1** botella, frasco (de perfume o similar). **2** biberón. || *s.sing.* **3 [the –]** (fam. y fig.) la botella, el alcohol, la bebida: *the bottle was always a strong attraction for her = la bebida fue siempre una tremenda atracción para ella.* **4** biberón, alimentación artificial, alimentación por biberón (de bebés). **5** (fam. y brit.) decisión, nervio, agallas: *have you got the bottle to tell her = ¿tienes agallas para decírselo?* || *v.t.* **6** envasar, embotellar. **7** poner en frascos, meter en frascos (especialmente fruta). || **8 to – out,** (fam. y brit.) cagarse de miedo, darle a uno una cagalera de miedo; no atreverse por falta de valor. **9 to – up,** reprimir, contener (una emoción fuerte). **10 to hit the –,** (fam.) beber demasiado, beber con exceso; empinar el codo. **11 on at/the –,** alimentado con biberón. **12 to take to the –,** (fam.) darse a la bebida.
bottled | 'bɒtld | *adj.* **1** embotellado, en botella, envasado. || **2 – gas,** gas en bombonas.
bottle-fed | 'bɒtlfed | *pret.* y *p.p.* de **bottle-feed.**
bottle-feed | 'bɒtlfiːd | [*pret.* y *p.p.* **bottle-fed**] *v.t.* e *i.* alimentar con biberón, alimentar artificialmente (a un bebé).
bottle-green | 'bɒtlgriːn | *adj.* (brit.) verde botella.
bottleneck | 'bɒtlnek | *s.c.* **1** estrechamiento, cuello de botella (especialmente en carreteras). **2** (fig.) obstáculo, dificultad.
bottle-opener | 'bɒtləupənər | *s.c.* abridor, abrebotellas.
bottle-party | 'bɒtlpɑːtɪ | *s.c.* fiesta donde cada invitado debe traer una botella de alguna bebida.
bottom | 'bɒtəm | *s.c.* **1 [– (of)]** parte inferior, parte de abajo: *the bottom of the tree = la parte inferior del árbol.* **2 [– (of)]** fondo (del mar, lago, bolso, etc.). **3 [– (of)]** final (parte más alejada del hablante): *the bottom of the street = el final de la calle.* **4 [– (of)]** pie (de una página). **5** (fig.) pantalón, pantalones (del pijama, bañador, etc.). **6** (fam.) culo, trasero. || *s.sing.* **7 [the –]** lo más bajo, lo último (en una escala cualquiera): *that's the bottom in this firm's salary scale = eso es lo más bajo en la escala salarial de esta empresa.* || *adj.* **8** inferior, más bajo, último (en una serie de capas o niveles): *the bottom book = el libro de abajo.* **9** (fig.) inferior, más bajo, último (socialmente, en categoría, etc.). || **10 at –,** en el fondo; en lo más íntimo de su ser. **11 at/from the – of one's heart,** en/desde el fondo del corazón de uno, con/de todo corazón. **12 to be/lie at the – of,** estar en el fondo de, estar detrás de, subyacer a: *jealousy is at the bottom of his anger = los celos se hallan en el fondo de su enfado.* **13 to bet one's – dollar,** apostar hasta el último centavo, apostar la última peseta. **14 – drawer,** (brit. y p.u.) ajuar. **15 – line,** (fam.) punto crucial, madre del cordero, quid. **16 to – out,** nivelarse (algo que estaba bajando): *the price of housing has bottomed out = el precio de la vivienda se ha nivelado.* **17 bottoms up,** (fam. y brit.) salud (antes de beber). **18 to get to the – of this/it,** llegar al fondo de algo, desentrañar (algo secreto). **19 the – drops/falls out (of),** FIN. el mercado deja de comprar (un producto), el mercado (de)... fracasa.
bottomless | 'bɒtəmlɪs | *adj.* **1** sin fondo, muy profundo, insondable. **2** (fig.) inacabable, interminable.
botulism | 'bɒtjulɪzəm | *s.i.* MED. botulismo.
boudoir | 'buːdwɑːr | | 'buːdwɔːr | *s.c.* (arc.) camarín, tocador (habitación para mujer).
bouffant | 'buːfɔːn | *s.c.* peinado abombado, estilo de peinado esponjado.
bougainvillaea | ˌbuːgən'vɪlɪə | *s.c.* e *i.* BOT. buganvilla.
bough | bau | *s.c.* (lit.) rama (de un árbol).
bought | bɔːt | *pret.* y *p.p. irreg.* de **buy.**
bouillon | 'buːjɔn | *s.c.* e *i.* GAST. caldo (normalmente de carne).
boulder | 'bəuldər | *s.c.* roca grande redonda.
boulevard | 'buːləvɑːd | (EE.UU.) | 'buləvɑːd | *s.c.* bulevar, rambla, paseo (entre árboles).
bounce | bauns | *v.i.* **1** botar, rebotar, dar un bote, dar botes (con una pelota). **2** (fig.) rebotar, reflejarse (la luz o el sonido). **3 [to – *prep.*]** (fam.) dar brincos, dar saltitos: *she bounced off the chair = ella dio un saltito bajándose de la silla.* **4** balancearse, flotar (hacia arriba y abajo): *the long hair bounced on her shoulders = el pelo largo se balan-*

ceaba sobre sus hombros. **5** FIN. rechazar, negarse a hacer efectivo (un cheque). **6 [to – (from)]** saltar, ir (de una idea a otra, de un trabajo a otro, etc.). || *v.t.* **7** botar (una pelota). **8** balancear, dar botes (a un niño sobre la rodilla). **9** (fig.) rebotar, reflejar (luz o sonido). **10** FIN. rechazar (cheque). || *s.c.* **11** bote, rebote (de pelota). **12** (fam.) brinco, saltito. || *s.i.* **13** (fam.) vitalidad, energía, vigor. **14** elasticidad (hacia arriba): *this carpet has got a lot of bounce = esta alfombra tiene mucha elasticidad.* || **15 to – back,** (fam.) salir de un estado depresivo, salir a flote (después de una desgracia).

bouncer | 'baʊnsər | *s.c.* (fam.) portero que expulsa a los borrachos o alborotadores.

bouncing | 'baʊnsɪŋ | *adj.* **[– (with)]** robusto, rebosante (de salud).

bouncy | 'baʊnsɪ | *adj.* **1** boyante (de energía). **2** que rebota bien. **3** (fig.) flexible, elástico.

bound | baʊnd | *pret.* y *p.p.* **1** de **bind.** || *adj.* **2 [– for]** con dirección a, en dirección a, destinado a, encaminado hacia. **3 [– (by/to)]** sujeto, obligado (por tratado o similar). **4** encuadernado (libro). || *s.c.* **5** salto, brinco. || *s.pl.* **6** límites, fronteras: *his joy had no bounds = su gozo no tenía límites.* || *v.t.* **7** rodear, limitar, poner límites a (físicamente). || *v.i.* **8 [to – *prep.*]** saltar, brincar: *he bounded off into the street = saltó rápidamente a la calle.* || **9 to be – to,** seguro que, por fuerza que: *it's bound to be cold tomorrow = seguro que hará frío mañana.* **10 -bound, a)** con destino a (en compuestos). **b)** obligado a estar en, confinado en (en compuestos): *housebound = confinado en casa.* **11 – up in,** (fam.) metido hasta las cejas en, absorto en (trabajo). **12 – up with,** relacionado con. **13 by leaps and bounds,** a grandes saltos; con gran rapidez. **14 to feel – to,** sentirse moralmente obligado a (hacer algo). **15 I am – to say/admit,** debo decir/admitir, reconocer. **16 I'll be –,** (p.u.) ciertamente, seguramente. **17 to know no bounds,** no conocer límites, no tener límites. **18 out of bounds,** prohibido; fuera de los límites permitidos.

boundary | 'baʊndrɪ | *s.c.* **1** frontera, límite. **2** (fig.) límite, frontera, confín, línea divisoria (entre ideas, áreas científicas, etc.).

bounder | 'baʊndər | *s.c.* (brit., fam., desp. y arc.) villano, tipo ruin.

boundless | 'baʊndlɪs | *adj.* ilimitado, infinito; vasto.

boundlessly | 'baʊndlɪslɪ | *adv.* ilimitadamente, infinitamente.

bounteous | 'baʊntɪəs | *adj.* (lit.) abundante, copioso; generoso.

bounteously | 'baʊntɪəslɪ | *adv.* (lit.) abundantemente, copiosamente; generosamente.

bountiful | 'baʊntɪfl | V. **bounteous.**

bounty | 'baʊntɪ | *s.c.* **1** recompensa; gratificación. || *s.c.* e *i.* **2** (lit.) regalo, dádiva, merced. || *s.sing.* **3** (lit.) generosidad, liberalidad, munificencia.

bouquet | bu'keɪ | *s.c.* **1 [– (of)]** ramo, ramillete (de flores). || *s.sing.* **2** fragancia, aroma (especialmente del vino y las flores).

bourbon | 'bɜːbən | *s.c.* e *i.* whisky (de maíz o de maíz y centeno, típico del estado de Kentucky en EE.UU.).

bourgeois | 'bɔːʒwɑː | (EE.UU.) | ˌbʊər'ʒwɑː | [*pl.* **bourgeois**] *s.c.* **1** burgués. || *adj.* **2** (desp.) mediocre, aburguesado, burgués. **2** POL. burgués (concepto del marxismo).

bourgeoisie | ˌbɔːʒwɑː'ziː | *s.sing.* POL. burguesía (en el marxismo).

bout | baʊt | *s.c.* **1 [– (of)]** ataque (de alguna enfermedad o sentimiento). **2 [– (of)]** ataque, arrebato (de actividad). **3** DEP. combate (de boxeo, lucha, etc.). || **'bout,** (fam.) acortamiento de **about.**

boutique | buː'tiːk | *s.c.* tienda pequeña de moda, boutique.

bovine | 'bəʊvaɪn | *adj.* **1** AGR. bovino, vacuno. **2** (fig. y desp.) brutote, lerdo, torpón.

bovver | 'bɒvər | *s.i.* (brit. y fam.) comportamiento agresivo, comportamiento violento.

bow | bəʊ | *s.c.* **1** lazo. **2** arco (arma). **3** MUS. arco (de violín y similar). || **4 to have two strings/a second string to one's –,** V. **string.**

bow | baʊ | *v.i.* **1 [to – (to)]** hacer una reverencia, saludar con una reverencia. **2 [to – (to)]** (fig.) doblegarse, ceder (ante una situación inevitable o parecido). || *v.t.* **3** inclinar, saludar mediante inclinación de (la cabeza). || *s.c.* **4** reverencia, saludo con una reverencia. **5** (también en *pl.*) MAR. proa. || **6 to – and scrape,** V. **scrape. 7 to – down (to),** hacer una reverencia muy respetuosa (ante). **8 to – in/out,** entrar/salir haciendo una reverencia. **9 to – out (of),** retirarse, salir (de alguna actividad profesional, política, etc.). **10 to take a –,** aceptar aplausos con una reverencia (actores o cantantes).

bowed | bəʊd | *adj.* curvado, en forma de arco.

bowed | baʊd | *adj.* **1** encorvado (por la edad, enfermedad, etc.). **2** inclinado (como signo de respeto).

bowdlerization | ˌbaʊdləraɪ'zeɪʃn | (EE.UU.) | ˌbaʊdlərɪ'zeɪʃn | (también **bowdlerisation**) *s.c.* e *i.* expurgación, mutilación (de un texto).

bowdlerize | 'baʊdləraɪz | (también **bowdlerise**) *v.t.* expurgar, mutilar, recortar (un texto).

bowel | 'baʊəl | *s.sing.* **1 [the –]** ANAT. el intestino. || *s.pl.* **2** intestinos, tripa. **3 [the – of]** (fig.) las entrañas de, lo más profundo de: *in the bowels of the earth = en las entrañas de la tierra.* || *adj.* **4** intestinal. || **5 – movement,** (euf.) defecación, deposición, evacuación. **6 to move/relieve/empty one's bowels,** (euf.) evacuar, deponer, defecar.

bower | baʊər | *s.c.* (lit.) **1** cenador, emparrado, glorieta. **2** (arc.) tocador, saloncito (de señora).

bowl | bəʊl | *s.c.* **1** tazón, bol, cuenco. **2** cazoleta (de pipa), taza (de retrete), cuenco, tazón (en general cualquier objeto con forma curvada donde se puede contener algo). **3** anfiteatro (en conciertos o teatro). **4** DEP. estadio. **5** DEP. bola (en cualquiera de las variantes del juego de los bolos). || *v.t.* **6** DEP. lanzar, tirar (en cricket o en bolos). **7** DEP. quitar de enmedio (al bateador en el cricket). **8** DEP. hacer, marcar (puntos). **9 [to – + *o.* + *prep.*]** enviar a gran velocidad, empujar a gran velocidad: *the children bowled the stones down the street = los chicos empujaban las piedras a gran velocidad por la calle.* || *v.i.* **10** bolear, lanzar la bola (en el cricket o los bolos). **11 [to – *prep.*]** ir a gran velocidad, deslizarse a toda velocidad. || **12 to – out,** DEP. poner fuera de juego (a un equipo o al bateador). **13 to – over, a)** derribar, tirar al suelo, arrollar. **b)** (fig.) dejar sorprendido/pasmado; aturdir: *her beauty bowled me over = su belleza me dejó pasmado.* **14 bowls,** DEP. bolos (normalmente al aire libre).

bow-legged | ˌbəʊ'legɪd | *adj.* estevado, patizambo, con las piernas torcidas.

bowler | 'bəʊlər | *s.c.* **1** DEP. lanzador (en cricket y bolos). **2** sombrero hongo. || **3 – hat,** sombrero hongo.

bowling | 'bəʊlɪŋ | *s.i.* **1** DEP. bolos (de bolera). **2** DEP. lanzamiento (de críquet). || **3 – alley, a)** bolera. **b)** pista de recorrido de la bola (en la bolera). **4 – green,** zona de juego de los bolos (al aire libre).

bowman | 'bəʊmən | [*pl.* **bowmen**] *s.c.* HIST. arquero.

bowmen | 'bəʊmən | *pl.irreg.* de **bowman.**

bow-tie | ˌbəʊ'taɪ | *s.c.* pajarita (en traje formal).

bow-window | ˌbəʊ'wɪndəʊ | *s.c.* ARQ. ventana curvada salediza, ventana mirador.

bow-wow | ˌbaʊ'waʊ | *s.c.* guau-guau (lenguaje de los niños).

box | bɒks | *s.c.* **1 [– (of)]** caja, cajita: *a box of matches = una caja de cerillas.* **2** cuadrado, casilla (en un impreso). **3** palco (teatro). **4** apartado, apartado de correos. **5** rinconcito, habitáculo (casa en serie y pequeña). **6** rectángulo prohibido (en aparcamientos). **7** protección (que cubre los genitales, especialmente para juegos duros). || *s.sing.* **8 [the –]** (fam. y brit.) la caja tonta, la tele. || *s.i.* **9** BOT. boj. || *v.i.* **10 [to – (against)]** DEP. boxear. || *v.t.* **11** DEP. pelear contra, boxear contra. || **12 -box,** caja, cabina, garito (en compuestos). **13 – camera,** FOT. cámara de cajón. **14 – girder,** ARQ. viga tubular. **15 to – in,** encajonar. **16 – junction,** zona de líneas a cuadros en un cruce (donde no se debe dejar el coche parado). **17 – lunch,** (EE.UU.) almuerzo (a base de sandwichs y fruta). **18 – number,** número de apartado de correos. **19 to – off,** tapar (haciendo un cubículo). **20 – pleat,** pliegue (en faldas).

OBS. Esta palabra, cuando es parte de un compuesto, puede aparecer sola con el significado del compuesto cuando el contexto es obvio: *box* en lugar de *telephone-box... box* en lugar de *post-box* y una larga lista.

boxcar | 'bɒkskɑːr | *s.c.* (EE.UU.) furgón de mercancías (tren).

boxed | 'bɒkst | *adj.* en cajas, puesto en cajas.

boxer | 'bɒksər | *s.c.* **1** DEP. boxeador. **2** ZOOL. perro bóxer, bóxer.

boxing | 'bɒksɪŋ | *s.i.* **1** DEP. boxeo. || **2 Boxing Day,** día 26 de Diciembre (se llama así por la tradición de cantar de puerta en puerta con una caja para que la gente ponga en ella el dinero).
boxing-glove | 'bɑksɪŋglʌv | *s.c.* guante de boxeo.
boxing-match | 'bɒksɪŋmætʃ | *s.c.* combate de boxeo.
box-office | 'bɒksofɪs | *s.c.* **1** taquilla (cine, teatro, etc.). || *s.sing.* **[the –]** (fig.) la taquilla (como éxito de taquilla). || *adj.* **3** taquillero, de taquilla: *a boxoffice success = un éxito de taquilla.*
boxroom | 'bɒksru:m | *s.c.* trastero, cuarto de los trastos.
boxwood | 'bɒkswud | *s.i.* madera de boj, boj.
boy | bɔɪ | *s.c.* **1** chico, muchacho, chaval. **2** (fam.) hijo. **3** (fam.) chaval; hombre (apelativo dado por una persona con autoridad): *that's one of my boys, take care = ése es uno de mis hombres, ten cuidado.* **4** (desp.) sirviente, chaval (especialmente con extranjeros o negros). || *s.pl.* **5 [the –]** los chicos, los muchachos (un grupo de la misma profesión, actividad, etc.): *we'll send this to the research boys = enviaremos esto a los chicos de investigación.* **6 [the –]** los chicos, los amigos, los compañeros (en un grupo informal de amigos). || *interj.* **7** vaya; mecachis. **8** chico, pequeño (manera de dirigirse a un animal macho). || **9 -boy,** chico (en compuestos): *the newspaper-boy = el chico de los periódicos.* **9 boys will be boys,** los chicos siempre serán chicos. **10 my –/my dear –/boys,** (p.u.) chaval, chico, muchacho/ chicos, muchachos: *hello, my dear boy = hola, muchacho.* **11 one of the boys,** uno de los de la panda, uno de los del grupo. **12 the boys/our boys,** los reclutas, los soldados, nuestros reclutas, nuestros soldados (del país de uno, especialmente durante una guerra): *our boys are coming back tomorrow = nuestros soldados regresan mañana.* **13 the boys in blue,** (fam. y brit.) los chicos de azul (la policía).
boycott | 'bɔɪkɒt | *v.t.* **1** hacer un boicot, boicotear. || *s.c.* **2 [– (of/against /on)]** boicot.
boyfriend | 'bɔɪfrend | *s.c.* novio, amigo especial.
boyhood | 'bɔɪhud | *s.i.* niñez, infancia.
boyish | 'bɔɪɪʃ | *adj.* **1** juvenil (hablando de un hombre). **2** de chico, de muchacho (hablando de mujeres): *a boyish appearance = un aire de chico.*
boyishly | 'bɔɪɪʃlɪ | *adv.* **1** juvenilmente (un hombre). **2** a manera de chico, de modo similar a un muchacho (una mujer).
bra | brɑ: | *s.c.* sostén.
brace | breɪs | *v.r.* **1 [to – oneself (for /inf.)]** prepararse; cobrar ánimo (para enfrentarse a algo negativo): *you have to brace yourself for the bad news = tienes que cobrar ánimo para enfrentarte a las malas noticias.* || *v.t.* **2** fortalecer, poner en tensión, poner en preparación (una parte del cuerpo). **3** apoyar, sostener (una parte del cuerpo en algún lugar). **4** asegurar, apuntalar (un objeto o parte del cuerpo). || *s.c.* **5** abrazadera, laña. **6** reforzamiento. **7** llave, corchete (en tipografía). **8** MED. aparato de ortodoncia. **9** [*pl.* **brace**] par (de caza). || **10 – and bit,** berbiquí. **11 braces,** (brit.) tirantes. **11 to – up,** animarse, cobrar ánimo, cobrar valor.
bracelet | 'breɪslɪt *s.c.* brazalete.
bracing | 'breɪsɪŋ | *adj.* fortificante, vigorizante (clima, lugar, etc.).
bracken | 'brækən | *s.i.* BOT. helecho.
bracket | 'brækɪt | *s.c.* **1** paréntesis. **2** categoría, grupo (especialmente en el tema fiscal): *I've gone into the upper bracket = he entrado en la categoría superior.* **3** soporte, escuadra (para estantes). || *v.t.* **4** poner entre paréntesis. **5 [to – *o.* (together/with)]** agrupar, clasificar, poner juntos: *she should be bracketed with the honest group in the class = ella debería ser incluida entre los buenos de la clase.*
brackish | 'brækɪʃ | *adj.* salobre (agua).
brad | bræd | *s.c.* punta (parecido a un clavo).
brag | bræg | [*ger.* **bragging,** *pret.* y *p.p.* **bragged**] *v.i.* **[to – (about/to/of)]** chulearse, jactarse, pavonearse.
braggart | 'brægət | *s.c.* (p.u. y desp.) fanfarrón, chulo.
Brahman | 'brɑ:mən | V. **Brahmin.**
Brahmin | 'brɑ:mɪn | *s.c.* REL. Brahmín (casta superior hindú).
braid | breɪd | *s.i.* **1** trenza, cinta, galón (en cortinas o similar). || *s.c.* **2** (p.u. o EE.UU.) trenza (del pelo). || *v.t.* **3** (p.u. o EE.UU.) trenzar, hacer trenzas en (el pelo).
braided | 'breɪdɪd | *adj.* **[– (with)]** trenzado (como adorno de ropa).
Braille | breɪl | *s.i.* Braille (escritura para ciegos).
brain | breɪn | *s.c.* **1** ANAT. cerebro. **2** (fig.) cabeza, mente: *there was great confusion in his brain = había una gran confusión en su cabeza.* **3** (fig. y fam.) genio, cabeza pensante. **4** (fig.) inteligencia (especialmente de algún tipo): *he has a very mathematical brain = tiene una inteligencia muy matemática.* || *s.pl.* **5** ANAT. sesos. **6** (fig.) inteligencia, cabeza, capacidad. **7 [the – (of/behind)]** (fam.) el cerebro (de un grupo, organización, etc.). || *v.t.* **8** (fam.) romper la crisma. || **9 to beat someone's brains out,** (fam.) darle a alguien unos golpes que le causen la muerte, matar a alguien a golpes. **10 to blow someone's brains out,** (fam.) levantarle a alguien la tapa de los sesos (con arma de fuego). **11 – death,** MED. muerte cerebral. **12 – fever,** MED. fiebre cerebral, inflamación febricular del cerebro. **13 brains trust,** (EE.UU. – **trust**), grupo de expertos, grupo de consejeros, grupo de asesores. **14 to have something on the –,** (desp. y fam.) darle vueltas a algo (en la cabeza). **15 to pick someone's brains,** (fam.) exprimir a alguien, sacar a alguien todo el jugo (cuando conoce muy bien un tema que le consultamos). **16 to rack one's brains,** V. **rack.**
brainchild | 'breɪntʃaɪld | *s.sing.* idea original, proyecto original: *the new petrol station is my brainchild = la nueva gasolinera fue idea mía.*
brain-drain | 'breɪndreɪn | *s.sing.* fuga de cerebros.
brainless | 'breɪnlɪs | *adj.* sin cabeza, tonto, atontado, estúpido.
brainstorm | 'breɪnstɔ:m | *s.c.* **1** (brit.) acceso de estupidez, ataque de locura transitorio. **2** (EE.UU.) idea brillante y repentina, idea genial.
brainstorming | 'breɪnstɔmɪŋ | *s.i.* método de resolución de problemas mediante la discusión de lo que piensa cada individuo dentro de un grupo.
brain-teaser | 'breɪnti:zər | *s.c.* rompecabezas; problema de difícil solución.
brainwash | 'breɪnwɒʃ | *v.t.* **[to – + *o.* + (into)]** lavar el cerebro.
brainwashing | 'breɪnwɒʃɪŋ | *s.i.* lavado de cerebro.
brainwave | 'breɪnweɪv | (EE.UU. **brainstorm**) *s.c.* idea genial, idea luminosa.
brainy | 'breɪnɪ | *adj.* (fam.) despierto, listo, inteligente.
braise | breɪz | *v.t.* GAST. dorar a fuego lento.
brake | breɪk | *s.c.* **1** MEC. freno. **2 [– (on/upon/off)]** (fig.) freno, parón, control. || *v.i.* **3** frenar, echar el freno. || *v.t.* **4** (fig.) frenar (el progreso o parecido). || **5 – fluid,** líquido de frenos (en vehículo). **6 to put a – on,** (fig.) poner el freno a (gasto excesivo, actividad perjudicial, etc.). **7 to take the brakes off,** (fig.) dar vía libre a (un proyecto o similar, después de haber estado parado).
brake-shoe | 'breɪkʃu: | *s.c.* MEC. zapata (del freno).
bramble | 'bræmbl | *s.c.* BOT. zarza, cambrón.
bran | bræn | *s.i.* salvado (normalmente del pan).
branch | brɑ:ntʃ | (EE.UU.) | bræntʃ | *s.c.* **1** rama (de árbol). **2** sucursal, agencia (de banco, empresa, etc.). **3** ramo, especialidad (de estudio o similar). **4** rama (de familia). **5** bifurcación, brazo (de río, carretera, etc.). **6** sección, división (de la estructura administrativa del Estado). || *v.i.* **7** bifurcarse. || **8 to – off, a)** separarse, salir, proceder: *a small road branches off at that point = una pequeña carretera se separa en ese punto.* **b)** (fig.) hacer una disgresión, cambiar momentáneamente de tema de conversación. **9 – office,** sucursal. **10 to – out,** ampliar el campo de operaciones, ampliar las actividades, lanzarse a una nueva actividad.
branch-line | 'brɑ:ntʃlaɪn *s.c.* ramal secundario (ferrocarril).
brand | brænd | *s.c.* **1** marca (registrada). **2** (fig.) tipo, manera, modo (de comportarse, pensar, etc.). **3** marca (en el ganado). **4** (lit.) tea, antorcha. || *v.t.* **5** marcar, poner una marca (al ganado). **6 [to – *o.* (as)]** (fig.) tachar, señalar, tildar: *the police branded him as a dangerous criminal = la policía le señaló como un criminal peligroso.* || **7 – name,** nombre de marca.
branded | 'brændɪd | *adj.* con marca (producto).
branding-iron | 'brændɪŋaɪən | *s.c.* hierro de marcar (ganado).
brandish | 'brændɪʃ | *v.t.* blandir, esgrimir (especialmente un arma).

brand-new | ˌbrænd'njuː | *adj.* nuevo, recién, totalmente nuevo.
brandy | 'brændɪ | *s.i.* **1** coñac, brandy. || **2 – butter,** GAST. mezcla de azúcar, mantequilla y coñac (que se come en Navidad).
brandy-snap | 'brændɪsnæp | *s.c.* GAST. galleta de gengibre.
brash | bræʃ | *adj.* (desp.) **1** impetuoso, temerario; insolente. **2** chillón (colores o vestimenta).
brashly | 'bræʃlɪ | *adv.* (desp.) **1** impetuosamente, temerariamente; insolentemente. **2** chillonamente (colores o vestimenta).
brashness | 'bræʃnɪs | *s.i.* (desp.) **1** impetuosidad; insolencia. **2** (lo) chillón (de ropa o colores).
brass | brɑːs | (EE.UU. | bræs) *s.i.* **1** latón. **2** (fam.) dinero, parné (especialmente en el Norte de Inglaterra). || *s.c.* **3** placa, placa conmemorativa (en latón). || *s.sing.* **4 [the –]** MUS. el metal (en una orquesta las trompetas y similar). || *adj.* **5** (fam.) insolente, descarado: *you have the brass cheek to tell me now! = ¡tienes el descaro de decírmelo ahora!* || **6 as bold as –,** V. **bold. 7 – band,** MUS. orquesta de metal. **8 brassed off (with),** (fam.) hasta las narices (de), harto (de). **9 – hat,** (brit. y fam.) MIL. oficial de alto rango. **10 – knuckles,** (EE.UU.) manopla. **11 – plate,** placa, rótulo (con el nombre y profesión, típico en puertas). **12 – rubbing,** copia en bronce. **13 to get down to – tacks,** (fam.) ir al grano, entrar en materia de verdad.
brasserie | 'bræsərɪ | *s.c.* cervecería; restaurante (pequeño).
brassière | 'bræsɪər | (EE.UU.) | brə'zɪər | *s.c.* (form. o p.u.) sostén, corpiño.
brassily | 'brɑːsɪlɪ | (EE.UU.) | 'bræsɪlɪ | *adv.* **1** chillonamente, estridentemente (sonido). **2** (desp.) desvergonzadamente, descaradamente (vestimenta, comportamiento, etc.).
brassiness | 'brɑːsɪnɪs | (EE.UU.) | 'bræsɪnɪs | *s.i.* **1** estridencia (sonido). **2** (desp.) desvergüenza, descaro (en ropa, comportamiento, etc.).
brass-monkey | 'brɑːsmʌnkɪ | *adj.* (fam. y brit.) (frío) que corta.
brasswork | 'brɑːswɜːk | *s.i.* objetos de latón.
brassy | 'brɑːsɪ | (EE.UU.) | 'bræsɪ | *adj.* **1** de color latón. **2** chillón, estridente (sonido). **3** (desp.) desvergonzado, descarado (en vestimenta, comportamiento, etc.).
brat | bræt | *s.c.* (fam. y desp.) malcriado (niño).
bravado | brə'vɑːdəʊ | *s.i.* bravata, baladronada.
brave | breɪv | *adj.* **1** valiente, esforzado. **2** (lit.) magnífico, espléndido. || *v.t.* **3** afrontar, arrostrar, encarar (una situación difícil). || *s.c.* **4** bravo, guerrero (indio). || **5 Brave New World,** utopía, mundo lleno de progreso y felicidad. **6 to – out,** encarar valientemente, afrontar con valentía. **7 to put a – face on,** poner al mal tiempo buena cara.
bravely | 'breɪvlɪ | *adv.* **1** valientemente, esforzadamente. **2** (lit.) magníficamente, espléndidamente.
bravery | 'breɪvərɪ | *s.i.* valentía, coraje.
bravo | ˌbrɑː'vəʊ | *interj.* (form.) bravo.
bravura | brə'vʊərə | *s.i.* (lit.) **1** excesivo adorno, excesiva apariencia. **2** MUS. ejecución brillante.
brawl | brɔːl | *s.c.* **1** riña, reyerta, pelea. || *v.i.* **2** pelear (especialmente con los puños).
brawn | brɔːn | *s.i.* **1** fuerza muscular. **2** GAST. carne en gelatina.
brawny | 'brɔːnɪ | *adj.* forzudo, musculoso.
bray | breɪ | *v.i.* **1** rebuznar (burro). **2** (fig. y desp.) sonar como un rebuzno. || *s.c.* **3** rebuzno.
brazen | 'breɪzn | *adj.* **1** descarado, desvergonzado. || **2 to – out,** afrontar descaradamente, salir con descaro (de una situación comprometida).
brazenly | 'breɪznlɪ | *adv.* descaradamente, desvergonzadamente.
brazier | 'breɪzɪər | *s.c.* brasero.
Brazil | brə'zɪl | *s.sing.* Brasil.
Brazilian | brə'zɪlɪən | *adj.* **1** brasileño. || *s.c.* **2** brasileño.
breach | briːtʃ | *s.c.* e *i.* **1** violación, incumplimiento (de acuerdo, contrato, etc.). || *s.c.* **2** ruptura, rompimiento (de una relación o similar). **3 [– (in)]** brecha, abertura (en muro, protección, etc.). || *v.t.* **4** violar, incumplir (acuerdo, ley, etc.). **5** abrir una brecha (especialmente en un muro, protección, etc.). || **6 – of promise,** (p.u.) DER. incumplimiento de compromiso matrimonial. **7 – of the peace,** DER. perturbación del orden público. **8 to step into the —,** meterse en la brecha (ayudando en alguna situación mala).
bread | bred | *s.i.* **1** pan. **2** (fig.) sustento, comida, pan. **3** (fam.) dinero, pasta, (Am.) plata. || **4 – and butter,** (fig.) **a)** sustento; pan y agua. **b)** básico y material, fundamental (materialmente): *most people are only interested in bread and buffer issues = la mayor parte de la gente sólo está interesada en temas básicos y materiales.* **5 to cast one's – upon the water/waters,** hacer el bien sin mirar a quién. **6 to know which side one's – is buttered on,** (fam.) saber lo que a uno le conviene, saber dónde le aprieta a uno el zapato. **7 the best thing since sliced –,** (fam.) lo nunca visto, el mejor invento desde la penicilina.
bread-bin | 'bredbɪn | *s.c.* panera.
bread-board | 'bredbɔːd | *s.c.* tabla para cortar el pan.
breadcrumb | 'bredkrʌm | *s.c.* (generalmente *pl.*) miga, miga de pan, migajas.
breaded | 'bredɪd | *adj.* GAST. cocinado con pan rallado, rebozado.
breadfruit | 'bredfruːt | *s.c.* e *i.* BOT. fruta del árbol del pan.
breadline | 'bredlaɪn | *s.sing.* **1** cola para la sopa boba. || **2 on the –,** pobre, mísero, en la miseria.
breadth | bretθ | *s.i.* **1 [– (of)]** anchura, ancho (físico). **2** envergadura, extensión. **3** liberalidad, carácter abierto (de una opinión o similar). || **4 the length and –,** V. **length.**
breadwinner | 'bredwɪnər | *s.c.* sostén económico de una familia (normalmente el padre).
break | breɪk | *v.* [*pret.irreg.* **broke,** *p.p.* **broken]** *t.* **1** romper, partir, quebrar. **2** MED. fracturar, romper (un hueso). **3** (fig.) romper, no cumplir (promesa), infringir (ley). **4** batir (un record, normalmente deportivo). **5** DEP. romper (el saque en tenis). **6** descifrar, romper (un código secreto o similar). **7** cambiar (un billete en moneda menor). **8** forzar (puerta, caja fuerte, etc.). **9** estropear, romper (aparato). **10** destrozar (la vida, carrera, etc. de alguien). **11** comunicar, dar (noticias). **12** amortiguar (la fuerza de algo). **13** interrumpir, romper (silencio, monotonía, etc.). **14** cortar, interrumpir (un proceso, línea, continuidad, etc.): *the trees broke the line of the horizon = los árboles interrumpían la línea del horizonte.* **15** cortar (piel): *the sword didn't break the skin = la espada no cortó la piel.* **16** poner fin a, romper (huelga laboral). **17** romper (relación amorosa, de amistad, etc.). **18 [to – +** *o.* **+ of]** quitar (un hábito, idea, etc.). **19** acabar con (una situación), destrozar (un sistema): *to break a deadlock = acabar con una situación de estancamiento.* || *i.* **20** romperse, partirse; quebrarse. **21** romperse, estropearse, averiarse (aparato). **22** comenzar, estallar (tormenta). **23** cambiar (la voz de un niño). **24** comenzar, amanecer, apuntar, rayar (un nuevo día). **25** cambiar (el tiempo atmosférico). **26 [to – (for)]** hacer una pausa, tomarse un descanso. **27** darse a conocer, anunciarse (noticias). **28** romper (olas). **29** AER. separarse, desplegarse. **30** disgregarse (multitud). || *s.c.* **31** MED. rotura, fractura. **32** interrupción (de un proceso, línea, etc.). **33** ruptura (de una relación, conexión, etc.). **34** DEP. ruptura (del saque en tenis); separación (de los boxeadores). **35** (fam.) oportunidad buena, casualidad ventajosa. **36** descanso; cambio (de actividad). **37** DEP. puntuación seguida, puntos conseguidos en serie (en billar). **38** claro (en las nubes, tráfico, etc.). **39** agujero, grieta, raja. || *s.i.* **40** (brit.) recreo (escolar). || **41 at the – of day,** al despuntar el día, al rayar el día. **42 to – away (from), a)** separar (de), apartarse (de) (físicamente). **b)** separarse (de), irse (de) (un grupo, colectivo, etc.). **43 to – camp,** V. **camp. 44 to – cover,** V. **cover. 45 to – down, a)** tirar abajo, derribar (físicamente). **b)** averiarse, estropearse (vehículo, maquinaria, etc.). **c)** fracasar, fallar (sistema, conversación, etc.). **d)** descomponerse (una sustancia). **e)** quitar, derribar, tirar (barreras culturales, obstáculos psicológicos, etc.). **f)** perder el control (de uno mismo y, normalmente, echarse a llorar). **g)** derrumbarse (mentalmente). **h)** analizar (una idea, dividiéndola en sus partes). **46 to – even,** ni ganar ni perder (económicamente). **47 to – free/loose/someone's hold, a)** soltarse, librarse (de una atadura o similar). **b)** (fig.) escaparse (para iniciar una nueva vida, un nuevo proyecto, etc.). **c)** desencadenarse, estallar (emociones,

situaciones apuradas, etc.). **48 to – fresh ground,** V. **ground. 49 to – in, a)** entrar (en un lugar rompiendo una puerta, ventana, etc.). **b)** acostumbrar gradualmente, dejar que alguien se haga gradualmente (a una nueva situación o parecido). **c)** ir usando, ir llevando (zapatos o botas nuevas hasta que se hacen cómodos). **d)** domar, amansar (especialmente caballos). **50 to – in (on),** interrumpir, cortar (conversación). **51 to – into, a)** entrar (en un lugar mediante el rompimiento de algún sistema de seguridad). **b)** dividir (en partes menores). **c)** echar mano de, empezar a utilizar (dinero ahorrado). **d)** comenzar a, iniciar, echarse a (correr, cantar, reír, etc.). **e)** interrumpir (un proceso, pensamiento, etc.). **f)** comenzar la nueva actividad de, iniciarse en (negocios, empresas, etc.). **52 to – off, a)** separar por completo, desprenderse por entero. **b)** interrumpir súbitamente, parar súbitamente (una actividad). **c)** romper (compromiso, acuerdo, etc.). **53 one's silence,** romper el silencio, interrumpir el período de silencio de uno (especialmente revelando un secreto). **54 to – one's step/pace,** cambiar de ritmo al caminar. **55 to – open,** forzar, abrir por la fuerza. **56 to – out, a)** escapar, huir (normalmente de una prisión o parecido). **b)** estallar (guerra, discusión, enfermedad, etc.). **57 to – out (in),** empezar a (sudar); salirle a uno (sarpullido). **58 to – out (of),** salir (de), escapar (de) (una situación negativa). **59 to – ranks,** V. **rank. 60 to – someone's heart,** V. **heart. 61 to – the bank, a)** hacer saltar la banca (en un juego). **b)** (fig. y fam.) ser una cantidad de dinero importante. **62 to – the ice,** V. **ice. 63 to – through, a)** penetrar a través de, abrirse paso por. **b)** aparecer (algo antes oculto). **c)** vencer (dificultades). **64 to – up, a)** dividirse en trocitos, romperse en trocitos, partirse en trocitos. **b)** romper (la monotonía). **c)** separarse, disgregarse (en unidades más pequeñas): *the party broke up = el partido se disgregó.* **d)** acabar violentamente con, irrumpir violentamente (y acabar con algo). **e)** (brit. y fam.) comenzar las vacaciones escolares, iniciar las vacaciones escolares. **65 to – up (with),** romper (con), terminar (con) (una relación amorosa o amistosa). **66 to – waters,** V. **water. 67 to – with, a)** romper con (persona o grupo). **b)** apartarse de, romper con (tradición, cultura, etc.). **68 to make a –,** escaparse, huir (normalmente de la prisión).

breakable | 'breɪkəbl | *adj.* **1** frágil, quebradizo. || **2 breakables,** objetos frágiles, mercancía frágil.

breakage | 'breɪkɪdʒ | *s.c.* **1** rotura; objeto roto. || *s.i.* **2** (form.) rotura.

breakaway | 'breɪkəweɪ | *s.c.* **1** (normalmente *sing.*) separación, ruptura (de un grupo, partido, asociación, etc.). || *adj.* **2** disidente.

break-dancing | 'breɪkdɑːnsɪŋ | *s.i.* baile break, estilo de baile break.

breakdown | 'breɪkdaʊn | *s.c.* **1** fracaso, fallo (de plan, proyecto, acuerdo, etc.). **2** avería (de vehículo o maquinaria). **3 [– (of)]** análisis (dividiendo en sus características). **4** depresión (mental). **5** finalización, terminación (de ideas, tradiciones, etc.): *the breakdown of castes in India = el fin de las castas en la India.*

breaker | 'breɪkər | *s.c.* ola grande, ola gigantesca.

breakfast | 'brekfəst | *s.c.* e *i.* **1** desayuno. || *v.i.* **2** (lit. o arc.) desayunar. || **3 – television,** TV. programa televisivo matutino. **4 the – table,** (fig.) la mesa del desayuno.

break-in | 'breɪkɪn | *s.c.* entrada forzada, entrada violenta (en un edificio).

breakneck | 'breɪknek | *adj.* arriesgada, vertiginosa (velocidad).

breakthrough | 'breɪkθruː | *s.c.* avance, adelanto, progreso: *a new breakthrough in medicine = un nuevo avance en la medicina.*

break-up | 'breɪkʌp | *s.c.* **1** ruptura (de un matrimonio). **2** destrozo, demolición, división. || *s.sing.* **3 [– of]** final de, finalización de. || *s.c.* e *i.* **4** disgregación (de un grupo, asociación, etc.).

breakwater | 'breɪkwɔːtər | *s.c.* rompeolas.

breast | brest | *s.c.* **1** pecho, seno, mama. **2** pecho (de hombre). **3** pechuga (de ave). **4** (lit.) pecho, corazón (como receptáculo de sentimientos). || *s.sing.* **5 [the –]** la parte delantera (de camisas o similar). || *s.c.* e *i.* **6** pechuga (como carne). || **7 to make a clean – of,** confesar, reconocer con toda franqueza (una culpa).

breastbone | 'brestbəʊn | *s.c.* ANAT. esternón.

breast-fed | 'brestfed | *pret.* y *p.p.* **1** de **breast-feed.** || *adj.* **2** alimentado naturalmente, alimentado con el pecho, amamantado.

breast-feed | 'brestfiːd | [*pret.* y *p.p. irreg.* **breast-fed**] *v.t.* e *i.* dar de mamar, alimentar con leche materna, amamantar, dar el pecho.

breast-feeding | 'brestfiːdɪŋ | *s.i.* alimentación natural, alimentación de la propia madre.

breast-high | ˌbrest'haɪ | *adj.* a la altura del pecho.

breastplate | 'brestpleɪt | *s.c.* peto (armadura).

breast-pocket | ˌbrest'pɒkɪt | *s.c.* bolsillo del pecho.

breaststroke | 'breststrəʊk | *s.i.* DEP. braza, estilo de braza (en la natación).

breastwork | 'brestwɜːk | *s.i.* MIL. parapeto, fortificación (de poca altura).

breath | breθ | *s.c.* **1** respiración, aliento. || *s.sing.* **2 [– of]** soplo de (aire). **3** (fig. y lit.) murmullo, pizca (pequeña cantidad). || *s.i.* **4** aliento, fuelle. || **5 a – of air,** un soplo de aire: *a breath of fresh air = un soplo de aire fresco.* **6 bad –,** mal aliento. **7 to catch one's –, a)** tomar aliento, recobrar el aliento. **b)** quedarse sin aliento (por la sorpresa, miedo, etc.). **8 to draw –,** tomar aire: *some swimmers can be under water for three minutes without drawing breath = algunos nadadores pueden estar bajo el agua durante tres minutos sin tomar aire.* **9 to get one's – back,** recuperar el aliento, recobrar el aliento, recobrarse. **10 to hold one's –,** contener la respiración, contener el aliento. **11 in the same –,** al mismo tiempo, simultáneamente (diciendo dos cosas contrarias). **12 out of –,** sin aliento, sin resuello. **13 to save one's –,** ahorrar palabras. **14 short of –,** con dificultad en la respiración, con falta de resuello. **15 to take a –,** tomar aire, inspirar. **16 to take one's – away,** dejar sin aliento, dejar sin resuello; (fig.) dejar sorprendido. **17 the – of life,** (fig.) lo más vital, lo más esencial, lo más importante (para alguien). **18 under one's –,** en voz baja. **19 to waste one's –,** gastar saliva, malgastar saliva. **20 with bated –,** V. **bated. 21 with one's dying /last –,** con el último suspiro de uno.

breathable | 'breθəbl | *adj.* respirable.

breathalyze | 'breθəlaɪz | (también **breathalyse**) *v.t.* (brit.) comprobar el contenido de alcohol en el aliento de alguien.

Breathalyzer | 'breθəlaɪzər | (también **Breathalyser**) *s.c.* (brit.) aparato medidor del contenido de alcohol en el aliento de una persona (marca registrada).

breathe | briːð | *v.i.* **1** respirar, tomar aire. **2** respirar, dejar que se airee (el vino). || *v.t.* **3** respirar, tomar (aire). **4** emanar, emitir, soltar (humo o similar). **5** susurrar, decir en susurros. **6 [to – + *o.* + (into)]** inspirar, infundir (confianza u otra emoción). || **7 to – again/(more) easily,** respirar tranquilo, relajarse (tras una experiencia preocupante). **8 to – down someone's neck,** seguirle a alguien demasiado cerca, estar detrás de alguien (para controlar de cerca lo que hace). **9 to – in,** tomar aire, inhalar, aspirar. **10 to – one's last,** (lit.) exhalar el último suspiro. **11 to – out,** exhalar, espirar.

breather | 'briːðər | *s.c.* (fam.) descanso, momento de respiro, respiro, pausa.

breathing | 'briːðɪŋ | *s.i.* respiración.

breathing-space | 'briːðɪŋspeɪs | *s.c.* respiro, pausa.

breathless | 'breθlɪs | *adj.* **1** jadeante, falto de aliento, sofocado. **2** (fig.) estupefacto; intenso, extremo (interés, temor, etc.).

breathlessly | 'breθlɪslɪ | *adv.* jadeantemente, sofocadamente. **2** (fig.) de modo estupefacto; intensamente, extremadamente (interés, temor, etc.).

breathlessness | 'breθlɪsnɪs | *s.i.* **1** estado sofocado, sofoco, jadeo. **2** (fig.) intensidad (de interés, temor, etc.).

breathtaking | 'breθteɪkɪŋ | *adj.* imponente, impresionante.

breathtakingly | 'breθteɪkɪŋlɪ | *adv.* imponentemente, impresionantemente, asombrosamente.

bred | bred | *pret.* y *p.p.irreg.* de **breed.**

breech | briːtʃ | *s.c.* **1** recámara (de un arma de fuego). || **2 – birth,** MED. parto de nalgas.

breeches | 'brɪtʃɪz | *s.pl.* pantalones hasta la rodilla, pantalones bombachos, pantalones de montar (a caballo).

breed | briːd | *v.* [*pret.* y *p.p.irreg.* **bred**] *t.* **1** criar (ganado); injertar (plantas). **2 [to – + *o.* + (for/*inf.*)]** educar, criar, enseñar (desde muy pequeño): *he was bred for the military academy = se le educó para la academia militar.* **3** (fig.) producir, engendrar (una situación, sentimiento, etc.). || *i.* **4** reproducirse, procrear (animales). || *s.c.* **5** casta, especie, raza (de animal). **6** (fig.) raza, tipo, clase (de persona). || **7 born and bred,** nacido y criado (en un lugar o acorde con una ideología).

breeder | 'bri:dər | *s.c.* criador (de perros, especialmente).

breeding | 'bri:dɪŋ | *s.i.* **1** reproducción, cría, cruce (de animales). **2** clase, buena educación (especialmente en la alta sociedad).

breeding-ground | 'bri:dɪŋgraʊnd | *s.c.* **1** criadero; zona protegida para la reproducción animal. **2** (fig.) semillero, criadero (de personas con una determinada formación o comportamiento): *a breeding-ground for general managers = un semillero de directores generales.*

breeze | bri:z | *s.c.* **1** brisa, viento suave. || *s.sing.* **2** (fam.) algo tirado, algo chupado (muy fácil de hacer). || *v.i.* **3 [to – *prep.*]** ir como Pedro por su casa, ir sin problemas: *she breezed into my room = entró en mi habitación sin problemas.* || **4 to shoot the –,** (EE.UU. y fam.) charlar, mover la sinhueso.

breeze-block | 'bri:zblɒk | *s.c.* e *i.* ARQ. ladrillo ligero.

breezeway | 'bri:zweɪ | *s.c.* (EE.UU.) pasaje (entre dos edificios).

breezily | 'bri:zɪlɪ | *adv.* jovialmente, despreocupadamente, animadamente, alegremente.

breeziness | 'bri:zɪnɪs | *s.i.* **1** presencia de brisa, presencia de viento ligero. **2** alegría, jovialidad, despreocupación.

breezy | 'bri:zɪ | *adj.* **1** con viento suave, con brisa. **2** jovial, alegre, despreocupado, animado.

brethren | 'breðrɪn | [no tiene *sing.*] *s.pl.* (p.u.) REL. hermanos.

breve | bri:v | *s.c.* MUS. breve.

breviary | 'bri:vɪərɪ | (EE.UU.) | 'bri:vɪerɪ | *s.c.* REL. breviario.

brevity | 'brevɪtɪ | *s.i.* **1** brevedad (tiempo). **2** concisión (al hablar).

brew | bru: | *v.i.* **1** hacerse, posarse bien (té o café). **2** (fig.) cocerse (una situación): *something is brewing in high places = algo se está cociendo en las alturas.* || *v.t.* **3** hacer, preparar (té o café). **4** fabricar, hacer (cerveza). || *s.c.* **5** (fam.) brebaje (cerveza). **6** infusión, brebaje (de hierbas exóticas normalmente). || **7 to – up, a)** (fam. y brit.) hacer, preparar (té). **b)** tramar(se), urdir(se) (una situación).

brewer | 'bru:ər | *s.c.* fabricante de cerveza, cervecero.

brewery | 'brʊərɪ | *s.c.* fábrica de cerveza.

briar | 'braɪər | (también **brier**) *s.c.* BOT. zarza, brezo.

bribe | braɪb | *s.c.* **1** soborno. || *v.t.* **2** sobornar: *he bribed his way out of prison = salió de la cárcel a base de sobornar.*

bribery | 'braɪbərɪ | *s.i.* soborno.

bric-a-brac | 'brɪkəbræk | *s.i.* cachivaches (ornamentales).

brick | brɪk | *s.c.* **1** ladrillo. **2** bloque, corte (helado). **3** (fam., brit. y p.u.) maravilla, cielo (de persona). || *s.i.* **4** ladrillo. || **5 to – in,** rodear de ladrillo, cerrar con ladrillos. **6 to – off,** tapar con ladrillos. **7 to – up,** cerrar con ladrillo por completo (una ventana, por ejemplo). **8 to come down on someone like a ton of bricks,** (fam.) cantar las cuarenta a alguien, dar una reprimenda de aúpa a alguien. **9 to make bricks without straw,** V. **straw.**

bricklayer | 'brɪkleər | *s.c.* albañil.

brickwork | 'brɪkwɜ:k | *s.i.* trabajo de albañilería, enladrillado: *the brickwork in this building is pretty lousy = el enladrillado en este edificio es bastante malo.*

brickyard | 'brɪkjɑ:d | *s.c.* fábrica de ladrillos.

bridal | 'braɪdl | *adj.* nupcial, de boda.

bride | braɪd | *s.c.* novia, prometida, desposada.

bridegroom | braɪdgrɒm | | braɪd gru:m | *s.c.* novio, prometido.

bridesmaid | 'braɪdzmeɪd | *s.c.* dama de honor (de la novia).

bride-to-be | 'braɪdtubi: | *s.c.* futura esposa.

bridge | brɪdʒ | *s.c.* **1** puente. **2** (fig.) puente, nexo de unión: *a bridge between the conservatives and the socialists = un nexo de unión entre los conservadores y los socialistas.* **3** ANAT. caballete (de la nariz). **4** MAR. puente (de un barco). **5** MUS. puente (de un violín). **6** puente (en los dientes). **7** puente (gafas). || *s.i.* **8** bridge (juego de cartas). || *v.t.* **9** tender un puente sobre, construir un puente sobre. **10** (fig.) abarcar, extenderse sobre (la vida, el trabajo de alguien): *my grandfather's life bridged four generations = la vida de mi abuelo abarcó cuatro generaciones.* **11** (fig.) salvar (distancias, separación, etc.): *the gulf between their two worlds could not be bridged = la separación entre sus dos mundos no podía salvarse.* || **12 to – the/a gap, a)** salvar las diferencias, acortar la separación (entre personas). **b)** llenar un vacío. **13 to burn one's bridges,** quemar las naves. **14 to cross one's bridges when one comes to them,** encararse con los problemas cuando existan, solucionar los problemas cuando lleguen. **15 water under the –,** V. **water.**

bridgehead | 'brɪdʒhed | *s.c.* MIL. cabeza de puente.

bridging | 'brɪdʒɪŋ | *s.i.* **1** ARQ. puntales, puntales de refuerzo. || **2 – loan,** FIN. crédito puente.

bridle | 'braɪdl | *s.c.* **1** brida, freno (para caballo). || *v.t.* **2** embridar (caballo). **3** (fig.) refrenar, dominar (pasiones, sentimientos, etc.). || *v.i.* **4 [to – (at/with)]** irritarse; ofenderse: *she bridled at my suggestion = ella se ofendió por mi sugerencia.* **5** erguirse con desdén, erguirse desdeñosamente.

bridlepath | 'braɪdlpɑ:θ | (también **bridleway**) *s.c.* camino de caballos, camino de herradura.

bridleway | 'braɪdlweɪ | V. **bridlepath.**

brief | bri:f | *adj.* **1** breve, corto. **2** conciso, sucinto (al hablar o escribir). **3** muy corta (falda). **4** brusco, cortante. || *s.c.* **5** (form.) instrucción, encargo. **6** DER. informe, alegato, escrito. **7** REL. breve. || *v.t.* **8** informar, poner al corriente, dar instrucciones. || **9 briefs,** calzoncillos cortos, bragas cortas. **10 to hold no – for,** (form.) tener en poco, no apoyar. **11 in –,** en pocas palabras, en resumen.

briefcase | 'bri:fkeɪs | *s.c.* cartera, cartera portafolio.

briefing | 'bri:fɪŋ | *s.c.* e *i.* **1** sesión informativa, reunión informativa. || *s.c.* **2** instrucción, información, informe.

briefly | 'bri:flɪ | *adv.* **1** brevemente, en poco tiempo. **2** concisamente, sucintamente. **3** en resumen, ateniéndose a los detalles fundamentales.

brier V. **briar.**

brig | brɪg | *s.c.* **1** MAR. bergantín. **2** (EE.UU.) buque prisión.

brigade | brɪ'geɪd | [– *v.sing./pl.*] *s.c.* **1** MIL. brigada. **2** grupo de gente organizada para una actividad especial.

brigadier | ˌbrɪgə'dɪər | *s.c.* (brit.) MIL. general de brigada.

brigand | 'brɪgənd | *s.c.* (lit.) bandolero.

bright | braɪt | *adj.* **1** brillante, colorido, lleno de color. **2** brillante, fuerte (color). **3** brillante (idea). **4** brillante, resplandeciente (tiempo, sol, etc.). **5** brillante, inteligente. **6** lleno de luz (lugar). **7** alegre, vivo. **8** prometedor, brillante (futuro). **9** brillante, reluciente (agua o metal). || **10 as – as a button,** más listo que el hambre. **11 – and early,** a primera hora de la mañana. **12 – lights,** vida atrayente, vida de la gran ciudad. **12 – spark,** (fam.) listillo. **13 to look on the – side,** mirar el lado bueno.

brighten | 'braɪtn | *v.i.* **1** animarse, alegrarse (cara, expresión, etc.), encenderse (ojos). **2** hacerse más intensa, hacerse más fuerte (luz). **3** mejorar, parecer menos negra (una situación). **4** mejorar (tiempo). **5** iluminarse, llenarse de luz (lugar). || *v.t.* **6** dar mayor colorido, alegrar, animar (lugar). **7** abrillantar (metal). **8** iluminar, llenar de luz (lugar). **9** mejorar, alegrar, dar animación (a una situación): *your arrival will brighten his life = tu llegada alegrará su vida.* || **10 to – up, a)** animarse, alegrarse (cara, expresión, etc.). **b)** dar mayor colorido, alegrar, animar (lugar). **c)** mejorar, alegrar, dar animación (a una situación). **d)** mejorar, parecer menos negra (situación). **e)** mejorar (tiempo). **f)** abrillantar (metal).

brightly | 'braɪtlɪ | *adv.* **1** brillantemente, con gran colorido. **2** brillantemente, de color intenso. **3** con gran fuerza, con fuerte resplandor. **4** alegremente, vivamente.

brightness | 'braɪtnɪs | *s.i.* **1** brillo, brillantez. **2** fuerza, intensidad (de un color o luz). **3** ingenio, inteligencia. **4** alegría, viveza.

brill | brɪl | *s.c.* **1** ZOOL. rodaballo (pez). || *interj.* **2** (fam. y brit.) guay, chupi.

brilliance | 'brɪljəns | (también **brilliancy**) *s.c.* **1** ingenio, inteligencia, brillantez (mental). **2** brillo, brillantez (de color, luz, etc.).

brilliancy | 'brɪlɪənsɪ | V. **brilliance.**

brilliant | 'brɪljənt | *adj.* **1** magnífico, soberbio, sobresaliente (en inteligencia, ideas, obras, etc.). **2** prometedor, brillante, espléndido (futuro). **3** brillante (color). **4** luminoso, lleno de luz. **5**

radiante (sonrisa). || *interj.* **6** magnífico, estupendo.
brilliantly | 'brɪljəntlɪ | *adv.* **1** magníficamente, soberbiamente, de manera sobresaliente. **2** prometedoramente, brillantemente, espléndidamente (futuro). **3** brillantemente (color). **4** luminosamente, con luz intensa. **5** radiantemente (sonreír).
brim | brɪm | *s.c.* **1** borde (de un recipiente); ala (de sombrero). || *v.i.* **2** **[to – (with)]** estar lleno (de un líquido). **3** **[to – (with)]** (fig.) rebosar, estar lleno (de alegría, animación, ideas, etc.). || **4 to – over, a)** estar lleno hasta arriba (de un líquido). **b)** (fig.) rebosar, desbordarse (de alegría, ideas, etc.). **5 to the –,** hasta el mismo borde, hasta arriba (lleno).
brimful | ˌbrɪm'fʊl | *adj.* **1** **[– of]** lleno hasta arriba de, rebosante de (líquido). **2** **[– of]** (fig.) rebosante de, desbordante de (sentimientos, ideas, etc.).
brimming | 'brɪmɪŋ | *adj.* **1** **[– (with)]** lleno hasta arriba, rebosante (de líquido). **2** **[– (with)]** (fig.) rebosante, desbordante (de ideas, sentimientos, etc.).
brimstone | 'brɪmstəʊn | *s.i.* **1** (arc.) azufre. || **2 fire and –,** (lit.) fuego y azufre, azufre hirviendo.
brine | braɪn | *s.i.* salmuera.
bring | brɪŋ | [*pret.* y *p.p. irreg.* **brought**] *v.t.* **1** traer: *bring me some coffee: tráeme café.* **2** llevar consigo, llevar, traer consigo: *bring the ruler to class = lleva la regla a clase.* **3** traer (a un sitio): *what brings you here? = ¿qué te trae por aquí?* **4** **[to – + *o.* + (to/for)]** producir, crear, traer (una cualidad a algo): *I want to bring happiness to you = quiero traerte felicidad.* **5** alcanzar (un precio). **6** introducir (algo como totalmente nuevo): *my firm brought new farming methods = mi empresa introdujo nuevos métodos de cultivo.* **7** **[to – + *o.* + (from)]** provocar, causar (reacción positiva o negativa): *my comment brought a remark from him = mi comentario provocó un comentario por parte de él.* **8** **[to – + *o.* + *prep.*]** meter, llevar, empujar (a alguien a una situación determinada): *it all brought him into conflict with the local police = todo ello le llevó a entrar en conflicto con la policía local.* **9** llevar, traer a colación (para mencionar algo). **10** traer (un espectáculo, programa televisivo, etc.). **11** causar, ser causa de: *the wind brought the root crashing to the ground = el viento fue la causa de que el tejado cayera estrepitosamente al suelo.* **12** traer, causar, ocasionar (el tiempo, un sentimiento, etc.): *anger brought tears to her eyes = la ira trajo lágrimas a sus ojos.* **13** **[to – + *o.* + up/down]** hacer subir/hacer bajar, elevar/bajar (el precio). **14** **[to – + *o.* + (on/to)]** traer, causar (algo negativo sobre alguien): *she brought shame on her family = ella trajo la vergüenza sobre su familia.* **15** **[to – + *o.* + (against)]** DER. formular (cargos). || *v.r.* **16** **[to – *inf.*]** hacerse a la idea de, convencerse de: *he couldn't bring himself to greet him as if nothing had happened = no pudo hacerse a la idea de saludarle como si nada hubiera ocurrido.* || **17 to – about,** causar, ocasionar, acarrear: *he didn't bring about the situation = él no ocasionó la situación.* **18 to – along,** traer, traer consigo (especialmente a casa de otra persona). **19 to – back, a)** evocar, traer al pensamiento (recuerdo). **b)** revivir, reintroducir, reimplantar (una tradición, estilo, etc.). **20 to – down, a)** derribar, tirar (físicamente). **b)** derribar (gobierno). **21 to – evidence (against),** DER. traer pruebas palpables (contra), sacar a la luz pruebas (contra). **22 to – forth, a)** (form.) traer a colación, poner de manifiesto, deparar. **b)** (lit. o p.u.) dar a luz (a un bebé). **23 to – forward, a)** poner sobre el tapete (para su discusión). **b)** COM. transferir, llevar un saldo (a la siguiente página). **24 to – forward (to),** adelantar (en la fecha). **25 to – in, a)** POL. introducir (una regulación, ley, etc.). **b)** producir, rendir (dinero). **c)** DER. pronunciar (un veredicto). **d)** arrestar (la policía). **e)** recoger (cosecha). **26 to – in/into, a)** invitar a participar en (como experto). **b)** mencionar, incluir (tema). **27 to – off,** (fam.) conseguir, lograr (algo difícil): *rescuing him was difficult, but we brought it off = rescatarle era difícil, pero lo logramos.* **28 to – on, a)** causar, ocasionar (enfermedad, dolor, etc.). **b)** (p.u.) formar, entrenar, sacar (personas). **29 to – out, a)** sacar (nuevo producto). **b)** decir, pronunciar (con dificultad). **c)** revelar, mostrar, sacar a relucir (cualidades o vicios que normalmente no se notan). **d)** poner de manifiesto, revelar (algo en una obra artística). **e)** hacer que alguien hable, hacer que alguien tímido se abra. **30 to – out in,** ocasionar (algún tipo de manchas en la piel). **31 to – round, a)** hacer volver en sí (a una persona inconsciente). **32 to – round (to),** hacer cambiar de opinión, convencer. **33 to – something into being,** V. **being. 34 to – something to an end/halt/stop,** parar algo, acabar con algo, poner fin a. **35 to – the house down,** V. **house. 36 to – to,** hacer volver en sí (a una persona inconsciente). **37 to – up, a)** educar, formar (el carácter). **b)** (fam.) vomitar, devolver. **c)** sacar, traer a colación (un tema).
bring-and-buy sale | 'brɪŋənbaɪseɪl | *s.c.* (brit.) mercadillo familiar.
brink | brɪŋk | *s.sing.* **1** (lit.) borde (de un precipicio o parecido). || **2 on/from the – (of),** al/del borde (de), a punto de: *on the brink of war = al borde de la guerra.*
brinkmanship | 'brɪŋkmənʃɪp | *s.i.* POL. política arriesgada, política que raya el límite, la crisis.
briny | 'braɪnɪ | *adj.* salado; (lit.) salobre (agua).
briquette | brɪ'ket | *s.c.* briqueta (de carbón o similar).
brisk | brɪsk | *adj.* **1** enérgico, activo, vigoroso (cualidad personal). **2** rápido, vigoroso (ritmo de hacer cosas). **3** continuo, abundante (negocio, trato comercial, etc.). **4** vigorizante, tonificante (tiempo atmosférico).
brisket | 'brɪskɪt | *s.i.* falda (de una res).
briskly | 'brɪsklɪ | *adv.* **1** enérgicamente, activamente, vigorosamente. **2** rápidamente, con vigor (actuar). **3** continuamente, abundantemente (negocios): *business was going briskly = el negocio funcionaba de una manera continua.* **4** de manera que tonifica (tiempo atmosférico).
briskness | 'brɪsknɪs | *s.i.* **1** energía, actividad, vigor. **2** rapidez, velocidad, vigor. **3** abundancia (de negocios). **4** (lo) vigorizante, (lo) tonificante (del tiempo atmosférico).
bristle | 'brɪsl | *v.i.* **1** ponerse de punta, erizarse (el pelo). **2** **[to – (at)]** encolerizarse, montar en cólera. || *s.c.* **3** [normalmente *pl.*] cerda (pelo de animal). **4** [normalmente *pl.*] (fig.) pelo fuerte (especialmente después del afeitado). || *s.i.* **5** cerda, pelo fuerte. || **6 to – with, a)** estar cubierto de, estar lleno de, estar erizado (objetos alargados). **b)** (fam. y brit.) estar abarrotado de, estar hasta arriba de, estar a más no poder de.
bristly | 'brɪslɪ | *adj.* **1** como con espinos, como alambre (pelo). **2** crecida de varios días, sin afeitar durante varios días (barba).
Brit | brɪt | *s.c.* (fam.) británico, inglés.
Britain | 'brɪtn | *s.sing.* Gran Bretaña.
British | 'brɪtɪʃ | *adj.* **1** británico. || **2 – English,** inglés británico. **3 the –,** los británicos. **4 the – Isles,** GEOG. las Islas Británicas.
Britisher | 'brɪtɪʃər | *s.c.* (fam. y EE.UU.) británico, inglés.
Briton | 'brɪtn | *s.c.* britano, británico.
brittle | 'brɪtl | *adj.* **1** quebradizo, rompible, frágil (objeto). **2** (fig.) frágil, débil, no asentado (costumbres, relación, sistema, etc.). **3** duro, insensible, hosco (persona). **4** seco, duro (sonido).
brittleness | 'brɪtlnɪs | *s.i.* **1** fragilidad. **2** (fig.) fragilidad, debilidad (de una relación, hábito, modo de vida, etc.). **3** dureza, insensibilidad, hosquedad (persona). **4** sequedad, dureza (sonido).
broach | brəʊtʃ | *v.t.* **1** abordar, sacar (un tema de conversación, discusión, etc.). **2** (form. o hum.) abrir, descorchar (botella); espitar (cuba).
broad | brɔːd | *adj.* **1** ancho, amplio. **2** extenso, grande, amplio. **3** amplia (sonrisa). **4** amplio, extenso: *a broad range of subjects = una amplia gama de temas.* **5** general, amplio (término o expresión). **6** pronunciado, marcado (acento, forma de hablar). **7** evidente, claro, obvio: *a broad hint = una indirecta obvia.* **8** liberal, abierto (de ideas). **9** comprehensivo, general, amplio, abarcador: *a broad appeal = una llamada general.* || *s.c.* **10** (fam. y EE.UU.) tía, moza. || **11 – bean,** (brit.) AGR. haba cochinera. **12 Broad Church,** REL. grupo liberal anglicano. **13 – in the beam,** V. **beam. 14 – jump,** (EE.UU.) DEP. salto de longitud. **15 in – daylight,** a plena luz del día, a plena luz del sol.
broadcast | 'brɔːdkɑːst | (EE.UU.) | 'brɔːdkæst | [*pret.* y *p.p.* **broadcast** o **broadcasted**] *v.t.* y *i.* **1** RAD. emitir, radiar. **2** TV. transmitir, televisar. || *v.t.* **3** (p.u.) anunciar, decir, informar. || *s.c.* **4** RAD. TV. emisión, transmisión;

programa de radio, programa de televisión.
broadcaster | 'brɔːdkɑːstər | *s.c.* RAD. TV. locutor, periodista de televisión, entrevistador, presentador.
broadcasting | 'brɔːdkɑːstɪŋ | *s.i.* RAD. TV. transmisión, radiodifusión.
broaden | 'brɔːdn | *v.i.* **1** ensancharse, hacerse más ancho. **2** ampliarse, hacerse más grande (cualquier cosa o fenómeno). **3** generalizarse (una experiencia). || *v.t.* **4** ampliar, hacer más grande (cualquier cosa o fenómeno). **5** generalizar (una experiencia); abarcar (a mucha gente una experiencia). || **6 to – one's mind,** ampliar las miras de uno, educar el pensamiento. **7 to – out, a)** ensancharse, ampliarse (físicamente). **b)** ampliar(se), generalizar(se) (con el fin de incluir el máximo número de elementos o personas).
broadly | 'brɔːdlɪ | *adv.* **1** en general, en sentido amplio: *this is, broadly, what I'm fighting for = esto es, en sentido amplio, por lo que estoy luchando.* **2** ampliamente, en sus aspectos generales. **3** ampliamente, abiertamente (modo de sonreír). || **4 – speaking,** hablando en general, hablando de modo general.
broadly-based | 'brɔːdlɪbeɪst | *adj.* de amplia base.
broadminded | ˌbrɔːd'maɪnded | *adj.* liberal, tolerante; de miras amplias.
broadmindedness | ˌbrɔːd'maɪndɪdnɪs | *s.i.* tolerancia; amplitud de miras.
broadsheet | 'brɔːdʃiːt | *s.c.* (brit.) **1** PED. periódico de una hoja. **2** folleto de propaganda de una hoja.
broadside | 'brɔːdsaɪd | *s.c.* **1** MIL. andanada de costado, descarga de costado (de un barco). **2** (fig.) andanada, retahíla (de críticas, insultos, etc.).
brocade | brə'keɪd | *s.i.* brocado.
broccoli | 'brɒkəlɪ | *s.i.* GAST. brócoli.
brochure | 'brəʊʃər | (EE.UU.) | brəʊ'ʃʊər | *s.c.* folleto, panfleto.
brogue | brəʊg | *s.sing.* **1** acento, acento regional (especialmente el irlandés). || *s.c.* **2** [normalmente *pl.*] zapato grueso.
broil | brɔɪl | *v.t.* GAST. asar a la parrilla.
broiler | 'brɔɪlər | *s.c.* **1** parrilla. **2** pollo joven, pollo tierno.
broiling | 'brɔɪlɪŋ | *adj.* (fam. y EE.UU.) sofocante, tórrido.
broke | brəʊk | *pret.irreg.* **1** de **break.** || *adj.* **2** (fam.) sin un céntimo, sin una perra. || **3 to go –,** (fam.) quedarse sin un duro, quedarse sin pasta. **4 to go for –,** (fam.) arriesgar el pellejo, poner toda la carne en el asador (para conseguir un objetivo concreto).
broken | brəʊkən | *p.p.irreg.* **1** de **break.** || *adj.* **2** roto, fragmentado, quebrado. **3** roto, fracturado (hueso). **4** averiado, estropeado (maquinaria). **5** chapurreado (idioma). **6** interrumpido (una línea, proceso, etc.). **7** destrozado (física o mentalmente). **8** violado, incumplido (contrato, acuerdo, etc.). **9** roto, acabado (matrimonio, amistad, etc.). **10** accidentado (terreno); turbulenta (agua). || **11 – home,** hogar roto, familia separada, familia de padres divorciados.
broken-down | ˌbrəʊkən'daʊn | *adj.* **1** averiado, estropeado (maquinaria, vehículo, etc.). **2** derruido, en ruinas.
broken-hearted | ˌbrəʊkən'hɑːtɪd | *adj.* con el corazón destrozado, traspasado de dolor.
broker | 'brəʊkər | *s.c.* FIN. agente de bolsa, corredor de bolsa.
brokerage | 'brəʊkərɪdʒ | *s.i.* FIN. comisión, corretaje.
brolly | 'brɒlɪ | *s.c.* (fam. y brit.) paraguas.
bromide | 'brəʊmaɪd | *s.c.* e *i.* **1** QUIM. bromuro. **2** (fig. y form.) trivialidad, cliché.
bromine | 'brəʊmiːn | *s.i.* QUIM. bromo.
bronchial | 'brɒŋkɪəl | *adj.* **1** MED. bronquial. **2** (fam.) de bronquitis, como bronquitis. || **3 – tube,** ANAT. bronquio.
bronchitis | brɒŋ'kaɪtɪs | *s.i.* MED. bronquitis.
bronco | 'brɒŋkəʊ | *s.c.* potro semisalvaje.
brontosaurus | ˌbrɒntə'sɔːrəs | *s.c.* ZOOL. brontosauro.
bronze | brɒnz | *s.i.* **1** MET. bronce. **2** color de bronce. || *s.c.* **3** (fig.) estatua de bronce. || *adj.* **4** de bronce. || **5 – medal,** medalla de bronce. **6 the Bronze Age,** HIST. la Edad de Bronce.
bronzed | brɒnzd | *adj.* bronceado (por el sol).
brooch | brəʊts | *s.c.* broche (de adorno).
brood | bruːd | *v.i.* **1 [to – (about)]** cavilar, dar vueltas a. **2** (form.) cernerse, pender (sobre algún sitio). || *s.c.* **3 [– *v.sing./pl.*]** nidada (de pájaros). **4 [– *v.sing./pl.*]** (fig. y hum.) prole, tribu (de niños). || **5 to – on/over,** pensar continuamente, no quitarse de la cabeza (algo negativo).
brooding | 'bruːdɪŋ | *adj.* **1** amenazante, preocupante. || *s.i.* **2** (fam.) cavilación. || **3 broodings,** (fam.) cavilaciones.
broodily | 'bruːdɪlɪ | *adv.* melancólicamente, tristonamente.
broodiness | 'bruːdɪnɪs | *s.i.* melancolía, tristeza.
brood-mare | 'bruːdmeə | *s.c.* ZOOL. yegua de cría.
broody | 'bruːdɪ | *adj.* **1** melancólico, tristón. **2** clueca, a punto de incubar (gallina). **3** (fam. y brit.) deseosa de tener un niño (mujer).
brook | brʊk | *s.c.* **1** arroyo. || *v.t.* **2** (form.) tolerar (discusión, contradicción, tardanza, etc.).
broom | bruːm | *s.c.* **1** escoba. || *s.i.* **2** BOT. retama, hiniesta.
broomstick | 'bruːmstɪk | *s.c.* palo de la escoba.
broth | brɒθ | (EE.UU.) | brɔːθ | *s.i.* GAST. **1** caldo, sopa. **2** consomé. || **3 too many cooks spoil the –,** V. **cook.**
brothel | 'brɒθl | *s.c.* burdel, casa de citas.
brother | 'brʌðər | *s.c.* **1** hermano. **2** (fig.) semejante, compañero, amigo, hermano: *all men should be brothers = todos los hombres deberían ser hermanos.* **3** (fam.) macho, tío, hermano (especialmente entre los negros americanos). **4 [– (to/of)]** parecido, relacionado, semejante (un animal a otro, por ejemplo). **5** [*pl.* **brethren**] REL. hermano (miembro de una congregación religiosa). || *interj.* **6** (p.u.) ¡jolines! || **7 brothers in arms,** compañeros de armas, compañeros en la guerra.
brotherhood | 'brʌðəhʊd | *s.i.* **1** hermandad, fraternidad. || *s.c.* **2 [– (of)]** hermandad, gremio, sindicato (asociación). **3 [– (of)]** REL. hermandad (monjes).
brother-in-law | 'brʌðərɪnlɔː | *s.c.* cuñado.
brotherliness | 'brʌðəlɪnɪs | *s.i.* fraternidad (sentimiento o actitud).
brotherly | 'brʌðəlɪ | *adj.* fraternal, fraterno.
brougham | 'bruːəm | *s.c.* berlina (coche de caballos).
brought | brɔːt | *pret.* y *p.p.irreg.* **1** de **buy.** || **2 well/badly brought up,** bien/ mal educado.
brouhaha | 'bruːhɑːhɑː | (EE.UU.) | bruː'hɑːhɑː | *s.i.* (fam.) follón, alboroto.
brow | braʊ | *s.sing.* **1** frente. || *s.c.* **2** (p.u.) ceja. **3 [– (of)]** cresta (de una elevación del terreno).
browbeat | 'braʊbiːt | *v.t.* [*pret.irreg.* **browbeat,** *p.p.* **browbeaten**] intimidar, amedrentar.
browbeaten | 'braʊbiːtn | *p.p.irreg.* **1** de **browbeat.** || *adj.* **2** amilanado, acobardado, intimidado, amedrentado.
brown | braʊn | *adj.* **1** marrón, castaño, pardo. **2** moreno, tostado (por el sol). **3** cobrizo (de raza). || *s.i.* **4** marrón, castaño. **5** moreno (del sol). || *v.t.* e *i.* **6** tostar(se); GAST. dorar(se). || **7 as – as a berry,** (brit.) con un magnífico moreno. **8 – bear,** ZOOL. oso pardo. **9 – bread,** pan integral. **10 browned off (with),** (fam. y brit.) harto (de), cansado (de), hasta las narices (de). **11 – paper,** papel de envolver, papel de estraza. **12 – rice,** arroz sin descascarillar, arroz integral. **13 – sugar,** azúcar moreno. **14 in a – study,** ensimismado por completo, ensimismado con los propios pensamientos.
brownie | 'braʊnɪ | *s.c.* **1** (EE.UU.) bizcocho de chocolate con avellanas. **2** niña exploradora (equivalente de Boy Scout). || **3 Brownie Guide,** niña exploradora. **4 – points,** (fam.) buenas acciones; puntos a favor.
brownish | 'braʊnɪʃ | *adj.* tirando a marrón, parduzco.
brownstone | 'braʊnstəʊn | *s.i.* **1** piedra arenisca. || *s.c.* **2** (EE.UU.) residencia, casa (construida con piedra arenisca).
browse | braʊz | *v.i.* **1 [to – (through)]** hojear, echar un vistazo (a un libro). **2** curiosear. **3** pacer, ramonear (ganado). || *s.c.* **4** vistazo relajado, mirada curiosa relajada: *a browse in the big bookshops = un vistazo relajado a las librerías.*
bruise | bruːz | *s.c.* **1** cardenal, magulladura, moratón. **2** trozo pocho (fruta). || *v.t.* e *i.* **3** magullar(se), contusionar(se), amoratar(se). **4** poner(se) pocha (fruta). || *v.t.* **5** [normalmente *pas.*] herir (sentimientos).
bruised | bruːzd | *adj.* **1** amoratado, magullado. **2** pocha (fruta).
bruiser | 'bruːzər | *s.c.* (fam.) matón (alguien que goza peleando).

bruising | 'bru:zɪŋ | *adj.* **1** hiriente (experiencia). || *s.i.* **2** contusión causante de cardenales, magulladuras.
brunch | brʌntʃ | *s.c.* e *i.* (fam. y EE.UU.) desayuno tarde, almuerzo (especialmente cuando uno se levanta muy tarde).
brunette | bru:'net | *s.c.* morena (mujer).
brunt | brʌnt | **to bear/take the – (of),** llevar el peso (de), aguantar lo peor (de): *your soldiers will bear the brunt of the enemy attack = sus soldados aguantarán lo peor del ataque enemigo.*
brush | brʌʃ | *s.c.* **1** cepillo (para distintas tareas). **2** brocha (para pintar). **3** ART. pincel. **4 [– with]** roce con, escaramuza con (algo o alguien). **5** cola (de zorro). || *s.sing.* **6 [a –]** cepillado, restregón. || *s.i.* **7** (EE.UU.) BOT. monte bajo. **8** maleza, rastrojo. || *v.t.* **9** cepillar, dar un cepillado a. **10 [to – *prep.*]** quitar, echar, apartar (con la mano en un movimiento parecido al del cepillo): *she brushed her hair back = se echó el pelo hacia atrás.* || *v.t.* e *i.* **11** rozar con, rozarse con (físicamente). || **12 to – aside,** apartar de la atención, apartar del pensamiento; no hacer caso (a pensamiento, sentimiento, etc.). **12 to – by,** pasar rozando (normalmente sin hacer caso). **13 to – down,** limpiar bien, quitarse la suciedad (con las manos o un cepillo). **14 to – off,** hacer caso omiso de, apartar (a una persona). **15 to – past,** pasar rozando (normalmente sin hacer caso). **16 to – up/to – up on,** ponerse al día en (materia de estudio).
brushed | brʌʃt | *adj.* tratado (tejido).
brushoff | 'brʌʃɑf | **to give someone the –,** (fam.) tratar desconsideradamente a alguien, tratar a alguien a patadas.
brush-up | 'brʌʃʌp | *s.c.* **1** restregón (para limpiarse). **2** repaso, puesta al día (en una materia de estudio).
brushwood | 'brʌʃwud | *s.i.* **1** BOT. monte bajo. **2** maleza, rastrojos.
brushwork | 'brʌʃwə:k | *s.i.* ART. técnica de pincel, técnica de pintar.
brusque | bru:sk | (EE.UU.) | brʌsk | *adj.* brusco, áspero; rudo.
brusquely | 'bru:sklɪ | (EE.UU.) | 'brʌsklɪ | *adv.* bruscamente, ásperamente; rudamente.
brusqueness | 'bru:sknɪss | (EE.UU.) | 'brʌsknɪs | *s.i.* brusquedad, aspereza; rudeza.
brussels sprout | 'brʌslzpraut | *s.c.* col de bruselas.
brutal | 'bru:tl | *adj.* **1** brutal, bestial, salvaje. **2** salvaje (sinceridad o similar). **3** crudo, sin paliativos, despiadado (como énfasis de algo negativo): *brutal competition = competencia despiadada.* **4** cruel, duro (tiempo atmosférico).
brutalise V. **brutalize.**
brutality | bru:'tælɪtɪ | *s.i.* **1** brutalidad, salvajismo. || *s.c.* **2** atrocidad, ejemplo de brutalidad.
brutalize | 'bru:təlaɪz | (también **brutalise**) *v.t.* embrutecer, quitar la sensibilidad.
brutally | 'bru:təlɪ | *adv.* **1** brutalmente, bestialmente, salvajemente. **2** salvajemente (sincero o similar). **3** crudamente, despiadadamente (enfatizando algo negativo). **4** cruelmente, duramente (del tiempo atmosférico).
brute | bru:t | *s.c.* **1** bruto, bestia (persona o animal). || *adj.* **2** bruta (fuerza). **3** tosco, grosero; brutal: *brute stupidity = estupidez tosca.*
brutish | 'bru:tɪʃ | *adj.* cruel, tosco, grosero.
brutishly | 'bru:tɪʃlɪ | *adv.* cruelmente, toscamente, groseramente.
bubble | 'bʌbl | *s.c.* **1** burbuja. **2** pompa de jabón. **3** ARQ. campana de vidrio. **4** (fig.) burbujeo. || *v.i.* **5** burbujear, hacer burbujas (visual y auditivamente). **6** cocerse, formarse el fermento de, bullir (una situación): *at that time new ideas were bubbling = en esa época estaba naciendo el fermento de nuevas ideas.* **7 [to – with]** rebosar de (felicidad u otro sentimiento agradable). || **8 to blow bubbles,** hacer pompas de jabón. **9 – and squeak,** (brit.) GAST. mezcla de patatas con repollo. **10 – bath, a)** baño espumoso. **b)** gel espumoso de baño. **11 to – over (with),** rebosar de (felicidad u otro sentimiento positivo). **12 to – up,** subir burbujeando, llegar hasta el borde con burbujas. **13 the – burst/it burst like a –/etc.,** la ilusión se deshizo, se derrumbó el castillo de arena, la fantasía fracasó.
bubblegum | 'bʌblgʌm | *s.i.* chicle (especialmente el de globos).
bubbly | 'bʌblɪ | *adj.* **1** burbujeante, chispeante (bebida). **2** (fam.) llena de vida, llena de chispa (persona). || *s.i.* **3** (fam.) champagne.
buccaneer | ˌbʌkə'nɪər | *s.i.* **1** bucanero, pirata, filibustero. **2** (fig.) empresario desalmado; persona sin escrúpulos.
buccaneering | ˌbʌkə'nɪərɪŋ | *adj.* arriesgado, que se expone (a perder dinero).
buck | bʌk | *s.c.* **1** (fam.) dólar. **2** ZOOL. ciervo, gamo; conejo macho. || *v.i.* **3** encabritarse, corcovear (caballo). || *v.t.* **4** (fam.) esquivar, quitarse de encima, evitar (un problema). || *adj.* **5** protuberantes, de conejo (dientes superiores). || **6 to – up,** (fam.) **a)** animar(se), subir (la moral). **b)** alegrarse. **c)** apresurarse, darse prisa. **7 to – one's ideas up,** comportarse de forma más positiva, comportarse con más seriedad; tomarse más en serio las cosas. **8 to make a fast/quick –,** (fam.) ganar una fortuna (de manera deshonesta especialmente). **9 to pass the –,** (fam.) rechazar la responsabilidad, no cargarse el muerto. **10 the – stops here,** aceptar la responsabilidad, cargarse el muerto.
bucked | bʌkt | *adj.* (fam.) animado, contento (por el elogio de otro).
bucket | 'bʌkɪt | *s.c.* **1** cubo, balde. **2** MEC. cubeta (de una máquina). || *v.i.* **3** (fam.) llover a mares. || *s.pl.* **4** (fam.) montones, a montones. || **5 to – down,** (fam.) llover a cántaros, llover a mares. **6 – seat,** asiento acolchado. **7 – shop,** (brit.) agencia de viajes especializada en vuelos baratos. **8 to kick the –,** (fam.) estirar la pata.
bucketful | 'bʌkɪtful | *s.c.* cubo (contenido).
buckle | 'bʌkl | *s.c.* **1** hebilla. || *v.t.* **2** abrochar (objeto con hebilla). **3** abombar, curvar (por la fuerza o el calor). || *v.i.* **4** abombarse, curvarse (por la fuerza o el calor). **5** ceder, no sostener (las piernas o brazos). || **6 to – down (to),** ponerse a trabajar seriamente (en), dedicarse seriamente (a), dedicarse con empeño (a). **7 to – in/into,** sujetar, sujetar a (mediante hebilla). **8 to – on,** ponerse (algo con hebillas). **9 to – to,** (fam.) arreglárselas como uno pueda.
buckshot | 'bʌkʃɒt | *s.i.* posta, perdigón.
buckskin | 'bʌkskɪn | *s.i.* **1** ante, piel de ante. || *s.pl.* **2** pantalones de ante, pantalones de piel de ante: *a pair of buckskins.*
buck-toothed | 'bʌktu:θt | *adj.* dentón, con los dientes protuberantes.
buckwheat | 'bʌkwi:t | (EE.UU.) | 'bʌkhwi:t | *s.i.* AGR. **1** alforfón, trigo sarraceno. || **2 – flour,** harina de trigo sarraceno.
bucolic | bju:'kɒlɪk | *adj* (lit.) bucólico, pastoril.
bud | bʌd | *s.c.* **1** BOT. brote, yema, capullo. **2** (fam. y EE.UU.) macho, colega, tío, chaval. **3** palito, bastoncillo (normalmente de algodón y para limpiarse los oídos). || *v.i.* **4** echar brotes, echar capullos. || **5 in –,** en ciernes, con brotes (plantas). **6 to nip in the –,** cortar de raíz (antes de que se desarrolle).
Buddha | 'budə | *s.sing.* **1** REL. Buda (fundador del budismo). || *s.c.* **2** estatua de Buda.
Buddhism | 'budɪzəm | *s.i.* REL. budismo.
Buddhist | 'budɪst | REL. *s.c.* **1** budista. || *adj.* **2** budista.
budding | 'bʌdɪŋ | *adj.* prometedor, en ciernes (artista, intelectual, etc.).
buddy | 'bʌdɪ | *s.c.* (fam. y EE.UU.) colega, compañero, macho, tío.
budge | bʌdʒ | *v.i.* **1** ceder, moverse lo más mínimo (físicamente). **2** (fig.) ceder lo más mínimo, admitir el más mínimo compromiso (en un asunto). || *v.t.* **3** hacer moverse un poco, hacer ceder un poco (físicamente). || **4 to – up,** (fam.) correrse un poquito, hacer un poquito de sitio (en un asiento o similar).
budgerigar | 'bʌdʒərɪgər | V. **budgie.**
budget | 'bʌdʒɪt | *s.c.* **1** presupuesto. || *v.i.* **2** hacer un presupuesto, presupuestar. || *adj.* **3** económico, asequible (especialmente en el lenguaje publicitario). || **4 – account,** FIN. cuenta comercial con una tienda; cuenta bancaria de gastos corrientes. **5 to – for,** tener en cuenta, contar en el presupuesto con. **6 to – one's time,** organizarse el tiempo.
budgetary | 'bʌdʒɪtɪrɪ | (EE.UU.) | 'bʌdʒɪterɪ | *adj.* presupuestario.
budgeting | 'bʌdʒɪtɪŋ | *s.i.* elaboración de un presupuesto.
budgie | 'bʌdʒɪ | (también **budgerigar**) *s.c.* ZOOL. periquito (ave).
buff | bʌf | *adj.* **1** color cuero, color ante. || *s.c.* **2** (fam.) enamorado, entusiasta; experto: *he's a science-fiction buff = es un entusiasta de la ciencia ficción.* || *v.t.* **3** pulir (uñas, zapatos,

etc.). || **4 in the –,** (hum. y p.u.) en cueros, en pelota viva.
buffalo | 'bʌfələʊ | [*pl.* **buffalo** o **buffaloes**] *s.c.* ZOOL. búfalo.
buffer | 'bʌfər | *s.c.* **1** MEC. amortiguador, tope; parachoques. **2** (fig.) protección; salvaguardia: *that's a good buffer against poverty and hunger = ésa es una buena protección contra la pobreza y el hambre.* **3 [old –]** (p.u.) carca, retrógrado.
buffet | 'bʊfeɪ | (EE.UU.) | bə'feɪ | *s.c.* **1** cafetería, cantina (típica de las estaciones de tren y autobuses). **2** vagón restaurante, vagón comedor (en un tren). **3** buffet (comida de pie). || **4 – car,** vagón restaurante, vagón comedor (en un tren).
buffet | 'bʌfɪt | *s.c.* **1** (form.) bofetada. || *v.t.* **2** (form.) abofetear, dar una bofetada. **3** (form. y fig.) golpear (la vida, una experiencia, etc.). **4** zarandear (el viento o el mar).
buffeting | 'bʌfɪtɪŋ | *s.i.* zarandeo, golpeteo (del mar o el viento).
buffoon | bə'fu:n | *s.c.* (p.u.) bufón.
buffoonery | bə'fu:nərɪ | *s.i.* (p.u.) bufonada.
bug | bʌg | *s.c.* **1** bicho, insecto. **2** virus, microbio, germen (causante de enfermedad). **3** INF. virus. **4** micrófono oculto. **5** (fam.) gusanillo (interés por algo). || *v.t.* **6** poner micrófonos ocultos en. **7** (fam.) sacar de quicio, volver tarumba. || **8 to be bitten by a –,** (fam.) entrarle a uno el gusanillo; tomarle gusto a algo.
bugbear | 'bʌgbeər | *s.c.* terror, coco, fantasma: *stagnation is the developed countries' bugbear = el fantasma de los países desarrollados es el estancamiento.*
bugger | 'bʌgər | (vulg.) *s.c.* **1** cabrón, hijo puta. **2** cabroncete (con cierto cariño). **3** agilipollado (tonto). **4** DER. sodomita. || *v.t.* **5** tener relaciones sexuales anales con. || *s.sing.* **6 [a –]** una jodienda, una cabronada (algo difícil de hacer). || **7 –/– it!,** ¡joder! **8 – ...!,** ¡a la puta mierda con...! **9 to – about/around,** andar por ahí jodiendo al personal. **10 – all!,** ¡a la puta mierda con todo! **11 – me!,** ¡no jodas! (sorpresa). **12 – off,** ir a tomar por culo, salir echando leches (irse rápidamente). **13 to – up,** joder el invento, mandar algo a tomar por culo. **14 not to give/mind a –,** importar un huevo, importar una mierda. **15 poor bugger,** pobre cabrón, pobrecillo hijo puta (con cierta pena).
buggered | 'bʌgəd | (vulg.) *adj.* **1** jodido, machacado, exhausto. **2** jodido, a tomar por culo, changado. || **3 ... be –,** a la puta mierda con..., que... se vaya a tomar por culo: *the job be buggered! = ¡que el trabajo se vaya a tomar por culo!* **4 I'll be –!,** ¡joder! (enorme sorpresa). **5 I'll be – if,** que me jodan si.
buggery | 'bʌgərɪ | *s.i.* sodomía.
buggy | 'bʌgɪ | *s.c.* **1** calesa (coche de caballos). **2** cochecito de bebé.
bugle | 'bju:gl | *s.c.* MUS. corneta.
bugler | 'bju:glər | *s.c.* MIL. corneta (soldado).
build | bɪld | *v.t.* [*pret.* y *p.p.irreg.* **built**] **1** construir, edificar. **2** (fig.) erigir, levantar (una nueva sociedad, organización, etc.). || *s.sing.* **3** figura, tipo (físico). || **4 to – into, a)** incorporar; construir dentro de (roca, por ejemplo). **b)** ser parte integrante de, estar profundamente asentado en: *inequality is built into our society = la desigualdad está profundamente asentada en nuestra sociedad.* **5 to – on/upon, a)** basar en, fundamentar en: *our policy is built on the belief in democracy = nuestra política está fundamentada en la creencia en la democracia.* **b)** explotar, aprovechar al máximo (un éxito). **6 to – up, a)** reunir (una colección). **b)** acumular(se), hacerse mayor, aumentar(se): *traffic is building up this morning = esta mañana está aumentando el tráfico.* **c)** fortalecer (la salud, el cuerpo, etc.). **d)** aumentar, dar más (confianza, moral, etc.). **e)** dar moral, dar coba. **f)** edificar, urbanizar completamente (un espacio). **g)** hacerse (una clientela). **7 Rome was not built in a day,** Roma no se construyó en un día; Zamora no se tomó en una hora.
builder | 'bɪldər | *s.c.* contratista de obras, especialista de la construcción, aparejador.
building | 'bɪldɪŋ | *s.c.* **1** edificio, construcción. || *s.i.* **2** construcción, edificación. || **3 – block,** componente (de algo). **4 – site,** solar. **5 – society,** (brit.) banco hipotecario.
build-up | 'bɪldʌp | *s.c.* **1** aumento, incremento (de cualquier cosa). **2** MIL. concentración (de tropas, fuego, munición, etc.). **3 [– to]** el preludio de, la parte anterior a: *the build-up to the confrontation = el preludio de la confrontación.* || *s.c.* e *i.* **4** propaganda, publicidad (de apoyo).
built | bɪlt | *pret.* y *p.p.irreg.* **1** de **build.** || *adj.* **2** construido. **3** formado (corporalmente): *a heavily built = una constitución corpulenta.*
built-in | ˌbɪlt'ɪn | *adj.* **1** empotrado (armario). **2** MEC. incorporado, integrado: *a built-in microphone.*
built-up | ˌbɪlt'ʌp | *adj.* **1** edificado, construido, urbanizado (espacio). **2** reforzado (zapato, especialmente para parecer más alto).
bulb | bʌlb | *s.c.* **1** ELEC. bombilla. **2** BOT. bulbo, tubérculo. **3** (fig.) esfera, ampolleta (de algún objeto).
bulbous | 'bʌlbəs | *adj.* bulboso, regordete, inflado, parecido a un bulbo.
Bulgaria | bʌl'geərɪə | *s.sing.* Bulgaria.
Bulgarian | bʌl'geərɪən | *s.c.* **1** búlgaro. || *adj.* **2** búlgaro. || *s.i.* **3** búlgaro (idioma).
bulge | bʌldʒ | *s.c.* **1** protuberancia, bulto (en una superficie). **2** (fam.) aumento transitorio: *the population bulge = aumento transitorio de la población.* || *v.i.* **3** hincharse, abultarse, formar protuberancias. **4 [to – (with)]** (fam. y fig.) estallar (por estar demasiado lleno).
bulging | 'bʌldʒɪŋ | *adj.* **1** hinchado, inflado, que sobresale notablemente. **2** (fam. y fig.) que estalla (por demasiado lleno).
bulk | bʌlk | *s.c.* **1 [– (of)]** masa, mole (cualquier objeto grande). **2** corpachón (de persona). || *s.i.* **3** grandes proporciones (de una persona). || *s.sing.* **4** mayor parte, mayoría, grueso: *the bulk of his work = la mayor parte de su obra.* || *adj.* **5** a granel, al por mayor. || **6 to – buy,** comprar al por mayor, comprar grandes cantidades. **7 to – large,** (lit.) alzarse imponente. **8 in –,** a granel, al por mayor.
bulkhead | 'bʌlkhed | *s.c.* ARQ. mampara, tabique (en un avión, construcción, etc.).
bulky | 'bʌlkɪ | *adj.* **1** voluminoso, pesado, difícil de mover (objeto). **2** voluminoso, grande (animales o personas).
bull | bʊl | *s.c.* **1** ZOOL. toro. **2** ZOOL. macho (elefante, ballena, etc.). **3** (fig.) fortachón, hombrón. **4** REL. bula. **5** centro de un blanco. **6** FIN. inversión que juega al alza. **7** (fam. y EE.UU.) poli. || *s.i.* **8** (fam.) bobada, chorrada. || **9 – market,** FIN. mercado alcista. **10 – terrier,** ZOOL. terrier (perro). **11 like a – in a china shop,** como un elefante en una tienda de porcelana. **12 to take the – by the horns,** V. **horn.**
bulldog | 'bʌldɒg | *s.c.* **1** ZOOL. bulldog (perro). || **2 – clip,** clip grande.
bulldoze | 'bʊldəʊz | *v.t.* **1** excavar con una máquina excavadora, nivelar con una excavadora, tirar con una excavadora. **2 [to – *o.* (into)]** obligar, intimidar (con malos modos).
bulldozer | 'bʊldəʊzər | *s.c.* MEC. máquina excavadora, bulldozer.
bullet | 'bʊlɪt | *s.c.* **1** bala, proyectil, cartucho. || **2 to bite the –,** a lo hecho pecho; arrostrar las consecuencias de los actos de uno.
bulletin | 'bʊlətɪn | *s.c.* **1** RAD. boletín (normalmente informativo). **2** parte, comunicado (oficial). **3** revista, boletín, publicación periódica. || **4 – board,** (EE.UU.) tablón de anuncios.
bullet-proof | 'bʊlɪtpru:f | *adj.* antibalas.
bullfight | 'bʊlfaɪt | *s.c.* corrida de toros.
bullfighter | 'bʊlfaɪtər | *s.c.* torero.
bullfighting | 'bʊlfaɪtɪŋ | *s.i.* toreo.
bullfinch | 'bʊlfɪntʃ | *s.c.* ZOOL. pinzón real (ave).
bullfrog | 'bʊlfrɒg | *s.c.* ZOOL. rana toro.
bullhorn | 'bʊlhɔ:n | *s.c.* (EE.UU.) megáfono.
bullion | 'bʊljən | *s.i.* oro en lingotes, plata en lingotes.
bullish | 'bʊlɪʃ | *adj.* FIN. en alza.
bullock | 'bʊlək | *s.c.* novillo castrado.
bullring | 'bʊlrɪŋ | *s.c.* plaza de toros; ruedo (terreno circular donde se realiza la lidia).
bull's-eye | 'bʊlzaɪ | *s.c.* **1** blanco, centro del blanco. **2** acierto en el blanco, blanco.
bullshit | 'bʊlʃɪt | (vulg.) *s.i.* **1** mierda, chorrada, gilipollez. || *v.t.* e *i.* **2** tomar el pelo, pensar que alguien es gilipollas. || *interj.* **3** vaya gilipollez.
bully | 'bʊlɪ | *s.c.* **1** (desp.) matón, chulo. || *v.t.* e *i.* **2** comportarse como un

matón, comportarse como un matón con, chulear(se). || *v.t.* **3 [to – + *o.* + (into)]** amedrentar, intimidar, obligar por miedo (a hacer algo). || **4 – boy,** matón, canalla a sueldo. **5 – for you /him/etc.,** (fam.) y qué, vaya cosa, no es para tanto (disminuyendo la importancia de algo).
bullying | 'bʊlɪɪŋ | *s.i.* actuación de matón, actuación de chulo.
bulrush | 'bʊlrʌʃ | *s.c.* BOT. espadaña.
bulwark | 'bʊlwək | *s.c.* **1 [– (of/ against)]** baluarte, bastión. **2** (fig.) baluarte, defensor, defensa. **3** (normalmente *pl.*) MAR. rompeolas.
bum | bʌm | (fam.) *s.c.* **1** vago, holgazán. **2** vagabundo, correcaminos. **3** caca, mierda (persona que no hace bien algo). **4** (brit.) culo, trasero. || *adj.* **5** inútil, de mierda: *a bum radio = una radio de mierda.* || *v.i.* **6 [to – + *o.* + (off)]** gorronear, sablear. || **7 to – about/ around, a)** vagabundear por el mundo, ir por ahí en plan vagabundo. **b)** holgazanear, estar mano sobre mano, hacer el vago.
bumble | 'bʌmbl | *v.i.* **1 [to – (about)]** hablar torpemente, trabucarse al hablar, pronunciar a tropezones. **2** andar torpemente, caminar a tropezones.
bumblebee | 'bʌmblbiː | *s.c.* ZOOL. abejorro.
bumbling | 'bʌmblɪŋ | *adj.* inepto, chapucero, incapaz.
bumf | bʌmf | (también **bumph**) *s.i.* (brit. y fam.) papeleo inútil; papeles para la basura.
bummer | 'bʌmər | *s.c.* (fam.) asco, incordio (algo).
bump | bʌmp | *s.c.* **1** choque, topetón, encontronazo. **2** golpe, porrazo (sonido). **3** bache (en carretera). **4** chichón (en el cuerpo). || *v.i.* **5** ir dando tumbos, ir dando botes (en un vehículo). **6 [to – (into)]** chocar, darse un golpe. || *v.t.* **7** golpear, dar un golpe (inconscientemente). || **8 to – into,** encontrarse con (por casualidad). **9 to – off,** (fam.) liquidar, matar, despachar. **10 to – up,** (fam.) subir, aumentar (alguna cantidad). **11 to – up against,** hacerse amigos, entablar una amistad casual.
bumper | 'bʌmpər | *s.c.* **1** parachoques (en vehículo). **2** (EE.UU.) amortiguador (de tren). || *adj.* **3** abundante, magnífica (cosecha). || **4 – to –,** uno pegado a otro, pegados (vehículos).
bumph V. **bumf.**
bumpily | 'bʌmpɪlɪ | *adv.* accidentalmente, incómodamente (viaje).
bumpiness | 'bʌmpɪnɪs | *s.i.* (lo) accidentado, (lo) incómodo (de un viaje).
bumpkin | 'bʌmpkɪn | *s.c.* (fam.) alcornoque; palurdo, patán.
bumptious | 'bʌmpʃəs | *adj.* (desp.) presuntuoso, engreído, pedante.
bumptiously | 'bʌmpʃəslɪ | *adv.* (desp.) engreídamente, pedantemente, con pedantería.
bumptiousness | 'bʌmpʃəsnɪs | *s.i.* (desp.) engreimiento, pedantería.
bumpy | 'bʌmpɪ | *adj.* **1** accidentado, lleno de baches (camino o similar). **2** incómodo, accidentado (viaje por caminos malos).
bun | bʌn | *s.c.* **1** GAST. bollo, panecillo dulce. **2** moño (estilo de peinado). || **3 to have (got) a – in the oven,** (vulg.) estar preñada, tener un bebé en la barriga.
bunch | bʌntʃ | *s.c.* **1** racimo (de fruta). **2** ramo (de flores). **3** manojo, puñado (de cualquier objeto). **4** grupo (de personas). || *v.t.* e *i.* **5 [to – + *o.* + (up/together)]** amontonar(se), agrupar(se); juntar(se). || **6 in bunches,** en dos coletas grandes (pelo). **7 the best of a bad –,** el tuerto en el reino de los ciegos, lo mejorcito dentro de un grupo malo. **8 the pick of the –/the best of the –,** lo mejor de lo que hay, lo mejorcito que hay.
bundle | 'bʌndl | *s.c.* **1** tajo (atado). **2** fardo, bulto, paquete. **3** (fam.) fastidio (persona, especialmente bebés). || *v.t.* **4 [to – *prep.*]** meter, empujar, lanzar (con rapidez y fuerza): *the kidnappers bundled the minister into the car = los secuestradores metieron al ministro a la fuerza en el coche.* || **5 a – of fun/joy/ mischief/etc.,** (fam.) divertidísimo/contentísimo/malísimo/etc., lleno de diversión/lleno de alegría/lleno de travesura/etc. **6 a – of nerves,** un manojo de nervios. **7 to – off (to),** salir a toda prisa (a), marcharse rápidamente (hacia). **8 to – up, a)** arroparse, abrigarse, **b)** juntar, amontonar. **9 to go a – on,** (fam.) chiflar a uno, encantar a uno.
bung | bʌŋ | *s.c.* **1** tapón, bitoque (normalmente de un barril, botella o similar). || *v.t.* **2** (brit. y fam.) tirar, echar (descuidadamente): *bung it in the drawer = tirarlo al cajón.* || **3 bunged up,** (fam.) taponado, tupido.
bungalow | 'bʌŋgələʊ | *s.c.* chalé, bungalow (de una sola planta).
bungle | 'bʌŋgl | *v.t.* e *i.* echar(se) a perder, hacer una chapuza.
bungled | 'bʌŋgld | *adj.* chapucero, hecho una chapuza.
bungling | 'bʌŋglɪŋ | *adj.* chapucero.
bungler | 'bʌnglər | *s.c.* chapuzas; incompetente.
bunion | 'bʌnjən | *s.c.* juanete (en el pie).
bunk | bʌŋk | *s.c.* **1** litera, camastro (típico de barcos, trenes, etc.). || *s.i.* **2** (fam.) palabrería insulsa, bobadas. || **3 – bed,** litera. **4 to do a –,** despedirse a la francesa, irse sin decir nada a nadie.
bunker | 'bʌŋkər | *s.c.* **1** MIL. búnker, refugio subterráneo. **2** DEP. arenal (en el golf).
bunny | 'bʌnɪ | *s.c.* **1** conejito (lenguaje de niños). || **2 – girl,** chica de club nocturno. **3 – rabbit,** conejito (lenguaje de niños).
bunting | 'bʌntɪŋ | *s.i.* banderitas para colgar de adorno.
buoy | bɔɪ | *s.c.* **1** MAR. boya. || **2 to – up,** dar ánimos, animar, alentar.
buoyancy | 'bɔɪənsɪ | *s.i.* **1** FIS. flotabilidad, capacidad de flotar (en líquido o aire). **2** empuje, ánimo, optimismo.
buoyant | 'bɔɪənt | *adj.* **1** flotante. **2** boyante, lleno de alegría, animado. **3** boyante (economía).
buoyantly | 'bɔɪəntlɪ | *adv.* **1** con ligereza, con un flotar suave. **2** animadamente, boyantemente.
burble | 'bəːbl | *v.i.* **1** borbotar, borbotear (sonido). **2** farfullar (hablar mal).
burden | 'bəːdn | (form.) *s.c.* **1** peso, carga (físico). **2** (fig.) gran responsabilidad, peso (mental). || *s.sing.* **3 [the – of]** el mensaje principal de, el sentido primario de (una obra de arte). || *v.t.* **4 [to – + *o.* + (with)]** apesadumbrar, agobiar. || **5 the – of proof,** el peso de la prueba, la carga de la prueba.
burdened | 'bəːdnd | *adj* (form.) **1 [– (with/by)]** aplastado bajo el peso, cargado (con algún objeto). **2 [– with/by]** apesadumbrado con, agobiado por.
burdensome | 'bəːdnsəm *adj.* (form.) gravoso, oneroso.
bureau | 'bjʊərəʊ | (EE.UU.) | bjʊ'rəʊ | [*pl.* **bureaux** o **bureaus**] *s.c.* **1** (EE.UU.) POL. organismo estatal, instituto estatal (de alguna especialidad). **2** (EE.UU.) sucursal, delegación (de una empresa, asociación, etc.). **3** (EE.UU.) cómoda, (mueble). **4** (brit.) escritorio.
bureaucracy | bjʊə'rɒkrəsɪ | *s.i.* **1** (desp.) burocracia. || *s.c.* **2** burocracia, sistema burocrático, sistema administrativo. || *s.sing.* **3 [the –]** la burocracia, los burócratas.
bureaucrat | 'bjʊərəkræt | *s.c.* (a veces desp.) burócrata.
bureaucratic | ˌbjʊərə'krætɪk | *adj.* **1** (desp.) burocrático. **2** administrativo, burocrático.
bureaucratically | ˌbjʊərə'krætɪklɪ | *adv.* **1** (desp.) burocráticamente. **2** administrativamente, burocráticamente.
bureaux | 'bjʊərəʊz | *pl.irreg.* de **bureau.**
burgeon | 'bəːdʒən | *v.i.* (lit.) florecer, crecer esplendorosamente (plantas, vida, etc.).
burgeoning | 'bəːdʒənɪŋ | *adj.* (lit.) floreciente; creciente, esplendorosa: *burgeoning industries.*
burger | 'bəːgər | *s.c.* **1** (fam.) hamburguesa. || **2 -burger,** hamburguesa (en compuestos): *cheeseburger.*
burgher | 'bəːgər | *s.c.* (arc.) burgués, pequeño comerciante, ciudadano.
burglar | 'bəːglər | *s.c.* ladrón de casas, caco.
burglar-alarm | 'bəːgləəlɑːrm | *s.c.* alarma antirrobo (en casa).
burglarize | 'bəːgləraɪz | (también **burglarise**) *v.t.* (EE.UU.) robar (casa o edificio).
burglary | 'bəːglərɪ | *s.c.* e *i.* robo casero, robo en casa; DER. robo con allanamiento de morada.
burgle | 'bəːgl | *v.t.* (brit.) robar (casa o edificio).
burial | 'berɪəl | *s.c.* **1** MAR. sepelio. || *s.c.* e *i.* **2** funeral, sepelio, enterramiento. || **3 – ground,** camposanto, cementerio.
burlesque | bəː'lesk | *s.c.* e *i.* LIT. **1** parodia, farsa (novela, ensayo, etc.). **2** comedia de variedades, espectáculo de variedades (típico de principios de siglo).
burliness | 'bəːlɪnɪs | *s.i.* corpulencia, robustez.
burly | 'bəːlɪ | *adj.* corpulento, robusto, fornido.
Burma | 'bəːmə | *s.sing.* Birmania.
Burmese | ˌbəː'miːz | *adj.* **1** birmano (cultura, costumbres, etc.). || *s.c.* **2** birmano (habitante). || *s.i.* **3** birmano (idioma).

burn | bɜːn | *v.* [*pret.* y *p.p.* **burned** o **burnt**] *t.* **1** quemar, incendiar (persona o cosa). **2** quemar, estropear (comida). **3** quemar, abrasar (una parte del cuerpo). **4** quemar, usar, consumir (combustible). **5** quemar, tostar (la piel por el sol). **6** quemar, incinerar (desechos, cadáveres, etc.). **7** matar mediante el fuego, quemar en la hoguera, quemar. || *i.* **8** quemarse, arder: *the house was burning the whole night = la casa estuvo ardiendo toda la noche.* **9** quemarse, estropearse (comida). **10** quemarse, usarse, consumirse (combustible). **11** quemarse, tostarse (la piel por el sol). **12** (fig.) arder, quemar, doler agudamente (como por el fuego): *his forehead was burning = la frente le ardía.* **13** **[to – *inf.*]** (fig.) arder en deseos de, anhelar, desear ardientemente. **14** arder, estar enrojecido, estar encendido (la cara por algún sentimiento). **15** **[to – with]** arder de, consumirse por (alguna emoción fuerte). **16** (fig.) brillar con fuerza, refulgir, despedir brillo, despedir gran cantidad de luz. || *r.* **17** quemarse, abrasarse. || *s.c.* **18** quemadura (en el cuerpo). || **19 to be burned alive/to death,** ser quemado vivo/morir en un incendio. **20 to – a hole,** hacer un agujero (el fuego). **21 to – down,** destrozar, arrasar (el fuego). **22 to – one's bridges,** V. **bridge.** **23 to – oneself out,** (fam.) agotarse, quedarse destrozado físicamente, quedar exhausto (por cansancio o enfermedad). **24 to – out, a)** apagar(se), agotar(se), extinguir(se) (el fuego). **b)** fundir(se), quedar(se) inservible (maquinaria). **25 to – the candle at both ends,** V. **candle.** **26 to – the midnight oil,** V. **midnight.** **27 to – to a crisp, a)** GAST. quemar por todos los lados (carne o similar). **b)** (fig.) achicharrar, dejar como un tizón. **28 to – to the ground,** arrasar (el fuego), destruir por completo (casas o edificios). **29 to – up, a)** quedar deshecho por el fuego, quedar destrozado por el calor. **b)** consumir mucho, quemar gran cantidad de (combustible).

burned | bɜːnd | | bɜːnt | *pret.* y *p.p.* **1** de **burn.** || **2 – out,** V. **burn-out.**

burner | 'bɜːnər | *s.c.* **1** quemador (de cualquier máquina). || **2 bunsen –,** mechero Bunsen (en laboratorios). **3 to put something on the back –,** aparcar algo momentáneamente, dejar algo para más tarde.

burning | 'bɜːnɪŋ | *s.i.* **1** quemado: *it smells of burning = huele a quemado.* **2** quema, destrozo: *the burning of cars = la quema de coches.* || *adj.* **3** ardiente, abrasador (dolor, sensación, etc.). **4** candente (tema de actualidad o similar): *a burning question = una cuestión candente.* **5** (fig.) ardiente, apasionado; extremo: *a burning desire = un deseo ardiente.* **6** brillante; como un ascua (con el color rojo o el naranja). || **7 – hot,** achicharrante, abrasador.

burnish | 'bɜːnɪʃ | *v.t.* (lit.) bruñir (metales).

burnished | 'bɜːnɪʃt | *adj.* (lit.) bruñido, refulgente.

burnt | bɜːnt | *pret.* y *p.p.irreg.* **1** de **burn.** || *adj.* **2** quemado, consumido por el fuego, incinerado: *a burnt piece of paper = un trozo de papel quemado.* || **3 – offering, a)** REL. sacrificio por el fuego, sacrificio de animal en el fuego. **b)** (hum.) comida quemada accidentalmente.

burnt-out | 'bɜːntaʊt | *adj.* **1** destrozado, quemado totalmente (objeto). **2** (fam. y fig.) exhausto, agotado, destrozado (física y mentalmente).

burp | bɜːp | *v.i.* **1** eructar, echar el aire, lanzar eructos. || *v.t.* **2** hacer eructar (a un bebé). || *s.c.* **3** eructo.

burr | bɜːr | *s.c.* **1** (también **bur**) BOT. carda. **2** runruneo (especialmente de motor). **3** FON. un sonido de erre especial (en dialectos, por ejemplo). || *v.i.* **4** hacer un runruneo (motor o similar).

burrow | 'bʌrəʊ | *s.c.* **1** madriguera, conejera, agujero (como guarida de algunos animales). || *v.i.* **2** hacer un túnel; excavar una madriguera. **3** buscar, rebuscar. **4** (fig.) acurrucarse, hacerse un ovillo (especialmente buscando calor). || **5** excavar, hacer excavando (una madriguera, agujero, etc.).

bursar | 'bɜːsər | *s.c.* gerente, secretario de finanzas (de institución educativa).

bursary | 'bɜːsərɪ | *s.c.* beca, ayuda al estudio.

burst | bɜːst | *v.* [*pret.* y *p.p.irreg.* **burst**] *t.* **1** explotar, hacer estallar, reventar (objeto). **2** arrollar, reventar con gran fuerza. || *i.* **3** estallar, reventarse, explotar. **4** hacer explosión (bomba o similar). **5** (fig.) aparecer en escena repentinamente, irrumpir, entrar súbitamente en escena (un fenómeno sociológico, invento científico, etc.). **6** **[to – (with)]** (fig.) estallar (con alguna emoción fuerte). **7** **[to – *prep.*]** irrumpir, ir volando, moverse a gran velocidad: *the police burst into the room = la policía irrumpió en la habitación.* || *s.c.* **8** reventón (de neumático, cañería, etc.). **9** **[– (of)]** arrebato (de actividad), impulso, estallido. **10** **[– (of)]** andanada, ráfaga (de disparos). **11** **[– of]** ataque de, arrebato de (emociones fuertes). || **12 to – apart,** abrirse con fuerza, abrirse de par en par, ceder violentamente. **13 to – in on,** hacer una entrada violenta en la habitación de (alguien). **14 to – into, a)** romper en, estallar de (llanto, risa, etc.). **b)** brotar repentinamente, brotar súbitamente (plantas, flores, etc.). **15 to – into flame,** V. **flame.** **16 to – open,** abrirse violentamente. **17 to – out, a)** romper en, estallar de (risa, llanto, etc.). **b)** lanzar un exabrupto, lanzar una exclamación.

bursting | 'bɜːstɪŋ | *adj.* **1** **[– (with)]** rebosante, hasta arriba, abarrotado. **2** [– *inf.*] (fam. y fig.) reventado por, deseandito de. **3** **[– (with)]** (fig.) reventando, lleno de (alguna cualidad positiva). **4** (fam.) reventado (por la necesidad de orinar). || **5 – at the seams,** (fam.) hasta la bandera, reventando, lleno hasta arriba.

burton | 'bɜːtn | (brit, vulg. y p.u.) **to go for a –, a)** irse al carajo, irse al cuerno (no resultar). **b)** pegarse un tortazo, darse un porrazo.

Burundi | bə'rʊndɪ | *s.sing.* Burundi.

Burundian | bʊ'rʊndɪən | *adj.* **1** de Burundi. || *s.c.* **2** burundés.

bury 'berɪ | *v.t.* **1** enterrar, sepultar, poner bajo tierra. **2** (euf.) enterrar, sufrir la muerte de (un ser querido): *I've buried three brothers = he sufrido la muerte de tres hermanos.* **3** esconder, ocultar. **4** (normalmente pasiva) cubrir, enterrar: *he was buried in snow = estaba cubierto por la nieve.* **5** dejar a un lado (diferencias personales), olvidar (agravios). **6** ocultar, esconder (cara o cabeza). || *v.i.* **7** incrustarse (una bala o similar). **8** aislarse, quedarse voluntariamente aislado. **9** **[to – in]** concentrarse en, quedarse absorto con/en, sumergirse en (lectura, estudio, etc.). || **10 to – away,** esconderse totalmente, quedar casi escondido a la vista de, ocultarse a medias. **11 to – the hatchet,** V. **hatchet.**

burying-ground | 'berɪŋgraʊnd | (también **burying place**) *s.c.* camposanto, cementerio.

bus bʌs | [(EE.UU. a veces) *pl.* **busses**] *s.c.* **1** autobús. || [(brit.) *ger.* **bussing,** *pret.* y *p.p.* **bussed**] *v.t.* **2** llevar en autobús, transportar en autobús. **3** (EE.UU.) POL. llevar a la escuela en autobús (para mezclar blancos con negros). || *v.i.* **4** ir en autobús, viajar en autobús. || **5 – conductor,** cobrador, cobrador de autobús. **6 by –,** en autobús.

busby | 'bʌzbɪ | *s.c.* MIL. morrión.

bush | bʊʃ | *s.c.* **1** arbusto, matorral. **2** **[– of]** (fig.) mata de (pelo). || *s.sing.* **3** **[the –]** GEOG. la maleza, la región de monte bajo, el matorral (en zonas de Australia y Africa). || **4 to beat about the –,** andarse por las ramas, andarse con rodeos, no ir al grano. **5 – telegraph,** (fam.) radio macuto.

bushbaby | 'bʊʃbeɪbɪ | *s.c.* ZOOL. galago (tipo de mono).

bushed | bʊʃt | *adj.* (fam. y EE.UU.) tirado, agotado, roto.

bushel | 'bʊʃl | *s.c.* **1** celemín (medida de volumen, especialmente con granos, de 35/36 litros). || **2 to hide one's light /talent/etc. under a –,** no darse bombo.

bushy | 'bʊʃɪ | *adj.* poblado (cejas), espeso (matorral), tupido (bosque).

busily | 'bɪzɪlɪ | *adv.* activamente, diligentemente, afanosamente.

business | 'bɪznɪs | *s.i.* **1** negocio, negocios. **2** negocio, comercio, actividad comercial, actividad profesional: *don't phone during business hours = no llames por teléfono durante horas de actividad profesional.* **3** (fam.) cosas importantes, temas importantes: *let's talk business = vamos a hablar de cosas importantes.* **4** asuntos, cosas: *all kind of business = todo tipo de asuntos.* || *s.c.* **5** empresa, compañía, firma comercial, negocio. || *s.sing.* **6** **[the –]** la actividad, el negocio; el mundo, el campo (de los negocios): *the publishing business = el campo de la edición.* **7** asunto de, asunto, cosa, cosa de: *this strike business = este asunto de la huelga.* **8** asunto, tema personal, preocupación individual: *that's my business = ese es mi asunto.* || **9 to be in –,** (fam.) estar totalmente preparado, estar listo. **10 – address,** dirección profesional, señas del trabajo. **11 – card,** tarjeta profesional. **12 – end,** (fam.) el lado malo, el extremo

puntiagudo (de un arma). **13 – is –,** los negocios son los negocios. **14 – studies,** empresariales, estudios empresariales. **15 to do its –,** (fam. y euf.) hacer caca, ensuciarse (un animal). **16 funny –,** V. **funny. 17 to have no – (to),** [+ *inf.*] no tener ningún derecho (a), no tener por qué. **18 in –,** en activo, en funcionamiento (una empresa). **19 like nobody's –,** (fam.) a todo meter (velocidad), de manera brutal (dolor); como nadie se puede imaginar. **20 to mean –,** (fam.) estar en plan serio, actuar en serio. **21 mind your own –,** (fam.) métete en tus cosas, no tiene nada que ver contigo. **22 none of somebody's –,** no te/le/etc., importa, a ti qué te importa, etc. **23 on –,** de negocios (viaje). **24 out of –,** sin actividad, sin negocio, sin posibilidad de negocio.
businesslike | 'bɪznɪslaɪk | *adj.* metódico, eficaz, eficiente, bien organizado (en su forma de trabajar).
businessman | 'bɪznɪsmæn | [*pl.* **businessmen**] *s.c.* hombre de negocios, empresario.
businessmen | 'bɪznɪsmən | *pl.* de **businessman.**
businesswoman | 'bɪznɪswumn | [*pl.* **businesswomen**] *s.c.* mujer empresaria, mujer de negocios.
businesswomen | 'bɪznɪswɪmn | *pl.* de **businesswoman.**
busk | bʌsk | *v.i.* (brit.) ganarse la vida cantando por las calles.
busker | 'bʌskər | *s.c.* (brit.) cantante callejero.
busking | 'bʌskɪŋ | *s.i.* (brit.) (el) ganarse la vida de cantante callejero.
busman | bʌsmən | [*pl.* **busmen**] *s.c.* **1** empleado de autobús. || **2 busman's holiday,** día de fiesta que uno pasa trabajando.
busmen | 'bʌsmən | *pl.* de **busman.**
bus-shelter | 'bʌsʃeltər | *s.c.* parada de autobús cubierta.
bus-stop | 'bʌsstɒp | *s.c.* parada de autobús.
bust | bʌst | *v.t.* [*pret.* y *p.p.irreg.* **bust** o **busted**] **1** (fam.) romper, destrozar. **2** (fam.) arrestar (por parte de la policía). **3** (fam.) hacer una redada en. || *adj.* **4** (fam.) roto, escachifollado. || *s.c.* **5** ART. busto, escultura de busto. **6** busto, pecho (de mujer). || *s.i.* **7** busto, medida del busto. || **8 to – out,** (fam.) escaparse violentamente, escaparse por la fuerza (de prisión o similar). **9 to – up,** (fam.) estropear, fastidiar (un acontecimiento). **10 to – up (with),** acabar una relación amorosa (con), terminar (con), acabar (con). **11 to go –,** (fam.) entrar en bancarrota, irse a la ruina.
buster | 'bʌstər | *s.c.* (fam.) machote, tío.
bustle | 'bʌsl | *v.i.* **1 [to – (about/around)]** moverse apresuradamente; trabajar con prisas. **2** ir apresuradamente, darse prisa, apresurarse. || *s.i.* **3** bullicio, animación. || *s.c.* **4** almohadilla (para mantener la falda levantada en la vestimenta femenina del siglo XIX).
bustling | 'bʌslɪŋ | *adj.* **1** activo, vivaz, enérgico (persona). **2 [– (with)]** con el bullicio (de algo o alguien): *bustling with people = con el bullicio de la gente.*
bust-up | 'bʌstʌp | *s.c.* (fam.) **1** pelea (entre amantes). **2** lucha, pelea, riña (física).
busty | 'bʌstɪ | *adj.* (fam.) pechugona, con buena delantera.
busy | 'bɪzɪ | *adj.* **1** ocupado, atareado. **2** activo, ocupado, con una apretada agenda. **3** concurrido, con mucha actividad (carretera, tiempo, etc.). **4 [–** *ger.***]** atareado, sin parar, sin pausa: *I was busy revising the book = estuve atareado revisando el libro.* **5** comunicando (teléfono). **6** ART. intricado, recargado (una pintura, escultura, diseño, etc.). || *v.r.* **7** estar activo; ocuparse (con alguna actividad).
busybody | 'bɪzɪbɒdɪ | *s.c.* (fam. y desp.) entremetido, chismoso.
but | bʌt, | bət | *conj.* **1** pero, mas, sin embargo: *I'm tired but I'll walk on = estoy cansado pero continuaré caminando.* **2 [***neg.* **–]** sino: *I'm not angry but disappointed = no estoy airado sino desilusionado.* **3** sólo que: *the dog was like a wolf but smaller = el perro era como un lobo sólo que más pequeño.* **4** pero es que (como énfasis): *nothing, but nothing will make me change my mind = nada, pero es que nada me hará cambiar de opinión.* || *prep.* **5** con la excepción de, menos: *I can't drink anything but water = no puedo beber nada más que agua.* || *adv.* **6** sólo, únicamente: *you can but pray = únicamente puedes rezar.* || *s.pl.* **7** peros: *you are coming at ten and no buts = vendrás a las diez y nada de peros.* || **8 all –,** casi: *I'm all but dead = estoy casi muerto.* **9 anything –,** V. **anything. 10 – for,** si no fuera por, de no ser por: *but for you I wouldn't want to live = si no fuera por ti no querría vivir.* **11 – then,** sin embargo, pero por otra parte. **12 cannot/couldn't –,** no tener más remedio que, no tener más salida que, no poder por menos que. **13 last – one,** V. **last. 14 not only... – also,** V. **only.**
butane | 'bjuːteɪn | *s.i.* QUIM. butano.
butch | butʃ | *adj.* **1** machote, varonil. **2** (vulg.) lesbiana.
butcher | 'butʃər | *s.c.* **1** carnicero. **2** (fig.) asesino, sanguinario, carnicero. || *v.t.* **3** matar (animales). **4** asesinar, matar sanguinariamente (personas). || **5 the butcher's,** la carnicería.
butchery | 'butʃərɪ | *s.i.* **1** de carnicero, de la actividad de carnicero. **2** carnicería, matanza. || *s.c.* **3** (arc.) carnicería.
butler | 'bʌtlər | *s.c.* mayordomo.
butt | bʌt | *s.c.* **1 [– (of)]** culata (de un arma). **2** colilla (de cigarrillo). **3** barrica, tonel. **4** (EE.UU. y fam.) culo, trasero. || *s.sing.* **5 [the –]** el blanco (de insultos, bromas, etc.). || *v.t.* e *i.* **6** embestir, topar, dar un topetazo. || **7 to – in,** (desp.) interrumpir groseramente, entrometerse. **8 to – one's way,** irrumpir como un elefante, empujar como un toro (en un sitio).
butter | 'bʌtər | *s.i.* **1** mantequilla (de leche u otro producto). | *v.t.* **2** untar con mantequilla, poner mantequilla en. || **3 to – up,** (fam.) hacer la pelota a, adular, lisonjear. **4 – wouldn't melt in someone's mouth,** ser una mosquita muerta. **5 to know which side one's bread is buttered on,** V. **bread.**
buttercup | 'bʌtəkʌp | *s.c.* BOT. botón de oro, ranúnculo.
buttered | 'bʌtəd | *adj.* untado con mantequilla.
butterfingers | 'bʌtəfɪŋgəz | *interj.* (hum.) manazas.
butterfly | 'bʌtəflaɪ | *s.c.* **1** ZOOL. mariposa. || **2 to have butterflies in one's stomach,** (fam.) tener los nervios un poco de punta, tener cosquillas en el estómago. **3 the –/the – stroke,** DEP. el estilo mariposa.
buttermilk | 'bʌtəmɪlk | *s.i.* suero de la leche.
butterscotch | 'bʌtəskɒtʃ | *s.c.* e *i.* GAST. caramelo (hecho de azúcar y mantequilla).
buttery | 'bʌtərɪ | *adj.* **1** cremoso, mantecoso. || *s.c.* **2** cafetería (en algunas universidades).
buttock | 'bʌtək | *s.c.* [normalmente *pl.*] ANAT. glúteo.
button | 'bʌtn | *s.c.* **1** botón (de ropa). **2** botón, pulsador (para cualquier mecanismo). **3** (EE.UU.) chapa, insignia (redonda). || *v.t.* **4** abotonar, abrochar (con botones). || **5 to – up,** abrochar de arriba a abajo, abrochar bien. **6 to – up/to – one's tip,** (EE.UU. y fam.) callarse/punto en boca.
button-down | 'bʌtndaun | *adj.* con botones en el cuello (camisa).
buttonhole | 'bʌtnhəul | *s.c.* **1** ojal. **2** (brit.) flor de ojal, flor en el ojal. || *v.t.* **3** arrinconar, detener, retener (casi por la fuerza).
buttress | 'bʌtrɪs | *s.c.* **1** ARQ. contrafuerte, botarel. || *v.t.* **2** fortalecer, poner un contrafuerte en (pared). **3** reforzar, apuntalar (un concepto, sistema, etc.).
buxom | 'bʌksəm | *adj.* de carnes prietas, voluptuosa (mujer).
buy | baɪ | *v.t.* [*pret.* y *p.p.irreg.* **bought**] **1** comprar, adquirir. **2** comprar, sobornar (persona). **3** pagar: *I'll give my children the best education I can buy for them = daré a mis hijos la mejor educación que les pueda pagar.* **4** ganar (tiempo o similar). **5** invitar (a una copa). **6** (fam.) creer, tragar, aceptar. | *s.c.* **7** compra, adquisición. || **8 to – in,** hacer acopio de, comprar grandes cantidades de (normalmente comida). **9 to – into,** comprar parte de (normalmente una empresa). **10 to – off,** sobornar, comprar (personas). **11 to – out,** comprar toda la participación de (alguien en una empresa). **12 to oneself out (of),** salirse mediante el pago de dinero (del ejército). **13 to – over,** sobornar, comprar (personas). **14 to – up,** amasar, hacer acopio, comprar gran cantidad de (tierras, propiedades, etc.).
buyer | baɪər | *s.c.* **1** comprador. **2** COM. agente de compras, jefe de compras (de una empresa, almacén, etc.). || **3 a buyer's market,** ECON. un mercado de precios bajos, un mercado favorable al comprador.
buzz | bʌz | *s.c.* **1** zumbido (de insectos, sonidos humanos, aparatos, etc.). || *v.i.* **2** zumbar, dar zumbidos, emitir zumbidos. **3 [to – around/about]** moverse

dando zumbidos, ir dando zumbidos; revolotear dando zumbidos. **4 [to – (with)]** bullir, llenar de murmullos (un espacio). **5** revolotear, dar vueltas (pensamientos en la cabeza). **6** zumbar (oídos). || *v.t.* **7** (fam.) llamar por teléfono interior. **8** pasar volando cerca de, volar cerca de. || *s.sing.* **9 [the –]** (fam.) lo último (de noticias). **10 [– (of)]** zumbido continuo (de conversación). **11** (fam.) ambiente, vida (actividad excitante). || **12 to – off,** (fam.) [siempre en imperativo] irse a la mierda, irse a la porra, irse al infierno. **13 – word,** (fam.) palabra de moda. **14 to give somebody a –,** (fam.) dar un telefonazo a alguien.

buzzard | 'bʌzəd | *s.c.* ZOOL. buitre.

buzzer | 'bʌzər | *s.c.* ELEC. timbre.

buzzing | 'bʌzɪŋ | *s.i.* zumbido, sonido zumbante.

by | baɪ | *prep.* **1** junto, al lado de: *I was standing by the door = estaba de pie junto a la puerta.* **2** por, a través de (una puerta o ventana): *he came in by the back door = él entró por la puerta de atrás.* **3** en (medio de transporte): *by train = en tren.* **4** [en *pas.*] por (agente): *he was killed by his own father = fue asesinado por su propio padre.* **5** según, por (ley, reglamento, medida internacional, etc.): *you are my wife by law = eres mi esposa según la ley.* **6** por, de (escrito, cantado, etc.): *a book by Cervantes = un libro de Cervantes.* **7** por delante de: *he rushed by us = él pasó a toda velocidad por delante de nosotros.* **8** [+ *ger.*] a base de: *by studying you'll pass = a base de estudiar aprobarás.* **9** por parte de: *the use of drugs by children = el consumo de drogas por los niños.* **10** por (a causa de): *by chance = por casualidad.* **11** MAT. por (multiplicación y división). **12 [– *num.*]** por, a: *he's earning money by the millions = está ganando dinero a millones.* **13** más o menos a, más o menos en; justo antes de (tiempo): *I want that by Monday = quiero eso más o menos el Lunes.* **14 [– the]** de (una parte del cuerpo): *I caught her by the hand = la agarré de la mano.* **15** con (refiriéndose a algo dicho): *what do you mean by that word? = ¿qué quieres decir con ese término?* **16** por, según (características de la personalidad): *he's, by nature, a swimmer = él es, por naturaleza, un nadador.* **17 [*s.* + – + *s.*]** a, tras: *day by day = día tras día; bit by bit = poquito a poquito.* || **18 all – oneself/– oneself, a)** a solas, solo, sin compañía. **b)** sin ayuda de nadie, solo. **19 – all means,** V. **mean. 20 – and –,** (p.u.) poco tiempo después, un poco más tarde. **21 – and large,** V. **large. 22 – day/– night,** por el día/por la noche. **23 side – side,** V. **side.** OBS. Esta palabra tiene un sentido adverbial de difícil traducción: **24** expresa que algo o alguien, en su movimiento físico, pasa por delante: *the cars sped by = los coches pasaron por delante a toda velocidad.*

bye | baɪ | *interj.* (fam.) adiós.

bye-bye | ˌbaɪ'baɪ | *interj.* (fam.) adiós.

bye-byes | 'baɪbaɪz | **to go to –,** (fam.) dormirse (lenguaje de niños).

byelaw V. **by-law.**

by-election | 'baɪɪlekʃn | *s.c.* POL. elección local, elección para un solo escaño.

bygone | 'baɪgɒn | *adj.* **1** pasado, antaño. || **2 let bygones be bygones,** lo pasado pasado está, olvidemos lo pasado.

by-law | 'baɪlɔː | (también **byelaw**) *s.c.* ley local, ley de ámbito local.

by-line | 'baɪlaɪn | *s.c.* PER. línea con el nombre del autor de un artículo.

bypass | 'baɪpɑːs | (EE.UU.) | baɪpæs | *v.t.* **1** circunvalar (una ciudad). **2** construir para circunvalación (una carretera). **3** evitar, esquivar (alguien en autoridad, un tema de difícil solución, etc.). **4** MED. hacer una derivación coronaria, hacer un bypass. || *s.c.* **5** carretera de circunvalación. || *adj.* **6** MED. de desviación coronaria, de bypass.

by-play | 'baɪpleɪ | *s.i.* juego escénico secundario.

by-product | 'baɪprɒdʌkt | *s.c.* **1 [– (of)]** subproducto, derivado, producto secundario. **2 [– (of)]** (fig.) efecto secundario.

bystander | 'baɪstændər | *s.c.* espectador, curioso.

byte | baɪt | *s.c.* INF. byte, unidad de memoria.

byway | 'baɪweɪ | *s.c.* camino secundario, carretera secundaria.

byword | 'baɪwəːd | *s.c.* **1** sobrenombre, apodo. **2 [– for]** símbolo de; prototipo de.

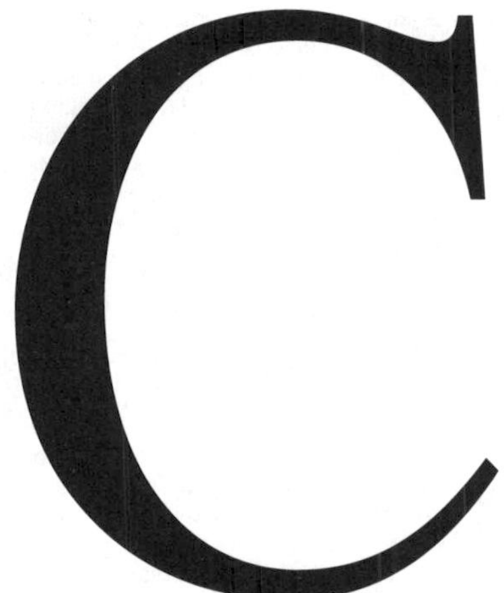

c, C | siː | *s.c.* **1** c, C tercera letra del alfabeto inglés. || *s.c.* e *i.* **2** MUS. do. **3** suficiente, aprobado (en el sistema académico inglés).
OBS. Esta letra sirve como abreviatura de muchos términos: **century, Celsius, copyright,** etc.
cab | kæb | *s.c.* **1** taxi. **2** cabina, cabina del conductor (de un camión o tren). || **3 by –,** en taxi.
cabal | kɪ'bæl | *s.c.* [+ *v.sing./pl.*] cábala, camarilla.
cabaret | 'kæbəreɪ | (EE.UU.) | ˌkæbə'reɪ | *s.i.* **1** cabaret. || *s.c.* **2** espectáculo de cabaret, show de cabaret. **3** cabaret, club nocturno.
cabbage | 'kæbɪʊʒ | *s.c.* e *i.* **1** BOT. repollo, berza. || *s.c.* **2** (brit. y fam.) muermo, pasota (persona sin intereses en la vida). **3** (brit. y fam.) vegetal (persona sin facultades mentales).
cabby | 'kæbɪ | (también **cabbie**) *s.c.* (brit. y p.u.) taxista, conductor de taxi.
cabin | 'kæbɪn | *s.c.* **1** MAR. camarote. **2** AER. cabina (de avión). **3** cabaña, cabaña de madera. || **4 – boy,** MAR. chico, camarero; grumete. **5 – class,** segunda clase (en barco). **6 – cruiser,** MAR. barco de recreo con camarote, yate de motor con camarote.
cabinet | 'kæbɪnɪt | *s.c.* **1** armario pequeño; vitrina. || **2 the Cabinet,** el Gobierno, el ejecutivo. **3 in cabinet,** POL. en el consejo de ministros.
cabinet-maker | 'kæbɪnɪtmeɪkər | *s.c.* ebanista.
cable | 'keɪbl | *s.c.* **1** cable, maroma. **2** ELEC. cable (transmisor). **3** telegrama, cablegrama. || *v.t.* **4** enviar un cablegrama, enviar un telegrama. **5** hacer un envío postal, enviar un giro postal (de dinero). || **6 – car,** vagón funicular. **7 – railway,** funicular. **8 – television,** TV, televisión por cable.
caboose | kə'buːs | *s.c.* **1** furgón de cola. **2** MAR. cocina, fogón (de barco).

cacao | kə'kaːeʊ | | kə'keɪəʊ | *s.c.* **1** (también **cacao-bean**) semilla de cacao. **2** (también **cacao-tree**) árbol de cacao.
cache | kæʃ | *s.c.* alijo (de armas o drogas).
cachet | 'kæʃeɪ | (EE.UU.) | kæ'ʃeɪ | *s.sing.* (form. o lit.) prestigio, distinción; sello distintivo.
cackle | 'kækl | *v.i.* **1** cacarear (gallina). **2** reírse con un cierto cacareo. || *s.sing.* **3 [a –]** una risa aguda. || **4 cut the –,** (fam.) cállate, corta el rollo.
cacophonous | kə'kɒfənəs | *adj.* cacofónico.
cacophony | kə'kɒfənɪ | *s.i.* cacofonía.
cacti | 'kæktaɪ | *pl.* de **cactus.**
cactus | 'kæktəs | [*pl.* **cactuses** o **cacti**] *s.c.* BOT. cacto.
cad | kæd | *s.c.* (fam. y p.u.) caradura, sinvergüenza.
caddish | 'kædɪʃ | *adj.* (fam. y p.u.) canallesco, típico de un sinvergüenza.
cadaver | kə'dɑːvər | | kə'deɪvə | (EE.UU.) | kə'dævər | *s.c.* (form. y EE.UU.) MED. cadáver.
cadaverous | kə'dævərəs | *adj.* cadavérico (de apariencia).
caddie | 'kædɪ | (también **caddy**) *s.c.* **1** cadi (portador de los palos en el golf). || *v.i.* **2** hacer de cadi, actuar como cadi.
cadence | 'keɪdns | *s.c.* **1** cadencia, modulación (de la voz). **2** ritmo, cadencia (del sonido). **3** MUS. cadencia.
cadenza | kə'denzə | *s.c.* MUS. cadencia (para solista).
cadet | kə'det | *s.c.* MIL. cadete.
cadge | kædʒ | (desp., fam. y brit.) *v.i.* **1** gorronear, sablear, vivir de gorra. || *v.t.* **2** [**to – +** *o.* **+ from/off**] sacar de gorra, sablear: *he cadged a few drinks off me = me sacó varias copas de gorra.*
cadger | 'kædʒər | *s.c.* (desp., fam. y brit.) gorrón.
cadmium | 'kædmɪəm | *s.i.* QUIM. cadmio.

cadre | 'kɑːdə | (EE.UU.) | 'kædrɪ | *s.c.* [+ *v.sing./pl.*] cuadro de dirigentes, cuadro de líderes, grupo directivo (en la política, administración, ejército, etc.).
Caesarean | sɪ'zeərɪən | (también **Cesarian** o **Caesarean section**) *s.c.* MED. cesárea.
caesura | sɪ'zjʊərə | (EE.UU.) | sɪ'ʒʊərə | *s.c.* LIT. cesura.
café | 'kæfeɪ, (EE.UU.) | kæ'feɪ | *s.c.* café (de bebidas —en Inglaterra sin alcohol— y comidas ligeras).
cafeteria | ˌkæfɪ'tɪərɪə | *s.c.* autoservicio; cafetería (en el lugar de trabajo).
caffeine | 'kæfiːn | *s.i.* cafeína.
caftan | 'kæftæn | | kəf'tɑːn | (también **kaftan**) *s.c.* **1** caftán (vestimenta árabe). **2** túnica, manto (de señora).
cage | keɪdʒ | *s.c.* **1** jaula. **2** MIN. montacargas, ascensor (en una mina). || *v.t.* **3** meter en una jaula, enjaular.
caged | keɪdʒt | *adj.* enjaulado (animal).
cagey | 'keɪdʒɪ | *adj.* [*comp.* **cagier,** *super.* **cagiest**] (fam.) cauteloso, prevenido; astuto.
cagily | 'keɪdʒɪlɪ | *adv.* (fam.) cautelosamente, prevenidamente; astutamente.
caginess | 'keɪdʒɪnɪs | (también **cageyness**) *s.i.* (fam.) cautela, prevención; astucia.
cagoule | kə'guːl | *s.c.* chubasquero.
cahoots | kə'huːts | **in – with,** (fam.) confabulado con, compinchado con.
caiman V. **cayman.**
cairn | keən | *s.c.* mojón, montón de piedras (que señala límites, un monumento, etc.).
cajole | kə'dʒəʊl | *v.t.* [**to – +** *o.* **+ (into/out of)**] engatusar, camelar, persuadir con lisonjas: *we cajoled them into going away with us = les persuadimos con lisonjas para que se vinieran con nosotros.*
cajolery | kə'dʒəʊlərɪ | *s.c.* halagos, lisonjas.

cake | keɪk | *s.c.* e *i.* **1** pastel, tarta, bizcocho; pastelillo. || *s.c.* **2** GAST. pastel (comida con la forma de pastel): *fish cakes = pasteles de pescado.* **3 [– of]** trozo de, barra de (jabón o cera). || *v.t.* **4 [to – + *o.* + with]** cubrir con, manchar con (algo endurecido): *your shoes are caked with mud = tus zapatos están cubiertos de barro.* || *v.i.* **5 [to – (on/in)]** ponerse sólido, endurecerse, hacerse duro, solidificarse (un líquido); coagularse (la sangre): *the blood had caked = la sangre se había coagulado.* || **6 a piece of –,** (fam.) una bicoca, tirado, chollo (algo muy fácil). **7 cakes and ale,** (fam.) color de rosa, puro placer: *life is not all cakes and ale = la vida no es todo color de rosa.* **8 to get/want/etc. a slice/share of the –,** conseguir/querer un trozo/parte del pastel (de los beneficios de una empresa, un trabajo colectivo, etc.). **9 to have one's – and eat it,** (fam.) oír misa y andar en la procesión, repicar y oír misa. **10 to sell like hot cakes,** (fam.) venderse como rosquillas. **11 the icing on the –,** V. **icing.**

calamine | 'kæləmaɪn | (también **calamine lotion**) *s.i.* QUIM. calamina (para las quemaduras).

calamitous | kə'læmɪtəs | *adj.* (a veces hum.) calamitoso, catastrófico, desastroso.

calamity | kə'læmɪtɪ | *s.c.* e *i.* calamidad, catástrofe, desastre.

calcification | ˌkælsɪfɪ'keɪʃn | *s.i.* calcificación.

calcify | 'kælsɪfaɪ | *v.t.* e *i.* calcificar(se).

calcination | ˌkælsɪ'neɪʃn | *s.i.* calcinación.

calcine | 'kælsaɪn | *v.t.* e *i.* calcinar(se).

calcium | 'kælsɪəm | *s.i.* QUIM. calcio.

calculate | 'kælkjuleɪt | *v.t.* e *i.* **1** calcular, estimar, hacer cálculos. || *v.t.* **2** determinar, fijar: *we must calculate all the possible consequences = debemos determinar todas las posibles consecuencias.* || **3 to be =N to,** [+ *inf.*] tener el propósito de, tener la finalidad de, tener la consecuencia segura de, tener la intención de: *the strike is calculated to last for a long time = la huelga tiene el propósito de durar mucho tiempo.* **4 to be scarcely calculated to,** [+ *inf.*] no estar de ninguna manera pensado para: *it's scarcely calculated to help the firm = no está de ninguna manera pensado para ayudar a la empresa.*

calculated | 'kælkjuleɪtɪd | *adj.* **1** premeditado, deliberado (comportamiento negativo). **2** muy pensado, muy meditado (riesgo).

calculating | 'kælkjuleɪtɪŋ | *adj.* (desp.) calculador, astuto.

calculation | ˌkælkju'leɪʃn | *s.c.* e *i.* **1** cálculo, cómputo, operación matemática. || *s.c.* **2** estimación, cálculo sopesado. || *s.i.* **3** (desp.) astucia, cálculo (egoísta).

calculator | 'kælkjuleɪtər | *s.c.* ELECTR. calculadora.

calculus | 'kælkjuləs | *s.i.* MAT. cálculo.

caldron V. **cauldron.**

calendar | 'kælɪndər | *s.c.* **1** calendario. **2** (fig.) calendario, agenda (de eventos, actuaciones, actividades, etc.). **3** [normalmente *sing.*] calendario, sistema de contabilizar el tiempo: *the Muslim calendar = el calendario musulmán.* || **4 – month,** mes de calendario (no lunar). **5 – year,** año civil.

calf | kɑːf | (EE.UU.) | kæf | [*pl.* **calves**] *s.c.* **1** ZOOL. carnero, ternero, novillo. **2** ZOOL. cría joven (de elefante, jirafa y otros mamíferos grandes). **3** ANAT. pantorrilla, muslo. || *s.i.* **4** (también **calfskin**) piel de ternero, piel de becerro. || **5 – love,** amor juvenil, amor adolescente. **6 in/with –,** preñada (una vaca). **7 to kill the fatted –,** celebrar una fiesta por todo lo alto, festejar a lo grande.

caliber V. **calibre.**

calibrate | 'kælɪbreɪt | *v.t.* MEC. calibrar, graduar (un instrumento).

calibration | ˌkælɪ'breɪʃn | *s.i.* MEC. calibración, graduación (de un instrumento).

calibre | 'kælɪbər | (EE.UU. **caliber**) *s.c.* **1** MEC. calibre (de un arma de fuego). || *s.i.* **2** (fig.) calidad, carácter, calibre (de una persona, institución, etc.).

calico | 'kælɪkəu | *s.i.* percal (tela).

caliper V. **calliper.**

caliph | 'keɪlɪf | (también **calif**) *s.c.* HIST. califa.

calisthenics V. **callisthenics.**

call | kɔːl | *v.t.* **1** llamar, poner el nombre de, dar el nombre de (persona u objeto). **2** llamar, denominar, etiquetar: *the minister called the students revolutionaries = el ministro etiquetó a los estudiantes de revolucionarios.* **3** convocar (reunión, conferencia, etc.). **4** llamar, hacer venir: *call everybody, everything is ready = llama a todos, todo está listo.* **5** llamar por teléfono, telefonear, llamar. **6** llamar en voz alta, levantar la voz, llamar (con un grito). **7** decir en voz alta (un nombre o número): *I'll call the numbers one by one = diré los números en voz alta uno a uno.* **8** DER. requerir (para aparecer en juicio). **9 [to – it...]** decir (como aproximación o sugerencia): *you owe me, let's call it a meal at Maxim's = me debes, digamos que una comida en el restaurante Maxim.* **10** escoger, decir (al echar suertes): *he called heads and lost = él escogió carta y perdió.* || *v.i.* **11** telefonear, llamar por teléfono. **12 [to – (on/at)]** visitar, pasar por (la casa, oficina, etc. de alguien). **13** parar, tener parada, pasar por (un tren, autobús, etc.): *the train calls at every station = el tren para en todas las estaciones.* **14 [to – for/to/from]** llamar en voz alta en busca de/a/desde: *he called for an ambulance = él llamó en busca de una ambulancia.* **15** escoger, decir (al echar suertes). || *s.c.* **16** llamada en voz alta, grito. **17** llamada telefónica. **18** visita. **19** requerimiento, llamada (a un doctor, por ejemplo). **20 [– (for)]** demanda, petición, requerimiento (de ayuda, justicia, etc.). **21** ZOOL. sonido característico, canto, reclamo (de un ave u otro animal). **22** DEP. decisión (de un árbitro). || *s.i.* **23 [– for]** necesidad de: *there was no call for insults = no hay ninguna necesidad de insultar.* || *s.sing.* **24 [the – (of)]** llamada, la atracción (de la naturaleza, lo desconocido, nuevo, etc.). **25 [– (of)]** llamada, vocación (religiosa, por ejemplo). || *v.r.* **26** creerse, proclamarse, (algo que puede ser falso): *he calls himself a progressive = él se cree progresista.* || **27 a – of nature,** V. **nature. 28 to be/feel called to,** tener vocación a, sentirse llamado a (una actividad religiosa, filantrópica, etc.). **29 to – a halt,** V. **halt. 30 to – a spade a spade,** V. **spade. 31 to – back, a)** devolver la llamada; volver a llamar (telefónicamente). **b)** hacer regresar, pedir que regrese (alguien). **32 to – down something (on),** (form.) implorar que algo (desgraciado) caiga (sobre), pedir al cielo que algo (malo) suceda (a). **33 to – for, a)** pasar a recoger a (alguien en su casa). **b)** ir a buscar, ir a reclamar (algún objeto). **c)** demandar, requerir, exigir. **d)** reclamar, exigir, necesitar: *this situation calls for imagination = esta situación necesita imaginación.* **34 to – forth,** (form.) inspirar, provocar (un sentimiento, reacción). **35 to – in, a)** hacer venir, requerir la presencia de: *call the doctor in = haz venir al médico.* **b)** requerir la devolución de. **c)** llamar al trabajo, llamar a casa (normalmente para avisar de algo). **36 to – it a day,** V. **day. 37 to – it quits,** V. **quit. 38 to – off, a)** cancelar, anular. **b)** llamar (a un perro especialmente) para que deje de atacar. **39 to – on/upon, a)** pedir, exigir (a alguien que haga algo). **b)** recurrir a (fuerza, esperanza, valentía, etc.). **40 ...to – one's own, ...** que uno pueda decir es suyo: *he hasn't got anything to call his own = él no tenía nada que pudiera decir que era suyo.* **41 to – out, a)** gritar, chillar, dar gritos fuertes. **b)** hacer salir, requerir la presencia de (alguna institución para ayudar): *the government called out the army = el gobierno hizo salir al ejército.* **c)** ordenar ir a la huelga, mandar comenzar una huelga. **42 to – out for,** requerir gritos, pedir a gritos (algún tipo de reacción): *apartheid calls out for all-out opposition = el sistema racista pide a gritos una oposición total.* **43 to – someone names,** insultar a alguien. **44 to – someone's bluff,** V. **bluff. 45 to – someone to order,** (form.) llamar al orden a alguien (en una reunión, asamblea, etc.). **46 to – something into question,** V. **question. 47 to – something to mind,** V. **mind. 48 to – the tune,** V. **tune. 49 to – up, a)** (fam.) dar un telefonazo, contactar por teléfono con. **b)** evocar, rememorar, venir a la cabeza (un recuerdo). **c)** llamar al servicio militar, llamar a filas, reclutar. **d)** INF. acceder a (información). **e)** DEP. requerir el servicio de (en un deporte). **50 to have first – on,** tener prioridad sobre. *I have first call on my dentist, because he is my son = tengo prioridad en el dentista porque es mi hijo.* **51 on –,** de guardia (médico), en situación de espera activa (bomberos, ejército, etc.).

call-box | 'kɔːlbɒks | *s.c.* cabina telefónica.

caller | 'kɔːlər | *s.c.* **1** visitante, visita (persona). **2** persona que llama por teléfono, persona que ha llamado por teléfono.

call-girl | 'kɔːlgəːl | *s.c.* prostituta, (que establece citas por teléfono).

calligraphy | kə'lɪgrəfɪ | *s.i.* caligrafía.

calling | 'kɔːlɪŋ | *s.sing.* **1** REL. vocación. **2** vocación profesional, ocupación.

calliper | 'kælɪpər | (también **caliper**) *s.c.* **1** (usualmente *pl.*) MEC. calibrador, compás de calibres (aparato medidor de anchos circulares). **2** (usualmente *pl.*) soporte ortopédico (para personas con problemas en las piernas).

callisthenics | ˌkælɪs'θenɪks | (también **calisthenics**) *s.pl.* calistenia, ejercicios físicos suaves.

callosity | kæ'lɒsətɪ | *s.c.* e *i.* (form.) callosidad, zona endurecida de la piel.

callous | 'kæləs | *adj.* **1** con callo, encallecido (piel). **2** (fig.) insensible, cruel.

calloused | 'kæləsd | *adj.* lleno de callos (piel).

callously | 'kæləslɪ | *adv.* insensiblemente, cruelmente.

callousness | 'kæləsnɪs | *s.i.* insensibilidad, crueldad.

callow | 'kæləʊ | *adj.* inexperto, novato, inmaduro.

callowness | 'kæləʊnɪs | *s.i.* inexperiencia, inmadurez.

call-up | 'kɔːlʌp | *adj.* MIL. **1** (brit.) orden de movilización, orden de reclutamiento, llamamiento a filas. || *s.c.* **2** reclutamiento (número de reclutas).

callus | 'kæləs | *s.c.* MED. callo.

calm | kɑːm, (EE.UU.) | kɑːlm | *adj.* **1** sereno, tranquilo. **2** en calma (el mar). **3** calmado, sin viento (tiempo atmosférico). || *s.i.* **4** calma, paz, serenidad (de un lugar normalmente). || *s.c.* **5** calma (del tiempo atmosférico). || *v.t.* **6** calmar, serenar (el tiempo atmosférico). **7** calmar, serenar (a alguien). || *v.i.* **8** calmarse, serenarse (el tiempo). || *v.r.* **9** calmarse, serenarse (alguien). || **10 to – down,** recobrar la calma, serenar(se), calmar(se).

calmly | 'kɑːmlɪ | *adv.* serenamente, tranquilamente.

calmness | 'kɑːmnɪs | *s.i.* serenidad, tranquilidad (cualidad personal).

calorie | 'kælərɪ | *s.c.* **1** FIS. caloría (medida del calor). **2** QUIM. caloría (en los alimentos).

calorific | ˌkælə'rɪfɪk | *adj.* calorífico: *calorific value = valor calorífico.*

calumniate | kə'lʌmnɪeɪt | *v.t.* (form.) calumniar.

calumnious | kə'lʌmnɪəs | *adj.* (form.) calumnioso.

calumny | 'kæləmnɪ | *s.c.* e *i.* (form.) calumnia.

calvary | 'kælvərɪ | *s.c.* REL. calvario.

calve | kɑːv | (EE.UU.) | kæv | *v.i.* parir (una vaca).

calves | kɑːvz | *pl.* de **calf.**

Calvinism | 'kælvɪnɪzəm | *s.i.* REL. calvinismo.

Calvinist | 'kælvɪnɪst | *s.c.* REL. calvinista.

calypso | kə'lɪpsəʊ | *s.c.* MUS. calipso.

cam | kæm | *s.c.* MEC. leva, cama.

camaraderie | ˌkæmə'rɑːdərɪ | (EE.UU.) | ˌkæmə'rædərɪ | *s.i.* camaradería, compañerismo.

cambric | 'keɪmbrɪk | *s.i.* holanda, batista (tejido).

came | keɪm | *pret.irreg.* de **come.**

camel | 'kæml | *s.c.* **1** ZOOL. camello. || **2 – hair,** pelo de camello.

camellia | kə'miːlɪə | *s.c.* BOT. camelia.

cameo | 'kæmɪəʊ | *s.c.* **1** camafeo (adorno). **2** (fig.) papel secundario brillante en una película u obra de teatro.

camera | 'kæmərə | *s.c.* **1** FOT. cámara, máquina fotográfica. **2** TV. cámara. || **3 in –,** DER. en sesión a puerta cerrada. **4 on –,** TV. en pantalla.

cameraman | 'kæmərəmæn | [*pl.* **cameramen**] *s.c.* TV. cameraman.

cameramen | 'kæmərəmən | *pl.* de **cameraman.**

camera-shy | 'kæmərəʃaɪ | *adj.* nervioso ante la cámara.

Cameroon | ˌkæmə'ruːn | *s.sing.* Camerún.

Cameroonian | ˌkæmə'ruːnɪən | *s.c.* **1** camerunés. || *adj.* **2** camerunés.

camomile | 'kæməmaɪl | (también **chamomile**) *s.i.* BOT. manzanilla.

camouflage | 'kæməflɑːʒ | *s.i.* **1** MIL. camuflaje. **2** camuflaje, ocultamiento, enmascaramiento. **3** (fig.) pantalla, engaño. || *v.t.* **4** MIL. camuflar. **5** (fig.) ocultar, fingir, esconder (sentimientos, riqueza, etc.).

camp | kæmp | *s.c.* **1** campamento (de tiendas de campaña). **2** MIL. campamento. **3** campo (de refugiados, prisioneros de guerra, etc.). **4** (fig.) campo, lado, facción (ideológica, religiosa, etc.). || *s.i.* **5** (fam.) frivolidad, banalidad, superficialidad. || *adj.* **6** (fam.) afectado, rebuscado, cursi. **7** (fam. y desp.) afeminado. || *v.i.* **8** acampar. || **9 to break –,** levantar el campamento. **10 to – it up,** (fam. y brit.) actuar de manera exagerada, comportarse de modo exagerado. **11 to – out,** dormir en tienda de campaña. **12 to make –,** fijar el campamento, acampar.

campaign | kæm'peɪn | *s.c.* **1** campaña (política, social, empresarial, etc.). **2** MIL. campaña, expedición militar. | *v.i.* **3** hacer una campaña (política o de otra clase).

campaigner | kæm'peɪnər | *s.c.* **1** luchador de campaña, propagandista. || **2 old –,** veterano, viejo lobo (en alguna actividad).

camp-bed | ˌkæmp'bed | *s.c.* cama de campaña, cama plegable.

camper | 'kæmpə | *s.c.* **1** campista, excursionista. **2** rulot, remolque, campera.

camp-fire | 'kæmpfaɪə | *s.c.* fuego de campamento.

camp-follower | 'kæmpfɒləʊər | *s.c.* **1** seguidor (de una causa). **2** MIL. acompañante de un ejército.

campground | 'kæmpgraʊnd | V. **campsite.**

camphor | 'kæmfər | *s.i.* QUIM. alcanfor.

camping-site | 'kæmpɪŋsaɪt | V. **campsite.**

campsite | 'kæmpsaɪt | *s.c.* camping.

campus | 'kæmpəs | *s.c.* campus (de una universidad).

can | kæn | (forma relajada | kən, kn) [*pret.irreg.* **could**] *v.i.* **1** poder: *today we can't go to the cinema = hoy no podemos ir al cine.* **2** poder (permiso): *can I take your newspaper? = ¿puedo cogerte el periódico?* **3** saber (tener los conocimientos o destrezas necesarias): *I can play the piano very well = sé tocar muy bien el piano.* || **4 can't,** no es posible que, no puede, no debe (haciendo una suposición): *but he can't be fifty, he must be much older = pero no es posible que tenga cincuenta años, debe ser mucho más viejo.* OBS. Este verbo no tiene más tiempos. Cuando se quiere expresar su significado en otros tiempos se debe utilizar la fórmula lingüística **to be able to** + *inf.*: *tomorrow I'll be able to see you = mañana te podré ver.*

can | kæn | [ger. **canning,** *pret.* y *p.p.* **canned**] *v.t.* **1** enlatar, envasar, poner en conserva. || *s.c.* **2** bote, lata (para conservas, pinturas, etc.). **3** bidón (de petróleo). || *s.sing.* (EE.UU.) **4 [the –]** la cárcel. **5 [the –]** el retrete, el water. || **6 to carry the –,** (fam. y brit.) pagar el pato. **7 in the –,** (fam.) en el bote, completamente terminado.

Canada | 'kænədə | *s.sing.* Canadá.

Canadian | kə'neɪdɪən | *s.c.* **1** canadiense (habitante). || *adj.* **2** canadiense (cultura, variante lingüística, etc.).

canal | kə'næl | *s.c.* **1** canal (hecho por el hombre). **2** ANAT. conducto, canal. || **3 – boat,** barcaza.

canalise V. **canalize.**

canalization | ˌkænəlaɪ'zeɪʃn | (EE.UU.) | ˌkænəlɪ'zeɪʃn | (también **canalisation**) *s.i.* (form.) canalización (de aguas, energías, etc.).

canalize | 'kænəlaɪz | *v.t.* (form.) **1** canalizar (aguas). **2** (fig.) canalizar (energías, esfuerzos, etc.).

canapé | 'kænəpeɪ | (EE.UU.) | ˌkænə'peɪ | *s.c.* GAST. canapé.

canard | kæ'nɑːd | | 'kænɑːd | *s.c.* bulo, patraña, noticia falsa.

canary | kə'neərɪ | *s.c.* **1** ZOOL. canario. || **2 – yellow,** amarillo claro.

can-can | 'kænkæn | *s.c.* (normalmente *sing.*) cancán (baile).

cancel | 'kænsl | *v.t.* **1** cancelar, anular (evento, reserva, etc.). **2** invalidar, anular (contrato). **3** tachar, borrar (escrito). || **4 to – out,** anularse mutuamente, neutralizarse.

cancellation | ˌkænsə'leɪʃn | *s.c.* e *i.* cancelación, anulación.

cancer | 'kænsər | *s.c.* e *i.* **1** MED. cáncer. || *s.c.* **2** (form. y fig.) cáncer.

cancerous | 'kænsərəs | *adj.* MED. cancerígeno.

candelabra | ˌkændɪ'lɑːbrə | V. **candelabrum.**

candelabrum | ˌkændɪ'lɑːbrəm | (también **candelabra**) [*pl.* **candelabra** o **candelabras**] *s.c.* candelabro.

candid | 'kændɪd | *adj.* franco, sincero.

candidacy | 'kændɪdəsɪ | (también **candidature**) *s.i.* candidatura.

candidate | 'kændɪdət | (EE.UU.) | 'kændɪdeɪt | *s.c.* **1** POL. candidato. **2** opositor, aspirante (persona que hace un examen). **3** (fig.) candidato (cosa o persona): *my firm is a possible candidate for the next prize = mi empresa es un candidato posible para el siguiente premio.*

candidature | 'kændɪdətʃər | V. **candidacy.**

candidly | 'kændɪdlɪ | *adv.* francamente, sinceramente.

candidness | 'kændɪdnɪs | *s.i.* franqueza, sinceridad.

candied | 'kændɪd | *adj.* GAST. azucarado, con caramelo.

candle | 'kændl | *s.c.* **1** vela. || (fam.) **2 to burn the – at both ends,** trasnochar y madrugar, gastar todas las fuerzas de uno, pasarse trabajando. **3 not to hold a – to,** no llegar a la suela del zapato de. **4 the game is not worth the –,** el resultado no merece la pena, el resultado no está en consonancia con el esfuerzo desarrollado.

candlelight | 'kændllaɪt | *s.i.* luz de vela.

candlelit | 'kændllɪt | *adj.* iluminado con velas.

candlestick | 'kændlstɪk | *s.c.* candelero, palmatoria.

candour | 'kændər | (EE.UU. **candor**) *s.i.* franqueza, sinceridad.

candy | 'kændɪ | *s.c.* e *i.* **1** (EE.UU.) caramelo, dulce. || **2 – floss,** (brit.) dulce de hilos.

candy-striped | 'kændɪstraɪpt | *adj.* rayado (blanco y rojo o rosa).

cane | keɪn | *s.i.* **1** BOT. caña. **2** caña, bejuco (para muebles). || *s.c.* **3** caña. **4** vara (para golpear). **5** bastón, báculo (como apoyo). || *s.sing.* **6 [the –]** la vara, el palo (castigo corporal en escuelas británicas). || *v.t.* **7** dar con la vara, pegar con la vara (como castigo escolar).

canine | 'kæɪnaɪn | *adj.* **1** canino. || *s.c.* **2** (form.) canino (perro). **3** colmillo. || **4 – tooth,** colmillo.

canister | 'kænɪstər | *s.c.* **1** bote, lata (para guardar té, café, etc.). **2** aerosol, bote de aerosol (con algún tipo de gas, crema, etc.).

canker | 'kæŋkər | *s.i.* **1** BOT. cancro. **2** MED. llaga, úlcera (en la boca). || *s.c.* **3** (form. y fig.) llaga, úlcera, cáncer (en la sociedad, asociación, etc.).

cannabis | 'kænəbɪs | *s.i.* marihuana.

canned | kænd | *adj.* **1** enlatado, en bote (comida, bebida, etc.). **2** (desp.) enlatado, en conserva (música, aplausos, etc.). **3** (fam.) trompa, bebido.

cannery | 'kænərɪ | *s.c.* fábrica de conservas.

canning | 'kænɪŋ | *s.i.* enlatado.

cannibal | 'kænɪbl | *s.c.* **1** caníbal (humanos). **2** caníbal (animal).

cannibalise V. **cannibalize.**

cannibalism | 'kænɪbəlɪzəm | *s.i.* canibalismo.

cannibalize | 'kænɪbəlaɪz | (también **cannibalise**) *v.t.* MEC. desmontar piezas viejas (para reparar otro coche).

cannon | 'kænən | [*pl.* **cannon** o **cannons**] *s.c.* MIL. **1** HIST. cañón de ruedas. **2** AER. ametralladora automática (en un avión). || **3 – ball,** MIL. bola de cañón. **4 – fodder,** (fig.) carne de cañón. **5 to – into,** estrellarse contra, darse con gran fuerza contra, chocarse violentamente contra.

cannonade | ˌkænə'neɪd | *s.c.* MIL. andanada (de cañón).

cannot | 'kænɒt | *contrac.* de **can** y **not.**

cannily | 'kænɪlɪ | *adv.* cautamente, sagazmente, astutamente.

canniness | 'kænɪnɪs | *s.i.* cautela, sagacidad, astucia.

canny | 'kænɪ | *adj.* cauto, sagaz, astuto.

canoe | kə'nuː | *s.c.* canoa.

canoeing | kə'nuːɪŋ | *s.i.* DEP. remo.

canon | 'kænən | *s.c.* **1** REL. canónigo. **2** (form.) principio, regla (de una ideología, de un arte, etc.). **3** LIT. canon, corpus (de un autor, de la Biblia, etc.). || **4 – law,** DER. código de derecho canónico.

canonical | kə'nɒnɪkl | *adj.* canónico.

canonise V. **canonize.**

canonization | ˌkænənaɪ'zeɪʃn | (EE.UU.)ˌkænənɪ'zeɪʃn | (también **canonisation**) *s.c.* e *i.* REL. canonización.

canonize | 'kænənaɪz | (también **canonise**) *v.t.* REL. canonizar.

canoodle | kə'nuːdl | *v.i.* (brit. y fam.) besuquearse.

canopied | 'kænəpɪd | *adj.* cubierto por toldo (balcón), cubierto por baldaquín (mueble).

canopy | 'kænəpɪ | *s.c.* **1** toldo; badalquín. **2** (fig.) bóveda (algo que cubre un espacio): *the canopy of leaves = la bóveda de las hojas.*

cant | kænt | *s.i.* tópico, trivialidad, hipocresía.

can't | kɑːnt | (EE.UU.) | kænt | *contrac.* de **can** y **not.**

cantankerous | kæn'tæŋkərəs | *adj.* arisco, irritable, malhumorado, pendenciero.

cantankerously | kæn'tæŋkərəslɪ | *adv.* ariscamente, irritablemente, malhumoradamente, pendencieramente.

cantata | kæn'tɑːtə | *s.c.* MUS. cantata.

canteen | kæn'tiːn | *s.c.* **1** cafetería, comedor (en el lugar de trabajo). **2** (brit.) juego (de cubertería). **3** cantimplora. **4** cocina de campaña (especialmente para militares).

canter | 'kæntər | *v.i.* **1** trotar a buena velocidad, trotar con energía. || *s.c.* **2** medio galope, trote vivaz. || **3 at a –,** con facilidad, sin esfuerzo; a buen ritmo y sin agobio.

canticle | 'kæntɪkl | *s.c.* REL. cántico litúrgico.

cantilever | 'kæntɪliːvər | *s.c.* **1** ARQ. viga voladiza, ménsula. || **2 – bridge,** ARQ. puente voladizo.

canto | 'kæntəu | *s.c.* LIT. canto, capítulo de poema épico.

canton | 'kæntɒn | *s.c.* POL. cantón (típico de algunos países, como Suiza).

cantonment | kən'tuːnmənt |, (EE.UU.) | kæn'təunmənt | *s.c.* MIL. acantonamiento, acuartelamiento temporal.

canvas | 'kænvəs | *s.i.* **1** lona (para tiendas de campaña, velas, etc.). || *s.c.* e *i.* **2** ART. lienzo (para pintura). || *s.c.* **3** ART. lienzo, cuadro. || **4 under –,** en tienda de campaña (viviendo).

canvass | 'kænvəs | *v.t.* **1** POL. dar propaganda, ofrecer explicaciones propagandísticas (casa por casa). **2** investigar la opinión, encuestar. || *v.i.* **3** POL. hacer propaganda (casa por casa). || *s.c.* **4** POL. propaganda directa en casa, propaganda directa.

canvassing | 'kænvəsɪŋ | *s.i.* POL. actividad propagandística.

canyon | 'kænjən | *s.c.* GEOG. cañón.

cap | kæp | *s.c.* **1** gorra, gorro. **2** tapa (de botella o similar). **3** capuchón (de pluma o bolígrafo). **4** (fam.) capuchón, diafragma (anticonceptivo). **5** GEOG. casquete (especialmente polar). **6** (brit.) DEP. gorra de selección (para ser parte del equipo). **7** cápsula de pólvora, pistón (en pistolas de juguete). || *v.t.* **8 [to – + *o.* + (with)]** coronar, rematar (poniendo algo en la parte superior). **9** DEP. conceder la gorra de selección. **10** rematar, poner como remate (de una actuación o similar). || **11 – in hand,** con la cabeza gacha, en actitud de súplica. **12 if the – fits,** aplícate el cuento.

capability | ˌkeɪpə'bɪlɪtɪ | *s.c.* e *i.* **1** capacidad, competencia, aptitud. **2** POL. capacidad (militar, nuclear, etc., de un país). || **3 capabilities,** capacidad, competencia, aptitud.

capable | 'keɪpəbl | *adj.* **1 [– of]** capaz de: *he is capable of killing himself = es capaz de suicidarse.* **2** capaz, competente (persona).

capably | 'keɪpəblɪ | *adv.* capazmente, competentemente.

capacious | kə'peɪʃəs | *adj.* espacioso, de gran cabida, capaz.

capaciousness | kə'peɪʃəsnɪs | *s.i.* cabida, capacidad.

capacity | kə'pæsɪtɪ | *s.i.* **1** capacidad (de volumen físico). **2** capacidad, aguante (de beber o comer). **3** ECON.

capacidad productiva, rendimiento máximo. || *s.c.* **4** capacidad, potencialidad (para hacer algo): *the capacity to read is basic = la capacidad de leer es fundamental.* **5** habilidad, aptitud, capacidad. || *s.c.* e *i.* **6** cilindrada (vehículos). || *adj.* **7** lleno hasta arriba, totalmente lleno, que abarrota (un teatro, estadios, etc.): *a capacity crowd = una multitud que abarrotaba...* || **8 filled to –,** lleno hasta arriba, lleno a más no poder. **9 in a ... –/in someone's – as,** en calidad de: *in my capacity as a teacher = en calidad de profesor.*

cape | keɪp | *s.c.* **1** GEOG. cabo. **2** capa, túnica (de vestir o de torear).

caper | 'keɪpər | *v.i.* **1** brincar, dar saltos, hacer cabriolas (de alegría o emoción similar). || *s.c.* **2** (fam.) embrollo, lío (criminal). **3** (p.u.) travesura, broma. **4** BOT. alcaparra. || **5 and all that –,** y todo ese engorro (algo molesto e innecesario). **6 to cut a –,** dar saltos, ir dando cabriolas.

capercaillie | ˌkæpə'keɪlɪ | (también **capercailzie**) *s.c.* ZOOL. urogallo.

capillary | kə'pɪlərɪ | (EE.UU.) | 'kæpɪlərɪ | *s.c.* **1** vaso capilar, vena capilar, capilar. || *adj.* **2** capilar, muy fino. || **3 – attraction,** FIS. fuerza capilar, atracción capilar.

capital | 'kæpɪtl | *s.c.* **1** GEOG. capital (de una nación). **2** (fig.) centro, capital (de la moda, arte, etc.). **3** GRAM. mayúscula. **4** ARQ. capitel, base. || *s.i.* **5** ECON. capital, dinero, fondos. **6** (fig.) capital, conocimiento, aptitud (de una persona): *don't waste your academic capital = no malgastes tu conocimiento académico.* || *s.sing.* **7** FIN. capital (no intereses). || *adj.* **8** FIN. de capital: *capital investment = inversión de capital.* **9** GRAM. mayúscula (letra). **10** DER. capital (de un crimen muy grave). **11** (fam. y p.u.) maravilloso, fantástico, magnífico. || **12 – gains,** FIN. ganancia (sobre inversión). **13 – gains tax,** FIN. impuesto sobre ganancias del capital. **14 – goods,** ECON. bienes de equipo. **15 – intensive,** ECON. necesitado de una fuerte inversión (industria). **16 – punishment,** DER. pena capital. **17 in capitals/in – letters,** en mayúsculas. **18 to make – out of/of,** sacar gran partido de, aprovecharse de. **19 with a – ...,** (fam.) en un sentido importante, en su significado esencial (queriendo marcar la relevancia del tema): *I'm talking about Art with a capital letter = estoy hablando del arte en su significado esencial.*

capitalise V. **capitalize.**

capitalism | 'kæpɪtəlɪzəm | *s.i.* POL. capitalismo.

capitalist | 'kæpɪtəlɪst | *s.c.* **1** POL. capitalista. **2** empresario, capitalista. || *adj.* **3** POL. capitalista: *capitalist society.* **4** (desp.) POL. capitalista, opresor.

capitalistic | ˌkæpɪtə'lɪstɪk | *adj.* (desp.) capitalista.

capitalization | ˌkæpɪtəlaɪ'zeɪʃn | (EE.UU.) | ˌkæpɪtəlɪ'zeɪʃn | (también **capitalisation**) *s.i.* FIN. capitalización.

capitalize | 'kəpɪtəlaɪz | (también **capitalise**) *v.i.* **1 [to – (on/upon)]** capitalizar, sacar partido de (una situación). || *v.t.* **2** poner mayúsculas. **3** FIN. convertir en capital, convertir algo en dinero vendiéndolo.

capitulate | kə'pɪtʃuleɪt | *v.i.* **[to – (to)]** capitular, rendirse, ceder.

capitulation | kəˌpɪtʃu'leɪʃn | *s.c.* e *i.* capitulación, rendición, cesión.

capon | 'keɪpən | *s.c.* capón (gallo).

caprice | kə'priːs | *s.c.* **1** antojo, capricho. **2** MUS. capricho. || **3** capricho, humor, veleidad (estado de ánimo personal).

capricious | kə'prɪʃəs | *adj.* **1** caprichoso, antojadizo, veleidoso. **2** (fig.) cambiante, impredecible, caprichoso (tiempo atmosférico).

capriciously | kə'prɪʃəslɪ | *adv.* caprichosamente, antojadizamente, veleidosamente.

capriciousness | kə'prɪʃəsnɪs | *s.i.* (lo) caprichoso, (lo) antojadizo, (lo) veleidoso.

Capricorn | 'kæprɪkɔːn | *s.sing.* Capricornio.

capsicum | 'kæpsɪkəm | *s.c.* e *i.* BOT. pimiento, guindilla; (Am.) ají.

capsize | kæp'saɪz | (EE.UU.) | 'kæpsaɪz | *v.t.* e *i.* MAR. zozobrar, volcar.

capsule | 'kæpsjuːl | (EE.UU.) | 'kæpsl | *s.c.* **1** MED. cápsula (de medicina). **2** BOT. cápsula (donde están las semillas). **3** ASTR. cápsula (espacial). || *adj.* **4** breve, conciso (como una cápsula).

captain | 'kæptɪn | *s.c.* **1** MIL. capitán. **2** DEP. capitán (de un equipo). || *v.t.* **3** capitanear, liderar. || **4 a – of industry,** (fam.) un gran industrial.

caption | 'kæpʃn | *s.c.* **1** PER. encabezamiento, titular. **2** pie, leyenda (de una fotografía, ilustración, etc.). || *v.t.* **3** titular; poner un pie, poner una leyenda (a una fotografía, ilustración o similar).

captious | 'kæpʃəs | *adj.* (form.) capcioso, insidioso, falaz.

captiously | 'kæpʃəslɪ | *adv.* (form.) capciosamente, insidiosamente, falazmente.

captiousness | 'kæpʃəsnɪs | *s.i.* (form.) insidia, falacia.

captivate | 'kæptɪveɪt | *v.t.* fascinar, cautivar (atención o similar).

captivating | 'kæptɪveɪtɪŋ | *adj.* fascinante, cautivante.

captivation | ˌkæptɪ'veɪʃn | *s.i.* encanto, fascinación (que alguien tiene).

captive | 'kæptɪv | *s.c.* **1** cautivo, prisionero. || *adj.* **2** cautivo, prisionero. || **3 – audience,** espectadores fascinados, espectadores encantados. **4 to hold someone –,** mantener a alguien prisionero. **5 to take someone –,** coger a alguien prisionero.

captivity | kæp'tɪvɪtɪ | *s.i.* cautividad, cautiverio.

captor | 'kæptər | *s.c.* aprehensor, persona que hace prisioneros.

capture | 'kæptʃər | *v.t.* **1** MIL. capturar, apresar. **2** MIL. capturar, tomar, conquistar (una posición, pueblo, etc.). **3** capturar (animales). **4** ganar, ganarse, controlar: *we must capture the support of old-age pensioners = debemos ganarnos el apoyo de los pensionistas.* **5** captar, reproducir fielmente (mediante música, pintura, escrito, etc.).

car | kɑːr | (EE.UU. **automobile**) *s.c.* **1** coche; (Am.) carro. **2** (brit.) vagón (de tren): *a sleeping car = un vagón cama.* **3** (EE.UU.) vagón (de pasajeros).

carate | kə'ræf | *s.c.* garrafa.

caramel | 'kærəmel | *s.i.* **1** GAST. caramelo. || *s.c.* **2** dulce, caramelo.

carat | 'kærət | (también **karat**) *s.c.* quilate (para medir oro y diamante).

caravan | 'kærəvæn | *s.c.* **1** (brit.) rulot. **2** caravana (en el desierto).

caravanning | 'kærəvænɪŋ | *s.i.* viaje en rulot (normalmente vacacional).

caravanserai | ˌkærə'vænsəraɪ | *s.c.* **1 posada para caravanas (típico de los parajes desérticos).** **2** (fig.) **[– (of)]** follón, estruendo, agitación (de personas o cosas arremolinadas y ruidosas).

caraway | 'kærəweɪ | *s.i.* BOT. alcaravea.

carbine | 'kɑːbaɪn | *s.c.* carabina (arma de fuego).

carbohydrate | ˌkɑːbəu'haɪdreɪt | *s.c.* e *i.* QUIM. hidrato de carbono.

carbolic acid | kɑːˌbɒlɪk'æsɪd | *s.i.* QUIM. ácido carbólico.

carbon | 'kɑːbən | *s.i.* **1** QUIM. carbono. || *s.c.* **2** papel carbón. **3** copia hecha en papel carbón. || **4 – copy, a)** copia hecha en papel carbón. **b)** réplica exacta, copia exacta (de persona o cosa). **5 – dating,** fijación de fecha por el método del carbono, determinación de la edad por el carbono (de un objeto). **6 – dioxide,** QUIM. dióxido de carbono. **7 – monoxide,** QUIM. monóxido de carbono. **8 – paper,** papel carbón.

carbonated | 'kɑːbəneɪtɪd | *adj.* (form.) carbonatada (agua).

carbuncle | 'kɑːbʌŋkl | *s.c.* **1** MED. carbunco, grano, furúnculo. **2** MIN. carbúnculo (tipo de piedra preciosa parecida al rubí).

carburettor | ˌkɑːbə'retər | (EE.UU. **carburetor**) | 'kɑːrbəreɪtər | *s.c.* MEC. carburador.

carcass | 'kɑːkəs | (también **carcase**) *s.c.* **1** animal muerto; esqueleto (de animal). **2** (fig., fam. y hum. o desp.) corpachón; culo: *take your carcass out of this room = saca el culo de esta habitación.*

carcinogen | kɑː'sɪnədʒen | *s.c.* agente cancerígeno, sustancia cancerígena.

carcinogenic | ˌkɑːsɪnə'dʒenɪk | *adj.* cancerígeno.

carcinoma | ˌkɑːsɪ'nəumə | [*pl.* **carcinomas** o **carcinomata**] *s.c.* MED. carcinoma.

carcinomata | ˌkɑːsɪ'nəʊmətə | *pl.* de **carcinoma.**
card | kɑːd | *s.c.* **1** tarjeta (con señas de una empresa, persona, etc.). **2** carnet, tarjeta (documento oficial). **3** tarjeta (de felicitación o similar). **4** postal (correos). **5** cuartilla, tarjeta, tarjetita (para escribir información). **6** carta, naipe (para juego). **7** (p.u.) tipo gracioso, tipo algo excéntrico. **8** (fig.) ventaja, carta: *I have still got a card my enemies don't know about = yo todavía tengo una carta que mis enemigos no conocen.* || *s.i.* **9** cartulina, papel cartulina. || *s.pl.* **10** cartas (juego). || **11 – index,** fichero. **12 – sharp/– sharper,** tahúr. **13 – vote,** voto colectivo (especialmente en el mundo sindical). **14 to hold/keep one's cards close to one's chest,** comportarse con sigilo sobre las intenciones de uno, mantener los planes de uno en secreto. **15 house of cards,** (fig.) castillo de naipes. **16 to lay/put one's cards on the table,** poner las cartas sobre la mesa. **17 on the cards,** (fam.) probable, casi seguro (de ocurrir). **18 to play one's cards right,** obrar con cuidado, actuar con la debida cautela.
cardamom | 'kɑːdəməm | *s.i.* BOT. cardamomo (una especia).
cardboard | 'kɑːdbɔːd | *s.i.* **1** cartón. || *adj.* **2** (fig.) falso, de cartón, de bisutería (personas, sentimientos, etc.).
card-carrying | 'kɑːdkærɪɪŋ | *adj.* oficialmente inscrito, con carnet: *I am a card-carrying member of the Communist Party = soy un miembro del Partido Comunista con carnet.*
cardiac | 'kɑːdɪæk | *adj.* MED. **1** cardíaco. || **2 – arrest,** paro cardíaco.
cardigan | 'kɑːdɪgən | *s.c.* chaqueta de punto, chaqueta de lana.
cardinal | 'kɑːdɪnl | *s.c.* **1** MAT. número cardinal. **2** REL. cardenal. || *adj.* **3** (form.) cardinal, fundamental, esencial, capital. || **4 – number,** MAT. número cardinal. **5 – point,** GEOG. punto cardinal. **6 – sin, a)** REL. pecado capital. **b)** (fig. y hum.) crimen capital, equivocación importante.
card-table | 'kɑːdteɪbl | *s.c.* mesa de naipes, mesa para jugar a las cartas.
care | keər | *s.i.* **1** cuidado, precisión, atención, esmero: *drink this with a lot of care = bébete esto con mucho cuidado.* **2** atención, cuidado (médico, especialmente hacia personas). || *s.c.* e *i.* **3** preocupación, inquietud: *I have no cares in this world = no tengo preocupaciones en mi vida.* || *v.i.* **4** importar, preocupar(se), inquietar(se): *I don't care what you think about me = no me preocupa lo que pienses de mí.* **5 [to – (for/ about)]** tener cariño, amar; estar dispuesto a amar: *I still care a lot for her = todavía le quiero mucho.* **6 [to – inf./for]** querer, dar la gana, apetecer: *I have a job for him, if he cared to take it = tengo un empleo para él, si quisiera cogerlo; would you care for an apple? = ¿te apetece una manzana?* || **7 to – for, a)** cuidar, atender (algo o alguien). **b)** apetecer, gustar; querer: *I don't care for drink = no me gusta la bebida.* **8 for all I –,** (fam.) me resulta indiferente, no me importa nada, me da lo mismo. **9 in –/into –,** dentro de una institución de atención al niño/anciano/ etc.: *she's been in care all her life = ella lleva toda su vida en instituciones de atención a niños.* **10 I/you/ etc. couldn't – less,** (fam.) me/te importa un pimiento, me/te importa un pepino, me/te importa un pito. **11 take –/take – of yourself,** (fam.) cuídate (despedida en carta o hablando). **12 to take – of, a)** cuidar, atender, encargarse de (persona). **b)** encargarse de, ocuparse de (algo). **13 to take – of oneself,** cuidar uno de sí mismo, protegerse uno a sí mismo. **14 to take – to,** [+ *inf.*] esforzarse por, empeñarse en. **15 who cares?,** (fam.) no me importa, no me preocupa lo más mínimo.
careen | kə'riːn | *v.i.* **1** MAR. carenar, enquillar. **2** (EE.UU.) ir dando tumbos (especialmente vehículos).
career | kə'rɪər | *s.c.* **1** trayecto profesional, carrera profesional: *my career in teaching started in 1974 = mi carrera profesional en la enseñanza comenzó en 1974.* **2** vida, curso vital. || *adj.* **3** profesional, por profesión. || *v.i.* **4** ir a gran velocidad sin control. || **5 – girl/woman,** chica/mujer profesional, chica/mujer dedicada a una profesión, chica/ mujer cuya prioridad es el desempeño de trabajo remunerado. **6 careers,** de orientación profesional, de orientación vocacional: *a careers advice department = un departamento para consejos sobre la orientación vocacional.*
careerist | kə'rɪərɪst | *s.c.* (desp.) persona agresiva en su trabajo; arribista.
carefree | 'keəfriː | *adj.* sin preocupaciones, sin problemas, libre de preocupaciones.
careful | 'keəfl | *adj.* **1** cuidadoso, cauteloso, prudente. **2** cuidadoso, escrupuloso, meticuloso, esmerado (en el trabajo, por ejemplo). **3** cuidadoso, ahorrativo (con el dinero). || **4 –!/be –!,** ¡ten cuidado!, ¡cuidado!
carefully | 'keəfəlɪ | *adv.* **1** cuidadosamente, cautelosamente, prudentemente. **2** cuidadosamente, escrupulosamente, meticulosamente, esmeradamente (trabajando, por ejemplo). **3** cuidadosamente, ahorrativamente (dinero).
carefulness | 'keəflnɪs | *s.i.* **1** cuidado, cautela. **2** escrupulosidad, meticulosidad (en el trabajo o similar).
careless | 'keəlɪs | *adj.* **1** descuidado, negligente, inconsciente. **2** descuidado, relajado, espontáneo (forma de vestir, reír, mirar, etc.). **3** descuidado, irresponsable (con el dinero).
carelessly | 'keəlɪslɪ | *adv.* **1** descuidadamente, negligentemente, inconscientemente. **2** descuidadamente, relajadamente, espontáneamente (cualquier acto). **3** descuidadamente, irresponsablemente (con el dinero).
carelessness | 'keəlɪsnɪs | *s.i.* **1** descuido, negligencia, inconsciencia. **2** relajo, espontaneidad (de un acto). **3** descuido, irresponsabilidad (en el uso del dinero).
caress | kə'res | *v.t.* **1** acariciar. || *s.c.* **2** caricia.
caretaker | 'keəteɪkər | *s.c.* **1** portero, guardia. || *adj.* **2** interino, provisional (gobierno, cargo oficial, administracion, etc.).
careworn | 'keəwɔːn | *adj.* agobiado, lleno de ansiedad.
carfare | 'kɑːfeər | *s.c.* (EE.UU.) precio del trayecto (en autobús o similar).
cargo | 'kɑːgəʊ | [*pl.* **cargoes**] *s.c.* e *i.* cargamento, carga.
caribou | 'kærɪbuː | [*pl.* **caribou** o **caribous**] *s.c.* ZOOL. caribú.
caricature | 'kærɪkətjʊər | *s.c.* e *i.* **1** caricatura. || *s.c.* **2 [– (of)]** (fig.) caricatura, remedo. || *v.t.* **3** caricaturizar, hacer una caricatura de.
caricatured | 'kærɪkətjʊəd | *adj.* caricaturizado, de caricatura, grotesco.
caricaturist | 'kærɪkətjʊərɪst | *s.c.* caricaturista.
caries | 'keəriːz | *s.i.* MED. caries.
caring | keərɪŋ | *s.i.* **1** cariño, afecto. **2** compasión, actitud servicial. || *adj.* **3** compasivo. **4** al cuidado de los necesitados/enfermos/mayores: *a caring agency = una agencia al cuidado de los necesitados.*
carmine | 'kɑːmaɪn | *s.i.* carmín (color).
carnage | 'kɑːnɪdʒ | *s.i.* matanza, carnicería (de personas).
carnal | 'kɑːnl | *adj.* **1** (form. o lit.) carnal. || **2 – knowledge,** (form.) conocimiento carnal, coito.
carnation | kɑː'neɪʃn | *s.c.* BOT. clavel.
carnival | 'kɑːnɪvl | *s.c.* carnaval.
carnivore | 'kɑːnɪvɔːr | *s.c.* BIOL. carnívoro.
carob | | *s.c.* BOT. algarrobo.
carol | 'kærəl | *s.c.* **1** MUS. villancico. || *v.i.* **2** (arc.) MUS. cantar alegremente (personas o pájaros). || **3 to go carolling,** ir a cantar villancicos para conseguir el aguinaldo.
carotid | kə'rɒtɪd | ANAT. *adj.* **1** carótida. || **2 – artery,** arteria carótida.
carouse | kə'raʊz | *v.i.* (p.u.) ir de juerga, ir de jarana.
carousel | ˌkærʊ'sel | (EE.UU. **carrousel**) *s.c.* **1** (EE.UU.) tiovivo. **2** cinta transportadora de equipajes (en un aeropuerto).
carp | kɑːp | [*pl.* **carp**] *s.c.* **1** ZOOL. carpa (pez). || *v.i.* **2 [to – (at/about)]** quejarse.
car-park | 'kɑːpɑːk | *s.c.* aparcamiento de coches, parking.
carpenter | 'kɑːpəntər | *s.c.* carpintero.
carpentry | 'kɑːpəntrɪ | *s.i.* carpintería.
carpet | 'kɑːpɪt | *s.c.* **1** alfombra. **2** (fig.) tapiz, alfombra (de cualquier

cosa). || *v.t.* **3** alfombrar. **4** (fig.) tapizar, alfombrar. || **5 – slipper,** zapatillas. **6 – sweeper,** escoba para barrer la alfombra. **7 on the –,** (fam.) a punto de recibir una regañina. **6 to sweep something under the –,** V. **sweep.**

carpetbagger | 'kɑːpɪtbægər | *s.c.* (EE.UU. y desp.) político de fuera de la localidad.

carpeted | 'kɑːpɪtɪd | *adj.* alfombrado.

carriage | 'kærɪdʒ | *s.c.* **1** (brit.) vagón (de tren). **2** coche de caballos, carruaje. **3** MEC. carro (de una máquina de escribir o similar). || *s.i.* **4** transporte, costo de transporte. **5** porte, postura (de una persona).

carriageway | 'kærɪdʒweɪ | *s.c.* (brit.) carril (de una carretera).

carrier | 'kærɪər | *s.c.* **1** transportista, transportador, empresa de transporte. **2** MIL. portaaviones. **3** MED. portador (de gérmenes, bacterias, etc.). **4** MEC. soporte transportador, soporte portador (en cualquier mecanismo). || **5 – bag,** (brit.) bolsa (para las compras). **6 – pigeon,** ZOOL. paloma mensajera.

carrillon | kə'rɪljən | (EE.UU.) | 'kærəlɒn | *s.c.* MUS. carrillón.

carrion | 'kærɪən | *s.i.* carroña.

carrot | 'kærət | *s.c.* e *i.* **1** zanahoria. || *s.c.* **2** (fig.) incentivo.

carroty | 'kærətɪ | *adj.* pelirrojo.

carry | 'kærɪ | *v.t.* **1** transportar, llevar, llevar en brazos. **2** MED. portar, transmitir (enfermedades, microbios, etc.). **3** PER. publicar (noticia, artículo, etc.). **4** POL. ganar en, conseguir los votos de (distrito, circunscripción, etc.): *he only carried one State = sólo ganó en un Estado.* **5** llevar aparejado, acarrear, significar (un castigo). **6** aprobar, pasar (moción, acuerdo, etc.). **7** soportar el peso de, aguantar todo el trabajo de (peso físico, responsabilidad grande, etc.): *he carried the office = él llevaba el peso de la oficina.* **8** conllevar, tener en sí (como consecuencia): *political power carries a lot of responsibility = el poder político conlleva mucha responsabilidad.* **9 [to – + *o.* + through]** llevar a término, aguantar durante (algo desagradable): *this money will help to carry you through the winter = este dinero te ayudará a aguantar durante el invierno.* **10 [to – + *o.* + with]** convencer, entusiasmar: *he carried everybody with him = él entusiasmó a todos.* **11** (p.u.) estar embarazada de: *I was carrying John when I finished the course = yo estaba embarazada de John cuando acabé el curso.* **12** desarrollar, llevar hasta (ideas, planes, etc.): *he carried that idea to its logical conclusion = llevó esa idea a su conclusión lógica.* **13** tener (en una tienda): *we don't carry post-cards = no tenemos postales.* || *v.i.* **14** oírse, llegar (sonidos y recorridos de distancias). || *v.r.* **15** moverse, andar, tener una postura (corporalmente). || **16 to be/get carried away,** perder el control (por emoción, pasión, etc.). **17 to – a load/burden,** llevar un peso encima, tener como una losa encima (de excesivo trabajo, responsabilidad, etc.). **18 to – coals to Newcastle,** V. **coal. 19 to – everything before one/to – all before one,** vencer todos los obstáculos ante uno, arrollar todos los obstáculos ante uno. **20 to – in one's head/mind,** retener en la cabeza (sin necesidad de escribirlo o parecido). **21 to – off, a)** llevarse, ganar, alzarse con (un premio). **b)** salir airoso en: *he carried everything off = salió airoso en todo.* **22 to – on, a)** continuar, no parar, no cesar (de hacer algo). **b)** (fam.) ponerse (de un determinado humor): *the way he carried on about politics! = ¡cómo se puso con la política!* **c)** seguir, llevar a cabo, conducir (una actividad): *my study on lions could not be carried on = mi estudio sobre los leones no pudo ser llevado a cabo.* **23 to – on (with),** (fam., p.u. y desp.) tener una relación amorosa ilícita (con). **24 to – out,** llevar a cabo, cumplir, realizar: *I want my orders carried out to the letter = quiero que mis órdenes se cumplan al pie de la letra.* **25 to – over,** llevar hasta, seguir haciendo uso de: *we must not carry our adolescent dreams over into adulthood = no debemos seguir haciendo uso de nuestros sueños adolescentes en la edad madura.* **26 to – the can,** V. **can. 27 to – the day,** llevarse el triunfo, conseguir la victoria, triunfar. **28 to – through,** sacar a flote, hacer que salga algo adelante, llevar a buen término (especialmente lo que es difícil). **29 to – weigh/to – a lot of weight,** tener peso, tener influencia, gozar de influencias (persona u opinión).

carry-all | 'kærɪɔːl | *s.c.* (EE.UU.) bolsa grande, cesta grande.

carrycot | 'kærɪkɒt | *s.c.* (brit.) cestillo, capazo (para bebés).

carry-on | 'kærɪɒn | *s.sing.* (fam., brit. y desp.) comportamiento exagerado, lío, conmoción.

carsick | 'kɑːsɪk | *adj.* mareado (yendo en coche).

carsickness | 'kɑːsɪknɪs | *s.i.* mareo (causado por coche).

cart | kɑːt | *s.i.* **1** carro, carromato, carreta (tirada por animales). **2** pequeña berlina (para personas). **3** carretilla (de mano). || *v.t.* **4** llevar en carro, transportar en carro. **5** (fam.) ir tirando de (persona o cosa con dificultad). || **6 to – off,** arrastrar, llevarse a rastras. **7 to put the – before the horse,** hacer las cosas al revés, tomar el rábano por las hojas.

carte blanche | ˌkɑːt'blɒnʃ | *s.i.* [;ms + *inf.*] carta blanca.

cartel | kɑː'tel | *s.c.* FIN. cartel (para control de precios y de la competencia).

carthorse | 'kɑːthɔːs | *s.c.* caballo de tiro.

cartilage | 'kɑːtɪlɪdʒ | *s.c.* e *i.* ANAT. cartílago.

cartilaginous | ˌkɑːtɪ'lædʒɪnəs | *adj.* ANAT. cartilaginoso.

cart-load | 'kɑːtləʊd | *s.c.* carretada (cantidad que transporta un carro).

cartographer | kɑː'tɒgrəfər | *s.c.* cartógrafo.

cartography | kɑː'tɒgrəfɪ | *s.i.* cartografía.

carton | 'kɑːtən | *s.c.* **1** caja de cartón. **2** envase (para líquidos).

cartoon | kɑː'tuːn | *s.c.* **1** PER. chiste, viñeta de humor, caricatura. **2** dibujo animado. **3** (brit.) PER. historieta de dibujos, historieta humorística, tira cómica (en periódicos). **4** ART. cartón (esbozo preliminar).

cartoonist | kɑː'tuːnɪst | *s.c.* PER. dibujante cómico.

cartridge | 'kɑːtrɪdʒ | *s.c.* **1** cartucho. **2** brazo del tocadiscos. **3** recambio (de bolígrafo o pluma). **4** FOT. cartucho. || **5 – paper,** papel de dibujo (duro).

cartridge-belt | 'kɑːtrɪdʒbelt | *s.c.* canana, cartuchera.

cartwheel | 'kɑːtwiːl | *s.c.* **1** rueda, rueda de carro. **2** pirueta de lado, pirueta mortal de lado. || *v.i.* **3** dar piruetas, hacer piruetas.

carve | kɑːv | *v.t.* **1** ART. tallar, cincelar (escultura). **2** (fig.) tallar, cincelar, labrar (el viento, la lluvia, etc.). || *v.t.* e *i.* **3** tallar, grabar (en madera, metal, etc.). **4** trinchar (carne). | **5 to – out,** (fam.) labrarse (una carrera, una vida, etc.). **6 to – out (of),** abrir un espacio, excavar un sitio libre (para hacer una obra). **7 to – up, a)** (fam. y fig.) acuchillar, herir a cuchilladas. **b)** trocear, cortar en trozos.

carving | 'kɑːvɪŋ | *s.i.* **1** talla (de objetos como adorno). || *s.c.* e *i.* **2** grabado (en madera, metal, etc.). || *s.c.* **3** escultura, escultura pequeña. || **4 – knife,** cuchillo de trinchar, trinchante.

cascade | kæ'skeɪd | *s.c.* **1** cascada, salto de agua. **2** (lit. y fig.) cascada, como en cascada (pelo o parecido). || *v.i.* **3** caer en cascada (agua). **4** (lit. y fig.) caer como en cascada (pelo o parecido).

case | keɪs | *s.c.* **1** caso, situación: *this is not our case = éste no es nuestro caso.* **2** caso, ejemplo, caso concreto. **3** caja. **4** maleta. **5** MED. caso. **6** GRAM. caso. **7** vitrina. **8** caja de 12 unidades (de bebida). **9** DER. caso. **10** BOT. vaina (donde están las semillas). **11** estuche, funda (de una guitarra, joya, etc.). **12** caso (policíaco). **13** caso (persona): *he is a hopeless case = él es un caso sin esperanza.* **14 [– (for/against)]** DER. evidencia, pruebas. **15 [– (for/against)]** hechos, argumentos: *there's a very good case for the installation of nuclear plants = hay muy buenos argumentos a favor de la instalación de centrales nucleares.* || *s.sing.* **16 [a –]** (fam.) un caso, un poema. || *v.t.* **17 [to – + *o.* + in]** enfundar en; revestir de (cubriendo el objeto): *the castle was cased in fog = el castillo estaba envuelto en niebla.* **18** (fam.) inspeccionar (lugar donde se piensa robar). || **19 as the – may be/ wha-**

tever the – may be, según salga la cosa, según el caso (no hay seguridad de lo que ocurrirá). **20 to be a – in point,** ser un ejemplo que hace al caso. **21 to be a – of,** ser una situación real de: *it is a case of not being able how to study it = es una situación real de no saber cómo estudiarlo.* **22 to be the –,** ser el caso, ser la realidad, ser la situación real. **23 – history,** historial, antecedentes; MED. historial, historia clínica. **24 – law,** DER. derecho consuetudinario, jurisprudencia. **25 in any case, a)** en cualquier caso, en todo caso; además: *he was tired and, in any case, it was too late = estaba cansado y, en cualquier caso, era demasiado tarde.* **b)** al menos, por lo menos: *his teachings or in any case his example were very influential = sus enseñanzas o al menos su ejemplo fueron de gran influencia.* **26 in –,** por si acaso, por si: *get ready in case she arrives = prepárate por si llega ella.* **27 in – of,** en caso de, por si hubiera: *in case of an emergency = por si hubiera una emergencia.* **28 in many/quite a lot/etc. cases,** en muchos/bastantes/etc. casos, en muchas/bastantes/etc. ocasiones. **29 in no –,** en ningún caso, en ninguna ocasión. **30 in that –/in which –,** en ese caso/en cuyo caso, en esa circunstancia/en cuya circunstancia. **31 to make a –/to make out a – (for/against),** presentar argumentos convincentes (a favor/en contra), establecer un punto de vista convincentemente (a favor/en contra). **32 to make one's –/to make the – (for/ against),** demostrar el punto de vista de uno (a favor/en contra).

casebook | 'keɪsbʊk | *s.c.* registro, diario (de personas tratadas por un médico, detective, etc.).

casement | 'keɪsmənt | (también **casement window**) *s.c.* ventana batiente, ventana a bisagra.

case-study | 'keɪsstʌdɪ | *s.c.* estudio monográfico, estudio específico, estudio especializado (sobre cualquier tema).

casework | 'keɪswəːk | *s.i.* trabajo de asistencia social, trabajo de rehabilitación social.

caseworker | 'keɪswəːkər | *s.c.* asistente social.

cash | kæʃ | *s.i.* **1** dinero en efectivo, dinero contante y sonante. **2** (fam.) dinero, parné. || *v.t.* **3** hacer efectivo (cheque o similar). || **4 – crop,** AGR. producción agrícola de rápida venta, cultivo de venta inmediata (no para consumición del granjero). **5 – dispenser,** FIN. cajero automático. **6 – down,** al contado. **7 – flow,** FIN. cash flow, flujo de efectivo, movimiento de dinero. **8 to – in (on),** sacar tajada de, aprovecharse astutamente de. **9 – on delivery,** COM. pago contra recepción. **10 – register,** caja registradora. **11 in –,** en efectivo, en dinero contante y sonante.

cash-and-carry | ˌkæʃən'kærɪ | *s.c.* tienda al por mayor.

cashbook | 'kæʃbʊk | *s.c.* COM. libro de caja.

cash-box | 'kæʃbɒks | *s.c.* caja (del dinero).

cash-desk | 'kæʃdesk | *s.c.* caja (donde uno paga).

cashier | kæ'ʃɪər | *s.c.* **1** cajero, caja. || *v.t.* **2** MIL. separar del servicio, dar la baja, despedir (del ejército).

cashmere | ˌkæʃ'mɪər | *s.i.* cachemira.

cashpoint | 'kæʃpɔɪnt | cajero automático.

casing | 'keɪsɪŋ | *s.c.* envoltura, revestimiento.

casino | kə'siːnəʊ | *s.c.* casino.

cask | kɑːsk | (EE.UU.) | kæsk | *s.c.* tonel, barril.

casket | 'kɑːskɪt | (EE.UU.) | 'kæskɪt | *s.c.* **1** cofrecito, cajita, arquilla, joyero (especialmente para cosas valiosas). **2** (EE.UU.) ataúd.

cassava | kə'sɑːvə | *s.i.* BOT. mandioca.

casserole | 'kæsərəʊl | *s.c.* **1** cazuela. || *s.c.* e *i.* **2** GAST. plato de una mezcla de verdura y carne o pescado cocinado lentamente al horno. || *v.t.* **3** GAST. cocinar a la cazuela (carne o pescado).

cassette | kə'set | *s.c.* **1** casete, cinta. **2** magnetofón, caset (aparato). || **3 – player/– recorder,** magnetofón/grabadora.

cassock | 'kæsək | *s.c.* sotana.

cast | kɑːst | (EE.UU.) | kæst | *v.* [*pret.* y *p.p. irreg.* **cast**] *t.* **1** echar, lanzar (mirada, vista, ojos, etc.). **2** BIOL. mudar de (piel o similar por parte de ciertos animales). **3** formar, moldear (objetos); vaciar (esculturas). **4 [to – + *o.* + (as)]** ART. dar un papel, conceder un papel (en teatro, cine, etc.): *I was cast as the teacher = me dieron el papel del profesor.* **5 [to – + *o.* + (on)]** echar (maldición, encantamiento, etc.). **6** DEP. lanzar, tirar (la caña al pescar). **7 [to – + *o.* + (on/upon)]** arrojar (dudas, sospechas, etc.). **8** (lit.) lanzar, echar, arrojar (luz o sombra). **9** (form. o lit.) arrojar, tirar, echar (algo o alguien). **10 [to – + *o.* + as/in]** describir como, poner la etiqueta de: *how can you cast your workmates as bums? = ¿cómo puedes poner a tus compañeros la etiqueta de vagos?* **11** (form.) quitarse, echar fuera de sí (un pensamiento negativo o similar). || *i.* **12** DEP. hacer un lanzamiento (de la caña de pescar). || *s.c.* **13** [=N *v.sing./pl.*] reparto (de actores). **14** DEP. lanzamiento (con la caña de pescar). **15** molde, forma: *a cast of my wife's hands = un molde de las manos de mi mujer.* **16** molde (objeto). **17** MED. escayola, vendaje enyesado (para roturas, esguinces, etc.). **18** ligera bizquera. **19 [– of]** (form.) clase de, tipo de (carácter, actitud mental, etc.). || **20 to be – in the same mould/in someone's mould,** V. **mould. 21 to – about/around (for),** (form.) intentar dar (con), buscar rápidamente (una expresión afortunada, la palabra correcta, etc.). **22 to – anchor,** V. **anchor. 23 to – aside,** rechazar, apartar (algo o alguien). **24 to – a vote,** depositar un voto, votar. **25 to – away,** (lit.) descartar, desembarazarse de, arrojar fuera de uno. **26 to – down,** (form.) echar abajo, rebajar (normalmente de categoría, clase social, etc.). **27 to – lots,** V. **lot. 28 to – off, a)** quitarse de encima, desechar, arrojar lejos (porque no deja progresar). **b)** MAR. levar anclas; quitar amarras. **c)** menguar (en costura). **29 to – on,** echar puntos (comenzar la labor de costura). **30 to – one's eye over something,** V. **eye. 31 to – one's mind back,** rememorar, recordar. **32 to – one's net wider,** V. **net. 33 to – one's spell on,** encantar, fascinar, dejar maravillado. **34 to – out,** (lit.) arrojar del lado de uno, expulsar del lado de uno. **35 to – pearls before swine,** V. **pearl. 36 to – up,** arrojar (el mar restos de naufragio, animales muertos, etc.). **37 the die is –,** V. **die.**

castanet | ˌkæstə'net | *s.c.* castañuela.

castaway | 'kɑːstəweɪ | (EE.UU.) | 'kæstəweɪ | *s.c.* náufrago.

caste | kɑːst | *s.c.* e *i.* **1** casta (especialmente en la India). **2** (fig.) casta, clase. || **3 to lose –,** perder el prestigio social, descender en la escala social.

caster V. **castor.**

castigate | 'kæstɪgeɪt | *v.t.* (form.) reprobar, censurar.

castigation | ˌkæstɪ'geɪʃn | *s.c.* e *i.* (form.) reprobación, censura.

casting | 'kɑːstɪŋ | (EE.UU.) | 'kæstɪŋ | *s.c.* **1** MET. fundición, pieza de fundición, molde fundido. || **2 – vote,** voto de calidad (del presidente).

cast-iron | ˌkɑːst'aɪən | (EE.UU.) | ˌkæst'aɪərn | *s.i.* **1** MET. hierro fundido. || *adj.* **2** irrefutable (excusa, coartada, etc.).

castle | 'kɑːsl | (EE.UU.) | 'kæsl | *s.c.* **1** castillo, fortaleza. **2** torre (en el ajedrez). || **3 an Englishman's home is his –,** la casa de un inglés es su refugio privado. **4 castles in the air,** castillos en el aire.

cast-off | 'kɑːstɒf | (EE.UU.) | 'kæstɒf | *adj.* **1** para tirar, inservible, viejo y sucio (especialmente de la ropa). **2** rechazado, no querido (un viejo, por ejemplo). || *s.c.* **3** ropa vieja.

castor | 'kɑːstər | (EE.UU.) | 'kæstər | (también **caster**) *s.c.* **1** MEC. ruedecilla. || **2 – oil,** aceite de ricino. **3 – sugar** (también **caster sugar**), azúcar extrafino.

castrate | kæs'treɪt | (EE.UU.) | 'kæstreɪt | *v.t.* castrar.

castration | kæs'treɪʃn | (EE.UU.) | 'kæstreɪʃn | *s.i.* castración.

casual | 'kæʒʊəl | *adj.* **1** casual, fortuito, no planeado, no intencionado. **2** casual, distraido, superficial: *a casual look = una mirada distraida.* **3** indiferente, despreocupado (cualidad personal). **4** informal (ropa). **5** temporal, eventual (trabajo no fijo).

casually | 'kæʒʊəlɪ | *adv.* **1** casualmente, fortuitamente. **2** casualmente, desinteresadamente, superficialmente. **3** indiferentemente, despreocupadamente (forma de comportarse). **4** informalmente (forma de vestir).

casualness | 'kæʒʊəlnɪs | *s.i.* indiferencia, despreocupación (cualidad personal).

casualty | 'kæʒʊəltɪ | *s.c.* **1** MIL. baja. **2** víctima, accidentado grave. **3 [– of]** (fig.) víctima de: *she was the first casualty of the political campaign = ella fue la primera víctima de la campaña política.* || *s.i.* **4** accidentes: *the casualty ward = la sección de accidentes.*

casuistry | 'kæzjʊɪstrɪ | *s.i.* (form.) FIL. casuística.

cat | kæt | *s.c.* **1** gato. **2** ZOOL. felino (león, tigre, etc.). || **3 a game of – and mouse,** el juego del gato y del ratón (una persona con poder burlándose de otra indefensa). **4 curiosity killed the –,** la curiosidad mató al gato (significando que no hay que ser curiosos). **5 has the – got your tongue?,** V. **tongue. 6 to let the – out of the bag,** revelar el secreto, soltar el secreto. **7 like – and dog,** como el perro y el gato; siempre peleándose. **8 to look like something the – brought in/dragged in,** tener una pinta de sucio que no va más. **9 look what the – has brought in,** mira quién ha venido (con sorpresa alegre). **10 to rain cats and dogs,** V. **rain. 11 to set the – among the pigeons,** V. **pigeon. 12 there are more ways than one to skin a –,** hay muchas maneras de hacer las cosas (no se puede ser dogmático). **13 there's not enough room to swing a –,** no cabe ni un alfiler, no hay sitio ni para respirar. **14 while the – is away, the mice will play,** mientras los gatos duermen, los ratones bailan.

cataclysm | 'kætaklɪzəm | *sc* **1** cataclismo (natural). **2** (fig.) cataclismo (político, social, etc.).

cataclysmic | ˌkætə'klɪzmɪk | *adj.* catastrófico, desastroso.

catacombs | 'kætəkuːmz | (EE.UU.) | 'kætəkəumz | *s.pl.* catacumbas.

catalepsy | 'kætəlepsɪ | *s.i.* MED. catalepsia.

cataleptic | ˌkætə'leptɪk | MED. *adj.* **1** cataléptico. || *s.c.* **2** cataléptico.

catalog | 'kætəlɒg | (*brit.* **catalogue** | 'kætəlɔːg) *s.c.* **1** catálogo (de una exposición, tienda, etc.). **2 [– of]** (fig.) serie de, enumeración de. || *v.t.* **3** catalogar (libros, cuadros, etc.). **4** (fig.) enumerar, hacer una enumeración de.

catalysis | kə'tælɪsɪs | *s.i.* QUIM. catálisis.

catalytic | ˌkætə'lɪtɪk | *adj.* QUIM. catalítico.

catalyst | 'kætəlɪst | *s.c.* **1** QUIM. catalizador. **2** (fig.) catalizador (de un hecho histórico, acontecimiento político, etc.).

catamaran | ˌkætəmə'ræn | *s.c.* MAR. catamarán.

catapult | 'kætəpʌlt | *s.c.* **1** (brit.) tirador (de un chico). **2** AER. lanzador (de aviones en un portaaviones). **3** HIST. catapulta (antigua). || *v.t.* **4** catapultar, lanzar. **5** (fig.) catapultar inesperadamente (a la fama, a un puesto superior, etc.). || *v.i.* **6** lanzarse violentamente, catapultarse.

cataract | 'kætərækt | *s.c.* **1** MED. catarata (ocular). **2** GEOG. catarata.

catarrh | kə'tɒː | *s.i.* MED. catarro con mucosidad.

catastrophe | kə'tæstrəfɪ | *s.c.* catástrofe, desastre.

catastrophic | ˌkætə'strɒfɪk | *adj.* catastrófico, desastroso.

catastrophically | ˌkætə'strɒfɪkəlɪ | *adv.* catastróficamente, desastrosamente.

catcall | 'kætkɔːl | *s.c.* silbido, abucheo, silbatina (en contra).

catch | kætʃ | *v.* [*pret.* y *p.p. irreg.* **caught**] *t.* **1** coger, capturar, agarrar. **2** coger, prender, capturar (a un criminal). **3** pillarse (dedo o similar). **4** coger (a alguien haciendo algo). **5** dar con, coger (a una persona a la que se está buscando). **6** coger, agarrar (autobús, tren, etc.). **7** contraer, coger (enfermedad). **8** coger, oír (algo que se ha dicho). **9** dar sobre (la luz): *the morning light caught the dew on the grass = la luz matutina dio sobre la escarcha en la hierba.* **10** captar, apresar (un ambiente, paisaje, etc.). **11** adoptar, ser influenciado por (sentimientos de otros): *after a few minutes I started to catch her nerves = después de unos minutos comencé a ser influenciado por sus nervios.* **12** llevarse, arrastrar (el viento o el agua). **13** notar, coger, darse cuenta de (una mirada, suspiro, sentimiento, etc.). **14** (fam.) no perderse (un programa, película, espectáculo, etc.). **15** dar, atizar, pegar (en una parte del cuerpo): *the blow caught him on the head = el golpe le pegó en la cabeza.* **16** atraer, captar (la atención, el interés, etc.). **17 [to – + *o.* + without]** coger, pillar (a alguien) sin: *the teacher caught him without his tie = el profesor le pilló sin la corbata.* **18** captar, entender, comprender: *I caught his hint = comprendí su indirecta.* || *i.* **19** engancharse, enredarse, cogerse (la ropa, una extremidad corporal, etc.). || *r.* **20** contenerse, controlarse (para no hacer o decir algo): *I was going to hit him but I caught myself = iba a pegarle pero me controlé.* **21** encontrarse (a sí mismo haciendo algo inconscientemente): *I suddenly caught myself climbing the tree = de repente me encontré trepando el árbol.* || *s.c.* **22** pesca, cantidad de peces atrapados. **23** cogida, acto de agarrar, acto de coger. **24** MEC. pasador, retén, pestillo. || *s.sing.* **25** (fam.) trampa, truco, engañifa: *there's no catch in this situation = no hay trampa en esta situación.* **26** nudo (en la garganta), voz entrecortada. || *s.i.* **27** coger (cualquier juego a coger a otro o atrapar una pelota). || **28 to be caught in,** estar atrapado en, quedar atrapado en (situación difícil, tormenta, etc.). **29 to be caught out,** coger fuera de juego, coger desprevenido (un acontecimiento reciente). **30 to be caught short,** V. **short. 31 to – a glimpse of/to – sight of,** ver momentáneamente, ver fugazmente. **32 to – at,** agarrar, echar mano de (agarrando). **33 to – fire,** V. **fire. 34 to – hold of,** V. **hold. 35 to – on,** (fam.) hacerse popular, ponerse de moda. **36 to – on (to),** (fam.) entender, comprender, coger. **37 to – one's breath,** V. **breath. 38 to =N out,** coger desprevenido, coger (en un renuncio, equivocación, etc.). **39 to – someone's eye,** V. **eye. 40 to – the light/sunlight,** reflejarse a la luz, brillar a la luz. **41 to – the post,** coger al cartero (antes de que vacíe el buzón). **42 to – the sun,** V. **sun. 43 Catch-22,** situación en la que no se puede avanzar, situación en la que hay un círculo vicioso que impide el progreso. **44 to – up (on/with),** recuperar, ponerse al corriente (trabajo, falta de sueño, etc.). **45 to – up (with),** alcanzar, llegar al mismo nivel que, llegar a la altura de (física o intelectualmente). **46 to – up with, a)** arrestar, dar finalmente con (un criminal). **b)** afectar, alcanzar (algo desagradable): *don't laugh, some problems will catch up with you soon = no te rías, algunos problemas te afectarán pronto a ti también.* **47 you'll – it,** (fam. y p.u.) te la vas a cargar. **48 you wouldn't – me...,** (fam.) a mí no me cogerás (haciendo algo que el hablante no desea).

catcher | 'kætʃər | *s.c.* DEP. receptor, catcher (en el béisbol).

catching | 'kætʃɪŋ | *adj.* contagioso, infeccioso (enfermedad).

catchment area | 'kætʃmənt,eərɪə | *s.c.* zona de influencia (de un hospital, escuela, etc.).

catchphrase | 'kætʃfreɪz | *s.c.* frase atrayente, eslogan, frase pegadiza (de la publicidad, propaganda política, etc.).

catchy | 'kætʃɪ | *adj.* pegadizo (música o similar).

catechism | 'kætəkɪzəm | *s.c.* REL. catecismo.

categorical | ˌkætɪ'gɒrɪkl | (EE.UU.) | ˌkætə'gɔːrɪkl | *adj.* categórico, rotundo.

categorically | ˌkætɪ'gɒrɪklɪ | (EE.UU.) | ˌkætə'gɔːrɪklɪ | *adv.* categóricamente, rotundamente.

categorization | ˌkætɪgərɪ'zeɪʃn | (EE.UU.) | ˌkætɪgerɪ'zeɪʃn | (también **categorisation**) *s.c.* e *i.* categorización, agrupamiento, clasificación.

categorize | 'kætɪgəraɪz | (también **categorise**) *v.t.* categorizar, clasificar, agrupar.

category | 'kætɪgərɪ | (EE.UU.) | 'kætəgɔːrɪ | *s.c.* categoría (clase).

cater | 'keɪtər | *v.i.* **1 [to – to/for]** intentar complacer a, intentar satisfacer los deseos de. **2 [to – for]** proveer de comida y bebida a, abastecer a (especialmente en acontecimientos sociales).

caterer | 'keɪtərər | *s.c.* abastecedor, proveedor (especialmente referido a banquetes).

catering | 'keɪtərɪŋ | *s.i.* organización de banquetes; suministro, abastecimiento (de fiestas).

caterpillar | 'kætəpɪlər | *s.c.* 1 BIOL. oruga. || 2 **– tracks,** cadenas (de un tanque o similar). 3 **– tractor,** tractor oruga.
caterwaul | 'kætəwɔːl | *v.i.* 1 chillar estridentemente. || *s.sing.* 2 chillido estridente.
catfish | 'kætfɪʃ | *s.c.* ZOOL. barbo; (Am.) bagre.
catharsis | kə'θɑːsɪs | *s.i.* (form.) LIT. catarsis.
cathartic | kə'θɑːtɪk | *adj.* (form.) LIT. catártico.
cathedral | kə'θiːdrəl | *s.c.* catedral.
cathode | 'kæθəʊd | ELECTR. *s.c.* 1 cátodo. || 2 **cathode-ray tube,** tubo de rayos catódicos.
Catholic | 'kæθəlɪk | *s.c.* 1 REL. católico. || *adj.* 2 REL. católico. || 3 **catholic,** (form.) universal, amplio, general.
Catholicism | kə'θɒləsɪzəm | *s.i.* REL. catolicismo.
catkin | 'kætkɪn | *s.c.* BOT. amento, candelilla.
catnap | 'kætnæp | (fam.) *s.c.* 1 sueñecito, cabezada. || *v.i.* 2 dar una cabezada, echar un sueñecito.
cat's-cradle | ˌkætskreɪdl | *s.c.* e *i.* cunita (juego o forma).
cat's-eye | 'kætsaɪ | *s.c.* baliza luminosa de carretera.
cat's-paw | 'kætspɔː | *s.c.* (p.u. y fig.) lacayo.
cat-suit | 'kætsuːt | *s.c.* mono (para mujeres).
catsup | 'kætsəp | *s.i.* ketchup, salsa de tomate.
cattle | 'kætl | *s.pl.* ganado.
cattle-grid | 'kætlgrɪd | *s.c.* enrejado para evitar el paso de ganado.
cattleman | 'kætlmæn | *s.c.* ganadero.
cattle-market | 'kætlmɑːkɪt | *s.c.* 1 mercado de ganado. 2 (desp. y fig.) mercado de carne, mercado sexual (referido a mujeres, especialmente en concursos de belleza).
cattily | 'kætɪlɪ | *adv.* (desp.) maliciosamente, rencorosamente (de mujeres).
cattiness | 'kætɪnɪs | *s.i.* (desp.) malicia, rencor (normalmente mujeres).
catty | 'kætɪ | *adj.* (desp.) maliciosa, rencorosa.
catwalk | 'kætwɔːk | *s.c.* 1 pasarela (para modelos). 2 ARQ. pasarela (entre dos edificios, o partes del mismo edificio).
caucus | 'kɔːkəs | *s.c.* POL. 1 consejo político (de un partido). 2 reunión política. 3 (EE.UU.) comisión electoral (dentro de un partido).
caught | kɔːt | *pret.* y *p.p. irreg.* 1 de **catch.** || 2 **to be – up in,** estar metido en, estar comprometido en.
cauldron | 'kɔːldrən | (también **caldron**) *s.c.* caldero.
cauliflower | 'kɒlɪflaʊər, (EE.UU.) | 'kɔːlɪflaʊər | *s.c.* e *i.* BOT. coliflor.
causal | 'kɔːzl | *adj.* 1 FIL. causal. 2 GRAM. causal.
causality | kɔː'zælɪtɪ | (también **causation**) *s.i.* FIL. causalidad.
causally | 'kɔːzəlɪ | *adv.* como causa.
causation | kɔː'zeɪʃn | V. **causality.**
causative | 'kɔːzətɪv | *adj.* 1 FIL. causativo. 2 GRAM. causativo.
cause | kɔːz | *s.c.* 1 causa, motivo. 2 causa (especialmente política). 3 DER. causa. || *s.i.* 4 [– *inf.*/*for*] motivo de, razón de, causa de. || *v.t.* 5 causar, ocasionar, provocar, motivar. || 6 **a lost –,** V. **lost.** 7 **– célèbre,** causa célebre, caso famoso, caso muy conocido. 8 **in/for a good –,** por una buena causa, por una causa noble.
causeway | 'kɔːzweɪ | *s.c.* calzada (carretera elevada).
caustic | 'kɔːstɪk | *adj.* 1 corrosivo, cáustico. 2 (fig.) cáustico, mordaz (comentario). || 3 **– soda,** QUIM. sosa cáustica.
caustically | 'kɔːstɪklɪ | *adv.* cáusticamente, mordazmente (comentario).
cauterize | 'kɔːtəraɪz | (también **cauterise**) *v.t.* cauterizar (herida).
caution | 'kɔːʃn | *s.i.* 1 prevención, cautela, prudencia, precaución. || *s.c.* 2 aviso, advertencia, amonestación. 3 DER. amonestación. || *v.t.* 4 avisar, advertir (a alguien de un peligro, problema, etc.). 5 DER. amonestar, hacer una amonestación formal. || 5 **to throw – to the winds,** V. **wind.**
cautionary | 'kɔːʃənərɪ | (EE.UU.) | 'kɔːʃənerɪ | *adj.* aleccionador, admonitorio, de escarmiento.
cautious | 'kɔːʃəs | *adj.* cuidadoso, cauteloso, precavido, prudente.
cautiously | 'kɔːʃəslɪ | *adv.* cuidadosamente, cautelosamente, precavidamente, prudentemente.
cautiousness | 'kɔːʃəsnɪs | *s.i.* cuidado, cautela, precaución, prudencia.
cavalcade | ˌkævl'keɪd | *s.c.* cabalgata, desfile (con caballos).
cavalier | ˌkævə'lɪər | *adj.* 1 arrogante, desdeñoso, altivo. || *s.c.* 2 (hum.) galán (acompañando a una dama). || 3 **Cavalier,** HIST. partidario del Rey Carlos I en la Guerra Civil inglesa.
cavalry | 'kævlrɪ | *s.sing.* **[the –]** MIL. la caballería (en caballos o tanques).
cave | keɪv | *s.c.* 1 cueva, caverna. || 2 **to – in, a)** derrumbarse, ceder (un techo). **b)** (fig.) rendirse, ceder, capitular.
caveat | 'kævɪæt | | 'keɪvɪæt | *s.c.* 1 (form.) advertencia, precaución. 2 DER. notificación, notificación de suspensión.
cave-in | 'keɪvɪn | *s.c.* derrumbamiento, derrumbe (de un techo o similar).
caveman | 'keɪvmæn | [*pl.irreg.* **cavemen**] *s.c.* 1 hombre de las cavernas. 2 (fig. y fam.) bruto, bestia.
cavemen | 'keɪvmən | *pl.irreg.* de **caveman.**
cavern | 'kævən | *s.c.* gruta, caverna (grande).
cavernous | 'kævənəs | *adj.* cavernoso (espacio, ojos, etc.).
caviar | 'kævɪɑːr | | kə'vɪɑːr | (también **caviare**) *s.i.* 1 caviar. || 2 **to be – to the general,** (hum. o p.u.) ser demasiado exquisito para paladares rudos.
cavil | 'kævɪl | (form.) *v.i.* 1 **[to – (at)]** poner reparos. || *s.c.* 2 reparo, crítica trivial.
cavity | 'kævɪtɪ | *s.c.* 1 cavidad, oquedad, hueco. 2 MED. caries. || 3 **– wall,** ARQ. pared doble (con espacio en medio).
cavort | kə'vɔːt | *v.i.* hacer cabriolas, dar saltos, retozar.
caw | kɔː | *v.i.* 1 graznar (ciertas aves). || *s.c.* 2 graznido.
cayenne | keɪ'en | (también **cayenne pepper**) *s.i.* pimentón (un tipo).
cayman | 'keɪmən | (también **caiman**) *s.c.* ZOOL. caimán.
cease | siːs | (form.) *v.i.* 1 cesar, terminar. 2 **[to –** *inf.*/*ger.***]** dejar de, cesar de: *he ceased to be a member last year = dejó de ser miembro el año pasado.* || *v.t.* 3 cesar, suspender (publicación, apoyo, etc.). || 4 **without –,** incesantemente, sin respiro.
ceasefire | ˌsiːs'faɪər | *s.c.* 1 MIL. alto el fuego, cese el fuego. 2 POL. suspensión de hostilidades, tregua.
ceaseless | 'siːslɪs | *adj.* (form.) continuo, incesante, perenne.
ceaselessly | 'siːslɪslɪ | *adv.* (form.) continuamente, incesantemente, perennemente.
cedar | 'siːdər | BOT. *s.c.* 1 cedro. || *s.i.* 2 madera de cedro, cedro.
cede | siːd | *v.t.* e *i.* ceder, entregar (obligado).
cedilla | sɪ'dɪlə | *s.c.* GRAM. cedilla.
ceiling | 'siːlɪŋ | *s.c.* 1 techo (de una habitación). 2 **[– (on)]** techo, límite. 3 AER. techo, máxima altura (de vuelo). || 4 **to hit the –,** V. **hit.**
celebrant | 'selɪbrənt | *s.c.* REL. celebrante.
celebrate | 'selɪbreɪt | *v.t.* 1 celebrar, festejar, conmemorar (fiesta, acontecimiento, etc.). 2 REL. celebrar, decir (misa). 3 **[to – +** *o.* **+ as/for]** (form.) aclamar como, exaltar por: *they celebrated him as the best living writer = lo aclamaron como el mejor escritor vivo.* || *v.i.* 4 hacer fiesta, festejar.
celebrated | 'selɪbreɪtɪd | *adj.* **[– (for)]** famoso, célebre.
celebration | ˌselɪ'breɪʃn | *s.c.* e *i.* 1 celebración, festejo, conmemoración. || *s.i.* 2 (form.) alabanza, aclamación, exaltación (de algo o alguien).
celebratory | sɪ'lebrətərɪ | *adj.* (form.) conmemorativo.
celebrity | sɪ'lebrɪtɪ | *s.c.* 1 celebridad, persona célebre. || *s.i.* 2 fama, celebridad.
celerity | sɪ'lerɪtɪ | *s.i.* (form.) rapidez, celeridad.
celery | 'selərɪ | *s.i.* BOT. apio.
celestial | sɪ'lestɪəl | (EE.UU.) | sɪ'lestʃl | *adj.* 1 celestial, del espacio. 2 (lit.) celeste, celestial, divino.
celibacy | 'selɪbəsɪ | *s.i.* 1 celibato (normalmente religioso). 2 continencia (por un tiempo).
celibate | 'selɪbɪt | *adj.* 1 célibe (normalmente religioso). 2 casto, continen-

te, virgen (durante un tiempo). || *s.c.* **3** célibe (religioso). **4** persona virgen/casta (durante un tiempo).
cell | sel | *s.c.* **1** BIOL. célula. **2** celda (prisión). **3** REL. celda. **4** POL. célula (revolucionaria o similar). **5** BIOL. celda, celdilla (abejas). **6** ELEC. célula, elemento.
cellar | 'selər | *s.c.* **1** sótano. **2** bodega (donde se guarda el vino).
cellist | 'tʃelɪst | *s.c.* MUS. violoncelista, concertista de violoncelo.
cello | 'tʃeləu | *s.c.* MUS. violoncelo.
cellophane | 'seləfeɪn | *s.i.* celofán (marca registrada).
cellular | 'seljulər | *adj.* **1** BIOL. celular. **2** térmica (prendas de abrigo, ropa, mantas, etc.).
celluloid | 'seljulɔɪd | *s.i.* **1** QUIM. celuloide (tipo de plástico). **2** (lit.) del cine, celuloide. || **3 on –,** (lit. y p.u.) en el cine, en las películas, sobre el celuloide.
cellulose | 'seljuləus | *s.i.* QUIM. celulosa.
Celsius | 'selsɪəs | *s.i.* FIS. centígrado.
Celt | kelt | (EE.UU.) | selt | *s.c.* **1** HIST. celta. **2** irlandés, galés, escocés (moderno).
Celtic | 'keltɪk | (EE.UU.) | 'seltɪk | *adj.* **1** celta (costumbres, historia, etc.). || *s.i.* **2** celta, irlandés, escocés (idioma).
cement | sə'ment | *s.i.* **1** cemento. **2** pegamento (un tipo). || *s.c.* **3** (fig.) vínculo (lo que une a personas en un grupo). || *v.t.* **4** poner cemento en, echar cemento en. **5** pegar, aglutinar (físicamente). **6** (fig.) fortalecer, consolidar, cimentar (acuerdo, relación, etc.). || **7 – mixer, a)** mezcladora de cemento, hormigonera. **b)** camión hormigonera.
cemetery | 'semɪtrɪ | (EE.UU.) | 'semәterɪ | *s.c.* cementerio (alejado de una iglesia).
cenotaph | 'senətɑːf | (EE.UU.) | 'senətæf | *s.c.* ART. cenotafio, memorial, monumento a los caídos.
censor | 'sensər | *s.c.* **1** censor (de películas, libros, etc.). || *v.t.* **2** censurar (película, libro, etc.).
censorious | sen'sɔːrɪəs | *adj.* **[– (of)]** crítico, censurador, reprobador.
censoriously | sen'sɔːrɪəslɪ | *adv.* críticamente, censuradoramente, reprobadoramente.
censoriousness | sen'sɔːrɪəsnɪs | *s.i.* crítica, censura, reprobación.
censorship | 'sensəʃɪp | *s.i.* **[– (of)]** censura (de películas, libros, etc.).
censure | 'senʃər | *s.i.* **1** censura, crítica despiadada, reprobación fuerte. || *v.t.* **2** criticar, censurar, condenar.
census | 'sensəs | *s.c.* censo; empadronamiento.
cent | sent | *s.c.* **1** centavo (de muchas monedas). || **2 cent-/centi,** centi- (en compuestos). **3 per –,** V. **per.**
centaur | 'sentɔːr | *s.c.* centauro.
centenarian | ˌsentɪ'neərɪən | *adj.* **1** centenario. || *s.c.* **2** centenario.
centenary | sen'tiːnərɪ | (EE.UU.) | 'sentənerɪ | (también form. **centennial**) *s.c.* centenario.
centennial | sen'tenɪəl | V. **centenary.**
center | 'sentər | V. **centre.**
centigrade | 'sentɪgreɪd | *s.i.* centígrado.
centilitre | 'sentɪliːtər | (EE.UU. **centiliter**) *s.c.* centilitro.
centimetre | 'sentɪmiːtər | (EE.UU. **centimeter**) *s.c.* centímetro.
centipede | 'sentɪpiːd | *s.c.* ZOOL. ciempiés.
central | 'sentrəl | *adj.* **1** central (en el espacio). **2** céntrico, cercano al centro. **3** importante, principal, central. **4** POL. central: *central committee = comité central.* || **5 – bank,** FIN. banco central, banco estatal. **6 – government,** POL. gobierno central. **7 – heating,** calefacción central. **8 – nervous system,** ANAT. sistema nervioso central. **9 – processor,** INF. procesador central.
centralise V. **centralize.**
centralism | 'sentrəlɪzəm | *s.i.* centralismo (principalmente en sentido político).
centralist | 'sentrəlɪst | *s.c.* **1** centralista. || *adj.* **2** centralista.
centrality | sən'trælətɪ | *s.i.* (form.) **1** posición central. **2** suma importancia, situación primordial.
centralization | ˌsentrəlaɪ'zeɪʃn | (EE.UU.) ;pbsentrQlZ[zeZ;itn | (también **centralisation**) *s.i.* centralización.
centralize | 'sentrəlaɪz | (también **centralise**) *v.t.* e *i.* **centralizar(se).**
centralized | 'sentrəlaɪzd | (también **centralised**) *adj.* centralizado.
centrally | 'sentrəllɪ | *adv.* **1** centralmente, en posición central. **2** céntricamente. **3** principalmente, primordialmente. **4** POL. centralmente. || **5 – heated,** con calefacción central.
centre | 'sentə | (EE.UU. **center**) *s.c.* **1** **[– (of)]** centro. **2** centro (de salud, datos, orientación, etc.). **3** zona, región (industrial o de otra actividad). **4** **[– (of)]** centro (de la atención o interés). **5** **[– (of)]** meollo, centro. **6** meollo, cogollo, centro (de una fruta, comida, etc.). **7** GEOM. centro geométrico, centro. **8** DEP. centro (persona o movimiento del balón). || *s.sing.* **9** **[the –]** POL. el centro. || *v.t.* **10** centrar, poner en el centro. || *adj.* **11** del centro, de la parte del centro. **12** POL. centrista. || **13 to – around/round,** centrarse en, basarse en. **14 – of gravity,** FIS. centro de gravedad. **15 to – on,** concentrar(se) en, girar alrededor de. **16 – spread,** PER. páginas centrales.
centred | 'sentəd | (EE.UU. **centered**) *adj.* **[– (in)]** basado, fundamentado: *a pupil centred approach = un enfoque basado en el alumno.*
centre-forward | ˌsentə'fɔːwəd | *s.c.* DEP. delantero centro.
centre-half | ˌsentə'hɑːf | *s.c.* DEP. defensa central.
centrepiece | 'sentəpiːs | *s.c.* **1** decoración central (normalmente en la mesa). || *s.sing.* **2** (fig.) atracción principal.
centrifugal | sen'trɪfjugl | | ˌsentrɪ'fjuːgl | *adj.* **1** centrífugo. || **2 – force,** FIS. fuerza centrífuga.
centripetal | sen'trɪpɪtl | | ˌsentrɪ'piːtl | *adj.* **1** centrípeto. || **2 – force,** FIS. fuerza centrípeta.
centrist | 'sentrɪst | POL. *s.c.* **1** centrista. || *adj.* **2** centrista, equilibrado.
centrism | 'sentrɪzəm | *s.i.* POL. centrismo.
centurion | sen'tjuərɪən | (EE.UU.) | sen'tuərɪən | *s.c.* HIST. centurión.
century | 'sentʃərɪ | *s.c.* **1** siglo. || **2 the turn of the –,** V. **turn.**
ceramic | sɪ'ræmɪk | *s.i.* **1** cerámica. || *s.c.* **2** objeto de cerámica. || *adj.* **3** de cerámica. || *s.pl.* **4** ART. arte de la cerámica.
cereal | 'sɪərɪəl | *s.c.* e *i.* **1** AGR. cereal. **2** cereal (para comer).
cerebral | 'serɪbrəl | (EE.UU.) | sə'riːbrəl | *adj.* **1** cerebral, del cerebro. **2** (fig.) cerebral, reflexivo. || **3 – palsy,** MED. parálisis cerebral.
cerebra | 'serɪbrə | *pl.* de **cerebrum.**
cerebrum | 'serɪbrəm | [*pl.* **cerebrums** o **cerebra**] *s.c.* ANAT. cerebro.
ceremonial | ˌserɪ'məunɪəl | *adj.* **1** ceremonial. || *s.i.* **2** ceremonial, rito, ritual.
ceremonially | ˌserɪ'məunɪəlɪ | *adv.* ceremonialmente, con gran ceremonia.
ceremonious | ˌserɪ'məunɪəs | *adj.* ceremonioso.
ceremoniously | ˌserɪ'məunɪəslɪ | *adv.* ceremoniosamente.
ceremony | 'serɪmənɪ | (EE.UU.) | 'serɪməunɪ | *s.c.* **1** ceremonia, rito, ritual. || *s.i.* **2** ceremonia (trato formal). || **3 to stand on –,** hacer cumplidos, estar en plan ceremonial. **4 without –,** sin ceremonias.
cert | səːt | *s.c.* (fam. y brit.) cosa segura, cosa cierta.
certain | 'səːtn | *adj.* **1** seguro, cierto. **2** **[– + *inf.*/of]** seguro de: *I am certain to pass = estoy seguro de aprobar.* **3** cierto, alguno: *certain people are interested in political upheaval = ciertas personas están interesadas en la intranquilidad política.* **4** **[a –]** un cierto (persona, sentimiento, cosa, etc.); un tal (persona). || *pron.* **5** **[– of]** algunos de, determinados: *certain of our students don't pass the exams = algunos estudiantes no aprueban los exámenes.* || **6 for –,** con toda seguridad, a ciencia cierta. **7 to make – (of),** asegurarse (de), cerciorarse (de). **8 to make – (that),** asegurarse (de que), cerciorarse (de que). **9 to a – degree/extent,** hasta cierto punto.
certainly | 'səːtnlɪ | *adv.* **1** ciertamente, seguro, por supuesto, claro (contestando a una pregunta). **2** ciertamente, seguramente, con toda seguridad, sin duda. || **3 – not,** ciertamente que no, claro que no, por supuesto que no.
certainty | 'səːtntɪ | *s.i.* **1** certeza, seguridad, certidumbre. **2** **[– (of)]** certeza, inevitabilidad. || *s.c.* **3** cosa cierta, cosa segura, resultado inevitable: *war is a certainty = la guerra es cosa segura.*
certifiable | ˌsəːtɪ'faɪbl | *adj.* MED. demente, para encerrar.
certificate | sə'tɪfɪkɪt | *s.c.* **1** certificado, partida (documento oficial). **2** diplo-

ma (título académico de menor importancia). || **3 Certificate of Secondary Education,** título de Bachiller (algo menos que el Bachiller Superior español).
certification | ˌsəːtɪfɪ'keɪʃən | *s.i.* certificación.
certified | 'səːtɪfaɪd | *adj.* **1** titulado, con diploma adecuado: *a certified nurse = una enfermera titulada.* || **2 – cheque,** (EE.UU.) COM. cheque garantizado, cheque certificado (por un banco).
certify | 'səːtɪfaɪ | *v.t.* **1** certificar (mediante documento oficial); declarar oficialmente. **2** dar un título, conceder un título (que capacite para ejercer una determinada actividad). **3** MED. declarar demente, certificar la incapacidad mental.
certitude | 'səːtɪtjuːd | (EE.UU.) | 'səːtɪtuːd | *s.i.* (form.) certeza.
cervical | sə'vaɪkl | (EE.UU.) | səːvɪkl | *adj.* ANAT. **1** cervical (parte de la columna vertebral). **2** cervical (de la zona vaginal).
cervices | 'səːvɪsiːz | *pl.* de **cervix.**
cervix | 'səːvɪks | [*pl.* **cervixes** o **cervices**] *s.c.* ANAT. cerviz (entrada a la vagina).
Cesarian (también **Cesarean**), V. **Caesarean.**
cessation | se'seɪʃn | *s.c.* e *i.* **[– of]** (form.) cese de, suspensión de.
cesspit | 'sespɪt | (también **cesspool**) *s.c.* pozo negro, sentina.
cesspool | 'sespuːl | V. **cesspit.**
cha-cha | 'tʃɑːtʃɑː | (también **cha-cha-cha**) *s.c.* MUS. chachachá.
Chad | tʃæd | *s.sing.* Chad.
Chadian | 'tʃædɪən | *adj.* **1** chadiano. || *s.c.* **2** chadiano.
chafe | tʃeɪf | *v.i.* **1** irritarse (la piel). **2 [to – at/under]** irritarse por, enfadarse por. || *v.t.* **3** irritar (la piel). || *s.c.* **4** irritación (de la piel).
chaff | tʃɑːf | (EE.UU.) | tʃæf | *s.i.* **1** barcia, paja desmenuzada. || **2 to separate/sift the wheat from the –,** separar la paja del grano; (fig.) coger lo bueno y tirar lo malo (de cualquier cosa, persona, acontecimiento, etc.).
chaffinch | 'tʃæfɪntʃ | *s.c.* ZOOL. pinzón, pinzón vulgar (ave).
chagrin | 'ʃægrɪn | (EE.UU.) | ʃəːgriːn | (form.) *s.i.* **1** desazón, disgusto; pesadumbre. || *v.t.* **2** (normalmente *pas.*) disgustarse, desazonarse.
chain | tʃeɪn | *s.c.* e *i.* **1** cadena (de eslabones o similar). || *s.c.* **2** (fig.) cadena, atadura, grillete: *the chains of ignorance = las ataduras de la ignorancia.* **3** (fig.) cadena (de establecimientos comerciales). **4** cordillera, cadena (de montañas). **5** serie, cadena (de acontecimientos, entrevistas, etc.). || *s.pl.* **6** cadenas, grilletes (de prisionero). || *v.t.* **7** encadenar, aherrojar. **8 [to – + *o.* + (to)]** (fig.) confinar, limitar (a un espacio, actividad, etc.). || **9 – letter,** carta de una cadena de buena suerte (supersticiosa). **10 – reaction,** reacción en cadena. **11 – store,** sucursal de una cadena de tiendas. **12 to – up,** encadenar, sujetar con cadenas. **13 in chains,** encadenado, sujeto, atado con cadenas.
chain-mail | 'tʃeɪnmeɪl | *s.c.* cota de malla.
chain-saw | 'tʃeɪnsɔː | *s.c.* MEC. sierra de cadena.
chain-smoke | 'tʃeɪnsməuk | *v.t.* e *i.* fumar un cigarrillo tras otro.
chain-smoker | 'tʃeɪnsməukər | *s.c.* fumador que enciende un cigarrillo tras otro.
chair | tʃeər | *s.c.* **1** silla. **2** cátedra (universitaria). || *s.sing.* **3 [the –]** el presidente, la presidencia (de una reunión o similar). **4 [the –]** (fam.) la silla eléctrica. || *v.t.* **5** actuar de presidente de (una reunión o similar). || **6 in the –,** presidiendo, en la presidencia (de una reunión o similar).
chairlift | 'tʃeəlɪft | *s.c.* telesilla.
chairman | 'tʃeəmən | [*pl.* **chairmen**] *s.c.* **1** presidente (de reunión o similar). **2** POL. presidente (de la nación u organismo oficial). **3 [– (of)]** (brit.) COM. presidente (de una empresa).
chairmanship | 'tʃeəmənʃɪp | *s.sing.* presidencia.
chairmen | 'tʃeəmən | *pl.* de **chairman.**
chairperson | 'tʃeəpəːsn | *s.c.* presidente (cuando no se quiere reflejar el sexo).
chairwoman | 'tʃeəwumən | [*pl.* **chairwomen**] *s.c.* presidenta.
chairwomen | 'tʃeəwɪmɪn | *pl.* de **chairwoman.**
chaise-longue ˌʃeɪz'lɒŋ | (EE.UU.) ˌʃeɪz'lɔːŋ | [*pl.* **chaises-longues**] *s.c.* tumbona.
chaises-longues ˌʃeɪz'lɒŋ | (EE.UU.) ˌʃeɪz'lɔːŋ | *pl.* de **chaise-longue.**
chalet | 'ʃæleɪ | *s.c.* **1** casa de campo, chalet. **2** cabaña.
chalice | 'tʃælɪs | *s.c.* REL. cáliz.
chalk | tʃɔːk | *s.i.* **1** GEOL. tiza. || *s.c.* e *i.* **2** tiza (para escribir en la pizarra). || *v.t.* e *i.* **3** escribir con tiza, señalar con tiza, dibujar con tiza. || **4 by a long –,** [con *neg.*] ni mucho menos, ni de lejos. **5 – and cheese/different as – and cheese,** diferentes como el agua y el vino, totalmente y radicalmente distintos. **6 to – up,** apuntar(se), anotar(se) (victorias, puntos, etc.).
chalky | 'tʃɔːkɪ | *adj.* calcáreo (agua), como tiza (cualquier objeto).
challenge | 'tʃælɪndʒ | *v.t.* **1 [to – + *o.* (+ *inf.*)]** desafiar, retar. **2** MIL. dar el alto a. **3** cuestionar, disputar, poner en cuestión (una idea, aseveración, etc.). **4** DER. poner objeciones (especialmente a un miembro de un jurado). || *s.c.* **5** reto, desafío. || *s.c.* e *i.* **6** MIL. alto. **7** cuestionamiento, duda. **8** incentivo, estímulo: *we need new challenges = necesitamos nuevos estímulos.* **9** DER. objeción formal (especialmente a un miembro de un jurado).
challenger | 'tʃælɪndʒər | *s.c.* retador, contrincante (contra el que detenta el primer lugar).
challenging | 'tʃælɪndʒɪŋ | *adj.* **1** arduo, difícil, exigente (tarea). **2** desafiante; estimulante.
challengingly | 'tʃælɪndʒɪŋlɪ | *adv.* **1** arduamente, difícilmente, exigentemente. **2** con desafío, desafiantemente; estimulantemente.
chamber | 'tʃeɪmbər | *s.c.* **1** (arc.) cámara, aposento. **2** cámara (de tortura, gas, etc.). **3** recámara (de arma de fuego). **4** FIS. cámara (para experimentos). **5** ANAT. cavidad anatómica (de cualquier órgano). **6** POL. cámara (de diputados). **7 [– of]** cámara de (comercio). || *s.pl.* DER. **8** despacho (de juez o magistrado). **9** corte menor. || **10 – concert,** MUS. concierto de música de cámara. **11 – music,** MUS. música de cámara. **12 – orchestra,** MUS. orquesta de cámara.
chamberlain | 'tʃeɪmbəlɪn | *s.c.* (arc.) chambelán.
chambermaid | 'tʃeɪmbəmeɪd | *s.c.* camarera, sirvienta (en un hotel).
chamber-pot | 'tʃeɪmbəpɒt | *s.c.* orinal.
chameleon | kə'miːlɪən | *s.c.* ZOOL. camaleón.
chammy | 'ʃæmɪ | *s.c.* (fam.) gamuza (para limpiar).
chamois | 'ʃæmwɑː | (EE.UU.) | 'ʃæmɪ | [*pl.* **chamois**] *s.c.* **1** gamuza (para limpiar). **2** ZOOL. gamuza (pequeño antílope). || **3 – leather,** gamuza (para limpiar).
chamomile V. **camomile.**
champ | tʃæmp | *s.c.* **1** (fam.) campeón. || *v.i.* **2** tascar (caballos); mascar, mordisquear (animales). **3** impacientarse. || *v.t.* **4** mordisquear (animales). || **5 to – at the bit,** volverse loco de impaciencia, morder la mesa de impaciencia.
champagne | ʃæm'peɪn | *s.i.* champán.
champion | 'tʃæmpɪən | *s.c.* **1** campeón, ganador, vencedor (persona o animal). **2 [– (of)]** (fig.) defensor, paladín (de persona, causa, etc.). || *v.t.* **3** defender, apoyar, abogar por (causa, persona, principio, etc.).
championship | 'tʃæmpɪənʃɪp | *s.c.* **1** DEP. campeonato. || *s.i.* **2** defensa, apoyo (de una causa o similar).
chance | tʃɑːns | (EE.UU.) | tʃæns | *s.c.* e *i.* **1** posibilidad, probabilidad; (Am.) chance: *they haven't got a chance of beating the other team = no tienen ninguna posibilidad de ganar al otro equipo.* || *s.c.* **2** [;ms *inf.*/**of**] oportunidad de, ocasión de: *the extra money gave us the chance to buy some more furniture = el dinero extra nos dio la oportunidad de comprar más muebles.* **3** riesgo, peligro, posibilidad comprometida. || *s.i.* **4** suerte, fortuna, destino, casualidad: *that was pure chance = eso fue pura casualidad.* || *v.t.* **5** arriesgarse a, correr el riesgo de. || *v.i.* **6 [to =N *inf.*]** dar la casualidad de, ocurrir por casualidad que, acaecer: *she chanced to come later and explain everything = dio la casualidad de que ella vino más tarde y lo explicó todo.* || *adj.* **7** casual, fortuito, accidental. || **8 by any –,** [con

interr.] por casualidad, por alguna coincidencia casual. **9 by –/by pure –/by sheer –,** por suerte, por fortuna, por pura chiripa, por pura casualidad. **10 to – on/upon,** tropezarse inesperadamente con, encontrarse fortuitamente con (alguien o algo). **11 to stand a –,** tener una posibilidad, tener un mínimo de posibilidad. **12 to take a – on,** arriesgarse, aceptar un riesgo. **13 to take chances,** arriesgarse demasiado, jugársela. **14 to take one's chances,** aprovechar las oportunidades de uno, no dejar pasar las oportunidades de uno.

chancel | 'tʃɑːnsl | (EE.UU.) | 'tʃænsl | *s.c.* REL. presbiterio, antealtar.

chancellery | 'tʃɑːnsələrɪ | (EE.UU.) | 'tʃænsələrɪ | *s.c.* POL. cancillería.

chancellor | 'tʃɑːnsələr | (EE.UU.) | 'tʃænsələːr | *s.c.* **1** POL. canciller (en Centroeuropa). **2** (brit.) rector honorífico (de una universidad). **3** POL. Ministro de Hacienda y Economía. || **4 Chancellor of the Exchequer,** POL. Ministro de Hacienda y Economía.

chancery | 'tʃɑːnsərɪ | (EE.UU.) | 'tʃænsərɪ | *s.c.* **1** (brit.) DER. tribunal superior. **2** archivo de documentos oficiales. **3** (EE.UU.) DER. tribunal de paz, juzgado de paz.

chancily | 'tʃɑːnsɪlɪ | *adv.* (fam.) de manera arriesgada, con riesgo, con peligro.

chancy | 'tʃɑːnsɪ | *adj.* (fam.) arriesgado, peligroso.

chandelier | ˌʃændə'lɪər | *s.c.* araña (candelabro con luces colgando del techo).

change | tʃeɪndʒ | *v.t.* e *i.* **1** cambiar(se), variar(se), hacerse diferente: *things have changed in this city = las cosas han cambiado en esta ciudad.* **2** transbordar, cambiar de (autobús, tren, etc.). **3** cambiar de (marcha o piñón), cambiar. || *v.t.* **4** cambiar (dinero en calderilla o en moneda extranjera). **5 [to – + *o.* + (for)]** cambiar, trocar, reemplazar. **6** cambiar de sitio, cambiar de lugar (un objeto). **7** cambiar, mudar (ropa). **8** cambiar (a un bebé). **9** cambiar (la cama). || *v.i.* **10 [to – (into/out of)]** cambiarse (de ropa). **11** cambiar de dirección (el viento). **12 [to – (to)]** cambiar (de un color, de estación, etc.). || *s.c.* e *i.* **13** cambio, alteración: *lots of changes took place = muchos cambios tuvieron lugar.* || *s.c.* **14 [– (of)]** cambio, recambio. **15** transbordo, cambio (de transporte). **16** cambio (de marcha en un vehículo). **17 [– of] muda de, cambio de (ropa).** || *s.i.* **18** cambio, vuelta (dinero). **19** calderilla, monedas sueltas. **20 [– for]** cambio de (una cantidad de dinero). || **21 all –!,** ¡todos deben bajarse! (de medio de transporte que ya no sigue). **22 to – direction,** cambiar de dirección. **23 to – down,** reducir la marcha (en un vehículo). **24 to – hands,** V. **hand. 25 – of direction,** cambio de dirección (físico o mental). **26 – of life,** menopausia. **27 to – one's mind,** V. **mind. 28 to – one's tune,** V. **tune. 29 to – over,** intercambiar (puestos, tareas, etc.). **30 to – over (from/to),** pasarse (de/a), cambiar (de/a). **31 to – tack,** V. **tack. 32 to – the subject,** V. **subject. 33 to – up,** cambiar de marcha (de una corta a otra larga). **34 for a –,** para variar. **35 to get no – from/out of,** (fam.) no conseguir sacar nada de (alguien). **36 to make a –,** significar algo para mejor, ser un cambio para mejor: *your coming to classes makes a change = el que vengas a clase es un cambio para mejor.* **37 to ring the changes,** V. **ring.**

changeable | 'tʃeɪndʒəbl | *adj.* variable, inestable (de carácter, tiempo, etc.).

changeless | 'tʃeɪndʒlɪs | *adj.* inmutable, invariable.

changeling | 'tʃeɪndʒlɪŋ | *s.c.* niño cambiado por otro.

changeover | 'tʃeɪndʒəuvər | *s.c.* **[– (to)]** cambio (de empleo, de partido político, etc.).

channel | 'tʃænl | *s.c.* **1** TV. canal. **2** RAD. canal. **3** canal (de comunicación, información, etc.). **4** canal (de irrigación o similar). **5** canal marítimo (de transporte). **6** conducto, ranura. || *v.t.* **7** canalizar (dinero, ayuda, etc.). || **8 the Channel/the English Channel,** GEOG. el Canal de la Mancha.

chant | tʃɑːnt | *s.c.* **1** sonsonete, repetición cantada. **2** REL. canto, salmodia, cántico. || *v.t.* e *i.* **3** repetir incansablemente, repetir gritando al unísono. **4** REL. salmodiar, cantar cánticos religiosos.

chaos | 'keɪɒs | *s.i.* caos, confusión, desorden.

chaotic | keɪ'ɒtɪk | *adj.* caótico, confuso, desordenado.

chap | tʃæp | *s.c.* (fam. y brit.) tipo, compañero, amigo, macho, tío, colega.

chapel | 'tʃæpl | *s.c.* REL. **1** capilla. **2** templo protestante. **3** capítulo, gremio (de trabajadores). **4** (EE.UU.) sección (de un club, asociación, etc.). || *adj.* **3** protestante (en contraposición con iglesias establecidas).

chaperon | 'ʃæpərəun | (también **chaperone**) *s.c.* **1** carabina (acompañante). **2** acompañante, jefe de grupo (de niños o similar). || *v.t.* **3** ir de carabina con. **4** acompañar, escoltar (a un grupo de menores o similar).

chaplain | 'tʃæplɪn | *s.c.* **[– (to/of)]** capellán.

chaplaincy | 'tʃæplɪnsɪ | *s.c.* **1** capellanía (lugar). || *s.i.* **2** capellanía.

chapped | tʃæpt | *adj.* agrietada (piel).

chapter | 'tʃæptər | *s.c.* **1** capítulo (de un libro). **2** (fig.) capítulo, período (de la vida o similar). **3** capítulo (de una sociedad secreta, especialmente). **4** REL. cabildo (de una catedral). || **5 a – of accidentes,** una serie de desgracias. **6 – and verse,** con pelos y señales.

chapter-house | 'tʃæptəhaus | *s.c.* REL. sala capitular.

char | tʃɑːr | [*ger.* **charring,** *pret.* y *p.p.* **charred**] *v.i.* **1** (p.u.) estar de limpiadora, trabajar como señora de la limpieza. || *s.i.* **2** (brit., fam. y p.u.) té. || *s.c.* **3** (p.u.) mujer de la limpieza, señora de la limpieza, limpiadora.

character | 'kærəktər | *s.c.* **1** carácter, personalidad. **2** LIT. personaje, carácter (en cualquier obra literaria). **3** tipo, sujeto: *he's an eccentric character = es un sujeto excéntrico.* **4** tipo, letra, carácter tipográfico. **5** FILOL. carácter, ideograma (en idiomas como el chino y otros). || *s.i.* **6** carácter, personalidad (como cosa positiva). **7** índole, naturaleza, carácter: *the stupid character of some high officials = la naturaleza estúpida de algunos altos cargos.* **8** reputación, buen nombre. || **9 – actor/actress,** actor/actriz especializado/a en papeles excéntricos. **10 – assassination,** destrozo despiadado del buen nombre de alguien, murmuración y calumnia cruel sobre alguien. **11 in –,** en su papel, en consonancia (con su carácter). **12 out of –,** nada característico, de ningún modo en consonancia (con su carácter). **13 the ... –,** la idiosincrasia..., la forma de ser...: *the Chinese character = la idiosincrasia china.*

characterise V. **characterize.**

characteristic | ˌkærəktə'rɪstɪk | *adj.* **1 [– (of)]** característico, peculiar, típico, propio. || *s.c.* **2 [– (of)]** característica, peculiaridad, rasgo distintivo.

characteristically | ˌkærəktə'rɪstɪklɪ | *adv.* característicamente, especialmente, peculiarmente, típicamente, propiamente.

characterization | ˌkærəktəraɪ'zeɪʃn | (también **characterisation**) *s.i.* LIT. caracterización; presentación, representación (de un hecho, persona, etc.).

characterize | 'kærəktəraɪz | (también **characterise**) *v.t.* **1** caracterizar, ser típico de, ser propio de. **2 [to – + *o.* + (as)]** describir, caracterizar.

characterless | 'kærəktəlɪs | *adj.* (desp.) sin carácter, sin personalidad (lugar o persona).

charade | ʃə'rɑːd | (EE.UU.) | ʃə'reɪd | *s.c.* e *i.* **1** charada, acertijo (juego). || *s.c.* **2 [– (of)]** (fig.) charada, espectáculo absurdo.

charcoal | 'tʃɑːkəul | *s.i.* **1** carbón vegetal, carbón de leña. **2** ART. carboncillo (forma de dibujar).

charge | tʃɑːdʒ | *v.t.* **1** cobrar, pedir (dinero). **2 [to – + *o.* + (with)]** DER. acusar formalmente (de algún delito). **3** ELEC. cargar, recargar (batería). **4 [to – + *o.* + *inf.*]** (form.) encargar, recomendar, encomendar: *I charged him to take care of his little sister = yo le encomendé que cuidara de su hermanita.* **5** MIL. cargar (arma). || *v.i.* **6** cobrar (dinero). **7** MIL. cargar, lanzarse al ataque, lanzarse a la carga. **8 [to – + *prep.*]** ir a toda velocidad, ir disparado; atacar velozmente, dirigirse en ataque: *the elephants charged at the group = los elefantes atacaron velozmente contra el grupo.* || *s.c.* **9** cobro, precio, costo. **10 [– (against)]** DER.

acusación formal. **11** (form.) responsabilidad (persona); persona a cargo. **12** MIL. carga explosiva. **13** FIS. carga, carga eléctrica. || *s.i.* **14** cometido, encargo, responsabilidad: *hundreds of students under my charge = cientos de estudiantes bajo mi responsabilidad.* || *s.c.* e *i.* **15** MIL. ataque, carga. **16** ataque (de animal o jugador). || **17 – hand,** ayudante de capataz. **18 – nurse,** enfermera jefe de sección hospitalaria. **19 – sheet,** DER. pliego de cargos, pliego de acusaciones. **20 to – to someone's account,** cargárselo a la cuenta de alguien (gasto o similar). **21 to – up,** ELEC. cargar, recargar (batería). **22 free of –,** gratis, totalmente gratis. **23 in – (of),** a cargo (de) (persona o cosa). **24 to reverse the charges,** V. **reverse. 25 to take –,** asumir el mando. **26 to take – of,** hacerse cargo de, encargarse de.

chargeable | 'tʃɑːdʒəbl | *adj.* **1** FIN. imponible, que se puede cobrar un impuesto sobre ello. **2** deducible, que se puede descontar de la declaración. **3** DER. imputable (crimen). **4** a cobrar, se puede cobrar (dinero).

charged | tʃɑːdʒt | *adj.* **1** ELEC. cargada (batería). **2 [– (with)]** (fig.) impregnado, saturado, cargado (de emoción o similar).

chargé d'affaires | ,ʃɑːʒeɪdæ'feər | [*pl.* **chargés d'affaires**] *s.c.* POL. encargado de negocios (diplomático).

charger | 'tʃɑːdʒər | *s.c.* **1** ELEC. cargador. **2** MIL. caballo de guerra.

chariot | 'tʃærɪət | *s.c.* HIST. cuádriga.

charioteer | ,tʃærɪə'tɪər | *s.c.* HIST. conductor de cuádriga.

charisma | kæ'rɪzmə | *s.i.* **1** carisma, atracción. || *s.c.* **2** REL. carisma.

charismatic | ,kærɪz'mætɪk | *adj.* **1** carismático, atrayente, de gran atracción. **2** REL. carismático.

charismatically | ,kærɪz'mætɪklɪ | *adv.* carismáticamente.

charitable | 'tʃærətəbl | *adj.* **1** caritativo, generoso (persona). **2** benéfico, caritativo (organización).

charitably | 'tʃærətəblɪ | *adv.* caritativamente, generosamente.

charity | 'tʃærɪtɪ | *s.i.* **1** caridad, generosidad, benevolencia. **2** limosna. || *s.c.* **3** asociación benéfica, asociación sin ánimo de lucro. || **4 – begins at home,** la caridad empieza en casa, la caridad empieza en uno mismo.

charlady | 'tʃɑːleɪdɪ | V. **charwoman.**

charlatan | 'ʃɑːlətən | *s.c.* (desp.) farsante, embaucador; curandero falso.

charleston | 'tʃɑːlstən | *s.c.* MUS. charlestón.

charlie | 'tʃɑːlɪ | *s.c.* (brit. y fam.) bobalicón.

charm | tʃɑːm | *s.c.* e *i.* **1** encanto, atracción, fascinación. || *s.c.* **2** amuleto. **3** palabra mágica, hechizo (palabra). **5** encanto, atractivo (especialmente de una mujer). || *v.t.* **5** encantar, fascinar, hechizar. || **6 to lead/have a charmed life,** tener suerte para todo. **7 to work like a –,** (fam.) funcionar como por magia, funcionar estupendamente, funcionar a la perfección.

charmer | 'tʃɑːmər | *s.c.* persona fascinante (para el otro sexo).

charming | 'tʃɑːmɪŋ | *adj.* fascinante, seductor, encantador.

charmingly | 'tʃɑːmɪŋlɪ | *adv.* fascinantemente, encantadoramente, seductoramente.

charred | tʃɑːd | *adj.* quemado, chamuscado.

chart | tʃɑːt | *s.c.* **1** gráfico, cuadro de gráficos. **2** carta geográfica; carta astronómica. || *v.t.* **3** hacer un mapa de, trazar un mapa de. **4** recoger, reseñar, anotar, dejar registrado (el desarrollo de algo). **5** planear, planificar (una actividad o similar). || **6 the charts,** MUS. las listas de los mejores (discos).

charter | 'tʃɑːtər | *s.c.* POL. carta (de derechos o similar). **2** estatuto (de una Universidad u otra institución). **3** constitución, estatutos fundacionales. || *adj.* **4** charter, especial, no regular (vuelo). || *v.t.* **5** alquilar los servicios de, contratar, fletar (avión no regular). **6** conceder una carta constitucional, otorgar una carta de estatutos. || **7 chartered surveyor/accountant,** topógrafo colegiado / contable titulado.

charwoman | 'tʃɑːwʊmən | (también **charlady** o **char**) [*pl.* **charwomen**] *s.c.* (p.u.) señora de la limpieza.

charwomen | 'tʃɑːwɪmɪn | *pl.* de **charwoman.**

charily | 'tʃeərɪlɪ | *adv.* **1** cautelosamente, cuidadosamente, de manera recelosa. **2** parcamente (elogiar o similar).

chary | 'tʃeərɪ | *adj.* **[– (of)] 1** cauteloso, cuidadoso, receloso; poco dispuesto. **2** parco (en elogios o similar).

chase | tʃeɪs | *v.t.* **1** perseguir, dar caza, acosar, ir tras de (dando caza). **2 [to – + *o.* + *prep.*]** expulsar, ahuyentar: *we chased the enemy from the village = expulsamos al enemigo del pueblo.* **3** (fig.) ir tras de, perseguir (empleo, éxito, dinero, etc.). **4** (fig.) ir tras de, perseguir (mujeres). || *v.i.* **5 [to – after]** perseguir, dar caza, acosar, ir tras de (dando caza). **6 [to – after]** (fig.) ir tras de, perseguir (empleo, éxito, dinero, etc.). **7 [to – + *prep.*]** ir corriendo, ir de prisa, apresurarse. || **8 to – up,** (brit. y fam.) **a)** ir a por (alguien que debe dinero, servicio, favor, etc.): *chase him up and ask him to give you the tests = ve a por él y pídele que te dé los exámenes.* **b)** ir tras de, acelerar (algo retrasado que es necesario). **9 to give –,** dar caza, perseguir. **10 to give up the –,** abandonar la caza, abandonar la persecución.

chaser | 'tʃeɪsər | *s.c.* **1** caballo saltador (de obstáculos). **2** (fam.) bebida que acompaña (a otra bebida, pero en distinto vaso). **3** perseguidor, cazador (persona).

chasm | 'kæzəm | *s.c.* **1** abismo, precipicio, grieta. **2 [– (between/in)]** (fig.) abismo, gran distancia, diferencia abismal (de posturas, intereses, etc.).

chassis | 'ʃæsɪ | [*pl.* **chassis** | 'ʃæsɪz] *s.c.* chasis (vehículo), armazón (aparato electrónico).

chaste | tʃeɪst | *adj.* **1** (p.u.) casto, virgen. **2** casto, púdico. **3** fiel (a marido o mujer). **4** sencillo, simple (sin decoración barroca).

chastely | 'tʃeɪstlɪ | *adv.* **1** castamente, púdicamente. **2** fielmente (a una persona). **3** sencillamente, simplemente, con sencillez (no barroco en su estilo o decoración).

chasten | 'tʃeɪsn | *v.t.* (p.u.) corregir, dar una reprimenda, disciplinar.

chastise | tʃæ'staɪz | *v.t.* **1** (form.) llamar la atención, corregir. **2** (p.u.) castigar (físicamente).

chastisement | tʃæ'staɪzmənt | | 'tʃæstɪzmənt | *s.c.* e *i.* **1** (form.) corrección, reprimenda, llamada de atención. **2** (p.u.) castigo (físico).

chastity | 'tʃæstɪtɪ | *s.i.* castidad, pureza (en el sentido sexual).

chat | tʃæt | [*ger.* **chatting,** *pret.* y *p.p.* **chatted**] *v.i.* **1 [to – (about/to/with)]** charlar, conversar; (Am.) platicar (informalmente). || *s.c.* e *i.* **2** charla, conversación; (Am.) plática (informal). || **3 – show,** TV. programa de entrevistas. **4 to – up,** (fam. y brit.) hacer conversación con, charlar con (normalmente para seguir una relación).

chattel | 'tʃætl | **someone's goods and chattels,** (p.u.) bienes y posesiones de alguien.

chatter | 'tʃætər | *v.i.* **1** charlar, chacharear, parlotear, cotorrear. **2** chillar (pájaros y monos). **3** castañetear (dientes); traquetear (máquina). || *s.i.* **4** charla, chachareo, parloteo, cotorreo. **5** chillido (de ciertos animales). **6 [– of]** castañeteo, traqueteo (de máquinas).

chatterbox | 'tʃætəbɒks | *s.c.* parlanchín, parlanchina, cotorra (persona).

chatterer | 'tʃætərər | V. **chatterbox.**

chattily | 'tʃætɪlɪ | *adv.* **1** locuazmente, en conversación. **2** informalmente, en tono conversacional.

chattiness | 'tʃætɪnɪs | *s.i.* **1** locuacidad. **2** informalidad (tono de un escrito o conversación).

chatty | 'tʃætɪ | *adj.* **1** locuaz, conversacional. **2** informal, sencillo (forma de escribir o hablar).

chauffeur | 'ʃəʊfər | (EE.UU.) | ʃəʊ'fɜːr | *s.c.* **1** chófer, conductor (privado). || *v.t.* **2** llevar en coche, hacer de chófer para (alguien, como trabajo).

chauvinism | 'ʃəʊvɪnɪzəm | *s.i.* (desp.) chauvinismo, patrioterismo.

chauvinist | ,ʃəʊvɪnɪst | *s.c.* (desp.) chauvinista, patriotero.

chauvinistic | ,ʃəʊvɪ'nɪstɪk | *adj.* (desp.) chauvinista, patriotero.

chauvinistically | ,ʃəʊvɪ'nɪstɪklɪ | *adv.* (desp.) patrioteramente.

cheap | tʃiːp | *adj.* **1** barato, económico, de bajo precio. **2** baratero, de baja calidad, de mala calidad. **3** reducido, económico (billete, entrada, etc.). **4** (desp.) barato, a precios abusivos, a precios de explotación: *cheap labour = mano de obra barata.* **5** (desp.) bajo, vulgar, despreciable (comportamiento general de una persona). || *adv.* **6** a precio asequible, a bajo precio. || **7 – and nasty,** (desp.) de bajo precio e igual calidad. **8 – at the price,** barato a la larga, a pesar del precio alto. **9 to go –,** (fam.) dedicarse a productos baratos (una tienda). **10 on the –,** (fam. y desp.) con un descuento considerable, en plan barato. **11 someone's life is –,** la vida de alguien no merece la pena, la vida de alguien no vale nada.

cheapen | 'tʃiːpən | *v.t.* **1** abaratar, reducir el precio de. **2** (desp.) vulgarizar, depreciar (la valía de alguien). || *v.r.* **3** rebajarse, hacer cosas indignas de uno.

cheaply | 'tʃiːplɪ | *adv.* **1** a bajo precio, a precio reducido, económicamente. **2** (desp.) vulgarmente, vilmente (comportarse en general).

cheat | tʃiːt | (desp.) *v.i.* **1** engañar, hacer trampas. || *v.t.* **2 [to – + *o.* + of/out of]** estafar, timar, quitar mediante un timo: *I was cheated out of 20.000 pesetas = me timaron 20.000 pesetas.* || *s.c.* **3** tramposo, timador. **4** trampa, timo. || **5 to – on,** (fam.) **a)** engañar, ser infiel (en el amor), **b)** engañar, timar (con falsedades, mentiras, etc.). **6 to feel cheated,** sentirse privado de algo a lo que uno tiene derecho, tener la sensación de quedar sin lo merecido.

cheating | 'tʃiːtɪŋ | *s.i.* trampa, engaño.

check | tʃek | *v.t.* **1** comprobar, examinar. **2** frenar, controlar (algo o alguien); reprimir (sentimientos). || *v.i.* **3** hacer una comprobación, llevar a cabo un examen. **4 [to – on]** verificar, comprobar: *he checked on the baby = comprobó si el bebé estaba bien.* **5 [to – (with)]** estar acorde, ser acorde, acordar, cuadrar (una información, dato, etc., con otro). || *v.r.* **6** frenarse, pararse, controlarse. || *s.c.* **7** (EE.UU.) cuenta, nota (en restaurante o similar). **8 [– (on)]** inspección, comprobación, examen. || *s.c.* e *i.* **9** tela de cuadros. || *adj.* **10** a cuadros. || *s.pl.* **11** cuadros (tejido). || **12 to double –,** hacer una segunda comprobación. **13 –,** jaque (en el ajedrez). **14 to – in, a)** inscribir(se) (en un hotel o similar). **b)** facturar, (Am.) chequear (equipajes). **15 to – off,** comprobar uno a uno, marcar uno a uno, apuntar uno a uno. **16 to – out, a)** comprobar completamente, hacer una comprobación minuciosa. **b)** salir, irse (de un hotel mediante el pago y la devolución de llaves). **c)** (fam.) investigar, hacer una investigación (sobre alguien). **17 to – up (on),** hacer una comprobación (sobre), hacer una investigación (sobre). **18 in –,** en jaque. **19 to keep/hold something/someone in –,** mantener a algo/alguien a raya. **continous —,** tablas, en jaque continuo.

checkbook V. **chequebook.**

checked | tʃekt | *adj.* a cuadros, con cuadros.

checker | 'tʃekər | *s.c.* **1** inspector, verificador. || **2 checkers,** (EE.UU.) damas (juego).

checkered V. **chequered.**

check-in | 'tʃekɪn | *s.c.* **1** mostrador, mostrador de facturación (en un aeropuerto). **2** facturación: *check-in time = hora de facturación.*

checking | 'tʃekɪŋ | *s.i.* **1** comprobación (acto de comprobar). **2 – account,** (EE.UU.) FIN. cuenta corriente.

checklist | 'tʃeklɪst | *s.c.* lista de comprobación, (Am.) lista de chequeo.

checkmate | 'tʃekmeɪt | *s.i.* **1** jaque y mate (en ajedrez). **2** (fig.) situación de jaque y mate, situación peligrosa estacionaria; callejón sin salida. || *v.t.* **3** dar un jaque y mate (en ajedrez). **4** (fig.) poner en un callejón sin salida; frustrar (planes o similar).

checkout | 'tʃekaʊt | *s.c.* **1** salida, marcha (de un hotel). **2** cajero (en un supermercado).

checkpoint | 'tʃekpɔɪnt | *s.c.* punto de control, punto de inspección (normalmente en las fronteras entre países).

checkroom | 'tʃekrum | *s.c.* (EE.UU.) guardarropa.

check-up | 'tʃekʌp | *s.c.* MED. chequeo completo, chequeo.

cheek | tʃiːk | *s.c.* **1** mejilla, carrillo. **2** (fam.) nalga, culo. || *s.i.* **3** insolencia, cara, descaro. || *v.t.* **4** tratar descaradamente, tratar con desprecio. | **5 – by jowl,** V. **jowl. 6 to have the –, [=N + *inf.*]** tener la cara de, tener el descaro de. **7 tongue in –,** V. **tongue. 8 to turn the other –,** aguantar sin responder violentamente.

cheekbone | 'tʃiːkbəun | *s.c.* ANAT. pómulo.

cheekily | 'tʃiːkɪlɪ | *adv.* descaradamente, irrespetuosamente, impertinentemente.

cheekiness | 'tʃiːkɪnɪs | *s.i.* descaro, impertinencia.

cheeky | 'tʃiːkɪ | *adj.* descarado, irrespetuoso, impertinente (personas o acciones).

cheep | tʃiːp | *v.i.* piar, hacer pío (pájaros).

cheer | tʃɪər | *v.t.* e *i.* **1** dar ánimos, alentar; vitorear. || *v.t.* **2** alegrar, animar (especialmente después de tristezas o dificultades). || *s.c.* **3** gritos de ánimo, vítores, hurras; aplausos: *three cheers for the President = tres hurras por el Presidente.* || *s.i.* **4** (p.u.) gozo, alegría; buen humor. || **5 to – on,** animar mediante gritos de entusiasmo, dar muchos ánimos (a alguien en su acción). **6 cheers, a)** salud, a tu salud (en un brindis). **b)** (brit. y fam.) gracias, **c)** (brit. y fam.) adiós, hasta luego. **7 to – up,** alegrarse, animarse; tomar nuevas fuerzas de ánimo.

cheerful | 'tʃɪəfl | *adj.* **1** alegre, jovial, animado, de buen humor. **2** alegre, de agradable aspecto, de agradable enfoque (habitación, paisaje, libro, etc.). **3** alegre, entusiasta (en alguna actividad o trabajo). **4** frívolo, superficialmente alegre, tontamente alegre, alegre (cuando no debería estarlo).

cheerfully | 'tʃɪəfəlɪ | *adv.* **1** alegremente, jovialmente, animadamente. **2** alegremente, con alegría en su aspecto, con alegría en su enfoque. **3** alegremente, entusiásticamente (la manera de trabajar o acometer una actividad). **4** frívolamente, alegremente (sin pensar con la debida seriedad).

cheerfulness | 'tʃɪəfəlnɪs | *s.i.* **1** alegría, jovialidad, animación. **2** aspecto alegre, enfoque alegre (de un lugar, una obra de arte, etc.). **3** alegría, entusiasmo (en una actividad). **4** frivolidad, alegría superficial, alegría tonta (cuando no hay razón).

cheerily | 'tʃɪərɪlɪ | *adv.* alegremente, jovialmente, animadamente.

cheeriness | 'tʃɪərɪnɪs | *s.i.* alegría, jovialidad, animación.

cheering | 'tʃɪərɪŋ | *adj.* **1** esperanzador, que anima, que da ánimos: *cheering news = noticias que animan.* || *s.i.* **2** griterío, vítores, vivas.

cheerio | ˌtʃɪərɪ'əʊ | *interj.* (brit. y fam.) adiós, hasta luego, (Am.) chao.

cheerleader | 'tʃɪəliːdər | *s.c.* (EE.UU.) animador, organizador del apoyo (a un equipo o similar).

cheerless | 'tʃɪəlɪs | *adj.* sombrío, triste, melancólico; inhospitalario: *a cheerless afternoon.*

cheerlessly | 'tʃɪəlɪslɪ | *adv.* sombríamente, tristemente, melancólicamente.

cheerlessness | 'tʃɪəlɪsnɪs | *s.i.* tristeza, melancolía (lugar, tiempo, etc.).

cheery | 'tʃɪərɪ | *adj.* alegre, jovial, animado.

cheese | tʃiːz | *s.c.* e *i.* **1** queso. || **2 to be cheesed off (with),** (fam. y brit.) estar hasta las narices (de), estar harto (de). **3 chalk and –,** V. **chalk. 4 say –,** un pajarito; sonría por favor (antes de hacer una foto).

cheeseboard | 'tʃiːzbɔːd | *s.c.* **1** plato con quesos distintos. || *s.sing.* **2 [the –]** los quesos (como parte final de una comida).

cheeseburger | 'tʃiːzbəːgər | *s.c.* GAST. hamburguesa de queso.

cheesecake | 'tʃiːzkeɪk | *s.c.* e *i.* **1** GAST. torta de queso, pastel de queso. || *s.i.* **2** (vulg.) muslamen, tetamen (en publicidad con mujeres semidesnudas).

cheesecloth | 'tʃiːzklɒθ | (EE.UU.) | 'tʃiːzklɔːθ | *s.i.* estopilla (tipo de tela fina).

cheese-paring | 'tʃiːzpeərɪŋ | (desp.) *s.i.* **1** tacañería, economías de miseria. || *adj.* **2** tacaño, miserable.

cheesy | 'tʃiːzɪ | *adj.* parecido al queso.

cheetah | 'tʃiːtə | *s.c.* ZOOL. leopardo pequeño.

chef | ʃef | *s.c.* cocinero profesional, chef, jefe de cocina.

chemical | 'kemɪkl | *adj.* **1** químico. || *s.c.* **2** producto químico. | **3 – engineer,** ingeniero químico. **4 – engineering,** ingeniería química. **5 – warfare,** guerra química.

chemically | ’kemɪklɪ | *adv.* químicamente.

chemist | ’kemɪst | *s.c.* **1** químico, experto en química. **2** (brit.) farmacéutico. || **3 the –/the chemist's,** (brit.) la farmacia.

chemistry | ’kemɪstrɪ | *s.i.* **1** química (estudio científico). **2 [the – of]** la reacción/característica/propiedad química de (una sustancia). **3** (fam. y fig.) manera de relacionarse, modo de tratarse, relación mutua (dos personas en un trabajo o relación personal): *there's very good chemistry between them = hay una buena relación entre ellos.*

chemotherapy | ˌkəːməʊ’θerəpɪ | *s.i.* MED. quimioterapia.

chenille | ʃə’niːl | *s.i.* **1** felpilla (tipo de tejido). **2** adorno de felpilla, cordón de felpilla (especialmente en muebles).

cheque | tʃek | (EE.UU. **check**) FIN. *s.c.* **1** cheque. || **2 by –,** por cheque. **3 – card,** (brit.) tarjeta que certifica la validez de cheques.

chequebook | ’tʃekbʊk | (EE.UU. **checkbook**) *s.c.* talonario.

chequered | ’tʃekəd | (EE.UU. **chekered**) *adj.* **1** accidentado, lleno de altibajos, lleno de vicisitudes (la historia de una persona o similar). **2** a cuadros de diferentes colores.

cherish | ’tʃerɪʃ | *v.t.* **1** albergar, abrigar, acariciar (esperanzas o recuerdos). **2** apreciar, estimar, valorar (privilegios o derechos). **3** querer, amar (con gran afecto y cariño).

cherished | ’tʃerɪʃt | *adj.* estimado, valorado, apreciado (recuerdos, derechos, privilegios, etc.).

cheroot | ʃə’ruːt | *s.c.* purito, puro pequeño.

cherry | ’tʃerɪ | *s.c.* **1** cereza. **2** BOT. cerezo. || *adj.* **3** color cereza, rojo fuerte. || **4 another/a second bite at the –,** (fam.) tener una segunda oportunidad, gozar de otra oportunidad. **5 – red,** color cereza, rojo fuerte. **6 – tree,** BOT. cerezo.

cherub | ’tʃerəb | [*pl.* **cherubs** o **cherubim**] *s.c.* **1** REL. querubín. **2** ART. figuras de ángeles. **3** (fig.) angelito, pequeñín (sólo niños).

cherubic | tʃɪ’ruːbɪk | *adj.* (lit.) inocente, angelical (sólo niños).

cherubim | ’tʃerəbɪm | *pl.* de **cherub.**

chervil | ’tʃəːvɪl | *s.i.* BOT. perifollo, cerafolio.

chess | tʃes | *s.i.* ajedrez.

chessboard | ’tʃesbɔːd | *s.c.* tablero de ajedrez.

chessman | ’tʃesmæn | [*pl.* **chessmen**] *s.c.* pieza (de ajedrez).

chessmen | ’tʃesmən | *pl.* de **chessman.**

chest | tʃest | *s.c.* **1** ANAT. pecho, tórax. **2** baúl, arcón. || **3 – of drawers,** cómoda. **4 to get something off one's –,** (fam.) desahogarse, quitarse un peso de encima, decir cuatro verdades.

chestnut | ’tʃesnʌt | *s.c.* **1** BOT. castaño. **2** castaña. || *adj.* **3** de color castaño, castaño. || **4 – brown,** castaño, de color castaño. **5 – tree,** BOT. castaño. **6 old –,** (fam.) historia de siempre, cuento archiconocido, historia superconocida.

chestiness | ’tʃestɪnɪs | *s.i.* **1** voluminosidad pectoral (especialmente mujeres). **2** mucosidad, problemas de pecho, problemas de bronquios.

chesty | ’tʃestɪ | *adj.* **1** de pecho voluminoso (especialmente mujeres). **2** cargado (por un catarro); fluida, con flema (tos).

chevron | ’ʃevrən | *s.c.* **1** MIL. galón (indicador de rango). **2** (fig.) forma de galón, curva siguiendo la forma de un galón (derecho o revés).

chew | tʃuː | *v.t.* e *i.* **1** masticar, mascar. || *v.i.* **2 [to – at/on]** mascar, comer poco a poco (haciendo un agujero, por ejemplo). **3 [to – on/over]** (fam.) rumiar, pensar, meditar, dar vueltas (a un problema o similar). || *s.c.* **4** bocado (como acción de masticar). **5** caramelo duro (que en la boca se pone blando). || **6 to bite off more than one can –,** V. **bite. 7 to – the cud,** V. **cud. 8 to – the fat/rag,** (fam.) refunfuñar. **9 to – up,** masticar bien, masticar como es debido.

chewing-gum | ’tʃuːɪŋgʌm | *s.i.* goma de mascar, chicle.

chewy | ’tʃuːɪ | *adj.* (fam.) tirando a duro, correoso (alimento).

chic | tʃɪk | *adj.* **1** chic, fino, elegante. || *s.i.* **2** elegancia, estilo, finura.

chicanery | ʃɪ’keɪnərɪ | *s.c.* e *i.* (form.) trapacería, argucia; embrollo.

chick | tʃɪk | *s.c.* **1** pajarito, cría (de ave). **2** (p.u.) mozuela.

chicken | ’tʃɪkɪn | *s.c.* e *i.* **1** pollo (animal y su carne). **2** (fam.) miedica, gallina. || *adj.* **3** (fam.) miedica, gallina. || **4 a – and egg situation,** una situación de la pescadilla que se muerde la cola. **5 to be no –/to be no spring –,** no ser ya joven, no ser ninguna jovencita (de mujeres especialmente). **6 to – out,** (fam. y desp.) no atreverse a hacer (algo), tener demasiado miedo (de hacer algo): *he wanted to climb the mountain but chickened out at the last minute = quería subir la montaña pero en el último minuto no se atrevió a hacerlo.* **7 don't count your chickens/don't count your chickens before they're hatched,** (fam.) no te adelantes a los acontecimientos, no te ocurra lo del cuento de la lechera.

chickenfeed | ’tʃɪkɪnfiːd | *s.i.* **1** pienso para pollos. **2** (fig. y fam.) pequeñez (de dinero).

chickenpox | ’tʃɪkɪnpɒks | *s.i.* MED. varicela.

chickpea | ’tʃɪkpiː | *s.c.* BOT. garbanzo.

chickweed | ’tʃɪkwiːd | *s.i.* BOT. pamplina, álsine.

chicory | ’tʃɪkərɪ | *s.i.* **1** BOT. achicoria. **2** achicoria (como bebida).

chid | tʃɪd | *pret.* y *p.p.* de **chide.**

chidden | ’tʃɪdn | *p.p.* de **chide.**

chide | tʃaɪd | *v.t.* [*pret.* **chided** o **chid,** *p.p.* **chided, chid** o **chidden**] (p.u.) regañar, dar una regañina, reprender.

chief | tʃiːf | *s.c.* **1** jefe, director (de policía o departamento gubernamental). **2** jefe (de una tribu). **3** (fam.) jefe (forma de llamar a una persona con alguna autoridad): *yes, chief = sí, jefe.* || *adj.* **4** principal, más importante, fundamental. **5** superior, primero (en rango o categoría): *his chief cashier = su cajero primero.* || **6 Chief Constable,** (brit.) Comisario Jefe. **7 Chief Justice,** DER. Presidente de Tribunal. **8 Chief of Staff,** MIL. Jefe del Estado Mayor. **9 in-chief,** en jefe (en compuestos): *commander-in-chief = comandante en jefe.* **10 too many chiefs and not enough Indians/all chiefs and no Indians,** (fam. y desp.) demasiados mandamases y muy pocos mandados (con la consecuencia de no sacar las cosas bien).

chiefly | ’tʃiːflɪ | *adv.* **1** principalmente, fundamentalmente. **2** en su mayor parte, principalmente: *plastic is chiefly made of petrol = el plástico está en su mayor parte hecho de petróleo.*

chieftain | ’tʃiːftən | *s.c.* jefe, caudillo (de una tribu).

chiffon | ’ʃɪfɒn | (EE.UU.) | ʃɪ’fɒn | *s.i.* chifón, gasa (tejido finísimo).

chihuahua | tʃɪ’wɑːwɑ | (EE.UU.) | tʃɪ’wɑːwɑː | *s.c.* chiguagua (tipo de perro mejicano).

chilblain | ’tʃɪlbleɪn | *s.c.* sabañón.

child | tʃaɪld | [*pl.irreg.* **children**] *s.c.* **1** chico, chica, niño, niña (entre 0 y 14 años aproximadamente). **2** hijo, hija, chico, chica: *she's an only child = ella es hija única.* **3** (desp.) niño, niñato (persona mayor comportándose mal). **4 [– of]** (fig. y form.) producto de, resultado de, hijo de (alguien): *he was a child of his century = él fue producto de su siglo.* || **5 – benefit,** (brit.) ayuda familiar por hijo. **6 – prodigy,** niño prodigio, prodigio de niño. **7 child's play,** (fam.) juego de niños, tirado, facilón. **8 the – is father of the man,** las experiencias de la infancia dejan una marca imborrable. **9 with –,** (arc.) encinta, embarazada.

childbearing | ’tʃaɪldbeərɪŋ | *s.i.* **1** maternidad, parto. || *adj.* **2** capaz de procrear, capaz de dar a luz, en edad de tener hijos: *a childbearing woman.*

childbirth | ’tʃaɪldbəːθ | *s.i.* MED. parto, alumbramiento.

childhood | ’tʃaɪldhʊd | *s.c.* e *i.* **1** infancia, niñez. || **2 to be in one's second –,** estar en la segunda infancia (por demasiado viejo).

childish | ’tʃaɪldɪʃ | *adj.* **1** de niño, típico de un niño. **2** (desp.) pueril, infantil, infantiloide.

childishly | ’tʃaɪldɪʃlɪ | *adv.* (desp.) puerilmente, infantilmente.

childishness | ’tʃaɪldɪʃnɪs | *s.i.* (desp.) puerilidad, infantilismo.

childless | ’tʃaɪldlɪs | *adj.* sin hijos, sin descendencia.

childlike | 'tʃaɪldlaɪk | *adj.* inocente, infantil, característico de un niño, igual que un niño.
childminder | 'tʃaɪldmaɪndər | *s.c.* (brit.) niñera, cuidadora de niños.
childminding | 'tʃaɪldmaɪndɪŋ | *s.i.* (brit.) cuidado de niños.
childproof | 'tʃaɪldpruːf | *adj.* a prueba de accidentes infantiles.
children | 'tʃɪldrən | *pl.* 1 de **child.** || 2 **children's home,** refugio para niños maltratados.
Chile | 'tʃɪlɪ | *s.sing.* Chile.
Chilean | 'tʃɪlɪən | *s.c.* 1 chileno. || *adj.* 2 chileno.
chili V. **chilli.**
chill | tʃɪl | *v.t.* e *i.* 1 enfriar(se), refrigerar(se) (comida o bebida). || *v.t.* 2 helar, congelar. 3 (fig.) enfriar, hacer disminuir (ánimo, entusiasmo, etc.). 4 (lit.) horrorizar, asustar horriblemente. || *s.c.* 5 resfriado, enfriamiento. 6 (fig.) escalofrío. 7 (normalmente *sing.*) frialdad, frío (desagradable). || *adj.* 7 frío, desagradable (tiempo). 8 horrible, que asusta, que horroriza: *a chill reminder of war = un recuerdo horrible de la guerra.* || 9 **to be chilled to the bone/to the marrow,** estar muerto de frío, tener metido el frío hasta los huesos. 10 **to take the chill off something,** calentar un poquito algo (hasta que pierda el exceso de frialdad).
chilli | 'tʃɪlɪ | (EE.UU. **chili**) *s.c.* e *i.* 1 BOT. chile, guindilla. || 2 **=N con carne,** GAST. carne picada con chile. 3 **– powder,** pimienta picante.
chilliness | 'tʃɪlɪnɪs | *s.i.* 1 frío, frialdad. 2 (fig.) frialdad (de trato).
chilling | 'tʃɪlɪŋ | *adj.* 1 horrible, horripilante, aterrador. 2 helador (tiempo atmosférico).
chillingly | 'tʃɪlɪŋlɪ | *adv.* horriblemente, de manera horripilante, aterradoramente.
chilly | 'tʃɪlɪ | *adj.* 1 frío, desagradable, desapacible (tiempo). 2 frío, helado, congelado (sentimiento físico de una persona). 3 (fig.) frío, hostil (en las relaciones humanas).
chimaera V. **chimera.**
chime | tʃaɪm | *v.i.* 1 repicar, tañer (campanas o similar). || *v.t.* 2 dar (horas de reloj mediante campanadas o similar sonido). || *s.c.* 3 sonsonete, carrillón (de campanas, relojes, etc.). || *s.pl.* 4 carrillón, campanas (objetos que hacen un ruido de campanillas o parecido): *door chimes = campanillas de la puerta.* || 5 **to – in (with),** secundar, asentir (diciendo): *she always chimes in with "quite, quite" = ella siempre asiente diciendo "sí, claro".* 6 **to – in with,** estar en armonía con, concordar con (dos cosas).
chimera | kaɪ'mɪərə | (también **chimaera**) *s.c.* 1 quimera (animal mitológico hecho de distintas partes de otros animales). 2 (fig.) quimera, ilusión, cosa imposible.
chimerical | kaɪ'merɪkl | *adj.* quimérico, imposible.
chiming | 'tʃaɪmɪŋ | *s.sing.* **[– (of)]** campanilleo, sonido suave (parecido a campanillas).
chimney | tʃɪmnɪ | *s.c.* 1 chimenea (parte alargada a la vista sobre los tejados). 2 tubo de protección, cristal de protección (de una lámpara). 3 GEOL. chimenea, grieta (en montañas). || 4 **to smoke like a –,** fumar como un carretero.
chimney-breast | 'tʃɪmnɪbrest | *s.c.* (brit.) ARQ. manto de chimenea.
chimney-pot | 'tʃɪmnɪpɒt | *s.c.* ARQ. cañón de chimenea.
chimney-stack | 'tʃɪmnɪstæk | *s.c.* (brit.) ARQ. fuste de chimenea (donde se ven varios juntos).
chimneysweep | 'tʃɪmnɪswiːp | *s.c.* deshollinador.
chimp | tʃɪmp | *s.c.* (fam.) chimpancé.
chimpanzee | ˌtʃɪmpæn'ziː | | ˌtʃimpænziː | *s.c.* ZOOL. chimpancé.
chin | tʃɪn | *s.c.* 1 barbilla, mentón. || 2 **to keep one's – up,** (fam.) no desanimarse, mantener el tipo. 3 **to take it on the –,** (fam.) tomar algo como un hombre, aguantar el golpe como un hombre.
china | 'tʃaɪnə | *s.i.* 1 porcelana china, porcelana fina. 2 objetos de porcelana china. || *s.sing.* 3 **[the –]** la vajilla de porcelana, la porcelana (platos y demás). || 4 **like a bull in a – shop,** V. **bull.** 5 **China,** China. 6 **China's tea,** té chino.
Chinese | 'tʃaɪ'niːz | *adj.* 1 chino, de la China. || *s.i.* 2 chino (idioma). || *s.c.* 3 chino (de procedencia). 4 (brit. y fam.) comida china. || 5 **– puzzle,** rompecabezas chino (con objetos que entran dentro de otros).
chink | tʃɪnk | *s.c.* 1 grieta, hendidura, resquicio, abertura pequeña. 2 tintineo, tintín, sonido suave metálico. || *v.i.* 3 tintinear (sonido metálico). || 4 **a – in one's armour,** punto débil en la personalidad de uno, talón de Aquiles. 5 **Chink,** (vulg. y desp.) chino.
chinless | 'tʃɪnlɪs | *adj.* sin personalidad, sin fuerza de carácter.
chintz | tʃɪnts | *s.i.* cretona (tejido).
chintzy | 'tʃɪntsɪ | *adj.* con cretona, de oropel.
chinwag | 'tʃɪnwæg | *s.sing.* **[a –]** (fam.) una parrafada larga, una charla larga y distendida.
chip | tʃɪp | [*ger.* **chipping,** *pret.* y *p.p.* **chipped**] *v.t.* e *i.* 1 astillar(se), desconchar(se), desportillar(se), causar un pequeño desperfecto, hacerse un pequeño desperfecto. || *s.c.* 2 (brit.) patata, (Am.) papa (frita y alargada). 3 desportilladura, pedacito roto, astilla. 4 (EE.UU.) patata frita (de las que vienen en bolsa). 5 ficha (especialmente en los casinos). 6 INF. chip, microchip. 7 (fam.) pequeño desperfecto (en un objeto). || *s.sing.* 8 **[the –]** (fig.) el mundo del microchip, la tecnología del microchip. || 9 **a – off the old block,** (fam.) de tal palo tal astilla. 10 **a – on one's shoulder,** (fam.) estar resentido, tener algún rencor secreto. 11 **to – in,** (fam.) a) contribuir, ir a partes iguales (en algún gasto). b) interrumpir (conversación). 12 **to – off,** quitar, desportillar poco a poco (empapelado, capa de pintura, etc.). 13 **– shop,** (brit.) tienda de patatas fritas y pescado/trozos de carne/etc. (que normalmente se lleva a casa, ya hecho, a comer). 14 **to have had one's chips,** (fam.) acabarse las oportunidades para uno, no tener más oportunidad. 15 **potato chips,** (EE.UU.) patatas fritas (de las que van en bolsa). 16 **the silicon =N,** (fig.) la tecnología moderna de los ordenadores. 17 **when the chips are down,** (fam.) cuando las cosas se ponen serias, cuando llega el momento (de algo importante o serio).
chipboard | 'tʃɪpbɔːd | *s.i.* aglomerado.
chipmunk | 'tʃɪpmʌŋk | *s.c.* ZOOL. ardilla listada.
chipped | tʃɪpt | *adj.* desconchado, astillado, desportillado (objeto).
chippings | 'tʃɪpɪŋgz | *s.pl.* gravilla (en las carreteras): *loose chippings = gravilla suelta.*
chiropodist | kɪ'rɒpədɪst | (EE.UU. **podiatrist**) *s.c.* pedicuro, callista.
chiropody | kɪ'rɒpədɪ | (EE.UU. **podiatry**) pedicura.
chiropractor | 'kaɪərəuˈpræktər | *s.c.* quiropráctico.
chirp | tʃəːp | *v.i.* 1 gorjear, piar, hacer cri-cri (pájaros y algunos insectos). || *v.t.* e *i.* 2 (fig.) decir jovialmente, pronunciar alegremente: *she chirped goodbye and left = ella dijo adiós jovialmente y se marchó.* || *s.c.* 3 gorjeo, sonido como cri-cri.
chirpily | 'tʃəːpɪlɪ | *adv.* (brit. y fam.) jovialmente, alegremente.
chirpiness | 'tʃəːpɪnɪs | *s.i.* (brit. y fam.) jovialidad, alegría.
chirpy | 'tʃəːpɪ | *adj.* (brit. y fam.) jovial, alegre.
chirrup | 'tʃɪrəp | *v.i.* 1 hacer pío, gorjear, hacer cri-cri. || *s.c.* 2 gorjeo, pío.
chisel | 'tʃɪzl | [brit. *ger.* **chiselling,** *pret.* y *p.p.* **chiselled;** EE.UU. *ger.* **chiseling,** *pret.* y *p.p.* **chiseled**] *v.t.* 1 cincelar, tallar (piedra, madera, etc.). || *s.c.* 2 cincel; formón.
chiseller | 'tʃɪzlər | (EE.UU. **chiseler**) *s.c.* (fam.) engañabobos, oportunista (en el engaño), tramposo.
chit | tʃɪt | *s.c.* 1 vale, nota de autorización (de alguien con cierta capacidad oficial). 2 (p.u. y desp.) jovenzuela, mozuela.
chit-chat | 'tʃɪttʃæt | *s.i.* (fam.) charla, parloteo, cháchara.
chitter | 'tʃɪtər | *v.i.* gorjear repetidamente, lanzar sonidos agudos repetitivos (pájaros y algunos insectos).
chitty | 'tʃɪtɪ | *s.c.* (fam.) vale, nota de autorización.
chivalrous | 'ʃɪvəlrəs | *adj.* galante, caballeroso, cortés (hombres).
chivalrously | 'ʃɪvlrəslɪ | *adv.* galantemente, caballerosamente, cortésmente (forma de actuar hombres).

chivalry | 'ʃɪvəlrɪ | *s.i.* **1** HIST. código de caballería, sistema medieval de la caballería. **2** caballerosidad, cortesía.
chives | tʃaɪvz | BOT. *s.i.* **1** cebollino, cebolleta. || *s.pl.* **2** hojas de cebolleta.
chivvy | 'tʃɪvɪ | (también **chivy**) *v.t.* (fam.) acosar, atormentar, fastidiar (a alguien para que lleve a cabo algo).
chloride | 'klɔːraɪd | *s.c.* e *i.* QUIM. cloruro.
chlorinate | 'klɔːrɪneɪt | *v.t.* tratar con cloro, echar cloro.
chlorinated | 'klɔːrɪneɪtɪd | *adj.* tratado con cloro, clorado.
chlorination | ˌklɔːrɪ'neɪʃn | *s.i.* cloración.
chlorine | 'klɔːriːn | *s.i.* QUIM. cloro.
chloroform | 'klɒrəfɔːm: ˌɛɛ.ʊʊ.ˌ | 'klɔːrəfɔːm | *s.i.* **1** QUIM. cloroformo. || *v.t.* **2** anestesiar con cloroformo, cloroformizar.
chlorophyll | 'klɒrəfɪl | (EE.UU.) | 'klɔːrəfɪl | *s.i.* BOT. clorofila.
choc-ice | 'tʃɒkaɪs | *s.c.* helado de chocolate.
chock | ›ɪtʃɒk | *s.c.* chocolate.
chock-a-block | ˌtʃɒkə'blɒk | *adj.* **[– (with)]** abarrotado, de bote en bote.
chock-full | tʃɒk'fʊl | *adj.* **[– (of)]** (fam.) plagado, lleno.
chocolate | 'tʃɒklɪt | *s.i.* **1** chocolate (sólido o líquido). || *s.c.* **2** chocolatina, bombón. || *adj.* **3** color chocolate. || **4 – éclair,** GAST. tarta de chocolate, relámpago de chocolate.
chocolate-box | 'tʃɒklɪtbɒks | *s.c.* caja de bombones, caja de chocolatinas.
choice | tʃɔɪs | *s.c.* **1** elección (entre una cosa u otra): *the choice of food = la elección de comida.* **2** opción, posibilidad de elección. **3** preferencia: *my choice for a house = mi preferencia por una vivienda.* || *adj.* **4** selecto, de gran calidad. || **5 to have no – (but),** no tener más remedio (que), no tener otra alternativa (más que). **6 it's your –,** es tu propia decisión, es lo que tú quieres. **7 of one's –,** de la elección de uno: *that's the book of my choice = ése es el libro de mi elección.*
choir | 'kwaɪər | *s.c.* **1** MUS. coro. **2** ARQ. coro. || **3 – school,** escuela catedralicia; escuela aneja (a una institución universitaria).
choirboy | 'kwaɪəbɔɪ | *s.c.* niño cantor, niño de coro.
choirmaster | 'kwaɪəmɒːstər | *s.c.* director de coro, maestro de coro.
choke | tʃəuk | *v.t.* **1** ahogar, sofocar, asfixiar: *the lack of air almost choked me = la falta de aire casi me asfixió.* **2** estrangular, ahogar (violentamente). **3** abarrotar, taponar, atascar. || *v.i.* **4** ahogarse, sofocarse, asfixiarse. || *s.c.* **5** ahogo, sofoco, asfixia. **6** MEC. estárter; obturador, (Am.) choc. || *s.i.* **7** aire (mediante el estárter de un vehículo). || **8 to – back,** contener, ahogar (emociones, lágrimas, etc.).
choked | tʃəukt | *adj.* **1** ahogada (voz, sonido, etc.). **2** sofocado (por la ira, enfado, etc.).
choker | 'tʃəukər | *s.c.* collar ajustado (de mujer).
choking | 'tʃəukɪŋ | *adj.* sofocante, asfixiante: *chocking dust = polvo sofocante.*
cholera | 'kɒlərə | *s.i.* MED. cólera.
choleric | 'kɒlərɪk | *adj.* colérico, de mal genio.
cholesterol | kə'lestərɒl | *s.i.* QUIM. colesterol.
chomp | tʃɒmp | *v.t.* e *i.* (fam.) mascar ruidosamente, masticar con gran ruido (comida).
choose | tʃuːz | *v.* [*pret.* **chose,** *p.p.* **chosen**] t. **1** escoger, elegir, seleccionar. **2** optar por, decidir por. || *i.* **3** escoger, elegir. **4** apetecer: *do as you choose = haz lo que te apetezca.* **5 [to – +** *inf.*] decidir, preferir: *he chose to start soon = decidió empezar pronto.* || **6 little/not much to – between...,** poco/no mucho que elegir entre..., no hay gran diferencia entre... **7 to pick and –,** V. **pick.**
choosy | 'tʃuːzɪ | *adj.* (fam.) melindroso, delicado, quisquilloso.
chop | tʃɒp | [*ger.* **chopping,** *pret.* y *p.p.* **chopped**] *v.t.* **1** cortar, tajar. **2** hacer rajas de, cortar en rajas (alimentos). **3** dar un golpe de karate. **4** (fam.) reducir, recortar (gastos). || *v.i.* **5** cortar, tajar. **6** dar un golpe de karate. || *s.c.* **7** tajo, golpe de tajo. **8** chuleta (de carne). **9** golpe, golpe de karate. || **10 to – and change,** (fam.) vacilar interminablemente, cambiar constantemente de opinión. **11 – suey,** GAST. chop suey. **12 for the –,** (brit. y fam.) destinado a desaparecer, destinado a caer: *the social programs will be the first for the chop = los programas sociales serán los primeros destinados a desaparecer.* **13 to get/to be given the –,** (brit. y fam.) ser despedido (del trabajo).
chopper | 'tʃɒpər | *s.c.* helicóptero.
choppy | 'tʃɒpɪ | *adj.* agitado, picado (mar).
chopstick | 'tʃɒpstɪk | *s.c.* palillo (para comer en China).
choral | 'kɔːrəl | *adj.* MUS. coral.
chord | kɔːd | *s.c.* **1** MUS. acorde. **2** GEOM. cuerda. || **3 to strike/touch a –,** dar con el tono adecuado, dar con la fibra sensible (para alguien).
chore | tʃɔː | *s.c.* tarea, faena, quehacer (especialmente cuando es desagradable).
choreograph | 'kɒrɪəgræːf | | 'kɒrɪəgræf | (EE.UU.) | 'kɔːrɪəgræf | *v.t.* e *i.* **1** hacer la coreografía (en un ballet o similar). || *v.t.* **2** (normalmente *pas.*) montar artificialmente, hacer un montaje artificial de.
choreographer | ˌkɒrɪ'ɒgrəfər | (EE.UU.) | ˌkɔːrɪ'ɒgrəfər | *s.c.* coreógrafo.
choreographic | ˌkɒrɪə'græfɪk | (EE.UU.) | ˌkɔːrɪə'græfɪk | *adj.* coreográfico.
choreography | ˌkɒrɪ'ɒgrəfɪ | (EE.UU.) | kɔːrɪ'ɒgrəfɪ | *s.i.* coreografía.
chorister | 'kɒrɪstər | (EE.UU.) | 'kɔːrɪstər | *s.c.* miembro de un coro.
chortle | 'tʃɔːtl | *v.i.* **1** reír entre dientes, reír ahogadamente (con placer). || *s.c.* **2** risa entre dientes, risa ahogada.
chorus | 'kɔːrəs | *s.c.* **1** MUS. coro (grupo). **2** MUS. coro (composición). **3** MUS. refrán, estribillo. **4 [– (of)]** (fig.) coro (de misma opinión, sentimiento, etc.). **5 [– (of)]** (fig.) coro (de canto de animales). || *v.t.* **6** decir a coro, decir al unísono. || **7 – girl,** corista. **8 in –,** al unísono.
chose | 'tʃəuz | *pret.irreg.* de **choose.**
chosen | 'tʃəuzn | *p.p.irreg.* **1** de **choose.** || *adj.* **2** elegido, seleccionado; querido, deseado. || **3 the – few,** la minoría, los menos, los pocos elegidos (por la fortuna).
chow | tʃau | *s.c.* **1** ZOOL. perro chino. || *s.i.* **2** (fam.) comida.
chowder | 'tʃəudər | *s.i.* GAST. sopa de pescado.
Christ | kraɪst | *s.sing.* **1** REL. Cristo. || *interj.* **2** Dios mío.
christen | 'krɪsn | *v.t.* **1** REL. bautizar. **2** nombrar, dar un nombre a. **3** (fam.) utilizar por primera vez.
Christendom | 'krɪsndəm | *s.sing.* HIST. Cristiandad.
christening | 'krɪsnɪŋ | *s.c.* REL. bautismo, bautizo.
Christian | 'krɪstɪən | *s.c.* **1** REL. cristiano. || *adj.* **2** REL. cristiano. **3** (fig.) bueno, virtuoso, cristiano. || **4 – name,** nombre propio.
Christianity | ˌkrɪstɪ'ænɪtɪ | *s.i.* REL. cristianismo.
Christmas | 'krɪsməs | *s.c.* e *i.* REL. Navidad. || **2 – Day,** día de Navidad. **3 – Eve,** Nochebuena. **4 – pudding,** pastel de Navidad. **5 – tree,** árbol de Navidad.
chrome | krəum | (también **chromium**) *s.i.* MIN. cromo.
chromium | 'krəumɪəm | V. **chrome.**
chromosome | 'krəuməsəum | *s.c.* BIOQUIM. cromosoma.
chronic | 'krɒnɪk | *adj.* **1** crónico (enfermedad o similar). **2** habitual, crónico, empedernido, inveterado (en sus hábitos negativos). **3** severo (problema o situación): *chronic unemployment.*
chronically | 'krɒnɪklɪ | *adv.* **1** crónicamente, de manera repetitiva. **2** severamente (de un problema o situación).
chronicle | 'krɒnɪkl | *s.c.* **1** crónica, historia. || *v.t.* **2** hacer la crónica de, narrar. || **3 Chronicle,** PER. Crónica (formando parte del nombre de un periódico).
chronological | ˌkrɒnə'lɒdʒɪkl | *adj.* **1** cronológico, secuencial. **2** real, cronológica (edad).
chronologically | ˌkrɒnə'lɒdʒɪklɪ | *adv.* **1** cronológicamente, en orden cronológico. **2** realmente (de la edad).
chronology | krə'nɒlədʒɪ | *s.i.* **[– (of)]** cronología, secuencia.
chrysalis | 'krɪsəlɪs | *s.c.* BIOL. crisálida.
chrysanthemum | krɪ'sænθəməm | *s.c.* BOT. crisantemo.
chubbiness | 'tʃʌbɪnɪs | *s.i.* (lo) regordete (de una cara, cuerpo, etc.).

chubby | 'tʃʌbɪ | *adj.* regordete, rellenito.
chuck | tʃʌk | (fam.) *v.t.* **1** arrojar, tirar, echar. **2** (brit.) dejar plantado, plantar (a alguien). (a un novio o novia). **3** abandonar, dejar (un empleo, actividad, etc.). || **4 to – away/out,** tirar, arrojar (algo que no se desea). **5 – steak,** filete de lomo.
chuckle | 'tʃʌkl | *v.i.* **1** reírse ahogadamente, reírse para uno mismo. || *s.c.* **2** risa ahogada, risa sofocada, risa para uno mismo.
chuffed | tʃʌft | *adj.* **[– (about)]** (brit. y fam.) encantado, contentísimo.
chug | tʃʌg | [*ger.* **chugging,** *pret.* y *p.p.* **chugged**] *v.i.* **1** hacer ruidos de explosión repetidamente. **2 [to – + *prep.*]** moverse haciendo ruidos de explosión repetitivos. || *s.c.* **3** ruido explosivo, explosión pequeña.
chum | tʃʌm | (fam. y p.u.) *s.c.* **1** macho, compinche, amigote. || **2 to – up (with),** hacerse amigo (de), compadrear (con).
chummily | 'tʃʌmɪlɪ | *adv.* simpáticamente, amigablemente.
chumminess | 'tʃʌmɪnɪs | *s.i.* simpatía, buenos sentimientos de amistad.
chummy | 'tʃʌmɪ | *adj.* (fam. y p.u.) simpático, amigable.
chump | 'tʃʌmp | *s.c.* (fam.) bobo, bobalicón.
chunk | 'tʃʌŋk | *s.c.* **1** trozo, pedazo. **2 [– (of)]** (fam.) porción sustancial.
chunky | 'tʃʌŋkɪ | *adj.* **1** fornido, cuadrado (persona). **2** macizo, sólido (objeto).
church | tʃɜːtʃ | *s.c.* **1** iglesia, templo. || *s.sing.* **2** REL. iglesia, grupo religioso. || **3 Church of England,** REL. Iglesia de Inglaterra, iglesia anglicana. **4 to go to –,** ir a la iglesia, ir a misa. **5 the Church/the –,** REL. la iglesia (sus componentes o su jerarquía).
churchgoer | 'tʃɜːtʃgəʊər | *s.c.* practicante, fiel (que va a misa).
churchman | 'tʃɜːtʃmən | [*pl.* **churchmen**] *s.c.* clérigo.
churchmen | 'tʃeːtʃmən | *pl.* de **churchman.**
churchwarden | tʃɜːtʃ'wɔːdən | *s.c.* REL. laico ayudante del cura (en la iglesia de Inglaterra).
churchyard | 'tʃɜːtʃjɑːd | *s.c.* cementerio de la iglesia (alrededor del edificio).
churlish | 'tʃɜːlɪʃ | *adj.* maleducado, grosero, intratable.
churlishly | 'tʃɜːlɪʃlɪ | *adv.* maleducadamente, groseramente, intratablemente.
churlishness | 'tʃɜːlɪʃnɪs | *s.i.* grosería, intratabilidad.
churn | tʃɜːn | *v.t.* **1** batir (leche, nata, etc.). || *v.t.* e *i.* **2** agitar(se), remover(se), revolver(se) (lodo, agua, etc.). || *v.i.* **3** (fam.) dar vuelcos (el estómago a punto de vomitar). || *s.c.* **4** mantequera (donde se hace mantequilla). || **5 to – out,** (desp.) hacer como churros. **6 to – up, a)** agitar con fuerza, remover violentamente, revolver por completo. **b)** (fam.) sacar de quicio, volver loco de ira, poner malo.
churning | 'tʃɜːnɪŋ | *s.i.* revuelco (en el estómago).
chute | ʃuːt | *s.c.* **1** tobogán, rampa de caída (para enviar mercancía con rapidez). **2** (fam.) paracaídas.
chutney | 'tʃʌtnɪ | *s.i.* GAST. condimento de especias.
cicada | sɪ'kɑːdə | *s.c.* ZOOL. cigarra.
cider | 'saɪdər | *s.i.* sidra.
cigar | sɪ'gɑːr | *s.c.* puro.
cigarette | ˌsɪgə'ret | (EE.UU.) | 'sɪgərət | *s.c.* **1** cigarrillo, pitillo. || **2 – end,** colilla. **3 – case,** pitillera. **4 – holder,** boquilla. **5 – lighter,** encendedor, mechero. **6 – paper,** papel de fumar.
cinch | sɪntʃ | *s.sing.* (fam.) cosa chupada, cosa tirada.
cinder | 'sɪndər | *s.c.* **1** (normalmente *pl.*) carbonilla, pavesa. || **2 to burn to a –,** quemar por completo, dejar hecho cenizas. **3 – track,** DEP. pista de atletismo de ceniza.
cine-camera | 'sɪnɪkæmərə | *s.c.* FOT. cámara de cine.
cinema | 'sɪnəmɑː | | 'sɪnəmə | *s.c.* **1** cine (lugar). || *s.i.* **2** ART. cine.
cinematic | ˌsɪnə'mætɪk | *adj.* del cine, cinematográfico.
cinematography | ˌsɪnəmə'tɒgrəfɪ | *s.i.* cinematografía.
cinnamon | 'sɪnəmən | *s.i.* BOT. canela.
cipher | 'saɪfər | (también **cypher**) *s.c.* **1** cifra, clave, código secreto. **2** mensaje cifrado, mensaje en clave. **3** (fam. y desp.) cero a la izquierda (persona sin importancia). || **4 in –,** en clave, cifrado.
ciphered | 'saɪfəd | *adj.* (forrm.) cifrado, escrito con código secreto.
circa | 'səkə | *prep.* (form.) cerca de, alrededor de, aproximadamente en (en el tiempo).
circle | 'sɜːkl | *s.c.* **1** círculo. **2 [– (of)]** círculo, redondel (cualquier forma). **3 [– (of)]** círculo, grupo (de personas). **4** GEOM. circunferencia. || *v.t.* **5** dar vueltas a, rodear, circundar. **6** hacer un círculo en, dibujar un círculo en, enmarcar dentro de un círculo. || *v.i.* **7** dar vueltas, girar alrededor: *the plane circled for hours = el avión dio vueltas durante horas.* || *s.sing.* **8 [the –]** arriba, anfiteatro (en un cine o teatro). || **9 to come full –,** acabar en el punto de partida, volver al mismo punto de partida (en un debate, situación, etc.). **10 to go round in circles,** (fam.) no avanzar nada, dar vueltas sin llegar a nada (en una discusión, problema o en un movimiento físico). **11 to run round in circles,** (fam.) ir por la vida corriendo sin parar (especialmente cuando no sirve para nada).
circlet | 'səklɪt | *s.c.* **[– (of)]** corona (de joyas, flores, etc., como adorno).
circuit | 'sɜːkɪt | *s.c.* **1** ELECTR. circuito. **2** gira, recorrido (de un lugar o serie de lugares con alguna característica común). **3** vuelta, recorrido en círculo (física). **4** circuito (de carreras). **5** DER. recorrido (de un juez cuya función es pasar cada cierto tiempo por ciertos lugares).
circuit-breaker | 'sɜːkɪtbreɪkər | *s.c.* ELECTR. interruptor automático.
circuitous | sə'kjuːɪtəs | *adj.* (form. o lit.) indirecta, tortuosa (ruta).
circuitously | sə'kjuːɪtəslɪ | *adv.* (form. o lit.) indirectamente, sin seguir un camino recto, tortuosamente, sinuosamente (en la ruta).
circuitry | 'sɜːkɪtrɪ | *s.i.* ELECTR. sistema de circuitos.
circular | 'sɜːkjʊlər | *adj.* **1** circular, redondo. **2** en círculo (un viaje que vuelve al punto de partida por distinto trayecto). **3** fallido, tortuoso, ilógico (forma de razonar). **4** enviada a muchas personas (circular, propaganda, etc.). || *s.c.* **5** circular (administrativa), propaganda enviada a muchas personas.
circularity | ˌsɜːkjʊ'lærɪtɪ | *s.i.* tortuosidad, falta de lógica (en el razonamiento).
circulate | 'sɜːkjʊleɪt | *v.t.* e *i.* **1** divulgar(se), propagar(se), circular (información, escritos, rumores, historias, etc.). **2** pasar, repartir, circular (comida o bebida en alguna ocasión social). **3** mover(se), circular (aire, refrigeración, sangre dentro del cuerpo, etc.). || *v.i.* **4** mezclarse, entremezclarse (con gente, especialmente en una fiesta o situación parecida). **5** moverse con fluidez, circular fácilmente (tráfico).
circulation | ˌsɜːkjʊ'leɪʃn | *s.c.* **1** PER. volumen de venta, número de ejemplares vendidos (periódicos, revistas, etc.). **2** movimiento, circulación (del aire o tráfico). || *s.sing.* **3** ANAT. circulación (de la sangre). || *s.i.* **4** ECON. circulación (de dinero). || **5 in – again/back in –,** de vuelta en el trabajo, de vuelta en la vida normal (especialmente después de enfermedad).
circulatory | ˌsɜːkjʊ'leɪtərɪ | (EE.UU.) | 'sɜːkjələtɔːrɪ | *adj.* MED. circulatorio (de la sangre).
circumcise | 'sɜːkəmsaɪz | *v.t.* circuncidar.
circumcision | ˌsɜːkəm'sɪʒn | *s.c.* e *i.* circuncisión.
circumference | sə'kʌmfərəns | *s.c.* **1** circunferencia, borde de un círculo. **2** circunferencia, longitud de una circunferencia.
circumflex | 'sɜːkəmfleks GRAM. *adj.* **1** circunflejo. || **2 – accent,** acento circunflejo.
circumlocution | ˌsɜːkəmlə'kjuːʃn | *s.c.* e *i.* (form.) circunloquio.
circumscribe | 'sɜːkəmskraɪb | *v.t.* **1** (form.) circunscribir, limitar. **2** GEOM. circunscribir, delinear.
circumspect | 'sɜːkəmspekt | *adj.* (form.) circunspecto, discreto, prudente.
circumspectly | 'sɜːkəmspektlɪ | *adv.* (form.) de modo circunspecto, discretamente, prudentemente.
circumspection | ˌsɜːkəm'spekʃn | *s.i.* (form.) circunspección, discreción, prudencia.

circumstance | 'sɑːkəmstəns | *s.i.* **1** (form.) circunstancia, fatalidad. || *s.pl.* **2** circunstancias, situación; posición. || **3 in/under the circumstances,** vistas las circunstancias, dada la situación existente, dadas las circunstancias. **4 under no circumstances,** bajo ningún supuesto, bajo ninguna circunstancia, de ninguna manera.
circumstantial | ˌsɑːkəm'stænʃl | *adj.* (form.) **1** completa, minuciosa (descripción). **2** circunstancial (prueba).
circumstantially | ˌsɑːkəm'stænʃəlɪ | *adv.* (form.) **1** minuciosamente, detalladamente (en una descripción). **2** circunstancialmente (prueba).
circumvent | ˌsɑːkəm'vent | *v.t.* (form.) **1** salvar, burlar, evitar, rodear (reglas, restricciones, etc.). **2** ser más listo que, burlar (a una persona).
circus | 'sɑːkəs | *s.c.* **1** circo. **2** HIST. circo romano. **3** (fam. y fig.) circo, cachondeo. || *s.sing.* **4 [the –]** ART. el circo. || *adj.* circense.
cirrhosis | sɪ'rəusɪs | *s.i.* MED. cirrosis.
cirri | 'sɪraɪ | *pl.* de **cirrus.**
cirrus | 'sɪrəs | [*pl.* **cirri**] *s.c.* e *i.* cirro (tipo de nube).
cissy V. **sissy.**
cistern | 'sɪstən | *s.c.* **1** cisterna (en un servicio). **2** tanque de agua, aljibe, depósito de agua (normalmente en un tejado).
citadel | 'sɪtədl | *s.c.* **1** fortaleza, ciudadela, alcázar. **2** (fig. y lit.) reducto, baluarte (ambiente difícil de penetrar): *the citadel of executives = el reducto de los ejecutivos.*
citation | saɪ'teɪʃn | *s.c.* (form.) **1** mención honorífica (especialmente por un acto de valentía en el ejército). **2** mención, cita (literaria). **3** DER. aviso de presentación a juicio, citación judicial.
cite | saɪt | *v.t.* (form.) **1** citar, entrar una cita de, mencionar (literariamente o como ejemplo de lo que se está diciendo). **2** DER. hacer una mención oficial, mencionar oficialmente. **3** DER. citar, hacer comparecer (en juicio). **4** mencionar honoríficamente (especialmente en un contexto militar).
citizen | 'sɪtɪzn | *s.c.* **1** ciudadano. **2** habitante (de una localidad). || **3 citizen's arrest,** DER. arresto llevado a cabo por un ciudadano (no un policía). **4 citizen's band,** RAD. banda de uso común (especialmente los camioneros).
citizenry | 'sɪtɪznrɪ | *s.i.* [=N *v.sing./pl.*] (lit.) ciudadanía (la gente).
citizenship | 'sɪtɪznʃɪp | *s.i.* **1** nacionalidad. **2** ciudadanía (como pertenencia a una comunidad).
citric acid | ˌsɪtrɪk'æsɪd | *s.i.* QUIM. ácido cítrico.
citrus | 'sɪtrəs | *s.c.* **1** BOT. agrio, producto agrio. || **2 – fruit,** cítrico.
city | 'sɪtɪ | *s.c.* **1** ciudad (normalmente con catedral). || *s.sing.* **2 [the –]** la ciudad entera, toda la ciudad (sus habitantes). || **3 – hall,** Ayuntamiento. **4 the City, a)** la zona céntrica comercial de Londres. **b)** (fig.) FIN. el mundo financiero de Londres.
civic | 'sɪvɪk | *adj.* **1** POL. municipal, local. **2** cívico, con sentido del bien común.
civics | 'sɪvɪks | *s.i.* POL. política local (como estudio).
civies V. **civvies.**
civil | 'sɪvl | *adj.* **1** civil, público. **2** civil (no militar). **3** educado, cortés, urbano. **4** DER. civil (no criminal). || **5 – defence,** protección civil, defensa civil. **6 – defences,** MIL. defensas civiles, seguridad civil (en tiempo de guerra). **7 – disobedience,** POL. desobediencia civil. **8 – divorce,** DER. divorcio civil. **9 – engineer,** ingeniero civil, ingeniero de caminos. **10 – engineering,** ingeniería civil. **11 – law,** DER. derecho civil. **12 – liberty,** libertades, libertad ciudadana. **13 – list,** (brit.) presupuesto de la Casa Real. **14 – marriage,** matrimonio civil. **15 – rights,** derechos civiles, garantías constitucionales. **16 – servant,** funcionario público. **17 Civil Service,** administración pública, administración del estado. **18 – war,** guerra civil.
civilly | 'sɪvəlɪ | *adv.* con urbanidad, cortésmente, educadamente.
civilian | sɪ'vɪlɪən | *s.c.* civil (no militar).
civilise V. **civilize.**
civility | sɪ'vɪlɪtɪ | (form.) *s.c.* e *i.* **1** urbanidad, buena educación, cortesía. || **2 civilities,** fórmulas de cortesía, fórmulas de urbanidad.
civilization | ˌsɪvəlaɪ'zeɪʃn | (EE.UU.) | ˌsɪvəlɪ'zeɪʃn | (también **civilisation**) *s.c.* e *i.* **1** HIST. civilización. || *s.i.* **2** civilización (estado de modernidad). **3** (hum.) civilización, vida moderna, vida cómoda. **4** civilización, buenas maneras, urbanidad. **5** civilización, humanidad, mundo civilizado.
civilize | 'sɪvəlaɪz | (también **civilise**) *v.t.* **1** civilizar. **2** (fig.) embellecer, hacer civilizado, poner con todas las comodidades (lugar).
civilized | 'sɪvɪlaɪzd | (también **civilised**) *adj.* **1** civilizado. **2** (fig.) embellecido, acondicionado con todas las comodidades (lugar). **3** refinado, civilizado (en sus maneras).
civilizing | ˌsɪvɪ'laɪzɪŋ | (también **civilising**) *adj.* civilizador, modernizador: *civilizing influences = influencias modernizadoras.*
civvies | 'sɪvɪz | (también **civies**) *s.pl.* (fam.) traje de paisano.
clack | klæk | *v.t.* e *i.* **1** hacer un ruido seco, hacer clac. || *s.c.* **2** ruido seco, golpe seco. || **3 to – one's tongue,** decir chismes, murmurar.
clad | klæd | *adj.* **[– (in)]** (p.u. o lit.) vestido, ataviado.
cladding | 'klædɪŋ | *s.i.* ARQ. revestimiento.
claim | kleɪm | *v.t.* **1** aseverar, asegurar, mantener: *he claimed he hadn't gone in to rob = él mantuvo que no había entrado a robar.* **2** solicitar, pedir, reclamar (atención): *my son claimed all my attention = mi hijo reclamó toda mi atención.* **3** demandar, exigir (derechos, dineros, ayuda, etc.): *the students claimed higher grants = los estudiantes demandaron becas más elevadas.* **4** alegar, afirmar, sostener (la inocencia de una persona). **5** cobrarse (víctimas). || *v.i.* **6 [to – for/on/to]** exigir, demandar (cualquier beneficio, derecho o similar): *I want to claim for children's allowances = quiero exigir la ayuda familiar por hijos.* || *s.c.* **7** aseveración, afirmación. **8 [– for]** demanda de, exigencia de (dinero, derechos, etc.). **9 [– on/upon/to/of]** derecho a, título a (una propiedad, beneficio, reconocimiento de algo, etc.). **10** reclamación, denuncio (especialmente de minas de metales preciosos). || **11 to – responsibility/credit (for),** responsabilizarse (de), aceptar decididamente la responsabilidad (de) (algo de lo que uno se puede enorgullecer). **12 to lay – to,** (form.) reclamar, reclamar la soberanía sobre, reclamar la posesión de. **13 to stake a –,** V. **stake.**
claimant | 'kleɪmənt | *s.c.* DER. demandante.
clairvoyance | kleə'vɔɪəns | *s.i.* clarividencia.
clairvoyant | kleə'vɔɪənt | *s.c.* **1** clarividente. || *adj.* **2** clarividente.
clam | klæm | *s.c.* **1** ZOOL. almeja. || **2 to – up,** (fam.) callarse como un muerto, no decir ni pío. **3 to shut up like a –,** (fam.) negarse a seguir hablando, negarse a hablar, cerrar el pico.
clamber | 'klæmbər | *v.i.* **1** encaramarse a gatas, gatear, trepar a gatas. || *s.c.* **2** recorrido a gatas, movimiento a gatas.
clammily | 'klæmɪlɪ | *adv.* pegajosamente (por la humedad).
clamminess | 'klæmɪnɪs | *s.i.* humedad pegajosa.
clammy | klæmɪ | *adj.* pegajoso (por la humedad).
clamorous | 'klæmərəs | *adj.* (form.) estridente, tumultuoso; vociferante.
clamor | 'klæmər | (*brit.* **clamour**) (form. o lit.) *s.i.* **1 [– (for)]** clamor (a favor de alguna medida, castigo, etc.). || *v.i.* **2 [to – for]** clamar por, demandar enérgicamente, exigir ruidosamente. **3** gritar, vociferar. || *s.c.* e *i.* **4** algarada, algarabía, vocerío, griterío.
clamp | klæmp | *s.c.* **1** MEC. abrazadera; laña; tornillo de ajuste. || *v.t.* **2** sujetar fuertemente, agarrar firmemente (como una abrazadera): *they clamped the two legs together = ellos sujetaron las dos patas fuertemente.* **3** apretar violentamente (ojos o labios). || **4 to – down (on),** apretar las clavijas (a); intentar acabar (con) (una situación mala): *the police are ready to clamp down on hooligans = la policía está dispuesta a apretar las clavijas a los gamberros.*

clampdown | 'klæmpdaʊn | *s.c.* **[– (on)]** restricción, prohibición, dificultación.
clan | klæn | *s.c.* **1** HIST. clan (en Escocia). **2** (fig. o hum.) clan (de una familia o grupo de personas).
clandestine | klæn'destɪn | *adj.* (form.) clandestino, furtivo, subrepticio.
clang | klæŋ | *v.t.* e *i.* **1** hacer un ruido fuerte (metálico). || *s.c.* **2** ruido fuerte, ruido estruendoso (metálico).
clanger | 'klæŋər | **to drop a –,** (brit. y fam.) meter la pata hasta el correjón, meter la pata estruendosamente.
clangour | 'klæŋgər | (EE.UU. **clangor**) *s.i.* (form.) estrépito continuo, estruendo inacabable.
clank | klæŋk | *v.t.* e *i.* **1** hacer un ruido metálico por choque, resonar metálicamente con gran estruendo. || *s.sing.* **2** sonido estruendoso metálico, choque estruendoso (metálico).
clannish | 'klænɪʃ | *adj.* (desp.) exclusivista, fiel sólo a su grupo, amigo de capillas.
clap | klæp | [ger. **clapping,** *pret.* y *p.p.* **clapped**] *v.t.* e *i.* **1** aplaudir; batir, dar (palmas). || *v.t.* **2** golpear, dar una palmada (en la espalda, especialmente). **3** poner con fuerza (en un lugar): *he clapped his hat on = se puso con fuerza el sombrero.* **4** (fam.) meter, empujar (a alguien en la prisión). || *s.c.* **5** aplauso. **6** golpe, palmada (típicamente en la espalda). || *s.sing.* **7 [the –]** (fam.) la sífilis, la gonorrea. || **8 a – of thunder,** un trueno. **9 to – eyes on someone,** V. **eye. 10 to – hands on,** (brit. y fam.) coger in fraganti, coger con las manos en la masa.
clapboard | 'klæpbɔːd | *s.c.* (EE.UU.) tabla, tablero (alargado).
clapped-out | 'klæptaʊt | *adj.* (brit. y fam.) fastidiada (cosa); medio muerto de cansancio (persona).
clapper | 'klæpər | *s.c.* **1** badajo (de campana). || **2 like the clappers,** (brit. y fam.) a toda pastilla, a todo meter.
clapperboard | 'klæpəbɔːd | *s.c.* claqueta (en el cine).
claptrap | 'klæptræp | *s.i.* (fam.) bobadas, tonterías, chorradas (dichas).
claret | 'klærət | *s.c.* e *i.* clarete (vino).
clarification | ˌklærɪfɪ'keɪʃn | *s.c.* e *i.* clarificación, esclarecimiento, aclaración.
clarified | 'klærɪfaɪd | *adj.* GAST. clarificado, limpiado (mediante calor).
clarify | 'klærɪfaɪ | *v.t.* **1** (form.) aclarar, esclarecer, poner en claro. **2** GAST. clarificar, limpiar de impurezas (mediante calor).
clarinet | ˌklærə'net | *s.c.* MUS. clarinete.
clarinettist | ˌklærə'netɪst | *s.c.* MUS. clarinetista.
clarion | 'klærɪən | *adj.* **1** sonoro, fuerte y claro (sonido). || **2 – call,** (lit.) llamada, exhortación (a hacer algo).
clarity | 'klærɪtɪ | *s.i.* **1** claridad, nitidez (de dibujo o sonido). **2** lucidez (de pensamiento, razonamiento, etc.). **3 [– (of)]** claridad, nitidez (de una explicación o similar).
clash | klæʃ | *v.i.* **1 [to – (with)]** chocar, pelear, reñir (personas). **2 [to – (with)]** chocar, entrar en conflicto, encontrarse (ideas, creencias, etc.). **3 [to – (with)]** no ir bien juntos, desentonar (ropa, colores, estilos, etc.). **4 [to – (with)]** coincidir, concurrir (dos acontecimientos, fechas, citas, etc.). **5** darse con estruendo, chocar sonoramente. || *v.t.* **6** hacer sonar estruendosamente. || *s.c.* **7 [– (between/with/of/over)]** riña, desacuerdo, pelea, encontronazo. **8** conflicto, encontronazo, choque (de culturas, creencias, etc.). **9** estruendo, golpetazo, ruido atronador. **10** faltos de armonía, que desentonan (de colores, estilos, etc.). **11** coincidencia (de fechas o similar).
clasp | klɑːsp | (EE.UU.) | klæsp | *v.t.* **1** agarrar con fuerza, abrazar estrechamente, estrechar, apretar. **2** abrochar, mantener abrochado. || *s.c.* **3** broche, cierre. **4** abrazo fuerte, apretón. || **5 – knife,** navaja de muelle.
class | klɑːs, (EE.UU.) | klæs | *s.c.* **1** clase, grupo de estudiantes. **2** clase, clase social. **3** BIOL. clase, grupo, categoría (de animales). **4** clase, categoría (de cosas): *a new class of detergents = una nueva clase de detergentes.* || *s.c.* e *i.* **5** clase, lección (académica). **6** clase, calidad (en productos, viajes, etc.). || *s.i.* **7** (brit.) de honor (de resultado académico): *first class honours = matrícula de honor.* **8** clase, estilo: *she's got class = ella tiene clase.* || *s.sing.* **9** (EE.UU.) generación, promoción (estudiantil). || *v.t.* **10** clasificar, agrupar. || **11 in a – of one's own/by itself,** único en su género, sin parangón. **12 in the same – (as),** en la misma clase (que), en la misma categoría (que); de la misma calidad (que). **13 the – struggle,** POL. la lucha de clases.
class-conscious | 'klɑːskɒnʃəs | (EE.UU.) | 'klæskɒnʃəs | *adj.* con conciencia de clase.
class-consciousness | 'klɑːskɒnʃəsnɪs | (EE.UU.) | klæskɒnʃəsnɪs | *s.i.* conciencia de clase.
classic | 'klæsɪk | *adj.* **1** ART. clásico. **2** clásico, típico: *the classic Spaniard = el español clásico.* **3** clásico, definitivo (obra de arte). || *s.c.* **4** LIT. clásico, obra maestra.
classical | 'klæsɪkl | *adj.* **1** clásico, tradicional, de siempre. **2** FILOL. clásico (variante idiomática). **3** MUS. clásica (música). **4** HIST. clásico (de la época grecorromana). **5** refinado, clásico, sencillo (estilo, belleza, adornos, etc.).
classically | 'klæsɪkəlɪ | *adv.* **1** clásicamente, típicamente. **2** refinadamente, clásicamente, sencillamente (en estilo, belleza, etc.).
classicism | 'klæsɪsɪzəm | *s.i.* ART. clasicismo.
classicist | 'klæsɪsɪst | *s.c.* especialista en estudios clásicos.
classics | 'klæsɪks | *s.i.* clásicas, estudios clásicos.
classification | ˌklæsɪfɪ'keɪʃn | *s.c.* e *i.* clasificación, tipificación, categorización.
classified | 'klæsɪfaɪd | *adj.* **1** clasificado, por grupos (una lista). **2** oficialmente secreta (información estatal). || **3 – advertisements,** PER. anuncios por palabras.
classify | 'klæsɪfaɪ | *v.t.* clasificar, poner en grupos ordenados.
classless | 'klɑːslɪs | (EE.UU.) | 'klæslɪs | *adj.* sin clases, igualitaria (sociedad).
classmate | 'klɑːsmeɪt | (EE.UU.) | 'klæsmeɪt | *s.c.* compañero de clase, condiscípulo, compañero de aula.
classroom | 'klɑːsrum | (EE.UU.) | 'klæsrum | *s.c.* aula, clase.
classy | 'klɑːsɪ, (EE.UU.) | 'klæsɪ | *adj.* (fam.) excelente, de mucho pisto, de gran postín.
clatter | 'klætər | *v.t.* e *i.* **1** hacer ruidos repetitivos, golpetear, tabletear. **2 [to – + *prep.*]** moverse haciendo ruidos repetitivos, hacer ruidos repetitivos (con una máquina, por ejemplo). || *s.sing.* **3** golpeteo, traqueteo, ruido repetitivo.
clause | klɔːz | *s.c.* **1** GRAM. oración (subordinada o principal). **2** DER. cláusula.
claustrophobia | ˌklɔːstrə'fəubɪə | *s.i.* PSIQ. claustrofobia.
claustrophobic | ˌklɔːstrə'fəubɪk | *adj.* **1** claustrofóbico, causante de claustrofobia (situación). **2** PSIQ. claustrófobo (persona).
clavichord | 'klævɪkɔːd | *s.c.* MUS. clavicordio.
claw | klɔː | *s.c.* **1** garra, zarpa, uña (en animales); tenaza (en marisco). || *v.t.* **2** hincar las garras en, atrapar. || **3 to – at,** echar zarpazos, tirar coces. **4 to – back,** (brit.) recuperar, volver a tomar (especialmente el gobierno dinero de los ciudadanos previamente concedido por él). **5 to – one's way,** abrirse camino en la vida a base de zarpazos (a los que están alrededor). **6 to get one's claws into,** (fam.) atacar con furor a, echar los zarpazos de uno encima de (especialmente por parte de mujeres).
clay | kleɪ | *s.i.* **1** arcilla. || **2 – pigeon,** tiro al plato. **3 to have feet of –,** tener pies de barro.
clean | kliːn | *adj.* **1** limpio, aseado. **2** FIS. limpio, sin radioactividad, descontaminado. **3** blanco, en blanco, sin usar (papel). **4** limpia, sin mancha (reputación, fama, etc.). **5** en limpio (no en borrador). **6** limpio (juego). **7** limpio, puro, saludable (aire, agua, etc.). **8** radical, completo, total (cambio vital o parecido): *a clean break = un cambio radical.* **9** limpia, honesta (vida). **10** limpio, nítido, perfectamente perceptible (sonido). **11** de formas suaves, de dimensiones adecuadas, bien definido, de formas elegantes: *an aeroplane with clean lines = un avión con líneas de*

formas elegantes. **12** REL. limpio, puro (especialmente en el Judaísmo la comida y los objetos). **13** grácil, hábil (movimiento). **14** limpio, fino (en la acción): *just a clean shot in the head = un tiro limpio en la cabeza.* || *adv.* (fam.) **15** completamente, totalmente, por completo: *I'm sorry, I'd clean forgotten = perdona, lo había olvidado por completo.* **16** justo; limpiamente: *the bullet went clean into her heart = la bala entró limpiamente en su corazón.* || *v.t.* **17** limpiar, asear. **18** limpiar, pelar (comida). || *v.i.* **19** hacer la limpieza (en una casa). || *s.sing.* **20** **[a –]** una buena limpieza. || **21 a – bill of health,** V. **bill. 22 as – as a whistle,** más limpio que una patena. **23 – as a new pin,** (fam.) tan limpio como un espejo. **24 to – down,** limpiar de arriba a abajo, limpiar a base de buenos restregones (casa, estancia, etc.). **25 to – out, a)** (fam.) dejar limpio (robando). **b)** vaciar (para limpiar). **26 to – up, a)** limpiarse bien, lavarse bien (normalmente después de estar muy sucio). **b)** dejar bien limpio, dar una buena limpieza (a un lugar). **c)** (fam.) ponerse las botas, sacar una buena tajada (de dinero). **d)** limpiar, hacer una buena batida (llevándose a los malhechores de un sitio). **27 to – up after,** poner en orden lo que otros dejan mal, limpiar lo que otros ensucian. **28 to come –,** (fam.) desembuchar, cantar todo lo que se sabe, confesar todo. **29 to make a – sweep,** V. **sweep.**

clean-cut | ˌkliːnkʌt | *adj.* **1** limpio, de buen aspecto (persona). **2** perfectamente definido, perfectamente delimitado: *a world of clean-cut choices = un mundo de elecciones perfectamente definidas.* **3** bien dibujado, claramente trazado (una línea, punto, letra, etc.).

cleaner | 'kliːnə | *s.c.* **1** limpiador, limpiadora, empleado de limpieza. **2** aspiradora. **3** quitamanchas, limpiatodo. **4** tintorero, lavandero. || **5 to take somebody to the cleaner's,** (fam.) **a)** dar un rapapolvo a alguien de aúpa. **b)** dejar a alguien sin un duro, dejar a uno pelado. **6 the –/the cleaner's,** la tintorería, la tienda de limpieza en seco.

cleaning | 'kliːnɪŋ | *s.i.* **1** limpieza, aseo. || **2 – woman/lady,** mujer de la limpieza, asistenta.

cleanliness | 'klenlɪnɪs | *s.i.* pulcritud, limpieza personal, aseo personal.

cleanly | 'klenlɪ | *adj.* **1** pulcro, limpio, aseado (persona). || | 'kliːnlɪ | *adv.* **1** limpiamente, con gran suavidad (acción).

cleanse | klenz | *v.t.* **1** MED. limpiar, desinfectar (herida). **2 [to – +** *o.* **+ (from /of)]** (form.) limpiar (en un sentido espiritual, o no físico).

cleanser | 'klenzər | *s.c.* e *i.* crema limpiadora, sustancia limpiadora (especialmente de la piel).

clean-shaven | ˌkliːn'ʃeɪvn | *adj.* bien afeitado, sin barba alguna.

cleanup | 'kliːnʌp | *s.sing.* limpieza total, eliminación completa de suciedad.

clear | klɪər | *adj.* **1** claro, diáfano, fácil (de comprensión). **2** claro, límpido (luz). **3** claro (de ver u oír). **4** evidente, claro, obvio: *it's clear she's angry = es evidente que está muy enfadada.* **5** transparente (cualquier material). **6** lúcido, claro, rotundo (pensamiento). **7** brillante, resplandeciente (luz o color). **8** libre, despejado, sin tráfico (carretera, camino, etc.). **9** libre de culpa, tranquila (conciencia). **10** claro, limpio (ojos, mirada, etc.). **11** neto, libre de otros gastos (interés, beneficio, etc.). **12** limpia, clara, sin manchas (piel). **13** libre, vacío, sin compromisos; entero (agenda, día, etc.). || *adv.* **14** con toda claridad, por completo (sonidos y acciones): *the captain could hear the sergeant loud and clear = el capitán podía oír al sargento como de cerca, con toda claridad.* || *adj.* y *adv.* **15 [– of]** sin contacto con, separado de, alejado de, sin tocar: *the aeroplane climbed clear of the trees = el avión se elevó sin tocar los árboles.* || *v.t.* **16** quitar, despejar, limpiar, quitar de enmedio: *clear the table = quita la mesa.* **17** desbloquear, destapar, dejar libre (conducto, carretera, espacio, etc.). **18** dar el visto bueno, dejar pasar, aprobar (método, proyecto, documento, persona para un trabajo, etc.). **19** salvar (un obstáculo, especialmente en un acontecimiento deportivo). **20** despejar (la cabeza). **21** sacar en limpio, embolsarse, sacar limpio (cantidades de dinero). **22** sacar adelante (tareas). **23** permitir el paso; permitir el despegue (avión); permitir la salida (de alguien o de un vehículo). **24** declarar inocente, absolver. || *v.i.* **25** despejarse, volver a una expresión normal (la cara, después de una emoción fuerte). **26** quitar de enmedio (objetos). || *v.t.* e *i.* **27** aclarar(se), hacer(se) transparente, limpiar(se) (un líquido). **28** aclarar(se), limpiar(se) (la piel). **29** FIN. aceptar(se) (el valor de un cheque). **30** aclarar(se), despejar(se) (tiempo atmosférico). || **31 to be –,** estar seguro, estar convencido; entender, comprender: *I am not clear about the whole thing = no entiendo toda la cuestión.* **32 – as a bell,** de un sonido diáfano. **33 – as day,** más claro que el sol, más claro que el agua. **34 – as mud,** nada claro, más bien turbio. **35 to – away,** quitar las cosas de enmedio, guardar las cosas (después de utilizarlas). **36 to – off,** (brit. y fam.) irse a freir espárragos, irse a la porra. **37 to – one's throat,** aclarar la garganta, aclarar la voz, carraspear. **38 to – out, a)** vaciar, limpiar, hacer limpieza (tirando lo innecesario). **b)** (fam.) irse de, marcharse de; largarse. **c)** tirar (lo innecesario). **39 to – the air,** V. **air. 40 to – the decks,** V. **deck. 41 to – up, a)** aclarar, solucionar (malentendido, problema, etc.). **b)** dejar las cosas en su sitio, dejar todo colocado. **c)** mejorar (un problema de salud o de tiempo atmosférico): *his dry cough is clearing up = su tos seca está mejorando.* **42 to get something –,** comprender, entender, captar. **43 in the –,** (fam.) libre de sospecha, limpio, sin mancha. **44 is that –?,** ¿entendido?, ¿me explico? (demostrando autoridad). **45 to make oneself –/to make it –,** explicarse con toda claridad, dejar las cosas diáfanas. **46 to stay/steer – (of),** evitar cualquier contacto (con), no rozarse tan siquiera (con). **47 the coast is –,** V. **coast.**

clearance | 'klɪərəns | *s.c.* e *i.* **1** despeje, roza, derrumbamiento (casas); tala (bosque): *slum clearance = derrumbamiento de chabolas.* || *s.i.* **2** permiso oficial, visto bueno (para entrar o salir de un país, aeropuerto, lugar, etc., o para emprender alguna acción oficial). || *s.c.* **3** DEP. despeje (de peligro de gol). || **3 – sale,** liquidación de existencias, liquidación total, venta a precios de saldo (normalmente porque la tienda va a cerrar).

clear-cut | ˌklɪə'kʌt | *adj.* clarísimo, meridiano, obvio (a la inteligencia).

clear-headed | ˌklɪə'hedɪd | *adj.* sereno, racional, perspicaz.

clear-headedly | ˌklɪə'hedɪdlɪ | *adv.* serenamente, racionalmente, perspicazmente.

clear-headedness | ˌklɪə'hedɪdnɪs | *s.i.* serenidad, racionalidad, perspicacia.

clearing | 'klɪərɪŋ | *s.c.* **1** claro (en un bosque o similar). || *s.i.* **2** limpieza total, limpieza, puesta en orden (de objetos). || **3 – bank,** (brit.) FIN. banco en contacto con la oficina de compensación interbancaria. **4 – house, a)** FIN. oficina de compensación interbancaria. **b)** centro de distribución (especialmente de información a escala nacional). **5 – up,** arreglo total, limpieza total, puesta de cada cosa en su sitio.

clearly | 'klɪəlɪ | *adv.* **1** claramente, diáfanamente, fácilmente (para la comprensión). **2** evidentemente, obviamente, con toda claridad. **3** claramente, nítidamente (en cuanto a la vista o al oído). **4** lúcidamente, con claridad de pensamiento: *think clearly = piensa con lucidez.* **5** claramente, rotundamente, sin ninguna ambigüedad.

clearness | 'klɪənɪs | *s.i.* **1** claridad (de visión o sonido). **2** claridad, lucidez (de pensamiento).

clear-out | 'klɪəraʊt | *s.sing.* (brit. y fam.) limpieza total, arreglo total.

clear-sighted | ˌklɪə'saɪtɪd | *adj.* clarividente, perspicaz, penetrante.

clear-sightedness | ˌklɪə'saɪtɪdnɪs | *s.i.* clarividencia, perspicacia, penetración (de pensamiento).

clearway | 'klɪəweɪ | *s.c.* (brit.) autovía, carretera donde no se puede parar (sin ser autopista).

cleavage | 'kliːvɪdʒ | *s.c.* e *i.* **1** escote, hendidura (espacio entre los senos de una mujer). || *s.c.* **2 [– (between)]** divi-

sión, desunión, separación (entre personas u objetos).
cleave | kliːv | (form. o lit.) *v.* [*pret.* **cleaved** o **clove,** *p.p.* **cleaved, cloven** o **cleft**] *t.* **1** hendir, partir, dividir. **2** unir, pegar, adherir (una cosa a otra). || *i.* **3 [to – in]** partirse en, dividirse en. **4 [to – to]** adherirse a, pegarse a. **5 [to – to]** (desp.) no separarse de, no alejarse de (un enfoque, idea, hábito mental, etc.).
cleaver | 'kliːvər | *s.c.* cuchillo de carnicero.
clef | klef | *s.c.* MUS. clave.
cleft | kleft | *p.p.* **1** de **cleave.** || *s.c.* **2** (lit.) hendidura, grieta (en la roca o suelo). || **3 – palate,** ANAT. fisura del paladar. **4 in a – stick,** (brit. y fam.) en un brete, en una situación difícil, en un apuro.
clematis | 'klemətɪs, | klə'meɪtɪs | *s.i.* BOT. clemátide.
clemency | 'klemənsɪ | *s.i.* (form.) clemencia (en el tiempo atmosférico o en una persona).
clench | klentʃ | *v.t.* **1** agarrar con fuerza, apretar con fuerza (algo en la mano). **2** apretar rabiosamente, apretar violentamente (los puños, dientes, etc.).
clergy | 'kləːdʒɪ | *s.pl.* REL. clérigos, clero.
clergyman | 'kləːdʒɪmən | [*pl.* **clergymen**] *s.c.* REL. clérigo, cura; ministro (de cualquier religión).
clergymen | 'kləːdʒɪmən | *pl.* de **clergyman.**
cleric | 'klerɪk | *s.c.* REL. clérigo, eclesiástico.
clerical | 'klerɪkl | *adj.* **1** REL. clerical, religioso, eclesiástico (referido a los clérigos). **2** de oficina, administrativo.
clerk | klɑːk | (EE.UU.) | klɜːrk | *s.c.* **1** administrativo, oficinista; escribiente. **2** (EE.UU.) recepcionista. **3** (EE.UU.) vendedor, dependiente.
clever | 'klevər | *adj.* **1** listo, despierto, inteligente. **2** hábil, diestro (en alguna actividad). **3** ingenioso (invención, mecanismo, libro, etc.). **4** avispado, listillo (con cierto tono peyorativo). || **5 – Dick,** (fam. y desp.) sabelotodo. **6 too – by half,** (brit., desp. y fam.) pasarse de listo, actitud de pasarse de listo.
cleverly | 'klevəlɪ | *adv.* **1** inteligentemente. **2** hábilmente, diestramente. **3** ingeniosamente. **4** avispadamente.
cleverness | 'klevənɪs | *s.i.* **1** inteligencia. **2** habilidad, destreza. **3** ingenio. **4** astucia (algo peyorativa).
cliché | 'kliːʃeɪ | (EE.UU.) | kliː'ʃeɪ | (también **cliche**) *s.c.* (desp.) cliché, frase manida, tópico, lugar común.
click | klɪk | *v.i.* **1** hacer "clic". **2** (fam.) caer en la cuenta repentinamente, darse cuenta súbitamente; hacer "clic" (una idea en la cabeza). **3** (fam.) caerse bien (dos personas al conocerse). || *v.t.* **4** chasquear, chascar (dedos); hacer un ruido seco, hacer un ruido como un "clic". || *s.c.* e *i.* **5** chasquido, "clic", ruido seco. || **6 to – one's heels,** V. **heel.**
client | 'klaɪənt | *s.c.* cliente.
clientele | ˌkliːən'tel | *s.sing.* [=N *v.sing./pl.*] clientela.
cliff | klɪf | *s.c.* GEOL. despeñadero, precipicio, risco.
cliff-hanger | 'klɪfhæŋgər | *s.c.* (fam.) momento crucial, momento emocionante (en cualquier situación).
climactic | klaɪ'mæktɪk | *adj.* culminante, decisivo (momento).
climate | 'klaɪmɪt | *s.c.* e *i.* **1** clima. **2** (fig.) clima, ambiente (en un lugar, país, grupo, etc.).
climatic | klaɪ'mætɪk | *adj.* climático (del clima).
climax | 'klaɪmæks | *s.i.* **1** culminación, punto cumbre, cumbre; LIT. clímax. **2** orgasmo, clímax. || *v.t.* e *i.* **4** (form.) culminar, llegar a un punto álgido.
climb | klaɪm | *v.t.* e *i.* **1** trepar, escalar. **2** [**to – +** *prep.*] moverse con dificultad, hacer un movimiento algo torpe: *they climbed into the waiting van = se subieron dificultosamente a la furgoneta que les esperaba.* **3** subir, trepar, ascender (en el mundo social). || *v.i.* **4** incrementarse, ascender de valor (económicamente). || *s.c.* **5** escalada, subida. **6** elevación, subida (monte). **7** ascenso, subida (social). || **8 to – down,** desdecirse, cambiar de opinión (admitiendo la del contrario), volverse atrás. **9 to – on the bandwagon,** V. **bandwagon.**
climb-down | 'klaɪmdaʊn | *s.c.* cambio de opinión, cambio de punto de vista (admitiendo la del contrario).
climber | 'klaɪmər | *s.c.* **1** DEP. montañista, escalador. **2** BOT. planta trepadora. **3** trepador (cualquier animal o persona): *my son is a good climber = mi hijo es un buen trepador.*
climbing | 'klaɪmɪŋ | *s.i.* DEP. montañismo.
climbing-frame | 'klaɪmɪŋfreɪm | *s.c.* estructura para juego de trepar (de niños).
clime | klaɪm | *s.c.* (lit. o p.u.) clima.
clinch | klɪntʃ | *v.t.* llegar a, alcanzar finalmente, remachar (acuerdo).
clincher | 'klɪntʃər | *s.c.* argumento decisorio.
clinching | 'klɪntʃɪŋ | *adj.* decisorio (para llegar a un acuerdo).
cling | klɪŋ | *v.i.* [*pret.* y *p.p. irreg.* **clung**] **1 [to – to]** adherirse a, pegarse a, no soltar a. **2 [to – to]** (desp.) no dejar ni a sol ni a sombra a (una persona); aferrarse a (una tradición, modo de comportarse, etc.).
clinging | 'klɪŋɪŋ | *adj.* **1** apretada, estrecha (ropa). **2** mimoso, que no deja a alguien ni a sol ni a sombra (especialmente un niño).
clinic | 'klɪnɪk | *s.c.* **1** clínica, centro médico. **2** período de enseñanza práctica (en especialidades médicas). **3** médico de clínica.
clinical | 'klɪnɪkl | *adj.* **1** MED. clínico (no teórico), hospitalario. **2** (desp.) aséptico, frío, desapasionado. **3** monacal, desnudo (habitación, estancia, etc.). || **4 – thermometer,** termómetro clínico.
clinically | 'klɪnɪklɪ | *adv.* **1** clínicamente. **2** (desp.) asépticamente, desapasionadamente, fríamente. **3** monacalmente, desnudamente.
clink | klɪŋk | *v.i.* **1** tintinear, hacer un sonido como tin-tin (típico en cristal, loza y metal). || *s.c.* **2** tintineo, tin-tin. | *s.sing.* **3 [the –]** (brit. y fam.) la cárcel.
clinker | 'klɪŋkər | *s.i.* escoria.
clip | klɪp | [*ger.* **clipping,** *pret.* y *p.p.* **clipped**] *v.t.* **1** recortar, cortar un trozo de, pegar un tijeretazo a. **2** dar un golpe, dar un revés, dar un cachete. **3** picar (un billete). **4** sujetar con un "clip". **5** reducir un poquito, quitar un poquito, recortar. **6** recortar, omitir (letras o palabras al hablar). || *v.i.* **7 [to – (to)]** sujetar. || *s.c.* **8** "clip", sujetapapeles. **9** tijeretazo, recorte. **10** golpetazo, cachete, revés. **11** MEC. pinza. **12** MIL. cargador. **13** avance, trozo (de película). || **14 at a –/at a fast –,** a toda pastilla, a todo meter. **15 – joint,** (fam.) cabaret de mala muerte carísimo. **16 to – someone's wings,** cortar las alas a alguien, no dar libertad a alguien.
clipboard | 'klɪpbɔːd | *s.c.* tablilla de apoyo (para escribir).
clip-clop | 'klɪpklop | *s.sing.* sonido de los cascos (de caballos).
clip-on | 'klɪpon | *adj.* de quita y pon: *clip-on ear-rings = pendientes de quita y pon.*
clipped | klɪpt | *adj.* **1** bien cortado, bien arreglado (pelo). **2** entrecortado (manera de hablar). **3** (fig.) escueto, lacónico (estilo de hablar o escribir).
clipper | 'klɪpər | *s.c.* MAR. clíper (barco veloz).
clippers | 'klɪpəz | *s.pl.* **1** maquinilla para cortar el pelo. **2** cortaúñas.
clipping | 'klɪpɪŋ | *s.c.* **1** recorte (de periódico). **2** (normalmente *pl.*) trozo cortado (de uñas, pelo, etc.).
clique | kliːk | *s.c.* [*v.sing./pl.*] (desp.) camarilla.
cliquey | 'kliːkɪ | *adj.* (desp.) exclusivo, exclusivista, típico de camarilla.
clitoris | 'klɪtərɪs | *s.c.* (normalmente *sing.*) ANAT. clítoris.
cloak | kləʊk | *s.c.* **1** capa, manto (prenda de vestir). **2** (normalmente *sing.*) (fig.) manto (de nieve, abrojo o cualquier objeto); pretexto, excusa: *the cloak of secrecy = el pretexto de la necesidad de secreto.* || *v.t.* **3** cubrir, esconder, ocultar, disimular.
cloak-and-dagger | ˌkləʊkən'dæʒər | *adj.* de capa y espada; de aventuras (con elementos de secretos e intriga).
cloakroom | 'kləʊkrʊm | *s.c.* **1** guardarropa. **2** (euf.) servicios, lavabo, (Am.) baño.
clobber | 'klɒbər | (fam.) *v.t.* **1** atizar, pegar, sacudir. **2** (fig.) dar una buena tunda, pegar duro (en deporte, política, discusiones, etc.). || *s.i.* **3** bártulos, pertenencias, equipo (ropa e instrumental).

cloche | klɒʃ | *s.c.* **1** sombrero en forma de campana. **2** protección de tiestos (en forma de campana y de plástico o cristal).
clock | klɒk | *s.c.* **1** reloj (no portátil). **2** cronómetro. **3** reloj para fichar. || *s.sing.* **4** cuentakilómetros. || *v.t.* **5** cronometrar, tomar la velocidad, tomar el tiempo (de un coche, atleta, etc.). **6** (brit. y fam.) atizar, soltar un sopapo. || **7 against the –,** contra reloj. **8 around /round the –,** sin parar, veinticuatro horas seguidas. **9 by the –/according to the –,** con total exactitud horaria, según la hora exacta. **10 to – in/on,** fichar a la entrada (del trabajo). **11 to – in (at),** quedar registrado (con) (un peso, medida, etc.). **12 to – off/out,** fichar a la salida (del trabajo). **13 to – up,** acumular, llegar hasta (una cantidad normalmente grande de algo). **14 to keep one's eyes on the –/to watch the –,** (fam.) estar pendiente del reloj, estar pendiente de la hora (para dejar de trabajar). **15 to put the – forward, a)** adelantar la hora. **b)** (fig.) ir en el pensamiento al futuro, imaginar el futuro. **16 to put/turn the – back,** (desp.) actuar retrógradamente, revertir a estilos pasados. **17 to set the – back,** retrasar la hora. **18 twenty-four hour –,** modo numérico de expresar la hora en un ciclo de 24 horas (típico de los horarios de transportes): *at 20.00 = a las veinte (a las ocho de la tarde).*
clockwise | 'klɒkwaɪz | *adj.* y *adv.* en el sentido de las manillas del reloj, en la dirección de las manillas del reloj.
clockwork | 'klɒkwəːk | *adj.* **1** mecánico, de cuerda. || *s.i.* **2** mecanismo de relojería. || **3 like –,** como un reloj, sin tardanza ni problemas.
clod | klɒd | *s.c.* **1** (lit. o p.u.) terrón. **2** (fam.) zoquete, estúpido.
clog | klɒg | [*ger.* **clogging,** *pret.* y *p.p.* **clogged**] *v.t.* **1** atascar, obstruir, atorar, tupir. || *s.c.* **2** (normalmente *pl.*) zueco. || **3 to – up (with),** atascar(se) (con), obstruir(se) (con), atorar(se) (con), tupir(se) (con).
clogged | klɒgd | *adj.* atascado, obstruido, atorado, tupido.
cloister | 'klɔɪstər | *s.c.* **1** ARQ. claustro. **2** convento, monasterio. || *s.sing.* **3** (fig.) vida de claustro, claustro. || *v.r.* **4** (form.) enclaustrarse, *s.sing.* **3** (fig.) vida de claustro, claustro. || *v.r.* **4** (form.) enclaustrarse, alejarse del mundo.
cloistered | 'klɔɪstəd | *adj.* de ermitaño, enclaustrador; recluida (vida).
clone | kləun | BIOQUIM. *s.c.* **1** clon. || *v.t.* **2** hacer una copia clónica (de un animal o planta).
cloning | 'kləunɪŋ | *s.i.* manipulación clónica.
clonk | 'klɒŋk | (fam.) *v.t.* e *i.* **1** hacer un ruido fuerte y seco. || *s.c.* **2** ruido fuerte y seco.
close | kləus | *v.t.* e *i.* **1** cerrar(se). **2** cerrar(se), acabar(se), concluir(se) (tienda, fábrica, período de trabajo). **3** cerrar(se) (una herida). || *v.t.* **4** cerrar el paso de, bloquear, cerrar. **5** cerrar, concluir, dar por terminado (un caso, discusión, conversación, etc.). **6** FIN. liquidar, cerrar (cuenta). **7** acortar, disminuir (una distancia, separación, etc.). || *v.i.* **8 [to – (on)]** acercarse, ganar terreno. **9** FIN. terminar, cerrar (un valor bursátil). || *s.sing.* **10 [the – (of)]** (form.) la terminación, el final, la conclusión; el cierre (de alguna actividad o período). || | kləus | *adj.* **11 [– (to)]** cerca, cercano, próximo, junto. **12 [– (to)]** (fig.) próximo, al borde de (un ataque, lágrimas, un acuerdo, etc.). **13 [– to]** cercano a, casi igual que (en ideas, creencias, sentimientos, etc.): *a look close to admiration = una mirada cercana a la admiración.* **14 [– (to)]** (fig.) encariñado, unido: *I feel very close to him = me siento muy unido a él.* **15** íntimo (amigo); cercano (pariente); confidencial (consejero). **16** cuidadosa, minuciosa, detenida (inspección, mirada, etc.). **17** ajustado, reñido (resultado de una votación o de una competición deportiva). **18** callado, reservado (que no quiere hablar). **19** apretada (letra). **20** (brit.) densa, cargada (atmósfera). **21** continuo, ininterrumpido (contacto, relación, etc.). || *adv.* **22** cerca: *they stood near = permanecieron de pie cerca.* || *s.c.* **23** callejón (normalmente en barrios residenciales). || **24 a – eye/watch (on),** una vigilancia estricta (sobre), un cuidado estricto (sobre). **25 a – shave/thing/call,** (fam.) una escapada por los pelos, una ocasión de peligro salvada por los pelos, una posibilidad de accidente salvada por los pelos. **26 at – range/quarters,** de cerca, a quemarropa. **27 to bring something closer to home,** V. **home. 28 to bring something to a –/to come to a –/to draw to a –,** acercarse a su final, terminar, finalizar, darse por terminado. **28 to – a deal,** cerrar un trato, cerrar un acuerdo de negocio. **30 – by/– at hand/– to hand,** a mano, muy cerca. **31 to – down, a)** TV. cerrar la emisión. **b)** cerrar por completo, liquidar (negocio). **32 to – in,** acortarse (los días). **33 to – in (on/upon), acercarse (sobre), echarse encima (de) (con cierta idea de ataque). 34 to – off,** dejar fuera de límites; clausurar (parte de un edificio o similar), cerrar al tráfico (una carretera). **35 to – one's eyes to something,** V. **eye. 36 to – ranks,** V. **rank. 37 – season,** veda (de caza y pesca). **38 to – the door on something,** V. **door. 39 – to/on,** cerca de, aproximadamente, casi (con una cantidad). **40 – to the bone,** V. **bone. 41 to – up, a)** apretarse unos contra otros, correrse (para dejar sitio). **b)** cerrar por completo, cerrar bien (un lugar porque se va a faltar de él un tiempo). **42 – up/to,** de cerca, muy de cerca, a dos dedos de distancia. **43 that was –,** casi me doy, casi me la pego. **44 the closest thing (to),** la cosa más parecida (a), lo más parecido (a) (para objetos y personas).
close-cropped | ˌkləus'krɒpt | *adj.* rapado (pelo).
closed | kləust | *adj.* **1** cerrado (un objeto). **2** cerrado, acabado, concluido (negocio, tienda, etc.). **3** cerrado, exclusivista, de horizonte corto (persona). || **4 a – book,** (fig.) un misterio. **5 behind – doors,** en secreto, a puerta cerrada. **6 – circuit,** ELEC. circuito cerrado. **7 closed-circuit television,** TV. televisión de circuito cerrado. **8 – season,** (EE.UU.) veda. **9 – shop,** lugar de trabajo de sindicación obligatoria a un mismo sindicato. **10 to have a – mind,** V. **mind.**
closedown | 'kləuzdaun | *s.c.* e *i.* TV. cierre de emisión.
close-fitting | ˌkləus'fɪtɪŋ | *adj.* ajustado, ceñido (ropa).
close-knit | ˌkləus'nɪt | *adj.* muy unido, muy integrado, muy homogéneo (grupo de personas con las mismas creencias, ideas, etc.).
closely | 'kləuslɪ | *adv.* **1** apretadamente, densamente (alrededor). **2** atentamente, con mucho cuidado (mirar o escuchar). **3** estrechamente (relacionado). **4** confidencialmente, estrechamente, compactamente (manera de trabajar o cooperar con otros). **5** exactamente, igualmente, parecidamente. **6** apretadamente (letra escrita).
closeness | 'kləusnɪs | *s.i.* **1** intimidad (entre amigos). **2** (brit.) falta de ventilación. **3** cercanía, proximidad.
close-run | ˌkləus'rʌn | *adj.* reñido (competición, elección, etc.).
close-set | ˌkləus'set | *adj.* muy juntos (ojos).
closet | 'klɒzɪt | *s.c.* **1** retrete rudimentario, servicio sin agua. **2** (p.u.) cámara, gabinete. **3** (EE.UU.) armario, alacena. || *adj.* **4** secreto, tapado, privado: *a closet revolutionary = un revolucionario secreto.* || *v.r.* **5** encerrarse, esconderse (con la puerta cerrada por alguna actividad). || **6 to come out of the –,** salir a la luz pública, darse a conocer públicamente, descubrirse (especialmente algún vergonzoso secreto).
closeted | 'klɒzɪtɪd | *adj.* encerrado, cerrado a cal y canto, a puerta cerrada: *I was closeted in my study for hours until I finished the book = estuve encerrado a cal y canto en mi estudio hasta que terminé el libro.*
close-up | 'kleusʌp | *s.c.* FOT. primer plano.
closing | 'kləusɪŋ | *adj.* **1** final, de cierre: *closing date = fecha final.* || **2 – time,** hora de cerrar, hora de cierre (en un establecimiento público).
closure | 'kləuʒə | *s.c.* e *i.* **1** cierre, terminación, clausura (de un negocio). || *s.c.* **2** (normalmente *sing.*) bloqueo, cierre, obstrucción (de carreteras, canales, etc.). **3** POL. cierre (de un debate en el Parlamento). **4** mecanismo de cierre (de una bolsa o parecido objeto).
clot | | [ger. **clotting,** *pret.* y *p.p.* **clotted**] *v.t.* e *i.* **1** coagular(se), solidificar(se)

(sangre u otro líquido). || *s.c.* **2** coágulo (de sangre o similar). **3** (brit., fam. y hum.) bobo, simplón, lelo. || **4 clotted cream,** (brit.) GAST. nata espesa (típica del Sur de Inglaterra).
cloth | klɒθ, (EE.UU.) | klɔːθ | [*pl.* **cloths** | klɒθs, (EE.UU.) | klɔːsz] *s.i.* **1** paño, tela, género. || *s.c.* **2** trapo, paño (para limpiar, por ejemplo). || *s.sing.* **3** **[the –]** (fig.) REL. la sotana; el clero. || **4 – cap,** (brit.) gorra de paño. **5 to cut one's coat according to one's cloth,** V. **coat.**
clothe | kləuð | *v.t.* **1** vestir, cubrir (con ropa). **2** recubrir, cubrir.
clothed | kləuðd | *adj.* **1** **[– (in)]** vestido, cubierto (por ropa). **2** **[– (in)]** cubierto, recubierto (por cualquier otra cosa).
clothes | kləuðz | *s.pl.* ropa, vestimenta, indumentaria.
clothes-basket | 'kləuðzbɑːskɪt | *s.c.* canasta de la ropa.
clothes-horse | 'kləuðzhɔːs | *s.c.* **1** secarropa de alambres, estructura metálica para secar ropa dentro de casa. **2** (desp.) presumido, pendiente de su ropa (especialmente mujeres).
clothes-line | 'kləuðzlaɪn | *s.c.* tendedero.
clothes-peg | 'kləuðzpeg | (EE.UU. **clothes -pin**) *s.c.* pinza (para tender ropa).
clothes-pin | 'kləuðzpɪn | V. **clothes-peg.**
clothing | 'kləuðɪŋ | *s.i.* **1** ropa, ropaje, tipo de ropa. || *adj.* **2** textil, de tejidos.
cloud | klaud | *s.c.* e *i.* **1** nube (atmosférica). || *s.c.* **2** nube (de humo, polvo, etc.). **3** (fig.) nube (de insectos o pájaros). || *v.t.* e *i.* **4** nublar(se), enturbiar(se), oscurecer(se) (la visión). **5** empañar(se) (cristal). || *v.t.* **6** confundir, oscurecer (el planteamiento de un asunto, la inteligencia, etc.). **7** oscurecer, nublar (situación); estropear (vida). || **8 to – over, a)** nublarse, llenarse de nubes (el cielo). **b)** ensombrecerse, nublarse (la expresión facial). **9 to have one's head in the clouds,** (desp. y fam.) tener la cabeza en las nubes, tener la imaginación desbocada. **10 on – nine,** (fam.) por las nubes, a medio metro del suelo (de felicidad). **11 under a –,** (fam.) bajo sospecha, en desgracia.
cloudburst | 'klaudəːst | *s.c.* chaparrón, aguacero.
cloud-cuckoo-land | klaud'kuːkulænd | **in –,** (fam. y desp.) en la inopia.
cloudiness | 'klaudɪnɪs | *s.i.* nubosidad.
cloudless | 'klaudlɪs | *adj.* despejado, sin nubes, sin una sola nube.
cloudy | 'klaudɪ | *adj.* **1** nuboso, nublado, encapotado (cielo). **2** oscuro, turbio (líquido). **3** desdibujado, oscuro, complicado (pensamiento, ideas, etc.).
clout | klaut | (fam.) *v.t.* **1** atizar, pegar, sacudir. || *s.c.* **2** sopapo, tortazo (fuerte). || *s.i.* **3** influencia, poder, fuerza (sindical, política, social, etc.).
clove | kləuv | *pret.irreg.* **1** de **cleave.** || *s.c.* **2** **[– (of)]** diente (de ajo). **3** (normalmente *pl.*) BOT. clavo.
cloven | 'kləuvn | *p.p.irreg.* **1** de **cleave.** || **2 – hoof,** pezuña hendida, pezuña partida en dos (típica de caballos, vacas, etc.).
clover | 'kləuvər | *s.c.* **1** BOT. trébol. || **2 in –,** (fam.) a cuerpo de rey, en la abundancia (vivir).
clown | klaun | *s.c.* **1** payaso. **2** (fig.) payaso, bufón; bromista. **3** (desp.) idiota, patán. || *v.i.* **4** hacer el payaso, hacer el bufón. || **5 to – around,** hacer el payaso, ir por ahí haciendo el payaso. **6 to make a =N of one-self,** hacer el ridículo, convertirse en el hazmerreír.
clownish | 'klaunɪʃ | *adj.* de payaso, bufonesco.
cloying | 'klɔɪɪŋ | *adj.* empalagoso (demasiado dulce).
cloyingly | klɔɪɪŋlɪ | *adv.* empalagosamente.
club | klʌb | [*ger.* **clubbing,** *pret.* y *p.p.* **clubbing]** *v.t.* **1** golpear, dar bastonazos, golpear con un objeto contundente. || *s.c.* **2** asociación, peña, club. **3** porra, bastón, garrote, maza. **4** DEP. palo de golf. || *s.pl.* **5** bastos. || **6 to – together (for/to),** (brit.) pagar a escote. **7 golf –,** DEP. palo de golf.
clubhouse | 'klʌbhaus | *s.c.* sede del club.
cluck | klʌk | *v.i.* **1** cloquear (gallina). **2** (fig.) hacer ruidos desaprobatorios, expresar el desacuerdo con sonidos desaprobatorios. || *s.c.* **3** chasquido desaprobatorio (con la lengua o labios). **4** chasquido de placer, sonido de deleite (onomatopéyico). || **5 to – over, a)** chasquear la lengua desaprobatoriamente. **b)** chasquear de placer.
clue | kluː | *s.c.* **1** **[– (to)]** pista, indicio (para la solución de algo). **2** explicación (de los crucigramas). || **3 not to have a —**, no tener la menor idea, no tener ni idea.
clued-up | 'kluːdʌp | *adj.* (fam.) muy puesto, al tanto; bien informado.
clueless | 'kluːlɪs | *adj.* (fam. y desp.) sin la menor idea, en la higuera.
clump | klʌmp | *s.c.* **1** **[=N + *v.sing./pl.*]** masa, grupo, conjunto (de árboles o similar). **2** trozo de tierra, terrón. **3** pisada, patadón (fuerte en el suelo). || **4 to – around/about,** ir dando fuertes pisadas. **5 to – down,** caer(se) pesadamente, caer haciendo un ruido fuerte. **6 to – together,** agruparse, estar juntas (personas o cosas).
clumsily | 'klʌmzɪlɪ | *adv.* **1** torpemente, desmañadamente. **2** incómodamente, toscamente, chapuceramente (hecho). **3** desatinadamente, torpemente (dicho o hecho por parte de una persona).
clumsiness | 'klʌmzɪnɪs | *s.i.* **1** torpeza, falta de maña. **2** incomodidad, tosquedad (de un objeto). **3** torpeza (verbal); insensibilidad (en el actuar).
clumsy | 'klʌmzɪ | *adj.* **1** torpe, desmañado. **2** incómodo, tosco, mal hecho, chapucero (objeto). **3** desatinado, torpe (comentario o acción).
clung | klʌŋ | *pret.* y *p.p. irreg.* de **cling.**
clunk | klʌŋk | *s.c.* **1** golpe apagado, sonido apagado metálico. || *v.i.* **2** hacer un ruido apagado metálico.
cluster | 'klʌstər | *s.c.* **1** hato, racimo, montón (de personas o cosas). || *v.i.* **2** apiñarse, arremolinarse, agruparse (personas o cosas).
clutch | klʌtʃ | *v.t.* **1** agarrar ávidamente, sujetar con fuerza, echar mano a. || *s.c.* **2** agarro, asimiento (acto de agarrar). **3** MEC. embrague. **4** BIOL. nidada (de ave). **5** sucesión, serie (de cosas). || *s.pl.* **6** garras, poder: *in the enemy's clutches = en poder del enemigo.* || **7 to – at, a)** agarrarse fuertemente, sujetarse con fuerza. **b)** echar mano de (una excusa, explicación, etc.). **8 to – at straws,** V. **straw. 9 – bag,** bolsa sin asas.
clutter | 'klʌtər | *s.i.* **1** desorden, desbarajuste, confusión (de objetos, especialmente innecesarios). || *v.t.* **2** **[to – + *o.* + (with)]** abarrotar sin orden, amontonar excesivamente. || **3 to – up,** llenar de cosas innecesarias, atestar desordenadamente.
cluttered | 'klʌtəd | *adj.* amontonado desordenadamente, abarrotado (sin orden).
coach | kəutʃ | *s.c.* **1** (brit.) autobús, autocar. **2** DEP. entrenador. **3** profesor particular, tutor particular. **4** (brit.) vagón (de tren). **5** diligencia, carroza, carruaje. || *v.t.* e *i.* **6** DEP. entrenar, hacer de entrenador, trabajar de entrenador. **7** dar clases particulares, trabajar dando clases particulares. **8 by –,** en autocar, en autobús. **9 – park,** parking especial para autobuses. **10 – station,** estación de autobuses.
coach-and-fours | 'kəutʃənfɔːz | *s.c.* carruaje de cuatro caballos.
coachload | 'kəutʃləud | *s.c.* autobús lleno de pasajeros, autobús lleno.
coachman | 'kəutʃmən | [*pl.* **coachmen]** *s.c.* cochero (en carruaje).
coachmen | 'kəutʃmən | *pl.* de **coachman.**
coagulate | kəu'ægjuleɪt | *v.t.* e *i.* coagular(se).
coagulation | kəu,ægju'leɪʃn | *s.i.* coagulación.
coal | kəul | *s.i.* **1** carbón. || *s.c.* **2** bola de carbón, trozo de carbón. || **3 – gas,** QUIM. gas de hulla. **4 – oil,** (EE.UU.) parafina. **5 – tar,** QUIM. alquitrán mineral. **6 to haul/drag someone over the coals,** (fam.) dar una regañina de aúpa, reprender con gran severidad. **7 to take/carry coals to Newcastle,** echar agua en el mar, vendimiar y llevar uvas de postre.
coal-black | 'kəulblæk | *adj.* negro como el carbón, negro como el azabache.
coalesce | ˌkəuə'les | *v.i.* (form.) fundirse, unirse (dos cosas).
coalescence | ˌkəuə'lesns | *s.i.* (form.) fusión, unión.
coalface | 'kəulfeɪs | *s.c.* MIN. frente de extracción del carbón.

coalfield | 'kəʊlfiːld | *s.c.* MIN. yacimiento de carbón.
coalition | ˌkəʊə'lɪʃn | *s.c.* **1** POL. coalición (de gobierno). **2** alianza, liga.
coalman | 'kəʊlmən | [*pl.* **coalmen**] *s.c.* carbonero.
coalmen | 'kəʊlmən | *pl.* de **coalman.**
oalminer | 'kəʊlmaɪnər | *s.c.* minero.
oal-scuttle | 'kəʊlskʌtl | *s.c.* cubo de carbón.
coarse | kɔːs | *adj.* **1** tosco, ordinario, grueso (al tacto). **2** vulgar, rudo, basto, ordinario, grosero (persona). **3** de poca calidad, ordinario (comida o bebida). || **4 – fishing,** DEP. pesca de agua dulce (excluyendo salmón y trucha).
coarsely | 'kɔːslɪ | *adv.* **1** toscamente, groseramente, vulgarmente, rudamente. **2** toscamente (hecho, tejido, etc.).
coarsen | 'kɔːsn | *v.t.* e *i.* hacer(se) tosco, hacer(se) ordinario.
coarseness | 'kɔːsnɪs | *s.i.* **1** tosquedad, ordinariez (al tacto). **2** grosería, vulgaridad (de una persona). **3** ordinariez (de comida o bebida).
coast | kəʊst | *s.c.* **1** costa, litoral. || *v.i.* **2** deslizarse, marchar con cierta inercia; ir en punto muerto (vehículo). **3** (fam.) hacer las cosas sin esfuerzo. || **4 to – along,** (fam.) marchar sin esfuerzo, deslizarse sin esfuerzo, funcionar con facilidad (en la vida). **5 from – to –,** de costa a costa. **6 off the –,** alejado de la costa un poco, justo apartado de la costa. **7 the – is clear,** no hay moros en la costa, no hay peligro alguno.
coastal | kəʊstəl | *adj.* costero.
coaster | 'kəʊstər | *s.c.* **1** posavasos. **2** MAR. barco de cabotaje.
coastguard | 'kəʊstgɑːd | *s.c.* **1** guardacostas. || *s.sing.* **2** **[the –]** la guardia costera, el servicio de guardacostas.
coastline | 'kəʊstlaɪn | *s.c.* litoral, línea de la costa.
coat | kəʊt | *s.c.* **1** abrigo, chaquetón, (Am.) saco. **2** chaqueta. **3** piel, pelaje (de un animal). **4** **[– (of)]** capa (de pintura o similar). || *v.t.* **5** **[to – + *o* + (with)]** poner una capa en, cubrir, revestir. || **6 – of arms,** escudo de armas. **7 – of mail,** cota de malla. **8 to cut one's – according to one's cloth,** adaptarse a las condiciones reales de uno (económicas, sociales, etc.).
coat-hanger | 'kəʊthæŋgər | *s.c.* colgador, perchero.
coating | 'kəʊtɪŋ | *s.c.* baño, capa fina.
coattails | 'kəʊteɪlz | *s.pl.* **1** faldones, faldillas (de un frac). || **2 to ride on someone/something's –,** (fam.) subirse al carro de alguien; aprovecharse de lo que ya alguien ha hecho.
co-author | kəʊ'ɔːθər | *s.c.* coautor.
coax | kəʊks | *v.t.* **1** **[to – + *o.* + *inf.*/into/out of]** inducir, instar, intentar persuadir. **2** sonsacar, sacar mediante halagos. **3** intentar hacer funcionar suavemente (una máquina o mecanismo).
coaxing | 'kəʊksɪŋ | *adj.* **1** halagador. || *s.c.* **2** tratamiento suave (de una máquina o similar).
cob | kɒb | *s.c.* (brit.) pan (redondo).
cobalt | 'kəʊbɔːlt | *s.i.* **1** QUIM. cobalto. || *adj.* **2** verde azulado, color verde azulado.
cobber | 'kɒbər | *s.c.* (fam.) macho (en Australia).
cobble | 'kɒbl | *s.c.* **1** adoquín. || **2 to – together,** (fam. y desp.) sacar a trancas y barrancas, parir malamente (un documento, un acuerdo, un proyecto, etc.).
cobbled | 'kɒbld | *adj.* adoquinado, empedrado (calle).
cobbler | 'kɒblər | *s.c.* **1** (p.u.) zapatero remendón. || **2 cobblers,** (brit. y fam.) chorrada, estupidez, memez.
cobblestone | 'kɒblstəʊn | *s.c.* adoquín (calle).
cobra | 'kəʊbrə | *s.c.* ZOOL. cobra.
cobweb | 'kɒbweb | *s.c.* e *i.* **1** telaraña. || **2 to blow the cobwebs away/to clear away the cobwebs,** desentumecerse mentalmente, airear la mente.
cobwebbed | 'kɒbwebd | *adj.* cubierto de telarañas.
cocaine | kə'keɪn | *s.i.* QUIM. cocaína.
coccyx | 'kɒksɪks | *s.c.* ANAT. coxis.
cock | kɒk | *s.c.* **1** gallo. **2** pájaro macho (de cualquier especie). **3** (vulg.) picha, polla. **4** (fam.) tío, gallito, machote. **5** espita, grifo, llave. || *s.i.* **6** (vulg.) gilipollez. || *v.t.* **7** levantar, enderezar, dirigir (parte del cuerpo). **8** montar (arma). || **9 to – an ear,** dirigir el oído atentamente, escuchar con mucha atención, aguzar el oído. **10 to – up,** estropear, fastidiar. **11 to keep one's ears/eyes cocked,** mantener la mirada/oído vigilante, mantenerse alerta (visual y auditivamente). **12 the – of the walk,** (desp.) el chulo del barrio, el gallito del barrio, el jefe del cotarro.
cock-a-hoop | ˌkɒkə'huːp | *adj.* **[– (about)] (fam.) jubiloso, encantado, contentísimo.**
cockatoo | ˌkɒkə'tuː | *s.c.* ZOOL. cacatúa.
cockcrow | 'kɒkrəʊ | (lit.) *s.i.* **1** canto del gallo. || **2 at –,** al amanecer, con el canto del gallo.
cocked | kɒkt | *adj.* **1** montado (arma). || **2 – hat,** sombrero de tres picos (en algunos uniformes militares). **3 to knock/beat into a – hat,** dejar tirado, dar quince y raya; ser infinitamente superior.
cockerel | 'kɒkrəl | *s.c.* gallito, gallo joven.
cocker | 'kɒkər | (también **cocker spaniel**) *s.c.* ZOOL. perro cocker, pachón inglés.
cockeyed | 'kɒkaɪd | *adj.* **1** bizco (de ojos). **2** sesgado, torcido. **3** alocado, demencial (plan, proyecto, etc.).
cockfight | 'kɒkfaɪt | *s.c.* pelea de gallos.
cockily | 'kɒkɪlɪ | *adv.* (fam.) presumidamente, petulantemente, con chulería.
cockiness | 'kɒkɪnɪs | *s.i.* (fam.) petulancia, chulería.
cockle | 'kɒkl | *s.c.* **1** berberecho. || **2 to warm the cockles of one's heart,** dar gran satisfacción a uno, dar una gran alegría a uno.
cockleshell | 'kɒklʃel | *s.c.* **1** concha de berberecho. **2** bote ligero.
cockney | 'kɒknɪ | *s.c.* **1** londinense nativo. || *s.i.* **2** dialecto popular del este de Londres.
cockpit | 'kɒkpɪt | *s.c.* **1** AER. cabina del piloto. **2** asiento del conductor (en coche de carreras). **3** cancha, arena, palestra (lugar donde se dirimen diferencias).
cockroach | 'kɒkrəʊtʃ | *s.c.* ZOOL. cucaracha.
cockscomb | 'kɒkskəʊm | *s.c.* cresta (de gallo).
cocksure | kɒk'ʃɔː | *adj.* (desp.) engreído, arrogante.
cocktail | 'kɒkteɪl | *s.c.* **1** cóctel. **2** GAST. cóctel (de mariscos u otras variedades). **3** (fig.) combinación, mezcla, cóctel (de cosas). || *adj.* **4** de cóctel (ropa, estilo, etc.).
cock-up | 'kɒkʌp | *s.c.* (fam.) estropicio, follón.
cocky | 'kɒkɪ | *adj.* (fam.) presumido, petulante, chuleta.
cocoa | 'kəʊkəʊ | *s.i.* **1** cacao, chocolate. || *s.c.* **2** taza de cacao, taza de chocolate. || *adj.* **3** color chocolate, chocolate.
coconut | 'kəʊkənʌt | *s.c.* **1** BOT. coco. || *s.i.* **2** coco, fruta de coco. || **3 – matting,** estera de cocotero. **4 – palm,** BOT. cocotero. **5 – shy,** tiro al coco (en barraca de feria).
cocoon | kə'kuːn | *s.c.* **1** capullo (de gusano de seda). **2** **[– (of)]** (fig.) protección, envoltorio (físico o espiritual). || *v.t.* **3** **[to – + *o.* + (in)]** cubrir, tapar, proteger.
cocooned | kə'kuːnd | *adj.* aislado, escondido.
cod | kɒd | [*pl.* **cod**] *s.c.* e *i.* ZOOL. bacalao, abadejo (pez). || **2 – liver oil,** aceite de hígado de bacalao.
coda | 'kəʊdə | *s.c.* **1** MUS. refrán, parte repetitiva (de una canción). **2** LIT. epílogo (de un libro).
coddle | 'kɒdl | *v.t.* **1** GAST. cocer a fuego lento. **2** mimar, consentir, superproteger.
code | kəʊd | *s.c.* **1** código, conjunto de principios. **2** código, clave (secreta). **3** código postal. **4** código numérico, código simbólico (de cualquier clase: telefónico, de comunicación, etc.). || *v.t.* **5** cifrar, componer en clave. **6** (fig.) expresar crípticamente (una opinión). || **7 – of practice,** código de conducta (en una determinada profesión). **8 in –,** cifrado, en cifra, en código secreto.
code-book | 'kəʊdbʊk | *s.c.* libro con clave del código secreto.
codeine | 'kəʊdiːn | *s.i.* QUIM. codeína.
code-name | 'kəʊdneɪm | *s.c.* nombre secreto, nombre en clave (de una operación militar, policial, etc.).
code-named | 'kəʊdneɪmd | *adj.* con el nombre secreto de.
code-word | 'kəʊdwɜːd | *s.c.* palabra en clave.

codex | 'kəʊdeks | [*pl.* **codices**] *s.c.* HIST. códice.
codger | 'kɒdʒər | *s.c.* (fam.) viejo excéntrico, tipo raro.
codices | 'kɑʊdɪsiːz | *pl.* de **codex.**
codicil | 'kɑʊdɪsɪl | (EE.UU.) | 'kɒdəsl | *s.c.* DER. codicilo.
codification | ˌkəʊdɪfɪ'keɪʃn | (EE.UU.) | ˌkɒdɪfɪ'keɪʃn | *s.i.* codificación.
codify | 'kəʊdɪfaɪ | (EE.UU.) | 'kɒdifaɪ | *v.t.* codificar.
codswallop | 'kɒdzwæləp | *s.i.* (brit. y fam.) chorrada, despropósito.
co-ed | ˌkəʊ'ed | *adj.* mixta (escuela).
co-education | ˌkəʊedʒʊ'keɪʃn | *s.i.* coeducación.
co-educational | ˌkəʊedʒʊ'keɪʃənl | *adj.* mixta (educación).
coefficient | ˌkəʊɪ'fɪʃnt | *s.c.* MAT. coeficiente.
coerce | kəʊ'əːs | *v.t.* **[to – +** *o.* **+ (into)]** (form.) coaccionar, forzar, obligar, hacer coacción.
coercion | kəʊ'əːʃn | (EE.UU.) | kəʊ'ɜːʒn | *s.i.* coacción, coerción.
coercive | kəʊ'əːsɪv | *adj.* coercitivo.
coexist | ˌkəʊɪg'zɪst | *v.i.* **[to – (with)]** coexistir; convivir.
coexistence | ˌkəʊɪg'zɪstəns | *s.i.* coexistencia.
coffee | 'kɒfɪ | (EE.UU.) | 'kɔːfɪ | *s.c.* e *i.* **1** café. || *s.i.* **2** BOT. café (planta). || *adj.* **3** color café. || **4 – bean,** grano de café. **5 – grinder,** molinillo de café. **6 – shop,** (EE.UU.) cafetería, salón de café. **7 – tree,** BOT. árbol del café.
coffee-bar | 'kɒfɪbɑːr | *s.c.* (brit.) cafetería.
coffee-break | 'kɒfɪbreɪk | *s.c.* pausa para tomar un café, descanso para el café (en casa o en el trabajo).
coffee-cup | 'kɒfɪkʌp | *s.c.* taza de café, taza para café.
coffee-house | 'kɒfɪhaʊs | *s.c.* HIST. café (típico del siglo XVIII en Londres).
coffee-mill | 'kɒfɪmɪl | *s.c.* molinillo de café.
coffee-morning | 'kɒfɪmɔːnɪŋ | *s.c.* reunión social donde se toma café (normalmente para recaudar fondos para organizaciones caritativas).
coffeepot | 'kɒfɪpɒt | *s.c.* cafetera.
coffee-table | 'kɒfɪteɪbl | *s.c.* **1** mesa para café, mesita de café. || **2 – book,** libro grande (normalmente con grabados atrayentes) que se coloca en la mesita del café.
coffer | 'kɒfər | *s.c.* **1** cofre (donde se guardan joyas). || *s.pl.* **2** fondos, tesorería (de una organización o similar).
coffin | 'kɒfɪn | *s.c.* **1** ataúd. || **2 a nail in somebody's/something's –,** (fig.) un clavo en el ataúd de alguien o algo; información que ayuda a destrozar la carrera de alguien o alguna asociación.
cog | kɒg | *s.c.* **1** MEC. diente (de una rueda). || **2 a – in the machine/wheel,** (fam.) una pieza de un mecanismo, una parte necesaria aunque pequeña en un entramado; una parte insignificante en un todo.
cog-wheel | 'kɒgwiːl | *s.c.* MEC. rueda dentada.
cogency | 'kəʊdʒənsɪ | *s.i.* (form.) fuerza, lógica (de un argumento).
cogent | 'kəʊdʒənt | *adj.* (form.) convincente, de lógica irresistible.
cogently | 'kəʊdʒəntlɪ | *adv.* (form.) convincentemente, irresistiblemente (en sus argumentos).
cogitate | 'kɒdʒɪteɪt | *v.i.* **[to – (about)]** (form.) cogitar, reflexionar.
cogitation | ˌkɒdʒɪ'teɪʃn | *s.i.* (form.) cogitación, reflexión.
cognac | 'kɒnjæk | *s.c.* e *i.* coñac.
cognate | 'kɒgneɪt | *adj.* FILOL. afín, relacionado, pariente (idiomas o palabras).
cognisance V. **cognizance.**
cognisant V. **cognizant.**
cognition | kɒg'nɪʃn | *s.i.* PSIC. cognición, proceso de conocimiento.
cognitive | 'kɒgnɪtɪv | *adj.* PSIC. cognitivo.
cognizance | 'kɒgnɪzəns | (también **cognisance**) (form.) *s.i.* **1 [– (of)]** conocimiento, conciencia: *no cognizance of that theory = ningún conocimiento de esa teoría.* || **2 to take – of,** darse cuenta de, ser consciente de, estar atento a.
cognizant | 'kɒgnɪzənt | (también **cognisant**) *adj.* **[– of]** (form.) consciente de, sabedor de.
cognoscenti | ˌkɒnjə'ʃentɪ | *s.pl.* (form.) expertos, conocedores (de cualquier tema).
cohabit | kəʊ'hæbɪt | *v.i.* **[to – (with)]** (form.) cohabitar (hombre y mujer).
cohabitation | ˌkəʊhæbɪ'teɪʃn | *s.i.* **[– (with)]** (form.) cohabitación (entre un hombre y una mujer).
cohere | kəʊ'hɪər | *v.i.* (form.) **1** tener coherencia, tener sentido, tener lógica. **2** pegarse, adherirse (físicamente).
coherence | ˌkəʊ'hɪərəns | *s.i.* **1** coherencia, lógica. **2** unión, solidez (de un grupo).
coherent | ˌkəʊ'hɪərənt | *adj.* **1** coherente, lógico, razonable. **2** harmonioso, bien entramado (un edificio, por ejemplo). **3** unido, consistente (grupo).
coherently | ˌkəʊ'hɪərəntlɪ | *adv.* **1** coherentemente, lógicamente, razonablemente. **2** armoniosamente (la manera de construir algo o actividad parecida).
cohesion | kəʊ'hiːʒn | *s.i.* **1** cohesión, armonía, unidad (en un grupo).
cohesive | kəʊ'hiːsɪv | *adj.* armonioso, unificador.
cohesively | kəʊ'hiːsɪvlɪ | *adv.* armoniosamente, unificadoramente.
cohesiveness | kəʊ'hiːsɪvnɪs | *s.i.* armonía, unidad.
cohort | 'kəʊhɔːt | *s.c.* **1** HIST. cohorte (unidad militar romana). **2 [– (of)]** cohorte, legión; grupo de apoyo.
coiffure | kwɑː'fəː | *s.c.* (form.) peinado, estilo de peinado.
coil | kɔɪl | *s.c.* **1** rollo (de cuerda, alambre, etc.). **2** vuelta, rosca, bucle. **3** erizo (del pelo). **4** ELEC. bobina, carrete. **5** anillo (de serpiente). **6** MED. dispositivo en forma serpentina intrauterino (como anticonceptivo). || *v.i.* **7 [to – (around)]** enroscarse, enrollarse. **8** moverse en espiral (humo, serpiente, etc.). || *v.t.* **9** enroscar, enrollar. || **10 to – up,** enrollar totalmente, enrollar bien (una cuerda, manguera, etc.).
coiled | kɔɪld | *adj.* enroscado, enrollado.
coin | kɔɪn | *s.c.* **1** moneda. || *s.i.* **2** metálico, moneda, dinero en forma de moneda. || *v.t.* **3** acuñar (moneda). **4** (fig.) acuñar, inventar, crear (palabras, frases, etc.). || **5 to – a phrase,** (hum.) diciéndolo de una manera totalmente original, expresándolo con palabras nuevas (cuando se acaba de utilizar un tópico). **6 – box,** (brit.) cabina telefónica (que funciona con monedas). **7 to – money/it,** (fam.) hacerse de oro, ganar dinero a espuertas. **8 to pay someone back in their own –,** pagar a alguien con la misma moneda. **9 the other side of the –,** el otro lado de la moneda; el otro aspecto del problema. **10 two sides of the same –,** las dos caras de una misma moneda; los dos lados de un mismo tema.
coinage | 'kɔɪnɪdʒ | *s.i.* **1** sistema monetario, moneda (de un país). **2** acuñación, ideación, invención (de palabras). || *s.c.* **3** palabra inventada, frase inventada.
coincide | ˌkəʊɪn'saɪd | *v.i.* **1 [to – (with)]** coincidir, ocurrir al mismo tiempo. **2 [to – (with)]** coincidir, estar de acuerdo (en opinión). **3 [to – (with)]** coincidir físicamente, unirse.
coincidence | kəʊ'ɪnsɪdəns | *s.c.* e *i.* **1** coincidencia, casualidad. || *s.sing.* **2 [the – of]** (form.) la coincidencia de, la identidad de.
coincident | kəʊ'ɪnsɪdənt | *adj.* **[– (with)]** (form.) igual, idéntico.
coincidental | kəʊˌɪnsɪ'dentl | *adj.* **1** fortuito, casual, accidental. **2** V. **coincident.**
coincidentally | kəʊˌɪnsɪ'dentəlɪ | *adv.* fortuitamente, casualmente, accidentalmente.
coir | kɔɪə | *s.i.* fibra de corteza de coco (para cuerdas).
coitus | kəʊɪtəs | *s.i.* (form.) coito.
coke | kəʊk | *s.i.* **1** MIN. cok, coque. **2** (fam.) coca (cocaína). || **3 Coke,** (fam.) Coca-Cola (marca registrada).
cola | 'kəʊlə | *s.c.* **1** BOT. cola. || *s.i.* **2** cola (bebida).
colander | 'kʌləndər | *s.c.* colador, escurridor (objeto de la cocina).
cold | kəʊld | *adj.* **1** frío, helado: *it's cold.* **2** frío, helado (en el cuerpo): *I'm cold = tengo frío/estoy helado.* **3** (desp.) frío, indiferente, insensible (persona). **4** fría (comida específicamente hecha para comer así). **5** frío (color). **6** débil, imperceptible (rastro, pista, etc.). **7** frío, alejado (de lo que se debe acertar): *no, you are cold = no, frío, frío.* ||

s.i. **8** frío (tiempo). || *adv.* **9** inesperadamente, sin preparación: *don't do that cold = no hagas eso sin preparación.* || *s.c.* **10** resfriado, constipado. || **11 to blow hot and –,** V. **hot. 12 to catch –,** coger un resfriado, coger un constipado. **13 – chisel,** cortafrío. **14 – cream,** crema para la piel, crema para el cutis (en mujeres). **15 – cuts,** (EE.UU.) fiambres. **16 – fish,** (fam.) tipo frío, tipo indiferente. **17 – frame,** vivero pequeño (para plantas). **18 – front,** frente frío (en meteorología). **19 – snap,** ola de frío repentina. **20 – sore,** MED. afta labial por constipado. **21 – storage,** almacenaje refrigerado. **22 – store,** almacén de refrigeración. **23 – sweat,** sudor frío. **24 – turkey,** (fam. y EE.UU.) mono (cuando se deja de tomar droga). **25 – war,** POL. guerra fría. **26 to have/get – feet,** (fam.) dar pánico repentino, asustarse ante algo. **27 in – blood,** V. **blood. 28 to leave somebody –,** dejar a alguien frío, no provocar ninguna emoción en alguien. **29 left out in the –/to find oneself out in the –,** dejado al margen/encontrarse dejado al margen (por un grupo). **30 to make one's blood run –,** V. **blood. 31 out –,** inconsciente, sin sentido (especialmente por haber sido golpeado). **32 to put into – storage,** dejar por el momento, abandonar temporalmente (una idea, plan, proyecto, etc.). **33 to throw/pour – water on something,** V. **wrater. 33 with –,** de frío, por el frío: *I'm sick with cold = estoy enfermo de frío.*

cold-blooded | ˌkəʊld'blʌdɪd | *adj.* **1** BIOL. de sangre fría (reptiles). **2** cruel, desalmado, insensible, despiadado.

cold-bloodedly | ˌkəʊld'blʌdɪdlɪ | *adv.* cruelmente, desalmadamente, insensiblemente, despiadadamente.

cold-hearted .

coldly | 'kəʊldlɪ | *adv.* (desp.) fríamente, insensiblemente, indiferentemente (actitud alejada de personas).

coldness | 'kəʊldnɪs | *s.i.* **1** frialdad (del tiempo). **2** (desp.) frialdad, indiferencia, insensibilidad.

cold-shoulder | ˌkəʊld'ʃəʊldər | *v.t.* dar la espalda, no hacer caso, dejar a un lado.

coleslaw | 'kəʊlslɔː | *s.i.* GAST. ensalada fría de verduras con mayonesa.

colic | 'kɒlɪk | *s.i.* MED. cólico, malestar estomacal.

colicky | 'kɒlɪkɪ | *adj.* aquejado de cólico, con malestar estomacal.

colitis | kɒ'laɪtɪs | *s.i.* MED. colitis.

collaborate | kə'læbəreɪt | *v.i.* **1 [to – (with/in)]** colaborar. **2 [to – (with)]** (desp.) cooperar, colaborar (con el enemigo).

collaboration | kəˌlæbə'reɪʃn | *s.i.* **1** colaboración, cooperación. || **2 in – (with),** en colaboración (con), en cooperación (con), en conjunción (con).

collaborative | kə'læbərətɪv | *adj.* (form.) conjunto, de más de una persona (trabajo, obra de arte, etc.).

collaboratively | kə'læbərətɪvlɪ | *adv.* (form.) conjuntamente, con la colaboración de más de una persona.

collaborator | kə'læbəreɪtər | *s.c.* **1** colaborador, cooperador. **2** (desp.) colaboracionista, colaborador (con el enemigo).

collage | 'kɒlɑːʒ | (EE.UU.) | kə'lɑːʒ | *s.i.* **1** ART. montaje, collage. || *s.c.* **2** ART. cuadro de collage. **3 [– (of)]** (fig.) mezcla, collage (de diversas cosas).

collapse | kə'læps | *v.i.* **1** derrumbarse, colapsarse, desplomarse (edificios, puentes, etc.). **2** hundirse hacia dentro, deformarse: *the parachute collapsed = el paracaídas se deformó.* **3** desmoronarse, hundirse, fracasar (institución, sistema, tradición, etc.). **4** quedar exhausto, derrumbarse por falta de fuerzas, agotarse por completo. **5** caer inconsciente, sufrir un colapso. **6** tirarse, hundirse (movimiento físico causado por agotamiento): *they collapsed on the beds = se tiraron en las camas.* **7** derrumbarse, desmoronarse, desplomarse (moneda, economía, etc.). **8** plegarse (silla o similar). || *v.t.* **9** hacer más corto, comprimir (un escrito). **10** plegar (un objeto plegable). || *s.i.* **11** derrumbamiento, desplome, desmoronamiento (de un edificio o similar). **12** agotamiento, postración. || *s.c.* e *i.* **13** desintegración, fracaso, hundimiento (de una institución o similar). **14** desmayo, pérdida de conocimiento, colapso.

collapsible | kə'læpsɪbl | *adj.* plegable (objeto).

collar | 'kɒlər | *s.c.* **1** cuello (de prenda de vestir). **2** collar (de animal). **3** MEC. anillo, aro. || *s.i.* **4** pescuezo (como carne para consumir). || *v.t.* **5** agarrar, capturar, coger, atrapar. **6** no dejar ir, agarrar (a alguien para hablar con él). || **7 to get hot under the – (about),** (fam.) sulfurarse (por), indignarse (por).

collarbone | 'kɒləbəʊn | *s.c.* ANAT. clavícula.

collate | kɒ'leɪt | *v.t.* cotejar, confrontar, comparar.

collateral | kɒ'lætərəl | (form.) *adj.* **1** colateral, paralelo. **2** FIN. colateral, garantía (en operaciones monetarias). **3** colateral (pariente).

collation | kə'leɪʃn | *s.c.* e *i.* **1** cotejo, comparación. || *s.c.* **2** (form.) colación, refrigerio (comida ligera).

colleague | 'kɒliːg | *s.c.* colega, compañero (en un trabajo o especialidad profesional o científica).

collect | kə'lekt | *v.t.* **1** coleccionar. **2** juntar, reunir, hacer acopio de: *collect the glasses for later = reúne los vasos para más tarde.* **3** recoger, ir por (personas o cosas): *today I'll collect the children = hoy recogeré a los niños.* **4** coger, recoger, recaudar, cobrar (dinero): *in Ireland you collect your pension at the post office = en Irlanda cobras la pensión en correos.* **5** acumular (polvo, suciedad, etc.). **6** atraer (luz, calor, etc.): *this device collects heat from the sun = este mecanismo atrae el calor del sol.* **7** serenar (pensamientos); recobrar (la calma). || *v.i.* **8** reunirse, congregarse, acumularse (personas o cosas). **9** recoger dinero, ir recogiendo dinero (para caridad, por ejemplo). || *v.r.* **10** serenarse, recobrarse, reponerse (mentalmente). || *adj.* y *adv.* **11** (EE.UU.) cobro revertido. || | 'kɒlekt | *s.c.* **12** REL. colecta (oración). || **13 to – up,** recoger bien, recoger completamente (instrumental, pertenencias, etc.).

collected | kə'lektɪd | *adj.* **1** LIT. completas (obras). **2** (form.) sosegado, sereno.

collectedly | kə'lektɪdlɪ | *adj.* (form.) con sosiego, con serenidad.

collecting | kə'lektɪŋ | *s.i.* **1** coleccionismo. || *adj.* **2** para la colección, de recoger (dinero): *the collecting box = la caja de recoger (dinero).*

collection | kə'lekʃn | *s.c.* **1** colección (de objetos). **2** LIT. colección, antología, compilación. **3** MUS. colección, recopilación. **4** recogida (postal). **5** colección, grupo, reunión (de personas o cosas). **6** REL. colecta, cuestación (de dinero). || *s.c.* e *i.* **7** colecta, recaudación (de impuestos, de dinero destinado a una obra de caridad, etc.). **8** recogida, (de cualquier objeto): *that shop makes collections in your house = esa tienda tiene servicio de recogida a domicilio.*

collective | kə'lektɪv | *adj.* **1** colectivo, conjunto. **2** colectiva (granja u otro tipo de negocio). **3** GRAM. colectivo (tipo de sustantivo). || *s.c.* **4** [*v.sing./pl.*] cooperativa, grupo colectivo de propiedad. || **5 – bargaining,** negociación colectiva (laboral). **6 – ownership,** propiedad colectiva.

collectively | kə'lektɪvlɪ | *adv.* colectivamente, conjuntamente.

collectivise V. **collectivize.**

collectivism | kə'lektɪvɪzəm | *s.i.* POL. colectivismo.

collectivist | kə'lektɪvɪst | POL. *s.c.* **1** colectivista. || *adj.* **2** colectivista.

collectivize | kə'lektɪvaɪz | (también **collectivise**) *v.t.* estatalizar, colectivizar.

collectivized | kə'lektɪvaɪzd | (también **collectivised**) *adj.* estatalizado, colectivizado.

collectivization | kəˌlektɪvaɪ'zeɪʃn | (EE.UU.) | kəˌlecktɪvɪʒeɪʃn | (también **collectivisation**) *s.i.* colectivización, estatalización.

collector | kə'lektər | *s.c.* **1** coleccionista. **2** cobrador, recaudador (de cosas variadas: deudas, alquileres, billetes, etc.). || **3 collector's item,** pieza única, sueño de coleccionista.

colleen | 'kɒliːn | *s.c.* chica (en Irlanda).

college | 'kɒlɪdʒ | *s.c.* **1** institución de enseñanza superior. **2** (brit.) facultad universitaria (en Oxford, Cambridge y Londres). **3** escuela femenina privada de enseñanza secundaria. **4 [– of]** colegio de (profesional): *College of Surgeons = Colegio de Cirujanos.*

collegiate | kə'liːdʒɪɪt | *adj.* **1** universitario; colegial. || **2 – university,** universidad dividida en facultades (como Oxford, Cambridge y Londres).

collide | kə'laɪd | *v.i.* **1 [to – (with)]** chocar violentamente, colisionar con fuerza. **2 [to – (with)]** (fig.) entrar en conflicto, chocar (grupos con intereses encontrados).
collie | 'kɒlɪ | *s.c.* perro pastor escocés, collie.
colliery | 'kɒlɪərɪ | *s.c.* (brit.) MIN. mina de carbón.
collision | kə'lɪʒn | *s.c.* e *i.* **1 [– (between/with)]** colisión, choque violento. **2 [– (between/with)]** conflicto, choque de pareceres. || **3 – course (with), a)** trayectoria de choque, trayectoria de colisión. **b)** de camino a la confrontación, camino de un conflicto.
collocate | 'kɒləkeɪt | FILOL. *s.c.* **1** palabra parte de una colocación lingüística. || | 'kɒləkeɪt | *v.i.* **2 [to – (with)]** formar colocación lingüística.
collocation | ˌkɒlə'keɪʃn | *s.i.* FILOL. colocación lingüística.
colloquial | kə'ləʊkwɪəl | *adj.* FILOL. coloquial, informal, familiar (nivel de lenguaje).
colloquialism | kə'ləʊkwɪəlɪzəm | *s.c.* FILOL. coloquialismo.
colloquially | kə'ləʊkwɪəlɪ | *adv.* coloquialmente, informalmente, familiarmente.
colloquia | kə'ləʊkwɪə | *pl.* de **colloquium.**
colloquium | kə'ləʊkwɪəm | [*pl.* **colloquia**] *s.c.* (form.) seminario científico, pequeño congreso de especialistas.
colloquy | 'kɒləkwɪ | *s.c.* e *i.* (form.) coloquio.
collude | kə'luːd | *v.i.* **[to – (with)]** conspirar, confabularse.
collusion | kə'luːʒn | *s.i.* **[– (with)]** (form.) confabulación, conspiración.
collywobbles | 'kɒlɪwɒblz | **the –,** (fam.) tembladera (nervios).
cologne | kə'ləʊn | *s.i.* colonia.
Colombia | kə'lɒmbɪə | *s.sing.* Colombia.
Colombian | kə'lɒmbɪən | *s.c.* colombiano. || *adj.* **2** colombiano.
colon | 'kəʊlən | *s.c.* **1** ANAT. colon. **2** dos puntos (en ortografía).
colonel | 'kɜːnl | *s.c.* MIL. coronel.
colonial | kə'ləʊnɪəl | *adj.* **1** colonial. **2** ARQ. estilo colonial. **3** ZOOL. colonial (insectos que viven en colonias). || *s.c.* **4** habitante de las colonias, colonial.
colonialism | kə'ləʊnɪəlɪzəm | *s.i.* POL. colonialismo.
colonialist | kə'ləʊnɪəlɪst | *s.c.* **1** colonialista. || *adj.* **2** colonialista.
colonist | 'kɒlənɪst | *s.c.* colono.
colonization | ˌkɒlənaɪ'zeɪʃn | (EE.UU.) | ˌkɒlənɪ'zeɪʃn | (también **colonisation**) *s.i.* colonización.
colonize | 'kɒlənaɪz | (también **colonise**) *v.t.* e *i.* **1** colonizar, establecer colonias. **2** ZOOL. colonizar (un lugar por parte de insectos).
colonized | 'kɒlənaɪzd | (también **colonised**) *adj.* **1** colonizado. **2** colonizado (por insectos).
colonizing | 'kɒlənaɪzɪŋ | (también **colonising**) *adj.* colonizador (país).
colonnade | ˌkɒlə'neɪd | *s.c.* ARQ. columnata.
colony | 'kɒlənɪ | *s.c.* **1** POL. colonia (país). **2** ZOOL. colonia (de insectos). **3** colonia, asentamiento (específico): *the leper colony = colonia de leprosos.* || **4 the colonies,** (brit. y p.u.) HIST. las colonias (de Gran Bretaña).
color V. **colour.**
coloration | ˌkʌlə'reɪʃn | *s.i.* coloración (de algo o algún animal).
coloratura | ˌkɒlərə'tʊərə | MUS. *s.i.* **1** floreo, estilo floreado de cantar. **2** cantante especializada en floreos (mujer).
colossal | kə'lɒsl | *adj.* colosal, inmenso.
colossally | kə'lɒsəlɪ | *adv.* colosalmente, inmensamente.
colossi | kə'lɒsaɪ | *pl.* de **colossus.**
colossus | kə'lɒsəs | [*pl.* **colossuses** o **colossi**] *s.c.* **1** ART. coloso (estatua). **2** (fam.) coloso, persona de gran estatura (moral, política, etc.).
colour | 'kʌlər | (EE.UU. **color**) *s.c.* **1** color. **2** color, tinte, colorante. || *s.i.* **3** color, colorido (como efecto general). **4** color (de una persona). **5** color (como consecuencia de salud corporal). **6** color, aspecto, atracción (calidad que hace algo más interesante). || *adj.* **7** de color, en color: *colour television = televisión en color.* || *s.pl.* **8** (fig.) colores, bandera. **9** DEP. colores (de un equipo). || *v.t.* **10** colorear, pintar. **11** colorear, afectar (la forma de pensar). || *v.i.* **12** colorearse. **13** ponerse colorado, enrojecer (la cara). || **14 color line,** (EE.UU.) línea de prohibición de entrada a personas de color. **15 – fast,** de color fijo (ropa). **16 – scheme,** combinación de colores (de decoración). **17 – supplement,** (brit.) PER. suplemento de color. **18 to – up,** ponerse muy colorado, sonrojarse. **19 to have a high –,** tener los colores demasiado subidos, estar demasiado sofocado (con sentido de falta de salud). **20 in –/in full –,** con color, a pleno color, en color, a todo color (revista, película, etc.). **21 to nail one's colors to the mast,** mantenerse firme en el punto de vista de uno, no estar dispuesto a ceder en la opinión de uno. **22 to see someone in their true colors,** caer en la cuenta del verdadero carácter de alguien. **23 to show one's true colors,** mostrar el verdadero carácter de uno, destaparse. **24 with flying colors,** brillantemente, magníficamente, triunfalmente.
colour-bar | 'kʌləbɑːr | *s.sing.* barrera de color (problema de racismo).
colour-blind | 'kʌləblaɪnd | *adj.* daltónico.
colour-blindness | 'kʌləblaɪndnɪs | *s.i.* MED. daltonismo.
colour-coded | 'kʌləkəʊdɪd | *adj.* con distintos colores, con un distinto código de color.
coloured | 'kʌləd | (EE.UU **colored**) *adj.* **1** de distintos colores, de diferentes colores: *all sorts of coloured birds = todo tipo de pájaros de distintos colores.* **2** de color (no blancos). **3** mestizo (en Suráfrica). || *s.c.* **4** negro, persona de color. **5** mestizo (en Suráfrica).
colourful | 'kʌləfl | (EE.UU **colorful**) *adj.* **1** lleno de colorido, con colorido. **2** llamativo, excéntrico (personalidad). **3** atrayente, brillante, con colores (historia).
colourfully | 'kʌləfəlɪ | (EE.UU. **colorfully**) *adv.* brillantemente, con gran cantidad de colores, con mucho colorido.
colouring | 'kʌlərɪŋ | (EE.UU. **coloring**) *s.i.* **1** coloración, colorido (de algo). **2** QUIM. colorante. || *s.sing.* **3** color, coloración (de la piel, pelo, ojos, etc.).
colourless | 'kʌləlɪs | (EE.UU. **colorless**) *adj.* **1** incoloro, sin color. **2** deslucido, apagado; aburrido.
colt | kəʊlt | *s.c.* potro.
coltish | 'kəʊtɪʃ | *adj.* retozón, juguetón, lleno de energía.
columbine | 'kɒləmbaɪn | *s.c.* BOT. aguileña, pajarilla.
column | 'kɒləm | *s.c.* **1** columna, pilar. **2 [– of]** columna de (humo o similar). **3** columna (formación en fila). **4** PER. columna (de un periódico). **5** PER. columna (periódica).
columnist | 'kɒləmnɪst | *s.c.* PER. columnista.
coma | 'kəʊmə | *s.c.* MED. coma.
comatose | 'kəʊmətəʊs | *adj.* **1** MED. comatoso. **2** (fam.) medio tirado, medio muerto (por cansancio o bebida).
comb | kəʊm | *s.c.* **1** peine. || *v.t.* **2** peinar. **3 [to – + *o.* + (for)]** peinar, investigar, registrar (lugares). || *s.sing.* **4 [a –]** un peinado. || **5 to – out,** desenredar, desenmarañar.
combat | 'kɒmbæt | *s.c.* e *i.* **1** combate, lucha, pelea. || *v.t.* **2** luchar contra, combatir contra, pelear contra.
combatant | 'kɒmbətənt | *s.c.* MIL. combatiente.
combative | 'kɒmbətɪv | *adj.* combativo, belicoso.
combatively | 'kɒmbətɪvlɪ | *adv.* combativamente, belicosamente.
combination | ˌkɒmbɪ'neɪʃn | *s.i.* **1** combinación. || *s.c.* **2** combinación. **3** combinación, clave (para cerraduras). **4** (brit.) moto y sidecar. || *s.pl.* **5** calzoncillos largos y camiseta de manga larga. || **6 – lock,** cerradura de combinación numérica. **7 in – with,** en combinación con.
combine | kəm'baɪn | *v.t.* e *i.* **1** combinar(se), mezclar(se). **2** unir(se) (dos empresas, dos organizaciones, etc.). || *v.t.* **3** combinar (dos cualidades, características, actividades, etc.). || | 'kɒmbaɪn | *s.c.* **4** agrupación, asociación. || **5 – harvester,** AGR. cosechadora.
combined | kəm'baɪnd | *adj.* **1 [– (with)] combinado:** *your knowledge combined with my expertise = tu cono-*

cimiento combinado con mi experiencia. **2** conjunta (operación o similar).

combustible | kəm'bʌstəbl | *adj.* (form.) combustible.

combustion | kəm'bʌstʃən | *s.i.* QUIM. combustión.

come | kʌm | *v.* [*pret.irreg.* **came,** *p.p.* [illegible]] *i.* **1** venir (hacia uno): *he came towards me = vino hacia mí.* **2** llegar, arribar: *he has come = ha llegado.* **3** ir, acercarse (a la persona que le llama o con quien está hablando): *I'm coming downstairs in a minute, John = voy abajo en un minuto, Juan.* **4 [to – from]** ser de, ser originario de, proceder de (país, ciudad, etc.): *where do you come from? = ¿de dónde eres?* **5 [to – to]** alcanzar la cantidad de; llegar hasta, costar (cantidad): *the meal came to 50 pounds = la comida costó 50 libras.* **6 [to – to]** alcanzar, llegar a, lograr (poder, influencia, etc.). **7 [to – into]** aparecer ante (la mirada, ojos, etc.): *the village came into view = el pueblo apareció ante la vista.* **8** ir ocurriendo, ir teniendo lugar, ir desarrollándose: *my hate came gradually = mi odio fue desarrollándose gradualmente.* **9 [to – +** *inf.*] llegar a ocurrir, suceder: *how did you come to like her? = ¿cómo sucedió el que te gustara ella?* **10 [to – +** *ger.*] venir, ir (a una actividad deportiva): *come fishing tomorrow = ven de pesca mañana.* **11** [=N *num.ord.*/expresión temporal] suceder, ocurrir; llegar, ser: *she came first in her class = ella fue la primera de su clase.* **12** (fam.) alcanzar un orgasmo, lograr un orgasmo. **13 [to – of]** proceder de, ser de (linaje, familia, etc.). **14 [to – before]** presentarse ante, aparecer ante (tribunal, investigación, etc.). **15 [to – to]** llegar a, comenzar a tocar (un tema, un aspecto científico, etc. que se está estudiando). **16 [to – in]** venir en, fabricarse en (diferentes tamaños, estilos, colores, etc.): *shirts come in three sizes only = las camisas únicamente se fabrican en tres tamaños.* **17** [sin *suj.*] (fam.) cuando vengan, cuando llegue (tiempo): *come the exams they won't go out = cuando lleguen los exámenes no saldrán.* || *t.* **18 [to – +** *o.* **+ with]** (fam.) hacerse el... con: *don't come the innocent with me = no te hagas el inocente conmigo.* || **19 as... as they come,** (fam.) más... que hecho de encargo: *those girls were as cheeky as they come = esas chicas eran más descaradas que hechas de encargo.* **20 –,** ánimo, venga: *come, don't cry = venga, no llores.* **21 to – about,** surgir, llegar a ocurrir: *how did the problem come about = ¿cómo surgió el problema?* **22 to – across, a)** darse con, encontrarse con, toparse con (algo o alguien inesperadamente). **b)** comunicarse, transmitirse, dar una impresión: *I'm afraid he didn't come across the way he wanted = me temo que no dio la impresión que él quería.* **23 to – across (as),** dar una imagen (de): *she comes across as a lovely person = ella da la imagen de ser una persona estupenda.* **24 to – across (with),** (p.u. y fam.) dar, soltar (dinero o similar). **25 – again?,** ¿cómo?, ¿qué? (con cierta sorpresa ante lo que se ha escuchado). **26 – along, a)** venga, que no pasa nada, ánimo (ante algo que no gusta). **b)** venga, de prisa, que no tenemos tiempo. **27 to – along, a)** aparecer inesperadamente, venir sin esperarlo. **b)** desarrollarse, progresar, avanzar (en conocimientos, salud, etc.): *the baby is coming along fine = el bebé está desarrollándose estupendamente.* **28 to – and go,** venir e ir, cambiar continuamente: *people come and go here = aquí la gente cambia continuamente.* **29 to – apart,** destrozarse, hacerse añicos, romperse en pedazos. **30 to – around, a)** V. **to — round. b)** (brit.) darse una vuelta por, pasar por (la casa de alguien). **31 to – at, a)** dirigirse amenazadoramente contra, ir en actitud de ataque contra. **b)** bombardear, acudir caóticamente (ideas, imágenes, etc., a la mente). **32 to – away (from),** separarse (de), desunirse (de), despegarse (de) (físicamente). **33 to – away (with),** irse (con), marcharse (con) (una impresión, sentimiento, etc.). **34 to – back, a)** regresar, volver, retornar. **b)** volverse a poner de moda, volver a pegar, volver a estar en uso. **c)** reintroducir, volver a tener vigencia (una tradición, ley, etc.). **35 to – back (to), a)** volver (a), echar mano nuevamente (de) (un tema, explicación, idea, etc.). **b)** regresar a la memoria, volver a la mente (recuerdos, imágenes, etc.). **36 to – between,** meterse en medio de, interponerse entre (amigos, pareja, etc.). **37 to – by,** encontrarse con, toparse con, ganar, lograr (algo): *money is difficult to come by = el dinero es difícil de ganar.* **38 –, –,** venga ya, no digas disparates, de ninguna manera (desacuerdo). **39 to – down, a)** disminuir, decrecer (una cantidad). **b)** dar en tierra, caer, desplomarse. **c)** (brit.) dejar la universidad, acabar una licenciatura universitaria. **d)** caer (lluvia, nieve, etc.). **40 to – down in the world,** perder la fortuna. **41 to – down (to),** bajar (a) (un lugar más al sur). **42 to – down (to/from),** ser pasada (a/de), ser transmitida (a/de) (una tradición, costumbre, historia, etc.). **43 to – down on,** reprochar, echar la culpa, regañar. **44 to – down to,** reducirse básicamente (una cuestión, problema, etc.). **45 to – with,** enfermar de. **46 to – for, a)** venir a por, venir a buscar (algo o alguien). **b)** ir a por, venir a por, dirigirse amenazadoramente a: *he came for me with clenched fists = fue a por mí con los puños apretados.* **47 to – forward,** presentarse voluntariamente, estar dispuesto voluntariamente, ofrecerse voluntario, ofrecerse voluntariamente. **48 to – forward with,** ofrecer (sugerencias, soluciones, propuestas, etc.): *he hasn't come forward with a single proposal = no ha ofrecido ni una propuesta.* **49 to – from,** proceder de, ser de (un ambiente, familia, etc.). **50 to – in, a)** llegar (tren, barco, avión, etc.). **b)** MAR. subir (marea). **c)** POL. entrar en funciones, acceder al poder, conseguir gobernar (partido). **d)** llegar, difundirse (noticias). **e)** ingresar, ganar de sueldo. **f)** interrumpir, tomar la palabra, aportar las ideas de uno (en una conversación, debate, etc.). **g)** pintar, aportar un granito de arena (en un plan, proyecto, etc.): *where do I come in? = ¿en qué punto aporto yo mi granito de arena?* **h)** ponerse de moda, pegar fuerte. **i)** haber gran cantidad, haber mucho (por ser la época de algún producto): *apples haven't come in yet = no hay gran cantidad de manzanas todavía.* **j)** participar, entrar en (negocios, acuerdos, etc.). **51 to – in/into,** entrar en, venir dentro. **52 to – in for,** ser el blanco de (críticas, insultos, etc.). **53 to – into,** heredar (posesiones). **54 to – into it,** entrar en el tema, ser parte del tema, entrar en ello, hacer al caso: *as far as she is concerned money doesn't come into it = en lo que afecta a ella, el dinero no es parte del tema.* **55 to – into line,** V. **line. 56 to – into one's own,** empezar a destacar, comenzar a hacer valer los propios méritos. **57 to – into play,** V. **play. 58 to – of age,** alcanzar la mayoría de edad, llegar a la mayoría de edad. **59 to – off, a)** dejar de tomar, dejar el hábito de (bebida, tabaco, etc.). **b)** separarse, desprenderse (físicamente). **c)** salir bien, resultar un éxito: *the party came off fine = la fiesta resultó un éxito total.* **d)** quitar de la cartelera (película, obra de teatro, etc.). **e)** tener lugar, ocurrir como previsto, efectuarse (cualquier acontecimiento). **f)** salir, resultar, acabar (bien, mal, regular, etc.). **60 – off it!,** (fam.) ¡anda ya!, ¡no me digas! (en desacuerdo). **61 – on, a)** venga, vamos, ánimo. **b)** de prisa, vamos ya, no demores. **c)** por favor, venga, no seas así (con queja o enfado). **62 to – on, a)** desarrollarse, crecer, progresar (en conocimientos, salud, trabajo, etc.). **b)** empezar (una enfermedad): *I feel the "flu" coming on = siento que me empieza la gripe.* **c)** aparecer (en película); entrar en (escena). **d)** encontrarse, dar con (algo o alguien, bastante inesperadamente). **e)** encenderse, darse (luz, calefacción, etc.). **63 to – one's way,** V. **way. 64 to – on to,** volver la atención a, dirigir la atención a (tema, idea, punto de vista, etc.). **65 to – out, a)** salir a la luz, revelarse (algo secreto, el resultado de una investigación o similar). **b)** publicarse, ver la luz, salir a la luz (libro). **c)** parecer, sonar, tener el marchamo de (una frase dicha). **d)** (brit.) hacer huelga, comenzar una huelga, ponerse en huelga. **e)** salir (sol, estrellas o luna). **f)** FOT. salir. **g)** desaparecer, quitarse, irse (manchas); debilitarse (color). **h)** reconocer ser, declararse (algo con visos de ocultamiento como, por ejemplo, homosexual). **i)** salir, resultar, acabar (como final de un proceso): *he came out on top = acabó vencedor.* **66 to – out (for/against),** declararse (a favor de/en contra de), reconocer públicamente estar (a favor de/en contra de). **67 to – out in,** quedar cubierto de (sudor, granos, etc.). **68 to – out of,** salir de, proceder de, originarse en, surgir de: *a lot of good has come out of medical research = muchas cosas buenas han salido de la investigación médica.* **69 to – out of oneself/to – out of one's shell,** salir de uno mismo, salir del cascarón. **70 to – out with,** soltar, decir repentina e inesperadamente. **71 to – over, a)** ocurrir, suceder, afectar (a alguien, que empieza a comportarse extrañamente): *something strange has come over him = algo extraño le ha sucedido.* **b)** venir aquí, acercarse aquí (de un país al país donde se está): *come over for Christmas = venid aquí a pasar la Navidad (una persona, por ejemplo en Francia, dice esto a otra en Inglaterra).* **c)** dejarse caer (por la casa de otra persona). **d)** dar una impresión; resultar (simpático, amable, maleducado, etc.). **e)** transmitirse, comunicarse (una idea, proyecto, etc.): *his ideas didn't come over in the proper way = sus ideas no fueron comunicadas de la manera adecuada.* **f)** (fam.) ponerse (enfermo, tonto, etc.): *she came over nervous at the meeting = se puso nerviosa en la reunión.* **72 to – round, a)** recuperarse, volver en sí (de un desmayo). **b)** acercarse, pasar por (casa de otro). **c)** llegar, llegar el momento de: *when the next meeting comes round call me = cuando llegue el momento de la próxima reunión llámame.* **73 to – round (to), a)** llegar a apreciar (a), llegar a respetar (a), llegar a tener cariño (a) (alguien que antes se despreciaba). **b)** ponerse al lado (de), dejarse convencer (por) (cambiando la opinión de uno en favor de la del otro). **74 to – through, a)** pasar por, sufrir (una situación difícil). **b)** darse a conocer (persona); transmitirse (una sensación). **c)** llegar (documento oficial o similar). **75 to – through (with),** producir finalmente, sacar a la luz (algo esperado): *he came through with the play = finalmente sacó a la luz la obra de teatro.* **76 to – to,** recobrar el conocimiento (después de un desmayo). **77 to – to a head,** V. **head. 78 to – to grips with,** V. **grip. 79 to – to life,** V. **life. 80 to – to light,** V. **light. 81 to – to mind,** V. **mind. 82 to – to pass,** V. **pass. 83 to – to terms with,** V. **term. 84 to – to the fore,** V. **fore. 85 – to think of it/when you – to think of it,** puestos a pensar con seriedad, puestos a reflexionar con detenimiento, si nos ponemos a pensar un poco seriamente (especialmente cuando antes no se ha hecho). **86 to – under, a)** ser responsabilidad de, ser competencia de. **b)** ser el blanco de, sufrir (críticas, insultos, etc.) **c)** estar clasificado bajo, estar bajo, estar agrupado bajo (en una lista, libro o similar). **87 to – up, a)** salir a colación (en una conversación). **b)** surgir inesperadamente (asunto o problema): *I can't see you, something has come up = no te puedo ver, ha surgido algo inesperadamente.* **c)** subir en la vida, ascender en la sociedad; mejorar en la vida: *he has come up by himself = él ha subido en la vida sin ayuda de nadie.* **d)** salir (sol o luna). **e)** nacer, crecer (plantas). **f)** surgir la oportunidad de (un empleo). **g)** DER. ser presentado (un caso ante un tribunal). **h)** intensificarse, hacerse más fuerte (la luz, el calor, etc.). **88 to – up (for),** POL. presentarse (a), presentarse de candidato (a). **89 to – up (to),** acercarse (a), aproximarse (a) (en el espacio). **90 to – up against,** darse de bruces con, encontrarse con, ser confrontado por (un problema). **91 to – up in the world,** ascender puestos en la vida, mejorar de posición social, subir en la sociedad. **92 to – upon, a)** darse de bruces con, topar con, encontrarse inesperadamente con (algo o alguien). **b)** ocurrírsele (a uno una idea repentina o similar). **93 to – up to, a)** acercarse, aproximarse (una fecha, una hora, etc.). **b)** llegar al nivel de, alcanzar el nivel de (en calidad). **94 to – up to scratch,** V. **scratch. 95 to – up with, a)** sugerir, proponer (plan o similar). **b)** sacar, aportar (dinero). **96 – what may,** pase lo que pase, ocurra lo que ocurra. **97 to get what is coming to one,** (fam.) recibir lo que uno se merece. **98 to have it coming to one,** (fam.) sufrir las consecuencias merecidas, tener que aguantar las consecuencias. **99 to have one's tea/coffee/etc. as it comes,** tomar el té/café/etc., sin preferencias especiales (de concentrado o suave). **100 how –?/how – ...?,** ¿cómo es eso?/¿cómo es posible que...? **101 if it comes to that,** si nos ponemos todos así, si hay que decirlo todo, si es que hemos llegado a esto (en un contraataque a una acusación): *well, if it comes to that I must say you didn't help me at all = bueno, si hemos llegado a esto, debo decir que no me ayudaste en absoluto.* **102 not to know whether one is coming or going,** estar totalmente desconcertado, no saber por dónde va uno, no saber qué hacer primero. **103 to –,** en adelante, en el futuro (en el tiempo): *for a long time to come = durante mucho tiempo en el futuro.* **104 what is it all coming to?,** ¿qué está ocurriendo en este mundo?, ¿a dónde vamos a ir a parar? **105 when it comes to,** cuando llega el momento crucial de, cuando se trata de: *when it comes to helping out nobody like my father = cuando llega el momento de echar una mano, nadie como mi padre.* OBS. Este verbo tiene los siguientes matices de difícil explicación: **106** expresa la idea de cambio: *my dreams haven't come true yet = mis sueños no se han hecho realidad todavía; the lid finally came unstuck = la tapadera finalmente se despegó.* **107** con las preposiciones **to** e **into** adquiere el significado de la palabra que le sigue: *the car came to a stop = el coche se paró; the whole thing didn't come into being because of her = todo el montaje no llegó a nada a causa de ella.*

comeback | 'kʌmbæk | *s.c.* **1** reaparición (de moda o similar). **2** (fam.) respuesta, contestación (a acusación, insulto, etc.). **3** (fam.) manera de recuperar (algo material). || **4 to make/stage a –,** volver al candelero, volver a la luz pública (un actor, por ejemplo).

comedian | kə'mi:dɪən | *s.c.* **1** (p.u.) comediante (profesión). **2** cómico (que cuenta chistes o similar).

comedienne | kə,mi:dɪ'en | *s.c.* cómica. V. **comedian 2.**

comedown | 'kʌmdaʊn | *s.sing.* (fam.) humillación, salto hacia atrás, bajón (en categoría, estilo, etc.).

comedy | 'kɒmɪdɪ | *s.c.* e *i.* **1** ART. comedia. || *s.i.* **2** comedia, humor.

comeliness | 'kʌmlɪnɪs | *s.i.* (p.u.) atracción, belleza (mujeres).

comely | 'kʌmlɪ | *adj.* (p.u.) atractiva, bien parecida (especialmente refiriéndose a mujeres).

come-on | 'kʌmɒn | *s.c.* (desp.) invitación, grito de ánimo, incitación (a hacer algo negativo). **— on!** ¡vamos! ¡date prisa!.

comer | 'kʌmər | *s.c.* **1** (normalmente *pl.*) el que llega, persona que llega: *we don't want any late-comers = no queremos personas que lleguen tarde.* || **2 all comers,** todos los aspirantes, todos los contendientes (a quitar el primer puesto a otro, normalmente en el deporte).

comet | 'kɒmɪt | *s.c.* ASTR. cometa.

come-uppance | kʌm'ʌpəns | *s.sing.* (fam.) castigo merecido, castigo justo: *in the end you'll get your come-uppance = al final recibirás el castigo que mereces.*

comfort | 'kʌmfət | *s.i.* **1** comodidad, confort; bienestar. || *s.c.* e *i.* **2** consuelo, solaz, alivio. || *s.c.* **3** (normalmente *pl.*) comodidad, detalles de comodidad, cosas agradables (de la vida): *the comforts of modern life = las comodidades de la vida moderna.* || *v.t.* **4** consolar, dar consuelo; confortar. || **5 cold –,** triste consuelo, falso consuelo (que no mejora una situación negativa). **6 – station,** (EE.UU. y euf.) servicios públicos, lavabos. **7 creature comforts,** V. **creature. 7 too ... for –,** demasiado ... como para estar a gusto, demasiado ... como para sentirse cómodo: *this is too strange for comfort = esto es demasiado extraño como para estar a gusto.*

comfortable | 'kʌmftəbl | (EE.UU.) | 'kʌmfərtəbl | *adj.* **1** cómodo, confortable (físicamente). **2** adecuado, cómodo, holgado (con suficientes ingresos). **3** cómodo, a gusto (sensación personal). **4** bien, con estado de salud satisfactorio (especialmente después de una enfermedad). **5** holgada, suficiente (mayoría de gobierno, de decisión, etc.). **6** fácil, cómodo, sin exigencia (trabajo, tarea, responsabilidad, etc.). **7** con la que es fácil comunicarse, amable (cualidad personal). **8** (desp.) comodón, facilón (en una opinión, creencia, etc.): *I don't like his comfortable religious life = no me gusta su vida religiosa comodona.*

comfortably | 'kʌmftəblɪ | *adv.* **1** cómodamente, confortablemente. **2** adecuadamente, holgadamente (en los medios materiales de la vida). **3** holgadamente, con un margen suficiente (con mayoría en decisiones políticas, de empresa, asociativas, etc.). **4** fácilmente, cómodamente, sin exigencia alguna (trabajo, tarea, responsabilidad, etc.). || **5 – off,** muy bien económicamente, con ingresos muy adecuados.

comforter | 'kʌmfətər | *s.c.* **1** consolador, objeto de consuelo/alivio. **2** (EE.UU.) colcha. **3** (brit.) chupete. **4** (p.u. y brit.) bufanda de lana.

comforting | 'kʌmfətɪŋ | *adj.* consolador: *comforting words = palabras consoladoras.*

comfortless | 'kʌmfətlɪs | *adj.* incómodo, sin comodidad (física).

comfy | 'kʌmfɪ | *adj.* (fam.) cómodo, a gusto, confortable.

comic | 'kɒmɪk | *adj.* **1** cómico, divertido. || *s.c.* **2** cómico, comediante. **3** (brit.) tebeo, cómic, historieta. || **4 – book,** (EE.UU.) tebeo, cómic, historieta. **5 – opera,** ART. ópera cómica. **6 – strip,** PER. tira cómica, historieta cómica en viñetas.

comical | 'kɒmɪkl | *adj.* gracioso, divertido, cómico.

comically | 'kɒmɪklɪ | *adv.* graciosamente, divertidamente, cómicamente.

coming | 'kʌmɪŋ | *adj.* **1** venidero, próximo (en el tiempo). || **2 – of age,** mayoría de edad. **3 comings and goings,** (fam.) idas y venidas, ir y venir, ajetreo.

comma | 'kɒmə | *s.c.* GRAM. coma (signo de puntuación).

command | kə'mɑːnd | (EE.UU.) | kəmænd | *v.t.* **1 [to – + *o.* + (*inf.*)]** mandar, ordenar, dar instrucciones. **2** merecer, obtener (por prestigio): *to command obedience = merecer obediencia (ser obedecido).* **3** estar en control de, controlar totalmente (los mares, ciertas zonas, etc., especialmente en el sentido militar). **4** MIL. estar al mando de. **5** (fig.) dominar, disfrutar de (una vista, paisaje o similar): *you command a beautiful view from here = disfrutas de una vista magnífica aquí.* || *v.i.* **6** dar órdenes, mandar. **7** MIL. ser el comandante en jefe, estar al mando. || *s.c.* e *i.* **8** mandato, orden; mando. || *s.i.* **9** MIL. mando. **10 [– of]** control de, dominio de. **11 [– of]** conocimiento de, manejo de, destreza en (una ciencia, idioma, etc.). || *s.c.* **12** INF. comando. **13 [=N *v.sing./pl.*]** MIL. grupo de oficiales al mando, mando, grupo de mando. **14** [=N *v.sing./pl.*] MIL. grupo de soldados bajo mando. || *s.sing.* **15** vista, panorámica. || **16 at one's –,** a la disposición de uno, bajo el dominio de uno, bajo el control de uno (una habilidad o capacidad intelectual): *he has three languages at his command = tiene tres idiomas a su disposición.* **17 Command,** MIL. mando, comandancia, grupo (del Ejército de Tierra o Aire). **18 – post,** MIL. puesto de mando. **19 in – (of),** controlando, en posición de control (sobre), con control (sobre): *he wasn't in control of his faculties = él no tenía control sobre sus facultades.* **20 second/third/etc. in –,** segundo/tercero/etc., de a bordo, segundo/ tercero/etc., en la cadena del mando (no solamente en el contexto militar).

commandant | ˌkɒmən'dænt | *s.c.* MIL. comandante, jefe (de una plaza, puesto, etc.).

commandeer | ˌkɒmən'dɪər | *v.t.* MIL. requisar, confiscar. **2** (desp. y fig.) confiscar, apoderarse de, coger (algo de alguien menos poderoso) tomar, apropiarse.

commander | kə'mɑːndər | (EE.UU.) | kə'mændər | *s.c.* MIL. **1** comandante (categoría). **2** capitán de fragata.

commander-in-chief | kəˌmɑːndərɪn'tʃiːf | (EE.UU.) | kəˌmændərɪn'tʃiːf | [*pl.* **commanders-in-chief**] *s.c.* MIL. jefe supremo, comandante en jefe.

commanding | kə'mɑːndɪŋ | (EE.UU.) | kə'mændɪŋ | *adj.* **1** dominante (posición física o de influencia). **2** impresionante, autoritario, imponente (voz, gesto, apariencia, etc.). **3** MIL. autorizado. || **4 – officer,** MIL. oficial de mando.

commandingly | kə'maːndɪŋlɪ | *adv.* impresionantemente, con autoridad, imponentemente.

commandment | kə'mɑːndmənt | (EE.UU.) | kə'mændmənt | *s.c.* REL. mandamiento.

commando | kə'mɑːndəʊ | (EE.UU.) | kə'mændəʊ | *s.c.* MIL. **1** grupo de comandos, pelotón de comandos. **2** comando.

commemorate | kə'meməreɪt | *v.t.* **1** conmemorar, celebrar (algo). **2** conmemorar, inmortalizar (un monumento).

commemoration | kəˌmemə'reɪʃn | *s.c.* e *i.* conmemoración.

commemorative | kə'memərətɪv | (EE.UU.) | kə'meməreɪtɪv | *adj.* conmemorativo.

commence | kə'mens | (form.) *v.t.* e *i.* comenzar, iniciar.

commencement | kə'mensmənt | *s.i.* **1** comienzo, inicio. || **2 Commencement,** (EE.UU.) día de licenciatura (en la Universidad).

commend | kə'mend | *v.t.* **1 [to – + *o.* + (for/to)]** alabar, aplaudir. **2 [to – + *o.* + (to/as)]** recomendar. || *v.r.* **3 [to – (to)]** aprobar, resultar aceptable, resultar adecuado: *the plan commends itself to me = el plan me resulta adecuado.*

commendable | kə'mendəbl | *adj.* alabable, digno de encomio, loable.

commendably | kə'mendəblɪ | *adv.* loablemente, meritoriamente.

commendation | ˌkɒmen'deɪʃn | *s.c.* e *i.* aplauso, alabanza.

commensurate | kə'menʃərət | *adj.* **[– (with)]** (form.) equivalente, correspondiente.

comment | 'kɒment | *v.i.* **1 [to – (on/upon)]** comentar, hacer un comentario. || *s.c.* e *i.* **2** comentario, glosa, observación. | **3 no –,** sin comentarios.

commentary | 'kɒməntrɪ | (EE.UU.) | 'kɒmənterɪ | *s.c.* **1 [– (on)]** TV. comentario, descripción. || *s.c.* e *i.* **2** comentario, nota explicativa.

commentate | 'kɒmenteɪt | *v.i.* TV. hacer comentarios, comentar (un acontecimiento).

commentator | 'kɒmenteɪtər | *s.c.* **1** TV. comentarista, narrador. **2** experto, comentarista (de temas intelectuales).

commerce | 'kɒməːs | *s.i.* **1** comercio. **2** (fig.) intercambio, trato, comunicación.

commercial | kə'məːʃl | *adj.* **1** comercial. **2** financiero, comercial (éxito o fracaso). **3** comercial, privado (radio o televisión). **4** industrial, en grandes cantidades (producción). **5** comercial (que está en venta). || *s.c.* **6** TV. RAD. comercial, anuncio. || **7 – art,** publicidad. **8 – artist,** publicista, diseñador de publicidad. **9 – bank,** FIN. banco comercial. **10 – traveller,** (EE.UU. **traveler**), viajante de comercio. **11 – vehicle,** vehículo de transporte público, vehículo de transporte de mercancías.

commercialise V. **commercialize.**

commercialism | kə'məːʃəlɪzəm | *s.i.* (desp.) comercialismo.

commercialization | kəˌməʃəlaɪ'zeɪʃn | (EE.UU.) | kəˌməʃəlɪ'zeɪʃn | (también **commercialisation**) *s.i.* comercialización.

commercialize | kə'məːʃəlaɪz | (también **commercialise**) *v.t.* comercializar.

commercialized | kə'məːʃəlaɪzd | (también **commercialised**) *adj.* (desp.) comercializado.

commercially | kə'məːʃəlɪ | *adv.* comercialmente.

commie | 'kɒmɪ | *s.c.* (fam. y pey.) rojo, comunista.

commiserate | kə'mɪzəreɪt | *v.i.* **[to – (with)]** (form.) apiadarse, compadecerse, sentir lástima.

commiseration | kəˌmɪzə'reɪʃn | *s.i.* **1** conmiseración, compasión. || **2 commiserations,** (form.) lo siento, mi más sentido pésame.

commissar | 'kɒmɪsɑː | *s.c.* POL. comisario, comisario político.

commissariat | ˌkəmɪ'seərɪət | *s.c.* **[=N *v.sing./pl.*]** MIL. intendencia.

commissary | 'kɒmɪsərɪ | *s.c.* (EE.UU.) MIL. economato.

commission | kə'mɪʃn | *s.c.* e *i.* **1** comisión (económica). || *s.c.* **2** encargo, cometido, misión. **3** encargo (de trabajo). **4** MIL. nombramiento (de un oficial). **5** [+ *v.sing./pl.*] comisión, comité. || *s.i.* **6** (form.) comisión, ejecución (de un crimen). || *v.t.* **7** encargar (hacer algo). **8** (normalmente *pas.*) MIL. nombrar oficial. || **9 commissioned officer,** oficial nombrado administrativamente. **10 on/by –,** a comisión. **11 out of –,** fuera de servicio (que no funciona).
commissionaire | kə,mɪʃə'neər | *s.c.* portero (de hotel, teatro, cine, etc.).
commissioner | kə'mɪʃənər | *s.c.* jefe de policía; jefe de servicio (en algún departamento administrativo).
commit | kə'mɪt | [*ger.* **committing,** *pret.* y *p.p.* **committed**] *v.t.* **1** cometer (crimen o similar). **2 [to – + *o.* + (to)]** confinar, recluir (en hospital, manicomio, etc.). **3 [to – + *o.* + (to)]** consignar, depositar (dinero); dedicar (esfuerzos); empeñar (medios materiales); MIL. enviar (tropas): *I don't want to commit the company's resources to that project = no quiero empeñar los recursos de la empresa en ese proyecto.* || *v.r.* **4 [to – (to)]** comprometerse, obligarse (a hacer algo). **5** comprometerse, (fam.) mojarse (en algo personal). || **6 to – suicide,** suicidarse. **7 to – to memory,** aprender de memoria; recurrir a la memoria. **8 to – to paper,** poner por escrito.
commitment | kə'mɪtmənt | *s.i.* **1** dedicación, lealtad: *my commitment to freedom = mi dedicación a la causa de la libertad.* || *s.c.* **2** responsabilidad, obligación. **3** compromiso (porque se ha prometido).
committal | kə'mɪtl | *s.i.* confinamiento, reclusión (en prisión, manicomio, etc.).
committed | kə'mɪtɪd | *adj.* comprometido (en alguna ideología o similar).
committee | kə'mɪtɪ | *s.c.* [+ *v.sing./pl.*] comité, comisión (de trabajo, de algún tema administrativo, etc.).
commode | kə'məʊd | *s.c.* (arc.) silla, retrete, sillico.
commodious | kə'məʊdɪəs | *adj.* (form.) cómodo, espacioso, amplio.
commodity | kə'mɒdɪtɪ | *s.c.* FIN. producto, mercancía.
commodore | 'kɒmədɔː | *s.c.* MAR. MIL. comodoro.
common | 'kɒmən | *adj.* **1** común, general, normal (no único o especial). **2 [– (to)]** compartido, común: *the wish for happiness is common to all peoples = el deseo de la felicidad es compartido por todas las gentes.* **3** medio, ordinario, común; MIL. raso. **4** BIOL. común (especies animales). **5** (fam. y desp.) soez, ordinario (cualidad personal). || *s.c.* **6** (brit.) espacio verde, zona verde; parque público. || **7 – cold,** MED. resfriado común. **8 – denominator,** MAT. común denominador. **9 – ground,** puntos compartidos, puntos de acuerdo (en discusión). **10 – land,** terreno comunal, mancomunidad. **11 – law,** DER. jurisprudencia. **12 Common Market,** POL. ECON. Mercado Común. **13 – noun,** GRAM. sustantivo, nombre común. **14 – or garden,** común, nada extraño, ordinario, de todos los días. **15 – room,** sala de recreo (en un establecimiento de enseñanza). **16 Commons,** (brit.) POL. Cámara Baja. **17 – sense,** sentido común. **18 for the – good,** para bien de todos, a favor del bien común. **19 to have in –,** compartir, tener en común (características). **20 in – (with),** en común (con), compartido (con). **21 to make – cause,** (form.) hacer causa común. **22 the – touch,** don de gentes.
commoner | 'kɒmənər | *s.c.* **1** HIST. plebeyo (no aristócrata). **2** miembro de la Cámara de los Comunes.
common-law | ,kɒmən'lɔː | *adj.* DER. no oficial, por mero acuerdo (por ejemplo, matrimonio no oficial): *his common-law wife = su mujer no oficial (con la que convive sin estar casado oficialmente.*
commonly | 'kɒmənlɪ | *adv.* **1** comúnmente, generalmente, normalmente. **2** (fam. y desp.) soezmente, con bastante ordinariez.
commonplace | 'kɒmənpleɪs | *adj.* **1** (normalmente desp.) trivial, vulgar, ordinario. || *s.c.* **2** lugar común, cliché. **3** (normalmente *sing.*) acontecimiento frecuente, cosa normal, cosa habitual.
commonwealth | 'kɒmənwelθ | *s.c.* **1** (form. o arc.) POL. estado, república, nación común. || **2 the Commonwealth,** POL. la Commonwealth, la Mancomunidad británica de naciones (antiguas colonias británicas que mantienen ciertos contactos entre ellas).
commotion | kə'məʊʃn | *s.i.* conmoción, follón, tumulto.
communal | 'kɒmjʊnl | | kə'mjuːnl | *adj.* **1** común, público (no privado). **2** comunal, colectivo.
communally | 'kɒmjʊnəlɪ | *adv.* **1** públicamente, en comunidad. **2** colectivamente, comunalmente.
commune | 'kɒmjuːn | *s.c.* **1** [+ *v.sing./pl.*] comuna. || | kə'mjuːn | *v.i.* **2 [to – with]** comunicarse con, conversar con (amigos, la naturaleza, etc.).
communicant | kə'mjuːnɪkənt | *s.c.* REL. persona que comulga.
communicate | kə'mjuːnɪkeɪt | *v.i.* **1 [to – (with)]** comunicarse, relacionarse. **2 [to – (with)]** relacionarse, tener contacto (personas). **3 [to – (with)]** (form.) escribirse, estar en contacto por carta. || *v.t.* **4** comunicar, transmitir (ideas, sentimientos, etc.).
communicating | kə'mjuːnɪkeɪtɪŋ | *adj.* que se comunican, comunicantes (físicamente).
communication | kə,mjuːnɪ'keɪʃn | *s.i.* **1** comunicación; transmisión. || *s.c.* **2** (form.) mensaje, carta, comunicación. || *s.pl.* **3** comunicaciones, sistema de comunicación. || **4 to be in – with,** estar en contacto con, tener contacto habitual con. **5 – cord,** (brit.) timbre de alarma (en un tren o similar).
communicative | kə'mjuːnɪkətɪv | *adj.* **1** comunicativo, de la comunicación. **2** hablador, expansivo, comunicativo.
communion | kə'mjuːnɪən | *s.i.* REL. comunión. **2** (form.) comunión (de ideas, un mismo espíritu, etc.). || *s.c.* **[– (of)]** comunidad, hermandad (de personas, especialmente de las mismas creencias religiosas).
communiqué | kə'mjuːnɪkeɪ, (EE.UU.) | kə,mjuːnə'keɪ | *s.c.* comunicado, comunicado oficial, comunicado de prensa.
communism | 'kɒmjʊnɪzəm | *s.i.* POL. comunismo.
communist | 'kɒmjʊnɪst | *s.c.* POL. **1** comunista. || *adj.* **2** comunista. || **3 the Communist Party,** el Partido Comunista.
community | kə'mjuːnɪtɪ | *s.sing.* **1 [the –]** la comunidad, la sociedad. **2 [the –]** POL. la comunidad, el acuerdo entre naciones, el pacto entre naciones. || *s.c.* **3 [=N *v.sing./pl.*]** comunidad, agrupación (de cualquier grupo humano nacional, religioso, social, etc.). **4** BIOL. comunidad (de animales). || *s.i.* **5** comunidad, hermandad: *a feeling of community = un sentimiento de hermandad.* || **6 – centre,** centro social (para la vecindad). **7 – chest,** (EE.UU.) fondo para beneficencia local. **8 – home,** (brit.) centro de reinserción social. **9 – policing,** policía de barrio. **10 – service,** servicio a la comunidad (sistema de trabajo para delincuentes, en vez de la prisión).
commute | kə'mjuːt | *v.i.* **1** hacer un largo recorrido diario de casa al trabajo y viceversa. || *v.t.* **2** conmutar (pena de muerte). **3** conmutar, intercambiar (normalmente una pensión por un pago de una sola vez).
commuter | kə'mjuːtər | *s.c.* persona que tiene que viajar diariamente una cierta distancia para ir al trabajo.
compact | kɒm'pækt | *adj.* **1** compacto, apretado. **2** conciso (estilo). **3** ajustado, compacto, con todo en un espacio mínimo (piso, coche, etc.). || *v.t.* **4** (form.) apretar fuertemente, comprimir con fuerza. || | 'kɒmpækt | *s.c.* **5** polvera (de mujer). || **6 – disc,** ELECTR. compacto, compact disc.
compactly | kəm'pæktlɪ | *adv.* **1** apretadamente, compactamente. **2** concisamente, brevemente (expresado).
compactness | kəm'pæktlɪ | *s.i.* **1** (lo) compacto. **2** concisión, brevedad (de estilo).
companion | kəm'pænɪən | *s.c.* **1** compañero (personal o animal). **2** acompañante, dama de compañía (chica joven que acompaña a una mujer mayor). **3** volumen adicional, volumen que va (con otro, hablando de libros).
companionable | kəm'pænɪəbl | *adj.* sociable, afable, simpático, abierto.

companionship | kəm'pænɪənʃɪp | *s.i.* compañerismo, camaradería.
companionway | kəm'pænɪənweɪ | *s.c.* MAR. escalera de cámara.
company | 'kʌmpənɪ | *s.c.* **1** [— *v.sing.* /*pl.*] FIN. empresa, compañía. **2** [+ *v.sing.*/*pl.*] MIL. compañía. **3** [+ *v.sing.*/*pl.*] ART. compañía (de actores). || *s.i.* **4** compañía: *I can use your company = puedo apreciar tu compañía.* **5** **[the –]** el personal, el acompañamiento, la compañía (en una fiesta u ocasión social). || **6 and –,** (fam. y desp.) y demás calaña, y los secuaces. **7 in –,** acompañado, con otras personas (no solo). **8 in – with,** junto con otros, al mismo tiempo que otros: *in company with many others, I believe in God = junto con muchos otros, creo en Dios.* **9 in good –,** con buena compañía, con buena gente, al igual que mucha buena gente (en opiniones, creencias, etc.). **10 to keep –,** asociarse con, ir en compañía de: *he keeps bad companies = él se asocia con mala gente.* **11 to keep someone –,** acompañar a alguien (para que no esté solo). **12 to part – (with), a)** separarse (de), despedirse (de). **b)** no estar de acuerdo (con). **c)** (hum.) separarse (de), desunirse (de), desconectarse (de) (físicamente): *when you ride that bicycle don't part company with it = cuando montes en esa bicicleta no te separes de ella (no te caigas).* **13 two's –, three's a crowd,** hay que dejar a la gente tranquila y con su vida privada sin estar presente (especialmente a las parejas).
comparability | ˌkəmpərə'bɪlɪtɪ | *s.i.* equivalencia; valor.
comparable | 'kɒmpərəbl | *adj.* **1 [– (to/with)]** comparable, igual, no menos. **2 [– (to/with)]** equivalente, comparable.
comparably | 'kɒmpərəblɪ | *adv.* comparablemente, igualmente.
comparative | kəm'pærətɪv | *adj.* **1** relativo: *we live in comparative comfort = vivimos con una comodidad relativa.* **2** comparativo, comparado (donde se compara algo). **3** GRAM. comparativo. || *s.c.* **4** GRAM. comparativo.
comparatively | kəm'pærətɪvlɪ | *adv.* en comparación, relativamente: *that's comparatively expensive = eso es relativamente caro.*
compare | kəm'peər | *v.t.* **1** comparar, cotejar. **2 [to – + *o.* + (to)]** equiparar, comparar (señalando la similitud). || *v.i.* **3 [to – with]** resultar la comparación de, ser la comparación de: *how does your book compare with Whitney's? = ¿cómo resulta la comparación de tu libro con el de Whitney?* || **4 beyond –,** (lit.) por encima de cualquier comparación, impar. **5 compared with/to,** comparado con, contrastado con. **6 to – favourably/unfavourably (with),** no ser menos (que)/ser peor (que). **7 to – notes,** V. **note. 8 not to – (with),** no tener ni comparación (con); ser claramente inferior (a).
comparison | kəm'pærɪsn | *s.c.* e *i.* **1** comparación, cotejación. **2** equiparación, igualación. || **3 in/by –,** en contraste. **4 in – to/with,** en comparación con, comparado con. **5 to stand/bear – (with),** poder compararse (con); no ser inferior en nada (a). **6 there's no –,** ni punto de comparación.
compartment | kəm'pɑːtmənt | *s.c.* **1** compartimento (especialmente en un tren). **2** sección, división (dentro de un todo): *there are three compartments in my desk drawer = hay tres secciones en el cajón de mi escritorio.*
compartmentalize | kəmpɑːt'mentəlaɪz | (también **compartmentalise**) *v.t.* dividir en secciones, dividir en compartimentos; separar en categorías.
compartmentalized | kəmpɑːt'mentəlaɪzd | (también **compartmentalised**) *adj.* compartimentado, dividido; separado en categorías.
compass | 'kʌmpəs | *s.c.* **1** brújula. **2 [a pair of –]** un compás. || *s.i.* **3** extensión, alcance; ámbito: *the compass of the mind = el alcance de la mente.* || **4 – point,** punto del compás (brújula).
compassion | kəm'pæʃn | *s.i.* compasión, conmiseración.
compassionate | kəm'pæʃənɪt | *adj.* **1** compasivo. || **2 – leave,** permiso especial, permiso extraordinario (por cuestiones familiares serias).
compassionately | kəm'pæʃənɪtlɪ | *adv.* compasivamente.
compatibility | kəm'pætə'bɪlɪtɪ | *s.i.* **1 [– (with/of/between)]** compatibilidad (de caracteres, creencias, sistemas, etc.). **2 [– (with/of/between)]** INF. compatibilidad.
compatible | kəm'pætəbl | *adj.* **1 [– (with)]** compatible (carácter, objeto, creencia). **2 [– (with)]** INF. compatible.
compatibly | kəm'pætəblɪ | *adv.* compatiblemente.
compatriot | kəm'pætrɪət | (EE.UU.) | kəm'peɪtrɪət | *s.c.* compatriota.
compel | kəm'pel | [*ger.* **compelling,** *pret.* y *p.p.* **compelled**] *v.t.* **1 [to – + *o. inf.*]** obligar, forzar. **2** exigir (respeto, ayuda y otras actitudes y acciones).
compelling | kəm'pelɪŋ | *adj.* **1** convincente; apremiante. **2** irresistible, interesantísimo (historia, novela, etc.).
compensate | 'kɒmpenseɪt | *v.t.* **1 [to – + *o.* + (for)]** compensar, remunerar, indemnizar. || *v.i.* **2 [to – for]** compensar: *blind people develop a very good sense of smell to compensate for their blindness = los ciegos desarrollan mucho el sentido del olfato para compensar su ceguera.*
compensation | ˌkɒmpen'seɪʃn | *s.i.* **1** indemnización, reparación. || *s.c.* e *i.* **2** compensación, recompensa (no económica): *I work hard, but I have compensations = trabajo duro pero tengo recompensas.*
compensatory | ˌkɒmpen'seɪtərɪ | (EE.UU.) | kəm'pensətɔːrɪ | *adj.* **1** de indemnización, de reparación. **2** compensatorio (educación, tratamiento social, etc.).
compere | 'kɒmpeər | (también **compère**) (brit.) *s.c.* **1** presentador (de un espectáculo). || *v.t.* e *i.* **2** presentar (espectáculo); hacer de presentador.
compete | kəm'piːt | *v.i.* **1** competir, rivalizar. **2** DEP. participar en competición. **3** tener opiniones irreconciliables, dar explicaciones irreconciliables. **4 [to – with]** tener tanta fuerza como, tener tanta intensidad como (un olor, sabor, ruido, etc.).
competence | 'kɒmpɪtəns | *s.i.* **1** capacidad (de una persona en algo). **2** DER. competencia.
competent | 'kɒmpɪtənt | *adj.* **1** competente, capaz. **2** adecuado, suficiente (pero no de calidad superior).
competently | 'kɒmpɪtəntlɪ | *adv.* **1** competentemente, capazmente. **2** adecuadamente, suficientemente.
competing | kəm'piːtɪŋ | *adj.* irreconciliable, opuesto (ideas, creencias, análisis, etc.).
competition | ˌkɒmpə'tɪʃn | *s.i.* **1** competencia, rivalidad. || **2** competición (deportiva o de otra clase). || *s.sing.* **3 [the –]** la competencia (especialmente comercial).
competitive | kəm'petɪtɪv | *adj.* **1** competitivo (ambiente, estilo de vida, etc.); selectivo (examen). **2** económico, competitivo (de precio). **3** ambicioso, luchador, agresivo (por ser mejor que otros).
competitively | kəm'petɪtɪvlɪ | *adv.* **1** económicamente, competitivamente (valorado). **2** ambiciosamente, agresivamente (modo de comportamiento que quiere destacar).
competitiveness | kəm'petɪtɪvnɪs | *s.i.* ambición, agresividad (por ser el mejor).
competitor | kəm'petɪtər | *s.c.* **1** DEP. participante, rival. **2** competidor (especialmente comercial).
compilation | ˌkɒmpɪ'leɪʃn | *s.c.* e *i.* recopilación.
compile | kəm'paɪl | *v.t.* **1** recopilar. **2** INF. trasvasar (instrucciones a programa concreto).
compiler | kəm'paɪlər | *s.c.* recopilador.
complacency | kəm'pleɪsnsɪ | (también **complacence**) *s.i.* (desp.) complacencia, autosatisfacción.
complacent | kəm'pleɪsnt | *adj.* **[– (about)]** (desp.) complacido, satisfecho con uno mismo.
complacently | kəm'pleɪsntlɪ | *adv.* (desp.) con complacencia, con un falso sentimiento de satisfacción.
complain | kəm'pleɪn | *v.t.* **1 [to – (to *o.*/about/of)]** quejarse, lamentarse. **2 [to – of]** quejarse de (un dolor, enfermedad, etc.). **3** DER. hacer una denuncia.
complainant | kəm'pleɪnənt | *s.c.* DER. demandante.
complaint | kəm'pleɪnt | *s.c.* e *i.* **1** queja, crítica, objeción. **2** DER. denun-

cia, demanda, reclamación. || *s.c.* **3** mal, enfermedad, dolencia.
complaisance | kəm'pleɪzəns | *s.i.* (form.) cortesía, deferencia; complacencia (especialmente del marido engañado por su mujer).
complaisant | kəm'pleɪzənt | *adj.* (form.) cortés, deferente; complaciente. V. **complaisance.**
complement | 'kɒmplɪmənt | *v.t.* **1** complementar, completar. || *s.c.* **2 [– (to)]** complemento. **3** GRAM. complemento. **4** MAR. tripulación. **5** necesidades, dotación, cuota (de puestos de trabajo ofertados o similar). || **6 full – (of),** total (de), cuota total (de).
complementary | ˌkɒmplɪ'mentrɪ | *adj.* **1 [– (to)]** complementario. || **2 – angle,** GEOM. ángulo complementario. **3 – colour,** FIS. color complementario.
complete | kəm'pli:t | *adj.* **1** completo, total, absoluto. **2** entero (no una parte únicamente). **3** perfecto: *he's the complete teacher = es el profesor perfecto.* **4** completo (con todos sus miembros o partes). **5** terminado, completado. || *v.t.* **6** completar, acabar, terminar. **7** rellenar por completo (un documento, solicitud, etc.). **8** completar (un número de personas o cosas): *we need one more to complete the team = necesitamos uno más para completar el equipo.* || **9 – with,** incluyendo también, con... y todo: *a house complete with a sauna = una casa con sauna y todo.*
completely | kəm'pli:tlɪ | *adv.* completamente, totalmente, absolutamente.
completeness | kəm'pli:tnɪs | *s.i.* integridad (de todas sus partes).
completion | kəm'pli:ʃn | *s.i.* terminación, finalización, consumación, cumplimiento.
complex | 'kɒmpleks | (EE.UU.) | kəm'pleks | *adj.* **1** complejo, intrincado. **2** complejo, difícil de entender, complicado. || *s.c.* **3** PSIQ. complejo. **3** ARQ. complejo (industrial, de casas, etc.). **5** (fig.) enmarañamiento, conjunto complejo (de cosas, elementos, teorías, etc.).
complexion | kəm'plekʃn | *s.c.* **1** cutis, tez. || *s.i.* **2** (form.) naturaleza, carácter (de cualquier cosa).
complexity | kəm'pleksɪtɪ | *s.i.* **1** complejidad. || *s.pl.* **2 [the – of]** las complejidades de.
compliance | kəm'plaɪəns | *s.i.* **[– (with)]** (form.) sumisión, acatamiento interior; obediencia.
compliant | kəm'plaɪənt | *adj.* **[– (to/with)]** (form.) sumiso; obediente.
complicate | 'kɒmplɪkeɪt | *v.t.* complicar.
complicated | 'kɒmplɪkeɪtɪd | *adj.* complicado, intrincado; enmarañado.
complication | ˌkɒmplɪ'keɪʃn | *s.c.* **1** complicación; dificultad. **2** (normalmente *pl.*) MED. complicación.
complicity | kəm'plɪsɪtɪ | *s.i.* (form.) complicidad.
compliment | 'kɒmplɪmənt | *s.c.* **1** cumplido, lisonja. || *v.t.* **2 [to – + *o.* + (on/for)]** cumplimentar, felicitar; lisonjear. || **3 a left-handed –,** un cumplido envenenado. **4 to return the –,** devolver el cumplido (que puede ser malo). **5 to send/pay one's compliments,** enviar los saludos de uno. **6 with one's compliments,** con los saludos de uno, con los mejores deseos de uno.
complimentary | ˌkɒmplɪ'mentrɪ | *adj.* **1** halagador (comentario o similar). **2** de regalo (un billete, libro, etc., como propaganda).
comply | kəm'plaɪ | *v.i.* **[to – with]** obedecer, acatar.
component | kəm'pəunənt | *s.c.* **1** componente, elemento, ingrediente. || *adj.* **2** constituyente, componente.
comport | kəm'pɔ:t | *v.r.* (form.) comportarse, conducirse (persona).
compose | kəm'pəuz | *v.t.* **1** componer, constituir (diversas partes un todo). **2** MUS. componer. **3** LIT. escribir, componer. **4** ART. arreglar, hacer una composición de, componer (elementos decorativos, arquitectónicos, etc.). || *v.r.* **5** calmarse, sosegarse, tranquilizarse. || **6 to be composed of,** estar compuesto de, estar constituido por, estar formado por.
composed | kəm'pəuzd | *adj.* sosegado, calmado, tranquilizado.
composedly | kəm'pəuzɪdlɪ | *adv.* sosegadamente, con calma, con tranquilidad.
composer | kəm'pəuzər | *s.c.* MUS. compositor.
composite | 'kɒmpəzɪt | *adj.* **1** compuesto (con diversas partes en él): *a composite substance = sustancia compuesta.* || *s.c.* **2 [– (of)]** mezcla, síntesis, conjunto.
composition | ˌkɒmpə'zɪʃn | *s.i.* **1** composición (de cualquier cosa). **2** MUS. composición, creación. **3** ART. ordenamiento, arreglo global, conjunto. || **4** MUS. composición, pieza (concreta). **5** ensayo, redacción (de escuela). **6** ART. composición, arreglo global (de una fotografía, escultura, etc.), creación, montage.
compositor | kəm'pɒzɪtər | *s.c.* cajista, impresor.
compost | 'kɒmpɒst | AGR. *s.i.* **1** abono vegetal, abono de estiércol. || *v.t.* **2** abonar con abono vegetal, abonar con abono de estiércol.
composure | kəm'pəuʒər | *s.i.* (form.) serenidad, calma.
compote | 'kɒmpəut | *s.i.* GAST. compota.
compound | 'kɒmpaund | *s.c.* **1** QUIM. compuesto. **2** GRAM. compuesto. **3** recinto (militar), recinto de seguridad (prisión), recinto (de otros tipos). **4** mezcla: *a compound of envy and jealousy = una mezcla de envidia y celos.* || *adj.* **5** compuesto. || | kəm'paund | *v.t.* **6** componer, combinar, mezclar. **7** agravar (problema, error, etc.). || **8 to be compounded (from/of),** estar formado (por/de), estar compuesto (por/de). **9 – fracture,** MED. fractura abierta. **10 – interest,** FIN. interés compuesto. **11 – sentence,** GRAM. oración compuesta.
comprehend | ˌkɒmprɪ'hend | *v.t.* e *i.* comprender, entender.
comprehensibility | kɒmprɪˌhensə'bɪlɪtɪ | *s.i.* comprensibilidad.
comprehensible | ˌkɒmprɪ'hensəbl | *adj.* comprensible.
comprehensibly | ˌkɒmprɪ'hensɪblɪ | *adv.* comprensiblemente.
comprehension | ˌkɒmprɪ'henʃn | *s.i.* **1** comprensión, entendimiento. || *s.c.* **2** FILOL. ejercicio de comprensión.
comprehensive | ˌkɒmprɪ'hensɪv | *adj.* **1** amplio, comprensivo, abarcador, que incluye todo. **2** (brit.) sin distinción de bachillerato y formación profesional (escuela). || *s.c.* **3** (fam. y brit.) escuela comprensiva.
compress | kɒm'pres | *v.t.* **1** comprimir, apretar. **2** comprimir (tiempo). **3** abreviar, condensar (escrito). || *v.i.* **4** comprimirse, apretarse. || *s.c.* **4** compresa (para bajar la fiebre).
compression | kəm'preʃn | *s.i.* **1** compresión. **2** compresión (de tiempo). **3** condensación, reducción (de un escrito).
compressor | kəm'presər | *s.c.* MEC. compresor.
comprise | kəm'praɪz | *v.t.* **1** comprender, incluir. **2** constituir (un colectivo): *Spanish students comprise 5% of the total = los estudiantes españoles constituyen el 5% del total.* || **3 to be comprised of,** constar de.
compromise | 'kɒmprəmaɪz | *s.c.* e *i.* **1** compromiso, acuerdo. || **2 [– between]** punto medio entre. || *v.i.* **3** llegar a un compromiso, llegar a un acuerdo. || *v.t.* **4** poner en duda, poner en tela de juicio (creencias, principios, etc.). || *v.r.* **5** comprometerse (haciendo algo negativo).
compromising | 'kɒmprəmaɪzɪŋ | *adj.* comprometedor.
compulsion | kəm'pʌlʃn | *s.i.* **1** coacción, obligación. || *s.c.* **2** compulsión, deseo irreprimible.
compulsive | kəm'pʌlsɪv | *adj.* **1** compulsivo, irreprimible (deseo o similar). **2** irresistible, interensantísimo (libro, película, etc.).
compulsively | kəm'pʌlsɪvlɪ | *adv.* **1** compulsivamente, irreprimiblemente (de deseos fuertes). **2** irresistiblemente, interesantísimamente (de películas, libros, etc.).
compulsorily | kəm'pʌlsərəlɪ | *adv.* obligatoriamente.
compulsory | kəm'pʌlsərɪ | *adj.* obligatorio.
compunction | kəm'pʌŋkʃn | *s.i.* (form.) compunción, remordimiento, contrición.
computation | ˌkɒmpju:'teɪʃn | *s.c.* e *i.* MAT. cálculo, cómputo.
compute | kəm'pju:t | *v.t.* calcular, computar.
computer | kəm'pju:tər | *s.c.* INF. ordenador, computadora.

computerise V. **computerize.**
computerization | kəm,pjuːtəraɪ'zeɪʃn | (EE.UU.) | kəm,pjuːtərɪ'zeɪʃn | (también **computerisation**) *s.i.* informatización.
computerize | kəm'pjuːtəraɪz | (también **computerise**) *v.t.* **1** informatizar. **2** meter en el ordenador (datos, información, etc.).
computerized | kəm'pjuːtəraɪzd | (también **computerised**) *adj.* informatizado (oficina, proceso, etc.).
computing | kəm'pjuːtɪŋ | *s.i.* informática (como creación y uso de programas).
comrade | 'kɒmrɪd | (EE.UU.) | 'kɒmræd | *s.c.* **1** camarada, compañero (de ideología). **2** (p.u.) amigo. || **3 – in arms,** compañero de armas.
comradely | 'kɒmreɪdlɪ | *adj.* amigable.
comradeship | 'kɒmrɪdʃɪp | *s.i.* camaradería, compañerismo.
con | kɒn | [*ger.* **conning,** *pret.* y *p.p.* **conned**] (fam.) *v.t.* **1 [to – +** *o.* **+ (into/out of)]** persuadir, engañar: *I conned her out of all her money = le saqué todo el dinero mediante engaños.* || *s.c.* **2** timo. **3** engaño. **4** convicto, presidiario. || **5 prons and cons,** V. **pro.**
concatenation | kən,kætɪ'neɪʃn | *s.i.* **[– of]** (form.) concatenación de, sucesión de, serie de.
concave | 'kɒŋkeɪv | *adj.* cóncavo.
conceal | kən'siːl | *v.t.* **1** ocultar, esconder. **2 [to – +** *o.* **+ (from)]** disimular, ocultar (información, sentimientos, etc.).
concealment | kən'siːlmənt | *s.i.* **1** ocultamiento. **2** disimulo, ocultamiento (de sentimientos, información, etc.).
concede | kən'siːd | (form.) *v.t.* **1** conceder, admitir (error o similar). **2** ceder, rendir (una posesión). **3** conceder, otorgar (derechos, privilegios, etc.). **4** DEP. conceder (un punto, un gol, etc.). || **5 to – defeat,** admitir la derrota.
conceit | kən'siːt | *s.i.* **1** engreimiento, vanidad, presunción, arrogancia. **2** LIT. metáfora ingeniosa.
conceited | kən'siːtɪd | *adj.* **[– (about)]** engreído, vanidoso, presumido, presuntuoso.
conceitedly | kən'siːtɪdlɪ | *adv.* engreídamente, vanidosamente, con presunción, presuntuosamente.
conceivable | kən'siːvəbl | *adj.* concebible, imaginable.
conceivably | kən'siːvəblɪ | *adv.* concebiblemente, imaginablemente.
conceive | kən'siːv | *v.t.* **1** concebir, idear, formarse una idea de. **2** ver, creer, pensar: *we should do what we conceive to be right = debemos hacer lo que pensamos que es correcto.* **3** concebir (un niño). || *v.i.* **4 [to – of]** concebir, imaginar. **5** quedar embarazada.
concentrate | 'kɒnsntreɪt | *v.i.* **1 [to – (on)]** concentrarse. **2** concentrarse, agruparse (físicamente). || *v.t.* **3** concentrar (atención, energías, etc.). **4** concentrar, agrupar (objetos, casas, edificios): *the government should concentrate all textile industries = el gobierno debería concentrar todas las industrias textiles.* || *s.i.* **5** concentrado (líquido). || **6 to – the mind,** agudizar la mente, agudizar el pensamiento.
concentrated | 'kɒnsntreɪtɪd | *adj.* **1** concentrado (líquido o sustancia). **2** reconcentrado, pensativo.
concentration | ,kɒnsn'treɪʃn | *s.i.* **1** concentración, intensidad (de pensamiento). **2 [– on]** concentración sobre, dedicación a (un tema). || *s.c.* e *i.* **3** concentración, acumulación (de dinero, gentes, etc.). || *s.c.* **4 [– of]** QUIM. concentración de (sustancias). || **5 – camp,** campo de concentración.
concentric | kən'sentrɪk | *adj.* concéntrico.
concept | 'kɒnsept | *s.c.* concepto.
conception | kən'sepʃn | *s.c.* **1** concepción, noción. || *s.i.* **2** concepción, formulación, ideación (de un plan o similar). **3** MED. concepción (de un niño por parte de una mujer).
conceptual | kən'septʃuəl | *adj.* PSIC. conceptual, nocional.
conceptualize | kən'septʃəlaɪz | (también conceptualise) *v.t.* FIL. conceptualizar.
concern | kən'sɜːn | *v.t.* **1** concernir, atañer, incumbir. **2** preocupar, afectar. **3** tratar de, versar sobre (libro, película, etc.). || *v.r.* **4 [to – about]** preocuparse por (una persona). **5 [to – (with)]** interesarse. || *s.c.* e *i.* **6** preocupación. || *s.c.* **7** empresa, grupo empresarial, firma comercial. || *s.i.* **8 [– (for)]** consideración, cuidado, atención: *he showed a lot of concern for me = me mostró mucha consideración.* || *s.sing.* **9** responsabilidad, asunto: *that field is my concern = ese campo de trabajo es responsabilidad mía.* || **10 a going –,** una empresa a pleno rendimiento, una empresa que funciona plenamente. **11 as far as I/you/etc. am concerned,** en lo que a mí respecta, en cuanto alcanza mi responsabilidad. **12 as far as ... is concerned/where ... is concerned,** en lo que afecta a..., en lo que respecta a. **13 none of one's –,** tema que no es asunto de uno, tema que a uno no le tiene porqué importar. **14 of –, a)** preocupante, inquietante. **b)** interés, importancia, cierta consideración. **15 to whom it may –,** a quien le pueda interesar.
concerned | kən'sɜːnd | *adj.* **1** preocupado. **2** interesado, con especial interés (por algo o alguien). || **3 the people /teachers/etc. –,** las personas/profesores /etc. a quienes atañe esto.
concernedly | kən'sɜːnɪdlɪ | *adv.* preocupadamente.
concerning | kən'sɜːnɪŋ | *prep.* tocante a, concerniente a, en cuanto a.
concert | 'kɒnsət | *s.c.* **1** MUS. concierto. || **2 at – pitch,** con una perfecta preparación, perfectamente dispuesto. **3 in –, a)** MUS. en concierto. **b)** (form.) en concierto, en conjunción (con otras personas).
concerted | kən'sɜːtɪd *adj.* **1** concertado (plan, esfuerzos, etc.). **2** serio, decidido.
concert-goer | 'kɒnsətgəuər | *s.c.* MUS. aficionado (a conciertos).
concertina | ,kɒnsə'tiːnə | *s.c.* **1** MUS. concertina. || *v.i.* **2** (fig.) ponerse como un acordeón (un objeto).
concertmaster | ,kɒnsət'mæstər | *s.c.* (EE.UU.) MUS. director de orquesta.
concerto | kən'tʃeətəu | | kənt'ʃɜːtəu | *s.c.* MUS. concierto (pieza musical).
concession | kən'seʃn | *s.c.* **1** concesión. **2** (normalmente *pl.*) concesión, privilegio de explotación (por ejemplo, pozos petrolíferos). || *s.i.* **3** (form.) concesión, entrega, cesión.
conch | kɒntʃ | *s.c.* **1** MAR. caracola. **2** concha (de cualquier especie marina).
concierge | ,kɒnsɪ'eəʒ | *s.c.* conserje, portero (especialmente en casas).
conciliate | kən'sɪlɪeɪt | *v.t.* e *i.* conciliar(se), calmar(se), apaciguar(se).
conciliation | kən,sɪlɪ'eɪʃn | *s.i.* reconciliación, conciliación, apaciguamiento.
conciliatory | kən'sɪlɪətərɪ, (EE.UU.) | kən'sɪlɪətɔːrɪ | *adj.* conciliatorio, apaciguador.
concise | kən'saɪs | *adj.* **1** sucinto, conciso. **2** LIT. básico, resumido (en libros como diccionarios y similares).
concisely | kən'saɪslɪ | *adv.* sucintamente, concisamente.
conciseness | kən'saɪsnɪs | *s.i.* concisión, brevedad.
conclave | 'kɒŋkleɪv | REL. *s.c.* **1** cónclave. || **2 in –,** en cónclave.
conclude | kən'kluːd | *v.i.* **1 [to – (from)]** concluir, sacar en conclusión. **2 [to – (with)]** (form.) concluir, dar por terminado (al hablar en público). **3** (form.) concluirse, terminarse, finalizarse, cerrarse. || *v.t.* **4** (form.) concluir, terminar, finalizar, cerrar. **5** firmar, acordar (tratado o parecido).
concluding | kən'kluːdɪŋ | *adj.* final (palabra, comentario, etc. en un discurso público).
conclusion | kən'kluːʒn | *s.c.* **1** conclusión, determinación final, razonamiento final. || *s.sing.* **2** final, finalización, cierre. **3 [– (of)]** acuerdo, firma (de un tratado o similar). || **4 a foregone –,** un resultado inevitable, un final cantado. **5 in –,** en conclusión, en suma. **6 to jump to a –/conclusions,** sacar conclusiones precipitadas.
conclusive | kən'kluːsɪv | *adj.* concluyente, decisivo, convincente.
conclusively | kən'kluːsɪvlɪ | *adv.* concluyentemente, decisivamente, convincentemente.
concoct | kən'kɒkt | *v.t.* **1** confeccionar, hacer (con distintos elementos y normalmente comida). **2** tramar, urdir (historias falsas, mentiras, etc.).
concoction | kən'kɒkʃn | *s.c.* e *i.* mezcolanza, extraña mezcla.

concomitant | kən'kɒmɪtənt | (form.) *adj.* **1 [– (with)]** acompañante, concomitante. || *s.c.* **2** fenómeno que acompaña, circunstancia concomitante.

concord | 'kɒŋkɔːd | *s.i.* **1** (form.) concordia, armonía. **2** GRAM. concordancia.

concordance | kən'kɔːdəns | *s.i.* **1** (form.) concordancia, similitud, conformidad. || *s.c.* **2** índice alfabético de temas. || **3 in – with,** en concordancia con, compatible con.

concourse | 'kɒŋkɔːs | *s.c.* **1** ARQ. vestíbulo abierto (en un gran edificio). **2 [=N** *v.sing./pl.*] (form.) concurrencia (de personas).

concrete | 'kɒŋkriːt | *adj.* **1** concreto, particular. **2** concreto, tangible, sólido. || *s.i.* **3** cemento, hormigón (Am.) concreto. || *v.t.* **4** cementar, echar cemento a. || **5 – mixer,** hormigonera. **6 prestressed –,** hormigón prensado. **7 reinforced –,** hormigón armado, hormigón reforzado.

concretely | 'kɒŋkriːtlɪ | *adv.* concretamente, específicamente, particularmente.

concubine | 'kɒŋkjubaɪn | *s.c.* concubina.

concupiscence | kən'kjuːpɪsns | *s.i.* (form.) concupiscencia.

concur | kən'kəːr | [*ger.* **concurring,** *pret.* y *p.p.* **concurred**] *v.i.* **[to – (with)]** (form.) concurrir, convenir, concordar, estar de acuerdo.

concurrence | kən'kʌrəns | *s.i.* **1** coincidencia temporal. || *s.sing.* **2** (form.) consentimiento, acuerdo.

concurrent | kən'kʌrənt | *adj.* coincidente, concurrente.

concurrently | kən'kʌrəntlɪ | *adv.* al mismo tiempo, concurrentemente.

concuss | kən'kʌs | *v.t.* golpear con fuerza (normalmente en una parte del cuerpo).

concussion | kən'kʌʃn | *s.i.* MED. concusión.

condemn | kən'dem | *v.t.* **1** condenar, denunciar, censurar, desaprobar. **2** DER. condenar, sentenciar (a una pena). **3** declarar cerrado (edificio); declarar (malo, por ejemplo un producto alimenticio). **4** (fig.) condenar de por vida, condenar (a un trabajo no querido, a alguna situación desagradable). **5** condenar (las propias palabras o hechos de uno).

condemnation | ˌkɒndem'neɪʃn | *s.c.* e *i.* **1** censura, condena, denuncia. || *s.sing.* **2 [– (of)]** condena (de algo concreto muy negativo).

condemnatory | ˌkɒndem'neɪtərɪ | | kən'demnətərɪ | *adj.* condenatorio.

condemned | kən'demd | *adj.* **1** DER. condenado. || **2 – cell,** celda de los condenados a muerte.

condensation | ˌkɒnden'seɪʃn | *s.c.* e *i.* **1** condensación (del agua). || *s.i.* **2** condensación (de un escrito o similar).

condense | kən'dens | *v.t.* e *i.* **1** condensar(se) (agua). || *v.t.* **2 [to – + *o.* + (into/to)]** condensar (un escrito o similar). || **3 condensed milk,** leche condensada.

condescend | ˌkɒndɪ'send | *v.i.* **1 [to – (to)]** ser condescendiente, comportarse condescendientemente. **2 [to – *inf.*]** tener la condescendencia de, dignarse a.

condescending | ˌkɒndɪ'sendɪŋ | *adj.* condescendiente. **2** superior, lleno de superioridad.

condescendingly | ˌkɒndɪ'sendɪŋlɪ | *adv.* condescendientemente.

condescension | ˌkɒndɪ'senʃn | *s.i.* condescendencia.

condiment | 'kɒndɪmənt | *s.c.* condimento.

condition | kən'dɪʃn | *s.sing.* **1** condición, situación. **2** (form.) condición: *human condition = condición humana.* || *s.i.* **3** condición, estado (cualidad física). **4** estado de salud, condición física. || *s.c.* **5 [– (for)]** requerimiento, condición sine qua non. **6 [– (of)]** estipulación, condición (de un empleo o similar). **7** enfermedad, mal. || *s.pl.* **8** circunstancias, situación. **9** condiciones (de vida): *living conditions = condiciones de vida.* || *v.t.* **10** acondicionar (pelo). **11** condicionar, marcar (el carácter durante largo tiempo): *she was conditioned by her father's character = quedó marcada por el carácter de su padre.* || **12 to be conditioned by,** (form.) estar sujeto a (reglas, estipulaciones, leyes, cláusulas, etc.). **13 to be in no –, [=N *inf.*]** estar en un estado capaz de, no estar en condiciones de. **14 on – that,** con la condición de que, con tal de que, siempre que. **15 out of –,** desentrenado, no en forma física.

conditional | kən'dɪʃənl | *adj.* **1 [– (on/upon)]** condicionado, dependiente (de otra circunstancia). **2** GRAM. condicional. || **3 to be – on/upon,** depender de, estar condicionado a: *the outcome is conditional on how much we are all ready to compromise = el resultado depende de hasta qué punto estemos todos dispuestos a ceder.*

conditionally | kən'dɪʃənəlɪ | *adv.* condicionalmente.

conditioner | kən'dɪʃənər | *s.c.* e *i.* **1** acondicionador (de cabello). **2** suavizante (de ropa).

conditioning | kən'dɪʃənɪŋ | *s.i.* PSIC. condicionamiento.

condole | kən'dəul | *v.i.* **[to – (with)]** (form.) condolerse, compadecerse.

condolence | kən'dəuləns | *s.i.* **1** pésame, condolencia. || **2 condolences,** pésame: *she didn't even offer me her condolences = ni siquiera me dio el pésame.* **3 my condolences,** le acompaño en el sentimiento.

condom | 'kɒndəm | *s.c.* condón, preservativo.

condominium | ˌkɒndə'mɪnɪəm | *s.c.* (EE.UU.) bloque de apartamentos.

condone | kən'dəun | *v.t.* perdonar, condonar.

condor | 'kɒndɔːr | *s.c.* ZOOL. cóndor.

conducive | kən'djuːsɪv | (EE.UU.) | kən'duːsɪv | *adj.* **[– to]** conducente a, favorable a.

conduct | 'kɒndʌkt | *s.i.* **1** conducta, comportamiento (en cuanto a la moralidad). || *s.sing.* **2 [the – of]** la forma de llevar, la manera de gestionar, la manera de proceder (en alguna actividad). || | kən'dʌkt | *v.t.* **3** conducir, llevar (actividad, tarea, etc.). **4** guiar, conducir, llevar (a un sitio). || *v.t.* e *i.* **5** MUS. dirigi[r] (orquesta). **6** ELEC. conducir (electrici[-] dad). || *v.r.* **7** (form.) conducirse, comportarse. || **8 conducted tour,** viaje con guía, visita con guía.

conduction | kən'dʌkʃn | *s.i.* ELEC. conducción.

conductor | kən'dʌktər | *s.c.* **1** MUS. director (de orquesta). **2** (brit.) cobrador (autobús); (EE.UU.) revisor (tren). **3** ELEC. conductor.

conductress | kən'dʌktrɪs | *s.c.* (brit.) cobradora (autobús).

conduit | 'kɒndɪt | (EE.UU.) | 'kɒndjuːɪt | 'kɒndwɪt | *s.c.* conducto, tubería de conducción (de agua, cables eléctricos, etc.).

cone | kəun | *s.c.* **1** GEOM. cono. **2** (fig.) cono, forma cónica (cualquier objeto con esa forma). **3** cucurucho (helado). **4** BOT. piña (de pino o árbol con fruto de forma similar). || **5 to – off,** cerrar al tráfico, cerrar a los coches (carretera, zona, etc.).

coney V. **cony.**

confection | kən'fekʃn | *s.c.* **1** confitura, producto de confitería, dulce, confite. **2** hechura, confección, creación (de ropa, especialmente llamativa).

confectioner | kən'fekʃənər | *s.c.* confitero, pastelero.

confectionery | kən'fekʃənərɪ | (EE.UU.) | kən'fekʃənerɪ | *s.i.* **1** dulces, productos de confitería. **2** repostería, confitería (especialidad).

confederacy | kən'fedərəsɪ | *s.c.* **1** POL. confederación, alianza, liga de naciones. **2 the Southern Confederacy,** HIST. la Confederación sureña (en 1860, en los Estados Unidos).

confederate | kən'fedərət | *adj.* **1** POL. confederado, aliado (naciones). || *s.c.* **2** cómplice, compinche (en actividad ilegal o secreta). || **3 Confederate,** HIST. confederado (soldado). **4 Confederate States,** HIST. Estados confederados (que quisieron separarse del resto de los Estados Unidos en 1860).

confederation | kənˌfedə'reɪʃn | *s.c.* e *i.* confederación, alianza (de estados, grupos industriales, asociaciones).

confer | kən'fəːr | [*ger.* **conferring,** *pret.* y *p.p.* **conferred**] *v.i.* **1 [to – (with)]** consultar (comentar un tema). || *v.t.* **2 [to – + *o.* + (on/upon)]** (form.) otorgar, conferir, conceder.

conference | 'kɒnfərəns | *s.c.* **1** discusión, reunión, junta, deliberación. **2** congreso (sobre algún tema). || **3 in –,** en una reunión, en una junta.

confess | kən'fes | *v.t.* **1** confesar, admitir (crimen). **2** admitir, reconocer: *I confess I haven't lived up to my parents'* *expectations = reconozco no he llegado a la altura que esperaban mis padres de mí.* **3** REL. confesar (pecados). || *v.i.* **4 [to – to]** admitir, reconocer. **5 [to – (to)]** hacer una confesión, confesar, admitir (crimen). **6** REL. hacer una confesión, confesarse. || **7 I –/I must –,** reconocer/deber decir (con cierto matiz de disculpa): *I must confess I am flabbergasted = debo decir que estoy alucinado.*

confessed | kən'fest | *adj.* declarado, patente: *a confessed alcoholic = un alcohólico declarado.*

confessedly | kən'fesɪdlɪ | *adv.* declaradamente (por uno mismo).

confession | kən'feʃn | *s.c.* e *i.* **1** confesión, admisión, reconocimiento (de algo mal hecho). **2** REL. confesión, penitencia. || *s.c.* **3** REL. profesión (de fe). **4** declaración, confesión (formal u oficial): *sign your confession = firma tu confesión.* || *s.pl.* **5** secretos, secretos inconfesables (en títulos de libros): *confessions of a window-cleaner = los secretos inconfesables de un limpiaventanas.*

confessional | kən'feʃənl | *s.c.* REL. confesional.

confessor | kən'fesər | *s.c.* REL. confesor (sacerdote).

confetti | kən'fetɪ | *s.i.* confeti.

confidant | ˌkɒnfɪ'dænt | *s.c.* (form.) amigo íntimo, confidente (persona con la cual uno habla de cosas íntimas, importantes, etc.).

confidante | ˌkɒnfɪ'dænt | *s.c.* (form.) amiga íntima, V. **confidant.**

confide | kən'faɪd | *v.t.* **[to – + *o.* + (to)]** confiar, revelar, confesar. **2 [to – + *o.* + to]** (form.) confiar a, dar a (como signo de confianza). || **3 to – in,** confiar en (contando un secreto o algo íntimo).

confidence | 'kɒnfɪdəns | *s.i.* **1** confianza, fe (en algo o alguien). **2** confidencia; secreto: *breach of confidence = revelación de un secreto.* **3** seguridad, confianza (en uno mismo). || *s.c.* **4** confidencia, comunicación reservada, información secreta. || **5 – man,** (form.) timador, estafador. **6 – trick,** (form.) fraude, timo, embaucamiento. **7 in –,** en plan de secreto, como información reservada. **8 to take into one's –,** confiar en, depositar la confianza de uno en, tener confianza en.

confident | 'kɒnfɪdənt | *adj.* **1** seguro: *I am confident I'll win = estoy seguro de que ganaré.* **2** confiado, seguro de uno mismo.

confidential | ˌkɒnfɪ'denʃl | *adj.* **1** confidencial, secreto. **2** de confianza (un empleado o amigo): *a confidential maid = una criada de confianza.* **3** reservado, confidencial (tono, forma de hablar, etc.).

confidentiality | ˌkɒnfɪˌdenʃɪ'ælɪtɪ | *s.i.* secreto, capacidad de mantener secreto (algo), discreción.

confidentially | ˌkɒnfɪ'denʃəlɪ | *adv.* **1** confidencialmente, secretamente. **2** reservadamente, confidencialmente (hablar). **3** en secreto, entre nosotros, en confianza.

confidently | 'kɒnfɪdəntlɪ | *adv.* **1** seguramente, con certeza. **2** con confianza en uno mismo, con seguridad en uno mismo.

confiding | kən'faɪdɪŋ | *adj.* confiado (persona que confía en otra).

confidingly | kən'faɪdɪŋlɪ | *adv.* confiadamente.

configuration | kənˌfɪgə'reɪʃn | (EE.UU.) | kənˌfɪgjʊ'reɪʃnl | *s.c.* (form.) configuración, figura, forma.

confine | kən'faɪn | *v.t.* **1** confinar, encerrar, recluir (en prisión, manicomio o similar). **2 [to – + *o.* + to]** limitar a, confinar a, restringir a: *I wish you confined your criticism to the people at the top = desearía que limitaras tus críticas a los mandamases.* || *v.r.* **3 [to – to]** limitarse a.

confined | kən'faɪnd | *adj.* cerrado, limitado, restringido, confinado (espacialmente).

confinement | kən'faɪnmənt | *s.i.* **1** reclusión, confinamiento. || *s.c.* e *i.* MED. parto, sobreparto (antes y durante el parto).

confines | 'kɒnfaɪnz | *s.pl.* **[– of]** (form.) límites de, confines de (física y figurativamente): *whithin the confines of family life = dentro de los límites de la vida de familia.*

confirm | kən'fəːm | *v.t.* **1** confirmar, ratificar, corroborar. **2** confirmar, acordar definitivamente (una fecha, reunión, etc.). **3** REL. confirmar. **4** fortalecer, confirmar (posición de poder, situación social, etc.). **5 [to – + *o.* + in]** confirmar en, asegurar en (opinión, creencia, etc.).

confirmation | ˌkɒnfə'meɪʃn | *s.c.* e *i.* **1** confirmación, ratificación, corroboración. **2** confirmación, acuerdo final (de una fecha, reunión, compromiso, etc.). **3** REL. confirmación.

confirmed | kən'fəːmd | *adj.* declarado, inveterado (fumador, bebedor u otros hábitos).

confiscate | 'kɒnfɪskeɪt | *v.t.* confiscar.

confiscation | ˌkɒnfɪ'skeɪʃn | *s.c.* e *i.* confiscación.

conflagration | ˌkɒnflə'greɪʃn | *s.c.* (form.) gran incendio.

conflate | kən'fleɪt | *v.t.* (form.) fundir, combinar (dos ideas, escritos, etc., en uno).

conflation | kən'fleɪʃn | *s.c.* e *i.* **[– of]** (form.) fusión de, combinación de.

conflict | 'kɒnflɪkt | *s.c.* e *i.* **1** conflicto, lucha, pelea, contienda, combate (físico). **2** (fig.) conflicto, desacuerdo (político, social, etc.). **3** choque, conflicto (de intereses, por ejemplo). || *s.i.* **4** agitación anímica, conflicto mental (estado del pensamiento). || | kən'flɪkt | *v.i.* **5 [to – (with)]** chocar, entrar en conflicto. || **6 to bring into – (with),** hacer chocar (con), hacer entrar en conflicto (con). **7 to come into – (with),** entrar en conflicto (con), chocar (con). **8 in –,** opuesto, contrario. **9 in – (with),** en pugna (con), en desacuerdo (con).

conflicting | kən'flɪktɪŋ | *adj.* contrario, opuesto (interés, idea, etc.).

confluence | 'kɒnflʊəns | *s.c.* **1 [– (of)]** confluencia (especialmente de dos ríos). | *s.sing.* **2 [– (of)]** (form.) confluencia, unión (de fenómenos, aspectos y de elementos físicos).

conform | kən'fɔːm | *v.i.* **1** acomodarse, conformarse (con una solución, situación real, etc.): *at the beginning he didn't want to, but in the end he conformed = al principio no quería, pero al final se conformó.* **2 [to – to/with]** obedecer, acatar (ley o similar). **3 [to – to/with]** acomodarse a, ajustarse a (una idea, opinión, estilo, etc.).

conformist | kən'fɔːmɪst | *s.c.* **1** conformista. || *adj.* **2** conformista.

conformity | kən'fɔːmɪtɪ | *s.i.* **1** conformidad; avenencia. || **2 in – with/to,** de acuerdo con, conforme a.

confound | kən'faʊnd | *v.t.* **1** dejar perplejo, confundir. || **2 – it!,** ¡maldita sea! **3 – you!,** ¡vete a la porra!

confounded | kən'faʊndɪd | *adj.* maldito, fastidioso, odioso.

confront | kən'frʌnt | *v.t.* **1** afrontar, plantar cara (a problemas). **2** enfrentarse a (algo desagradable). **3** encararse con, hacer frente a (persona). **4 [to – + *o.* + with]** exponer los hechos irrefutables, confrontar con: *I confronted her with the blood stains = la expuse el hecho irrefutable de las manchas de sangre.*

confrontation | ˌkɒnfrən'teɪʃn | *s.c.* e *i.* confrontación, enfrentamiento (físico o verbal).

confuse | kən'fjuːz | *v.t.* **1** confundir, mezclar. **2** desconcertar, desorientar (a una persona). **3** oscurecer, complicar (situación o problema).

confused | kən'fjuːzd | *adj.* **1** confuso, desordenado, entremezclado (algo). **2** confundido, desorientado, desconcertado (persona).

confusedly | kən'fjuːzɪdlɪ | *adv.* **1** confusamente, desordenadamente, entremezcladamente. **2** desorientadamente, desconcertadamente.

confusing | kən'fjuːzɪŋ | *adj.* desconcertante, desorientador.

confusingly | kən'fjuːzɪŋlɪ | *adv.* desconcertadamente.

confusion | kən'fjuːʒn | *s.i.* **1** confusión, desorden, caos. **2** confusión, malentendido. **3** confusión (entre una cosa o persona y otra). **4** confusión, desconcierto, desorientación (mental). **5** confusión, vergüenza (personal).

congeal | kən'dʒiːl | *v.t.* e i. cuajar(se), coagular(se) (líquidos).

congenial | kən'dʒiːnɪəl | *adj.* **1** agradable, sociable, simpático. **2** compatible, congenial, adecuado (a la salud, trabajo, etc. de uno): *a congenial climate = un clima adecuado (a uno).*

congenially | kən'dʒiːnɪəlɪ | *adv.* agradablemente, sociablemente, simpáticamente.
congenital | kən'dʒenɪtl | *adj.* **1** MED. congénito, de nacimiento. **2** (fig.) de siempre, congénito (gustos, aficiones, manías, etc.).
congenitally | kən'dʒenɪtəlɪ | *adv.* congénitamente, hereditariamente.
congested | kən'dʒestɪd | *adj.* **1** congestionado, transitado (carretera). **2** congestionado (con mucha mucosidad).
congestion | kən'dʒestʃən | *s.i.* **1** congestión (de tráfico). **2** MED. congestión, mucosidad excesiva.
conglomerate | kən'glɒmərət | *s.c.* (form.) **1** COM. conglomerado (de empresas). **2** mezcla, conglomerado, unión desordenada.
conglomeration | kənˌglɒmə'reɪʃn | *s.c.* mezcolanza (de personas, teorías, cosas, etc., especialmente sin orden ni concierto).
congrats | kən'græts | *interj.* (fam.) enhorabuena, felicidades.
congratulate | kən'grætʃuleɪt | *v.t.* **1 [to – + *o.* + (on/for)]** felicitar, dar la enhorabuena, cumplimentar. || *v.r.* **2 [to – (on/for)]** felicitarse, congratularse.
congratulation | kənˌgrætʃu'leɪʃn | *s.i.* **1** felicitación, enhorabuena. || **2 congratulations,** felicidades, enhorabuena.
congratulatory | kən'grætʃulətərɪ | (EE.UU.) | kən'grætʃulətɔːrɪ | *adj.* congratulatorio, de felicitación.
congregate | 'kɒŋgrɪgeɪt | *v.i.* congregarse, reunirse (personas en gran número).
congregation | ˌkɒŋgrɪ'geɪʃn | *s.c.* **[=N *v.sing./pl.*]** REL. congregación.
congress | 'kɒŋgres | (EE.UU.) | 'kɒŋgrəs | *s.c.* e *i.* **1** congreso, convención (político, sindical, profesional, etc.). || **2 Congress,** (EE.UU.) POL. Congreso (cámara baja americana).
congressional | kən'greʃənl | *adj.* (EE.UU.) POL. del congreso.
congressman | 'kɒŋgrəsmən | [*pl.* **congressmen**] *s.c.* (EE.UU.) POL. congresista, representante, diputado.
congressmen | 'kɒŋgrəsmən | *pl.* de **congressman.**
congresswoman | 'kɒŋgrəswumən | [*pl.* **congresswomen**] *s.c.* (EE.UU.) POL. congresista, diputada.
congresswomen | kɒŋgrəswɪmɪn | *pl.* de **congresswoman.**
congruence | 'kɒŋgruəns | *s.i.* (form.) concordancia, congruencia (entre dos cosas).
congruent | 'kɒŋgruənt | *adj.* **[– (with)]** (form.) congruente, concordante (dos cosas).
conical | 'kɒnɪkl | *adj.* cónico.
conifer | 'kɒnɪfər | | 'kəunɪfə | *s.c.* BOT. conífero.
coniferous | kə'nɪfərəs | (EE.UU.) | kəu'nɪfərəs | *adj.* BOT. conífero.
conjectural | kən'dʒektʃərəl | *adj.* hipotético, de pura conjetura.
conjecture | kən'dʒektʃər | *s.c.* e *i.* **1** conjetura, suposición, especulación. || *v.i.* **2** conjeturar, suponer, especular.
conjugal | 'kɒndʒugl | *adj.* (form.) conyugal, marital.
conjunction | kən'dʒʌŋkʃn | *s.c.* **1 [– (of)]** conjunción (de características, cosas, rasgos, etc.). **2** GRAM conjunción. || **3 in – (with),** en conjunción (con), conjuntamente (con).
conjunctivitis | kɒŋˌdʒʌŋktɪvaɪtɪs | *s.i.* MED. conjuntivitis.
conjure | 'kʌndʒər | *v.t.* **1 [to – (up)]** invocar, hacer venir por magia, hacer aparecer por magia. **2** (arc. y form.) conjurar: *I conjure you, go = te conjuro, vete.* || **3 a name to – with,** un nombre con el que contar, un nombre de gran prestigio. **4 to – up,** evocar (memoria, imagen, etc.).
conjurer | 'kʌndʒərər | (también **conjuror**) *s.c.* mago, prestidigitador.
conjuring | 'kʌndʒərɪŋ | *s.i.* **1** trucos de manos. || **2 – trick,** truco de magia, juego de manos.
conk | kɒŋk | (brit. y fam.) *s.c.* **1** napias, narizotas. || **2 to – out,** fastidiarse, estropearse.
conker | 'kɒŋkər | *s.c.* **1** BOT. castaño de Indias. || **2 conkers,** juego a romper la castaña del compañero.
connect | kə'nekt | *v.t.* **1 [to – + *o.* + (to)]** conectar, juntar, unir. **2** comunicar (por teléfono, por parte de una operadora). **3 [to – + *o.* + (to/with)]** asociar, relacionar: *I would never have connected you with John = nunca te hubiera relacionado con John.* || *v.i.* **4 [to – (with)]** conectar (un medio de transporte con otro). || **5 connecting road,** biela.
connected | kə'nektɪd | *adj.* **1 [– (with)]** conectado, asociado, relacionado (con cosas, asociaciones, hechos, etc.). **2 [– (with/to)]** emparentado.
connecting | kə'nektɪŋ | *adj.* que comunica (especialmente puerta entre dos habitaciones).
connection | kə'nekʃn | (también **connexion**) *s.c.* **1 [– (with/to/between)]** conexión, relación (de dos cosas). **2** conexión, junta (de tuberías, cables, etc.). **3** enlace, conexión (en un viaje). **4** (normalmente *pl.*) conexión personal, conexión profesional. **5** (normalmente *pl.*) pariente. || **6 in – with,** relacionado con, con respecto a. **7 in this/that –,** en este/ese sentido, con respecto a esto/eso (refiriéndose a algo que se ha mencionado antes).
connivance | kə'naɪvəns | *s.i.* (desp.) confabulación, connivencia.
connive | kə'naɪv | *v.i.* **1 [to – at]** consentir, tolerar (algo malo). **2 [to – (with)]** (desp.) confabularse, conspirar.
conniving | kə'naɪvɪŋ | *adj.* conspirador, urdidor (de engaños).
connoisseur | ˌkɒnə'sɜːr | *s.c.* gran conocedor, experto (especialmente de comida, bebida y otros placeres).
connotation | ˌkɒnə'teɪʃn | *s.c.* connotación.
connote | kə'nəut | *v.t.* (form.) connotar, sugerir (una palabra).
connubial | kə'njuːbɪəl | (EE.UU.) | kə'nuːbɪəl | *adj.* (form.) conyugal, matrimonial.
conquer | 'kɒŋkər | *v.t.* e *i.* **1** conquistar (otro país). **2** (fig.) conquistar (a una mujer o viceversa); ganar la admiración (de personas). **3** dominar, vencer, superar (plagas de la humanidad, obstáculos en el progreso, etc.).
conqueror | 'kɒŋkərər | *s.c.* HIST. conquistador.
conquest | 'kɒŋkwest | *s.i.* **1** conquista (de un país). || *s.c.* **2** conquista, terreno conquistado. **3 [– (of)]** (fig.) conquista, admiración (de personas del otro sexo, de grupos sociales, etc.). || *s.sing.* **4 [the – of]** la conquista (de algo serio y grande), el control de (una enfermedad).
conscience | 'kɒnʃəns | *s.c.* **1** FIL. conciencia (ética). **2** remordimiento, conciencia (cuando remuerde): *problems of conscience.* || **3 a bad/guilty –,** una mala conciencia, una conciencia que remuerde. **4 in all/good –,** en verdad, en conciencia, en justicia. **5 on one's –,** pesando sobre la conciencia de uno, como cargo de conciencia de uno. || **6 – money,** dinero que se paga después que se debería porque la conciencia remuerde.
conscience-stricken | 'kɒnʃənsstrɪkən | *adj.* lleno de remordimientos.
conscientious | ˌkɒnʃɪ'enʃəs | *adj.* **1** concienzudo, meticuloso, cuidadoso (persona o su manera de hacer algo). || **2 – objector,** MIL. objetor de conciencia.
conscientiously | ˌkɒnʃɪ'enʃəslɪ | *adv.* concienzudamente, meticulosamente, cuidadosamente.
conscientiousness | ˌkɒnʃɪ'enʃəsnɪs | *s.i.* meticulosidad, cuidado (en hacer algo muy bien).
conscious | 'kɒnʃəs | *adj.* **1 [– of]** consciente de, sabedor de (verdad, hecho, evidencia, etc.). **2** consciente, deliberado, intencional (poniendo en ello la voluntad). **3** consciente, en estado de consciencia (no dormido o parecido). **4** PSIC. consciente (pensamientos, recuerdos, imágenes mentales, etc. que tenemos conscientemente). **5** POL. consciente, alerta (en temas políticos, sociales o similares). || *s.sing.* **6 [the –]** PSIC. el consciente (que se opone al inconsciente). || **7 – conscious,** consciente de (en compuestos): *class-conscious = consciente de la división en clases (de la sociedad).*
consciously | 'kɒnʃəslɪ | *adv.* **1** conscientemente. **2** deliberadamente, intencionalmente.
consciousness | 'kɒnʃəsnɪs | *s.i.* **1** conciencia, conocimiento (dándose cuenta de la realidad). **2** conciencia, mentalidad (de un grupo de personas): *the American consciousness = la mentalidad americana.* **4** PSIC. mente, cabeza (entendida como receptora de impulsos). **5** conciencia (política, eco-

lógica, etc.). || **6 to lose –,** perder el conocimiento, desmayarse. **7 to regain –,** recobrar el conocimiento, volver en sí.
conscript | 'kɒnscrɪpt | *s.c.* **1** MIL. recluta, quinto. || | kən'skrɪpt | *v.t.* **2** MIL. alistar, reclutar. **3** (fig.) obligar por la fuerza a trabajar.
conscripted | kən'skrɪptɪd | *adj.* **1** MIL. alistado, reclutado. **2** obligado por la fuerza a trabajar.
conscription | kən'skrɪpʃn | *s.i.* MIL. reclutamiento, alistamiento.
consecrate | 'kɒnsɪkreɪt | *v.t.* **1** REL. consagrar (sitio). **2** REL. consagrar, ordenar (sacerdotes). **3 [to – +** *o.* **+ (to)]** (fig.) consagrar, dedicar (un día a la memoria de alguien o algo heroico).
consecrated | 'kɒnsɪkreɪtɪd | *adj.* consagrado (sitio, persona, etc.).
consecration | ˌkɒnsɪ'kreɪʃn | *s.i.* REL. consagración.
consecutive | kən'sekjutɪv | *adj.* consecutivo.
consecutively | kən'sekjutɪvlɪ | *adv.* consecutivamente.
consensus | kən'sensəs | *s.i.* consenso.
consent | kən'sent | *s.i.* **1** consentimiento, permiso. **2** consentimiento, acuerdo. || *v.i.* **3 [to – to/***inf.***]** consentir en, acceder a. || **4 with one –,** (arc.) unánimemente.
consenting | kən'sentɪŋ | *adj.* capaz de dar su consentimiento (especialmente en relaciones sexuales).
consequence | 'kɒnsɪkwəns, (EE.UU.) | 'kɒnsɪkwens | *s.c.* **1** consecuencia, resultado. || **2 in –,** en consecuencia, por consiguiente. **3 in – of,** de resultas de. **4 of –,** de importancia, de gran significado. **5 to take/suffer the consequences,** sufrir las consecuencias, aguantar las consecuencias.
consequent | 'kɒnsɪkwənt | *adj.* consecuente, consiguiente.
consequential | ˌkɒnsɪ'kwenʃl | *adj.* (form.) 1 significante, de consecuencia. **2** consecuente, consiguiente.
consequentially | ˌkɒnsɪ'kwenʃəlɪ | *adv.* (form.) **1** significantemente, de importancia. **2** consecuentemente, consiguientemente.
consequently | 'kɒnsɪkwəntlɪ | *adv.* consecuentemente, consiguientemente.
conservation | ˌkɒnsə'veɪʃn | *s.i.* **1** conservación (animal, de plantas, etc.). **2** conservación (de arte, edificios, etc.). **3** FIS. conservación (de energía y otros conceptos físicos). **4** ahorro (de energía o similar).
conservationist | ˌkɒnsə'veɪʃənɪst | *s.c.* conservacionista, ecologista.
conservatism | kən'sɜːvətɪzəm | *s.i.* **1** POL. conservadurismo, tradicionalismo. **2** (desp.) conservadurismo. || **3 Conservatism,** (brit.) POL. Partido Conservador.
conservative | kən'sɜːvətɪv | *adj.* **1** POL. conservador. **2** (desp.) conservador, reaccionario, tradicionalista. **3** conservador (cálculo). **4** conservador (en estilo, vestimenta, gustos, etc.). || **5 Conservative,** POL. conservador, miembro del partido conservador. **6 Conservative Party,** POL. Partido Conservador (especialmente el de Gran Bretaña).
conservatively | kən'sɜːvətɪvlɪ | *adv.* **1** POL. conservadoramente. **2** tradicionalmente, conservadoramente, reaccionariamente.
conservatory | kən'sɜːvətrɪ | (EE.UU.) | kən'sɜːvətɔːrɪ | *s.c.* **1** invernadero (para plantas). **2** MUS. conservatorio.
conserve | kən'sɜːv | *v.t.* **1** conservar, preservar. **2** conservar, ahorrar. || | 'kɒnsɜːv | *s.i.* **3** compota, conserva (como mermelada).
consider | kən'sɪdər | *v.t.* **1** considerar, juzgar, estimar. **2** pensar en, reflexionar sobre. **3 [to –** *ger./s.***]** pensar en, aceptar la consideración de, tener en cuenta de. **4** debatir, considerar, discutir (algo en una reunión de personas). **5** examinar, estudiar (visualmente). || *v.r.* **6** considerarse, verse a sí mismos (de una manera u otra). || **7 all things considered,** teniendo todas las circunstancias en cuenta, considerando todos los puntos.
considerable | kən'sɪdərəbl | *adj.* considerable, sustancial, notable (en tamaño, grado o similar).
considerably | kən'sɪdərəblɪ | *adv.* considerablemente, sustancialmente, notablemente.
considerate | kən'sɪdərɪt | *adj.* considerado, atento, educado (en formas cívicas o sociales).
considerately | kən'sɪdərɪtlɪ | *adv.* consideradamente, atentamente, educadamente.
consideration | kənˌsɪdə'reɪʃn | *s.i.* **1** consideración, estudio detenido. **2** consideración, atención (hacia alguien). || *s.c.* **3** factor, consideración. || **4 of no /little –,** de ninguna/poca importancia, de ninguna/poca significación. **5 to take into –,** tomar en consideración, tener en cuenta. **6 under –,** en estudio, en discusión todavía.
considered | kən'sɪdəd | *adj.* **1** pensado, meditado, estudiado. **2** apreciado: *a highly considered writer = un escritor muy apreciado.*
considering | kən'sɪdrɪŋ | *conj.* **1** considerando que, teniendo en cuenta que. || *adv.* **2** (fam.) teniendo en cuenta todo (como contraste): *she's all right considering = ella está bien teniendo en cuenta todo.*
consign | kən'saɪn | *v.t.* (form.) **1 [to – +** *o.* **+ to]** relegar a (algo no deseado a un sitio). **2 [to – +** *o.* **+ to]** encomendar a, destinar a, poner. **3** enviar, dirigir, consignar (mercancías).
consignment | kən'saɪnmənt | *s.c.* **[– (of)]** (form.) envío (de mercancías).
consist | kən'sɪst | *v.i.* **1 [to – of]** constar de, estar compuesto de, estar constituido por. **2 [to – in]** consistir en: *the games consist in retaining the ball as long as you can = el juego consiste en retener la pelota tanto tiempo como puedas.*
consistency | kən'sɪstənsɪ | *s.i.* **1** consistencia (de una sustancia). **2** coherencia, consistencia (en opiniones o similar). || *s.c.* **3** consistencia (de sustancias).
consistent | kən'sɪstənt | *adj.* **1** consistente, constante (que no cambia). **2 [– (with)]** consistente, consecuente, coherente.
consistently | kən'sɪstəntlɪ | *adv.* consistentemente, constantemente (sin variación).
consolation | ˌkɒnsə'leɪʃn | *s.c.* e *i.* **1** consolación, consuelo. || **2 – prize,** premio de consolación.
console | kən'səul | *v.t.* **1** consolar. || | 'kɒnsəul | *s.c.* **2** MEC. panel de instrumentos, tablero de mandos. **3** consola, caja (donde se guarda un televisor, ordenador, etc.).
consolidate | kən'sɒlɪdeɪt | *v.t.* e *i.* **1** consolidar, reforzar (poder, posición, categoría, etc.). **2** COM. fusionar(se), amalgamar(se) (empresas).
consolidation | kənˌsɒlɪ'deɪʃn | *s.i.* **1** consolidación, reforzamiento. **2** COM. fusión, amalgamamiento (de empresas).
consommé | kən'sɒmeɪ | (EE.UU.) | ˌkɒnsə'meɪ | *s.i.* GAST. consomé.
consonant | 'kɒnsənənt | *s.c.* **1** FON. consonante. || *adj.* **2 [– with]** (form.) en consonancia con, conforme con.
consort | 'kɒnsɔːt | *s.c.* **1** príncipe consorte, princesa consorte. || | kən'sɔːt | *v.i.* **2 [to – with/together]** (desp.) concharbarse con, asociarse con (para algo malo).
consortia | kən'sɔːtɪə | (EE.UU.) | kən'sɔːrʃɪə | *pl.* de **consortium.**
consortium | kən'sɔːtɪəm | (EE.UU.) | kən'sɔːrʃɪəm | [*pl.* **consortiums** o **consortia**] *s.c.* COM. consorcio.
conspicuous | kən'spɪkjuəs | *adj.* **1** conspicuo, llamativo, sobresaliente (por alguna razón). || **2 to be – by one's absence,** brillar por su ausencia.
conspicuously | kən'spɪkjuəslɪ | *adv.* llamativamente, visiblemente, notoriamente.
conspicuousness | kən'spɪkjuəsnɪs | *s.i.* notoriedad, (lo) sobresaliente, (lo) llamativo.
conspiracy | kən'spɪrəsɪ | *s.c.* e *i.* **1** conspiración, conjura, conjuración (normalmente política). || *s.c.* **2** complot, conspiración. || **3 a – of silence,** una conspiración de silencio.
conspirator | kən'spɪrətər | *s.c.* conspirador.
conspiratorial | kənˌspɪrə'tɔːrɪəl | *adj.* de conspirador, secreto.
conspiratorially | kənˌspɪrə'tɔːrɪəllɪ | *adv.* como conspiradores, secretamente.
conspire | kən'spaɪər | *v.i.* **1** conspirar, tramar un complot, conjurarse (normalmente con fines políticos). **2** (fig.) aunarse, combinarse (cosas que llevan a un resultado): *strange things conspired against us = cosas extrañas se aunaron en contra nuestra.*

constable | 'kʌnstəbl | (EE.UU.) | 'kɔnstəbl | *s.c.* (brit.) policía, número de la policía.
constabulary | kən'stæbjʊlərɪ | (EE.UU.) | kən'stæbjʊlerɪ | *s.c.* (brit.) policía local (distrito).
constancy | 'kɒnstənsɪ | *s.i.* **1** constancia, perseverancia. **2** lealtad, fidelidad, constancia (especialmente en el matrimonio).
constant | 'kɒnstənt | *adj.* **1** constante (en el tiempo). **2** leal, fiel (calificación de una persona). **3** constante, al mismo nivel, invariable. || *s.c.* **4** FIS. constante. **5** MAT. constante. **6** elemento constante, característica constante, cosa constante.
constantly | 'kɒnstəntlɪ | *adv.* constantemente.
constellation | ˌkɒnstə'leɪʃn | *s.c.* **1** ASTR. constelación. **2** **[– of]** (form. y fig.) conjunto de, lista de (razones, excusas, etc.).
consternation | ˌkɒnstə'neɪʃn | *s.i.* consternación.
constipated | 'kɒnstɪpeɪtɪd | *adj.* estreñido.
constipation | ˌkɒnstɪ'peɪʃn | *s.i.* MED. estreñimiento.
constituency | kən'stɪtjʊənsɪ | *s.c.* POL. **1** distrito electoral. **2** **[=N** *v.sing./pl.***]** votantes de un distrito electoral.
constituent | kən'stɪtjʊənt | *s.c.* **1** POL. votante (de un distrito electoral). **2** ingrediente, componente (de una mezcla o sustancia). || *adj.* **3** componente, constituyente. || **4 – assembly,** POL. asamblea constituyente.
constitute | 'kɒnstɪtjuːt | *v.t.* **1** constituir, representar, formar. **2** constituir, componer (una cantidad): *Africans constitute the whole population = los africanos constituyen toda la población.* **3** (form.) formar, establecer, integrar: *the committee was constituted by males = el comité estaba integrado por hombres.*
constitution | ˌkɒnstɪ'tjuːʃn | (EE.UU.) | kɒnstɪ'tuːʃn | *s.c.* **1** DER. constitución. **2** constitución (salud). || *s.sing.* **3** **[the – of]** la constitución de, la formación de, el establecimiento de (algo hecho de diversas partes): *the constitution of the board = la constitución del consejo.*
constitutional | ˌkɒnstɪ'tjuːʃənl | (EE.UU.) | ˌkɒnstɪ'tuːʃənl | *adj.* **1** DER. constitucional. **2** de la constitución física. || *s.c.* **3** (hum. o p.u.) paseo.
constitutionalism | ˌkɒnstɪ'tjuːʃənəlɪzəm | (EE.UU.) | ˌkɒnstɪ'tuːʃənəlɪzəm | *s.i.* POL. constitucionalismo.
constitutionally | ˌkɒnstɪ'tjuːʃənəlɪ | (EE.UU.) | ˌkɒnstɪ'tuːʃənəlɪ | *adv.* **1** DER. constitucionalmente. **2** por constitución física.
constrain | kən'streɪn | *v.t.* **1** constreñir, compeler, obligar. **2** restringir, inhibir.
constrained | kən'streɪnd | *adj.* **1** obligado, constreñido (a algo). **2** forzado, artificial (sonrisa, voz, etc.).
constraint | kən'streɪnt | *s.i.* **1** coacción, compulsión. **2** (form.) forma forzada (de reír, mirar, hablar, etc.). || *s.c.* **3** **[– (on/of)]** obligación, limitación (a lo que se puede hacer).
constrict | kən'strɪkt | *v.t.* **1** comprimir, hacer encoger, apretar (físicamente). **2** limitar, constreñir (lo que se puede hacer).
constricted | kən'strɪktɪd | *adj.* limitado, constreñido.
constricting | kən'strɪktɪŋ | *adj.* **1** apretado, comprimido (físicamente). **2** limitador (de la acción o libertad de alguien).
constriction | kən'strɪkʃn | *s.i.* **1** constricción, contracción (física). **2** limitación (de la acción de alguien). || *s.c.* **3** limitación, restricción. || *s.sing.* **4** MED. sensación de algo apretando (en pecho o garganta).
construct | kən'strʌkt | *v.t.* **1** construir, hacer. **2** componer, hacer, construir, formular (idea, sistema, escrito, etc.). || | 'kɒnstrʌkt | *s.c.* **3** (form.) creación, fabricación (cosa construida). **4** idea, concepto, construcción mental.
construction | kən'strʌkʃn | *s.i.* **1** construcción, obras públicas. **2** formación, construcción, creación (de maquinaria o parecido uniendo partes diferentes). **3** **[– (of)]** estructura, estructuración. || *s.c.* **4** construcción, creación (cualquier cosa). **5** (form.) interpretación (de algo dicho, escrito, etc.). **6** GRAM. estructura. || **7 of simple/solid/etc. –,** de construcción sencilla/sólida/etc.
constructive | kən'strʌktɪv | *adj.* constructivo, positivo (sugerencia o similar).
constructively | kən'strʌktɪvlɪ | *adv.* constructivamente, positivamente.
construe | kən'struː | *v.t.* (form.) interpretar, explicar (situación, acontecimiento, palabras, etc.).
consul | 'kɒnsl | *s.c.* cónsul.
consular | 'kɒnsjʊlər | (EE.UU.) | 'kɒnsələr | *adj.* consular.
consulate | 'kɒnsjʊlət | (EE.UU.) | 'kɒnsələt | *s.c.* consulado.
consult | kən'sʌlt | *v.t.* **1** consultar (alguien o algo). || *v.i.* **2** **[to – (with)]** hablar, discutir, consultar, entrar en consultas. || **3 consulting room,** sala de consulta (de un médico).
consultancy | kən'sʌltənsɪ | *s.c.* e *i.* COM. "consulting", asesoría de empresas. || *s.c.* **2** MED. puesto de médico especialista hospitalario.
consultant | kən'sʌltənt | *s.c.* **1** MED. especialista hospitalario. **2** COM. asesor de empresas, asesor.
consultation | ˌkɒnsl'teɪʃn | *s.c.* e *i.* **1** **[– (about/with)]** reunión, consulta. || *s.i.* **2** consulta (de libros).
consultative | kən'sʌltətɪv | *adj.* consultivo, asesor.
consume | kən'sjuːm | (EE.UU.) | kən'suːm | *v.t.* **1** consumir (comer o beber). **2** consumir (tipos de energías). **3** consumir, destrozar (por el fuego). **4** (fig.) consumir, estar consumido por (sentimientos o deseos).
consumer | kən'sjuːmər | (EE.UU.) | kən'suːmər | *s.c.* **1** consumidor. || **2 – goods,** artículos de consumo.
consumerism | kən'sjuːmərɪzəm | (EE.UU.) | kən'suːmərɪzəm | *s.i.* consumismo.
consuming | kən'sjuːmɪŋ | *adj.* dominante, obsesivo, avasallador.
consummate | kən'sʌmət | (form.) *adj.* **1** consumado (en alguna habilidad o aspecto). || | 'kɒnsəmeɪt | *v.t.* **2** consumar (matrimonio). **3** completar, acabar, perfeccionar.
consummation | ˌkɒnsə'meɪʃn | *s.i.* **1** consumación (de matrimonio). **2** acabamiento, consumación, perfeccionamiento.
consumption | kən'sʌmpʃn | *s.i.* **1** consumo (de comida, energía, etc.). **2** (p.u.) MED. tisis. || **3 for someone's –,** para consumo de alguien, específicamente para consumo de alguien.
consumptive | kən'sʌmptɪv | (p.u.) *adj.* **1** tísico. || *s.c.* **2** tísico.
contact | 'kɒntækt | *s.c.* e *i.* **1** **[– (with /between)]** contacto, contacto físico. **2** contacto (de miradas). || *s.i.* **3** contacto, comunicación, transmisión. || *s.c.* **4** contacto (persona). **5** ELEC. contacto, conexión. || | kən'tækt | | 'kɒntækt | *v.t.* **6** contactar con, ponerse en contacto con. || **7 – lens,** lente de contacto. **8 to lose – (with),** perder el contacto (con). **9 to make – (with),** establecer contacto (con), contactar (con).
contagion | kən'teɪdʒən | *s.i.* **1** MED. contagio, contaminación. **2** (fig.) contagio, contaminación (de ideas, teorías, etc. negativas). || *s.c.* **3** MED. enfermedad contagiosa.
contagious | kən'teɪdʒəs | *adj.* **1** MED. contagioso, infeccioso (enfermedad o enfermo). **2** (fig.) contagioso (ideas, teorías, actitudes, etc., pero no necesariamente negativas).
contagiously | kən'teɪdʒəslɪ | *adv.* **1** MED. contagiosamente. **2** (fig.) contagiosamente (acción que se transmite a otros).
contain | kən'teɪn | *v.t.* **1** contener (un volumen). **2** contener, tener (cantidad): *this contains a tiny percentage of gold = esto contiene un pequeño porcentaje de oro.* **3** contener, tener, incluir (ideas, imágenes, verdades, etc.): *this book contains a lot of information on Asia = este libro incluye muchísima información sobre Asia.* **4** contener, controlar, refrenar (algo negativo, un peligro o un sentimiento que se desborda). **5** MAT. ser exactamente divisible por. **6** (normalmente *pas.*) (form.) contener, limitar (físicamente). || *v.r.* **7** refrenarse, contenerse (para no mostrar sentimientos).
contained | kən'teɪnd | *adj.* sereno, que refrena sus sentimientos.
container | kən'teɪnər | *s.c.* **1** recipiente, envase, caja. **2** contenedor (que se transporta en camiones). || **3 – ship,** MAR. buque de contenedores, barco transportador de contenedores.

containment | kən'teɪnmənt | *s.i.* POL. contención, política de contención (de otro país). **2** contención, represamiento (de una sustancia).
contaminant | kən'tæmɪnənt | *s.c.* (form.) contaminante.
contaminate | kən'tæmɪneɪt | *v.t.* **1** contaminar, causar polución en. **2** contaminar radioactivamente. **3** (fig.) contaminar (las mentes).
contaminated | kən'tæmɪneɪtɪd | *adj.* **1** contaminado, poluto. **2** contaminado por radioactividad. **3** (fig.) contaminado (el pensamiento por teorías malignas).
contamination | kən,tæmɪ'neɪʃn | *s.i.* **1** contaminación, polución. **2** contaminación radioactiva. **3** (fig.) contaminación (de las mentes).
contemplate | 'kɒntempleɪt | *v.t.* e *i.* **1** pensar (sobre), reflexionar (sobre), meditar (sobre). **2** proyectar, tener la intención de, entrar en los planes de uno: *are you contemplating retirement?* = *¿entra en tus planes la jubilación?* || *v.t.* **3** contemplar, mirar detenidamente (con la vista).
contemplation | ,kɒntem'pleɪʃn | *s.i.* **1** contemplación (mirada). **2** intención, proyecto, consideración (de llevar algo a cabo). || *s.c.* e *i.* **3** reflexión, mediación (sobre algo).
contemplative | kən'templətɪv | | 'kɒntempleɪtɪv | *adj.* **1** pensativo (persona). **2** REL. contemplativo (de las órdenes contemplativas).
contemplatively | kən'templətɪvlɪ | [k=fntempleZtZvlZ | *adv.* pensativamente; de manera contemplativa.
contemporaneous | kən,tempə'reɪnɪəs | *adj.* (form.) contemporáneo.
contemporary | kən'temprərɪ | (EE.UU.) | kən'tempərərɪ | *adj.* **1** contemporáneo. **2** de la misma época, del mismo tiempo (dentro del pasado): *a contemporary novel of Shakespeare's* = *una novela de la misma época de Shakespeare.* || *s.c.* **3** contemporáneo, coetáneo.
contempt | kən'tempt | *s.i.* **1** **[– (for)]** desprecio, desdén. **2** DER. desacato. || **3 beneath –/beneath one's –,** absolutamente despreciable. **4 – of court,** DER. desacato al tribunal. **5 to hold in –,** despreciar, tener por despreciable.
contemptible | kən'temptəbl | *adj.* despreciable, vil.
contemptuous | kən'temptʃʊəs | *adj.* (form.) desdeñoso, despectivo.
contemptuously | kən'temptʃʊəslɪ | *adv.* (form.) desdeñosamente, despectivamente.
contend | kən'tend | *v.t.* **1** (form.) sostener, mantener, afirmar (una idea, creencia, etc.). || *v.i.* **2** **[to – with/ against]** luchar, rivalizar, pugnar (con una dificultad, problema, etc.). **3** **[to – with]** competir, contender, luchar (con alguien).
contender | kən'tendər | *s.c.* competidor, contendiente.
contending | kən'tendɪŋ | *adj.* rival, opuesto, contendiente.
content | 'kɒntent | *s.c.* **1** contenido (sustancia): *calcium content* = *contenido de calcio.* || *s.i.* **2** contenido (de un programa, escrito, película, etc.). || *s.pl.* **3** contenidos (de un recipiente, escrito, etc.). **4** índice de materias (en un libro).
content | kən'tent | *adj.* **1** **[– *inf.*/*with*]** contento de/con, feliz de/con. **2** alegre, satisfecho, contento. || *v.t.* **3** satisfacer, contentar. || *v.r.* **4** **[to – with]** contentarse con, sentirse satisfecho con (excluyendo otra cosa). || *s.i.* **5** (lit.) contento, satisfacción. || **6 to one's heart's –,** V. **heart.**
contented | kən'tentɪd | *adj.* satisfecho, contento, contentado (con lo que uno tiene).
contentedly | kən'tentɪdlɪ | *adv.* con satisfacción, con contento.
contention | kən'tenʃn | (form.) *s.c.* **1** argumento, punto de vista, forma de ver las cosas. || *s.i.* **2** contención, disputa. || **3 in –,** en pugna, en rivalidad, en competencia.
contentious | kən'tenʃəs | *adj.* (form.) **1** conflictivo, causante de controversia, polémico (tema, problema, etc.). **2** pendenciero (cualidad personal).
contentment | kən'tentmənt | *s.i.* satisfacción, alegría, contentamiento.
contest | 'kɒntest | *s.c.* **1** certamen, concurso, lid, competición. **2** lucha, pelea, contienda (por el poder o control de algo). || | kən'test | *v.t.* **3** disputar (una elección política, concurso, etc.). **4** impugnar, rechazar (normalmente mediante acción legal una declaración, resultado, etc.).
contestant | kən'testənt | *s.c.* **1** concursante, participante (en certamen, concurso o similar). **2** candidato (a un puesto de cualquier clase).
context | 'kɒntekst | *s.c.* **1** contexto, situación (de cualquier acontecimiento). **2** contexto (lingüístico). || **3 in/into –,** en contexto, en su contexto. **4 out of –,** fuera de contexto.
contextual | kən'tekstʃʊəl | *adj.* contextual, del contexto.
contiguous | kən'tɪgjʊəs | *adj.* **[– (to /with)]** (form.) contiguo, colindante.
continence | 'kɒntɪnəns | *s.i.* **1** (form.) continencia (especialmente sexual). **2** MED. continencia (de la orina).
continent | 'kɒntɪnənt | *s.c.* **1** GEOG. continente. || *adj.* **2** (form.) continente (especialmente en el tema sexual). **3** MED. continente, con control (de su vejiga urinaria). || **4 the Continent,** (brit.) Europa, el resto de Europa (la manera en que los británicos llaman a la parte continental de Europa).
continental | ,kɒntɪ'nentl | *adj.* **1** GEOG. continental. **2** (brit.) continental, del resto de Europa. || *s.c.* **3** (fam. y brit.) europeo, persona del continente europeo. || **4 – breakfast,** (brit.) desayuno muy ligero (normalmente un café y un bollo). **5 – drift,** GEOG. deriva de los continentes. **6 – quilt,** (brit.) edredón. **7 – shelf,** GEOG. plataforma continental.
contingency | kən'tɪndʒənsɪ | *s.c.* (form.) contingencia, eventualidad.
contingent | kən'tɪndʒənt | (form.) *s.c.* **1** MIL. contingente. **2** (fig.) contingente, grupo (representante ante un congreso, asociación, etc.). || *adj.* **3** FIL. contingente. || **4 to be – on,** depender de: *the outing was contingent on Mrs. Jones's health* = *la excursión dependía de la salud de Mrs Jones.*
continual | kən'tɪnjʊəl | *adj.* **1** continuo, constante (con pequeños descansos entre medias). **2** repetitivo.
continually | kən'tɪnjʊəlɪ | *adv.* **1** continuamente, constantemente. **2** repetitivamente.
continuance | kən'tɪnjʊəns | *s.i.* (form.) continuación, prolongación, permanencia.
continuation | kən,tɪnjʊ'eɪʃn | *s.i.* **1** prolongación, permanencia. **2** extensión, continuación (añadiendo algo a algo ya existente).
continue | kən'tinju: | *v.i.* **1** **[to – *ger.*/*inf.*]** continuar, seguir, proseguir. **2** **[to – *prep.*]** continuar, seguir (movimiento). **3** **[to – with]** continuar con, seguir con (algo). **4** continuar, seguir, extenderse más allá (una carretera o similar). || *v.t.* e *i.* **5** continuar, seguir (un proceso, suceso, etc.): *I want to continue my training in Canada* = *quiero continuar mi preparación en Canadá.* **6** durar, continuar (en el tiempo). || **6 continued on,** continúa en (tal página). **7 to be continued,** continuará (película, novela, etc.).
continuity | ,kɒntɪ'nju:ɪtɪ | (EE.UU.) | ,kɒntɪ'nu:ətɪ | *s.c.* e *i.* **1** continuidad, permanencia. || *s.i.* **2** continuidad, conexión, lógica, unión (entre dos elementos, especialmente artísticos). **3** TV. continuidad.
continuous | kən'tɪnjʊəs | *adj.* **1** continuo, incesante, ininterrumpido (sin descanso). **2** GEOM. continua (línea). **3** GRAM. continuo.
continuously | kən'tɪnjʊəslɪ | *adv.* continuamente, incesantemente, ininterrumpidamente (sin descanso).
continuum | kən'tɪnjʊəm | *s.sing.* (form.) continuo, solución de continuidad.
contort | kən'tɔ:t | *v.t.* e *i.* **1** retorcer(se) (cuerpo). **2** demudar(se) (rostro).
contorted | kən'tɔ:tɪd | *adj.* **1** retorcido (cuerpo). **2** demudado (cara).
contortion | kən'tɔ:ʃn | *s.c.* e *i.* **1** retorcimiento, contorsión (del cuerpo). **2** demudación, desfiguración (de la cara).
contortionist | kən'tɔ:ʃənɪst | *s.c.* contorsionista.
contour | 'kɒntʊər | *s.c.* **1** perfil, contorno (de algo). **2** (también **contour line**) GEOG. isohipsa, curva de nivel. || **3 – map,** GEOG. mapa acotado.
contraband | 'kɒntrəbænd | *s.i.* **1** contrabando. || *adj.* **2** de contrabando.

contraception | ˌkɒntrə'sepʃn | *s.i.* MED. contracepción.
contraceptive | ˌkɒntrə'septɪv | MED. *s.c.* 1 anticonceptivo, contraceptivo. || *adj.* 2 anticonceptivo. || 3 – **pill,** píldora anticonceptiva.
contract | 'kɒntrækt | *s.c.* 1 contrato, convenio (oficial o legal). || 2 **to put work out to –,** COM. subcontratar una obra, hacer una subcontrata en una obra. 3 **under – (to),** bajo contrato con, ligado por contrato a.
contract | kən'trækt | *v.t.* 1 contraer, tensar, poner en tensión (músculos). 2 (form.) contraer (enfermedad). 3 (form.) contraer (matrimonio). || *v.i.* 4 contraerse, tensarse (músculos). 5 contraerse, disminuir (sustancia, metal, etc.). 6 ECON. contraerse, debilitarse (la economía). 7 **[to –** *inf./with***]** (form.) estipular mediante contrato con, acordar mediante contrato con. || 8 **to – in (to),** DER. entrar en la licitación (de), entrar en el concurso público (por) (llevar a cabo una obra de algún tipo). 9 **to – out (of),** DER. salirse de un plan (de), no querer tomar parte en un plan (de) (pensiones, ayudas, becas, etc.). 10 **to – out (to),** subcontratar (a), ceder en régimen de subcontrata (a).
contraction | kən'trækʃn | *s.c.* 1 GRAM. contracción. 2 MED. contracción (del útero al dar a luz). || *s.i.* 3 ECON. contracción, debilitamiento. 4 contracción, empequeñecimiento (de un metal, por ejemplo, por el calor). || *s.c.* e *i.* 5 contracción, tensión (muscular).
contractor | kən'træktər | | 'kɒntræktə | *s.c.* contratista (de obras).
contractual | kən'træktʃʊəl | *adj.* (form.) contractual.
contractually | kən'træktʃʊəlɪ | *adv.* (form.) por contrato, mediante contrato.
contradict | ˌkɒntrə'dɪkt | *v.t.* 1 contradecir, refutar, disputar, oponerse. || *v.r.* 2 contradecirse, oponerse.
contradiction | ˌkɒntrə'dɪkʃn | *s.c.* e *i.* 1 contradicción, inconsistencia. || 2 **a – in terms,** contradicción, incompatibiliad de términos.
contradictory | ˌkɒntrə'dɪktərɪ | *adj.* contradictorio, inconsistente, incompatible.
contraindication | ˌkɒntrəɪndɪ'keɪʃn | *s.c.* MED. contraindicación.
contralto | kən'træltəʊ | MUS. *s.c.* 1 cantante de contralto, contralto. || *s.sing.* 2 contralto, voz de contralto. || *adj.* 3 de contralto, contralto.
contraption | kən'træpʃn | *s.c.* (fam.) artilugio.
contrapuntal | ˌkɒntrə'pʌntl | *adj.* MUS. de contrapunto.
contrary | 'kɒntrərɪ | (EE.UU.) | 'kɒntrerɪ | *adj.* 1 **[– (to)]** opuesto, contrario (actitud, pensamiento, ideas, etc.). || 2 **– to,** en contra de, en oposición a. 3 **on the –,** por el contrario, al contrario, al revés. 4 **to the –,** en contra, en su contra (contradiciendo algo anterior).
contrary | kən'treərɪ | *adj.* (desp.) terco, díscolo, recalcitrante, que lleva siempre la contraria.
contrarily | kən'treərɪlɪ | *adv.* (desp.) tercamente, díscolamente, recalcitrantemente.
contrariness | kən'treərɪnɪs | *s.i.* (desp.) terquedad.
contrast | kən'trɑːst | (EE.UU.) | kən'træst | *v.t.* 1 **[to – +** *o.* **+ (to/with)]** contrastar, contraponer, comparar. || *v.i.* 2 contrastar, no casar, estar en contraste. || **contrast** | 'kɒntrɑːst | (EE.UU.) | 'kɒntræst | *s.c.* 3 **[– (to/with)]** contraste, cambio total, diferencia absoluta. || *s.i.* 4 TV. contraste. || *s.c.* e *i.* 5 **[– (between/with)]** contraste, disparidad. || 6 **by – (to)/in – (with),** en contraste (con), en oposición (con); por contra. 7 **in – (with/to),** completamente distinto (a), completamente opuesto (a).
contrasting | kən'trɑːstɪŋ | *adj.* contrastante.
contravene | ˌkɒntrə'viːn | *v.t.* (form.) 1 contravenir, desobedecer, infringir (orden, regla, etc.). 2 oponerse a, estar en desacuerdo con (teorías, documentos, palabras, etc.) que se oponen.
contravention | ˌkɒntrə'venʃn | *s.c.* e *i.* **[– (of)]** (form.) infracción, desobediencia (de ley o similar).
contretemps | 'kɒntrətɒm | [*pl.* **contretemps**] *s.c.* (form. o lit.) contratiempo.
contribute | kən'trɪbjuːt | *v.t.* e *i.* 1 **[to – (to/towards)]** contribuir, aportar, poner un granito de arena (diciendo o haciendo cosas). 2 **[to – (to)]** contribuir, aportar (medios materiales). 3 **[to – (to)]** contribuir (artículos o escritos en general). || *v.i.* 4 **[to – to]** contribuir a, influir positivamente en, ser la causa fundamental de: *you have contributed to the feeling of hate = has sido la causa fundamental del sentimiento de odio.*
contributing | kən'trɪbjuːtɪŋ | *adj.* de gran influencia, influyente (como una de las causas de una situación).
contribution | ˌkɒntrɪ'bjuːʃn | *s.c.* 1 contribución (material o monetaria). 2 (brit.) derecho pasivo (de pensión). 3 contribución (literaria). || *s.i.* 4 **[– (of)]** contribución, aportación (material).
contributor | kən'trɪbjuːtər | *s.c.* 1 **[– (to)]** colaborador (literario). 2 **[– (to)]** causa, origen. 3 **[– (to)]** donante (de dinero).
contributory | kən'trɪbjʊtərɪ | (EE.UU.) | kən'trɪbjʊtɔːrɪ | *adj.* 1 contributivo, causante, influyente (factor, elemento, etc.). 2 a base de aportaciones periódicas (pensión o similar).
contrite | 'kɒntraɪt | *adj.* contrito, arrepentido, pesaroso.
contritely | 'kɒntraɪtlɪ | *adv.* con contrición, con arrepentimiento.
contrition | kən'trɪʃn | *s.i.* arrepentimiento, contrición.
contrivance | kən'traɪvəns | *s.c.* 1 artilugio, aparato extraño, ingenio mecánico. 2 (desp.) maquinación, treta (para beneficiarse uno). || *s.i.* 3 (form.) maniobras, estratagemas.
contrive | kən'traɪv | *v.t.* 1 efectuar, lograr llevar a cabo, idear (algo). 2 inventar (máquina, dispositivo, etc.). || *v.i.* 3 **[to –** *inf.***]** lograr, conseguir. 4 **[to –** *inf.***]** (form. o hum.) ingeniárselas (para hacer algo bobo).
contrived | kən'traɪvd | *adj.* (desp.) artificial, artificioso, antinatural (cosa u obra de arte).
control | kən'trəʊl | *v.t.* 1 controlar, estar al mando de (situación, país, etc.). 2 controlar (enfermedad). 3 controlar, dominar (gesto, voz, etc.). 4 controlar, verificar, regular (resultados, maquinaria, cuentas, etc.). 5 controlar, dominar (mecanismos sociales, económicos, etc.). || *v.r.* 6 controlarse, dominarse (carácter, sentimientos, etc.). || *s.i.* 7 **[– (of/over)]** control (de una situación, país, etc.). 8 **[– (of/over)]** control, dominio (de la vida, vehículo o similar). 9 **[– (of)]** control, dominio (de sentimientos, reacciones, etc.). 10 inspección, verificación, control (de un proceso o tarea). || *s.c.* 11 control, botón. 12 (normalmente *pl.*) control, limitación (a fenómenos económicos, sociales, etc. por parte de un gobierno). 13 (normalmente *sing.*) control (de pasaportes o similar en un aeropuerto). || 14 **at the controls (of),** en los controles (de), al mando (de), en el puesto de mando (de) (un vehículo o similar con botones). 15 **beyond/outside one's –,** fuera del control de uno, más allá del control de uno. 16 **– tower,** AER. torre de control. 17 **in – (of),** con control (de), controlando (un proceso, reacción, etc.). 18 **out of –,** sin control, descontrolado, fuera de control. 19 **under –,** bajo control, controlado. 20 **under one's –,** bajo el control de uno.
controllable | kən'trəʊləbl | *adj.* controlable, dominable.
controlled | kən'trəʊld | *adj.* 1 controlado, regulado, dominado. 2 sereno, en calma.
controller | kən'trəʊlər | *s.c.* 1 interventor (de cuentas). 2 director, superintendente (jefe de una parte de una organización).
controlling | kən'trəʊlɪŋ | *adj.* 1 que da control, que da dominio. || 2 **– interest,** COM. capital mayoritario (dentro de una empresa).
controversial | ˌkɒntrəvəːʃl | *adj.* polémico, discutible (persona o asunto).
controversially | ˌkɒntrəvəːʃəlɪ | *adv.* polémicamente, discutiblemente.
controversy | 'kɒntrəvəːsɪ | | kən'trɒvəsɪ | *s.c.* e *i.* controversia, polémica.
contusion | kən'tjuːʒn (EE.UU.) | kən'tuːʒn | *s.c.* e *i.* MED. contusión, golpe fuerte, magullamiento.
conundrum | kə'nʌndrəm | *s.c.* (form. o p.u.) 1 asunto intricado, enigma. 2 acertijo.
conurbation | ˌkɒnəː'beɪʃn | *s.c.* (form.) conurbación, ciudad extendida,

gran ciudad (que ha englobado pequeñas ciudades de alrededor).
convalesce | ˌkɒnvə'les | *v.i.* **[to – (from)] convalecer.**
convalescence | ˌkɒnvə'lesns | *s.i.* convalecencia.
convalescent | ˌkɒnvə'lesnt | *adj.* **1** convaleciente. || *s.c.* **2** convaleciente, paciente en proceso de recuperación.
convection | kən'vekʃn | *s.i.* FIS. convección.
convector | kən'vektər | (también **convector heater**) *s.c.* MEC. calentador por aire.
convene | kən'viːn | (form.) *v.t.* **1** convocar, citar (reunión o similar). || *v.i.* **2** reunirse, juntarse (en una reunión).
convener V. **convenor.**
convenience | kən'viːnɪəns | *s.i.* **1** conveniencia, provecho, utilidad. || *s.c.* **2** cosa conveniente, asunto provechoso. **2** (normalmente *pl.*) (form.) lavabo público, servicios. || **4 at one's –,** cuando le venga bien a uno, cuando guste uno. **5 at one's earliest –,** (form.) con la mayor brevedad, tan pronto como le sea posible a uno. **6 – food,** GAST. comida precocinada, comida rápida (en conservas o similar).
convenient | kən'viːnɪənt | *adj.* **1** conveniente, adecuado, oportuno, apropiado. **2** conveniente (por estar cerca).
conveniently | kən'viːnɪəntlɪ | *adv.* **1** convenientemente, adecuadamente, oportunamente, apropiadamente. **2** convenientemente (cerca).
convenor | kən'viːnər | (también **convener**) *s.c.* **1** convocante (a una reunión). **2** (brit.) presidente de comisión sindical.
convent | 'kɒnvənt | (EE.UU.) | 'kɒnvent | *s.c.* **1** REL. convento. || **2 – school,** escuela de monjas.
convention | kən'venʃn | *s.c.* e *i.* **1** convención, costumbre. || *s.c.* **2** convención, convención artística. **3** POL. convención, acuerdo internacional. **4** convención, congreso, asamblea.
conventional | kən'venʃənl | *adj.* **1** convencional, acostumbrado. **2** tradicional, viejo, antiguo (método, forma, sistema, etc.). **3** MIL. convencional, no nuclear. || **4 the – wisdom,** (form.) la opinión convencional.
conventionality | kənˌvenʃən'ælətɪ | *s.i.* convencionalismo, formalismo.
conventionally | kən'venʃənəlɪ | *adv.* **1** convencionalmente, como costumbre. **2** tradicionalmente, antiguamente.
converge | kən'vəːdʒ | *v.i.* **1** converger, unirse (caminos o similar). **2** converger, unirse (tendencias, fenómenos, etc.). **3 [to – in/on/upon]** reunirse, converger (gentes o vehículos en la misma dirección).
convergence | kən'vəːdʒəns | *s.c.* e *i.* **[– (of/between)]** (form.) fusión, convergencia.
conversant | kən'vəːsnt | *adj.* **[– with]** (form.) familiarizado con, al corriente de, experto en.
conversation | ˌkɒnvə'seɪʃn | *s.c.* e *i.* **1** conversación. || **2 in –,** en conversación, conversando, charlando. **3 to make –,** dar conversación, charla, (Am.) platicar.
conversational | ˌkɒnvə'seɪʃənl | *adj.* conversacional; coloquial.
conversationalist | ˌkɒnvə'seɪʃənəlɪst | *s.c.* hablador, conversador.
converse | kən'vəːs | (form.) *v.i.* **1 [to – (with)]** conversar, hablar, (Am.) platicar. || | 'kɒnvəːs | *adj.* **2** inverso, opuesto. || *s.sing.* **3 [the – (of)]** lo contrario, lo opuesto.
conversely | 'kɒnvəːslɪ | *adv.* a la inversa.
conversion | kən'vəːʃn, (EE.UU.) | kən'vəːrʒn | *s.c.* e *i.* **1** conversión (cambio en otra forma). **2** COM. conversión, cambio (de divisas). **3 [– (from/to)]** REL. conversión. **4** DEP. transformación (en algunos deportes). **5** MAT. conversión.
convert | 'kɒnvəːt | *s.c.* **1** converso (normalmente religioso). || | kən'vɜːt | *v.t.* e *i.* **2 [to – + *o.* + (from/into/to)]** transformar (una cosa en otra). **3** REL. convertir(se). **4** DEP. transformar. || *v.t.* **5 [to – + *o.* + (into/to)]** transformar, convertir (una cantidad a otra). **6 [to – + *o.* + (from/to)]** transformar, adaptar (un sistema). **7** reformar, modificar (edificio).
converted | kən'vəːtɪd | *adj.* reformada (casa).
converter | kən'vəːtər | (también **convertor**) *s.c.* ELEC. convertidor.
convertible | kən'vəːtəbl | *s.c.* **1** descapotable (coche). || *adj.* **2** FIN. convertible (dinero). **3** adaptable, convertible, transformable (objeto).
convertor V. **converter.**
convex | 'kɒnveks | *adj.* GEOM. convexo.
convey | kən'veɪ | *v.t.* **1** llevar, transmitir (un significado, una idea, etc.). **2** (form.) transportar, conducir, llevar. **3** (form.) transmitir (propiedad).
conveyance | kən'veɪəns | *s.c.* **1** (p.u.) medio de transporte. **2** DER. escritura de traspaso.
conveyancing | kən'veɪənsɪŋ | *s.i.* DER. (brit.) transmisión de propiedad.
conveyor | kən'veɪər | *s.c.* **1** portador, transportador. || **2 – belt,** MEC. cinta transportadora.
convict | 'kɒnvɪkt | *s.c.* **1** convicto, presidiario. | kən'vɪkt | *v.t.* **2 [to – + *o.* (of/for)]** condenar a la cárcel, declarar culpable.
conviction | kən'vɪkʃn | *s.c.* e *i.* **1** convicción, convencimiento. **2 [– (of/for)]** condena. || **3 to carry –,** ser convincente, ser creíble.
convince | kən'vɪns | *v.t.* convencer, persuadir.
convinced | kən'vɪnst | *adj.* **1** convencido, persuadido: *I'm convinced that he's dead = estoy convencido de que está muerto.* **2** convencido (de una religión).
convincing | kən'vɪnsɪŋ | *adj.* convincente, persuasivo.
convincingly | kən'vɪnsɪŋlɪ | *adv.* convincentemente, persuasivamente.
convivial | kən'vɪvɪəl | *adj.* **1** jovial, alegre, festivo. **2** (form.) sociable, amigable.
conviviality | kənˌvɪvɪ'ælɪtɪ | *s.i.* jovialidad, buen humor.
convivially | kən'vɪvɪəlɪ | *adv.* jovialmente, festivamente, alegremente.
convocation | ˌkɒnvə'keɪʃn | (form.) *s.sing.* **1 [– (of)]** convocación, convocatoria (de una asamblea, especialmente). || *s.c.* **2** asamblea.
convoluted | 'kɒnvəluːtɪd | *adj.* (form.) **1** curvado, con muchas curvas. **2** (fig.) complicado, intricado, tortuoso.
convolution | ˌkɒnvə'luːʃn | *s.c.* (form.) circunvolución, curva.
convoy | 'kɒnvɔɪ | *s.c.* convoy.
convulse | kən'vʌls | (form.) *v.i.* **1** agitarse violentamente, tener convulsiones. || *v.t.* **2** hacer desternillarse (de risa).
convulsion | kən'vʌlʃn | *s.c.* **1** MED. convulsión, espasmo. **2** (fig.) conmoción, agitación. **3** (normalmente *pl.*) ataque de risa irreprimible.
convulsive | kən'vʌlsɪv | *adj.* **1** convulso, espasmódico (movimiento). **2** MED. convulsivo (enfermedad que causa espasmos).
convulsively | kən'vʌlsɪvlɪ | *adv.* convulsivamente, espasmódicamente.
cony | 'kəunɪ | *s.c.* **1** (arc.) conejo. || *s.i.* **2** piel de conejo para abrigos.
coo | kuː | *v.i.* **1** arrullar (sonido de las palomas). || *v.t.* e *i.* **2** (fig.) arrullar, hablar como con arrullos, decir en arrullos. || *interj.* **3** (brit.) vaya (como sorpresa).
cooing | kuːɪŋ | *s.i.* **1** sonido arrullador, arrullos. || *adj.* **2** arrullador (sonido de voces).
cook | kuk | *v.t.* e *i.* **1** cocinar, guisar. || *v.t.* **2** (fam.) falsear (cuentas, escritos, etc.). || *v.i.* **3** (fam.) tramar, maquinar. || *s.c.* **4** cocinero. || **5 to – the books,** (desp. y fam.) falsificar las cuentas, falsear los libros. **6 to – up,** (fam.) maquinar, urdir (trampas o similar). **7 too many cooks/too many cooks spoil the broth,** demasiadas manos/demasiados cocineros arruinan el puchero.
cookbook | 'kukbuk | *s.c.* libro de recetas, recetario, libro de cocina.
cooked | kukt | *adj.* cocinado, guisado.
cooker | 'kukər | *s.c.* **1** cocina (el electrodoméstico). **2** (fam. y brit.) manzana para repostería (no para comer).
cookery | 'kukərɪ | *s.i.* **1** arte culinario, arte de la cocina. || **2 – book,** libro de cocina, libro de recetas.
cookie | 'kukɪ | *s.c.* **1** (EE.UU.) galleta. || **2 that's the way the – crumbles,** (fam.) así es la vida, las cosas son así.
cooking | 'kukɪŋ | *s.i.* **1** cocina, arte culinario. || *adj.* **2** de cocinar, para cocinar (aceite, vino, etc.).
cool | kuːl | *adj.* **1** fresco (moderadamente frío). **2** sereno, tranquilo. **3** indiferente, distante. **4** (fam.) fenómeno. **5**

(fam.) ni más ni menos que (cantidad). **6** frío (color, especialmente el verde y azul). || *v.t.* e *i.* **7** enfriar(se), refrescar(se). **8** moderar(se), apaciguar(se) (un sentimiento o emoción). || *s.sing.* **9 [the –]** el fresco, el frío. || **10 – as a cucumber,** V. **cucumber. 11 to – down, a)** enfriar(se), refrescar(se). **b)** calmar(se), serenar(se). **12 – it,** (fam.) cálmate, tranquilo. **13 to – off,** enfriarse rápidamente, ponerse frío rápidamente. (fig.) perder entusiasmo, entibiarse. **14 to – one's heels,** V. **heel. 15 to keep one's –,** (fam.) mantener la calma, mantener la serenidad. **16 to lose one's –,** (fam.) montar en cólera, ponerse malo (de ira). **17 to play it –,** (fam.) tomárselo con calma.

coolant | 'kuːlənt | *s.c.* e *i.* líquido de refrigeración.

cooler | 'kuːlər | *s.c.* **1** nevera portátil. || *s.sing.* **2** (fam.) cárcel, (Am.) cana.

coolie | 'kuːlɪ | *s.c.* (p.u.) culi (portador asiático).

cooling | 'kuːlɪŋ | *s.i.* **1** enfriamiento (hacer más frío). || *adj.* **2** refrescante. || **3 cooling-off period,** período de tregua (en las negociaciones sindicales). **4 – tower,** torre de refrigeración.

coolly | 'kuːlɪ | *adv.* serenamente, tranquilamente.

coolness | 'kuːlnɪs | *s.i.* **1** frescor, frío. **2** serenidad, tranquilidad. **3** indiferencia, distanciamiento (en el carácter de alguien).

coop | kuːp | *s.c.* **1** jaula (para gallinas, conejos, etc.). || **2 to – up,** enjaular, encerrar.

co-op | 'kəuɒp | *s.c.* (fam.) cooperativa.

cooperate | kəu'ɒpəreɪt | *v.i.* **[to – (with)]** cooperar, colaborar.

co-operation | kəu,ɒpə'reɪʃn | *s.i.* cooperación, colaboración.

cooperative | kəu'ɒpərətɪv | *s.c.* **1** cooperativa. || *adj.* **2** cooperativo, colaborador. **3** servicial, dispuesto (a ayudar). || **4 – society,** (brit.) tienda de la cooperativa, almacén en régimen de cooperativa.

cooperatively | kəu'ɒpərətɪvlɪ | *adv.* **1** cooperativamente, con toda cooperación. **2** de manera servicial, en plan colaborador, dispuesto (a ayudar).

co-opt | kəu'ɒpt | *v.t.* (form.) elegir, nombrar (miembros de un comité).

co-option | kəu'ɒpʃn | *s.i.* (form.) elección, nombramiento.

coordinate | ,kəu'ɔːdɪneɪt | *v.t.* **1** coordinar. **2** coordinar, controlar (movimientos del cuerpo). || | kəu'ɔːdɪnət | *s.c.* **3** (normalmente *pl.*) MAT. coordenada. **4 coordinating conjunction,** GRAM. conjunción copulativa.

co-ordinator | ,kəu'ɔːdɪneɪtər | *s.c.* **[– (of)]** coordinador (de un proyecto o actividad).

coot | kuːt | *s.c.* **1** ZOOL. fúlica, focha (ave). **2** (p.u. y brit.) bobalicón.

cop | kɒp | (fam.) *s.c.* **1** poli. || *v.t.* **2** recibir, apechar con, sufrir (algo desagradable). || **3 to – hold (of),** (brit.) echar mano (a), agarrar, sostener, sujetar (algo). **4 to – it,** ganárselas, irlas a pagar: *if I catch you asleep again, you'll cop it = si te encuentro otra vez dormida me las vas a pagar.* **5 to – out (of),** (desp.) escaquearse (de), rajarse (de) (hacer algo). **6 cops and robbers,** policías y ladrones (juego de niños). **7 not much –,** (brit.) no gran cosa, una porquería (de calidad o interés).

cope | kəup | *v.i.* **1 [to – with]** arreglárselas con, solucionar (dificultad, problema, etc.). || *s.c.* **2** REL. capa consistorial, capa pluvial (de un cura).

copier | 'kɒpɪər | *s.c.* copiadora, fotocopiadora.

copilot | ,kəu'paɪlət | *s.c.* copiloto.

coping | 'kəupɪŋ | *s.c.* e *i.* ARQ. albardilla, remate.

copious | 'kəupɪəs | *adj.* copioso, abundante, cuantioso.

copiously | 'kəupɪəslɪ | *adv.* copiosamente, abundantemente, cuantiosamente.

cop-out | 'kɒpaut *s.c.* (fam. y desp.) salida por la tangente, evasión del tema, miedo a encararse con la responsabilidad de uno.

copper | 'kɒpər | *s.i.* **1** QUIM. cobre. || *s.c.* **2** (fam. y brit.) poli. **3** caldero (de cobre). **4** perra (dinero insignificante). || *adj.* **4** cobre (color). || **5 – beech,** BOT. haya roja.

copperplate | ,kɒpə'pleɪt | *s.i.* caligrafía nítida y algo barroca.

coppice | 'kɒpɪs, V. **copse.**

copse | kɒps | (también **coppice**) *s.c.* bosquecillo.

Copt | kɒpt | *s.c.* REL. copto.

Coptic | 'kɒptɪk | REL. *adj.* **1** copto. || **2 the Coptic Church,** la Iglesia copta.

copula | 'kɒpjulə | *s.c.* GRAM. cópula.

copulate | 'kɒpjuleɪt | *v.i.* **[to – (with)]** (form.) BIOL. copular (sexualmente, los animales); copular, tener relaciones sexuales (personas).

copulation | ,kɒpju'leɪʃn | *s.i.* copulación, coito.

copy | 'kɒpɪ | *s.c.* **1** copia, duplicado, reproducción. **2** ejemplar (de un libro, periódico, etc.). || *s.i.* **3** material escrito. **4** PER. material digno de publicación. || *v.t.* **5** copiar, reproducir exactamente. **6** copiar, imitar. || *v.t.* e *i.* **7** copiar (en exámenes). || **8 to – down/out,** copiar, reproducir con toda exactitud.

copybook | 'kɒpɪbuk | *s.c.* **1** cuaderno de copia. || *adj.* **2** de libro, llevado a cabo con toda perfección. || **3 to blot one's –,** manchar la reputación de uno, meter la pata de manera trascendental.

copycat | 'kɒpɪkæt | *s.c.* (fam. y hum.) mono imitador, imitador.

copyright | 'kɒpɪraɪt | *s.c.* e *i.* DER. copyright, derechos de propiedad intelectual.

copywriter | 'kɒpɪraɪtər | *s.c.* publicista, escritor de anuncios.

coquetry | 'kɒkɪtrɪ | *s.i.* (form. o lit.) coquetería.

coquette | kə'ket | | kɒ'ket | *s.c.* (form.) coqueta (mujer).

coquettish | kə'ketɪʃ | *adj.* (form.) coquetón, coquetona.

coquettishly | kə'ketɪʃlɪ | *adv.* (form.) coquetonamente, con coquetería.

cor | kɔːr | *interj.* **1** ¡o! (sorpresa o impresión). || **2 – blimey,** (p.u.) ¡qué bárbaro!

coral | 'kɒrəl | (EE.UU.) | 'kɔːrəl | *s.* **1** BIOL. coral. || *s.c.* **2** ZOOL. coral. || *adj.* **3** coralino (color). || **4 – reef,** GEOL. arrecife de coral.

corbel | 'kɔːbl | *s.c.* ARQ. voladizo.

cord | kɔːd | *s.c.* e *i.* **1** cordel, cuerda fina. || *s.c.* **2** ELEC. cable. || *adj.* **3** de pana. || *s.p.* **4 [a pair of –]** (fam.) un par de pantalones de pana.

cordial | 'kɔːdɪəl | (EE.UU.) | 'kɔːrdəəl | *adj.* **1** cordial, amistoso. **2** (form.) fuerte (odio o similar): *cordial dislike = antipatía fuerte.* || *s.c.* e *i.* **3** (brit.) cordial (bebida estimulante de zumo de frutas).

cordiality | ,kɔːdɪ'ælɪtɪ | (EE.UU.) | ,kɔːrdər'ælɪtɪ | *s.i.* cordialidad, afabilidad.

cordially | 'kɔːdɪəlɪ | (EE.UU.) | 'kɔːrdəəlɪ | *adv.* **1** cordialmente, amistosamente. **2** fuertemente (con algo negativo). V. **cordial 2.**

cordite | 'kɔːdaɪt | *s.i.* QUIM. cordita (explosivo).

cordon | 'kɔːdn | *s.c.* **1** cordón (policial o parecido). || **2 – bleu,** de primera calidad. **3 to – off,** acordonar (zona).

corduroy | 'kɔːdərɔɪ | *s.i.* **1** pana (tejido). || *s.pl.* **2** (p.u.) pantalones de pana.

core | kɔː | *s.c.* **1** corazón (fruta). **2** centro, parte central, núcleo (de cualquier objeto o lugar). || *s.sing.* **3 [– (of)]** grupo esencial, minoría dirigente. **4** meollo, punto principal, punto esencial, punto central. || *v.t.* **5** quitar el corazón (de fruta). || **6 to the –,** (form.) hasta la médula, hasta lo más íntimo.

coriander | ,kɒrɪ'ændər | (EE.UU.) | kɔːrɪ'ændər | *s.i.* BOT. coriandro, cilantro.

cork | kɔːk | *s.i.* **1** BOT. corcho. || *s.c.* **2** corcho (de una botella). | *v.t.* **3** poner un corcho (a una botella). || **4 to – up,** cerrar bien con corcho (una botella).

corkscrew | 'kɔːkskruː | *s.c.* sacacorchos.

cormorant | 'kɔːmərənt | *s.c.* ZOOL. cormorán (ave).

corn | kɔːn | *s.i.* **1** (brit.) cereal, trigo, grano. **2** (EE.UU.) maíz. **3** (fam.) pura sensiblería (especialmente en espectáculos). || *s.c.* **4** callo (en el pie). || **5 corned beef,** carne de ternera en lata. **6 – on the cob,** mazorca de maíz (para comer).

cornea | 'kɔːnɪə | *s.c.* ANAT. córnea.

corner | 'kɔːnər | *s.c.* **1** esquina, ángulo, rincón. **2** comisura (de los labios). **3** recodo, curva (parte de una carretera o conjunción de dos calles). **4** DEP. saque de esquina, córner. **5** (fig.) rincón, lugar apartado, lugar lejano (del mundo). || *v.t.* **6** atrapar, poner en una situación comprometida. **7** monopolizar, apoderarse de la mayor parte de (algo en el mercado). || *v.i.* **8** coger las curvas (vehículo). || **9 to be in a tight –,** estar en una situación comprometida, estar en una situación difícil, estar en un aprieto. **10 – shop,** tienda de la esquina. **11 to cut corners,** reducir gastos como sea, hacer peor lo que se podría hacer mejor (por ahorrar tiempo o dinero). **12 to cut the –,** atajar por en medio (de una zona, en lugar de seguir el borde). **13 in/into a –,** en un aprieto, en una situación difícil. **14 just around the –,** justo a la vuelta de la esquina, justo al lado. **15 to make a – in,** hacer avances en, apoderarse de, ganar el control de (un producto). **16 to turn the –,** doblar la esquina.

cornered | 'kɔːnəd | *adj.* atrapado, acorralado.

cornerstone | 'kɔːnəstəʊn | *s.c.* **1** ARQ. piedra angular, primera piedra (de un edificio). **2** (fig.) piedra angular, punto de apoyo.

cornet | 'kɔːnɪt | *s.c.* **1** MUS. corneta. **2** cucurucho (helado).

cornfield | 'kɔːnfiːld | *s.c.* AGR. campo de maíz.

cornflake | 'kɔːnfleɪk | *s.c.* copo de maíz.

cornflour | 'kɔːnflaʊər | *s.i.* harina de maíz.

cornflower | 'kɔːnflaʊər | *s.c.* BOT. aciano, liebrecilla.

cornice | 'kɔːnɪs | *s.c.* ARQ. cornisa.

cornucopia | ˌkɔːnjʊ'kəʊpɪə | *s.sing.* **[– of]** (form. o hum.) abundancia de, riqueza de.

corny | kɔːnɪ | *adj.* (fam. y desp.) **1** trillado, muy visto. **2** sentimentaloide, sensiblero.

corollary | kə'rɒlərɪ | (EE.UU.) | 'kɒrəlerɪ | *s.c.* **[– (to/of)]** (form.) corolario, consecuencia.

corona | kə'rəʊnə | *s.c.* ASTR. corona, halo (alrededor de la luna).

coronary | 'kɒrənrɪ | (EE.UU.) | 'kɔːrənerɪ | MED. *s.c.* **1** ataque al corazón. || **2 – attack,** ataque al corazón. **3 – thrombosis,** trombosis coronaria.

coronation | ˌkɒrə'neɪʃn | (EE.UU.) | ˌkɔːrə'neɪʃn | *s.c.* coronación (de un rey o reina).

coroner | 'kɒrənər | (EE.UU.) | 'kɔːrənər | *s.c.* DER. juez de instrucción de una causa por muerte violenta.

coronet | 'kɒrənɪt | (EE.UU.) | 'kɔːrənet | *s.c.* diadema, pequeña corona.

corpora | 'kɔːpərə | *pl.* de **corpus.**

corporal | 'kɔːpərəl | *adj.* **1** corporal, físico, del cuerpo. || *s.c.* **2** MIL. cabo. || **3 – punishment,** castigo corporal, castigo físico.

corporate | 'kɔːpərət | *adj.* **1** COM. empresarial. **2** colectivo, grupal.

corporately | 'kɔːpərətlɪ | *adv.* colectivamente, como grupo.

corporation | ˌkɔːpə'reɪʃn | *s.c.* **1** COM. gran empresa. **2 [=N** *v.sing./pl.*] (brit.) POL. corporación municipal, ayuntamiento. || **3 – tax,** FIN. impuesto sobre sociedades.

corporeal | kɔː'pɔːrɪəl | *adj.* (form.) corpóreo, material, tangible.

corps | kɔː | [*pl.* **corps**] *s.c.* **1** cuerpo (como parte organizada especialmente de la administración pública): *diplomatic corps = cuerpo diplomático.* **2** MIL. cuerpo (de ejército).

corpse | kɔːps | *s.c.* cadáver.

corpulence | 'kɔːpjʊləns | *s.i.* (form.) corpulencia.

corpulent | 'kɔːpjʊlənt | *adj.* (form.) corpulento, grueso.

corpus | 'kɔːpəs | [*pl.* **corpuses** o **corpora**] *s.c.* (form.) corpus, colección (de escritos).

corpuscle | 'kɔːpʌsl | *s.c.* ANAT. glóbulo (rojo o blanco).

corral | kə'rɑːl | (EE.UU.) | kə'ræl | (EE.UU.) *s.c.* **1** corral, cercado (para ganado). || *v.t.* **2** llevar al corral, encerrar en el corral (al ganado).

correct | kə'rekt | *adj.* **1** correcto. **2** en lo cierto: *I am correct = estoy en lo cierto.* **3** apropiado, correcto, debido (curso de acción). **4** correcto, educado (cualidad personal). **5** adecuado, apropiado, correcto (conducta). || *v.t.* **6** corregir, rectificar, subsanar (algo o alguien). **7** corregir, rectificar (un mal, enfermedad, etc.). || **8 correcting fluid,** sustancia correctora (dentro de un lápiz corrector). **9 – me if I'm wrong,** corrígeme si me equivoco. **10 I stand corrected,** (form.) admito la corrección, admito mi equivocación.

correction | kə'rekʃn | *s.c.* e *i.* **1** corrección, rectificación. || *s.c.* **2** corrección, tachadura (en el trabajo escolar). || *s.i.* **3** (p.u.) castigo (referido a reformatorios para los jóvenes).

corrective | kə'rektɪv | *adj.* **1** corrector. || *s.c.* **2 [– (to)]** ajuste, elemento corrector.

correctly | kə'rektlɪ | *adv.* **1** correctamente. **2** apropiadamente, debidamente, correctamente. **3** correctamente, educadamente. **4** adecuadamente, como es debido (conducta).

correctness | kə'rektnɪs | *s.i.* **1** exactitud. **2** buena educación, buenas maneras.

correlate | 'kɒrəleɪt | (EE.UU.) | 'kɔːrəleɪt | *v.t.* **1** (normalmente *pas.*) relacionarse estrechamente. || *v.i.* **2 [to – with]** estar en estrecha relación con.

correlation | ˌkɒrə'leɪʃn | (EE.UU.) | ˌkɔːrə'leɪʃn | *s.i.* correlación.

correlative | kɒ'relətɪv | *adj.* (form.) correlativo.

correspond | ˌkɒrɪ'spɒnd | (EE.UU.) | ˌkɔːrɪ'spɒnd | *v.i.* **1 [to – (to/with)]** corresponderse (hechos, números, etc.). **2 [to – (with)]** mantener correspondencia.

correspondence | ˌkɒrɪ'spɒndəns | (EE.UU.) | ˌkɔːrɪ'spɒndəns | *s.i.* **1** correspondencia (cartas). || *s.c.* e *i.* **2 [– (between /with)]** correspondencia, relación. || **3 – course,** curso por correspondencia.

correspondent | ˌkɒrɪ'spɒndənt | (EE.UU.) | ˌkɔːrɪ'spɒndənt | *s.c.* **1** PER. corresponsal (del extranjero), periodista especializado (en economía, educación, etc.). **2** escritor de cartas.

corresponding | ˌkɒrɪ'spɒndɪŋ | (EE.UU.) | ˌkɔːrɪ'spɒndɪŋ | *adj.* **1** correspondiente. **2** equivalente (título, cantidad, etc.).

correspondingly | ˌkɒrɪ'spɒndɪŋlɪ | (EE.UU.) | ˌkɔːrɪ'spɒndɪŋlɪ | *adv.* correspondientemente.

corridor | 'kɒrɪdɔːr | (EE.UU.) | 'kɔːrɪdɔːr | *s.c.* **1** pasillo. **2** POL. pasillo, corredor (zona de un país que atraviesa otro). || **3 corridors of power,** pasillos del poder.

corroborate | kə'rɒbəreɪt | *v.t.* corroborar, confirmar.

corroboration | kəˌrɒbə'reɪʃn | *s.i.* corroboración, confirmación.

corroborative | kə'rɒbərətɪv | (EE.UU.) | kə'rɒbəreɪtɪv | *adj.* corroborante, confirmativo.

corrode | kə'rəʊd | *v.t.* e *i.* **1** corroer(se), oxidar(se). || *v.t.* **2** (lit. y fig.) corroer (un sentimiento, pasión, etc.).

corroded | kə'rəʊdɪd | *adj.* corroído, oxidado.

corroding | kə'rəʊdɪŋ | *adj.* oxidante, causante de corrosión.

corrosion | kə'rəʊʒn | *s.i.* corrosión, oxidación, desgaste.

corrosive | kə'rəʊsɪv | *adj.* **1** corrosivo. **2** (fig.) mordaz, cáustico. **3** causante de daño a largo plazo (una política económica, educativa, etc.).

corrugated | 'kɒrəgeɪtɪd | *adj.* **1** acanalado (para que sea más fuerte cualquier material). || **2 – iron,** hierro corrugado, hierro acanalado.

corrupt | kə'rʌpt | *adj.* **1** corrupto, deshonesto (en cuestiones de dinero). **2** corrupto, pervertido, depravado. **3** viciado, con errores (texto). || *v.t.* e *i.* **4** corromper(se) (con dinero, poder, etc.). **5** corromper(se), depravar(se). || *v.t.* **6** DER. pervertir (especialmente a alguien menor). || *v.i.* **7** corromperse, entrar en corrupción (cuerpo o similar).

corruption | kə'rʌpʃn | *s.i.* **1** corrupción, deshonestidad (en asuntos de dinero, poder, etc.). **2** BIOL. corrupción, putrefacción. **3** DER. corrupción (por ejemplo, de menores).

corsage | kɔː'sɑːʒ | *s.c.* **[– (of)]** ramillete (que las mujeres sujetan al pecho como adorno).

corset | 'kɔːsɪt | *s.c.* **1** corsé. **2** MED. corsé (ortopédico).

cortege | kɔː'teɪʒ | (también **cortège**) *s.c.* **[=N** *v.sing./pl.*] cortejo.

cortex | 'kɔːteks | [*pl.* **cortices**] *s.c.* ANAT. corteza del cerebro.

cortices | 'kɔːtɪsiːz | *pl.* de **cortex.**

cortisone | 'kɔːtɪzəʊn | *s.i.* QUIM. cortisona.

cosh | kɒʃ | (brit.) *s.c.* **1** cachiporra. || *v.t.* **2** pegar un cachiporrazo.

cosine | 'kəʊsaɪn | *s.c.* MAT. coseno.

cosmetic | kɒz'metɪk | *s.c.* **1** cosmético. || *adj.* **2** (fig.) superficial, poco profundo. || **3 – surgery,** MED. cirugía plástica, cirugía reparadora.

cosmic | 'kɒzmɪk | *adj.* **1** cósmico. **2** (fig.) mundial, total. || **3 – ray,** ASTR. rayo cósmico.

cosmology | koz'mɒlədʒɪ | *s.c.* e *i.* cosmología.

cosmonaut | 'kɒzmənɔːt | *s.c.* cosmonauta.

cosmopolitan | ˌkɒzmə'pɒlɪtən | *adj.* **1** cosmopolita, internacional. || *s.c.* **2** cosmopolita, ciudadano del mundo.

cosmos | 'kɒzmɒs | *s.sing.* **[the –]** ASTR. el cosmos.

cosset | 'kɒsɪt | *v.t.* (desp.) mimar, estropear con mimos.

cosseted | 'kɒsɪtɪd | *adj.* (desp.) mimado.

cost | kɒst | (EE.UU.) | kɔːst | *v.t.* [*pret.* y *p.p.irreg.* **cost**] **1** costar (dinero). **2** costar (la vida, la reputación, etc.): *the mistake cost him his promotion = su equivocación le costó su ascenso.* **3** (fam.) costar un potosí. || *s.c.* **4** costo, precio. || *s.sing.* **5** (fig.) precio, coste (en vidas humanas, sufrimiento, etc.). || *s.pl.* **6** costos, gastos. || **7 at all –/at all costs,** a toda costa, cueste lo que cueste (en dinero o esfuerzo). **8 at any –,** a cualquier precio. **9 at –,** COM. a precio de coste. **10 – accountant,** COM. contable. **11 – accounting,** ECON. contabilidad financiera. **12 to – money,** costar dinero, no ser gratis (normalmente indica que no se puede comprar). **13 – of living,** ECON. coste de la vida. **14 – price,** COM. precio de coste. **15 to – somebody dear,** V. **dear. 16 to count the – (of),** calcular el gasto (de), calcular el esfuerzo (de), calcular el riesgo (de). **17 to one's –,** a expensas de uno, en la propia carne de uno.

co-star | 'kəustɑː | *s.c.* **1** actor acompañante, actriz acompañante. || *v.t.* **2** presentar la actuación conjunta de. || *v.i.* **3 [to – (with)]** actuar, hacer una película.

Costa Rica | ˌkɒstə'riːkə | *s.sing.* Costa Rica.

Costa Rican | ˌkɒstə'riːkən | *adj.* **1** costarricense. || *s.c.* **2** costarricense.

cost-effective | ˌkɒstɪ'fektɪv | *adj.* económico, rentable.

costing | 'kɒstɪŋ | (EE.UU.) | 'kɔːstɪŋ | *s.c.* e *i.* cálculo del coste.

costliness | 'kɒstlɪnɪs | (EE.UU.) | 'kɔːstlɪnɪs | *s.i.* carestía.

costly | 'kɒstlɪ | (EE.UU.) | 'kɔːstlɪ | *adj.* costoso, caro.

cost-plus | 'kɒstplʌs | *adj.* FIN. costo de producción más margen.

costume | 'kɒstjuːm | (EE.UU.) | 'kɒs↓tuːm | *s.c.* **1** traje, vestido (en teatro, película, etc.). || *s.i.* **2** vestuario (de película, obra de teatro, etc.). **3** HIST. vestimenta de la época. || *adj.* **4** de trajes de la época (en teatro, cine, etc.). || **5 – jewellery,** bisutería.

costumier | kɒ'stjuːmɪər | (EE.UU.) | kɒ'stuːmɪər | *s.c.* sastre (de cine, teatro, etc.).

cosily | 'kəuzɪlɪ | (EE.UU. **cozily**) *adv.* **1** acogedoramente, agradablemente, cómodamente. **2** íntimamente, amistosamente.

cosiness | 'kəuzɪnɪs | (EE.UU.) *s.i.* **1** comodidad, amenidad. **2** intimidad.

cosy | 'kəuzɪ | (EE.UU. **cozy**) *adj.* **1** acogedor, agradable, cómodo (habitación, persona, etc.). **2** íntimo, amistoso (charla, ambiente, etc.). || *s.c.* **3** protector del calor (de una tetera o similar).

cot | kɒt | *s.c.* **1** (brit.) cuna. **2** (EE.UU.) cama portátil, cama plegable. || **3 – death,** MED. muerte de cuna.

coterie | 'kəutərɪ | *s.c.* [=N *v.sing./pl.*] (form.) tertulia; círculo.

cottage | 'kɒtɪdʒ | *s.c.* **1** casa rural, casa antigua rural. || **2 – cheese,** GAST. requesón. **3 – industry,** industria casera (normalmente textil o de alfarería). **4 – loaf,** (brit.) pan rural. **5 – pie,** (brit.) GAST. carne picada con patatas.

cottager | 'kɒtɪdʒər | *s.c.* persona que vive en una casa rural.

cotton | 'kɒtn | *s.i.* **1** algodón. **2** (brit.) hilo de algodón. || *s.pl.* **3** prendas de algodón. || **4 – candy,** (EE.UU.) algodón de azúcar. **5 to – on (to),** (fam.) tener pesquis, darse cuenta (de), caer en la cuenta (de).

cottonwool | ˌkɒtn'wul | *s.i.* algodón (para usos médicos).

couch | kautʃ | *s.c.* **1** sofá, diván. **2** diván (del psiquiatra). || *s.sing.* **3 [the –]** (fam.) PSIQ. el diván (como símbolo de problemas mentales). || *v.t.* **4 [to – + *o.* + (in)]** expresar, formular (pensamiento en lenguaje). || *v.i.* **5** ponerse al acecho, ponerse en actitud de ataque (animal). || **6 – grass,** BOT. grama, bermuda.

couchette | kuː'ʃet | *s.c.* litera (de tren o barco).

cougar | 'kuːgər | *s.c.* ZOOL. puma.

cough | kɒf | (EE.UU.) | kɔːf | *v.i.* **1** toser. **2** hacer ruidos como tos (maquinaria). || *v.t.* **3** toser, expulsar, escupir (sangre u otra sustancia). || *s.c.* **4** tos. || **5 to – up, a)** toser con fuerza expulsando algo, expectorar (cualquier sustancia). **b)** (fam.) soltar la pasta, aflojar la cartera.

coughing | 'kɒfɪŋ | *s.i.* ataque de tos.

could | kud | (forma relajada | kəd) *pret. irreg.* **1** de **can.** | *v.i.* **2** podría: *could I bother you for a minute? = ¿podría molestarte un minuto?* || **3 – do with,** V. **do. 4 I couldn't,** no, muchas gracias, no, no podría con más (forma de rechazar cortésmente invitación a comer más).

OBS. Esta forma tiene significados en pasado y otros usos paralelos a los de su forma de presente **can.**

couldn't | 'kudnt | *contr.* de **could** y **not.**

could've | 'kudəv | *contr.* de **could** y **have.**

council | 'kaunsl | *s.c.* **1** [=N *v.sing./pl.*] (brit.) POL. consejo local, diputación provincial. **2** [=N *v.sing./pl.*] consejo (de iglesia, asociación, etc.). **3** POL. conferencia, junta (de algún tema gubernativo específico). || **4 – house/flat,** vivienda social (casa o piso). **5 – of war,** POL. junta de defensa.

councillor | 'kaunsələr (EE.UU. **councilor**) *s.c.* (brit.) POL. diputado provincial, consejero local.

counsel | 'kaunsl | *s.i.* **1** (form.) consejo, sugerencia. || *s.c.* e *i.* **2** DER. asesor legal, abogado. || *v.t.* **3** dar un consejo, ofrecer una sugerencia. **4** (form.) aconsejar (un tipo de acción). **5 [to – + *o.* + *inf.*/(against/on)]** (form.) aconsejar, sugerir: *I counselled them against giving money to Jim = yo les aconsejé en contra de dar dinero a Jim.* || *v.i.* **6 [to – about/on]** aconsejar sobre. || **7 to keep one's own –,** (form.) guardar silencio, callar. **8 to take –/to take – together,** (form.) consultar (pidiendo consejo sobre un problema).

counselling | 'kaunsəlɪŋ | (EE.UU. **counseling**) *s.i.* asesoramiento personal, ayuda psicológica, asistencia psiquiátrica.

counsellor | 'kaunsələr | (EE.UU. **counselor**) *s.c.* consejero (especialmente en temas psicológicos).

count | kaunt | *v.t.* **1** contar (números); incluir (detalles, elementos, propiedades). **2** contar, considerar, estimar (expresa la importancia de algo o alguien): *I don't count him as one of us = no le considero uno de nosotros.* || *v.i.* **3** contar, hacer cálculos. **4** importar, tener importancia, contar: *what counts is him = lo que cuenta es él.* **5 [to – for]** contar para, significar, valer: *he counts for nothing = él no cuenta para nada.* || *s.c.* **6** cifra, cálculo: *the official count of the accident was high = la cifra oficial del accidente fue alta.* **7** DEP. cuenta (en boxeo). **8** nivel (de alguna sustancia en un análisis). **9** DER. cargo, acusación. **10** aspecto, punto (de discusión): *I disagree with you on all counts = estoy en desacuerdo contigo en todos los puntos.* **11** conde (título nobiliario). || *v.r.* **12** verse uno a sí mismo como, considerarse: *I count myself very lucky to have him as friend = me considero afortunado de tenerle como amigo.* || **13 to be counted,** ser considerado (algo). **14 to – against,** ir en contra, influir en contra, pesar en contra. **15 to – in,** incluir, contar con (alguien). **16 – noun,** GRAM. sustantivo contable. **17 to – on,** contar con, depender de (algo). **18 to – on/upon,** contar con, confiar en, depender de (alguien). **19 to – one's blessings,** V. **blessing. 20 to – one's chickens,** V. **chicken. 21 to – out, a)** contar con detenimiento, contar uno por uno (especialmente dinero). **b)** DEP. acabar la cuenta de diez (boxeo). **c)** excluir, no contar con (alguien). **22 to – the cost,** V. **cost. 23 to – towards,** tenerse en cuenta para, contabilizarse para (hablando de dinero). **24 to – up, contar hasta el final, contar todos, ir añadiendo (en una cuenta). 25 to keep – (of),** llevar la cuenta (de). **26 to lose – (of),** perder la cuenta (de). **27 not coun-**

ting, sin contar, excluyendo. **28 out for the –,** (fam.) inconsciente, noqueado.
countable | 'kauntəbl | *adj.* **1** contable, que se puede contar. || **2 – noun,** GRAM. sustantivo contable.
countdown | 'kauntdaun | *s.c.* cuenta atrás.
countenance | 'kauntənəns | *s.c.* **1** (lit.) expresión facial, rostro, semblante. || *v.t.* **2** (form.) tolerar, aprobar, sancionar. || **3 to keep one's –,** (form.) mantenerse serio (especialmente por no reírse).
counter | 'kauntər | *s.c.* **1** mostrador (de cualquier tienda). **2** ficha (en algunos juegos de mesa). || *v.t.* **3** contradecir, contestar a (con palabras). **4 [to – + *o.* + (by/with)]** combatir, oponerse a (una determinada política, acción o similar). || *v.i.* **5 [to – (by/with)]** replicar, oponerse (con palabras). || **6 counter-,** contra (en compuesto): *counterinsurgency = medidas antiinsurreccionales.* **7 to run – to,** estar en contra de, ser contrario de (algo en contra de otra cosa): *your actions runs counter to your beliefs = tus acciones están en contra de tus creencias.* **8 under the –,** a escondidas, subrepticiamente, por la trastienda, por debajo del tapete.
counteract | ˌkauntə'rækt | *v.t.* contrarrestar, neutralizar.
counter-attack | 'kauntərətæk | *v.t.* e *i.* **1** contraatacar. || *s.c.* **2** contraataque.
counterbalance | 'kauntəbæləns | *v.t.* **1** compensar, equilibrar. || *s.c.* **2** contrapeso, contrabalanza.
counterclockwise | ˌkauntə'klɒkwaiz | *adj.* y *adv.* (EE.UU.) en sentido contrario a las manillas del reloj.
counter-espionage | ˌkauntər'espɪənɑːʒ | *s.i.* contraespionaje.
counterfeit | 'kauntəfɪt | *adj.* **1** falsificado, falso (dinero o similar). || *v.t.* **2** falsificar.
counterfeiter | 'kauntəfɪtər | *s.c.* falsificador.
counterfoil | 'kauntəfɔɪl | *s.c.* resguardo, matriz (de cheques, billetes, etc.).
countermand | ˌkauntə'mɑːnd | (EE.UU.) | ˌkauntə'mænd | *v.t.* cancelar (un pedido, pidiendo otro).
countermeasure | ˌkauntəmeʒər | *s.c.* contramedida, medida en contra.
counterpane | 'kauntəpeɪn | *s.c.* (form.) colcha de adorno, cubrecama.
counterpart | 'kauntəpɑːt | *s.c.* homólogo (personas).
counterpoint | 'kauntəpɔɪnt | *s.i.* MUS. contrapunto.
counter-productive | kauntəprə'dʌktɪv | *adj.* contraproducente.
counter-productively | kauntəprə'dʌktɪvlɪ | *adv.* de manera contraproducente.
counter-revolution | ˌkauntəˌrevə'luːʃn | *s.c.* contrarrevolución.
counter-revolutionary | ˌka'untəˌrevə'luːʃənərɪ | (EE.UU.) | ˌkauntə'ˌrevə'luːʃənərɪ | adj. **1** contrarrevolucionario. || **2** elemento contrarrevolucionario.
countersign | 'kauntəsaɪn | *v.t.* refrendar, aprobar, dar la aprobación.
countess | 'kauntɪs | *s.c.* condesa (título nobiliario).
countless | 'kauntlɪs | *adj.* sin cuento, incontable, innumerable.
country | 'kʌntrɪ | *s.c.* **1** país, nación, territorio nacional. || *s.sing.* **2 [the –]** la nación (la población). **3 [the –]** el campo (opuesto a la ciudad). || *adj.* **4** rural, del campo. **5** MUS. country (tipo de música americana). || *s.i.* **6** región, distrito, territorio: *this is lake country = ésta es región de lagos.* || **7 a – cousin,** (fam.) un alcornoque, un provinciano, un pueblerino (ignorante de los modos de la ciudad). **8 across –,** a través del campo (sin utilizar carreteras). **9 – and western,** MUS. música country. **10 – club,** club de campo. **11 – dancing,** (brit.) baile regional. **12 – house,** casa de campo (especialmente de alto nivel). **13 – seat,** casa solariega, finca (de alguien de la ciudad). **14 to go to the –,** (brit.) convocar elecciones generales. **15 one's line of –,** (fam.) tema en el que uno está puesto, asunto del que uno sabe mucho.
countryman | 'kʌntrɪmən | [*pl.* **countrymen**] *s.c.* **1** campesino, granjero. **2** compatriota.
countrymen | 'kʌntrɪmən | *pl.* de **countryman.**
countryside | 'kʌntrɪsaɪd | *s.i.* campo, campiña.
countrywoman | 'kʌntrɪwumən | [*pl.* **countrywomen**] *s.c.* campesina.
countrywomen | 'kʌntrɪwɪmɪn | *pl.* de **countrywoman.**
county | 'kauntɪ | *s.c.* **1** condado (como la provincia en España). || *adj.* **2** (fam. y brit.) pijo, de clase alta. || **3 – council,** POL. diputación provincial. **4 – town,** (brit.) capital de provincia. **5 – seat,** (EE.UU.) capital de provincia.
coup | kuː | *s.c.* POL. golpe de Estado. **2** golpe maestro. || **3 – de grace,** (form.) golpe de gracia. **4 – d'état,** POL. golpe de Estado.
coupé | 'kuːpeɪ | (EE.UU. **coupe**) *s.c.* cupé (coche).
couple | 'kʌpl | *s.c.* **1 [=N *v.sing./pl.*]** pareja. || *v.t.* **2 [to – + *o.* + to/together]** empalmar a, acoplar a (una cosa a otra). **3 [to – + *o.* + with]** unir con, asociar con (otro fenómeno, acción, etc.). || *v.i.* **4** (lit.) copular, copularse.
couplet | 'kʌplɪt | *s.c.* LIT. pareado.
coupling | 'kʌplɪŋ | *s.c.* e *i.* copulación, pareo (sexual).
coupon | 'kuːpɒn | *s.c.* **1** cupón, vale (de descuento, publicidad, etc.). **2** boleto (de apuestas).
courage | 'kʌrɪdʒ | *s.i.* **1** coraje, valentía, valor, intrepidez. || **2 to have the – of one's convictions,** tener el valor para poner en práctica las convicciones de uno. **3 to pluck up –,** V. **pluck. 4 to screw up one's –,** V. **screw. 5 to take –,** animarse, cobrar ánimo. **6 to take one's – in both hands,** armarse de valor (para algo de lo que uno tiene miedo).
courageous | kə'reɪdʒəs | *adj.* valiente, intrépido, arrojado.
courageously | kə'reɪdʒəslɪ | *adv.* valientemente, intrépidamente, arrojadamente.
courgette | kɔː'ʒet | *s.c.* (brit.) BOT. calabacín.
courier | 'kurɪər | *s.c.* **1** mensajero. **2** guía (de turismo).
course | kɔːs | *s.c.* **1** curso (educativo). **2** curso, dirección, rumbo. **3** GEOL. curso (de un río). **4** plato (de una comida). **5 [– of]** MED. tratamiento de, serie de (medicamento). **6** DEP. pista (de algunos deportes, como el golf). **7** forma de actuar, medida: *what course is the best now? = ¿cuál es la mejor forma de actuar ahora?* **8** ARQ. hilada. || *adv.* **9** (fam.) por supuesto, desde luego, claro. || *v.i.* **10** (lit.) recorrer, fluir (un líquido). || *s.sing.* **11 [the – of]** el curso de (la historia, el progreso, etc.). || **12 as a matter of –,** como algo muy normal, como algo muy corriente, sin nada especial. **13 – of action,** línea de actuación, forma de proceder, proceder. **14 in – of,** en vías de (cuando se está haciendo algo en ese momento). **15 in due –,** V. **due. 16 in the – of,** durante, en el transcurso de. **17 in the – of time,** con el transcurso del tiempo, con el paso del tiempo, a la larga. **18 in the ordinary/normal/etc. – of things/events/etc.,** como cosa normal, de una manera normal, siempre que no ocurra nada extraordinario. **19 of –,** por supuesto, ciertamente, claro, desde luego, naturalmente (expresando sorpresa, seguridad, afirmación, etc.). **20 of – not,** por supuesto que no, claro que no, desde luego que no, ciertamente que no. **21 off –,** despistado, fuera del rumbo correcto. **22 on –,** con el rumbo correcto; en su rumbo. **23 to run/take its –,** seguir su curso (de una manera natural). **24 to stick/stay the –,** aguantar hasta el final.
coursing | 'kɔːsɪŋ | *s.i.* caza con perros.
court | kɔːt | *s.c.* **1** DER. tribunal, juzgado, corte judicial. **2** patio. **3** DEP. pista (de tenis o similar). **4** corte (de un rey). || *v.t.* **5** (p.u.) cortejar, hacer la corte a. **6** exponerse a (un desastre, muerte, castigo, etc.). **7** (lit.) solicitar, procurar (favor, oportunidad, etc.). || *v.i.* **8** (p.u.) salir de novios, pasar el tiempo juntos en plan de novios. || **9 at –,** en la corte (de un rey). **10 – of appeal,** DER. tribunal de apelación. **11 – of inquiry,** comisión de investigación. **12 – of law,** DER. tribunal legal, corte de justicia. **13 to go to –/to take someone to –,** DER. acudir a los tribunales/llevar a alguien ante los tribunales. **14 to hold –,** lanzar las parrafadas de uno. **15 in –,** DER. en los tribunales. **16 to laugh someone out of –,** burlarse de las opiniones de alguien, poner en ridículo a alguien por sus opiniones. **17**

out of –, sin recurso a los tribunales, al margen de estos.
corteous | 'kɜːtɪəs | *adj.* **[– (to)]** atento, cortés, correcto.
courteously | 'kɜːtɪəslɪ | *adv.* atentamente, cortésmente, correctamente.
courtesan | ˌkɔːtɪ'zæn | (EE.UU.) | 'kɔːtɪzn | *s.c.* HIST. cortesana, meretriz.
courtesy | 'kɜːtəsɪ | *s.i.* **1** cortesía, buenas maneras, gentileza. || *s.pl.* **2** detalles de cortesía, atenciones. || **3 by – of,** (form.) gracias a, con permiso de. **4 – title,** título de cortesía.
courthouse | ˌkɔːthaus | *s.c.* (EE.UU.) DER. palacio de justicia.
courtier | 'kɔːtɪər | *s.c.* HIST. cortesano (acompañante de palacio).
courting | 'kɔːtɪŋ | *s.i.* cortejo (entre hombre y mujer).
courtliness | 'kɔːtlɪnɪs | *s.i.* fineza, cortesía.
courtly | 'kɔːtlɪ | *adj.* fino, detallista; distinguido.
court-martial | ˌkɔːt'mɑːʃl | [*pl.* **courts martial**] MIL. *s.c.* **1** consejo de guerra. || *v.t.* **2** llevar a un consejo de guerra.
courtroom | 'kɔːtrum | *s.c.* DER. sala de tribunal.
courtship | 'kɔːtʃɪp | *s.i.* cortejeo, galanteo, noviazgo.
courtyard | 'kɔːtjɑːd | *s.c.* patio.
cousin | 'kʌzn | *s.c.* **1** primo. **2** compañero, camarada, amigo. || **3 first – once removed,** V. **removed.**
couture | kuː'tuə | *s.i.* alta costura.
couturier | kuː'tuərɪeɪ | *s.c.* diseñador de moda.
cove | kəuv | *s.c.* GEOG. cala, caleta.
covenant | 'kʌvənənt | *s.c.* **1** DER. contrato, pacto. **2** (form.) contribución periódica a una obra de caridad. || **3 the Covenant,** REL. la Alianza.
Coventry | 'kɒvəntrɪ | **to send someone to –,** hacer a alguien el vacío, no querer tener nada que ver con alguien.
cover | 'kʌvər | *v.t.* **1** cubrir, tapar (poner encima). **2** cubrir, ocupar (una zona). **3** PER. informar sobre, cubrir la información sobre. **4** debatir, hablar sobre. **5** cubrir, recorrer (distancia). **6** MIL. proteger, escoltar. **7** hacer frente (a gastos económicos). **8** cubrir, revestir (con algo). **9** apuntar, tener cubierto (por un arma). **10** cubrir, incluir (un seguro, ciertos supuestos). **11** cubrir (un animal macho a una hembra). **12** aplicar, entrar en el ámbito de (una ley). || *s.c.* **13** cubierta, tapa, funda (de muchos objetos). **14** tapa, cubierta (de un libro). **15** tapadera (de algo deshonesto). || *s.i.* **16** refugio, escondite. **17** MIL. protección (aérea, antisubmarinista, etc.). **18** protección (de una póliza de seguros). **19** protección (arbustos o similar). || *s.pl.* **20 [the –]** la ropa de sobrecama. || **21 to be covered (with/in),** estar inundado (por), estar desbordado (por) (sentimientos, pasiones, etc.). **22 to break –,** abandonar el refugio, dejar la protección. **23 – charge,** pago extra (algunos establecimientos de lujo). **24 – girl,** PER. modelo de portada de revista. **25 to – up, a)** cubrir completamente, tapar por completo. **b)** tapar (escándalo o similar). **26 to take –,** refugiarse, ponerse a cubierto (del tiempo o fuego de armas). **27 under –,** bajo cubierto, bajo protección. **28 under – of,** bajo la protección de, al abrigo de. **29 under plain –,** en un sobre con sólo el nombre y la dirección (típico de las empresas). **30 under separate –,** por correo aparte.
coverage | 'kʌvərɪdʒ | *s.i.* PER. reportaje, cobertura.
covered | 'kʌvəd | *adj.* tapado, dentro de una funda, cubierto.
covering | 'kʌvərɪŋ | *s.c.* e *i.* **1** cubierta, envoltura. || **2 – letter,** carta acompañante, carta que acompaña (otro paquete, otra carta, etc.).
coverlet | 'kʌvəlɪt | *s.c.* (form.) colcha, sobrecama.
covert | 'kʌvət | (EE.UU.) | 'kəuvəːrt | *adj.* **1** (form.) secreto, furtivo, disimulado. || *s.c.* **2** espesura (vegetal).
covertly | 'kʌvətlɪ | (EE.UU.) | 'kəuvəːrtlɪ | *adv.* (form.) secretamente, furtivamente, disimuladamente.
cover-up | 'kʌvərʌp | *s.c.* encubrimiento, tapadera (de algo malo).
covet | 'kʌvɪt | *v.t.* (form.) codiciar, ambicionar.
covetous | 'kʌvɪtəs | *adj.* (form.) codicioso, ambicioso, avaricioso.
covetously | 'kʌvɪtəslɪ | *adv.* (form.) codiciosamente, ambiciosamente, avariciosamente.
covetousness | 'kʌvɪtəsnɪs | *s.i.* (form.) codicia, avaricia, ambición.
cow | kau | *s.c.* **1** vaca. **2** ZOOL. hembra (de animales grandes). **3** (fam.) adefesio de mujer, bruja. || *v.t.* **4** [normalmente *pas.*] acobardar, amedrentar, intimidar. || **5 till the cows come home,** hasta que las ranas críen pelo.
coward | 'kauəd | *s.c.* (desp.) cobarde.
cowardice | 'kauədɪs | *s.i.* (desp.) cobardía.
cowardly | 'kauədlɪ | *adj.* (desp.) cobarde.
cowboy | 'kaubɔɪ | *s.c.* **1** vaquero. **2** (brit. y fam.) pirata (en alguna profesión). || **3 cowboys and Indians,** vaqueros e indios (juego de niños).
cowed | kaud | *adj.* acobardado, amedrentado, intimidado.
cower | 'kauər | *v.i.* agazaparse con miedo, encogerse de temor.
cowhide | 'kauhaɪd | *s.i.* cuero de vaca, piel de vaca.
cowl | kaul | *s.c.* **1** ARQ. sombrerete (de chimenea). **2** capucha (especialmente del hábito de un monje).
cowman | 'kaumən | [*pl.* **cowmen**] *s.c.* vaquero.
cowmen | 'kaumən | *pl.* de **cowman.**
cowpat | 'kaupæt | *s.c.* boñiga.
cowshed | 'kauʃed | *s.c.* establo (para vacas).
cowslip | 'kauslɪp | *s.c.* BOT. prímula.
coy | kɔɪ | *adj.* **1** tímido, esquivo. **2** evasivo, reservado (que no quiere hablar).
coyly | 'kɔɪlɪ | *adv.* **1** tímidamente, esquivamente. **2** evasivamente, reservadamente.
coyness | 'kɔɪnɪs | *s.i.* **1** timidez, esquivez. **2** reserva, silencio.
coyote | kɔɪ'əutɪ | (EE.UU.) | 'kaɪəut *s.c.* ZOOL. coyote.
cozily V. **cosily.**
coziness V. **cosiness.**
cozy V. **cosy.**
crab | kræb | *s.c.* e *i.* cangrejo.
crab-apple | 'kræbæpl | *s.c.* e *i.* BOT. manzano silvestre.
crabbed | 'kræbd | | kræbd | *adj.* **1** apretado (forma de escribir). **2** (p.u.) malhumorado.
crabby | 'kræbɪ | *adj.* (fam.) malhumorado.
crabwise | 'kræbwaɪz | *adv.* con el movimiento del cangrejo.
crack | kræk | *v.t.* e *i.* **1** romper(se) un poco, hacer(se) una rajita. **2** crujir (sonido). || *v.t.* **3** darse un golpe fuerte en (parte del cuerpo). **4** contar (chistes). **5** abrir (rompiendo un huevo, nuez, etc.). **6** (fam.) solucionar (problemas, dificultades, etc.). **7** abrir (una caja fuerte). || *v.i.* **8** resquebrajarse, romperse (la voz). **9** romperse por dentro, trastornarse mentalmente. **10** traicionar (a uno los nervios). || *s.c.* **11** raja, hendidura, grieta. **12** chasquido, crujido (sonido). **13** descascarillado, pequeño imperfecto (en un objeto). **14** chascarrillo, chiste. **15 [– (at)]** (fam.) intento: *I'll take a crack at that game = haré un intento en ese juego.* | *s.i.* **16** (fam.) droga, crack. || *adj.* **17** de primera, superior, excelente: *a crack team = un equipo de primera.* || **18 a fair – of the whip,** una oportunidad en igualdad de condiciones. **19 at the – of dawn,** (fam.) al amanecer, a primera hora de la mañana. **20 to – down (on),** reprimir con fuerza, actuar duramente (contra). **21 – shot,** tirador de primera, tirador con una puntería excelente. **22 to – up,** hacerse pedazos (interiormente), desmoronarse, perder el control de los nervios. **23 to get cracking,** (fam.) poner manos a la obra, no estarse mano sobre mano. **24 to have a crack at,** (fam.) probar, intentar. **25 to paste/paper over the cracks,** poner una enorme tapadera, ocultar los defectos, correr un tupido velo (delante de algo negativo e incluso deshonesto). **26 something/someone is/was/etc. not all/everything they are cracked up to be,** (fam.) algo/alguien no es/fue/etc. todo lo que uno esperaba de ellos. **27 the – of doom,** el final del mundo: *I don't want to wait until the crack of doom = no quiero esperar hasta el fin del mundo.*
crackdown | 'krækdaun | *s.c.* **[– (on)]** medida de fuerza, medida enérgica.

cracked | krækt | *adj.* **1** con algún desperfecto, con algún pequeño descascarillado. **2** cascada (voz). **3** (fam.) loquete, chalado, (Am.) tarado.

cracker | 'krækər | *s.c.* **1** galletita (de aperitivo). **2** petardo. **3** cascanueces (objeto para hacer ruido en fiestas). **4** (fam. y brit.) maravilla, belleza (mujer o gesta deportiva). || **5 crackers,** (fam. y brit.) chiflado, ido.

cracking | 'krækɪŋ | (fam.) *adj.* **1** de primera, de fábula. || **2 at a – pace,** a una velocidad de aúpa.

crackle | 'krækl | *v.i.* **1** chisporrotear, crepitar. || *s.c.* e *i.* **2** chisporroteo.

crackling | 'kræklɪŋ | *s.i.* **1** ruido de chisporroteo, sonido de chisporroteo. **2** GAST. chicharrones.

crackpot | 'krækpɒt | (fam.) *s.c.* **1** tipo chiflado, tipo en las nubes. || *adj.* **2** alocado, chiflado (con ideas excéntricas).

crack-up | 'krækʌp | *s.c.* (fam.) desmoronamiento mental, ataque de nervios.

cradle | 'kreɪdl | *s.c.* **1** cuna (de bebé). **2** horquilla, gancho (de teléfono). **3** plataforma colgante (para pintar el exterior de algo, por ejemplo). **4 [the – of]** (fig.) el origen de, la cuna de: *this land is the cradle of the American Civil War = este territorio es la cuna de la Guerra Civil americana.* || *v.t.* **5** acunar, sostener en los brazos. || **6 from the – to the grave,** desde la cuna a la tumba, desde el nacimiento hasta la muerte.

cradle-snatcher | 'kreɪdlsnætʃər | *s.c.* (brit., fam. y desp.) viejales, viejo verde que va tras las jovencitas.

craft | krɑːft | (EE.UU.) | kræft | *s.c.* **1** trabajo manual, trabajo de artesanía. **2** ocupación, trabajo: *I haven't learnt the ins and outs of my craft = todavía no he aprendido los pormenores de mi trabajo.* **3** nave, embarcación (aérea o marítima). || *s.i.* **4** destreza manual, habilidad manual. **5** (p.u.) astucia, artimaña. || *v.t.* **6** (normalmente *pas.*) hacer con gran destreza: *the descriptions are beautifully crafted = las descripciones están bellísimamente escritas.*

craftily | 'krɑːftɪlɪ | (EE.UU.) | 'kræftɪlɪ | *adv.* (desp.) astutamente, de manera taimada, ladinamente.

craftiness | 'krɑːftɪnɪs | (EE.UU.) | 'kræftɪnɪs | *s.i.* (desp.) astucia, malas mañas.

craftsman | 'krɑːftsmən | (EE.UU.) | 'kræftsmən | [*pl.* **craftsmen**] *s.c.* **1** artesano, especialista en manualidades. 2 (fig.) maestro (en algo).

craftsmanship | 'krɑːftsmənʃɪp | (EE.UU.) | 'kræftsmənʃɪp | *s.i.* **1** artesanía. **2** acabado, calidad del acabado.

craftsmen | 'krɑːftsmən | (EE.UU.) | 'kræftsmən | *pl.* de **craftsman.**

craftswoman | 'krɑːftswʊmən | (EE.UU.) | 'kræftswʊmən | [*pl.* **craftswomen**] *s.c.* mujer artista (en artesanías).

craftswomen | 'krɑːftswɪmɪn | (EE.UU.) | 'kræftswɪmɪn | *pl.* de **craftswoman.**

crafty | 'krɑːftɪ | (EE.UU.) | 'kræftɪ | *adj.* (desp.) astuto, taimado, ladino.

crag | kræg | *s.c.* GEOG. despeñadero, risco.

craggy | 'krægɪ | *adj.* **1** escarpado, rocoso, peñascoso, escabroso (físicamente). **2** de facciones duras, de facciones marcadas.

cram | kræm | [*ger.* **cramming,** *pret.* y *p.p.* **crammed**] *v.t.* **1** llenar hasta arriba, atestar, abarrotar, meter (llenándolo hasta arriba): *I crammed all the children into the car = metí a todos los chicos en el coche.* || *v.i.* **2 [to – (for)]** (fam.) empollar (estudio).

crammed | kræmd | *adj.* **[– with/full of]** abarrotado de, hasta arriba de.

cramp | kræmp | *s.i.* **1** [también *pl.*] calambre (muscular). || *v.i.* **2** sufrir un calambre. || *v.t.* **3** entorpecer, restringir (un sentimiento, destreza, etc.) || **4 to – someone's style,** (fam.) cohibir, cortar las alas a alguien.

cramped | kræmpt | *adj.* **1** apretado, sin espacio libre, estrecho. **2** apretada, indescifrable (letra). || **3 – for room/space,** sin espacio libre alguno, como sardinas en lata.

cranberry | 'krænbərɪ | (EE.UU.) | 'krænberɪ | *s.c.* BOT. ráspano, arándano.

crane | kreɪn | *s.c.* ZOOL. grulla (ave). **2** MEC. grúa. || *v.t.* e *i.* **3** estirar(se) (normalmente el cuello o cabeza, queriendo ver algo).

cranefly | 'kreɪnflaɪ | *s.c.* ZOOL. típula (insecto).

crania | 'kreɪnɪə | *pl.* de **cranium.**

cranial | 'kreɪnɪəl | *adj.* craneal, craneano.

cranium | 'kreɪnɪəm | [*pl.* **craniums** o **crania**] *s.c.* BIOL. cráneo.

crank | kræŋk | *s.c.* **1** MEC. manivela, manubrio. **2** (desp.) maniático (en cualquier tema). || *v.t.* **3** mover mediante manivela. || **4 to – up/to – the engine,** arrancar un vehículo con un golpe de manivela.

crankshaft | 'kræŋkʃɑːft | (EE.UU.) | 'kræŋkʃæft | *s.c.* MEC. cigüeñal.

cranky | 'kræŋkɪ | *adj.* (fam. y desp.) **1** excéntrico, raro, estrafalario. **2** (EE.UU.) (vulg.) cabreado.

cranny | 'kænɪ | *s.c.* **1** raja minúscula, grieta pequeña (en pared, roca, etc.). **2 every nook and –,** V. **nook.**

crap | kræp | *s.i.* **1** (vulg.) mierda, caca. **2** (vulg. y fig.) mierda, caca (cosas que no sirven, libro, película, lo que otra persona dice, etc.). || *v.i.* **3** (vulg.) cagar. || *s.sing.* **4** (vulg.) cagada (acción). || **5 craps/–,** (EE.UU.) juego a dos dados.

crape V. **crepe.**

crappy | 'kræpɪ | *adj.* (vulg.) asqueroso, de mierda.

crash | kræʃ | *v.i.* **1** estrellarse, chocar (especialmente vehículo). **2** golpear con fuerza y ruido, estrellarse con fuerza y ruido: *the tree crashed on to the house = el árbol golpeó con fuerza y estrépito la casa.* **3** caer con fuerza y estrépito: *the glass crashed to the floor = el vaso cayó con fuerza y estrépito al suelo.* **4** COM. hundirse estrepitosamente (empresa). **5 [to – (out)]** retumbar con fuerza, oírse con gran estrépito. **6 [to – through]** abrirse paso violentamente, abrirse paso por en medio (de algo difícil de atravesar). **7** (fam. y EE.UU.) quedarse a dormir transitoriamente, pasar una noche como sea (en la casa de alguien). || *v.t.* **8** estrellar, chocar (un vehículo). **9** (fam.) colarse en, meterse sin ser invitado en. || *s.c.* **10** choque, colisión (de vehículos). **11** estrépito, estampido, estallido. **12** COM. quiebra súbita, bancarrota total. || **13 – barrier,** (brit.) valla protectora (no fija). **14 – course (in),** curso intensivo (en). **15 – helmet,** casco, casco protector (típico de un motorista).

crashing | 'kræʃɪŋ | *adj.* (fam. y desp.) perfecto, completo; inaguantable: *he's a crashing bore = es un perfecto aburrimiento.*

crashingly | 'kræʃɪŋlɪ | *adv.* (fam. y desp.) perfectamente, completamente; inaguantablemente.

crash-landing | ˌkræʃ'lændɪŋ | *s.c.* AER. aterrizaje de emergencia, aterrizaje forzoso.

crass | kræs | *adj.* (form. y desp.) **1** craso, completo. **2** estúpido, insensato.

crassly | 'kræslɪ | *adv.* (form. y desp.) **1** completamente, por completo. **2** estúpidamente, insensatamente.

crassness | 'kræsnɪs | *s.i.* (form. y desp.) **1** enormidad (de un error, comentario, etc.). **2** estupidez, insensatez.

crate | kreɪt | *s.c.* **1** caja de madera, cajón de embalaje, (Am.) jaba. **2** caja, cajón (para botellas de todo tipo). **3** (fam.) armatoste, cacharro (coche o avión viejo). || *v.t.* **4** embalar (en caja). || **5 to – up,** embalar totalmente, hacer un embalaje completo de (un objeto).

crater | 'kreɪtər | *s.c.* GEOL. cráter.

cravat | krə'væt | *s.c.* fular, pañuelo de cuello (para hombres).

crave | kreɪv | *v.t.* **1** ansiar, anhelar. || *v.i.* **2 [to – for]** ansiar, anhelar.

craven | 'kreɪvn | *adj.* (form. y desp.) amilanado, acobardado, pusilánime.

cravenly | 'kreɪvnlɪ | *adv.* (form. y desp.) acobardadamente, con pusilanimidad.

craving | 'kreɪvɪŋ | *s.c.* **1[– (for/*inf.*)]** anhelo, ansia, deseo fuerte.

crawl | krɔːl | *v.i.* **1** reptar, andar a gatas, arrastrarse. **2** marchar lentísimamente, andar a paso de tortuga (vehículos). **3 [to – (to)]** (desp. y fam.) hacer la pelota; humillarse. || *s.sing.* **4 [a –]** un paso de tortuga, una marcha lentísima (en un vehículo). **5 [the –]** DEP. el crol (forma de nadar). || **6 to make one's skin –,** (fam.) ponerle la carne de gallina a uno, dar repeluz a uno (de asco).

crawler | 'krɔːlər | *s.c.* (fam. y desp.) pelota, tipo servil.

crawling | 'krɔːlɪŋ | *adj.* **1 [– with]** (fam.) infectado de, abarrotado de, atestado de. **2** reptante, que se arrastra por el suelo.

crayfish | 'kreɪfɪʃ | [*pl.* **crayfish**] *s.c.* ZOOL. ástaco, cangrejo de río.

crayon | 'kreɪən | *s.c.* e *i.* **1** lápiz de color. || *v.t.* e *i.* **2** dibujar con lápices de colores.

craze | kreɪz | *s.c.* furor, delirio (moda pasajera).

crazed | kreɪzd | *adj.* **1** enajenado, enloquecido. **2** agrietado, cuarteado (superficie).

crazily | 'kreɪzɪlɪ | *adv.* locamente, lunáticamente, alocadamente.

craziness | 'kreɪzɪnɪs | *s.i.* locura.

crazy | 'kreɪzɪ | (fam.) *adj.* **1** loco, lunático, majareta. **2 [– about]** loco por, interesadísimo por, chalado por (algo o alguien). || *s.c.* **3** (EE.UU.) loco, chalado. || **4 – paving,** (brit.) empedrado irregular, enlosado irregular. **5 to drive/make someone –,** volver a alguien loco, volver a alguien majara. **6 like –,** (fam.) como un loco (forma de trabajar, correr y otras acciones).

creak | kriːk | *v.t.* e *i.* **1** rechinar, chirriar. || *s.c.* **2** chirrido.

creakily | 'kriːkɪlɪ | *adv.* con sonidos chirriantes.

creaking | 'kriːkɪŋ | *s.c.* e *i.* sonidos chirriantes.

creaky | 'kriːkɪ | *adj.* chirriante, crujiente.

cream | kriːm | *s.i.* **1** nata, crema (natural o artificial). **2** crema (cutánea). **3** crema (color). || *s.c.* **4** bollo con nata, pastel de crema. || *s.sing.* **5 [a –]** GAST. crema (mezcla de líquido y sólido). **6 [the – (of)]** (fig.) la élite, la crema y nata. || *adj.* **7** de color crema. || *v.t.* **8 [to – +** *o.* **+ (with)]** GAST. batir, hacer crema de (mezclas). || **9 – cheese,** GAST. queso blanco de nata. **10 – cracker,** GAST. galleta salada. **11 to – off,** separar, seleccionar (de entre muchos para un trato especial): *here we never cream off the best pupils for intensive lessons = aquí nunca seleccionamos a los mejores alumnos para darles lecciones intensivas.* **12 – of tartar,** QUIM. crémor tártaro. **13 – tea,** (brit.) té con bollos.

creamy | 'kriːmɪ | *adj.* **1** cremoso, como crema. **2** lleno de nata, lleno de crema.

crease | kriːs | *v.t.* e *i.* **1** arrugar(se), hacer(se) arrugas (ropa especialmente). **2** arrugar (alguna parte de la cara). || *s.c.* **3** raya (de los pantalones). || *s.pl.* **4** arrugas (de ropa, cara, etc.). || *v.t.* **5** (fam.) hacer reír. || **6 to – up,** (fam.) hacer desternillarse de risa.

creased | kriːst | *adj.* arrugado (ropa o parecido).

create | kriː'eɪt | *v.t.* **1** crear. **2** crear, causar, producir (consecuencia, resultado, pensamiento, imagen, etc.). **3** crear, inventar (cualquier cosa o fenómeno). || *v.i.* **4** (brit. y fam.) armar un follón, cogerse un enfado ruidoso.

creation | kriː'eɪʃn | *s.i.* **1 [– (of)]** creación, producción. **2 [the –]** REL. la creación. **3** ASTR. creación, universo, cosmos. || *s.c.* **4** creación, producción artística, producto de arte. **5** (fig. y a veces hum.) creación, imagen, cosa (cualquier cosa que se hace).

creative | kriː'eɪtɪv | *adj.* **1** creativo, imaginativo (especialmente en el arte). **2** inventivo, creativo, novedoso.

creatively | kriː'eɪtɪvlɪ | *adv.* **1** creativamente, imaginativamente (en el arte). **2** inventivamente, creativamente, novedosamente.

creativity | ˌkriːeɪ'tɪvɪtɪ | *s.i.* creatividad.

creator | krɪː'eɪtər | *s.c.* **1** creador, inventor. || **2 the Creator,** REL. el Creador.

creature | 'kriːtʃər | *s.c.* **1** criatura. **2** (lit.) criatura, persona, hombre, mujer (enfatizando una cualidad): *she's a beautiful creature = es una mujer bellísima.* || **3 a – of habit,** V. **habit. 4 – comforts,** las comodidades necesarias de la vida (cama caliente, un techo, etc.). **5 somebody's –,** (form. y desp.) el instrumento de alguien, el lacayo de alguien.

crèche | kreɪʃ | | kreʃ | *s.c.* (brit.) casa cuna, jardín de infancia.

credence | 'kriːdns | *s.i.* (form.) crédito, credibilidad.

credentials | krɪ'denʃlz | *s.pl.* **1** credenciales, documentos de identidad. **2** (fig.) credenciales, referencias, méritos (como reputación).

credibility | ˌkredə'bɪlɪtɪ | *s.i.* **1** credibilidad, verosimilitud. || **3 – gap,** inconsistencia, incoherencia.

credible | 'kredəbl | *adj.* convincente, creíble, verosímil (algo o alguien).

credibly | 'kredəblɪ | *adv.* convincentemente, creíblemente, verosímilmente.

credit | 'kredɪt | *s.i.* **1** COM. crédito. **2** crédito, solvencia, confianza (en que se devolverá lo que se debe): *his credit is no longer good = el crédito de él no es firme.* **3 [– (for)]** fama, honor, crédito, reconocimiento público. **4** credibilidad, crédito. || *s.c.* **5** FIN. ingreso, asiento. **6** crédito, punto (en el sistema de Educación Superior). || *s.pl.* **7** TV. títulos de crédito (también en el cine, música, etc.). || *adj.* **8** en números negros, con crédito. || *v.t.* **9 [to – +** *o.* **+ (to/with)]** FIN. abonar en, ingresar en (cuenta). **10 [to – +** *o.* **+ with]** atribuir el mérito de, reconocer: *these savages credit us with all sorts of powers = estos salvajes nos atribuyen el mérito de tener todo tipo de poderes.* **11 [to – +** *o.* **+ to/with]** reconocer (pagos, contribuciones, etc.). **12** creer, dar crédito a. || **13 a – to,** un orgullo para. **14 to be credited with/to,** atribuírsele (la autoría de una obra de arte, el comienzo de un partido político u otra acción notable). **15 – account,** FIN. credicuenta, cuenta a crédito. **16 – card,** FIN. tarjeta de crédito. **17 – note,** COM. nota de crédito. **18 – rating,** COM. límite de crédito. **19 – transfer,** FIN. transferencia bancaria. **20 to do someone –,** decir mucho a favor de alguien. **21 to give someone – for,** creer a alguien con, dar a alguien crédito por, conceder crédito a alguien por: *I gave you credit for mo[re] capacity of effort = yo te creía con má[s] capacidad para el esfuerzo.* **22 in –,** FIN. en números negros, con superávit. **23 on –,** a crédito, a plazos. **24 on the – side,** en el haber (en cuanto a virtudes, cualidades, etc.). **25 to one's –,** en el haber de uno. **26 to someone's –,** en el haber de alguien, a favor de alguien.

creditable | 'kredɪtəbl | *adj.* **1** magnífico, excelente, digno de crédito. **2** respetable, loable (conducta).

creditably | 'kredɪtəblɪ | *adv.* **1** magníficamente, excelentemente. **2** loablemente, respetablemente.

creditor | 'kredɪtər | *s.c.* COM. acreedor.

credit-worthiness | 'kredɪtwɜːθɪnɪs | *s.i.* solvencia.

credit-worthy | 'kredɪtwɜːθɪ | *adj.* solvente.

credo | 'kriːdəʊ | | 'kreɪdəʊ | *s.c.* (form.) credo (político, social, etc.).

credulity | krɪ'djuːlətɪ | (EE.UU.) | krɪ'duːlətɪ | *s.i.* credulidad.

credulous | 'kredjʊləs | (EE.UU.) | 'kredʒələs | *adj.* crédulo.

creed | kriːd | *s.c.* **1** credo (conjunto de creencias). **2** REL. credo, doctrina religiosa. || **3 the Creed,** REL. el Credo.

creek | kriːk | *s.c.* **1** (brit.) cala, ensenada. **2** (EE.UU.) riachuelo, arroyo. || **3 up the –,** (fam.) en apuros, con apuros, con el agua al cuello.

creel | kriːl | *s.c.* cesta de pescador.

creep | kriːp | *v.i.* [*pret.* y *p.p.irreg.* **crept**] **1** deslizarse, arrastrarse, moverse (sin apenas ruido). **2** (lit.) avanzar imperceptiblemente (nube, sombra, etc.). **3 [to – into]** (lit.) deslizarse dentro de, meterse subrepticiamente dentro de (el pensamiento, corazón, alma, etc.). **4 [to – up]** trepar (plantas). || *s.c.* **5** (fam.) cobista, pelotillero. || **6 to – in,** entrar poco a poco, penetrar poco a poco (una costumbre, palabra nueva, etc.). **7 to – up on, a)** acercarse inadvertidamente a, aproximarse sigilosamente a (alguien). **b)** penetrar poco a poco en, insinuarse gradualmente, comenzar a notarse (un sentimiento o sensación). **8 to give one the creeps,** (fam.) **a)** poner a uno enfermo, poner a uno malo, dar a uno asco (otra persona). **b)** dar a uno pavor, sobrecoger a uno de miedo, horripilar a uno. **9 to make one's flesh –,** (fam.) poner a uno la carne de gallina.

creeper | 'kriːpər | *s.c.* BOT. planta trepadora.

creeping | 'kriːpɪŋ | *adj.* **1** trepadora (cualquier planta con esa característica). **2** progresivo, gradual (que ocurre poco a poco).

creepy | ˈkriːpɪ | *adj.* (fam.) tétrico, horripilante.

creepy-crawly | ˌkriːpɪˈkrɔːlɪ | *s.c.* (fam.) bicho, insecto.

cremate | krɪˈmeɪt | *v.t.* incinerar (cadáver).

cremation | krɪˈmeɪʃn | *s.c.* incineración (servicio funerario).

crematoria | ˌkreməˈtɔːrɪə | *pl.* de **crematorium.**

crematorium | ˌkreməˈtɔːrɪəm | [*pl.* **crematoria** o **crematoriums**] *s.c.* horno crematorio.

creole | ˈkriːəʊl | *s.c.* **1** francés criollo, criollo (idioma). **2** HIST. criollo.

creosote | ˈkrɪəsəʊt | *s.i.* **1** QUIM. creosota (para la madera). || *v.t.* **2** pintar con creosota, recubrir con creosota.

crepe | kreɪp | (también **crape**) *s.i.* **1** crespón (tejido). **2** crepé (en zapatos). || **3 – paper,** papel de crepé.

crept | krept | *pret.* y *p.p.irreg.* de **creep.**

crescendi | krɪˈʃendiː | *pl.* de **crescendo.**

crescendo | krɪˈʃendəʊ | [*pl.* **crescendos** o **crescendi**] *s.c.* **1** MUS. crescendo. **2** (fig. y lit.) punto álgido, punto cumbre. || *adj.* y *adv.* **3** en crescendo.

crescent | ˈkresnt | *s.c.* **1** calle (curvada). **2** casas (en una calle curvada). **3** semicírculo, forma de media luna. || **4 the Crescent,** REL. (fig.) la Media Luna.

cress | kres | *s.i.* BOT. mastuerzo, berro.

crest | krest | *s.c.* **1** cresta (de ola). **2** cresta (en la cabeza de ciertos pájaros). **3** cimera, blasón (en la heráldica). || **4 on the – of a wave,** en la cresta de la ola (en un momento de gran éxito).

crested | ˈkrestɪd | *adj.* con cresta (pájaro).

crestfallen | ˈkrestfɔːlən | *adj.* abatido, alicaído, cabizbajo.

cretin | ˈkretɪn | (EE.UU.) | ˈkriːtn | *s.c.* subnormal (uso ofensivo).

cretinous | ˈkretɪnəs | (EE.UU.) | kriːtɪnəs | *adj.* subnormal.

crevasse | krɪˈvæs | *s.c.* GEOL. fisura de glaciar, grieta de glaciar.

crevice | ˈkrevɪs | *s.c.* hendedura, grieta rocosa.

crew | kruː | *s.c.* **1** [=N *v.sing./pl.*] tripulación (de barco, avión, etc.). **2** [=N *v.sing./pl.*] equipo técnico, equipo de especialistas. **3** (desp.) pandilla, banda. || **4 – cut,** corte de pelo a cepillo, corte de pelo a rape.

crewman | ˈkruːmən | [*pl.* **crewmen**] *s.c.* tripulante.

crewmen | ˈkruːmən | *pl.* de **crewman.**

crib | krɪb | *s.c.* **1** (EE.UU.) cuna. **2** [– (from)] plagio, copia. **3** chuleta (de la que copiar). **4** REL. nacimiento de Cristo (escena de la Navidad). || *v.t.* e *i.* **5** (desp.) copiar, plagiar. || *s.i.* **6** V. **cribbage.**

cribbage | ˈkrɪbɪdʒ | *s.i.* juego de cartas.

crick | krɪk | *v.t.* **1** dar dolor en, causar tortícolis (el cuello o espalda). || *s.c.* **2** dolor, tortícolis.

cricket | ˈkrɪkɪt | *s.i.* **1** DEP. cricket (juego parecido al béisbol). || *s.c.* **2** ZOOL. grillo. || **3 not –,** (p.u. y brit.) no es juego limpio.

cricketer | ˈkrɪkɪtər | *s.c.* DEP. jugador de cricket.

crier | ˈkraɪər | (también **town crier**) *s.c.* pregonero.

crikey | ˈkraɪkɪ | *interj.* (brit., fam. y p.u.) pardiez, vaya, toma ya (sorpresa).

crime | kraɪm | *s.c.* e *i.* **1** crimen, delito, fechoría (castigable). **2** (fig.) crimen, acción feísima.

criminal | ˈkrɪmɪnl | *adj.* **1** criminal, delictivo. **2** (fig.) fatal, horrible, criminal. || *s.c.* **3** criminal, delincuente.

criminality | ˌkrɪmɪˈnælətɪ | *s.i.* criminalidad, delincuencia.

criminally | ˈkrɪmɪnəlɪ | *adv.* **1** criminalmente, delictivamente. **2** (fig.) fatalmente, horriblemente, criminalmente.

criminologist | ˌkrɪmɪˈnɒlədʒɪst | *s.c.* criminalista, experto en criminología.

criminology | ˌkrɪmɪˈnɒlədʒɪ | *s.i.* criminología.

crimp | krɪmp | *v.t.* **1** rizar (pelo). **2** ondular (tejidos, platos de comida, etc.).

crimped | krɪmpt | *adj.* **1** rizado (pelo). **2** ondulado (algún objeto o cosa).

crimson | ˈkrɪmzn | *adj.* **1** carmesí (color). **2** rojo, enrojecido (de ira o vergüenza). || *s.i.* **3** color carmesí.

cringe | krɪndʒ | *v.i.* **1** agacharse, encogerse, recular (con miedo). **2** (fig.) encogerse (por la vergüenza).

crinkle | ˈkrɪŋkl | *v.t.* e *i.* **1** plegar(se), arrugar(se) un poco. || *s.c.* **2** (normalmente *pl.*) pliegue, arruga leve (en la piel u otra superficie).

crinkled | ˈkrɪŋkld | *adj.* plegado, arrugado (cualquier objeto o superficie).

crinkly | ˈkrɪŋklɪ | *adj.* en pliegues, con pequeñas arrugas.

crinoline | ˈkrɪnəlɪn | *s.c.* (p.u.) miriñaque (usado debajo de faldas).

cripple | ˈkrɪpl | *s.c.* **1** lisiado, tullido, inválido. **2** desfavorecido (socialmente); inválido (mental). || *v.t.* **3** tullir, lisiar, dejar inválido. **4** (form. o lit.) aherrojar, incapacitar, paralizar (una organización, estado, etc.).

crippled | ˈkrɪpld | *adj.* **1** inválido, tullido. **2** (fig.) incapacitado, paralizado (país, organización, etc.) || **3 the –,** los tullidos, los inválidos, los incapacitados.

crippling | ˈkrɪplɪŋ | *adj.* **1** incapacitadora, que deja inválido (enfermedad, accidente, etc.). **2** paralizante, agobiante, demoledor (impuesto, precio, etc.).

crises | ˈkraɪsiːz | *pl.* de **crisis.**

crisis | ˈkraɪsɪs | *s.c.* e *i.* **1** crisis, emergencia. || *s.c.* **2** crisis, punto crucial (en la vida o similar).

crisp | krɪsp | *adj.* **1** crujiente, tostado, frito en su punto (de comida). **2** fresco y crujiente (verdura y fruta). **3** sin arrugas, fino (papel); bien planchada (ropa). **4** firme, duro (aunque esté algo quebradizo, especialmente con nieve o escarcha). **5** vigorizante (tiempo, viento, etc.). **6** sucinto (escrito o discurso). **7** (desp.) brusco, desconsiderado (persona). || **8 burnt to a –,** quemado, tostado (especialmente por el sol). **9 crisps,** (brit.) patatas fritas (de paquete), (Am.) papas fritas.

crisply | ˈkrɪsplɪ | *adv.* **1** sucintamente (en palabras). **2** (desp.) bruscamente, desconsideradamente.

crispness | ˈkrɪspnɪs | *s.i.* **1** vigor (en el tiempo, viento, etc.). **2** precisión (en el lenguaje). **3** (desp.) brusquedad, desconsideración. **4** (lo) tostado, (lo) bien frito.

crispy | ˈkrɪspɪ | *adj.* churruscadito (bien frito).

criss-cross | ˈkrɪskrɒs | *v.t.* e *i.* **1** cruzar de un lado a otro, ir de aquí para allá. || *adj.* **2** entrecruzado, enmarañado (diseño o patrón). || *s.c.* **3** red de líneas cruzadas, entrecruzamiento.

criteria | kraɪˈtɪərɪə | *pl.* de **criterion.**

criterion | kraɪˈtɪərɪən | [*pl.* **criteria**] *s.c.* criterio, norma (por la que uno juzga).

critic | ˈkrɪtɪk | *s.c.* **1** ART. crítico (de cualquier tipo de arte). **2** crítico, oponente, contrario.

critical | ˈkrɪtɪkl | *adj.* **1** crítico, crucial (momento o situación). **2** [– (of)] crítico, censurador. **3** peligroso (especialmente de enfermedades). **4** LIT. crítico. **5** analítico (forma de ver el mundo o un acontecimiento).

critically | ˈkrɪtɪklɪ | *adv.* **1** críticamente, crucialmente (importancia). **2** críticamente, censuradoramente. **3** peligrosamente, arriesgadamente. **4** analíticamente (estudiar, ver, pensar, etc.).

criticise V. **criticize.**

criticism | krɪtɪsɪzəm | *s.c.* e *i.* **1** crítica, censura, comentario crítico. **2** LIT. crítica literaria.

criticize | ˈkrɪtɪsaɪz | (también **criticise**) *v.t.* **1** criticar, censurar. **2** analizar, evaluar.

critique | krɪˈtiːk | *s.c.* LIT. crítica, escrito crítico, ensayo crítico, análisis (de cualquier fenómeno).

croak | krəʊk | *v.i.* **1** croar (rana); graznar (cuervo). **2** hablar como graznando, hablar con voz ronca, gruñir. **3** (fam.) estirar la pata, diñarla. || *v.t.* **4** decir con voz ronca, gruñir. || *s.c.* **5** graznido (cuervo); canto (rana). **6** gruñido, sonido ronco (hablando).

crochet | ˈkrəʊʃeɪ | (EE.UU.) | krəʊˈʃeɪ | *s.i.* **1** labor de ganchillo, croché. || *v.t.* e *i.* **2** hacer labor de ganchillo, hacer en croché.

crock | krɒk | *s.c.* **1** [– (of)] olla de barro, tarro de barro. **2** (normalmente *pl.*) loza, objetos de loza. **3** (fam. y brit.) cacharro (vehículo). **4** (fam. y brit.) viejales, carcamal.

crockery | ˈkrɒkərɪ | *s.i.* loza, vasija de loza.

crocodile | ˈkrɒkədaɪl | *s.c.* **1** ZOOL. cocodrilo. **2** (brit. y fam.) fila de escolares. || **3 – tears,** lágrimas de cocodrilo.

crocus | 'krəukəs | *s.c.* BOT. azafrán.
croissant | 'krwʌsɑŋ | *s.c.* cruasán.
crone | krəun | *s.c.* (fam. y desp.) arpía, vieja bruja.
crony | 'krəunɪ | *s.c.* (fam. y desp.) amigote, compinche.
crook | kruk | *s.c.* **1** (fam.) maleante, tramposo, ladrón. **2** báculo, cayado (especialmente el de un obispo). **3 [– of]** curva de, pliegue de, recodo de (un brazo, camino, río, etc.). || *v.t.* **4** doblar, torcer (especialmente un dedo o el brazo). || **5 by hook or by =N,** V. **hook.**
crooked | 'krukɪd | *adj.* **1** doblado, encorvado, torcido (objeto cuerpo). **2** (fam.) deshonesto, tramposo, corrupto. **3** torcida (sonrisa).
crookedly | 'krukɪdlɪ | *adv.* **1** encorvadamente, torcidamente. **2** corruptamente, tramposamente, deshonestamente. **3** torcidamente (sonreír).
crookedness | 'krukɪdnɪs | *s.i.* **1** sinuosidad (física). **2** deshonestidad, corrupción, trampa.
croon | kru:n | *v.t.* e *i.* **1** cantar dulcemente, cantar melodiosamente, cantar susurrando. **2** decir suavemente, hablar en voz baja y susurrante.
crooner | 'kru:nər | *s.c.* cantante de canciones melódicas y susurrantes (especialmente en los años 30 y 40).
crop | krɒp | *s.c.* **1** AGR. cultivo. **2** AGR. cosecha. **3** (fam. y hum.) montón, lote: *a thick crop of hair = un montón de pelo fuerte.* **4** buche (de algunas aves). || *v.t.* **5** AGR. cosechar, sacar cosechas de. **6** AGR. cultivar, llevar a cabo el cultivo de. **7** recortar (una foto, por ejemplo). **8** cortar muy corto (el pelo). **9** pacer, comer (animales). || *v.i.* **10** dedicarse a producir, dedicarse a cosechar. || *s.sing.* **11 [a –]** un corte de pelo corto. || **12 to – up,** (fam.) surgir, aparecer, salir (normalmente un problema o dificultad).
cropper | 'krɒpər | *s.c.* **1** cultivo: *a bad cropper.* || **2 to come a –,** (fam.) **a)** darse un porrazo, coger una liebre. **b)** fallar estrepitosamente, fracasar, salir fatal.
croquet | 'krəukeɪ | *s.i.* DEP. croquet.
croquette | krəu'ket | *s.c.* GAST. croqueta.
cross | krɒs | (EE.UU.) | krɔ:s | *s.c.* **1** cruz. **2** (fig.) cruz, carga pesada vital. **3** cruce, híbrido (animal o planta). **4** cruz, señal (en escrito). || *v.t.* e *i.* **5** cruzar (un espacio). **6** entrecruzar(se), cruzar(se) (caminos o parecido). || *v.t.* **7** cruzar, pasar por, pasar cruzando por. **8** cruzar (una expresión momentáneamente por la cara). **9** vencer, cruzar (obstáculos, impedimentos sociales, prejuicios, etc.). **10** cruzar (piernas o brazos). **11** FIN. cruzar (cheque). **12** (form. o lit.) irritar, cruzarse en el camino de (alguien). **13** BIOL. cruzar (animales o plantas). || *v.r.* **14** REL. santiguarse, hacer la señal de la cruz. || *adj.* **15** enfadado, enojado, malhumorado. || **16 to be cut on the –,** ser cortado al sesgo (tejido). **17 – my heart,** V. **heart. 18 to – off/out,** tachar (en un escrito). **19 to – one's fingers,** cruzar los dedos de uno. **20 to – one's mind,** pasar por la cabeza, pasar por la mente. **21 to – someone's palm with silver,** V. **palm. 22 to – someone's path,** V. **path. 23 to – that bridge when one comes to it,** V. **bridge. 24 the Cross,** REL. la Cruz, el Crucifijo.
crossbar | 'krɒsbɑ:r | (EE.UU.) | 'krɔ:sbɑ:r | *s.c.* **1** larguero (de una portería). **2** tubo horizontal (de una bicicleta).
crossbones | 'krɒsbəunz | (EE.UU.) 'krɔ:sbəunz | V. **skull and crossbones.**
crossbow | 'krɒsbəu | (EE.UU.) | 'krɔ:sbəu | *s.c.* ballesta.
cross-check | ˌkrɒs'tʃek | (EE.UU.) | ˌkrɔ:s'tʃek | *v.t.* comprobar varias veces.
cross-country | ˌkrɒs'kʌntrɪ | (EE.UU.) | ˌkrɔ:s'kʌntrɪ | *adj.* y *adv.* **1** campo a través. || **2 – race,** DEP. carrera de cross, carrera de campo a través.
cross-examination | ˌkrɒsɪgzæmɪ'neɪʃn | (EE.UU.) | ˌkrɔ:sɪgˌzæmɪ'neɪʃn | *s.c.* e *i.* interrogatorio profundo, interrogatorio minucioso.
cross-examine | ˌkrɒsɪg'zæmɪn | (EE.UU.) ˌkrɔ:sɪg'zæmɪn | *v.t.* hacer un interrogatorio riguroso, preguntar toda clase de detalles.
cross-eyed | 'krɒsaɪd | (EE.UU.) | 'krɔ:saɪd | *adj.* bizco.
crossfire | 'krɒsfaɪər | (EE.UU.) | 'krɔ:sfaɪər | *s.i.* MIL. fuego cruzado. || **2 to be caught in the –,** quedar atrapado en medio (de una discusión o parecido).
crossing | 'krɒsɪŋ | (EE.UU.) | 'krɔ:sɪŋ | *s.c.* **1** cruce, lugar de cruce (para peatones). **2** MAR. travesía. **3** intersección, cruce (especialmente de carretera con vía férrea).
cross-legged | ˌkrɒs'legd | (EE.UU.) | ˌkrɔ:s'legd | *adj.* y *adv.* con las piernas cruzadas.
crossly | 'krɒslɪ | (EE.UU.) | 'krɔ:slɪ | *adv.* malhumoradamente, enfadadamente, airadamente.
crossness | 'krɒsnɪs | (EE.UU.) | 'krɔ:snɪs | *s.i.* mal humor, enfado.
cross-purposes | ˌkrɒs'pɜ:pəsɪz | (EE.UU.) ˌkrɔ:s'pɜ:pəsɪz | **at –,** en una situación de no escucharse mutuamente, sin entenderse.
cross-question | ˌkrɒs'kwestʃən | (EE.UU.) ˌkrɒs'kwestʃən | *v.t.* hacer todo tipo de preguntas.
cross-reference | ˌkrɒs'refrəns | (EE.UU.) ˌkrɔ:s'refrəns | *s.c.* **1** referencia cruzada (en libro). || *v.t.* **2** hacer referencias cruzadas en.
cross-roads | 'krɒsrəudz | (EE.UU.) | 'krɔ:srəudz | [*pl.* **cross-roads**] *s.c.* **1** cruce de carreteras. | **2 at a –,** en una encrucijada.
cross-section | ˌkrɒs'sekʃn | (EE.UU.) | ˌkrɔ:s'sekʃn | *s.c.* **1** corte transversal. **2 [– of]** muestra representativa de (opiniones o similar).
crosswind | 'krɒswɪnd | (EE.UU.) | 'krɔ:swɪnd | *s.c.* viento de costado.
crosswise | 'krɒswaɪz | (EE.UU.) | 'krɔ:swaɪz | *adv.* diagonalmente, transversalmente, al través.
crossword | 'krɒswɜ:d (EE.UU.) | 'krɔ:swɜ:d | (también **crossword puzzle**) *s.c.* crucigrama.
crotch | krɒtʃ | *s.c.* **1** ANAT. entrepierna, horcajadura. **2** entrepierna (de unos pantalones).
crotchet | 'krɒtʃɪt | *s.c.* MUS. negra.
crotchety | 'krɒtʃɪtɪ | *adj.* (fam.) caprichoso, inaguantable.
crouch | krautʃ | *v.i.* **1** acuclillarse, agazaparse. **2 [to – over]** doblarse sobre, inclinarse por encima de. || *s.c.* **3** posición de cuclillas.
croup | kru:p | *s.i.* MED. crup (tos y ahogos).
croupier | 'kru:pɪəɪ | *s.c.* crupier.
crow | krəu | *s.c.* **1** ZOOL. cuervo, grajo. || *v.i.* **2** cantar (el gallo). **3** emitir sonidos placenteros (bebés). **4 [to – over/ about]** (fam. y a veces desp.) exultar por, gozarse por. || **5 as the – flies,** en línea recta. **6 crow's feet,** patas de gallo.
crowbar | 'krəubɑ: | *s.c.* MEC. palanca.
crowd | kraud | *s.c.* **1** multitud, muchedumbre. **2** pandilla (de amigos). || *v.t.* **3** abarrotar, llenar hasta arriba. **4 [to – +** *o.* **+ in/into]** meter en (hasta llenar). **5** (fam.) vigilar, dar la lata, estar demasiado encima de. || *v.i.* **6 [to – about /round]** congregarse alrededor de, amontonarse alrededor de. **7 [to – in/into]** entrar en grupo en, meterse en grupo dentro de. || **8 a whole – of /crowds of/a – of,** (fam.) un montón de, una pila de. **9 to – in (on),** inundar a (alguien, recuerdos, sentimientos, etc.). **10 to – out,** dejar fuera aposta, dejar sin sitio a propósito. **11 to follow the –/to move with the –/to go with the –,** (fam. y desp.) seguir a la masa, hacer lo que hace la masa. **12 join the –!** (fam.) ¡ya eres uno de los nuestros! (cuando hay coincidencia de experiencia). **13 two's company three's a –,** V. **company.**
crowded | 'kraudɪd | *adj.* **1 [– (with)]** abarrotado, atestado. **2** apretado, apiñado (personas). **3 [– (with)]** (fig.) abarrotado (de sentimientos, ideas, etc.).
crowing | 'krəuɪŋ | *s.i.* canto (del gallo).
crown | kraun | *s.c.* **1** corona. **2** corona, adorno (de flores u otra cosa). **3** coronilla (de la cabeza). **4** copa (del sombrero). **5** cumbre (de colina). **6** corona (moneda). **7** MED. funda (de diente). || *s.sing.* **8** cumbre, cima (de una carrera, por ejemplo). || *v.t.* **9** coronar. **10** MED. poner una funda a (diente). **11** coronar, rematar (tarde, actuación, etc.). **12** (lit.) rematar, culminar (físicamente): *all those objects crowned with gold = todos esos objetos rematados con oro.* **13** (fam.) dar un capón, atizar un capón. || **14 – court,** (brit.) DER. tribunal con jurado. **15 crowned head,** (fig.) monarca. **16 – jewels,** joyas de la corona. **17 Crown Prince,** príncipe heredero. **18 Crown Princess, a)** princesa heredera. **b)** esposa del príncipe heredero. **19 to – it all,** para

colmo de desgracias, para remate. **20 the Crown,** POL. la Corona, la Monarquía.
crowning | 'kraʊnɪŋ | *adj.* supremo, más importante (libro, acción, etc.).
crucial | 'kru:ʃl | *adj.* crucial, esencial, fundamental.
crucially | 'kru:ʃəlɪ | *adv.* crucialmente, esencialmente, fundamentalmente.
crucible | 'kru:sɪbl | *s.c.* crisol.
crucifix | 'kru:sɪfɪks | *s.c.* crucifijo.
crucifixion | ˌkru:sɪ'fɪkʃn | *s.c.* e *i.* **1** crucifixión. || **2 the Crucifixion,** REL. la Crucifixión.
crucify | 'kru:sɪfaɪ | *v.t.* **1** crucificar. **2** (fam.) hacer pasar canutas, castigar el hígado, dejar hecho uno caca (indicando castigo).
crude | kru:d | *adj.* **1** tosco, simplón, imperfecto (objeto). **2** grosero, ordinario, vulgar. **3** (desp.) simplona, inculta (idea, proposición, etc.). || **4 – oil,** crudo.
crudely | 'kru:dlɪ | *adv.* **1** toscamente, imperfectamente (hecho). **2** groseramente, ordinariamente, vulgarmente. **3** (desp.) simplonamente, incultamente.
crudeness | 'kru:dnɪs | *s.i.* (desp.) simplonería, incultura.
crudity | 'kru:dɪtɪ | *s.i.* **1** tosquedad, ramplonería, imperfección (en objetos). **2** grosería, ordinariez, vulgaridad.
cruel | 'krʊəl | *adj.* **1 [– (to)]** cruel, despiadado. **2** inclemente, duro (mundo, tiempo, enfermedad, etc.).
cruelly | 'krʊəlɪ | *adv.* **1** cruelmente, despiadadamente. **2** inclementemente, duramente.
cruelty | 'krʊəltɪ | *adv.* **1** cruelmente, despiadadamente. **2** inclementemente, duramente.
cruelty | 'krʊəltɪ | *s.c.* e *i.* crueldad, barbaridad.
cruet | 'kru:ɪt | *s.c.* angarillas, vinagreras (de servicio de mesa).
cruise | kru:z | *v.i.* **1** hacer un crucero, viajar en un crucero. **2** circular a velocidad constante, andar a paso constante. || *s.c.* **3** MAR. crucero, viaje turístico por mar. || **4 – missile,** MIL. mísil de crucero.
cruiser | 'kru:zər | *s.c.* MAR. MIL. crucero.
crumb | krʌmb | *s.c.* **1** [normalmente *pl.*] miga, migaja. **2** migaja (de dinero, información, etc.). || **3 crumbs,** (brit. y p.u.) ¡mecachis!
crumble | 'krʌmbl | *v.t.* e *i.* **1** desmenuzar(se), desmigajar(se). || *v.i.* **2** desmoronarse, caer poco a poco (edificios antiguos o similar). **3** desintegrarse, deshacerse (algo intangible, como una organización). || *s.c.* **4** GAST. pastel al horno. || **5 that's the way the cookie crumbles** V. **cookie.**
crumbly | 'krʌmblɪ | *adj.* desmenuzable, fácil de deshacerse.
crummy | 'krʌmɪ | *adj.* (fam.) mísero, de mala muerte (baja calidad).
crumpet | 'krʌmpɪt | *s.c.* **1** GAST. buñuelo. || *s.i.* **2** tía buena (uso algo ofensivo hacia las mujeres).
crumple | 'krʌmpl | *v.t.* e *i.* **1** arrugar(se), estrujar(se). || *v.i.* **2** desplomarse (por fuerte emoción o parecido). || **3 to – up,** hacer una bola arrugada de (algún objeto).
crunch | krʌntʃ | *v.t.* e *i.* **1** masticar ruidosamente. **2** hacer un ruido ronzante (como de ser aplastado, por ejemplo, el cristal). || *s.c.* **3** sonido de aplastamiento de cristal, crujido. || **4 when/if it comes to the –,** (fam.) cuando llega el momento de la verdad.
crunchy | 'krʌntʃɪ | *adj.* crujiente (comida o superficie adecuada para un ruido como de crujir o aplastar).
crusade | kru:'seɪd | *s.c.* **1** HIST. cruzada. **2** (fig.) cruzada, lucha moral, campaña. || *v.i.* **3** emprender una cruzada.
crusader | kru:'seɪdər | *s.c.* **1** cruzado. **2** (fig.) cruzado, persona que hace campaña por una idea.
crush | krʌʃ | *v.t.* **1** apretar, aplastar, estrujar. **2** hacer polvo, convertir en polvo (físicamente). **3** aplastar, destrozar (al enemigo). **4** desolar, dejar destrozado (noticia mala o parecido). || *v.t.* e *i.* **5** arrugar(se) (ropa, papel, etc.). || *s.c.* **6** gentío, muchedumbre. **7 [– (on)]** (fam.) pasión voraz, amorío (típico de quinceañeras). || **8 to be crushed,** ser apretujado, ser aplastado, ser estrujado (físicamente). **9 – barrier,** (brit.) barrera de seguridad.
crushed | krʌʃt | *adj.* desolado, destrozado (por mala noticia o similar).
crushing | 'krʌʃɪŋ | *adj.* **1** devastadora (noticia o similar). **2** aplastante (victoria o parecido).
crust | krʌst | *s.c.* e *i.* **1** corteza (de pan). || *s.c.* **2** costra, capa exterior (de algo). **3** GEOL. corteza (terrestre).
crustacean | krʌ'steɪʃn | *s.c.* BIOL. crustáceo.
crusted | 'krʌstɪd | *adj.* **[– (with)]** cubierto con una costra.
crusty | 'krʌstɪ | *adj.* **1** de corteza dura, crujiente. **2** (fam.) irritable, áspero.
crutch | krʌtʃ | *s.c.* **1** muleta. **2** (fig.) sostén, soporte (persona). **3** V. **crotch.**
crux | krʌks | *s.sing.* **[the – of]** el quid de, el punto esencial de.
cry | kraɪ | *v.i.* **1** llorar (con algún ruido). **2** gritar, lanzar un grito, exclamar. **3 [to – out]** dar un grito fuerte, exclamar con fuerza. **4** lanzar aullidos (animales). || *s.c.* **5** grito, exclamación. **6** aullido (de animal). || *s.sing.* **7** llanto, sesión de llanto. || **8 a far – (from),** a millas de distancia, absolutamente distinto. **9 to – down,** (fam.) empequeñecer, desacreditar (lo que hace alguien). **10 to – off,** (fam.) rajarse (no querer hacer lo prometido). **11 to – oneself to sleep,** dormirse llorando, llorar tanto que uno se duerme. **12 to – one's eyes out,** darse una buena sesión de llorar, llorar como una magdalena. **13 to – out against,** ponerse violentamente en contra de, oponerse con fuerza a. **14 to – out for,** solicitar decididamente, exigir con fuerza. **15 for crying out loud,** (fam.) para echarse a llorar, de pena. **16 in full –, a)** apasionado con lo que decía, en la mitad de una apasionada charla. **b)** en plena persecución (animales).
cry-baby | 'kraɪbeɪbɪ | *s.c.* (fam. y desp.) llorica.
crying | 'kraɪɪŋ | *s.i.* **1** lloro, llanto. || *adj.* **2** perentorio, urgente (necesidad o similar). || **3 a – shame,** una vergüenza escandalosa.
crypt | krɪpt | *s.c.* ARQ. cripta.
cryptic | 'krɪptɪk | *adj.* enigmático, misterioso, críptico.
cryptically | 'krɪptɪklɪ | *adv.* enigmáticamente, misteriosamente, crípticamente.
crystal | 'krɪstl | *s.i.* **1** MIN. cristal. **2** cristal, cristal duro, cristal de calidad, vidrio (para objetos, como vasos). || *s.c.* **3** MIN. cristal. **4** joya, gema. **5** (EE.UU.) esfera (del reloj). || *adj.* **6** (lit.) transparente, purísimo. || **7 – ball,** bola de cristal (de las adivinas). **8 – clear, a)** puro, inmaculado (el aire, por ejemplo). **b)** clarísimo, evidente, sin lugar a ninguna duda.
crystalline | 'krɪstəlaɪn | *adj.* **1** QUIM. cristalino. **2** (fig.) cristalino, transparente, puro.
crystallization | ˌkrɪstəlaɪ'zeɪʃn | (EE.UU.) | ˌkrɪstə'lɪ'zeɪʃn | (también crystallisation) *s.i.* cristalización.
crystallize | 'krɪstəlaɪz | (también **crystallise**) *v.t.* e *i.* **1** cristalizar(se). **2** (fig.) cristalizar(se), cuajar(se), hacer(se), realidad.
crystallized | 'krɪstəlaɪzd | (también **crystallised**) *adj.* escarchada (fruta).
cub | kʌb | *s.c.* **1** cachorro (de felinos especialmente). **2** chaval explorador. || **3 – reporter,** PER. periodista en prácticas (joven). **4 – scout,** explorador (de 8 a 11 años).
Cuba | 'kju:bə | *s.sing.* Cuba.
Cuban | 'kju:bən | *adj.* **1** cubano. || *s.c.* **2** cubano.
cubby-hole | 'kʌbɪhəʊl | *s.c.* cuartito, chiribitil.
cube | kju:b | *s.c.* **1** GEOM. cuadrado. **2** trocito cuadrado, terrón (de azúcar). **3** MAT. cubo, tercera potencia. || *v.t.* **4** (normalmente pasiva) MAT. elevar al cubo. || **5 – root,** MAT. raíz cúbica.
cubic | 'kju:bɪk | *adj.* **1** GEOM. cúbico. **2** MAT. cúbico.
cubicle | 'kju:bɪkl | *s.c.* cubículo, compartimento (donde cambiarse la ropa o similar).
cubism | 'kju:bɪzəm | *s.i.* ART. cubismo.
cubist | 'kju:bɪst | *s.c.* ART. cubista.
cuckold | 'kʌkəʊld | (lit. o p.u.) *s.c.* **1** cornudo (marido). || *v.t.* **2** poner los cuernos a (marido).
cuckoo | 'kʊku: | *s.c.* ZOOL. cuclillo, cucú. || *adj.* **2** (fam.) como una cabra. || **3 –,** cucú (sonido). **4 – clock,** reloj de cucú.
cucumber | 'kju:kʌmbər | *s.c.* **1** BOT. pepino. || **2 as cool as a –,** (fam.) tan fres-

co como una lechuga (sin preocupación).

cud | kʌd | *s.i.* **1** bolo (de rumiantes). || **2 to chew the –, a)** rumiar. **b)** (fig.) rumiar, reflexionar,meditar.

cuddle | 'kʌdl | *v.t.* e *i.* **1** hacer mimos, abrazar con cariño, acurrucar. || *s.c.* **2** abrazo cariñoso, mimo, acción de acurrucar. || **3 to – up,** (fam.) acurrucarse.

cuddly | 'kʌdlɪ | *adj.* blando, que dan ganas de abrazarlo.

cudgel | 'kʌdʒl | *s.c.* **1** estaca, porra. || *v.t.* **2** aporrear, dar golpes repetitivos con una porra. **3** maltratar de palabra, insultar descaradamente. || **4 to – one's brains,** (fam.) devanarse los sesos (para recordar). **5 to take up/carry cudgels/the – (for),** salir en defensa (de), estar dispuestos a luchar (por).

cue | kjuː | *s.c.* **1** indirecta, aviso, indicación, señal (para hacer algo). **2** pie, apunte, entrada (del apuntador en teatro). **3** taco (de billar). || *v.t.* **4** dar entrada (a un actor). || **5 on –,** en el preciso instante, en el momento justo. **6 to take one's – (from),** seguir el ejemplo (de).

cuff | kʌf | *s.c.* **1** puño (de prenda de vestir). **2** (EE.UU.) vuelta, doblez (de pantalón). **3** (normalmente *pl.*) esposa, grillete. **4** (normalmente *sing.*) (fam.) torta. || *v.t.* **5** esposar, poner las esposas. **6** (fam.) dar una torta. || **7 off the –,** improvisadamente, sin pensarlo, de improviso.

cufflink | 'kʌflɪŋk | *s.c.* (normalmente *pl.*) gemelo (para el puño de la camisa).

cuisine | kwɪ'ziːn | *s.i.* cocina, estilo de cocinar.

cul-de-sac | 'kʌldəsæk | *s.c.* **1** callejón sin salida. || *s.sing.* **2** (fig.) lugar sin vida.

culinary | 'kʌlɪnərɪ | (EE.UU.) | 'kʌlɪnerɪ | *adj.* culinario.

cull | kʌl | *v.t.* **1 [to – + *o.* + (from)]** entresacar (información, ideas, etc.). **2** hacer una selección (matando a los animales débiles en un rebaño). || *s.c.* **3** selección, matanza de selección.

culminate | 'kʌlmɪneɪt | *v.i.* **[to – in]** culminar en, acabar en.

culmination | ˌkʌlmɪ'neɪʃn | *s.sing.* **[the – of]** la culminación de, el no va más de.

culottes | kjuː'lɒts | *s.pl.* **[(a pair of) –]** falda pantalón.

culpability | ˌkʌlpə'bɪlɪtɪ | *s.i.* (form.) culpabilidad.

culpable | 'kʌlpəbl | *adj.* (form.) culpable.

culprit | 'kʌlprɪt | *s.c.* culpable, reo, delincuente (persona o cosa).

cult | kʌlt | *s.c.* **1 [– (of)]** REL. culto. **2 [– (of)]** (fig.) culto, canonización (de algo o alguien).

cultivate | 'kʌltɪveɪt | *v.t.* **1** cultivar (tierra). **2** (fig.) fomentar, cultivar (sentimientos, ideas, etc.). **3** mejorar (los conocimientos intelectuales): *to cultivate one's mind = mejorarel intelecto.* **4** (desp.) ganarse la amis-tad de (para fines malos).

cultivated | 'kʌltɪveɪtɪd | *adj.* **1** cultivada, labrada (tierra). **2** refinado, educado (intelectualmente).

cultivation | ˌkʌltɪ'veɪʃn | *s.i.* **1** cultivo (de la tierra). **2 [– of]** cultivo de, fomento de, mejora de (ideas, sentimientos, etc.). **3 [– of]** (desp.) cultivo de (amistad para fines malos).

cultivator | 'kʌltɪveɪtər | *s.c.* **1** labrador. **2** MEC. máquina labradora.

cultural | 'kʌltʃərəl | *adj.* **1** cultural. **2** artístico, cultural. || **3 – desert,** (fam.) desierto cultural.

culturally | 'kʌltʃərəlɪ | *adv.* **1** culturalmente. **2** artísticamente.

culture | 'kʌltʃər | *s.c.* e *i.* **1** cultura, civilización: *different cultures.* | *s.i.* **2** cultura. **3** cultura, arte. **4** cultura, preparación (física, mental, etc.). **5** cultura, buena educación. || *s.c.* **6** cultura, civilización (concreta). **7** BIOL. cultivo (de distintos tipos de células y microorganismos). || *v.t.* **8** BIOL. cultivar, hacer cultivos de. || **9 – shock,** choque cultural, falta de acoplamiento a una cultura extraña.

cultured | 'kʌltʃəd | *adj.* **1** educado, cultivado, refinado. || **2 – pearl,** perla cultivada.

culvert | 'kʌlvət | *s.c.* atarjea.

cumbersome | 'kʌmbəsəm | *adj.* **1** embarazoso, engorroso, incómodo, molesto de manejar. **2** torpe, pesado (funcionamiento, proceso, actividad, etc.).

cumin | 'kʌmɪn | (también **cummin**) *s.i.* comino (especia).

cummerbund | 'kʌməbʌnd | *s.c.* faja de frac.

cumulative | 'kjuːmjulətɪv | (EE.UU.) | 'kjuːmjuleɪtɪv | *adj.* acumulativo.

cumulatively | 'kjuːmjulətɪv | (EE.UU.) | 'kjuːmjuleɪtɪvlɪ | *adv.* acumulativamente.

cumuli | 'kjuːmjulaɪ | *pl.* de **cumulus.**

cumulus | 'kjuːmələs | [*pl.* **cumuli**] *s.c.* e *i.* cúmulo (nube).

cunning | 'kʌnɪŋ | *s.i.* **1** (desp.) astucia, sagacidad. || *adj.* **2** (desp.) astuto, sagaz. **3** inteligente, ingenioso, hábil. **4** (EE.UU.) lindo, mono.

cunningly | 'kʌnɪŋlɪ | *adv.* **1** (desp.) astutamente, sagazmente. **2** inteligentemente, ingeniosamente, hábilmente.

cunt | kʌnt | *s.c.* (vulg.) **1** coño. **2** gilipollas, coñazo.

cup | kʌp | *s.c.* **1** taza. **2** copa (trofeo). **3** objeto con forma de copa. || *s.sing.* **4** DEP. copa (en distintos deportes): *the cup final.* || *v.t.* **5** ahuecar la mano en forma de copa. || *s.i.* **6** ponche (de distintos tipos). || **7 not one's – of tea,** V. **tea.**

cupboard | 'kʌbəd | *s.c.* **1** armario, alacena. || **2 a skeleton in the –,** V. **skeleton. 3 – love,** amor interesado, amor egoísta.

cupful | 'kʌpful | *s.c.* taza (contenido): *a cupful of this medicine.*

cupid | 'kjuːpɪd | *s.c.* **1** ART. figura de cupido, niño cupido. || **2 Cupid,** Cupido (símbolo del enamoramiento).

cupidity | kjuː'pɪdɪtɪ | *s.i.* (form.) avaricia, codicia (especialmente de cosas materiales).

cupola | 'kjuːpələ | *s.c.* ARQ. cúpula.

cuppa | 'kʌpə | *s.c.* (brit. y fam.) tacita de té.

cup-tie | 'kʌptaɪ | *s.c.* DEP. semifinal a un sólo partido.

curable | 'kjuərəbl | *adj.* curable, que se puede curar.

curacy | 'kjuərəsɪ | *s.i.* REL. curato (de la Iglesia Anglicana).

curate | 'kjuərət | *s.c.* REL. cura ayudante, coadjutor (en Anglicanismo). || **2 a curate's egg,** V. **egg.**

curative | 'kjuərətɪv | *adj.* curativo.

curator | kjuə'reɪtər | *s.c.* conservador (de museo).

curb | kəːb | *v.t.* **1** contener, refrenar (algo o alguien). || *s.c.* **2 [– (on)]** freno, restricción. **3** (EE.UU.) cera, bordillo.

curd | kəːd | *s.c.* cuajada; grumo de sustancia cuajada.

curdle | 'kəːdl | *v.t.* e *i.* **1** cuajar(se) (especialmente la leche). || **2 to – one's blood/one's blood curdles/etc.,** helársele a uno la sangre.

cure | kjuər | *v.t.* e *i.* **1** curar, sanar. **2** curar(se) (tabaco, piel, etc.). || *v.t.* **3** curar, resolver, salvar (problema, dificultad, etc.). **4 [to – + *o.* + of]** quitar, curar de (vicio, hábito, etc.). || *s.c.* **5 [– (for)]** cura, remedio (médico). **6 [– (of)]** curación. **7 [– (of)]** (fig.) cura, cuidado (de almas). || *s.c.* e *i.* **8 [– (for)]** solución, resolución.

cure-all | 'kjuərɔːl | *s.c.* panacea.

curfew | 'kəːfjuː | *s.c.* toque de queda.

curio | kjuərɪəu | *s.c.* objeto curioso, objeto para coleccionista.

curiosity | ˌkjuərɪ'ɒsɪətɪ | *s.i.* **1** curiosidad, interés. **2** (desp.) curiosidad, espíritu inquisitorio. || *s.c.* **3** objeto de interés. **4** tipo raro (pasado de moda). || **5 – killed the cat,** por la boca muere el pez.

curious | 'kjuərɪəs | *adj.* **1** curioso, interesado (en saber más). **2** (desp.) entrometido, curioso. **3** extraño, curioso (cosa o acontecimiento).

curiously | 'kjuərɪəslɪ | *adv.* **1** curiosamente, interesadamente. **2** (desp.) entrometidamente, curiosamente. **3** extrañamente, curiosamente.

curl | kəːl | *s.c.* **1** rizo (de pelo). **2** espiral, bucle (de humo o similar). || *s.sing.* **3** mueca, torcimiento (de labios). || *s.i.* **4** rizado (de pelo). || *v.t.* **5** rizar (el pelo). || *v.t.* e *i.* **6** retorcer(se), hacer(se) espirales. || *v.i.* **7** enroscarse, enrollarse (posición del cuerpo). **8** rizarse, formarse rizos (el pelo). **9** ondularse, levantarse los bordes (papel o similar). || **10 to – into a ball,** hacerse una bola, enroscarse como una madeja. **11 to – one's lips,** fruncir los labios. **12 to – up,** enrollarse por completo, hacerse una bola, ondearse hacia arriba (persona o cosa).

curler | 'kəːlər | *s.c.* rulo

curlew | 'kəːljuː | *s.c.* ZOOL. sarapico (ave).

curling | 'kəːlɪŋ | *s.i.* **1** juego escocés sobre hielo. || **2 – tongs,** tenacillas (para rizar el pelo).

curly | 'kəːlɪ | *adj.* **1** rizado (pelo). **2** (fam.) curvado, circular, ondulado.

currant | 'kʌrənt | *s.c.* BOT. **1** grosella. **2** pasa de Corinto.

currency | 'kʌrənsɪ | *s.c.* e *i.* FIN. moneda (sistema monetario de un país). || *s.i.* **2** uso general, aceptación (de una palabra, idea, etc.).

current | 'kʌrənt | *adj.* **1** actual, moderno, en curso, del presente. **2** aceptada, de uso corriente (palabra, idea, etc.). || *s.c.* **3** corriente (de agua). **4** corriente (de opinión). **5** corriente (de aire). **6** ELEC. corriente. || **7 – account,** FIN. cuenta corriente. **8 – affairs, a)** acontecimientos del día, sucesos habituales. **b)** temas de actualidad (como asignatura).

currently | 'kʌrəntlɪ | *adv.* actualmente, modernamente, durante el presente.

curricula | kə'rɪkjʊlə | *pl.* de **curriculum.**

curriculum | kə'rɪkjʊləm | [*pl.* **curriculums** o **curricula**] *s.c.* **1** currículo, plan de estudios (asignaturas). || **2 – vitae,** curriculum vitae.

curried | 'kʌrɪd | *adj.* GAST. con curry.

curry | 'kʌrɪ | *s.i.* **1** GAST. curry. || *v.t.* **2** cocinar condimentando con curry. **3** almohazar (caballos). || **4 to – favour (with),** (desp.) congraciarse vilmente (con), hacer la pelota (a). **5 – powder,** GAST. curry en polvo.

curse | kəːs | *v.i.* **1** decir palabrotas, maldecir. || *v.t.* **2 [to – + *o.* + (for)]** insultar, maldecir. **3** quejarse con palabrotas de, maldecir. || *s.c.* **4** palabrota, obscenidad. **5 [– (on/upon)]** maldición. **6 [– (of)]** azote, calamidad. || *s.sing.* **7 [the –]** (fam. y p.u.) el período.

cursed | 'kəːsɪd | *adj.* **1** maldito (causado por una maldición). || **2 to be – with,** estar afligido por, tener que aguantar.

cursedly | 'kəːsɪdlɪ | *adv.* malditamente.

cursive | 'kəːsɪv | *adj.* cursiva (tipo de letra).

cursor | 'kəːsər | *s.c.* INF. cursor.

cursorily | 'kəːsərəlɪ | *adv.* (a veces desp.) superficialmente, sin interés.

cursory | 'kəːsərɪ | *adj.* (a veces desp.) superficial, desinteresado.

curt | kəːt | *adj.* (desp.) brusco, seco.

curtail | kəː'teɪl | *v.t.* **1** reducir, cortar, cercenar (especialmente gastos). **2** restringir (poder, libertad, etc.).

curtailment | kəː'teɪlmənt | *s.i.* **[– of]** (form.) reducción de, recorte de, restricción de (libertad, crédito, etc.).

curtain | 'kəːtn | *s.c.* **1** cortina (de tela, plástico, etc.). **2** ART. cortina (en el teatro). || *s.sing.* **3** (fig.) tiempo de comienzo (en el teatro). || *s.i.* **4** (fig.) cortina, pantalla (de humo, mentiras, obstáculos, etc.). || **5 – call,** salida al escenario a recibir aplausos. **6 to – off,** separar con cortinas, dividir con cortinas (una parte de una habitación). **7 – for,** (fam.) se acabó para, se terminó lo que se daba para. **8 the last/final –,** la última representación.

curtained | 'kəːtnd | *adj.* acortinado, con visillos.

curtain-raiser | 'kəːtnreɪzər | *s.c.* **1** comedia corta, preludio (en teatro). **2** (fig.) prólogo, preludio (de algo más importante).

curtly | 'kəːtlɪ | *adv.* (desp.) bruscamente, secamente.

curtness | 'kəːtnɪs | *s.i.* (desp.) brusquedad, sequedad.

curtsy | 'kəːtsɪ | (también **curtsey**) *v.i.* **1 [to – (to)]** hacer una reverencia. || *s.c.* **2** reverencia (corporal).

curvaceous | kəː'veɪʃəs | *adj.* curvilíneo (especialmente del cuerpo de una mujer).

curvature | 'kəːvətʃər | *s.i.* **[– (of)]** GEOM. curvatura.

curve | kəːv | *s.c.* **1** curva. || *s.pl.* **2** (fam.) curvas (de una mujer). || *v.i.* **3** curvarse, hacer una curva. **4** moverse haciendo curvas.

curved | kəːvd | *adj.* curvado.

curving | 'kəːvɪŋ | *adj.* que hace curvas (carretera).

curvy | 'kəːvɪ | *adj.* (fam.) **1** curvado, combado. **2** con magníficas curvas (mujer).

cushion | 'kʊʃn | *s.c.* **1** cojín, almohadilla. **2** parte blanda, parte suave (de cualquier objeto). **3** amortiguador (algo que hace de amortiguador). || *v.t.* **4** amortiguar (un golpe, caída, etc.). **5** disminuir el impacto, amortiguar (algún resultado negativo): *to cushion the blow of the price increase = amortiguar el golpe del incremento de precios.*

cushy | 'kʊʃɪ | (fam.) *adj.* **1** segurito, cómodo, fácil (trabajo, tarea, etc.). **2 a – number,** chollo.

cuss | kʌs | (p.u. y fam.) V. **curse.**

cussed | 'kʌsɪd | *adj.* obstinado, terco.

cussedly | 'kʌsɪdlɪ | *adv.* obstinadamente, tercamente.

cussedness | 'kʌsɪdnɪs | *s.i.* obstinación, terquedad.

custard | 'kʌstəd | GAST. *s.i.* **1** natilla. || **2 – pie/tart,** torta de crema.

custodial | kʌ'stəʊdɪəl | *adj.* DER. de prisión.

custodian | kʌ'stəʊdɪən | *s.c.* guarda, guardián.

custody | 'kʌstədɪ | *s.i.* **1** DER. custodia. || **2 in –,** en prisión.

custom | 'kʌstəm | *s.c.* **1** costumbre, usanza. || *s.i.* **2** (form.) clientela, parroquia (de tienda). || **3 customs,** aduana. **4 – house,** aduana (sitio). **5 – union,** POL. unión aduanera (entre países).

customarily | 'kʌstəmərəlɪ | (EE.UU.) | kʌstə'merəlɪ | *adv.* según costumbre, habitualmente, usualmente.

customary | 'kʌstəmərɪ | (EE.UU.) | 'kʌstəmerɪ | *adj.* acostumbrado, usual, habitual.

custom-built | ˌkʌstəm'bɪlt | *adj.* hecho a medida.

customer | 'kʌstəmər | *s.c.* **1** cliente, parroquiano. **2** [*adj.* + ;ms] (fam.) tipo, sujeto: *a cool customer = un tipo frío.*

customize | 'kʌstəmaɪz | (también **customise**) *v.t.* hacer a gusto del comprador, retocar a gusto del comprador.

custom-made | ˌkʌstom'meɪd | V. **custom-built.**

cut | kʌt | *v.* [*pret.* y *p.p.irreg.* **cut**] *t.* **1** cortar. **2** reducir, cortar (gastos). **3** cortar, cercenar (trozos de escrito o similar). **4** negar el saludo: *if he gets angry he will cut you for a week = si se coge un buen enfado te niega el saludo durante una semana.* **5** dejar (de hacer algo que se hacía): *I'm going to cut private classes = voy a dejar las clases particulares.* **6** MUS. hacer, grabar (disco). **7** cortar (cartas). **8** salirle (un diente a un bebé). **9** cortar (pelo, uñas, etc.). **10** cortar, recortar (hierba). **11** dividir, cortar (algo en dos partes). **12** pulir, cortar (joya). **13** tallar, grabar (metal, madera, etc.). **14** cortar (vestido). **15** afectar, dar en lo vivo (un comentario, palabra, etc.): *my words cut him deeply = mis palabras le afectaron profundamente.* || *i.* **16** cortar, tener filo: *this knife cuts very well = este cuchillo corta muy bien.* **17 [to – into]** pegar un corte, cortar, rajar. **18 [to – through]** atravesar, cortar (agua en barco). **19 [to – across/through]** cruzar por (un lugar, normalmente queriendo un atajo). || *r.* **20** cortarse, herirse. || *s.c.* **21** corte, raja. **22** corte, herida. **23** recorte, reducción (de impuestos, salarios, etc.). **24** corte (en película o similar). **25** tajada, trozo (de carne). **26** corte (de pelo). || *s.sing.* **27** (fam.) tajada, comisión (en un negocio deshonesto). || *adj.* **28** cortado, hecho rebanada (cualquier cosa). **29** herida, cortada, con corte. **30** cortado, hecho (vestimenta): *a beautifully cut blouse = una blusa hecha primorosamente.* **31** pulido, cortado (joya). || **32 a – above,** ser superior a, ser mejor que. **33 –!,** ¡corten! **34 to – across,** rebasar las diferencias, superar las diferencias (diferencias posibles por su importancia): *racism cuts across all parties = el racismo supera las diferencias de todos los partidos.* **35 to – a... figure,** tener una pinta...: *he cuts a slim figure in that suit = tiene una pinta muy delgada con ese traje.* **36 to – a long story short,** para ser breve. **37 to – and run,** (fam. y desp.) salir pitando, huir con el rabo entre las piernas. **38 to – back (on),** recortar gastos, reducir el gasto (en). **39 to – both ways,** tener doble filo (un problema, situación, etc.). **40 to – down,** cortar (árbol). **41 to – down (on),** reducir el consumo de, tomar menos (de): *I have to cut down on fat = tengo que reducir el consumo de grasa.* **42 to – to size,** dejar en su sitio (humillar). **43 to – in,** interrumpir. **44 to – no ice,** V. **ice. 45 to – off, a)** cortar (pelo, cuando es largo). **b)**

interrumpir, no dejar continuar, no dejar hablar. **c)** desconectar (en conversación telefónica). **d)** interrumpir el suministro de (agua, electricidad, etc.). **46 to – off (from),** aislar (de). **47 to – off your nose to spit in your face,** V. **nose. 48 to – one's losses,** V. **loss. 49 to – out, a)** recortar (un artículo de periódico, por ejemplo). **b)** calarse (motor). **c)** dejar, abandonar, desechar (hábito, costumbre, conversación, etc.): *do not argue, cut it out = no discutas, déjalo.* **d)** censurar, cortar, dejar fuera. **e)** tapar, ocultar, no dejar pasar (una vista, la luz, etc.). **50 – out (to/for),** hecho para, destinado por la providencia para: *I'm not cut out to become a policeman = no estoy hecho para ser policía.* **51 to – out (of),** excluir (de), quitar (de) (una actividad). **52 to – someone dead,** no hacer caso alguno a alguien, no saludar a alguien, ignorar a alguien. **52 to – someone out of one's will,** desheredar, dejar fuera del testamento de uno a alguien. **53 to – someone short,** dejar con la palabra en la boca, interrumpir. **54 to – up,** hacer cachitos, cortar en pedazos pequeños. **55 – up (about),** disgustado (acerca de), afectado (por). **56 to have one's work – out,** V. **work.**

cut-and-dried | 'kʌtəndaɪd | *adj.* preparado, arreglado, convenido (plan, acuerdo, actividad, etc.).

cutback | 'kʌtbæk | *s.c.* **[– (in)]** reducción (especialmente de personal).

cute | kjuːt | *adj.* (EE.UU.) **1** mono, (Am.) lindo. **2** atractivo (desde un punto de vista sexual). **3** listo, despierto, agudo (de inteligencia).

cutely | 'kjuːtlɪ | *adv.* (EE.UU.) **1** preciosamente, (Am.) lindamente. **2** inteligentemente, agudamente.

cuteness | 'kjuːtnɪs | *s.i.* (EE.UU.) **1** monería, (Am.) lindeza. **2** atracción (sexual). **3** inteligencia, agudeza.

cut-glass | ˌkʌt'glɑːs | *adj.* **1** de cristal tallado. **2** (fam.) de habla refinada. || *s.i.* **3** cristal tallado.

cutlass | 'kʌtləs | *s.c.* alfanje.

cutlery | 'kʌtlərɪ | *s.i.* cubertería.

cutlet | 'kʌtlɪt | *s.c.* costilla.

cut-off | 'kʌtɒf | (también **cut-off point**) *s.c.* límite, máximo.

cut-out | 'kʌtaʊt | *s.c.* **1** recorte (de periódico y similar). **2** válvula de seguridad, cortacircuito de seguridad.

cut-price | ˌkʌt'praɪs | *adj.* de rebajas, de recorte de precios.

cutter | 'kʌtər | *s.c.* **1** cuter, cortador, aparato cortador. **2** MAR. balandra, cúter. **3** cortador, sastre (de trajes). || *s.pl.* **4** tijeras grandes.

cut-throat | 'kʌtərəʊt | *adj.* despiadado, cruel.

cutting | 'kʌtɪŋ | *s.c.* **1** recorte (de periódico o similar). **2** BOT. injerto (que se corta para otro sitio). **3** corte (en una montaña para el paso del tren). || *adj.* **4** sarcástico, despiadado (que hiere). || **5 – room,** TV. montaje, sala de montaje.

cuttingly | 'kʌtɪŋlɪ | *adv.* sarcásticamente, despiadadamente.

cuttlefish | 'kʌtlfɪsh | [*pl.* **cuttlefish** o **cuttlefishes**] *s.c.* ZOOL. sepia, jibia.

cyanide | 'saɪənaɪd | *s.i.* QUIM. cianuro.

cybernetics | ˌsaɪbə'netɪks | *s.i.* cibernética.

cyclamen | 'sɪkləmən | (EE.UU.) | 'saɪkləmən | *s.c.* e *i.* BOT. ciclamino.

cycle | 'saɪkl | *v.i.* **1** ir en bicicleta. || *s.c.* **2** bicicleta. **3** (EE.UU.) motocicleta. **4** ciclo, secuencia, repetición. **5** ciclo, vuelta. **6** LIT. ciclo (de novelas o parecido).

cyclic | 'saɪklɪk | (también **cyclical**) *adj.* cíclico.

cyclical | 'saɪklɪkl | V. **cyclic.**

cyclically | 'saɪklɪkəlɪ | *adv.* cíclicamente.

cyclist | 'saɪklɪst | *s.c.* ciclista.

cyclone | 'saɪkləʊn | *s.c.* ciclón.

cygnet | 'sɪgnɪt | *s.c.* ZOOL. cisne joven.

cylinder | 'sɪlɪndər | *s.c.* **1** GEOM. cilindro. **2** MEC. cilindro (de un motor de vehículo). || **3 working/firing on all cylinders,** (fam.) trabajando a todo trapo, funcionando a pedir de boca.

cylindrical | sɪ'lɪndrɪkl | *adj.* GEOM. cilíndrico.

cymbal | 'sɪmbl | *s.c.* MUS. címbalo.

cynic | 'sɪnɪk | *s.c.* cínico.

cynical | 'sɪnɪkl | *adj.* cínico, desengañado.

cynically | 'sɪnɪklɪ | *adv.* cínicamente, con un gran desengaño.

cynicism | 'sɪnɪsɪzəm | *s.i.* cinismo.

cypher, V. **cipher.**

cyphered, V. **ciphered.**

cypress | 'saɪprəs | [*pl.* **cypresses** o **cypress**] *s.c.* **1** BOT. ciprés. || *s.i.* **2** madera de ciprés, ciprés.

Cypriot | 'sɪprɪət | *s.c.* **1** chipriota. || *adj.* **2** chipriota.

Cyprus | 'saɪprəs | *s.sing.* Chipre.

cyst | sɪst | *s.c.* MED. quiste.

cystitis | sɪ'staɪtɪs | *s.i.* MED. cistitis.

czar V. **tsar.**

czarina V. **tsarina.**

czarist V. **tsarist.**

Czech | tʃek | *s.c.* **1** checo, checoslovaco. || *s.i.* **2** checo (idioma). || *adj.* **3** checo, checoslovaco.

Czechoslovak | ˌtʃekəʊ'sləʊvæk | (también **Czechoslovakian**) *adj.* checoslovaco.

Czechoslovakia | ˌtʃekəʊslə'vækɪə | *s.sing.* Checoslovaquia.

Czechoslovakian | ˌtʃəkəʊlə'vækɪən | V. **Czechoslovak.**

d, D | diː | *s.c.* **1** d (cuarta letra del alfabeto inglés). || *s.c.* e *i.* **2** MUS. Re. **3** insuficiente, suspenso (nota académica).
OBS. Esta letra se puede utilizar como abreviatura de palabras como: **daughter, died, delete, dimension, penny** (en el sistema monetario vigente en Inglaterra antes de 1971).
'd o **d'** son contracciones verbales de **had** y **would** y de **do.**
Finalmente, esta letra aparece como sufijo en la terminación del pasado y participio de los verbos regulares.
dab | dæb | [ger. **dabbing,** *pret.* y *p.p.* **dabbed**] *v.t.* **1** dar toques ligeros, aplicar con toques suaves: *I dabbed the table with a strong cleaner = apliqué una sustancia fuerte en la mesa con toques suaves.* || *s.c.* **2** toquecito ligero, pincelada suave. **3** ZOOL. lenguado. || **4 to – at,** dar toques ligeros en. **5 a – hand at,** (brit. y fam.) un manitas en. **6 dabs,** (brit. y fam.) huellas (dactilares).
dabble | 'dæbl | *v.i.* **1 [to – (in)]** tener un interés superficial, meterse frívolamente: *he dabbled in politics = se metió de manera frívola en política.* || *v.t.* **2** mojar; chapotear: *dabble your handkerchief in the water = moja el pañuelo en el agua.*
dabbler | 'dæblər | *s.c.* (desp.) aficionado, diletante.
dace | deɪs | [*pl.* **dace**] *s.c.* ZOOL. albur, dardo, breca (pez de agua dulce).
dacha | 'dætʃə | *s.c.* dacha (casa chalet rusa en el campo).
dachshund | 'dækshʊnd | *s.c.* ZOOL. perro tejonero, dachshund.
dad | dæd | *s.c.* (fam.) papá.
daddy | 'dædɪ | *s.c.* (fam.) papá, papaíto.
daddy-longlegs | dædɪ'lɒŋlegz | [*pl.* **daddy-longlegs**] *s.c.* ZOOL. segador, típula (insecto con patas muy largas).
daddy-o | 'dædɪəʊ | *s.c.* (fam.) tío, colega, jefe (en los años 60).
dado | 'deɪdəʊ | *s.c.* ARQ. friso, dado.
daffodil | 'dæfədɪl | *s.c.* BOT. narciso.
daft | dɑːft | *adj.* (brit. y fam.) **1** estúpido, bobo; chiflado. **2 [– (about)]** (fig.) chiflado: *I'm daft about her = estoy chiflado por ella.*
dagger | 'dægər | *s.c.* **1** daga. || **2 at daggers drawn,** en desacuerdo total (casi violento). **3 to look daggers at,** atravesar con la mirada a.
dago | 'deɪgəʊ | *s.c.* (desp.) sudaca, macho hispánico, latino idiota (usado ofensivamente con gente mediterránea y sudamericana en general).
dahlia | 'deɪlɪə | *s.c.* BOT. dalia.
daily | 'deɪlɪ | *adj.* **1** diario: *a daily delivery = un reparto diario.* **2** por día, al día. || *s.c.* **3** periódico diario (no se publica los domingos). **4** (brit. y fam.) asistenta. || *adv.* **5** diariamente.
daintily | 'deɪntɪlɪ | *adv.* refinadamente; primorosamente.
dainty | 'deɪntɪ | *adj.* refinado; primoroso (normalmente para describir a mujeres): *a dainty little woman = una mujer pequeña y refinada.*
daiquiri | 'dækərɪ | *s.c.* daiquiri (bebida de cocktail).
dairy | 'deərɪ | *s.c.* **1** lechería. **2** vaquería; quesería. || *s.i.* **3** lácteo, de leche: *dairy products.*
dairy-farm | 'deərɪfɑːm | *s.c.* granja lechera.
dairymaid | 'dearimeɪd | *s.c.* (arc.) lechera, vaquera.
dairyman | 'deərɪmən | *s.c.* lechero.
dais | 'deɪɪs | *s.c.* estrado.
daisy | 'deɪzɪ | *s.c.* **1** BOT. margarita. || **2 to be pushing up the daisies,** (hum. y fam.) estar criando margaritas. **3 fresh as a –,** V. **fresh.**
daisy-chain | 'deɪzɪtʃeɪn | *s.c.* (brit.) guirnalda (hecha con margaritas).
daisywheel | 'deɪzɪwiːl | *s.c.* INF. margarita.
dale | deɪl | *s.c.* **1** (arc.) valle. || **2 up hill and down –,** por una ruta laboriosa, por una ruta penosa.
dalliance | 'dælɪəns | *s.i.* (p.u.) coqueteo; retozo.
dally | 'dælɪ | *v.i.* **1** (p.u.) demorarse; holgar. **2 [to – with]** acariciar, juguetear con (ideas, proyectos, etc.). **3 [to – with]** (p.u.) coquetear con.
Dalmatian | dæl'meɪʃn | *s.c.* ZOOL. dálmata (raza canina).
dam | dæm | *s.c.* **1** presa; dique. **2** pantano, embalse. **3** ZOOL. madre (de animales cuadrúpedos). || *v.t.* **4** embalsar, represar (agua). || **5 to – up, a)** parar el curso (de un río, etc.) con una presa. **b)** (fig.) bloquear; ocultar (sentimientos).
damage | 'dæmɪdʒ | *v.t.* **1** dañar, estropear; deteriorar. || *s.i.* **2** daño, avería; deterioro. || **3 damages,** DER. daños y perjuicios. **4 the – is done,** no hay nada que hacer; el daño está hecho. **5 what's the –?,** (fam.) ¿cuánto te debo por el daño/deterioro?
damaging | 'dæmɪdʒɪŋ | *adj.* **[– (to)]** dañino, perjudicial.
damask | 'dæməsk | *s.i.* damasco.
dame | deɪm | *s.c.* **1** (EE.UU. y fam.) dama, señora.
dammit V. **damn.**
damn | dæm | *adj.* **1** maldito, condenado (muy usado en el lenguaje coloquial): *he is a damn fool = es un condenado estúpido.* || *adv.* **2** (fam.) muy; requete: *I'm damn good at Maths = soy requetebueno en mates.* || *interj.* (vulg.) **3 ¡mierda!** || **4 as near as damn it,** (fam.) casi; por lo menos. **5 to be damned for,** ser culpado de, ser condenado por. **6 damn you,** ¡maldito tú! **7 damn it, dammit,** (vulg.) ¡mierda podrida! **8 to give /care a damn,** (fam.) importar un bledo. **9 not to be worth a damn,** (fam.) no valer un pimiento/céntimo (dinero).
damnable | 'dæmnəbl | *adj.* (p.u.) detestable, execrable.
damnably | 'dæmnəblɪ | *adv.* (p.u.) detestablemente, execrablemente.

damnation | dæm'neɪʃn | *s.i.* **1** REL. condenación. || *interj.* **2** (p.u.) ¡pardiez!, ¡por Júpiter!
damned | dæmd | *adj.* **1** (fam.) maldito, condenado. **2** REL. condenado. || *adv.* **3** (fam.) muy (lo importante es el énfasis). || **4 to be – it,** (fam.) jamás, nunca, ni por asomo. **5 damnedest,** (fam. y p.u.) más alucinante, más sorprendente: *he's the damnedest artist I've ever met = él es el artista más sorprendente que he conocido jamás.* **6 to do one's damnedest,** hacer todo lo que uno pueda de verdad. **7 I'll be –/I'm –,** ¡mecachis!; ¡y un jamón!
damning | 'dæmɪŋ | *adj.* concluyente; irrecusable.
damp | dæmp | *adj.* **1** húmedo, mojado (con un sentido desagradable). || *s.i.* **2** humedad (desagradable). || *v.t.* **3** mojar ligeramente, humedecer. || **4 – down, a)** moderar; amortiguar (la fuerza, violencia, ánimo, etc.). **b)** cubrir (el fuego). **5 – squib,** V. **squib.**
damp-course | 'dæmpkɔːs | *s.c.* ARQ. hilada de ladrillos (antihumedad).
dampen | 'dæmpən | *v.t.* **1** mojar ligeramente, humedecer. **2** moderar; amortiguar (la fuerza, violencia, ánimo, etc.).
damper | 'dæmpər | *s.c.* **1** regulador de tiro (chimenea). **2** MUS. apagador; sordina. || **3 to act as a – on/to put a – on,** (fam.) desanimar, desalentar.
dampness | 'dæmpnɪs | *s.i.* humedad.
damsel | 'dæmzl | *s.c.* (arc. y lit.) doncella.
dance | dɑːns | *v.i.* **1** bailar, danzar. **2** (fig.) brincar, saltar (de gozo). || *v.t.* **3** bailar (un baile, una danza). || *s.c.* **4** baile, danza. **5** baile, fiesta. || *s.i.* **6** baile, danza. || **7 to – attendance on,** estar excesivamente pendiente de, tratar con excesiva deferencia. **8 – studio, estudio de baile. 9 to – to someone's tune,** V. **tune. 10 to lead someone a merry/pretty –,** poner muchas dificultades a alguien, hacer a alguien las cosas difíciles. **11 to make a song and – about something,** V. **song.**
dance-floor | 'dɑːnsflɔːr | *s.c.* pista de baile.
dance-hall | 'dɑːnshɔːl | *s.c.* salón de baile.
dancer | 'dɑːnsər | *s.c.* bailarín.
dancing | 'dɑːnsɪŋ | *s.i.* **1** baile (como actividad): *dancing is my profession = el baile es mi profesión.* || *adj.* **2** alegres; danzarines (ojos).
dancing-girl |'dɑːnsɪŋgɜːl | *s.c.* bailarina.
dancing-partner | 'dɑːnsɪŋ'pɑːtnər | *s.c.* pareja de baile.
dandelion | 'dændɪlaɪən | *s.c.* BOT. diente de león.
dandified | 'dændɪfaɪd | *adj.* (p.u.) presumido, petimetre (sólo para hombres).
dandle | 'dændl | *v.t.* mecer; mover repetidamente sobre las rodillas (niño).
dandruff | 'dændrəf | *s.i.* caspa.
dandy | 'dændɪ | *s.c.* **1** (p.u. y desp.) petimetre. || *adj.* **2** (fam. y EE.UU.) chupi; de rechupete.

Dane | deɪn | *s.c.* danés.
danger | 'deɪndʒər | *s.i.* **1** peligro; riesgo. || *s.c.* **2** peligro. || **3 – money,** compensación por trabajo peligroso, plus de peligrosidad. **4 on the – list,** en peligro de muerte. **5 out of –,** fuera de peligro. **6 there's no – of that,** no hay peligro de que eso ocurra.
dangerous | 'deɪndʒərəs | *adj.* peligroso.
dangerously | 'deɪndʒərəslɪ | *adv.* peligrosamente.
dangle | 'dæŋgl | *v.t.* **1** balancear; colgar, suspender (algo sujeto por un solo extremo). **2 [to – (in front of/before)]** ofrecer como cebo. || *v.i.* **3** pender, colgar. || **4 to keep someone dangling,** (fam.) mantener en suspenso a alguien.
Danish | 'deɪnɪʃ | *adj.* **1** danés. || *s.i.* **2** danés (idioma). || **3 – pastry,** GAST. pastel de frutas o nueces.
dank | dæŋk | *adj.* húmedo; malsano (con un sentido muy negativo).
dapper | 'dæpər | *adj.* pulcro, aseado; apuesto.
dappled | 'dæpld | *adj.* moteado.
dare | deər | *v.i.* **1** atreverse, osar. || *v.t.* **2** desafiar. || *s.c.* **3** desafío. || **4 – I say it,** me temo, debo decir a mi pesar. **5 don't you –,** no te atrevas, no te arriesgues. **6 how – you,** cómo te atreves. **7 I dare say/I daresay,** supongo, me parece.
OBS. Este verbo puede utilizarse sin auxiliar en el sentido de la correspondencia: **1:** *I dare not go now = no me atrevo a irme ahora.*
daredevil | 'deədevl | *s.c.* temerario, atrevido, osado.
daren't | 'deərənt | *contr.* de **dare** y **not.**
daring | 'deərɪŋ | *s.i.* **1** atrevimiento, osadía. || *adj.* **2** atrevido, osado.
daringly | 'deərɪŋlɪ | *adv.* atrevidamente, osadamente.
dark | dɑːk | *adj.* **1** oscuro. **2** oscuro; negro (pelo, ojos, etc.). **3** sombrío; misterioso (lugar, época). **4** triste; sombrío (ideas, pensamientos, etc.). **5** siniestro; malvado (mirada o comentario). || *s.i.* **6** oscuridad. || **7 after –,** después del anochecer/puesta de sol. **8 before –,** antes de que oscurezca, antes del anochecer, antes de la puesta del sol. **9 – age,** edad oscura, edad de retroceso. **10 – glasses,** gafas de sol. **11 – horse,** persona misteriosa (de la que no se sabe casi nada): *he's a dark horse = él es una persona misteriosa.* **12 in the –,** ignorante: *I'm in the dark about what you say = soy ignorante de lo que dices.* **13 to keep something –,** mantener algo en secreto, no revelar algo.
darken | 'dɑːkən | *v.t.* **1** oscurecer, ensombrecer; ennegrecer. **2** entristecer, ensombrecer: *her death darkened his life = la muerte de ella ensombreció su vida.* || *v.i.* **3** oscurecerse, ensombrecerse; ennegrecerse. || **4 never to – one's door again,** (arc. y lit.) nunca volver a pisar el umbral de la casa de uno.
darkie | 'dɑːkɪ | (también **darky**) *s.c.* (desp.) negro.

darkish | 'dɑːkɪʃ | *adj.* tirando a oscuro/moreno.
darkness | 'dɑːknɪs | *s.i.* oscuridad.
darkroom | 'dɑːkrum | *s.c.* FOT. cuarto oscuro.
darling | 'dɑːlɪŋ | *s.c.* **1** querido, cariño: *good morning, darling = buenos días, cariño.* **2** favorito, preferido: *she's the teachers' darling = ella es la favorita de los profesores.* || *adj.* **3** encantador. **4** amado, querido. || **5 a –,** un ángel. **6 be a –,** por favor; sé bueno: *be a darling and bring me a glass of water = sé bueno y tráeme un vaso de agua.*
darn | dɑːn | *v.t.* **1** zurcir. || *s.c.* **2** zurcido, zurcidura. || *adj.* **3** (euf. y fam.) maldito, condenado: *I hate this darn car = odio este maldito coche.* || *adv.* **4** (euf. y fam.) condenadamente. || **5 darned,** maldito, condenado. **6 – it!,** (fam. y euf.) ¡porras!
darning | 'dɑːnɪŋ | *s.i.* cosas para zurcir; ropa para zurcir.
dart | dɑːt | *v.i.* **1** lanzarse; precipitarse (con gran rapidez): *he darted aside = se lanzó a un lado.* || *v.t.* **2** lanzar (una mirada). || *s.c.* **3** movimiento rápido, sprint. **4** dardo, saeta. **5** sisa, pinza (en vestidos). || **6 darts,** dardos (juego).
dartboard | 'dɑːtbɔːd | *s.c.* blanco (en el juego de los dardos).
dash | dæʃ | *v.i.* **1** ir a toda velocidad, esprintar. || *v.t.* **2** arrojar (con gran violencia). **3** destrozar, hacer añicos (esperanzas, ilusiones, etc.). || *s.c.* **4** sprint, carrera rápida. **5** guión (trazo horizontal). **6** RAD. raya (del sistema Morse). **7** pincelada; toque: *a dash of red.* **8** pizca; chorrito: *a dash of rum.* **9** V. **dashboard.** || *s.i.* **10** (p.u.) donaire, garbo. || **11 to cut a –,** (p.u.) tener garbo. **12 –!/– it!/– it all,** (p.u. y fam.) ¡porras! **13 to –/shatter someone's hopes,** destrozar las expectativas/esperanzas de alguien. **14 to – off,** escribir a toda velocidad y chapuceramente. **15 to make a – for it,** salir pitando/a toda velocidad. **16 must –/to have to –,** tener que darse prisa.
dashboard | 'dæʃbɔːd | *s.c.* TEC. tablero de instrumentos, consola.
dashing | 'dæʃɪŋ | *adj.* elegante.
dastardly | 'dæstədlɪ | *adj.* (arc.) vil.
data | 'deɪtə | [*sing.* **datum**] *s.pl.* **1** datos. || *s.i.* **2** información.
data-bank | 'deɪtəbæŋk | *s.c.* INF. banco de datos.
database | 'deɪtəbeɪs | *s.c.* INF. base de datos.
data-processing | 'deɪtəprəusesɪŋ | *s.i.* INF. proceso de datos.
date | deɪt | *s.c.* **1** fecha, día. **2** cita, compromiso. **3** cita (con persona del sexo opuesto). **4** (EE.UU.) persona (del otro sexo con quien se sale). **5** BOT. dátil (fruta y árbol). || *v.t.* **6** fechar, poner la fecha. **7** revelar la edad. **8** (EE.UU.) salir con (persona del otro sexo). || *v.i.* **9** pasarse de moda. || **10 at a later –/at some future –,** más adelante, en el futuro. **11 to – back,** remontarse (en el tiempo): *the car dates back to the 1930's = el coche se remonta a los años 30.* **12 to**

– from, datar de. **13 – of birth,** fecha de nacimiento. **14 – palm,** BOT. palmera de dátiles. **15 to –,** hasta la fecha, hasta ahora.
dated | 'deɪtɪd | *adj.* anticuado.
dative | 'deɪtɪv | *adj.* **1** GRAM. dativo. || *s.c.* **2** GRAM. dativo.
daub | dɔːb | *v.t.* pintarrajear; poner (alguna sustancia en una superficie cualquiera con rapidez y descuido).
daughter | dɔːtər | *s.c.* **1** hija. **2** (fig.) originaria: *she's a daughter of Dublin = ella es originaria de Dublín.* || *adj.* **3** derivada: *Latin has five daughter languages = el latín tiene cinco lenguas derivadas.*
daughter-in-law | 'dɔːtərɪnlɔː | *s.c.* nuera, hija política.
daunt | dɔːnt | *v.t.* acobardar, atemorizar, intimidar.
daunting | 'dɔːntɪŋ | *adj.* intimidante, atemorizador.
dauntless | 'dɔːntlɪs | *adj.* intrépido; arrojado.
dauntlessly | 'dɔːntlɪslɪ | *adv.* intrépidamente.
dawdle | 'dɔːdl | *v.i.* demorarse; haraganear.
dawdler | 'dɔːdlər | *s.c.* holgazán, haragán.
dawn | dɔːn | *s.c.* e *i.* **1** aurora, alba, amanecer. **2** (fig.) aurora, albor, principio. || *v.i.* **3** amanecer, hacerse de día. **4** (fig. y lit.) amanecer, despertar (un nuevo período literario, una nueva época histórica). || **5 – chorus,** el canto de los pájaros al alba. **6 to – on/upon,** darse cuenta, caer en la cuenta, comenzar a entender.
day | dei | *s.c.* **1** día. **2** (fig.) día, época, tiempo: *the day of the typewriter is gone = la época de las máquinas de escribir ha pasado.* || *s.c.* e *i.* **3** día (contrapuesto a noche). || **4 any – now,** en cualquier momento/instante; un día de estos. **5 to call it a –,** (fam.) dejarlo por hoy, dejar la tarea por hoy. **6 – and night/night and –,** día y noche; a todas horas, continuamente. **7 – care,** cuidado de niños, en régimen de guardería. **8 – care centre,** guardería. **9 – in, – out,** un día sí y otro también; todos los días. **10 – nursery,** guardería, casa cuna. **11 – off,** día libre (del trabajo). **12 – of reckoning,** momento de rendir cuentas; día del juicio final. **13 – return,** (brit.) billete de ida y vuelta en el mismo día. **14 – school,** escuela sin residencia. **15 in this – and age,** en estos tiempos. **16 it's early days yet,** V. **early. 17 to make a – of it,** (fam.) continuar/no parar en todo el día (una actividad placentera que se ha comenzado). **18 to make one's –,** (fam.) poner contento/feliz a uno: *your news has made my day = tus noticias me han puesto feliz.* **19 one –,** un día (cualquiera). **20 one –/some –/one of these days,** un día de estos, un día (en el futuro). **21 one of those days,** (fam.) un día aciago. **22 to pass the time of –,** V. **time. 23 that'll be the –,** (fam.) ese día no llegará (contestando negativamente el comentario de alguien). **24 the good old days,** los buenos tiempos pasados. **25 the other –,** V. **other. 26 those were the days,** ¡qué tiempos aquellos! (con sentido positivo). **27 to the –,** exactamente (con expresión temporal). **28 to this –,** hasta el día de hoy. **29 to win/lose the –,** ganar/perder finalmente, ganar/perder en última instancia.
daybook | 'deɪbʊk | *s.c.* ECON. diario (de contabilidad).
daybreak | 'deɪbreɪk | *s.i.* alba, amanecer.
daydream | 'deɪdrɪːm | *s.c.* **1** ensueño. **2** ilusión (improbable). || *v.i.* **3 [to – (about/of)]** fantasear.
daylight | 'deɪlaɪt | *s.i.* **1** luz, luz del día. || **2 – robbery,** (fam.) atraco a mano armada (exageración cuando un lugar es demasiado caro). **3 – saving,** ahorro de luz mediante cambio horario. **4 in broad –,** a plena luz, a pleno día. **5 to knock/beat the living daylights out of someone,** (fam.) pegarle una paliza a alguien. **6 to scare the living daylights out of someone,** dar un miedo horrible a alguien, asustar muchísimo a alguien.
day-pupil | 'deɪpjuːpl | *s.c.* alumno no residente (en una escuela con residencia como parte esencial).
day-release | ˌdeɪrɪ'lɪːs | *s.i.* (Brit.) día de estudio para obreros (dentro de un sistema británico de obreros perfeccionándose en su trabajo).
daytime | 'deɪtaɪm | *s.i.* día (desde salida hasta puesta del sol).
day-to-day | ˌdeɪtə'deɪ | *adj.* cotidiano; rutinario.
day-trip | 'deɪtrɪp | *s.c.* excursión, salida de un día.
day-tripper | 'deɪtrɪpər | *s.c.* excursionista (de un solo día).
daze | deɪz | *v.t.* **1** (sólo voz pasiva) estar/quedar aturdido; atontado. || **2 in a –,** aturdido; atontado.
dazed | deɪzd | *adj.* aturdido; atontado.
dazzle | 'dæzl | *v.t.* **1** deslumbrar (por el brillo de la luz). **2** (fig.) deslumbrar (a causa de la belleza, inteligencia, etc.). || *s.i.* **3** brillo deslumbrante. **4** (fig.) brillo; atractivo: *the dazzle of high society = el atractivo de la alta sociedad.*
dazzling | 'dæzlɪŋ | *adj.* **1** deslumbrante; impresionante; fascinante. **2** cegador; deslumbrante.
D-day | 'diːdeɪ | *s.i.* día D, día importante (para algún hecho trascendental).
deacon | 'dɪːkən | *s.c.* REL. diácono (en iglesias protestantes).
deaconess | 'dɪːkənəs | *s.c.* REL. diaconisa (en el protestantismo).
deactivate | dɪ'ːæktɪveɪt | *v.t.* desactivar (una bomba, objeto, etc.).
dead | ded | *adj.* **1** muerto, difunto. **2** estéril (tierra); muerta, estancada (agua). **3** insensible; entumecido: *my foot has gone dead = se me ha quedado insensible el pie.* **4** (fam.) exhausto, agotado, muerto. **5** inactivo; muerto (lugar). **6** ELEC. sin corriente; sin línea. **7 [– (to)]** indiferente; insensible: *he is dead to his wife's serious problems = él es indiferente a los serios problemas de su mujer.* **8** apagado; acabado (tema, fuego o cualquier cosa que ya no se puede usar). **9** apagado; opaco (sonido o color). **10** absoluto, completo (silencio, centro, parada). **11** FIN. inactivo, muerto (capital, cuenta, etc.) || *adv.* **12** (fam.) exactamente: *dead at 12 O'clock.* **13** (fam.) muy, pero que muy: *dead lucky = pero que muy afortunado.* || *s.i.* **14** más profundo (de la noche o invierno). || **15 a – loss,** V. **loss. 16 as – as a doornail,** más muerto que mi abuela. **17 – duck,** (brit. y fam.) plan destinado al fracaso. **18 – from the neck up,** (fam.) bobo, imbécil. **19 – heat,** empate muy ajustado; llegada al unísono. **20 – to the world,** (fam.) frito, cocido; dormido. **21 half –,** medio muerto (con cansancio o enfermedad). **22 over my – body,** sobre mi cadáver. **23 to rise/be raised from the –,** (lit.) resucitar de entre los muertos. **24 the –,** los muertos. **25 I wouldn't be seen –,** (fam.) jamás me dejaría ver (en un sitio malo, con una persona que se dedica a la delincuencia, etc.).
deadbeat | 'dedbiːt | *s.c.* **1** (EE.UU. y fam.) hippy. || *adj.* **2** (brit. y fam.) machacado, agotado.
deaden | 'dedn | *v.t.* amortiguar; aliviar, amortecer (sonido, sensación).
dead-end | 'dedend | *s.c.* **1** callejón sin salida. **2** (fig.) callejón sin salida.
deadening | 'dednɪŋ | *adj.* mortecino; sin interés.
deadline | 'dedlaɪn | *s.c.* fin/cierre de plazo; fecha señalada.
deadlock | 'dedlɒk | *s.i.* punto muerto; estancamiento: *the talks ended in deadlock = las conversaciones finalizaron en un punto muerto.*
deadlocked | 'dedlɒkt | *adj.* en un punto muerto, estancado.
deadly | 'dedlɪ | *adj.* **1** mortífero, letal, mortal. **2** devastador; implacable (crítica, comentario, etc.). **3** (fam.) un rollo, un rollazo. **4** absoluto, completo (con un matiz desagradable). || *adv.* **5** (desp.) horriblemente; extremadamente.
deadpan | 'dedpæn | *adj.* **1** impasible; inexpresivo. || *adv.* **2** impasiblemente; inexpresivamente.
dead-weight | ˌded'weɪt | *s.c.* **1** peso muerto.
deadwood | 'dedwʊd | *s.i.* gente inútil (en una empresa, institución, etc.).
deaf | def | *adj.* **1** sordo. **2 [– (to)]** sordo; insensible. || **3 as – as a post,** tan sordo como una tapia. **4 – and dumb,** sordomudo. **5 to fall on – ears,** caer en saco roto. **6 to turn a – ear,** hacer caso omiso.
deaf-aid | 'defeɪd | *s.c.* (brit.) aparato para el oído, audífono.
deafen | 'defn | *v.t.* ensordecer; atronar.
deafening | 'defnɪŋ | *adj.* ensordecedor; atronador.
deaf-mute | 'def'mjuːt | *s.c.* sordomudo.
deafness | 'defnɪs | *s.i.* sordera.
deal | diːl | *s.c.* **1** contrato; pacto, acuerdo. **2** trato, tratamiento: *the wor-*

kers should get a better deal = los trabajadores deberían recibir un mejor trato. || *v.t.* **[dealt, dealt]** **3** dar, asestar (un golpe). **4** dar, repartir (las cartas). || *cuant.* **5** (fam.) mucho, bastante: *a deal of money.* || *s.i.* **6** turno (de dar cartas). || **7 a great/good –,** mucho, muchos. **8 big –,** (fam.) ¿y qué?; pues vaya cosa. **9 to – in,** comerciar en. **10 to – out, a)** dar, repartir (cartas). **b)** dar, imponer (castigo). **11 to – with, a)** encargarse de. **b)** tratar de, versar sobre (libro, película, etc.). **c)** tener trato con (empresa, persona, etc.).

dealer | 'diːlər | *s.c.* **1** comerciante, negociante, traficante. **2** traficante de drogas. **3** repartidor, el que da (las cartas).

dealings | 'diːlɪŋz | *s.pl.* **[– (with)]** trato; transacciones, negocios.

dealt | delt | *pret.* y *p.p.* de **deal.**

dean | diːn | *s.c.* **1** decano (Universidad). **2** deán (eclesiástico).

deanery | 'diːnərɪ | *s.c.* deanato, domicilio del deán.

dear | dɪər | *adj.* **1** querido, apreciado. **2** querido, estimado (encabezando cartas). **3** caro, costoso. **4 [– (to)]** querido, preciado: *my brother is very dear to me = mi hermano es para mí muy querido.* || *s.c.* **5** querido: *hello, dear!,* **6** encanto: *she's a dear = ella es un encanto.* || **7 to cost someone –,** costar caro a alguien (con gran esfuerzo y dolor). **8 –!/oh –!/– me!,** ¡caramba!; ¡Dios mío! **9 dearest, a)** cariño, lucero. **b)** preciado, más preciado.

dearie | 'dɪərɪ | (fam.) *s.c.* **1** cariño, pequeño (de manera condescendiente). || **2 – me,** ¡caramba!

dearly | 'dɪəlɪ | *adv.* **1** profundamente; con gran cariño. || **2 to pay –,** pagar caro (con sufrimiento).

dearth | dɜːθ | *s.i.* escasez.

death | deθ | *s.c.* e *i.* **1** muerte, defunción. **2** (fig.) fin (de una costumbre, de una institución, etc.). || **3 at –'s door,** a las puertas de la muerte. **4 to be put to –, ser ejecutado; ser muerto. 5 bored to –,** muerto de aburrimiento; muy aburrido. **6 to catch one's –/to catch one's – of cold,** (fam.) morirse de frío. **7 – certificate,** certificado de defunción. **8 – penalty,** pena de muerte. **9 – row,** (EE.UU.) celdas de los que están esperando ser ajusticiados. **10 – sentence,** DER. sentencia de muerte. **11 death-watch beetle,** V. **beetle. 12 fight to the –,** lucha a muerte. **13 to fight to the –,** luchar a muerte. **14 to frighten/scare/ worry someone to –,** asustar/preocupar a alguien muchísimo. **15 like – warmed up,** (fam.) fatal; como un muerto. **16 sick to –,** malo, enfermo (por enfado). **17 to work someone to –,** matar a alguien a trabajar. **18 someone will be the – of someone else,** alguien va a matar a disgustos a alguna otra persona: *you'll be the death of your mother = vas a matar a tu madre a disgustos.*

deathbed | 'deθbed | *s.c.* **1** lecho de muerte. || **2 on someone's –,** en el lecho de muerte de alguien; justo antes de morir.

deathblow | 'deθbləʊ | *s.c.* golpe mortal, golpe de muerte.

death-duty | 'deθdjuːtɪ | *s.c.* DER. impuesto sobre sucesiones, impuesto sobre herencias.

death-knell | 'deθnel | *s. sing.* **1** toque a muerto. **2** (fig.) golpe de gracia.

deathly | 'deθlɪ | *adj.* mortal, de muerte.

death-mask | 'deθmɑːsk | *s.c.* mascarilla (de alguien muerto).

death-throes | 'deθrəʊs | *s. pl.* **1** agonía. **2** (fig.) últimas (de un plan, proyecto, etc.).

death-toll | 'deθtəʊl | *s.c.* número de muertes/muertos (en un accidente o similar).

death-trap | 'deθtræp | *s.c.* trampa mortal; sitio peligroso (teatro sin salida de incendios, etc.).

death-warrant | 'deθwɒrənt | *s.c.* **1** sentencia de muerte. || **2 to sign one's own –,** firmar la sentencia de muerte de uno.

death-wish | 'deθwɪʃ | *s. sing.* deseo tendente al suicidio, deseo de asesinar a alguien (normalmente subconsciente).

deb | deb | V. **debutante.**

debacle | deɪ'bɑːkl | *s.c.* debacle; MIL. derrota.

debar | dɪ'bɑːr | **[debarring, debarred]** *v.t.* **[to – from]** (form.) DER. prohibir; excluir de.

debase | dɪ'beɪs | *v.t.* **1** degradar; envilecer. || *v.r.* **2** degradarse; envilecerse.

debasement | dɪ'beɪsmənt | *s.i.* degradación; envilecimiento.

debatable | dɪ'beɪtəbl | *adj.* discutible.

debate | dɪ'beɪt | *s.c.* e *i.* **1** debate, discusión. || *v.t.* **2** debatir, discutir: *debate a point.* || *v.i.* **3 [to – (with)]** debatir, discutir. || **4 in –,** en discusión; en duda. **5 open to –,** sin dilucidar.

debated | dɪ'beɪtɪd | *adj.* discutido, debatido.

debating | dɪ'beɪtɪŋ | *s.i.* debate: *the art of debating = el arte del debate.*

debater | dɪ'beɪtər | *s.c.* polemista.

debauch | dɪ'bɔːtʃ | *v.t.* corromper, pervertir.

debauched | dɪ'bɔːtʃt | *adj.* depravado, degenerado.

debauchery | dɪ'bɔːtʃərɪ | *s.i.* depravación (especialmente en temas sexuales y alcoholismo).

debenture | dɪ'bentʃər | *s.c.* FIN. obligación.

debilitate | dɪ'bɪlɪteɪt | *v.t.* debilitar.

debilitated | dɪ'bɪlɪ'teɪtɪd | *adj.* debilitado.

debilitating | dɪ'bɪlɪteɪtɪŋ *adj.* debilitador.

debility | dɪ'bɪlɪtɪ | *s.i.* debilidad.

debit | 'debɪt | FIN. *v.t.* **1** cargar (en la cuenta de alguien). || *s.c.* **2** débito, debe, cargo. || **3 – note,** nota de débito.

debonair | debə'neər | *adj.* gallardo; garboso; jovial.

debrief | diː'briːf | *v.t.* interrogar (a diplomáticos, políticos, etc. sobre su misión).

debriefing | diː'briːfɪŋ | *s.i.* interrogación, interrogamiento.

debris | 'deɪbriː | *s.i.* restos; escombros.

debt | det | *s.c.* e *i.* **1** deuda (personal, empresarial o gubernamental). || *s.c.* **2** (fig.) deuda (sentimiento de agradecimiento). || **3 – collector,** FIN. agente de cobro de deudas. **4 debt-service ratio,** FIN. ratio de servicio de la deuda. **5 – servicing,** FIN. servicio de la deuda. **6 to get into –,** endeudarse. **4 in –,** endeudado. **5 in someone's –,** (form.) en deuda con alguien (de agradecimiento). **6 out of –,** libre de deudas. **7 to run up a –/debts,** contraer una deuda/deudas.

debtor | 'detər | *s.c.* deudor.

debug | diː'bʌg | *v.t.* INF. quitar el virus (a un programa para ordenador).

debunk | diː'bʌŋk | *v.t.* desprestigiar; bajar del pedestal.

debut | 'deɪbuː | *s.c.* debut.

debutante | 'debjuːtɑːnt | *s.c.* (p.u.) debutante (mujer joven que es presentada en sociedad).

decade | 'dekeid | *s.c.* década, decenio.

decadence | 'dekədəns | *s.i.* decadencia.

decadent | 'dekədənt | *adj* (desp.) decadente.

decaffeinated | diː'kæfɪneɪtɪd | *adj.* descafeinado.

decamp | dɪ'kæmp | *v.i.* irse (secreta y rápidamente).

decant | dɪ'kænt | *v.t.* trasegar, decantar.

decanter | dɪ'kæntər | *s.c.* jarra.

decapitate | dɪ'kæpɪteɪt | *v.t.* (form.) decapitar, descabezar.

decapitation | dɪkæpɪ'teɪʃn | *s.i.* (form.) decapitación, descabezamiento.

decathlon | dɪ'kæθlən | *s.c.* DEP. decathlón.

decay | dɪ'keɪ | *v.i.* **1** corromperse, pudrirse; descomponerse. **2** (fig.) decaer, deteriorarse. || *s.i.* **3** descomposición (del cuerpo, de plantas, etc.). **4** decadencia, deterioro (de la sociedad, instituciones, etc.).

decayed | dɪ'keɪd | *adj.* podrido, corrupto; descompuesto.

decaying | dɪ'keɪŋ | *adj.* **1** en descomposición (un cuerpo, un animal, etc.). **2** decadente, en decadencia (una institución o similar).

decease | dɪ'siːs | *s.sing.* DER. deceso, defunción.

deceased | dɪ'siːsd | *s.sing.* **1** DER. difunto, fallecido. || *adj.* **2** (form.) difunto, fallecido: *the deceased girl is theirs = la chica fallecida es la suya.*

deceit | dɪ'siːt | *s.i.* engaño, duplicidad.

deceitful | dɪ'siːtfl | *adj.* engañoso, falaz.

deceitfully | dɪ'siːtfʊlɪ | *adv.* engañosamente, falazmente.

deceitfulness | dɪ'siːtfʊlnɪs | *s.i.* engaño, falacia.

deceive | dɪ'siːv | *v.t.* **1 [to – (into)]** engañar, embaucar: *he deceived me into lending him the car = me engañó para que le prestara el coche.* || *v.r.* **2** engañarse.

decelerate | diː'seləreɪt | *v.i.* disminuir la velocidad.

deceleration | ˌdiːseləˈreiʃn | *s.i.* desaceleración, disminución de velocidad.
December | dɪˈsembər | *s.i.* Diciembre.
decency | ˈdiːsnsɪ | *s.i.* **1** decoro, decencia; pudor. **2** honradez; decencia; bondad. || **3 decencies,** (form.) modales corteses, buenos modales. **4 to have the –,** [— *inf.*] tener la educación: *at least have the decency to invite her = por lo menos ten la educación de invitarla.*
decent | ˈdiːsnt | *adj.* **1** apropiado, adecuado, como es debido. **2** decoroso, decente (expresando lo moralmente correcto). **3** (hum.) vestido, cubierto. **4** honrado, decente. **5 [– of]** (fam.) detallista/gentil por parte de: *that was very decent of him = eso fue muy detallista por parte de él.* || **6 to do the – thing,** comportarse como es debido (a pesar de que pueda haber desgana): *after all she's done for you, do the decent thing and thank her = después de todo lo que ella ha hecho por ti, compórtate como es debido y agradéceselo.*
decentralization | ˌdiːsentrəlaɪˈzeiʃn | *s.i.* descentralización.
decentralize | ˌdiːˈsentrəlaɪz | (también **decentralise**) *v.t.* descentralizar.
decentralized | ˌdiːˈsentrəlaɪzd | *adj.* descentralizado.
deception | dɪˈsepʃn | *s.c.* e *i.* engaño; fraude.
deceptive | dɪˈseptɪv | *adj.* engañoso.
deceptively | dɪˈseptɪvlɪ | *adv.* engañosamente.
decibel | ˈdesɪbel | *s.c.* FIS. decibelio (unidad para medir sonido).
decide | dɪˈsaɪd | *v.i.* **1 [to – *inf.*]** decidir, tomar la decisión de. **2** llegar a la conclusión de que: *the editorial decided that the Americans were wrong = el editorial llegó a la conclusión de que los americanos no tenían razón.* || *v.t.* **3 [to – *o.d. inf.*]** decidir, hacer decidir; persuadir: *his words decided me to leave = sus palabras me persuadieron a marcharme.* **4** decidir, sentenciar (un partido, un debate, etc.). **5** decidir, resolver (por dictamen, decreto o similar). **6 to – on/upon,** optar por.
decided | dɪˈsaɪdɪd | *adj.* claro, rotundo, obvio: *I have very decided ideas about politics = tengo ideas muy claras sobre la política.*
decidedly | dɪˈsaɪdɪdlɪ | *adv.* **1** claramente, rotundamente, obviamente. **2** con gran fuerza, con gran énfasis = de una manera rotunda. (una manera de decir, de hablar).
deciduous | dɪˈsɪdjuəs | *adj.* BOT. caduco (que pierde hojas en otoño).
decimal | ˈdesiml | MAT. *adj.* **1** decimat: *decimal system = sistema decimal.* || *s.c.* **2** decimal. || **3 – point,** punto decimal.
decimalization | ˌdesɪməlaɪˈzeɪʃn | *s.i.* conversión al sistema decimal.
decimalize | ˈdesɪməlaɪz | (también **decimalise**) *v.t.* convertir al sistema decimal.
decimate | ˈdesɪmeɪt | *v.t.* diezmar.
decimation | desɪˈmeɪʃn | *s.i.* **[– of]** pérdida de gran parte de.
decipher | dɪˈsaɪfər | *v.t.* descifrar.
decision | dɪˈsɪʒn | *s.c.* **1 [– (on/about)]** decisión, resolución. || *s.i.* **2** decisión, determinación, firmeza.
decision-making | dɪˈsɪʒnmeɪkɪŋ | *s.i.* capacidad de decisión, toma de decisión.
decisive | dɪˈsaɪsɪv | *adj.* **1** concluyente, terminante, decisivo. **2** decidido, firme (característica de una persona).
decisively | dɪˈsəɪsɪvlɪ | *adv.* **1** concluyentemente, terminantemente, decisivamente. **2** decididamente, firmemente.
decisiveness | dɪˈsaɪsɪvnɪs | *s.i.* firmeza, decisión.
deck | dek | *s.c.* **1** plataforma, nivel (en un autobús, tranvía, etc. de más de un piso). **2** plato (de un tocadiscos). **3** baraja (de cartas). || *s.sing.* **4** MAR. cubierta. || *v.t.* **5** (p.u.) engalanar; decorar. **6** (fam. y EE.UU.) derribar (de un golpe). || **7 below decks,** MAR. bajo cubierta. **8 to clear the decks,** (fam.) despejar la mesa de trabajo (preparándose para otro asunto). **9 to – out,** embellecer, engalanar, ataviar espléndidamente: *the hall was decked out for the occasion = el salón estaba engalanado para la ocasión.* **10 to hit the –,** (fam.) dar con los huesos en tierra.
deckchair | ˈdektʃeər | *s.c.* hamaca; silla de cubierta.
deckhand | ˈdekhænd | *s.c.* MAR. mozo de cubierta.
declaim | dɪˈkleɪm | *v.t.* **1** declamar, hablar grandiosamente. **2** (fig.) arengar, lanzar una perorata. **3** recitar, leer dramáticamente (poesía o similar).
declamation | ˌdekləˈmeɪʃn | *s.i.* **1** recitación, declamación (de poesía o similar). || *s.c.* **2** arenga; discurso grandioso.
declamatory | dɪˈklæmətərɪ | *adj.* grandioso, dramático (un discurso o escrito).
declaration | ˌdekləˈreɪʃn | *s.c.* **1 [– (of)]** declaración, manifestación. **2 [– (of)]** declaración (formal), manifiesto: *Declaration of Independence.* **3** DER. declaración, primer alegato.
declaratory | ˌdəklərəˈtɒrɪ | *adj.* firme, seguro (tono de un discurso, escrito, etc.).
declare | dɪˈkleər | *v.t.* **1** declarar, aseverar, afirmar. **2** declarar (en Aduanas, ante Hacienda, etc.). **3** proclamar, declarar (una intención o similar): *the party declared its support for the President = el partido proclamó su apoyo al Presidente.* || *v.r.* **4** manifestar su opinión, declararse (sobre un asunto). || **5 to – against,** oponerse a, estar en contra de (mediante declaración). **6 to – for,** estar a favor de, apoyar (mediante declaración). **7 (Well), I –,** (p.u.) ¡no me digas!
declared | dɪˈkleəd | *adj.* declarado (que no lo oculta): *he's a declared communist = es un comunista declarado.*
declassification | ˌdiːklæsɪfɪˈkeɪʃn | *s.i.* permiso de publicación de documentación oficial secreta (hasta entonces).
declassify | ˌdiːklæsɪfaɪ | *v.t.* permitir la publicación de documentación oficial secreta (hasta entonces).
decline | dɪˈklaɪn | *v.i.* **1** declinar, disminuir (la importancia, cantidad o similar de algo): *the unions' power is declining = el poder de los sindicatos está declinando.* || *v.t.* **2 [to – + *o.d./inf.*]** (form.) declinar, no aceptar. || *s.c.* e *i.* **3** disminución, descenso. || **4 to fall/go into (a) –,** empezar a debilitarse, perder fuerza. **5 on the decline,** en decadencia.
declining | dɪˈklaɪnɪŋ | *adj.* cada vez más débil.
decode | ˌdiːˈkəud | *v.t.* descifrar.
decoder | diːˈkəudər | *s.c.* **1** experto en descifrar. **2** ELECTR. aparato descifrador (de una señal electrónica).
décolletage | ˌdeɪkɒlˈtɑːʒ | *s.sing.* escote atrevido.
décolleté | deɪˈkɒlteɪ | (también **décolletée**) *s.c.* **1** escote atrevido (el hecho de llevarlo). || *adj.* **2** muy escotada.
decolonization | ˌdiːkɒlənaiˈzeɪʃn | *s.i.* POL. descolonización.
decolonize | ˌdɪːkɒlənaɪz | (también **decolonise**) *v.t.* POL. descolonizar.
decompose | ˌdiːkəmˈpəuz | *v.i.* descomponerse, pudrirse.
decomposition | ˌdiːkɒmpəˈzɪʃn | *s.i.* descomposición, putrefacción.
decompression | ˌdiːkəmˈpreʃn | FIS. *s.i.* **1** descompresión. || **2 – chamber,** cámara de descompresión.
decongestant | ˌdiːkənˈdʒestənt | *s.c.* MED. mucolítico.
decontaminate | ˌdiːkənˈtæmɪneɪt | *v.t.* desinfectar, descontaminar.
decontamination | ˌdiːkəntæmɪˈneɪʃn | *s.i.* desinfección, descontaminación.
decor | ˈdeɪkɔːr | *s.i.* decoración, decorado (del teatro).
decorate | ˈdekəreɪt | *v.t.* **1** decorar, adornar. **2** mejorar (una habitación con una capa nueva de pintura, nuevo empapelado, etc.). || **3 to be decorated,** ser condecorado.
decorating | ˌdekəˈreɪtɪŋ | *s.i.* decoración, mejora (de una habitación).
decoration | ˌdekəˈreɪʃn | *s.c.* **1** condecoración. || *s.c.* e *i.* **2** decoración, ornamentación, adorno.
decorative | ˈdekərətɪv | *adj.* ornamental, decorativo.
decorator | ˌdekəreɪtər | *s.c.* decorador.
decorous | ˈdekərəs | *adj.* decoroso, correcto, apropiado (de conducta).
decorously | ˌdekərəslɪ | *adv.* decorosamente, correctamente, apropiadamente.
decorum | dɪˈkɔːrəm | *s.i.* (form.) decoro, corrección.
decoy | ˈdiːkɔɪ | *s.c.* **1** señuelo, añagaza. **2** reclamo (en la caza). || *v.t.* **3** engañar (mediante algún tipo de señuelo o similar), desviar de su objetivo.
decrease | dɪˈkriːs | *v.t.* e *i.* **1** disminuir(se), decrecer(se), aminorar(se). || *s.c.* **2 [– (of/in)]** disminución, decrecimiento.

decreasing | dɪ'kriːsɪŋ | *adj.* decreciente, cada vez menor.
decreasingly | dɪ'kriːsɪŋlɪ | *adv.* decrecientemente.
decree | dɪ'kriː | *v.t.* **1** decretar. || *s.c.* **2** decreto. **3** (EE.UU.) DER. edicto (proveniente de un tribunal). || **4 – absolute,** DER. decreto final de divorcio (que finaliza el matrimonio). **5 – nisi,** DER. orden preliminar de divorcio.
decrepit | dɪ'krepɪt | *adj.* decrépito.
decrepitude | dɪ'krepɪtjuːd | *s.i.* (form.) decrepitud.
decry | dɪkraɪ | *v.t.* (form.) desaprobar, censurar.
dedicate | 'dedɪkeɪt | *v.t.* **1** dedicar (un libro), consagrar (un monumento, etc.) || *v.r.* **3 [to – to]** dedicarse a, consagrarse a.
dedicated | ˌ'dedɪ'keɪtɪd | *adj.* **1** de gran dedicación; comprometido: *he's a dedicated teacher = es un profesor de gran dedicación.* **2 [– to]** dedicado a, comprometido con.
dedication | ˌdedɪ'keɪʃn | *s.i.* **1** dedicación; esmero; compromiso. || *s.c.* **2** dedicatoria (en un libro o similar). **3** consagración (de una iglesia, etc.).
deduce | dɪ'djuːs | *v.t.* **1** deducir, sacar como conclusión. **2** FIL. deducir, inferir.
deduct | dɪ̀dʌkt | *v.t.* substraer, deducir, restar.
deduction | dɪ̀dʌkʃn | *s.c.* **1** deducción, conclusión. || *s.c.* e *i.* **2** FIL. deducción, inferencia. **3** deducción, descuento.
deductive | dɪ'dʌktɪv | *adj.* FIL. deductivo.
deed | diːd | *s.c.* **1** hecho (no palabra). **2** hazaña, proeza. **3** DER. escritura (especialmente de propiedad). || **4 – poll,** DER. escritura legal de cambio de nombre. **5 to do one's good – for the day,** (fam.) hacer el acto bueno del día. **6 in word and –,** de palabra y obra.
deed-box | 'diːdbɒks | *s.c.* caja fuerte (para documentos legales).
deem | diːm | *v.t.* **[to – *inf.*]** (form.) juzgar, considerar: *he wasn't deemed to be fit for the post = no se consideró que fuera la persona adecuada para el puesto.*
deep | diːp | *adj.* **1** profundo, hondo (río, lago, etc.). **2** profundo (superficie a lo ancho): *the new wardrobe is very deep = el armario nuevo es muy profundo.* **3** DEP. profundo (hacia el límite del campo contrario). **4** de profundidad, de hondo (con medidas): *the canal is 10 feet deep = el canal tiene 10 pies de profundidad.* **5** grave, serio; profundo (dando énfasis a la importancia, gravedad, etc. de algo): *I'm in deep economic trouble = estoy en una problemática económica grave.* **6** profundo, reparador (sueño). **7** intenso, oscuro (color). **8** grave, profundo (sonido, voz, etc.). **9** profundo, insondable (carácter de una persona). **10** penetrante, profunda (mirada). **11** a pleno pulmón, profundo (suspiro, toma de aire, etc.) || *adv.* **12** profundamente: *they dived deep = ellos se sumergieron profundamente.* **13** [*num.* –] de... en fondo: *they stood four deep = permanecieron de pie de cuatro en fondo.* **14** en lo más profundo, en lo más interior (como sentimiento). **15** penetrantemente (mirada). **16 [– (in/into)]** hasta arriba, profundamente (endeudado). || *s.sing.* **17** (lit.) piélago. || **18 – down,** en lo más íntimo, interiormente. **19 – freeze,** congelador. **20 – in thought,** ensimismado, absorto. **21 deeps,** (p.u.) profundidades (de la tierra). **22 to go /run –,** estar muy profundo (problema), ser muy serio (cualquier cosa): *the controversy runs deep = la controversia es muy seria.* **23 to go off the – end,** (fam.) convertirse en un basilisco, volverse loco de enfado. **24 in – mourning,** en luto riguroso. **25 in – water,** en líos, con problemas. **26 to jump in at the – end,** aceptar la peor parte (de algo). **27 still waters run –,** del agua mansa me libre Dios. **28 to take a – breath,** aspirar profundamente. **29 to throw somebody in at the – end,** poner a alguien en un brete.
deep-chested | 'diːptʃestɪd | *adj.* ancho de pecho.
deepen | 'diːpən | *v.t.* **1** hacer más profundo. **2** profundizar (conocimientos). **3** poner grave (la voz). || *v.i.* **4** hacerse más profundo. **5** adquirir tintes más oscuros; intensificarse (un problema). **6** ampliarse (conocimientos). **7** ponerse más grave (voz). **8 [to – (in/into)]** hacerse más oscuro (luz o color): *the day deepened = el día se hizo más oscuro.*
deep-fry | ˌdiːp'fraɪ | *v.t.* freír en mucho aceite (o sucedáneo).
deeply | diːplɪ | *adv.* **1** profundamente, hondamente. **2** profundamente, seriamente: *I love you deeply = te amo profundamente.* **3** reparadoramente, profundamente (sueño). **4** intensamente, profundamente (mirada). **5** a pleno pulmón, profundamente (suspiro o similar).
deep-rooted | ˌdiːp'ruːtɪd | *adj.* enraizado, muy arraigado (creencias, opiniones, etc.).
deep-sea | 'diːpsiː | *adj.* de aguas profundas, de alta mar: *deep-sea diving = submarinismo de aguas profundas.*
deep-seated | ˌdiːp'siːtɪd | *adj.* muy arraigado, inveterado.
deep-set | 'diːpset | *adj.* hundido (ojos).
deer | dɪər | [*pl.* **deer**] *s.c.* ZOOL. ciervo, venado.
deerskin | 'dɪəskɪn | *s.i.* de piel de ciervo; cuero de venado.
deerstalker | 'dɪəstɔːkər | *s.c.* gorra de cazador (con visera atrás y delante).
de-escalate | ˌdiː'eskəleɪt | *v.t.* e *i.* reducir(se), aminorar(se) (un problema).
de-escalation | diːˌeskə'leɪʃn | *s.i.* reducción de tensión (en una situación ya de por sí mala).
deface | dɪ'feɪs | *v.t.* emborronar, desfigurar; estropear (algo escrito o pintado): *the picture of the Prime Minister was defaced = el retrato del Primer Ministro fue desfigurado.*
defacement | dɪ'feɪsmənt | *s.i.* emborronamiento, desfiguración.
de facto | ˌdeɪ'fæktəu | *adj.* y *adv.* (form.) de hecho, de facto.
defamation | ˌdefə'meɪʃn | *s.i.* (form.) difamación, calumnia.
defamatory | dɪ'fæmətrɪ | *adj.* (form.) difamatorio, calumnioso.
defame | dɪ'feɪm | *v.t.* (form.) difamar, calumniar.
default | dɪ'fɔːlt | *v.i.* **1 [to – (in/on)]** DER. no aparecer (en un juicio), no pagar (un contrato o similar). || *s.i.* **2** DER. incumplimiento (de contrato), ausencia (de un juicio). || **3 by –, a)** DER. en rebeldía. **b)** por ausencia (de algo que habría cambiado la situación). **4 in – of,** (form.) por falta de.
defaulter | dɪ'fɔːltər | *s.c.* **1** incumplidor, deudor, ausente. **2** (brit.) soldado perseguido (culpable de algún delito de índole militar).
defeat | dɪ'fiːt | *v.t.* **1** derrotar, vencer, ganar (en deporte, elecciones, batallas, etc.). **2** desesperar, frustrar (con un problema difícil). **3** desbaratar, anular, hacer fracasar: *the students defeated the goals of the program = los estudiantes hicieron fracasar los objetivos del programa.* || *s.c.* **4** derrota, fracaso. || *s.i.* **5** derrota, frustración.
defeatism | dɪ'fiːtɪzəm | *s.i.* derrotismo.
defeatist | dɪ'fiːtɪst | *s.c.* **1** derrotista. || *adj.* **2** derrotista.
defecate | 'defəkeɪt | *v.i.* (form.) defecar, evacuar (el vientre).
defecation | ˌdefəkeɪʃn | *s.i.* (form.) defecación.
defect | 'diːfekt | *s.c.* **1 [– (in/of)]** defecto, desperfecto, imperfección. || | dɪ'fekt | *v.i.* **2 [to – (from/to)]** abandonar, desertar (el propio país, partido, etc. para pasar a otro país, al bando contrario).
defection | dɪ'fekʃn | *s.c.* e *i.* deserción, defección, abandono.
defective | dɪ'fektɪv | *adj.* **1** defectuoso, imperfecto. **2** GRAM. defectivo (verbo carente de todos los tiempos).
defector | dɪ'fektər | *s.c.* desertor, tránsfuga.
defence | dɪ'fens | (EE.UU. **defense**) *s.i.* **1** defensa, protección. **2** POL. defensa, sistema de defensa (de una nación). || *s.c.* **3 [– (of/against)]** defensa, escudo, protección. **4 [– (of/against)]** justificación, defensa (de una idea, tesis, etc.). **5** DER. defensa. **6** DEP. defensa. || *s.sing.* **7** DER. defensa, abogado defensor. || **8 – mechanism,** mecanismo de defensa. **9 defences,** MIL. defensas.
defenceless | dɪ'fenslɪs | (EE.UU. **defenseless**) *adj.* indefenso, desamparado, sin posibilidad de defensa.
defencelessness | dɪ'fenslɪsnɪs | (EE.UU. defenselessness) *s.i.* situación de desamparo, situación de indefensión.
defend | dɪ'fend | *v.t.* **1** defender, proteger. **2** DER. defender. **3** DEP. defender (un título o similar). || *v.r.* **4** defenderse, protegerse (en todos los sentidos).

defendant | dɪ'fendənt | *s.c.* DER. acusado, demandado.
defender | dɪ'fendər | *s.c.* **1 [– (of)]** defensor, protector; campeón. **2** DEP. defensor.
defensible | dɪ'fensəbl | *adj.* defendible.
defensive | dɪ'fensɪv | *adj.* **1** defensivo, de defensa, de protección. **2** defensiva (actitud personal): *she always has this stupid defensive tone = siempre tiene un tono defensivo estúpido.* || **3 on the –,** a la defensiva.
defensively | dɪfensɪvlɪ | *adv.* a la defensiva.
defensiveness | dɪ'fensɪvnɪs | *s.i.* actitud defensiva.
defer | dɪ'fɜːr | **[deferring, deferred]** *v.t.* **1 [to – *o.d./gerundio*]** diferir, retrasar; dilatar. || *v.i.* **2 [to – to]** someterse a, deferir ante (una persona que merece respeto).
deference | 'defərəns | *s.i.* **1 [– (to)]** deferencia, acatamiento. || **2 in – to,** por deferencia a, por consideración con.
deferential | ˌdefə'renʃl | *adj.* deferente, respetuoso.
deferentially | ˌdefə'renʃlɪ | *adv.* deferentemente, respetuosamente.
deferment | dɪ'fɜːmənt | *s.c.* e *i.* (form.) aplazamiento.
deferral | dɪ'fɜːrəl | V. **deferment.**
deferred | dɪ'fɜːd | *adj.* **1** aplazado, retrasado. || **2 – payment,** pago aplazado, pago a plazos. **3 – shares,** FIN. acciones de pago atrasado. **4 – stock,** FIN. paquete de acciones de pago diferido.
defiance | dɪ'faɪəns | *s.i.* **1** provocación, desafío, reto. || **2 in – of,** a despecho de, como provocación para.
defiant | dɪ'faɪənt | *adj.* provocador, insolente.
defiantly | dɪ'faiəntlɪ | *adv.* provocadoramente, insolentemente.
deficiency | dɪ'fɪʃnsɪ | *s.c.* e *i.* **1 [– (in)]** deficiencia, carencia (física). **2** imperfección, falta: *his deficiencies are obvious = sus imperfecciones son clarísimas.*
deficient | dɪ'fɪʃnt | *adj.* **1 [– (in)]** deficiente, carente, insuficiente (en alguna cosa necesaria). **2** imperfecto, falto.
deficit | 'defɪsɪt | FIN. *s.c.* **1** déficit, descubierto. || **2 in –,** al descubierto, con deudas.
defile | dɪ'faɪl | *v.t.* **1** profanar, mancillar. || | 'diːfaɪl | *s.c.* **2** (lit.) desfiladero, garganta entre montañas.
definable | dɪ'faɪnəbl | *adj.* definible.
define | dɪ'faɪn | *v.t.* **1** definir (una situación, una palabra, etc.). || **2 to be defined,** marcarse en silueta, delinearse: *the roofs were defined in the horizon = los tejados se delineaban en el horizonte.*
defined | dɪ'faind | *adj.* definido, clarificado, explicado.
definite | 'defɪnət | *adj.* **1** determinado, fijo, asegurado. **2** preciso, claro (en su forma o características): *I have a definite task = tengo una tarea precisa.* **3** cierto, determinado (sin duda alguna). **4** firme (en comportamiento): *he is a definite teacher = es un profesor firme.* || **5 – article,** GRAM. artículo determinado.
definitely | 'defɪnətlɪ | *adv.* **1** fijamente; ciertamente. **2** por supuesto (en contestaciones muy afirmativas).
definition | ˌdefɪ'nɪʃn | *s.c.* **1** definición. || *s.i.* **2** nitidez, claridad, definición. || **3 by –,** por definición.
definitive | dɪ'fɪnətɪv | *adj.* definitivo, concluyente.
definitively | dɪ'fɪnətɪvlɪ | *adv.* definitivamente, en definitiva.
deflate | dɪ'fleɪt | *v.t.* **1** rebajar, disminuir (reputación, importancia, etc.). **2** ECON. enfriar (la economía). **3** desinflar (un globo o similar). || *v.i.* **4** desinflarse (un globo).
deflated | dɪ'fleɪtɪd | *adj.* desinflado, sin ánimos (de espíritu).
deflation | dɪ'fleɪʃn | *s.i.* **1** ECON. deflación, enfriamiento. **2** desánimo, desilusión.
deflationary | ˌdiː'fleɪʃnərɪ | *adj.* ECON. deflacionario, de enfriamiento.
deflect | dɪ'flekt | *v.t.* **1** desviar, apartar (críticas o similar). **2 [to – (from)]** apartar, desviar: *the new job deflected him from his family duties = el nuevo empleo le apartó de sus deberes familiares.* **3** despejar, echar a un lado, empujar a un lado, desviar (en deporte, experimentos físicos, etc.). || *v.i.* **4** desviarse, apartarse.
deflection | dɪ'flekʃn | *s.c.* e *i.* **1** desvío, desviación. || *s.c.* **2** FIS. desviación.
deflower | ˌdiː'flauər | *v.t.* (lit.) desflorar (a una virgen).
defoliant | ˌdiː'fəulɪənt | *s.c.* QUIM. defoliante.
defoliate | ˌdiː'feulɪeɪt | *v.t.* deshojar (plantas, árboles, etc.).
defoliation | ˌdiːfəulɪ'eɪʃn | *s.i.* defoliación.
deforest | ˌdiː'fɒrɪst | *v.t.* desforestar, talar.
deforestation | diːfɒrɪ'steɪʃn | *s.i.* desforestación, tala.
deform | dɪ'fɔːm | *v.t.* **1** deformar, desfigurar. **2** distorsionar, deformar (la realidad que sea).
deformed | dɪ'fɔːmd | *adj.* deforme, desfigurado.
deformation | ˌdiːfɔː'meiʃn | *s.c.* e *i.* deformación, desfiguración.
deformity | dɪ'fɔːmətɪ | *s.c.* e *i.* deformidad.
defraud | dɪfrɔːd | *v.t.* **[to – of]** estafar, defraudar: *he defrauded all of his employees of their social security payments = estafó a todos sus empleados los pagos de la seguridad social.*
defray | dɪ'freɪ | *v.t.* (form.) sufragar, costear (gastos o similar).
defrost | ˌdiː'frɒst | *v.t.* e *i.* **1** descongelar(se), deshelar(se) (un frigorífico, comida congelada, etc.). || *v.r.* **2** descongelarse.
deft | deft | *adj.* **1** hábil, diestro, ducho (con las manos o movimientos corporales). **2 [– (at)]** (fig.) hábil, experto (con personas, situaciones, etc.).
deftly | deftlɪ | *adv.* **1** hábilmente, con destreza (física). **2** expertamente, hábilmente (trato de personas o similar).
deftness | 'deftnɪs | *s.i.* **1** habilidad, destreza, maña (física). **2** habilidad, experiencia (con personas, situaciones, etc.).
defunct | dɪ'fʌŋkt | *adj.* **1** (form.) difunto (persona). **2** inactivo, inexistente (programa, sistema, industria, etc.).
defuse | ˌdiː'fjuːz | *v.t.* **1** neutralizar (una situación problemática). **2** desactivar (bomba o similar).
defy | dɪ'faɪ | *v.t.* **1** desafiar, retar; desobedecer. **2 [to – + *o.d.* + to + *inf.*]** desafiar, retar. **3** no admitir, no permitir (descripción, comprensión, análisis, etc.): *her beauty defies description = su belleza no admite una descripción.*
degeneracy | dɪ'dʒenərəsɪ | *s.i.* decadencia, degradación, depravación.
degenerate | dɪ'dʒenərɪt | *adj.* **1** (desp.) degenerado, depravado. || *s.c.* **2** degenerado, depravado. || | dɪ'dʒenəreɪt | *v.i.* **3 [to – (into/to)]** degenerar, degradarse.
degeneration | dɪˌdʒenə'reɪʃn | *s.i.* degeneración, deterioro.
degenerative | dɪˌdʒe'nerətɪv | *adj.* degenerativo.
degradation | ˌdegrə'deɪʃn | *s.i.* **1** degradación, miseria extrema. **2** envilecimiento. **3** deterioro.
degrade | dɪ'greɪd | *v.t.* **1** envilecer, degradar: *a book which degrades History = un libro que envilece la Historia.* **2** deteriorar, empeorar. || *v.r.* **3** envilecerse, degradarse.
degrading | dɪgreɪdɪŋ | *adj.* degradante, envilecedor.
degree | dɪ'griː | *s.c.* **1** FIS. grado (de temperatura). **2** GEOM. grado. **3** grado, punto; graduación: *we are all guilty in different degrees = somos todos culpables en grados diferentes.* **4** título, grado (académico). || **5 by degrees,** gradualmente, poco a poco. **6 to a/some –,** hasta cierto punto, en cierta medida.
OBS: Esta palabra entra en compuestos numéricos para cuantificar hasta qué punto ha sucedido algo: **7** (EE.UU.) DER. grado de criminalidad: *first-degree murder = asesinato en primer grado.* **8** en quemaduras: *third-degree burns = quemaduras de tercer grado.*
dehumanization | diː'hjuːmənər'zeɪʃn | *s.i.* deshumanización, embrutecimiento.
dehumanize | ˌdiː'hjuːmənaɪz | (también dehumanise) *v.t.* **1** deshumanizar, embrutecer. || **2 to be dehumanized:** quedar deshumanizado, estar deshumanizado (actividad humana como el trabajo o similar).
dehumanizing | ˌdiː'hjuːmənaizɪŋ | *adj.* embrutecedor, que deshumaniza.
dehydrate | ˌdiː'haɪdreɪt | *v.t.* deshidratar, desecar.
dehydrated | ˌdiːhaɪ'dreɪtɪd | *adj.* deshidratado, sin ninguna agua.
dehydration | ˌdiːhaɪ'dreɪʃn | *s.i.* deshidratación, desecación.
deification | ˌdiːɪfɪ'keɪʃn | *s.i.* (form.) deificación, divinización.

deify | 'di:ɪfaɪ | *v.t.* (form.) deificar, divinizar.
deign | deɪn | *v.t.* **[to –** *inf.***]** dignarse a, condescender en.
deism | 'di:ɪzəm | *s.i.* REL. deísmo (creencia en la fe como base fundamental de la religión).
deist | 'di:ɪst | *s.c.* REL. deísta.
deity | 'di:ɪtɪ | *s.c.* deidad, dios, diosa.
déjà vu | ˌdeɪʒɑ:'vju: | *s.i.* vulgaridad repetitiva, ilusión cansina (sentimiento de haber experimentado lo que está ocurriendo en el presente).
dejected | dɪ'dʒektɪd | *adj.* abatido, desalentado, desanimado.
dejectedly | dɪ'dʒektɪdlɪ | *adv.* abatidamente, desalentadamente, con gran desánimo.
dejection | dɪ'dʒekʃn | *s.i.* abatimiento, desánimo.
de jure | ˌdeɪ'dʒʊərɪ | *adj.* DER. de derecho, en teoría.
dekko | 'dekəʊ | **to have a – at,** (fam. y brit.) echar un vistazo a.
delay | dɪ'leɪ | *v.t.* **1** atrasar, retardar. **2** **[to –** *ger.***]** retardar, posponer, atrasar: *don't delay starting the legal procedure = no atrases el comenzar el procedimiento judicial.* || *v.i.* **3** atrasarse, retardarse, demorarse. || *s.c.* e *i.* **4** retraso, demora, tardanza. || **5 delayed-action,** de acción retardada. **6 without –,** sin dilación, sin tardanza, sin demora.
delaying | dɪ'leɪɪŋ | *adj.* dilatorio: *delaying tactics.*
delectable | dɪ'lektəbl | *adj.* **1** (fam. y lit.) atrayente, atractivo (sexualmente). **2** delicioso, deleitoso.
delectation | ˌdi:lek'teɪʃn | *s.i.* (form.) goce, fruición, deleite.
delegate | 'delɪgɪt | *s.c.* **1** delegado, comisionado. || | 'delɪgeɪt | *v.t.* **2** delegar, comisionar. **3** **[to –** *o.d.* **+ to +** *inf.***]** comisionar para, autorizar para.
delegation | ˌdelɪ'geɪʃn | *s.c.* **1** delegación (grupo de delegados). || *s.i.* **2** delegación, diputación.
delete | dɪ'li:t | *v.t.* borrar, suprimir, tachar.
deleterious | ˌdelɪ'tɪərɪəs | *adj.* (form.) nocivo, pernicioso.
deletion | dɪ'li:ʃn | *s.c.* e *i.* supresión (de algo escrito).
deliberate | dɪ'lɪbərɪt | *adj.* **1** deliberado, intencional. **2** pausado, deliberado (movimiento). || | dɪ'lɪbəreɪt | *v.i.* **3** deliberar, meditar, considerar.
deliberately | dɪ'lɪbərɪtlɪ | *adv.* **1** deliberadamente, intencionalmente. **2** pausadamente, deliberadamente.
deliberation | dɪˌlɪbə'reɪʃn | *s.i.* **1** deliberación, meditación, consideración. **2** pausa, deliberación. || **3 deliberations,** deliberaciones. **4 with –,** con deliberación, con pausa.
deliberative | ˌdɪlɪ'berətɪv | *adj.* de deliberación, de reflexión.
delicacy | ˌdelɪkəsɪ | *s.i.* **1** delicadeza, gentileza. **2** delicadeza, carácter delicado (de una cuestión). **3** tacto, finura. || *s.c.* **4** manjar, bocado exquisito.
delicate | 'delɪkɪt | *adj.* **1** delicado, fino, exquisito. **2** delicado (de salud). **3** modesto, pudoroso. **4** delicado, suave (de olor, sabor, color, etc.). **5** frágil, delicado. **6** cauto, delicado (con sus palabras). **7** delicado, sensible (un objeto). **8** delicado, precario (situación).
delicately | 'delɪkɪtlɪ | *adv.* **1** delicadamente, finamente, exquisitamente. **2** cautamente, delicadamente (con palabras). **3** delicadamente, precariamente.
delicatessen | ˌdelɪkə'tesn | *s.c.* mantequería, fiambrería.
delicious. | dɪ'lɪʃəs | *adj.* **1** delicioso, exquisito (comida). **2** (fig.) agradable, placentero: *a delicious girl = una chica agradable.*
deliciously | dɪ'lɪʃəslɪ | *adv.* **1** deliciosamente, exquisitamente. **2** agradablemente, placenteramente.
delight | dɪ'laɪt | *s.i.* **1** deleite, delicia; placer. || *s.i.* **2** encanto, placer. || *v.t.* **3** complacer, dar placer. || *v.i.* **4 [to – in/at]** complacerse en, alegrarse con. || **5 to be delighted,** darle a uno mucha alegría: *I was delighted to hear the news = me dio mucha alegría oír las noticias.* **6 to take –/a – (in),** deleitarse (en).
delighted | dɪ'laɪtɪd | *adj.* encantado, muy contento.
delightedly | dɪ'laɪtɪdlɪ | *adv.* con gran deleite, con gran placer.
delightful | dɪ'laɪtfl | *adj.* encantador, delicioso.
delightfully | dɪ'laɪtfəlɪ | *adv.* encantadoramente, deliciosamente.
delimit | di:'lɪmɪt | *v.t.* (form.) delimitar, deslindar.
delineate | dɪ'lɪnɪeɪt | *v.t.* (form.) describir; trazar, bosquejar.
delineation | dɪ'lɪnɪ'eɪʃn | *s.i.* y *c.* (form.) descripción; bosquejo, esbozo.
delinquency | dɪ'lɪŋkwənsɪ | *s.i.* y *c.* delincuencia, criminalidad.
delinquent | dɪ'lɪŋkwənt | *adj.* **1** delincuente, criminal. || *s.c.* **2** delincuente, criminal.
delirious | dɪ'lɪrɪəs | *adj.* **1** desvariado, delirante. **2** (fig.) lleno de éxtasis.
deliriously | dɪ'lɪrɪəslɪ | *adv.* delirantemente, en desvarío.
delirium | dɪ'lɪrɪəm | *s.i.* **1** delirio, desvarío. **2** (fig.) éxtasis. || **3 – tremens,** delirium tremens.
deliver | dɪ'lɪvər | *v.t.* **1** repartir, distribuir (casa por casa). **2** dar, pronunciar (discurso, sermón, etc.). **3** ayudar en el parto de. **4** (form.) entregar. **5** (lit.) dar, asestar (golpe). **6 [to – (from)]** (form.) librar, libertar. **7** cumplir, ofrecer resultados: *the party failed to deliver = el partido no ofreció resultados.* || *v.i.* **8** hacer una entrega, realizar distribución (casa por casa). || **9 to be delivered of,** (form.) dar a luz (a un bebé). **10 to – the goods,** cumplir lo prometido, cumplir lo pactado.
deliverance | dɪ'lɪvərəns | *s.i.* (p.u.) liberación, salvación.
delivery | dɪ'lɪvərɪ | *s.i.* y *c.* **1** reparto (casa por casa). **2** parto, alumbramiento. || *s.c.* **3** entrega (de un pedido). || *s.i.* **4** modo, forma, estilo (de expresarse). **5** **[– (from)]** (lit.) liberación, salvación. || **6 – note,** (brit.) albarán de entrega. **7 – truck,** (EE.UU.) camión/furgoneta de reparto. **8 – van,** (brit.) furgoneta de reparto. **9 to take – of,** recibir una entrega de.
dell | del | *s.c.* (lit.) valle (pequeño y arbolado).
delouse | ˌdi:'laʊs | *v.t.* despiojar.
delphinium | del'fɪnɪəm | *s.c.* BOT. delfinio, espuela de caballero.
delta | 'deltə | *s.c.* **1** GEOG. delta (de un río). || **2 Delta,** delta (cuarta letra del alfabeto griego). **3 – wing aircraft,** DEP. ala delta.
delude | dɪ'lu:d | *v.t.* y *r.* engañar(se); despistar(se).
deluge | 'delju:dʒ | *s.c.* **1** diluvio, inundación. **2 [a – of]** (fig.) un torrente de (palabras, cartas y muchas cosas más). || *v.t.* **3** inundar, anegar. || **4 to be deluged (with),** ser inundado (por/de): *we were deluged with petitions = fuimos inundados de peticiones.*
delusion | dɪ'lu:ʒn | *s.c.* e *i.* **1** falsa ilusión. || **2 delusions of grandeur,** delirios de grandeza.
delusive | dɪ'lu:sɪv | *adj.* engañoso, falaz.
de luxe | də'lʌks | *adj.* de lujo, lujoso.
delve | delv | *v.i.* **1 [to – (in/into)]** sondear, ahondar: *I must delve into this matter = debo ahondar en este asunto.* **2** revolver (buscando).
demagnetize | ˌdi:'mægnɪtaɪz | (también **demagnetise**) *v.t.* desmagnetizar, quitar la propiedad de imantación.
demagogic | ˌdemə'gɪk | *adj.* (desp.) demagógico.
demagogue | 'deməgɒg | *s.c.* (desp.) demagogo.
demagogy | 'deməgɒgɪ | *s.i.* POL. demagogia.
demand | dɪ'mɑ:nd | *v.t.* **1** exigir, reclamar. **2** requerir, necesitar: *the situation demands a leader = la situación requiere un líder.* **3** exigir saber, preguntar con gran exigencia: *what are you doing here? he demanded = ¿qué estás haciendo aquí? exigió saber.* || *s.c.* **4** exigencia, reclamación. || *s.i.* **5 [– (for)]** demanda: *the demand for foreign currency = la demanda de moneda extranjera.* || **6 demands,** demandas, exigencias, requerimientos. **7 in (great) –,** en (gran) demanda. **8 to make demands on/of,** exigir un gran esfuerzo de: *this new technique makes tremendous demands on the workers = esta nueva técnica exige un gran esfuerzo de los trabajadores.* **9 on –,** a petición (sin más trámites): *abortion on demand.*
demanding | dɪ'mɑ:ndɪŋ | *adj.* **1** agotador; absorbente (tarea). **2** exigente, duro (persona).
demarcate | 'di:mɑ:keɪt | *v.t.* (form.) demarcar, delimitar.
demarcation | ˌdi:mɑ:'keɪʃn | *s.i.* demarcación, deslinde.
demean | dɪ'mi:n | *v.t.* y *r.* abajar(se), humillar(se), degradar(se).

demeaning | dɪ'miːnɪŋ | *adj.* humillante, degradante.
demeanour | dɪ'miːnər | (EE.UU. **demeanor**) *s.i.* (form.) porte, proceder; conducta.
demented | dɪ'mentɪd | *adj.* demente, loco.
dementedly | dɪ'mentɪdlɪ | *adv.* locamente.
dementia | dɪ'menʃə | *s.i.* MED. demencia.
demerit | diː'merɪt | *s.c.* (form.) demérito, desmerecimiento.
demijohn | 'demɪdʒɒn | *s.c.* garrafón.
demilitarization | ˌdiːˌmɪlɪtəraɪ'zeɪʃn | *s.i.* desmilitarización.
demilitarize | ˌdiː'mɪlɪtəraɪz | (también **demilitarise**) *v.t.* desmilitarizar.
demise | dɪ'maɪz | *s.sing.* **1** defunción, muerte (no de una persona). **2** (form. y p.u.) fallecimiento (de alguien).
demist | ˌdiː'mɪst | *v.t.* desempañar (los cristales de un vehículo).
demo | 'deməʊ | *s.c.* (brit. y fam.) V. **demonstration.**
demob | ˌdiː'mɒb | *v.t.* (brit. y fam.) V. **demobilize.**
demobilization | ˌdiːˌməʊbəlaɪ'zeɪʃn | *s.i.* MIL. desmovilización, licenciamiento.
demobilize | diː'məʊbəlaɪz | (también **demobilise**) *v.t.* MIL. desmovilizar, licenciar.
democracy | dɪ'mɒkrəsɪ | *s.i.* **1** POL. democracia. **2** sistema democrático (en una empresa, en una casa, etc.). || *s.c.* **3** país democrático, democracia.
democrat | 'deməkræt | *s.c.* **1** (EE.UU.) seguidor del partido demócrata. **2** demócrata.
democratic | ˌdemə'krætɪk | *adj.* **1** democrático (como sistema de gobierno y postura respetuosa con los deseos de la mayoría). || **2 Democratic,** (EE.UU.) demócrata (del partido estadounidense).
democratically | ˌdemə'krætɪklɪ | *adv.* democráticamente.
democratization | dɪˌmɒkrətaɪ'zeɪʃn | *s.i.* (form.) democratización.
democratize | dɪ'mɒkrətaɪz | (también **democratise**) *v.t.* (form.) democratizar, hacer democrático.
demographer | dɪ'mɒgrəfər | *s.c.* demógrafo.
demographic | ˌdemə'græfɪk | *adj.* demográfico.
demography | dɪmɒgrəfɪ | *s.i.* demografía.
demolish | dɪ'mɒlɪʃ | *v.t.* **1** derribar, derruir. **2** (fig.) demoler, destruir (argumentos, ideas, creencias, etc.).
demolition | ˌdemə'lɪʃn | *s.c.* e *i.* **1** derribo, demolición. **2** (fig.) refutación demoledora (de argumentos, creencias, etc.).
demon | 'diːmən | *s.c.* **1** demonio, diablo, espíritu maligno. **2** (fig.) persona incansable (en el trabajo, deporte, etc.), león: *I've been studying like a demon = he estado estudiando como un león.*
demoniac | dɪ'məʊnɪæk | (también **demoniacal**) *adj.* **1** demoníaco, maligno. **2** (fig.) brutal, salvaje, endemoniado (una actividad).
demonic | diː'mɒnɪk | *adj.* diabólico, demoníaco.
demonstrable | 'demənstrəbl | *adj.* demostrable.
demonstrably | 'demənstrəblɪ | *adv.* demostrablemente.
demonstrate | 'demənstreɪt | *v.t.* **1** demostrar, probar. **2** demostrar, mostrar (el funcionamiento de un objeto). **3** demostrar, revelar, exhibir (un sentimiento, habilidad, etc.). || *v.i.* **4** manifestarse, hacer una manifestación, ir de manifestación (política, social, etc.).
demonstration | ˌdemən'streɪʃn | *s.c.* **1** manifestación (política o similar). **2** 1demostración (del uso de un objeto). || *s.c.* e *i.* **3** demostración, prueba. **4** revelación, exhibición (de sentimientos o similar).
demonstrative | dɪ'mɒnstrətɪv | *adj.* **1** efusivo, expansivo, abierto (con sus sentimientos, emociones, etc.). || *s.c.* **2** GRAM. demostrativo.
demonstrator | 'demənstreɪtər | *s.c.* **1** manifestante (político o similar). **2** vendedor (que demuestra el uso de algo).
demoralization | dɪˌmɒrəlaɪ'zeɪʃn | *s.i.* desmoralización.
demoralize | dɪ'mɒrəlaɪz | (también **demoralise**) *v.t.* desmoralizar.
demoralized | dɪ'mɒrəlaɪzd | *adj.* desmoralizado, desalentado.
demote | ˌdiː'məʊt | *v.t.* degradar, rebajar (de categoría).
demotion | ˌdiː'məʊʃn | *s.c.* e *i.* degradación, descensión (en categoría).
demotic | dɪ'mɒtɪk | *adj.* **1** (form.) demótico, popular. || *s.i.* **2** griego moderno (idioma).
demur | dɪ'mɜːr | (form.) *v.i.* **1** poner reparos, objetar. || **2 without –,** sin objeción.
demure | dɪ'mjʊər | *adj.* tímido, reservado, pacato (especialmente de mujeres y niños).
demurely | dɪ'mjʊəlɪ | *adv.* tímidamente, reservadamente.
demystification | ˌdiːˌmɪstɪfɪ'keɪʃn | *s.i.* desmitificación.
demystify | ˌdiː'mɪstɪfaɪ | *v.t.* desmitificar.
den | den | *s.c.* **1** madriguera (de algunos animales). **2** cuarto de trabajo, rincón privado. **3 [– (of)]** cubil, guarida, escondrijo.
denationalization | ˌdiːˌnæʃənəlaɪ'zeɪʃn | *s.i.* privatización, desnacionalización (de algo en manos estables).
denationalize | ˌdiː'næʃənəlaɪz | (también **denationalise**) *v.t.* privatizar, desnacionalizar (algo estatal).
denial | dɪ'naɪəl | *s.c.* **1** negativa, denegación; desmentida. || *s.i.* **2 [– (of)]** rechazo, repudiación: *denial of freedom = rechazo de la libertad.*
denier | 'denɪər | *s.i.* diner (unidad de medida con ciertos tejidos).
denigrate | 'denɪgreɪt | *v.t.* denigrar; mancillar, minimizar (la reputación).
denigration | ˌdenɪ'greɪʃn | *s.i.* **[– (of)]** denigración, minimización (de reputación o similar).
denim | 'denɪm | *s.i.* **1** tejido de vaqueros, dril de algodón. || **2 denims,** pantalones vaqueros; ropa vaquera.
denizen | 'denɪzn | *s.c.* **[– (of)]** (lit.) residente, oriundo (personas, animales, plantas).
denomination | dɪˌnɒmɪ'neɪʃn | *s.c.* REL. denominación, religión, creencia.
denominational | dɪˌnɒmɪ'neɪʃənl | *adj.* religioso, de una religión.
denominator | dɪ'nɒmɪneɪtər | *s.c.* MAT. denominador.
denotation | dɪnə'teɪʃn | *s.i.* denotación, designación.
denote | dɪ'nəʊt | *v.t.* **1** denotar, indicar, designar. **2** representar, simbolizar, significar: *that sign denotes danger = ese signo significa peligro.*
denouement | ˌdeɪ'nuːmɒŋ | (también **dénouement**) *s.c.* desenlace, solución final.
denounce | dɪ'naʊns | *v.t.* denunciar, censurar, condenar.
dense | dens | *adj.* **1** denso, apretado, compacto. **2** opaco, denso (humo o niebla). **3** denso (libro o película difícil de entender). **4** (fam.) bobo, lento, torpe.
density | 'densətɪ | *s.i.* e *c.* **1** densidad, concentración (de población). **2** FIS. densidad (de un cuerpo). || *s.i.* **3** densidad; dificultad (de libro, película, etc.).
densely | 'denslɪ | *adv.* **1** densamente, apretadamente, de manera compacta.
dent | dent | *v.t.* **1** abollar (vehículo). **2** hacer un impacto en, mellar (orgullo, ideas preconcebidas, etc.). || *s.c.* **3** abolladura, golpe (en vehículo). || **4 to make a – in,** hacer mella en.
dental | 'dentl | *adj.* dental.
dented | 'dentɪd | *adj.* abollado, mellado (vehículo).
dentist | 'dentɪst | *s.c.* **1** dentista. | **2 the dentist's,** la clínica dental, la consulta del dentista.
dentistry | 'dentɪstrɪ | *s.i.* cirugía dental, odontología.
dentures | 'dentʃəs | *s.pl.* dentadura postiza.
denude | dɪ'njuːd | *v.t.* **1 [to – *o.d.* + of]** quitar: *denude both beds of the sheets = quita las sábanas de ambas camas.* **2** desnudar, despojar, desposeer (un país, un paisaje, etc.).
denuded | dɪ'njuːdɪd | *adj.* **1** desnudo, sin sábanas (y otras formas de cubiertas). **2** despojado, desposeído.
denunciation | dɪˌnʌnsɪ'eɪʃn | *s.c.* e *i.* **[– (of)]** condena, denuncia.
deny | dɪ'naɪ | *v.t.* **1** negar; rechazar. **2 [to – *ger.*]** negar (hacer algo). **3** denegar, no permitir (a una persona algo). **4** (p.u.) negar, repudiar (a una persona).
deodorant | diː'əʊdərənt | *s.c.* desodorante.
deodorize | diː'əʊdəraɪz | (también **deodorise**) *v.t.* (form.) desodorizar.

deodorized | diː'əudəraɪzd | *adj.* (form.) con desodorante, desodorizado.
depart | dɪ'pɑːt | *v.i.* **1** ir, irse, marcharse. **2 [to – from]** apartarse de, desviarse de (una tradición, costumbre, etc.).
departed | dɪ'pɑːtɪd | *adj.* **1** (form.) difunto, fallecido. || *s.sing.* **2** difunto.
department | dɪ'pɑːtmənt | *s.c.* **1** sección, departamento, seminario (de hospital, universidad, etc.). **2** POL. Ministerio; Secretaría de Estado. || **3 to be one's –,** (fam.) ser el tema de uno. **4 – store,** gran almacén, grandes almacenes.
departmental | ˌdiːpɑːt'mentl | *adj.* de sección, de departamento: *a departmental meeting = una reunión del departamento.*
departure | dɪ'pɑːtʃər | *s.c.* e *i.* **1** marcha, salida, partida. **2 [– (from)]** desviación, alejamiento. || *s.c.* **3** derrotero, rumbo (nuevo en algún aspecto de la vida): *a new departure in my life = un nuevo rumbo en mi vida.*
depend | dɪ'pend | *v.i.* **1 [to – on/upon]** depender de, confiar en, contar con (en muchos sentidos). **2 [to – (on)]** depender: *will you do it for me? It depends = ¿lo harás por mí? Depende.* || **3 depending on,** según.
dependability | dɪˌpendə'bɪlɪtɪ | *s.i.* formalidad.
dependable | dɪ'pendəbl | *adj.* formal, responsable, seguro (que puedes contar con él).
dependably | dɪ'pendəblɪ | *adv.* formalmente, responsablemente, con seguridad.
dependant | dɪ'pendənt | (también **dependent**) *s.c.* persona a cargo, persona dependiente (ancianos, niños, etc.).
dependence | dɪ'pendəns | (EE.UU. **dependance**) *s.i.* **1 [– (on/upon)]** dependencia, necesidad (de drogas, materia prima, etc.). **2 [– (on/upon)]** apoyo, sostén (persona): *his dependence on his wife = el sostén de su mujer para él.*
dependency | dɪ'pendənsɪ | *s.c.* colonia, posesión (país).
dependent | dɪ'pendənt | *adj.* **[– on/upon]** dependiente de, necesitado de, sujeto a.
depict | dɪ'pɪkt | *v.t.* retratar, pintar (persona, situación, etc.).
depiction | dɪ'pɪkʃn | *s.c.* retrato, pintura; descripción.
depilatory | dɪ'pɪlətrɪ | *adj.* depilatorio.
deplete | dɪ'pliːt | *v.t.* reducir drásticamente, agotar (la cantidad de algo).
depletion | dɪ'pliːʃn | *s.i.* reducción drástica, agotamiento.
deplorable | dɪ'plɔːrəbl | *adj.* deplorable, lamentable.
deplorably | dɪ'plɔːrəblɪ | *adv.* deplorablemente, lamentablemente.
deplore | dɪ'plɔː | *v.t.* (form.) deplorar, lamentar.
deploy | dɪ'plɔɪ | *v.t.* **1** MIL. desplegar (tanques, buques, etc.). **2** (fig.) estructurar, ordenar, desplegar (para utilización eficaz): *the Ministry deployed the best experts = el Ministerio desplegó los mejores expertos.*
deployment | dɪ'plɔɪmənt | *s.i.* **1** MIL. despliegue. **3** (fig.) estructuración, ordenamiento, despliegue.
depopulate | ˌdiː'pɒpjuleɪt | *v.t.* despoblar.
depopulated | ˌdiː'pɒpjuleɪtɪd | *adj.* despoblado.
depopulation | ˌdiːpˌpju'leɪʃn | *s.i.* despoblación.
deport | dɪ'pɔːt | *v.t.* deportar, expulsar.
deportation | ˌdiːpɔː'teɪʃn | *s.c.* e *i.* deportación, expulsión.
deportment | dɪ'pɔːtmənt | *s.i.* (p.u.) porte; conducta.
depose | dɪ'pəuz | *v.t.* destituir, deponer, destronar.
deposit | dɪ'pɒzɪt | *s.c.* **1** FIN. depósito, depósito bancario. **2** señal, desembolso inicial. **3** fianza (del alquiler de pisos o coches). **4** (brit.) POL. pago de fianza política (que los candidatos al Parlamento recuperan si consiguen el 15%). **5** GEOL. sedimento, depósito de sedimento. || *v.t.* **6** GEOL. sedimentar, posar (arena, tierra, etc.). **7** depositar (dinero, joyas o similar). **8** dejar en depósito (en lugar seguro). **9** dejar caer, dejar (en un sitio): *the wind deposited the dead leaves all over the place = el viento dejó caer las hojas muertas por todo el lugar.* || **10 – account,** FIN. cuenta a depósito, cuenta a largo plazo. **11 on –,** FIN. en depósito (dinero, joyas, o similar).
deposition | ˌdepə'zɪʃn | *s.i.* **1** GEOL. sedimentación. **2** POL. destitución. **3** DER. testimonio escrito.
depot | 'depəu | *s.c.* **1** almacén (de mercancías). **2** depósito, cochera (para tren y autobús). **3** (EE.UU.) estación (de tren o autobús).
deprave | dɪ'preɪv | *v.t.* depravar, corromper.
depraved | dɪ'preɪvd | *adj.* depravado, corrupto.
depravity | dɪ'prævɪtɪ | *s.i.* corrupción, depravación.
deprecate | 'deprɪkeɪt | *v.t.* (form.) desaprobar, condenar.
deprecating | depr'keɪtɪŋ | *adj.* desaprobatorio, condenatorio.
deprecatingly | deprɪ'keɪtɪŋlɪ | *adv.* con desaprobación.
deprecatory | ˌdeprɪ'keɪtərɪ | V. **deprecating.**
depreciate | dɪ'priːʃɪeɪt | *v.i.* depreciarse, desvalorizarse.
depreciation | dɪˌpriːʃɪ'eɪʃn | *s.i.* depreciación, desvalorización.
depredation | ˌdeprɪ'deɪʃn | *s.c.* e *i.* depredación, pillaje.
depress | dɪ'pres | *v.t.* **1** deprimir, dar mucha tristeza. **2** reducir, disminuir (precios, salarios, etc.).
depressed | dɪ'prest | *adj.* **1** deprimido, entristecido. **2** hundido, deprimido (en su parte central). **3** empobrecido, deprimido (económicamente).
depressing | dɪ'presɪŋ | *adj.* deprimente, entristecedor.
depressingly | dɪ'presɪŋlɪ | *adv.* deprimentemente.
depression | ˌdɪ'preʃn | *s.i.* y *c.* **1** PSIQ. depresión. || *s.c.* **2** ECON. depresión. **3** hundimiento, aplanamiento, depresión (física). **4** borrasca, zona de presión baja.
depressive | dɪ'presɪv | *adj.* **1** deprimente, desalentador. || *s.c.* **2** PSIQ. depresivo (persona).
deprivation | ˌdeprɪ'veɪʃn | *s.i.* y *c.* privación, carencia (de bienes).
deprive | dɪ'praɪv | *v.t.* **[to – o.d. + (of)]** privar, desposeer.
deprived | dɪ'praɪvd | *adj.* necesitado, menesteroso, sin las ventajas sociales normales.
depth | depθ | *s.i.* y *c.* **1** profundidad (vertical y horizontal). || *s.i.* **2** intensidad, profundidad (de una emoción o situación). **3** profundidad, extensión (de conocimientos). **4** gravedad, profundidad (sonido). **5** oscuridad (color). || **6 – charge,** MIL. carga de profundidad. **7 – of field,** FOT. profundidad de campo. **8 depths, a)** partes remotas (en el campo). **b)** aspectos íntimos. **c)** (lit.) profundidades, abismos (del mar y la tierra). **9 in –,** en profundidad, con gran detalle. **10 in the depths of,** en pleno...: *in the depths of despair = en plena desesperación.* **11 out of one's –, a)** sin hacer pie, donde no se hace pie. **b)** (fig.) fuera del ambiente de uno.
deputation | ˌdepju'teɪʃn | *s.c.* delegación (grupo de personas).
depute | dɪ'pjuːt | *v.t.* **[to – (for)]** (form.) encargar, dar un encargo.
deputize | 'depjutaɪz | (también **deputise**) *v.i.* **[to – (for)]** delegar, suplir.
deputy | 'depjutɪ | *s.c.* **1** suplente. **2** ayudante, vice.
derail | dɪ'reɪl | *v.t.* descarrilar.
derailment | dɪ'reɪlmənt | *s.c.* e *i.* descarrilamiento.
deranged | dɪ'reɪndʒd | *adj.* trastornado, loco.
derangement | dɪ'reɪndʒmənt | *s.i.* (p.u.) trastorno mental, locura.
derby | 'dɑːbɪ | *s.c.* **1** DEP. derby. **2** (EE.UU.) bombín (sombrero). || **3 Derby:** Derby (carrera famosa de caballos).
derelict | 'derɪlɪkt | *adj.* **1** abandonado, en mal estado (edificio o similar). || *s.c.* **2** vago, pelagatos.
dereliction | ˌderɪ'likʃn | *s.i.* **1** abandono (edificio o similar). || **2 – of duty,** (form.) abandono del deber.
deride | dɪ'raɪd | *v.t.* ridiculizar, escarnecer, mofarse de.
de rigueur | dərɪ'gəːr | *adj.* de rigor, necesario, fundamental.
derision | dɪ'rɪʒn | *s.i.* escarnio, burla, mofa.
derisive | dɪ'raɪsɪv | *adj.* burlón, lleno de escarnio.
derisively | dɪ'raɪsɪvlɪ | *adv.* burlonamente, con escarnio, con mofa.
derisory | dɪ'raɪsərɪ | *adj.* irrisorio, ridículo (algo): *a derisory budget = un presupuesto irrisorio.*
derivation | ˌderɪ'veɪʃn | *s.c.* e *i.* FILOL. derivación (de palabras).

derivative | dɪ'rɪvətɪv | *adj.* **1** (desp.) copiado, no original. || *s.c.* **2** derivado: *this word is a derivative = esta palabra es un derivado.*

derive | dɪ'raɪv | *v.i.* **1 [to – from]** *derivar de, originarse en (una palabra, una costumbre, etc.).* || *v.t.* **2 [to – *o.d.* + (from)]** (form.) obtener, sacar: *I derive great joy from my hobby = saco gran gozo a mi hobby.*

dermatitis | ˌdɜːmə'taɪtɪs | *s.i.* MED. dermatitis.

derogatory | dɪ'rɒgətrɪ | *adj.* despectivo, desdeñoso, despreciativo.

derrick | 'derɪk | *s.c.* **1** grúa, cabria. **2** torre de taladrar (para la extracción de petróleo).

derv | dɜːv | *s.i.* diesel.

dervish | 'dɜːvɪʃ | *s.c.* derviche (miembro de una secta musulmana que se caracteriza por su enérgica danza).

descale | ˌdiː'skeɪl | *v.t.* quitar el óxido (de tetera, etc.).

descant | 'deskænt | *s.c.* MUS. contrapunto.

descend | dɪ'send | *v.i.* **1** (form.) descender, bajar. **2 [to – to]** bajarse hasta, rebajarse a. **3 [to – on/upon]** caer sobre; invadir. **4** (lit.) caer, descender (la noche, el crepúsculo, etc.). **5 [to – from]** descender de, provenir de (familia, tribu, etc.). **6 [to – on/upon]** caer sobre, descender sobre (personas un sentimiento, una sensación, etc.). || *v.t.* **7** bajar (algo).

descendant | dɪ'sendənt | *s.c.* descendiente.

descended | dɪ'sendɪd | *adj.* **[– from]** descendiente de.

descending | dɪ'sendɪŋ | *adj.* descendiente (objeto).

descent | dɪ'sent | *s.c.* **1** descenso, bajada. **2** cuesta, declive, pendiente. || *s.sing.* **3** descenso (de categoría o similar). **4** rebajamiento (moral). || *s.i.* **5** ascendencia, origen (de una familia, individuo, etc.).

describe | dɪ'skraɪb | *v.t.* **1** describir (físicamente). **2** describir, narrar, relatar. **3 [to – *o.d.* + as]** describir (ideas, cualidades, etc.): *he described her as being stupid = la describió como estúpida.* **4** (form.) trazar, dibujar: *the arrow described an elongated curve = la flecha trazó una curva alargada.*

description | dɪ'skrɪpʃn | *s.c.* **1** descripción, relato, narración. || *s.i.* **2** descripción, explicación. || *s.sing.* **3** tipo, clase. || **4 beyond/past –,** más allá de todo lo imaginado; no puedes ni imaginarlo.

descriptive | dɪ'skrɪptɪv | *adj.* **1** descriptivo (explicativo). **2** descriptivo (ciencia): *descriptive linguistics.*

descriptively | dɪ'skrɪptɪvlɪ | *adv.* descriptivamente.

desecrate | 'desɪkreɪt | *v.t.* profanar.

desecration | ˌdesɪ'kreɪʃn | *s.i.* profanación.

desegregate | ˌdiː'segrɪgeɪt | *v.t.* abolir la segregación de razas.

desegregation | ˌdiːˌsegrɪ'geɪʃn | *s.i.* abolición de la segregación de razas.

desensitize | ˌdiː'sensɪtaɪz | (también **desensitise**) *v.t.* insensibilizar.

desert | 'dezət | *s.c.* **1** desierto. **2** (fig.) páramo, baldío, yermo. || *v.t.* | dɪ'zɜːt | **3** abandonar (un lugar, una persona, etc.). **4** MIL. desertar. **5** fallar, abandonar: *my courage deserted me = mi coraje me falló.* || *v.i.* **6** MIL. desertar. || **7 – island,** isla desierta. **8 just deserts,** su merecido.

deserted | dɪ'zɜːtɪd | *adj.* abandonado.

deserter | dɪ'zɜːtər | *s.c.* MIL. desertor.

desertion | dɪ'zɜːʃn | *s.i.* **1** deserción, abandono (de un partido, de una ideología, etc.). || *s.c.* e *i.* **2** abandono (del hogar, de una persona, etc.). **3** MIL. deserción.

deserve | dɪ'zɜːv | *v.t.* merecer.

deserved | dɪ'zɜːvd | *adj.* merecido.

deservedly | dɪ'zɜːvɪdlɪ | *adv.* merecidamente.

deserving | dɪ'zɜːvɪŋ | (form.) *adj.* **1** meritorio, de mérito, digno. || **2 – of,** digno de, merecedor de.

desiccated | 'desɪkeɪtɪd | *adj.* **1** desecado (comida para que dure). **2** (form.) reseco, sin humedad.

desiccation | ˌdesɪ'keɪʃn | *s.i.* (form.) desecación, deshidratación.

design | dɪ'zaɪn | *v.t.* **1** diseñar (casa, producto, etc.). **2** concebir, idear; inventar. || *s.c.* **3** diseño, dibujo; patrón. **4** propósito, designio, intención. || *s.i.* **5** diseño (de objetos o similar). || **6 to be designed, [for/to *inf.*]** estar destinado a: *his products are designed for children = sus productos están destinados a niños.* **7 by –,** intencionadamente, intencionalmente. **8 to have designs on,** tener la mira puesta en.

designate | 'dezɪgnɪt | *adj.* **1** [*s.* + –] designado, electo. || | 'dezɪgneɪt | *v.t.* **2** designar, nombrar. **3 [to – *o.d.* + as]** destinar... para, denominar... para.

designation | ˌdezɪg'neɪʃn | (form.) *s.c.* **1** designación, nombre, descripción. || *s.i.* **2** designación, denominación.

designer | dɪ'zaɪnər | *s.c.* diseñador.

designing | dɪ'zaɪnɪŋ | *s.i.* **1** diseño, arte del diseño. || *adj.* **2** (desp.) intrigante, maquinador.

desirability | dɪˌzaɪərə'bɪlɪtɪ | *s.i.* **1** valor, conveniencia (de la existencia de algo). **2** atracción sexual.

desirable | dɪ'zaɪərəbl | *adj.* **1** deseable, conveniente, apetecible. **2** atractiva, atrayente (sexualmente).

desirably | dɪ'zaɪərəblɪ | *adv.* convenientemente, apeteciblemente.

desire | dɪ'zaɪər | *v.t.* **1** desear, anhelar, querer (con gran fuerza). **2** desear (a una mujer). || *s.c.* **3** deseo, anhelo. || *s.c.* e *i.* **4 [– (for)]** deseo, apetencia (sexual). **5 to be one's heart's –,** (lit.) ser la cosa más querida de uno. **6 to leave much/a lot/a great deal to be desired,** dejar mucho que desear.

desired | dɪ'zaɪəd | *adj.* deseado, querido: *the desired effect = el resultado deseado.*

desirous | dɪ'zaɪərəs | *adj.* **[– of]** (form.) deseoso de.

desist | dɪ'zɪst | *v.i.* **[to – (from)]** (form.) desistir.

desk | desk | *s.c.* **1** mesa de trabajo, pupitre. **2** mostrador: *information desk.* **3** (fig.) sección, departamento (en un periódico o ministerio). || **4 – clerk,** (EE.UU.) recepcionista (de hotel).

desk-top | 'desktɒp | *s.c.* **1** parte superior de una mesa de trabajo. || *adj.* **2** para/de la parte superior de una mesa de trabajo. || **3 – publishing,** PER. impresión por microcomputadora (normalmente láser).

desolate | 'desəlɪt | *adj.* **1** desolado, desierto, solitario. **2** desolado, afligido, sombrío. || | 'desəleɪt | *v.t.* **3** (lit.) desolar, devastar, arrasar.

desolated | 'desəleɪtɪd | *adj.* **1** devastado, arrasado, desolado. **2 [– (at/by)]** desolado, afligido, desconsolado.

desolation | ˌdesə'leɪʃn | *s.i.* **1** desolación, abandono. **2** devastación. **3** aflicción, desconsuelo.

despair | dɪ'speər | *s.i.* **1** desesperación, desesperanza. || *v.i.* **2 [to – (at)]** desesperarse. **3 [to – of]** abandonar la esperanza de. || **4 in –,** totalmente desesperado, lleno de desesperación.

despairing | dɪ'speərɪŋ | *adj.* desesperado, abatido.

despairingly | dɪ'speərɪŋlɪ | *adv.* desesperadamente, abatidamente.

despatch | dɪ'spætʃ | V. **dispatch.**

desperado | ˌdespə'rɑːdəʊ | [*pl.* **desperados/desperadoes**] *s.c.* (p.u.) malhechor, bandido (que está desesperado).

desperate | 'despərɪt | *adj.* **1** desesperado, desesperanzado. **2** desesperado, peligroso, crítico (persona, situación, etc.). **3 [– for/to + *inf.*]** necesitado urgentemente de/urgido para. **4** desesperado, temerario.

desperately | 'despərɪtlɪ | *adv.* **1** desesperadamente, temerariamente. **2** muy, enormemente, seriamente, desesperadamente: *she was desperately ill = ella estaba muy enferma.*

desperation | ˌdespə'reɪʃn | *s.i.* desesperación.

despicable | dɪ'spɪkəbl | *adj.* (desp.) despreciable, vil.

despicably | dɪ'spɪkəblɪ | *adv.* (desp.) despreciablemente, vilmente.

despise | dɪ'spaɪz | *v.t.* despreciar, desdeñar.

despite | dɪ'spaɪt | *prep.* **1** a pesar de. || **2 – oneself,** a pesar de los gustos/ideas/sentimientos de uno.

despoil | dɪ'spɔɪl | *v.t.* (form.) despojar.

despondency | dɪ'spɒndənsɪ | *s.i.* (form.) desaliento, desánimo; melancolía.

despondent | dɪ'spɒndənt | *adj.* (form.) desanimado, desalentado, melancólico.

despondently | dɪ'spɒndəntlɪ | *adv.* (form.) sin ánimo; melancólicamente.

despot | 'despɒt | *s.c.* déspota.

despotic | dɪ'spɒtɪk | *adj.* despótico.

despotism | 'despətɪzəm | *s.i.* POL. despotismo.

dessert | dɪ'zɜːt | *s.c.* e *i.* postre.

dessertspoon | dɪˌzɜːt'spuːn | *s.c.* **1** cucharilla de postre. **2** cucharada de postre.
destination | 'destɪ'neɪʃn | *s.c.* destino (lugar).
destined | 'destɪnd | *adj.* **1** **[– for]** con destino a. **2** **[– for/to +** *inf.***]** destinado para/a.
destiny | 'destɪnɪ | *s.c.* e *i.* destino, sino.
destitute | 'destɪtjuːt | *adj.* (form.) necesitado, indigente.
destitution | ˌdestɪ'tjuːʃn | *s.i.* (form.) indigencia, pobreza abyecta.
destroy | dɪ'strɔɪ | *v.t.* **1** destrozar, destruir. **2** matar, sacrificar (animales). **3** dejar destrozado, destrozar (la vida de alguien).
destroyer | dɪ'strɔɪər | *s.c.* **1** MAR. destructor. **2** fuerza destructora; persona destructora.
destruction | dɪ'strʌkʃn | *s.i.* destrucción, aniquilamiento.
destructive | dɪ'strʌktɪv | *adj.* destructivo, destructor.
destructively | dɪ'strʌktɪvlɪ | *adv.* destructivamente, destructoramente.
destructiveness | dɪ'strʌktɪvnɪs | *s.i.* destructividad, capacidad destructora.
desultorily | 'desəltrɪlɪ | *adv.* (form.) desganadamente, sin muchas ganas.
desultory | 'desəltrɪ | *adj.* (form.) irregular, esporádico, indiferente.
detach | dɪ'tætʃ | *v.t.* **1** **[to – (from)]** separar, apartar. || *v.r.* **2** **[to – (from)]** apartarse; descomprometerse. **3** **[to – from]** (form.) irse de, marcharse de, abandonar.
detachable | dɪ'tætʃəbl | *adj.* desmontable.
detached | dɪ'tætʃt | *adj.* **1** separada, independiente (casa rodeada de espacio libre). **2** separado, aislado (objeto). **3** indiferente, no comprometido.
detachment | dɪ'tætʃmənt | *s.i.* **1** desinterés, indiferencia. || *s.c.* **2** MIL. destacamento.
detail | 'diːteɪl | *s.c.* **1** **[– (of/about)]** detalle, pormenor. **2** minucia. **3** detalle (de un cuadro). **4** MIL. grupo/destacamento (con un objetivo). || *s.i.* **5** detalle. || *v.t.* **6** detallar, dar detalles. **7** **[to –** *o.d.* **+** *inf.***]** asignar (para alguna tarea). || **8** **details,** detalles; información. **9** **to go into (the) –/details,** entrar en detalles, entrar en pormenores. **10** **in –,** en detalle, con todo detalle.
detailed | 'diːteɪld | *adj.* detallado.
detain | dɪ'teɪn | *v.t.* **1** detener, arrestar. **2** retardar, retener.
detainee | ˌdiːteɪ'niː | *s.c.* detenido.
detect | dɪ'tekt | *v.t.* **1** detectar. **2** percibir, advertir.
detectable | dɪ'tektəbl | *adj.* detectable, perceptible.
detection | dɪ'tekʃn | *s.i.* **1** detección. **2** investigación, averiguación: *crime detection = investigación del crimen.*
detective | dɪ'tektɪv | *s.c.* **1** detective (privado). || **2** **Detective,** Detective (título oficial de la policía).
detector | dɪ'tektər | *s.c.* detector (objeto).
detente | ˌdeɪ'tɑːnt | (también **détente**) *s.i.* (form.) POL. detente.
detention | dɪ'tenʃn | *s.i.* **1** detención, arresto. || *s.c.* e *i.* **2** castigo escolar (quedarse más tiempo en la escuela). || **3** **– centre,** reformatorio.
deter | dɪ'tɜːr | *v.t.* **[to – (from)]** disuadir, desanimar: *his insults didn't deter me from going in = sus insultos no me disuadieron de entrar.*
detergent | dɪ'tɜːdʒənt | *s.c.* e *i.* detergente.
deteriorate | dɪ'tɪərɪəreɪt | *v.i.* deteriorarse, desmejorarse, empeorar.
deterioration | dɪˌtɪərɪə'reɪʃn | *s.i.* deterioro, desmejora, empeoramiento.
determinant | dɪ'tɜːmɪnənt | *s.c.* (form.) determinante.
determination | dɪˌtɜːmɪ'neɪʃn | *s.i.* **1** determinación, resolución, firmeza. || *s.sing.* **2** fijación, determinación (de cantidades o similar).
determine | dɪ'tɜːmɪn | *v.t.* **1** determinar, decidir, resolver. **2** determinar, asegurarse de: *with a blood analysis we'll determine it's not serious = con un análisis de sangre nos aseguraremos de que no es grave.* **3** fijar, establecer (una fecha, una acción, etc.). **4** **[to –** *inf.***]** (form.) tomar la decisión de, tomar la firme resolución de.
determined | dɪ'tɜːmɪnd | *adj.* **1** decidido (cualidad personal). **2** **[–** *inf.***]** resuelto a, decidido a.
determinedly | dɪ'tɜːmɪndlɪ | *adv.* de manera resuelta, con decisión.
determiner | dɪ'tɜːmɪnər | *s.c.* GRAM. determinador.
determinism | dɪ'tɜːmɪnɪzəm | *s.i.* determinismo.
determinist | dɪ'tɜːmɪnɪst | *s.c.* determinista.
deterministic | dɪˌtɜːmɪ'nɪstɪk | *adj.* determinista.
deterrence | dɪ'terəns | *s.i.* POL. disuasión (equilibrio armamentístico).
deterrent | dɪ'terənt | *s.c.* **1** disuasión (a no hacer algo). **2** MIL. arma disuasiva (normalmente nuclear). || *adj.* **3** disuasivo.
detest | dɪ'test | *v.t.* detestar, aborrecer, odiar.
detestable | dɪ'testəbl | *adj.* detestable, aborrecible, odioso.
detestation | ˌdiːte'steɪʃn | *s.i.* aborrecimiento, odio.
dethrone | ˌdiː'θrəun | *v.t.* destronar; derrocar.
detonate | 'detəneɪt | *v.t.* e *i.* detonar, explotar, hacer detonar.
detonation | ˌdetə'neɪʃn | *s.c.* e *i.* detonación, estallido.
detonator | 'detəneɪtər | *s.c.* detonador.
detour | 'diːtuər | *s.c.* rodeo, desvío.
detract | dɪ'trækt | *v.i.* **[to – from]** disminuir; desmerecer: *his stupidity does not detract from his achievement = su estupidez no disminuye su logro.*
detractor | dɪ'træktər | *s.c.* detractor.
detriment | 'detrɪmənt | *s.i.* **1** detrimento, daño. || **2** **to someone's –/to the – of,** para detrimento de alguien/para detrimento de, para perjuicio de. **3** **without – to,** sin detrimento para, sin daño para, sin perjuicio para.
detrimental | ˌdetrɪ'mentl | *adj.* **[– (to)]** dañino, perjudicial, nocivo.
detritus | dɪ'traɪtəs | *s.i.* detritus, basura.
deuce | djuːs | *s.i.* y *c.* DEP. cuarenta iguales (en el tenis).
devaluation | ˌdiːvælju'eɪʃn | *s.c.* e *i.* ECON. devaluación, depreciación.
devalue | ˌdiː'væljuː | *v.t.* **1** desvalorizar, devaluar. **2** ECON. depreciar, devaluar (moneda).
devalued | ˌdiː'væljuːd | *adj.* desvalorizado, devaluado.
devastate | 'devəsteɪt | *v.t.* devastar, desolar, arrasar.
devastated | 'devəsteɪtɪd | *adj.* desolado, abrumado.
devastating | 'devəsteɪtɪŋ | *adj.* **1** devastador, desastroso. **2** (fig.) devastador (comentario, crítica, etc.). **3** abrumador, desolador. **4** (fam.) brillante, maravilloso; precioso.
devastatingly | ˌdevəs'teɪtɪŋlɪ | *adv.* **1** con crítica brillante. **2** (fam.) maravillosamente, brillantemente: *a devastatingly beautiful woman = una mujer maravillosamente hermosa.*
devastation | ˌdevəs'teɪʃn | *s.i.* y *c.* asolación, arrasamiento, destrozo.
develop | dɪ'veləp | *v.i.* **1** desarrollarse, evolucionar, crecer. **2** desarrollarse, hacerse más avanzado (país, región, etc.). **3** cobrar fuerza, crecer (problema, dificultad, crisis, etc.). || *v.t.* **4** desarrollar, hacer crecer, hacer avanzar (un negocio o similar). **5** MÚS. arreglar. **6** FOT. revelar. **7** adquirir, adoptar (un hábito o similar). **8** afianzar, asegurar; perfeccionar (capacidades, habilidades, etc.): *I must develop my French = debo perfeccionar mi francés.* **9** urbanizar (terrenos). **10** contraer, coger, sufrir (enfermedad, desperfecto, etc.). **11** desarrollar; clarificar (una historia, un carácter, etc.). **12** mejorar, perfeccionar (técnica, máquina, proceso, etc.). **13** formular, exponer; ampliar (ideas, métodos, etc.).
developed | dɪ'veləpt | *adj.* **1** desarrollado (país o similar). **2** formado, desarrollado (cuerpo, planta, etc.). **3** desarrollado, formulado; ampliado (idea, método, etc.).
developer | dɪ'veləpər | *s.c.* **1** urbanizador, agente inmobiliario. **2** creador; diseñador (de un producto, idea, etc.). || *s.i.* **3** FOT. revelador, sustancia para revelación.
developing | dɪ'veləpɪŋ | *adj.* en vías de desarrollo (países).
development | dɪ'veləpmənt | *s.i.* **1** desarrollo, crecimiento (de personas, cosas o países). **2** mejora, perfeccionamiento (de zonas, fábricas, etc.). || *s.c.* e *i.* **3** innovación, investigación. || *s.c.* **4** POL. cambio, nueva situación, novedad (en un país). **5** urbanización.
developmental | dɪˌveləp'mentəl | *adj.* de desarrollo, para el desarrollo.

deviance | 'di:vɪəns | *s.i.* desviación, disconformidad (comportamiento diferente).
deviant | 'di:vɪənt | *adj.* **1** inconformista, desviacionista (comportamiento). || *s.c.* **2** inconformista.
deviate | 'di:vɪeɪt | *v.i.* **[to – (from)]** desviarse, apartarse (en comportamiento).
deviation | ˌdi:vɪ'eɪʃn | *s.c.* e *i.* **1** desviación, disconformidad (en comportamiento o ideas). || **2** MAT. desviación (concepto estadístico).
device | dɪ'vaɪs | *s.c.* **1** ingenio, dispositivo, artefacto. **2** (fig.) ardid, estratagema. **3** LIT. figura (de estilo), mecanismo. || **4 to leave someone to their own devices,** dejar a alguien que se las arregle sólo, dejar a alguien que decida lo que le apetezca.
devil | 'devl | *s.c.* **1** espíritu maligno, diablo. **2** (fam.) diablillo (niños), demonio. **3** [*adj.* **–]** tipo: *a lucky devil = un tipo afortunado.* || *v.t.* **4** sazonar fuertemente. || *v.i.* **5 [to – for]** (brit.) trabajar de aprendiz para un abogado. || **6 a – of a,** un dificilísimo; un asco de: *a devil of a job = un asco de trabajo.* **7 be a –,** cae en la tentación; adelante con ello. **8 better the – you know than the – you don't know,** más vale lo malo conocido que lo bueno por conocer. **9 between the – and the deep blue sea,** entre la espada y la pared. **10 devil's advocate,** abogado de diablo. **11 to give the – his due,** para ser justo hasta con los enemigos. **12 go to the –!,** (p.u.) ¡vete a la porra! **13 to have the luck of the –,** (fam.) tener potra, tener muchísima suerte. **14 like the –,** (fam.) como un poseso. **15 to play the – with,** (fam.) arruinar, destrozar, chafar. **16 to raise the –,** (p.u.) armar la de San Quintín, armar una buena. **17 talk of the –,** hablando del rey de Roma. **18 ... the –!,** ¡...diablos!, ¡...narices!: *what the devil are you laughing at? = ¿de qué narices te estás riendo?* **19 the – ...!,** (fam.) ¡ni hablar!: *I'm going out now, daddy. The devil you are = salgo por ahí ahora, papá. ¡Ni hablar!.* **20 the Devil,** REL. el Diablo, Satanás. **21 the – looks after his own,** la fortuna sonríe a los peores. **22 the – makes work for idle hands,** la pereza es el principio de muchos vicios. **23 the – of a time,** gran dificultad; follón: *I had the devil of a time trying to understand that Chinese girl = tuve gran dificultad intentando entender a esa china.* **24 the – take the hindmost,** el que se quede en zaga, con el diablo se las haya. **25 there will be the – to pay,** (fam.) habrá una de todos los diablos.
devilish | 'devlɪʃ | *adj.* **1** perverso, malvado. || *adv.* **2** extremadamente, muy; diabólicamente: *devilish difficult.*
devilishly | 'devlɪʃlɪ | *adv.* perversamente, diabólicamente.
devil-may-care | 'devlmeɪkeər | *adj.* despreocupado, viva la Virgen (actitud): *devil-may-care attitude.*
devilry | 'devlrɪ | *s.i.* (p.u.) diablura.
devious | 'di:vɪəs | *adj.* **1** taimado, engañoso (persona y conducta). **2** tortuoso (camino, carretera, etc.).
deviousness | 'di:vɪəsnɪs | *s.i.* engaño, tortuosidad.
devise | dɪ'vaɪs | *v.t.* idear, concebir; inventar (plan, máquina, método, etc.).
devoid | dɪ'vɔɪd | *adj.* **[– of]** falto de; desprovisto de.
devolution | ˌdi:və'lu:ʃn | *s.i.* POL. descentralización; transferencia (de autoridad desde el centro a la periferia o secciones administrativas menores).
devolve | dɪ'vɒlv | *v.t.* **1** transferir; pasar (una responsabilidad o similar). || *v.i.* **2 [to – on/upon]** incumbir a, tocar a (alguien nuevo decidir).
devote | dɪ'vəʊt | *v.t.* e *i.* **[to – (to)]** dedicar(se): *I devoted all my time to her = dediqué todo mi tiempo a ella.*
devoted | dɪ'vəʊtɪd | *adj.* **1 [– (to)]** enamorado; leal, fiel. **2** continuado, intenso (en una actividad).
devotee | ˌdevəʊ'ti: | *s.c.* **1** REL. creyente, devoto. **2 [– (of)]** (fig.) entusiasta, fanático.
devotion | dɪ'vəʊʃn | *s.i.* **1 [– (to)]** devoción, dedicación: *devotion to one's husband = dedicación al marido de una.* **2** REL. devoción. || **3 devotions,** REL. oraciones, devociones personales.
devotional | dɪ'vəʊʃənl | *adj.* REL. religioso, piadoso, devoto.
devour | dɪ'vaʊər | *v.t.* **1** devorar, comer. **2** (fig.) devorar (un libro o similar). || **3 to be devoured by:** estar consumido por (emoción, sentimiento, etc.).
devouring | dɪ'vaʊərɪŋ | *adj.* absorbente, arrollador (actividad, interés, etc.).
devout | dɪ'vaʊt | REL. *adj.* **1** devoto, piadoso. || **2 the –,** los devotos.
devoutly | dɪ'vaʊtlɪ | *adv.* **1** REL. devotamente, piadosamente. **2** (form.) sinceramente.
dew | dju: | *s.i.* rocío.
dewlap | 'dju:læp | *s.c.* papada (de algunos animales).
dewy | 'dju:ɪ | *adj.* húmedo con el rocío.
dewy-eyed | ˌdju:ɪ'aɪd | *adj.* inocente, ingenuo.
dexterity | dek'sterɪtɪ | *s.i.* destreza, maña, agilidad manual.
dexterous | 'dekstrəs | (también **dextrous**) *adj.* mañoso, ágil con las manos, diestro.
dexterously | 'dekstrəslɪ | (también **dextrously**) *adv.* mañosamente, diestramente.
dextrose | 'dekstrəʊs | *adj.* QUIM. dextrosa.
diabetes | ˌdaɪə'bi:ti:z | *s.i.* MED. diabetes.
diabetic | ˌdaɪə'bɪtɪk | MED. *adj.* **1** diabético. || *s.c.* **2** diabético.
diabolic | ˌdaɪə'bɒlɪk | *adj.* REL. (form.) del Diablo, diabólico.
diabolical | ˌdaɪə'bɒlɪkl | *adj.* (fam.) **1** diabólico, malísimo, molestísimo. **2** increíble (énfasis para expresar algo extremo o de mala calidad).
diabolically | ˌdaɪə'bɒlɪklɪ | *adv.* molestísimamente, malísimamente, diabólicamente: *diabolically difficult.*
diadem | 'daɪədem | *s.c.* corona pequeña (con gemas en ella).
diagnose | ˌdaɪəgnəʊz | *v.t.* diagnosticar (enfermedad o problema).
diagnosis | ˌdaɪəg'nəʊsɪs | (*pl.* **diagnoses**) *s.c.* e *i.* diagnóstico.
diagnostic | ˌdaɪəg'nɒstɪk | *adj.* de diagnóstico, para diagnóstico.
diagonal | daɪ'ægənl | GEOM. *adj.* **1** diagonal. || *s.c.* **2** diagonal.
diagonally | daɪ'ægənəlɪ | *adv.* diagonalmente.
diagram | 'daɪəgræm | *s.c.* diagrama.
diagrammatic | ˌdaɪəgrə'mætɪk | *adj.* de diagrama, en forma de diagrama.
dial | 'daɪəl | *v.t.* e *i.* **1** marcar (teléfono). | *s.c.* **2** estera (de algún aparato). **3** mando, dial (de aparatos). **4** disco (de marcar el teléfono). || **5 dialling code,** prefijo telefónico. **6 dialling tone,** tono de marcar. **7 – tone,** (EE.UU.) tono de marcar.
dialect | 'daɪəlekt | *s.c.* dialecto.
dialectic | ˌdaɪə'lektɪk | *s.sing.* **1** FIL. dialéctica. **2** dialéctica. **2** dialéctica, juego dialéctico, tensión dialéctica. || **3 dialectics,** FIL. dialéctica (como disciplina).
dialectical | ˌdaɪə'lektɪkl | *adj.* FIL. dialéctico.
dialogue | 'daɪəlɒg | (EE.UU. **dialog**) *s.c.* e *i.* **1** diálogo. || *s.c.* **2** conversación, diálogo, intercambio.
diameter | daɪ'æmɪtər | *s.c.* GEOM. diámetro.
diametrically | ˌdaɪə'metrɪklɪ | *adv.* diamétricamente, totalmente (oposición).
diamond | 'daɪəmənd | *s.c.* **1** diamante. **2** GEOM. rombo. || **3 – jubilee,** sexagésimo aniversario (de algún acontecimiento). **4 diamonds, a)** joyas (con diamantes). **b)** rombos, diamantes (en una baraja). **5 – wedding,** sexagésimo aniversario de boda.
diaper | 'daɪəpər | *s.c.* (EE.UU.) pañal, pico.
diaphanous | daɪ'æfənəs | *adj.* transparente, diáfano.
diaphragm | 'daɪəfræm | *s.c.* **1** ANAT. diafragma. **2** diafragma (ingenio anticonceptivo).
diarist | 'daɪərɪst | *s.c.* diarista, escritor de diario.
diarrhoea | ˌdaɪə'rɪə | (EE.UU. **diarrhea**) *s.i.* MED. diarrea.
diary | 'daɪərɪ | *s.c.* **1** diario. || **2 to keep a –,** guardar un diario, escribir un diario.
diaspora | daɪ'æspərə | *s.sing.* (form.) diáspora.
diatribe | 'daɪətraɪb | *s.c.* diatriba.
dice | daɪs | (pl. **dice**) *s.c.* **1** dado. || *s.i.* **2** dados (juego). || *v.t.* **3** trocear en cubitos (carne). || **4 to – with death,** jugar con la muerte.
diced | daɪsd | *adj.* troceado en cubitos.
dicey | 'daɪsɪ | *adj.* (fam.) peligroso; incierto.

dichotomy | daɪ'kɒtəmɪ | *s.c.* (form.) dicotomía.

dick | dɪk | *s.c.* **1** (fam. y vulg.) pene; polla. **2** (fam., p.u. y EE.UU.) polizonte, detective.

dickens | 'dɪkɪns | **the dickens,** (fam. y p.u.) porras, canutos (en expresiones con **what, where,** etc.): *what the dickens are you looking at? = ¿qué porras estás mirando?*

Dickensian | dɪ'kenzɪən | *adj.* de la época de Dickens.

dicky | 'dɪkɪ | *s.c.* **1** pechera postiza. || *adj.* **2** (fam.) debilucho.

dicky-bird | 'dɪkɪbɜːd | *s.c.* **1** pajarito (lenguaje para niños). || **2 not to say a –,** (fam.) no decir ni pío.

dictate | dɪk'teɪt | *v.t.* **1** dictar (una carta o similar). **2** mandar, dictar, ordenar. || *v.i.* **2 [to – to]** ordenar a, dar órdenes a. || | 'dɪkteɪt | *s.c.* **4** orden, precepto, mandato. **5** dictado (de la conciencia o similar).

dictation | dɪk'teɪʃn | *s.i.* **1** dictado (de carta o similar). **2** mandato, dictado. || *s.c.* e *i.* **3** dictado (como ejercicio). || **4 to take –,** escribir al dictado, tomar dictado.

dictator | dɪk'teɪtər | *s.c.* (desp.) POL. dictador. **2** (fig.) tirano, dictador.

dictatorial | ˌdɪktə'tɔːrɪəl | *adj.* **1** POL. dictatorial. **2** (fig.) dictatorial, despótico, tiránico.

dictatorship | dɪk'teɪtəʃɪp | POL. *s.c.* **1** dictadura (país). || *s.i.* **2** dictadura (sistema político). || *s.c.* e *i.* **3** dictadura (gobierno).

diction | 'dɪkʃn | *s.i.* dicción (claridad de sonido).

dictionary | 'dɪkʃənrɪ | *s.c.* diccionario (de un idioma o especialidad).

dictum | 'dɪktəm | (pl. **dictums/dicta**) *s.c.* **1** máxima: *a wise dictum = una máxima sabia.* **2** declaración, exhortación (de alguien en autoridad). || **3** DER. dictamen.

did | dɪd | *pret.* de **do.**

didactic | dɪ'dæktɪk | *adj.* didáctico.

didactically | dɪ'dæktɪklɪ | *adv.* didácticamente.

diddle | 'dɪdl | *v.t.* (fam. y brit.) estafar, engañar.

didn't | 'dɪdənt | *contr.* de **did** y **not.**

die | daɪ | (*ger.* **dying**) *v.i.* **1** morir. **2** apagarse, apagarse poco a poco (una máquina, un fuego, un sentimiento, etc.). || *v.t.* **4 [=N death]** sufrir, morir de: *he died a horrible death = sufrió una muerte horrible.* || *s.c.* **4** MEC. troquel, molde. || **5 to be dying,** estarse muriendo, estar muy enfermo, estar en las últimas. **6 to be dying for,** (fam.) estar deseando tomar/beber/etc.: *I'm dying for a glass of beer = estoy deseando tomar un vaso de cerveza.* **7 to be dying of,** (fam.) estar muriéndose de (sed, hambre, etc.). **8 to be dying to, [=N *inf.*]** (fam.) estar deseando, morirse por. **9 to – away,** apagarse, ir desapareciendo (ruidos o sonidos). **10 to – back,** ponerse mustia, caer la hoja (de una planta). **11 to – down,** hacerse menor, amortiguarse, debilitarse: *the storm has died down = la tormenta se ha debilitado.* **12 to – hard,** aguantar, resistir, perdurar (ideas, tradiciones, costumbres, etc.). **13 to – in harness,** morir trabajando. **14 to – in one's bed,** morir en la cama de uno, morir de viejo, morir de manera natural. **15 to – laughing,** (fam.) morirse de risa. **16 to – like flies,** morir como moscas. **17 to – off,** morir uno a uno: *all my friends have died off = todos mis amigos han muerto uno a uno.* **18 to – out,** desaparecer gradualmente, extinguirse. **19 I/you/etc. nearly died/could have died,** (fam.) era para morirse (de sorpresa, horror, vergüenza, etc.), sentir (sorpresa, horror, vergüenza, etc.). **20 the – is cast,** la suerte está echada.

diehard | 'daɪhɑːd | *s.c.* reaccionario, intransigente, inmovilista.

diesel | 'diːzl | *s.i.* **1** gasoil, diesel. || *s.c.* **2** coche de gasoil, vehículo de gasoil. || **3 – engine,** MEC. motor de gasoil. **4 – oil,** gasoil, aceite pesado.

diet | 'daɪət | *s.c.* **1** dieta (comida habitual). **2** dieta, régimen, régimen alimenticio. || *s.i.* **3** dieta, sistema alimenticio. || *v.i.* **4** comer siguiendo una dieta/régimen. || *adj.* **5** de dieta, dietético, de régimen. || *s.sing.* **6** (fig.) ración: *the usual diet of stupid ideas = la ración usual de ideas estúpidas.* || **7 to be on a –,** estar a dieta, estar a régimen. **8 to go on a –,** comenzar una dieta. **9 to put somebody on a –,** poner a régimen a alguien.

dietary | 'daɪətərɪ | *adj.* de comer, alimenticio, dietético: *dietary traditions.*

dietetics | ˌdaɪə'tetɪks | *s.i.* dietética (como ciencia).

dietician | ˌdaɪə'tɪʃn | *s.c.* dietista, dietético, experto en dietas.

differ | 'dɪfər | *v.i.* **1 [to – (from)]** diferir, ser diferente. **2** disentir, discrepar. || **3 to agree to –,** estar de acuerdo en discrepar. **4 I beg to –,** (form.) siento no estar de acuerdo, siento discrepar.

difference | 'dɪfrəns | *s.c.* e *i.* **1** diferencia, disimilitud, desemejanza. || *s.c.* **2** diferencia de opinión, discrepancia, disputa. || *s.sing.* **3 [– (between)]** diferencia (numérica). || **4 to make all the –,** significar mucho, ayudar mucho: *your help makes all the difference = tu ayuda significa mucho.* **5 to make no –/not to make any –,** no tener importancia, no tener relevancia, dar lo mismo. **6 to split the –,** partir la diferencia, dividir la diferencia (en una transacción). **7 with a –,** con una diferencia a su favor distinto, no como los demás, a su modo: *she's a doctor with a difference = es una doctora distinta* (que tiene algo especial).

different | 'dɪfrənt | *adj.* **1 [– (from/to)]** diferente, distinto. **2** diferente, especial (en su diferencia), original.

differential | ˌdɪfə'renʃl | *s.c.* **1** MAT. diferencial. **2** (brit.) diferencial (de sueldo en una misma empresa por distinto tipo de trabajo).

differentiate | ˌdɪfə'renʃɪeɪt | *v.t.* **1 [to – (from)]** diferenciar, distinguir. || *v.i.* **2 [to – between]** distinguir entre.

differentiation | ˌdɪfərenʃɪ'eɪʃn | *s.i.* diferenciación.

differently | 'dɪfrəntlɪ | *adv.* de modo distinto, de modo diferente.

difficult | 'dɪfɪkəlt | *adj.* **1** difícil, no fácil. **2** terco, obstinado, difícil.

difficulty | 'dɪfɪkəltɪ | *s.c.* e *i.* **1** dificultad. || **2 to have/find –,** tener dificultad, encontrar difícil. **3 in –/in difficulties,** con problemas (de todo tipo). **4 with –,** con dificultad.

diffidence | 'dɪfɪdəns | *s.i.* reserva, timidez natural.

diffident | 'dɪfɪdənt | *adj.* reservado, comedido; tímido.

diffidently | 'dɪfɪdəntlɪ | *adv.* reservadamente, comedidamente; tímidamente.

diffuse | dɪ'fjuːs | *v.t.* **1** esparcir, difundir (luz). **2** difundir, propagar (información, conocimientos, etc.). || *v.i.* **3** esparcirse, difundirse (luz). **4** difundirse, propagarse (información, conocimientos, etc.). **5** diluirse, disolverse (un líquido o gas). || | dɪ'fjuːs | *adj.* **6** impreciso, vago, difuso. **7** esparcido, difuso (luz); descentralizado (organización).

diffusion | dɪ'fjuːʒn | *s.i.* **1** difusión, propagación (de información, conocimientos, etc.). **2** disolución (líquido o gas).

dig | dɪg | *v.* [*ger.* **digging,** *pret.* y *p.p.* **dug**] *t.* **1** cavar, excavar. **2** (fig.) meter, introducir (con cierta fuerza una cosa dentro de otra): *I dug my elbow into his side = metí mi codo en su costado.* **3** (fam. y p.u.) comprender, captar; apreciar. || *i.* **4** hacer un hoyo. **5 [to – into]** pegar un golpe a; meterse en: *this is digging into my neck = esto se está metiendo en mi cuello.* **6 [to – (into)]** buscar, rebuscar, meter la mano (en un sitio). || *s.c.* **7** (fam.) indirecta. **8** golpe, toque fuerte. **9** excavación arqueológica. || *s.sing.* trabajo de cavar (en el jardín normalmente): *this garden needs a dig = este jardín necesita trabajo de cavar.* || **10 to – at,** tirar una indirecta a. **11 to – in, a)** (brit. y fam.) comer, jamar. **b)** MIL. atrincherarse. **12 to – into/in,** mezclar; añadir (algo a la tierra). **13 to – oneself in:** MIL. atrincherarse. **14 to – one's heels in,** V. **heel. 15 to – out, a)** sacar (con cierta dificultad). **b)** descubrir, desentrañar, sacar fuera. **16 digs,** (brit.) alojamiento, pensión. **17 to – up, a)** desenterrar. **b)** sacar a la luz, desenterrar (información, hechos, etc. ocultos).

digest | daɪ'dʒest | *v.t.* **1** digerir (comida). **2** (fig.) asimilar (información o similar). || *s.c.* **3** compendio, resumen.

digestible | dɪ'dʒestəbl | *adj.* digerible, digestible (comida).

digestion | dɪ'dʒestʃən | *s.c.* e *i.* digestión.

digestive | dɪ'dʒestɪv | *adj.* digerible, digestible (comida).

digger | 'dɪgər | *s.c.* excavadora (máquina).

digit | 'dɪdʒɪt | *s.c.* **1** MAT. dígito. **2** (form.) dedo (de la mano o pie).

digital | 'dɪdʒɪtl | *adj.* **1** digital (que muestra números). || **2 – computer,** INF. ordenador digital, computadora digital. **3 – recording,** grabación digital.
dignified | 'dɪgnɪfaɪd | *adj.* digno, serio, señorial.
dignify | 'dɪgnɪfaɪ | *v.t.* **1** ennoblecer, dar un toque de distinción a. **2** dignificar (algo más de allá de lo merecido).
dignitary | 'dɪgnɪtərɪ | *s.c.* dignatario (de alguna institución relevante).
dignity | 'dɪgnɪtɪ | *s.i.* **1** dignidad, excelencia, señorío. || *s.sing.* **2** dignidad personal: *my dignity doesn't allow me to dance like that = mi dignidad personal no me permite bailar así.* || **3 beneath one's –,** impropio de uno. **4 to stand on one's –,** ponerse en su lugar, hacerse respetar.
digress | daɪ'gres | *v.i.* **[to – (from)]** apartarse (del tema), hacer una digresión.
digression | daɪ'greʃn | *s.c.* e *i.* digresión.
dike | daɪk | V. **dyke.**
dilapidated | dɪ'læpɪdeɪtɪd | *adj.* ruinoso, (edificio o similar).
dilate | daɪ'leɪt | *v.t.* e *i.* dilatar(se) (ojos).
dilated | daɪ'leɪtɪd | *adj.* dilatado (ojos).
dilatory | 'dɪlətərɪ | *adj.* (form.) tardo, dilatorio.
dilemma | dɪ'lemə | *s.c.* **1** dilema. || **2 on the horns of a –,** V. **horn.**
dilettante | ˌdɪlɪ'tæntɪ | (*pl.* **dilettantes /dilettanti**) *s.c.* (desp.) diletante, aficionado.
diligence | 'dɪlɪdʒəns | *s.i.* diligencia, esmero.
diligent | 'dɪlɪdʒənt | *adj.* diligente, esmerado.
diligently | 'dɪlɪdʒəntlɪ | *adv.* diligentemente, esmeradamente.
dill | dɪl | *s.i.* BOT. eneldo.
dilly-dally | 'dɪlɪdælɪ | *v.i.* (fam.) perder el tiempo, estar mano sobre mano.
dilute | daɪlju:t | *v.t.* **1** diluir, desleir, aguar. **2** (fig.) adulterar, aguar (principios, creencias, etc.). || *adj.* **3** diluido, aguado.
dilution | daɪ'lju:ʃn | *s.i.* adulteración.
dim | dɪm | *adj.* **1** débil, opaco, mortecino (luz). **2** indistinto, poco claro, confuso (el objeto que se mira). **3** deslavazado, confuso (pensamiento, recuerdo, etc.). **4** oscuro, negro (futuro). **5** (fam.) lerdo, bobalicón. **6** velado, oscurecido (ojos, mirada, etc.). || *v.i.* **7** oscurecerse, amortiguarse (luz). **8** desvanecerse, apagarse (emociones, pensamientos, recuerdos, etc.). || *v.t.* **9** oscurecer, amortiguar (luz). **10** velar, empañar (la mirada): *tears dimmed my eyes = las lágrimas velaron mis ojos.* || **11 to be dimmed,** desvanecerse, apagarse (emociones, pensamientos, recuerdos, etc.). **12 to take a – view of,** V. **view.**
dime | daɪm | *s.c.* moneda de 10 centavos de dólar.
dimension | dɪ'menʃn | *s.c.* **1** dimensión, ángulo, aspecto. **2** GEOM. dimensión (espacial). || **3 dimensions, a)** dimensiones, tamaño. **b)** extensión, dimensión: *the dimensions of the problem = la extensión del problema.* **4 fourth –,** FIS. cuarta dimensión (el tiempo).
diminish | dɪ'mɪnɪʃ | *v.i.* **1** disminuir, decrecer, aminorarse. || *v.t.* **2** reducir, aminorar. **3** degradar, rebajar, empequeñecer (algo o alguien).
diminished | dɪ'mɪnɪʃt | *adj.* **1** disminuido, aminorado, debilitado. || **2 – responsibility,** DER. capacidad disminuida. **3 – returns,** ECON. utilidad decreciente.
diminishing | dɪ'mɪnɪʃɪŋ | *adj.* decreciente, en declive, en descenso.
diminution | ˌdɪmɪ'nju:ʃn | *s.i.* **[– (of/in)]** disminución, reducción, merma.
diminutive | dɪ'mɪnjʊtɪv | *adj.* **1** diminutivo. **2** diminuto, menudo.
dimly | 'dɪmlɪ | *adv.* **1** débilmente, mortecinamente, opacamente (luz). **2** deslavazadamente, confusamente (pensamientos o recuerdos).
dimmer | 'dɪmər | *s.c.* **1** reductor de luz. || **2 – switch,** reductor de luz.
dimness | 'dɪmnɪs | *s.i.* oscurecimiento, opacidad (luz).
dimple | 'dɪmpl | *s.c.* hoyito, hoyuelo (en la cara, especialmente al sonreír).
dimpled | 'dɪmpld | *adj.* con hoyitos, con hoyuelos (cara y otras superficies).
dimwit | 'dɪmwɪt | *s.c.* (fam.) imbécil, bobo.
din | dɪn | *s.c.* **1** estruendo, ruido, follón. || **2 to – into,** meter/enseñar a base de repetir: *the teacher dinned the idea into the children = el profesor les metió la idea a los chicos a base de repetírsela.*
dine | daɪn | (form.) *v.i.* **1** cenar, comer. || **2 to – in,** comer en casa, cenar en casa. **3 to – off/on,** (p.u.) tomar, comer: *they dined on horse meat = tomaron carne de caballo.* **4 to – out,** comer fuera, comer fuera de casa. **5 to – out on,** comentar durante la comida, hablar de... durante la comida.
diner | 'daɪnər | *s.c.* **1** comensal, cliente (en restaurante). **2** (EE.UU.) fonda, restaurante popular. **3** vagón restaurante (en un tren).
ding-dong | ˌdɪŋ'dɒŋ | *s.c.* e *i.* **1** ding-dong, talán, talán (sonido onomatopéyico de campanas o similar). || *adj.* **2** reñido (partido deportivo o similar). || *s.sing.* **3** riña, pelea (ruidosa).
dinghy | 'dɪŋgɪ | MAR. *s.c.* **1** esquife, bote: *sailing dinghy = bote de vela.* **2** lancha: *inflatable dinghy = lancha de rescate.*
dinginess | 'dɪndʒɪnɪs | *s.i.* suciedad, deslustre (tejido o edificio).
dingo | 'dɪŋgəʊ | (*pl.* **dingoes**) *s.c.* dingo (perro salvaje australiano).
dingy | 'dɪŋdʒɪ | *adj.* **1** sucio, deslustrado (ropa o tejido). **2** oscuro, sombrío (lugar o edificio).
dining-car | 'daɪnɪŋkɑ: | *s.c.* vagón restaurante (en un tren).
dining-room | 'daɪnɪŋru:m | *s.c.* comedor (en casa o en un hotel).
dining-table | 'daɪnɪŋteɪbl | *s.c.* mesa del comedor.
dinner | 'dɪnər | *s.c.* e *i.* **1** comida principal (del día); cena (para la clase media); comida de mediodía (para la clase obrera). || *s.c.* **2** banquete, cena (de celebración social). **3** cena (reunión social de amigos).
dinner-dance | 'dɪnədɑ:ns | *s.c.* cena y baile.
dinner-jacket | 'dɪnədʒækɪt | *s.c.* smoking, esmoquin.
dinner-party | 'dɪnəpɑ:tɪ | *s.c.* cena (como ocasión de reunión social).
dinner-service | 'dɪnəsəvɪs | *s.c.* vajilla.
dinner-table | 'dɪnəteɪbl | *s.c.* **1** mesa del comedor. || *s.sing.* **2** conversación de mesa, charla durante la comida.
dinnertime | 'dɪnətaɪm | *s.i.* hora de la cena, hora de la comida.
dinosaur | 'daɪnəsɔ: | *s.c.* ZOOL. dinosaurio.
dint dɪnt | *s.c.* **1** abolladura. || **2 by – of,** (p.u.) a fuerza de, a base de.
diocesan | daɪ'ɒsɪsn | *adj.* REL. diocesano.
diocese | 'daɪəsɪs | *s.c.* REL. diócesis.
dip | dɪp | *v.t.* **1** mojar, humedecer, meter (en un líquido). **2** (brit.) dar/poner la corta (luz de un vehículo). **3** bañar (animales en desinfectante). || *v.i.* **4 [to – (in/into)]** mojarse, humedecerse, meterse (en un líquido). **5** bajar, descender (carretera, camino, etc.). **6** zambullirse, bajar velozmente (pájaro, avión, etc.). **7 [to – under/below]** bajar por debajo de, descender por debajo de (hablando de cantidades, porcentajes, etc.). **8 [to – in/into]** meter (la mano, cuchara, etc.) en: *they dipped into the pot with their spoons = metieron sus cucharas en la cacerola.* **9 [to – in/into]** hojear, leer superficialmente (un libro). || *s.c.* **10** bajada, descenso, depresión (de un camino o similar). **11** zambullida, bajada veloz (pájaro, avión, etc.). **12** chapuzón. **13** baño desinfectante (para animales). **14** GAST. salsa (para verduras crudas o galletas). **15** hojeada, lectura superficial (a un libro). **16** caída, descenso (de una cantidad, porcentaje, etc.). || **17 to – in,** empezar a servirse (comida), no tener remilgos (para servirse comida o similar). **18 to – into one's savings/purse/pocket,** rascarse el bolsillo; gastar dinero.
diphteria | dɪf'θɪərɪə | *s.i.* MED. difteria.
diphthong | 'dɪfθɒŋ | *s.c.* FON. diptongo.
diploma | dɪ'pləʊmə | *s.c.* diploma.
diplomacy | di'pləʊməsɪ | *s.i.* **1** diplomacia. **2** (fig.) tacto, diplomacia, discreción.
diplomat | 'dɪpləmæt | *s.c.* **1** diplomático. **2** (fig.) diplomático, persona discreta.
diplomatic | ˌdɪplə'mætɪk | *adj.* **1** diplomático. **2** (fig.) diplomático, discreto. || **3 – bag,** valija diplomática. **4 – corps,** cuerpo diplomático. **5 – immunity,** inmunidad diplomática. **6 – service,** servicio diplomático.

diplomatically | ˌdɪplə'mætɪklɪ | *adv.* diplomáticamente, discretamente.
dipper | 'dɪpər | *s.c.* cazo.
dipping | 'dɪpɪŋ | *s.i.* desinfectación (de animales).
dipstick | 'dɪpstɪk | *s.c.* varilla (para medir profundidad).
dire | 'daɪər | *adj.* **1** horrendo, calamitoso, fatal (enfatizando lo serio de una situación): *I'm in a dire situation = estoy en una situación fatal.* **2 – straits,** situación difícil; posición insostenible.
direct | dɪ'rekt | *adj.* **1** directo, derecho, recto. **2** inmediato, directo (acción). **3** claro, inequívoco, directo (sin duda alguna): *direct answer = contestación inequívoca.* **4** franco, abierto, sincero (cualidad personal). **5** de lleno, directo, pleno (luz, rayos del sol, calor, etc.): *in direct sunlight = a pleno sol.* **6** directo (descendiente de alguien). || *adv.* **7** directamente: *I'll go to London direct = iré a Londres directamente.* || *v.t.* **8** dirigir, encabezar (un proyecto, un equipo de personas, etc.). **9** dirigir (película o similar). **10 [to – + *o.* + *inf.*]** (form.) ordenar, mandar. **11 [to – + *o.* + (to)]** indicar, señalar (dónde está un lugar). **12 [to – *o.* + (at/to/towards)]** (form.) dirigir, sobreescribir (carta o similar). **13 [to – *o.* + (at/to/towards)]** dirigir, centrar (atención, esfuerzo, etc.). **14 [to – *o.* + (at/to/towards/against)]** dirigir (miradas, palabras, etc.). || **15 – action,** acción directa (especialmente huelgas o similar). **16 – current,** ELEC. corriente continua. **17 – hit,** blanco, impacto de lleno, impacto directo. **18 – object,** GRAM. complemento directo. **19 – rule,** POL. gobierno centralizado; gobierno central (cuando antes se tenía algo de autonomía): *Northern Ireland is now under direct rule from London = Irlanda del Norte está ahora bajo el gobierno central de Londres.* **20 – tax,** ECON. impuesto directo. **21 – taxation,** ECON. impuestación directa, sistema de impuestos directos.
direction | dɪ'rekʃn | *s.c.* **1** dirección, trayectoria, sentido. **2** dirección, orientación (de la economía, de las leyes, de la educación, etc.). || *s.c.* **3** dirección, gobierno, supervisión (de un libro, proyecto, etc.). || *s.sing.* **4** dirección (de una película, obra de teatro o similar). || **5 directions,** instrucciones (para hacer algo), rumbo (para un lugar). **6 sense of –,** sentido de la orientación (espacial).
directional | dɪ'rekʃənl | *adj.* **1** TEC. direccional, que marca la dirección. **2** RAD. direccional, de orientación (según la orientación recibe señales mejor o no).
directive | dɪ'rektɪv | *s.c.* (form.) directiva, orden, instrucción.
directly | dɪ'rektlɪ: daɪ'rektlɪ | *adv.* **1** directamente, exactamente: *directly under = exactamente debajo.* **2** inmediatamente, en seguida. **3** en poco tiempo: *they'll arrive directly = llegarán en poco tiempo.* **4** directamente, sin interferencia, sin más: *go directly to the headmaster = ve sin más al director.* **5** francamente, sinceramente. || *conj.* **6** inmediatamente que, tan pronto como, en cuanto.
directness | dɪ'rektnɪs | *s.i.* franqueza, sinceridad.
director | dɪ'rektər, daɪ'rektər | *s.c.* **1** director (de cualquier organización), consejero (de una empresa). **2** director (de cine, teatro o similar). || **3 Director of Public Prosecutions,** POL. Fiscal General del Estado.
directorate | dɪ'rektərət | *s.c.* **1** directiva (de empresa). **2** departamento, Dirección General (de la administración).
director-general | dɪˌrektə'dʒenrəl | [*pl.* **director-generals** o **directors-general**] *s.c.* Presidente, Director General (de una gran organización).
directorial | dɪrək'tɔːrɪəl | *adj.* directorio, de director.
directorship | dɪ'rektəʃɪp | *s.c.* cargo de director.
directory | dɪ'rektərɪ | *s.c.* **1** guía (de teléfonos), directorio (de empresas o similar). || **2 – enquiries,** centralita de información.
dirge | dɜːdʒ | *s.c.* endecha, canto fúnebre.
dirigible | 'dɪrɪdʒəbl | *s.c.* AER. dirigible.
dirt | dɜːt | *s.i.* **1** suciedad, mugre, inmundicia. **2** tierra, polvo (en su aspecto sucio). || *s.c.* **3** excremento (de animales). || *s.sing.* **4** (fam.) escándalo, chisme de escándalo. **5** (fig.) bajeza, sordidez (especialmente en asuntos sexuales). || **6 as common/cheap as –,** guarra, vulgar. **7 – farmer,** (EE.UU.) labrador sin asalariados (que cultiva su propia tierra sólo). **8 – road,** (EE.UU.) carretera de tierra (de segunda clase). **9 – track,** carretera de tierra (de segunda clase). **10 to fling/throw – at,** lanzar denuestos contra, insultar asquerosamente a. **11 to treat somebody like –,** tratar a alguien mal, tratar a alguien como si fuera basura.
dirt-cheap | ˌdɜːt'ʃiːp | *adj.* y *adv.* **1** (fam.) tirado, baratísimo.
dirty | 'dɜːtɪ | *adj.* **1** sucio, mugriento, inmundo. **2** (desp.) sucio, asqueroso, infame (acción, pensamiento, etc.). **3** indecente, obsceno, sucio (referido al tema del sexo, vulgarmente). **4** deshonesto, sórdido, sucio (acciones humanas): *a dirty player = un jugador sucio.* **5** (fam.) rencorosa, malévola (mirada). **6** grisáceo, sucio (para colores). **7** (fam.) asqueroso, sucio, (como énfasis): *you're a dirty idiot = eres un asqueroso idiota.* **8** desapacible, lluvioso (tiempo). || *v.t.* **9** ensuciar, manchar. || **10 a – word,** tabú, algo que no se quiere oír: *David has become a dirty word for her = David se ha convertido en un tabú para ella.* **11 – old man,** (fam.) viejo verde. **12 – weekend,** (fam.) fin de semana dedicado al sexo; fin de semana de cana al aire. **13 to do somebody's – work,** hacerle el trabajo sucio a alguien. **14 to do the – on,** (fam. y brit.) hacerle una mala pasada a.
disability | ˌdɪsə'bɪlɪtɪ | *s.c.* **1** handicap, problema físico, problema psicológico, minusvalía (de todo tipo). || *s.i.* **2** (form.) incapacidad, invalidez.
disable | dɪs'eɪbl | *v.t.* incapacitar (mentalmente, físicamente, etc.).
disabled | dɪs'eɪbəld | *adj.* **1** minusválido, incapacitado. || **2 the –,** los minusválidos.
disablement | dɪs'eɪbəlmənt | *s.i.* incapacitación, inhabilitación.
disabuse | ˌdɪsə'bjuːz | *v.t.* **[to – + *o.* + (of)]** (form.) desengañar, sacar de un error.
disadvantage | ˌdɪsəd'vɑːntɪdʒ | *s.c.* **1** desventaja, detrimento. || **2 at a –,** en desventaja. **3 to be/work to one's –,** ir en contra de uno, crear dificultades para uno. **4 to put one at a –,** ponerle a uno en desventaja, causarle a uno detrimento.
disadvantaged | ˌdɪsəd'vɑːntɪdʒd | *adj.* de condición social baja, de situación económica mala: *disadvantaged families.*
disadvantageous | ˌdɪsædvɑːn'teɪdʒəs | *adj.* **[– (to)]** desventajoso, desfavorable.
disaffected | ˌdɪsə'fektɪd | *adj.* desafecto; desleal (a alguna causa).
disaffection | ˌdɪsə'fekʃn | *s.i.* rebeldía; deslealtad (a alguna causa).
disagree | ˌdɪsə'griː | *v.i.* **1 [to – (with/about/over)]** estar en desacuerdo, disentir, discrepar. **2 [to – (with)]** no casar (cantidades, balances, versiones, etc.): *the two stories disagree = las dos historias no casan.* **3 [to – (with)]** desaprobar, no aprobar, oponerse. **4 [to – (with)]** (fam.) sentar mal, caer mal (comida o bebida).
disagreeable | ˌdɪsə'griːəbl | *adj.* desagradable, displicente, ingrato (algo o alguien).
disagreeably | ˌdɪsə'griːəblɪ | *adv.* desagradablemente, displicentemente, ingratamente.
disagreement | ˌdɪsə'griːmənt | *s.c.* **1** desacuerdo, pelea verbal, disputa. || *s.i.* **2** desacuerdo, disconformidad. || *s.c.* e *i.* **3** falta de acuerdo (en cifras o similar). || **4 in –,** en desacuerdo.
disallow | ˌdɪsə'laʊ | *v.t.* anular (un gol), no aceptar (un dictamen, informe, etc.).
disappear | ˌdɪsə'pɪər | *v.i.* **1** desaparecer, perderse de vista. **2** extinguirse, desaparecer (vida, instituciones, acuerdos, etc.).
disappearance | ˌdɪsə'pɪərəns | *s.c.* e *i.* **1** desaparición (de personas). || *s.sing.* **2** pérdida, desaparición (de cosas). || *s.i.* **3** extinción, desaparición (especie, animal, objeto, etc.).
disappoint | ˌdɪsə'pɔɪnt | *v.t.* **1** decepcionar, defraudar; desilusionar.
disappointed | ˌdɪsə'pɔɪntɪd | *adj.* **[– (in/with/at)/ + *inf.*]** decepcionado, desilusionado: *I was very disappointed at his failure = quedé muy decepcionado por su fracaso.*
disappointing | ˌdɪsə'pɔɪntɪŋ | *adj.* decepcionante.

disappointingly | ˌdɪsəˈpɔɪntɪŋlɪ | *adv.* decepcionantemente.

disappointment | ˌdɪsəˈpɔɪntmənt | *s.c.* e *i.* desilusión, decepción (cosa o persona): *he was a great disappointment = él significó una gran decepción.*

disapproval | ˌdɪsəˈpruːvl | *s.i.* **[– (of)]** desaprobación, condenación.

disapprove | ˌdɪsəˈpruːv | *v.i.* **[to – of]** desaprobar, condenar.

disapproving | ˌdɪsəˈpruːvɪŋ | *adj.* condenatorio, de desaprobación.

disapprovingly | ˌdɪsəˈpruːvɪŋlɪ | *adv.* de manera condenatoria.

disarm | dɪsˈɑːm | *v.t.* **1** desarmar, quitar las armas. **2** (fig.) desarmar, neutralizar (críticas). **3** apaciguar (a alguien enfadado o similar). || *v.i.* **4** desarmarse (especialmente un país).

disarmament | dɪsˈɑːməmənt | *s.i.* desarme.

disarmer | dɪsˈɑːmər | *s.c.* pacifista, desarmamentista.

disarming | dɪsˈɑːmɪŋ | *adj.* apaciguador, cautivador.

disarmingly | dɪsˈɑːmɪŋlɪ | *adv.* apaciguadoramente, cautivadoramente.

disarrange | ˌdɪsəˈreɪndʒ | *v.t.* desarreglar, descomponer, desbarajustar (planes, cosas ordenadas, etc.).

disarray | ˌdɪsəˈreɪ | *s.i.* **1** desorden, confusión, desaliño. || **2 in –, a)** descompuesto, desorganizado (un ejército, empresa, etc.). **b)** desaliñado (ropa), despeinado (pelo).

disassociate | ˌdɪsəˈsəʊʃɪeɪt | *v.r.* **[to – (from)]** disociarse, separarse.

disaster | dɪˈzɑːstər | *s.c.* **1** desastre, catástrofe (natural). **2** (fig.) desastre, estropicio. || *s.i.* **3** calamidad, desastre. || **4 – area,** zona catastrófica.

disastrous | dɪˈzɑːstrəs | *adj.* catastrófico, calamitoso, desastroso.

disastrously | dɪˈzɑːstrəslɪ | *adv.* catastróficamente, calamitosamente, desastrosamente.

disavow | ˌdɪsəˈvaʊ | *v.t.* (form.) desautorizar; repudiar.

disband | dɪsˈbænd | *v.t.* e *i.* disolver(se) (organización, institución, etc.).

disbelief | ˌdɪsbɪˈliːf | *s.i.* incredulidad; escepticismo.

disbelieve | ˌdɪsbɪˈliːv | *v.t.* **1** no creer en, desconfiar de. || *v.i.* **2 [to – in]** no creer en.

disburse | dɪsˈbɜːs | *v.t.* (form.) desembolsar (dinero).

disbursement | dɪsˈbɜːsmənt | *s.c.* e *i.* (form.) desembolso (de dinero).

disc | dɪsk | (EE.UU. **disk**) *v.t.* **1** disco (cualquier objeto con esa forma). **2** ANAT. disco (de la columna). **3** MUS. disco. || **4 – brake,** freno de disco. **5 – jockey,** pinchadiscos, disc jockey.

discard | dɪˈskɑːd | *v.t.* descartar, desechar; tirar.

discarded | dɪˈskɑːdɪd | *adj.* descartado, desechado; tirado: *discarded food = comida tirada.*

discern | dɪˈsɜːn | (form.) *v.t.* **1** percibir, discernir, darse cuenta de. **2** distinguir (con la vista).

discernible | dɪˈsɜːnɪbl | *adj.* perceptible, visible.

discernibly | dɪˈsɜːnərblɪ | *adv.* perceptiblemente, visiblemente.

discerning | dɪˈsɜːnɪŋ | *adj.* perspicaz, juicioso, discernidor.

discernment | dɪˈsɜːnmənt | *s.i.* discernimiento, perspicacia.

discharge | dɪsˈtʃɑːdʒ | *v.t.* **1** licenciar (del ejército), dar el alta (médico), poner en libertad. **2** (normalmente pasiva) despedir (del trabajo). **3** (p.u.) disparar. **4** (form.) pagar, saldar, cancelar (deuda). **5** (form.) librar, expulsar, sacar, descargar: *the big trawlers discharged tons of fish = los grandes barcos de pesca descargaron toneladas de pescado.* **6** (form.) desempeñar, ejecutar (tareas, responsabilidades, etc.). || *s.c.* e *i.* **7** MED. secreción. **8** (form.) derrame, descarga (de algún líquido o sustancia). **9 [– (from)]** alta (médica), puesta en libertad, licenciamiento (del ejército). **10** (form.) despido (del trabajo). **11** (form.) desempeño (de tareas). **12** ELEC. descarga.

disciple | dɪˈsaɪpl | *s.c.* discípulo, seguidor.

disciplinarian | ˌdɪsɪplɪˈneərɪən | *s.c.* autoritario, partidario de la disciplina férrea.

disciplinary | ˈdɪsɪplɪnərɪ | *adj.* disciplinario.

discipline | ˈdɪsɪplɪn | *s.i.* **1** disciplina, orden, autoridad. **2** autocontrol, disciplina. || *s.c.* e *i.* **3** disciplina (de una situación), regla (de un estado), imposición (de una acción): *I need the discipline of having to get up at a fixed time = necesito la imposición de tener que levantarme a hora fija.* || *s.c.* **4** (form.) disciplina, asignatura (de estudio). || *v.t.* **5** castigar, corregir, disciplinar. **6** disciplinar, entrenar. || *v.r.* **7** disciplinarse, entrenarse.

disciplined | ˈdɪsɪplɪnd | *adj.* **1** ordenado, disciplinado, organizado (organización, sistema, actividad, etc.). **2** con autocontrol.

disclaim | dɪsˈkleɪm | *v.t.* (form.) rechazar, repudiar, desaprobar (responsabilidades, planes, informaciones, etc.).

disclaimer | dɪsˈkleɪmər | *s.c.* (form.) negación, rechazo (en forma de declaración).

disclose | dɪsˈkləʊz | *v.t.* revelar, descubrir (información secreta u objeto tapado).

disclosure | dɪsˈkləʊʒər | *s.i.* **1** revelación (de información). || *s.c.* **2** información, revelación.

disco | ˈdɪskəʊ | *s.c.* discoteca.

discoloration | ˌdɪskʌləˈreɪʃn | *s.i.* descoloramiento.

discolour | dɪsˈkʌlər | (EE.UU. **discolor**) *v.t.* e *i.* descolorar(se).

discoloured | dɪsˈkʌləd | (EE.UU. **discolored**) *adj.* descolorido.

discomfit | dɪsˈkʌmfɪt | *v.t.* (normalmente pasiva) (lit.) desconcertar, turbar.

discomfiture | dɪsˈkʌmfɪtʃər | *s.i.* (lit.) turbación, desconcierto.

discomfort | dɪsˈkʌmfət | *s.i.* **1** malestar, molestia (física). **2** incomodidad, inquietud. || *s.c.* **3** incomodidad, falta de comodidad.

disconcert | ˌdɪskənˈsɜːt | *v.t.* turbar, incomodar, desconcertar.

disconcerting | ˌdɪskənˈsɜːtɪŋ | *adj.* turbador, desconcertante.

disconcertingly | ˌdɪskənˈsɜːtɪŋlɪ | *adv.* turbadoramente, desconcertantemente.

disconnect | ˌdɪskəˈnekt | *v.t.* **1 [to – + *o.* + (from)]** desconectar, separar, desunir. **2** desconectar, apagar. **3** cortar (luz, teléfono, etc., especialmente por no pagar).

disconnected | ˌdɪskəˈnektɪd | *adj.* inconexo, incoherente, deslavazado (forma de hablar).

disconsolate | dɪsˈkɒnsəlɪt | *adj.* desconsolado, desolado, inconsolable.

disconsolately | dɪsˈkɒnsəlɪtlɪ | *adv.* desconsoladamente, desoladamente, inconsolablemente.

discontent | ˌdɪskənˈtent | *s.i.* **1** descontento, insatisfacción. || **2 discontents,** (form.) agravios.

discontented | ˌdɪskənˈtentɪd | *adj.* **[– (with)]** descontento, insatisfecho.

discontentedly | ˌdɪskənˈtentɪdlɪ | *adv.* con descontento, sin satisfacción.

discontinue | ˌdɪskənˈtɪnjuː | *v.t.* suspender, interrumpir, anular.

discontinuity | ˌdɪskəntɪˈnjuːɪtɪ | *s.i.* y *c.* (form.) discontinuidad; interrupción (en un proceso o similar).

discontinuous | ˌdɪskənˈtɪnjʊəs | *adj.* interrumpido, con interrupciones.

discord | ˈdɪskɔːd | *s.i.* **1** discordia, desacuerdo, desavenencia. || *s.c.* **2** MUS. disonancia.

discordant | dɪˈskɔːdənt | *adj.* **1** discordante, discrepante. **2** MUS. disonante.

discotheque | ˈdɪskətek | *s.c.* discoteca. V. **disco.**

discount | dɪsˈkaʊnt | *s.c.* **1** desacuerdo, rebaja. || *v.t.* **2** descontar, rebajar (un porcentaje de un precio). **3** (con pronunciación) despreciar, desestimar, descartar (una idea, teoría, etc.).

discourage | dɪˈskʌrɪdʒ | *v.t.* **1** descorazonar, desanimar. **2 [to – + *o.* + (from)]** disuadir.

discouraged | dɪˈskʌrɪdʒt | *adj.* descorazonado, desanimado.

discouragement | dɪˈskʌrɪdʒmənt | *s.i.* **1** desánimo, desaliento. || *s.c.* **2** disuasión; estorbo.

discouraging | dɪˈskʌrɪdʒɪŋ | *adj.* desalentador, descorazonador.

discourse | ˈdɪskɔːs | (form.) *s.c.* **1** disquisición; disertación. || *s.i.* **2** conversación, plática. || *v.i.* **3 [to – (on)]** platicar, disertar, hablar.

discourteous | dɪsˈkɜːtɪəs | *adj.* (form.) descortés, desatento, grosero.

discourteously | dɪsˈkɜːtɪəslɪ | *adv.* (form.) de manera descortés, groseramente.

discoutesy | dɪsˈkɜːtɪsɪ | *s.i.* (form.) descortesía, desatención, grosería.

discover | dɪsˈkʌvər | *v.t.* **1** descubrir. **2** descubrir, hallar, encontrar. **3** descubrir

(un nuevo invento, nueva tierra, etc.). **4** descubrir (un talento, un actor, escritor, etc.).
discoverer | dɪs'kʌvərər | *s.c.* **[– (of)]** descubridor; inventor.
discovery | dɪs'kʌvərɪ | *s.c.* **1** descubrimiento. **2** hallazgo, descubrimiento. **3** revelación, descubrimiento (de talento en las artes). || *s.i.* **4** descubrimiento, hallazgo (de nuevos caminos científicos o similar).
discredit | dɪs'kredɪt | (form.) **1** desacreditar, desprestigiar. **2** cuestionar, dudar de (ideas, creencias, etc.). || **3 to one's –,** para discrédito de uno, para desprestigio de uno.
discredited | dɪs'kredɪtɪd | *adj.* **1** desacreditado, desprestigiado. **2** cuestionado.
discreditable | dɪs'kredɪtəbl | *adj.* (form. y desp.) vergonzoso, desdoroso, deshonroso.
discreet | dɪ'skriːt | *adj.* **1** discreto, mesurado, moderado. **2** prudente, cuidadoso. **3** discreto (que no atrae la atención).
discreetly | dɪ'skriːtlɪ | *adv.* discretamente, mesuradamente, moderadamente.
discrepancy | dɪ'skrepənsɪ | *s.c.* **[– (between/in)]** discrepancia.
discrete | dɪ'skriːt | *adj.* inconexo, deslavazado.
discretion | dɪ'skreʃn | *s.i.* **1** discreción, tacto. **2** arbitrio, albedrío. || **3 at the – of,** a juicio de, según el deseo de.
discretionary | dɪ'skreʃənərɪ | *adj.* discrecional.
discriminate | dɪ'skrɪmɪneɪt | *v.i.* **1 [to – (between/among)]** distinguir, diferenciar. **2 [to – (against/in favour of)]** discriminar, hacer discriminación.
discriminating | dɪ'skrɪmɪneɪtɪŋ | *adj.* exigente, que muestra buen gusto.
discrimination | dɪˌskrɪmɪ'neɪʃn | *s.i.* **1** (desp.) discriminación. **2** diferenciación, distinción (entre dos cosas). **3** buen gusto; exigencia de calidad.
discriminatory | dɪ'skrɪmɪnətərɪ | *adj.* discriminatorio, parcial, injusto.
discursive | dɪ'skəːsɪv | *adj.* (form.) digresivo, divagante.
discus | 'dɪskəs | DEP. *s.c.* **1** disco (objeto). || *s.sing.* **2** disco (acontecimiento deportivo).
discuss | dɪ'skʌs | *v.t.* discutir, tratar, debatir (por palabra o escrito).
discussion | dɪ'skʌʃn | *s.c.* e *i.* **1** debate, discusión; polémica. || **2 under –,** siendo discutido, siendo debatido.
disdain | dɪs'deɪn | *s.i.* **1 [– (for)]** desdén, menosprecio. || *v.t.* **2** despreciar, desdeñar.
disdainful | dɪs'deɪnfl | *adj.* **[– (of)]** desdeñoso, despectivo.
disdainfully | dɪs'deɪnfəlɪ | *adv.* desdeñosamente, despectivamente.
disease | dɪ'ziːz | *s.c.* e *i.* enfermedad, mal, dolencia.
diseased | dɪ'ziːzd | *adj.* **1** enfermo, achacoso. **2** enfermo, morboso (de mente).
disembark | ˌdɪsɪm'bɑːk | *v.i.* **1 [to – (from)]** desembarcar. || *v.t.* **2** descargar, desembarcar (mercancías).
disembarkation | ˌdɪsembɑː'keɪʃn | *s.i.* **1** desembarco. **2** desembarque, descarga (de mercancías).
disembodied | ˌdɪsɪm'bɒdɪd | *adj.* incorpóreo, sin cuerpo.
disembowel | ˌdɪsɪm'baʊəl | *v.t.* destripar (animales o personas).
disenchanted | ˌdɪsɪn'tʃɑːntɪd | *adj.* desencantado, desilusionado.
disenchantment | ˌdɪsɪn'tʃɑːntmənt | *s.i.* desencanto, desilusión.
disenfranchise | ˌdɪsɪn'fræntʃaɪz | *v.t.* privar de derechos (como de votación para elecciones y otros).
disengage | ˌdɪsɪn'geɪdʒ | *v.t.* **1 [to – + *o.* + (from)]** desasir, soltar, librar. || *v.i.* **2** MIL. retirarse del combate, cesar el combate.
disengagement | ˌdɪsɪn'geɪdʒmənt | *s.i.* **[– (from)]** ruptura de compromiso.
disentangle | ˌdɪsɪn'tæŋgl | *v.t.* desenredar, desembrollar, desenmarañar.
disequilibrium | ˌdɪsiːkwɪ'lɪbrɪəm | *s.i.* (form.) inestabilidad.
disestablish | ˌdɪsɪ'stæblɪʃ | *v.t.* (form.) separar del Estado (la Iglesia).
disestablishment | ˌdɪsɪ'stæblɪʃmənt | *s.i.* (form.) separación del Estado (por parte de la Iglesia).
disfavour | ˌdɪs'feɪvər | (EE.UU. **disfavor**) (form. y p.u.) *s.i.* **1** desagrado, desaprobación. **2** desgracia, desprestigio. || *s.c.* **3** faena, mala pasada. || **4 to fall into – with,** caer en desgracia con.
disfigure | ˌdɪs'fɪgər | *v.t.* **1** desfigurar, deformar. **2** (fig.) afear, estropear (el paisaje, un objeto de arte, etc.).
disfigurement | dɪs'fɪgəmənt | *s.c.* desfiguramiento, deformidad.
disgorge | dɪs'gɔːdʒ | *v.t.* vomitar, verter, arrojar fuera de sí (en sentido figurado y normal): *the buildings disgorged thousands of people at 6.30 = los edificios vomitaron miles de personas a las 6.30.*
disgrace | dɪs'greɪs | *s.i.* **1** desgracia, ignominia, oprobio. || *s.sing.* **2** vergüenza: *the new tax is a disgrace = el impuesto nuevo es una vergüenza.* || *v.t.* y *r.* **3** deshonrar(se), desacreditar(se). || **4 to be a – to,** ser una deshonra para, ser una vergüenza para. **5 to bring – on,** deshonrar, traer deshonra sobre. **6 to fall into –,** caer en desgracia. **7 in –,** en desgracia, desacreditado.
disgraceful | dɪs'greɪsfl | *adj.* deshonroso, vergonzoso, ignominioso.
disgracefully | dɪs'greɪsfəlɪ | *adv.* deshonrosamente, vergonzosamente, ignominiosamente.
disgruntled | dɪs'grʌntld | *adj.* malhumorado, descontento.
disguise | dɪs'gaɪz | *s.c.* **1** disfraz. || *s.i.* **2** enmascaramiento, simulación, disfraz. || *v.r.* **3 [to – (as/with)]** disfrazarse. || *v.t.* **4** disfrazar, enmascarar. **5** (fig.) ocultar, solapar; desfigurar. || **6 a blessing in –,** no hay mal que por bien no venga. **7 to be disguised as/with,** ir disfrazado de/con. **8 in –,** disfrazado.
disgust | dɪs'gʌst | *v.t.* **1** repugnar, dar asco, inspirar aversión: *he disgusts me.* || *s.i.* **2** repugnancia, aversión, asco. || **3 in –,** con repugnancia, con asco, asqueado.
disgusted | dɪs'gʌstɪd | *adj.* asqueado; hastiado.
disgustedly | dɪs'gʌstɪdlɪ | *adv.* asqueadamente, con asco, desagradablemente.
disgusting | dɪs'gʌstɪŋ | *adj.* (desp.) repugnante, asqueroso; desagradable, horrible.
disgustingly | dɪs'gʌstɪŋlɪ | *adv.* (desp.) repugnadamente, asquerosamente; desagradablemente, horriblemente.
dish | dɪʃ | *s.c.* **1** plato; fuente. **2** (fig.) plato (el contenido de comida). || *s.sing.* **3** (fam. y brit.) tío bueno, tía buena: *she's quite a dish = es una tía bastante buena.* || *v.t.* **4** (fam. y brit.) destrozar, tirar por el suelo (esperanzas, ilusiones). || **5 dishes,** vajilla; platos: *wash the dishes = lavar los platos.* **6 to – it out,** (fam.) liarse a porrazos; pegar fuerte y bien. **7 to – out,** (fam.) **a)** servir (comida). **b)** infligir (castigo, crítica, etc.). **c)** dar, entregar, distribuir (generosamente). **d)** soltar, lanzar (cosas desagradables para que otras personas las hagan): *the boss dished out a lot of work yesterday = el jefe nos soltó mucho trabajo ayer.* **8 to – the dirt,** (fam. y brit.) mencionar escándalos, sacar a la luz escándalos (sobre alguien): *she's always dishing the dirt about me = ellas siempre están sacando a la luz escándalos sobre mí.* **9 to – up,** (fam.) servir, poner (comida en el plato).
disharmony | dɪs'hɑːmənɪ | *s.i.* (form.) falta de armonía, tensión.
dishcloth | 'dɪʃklɒθ | *s.c.* paño de cocina (para secar platos).
disheartened | dɪs'hɑːtnd | *adj.* desalentado, desanimado, descorazonado.
disheartening | dɪs'hɑːtnɪŋ | *adj.* desalentador, descorazonador.
dishevelled | dɪ'ʃevld | *adj.* despeinado; desaliñado (ropa, pelo o apariencia general).
dishonest | dɪsnɒɪst | *adj.* fraudulento, falso; ímprobo.
dishonestly | dɪs'ɒnɪstlɪ | *adv.* fraudulentamente, falsamente.
dishonesty | dɪsnɒɪstɪ | *s.i.* falta de honradez, improbidad.
dishonour | dɪsnɒər | (EE.UU. **dishonor**) (form.) *s.i.* **1** deshonor, ignominia. || *v.t.* **2** deshonrar; afrentar. **3** FIN. rechazar, rehusar el pago de (un cheque, por parte de un banco).
dishonourable | dɪsnɒərəbl | *adj.* (desp.) deshonroso, ignominioso.
dishonourably | dɪsnɒərəblɪ | *adv.* (desp.) deshonradamente, ignominiosamente.
dishwasher | 'dɪʃwɒʃər | *s.c.* lavaplatos, lavavajillas.
dishwater | 'dɪʃwɔːtər | *s.i.* **1** agua de fregar, agua sucia (después del fregado). || **2 as weak as –/like –,** no suficientemente fuerte (el té).

dishy | 'dɪʃɪ | *adj.* (fam. y brit.) bueno, buena. V. **dish 3.**
disillusion | ˌdɪsɪl'luːzn | *v.t.* **1** desencantar, desilusionar. || *s.i.* **2** V. **disillusionment.**
disillusioned | ˌdɪsɪl'luːznd | *adj.* desilusionado, desencantado.
disillusionment | ˌdɪsɪl'luːznmənt | *s.i.* desilusión, desencanto.
disincentive | ˌdɪsɪn'sentɪv | *s.c.* **[– (to)]** (form.) freno, falta de incentivo.
disinclination | ˌdɪsɪnklɪ'neɪʃn | *s.i.* (form.) renuencia; aversión.
disinclined | ˌdɪsɪn'klaɪnd | *adj.* maldispuesto, poco dispuesto.
disinfect | ˌdɪsɪn'fekt | *v.t.* desinfectar.
disinfectant | ˌdɪsɪn'fektənt | *s.c.* e *i.* desinfectante.
disinfection | ˌdɪsɪn'fekʃn | *s.i.* desinfección.
disinformation | dɪs'ɪnfə'meɪʃn | *s.i.* desinformación.
disingenuous | ˌdɪsɪn'dʒenjʊəs | *adj.* falso, doble, solapado.
disingenuously | ˌdɪsɪn'dʒenjʊəslɪ | *adv.* falsamente, con doblez.
disinherit | ˌdɪsɪn'herɪt | *v.t.* (form.) desheredar.
disinherited | ˌdɪsɪn'herɪtɪd | *adj.* (form.) desheredado (cultural o socialmente).
disintegrate | dɪs'ɪntɪgreɪt | *v.i.* **1** desintegrarse; deshacerse. **2** (fig.) desmoronarse, hacerse añicos.
disintegration | dɪsˌɪntɪ'greɪʃn | *s.i.* **1** desintegración, desaparición. **2** (fig.) desmoronamiento, hacerse añicos.
disinter | ˌdɪsɪn'tɜːr | *v.t.* **1** (hum.) resucitar, dar nueva vida. **2** desenterrar, exhumar.
disinterest | dɪs'ɪntrəst | *s.i.* desinterés.
disinterested | dɪs'ɪntrɪstɪd | *adj.* **1** desinteresado, indiferente. **2** imparcial, objetivo.
disinterestedly | dɪs'ɪntrəstɪdlɪ | *adv.* **1** desinteresadamente, indiferentemente. **2** imparcialmente, objetivamente.
disinterestedness | dɪs'ɪntrəstɪdnɪs | *s.i.* imparcialidad, objetividad.
disjointed | dɪs'dʒɔɪntɪd | *adj.* inconexo, incoherente; desordenado (en las ideas, forma de hablar, etc.).
disk | dɪsk | *s.c.* **1** INF. disco, diskette. **2** V. **disc.**
dislike | dɪs'laɪk | *v.t.* **1** tener aversión a, no gustar. || *s.i.* **2** aversión, antipatía. || **3 dislikes,** fobias; antipatías. **4 to take a – to,** tomar aversión a, coger manía a, caerle mal a uno: *I took an immediate dislike to him = él me cayó mal inmediatamente.*
dislocate | 'dɪsləkeɪt | *v.t.* **1** dislocar, descoyuntar. **2** trastornar; dar al traste con (planes, negocios, rutinas, etc.).
dislocation | ˌdɪslə'keɪʃn | *s.i.* desarreglo; trastorno.
dislodge | dɪs'lɒdʒ | *v.t.* desalojar, sacar (algo de un sitio, con mucho esfuerzo): *he dislodged the small fish-bone from his teeth = sacó la pequeña espina de sus dientes.*

disloyal | dɪs'lɔɪəl | *adv.* **[– (to)]** desleal, infiel.
disloyalty | dɪs'lɔɪəltɪ | *s.i.* deslealtad, infidelidad.
dismal | 'dɪzməl | *adj.* **1** deprimente, lúgubre. **2** miserable, fatal (de calidad): *what a dismal place! = ¡qué lugar tan miserable!*
dismally | 'dɪzməlɪ | *adv.* de manera deprimente, de manera lúgubre.
dismantle | dɪs'mæntl | *v.t.* **1** desmontar, desarmar. **2** (fig.) desmantelar (una institución, organización, sistema, etc.).
dismay | dɪs'meɪ | *v.t.* **1** consternar; desalentar. || *s.i.* **2** consternación; desaliento. || **3 to one's –,** para consternación de uno.
dismember | dɪs'membər | (form.) *v.t.* **1** desmembrar, despedazar. **2** (fig.) dividir, desmembrar (un imperio, país o similar).
dismemberment | dɪs'membəmənt | (form.) *s.i.* **1** desmembramiento. **2** (fig.) división, desmembramiento (de un imperio, país o similar).
dismiss | dɪs'mɪs | *v.t.* **1** despedir (del trabajo), destituir (de un cargo público), licenciar (del ejército). **2** desechar; alejar (pensamiento, deseo, ocurrencia, etc.). **3** dejar ir, dar permiso para irse: *the teacher dismissed everybody but Mary = la profesora dejó ir a todos menos a Mary.* **4** MIL. romper filas. **5** DER. sobreseer.
dismissal | dɪs'mɪsl | *s.c.* e *i.* **1 [– (of/from)]** despido (del trabajo). || *s.i.* **2** rechazo (de un plan, idea, ocurrencia, etc.).
dismissive | dɪs'mɪsɪv | *adj.* **[– (of)]** despectivo, desdeñoso.
dismissively | dɪs'mɪsɪvlɪ | *adv.* despectivamente, desdeñosamente.
dismount | ˌdɪs'maʊnt | *v.i.* **[to – (from)]** (form. y hum. a veces) apearse, desmontar.
disobedience | ˌdɪsə'biːdɪəns | *s.i.* desobediencia.
disobedient | ˌdɪsə'biːdɪənt | *adj.* desobediente.
disobey | ˌdɪsə'beɪ | *v.t.* desobedecer.
disobliging | ˌdɪsə'blaɪdʒɪŋ | *adj.* poco servicial; desagradable, ofensivo.
disorder | dɪs'ɔːdər | *s.i.* **1** desorden, desbarajuste. **2** alboroto, desorden (público). || *s.c.* e *i.* **3** MED. trastorno: *mental disorder.* || **4 disorders,** desórdenes, alborotos (públicos).
disordered | dɪs'ɔːdəd | *adj.* **1** desordenado (una habitación o similar). **2** MED. trastornado.
disorderly | dɪs'ɔːdəlɪ | *adj.* **1** desordenado (objetos). **2** alborotador, turbulento; escandaloso. || **3 drunk and –,** DER. alteración del orden público y embriaguez.
disorganization | dɪsˌɔːgənaɪ'zeɪʃn | *s.i.* desorganización.
disorganize | dɪs'ɔːgənaɪz | (también **disorganise**) *v.t.* desorganizar.
disorganized | dɪsˌɔːgənaɪzd | *adj.* desorganizado.

disorientate | dɪs'ɔːrɪənteɪt | (también **disorient**) *v.t.* desorientar.
disorientated | dɪs'ɔːrɪənteɪtɪd | *adj.* desorientado.
disorientation | dɪsˌɔːrɪən'teɪʃn | *s.i.* desorientación.
disown | dɪs'əʊn | *v.t.* repudiar, no reconocer, rechazar: *his grandfather disowned her = su abuelo la repudió.*
disparage | dɪ'spærɪdʒ | *v.t.* (form.) menospreciar; denigrar.
disparagement | dɪ'spærɪdʒmənt | *s.i.* (form.) menosprecio; descrédito.
disparaging | dɪ'spærɪdʒɪŋ | *adj.* menospreciativo, despreciativo.
disparagingly | dɪ'spærɪdʒɪŋlɪ | *adv.* despreciativamente.
disparate | 'dɪspərɪt | *adj.* (form.) desemejante, desigual.
disparity | dɪ'spærɪtɪ | *s.c.* e *i.* **[– (between/in)]** (form.) disparidad, desemejanza, desigualdad.
dispassionate | dɪ'spæʃənɪt | *adj.* desapasionado; imparcial.
dispassionately | dɪ'spæʃənɪtlɪ | *adv.* desapasionadamente; imparcialmente.
dispatch | dɪ'spætʃ | (también **despatch**) *s.c.* **1** PER. crónica (de otra ciudad o del extranjero). **2** MIL. despacho, mensaje, envío. || *v.t.* **3** (form.) enviar, despachar (algo o alguien). **4** (p.u.) matar, despachar. **5** (p.u.) despachar (una tarea). || *s.sing.* **6** (form.) envío (de tropas, equipos o similar). || *s.i.* **7** (p.u.) prontitud, diligencia. | **8 to be mentioned in dispatches,** MIL. ser recomendado para una mención especial/una medalla.
dispatch-rider | dɪ'spætʃraɪdər | *s.c.* MIL. mensajero motorizado.
dispel | dɪ'spel | *v.t.* disipar; quitar de la cabeza (pensamientos o similar).
dispensable | dɪ'spensəbl | *adj.* dispensable, prescindible.
dispensary | dɪ'spensərɪ | *s.c.* MED. dispensario (de medicinas), botiquín.
dispensation | ˌdɪspen'seɪʃn | (form.) *s.i.* **1** dispensación, administración (de justicia, tratamiento médico, etc.). **2** permiso especial, dispensa. || *s.c.* **3** REL. dispensa. **4** exención, permiso, dispensa (en cualquier ámbito). **5** régimen, plan, designio (religioso o político): *before the new dispensation = antes del nuevo régimen.*
dispense | dɪ'spens | *v.t.* **1** (form.) distribuir, repartir. **2** preparar, hacer (medicinas). **3** (form.) administrar, aplicar (sistema público de algo). || **4 to – with,** prescindir de, eliminar.
dispenser | dɪ'spensər | *s.c.* máquina automática (con cosas para adquirir mediante introducción de una moneda o presión de un botón).
dispersal | dɪ'spɜːsl | *s.i.* dispersión (de cosas o personas).
disperse | dɪ'spɜːs | *v.t.* e *i.* dispersar(se), esparcir(se).
dispersed | dɪ'spɜːsd | *adj.* esparcido, dispersado.
dispersion | dɪ'spɜːʃn | *s.i.* dispersión.
dispirited | dɪ'spɪrɪtɪd | *adj.* desanimado, desalentado, abatido.

dispiritedly | dɪ'spɪrɪtɪdlɪ | *adv.* con desánimo, abatidamente, desalentadamente.

dispiriting | dɪ'spɪrɪtɪŋ | *adj.* desalentador; deprimente.

displace | dɪs'pleɪs | *v.t.* **1** desplazar; desalojar. **2** (form.) sustituir, reemplazar. || **3 to be displaced,** ser desplazado del entorno familiar habitual. **4 displaced person,** (p.u.) refugiado.

displacement | dɪs'pleɪsmənt | *s.i.* **1** sustitución (de una cosa por otra). **2** desalojo, expulsión (de gente). **3** FIS. desplazamiento.

display | dɪ'spleɪ | *v.t.* **1** exhibir, exponer. **2** lucir, hacer ostentación de. **3** demostrar, revelar (emoción, virtud, cualidad, etc.). **4** INF. enseñar, mostrar (la pantalla del monitor). || *s.c.* **5** escaparate, exposición. **6** exhibición, demostración (como espectáculo). **7** INF. pantalla. **8** demostración (de sentimientos o similar). || *s.i.* **9** exhibición (de objetos). **10 on –,** a la vista, en exhibición.

displease | dɪs'pliːz | *v.t.* disgustar, enojar; desagradar.

displeased | dɪs'pliːzd | *adj.* **[– (with)]** disgustado, enojado.

displeasure | dɪs'pleʒər | *s.i.* enojo, desagrado, disgusto.

disport | dɪ'spɔːt | *v.r.* (p.u. y hum.) divertirse, retozar.

disposable | dɪ'spəuzəbl | *adj.* **1** desechable: *disposable nappies = braguitas de bebé desechables.* **2** a disposición, neto (sueldo o similar). **3** disponible, a su disposición.

disposal | dɪ'spəuzl | *s.i.* **1 [– (of)]** eliminación (de basura, productos peligrosos, etc.). || **2 at one's –,** a la disposición de uno.

dispose | dɪ'spəuz | **1 – of,** desembarazarse de, deshacerse de (algo). **2 – of,** decidir, resolver. **3 – of,** eliminar, matar, quitar de enmedio.

disposed | dɪ'spəuzd | *adj.* **1 [– inf.]** dispuesto, decidido. **2** (form.) ordenado, colocado, dispuesto. || **3 to be well/favourably – to,** estar bien dispuesto hacia, estar a favor de: *she's favourably disposed to your plan = está a favor de tu plan.*

disposition | ˌdɪspə'zɪʃn | (form.) *s.i.* **1** constitución, carácter. **2** tendencia, inclinación. || *s.c.* **3 [– (of)]** ordenación, colocación, disposición.

dispossess | ˌdɪspə'zes | *v.t.* **[to – + *o.* + (of)]** desposeer, privar.

dispossessed | ˌdɪspə'zesd | *adj.* **1** desposeído. || **2 the –,** los desposeídos, los pobres, los que no tienen nada.

disproportion | ˌdɪsprə'pɔːʃn | *s.c.* e *i.* **[– (between)]** (form.) disparidad; desproporción.

disproportionate | ˌdɪsprə'pɔːʃənɪt | *adj.* desproporcionado; desigual, dispar.

disproportionately | ˌdɪsprə'pɔːʃənɪtlɪ | *adv.* desproporcionadamente; desigualmente.

disprove | ˌdɪs'pruːv | *v.t.* refutar, rebatir.

disputation | ˌdɪspjuː'teɪʃn | (form.) *s.i.* y *c.* disputa, debate, polémica.

dispute | dɪ'spjuːt | *s.c.* **1** conflicto (laboral). **2** debate, polémica. **3** disputa; conflicto (armado). || *s.i.* **4** litigio, disputa. || *v.i.* **5 [to – (with)]** debatir, argüir, disputar. || *v.t.* **6** cuestionar, disputar (un hecho, una teoría, una declaración, etc.). **7** contender por, disputarse (un terreno, un trozo de comida, etc.). || **8 beyond –,** irrefutable, innegable. **9 in –,** disputado. **10 industrial –,** huelga. **11 without –,** sin disputa.

disqualification | dɪsˌkwɒlɪfɪ'keɪʃn | *s.c.* e *i.* **[– (from)]** descalificación, inhabilitación.

disqualify | dɪs'kwɒlɪfaɪ | *v.t.* **[to – + *o.* + (from)]** descalificar, inhabilitar.

disquiet | dɪs'kwaɪət | (form.) *s.i.* **1** desasosiego, intranquilidad. || *v.t.* **2** desasosegar, intranquilizar, inquietar.

disquieting | dɪs'kwaɪətɪŋ | *adj.* (form.) inquietante.

disquisition | ˌdɪskwɪ'zɪʃn | *s.c.* (form.) disertación, disquisición.

disregard | ˌdɪsrɪ'gɑːd | *v.t.* **1** hacer caso omiso de, pasar por alto; descuidar. || *s.i.* **2 [– (of/for)]** descuido, desatención.

disrepair | ˌdɪsrɪ'peər | *s.i.* **1** mal estado. || **2 in –,** en mal estado.

disreputable | dɪs'repjutəbl | *adj.* de mala fama; vergonzoso, deshonroso.

disrepute | ˌdɪsrɪ'pjuːt | *s.i.* **1** descrédito, desprestigio. || **2 to bring/fall into –,** desacreditar, desprestigiar. **3 in –,** desprestigiado, desacreditado.

disrespect | ˌdɪsrɪ'spekt | *s.i.* descortesía, falta de respeto.

disrespectful | ˌdɪsrɪ'spektfl | *adj.* irrespetuoso, irreverente, descortés.

disrespectfully | ˌdɪsrɪ'spektfəlɪ | *adv.* irrespetuosamente, irreverentemente, descortésmente.

disrobe | dɪs'rəub | *v.t.* e *i.* (form. y hum. a veces) desvestir(se).

disrupt | dɪs'rʌpt | *v.t.* desbaratar, desorganizar (acontecimiento o similar).

disruption | dɪs'rʌpʃn | *s.c.* e *i.* desorganización; interrupción.

disruptive | dɪs'rʌptɪv | *adj.* destructivo; perjudicial.

disruptively | dɪs'rʌptɪvlɪ | *adv.* destructivamente; perjudicialmente.

dissatisfaction | dɪ'sætɪs'fækʃn | *s.i.* **[– (with)]** insatisfacción, descontento.

dissatisfied | dɪ'sætɪsfaɪd | *adj.* insatisfecho.

dissect | dɪ'sekt | *v.t.* **1** disecar. **2** (fig.) analizar minuciosamente.

dissection | dɪ'sekʃn | *s.c.* e *i.* **1** disección. || *s.i.* **2** (fig. y form.) análisis minucioso.

dissemble | dɪ'sembl | *v.i.* (lit.) disimular; actuar hipócritamente.

disseminate | dɪ'semɪneɪt | *v.t.* diseminar, difundir (información, conocimientos, etc.).

dissemination | dɪˌsemɪ'neɪʃn | *s.i.* difusión, divulgación.

dissension | dɪ'senʃn | *s.i.* disensión, desacuerdo, discordia.

dissent | dɪ'sent | *v.i.* **1** discrepar, disentir. **2 [to – from]** (form.) estar en desacuerdo con. || *s.i.* **3** disentimiento, discrepancia; disidencia.

dissenter | dɪ'sentər | *s.c.* **1** disidente. || **2 Dissenter,** REL. no conformista (que no es anglicano).

dissenting | dɪ'sentɪŋ | *adj.* discrepante.

dissertation | ˌdɪsə'teɪʃn | *s.c.* **1** tesis, tesina (trabajo académico). **2** disertación (escrito o discurso).

disservice | dɪs'sɜːvɪs | *s.c.* **1** mal servicio, perjuicio. || **2 to do a –,** perjudicar.

dissident | 'dɪsɪdənt | *s.c.* **1** disidente. || *adj.* **2** disidente.

dissimilar | dɪ'sɪmɪlər | *adj.* **[– (to/from/in)]** diferente, distinto, desemejante.

dissimilarity | ˌdɪsɪmɪ'lærɪtɪ | *s.c.* e *i.* **[– (between/in)]** diferencia, desemejanza; diversidad.

dissimulate | dɪ'sɪmjuleɪt | *v.t.* e *i.* (form.) disimular, fingir.

dissimulation | dɪˌsɪmju'leɪʃn | *s.i.* (form.) disimulo, fingimiento.

dissipate | 'dɪsɪpeɪt | (form.) *v.t.* **1** desvanecer, disipar. **2** malgastar, desperdiciar, derrochar (dinero, tiempo, energía, etc.). || *v.i.* **3** desvanecerse, disiparse.

dissipated | ˌdɪsɪ'peɪtɪd | *adj.* disoluto, vicioso.

dissipation | ˌdɪsɪ'peɪʃn | *s.i.* **1** (form.) disipación, desaparición. **2** (form.) derroche, desperdicio. **3** vicio; libertinaje.

dissociate | dɪ'səuʃɪeɪt | *v.t.* **1 [to – + *o.* + (from)]** separar, disociar. || *v.r.* **2 [to – (from)]** separarse, disociarse.

dissolute | 'dɪsəluːt | *adj.* (desp.) disoluto, libertino.

dissolution | ˌdɪsə'luːʃn | *s.i.* **1 [– (of)]** disolución (del Parlamento o parecido). **2 [– (of)]** disolución; debilitamiento, degradación. || *s.c.* **3** disolución (de contrato, matrimonio, etc.).

dissolve | dɪ'zɒlv | *v.t.* **1** disolver (en un líquido). **2** (fig.) disolver (Parlamento, matrimonio, contrato, etc.). || *v.i.* **3** disolverse (en líquido). **4** desvanecerse, debilitarse. || **5 to – into,** deshacerse en (risas o lágrimas).

dissolved | dɪ'zɒlvd | *adj.* disuelto (algo en un líquido).

dissonance | 'dɪsənəns | *s.i.* (form.) disonancia.

dissuade | dɪ'sweɪd | *v.t.* **[to – + *o.* + (from)]** disuadir, desaconsejar.

distance | 'dɪstəns | *s.c.* e *i.* **1** distancia. || *s.i.* **2** lejanía; alejamiento. **3** (fig. y form.) reserva, frialdad, distanciamiento. || *v.r.* **4 [to – (from)]** distanciarse, alejarse. || *v.t.* **5** distanciar, alejar, apartar. || **6 at a –,** a distancia, a cierta distancia. **7 from a –,** desde lejos. **8 to go the –,** (fam.) DEP. completar (un partido, una carrera, etc.). **9 in the –,** a lo lejos. **10 to keep one's –, a)** mantenerse a distancia, no mezclarse. **b)** (p.u.) no acercarse, quedarse a cierta distancia.

distant | ’dɪstənt | *adj.* **1** distante, alejado, lejano, remoto (lugar, tiempo, viaje, pariente, etc.). **2** reservado, esquivo; frío. **3** abstraído: *a distant look.*
distantly | ’dɪstəntlɪ | *adj.* **1** a lo lejos, de lejos, en lontananza. **2** (lit.) en un lugar lejano. **3** lejanamente (emparentado). **4** reservadamente, fríamente. **5** abstraídamente.
distaste | dɪs’teɪst | *s.i.* aversión, repugnancia.
distasteful | dɪs’teɪstfl | *adj.* desagradable, repugnante.
distastefully | dɪs’teɪstfəlɪ | *adv.* desagradablemente, repugnantemente.
distemper | dɪ’stempər | *s.i.* **1** moquillo (enfermedad canina). **2** temple, pintura al temple.
distend | dɪ’stend | *v.t.* e *i.* (form.) MED. agrandar(se), hinchar(se), dilatar(se).
distended | dɪ’stendɪd | *adj.* (form.) MED. hinchado, dilatado.
distension | dɪ’stenʃn | (EE.UU. **distention**) *s.c.* e *i.* MED. hinchazón, dilatación.
distil | dɪ’stɪl | (EE.UU. **distill**) *v.t.* **1** destilar (líquido). **2 [to – + *o.* + (from)]** (fig.) extraer, sacar, entresacar: *his novel was distilled from his experiences in China = su novela fue sacada de sus experiencias en China.*
distillation | ˌdɪstɪ’leɪʃn | *s.i.* **1** destilación, destilado (líquido). || *s.c.* **2** (fig.) extracción, extracto, esencia.
distilled | dɪ’stɪld | *adj.* **1** destilado (líquido). **2** (fig.) extraído, entresacado (de la experiencia, del pensamiento, etc.).
distiller | dɪ’stɪlər | *s.c.* destilador; fabricante de bebidas alcohólicas.
distillery | dɪ’stɪlərɪ | *s.c.* destilería; fábrica de bebidas alcohólicas.
distinct | dɪ’stɪŋkt | *adj.* **1 [– (from)]** distinto, diferente, diverso. **2** nítido, claro (a la vista o al pensamiento). **3** indudable, inconfundible: *a distinct possibility.* || **4 as – from,** opuesto a; distinto a, distinto de.
distinction | dɪ’stɪŋkʃn | *s.c.* **1** distinción, diferenciación, diferencia. **2** mención especial (académicamente); matrícula de honor. || *s.i.* **3** distinción: *a man of distinction.* || *s.c.* e *i.* **4** honor, distinción: *I had the distinction of being the first boy to climb the Mount Blanc = yo tuve el honor de ser el primer muchacho que subió al Mont Blanc.* || **5 to draw/ make a –,** distinguir, hacer una distinción.
distinctive | dɪ’stɪŋktɪv | *adj.* característico, distintivo.
distinctively | dɪ’stɪŋktɪvlɪ | *adv.* característicamente, distintivamente.
distinctiveness | dɪ’stɪŋktɪvnɪs | *s.i.* (lo) característico, (lo) distintivo.
distinctly | dɪ’stɪŋktlɪ | *adv.* **1** claramente, nítidamente, inconfundiblemente. **2** indudablemente, marcadamente, positivamente: *he looks distinctly drunk = parece indudablemente bebido.*
distinguish | dɪ’stɪŋgwɪʃ | *v.t.* **1 [to – + *o.* + (from)]** distinguir, diferenciar. **2** divisar, distinguir (con la mirada). || *v.r.* **3** descollar, lucirse, distinguirse (en el arte, milicia, estudios, etc.). || *v.i.* **4 [to – between]** distinguir entre, diferenciar entre.
distinguishable | dɪ’stɪŋgwɪʃəbl | *adj.* **1 [– (from)]** distinguible, diferenciable. **2** perceptible, discernible.
distinguished | dɪ’stɪŋgwɪʃt | *adj.* distinguido, prestigioso, ilustre.
distort | dɪ’stɔːt | *v.t.* **1** deformar, distorsionar, tergiversar (hechos, imágenes, etc.). || *v.i.* **2** deformarse, distorsionarse, retorcerse (objeto).
distorted | dɪ’stɔːtɪd | *adj.* deformado, distorsionado, retorcido (objeto).
distorting | dɪ’stɔːtɪŋ | *adj.* deformador, distorsionador, tergiversador: *a distorting mirror = un espejo deformador.*
distortion | dɪ’stɔːʃn | *s.c.* e *i.* deformación, distorsión, tergiversación.
distract | dɪ’strækt | *v.t.* distraer, apartar (atención).
distracted | dɪ’stræktɪd | *adj.* distraído, aturdido; trastornado.
distractedly | dɪ’stræktɪdlɪ | *adv.* distraídamente, aturdidamente; trastornadamente.
distraction | dɪ’strækʃn | *s.c.* e *i.* **1** distracción, entretenimiento. || **2 to drive somebody to –,** sacar a alguien de sus casillas.
distraught | dɪ’strɔːt | *adj.* perturbado, aturdido, ido.
distress | dɪ’stres | *v.t.* **1** angustiar, afligir; apenar. || *s.i.* **2** angustia, aflicción, congoja. **3** apuro, necesidad perentoria, escasez. **4** dolor, sufrimiento. **5** situación de emergencia; socorro: *a distress signal = una señal de socorro.*
distressed | dɪ’stresd | *adj.* **1** angustiado, afligido, acongojado. **2** dolido, con gran sufrimiento.
distressful | dɪ’stresfl | *adj.* angustioso, penoso.
distressfully | dɪ’stresfəlɪ | V. **distressingly.**
distressing | dɪ’stresɪŋ | *adj.* inquietante, angustioso.
distressingly | dɪ’stresɪŋlɪ | *adv.* angustiosamente, penosamente.
distribute | dɪ’strɪbjuːt | *v.t.* **1** distribuir, repartir. **2** colocar, distribuir (por ejemplo, muebles en una habitación).
distribution | ˌdɪstrɪ’bjuːʃn | *s.c.* e *i.* distribución, reparto, repartición.
distributor | dɪ’strɪbjʊtər | *s.c.* **1** distribuidor (de cualquier género). **2** MEC. distribuidor (en un motor).
district | ’dɪstrɪkt | *s.c.* **1** distrito, comarca, zona (de una ciudad o área). || *s.sing.* **2** localidad (zona alrededor de un pueblo o calle). || **3 – attorney,** (EE.UU.) fiscal del distrito. **4 – nurse,** (brit.) enfermera visitadora.
distrust | dɪs’trʌst | *v.t.* **1** desconfiar de, recelar de. || *s.i.* **2 [– (of)]** desconfianza, recelo.
distrusted | dɪs’trʌstɪd | *adj.* en quien no se confía: *the most distrusted Minister in the Cabinet = el Ministro en quien se confía menos del Gobierno.*
distrustful | dɪs’trʌstfʊl | *adj.* **[– (of)]** receloso, desconfiado.
disturb | dɪ’stəːb | *v.t.* **1** molestar, perturbar. **2** turbar, inquietar. **3** alterar, desordenar, desarreglar (objetos o similar). || **4 to – the peace,** DER. alterar el orden público.
disturbance | dɪ’stəːbəns | *s.i.* **1** turbación, alteración: *I don’t want the least disturbance here = no quiero la menor alteración aquí.* || *s.c.* **2** conmoción, revuelo, alboroto.
disturbed | dɪ’stəːbd | *adj.* **1** desequilibrado (mentalmente). **2** afectado (por la preocupación, ansia o similar). **3** insatisfactorio, carente de armonía; agitado: *disturbed adolescence = adolescencia agitada.*
disturbing | dɪ’stəːbɪŋ | *adj.* inquietante, perturbador, preocupante.
disturbingly | dɪ’stəːbɪŋlɪ | *adv.* inquietantemente, perturbadoramente, preocupadamente.
disunite | ˌdɪsjuː’nait | *v.t.* (form.) desunir, separar, dividir (personas).
disunited | ˌdɪsjuːnaɪtɪd | *adj.* (form.) desunido, separado, dividido (personas).
disunity | dɪs’juːnɪtɪ | *s.i.* **[– (in/within /among)]** (form.) desunión, discordia, desavenencia.
disuse | dɪs’juːs | *s.i.* **1** desuso, abandono. || **2 to fall into –,** caer en desuso.
disused | dɪs’juːzd | *adj.* abandonado, deshabitado, sin ninguna clase de funcionamiento (especialmente los edificios).
ditch | dɪtʃ | *s.c.* **1** cuneta, badén, zanja. || *v.t.* **2** (fam.) despedir, cortar (una relación amorosa), tirar (objeto no deseado).
ditchwater | ’dɪtʃwɔːtər | **as dull as –,** (fam. y p.u.) pesado, latoso, aburridísimo.
dither | ’dɪðər | *v.i.* **1 [to – (about)]** vacilar, dudar. || **2 in a –/all of a –,** (fam.) nerviosísimo, agitadísimo.
ditto | ’dɪtəʊ | *adj.* **1** ídem, lo mismo (en listas escritas). || *adv.* **2** (fam.) ídem de ídem, ídem.
ditty | ’dɪtɪ | *s.c.* MUS. cancioneta, cantinela.
diuretic | ˌdaɪjʊ’retɪk | MED. *adj.* **1** diurético. || *s.c.* **2** diurético.
diurnal | daɪ’əːnl | *adj.* (form.) diurno.
divan | dɪ’væn | *s.c.* **1** cama turca. **2** otomana. || **3 – bed,** cama turca.
dive | daɪv | [EE.UU. *pret.* **dove**] *v.i.* **1 [to – (into)]** zambullirse, tirarse, saltar (al agua). **2** bucear; sumergirse. **3** lanzarse en picado, picar. **4** lanzarse, tirarse, meterse (en cualquier dirección o lugar). **5 [to – in/into]** (fig.) meterse de lleno en, abordar (una actividad). **6 [to – into]** meter la mano velozmente en (buscando algo). || *s.c.* **7** zambullida. **8** picado, lanzamiento en picado. **10** estirada, salto (a por algo). **11** (fam. y desp.) tugurio, tasca. || **11 to – for cover,** buscar cobijo de un salto, esconderse

del ataque de un salto. **12 – in!,** ¡a comer!
dive-bomb | 'daɪvɒm | *v.t.* MIL. bombardear en picado.
dive-bomber | 'daɪvɒmər | *s.c.* MIL. cazabombardero.
diver | 'daɪvər | *s.c.* **1** buzo. **2** saltador (de trampolín).
diverge | daɪ'vɜːdʒ | *v.i.* **1** divergir; ser diferente. **2 [to – from]** desviarse de (la verdad, un modelo, etc.). **3 [to – (from)]** separarse, divergir (carreteras, caminos o similar).
divergence | daɪ'vɜːdʒəns | *s.c.* e *i.* divergencia; desacuerdo.
divergent | daɪ'vɜːdʒənt | *adj.* divergente; diferente.
divers | 'daɪvəz | *adj.* (p.u. y form.) diverso, vario.
diverse | daɪ'vɜːs | *adj.* diverso, variado.
diversification | daɪˌvɜːsɪfɪ'keɪʃn | *s.i.* diversificación.
diversify | daɪ'vɜːsɪfaɪ | *v.t.* e *i.* diversificar(se).
diversion | daɪ'vɜːʃn | *s.c.* **1** distracción (que distrae la atención). **2** desviación (de tráfico). **3** MIL. maniobra de distracción. **4** (p.u.) diversión, entretenimiento, pasatiempo. **5** desviación (de un objetivo): *the diversion of funds = la desviación de dinero.*
diversionary | daɪ'vɜːʃənərɪ | *adj.* de distracción (maniobra, táctica, etc.).
diversity | daɪ'vɜːsətɪ | *s.i.* y *c.* diversidad, variedad. || *s.i.* **2** divergencia, desemejanza.
divert | daɪ'vɜːt | *v.t.* **1** desviar (recursos, tráfico, tropas, etc.). || *v.r.* **2** (p.u.) distraerse, entretenerse.
divest | daɪ'vest | (form.) *v.r.* **1 [to – of]** despojarse de, librarse de (ropa, valores, creencias, etc.). || *v.t.* **2 [to – + *o.* + of]** despojar, quitar (función, rol, etc.).
divide | dɪ'vaɪd | *v.t.* **1** dividir, partir. **2 [to – + *o.* + (among/between)]** repartir. **3** (fig.) separar, desunir, dividir. **4 [to – + *o.* + (into/by)]** MAT. dividir. || *v.i.* **5** dividirse, partirse. **6** separarse, desunirse, dividirse. **7 [to – into/by]** dividir en/por (matemáticamente). || *s.c.* **8** (EE.UU.) GEOL. divisoria (tierra entre dos cuencas fluviales). **9** división, separación (de clases sociales, grupos o similar). **10** (fig.) acontecimiento decisorio, hecho de gran importancia: *the invention of the steam engine was a great divide in our history = la invención de la máquina de vapor fue un hecho de gran importancia en nuestra historia.* || **11 to be divided in/into,** estar dividido en, dividirse en (partes, trozos, secciones, etc.). **12 – and rule,** divide y vencerás. **13 to – off,** aislar, separar totalmente (formando una barrera). **14 to – up, a)** fragmentar, trocear. **b)** repartir equitativamente.
divided | dɪ'vaɪdɪd | *adj.* **1 [– (on/over)]** dividido, desunido. **2** de diferente parecer, opuesto, encontrado: *there was a divided opinion on the issue = hubo opiniones encontradas sobre el tema.*
dividend | 'dɪvɪdend | *s.c.* **1** FIN. dividendo. **2** (fig.) beneficio, ganancia (especialmente inesperado). || **3 to pay dividends,** traer beneficios, dar ventajas, beneficiar (especialmente en el futuro).
divider | dɪ'vaɪdər | *s.c.* **1** barrera, separación: *a social divider.* || **2 dividers,** compás de división, compás de puntas.
dividing line | dɪ'vaɪdɪŋlaɪn | *s.c.* **[– (between)]** línea divisoria.
divination | ˌdɪvɪ'neɪʃn | *s.i.* adivinación.
divine | dɪ'vaɪn | *adj.* **1** divino. **2** (fam. y p.u.) sublime, fantástico, divino. || *s.c.* **3** teólogo. || *v.t.* **4** (lit.) adivinar.
divinely | dɪ'vaɪnlɪ | *adv.* **1** sobrenaturalmente. **2** (fam. y p.u.) divinamente, fantásticamente.
diving | 'daɪvɪŋ | *s.i.* **1** DEP. submarinismo. **2** DEP. saltos de trampolín.
diving-board | 'daɪvɪŋbɔːd | *s.c.* trampolín.
diving-suit | 'daɪvɪŋsjuːt | *s.c.* traje de buzo.
divinity | dɪ'vɪnɪtɪ | *s.i.* **1** teología. **2** divinidad, deidad. || *s.c.* **3** divinidad, dios, diosa.
divisible | dɪ'vɪzəbl | *adj.* **1 [– (by)]** MAT. divisible. **2 [– (into/from)]** divisible, fragmentable.
division | dɪ'vɪʒn | *s.i.* **1** división, distribución. **2 [– (into)]** separación, división. **3** MAT. división. || *s.c.* **4** (fig.) discordia, desunión, división (en ideas, creencias, etc.). **5** ramo, departamento (dentro de una empresa o similar). **6** MIL. división. **7** DEP. división, categoría (en el fútbol, baloncesto, etc.). **8** sección, compartimento; hueco (dentro de una caja, bolso o similar). || *s.c.* e *i.* **9** (brit.) POL. votación, voto (sistema del Parlamento británico). || **10 – of labour,** reparto de responsabilidades laborales. **11 – sign,** MAT. signo de división. **12 without –,** (brit.) por unanimidad.
divisional | dɪ'vɪʒənl | *adj.* **1** MIL. de división. **2** departamental (en una empresa).
divisive | dɪ'vaɪsɪv | *adj.* disgregador, separador.
divorce | dɪ'vɔːs | *s.c.* e *i.* **1** divorcio. || *s.i.* **2 [of – (of/between)]** (fig.) divorcio, separación: *divorce between family and school = separación entre la familia y la escuela.* || *v.t.* **3** divorciarse, divorciarse de. **4 [to – + *o.* + (from)]** (fig.) separar, disociar: *you should divorce your financial interests from your involvement with the party = deberías disociar tus intereses económicos de tu participación en el partido.*
divorced | dɪ'vɔːst | *adj.* **1** divorciado. **2 [– (from)]** (fig.) separado, disociado: *divorced from reality = separado de la realidad.*
divorcee | dɪ'vɔː'siː | *s.c.* divorciado, divorciada.
divulge | daɪ'vʌldʒ | *v.t.* revelar, divulgar.
D.I.Y. | ˌdiːaɪ'waɪ | *s.i.* hágalo Vd. mismo; bricolage (siglas de **do-it-yourself**): *a D.I.Y. kit = un conjunto de instrumentos de bricolage.*
dizzily | 'dɪzɪlɪ | *adv.* aturdidamente; vertiginosamente.
dizziness | 'dɪzɪnɪs | *s.i.* **1** mareo, vértigo. **2** aturdimiento.
dizzy | 'dɪzɪ | *adj.* **1** mareado. **2 [– (with)]** confuso; aturdido. **3** vertiginoso (altura, nivel, etc.): *the climbers reached a dizzy height of 8.000 metres = los escaladores alcanzaron una altura vertiginosa de 8.000 metros.* || *v.t.* **4** marear; aturdir.
D.J. | 'diː'dʒeɪ | *s.c.* disc jockey (siglas de **disc jockey**).
djinn | dʒɪn | *s.c.* genio, geniecillo (especialmente en cuentos orientales).
DNA | ˌdiːen'eɪ | *s.i.* BIOL. ácido desoxiribonucleico (siglas de deoxyribonucleic acid).
do | duː | *v.* [*pret.* **did,** *p.p.* **done**] *t.* **1** hacer; realizar, ejecutar: *I'm not doing much work lately = no estoy haciendo mucho trabajo últimamente.* **2** estudiar (un tema, una asignatura, etc.). **3** visitar (un museo, ciudad o similar, de turista). **4 [to – + *o.* + (about)]** hacer, solucionar: *we'll do everything possible about your problem = haremos todo lo posible sobre su problema.* **5** causar, hacer: *to do harm = causar daño.* **6** dedicarse a (trabajo), hacer, trabajar: *what do you do? = ¿en qué trabajas?* **7 [to – + *o.* + (with)]** hacer (expresando utilización): *what are you going to do with that? = ¿qué vas a hacer con eso?* **8** hacer de (con mímica): *he does the teacher very well = hace de profesor muy bien.* **9** (fam.) matar, destrozar: *I'll do you! = ¡te mataré!* **10** ofrecer, ofertar: *do you do paperbacks? = ¿ofrece Vd. libros de bolsillo?* **11** correr a, ir a (velocidad). **12** servir, ser suficiente: *this will do me = esto me servirá.* **13** arreglar, limpiar: *do this room = arregla esta habitación.* **14** hacer (una tarea concreta): *do your hair = péinate.* || *i.* **15 [to – for]** hacer bien, mejorar: *this shirt does a lot for you = esta camisa te mejora mucho.* **16 [to – *adv.*]** salirle a uno, tener éxito: *I did very well in my exam = me salió muy bien el examen.* **17** servir: *this will do = esto servirá.* || *s.c.* **18** (fam.) fiesta, festejo. || **19 badly done by,** mal tratado. **20 can – for,** poder hacer por: *what can I do for you? = ¿qué puedo hacer por ti?* **21 could – with,** venir bien: *I could do with some sleep = me vendría bien dormir un poco.* **22 – as you would be done by,** haz a los otros lo que quieras que te hagan a ti. **23 to – away with,** librarse de, acabar con. **24 to – down,** (fam.) desacreditar. **25 to – for,** (fam.) destrozar, liquidar. **26 to – in,** (fam.) matar. **27 done in,** (fam.) agotado, roto, destrozado: *after so much work, I'm done in = después de tanto trabajo estoy destrozado.* **28 to – one's best,** hacer lo que uno buenamente pueda. **29 to – out, a)** (fam.) hacer limpieza total de (un objeto). **b)** (fam.) decorar, arreglar perfectamente. **30 to – out of,** (fam.) privar de, quitar (con engaño). **31 to – over, a)** (EE.UU. y fam.) rehacer. **b)** (EE.UU. y fam.) rede-

corar. **c)** (fam.) robar (en un lugar). **d)** (fam.) dar una paliza. **32 dos and don'ts,** (lo) que se debe y no se debe hacer; las reglas. **33 to – up, a)** atar (zapatos), abrochar (botones). **b)** arreglarse (el pelo y normalmente una mujer). **c)** renovar (edificio). **d)** embellecer, poner bonito (un paquete, un regalo, etc.). **34 to – without,** arreglárselas sin, vivir sin: *I can't do without tea = no puedo vivir sin té.* **35 easier said than done,** V. **easy. 36 to have to – with/to be to – with,** tener que ver con, tener relación con. **37 how – you –?,** ¿cómo está Vd.?; encantado (tanto el saludo como la respuesta). **38 how someone is/was/etc. doing,** cómo le va a alguien (en la vida). **39 in Rome – as the Roman –,** dondequiera que fueres, haz lo que vieres. **40 to make –,** V. **make. 41 no sooner said than done,** V. **soon. 42 that will –,** vale ya, no más, ya no más (a un niño que molesta o hace algo mal). **43 that will not –/that will never –,** eso no servirá para nada. **44 the (best) thing to –,** la mejor idea, lo mejor: *the best thing to do is to get married soon = lo mejor es casarse pronto.* **45 what someone/something is/was, etc. doing,** qué hace alguien/algo, a qué viene que alguien/algo esté (con sorpresa). **46 what someone did with,** qué hizo alguien con, dónde puso alguien. **47 would – well,** lo mejor que puede hacer, haría bien en: *she would do well not to see him again = lo mejor que puede hacer es no verle más.*
OBS. Este verbo sirve de auxiliar para hacer las formas interrogativas y negativas del presente y del pasado de todos los verbos del inglés (menos los verbos llamados defectivos y los verbos **to be** y **to have,** este último en algunos casos sólo).
Además, el verbo sirve para hacer las siguientes precisiones: **48** señala el énfasis en la forma afirmativa del presente, pasado y el imperativo: *do come in = haz el favor de entrar; I did see you last night = claro que te vi ayer por la noche.* **49** indica una contestación o añadido muy escueto a una pregunta o comentario: *did you go yesterday? yes, I did = ¿te fuiste ayer? sí; I like wine but my brother doesn't = me gusta el vino pero a mi hermano no; you studied in London, didn't you? = estudiaste en Londres, ¿no?*

doc | dɒk | *s.c.* (fam.) doctor.

docile | 'dəʊsaɪl | *adj.* dócil, sumiso.

docilely | dəʊsaɪllɪ | *adv.* dócilmente, sumisamente.

docility | dəʊ'sɪlɪtɪ | *s.i.* docilidad, sumisión.

dock | dɒk | *s.c.* **1** muelle, dársena, desembarcadero. || *s.c.* e *i.* **2** BOT. romaza. || *s.sing.* **3** banquillo (del acusado). || *v.t.* **4** poner en dique (un barco). **5** deducir, descontar (del sueldo). **6** cercenar, desmochar (la cola de un animal). **7** acoplar (aviones en vuelo). || *v.i.* **8** entrar en dique (un barco). **9** acoplarse (aviones en vuelo). || **10 docks,** muelles. **11 in –,** en el dique seco (un barco).

docker | 'dɒkər | *s.c.* estibador, trabajador portuario.

docket | 'dɒkɪt | (brit.) *s.c.* **1** etiqueta, rótulo, marbete. || *v.t.* **2** etiquetar, poner rótulo.

dockland | 'dɒklænd | *s.c.* e *i.* distrito de los muelles, zona del puerto.

dockworker | ˌdɒk'wɜːkər | *s.c.* estibador, trabajador portuario.

dockyard | 'dɒkjɑːd | *s.c.* muelle; puerto.

doctor | 'dɒktər | *s.c.* **1** doctor, médico. **2** doctor (después de la tesis doctoral). || *v.t.* **3** manipular, alterar, falsear. **4** medicinar, tratar (a personas). **5** castrar (especialmente gatos y perros). **6** drogar, añadir alcohol a (una bebida).

doctoral | 'dɒktərəl | *adj.* doctoral: *a doctoral thesis.*

doctorate | 'dɒktərɪt | *s.c.* doctorado (rango académico).

doctrinaire | ˌdɒktrɪ'neər | *adj.* (form. y desp.) doctrinario.

doctrinal | dɒk'traɪnl | *adj.* (form.) doctrinal.

doctrine | 'dɒktrɪn | *s.c.* e *i.* doctrina, credo (político, religioso, etc.).

document | 'dɒkjʊmənt | *s.c.* **1** documento. || *v.t.* **2** documentar con pruebas fehacientes.

documentary | ˌdɒkjʊ'mentrɪ | *s.c.* **1** documental (especialmente películas). || *adj.* **2** documental, basado en documentos.

documentation | ˌdɒkjumen'teɪʃn | *s.i.* documentación.

dodder | 'dɒdər | *v.i.* chochear; tambalearse (como un viejo al andar).

doddering | 'dɒdərɪŋ | *adj.* chocheante; inseguro (como un viejo al andar).

doddery | 'dɒdərɪ | *adj.* chocho; inseguro, senil.

doddle | 'dɒdl | *s.sing.* (fam.) una tarea chupada; coser y cantar: *this is a doddle = esto es coser y cantar.*

dodge | dɒdʒ | *v.i.* **1** esquivar el cuerpo, hurtar el cuerpo, regatear. || *v.t.* **2** esquivar, evitar (un golpe o similar). **3** (fig.) esquivar, eludir (un tema o similar). **4** evitar (algo desagradable): *to dodge work.* || *s.c.* **5** regate (para esquivar algo o alguien). **6** truco, maniobra, artificio (para evitar algo).

dodgem | 'dɒdʒəm | (brit.) *s.c.* **1** coche que choca, coche de choque. || **2 – car,** coche que choca, coche de choque.

dodger | 'dɒdʒər | *s.c.* evasor, persona que evita (impuestos y otras obligaciones): *draft dodger = persona que evita ir al servicio militar.*

dodgy | 'dɒdʒɪ | (fam.) *adj.* **1** tramposo (persona). **2** incierto, peligroso.

dodo | 'dəʊdəʊ | (*pl.* **dodos** o **dodoes**) *s.c.* **1** ZOOL. dodo (ave extinta). **2** (fam.) bobo, lelo. || **3 as dead as a –,** más muerto que mi abuela.

doe | dəʊ | *s.c.* ZOOL. gama; coneja.

doer | 'duːər | *s.c.* persona activa, persona de gran actividad.

does | dʌz | [tercera persona *sing.* del verbo **to do**].

doesn't | 'dʌzənt | [*contr.* de **does** y **not**].

doff | dɒf | *v.t.* (p.u.) quitarse (el sombrero o el abrigo).

dog | dɒg | *s.c.* **1** perro. **2** macho de lobo, macho de zorro. **3** (fam.) rata, canalla. **4** (EE.UU. y fam.) caca, porquería (algo de mala calidad). || *v.t.* **5** seguirle los pasos a, ir tras los pasos de, ir pegado detrás de. **6** acosar, atacar como una plaga (problemas, dificultades, etc.). || **7 a dog's life,** una vida de perros. **8 – eats –,** competencia despiadada. **9 every – has its day,** a cada uno le llega su turno (para la buena suerte). **10 to give a – a bad name,** calumnia que algo queda. **11 to go to the dogs,** echarse a perder, irse a la porra. **12 let sleeping dogs lie,** deja lo bueno en paz, más vale no meneallo. **13 like a dog's dinner,** (brit. y fam.) llamativamente, de punta en blanco. **14 like cat and dog,** V. **cat. 15 love me, love my –,** quien quiere a Beltrán quiere a su can. **16 to put on the –,** (EE.UU.) darse aires, creerse alguien importante. **17 the dogs,** los galgos, el canódromo (donde hay apuestas). **18 to treat like a –,** tratar a palos, tratar muy mal. **19 you can't teach an old – new tricks,** loro viejo no aprende a hablar.

dogcart | 'dɒgkɑːt | *s.c.* dócar, carruaje ligero.

dog-collar | 'dɒgkɒlər | *s.c.* **1** collar de perro. **2** (fam.) alzacuellos (de cura u otro ministro religioso).

dog-eared | 'dɒgjəd | *adj.* usado (libro con las puntas dobladas).

dogfight | 'dɒgfaɪt | *s.c.* **1** pelea de perros (especialmente organizada). **2** AER. combate aéreo (confuso y equilibrado).

dogfish | 'dɒgfɪʃ | (*pl.* **dogfish**) *s.c.* cazón (tiburón pequeño).

dogged | 'dɒgɪd | *adj.* tenaz, obstinado, terco.

doggedly | 'dɒgɪdlɪ | *adv.* tenazmente, obstinadamente, tercamente.

doggedness | 'dɒgɪdnɪs | *s.i.* tenacidad, obstinación, terquedad.

doggerel | 'dɒgərəl | *s.i.* chabacanería, ramplonería (en versos especialmente); coplas de ciego.

doggie | 'dəʊgɪ | (también **doggy**) *s.c.* perrito, gau-gau (de niños).

doggie-paddle | 'dəʊgɪpædl | (también **dog-paddle**) *s.i.* (fam.) estilo de natación como un perro.

doggo | 'dɒgəʊ | **to lie doggo,** (fam.) no mover un dedo, estarse muy quieto (sin emitir sonido alguno).

doggone | 'dɒgɒn | *adj.* (EE.UU. y fam.) maldito: *that's a doggone lie = esa es una maldita mentira.*

dog-house | 'dɒghaʊs | *s.c.* **1** (EE.UU.) casita para el perro. || **2 to be in the –,** (fam.) estar en desgracia.

dogleg | 'dɒgleg | *s.c.* curva cerrada.

dogma | 'dɒgmə | *s.c.* e *i.* dogma.

dogmatic | dɒg'mætɪk | *adj.* dogmático.

dogmatically | dɒg'mætɪklɪ | *adv.* dogmáticamente.

dogmatism | 'dɒgmətɪzəm | *s.i.* dogmatismo.
dogmatist | 'dɒgmətɪst | *s.c.* dogmático.
dogmatize | 'dɒgmətaɪz | (también **dogmatise**) *v.t.* (form.) dogmatizar.
do-gooder | ˌduː'gʊdər | *s.c.* (desp.) filántropo; bienhechor torpe.
dogsbody | 'dɒgzbɒdɪ | *s.c.* (brit. y fam.) criado de todos, pupas (a quien le toca la parte peor del trabajo).
dog-tired | 'dɒgtaɪəd | *adj.* (fam.) tirado, machacado, rendido.
doily | 'dɔɪlɪ | *s.c.* servilleta para adorno, paño para platos.
doings | 'duːɪŋz | *s.pl.* **1** actividades (en general). **2** chisme: *give me the doings = dame el chisme.*
do-it-yourself | ˌduːɪtjɔː'self | V. **D.I.Y.**
doldrums | 'dɒldrəmz | *s.pl.* **1** calmas de la zona ecuatorial. || **2 in the –,** estancado, sin actividad alguna, sin vida.
dole | dəʊl | *s.sing.* **1** (brit.) paro, subsidio de paro. || **2 to be on the –,** estar en el paro. **3 to – out,** repartir, distribuir (cosas en un grupo).
doleful | 'deʊlfl | *adj.* triste, lúgubre, lastimoso (personas y formas).
dolefully | 'dəʊlfəlɪ | *adv.* tristemente, lúgubremente, lastimosamente.
doll | dɒl | *s.c.* **1** muñeca (juguete). **2** (EE.UU. y fam.) chavala, moza; muchacha, chica. || **3 dolled up,** (fam.) mona, guapa (con vestidos). **4 doll's house,** casa de muñecas (juguete). **5 to – up,** (fam.) ponerse mona (con vestidos).
dollar | 'dɒlər | *s.c.* dólar (unidad monetaria estadounidense).
dollop | 'dɒləp | *s.c.* pegote, montón (de comida casi como puré): *a dollop of butter on top of the maize = un pegote de mantequilla encima del maíz.*
dolly | 'dɒlɪ | *s.c.* **1** muñeca (juguete). **2** (brit. y fam.) muñeca (chica presumida). || **3 – girl,** (brit. y fam.) muñeca (chica presumida).
dolphin | 'dɒlfɪn | *s.c.* ZOOL. delfín.
dolt | dəʊlt | *s.c.* imbécil, tonto; bobalicón.
domain | dəʊ'meɪn | *s.c.* **1** área, campo, esfera (intelectual): *in the domain of linguistics = en el campo de la lingüística.* **2** área de influencia, reino, dominio, territorio (de una persona o animal).
dome | dəʊm | *s.c.* **1** ARQ. cúpula. **2** (fig.) cima redondeada (de una montaña), cabeza (de una persona), bóveda (del cielo).
domed | dəʊmd | *adj.* en forma de cúpula.
domestic | də'mestɪk | *adj.* **1** interno (de un país). **2** doméstico (de una casa). **3** casero, hogareño. **4** doméstico (de un animal). || *s.c.* **5** criado, criada, servicio. || **6 – help,** criado, criada, servicio. **7 – science,** hogar (asignatura).
domestically | də'mestɪklɪ | *adv.* **1** internamente, nacionalmente (asuntos de un país). **2** hogareñamente. **3** domésticamente.
domesticate | də'mestɪkeɪt | *v.t.* **1** domesticar, amaestrar, amansar (animales o plantas). **2** (fig.) civilizar (en el comportamiento en casa); acostumbrar a ayudar en casa.
domesticated | də'mestɪ'keɪtɪd | *adj.* **1** domesticado, amaestrado (animales y plantas). **2** civilizado; concienzado a ayudar en casa.
domestication | dəˌmestɪ'keɪʃn | *s.i.* amaestramiento, amansamiento.
domesticity | 'dəʊme'stɪsɪtɪ | *s.i.* estado hogareño, estilo casero.
domicile | 'dɒmɪsaɪl | *s.c.* (form.) residencia, domicilio.
domiciled | 'dɒmɪsaɪld | *adj.* (form.) domiciliado.
dominance | 'dɒmɪnəns | *s.i.* **1** importancia, prominencia (en una situación). **2 [– (of/over)]** dominio, predominio.
dominant | 'dɒmɪnənt | *adj.* **1** predominante, prominente. **2** dominante (cualidad personal).
dominate | 'dɒmɪneɪt | *v.t.* **1** regir, dominar (una situación o país). **2** dominar, tener dominio sobre, ejercer control sobre (personas). **3** (fig.) dominar, sobresalir por encima de (en un paisaje). || *v.i.* **4** dominar, ejercer dominio.
dominating | ˌdɒmɪ'neɪtɪŋ | *adj.* de fuerte personalidad, con una personalidad dominadora.
domination | ˌdɒmɪ'neɪʃn | *s.i.* control, dominio (de una situación, país o personas).
domineering | ˌdɒmɪ'nɪərɪŋ | *adj.* avasallador, mandón, tiránico.
Dominican | də'mɪnɪkən | *adj.* **1** dominico (de la orden religiosa). **2** dominicano (del país). || **3 – Republic,** República Dominicana.
dominion | də'mɪnɪən | *s.i.* **1 [– (over)]** control, soberanía, dominio. || *s.c.* **2** territorio, zona aérea (de dominio o control). || **3 Dominion,** POL. colonia con autogobierno (dentro del sistema de la Commonwealth antiguo).
domino | 'dɒmɪnəʊ | (*pl.* **dominoes**) *s.c.* **1** ficha de dominó. || **2 dominoes,** dominó (juego). **3 – effect,** efecto dominó (en política u otros campos).
don | dɒn | [*ger.* **donning,** *put.* y *p.p.* **donned**] *v.t.* **1** (lit.) ponerse (ropa). || *s.c.* **2** profesor titular (de universidad).
donate | dəʊ'neɪt | *v.t.* donar; regalar.
donation | dəʊ'neɪʃn | *s.i.* **1** donación. || **2 [– (to/from)]** donación, dádiva; regalo.
done | dʌn | *adj.* **1** completado, realizado, hecho. **2** (fam.) socialmente aceptable: *picking your nose is not done = meterse el dedo en la nariz no es socialmente aceptable.* || **3 –,** trato hecho. **4 – to a turn,** V. **turn. 5 over and – with,** totalmente acabado; punto final. **6 what is – cannot be undone,** a lo hecho pecho.
OBS. Esta palabra también es el *p.p.* del verbo **do.**
Don Juan | ˌdɒn'dʒuːən | *s.c.* Don Juan, seductor.
donkey | 'dɒŋkɪ | *s.c.* **1** burro, asno, borrico. || **2 – work,** (fam.) trabajo pesado, trabajo aburrido. **3 donkey's years,** (fam.) muchísimos años. **4 to talk the hind legs off a –,** (fam.) hablar por los codos; no dejar meter baza.
donkey-jacket | 'dɒŋkɪdʒækɪt | *s.c.* gabardo (de trabajo).
donnish | 'dɒnɪʃ | *adj.* (brit.) erudito; estudioso.
donor | 'dəʊnər | *s.c* **1** donante (de sangre, órganos, etc.). **2** benefactor, donador (de dinero o similar).
Don Quixote | ˌdɒn'kwɪksət | *s.c.* Quijote; idealista.
don't | dəʊnt | *contr.* de **do** y **not.**
doodah | 'duːdɑː | *s.c.* chisme, como se llame (cuando no se da con la palabra exacta de un objeto).
doodle | 'duːdl | *v.i.* **1** garabatear, hacer garabatos. || *s.c.* **2** garabatos.
doom | duːm | *v.t.* **1 [to – + *o.* + (to)]** condenar, sentenciar (a algo negativo). || *s.c.* **2** fatalidad, sino. || **3 to be doomed, [=N *inf.*]** estar llamado a, estar destinado a: *the plan was doomed to fail = el plan estaba destinado a fracasar.*
doomed | duːmd | *adj.* **[– (+ *inf.*to)]** condenado. **2** sentenciado, destinado al fracaso: *your project is doomed = tu plan está destinado al fracaso.*
Doomsday | 'duːmzdeɪ | *s.sing.* **1** REL. Día del Juicio Final. || **2 doomsday,** (fig.) época de problemas serios. **3 till doomsday,** hasta el día del fin del mundo (indicando muchísimo tiempo).
door | dɔː | *s.c.* **1** puerta. **2** (fig.) entrada, acceso. || **3 to answer the –,** abrir la puerta (después que alguien ha llamado). **4 at death's door,** V. **death. 5 to close the – on,** cerrar la puerta a (una posibilidad o similar). **6 from – to –,** de puerta en puerta, de puerta a puerta. **7 to get in by the back –,** entrar (en un trabajo) por enchufe, conseguir mediante influencias. **8 to lay at someone's –,** echar la culpa a alguien; cargar el muerto a alguien. **9 next door,** vecinos. **10 on the –,** de portero (especialmente de un club nocturno o similar). **11 to open the – to,** abrir la puerta a; hacer posible. **12 out of doors,** fuera, en el exterior, al aire libre. **13 to see to the –,** acompañar a la puerta. **14 to show someone the –,** echar a alguien fuera (con enfado), enseñarle a alguien la puerta. **15 to shut/slam the – in somebody's face,** dar con la puerta en las narices a alguien. **16 the – to,** la puerta a: *the door to serious negotiations = la puerta a negociaciones serias.* **17 two/three doors up/down,** (fam.) dos/tres puertas más arriba/más abajo de la calle.
doorbell | 'dɔːbel | *s.c.* timbre, campanilla.
door-frame | 'dɔːfreɪm | *s.c.* enmarcado, marco de la puerta.
door-handle | 'dɔːhændl | *s.c.* picaporte.
doorkeeper | 'dɔːkiːpər | *s.c.* conserje; portero. V. **doorman.**
doorknob | 'dɔːnɒb | *s.c.* pomo, tirador (de puerta).
door-knocker | 'dɔːnɒkər | V. **knocker 1.**
doorman | 'dɔːmən | (*pl.* **doormen**) *s.c.* portero.

doormat | 'dɔːmæt | *s.c.* **1** felpudo. **2** (fig. y fam.) sufrido, persona con gran aguante (de no rechistar ante abusos contra él).
doornail | 'dɔːneɪl | *s.c.* **1** (arc.) clavo de puerta de gran tamaño. || **2 as dead as a –,** V. **dead.**
door-plate | 'dɔːpleɪt | *s.c.* placa, rótulo (de un médico, abogado, etc.).
doorstep | 'dɔːstep | *s.c.* **1** umbral, peldaño (de puerta). || **2 on one's –,** al lado, al ladito.
doorstop | 'dɔːstɒp | *s.c.* tope para puertas.
door-to-door | ˌdɔːtə'dɔːr | *adj.* de puerta a puerta.
doorway | 'dɔːweɪ | *s.c.* entrada; portal.
dope | dəʊp | (fam.) *s.i.* **1** droga (ilegal). **2** medicina, narcótico. || *s.c.* **3** bobo, idiota. || *s.sing.* **4 [– (on)]** informes confidenciales: *I've got a lot of dope on him = tengo muchos informes confidenciales sobre él.* || *v.t.* **5** drogar, dopar. **6** echar narcótico en, adormecer con drogas. || **7 to be doped/to be doped up,** (argot) estar dopado, estar drogado, estar con el mono.
dopey | 'dəʊpɪ | (fam.) *adj.* **1** aletargado, adormilado, groggy. **2** atontado, embobado.
dorm | dɔːm | *s.c.* (fam.) (abreviatura de **dormitory**) dormitorio.
dormancy | 'dɔːmənsɪ | *s.i.* (form.) inactividad, estado de letargo.
dormant | 'dɔːmənt | *adj.* **1** inactivo; latente, en suspensión. || **2 to lie –,** estar inactivo, estar aletargado.
dormer | 'dɔːmər | *s.c.* **1** ventana abuhardillada. || **2 – window,** ventana abuhardillada.
dormitory | 'dɔːmɪtrɪ | *s.c.* **1** dormitorio (en una residencia o similar). **2** (EE.UU.) residencia estudiantil. || **3 – town/suburb,** (brit.) ciudad/barrio dormitorio.
dormouse | 'dɔːmaʊs | [*pl.* **doormice**] *s.c.* ZOOL. lirón.
dorsal | 'dɔːsl | *adj.* ANAT. dorsal (sólo con animales).
dosage | 'dəʊsɪdʒ | *s.c.* dosis, dosificación.
dose | dəʊs | *s.c.* **1** dosis, toma (de medicina). **2** (fig.) dosis, cantidad (de cualquier otra cosa): *my daily dose of reading = mi dosis diaria de lectura.* || *v.t.* y *r.* **3 [to – + *o.* + (with)]** administrar(se), medicar(se). || **4 to – up,** administrar una gran cantidad de medicina. **5 like a – of salts,** (fam.) a todo meter, a toda velocidad.
doss down | 'dɒsdaʊn | *v.i.* (fam. y brit.) pasar la noche (incómodamente).
dosser | 'dɒsər | *s.c.* (fam. y brit.) vagabundo.
doss-house | 'dɒshaʊs | *s.c.* (fam. y brit.) pensión de mala muerte.
dossier | 'dɒsɪeɪ | *s.c.* expediente, historial.
dot | dɒt | *s.c.* **1** punto (para cifras, para la "i", etc.). **2** punto, mota, puntito. **3** RAD. punto (del código Morse). || *v.t.* **4** poner el punto a (la letra "i"). **5** motear, salpicar: *small beautiful villages dot this region = pueblecitos preciosos salpican esta región.* || **6 to – the i's and cross the t's,** poner los puntos sobre las íes. **7 on the –,** en punto (puntualidad). **8 the year –,** (fam.) en tiempos de Maricastaña; hace muchísimo tiempo.
dotage | 'dəʊtɪdʒ | *s.i.* (fam.) **1** chochez. || **2 in one's –,** cuando uno chochee.
dote | dəʊt | *v.i.* **[to – on/upon]** adorar, idolatrar.
doting | 'dəʊtɪŋ | *adj.* excesivamente amoroso, amante en demasía: *she's a doting mother = es una madre excesivamente amorosa.*
dotted | 'dɒtɪd | *adj.* **1** discontinuo, punteado. **2** moteado, con puntos: *a dotted curtain = una cortina moteada.* **3 [– with]** moteado de, salpicado de (como puntos): *the mountain was dotted with villas = la montaña estaba salpicada de chalets de verano.* || **4 to sign on the – line,** formalizar el acuerdo, poner la firma oficial definitiva.
dotty | 'dɒtɪ | (brit. y fam.) *adj.* **1** excéntrico; loco. **2 [– about]** chiflado por, loco por: *he's dotty about old coins = está chiflado por las monedas viejas.*
double | 'dʌbl | *cuant.* **1** doble, el doble, el doble de: *I earn double the amount I was getting last year = gano el doble de la cantidad que ganaba el año pasado.* || *adj.* **2** doble, dos veces mayor. **3** doble (bebida). **4** doble, para una pareja (habitación, billete, etc.). **5** doble, dos (cosas hechas o compuestas con dos trozos iguales): *double door = doble puerta; double page ads = anuncios a dos páginas.* || *s.c.* **6** doble (bebida). **7** doble; sustituto (en películas o similar). || *adv.* **8** doble, en dos, doblemente: *to fold something double = doblar algo en dos.* || *v.t.* **9** doblar en dos. **10** doblar, duplicar (una cantidad). || *v.i.* **11** doblarse, duplicarse (una cantidad). **12** volverse bruscamente, cambiar de dirección rápidamente. **13 [to – as]** hacer de, servir de (además de su primera función): *the teacher used to double as a cleaner = la profesora solía hacer de limpiadora.* || **14 at/on the –,** (fam.) a paso ligero, rápidamente. **15 to bend –,** inclinar medio cuerpo, doblar medio cuerpo. **16 – agent,** agente doble. **17 to – back,** volver sobre sus pasos. **18 – bass,** MUS. contrabajo. **19 – bed,** cama doble, cama de matrimonio. **20 – bill,** programa doble (en cine o similar). **21 – bind,** dilema. **22 – bluff,** engaño por partida doble (cuando se dice la verdad sabiendo que el otro no se lo creerá). **23 – chin,** papada (expresando gordura). **24 – cream,** (brit.) GAST. nata espesa. **25 – date,** (EE.UU.) salida de dos parejas juntas. **26 – entry,** FIN. partida doble (en contabilidad). **27 – figures,** dos dígitos. **28 – first,** titulación con dos matrículas de honor. **29 – negative,** GRAM. doble negación. **30 – or quits,** doble o nada. **31 to – over,** retorcerse, desternillarse (de dolor, risa, etc.). **32 – pneumonia,** MED. pulmonía doble. **33 – room,** habitación doble. **34 doubles,** DEP. dobles (tenis o badminton). **35 – standard,** doble moral, distinta vara para medir (la licitud de actos). **36 – time,** doble paga. **37 to – up, a)** compartir el mismo coche/habitación, etc. **b)** retorcerse, desternillarse (de dolor, risa, etc.). **38 – vision,** MED. visión doble, diplopía. **39 to see –,** ver doble.
double-barrelled | ˌdʌbl'bærəld | *adj.* **1** de doble cañón (arma). **2** con apellido compuesto (por dos palabras).
double-book | ˌdʌbl'bʊk | *v.t.* hacer una reserva para más de una persona equivocadamente.
double-booking | ˌdʌbl'bʊkɪŋ | *s.c.* reserva para más de una persona equivocadamente.
double-breasted | ˌdʌbl'brestɪd | *adj.* cruzado, con doble hilera de botones.
double-check | ˌdʌbl'tʃek | *v.t.* e *i.* **1** comprobar dos veces, asegurarse. || *s.c.* **2** doble comprobación.
double-cross | ˌdʌbl'krɒs | (fam.) *v.t.* **1** traicionar, engañar, pasarse al enemigo, dar la espalda. || *s.c.* **2** traición, engaño.
double-dealing | ˌdʌbl'diːlɪŋ | *s.i.* duplicidad, doblez.
double-decker | ˌdʌbl'dekər | *s.c.* **1** autobús de dos pisos. || **2 – bus,** autobús de dos pisos.
double-Dutch | ˌdʌbl'dʌtʃ | *s.i.* (brit. y fam.) chino (algo que no se entiende hablado o escrito).
double-dyed | ˌdʌbl'daɪd | *adj.* (p.u.) inveterado, rematado; vil: *a double-dyed rogue = un canalla inveterado.*
double-edged | ˌdʌbl'edʒd | *adj.* **1** de dos filos. **2** (fig.) de dos filos.
double-entendre | ˌduːblɑːn'tɑːndr | *s.c.* (form. y lit.) de doble sentido (uno de los cuales suele ser sexual).
double-faced | ˌdʌbl'feɪst | *adj.* (desp.) hipócrita.
double-glaze | ˌdʌbl'gleɪz | *v.t.* poner dobles ventanas en.
double-glazing | ˌdʌbl'gleɪzɪŋ | *s.i.* doble ventana.
double-jointed | ˌdʌbl'dʒɔɪntɪd | *adj.* con articulación flexible (en dedos).
double-park | ˌdʌbl'pɑːk | *v.t.* e *i.* aparcar en doble fila.
double-quick | ˌdʌbl'kwɪk | *adj.* y *adv.* **1** con toda prontitud. || **2 in – time,** rapidísimamente, a la carrera.
double-stop | ˌdʌbl'stɒp | *v.i.* MUS. tocar dos notas al mismo tiempo (en instrumento de cuerda).
doublet | ˌdʌblɪt | *s.c.* casaca, jubón.
double-take | ˌdʌbl'teɪk | **to do a double-take,** reaccionar tarde, reaccionar con retraso.
double-talk | 'dʌbltɔːk | *s.i.* lenguaje engañoso; galimatías.
double-think | 'dʌblθɪŋk | *s.i.* pensamiento que admite lo contradictorio.
doubly | 'dʌblɪ | *adv.* **1** doblemente; especialmente. **2** por duplicado, dos veces, doblemente.
doubt | daʊt | *s.c.* e *i.* **1 [– (about)]** duda, incertidumbre. || *v.t.* **2** dudar de,

desconfiar de, dudar. || *v.i.* **3** tener dudas, dudar. || **4 beyond all –/beyond a –,** fuera de duda, fuera de toda duda. **5 to cast doubt (on),** arrojar dudas (sobre). **6 doubting Thomas,** incrédulo (como Santo Tomás). **7 to give someone the benefit of the –,** conceder a alguien el beneficio de la duda. **8 to have no – (about/of),** no tener duda alguna (sobre). **9 to have one's doubts (about),** tener las dudas de uno (sobre). **10 in –/open to –,** incierto, dudoso; en el aire. **11 to leave no –,** no dejar lugar a dudas. **12 no –,** sin duda, sin duda alguna. **13 no – about it,** sin lugar a dudas, absolutamente seguro. **14 there is no –/little –/not much –,** no hay duda, no hay duda alguna. **15 without –/without a –/without a slightest –,** sin duda, sin duda alguna.

doubter | 'dautər | *s.c.* incrédulo (especialmente sobre religión o ideología política).

doubtful | 'dautfl | *adj.* **1** dudoso, incierto. **2** dudoso, sospechoso (no parece verdadero). **3 [– about/of]** indeciso sobre, titubeante sobre: *I'm doubtful about my future = estoy indeciso sobre mi futuro.*

doubtfully | 'dautfəlı | *adv.* **1** dudosamente, inciertamente. **2** sospechosamente, dudosamente. **3** con titubeo, con indecisión.

doubtless | 'dautlıs | *adj.* indudable, cierto.

dough | dəu | *s.i.* **1** GAST. masa. || *s.c.* **2** (fam.) dinero, pasta, parné.

doughnut | 'dəunʌt | *s.c.* donut; buñuelo.

doughty | 'dautı | *adj.* (p.u.) valiente, esforzado.

doughy | 'dəuı | *adj.* pastoso (como la masa).

dour | duər | *adj.* hosco, malhumorado.

dourly | 'duəlı | *adv.* hoscamente, con mal humor.

douse | daus | (también **dowse**) *v.t.* **1** apagar, extinguir (una lámpara, fuego o similar). **2 [to – + *o.* + (in/with)]** empapar; remojar.

dove | dəuv | (EE.UU.) *p.p.* de **dive.**

dove | dʌv | *s.c.* **1** paloma, tórtola. **2** (fig.) paloma, pacifista.

dovecote | 'dʌvkɒt | *s.c.* palomar.

dove-grey | 'dʌvgreı | *adj.* grisáceo, gris de paloma.

dovetail | 'dʌvteıl | *v.i.* **1** encajar, ajustarse (una cosa en otra). || *s.c.* **2** cola de milano (en carpintería). || **3 – joint,** cola de milano.

dowager | 'dauədʒər | *s.c.* **1** viuda con título (heredado del marido). **2** (fam.) matrona respetable, señora mayor respetable.

dowdily | 'daudılı | *adv.* desaliñadamente, con ropas poco elegantes.

dowdiness | 'daudınıs | *s.i.* desaliño, vestir mal.

dowdy | 'daudı | *adj.* desaliñado, poco elegante.

dowel | 'dauəl | *s.c.* clavija, espiga (de carpintería).

down | daun | *prep.* **1** abajo, hacia abajo, abajo de: *they ran down the stairs = corrieron escaleras abajo.* || *adv.* **2** abajo, hacia abajo: *they all went down = todos fueron abajo.* || *adj.* **3** (fam.) deprimido, tristón. **4** escrito, puesto en papel. **5** INF. estropeado, sin posibilidad de funcionamiento. || *s.i.* **6** plumón, flojel (de pájaros). **7** pelusilla, vello fino. || *v.t.* **8** devorar, acabar con (comida o bebida, de manera rápida). **9** MIL. derribar (especialmente un avión enemigo). || **10 –!,** ¡al suelo! (a un perro). **11 – for,** apuntado a (una actividad o similar): *I'm down for basketball = estoy apuntado al baloncesto.* **12 Down's syndrome,** MED. síndrome de Down. **13 – to... go...,** fuera queda(n)...: *one player down, six to go = uno fuera, quedan seis.* **14 – with!,** ¡abajo, muera!: *down with the king! = ¡abajo el rey!* **15 to have a – on someone,** tener ojeriza a alguien, tener inquina contra alguien. **16 right – to/– to,** hasta el más mínimo (detalle o similar). **17 the Downs,** GEOG. las praderas sureñas, los llanos sureños. **18 up and –,** arriba y abajo, repetitivamente (en el espacio), continuo, de un lado a otro.

OBS. Esta palabra tiene múltiples matizaciones en sentidos preposicionales y adverbiales: **19** señala el movimiento hacia abajo sin necesidad de que se traduzca: *he sat down = él se sentó; the house was burnt down = la casa se quemó.* **20** indica acercamiento o alejamiento al suelo: *the knife is in the fourth drawer down = el cuchillo está en el cuarto cajón hacia el suelo.* **21** expresa recorrido o situación de arriba a abajo por una línea imaginaria: *I felt a chill run down my spine = sentí un escalofrío recorrerme la columna.* **22** matiza la colocación en una superficie: *put the cup down = pon la taza en la mesa.* **23** ayuda a matizar el sentido de comer o beber, especialmente cuando no se desea hacerlo: *she drank the medicine down = se bebió la medicina.* **24** (fam.) señala el sitio al que se va: *I'm going down the factory = me voy a la fábrica.* **25** tiene un uso geográfico no científico cuando se piensa que se va a un lugar que está más bajo o hacia el sur, aunque no sea estrictamente cierto: *we'll travel down to Málaga = viajaremos hacia el sur, hacia Málaga.* **26** viene a tener la significación de a lo largo hablando de calles o similar: *I was walking down the street = yo iba andando por la calle.* **27** indica la dirección hacia el mar de un río: *row down the stream = rema arroyo abajo.* **28** significa posición plegada o recogida de algo: *with the blinds down = con las persianas bajadas.* **29** expresa reducción de cantidades: *exports are down 10% = las exportaciones han bajado un 10%.* **30** en deportes y competiciones señala al perdedor: *the team were one down at the final whistle = el equipo perdía por uno cuando sonó el pitido del final del encuentro.* **31** (fam.) indica enfermedad: *I was down with the flu for a whole week = estuve enfermo de gripe durante una semana entera.* **32** expresa duración a lo largo del tiempo: *we owned this land down to my father's death = poseíamos esta tierra hasta la muerte de mi padre.*

down-and-out | 'daunənaut | *s.c.* vagabundo, pobre.

down-at-heel | 'daunəthi:l | *adj.* venido a menos, decaído.

downbeat | 'daunbi:t | *adj.* (fam.) sombrío, poco abierto (en la comunicación de sentimientos o noticias).

downcast | 'daunkɑ:st | *adj.* **1** abatido, alicaído, deprimido. **2** cabizbajo; bajada (la vista).

downer | 'daunər | (fam.) *s.c.* **1** calmante (medicina). || **2 on a –,** con la depre.

downfall | 'daunfɔ:l | *s.i.* caída, ruina (de una persona, institución, país, etc.).

downgrade | 'daungreıd | *v.t.* degradar, disminuir (en importancia, prestigio, etc.).

downhearted | ˌdaunhɑ:tıd | *adj.* descorazonado, desanimado.

downhill | ˌdaun'hıl | *adv.* **1** cuesta abajo, hacia abajo, abajo (con movimiento). **2** (fig.) en decadencia, en declive, cuesta abajo. || *adj.* **3** DEP. ladera abajo: *downhill skiing.* **4** (fig.) fácil, factible, asequible.

Downing Street | 'daunıŋ stri:t | *s.sing.* **1** casa del Primer Ministro. **2** (fig.) decisión/idea/política gubernamental; decisión/idea/política del Primer Ministro.

down-load | ˌdaun'ləud | *v.t.* INF. transferir, volcar (de un sistema mayor a otro menor).

down-market | ˌdaun'mɑ:kıt | *adj.* y *adv.* baratero, de menor calidad.

down-payment | ˌdaun'peımənt | *s.c.* entrada, señal; depósito.

downpour | 'daunpɔ:r | *s.c.* chaparrón, aguacero.

downright | 'daunraıt | *adj.* **1** completo, total: *he's a downright liar = es un mentiroso completo.* || *adv.* **2** completamente, totalmente.

downstairs | ˌdaun'steəz | *adv.* **1** abajo, hacia abajo, escaleras abajo. || *adj.* **2** abajo, abajo de las escaleras. **3** de abajo: *the downstairs toilet = el servicio de abajo.* **4** de abajo (vecino): *the man downstairs = el vecino de abajo.*

downstream | ˌdaun'stri:m | *adv.* río abajo, aguas abajo, corriente abajo.

down-to-earth | 'dauntəə:θ | *adj.* práctico, realista.

downtown | ˌdaun'taun | *adj.* y *adv.* del centro, al centro (donde están los almacenes, empresas, oficinas, espectáculos en una ciudad): *let's go downtown = vamos al centro.*

downtrodden | 'dauntr'dn | *adj.* oprimido, esclavizado, pisoteado.

downturn | 'dauntə:n | *s.c.* ECON. depresión, baja (tendencia depresiva de la economía).

down-under | ˌdaʊn'ʌndər | *adj.* (brit. y fam.) Australia: *I'm going down-under next year = me voy a Australia el próximo año.*

downward | 'daʊnwəd | *adj.* **1** hacia abajo. **2** (fig.) en declive, en decadencia.

downwards | 'daʊnwədz | (también **downward**) *adv.* **1** abajo, hacia abajo. **2** (fig.) en decadencia.

downwind | ˌdaʊn'wɪnd | *adv.* **1** a favor del viento. **2 [– (of)]** en el lado del viento (con respecto a un lugar por el que pasa primero el viento).

downy | 'daʊnɪ | *adj.* **1** lleno de plumas, lleno de plumón. **2** velloso, con vello, con pelusilla.

dowry | 'daʊərɪ | *s.c.* dote (para el matrimonio).

dowse | daʊz | *v.i.* **[to – for]** buscar (agua o metales preciosos) con varita.

dowser | 'daʊzər | *s.c.* Zahorí (del lugar de agua o metales preciosos).

doyen | 'dɔɪən | *s.c.* (form.) decano (de un grupo profesional).

doyenne | dɔɪ'en | *s.c.* (form.) decana (de un grupo profesional).

doze | dəʊz | *v.i.* **1** dormitar, medio dormir, dormir a medias; sestear. || *s.c.* **2** siesta, sueño corto, sueño ligero. || **3 to – off,** adormilarse, quedarse dormido con sueño ligero.

dozen | 'dʌzn | *s.c.* **1** [*art.* –] docena, docena de. || **2 a –/dozens (of),** montones, montones de; muchos. **3 baker's –, V. baker. 4 it is six of one and half a – of the other,** no hay diferencia, es igual, da lo mismo. **5 nineteen to the dozen,** V. **nineteen.**

dozy | 'dəʊzɪ | *adj.* **1** somnoliento, medio dormido, amodorrado, adormecido. **2** (fam.) lento de cascos, abobado.

drab | dræb | *adj.* **1** deslustrado, gris, monótono (cualquier cosa o idea). **2** pardusco. || **3 in dribs and drabs,** (fam.) en cantidades pequeñas, poco a poco, intermitentemente: *they arrived in dribs and drabs = llegaron intermitentemente.*

drabness | 'dræbnɪs | *s.i.* deslustre, monotonía.

drachma | 'drækmə | (*pl.* **drachmae** o **drachmas**) *s.c.* dracma (moneda griega).

draconian | drə'kəʊnɪən | *adj.* (desp.) draconiano (de leyes, políticas, etc.).

draft | drɑːft | *s.c.* **1** bosquejo, borrador, anteproyecto. **2** FIN. letra de cambio. || *s.sing.* **3** (EE.UU.) MIL. reclutamiento, conscripción. || *v.t.* **4** hacer un borrador de, bosquejar. **5** destacar, enviar un destacamento de: *the newspaper drafted two assistants to Paris = el periódico destacó a dos ayudantes a París.* || *v.i.* **6 [to – in]** hacer venir, hacer llegar (como destacamento). || **7 to be drafted,** (EE.UU.) MIL. ser llamado a filas, ser reclutado. **8 – beer,** cerveza de barril. **9 – dodger,** MIL. opositor al servicio militar. V. **draught.**

draft-card | 'drɑːfkɑːd | *s.c.* (EE.UU.) tarjeta de recluta, tarjeta de alistamiento (para que se presente a comenzar su servicio militar).

draftee | ˌdrɑːf'tiː | *s.c.* (EE.UU.) conscripto, recluta.

draftsman | 'drɑːftsmən | V. **draughtsman.**

draftsmanship | 'drɑːftmənʃɪp | V. **draughtsmanship.**

drafty | 'drɑːftɪ | V. **draughty.**

drag | dræg | *v.t.* **1** arrastrar, tirar (por el suelo con cierta dificultad). **2** (fig.) llevar a la fuerza. **3** caminar arrastrando, arrastrar (una pierna o similar). **4** rastrear, dragar (el fondo de un río, lago, etc.). **5** arrancar, tirar con fuerza: *I dragged him away from the murderer = tiré de él con fuerza lejos del asesino.* || *v.r.* **6** arrastrarse, tirar de uno mismo (con dificultad y gran esfuerzo): *wounded, she dragged herself upstairs = herida, se arrastró escaleras arriba.* **7 [to – away]** irse a desgana, alejarse sin quererlo: *I had to drag myself away from the party = tuve que irme a desgana de la fiesta.* || *v.i.* **8** ir arrastrando los pies, ir a desgana. **9** pasar lentamente, avanzar lentamente, avanzar tediosamente (el tiempo). || *s.c.* **10** (fam.) chupada, calada (a un cigarrillo). || *s.i.* **11** travestismo, espectáculo de travestismo. **12** FIS. resistencia (al avance). || *s.sing.* **13 [– (on)]** estorbo, traba. **14** (fam.) plasta, aburrimiento, pesadez. || **15 to – down, a)** rebajar de clase social, empujar hacia abajo en la sociedad. **b)** dejar deprimido, dejar sin fuerzas, dejar sin ganas: *the extra work dragged me down = el trabajo extra me dejó sin fuerzas.* **16 to – in,** traer a cuenta sin razón, traer por los pelos. **17 to – into,** meter sin necesidad en, meter sin razón en, mezclar indebidamente con: *don't drag religion into politics = no mezcles la religión con la política indebidamente.* **18 to – on/along,** ser interminable, transcurrir tediosamente: *the film dragged on for hours = la película transcurrió tediosamente durante horas.* **19 to – one's feet/heels,** actuar en plan remolón, arrastrar los pies (no haciendo nada). **20 to – out, a)** prolongar innecesariamente, alargar innecesariamente, dilatar. **b)** sacar, sonsacar (algo a alguien que no lo quería decir). **21 – pub,** pub con espectáculos de travestismo. **22 – race,** carrera de coches no oficial (en la que los coches luchan desde una misma salida para ver quién acelera más). **23 – racing,** carreras de coches no oficiales (V. **drag 22**). **24 to – up,** sacar a relucir: *you needn't have dragged my mistake up again = no tenías porque sacar a relucir mi error otra vez.* **25 in –,** vestido de mujer, travestido.

dragnet | 'drægnɪt | *s.c.* MAR. red barredera.

dragon | 'drægən | *s.c.* **1** dragón (animal mítico). **2** (fam.) vieja bruja.

dragonfly | 'drægənflaɪ | *s.c.* ZOOL. libélula.

dragoon | drə'guːn | *s.c.* **1** MIL. dragón (soldado a caballo). || **2 to – into,** obligar a, forzar a: *my mother dragooned me into studying music = mi madre me obligó a estudiar música.*

dragster | 'drægstər | *s.c.* MEC. coche preparado (para **drag races**).

drain | dreɪn | *v.t.* **1** drenar, desaguar. **2** chupar, tomar (líquido de algún sitio). **3** AGR. desecar (tierra). **4** vaciar totalmente, apurar (un vaso, botella o similar). **5** agotar, dejar exhausto. **6** consumir, gastar (energías, fuerzas, etc.). || *v.i.* **7** drenarse, desaguarse; vaciarse. **8** escurrir (platos); secarse. **9 [to – from]** desaparecer, irse (el color de la cara). **10 [to – away/out of]** deshacerse, derretirse, disiparse (un sentimiento o similar): *all my anger seemed to drain away when she smiled = toda mi cólera pareció derretirse cuando ella sonrió.* || *s.c.* **11** tubería de desagüe, sumidero. **12** desagüe, drenaje. || *s.sing.* **13 [– on]** (fig.) lastre para, carga para: *the country house is a drain on my salary = la casa de campo es un lastre para mi salario.* || **14 to be drained of,** empobrecer, agotar reservas: *the country is being drained of its natural wealth = al país se le están agotando las reservas de su riqueza natural.* **15 brain –,** V. **brain. 16 down the –,** tirado por la ventana. **17 to go down the –,** fracasar, irse a la porra (negocio o similar).

drainage | 'dreɪnɪdʒ | *s.i.* **1** alcantarillado; saneamiento. **2** sistema de desagüe, sistema de drenaje.

drainage-basin | 'dreɪnɪdʒbeɪsn | *s.c.* GEOL. cuenca (hidrográfica).

drained | 'dreɪnd | *adj.* agotado, deshecho (especialmente en la mente).

draining-board | 'dreɪnɪybɔːd | *s.c.* escurreplatos.

drainpipe | 'dreɪnpaɪp | *s.c.* tubo de desagüe, caño de desagüe.

drake | dreɪk | *s.c.* pato (macho).

dram | dræm | *s.c.* copita (medida escocesa para whisky).

drama | 'drɑːmə | *s.c.* **1** drama, obra dramática. **2** (fig.) drama, tragedia (de la vida). || *s.i.* **3** arte escénico, arte dramático, teatro. || *s.sing.* **4** (fig.) arte escénico, teatro (de la vida, política, altas finanzas, etc.).

dramatic | drə'mætɪk | *adj.* **1** teatral, del teatro, dramático. **2** (fig.) impresionante; dramático, trágico. || **3 – irony,** ironía dramática, ironía del destino (cuando los espectadores son más conscientes de lo que pasa que los actores).

dramatically | drə'mætɪklɪ | *adv.* **1** radicalmente, totalmente. **2** de manera impresionante, de manera dramática, dramáticamente.

dramatics | drə'mætɪks | *s.pl.* **1** arte dramático (como asignatura). **2** (fig.) dramatismo exagerado, gestos melodramáticos.

dramatis personae | ˌdræmətɪspɜː'səʊnai | *s.pl.* (form.) caracteres, personajes (de una obra de teatro).

dramatist | 'dræmətɪst | *s.c.* dramaturgo, escritor teatral.

dramatization | ˌdræmətaɪ'zeɪʃn | *s.c.* escenificación, puesta en escena.

dramatize | 'dræmətaɪz | (también **dramatise**) *v.t.* **1** escenificar, adaptar para la escena (una novela, historia, etc.). **2** (fig.) exagerar, poner acentos trágicos a (algo que realmente no los tiene).
drank | dræŋk | *pret.* de **drink.**
drape | dreɪp | *v.t.* **1** cubrir, vestir (con algún tipo de colgadura): *drape your shoulders with my jacket, it's cold = cubre tus hombros con mi chaqueta, hace frío.* **2** poner relajadamente, descansar (una parte del cuerpo en algún sitio). || *s.c.* **3** (EE.UU.) cortina. || **4 to be draped (with/in),** estar cubierto (con), estar adornado (con).
draper | 'dreɪpər | (brit.) *s.c.* **1** pañero, lencero, mercero. || **2 the draper's,** la mercería.
drapery | 'dreɪpərɪ | *s.i.* **1** (brit.) mercería. **2** cortinaje, tapicería. || **3 draperies, a)** cortinajes, tapicerías. **b)** colgaduras, adornos (de paño).
drastic | 'dræstɪk | *adj.* drástico, extremo, dramático.
drastically | 'dræstɪklɪ | *adv.* drásticamente, dramáticamente.
drat | dræt | (arc.) *interj.* **1** ¡maldita sea! || **2 – it!/– the man!,** ¡maldita sea!
draught | drɑːft | (EE.UU. **draft**) *s.c.* **1** corriente (de aire). **2** trago (de bebida). **3** (form. y p.u.) jarabe (medicinal). **4** (brit.) ficha (del juego de las damas). || *adj.* **5** de barril (cerveza). **6** de tiro, de carga, de tracción (animal). || **7 draughts,** damas (juego). **8 on –,** de barril (cerveza).
draughtboard | 'drɑːftbɔːd | *s.c.* (brit.) tablero (para juego de damas).
draughthorse | 'drɑːfthɔːs | *s.c.* caballo de tiro.
draughtsman | 'drɑːfsmən | (EE.UU. **draftsman**) *s.c.* **1** delineante. **2** dibujante.
draughtsmanship | 'drɑːftsmənʃɪp | (EE.UU. draftsmanship) *s.i.* estilo de dibujante.
draughty | drɑːftɪ | (EE.UU. **drafty**) *adj.* lleno de corrientes de aire.
draw | drɔː | *v.* [*pret.* **drew,** *p.p.* **drawn**] *t.* **1** dibujar, trazar. **2** tirar de (suavemente). **3** llevar (tranquilamente): *he drew me into the bedroom = me llevó a la habitación.* **4** sacar, inferir, extraer (una conclusión). **5** sacar (arma de su vaina). **6** cobrar (sueldo). **7** hacer (comparación, distinción, etc.). **8** atraer (por su interés). **9** FIN. hacer efectivo (un cheque). **10** (p.u.) sacar, extraer (una muela). **11** hacer un reintegro, sacar (dinero). **12** DEP. empatar, igualar (un partido). **13** tomar (inspiración de aire). **14** sacar (en un sorteo). **15 [to – + *o.* + (from)]** sacar: *I drew inspiration from her = saqué inspiración de ella.* **16** ganarse (una reacción): *he drew an angry hint = se ganó una indirecta colérica.* **17** echar, correr (cortinas o similar). **18** tirar de, arrastrar (carros, carrozas, etc.). **19** sacar (suavemente de algún sitio). || *i.* **20 [to – (with/against)]** DEP. empatar, igualar. **21 [to – away]** (form.) alejarse, irse. **22** posarse; absorberse (las hojas de té por el agua caliente): *wait for the tea to draw = espera a que el té se pose.* || *s.c.* **23** (fam.) atracción. **24** sorteo. **25** DEP. empate. || **26 at daggers drawn,** V. **dagger. 27 to beat someone to the –,** adelantarse a alguien en sacar el revólver. **28 to be drawn,** mojarse (en dar una opinión o similar): *he's always refused to be drawn about his opinions = siempre se ha negado a mojarse en cuanto a sus opiniones.* **29 to be quick/slow on the –, a)** ser rápido/lento para sacar el revólver. **b)** (fam.) entender las cosas rápidamente/ser lento de entendimiento. **30 to – a bead on,** (fam.) poner el ojo en, apuntar cuidadosamente a. **31 to – a blank,** (fam.) no tener éxito (en la búsqueda de alguien). **32 to – attention to something/to – someone's attention to something,** señalar algo/atraer la atención de alguien sobre algo. **33 to – back,** retroceder ante, huir (de una acción, decisión, etc.). **34 to – breath, a)** inspirar aire, tomar aire, respirar. **b)** (fig.) vivir, estar vivo. **35 to – in, a)** llegar, arribar (un barco). **b)** tomar una bocanada de aire, respirar profundamente. **c)** acortarse las tardes, hacerse de noche antes. **d)** hacer participar, meter (a alguien en una discusión, reunión, etc.): *we were discussing religion and I drew the priest in = estábamos hablando de la religión y metí en ello al cura.* **36 to – one's horns,** tomar precauciones (de índole económica), no pasarse en los gastos. **37 to – lots,** V. **lot. 38 to – near/closer,** acercarse (en el tiempo o espacio). **39 to – off,** extraer, sacar, chupar (líquidos). **40 to – on, a)** pasar (el tiempo): *the evening drew on = la tarde pasó.* **b)** hacer uso de, echar mano de. **c)** echar una calada (al cigarrillo o similar). **41 to – oneself up to one's full height,** estirarse todo lo largo que es uno. **42 to – one's first/last breath,** respirar por primera/última vez; nacer/morir. **43 to – out, a)** sacar a alguien de sí mismo, hacer hablar. **b)** partir, salir (un tren). **c)** sacar, sonsacar (alguna información de alguien). **d)** alargar, estirar (sonidos). **44 to – somebody's fire,** V. **fire. 45 to – somebody's/something's teeth/fangs,** hacer a alguien/algo inofensivo. **46 to – stumps,** DEP. acabar el juego, terminar el partido (cricket). **47 to – the line,** V. **line. 48 to – to an end/to a close,** acabar, terminar, tocar a su fin: *the lecture drew to an end = la conferencia terminó.* **49 to – trumps,** jugar a la pinta (en cartas, hasta que al adversario no le quede ninguna). **50 to – up, a)** pararse, detenerse (un vehículo). **b)** redactar, formular por escrito. **c)** acercar (silla o similar). **d)** *v.r.* estirarse. **51 to – upon,** usar, echar mano de (algo con una finalidad determinada). **52 the luck of the –,** por pura suerte.
drawback | 'drɔːbæk | *s.c.* inconveniente, desventaja; impedimento.
drawbridge | 'drɔbrɪdʒ | *s.c.* puente levadizo.
drawer | drə'ər | *s.c.* **1** cajón. **2** dibujante, bocetista. **3** FIN. librador (de un cheque o similar). || **4 drawers,** (p.u.) bragas.
drawing | 'drɔːɪŋ | *s.c.* **1** dibujo, boceto. || *s.i.* **2** dibujo (como asignatura).
drawing-board | 'drɔːɪŋbɔːd | *s.c.* **1** tablero de dibujo, tablero de delineación. || **2 back to the –,** a volver a hacerlo, a repetirlo.
drawing-pin | 'drɔːɪŋpɪn | *s.c.* (brit.) chincheta.
drawing-room | 'drəːɪŋrum | *s.c.* (p.u.) salón, sala de estar.
drawl | drɔːl | *v.i.* **1** pronunciar lenta y pesadamente, arrastrar las palabras. || *s.sing.* **2** pronunciación lenta, arrastre de palabras.
drawn | drɔːn | *p.p.* **1** de **draw.** || *adj.* **2** echado, corrido (cortinas o similar). **3** contraído, tenso (en las facciones de la cara).
OBS. Esta palabra sirve para compuestos en los que se expresa la siguiente matización: **4** el medio de tracción empleado: *a horse-drawn cart = un carromato tirado por caballos.*
drawn-out | 'drɔːnaut | *adj.* interminable, inacabable.
drawstring | 'drɔːstrɪŋ | *s.c.* cordel, cuerda, cinta (que al tirar de ella cierra una bolsa o algo similar).
dray | dreɪ | *s.c.* carreta (plana), carreta pesada.
dray-horse | 'dreɪhɔːs | *s.c.* caballo de tiro, caballo de carreta (capaz de tirar de grandes pesos).
dread | dred | *v.t.* **1** temer, tener miedo de. || *s.i.* **2** temor, pavor, espanto. || *adj.* **3** (arc.) temido, espantoso. || **4 to – to think,** tener miedo de pensar, temer imaginar, dar miedo pensar: *I dread to think what the children are doing alone in the house = me da miedo pensar lo que los chicos están haciendo solos en la casa.*
dreaded | dredɪd | *adj.* temido: *he is dreaded in his own house = es temido en su propia casa.*
dreadful | 'dredfl | *adj.* **1** fatal, horrible, malísimo, desagradable: *dreadful weather = tiempo desagradable; dreadful traffic.* **2** terrible; increíble (como énfasis de algo malo): *a dreadful mess = un follón increíble.*
dreadfully | 'dredfəlɪ | *adv.* **1** horriblemente, desagradablemente: *she wrote dreadfully = escribía horriblemente.* **2** muy (enfático): *she was dreadfully saddened by his death = estaba muy entristecida por la muerte de él.*
dream | driːm | *v.* [*pret.* y *p.p.* **dreamed** o **dreamt**] *i.* **1 [to – (of/about)]** (fig.) soñar, fantasear. || *t.* **3** soñar. | *s.c.* **4 [– (of/about)]** sueño. **5** (fig.) sueño, ilusión. **6** (fig.) sueño, ambición. || *s.c.* e *i.* **7** ensoñación, ensueño. || *s.sing.* **8** sueño, paraíso: *this place is a single man's dream = este lugar es un paraíso para un soltero.* **9** (fam.) maravilla, de sueño: *the house is a dream = la casa es una maravilla.* || *adj.* **10** de ensueño, fabuloso, ideal: *a dream world = un mundo ideal.* || **11 beyond one's wildest dreams,** mucho más de lo que se esperaba, que-

darse corto (en los sueños, deseos, etc.). **12 to – a –,** soñar, tener un sueño. **13 to – up,** idear, concebir (un plan, idea, proyecto, etc.). **14 I/you/etc. never dreamed,** nunca se me/te/etc. pasó por la cabeza. **15 I/you/etc. would not – of/would never – of,** ni en sueños se me/te/etc. ocurriría. **16 in one's wildest dreams,** en la imaginación desbocada de uno. **17 like a –,** como un sueño; perfectamente, con total perfección. **18 the (thing or person) of one's dreams,** el (cosa o persona) de los sueños de uno.

dreamer | 'driːmər | *s.c.* soñador, visionario.

dreamily | 'driːmɪlɪ | *adv.* ensoñadoramente, como en ensueño.

dreaminess | 'driːmɪnɪs | *s.i.* languidez, estado de ensueño.

dreamland | 'driːmlænd | *s.sing.* **1** tierra de fantasía, país de ensueños. || **2 to be in –,** estar en la luna, no estar en la realidad.

dreamless | 'driːmlɪs | *adj.* reparador (sueño).

dreamlike | 'driːmlaɪk | *adj.* irreal, como en un sueño.

dreamt | dremt | *pret.* y *p.p.* de **dream.**

dreamy | 'driːmɪ | *adj.* **1** ensoñador, soñador. **2** ida, distraída (mirada). **3** tenue, vago, nebuloso (sonido o visión). **4** (fam.) maravilloso, encantador, fantástico.

drearily | 'drɪərɪlɪ | *adv.* melancólicamente, monótonamente, tristemente.

dreariness | 'drɪərɪnɪs | *s.i.* melancolía, monotonía, tristeza.

dreary | 'drɪərɪ | *adj.* melancólico, monótono, triste.

dredge | dredʒ | *v.t.* **1** dragar, rastrear (puerto, río o similar). || **2 to – up,** desempolvar (conocimientos, recuerdos, etc.).

dredger | 'dredʒər | *s.c.* MAR. draga.

dregs | dregz | *s.pl.* **1** posos, sedimento. **2** (fig.) escoria: *the dregs of society = la escoria de la sociedad.*

drench | drentʃ | *v.t.* empapar.

drenched | drentʃt | *adj.* empapado.

drenching | 'drentʃɪŋ | *adj.* torrencial (lluvia).

dress | dres | *s.c.* **1** vestido, traje de mujer. || *s.i.* **2** ropa, vestimenta, atuendo. || *v.t.* **3** vestir. **4** limpiar, destripar. **5** aliñar, aderezar (ensalada). **6** cuidar (una herida). || *v.i.* **7** vestirse. **8 [to – for]** vestirse para, ataviarse para, prepararse para: *I dressed for the party = me vestí para la fiesta.* || *v.r.* **9** vestirse. || **10 to – down, a)** (brit.) vestir un poco informalmente (cuando uno está acostumbrado al estilo formal). **b)** regañar, calentar las orejas. **11 – uniform,** MIL. uniforme de gala. **12 to – up, a)** disfrazarse. **b)** vestirse de etiqueta, endomingarse. **c)** (fig.) embellecer, adornar.

dressage | 'dresɑːʒ | *s.i.* DEP. doma de exhibición (en los caballos).

dress-circle | 'dressəːkl | *s.sing.* principal (primer piso en teatros).

dressed | drest | *adj.* **1** vestido (no desnudo). **2 [– (in)]** vestido, ataviado. || **3 all – up,** vestido como un rey, vestido con elegancia. **4 – like a dog's dinner,** (fam.) emperifollado, emperejilado. **5 – to kill,** (fam.) impresionantemente vestido (normalmente para llamar la atención del otro sexo). **6 – up, a)** disfrazado. **b)** (fig.) embellecido, adornado. **7 – up to the nines,** de punta en blanco. **8 to get –,** vestirse.

dresser | 'dresər | *s.c.* **1** (fam.) persona (en cuanto a su gusto de vestir): *she's a hopeless dresser = ella es una persona que viste fatal.* **2** ayuda de cámara (en el teatro persona que ayuda a los actores a vestirse). **3** (brit.) armario (especialmente de cocina). **4** (EE.UU.) cómoda, tocador. **5** MED. ayudante de cirujano.

dressing | 'dresɪŋ | *s.c.* **1** venda, vendaje. || *s.i.* **2** aliño, aderezo. || **3 – station,** MIL. hospital de campaña de primeras curas.

dressing-down | ˌdresɪŋ'daʊn | *s.sing.* regañina, reprimenda.

dressing-gown | 'dresɪŋgaʊn | *s.c.* bata, batín, salto de cama.

dressing-room | 'dresɪŋruːm | *s.c.* camarín, camerino, vestidor.

dressing-table | 'dresɪŋteɪbl | *s.c.* tocador.

dressing-up | 'dresɪŋʌp | *s.i.* juego de disfraces (de niños).

dressmaker | 'dresmeɪkər | *s.c.* modista, costurera.

dressmaking | 'dresmeɪkɪŋ | *s.i.* corte y confección.

dress-rehearsal | 'dresrɪhəːsl | *s.c.* ensayo general.

dress-shirt | 'dresʃəːt | *s.c.* camisa de frac, camisa de etiqueta.

dressy | 'dresɪ | (fam.) *adj.* **1** elegante, de etiqueta. **2** acicalado, peripuesto (persona). **3** vistoso, elegante (ropa).

drew | druː | *pret.* de **draw.**

dribble | 'drɪbl | *v.i.* **1** gotear. **2** babear (especialmente bebés). **3** ir en grupos, ir en pandillas. || *v.t.* **4** driblar, esquivar mediante un giro de cintura. **5** dejar gotear. || *s.c.* **6** gota, gotita, chorrito. || *s.i.* **7** babas (saliva).

driblet | 'drɪblɪt | *s.c.* pizca, gota: *in driblets = a gotas.*

dried | draɪd | *adj.* **1** seco (comida en general). || **2 – fruit,** frutos secos.

dried-up | 'draɪdʌp | *adj.* acartonado, apergaminado (apariencia de personas mayores en general).

drift | drɪft | *v.i.* **1** MAR. flotar a la deriva. **2** ir sin rumbo fijo (en la vida). **3** dejarse llevar, no tener objetivo fijo: *the association drifted for years = la asociación no tuvo objetivo fijo durante años.* **4** amontonarse (la nieve). || *s.i.* **5** flujo, corriente (del agua). || *s.c.* **6** montón irregular, amontonamiento. **7** tenor; significado (de una conversación). **8 [– (of)]** flujo, dirección, movimiento (de gente o animales). **9** nube (de polvo, tierra, arena, etc.). || *s.sing.* **10** tendencia (como cambio): *there was a general drift towards better education = hubo una tendencia general hacia una mejor educación.* || **11 to – off,** quedarse dormido. **12 to get the – of,** comprender el significado de.

drifter | 'drɪftər | *s.c.* vagabundo.

drift-ice | 'drɪftaɪs | *s.i.* hielo flotante.

drift-net | 'drɪftnet | *s.c.* MAR. red rastrera.

driftwood | 'drɪftwʊd | *s.i.* madera de deriva.

drill | drɪl | *s.c.* **1** taladradora. **2** ejercicio de repetición (especialmente en la enseñanza de idiomas). **3** instrucción, adiestramiento, ejercicio: *a fire drill = un ejercicio contra incendios.* **4** ZOOL. dril (mono). || *s.c.* e *i.* **5** MIL. entrenamiento, instrucción. || *s.i.* **6** algodón de dril. || *s.sing.* **7** (p.u. y brit.) procedimiento correcto, conducta correcta: *what is the drill for claiming travelling expenses? = ¿cuál es el procedimiento correcto para reclamar dietas de viaje?* || *v.t.* **8** taladrar. **9 [to – (in)]** adiestrar, entrenar (mediante ejercicios repetitivos). **10** MIL. instruir, entrenar. || *v.i.* **11 [to – (into)]** hacer un agujero. **12 [to – for]** excavar en busca de, perforar en busca de. **13** MIL. hacer la instrucción. || **14 to – into,** meter a base de ejercicios repetitivos.

drily | 'draɪlɪ | *adv.* con sequedad (en la voz).

drink | drɪŋk | *v.* [*pret.* **drank,** *p.p.* **drunk**] *t.* **1** beber. || *i.* **2** beber (alcohol): *do you drink? = ¿bebes?* || *r.* **3 [to – into/to]** beber hasta (algún estado mental): *last night I drank myself stupid = ayer por la noche bebí hasta quedar atontado.* || *s.c.* **4** copa (algo de bebida). **5** copa (de algo alcohólico). **6** trago || *s.i.* **7** bebida (especialmente alcohólica). || *s.sing.* **8** (fam.) mar. || **9 to be the worse for –,** estar beodo, estar borracho. **10 to – in,** absorber, beberse (información o similar). **11 to – like a fish,** beber como un cosaco. **12 to – someone's health,** V. **health. 13 to – someone under the table,** hacer emborracharse a alguien. **14 to – to,** brindar por. **15 to – up,** acabar la bebida, beberse todo de un trago. **16 to take to –,** darse a la bebida. **17 what are you drinking?,** ¿qué quieres tomar?, ¿qué bebes?

drinkable | 'drɪŋkəbl | *adj.* **1** potable. **2** bueno, aceptable, agradable (bebida).

drinker | 'drɪŋkər | *s.c.* **1** bebedor (de alcohol). **2** bebedor de: *I'm a tea drinker = yo soy bebedor de té.*

drinking | 'drɪnkɪŋ | *s.i.* **1** bebida, acción de beber: *there was a lot of drinking at the party = se bebió mucho en la fiesta.* || *adj.* **2** de la bebida, consumo de bebidas: *drinking laws = leyes del consumo de bebidas.* **3** bebedor.

drinking-fountain | 'drɪŋkɪŋfaʊntən | *s.c.* fuente.

drinking-song | 'drɪŋkɪŋsˈŋ | *s.c.* canción de taberna.

drinking-water | 'drɪŋkɪŋwɔːtər | *s.i.* agua potable.

drip | drɪp | *s.c.* **1** goteo. **2** gotera. **3** MED. gota a gota. **4** (fam.) pelma, pelmazo, pesado. || *v.i.* **5** gotear, caer gota a

gota. **6** rezumar, chorrear. || *v.t.* **7** hacer caer gota a gota.
drip-dry | ˌdrɪp'draɪ | *adj.* de secado rápido (ropa).
dripping | 'drɪpɪŋ | *s.i.* **1** grasa (que cae al freír o asar). || *adj.* **2** empapado, calado. || **3 – wet,** calado por completo, empapado totalmente.
drive | draɪv | *v.* [*pret.* **drove,** *p.p.* **driven**] *t.* **1** conducir (vehículo). **2** llevar (a alguien en un vehículo). **3** impulsar, accionar (una máquina o similar). **4** meter, clavar: *she drove the nail into the wall with difficulty = clavó el clavo dentro de la pared con dificultad.* **5** impulsar, golpear (el balón). **6** empujar, soplar, inclinar (el viento a la lluvia o nieve): *the wind was driving the snow into our faces = el viento soplaba la nieve contra nuestros rostros.* **7** empujar, impulsar, hacer ir, forzar (en una dirección): *we drove the cattle into the yard = hicimos ir al ganado dentro del patio.* **8** impulsar, arrastrar (un sentimiento o deseo): *she was driven by jealousy = ella estaba impulsada por los celos.* **9** llevar a, conducir a; volver (como cambio de situación, tanto anímica como económica o social, etc.): *she's driving me mad = ella me está volviendo loco; the new ventures drove the company into bankruptcy = las nuevas operaciones arriesgadas llevaron a la empresa a la bancarrota.* || *i.* **10** conducir, llevar el coche, viajar en coche. || *s.c.* **11** paseo en coche, viaje en coche. **12** acceso particular, camino particular (dentro de los límites de una casa particular). **13** instinto, impulso natural: *sex drive = instinto sexual.* **14** DEP. draiv, golpe al ras de la red (especialmente en el tenis). **15** MIL. ataque, avance. || *s.i.* **16** ímpetu, agresividad: *you need a lot of drive in this job = se necesita mucha agresividad en este trabajo.* || *sing.* **17** MEC. tracción, mecanismo de transmisión: *front wheel drive = tracción delantera.* **18** campaña (de un grupo social para algo): *the anti-drug drive = la campaña antidroga.* **19** avenida, camino (como nombre de una calle). || **20 to be driving at, [what =N** estructura] querer decir, insinuar: *what are you driving at? = ¿qué insinúas?* **21 to – a coach and horses through something,** no hacer el menor caso a algo (normalmente una ley o similar). **22 to – a hard bargain,** hacer un buen negocio. **23 to – away,** alejar, echar, librarse: *your hints drove him away = tus indirectas le echaron.* **24 to – a wedge between,** enemistar, romper la relación entre (dos personas amigas). **25 to – home,** hacer entender, hacer comprender: *I think I drove home to him that he had to study seriously = me parece que le hice comprender que tenía que estudiar seriamente.* **26 to – off,** repeler, ahuyentar. **27 to – out,** arrojar, echar, expulsar: *to drive out the evil spirits = arrojar a los malos espíritus.*
drive-in | 'draɪvɪn | *s.c.* **1** parador, restaurante para automovilistas, cine para automovilistas (no hay que bajarse del coche). || *adj.* **2** de automovilista: *a drive-in bank = un banco para automovilistas.*
drivel | 'drɪvl | (fam.) *s.i.* **1** estupideces, bobadas. || **2 to – on,** no parar de decir bobadas.
driven | 'drɪvn | *p.p.* de **drive.**
driver | 'draɪvər | *s.c.* **1** conductor. || **2 driver's licence** (EE.UU. **driver's license**), carnet de conducir. **3 in the driver's seat,** en una posición de autoridad, con el control.
drive-shaft | 'draɪvʃɑːft | *s.c.* MEC. árbol propulsor, eje transmisor.
driveway | 'draɪvweɪ | *s.c.* camino particular, camino de acceso (a una casa particular).
driving | 'draɪvɪŋ | *s.i.* **1** conducción. || *adj.* **2** del conductor, del lado del conductor: *the driving seat = el asiento del conductor.* **3** dinámico, enérgico (cualidad personal). **4** violento, torrencial (de lluvia y nieve). || **5 – school,** autoescuela. **6 in the – seat,** con el control de la situación.
driving-belt | 'draɪvɪŋbelt | *s.c.* MEC. correa de transmisión.
driving-licence | 'draɪvɪŋlaɪsəns | V. **driver 2.**
driving-test | 'draɪvɪŋtest | *s.c.* examen de conducir.
drizzle | 'drɪzl | *v.i.* **1** chispear, lloviznar (lluvia). || *s.i.* **2** lluvia fina, llovizna, chirimiri.
drizzly | 'drɪzlɪ | *adj.* de llovizna, con llovizna.
droll | drəul | *adj.* (p.u.) divertido, gracioso (algo o alguien).
drollery | drəulərɪ | *s.i.* (p.u.) gracia.
dromedary | 'drɒmədərɪ | *s.c.* ZOOL. dromedario (una joroba).
drone | 'drəun | *v.i.* **1** zumbar (sonido). **2** (fig.) hablar monótonamente. || *s.sing.* **3** zumbido; tono monótono. || *s.c.* **4** ZOOL. zángano. || **5 to – on,** hablar interminablemente en tono monótono, dar la tabarra.
drool | druːl | *v.i.* **1** babear incontroladamente. **2 [to – (over/at)]** (fam.) caérsele a uno la baba (con placer, admiración, etc.). || *s.i.* **3** saliva.
droop | druːp | *v.i.* **1** inclinarse, pender, colgar (perdiendo la verticalidad connatural del objeto que sea): *the willow drooped over the river = el sauce se inclinaba sobre el río.* **2** (fig.) decaer, languidecer, marchitarse.
drooping | druːpɪŋ | *adj.* inclinado; caído (párpados, hombros, etc.).
droopy | druːpɪ | *adj.* lánguido, flojo, fláccido.
drop | drɒp | *ger.* [**dropping,** *pret.* y *p.p.* **droppied**] *v.t.* **1** dejar caer, tirar (involuntariamente): *don't drop it = no lo tires.* **2** dejar caer, tirar, soltar (voluntariamente): *drop your gun = suelta la pistola.* **3** dejar caer (un comentario, una indirecta, etc.). **4** excluir (de un equipo o similar). **5** no pronunciar, no decir: *he drops the "g" sound in playing = él no pronuncia el sonido "g" en "playing".* **6** dejar caer (un punto mientras hace calceta). **7** (fam.) dejar de tener contactos con, dejar de tener amistad con. **8** bajar (la voz). **9** dejar (algo o alguien en un sitio): *drop me at the station on your way to work = déjame en la estación de camino al trabajo.* **10** dejar, abandonar (idea, discusión, tarea, etc.): *don't go on insulting me, drop it! = no sigas insultándome, ¡déjalo ya!* **11** DEP. conceder, perder (un punto, un juego, etc.). **12** (fam.) mandar, escribir (tarjeta, carta, nota, etc.). || *v.i.* **13** caer, caerse: *the knife dropped out the pocket = el cuchillo se cayó del bolsillo.* **14** (fig.) derrumbarse, desplomarse, caer destrozado (por la enfermedad, agotamiento, etc.). **15** descender, bajar, hacer una bajada (camino, carretera, paisaje, etc.). **16** dejarse caer (en un sitio o posición del cuerpo): *I dropped into the armchair = me dejé caer en el sillón.* **17 [to – to]** quedar relegado a, descender a (en una competición): *he dropped to second place after leading for days = él descendió a la segunda posición después de ir el primero durante días.* **18** disminuir, reducirse (una cantidad). **19** descender, bajar (la voz). || *s.c.* **20** gota (de líquido). **21** (fam.) gota, gotita, pizca (de líquido). **22** caída, descenso (en una cantidad). **23** caramelo (redondo y pequeño). **24** lanzamiento (de algo, especialmente desde un avión). **25** (fam.) buzón (para cartas, mensajes, notas, etc.). || *s.sing.* **26** declive, pendiente, caída. || **27 a – in the ocean,** una gota de agua en el mar; es tan poco que no tiene importancia. **28 at the – of a hat,** al instante, en el acto. **29 to – a brick/a clanger,** meter la pata hasta el corvejón. **30 to – away,** debilitarse, decaer; languidecer. **31 to – back,** quedarse retrasado, quedarse atrás. **32 to – by,** (fam.) pasarse por (casa de alguien). **33 to – dead,** desplomarse sin vida (repentinamente). **34 – dead!,** (fam.) ¡vete al cuerno!, ¡vete a tomar vientos! **35 to – in,** (fam.) visitar inesperadamente, dejarse caer (por casa de alguien). **36 to – off, a)** quedarse dormido (sin intención). **b)** llevar y dejar (en un vehículo): *if you like, I'll drop you off at the cinema = si quieres te llevo y te dejo en el cine.* **c)** decaer, ir a menos, decrecer (el interés, el apoyo, etc.). **37 to – out, a)** salir, abandonar (una institución o grupo). **b)** dejar de utilizarse, desaparecer (una palabra en un idioma). **38 to – round,** (fam.) **a)** ir a ver sin avisar, hacer una visita casual. **b)** acercar (algo a alguien): *I can drop your shopping round later = puedo acercarte las compras luego.* **39 drops,** MED. gotas (de cualquier medicina).
droplet | 'drɒplɪt | *s.c.* gotita.
dropout | 'drɒpaut | (fam. y desp.) *s.c.* **1** estudiante que abandona/abandonó (sus estudios antes de acabar la carrera). **2** hippy, antisocial: *Hamlet is a dro-*

pout at heart = en el fondo Hamlet es un antisocial.
dropper | 'drɒpər | *s.c.* MED. cuentagotas.
droppings | 'drɒpɪŋz | *s.pl.* deyecciones, excrementos (de animales pequeños, domésticos).
dropsy | 'drɒpsɪ | *s.i.* MED. hidropesía.
dross | drɒs | *s.i.* **1** MET. escoria, impureza (después del fundido de metales). **2** (fig.) porquería, basura.
drought | draʊt | *s.c.* e *i.* sequía.
drove | drəʊv | *p.p.* **1** del verbo **drive.** || *s.c.* **2** multitud, muchedumbre. **3** manada, rebaño, piara. || **4 in droves,** en tropel (de gente), a montones (cosas).
drown | draʊn | *v.i.* **1** ahogarse. || *v.t.* **2** ahogar. **3** inundar, anegar (un lugar). **4** empapar (una comida o bebida con algún condimento que apague su sabor): *he drowned his meat in tomato sauce = él empapó la carne en salsa de tomate.* **5** ahogar (sonido o ruido). || **6 to – one's sorrows,** ahogar las penas de uno (en alcohol). **7 to – out,** ahogar por completo (ruido o sonido).
drowse | draʊz | *v.i.* sestear, dormitar; amodorrarse.
drowsily | 'draʊzɪlɪ | *adv.* adormecidamente, somnolientamente.
drowsiness | 'draʊzɪnɪs | *s.i.* somnolencia, modorra.
drowsy | 'draʊzɪ | *adj.* **1** amodorrado, adormecido. **2** adormecedor, relajante.
drub | drʌb | [*ger.* **drubbing,** *pret.* y *p.p.* **drubbed**] *v.t.* (fam.) zurrar.
drubbing | 'drʌbɪŋ | (fam.) *s.i.* **1** zurra. || **2 to get a good –,** recibir una zurra; perder miserablemente. **3 to give a good –,** dar una paliza; vencer con claridad.
drudge | drʌdʒ | *s.c.* persona que hace trabajo aburrido.
drudgery | 'drʌdʒərɪ | *s.i.* trabajo pesado, labor pesada.
drug | drʌg | [**drugged, drugging**] *v.t.* **1** drogar, narcotizar, administrar un narcótico. **2** drogar, poner un narcótico en (comida o bebida). || *s.c.* **3** droga, narcótico. **4** droga, estupefaciente (sustancia ilegal). **5** (fig.) droga, afición favorita. || **6 a – on the market,** (fam.) objeto invendible, algo que nadie quiere comprar. **7 – addict,** drogadicto. **8 – dealer/pusher,** camello, vendedor de drogas.
drugged | drʌgd | *adj.* drogado, narcotizado.
druggist | 'drʌgɪst | *s.c.* (EE.UU.) **1** farmacéutico. **2** farmacia.
drugstore | 'drʌgstɔːr | *s.c.* (EE.UU.) drugstore, tienda de artículos varios.
druid | 'druːɪd | *s.c.* druida.
drum | drʌm | [*ger.* **drumming,** *pret.* y *p.p.* **drummed**] *v.t.* **1** tamborilear (con los dedos): *he was so nervous he didn't stop drumming his fingers on the table = estaba tan nervioso que no paró de tamborilear los dedos sobre la mesa.* || *v.i.* **2** tocar el tambor. **3** (fig.) golpear repetidamente: *the rain drummed loudly on the tin roof = la lluvia golpeaba repetidamente el tejado de hojalata con un fuerte sonido.* || *s.c.* **4** MUS. tambor. **5** bidón. **6** MEC. cilindro, tambor. || **7 to – into,** meter a fuerza de repetir, hacer aprender a base de repeticiones. **8 – major,** MIL. tambor mayor. **9 – majorette,** majorette jefe. **10 to – out,** expulsar, echar ignominiosamente (de una asociación o similar). **11 to – up,** reunir, organizar (apoyo): *he drummed up support for the party everywhere he went = organizaba apoyo para el partido dondequiera que fuese.*
drumbeat | 'drʌmbiːt | *s.c.* golpe de tambor, toque de tambor.
drummer | 'drʌmər | *s.c.* tambor (persona), percusionista.
drumming | 'drʌmɪŋ | *s.i.* **1** tamboreo. **2** repicoteo, martilleo (sonido repetitivo sobre alguna superficie).
drum-roll | 'drʌmrəʊl | *s.c.* redoble de tambor.
drumstick | 'drʌmstɪk | *s.c.* **1** palillo de tambor. **2** muslo de ave (cocinada).
drunk | drʌŋk | *p.p.* **1** de **drink.** || *adj.* **2** borracho, bebido. **3 [– with/on]** borracho de: *drunk with pleasure = borracho de placer.* || *s.c.* **4** borracho, borrachín. **5** alcohólico, bebedor.
drunkard | 'drʌŋkəd | *s.c.* (desp.) borracho, alcohólico, bebedor.
drunken | 'drʌŋkən | *adj.* **1** borracho, ebrio. **2** de borrachos, de borrachera: *a drunken party = una fiesta de borrachos.*
drunkenly | 'drʌŋkənlɪ | *adv.* ebriamente.
drunkenness | 'drʌŋkənnɪs | *s.i.* embriaguez.
dry | draɪ | *adj.* **1** seco (no mojado). **2** seco, desecado (lago, río, etc.). **3** seco, sin explotación (pozo de petróleo). **4** sin leche (vaca o mujer). **5** sin lágrimas. **6** (fam.) sediento. **7** (fam.) sin bebidas alcohólicas. **8** seca, agarrada (tos). **9** irónico (humor). **10** seca (voz). **11** falto de inspiración, sin inspiración (obra escrita, discurso o similar). **12** sin mantequilla (pan). **13** seco (vino). **14** seco (ruido). || *v.t.* **15** secar. || *v.i.* **16** secarse. **17** olvidar su papel (un actor). || **18 as – as a bone,** más seco que un muerto, totalmente seco. **19 as – as dust,** un plomazo (de aburrido). **20 – battery,** ELEC. batería seca. **21 – cell,** ELEC. elemento seco, pila seca. **22 – dock,** MAR. dique seco (donde se repara un barco). **23 – ginger,** jengibre seco. **24 – goods,** (EE.UU.) artículos de lencería /mercería. **25 – ice,** nieve carbónica. **26 – land,** tierra firme. **27 – measure,** medida de mercería. **28 to – off,** desecarse totalmente. **29 to – out, a)** desecarse totalmente. **b)** (fam.) dejar de beber. **30 – rot,** putrefacción, podredumbre. **31 – run,** (fam.) ensayo, prueba. **32 to – up, a)** secarse, quedarse seco. **b)** no dar más de sí (un pozo o similar). **c)** secar (los platos). **d)** quedarse con la mente en blanco (mientras está hablando). **33 – up!,** ¡cállate!, ¡cierra el pico! **34 not a – eye in the house,** (fam.) todo el mundo estaba llorando.
dry-clean | ˌdraɪ'kliːn | *v.t.* limpiar en seco, hacer limpieza en seco de.
dry-cleaner | ˌdraɪ'kliːnər | *s.c.* **1** tintorero, limpiador en seco. **2** tintorería, tienda de limpieza en seco. || **3 dry-cleaner's,** tienda de limpieza en seco.
dry-cleaning | ˌdraɪ'kliːnɪŋ | *s.i.* **1** limpieza en seco. **2** ropa para limpieza en seco.
dryer | draɪər | *s.c.* **1** secador (para el pelo). **2** secadora (para ropa).
dry-eyed | ˌdraɪ'aɪd | *adj.* sin una lágrima.
drying-up | 'draɪŋʌp | *s.i.* secado (de platos).
dryness | 'draɪnɪs | *s.i.* **1** sequedad, aridez. **2** ironía.
dry-stone | 'draɪstəʊn | *adj.* **1** de piedras sin cemento. || **2 – wall,** pared de piedras sin cemento.
DT's | ˌdiː'tiːz | *s.pl.* temblores (siglas de Delirium Tremens).
dual | 'djuːəl | *adj.* **1** dual, doble. || **2 – carriageway,** (brit.) autopista.
dualism | djuːə'lɪzəm | *s.i.* (form.) dualismo.
duality | djuː'ælɪtɪ | *s.i.* (form.) dualidad.
dub | dʌb | *v.t.* **1** denominar, bautizar, llamar: *they dubbed him the king = le llamaron el rey.* **2** doblar (películas).
dubbin | 'dʌbɪn | *s.i.* (brit.) adobo impermeable (para el cuero).
dubbing | 'dʌbɪŋ | *s.i.* doblaje (de películas).
dubious | 'djuːbɪəs | *adj.* **1** dudoso, sospechoso. **2** indeciso, irresoluto. **3** (desp.) dudoso: *he's a man of dubious morals = es un hombre de moral dudosa.*
dubiously | 'djuːbɪəslɪ | *adv.* indecisamente, irresolutamente.
ducal | 'djuːkl | *adj.* ducal.
duchess | 'dʌtʃɪs | *s.c.* duquesa.
duchy | 'dʌtʃɪ | *s.c.* ducado.
duck | dʌk | *s.c.* **1** pato. **2** pata (hembra). || *s.i.* **3** pato (carne). || *v.t.* **4** esquivar, evitar (golpe o similar). **5** sumergir (la cabeza especialmente). **6** hundir (la cabeza de alguien en agua). **7** (fig.) esquivar, evitar (responsabilidad o algo parecido). || *v.i.* **8** agacharse (esquivando). **9** zambullirse (en el agua). **10** lanzarse, tirarse (normalmente evitando algún peligro). || **11 to – out,** remolonear, esquivar (algo que es obligación hacer). **12 ducks and drakes,** ranas (juego de tirar piedras que reboten en el agua). **13 like water off a duck's back,** sin producir efecto alguno, como quien oye llover. **14 to play ducks and drakes with something,** (fam.) tirar algo por los suelos, desperdiciar algo malamente. **15 to take to something like a – to water,** hallarse en su elemento con, dársele de maravillas algo a uno.
ducking | 'dʌkɪŋ | *s.c.* aguadilla.
duckling | 'dʌklɪŋ | *s.c.* patito.
duct | dʌkt | *s.c.* **1** tubería, tubo, conducto. **2** ANAT. conducto.
dud | dʌd | *adj.* **1** inútil, inoperativo: *a dud hand-grenade = una granada de mano inoperativa.* || *s.c.* **2** cosa inútil, inutilidad: *that's a dud = eso es una*

inutilidad. || **3 – cheque,** FIN. cheque sin fondos.

dude | djuːd | (EE.UU.) *s.c.* **1** (p.u.) chorvo, fulano, tío. **2** chulo negro. || **3 – ranch,** camping de recreo, rancho de recreo.

dudgeon | 'dʌdʒən | **in high dudgeon,** hecho un basilisco.

due | djuː | *adj.* **1** debido, merecido: *due attention = debida atención.* **2 [– (to)]** debido, acordado. || *prep.* **3** (EE.UU.) debido a, acordado con. || *adv.* **4** directamente (con puntos cardinales): *due south = directamente al sur.* || **5 to be due to,** deber; suponerse que: *the train is due to leave soon = el tren debe salir pronto.* **6 credit where credit's –,** dando a cada uno su merecido, a fuer de sinceros. **7 dues,** cuotas (de asociación, sindicato o similar). **8 – to,** debido a. **9 to give someone their –,** dar a alguien lo que le corresponde/lo que es de justicia. **10 in – course,** a su debido momento. **11 with – respect,** con el debido respeto.

duel | 'djuːəl | *s.c.* **1** duelo (entre dos personas). **2** combate, lucha, duelo. || *v.i.* **3** luchar en un duelo.

duet | djuː'et | *s.c.* MUS. dúo.

duff | dʌf | (fam. y brit.) *adj.* **1** falso; inútil. || **2 to – up,** dar una tunda, atizar duro.

duffel | 'dʌfl | (también **duffle**) *s.c.* trenca.

duffel-bag | 'dʌflbæg | *s.c.* talego, bolsa de efectos personales (especialmente para su uso militar).

duffel-coat | 'dʌflkəʊt | *s.c.* trenca.

duffer | 'dʌfər | *s.c.* (fam.) zoquete.

dug | dʌg | *pret.* y *p.p.* de **dig.**

dugout | 'dʌgaʊt | *s.c.* **1** piragua, canoa. **2** MIL. trinchera cubierta.

duke | djuːk | *s.c.* duque.

dukedom | 'djuːkdəm | *s.i.* ducado.

dulcet | 'dʌlsɪt | *adj.* (lit. y a veces hum.) melifluo; melodioso.

dull | dʌl | *adj.* **1** aburrido, tedioso, monótono. **2** lerdo, lento, embotado (sin reacción anímica animada). **3** opaco, deslustrado (color). **4** gris, nublado (tiempo). **5** apagado, sordo (sonido). **6** (form.) romo, sin punta. **7** torpe, tardo (de entendimiento). **8** apagado, sordo (dolor). || *v.t.* **9** embotar, entorpecer; mitigar (los sentidos, sentimientos, dolores, etc.). **10** oscurecer, opacar, empañar: *the clouds dulled the moon's light = las nubes oscurecieron la luz de la luna.* || *v.i.* **11** oscurecerse, opacarse, empañarse.

dullard | 'dʌləd | *s.c.* (arc.) lerdo, estúpido.

dully | 'dʌlɪ | *adv.* **1** sordamente, apagadamente (sonido o dolor). **2** opacamente. **3** sin vivacidad.

dullness | 'dʌlnɪs | *s.i.* **1** aburrimiento, tedio, monotonía. **2** estupidez, torpeza. **3** deslustre, opacidad.

duly | 'djuːlɪ | *adv.* **1** debidamente, correctamente. **2** apropiadamente, en su momento adecuado.

dumb | dʌm | *adj.* **1** mudo. **2** (fig.) mudo, callado, silencioso (por la sorpresa, el temor, etc.). **3** (fam.) atontado, embobado. **4** reticente, contenido: *a dumb anger = una cólera contenida.* **5** (fam. y desp.) estúpido, bobo. **6** mudo, que no habla (referido a los animales). || **7 – show,** espectáculo de mimo. **8 – waiter,** montacargas (en restaurantes). **9 to strike somebody –,** dejar sin habla.

dumbbell | 'dʌmbel | *s.c.* **1** barra con pesas. **2** (fam. y EE.UU.) zopenco.

dumbfounded | dʌm'faʊndɪd | *adj.* atónito, pasmado.

dumbly | 'dʌmlɪ | *adv.* en silencio, silenciosamente.

dumbo | 'dʌmbəʊ | *s.c.* (fam.) bobo.

dumbstruck | 'dʌmstrʌk | *adj.* atónito, pasmado.

dum-dum | 'dʌmdʌm | *s.c.* **1** bala de expansión, bala dum-dum. || **2 – bullet,** bala de expansión, bala dum-dum.

dummy | 'dʌmɪ | *s.c.* **1** maniquí (en los escaparates de las tiendas). **2** (brit.) chupete. **3** imitación, modelo (de cualquier cosa). **4** (fam.) imbécil. || *adj.* **5** falso, postizo. || **6 – ammunition,** MIL. munición de fogueo. **7 – run,** prueba (con una máquina nueva).

dump | dʌmp | *v.t.* **1** tirar, arrojar, deshacerse de. **2** (fam.) dejar (desde un vehículo a una persona). **3** ECON. hacer dumping (vender por debajo del precio de coste). **4** FIN. volcar. || *s.c.* **5** basurero. **6** MIL. depósito. **7** INF. volcado. **8** (fam.) pocilga; chabola. || **9 down in the dumps,** (fam.) por los suelos (de falta de ánimo). **10 – truck,** volquete, camión de volteo.

dumper-truck | 'dʌmpətrʌk | *s.c.* volquete, camión de volteo.

dumping | 'dʌmpɪŋ | *s.i.* **1** ECON. dumping, inundación del mercado con precios bajos. **2** arrojado, vaciado, descarga. || **3 – ground,** basurero (especialmente no autorizado).

dumpling | 'dʌmplɪŋ | *s.c.* GAST. **1** bola de masa. **2** fruta envuelta en masa dulce.

dumpy | 'dʌmpɪ | *adj.* regordete.

dun | dʌn | *adj.* pardo.

dunce | dʌns | *s.c.* (desp.) burro, zopenco, zoquete.

dune | djuːn | *s.c.* duna.

dung | dʌŋ | *s.i.* excremento; estiércol.

dunghill | 'dʌŋhɪl | *s.c.* estercolero.

dungarees | ˌdʌŋgə'riːz | *s.pl.* mono, traje de faena.

dungeon | 'dʌndʒən | *s.c.* mazmorra.

dunk | dʌŋk | *v.t.* **1** mojar (algo en un líquido antes de comerlo). **2 [to – +** *o.* **+ (in)]** remojar, poner en remojo.

duo | 'djuːəʊ | *s.c.* **1** MUS. dúo. **2** (fam.) pareja, dúo.

duodenal | ˌdjuːə'diːnl | *adj.* ANAT. duodenal.

duodenum | ˌdjuːə'diːnəm | *s.c.* ANAT. duodeno.

dupe | djuːp | *s.c.* **1** primo, incauto, inocentón. || *v.t.* **2 [to – +** *o.* **+ (into)]** embaucar, timar.

duplex | 'djuːpleks | *adj.* **1** TEC. dual, doble. **2** (EE.UU.) casa. **3** (EE.UU.) dúplex (piso con dos niveles).

duplicate | 'djuːplɪkeɪt | *v.t.* **1** fotocopiar, copiar. **2** reproducir, repetir. || | 'djuːplɪkət | *adj.* **3** duplicado, doble. || *s.c.* **4** duplicado, copia. || **5 in –,** por duplicado.

duplication | ˌdjuːplɪ'keɪʃn | *s.i.* duplicación, duplicado.

duplicator | ˌdjuːplɪ'keɪtər | *s.c.* multicopista.

duplicity | djuː'plɪsətɪ | *s.i.* duplicidad, doblez, engaño.

durability | 'djʊərə'bɪlɪtɪ | *s.i.* aguante, resistencia, durabilidad.

durable | 'djʊərəbl | *adj.* fuerte, resistente, durable.

durables | 'djʊərəblz | *s.pl.* objetos no perecederos (como los electrodomésticos).

duration | djʊ'reɪʃn | *s.sing.* **1** duración. || **2 for the –,** mientras esto dure: *I'll be around for the duration = estaré por aquí mientras esto dure.*

duress | djʊ'res | *s.i.* **[under –]** bajo coacción.

during | 'djʊərɪŋ | *prep.* **1** durante. **2** en el transcurso de: *she gave birth during the night = dio a luz en el transcurso de la noche.*

dusk | dʌsk | *s.sing.* e *i.* (lit.) crepúsculo, anochecer.

duskiness | 'dʌskɪnɪs | *s.i.* (lit.) oscuridad, luz de la anochecida.

dusky | 'dʌskɪ | *adj.* (form. y lit.) **1** oscuro. **2** negruzco, oscuro (pelo).

dust | dʌst | *s.i.* **1** polvo (dentro y fuera de casa). **2** polvillo (de metales), serrín (de madera). || *v.t.* **3** quitar el polvo a. **4** empolvarse (especialmente la cara). **5** echar polvo (medicinal, de condimento, etc.) sobre. || *v.i.* **6** limpiar el polvo. || **7 to allow/let the – to settle,** (fam.) dejar que se calmen los ánimos, dejar que se pasen las cosas. **8 to bite the –,** (fam. y hum.) morder el polvo. **9 – bowl,** zona de sequía. **10 to – down,** cepillar el polvo, limpiar el polvo. **11 to – off,** quitar la suciedad totalmente. **12 to throw – in somebody's eyes,** cegar a alguien, engañarle. **13 when the – has settled,** cuando se pueda ver claro.

dustbin | 'dʌstbɪn | *s.c.* (brit.) cubo de la basura.

dustcart | 'dʌstkɑːt | *s.c.* (brit.) camión de la basura.

dust-cover | 'dʌstkʌvər | V. **dust-jacket.**

duster | 'dʌstər | *s.c.* paño guardapolvo, guardapolvo.

dust-jacket | 'dʌstdʒækɪt | *s.c.* sobrecubierta (de un libro).

dustman | 'dʌstmən | *s.c.* (brit.) basurero.

dustpan | 'dʌstpæn | *s.c.* cogedor.

dustsheet | 'dʌstʃiːt | *s.c.* (brit.) sábana guardapolvo.

dustup | 'dʌstʌp | *s.c.* (fam.) pelea, riña.

dusty | 'dʌstɪ | *adj.* **1** polvoriento, empolvado. **2** gris monótono. || **3 a – answer,** (fam.) una respuesta negativa. **4 not so –,** (fam. brit. y p.u.) tirando, bastante bien.

Dutch | dʌtʃ | *adj.* **1** holandés. | *s.i.* **2** holandés (idioma). || **3 – courage,** (fam.)

la valentía del alcohol. **4 to go –,** (fam.) pagar cada uno lo suyo. **5 the –,** los holandeses.
Dutchman | 'dʌtʃmən | *s.c.* holandés.
Dutchwoman | 'dʌtʃwʊmən | *s.c.* holandesa.
dutiful | 'djuːtɪfl | *adj.* cumplidor, obediente, sumiso.
dutifully | 'djuːtɪfəlɪ | *adv.* cumplidoramente, obedientemente, sumisamente.
duty | 'djuːtɪ | *s.i.* **1** tarea, trabajo, obligación laboral. || *s.c.* **2** tarea específica, deber concreto: *my duties as a policeman are very important to me = mis deberes concretos como policía son muy importantes para mí.* **3** deber, obligación. || *s.c.* e *i.* **4** arancel, impuesto. || **5 off –,** libre de servicio, fuera de servicio. **6 on –,** de servicio, MIL. de guardia.
duty-bound | ˌdjuːtɪ'baʊnd | *adj.* [– *inf.*] (form.) obligado por sentido del deber: *you're duty-bound to help your sick mother = estás obligado por sentido del deber a ayudar a tu madre enferma.*
duty-free | ˌdjuːtɪ'friː | *adj.* y *adv.* **1** libre de impuestos. || **2 – shop,** tienda con artículos libres de impuestos (típica de los aeropuertos).
duvet | 'duːveɪ | *s.c.* **1** edredón. || **3 – cover,** funda de edredón (lavable).
dwarf | dwɔːf | (*pl.* **dwarfs** o **dwarves**) *s.c.* **1** enano, persona enana. **2** enano, duende. || *adj.* **3** de miniatura, liliputiense, diminuto. || *v.t.* **4** empequeñecer, hacer que parezca pequeño: *the new building dwarfs the old school = el nuevo edificio hace que la vieja escuela parezca pequeña.*
dwarfish | 'dwɔfɪʃ | *adj.* diminuto, pequeño, enano.
dwell | dwel | *v.* [*pret.* y *p.p.* **dwelled** o **dwelt**] *i.* **1** (form.) morar, habitar, residir. || **2 to – on/upon,** explayarse en, dedicar mucho tiempo a, meditar sobre: *he dwelt on his unhappy childhood far too long = él se explayó acerca de su niñez infeliz durante muchísimo tiempo.*
dweller | 'dwelər | *s.c.* residente, habitante: *a city dweller.*
dwelling | 'dwelɪŋ | (form. y p.u.) *s.c.* **1** residencia, lugar de residencia. || **2 – place,** residencia, lugar de residencia.
dwelt | dwelt | V. **dwell.**
dwindle | 'dwɪndl | *v.i.* disminuir, menguar.
dwindling | 'dwɪndlɪŋ | *adj.* cada vez más pequeño, decreciente.
dye | daɪ | *v.t.* **1** teñir. || *s.c.* **2** tinte (para teñir). || **3 of the blackest/deepest –,** (p.u.) de la peor calaña.
dyed | daɪd | *adj.* teñido (pelo).
dyed-in-the-wool | ˌdaɪdɪnðə'wʊl | *adj.* acérrimo, intransigente: *I'm a dyed-in-the-wool conservative = soy un conservador acérrimo.*
dyer | daɪər | *s.c.* tintorero.
dying | daɪŋ | *ger.* **1** de **die.** || *adj.* **2** moribundo, agonizante. **3** en las últimas, sin futuro (industria, tradición, etc.). **4** último (suspiro o parecido). || **5 the –,** los agonizantes, los moribundos; los enfermos terminales.
dyke | daɪk | (también **dike**) *s.c.* **1** dique. **2** (vulg.) lesbiana.
dynamic | daɪ'næmɪk | *adj.* **1** dinámico; enérgico. **2** FIS. dinámico. || *s.c.* **3** HIS. dinámica, tendencia histórica, fuerza histórica.
dynamically | daɪ'næmɪkəlɪ | *adv.* **1** con dinamismo, dinámicamente; enérgicamente. **2** FIS. dinámicamente.
dynamics | daɪ'næmɪks | *s.i.* FIS. dinámica.
dynamism | 'daɪnəmɪzəm | *s.i.* dinamismo (cualidad personal positiva).
dynamite | 'daɪnəmaɪt | *s.i.* **1** dinamita. **2** (fig.) dinamita, dinamita pura. || *v.t.* **3** dinamitar.
dynamo | 'daɪnəməʊ | *s.c.* **1** MEC. dinamo. **2** (fig.) máquina: *that fellow is a dynamo = ese tío es una máquina.*
dynastic | dɪ'næstɪk | *adj.* dinástico.
dynasty | 'dɪnəstɪ | *s.c.* **1** dinastía (personas). **2** HIS. dinastía (época histórica).
dysentery | 'dɪsəntrɪ | *s.i.* MED. disentería.
dyslexia | dɪs'leksɪə | *adj.* MED. dislexia.
dyslexic | dɪs'leksɪk | *adj.* MED. disléxico.
dyspepsia | dɪs'pepsɪə | *s.i.* MED. dispepsia.
dyspeptic | dɪs'peptɪk | *adj.* MED. dispéptico.
dystrophy | 'dɪstrəfɪ | MED. *s.i.* **1** distrofia. || **2 muscular –,** distrofia muscular.

e, E | iː | *s.c.* **1** e, E (quinta letra del alfabeto inglés). || *s.c.* e *i.* **2** MUS. Mi. || **3 E number,** código E (que indica los aditivos de comida y bebida).
OBS. Esta letra sirve como sigla para muchas palabras como **English, east, earth,** etc.
each | iːtʃ | *adj.indef.* **1 [– + *v./s.sing*]** cada (con una sola unidad): *he made a sentence for each picture = hizo una frase para cada dibujo.* || *pron.* **2** cada uno: *we each had a surprise = cada uno de nosotros recibió una sorpresa.* **3 [– of]** cada uno de: *each of them knows English = cada uno de ellos sabe inglés.* || *adv.* **4** cada uno, por persona, por cabeza: *they bought one each = compraron uno por cabeza.* || **5 – and every,** todos y cada uno: *each and every house = todas y cada una de las casas.* **6 – other,** uno al otro, mutuamente, se: *Mary and John love each other = Mary y John se quieren.*
eager | ’iːgər | *adj.* **1 [– (for/*inf.*)]** ansioso, impaciente, deseoso, ávido: *he was eager to help = estaba ansioso por ayudar.* **2** excitado, ansioso, entusiasmado. || **3 – beaver,** V. **beaver.**
eagerly | ’iːgəlɪ | *adv.* ansiosamente, excitadamente, entusiásticamente; con impaciencia.
eagerness | ’iːgənɪs | *s.i.* **1 [– (for/*inf.*)]** ansia, impaciencia, avidez. **2** entusiasmo, excitación.
eagle | ’iːgl | *s.c.* **1** ZOOL. águila. **2** DEP. “eagle” (en golf una tarjeta de dos por debajo del par). || **3 – eye,** vista de lince. **4 golden –,** ZOOL. águila real.
eagle-eyed | ˌiːgl’aɪd | *adj.* con vista de lince.
eaglet | ’iːglɪt | *s.c.* ZOOL. aguilucho.
ear | ɪər | *s.c.* **1** oreja, oído. **2** BOT. espiga (de cualquier cereal). || *s.sing.* **3 [– (for)]** oído, aptitud (para la música, los idiomas o similar). || *s.c.* e *i.* **4** (fig.) atención, predisposición: *he listened with a willing ear = escuchó con buena predisposición.* || **5 a flea in the –,** V. **flea. 6 a thick –,** (brit.) un ojo morado. **7 to be all ears,** ser todo oídos, estar totalmente dispuesto a escuchar. **8 to box someone's ears,** V. **box. 9 -eared,** con orejas, de orejas (en compuestos): *big-eared = de grandes orejas.* **10 in one – and out the other,** entra por un oído y sale por el otro. **11 to keep/ have one's – to the ground,** estar al tanto de todo, estar alerta. **12 out on one's –,** en la calle, despedido, sin trabajo. **13 to play by –,** tocar de oído. **14 to play it by –,** improvisar, tocar de oído (en un sentido figurado). **15 to turn a deaf –,** hacer oídos sordos, hacerse el sordo, cerrar los oídos. **16 up to one's ears in,** hasta arriba en, cubierto completamente por, hundido en: *up to my ears in glue = cubierto completamente de pegamento.* **17 wet behind the ears,** V. **wet. 18 with only half an –,** sin prestar una atención total.
earache | ’ɪəreɪk | *s.i.* y *sing.* dolor de oídos.
eardrop | ’ɪədrɒp | *s.c.* [generalmente *pl.*] gota para los oídos.
eardrum | ’ɪədrʌm | (también **drum**) *s.c.* ANAT. tímpano.
earful | ’ɪəfʊl | **to give/get an –,** (fam.) regañar/recibir una regañina.
earl | əːl | (*f.* **countess**) *s.c.* **1** conde. || **2 Earl,** Conde (en títulos nobiliarios).
earldom | ’əːldəm | *s.i.* condición de conde, dominio del conde, condado.
earlier | ’əːlɪər | *comp.* **1** de **early.** || *adj.* **2** anterior, antiguo. || *adv.* **3** antiguamente, anteriormente.
earliest | ’əːlɪəst | *super.* **1** de **early.** || *adj.* **2** primero, primerizo. || **3 at one's – convenience,** (form.) COM. tan pronto como (le) sea posible (especialmente utilizado en cartas comerciales). **4 at the –,** lo más pronto posible; cuanto antes.
earliness | ’əːlɪnɪs | *s.i.* prontitud, presteza; precocidad.
earlobe | ’ɪələʊb | *s.c.* ANAT. lóbulo (de la oreja).
early | ’əːlɪ | [*comp.* **earlier,** *super.* **earliest**] *adj.* **1** temprano: *very early.* **2** a principios de, en los primeros días/semanas/meses/etc.: *in early March = en los primeros días de Marzo.* **3** temprano, tierno (edad), prematuro (al principio de la vida de alguien): *at an early age = en una edad tierna.* **4** prematuro (que ocurre antes de lo esperado): *an early death = una muerte prematura.* || *adv.* **5** temprano, tempranamente. **6** en los primeros días/semanas/meses/etc. **7** prematuramente (antes de lo esperado). **8** con antelación, con adelanto: *he arrived early = llegó con adelanto.* || **9 an – bird,** (hum.) un tipo madrugador. **10 an – riser,** un madrugador, una persona madrugadora. **11 as – as,** incluso en, hasta en, ya: *as early as 1970 I had known about it = ya en 1970 yo sabía eso.* **12 – closing,** que cierra temprano (cuando las tiendas cierran antes que otros días para descanso del personal). **13 – days,** (brit. y fam.) demasiado pronto, demasiado temprano (para una decisión, un proyecto, un resultado, etc.). **14 – to bed, and – to rise (makes a man healthy, wealthy and wise),** al que madruga, Dios le ayuda, llevar una vida sana da larga vida y felicidad. **15 to keep – hours,** ser comedido en las horas de dormir, tener cuidado de dormir suficiente; irse pronto a la cama y levantarse temprano. **16 the – bird catches the worm,** al que madruga, Dios le ayuda. **17 the – hours,** las primeras horas del día, la madrugada.
early-warning | ˌəːlɪ’wɔːnɪŋ | *adj.* de aviso previo.
earmark | ’ɪəmɑːk | *v.t.* **1 [to – + *o.* + (for)]** designar, destinar (algo para alguna finalidad). || **2 earmarks (of),** señales (de), marcas (de): *this has the earmarks of a gradual and slow evolution = esto de señales de ser una evolución gradual y lenta.*

earmuff | 'ɪəmʌf | *s.c.* [generalmente *pl.*] orejera (para protección contra el frío).

earn | ɜːn | *v.t.* **1** ganar (dinero, salario, etc.). **2** ganar, devengar (intereses, beneficios, etc.): *the money earns a good interest = el dinero devenga un buen interés.* **3** (fig.) merecer, granjearse, ganar (reputación, honor, etc.): *his good works earned him a lot of respect = sus buenas obras le granjearon mucho respeto.* || **4 to –/turn an honest penny,** ganarse la vida honradamente. **5 to – one's keep,** ganar lo suficiente para vivir. **6 to – one's living,** ganarse la vida, ganarse el pan.

earner | 'ɜːnər | *s.c.* receptor (de un sueldo), proveedor (de una familia), productor (de intereses): *that deposit account is a good earner = esa cuenta a plazo fijo es una buena productora (de intereses).*

earnest | 'ɜːnɪst | *adj.* **1** serio, formal; ferroroso, ardiente || *s.sing.* **2** pago (a cuenta). **3** (fig.) prenda, fianza, señal. || **4 in –,** en serio, de manera seria; de veras.

earnestly | 'ɜːnɪstlɪ | *adv.* **1** seriamente, con formalidad. **2** con toda seriedad, definitivamente; sin falsos comienzos.

earnestness | 'ɜːnɪstnɪs | *s.i.* seriedad, formalidad.

earnings | 'ɜːnɪŋz | *s.pl.* ingresos.

earnings-related | ˌɜːnɪŋzrɪleɪtɪd | *adj.* relacionado con los ingresos, en conexión con los ingresos.

earphone | 'ɪəfəʊn | *s.c.* [generalmente *pl.*] auricular (para escuchar música u otras cosas).

earpiece | 'ɪəpiːs | *s.c.* **1** audífono. **2** patillas (de las gafas).

earplug | 'ɪəplʌg | *s.c.* tapón para los oídos.

earring | 'ɪərɪŋ | *s.c.* pendiente, arete, zarcillo.

earshot | 'ɪəʃɒt | *s.c.* **within –/out of –,** al alcance del oído/fuera del alcance del oído.

ear-splitting | 'ɪəsplɪtɪŋ | *adj.* ensordecedor, atronador, estridente, que rompe los tímpanos.

earth | ɜːθ | *s.sing.* **1 [the –]** la tierra (el planeta). **2 [the –]** la tierra, la superficie terrestre. || *s.c.* **3** madriguera (de un zorro o parecido). **4** [generalmente *sing.*] ELEC. toma de tierra (en un enchufe). || *s.i.* **5** tierra, suelo: *red earth is common here = la tierra rojiza es normal aquí.* || *v.t.* **6** (brit.) ELEC. conectar la toma de tierra, hacer que la toma de tierra quede conectada. || **7 to come back to –,** regresar a la tierra, volver a la realidad, bajarse de las nubes (dejándose de fantasías). **8 to – up,** enterrar, cubrir con tierra (las raíces o similar, normalmente de plantas). **9 to go to –,** esconderse, dispersarse y desaparecer. **10 hell on –,** V. **hell. 11 like nothing on –,** (fam.) como nada en el mundo, de una manera impresionante (normalmente tiene sentido negativo): *he cried like nothing on earth = lloró de una manera impresionante.* **12 to move heaven and –,** V. **heaven. 13 on –, a) [what –] porras, demonios, narices:** *what on earth are you doing? = ¿qué demonios estás haciendo?* **b)** en este mundo, del mundo, de todo el mundo: *this is the best food on earth = esta es la mejor comida del mundo.* **14 to pay/cost/etc. the –,** pagar/costar un potosí, pagar una fortuna/costar una fortuna. **15 to promise someone the –,** prometer a alguien el oro y el moro. **16 to run someone/something to –,** dar con alguien/algo, encontrar alguien/algo finalmente (después de una larga búsqueda). **17 the ends of the –,** los confines del mundo, los lugares más recónditos de la tierra. **18 the salt of the –,** V. **salt.**

earthbound | 'ɜːθbaʊnd | *adj.* **1** incapaz de volar, pegado irremisiblemente a la tierra. **2** (fig.) pedestre, prosaico.

earthen | 'ɜːθn | *adj.* **1** de arcilla, de barro (cocido). **2** de tierra (dura).

earthenware | 'ɜːθnweər | *adj.* **1** de arcilla, de barro (cocido). || *s.i.* **2** objetos de loza, objetos de alfarería.

earthiness | 'ɜːθɪnɪs | *s.i.* desenfado, sinceridad natural (virtudes positivas).

earthly | 'ɜːθlɪ | *adj.* **1** terrenal, terreno, terrestre (no espiritual o etéreo). **2** [con *neg.*] (fam.) lo más mínimo; posible, concebible: *there's no earthly use in that = eso no sirve lo más mínimo.* || **3 not to have an –,** (brit. y fam.) no tener ni remota idea.

earthquake | 'ɜːθkweɪk | *s.c.* terremoto.

earth-shattering | 'ɜːθʃætərɪŋ | *adj.* importantísimo, de la máxima trascendencia (noticia, descubrimiento, etc.).

earthwork | 'ɜːθwɜːk | *s.c.* terraplén de fortificación.

earthworm | 'əθwɜːm | *s.c.* ZOOL. lombriz.

earthy | 'ɜːθɪ | *adj.* **1** terroso, parecido a tierra, como de tierra. **2** desenfadado, sincero, natural, abierto: *my wife is a lovely earthy italian = mi mujer es una italiana preciosa y desenfadada.*

ear-trumpet | 'ɪətrʌmpɪt | *s.c.* trompetilla (para sordos).

earwig | 'ɪəwɪg | *s.c.* ZOOL. tijereta.

ease | iːz | *s.i.* **1 [– (of/with)]** facilidad. **2** comodidad, confort, desahogo. || *v.t.* **3** aliviar (dolor), disminuir (tensiones), mejorar (una situación mala). **4** mitigar, moderar. **5** dejar caer, poner, colocarse (un objeto en algún sitio con lentitud y cuidado): *I eased the body into the box = puse el cuerpo en la caja cuidadosamente.* || *v.r.* **6** dejarse caer, ponerse, colocarse (con lentitud y cuidado): *he eased himself into the armchair = se dejó caer cuidadosamente en el sillón.* || *v.i.* **7** mitigarse, moderarse (tensiones, conflictos, etc.). || **8 at –/at one's –,** relajado, cómodo, a gusto. **9 at –/stand at –,** MIL. ¡descanso! **10 to – off,** aflojar, apaciguarse, disminuir (la cantidad, velocidad, intensidad, etc., de algo). **11 to – up,** aflojar, apaciguarse, disminuir (la cantidad, velocidad, intensidad, etc. de algo). **12 to – up on,** (fam.) tratar con menos rigor, tratar con más relajación. **13 ill at –,** nervioso, incómodo: *I felt ill at ease while he was around = me sentí incómodo mientras él estuvo por allí.* **14 to take one's –,** relajarse. **15 with –,** con facilidad, con soltura, sin dificultad.

easel | 'iːzl | *s.c.* atril, caballete.

easily | 'iːzɪlɪ | *adv.* **1** fácilmente, sencillamente. **2** relajadamente, sin excesivas tensiones. **3** sobradamente, con mucho (como énfasis): *that's easily the cheapest car in the world = ese es con mucho el coche más barato del mundo.* 4 probablemente, con toda probabilidad: *the flu could easily leave half the school empty = la gripe podría con toda probabilidad dejar la mitad de la escuela vacía.* **5** con demasiada facilidad, con demasiada rapidez: *you get angry easily = te enfadas con demasiada facilidad.* || **6 more – said than done,** V. **easy 9.**

easiness | 'iːzɪnɪs | *s.i.* facilidad, sencillez.

east | iːst | *s.sing.* **1 [(the) –]** este (punto cardinal). || *adv.* **2** hacia el este, en dirección al este: *travel east.* || **3** este, del oeste: *east coast; east wind = viento del este.* || **4 East German,** alemán oriental, alemán del este. **5 East Germany,** Alemania Oriental, Alemania del Este. **6 the East,** GEOG. **a)** países del Este de Europa. **b)** el Oriente (China, Japón, India...).

eastbound | 'iːstbaʊnd | *adj.* con dirección al este, con rumbo al este.

Easter | 'iːstər | *s.i.* **1** Semana Santa, Pascua. || **2 – egg,** huevo de Pascua. **3 – Sunday,** REL. domingo de Resurrección.

easterly | 'iːstəlɪ | *adj.* **1** oriental, hacia el este. **2** de levante (viento).

eastern | 'iːstən | *adj.* **1** oriental, del este (orientación de una extensión geográfica). **2** oriental, del oriente: *eastern culture.* **3** POL. del este (referido a los países del Este de Europa).

easterner | 'iːstənər | *s.c.* oriental (especialmente los de esa región en Estados Unidos).

easternmost | 'iːstənməʊst | *adj.* más hacia el este, más oriental.

eastward | 'iːstwəd | (también **eastwards**) *adj.* y *adv.* hacia el este, en dirección al este; del este.

easy | 'iːzɪ | *adj.* **1** fácil, sencillo. **2** relajado. **3 [– (on)]** (fam.) bueno para, agradable para: *this kind of music is easy on the ears = este tipo de música es agradable a los oídos.* **4** sencillo, cómodo, sin complicaciones, sin preocupaciones: *an easy life = una vida sin preocupaciones.* **5** propicio (víctima), fácil (presa). **6** (desp. y fam.) chupado, tirado. || **7 as – as pie,** (fam.) chupado, tirado; un niño lo podría hacer. **8 to be – about, a)** (fam. y brit.) no tener una preferencia clara por, darle a uno lo mismo (hacer una cosa u otra). **b)** [con *neg.*] encontrarse cómodo con, encontrarse a gusto con: *I have never been easy about Freudian theories = nunca me he encontrado a gusto con las teorías freudianas.* **9 easier said than done,** es más facil predicar que dar trigo, se dice mejor que se hace. **10 – chair,** butacón, poltrona, sillón. **11 – come, – gone,** (fam.) feliz cuando tiene dinero y feliz cuando no, despreocupado por las cosas materiales, así como viene el dinero se va. **12 – does it,** (fam.) cuidado, dale despacio, ve con cuidado, no te apresures. **13 – touch,** (fam.) toque suave, toque delicado. **14 far from –/none too –/no – task,** nada fácil, demasiado difícil. **15 to go – on,** (fam.) utilizar con parquedad, tomar con moderación, economizar, no pasarse en (usar, tomar, etc., algo): *go easy on the milk, the milkman is not coming tomorrow = economiza la leche, el lechero no viene mañana.* **16 to stand –,** MIL. estar en posición de descanso. **17 to take it/things –,** tomárselo con calma, tomar las cosas con calma. **18 too –,** demasiado fácil, no cuesta nada (con matiz negativo): *it's too easy to offer your help when you know it is not needed = no cuesta nada ofrecer tu ayuda cuando sabes que no es necesaria.* **19 woman of – virtue,** mujer fácil, mujer de vida fácil.

easy-going | ˌiːzɪ'gəuɪŋ | *adj.* acomodadizo, plácido, de disposición despreocupada.

eat | iːt | *v.* [*pret.* **ate,** *p.p.* **eaten**] *t.* **1** comer, tomar, ingerir. **2** (fam.) corroer por dentro, intranquilizar: *what's eating you = ¿qué te está corroyendo por dentro?* || *i.* **3** comer, hacer la comida (del día). || *s.pl.* **4** (fam.) comida. || **5 to – away,** desgastar poco a poco, corroer gradualmente. **6 to – humble pie,** V. **humble. 7 to – in,** comer en casa. **8 to – into, a)** corroer, desgastar. **b)** mermar, hacer estragos en (energía, ahorros, etc.). **9 to – like a horse,** (fam.) comer como un lobo, comer muchísimo. **10 to – one's hat,** V. **hat. 11 to – one's heart out,** sufrir amargamente, sufrir sin rechistar, sufrir en silencio. **12 to – one's words,** V. **word. 13 to – out,** comer fuera de casa, comer fuera, comer en un restaurante. **14 to – someone out of house and home,** V. **house. 15 to – up, a)** comer todo, devorar, acabar con todo. **b)** absorber, hacer desaparecer, deshacerse de (cosas en grandes cantidades): *the new job is eating up all my spare time = el empleo nuevo me absorbe todo el tiempo libre.* **c)** (generalmente pasiva) (fam. y desp.) corroer, reconcomer (la envidia, los celos, el deseo, etc.). **16 to have someone eating out of one's hand,** (fam.) tener a alguien en el poder de uno, poder hacer con alguien lo que uno quiera (porque lo tiene en su poder). **17 I could – a horse,** (fam.) tengo un hambre de lobo, tengo un hambre atroz, me muero de hambre.

eatable | 'iːtəbl | *adj.* comestible, que se puede comer.

eaten | 'iːtn | V. **eat.**

eater | 'iːtər | *s.c.* **1** comedor; devorador: *this baby is a bad eater = este bebé es mal comedor.* **2** (fam.) fruta de mesa.

eating | 'iːtɪŋ | *adj.* comestible (sólo referido a fruta que se puede comer cruda). V. **eater 2.**

eating-house | 'iːtɪŋhauz | *s.c.* (también **eating-place**) *s.c.* casa de comidas, restaurante.

eating-place | 'iːtɪŋpleɪs | V. **eating-house.**

eau-de-cologne | ˌəudəkə'ləun | (también **cologne**) *s.i.* agua de colonia, colonia.

eaves | iːvz | *s.pl.* ARQ. aleros (de un tejado).

eavesdrop | 'iːvzdrɒp | [*ger.* **eavesdropping,** *p.p.* **eavesdropped**] *v.i.* **[to – (on)]** llevar a cabo una escucha, escuchar furtiva y secretamente, escuchar a escondidas.

eavesdropper | 'iːvzdrɒpər | *s.c.* espía (en forma de escucha).

ebb | eb | *v.i.* **1** bajar, menguar (la marea). **2** (lit. y fig.) decaer, menguar, declinar (la fuerza, los sentimientos, etc. de una persona). || *s.sing.* **3 [(the) –]** reflujo (de la marea). || **4 at a low –,** en un punto bajo, en franca decadencia, muy decaído (en ánimo, fortuna, etc.). **5 to – away, a)** bajar, menguar (la marea). **b)** (fig.) disminuir, decaer (sentimientos). **6 – tide,** marea baja. **7 on the –,** en mengua (la marea). **8 the – and flow of,** el flujo y reflujo, las subidas y bajadas (de la suerte, vida, progreso, etc.).

ebony | 'ebənɪ | *s.c.* **1** BOT. ébano. || *s.i.* **2** madera de ébano, ébano. || *adj.* **3** ébano, de color de ébano, de ébano. **4** de ébano (muebles).

ebullience | ɪ'bʌlɪəns | *s.i.* (form.) exaltación, efervescencia, ebullición, exuberancia (de personas).

ebullient | ɪ'bʌlɪənt | | ɪ'bulɪənt | *adj.* (form.) exaltado, efervescente, en ebullición, exuberante (de personas).

ebulliently | ɪ'bʌlɪəntlɪ | *adv.* (form.) exaltadamente, efervescentemente, con gran ebullición, exuberantemente.

eccentric | ɪk'sentrɪk | *adj.* **1** excéntrico, extravagante, no convencional. || *s.c.* **2** excéntrico, extravagante.

eccentrically | ɪk'sentrɪklɪ | *adv.* excéntricamente, extravagantemente, sin ningún convencionalismo.

eccentricity | ˌeksen'trɪsɪtɪ | *s.i.* **1** excentricidad, extravagancia. || *s.c.* **2** (generalmente *pl.*) excentricidad (de una persona concreta): *I don't mind my grandfather's eccentricities = no me importan las excentricidades de mi abuelo.*

ecclesiastic | ɪˌkliːzɪ'æstɪk | *s.c.* (form. y p.u.) eclesiástico, clérigo.

ecclesiastical | ɪˌklɪːzɪ'æstɪkl | *adj.* eclesiástico.

ecclesiastically | ɪˌkliːzɪ'æstɪklɪ | *adv.* eclesiásticamente, desde una óptica eclesiástica.

echelon | 'eʃəlɒn *s.c.* **1** categoría, grado (en una organización). **2** MIL. escalonamiento (orden de formación).

echo | 'ekəu | [*pl.* **echoes**] *s.c.* **1** eco. **2 [– (of)]** (fig.) repetición, eco. **3 [– (of)]** eco, trazo (que le recuerda otra cosa a uno): *there are echoes of romanticism in his work = hay ecos del romanticismo en su obra.* || *v.i.* **4** hacer eco, reverberar. **5** resonar, estar lleno de ecos (un lugar). **6** (fig.) resonar, oírse, estar en candelero (un tema de actualidad, una noticia, etc.). || *v.t.* **7** hacerse eco de, repetir, reproducir (lo que otro ha dicho, escrito, pintado, etc.): *he echoed my words = él se hizo eco de mis palabras; the rhythm echoes the African dances = el ritmo reproduce las danzas africanas.* || **8 to the –,** (arc.) con gran volumen durante mucho tiempo; repetidamente.

echoing | 'ekəuɪŋ | *adj.* resonante, reverberante, que hace eco.

echo-sounder | 'ekəusaundər | *s.c.* MAR. onda acústica, sonar.

éclair | ɪ'kleər | | eɪ'kleər | (también **chocolate éclair**) *s.c.* GAST. pastel relleno de crema y recubierto de chocolate.

éclat | 'eɪklɑː | (EE.UU. | eɪ'klɑː | *s.i.* **1** gran éxito, gran resonancia. **2** aplauso, aclamación.

eclectic | ɪ'klektɪk | (form.) *adj.* **1** ecléctico. || *s.c.* **2** ecléctico.

eclectically | ɪ'klektɪklɪ | *adv.* (form.) eclécticamente.

eclecticism | ɪ'klektɪsɪzəm | *s.i.* (form.) FIL. eclecticismo.

eclipse | ɪ'klɪps | *s.c.* **1** ASTR. eclipse. || *s.sing.* **2** (fig.) eclipse, desaparición, oscurecimiento; pérdida de influencia. || *v.t.* **3** ASTR. eclipsar. **4** (fig.) eclipsar, dejar empequeñecido, hacer que no se noten los demás. || **5 in/into –,** en decadencia, en proceso de desaparición, en vías de desaparecer.

eco- | iːkɒ | *prefijo* eco (para compuestos que tengan relación con la ecología): *ecotype.*

ecological | ˌiːkə'lɒdʒɪkl | *adj.* **1** BIOL. ecológico. **2** POL. verde, ecológico.

ecologically | ˌiːkə'lɒdʒɪklɪ | *adv.* ecológicamente, desde el punto de vista del equilibrio de la naturaleza.

ecologist | iː'kɒlədʒɪst | *s.c.* **1** BIOL. experto en ecología, ecólogo. **2** POL. verde, miembro del partido ecologista.

ecology | iː'kɒlədʒɪ | *s.i.* **1** BIOL. ecología. || **2 the Ecology Party,** (también **the Green Party**) POL. el partido verde, el partido ecologista.

economic | ˌiːkə'nɒmɪk | | ˌekə'nɒmɪk | *adj.* **1** económico, financiero: *the economic system.* **2** económico, que cueste poco, que cueste lo justo.

economical | ˌiːkə'nɒmɪkl | | ˌekə'nɒmɪkl | *adj.* **1** barato, económico. **2** cuidadoso con el dinero, frugal, consciente del gasto. **3** eficiente, ajustado (uso de tiempo, energías, etc.).

economically | ˌiːkə'nɒmɪklɪ | | ˌekə'nɒklɪ | *adv.* **1** económicamente, desde el punto de vista económico. **2** económicamente, sin demasiado gasto, módicamente. **3** frugalmente, cuidadosamente con el dinero. **4** eficientemente, ajustadamente (en el uso del tiempo, energías, etc.).

economics | ˌiːkəˈnɒmɪks | ˌekəˈnɒmɪks | *s.i.* **1** economía (como ciencia). || *s.pl.* **2** economía, medidas económicas.

economise V. **economize.**

economist | ɪˈkɒnəmɪst | *s.c.* economista.

economize | ɪˈkɒnəmaɪz | (también **economise**) *v.i.* **[to – (on)]** economizar, reducir costes, ahorrar.

economy | ɪˈkɒnəmɪ | *s.c.* **1** economía, sistema económico. **2** (generalmente *pl.*) ahorro, economía, reducción de costes. **3** [generalmente *sing.*] estado económico, situación económica, economía (de un país, región, etc.). || *s.i.* **4** ahorro, reducción de costes, economía, frugalidad: *the situation is bad, we need a lot of economy = la situación está mal, necesitamos mucho ahorro.* **5** **[– (of)]** (fig.) ahorro, uso inteligente, uso cuidadoso (del tiempo, idioma, energías, etc.). || *adj.* **6** ahorrativo, económico (en ofertas de tiendas, de viajes, etc.): *economy class = clase económica.*

ecosystem | ˈiːkəʊsɪstəm | *s.c.* BIOL. ecosistema.

ecstasy | ˈekstəsɪ | *s.c.* e *i.* **1** éxtasis, arrobamiento, embeleso. **2** rapto, frenesí, delirio, ataque agudo (de algún sentimiento o pasión): *an ecstasy of delight = un rapto de gozo.* || **3 to go into ecstasies (about),** caer en un éxtasis (sobre), llegar a un éxtasis (acerca de). **4 in ecstasies,** en puro éxtasis, en arrobamiento.

ecstatic | ɪkˈstætɪk | *adj.* eufórico, embelesado, de puro éxtasis: *an ecstatic performance = una actuación de puro éxtasis.*

ecstatically | ɪkˈstætɪklɪ | *adv.* eufóricamente, embelesadamente, lleno de puro éxtasis.

ectoplasm | ˈektəplæzəm | *s.i.* **1** BIOL. ectoplasma. **2** emanación del médium (en el espiritismo).

ECU | | *s.c.* ecu (siglas de "European Currency Unit").

Ecuador | ˈekwədɔːr | *s.sing.* Ecuador.

Ecuadorian | ˌekwəˈdɔːrɪən | *adj.* **1** ecuatoriano, de Ecuador. || *s.c.* **2** ecuatoriano.

ecumenical | ˌiːkjuːˈmenɪkl | (también **oecumenical**) (form.) REL. *adj.* **1** ecuménico. || **2 – council,** concilio ecuménico (expresando la universalidad de la iglesia).

ecumenically | ˌiːkjuːˈmenɪklɪ | *adv.* ecuménicamente.

ecumenicism | ɪˈkjuːmənɪsɪzəm | (también **ecumenism**) *s.i.* REL. ecumenismo.

ecumenism | ɪˈkjuːmənɪzəm | V. **ecumenicism.**

eczema | ˈeksɪmə | (EE.UU.)ɪgˈziːmə | *s.i.* MED. eczema.

eddy | ˈedɪ | *v.i.* **1** remolinear, revolotear, arremolinarse (sin rumbo o propósito fijo). || *s.c.* **2** remolino, revoloteo (del agua, viento, polvo, etc.).

edelweiss | ˈeɪdlvaɪs | [*pl.* **edelweiss**] *s.c.* BOT. edelweiss.

Eden | ˈiːdn | *s.sing.* REL. Edén.

edge | edʒ | *s.c.* **1 [– (of)]** borde, límite, margen (de cualquier espacio físico). **2** filo (de un cuchillo o similar). **3 [– (of)]** borde (parte fina de un objeto): *on the edge of the board = sobre el borde del encerado.* || *s.sing.* **4 [the – (of)]** el borde, el límite (de una situación): *to the edge of war = al borde de la guerra.* **5 [– (over)]** ventaja, prioridad: *the economy has an edge over anything else = la economía tiene prioridad por encima de cualquier otra cosa.* **6 [an – (to)]** deje, sabor, acento cortante (en la voz, tono o similar). || *v.t.* **7** bordear, ribetear, poner bordes en. **8** empujar poco a poco, trasladar gradualmente (un objeto): *I edged my chair away from the sleeping snake = empujé poco a poco mi silla lejos de la serpiente dormida.* || *v.i.* **9** moverse poco a poco; acercarse/alejarse poco a poco (dependiendo de la preposición). || **10 -edged,** de borde, de lado, de filo (en compuestos): *a new five-edged coin = una nueva moneda de cinco lados.* **11 on –,** en tensión, con los nervios de punta. **12 to set somebody's teeth on –,** poner los nervios de punta, irritar a alguien en gran manera. **13 to take the – off,** suavizar, mitigar (un enfado o similar); quitar hierro a (una situación desagradable). **14 to take the – off one's appetite,** engañar el hambre (comiendo un poquito).

edgeways | ˈedʒweɪz | (también **edgewise**) *adv.* **1** de filo, de canto. || **2 to get a word in –,** (generalmente *neg.*) meter baza (hablando): *she didn't let me get a word in edgeways = ella no me dejó meter baza.*

edgewise | ˈedʒwaɪz | V. **edgeways.**

edgily | ˈedʒɪlɪ | *adv.* (fam.) nerviosamente, con inquietud.

edginess | ˈedʒɪnɪs | *s.i.* (fam.) nerviosismo, inquietud, intranquilidad.

edging | ˈedʒɪŋ | *s.c.* reborde, orla, margen.

edging-shears | ˈedʒɪŋʃɪəz | *s.pl.* tijeras de jardinero para los bordes.

edgy | ˈedʒɪ | *adj.* (fam.) nervioso, inquieto.

edibility | ˌedɪˈbɪlɪtɪ | *s.i.* condición de ser comestible, no nocividad (de un alimento).

edible | ˈedɪbl | *adj.* comestible, comible.

edict | ˈiːdɪkt | (form.) *s.c.* **1** instrucción oficial, mandato oficial. **2** decreto, ordenanza, edicto (gubernamental o de autoridad equivalente).

edification | ˌedɪfɪˈkeɪʃn | *s.i.* (form. o hum.) edificación, enseñanza (moral).

edifice | ˈedɪfɪs | *s.c.* **1** edificio, construcción (especialmente cuando es imponente). **2** (fig. y fam.) estructura, edificio, entramado (en sentido intangible): *the edifice of his ideas fell apart = el entramado de sus ideas se desmoronó.*

edify | ˈedɪfaɪ | *v.t.* (form.) instruir, enseñar, edificar, aleccionar (especialmente con un sentido ético).

edifying | ˈedɪfaɪɪŋ | *adj.* (form.) edificante, ejemplar, aleccionador, instructivo (desde el punto de vista del ejemplo).

edit | ˈedɪt | *v.t.* **1** corregir, anotar, preparar para su publicación (un texto). **2** dirigir una colección (de artículos dentro de un mismo libro o de libros): *I'll edit the whole collection = yo dirigiré toda la colección.* **3** PER. dirigir (una publicación como periódico, revista, etc.). **4** TV. montar, hacer el montaje de (película o similar). **6** INF. editar (un texto para su procesamiento por ordenador). || *v.i.* **5** corregir, hacer correcciones, hacer los preparativos para la publicación (de textos). || *s.c.* **6** corrección, arreglo, preparación para publicación (de un texto). || **7 to – out,** cortar, borrar, suprimir (de un texto o película).

edited | ˈedɪtɪd | *adj.* corregido, anotado, arreglado, preparado (textos).

editing | ˈedɪtɪŋ | *s.i.* corrección, anotación, preparación (de textos).

edition | ɪˈdɪʃn | *s.c.* **1** edición (de cualquier tipo de texto): *the morning edition of this newspaper = la edición de la mañana de este periódico.* **2** tirada, edición: *there have been three editions of this book so far = ha habido hasta ahora tres ediciones de este libro.* **3 [– (of)]** TV. programa (uno dentro de una serie).

editor | ˈedɪtər | *s.c.* **1** PER. director. **2** PER. jefe de sección (con el nombre de la sección bajo su cargo): *the sports editor.* **3** TV. jefe de montaje. **4** corrector; compilador, coordinador (de una obra literaria). **5** INF. editor de textos (programa).

editorial | ˌedɪˈtɔːrɪəl | *s.c.* **1** PER. editorial. || *adj.* **2** editorial (en cuanto tiene que ver con textos). **3** editorial (en cuanto a la dirección de una publicación): *the editorial policy is not coherent = la trayectoria editorial no es coherente.* || **4 – staff,** PER. redacción.

editorialise V. **editorialize.**

editorialize | ˌedɪˈtɔːrɪəlaɪz | (también **editorialise**) *v.i.* PER. hacer comentarios de matiz subjetivo (especialmente en artículos que deberían ser neutros y objetivos).

editorializing | ˌedɪˈtɔːrɪəˈlaɪzɪŋ | (también **editorialising**) (desp.) *adj.* **1** subjetivo (especialmente en artículos que se espera que sean objetivos). || *s.i.* **2** comentarios subjetivos (cuando especialmente no deberían serlo).

editorially | ˌedɪˈtɔːrɪəlɪ | *adv.* en cuanto a su política editorial (en el sentido de la opinión oficial de una publicación).

editorship | 'edɪtəʃɪp | *s.i.* PER. dirección.
educate | 'edjʊkeɪt | *v.t.* **1** educar (intelectualmente), instruir, formar (la mente). **2** pagar una educación, dar una educación (intelectual, por parte de los padres: *I will try to earn enough to be able to educate my children in the best schools = intentaré ganar lo suficiente para poder educar a mis hijos en las mejores escuelas.* **3** formar, informar, educar (para la mejora): *we must educate parents now = debemos educar a los padres ahora.*
educated | 'edjʊkeɪtɪd | *adj.* **1** educado (intelectualmente), instruido. || **2 an – guess,** una suposición fundada, una adivinanza probable.
education | ˌedjʊ'keɪʃn | *s.i.* **1** educación, instrucción (sistema). **2** educación, formación (intelectual): *I am worried about your education = estoy preocupado por tu educación.* **3** pedagogía, teoría de la educación.
educational | ˌedjʊ'keɪʃənl | *adj.* **1** educativo, de la educación. **2** instructivo, educativo, formativo: *the program was very educational = el programa fue muy instructivo.*
educationalist | ˌedjʊ'keɪʃənəlɪst | (también **educationist**) *s.c.* especialista en educación, experto en educación, pedagogo.
educationally | ˌedjʊ'keɪʃənəlɪ | *adv.* educativamente.
educationist | ˌedjʊ'keɪʃənɪst | V. **educationalist.**
educative | 'edjʊkətɪv | *adj.* educativo, instructivo, formativo. V. **educational.**
educator | 'edjʊkeɪtər | *s.c.* pedagogo, experto en educación; profesor.
Edwardian | e'dwɔːdɪən | *adj.* ARQ. eduardiano, de la época eduardiana (de principios de siglo).
EEC | ˌiːiː'siː | *s.sing.* **[the –]** la CEE (European Economic Community).
eel | iːl | *s.c.* ZOOL. anguila.
e'er | eər | *adv.* (lit.) jamás, nunca (forma poética de **ever).**
eerie | 'ɪərɪ | (también **eery**) *adj.* misterioso, fantástico, extraño (con sentimiento de miedo).
eerily | 'ɪərɪlɪ | *adv.* misteriosamente, fantásticamente, extrañamente.
eery V. **eerie.**
eff | ef | *v.i.* **– off,** (euf.) irse a la porra (para no utilizar **fuck**).
effing | 'efɪŋ | *adj.* (euf.) asqueroso, desagradable, de asco (para no utilizar **fucking**).
efface | ɪ'feɪs | *v.t.* **1** borrar, hacer olvidar (una equivocación, un sentimiento desagradable, etc.); eclipsar (una mala impresión). **2** (form.) borrar, hacer desaparecer (físicamente). || *v.r.* **3** retirarse de la escena, no hacerse notar, pasar inadvertido (como actitud de humildad): *I try to efface myself when there are other higher officials = yo intento pasar inadvertido cuando hay otros empleados de mayor categoría.*
effacement | ɪ'feɪsmənt | *s.i.* **1** borrado, tachadura; desaparición (física). **2** modestia, humildad, discreción.
effect | ɪ'fekt | *s.c.* **1 [– (on)]** efecto, resultado, consecuencia. **2** sensación, efectos, resultado (corporal): *under the effect of the strong drug = bajo los efectos de la fuerte droga.* **3** (generalmente *sing.*) efecto final, efecto total, efecto, impacto total: *if you put the vase on that table you will spoil the effect = si pones el jarrón en esa mesa estropearás el efecto total.* || *s.i.* **4** resultado, impacto, consecuencia. || *s.pl.* **5** (form.) efectos personales, posesiones personales, pertenencias. **6** efectos especiales (de una película, entendidos en general, sin distinguir los de sonido de los de escenario, etc.). || *v.t.* **7** (form.) efectuar, ejecutar, llevar a cabo. || **8 for –,** para causar efecto, para mayor dramatismo, para impresionar. **9 in –,** en efecto, efectivamente, en realidad. **10 to put /bring/carry something into –,** poner en marcha algo, llevar a cabo algo, hacer realidad algo. **11 to take –,** hacer efecto (una medicina, una medida económica, un plan de acción social, etc.). **12 to take –/come into –/go into –,** tener efecto, entrar en vigor (ley o similar). **13 to good/great/etc. –,** con buen resultado, con magníficos resultados. **14 to no/little/etc. –,** sin resultados, sin resultado alguno, inútilmente. **15 to the – that,** en el sentido de que, apuntando a que, indicando que: *he repeated what Frank had said to the effect that he wasn't up to the job = él repitió lo que Frank había dicho apuntando a que no estaba capacitado para el empleo.* **16 to this/that –,** en este/ese sentido. **17 with immediate –/with –,** con efecto inmediato.
effective | ɪ'fektɪv | *adj.* **1** efectivo, eficaz, con resultados. **2** efectivo, impactante, impresionante, de impresión: *giving the money to the poor was an effective gesture = dar el dinero a los pobres fue un gesto impactante.* **3** real, efectivo (no teórico): *the effective boss = el jefe real.* **4** operativo, en vigor (una ley, acuerdo, etc.).
effectively | ɪ'fektɪvlɪ | *adv.* **1** efectivamente, en efecto, en realidad. **2** eficientemente, eficazmente.
effectiveness | ɪ'fektɪvnɪs | *s.i.* **1** eficacia. **2** impresión, impacto (de una acción llamativa). **3** vigencia (de una ley, acuerdo, etc.).
effectual | ɪ'fektʃʊəl | *adj.* (form.) efectivo, eficaz; válido.
effectually | ɪ'fektʃʊəlɪ | *adv.* (form.) efectivamente, eficazmente; válidamente.
effeminacy | ɪ'femɪnəsɪ | *s.i.* (desp.) afeminamiento, afeminación.
effeminate | ɪ'femɪnɪt | *adj.* (desp.) afeminado.
effeminately | ɪ'femɪnətlɪ | *adv.* (desp.) afeminadamente.
effervesce | ˌefə'ves | *v.i.* **1** hacer efervescencia (cualquier líquido). **2 [to – (with)]** (form.) bullir, estar eufórico (de alegría o similar).
effervescence | ˌefə'vesns | *s.i.* **1** efervescencia (en líquidos). **2** (fig.) efervescencia, euforia (de sentimientos).
effervescent | ˌefə'vesnt | *adj.* **1** efervescente (líquido). **2** (fig.) eufórico, lleno de euforia.
effete | ɪ'fiːt | *adj.* (desp.) incapaz, decadente, debilucho.
effeteness | ɪ'fiːtnɪs | *s.i.* (desp.) incapacidad, decadencia, debilidad.
efficacious | ˌefɪ'keɪʃəs | *adj.* (form.) eficaz, con buenos resultados (nunca hablando de personas).
efficaciously | ˌefɪ'keɪʃəslɪ | *adv.* (form.) eficazmente (nunca sobre acciones de personas).
efficacy | 'efɪkəsɪ | *s.i.* eficacia (nunca de una persona).
efficiency | ɪ'fɪʃnsɪ | *s.i.* **1** eficiencia, profesionalidad, competencia. || *s.c.* e *i.* **2** FIS. eficiencia, rendimiento.
efficient | ɪ'fɪʃnt | *adj.* eficaz, eficiente, profesional, competente.
efficiently | ɪ'fɪʃntlɪ | *adv.* eficazmente, eficientemente, profesionalmente, competentemente.
effigy | 'efɪdʒɪ | *s.c.* **1** (form.) efigie, escultura. **2** muñeco, pelele, efigie: *there were effigies of the most important authors lying on the ground = había esculturas de los autores más importantes tiradas por el suelo.* || **3 in –,** en efigie, en forma de muñeco.
efflorescence | ˌeflɔː'resns | *s.i.* (lit.) **1** florecimiento. **2** (fig.) florecimiento, época de florecimiento (de la literatura, artes, etc.).
efflorescent | ˌeflɔː'resnt | *adj.* (lit.) **1** floreciente. **2** (fig.) floreciente, boyante (en el arte o similar).
effluent | 'eflʊənt | *s.c.* e *i.* (form.) desperdicio (en estado líquido).
effort | 'efət | *s.c.* **1** esfuerzo. **2** sacrificio, campaña de esfuerzo: *the war effort = la campaña de esfuerzo para la guerra.* **3** intento (fallido), obra (de mala calidad), esfuerzo infructuoso (de hacer algo). || *s.i.* **4** esfuerzo. **5** dificultad, sacrificio: *after so many months in bed he walked with effort = después de tantos meses en la cama caminaba con dificultad.* || **6 an – of will,** un esfuerzo de la voluntad. **7 to be worth the –,** valer la pena el esfuerzo, valer la pena el sacrificio. **8 to make the –,** hacer esfuerzos, poner de la parte de uno: *he never makes the effort to talk = nunca pone de su parte para hablar.*
effortless | 'efətlɪs | *adj.* **1** sin esfuerzo, sin sacrificio. **2** fácil, de manera natural: *he has an incredibly effortless style of writing = tiene un estilo de escribir increíblemente fácil.*
effortlessly | 'efətlɪslɪ | *adv.* de manera fácil, fácilmente, sin esfuerzo alguno.
effortlessness | 'efətlɪsnɪs | *s.i.* facilidad, ausencia de esfuerzo, ausencia de sacrificio.

effrontery | ɪ'frʌntərɪ | *s.i.* descaro, insolencia, desfachatez.
effulgence | ɪ'fʌldʒəns | *s.i.* (lit.) refulgencia, resplandor (de luz).
effusion | ɪ'fju:ʒn | *s.c.* e *i.* (lit. o form.) **1** efusión (de líquido, gas, luz, etc.). **2** (fig.) efusión, desahogo (de sentimientos, emociones, ideas, etc.).
effusive | ɪ'fju:sɪv | *adj.* efusivo, expansivo (especialmente de sentimientos).
effusively | ɪ'fju:sɪvlɪ | *adv.* efusivamente, expansivamente (en sentimientos).
effusiveness | ɪ'fju:sɪvnɪs | *s.i.* efusividad, naturaleza efusiva.
e.g. | ˌi:'dʒi: | (*abreviatura* de **exempli gratia**) por ejemplo, es decir.
egalitarian | ɪ'gælɪ'teərɪən | *adj.* **1** igualitario. || *s.c.* **2** igualitario, creyente en el igualitarismo.
egalitarianism | ɪˌgælɪ'teərɪənɪzəm | *s.i.* POL. igualitarismo.
egg | eg | *s.c.* **1** huevo. **2** BIOL. óvulo, huevo (del aparato reproductor femenino). || *s.c.* e *i.* **3** huevo (como comida). || **4 a chicken and – situation,** V. **chicken. 5 a curate's —,** (brit. y desp.) algo que no es ni fu ni fa, ni chicha ni limoná. **6 a bad –,** (p.u. o hum.) una mala persona, un tipo de cuidado. **7 as sure as eggs is eggs,** con toda seguridad, con total certeza, sin ningún género de dudas. **8 don't teach your grandmother to suck eggs,** (brit.) no hay que enseñar al maestro lo que sabe muy bien. **9 to – on,** azuzar, incitar, animar (a alguien a hacer algo). **10 to have – on one's face,** aparecer como un estúpido, hacer el tonto públicamente. **11 to put all one's eggs in one basket,** poner toda la carne en el asador; diversificar los esfuerzos de uno, arriesgar todo al mismo caballo. **12 to walk on eggs,** actuar con precaución, andarse con cuidado.
egg-beater | 'egbi:tər | V. **egg-whisk.**
egg-cup | 'egkʌp | *s.c.* huevera (recipiente donde se sirven los huevos pasados por agua).
egghead | 'eghed | *s.c.* (fam. y desp.) cabeza pensante, intelectual, cabeza hueca.
egg-plant | 'egplænt | (brit. **aubergine**) *s.c.* e *i.* (EE.UU.) berenjena.
eggshell | 'egʃel | *s.c.* e *i.* **1** cáscara (de huevo). || *adj.* **2** fino; frágil (como la cáscara de un huevo). **3** lustroso; indistinto (de color): *eggshell paint = pintura ni mate ni brillante.*
egg-timer | 'egtaɪmər | *s.c.* reloj de arena (típico para medir el tiempo de cocción de un huevo).
egg-whisk | 'egwɪsk | (también **egg-beater**) *s.c.* batidor de huevos (manual).
eglantine | 'egləntaɪn | (también **sweet-briar**) *s.i.* BOT. eglantina.
ego | 'egəʊ | (EE.UU. | 'i:gəʊ) *s.c.* **1** (fam.) ego, autoestima. **2** PSIC. ego.
egocentric | ˌegəʊ'sentrɪk | *adj.* egocéntrico.
egocentricity | ˌegəʊsən'trɪsətɪ | *s.i.* egocentrismo.
egoism | 'egəʊɪzəm | (EE.UU. | 'i:gəʊɪzəm) V. **egotism.**
egoist | 'egəʊɪst | (EE.UU. | 'i:gəʊɪst) V. egotist.
egoistic | ˌegəʊ'ɪstɪk | (EE.UU. | ˌi:gəʊ'ɪstɪk) V. **egotistic.**
egomania | ˌegəʊ'meɪnɪə | *s.i.* PSIQ. preocupación obsesiva por el propio yo.
egomaniac | ˌegəʊ'meɪnɪək | *s.c.* PSIQ. maníaco obsesivo del yo.
egotism | 'egəʊtɪzəm | (EE.UU. | 'i:gəʊtɪzəm) *s.i.* **1** (desp.) egoísmo. **2** FIL. egocentrismo.
egotist | 'egəʊtɪst | (EE.UU. | 'i:gəʊtɪst) *s.c.* egoísta.
egotistic | ˌegə'tɪstɪk | (EE.UU. | ˌi:gətɪstɪk) (también **egotistical**) *adj.* egoísta.
egotistical | ˌegə'tɪstɪkl | | ˌi:gə'tɪstɪkl | V. **egotistic.**
egotistically | ˌegə'tɪstɪklɪ | *adv.* egoístamente, egoísticamente.
ego-trip | 'egəʊtrɪp | *s.c.* (desp.) acción pensando en uno mismo, actitud ególatra.
egregious | ɪ'gri:dʒəs | *adj.* (form.) egregio, insigne; atroz (normalmente para algo negativo).
egregiously | ɪ'gri:dʒɪəslɪ | *adv.* (form.) insignemente; atrozmente.
egress | 'i:gres | *s.i.* **1** (form. y p.u.) salida. || *s.c.* **2** DER. salida, derecho de salida.
egret | 'i:grɪt | *s.c.* ZOOL. airón, penacho (tipo de ave).
Egypt | 'i:dʒɪpt | *s.sing.* Egipto.
Egyptian | ɪ'dʒɪpʃn | *adj.* **1** egipcio (cultura). || *s.c.* **2** egipcio (habitante).
eh | eɪ | *interj.* **1** ¿eh?, ¿no? (expresando contestación o búsqueda de acuerdo): *that looks beautiful, eh? = eso tiene una apariencia bellísima, ¿no?* **2** ¿eh?, ¿cómo? (queriendo que se repita algo porque no se ha entendido).
eiderdown | 'aɪdədaʊn | *s.c.* edredón.
eight | eɪt | *num. card.* **1** ocho. || *s.c.* **2** DEP. ocho, embarcación de ocho remeros. || **3 eight-,** de ocho (en compuestos): *eight-sided = de ocho lados.* **4 to have one over the —,** (fam.) estar chispa, estar un poco bebido.
eighteen | eɪ'ti:n | *num.card.* dieciocho.
eighteenth | ˌeɪ'ti:nθ | *num.ord.* décimo octavo.
OBS. Se utiliza con los siglos y con las fechas: *the eighteenth century = el siglo dieciocho; my birthday is on the eighteenth = mi cumpleaños cae el dieciocho.*
eighth | eɪtθ | *num.ord.* **1** octavo. || *s.c.* **2** octavo, octava parte. || **3 – note,** (EE.UU.) MUS. corchea.
eightieth | 'eɪtɪəθ | *num.ord.* octogésimo.
eightsome | 'eɪtsəm | *s.sing.* **1** grupo de ocho personas. || **2 – reel,** MUS. baile escocés.
eighty | 'eɪtɪ | *num.card.* **1** ochenta. || **2 in one's eighties,** de unos ochenta años, entre ochenta y noventa años. **3 the eighties,** en la década de los ochenta, en los años ochenta.
eisteddfod | ˌaɪ'steðvɒd | *s.c.* festival galés de las artes (música, poesía, etc.).
either | 'aɪðər | (EE.UU. | 'i:ðər | *adv.* **1** [con *neg.*] tampoco (se coloca al final de la oración): *"I don't like coffee", "I don't like coffee either" = "no me gusta el café", "no me gusta el café tampoco".* **2** [con *neg.*] además (se coloca al final de la oración): *I wasn't in a mood to laugh either = yo además no estaba de humor para reír.* || *pron.* **3** cualquiera (de dos), uno de los dos: *there are two cakes and you can eat either = hay dos pasteles y puedes comer cualquiera de los dos.* **4 [– of]** cualquiera de (dos): *either of you can do it = cualquiera de vosotros dos puede hacerlo.* **5** [con *neg.*] ninguno (de dos): *"there is fish or meat", "I don't want either" = "hay pescado o carne", "no quiero ninguna de las dos cosas".* || *adj.* **6** cualquier (de dos): *on either side of the street you can buy crisps = en cualquiera de los dos lados de la calle puedes comprar patatas fritas.* **7** [con *neg.*] ninguno (de dos): *there was no sound coming from either boy = ninguno de los dos chicos emitía sonido alguno.* **8 [– *sing.*]** ambos, los dos: *there was a lot of noise in either room = había muchísimo ruido en las dos habitaciones.* || OBS. Esta palabra tiene un uso como conjunción con la siguiente estructura: **9 either... or...,** o... o... (a veces no es necesario traducir el primer elemento): *either you say something more intelligent or you shut up = o dices algo más inteligente o te callas.* **10** [con *neg.*] ni... ni... (a veces no es necesario traducir el primer elemento): *I am not ready either for a job or for the University = no estoy preparado ni para un empleo ni para la Universidad.*
ejaculate | ɪ'dʒækjʊleɪt | *v.t.* e *i.* **1** FISIOL. eyacular (semen). **2** (form.) exclamar, utilizar expletivos, proferir exclamaciones.
ejaculation | ɪˌdʒækjʊ'leɪʃn | *s.i.* **1** FISIOL. eyaculación (de semen). **2** (form.) exclamación.
eject | ɪ'dʒekt | *v.t.* **1** expeler, lanzar, expulsar: *they were laughing and were ejected from the classroom = se estaban riendo y les expulsaron de la clase.* **2** AER. lanzar, expeler (de un avión que se va a estrellar).
ejection | ɪ'dʒekʃn | *s.i.* **1** expulsión, acto de expeler, lanzamiento. **2** AER. expulsión (de un avión en peligro). || **3 – seat,** (EE.UU.) AER. asiento de lanzamiento, asiento proyectable.
ejector seat | ɪ'dʒektəsi:t | (brit.) V. **ejection 3.**
eke | i:k | **1 to – out,** estirar (el dinero u otro bien), complementar, suplir (algo de por sí escaso), hacer durar: *they eked out their supply of petrol = ellos hicieron durar su suministro de gasolina.* **2**

to – out a living/an existence, ganarse la vida a duras penas.

elaborate | ɪ'læbərɪt | *adj.* **1** elaborado, complicado, complejo, intricado. **2** ornado, muy trabajado (artísticamente). **3** detallado, esmerado (plan, método, preparación, etc.). || | ɪ'læbəreɪt | *v.t.* **4** detallar, explicar con detalle. **5** desarrollar con gran esmero, refinar (una teoría o similar). || *v.i.* **6 [to – on]** detallar, explicar con detalle.

elaborately | ɪ'læbərɪtlɪ | *adv.* **1** elaboradamente, complicadamente, complejamente, intrincadamente. **2** ornadamente, trabajadamente (algún objeto artístico). **3** detalladamente, esmeradamente (desarrollar un plan o similar).

elaborateness | ɪ'læbərətnɪs | *s.i.* **1** complejidad. **2** perfección, primor (en el arte). **3** esmero (en la elaboración de un proyecto o similar).

elaboration | ɪ,læbə'reɪʃn | *s.i.* **1** explicación detallada, desarrollo total. **2** refinamiento (de una teoría o similar). || *s.c.* **3** (generalmente *pl.*) detalle prolijo, adición excesiva, añadido innecesario.

élan | eɪ'lɑːn | | eɪ'læn | *s.i.* (lit.) brío; donaire.

eland | 'iːlənd | *s.c.* ZOOL. antílope (africano).

elapse | ɪ'læps | *v.i.* (form.) transcurrir (tiempo).

elastic | ɪ'læstɪk | *adj.* **1** elástico, flexible (físicamente). **2** (fig.) adaptable, flexible (ideas o similar). || *s.i.* **3** elástico (material). || **4 – band,** V. **rubber band.**

elasticated | ɪ'læstɪkeɪtɪd | *adj.* con elástico (ropa).

elasticity | ,elæ'stɪsɪtɪ | *s.i.* **1** elasticidad. **2** (fig.) flexibilidad, adaptabilidad (a nuevas circunstancias o situaciones).

elated | ɪ'leɪtɪd | *adj.* regocijado, alborozado, gozoso.

elatedly | ɪ'leɪtɪdlɪ | *adv.* regocijadamente, alborozadamente, gozosamente.

elation | ɪ'leɪʃn | *s.i.* júbilo, alborozo.

elbow | 'elbəʊ | *s.c.* **1** codo. **2** (fig.) codo, codillo, curvatura (en tuberías u otros objetos). || *v.t.* **3** utilizar los codos (por ejemplo, para abrirse camino): *I elbowed my way to the front = me abrí camino con los codos hasta la parte delantera.* || **4 at one's –,** a la mano, muy cerca, al lado. **5 to get the –,** (fam.) ser rechazado, mandado al cuerno. **6 to give someone the –,** dar esquinazo, dejar plantado, rechazar totalmente a alguien. **7 out at the elbows, a)** raído en los codos, desgastado en los codos. **b)** mal vestido (persona).

elbow-grease | 'elbəʊgriːz | *s.i.* (fam.) ahínco (en el trabajo manual).

elbow-room | 'elbəʊrʊm | *s.i.* (fam.) espacio libre; libertad de acción.

elder | 'eldər | *comp.irr.* **1** de **old.** || *adj.* **2** mayor: *my elder daughter = mi hija mayor.* || *s.c.* **3** mayor: *we must respect our elders = debemos respetar a nuestros mayores.* **4** REL. anciano venerable (en algunas iglesias). **5** BOT. saúco. || **6 – statesman, a)** estadista de prestigio, estadista ilustre, **b)** (fig.) jubilado de prestigio (en una empresa, institución, etc.).

elderberry | 'eldəbrɪ | *s.c.* **1** BOT. baya (de saúco). || **2 – wine,** vino de baya.

elderly | 'eldəlɪ | *adj.* **1** metido en años, mayor, de avanzada edad. **2** anticuado (un objeto). || **3 the –,** los mayores, los miembros de la tercera edad.

eldest | 'eldɪst | *super.irr.* **1** de **old.** || *adj.* **2** mayor (más viejo). || *s.sing.* **3** (fam.) el hijo mayor, la hija mayor.

eldorado | ,eldə'rɑːdəʊ | *s.c.* El Dorado, paraíso imaginario.

elect | ɪ'lekt | *v.t.* **1** elegir, escoger, seleccionar. || *v.i.* **2 [to – *inf.*]** (form.) apetecer, optar por: *I elected to leave before the end = opté por irme antes del final.* || *adj.* **3 [*s.* –]** electo: *the President elect = el Presidente electo.* || **4 the –,** los elegidos, los escogidos.

elected | ɪ'lektɪd | *adj.* elegido (por el pueblo).

election | ɪ'lekʃn | *s.c.* e *i.* **1** elección. || *s.sing.* **2** nombramiento, elección (normalmente a un puesto de carácter político).

electioneering | ɪ,lekʃə'nɪərɪŋ | *s.i.* POL. campaña electoral.

elective | ɪ'lektɪv | *adj.* **1** de elección democrática: *an elective post = un puesto de elección democrática.* **2** (EE.UU.) optativo, no obligatorio (estudio). || *s.c.* **3** (EE.UU.) materia optativa, asignatura optativa.

elector | ɪ'lektər | *s.c.* POL. elector.

electoral | ɪ'lektərəl | *adj.* **1** electoral. || **2 – register/roll,** lista de electores, lista de personas con derecho al voto, lista oficial de electores.

electorally | ɪ'lektərəlɪ | *adv.* electoralmente.

electorate | ɪ'lektərɪt | *s.c.* (generalmente *sing.*) electorado.

electric | ɪ'lektrɪk | *adj.* **1** eléctrico (producido o que produce electricidad). **2** (fig.) electrizante, excitante (situación, ambiente, etc.). || **3 – blanket,** manta eléctrica. **4 – chair,** silla eléctrica. **5 – eye,** FOT. célula fotoeléctrica. **6 – field,** FIS. campo eléctrico. **7 – razor,** máquina de afeitar eléctrica. **8 – shock,** sacudida eléctrica, choque eléctrico. **9 – storm,** tormenta eléctrica.

electrical | ɪ'lektrɪkl | *adj.* eléctrico (objeto, componente, sistema, etc.).

electrically | ɪ'lektrɪklɪ | *adv.* eléctricamente, desde el punto de vista de la electricidad.

electric-blue | ɪ'lektrɪkbluː | *adj.* **1** azul acero. || *s.i.* **2** color azul acero, azul acero.

electrician | ɪ,lek'trɪʃn | *s.c.* electricista.

electricity | ɪ,lek'trɪsɪtɪ | *s.i.* electricidad.

electrification | ɪ,lektrɪfɪ'keɪʃn | *s.i.* electrificación.

electrified | ɪ'lektrɪfaɪd | *adj.* electrificado (una valla, por ejemplo).

electrify | ɪ'lektrɪfaɪ | *v.t.* **1** electrificar, instalar la electricidad. **2** cargar con electricidad, suministrar corriente eléctrica (a una valla o similar). **3** (fig.) electrizar, exaltar (ánimos).

electrifying | ɪ'lektrɪfaɪɪŋ | *adj.* electrizante, excitante.

electro- | ɪ'lektrəʊ | *prefijo* **electro-:** *electrobiology.*

electrocardiogram | ɪ,lektrəʊ'kɑːdɪəʊgræm | *s.c.* MED. electrocardiograma.

electrocardiograph | ɪ,lektrəʊ'kɑːdɪəʊgrɑːf | *s.c.* MED. electrocardiógrafo.

electrochemistry | ɪ,lektrəʊ'kemɪstrɪ | *s.i.* electroquímica.

electrocute | ɪ'lektrəkjuːt | *v.t.* **1** electrocutar (matar con carga eléctrica). || *v.r.* **2** electrocutarse (accidentalmente).

electrocution | ɪ,lektrə'kjuːʃn | *s.i.* electrocución.

electrode | ɪ'lektrəʊd | *s.c.* ELEC. electrodo.

electroencephalogram | ɪ,lektrəʊen'sefələgræm | *s.c.* MED. electroencefalograma.

electroencephalograph | ɪ,lektrəʊen'sefələgrɑːf | (EE.UU. ɪ,lektrəʊen'sefələgræf | *s.c.* MED. electroencefalógrafo.

electrolysis | ,ɪlek'trɒlɪsɪs | *s.i.* **1** FIS. electrólisis. **2** electrólisis (método de depilación).

electrolyte | ɪ'lektrəlaɪt | *s.c.* FIS. electrólito.

electromagnet | ɪ,lektrəʊ'mægnɪt | *s.c.* FIS. electromagneto.

electromagnetic | ɪ,lektrəʊmæg'netɪk | *adj.* FIS. electromagnético.

electromagnetism | ɪ,lektrəʊ'mægnətɪzəm | *s.i.* FIS. electromagnetismo.

electron | ɪ'lektrɒn | *s.c.* **1** FIS. electrón. || **2 – microscope,** microscopio de electrones.

electronic | ,ɪlek'trɒnɪk | *adj.* **1** electrónico. || **2 – mail,** INF. trasvase de información por ordenador.

electronically | ,ɪlek'trɒnɪklɪ | *adv.* electrónicamente.

electronics | ,ɪlek'trɒnɪks | *s.i.* **1** electrónica. || *s.pl.* **2** objetos electrónicos, mecanismos electrónicos.

electroplate | ɪ'lektrəpleɪt | *v.t.* galvanizar (mediante galvanoplastia).

elegance | 'elɪgəns | *s.i.* elegancia.

elegant | 'elɪgənt | *adj.* **1** elegante. **2** refinado, bien meditado (plan, idea, etc.).

elegantly | 'elɪgəntlɪ | *adv.* **1** elegantemente. **2** refinadamente, con buena preparación (manera de idear un plan o similar).

elegiac | ,elɪ'dʒaɪək | *adj.* (lit.) elegíaco.

elegy | 'elədʒɪ | *s.c.* LIT. elegía.

element | 'elɪmənt | *s.c.* **1** elemento, componente, ingrediente. **2** elemento, característica, factor: *let's not forget the human element in our plans = no olvidemos el elemento humano en nuestros planes.* **3** QUIM. elemento. **4** ELEC. elemento, resistencia. **5** (normalmente *pl.*) elemento (persona o individuo). || *s.pl.* **6** puntos elementales, puntos básicos (de una asignatura o similar). **7 [the –]** (form.) los elementos (fenómenos atmosféricos naturales). || *s.sing.* e *i.* **8 [(an) – of]** partícula de, grano de, algo de (verdad, virtud, etc.): *there was an element of fear in his voice = había un algo de miedo en su voz.* || **9 in one's –,** en el elemento de uno. **10 out of one's –,** fuera del elemento de uno.

elemental | ˌelɪ'mentl | *adj.* (lit.) elemental, primario.

elementary | ˌelɪ'mentrɪ | *adj.* **1** elemental, básico (por ejemplo, en estudios). || **2 – particle,** FIS. partícula elemental. **3 – school,** (EE.UU.) escuela primaria (los 6 u 8 primeros años).

elephant | 'elɪfənt | *s.c.* **1** ZOOL. elefante. || **2 a white –,** V. **white. 3 elephants never forget,** los elefantes nunca olvidan, los elefantes tienen buena memoria.

elephantine | ˌelɪ'fæntaɪn | (EE.UU. | ˌelɪ'fæntiːn) *adj.* (desp.) torpe, pesado, torpón.

elephantiasis | ˌelɪfən'taɪəsɪs | *s.i.* MED. elefantiasis.

elevate | 'elɪveɪt | *v.t.* **1** elevar, empujar hacia arriba (físicamente). **2 [to – + *o.* + (to/into)]** elevar, alzar, ascender (a una posición oficial, estatus, etc.). **3** (fig.) ennoblecer, exaltar, elevar de temperatura moral/intelectual.

elevated | 'elɪveɪtɪd | *adj.* **1** elevado, a más alto nivel (físico). **2** elevado, ascendido (en la profesión, en categoría social, etc.). **3** (fig.) elevado, ennoblecido, exaltado. || **4 – railway/railroad,** (EE.UU.) ferrocarril elevado.

elevating | 'elɪveɪtɪŋ | *adj.* (form.) eminente, excelso, que ennoblece.

elevation | ˌelɪ'veɪʃn | *s.c.* **1** elevación, altura (física). **2** GEOL. elevación, altiplano, colina. **3** ARQ. alzado (de un edificio). || *s.sing.* **4 [– to]** ascenso a (mayor categoría profesional), nombramiento a (puesto). **5 [the – of]** (fig.) la elevación de, la exaltación de, el ennoblecimiento de. || **6 the Elevation,** REL. la Elevación.

elevator | 'elɪveɪtər | *s.c.* **1** (EE.UU.) ascensor. **2** montacargas, elevador (de cajas, etc. en un almacén o similar). **3** AER. timón de profundidad. **4** silo (para el grano).

eleven | ɪ'levn | *num.card.* **1** once. **2** DEP. once (de fútbol u otro deporte de once jugadores). || **3 eleven-,** de once (en compuestos): *an eleven-mile drive = un paseo de once millas en coche.*

eleven-plus | ɪˌlevn'plʌs | *s.sing.* (brit.) examen de ingreso (en el Bachillerato, ya no en uso).

eleventh | ɪ'levnθ | *num.ord.* **1** decimoprimero, onceavo. || *s.c.* **2** onceava parte. || **3 the – hour,** en el último momento, a ultimísima hora.

elevenses | ɪ'levnzɪz | *s.pl.* **[=N *v.sing.*]** (brit. y fam.) tentenpié, tapa, refrigerio (típico de la mitad de la mañana).

elf | elf | [*pl.* **elves**] *s.c.* LIT. elfo (figura imaginaria).

elfin | 'elfɪn | *adj.* **1** de duende, traviesillo. **2** mágico, encantador.

elfish | 'elfɪʃ | *adj.* de diablillo, de elfo, travieso.

elicit | ɪ'lɪsɪt | *v.t.* **1 [to – + *o.* + (from)]** provocar, producir, sacar (cualquier reacción): *his shouts elicited tears from her = sus gritos provocaron lágrimas en ella.* **2** (form.) sonsacar (información con preguntas inteligentes).

elide | ɪ'laɪd | *v.t.* FILOL. omitir, suprimir, no pronunciar (una letra o sonido).

eligibility | ˌelɪdʒə'bɪlɪtɪ | *s.i.* **1** elegibilidad, idoneidad (para ser elegido). **2** aceptabilidad, buen partido (para el matrimonio).

eligible | 'elɪdʒəbl | *adj.* **1 [– (for/*inf.*)]** idóneo, apto: *he's not eligible for the grant = no es apto para la beca.* **2** aceptable, de buen partido (para el matrimonio).

eliminate | ɪ'lɪmɪneɪt | *v.t.* **1** (form.) eliminar, erradicar, suprimir. **2** (fam.) eliminar, liquidar, quitar de enmedio (matando). **3** (form.) borrar, eliminar (de una competición).

elimination | ɪˌlɪmɪ'neɪʃn | *s.i.* **1** (form.) erradicación, supresión, eliminación. **2** (fam.) liquidación, eliminación (matando).

elision | ɪ'lɪʒn | *s.i.* FILOL. elisión, omisión.

elite | eɪ'liːt | *s.c.* **1** élite. || *adj.* **2** elitista, selecto.

elitism | eɪ'liːtɪzəm | *s.i.* (a menudo desp.) elitismo.

elitist | eɪ'liːtɪst | (a veces desp.) *s.c.* **1** elitista. || *adj.* **2** elitista, selectista.

elixir | ɪ'lɪksər | *s.c.* e *i.* **1 [– (of)]** elixir. **2** (normalmente *sing.*) (fig. y hum.) bebercio, combustible alcohólico, jarabito.

Elizabethan | ɪˌlɪzə'biːθən | *adj.* isabelino (referente al reinado de Isabel I).

elk | elk | [*pl.* **elk** o **elks**] *s.c.* ZOOL. alce.

ellipse | ɪ'lɪps | *s.c.* GEOM. elipse.

ellipsis | ɪ'lɪpsɪs | *s.c.* e *i.* FILOL. elipsis.

elliptic | ɪ'lɪptɪk | (también **elliptical**) *adj.* **1** GEOM. en forma de elipse. **2** LIT. lleno de elipsis.

elliptical | ɪ'lɪptɪkl | V. **elliptic.**

elliptically | ɪ'lɪptɪklɪ | *adv.* **1** GEOM. elípticamente, con forma de elipse. **2** LIT. elípticamente, con elipsis.

elm | elm | BOT. *s.c.* e *i.* **1** olmo. || **2 – tree,** olmo.

elocution | ˌelə'kjuːʃn | *s.i.* arte de hablar, declamación, locución.

elocutionary | ˌelə'kjuːʃənərɪ | (EE.UU. | ˌelə'kjuːʃənerɪ) *adj.* declamatorio.

elocutionist | ˌelə'kjuːʃənɪst | *s.c.* logopeda, experto en declamación, profesor de elocución.

elongate | 'iːlɒŋgeɪt | (EE.UU. | ɪ'lɔːŋgeɪt) *v.t.* e *i.* (form.) alargar(se).

elongated | 'iːlɒŋgeɪtɪd | | ɪ'lɔːŋgeɪtɪd | *adj.* (form.) alargado.

elongation | ˌiːlɒŋ'geɪʃn | | ɪˌlɔːŋ'geɪʃn | *s.c.* e *i.* (form.) alargamiento, prolongación.

elope | ɪ'ləʊp | *v.i.* **1** escaparse, evadirse, huir. **2 [to – with]** fugarse con (una mujer).

elopement | ɪ'ləʊpmənt | *s.c.* e *i.* huida, fuga (de dos amantes).

eloquence | 'eləkwəns | *s.i.* elocuencia, oratoria convincente.

eloquent | 'eləkwənt | *adj.* **1** elocuente; convincente. **2** (fig.) expresivo (en el rostro o de otra manera exterior).

eloquently | 'eləkwəntlɪ | *adv.* **1** elocuentemente; convincentemente. **2** expresivamente (de forma visible).

El Salvador | el'sælvədɔːr | *s.sing.* El Salvador.

else | els | *adv.* **1 [what/etc. –]** qué/etc. más, qué otra cosa: *what else do you want? = ¿qué otra cosa desea?* || **2 if nothing –,** por lo menos, a falta de otra cosa. **3 or –,** si no: **a)** *stop drinking or else I'll leave you = deja de beber, si no te dejaré.* **b)** o si no, o en otro caso, o quizá: *I think I drank coffee or else tea = me parece que bebí café o quizá té.* **c)** (fam.) o si no... (indicando amenaza): *shut up or else = cállate o si no...* OBS. Esta palabra adquiere diversas posibles traducciones detrás de términos que indiquen las siguientes matizaciones: **4** lugar: *I put the book somewhere else = puse el libro en algún otro sitio.* **5** modo: *how else am I going to learn German? = ¿de qué otra manera voy a aprender alemán?*

elsewhere | ˌels'weər | *adv.* en algún otro sitio, en otro sitio, a otro sitio: *I will go elsewhere if I am not welcomed here = iré a otro sitio si no soy bién recibido aquí.*

elucidate | ɪ'luːsɪdeɪt | *v.t.* (form.) elucidar, poner en claro.

elucidation | ɪˌluːsɪ'deɪʃn | *s.i.* (form.) elucidación, aclaración.

elude | ɪ'luːd | *v.t.* (form.) **1** eludir, esquivar, evitar (algo o alguien). **2** escapársele a uno, no entender, no comprender: *that type of mathematics eludes me = ese tipo de matemáticas se me escapa.*

elusive | ɪ'luːsɪv | *adj.* esquivo, escurridizo (difícil de entender, recordar, etc.): *that's an elusive answer = esa es una contestación esquiva.*

elusively | ɪ'luːsɪvlɪ | *adv.* esquivamente, escurridizamente.

elusiveness | ɪ'luːsɪvnɪs | *s.i.* esquivez.

elves | elvz | *pl.* de **elf.**

emaciated | ɪ'meɪʃɪeɪtɪd | *adj.* esquelético, en los huesos.

emaciation | ɪˌmeɪsɪ'eɪʃn | *s.i.* demacración.

emanate | 'eməneɪt | *v.i.* **1 [to – from]** (form.) brotar de, surgir de, proceder de (los pensamientos, los sentimientos, etc.). || *v.t.* **2** irradiar, emitir (deseos, ideas, pensamientos, etc.).

emanation | ˌemə'neɪʃn | *s.i.* (form.) emanación, efluvio.

emancipate | ɪ'mænsɪpeɪt | *v.t.* (form.) emancipar, libertar.

emancipation | ɪˌmænsɪ'peɪʃn | *s.i.* **[– (of)]** emancipación.

emasculate | ɪ'mæskjʊleɪt | *v.t.* (form.) **1** castrar. **2** (fig.) debilitar, enervar (quitando la fuerza).

emasculation | ɪˌmæskju'leɪʃn | *s.i.* (form.) **1** castración. **2** (fig.) debilitamiento, enervación.

embalm | ɪm'bɑːm | (EE.UU. | ɪm'bɑːlm *v.t.* **1** embalsamar. **2** perfumar, llenar de bálsamo.

embalmer | ɪm'bɑːmər | (EE.UU. | ɪm'bɑːlmə *s.c.* embalsamador.

embalmment | ɪm'bɑːmmənt | (EE.UU. | ɪm'bɑːlmmənt) *s.i.* embalsamamiento.

embankment | ɪm'bæŋkmənt | *s.c.* malecón, dique, terraplén (de protección de algún tipo).

embargo | ɪm'bɑːgəu | *s.c.* e *i.* **1** **[– (on)]** embargo. || *v.t.* **2** embargar. **3** requisar (especialmente en tiempo de guerra).

embark | ɪm'bɑːk | *v.i.* **1** embarcar, subir a un barco. || **2 to be embarked on,** estar embarcado en, estar metido en (alguna actividad o proyecto). **3 to – on,** embarcarse en, meterse en (una empresa, un proyecto, etc., especialmente cuando es difícil).

embarkation | ˌembɑː'keɪʃn | *s.c.* e *i.* embarque.

embarrass | ɪm'bærəs | *v.t.* **1** avergonzar, hacer enrojecer. **2** POL. poner en apuros (con un escándalo o similar). **3** turbar; desconcertar.

embarrassed | ɪm'bærəst | *adj.* **1** avergonzado, puesto en evidencia. **2** incómodo, desconcertado (actos).

embarrassing | ɪm'bærəsɪŋ | *adj.* vergonzoso, embarazoso; desconcertante: *an embarrassing situation = una situación embarazosa.*

embarrassingly | ɪm'bærəsɪŋlɪ | *adv.* vergonzosamente, embarazosamente; desconcertadamente.

embarrassment | ɪm'bærəsmənt | *s.i.* **1** **[– (at/of)]** vergüenza; turbación. **2** incomodidad, apuro (económico): desconcierto. || *s.c.* **3** POL. vergüenza, vergüenza política. || *s.sing.* **4** estorbo, impedimento (persona): *he's an embarrassment to his family = es un estorbo para su familia.* || **5 an – of riches,** un montón de cosas buenas, demasiada cantidad de cosas buenas.

embassy | 'embəsɪ | *s.c.* embajada.

embattled | ɪm'bætld | *adj.* **1** MIL. cercado, sitiado. **2** (fig.) rodeado de dificultades, asediado por los problemas: *the party has been embattled for years = el partido ha estado asediado por los problemas durante años.*

embed | ɪm'bed | [*ger.* **embedding,** *pret.* y *p.p.* **embedded**] *v.t.* **1** **[to – + *o.* + (in)]** incrustar, empotrar (un objeto en algún sitio o sustancia). || **2 to be embedded in,** estar enraizado en, estar profundamente asentado en (una persona o sociedad una costumbre o similar).

embellish | ɪm'belɪʃ | *v.t.* **1** **[to – + *o.* + (with)]** embellecer; ornamentar. **2** (fig.) exagerar, adornar (con detalles inventados).

embellished | ɪm'belɪʃt | *adj.* **1** embellecido; ornamentado. **2** (fig.) exagerado, adornado, embellecido (con detalles inventados).

embellishment | ɪm'belɪʃmənt | *s.c.* e *i.* **1** embellecimiento; ornamentación. || *s.c.* **2** (fig.) exageración (con detalles inventados).

ember | 'embər | *s.c.* (generalmente *pl.*) ascua, brasa, pavesa.

embezzle | ɪm'bezl | *v.t.* e *i.* malversar, apropiarse ilícitamente de (fondos, dinero, etc.).

embezzlement | ɪm'bezlmənt | *s.i.* malversación, desfalco (de dinero).

embezzler | ɪm'bezlər | *s.c.* malversador.

embitter | ɪm'bɪtər | *v.t.* amargar (carácter); envenenar (relaciones humanas).

embittered | ɪm'bɪtəd | *adj.* amargado.

embittering | ɪm'bɪtərɪŋ | *adj.* causante de amargura.

embitterment | ɪm'bɪtəmənt | *s.i.* (form.) amargura.

emblazon | ɪm'bleɪzən | *v.t.* adornar con, engalanar con (especialmente grabándolo en su superficie): *his shield was emblazoned with a bright sun = su escudo estaba adornado con un sol brillante.*

emblazonment | ɪm'bleɪzənmənt | *s.i.* engalanamiento, grabación de adorno, acción de blasonar.

emblem | 'embləm | *s.c.* **1** emblema, insignia (simbolizando algo). **2** (fig.) símbolo, signo (de una cualidad, virtud o parecido).

emblematic | ˌemblə'mætɪk | *adj.* (form.) emblemático, simbólico.

embody | ɪm'bɒdɪ | *v.t.* **1** encarnar, personificar. **2** incluir, comprender, englobar.

embodiment | ɪm'bɒdɪmənt | *s.sing.* personificación, encarnación.

embolden | ɪm'bəuldən | *v.t.* animar, envalentonar.

emboldened | ɪm'bəuldənd | *adj.* animado, envalentonado.

embolism | 'embəlɪzəm | *s.c.* MED. embolia.

embossed | ɪm'bɒst | | ɪm'bɔːst | *adj.* grabado en relieve, tallado en relieve, repujado.

embrace | ɪm'breɪs | *v.t.* e *i.* **1** abrazar, dar un abrazo. || *v.t.* **2** (fig.) abrazar, adoptar, aceptar (una fe, ideología, etc.). **3** abarcar, comprender, incluir: *this concept embraces all the possible colours = este concepto abarca todos los colores posibles.* || *s.c.* **4** abrazo.

embrasure | ɪm'breɪʒər | *s.c.* **1** tronera, cañonera, saetera (en una muralla o pared). **2** ARQ. alféizar; vano, hueco (para ventana o puerta).

embrocation | ˌembrə'keɪʃn | *s.i.* linimento.

embroider | ɪm'brɔɪdər | *v.t.* **1** bordar, recamar. **2** (fig.) embellecer (una historia o similar con añadidos imaginados). || *v.i.* **3** bordar, recamar. **4 [to – on]** embellecer, adornar (una historia con detalles imaginados).

embroidered | ɪm'brɔɪdəd | *adj.* **1** bordado, recamado. **2** (fig.) embellecido, adornado (con detalles imaginados).

embroidery | ɪm'brɔɪdərɪ | *s.c.* e *i.* **1** bordado, labor de bordado. **2** (fig.) adorno, añadidos innecesarios (a una historia, relato, anécdota, etc.).

embroil | ɪm'brɔɪl | *v.t.* **1** **[to – + *o.* + (with/in)]** embrollar, enredar (en un asunto desagradable): *I don't want to embroil you in my personal problems = no deseo embrollarte en mis problemas personales.* || **2 to get/become embroiled with,** mezclarse en, verse mezclado, involucrarse con (alguna persona).

embryo | 'embrɪəu | *s.c.* **1** BIOL. embrión. **2** (fig.) embrión, germen (un proyecto, plan o similar). || *adj.* **3** embrionario, en germen, en embrión. || **4 in –,** en embrión, en germen (planes o similar).

embryologist | ˌembrɪ'ɒlədʒɪst | *s.c.* embriólogo, experto en embriología.

embryology | ˌembrɪ'ɒlədʒɪ | *s.i.* embriología.

embryonic | ˌembrɪ'ɒnɪk | *adj.* (form.) embrionario (seres o planes).

emcee | ˌem'siː | *s.c.* **1** maestro de ceremonias (de un espectáculo artístico). || *v.t.* e *i.* **2** hacer de maestro de ceremonias; llevar (un espectáculo).

emend | ɪ'mend | *v.t.* enmendar, corregir (un escrito).

emendation | ˌiːmen'deɪʃn | *s.c.* e *i.* corrección, enmienda (en un escrito).

emerald | 'emərəld | *s.c.* **1** MIN. esmeralda. || *adj.* **2** esmeralda (color). || **3 – green,** esmeralda, verde esmeralda. **4 the Emerald Isle,** (fig.) Irlanda.

emerge | ɪ'mɜːdʒ | *v.i.* **1** **[to – (from/out of)]** surgir, emerger (de un lugar cerrado, del agua, etc.): *the problems only emerged later = los problemas sólo surgieron más tarde.* **2** surgir, aparecer (gradualmente): *banks emerged during the nineteenth century = los bancos aparecieron durante el siglo diecinueve.* **3 [to – from]** surgir de, salir de (un estado mental, una experiencia difícil o situaciones similares). **4 [to – that...]** salir a la luz que, resultar que: *it emerged that he was going out with different women = salió a la luz que él estaba saliendo con distintas mujeres.*

emergence | ɪ'mɜːdʒəns | *s.sing.* **[– (of)]** aparición, surgimiento.

emergency | ɪ'mɜːdʒənsɪ | *s.c.* **1** emergencia, urgencia, apuro, aprieto. || *adj.* **2** de emergencia, de urgencia: *emergency landing = aterrizaje de emergencia.* || **3 – services,** servicios de protección civil (bomberos, ambulancias, etc.).

emergent | ɪ'mɜːdʒənt | *adj.* (form.) **1** POL. que emerge, que aparece, naciente (en la escena mundial): *emergent countries = países que aparecen en la escena mundial.* **2** en proceso de aparición, cada vez más patente: *an emergent new ruling class = una clase dirigente nueva en proceso de aparición.*

emeritus | ɪ'merɪtəs | *adj.* **1** emérito, honorario (especialmente un profesor universitario jubilado). || **2 Emeritus,** emérito (como título o forma de respeto).

emery | 'emərɪ | *s.i.* **1** MIN. esmeril. || **2 – board,** lima (de uñas).

emery-paper | 'emərɪpeɪpər | *s.c.* e *i.* lija, papel de lija, papel de esmeril.

emetic | ɪ'metɪk | MED. *s.c.* **1** vomitivo. || *adj.* **2** vomitivo.

emigrant | 'emɪgrənt | *s.c.* emigrante, emigrado.

emigrate | 'emɪgreɪt | *v.i.* **[to – (to /from)]** emigrar, irse a vivir al extranjero; expatriarse.

emigration | ˌemɪ'greɪʃn | *s.i.* emigración.

émigré | 'emɪgreɪ | *s.c.* (form. o lit.) emigrado, expatriado.

eminence | 'emɪnəns | *s.i.* **1** altura, eminencia, importancia (normalmente de índole intelectual): *he rose to eminence when he was still a young man = él alcanzó gran eminencia cuando todavía era un hombre joven.* || **2 Your/His Eminence,** REL. Su Eminencia (forma de dirigirse a cardenales de la religión católica).

eminent | 'emɪnənt | *adj.* **1** eminente, importante, distinguido (especialmente referido al ejercicio profesional). **2** (form.) sobresaliente, notable (de cualidades personales): *a man of eminent goodness = un hombre de bondad sobresaliente.* || **3 – domain,** DER. derecho de expropiación.

eminently | 'emɪnəntlɪ | *adv.* (form.) notablemente, de manera sobresaliente, destacadamente.

emir | e'mɪər | (también **amir**) *s.c.* emir.

emirate | e'mɪəreɪt | *s.c.* emirato.

emissary | 'emɪsərɪ | *s.c.* (form.) emisario.

emission | ɪ'mɪʃn | *s.c.* e *i.* (form.) emisión, emanación, escape (de gas, líquido, luz, etc.).

emit | ɪ'mɪt | [*ger.* **emitting,** *pret.* y *p.p.* **emitted]** *v.t.* (form.) emitir, despedir (luz, sonidos, sustancias, etc.); dar (grito).

emitter | ɪ'mɪtər | *s.c.* RAD. emisor.

emollient | ɪ'mɒlɪənt | (form.) *adj.* **1** suavizante (crema). || *s.c.* **2** crema suavizante, emoliente.

emolument | ɪ'mɒljumənt | *s.c.* (normalmente *pl.*) (form.) emolumento, estipendio.

emotion | ɪ'məuʃn | *s.c.* e *i.* **1** emoción, sentimiento. || *s.i.* **2** emoción, pasión, sentimientos (en contraste con la razón).

emotional | ɪ'məuʃənl | *adj.* **1** emocional, del sentimiento. **2** cargada de emoción, emotiva (una situación). **3** impresionable, sensible, sentimental, emocional (característica personal). || **4 to be/get/become, etc. –,** dar rienda suelta a los sentimientos, no contener los sentimientos. **5 – life,** vida afectiva.

emotionalism | ɪ'məuʃənəlɪzəm | *s.i.* emocionalismo, sentimentalismo.

emotionally | ɪ'məuʃənəlɪ | *adv.* **1** emocionalmente, sentimentalmente. **2** emotivamente (de situaciones). **3** impresionablemente, sensiblemente, de manera sentimental, en lo que respecta a los sentimientos.

emotionless | ɪ'məuʃnlɪs | *adj.* sin emoción, sin sentimientos.

emotive | ɪ'məutɪv | *adj.* emotivo, lleno de emoción, conmovedor.

empanel | ɪm'pænl | (también **impanel**) *v.t.* (form.) DER. nombrar para un jurado.

empathize | 'empəθaɪz | (también **empathise**) *v.i.* **[to – (with)]** hacerse cargo; sentir una cierta empatía: *I can empathize with your feelings = puedo hacerme cargo de tus sentimientos.*

empathy | 'empəθɪ | *s.i.* empatía.

emperor | 'empərər | *s.c.* emperador.

emphases | 'emfəsiːz | *pl.* de **emphasis.**

emphasis | 'emfəsɪs | [*pl.* **emphases**] *s.c.* e *i.* **1** énfasis, acento, relieve. **2** GRAM. énfasis, intensidad.

emphasize | 'emfəsaɪz | (también **emphasise**) *v.t.* enfatizar, subrayar, poner el énfasis en.

emphatic | ɪm'fætɪk | *adj.* **1** tajante, lleno de énfasis, fuerte, categórico (cualidad personal, opinión, comentario, etc.). **2** enfático, acentuado (modo de hablar).

emphatically | ɪm'fætɪklɪ | *adv.* **1** enfáticamente, con mucho énfasis, fuertemente. **2** manifiestamente, evidentemente (enfatizando la evidencia de algo): *she is emphatically different from the others = ella es manifiestamente diferente de los otros.*

emphysema | ˌemfɪ'siːmə | *s.i.* MED. enfisema.

empire | 'empaɪər | *s.c.* **1** imperio. **2** (fig.) imperio, emporio (de índole comercial): *a building empire = un imperio inmobiliario.*

empirical | ɪm'pɪrɪkl | *adj.* empírico.

empirically | ɪm'pɪrɪklɪ | *adv.* empíricamente, de modo práctico.

empiricism | ɪm'pɪrɪsɪzəm | *s.i.* FIL. empirismo.

empiricist | ɪm'pɪrɪsɪst | *s.c.* FIL. empírico.

emplacement | ɪm'pleɪsmənt | *s.c.* MIL. emplazamiento, ubicación, posición (especialmente de un cañón pesado y fortificada).

employ | ɪm'plɔɪ | *v.t.* **1** dar trabajo a, dar empleo a, emplear. **2** (form.) usar, utilizar, emplear: *I employed all my time to do the job = utilicé todo mi tiempo para hacer la tarea.* || *s.i.* **3** (form.) servicio, empleo: *I left their employ two years ago = dejé su servicio hace dos años.* || **4 to be better employed, [=N** *ger.***]** valer más, ser más útil: *you would be better employed doing something else = serías más útil haciendo cualquier otra cosa.* **5 in someone's –,** (form.) al servicio de alguien.

employable | ɪm'plɔɪəbl | *adj.* **1** utilizable. **2** que puede ser empleado: *that man isn't really employable, he has a drink problem = ese hombre en realidad no puede ser empleado, tiene problemas con la bebida.*

employee | ˌemplɔɪ'iː | *s.c.* empleado, trabajador.

employer | ɪm'plɔɪər | *s.c.* patrono, empresario.

employment | ɪm'plɔɪmənt | *s.i.* **1** empleo, trabajo, ocupación, contratación. **2** uso, utilización, empleo: *the employment of chemical weapons = el uso de armas químicas.* || **3 – agency,** agencia de empleo, agencia de colocación.

emporia | ɪm'pɔːrɪə | V. **emporium.**

emporium | ɪm'pɔːrɪəm | [*pl.* **emporiums** o **emporia**] *s.c.* (form. o p.u.) **1** grandes almacenes. **2** (EE.UU.) bazar, tienda grande.

empower | ɪm'pauər | *v.t.* (form.) facultar, autorizar, permitir: *the new law empowers the local authorities to increase taxes 20% = la nueva ley faculta a las autoridades locales para elevar los impuestos un 20%.*

empress | 'emprɪs | *s.c.* emperatriz.

emptiness | 'emptɪnɪs | *s.i.* **1** vacío, espacio vacío: *the emptiness of the house unnerved her = el vacío de la casa le causó zozobra.* **2** (fig.) vacío, vacuidad, vaciedad (como sentimiento). || *s.c.* **3** (normalmente *sing.*) (lit.) extensión, paisaje (vacío); páramo (sin nada o nadie).

empty | 'emptɪ | *adj.* **1** vacío; desocupado: *an empty house = una casa vacía.* **2 [– of]** (a veces *form.*) sin: *our account is empty of money = nuestra cuenta está sin dinero.* **3** hueco, vano, inútil (palabras, gestos, vida, etc.). **4** vacío, sin palabras, sin nada dentro (sentimiento). || *v.t.* **5** vaciar, verter (el contenido de cualquier cosa). **6** vaciar, desalojar, echar afuera (porque no es lo suficientemente interesante): *his lectures emptied the hall = sus clases magistrales vaciaban el salón.* || *v.i.* **7** vaciarse, verterse. **8 [to – into]** desembocar en, desaguar en (ríos). || **9 empties,** botellas vacías. **10 on an – stomach,** con el estómago vacío, en un estómago vacío.

empty-handed | ˌemptɪ'hændɪd | *adj.* con las manos vacías; sin resultado positivo alguno.

empty-headed | ˌemptɪ'hedɪd | *adj.* cabeza de chorlito, frívolo, necio.

Empyrean | empɪ'riːən | *s.sing.* (lit.) firmamento.

emu | 'iːmjuː | *s.c.* ZOOL. emú (un tipo de avestruz australiana).

emulate | 'emjuleɪt | *v.t.* (form.) emular, imitar.

emulation | ˌemju'leɪʃn | *s.i.* emulación, imitación.

emulsifier | ɪ'mʌlsɪfaɪər | *s.c.* QUIM. emulsionador, sustancia emulsiva.

emulsify | ɪ'mʌlsɪfaɪ | *v.t.* e *i.* QUIM. emulsionar(se).

emulsion | ɪ'mʌlʃn | *s.c.* e *i.* FOT. emulsión. || *s.i.* **2** pintura mate. || *v.t.* **3** pintar con pintura mate. || **4 – paint,** pintura mate.

enable | ɪ'neɪbl | *v.t.* **1** permitir, capacitar, posibilitar: *this medicine will enable you to sleep = esta medicina le permitirá dormir.* **2** autorizar, permitir (como contrario de prohibir).

enabling | ɪ'neɪblɪŋ | *adj.* que conceda más derechos, que otorgue más autoridad: *enabling legislation.*

enact | ɪ'nækt | *v.t.* **1** DER. promulgar, sancionar, decretar. **2** (form.) representar, hacer (una obra de teatro, una historia, etc.).

enactment | ɪ'næktmənt | *s.c.* e *i.* **1** DER. promulgación (de una ley o equivalente). || *s.i.* **2** (form.) representación (de obra de teatro, historia, etc.).

enamel | ɪ'næml | (brit. **enamelling, enamelled;** EE.UU. **enameling, enamelled**) *v.t.* **1** esmaltar, pintar con esmalte. || *s.i.* **2** esmalte. **3** MED. esmalte (de la dentadura).

enamelled | ɪ'næmld | (EE.UU. **enameled**) *adj.* esmaltado.

enamoured | ɪ'næməd | (EE.UU. **enamored**) *adj.* (form.) **1 [– (of)]** fascinado, cautivado (con algún tema, arte, etc.). **2 [– (of)]** enamorado, prendado (de una persona).

en bloc | ˌɒn'blɒk | *adv.* en bloque, al unísono; todos juntos (tomado del francés).

encamp | ɪn'kæmp | *v.i.* (form.) acampar, fijar el campamento.

encampment | ɪn'kæmpmənt | *s.c.* (form.) campamento.

encapsulate | ɪn'kæpsjuleɪt | *v.t.* (form.) narrar de forma resumida, abarcar, incluir (en un pequeño comentario, símbolo, hecho, etc.): *the story encapsulates the fighting spirit of the Irish = la historia narra de forma resumida el espíritu de lucha de los irlandeses.*

encase | ɪn'keɪs | *v.t.* (form.) encerrar, revestir (un objeto otro objeto).

encephalitis | ˌensefə'laɪtɪs | *s.i.* MED. encefalitis.

encephalogram | ˌensefələ'græm | *s.c.* MED. encefalograma.

enchant | ɪn'tʃɑːnt | (EE.UU. | ɪn'tʃænt) *v.t.* **1** encantar, hechizar. **2** (fig.) encantar, deleitar.

enchanted | ɪn'tʃɑːntɪd | *adj.* **1** encantado, hechizado. **2** (fig.) deleitado, transportado de placer: *we were enchanted by the beautiful scenery = fuimos transportados de placer por el bellísimo paisaje.*

enchanter | ɪn'tʃɑːntər | *s.c.* hechicero, brujo, encantador.

enchanting | ɪn'tʃɑːntɪŋ | *adj.* encantador, fascinante.

enchantingly | ɪn'tʃɑːntɪŋlɪ | *adv.* encantadoramente, fascinantemente, de manera fascinante.

enchantment | ɪn'tʃɑːntmənt | *s.i.* **1** encanto, magia, embeleso, fascinación. || *s.c.* **2** hechizo, encantamiento.

enchantress | ɪn'tʃɑːntrɪs | *s.c.* **1** bruja, hechicera. **2** (fig.) seductora, vampiresa, hechicera.

encircle | ɪn'sɜːkl | *v.t.* **1** rodear, circundar, circunvalar. **2** MIL. envolver, poner cerco a.

encirclement | ɪn'sɜːklmənt | *s.i.* **1** circunvalación, rodeo. **2** MIL. envolvimiento, cerco.

enclave | 'enkleɪv | *s.c.* enclave; zona.

enclose | ɪn'kləuz | *v.t.* **1 [to – + *o.* + (in/with)]** cercar, encerrar. **2 [to – + *o.* + (in/with)]** adjuntar, incluir (dentro de un sobre).

enclosed | ɪn'kləuzd | *adj.* **1** cercado, encerrado. **2** adjuntado, incluido (dentro de un sobre). **3** (fig.) cerrado en sí mismo (una comunidad, existencia personal, etc.).

enclosure | ɪn'kləuʒər | *s.c.* **1** cercado, cercamiento, encerramiento. **2** documento adjunto, carta adjunta, anexo.

encode | ɪn'kəud | *v.t.* **1** codificar, poner en clave. **2** INF. poner en un determinado código (datos para su proceso).

encomia | ɪn'kəumɪə | V. **encomium.**

encomium | ɪn'kəumɪəm | [*pl.* **encomiums** o **encomia**] *s.c.* (form.) encomio, elogio.

encompass | ɪn'kʌmpəs | *v.t.* **1** cubrir totalmente, abarcar por entero (un espacio físico). **2** incluir, abarcar (un tema, actividad, etc.).

encore | 'ɒŋkɔː | *interj.* **1** otra vez, ¡bis! (en espectáculos cuando se quiere una actuación extra al final). || *s.c.* **2** repetición (de actuación). || *v.t.* **3** pedir una repetición de la actuación.

encounter | ɪn'kauntər | *v.t.* **1** (form.) encontrarse con, toparse con (alguien). **2** encontrar, tropezar con (dificultades, problemas, etc.). **3** experimentar, encontrar por primera vez en la vida: *the Apaches encountered Franciscan monks in the 18th century = los Apaches encontraron por primera vez en la vida monjes franciscanos en el siglo dieciocho.* || *s.c.* **4 [– (with)]** encuentro (inesperado o casual). **5 [– (with/between)]** encuentro, choque (con peligro). **6 [– (with)]** experiencia, encuentro (como experiencia primeriza).

encourage | ɪn'kʌrɪdʒ | *v.t.* **1 [to – + *o.* + *inf.*]** animar, alentar. **2** fomentar, estimular (una actividad).

encouraged | ɪn'kʌrɪdʒt | *adj.* animado, alentado, estimulado.

encouragement | ɪn'kʌrɪdʒmənt | *s.i.* ánimo, aliento, estímulo.

encouraging | ɪn'kʌrɪdʒɪŋ | *adj.* halagüeño, alentador, que anima.

encouragingly | ɪn'kʌrɪdʒɪŋlɪ | *adv.* halagüeñamente, alentadoramente.

encroach | ɪn'krəutʃ | *v.i.* (form.) **1 [to – on/upon]** invadir, usurpar (tierras, derechos, propiedades, etc.). **2 [to – on/upon]** ocupar, robar (tierra por algún agente geofísico): *the sea encroached on the land in Holland = el mar ocupaba tierra en Holanda.*

encroachment | ɪn'krəutʃmənt | *s.c.* e *i.* (form.) **1 [– (of/on/upon)]** invasión, usurpación (de tierras, derechos, propiedades, etc.). **2 [– (of/on/upon)]** ocupación (de tierra por algo).

encrust | ɪn'krʌst | *v.t.* e *i.* incrustar(se), cubrir(se) con incrustaciones.

encrustation | ənˌkrʌst'eɪʃn | *s.c.* e *i.* incrustación; capa (de alguna sustancia): *encrustations of lime in a teapot = capas de cal en una tetera.*

encrusted | ɪn'krʌstɪd | *adj.* **[– (with)]** incrustado (con algún adorno); cubierto (por algo): *the mountains in the distance incrusted with snow = las montañas a lo lejos cubiertas por la nieve.*

encumber | ɪn'kʌmbər | *v.t.* **1** recargar, sobrecargar; estorbar: *I can't encumber my husband with all the children while I go out shopping = yo no puedo estorbar a mi marido con todos los niños mientras me voy de compras.* **2** (fig. y desp.) abarrotar, sobrecargar (un espacio con cosas inútiles).

encumbrance | ɪn'kʌmbrəns | *s.c.* estorbo, impedimento.

encyclical | ɪn'sɪklɪkl | *s.c.* REL. encíclica.

encyclopedia | ɪnˌsaɪklə'piːdɪə | (también **encyclopaedia**) *s.c.* enciclopedia.

encyclopedic | ɪnˌsaɪklə'piːdɪk | (también **encyclopaedic**) *adj.* enciclopédico, comprehensivo, exhaustivo.

end | end | *s.sing.* **1** fin, final: *at the end of the month = al final del mes.* || *s.c.* **2** [normalmente *sing.* **(to/of)**] finalización, término, final: *an end to war = finalización de la guerra.* **3** objetivo, finalidad, propósito, fin. **4** extremo, punta: *to the other end of the street = a la otra punta de la calle.* **5** resto, sobrante (de algo usado cuando tiene forma alargada): *the burnt ends of cigarettes.* **6** aspecto, área (de un negocio o similar): *I'll take over the marketing end = yo me ocuparé del área de marketing.* **7** (lit. y euf.) muerte, fin. || *v.i.* **8** finalizar, terminar, acabar. **9 [to – with/in]** terminar en (hablando de objetos): *the sword ends in a very sharp point = la espada termina con una punta muy afilada.* **10 [to – (on/with)]** concluir, terminarse (discurso, escrito, obra de teatro, etc.). || *v.t.* **11** terminar, finalizar, acabar. **12** concluir (discurso, escrito, obra de teatro, etc.). || **13 a means to an –,** V. **means. 14 an – in itself,** un fin en sí mismo. **15 at an –,** finalizado, acabado. **16 at one's wits' –,** V. **wit. 17 at the – of one's tether,** V. **tether. 18 at the – of the day,** finalmente, después de todo. **19 to be at a loose —,** V. **loose. 20 to be at the – of,** tener agotado/a el/la (paciencia u otra virtud): *I'm at the end of my patience = tengo agotada la paciencia.* **21 to be on the receiving –,** V. **receive. 22 to be the –,** (fam. y brit.) ser el final, ser el colmo. **23 to burn the candle at both ends,** V. **candle. 24 to come to an –,** finalizar, terminar; cesar. **25 to – it all,**

(euf.) suicidarse. **26 to – up, a)** acabar, ir a parar: *he ended up in the army = él acabó en el ejército.* **b) [=N** *ger.***]** terminar, acabar (de una manera inesperada): *after the argument I ended up drinking in a bar = después de la pelea acabé bebiendo en un bar.* **27 from beginning to –,** de principio a fin, de cabo a rabo. **28 to get the wrong – of the stick,** V. **stick. 29 to go off the deep –,** V. **deep. 30 in at the deep –,** V. **deep. 31 in the –,** al final, finalmente, a la larga. **32 to keep/hold one's – up,** defenderse, no ceder cobardemente, cumplir con la parte de uno. **33 to make ends meet,** arreglárselas económicamente, hacer llegar el dinero. **34 to make one's hair stand on –,** V. **hair. 35 no –,** (fam.) un montón, muchísimo. **36 on –, a)** vertical, verticalmente, en vertical. **b)** de manera continuada, continuamente, sin parar. **37 to put an – to,** poner término a, acabar con: *I'm quite ready to put an end to this stupidity = estoy totalmente dispuesto a poner término a esta estupidez.* **38 the – justifies the means,** el fin justifica los medios. **39 the – of the road,** V. **road. 40 the – of the world,** el fin del mundo, un cataclismo, una tragedia: *failing a subject is not the end of the world = el suspender una asignatura no es el fin del mundo.* **41 the ends of the earth,** lejísimos, los confines de la tierra. **42 the thin – of the wedge,** V. **wedge. 43 to the bitter/very –,** hasta el final, hasta el fin: *we'll fight to the bitter end = lucharemos hasta el final.* **44 to the – of time,** hasta siempre, siempre, por siempre: *I'll love her to the end of time = la querré siempre.* **45 without –,** sin fin, sin final.

endanger | ɪn'deɪndʒər | *v.t.* poner en peligro, comprometer, hacer peligrar.

endangered | ɪn'deɪndʒəd | *adj.* en peligro (de extinción especialmente): *an endangered species = una especie en peligro.*

endear | ɪn'dɪər | *v.t.* **1** hacer querer, encariñar con: *her sweet ways have endeared her to me = su forma de comportarse tan delicada me ha encariñado con ella.*

endearing | ɪn'dɪərɪŋ | *adj.* cautivador, atractivo, atrayente.

endearingly | ɪn'dɪərɪŋlɪ | *adv.* cautivadoramente, atrayentemente; cariñosamente.

endearment | ɪn'dɪəmənt | *s.c.* e *i.* palabra cariñosa, término cariñoso: *he murmured endearments into her ear = murmuró palabras cariñosas en su oído.*

endeavour | ɪn'devər | (EE.UU. **endeavor**) (form.) *s.c.* **1** empeño, esfuerzo, tentativa. || *s.i.* **2** empeño, esfuerzo. || *v.i.* **3 [=N** *inf.***]** esforzarse por, procurar con esfuerzo: *I endeavoured o un-derstand but I couldn't = yo me esforcé por entender pero no pude.*

endemic | en'demɪk | *adj.* **[– (to/in)]** (form.) endémico.

ending | 'endɪŋ | *s.sing.* **1** final, finalización. || *s.c.* **2** final: *a happy ending = un final feliz.* **3** GRAM. terminación, desinencia (de una palabra). **4** terminación; extremo.

endive | 'endɪv | (EE.UU. | 'endaɪv) *s.c.* e *i.* BOT. **1** escarola. **2** (EE.UU.) achicoria.

endless | 'endlɪs | *adj.* interminable, sin fin, sin término (temporalmente o en extensión).

endlessly | 'endlɪslɪ | *adv.* interminablemente, sin parar, continuamente.

endocrine | 'endəkrɪn | FISIOL. *adj.* **1** endocrino. || **2 – gland,** glándula endocrina.

endorse | ɪn'dɔːs | *v.t.* **1** apoyar, aprobar (un plan o similar). **2** FIN. endosar, respaldar (un cheque). **3** marcar, confirmar, respaldar (un documento). **4** (brit.) señalar infracciones (en el carnet de conducir).

endorsement | ɪn'dɔːsmənt | *s.c.* e *i.* **1 [– (of)]** apoyo, aprobación (de un plan o similar). **2 [– (of)]** nota de inhabilitación (en un carnet de conducir). **3 [– (of)]** FIN. confirmación, respaldo (de cheque o equivalente).

endow | ɪn'daʊ | *v.t.* **1** donar, entregar una donación (normalmente una cantidad fija durante mucho tiempo). **2 [to – +** *o.* **+ with]** dotar de: *God has endowed her with beauty = Dios le ha dotado de belleza.*

endowment | ɪn'daʊmənt | *s.c.* **1** contribución económica, dotación a una fundación (o equivalente). **2** (form.) parte, dote (de inteligencia u otra cualidad). || **3 – policy,** póliza de seguro.

end-product | 'end prɒdʌkt | *s.c.* producto final.

end-result | 'endrɪzʌlt | *s.c.* resultado final.

endued | ɪn'djuːd | (EE.UU. | ɪn'duːd) *adj.* **[– with]** (form.) dotado de.

endurable | ɪn'djʊrəbl | *adj.* soportable, tolerable, que se puede aguantar.

endurance | ɪn'djʊərəns | *s.i.* aguante, resistencia; paciencia.

endure | ɪn'djʊər | *v.t.* **1** aguantar, resistir, sobrellevar. || *v.i.* **2** perdurar, aguantar el paso del tiempo.

enduring | ɪn'djʊərɪŋ | *adj.* perdurable, permanente, resistente.

enduringly | ɪn'djʊərɪŋlɪ | *adv.* perdurablemente, permanentemente, resistentemente.

endways | 'endweɪz | (también **endwise**) *adv.* **1** extremidad con extremidad. **2** con la parte trasera hacia delante.

endwise | 'endwaɪz | V. **endways.**

enema | 'enɪmə | *s.c.* MED. enema.

enemy | 'enɪmɪ | *s.c.* **1** enemigo, adversario, antagonista. **2** MIL. enemigo. **3 [– (of)]** (fig.) enemigo: *the enemy of science is ignorance = el enemigo de la ciencia es la ignorancia.*

energetic | ˌenə'dʒetɪk | *adj.* enérgico, vigoroso (persona o actividad).

energetically | ˌenə'dʒetɪklɪ | *adv.* enérgicamente, activamente, vigorosamente.

energize | 'enədʒaɪz | (también **energise**) *v.t.* **1** dar vigor a, dar energía a. **2** ELEC. energizar.

energy | 'enədʒɪ | *s.i.* **1** energía, vigor; fuerza. **2** vigor, tesón (como cualidad positiva). **3** energía (en forma de petróleo, carbón, etc.). || **4 energies,** energías, esfuerzos.

enervated | 'enəveɪtɪd | *adj.* debilitado, sin fuerzas, falto de vigor.

enervating | 'enəveɪtɪŋ | *adj.* debilitante; deprimente.

enfant terrible | ˌɒnfɒnte'riːbl | *s.c.* (lit.) enfant terrible.

enfeebled | ɪn'fiːbld | *adj.* debilitado (físicamente).

enfold | ɪn'fəʊld | *v.t.* (form.) **1 [to – +** *o.* **+ (in)]** abrazar, estrechar (entre los brazos). **2 [to – +** *o.* **+ (in)]** envolver, cubrir, rodear (totalmente): *fog enfolded me = el temor me envolvió.*

enforce | ɪn'fɔːs | *v.t.* **1** imponer, hacer valer (una ley, la autoridad, etc.). **2** exigir, demandar, forzar: *I'm going to enforce discipline here = voy a exigir disciplina aquí.*

enforceable | ɪn'fɔːsəbl | *adj.* **[– (by)]** exigible, que se puede hacer cumplir: *an enforceable contract.*

enforced | ɪn'fɔːst | *adj.* inevitable, obligado, forzoso: *enforced inactivity.*

enforcement | ɪn'fɔːsmənt | *s.i.* **[– (of)]** imposición (de una ley, modo de actuar, etc.); exigencia (de un comportamiento determinado o similar).

enfranchise | ɪn'fræntʃaɪz | *v.t.* (form.) **1** conceder derechos de sufragio. **2** libertar, dar la libertad (a esclavos).

enfranchisement | ɪn'fræntʃɪzmənt | *s.i.* (form.) **1** concesión del derecho de sufragio. **2** manumisión, liberación, puesta en libertad (a esclavos).

engage | ɪn'geɪdʒ | (form.) *v.i.* **1 [to – in/on/upon]** meterse en, participar en, ocuparse de (asuntos de cualquier tipo): *he's been engaged in politics for a year = lleva un año metido en política.* **2** MIL. entablar batalla, trabarse en combate. **3 [to – (with)]** MEC. encajar, acoplarse (piezas, mecanismos, etc.). || *v.t.* **4** captar, atraer (la atención, el interés, etc.); cautivar. **5** alquilar (servicios de alguien), contratar (a una persona). **6** MIL. entablar batalla con: *our forces engaged the enemy = nuestras fuerzas entablaron batalla con el enemigo.* **7** MEC. acoplar, hacer engranar. || **8 to — someone in conversation/gossip/etc.,** comenzar una conversación/murmuración con alguien.

engaged | ɪn'geɪdʒd | *adj.* **1 [– (to)]** prometido (para casarse). **2** ocupado (un servicio o similar). **3** comunicando (teléfono). **4** ocupado, comprometido, con otro compromiso: *I can't see you, I'm engaged somewhere else = no puedo verte, tengo un compromiso en otro sitio.*

engagement | ɪn'geɪdʒmənt | *s.c.* **1** compromiso (para casarse). **2** (form.) cita, compromiso. **3** obligación profesional, compromiso profesional: *my last engagement was in Paris = mi último compromiso profesional fue en París.* **4** tiempo de compromiso (para casarse). **5** MIL. acción militar, batalla. || *s.i.* **5** contratación, empleo: *the firm can't carry out the engagement of new workers = la empresa no puede llevar a cabo la contratación de nuevos trabajadores.* **6** MEC. acople, ajuste. || **7 – ring,** anillo de compromiso, anillo de prometida. **8 engagements,** (form.) FIN. compromisos financieros, deudas (especialmente cuando constan por escrito).

engaging | ɪn'geɪdʒɪŋ | *adj.* cautivador, atrayente, simpático (sólo para personas).

engagingly | ɪn'geɪdʒɪŋlɪ | *adv.* cautivadoramente, simpáticamente.

engender | ɪn'dʒendər | *v.t.* (form.) engendrar, causar, producir.

engine | 'endʒɪn | *s.c.* **1** motor (en cualquier tipo de ingenio mecánico). **2** locomotora, máquina (en trenes). **3** (arc. y fig.) maquinaria, instrumento mecánico: *engines of war = maquinaria de guerra.*

engine-driver | 'endʒɪndraɪvər | *s.c.* (brit.) conductor de tren, maquinista.

engineer | ˌendʒɪ'nɪər | *s.c.* **1** ingeniero. **2** especialista, trabajador especializado (especialmente en la rama eléctrica o electrónica). **3** (EE.UU.) conductor de tren, maquinista. || *v.t.* **4** construir, hacer (con conocimientos de ingeniería). **5** (fam.) fraguar, tramar, agenciarse (para propio provecho): *he engineered the firing of the two workers = él tramó el despido de los dos trabajadores.*

engineering | ˌendʒɪ'nɪərɪŋ | *s.i.* ingeniería (como asignatura y como trabajo o actividad).

English | 'ɪŋglɪʃ | *adj.* **1** inglés (idioma, cultura, etc.). || *s.i.* **2** inglés (idioma o asignatura). || **3 – breakfast,** desayuno inglés (fuerte y copioso). **4 in plain –,** en cristiano, con claridad, sin rodeos: *if you wanted to go out, why didn't you say so in plain English? = si querías salir, ¿por qué no lo dijiste con claridad?* **5 the –,** los ingleses (muchas veces erróneamente se incluye a los escoceses, galeses, irlandeses). **6 the – Channel,** GEOG. el Canal de la Mancha. **7 the Queen's/King's –,** el inglés correcto, el tipo de inglés más correcto.

Englishman | 'ɪŋglɪʃmən | [*pl.* **Englishmen**] *s.c.* **1** inglés. || **2 an Englishman's home is his castle,** la casa de un inglés es sagrada (proverbio que indica el gusto de los ingleses por su vida privada).

Englishwoman | 'ɪŋglɪʃwʊmən | [*pl.* **Englishwomen**] *s.c.* inglesa.

engrave | ɪn'greɪv | *v.t.* **1** grabar, burilar: *I want to engrave my father's name on the pipe = quiero grabar el nombre de mi padre en la pipa.* **2** (fig.) grabar, imprimir (en la mente, memoria o similar).

engraved | ɪn'greɪvd | *adj.* **1** grabado, burilado. **2** (fig.) grabado, impreso (en la mente, memoria o similar).

engraver | ɪn'greɪvər | *s.c.* grabador.

engraving | ɪn'greɪvɪŋ | *s.c.* **1** grabado, lámina grabada. || *s.i.* **2** grabación, método de grabación, arte de grabación.

engross | ɪn'grəʊs | *v.t.* **1** DER. redactar un documento con claridad, redactar un documento con letras grandes. **2** (normalmente en pasiva) absorber (la atención): *I was engrossed in my new book = estaba absorto en mi libro.*

engrossed | ɪn'grəʊst | *adj.* **[– (in)]** absorto, enfrascado.

engrossing | ɪn'grəʊsɪŋ | *adj.* absorbente, fascinante.

engulf | ɪn'gʌlf | *v.t.* **1** cubrir totalmente, sumir por completo (especialmente por el mar, las llamas, etc.). **2** (fig.) sumergir, sumir (en el silencio, oscuridad, ignorancia, etc.).

enhance | ɪn'hɑːns | (EE.UU. | ɪn'hæns) *v.t.* realzar, aumentar, mejorar (reputación, estatus, cualidades, etc. de personas o cosas).

enhancement | ɪn'hɑːnsmənt | *s.c.* e *i.* realce, aumento, mejora.

enigma | ɪ'nɪgmə | *s.c.* enigma, misterio.

enigmatic | ˌenɪg'mætɪk | *adj.* enigmático, misterioso.

enigmatically | ˌenɪg'mætɪklɪ | *adv.* enigmáticamente, misteriosamente.

enjoin | ɪn'dʒɔɪn | *v.t.* (form.) **1 [to – +** *o.* **+** *inf.***]** ordenar, prescribir (especialmente con autoridad). **2 [to – +** *o.* **+ (on/upon)]** imponer, mandar.

enjoy | ɪn'dʒɔɪ | *v.t.* **1** disfrutar de/con, pasarlo bien con, gozar de/con, gustar mucho: *enjoy the film = disfruta de la película.* **2 [to –** *ger.***]** disfrutar, gozar, pasarlo bien: *I enjoyed talking to him = lo pasé bien hablando con él.* **3** disfrutar de, gozar de (alto nivel de vida, privilegios, etc.). || *v.r.* **4** divertirse, pasarlo bien.

enjoyable | ɪn'dʒɔɪəbl | *adj.* divertido, grato, agradable.

enjoyably | ɪn'dʒɔɪəblɪ | *adv.* gratamente, agradablemente, con gran diversión.

enjoyment | ɪn'dʒɔɪmənt | *s.i.* **1** disfrute, goce. **2** uso, disfrute (de un buen nivel de vida, posición acomodada, etc.). || *s.c.* **3** disfrute, placer: *reading is one of my most cherished enjoyments = la lectura es uno de mis más queridos placeres.*

enkindle | ɪn'kɪndl | *v.t.* (form. y arc.) avivar, inflamar (pasiones o similar).

enlarge | ɪn'lɑːdʒ | *v.t.* **1** aumentar, agrandar, extender, hacer más grande. **2** FOT. ampliar. || *v.i.* **3** aumentarse, agrandarse, extenderse, hacerse más grande. || **4 to – on,** elaborar algo más, explicar con más detalle (algo que se ha dicho o escrito): *could you enlarge on that point? = ¿podrías elaborar algo más ese punto?*

enlargement | ɪn'lɑːdʒmənt | *s.c.* **1** FOT. ampliación. || *s.i.* **2** agrandamiento, aumento. || *s.sing.* **3 [the – of]** el aumento de, la expansión de, el agrandamiento de.

enlarger | ɪn'lɑːdʒər | *s.c.* FOT. ampliadora.

enlighten | ɪn'laɪtn | *v.t.* aclarar, esclarecer (ayudando a entender); ilustrar (cuestiones de cultura, información, conocimiento, etc.).

enlightened | ɪn'laɪtnd | *adj.* culto, civilizado, bien informado, sin prejuicios arcaicos.

enlightening | ɪn'laɪtnɪŋ | *adj.* aclaratorio, instructivo, con la información adecuada.

enlightenment | ɪn'laɪtnmənt | *s.i.* **1** cultura, ilustración, esclarecimiento. || **2 the Age of Enlightenment,** HIST. el Siglo de las Luces. **3 the Enlightenment,** HIST. la Ilustración.

enlist | ɪn'lɪst | *v.t.* **1** MIL. alistar, reclutar. **2** (fig.) conseguir, asegurarse (la cooperación, ayuda, etc. de alguien); reclutar (gente, normalmente para un trabajo). || *v.i.* **3 [to – (in/into)]** MIL. alistarse, enrolarse.

enlisted | ɪn'lɪstɪd | *adj.* (EE.UU.) MIL. enrolado, alistado.

enlistment | ɪn'lɪstmənt | *s.c.* e *i.* **1** MIL. alistamiento, reclutamiento. **2** (fig.) reclutamiento, contratación.

enliven | ɪn'laɪvn | *v.t.* animar, dar vida a, avivar (una fiesta, un acontecimiento, una reunión, etc.).

en masse | ˌɒn'mæs | *adv.* en masa, como un solo hombre (del francés).

enmeshed | ɪn'meʃt | *adj.* **[– (in)]** enredado, enmarañado (involuntariamente en una situación no deseada).

enmity | 'enmətɪ | *s.c.* e *i.* enemistad, hostilidad.

ennoble | ɪ'nəʊbl | *v.t.* (form.) **1** hacer noble, dar un título nobiliario. **2** (fig.) ennoblecer, elevar, dignificar.

ennoblement | ɪ'nəʊblmənt | *s.i.* (form.) **1** concesión de un título nobiliario. **2** (fig.) ennoblecimiento, dignificación.

ennui | ɒn'wiː | *s.i.* (lit.) tedio, fastidio, displicencia.

enormity | ɪ'nɔːmɪtɪ | *s.sing.* **1 [the – (of)]** la enormidad, la magnitud, la seriedad (de una situación, problema, etc.). || *s.i.* **2** monstruosidad, atrocidad (de un crimen o parecido). | **3 enormities,** (form.) monstruosidades, atrocidades.

enormous | ɪ'nɔːməs | *adj.* **1** enorme, inmenso, descomunal, desmesurado. || *int.* **2** enorme (intensificando la extensión o gran tamaño de algo o de algún sentimiento): *an enormous pleasure = un placer enorme.*

enormously | ɪ'nɔːməslɪ | *adv.* enormemente, inmensamente, descomunalmente, desmesuradamente.

enough | ɪ'nʌf | *adv.* **1** bastante, suficiente, suficientemente: *this is enough, I don't want any more = esto es suficiente, no quiero más.* **2 [***adj.* **–]** suficientemente, lo suficientemente: *is my explanation clear enough? = ¿es mi* *explicación lo suficientemente clara?* || *adj.* **3** suficiente, bastante: *have you get enough money? = ¿tiene Vd. suficiente dinero?* **4** **[***s.* **–]** (form.) suficientemente, lo bastante: *he's man enough to fight you = él es lo bastante hombre para pelear contigo.* || *pron.* **5** **[– (of)]** suficiente, bastante: *I've eaten enough of the meat, you have the rest = he comido suficiente carne, come tú el resto.* **6** **[– of]** suficiente, bastante (con matiz negativo): *I've seen enough of you, go! = ya te he visto bastante, ¡vete!* || **7 – is –,** vale ya, no más, ya es suficiente. **8 – said,** ya no hay que decir más, no digamos más. **9 fair –,** V. **fair.** **10 to have had – (of),** ya estoy hasta la coronilla (de), estoy harto (de). **11 oddly –/strangely –/funnily –/interestingly –/etc.,** curiosamente, extrañamente (matiza una información o comentario intensificando un poco). **12 sure –,** V. **sure.** **13 that's –,** ya vale, eso es suficiente (especialmente con un niño).

en passant | ˌɒn'pæsɒn | *adv.* (lit.) de pasada, de paso (origen francés).

enquire V. **inquire.**

enquirer V. **inquirer.**

enquiry V. **inquiry.**

enrage | ɪn'reɪdʒ | *v.t.* enfurecer, encolerizar.

enraged | ɪn'reɪdʒt | *adj.* enfurecido, encolerizado.

enraptured | ɪn'ræptʃəd | *adj.* (lit.) arrobado, embelesado, extasiado.

enrich | ɪn'rɪtʃ | *v.t.* **1** enriquecer. **2** **[to – +** *o.* **+ (with)]** (fig.) enriquecer, mejorar, embellecer: *enrich this soil with fertilizer = enriquece esta tierra con fertilizante.*

enriched | ɪn'rɪtʃt | *adj.* enriquecido (con vitaminas o alguna cosa buena).

enrichment | ɪn'rɪtʃmənt | *s.i.* enriquecimiento, mejora, aumento de calidad.

enrol | ɪn'rəʊl | (EE.UU. **enroll**) *v.t.* e *i.* apuntar(se), inscribir(se), matricular(se).

enrolment | ɪn'rəʊlmənt | *s.i.* **1** matriculación, inscripción. **2** matrícula (número de personas matriculadas).

en route | ˌɒn'ruːt | *adv.* en el camino, en la ruta (origen francés).

ensconce | ɪn'skɒns | *v.r.* **[to – (in/at)]** (form.) acomodarse, asentarse, situarse.

ensemble | ɒn'sɒmbl | *s.c.* **1** grupo, conjunto, colectividad. **2** conjunto, combinación (de vestir): *she was wearing a lovely ensemble = ella llevaba un conjunto precioso.* **3** MUS. grupo musical, conjunto musical.

enshrine | ɪn'ʃraɪn | *v.t.* (form.) venerar, establecer como principio fundamental: *our constitution enshrines the right to life = nuestra constitución establece el derecho a la vida.*

enshroud | ɪn'ʃraʊd | *v.t.* (form. y lit.) ocultar, tapar totalmente, velar.

ensign | 'ensən | *s.c.* **1** enseña, pabellón, bandera, insignia. **2** (EE.UU.) alférez de navío. **3** (brit.) portaestandarte (cargo de rango de oficial en el siglo pasado).

enslave | ɪn'sleɪv | *v.t.* **1** esclavizar, convertir en un esclavo. **2** (fig.) dominar, esclavizar: *drugs enslave many young people today = las drogas dominan a muchos jóvenes hoy.*

enslavement | ɪn'sleɪvmənt | *s.i.* **1** esclavitud. **2** **[– (to)]** (fig.) dominio, esclavitud, servidumbre.

ensnare | ɪn'sneər | *v.t.* **1** atrapar (a un animal). **2** (fig.) seducir, engañar.

ensue | ɪn'sjuː | (EE.UU. | ɪn'suː) *v.i.* **[to – (from)]** resultar, seguirse, sobrevenir, tener lugar a continuación: *a discussion ensued = a continuación tuvo lugar un debate.*

ensuing | ɪn'sjuːɪŋ | *adj.* resultante, siguiente.

en suite | ˌɒn'swiːt | *adv.* en conjunto, unido (expresión de origen francés).

ensure | ɪn'ʃɔːr | (EE.UU. **insure**) *v.t.* **[to – (that/***o.***)]** asegurar, garantizar: *this new lock ensures that the place will be safe = este candado garantiza que el lugar estará a salvo.*

entail | ɪn'teɪl | *v.t.* **1** significar, conllevar, acarrear. **2** DER. vincular, sujetar a vínculo (bienes, propiedades, etc.). || *s.c.* e *i.* **3** DER. vínculo, sujeción a vínculo (de bienes, propiedades, etc.).

entangle | ɪn'tæŋgl | *v.t.* **1** enredar, enmarañar (una cuerda, cordón, etc.). || **2 to be entangled in,** (fig.) estar embrollado en (problemas, crisis, situaciones difíciles). **3 to be entangled with,** (fig.) estar enredado con, estar mezclado con (personas de otro sexo, criminales, etc.).

entanglement | ɪn'tæŋglmənt | *s.i.* **1** enredo, enmarañamiento. || *s.c.* **2** (normalmente *pl.*) enredo, embrollo (en problemas de cualquier tipo). || **3 entanglements,** MIL. alambradas.

entente | ɒn'tɒnt | *s.c.* e *i.* **1** convenio, pacto. **2** alianza (de países). || **3 – cordiale,** entendimiento cordial, entente cordial (entre países).

enter | 'entər | (form.) *v.t.* **1** entrar en, introducirse en, penetrar en. **2** entrar en, unirse a (una organización, institución o similar). **3** participar en, registrarse en (un acontecimiento deportivo, examen o similar). **4** registrar, apuntar, anotar (en un libro de contabilidad, diario, etc.). **5** (fig.) entrar en, meterse en, introducirse (en la voz, en la vida, etc.). || *v.i.* **6** entrar en escena (en el teatro). || **7 to – a protest/plea/etc.,** formular una protesta/petición de gracia/etc. **8 to – for,** apuntar(se), inscribir(se) (en una carrera, competición o similar). **9 to – into, a)** participar en, meterse en, entrar en (algo problemático y largo): *we'll enter into fresh high level conversations = entraremos en nuevas conversaciones de alto nivel.* **b)** afectar, entrar en, tener que ver con (señalando un factor necesario en algo): *money considerations don't enter into my decision at all = las consideraciones monetarias no afectan en absoluto mi decisión.* **10 to – one's head,** pasársele a uno por la cabeza, ocurrírsele a uno. **11 to – the lists,** V. **list.** **12 to – upon, a)** embarcarse en, emprender (un proyecto, plan, etc.): *we're going to enter upon a partnership with them = vamos a embarcarnos en un proyecto común con ellos.* **b)** DER. tomar posesión de, hacerse cargo de (una herencia u otra obligación legal).

enteric | en'terɪk | *adj.* MED. entérico, intestinal.

enteritis | ˌentə'raɪtɪs | *s.i.* MED. enteritis, inflamación intestinal.

enterprise | 'entəpraɪz | *s.c.* **1** empresa, proyecto, aventura (especialmente nuevo y difícil): *my new enterprise = mi proyecto nuevo.* **2** empresa, negocio, compañía. || *s.i.* **3** iniciativa, resolución, empuje (cualidades positivas). **4** empresa, espíritu de empresa (en el sentido comercial).

enterprising | 'entəpraɪzɪŋ | *adj.* emprendedor, acometedor; decidido.

enterprisingly | 'entəpraɪzɪŋlɪ | *adv.* con espíritu emprendedor, con ánimo emprendedor; decididamente.

entertain | ˌentə'teɪn | *v.t.* **1** agasajar; invitar a casa (a comer, una copa o similar). **2** divertir, hacer pasarlo bien; distraer (con un espectáculo agradable). **3** (fig.) abrigar, acariciar (ideas, proyectos, sueños, etc.): *going abroad is a dream I've always entertained = salir al extranjero es un sueño que siempre he acariciado.* **4** (form.) considerar, estudiar, plantearse: *I refuse to entertain that stupid idea = me niego a considerar esa idea estúpida.* || *v.i.* **5** dar fiestas (en la casa propia), recibir invitados (con gusto). **6** divertir, hacer pasarlo bien; distraer (con un espectáculo agradable).

entertainer | ˌentə'teɪnər | *s.c.* anfitrión, animador, director de un espectáculo.

entertaining | ˌentə'teɪnɪŋ | *adj.* entretenido, divertido, gracioso.

entertainingly | ˌentə'teɪnɪŋlɪ | *adv.* entretenidamente, divertidamente, con mucha gracia.

entertainment | ˌentə'teɪnmənt | *s.i.* **1** diversión, entretenimiento. || *s.c.* **2** espectáculo (de cine, teatro, etc.).

enthral | ɪn'θrɔːl | (EE.UU. **enthrall**) *v.t.* cautivar, hechizar, encantar: *his speech enthralled me = su discurso me cautivó.*

enthralling | ɪn'θrɔːlɪŋ | *adj.* cautivador, encantador: *an enthralling look = una mirada cautivadora.*

enthralment | ɪn'θrɔːlmənt | (EE.UU. **enthrallment**) *s.i.* hechizo, encantamiento, subyugación.

enthrone | ɪn'θrəʊn | *v.t.* (form.) **1** entronizar (a un rey o similar). **2** (fig.) entronizar, dar prominencia (a una idea).

enthronement | ɪn'θrəʊnmənt | *s.c.* (form.) **1** entronización. || *s.sing.* **2** (fig.) entronización, prominencia, elevación.

enthuse | ɪn'θjuːz | *v.i.* **1** **[to – over/about]** entusiasmarse por, volverse loco

por (en sentido muy positivo). **2** decir con entusiasmo, decir animadamente: *I've passed, he enthused = he aprobado, dijo él con entusiasmo.* || *v.t.* **3** entusiasmar, animar en gran manera.
enthusiasm | ɪn'θjuːzɪæzəm | *s.c.* e *i.* **1** **[– (for)]** entusiasmo. || *s.c.* **2** pasión, entusiasmo, interés sumo.
enthusiast | ɪn'θjuːzɪæst | *s.c.* entusiasta, apasionado.
enthusiastic | ɪn,θjuːzɪ'æstɪk | *adj.* entusiasmado, lleno de entusiasmo, entusiasta.
enthusiastically | ɪn,θjuːzɪ'æstɪklɪ | *adv.* de manera entusiasta, con gran entusiasmo.
entice | ɪn'taɪs | *v.t.* seducir, engatusar, atraer con engaño, tentar.
enticement | ɪn'taɪsmənt | *s.c.* e *i.* tentación, seducción, engatusamiento.
enticing | ɪn'taɪsɪŋ | *adj.* tentador, seductor, engatusador.
enticingly | ɪn'taɪsɪŋlɪ | *adv.* tentadoramente, seductoramente, incitadoramente.
entire | ɪn'taɪər | *adj.* entero, completo, todo (en el espacio y tiempo).
entirely | ɪn'taɪəlɪ | *adv.* **1** exclusivamente: *the school is attended entirely by black children = la escuela es frecuentada exclusivamente por chicos negros.* **2** enteramente, totalmente, completamente (en el espacio y tiempo).
entirety | ɪn'taɪərətɪ | **in its –,** íntegramente, enteramente, en su totalidad.
entitle | ɪn'taɪtl | *v.t.* **1** (normalmente pasiva) titular. **2** habilitar, autorizar, acreditar, permitir: *this law entitles me to act as your father = esta ley me autoriza a actuar como tu padre.*
entitlement | ɪn'taɪtlmənt | *s.c.* e *i.* (form.) autorización, permiso, derecho.
entity | 'entɪtɪ | *s.c.* e *i.* **1** (form.) entidad, ente. **2** FIL. entidad (del ser).
entomb | ɪn'tuːm | *v.t.* (form.) sepultar, enterrar (en sentido real y figurado).
entombment | ɪn'tuːmmənt | *s.i.* (form.) enterramiento.
entomological | ,entəmə'lɒdʒɪkl | *adj.* entomológico.
entomologist | ,entə'mɒlədʒɪst | *s.c.* entomólogo.
entomology | ,entə'mɒlədʒɪ | *s.i.* entomología.
entourage | ,ɒntʊ'rɑːʒ | *s.c.* cortejo, séquito, acompañantes.
entrails | 'entreɪlz | *s.pl.* entrañas, tripas, vísceras.
entrance | 'entrəns | *s.c.* **1** **[– (to/into/of)]** entrada, acceso. **2** entrada, llegada (de una persona en un sitio). **3** ART. entrada en escena, aparición en escena, salida a escena (en el teatro). || *s.i.* **4** **[– (to/into)]** entrada, acceso: *you gain entrance to the building through the back = se accede al edificio por la parte posterior.* **5** **[– (to/into)]** admisión, ingreso (en una profesión, asociación, puesto político, lugar académico, etc.). || | ɪn'trɑːns, (EE.UU. | ɪn'træns) *v.t.* **6** [normalmente *pas.*] fascinar, encantar. || **7 – fee,** cuota de entrada, pago de ingreso, billete (de entrada en espectáculo), derechos de admisión.
entranced | ɪn'trɑːnst | *adj.* fascinado, encantado.
entrancing | ɪn'trɑːnsɪŋ | *adj.* fascinante.
entrant | 'entrənt | *s.c.* **1** persona recién ingresada, ingreso, miembro nuevo (en una asociación, universidad, etc.). **2** concursante (en cualquier tipo de concurso).
entrap | ɪn'træp | [*ger.* **entrapping,** *pret.* y *p.p.* **entrapped**] *v.t.* (form.) atrapar, hacer caer en una trampa; engañar.
entrapment | ɪn'træpmənt | *s.c.* e *i.* (form.) DER. arresto ilegal (realizado utilizando algún tipo de trampa no admitida por los jueces).
entreat | ɪn'triːt | *v.t.* **[to – + *o.* + (*inf.*)]** (form.) implorar, suplicar.
entreating | ɪn'triːtɪŋ | *adj.* suplicante, implorante.
entreatingly | ɪn'triːtɪŋlɪ | *adv.* en actitud de súplica.
entreaty | ɪn'triːtɪ | *s.c.* e *i.* (form.) súplica.
entrée | 'ɒntreɪ | (form.) *s.sing.* **1** entrada, admisión (en círculos de clase alta, en la casa de alguien, etc.). || *s.c.* **2** GAST. plato principal, plato más importante (de una comida).
entrench | ɪn'trentʃ | *v.t.* **1** (normalmente pasiva) MIL. atrincherar, fortalecer. **2** (fig.) fortalecer, afianzar (la posición de uno en una empresa, institución, etc.).
entrenched | ɪn'trentʃt | *adj.* fortalecido, afianzado; enraizado, arraigado.
entrenchment | ɪn'trentʃmənt | *s.c.* MIL. trinchera, atrincheramiento.
entrepreneur | ,ɒntrəprə'nɜːr | *s.c.* empresario, hombre de negocios.
entrepreneurial | ,ɒntrəprə'nɜːrɪəl | *adj.* empresarial, con iniciativa empresarial.
entropy | 'entrəpɪ | *s.i.* (form.) entropía; caos, desorden.
entrust | ɪn'trʌst | *v.t.* **[to – + *o.* + to /with]** confiar, encomendar, encargar: *I entrusted my wife with the message = confié a mi mujer el encargo.*
entry | 'entrɪ | *s.c.* **1** entrada (físicamente hablando). **2** llegada, entrada (de alguien). **3** anotación (en un diario o similar). **4** COM. asiento (de contabilidad). **5** INF. dato. **6** FILOL. entrada, artículo (en diccionario o enciclopedia). **7** participante, participación (persona o cosa que entran en un concurso o competición). || *s.sing.* **8** lista total de participantes (en competición); lista de miembros nuevos (en institución académica o similar). || *s.i.* **9** acceso, admisión, entrada (física). **10** admisión, ingreso (en asociación, institución, etc.). **11** participación, registro de participación (en competición o similar). **12** INF. input. || **13 – fee,** cuota de ingreso, derechos de admisión, billete (para espectáculos). **14 no –,** prohibida la entrada.
entryism | 'entrɪɪzəm | *s.i.* POL. submarinismo, entrismo (en un partido para controlarlo).
entwine | ɪn'twaɪn | *v.t.* e *i.* entrelazar(se) (los dedos, por ejemplo).
enumerate | ɪ'njuːməreɪt | *v.t.* enumerar, contar.
enumeration | ɪ,njuːmə'reɪʃn | *s.i.* enumeración.
enunciate | ɪ'nʌnsɪeɪt | (form.) *v.t.* **1** pronunciar, articular la pronunciación de. **2** expresar, proclamar (pensamientos, principios, etc.): *I always try to enunciate my opinions in the clearest way possible = siempre intento expresar mis opiniones en la forma más clara posible.* || *v.i.* **3** pronunciar, articular (sonidos), tener una dicción (buena, mala, etc.): *my teacher enunciates extremely well = mi profesor tiene una dicción magnífica.*
enunciation | ɪ,nʌnsɪ'eɪʃn | *s.i.* **1** pronunciación, dicción, articulación (de sonidos). **2** expresión, proclamación (de principios, intenciones, etc.).
envelop | ɪn'veləp | *v.t.* envolver, cubrir, rodear (real y figurativamente): *the mist enveloped the mountains = la neblina envolvía las montañas.*
envelope | 'envələʊp | *s.c.* sobre (para cartas).
envelopment | ɪn'veləpmənt | *s.i.* envolvimiento.
enviable | 'envɪabl | *adj.* envidiable, magnífico.
enviably | 'envɪəblɪ | *adv.* envidiablemente, magníficamente.
envious | 'envɪəs | *adj.* envidioso.
enviously | 'envɪəslɪ | *adv.* envidiosamente, con envidia.
environment | ɪn'vaɪərənmənt | *s.sing.* **1** **[the –]** el medio ambiente, el ambiente (natural). || *s.c.* e *i.* **2** ambiente, circunstancia, medio (de una persona). || *s.c.* **3** BIOL. hábitat, medio, medio ambiente (de una especie biológica).
environmental | ɪn,vaɪərən'mentl | *adj.* ambiental.
environmentally | ɪn,vaɪərən'mentəlɪ | *adv.* ambientalmente.
environmentalist | ɪn,vaɪərən'mentəlɪst | *s.c.* **1** persona que quiere proteger el medio ambiente. || *adj.* **2** de protección del medio ambiente: *an environmentalist attitude = una actitud de protección del medio ambiente.*
environs | ɪn'vaɪərənz | *s.pl.* (form.) alrededores, zonas próximas.
envisage | ɪn'vɪzɪdʒ | (EE.UU. **envision**) *v.t.* concebir, imaginar.
envision | ɪn'vɪʒən | V. **envisage.**
envoy | 'envɔɪ | *s.c.* **1** mensajero, enviado. **2** POL. representante diplomático (con rango inferior al de embajador).
envy | 'envɪ | *s.i.* **1** envidia. || *v.t.* **2** envidiar, tener envidia de, sentir envidia por. || **3 to be the – of,** ser la envidia de: *my new washing-machine is the envy of all my neighbours = mi lavadora nueva es la envidia de todos mis vecinos.* **4** **green with –,** V. **green.**

enzyme | 'enzaɪm | *s.c.* BIOQ. enzima.
eon V. **aeon.**
EP | ˌiː'piː | *s.c.* single, disco de corta duración (Extended Play).
epaulet | 'pəlet | (también **epaulette**) *s.c.* charretera.
epaulette, V. **epaulet.**
épée | 'eɪpeɪ | *s.c.* DEP. espada (usada en la esgrima).
ephemera | ɪ'femərə | *s.pl.* cosas efímeras. ephemeral | ɪ'femərəl | *adj.* (lit.) efímero, transitorio.
epic | 'epɪk | *s.c.* **1** LIT. épica. || *adj.* **2** (fig.) épico, grandioso.
epicenter V. **epicentre.**
epicentre | 'epɪsentər | (EE.UU. **epicenter**) *s.c.* GEOL. epicentro (de un terremoto).
epicure | 'epɪkjʊər | *s.c.* **1** FIL. epicúreo. **2** (fig.) gurmet, amante de la buena mesa.
epicurean | ˌepɪkjʊ'riːən | *adj.* lujoso, placentero (comida, fiesta, etc.).
epidemic | ˌepɪ'demɪk | *s.c.* **1** MED. epidemia. **2** (fig.) epidemia, ola (algo que a todo el mundo le da por hacer).
epidermis | ˌepɪ'dɜːmɪs | *s.sing.* ANAT. epidermis.
epidural | ˌepɪ'djʊərəl | MED. *s.c.* **1** epidural (tipo de anestesia mediante inyección en la espina dorsal). || *adj.* **2** epidural.
epiglottides | ˌepɪ'glɒtɪdiːz | *pl.* de **epiglottis.**
epiglottis | ˌepɪ'glɒtɪs | [*pl.* **epiglottides** o **epiglottises**] *s.c.* ANAT. epiglotis.
epigram | 'epɪgræm | *s.c.* LIT. epigrama (poema corto).
epigrammatic | ˌepɪgrə'mætɪk | *adj.* epigramático, corto e ingenioso.
epigraph | 'epɪgræf | *s.c.* epígrafe.
epilepsy | 'epɪlepsɪ | *s.i.* MED. epilepsia.
epileptic | 'epɪ'leptɪk | MED. *adj.* **1** epiléptico. || *s.c.* **2** epiléptico (persona).
epilog | 'epɪlɔːg | V. **epilogue.**
epilogue | 'epɪlɒg | (EE.UU. **epilog**) *s.c.* LIT. epílogo.
Epiphany | ɪ'pɪfənɪ | *s.sing.* REL. Epifanía.
episcopal | ɪ'pɪskəpl | *adj.* **1** (form.) episcopal. || **2 Episcopal,** Episcopal (de la denominación protestante).
Episcopalian | ɪˌpɪskə'peɪlɪən | REL. *adj.* **1** episcopaliano. || *s.c.* **2** episcopaliano (miembro de la iglesia episcopal).
episiotomy | əˌpiːzɪ'ɒtəmɪ | *s.c.* MED. corte vaginal (para ayudar a la mujer en el parto).
episode | 'epɪsəʊd | *s.c.* **1** episodio: *there is a tragic episode in my life = hay un episodio trágico en mi vida.* **2** TV. capítulo, parte (de una serie).
episodic | ˌepɪ'sɒdɪk | *adj.* (form.) episódico.
epistemology | ɪˌpɪstə'mɒlədʒɪ | *s.c.* FIL. epistemología.
epistle | ɪ'pɪsl | *s.c.* **1** (form.) epístola, misiva. || **2 Epistle,** REL. Epístola.
epistolary | ɪ'pɪstələrɪ | (EE.UU. | ɪ'pɪstəlerɪ) *adj.* (form.) epistolar.
epitaph | 'epɪtɑːf | (EE.UU. | 'epɪtæf) *s.c.* epitafio.
epithelia | ˌəpɪ'θelɪə | *pl.* de **epithelium.**
epithelium | ˌəpɪ'θelɪəm | [*pl.* **epitheliums** o **epithelia**] *s.c.* BIOL. epitelio.
epithet | 'epɪθet | *s.c.* GRAM. epíteto.
epitome | ɪ'pɪtəmɪ | *s.sing.* **1** (lit.) epítome, compendio, extracto, sumario. **2** modelo, ejemplo: *the epitome of grace = la gracia misma.*
epitomize | ɪ'pɪtəmaɪz | *v.t.* **1** (brit.) tipificar, ejemplificar. **2** resumir, compendiar, ser el epítome de.
epoch | 'iːpɒk | *s.c.* **1** época, período. **2** GEOL. era. **3** HIST. edad. || **4 to mark an –,** marcar época.
epoch-making | 'iːpɒkˌmeɪkɪŋ | *adj.* memorable, trascendental, que hace época, importantísimo.
Epson salts | ˌepsəm'sɔːlts | *s.pl.* sales de Epson, epsomita, sal de la higuera, sulfato de magnesio natural.
equable | 'ekwəbl | *adj.* **1** ecuánime, tranquilo, afable (una persona). **2** equilibrado, calmado, sosegado (el carácter). **3** estable, constante (el tiempo atmosférico).
equably | 'ekwəblɪ | *adv.* **1** ecuánimemente, afablemente, tranquilamente. **2** equilibradamente, sosegadamente, calmadamente. **3** establemente (el tiempo atmosférico).
equal | 'iːkwəl | (brit. **equall**) *adj.* **1** igual, idéntico, comparable: *equal in value = de igual valor.* **2** tanto, mismo. **3** equitativo (un tratamiento). **4** (arc.) imparcial, justo. **5** (arc.) ecuánime, tranquilo, sosegado. **6** (arc.) liso, a nivel, parejo. || *s.c.* **7** igual, par, semejante (una persona, un número, un tamaño): *her equals = sus semejantes (de ella).* || *v.t.* **8** igualar, nivelar, poner al mismo nivel, emparejar. **9** equivaler a. || **10 to be – to,** ser igual a, equivaler a. **11 to be – to doing something,** tener fuerzas para algo, ser capaz de algo, poder desempeñar algo. **12 to have no –,** no tener igual, no tener parangón. **13 on – terms,** en términos de igualdad. **14 other things being –,** si las circunstancias no cambian. || **15 without –,** sin par, sin igual.
equality | iː'kwɒlɪtɪ | | ɪ'kɑːlətɪ | *s.i.* igualdad, paridad, uniformidad.
equalization | ˌiːkwəlaɪ'zeɪʃn | (EE.UU. | ˌiːkwəlɪ'zeɪʃn) (también **equalisation**) *s.i.* igualamiento, igualación.
equalize | 'iːkwəlaɪz | (brit. **equalise**) *v.t.* **1** igualar. **2** emparejar, uniformar. || *v.i.* **3** (brit.) equilibrar, nivelar. **4** DEP. (brit.) empatar.
equalizer | 'iːkwəlaɪzər | *s.c.* **1** (brit.) DEP. empate. **2** balance, equilibrio. **3** MEC. balancín, compensador. **4** ELECTR. ecualizador. **5** (EE.UU. y argot) revólver, pistola, arma, pipa.
equanimity | ˌekwə'nɪmɪtɪ | *s.i.* (lit.) ecuanimidad, calma, equilibrio.
equate | ɪ'kweɪt | *v.t.* **1** comparar, considerar equivalente, considerar idéntico. **2** tratar de igual modo, tratar de igual a igual. || *v.i.* **3** ser igual, corresponder, parecer igual.
equation | ɪ'kweɪʒn | *s.c.* **1** MAT. ecuación. || *s.i.* **2** (lit.) equilibrio, balance, igualdad.
equator | ɪ'kweɪtər | *s.* GEOGR. ecuador, línea del ecuador (gen. en mayúscula).
equatorial | ˌekwə'tɔːrɪəl | *adj.* **1** ecuatorial (posición). **2** ecuatorial, muy caluroso (clima).
equerry | ɪ'kwerɪ | | 'ekwərɪ | *s.c.* ayuda de cámara (en la casa real británica).
equestrian | ɪ'kwestrɪən | *adj.* **1** ecuestre. || *s.c.* **2** jinete.
equi- | 'iːkwɪ | *prefijo* equi-.
equidistant | ˌiːkwɪ'dɪstənt | *adj.* **1** equidistante, a la misma distancia.
equilateral | ˌiːkwɪ'lætərəl | *adj.* **1** GEOM. equilátero. || *s.c.* **2** GEOM. lado equilátero. **3** GEOM. triángulo equilátero.
equilibrium | | [*pl.* **equilibria** o **equilibriums**] *s.c.* e *i.* **1** (lit.) equilibrio, balance, serenidad, aplomo (emocional). **2** FIS. equilibrio.
equine | 'ekwaɪn | *adj.* de caballo, equino.
equinoctial | ˌiːkwɪ'nɒkʃl | *adj.* ASTR. equinoccial.
equinox | 'iːkwɪnɒks | | 'ekwɪnɒks | *s.sing.* ASTR. equinoccio.
equip | ɪ'kwɪp | *v.t.* **1 [to – (with/for)]** equipar, proveer de, aviar con. **2 [to – (for)]** preparar (para), dotar (para) (un trabajo, una materia). **3** (EE.UU.) vestirse de etiqueta, endomingarse.
equipment | ɪ'kwɪpmənt | *s.i.* **1** equipo, pertrechos, aparatos (gen. de tipo técnico). **2** (p.u.) equipaje. **3** capacidad, aptitud, eficiencia. **4** dotación, equipamiento. **5** TEC. equipo rodante, material móvil.
equipoise | 'ekwɪpɔɪz | *s.i.* (form.) equilibrio, autocontrol (mental).
equitable | 'ekwɪtəbl | *adj.* equitativo, justo, razonable, imparcial.
equitably | 'ekwɪtəblɪ | *adv.* equitativamente, razonablemente, con justicia.
equity | 'ekwɪtɪ | *s.i.* **1** (lit.) equidad, imparcialidad, justicia. **2** DER. derecho natural, justicia natural, equidad. || **3** COM. acciones de interés variable, acciones de dividendo no fijo.
equivalence | ɪ'kwɪvələns | *s.i.* **1** equivalencia, correspondencia, igualdad. **2** MAT. equivalencia.
equivalent | ɪ'kwɪvələnt | *adj.* **1** equivalente. || *s.c.* **2** equivalente. || **3 to be – to,** equivaler a.
equivocal | ɪ'kwɪvəkl | *adj.* **1** equívoco, dudoso, ambiguo, vago (palabras, opiniones). **2** sospechoso, misterioso, incierto (el comportamiento, un acontecimiento). **3** discutible, controvertido.
equivocate | ɪ'kwɪvəkeɪt | *v.i.* **1** (lit.) hablar con ambigüedad, expresarse de forma equívoca (con intención). **2** soslayar el tema, ser poco explícito.
equivocation | ɪˌkwɪvə'keɪʃn | (form.) *s.c.* **1** ambigüedad (del lenguaje). || *s.i.* **2** uso equívoco del lenguaje.
era | 'ɪərə | *s.c.* **1** HIST. era, período histórico, edad, época. **2** GEOL. era, edad.

eradiate | ɪ'reɪdɪeɪt | *v.t.* irradiar, radiar.
eradication | ɪˌreɪdɪ'keɪʃn | *s.i.* **1** erradicación, supresión, extirpación, eliminación.
eradicator | ɪ'rædɪkeɪtər | *s.c.* quitamanchas.
erase | ɪ'reɪz | | ɪ'reɪs | *v.t.* **1** (lit.) borrar (del papel, de una cinta magnetofónica, etc...). **2** (fig.) borrar, eliminar, hacer desaparecer (de la mente).
eraser | ɪ'reɪzər | | ɪ'reɪsər | *s.c.* **1** (EE.UU. y fam.) goma de borrar. **2** borrador.
erasure | ɪ'reɪʒər | *s.c.* **1** (lit.) borradura, tachadura, raspadura. || *s.i.* **2** destrucción, eliminación, supresión.
ere | eə | *prep.* (arc.) **1** antes de. || *conj.* **2** antes de que.
erect | ɪ'rekt | *adj.* **1** erecto, erguido, derecho, vertical. **2** FISIOL. erecto, en estado de erección. **3** erizado, de punta (el pelo). **4** (arc.) alerta, despierto. || *v.t.* **5** erigir, elevar, levantar, construir (un edificio). **6** (fig.) establecer, constituir. **7** MAT. construir sobre una base. **8** MEC. montar.
erectile | ɪ'rektaɪl | (EE.UU. | ɪ'rektɪl) *adj.* FISIOL. eréctil.
erection | ɪ'rekʃn | *s.i.* **1** construcción, edificación. **2** MEC. montaje. || *s.c.* **3** estructura, construcción, edificio. || *s.c.* e *i.* **4** FISIOL. erección. **5** (fig.) constitución, establecimiento.
erectness | ɪ'rektnɪs | *s.i.* erguimiento.
erg | ɜːg | *s.* **1** FIS. ergio.
ergonomics | ˌɜːgəʊ'nɒmɪks | | ˌɜːrgə'nɑːmɪks | *s.i.* TEC. ergonomía.
ermine | 'ɜːmɪn | *s.i.* **1** armiño (piel). || *s.c.* **2** ZOOL. armiño.
erode | ɪ'rəʊd | *v.t.* **1** GEOL. erosionar, causar erosión. **2** raer, corroer, desgastar. || *v.i.* **3** GEOL. erosionarse. **4** desgastarse, raerse, corroerse.
erogenous | ɪ'rɒdʒənəs | *adj.* erógeno: *erogenous zones = zonas erógenas.*
erosion | ɪ'rəʊʒn | *s.i.* **1** GEOL. erosión. **2** erosión, desgaste. **3** (fig.) erosión, desgaste.
erosive | ɪ'rəʊsɪv | *adj.* GEOL. erosivo.
erotic | ɪ'rɒtɪk | *adj.* erótico (generalmente aplicado a obras de arte).
erotica | ɪ'rɒtɪkə | *s.pl.* material erótico.
erotically | ɪ'rɒtɪklɪ | *adv.* eróticamente.
eroticism | ɪ'rɒtɪsɪzəm | *s.i.* erotismo, lo erótico.
err | ɜːr | *v.i.* **1** (lit.) errar, equivocarse, cometer errores. **2** pecar, ir por mal camino, descarriarse. || **3 to – on the side of,** pecar por exceso de. **4 to – is human, to forgive divine,** equivocarse es humano, perdonar, divino.
errand | 'erənd | *s.c.* **1** recado, encargo, mandado. **2** (arc.) misión, embajada. || **3 to go on/to run errands for,** hacer recados para, hacer encargos para, llevar recados a. **4 – of mercy,** tentativa de salvamento. **5 – boy,** mensajero, recadero, mandadero. **6 a fool's –,** V. **fool.**
errant | 'erənt | *adj.* **1** (lit. o hum.) errante, errabundo, andante: *knight errant = caballero andante.* **2** descarriado, desorientado. **3** (fig.) descarriado, infiel.
erratic | ɪ'rætɪk | *adj.* **1** irregular, inconstante. **2** voluble, caprichoso (de carácter). **3** excéntrico (de comportamiento). **4** desigual, poco uniforme (resultados). **5** MED. errático.
erratically | ɪ'rætɪkəlɪ | *adv.* **1** irregularmente, de modo inconstante. **2** excéntricamente, caprichosamente. **3** desigualmente. **4** erráticamente.
erroneous | ɪ'rəʊnɪəs | *adj.* (lit.) erróneo, incorrecto, equivocado.
erroneously | ɪ'rəʊnjəslɪ | *adv.* (lit.) erróneamente, equivocadamente.
error | 'erər | *s.c.* e *i.* **1** (lit.) error, equivocación. **2** transgresión, descarrío. **3** ofensa, falta. **4** MAT. error. || **5 by/in –,** por equivocación, por error. **6 errors and omissions excepted,** salvo error u omisión. **7 to see the – of one's ways,** reconocer los propios errores, reconocer las faltas en que uno ha incurrido. **7 trial and –,** V. **trial.**
OBS. **error** es más literario que **mistake** y sugiere algo mal hecho moralmente. En ciertas frases hechas, solo puede utilizarse uno de ellos.
ersazt | 'eəzæts | *adj.* (desp.) sucedáneo, sustituto, artificial.
erstwhile | 'ɜːstwaɪl | *adj.* **1** (lit. y arc.) anterior, de otro tiempo, antiguo: *her erstwhile husband = su anterior marido (de ella).*
erudite | 'eruːdaɪt | *adj.* (lit.) erudito, culto, instruido, versado.
eruditely | 'eruːdaɪtlɪ | *adv.* eruditamente, cultamente (en la entrada **escape**) || **13 – clause,** DER. cláusula de liberación de obligaciones. **14 – velocity,** FIS. velocidad de escape. **15 to make good one's –,** escapar sin ser visto, escapar con éxito.
erudition | ˌeruː'dɪʃn | *s.i.* (lit.) erudición, cultura, conocimientos.
erupt | ɪ'rʌpt | *v.i.* **1** GEOL. entrar en erupción, hacer erupción, estar en erupción. **2** estallar (un fuego). **3** (fig.) estallar, explotar, brotar (la violencia). **4** MED. tener una erupción, salir (manchas, granos). **5** salir (un diente). **6** interrumpir (en un lugar). || *v.t.* **7** arrojar (lava).
eruption | ɪ'rʌpʃn | *s.c.* e *i.* **1** GEOL. erupción. **2** MED. erupción, brote. **3** (fig.) estallido, brote, explosión (de violencia, de pasión).
escalate | 'eskəleɪt | *v.t.* e *i.* **1** intensificar(se), extender(se). **2** subir, aumentar, ascender (los precios). **3** empeorar, agravarse (una situación).
escalation | ˌeskə'leɪʃn | *s.c.* e *i.* **1** escalada, intensificación, extensión. **2** ascenso, aumento (de los precios). **3** empeoramiento (de una situación).
escalator | 'eskəleɪtər | *s.c.* (brit.) escalera mecánica.
escapade | ˌeskə'peɪd | *s.c.* escapada, aventura, travesura.
escape | ɪ'skeɪp | *v.i.* **1** escaparse, huir, fugarse (una persona). **2** escaparse, salirse, (un líquido, gas). **3** crecer de forma silvestre (las plantas). || *v.t.* **4** salvarse de, librarse de, escaparse de (algo peligroso o desagradable). **5** evitar, eludir (a una persona, una actividad). **6** escapársele a uno, pasársele desapercibido, olvidársele: *your name escapes me = se me ha olvidado tu nombre.* **7** escapar a, burlar (la vigilancia). || *s.c.* e *i.* **8** evasión, fuga, huida. **9** escape, fuga (de líquido, de gas). **10** escapatoria. **11** (fig.) evasión. **12** planta silvestre.
escapee | ɪˌskeɪ'piː | *s.c.* persona escapada, fugado.
escapism | ɪ'skeɪpɪzəm | *s.i.* (desp.) evasión.
escapist | ɪ'skeɪpɪst | *adj.* **1** que se evade o fomenta la evasión. *s.c.* **2** persona que se evade.
escapologist | ˌeskə'pɒlədʒɪst | *s.c.* contorsionista (especializado en salirse de sitios bien cerrados, sujetos con cadenas, etc.).
escapology | ˌeskə'pɒlədʒɪ | *s.i.* contorsionismo. V. **escapologist.**
escarpment | ɪ'skɑːpmənt | *s.c.* **1** acantilado. **2** zona escarpada, escarpadura.
eschatology | ˌeskə'tɒlədʒɪ | *s.i.* REL. escatología.
eschew | ɪs'tʃuː | *v.t.* (form.) abstenerse, evitar, renunciar, rehuir, esquivar.
escort | e'skɔːt | *s.c.* **1** MIL. escolta. **2** MAR. convoy, escolta. **3** acompañamiento, pareja (para una fiesta). || | 'eskɔːt | *v.t.* **4** MIL. escoltar. **5** MAR. convoyar, escoltar. **6** acompañar (a una fiesta).
escritoire | ˌeskrɪ'twɑː | *s.c.* escritorio.
escrow | 'esˌkrou | *s.c.* **1** DER. plica, depósito, fideicomiso. || **2 in –,** en depósito, en custodia.
escutcheon | ɪ'skʌtʃən | *s.c.* **1** blasón, emblema, escudo de armas. **2** placa de protección, escudo (de una cerradura). **3** MAR. espejo de popa. **4** (fig.) honor, reputación.
Eskimo | 'eskɪməʊ | [*pl.* **Eskimo** o **Eskimos**] *s.c.* **1** esquimal (raza). **2** esquimal (idioma). || *adj.* **3** esquimal.
esophagus V. **oesophagus.**
esoteric | ˌesəʊ'terɪk | *adj.* **1** esotérico, oculto, secreto. **2** confidencial, privado.
especial | ɪ'spəʃl | *adj.* (lit.) especial, particular.
especially | ɪ'spəʃəlɪ | *adv.* **1** especialmente, particularmente, en particular. **2** ante todo, sobre todo: *especially if I go = sobre todo si voy.*
espionage | ˌespɪə'nɑːʒ | | ˌespjə'nɑːʒ | *s.i.* espionaje.
esplanade | ˌesplə'neɪd | *s.c.* explanada, paseo marítimo.
espousal | ɪ'spauzl | *s.i.* **[– of]** adopción de (una ideología, causa, etc.).
et al | ˌet'æl | *abreviatura* (fam.) y otros, y otras.
espouse | ɪ'spauz | *v.t.* **1** (lit.) apoyar, adherirse, abrazar (una causa, una idea). **2** (lit.) desposar, casarse con. **3** casar a, dar en matrimonio.
espresso | e'spresəʊ | [*pl.* **espressos**] *s.c.* e *i.* café exprés, café de cafetera a presión.

esprit de corps | ˌespriːdə'kɔrː | *s.i.* espíritu de cuerpo, espíritu de equipo; solidaridad, lealtad.

espy | ɪ'spaɪ | *v.t.* (lit.) divisar, vislumbrar.

esquire | ɪ'skwaɪər | *s.c.* **1** (brit. y p.u.) señor, don (título de cortesía después del nombre y apellido en la correspondencia): *Charles Starmer Esq.* = *Don Charles Starmer.* **2** HIST. escudero. **3** (brit.) noble (de rango menor).

essay | 'eseɪ | *s.c.* **1** LIT. ensayo. **2** ensayo, composición (escolar). **3** (p.u.) tentativa, prueba, intento. **4** muestra, ejemplo. || *v.t.* **5** (p.u.) intentar, probar, ensayar. **6** someter a prueba, probar (a alguien).

essayist | 'eseɪst | *s.c.* LIT. ensayista.

essence | 'esns | *s.sing.* **1** FIL. esencia, naturaleza intrínseca. **2 [the –]** lo esencial, lo fundamental, el alma. **3** QUIM. esencia, extracto. || **4 in –,** esencialmente, fundamentalmente. **5 of the –,** fundamental, indispensable, esencial.

essential | ɪ'senʃl | *adj.* **1** esencial, básico, indispensable. **2** FIL. intrínseco, inherente. || *s.c.* **3** parte esencial, elemento imprescindible; [*pl.*] elementos fundamentales, factores más importantes. || **4 in essentials/in all essentials,** básicamente, esencialmente. **5 to stick to the essentials,** ir al grano.

essentially | ɪ'senʃəlɪ | *adv.* **1** esencialmente, básicamente. **2** necesariamente.

establish | ɪ'stæblɪʃ | *v.t.* **1** establecer, instituir, crear, fundar (un negocio, una sociedad, una teoría). **2** establecer, implantar, crear (un precedente). **3** arraigar (en un estado o posición). **4** probar, demostrar (un hecho). **5** (gen. pasiva) reconocer, oficializar (una religión). **6** promulgar, introducir, establecer (una ley). **7** establecer, tomar (contacto). || *v.r.* **8 [to – oneself]** establecerse, asentarse (en una posición, o estado).

established | ɪ'stæblɪʃt | *adj.* **1** sólido, arraigado (una costumbre, un negocio). **2** probado, conocido (un hecho). **3** oficial (una religión). **4** de plantilla, fijo (un empleado).

establishment | ɪ'stæblɪʃmənt | *s.i.* **1** establecimiento, creación, fundación. || *s.c.* **2** establecimiento, negocio, casa, club. **3** MIL. fuerzas, efectivos. **4 Establishment,** clase dirigente, grupo dirigente (político, profesional). **5 Establishment,** (brit.) Iglesia Anglicana, iglesia oficial. **6** plantilla, personal. **7** servidumbre.

estate | ɪ'steɪt | *s.c.* **1** finca, hacienda, heredad. **2** (brit.) barrio, barriada, zona, polígono (de viviendas, industrial). **3** DER. relictos, herencia, bienes. **4** propiedades, fortuna, bienes (raíces, inmuebles). **5** (arc.) posición social, condición, estado (clero, nobleza, el pueblo). **6** pompa, ostentación. || **7 – administration,** DER. administración de una herencia. **8 – duty/tax,** impuesto de sucesión. **9 – probate,** DER. adjudicación de la herencia, del patrimonio. **10 the fourth –,** (fam.) el cuarto poder, (la prensa).

esteem | ɪ'stiːm | *s.i.* **1** (lit.) estima, respeto, consideración, aprecio. **2** (arc.) juicio, opinión. || *v.t.* **3** (lit.) estimar, apreciar, respetar, admirar, considerar. **4 [to – + *o.* + *adj.*/*s.*]** (lit. y p.u.) considerar, valorar, creer: *I esteem it worth* = *considero que merece la pena.* || **5 to hold someone in –,** tener a uno en estima.

esthete | 'iːsəiːt | (EE.UU. **aesthete**) *s.c.* esteta, amante de la belleza.

Esthonia, Estonia | e'stəunjə | *s.* Estonia (república soviética).

Esthonian, Estonian | e'stəunjən | *s.c.* **1** estonio (de origen). **2** estonio (idioma). || *adj.* **3** estonio.

estimable | 'estɪməbl | *adj.* **1** (p.u.) estimable, apreciable, admirable. **2** apreciado, admirado.

estimate | 'estɪmɪt | *v.t.* **1 [to – (at)]** calcular, valorar, tasar. **2** calcular, juzgar, presuponer. || *v.i.* **3 [to – (for)]** presupuestar, hacer un presupuesto. || *s.c.* **4** cálculo, evaluación, valoración, tasación. **5** presupuesto. **6** juicio, suposición, opinión. || **7 at a rough –,** haciendo un cálculo aproximado.

estimation | ˌestɪ'meɪʃn | *s.i.* **1** (lit.) juicio, opinión, impresión. **2** estima, aprecio. || *s.c.* **3** cálculo, valoración, tasación. || **4 to go up/down in someone's –,** subir/bajar en la estima de alguien, mejorar/empeorar en la opinión de alguien.

estrange | ɪ'streɪndʒ | *v.t.* **1 [to – from]** separarse de, apartarse de, enemistarse con, enajenar.

estrangement | ɪ'streɪndʒmənt | *s.c.* e *i.* extrañamiento, separación, alejamiento, desavenencia.

estuary | 'estjuərɪ | *s.c.* GEOGR. estuario.

etcetera | ɪt'setərə | *adv.* **1** etcétera, así sucesivamente. || *s.pl.* **2** extras, adornos.

etch | etʃ | *v.t.* e *i.* **1** grabar al aguafuerte. **2** (fig.) grabarse (en la memoria).

etcher | 'etʃər | *s.c.* grabador.

etching | etʃɪŋ | *s.c.* e *i.* aguafuerte, grabado al aguafuerte.

eternal | iːtəːnl | *adj.* **1** eterno, sempiterno. **2** perpetuo, perenne, interminable. **3** (fig.) constante, incesante. **4** inmutable, absoluto (un valor, una verdad). || *s.* **5 the Eternal,** el Padre Eterno, el Eterno. || **6 the – triangle,** el triángulo amoroso típico.

eternally | iːtəːnlɪ | *adv.* eternamente, constantemente, perpetuamente, por siempre.

eternity | iː'təːnɪtɪ | *s.i.* **1** eternidad. **2** (fig.) eternidad, siglos, mucho tiempo: *it seemed like an eternity* = *parecía que no iba a acabar jamás.*

ether | 'iːθər | *s.i.* **1** éter; espacio. **2** QUIM. éter.

ethereal | iː'θɪərɪəl | *adj.* **1** etéreo, celestial, sublime, sutil. **2** QUIM. etéreo, con éter, de éter.

ethic | 'eθɪk | *s.sing.* sistema moral, ética: *the Christian ethic* = *la ética cristiana.*

ethical | 'eθɪkl | *adj.* **1** [no *comp.*] ético, moral. **2** honrado.

ethically | 'eθɪklɪ | *adv.* **1** éticamente, moralmente. **2** honradamente.

ethics | 'eθɪks | *s.i.* **1** FIL. [– *v.sing.*/*pl.*] ética, moral. **2** moralidad, honradez, principios éticos.

Ethiopia | ˌiːθɪ'əupjə | *s.sing.* Etiopía.

Ethiopian | ˌiːθɪ'əupjən | *adj.* **1** etíope, etiope. || *s.c.* **2** etíope, etiope.

ethnic | 'eθnɪk | *adj.* étnico, racial.

ethnically | 'eθnɪklɪ | *adv.* étnicamente, racialmente.

ethnographer | eθ'nɒgrəfər | *s.c.* etnógrafo.

ethnographic | ˌeθnə'græfɪk | *adj.* etnográfico.

ethnography | ˌeθnəu'græfɪ | *s.i.* etnografía.

ethnological | ˌeθnə'lɒdʒɪkl | *adj.* etnológico.

ethnologist | eθ'nɒlədʒɪst | *s.c.* etnólogo.

ethnology | eθ'nɒlədʒɪ | *s.i.* etnología.

ethos | 'iːθɒs | *s.sing.* carácter distintivo, rasgo distintivo (de un grupo humano o cultural).

ethyl | 'eθɪl | *s.i.* **1** QUIM. etilo. || **2 – alcohol,** alcohol etílico. **3 – chloride,** QUIM. cloruro etílico.

etiolated | 'iːtɪəuleɪtɪd | *adj.* **1** BOT. descolorido por falta de luz. **2** (form.) pálido, blanquecino (personas).

etiquette | 'etɪket | *s.i.* **1** etiqueta, protocolo, convencionalismo, comportamiento social. **2** honor profesional, decoro profesional.

Etruscan | ɪ'trʌskən | *adj.* **1** HIST. etrusco. | *s.c.* **2** HIST. etrusco (habitante de Etruria). **3** etrusco (idioma).

etymological | ˌetɪmə'lɒdʒɪkl | *adj.* etimológico.

etymologist | ˌetɪ'mɒlədʒɪst | *s.c.* etimólogo.

etymology | ˌetɪ'mɒlədʒɪ | *s.i.* **1** etimología (ciencia). || *s.c.* **2** etimología (de una palabra).

eucalypti | ˌjuːkə'lɪptaɪ | *pl.* de **eucalyptus.**

eucalyptus | ˌjuːkə'lɪptəs | [*pl.* **eucalyptuses** o **eucalypti**] *s.c.* e *i.* BOT. eucalipto.

Eucharist | 'juːkərɪst | *s.c.sing.* REL. Eucaristía.

eugenist | juːdʒenɪst | *s.c.* MED. versado en eugenesia.

eugenics | juː'dʒenɪk | *s.i.* **1** eugenesia.

eulogize | 'juːlədʒaɪz | *v.t.* e *i.* (form.) alabar, cantar las alabanzas de.

eulogy | 'juːlədʒɪ | *s.c.* e *i.* (lit.) panegírico, apología, alabanza, elogio, encomio.

eunuch | 'juːnək | *s.c.* **1** eunuco, castrado. **2** (fig.) don nadie, segundón, figurón (un político).

euphemism | 'juːfɪmɪzəm | *s.c.* e *i.* RET. eufemismo.

euphemistic | ˌjuːfə'mɪstɪk | *adj.* eufemístico (lenguaje).

euphemistically | ˌjuːfəmɪstɪklɪ | *adv.* eufemísticamente.

euphonic | juː'fɒnɪk | *adj.* RET. eufónico.

euphoria | juː'fɔrɪə | *s.i.* euforia, entusiasmo, optimismo, exaltación, alegría.
euphoric | juː'fɒrɪk | *adj.* eufórico, entusiasta, optimista, exaltado, alegre.
Eurasian | jʊə'reɪʒjən | *adj.* eurásico.
eureka | jʊə'riːkə | *interj.* eureka, lo encontré.
Euro bond | 'jʊərəˌbɒnd | *s.c.* COM. eurobono, bono de la Comunidad Económica Europea.
Eurodollar | ˌjʊərə'dɒlər | *s.c.* COM. eurodólar.
Europe | 'jʊərəp | *s.sing.* Europa.
European | ˌjʊərə'piːən | *adj.* **1** europeo, de Europa. || *s.c.* **2** europeo (ciudadano).
Eurovision | 'jʊərəʊˌvɪʒn | *s.sing.* TV. Eurovisión.
Eurydice | jʊə'rɪdɪsiː | *s.sing.* MIT. Eurídice (esposa de Orfeo).
euthanasia | ˌjuːθə'neɪzjə | *s.i.* (euf.) eutanasia, muerte sin dolor.
evacuate | ɪ'vækjʊeɪt | *v.t.* **1** evacuar, desalojar, vaciar, desocupar (un edificio, una ciudad). **2** (lit.) evacuar, expeler (excrementos).
evacuation | ɪˌvækjʊ'eɪʃn | *s.c.* e *i.* **1** evacuación, desalojo. **2** (form.) defecación.
evacuee | ɪˌvækjuː'iː | *s.c.* evacuado, desalojado (una persona).
evade | ɪ'veɪd | *v.t.* **1** (desp.) evadir, eludir, rehuir, esquivar (responsabilidades, una respuesta). **2** defraudar, evadir (impuestos). **3** escaparse de, esquivar a (un perseguidor).
evaluate | ɪ'væljʊeɪt | *v.t.* **1** evaluar, valorar, tasar, calcular. **2** evaluar (el rendimiento escolar). **3** MAT. calcular, hallar el valor numérico. **4** interpretar.
evaluation | ɪˌvæljʊ'eɪʃn | *s.c.* **1** evaluación, valoración, cálculo. **2** evaluación (del rendimiento escolar). **3** interpretación.
evanescent | ˌiːvə'nesnt | *adj.* (lit.) evanescente, efímero, breve, pasajero.
evangelic(al) | ˌiːvæn'dʒelɪkl | *adj.* REL. evangélico (generalmente en mayúscula).
evangelise V. **evangelize.**
evangelism | ɪ'vændʒəlɪzəm | *s.i.* evangelismo, proselitismo cristiano.
evangelist | ɪ'vændʒəlɪst | REL. *s.c.* **1** evangelista. **2** evangelizador.
evangelize | ɪ'vændʒəlaɪz | (también **evangelise**) *v.t.* e *i.* **1** evangelizar, predicar el evangelio. **2** convertirse al cristianismo.
evaporate | ɪ'væpəreɪt | *v.t.* e *i.* **1** evaporar. **2** (fig.) evaporarse, desaparecer.
evaporation | ɪˌvæpə'reɪʃn | *s.i.* evaporación.
evasion | ɪ'veɪʒn | *s.c.* e *i.* **1** evasión, fuga (especialmente de algo a lo que obliga la ley). **2** evasiva (no contestar con claridad).
evasive | ɪ'veɪsɪv | *adj.* (desp.) evasivo.
evasively | ɪ'veɪsɪvlɪ | *adv.* evasivamente, de modo evasivo.
evasiveness | ɪ'veɪsɪvnɪs | *s.i.* tono evasivo.
eve | iːv | *s.sing.* **1** Eva (con mayúscula). || *s.i.* **1** víspera, vigilia. **2** (lit.) atardecer, anochecer. || **3 Christmas Eve,** Nochebuena. **4 New Year's Eve,** Nochevieja.
even | 'iːvn | *adj.* **1** incluso, hasta, aún: *even when I sleep = hasta cuando duermo.* **2** [*v.neg* /**not –**] ni siquiera: *she couldn't even talk = ni siquiera podía hablar.* **3** aún, todavía (para enfatizar una comparación): *she's even better al Maths = (ella) aún es mejor en Matemáticas.* **4** incluso, verdaderamente, más aun, se diría (que): *he seemed pleased, even amused = parecía encantado, más aun, divertido.* || *adj.* **5** llano, liso, plano. **6** nivelado, paralelo, al ras. **7** ajustado, balanceado (cuentas). **8** empatado, igual, igualado, parejo. **9** MAT. par, divisible por dos. **10** regular, constante, uniforme. **11** apacible, ecuánime, tranquilo (de carácter). || *s.i.* **12** (lit.) tarde. || *v.t.* e *i.* **13 [to – out]** igualar, nivelar, emparejar. || *v.t.* **14 [to – up]** nivelar, balancear, ajustar (cuentas). || **15 an – chance,** un 50% de probabilidades. **16 to be – with,** estar empatado con, tener los mismos tantos que, estar mano a mano con (en el juego); (fig.) estar en paz con, haberse vengado de. **17 to break –,** no tener ganancias pero tampoco pérdidas, recuperar gastos, salir sin ganar ni perder (en un negocio). **18 – as,** al igual que, lo mismo que; en el mismo momento que. **19 – if/ though,** aunque, aun cuando. **20 – so,** aun así, sin embargo. **21 to get – with,** vengarse de, desquitarse de.
even-handed | ˌiːvn'hændɪd | *adj.* imparcial, equitativo, justo.
even-handedly | ˌiːvn'hændɪdlɪ | *adv.* imparcialmente, equitativamente, con justicia.
even-handedness | ˌiːvn'hændɪdnɪs | *s.i.* imparcialidad.
evening | 'iːvnɪŋ | *s.c.* e *i.* **1** tarde, atardecer, anochecer. **2** noche (antes de acostarse). **3** (fig.) ocaso, final. || *s.c.* **4** velada, noche. || *adj.atr.* **5** de etiqueta, de noche, elegante (un traje). **6** nocturno, vespertino (clases, periódicos, estrellas). || **7 evenings,** generalmente por la tarde, regularmente por la tarde. **8 Evening Star,** Venus.
evenly | 'iːvnlɪ | *adv.* **1** lisamente, por igual, uniformemente. **2** imparcialmente, equitativamente. **3** suavemente, apaciblemente, sin alteración.
evenness | 'iːvnnɪs | *s.i.* **1** lisura, uniformidad, igualdad. **2** imparcialidad, equidad. **3** suavidad, serenidad, ecuanimidad.
event | ɪ'vent | *s.c.* **1** acontecimiento, evento. **2** suceso, incidente. **3** DEP. prueba, competición. || **4 at all events,** a pesar de todo, por lo menos, en todo caso. **5 in any –,** en cualquier caso, en todo caso. **6** (brit.) **in the –,** en ese momento, en el caso de, cuando se pone uno a ello. **7 in the – of,** en caso de.
even-tempered | ˌiːvn'tempəd | *adj.* apacible, sosegado, sereno, ecuánime, tranquilo.
eventful | ɪ'ventfəl | *adj.* **1** azaroso, pleno de acontecimientos, ajetreado, accidentado. **2** memorable, inolvidable, emocionante. **3** importante, vital, trascendental.
eventual | ɪ'ventʃʊəl | *adj.* **1** final, definitivo, subsiguiente, consiguiente. **2** eventual, casual, fortuito.
eventuality | ɪˌventʃʊ'ælɪtɪ | *s.c.* (lit.) eventualidad, posibilidad, contingencia (gen. desagradable).
eventually | ɪ'ventʃʊəlɪ | *adv.* a la larga, finalmente.
ever | 'evər | *adv.* **1** [en frases interrogativas y condicionales] alguna vez, una vez, en algún momento: *have you ever been to London? = ¿has estado en Londres alguna vez?; if you ever come... = si vienes alguna vez...?* **2** [en frases negativas, con comparativos, superlativos] nunca, jamás, en la vida, en ningún momento: *I' ve never been there = no he estado allí jamás; funnier than ever = más divertido que nunca.* **3** siempre: *they lived happily ever after = y por siempre vivieron felices; the best ever seen = el mejor que se ha visto jamás.* **4** (EE.UU. y fam.) absolutamente, totalmente (para dar énfasis a una exclamación): *was he ever annoyed! = ¡qué irritado estaba!* **5** (para dar énfasis a una pregunta, mostrar sorpresa, etc...; a veces se traduce por "poder" o no se traduce): *why ever did you do that? = ¿cómo pudiste hacer eso?* || **all someone =N does,** lo único que hace uno. **7 as =N,** como siempre. **8 =N since,** desde entonces. **9 =N so/such,** tan, muy, sumamente: *she' s ever so rude! = ¡es tan maleducada!* **10 hardly/scarcely =N, casi nunca.** **11 yours =N, / =N yours,** (fam.) recibe un abrazo (como despedida en una carta).
everglade | 'evəˌgleɪd | *s.i.* terreno pantanoso cubierto de hierbas altas (al sur de Florida en EE.UU.).
evergreen | 'evəgriːn | *adj* **1** BOT. de hoja perenne, siempre verde. **2** (fig.) de siempre, que no pasa de moda: *evergreen songs = canciones de siempre.* || *s.c.* **3** BOT. árbol de hoja perenne, arbusto de hoja siempre verde. || *s.pl.* **4** ramas verdes, hojas verdes (usadas en decoración). || **5 – oak,** encina.
ever-growing | ˌevə'grəʊɪŋ | *adj.* en continuo aumento.
everlasting | ˌevə'lɑːstɪŋ | *adj.* **1** (lit.) eterno, sin fin, perpetuo. **2** (desp.) interminable, aburrido, tedioso. **3** BOT. duradero, perdurable (el color, la forma). || *s.c.* **4 The Everlasting,** El Eterno, Dios. **5** eternidad. **6** BOT. siempreviva.
everlastingly | ˌevə'lɑːstɪŋlɪ | *adv.* **1** eternamente, perpetuamente. **2** interminablemente, tediosamente.
evermore | ˌevə'mɔːr | *adv.* **1** (lit.) eternamente, para siempre. || **2 for –,** por siempre jamás.

every | 'evrɪ | *adj.* **1** [– *s.c.*] cada: *every time = cada vez.* **2** todos los, todos y cada uno de: *every day = todos los días.* **3** todo: *every student = todo alumno.* **4** absoluto, completo, todo: *there's every chance = existe la absoluta posibilidad.* || **5 – bit,** todo, absolutamente todo. **6 – bit as** + *adj.* + **as someone/something,** tan, todo lo + *adj.* + que: *every bit as clever as John = tan inteligente como John.* **7** (fam.) **– last,** todo, hasta el fondo, hasta el final. **8 – man for himself,** cada uno por su cuenta, sálvese quien pueda. **9 – now and then/again,** todo, hasta el fondo, hasta el final. **10 – other day,** un día sí y otro no, cada dos días. **11 – so often,** alguna que otra vez, cada cierto tiempo. **12** (fam.) **– which way,** desordenadamente, de cualquier modo, por todas partes.

everybody | 'evrɪˌbɒdɪ | | 'evrɪbɑːdɪ | *pron.* **1** todos, todo el mundo, cada cual. || **2 – for himself,** cada uno por su cuenta, sálvese quien pueda.

everyday | 'evrɪdeɪ | *adj.* **1** ordinario, corriente, común, acostumbrado. **2** de todos los días, cotidiano, diario. **3** rutinario. **4** vulgar, corriente.

everyone | 'evrɪwʌn | V. **everybody.**

everyplace | 'evrɪpleɪs | V. **everywhere.**

everything | 'evrɪθɪŋ | *pron.* **1** [– *v.sing.*] todo, todas las cosas. **2** el todo, lo más importante. || **3 and –,** (fam.) etcétera, y todo lo demás.

everywhere | 'evrɪweər | (EE.UU. **everyplace**) *adv.* **1** en todas partes, por todas partes, a todas partes.

evict | ɪ'vɪkt | *v.t.* DER. desahuciar, echar a la calle (a un inquilino).

eviction | ɪ'vɪkʃn | *s.c.* e *i.* desahucio.

evidence | 'evɪdəns | *s.i.* **1** DER. evidencia, prueba (de culpabilidad). **2** DER. testimonio, testificación, declaración. **3** evidencia, certeza, seguridad, convicción. || **4 documentary –,** prueba documental. **5 to give –,** DER. declarar, testimoniar, testificar. **6 to hold –,** DER. levantar atestado, tomar declaración. **7 in –,** a la vista, visible, manifiesto, notorio. **8 to show –,** presentar indicios, presentar señales. **9** (EE.UU.) **to turn estate's –,**(brit.) **to turn King's/Queen's –,** declarar contra los cómplices.

evident | 'evɪdənt | *adj.* **1** evidente, claro, obvio, patente. || **2 to be – (that),** ser obvio que, ser manifiesto que. **3 to be – in,** manifestarse en.

evidently | 'evɪdəntlɪ | *adv.* evidentemente, obviamente, patentemente, manifiestamente.

evil | 'iːvl | *adj.* **1** (lit.) maligno, perverso, malvado. **2** diabólico, viperino. **3** (fam.) desagradable, fétido, horrible (un olor). **4** aciago, desgraciado (una circunstancia, un día). || *s.c.* e *i.* **5** (lit.) mal, maldad. **6** desgracia. || **7 the Evil,** el Maligno, el Demonio. **8 the root of all –,** la causa de todos los males.

evildoer | ˌiːvl'duːər | *s.c.* malhechor, malvado, perverso.

evil-minded | ˌiːvl'maɪndɪd | *adj.* malintencionado, mal pensado.

evil-smelling | ˌiːvl'smelɪŋ | *adj.* fétido, maloliente.

evince | ɪ'vɪns | *v.t.* (lit.) revelar, mostrar, manifestar (un sentimiento, una cualidad).

eviscerate | ɪ'vɪsəreɪt | *v.t.* **1** (lit.) destripar, desentrañar. **2** MED. vaciar, remover (la cuenca del ojo). **3** MED. extirpar (un órgano).

evocation | ˌiːvəʊ'keɪʃn | *s.c.* e *i.* (form.) evocación, rememoración.

evocative | ɪ'vɒkətɪv | | ɪ'vɑːkətɪv | *adj.* evocador, sugerente, sugestivo.

evoke | ɪ'vəʊk | *v.t.* (lit.) evocar, sugerir (sentimientos, memorias).

evolution | ˌiːvə'luːʃn | (EE.UU. | ˌevə'luːʃn) *s.i.* **1** BIOL. evolución. **2** proceso, evolución (de un hecho en la historia o similar).

evolutionary | ˌiːvə'luːʃnərɪ | | ˌevə'luːʃənerɪ | *adj.* evolucionista, evolutivo.

evolve | ɪ'vɒlv | *v.t.* e *i.* **1** BIOL. evolucionar. **2** desarrollar, evolucionar. **3** producir, emitir, arrojar (calor).

ewe | juː | *s.c.* oveja (vieja).

exacerbate | ek'sæsəbeɪt | *v.t.* **1** (lit.) exacerbar, agravar (un dolor). **2** (lit.) irritar, alterar, enfurecer.

exact | ɪg'zækt | *adj.* **1** exacto, preciso. **2** certero, meticuloso, exacto. || *v.t.* **3** (lit.) exigir, demandar, requerir (por la fuerza, con amenazas). **4** imponer (por la fuerza).

exacting | ɪg'zæktɪŋ | *adj.* riguroso, severo (persona o tarea).

exactitude | ɪg'zæktɪtjuːd | *s.i.* **1** exactitud, precisión. **2** meticulosidad.

exactly | ɪg'zæktlɪ | *adv.* **1** **[what/where/who –]** exactamente, con precisión. **2** en punto (una hora). **3** realmente, en concreto (añade énfasis a lo anterior). **4** ¡exactamente!, ¡claro! || **5 no –,** no precisamente, no que digamos: *she's not exactly clever = no es lista que digamos.*

exactness | ɪg'zæktnɪs | *s.i.* **1** exactitud, precisión. **2** meticulosidad.

exaggerate | ɪg'zædʒəreɪt | *v.t.* e *i.* exagerar, ponderar.

exaggerated | ɪg'zædʒəreɪtɪd | *adj.* exagerado, engrandecido.

exaggeratedly | ɪg'zædʒəreɪtɪdlɪ | *adv.* exageradamente.

exaggeration | ɪg'zædʒəreɪʃn | *s.c.* e *i.* exageración.

exalt | ɪg'zɔːlt | *v.t.* **1** (form.) exaltar, alabar, glorificar, ensalzar, engrandecer. **2** elevar (de rango).

exaltation | ˌegzɔːl'teɪʃn | *s.i.* **1** (lit.) exaltación, enaltecimiento, glorificación. **2** exaltación, éxtasis, arrebato.

exalted | ɪg'zɔːltɪd | *adj.* **1** eminente, prominente. **2** elevado, sublime. **3** (lit.) exaltado, pleno de felicidad, pleno de júbilo.

exam | ɪg'zæm | *s.c.* (fam.) examen (oral o escrito).

examination | ɪgˌzæmɪ'neɪʃn | *s.c.,* **1** (form.) examen (académico). || *s.c.* e *i.* **2** MED. examen, reconocimiento. **3** DER. interrogatorio. **4** investigación, análisis. **5** inspección, revisión. **6** registro. || **7 under –,** sujeto a investigación, sujeto a análisis.

examine | ɪg'zæmɪn | *v.t.* **1** examinar (académicamente). **2** MED. examinar, hacer un reconocimiento. **3** registrar, inspeccionar (el equipaje en aduanas). **4** inspeccionar, investigar (libros de contabilidad). **5** DER. interrogar (a un testigo). **6** analizar, estudiar (un contrato, un programa político).

examinee | ɪgˌzæmɪ'niː | *s.c.* examinando.

examiner | ɪg'zæmɪnər | *s.c.* examinador.

example | ɪg'zɑːmpl | *s.c.* **1** ejemplo, muestra, ejemplar, tipo. **2** ejemplo, modelo (de comportamiento). **3** ejemplo, ilustración (después de una definición). **4** MAT. problema, ejercicio. || **5 to follow the –,** seguir el ejemplo. **6 for –,** por ejemplo. **7 to make an – of someone,** dar un castigo ejemplar a alguien. **8 to set an –,** dar ejemplo.

exasperate | ɪg'zæspəreɪt | *v.t.* (gen. pasiva) **1** exasperar, irritar, enfurecer, sacar de quicio. **2** agravar, intensificar.

exasperated | ɪg'zæspəreɪtɪd | *adj.* exasperado, irritado, enfurecido.

exasperating | ɪg'zæspəreɪtɪŋ | *adj.* irritante, exasperante, que saca a uno de quicio, que vuelve a uno loco, insoportable.

exasperation | ɪgˌzæspə'reɪʃn | *s.i.* exasperación, irritación, enojo.

excavate | 'ekskəveɪt | *v.t.* e *i.* **1** excavar, cavar (hoyos). **2** ARQ. excavar, desenterrar, descubrir.

excavation | ˌekskə'veɪʃn | *s.c.* e *i.* ARQ. excavación.

excavator | 'ekskəveɪtər | *s.c.* **1** excavador. **2 =N (steam shovel)** (EE.UU.) máquina excavadora, pala excavadora (mecánica).

exceed | ɪk'siːd | *v.t.* **1** exceder, pasar de, superar (una cantidad). **2** (desp.) sobrepasar, rebasar (un límite). **3** extralimitarse en, abusar de (derechos).

exceedingly | ɪk'siːdɪŋlɪ | *adv.* en extremo, sobremanera, extraordinariamente.

excel | ɪk'sel | *v.t.* e *i.* **1** (form.) sobresalir, ser superior, ser el mejor, distinguirse. || **2 to – oneself,** lucirse, hacer (algo) mejor que nunca.

excellence | 'eksələns | *s.i.* excelencia.

Excellency | 'eksələnsɪ | *s.* Excelencia (título honorífico para gente de Estado o de la Iglesia).

excellent | 'eksələnt | *adj.* excelente.

excellently | 'eksələntlɪ | *adv.* excelentemente.

except | ɪk'sept | *prep.* **1** excepto, salvo, aparte de, menos. **2** (fam.) pero, solo que (para dar una excusa): *I'd buy it, except it's too expensive = lo compraría, pero es demasiado caro.* **3** (arc.) a menos que. || *v.t.* **4** (form.) exceptuar, excluir. || *v.i.* **5** objetar a. || **6 – for,** aparte de, con excepción de, excepto, salvo:

except for restaurants... = salvo restaurantes... 7 (fam.) – **that,** salvo que, solo que.
excepting | ɪk'septɪŋ | *prep.* a menos que, salvo que, excepto.
exception | ɪk'sepʃn | *s.c.* e *i.* 1 excepción, salvedad. || 2 **to take – (to),** ofenderse (por), enfadarse (por), objetar (a). 3 **the – proves the rule,** la excepción confirma la regla. 4 **with the – of,** exceptuando, a excepción de. 5 **without –,** sin excepción.
exceptional | ɪk'sepʃənl | *adj.* 1 excepcional, extraordinario. 2 raro, poco frecuente.
exceptionally | ɪk'sepʃənəlɪ | *adv.* 1 excepcionalmente, extraordinariamente. 2 excepcionalmente, poco corrientemente, en pocos casos, en pocas ocasiones.
excerpt | 'eksə:pt | *s.c.* 1 extracto, cita, pasaje (de una obra literaria, musical, etc.). || *v.t.* 2 seleccionar, extractar, citar.
excess | ɪk'ses | *s.c.* e *i.* 1 exceso, demasía, abuso. 2 (form.) COM. superávit, excedente. 3 tropelía, abuso. 4 intemperancia, exceso (en la comida o la bebida). || *adj.* 5 excesivo, de más. 6 COM. excedentario, sobrante. 7 suplementario. 8 **in – of,** más que, superior a. 9 **to –,** en exceso, de sobra.
excessive | ɪk'sesɪv | *adj.* excesivo, exagerado, descomunal, desmedido.
excessively | ɪk'sesɪvlɪ | *adv.* excesivamente, exageradamente, desmedidamente.
exchange | ɪks'tʃeɪndʒ | *s.c.* e *i.* 1 cambio, intercambio, trueque (de ideas, mercancías). 2 canje, intercambio (de prisioneros). 3 COM. cambio (de divisas). 4 COM. tipo de cambio. 5 COM. documentos de cambio. 6 intercambio de golpes, palabras, disparos. || *s.c.* 7 intercambio (escolar). 8 ejemplar de canje. 9 central telefónica. 10 COM. mercado de valores, Bolsa. 11 bolsa de trabajo. 12 lonja, mercado, plaza. || *v.t.* 13 cambiar, intercambiar, canjear. || 14 **to – signs,** hacerse señales, intercambiar gestos. 15 **to – words,** cruzar palabras. 16 **in – for,** a cambio de. 17 **Stock Exchange,** FIN. Bolsa.
exchangeable | ɪks'tʃeɪndʒəbl | *adj.* intercambiable, canjeable, cambiable.
excise | 'eksaɪz | *s.i.* 1 COM. impuesto de consumo (en comercio interior). || *v.t.* 2 COM. gravar al consumo. 3 MED. extirpar, amputar, cortar, eliminar.
excision | ek'sɪʒn | *s.c.* e *i.* MED. escisión, amputación, extirpación, supresión.
excitability | ɪkˌsaɪtə'bɪlɪtɪ | *s.i.* excitabilidad.
excitable | ɪk'saɪtəbl | *adj.* excitable, nervioso, histérico.
excite | ɪk'saɪt | *v.t.* 1 excitar, poner nervioso, alterar. 2 alterar, enardecer, entusiasmar. 3 excitar, emocionar, apasionar (sexualmente). 4 (form.) suscitar, despertar, provocar (admiración, interés). 5 BIOL. estimular (órganos, tejidos). 6 FIS. excitar, activar, incrementar la energía.
excited | ɪk'saɪtɪd | *adj.* 1 alterado, agitado, nervioso. 2 ilusionado, emocionado, entusiasmado. 3 acalorado, nervioso, alborotado (los niños). 4 excitado, estimulado (sexualmente). 5 FIS. activado, excitado. || 6 **to be nothing to get –,** no ser ninguna maravilla, no ser nada del otro mundo. 7 **to get –,** emocionarse, ilusionarse.
excitedly | ɪk'saɪtɪdlɪ | *adv.* acaloradamente, con entusiasmo, con emoción, con excitación.
excitement | ɪk'saɪtmənt | *s.i.* 1 excitación, nerviosismo, alteración. 2 ilusión, emoción, entusiasmo. 3 alboroto, acaloramiento, conmoción. || *s.c.* 4 emoción: *after all the excitements = después de todas las emociones.*
exciting | ɪk'saɪtɪŋ | *adj.* apasionante, emocionante, excitante.
excitingly | ɪk'saɪtɪŋlɪ | *adv.* apasionadamente, emocionalmente, excitantemente.
exclaim | ɪk'skleɪm | *v.t.* e *i.* (form.) exclamar, proferir una exclamación (de alegría, sorpresa).
exclamation | ˌeksklə'meɪʃn | *s.c.* 1 exclamación, grito. 2 GRAM. interjección. || 3 **– mark/point,** signo de admiración.
exclamatory | ek'sklæmətərɪ | *adj.* exclamativo, exclamatorio.
exclude | ɪk'sklu:d | *v.t.* 1 **[to – (from)]** excluir (de), exceptuar (de). 2 impedir, prohibir (el paso). 3 rechazar, omitir, no tomar en consideración (una razón, una posibilidad).
excluding | ɪk'sklu:dɪŋ | *prep.* con la exclusión de, con la excepción de.
exclusion | ɪk'sklu:ʒn | *s.i.* 1 exclusión, omisión. || 2 **to the – of,** excluyendo, con exclusión de, excepto.
exclusive | ɪk'sklu:sɪv | *adj.* 1 selecto, elegante, distinguido. 2 exclusivo, único (uso, propiedad). 3 incompatible, excluyente. || *s.c.* 4 exclusiva (una noticia, una venta). || 5 **– of,** sin, sin tomar en cuenta, excluyendo. 6 INF. – OR, O exclusivo.
exclusively | ɪk'sklu:sɪvlɪ | *adv.* exclusivamente, únicamente.
excomunicate | ˌekskə'mju:nɪkeɪt | *v.t.* 1 REL. excomulgar. || *adj.* 2 excomulgado.
excrement | 'ekskrɪmənt | *s.i.* (form.) excrementos, heces.
excrescence | ɪk'skresns | *s.c.* 1 (form.) excrecencia (en animales o plantas). 2 (fig.) bodrio, birria, espanto, horror.
excreta | ɪk'skri:tə | *s.i.* (form.) excreciones (corporales).
excrete | ek'skri:t | *v.t.* e *i.* (form.) excretar.
excruciating | ɪk'skru:ʃɪeɪtɪŋ | *adj.* 1 intenso, agudísimo, atroz (un dolor). 2 (fig.) penosísimo, fatal, espantoso (una actuación).
excruciatingly | ɪk'skru:ʃɪeɪtɪŋlɪ | *adv.* 1 agudísimamente, intensísimamente. 2 (fig.) dolorosamente, penosamente, fatal, de morirse de risa.
exculpate | 'ekskʌlpeɪt | *v.t.* (form.) exculpar, exonerar, disculpar.
excursion | ɪk'skə:ʃən | | ɪk'skə:ʒən | *s.c.* 1 excursión, paseo, salida. 2 incursión. 3 divergencia, disgresión. 4 MIL. expedición. || 5 **– ticket,** billete de excursión.
excusable | ɪk'skju:zəbl | *adj.* excusable, disculpable, perdonable.
excuse | ɪk'skju:s | *v.t.* 1 excusar, perdonar, disculpar. 2 justificar, defender (un comportamiento, un error). 3 excusar, eximir, dispensar (de un trabajo). 4 (euf.) (gen. pasiva) dar permiso, permitir (ir al retrete los niños en la escuela). 5 dejar salir. || *s.c.* 6 excusa, pretexto, disculpa. 7 razón, justificación. || 8 **by way of –/in –,** como pretexto, como excusa, como justificación. 9 **– me,** perdone, lo siento (al interrumpir a alguien); perdone, por favor (al abrirse paso); con permiso, disculpe (al abandonar un lugar). 10 **to make one's/ someone's excuses,** presentar excusas (por sí mismo o por otro).
execrable | 'eksɪkrəbl | *adj.* (form.) execrable, abominable.
executant | ɪg'zekjutənt | *s.c.* MUS. (form.) intérprete, ejecutante.
execute | 'eksɪkju:t | *v.t.* 1 ejecutar, ajusticiar. 2 (form.) ejecutar, realizar, cumplir, llevar a cabo (un trabajo, una orden). 3 MUS. interpretar, ejecutar. 4 DER. cumplir una disposición testamentaria.
execution | ˌeksɪ'kju:ʃn | *s.c.* e *i.* 1 ejecución, ajusticiamiento. || *s.i.* 2 (form.) ejecución, cumplimiento, realización (de una orden, un plan). 3 MUS. (form.) interpretación, ejecución. 4 DER. cumplimiento de una disposición testamentaria. || 5 **– cycle,** INF. ciclo de ejecución. 6 **– time,** INF. tiempo de ejecución. 7 **– routine,** INF. rutina de supervisión de un sistema operativo.
executioner | ˌeksɪ'kju:ʃnər | *s.c.* 1 verdugo. 2 intérprete, ejecutante.
executive | ɪg'zekjutɪv | *adj.* 1 ejecutivo (poder). 2 ejecutivo, directivo, administrativo. 3 de ejecutivo, para ejecutivos: *executive chair = silla de ejecutivo.* || *s.c.* 4 ejecutivo, directivo, administrador. 5 **[the –]** el ejecutivo, el comité ejecutivo (de un gobierno, de un partido político).
executor | ɪg'zekjutər | *s.c.* 1 DER. albacea, testamentario. 2 ejecutor, ejecutante.
exegeses V. **exegesis.**
exegesis | ˌeksɪ'dʒi:sɪs | [*pl.* **exegeses**] *s.c.* e *i.* 1 exégesis, interpretación, análisis (de un texto, de la Biblia).
exemplary | ɪg'semplərɪ | *adj.* 1 ejemplar, extraordinario. 2 (form.) ejemplar (un castigo).
exemplification | ɪgˌzemplɪfɪ'keɪʃn | *s.c.* e *i.* ejemplificación.
exemplify | ɪg'zemplɪfaɪ | *v.t.* 1 ejemplificar, tipificar. 2 ilustrar, dar un ejem-

plo, servir de ejemplo. **3** DER. certificar, notificar.
exempt | ɪg'zempt | *adj.* **1** exento, excusado, exonerado. **2** aislado, separado. || *v.t.* **3 [to – from]** exentar de, exonerar de, eximir de, excusar de. **4** aislar, separar.
exemption | ɪg'zempʃn | *s.c.* e *i.* **1** exención, exoneración. **2** inmunidad; franquicia.
exercise | 'eksəsaɪz | *s.c.* e *i.* **1** ejercicio, entrenamiento, práctica. || *s.c.* **2** ejercicio, composición, deber (escolar). **3** MIL. maniobra, ejercicio. **4** tarea, trabajo, labor, obra. **5** ceremonia (académica). || *s.pl.* **6** REL. ejercicios espirituales. || *s.i.* **7** (form.) ejercicio, uso (de un derecho, de una facultad). || *v.t.* e *i.* **8** hacer ejercicio físico, entrenarse. **9** llevar a hacer ejercicio, sacar a pasear (a un animal). || *v.t.* **10** (form.) ejercer, usar, emplear (un derecho, una facultad, un poder). **11 [to – by/about]** (gen. pasiva) (form.) preocupar, angustiar, inquietar. **12** (gen. pasiva) irritarse, ofenderse. || **13 – book,** cuaderno, libreta.
exert | ɪg'zəːt | *v.t.* **1** utilizar, emplear, aplicar (la fuerza, autoridad). **2** ejercer (influencia, un derecho). || *v.r.* **3 [to – oneself]** esforzarse, afanarse, (por hacer) molestarse mucho (física o mentalmente).
exertion | ɪg'zəːʃn | *s.c.* e *i.* esfuerzo extenuante, trabajo excesivo.
exhalation | ˌekshə'leɪʃn | *s.c.* e *i.* exhalación (de aire).
exhale | eks'heɪl | *v.t.* e *i.* **1** exhalar, espirar (aire). **2** emitir, despedir (gas, vapor). **3** evaporar, disipar.
exhaust | ɪg'zɔːst | *v.t.* **1** estar exhausto, dejar exhausto, agotar, rendir. **2** agotar, consumir, gastar, acabar (las fuerzas, los recursos). **3** (fig.) consumir, agotar (un tema). **4** vaciar, sacar. **5** empobrecer (el suelo). || *v.i.* **6** escapar, salir, fugarse (el gas). || *s.c.* **7** tubo de escape. || *s.i.* **8** gases de escape. || **9** (brit.) – **pipe**/(EE.UU.) **tail pipe,** tubo de escape.
exhausting | ɪg'zɔːstɪŋ | *adj.* agotador, cansado.
exhaustion | ɪg'zɔːstʃən | *s.i.* agotamiento, cansancio.
exhaustive | ɪg'zɔːstɪv | *adj.* exhaustivo, minucioso.
exhaustively | ɪg'zɔːstɪvlɪ | *adv.* exhaustivamente.
exhibit | ɪg'zɪbɪt | *v.t.* e *i.* **1** exhibir, exponer, presentar al público (obras de arte). || *v.t.* **2** (form.) mostrar, manifestar, revelar (un sentimiento, una cualidad). || *s.c.* **3** obras de arte, objetos (de una exposición). **4** DER. prueba documental, prueba instrumental. **5** (EE.UU.) exposición, exhibición.
exhibition | ˌeksɪ'bɪʃn | *s.c.* **1** exposición, exhibición. **2** demostración, manifestación (de mal comportamiento, de habilidad, de talento). **3** comportamiento estúpido, ridículo. **4** (brit.) beca. || **5 – space,** COM. feria de muestras, stand de feria. **6 to make an – of oneself,** hacer el ridículo, dar el espectáculo. **7 on –,** en exposición, expuesto al público.
exhibitionism | ˌeksɪ'bɪʃnɪzəm | *s.i.* exhibicionismo.
exhibitionist | ˌeksɪ'bɪʃnɪst | *s.c.* **1** exhibicionista. || *adj.* **2** exhibicionista.
exhibitor | ɪg'zɪbɪtər | *s.c.* expositor, participante (en una exposición o feria).
exhilarate | ɪg'zɪləreɪt | *v.t.* **1** encantar, emocionar, regocijar, exaltar. **2** estimular, levantar el ánimo.
exhilarated | ɪg'zɪləreɪtɪd | *adj.* emocionado.
exhilaration | ɪgˌzɪlə'reɪʃn | *s.i.* **1** alegría, optimismo, emoción, entusiasmo. **2** efecto estimulante.
exhort | ɪg'zɔːt | *v.t.* **1** (form.) exhortar, incitar. **2** (form.) aconsejar, instar. || *v.i.* **3** (form.) urgir.
exhortation | ˌɪgzɔː'teɪʃn | *s.c.* e *i.* **1** (form.) exhortación, incitación. **2** (form.) invocación, persuasión. **3** (form.) exhortación, consejo.
exhumation | ˌekshjuː'meɪʃn | *s.c.* e *i.* (form.) exhumación (de cadáveres).
exhume | eks'hjuːm | | ɪg'zjuːm | | ɪk'sjuːm | *v.t.* **1** (form.) exhumar, desenterrar. **2** sacar a la luz (después de un período de oscuridad).
exigence, exigency | 'eksɪdʒəns | *s.c.* (gen. *pl.*) **1** (form.) exigencia, urgencia, emergencia. || *s.i.* **2** exigencia, requerimiento.
exigent | 'eksɪdʒənt | *adj.* **1** (form.) urgente. **2** exigente.
exiguous | eg'zɪgjʊəs | *adj.* **1** (form.) exiguo, reducido, escaso. **2** insignificante, diminuto.
exile | 'eksaɪl | *s.i.* **1** exilio, destierro, deportación. || *s.c.* **2** exiliado, desterrado, deportado. || *v.t.* **3** exiliar, deportar, desterrar.
exist | ɪg'zɪst | *v.i.* **1** existir, ser, haber. **2** subsistir, sobrevivir, vivir en condiciones penosas.
existence | ɪg'zɪstəns | *s.i.* **1** existencia: *the existence of God = la existencia de Dios.* **2** existencia, vida, subsistencia: *a miserable existence = una vida miserable.* || **3 to come into –,** salir a la luz, nacer, aparecer.
existent | ɪg'zɪstənt | *adj.* existente, en existencia, actual.
existential | egzɪ'stenʃl | *adj.* (form.) existencia.
existentialism | ˌegzɪ'stenʃəlɪzəm | *s.i.* existencialismo.
existentialist | ˌegzɪ'stenʃəlɪst | FIL. *s.c.* **1** existencialista. || *adj.* **2** existencialista.
existing | ɪg'zɪstɪŋ | *adj.* existente, actual, vigente.
exit | 'eksɪt | *s.c.* **1** salida, puerta de salida (escrito en puertas, salida de autopista, de estaciones, etc...). **2** salida, marcha, partida, abandono (de un lugar). **3** mutis, salida de escena (en teatro). **4** (fig.) muerte. **5** INF. salida. || *v.i.* **6** salir, partir, marchar. **7** salir a escena: *exit Macbeth... = sale Macbeth.* **8 – trigger,** disparo externo (en video).
OBS. en teatro **exit** y su plural **exeunt** se colocan ante sujeto, y la tercera persona del *sing.* no lleva s.
exodus | 'eksədəs | *s.sing.* **1** éxodo, emigración, salida masiva. **2** Exodus, Éxodo (libro del Pentateuco). **3 the Exodus,** el éxodo (salida de los Israelitas de Egipto).
exonerate | ɪg'zɒnəreɪt | *v.t.* **1 [to – (from)]** (form.) exonerar, exculpar, eximir (de culpa, de responsabilidad). **2** exonerar, eximir, excusar (de obligaciones).
exoneration | ɪgˌzɒnə'reɪʃn | *s.i.* **1** exoneración, exculpación, descargo (de culpa, de responsabilidad). **2** exención, liberación (de obligaciones).
exorbitant | ɪg'zɔbɪtənt | *adj.* exorbitante, desorbitado, excesivo, exagerado, desmesurado.
exorbitantly | ɪg'zɔːbɪtəntlɪ | *adv.* de manera exorbitante, desorbitada, desmesuradamente.
exorcise | 'eksɔːsaɪz | (EE.UU. **exorcize**) *v.t.* **1** exorcizar, conjurar (solemnemente). **2** (fig.) librarse de, desembarazarse de (un recuerdo).
exorcism | 'eksɔːsɪzəm | *s.c.* e *i.* **1** exorcismo, conjuro. **2** (fig.) liberación, erradicación (de un recuerdo).
exorcist | 'eksɔːsɪst | *s.c.* REL. exorcista.
exotic | ɪg'zɒtɪk | *adj.* exótico, extraño, fascinante.
exoticism | ɪg'zɒtɪsɪzəm | *s.i.* exotismo.
expand | ɪk'spænd | *v.t.* e *i.* **1** expandir, incrementar, agrandar, ensanchar (la forma). **2** dilatar, hinchar (el volumen). **3** incrementar, aumentar (el número). **4** alargar, detallar (una historia). **5** desplegar (las alas). **6** MAT. desarrollar. **7** COM. expandir, extender. || *v.i.* **8 [to – on/upon]** sentirse expansivo, hablar con confianza, desahogarse.
expander | ɪk'spændər | *s.c.* TV. extensor.
expanse | ɪk'spæns | *s.c.* **1** espacio, área, extensión (de tierra, mar, agua). **2** expansión.
expansion | ɪk'spænʃn | *s.i.* **1** expansión, ampliación, ensanche. || *s.i.* **2** expansión, complemento, desarrollo (de un libro). **3** MAT. desarrollo. **4** espacio, extensión. **5** INF. expansión.
expansionism | ɪk'spænʃənɪzəm | *s.i.* POL. expansionismo.
expansionist | ɪk'spænʃənɪst | *adj.* **1** (desp.) POL. expansionista.
expansive | ɪk'spænsɪv | *adj.* **1** expansivo, efusivo, hablador, eufórico. **2** (form.) grande, extenso, amplio. **3** espléndido, generoso.
expansively | ɪk'spænsɪvlɪ | *adv.* **1** expansivamente, efusivamente. **2** (form.) extensamente, ampliamente (en el espacio). **3** generosamente, espléndidamente.
expansiveness | ɪk'spænsɪvnɪs | *s.i.* **1** efusividad. **2** (form.) extensión, amplitud (espacial). **3** generosidad, esplendidez.

expatiate | ɪk'speɪʃɪeɪt | *v.i.* **[to – on/ upon/about]** (form.) explayarse en/sobre (un tema).
expatriate | eks'pætrɪət | *s.c.* **1** expatriado, exiliado, desterrado. || *v.t.* **2** expatriar, exiliar, desterrar. || *v.r.* **3** expatriarse, exiliarse.
expect | ɪk'spekt | *v.t.* **1** esperar, creer, pensar, anticipar (que algo sucederá). **2** figurarse, contar con (algo). **3** esperar, aguardar, contar con (algo). **4** (fam.) presumir, suponer, imaginar. **5** considerar obligatorio, requerir. || **6 to be expecting,** estar embarazada, estar encinta, esperar (un hijo). **7 only to be expected,** bastante lógico, es muy normal.
expectancy | ɪk'spektənsɪ | *s.i.* **1** expectativa, esperanza, posibilidad. **2** expectación. || **3 life –,** esperanza de vida.
expectant | ɪk'spektənt | *adj.* **1** expectante, ansioso, anhelante. **2** embarazada, futura madre, futuro padre.
expectantly | ɪk'spektəntlɪ | *adv.* a la expectativa, con expectación.
expectation | ˌekspek'teɪʃn | *s.c.* e *i.* **1** aspiración, expectativa, expectación. **2** índice, probabilidad (de vida). **3** [*pl.*] expectativas, perspectivas de heredar. || **4 against/contrary to all expectations,** contra todas las expectativas. **5 beyond our expectations,** más allá de toda esperanza, mejor de lo que esperábamos.
expectorant | ɪk'spektərənt | *s.c.* MED. expectorante, medicina para la tos.
expedience, expediency | ɪk'spiːdjəns | | ek'spiːdjənsɪ | *s.i.* **1** conveniencia, oportunidad, utilidad. **2** ventaja.
expedient | ɪk'spiːdjənt | *adj.* **1** conveniente, apropiado, útil, oportuno. **2** rápido, acelerado, urgente. || *s.c.* **3** recurso, medida.
expedite | 'ekspɪdaɪt | *v.t.* **1** (form.) acelerar, facilitar (un asunto). **2** actuar con rapidez y eficacia. **3** (form.) expedir, despachar, dar curso a (documentos oficiales, mercancías).
expedition | ˌekspɪ'dɪʃn | *s.c.* **1** [– *v.sing./pl.*] expedición, viaje, excursión. **2** MIL. expedición, grupo expedicionario. || *s.i.* **3** rapidez, prontitud.
expeditionary | ˌekspɪ'dɪʃənərɪ | | eks↓pɪ'dɪʃəneri | *adj.* MIL. expedicionario.
expeditious | ˌekspɪ'dɪʃəs | *adj.* (form.) expedito, rápido, pronto, veloz.
expeditiously | ˌekspɪ'dɪʃəslɪ | *adv.* (form.) expeditamente, con prontitud, velozmente.
expel | ɪk'spel | *v.t.* **1** expulsar, echar (de un país). **2** expulsar (de un centro escolar). **3** destituir, expulsar (de una organización). **4** (form.) expeler (aire).
expend | ɪk'spend | *v.t.* **1** (form.) consumir, dedicar, pasar (tiempo). **3** (form.) derrochar, gastar (energía, dinero, medios). **3** (form.) poner, pasar (cuidado).
expendable | ɪk'spendəbl | *adj.* **1** sacrificable, no esencial, prescindible (personas). **2** fungible, que se puede tirar (un material). || *s.c.* **3** material fungible. || **4** COM. **– merchandise,** mercancía desechable. **5 – money,** COM. dinero disponible. **6 – personnel,** COM. personal excedente (del que se puede prescindir). **7 – shares,** COM. acciones amortizables.
expenditure | ɪk'spendɪtʃər | *s.c.* e *i.* **1** gasto, desembolso (de dinero). **2** gasto, consumo, dedicación (de tiempo, energía).
expense | ɪk'spens | *s.c.* e *i.* **1** gasto, coste, dispendio (de dinero, de tiempo, de esfuerzo). **2** detrimento, menoscabo, quebranto (de salud). **3** costa, expensas. **4** [*pl.*] gastos, dietas (de trabajo). || **5 to spare no –/to go to a lot of –,** sin reparar en gastos, sin mirar el dinero. **6 at the – of,** a costa de, en detrimento de. **7 at someone's –,** a costa de alguien. **8 all expenses paid,** a gastos pagados, con dietas. **9 expenses accrued,** gastos acumulados. **10 – allowance,** dieta, gastos pagados. **11 – budget,** presupuesto de gastos. **12 – account,** cuenta de gastos a justificar, cuenta de gastos reembolsables.
expensive | ɪk'spensɪv | *adj.* caro, costoso, gravoso.
expensively | ɪk'spensɪvlɪ | *adv.* caramente, costosamente.
experience | ɪk'spɪərɪəns | *s.i.* **1** experiencia, práctica. || *s.c.* **2** experiencia, vivencia. || *v.t.* **3** experimentar, sufrir, sentir. **4** afrontar, enfrentarse a (una situación); tropezar con (dificultades).
experienced | ɪk'spɪərɪənst | *adj.* **1** experimentado, experto, con experiencia. **2** versado, entendido, erudito, culto.
experiment | ɪk'sperɪmənt | *s.c.* e *i.* **1** experimento, prueba, ensayo. || *v.i.* **2 [to – (on/with)]** experimentar, hacer experimentos, realizar pruebas (científicas). **3** experimentar, probar, intentar (un método, una idea).
experimental | ekˌsperɪ'mentl | *adj.* **1** experimental, de prueba. **2** empírico.
experimentally | ekˌsperɪ'mentlɪ | *adv.* experimentalmente, de manera experimental.
experimentation | ekˌsperɪmen'teɪʃn | *s.i.* experimentación, ensayo.
expert | 'ekspəːt | *s.c.* **1** experto, perito, avezado, diestro. **2** especialista, técnico. || *adj.* **3** experto, experimentado, versado. **4** especializado, altamente cualificado.
expertise | ˌekspəː'tiːz | *s.i.* **1** experiencia, pericia, conocimiento, habilidad. **2** juicio, criterio, apreciación, estimación.
expertly | 'ekspəːtlɪ | *adv.* con pericia, habilidosamente.
expiate | 'ekspɪeɪt | *v.t.* (form.) expiar, purgar, reparar, subsanar, remediar.
expiation | ˌekspɪ'eɪʃn | *s.i.* expiación, reparación (de culpas).
expiatory | 'ekspɪətərɪ | *adj.* expiatorio.
expiration | ˌekspɪ'reɪʃn | *s.i.* **1** expiración, finalización, terminación. **2** COM. vencimiento (de un plazo). **3** (lit.) muerte.
expire | ɪk'spaɪər | *v.i.* **1** expirar, terminar, finalizar. **2** COM. vencer (un plazo). **3** (lit.) expirar, morir. **4** expirar, exhalar (aire). **5** (arc.) emitir, despedir (vapor, olor, gas).
expiry | ɪk'spaɪərɪ | V. **expiration.**
explain | ɪk'spleɪn | *v.t.* e *i.* **1** explicar, aclarar, esclarecer. **2** interpretar. || *v.t.* **3** explicar, justificar, dar razones. || *v.r.* **4 to – oneself,** explicarse con detalle, hablar claro, justificarse. **5 to – away,** explicar convincentemente, disculpar con habilidad, justificar.
explainable | ɪk'spleɪnəbl | *adj.* **1** explicable. **2** justificable.
explanation | ˌeksplə'neɪʃn | *s.c.* e *i.* **1** [– **(of, for)**] explicación, aclaración, esclarecimiento. **2** justificación, explicación, disculpa.
explanatory | ɪk'splænətərɪ | *adj.* explicativo, aclaratorio, esclarecedor.
expletive | ɪk'spliːtɪv | | 'eksplətɪv | *s.c.* (form.) imprecación, juramento, taco, palabrota.
explicable | ɪk'splɪkəbl | *adj.* (form.) explicable.
explicit | ɪk'splɪsɪt | *adj.* **1** explícito, preciso, claro. **2** detallado, gráfico. **3** franco, sin reservas. || **4 – addressing,** INF. direccionamiento en que la tarjeta viene expresada. **5 – operand,** INF. operando no simbólico, explícito.
explicitly | ɪk'splɪsɪtlɪ | *adv.* **1** explícitamente, con precisión, con claridad. **2** gráficamente, detalladamente. **3** abiertamente.
explicitness | ɪk'splɪsɪtnɪs | *s.i.* claridad, precisión.
explode | ɪk'spləud | *v.t.* e *i.* **1** estallar, explosionar, hacer explosión, volar (una bomba). **2** (lit.) hacer eclosión, brotar (una flor, la luz). **3** (lit.) estallar (una tormenta). || *v.i.* **4 [to – (in/into/with)]** estallar (de ira); reventar, desternillarse (de risa). || *v.t.* **5** [gen. *pas.*] refutar, rebatir (una teoría).
exploit | ɪk'splɔɪt | *v.t.* **1** (desp.) explotar, utilizar, aprovecharse de (una persona). **2** explotar, sacar provecho a (la tierra, una idea, etc.). || | 'eksplɔɪt | *s.c.* **3** hazaña, gesta, proeza, heroicidad.
exploitable | ɪk'splɔɪtəbl | *adj.* **1** aprovechable, utilizable (recursos materiales). **2** explotable (gente).
exploitation | ˌeksplɔɪ'teɪʃn | *s.i.* explotación, aprovechamiento.
exploitative | ɪk'splɔɪtətɪv | *adj.* (form. y desp.) explotador.
exploiter | ɪk'splɔɪtər | *s.c.* explotador.
exploration | ˌeksplə'reɪʃn | *s.c.* e *i.* **1** exploración (viaje). **2** examen, investigación. **3** MED. exploración.
exploratory | ek'splɒrətərɪ | *adj.* exploratorio.
explore | ɪk'splɔ | *v.t.* **1** explorar, descubrir. **2** examinar, investigar, estudiar (posibilidades, un tema). **3** MED. explorar, auscultar, examinar.
explorer | ɪk'splɔːrər | *s.c.* **1** explorador, descubridor. **2** MED. sonda. **3** (EE.UU.) sonda espacial.
explosion | ɪk'spləuʒn | *s.c.* **1** explosión, estallido, detonación. **2** (fig.)

explosión, estallido (de ira, risas). **3** eclosión, brote.
explosive | ɪk'spləʊsɪv | *adj.* **1** explosivo. **2** (fig.) explosivo, fuerte, violento (el carácter). **3** controvertido, polémico (un tema). || *s.c.* e *i.* **4** explosivo, material explosivo. || **5 high –,** explosivo de gran potencia. **6 plastic –,** V. **plastic.**
explosively | ɪk'spləʊsɪvlɪ | *adv.* **1** con explosión, de manera detonante. **2** fuertemente, con fiereza (reacción de una persona).
explosiveness | ɪk'spləʊsɪvnɪs | *s.i.* delicadeza (de una situación que puede explotar).
exponent | ek'spəʊnənt | *s.c.* **1** exponente, defensor, partidario. **2** experto, versado. **3** MAT. exponente, índice. **4** INF. exponente. || *adj.* **5** explicativo.
export | ek'spɔːt | *v.t.* e *i.* **1** COM. exportar. **2** (fig.) exportar, extender (una idea). || | 'ekspɔːt | *s.i.* **3** COM. exportación. || *s.c.* **4** COM. producto para la exportación. || **5 – licence,** COM. licencia de exportación.
export-import bank | ˌekspɔːt'ɪmpɔːt bæŋk | *s.c.* COM. banco de exportación-importación.
exportable | ek'spɔːtəbl | *adj.* exportable.
exportation | ˌekspɔː'teɪʃn | *s.i.* **1** COM. exportación. || *s.c.* **2** COM. producto para exportación.
exporter | ek'spɔːtər | *s.c.* COM. exportador (una persona, un país).
expose | ɪk'spəʊz | *v.t.* **1** exponer, exhibir, mostrar, descubrir. **2** (fig.) exponer, arriesgar, aventurar, comprometer. **3** delatar, desenmascarar. **4** FOT. exponer (a la luz). **5** abandonar (a un niño). || *v.r.* **6** exhibir (un hombre, sus genitales).
exposed | ɪk'spəʊzd | *adj.* **1** expuesto, sin protección, al descubierto. || **2 to be – to,** estar expuesto a.
exposition | ˌekspəʊ'zɪʃn | *s.c.* e *i.* **1** exposición, explicación, comentario. || *s.c.* **2** exposición internacional, feria internacional (de productos industriales, obras de arte). **3** MUS. exordio, introducción (de una sonata, de una fuga). **4** abandono (de un niño).
expostulate | ɪk'spɒstjʊleɪt | *v.i.* **1** (form.) objetar, protestar, recriminar. **2** tratar de convencer, tratar de disuadir. **3** **[to – with]** reprender a, discutir con.
expostulation | ɪkˌspɒstjʊ'leɪʃn | *s.c.* e *i.* **1** (form.) objeción, protesta, recriminación. **2** disuasión.
exposure | ɪk'spəʊʒər | *s.c.* e *i.* **1** exposición, riesgo. **2** delación, revelación. || *s.c.* **3** FOT. fotografía, exposición: *one exposure left = queda una fotografía* (en la cámara fotográfica). || *s.i.* **4** hipotermia, frío: *died of exposure = murió de frío.* **5** frente, posición (de un edificio): *it has a western exposure = da a poniente.* **6** abandono (de un niño). || **7 – meter,** fotómetro.
expound | ɪk'spaʊnd | *v.t.* e *i.* **[to – (on)]** exponer, explicar, detallar (una idea).
express | ɪk'spres | *v.t.* **1** expresar, dar expresión, manifestar (una opinión). **2** transmitir, comunicar, dar a entender (a través del comportamiento, de una mirada). **3** (brit.) enviar por correo urgente, enviar por mensajero. **4 [to – (from/out)]** (form.) exprimir, extraer (zumo). **5** MAT. representar, expresar. || *v.r.* **6 [to – oneself]** expresarse. || *s.c.* **7** rápido, expreso (trenes, autobuses). || *s.i.* **8** (brit.) correo urgente, transporte urgente, servicio de urgencia. || *adv.* **9** por servicio urgente, por correo urgente, urgentemente. || *adj.* **10** rápido, urgente, expreso (un envío, un tren, etc.). **11** (form.) explícito, claro, preciso, expreso (un deseo, una orden). **12** específico, particular (un propósito).
expression | ɪk'spreʃn | *s.c.* e *i.* **1** expresión, manifestación. || *s.c.* **2** expresión, semblante, aspecto. **3** expresión, modismo, frase hecha. **4** MAT. representación. || *s.i.* **5** expresividad, emoción, sensibilidad, sentimiento (al actuar, al cantar). **6** expresión (de frutas). || **7 to give – to,** expresar, manifestar. **8 as an – of thanks,** en señal de agradecimiento.
expressionism | ɪk'spreʃnɪzəm | *s.i.* ART. expresionismo.
expressionist | ɪk'spreʃənɪst | *s.c.* ART. expresionista.
expressionless | ɪk'spreʃnlɪs | *adj.* inexpresivo, poco emotivo, sin sentimiento.
expressive | ɪk'spresɪv | *adj.* **1** (form.) significativo, expresivo, revelador, indicativo (de un sentimiento). **2** comunicativo.
expressiveness | ɪk'spresɪvnɪs | *s.i.* expresividad, intensidad de la expresión.
expressively | ɪk'spresɪvlɪ | *adv.* **1** expresamente, explícitamente, con claridad. **2** adrede, con el propósito de, con la intención de. || **3 to deny/prohibit –,** denegar o prohibir terminantemente.
expropriate | eks'prəʊprɪeɪt | *v.t.* **1** expropiar (legalmente). **2** desposeer, expoliar, despojar (ilegalmente).
expropriation | eksˌprəʊprɪ'eɪʃn | *s.c.* e *i.* **1** expropiación. **2** desposesión, expoliación.
expulsion | ɪk'spʌlʃn | *s.c.* e *i.* **1** expulsión (de un lugar, de un país). **2** expulsión, descarga.
expunge | ek'spʌndʒ | *v.t.* **1** (form.) borrar, tachar, destruir. **2** (fig. y form.) borrar (de la memoria).
expurgate | 'ekspəːgeɪt | *v.t.* expurgar, mutilar (una obra literaria).
exquisite | 'ekskwɪzɪt | *adj.* **1** exquisito, refinado, cortés. **2** delicado, sensible, bello. **3** (form.) intenso, vivo (un dolor, un placer). || *s.c.* **4** petimetre, elegante (en exceso).
exquisitely | 'ekskwɪzɪtlɪ | *adv.* **1** exquisitamente, refinadamente. **2** delicadamente, sensiblemente. **3** intensamente, agudamente.
ex-serviceman | ˌeks'səːvɪsmæn | [*pl.* **ex-servicemen**] *s.c.* (brit.) excombatiente.
extant | ek'stænt | *adj.* **1** (form.) existente, en existencia (un documento, una obra artística, literaria). **2** vigente (una ley).
extemporary | ɪk'stempərərɪ | *adj.* improvisado, sin preparación previa.
extempore | ek'stempərɪ | *adj.* **1** improvisado, sin preparación previa. || *adv.* **2** de improviso, sin preparación.
extemporize | ɪk'stempəraɪz | (también **extemporise**) *v.t.* **1** (form.) improvisar.
extend | ɪk'stend | *v.i.* **1 [to – *adv./prep.*]** extenderse, prolongarse (en el tiempo). **2** extenderse, abarcar, llegar hasta. **3** (fig.) incluir (a alguien): *this extends to you, too = esto también te incluye.* || *v.t.* **4** extender, alargar, ampliar, ensanchar, prolongar. **5** extender, estirar (los brazos). **6** desplegar, extender (las alas). **7** entregar, tender (algo a alguien). **8** (form.) ofrecer, brindar (ayuda, amistad). **9** COM. conceder (un crédito). **10** (gen. pasiva) forzarse a, desplegar todas las fuerzas. **11** adulterar, mezclar. **12** (brit.) DER. tasar, evaluar, valorar. **13** DER. embargar. || *v.r.* **14 [to – oneself]** rendir al máximo, trabajar al máximo. || **15 extended memory storage,** INF. almacenamiento ampliado de memoria. **16 extended operating system,** INF. sistema operativo extensivo (EOS).
extension | ɪk'stenʃn | *s.c.* e *i.* **1** extensión, prolongación, alargamiento. **2** prórroga, ampliación. || *s.c.* **3** ampliación, anexo (en una vivienda). **4** extensión telefónica. **5** teléfono supletorio. **6** cable alargador.
extensive | ɪk'stensɪv | *adj.* **1** extenso, enorme, amplio, vasto. **2** general, común. **3** frecuente.
extensively | ɪk'stensɪvlɪ | *adv.* **1** extensamente, muchísimo. **2** por todas partes. **3** totalmente, completamente: *extensively modified = completamente modificado.*
extent | ɪk'stent | *s.i.* **1** extensión, dimensión, área. **2** (fig.) magnitud, amplitud (de conocimientos). **3** importancia, alcance, medida (de daños, problemas). **4** límite. **5** (arc.) tasación, valoración. **6** DER. (brit.) embargo, ejecución de una deuda. || **7 to a certain/some –,** hasta cierto punto. **8 to such an –,** hasta tal punto. **9 to a large/great –,** en gran parte, en gran medida. **10 to the – of,** hasta el punto de.
extenuate | ek'stenjʊeɪt | *v.t.* **1** atenuar, reducir, mitigar, disminuir. **2** extenuar, debilitar.
extenuating | ek'stenjʊeɪtɪŋ | *adj.* **1** atenuante, paliativo: *extenuating circumstances = circunstancias atenuantes.*
extenuation | ɪkˌstenjʊ'eɪʃn | *s.i.* DER. atenuante.
exterior | ek'stɪərɪər | *adj.* **1** exterior, externo. || *s.c.* **2** exterior, aspecto exterior, apariencia. **3** ART. paisaje.
exterminate | ɪk'stəːmɪneɪt | *v.t.* exterminar, aniquilar.
extermination | ɪkˌstəːmɪ'neɪʃn | *s.i.* exterminación, aniquilación.

external | ek'stɜːnl | | ek'stɜːrnl | *adj.* **1** externo, exterior. **2** externo, superficial. || *s.pl.* **3** (form.) apariencias; partes externas. || **4 – line,** INF. línea externa. **5 – memory/storage,** INF. memoria o almacenamiento externo. **6 – name,** INF. nombre externo. **7 – procedure,** INF. procedimiento externo.

externally | ek'stɜː'nlɪ | *adv.* **1** externamente, exteriormente. **2** superficialmente.

externalize | ɪk'stɜːnəlaɪz | (también **externalise**) *v.t.* (form.) exteriorizar (pensamientos o similar).

extinct | ɪk'stɪŋkt | *adj.* **1** extinto, extinguido (una raza). **2** (fig.) desaparecida, destruida, abolida, suprimida, desaparecida (una costumbre). **3** inactivo (un volcán).

extinction | ɪk'stɪŋkʃn | *s.i.* **1** extinción. **2** desaparición, destrucción, abolición. **3** (form.) extinción (de un fuego).

extinguish | ɪk'stɪŋgwɪʃ | *v.t.* **1** (form.) extinguir, apagar. **2** (fig.) extinguir, desvanecer (una esperanza, la fe). **3** eclipsar, obscurecer. **4** DER. abolir, derogar, suprimir.

extinguisher | ɪk'stɪŋgwɪʃər | *s.c.* extintor.

extirpate | 'ekstɜːpeɪt | *v.t.* **1** (form.) erradicar, exterminar. **2** MED. extirpar. **3** arrancar de raíz, desarraigar.

extol | ɪk'stəʊl | *v.t.* (form.) ensalzar, alabar, elogiar, enaltecer, encomiar.

extort | ɪk'stɔːt | *v.t.* **1** extorsionar, obtener por la fuerza, conseguir con amenazas. **2** (lit.) arrancar (una promesa).

extortion | ɪk'stɔːʃn | *s.i.* **1** extorsión. **2** robo, atropello, atraco (referido al coste excesivo de algo).

extortionate | ɪk'stɔːʃnət | *adj.* **1** (desp.) exorbitante, exagerado, desorbitado (un precio). **2** de extorsión.

extortioner | ɪk'stɔːʃnər | *s.c.* usurpador, causante de extorsión; concusionario (un funcionario).

extortionist | ɪk'stɔːʃənɪst | V. **extortioner.**

extra | 'ekstrə | *adj.* **1** extra, adicional, suplementario. **2** extra, de recargo, aparte. **3** de recambio (piezas). **4** superior, óptimo. || *adv.* **5** extra, adicionalmente. **6** especialmente, excepcionalmente, en extremo: *extra kind = excepcionalmente amable.* **7** muy, más de lo normal: *extra dry = muy seco.* || *s.c.* **8** suplemento, recargo. **9** extra, gasto extraordinario. **10** sobrante, exceso. **12** especial (una edición de un periódico). **13** sustituto, suplente (un trabajador).

OBS. **extra** se utiliza como prefijo delante de *adj.* para formar otros *adj.*, gen. en publicidad: *extra large = más grande de lo normal; extra parliamentary groups = grupos extraparlamentarios.*

extract | ɪk'strækt | *v.t.* **1** extraer, sacar (un diente). **2** (fig.) arrancar, obtener por la fuerza (una confesión). **3** QUIM. extraer, sacar, obtener (por destilación, evaporación). **4** extractar, condensar, compendiar (una obra escrita). **5** MAT. extraer, calcular (una raíz). || | 'ekstrækt | *s.c.* **6** extracto, compendio, selección, pasaje (de una obra escrita). || *s.i.* **7** QUIM. extracto, esencia.

extraction | ɪk'strækʃn | *s.c.* e *i.* **1** extracción. **2** QUIM. extracción, obtención. || *s.i.* **3** extracción, origen, descendencia.

extractor | ɪk'stræktər | *s.c.* **1** extractor (un instrumento, una máquina). **2** exprimidor (de zumos). || **3 – fan,** extractor de humos.

extracurricular | ˌekstrəkə'rɪkjələr | *adj.* complementario, de actividades extraescolares (en la educación).

extraditable | 'ekstrədaɪtəbl | *adj.* DER. extraditable, sujeto a extradición.

extradite | 'ekstrədaɪt | *v.t.* **1** DER. extraditar, extradir. **2** obtener la extradición.

extradition | ˌekstrə'dɪʃn | *s.c.* e *i.* DER. extradición.

extramarital | ˌekstrə'mærɪtl | *adj.* (form.) adúltero.

extra-mural | ˌekstrə'mjʊərəl | *adj.* **1** de enseñanza de adultos (actividades de las universidades para adultos). **2** de fuera (actividades hacia fuera de una organización o institución cualquiera): *our extra-mural activities are very interesting = nuestras actividades externas son muy interesantes.*

extraneous | ek'streɪnjəs | *adj.* **1** irrelevante, intrascendente, sin importancia. **2** externo, extraño, exterior, ajeno.

extraordinarily | ɪk'strɔːdnrɪlɪ | | ɪkˌstrɔːrdn'erəlɪ | | ˌekstrə'ɔːrdnerəlɪ | *adv.* **1** extrañamente, extraordinariamente. **2** extremadamente.

extraordinary | ɪk'strɔːdnrɪ | | ɪk'strɔːrdnerɪ | | ˌekstrə'ɔːrdnerɪ | *adj.* **1** extraño, raro, increíble. **2** extraordinario, excepcional, notable. **3** (form.) extraordinaria (una junta, una reunión). **4** [*s.* + –] extraordinario, especial: *Embassador extraordinary = embajador extraordinario.*

extrapolation | ɪkˌstræpə'leɪʃn | (form.) *s.i.* **1** extrapolación, inferencia. || *s.c.* **2** [– (**from**)] proyección, cálculo (basado en puntos previos).

extraterrestrial | ˌekstrətə'restrɪəl | *adj.* **1** extraterrestre. || *s.c.* **2** extraterrestre.

extrasensory | ˌekstrə'sensərɪ | *adj.* extrasensorial.

extraterritorial | 'ekstrəˌterɪ'tɔːrɪəl | *adj.* **1** (form.) extraterritorial. **2** DER. con inmunidad (no sujeto a la jurisdicción local).

extravagance | ɪk'strævəgəns | *s.c.* e *i.* **1** (desp.) extravagancia, excentricidad. **2** (desp.) derroche, despilfarro.

extravagant | ɪk'strævəgənt | *adj.* **1** despilfarrador, derrochador. **2** lujoso. **3** exagerado, desorbitante (un precio). **4** (desp.) excentricidad, extravagancia.

extravagantly | ɪk'strævəgəntlɪ | *adv.* **1** extravagantemente, excéntricamente, de modo raro. **2** con derroche, con despilfarro. **3** lujosamente. **4** exageradamente, excesivamente.

extravaganza | ekˌstrævə'gænzə | *s.c.* espectáculo (costoso, elaborado, y de gran colorido).

extreme | ɪk'striːm | *adj.* **1** [no *comp.*] extremo, sumo, intenso, de más alto grado. **2** [no *comp.*] extremo, remoto, alejado. **3** (desp.) extremo, radical, inmoderado (de ideas). **4** drástico, severo. || *s.c.* **5** extremo, límite, cabo. **6** FIL. premisa mayor o menor (de un silogismo). **7** MAT. término primero o último (de una serie). || **8 to go from one – to the other,** pasar de un extremo a otro. **9 to go/be driven/carry/take to extremes,** excederse, ir muy lejos, tomar medidas extremas. **10 in the –,** en grado sumo.

extremely | ɪk'striːmlɪ | *adv.* extremadamente, excesivamente, sumamente.

extremism | ɪk'striːmɪzəm | *s.i.* (gen. desp.) extremismo, radicalismo (político).

extremist | ɪk'striːmɪst | *adj.* (gen. desp.) extremista, radical (de ideas políticas).

extremity | ɪk'stremɪtɪ | *s.i.* **1** (form.) extremo, más alto grado (de sufrimiento). **2** extremismo, radicalismo (político). || *s.c.* **3** (form.) extremo, punto más lejano. **4** punto extremo, alto grado. || *s.pl.* **5** ANAT. extremidades, miembros. **6** medidas extremas.

extricate | 'ekstrɪkeɪt | *v.t.* **1** [**to – from**] retirar de, liberar de, separar de, sacar de (entre escombros). **2** desenredar, desenmarañar, desembrollar. || *v.r.* **3** [**to – oneself**] (fig.) librarse, lograr salir (de una situación).

extrication | ˌekstrɪ'keɪʃn | *s.i.* **1** liberación, desembarazo (de algo o alguien, o en favor de alguien).

extrinsic | ek'strɪnsɪk | *adj.* **1** extrínseco, externo, extraño. **2** accesorio, no inherente.

extrovert, extravert | 'ekstrəʊvɜːt | *s.c.* **1** extrovertido, extravertido. **2** (fam.) alegre, activo, sociable. || *adj.* **3** extrovertido.

extrude | ɪk'struːd | *v.t.* e *i.* (form.) expulsar, echar afuera (a través de un pequeño orificio).

extrusion | ɪk'struːʒn | *s.c.* e *i.* (form.) expulsión, V. **extrude.**

exuberance | ɪg'zjuːbərəns | *s.i.* alegría, gozo; exuberancia.

exuberant | ɪg'zjuːbərənt | | ɪg'zuːbərənt | *adj.* **1** efusivo, entusiasta, eufórico, lleno de vida. **2** (fig.) espléndido, generoso. **3** exuberante, frondoso (una planta).

exude | ɪg'zjuːd | *v.t.* e *i.* **1** rezumar, destilar, exudar. **2** (fig.) destilar, transmitir (confianza, vitalidad).

exult | ɪg'zʌlt | *v.i.* (form.) [**to – at/in/over**] exultar, alegrarse en extremo, regocijarse, estar triunfante.

exultant | ɪg'zʌltənt | *adj.* (form.) exultante, jubiloso, triunfante.

exultation | ˌegzʌl'teɪʃn | *s.i.* (form.) exultación, júbilo, regocijo.

eye | aɪ | *s.c.* **1** ANAT. ojo. **2** vista, visión. **3** (fig.) vista, ojo, juicio, intuición. **4** ojo (de la aguja). **5** ojo, yema (de la patata). **6** ojo, centro (de la tormenta, del huracán). **7** presilla. **8** centro, foco. **9** opinión, punto de vista. **10** (fam.) detective, investigador. || *v.t.* **11** **[to – (up)]** mirar detenidamente, observar, echar una ojeada. || **12 an – for an –,** ojo por ojo. **13 to catch someone's –,** captar la atención de alguien, atraer la atención de alguien. **14 to cry one's eyes out,** llorar a mares, llorar a lágrima viva, llorar lágrimas de sangre. **15 to give the –/to make eyes at,** (fam.) lanzar miradas incitantes a, comer con los ojos a. **16 to have an – to/for the main chance,** estar a la que salta. **17 to have eyes in the back of one's head,** (fam.) ver a través de las paredes, tener ojos en el cogote. **18 in the eyes of,** en opinión de, a los ojos de. **19 in a pig's –,** (argot) ¡jamás!, ¡bajo ningún concepto! **20 to keep one's – on/out of,** echar una ojeada a, vigilar a; (fig.) no perder de vista a, estar atento a. **21 to keep one's eyes open /peeled skinned,** estar alerta, vigilar atentamente. **22 more than meets the –,** más complicado de lo que parece. **23 my –!** (argot y arc.) ¡sí, ya!, ¡y que más!, ¡anda ya! **24 one in the – for,** (fam.) una frustración, una desilusión. **25 only to have eyes for,** tener solamente ojos para. **26 to see – to –,** ver por los ojos de, llevarse excelentemente. **27 to shut /close one's eyes to,** cerrar los ojos a, ignorar. **28 someones eyes are too big for their stomach,** (hum.) antes se llena la tripa que el ojo. **29 under/before one's very eyes,** ante los propios ojos de uno. **30 up to the eyes/one's eyes in,** (fam.) atosigado, abrumado, hasta las narices (de trabajo). **31 with an – to,** con vistas a, con el propósito de, con la intención de. **32 with half an –,** (fam.) sin profundizar demasiado, a simple vista. **33 with one's eyes open,** con los ojos bien abiertos, a sabiendas. **34 black –,** V. **black. 35 electric –,** V. **electric. 36 evil –,** V. **evil. 37 magic –,** V. **magic. 38 to turn a blind –,** V. **blind. 39 to feast your eyes,** V. **to feast. 40 to look someone in the –,** V. **to look. 41 to meet someone in the –,** V. **to meet. 42 in the twinkling of an –,** V. **twinkling.**

eyeball | 'aɪbɔːl | *s.c.* **1** globo ocular. || *v.t.* **2** (EE.UU.) mirarse a la cara, mirarse de frente. || **3 – to –,** cara a cara, frente a frente.

eyebath | 'aɪbaːθ | [*pl.* **eyebaths**] *s.c.* ojera.

eyebrow | 'aɪbraʊ | *s.c.* **1** ceja. || **2 to raise one's –,** levantar las cejas, (desaprobadoramente, sorprendido). **3 up to one's eyebrows,** (fam.) muy ocupado, atosigado, abrumado, hasta el gorro, hasta la coronilla (de trabajo).

eye-catcher | 'aɪˌkætʃər | *s.c.* cosa que llama la atención.

eye-catching | 'aɪˌkætʃɪn | *adj.* que llama la atención, poco corriente, muy atractivo.

-eyed | aɪd | *adj.* [*adj.* – en compuestos] de ojos: *blue-eyed = de ojos azules.*

eyeful | 'aɪfʊl | *s.c.* **1** (fam.) una buena ojeada, un vistazo. **2** (fam.) persona interesante, persona atractiva (especialmente una mujer).

eyeglass | 'aɪglɑːs | | 'aɪglæs | *s.c.* **1** monóculo. **2** [*pl.*] (arc.) anteojos, gafas. **3** lavaojos.

eyelash | 'aɪlæʃ | *s.c.* pestaña.

eyelid | 'aɪlɪd | *s.c.* **1** párpado. || **2 without batting an –,** sin pestañear, sin inmutarse.

eye-opener | 'aɪˌəʊpnər | *s.sing.* **1** sorpresa, revelación. **2** (fam.) trago, bebida (alcohólica).

eyepiece | 'aɪpiːs | *s.c.* OPT. lente, ocular.

eyeshade | 'aɪˌʃeɪd | *s.c.* visera.

eyeshadow | 'aɪˌʃædəʊ | *s.c.* e *i.* sombreador de ojos, sombra de ojos (cosmético).

eyesight | 'aɪsaɪt | *s.i.* vista, alcance visual.

eyesore | 'aɪsɔː | *s.c.* engendro, cosa antiestética, monstruosidad, cosa que ofende la vista.

eyestrain | 'aɪstreɪn | *s.i.* MED. fatiga ocular, vista fatigada.

eyetooth | 'aɪtuːθ | [*pl.* **eyeteeth**] *s.c.* **1** canino, colmillo. || **2 to give one's eyeteeth for,** dar la luna por, dar todo el oro del mundo por.

eyewash | 'aɪwɒʃ | *s.i.* **1** MED. colirio, solución ocular. **2** (fam. y p.u.) bobada, engañabobos.

eyewitness | ˌaɪ'wɪtnɪs | *s.c.* testigo ocular, testigo presencial.

eyrie | 'aɪərɪ | *s.c.* **1** nido de ave rapaz; aguilera. **2** (fig.) fortaleza inexpugnable.

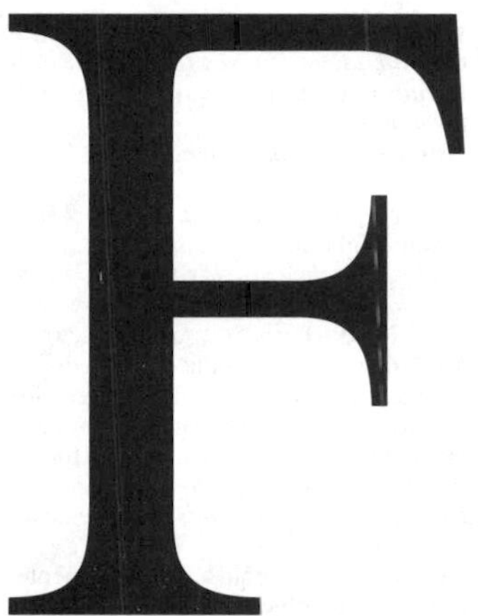

f, F | ef | *s.c.* **1** f, F (sexta letra del alfabeto inglés). || *s.c.* e *i.* **2** MUS. Fa.
OBS. Esta letra puede servir para señalar la abreviatura de gran número de palabras, entre ellas la más importante puede ser **3** la utilizada para indicar grados de temperatura Fahrenheit.
fab | fæb | *adj.* (fam.) fabuloso, magnífico.
fable | 'feɪbl | *s.c.* **1** LIT. fábula, fabulación. **2** (fig.) cuento, cuento chino, fábula.
fabled | 'feɪbld | *adj.* legendario, mítico.
fabric | 'fæbrɪk | *s.c.* e *i.* **1** tela, paño, tejido. || *s.sing.* **2 [(the) – (of)]** (fig.) base, fundamento: *the fabric of society.* **3** estructura, fábrica: *the fabric of this church is strong = la estructura de esta iglesia es fuerte.*
fabricate | 'fæbrɪkeɪt | *v.t.* **1** falsificar, inventar falsificando (evidencias, pruebas, etc.). **2** (form.) fabricar, manufacturar.
fabrication | ˌfæbrɪ'keɪʃn | (form.) *s.c.* e *i.* **1** invención, falsificación, mentira. || *s.i.* **2** fabricación, manufactura.
fabulous | 'fæbjʊləs | *adj.* **1** (fam.) fabuloso, extraordinario, fantástico. **2** legendario, mítico, de fábula (criaturas, lugares, monstruos, etc.).
fabulously | 'fæbjʊləslɪ | *adv.* fabulosamente, extraordinariamente, fantásticamente.
façade | fə'sɑːd | *s.c.* **1** ARQ. fachada, frente. || *s.sing.* **2** (fig.) apariencia pretenciosa, pretensión falsa: *we have a façade of unity, but it is not real = tenemos una apariencia pretenciosa de unidad, pero no es real.*
face | feɪs | *s.c.* **1** cara, rostro, faz (como parte anatómica). **2** (fig.) aspecto, cara, expresión facial: *a happy face.* **3** esfera (del reloj). **4** cara (de cartas o similar). **5** haz, derecho, parte delantera (de un objeto). **6** GEOG. cara, lado. || *s.sing.* **7** (lit.) faz, aspecto (de una ciudad, lugar, etc.). **8** cariz, apariencia: *the new technology has changed the face of my profession = la nueva tecnología ha cambiado la apariencia de mi profesión.* || *v.t.* **9** encarar, mirar hacia: *the house faces south = la casa mira hacia el sur.* **10** confrontar, colocarse ante: *I'm afraid to face the board of directors = tengo miedo de colocarme ante el consejo de dirección.* **11** plantar cara ante, enfrentarse a: *to face the problem.* **12** arrostrar, afrontar (peligros, acusaciones, etc.). **13** guarnecer (la parte delantera de un vestido). || **14 a long –,** una cara larga. **15 to be faced (with),** ser confrontado (con), tener que enfrentarse (a). **16 to blow up/explode in one's –,** (fam.) irse de las manos de uno, explotarle a uno el asunto entre las manos. **17 blue in the –, V. blue. 18 (I/etc.) can't/couldn't –,** (yo/etc.) no puedo/podría encarar, no puedo/podría tener que soportar. **19 to cut off one's nose to spite one's –,** V. **spite. 20 to disappear/vanish off the – of the earth,** desaparecer sin dejar rastro. **21 egg on one's –,** V. **egg. 22 – down,** cara abajo. **23 -faced,** con la cara (en compuestos): *a ruddy-faced youngster = un joven con la cara roja.* **24 to – down,** (EE.UU.) vencer con la mirada, vencer sin gritos sino con la mirada. **25 – lift, a)** lifting, estiramiento de la piel de la cara. **b)** (fig.) embellecimiento, mejora de la apariencia. **26 to – out,** (brit.) manejar, solucionar (un problema, crisis, una personalidad fuerte, etc.). **27 – pack,** mascarilla (de belleza). **28 – powder,** polvos para la cara, polvos de tocador. **29 – to – (with),** cara a cara (con), frente a frente (con) (problemas, dificultades, personas, etc.). **30 – up,** cara arriba. **31 to – up to,** encararse valientemente con. **32 to – the music,** (fam.) aguantar las consecuencias, aceptar las responsabilidades. **33 – value,** V. **value. 34 to fly in the – of,** desafiar, ir en contra de, oponerse resueltamente a. **35 to have the –,** (*inf.*), (fam.) tener el atrevimiento de, tener cara suficiente para. **36 in the – of,** ante; a pesar de: *she laughed in the face of death = ella se rió ante la muerte.* **37 to keep a straight –,** contener la risa, aguantar la carcajada. **38 let's – it,** admitámoslo, reconozcámoslo, seamos sinceros. **39 to look someone in the –,** mirar a alguien cara a cara. **40 to lose –,** quedar mal, perder prestigio. **41 loss of –,** pérdida de prestigio, ocasión de quedar mal. **42 to make/pull a –,** hacer una mueca (de disgusto, desafío, asco, etc.). **43 on the – of it,** a primera vista, según parece, según las apariencias. **44 to put on a brave/good –,** poner buena cara (cuando la procesión va por dentro). **45 to save –,** salvar las apariencias, no quedar mal. **46 to set one's – against,** oponerse fuertemente a, mostrarse muy contrario a. **47 to show one's –,** asomar la cara; mostrarse en público, aparecer en público. **48 to shut one's –,** V. **shut. 49 to shut/slam the door in someone's –,** V. **door. 50 slap in the –,** V. **slap. 51 the – of the earth/world,** todo el mundo, el mundo entero. **52 to someone's –,** a la cara de alguien; abierta y directamente. **53 to wipe the grin/smile off someone's –,** V. **wipe.**
face-cloth | 'feɪsklɒθ | *s.c.* toallita para la cara. V. **face-flannel.**
face-cream | 'feɪskriːm | *s.c.* crema facial.
face-flannel | 'feɪsflænl | *s.c.* (brit.) toallita para la cara (para el lavado).
faceless | 'feɪslɪs | *adj.* (desp.) desconocido, anónimo, sin cara: *faceless experts.*
face-saver | 'feɪsseɪvər | *s.c.* motivo/ocasión de salvar las apariencias.
face-saving | 'feɪs seɪvɪŋ | *adj.* para salvar las apariencias: *a face-saving gesture = un gesto para salvar las apariencias.*
facet | 'fæsɪt | *s.c.* **1 [– (of)]** faceta, aspecto. || **2 facets,** MIN. caras (de alguna piedra preciosa).

facetious | fə'siːʃəs | *adj.* frívolamente chistoso, pesadamente cómico.
facetiously | fə'siːʃəslɪ | *adv.* frívolamente, cómicamente (con cierto sentido negativo).
facial | 'feɪʃl | *adj.* **1** facial. || *s.c.* **2** tratamiento facial, masaje facial.
facially | 'feɪʃəlɪ | *adv.* facialmente, en la cara.
facile | 'fæsaɪl | *adj.* (desp.) facilón; superficial.
facilitate | fə'sɪlɪteɪt | *v.t.* (form.) facilitar.
facilitation | fəˌsɪlɪ'teɪʃn | *s.i.* (form.) facilitación.
facility | fə'sɪlɪtɪ | *s.c.* **1** ventaja extra, pequeño dispositivo de ayuda: *this hi-fi set has a wonderful facility: an extra tape deck = este equipo de alta fidelidad tiene una ventaja extra maravillosa: una pletina de más.* **2** (normalmente *pl.*) servicio, institución de fomento cultural, tienda para servicio público. || *s.c.* e *i.* **3 [– in/for]** facilidad en/para, habilidad en/para. || *s.i.* **4** facilidad: *with facility.*
facing | 'feɪsɪŋ | *s.i.* **1** guarnición (en ropa). || *s.c.* e *i.* **2** ARQ. revestimiento, paramento. || **3 facings,** vueltas (en ropa).
facsimile | fæk'sɪməlɪ | *s.c.* facsímil.
fact | fækt | *s.c.* e *i.* **1** hecho, realidad: *it's not a fiction, it's a fact = no es una entelequia, es un hecho.* || *s.c.* **2** dato; hecho concreto. || **3 as a matter of –,** en realidad, de hecho, realmente. **4 – sheet,** hoja de datos resumidos; resumen de datos esenciales (especialmente de noticias periodísticas). **5 for a –,** a ciencia cierta. **6 in –/in actual –/as a matter of –/in point of –,** de hecho, en realidad (como énfasis para introducir un desacuerdo): *you're right but in actual fact what Jimmy is saying is very true = tienes razón pero en realidad lo que dice Jimmy es muy cierto.* **7 in –/in point of –/in actual –,** de hecho, en realidad, además (como énfasis o introducción de un nuevo enfoque en la conversación). **8 is that a –?,** ¿es eso verdad?, ¿de verdad? **9 that's a –/and that's a –,** (fam.) eso es un hecho, esa es la realidad, así son las cosas. **10 the – is/the – of the matter is,** el hecho es que, la realidad es que. **11 the – remains,** sin embargo, a pesar de todo. **12 the facts of life,** las verdades de la vida, las realidades de la vida, los hechos de la vida (sobre el misterio de la procreación). **13 the – that/a – which/this –/etc.,** el hecho de que, un hecho que, este hecho (mencionado o a punto de mencionar).
fact-finding | 'fæktfaɪndɪŋ | *adj.* de investigación, de indagación.
faction | 'fækʃn | *s.c.* **1** [— *v.sing./pl.*] facción, camarilla (dentro de un grupo mayor). || *s.i.* **2** división, desacuerdo divisorio.
factious | 'fækʃəs | *adj.* partidista, sectario.
factitious | fæk'tɪʃəs | *adj.* (form.) artificial, artificioso.
factor | 'fæktər | *s.c.* **1** factor: *the human factor.* **2** MAT. factor, divisor. || *s.sing.* **3** grado, factor (en escalas distintas): *the factor 6 gives the highest protection = el factor 6 da la mayor protección.*
factorial | fæk'tɔːrɪəl | *adj.* MAT. factorial.
factory | 'fæktərɪ | *s.c.* **1** fábrica. **2** (fig. y hum.) fábrica: *this family is a factory of children, they already have 12 = esta familia es una fábrica de niños, ya tienen 12.* || **3 – farm,** AGR. granja factoría. **4 – farming,** AGR. producción mediante granjas factorías. **5 – floor,** (fig.) los obreros. **6 – ship,** MAR. barco factoría.
factotum | fæk'təutəm | *s.c.* (form.) factótum, persona que lo hace todo.
factual | 'fæktʃuəl | *adj.* real, exacto, objetivo.
factually | 'fæktʃuəlɪ | *adv.* realmente, exactamente, objetivamente.
faculty | 'fækltɪ | *s.c.* **1** facultad (sección de una Universidad). **2** (normalmente *pl.*) potencia, facultad (de pensar, sentir, etc.): *I am in possession of all my faculties = estoy en posesión de todas mis facultades.* **3 [– (for/of)]** aptitud, habilidad: *she has the faculty of listening to all the sides of an argument = ella posee la habilidad de escuchar todas las opiniones en una discusión.* || **4 the –,** [*v.sing./pl.*] el cuerpo docente (de una facultad).
fad | fæd | *s.c.* última novedad, moda pasajera, furor poco duradero: *the Chinese food fad = la moda pasajera de la comida china.*
faddish | 'fædɪʃ | *adj.* (desp.) caprichoso; seguidor de modas pasajeras.
faddy | 'fædɪ | *adj.* (fam. y desp.) tiquis-miquis (en la comida).
fade | feɪd | *v.t.* **1** descolorar, hacer desvanecer los colores: *the sun fades the carpets = el sol descolora las alfombras.* || *v.i.* **2** descolorarse. **3** desvanecerse, apagarse poco a poco (la señal). **6** decaer, disminuir (interés, sentimiento, etc.). **7** envejecer (en su exterior): *his looks have faded tremendously = su cara ha envejecido tremendamente.* **8** marchitarse (flores, plantas, etc.). **9** desaparecer (sonrisa). **10** deslizarse (a algún sitio sin ser notado). **11** (lit.) apagarse, morir. || *s.c.* **12** TV. disolvencia (lenta desaparición de una imagen). || **13 to – away, a)** desvanecerse, desaparecer, extinguirse (lenta y gradualmente): *my interest in her faded away after a few months = mi interés por ella desapareció después de unos cuantos meses.* **b)** morir lentamente. **14 to – in,** TV. aparecer en imagen poco a poco, oírse gradualmente. **15 to – out, a)** TV. desaparecer la imagen poco a poco, desvanecerse gradualmente (sonido). **b)** disolverse poco a poco hasta terminar, perder fuerza gradualmente hasta la desaparición total: *the rebellion faded out = la rebelión perdió fuerza gradualmente hasta la desaparición total.*
faded | feɪdɪd | *adj.* **1** descolorido (ropa, tejido, etc.). **2** desaparecido, obsoleto.
fade-in | 'feɪdɪn | *s.c.* TV. enfoque.
fade-out | 'feɪdaut | *s.c.* TV. desenfoque.
faeces | 'fiːsiːz | (EE.UU. **feces**) *s.i.* (form.) heces.
faecal | 'fiːkl | (EE.UU. **fecal**) *adj.* (form.) fecal.
faff | fæf | **– about/around,** (fam. y brit.) hacer el tonto, hacer el bobo (como actividad infructífera y desorganizada).
fag | fæg | *s.c.* **1** (fam. y brit.) pitillo, cigarrillo. **2** (EE.UU. y vulg.) marica, sarasa. **3** estudiante ayudante (de alumnos mayores en escuelas privadas de Gran Bretaña). || *s.sing.* **4** (fam.) faena pesada, trabajo duro. || *v.i.* **5 [to – (for)]** atender, servir (a un alumno de los mayores por parte de uno de los pequeños en escuelas privadas inglesas). || **6** (fam.) trabajar duramente, faenar brutalmente. || **7 to – out,** (fam.) agotar, dejar tirado (de cansancio).
fag-end | 'fægend | (fam.) *s.c.* **1** colilla (de cigarrillo). **2 [– of]** última parte de, parte final de: *I only saw the fag-end of the film = sólo vi la parte final de la película.*
fagged | fægd | (también **fagged out**) *adj.* (brit. y fam.) agotado, tirado, machacado.
faggot | 'fægət | *s.c.* **1** (p.u.) gavilla, haz de palos (para el fuego). **2** (fam. y EE.UU.) marica, sarasa, tipo de la acera de enfrente. **3** (normalmente *pl.*) (brit.) GAST. albóndigas.
Fahrenheit | 'færənhaɪt | *s.i.* FIS. Fahrenheit (medida de temperatura).
fail | feɪl | *v.i.* **1** suspender (asignaturas). **2** fracasar, fallar. **3 [to –** *inf.*] no lograr, fracasar en: *she failed to get the job = no logró conseguir el empleo.* **4** fallar, averiarse, dejar de funcionar. **5** cerrar, fracasar, quebrar (un negocio). **6** debilitarse, fallar, decaer (cualquier cosa): *light is beginning to fail = la luz está empezando a debilitarse.* **7** acabarse, terminarse (el suministro de algo): *water failed at the wrong time = el agua se terminó en el peor momento.* **8 [to – in]** fracasar en, fallar en (algo de la responsabilidad de uno): *you failed in your duty to your country = fracasó en el deber para con su país.* **9** irse, desaparecer (habilidad, cualidad personal, etc.): *at the last minute his courage failed = en el último minuto su valentía desapareció.* || *v.t.* **10** suspender (asignaturas). **11** fallar, desilusionar: *you've failed me again = me has desilusionado otra vez.* **12** abandonar, desertar: *strength failed me = la fuerza me abandonó.* || *s.c.* **13** suspenso. || **14 I – to see,** no logro entender, no logro ver. **15 without –, a)** sin falta, con toda seguridad. **b)** religiosamente, sin fallo alguno: *he pays without fail = paga religiosamente.* **16 words –,** las palabras no dan con, las palabras no aciertan con (el significado de algo que se quiere expresar).
failed | feɪld | *adj.* **1** fracasado, fallido: *failed plans.* **2** quebrado, fracasado (negocio o similar).

failing | 'feɪlɪŋ | *s.c.* **1** debilidad, defecto, fallo (personal o de un objeto). || *adj.* **2** declinante, en declive, que falla cada vez más: *failing health = salud en declive.* || **3 – that,** en caso de que no, si no es así, si no es posible: *put on your vest or, failing that, a thick shirt = ponte la camiseta o, si no es posible, una camisa gruesa.*

fail-safe | 'feɪlseɪf | *adj.* de seguridad, protector seguro: *a failsafe mechanism = un mecanismo de seguridad.*

failure | 'feɪlɪər | *s.c.* **1** fracaso (persona o cosa). || *s.i.* **2** fracaso, fallo, malogro. || *s.c.* e *i.* **3** [– *inf.*] fracaso en, fallo en: *their failure to control the ball shocked me = su fracaso en el control del balón me asombró.* **4** fracaso, quiebra (de negocio o similar). **5** fallo, deficiencia (en el funcionamiento de algo). **6** fallo, pérdida (de alguna capacidad o habilidad): *failure of understanding = fallo de comprensión.*

fain | feɪn | *adv.* (arc.) alegremente, gustosamente.

faint | feɪnt | *adj.* **1** tenue, débil, lánguido (color, sonido, etc.). **2** desfallecido, debilitado, mareado. **3** desmotivado, vago: *a faint attempt = un intento desmotivado.* || *s.c.* **4** desmayo, desfallecimiento. || *v.i.* **5** desmayarse, desfallecer. || **6 in a (dead) –,** desfallecido totalmente, desmayado por completo.

OBS. La forma de superlativo de este adjetivo es utilizada como un intensivo en oraciones negativas con el sentido: **7** mínimo, más mínimo, menor: *he hasn't got the faintest idead about it = no tiene la más mínima idea del asunto.*

faint-hearted | ˌfeɪnt'hɑːtɪd | *adj.* tímido, pusilánime, temeroso. || **2 the –,** los pusilánimes, los tímidos.

faint-heartedly | ˌfeɪnt'hɑːtɪdlɪ | *adv.* tímidamente, pusilánimemente, temerosamente.

faint-heartedness | ˌfeɪnt'hɑːtɪdnɪs | *s.i.* timidez, pusilanimidad, temor.

faintly | 'feɪntlɪ | *adv.* **1** ligeramente, tenuemente. **2** ligeramente, apenas (reduciendo el significado de otro adjetivo): *faintly mad = ligeramente loco.*

faintness | 'feɪntnɪs | *s.i.* **1** languidez, debilidad (de colores, sonidos, etc.). **2** desfallecimiento, estado de desmayo.

fair | feər | *adj.* **1** justo, imparcial, razonable: *a fair decision.* **2** rubio (de pelo). **3** considerable, adecuado (cantidad, tamaño, etc.): *a fair amount of money = una cantidad considerable de dinero.* **4** regular, aceptable, no mal: *her Italian is only fair = su italiano sólo es regular.* **5** blanca, pálida (piel). **6** agradable, bueno, favorable (tiempo atmosférico). **7** bueno, agudo, inteligente (pensamiento, ocurrencia, adivinanza, etc.): *a fair guess = una suposición aguda.* **8** (p.u.) precioso, bello, bonito (persona o lugar). || *s.c.* **9** (brit.) feria, parque (de atracciones). **10** fiesta, feria (de ganado, de algún producto específico, etc.). || **11 all is – in love and war,** en el amor y la guerra todo está permitido, en el amor y la guerra todo vale. **12 to be –/I must be –,** siendo justo, justo es reconocer, a fuer de justos. **13 by – means or foul,** a toda costa, a todo trance, como sea, por cualquier medio. **14 – and square, a)** honrada y abiertamente, con toda honradez. **b)** justo en el centro (de un blanco). **15 – copy,** copia en limpio. **16 – enough, a)** de acuerdo, vale. **b)** bastante bien, no está mal (razonable, pero...): *she's a good cook, fair enough, but she's a lousy mother = ella es una buena cocinera, bastante bien, pero es una madre fatal.* **17 – game,** blanco de críticas (persona). **18 – is –,** seamos responsables, tengamos comprensión. **19 – play,** juego limpio. **20 to play –,** jugar limpio. **21 the – sex,** (hum. y p.u.) el sexo débil; las mujeres.

fairground | 'feəgraʊnd | *s.c.* terreno de feria, zona de ferias.

fairly | 'feəlɪ | *adv.* **1** bastante (especialmente con adjetivos de sentido positivo y con poco énfasis): *you speak French fairly well = hablas francés bastante bien.* **2** razonablemente, con justicia. **3** (lit.) en gran manera; muchísimo: *the sea fairly played with the ship = el mar jugó en gran manera con el barco.*

fairness | 'feənɪs | *s.i.* **1** justicia, equidad, imparcialidad. **2** (lit.) belleza. **3** palidez, blancura (de tez). || **4 in – to/out of all –,** con toda justicia para/siendo justos.

fairway | 'feəweɪ | *s.c.* **1** DEP. calle (en el golf). **2** MAR. paso navegable, canalizo.

fair-weather | ˌfeə'weðər | *adj.* (desp.) mudadizo, inconstante: *a fair-weather friend = un amigo mudadizo.*

fairy | 'feərɪ | *s.c.* **1** hada: *a fairy story = una historia de hadas.* **2** (vulg.) maricón. || **3 – godmother,** hada madrina, bienhechora. **4 – lights,** bombillas de colorines (para decorar árboles de Navidad, etc.).

fairyland | 'feərɪlænd | *s.i.* **1** país de las hadas. **2** (fig.) mundo mágico, paisaje de encanto.

fairy-tale | 'feərɪteɪl | *s.c.* **1** cuento de hadas. **2** (fig.) patraña, embuste.

fait accompli | ˌfeɪtə'kɒmpliː | *s.c.* (form.) hecho consumado.

faith | feɪθ | *s.i.* **1** [– (in)] fe, confianza: *I have faith in you = tengo confianza en ti.* **2** REL. fe, creencia. || *s.c.* **3** REL. fe, religión: *the Catholic faith = la religión católica.* || **4 to break – with,** faltar a la palabra dada a, engañar. **5 in bad –,** de mala fe. **6 in good –,** de buena fe. **6 to keep – with,** cumplir la palabra dada a.

faith-cure | 'feɪθkjʊə | V. **faith-healing.**

faithful | 'feɪθfl | *adj.* **1** leal, fiel. **2** [– (to)] fiel (a la esposa, marido, etc.). **3** [– (to)] fiel, exacto (historia, dibujo, etc.): *that's a very faithful picture of your wife = ese es un dibujo muy exacto de tu mujer.* **4** [– (to)] firme, constante, muy fiel: *faithful watchers of the programme = espectadores constantes del programa.* || **5 faithfuls,** fieles, incondicionales, leales (de un partido, organización, etc.). **6 the faithfuls, a)** REL. los fieles. **b)** los leales, los incondicionales (de un partido o similar).

faithfully | 'feɪθfəlɪ | *adv.* **1** lealmente, fielmente. **2** con exactitud, fielmente. **3** constantemente, firmemente (en su línea de actuación). || **4 Yours –,** atentamente, le saluda atentamente (en cartas de registro formal).

faithfulness | 'feɪθfəlnɪs | *s.i.* **1** fidelidad, lealtad. **2** exactitud, fidelidad (a la verdad, a lo objetivo, etc.). **3** (fig.) lealtad (a la esposa o esposo). **4** constancia, fidelidad (a una línea de actuación o similar).

faith-healing | 'feɪθhiːlɪŋ | *s.i.* curación por fe (típico de ciertas variantes de protestantismo).

faithless | 'feɪθlɪs | *adj.* infiel, desleal; falso: *a faithless friend = un amigo desleal.*

faithlessly | 'feɪθlɪslɪ | *adv.* infielmente, deslealmente; falsamente.

faithlessness | 'feɪθlɪsnɪs | *s.i.* deslealtad, infidelidad.

fake | feɪk | *adj.* **1** falso, falsificado; fraudulento. || *s.c.* **2** falsificación (de cualquier objeto). **3** falso, farsante, impostor. || *v.t.* **4** falsificar (documentos, dinero, etc.). **5** (fig.) fingir, simular (un sentimiento o similar).

fakir | 'feɪkɪər | *s.c.* faquir.

falcon | 'fɔːlkən | *s.c.* ZOOL. halcón.

falconer | 'fɔːlkənər | *s.c.* cetrero, halconero.

falconry | 'fɔːlkənrɪ | *s.i.* cetrería.

fall | fɔːl | *v.* [*pret.* **fell,** *p.p.* **fallen**] *i.* **1** caer, caerse, desplomarse: *to fall down the stairs = caerse por las escaleras.* **2** caer, descender (agua, nieve, etc.). **3 [to – (into/out of)]** (fig.) desplomarse, caer como un fardo: *I didn't get into bed, I was so tired that I fell into it = no me metí en la cama, estaba tan cansado que me desplomé sobre ella.* **4** caer (la noche, la tarde, la oscuridad, etc.). **5** caer (en una fecha). **6 [to – (on)]** caer, dar en (un golpe): *the blow fell on his back = el golpe le dio en la espalda.* **7** cubrir, caer (luz, sombra, etc.): *the shadows fell over the house = las sombras cubrieron la casa.* **8** descender, caer (el silencio, la tristeza, la ansiedad, etc.): *an oppressive silence fell = descendió un silencio agobiante.* **9** desaparecer, irse, desplomarse (barreras de cualquier tipo entre personas). **10** descender, bajar, disminuir (una cantidad, valor, cifra, etc.): *our living standards have fallen = nuestro nivel de vida ha disminuido.* **11 [to – to]** descender hasta, colgar hasta (ropa o pelo): *his coat fell to the floor = su abrigo descendía hasta el suelo.* **12** POL. caer (un gobierno, una persona en autoridad, etc.). **13** convertirse en (paso de un estado a otro): *he had fallen a victim to despair = él se había convertido en una víctima de la desesperación.* **14** pertenecer a, caer dentro de (una clasificación, grupo o similar): *in this country, political scandals fall into the category of simple human failings = en este país los* *escándalos políticos caen dentro de la categoría de fallos humanos sencillos.* **15** DEP. caer (un palito del juego de críquet, lo que significa que un bateador debe irse). **16** caer, ser capturado (una ciudad, una empresa, etc.). **17** (lit.) morir, caer (especialmente en batalla). **18 [to – from]** (lit.) salir de (la boca): *no words of hate fell from my lips = ninguna palabra de odio salió de mis labios.* **19** (lit. y p.u.) pecar. **20** decrecer, disminuir (un sonido o similar). || *s.c.* **21** caída, desplome. **22** caída (de lluvia, nieve o similar). **23 [– in]** descenso de, caída de, bajada de: *the fall in the dollar = la bajada del dólar.* **24** DEP. caída (en alguna modalidad de lucha). **25** (EE.UU.) otoño. || *s.sing.* **26** POL. caída, colapso: *the fall of the tyrannical regime = la caída del régimen tiránico.* **27** caída, toma, conquista (de una ciudad, institución, empresa, etc.). **28 [– of]** caída de, forma de caída de (una cortina o similar). **29** (lit.) caída (de la noche, tarde, oscuridad, etc.). **30** declive, inclinación, pendiente. **31** ocurrencia (especialmente por el azar). **32 [– of]** caída de, pecado de: *the fall of man = el pecado del hombre.* || **33 to – about,** (fam.) desternillarse, partirse (de risa). **34 to – apart, a)** romperse en pedazos, deshacerse completamente (normalmente por estar viejo o en mal estado). **b)** deshacerse, desintegrarse (un sistema, organización, etc.). **c)** (fam.) quedarse deshecho, quedar destrozado (anímicamente): *he fell apart after his wife's death = él quedó destrozado después de la muerte de su mujer.* **35 to – asleep,** quedarse dormido, dormirse. **36 to – at somebody's feet,** echarse a los pies de alguien (en actitud de súplica). **37 to – away, a)** caerse (de una superficie donde debería estar pegado): *pieces of concrete had fallen away = se habían caído trozos de cemento.* **b)** declinar, reducirse (en número, fuerza, etc.): *the number of students has fallen away = el número de estudiantes ha declinado.* **c)** inclinarse, comenzar un declive (un camino, carretera o similar). **d)** cesar, desaparecer (un tipo de comportamiento): *his grand airs fell away gradually = sus afectaciones de grandeza cesaron gradualmente.* **e)** REL. separarse poco a poco: *she has fallen away from the faith = se ha separado poco a poco de la fe.* **38 to – back, a)** MIL. retroceder, replegarse. **b)** echarse hacia atrás (especialmente por una emoción fuerte como miedo o similar). **39 to – back on,** recurrir a (solución o similar): *I had to fall back on all my charm to calm her down = tuve que recurrir a todos mis encantos para calmarla.* **40 to – behind, a)** rezagarse, quedarse atrás, descolgarse. **b)** (fig.) retrasarse (en estudios o similar). **c)** (fig.) retrasarse, rezagarse (en pagos, velocidad de un proyecto, etc.). **41 to – by the wayside,** V. **wayside. 42 to – down, a)** caerse, caer al suelo. **b)** colapsarse, desmoronarse (un puente, edificio, etc.). **c)** (fig.) fracasar, no valer (idea, teoría, etc.). **43 to – flat,** V. **flat. 44 to – for,** (fam.) **a)** prendarse de, quedar cautivado por (persona del otro sexo). **b)** ser embaucado; tragarse (un cuento): *the poor fellow fell for the trick immediately = el pobre hombre se tragó el truco inmediatamente.* **45 to – foul of,** ponerse a malas con, enfadarse con, pelearse con. **46 to – from grace,** V. **grace. 47 – guy,** ingenuo, crédulo. **48 to – in, a)** desplomarse hacia dentro (un tejado o similar). **b)** MIL. ponerse en fila, formar, alinearse. **49 to – into, a)** iniciar, trabar (conversación, discusión, etc.). **b)** caer en (algún estado anímico). **c)** dividirse en, agruparse en: *this falls into three groups = esto se divide en tres grupos.* **d)** caer en (trampa o similar). **50 to – into place,** V. **place. 51 to – into step,** V. **step. 52 to – into the hands/clutches of,** caer en las manos/garras de; pasar a ser controlado por. **53 to – in with,** dar su conformidad a, estar de acuerdo con (idea, plan, etc.). **54 to – off, a)** caerse, caerse de (una superficie): *all the paintwork is falling off = toda la pintura se está cayendo.* **b)** decrecer, disminuir (una cantidad, cifra o similar). **55 to – on/upon, a)** caer accidentalmente encima (de). **b)** posarse en, descansar en (la mirada). **c)** caer sobre, echarse sobre (con idea de ataque). **d)** abrazarse: *my aunt fell on me, kissing me fifty times = mi tía se abrazó a mí, besándome cincuenta veces.* **e)** (lit.) embestir, asaltar (las penas, desgracias, etc.). **f)** ser responsabilidad de: *it falls on the teacher to organize some matches = es responsabilidad del profesor organizar algunos partidos.* **55 to – on one's feet,** caer de pie; tener mucha suerte. **57 to – open,** abrirse involuntariamente. **58 to – out, a)** caerse (pelo o dientes). **b)** MIL. romper filas, romper la formación. **c)** caerse accidentalmente (de cualquier tipo de recipiente). **d) [(with)]** pelearse, enemistarse, regañar (con alguien). **e)** ocurrir, suceder, resultar: *I'm happy about how everything fell out = estoy contento de cómo resultó todo.* **59 to – over, a)** caer (longitudinalmente). **60 to – over oneself,** (fam.) volverse loco por (hacer algo): *she was falling over herself to please him = ella se estaba volviendo loca por agradarle.* **61 to – short,** V. **short. 62 to – through,** fracasar, no salir: *the plan fell through = el plan no salió.* **63 to – to, a)** ser responsabilidad de, corresponder el deber de: *it falls to me to talk to her about her son's death = me corresponde a mí el deber de hablarle de la muerte de su hijo.* **b)** ponerse a (de manera tonta e inconveniente): *they fell to fighting after their failure = se pusieron a pelearse después de su fracaso.* **64 to – to bits/pieces,** hacerse pedazos, hacerse añicos. **65 to – to one's knees,** caer de rodillas, ponerse de rodillas (con sentimiento de gran respeto o algo similar). **66 pride comes before a –,** siempre hay soberbia antes del pecado. **67 to ride for a –,** presumir con orgullo (corriendo el peligro de una pronta caída). **68 someone's face falls/fell/etc.,** parecer desilusionado, entristecerse: *her face fell at the news = su cara se entristeció con las noticias.* **69 to stand or –,** valer o no valer (ideas, creencias, etc.). **70 the Fall,** REL. el Pecado Original, la Caída (de la humanidad). **71 the falls,** las cataratas, los saltos de agua.

fallacious | fə'leɪʃəs | *adj.* (form.) erróneo, falaz.

fallaciously | fə'leɪʃəslɪ | *adv.* (form.) erróneamente, falazmente.

fallacy | 'fæləsɪ | (form.) *s.c.* **1** error, idea errónea. || *s.c.* e *i.* **2** (fig.) defecto (en el razonamiento o lógica).

fallen | 'fɔːlən | *p.p.* **1** de **fall.** || *adj.* **2** caído, desmoronado. **3** (p.u.) deshonrada (mujer infiel). **4** (p.u. y lit.) REL. caído, pecador: *the fallen angels = los ángeles caídos.* || **5 – arches,** ANAT. pies planos. **6 the –,** (form.) los caídos (en batalla).

fallibility | ˌfælə'bɪlitɪ | *s.i.* (form.) falibilidad.

fallible | 'fæləbl | *adj.* (form.) falible.

falling | 'fɔːlɪŋ | *adj.* **1** decreciente, en disminución: *falling mortality rates = índices de mortalidad decreciente.* || **2 – star,** ASTR. meteoro, estrella fugaz.

falling-off | 'fɔːlɪŋɔf | *s.sing.* **[– (of/in)]** descenso, baja, disminución.

falling-out | 'fɔːlɪŋaʊt | *s.c.* pelea (verbal), desacuerdo fuerte.

fallout | 'fɔːlaʊt | *s.i.* FIS. escape (radioactivo).

fallow | 'fæləʊ | *adj.* **1** AGR. en barbecho (tierra). **2** (fig.) inactivo. || **3 – deer,** ZOOL. gamo, corzo.

false | fɔːls | *adj.* **1** falso, incorrecto. **2** falso, equivocado: *I was under a false impression = tenía una impresión equivocada.* **3** falso, postizo: *false teeth = dentadura postiza.* **4** (desp.) falso, engañoso, traicionero: *false promise = promesa engañosa.* **5** (desp.) desleal, falso, insincero: *false friends = amigos desleales.* || **6 to be – to,** (desp.) traicionar: *she was false to herself = se traicionó a sí misma.* **7 – alarm,** falsa alarma. **8 – bottom,** doble fondo (en una maleta o similar). **9 – move,** movimiento en falso. **10 – start, a)** DEP. salida en falso. **b)** comienzo inseguro, comienzo dubitativo (al principio de una conferencia, clase, etc.). **11 – step,** paso en falso. **12 in a – position,** en una situación comprometida, en una posición poco clara: *I was left in a false position after she came unexpectedly = quedé en una situación comprometida después de que ella apareciera inesperadamente.* **13 to play somebody –,** traicionar a alguien. **14 to strike/sound a – note,** decir una inconveniencia; meter la pata verbalmente. **15 under – colours, a)** MAR. bajo bandera falsa, bajo pabellón falso. **b)** (fig.) con pretextos falsos. **16 under – pretences,** V. **pretence.**

falsehood | 'fɔːlshʊd | *s.i.* **1** falsedad. || *s.c.* **2** (form.) mentira.

falsely | 'fɔːlslɪ | *adv.* **1** falsamente, incorrectamente. **2** (desp.) engañosamente, deslealmente, falsamente.

falseness | 'fɔːlsnɪs | *s.i.* (desp.) engaño, insinceridad.

falsetto | fɔːl'setəʊ | (*pl.* **falsettos**) *s.c.* e *i.* falsete.

falsies | 'fɔːlsɪz | *s.pl.* (fam.) senos postizos, rellenos postizos para los senos.

falsification | ˌfɔːlsɪfɪ'keɪʃn | *s.c.* e *i.* falsificación.

falsify | 'fɔːlsɪfaɪ | *v.t.* falsificar (especialmente documentos).

falsity | 'fɔːlsɪtɪ | *s.i.* y *c.* falsedad, mentira: *truth and falsity = la verdad y la mentira.*

falter | 'fɔːltər | *v.i.* **1 [to – (in)]** vacilar, titubear (sobre la acción a seguir). **2** tartamudear, balbucear. **3** tropezar, dar un traspié tras otro, tartalear. **4** perder fuerza, debilitarse, vacilar: *my father's interest in books never faltered = el interés de mi padre por los libros nunca se debilitó.* || *v.t.* **5** decir balbuceando.

faltering | 'fɔːtərɪŋ | *adj.* vacilante, titubeante.

falteringly | 'fɔːtərɪŋlɪ | *adv.* de forma vacilante, con titubeos.

fame | feɪm | *s.i.* fama, renombre.

famed | feɪmd | *adj.* **[– (for)]** renombrado, famoso, afamado.

familial | fəmɪlɪəl | *adj.* (form.) de familia, de la familia.

familiar | fə'mɪlɪər | *adj.* **1 [– (to)]** familiar, muy conocido. **2 [– (with)]** familiarizado: *I'm familiar with the type of problem = estoy familiarizado con el tipo de problema.* **3** familiar, íntimo (en el modo de comportarse con alguien). || *s.c.* **4** espíritu protector (en cuentos antiguos). || **5 to be on – terms (with),** tener confianza (con). **6 familiars,** (arc.) íntimos, amigos íntimos, compañeros íntimos.

familiarity | fəˌmɪlɪ'ærɪtɪ | *s.i.* **1** familiaridad, acostumbramiento. **2 [– (with)]** familiaridad, conocimiento. **3** confianza, intimidad. || **4 familiarities,** libertades (en el teatro). **5 familiarity breeds contempt,** la confianza da asco; lo conocido no se estima.

familiarization | fəˌmɪlɪəraɪ'zeɪʃn | *s.i.* familiarización, acostumbramiento, habituación.

familiarize | fə'mɪlɪəraɪz | (también **familiarise**) *v.t.* y *r.* **[to – with/to – *o.* + with]** familiarizar(se) con, habituar(se) a, hacerse a.

familiarly | fə'mɪlɪəlɪ | *adv.* con confianza, familiarmente.

family | 'fæmɪlɪ | *s.c.* **1** [*v.sing./pl.*] familia (en un sentido más amplio o más reducido). **2** (fig.) antepasados, familia: *my family has owned this land for centuries = mis antepasados han poseído esta tierra durante siglos.* **3** ZOOL. familia: *a member of the cat family = un miembro de la familia de los felinos.* **4** FILOL. familia, grupo (de lenguas). || *s.i.* **5** familia, linaje: *of good family = de buena familia.* || *adj.* **6** de familia, adecuado para una familia: *a family car.* || **7 – circle,** círculo familiar, medio familiar. **8 – doctor,** (brit.) MED. médico de familia, facultativo de medicina general. **9 – likeness,** semejanza familiar, parecido familiar. **10 – man,** padre de familia; hombre casero. **11 – name,** apellido. **12 – planning,** planificación familiar. **13 – tree,** árbol genealógico. **14 in the – way,** (fam.) embarazada, encinta. **15 to be in the – way,** (fam.) estar embarazada, encinta. **15 to put in the – way,** (fam.) dejar embarazada.

famine | 'fæmɪn | *s.c.* e *i.* hambre, hambruna (cuando la gente muere).

famished | 'fæmɪʃt | *adj.* (fam.) muerto de hambre, desmayado de hambre.

famous | 'feɪməs | *adj.* **[– (for)]** famoso, conocido, célebre.

famously | 'feɪməslɪ | *adv.* **1** más conocido, mejor conocido. || **2 to get on –,** llevarse magníficamente bien, llevarse de maravilla.

fan | fæn | *s.c.* **1** fan, hincha, admirador. **2** abanico. **3** MEC. ventilador. **4 [– (of)]** (fig.) forma en abanico. || *v.t.* **5** abanicar, dar aire. **6** avivar (un fuego). **7** (fig.) excitar, atizar (pasiones, odios, etc.). || *v.r.* **8** abanicarse. || **9 – belt,** MEC. correa del ventilador (en un vehículo). **10 – club,** club de fans, club de admiradores. **11 – heater,** calentador de aire. **12 – mail,** correo de admiradores. **13 to – out, a)** abrirse en abanico. **b)** esparcir, abrir, desplegar (alas o similar). **14 to – the flames,** V. **flame. 15 the shit hit the –,** (vulg.) se armó un follón del demonio.

fanatic | fə'nætɪk | *s.c.* **1** fanático, extremista. **2** (fig. y fam.) amante, fanático: *a television fanatic = un amante de la televisión.*

fanatical | fə'nætɪkl | (también **fanatic**) *adj.* fanático, extremista.

fanatically | fə'nætɪklɪ | *adv.* fanáticamente.

fanaticism | fə'nætɪsɪzəm | *s.i.* fanatismo, extremismo.

fancier | 'fænsɪər | *s.c.* **1** criador (de animales o plantas). || *comp.* **2** de **fancy.**

fanciful | 'fænsɪfl | *adj.* **1** fantasioso, imaginario; caprichoso. **2** (desp.) extravagante, fantástico: *fanciful art.*

fancifully | 'fænsɪfəlɪ | *adv.* **1** fantasiosamente, imaginariamente. **2** (desp.) extravagantemente, fantásticamente.

fancy | 'fænsɪ | *s.i.* **1** fantasía; imaginación (desbocada). || *s.c.* **2** (fam.) capricho, antojo. || *s.c.* e *i.* **3** (form.) fantasía, irrealidad. || *adj.* **4** (fam.) selecto, especialmente fino: *fancy food = comida especialmente fina.* **5** (fam.) lujoso, de fantasía: *a fancy place = un lugar de fantasía.* **6** (fam.) excesivo (en el precio). || *v.t.* **7 [to – *ger.*]** (fam.) apetecer: *I fancy a cake = me apetece un pastel.* **8** (fam.) agradar, gustar (especialmente referido al sexo). **9** imaginar(se), suponer: *I fancy that is the explanation = me imagino que ésa es la explicación.* || *v.r.* **10** (fam. y desp.) ser muy engreído, creerse alguien (guapo, inteligente, etc.). **11 [to – as]** (fam.) dárselas de, creerse: *he fancies himself as a dancer = se las da de bailarín.* **12 [to – *inf.*]** (fam.) imaginarse: *they fancy themselves to be doctors = se imaginan que son médicos.* || **13 fancies,** GAST. pastelillos dulces. **14 –!,** ¡fíjate!, ¡qué casualidad!, ¡vaya! **15 – ball,** baile de disfraces, fiesta con disfraces. **16 – dress,** disfraz. **17 – man,** (fam., desp. y p.u.) amante. **18 – woman,** (fam., desp. y p.u.) querida. **19 to take a – to,** (fam.) coger cariño a; aficionarse a: *the girl took a fancy to me = la niña me cogió cariño.* **20 to take/tickle one's –,** (fam.) cautivar a uno: *the sculpture tickled my fancy = la escultura me cautivó.*

fancy-free | ˌfænsɪ'friː | *adj.* **1** sin una preocupación, sin una responsabilidad. || **2 footloose and –,** V. **footloose.**

fandango | fæn'dæŋgəʊ | (*pl.* **fandangoes**) *s.c.* **1** MUS. fandango. **2** (fig.) tonterías, bobadas.

fanfare | 'fænfeər | *s.c.* MUS. toque de trompetas; bombo y platillos.

fang | fæŋ | *s.c.* (normalmente *pl.*) ANAT. colmillo (animales).

fanlight | 'fænlaɪt | *s.c.* ARQ. abanico, montante (ventanilla sobre una puerta).

fanny | 'fænɪ | *s.c.* **1** (EE.UU. y vulg.) culo. **2** (brit. y vulg.) coño.

fantasia | fæn'teɪzɪə | (también **fantasy**) *s.c.* MUS. fantasía (composición sin limitaciones de forma).

fantasize | 'fæntəsaɪz | (también **fantasise**) *v.t.* e *i.* **[to – (that/about)]** fantasear, soñar, imaginar (cosas imposibles): *she's always fantasizing about her future life = siempre está fantaseando sobre su vida futura.*

fantastic | fæn'tæstɪk | *adj.* **1** (fam.) fantástico, magnífico, maravilloso. **2** (fam.) fantástico, enorme, grandísimo (cantidad): *he gets a fantastic salary = tiene un sueldo fantástico.* **3** exótico, fantástico, imaginario: *a fantastic story = una historia imaginaria.* **4** increíble, extraordinario: *what a fantastic possibility! = ¡qué increíble posibilidad!* **5** fantástico, imposible (ideas, planes, proyectos, etc.).

fantastically | fæn'tæstɪklɪ | *adv.* **1** (fam.) fantásticamente, grandísimamente, enormemente. **2** exóticamente, fantásticamente, imaginariamente.

fantasy | 'fæntəsɪ | *s.c.* e *i.* fantasía, ensueño, imaginación.

far | fɑːr | (*comp.* **farther/further,** *super.* **farthest/furthest**) *adv.* **1** lejos, alejado, alejadamente. **2** lejos (en el futuro). **3** (fig.) a un punto avanzado: *the research has gone very far = la investigación ha llegado a un punto muy avanzado.* **4 [– *comp.*/too]** muy, mucho, muchísimo (como enfático): *he's far more intelligent than you = él es mucho más inteligente que tú.* || *adj.* **5** remoto, alejado, lejano: *the far west.* **6** de allá, del otro lado, del lado de más allá: *she lives in the far end of the village = ella vive en el extremo del otro lado del pueblo.* **7** POL. extremo: *he belongs to the far left = pertenece a la extrema izquierda.* || **8 a bit –/too –,** demasiado lejos, más allá de la raya, más allá del límite: *he has gone a bit far in his hate towards me = ha ido demasiado lejos en su odio hacia mí.* **9 a – cry from,** V. **cry. 10 as – as, a)** hasta (en el espacio): *walk as far as the traffic lights = camina hasta los semáforos.* **b)** hasta el extremo (que sea), hasta el punto (que sea): *control yourself as far as possible = contrólate hasta el punto que sea posible.* **c)** hasta (enfático o señalando hasta el grado de actuación que se quiere alcanzar): *I'm ready to go as far as divorce = estoy dispuesto a llegar hasta el divorcio.* **11 as/so – as somebody is concerned,** en lo que respecta a alguien, en lo que toca a alguien: *as far as I'm concerned he doesn't exist = en lo que toca a mí él no existe.* **12 as/so – as somebody knows/remembers,** que sepa/recuerde alguien: *as far as I remember he is Turkish = que yo recuerde él es turco.* **13 as/so – as it goes,** hasta cierto punto, hasta cierto grado (cuando algo es positivo pero no de manera absoluta). **14 as/so – as something goes/is concerned,** en lo que concierne a algo, en lo que respecta a algo. **15 by –/– and away,** con mucho, en gran manera, hasta un alto grado: *he is, by far, the best = él es el mejor con mucho.* **16 – be it from me,** (*inf.*), yo sería incapaz de: *far be it from me to deny it, but the story sounds too odd = sería incapaz de negarlo, pero la historia suena demasiado extraña.* **17 – from, a)** lejos de, alejado de; distinto de: *it's far from the truth = eso está muy alejado de la verdad.* **b)** no muy, no... nada: *that place is far from near = ese lugar no está nada cerca.* **18 – from it,** en absoluto: *are you tired? far from it = ¿estás cansado? en absoluto.* **19 – gone,** muy avanzado (cualquier estado): *he's far gone in his hopeless decay = está en un estado de decadencia avanzada.* **20 few and – between,** V. **few. 21 to go as/so – as,** ir hasta el extremo de. **22 to go –,** V. **go. 23 to go too –,** pasarse de la raya. **24 how –, a)** a qué distancia. **b)** hasta qué punto: *how far are you ready to go? = ¿hasta qué punto estás dispuesto a llegar?* **25 in so – as/insofar as,** en cuanto, en cuanto que, hasta el grado que, hasta el punto que. **26 not – wrong/not – out/not – off/not – short,** no muy alejado de la verdad, casi correcto. **27 so –, a)** hasta ahora, hasta este momento. **b)** hasta cierto sitio, hasta cierto punto (en el espacio). **28 so – so good,** hasta ahora bien. **29 the Far East,** GEOG. el Lejano Oriente. **30 thus –,** (form.) hasta ahora, hasta aquí.

faraway | 'fɑːəweɪ | *adj.* **1** alejado, distante. **2** (fig.) abstraído, distraído; ido.

farce | fɑːs | *s.c.* **1** LIT. farsa, entremés, sainete. **2** (fig. y desp.) farsa, tramoya: *this meeting is a farce = esta reunión es una farsa.* || *s.i.* **2** LIT. farsa, enredo (estilo de escribir).

farcical | 'fɑːsɪkl | *adj.* ridículo, absurdo, de sainete.

farcically | 'fɑːsɪklɪ | *adv.* ridículamente, absurdamente, en forma de sainete.

fare | feər | *s.c.* **1** precio del trayecto, tarifa del viaje (en autobús, taxi, etc.). **2** pasajero (en un taxi). || *s.i.* **3** (p.u.) comida, dieta. || *v.i.* **4** (p.u.) irle a uno (bien o mal).

fare-stage | 'feəsteɪdʒ | *s.c.* parada, etapa (en autobús).

farewell | ˌfeə'wel | (lit. y p.u.) *interj.* **1** adiós. || *s.c.* **2** despedida. || **3 to bid –,** despedirse, decir adiós.

far-fetched | ˌfɑː'fetʃt | *adj.* muy improbable, inverosímil.

far-flung | ˌfɑː'flʌŋg | *adj.* **1** vasto, extenso. **2** remoto, muy distante.

farinaceous | ˌfærɪ'n | *adj.* farináceo.

farm | fɑːm | *s.c.* **1** granja, explotación agrícola. **2** granja, explotación (de muchas variedades): *a fish farm.* || *v.t.* e *i.* **3** cultivar, labrar, trabajar en tareas agrícolas. || **4 to – out,** encargar, repartir (trabajos, tareas, etc., enviándoselos a alguien): *I get so many translations that I farm out some of them to friends = tengo tantas traducciones que reparto algunas entre los amigos.*

farmer | 'fɑːmər | *s.c.* granjero, agricultor.

farm-hand | 'fɑːmhænd | *s.c.* peón agrícola.

farmhouse | 'fɑːmhaus | *s.c.* casa (en una granja).

farming | 'fɑːmɪŋ | *s.i.* agricultura.

farmland | 'fɑːmlænd | *s.c.* e *i.* tierra de cultivo.

farmstead | 'fɑːmsted | *s.c.* granja (con todas sus dependencias).

farmyard | 'fɑːmjɑːd | *s.c.* corral.

far-off | 'fɑːrɔf | *adj.* y *adv.* distante, remoto (en el tiempo y en el espacio).

far-out | 'fɑːraut | *s.c.* **1** extraño, raro, grotesco: *it's far-out but true = es raro pero verdad.* **2** (fam.) de miedo, fantástico, fabuloso.

farrago | fə'rɑːgəu | (brit. *pl.* **farragos,** EE.UU. *pl.* **farragoes**) *s.c.* fárrago, mescolanza, mezcla: *a farrago of wild ideas = una mescolanza de ideas alocadas.*

far-reaching | ˌfɑː'riːtʃɪŋ | *adj.* de largo alcance, de gran repercusión: *farreaching consequences = consecuencias de gran repercusión.*

farrier | 'færɪər | *s.c.* herrador.

farrow | 'færəu | *v.i.* parir (sólo para cerdas).

far-seeing | ˌfɑː'siːɪŋ | *adj.* previsor, precavido.

far-sighted | ˌfɑː'saɪtɪd | *adj.* **1** prudente, sagaz, previsor. **2** (EE.UU.) hipermétrope.

far-sightedness | ˌfɑː'saɪtɪdnɪs | *s.i.* **1** prudencia, sagacidad, previsión. **2** (EE.UU.) MED. hipermetropía.

fart | fɑːt | (vulg.) *v.i.* **1** pedorrear, tirarse un pedo. || *s.c.* **2** pedo. **3** (fig.) imbécil, gilipollas (normalmente usado con gente mayor). **4** || **4 to – about /around,** hacer el tonto, hacer el gilipollas.

farther | 'fɑːðər | *comp.* de **far.**

farthest | 'fɑːðɪst | *super.* de **far.**

farthing | 'fɑːðɪŋ | *s.c.* **1** (brit.) cuarto de penique (moneda no usada en la actualidad). || **2 it doesn't matter a brass –/I don't care a brass –/etc.,** (fam. y p.u.) me importa un pimiento, me importa un comino.

fascia | 'feɪʃə | *s.c.* **1** ARQ. faja, imposta. **2** (form.) MEC. panel de mandos (en un vehículo).

fascinante | 'fæsɪneɪt | *v.t.* fascinar, hechizar, encantar.

fascinated | 'fæsɪneɪtɪd | *adj.* fascinado, hechizado, encantado.

fascinating | 'fæsɪneɪtɪŋ | *adj.* fascinante, hechizador, encantador.

fascinatingly | 'fæsɪneɪtɪŋlɪ | *adv.* fascinantemente, encantadoramente.

fascination | ˌfæsɪ'neɪʃn | *s.c.* e *i.* **1** fascinación, hechizo, encanto. **2 in –,** fascinado, hechizado, con gran fascinación: *I looked at her in fascination = la miré con gran fascinación.*

fascism | 'fʌʃɪzəm | (también **Fascism**) *s.i.* POL. fascismo.

fascist | 'fæʃɪst | (también **Fascist**) POL. *s.c.* **1** fascista. || *adj.* **2** fascista.

fashion | 'fæʃn | *s.c.* e *i.* **1** moda, boga, estilo de moda (en la ropa). **2** tendencia, moda: *the fashion now is to be liberal = la moda ahora es ser liberal.* || *s.c.* **3** manera, modo, estilo: *in a friendly fashion = de una manera amistosa.* || *v.t.* **4** (form.) moldear (las actitudes, carácter, etc., de alguien). **5** (form. y p.u.) formar, dar vida a (con las manos, como, por ejemplo, un escultor). || **6 after a –,** hasta cierto punto, un poco (no completamente bien): *I can swim after a fashion = sé nadar un poco.* **7 after the – of,** a manera de, con el estilo de (alguien): *he writes after the fashion of the '98 generation = escribe con el estilo de la generación del 98.* **8 all the –/rage,** (fam.) lo que pega, lo que se lleva (actualmente): *living in old houses is all the fashion = vivir en casas viejas es lo que se lleva.* **9 to come into –,** ponerse de moda. **10 to go out of –,** pasarse de moda. **11 in –,** de moda, en boga. **12 out of –,** pasado de moda. **13 to set the –,** dictar la moda.

fashionable | 'fæʃnəbl | *adj.* **1** de moda, en boga. **2** elegante, de buen tono: *a fashionable pub = un bar de buen tono.*

fashionably | 'fæʃnəblɪ | *adv.* con el estilo de moda.

fast | fɑːst | *adj.* **1** rápido, veloz. **2** (fig.) vivo, ágil: *fast steps = pasos vivos.* **3** DEP. rápida (pista). **4** rápido (carretera, carril o similar). **5** adelantado (reloj). **6** FOT. rápido, de alta sensibilidad (carrete). **7** permanente, fijo (colores de la ropa). **8** intensa (forma de vivir la vida, especialmente en gente joven). **9** (desp.) inmoral, disoluta (especialmente mujer). **10** rápido, inmediato: *a fast profit = un beneficio inmediato.* || *adv.* **11** rápidamente, velozmente. **12 —** (*ger.*), a toda velocidad, rápidamente: *we are fast realizing the importance of a good family education = nos estamos dando cuenta rápidamente de la importancia de una buena educación familiar.* **13**

vivamente, ágilmente: *her words tumbling out fast = sus palabras saliendo a borbotones.* **14** inmediatamente, rápidamente: *I want the letter fast on my desk = quiero la carta inmediatamente en mi mesa de despacho.* **15** firmemente, establemente (con la sujeción adecuada): *fix it fast = fíjalo firmemente.* || *v.i.* **16** REL. ayunar, hacer ayuno. || *s.c.* **17** REL. ayuno. || **18 as – as one's legs can carry one,** tan rápido como uno puede aguantar, tan rápido como uno puede soportar. **19 to break one's –,** romper el ayuno de uno. **20 – asleep,** dormido profundamente. **21 – breeder reactor,** FIS. reactor nuclear de plutonio. **22 – day,** día de ayuno. **23 hard and –,** V. **hard. 24 to hold –, a)** agarrar fuertemente, sujetar con fuerza. **b)** mantenerse firme (en opiniones, línea de actuación, etc.). **25 how –,** a qué velocidad. **26 to make a – buck,** V. **buck. 27 to make –,** amarrar, asegurar (mediante atadura). **28 not so –,** no tan rápido, quieto, calma. **29 to play – and loose,** tratar irresponsablemente, comportarse atolondradamente; jugar (con los sentimientos de otra persona). **30 to pull a – one,** (fam.) hacer una jugarreta, tomar el pelo (económicamente). **31 thick and –,** V. **thick.**

fasten | 'fɑːsn | *v.t.* **1** atar, sujetar, abrochar: *fasten your seat belts = abróchense los cinturones.* **2** (fig.) clavar (dientes, mirada, etc.), poner (manos): *I wish I could fasten my hands on him = ojalá pudiera ponerle las manos encima.* || *v.i.* **3** atarse, sujetarse, abrocharse: *this dress fastens at the back = este vestido se abrocha en la espalda.* || **4 to – on/ upon,** fijar(se) en (con la atención o el pensamiento): *he needed a scapegoat and he fastened on me = necesitaba una cabeza de turco y se fijó en mí.* **5 to – on to,** no separarse de, no irse del lado de. **6 to – up,** abrochar de arriba a abajo, sujetar totalmente.

fastener | 'fɑːsnər | *s.c.* mecanismo de cierre, mecanismo de abrochar (cualquier cosa que sujete, cierre, abroche, ate, etc.).

fastening | 'fɑːsnɪŋ | V. **fastener.**

fast-food | ˌfɑːst'fuːd | *s.i.* comida rápida; platos precocinados.

fastidious | fæ'stɪdɪəs | (form.) *adj.* **1** quisquilloso, exigente. **3** (desp.) descontentadizo, remilgado (en la limpieza de las cosas).

fastidiously | fæ'stɪdɪəslɪ | (form.) *adv.* **1** quisquillosamente, exigentemente. **2** (desp.) con patente descontento, remilgadamente.

fastidiousness | fæ'stɪdɪəsnɪs | (form.) *s.i.* **1** quisquillosidad, exigencia. **2** (desp.) remilgo, melindro (exagerado en la limpieza).

fastness | 'fɑːstnɪs | *s.i.* **1** rapidez, velocidad. **2** firmeza (de colores en la ropa). **3** firmeza, fijeza (de objetos sujetados a algún sitio). || *s.c.* **4** plaza fuerte, fortaleza.

fat | fæt | *adj.* **1** gordo, obeso. **2** grueso, ancho (libro o similar). **3** fértil, rica (tierra, suelo, etc.). **4** próspero, de abundancia (tiempo). **5** (fam.) pingüe, lucrativo, provechoso (económicamente). **6** estúpido, lerdo, torpe (inteligencia): *he can't get it into his fat head = no se lo puede meter en su torpe cabeza.* || *s.i.* **7** grasa, gordo. **8** GAST. manteca (para cocinar). || **9 a – lot of good,** (fam.) nada de nada, no vale para nada. **10 to chew the –/rag,** (fam.) charlar, (Am.) platicar. **11 – cat,** (fam. y EE.UU.) potentado. **12 – chance,** (fam.) ni en sueños, ni por asomo. **13 to grow fat (on),** (fig.) engordar con, hacerse rico con. **14 to run to –,** poner peso, engordar. **15 the – is in the fire,** (fam.) la situación es crítica. **16 the – of the land,** la opulencia, lo mejor de todo.

fatal | 'feɪtl | *adj.* **1** funesto, muy serio, muy significante (equivocación, decisión, fallo, defecto, etc.). **2** fatal, mortífero, mortal.

fatalism | 'feɪtəlɪzəm | *s.i.* fatalismo.

fatalist | 'feɪtəlɪst | *s.c.* fatalista.

fatalistic | ˌfeɪtə'lɪstɪk | *adj.* fatalista.

fatality | fə'tælətɪ | *s.c.* **1** fatalidad, calamidad, desgracia. || *s.i.* **2** fatalidad (sensación o creencia).

fatally | 'feɪtlɪ | *adv.* **1** funestamente, seriamente, significantemente. **3** fatalmente, mortíferamente, mortalmente.

fate | feɪt | *s.i.* **1** destino, hado, sino. || *s.c.* **2** suerte, fortuna (como sino): *she died in a car accident and her brother suffered a similar fate a few years later = ella murió en un accidente de coche y su hermano tuvo una suerte similar unos cuantos años después.* || **3 a – worse than death,** (hum.) una experiencia muy desagradable; un asunto muy serio. **4 to meet one's –,** encontrar la muerte. **5 the Fates,** LIT. las Parcas.

fated | 'feɪtɪd | *adj.* [– *inf.*] predestinado, destinado: *we are fated to love each other = estamos predestinados a amarnos.*

fateful | 'feɪtfl | *adj.* trascendental; fatídico: *the fateful moment = el momento trascendental.*

fatefully | 'feɪtfəlɪ | *adv.* trascendentalmente; fatídicamente.

fathead | 'fæthed | *s.c.* (vulg.) idiota, imbécil, palurdo.

father | 'fɑːðər | *s.c.* **1** padre, progenitor. **2 [(the) – (of)]** (fig.) padre, autor, inventor. || *v.t.* **3** engendrar, procrear (hijos). || **4 Father, a)** REL. Padre (Dios). **b)** padre (llamando al padre de uno). **c)** REL. padre (forma de llamar a un cura). **d)** (lit.) Padre (simbólicamente): *Father Time.* **5 Father Christmas,** Papá Noel. **6 – image,** PSIC. idealización del padre. **7 fathers, a)** antecesores. **b)** padres (de la patria o similar). **8 Father's Day,** el día del Padre (tercer Domingo de Junio). **9 from – to son,** de generación en generación, de padres a hijos. **10 like – like son,** de tal palo tal astilla. **11 the child is – of the man,** el hombre es el resultado de las vivencias infantiles.

father-figure | 'fɑːðəfɪgər | *s.c.* sustituto paternal (persona, especialmente mayor, a quien uno mira como a un padre).

fatherhood | 'fɑðəhʊd | *s.i.* paternidad.

father-in-law | 'fɑːðərɪnlɔː | *s.c.* suegro, padre político.

fatherland | 'fɑːðəlænd | *s.c.* patria.

fatherless | 'fɑːðəlɪs | *adj.* huérfano, sin padre.

fatherly | 'fɑːðəlɪ | *adj.* paternal.

fathom | 'fæðəm | *s.c.* **1** MAR. braza (medida de profundidad). || *v.t.* **2** desentrañar, resolver. || **3 to – out,** desentrañar, resolver.

fathomless | 'fæðəmlɪs | *adj.* insondable, impenetrable.

fatigue | fə'tiːg | *s.i.* **1** fatiga, cansancio. **2** (fig.) MET. fatiga (de los metales después del uso frecuente). || *v.t.* **3** (form.) fatigar, adoptar. || **4 fatigues,** MIL. traje de faena.

fatigued | fə'tiːgd | *adj.* fatigado, cansado, agotado.

fatless | 'fætlɪs | *adj.* sin grasa.

fatness | 'fætnɪs | *s.i.* **1** gordura, obesidad. **2** riqueza, abundancia.

fatso | 'fætsəʊ | *s.sing.* (fam.) regordete (como insulto o apodo).

fatstock | 'fætstɔk | *s.i.* ganado de engorde.

fatted | 'fætɪd | **to kill the – calf,** (p.u.) celebrar por lo grande la llegada de alguien.

fatten | 'fætn | *v.t.* e *i.* **1** engordar, cebar(se). **2** (fig.) hacer(se) rico. || **3 to – up,** engordar, cebar hasta su punto adecuado.

fattening | 'fætnɪŋ | *adj.* que engorda.

fattish | 'fætɪʃ | *adj.* regordete, rellenito.

fatty | 'fætɪ | *s.c.* **1** gordinflón. || *adj.* **2** grasiento, lleno de grasa. **3** ANAT. adiposo.

fatuity | fə'tjuːətɪ | *s.c.* e *i.* fatuidad, simpleza, estupidez.

fatuous | 'fætʃʊəs | *adj.* fatuo, necio, presumido.

fatuously | 'fætʃʊəslɪ | *adv.* fatuamente, neciamente, presumidamente.

fatuousness | 'fætʃʊəsnɪs | *s.i.* fatuidad, necedad.

faucet | 'fɔːsɪt | *s.c.* (EE.UU.) grifo.

fault | fɔːlt | *s.sing.* **1** culpa: *that's not my fault = no es culpa mía.* || *s.c.* **2** error, fallo, equivocación. **3** defecto (en el carácter, sistema, institución, máquina, etc.). **4** DEP. falta (en el tenis). **5** GEOL. falla. || *v.t.* **6 [to – *o.* (on/with)]** culpar, hallar defectos en. || **7 at –,** culpable. **8 to find – with,** desaprobar, censurar, criticar, poner peros a. **9 for all something/somebody's faults,** a pesar de los defectos de algo/alguien, a pesar de los fallos de algo/alguien. **10 to a –,** hasta la saciedad, hasta un grado extremo (hablando de cualidades personales).

faultfinding | 'fɔːltfaɪndɪŋ | *s.i.* crítica mezquina; reparos excesivos.

faultily | 'fɔːltɪlɪ | *adv.* defectuosamente (en el funcionamiento de una máquina o parecido).

faultless | 'fɔːltlɪs | *adj.* perfecto, impecable, sin falta alguna.

faultlessly | 'fɔːltlɪslɪ | *adv.* perfectamente, impecablemente.
faulty | fɔːltɪ | *adj.* defectuoso (máquina o similar).
faun | fɔːn | *s.c.* LIT. fauno.
fauna | 'fɔːnə | *s.pl.* ZOOL. fauna: *the flora and fauna of Spain.*
faux pas | ˌfəʊ'pɑː | (*pl.* **faux pas**) *s.c.* (form.) metedura de pata, paso en falso.
favour | 'feɪvər | (EE.UU. **favor**) *s.c.* **1** favor, servicio: *to do a favour = hacer un favor.* || *s.i.* **2** aprecio, favor, estimación: *I want to win your favour = quiero ganarme tu aprecio.* **3** favoritismo, privilegio. || *v.t.* **4** preferir, apoyar: *I favour Ian's option = yo prefiero la opción de Ian.* **5** favorecer, beneficiar: *the heat favoured the Mexican team = el calor beneficiaba al equipo mejicano.* **6** tratar con favoritismo, privilegiar. **7** (form.) honrar (con la atención, cuidado, presencia, etc.). || **8 do me a –!,** (fam.) ¡Por favor! (como queriendo decir que no). **9 favours,** (form.) favores (en el campo sexual). **10 in –,** a favor: *torture! I'm not in favour = ¡la tortura! yo no estoy a favor.* **11 in – of,** a favor de, en provecho de. **12 in someone's –,** a favor de alguien: *everything is in your favour = todo está a tu favor.* **13 out of –,** en desgracia, no grato.
favoured | 'feɪvəd | *adj.* **1** preferido, favorito, extendido. **2** privilegiado, favorecido (injustamente).
favourable | 'feɪvərəbl | *adj.* **1 [– (to)]** favorable, positivo. **2** beneficioso, favorable: *this is favourable for trade = esto es beneficioso para el comercio.*
favourably | 'feɪvərəblɪ | *adv.* **1** favorablemente, positivamente. **2** beneficiosamente.
favourite | 'feɪvərɪt | *adj.* **1** favorito, preferido, predilecto. || *s.c.* **2** favorito (en una elección, partido, etc.). **3** objeto favorito; bebida favorita. **4** favorito (persona).
favouritism | 'feɪvərɪtɪzəm | *s.i.* favoritismo, parcialidad.
fawn | fɔːn | *adj.* **1** amarillo-marrón; color piel. || *s.c.* ZOOL. cervatillo, gamo joven. || *v.i.* **3 [to – on]** adular, lisonjear. **4 [to – (on)]** saltar alegremente (un perro).
faze | feɪz | *v.t.* molestar, perturbar.
FBI | ˌefbiː'aɪ | *s.sing.* FBI, **Federal Bureau of Investigation.**
fealty | 'fiːəltɪ | *s.c.* e *i.* (arc.) HIS. lealtad, fidelidad (de un vasallo hacia su señor feudal).
fear | fɪər | *s.c.* e *i.* **1** temor, miedo. || *v.t.* **2 [to – *o./ger./inf.*]** temer, recelar de, tener miedo de. **3** tener mal presagio (de que algo malo va a ocurrir). || *v.i.* **4 [to – for]** temer por: *I fear for my father's life = temo por la vida de mi padre.* || **5 for –,** por temor, por miedo: *they never say anything for fear that the headmaster will fire them = nunca dicen nada por temor a que el director les despida.* **6 I fear so/not,** me temo que sí/no. **7 in – and trembling,** asustado y acobardado. **8 in – of,** temeroso de, acobardado ante; miedo de: *I am in fear of him = tengo miedo de él.* **9 never –/– not,** (form. y p.u.) pierda cuidado. **10 no –,** (fam.) en absoluto, jamás. **11 to put the – of God into,** dar un susto de muerte a.
fearful | 'fɪəfl | *adj.* **1** asustado, temeroso. **2** terrible, espantoso: *a fearful sight = una aparición espantosa.* **3** (fam.) tremendo, brutal (énfasis de lo negativo o malo de algo): *what fearful noise = qué ruido tan tremendo.*
fearfully | 'fɪəfəlɪ | *adv.* **1** con mucho miedo, temerosamente. **2** terriblemente, espantosamente. **3** (fam.) tremendamente, brutalmente: *the weather was fearfully hot = hacía un tiempo tremendamente caluroso.*
fearfulness |'fɪəflnɪs | *s.i.* miedo, temor, espanto.
fearless | 'fɪəlɪs | *adj.* intrépido, osado, arrojado.
fearlessly | 'fɪəlɪslɪ | *adv.* intrépidamente, osadamente, arrojadamente.
fearlessness | 'fɪəlɪsnɪs | *s.i.* intrepidez, osadía, arrojo.
fearsome | 'fɪəsəm | *adj.* (form.) temible, terrible, espantoso.
feasibility | ˌfiːzə'bɪlɪtɪ | *s.i.* viabilidad.
feasible | 'fiːzəbl | *adj.* viable, realizable, factible.
feasibly | 'fiːzəblɪ | *adv.* viablemente, factiblemente.
feast | fiːst | *s.c.* **1** festín, banquete. **2** REL. fiesta, día de fiesta, festividad. **3** (fig.) festejo, gozo, deleite. || *v.i.* **4** banquetear, comer como un rey. **5 [to – (on/off)]** darse un banquetazo. || *v.t.* **6** festejar, dar un banquete para. || **7 – day,** REL. festividad, día de fiesta. **8 to – one's eyes on/upon,** regalarse la vista con.
feasting | 'fiːstɪŋ | *s.i.* festejo, banqueteo.
feat | fiːt | *s.c.* proeza, hazaña.
feather | 'feðər | *s.c.* **1** pluma. || *v.t.* **2** cubrir con plumas, forrar con plumas. **3** poner horizontal (la pala de un remo). || **4 a – in one's cap,** motivo de orgullo. **5 birds of a –,** gente de la misma calaña, lobos de la misma camada. **6 birds of a – flock together,** Dios los cría y ellos se juntan. **7 – bed,** colchón de plumas, plumón. **8 – boa,** bufanda de plumas. **9 – duster,** plumero. **10 to – one's nest,** hacer su agosto, forrarse de dinero. **11 to show the white –,** revelar cobardía, mostrarse cobarde.
feather-bedding | ˌfeðə'bedɪŋ | *s.i.* (fam. y desp.) trabajo lento y retardado.
feather-brained | 'feðəbreɪnd | *adj.* bobo; casquivano.
feathered | 'feðəd | *adj.* con plumas.
featherweight | 'feðəweɪt | *s.c.* **1** DEP. luchador de peso pluma. **2** persona de poco peso. **3** (fig.) persona de poca importancia.
feathery | 'feðərɪ | *adj.* plumoso, lleno de plumas.
feature | 'fiːtʃər | *s.c.* **1 [– (of/in)]** característica, peculiaridad; aspecto. **2** GEOG. rasgo paisajístico, característica del paisaje. **3** TV. película de larga duración, largometraje. **4 [– (on)]** reportaje principal. **5 [– (on)]** RAD. programa especial. || *v.t.* **6** ofrecer, tener en su programa: *the exhibition features several paintings by my friend = la exposición tiene en su programa varios cuadros de mi amigo.* **7** destacar, promocionar, hacer resaltar. || *v.i.* **8 [to – in]** aparecer en, tener su lugar destacado en: *the same landscape features in both films = el mismo paisaje aparece en las dos películas.* || **9 features,** rasgos, facciones, fisonomía.
featureless | 'fiːtʃəlɪs | *adj.* sin rasgos sobresalientes, monótono, aburrido.
febrile | 'fiːbraɪl | *adj.* (lit.) febril.
February | 'februərɪ | *s.i.* febrero.
feces | 'fiːsiːz | V. **faeces.**
feckless | 'feklɪs | (form. y desp.) *adj.* **1** débil de carácter, indeciso. **2** irresponsable, incompetente, inconsciente: *feckless behaviour = conducta inconsciente.*
fecklessly | 'feklɪslɪ | (form. y desp.) *adv.* **1** indecisamente, con inseguridad. **2** irresponsablemente, incompetentemente, inconscientemente.
fecklessness | 'feklɪsnɪs | (form. y desp.) *s.i.* **1** indecisión, inseguridad (en el carácter). **2** incompetencia, irresponsabilidad, inconsciencia.
fecund | 'fiːkənd | *adj.* (lit.) fecundo.
fecundity | fɪ'kʌndətɪ | *s.i.* (lit.) fecundidad.
fed | fed | *pret.* y *p.p.* de **feed.**
federal | 'fedərəl | *adj.* **1** POL. federal. **2** central, nacional (en estados federales): *the Federal Government.* || **3 Federal Bureau of Investigation,** (EE.UU.) Oficina Central de la Policía Federal.
federalism | 'fedərəlɪzəm | *s.i.* POL. federalismo.
federalist | 'fedərəlɪst | *s.c.* POL. federalista.
federate | 'fedəreɪt | *v.t.* e *i.* POL. federar(se), formar una federación.
federation | ˌfedə'reɪʃn | *s.c.* **1** federación, agrupamiento. **2** POL. país federal, federación. || **3 Federation,** Federación (en el asociacionismo).
fed up | ˌfed'ʌp | *adj.* **[– (with/about)]** (fam.) harto, hastiado; aburrido: *I'm fed up with you = estoy harto de ti.*
fee | fiː | *s.c.* **1** honorarios (de un abogado, notario, médico o cualquier otra profesión). **2** derechos, matrícula, cuota (en una asociación): *school fee.* **3** DER. patrimonio, heredad. **4** HIS. feudo. || *v.t.* **5** (arc.) DER. contratar: *he feed a lawyer to act on his behalf = contrató a un abogado para actuar en su defensa.* || **6 entrance –,** cuota de admisión. **7 to hold in –,** DER. poseer de acuerdo con la ley, poseer legalmente. **8 membership –,** cuota de socio. **9 registration –,** derechos de matrícula (en el mundo académico).
feeble | 'fiːbl | *adj.* **1** débil, sin fuerzas, endeble: *a feeble old man = un débil anciano.* **2** tenue, débil (luz). **3** inaudible, imperceptible (sonido). **4** irresoluto; ineficaz.
feeble-minded | ˌfiːbl'maɪndɪd | *adj.* (euf.) retrasado mental, lento de entendimiento.

feebleness | 'fi:blnɪs | *s.i.* **1** debilidad, endeblez (personas, cosas, argumentos, etc.). **2** ineficacia; falta de definición (de una persona sobre un tema).

feebly | 'fi:blɪ | *adv.* **1** débilmente; tenuemente; inaudiblemente. **2** irresolutamente, ineficazmente.

feed | fi:d | *v.* [*pret.* y *p.p.* **fed**] *t.* **1** dar de comer, alimentar: *she's feeding the children = ella está dando de comer a los niños.* **2** introducir, meter, cargar (en cualquier tipo de máquina): *to feed ammunition into a gun = meter munición en una pistola.* **3** INF. introducir, meter (información en un ordenador). **4** nutrir, alimentar (una planta). **5** dar el pecho, dar de mamar: *she's feeding the baby = está dando de mamar al bebé.* **6** fomentar (un sentimiento), dar pábulo a (un rumor o comentario): *lack of information feeds rumours = la falta de información da pábulo a rumores.* **7** DEP. pasar, centrar (la pelota). **8** alimentar (un fuego). **9** (normalmente pasiva) recibir como afluente (un río o lago): *this lake is fed by several small mountain streams = este lago recibe como afluentes varios arroyos de montaña.* || *i.* **10 [to – (on/off)]** alimentarse, nutrirse. **11 [to – on]** (fig.) alimentarse de, crecer a base de: *hatred feeds on disillusionment = el odio se alimenta de desilusión.* || *s.i.* **12** pienso. || *s.c.* **13** comida (animales), toma (bebés). **14** (fam.) comida, comilona. **15** MEC. alimentación, mecanismo de alimentación (en cualquier tipo de máquina). || **16 to – a cold,** comer bien para luchar contra un catarro.

feedback | 'fi:dbæk | *s.i.* **1** información acerca del resultado de un proceso, feedback. **2** retroacción, realimentación, reacción: *the feedback from the machine helps us a lot to improve it = la reacción de la máquina nos ayuda mucho para mejorarla.*

feed-bag | 'fi:dbæg | *s.c.* (EE.UU.) morral.

feeder | 'fi:dər | *s.c.* **1** MEC. alimentador. **2** (brit.) biberón; babero. **3** [*adj.* –] que come: *our baby is a very slow feeder = nuestro pequeño es un bebé que come muy despacio.* **4** ramal secundario (en carreteras, vías de tren, etc.).

feeding | 'fi:dɪŋ | *s.c.* e *i.* **1** alimentación, alimento, nutrición. || **2 – ground,** zona de alimentos (para un determinado grupo de animales).

feeding-bottle | 'fi:dɪŋbɔtl | *s.c.* biberón.

feel | fi:l | *v.* [*pret.* y *p.p.* **felt**] *i.* **1** sentirse, encontrarse (bien, mal, enfermo, etc.). **2 [to – *adj.*]** dar la sensación de, parecer (al tacto): *this material feels rough = este tejido parece rugoso.* **3 [to – as if/like]** sentirse como si, sentirse como si fuera; parecer como si fuera: *it feels like summer = parece como si fuera verano; I feel as if I was seventy = me siento como si tuviera setenta años.* **4 [to – (about)]** opinar: *you know what I feel about Marxism = sabes lo que opino del marxismo.* || *t.* **5** sentir (emoción, estado físico, etc.): *I feel your father's death = siento la muerte de tu padre.* **6** palpar, tocar (con cierto cuidado): *I felt her cold face = toqué su cara fría.* **7** opinar, creer, parecerle a uno: *I feel your attitude is not correct = me parece que tu actitud no es la correcta.* **8** notar, sentir en su propia vida: *the children didn't notice the change = los niños no notaron el cambio.* **9 [to – *o.* + *inf.*]** *sentir, parecer: we felt it necessary to leave China = nos pareció necesario irnos de China.* || *v.r.* **10** darse cuenta de: *he felt himself getting red = se dio cuenta de que se estaba poniendo colorado.* || *s.sing.* **11** tacto (uno de los cinco sentidos). **12** ambiente, atmósfera: *the feel of a place = el ambiente de un lugar.* || **13 to – around,** buscar tanteando, buscar a tientas. **14 to – for, a)** sentir pena por, sentir compasión por, compadecer a. **a)** buscar a tientas. **15 to – like,** (*ger./o.*), apetecer, tener ganas de: *do you feel like an apple? = ¿te apetece una manzana?* **16 to – like rain/snow,** parecer que va a llover/nevar. **17 to – oneself,** sentirse bien, sentirse sano: *I don't feel myself today = no me siento bien.* **18 to – one's oats,** (fam.) sentirse fabulosamente, sentirse lleno de alegría. **19 to – one's way, a)** palpar (cuando no se ve bien), andar a tientas. **b)** actuar con precauciones (en unas conversaciones políticas, con una nueva amistad, etc.). **20 to – something in one's bones,** V. **bone. 21 to – the cold,** sufrir con el frío, no acostumbrarse al frío. **22 to – up to,** sentirse capaz de, sentirse capacitado para: *I don't feel up to more responsibilities = no me siento capacitado para más responsabilidades.* **23 to get the – of,** acostumbrarse a, hacerse a: *I haven't got the feel of the new job yet = todavía no me he hecho al nuevo trabajo.*

feeler | 'fi:lər | *s.c.* **1** ZOOL. antena, tentáculo, palpo (de animales). || **2 to put /have feelers out,** tantear, sondear (para ver la reacción de alguien).

feeler-gauge | 'fi:ləgeɪdʒ | *s.c.* MEC. calibrador de hojillas, indicador de holgura.

feeling | 'fi:lɪŋ | *s.c.* **1** sentimiento (de alegría, tristeza, ira, etc.). **2** sensación (de cansancio o cualquier otra cosa física). **3** impresión: *I have the feeling that she's angry = tengo la impresión de que ella está enfadadísima.* || *s.i.* **4** emoción, sentimiento: *she sings with feeling = ella canta con sentimiento.* **5** tacto, capacidad de tacto, sensación de tacto. **6 [– (for)]** simpatía, conmiseración. || *s.sing.* **7 [a – for]** un gusto especial por, un sentimiento especial por: *my son has a feeling for music = mi hijo tiene un gusto especial por la música.* **8** presentimiento, corazonada. **9** ambiente, atmósfera (especialmente de un libro o similar). || *s.c.* e *i.* **10** parecer, opinión. || *adj.* **11** sensible, tierno, compasivo. **12** lleno de sentimiento, conmovedor. || **13 bad –,** hostilidad, acritud. **14 feelings,** sentimientos (como conjunto de la parte emotiva de una persona): *please, don't hide your feelings from me = por favor, no me ocultes tus sentimientos.* **15 hard feelings,** resentimiento. **16 to have mixed feelings about,** no tener una idea definida sobre; estar intranquilo sobre. **17 to hurt someone's feelings,** herir los sentimientos de alguien. **18 I know the –,** sé a qué te refieres; conozco lo que sientes.

feelingly | 'fi:lɪŋlɪ | *adv.* con gran sentimiento, con mucha emoción.

feet | fi:t | *pl.* de **foot.**

feign | feɪn | *v.t.* (lit.) aparentar, fingir, simular.

feint | feɪnt | *s.c.* e *i.* **1** finta, amago, falso ataque. || *s.i.* **2** papel a rayas. || *v.t.* e *i.* **3** fintar, hacer una finta, hacer un amago.

feisty | 'faiːstɪ | *adj.* **1** (EE.UU. y fam.) lleno de energía, lleno de vida, lleno de fuerza. **2** (desp.) irritable, de mal genio.

feldspar | 'feldspɑr | *s.i.* MIN. feldespato.

felicitate | fi'lɪsɪteɪt | *v.t.* (lit.) felicitar, cumplimentar.

felicitation | fi'lɪsɪ'teɪʃn | *s.c.* e *i.* (lit.) felicitación, cumplimentación, parabién.

felicitous | fi'lɪsɪtəs | *adj.* (form. y lit.) afortunado, oportuno, bien expresado (palabras o imágenes).

felicity | fi'lɪsɪtɪ | *s.i.* **1** dicha, felicidad. **2** gracia, buen hacer. || **3 felicities,** palabras ocurrentes, ocurrencias, dicho bien expresado.

feline | 'fi:laɪn | *adj.* **1** ZOOL. felino. **2** (fig.) gatuno, felino; ágil. || *s.c.* **3** ZOOL. felino.

fell | fel | *pret.* **1** de **fall.** || *v.t.* **2** cortar (un árbol). **3** derribar, tirar al suelo (de un golpe). || *s.c.* **4** colina (especialmente en el norte de Inglaterra). || **5 with one – swoop,** V. **swoop.**

fellatio | fi'leɪʃi:əʊ | *s.i.* (form.) estimulación oral del pene.

fellow | 'feləʊ | (fam. también **fella/ feller**) *s.c.* **1** (fam.) tipo, socio, tío: *he's a nice fellow = es un tío majo.* **2** (fam.) novio, pareja. **3** miembro (de sociedades científicas o consejos académicos). **4** (EE.UU.) becario (una vez acabada una licenciatura). **5** (form.) par, congénere: *this is one of the socks, but where is its fellow? = este es uno de los calcetines, pero ¿dónde está su par?* || *adj.* **6** camarada de, compañero de: *my fellow workers = mis compañeros de trabajo.* || **7 fellow-,** con- (en compuestos): *fellow student = condiscípulo; fellow citizen = conciudadano... fellow countryman = compatriota.* **8 Fellow,** miembro (como título). **9 – feeling,** camaradería, compañerismo. **10 fellows,** compañeros; semejantes.

fellowship | 'feləʊʃɪp | *s.i.* **1** camaradería, compañerismo. **2** condición de socio (de algún tipo de asociación académica). || *s.c.* **3** sociedad, hermandad, fraternidad: *the fellowship of the Rose*

= *la hermandad de la Rosa.* **4** beca (después de la licenciatura). **5** puesto de becario universitario.
felon | 'felən | *s.c.* DER. criminal, delincuente (de importancia).
felonious | fe'ləʊnɪəs | DER. *adj.* **1** criminal. || **2 – assault,** asalto con propósito criminal. **3 – intent,** propósito criminal.
felony | 'felənɪ | *s.i.* y *c.* DER. crimen, delito mayor.
felt | felt | *pret.* y *p.p.* **1** de **feel.** || *s.i.* **2** fieltro.
felt-pen | ˌfelt'pen | V. **felt-tip.**
felt-tip | ˌfelt'tɪp | *s.c.* **1** rotulador. || **2 – pen,** rotulador.
female | 'fiːmeɪl | *s.c.* **1** hembra. **2** (form.) mujer, chica. || *adj.* **3** hembra, femenino. **4** MEC. hembra, matriz. **5** BOT. gineceo, pistilado.
feminine | 'femɪnɪn | *adj.* **1** femenino, de mujer. **2** femenina (como característica personal). **3** GRAM. femenino.
femeninity | ˌfemi'nɪnɪtɪ | *s.i.* **1** feminidad, sexo femenino. **2** feminidad (característica personal).
feminism | 'femɪnɪzəm | *s.i.* POL. feminismo.
feminist | 'femɪnɪst | POL. *s.c.* **1** feminista. || *adj.* **2** feminista.
femme fatale | ˌfæm fə'tɑːl | (*pl.* **femmes fatales**) *s.c.* mujer fatal, vampiresa.
femur | 'fiːmər | (*pl.* **femurs** o **femora**) *s.c.* ANAT. fémur.
fen | fen | *s.c.* e *i.* GEOG. marjal, ciénaga, pantano.
fence | fens | *s.c.* **1** valla, cerca. **2** DEP. obstáculo. **3** (fam.) receptor (de objetos robados). || *v.t.* **4** cercar, vallar. || *v.i.* **5** DEP. hacer esgrima, practicar esgrima. **6** (form.) lanzar evasivas; no comprometerse (de palabra). || **7 to come down on one side of the – or the other,** tomar partido por un bando u otro. **8 to come down on the right side of the –,** tomar partido por los vencedores; ponerse al sol que más calienta. **9 to – in, a)** vallar, encerrar (especialmente animales para evitar que se escapen). **b)** encajonar, ahogar (dentro de muy poco espacio). **10 to – off,** separar mediante cerca. **11 to sit on the –,** no comprometerse, estar a verlas venir, no querer mojarse.
fenced | fensd | *adj.* vallado, cercado; cerrado con valla, separado por medio de una valla.
fencer | 'fensər | *s.c.* DEP. esgrimista.
fencing | 'fensɪŋ | *s.i.* **1** DEP. esgrima. **2** material para cercados.
fend | fend | *v.t.* **1 to – for oneself,** valerse por sí mismo, ganarse la vida. **2 to – off, a)** defenderse contra, repeler; mantener a raya. **b)** (fig.) repeler, defenderse contra, rechazar (preguntas, críticas, etc.).
fender | 'fendər | *s.c.* **1** guardafuego (de una chimenea). **2** MAR. andullo, pallete (como protección contra un choque). **3** (EE.UU.) guardabarro; parachoque.
fennel | 'fenl | *s.i.* BOT. hinojo.
feral | 'fɪərəl | *adj.* (form.) salvaje, fiero (animales).
ferment | 'fɜːment | *s.i.* **1** agitación, tumulto. || | fə'ment | *v.t.* e *i.* **2** fermentar(se) (vino, fruta, masa, etc.).
fermented | fə'mentɪd | *adj.* fermentado (vino, fruta, masa, etc.).
fermentation | ˌfɜːmen'teɪʃn | *s.c.* e *i.* fermentación (proceso químico).
fern | fɜːn | (*pl.* **fern** o **ferns**) BOT. helecho.
ferocious | fə'rəʊʃəs | *adj.* **1** feroz, salvaje (animales, personas, guerras, etc.). **2** (fig.) feroz, terrorífico, brutal: *they used ferocious spears with spikes = utilizaron lanzas terroríficas con clavos; we've had ferocious heat lately = hemos sufrido un calor brutal últimamente.*
ferociously | fə'rəʊʃəslɪ | *adv.* **1** ferozmente, salvajemente. **2** ferozmente, terroríficamente, brutalmente.
ferocity | fə'rɒsɪtɪ | *s.i.* ferocidad, fiereza; crueldad.
ferret | 'ferɪt | *s.c.* **1** ZOOL. hurón. || *v.i.* **2 [to – about]** (fam.) husmear, hurgar, rebuscar (en busca de algo). || **3 to – out,** (fam.) descubrir, sacar a la luz (después de esfuerzo). **4 to go ferreting,** ir de caza de ratas o conejos con un hurón.
Ferris wheel | 'ferɪs wiːl | V. **wheel.**
ferroconcrete | ˌferəʊ'kɒŋkriːt | *s.i.* cemento armado, hormigón.
ferrous | 'ferəs | *adj.* MIN. ferroso, con hierro, de hierro.
ferrule | 'feruːl | *s.c.* MEC. férula, casquillo.
ferry | 'ferɪ | *s.c.* **1** ferry, transbordador. || *v.t.* **2** transportar (de una orilla a otra en un río, de un puerto a otro en un canal). **3** MIL. transportar (en barco o en avión).
ferryboat | 'ferɪbəʊt | *s.c.* barco transbordador, ferry.
ferryman | 'ferɪmən | *s.c.* encargado de ferry; guardián de una balsa (que lleva objetos o personas de orilla a orilla en tramos cortos).
fertile | 'fɜːtaɪl | *adj.* **1** fértil, feraz (tierra). **2** fecundo, fértil (persona o animal). **3** (fig.) fecundo, productivo (situación): *this is fertile ground for prostitution = este es terreno fecundo para la prostitución.* **4** fértil, creativo, creador: *to have a fertile imagination = tener una imaginación fértil.*
fertility | fə'tɪlitɪ | *s.i.* **1** fertilidad, fecundidad (de tierra, animales, personas). **2** (fig.) fertilidad, creatividad.
fertilization | ˌfɜːtəlaɪ'zeɪʃn | *s.i.* fertilización, fecundación.
fertilize | 'fɜːtəlaɪz | (también **fertilise**) **1** fertilizar, fecundar. **2** abonar, nutrir (la tierra).
fertilized | 'fɜːtəlaɪzd | *adj.* fertilizado, fecundado.
fertilizer | 'fɜːtəlaɪzər | *s.c.* e *i.* fertilizante, abono.
fervent | 'fɜːvənt | *adj.* ferviente, fervoroso.
fervently | 'fɜːvəntlɪ | *adv.* fervientemente, fervorosamente.
fervid | 'fɜːvɪd | *adj.* (form.) férvido, fervoroso.
fervour | 'fɜːvər | (EE.UU. **fervor**) *s.i.* (form.) fervor, celo, vehemencia.
festal | 'festl | *adj.* (form.) festivo.
fester | 'festər | *v.i.* **1** MED. supurar. **2** (fig.) deteriorarse; enconarse (una situación, etc.): *those slums are festering with violence = esos suburbios están deteriorándose con la violencia.*
festival | 'festivl | *s.c.* **1** festival, fiesta. || **2 Festival,** Festival, Certamen (con nombre propio).
festive | 'festɪv | *adj.* festivo, alegre.
festivity | fe'stɪvitɪ | *s.i.* **1** ambiente de fiesta, alegría. || **2 festivities,** celebraciones, fiestas.
festoom | fe'stuːn | *v.t.* adornar en forma de guirnaldas, adornar, engalanar.
fetal | 'fiːtl | V. **foetal.**
fetch | fetʃ | *v.t.* **1** traer, ir a por, ir a traer: *fetch the glasses = ve a por las copas.* **2** alcanzar un precio de: *this house can fetch more than 20 million = esta casa puede alcanzar un precio de más de 20 millones.* **3** (fam.) atizar, pegar (un golpe). **4** (p.u.) tomar (aliento), arrancar (lágrimas o suspiros). || **5 to – and carry,** llevar y traer; trajinar (en servicio de alguien). **6 to – up,** (EE.UU. y fam.) aparecer inesperadamente: *we knew through the papers that he had fetched up in Africa = supimos por los periódicos que él había aparecido inesperadamente en Africa.*
fetching | 'fetʃɪŋ | *adj.* atractivo, encantador.
fetchingly | 'fetʃɪŋlɪ | *adv.* atractivamente, encantadoramente.
fete | feɪt | (también **fête**) *s.c.* **1** fiesta (especialmente al aire libre y con algún fin caritativo de recaudación de fondos). || **2 to be feted,** ser agasajado, ser festejado.
fetid | 'fetɪd | *adj.* (form.) fétido, hediondo.
fetish | 'fetɪʃ | *s.c.* **1** PSIQ. fetiche. **2** (fig.) manía, obsesión: *bikes are almost a fetish with him = las bicicletas son casi una obsesión para él.*
fetishism | 'fetɪʃɪzəm | *s.i.* PSIQ. fetichismo.
fetishist | 'fetɪʃɪst | *s.c.* PSIQ. fetichista.
fetlook | 'fetlɒk | *s.c.* ZOOL. espolón, menudillo (parte de la anatomía caballar, encima de los cascos).
fetter | 'fetər | *v.t.* **1** aherrojar, sujetar con grilletes. **2** (fig.) inhibir; estorbar: *I hate fettering my students with all sorts of rules = odio inhibir a mis estudiantes con todo tipo de reglas.* || *s.c. pl.* **3** grilletes, pihuelas. **4** (fig.) estorbos, trabas. || **5 in fetters,** encadenado, con grilletes.
fettle | 'fetl | **in fine/good –,** (fam.) en perfectas condiciones físicas, en forma.
fetus | 'fiːtəs | V. **foetus.**
feud | fjuːd | *s.c.* **1** odio inveterado, disputa permanente (entre dos familias especialmente). || *v.i.* **2 [to – (with)]** luchar sin tregua, disputar sin descanso.
feudal | 'fjuːdl | *adj.* HIST. feudal.
feudalism | 'fjuːdəlɪzəm | *s.i.* HIST. feudalismo.

fever | 'fiːvər | *s.c.* e *i.* **1** MED. fiebre, calentura. || *s.c.* **2** (fig.) frenesí, agitación. || **3 at/to fever pitch,** (fam.) a/en un grado considerable de excitación, hasta el delirio.

fevered | 'fiːvəd | *adj.* **1** febril, con fiebre, ardiendo por la fiebre. **2** (fig.) febril, muy excitado.

feverish | 'fiːvərɪʃ | *adj.* **1** febril, calenturiento, con fiebre. **2** (fig.) desasosegado; excitadísimo.

feverishly | 'fiːvərɪʃlɪ | *adv.* febrilmente, desasosegadamente; con gran excitación, frenéticamente.

few | fjuː | *adj.* **1** pocos: *I have a few good friends here = tengo unos pocos buenos amigos aquí.* || *cuant.* **2** pocos (con sentido negativo): *there are few chances = hay pocas oportunidades.* **3** **[a –]** algunos, unos pocos: *I'll stay for a few weeks = me quedaré durante unas pocas semanas.* || *pron.* **4** pocos. **5 [a –]** algunos, unos cuantos: *we invited many but only a few came = invitamos a muchos pero solamente vinieron unos cuantos.* || **6 as – as,** únicamente; increíblemente sólo: *those insects live as few as 7 days = esos insectos únicamente viven 7 días.* **7 – and far between,** poquísimos, contadísimos: *facilities in this district are few and far between = los servicios en este distrito son contadísimos.* **8 to have a few/to have a few too many,** (fam.) estar borracho, pasarse en el alcohol. **9 no fever than,** nunca menos de (enfatizando una gran cantidad). **10 quite a –/a good –/not a –,** bastantes, un buen número, no pocos. **11 the –,** los menos, la minoría; los selectos. **12 the lucky –,** los afortunados, los privilegiados.

fey | feɪ | *adj.* fantasioso; excéntrico.

fez | fez | *s.c.* gorro de moro (rojo y con borla negra).

fiancé | fɪ'ɔnseɪ | *s.c.* prometido.

fiancée | fɪ'ɔnseɪ | *s.c.* prometida.

fiasco | fɪ'æskəʊ | (EE.UU. *pl.* **fiascoes** /brit. *pl.* **fiascos**) *s.c.* fracaso, fiasco, fallo total.

fiat | 'faɪæt | *s.c.* (form.) fiat, mandato, orden.

fib | fɪb | (fam.) *s.c.* **1** mentira, mentirijilla. || *v.i.* **2** decir mentiras, contar mentiras.

fibber | 'fɪbər | *s.c.* (fam.) embustero, mentiroso.

fibre | 'faɪbər | (EE.UU. **fiber**) *s.c.* **1** fibra, filamento (naturales o artificiales). **2** ANAT. fibra. || *s.i.* **3** GAST. fibra. **4** (fig.) temperamento, nervio, carácter. || *s.c.* e *i.* **5** hilo, tejido. || **6 – optic,** TEC. fibra óptica. **7 – optics,** TEC. transmisión por fibra óptica. **8 with every – of one's being,** con cada fibra del ser de uno; profundamente: *I love you with every fibre of my being = te quiero profundamente.*

fibreglass | 'faɪbəglɑːs | *s.i.* QUIM. fibra de vidrio.

fibrosis | faɪ'brəʊsɪs | *s.i.* MED. fibrosis.

fibrous | 'faɪbrəs | *adj.* **1** fibroso. || **2 – tissue,** ANAT. tejido fibroso.

fibula | 'fɪbjulə | (*pl.* **fibulae** o **fibulas**) *s.c.* ANAT. peroné.

fickle | fɪkl | *adj.* **1** (desp.) veleidoso, inestable, voluble. **2** (fig.) inestable, inconstante (el viento o el tiempo).

fickleness | 'fɪklnɪs | *s.i.* (desp.) veleidad, inconstancia, inestabilidad.

fiction | 'fɪkʃn | *s.i.* **1** ficción, irrealidad. **2** LIT. novelística, género de novela. || *s.c.* **3** ficción, mentira, entelequia.

fictional | 'fɪkʃənl | *adj.* **1** ficcional, irreal. **2** literario, novelesco. **3** ficticio, falso.

fictionalization | ˌfɪkʃənəlaɪ'zeɪʃn | *s.c.* e *i.* adaptación literaria.

fictionalize | 'fɪkʃənəlaɪz | (también **fictionalise**) *v.t.* adaptar (una historia real).

fictionalized | 'fɪkʃənəlaɪzd | *adj.* adaptado (que no cuenta toda la realidad).

fictitious | fɪk'tɪʃəs | *adj.* **1** falso, inexistente. **2** imaginario, inventado: *a fictitious character = un personaje imaginario.*

fiddle | 'fɪdl | *v.i.* **1 [to – with]** manosear (nerviosamente). **2 [to – with]** toquetear; manipular (sin conocimientos suficientes): *stop fiddling with the TV = deja de toquetear la televisión.* || *v.t.* **3** (fam.) falsificar: *to fiddle the books = falsificar los libros de las cuentas.* || *s.c.* **4** (fam.) MUS. violín. **5** (fam.) falsificación, fraude. || **6 to – about/around,** haraganear, malgastar el tiempo (emprendiendo cosas sin orden ni concierto). **7 to – about/around with,** trastocar, toquetear. **8 to – while Rome burns,** tocar la flauta (mientras algo grave sucede). **9 on the –,** metido en algo fraudulento, metido en chanchullos. **10 to play second – (to),** ser el segundón (de), ir de segundón (de).

fiddler | 'fɪdlər | *s.c.* **1** violinista (especialmente de música tradicional, no de orquesta). **2** (fam.) chanchullero; falsificador.

fiddlesticks | 'fɪdlstɪks | *interj.* (p.u.) tonterías, bobadas.

fiddling | 'fɪdlɪŋ | *s.i.* **1** prácticas fraudulentas; chanchullos. || *adj.* **2** nimio, poco importante.

fiddly | 'fɪdlɪ | *adj.* (fam.) difícil, complicado (de usar, manejar, etc.).

fidelity | fɪ'delɪtɪ | *s.i.* **1 [– (to)]** fidelidad, lealtad (a una persona). **2 [– (to)]** (form.) fidelidad, lealtad (a ideas, personas, etc.). **3** (form.) exactitud, fidelidad (de una traducción, adaptación, etc.).

fidget | 'fɪdʒɪt | *v.i.* **1** no parar de moverse, estar sin parar: *these boys are always fidgeting = estos chicos no paran de moverse.* **2 [to – with]** manosear, toquetear. || *s.c.* **3** (fig. y fam.) culo de mal asiento, lagartija. || **4 to be fidgeting,** (*inf.*), estar impaciente por: *I'm fidgeting to go = estoy impaciente por irme.* **5 to – about,** no parar en un mismo sitio, no parar de moverse de sitio. **6 to have the fidgets,** no parar en un mismo sitio, no parar de moverse de sitio. **7 the fidgets,** movimientos de impaciencia/inquietud/desasosiego: *she has the fidgets again = tiene otra vez los movimientos de impaciencia.*

fidgety | 'fɪdʒɪtɪ | *adj.* inquieto, intranquilo, impaciente.

fie | faɪ | *interj.* **[– on]** (arc.) vergüenza sobre, deshonra sobre: *fie on you! = ¡la vergüenza caiga sobre ti!*

fief | fiːf | *s.c.* HIST. feudo.

field | fiːld | *s.c.* **1** campo (acotado): *a wheat field = un campo de trigo.* **2** DEP. campo, terreno de juego. **3** MIN. yacimiento (de petróleo, de gas, de diamantes, etc.). **4** extensión, campo (de cualquier cosa como nieve, hielo, etc.). **5** FIS. campo (magnético, de gravedad, etc.). **6** especialidad, campo de investigación, ramo (de ciencia). **7** fondo (de una moneda, escudo o bandera). **8** FOT. campo (visual). **9** MIL. campo (de fuego). || *s.sing.* **10** MIL. campo, campo de batalla. **11 [– *v.sing./pl.*]** competidores, participantes (en una carrera o juego). || *adj.* **12** de campo, de campaña; de prácticas (señala un tipo de investigación in situ): *a field trip to study wild goats = un viaje de prácticas para estudiar cabras salvajes.* || *v.t.* **13** contestar satisfactoriamente (preguntas). **14** DEP. parar y devolver (la pelota en ciertos juegos). **15** DEP. sacar a jugar: *Real Madrid fielded a wonderful team = el Real Madrid sacó a jugar un equipo estupendo.* **16** poner en juego, poner a punto: *I can easily field a few repair teams = puedo fácilmente poner en juego unos cuantos equipos de reparación.* || *v.i.* **17** DEP. parar (la pelota). **18** DEP. jugar a la contra (en el béisbol o críquet). || **19 – event,** DEP. lanzamiento, salto (en el atletismo). **20 – hockey,** DEP. (EE.UU.) hockey. **21 – sports,** caza y pesca. **22 to have a – day,** divertirse de lo grande. **23 to hold/lead the –,** estar/ir a la cabeza (en alguna especialidad o actividad). **24 in the –,** al natural, en la práctica (no teórico). **25 to play the –,** (fam.) no comprometerse, estar sin compromiso (especialmente con el sexo opuesto). **26 to take the –, a)** MIL. empezar una campaña. **b)** DEP. salir al campo de juego.

field-day | 'fiːlddeɪ | *s.c.* **1** día de investigación práctica en el campo. **2** día de maniobras. **3** (EE.UU.) día de deportes (en escuela o universidad).

fielder | 'fiːldər | *s.c.* DEP. jardinero (en béisbol), servidor (en críquet).

field-glasses | 'fiːldglɑːsɪz | *s.pl* prismáticos, gemelos.

fieldmarshal | ˌfiːld'mɑːʃl | *s.c.* MIL. mariscal de campo.

fieldmouse | 'fiːldmaus | (*pl.* **fieldmice**) *s.c.* ZOOL. ratón de campo.

field-test | 'fiːldtest | *v.t.* **1** someter a prueba práctica, comprobar el funcionamiento práctico de. || *s.i.* **2** prueba práctica, prueba de funcionamiento práctico.

fieldwork | 'fiːldwəːk | *s.i.* **1** trabajo sobre el terreno, estudio práctico, investigación de campo, investigación sobre el terreno. **2** MIL. obras de fortificación temporal.

fiend | fiːnd | *s.c.* **1** (lit. y p.u.) monstruo, demonio, desalmado. **2** [*s.* –] (fam.) fanático de, entusiasta de, enamorado de: *she's a bodybuilding fiend = ella es una entusiasta del culturismo.*
fiendish | 'fiːndɪʃ | *adj.* **1** cruel, perverso; diabólico. **2** (fam. y fig.) diabólico, perverso (en su inteligencia). **3** (fam. y fig.) diabólico (en su complejidad).
fiendishly | 'fiːndɪʃlɪ | *adv.* **1** cruelmente, perversamente, diabólicamente. **2** (fam.) muy (intensificando la idea de dificultad).
fierce | fɪəs | *adj.* **1** fiero, feroz; agresivo. **2** inamovible, firme: *fierce loyalty = lealtad inamovible.* **3** intenso, fuerte: *fierce heat = calor intenso.*
fiercely | 'fɪəslɪ | *adv.* **1** agresivamente; ferozmente. **2** inamoviblemente, firmemente. **3** intensamente, fuertemente.
fierceness | 'fɪəsnɪs | *s.i.* **1** agresividad; ferocidad. **2** firmeza (en los sentimientos). **3** intensidad (de algo en su aspecto desagradable).
fiery | 'faɪərɪ | *adj.* **1** llameante, que arde. **2** enrojecido, rojo. **3** que quema, picante (de comida o bebida). **4** apasionado, temperamental; fogoso.
fiesta | fɪ'estə | *s.c.* fiesta, celebración; vacación (esta palabra tiene sabor latino por su procedencia).
fife | faɪf | *s.c.* MUS. pífano.
fifteen | ˌfɪf'tiːn | *num. ord.* **1** quinto, cinco (en fechas). || *s.c.* **2** MUS. quinta (intervalo). **3** quinto (fracción). || **4 – column,** POL. quinta columna. **5 – columnist,** POL. quintacolumnista.
fifthly | 'fɪfθlɪ | *adv.* en quinto lugar.
fiftieth | 'fɪftɪəθ | *num. ord.* quincuagésimo.
fifty | 'fɪftɪ | *num. card.* **1** cincuenta. || **2 in one's fifties,** en la cincuentena (edad). **2 the fifties, a)** los años cincuenta, la década de los cincuenta. **b)** la banda de los cincuenta grados (de temperatura).
fifty-fifty | ˌfɪftɪ'fɪftɪ | *adv.* **1** al cincuenta por ciento, a medias, a partes iguales. || *adj.* **2** del cincuenta por ciento, del cincuenta por ciento para cada uno. || **3 to go –,** ir a medias, ir a partes iguales.
fig | fɪg | *s.c.* **1** higo, breva. || **3 – tree,** BOT. higuera. **3 not to care/give a – (about),** no importar un comino, no importar un bledo: *I don't care a fig about her = ella me importa un bledo.*
fight | faɪt | *v.* [*pret.* y *p.p.* **fought**] *t.* **1** luchar contra, combatir; enfrentarse a: *we must fight desease = debemos luchar contra la enfermedad.* **2** MIL. luchar contra, batallar contra, pelear contra. **3** pelear con, pegarse con (especialmente niños). **4** DEP. batirse contra, enfrentarse a (en el boxeo). **5** reñir con, pelearse con (verbalmente). **6** POL. luchar por un escaño en (una elección). **7 [to – *o.* + for]** luchar contra... por, competir contra... por: *I fought Williams for the post of sales manager = competí contra Williams por el puesto de director de ventas.* **8** resistir, luchar contra (un sentimiento). **9** tomar parte en, participar (en una guerra, duelo, etc.). || *i.* **10 [to – (against)]** luchar, combatir: *I will always fight against ignorance = siempre lucharé contra la ignorancia.* **11 [to – for/*inf.*]** luchar por, pelear por: *fight for your rights = lucha por tus derechos.* **12 [to – (with/against)]** MIL. luchar, guerrear, batallar. **13 [to – (against)]** DEP. pelear, batirse, luchar (en el boxeo). **14 [to – (with/against)]** pegarse, pelearse (especialmente niños). || *s.c.* **15 [– (against)]** lucha, batalla. **16 [to – (for)]** lucha, batalla (por algo como libertad, derechos humanos, etc.). **17** MIL. lucha, batalla, pelea, combate. **18** pelea, riña, discusión a golpes. **19** discusión verbal, pelea (no a golpes). **20 [– (against)]** DEP. combate pugilístico, combate de boxeo. || *s.i.* **21** combatividad, ánimo combativo, brío. || **22 to – a losing battle,** V. **battle. 23 to – back, a)** repeler un ataque, responder a un ataque, defenderse de. **b)** resistir, reprimir (sentimientos o similar). **24 to – down,** resistir, reprimir (sentimientos o similar). **25 to – fire with fire,** V. **fire. 26 to – for one's life,** luchar por la vida de uno (cuando se está muy enfermo o en gran peligro). **28 to – like a tiger,** (fam.) luchar como un león, luchar como una fiera. **29 to – off, a)** repeler, rechazar (ataques). **b)** mantener a raya (sentimientos o similar). **30 to – one's way,** abrirse paso. **31 to – out,** dirimir mediante pelea. **32 to – shy of,** V. **shy. 33 to put up a –,** ofrecer resistencia, no amilanarse.
fighter | 'faɪtər | *s.c.* **1** luchador, combatiente, contrincante (en el deporte, milicia o similar). **2** (fig.) luchador (que no se rinde fácilmente). **3** MIL. caza (avión). || **4 – plane,** MIL. caza, avión de caza.
fighting | 'faɪtɪŋ | *s.i.* **1** MIL. combate, batalla, lucha. **2** peleas, luchas: *street fighting = peleas callejeras.* || **3 – chance,** buena probabilidad de sobrevivir, buena probabilidad de éxito. **4 – cock, a)** gallo de pelea. **b)** (fig.) persona pugnaz. **5 – fit,** magnífica salud.
figleaf | 'fɪgliːf | *s.c.* **1** hoja de higuera. **2** (fig.) hoja de parra (para ocultar el sexo en muchos cuadros).
figment | 'fɪgmənt | *s.c.* **[– (of)]** invención, ficción: *a figment of your imagination = una invención de tu imaginación.*
figurative | 'fɪgərətɪv | *adj.* **1** figurado, metafórico. **2** figurativo (de pintura y escultura).
figuratively | 'fɪgərətɪvlɪ | *adv.* figuradamente, metafóricamente.
figure | 'fɪgər | *s.c.* **1** cifra, dato; número: *the export figures = las cifras de la exportación.* **2** silueta, figura, tipo: *she's got a lovely figure = tiene un tipo precioso.* **3** ART. figura, dibujo (en cuadros o esculturas). **4** (fig.) figura, personaje, figura prominente. **5** símbolo: *mother figure = símbolo materno.* **6** GEOM. figura. **7** ilustración, dibujo (normalmente acompañando a texto). **8** figura (de baile). || *v.t.* **9** (EE.UU. y fam.) creer, imaginar, deducir: *I figure that is right = imagino que eso es correcto.* **10** (EE.UU. y p.u.) MAT. calcular, hacer cuentas aritméticas. || *v.i.* **11** (EE.UU. y p.u.) MAT. hacer cuentas aritméticas. **12 [to – in]** aparecer en, estar incluido en: *your city doesn't figure in my brochure = tu ciudad no aparece en mi folleto.* || **13 a fine – of a man/woman,** un hombre /mujer de imponente aspecto, un hombre/mujer de buena presencia. **14 to cut a –,** V. **cut. 15 double figures,** cifra de dos números: *inflation has gone beyond double figures in Argentina = la inflación ha sobrepasado la cifra de dos números en Argentina.* **16 – eight,** (EE.UU.) ocho (figura en el patinaje artístico). **17 – of eight,** ocho (figura en el patinaje artístico). **18 – of fun,** persona grotesca. **19 – of speech,** FILOL. tropo, figura de dicción, forma de expresión. **20 to – on,** (EE.UU. y fam.) contar con, entrar en los cálculos de uno: *I figure on getting the job very soon = cuento con lograr el empleo muy pronto.* **21 to – out,** (EE.UU. y fam.) **a)** calcular (una cantidad o similar). **b)** resolver; deducir: *I figured out she was lying = deducí que estaba mintiendo.* **22 figures,** (fam.) aritmética, cálculo. **23 – skating,** DEP. patinaje artístico. **24 to keep one's –,** guardar la línea, no engordar. **24 to lose one's –,** perder la línea, engordar. **25 to put a – on,** poner una cifra concreta a, decir con exactitud (una cantidad). **26 single figures,** cifra de un número (entre 0 y 9). **27 it/that figures,** eso es lógico, eso tiene sentido.
figurehead | 'fɪgəhed | *s.c.* **1** MAR. mascarón de proa. **2** (fig.) testaferro, títere, hombre de paja.
figurine | 'fɪgəriːn | *s.c.* estatuilla, figurina.
filament | 'fɪləmənt | *s.c.* **1** filamento, hilillo. **2** ELEC. filamento.
filch | fɪltʃ | *v.t.* (fam.) afanar, hurtar.
file | faɪl | *s.c.* **1** ficha, archivador, carpeta. **2** dossier, archivo. **3** lima (para las uñas). **4** INF. archivo. **5** fila, hilera, columna. || *v.t.* **6** archivar, fichar. **7** cursar, presentar oficialmente, entrar en el registro (solicitud, queja, etc.). **8** entregar, presentar, someter (informe o artículo periodístico). **9** limar. || *v.i.* **10** ir en fila, marchar en fila. **11 [to – for]** solicitar oficialmente, cursar la solicitud de: *to file for divorce = solicitar oficialmente divorcio.* **12** limarse. || **13 to – an appeal,** DER. presentar una apelación. **14 to – a suit,** DER. entablar juicio. **15 to – away, a)** archivar en su sitio. **b)** (fig.) anotar (para recordar más tarde). **16 (in) single –,** (en) fila india. **17 on –/on the files/on someone's files,** archivado, registrado.
filet | 'fɪleɪ | GAST. (EE.UU.) *s.c.* **1** filete de solomillo. || **2 – mignon,** filete de solomillo.
filial | 'fɪlɪəl | *adj.* filial.
filibuster | 'fɪlɪbʌstər | POL. (EE.UU.) *s.c.* **1** retraso; maniobra dilatoria (en el Congreso a base de alargar discursos). || *v.i.* **2** retrasar; dilatar (sesiones del Congreso).

filigree | 'fɪlɪgri: | *s.i.* filigrana.
filing-cabinet | 'faɪlɪŋ kæbɪnət | *s.c.* archivador (metálico).
filing-clerk | 'faɪlɪŋ klɑ:k | *s.c.* archivero; empleado administrativo.
filings | 'faɪlɪŋz | *s.pl.* virutas, limaduras (de diversos materiales).
Filipino | ˌfɪlɪ'pi:nəʊ | *adj.* **1** filipino (cultura, idioma, etc.). || *s.c.* **2** filipino.
fill | fɪl | *v.t.* **1** llenar (cualquier recipiente, caja o bolsa). **2** rellenar, tapar (hueco, agujero, etc.). **3** ocupar, llenar (un espacio, extensión, etc.). **4 [to – *o.* (with)]** embargar, llenar (de emoción o similar). **5 [to – *o.* (with)]** inundar (de luz, calor u olor). **6** llenar (el tiempo en alguna actividad). **7 [to – *o.* (with)]** (fig.) llenar (de ideas, deseos, etc.): *don't fill my head with complexes = no me llenes la cabeza de complejos.* **8** cumplir (requisitos, exigencias, etc.). **9** hacer (un papel, rol, etc.). **10** (EE.UU.) preparar (una bebida o similar). **11** MED. empastar (dientes). **12** MAR. hinchar (velas). **13** ocupar (un puesto de trabajo). || *v.i.* **14 [to – (with)]** llenarse. **15** MAR. hincharse (las velas). || *s.sing.* **16 [– (of)]** hartazgo, hartura; superabundancia. || *v.r.* **17 [to – (with)]** llenarse, hartarse (de comida, bebida, etc.). || **18 to – in, a)** rellenar (impresos). **b)** rellenar (hueco o agujero). **c)** utilizar (tiempo libre o tiempo de espera): *I filled in my time reading = utilicé mi tiempo leyendo.* **d)** rellenar (figura o dibujo con pintura o similar). **e)** poner al día, poner al corriente. **f)** (fam.) dar una tunda, atizar hasta en el carnet de identidad. **g) [to — (for)]** sustituir, ocupar el puesto (de). **19 to – out, a)** rellenar (impresos). **b)** engordar (no necesariamente con sentido negativo). **20 to – the bill,** V. **bill. 21 to – up, a)** llenar hasta arriba. **b)** llenar totalmente, ocupar todo el espacio de (cualquier volumen). **c)** rellenar sin despiste alguno, rellenar sin omisión (impresos). **d)** atiborrarse (de comida). **e)** ocupar, llenar (el tiempo con alguna actividad). **f)** hartar, saciar completamente, llenar: *this kind of food fills you up = este tipo de alimento te harta.* **g) [to — (with)]** llenarse (de): *the office filled up with shouting workers = la oficina se llenó de obreros que gritaban.* **22 to have one's – of,** hartarse de, saciarse de.
filled | fɪld | *adj.* **1** lleno, completo. **2 [– (with)]** embargado, lleno. || **3 -filled,** lleno de (en compuestos): *tear-filled eyes = ojos llenos de lágrimas.*
filler | 'fɪlər | *s.i.* relleno, tapaporos (para madera, grietas, etc.).
filler-cap | 'fɪləkæp | *s.c.* MEC. tapón de la gasolina (en un coche).
fillet | 'fɪlɪt | *s.c.* e *i.* **1** filete (de carne o pescado). || *v.t.* **2** cortar en filetes.
filling | 'fɪlɪŋ | *s.c.* **1** MED. empaste (de dientes). **2** GAST. relleno (en pasteles, carnes, etc.). **3** relleno (de almohadas o similar). || *adj.* **4** que llena mucho (comida). || **5 – station,** gasolinera, estación de servicio.
fillip | 'fɪlɪp | *s.c.* **1** estímulo, incentivo: *we need a fillip to our new business = necesitamos un estímulo para nuestro negocio nuevo.* **2** toquecito, tobita (con los dedos).
filly | 'fɪlɪ | *s.c.* potrilla, potranca.
film | fɪlm | *s.c.* **1** película, film. **2** capa, película, velo (de polvo, grasa, lágrimas, etc.) || *s.i.* **3** metraje (de película). **4** plástico fino para envolver. || *s.c.* e *i.* **5** FOT. film para fotos, película para fotos. **6** ART. cine (como arte). || *v.t.* **e** *i.* **7** filmar(se), coger(se) en película. || **8 – star,** estrella de cine. **9 – test,** prueba cinematográfica (para comprobar si una persona puede ser actor o actriz).
film-strip | 'fɪlmstrɪp | *s.c.* tira de película; diapositiva.
filmy | 'fɪlmɪ | *adj.* tenue, diáfano.
filter | 'fɪltər | *s.c.* **1** filtro (para filtrar alguna sustancia). **2** FIS. filtro (de sonido, luz, etc.). **3** ordenación, filtro (de tráfico). || *v.t.* **4** filtrar, colar (cualquier sustancia). || *v.i.* **5** filtrarse, colarse (de cualquier sustancia). **6** (fig.) filtrarse (luz o sonido). **7** (fig.) filtrarse (noticias, documentos secretos, información, etc.). **8** canalizar, organizar (el tráfico). || *adj.* **9** de filtro, emboquillado (cigarrillos). || **10 to – out,** quitar mediante filtrado, limpiar con un filtro.
filter-tip | 'fɪltətɪp | *s.c.* filtro, boquilla (en cigarrillos).
filter-tipped | 'fɪltətɪpt | *adj.* emboquillado, con filtro.
filth | fɪlθ | *s.i.* **1** suciedad extrema, mugre, inmundicia. **2** (fig.) lenguaje burdo, lenguaje obsceno. **3** (fig.) obscenidad, procacidad (en el sexo).
filthily | 'fɪlθɪlɪ | *adv.* **1** asquerosamente, con inmundicia. **2** (fig.) suciamente, obscenamente (en palabras). **3** (fig.) procazmente (en temas de sexo).
filthiness | 'fɪlθɪnɪs | *s.i.* suciedad, asquerosidad.
filthy | 'fɪlθɪ | *adj.* **1** asqueroso, mugriento. **2** obsceno, asqueroso, grosero (en el plano sexual). **3** (fam.) malo, lluvioso, de perros (tiempo atmosférico). || **4 – dirty,** asquerosamente sucio. **5 – rich,** (fam.) forrado, riquísimo.
fin | fɪn | *s.c.* ANAT. aleta (de peces).
final | 'faɪnl | *adj.* **1** final; último. **3** (fig.) definitivo, irrevocable: *final decision = decisión irrevocable.* **3** PER. última (edición). || *s.c.* **4** DEP. final (de un campeonato). **5** PER. edición final, última edición. || **6 finals, a)** exámenes finales. **b)** DEP. final (último encuentro).
finale | fɪ'nɑ:lɪ | *s.c.* **1** última escena, clímax (en un espectáculo). **3** MUS. final, último movimiento.
finalist | 'faɪnəlɪst | *s.c.* finalista (de deporte, concursos, etc.).
finality | faɪ'nælɪtɪ | *s.i.* finalidad, rotundidad: *to say with finality = decir con rotundidad.*
finalization | ˌfaɪnəlaɪ'zeɪʃn | *s.i.* retoque último.
finalize | 'faɪnəlaɪz | (también **finalise**) *v.t.* dar los últimos toques a, hacer la versión definitiva de (especialmente de contratos legales).
finally | 'faɪnəlɪ | *adv.* finalmente, por último; a la larga.
finance | 'faɪnæns | *s.i.* **1** finanzas, dinero: *we need more finance = necesitamos más dinero.* **2** ciencia financiera, finanzas. || *v.t.* **3** financiar, costear, proveer fondos para. || **4 finances,** fondos, fuentes (de ingresos).
financial | faɪ'nænʃl | *adj.* **1** financiero. || **2 – year,** ECON. ejercicio económico anual.
financially | faɪ'nænʃəlɪ | *adv.* financieramente.
financier | faɪ'nænsɪər | *s.c.* financiero (persona), empresa financiera.
finch | fɪntʃ | *s.c.* ZOOL. pinzón (especie de pájaro).
find | faɪnd | *v.* [*pret.* y *p.p.* **found**] *t.* **1** encontrar, descubrir, hallar: *I found a lovely restaurant unexpectedly = me encontré inesperadamente un restaurante precioso.* **2** encontrar, hallar (la respuesta a algo). **3 [to – that/*o.* + *inf.*]** encontrar que, descubrir que: *he found that he didn't know enough = descubrió que no sabía lo suficiente... I found him to be wrong often = descubrí que él estaba a menudo equivocado.* **4** encontrar, notar, observar: *communists, I find, are very idealistic = los comunistas, yo observo, son muy idealistas.* **5 [to – (in)]** encontrar (placer, alegría, etc. en alguna actividad). **6** DER. declarar (culpable o inocente). **7** alcanzar, encontrar, dar en (el objetivo). **8 [to – *o.* + (for/*inf.*)]** encontrar (dinero, tiempo, oportunidad, etc. para algo): *I couldn't find time to study for the exams = no pude encontrar tiempo para estudiar para los exámenes.* **9** (lit.) hallar; ver: *the night found him still drinking = la noche le halló bebiendo todavía.* **10** hallar, encontrar (como fórmula en cartas): *I hope this letter finds you happy and energetic = confío que esta carta te halle feliz y lleno de energía.* || *v.r.* **11** encontrarse inesperadamente: *I found myself crying = me encontré inesperadamente llorando.* **12** encontrarse (por ideas): *I find myself in agreement with you = me encuentro de acuerdo contigo.* || *s.c.* **13** descubrimiento, hallazgo (de carácter científico o similar). || *s.sing.* **14** hallazgo, descubrimiento (persona o lugar). || **15 all found,** todo incluido. **16 to be found,** encontrarse, existir, vivir: *this kind of animal is found only in Indonesia = esta clase de animal sólo se encuentra en Indonesia.* **17 to – expression in,** expresarse en forma de, encontrar expresión en forma de: *his anguish finally found expression in a flood of tears = su angustia se expresó en un mar de lágrimas.* **18 to – fault,** V. **fault. 19 to – favour,** V. **favour. 20 to – for,** DER. fallar a favor de. **21 to – it in one's heart,** sentirse capaz: *can you find it in your heart to forgive her? = ¿puedes sentirte capaz de perdonar?* **22 to – one's feet,** encontrarse a gusto (en una

situación nueva). **23 to – one's tongue,** V. **tongue. 24 to – one's way, a)** encontrar la forma de ir, encontrar el camino. **b)** acabar en (sólo hablando de cosas): *the aid found its way in the pockets of the military = la ayuda acabó en los bolsillos de los militares.* **25 to – out, a)** descubrir, averiguar. **b)** desenmascarar. **26 to – vanting,** encontrar deficiente, encontrar deficiencias en. **27 take me as you; me/you'll have to take us as you – us,** hay que aceptarme/nos como soy/somos.

finder | 'faɪndər | *s.c.* **1** descubridor, hallador, el que encuentra (algo). || **2 finders keepers,** el que se encuentra con algo se lo puede guardar.

finding | 'faɪndɪŋ | *s.c.* **1** descubrimiento, hallazgo. || **2 findings,** DER. veredicto, fallo.

fine | faɪn | *adj.* **1** estupendo, excelente, muy bueno, bien: *how are you? fine = ¿cómo está Vd.? bien.* **2** fino (estrecho o delgado): *a fine point = una punta fina.* **3** estupendo, excelente, magnífico (tiempo). **4** fino (en cuanto a lo pequeño): *fine dust = polvo fino.* **5** refinado, lindo, bonito (objeto). **6** sutil (distinción, detalle, etc.). **7** importante, grandioso: *I can't stand your fine friends = no puedo soportar a tus amigos importantes.* **8** (hum.) bonito, agradable: *what a fine way to thank me, with a kick! = vaya forma tan bonita de darme las gracias, ¡con una patada!* || *adv.* **9** estupendamente, magníficamente. || *s.c.* **10** multa. || *v.t.* **11** multar. || **12 to cut it a bit –,** dejar muy poco tiempo (para alguna actividad): *you're cutting it a bit fine, getting ready now = estás dejando muy poco tiempo, preparándote ahora.* **13 – art/– arts,** bellas artes. **14 to – down,** afinar; perfeccionar (teorías o similar). **15 – print,** letra pequeña (de un contrato o similar). **16 to get something down to a – art,** V. **art. 17 not to put too fine a point on it,** V. **point. 18 that's –/–,** vale, estupendo, de acuerdo.

finely | 'faɪnlɪ | *adv.* **1** estupendamente, magníficamente. **2** finamente. **3** sutilmente. **4** exquisitamente, refinadamente.

fineness | 'faɪnnɪs | *s.i.* **1** sutilidad. **2** fineza. **3** belleza (del tiempo atmosférico).

finery | 'faɪnərɪ | *s.i.* galas, adornos (de vestimenta y accesorios).

finesse | fɪ'nes | *s.i.* finura, tino, tacto.

fine-tooth comb | faɪn'tuːθkəʊm | *s.c.* **1** peine grueso. **2 to go over/through something with a –,** escudriñar minuciosamente, examinar atentamente.

finger | 'fɪŋgər | *s.c.* **1** dedo (únicamente de la mano). **2** dedo (de un guante o similar). **3** (fig.) columna, dedo (algo con forma de dedo): *a finger of land jutting into the sea = un dedo de tierra que se mete dentro del mar.* **4** dedo (medida de líquido). || *v.t.* **5** tocar, palpar (cuidadosamente con los dedos). **6** MUS. tocar (un instrumento). **7** (fam.) chivarse (a la policía). || **8 all fingers and thumbs,** más torpe que nada en el mundo; manazas. **9 to cross one's fingers,** V. **cross. 10 – bowl,** aguamanil (para lavarse los dedos durante una comida formal). **11 to get one's fingers burnt/to burn one's fingers,** meter la pata, pillarse los dedos. **12 to have a – in every/the pie,** estar metido en el asunto/todos los asuntos. **13 to have green fingers,** V. **green. 14 to lay a – on,** (normalmente en negativa) tocar a: *you mustn't lay a finger on my son = no debe Vd. tocar a mi hijo.* **15 to lift/raise a –,** mover un dedo (para ayudar). **16 to point the/a – at,** señalar con el dedo a (como culpable). **17 to point the – of scorn/suspicion/etc. at,** señalar con el dedo por desdén/sospecha/etc. a: *don't point the finger of scorn at me = no me señales con el dedo por desdén.* **18 to pull/get one's – out,** (fam.) empezar la faena, comenzar a trabajar. **19 to put one's – on,** acertar con, dar con (la solución, identificación, etc. de un problema): *you have just put your finger on the whole thing = acabas de acertar con todo el asunto.* **20 to put the – on someone,** (fam.) delatar a alguien (normalmente a la policía). **21 to slip through one's fingers,** escaparse entre los dedos (después de haber estado cerca de ello). **22 to twist someone round one's little –,** manejar a alguien como se desea. **23 to work one's fingers to the bone,** V. **bone.**

fingering | 'fɪŋgərɪŋ | *s.sing.* MUS. digitación, juego de los dedos (al tocar un instrumento).

fingermark | 'fɪŋgəmɑːk | *s.c.* señal (normalmente sucia de los dedos).

fingernail | 'fɪŋgəneɪl | *s.c.* uña.

finger-painting | 'fɪŋgəpeɪntɪŋ | *s.i.* y *c.* pintura con los dedos (de niños).

fingerprint | 'fɪŋgəprɪnt | *s.c.* **1** huella dactilar. || *v.t.* **2** coger/tomar las huellas. **3** poner una sustancia reveladora de huellas en (un objeto): *the police even fingerprinted the TV set = la policía incluso puso sustancia reveladora de huellas en el aparato de televisión.* || **4 to take somebody's fingerprints,** tomar las huellas de alguien.

fingertip | 'fɪŋgətɪp | *s.c.* **1** yema (del dedo). || **2 to have something at one's fingertips,** saber algo al dedillo. **3 to the fingertips/to one's fingertips,** de los pies a la cabeza.

finicky | 'fɪnɪkɪ | *adj.* (desp.) remilgado, melindroso.

finish | 'fɪnɪʃ | *v.t.* **1** acabar, terminar, finalizar (una comida, una actividad, etc.). **2** perfeccionar, pulir, acabar bien (un objeto). **3** concluir, acabar diciendo: *I love you she finished = te quiero, concluyó ella.* || *v.i.* **4** [— *ger.*] acabar de, terminar de: *I finished eating at 4 = terminé de comer a las 4.* **5** [— *num. ord.*] terminar, acabar; llegar (a la meta): *he finished second = llegó segundo.* **6** acabar, terminar, finalizar (una película, una conferencia, etc.). **7 [to – (by/with)]** terminar, acabar: *he finished with a joke = terminó con un chiste.* || *s.sing.* **8 [(the) – (of)]** finalización, final, fin, terminación. || *s.c.* **9** llegada, meta (de una carrera o similar). || *s.c.* e *i.* **10** acabado, perfección: *the table has a lovely finish = la mesa tiene un acabado precioso.* || **11 a fight to the –,** una lucha a muerte. **12 to fight to the –,** luchar a muerte. **13 finishing touches/a finishing touch (to),** toque final (a), toques finales (de). **14 to – off, a)** despachar, rematar, matar: *finish off that wounded horse = remata a ese caballo herido.* **b)** completar, acabar por completo, rematar (una tarea). **c)** concluir, terminar (una actuación, discurso, etc.). **d)** despachar, terminar (comida o bebida). **15 to – up, a)** acabar, terminar (como colofón a algo): *he finished up living with a rich widow twenty years older = acabó viviendo con una viuda rica veinte años mayor.* **b)** despachar, terminar (comida o bebida). **16 to – with,** terminar con, acabar con (algo); dejar a (una persona).

finished | 'fɪnɪʃt | *adj.* **1 [– (with)]** no interesado. **2 [– (with)]** finalizado: *I won't be finished for a while = no habré finalizado durante un rato.* **3** acabado (una persona). **4** perfeccionado, acabado, rematado (un objeto).

finishing school | 'fɪnɪʃɪŋ skuːl | V. **school.**

finite | 'faɪnaɪt | *adj.* **1** finito, limitado. **2** GRAM. finito (que tiene inflexiones).

fink | fɪŋk | *s.c.* (EE.UU., fam. y desp.) soplón, chivato.

Finland | 'fɪnlənd | *s.sing.* Finlandia.

Finn | fɪn | *s.c.* finés, finlandés.

Finnish | 'fɪnɪʃ | *adj.* **1** finés, finlandés (cultura, tradiciones, etc.). || *s.i.* **2** finés, finlandés (idioma).

fir | fəːr | *s.c.* BOT. **1** abeto. || **2 – tree,** abeto.

fire | 'faɪər | *s.i.* **1** fuego. **2** MIL. fuego, disparos. **3** (fig.) inspiración, entusiasmo, fuerza: *his fire and competence as a politician impressed us = su entusiasmo y buen hacer como político nos impresionaron.* **4** (fig.) críticas, ataques; disparos: *I don't mind his leftist fire = no me importan sus críticas izquierdistas.* || *s.c.* **5** fuego, hoguera. **6** placa (eléctrica o de gas). || *s.c.* e *i.* **7** fuego, incendio, destrucción por fuego. || *v.i.* **8** disparar, hacer fuego. **9** MEC. saltar la chispa (causando combustión en un motor). || *v.t.* **10** disparar (un arma, una bala, etc.). **11** despedir, echar del trabajo. **12 [to – (at)]** (fig.) lanzar, hacer (preguntas o similar muy rápidamente). **13** (fig.) inspirar, entusiasmar, apasionar. **14** cocer (en alfarería). || **15 to catch –,** encenderse, comenzar a arder. **16 to come under –,** ser criticado ferozmente, ser blanco de críticas feroces. **17 to draw the – of,** MIL. atraer los disparos/el fuego de. **18 the fat's in the –,** V. **fat. 19 to fight a –,** luchar contra un incendio. **20 to fight – with –,** utilizar los mismos medios que el enemigo. **21 to – away,** comenzar a hablar en contra, empezar a lanzar críticas, criticar sin reparos. **22 – drill,** simulacro de incendio. **23 – lighter,** trozo de material fácil de arder (para encender la chimenea o similar). **24 to – off,** disparar, lanzar (algún tipo de proyectil sofisticado). **25 – service,** servicio contraincendios. **26 – station,** estación de bomberos. **27 – trap,** edificio sin la debida seguridad en caso de incendio. **28 out of the frying pan into the –,** V. **frying. 29 to hang –,** demorarse (un asunto o similar). **30 to hold one's –,** MIL. dejar de disparar. **31 like a house on –,** V. **house. 32 line of –,** MIL. línea de fuego. **33 on –, a)** ardiendo, en llamas. **b)** abrasado, ardiendo (por la fiebre, dolor, etc.). **c)** excitado, ilusionado. **34 to open –,** abrir fuego, comenzar a disparar. **35 to play with –,** jugar con fuego. **36 to return –/to return someone's –,** MIL. contestar a los disparos /devolver el fuego de alguien. **37 to set – to/to set something on –,** prender fuego a/prender fuego a algo. **38 there's no smoke without –,** V. **smoke.**

OBS. Esta palabra en forma de participio sirve para formar compuestos: **39** expresando la energía con que funciona un determinado sistema o máquina: *an oil-tired machine = una máquina que funciona con petróleo.*

fire-alarm | 'faɪərəlɑːm | *s.c.* alarma de incendios.

firearm | 'faɪərɑːm | *s.c.* arma de fuego.

fireball | 'faɪəbɔːl | *s.c.* bola de fuego.

firebomb | 'faɪəbɔm | *s.c.* bomba incendiaria.

firebrand | 'faɪəbrænd | *s.c.* agitador, revolucionario.

firebreak | 'faɪəbreɪk | *s.c.* cortafuego.

firebrick | 'faɪəbrɪk | *s.c.* e *i.* ARQ. ladrillo refractario.

fire-brigade | 'faɪəbrɪgeɪd | *s.sing.* y *c.* los bomberos: *call the fire-brigade = llama a los bomberos.*

firecracker | 'faɪəkrækər | *s.c.* petardo.

fire-eater | 'faɪəriːtər | *s.c.* **1** pirófago (en un circo). **2** (fig.) buscapleitos.

fire-engine | 'faɪərendʒɪn | *s.c.* coche de bomberos, bomba de incendios.

fire-escape | 'faɪərɪskeɪp | *s.c.* escalera de emergencia, salida de incendios.

fire-extinguisher | 'faɪərɪkstɪŋgwɪʃər | *s.c.* extintor.

fire-fighter | 'faɪəfaɪtər | *s.c.* bombero.

fire-fighting | 'faɪəfaɪtɪŋ | *s.i.* extinción de incendios.

firefly | 'faɪəflaɪ | *s.c.* ZOOL. luciérnaga.

fireguard | 'faɪəgɑːd | *s.c.* pantalla guardafuego (en una chimenea).

fire-hydrant | 'faɪəhaɪdrənt | *s.c.* boca de riego contra incendios.

fire-irons | 'faɪəraɪənz | *s.pl.* utensilios para la chimenea (como el atizador, las tenazas, etc.).

firelight | 'faɪəlaɪt | *s.i.* luz del fuego: *in the firelight = a la luz del fuego.*

fireman | 'faɪəmən | *s.c.* bombero.

fireplace | 'faɪəpleɪs | *s.c.* chimenea; hogar (el sitio concreto donde se enciende el fuego).

fireplug | 'faɪəplʌg | *s.c.* (EE.UU.) boca de incendios.

firepower | 'faɪəpauər | *s.i.* MIL. potencia de fuego.

fireproof | 'faɪəpruːf | *adj.* **1** a prueba de fuego; incombustible. || *v.t.* **2** revestir, acondicionar (a prueba de fuego).

fire-raising | 'faɪəreɪzɪŋ | *s.i.* incendio provocado, incendio deliberado.

fire-sale | 'faɪəseɪl | *s.c.* liquidación por incendio (a precios bajísimos).

fireside | 'faɪəsaɪd | *s.c.* **1** fuego, hogar. || *adj.* **2** hogareño. | **3 by the –,** junto al fuego, al calor del hogar, al calor de la lumbre.

fire-storm | 'faɪəstɔːm | *s.c.* MIL. tormenta de fuego (cuando después de un bombardeo el aire caliente se eleva y nuevo aire acude con fuerza al vacío haciendo que el fuego sea peor).

fire-watching | 'faɪəwɔtʃɪŋ | *s.i.* vigilancia contra incendios.

firewater | 'faɪəwɔːtər | *s.i.* (fam.) licor (fuerte).

firewood | 'faɪəwud | *s.i.* leña; astillas.

firework | 'faɪəwəːk | *s.c.* **1** bengala. || **2 fireworks, a)** fuegos artificiales. **b)** (fig.) pelea, follón: *there will be fireworks when he finds out = habrá follón cuando él lo descubra.* **c)** exuberancia (verbal o escrita): *his fireworks don't impress me = no me impresiona su exuberancia.*

firing | 'faɪərɪŋ | *s.i.* y *c.* **1** acto de cocer (en alfarería). || *s.i.* **2** MIL. fuego. || **3 – line,** MIL. línea de fuego. **4 – squad,** pelotón de fusilamiento, pelotón de ejecución.

firm | fəːm | *s.c.* **1** empresa, compañía, firma comercial. || *adj.* **2** firme, sólido: *firm ground = tierra sólida.* **3** fijo, estable, seguro (que no se mueva). **4** firme, fuerte: *a firm grasp = un apretón fuerte.* **5** definitivo: *a firm decision.* **6** FIN. firme, constante (una moneda, un valor, un índice económico, etc.). **7** decidido; determinado (que no cambiará): *I'm firm about that = estoy decidido acerca de ello.* **8** cierto, seguro (evidencia, información, etc.). || *v.t.* **9** apretar, afirmar (tierra, arena, etc.). || **10 to – up, a)** COM. finiquitar (un contrato o similar). **b)** fortalecer, hacer firme (alguna parte del cuerpo). **11 to hold – to,** ser fiel a, ser leal a (principios, creencias, etc.). **12 to stand –,** mantenerse en sus trece, no vacilar; no ceder.

firmament | 'fəːməmənt | *s.sing.* (lit.) firmamento, cielo.

firmly | 'fəːmlɪ | *adv.* **1** firmemente, sólidamente. **2** fijamente, establemente, seguramente (que no se mueva). **3** firmemente, fuertemente. **4** decididamente, determinadamente.

firmness | 'fəːmnɪs | *s.i.* **1** firmeza, solidez, consistencia. **2** firmeza, fuerza. **3** rotundidad: *he said it with firmness in his voice = lo dijo con rotundidad en su voz.* **4** firmeza (en una decisión o similar).

first | fəːst | *num. ord.* **1** [— *sing.* o *pl.*] primero. || *adv.* **2** primero, primeramente, en primer lugar, por primera vez. || *s.c.* **3** primera vez: *it was a first for him = fue una primera vez para él.* **4 [(a) – (in)]** matrícula (en enseñanza superior solamente). || *s.i.* **5** primera (marcha de un vehículo). || **6 at –,** en primer lugar, en un principio. **7 at – hand,** de primera mano. **8 to come –,** ser lo primero, tener prioridad. **9 – aid,** primeros auxilios. **10 – and foremost,** V. **foremost. 11 – and last,** desde todos los puntos de vista. **12 – come, – served,** prioridad para el primero que llegue, el primero se lo queda. **13 – cousin,** primo hermano. **14 – floor, a)** (Brit.) primer piso. **b)** (EE.UU.) piso a nivel de la calle. **15 – fruits,** primeros frutos, primeros resultados. **16 – lady,** primera figura. **17 First Lady,** POL. primera dama. **18 – language,** lengua materna, idioma materno. **19 – name,** nombre de pila. **20 – night,** estreno (de una película, obra de teatro, etc.). **21 – off,** (fam.) primeramente, en primer lugar. **22 – offender,** DER. sin otros antecedentes penales; transgresor por primera vez. **23 – person,** LIT. primera persona (narración o similar). **24 – school,** escuela primaria (entre los 5 y los 8 años aproximadamente). **25 – thing,** antes que nada. **26 – things –,** lo primero es lo primero. **27 from – to last,** desde principio a fin. **28 from the –,** desde el comienzo, desde el principio. **29 not to know the – thing about,** no tener ni idea de, no tener ni repajolera idea de. **30 not to have the – idea about,** no entender lo más mínimo de. **31 to put someone/something —,** dar prioridad a alguien/algo, poner alguien /algo en primer lugar: *she put her children first = ella puso a sus hijos en primer lugar.*

first-born | 'fəːstbɔːn | (lit.) *s.sing.* **1** primogénito. || *adj.* **2** primogénito.

first-class | ˌfəːst'klɑːs | *adj.* **1** de primera clase; de gran calidad. || *adj.* y *adv.* **2** primera clase, de primera clase, en primera clase (en el tren, avión o en el correo).

first-degree | ˌfəːstdɪ'griː | *adj.* **1** MED. de primer grado (quemadura). **2** DER. en primer grado (asesinato).

first-ever | ˌfəːst'evər | *adj.* primerísimo; sin precedentes.

first-hand | ˌfəːst'hænd | *adj* y *adv.* de primera mano.

firstly | 'fəːstlɪ | *adv.* en primer lugar, primeramente.

first-nighter | ˌfəːst'naɪtər | *s.c.* persona que acude a los estrenos.

first-rate | ˌfəːst'reɪt | *adj.* de primera clase, de gran calidad.

fiscal | 'fɪskl | *adj.* **1** fiscal. || **2 – year,** año fiscal.

fish | fɪʃ | (*pl.* **fish** o **fishes**) *s.c.* **1** pez. || *s.i.* **2** pescado. || *v.t.* **3** pescar. **4 [to – (out/from)]** (fam.) sacar, extraer: *I fished my card out of the bag = extraje mi tarjeta del bolso.* || *v.i.* **5** pescar. **6 [to – for]** buscar (alabanza o información). || **7 an odd/queer –,** (fam.) un tipo raro/extraño. **8 to drink like a –,** (fam.) beber como un cosaco. **9 – and chips,** pescado con patatas fritas (comida muy popular). **10 – and chip shop,** tienda de pescado con patatas fritas (sólo dedicada a esto). **11 to – in troubled waters,** pescar en río revuelto. **12 to have other /bigger – to fry,** tener cosas más importantes que hacer. **13 like a – out of water,** como pez fuera del agua. **14 there are other – in the sea,** hay otras personas en el mundo, hay otros asuntos en la vida.

fishbone | 'fɪʃbəʊn | *s.c.* espina, raspa.

fishbowl | 'fɪʃbəʊl | *s.c.* pecera.

fishcake | 'fɪʃkeɪk | *s.c.* GAST. pastel de pescado y patatas.

fisherman | 'fɪʃəmən | *s.c.* pescador.

fishery | 'fɪʃərɪ | *s.c.* pesquería (zona rica en peces).

fish-finger | ˌfɪʃ'fɪŋgər | *s.c.* delicias de pescado (en forma alargada).

fishing | 'fɪʃɪŋ | *s.i.* pesca.

fishing-line | 'fɪʃɪŋlaɪn | *s.c.* sedal.

fishing-rod | 'fɪʃɪŋrɔd | *s.c.* caña de pescar.

fishing-tackle | 'fɪʃɪŋtækl | *s.i.* aparejo de pesca.

fish-knife | 'fɪʃnaɪf | *s.c.* cuchillo para el pescado (cubierto).

fishmonger | 'fɪʃmʌŋgər | (brit.) *s.c.* **1** pescadero. || **2 the fishmonger/the fishmonger's,** la pescadería.

fish-slice | 'fɪʃlaɪs | *s.c.* paleta para servir o cocinar pescado.

fishwife | 'fɪʃwaɪf | *s.c.* (desp. y fam.) verdulera.

fishy | 'fɪʃɪ | *adj.* **1** de pescado, a pescado (olor, sabor, etc.). **2** (fam.) sospechoso; dudoso. **3 there's something fishy here,** (fam.) aquí hay gato encerrado.

fission | 'fɪʃn | *s.i.* FIS. fisión: *nuclear fission.*

fissure | 'fɪʃər | *s.c.* fisura; grieta.

fist | fɪst | *s.c.* **1** puño: he shook his fist at me = me amenazó con el puño. || **2 hand over –,** V. **hand.**

fistful | 'fɪstfʊl | *s.c.* puñado: *a fistful of sand = un puñado de arena.*

fisticuffs | 'fɪstɪkʌfs | *s.pl.* (p.u.) puñetazos.

fit | fɪt | (a veces EE.UU. pasado y participio **fit**) *v.t.* **[fitting, fittted] 1** sentar bien, caer bien (ropa o similar). **2** ajustar, acoplar; colocar (en su sitio): *fit this here = coloca esto aquí.* **3** ir con, ajustarse a: *that fits my theory = eso se ajusta a mi teoría.* **4 [to – (in/into)]** acoplar, meter (dentro de una categoría o similar): *I can't fit your opinion into any system of thought = no puedo acoplar tu opinión dentro de ningún sistema de pensamiento.* **5 [to – (to/with)]** instalar; equipar: *fit a new lock to the door = instala un nuevo candado en la puerta.* **6 [to – (for/to + *inf.*)]** (lit.) adecuar; dar derecho: *being a refugee doesn't fit you to criticize everything = el ser un refugiado no te da derecho a criticar todo.* || *v.i.* **7** ajustarse, ir: *this fits well = esto se ajusta bien.* **8 [to – in]** caber, entrar: *all this can't fit in there = todo esto no puede entrar ahí.* || *adj.* **9** en forma, sano, fuerte. **10 [– (for/to + *inf.*)]** adecuado, conveniente; digno: *she's not fit to live = ella no es digna de vivir.* || *adj.* y *adv.* **10 [– *inf.*]** (fam.) como para, dispuesto a: *he looked fit to scream = él parecía dispuesto a aullar.* || *s.c.* **11** ataque (de rabia, risa, cólera, etc.). || *s.sing.* **12** encaje, talle (que queda bien una vestimenta): *it is a lovely fit = queda precioso.* || **13 as – as a fiddle,** (fam.) como un roble, en perfectas condiciones físicas. **14 to be fitted,** estar probándose ropa, hacerse pruebas en el sastre: *At the moment she's being fitted = en este momento se está haciendo pruebas en el sastre.* **15 fighting –,** V. **fighting. 16 to – in/into, a)** tener tiempo para (una actividad o persona). **b)** encajar en (un grupo o similar). **17 to – (someone) like a glove,** sentar (a alguien) muy bien. **18 to – out/up,** equipar por completo. **19 to fit the bill,** V. **bill. 20 to have a –,** sufrir un ataque (de cólera o enorme sorpresa). **21 in fits,** muerto (de risa). **22 in/by fits and starts,** a trancas y barrancas. **23 to see/think –,** tener a bien, parecerle a uno bien: *I saw fit to get my child out of that school = me pareció bien sacar a mi chico de esa escuela.*

fitful | 'fɪtfl | *adj.* intermitente, espasmódico; irregular: *fitful sleep = sueño intermitente.*

fitfully | 'fɪtfəlɪ | *adv.* intermitentemente, espasmódicamente; irregularmente.

fitment | 'fɪtmənt | *s.c.* mueble de acoplamiento.

fitted | 'fɪtɪd | *adj.* **1 [– (for/to + *inf.*)]** adecuado, idóneo: *I'm not fitted for this job = no soy la persona adecuada para este trabajo.* **2** hecho a medida (muebles, ropas, etc.). **3** empotrado (muebles). **4** amueblado, totalmente amueblado (especialmente la cocina y los dormitorios). **5** enmoquetado, alfombrado (de pared a pared). || **6 – sheet,** sábana bajera ajustable.

fitter | 'fɪtər | *s.c.* ajustador, montador.

fitting | 'fɪtɪŋ | *adj.* **1** conveniente, apropiado: *it is not fitting for you to sit there = no es apropiado que te sientes allí.* || *s.c.* **2** accesorio (como componentes de objetos). **3** prueba (de ropa). **4** (brit.) horma (para zapatos). || **5 fittings,** aparatos, instalaciones (de calefacción o de electrodomésticos, que se pueden poner o quitar en una casa).

OBS. **6 -fitting** es parte de un compuesto adjetival o adverbial que indica la forma en que sienta ropa o similar: *a fightfitting jacket = una chaqueta muy apretada.*

fittingly | 'fɪtɪŋlɪ | *adv.* convenientemente, apropiadamente.

five | faɪv | *num. card.* **1** cinco. || **2 – o'clock shadow,** barba de unas horas (que se empieza a notar). **3 fives,** DEP. juego de pelota a tres bandas.

fiver | 'faɪvər | *s.c.* (fam.) billete de cinco libras, billete de cinco dólares.

fix | fɪks | *v.t.* **1** fijar, sujetar, asegurar. **2** fijar, establecer, decidir (hora o lugar). **3** reparar (un objeto). **4** adecentar, preparar (un lugar, un detalle, etc.). **5** retocar, arreglar (pelo, maquillaje, etc.). **6** preparar (comida o bebida): *I'll fix you a drink = te prepararé una copa.* **7** organizar, planificar (cualquier cosa). **8** resolver, solucionar (cualquier asunto): *don't worry, I'll fix everything for you = no te preocupes, te lo resolveré todo.* **9 [to – (on/upon/with)]** fijar (la vista, atención, mirada, etc.). **10** QUIM. fijar (una sustancia volátil o gaseosa). **11** (fam.) arreglar (un asunto mediante soborno o similar). **12** (fam.) dar para el pelo, dar donde duele; acabar con (algo o alguien): *I'll fix you = acabaré contigo.* || *v.r.* **13** prepararse (comida o bebida). || *s.c.* **14** AER. punto de posición, determinación de posición (mediante compás, radar, etc.). **15** (fam.) pinchazo, picado; inyección de droga. **16** (fam.) aprieto, dificultad. || *s.sing.* **17** arreglo (mediante soborno). || **18 to – bayonets,** MIL. calar bayonetas. **19 to – on/ upon,** decidir, fijar (un asunto). **20 to – something in one's mind/brain,** fijar en la mente de uno, grabar en el cerebro de uno. **21 to – up, a)** arreglar, acondicionar (un piso, lugar, etc.). **b)** medio hacer, hacer provisionalmente. **c)** organizar (un viaje, salida, etc.), arreglar (una situación), adecentar (niños). **22 to – up with,** dar, proporcionar: *I can fix you all up with everything = puedo proporcionarles todo a todos.*

fixated | fɪk'seɪtɪd | *adj.* obsesionado, con la mente fija (en algo).

fixation | fɪk'seɪʃn | *s.c.* obsesión, manía.

fixative | 'fɪksətɪv | *s.c.* e *i.* QUIM. fijativo, fijador (sustancia que pega fuertemente).

fixed | fɪkst | *adj.* **1** fijo (posición, idea, mirada, etc.). **2** artificial, postizo (sonrisa, expresión facial). **3** (fam.) arreglado (mediante soborno o similar). || **4 – interest,** FIN. interés fijo, interés no variable. **5 no – abode/address,** (lit.) sin vivienda fija, sin casa permanente.

fixedly | 'fɪksɪdlɪ | *adv.* fijamente (mirada).

fixings | 'fɪksɪŋgz | *s.pl.* (EE.UU.) guarnición (en comidas).

fixity | 'fɪksɪtɪ | *s.i.* fijeza (de mirada, propósitos, etc.).

fixture | 'fɪkstʃər | *s.c.* **1** mueble (fijo en una casa): *fixtures and fittings = muebles fijos y muebles que se pueden quitar.* **2** (brit.) DEP. encuentro, partido, acontecimiento deportivo. **3** (fam.) incondicional, cliente permanente (persona que siempre está en el mismo lugar).

fizz | fɪz | *v.i.* **1** burbujear. **2** hacer un ruido/sonido suave sibilante (onomatopeya). || *s.i.* **3** efervescencia (de líquido o gas). **4** champán, vino espumoso.

fizzle | 'fɪzl | *v.i.* **1** chisporrotear (onomatopeya). || **2 to – out,** apagarse; acabar mal, fracasar.

fizzy | 'fɪzɪ | *adj.* efervescente, espumoso; con gas (en refrescos).

fjord | fjɔːd | (también **fiord**) *s.c.* GEOG. fiordo.

flab | flæb | *s.i.* (fam.) grasa, carne fofa (de una persona).

flabbergasted | 'flæbəgɑːstɪd | *adj.* asombrado, alucinado, lelo.

flabbiness | 'flæbɪnɪs | *s.i.* **1** fofez, flojedad. **2** abulia, sosez.
flabby | 'flæbɪ | *adj.* **1** fofo, blando, flojo, debilucho. **2** abúlico, soso.
flaccid | 'flæksɪd | *adj.* flácido.
flag | flæg | *s.c.* **1** bandera, pabellón, estandarte. **2** banderita: *there were lots of flags on the huge map = había muchísimas banderitas en el mapa enorme.* **3** símbolo de la patria, bandera: *under our flag = bajo nuestra bandera.* **4** losa, baldosa. || *s.sing.* **5** (fig.) estandarte; causa: *the flag of peace = la causa de la paz.* || **[flagging, flagged]** *v.i.* **6** decaer, debilitarse (ánimo o similar). || **7 to – down,** hacer señas para que pare un vehículo (normalmente un taxi). **8 to fly the –/to keep the – flying,** actuar con orgullo patriotero (especialmente en el extranjero). **9 with flags flying,** con gran triunfo, triunfalmente.
flag-day | 'flægdeɪ | *s.c.* día de la banderita (contra el cáncer u otra cosa).
flagellate | 'flædʒəleɪt | *v.t.* (lit.) **1** flagelar. **2** (fig.) criticar severamente.
flagellation | ˌflædʒə'leɪʃn | *s.i.* flagelación.
flagged | flægd | *adj.* enlosado, con baldosas.
flagging | 'flægɪŋ | *adj.* decreciente; cada vez más débil (ánimo o similar).
flagon | 'flægən | *s.c.* jarro grande.
flagpole | 'flægpəul | *s.c.* asta (de bandera).
flagrant | 'fleɪgrənt | *adj.* flagrante, notorio: *flagrant injustice.*
flagrantly | 'fleɪgrəntlɪ | *adv.* descaradamente, flagrantemente, notoriamente.
flagship | 'flægʃɪp | *s.c.* **1** MIL. buque insignia. **2** (fig.) modelo; bandera (refiriéndose a algo que es modelo dentro de una empresa o similar): *the firm's flagship is the clinic in London = el modelo de la empresa es la clínica de Londres.*
flagstaff | 'flægstɑːf | V. **flagpole.**
flagstone | 'flægstəun | *s.c.* losa, baldosa.
flag-waving | 'flægweɪvɪŋ | *s.i.* **1** patrioterismo; chovinismo. || *adj.* **2** patriotero; chovinista.
flail | fleɪl | *v.i.* **1** agitar (brazos o piernas). || *v.t.* **2** azotar (con un palo o similar). || *s.c.* **3** mayal, desgranador.
flair | fleər | *s.sing.* **1 [(a) – for]** capacidad para, talento para: *I have a flair for languages = tengo talento para los idiomas.* || *s.i.* **2** estilo; originalidad.
flak | flæk | *s.i.* **1** MIL. fuego antiaéreo. **2** (fam.) crítica; vituperios.
flake | fleɪk | *s.c.* **1** copo; escama; trocito: *flakes of snow... flakes of rust = copos de nieve... escamas de óxido.* || *v.t.* **2** trocear (comida). || *v.i.* **3** trocearse, partirse (en trozos pequeños), desprenderse en trocitos. || **4 to – out,** (fam.) quedar inconsciente/rendido: *when I finished the race I flaked out = cuando acabé la guerra quedé rendido.*
flaked | fleɪkt | *adj.* **1** troceado: *flaked fish.* **2 – out,** (fam.) agotado.
flak-jacket | 'flækdʒækɪt | *s.c.* chaleco antibalas.
flaky | 'fleɪkɪ | *adj.* **1** escamoso, desmenuzable, hojaldrado. || **2 – pastry,** GAST. masa de harina hojaldrada (para repostería).
flambé | 'flɑmbeɪ | *v.t.* GAST. cocinar con coñac quemado.
flamboyance | flæm'bɔɪəns | *s.i.* **1** extravagancia, ostentación. **2** vistosidad (de colores y formas).
flamboyant | flæm'bɔɪənt | *adj.* **1** extravagante, vistoso. **2** deslumbrante: *a flamboyant evening dress = un traje de noche deslumbrante.*
flame | fleɪm | *s.c.* e *i.* **1** llama. || *s.c.* **2** (lit.) llama; arrebato: *a flame of indignation = un arrebato de indignación.* || *v.i.* **3** llamear, echar llamas, despedir llamas. **4** brillar (con color rojo): *her cheeks flamed = sus mejillas brillaron enrojecidas.* || **5 in flames,** ardiendo, en llamas. **6 to burst into flames;** estar en llamas, arder súbitamente. **7 to fan the flames/to add fuel to the flames,** avivar la controversia, enconar el problema, echar leña al fuego. **8 to go up in flames,** ser presa de las llamas.
flamenco | flə'meŋkəu | *s.c.* e *i.* flamenco.
flameproof | 'fleɪmpruːf | *adj.* a prueba de incendios, contra fuego.
flame-thrower | 'fleɪmθrəuər | *s.c.* lanzallamas.
flaming | 'fleɪmɪŋ | *adj.* **1** llameante. **2** resplandeciente (sólo con el color rojo o muy similar). **3** apasionado (discusión o temperamento). **4** maldito, cochino (expresa un enfado que no alcanza a ser palabrota): *flaming teacher! = ¡maldito profesor!*
flamingo | flə'mɪŋgəu | *s.c.* ZOOL. flamenco.
flammable | 'flæməbl | *adj.* inflamable.
flan | flæn | *s.c.* GAST. bizcocho (con algún tipo de relleno).
flange | flændʒ | *s.c.* MEC. pestaña, brida, reborde.
flank | flæŋk | *s.c.* **1** costado, ijada (en animales). **2** MIL. flanco. **3** lado. || *v.t.* **4** flanquear; estar al lado de: *groups of savages flanked us = grupos de salvajes estaban a nuestros dos lados.*
flannel | 'flænl | *s.i.* **1** franela. **2** (fam.) lisonja, coba. || *s.c.* **3** (brit.) toallita (para el lavado personal). || *v.t.* **4** (fam.) dar coba: *in general, politicians flannel people = en general, los políticos dan coba a la gente.* || **5 flannels,** pantalones de franela (de hombres).
flannelette | ˌflænə'let | *s.i.* moletón, franela fina.
flap | flæp | *v.i.* **1** aletear, mover las alas: *the bird flapped.* **2** agitarse (en un movimiento parecido al aleteo): *the flag flapped = la bandera se agitó.* || *v.t.* **3** mover, agitar; batir: *he flapped his arms = agitó sus brazos.* || *s.c.* **4** solapa (o cualquier parte plegadiza de un objeto): *the flap of a table; the flap of a hat.* **5** AER. alerón. **6** aletazo, golpe de ala (o similar). || **7 in a –,** en un estado de conmoción/agitación/preocupación.
flapjack | 'flæpdʒæk | GAST. *s.i.* **1** (brit.) torta (hecha con mantequilla principalmente). || *s.c.* **2** (EE.UU.) torta (plana y rellena de dulce).
flare | fleər | *s.c.* **1** bengala. || **2 [to – (up)]** estallar (un conflicto); avivarse (un fuego). **3 [to – (out)]** ensancharse; acampanarse (una falda o similar). || **4 flares,** pantalones acampanados.
flared | fleəd | *adj.* acampanado (de pantalones).
flare-path | 'fleəpɑːθ | *s.c.* AER. baliza (señal luminosa de una pista de aterrizaje).
flare-up | 'fleərʌp | *s.c.* **1** llamarada. **2** estallido súbito (de cólera, de un conflicto, etc.).
flash | flæʃ | *v.i.* **1** destellar, fulgurar; relampaguear: *a light flashed in the distance = una luz destelló a lo lejos.* **2 [to – (by/past/through)]** pasar/moverse como un relámpago: *the car flashed past.* **3** (fig.) pasar como un rayo (una imagen, un pensamiento, etc.). **4** (fam.) exhibirse (públicamente). **5** brillar de cólera/emoción (los ojos). || *v.t.* **6** hacer destellar: *that car flashed its lights = ese coche hizo destellar sus luces.* **7** lanzar (una mirada o sonrisa). **8** mostrar rápidamente, enseñar en un instante: *I flashed my card at the policeman = mostré rápidamente mi carnet al policía.* **9** PER. transmitir (información o noticias). || *s.c.* **10** destello; fogonazo: *a flash of light.* **11** (EE.UU.) linterna. **12** instante; ráfaga (de algún estado de emoción): *a flash of anger = una ráfaga de cólera.* **13** franja (de color brillante). || *s.i.* **14** FOT. flash: *this camera has no flash.* || *adj.* **15** (fam.) chillón, llamativo. || **16 to – back (to),** retrotraerse (mentalmente); recordar. **17 – burn,** MED. quemadura (por la cercanía a un punto de explosión). **18 – in the pan,** destello de brillantez (mental y que no se repite). **19 in a –,** en un segundo, inmediatamente. **20 quick as a –,** rápida y agudamente.
flashback | 'flæʃbæk | *s.c.* **1** flashback, escena/narración retrospectiva. **2** recuerdo, rememoración.
flashbulb | 'flæʃbʌlb | *s.c.* FOT. flash, lamparilla (de una cámara).
flashcard | 'flæʃkɑːd | *s.c.* tarjeta, tarjetón (que muestra letras para enseñar a los niños a leer).
flashcube | 'flæʃkjuːb | *s.c.* FOT. juego de bombillas (para flash).
flasher | 'flæʃər | *s.c.* (fam.) **1** intermitente (de un coche). **2** exhibicionista.
flash-flood | 'flæʃflʌd | *s.c.* riada.
flashgun | 'flæʃgʌn | *s.c.* FOT. disparador de flash.
flashing | 'flæʃɪŋ | *s.i.* ARQ. capa de alquitrán antigua.
flashlight | 'flæʃlaɪt | *s.c.* **1** linterna. **2** (p.u.) FOT. flash. **3** luz intermitente, luz giratoria (de cualquier objeto).
flashpoint | 'flæʃpɔɪnt | *s.c.* **1** FIS. punto de ignición (de una sustancia). **2** sitio conflictivo, lugar de peligro. **3** momen-

to peligroso (en un conflicto en el que las cosas pueden empeorar).

flashy | 'flæʃɪ | *adj.* ostentoso, llamativo, relumbrón.

flask | flɑːsk | *s.c.* **1** frasco, botella de bolsillo, botellita. **2** (fam.) termo. **3** QUIM. matraz.

flat | flæt | *s.c.* **1** piso. **2** neumático pinchado. **3** parte plana (de un objeto). **4** MUS. bemol. || *adj.* **5** plano, horizontal, liso, llano. **6** achatado, bajo: *a flat box = una caja achatada.* **7** mate (en pintura). **8** rotundo; total (negativa, rechazo, etc.). **9** MUS. bemol. **10** monótono; neutro. **11** flojo (negocios, actividad económica). **12** insípido; aburrido (espectáculo, conferencia, etc.). **13** sin tacones; con tacones muy bajos. **14** desinflado; pinchado. **15** descargado (batería). **16** estándar, básico; uniforme (cantidad, cifra, etc.): *I pay a flat rate of 10% on my income = pago la cantidad uniforme de un 10% de mis ingresos.* **17** sin burbujas; sin fuerza (bebidas). || *adv.* **18** de plano, tumbado: *lie flat on your belly = échate tumbado sobre tu estómago.* || **19 and that's –,** y se acabó, y no hay más que hablar. **20 as – as a pancake,** extremadamente llano/liso. **21 to fall –,** fallar, fracasar; caer en el vacío: *the plan fell flat = el plan fracasó.* **22 – broke,** (fam.) sin un céntimo, sin blanca. **23 – cap,** gorra de paño. **24 – racing,** carreras de caballos sin obstáculos. **25 flats** (a veces **flat**), llanura; meseta. **26 on the –,** a nivel de la calle.

flat-chested | ˌflæt'tʃestɪd | *adj.* de poco pecho, de pecho plano.

flatfish | 'flætfɪʃ | *s.c.* ZOOL. pez pleuronecto (rodaballo, lenguado, etc.).

flat-footed | ˌflæt'fʊtɪd | *adj.* **1** de pies planos. **2** (fig.) torpón. **3** bruto, metepatas.

flatiron | flætaɪən | *s.c.* plancha (de estilo antiguo).

flatlet | 'flætlɪt | *s.c.* piso pequeño, apartamento.

flatly | 'flætlɪ | *adv.* **1** terminantemente, rotundamente. **2** neutralmente, sin emoción alguna.

flatmate | 'flætmeɪt | *s.c.* compañero de piso.

flatness | 'flætnɪs | *s.i.* **1** llanura, lo liso/llano. **2** monotonía, insipidez.

flatten | 'flætn | *v.t.* **1** aplastar, aplanar, allanar. **2** tirar al suelo a alguien (de un golpe). **3** (fig.) desconcertar: *His explanations flattened me = Sus explicaciones me desconcertaron.* || *v.r.* **4 [to – against]** apretarse contra, aplastarse contra: *she flattened herself against me = se apretó contra mí.* || *v.i.* **5** (a veces con **out**) aplastarse, aplanarse, allanarse. || **to – out,** AER. enderezarse, tomar la posición horizontal estándar.

flattened | 'flætənd | *adj.* aplastado; apretado.

flatter | 'flætər | *v.t.* **1** halagar, adular. **2** favorecer (ropa, descripción, fotografía, etc.): *this dress flatters you.* || *v.r.* **3** felicitarse, congratularse: *I flatter myself I am a good teacher = me felicito de ser un buen profesor.* || **4 to be flattered,** halagarle algo a uno: *I was flattered to be called a hero = me halagó que me llamaran héroe.*

flatterer | 'flætərər | *s.c.* adulador, piropeador.

flattering | 'flætərɪŋ | *adj.* halagador, lisonjero.

flatteringly | 'flætərɪŋlɪ | *adv.* halagadoramente, aduladoramente.

flattery | 'flætərɪ | *s.i.* adulación, halago.

flatties | 'flætɪz | *s.pl.* (fam.) zapatos planos.

flatulence | 'flætjʊləns | *s.i.* flatulencia, gases.

flatulent | 'flætjʊlənt | *adj.* flatulento.

flaunt | flɔːnt | *v.t.* ostentar, hacer ostentación de.

flautist | 'flɔːtɪst | *s.c.* MUS. flautista.

flavour | 'fleɪvər | (EE.UU. **flavor**) *s.i.* y *c.* **1** sabor, gusto. **2** (fig.) sabor, toque: *my guitar gave the party a Spanish flavour = mi guitarra dio a la fiesta un toque español.* || *v.t.* **3 [to – with]** condimentar con, sazonar con, dar un sabor especial a.

flavouring | 'fleɪvərɪŋ | *s.i.* e *c.* GAST. condimento, condimentación.

flavourless | 'fleɪvəlɪs | *adj.* insípido, soso (comidas, bebidas, etc.).

flaw | flɔː | *s.c.* **[– (in)]** desperfecto; defecto (en el carácter, objeto, proyecto).

flawed | flɔːd | *adj.* defectuoso, que tiene algún fallo.

flawless | 'flɔːlɪs | *adj.* perfecto; impecable.

flawlessly | 'flɔːlɪslɪ | *adv.* perfectamente; impecablemente.

flax | flæks | *s.i.* lino.

flaxen | 'flæksn | *adj.* pajizo: *flaxen hair.*

flay | fleɪ | *v.t.* **1** desollar, despellejar. **2** (fig.) despellejar (a golpes). **3** criticar severamente.

flea | fliː | *s.c.* **1** pulga. || **2 – market,** mercado de ocasiones de segunda mano. **3 to send someone away with a – in one's ear,** echar a alguien a cajas destempladas.

fleabite | 'fliːbaɪt | *s.c.* picadura de pulga.

fleapit | 'fliːpɪt | *s.c.* (brit. y fam.) cine o teatro de ínfima categoría.

fleck | flek | *s.c.* **1** punto, puntito, manchita: *there were flecks of white on his hair = había manchitas de color blanco en su pelo.* || **2 to be flecked with,** estar salpicado de manchitas/puntitos de.

fled | fled | V. **flee.**

fledgling | 'fledʒlɪŋ | *s.c.* **1** pájaro pequeño, cría de pájaro. || *adj.* **2** inexperto, bisoño.

flee | fliː | *v.* [*pret.* y *p.p.* **fled**] *t.* e *i.* huir de, escapar de.

fleece | fliːs | *s.c.* **1** vellón. **2** piel de lana de oveja. || *v.t.* **3** (fam.) desplumar (de dinero, propiedades, etc.).

fleecy | 'fliːsɪ | *adj.* **1** lanudo, de lana. **2** lanoso, como lana: *fleecy clouds = nubes como ovillos de lana.*

fleet | fliːt | *s.c.* flota (de barcos, de automóviles, etc.).

fleeting | 'fliːtɪŋ | *adj.* efímero, fugaz, pasajero.

Fleet Street | 'fliːt striːt | *s.sing.* la prensa (es la calle donde se asientan la mayor parte de los periódicos nacionales británicos): *Fleet Street is very powerful = la prensa es muy poderosa (la prensa en Inglaterra).*

Flemish | 'flemɪʃ | *adj.* **1** flamenco (de Flanders). || *s.i.* **2** flamenco (idioma).

flesh | fleʃ | *s.i.* **1** carne (de una persona o de animal cuando no está preparado para ser comido). **2** (fig.) cuerpo (especialmente desnudo). **3** pulpa, parte sin piel dura (de una fruta o similar). **4** carne (desde el punto de vista sexual): *pleasures of the flesh = placeres de la carne.* || **5 – and blood,** de carne y hueso; humano. **6 to – out,** V. **flesh 10. 7 – wound,** MED. herida superficial (que no daña órganos vitales). **8 in the –,** en persona. **9 one's (own) flesh and blood,** de la familia (propia) de uno. **10 to put – on something,** dar detalles que completen la información. **10 the spirit is willing but the – is weak,** el espíritu está pronto pero la carne es débil (proverbio).

flesh-coloured | 'fleʃkʌləd | *adj.* color carne.

fleshly | 'fleʃlɪ | *adj.* carnal, sensual.

fleshpot | 'fleʃpɔt | *s.c.* antro de placer.

fleshy | 'fleʃɪ | *adj.* **1** corpulento, tirando a gordo. **2** carnoso, de carne. **3** pulposo, con pulpa (frutas y similar).

flew | fluː | V. **fly.**

flex | fleks | *s.c.* e *i.* **1** cordón, hilo, cable (eléctrico). || *v.t.* **2** flexionar; doblar. **3** (EE.UU.) mostrar, hacer ostentación de (el poder, la fuerza, etc.).

flexibility | ˌfleksɪ'bɪlɪtɪ | *s.i.* **1** flexibilidad. **2** adaptabilidad.

flexible | 'fleksəbl | *adj.* **1** flexible, elástico. **2** adaptable.

flexibly | 'fleksəblɪ | *adv.* flexiblemente, elásticamentee.

flexitime | 'fleksɪtaɪm | *s.i.* horario flexible.

flibbertigibbet | ˌflɪbətɪ'dʒɪbɪt | *s.c.* casquivana, frivolona (especialmente con mujeres).

flick | flɪk | *v.t.* **1** dar un golpecito (como golpeando una canica con el dedo). **2** dar un latigazo (con cuerda, látigo, etc.). **3 [to – (through/back/over)]** pasar las páginas (sin parar, hacia atrás, hacia delante). **4 [to – (on/off)]** dar (encendiendo y apagando cosas eléctricas). || *v.i.* **5** moverse (con un movimiento repentino y corto). || *s.c.* **6** movimiento rápido y corto: *a flick of the wrist = un movimiento rápido de muñeca.* **7** golpecito. **8** latigazo. **9** ojeada rápida. || **10 flicks,** (fam. y p.u.) cine. **11 to – through,** echar una ojeada rápida, ojear rápidamente (a algo que tenga más de una página).

flicker | 'flɪkər | *v.i.* **1** parpadear; titilar (luz, llama, etc.). **2** (fig.) vibrar brevemente; fluctuar: *hope still flickered in* *his heart = la esperanza todavía vibraba débil en su corazón.* **3** oscilar; temblar: *flickering shadows = sombras que tiemblan.* || *v.t.* **4** hacer temblar, hacer oscilar. || *s.c.* **5** parpadeo. **6** fluctuación, vibración. **7** oscilación, temblor.

flick-knife | ’flɪknaɪf | *s.c.* navaja.

flier | flaɪər | V. **flyer.**

flight | flaɪt | *s.c.* **1** vuelo (de animal o avión). **2** bandada: *a flight of geese = una bandada de gansos.* **3** tramo (de escalera). **4** arrebato; vuelo (de la imaginación, de emoción, etc.). || *s.i.* **5** vuelo (el hecho o la acción de volar). **6** huida, fuga. || **7 – lieutenant,** MIL. teniente de aviación. **8 in –,** volando. **9 to put someone to –,** (p.u.) hacer huir, ahuyentar. **10 to take to –/to take –,** huir, escapar.

flight-deck | ’flaɪtdek | *s.c.* **1** cubierta de vuelo. **2** AER. compartimento de pilotaje.

flightless | ’flaɪtlɪs | *adj.* incapaz de volar.

flight-recorder | ’flaɪtrɪkɔːdər | *s.c.* AER. caja negra (de un avión).

flighty | ’flaɪtɪ | *adj.* frívolo, casquivano; veleidoso.

flimsily | ’flɪmzɪlɪ | *adv.* frágilmente, ligeramente, trivialmente.

flimsiness | ’flɪmzɪnɪs | *s.i.* fragilidad, endeblez.

flimsy | ’flɪmzɪ | *adj.* **1** frágil, endeble: *a flimsy house.* **2** fino, ligero: *a flimsy jacket.* **3** baladí, sin peso: *a flimsy excuse.* || *s.c.* e *i.* **4** papel cebolla.

flinch | flɪntʃ | *v.i.* **1** arredrarse; echarse para atrás (instintivamente): *he flinched when I raised my hand = se echó para atrás cuando levanté la mano.* **2 [to – (from)]** acobardarse; retroceder: *he didn’t flinch from killing his own brother = no se acobardó ante matar a su propio hermano.*

fling | flɪŋ | *v.* [*pret.* y *p.p.* **flung**] *t.* **1** arrojar, tirar (con mucha fuerza). **2** echar, agitar (una parte del cuerpo en alguna dirección). **3** tirar; poner (descuidadamente y con un poco de agresividad): *he flung his socks into the drawer = puso descuidadamente los calcetines en el cajón.* **4** decir (agresivamente): *shut up! he flung at her = ¡cállate! le dijo agresivamente.* || *r.* **5** arrojarse, tirarse, lanzarse. **6** meterse de lleno y enérgicamente en una actividad, ponerse a... con ahinco. || *s.c.* **7** (fam.) aventura amorosa, plan. **8** escape (actividad). || **9 to – off,** quitarse (ropa a toda velocidad). **10 to – on,** ponerse (ropa a toda velocidad). **11 to – out, a)** tirar (cosas que no se quieren). **b)** lanzar; decir (insultos, improperios, etc.).

flint | flɪnt | *s.c.* e *i.* **1** pedernal. || *s.c.* **2** piedra (de encendedor, en armas de fuego antiguas, etc.).

flintlock | ’flɪntlɔk | *s.c.* trabuco de chispa, fusil de chispa (del estilo antiguo).

flinty | ’flɪntɪ | *adj.* **1** de pedernal. **2** (fig.) inflexible; duro.

flip | flɪp | *v.t.* **1** dar, golpear (con un dedo). **2 [to – (on/off)]** dar (encendiendo o apagando objetos eléctricos). **3** tirar al aire (con un golpecito del pulgar): *he flipped a coin = tiró al aire una moneda.* || *v.i.* **4 [to – (through)]** pasar las hojas rápidamente (buscando algo en un libro, documento, etc.). **5** (fam.) enfurecerse. || *adj.* **6** petulante; frívolo. || *interj.* **7** (fam. y brit.) ¡mecachis!, ¡jolín!

flip-flop | ’flɪpflɔp | *s.c.* chancleta.

flippancy | ’flɪpənsɪ | *s.i.* frivolidad, ligereza.

flippant | ’flɪpənt | *adj.* frívolo, ligero.

flipper | ’flɪpər | *s.c.* **1** aleta (de mamífero que viva en el agua, no de pez). **2** aleta (para nadar).

flipping | ’flɪpɪŋ | *adj.* y *adv.* (fam. y brit.) condenado, maldito; condenadamente: *the flipping handle! = ¡el condenado mango!*

flip-side | ’flɪpsaɪd | *s.sing.* MUS. cara B (la menos importante en un disco).

flirt | flɜːt | *v.i.* **1 [to – (with)]** coquetear, flirtear. || *s.c.* **2** coqueta; galán. || **3 – with,** jugar con, considerar con ligereza (una idea, un plan, etc.): *he flirted with the idea of writing a novel = jugó con la idea de escribir una novela.*

flirtation | flɜː’teɪʃn | *s.c.* e *i.* **1** flirteo, coqueteo. **2** consideración frívola, jugueteo.

flirtatious | flɜː’teɪʃəs | *adj.* coqueta, provocador, provocadora.

flit | flɪt | *v.i.* **1** moverse rápidamente, pasar de una cosa a otra con gran velocidad: *the boys flitted into the room and suddenly they were gone = los chicos pasaron rápidamente dentro de la habitación y de repente desaparecieron.* **2** (fig.) pasar rápidamente (por el pensamiento, por la mente, por el gesto de la cara, etc.). || *s.c.* **3** (fam.) desaparición secreta.

float | fləʊt | *v.i.* **1** flotar. **2** (fig.) flotar (en el aire). **3** acercarse; andar (con cierta liviandad y estilo majestuoso): *the hostess floated to him = la anfitriona se acercó a él majestuosamente.* **4** (lit.) flotar; viajar (el sonido de una voz, de una canción). **5** ECON. quedar libre (el cambio de la moneda de un país). **6** vagar (sin sentido, sin finalidad). || *v.t.* **7** poner en el agua, poner a flote: *efforts to float the ship = esfuerzos para poner el barco a flote.* **8** lanzar; idear (un proyecto, un plan, una sugerencia). **9** FIN. sacar al público (bonos, acciones o similar). **10** ECON. flotar, no fijar (el cambio de una moneda nacional). || *s.c.* **11** flotador. **12** corcho (en una caña de pescar). **13** carroza (en un desfile). **14** cambio; monedas sueltas (en espera de clientes con necesidad de ello).

floating | ’fləʊtɪŋ | *adj.* **1** POL. indeciso: *floating vote = voto indeciso.* **2** GEOG. flotante: *floating population.*

flock | flɔk | *s.c.* **1** [– *v.sing./pl.*] rebaño, hato, manada. **2** multitud, gentío, tropel, muchedumbre. **3** REL. congregación, parroquia, grey. || *s.i.* **4** borra, vellón de lana, copo de algodón. **5** fieltro, fibra, pelillo (utilizado en la decoración de papel o tela). || *v.i.* **6 [to –** *adv./prep.***]** reunirse, congregarse, afluir, ir en tropel. || **7 birds of a feather – together,** V. **bird.**

floe | fləʊ | *s.c.* témpano, masa de hielo flotante.

flog | flɔg | *v.t.* **1** dar latigazos, azotar, flagelar. **2** (brit.) vender. || **3 to – a dead horse,** (fam.) perseguir lo imposible, desperdiciar energías (volviendo a algo ya tratado). **4 to – somebody/something to the ground,** (fam.) trabajar en exceso, matarse a trabajar (una persona), dejar algo inservible, usar en exceso, maltratar algo. **5 to – something to death,** (fam.) estropear, fastidiar, machacar (por repetición excesiva).

flogging | ’flɔgɪŋ | *s.c.* e *i.* **1** flagelación. **2** apaleamiento, zurra, azotaina.

flood | flʌd | *s.c.* e *i.* **1** inundación, diluvio. **2** desbordamiento, riada. **3** torrente, cantidad enorme (de cosas, personas). || *v.t.* e *i.* **4** inundar, anegar. **5** entrar o salir a raudales, en gran cantidad (la luz, gente). **6** saturar, inundar (el mercado). **7** abarrotar (un lugar). || *i.* **8** desbordarse (un río). || **9 before the Flood,** de tiempos de Maricastaña, antediluviano. **10 to – somebody out,** hacer abandonar, verse obligado a evacuar la vivienda (a causa de inundaciones). **11 in floods of tears,** llorando a mares, hecho un mar de lágrimas. **12 the Flood,** el Diluvio Universal.

floodgate | ’flʌdgeɪt | *s.c.* **1** (generalmente *pl.*) compuerta (de pantano, dique). || **2 to open the floodgates,** abrir cauces, aflojar la presión (después de un período de represión).

flooding | ’flʌdɪŋ | *s.i.* inundación.

floodlight | ’flʌdlaɪt | *s.c.* **1** foco, reflector (utilizado para iluminar edificios públicos). || *v.t. irr.* [*pret.* y *p.p.* **floodlighted** o **floodlit.**] **2** iluminar con focos o reflectores.

floodtide | flʌdtaɪd | *s.sing* **1** pleamar, marea creciente. **2** punto álgido, clímax.

floor | flɔːr | *s.c.* **1** suelo, pavimento, piso, firme. **2** piso (de un bloque). **3 [the – of +** *s.***]** el fondo, el lecho de (un río, valle). **4** hemiciclo (de un edificio público). || *v.t.* **5** pavimentar, solar, entarimar. **6** tumbar, derribar, echar a tierra (de un golpe). **7** vencer, derrotar. **8** desconcertar, confundir, asombrar, dejar sin capacidad de reacción: *floored by the events = desconcertados por los acontecimientos.* || **9 dance –,** pista de baile. **10 – polish,** cera abrillantadora para suelos. **11 – cloth,** bayeta. **12 – show,** espectáculo (de cabaret, sala de fiestas). **13 from the –,** del público, de la concurrencia: *questions from the floor = preguntas de la concurrencia.* **14 to go through the –,** bajar al mínimo, caer (los precios). **15** (brit.) **ground –,** (EE.UU.) **first –,** planta baja. **16 to have the –,** tener el uso de la palabra. **17 to hold the –,** estar en el uso de la palabra. **18 to take the –,** tomar la palabra.

floorboard | ’flɔːbɔːd | *s.c.* tablilla, tabla, plancha de madera.

floorwalker | 'flɔːˌwɔːkər | *s.c.* (EE.UU.) superintendente, supervisor de ventas (en grandes almacenes).

floozy | 'fluːzɪ | *s.c.* (fam.) putilla barata; callejera.

flop | flɒp | *v.i.* **1** **[to –** *adv./prep.***]** desplomarse, caer como un fardo, colapsar. **2** moverse torpemente, relajadamente. **3** (fam.) fracasar, tener poco éxito (un plan, una obra teatral). || *s.sing.* **4** sonido sordo (producido al desplomarse o caer algo al agua). || *s.c.* **5** (fam.) fracaso, fiasco, fallo.

flop-house | 'flɒphaus | *s.c.* (*pl.* **flop-houses**) (EE.UU.) hotelucho, pensión de mala muerte.

floppy | 'flɒpɪ | *adj.* **1** flexible, blando, fofo. **2** flojo, suelto, colgante (ropa). || **3** INF. **– disk,** disco flexible, diskette.

flora | 'flɔːrə | (*pl.* **floras** o **florae**) *s.c.* e *i.* flora.

floral | flɔːrəl | *adj.* floral.

florescence | flɒː'resns | *s.i.* BOT. floración, florescencia.

florid | flɒrɪd | *adj.* **1** recargado, florido (decoración, estilo). **2** arrebolado, encendido, subido de color, sanguíneo, rojo. **3** florido, cubierto de flores.

florin | flɒrɪn | *s.c.* **1** florín (holandés). **2** (arc.) florín (moneda de oro o plata).

florist | flɒrɪst | *s.c.* **1** florista. || **2** **florist's/florist's shop,** floristería.

floss | flɒs | *s.i.* borra, cadarzo.

flossy | 'flɒsɪ | *adj.* velloso; suave (al tacto).

flotation | fləʊ'teɪʃn | *s.c.* e *i.* **1** FIN. flotación, lanzamiento (de una empresa mediante la venta de acciones al público). || *s.i.* **2** flotación: *flotation tank = tanque de flotación.*

flotsam | flɒtəm | *s.i.* **1** DER. MAR. pecios, restos de naufragio. **2** desechos, basura (que flota en el mar o queda en la playa). || **3** **– and jetsam,** trastos, restos; transeúntes, vagabundos.

flounce | flauns | *s.c.* **1** cenefa, volante (en vestidos, cortinajes). **2** contoneo, contorsión, gesto de desdén. || *v.i.* **3** [– + *adv./prep.*] moverse exageradamente, violentamente; hacer aspavientos. **4** contonearse.

flounced | flaunst | *adj.* adornado, guarnecido con grecas o volantes.

flounder | flaundər | *v.i.* **1** caminar torpemente, moverse con dificultad, andar a duras penas. **2** perder el hilo, titubear. || *s.c.* **3** tropiezo, dificultad de movimiento. **4** platija, especie de lenguado.

flour | flauər | *s.i.* **1** harina. || *v.t.* **2** espolvorear con harina, echar harina. || **3** **– bin,** harinero, recipiente para la harina.

flourish | flʌrɪʃ | *v.i.* **1** crecer sanamente. **2** marchar bien, prosperar, tener éxito. || *v.t.* **3** blandir, esgrimir: *flourishing the documents = esgrimiendo los documentos.* || *s.c.* **4** gesto, movimiento, ademán (para atraer la atención). **5** floritura (en la escritura). **6** rúbrica. **7** MUS. toque de trompeta, floreo (para marcar la entrada de alguien importante).

flourishing | 'flʌrɪʃɪŋ | *adj.* floreciente, próspero.

floury | 'flauərɪ | *adj.* rebozado, enharinado, farináceo.

flout | flaut | **1** desobedecer, despreciar. **2** ir en contra, llevar la contraria.

flow | fləʊ | *s.c.* **1** corriente, flujo, caudal. **2** chorro. **3** (fig.) profusión (de ideas). **4** fluidez. **5** flujo, afluencia, raudal. **6** subida, flujo creciente de la marea. **7** ondulación, ondear: *the flow of her dress = el ondear de su vestido.* **8** menstruación. || *v.i.* **9** fluir, manar, brotar. **10** discurrir, correr (un líquido). **11** discurrir hacia, pasar, deslizarse (la gente). **12** subir (la marea). **13** **[to – from]** derivar, surgir, nacer de. **14** pasar, fluir (el tiempo). **15** flotar, ondear: *flags flowing = banderas ondeando.* **16** **[to – with]** rebosar, nadar en (la riqueza). || *t.* **17** inundar, anegar. || **18** **– chart,** COM. diagrama de movimiento, representación esquemática de una secuencia de operaciones; INF. ordinograma, diagrama de flujo. **19** **to – into,** desembocar en. **20** **to – together,** confluir. **21** **in full –,** sin parar de hablar, sin dejar meter baza.

flower | 'flauər | *s.c.* **1** flor, brote, capullo, planta. **2** **[the – of]** (lit.) la flor y nata, la crema: *the flower of the city = la flor y nata de la ciudad.* **3** QUIM. flor. || *v.i.* **4** florecer, dar flores. **5** (fig. y form.) desarrollarse, florecer, brotar (ideas). || **6** **– shop/– store,** floristería. **7** **– show,** concurso de floricultura. **8** **in –/into –,** en flor.

flowerbed | 'flauəbed | *s.c.* macizo, cuadro de flores.

flowered | flauəd | *adj.* con flores (paño o papel).

flowering | 'flaurɪŋ | *s.c.* **1** **[– (of)]** florecimiento (de una idea, estilo, etc.). || *adj.* **2** floreciente, en flor.

flowerpot | 'flauəpɔt | *s.c.* tiesto, maceta.

flowery | 'flauərɪ | *adj.* **1** floreado, de flores, floreteado: *a flowery fabric = una tela floreada.* **2** floral, fragante. **3** (fig.) florido, retórico, recargado, elaborado, barroco (estilo literario, pictórico).

flowing | 'fləʊɪŋ | *adj.* **1** ondulado, curvilíneo. **2** suelto, flotante. **3** fluido, deslizante.

flown | fləʊn | *p.p.* de **fly.**

flu | fluː | (también **influenza**) *s.i.* (fam.) gripe, influenza.

fluctuate | 'flʌktjʊeɪt | *v.i.* **1** fluctuar, oscilar, variar. || *v.t.* **2** hacer fluctuar, hacer variar, hacer oscilar.

fluctuation | ˌflʌktjʊ'eɪʃn | *s.c.* **1** fluctuación, oscilación, variación.

flue | fluː | *s.c.* **1** tubo de chimenea. **2** MEC. tubo, conducto. **3** MUS. cañón, tubo sonoro (en instrumentos de viento). **4** MAR. tipo de red barredera.

fluency | 'fluːənsɪ | *s.i.* fluidez, fluencia, facilidad de palabra, labia.

fluent | 'fluːənt | *adj.* **1** fluido, fluente, correcto (en una lengua, escritura). **2** inteligible, claro, rápido.

fluently | 'fluːəntlɪ | *adv.* **1** fluentemente, con fluidez. **2** elocuentemente, inteligiblemente, claramente.

fluff | flʌf | *s.i.* **1** (brit.) pelusa, borra, tamo. **2** plumón. **3** fracaso, chapuza; olvido (de texto en teatro). || *s.c.* **4** DEP. golpe defectuoso (en golf). || *v.t.* **5** **[to – (out/up)],** esponjar, ahuecar (el pelo o las plumas los animales). **6** ahuecar, mullir (cojines). **7** (fam.) arruinar, estropear, destrozar (algo por error). **8** olvidar (texto teatral, un actor).

fluffy | 'flʌfɪ | *adj.* **1** esponjoso, ahuecado, mullido. **2** cubierto de pelusa.

fluid | 'fluːɪd | *adj.* **1** líquido, fluido, fluente. **2** variable, susceptible de cambio: *a fluid arrangement = un plan susceptible de cambio.* **3** convertible en dinero. **4** dúctil, flexible, plegable. || *s.c.* e *i.* **5** MED. fluido, líquido. || **6** **a – ounce,** 0,0284 de litro (unidad de medida).

fluidity | fluː'ɪdətɪ | *s.i.* **1** fluidez, liquidez. **2** variabilidad, susceptibilidad de cambio.

fluke | fluːk | *s.c.* **1** (fam.) carambola, chiripa, suerte. **2** especie de platija o lenguado. **3** oreja (apéndice triangular de una flecha, ancla). **4** aleta (una de las dos en que termina la cola de la ballena o similar).

fluky | 'fluːkɪ | *adj.* **1** de chiripa, de carambola. **2** caprichoso, cambiante.

flummox | 'flʌməks | *v.t.* despistar, embrollar: *I'm flummoxed about what to do in my life = estoy despistado sobre qué hacer en mi vida.*

flung | flʌŋ | *pret.* y *p.p.* de **fling.**

flunk | flʌŋk | *v.t.* **1** (EE.UU. y fam.) suspender, fracasar en los estudios. **2** (EE.UU.) dar una mala nota, suspender (a un alumno). || *s.c.* **3** suspenso. || **4** (EE.UU.) **to – out,** expulsar o ser expulsado de un centro de estudios por bajo rendimiento.

flunkey | 'flʌŋkɪ | (también **flunky**) *adj.* (fam.) **1** lacayo. **2** (desp. y fig.) lacayo, adulador, pelota (típico servidor de personas importantes).

fluorescence | fluə'resns | *s.i.* fluorescencia, luminiscencia.

fluorescent | fluə'resnt | *adj.* fluorescente, luminiscente.

fluoridation | fluərɪ'deɪʃn | *s.i.* adición de fluoruro al agua.

fluoride | 'fluəraɪd | *s.i.* compuesto de fluoruro (para añadir al agua).

flurried | 'flʌrɪd | *adj.* aturdido, confundido, agitado (normalmente por las prisas y la desorganización).

flurry | 'flʌrɪ | *s.c.* **1** ráfaga, racha (de viento, nieve). **2** agitación, desasosiego, conmoción, desazón. **3** COM. subida o bajada repentina (de la bolsa). || *v.t.* **4** (generalmente *pas.*) aturdir, confundir, poner nervioso. || *v.i.* **5** moverse a ráfagas, a rachas. || **6** **a – of excitement,** un frenesí, una locura.

flush | flʌʃ | *s.c.* **1** limpieza, lavado, baldeo. **2** chorro de agua. **3** cadena de retrete. **4** rubor, sonrojo, sofoco. **5** **[– of]** ataque de, acceso de (ira). **6** **[– of]** abundancia de, crecimiento. **7** emoción, optimismo, alegría. **8** frescura, vigor. **9** mano de cartas del mismo palo. || *adj.* **10** TEC. nivelado, al ras, alineado. **11** **[–**

+ (with)] (fam.) rico, adinerado, opulento, repleto. || *v.t.* **12 [to — out]** lavar a chorros de agua, baldear. **13** tirar de la cadena (del retrete). **14 [to — *o.* + *adv./prep.*]** espantar, ahuyentar, forzar a salir de un escondite, sacar por la fuerza. || *v.t.* e *i.* **15** ruborizar(se), poner(se) colorado. || *adv.* **16 [– *prep.*]** directamente, de lleno: *flush on her face = de lleno en la cara (de ella).* **17** exactamente, a nivel de, a ras de. || **18 in the first – of,** en la flor de (la vida); en el emocionante momento de.

flushed | flʌʃt | *adj.* **[– (with)]** excitado (con alegría, emoción, etc.).

fluster | 'flʌstər | *s.i.* **1** nerviosismo, confusión, agitación, aturdimiento. || *v.t.* e *i.* **2** confundir(se), poner(se) nervioso, aturdir(se).

flute | fluːt | *s.c.* **1** MUS. flauta. **2** ARQ. estría, acanaladura. **3** pliegue, tabla, fuelle (en la ropa). || *v.t.* **4** tocar la flauta. **5** decorar con estrías, con acanaladuras.

fluted | 'fluːtɪd | *adj.* **1** estriado, acanalado, ondulado, estriado.

flutter | 'flʌtər | *s.* **1** revoloteo, aleteo, agitación. **2** pestañeo. **3** palpitación, latido. **4** estremecimiento, ansiedad, excitación, revuelo. **5** nerviosismo, confusión. **6** TEC. vibración. || *s.c.* **7** (generalmente *sing.*) (brit.) especulación, apuesta (en pequeñas cantidades). || *v.t.* e *i.* **8** revolotear, aletear. **9** pestañear. **10** ir de un lado a otro sin parar. **11** latir. || *v.i.* **12** ondear, volar al viento: *papers fluttering... = papeles revoloteando...*

fluty | fluːtɪ | *adj.* aflautado (tono).

flux | flʌks | *s.i.* **1** flujo, fluctuación, cambio continuo, transformación. **2** corriente, flujo. **3** MED. flujo, fluido. **4** FIS. fluido magnético. **5** MET. fundente (para soldar). || **7 in a state of –,** en estado de cambio permanente.

fly | flaɪ | *v.* [*irr.pret.* **flew,** *p.p.* **flown**] *i.* volar. **2** viajar en avión, volar. **3** flotar, ondear (al viento). **4** pasar rápidamente, moverse a gran velocidad, apresurarse. **5 [to – *adv./prep.*]** salir despedido: *it flew from his hand = salió despedido de su mano.* || *t.* **6** utilizar una línea aérea, volar con. **7** transportar o enviar por avión. **8** salvar un trayecto ultramarino, cruzar (en avión). || *t.* e *i.* **9** pilotar, manejar un avión. **10** ondear, flotar (al viento). **11 [to – from]** huir, escapar, evadirse (de la justicia, de un país). || *s.c.* **12** mosca. **13** mosca artificial (para pescar). **14** vuelo. **15** bragueta, pliegue (que cubre los botones). **16** (brit.) astuto, despierto, vivo, espabilado. **17** toldo. **18** bambalinas (teatro). **19** ancho de la bandera. **20** parte superior de la bandera (la más alejada del asta). **21** (brit.) calesa, cabriolé. || **22 a – in the ointment,** nimiedad, tontería (que estropea el encanto de un momento). **23 as the crow flies,** en línea recta. **24 to drop like flies,** caer como moscas. **25 to – a kite,** sondear la opinión, ver por donde sopla el viento. **26 to – in the face/in the teeth of,** desafiar a, retar a. **27 to – into a temper/into a rage,** montar en cólera, perder los estribos. **28 to – off the handle,** ponerse hecho un basilisco. **29 go – a kite!,** ¡vete y déjame en paz! **30 to let – at,** poner verde, agredir, insultar; disparar un proyectil. **31 to send something/somebody flying,** lanzar algo/a alguien de un puñetazo por los aires. **32 Spanish –,** afrodisíaco (cantharsis vesicatoria). **33 there are no flies in someone,** (brit.) no hay quien le tome el pelo, no tiene un pelo de tonto.

fly-by-night | 'faɪbaɪnaɪt | *adj.* **1** arribista, ambicioso, poco fiable, aprovechado (en negocios). **2** efímero, fugaz, temporal. || *s.c.* **3** tiburón, arribista.

flyaway | 'flaɪəweɪ | *adj.* voladizo (pelo).

flyblown | 'flaɪbləun | *adj.* cubierto con manchas.

flyby | 'flaɪbaɪ | (EE.UU. **flypast**) *s.c.* AER. exhibición de vuelo.

flycatcher | 'flaɪ,kætʃər | *s.c.* ZOOL. papamoscas, cazamoscas.

flyfishing | 'flaɪ,fɪʃɪŋ | *s.i.* pesca con mosca artificial.

flying | 'flaɪɪŋ | *adj.* **1** elevado, por los aires, por lo alto. **2** volante, volador. **3** breve, rápido. || *s.c.* **4** vuelo, viaje en avión. **5** pilotaje, navegación aérea. || **6 – boat,** hidroavión, hidroplano. **7 – bomb,** bomba teledirigida, bomba volante. **8 Flying Dutchman,** Holandés Errante (obra de Wagner); buque fantasma (según la leyenda aparece cerca del Cabo de Buena Esperanza durante la tormenta y presagia desastre). **9 – fish,** pez volador. **10 – machine,** máquina voladora (de comienzos de la aviación). **11 – time,** duración del vuelo. **12 to get off to a – start,** empezar con fuerza, con brío, con ganas.

flyleaf | 'flaɪliːf | (*s.pl.* **flyleaves**) *s.c.* guarda (imprenta).

flyover | flaɪ,əuvər | *s.* **1** (brit.) paso elevado, carretera a desnivel (en cruces de autopista). **2** (EE.UU.) vuelo rasante, a baja altura (en exhibiciones aéreas).

flypaper | 'flaɪ,peɪpər | *s.i.* tira de papel atrapamoscas.

flysheet | 'flaɪʃiːt | *s.c.* lona, cubierta (de una tienda de campaña).

flyswatter | 'flaɪ,swɔtər | *s.c.* pala matamoscas.

flyweight | 'flaɪweɪt | *s.* peso mosca (boxeo).

flywheel | 'flaɪwiːl | *s.* MEC. volante (regularizador del movimiento de una máquina).

foal | fəul | *s.c.* **1** potro, potrillo; cría de asno, pollino. || *v.i.* **2** parir (una yegua, una burra).

foam | fəum | *s.i.* **1** espuma. **2** espumarajo, espumajo. **3** (lit.) el mar. **4** poliexpan, aislante para embalaje. || *v.t.* e *i.* **5** espumajear, echar espumarajos. | **6 – at the mouth,** echar espuma por la boca; (fig.) echar chispas. || **7 – rubber,** caucho, espuma de caucho.

foamy | fəumɪ | *adj.* **1** focal, céntrico. || **2 – point,** OPT. punto focal, foco.

fob | fɒb | *s.c.* **1** leontina. || **2 to – off,** quitar de en medio con disculpas (a alguien), deshacerse con disculpas (de alguien). **3 to – off on,** encasquetar (una cosa a alguien especialmente con engaño): *I can't understand how she was able to fob her old typewriter on Jimmy = no puedo entender cómo pudo encasquetar a Jimmy la vieja máquina de escribir.*

focus | fəukəs | (*pl.* **focuses** o **foci,**) *s.c.* **1** FIS. foco. || *s.c.* e *i.* **2** foco, centro de atención, foco de interés, punto central, énfasis. **3** OPT. distancia focal. || *v.t.* e *i.* **4 [to – on]** enfocar. **5 [to – on]** centrar, concentrar, dirigir (la atención). || *v.t.* **6 [to – on]** enfocar, ajustar (una lente). || **7 in –,** enfocado. **8 out of –,** desenfocado.

fodder | fɒdər | *s.i.* **1** pasto, forraje pienso. **2** (fig. y desp.) carne, material, objeto. || *v.t.* **3** alimentar con forraje. || **4 cannon –,** V. **cannon.**

foe | fəu | *s.c.* (lit.) enemigo, adversario, oponente.

foetal | 'fiːtl | (también **fetal**) *adj.* MED. fetal.

foetus o **fetus** | fiːtəs | *s.c* MED. feto.

fog | fɔg | *s.c.* e *i.* **1** niebla, bruma, neblina. **2** FOT. velado. **3** confusión mental, desorientación. **4** segunda cosecha (de pasto). || *v.t.* e *i.* **5** cubrirse de niebla, envolver en niebla. **6** FOT. velar. **7 [to – up]** empañar (cristal). **8** aturdir, confundir, desorientar. || **9 – lamp,** faro antiniebla.

fog-bank | 'fɒgbæŋk | *s.c.* banco de niebla.

fogbound | 'fɒgbaund | *adj.* detenido por la niebla, inmovilizado por la niebla: *fogbound airport = aeropuerto inmovilizado por la niebla.*

fogey o **fogy** | fəugɪ | *s.c.* persona anticuada, pasada de moda, vejestorio.

foggy | 'fɒgɪ | *adj.* **1** brumoso, de niebla, nebuloso. **2** poco claro, confuso, nebuloso (un plan, idea, etc.). || **3 not to have the foggiest idea,** no tener ni la más remota idea.

foghorn | 'fɒghɔːn | | fɔːghɔːrn | *s.c.* **1** sirena, bocina (para prevenir accidentes en la niebla). || **2 a voice like a –,** una voz desagradable, fuerte, ronca, una voz como un camionero.

foible | 'fɔɪbl | *s.c.* **1** debilidad, manía, punto flaco, punto vulnerable. **2** parte más débil de la hoja de la espada (desde el centro a la punta).

foil | fɔɪl | *s.i.* **1** papel de aluminio, papel de plata. **2** hojuela, pan (de oro, de plata). || *s.c.* **3 [– to/for]** contraste, combinación (con otra cosa o persona): *a foil to tanned skin = un contraste con la piel morena.* **4** DEP. florete. **5** huella, pista, rastro (de animal). **6** realce, pan (bajo una gema falsa). **7** azogue (en espejos). **8** ARQ. lóbulo. || *v.t.* **9** envolver en papel de plata, de aluminio. **10** realzar, contrastar. **11** frustrar, hacer inútil (un plan, intento, etc.). **12** destruir, borrar, pisotear (huellas).

foist | fɔɪst | *v.t.* **1 [to – on]** imponer, obligar a, soportar. **2** introducir fraudulentamente, con engaño, colar algo. || **3 to – something off/on/upon somebody,**

vender engañosamente, colar algo a alguien.

fold | fəʊld | *s.c.* **1** doblez, pliegue, arruga. **2** hendidura, hueco (de un pliegue). **3** GEOL. (brit.) pliegue, plegamiento. **4** redil, aprisco. **5** (fig.) redil, filas. **6** MED. pliegue, doblez. || *v.t.* **7** plegar, doblar. **8** replegar, plegar, recoger (las alas). **9** cruzar, entrelazar, enlazar (los brazos, las manos, etc.). **10** **[to –** *prep./adv.*] cubrir, envolver. || *v.i.* **11** plegar, cerrar. **12** **[to – up]** fracasar financieramente, cerrar por mal funcionamiento (un negocio). **13** plegarse a, doblegarse a. || **14 to – somebody in,** abrazar, cubrir, envolver en. || **15 to – something in/into,** GAST. mezclar con (en cocina).

fold-away | 'fəʊdəweɪ | *adj.* plegable (que se hace más pequeño).

folded | 'fəʊldɪd | *adj.* **1** doblado, plegado. **2** cerrado (los pétalos de una flor).

folder | fəʊldər | *s.c.* **1** carpeta. **2** folleto propagandístico. **3** carterita (de cartón).

folding | fəʊldɪŋ | *adj.* **1** plegable, plegadizo. || **2 – chair,** silla de tijera, plegable. **3 – table,** mesa plegable.

fold-up | 'fəʊldʌp | *adj.* abatible, plegable.

foliage | 'fəʊlɪɪdʒ | *s.i.* follaje, fronda, hojas.

foliation | fəʊlɪ'eɪʃn | *s.i.* **1** foliación. **2** decoración, ornamentación a base de follaje. **3** foliación, paginación (de un libro). **4** laminación (de cristal o metal).

folio | fəʊlɪəʊ | *s.c.* **1** TEC. folio, hoja (de manuscrito, libro de contabilidad, etc.). **2** infolio, libro de tamaño folio. || *s.i.* **3** pliego de papel doblado en dos (que da lugar a cuatro páginas). **4** paginación, numeración de página. **5** DER. folio (unidad de un número específico de palabras en un documento). || *v.t.* **6** paginar, numerar páginas.

folk | fəʊk | *s.c.* **1** *pl.* gente, pueblo, tribu (referido a una pequeña comunidad o grupo étnico). **2** (EE.UU.) gente (en general). **3** parientes, familiares, padres. **4** amigos: *hello, folks! = ¡hola, amigos!* || *s.i.* **5** música tradicional, música popular. || *adj.* **6** tradicional, popular, folklórico (música). || **7 – dance,** baile folklórico. **8 – tale,** cuento popular.

folklore | fəʊklɔː | *s.i.* **1** folklore, tradiciones, creencias y leyendas de un pueblo. **2** estudio de la cultura de un determinado pueblo o grupo étnico.

folksong | 'fəʊsɒŋ | *s.c.* canción folklórica, tradicional, popular.

folksy | 'fəʊksɪ | *adj.* **1** (EE.UU.) informal, familiar (a veces artificialmente). **2** campechano, afable, sencillo, llano (de costumbres o trato).

follicle | 'fɔlɪkl | *s.c.* ANAT. folículo.

follow | 'fɔləʊ | *v.t.* e *i.* seguir, ir detrás de, perseguir. **2** imitar, copiar, seguir, aceptar: *they also followed her teachings = también siguieron sus enseñanzas.* **3** suceder, ir después de, seguir a. **4** **[to – (that)]** deducirse (que), desprenderse (de), resultar (que), derivar (de). || *v.t.* **5** seguir, proseguir, ir a lo largo de, ir en la misma dirección. **6** observar, espiar, acechar, seguir (con la mirada). **7** seguir, escuchar atentamente, atender, observar (instrucciones, una charla). **8** entender, comprender, seguir el hilo. **9** seguir, aceptar (un consejo, costumbres). **10** interesarse por, seguir, cursar (una materia). **11** tratar de, ser sobre: *it follows a couple who... = trata de una pareja que...* || **12 as follows,** como sigue, a saber (para introducir una lista, descripción...). **13 to –,** después, a continuación: *first soup, to follow a steak = primero sopa, a continuación un filete.* **14 to – in the footsteps of,** seguir el ejemplo de, seguir las huellas de. **15 to – on/upon,** ser el resultado de. **16 to – one's nose,** seguir el instinto, ir derecho a. **17 to – (something) through/out,** investigar a fondo, ir hasta el final (de una investigación). **18 to – something up,** perseguir con ahínco, llevar hasta las últimas consecuencias; reforzar, continuar algo. **19 to – suit,** imitar el ejemplo, hacer lo mismo que. **20 to – the herd/crowd,** dejarse llevar por la corriente. **21 to – through/out,** DEP. completar el movimiento (después de golpear la pelota en tenis, golf, etc.).

follower | 'fɒləʊər | *s.c.* **1** partidario, seguidor, discípulo, imitador (de un método, enseñanza, teoría). **2** DEP. hincha, partidario. **3** perseguidor. **4** subalterno, subordinado, criado. **6** MEC. polea, engranaje. || **6 followers,** séquito.

following | 'fɒləʊɪŋ | *adj.* **1** **[the –]** el siguiente, el próximo. **2** **[the –]** lo siguiente, los siguientes (al iniciar una lista). **3** MAR. de popa. || *s.c.* **4** (generalmente *sing.*) seguidores, partidarios. **5** cortejo, comitiva, séquito. || *prep.* **6** después de, a continuación de, a raíz de.

follow-through | fɒləʊ'θruː | *s.c.* **1** DEP. movimiento complementario, continuación de swing después del impacto (en tenis, golf, etc.). **2** movimiento complementario (de una acción o serie de acciones planeadas).

follow-up | fɒləʊ'ʌp | *adj.* **1** de seguimiento, complementario (como refuerzo de algo previamente hecho): *a follow-up visit = una visita de seguimiento.* || *s.c.* **2** seguimiento, continuación.

folly | 'fɒlɪ | *s.c.* e *i.* **1** locura, estupidez, insensatez. || *s.c.* **2** locura, desvarío, extravagancia, insensatez. **3** construcción o edificio extravagante (como elemento decorativo en parques, etc.).

foment | fəʊ'ment | *v.t.* (form.) **1** fomentar, avivar, instigar, provocar. **2** MED. aplicar fomentos, tratar (la piel) con paños calientes.

fomentation | fəʊmen'teɪʃn | *s.i.* (form.) **1** provocación, instigación. **2** aplicación de fomentos o paños calientes. **3** cataplasma, fomento.

fond | fɒnd | [*gen.* **to be – of**] *adj.* **1** afectuoso, cariñoso, tierno. **2** interesado en, aficionado a. **3** excesivamente indulgente. **4** enamorado. **5** ingenuo, absurdo, inocente, cándido. || **6 to become – of,** aficionarse a, tomar cariño a. **7 to grow – of,** interesarse cada vez más por.

fondant | 'fɒndənt | *s.c.* dulce de caramelo, dulce (especial para hacer diversos tipos de pasteles).

fondle | fɒndl | *v.t.* **1** acariciar. **2** (desp.) manosear, meter mano. **3** ser indulgente, ser solícito. || *v.i.* **4** mostrarse cariñoso.

fondly | 'fɒndlɪ | *adv.* **1** cariñosamente, afectuosamente, tiernamente. **2** estúpidamente, ingenuamente, inocentemente.

fondness | 'fɒndnɪs | *s.i.* **1** cariño, afecto, ternura. **2** afición, interés, inclinación.

fondue | 'fɒndjuː | *s.c.* e *i.* GAST. queso derretido, flan de queso.

font | fɒnt | *s.c.* **1** pila bautismal, pila de agua bendita. **2** depósito de una lámpara de aceite. **3** fuente, origen: *the font of all problems = el origen de todos los problemas.* **4** fuente, fundición (de tipos de imprenta). **5** INF. familia de caracteres de un tipo específico.

food | fuːd | *s.i.* **1** alimento, comida, manjar, vianda. **2** pasto. **3** **[– of]** pábulo, pasto, materia, alimento (intelectual). || *s.c.* e *i.* **4** alimentos, víveres, manjar: *baby foods = alimentos infantiles.* || **5 to be off one's –,** estar inapetente, tener pocas ganas de comer. **6 – for thought,** materia de reflexión, materia para pensar. **7 – poisoning,** intoxicación alimenticia, gastroenteritis, botulismo. **8 – value,** valor nutritivo, sustancia nutritiva.

food-mixer | 'fuːdmɪksər | *s.c.* batidora.

foodstuffs | 'fuːdstʌfs | *s.c.* e *i.* (eneralmente *pl.*) producto alimenticio, comida, víveres.

fool | fuːl | *s.c.* **1** tonto, idiota, necio, estúpido, imbécil, bobo. **2** **[– for]** loco por, enloquecido por (algo, alguien). **3** bufón, payaso (en el teatro, la corte). || *s.c.* e *i.* **4** (brit.) compota con crema (postre). || *v.t.* **5** engañar, embaucar. || *v.i.* **6** bromear, hacer el bobo. **7** jugar, juguetear (con algo peligroso). || *adj.* **8** (EE.UU.) estúpido, insensato, loco, imbécil. || **9 a fool's errand,** una empresa descabellada, una misión imposible. **10 any –,** nadie en absoluto. **11 to act/play the –,** hacer el tonto, comportarse como un niño. **12 to be nobody's –,** no tener un pelo de tonto, no dejarse engañar. **13 to – about/around,** perder el tiempo de forma estúpida, a lo tonto. **14 to – around with,** tontear con, estar liado con (personas casadas). **15 to – away,** malgastar, despilfarrar (tiempo, dinero). **16 to make a – of oneself,** hacer el ridículo, ponerse en ridículo. **17 to make a – of someone,** poner a alguien en ridículo, engañar a alguien. **18** (brit.) **(the) more – you,** más tonto eres. **19 no fooling,** sin bromas.

foolery | 'fuːlərɪ | *s.c.* e *i.* tontería, estupidez, bufonada.

foolhardiness | 'fuːlhɑːdɪnɪs | *s.i.* temeridad.

foolhardy | 'fuːlhɑːdɪ | *adj.* aventurado, arriesgado, temerario.

foolish | ’fu:lɪʃ | *adj.* descabellado, estúpido, tonto, disparatado, absurdo ridículo.
foolishly | ’fu:lɪʃlɪ | *adv.* tontamente, bobamente, estúpidamente.
foolishness | ’fu:lɪʃnɪs | *s.i.* estupidez, ridiculez, tontería, disparate, simpleza.
foolproof | ’fu:lpru:f | *adj.* **1** infalible, seguro: *a foolproof plan = un plan infalible.* **2** TEC. a prueba de impericia, a prueba de bomba. **3** fácil de entender, fácil de usar.
foolscap | ’fu:lskæp | *s.i.* **1** hoja de papel de tamaño de un folio. || *s.c.* | ’fulzkæp | **2** capirote, gorro de payaso, gorro de bufón (con campanillas en las puntas).
foot | fut | (*pl.* **feet**) *s.c.* **1** pie, pata. **2** pie, parte inferior, parte baja (de escalera, página, etc.). **3** pie (medida de longitud equivalente a 30.48 cm). **4** peal, pie (de calcetín, media). **5** LIT. pie, medida básica de ritmo. **6** MEC. prensatelas, pisacosturas (en máquinas de coser). **7** sedimento (de petróleo refinado). || *adj.* **8** de a pie, de infantería. || *v.i.* **9** caminar, ir a pie. **10** bailar. || *v.t.* **11** hacer a pie, ir andando (un trayecto). **12** pagar (una factura). **13** sumar una columna de cifras. || **14** *at your feet = encantado, a sus pies.* **15 to be on one's feet,** estar en pie, no parar de trabajar; estar bien de salud. **16 to be rushed off one's feet,** V. **rush. 17 to be under one's feet,** estar en medio, estorbar a alguien. **18 to drag one's feet,** V. **drag. 19 to fall on one's feet,** V. **fall. 20 feet of clay,** V. **clay. 21 fleet of –,** (lit.) de pies alados, alígero. **22 – brake,** MEC. freno de pie. **23 to get a – in the door,** estar en una situación de favor, tener puertas abiertas, tener cierta influencia, abrir brecha. **24 to get/rise to one's feet,** ponerse en pie, levantarse. **25 to have a – in both camps,** nadar entre dos aguas. **26 to have a – in the grave,** V. **grave. 27 to have /keep both feet on the ground,** ser realista, tener los pies en el suelo. **28 to have cold feet,** V. **cold. 29 to keep on one's feet,** mantenerse en pie, no tambalearse. **30 my –!,** ¡tonterías!, ¡qué disparate!, ¡no lo creo! **31 on –,** a pie, caminando. **32 to put a – wrong,** (brit.) cometer errores, meter la pata, hacer las cosas mal. **33 to put one's best – forward,** esmerarse, esforzarse, hacer lo posible por causar una buena impresión. **34 to put one's feet down,** (fig.) no ceder, adoptar una actitud firme. **35 to put one's feet up,** descansar con los pies apoyados en alto. **36** (brit.) **to put one's – in it/** (EE.UU.) **to put one's – in one's mouth,** meter la pata. **37 to set – in a place,** entrar en, poner pie en un lugar. **38 to stand on one's own (two) feet,** V. **stand. 39 to start off on the wrong –,** levantarse con el pie izquierdo, empezar mal. **40 to sweep someone off their feet,** enamorar perdidamente a alguien, volver loco a alguien. **41 to tide/bind someone hand and –,** V. **hand. 42 under –,** V. **under.**
foot-and-mouth disease | ’futən’mauθ dɪ’zi:z | *s.i.* fiebre aftosa, glosopeda.
football | ’futbɔ:l | *s.i.* **1** DEP. balompié, fútbol. **2** rugby. **3** fútbol americano. || *s.c.* **4** balón de fútbol. **5** pasatiempo, diversión, devaneo (una forma de iniciar una discusión generalmente política). || **6 – pool,** quiniela.
footballer | ’futbɔ:lər | *s.c.* DEP. futbolista.
footboard | ’futbɔ:d | *s.sing.* estribo, plataforma (para colocar los pies el cochero). **2** pie de cama, barandilla pie de cama.
footbridge | ’futbrɪdʒ | *s.c.* puente peatonal, pasarela.
footed | ’futɪd | *adj.* (en combinación con otra palabra). **1** de... patas, de... pies: *four-footed = de cuatro patas; cuadrúpedo.*
footfall | ’futfɔ:l | *s.c.* pisada, paso (sonido).
foothill | ’futhɪl | *s.c.* estribaciones, colina (en la base de grandes montañas).
footing | ’futɪŋ | *s.i.* **1** pie, balance, emplazamiento firme del pie, equilibrio; suelo, piso. **2** base, fundamento, nivel, términos, posición: *on equal footing = en términos de igualdad.* **3** cimientos, zarpa (de un edificio). **4** suma de una columna de cifras.
footlights | futlaɪts | *s.pl.* **1** candilejas, luces del proscenio. **2** (fig.) teatro, tablas.
footling | ’fu:tlɪŋ | *adj.* (arc. y desp.) nimio (excusa o similar).
footloose | ’futlu:s | *adj.* **1** sin obligaciones, libre de ir a cualquier parte. || **2 – and fancy-free,** libre como el viento, sin trabas.
footman | ’futmən | *s.c.* (*pl.* **footmen**) **1** mayordomo, criado, sirviente. **2** (arc.) soldado de infantería. **3** (arc.) peatón, caminante.
footmark | ’futmɑ:k | *s.c.* huella (de pisada).
footnote | ’futnəut | *s.c.* **1** nota a pie de página. **2** comentario adicional, información adicional. **3** detalle, acontecimiento posterior (a otro más importante). || *v.t.* **4** poner notas a pie de página. **5** añadir un comentario.
footpath | ’futpɑ:θ | *s.c.* sendero, camino, vereda.
footplate | ’futpleɪt | *s.c.* plataforma del maquinista (en trenes antiguos).
footprint | ’fut,prɪnt | *s.c.* (generalmente *pl.*) **1** huella, pisada, rastro.
footsie | ’futsɪ | **to play – with,** (fam.) flirtear con (a escondidas).
footslogging | ’futslɔgɪŋ | *s.i.* acción de patear las calles.
footsore | ’futsɔ: | *adj.* pies cansados, hinchados y doloridos.
footstep | ’futstep | *s.c.* **1** pisada, paso (sonido). **2** paso (longitud). **3** huella, pisada, rastro. || **4 to follow in the footsteps of,** seguir las huellas, seguir los pasos de (un predecesor).
footstool | ’futstu:l | *s.c.* escabel.
footway | ’futweɪ | *s.c.* vereda, caminito.
footwear | ’futweər | *s.i.* calzado.
footwork | ’futwə:k | *s.i.* **1** DEP. juego de pies, de piernas (boxeo, baile). **2** manejo, manipulación (de una situación).
fop | fɔp | *s.c.* (desp.) dandi, petimetre, mequetrefe.
foppish | fɒpɪʃ | *adj.* emperifollado, afectado en el vestir, presumido.
for | fɔ:r | | fər | *prep.* **1** para (destinado a): *this letter is for you = esta carta es para ti.* **2** para (una finalidad): *a liquid for cleaning ovens = un líquido para limpiar hornos.* **3** por, para (ayudar, beneficiar, mejorar una condición): *shall I open the door for you? = ¿te abro la puerta?; give him an aspirin for his headache = dale una aspirina para el dolor de cabeza.* **4** por, a causa de, debido a, con motivo de: *I congratulated her for the results = la felicité por los resultados.* **5** para, con ocasión de (una fecha): *invited for her birthday = invitados para su cumpleaños.* **6** para, por, durante (un tiempo, un espacio): *on holidays for 2 weeks = de vacaciones durante 2 semanas; we walked for miles = caminamos muchas millas.* **7** por, para, debido a, por lo que respecta a, por parte de: *not nice for a young boy to behave like that = no está bien que un joven se comporte así; Spain is famous for its oranges = España es famosa por sus naranjas.* **8** para, con el fin de (conseguir algo): *for details, write to personnel = para (obtener) más detalles, escriba al departamento de personal.* **9** por (una cantidad, un precio): *for $ 8 = por 8 dólares.* **10** por, como (representante de): *don't take me for an idiot = no me tomes por idiota.* **11** por, de, (como signo de, en representación de): *an MP for Bristol = un diputado por Bristol.* **12** por, a favor de, en defensa de, de acuerdo con: *are you for the new laws? = ¿estás a favor de las nuevas leyes?* **13** para, hacia, en dirección a: *we are leaving for Greece tomorrow = salimos hacia Grecia mañana.* **14** [*comp.* **–**] por, después de, como resultado de, a causa de: *you'll feel all the better for a few minutes rest = te sentirás mejor después de descansar unos minutos.* **15** para, considerando: *too hot for Spring = demasiado caluroso para ser primavera.* **16** [**– each/every +** número] por (para indicar correlación, correspondencia): *for every point you get $ 4 = por cada punto te dan 4 dólares.* **17** [**–** *s./pron./inf.* **+ to**] que, para que, de que: *it is necessary for him to come = es necesario que venga él; for a clever boy to cheat is incredible = el que un chico inteligente haga trampas es increíble.* || *conj.* **18** (form.) porque, ya que, puesto que: *I felt tired for I'd worked too hard = me sentía cansada ya que había trabajado demasiado.* || *prefijo.* **19** completamente, excesivamente (con efectos destructivos): *forworn = completamente destrozado.* || **20 free on rail,** COM. cargado y transportado en tren

libre de pagos adicionales (un producto). || **21 as –,** V. **as. 22 to be all –,** estar totalmente a favor de. **23 to be in – it,** (fam.) estar a punto de armarla, ser inevitable meterse en líos. **24 except –,** V. **except. 25 – a living,** para ganarse la vida. **26 – all,** V. **all. 27 – ever and a day,** por siempre jamás. **28 – one thing ...,** en primer lugar... **29 – example,** V. **example. 30 – instance,** V. **instance. 31 – the last/first time,** por primera o última vez. **32 that's... – you,** (desp.) típico de..., ese es el problema de...: *not even a letter, that's friends for you! = ni una carta, ¡ese es el problema de tener amigos!*

forage | fɒrɪdʒ | *s.i.* **1** forraje. **2** forrajeo, búsqueda de forraje. || *v.i.* **3** [– *adv./prep.*] forrajear, buscar forraje, buscar provisiones. **4** buscar concienzudamente, afanosamente.

foray | fɒreɪ | *s.c.* **1** incursión, razzia (por un pequeño grupo, para minar al enemigo). **2** aventura, incursión, intento inicial. || **3 [– (into)]** saquear, cometer actos de pillaje.

forbade | fə'bæd | *pret.* de **forbid.**

forbear | fɔː'beər | *v.t.* e *i. irr. pret.* **forbore,** *p.p.* **forborn. 1 [to – from +** *inf.***]/[to – to +** *ger.***]** contenerse, resistirse, abstenerse de, renunciar a. || *s.c.* **2** (EE.UU.) variante de **forebear,** (form.) progenitor, antecesor.

forbearance | fɔː'beərəns | *s.i.* **1** paciencia, dominio de uno mismo. **2** clemencia, indulgencia, amabilidad.

forbearing | fɔː'beərɪŋ | *adj.* paciente, indulgente, condescendiente.

forbid | fə'bɪd | *v.irr.pret.* **forbade,** *p.p.* **forbidden,** *t.* **1** prohibir (por ley). **2** prohibir, no permitir. **3** impedir, obstruir, obstaculizar, hacer imposible. || **4 God –!/Heaven –!,** Dios no lo quiera, no lo permita Dios.

forbidden | fə'bɪdn | *pret.* de **forbid.** || *adj.* **1** prohibido, vedado, ilícito (por ley, orden, regla). || **2 – ground/– territory,** terreno prohibido, tabú. **3 – fruit,** (fig.) fruta prohibida (cualquier cosa).

forbidding | fə'bɪdɪŋ | *adj.* **1** poco amistoso, desagradable, siniestro, repulsivo, aborrecible (de apariencia). **2** amenazante, formidable: *forbidding mountain = una montaña formidable.*

forbiddingly | fə'bɪdɪŋlɪ | *adv.* amenazantemente; siniestramente.

forbore | fɔː'bɔː | *pret.* de **forbear.**

force | fɔːs | *s.i.* **1** fuerza, energía, potencia, vigor. **2** fuerza, violencia. **3** fuerza, peso, influencia (de un argumento). || *s.c.* **4** influencia, fuerza, poder. **5** MIL. cuerpo, fuerza. **6** MIL. *pl.* el ejército, las fuerzas armadas. || *s.c.* e *i.* **7** FIS. fuerza. || *v.t.* **8 [to – on/upon/to]** forzar a, obligar a, coaccionar a, coercer a. **9** forzar, violentar (algo). **10** presionar (sobre un proceso). **11** forzar, aparentar, disimular (una sonrisa, opinión). **12** AGR. acelerar la maduración, hacer madurar a la fuerza (por calor). || **13 by – of circumstances,** debido a las circunstancias. **14 by – of habit,** por rutina, por la fuerza de la costumbre. **15 to – an entry/to – one's way,** entrar por la fuerza, abrirse paso a la fuerza. **16 to – back,** rechazar, hacer retroceder. **17 to – oneself to do something,** esforzarse enormemente por hacer algo, hacer un gran esfuerzo para hacer algo. **18 to – someone's hand,** obligar a obrar o revelar planes prematuramente, (fig.) hacer cantar a alguien. **19 to – something from/out of somebody,** lograr algo de alguien por la fuerza, sacar a alguien algo por la fuerza. **20 to – something on/ upon somebody,** imponer algo a alguien. **21 in –,** en gran número, en gran cantidad. **22** DER. **in/into –,** vigente, en vigor. **23 to join/combine forces with,** unir fuerzas con, aliarse con.

forced | fɔːst | *adj.* **1** forzoso, obligatorio. **2** falso forzado, fingido, afectado.

force-feed | 'fɔːsfiːd | *v.t.* alimentar forzadamente.

forceful | 'fɔːsful | *adv.* vigoroso, enérgico.

forcefully | 'fɔːsfəlɪ | *adv.* vigorosamente, enérgicamente.

forcefulness | 'fɔːsflnɪs | *s.i.* energía, temperamento vigoroso.

forceps | fɔːseps | *s.pl.* **1** MED. forceps. **2** tenacillas, pinzas. **3** ZOOL. tenacillas (en el abdomen de ciertos insectos).

forcible | 'fɔːsəbl | *adj.* **1** forzoso, por la fuerza, a la fuerza. **2** potente, vigoroso, poderoso, enérgico (tono de voz).

forcibly | 'fɔːsəblɪ | *adv.* enérgicamente, a la fuerza, violentamente.

ford | fɔːd | *s.c.* **1** vado (de río). || *v.t.* **2** vadear, atravesar un vado.

fore | fɔː | *adv.* **1** hacia delante, en la parte delantera. **2** MAR. a proa. || *adj.* **3** delantero, anterior. **4** MAR. de proa, proel. || *s.c.* **5** frente, delantera, cabeza (de vehículo, animal). **6** proa. || **7 to come to the –,** empezar a sobresalir, a destacar, estar en primer plano, en lugar destacado. **8 – and aft,** de proa a popa.

forearm | fɔːr'ɑːm | *s.c.* antebrazo.

forebode | fɔː'bəud | *v.t.* anunciar, presagiar, predecir, tener una premonición, presentir.

foreboding | fɔː'bəudɪŋ | *s.c.* e *i.* **1** premonición, presagio, corazonada. || *adj.* **2** agorero.

forecast | 'fɔːkɑːst | *v.irr.pret.* y *p.p.* **forecast** o **forecasted,** *t.* **1** pronosticar, predecir. || *s.c.* **2** pronóstico, presagio.

forecastle | 'fəuksl | *s.c.* castillo de proa.

foreclose | fɔː'kləuz | *v.t.* e *i.* DER. ejecutar (una hipoteca), privar del derecho de redimir una hipoteca.

forecourt | 'fɔːkɔːt | *s.c.* ARQ. pórtico (de un hotel o similar).

forefather | 'fɔːˌfɑːðər | *s.c.* (generalmente *pl.*) antecesor, antepasado.

forefinger | 'fɔːfɪŋgər | *s.c.* dedo índice.

forefront | 'fɔːfrʌnt | *s.sing.* **[the – of]** la vanguardia de, la primera línea de, el primer plano de.

foregoing | fɔ'gəuɪŋ | *adj.* **1** anterior, previo, precedente. || *s.c.* (generalmente *sing.*) **2** lo anterior, lo previo, lo que precede.

foregone | fɔː'gɒn | *p.p.* de **forego.** || *adj.* **1** previo, anterior, pasado. || **2 a – conclusion,** una conclusión previa, segura, sacada de antemano.

foreground | 'fɔgraund | *s.sing.* **1** primer plano, primer término, parte anterior (de un cuadro, fotografía, etc.). || **2** (fig.) **to be in the –,** estar en primer plano, ser el centro de atención, estar en el candelero.

forehand | 'fɔːhænd | *s.c.* **1** DEP. directo, derechazo (tenis, frontón). **2** (arc.) ventaja. || *adj.* **3** DEP. directo, derechazo. || *adv.* **4** directo.

forehead | 'fɔrɪd | *s.c.* frente (parte de la cara).

foreign | 'fɒrin | *adj.* **1** extranjero, exterior (ciudadano, ciudad, moneda, etc.): *Foreign Minister = ministro de Asuntos Exteriores,* extraño, ajeno, no natural, raro (en una persona). **3** (form.) extraño, exterior, externo, anormal: *a foreign body = un cuerpo extraño.*

foreigner | 'fɒrɪnər | *s.c.* extranjero.

foreknowledge | fɔː'nɒlɪdʒ | *s.i.* clarividencia, presciencia.

foreland | 'fɔːlənd | *s.c.* GEOG. cabo, punta, promontorio.

foreleg | 'fɔːleg | *s.c.* pata delantera (de un animal).

forelock | 'fɔːlɔk | *s.c.* mechón del flequillo (pelo).

foreman | 'fɔːmən | (*pl.* **foremen**) *s.c.* **1** capataz, encargado, maestro de obras. **2** DER. presidente del jurado.

foremost | 'fɔːməust | *adj.* **1 [the –]** el más importante, el principal, el que más sobresale. **2** primero, delantero. || *adv.* **3** en primer lugar.

forensic | fə'rensɪk | *adj.* DER. forense: *forensic medicine = medicina forense.*

foreordain | ˌfɔːrɔː'deɪn | *v.t.* (form.) REL. predestinar; preordinar.

forepart | 'fɔːpɑːt | *s.c.* **[– (of)]** (form.) parte delantera (especialmente de animales).

foreplay | 'fɔːpleɪ | *s.i.* muestras de cariño antes del acto sexual.

forerunner | 'fɔːˌrʌnər | *s.c.* **1** presagio. **2** precursor, predecesor, antecesor.

foresee | fɔː'siː | *v.irr.* [*pret.* **foresaw,** *p.p.* **foreseen**] *t.* predecir, prever.

foreseeable | fɔː'siːəbəl | *adj.* **1** previsible, probable. || **2 in the – future,** en el futuro próximo, hasta donde se puede ver, hasta donde se alcanza.

foreshadow | fɔː'ʃædəu | *v.t.* (lit.) anunciar, presagiar, prefigurar, prever.

foreshore | 'fɔːʃɔː | *s.c.* playa entre pleamar y bajamar.

foreshorten | fɔː'ʃɔːtn | *v.t.* **1** dibujar un escorzo, escorzar. **2** reducir, condensar, escorzar (objetos).

foresight | 'fɔːsaɪt | *s.i.* previsión, prudencia.

foreskin | 'fɔːskɪn | *s.c.* ANAT. prepucio.

forest | 'fɒrɪst | *s.c.* e *i.* **1** bosque, monte: *a dense forest = una selva.* **2** (fig.) montón, masa, bosque: *a forest of tall buildings = un bosque de altos edificios.* **3** forestal. || *v.t.* **4** plantar árboles, arbolar.

forestal | fɔː'stɔːl | *adj.* forestal.

forestall | fɔː'stɔːl | *v.t.* **1** prevenir, impedir, tomar medidas de precaución. **2** interceptar, anticiparse a (un plan). **3** acaparar, hacer acopio de (bienes para que suban de precio).

forester | 'fɔrɪstər | *s.c.* **1** guardabosques. **2** habitantes del bosque. **3** especie de polilla tropical.

forestry | 'fɔrɪstrɪ | *s.i.* **1** silvicultura, ciencia forestal. **2** terreno boscoso, terreno poblado de árboles.

foretaste | fɔː'teɪst | *s.c.* muestra, anticipo.

foretell | fɔː'tel | *v.irr.* [*pret.* y *p.p.* **foretold**] *t.* predecir, presagiar, vaticinar, adivinar, profetizar.

forethought | 'fɔːðɔːt | *s.i.* previsión, prevención, prudencia, premeditación.

forewarn | fɔː'wɔːn | *v.t.* **1 [to – of/against/about]** advertir de, prevenir sobre, precaver contra. || **2 forewarned is forearmed,** hombre precavido vale por dos.

foreword | 'fɔːwəːd | *s.c.* prólogo, introducción, prefacio, preámbulo, exordio, proemio.

forfeit | 'fɔːfɪt | *s.c.* **1** penalización, multa, precio. **2** pérdida, confiscación, castigo. **3** prenda. **4** *pl.* juego de las prendas. || *v.t.* **5** confiscar, perder como castigo (una cantidad, un derecho). || *adj.* **6** perdido, enajenado (por error, delito u ofensa).

forfeiture | 'fɔːfɪtʃər | *s.i.* **[– of]** pérdida, decomiso, prenda, multa de.

forgave | fə'geɪv | *pret.* de **forgive.**

forge | fɔːdʒ | *v.t.* **1** falsificar, falsear. **2** fraguar, forjar. **3** (fig.) fraguar, forjar, formar, inventar. || *v.i.* **4 [to – ahead]** moverse con ímpetu hacia adelante, avanzar con firmeza, adelantarse. || *s.c.* **6** fragua, forja. **7** fundición.

forger | 'fɔːdʒər | *s.c.* falsificador, falseador, falsario.

forgery | 'fɔːdʒərɪ | *s.c.* e *i.* falsificación (de cuadros, moneda, documentos).

forget | fə'get | *v.irr.pret.* **forgot,** p.p. **forgotten.** *t.* **1 [to – wh-/about]** olvidar, abandonar (por negligencia). **2 [to – *inf.*]** olvidarse de, dejar de: *I forgot what it was = olvidé que era; don't forget to close = no olvides/dejes de cerrar.* **3 [to – (that)]** olvidarse(le) a uno (que): *I forgot (that) he was coming = se me olvidó que venía (él).* || *v.i.* **4** olvidarse, no recordar. || **5 to – about,** descuidar, olvidarse de. **6 – it!,** déjalo, no te preocupes, no lo pienses más. **7 to – oneself,** perder los estribos, propasarse, extralimitarse; olvidarse de uno mismo.

forgetful | fə'getful | *adj.* **1** olvidadizo, desmemoriado, despistado. **2** poco atento, negligente, descuidado.

forgetfulness | fə'getfʊnɪs | *s.i.* olvido, descuido, despiste, falta de memoria.

forget-me-not | fə'getmɪnɔt | *s.c.* BOT. nomeolvides.

forgettable | fə'getəbl | *adj.* corriente, nada especial.

forgivable | fə'gɪvəbl | *adj.* disculpable, perdonable.

forgivably | fə'gɪvəblɪ | *adv.* disculpablemente.

forgive | fə'gɪv | *v.t.* e *irr.pret.* **forgave,** *p.p.* **forgiven. 1 [to – for]** perdonar (faltas, errores). **2** eximir, perdonar (deudas).

forgiven | fə'gɪvn | *p.p.* de **forgive.**

forgiveness | fəxgɪvnɪs | *s.i.* perdón, misericordia, indulgencia, clemencia.

forgiving | fə'gɪvɪŋ | *adj.* indulgente, misericordioso, clemente.

forgo o **forego** | fɔː'gəʊ | | fɔː'gəʊ | *v.t. irr. pret.* **forment,** *p.p.* **forgone. 1** renunciar a, privarse de. **2** desperdiciar, perder.

forgot | fə'gɔt | *pret.* de **forget.**

forgotten | fə'gɔtn | *p.p.* de **forget.**

fork | fɔːk | *s.c.* **1** tenedor. **2** horca, horquilla, bieldo (para labores de jardinería, del campo, etc.). **3** ramificación, bifurcación (de un río, carretera). **4** horqueta, ramificación, horcadura (de un árbol). **5** *pl.* MEC. horquilla (de bicicleta). || *v.t.* **6** trabajar con horca. || *v.i.* **7** bifurcarse, ramificarse. **8 [– *adv./prep.*]** tomar una bifurcación: *fork right at the lights = tuerce a la derecha en el semáforo.* || **9** (fam.) **to – something out,** desembolsar, aflojar, soltar (dinero). **10 to – up,** pagar de mala gana.

forked | fɔːkt | *adj.* **1** bífido. **2** bifurcado, ahorquillado. || **3 a – lightning,** rayo en zig-zag. **4 to speak with a – tongue,** tener una lengua viperina.

fork-lift truck | ˌfɔːklɪft'trʌk | *s.c.* carretilla elevadora.

forlorn | fə'lɔːn | *adj.* **1** (form.) desamparado, desgraciado, triste (persona). **2** abandonado, desierto: *a forlorn place = un lugar desierto.* **3** desesperado, vano, inútil: *a forlorn effort = un esfuerzo vano.*

forlornly | fə'lɔːnlɪ | *adv.* tristemente, desgraciadamente; con total desamparo.

form | fɔːm | *s.c.* **1** forma, sistema, tipo, clase. **2** formulario, hoja de inscripción, solicitud. **3** forma (gramatical). **4** (brit.) curso: *4th form = cuarto curso.* **5** forma, figura. **6** banqueta, taburete, banquillo. || *s.i.* **7** forma, estructura (de una obra de arte, literaria). **8** forma, estado físico, estado anímico. **9 [the –]** el procedimiento, la costumbre, la fórmula. **10** (arc.) educación, comportamiento. || *v.t.* e *i.* **11** formar, adiestrar, educar. **12** formar, desarrollar (hábitos, costumbres). **13** surgir, aparecer, formarse. || *v.t.* **14** formar, componer: *add an "s" to form the plural = añade una "s" para formar el plural.* **15** constituir, integrar, formar parte de. **16** organizar, formar, hacer (un equipo, una fila). || **17 a matter of –,** pura fórmula. **18 to fill in/out a –,** rellenar una solicitud/un formulario. **19 in any shape or –,** de ningún modo, de ninguna clase, de ningún tipo. **20 in great –,** muy animado. **21 off –,** desenfrenado, en baja forma. **22 on –,** en forma (física). **23 to take the – of,** mostrarse, manifestarse: *salmonella takes the form of... = la salmonela se manifiesta con...* **24 true to –,** como de costumbre, típico.

formal | 'fɔːml | *adj.* **1** formal, serio, correcto (lenguaje). **2** ceremonioso, solemne (comportamiento). **3** elegante, de etiqueta (ropa). **4** oficial, técnica: *a formal visit = una visita oficial.* **5** oficial (educación). **6** regular (de forma). **7** aparente, externo.

formaldehyde | fɔː'mældɪhaɪd | *s.i.* QUIM. formaldehído, aldehído fórmico.

formalism | 'fɔːməlɪzəm | *s.i.* ART. formalismo.

formalist | 'fɔːməlɪst | *s.c.* ART. formalista.

formality | fɔː'mælətɪ | *s.i.* **1** convencionalismo, formalidad, ceremoniosidad. || *s.c.* **2** legalismo, formalidad. **3** convencionalismo, formalismo.

formalize | 'fɔːməlaɪz | (también **formalise**) *v.t.* dar forma, concretar (ideas, planes, proyectos, etc.).

formally | 'fɔːməlɪ | *adv.* **1** formalmente, oficialmente. **2** elegantemente. **3** ceremoniosamente. **4** regularmente.

format | 'fɔːmæt | *s.c.* **1** formato, tamaño, forma (de un libro, revista). **2** TV. estructura general, plan. || *v.t.* **3** INF. formatear (diskettes, datos).

formation | fɔː'meɪʃn | *s.i.* formación, establecimiento, desarrollo (de hábitos, ideas). || *s.c.* e *i.* **2** orden, forma (de batalla, vuelo). **3** GEOL. formación, estructura.

formative | 'fɔːmətɪv | *adj.* **1** formativo. **2** GRAM. flexional, formante.

former | 'fɔːmər | *adj.* **1** previo, anterior. || *s.c.* **2 [the –]** el primero (de dos personas, cosas, etc., mencionadas): *I prefer the former = prefiero el primero (al segundo).* || **3 his – self,** el que siempre fue.

formerly | 'fɔːməlɪ | *adv.* antes, con anterioridad, previamente.

formic | 'fɔːmɪk | *adj.* QUIM. fórmico.

formidable | 'fɔːmɪdəbl | *adj.* **1** formidable, impresionante, asombroso, aterrador. **2** temible. **3** extremadamente difícil.

formidably | 'fɔːmɪdəblɪ | *adv.* formidablemente, impresionantemente, asombrosamente.

formless | 'fɔːmlɪs | *adj.* **1** informe, deforme. **2** (desp.) desordenado, desorganizado, nebuloso.

formula | 'fɔːmjʊlə | (*pl.* **formulas** o **formulae**) *s.c.* **1 [– (for)]** QUIM. fórmula. **2 [– (for)]** receta, fórmula (de cocina, de un preparado). **3** método, fórmula, plan, cliché. **4** (EE UU.) papilla. || *s.i.* **5 [– número]** coche de carreras (Fórmula 1); carrera de coches (de Fórmula 1).

formulaic | ˌfɔːmjʊ'leɪɪk | *adj.* formulista.

formulate | 'fɔːmjʊleɪt | *v.t.* **1** formular, expresar con exactitud (una idea, teoría, etc.). **2** inventar, concebir, elaborar (un plan, sugerencia, etc.).

formulation | fɔːmjʊ'leɪʃn | *s.c.* e *i.* **1** formulación, expresión exacta. **2** elaboración (de un plan, sugerencia, etc.).

fornicate | 'fɔːnɪkeɪt | *v.i.* **[to – with]** fornicar.

fornication | ˌfɔːnɪ'keɪʃn | *s.i.* fornicación.

forsake | fə'seɪk | *v.t.irr.pret.* **forsook,** *p.p.* **forsaken.** (lit.) **1** abandonar, dejar, renunciar, desertar. **2** repudiar.

forsaken | fə'seɪkən | *p.p.* de **forsake.** || *adj.* **1** abandonado, desamparado, desvalido. **2** repudiado.

forsook | fə'sʊk | *pret.* de **forsake.**

forswear | fɔː'sweər | *v.t.irr.pret.* **forswore,** *p.p.* **forsworn. 1 [to – (*ger.*)]** renunciar a, abandonar definitivamente (posesiones). **2** repudiar, rechazar. **3 [to – oneself]** perjurar, abjurar, jurar en vano.

forsythia | fɔː'saɪθjə | *s.i.* BOT. forsitia.

fort | fɔːt | *s.c.* **1** fuerte, fortaleza, fortín. || **2 to hold the –** (fig.) defender el puesto (asumiendo responsabilidades en ausencia de otros).

forte | 'fɔːtɪ | *s.c.* **1** (generalmente *sing.*) fuerte (algo en lo que una persona sobresale). **2** fuerte, alma (de la espada). || *adj.* **3** MUS. forte, fuerte, alto. || *adv.* **4** fuertemente, con fuerza.

forth | fɔːθ | *adv.* **1 [*v.* –]** (lit.) adelante, hacia adelante (lugar): *going forth into the river = adentrándose en el río.* **2** en adelante, en lo sucesivo: *from that time forth = de ese momento en adelante.* || **3 and so –,** V. **and. 4 back and –,** V. **back. 5 to bring –,** V. **bring. 6 to hold –,** V. **hold.**

forthcoming | ˌfɔːθ'kʌmɪŋ | *adj.* (no *comp.*) **1** próximo, venidero, futuro. **2** [*v.neg.* –] amistoso, comunicativo, amigable. **3** [*v.neg.* –] (fam.) disponible, a disposición de.

forthright | ˌfɔːθraɪt | *adj.* **1** espontáneo, directo, abierto, franco. **2** contundente, enérgico, terminante, rotundo.

forthwith | ˌfɔːθ'wɪθ | *adv.* (lit.) inmediatamente, en el acto, sin dilación.

fortieth | 'fɔːtɪəθ | *adj.num.ord.* **1** cuadragésimo. **2** cuarentavo, cuadragésimo (partitivo). || *s.num.ord.* **3** cuadragésimo.

fortification | ˌfɔːtɪfɪ'keɪʃn | *s.c.* **1** (generalmente *pl.*) fortificación. || *s.i.* **2** fortificación, fortaleza.

fortify | 'fɔːtɪfaɪ | *v.t.* **1** MIL. fortificar, reforzar (lugares). **2** fortalecer (la salud, el ánimo). **3** reafirmar, ratificar, confirmar, reforzar (una opinión, un punto de vista). **4** enriquecer (los alimentos): *fortified with A vitamin = enriquecido con vitamina A.* **5** encabezar, añadir grados (a un vino).

fortissimo | fɔː'tɪsɪməʊ | *adj.* y *adv.* MUS. fortissimo.

fortitude | 'fɔːtɪtjuːd | *s.i.* fortaleza de ánimo, entereza, valor.

fortnight | 'fɔːtnaɪt | *s.c.* quincena, quince días.

fortnightly | 'fɔːtˌnaɪtlɪ | *adj.* **1** quincenal. || *adv.* **2** quincenalmente.

FOR-TRAN | 'fɔːtræn | *s.i.* **1** INF. traductor de fórmulas. **2** lenguaje de programación científico.

fortress | 'fɔːtrɪs | *s.c.* fortaleza, plaza fuerte, fortín.

fortuitous | fɔː'tjuːɪtəs | *adj.* **1** casual, accidental, fortuito. **2** afortunado.

fortuitously | fɔː'tjuːɪtəslɪ | *adv.* casualmente, accidentalmente, fortuitamente.

fortunate | 'fɔːtʃnət | *adj.* **1** afortunado, con suerte, exitoso. **2** propicio, adecuado. || **3 to be –,** tener suerte.

fortunately | 'fɔːtʃnətlɪ | *adv.* afortunadamente, por suerte, felizmente.

fortune | 'fɔːtʃuːn | *s.c.* **1** fortuna, dineral. **2** (generalmente *pl.*) casualidades, azares, avatares. **3** buenaventura, suerte, fortuna, futuro. || *s.i.* **4** suerte, fortuna: *the fortune to live in the south = la suerte de vivir en el sur.* || **5 to be worth a –/to cost a –,** (fig.) valer una fortuna, costar un potosí, valer un ojo de la cara. **6 to marry a –,** (vulg.) dar un braguetazo. **7 to seek one's –,** V. **seek. 8 to tell the –,** echar la buenaventura.

fortuneteller | 'fɔːtʃəntelər | *s.c.* **1** adivina, pitonisa.

forty | 'fɔːtɪ | *adj.num.card.* **1** cuarenta. || *s.num.card.* **2** *pl.* **(the) forties,** (los) años cuarenta. || **3 to be in one's forties,** rondar los cuarenta y tantos.

fortyish | 'fɔːtɪɪʃ | *adj.* cuarentón, de aproximadamente cuarenta años.

forum | 'fɔːrəm | (*pl.* **forums** o **fora**) *s.c.* **1** HIST. foro. **2 [– (for)]** foro, tribuna, lugar de discusión.

forward | 'fɔːwəd | | 'fɔːrwərd | (también **forwards.**) *adv.* **1** adelante, hacia delante, hacia el frente. **2** hacia el final, hacia el fondo. **3** en adelante: *from the 9th forward = del 9 en adelante.* **4** a colación; de relieve. **5** MAR. a proa. || *adj.* **6** (no *comp.*) delantero, frontal. **7** progresivo (un movimiento). **8** de futuro, futuro, con fecha futura (un plan, una venta). **9** adelantado, avanzado (un trabajo, un plan). **10** precoz, adelantado (una persona). **11** progresista, avanzado (de ideas). **12** seguro de sí, confiado. **13** impertinente, descarado, atrevido. **14** ansioso, deseoso, impaciente. **15** MAR. de proa. **16** DEP. delantero. || *s.c.* **17** DEP. delantero. || *v.t.* **18** reenviar, reexpedir (una carta, un paquete). **19** (form.) enviar, expedir. **20** (form.) promover, activar, acelerar. || **21 to bring –,** V. **bring. 22 to look –,** V. **look. 23 to look – to,** V. **look.**

forward-looking | 'fɔːwədlʊkɪŋ | *adj.* avanzado de ideas, esperanzado en el futuro.

forwardness | 'fɔːwədnɪs | *s.i.* **1** adelantamiento. **2** avance, progreso, mejora. **3** atrevimiento, impertinencia, descaro. **4** precocidad, adelanto.

forwards | 'fɔːwədz | *adv.* V. **forward.**

fossil | 'fɒsl | *adj.* **1** fósil. || *s.c.* **2** fósil. **3** (fig.) fósil (persona). || **4 – fuel,** QUIM. energía fósil, petróleo de fósiles.

fosilization | ˌfɒsɪlaɪ'zeɪʃn | *s.i.* fosilización, osificación.

fosilized | 'fɒsɪlaɪz | *adj.* **1** fosilizado. **2** (fig.) fosilizado, anticuado, pasado de moda, carcamal, carroza.

foster | 'fɒstər | *v.t.* **1** adoptar, criar (hijos ajenos). **2** DER. acoger (hijos ajenos). **3** fomentar, promover, alentar. **4** alimentar (esperanzas). || *adj.* **5** acogido, adoptivo. **6** temporal, transitorio. || **7 – parents,** padres adoptivos.

fought | fɔːt | *pret.* y *p.p.* de **fight.**

foul | faʊl | *adj.* **1** molesto, repugnante, pútrido, fétido (olor). **2** grosero, obsceno, ofensivo (lenguaje). **3** brutal, violento, desagradable (carácter). **4** sucio, viciado (aire, agua). **5** tormentoso, desabrido, desapacible: *a foul winter day = un desapacible día de invierno.* **6** vil, cruel, indigno, malvado. **7** MAR. enredado, liado, enmarañado (un cabo, una cadena). **8** obstruido, atascado, bloqueado (un conducto). || *s.c.* **9 [– against/on]** falta, infracción contra. **10** obstrucción. || *v.t.* e *i.* **11** DEP. cometer falta, cometer infracción. **12** MAR. enredar, liar, enmarañar. || *v.t.* **13** (p.u.) manchar, ensuciar, defecar (animales). || **14 by fair means or –,** (lit.) quieras o no, por las buenas o por las malas. **15 to fall – of,** V. **fall. 16 to – out,** DEP. expulsar por faltas. **17 to – up,** desbaratar, frustrar (un plan).

foul-mouthed | 'faʊl'maʊðd | *adj.* (desp.) malhablado, grosero, soez, ordinario.

foul-smelling | 'faʊl'smelɪŋ | *adj.* pestilente, fétido, hediondo, nauseabundo.

foul-up | 'faʊlʌp | *s.c.* (fam.) desbarajuste.

found | faʊnd | *pret.* y *p.p.* de **find.** || *v.t.* **1** fundar, establecer. **2** constituir, instituir, crear, apoyar (con dinero). **3 [to – on/upon** y generalmente *pas.*] basar en, apoyar en, asentar en (un edificio, una opinión). **4** fundir metales, fabricar objetos por fundición.

foundation | faʊn'deɪʃn | *s.i.* **1** fundación, establecimiento, inicio. **2** fundamento, base (de una idea, opinión). || *s.c.* **3** fundación, institución, organización: *the Rockefeller foundation = la Fundación Rockefeller.* **4** *pl.* cimientos. **5** (fig.) fundamento, base: *no foundation in fact = sin fundamento.* || **6 – cream,** base de maquillaje. **7 – stone,** primera piedra, piedra angular. **8 to lay the foundations,** poner los cimientos.

founder | 'faʊndər | *s.c.* **1** fundador. || *v.i.* **2** MAR. (lit.) zozobrar, hundirse. **3** (fig.) fracasar, fallar, malograrse (un plan). **4** quedar inválido, quedar lisiado; caer, tropezar (un animal).

founding | 'faʊndɪŋ | *adj.* **1** fundador, iniciador. || **2 Founding Father,** Padre Fundador (asistente a la Convención Constitucional americana de 1787).

foundling | 'faʊdlɪŋ | *s.c.* (arc.) niño abandonado.

foundry | 'faʊndrɪ | *s.c.* **1** fundición. **2** arte de fundir metales.

fount | faʊnt | s.c. **1** (lit.) fuente, origen. **2** manantial, fuente. **3** TEC. conjunto o familia de letras (en imprenta). || **4 – of wisdom,** fuente de sabiduría.

fountain | 'faʊntɪn | *s.c.* **1** fuente artificial, surtidor. **2** manantial, fuente. **3** chorro, chorretada. **4** depósito de agua. **5** (fig. y lit.) fuente, origen. **6** (lit.) cascada. || **7 – pen,** pluma estilográfica.

fountain-head | ˌfaʊntɪn'hed | *s.c.* **1** manantial, nacimiento de un río. **2** fuente, origen.

four | fɔːr | *s.num.card.* **1** cuatro. **2** equipo de cuatro, juego de cuatro (personas o cosas). **3** bote de cuatro remos. || *adj.* **4** cuatro. || **5 a coach and –,** carruaje (tirado por cuatro caballos). **6 to make up a –,** formar un equipo de cuatro (para el juego). **7 on all fours,** a gatas, a cuatro patas. **8 to scatter to the – winds,** V. **scatter. 9 the – corners of the earth,** el último confín, los confines de la tierra.
four-door | 'fɔː'dɔːr | *adj.* de cuatro puertas: *a four-door car = un coche de cuatro puertas.*
four-engined | 'fɔːr'endʒɪnd | *adj.* cuatrimotor, tetramotor.
four-flusher | 'fɔː'flʌʃər | *s.c.* **1** farolero, fanfarrón (en póquer). **2** pretencioso, jactancioso.
fourfold | 'fɔːˌfəʊld | *adj.* **1** cuádruple. || *adv.* **2** cuatro veces.
four-footed | ˌfɔː'fʊtɪd | *adj.* ZOOL. cuadrúpedo, de cuatro patas.
four-poster | 'fɔːˌpəʊstər | *s.c.* cama de cuatro columnas (para sujetar un dosel).
fourteen | ˌfɔː'tiːn | *num.card.* catorce.
fourteenth | ˌfɔː'tiːnθ | *s.num.ord.* **1** decimocuarto. || *adj.* **2** decimocuarto.
fourth | fɔːθ | *num.ord.* **1** cuarto, cuarta parte. **2** MUS. cuarta. || **3 – dimension,** V. **dimension.** || **4 to make a –,** formar un equipo de cuatro (para juegos de cartas).
fourthly | fɔːθlɪ | *adv.* en cuarto lugar (al enumerar varios puntos, cosas, etc.).
four-wheel drive | ˌfɔːwiːl'draɪv | *s.i.* tracción a las cuatro ruedas, transmisión a las cuatro ruedas.
fowl | faʊl | *s.c.* **1** ave de corral. **2** ave (de caza). || *s.i.* **3** carne de ave de corral. || *v.i.* **4** cazar (aves).
fox | fɒks | *s.c.* **1** zorro, raposa. **2** (fig.) zorro, zorreras, cuco, artero. **3** MAR. cuerda corta, cabo corto. **4** (EE.UU.) vampiresa, mujer seductora, atractiva. || *s.i.* **5** piel de zorro. || *v.t.* **6** confundir, dejar perplejo. **7** despistar, distraer. **8** fermentar (la cerveza). **9** indio algonquino (de Wisconsin). || **10 – club,** cachorro de zorro, zorrillo. || **11 – terrier,** fox terrier (perro de compañía).
foxed | fɒkst | *adj.* **1** manchado, descolorido.
foxglove | 'fɒksglʌv | *s.c.* BOT. dedalera, digital.
foxhole | 'fɒkshəʊl | *s.c.* MIL. trinchera, hoyo de protección (individual).
foxhound | 'fɒkshaʊnd | *s.c.* perro raposero (para la caza del zorro).
foxhunting | 'fɒkshʌntɪŋ | *s.i.* DEP. caza del zorro.
foxtrot | 'fɒkstrɔt | *s.c.* **1** foxtrot (baile, música). **2** trote corto (de caballo). || *v.i.* **3** bailar el foxtrot.
foxy | 'fɒksɪ | *adj.* **1** zorro, astuto, taimado. **2** zorruno (de aspecto): *a foxy look = una mirada zorruna.* **3** rojizo. **4** descolorido, manchado. **5** agrio (bebidas, especialmente el vino). **6** (fam.) atractivo.
foyer | 'fɔɪeɪ | *s.c.* **1** vestíbulo (de hotel, teatro). **2** (EE.UU.) recibidor, vestíbulo (de la casa).

fracas | 'frækɑː | *s.c.* alboroto, disturbio, bronca, jaleo, altercado.
fraction | 'frækʃn | *s.c.* **1** MAT. fracción, quebrado. **2** fragmento, porción, fracción.
fractional | 'frækʃənl | *adj.* **1** MAT. fraccionario, quebrado. **2** minúsculo, insignificante. **3** fragmentado, fraccionado.
fractionally | 'frækʃənəlɪ | *adv.* fraccionadamente.
fractious | 'frækʃəs | *adj.* **1** irritable, malhumorado, quejica, rezongón (especialmente niños o ancianos). **2** díscolo, rebelde, desobediente, indisciplinado.
fracture | 'fræktʃər | *s.c.* **1** MED. fractura, rotura. **2** brecha, grieta, fisura. || *v.t.* e *i.* **3** fracturar, romper. **4** infringir, violar (reglas, restricciones). || **5 compound –,** fractura abierta. **6 simple –,** fractura simple (no manifiesta al exterior).
fragile | 'frædʒaɪl | *adj.* **1** frágil, quebradizo, delicado, rompible. **2** débil, delicado, enfermizo, enclenque. **3** flojo (después de una borrachera).
fragility | frə'dʒɪlɪtɪ | *s.i.* fragilidad, delicadeza.
fragment | 'frægmənt | *s.c.* **1** fragmento, trozo, pedazo, segmento. || *v.t.* e *i.* **2** dividir, fragmentar, hacer añicos, fraccionar.
fragmentary | 'frægməntərɪ | *adj.* fragmentario, incompleto, insuficiente, mutilado.
fragmentation | ˌfrægmen'teɪʃn | *s.i.* fragmentación.
fragmented | fræg'mentɪd | *adj.* fragmentado.
fragrance | 'freɪgrəns | *s.c.* fragancia, perfume, aroma.
fragrant | 'freɪgrənt | *adj.* fragante, aromático, perfumado, oloroso.
frail | freɪl | *adj.* **1** frágil, débil, delicado, endeble, enfermizo. **2** frágil, quebradizo, rompible, delicado. **3** moralmente débil. || *s.c.* **4** cesto de junco (para frutas).
frailty | 'freɪltɪ | *s.i.* **1** fragilidad, debilidad, delicadeza. || *s.c.* **2** debilidad, flaqueza (moral).
frame | freɪm | *s.c.* **1** marco, cerco, bastidor. **2** montura (de gafas). **3** esqueleto, cuerpo, figura. **4** forma (de una persona). **5** cuadro, estructura (de bicicleta). **6** invernadero, vivero cubierto. **7** estructura, sistema. **8** turno (de juego en billar, bolos, etc.). **9** fotograma (en cine). || *v.t.* **10** enmarcar, encuadrar, rodear. **11** formular, redactar, expresar (una ley). **12** (fam.) incriminar falsamente a un inocente. || **13 – of mind,** estado de ánimo.
frame-up | 'freɪmʌp | *s.c.* estratagema, treta, complot (para incriminar a un inocente).
framework | 'freɪmwəːk | *s.c.* **1** TEC. armazón, entramado, esqueleto. **2** (fig.) marco, estructura, sistema: *within the framework of free trade = en el marco del libre comercio.*
franc | frænk | *s.c.* franco (unidad monetaria).
France | frɑːns | *s.* Francia.

franchise | 'fræntʃaɪz | *s.c.* **1** COM. franquicia, permiso. **2** POL. sufragio, derecho de voto.
Franciscan | fræn'sɪskən | *s.c.* **1** franciscano. || *adj.* **2** franciscano.
francophile | 'fræŋkəʊfaɪl | *s.c.* **1** francófilo. || *adj.* **2** francófilo.
francofobe | 'fræŋkəʊfəʊb | *s.c.* **1** francófobo. || *adj.* **2** francófobo.
frank | fræŋk | *adj.* **1** franco, sincero, abierto, ingenuo. **2** claro, evidente, incuestionable, indiscutible. || *v.t.* **3** franquear, enviar gratis, tener o dar franquicia. **4** permitir libertad de movimiento.
frankfurt(er) | 'fræŋkfɒːtər | *s.c.* salchicha ahumada (alemana).
frankincense | 'fræŋkɪnsens | *s.i.* incienso, olíbano.
frankly | fræŋklɪ | *adv.* **1** abiertamente, francamente, sinceramente. **2** honestamente, de verdad.
frankness | 'frænknɪs | *s.i.* franqueza, sinceridad, candor, ingenuidad, llaneza.
frantic | 'fræntɪk | *adj.* **1** frenético, exaltado, enloquecido. **2** desesperado, furioso, violento, perturbado, loco.
frantically | 'fræntɪkəlɪ | *adv.* **1** frenéticamente, desesperadamente. **2** furiosamente.
fraternal | frə'təːnl | *adj.* **1** (lit. y p.u.) fraternal, fraterno. **2** fraternal (sociedad, asociación). **3** BIOL. dicigótico, biovular.
fraternity | frə'təːnɪtɪ | *s.c.* **1** sociedad, asociación (profesional): *the medical fraternity = la asociación médica.* || *s.i.* **2** (EE.UU.) asociación, club estudiantil masculino. **3** (p.u.) fraternidad, hermandad.
fraternization | ˌfrætənaɪ'zeɪʃn | *s.i.* **[– (with)]** confraternización, fraternización.
fraternize | 'frætənaɪz | (también **fraternise**) *v.i.* **1 [to – with]** confraternizar con, fraternizar con, congeniar. **2** (desp.) confraternizar. || **3 to – with the enemy,** confraternizar con el enemigo.
fraticidal | ˌfrætrɪʃsaɪdl | *adj.* fraticida.
fratricide | 'frætrɪsaɪd | *s.c.* **1** fratricida. || *s.i.* **2** fratricidio.
fraud | frɔːd | *s.c.* **1** fraudulencia, engaño, timo. **2** farsante, impostor. || *s.i.* **3** fraude, engaño.
fraudulence | 'frɔːdjʊləns | *s.i.* fraudulencia, fraude.
fraudulent | 'frɔːdjʊlənt | *adj.* fraudulento, engañoso.
fraught | frɔːt | *adj.* **1 [– with]** pleno de, lleno de, cargado de. **2** (fam.) preocupado, pleno de ansiedad.
fray | freɪ | *s.c.* **1** batalla, pelea, riña. || *v.t.* e *i.* **2** deshilachar, deshilar, desgastar, raer (los bordes de una tela). **3** irritar, exacerbar (los ánimos).
frazzle | 'fræzl | *s.i.* **1** agotamiento, cansancio (mental, físico). **2** desgaste, deshilachamiento. || *v.t.* **3** agotar física o mentalmente. || *v.i.* **4** deshilacharse, desgastarse, raerse. || **5 to beat someone to a –,** DEP. ganar fácilmente a uno, derrotar a uno por completo. **6 to be worn to a –,** (fig.) estar rendido de cansancio, estar

completamente agotado. **7 burnt to a –,** totalmente quemada (la comida).
frazzled | fræzld | *adj.* (fam.) **1** desgastado, agotado (persona). **2** quemado, tostado (por el sol).
freak | fri:k | *s.c.* **1** fenómeno, monstruo. **2** anormalidad, rareza, monstruosidad, mutación. **3** casualidad, fenómeno fortuito. **4** tipo extravagante, excéntrico, raro. **5** capricho, antojo. **6** (EE.UU.) hippy, drogadicto. **7** (EE.UU.) entusiasta, fanático, seguidor. || *adj.* **8** engaño, inesperado. || *v.t.* e *i.* **9** reaccionar de forma extraña al ingerir drogas (con alucinaciones, paranoia), (fig.) tener un mal viaje, coger un mal rollo. **10** comportarse irracionalmente, sin control. **11** sorprenderse en extremo.
freakish | 'fri:kɪʃ | *adj.* **1** raro, extraño, irracional. **2** caprichoso, imprevisible, casual.
freakishly | 'fri:kɪslɪ | *adv.* extrañamente, anormalmente.
freaky | 'fri:kɪ | *adj.* (fam.) extraño, anormal.
freckle | 'frekl | *s.c.* (generalmente *pl.*) peca.
freckled | 'frekld | *adj.* pecoso, cubierto de pecas.
Fred, Freddie, Freddy | fred | | fredɪ | | fredɪ | *s.* **1** apelativos familiares en lugar de **Frederick.**
Frederick | 'fredrɪk | *s.* Federico.
free | fri: | *adj.* **1** libre, independiente (hombre, institución o nación). **2** libre, en libertad. **3** libre, sin trabas (elección, acuerdo, prensa, opinión, traducción). **4** (no *comp.*) gratis, gratuito. **5** (no *comp.*) libre (período de tiempo). **6** vacante, libre, desocupado. **7** abierto, libre, no bloqueado (camino, conducto). **8** (no *comp.*) suelto, flojo (ropa, cuerda). **9 [– of/from]** exento de, libre de: *free of charge = libre de cargas.* **10** flexible, gracioso (movimiento). **11 [– with]** generoso, desprendido, derrochador. **13** (no *comp.*) QUIM. puro, no combinado. || *adv.* **14** gratis. **15** sin control, suelto, libre (un animal). **16** sin sujeción, sin fijación (tornillo). || *v.t.* **17 [– from/of]** liberar, libertar, poner en libertad: *free from prison = puesto en libertad.* **18 [– from]** rescatar, salvar de (escombros, pesos). **19 [– *o.* + *inf.*]** dejar en libertad para, en libertad de. **20** desenredar, soltar. **21** eximir, exentar (de cargas, impuestos). || **22 to be – with,** prodigarse, ser generoso. **23 to be – with one's money,** ser un manirroto. **24 to break –,** soltarse, desatarse. **25 feel –!,** ¡adelante!, ¡como si estuvieras en tu casa! **26 – and easy,** despreocupado, informal. **27 – form,** INF. forma libre. **28 – kick,** DEP. tiro libre. **29 – of duty,** COM. libre de derechos de aduana. **30 – on board,** COM. mercancía puesta en el puerto de origen. **31 – speech,** libertad de opinión. **32 – stack,** INF. área libre del stack. **33 – trade,** libre comercio, librecambio. **34 – trader,** librecambista. **35 – will,** libre elección, libre albedrío. **36 to give a – hand,** dar carta blanca, dar plenos poderes. **37 to let someone go –,** poner a alguien en libertad. **38 to make – with,** tomarse libertades, utilizar, tomar algo de otros como si fuera propio.
OBS. Se combina con nombres para formar otros adjetivos tomando el significado de sin, libre de: *error-free = sin, libre de error, trouble-free = sin problema,* etc.
freebie | 'fri:bi: | *s.c.* (fam.) chollo.
freedom | 'fri:dəm | *s.i.* **1** libertad. || *s.c.* **2 [– of/+ *inf.*]** libertad de (prensa, palabra, culto, etc...). **3 [– (from)]** inmunidad, impunidad. **4** desenvoltura, falta de modestia. || **5 to give the – of a city,** nombrar hijo adoptivo (honor concedido a personalidades).
free-fight | 'fri:'faɪt | *s.c.* **1** lucha libre: *free-fight champion = campeón de lucha libre.* **2** refriega, disputa, riña.
free-for-all | 'fri:fərˌɔ:l | *s.c.* (fam.) pelotera, altercado, disturbio, tumulto, alboroto.
freehold | 'fri:həʊld | *s.c.* e *i.* **1** dominio absoluto. || *adj.* **2** dominio absoluto: *freehold property = feudo, propiedad, dominio.* || *adv.* **3** en propiedad: *they bought it freehold = lo tienen en propiedad.*
freelance | 'fri:lɑ:ns | *s.c.* **1** trabajador por cuenta propia, independiente. **2** independiente políticamente (afín a las ideas de un partido, pero no adscrito a éste). || *adj.* **3** independiente. || *adv.* **4** independiente, por cuenta propia: *he worked freelance = trabajó como independiente.* || *v.t.* e *i.* **5** trabajar como independiente, por cuenta propia.
freely | 'fri:lɪ | *adv.* **1** libremente, gustosamente. **2** francamente, espontáneamente. **3** libremente, sin trabas, sin problemas: *freely available = fácil de conseguir.* **4** generosamente, en cantidad: *she spends freely = (ella) gasta en cantidad.*
freeman | 'fri:mən | (*pl.* **freemen**) *s.c.* **1** HIST. hombre libre, ciudadano libre. || **2 – of a city,** hijo adoptivo (de una ciudad).
Freemason | 'fri:ˌmeɪsn | *s.c.* francmasón, masón.
freemasonry | 'fri:ˌmeɪsnrɪ | *s.i.* **1** francmasonería, masonería. **3** (fig.) compañerismo, camaradería, fraternidad, hermandad.
free-standing | ˌfri:s'tændɪŋ | *adj.* sin fijación (muebles independientes).
freestyle | 'fri:staɪl | *s.i.* **1** DEP. libre (estilo específico de natación, esquí, etc.): *100 metre freestyle = 100 metros libres.* **2** DEP. libre, sin reglas (lucha). || *adj.* **3** libre. || *adv.* **4** libre, sin reglas.
freethinker | ˌfri:'θɪŋkər | *s.c.* librepensador.
freethinking | ˌfri:'θɪŋkɪŋ | *s.i.* librepensamiento.
free-way | 'fri:weɪ | *s.c.* (EE.UU.) autopista.
freewheel | ˌfri:wi:l | *v.i.* ir en punto neutro; ir sin dar pedales.
freewheeling | ˌfri:'wi:lɪŋ | *adj.* despreocupado; vivalavirgen.
freeze | fri:z | *v.irr.pret.* **froze,** *p.p.* **frozen** *t.* e *i.* **1** congelar, helar, solidificar: *the pool froze = el estanque se congeló.* **2** bloquear por congelación. **3** helar: *it will freeze tonight = esta noche helará.* **4** estar helado, morirse de frío: *I'm freezing cold = estoy totalmente helado.* **5** congelar, preservar (alimentos por congelación). **6** permanecer completamente inmóvil, parar en seco, paralizarse. || *t.* congelar, fijar, controlar: *salaries were frozen = se congelaron los salarios.* **8** congelar (la imagen en una película). || *s.c.* **9** helada. **10** congelación (de precios, salarios). || **11 deep –,** V. **deep. 12 to – in one's tracks,** quedar paralizado, totalmente inmóvil. **13 to – one's blood,** helársele a uno la sangre. **14 to – over,** congelarse una superficie. **15 to – to death,** morirse de frío. **16 frozen stiff,** tieso de frío, congelado.
freeze-frame | 'fri:zfreɪm | *s.c.* TV. **1** dispositivo de congelación de imagen (especialmente en un vídeo). **2** fotograma (de una película).
freezer | 'fri:zər | *s.c.* congelador.
freightage | freɪtɪdʒ | *s.i.* **1** COM. flete, carga, cargamento. **2** COM. capacidad de carga.
freighter | 'freɪtər | *s.c.* **1** MAR. buque de carga, carguero. **2** AER. avión de carga, avión de transportes pesados.
French | frentʃ | *s.c.* **1** francés (lengua). **2 [the –]** los franceses. || *adj.* **3** francés (nacionalidad). || **4 – bean,** judía verde, habichuela verde, (Am.) vainita. **5 – bread,** pan de barra. **6 – Canadian,** francocanadiense. **7 – door,** ARQ. puerta que da al jardín, puerta vidriera. **8 – dressing,** GAST. vinagreta, salsa de vinagreta, salsa francesa. **9 – fies,** patatas fritas alargadas. **10 – horns,** MUS. corno francés. **11 – loaf,** barra larga de pan. **12 – window,** ARQ. puerta-ventana de dos hojas.
Frenchman | 'frentʃmən | (*pl.* **Frenchmen**) *s.c.* francés (ciudadano).
Frenchwoman | 'frentʃwʊmən | (*pl.* **Frenchwomen**) *s.c.* francesa (ciudadana).
frenetic | frə'netɪk | *adj.* frenético, enloquecido, sobreexcitado.
frenzied | 'frenzɪd | *adj.* **1** frenético, desesperado, exasperado, sobreexcitado: *a frenzied rage = una rabia loca.* **2** enloquecido, histérico (gente, una multitud).
frenzy | 'frenzɪ | *s.c.* e *i.* (generalmente *sing.*) **1** frenesí, locura, desvarío. || *v.t.* **2** enfurecer, volver loco.
frequency | 'fri:kwənsɪ | *s.i.* **1** frecuencia, repetición. || *s.c.* e *i.* **2** MAT. frecuencia. || **3 high –,** ELECTR. alta frecuencia. **4 low –,** ELECTR. baja frecuencia.
frequent | 'fri:kwənt | *adj.* frecuente, repetido, habitual, usual, ordinario. || *v.t.* | fri:'kwənt | **2** frecuentar, visitar a menudo.
frequently | 'fri:kwəntlɪ | *adv.* frecuentemente, repetidamente.
fresco | 'freskəʊ | (*pl.* **frescos** o **frescoes**) *s.c.* e *i.* **1** fresco, pintura al fresco. || *v.t.* **2** pintar al fresco.
fresh | freʃ | *adj.* **1** fresco, natural, reciente (alimentos, flores). **2 [– from]**

(no *comp.*) recién llegado de, reciente. **3** (no *comp.*) dulce, potable (agua). **4** (no *comp.*) nuevo, diferente: *a fresh sheet of paper = una hoja nueva* (de papel). **5** fresco, reciente (recuerdos, memorias). **6** lozana, fresca (la tez). **7** saludable, vigoroso, rejuvenecido, descansado (aspecto). **8** puro (aire). **9** TEC. fuerte (viento). **10** (fam.) fresco, ventoso (tiempo atmosférico). **11 [– (with)]** (fam.) descarado, impertinente. || *adv.* **12** [– *adj.*] recientemente: *fresh baked bread = pan reciente; fresh cut flowers, flores recientemente cortadas.* || *v.t.* e *i.* **13 [to – up]** refrescar. || **14 as – as a daisy,** tan fresco como una rosa. **15 as – as paint,** fresco como una lechuga. **16 to be – out of something,** (EE.UU.) acabarse algo, no quedar nada de algo. **17 to break – ground,** empezar algo nuevo, explorar un campo nuevo.

freshen | 'freʃn | *v.t.* e *i.* **1** refrescar. **2** avivar (el viento). || **3 to – up,** asearse, refrescarse, arreglarse, ponerse atractivo (después de un largo día).

fresher | 'freʃər | *s.c.* (brit. y fam.) estudiante de primer año (en la Universidad).

freshly | freʃlı | *adv.* **1** [– *p.p.*] recientemente, últimamente. **2** descaradamente, con frescura, con impertinencia.

freshman | 'freʃmen | (*pl.* **freshmen**) *s.c.* **1** (brit.) estudiante de primer año (de Universidad o colegio superior). **2** (EE.UU.) estudiante de primer año (de escuela secundaria, Universidad o colegio superior). **3** principiante, novato.

freshness | freʃnıs | *s.i.* **1** frescura, frescor. **2** lozanía, verdor, vigor. **3** (fam.) descaro, impertinencia.

freshwater | 'freʃ,wɔːtər | *adj.* **1** de agua dulce: *freshwater fish = pescado de agua dulce.*

fret | fret | *v.t.* e *i.* **1 [to – (about/over)]** preocuparse, inquietarse (por pequeñeces). **2** corroer(se), raer(se), rasgar(se). || *v.t.* **3** (p.u.) agitar, ondear (el agua). **4** formar surcos (por erosión). **5** decorar con marquetería. || *s.c.* **6** irritación, nerviosismo, inquietud: *in a fret = en estado de irritación.* **7** roce, desgaste, rozadura. **8** traste (en instrumentos de cuerda). **9** greca, calado; decoración en relieve. || **10 to – away one's time,** pasar el tiempo consumiéndose de inquietud.

fretful | 'fretful | *adj.* incómodo, molesto, quejoso, irritable, impaciente.

fretfully | 'fretfulı | *adv.* impacientemente, inquietamente; de mal humor, de mala gana.

fretsaw | 'fretsɔː | *s.c.* sierra de marquetería, sierra de calados.

fretwork | 'fretwəːk | *s.i.* greca, adorno calado o en relieve.

Freudian | frɔıdjən | *adj.* **1** PSIC. freudiano. || **2 – slip,** lapsus.

friable | 'fraıəbl | *adj.* TEC. friable, desmenuzable, terroso (terreno).

friar | 'fraıər | *s.c.* **1** REL. fraile (de las órdenes mendicantes católicas). **2** fray (ante nombres propios).

fricassee | 'frıkəsiː | *s.c.* e *i.* GAST. fricasé; carne estofada.

fricative | 'frıkətıv | *s.c.* FON. **1** fricativa, consonante fricativa. || *adj.* **2** fricativo (sonido).

friction | 'frıkʃn | *s.i.* **1** MED. fricción, rozamiento, roce. **2** MEC. fricción, rozamiento. || *s.c.* e *i.* **3** desavenencia, desacuerdo, falta de armonía, disensión.

Friday | 'fraıdı | *s.c.* **1** viernes. || **2 girl –,** secretaria personal. **3 Good –,** REL. Viernes Santo. **4 man –,** secretario personal, hombre de confianza.

fridge | frıdʒ | *s.c.* (brit. y fam.) frigorífico, nevera, refrigerador.

fried | fraıd | *pret.* y *p.p.* de **fry.** || **2** *adj.* frito.

friend | frend | *s.c.* **1** amigo, compañero. **2 [– of/to]** partidario, aliado (de una causa); consejero, mecenas. **3** MIL. aliado, amigo. **4** gente de paz (en respuesta a un centinela). **5** (desp.) amigo (al mencionar a alguien con alguna particularidad desagradable). **6** REL. cuáquero. || **7 a – in need,** un verdadero amigo. **8 to be close friends (with),** ser amigos íntimos, estar a bien. **9 to be no – to,** no ser partidario de. **10 to have a – at court/to have friends in high places,** tener influencias, tener amistades en altas esferas. **11 to keep close friends (with),** estar en buenas relaciones/en buenos términos (con). **12 to make friends with,** hacer amistades, trabar amistades con. **13 my honourable –,** mi honorable amigo (utilizado en la Cámara de los Lores). **14 my learned –,** mi docto amigo (utilizado en los tribunales de Justicia por los abogados).

friendless | 'frendlıs | *adj.* sin amigos, solitario, desamparado, abandonado.

friendliness | 'frendlınıs | *s.i.* **1** amistad, simpatía, cordialidad, amabilidad. **2 [the –]** lo acogedor.

friendly | 'frendlı | *adj.* **1 [– to/towards]** amistoso, amable, cordial, afable (una persona). **2 [– with]** amigo de, en buenas relaciones con. **3** acogedor, agradable. **4** POL. aliado, amigo. **5** amistoso, cordial (tono de voz, relación). || *s.c.* **6** (brit.) partido amistoso, juego amistoso. || **7 – society,** ECON. (brit.) sociedad de ayuda mutua. **8 to get –,** (fam.) dirigir indirectas.

friendship | 'frendʃıp | *s.i.* **1** amistad, camaradería. || *s.c.* **2** amistad, amigo, camarada. || **3 to strike a –,** entablar una amistad, empezar a ser amigos.

Friesland | 'friːzlənd | *s.* **1** Frisia (región holandesa)

frieze | friːz | *s.c.* **1** ARQ. friso. **2** cenefa, greca.

frig | frıg | **[frigging, frigged] to – about/around,** (vulg.) hacer el gilipollas.

frigate | 'frıgıt | *s.c.* **1** MAR. fragata.

frigging | 'frıgıŋ | *adj.* (vulg.) jodido: *the frigging car, it's not going properly = el jodido coche, no funciona bien.*

fright | fraıt | *s.i.* **1** susto, sobresalto, miedo, terror. || *s.c.* **2** susto, miedo. **3** (fam.) espantajo, esperpento. || **4 to get the – of one's life,** pasar el mayor susto de la vida de uno. || **5 to take – at,** asustarse.

frighten | 'fraıtn | *v.t.* **1** asustar, aterrorizar, espantar, sobresaltar, alarmar. || **2 to be frightened by/of/at,** tener miedo de, estar asustado de. **3 to – away/off,** ahuyentar, espantar. **4 to – into** (*ger.*) forzar con amenazas. **5 to – someone out of** (*ger.*) intimidar a alguien. **6 to – the life/the wits out of somebody,** dar un susto de muerte a alguien.

frightened | 'fraıtnd | *adj.* **1** asustado, atemorizado, con miedo. || **2 to be – (of/*inf.*/that)** temer, tener miedo.

frightening | 'fraıtnıŋ | *adj.* aterrador, espantoso, alarmante.

frightful | 'fraıtful | *adj.* **1** espantoso, horrible, pavoroso. **2** (fam.) espantoso, pésimo, malísimo.

frightfully | 'fraıtfulı | *adv.* **1** espantosamente, terriblemente, tremendamente. **2** (fam.) muy, muchísimo, extremadamente: *I'm frightfully sorry = lo siento en el alma, muchísimo.*

frightfulness | 'fraıtfulnıs | *s.i.* horror, terror, pavor.

frigid | 'frıdʒıd | *adj.* **1** MED. frígido (sexualmente). **1** (fig.) indiferente, apático, frío. **3** TEC. (no *comp.*) helado, extremadamente frío (clima).

frigidity | frı'dʒıdıtı | *s.i.* **1** frigidez (sexual). **2** frialdad, frío (físico).

frill | frıl | *s.c.* **1** volante, adorno, chorrera. **2** guirnalda, papillote (para decorar las patas de las aves en cocina). **3** (fam.) *pl.* adorno superfluo, extravagante: *with no frills = sencillo, sin adornos superfluos.* **4** ZOOL. gola de plumas.

frilled | frıld | *adj.* con volantes.

frilly | 'frılı | *adj.* lleno de volantes.

fringe | frındʒ | *s.c.* **1** (brit.) flequillo. **2** fleco, orla, borla. **3** margen, borde (de un lago, bosque, grupo). **4** grupo marginal, extremista, o radical. **5** grupo de vanguardia. **6** OPT. franja oscura o brillante (producida por difracción de la luz). || *v.t.* **7** bordear, rodear. || **8 – benefits,** prestaciones sociales (que se dan en algunas empresas a ciertos trabajadores).

fringed | frındʒt | *adj.* **1** con flecos, con orlas, con borlas (ropa, cortinas, etc.). **2 [– with/by]** bordeado por, rodeado por (en forma de flequillo o fleco): *the house was fringed by lovely flowers = la casa estaba bordeada por flores preciosas.*

frippery | 'frıpərı | (también **fripperies**) *s.i.* (desp.) chorradas, fruslerías, perifollos (objetos inútiles).

frisk | frısk | *v.i.* **1** retozar, juguetear, brincar (animales). || *v.t.* **2** (fam.) cachear, registrar. || *s.c.* **3** cacheo, registro.

frisky | 'frıskı | *adj.* retozón, juguetón, activo (cachorros).

fritter | 'frıtər | *s.c.* **1** fruta o vegetal rebozado, buñuelo, frisuelo. || *v.t.* **2** desmenuzar, desmigajar. **3 [to – away]** desperdiciar, malgastar (dinero).

frivolity | frı'vɔlıtı | *s.i.* **1** (desp.) frivolidad, liviandad, futilidad, trivialidad, ligereza. || *s.c.* **2** *pl.* (desp.) frivolidades, trivialidades.

frivolous | 'frıvələs | *adj.* **1** (desp.) frívolo, vano, fútil. **2** superficial, trivial.

frizz | frɪz | *v.t.* **1** rizar (el pelo). || **2 a – of hair,** un montón de pelo rizado, pelo rizado.
frizzed | frɪzd | *adj.* arreglado con rizos, rizado (en peluquería).
frizzle | 'frɪzl | *v.t.* e *i.* freír(se), quemar(se) un poco, churruscar(se).
frizzled | frɪzld | *adj.* frito, churruscado, un poco quemado.
frizzy | 'frɪzɪ | *adj.* enmarañado; con rizos enmarañados (el pelo).
fro | frəʊ | *adv.* **1** atrás, hacia atrás. || **2 to and –,** de un lado a otro, de aquí para allá.
frock | frɒk | *s.c.* **1** (arc.) vestido (de mujer). **2** hábito, túnica, sayo. **3** camiseta de marinero.
frog | frɒg | *s.c.* **1** ZOOL. rana. **2** (fam. y desp.) francés. || **3** (fam.) **to have a – in one's throat,** padecer carraspera, tener ronquera.
frogman | 'frɒgmən | (*pl.* **frogmen**) *s.c.* hombre rana, buzo, buceador.
frog-march | 'frɒgmɑːtʃ | *v.t.* llevar por la fuerza, llevar casi en volandas por la fuerza (normalmente entre dos personas).
frolic | 'frɒlɪk | *s.c.* **1** retozo, jugueteo. **2** alegría, júbilo, regocijo. || *v.i.* **3** juguetear, retozar.
frolicsome | 'frɒlɪksəm | *adj.* **1** (lit.) retozón, juguetón, travieso. **2** alegre, jubiloso.
from | frɒm | | frəm | *prep.* **1** de, desde (un lugar específico, posición, condición, origen, ocasión, distancia): *from London to Manchester = desde Londres hasta Manchester; it's 5 miles from town = está a 5 millas de la ciudad; a letter from Mary = una carta de Mary.* **2** de, desde, a partir de (un punto en el tiempo, un precio): *from Monday to Sunday = de lunes a domingo; we start a month from Friday = empezamos del viernes en un mes.* **3** a, de (indica privación, exclusión): *keep away from the fire = aléjate del fuego; they separated the baby from its mother = separaron al niño de su madre.* **4** de, contra (un peligro): *saved from the fire = salvado del fuego.* **5** de, entre (para hacer una diferenciación): *to know right from wrong = distinguir entre el bien y el mal (el bien del mal).* **6** de, a partir de (un agente, un instrumento): *we get butter from milk = obtenemos mantequilla de la leche.* **7** por, a causa de, como resultado de: *they died from starvation = murieron de inanición.* **8** por, según, a juzgar por, considerando: *from what you say, it's too far = según lo que dices está demasiado lejos.* || **9 – A to Z,** de pe a pa, de principio a fin. **10 – now on,** de ahora en adelante.
frond | frɒnd | *s.c.* fronda, hoja (especialmente de palma).
front | frʌnt | *s.c.* **1** fachada, parte delantera, parte frontal: *the front of the building = la fachada del edificio.* **2** malecón, paseo marítimo, ribera. **3** frente de batalla, línea de combate. **4** frente (unión de fuerzas): *the Popular Front = el Frente Popular.* **5** área (de dificultad). **6** apariencia (de una persona), (fig.) cara, rostro. **7** pantalla, tapadera, cobertura (de algo ilegal). **8** FIS. frente (atmosférico): *a cold front = un frente frío.* **9** frente, testuz, testa (de un animal). **10** pechera. **11** (arc.) inicio, comienzo, principio. || *adj.* **12** primero, delantero, frontal: *the front page = primera página.* **13** dirigente, directivo. **14** FON. frontal (sonido). || *v.i.* **15 [to – onto]** dar a, mirar a: *fronting into the garden = que da al jardín.* || *v.t.* **16** cubrir, recubrir (una fachada): *they fronted it with tiles = recubrieron la fachada de azulejo.* **17** dirigir, estar al frente de. || **18 to be in –,** ir delante, ir en cabeza. **19 to come to the –,** empezar a destacar, empezar a ser famoso. **20 – feed,** INF. alimentador principal. **21 – feed platen,** rodillo alimentador (de prensa). **22 – room,** sala de estar, salón. **23 – wheel drive,** transmisión delantera. **24 in – of,** delante de, frente a. **25 out –,** entre el auditorio, entre los espectadores. **26 push one's way to the –,** abrirse camino hasta la primera fila. **27 to put on a bold –,** hacer de tripas corazón. **28 to put up a –,** disimular la verdad.
frontage | 'frʌntɪdʒ | *s.c.* **1** frente, vista, orientación. **2** fachada, frente. **3** DER. derecho de fachada.
frontal | 'frʌntl | *adj.* **1** MED. frontal, (músculo, hueso). **2** directo, de frente: *a frontal attack = un ataque frontal.* **3** FIS. frontal (en metereología).
front-bencher | frʌnt'bentʃər | *s.c.* POL. (brit.) parlamentario con cargo en el gobierno, parlamentario con responsabilidades gubernamentales.
frontier | 'frʌnˌtɪər | *s.c.* **1 [– between /with]** frontera con, límite con. **2 [the –]** (EE.UU.) región fronteriza, la frontera. || *adj.* **3** limítrofe, lindante. || **4 frontiers,** límite, frontera (entre lo conocido y lo desconocido).
frontiersman | 'frʌntɪəzmən | (*pl.* **frontiersmen**) *s.c.* explorador, colonizador (de las regiones habitadas en América del Norte).
frontispiece | 'frʌntɪspiːs | *s.c.* **1** (generalmente *sing.*) portada (de un libro). **2** ARQ. frontispicio.
front-line | ˌfrʌnt'laɪn | *s.c.* **1** MIL. línea de fuego, primera línea. || **2 in the –,** (fig.) en primera línea, en situaciones comprometidas.
front-runner | ˌfrʌnt'rʌnər | *s.c.* favorito (persona que todos piensan que pueda ganar en algún tipo de competición).
frost | frɒst | *s.i.* **1** escarcha, cencellada. || *s.c.* e *i.* **2** helada (condición o período atmosférico). || *v.t.* e *i.* **3 [to – over/up]** cubrirse de escarcha, escarcharse. || *v.t.* **4** esmerilar (el cristal). **5** (EE.UU.) escarchar: *frosted fruit = frutas escarchadas.* || **6 degrees of –,** grados bajo cero.
frostbite | 'frɒstbaɪt | *s.i.* **1** MED. congelación, entumecimiento (por frío). || *v.t.irr.* [*pret.* **frostbit,** *p.p.* **frostbitten**] MED. congelar, entumecer.
frostbitten | 'frɒstbɪtn | **1** *p.p.* de **frostbite.** || **2** *adj.* congelado.
frosted | 'frɒstɪd | *adj.* **1** empañado, mate (el cristal). **2** recubierto (por algo similar a la escarcha): *frosted with brilliants = recubierto de brillantes.* **3** (EE.UU.) escarchado, recubierto de azúcar escarchada.
frosting | 'frɒstɪŋ | *s.i.* **1** superficie opaca, superficie mate. **2** (EE.UU.) capa de escarcha, capa de azúcar escarchada (en pastelería, coctelería).
frosty | 'frɒstɪ | *adj.* **1** helado, muy frío. **2** cubierto de escarcha. **3** (fig.) frío, indiferente, poco amistoso, desaprobador.
froth | frɒθ | *s.i.* **1** espuma, burbuja, espumaje. **2** espumarajo, espumajo. **3** (desp.) trivialidad, frivolidad, fruslería. || *v.i.* **4** espumajear, producir espuma o burbujas. || **5 to – at the mouth,** (fig.) echar espuma por la boca, echar chispas, estar hecho un basilisco.
frothy | frɒθɪ | *adj.* espumoso (de cualquier líquido).
frown | fraʊn | *v.i.* **1** fruncir el ceño, fruncir el entrecejo, arrugar la frente. || *s.c.* **2** ceño, entrecejo. | **3 to – on/upon,** desaprobar, expresar desagrado.
frowning | 'fraʊnɪŋ | *adj.* ceñudo, malhumorado.
froze | frəʊz | *pret.* de **freeze.**
frozen | 'frəʊzn | *p.p.* de **freeze.** || *adj.* **1 [– over]** helado, cubierto de hielo, rodeado de hielo. **2** gélido, glacial, extremadamente frío. **3** rígido, duro (el terreno). **4** congelado (un alimento). **5** (fig.) petrificado, inmovilizado (por el pánico). **6** (fig.) poco amistoso, desdeñoso, frío. **7** congelado, fijo (un precio, el salario). **8** inmovilizado, sin posibilidad de liquidación (propiedades).
frugal | 'fruːgl | *adj.* **1** austero, ahorrador. **2** frugal, sobrio.
frugality | fruː'gælətɪ | *s.i.* **1** frugalidad, sobriedad, austeridad.
fruit | fruːt | *s.c.* e *i.* (*pl.* **fruit** o **fruits**) **1** fruta. **2** fruto. || *s.c.* **3** fruto, producto, alimento. **4** *pl.* frutos, resultados. **5** (EE.UU.) (fam.) homosexual, afeminado. || *v.i.* **6** dar fruto, producir frutas. || **7 to bear –,** dar frutos, obtener resultados. **8 – cup,** sangría. **9 – dish,** frutero. **10 – salad,** macedonia de frutas. **11 – salts,** sales de fruta. **12 – tree,** frutal, árbol frutal.
fruitcake | 'fruːtkeɪk | *s.c.* pastel de frutas secas.
fruitful | 'fruːtful | *adj.* **1** útil, provechoso. **2** productivo, fértil, fecundo.
fruitfully | 'fruːtfəlɪ | *adv.* fructíferamente, provechosamente.
fruition | fruː'ɪʃn | *s.i.* **1** fructificación, realización, cumplimiento (de planes, objetivos). **2** fructificación (de árboles, plantas). **3** alegría, complacencia (por la posesión de algo). || **4 to bring to –,** cumplirse, realizarse (los planes, objetivos).
fruitless | 'fruːtlɪs | *adj.* **1** vano, infructuoso, inútil, ineficaz. **2** improductivo.
fruity | 'fruːtɪ | *adj.* **1** afrutado. **2** profundo, sonoro (tono de voz). **3** meloso, empalagoso. **4** (fam.) verde, procaz.

frump | frʌmp | *s.c.* (fam.) mujer insulsa, aburrida, anticuada (de ideas, de ropa).
frustrate | frʌ'streɪt | *v.t.* **1** frustrar, defraudar. **2** invalidar, anular, hacer fallar (planes, esfuerzos).
frustrated | frʌ'streɪtɪd | *adj.* **1** frustrado (con sentimiento de frustración). **2** no llevado a cabo, frustrado (planes o similar).
frustrating | frʌs'treɪtɪŋ | *adj.* frustrante.
frustration | frʌ'streɪʃn | *s.i.* **1** frustración, desencanto. || *s.c.* **2** frustración.
fry | fraɪ | *v.t.* **1** freír. || *v.i.* **2** quemarse, asarse (de calor). **3** (EE.UU. y fam.) ser ejecutado (en la silla eléctrica). || *s.i.* **4** *pl.* pececillos, alevines. **5** cría (de animales).
frying pan | 'fraɪɪŋ,pæn | *s.c.* **1** sartén. || **2 out of the – into the fire,** de Guatemala a guatepeor.
fuchsia | 'fjuːʃə | *s.c.* BOT. fucsia.
fuck | fʌk | (vulg.) *v.t.* **1** follar, joder. || *interj.* **2** joder. || *s.c.* **3** jodida, follada (acción de joder o follar). || **4 to – about/around,** hacer el gilipollas a todo pasto. **5 – all,** nada en absoluto, ni jodiendo. **6 – off,** vete a joder por ahí, vete a la jodida mierda. **7 to – up,** joder (rompiendo o estropeando).
OBS. Esta palabra muy ofensiva se utiliza adjetival y adverbialmente de manera profusa por las personas que no les importa su alto grado de malsonancia. Como, por ejemplo: **8** *what the fuck are you doing here? = ¿qué coño estás haciendo aquí?*
fucking | 'fʌkɪŋ | *adj.* jodido, coño: *the fucking machine is not working = la jodida máquina no funciona.*
fuddled | 'fʌdl | *adj.* confuso, lento de reflejos, aturdido (gen. a causa del alcohol).
fuddy-duddy | 'fʌdɪdʌdɪ | (desp.) *s.c.* **1** tipo pomposo, tipo estirado. || *adj.* **2** pomposo, estirado.
fudge | fʌdʒ | *s.i.* **1** GAST. dulce de turrón. || *v.t.* **2** no decir claramente, dejar poco claras: *to fudge the issues = dejar los temas poco claros.*
fuel | fjʊəl | *s.i.* **1** combustible, carburante. || *s.c.* **2** combustible, carburante: *alternative fuels = carburantes alternativos.* || *v.t.* **3** (EE.UU.) aprovisionar, abastecer de combustible. **4** estimular, alentar. || **5** (fig.) **to add – to the flames,** echar leña al fuego. **6 – oil,** petróleo. **7 – tank,** depósito de combustible.
fug | fʌg | *s.sing.* (brit. y fam.) humo, atmósfera cargada.
fugitive | 'fjuːdʒətɪv | *adj.* **1** fugitivo. **2** efímero, breve, corto, fugaz. **3** pasajero, perecedero. **4** ininteligible, incomprensible, irretenible. **5** vagabundo, errante. || *s.c.* **6** fugitivo, prófugo: *a fugitive from justice = un fugitivo de la justicia.* **7** lo efímero, lo breve, lo fugaz.
fugue | fjuːg | *s.c.* e *i.* MUS. fuga.
fulcrum | 'fʌlkrəm | (*pl.* **fulcrums** o **fulcra**) *s.c.* **1** MEC. fulcro, punto de apoyo, soporte de la balanza.
fulfill | fʊl'fɪl | *v.t.* **1** llevar a cabo, cumplir, ejecutar (una promesa, una orden, una amenaza). **2** hacer el papel de, cumplir (una función). **3** satisfacer (una necesidad, un propósito). **4** cumplir, hacer realidad (planes, deseos). **5** desarrollar, expresar (habilidades, cualidades).
fulfilled | fʊl'fɪld | *adj.* satisfecho (lo contrario de frustrado).
fulfilling | fʊl'fɪlɪŋ | *adj.* placentero, que da satisfacción.
fulfillment | fʊl'fɪlmənt | *s.i.* **1** cumplimiento, ejecución (de una orden, una amenaza). **2** satisfacción, agrado, gratificación.
full | fʊl | *adj.* **1 [– of/up]** lleno, repleto, completo (un recipiente, un espacio, un período de tiempo). **2 [– (of)]** lleno, cargado, repleto: *full of lies = cargado de mentiras.* **3 [– up]** repleto, lleno, satisfecho (después de una comida). **4** todo, completo, detallado: *a full version = una versión completa.* **5 [at –]** máximo, todo: *at full speed = a toda velocidad.* **6** rollizo, rechoncho, carnoso, redondo. **7** amplio, ancho, suelto (la ropa). **8** intenso, profundo (el color). **9** fuerte, intenso (el sonido). **10** fuerte, concentrado (el sabor). **11** pleno: *a full life = una vida plena.* **12** de pleno derecho, titular: *a full Academy member = un miembro de la Academia de pleno derecho.* **13** pleno, total: *a policy of full employement = una política de pleno empleo.* || *adv.* **14** exactamente, directamente. **15** muy, bastante, perfectamente. || **16 at – blast,** V. **blast. 17 at – length,** cuan largo, todo lo largo, en toda su extensión. **18 at – pelt,** V. **pelt. 19 at – tilt,** V. **tilt. 20 to be – of oneself,** ser un engreído, ser un soberbio, ser un orgulloso. **21 to come – circle,** V. **circle. 22 – of beans,** V. **bean. 23 – to bursting,** hasta la bandera, de bote en bote. **24 – to the brim,** hasta el borde, completamente lleno (un recipiente). **25 – session,** sesión plenaria. **26 to have – hands,** V. **hand. 27 in –,** completamente, totalmente. **28 in – cry,** V. **cry. 29 in – swing,** V. **swing.**
full-back | 'fʊlbæk | *s.c.* DEP. defensa, defensor.
full-blooded | ,fʊl'blʌdɪd | *adj.* **1** viril, vigoroso. **2** de pura raza.
full-blown | ,fʊl'bləʊn | *adj.* **1** totalmente abierto, totalmente desarrollado (especialmente de flores). **2** (fig.) total, completo, acabado: *a full-blown attack = un ataque total.*
full-bodied | ,fʊl'bɒdɪd | *adj.* **1** corpulento. **2** rico, aromático (especialmente de los vinos).
fuller | 'fʊlər | *s.c.* **1** batanero, batán (limpiador de tejidos). || **2 fuller's earth,** tierra de batán, arcilla de batán.
full-face | ,fʊl'feɪs | *adj.* y *adv.* de lleno, de rostro entero.
full-fledged | ,fʊl'fledʒt | V. **fully-fledged.**
full-grown | ,fʊl'grəʊn | *adj.* maduro, crecido, con el desarrollo natural acabado (de animales o plantas).
full-length | ,fʊl'leŋθ | *adj.* **1** de cuerpo entero (retrato o espejo). **2** de largo normal (para libros o películas). **3** de suelo a pared (cortinas o parecido). || *adv.* **4** a todo lo largo (del cuerpo): *she was lying full-length on the carpet = estaba tumbada a todo lo largo sobre la alfombra.*
fullness | 'fʊlnɪs | *s.i.* **1** saciedad; abundancia. **2** redondez (de alguna parte del cuerpo). **3** riqueza (de sonido). **4** aroma pleno (de sabor). || **5 in the – of time,** en la plenitud de los tiempos; muy a la larga.
full-page | ,fʊl'peɪdʒ | *adj.* PER. de página entera (anuncio, artículo, etc.).
full-scale | ,fʊl'skeɪl | *adj.* **1** de g[illegible] envergadura, total: *full-scale war* [illegible] *guerra total.* **2** de tamaño natural.
full-size | ,fʊl'saɪz | (también **full-sized**) *adj.* **1** totalmente desarrollado. **2** de tamaño natural, de tamaño verdadero.
full-throated | ,fʊl'θrəʊtɪd | *adj.* fuerte, alto (sonidos como la risa, el grito, etc.).
full-time | ,fʊl'taɪm | *adj.* y *adv.* **1** a tiempo completo, de dedicación plena, de horario completo: *full-time students = estudiantes a tiempo completo.* || *s.i.* **2** DEP. tiempo, final (en algún juego como fútbol). || **3 a – job,** (fam.) tela marinera: *to take care of two babies is a full-time job = cuidar de dos bebés es tela marinera.*
fully | 'fʊlɪ | *adv.* **1** completamente, totalmente, enteramente. **2** de cabo a rabo, en su totalidad (sin omitir nada). **3** incluso, hasta (con cantidades): *fully 300 students have a grant here = hasta 300 estudiantes tienen beca aquí.*
fully-fledged | ,fʊlɪ'fledʒt | *adj.* **1** ANAT. ZOOL. totalmente plumado (de aves). **2** **[a – s.]** todo un: *a fully-fledged surgeon = todo un cirujano.*
fulminate | 'fʌlmɪneɪt | *v.i.* **[to – (at/against)]** tronar, criticar severamente.
fulmination | ,fʌlmɪ'neɪʃn | *s.c.* e *i.* crítica, ataque furibundo.
fulsome | 'fʊlsəm | *adj.* (desp.) exagerado, extravagante, de mal gusto (la manera de dar gracias, pedir perdón, etc.).
fulsomely | 'fʊlsəmlɪ | *adv.* (desp.) exageradamente, extravagantemente, con mal gusto.
fumble | 'fʌmbl | *v.i.* **1** manosear torpemente, toquetear con torpeza. **2** farfullar.
fume | fjuːm | *v.i.* **1** echar humo, emitir gases, humear. **2** (fig. y fam.) echar humo (por enfado), echar rayos, irritarse. || **3 fumes,** gases, humos, polución.
fumigate | 'fjuːmɪgeɪt | *v.t.* fumigar, desinfectar.
fumigation | ,fjuːmɪ'geɪʃn | *s.i.* fumigación.
fun | fʌn | *s.i.* **1** diversión, regocijo: *it's great fun to work with her = es una gran diversión trabajar con ella.* || *adj.* **2** divertido, gracioso (de personas). **3** (EE.UU. y fam.) divertido, gracioso (para personas y cosas). || **4 figure of –,**

V. **figure.** **5 for –/for the – of it/for the – of the thing,** (fam.) por pura diversión, por puro regocijo. **6 – and games,** (fam. y desp.) cachondeo excesivo: *his fun and games made me angry = su cachondeo excesivo me puso enfermo.* **7 to have –,** pasarlo bien, divertirse, pasar un buen rato. **8 in –/out of –,** de broma. **9 to make – of/poke – at,** burlarse de, reírse de. **10 to spoil the –,** aguar la fiesta. **11 what –!,** ¡qué diversión!, ¡qué divertido!

function | 'fʌŋkʃn | *s.c.* **1** función, objeto; *the function of power is to serve people = la función del poder es servir a la gente.* **2** solemnidad, cena formal, comida solemne. **3 [– of]** (form.) en función de, función de. **4** MAT. función, operación. **5** INF. función. || *s.i.* **6** funcionamiento. || *v.i.* **7 [to – (as)]** funcionar; operar; servir: *this functions as a lever = esto sirve de palanca.*

functional | 'fʌŋkʃənl | *adj.* **1** funcional, de funcionamiento. **2** práctico, funcional (muebles, diseños, etc.). **3** en funcionamiento, funcionando. **4** MED. funcional (que no afecta al órgano que está mal).

functionalism | 'fʌŋkʃənəlɪzəm | *s.i.* (form.) funcionalismo (visión de la realidad desde un enfoque práctico o utilitarista).

functionalist | 'fʌŋkʃənəlɪst | *s.c.* (form.) funcionalista, V. **functionalism.**

functionally | 'fʌŋkʃənəlɪ | *adv.* funcionalmente.

functionary | 'fʌŋkʃənərɪ | *s.c.* funcionario (gubernamental).

fund | fʌnd | *s.c.* **1** fondo, reserva; colecta especial (con algún propósito concreto). **2 [– of]** (fig.) acopio de, montón de: *he has an incredible fund of jokes = tiene un increíble acopio de chistes.* || *v.t.* **3** financiar, meter dinero en, dedicar fondos a. || **4 funds,** FIN. capital, dineros, fondos disponibles. **5 in funds,** (fam.) con dinero suficiente, con fondos adecuados.

fundamental | ˌfʌndə'mentl | *adj.* **1 [– (to)]** fundamental, esencial. **2** FIL. básico, fundamental. || **3 fundamentals,** principios básicos.

fundamentalism | ˌfʌndə'mentəlɪzəm | *s.i.* REL. fundamentalismo (interpretar al pie de la letra las Escrituras).

fundamentalist | ˌfʌndə'mentəlɪst | *s.c.* REL. fundamentalista, V. **fundamentalism.**

fundamentally | ˌfʌndə'mentəlɪ | *adv.* fundamentalmente, básicamente, esencialmente.

funding | 'fʌndɪŋ | *s.i.* financiación.

fund-raising | 'fʌndreɪzɪŋ | *s.i.* recogida de fondos, reunión de fondos.

funeral | 'fjuːnərəl | *s.c.* **1** funeral, exequias. || **2 – director,** (EE.UU.) responsable de funeraria. **3 – home,** (EE.UU.) funeraria. **4 – parlour,** (brit.) funeraria. **5 it's your –,** (fam.) allá te las apañes, soluciónalo tú que es asunto tuyo.

funerary | 'fjuːnərərɪ | *adj.* (form.) funerario, fúnebre.

funereal | fjuː'nɪərɪəl | *adj.* (desp.) funesto, lúgubre.

funfair | 'fʌnfeər | *s.c.* (brit.) parque de atracciones.

fungal | 'fʌŋgəl | *adj.* (form.) fungoideo, de hongos.

fungi | 'fʌŋgaɪ | V. **fungus.**

fungicide | 'fʌngɪsaɪd | *s.c.* e *i.* QUIM. fungicida.

fungoid | 'fʌŋgɔɪd | *adj.* (form. y lit.) fungoideo.

fungus | 'fʌŋgəs | (*pl.* **fungus, fungi, funguses**) *s.c.* e *i.* BOT. hongo.

funicular | fjuː'nɪkjʊlər | *s.c.* **1** funicular. || **2 – railway,** funicular.

funk | fʌŋk | *s.i.* **1** (p.u.) temor, miedo, amilanamiento. **2** MUS. música funk (cruce de jazz y blues). || *s.c.* **3** (p.u.) cobarde, cobardica. || *v.t.* **4** (p.u.) temer, tener miedo de.

funky | 'fʌŋkɪ | *adj.* **1** MUS. música funky. **2** (fam. y p.u.) chulo, chic.

funnel | 'fʌnl | *s.c.* **1** embudo. **2** MAR. chimenea (de barcos). **3** (fig.) túnel, embudo. || *v.t.* e *i.* **4** dirigir(se), encausar(se), canalizar(se), *we must funnel the weapons for the guerrillas through Amsterdam = debemos dirigir las armas para los guerrilleros a través de Amsterdam.*

funnily | 'fʌnɪlɪ | *adv.* **1** (fam.) extrañamente, raramente. || **2 – enough,** curiosamente: *she is, funnily enough, very sensitive = ella es, curiosamente, muy sensible.*

funny | 'fʌnɪ | *adj.* **1** extraño, raro, peculiar. **2** divertido, gracioso. **3** (fam.) un poco ido, un poquito loco. **4** (fam.) un poco enfermo, un poco mal. || **5 – bone,** (fam.) hueso de la risa. **6 – business,** (fam.) negocios sospechosos, negocios deshonestos. **7 to go –,** (fam.) escacharrarse. **8 the funnies,** (EE.UU. y fam.) PER. las tiras cómicas, las tiras de dibujos cómicos.

fur | fɜːr | *s.i.* **1** piel, pelaje (de animales). **2** (fig.) piel sintética. **3** MED. sarro, saburra (capa que se forma en la lengua). **4** sarro (en las teteras). || *s.c.* **5** piel, prenda de piel. || *s.c.* e *i.* **6** piel (en su uso para vestir): *a fur coat = un abrigo de pieles.* || *v.i.* **7** llenarse de sarro (teteras o tuberías). || **8 to – up,** llenarse por completo de sarro. **9 to make the – fly/to set the – flying,** armar follón, causar follón, causar discusiones.

furbelow | 'fɜːbɪləʊ | *s.c.* volante (en un vestido).

furbish | 'fɜːbɪʃ | *v.t.* (form.) renovar, restaurar.

furious | 'fjʊərɪəs | *adj.* **1** furioso, furibundo, colérico. **2** lleno de vigor, lleno de energía (en la manera de hacer algo).

furiously | 'fjʊərɪəslɪ | *adv.* **1** furiosamente, furibundamente, coléricamente. **3** vigorosamente, energéticamente (manera de hacer algo).

furl | fɜːl | *v.t.* cerrar, enrollar (paraguas, vela, bandera, etc.).

furled | fɜːld | *adj.* enrollado, cerrado (paraguas, vela, etc.).

furlong | 'fɜːlɒŋ | *s.c.* furlong (medida de longitud de unos 200 metros).

furlough | 'fɜːləʊ | *s.c.* e *i.* licencia, permiso (especialmente militar).

furnace | 'fɜːnɪs | *s.c.* **1** horno, caldera. || *s.sing.* **2** (fam.) horno (lugar de mucho calor).

furnish | 'fɜːnɪʃ | *v.t.* **1** amueblar. **2 [to – + *o.* + with]** (form.) proveer, suministrar.

furnished | 'fɜːnɪʃt | *adj.* **[– (with)]** amueblado.

furnishings | 'fɜːnɪʃɪŋgz | *s.pl.* muebles (incluyendo accesorios).

furniture | 'fɜːnɪtʃər | *s.i.* **1** mobiliario. || **2 part of the –,** (fam.) un mueble (algo a lo que uno se ha acostumbrado): *she's become part of the furniture after so long = ella se ha convertido en un mueble después de tanto tiempo.*

furore | fjʊ'rɔːrɪ | (EE.UU. **furor**) *s.sing.* furor, furia, rabia.

furrier | 'fʌrɪər | *s.c.* comerciante en pieles.

furrow | 'fʌrəʊ | *s.c.* **1** AGR. surco. **2** (fig.) surco, canal (en cualquier superficie plana). **3** arruga (en la cara). || *v.t.* **4** arrugar (la frente). **5** (lit.) hacer un surco en. || *v.i.* **6** arrugarse (la frente).

furrowed | 'fʌrəʊd | *adj.* arrugado (en la cara).

furry | 'fɜːrɪ | *adj.* **1** velloso, lanudo, peludo (animales). **2** parecido a piel, como piel (en objetos). **3** sarroso, lleno de sarro (lengua).

further | 'fɜːðər | (*comp.* de **far**) *adv.* **1** ulteriormente; más: *I have to study the matter further = tengo que estudiar más el tema.* **2** más avanzado; más allá: *I'll go further and say... = iré más allá y diré...* **3** (form.) lo que es más (al principio de una oración). **4** más lejos. **5** más (en el tiempo): *I won't delay you further = no te entretendré más.* || *adj.* **6** más, añadido: *a further problem is drugs = un problema añadido es la droga.* **7** alejado: *the further end of the street = el extremo alejado de la calle.* || *v.t.* **8** promover, fomentar, favorecer. || **9 – back,** más atrás, anteriormente (en el tiempo). **10 – education,** (brit.) educación de la tercera edad; educación universitaria no obligatoria. **11 – on,** más adelante, posteriormente (en el tiempo). **12 – to,** (form.) en lo que respecta a, en lo que se refiere a. **13 not to go any –,** no extenderse; no servir de modelo: *this rebellion must not go any further = esta rebelión no se debe extender.*

furtherance | 'fɜːðərəns | *s.i.* fomento, promoción.

furthermore | ˌfɜːðə'mɔː | *adv.* (form.) además, además de esto.

furthermost | ˌfɜːðə'məʊst | *adj.* lo más alejado, lo más distanciado.

furthest | 'fɜːðɪst | (*super.* de **far**) *adv.* y *adj.* **1** más, lo que más: *nowadays medicine has developed furthest = hoy en día la medicina se ha desarrollado la que más.* **2** más alejado, más distanciado.

furtive | 'fɜːtɪv | *adj.* furtivo, sigiloso, disimulado.

furtively | 'fɜːtɪvlɪ | *adv.* furtivamente, sigilosamente, disimuladamente, con disimulo.

furtiveness | ’fəːtɪvnɪs | *s.i.* sigilo, disimulo.
fury | ’fjʊərɪ | *s.i.* **1** furia, ira. || **2 in a –,** lleno de furia, lleno de ira. **3 like –,** (p.u.) como una furia.
fuse | fjuːz | *s.c.* **1** ELEC. fusible, interruptor fusible. **2** (brit. y fam.) fallo de fusible. **3** mecha (en explosivos). || *v.t.* e *i.* **4** (brit.) fundir(se), ir(se) (un fusible). **5** fundir(se), unir(se). **6** fundir(se) (metales). **7** (fig.) mezclar(se), combinar(se) (ideas, creencias, ideologías, etc.). || **8 – box,** ELEC. caja de fusibles. **9 – wire,** ELEC. cable de fusible.
fused | fjuːzd | *adj.* ELEC. con fusible.
fuselage | ’fjuːzəlɑːʒ | *s.c.* AER. fuselaje.
fusible | ’fjuːzəbl | *adj.* fundible, mezclable.
fusillade | ˌfjuːzə’leɪd | *s.sing.* **1** MIL. descarga, andanada. **2 [– of]** (fig.) andanada de, descarga de (críticas o similar).
fusion | ’fjuːʒn | *s.c.* **1** fusión, unión. || *s.i.* **2** fusión, síntesis. **3** FIS. fusión (atomica).
fuss | fʌs | *s.sing.* **1 [– (about/over)]** conmoción, follón. **2** estado nervioso, agitación. **3** (fam.) bronca, follón. || *v.i.* **4 [to – (about/over)]** inquietarse, agitarse. || *v.t.* **5** (fam. y EE.UU.) molestar, dar la lata. || **6 to – over,** prestar excesiva atención a. **7 to make/kick up a –,** (fam.) quejarse airadamente, armar un lío. **9 to make a – of,** (brit.) mimar a, tratar con mimos a, tratar con mucho cuidado.
fussily | ’fʌsɪlɪ | *adv.* **1** nerviosamente, agitadamente. **2** remilgadamente, melindrosamente (en el vestir).
fussiness | ’fʌsɪnɪs | *s.i.* remilgo, melindre.
fusspot | ’fʌspɔt | *s.c.* (fam.) preocupón.
fussy | ’fʌsɪ | *adj.* **1** nervioso, agitado (sobre pequeñeces). **2** remilgado, melindroso (en el vestir). || **3 I'm not –,** no me importa.
fusty | ’fʌstɪ | *adj.* **1** (desp.) anticuado, pasado de moda. **2** rancio (olor).
futile | ’fjuːtaɪl | *adj.* **1** fútil, vano, infructuoso. **2** insignificante, baladí (algo que se dice).
futility | fjuː’tɪlətɪ | *s.i.* futilidad, inutilidad.
future | ’fjuːtʃər | *s.sing.* **1** futuro, mañana. **2** tiempo futuro. **3** futuro, porvenir: *to have a future = tener un porvenir.* || *s.c.* **4** futuro profesional, futuro (visto como carrera): *my political future = mi futuro político.* || *adj.* **5** futuro: *a future generation = una generación del futuro.* **6** GRAM. futuro. || **7 for the –,** para el futuro, para el mañana. **8 futures,** COM. acciones, futuros. **9 in –,** en el futuro. **10 in the –,** en el futuro, en el mañana.
futurism | ’fjuːtʃərɪzəm | *s.i.* ART. futurismo.
futuristic | ’fjuːtʃərɪstɪk | *adj.* futurista.
fuzz | fʌz | *s.i.* **1** pelusa, vello. **2** pelo fosco. || **3 the —,** (fam.) la policía.
fuzzily | ’fʌzɪlɪ | *adv.* confusamente, con poca claridad (en los pensamientos).
fuzziness | ’fʌzɪnɪs | *s.i.* **1** vellosidad. **2** (lo) borroso, (lo) indistinto.
fuzzy | ’fʌzɪ | *adj.* **1** foscado, encrespado (pelo). **2** borroso, indistinto (en fotos o similar). **3** (fig.) borroso, poco claro (pensamientos). **4** con vello, cubierto de pelusa.

g, G | dʒiː | *s.c.* **1** g, G (séptima letra del alfabeto inglés). **2** MUS. sol. **3** MUS. clave de sol. **4** TEC. abreviatura de la gravedad, fuerza de la gravedad o de la aceleración. **5** abreviatura de gramo, galón y alemán (german). **6** (EE.UU. y fam.) billete de 1.000 dólares. || *adj.* **7** letra de clasificación para películas toleradas para menores.

gab | gæb | *v.i.* **1** (fam.) cotorrear, parlotear, charlar. || *s.i.* **2** cotorreo, parloteo. || **3 the gift of the –,** V. **gift.**

gabardine | 'gæbədiːn | (también **gabardine**) *s.i.* **1** gabardina (tela). || *s.c.* **2** gabardina (prenda), túnica (usada por los judíos en la E. Media).

gabble | gæbl | *v.t.* e *i.* **1** (fam.) barbullar, barbotear, hablar atropelladamente. **2** cloquear, graznar. || *s.i.* **3** (fam.) cháchara, cloqueo, parloteo.

gable | 'geɪbl | *s.c.* ARQ. gablete, aguilón.

gabled | 'geɪbld | *adj.* ARQ. de gablete, con gabletes.

gad | gæd | **(gadding, gadded), to – about/around,** (fam. y desp.) ir por ahí en busca de juerga, andar en busca de juerga.

gadabout | 'gædəbaʊt | *s.c.* (fam. y desp.) trotacalles, juerguista.

gadfly | 'gædflaɪ | *s.c.* **1** ZOOL. tábano, moscardón. **2** (fig. y desp.) latoso, pesado.

gadget | 'gædʒɪt | *s.c.* artilugio, artefacto, aparato, cachivache.

gadgetry | 'gædʒɪtrɪ | *s.i.* artilugios, artefactos (vistos como un todo).

Gael | geɪl | *s.c.* gaélico, habitante de Escocia, Irlanda e Isla de Man.

Gaelic | 'geɪlɪk | *adj.* **1** gaélico (lengua hablada en Escocia, Irlanda e Isla de Man).

gaff | gæf | *s.c.* **1** gancho, garfio, arpón de pesca (para el izado de peces). || **2 to blow the –,** (fam.) revelar el secreto, descubrir el pastel.

gaffe | gæf | *s.c.* metedura de pata, indiscreción.

gaffer | 'gæfər | *s.c.* (fam.) **1** (desp.) vejestorio, viejo. **2** (brit.) capataz, supervisor (de un grupo de obreros).

gag | gæg | *s.c.* **1** chiste, gracia, broma, efecto cómico. **2** morcilla (en teatro), payasada. **3** mordaza. **4** limitación, censura (de opinión). **5** MED. abrebocas (aparato de dentista). || *v.t.* **6** amordazar, poner mordaza. **7** (fig.) amordazar, hacer callar, censurar, acallar. **8** mantener la boca abierta (por medio de artilugio dentista). **9** bloquear, obstruir. || *v.i.* **10** sentir náuseas. **11** meter morcillas (en teatro). **12** contar chistes, hacer trucos, bromear.

gaga | 'gɑːgɑː | *adj.* (fam.) chiflado, chalado.

gage V. **gauge.**

gaggle | 'gægl | *s.c.* **1** manada (de gansos). **2** (fig.) grupo (ruidoso y normalmente de niños).

gaiety | 'geɪɪtɪ | *s.i.* **1** alegría, regocijo, alboroto, júbilo. **2** *pl.* diversión, festejo, animación. **3** adorno, atavío festivo.

gaily | 'geɪlɪ | *adv.* **1** alegremente, jovialmente. **2** vistosamente, brillantemente (vestido, coloreado, adornado, etc.).

gain | geɪn | *v.t.* e *i.* **1** (form.) **[– (by, from)]** ganar, conseguir, obtener, captar (algo útil o ventajoso). **2** adelantar(se) (un reloj). || *v.t.* **3** ganar, adquirir, subir de, incrementar, aumentar (de peso, en riqueza, etc.). **4** (form.) llegar a, alcanzar (un lugar, con esfuerzo). || *v.i.* **5 [– (on, upon)]** reducir distancias, acercarse, alcanzar. **6** aumentar el valor, subir, ganar en, progresar, mejorar (valor, fuerza, salud, etc.). || *s.i.* **7** ganancia, beneficio, provecho. || *s.c.* **8** aumento, subida, incremento. **9** compra, adquisición. **10** mejora, avance, ventaja. **11** ELECTR. amplificación, volumen. || **12 to – entry,** entrar, conseguir entrar. **13 to – ground,** ganar terreno (en fuerza, popularidad, aceptación). **14 ill-gotten gains,** ganancias o beneficios ilícitos.

gainer | geɪnər | *s.c.* **1** ganador. **2** DEP. salto mortal hacia atrás y entrada en el agua de pie (en natación).

gainful | 'geɪnfʊl | *adj.* lucrativo, remunerado, ventajoso, útil: *gainful employement = empleo remunerado.*

gainfully | 'geɪnfəlɪ | *adv.* lucrativamente, remuneradamente, ventajosamente.

gainsay | ˌgeɪn'seɪ | *v.* [*pret.* y *p.p.* **gainsaid**] *t.* (p.u. y form.) contradecir, negar.

gait | geɪt | *s.c.* **1** modo de andar particular. **2** paso, trote corto (caballo). || *v.t.* **3** adiestrar (al caballo) en el trote corto, en el paso.

gaiter 'geɪtər | *s.c.* **1** polaina, sobrebota (para montañeros, esquiadores). **2** botín con goma elástica en los laterales.

gal | gæl | *s.c.* (fam.) chica, muchacha.

gala | 'gɑːlə | *s.c.* **1** gala, celebración, festival, festejo (público): *a gala night = una fiesta nocturna.* **2** (brit.) DEP. certamen, competición, gala: *a swimming gala = una competición de natación.* || *adj.* **3** festivo, de gala.

galactic | gə'læktɪk | *adj.* **1** lácteo. **2** ASTR. galáctico.

galantine | 'gæləntiːn | *s.i.* GAST. galantina (carne blanca servida enrollada y fría).

galaxy | 'gæləksi | *s.c.* **1** ASTR. galaxia, constelación. **2 [– of]** (fig.) grupo de personas brillantes, constelación, pléyade: *a galaxy of writers = una pléyade de escritores.* || **3 the Galaxy,** ASTR. la Vía Láctea.

gale | geɪl | *s.c.* **1** galerna, vendaval, ventarrón, ventisca. **2** (arc.) brisa. **3** *pl.* [– **(of)**] estallido (de risas, de carcajadas): *gales of laughter = carcajadas, estallido de carcajadas.*

Galician | gə'lɪʃɪən | *adj.* **1** gallego. || *s.c.* **2** gallego (habitante de Galicia). **3** gallego (idioma).

Galilee | 'gælɪli: | *s.* **1** Galilea. **2** pórtico de iglesia, capilla (con minúscula).

gall | gɔ:l | *s.i.* **1** descaro, coraje, osadía, agallas. **2** rencor. **3** (arc.) bilis, hiel. **4** rozadura (especialmente de caballo). **5** exasperación, irritación. **6** BOT. agalla, gargal. **7** inflamación (causada por infección o daño). || *v.t.* **8** irritar, exasperar, molestar. **9** rozar, desollar. || *v.i.* **10** irritarse, molestarse, exasperarse. || **11 – bladder,** ANAT. vesícula biliar.

gallant | 'gælənt | *adj.* **1** (lit.) valeroso, valiente, heroico. **2** (lit.) galante, cortés, caballeroso, considerado. **3** majestuoso, imponente, deslumbrante. **4** (arc.) galán, galanteador, elegante. || *s.c.* e *i.* **5** (arc.) caballero, señor.

gallantly | 'gæləntlɪ | *adv.* **1** valerosamente, heroicamente. **2** galantemente, cortésmente, caballerosamente.

gallantry | 'gæləntrɪ | *s.c.* e *i.* **1** (lit.) heroísmo, valentía, valor. **2** galantería, cortesía, caballerosidad.

galleon | 'gælɪən | *s.c.* MAR. galeón.

gallery | 'gælərɪ | *s.c.* **1** galería de arte. **2** sala (de museo); museo, pinacoteca. **3** galería (de teatro). **4** tribuna. **5** (fig.) galería, espectadores, público. **6** galería, túnel, pasadizo subterráneo (de una mina, una cueva). **7** galería de tiro. **8** galería, balconada. **9** (EE.UU.) veranda, porche, pórtico. **10** MAR. galería (plataforma en barcos antiguos). || **11 to play to the –,** actuar para la galería.

galley | 'gælɪ | *s.c.* **1** MAR. galera. **2** cocina (de barco o avión). **3** galera (para formar la galerada en imprenta). || **4 – proof,** galerada, prueba de galera (en imprenta).

galley-slave | 'gælɪsleɪv | *s.c.* **1** galeote, esclavo de galera. **2** (fig.) esclavo (persona a quien se le obliga a trabajar mucho).

Gallic | 'gælɪk | *adj.* (form.) gálico, francés.

gallicism | 'gælɪsɪzəm | *s.c.* galicismo.

galling | 'gɔ:lɪŋ | *adj.* **1** irritante, exasperante, mortificante.

gallivant | ˌgælɪ'vænt | **to – about/around,** (desp. y p.u.) ir por ahí en plan de diversión, salir por ahí a divertirse.

gallon | 'gælən | *s.c.* galón (medida, brit. = 4,5 l., EE.UU. = 3,7 l.).

gallop | 'gæləp | *s.c.* **1** galope, galopada, paso rápido. || *v.t.* e *i.* **2** galopar, hacer galopar. **3** (fig.) ir de prisa, ir a galope. || **4 at a –,** a galope, galopar. **5 to break into a –,** echar a galopar.

galloping | 'gæləpɪŋ | *adj.* **1** galopante, rápido, creciente: *galloping inflation = inflación galopante.* **2** MED. galopante, de desarrollo acelerado.

gallows | 'gæləʊz | *s.c. sing.* y *pl.* **1** horca. **2** ejecución en la horca. || **3 – humour,** humor negro.

gallstone | 'gɔ:lstəʊn | *s.c.* cálculo biliar.

galore | gə'lɔ: | *adj.* muchísimo, en cantidad, a porrillo, en abundancia.

galosh | gə'lɒʃ | *s.c. gen. pl.* chanclos, botas de goma.

galumph | gə'lʌmf | *v.i.* (hum. y fam.) ir haciendo cabriolas, ir saltando alegremente (típico de niños): *the schoolboys galumphed into the yard = los escolares entraron en el patio haciendo cabriolas.*

galvanic | gæl'vænɪk | *adj.* **1** ELEC. galvánico. **2** (fig.) estimulante, convulsivo.

galvanism | 'gælvənɪzəm | *s.i.* ELEC. galvanismo.

galvanization | ˌgælvənaɪ'zeɪʃn | *s.i.* galvanización.

galvanize | 'gælvənaɪz | *v.t.* **1** galvanizar. **2 [to – into]** excitar, provocar, sacudir, espolear.

galvanized | 'gælvənaɪzd | *adj.* galvanizado.

gambit | 'gæmbɪt | *s.c.* **1** estratagema, táctica, maniobra. **2** gambito (en ajedrez).

gamble | 'gæmbl | *v.i.* **1 [to – (on/with)]** apostar (dinero, propiedades), aventurar en el juego: *gamble on the horses = apostar a los caballos.* **2** arriesgarse, especular (Bolsa). || *v.t.* **3 [to – (on)]** apostar en el juego, jugar. **4** arriesgar, especular (Bolsa). || *s.c.* **5 riesgo, empresa arriesgada, suerte.** **6** apuesta, jugada arriesgada. || **7 to – away,** perder en el juego.

gambler | 'gæmblər | *s.c.* jugador, tahúr.

gambling | 'gæmblɪŋ | *s.i.* **1** juego, apuesta (por dinero). **2** especulación. || **3 – den,** garito, casa de juego.

gambol | 'gæmbl | *v.i.* **1** saltar, brincar, retozar, juguetear. || *s.c.* **2** salto, brinco, cabriola, jugueteo.

game | geɪm | *s.c.* **1** juego, deporte; partido, partida. **2** juego, set, manga (parte de un partido). **3** torneo, certamen, competición, copa (en tenis, bridge). **4** *pl.* juegos: *Olympic Games = Juegos Olímpicos.* **5** diversión, entretenimiento, pasatiempo, juego: *lots of games, as dice, chess... = montones de juegos, como dados, ajedrez...* **6** profesión, negocio, situación: *new to the game of... = nuevo en el negocio de...* **7** estilo deportivo, actuación en el juego. **8** broma, truco. **9** estratagema, argucia, artimaña. || *s.i.* **10** caza, animal de caza. **11** presa (de burla, escarnio). || *adj.* **12** valeroso, animoso, determinado, resoluto. **13 [– (for)]** deseoso, atrevido, preparado: *are you game for a run = ¿estás listo para correr?* || *v.i.* **14** apostar, jugar (por dinero). **15 at their own –,** con sus mismos métodos. **16 to be on the –,** (brit.) ser del oficio (de la prostitución). **17 board games,** juegos de mesa. **18 fun and games,** V. **fun.** **19 – bird,** ave de caza. **20** (fig.) **to give the – away,** descubrir las cartas, descubrir el pastel. **21 to make – of,** ridiculizar, reírse de, burlarse de. **22 to play the –,** jugar limpio, observar las reglas. **23 the game's up,** se acabó todo, te he descubierto. **24 the name of the –,** V. **name.** **25 two can play at that –,** donde las dan las toman.

gamebag | 'gæɪmbæg | *s.c.* zurrón, morral (del cazador).

gamecock | 'gæɪmkɒk | *s.c.* gallo de pelea.

gamekeeper | 'gæɪmˌki:pər | *s.c.* guardabosques.

gamesmanship | 'geɪmzmənʃɪp | *s.i.* maestría, saber hacer, picardía (poniendo nervioso al contrincante sin salirse de las reglas).

gamely | 'geɪmlɪ | *adv.* animosamente, valerosamente.

gamete | 'gæmi:t | *s.c.* BIOL. gameto.

gametic | gə'metɪk | *adj.* BIOL. del gameto.

game-warden | 'geɪmwɔ:dən | *s.c.* guarda en una reserva; guardabosque.

gamin | gæmɪn | *s.c.* pilluelo, golfillo.

gamine | gæ'mi:n | *s.c.* **1** pilluela, golfilla. || **2 – haircut,** corte de pelo a lo garçon.

gaming | geɪmɪŋ | *s.i.* **1** juego, apuesta (gen. cartas o ruleta). || **2 – house,** garito, casa de juego.

gamma | 'gæmə | *s.c.* e *i.* **1** gamma (tercera letra del alfabeto griego, a veces utilizada como calificación escolar baja). **2** TV. grado de contraste (fotográfico; también en vídeo y fotografía). || **3 – correction,** corrección de gamma (TV, vídeo, fotografía). **4** FIS. **– rays,** rayos gamma.

gammon | 'gæmən | *s.i.* **1** (brit.) jamón (gen. carne de cerdo para freír o asar, a veces ahumada o curada). **2** juego doble (en backgammon). **3** (brit. y fam.) charlatanería, charla engañosa. || *v.t.* **4** ganar al backgammon. **5** MAR. trincar (el bauprés a la roda). || *v.i.* **6** hablar con engaño.

gammy | 'gæmɪ | *adj.* (fam. y brit.) chungo, en mal estado (un miembro del cuerpo), cojo (una pierna).

gamut | 'gæmət | *s.* **1** serie, gama, variedad. **2** MUS. escala musical. || **3 to run the – of something,** experimentar toda la variedad, serie o gama de algo: *she's run the gamut of all jobs = ha experimentado toda clase de trabajos.*

gamy, gamey | 'geɪmɪ | *adj.* **1** de sabor y olor bravío, fuerte (carne de caza). **2** bravucón, intrépido. **3** de mala fama, de mala reputación. **4** escandaloso.

gander | 'gændər | *s.c.* **1** ganso (macho). **2** simplón, tontarrón. **3** (fam.) ojeada, vistazo: *take a gander at this = echa una ojeada a esto.*

gang | gæŋ | *s.c.* **1** [– *v.sing.* o *pl.*] banda (de ladrones, criminales). **2** pandilla (de jóvenes peligrosos): *a gang of hell's Angels = una pandilla de ángeles del infierno.* **3** grupo, pandilla, cuadrilla (en gen, de jóvenes.). **4** cuadrilla, brigada (de trabajadores). **5** juego (de herramientas). || *v.i.* **6 [to – up/on/against]** conspirar contra, estar en contra de; atacar (en pandilla).

ganger | 'gæŋər | *s.c.* (brit.) capataz, jefe de grupo (de obreros).

gangland | 'gæŋlənd | *s.sing.* mundo del hampa, mundo del crimen organizado.

GHI

gangling | 'gæŋglɪŋ | (también **gangles**) *adj.* **1** desgarbado, larguirucho, delgaducho (gen. chicos).

ganglion | 'gæŋglɪən | [*pl.* **ganglions** o **ganglia**] *s.c.* ANAT. ganglio.

gangplank | 'gæŋplæŋk | *s.c.* **1** rampa, pasarela (de desembarque).

gangrene | 'gæŋgri:n | *s.i.* **1** MED. gangrena. || *v.t.* e *i.* **2** gangrenar(se).

gangrenous | 'gæŋgrɪnəs | *adj.* MED. gangrenoso.

gangster | 'gæŋstər | *s.c.* mafioso, hampón, ladrón, criminal.

gangway | 'gæŋweɪ | *s.c.* **1** pasadizo, pasaje. **2** pasarela, escalerilla. **3** (brit.) pasillo (de cine, autobús, etc.). **4** nivel (de una mina). **5** MAR. portalón. || **6 –!,** ¡abran paso!

gannet | 'gænɪt | *s.c.* ZOOL. alcatraz, planco (un tipo de pájaro).

gantry | 'gæntrɪ | *s.c.* MEC. estructura de soporte, caballete de soporte.

gaol | dʒeɪl | *s.c.* e *i.* **1** (brit.) cárcel, prisión.

gaolbird | 'dʒeɪlbə:d | *s.c.* (brit., fam. y p.u.) pájaro de cuenta, carne de prisión.

gaolbreak | 'dʒeɪlbreɪk | *s.c.* (brit.) huida de prisión.

gaoler | 'dʒeɪlər | *s.c.* (brit.) carcelero.

gap | gæp | *s.c.* **1** brecha, resquicio, boquete, abertura, espacio. **2** (fig.) hueco, vacío, laguna. **3** (fig.) intervalo (de tiempo). **4** espacio (en la escritura). **5** cañada, desfiladero. **6** INF. separación entre bloques de registros. || *v.t.* **7** abrir un espacio, hacer una brecha. || *v.i.* **8** abrirse. || **9 credibility –,** V. **credibility.** || **10 generation –,** diferencia generacional (de ideas, intereses).

gape | geɪp | *v.i.* **1 [to – at]** mirar boquiabierto, quedarse boquiabierto. **2** bostezar. **3** separarse, abrirse completamente. **4** (fig.) tener lagunas (en el discurso). || *s.i.* **5** ZOOL. anchura del espacio de las mandíbulas abiertas de los vertebrados. **6** ZOOL. peste aviar. **7** ataque de bostezos.

gaping | geɪpɪŋ | *adj.* **1** boquiabierto, embobado. **2** profundo, cavernoso.

gappy | 'gæpɪ | *adj.* desdentado.

gap-toothed | gæp'tu:θt | *adj.* **1** de dientes separados, malformados. **2** sin algún(algunos) diente(s).

garage | 'gærɑ:dʒ | | 'gærɪdʒ | | gə'rɑ:ʒ | *s.c.* **1** garaje. **2** garaje, taller de reparación (de vehículos), cochera. **3** gasolinera. || *v.t.* **4** guardar, dejar en un garaje.

garb | gɑ:b | *s.i.* **1** (lit. y fig.) vestimenta, vestiduras, ropajes: *doctor's garb = vestimenta de médicos.* || *v.t.* **2** (lit. y fig.) vestir, ir ataviado, ir de (un color): *she was garbed in white = ella iba de blanco.*

garbage | 'gɑ:bɪdʒ | *s.i.* **1** (EE.UU.) basura, desperdicios. **2** (brit. y fam.) tonterías, estupideces. **3** INF. información inservible, incorrecta. || **4 – can,** (EE.UU.) cubo de basura.

garble | 'gæ:bl | *v.t.* **1** distorsionar, falsear, mezclar (los hechos). **2** escoger, seleccionar, cribar. || *s.i.* **3** distorsión, falseamiento.

garbled | 'gɑ:bld | *adj.* confuso, distorsionado (especialmente un mensaje o información).

garden | 'gɑ:dn | *s.c.* **1** jardín. **2** huerto, huerta. **3** *pl.* parques, jardines públicos: *Kew Gardens.* **4** (fig.) vergel. || *v.i.* **5** cultivar el jardín, el huerto, trabajar en el jardín, en el huerto. || *adj.* **6** de jardín, de huerto. **7** corriente, ordinario. || **8** (brit.) **– party/** (EE.UU.) **– lawn party,** fiesta, recepción al aire libre. **9** (brit.) **to lead someone up the – path,** llevar a alguien al huerto, seducir, engañar.

gardener | 'gɑ:dnər | *s.c.* jardinero, hortelano.

gardenia | gɑ:'di:njə | *s.c.* BOT. gardenia.

gardening | 'gɑ:dnɪŋ | *s.i.* jardinería, horticultura.

gargantuan | gɑ:'gæntjuən | *adj.* enorme, gigantesco, inmenso, monstruoso: *a gargantuan meal = una comida pantagruélica.*

gargle | 'gɑ:gl | *s.c.* e *i.* **1** gárgaras. **2** gargarismo (con líquido medicinal). || *v.i.* **3** hacer gárgaras, aclarar, limpiar (la garganta) haciendo gárgaras.

gargoyle | 'gɑ:gɔɪl | *s.c.* ARQ. gárgola.

garish | 'geərɪʃ | *adj.* chillón, deslumbrante, llamativo, de mal gusto, exagerado (en colores).

garishly | 'geərɪʃlɪ | *adv.* chillonamente, deslumbrantemente, llamativamente (especialmente en colores).

garishness | 'geərɪʃnɪs | *s.i.* aspecto llamativo, aspecto chillón: *her garishness disgusts me = su aspecto chillón me disgusta.*

garland | 'gɑ:lənd | *s.c.* e *i.* **1** guirnalda (para adornar el cuello), corona de hojas y flores. **2** MAR. estrobo, arza. **3** antología (especialmente de poemas, baladas). || *v.t.* **4 [to – with]** enguirnaldar, adornar con guirnaldas. **5** formar, hacer guirnaldas.

garlic | 'gɑ:lɪk | *s.i.* ajo.

garlicky | 'gɑ:lɪkɪ | *adj.* con sabor a ajo.

garment | 'gɑ:mənt | *s.c.* **1** TEC. prenda de vestir (*gen.* externa). || *v.t.* **2** vestir.

garner | 'gɑ:nər | *v.t.* **1** (lit.) hacer acopio de, acumular, almacenar, recoger, adquirir. || *s.c.* **3** granero.

garnet | 'gɑ:nɪt | *s.c.* **1** granate (mineral). **2** granate (color). **3** MAR. aparejo del estrinque (para sujetar carga ligera).

garnish | 'gɑ:nɪʃ | *s.c.* e *i.* **1** aderezo, condimento, guarnición (cocina). **2** ornamento, embellecimiento, decoración. **3** DER. (fam.) tributo, cuota (con la que los presos extorsionan al recién encarcelado). || *v.t.* **4 [to – with]** aderezar, condimentar. **5** adornar, decorar.

garnishee | ˌgɑ:nɪ'ʃi: | DER. *v.t.* **1** embargar, ejecutar una deuda. **2** notificar un embargo. || *s.c.* **3** embargado. **4** tercero, tercerista.

garnishing | ˌgɑ:nɪ'ʃi:sŋ | *s.c.* e *i.* aderezo, adorno.

garnishment | 'gɑ:nɪʃmənt | *s.* **1** DER. embargo, ejecución de una deuda. **2** DER. notificación, citación. **3** adorno, ornamento.

garret | 'gærit | *s.c.* (lit.) buhardilla, desván.

garrison | 'gærɪsn | MIL. *s.c.* **1** [– *v.sing.* o *pl.*] guarnición, destacamento. **2** campamento, cuartel, guarnición. || *v.t.* **3** destacar (a una compañía), guarnicionar, guarnecer.

garrotte | gə'rɒt | | gə'rɑ:t | *s.c.* **1** garrote (de ejecución). **2** garrote vil. || *v.t.* **3** dar garrote vil, ejecutar con garrote vil. **4** estrangular.

garrulity | gæ'ru:litɪ | *s.i.* charlatanería, locuacidad.

garrulous | 'gærələs | *adj.* locuaz, charlatán, parlanchín.

garrulously | 'gærələslɪ | *adv.* locuazmente, parlanchinamente.

garter | 'gɑ:tər | *s.c.* **1** liga, banda elástica (para medias o calcetines). **2** (brit.) jarretera: *The Order of the Garter = la Orden de la Jarretera.* || *v.t.* **3** sujetar con liga o banda elástica. || **4 – belt,** liguero, portaligas. **5 to have someone's guts for garters,** (fam.) hacer picadillo a alguien, hacer trizas a alguien.

gas | gæs | [*pl.* **gases** o **gasses**] *s.c.* e *i.* **1** gas. **2** sustancia gaseosa. || *s.i.* **3** (EE.UU.) (fam.) gasolina. **4** anestésico gaseoso. **5** (EE.UU.) gas (en el estómago). **6** (EE.UU. y fam.) entretenimiento, diversión. **7** (brit. y fam.) cháchara, cotorreo, palique. || *v.t.* **8** gasear, asfixiar con gas. **9** echar gasolina. **10** (brit. y fam.) dar palique, cotorrear. || **11 – burner,** quemador de gas, mechero de gas. **12 – chamber,** cámara de gas. **13 – cooker,** cocina de gas. **14 – fire,** estufa de gas. **15 – fitter,** instalador de gas. **16 – jet,** llama de quemador de gas. **17 – main,** tubería maestra del gas. **18 – mask,** máscara de gas. **19 – meter,** contador del gas. **20 – oven,** horno de gas. **21 – ring,** quemador de gas (cocina), estufa de gas. **22 – stove,** cocina de gas. **23 – tank,** tanque de gas, de gasolina. **24 – tap,** llave de gas. **25 to step on the –,** apretar el acelerador.

gasbag | 'gæsbæg | *s.c.* (desp. y fam.) charlatán, parlanchín.

gaseous | 'gæsjəs | *adj.* **1** TEC. gaseoso, gaseiforme. **2** (fig.) inconcreto, tenue.

gash | gæʃ | *v.t.* **1** hacer un corte o herida profunda. || *s.c.* **2** brecha, corte profundo.

gasholder | 'gæsˌhəuldər | *s.c.* **1** bombona (de gas). **2** tanque de gas, gasómetro.

gaslight | 'gæslaɪt | *s.i.* **1** luz de gas. || *s.c.* **2** lámpara de gas, alumbrado de gas.

gas-lit | 'gæslɪt | *adj.* iluminado por luz de gas.

gasify | 'gæsɪfaɪ | *v.i.* convertirse en gas, gasificarse.

gasket | 'gæskɪt | *s.c.* MEC. junta, arandela.

gasman | 'gæsmæn | *s.c.* lector de contadores del gas.

gasoline | 'gæsəuli:n | *s.i.* (EE.UU.) gasolina.
gasometer | gæ'sɒmɪtər | *s.c.* gasómetro.
gasp | gɑ:sp | *v.i.* **1 [to – at/with/in]** cortarse la respiración, quedarse sin aliento, boquiabierto (por la sorpresa, susto). **2** jadear, resollar, respirar con dificultad. || *v.t.* **3 [to – out]** hablar entrecortadamente. || *s.c.* **4** jadeo, resuello. || **5 at the last –,** al borde de la asfixia, a punto de dar la última bocanada.
gassy | 'gæsɪ | *adj.* gaseoso, con mucho gas (especialmente bebidas con burbujas).
gastric | 'gæstrɪk | *adj.* MED. gástrico: *gastric juices = jugos gástricos.*
gastritis | gæ'straɪtɪs | *s.i.* **1** MED. gastritis, irritación/inflamación estomacal.
gastro-enteritis | ˌgæstrəuˌentə'raɪtɪs | *s.i.* MED. gastroenteritis.
gastronome | 'gæstrənəum | *s.c.* (hum.) gastrónomo.
gastronomic | ˌgæstrə'nɒmɪk | *adj.* gastronómico.
gastronomically | ˌgæstrə'nɒmɪklɪ | *adv.* gastronómicamente.
gastronomy | gæ'strɒnəmɪ | *s.i.* gastronomía.
gasworks | 'gæswə:ks | *s.c.*[– *v.sing./pl.*] fábrica de gas.
gat | gæt | *s.c.* **1** canal, pasaje (entre acantilados). **2** (EE.UU. y fam.) pistola, revólver. **3** (arc.) *pret.* de **get.**
gate | geɪt | *s.c.* **1** verja, cancela, portezuela, portón (de un cercado). **2** barrera (tren). **3** puerta de embarque (de aeropuerto). **4** compuerta, esclusa. **5** válvula, llave de paso (del gas). **6** (brit.) DEP. taquilla, entrada (ingresos por un partido). **7** MET. conducto de colada. **8** INF. puerta. **9** (arc.) camino, sendero, paso. **10** método, estilo. || *v.t.* **11** (brit.) castigar (con permanencia después del horario escolar). || **12** INF. **– file,** unidad de disco tipo puerta. **13** DEP. **– money,** recaudación. **14 to give someone the –, a)** despedir, dar el despido (del trabajo); **b)** dar calabazas (a un hombre).
gâteau | 'gætəu | [*pl.* **gateaus** o **gateaux**] *s.c.* e *i.* GAST. pastel, tarta.
gatecrash | 'geɪtkræʃ | *v.t.* entrar sin ser invitado, entrar de gorra, colarse.
gatehouse | 'geɪthaus | *s.c.* **1** casa del guarda (en mansiones, parques). **2** caseta del guardabarrera (del tren).
gatekeeper | 'geɪtˌki:pər | *s.c.* **1** guarda, portero. **2** guardabarrera.
gatepost | 'geɪtpəust | *s.c.* **1** pilar, poste (de una verja o portón). || **2 between you, me and the –,** confidencialmente, entre tú y yo, entre nosotros.
gateway | 'geɪtweɪ | *s.c.* **1** entrada, paso, puerta de acceso. **2** (fig.) **[the – to]** la puerta de, el camino hacia: *the gateway to success = la puerta del éxito.*
gather | 'gæðər | *v.t.* **1 [to – in/up]** (lit.) recoger (objetos). **2** recolectar. **3** conseguir, reunir, acumular (información, cualidades, dinero). **4** ganar, aumentar (velocidad). **5 [– (from)]** deducir, inferir, comprender, concluir. **6** cubrirse con, envolverse con (ropa). **7** fruncir, formar pliegues. **8** cobrar, reunir (aliento, fuerzas). **9** atraer, ser centro de atención. **10** (form.) abrazar. || *v.i.* **11 [– round]** reunirse, juntarse, congregarse. **12** acumularse, aumentarse, incrementarse. **13** MED. formar pus, supurar. || *s.* **14** pliegue, frunce. **15** cosecha, recolección. || **16 a rolling stone gathers no moss,** piedra que rueda no cría musgo. **17 – dust,** llenarse de polvo (por falta de uso).
gathering | 'gæðərɪŋ | *s.c.* **1** reunión, asamblea. **2** recolección, acopio. **3** pliegue, frunce. **4** MED. absceso.
gather-write | 'gæðəˌraɪt | *s.* INF. escritura agrupada, grabación agrupada.
gauche | gəuʃ | *adj.* patoso, torpe, falto de tacto, poco seguro de sí mismo.
gaudily | 'gɔdɪlɪ | *adv.* (desp.) ostentosamente, con demasiado brillo, chillonamente.
gaudiness | 'gɔ:dɪnɪs | *s.i.* (desp.) ostentación, vestir chillón.
gaudy | 'gɔ:dɪ | *adj.* **1** chillón, llamativo (color). **2** recargado.
gauge, gage | geɪdʒ | *s.c.* **1** calibre, calibrador. **2** pluviómetro. **3** manómetro. **4** medida, norma. **5** tamaño, capacidad, nivel. **6** ancho de vía, distancia entre dos ejes (en el tren). **7** MAR. calado. **8** MET. espesor, calibre (de una hoja de metal). **9** espesor (de un tejido). || *v.t.* **10 a)** medir con precisión. **b)** (fig.) calibrar. **11** estimar, juzgar. **12** mezclar en proporciones correctas (peso). **13** tallar, cortar (piedras, ladrillos). || **14 to – the right occasion,** elegir la ocasión propicia.
Gaul | gɔ:l | *s.* **1** HIST. Galicia. **2** galo, francés.
gaunt | gɔ:nt | *adj.* **1** flaco, delgaducho, chupado. **2** demacrado. **3** (fig.) desolado, desierto, yermo.
gauntlet | 'gɔ:ntlɪt | *s.c.* **1** guante de trabajo, protección. **2** HIST. MIL. guantelete, manopla. **3** (fig.) reto (a luchar, competir). || **4 to pick up the –,** aceptar el reto. **5 to run the –,** ser despreciado, tratado a baquetazos, sufrir malos tratos. **6 to throw down the –,** arrojar el guante (retar).
gauntness | 'gɔ:ntnɪs | *s.i.* flacura, extrema flacura.
gauze | gɔ:z | *s.i.* **1** gasa. **2** (EE.UU.) venda. **3** malla fina (de plástico o metal). **4** calina, bruma.
gauzy | 'gɔ:zɪ | *adj.* **1** brumoso; nebuloso. **2** diáfano, transparente.
gave | geiv | *pret.* de **give.**
gavel | 'gævl | *s.c.* **1** martillo, mazo (de jueces, subastadores). **2** mazo, maza (de albañil). **3** HIST. gavela, tributo medieval.
gawk | gɔ:k | *v.i.* **1 [to – at]** mirar boquiabierto, papar moscas. || *s.c.* **2** bobo, pánfilo.
gawkily | 'gɔ:kɪlɪ | *adv.* torpemente, desmañadamente, desganadamente.
gawkiness | 'gɔ:kɪnɪs | *s.i.* torpeza, desmaña.
gawky | 'gɔ:kɪ | *adj.* torpe, desganado, desgalichado.
gawp | gɔ:p | *v.i.* **[to – (at)]** (fam.) mirar con la boca abierta, mirar estúpidamente.
gay | geɪ | *adj.* **1** *pred.* homosexual (usado en medios homosexuales). **2** atractivo, alegre, vistoso (colores). **3** *atr.* divertido, festivo, alegre (personas). **4** libertino, dado a los placeres, licencioso. || *s.c.* **5** homosexual (*gen.* hombre). || **6 – lib/liberation,** movimiento de liberación gay.
gayness | 'geɪnɪs | *s.i.* homosexualidad.
gaze | geɪz | *v.i.* **1 [to –** *adv./prep.*] mirar fijamente, contemplar con asombro (a veces inconscientemente). || *s.c.* **2** mirada penetrante, fija. || **3 to meet someone's –,** cruzar una mirada con alguien.
gazebo | gə'zi:bəu | *s.c.* ARQ. mirador, mirador de torre.
gazelle | gə'zel | *s.c.* ZOOL. gacela.
gazette | gə'zet | *s.c.* **1** boletín (de carácter estatal u oficial). **2** gaceta (utilizado como nombre de un periódico). || *v.t.* **3** publicar en el boletín oficial. **4** [usualmente *pas.*] publicar un nombramiento en el boletín oficial (especialmente en el ámbito militar).
gazetteer | ˌgæzə'tɪər | *s.c.* **1** lista de lugares geográficos (en atlas, diccionarios). **2** (arc.) periodista, gacetillero.
gazump | gə'zʌmp | *v.t.* [usualmente *pas.*] (brit., fam. y desp.) engañar (subiendo el precio de la vivienda después de acordar una cantidad): *we've been gazumped, we won't buy the house = nos han engañado, no compraremos la casa.*
gazumper | gə'zʌmpər | *s.c.* (brit., fam. y desp.) mafioso, tramposo, aprovechado. V. **gazump.**
gazumping | gə'zʌmpɪŋ | *s.i.* (brit., fam. y desp.) práctica tramposa, práctica mafiosa. V. **gazump.**
gear | gɪər | *s.c.* **1** marcha, velocidad (de coches): *change gear = cambio de velocidad.* **2** cambio de piñón, de desarrollos (en una bicicleta). **3** MEC. engranaje, rueda dentada. **4** (fig.) actividad, ritmo, engranaje. || *s.i.* **5** equipo, ropa. **6** utensilios, instrumentos, bártulos. **7** aparejos (de animales, barcos). **8** tren, frenos (de aterrizaje). || *v.t.* **9** engranar. **10** meter una velocidad. **11 [– to,** *gen.pas.*] adaptarse, amoldarse (a una situación). || *v.i.* **12** engranarse. || **13** (brit.) **bottom –,** (EE.UU.) **low –,** primera velocidad. **14** [*gen.pas.*] **to – up,** (fam.) estar listo, estar preparado (con ansiedad). **15** (brit.) **– lever,** (EE.UU.) **– shift,** palanca de cambios (de velocidades). **16 in –,** con una marcha puesta; con el embrague puesto. **17 neutral –,** punto muerto.
gearbox | 'gɪəbɒks | *s.c.* **1** caja de cambios (automóvil). **2** MEC. caja de engranajes. **3** (fam.) idiota.
gear-change | 'gɪətʃeɪndʒ | *s.sing.* MEC. cambio de marcha, cambio de embra-

gue: *the gear-change works smoothly = el cambio de marcha funciona suavemente.*

gearwheel | gɪəwiːl | *s.c.* rueda dentada.

gecko | 'gekəʊ | *s.c.* ZOOL. salamanquesa, salamandra.

gee | dʒiː | *s.c.* **1** letra g. || *interj.* **2** (fam. y EE.UU.) ¡caramba! **3** (euf.) ¡Jesús! (expresa sorpresa). **4** (fig.) 10.000 dólares. || **5 to – somebody up,** (brit.) apretar, apurar, obligar (a hacer algo con amenazas). **6 – up!,** ¡arre!

gee-gee | 'dʒiːdʒiː | *s.* (fam.) caballito.

geese | giːs | *pl.* de **goose.**

geezer | 'giːzər | *s.c.* **1** (arc.) viejo, excéntrico, extraño, raro. **2** tipo, tío.

Geiger counter | 'gaɪgəkaʊntər | *s.c.* FIS. contador Geiger (detector de radioactividad).

geisha | 'geɪʃə | *s.c.* geisha.

gel | dʒel | *s.c.* e *i.* **1** gel. || *v.i.* **2** cuajar (en forma de gelatina). **3** (fig.) cuajar (ideas, proyectos, etc.).

gelatin(e) | dʒelə'tiːn | *s.i.* **1** (EE.UU.) gelatina.

gelatinous | dʒə'lætɪnəs | *adj.* **1** TEC. gelatinoso, viscoso, pegajoso.

geld | geld | *v.t.* **1** capar, castrar (a ciertos animales). || *s.* **2** HIST. impuesto (pagado a reyes anglosajones y normandos por los campesinos).

gelding | geldɪŋ | *s.c.* animal castrado (especialmente el caballo).

gelignite | dʒelɪgnaɪt | *s.i.* **1** gelignita (explosivo muy potente).

gem | dʒem | *s.c.* **1** gema, piedra preciosa o semipreciosa, joya. **2** (fig.) joya, tesoro (cosas, personas). **3** bizcocho, bollo, mollete. || *v.t.* **4** adornar con joyas.

Gemini | 'dʒemɪnaɪ | *s.* **1** ASTRON. Géminis, tercer signo del zodíaco. || *s.c.* **2** Géminis (persona de este signo).

gemstone | 'dʒemstəʊn | *s.c.* piedra preciosa (especialmente sin tallar).

gen | dʒen | (p.u., fam. y brit.) *s.i.* **1** **[the – on]** la información sobre. || **2 to – on,** obtener información sobre, ponerse al día sobre.

gendarme | 'ʒɒɑːndɑːm | *s.c.* gendarme, policía (*gen.* francés).

gender | 'dʒendər | *s.c.* e *i.* **1** GRAM. género (masculino, femenino o neutro). **2** TEC. sexo. || *v.t.* **3** (arc.) engendrar.

gene | dʒiːn | *s.c.* gene.

genealogical | ˌdʒiːnjə'lɒdʒɪkl | *adj.* genealógico.

genealogically | ˌdʒiːnɪə'lɒdʒɪklɪ | *adv.* genealógicamente, por genealogía.

genealogist | ˌdʒiːnɪ'ælədʒɪst | *s.c.* genealogista, estudioso de la genealogía.

genealogy | ˌdʒiːnɪ'ælədʒɪ | *s.i.* **1** genealogía. || *s.c.* **2** árbol genealógico, linaje.

genera | 'dʒenərə | *pl.* de **genus.**

genera | 'dʒenərə | V. **genus.**

general | 'dʒenərəl | *adj.* **1** general, corriente, común (algo que afecta a la mayoría): *the general public = la mayoría de la gente.* **2** general, total, ilimitado, no especializado (educación, conocimientos). **3** no cualificado, mixto (trabajo, cargo). **4** generalizado, extendido, usual, frecuente (un hecho). **5** vago, indefinido, no detallado (idea, descripción). **6** general, jefe principal (parte de un título): *Attorney General =* (brit.) *Fiscal de la Corona,* (EE.UU.) *Ministro de Justicia.* || *s.c.* **7** MIL. General. **8 [the –]** (arc.) el público. || **9 as a – rule,** por regla general. **10 – accounting,** contabilidad general. **11 – average,** pérdida enorme, total (seguros). **12 – balance,** balance general. **13 – coverage,** cobertura total. **14 – manager,** encargado jefe. **15 in –,** por lo general, en general.

generality | ˌdʒenə'rælitɪ | *s.c.* **1** generalidad, vaguedad. **2 [the – of]** la mayoría, la mayor parte. || *s.i.* **3** generalidad, carácter general.

generalization | ˌdʒenərəlaɪ'zeɪʃn | *s.c.* **1** (desp.) generalización, vaguedad. || *s.i.* **2** generalización.

generalize | 'dʒenərəlaɪz | *v.i.* **1** generalizar, hablar en general, hablar vagamente, sin detalles. **2** sacar conclusiones, formar conceptos (de forma inductiva). **3** MED. generalizarse, extenderse (enfermedad localizada). || *v.t.* **4** generalizar, aplicar extensamente (una ley).

generalized | 'dʒenrəlaɪzd | *adj.* generalizado, extendido.

generally | 'dʒenərəlɪ | *adv.* **1** generalmente, usualmente. **2** mayoritariamente, por la mayoría. || **3 – speaking,** en términos generales, generalmente hablando.

general-purpose |ˌdʒenrəl'pɜːpəʊz| *adj.* multiuso.

generalship | 'dʒenərəlʃɪp | *s.i.* **1** generalato. **2** don de mando. **3** táctica.

generate | 'dʒenəreit | *v.t.* **1** generar, producir (situación, sentimientos, riqueza). **2** TEC. generar (electricidad). **3** INF. producir (un programa).

generating station | 'dʒenəreɪtɪŋ 'steɪʃn | *s.c.* ELEC. planta, central eléctrica.

generation | ˌdʒenə'reɪʃn | *s.c.* **1** generación (período de tiempo). **2** [– *v.sing.* o *pl.*] generación (de personas o cosas): *new generation of computers = computadoras de nueva generación.* || *s.i.* **3** TEC. generación, producción, creación. || **4 the rising generations,** las nuevas generaciones.

generative | 'dʒenərətɪv | *adj.* **1** BIOL. generativo, procreador. **2** generativo: *generative grammar.*

generator | 'dʒenəreɪtər| *s.c.* **1** generador, dinamo. **2** generatriz. **3** INF. generador. || **4** TEC. **– lock,** modo de sincronización de un equipo de video.

generic | ˌdʒɪ'nerɪk | *adj.* **1** genérico, general, común. **2** BIOL. genérico, relativo a los genes. **3** (EE.UU.) sin marca registrada (por lo tanto sin protección legal).

generically | dʒɪ'nerɪklɪ | *adv.* genéricamente.

generosity | ˌdʒenə'rɒsɪtɪ | *s.c.* e *i.* generosidad.

generous | ˌdʒenərəs | *adj.* **1** generoso, dadivoso, espléndido, desinteresado. **2** altruista, magnánimo. **3** abundante (comida, regalos), espléndido, estupendo (ropa). **4** generoso (vino). **5** (arc.) de noble linaje.

generously | 'dʒenərəslɪ | *adv.* generosamente, espléndidamente, abundantemente.

genesis | 'dʒenɪsɪs | *s.* **1 [the – of]** el génesis de, el origen de. **2 Genesis,** REL. Génesis.

genetic | dʒɪ'netɪk | *adj.* **1** BIOL. genético. **2** genético, genesíaco. || **3 – engineering,** BIOL. ingeniería genética.

genetically | dʒɪ'netɪklɪ | *adv.* genéticamente.

geneticist | dʒɪ'netɪsɪst | *s.c.* persona especializada en genética.

genetics | dʒɪ'netɪks | *s.i.* genética.

genial | 'dʒiːnjəl | *adj.* **1** cordial, simpático, afable, amistoso. **2** (EE.UU. y p.u.) genial, brillante, ocurrente. **3** (EE.UU. y p.u.) matrimonial, nupcial. || *s.i.* **4** ANAT. geniano (relativo a la barbilla).

geniality | ˌdʒiːnɪ'ælitɪ | *s.i.* simpatía, cordialidad, afabilidad.

genially | 'dʒiːnɪəlɪ | *adv.* **1** cordialmente, afablemente, amistosamente. **2** brillantemente, ocurrentemente, genialmente.

genie | 'dʒiːnɪ | [*pl.* **genies** o **genii**] *s.c.* genio (típico de las historias arábigas).

genital(s) | 'dʒenɪtl(z) | *s.pl.* órganos genitales.

genitive | 'dʒenɪtɪv | *s.c.* **1** GRAM. genitivo (caso). || *adj.* **2** genitivo.

genius | 'dʒiːnjəs | *s.i.* **1** genio, inteligencia, talento, ingenio. || *s.c.* **2** genio, lumbrera, experto. **3 [a – for],** talento, habilidad. **4** influencia: *her evil genius = su influencia maligna.*

genned up | 'dʒendʌp | *adj.* (fam. y brit.) al tanto, bien informado, al loro.

genocide | 'dʒenəʊsaɪd | *s.i.* genocidio.

Genoese | ˌdʒenəʊ'iːz | *adj.* **1** genovés. || *s.c.* **2** genovés (natural de Génova).

genre | 'ʒɔːŋrə | *s.c.* **1** género, categoría, estilo. **2** (p.u.) clase, tipo.

gent | dʒent | *s.c.* **1** (brit., hum. y fam.) gentleman, hombre, tío, tipo, individuo. || **2 gents,** retrete de caballeros.

genteel | dʒen'tiːl | *adj.* **1** afectado, remilgado, pomposo. **2** (lit.) cortés, refinado, respetuoso. **3** (arc.) clase social alta.

genteelly | dʒen'tiːllɪ | *adv.* **1** remilgadamente, pomposamente, afectadamente. **2** (lit.) cortésmente, refinadamente, respetuosamente.

gentian | 'dʒenʃn | *s.c.* **1** BOT. genciana. || **2 – violet,** MED. tintura de genciana (para el tratamiento de quemaduras).

gentile | 'dʒentaɪl | *s.c.* **1** gentil, cristiano, no judío. || *adj.* **2** gentil, no judío.

gentility | dʒen'tɪlitɪ | *s.i.* **1** gentileza, cortesía, elegancia. **2** afectación, remilgo. **3** nobleza.

gentle | 'dʒentl | *adj.* **1** apacible, tranquilo, dulce (de carácter, comportamiento). **2** suave, gradual, moderado. **3** dócil, manejable (persona). **4** suave, ligero, lento, pausado (movimiento de voz, expresión. **5** agradable, benigno, apacible (tiempo). **6** suave, relajante (paisaje). **7** sin malicia, amable (comentario, chiste). **8** amable, querido (lector). **9** de buena familia, bien nacido. **10** (arc.) noble, caballeroso. || *v.t.* **11** suavizar, moderar. **12** domar, amansar (caballos). **13** (arc.) elevarse a la nobleza, ennoblecer. || **14 – does it!,** ¡con suavidad, con cuidado! (al manejar objetos frágiles). **15 the – sex,** el sexo débil.

gentleman | 'dʒentlmən | [*pl.* **gentlemen**] *s.c.* **1** caballero, señor, hombre de bien (posición social). **2** caballero, señor (comportamiento social). **3** *pl.* caballeros, señores (para encabezar cartas o al comienzo de un discurso). **4** señor, hombre (término respetuoso). **5** sirviente, paje. || **6 to be no –,** no ser un caballero, no ser educado. **7 gentlemen,** retrete de caballeros. **8 gentleman's agreement,** trato entre caballeros (de palabra).

gentlemanly | 'dʒentlmənlɪ | *adj.* caballeroso, cortés, educado (de comportamiento o posición social).

gentleness | 'dʒentlnɪs | *s.i.* **1** suavidad, dulzura, ternura. **2** docilidad, mansedumbre. **3** lentitud, calma. **4** bondad, amabilidad.

gentlewoman | 'dʒentlwʊmən | [*pl.* **gentlewomen**] *s.c.* (arc.) señora.

gently | 'dʒentlɪ | *adv.* **1** suavemente, dulcemente. **2** dócilmente. **3** poco a poco, lentamente. **4** amablemente, con bondad, con cariño.

gentrify | 'dʒentrɪfaɪ | *v.t.* (fam.) embellecer, acondicionar correctamente (una zona residencial).

gentry | 'dʒentrɪ | *s.i.* **1 [the –]** la aristocracia. **2** (brit.) la alta burguesía, clase acomodada. **3** gente, familia (de un grupo determinado).

genuflect | 'dʒenju:flekt | *v.i.* **1 [to – (before)]** hacer una genuflexión, doblar la rodilla (signo de respeto, reverencia).

genuflexion | ˌdʒenju:'flekʃn | *s.c.* e *i.* genuflexión.

genuine | 'dʒenjʊin | *adj.* **1** genuino, real, auténtico. **2** sincero, honesto, franco.

genuinely | 'dʒenjʊɪnlɪ | *adv.* **1** genuinamente, realmente, auténticamente. **2** sinceramente, honestamente, francamente.

genuineness | 'dʒenjʊɪnɪs | *s.i.* **1** autenticidad. **2** sinceridad, honestidad, franqueza.

genus | 'dʒi:nəs | *pl.* **genera,** *s.c.* TEC. género, clase, categoría, tipo, grupo.

geocentric | ˌdʒi:əʊ'sentrɪk | *adj.* geocéntrico.

geodesic | ˌdʒi:əʊ'desɪk | *adj.* MAT. geodésico.

geographer | dʒɪ'ɒgrəfər | *s.c.* geógrafo.

geographical | dʒɪə'græfɪkl | *adj.* **1** geográfico. || **2 – break out,** COM. ventas, salida en un lugar específico.

geographically | ˌdʒɪə'græfɪklɪ | *adv.* geográficamente.

geography | dʒɪ'ɒgrəfɪ | *s.i.* **1** geografía. **2** (fig.) geografía, emplazamiento, disposición (de un lugar).

geological | ˌdʒɪəʊ'lɒdʒɪkl | *adj.* geológico.

geologically | dʒɪə'lɒdʒɪklɪ | *adv.* geológicamente.

geologist | dʒɪ'ɒlədʒɪst | *s.c.* geólogo.

geology | dʒɪ'ɒlədʒɪ | *s.i.* **1** geología (ciencia, estudio). **2** geología (libro de texto).

geometric(al) | ˌdʒɪəʊ'metrɪkl | *adj.* **1** geométrico (relativo a la geometría). **2** geométrico, regular (formas). || **3 – distorsion,** TEC. distorsión geométrica (en vídeo). **4 – progression,** progresión geométrica.

geometrically | dʒɪə'metrɪklɪ | *adv.* geométricamente.

geometry | dʒɪ'ˋmitrɪ | *s.i.* **1** geometría. **2** configuración geométrica (de un objeto). || **3 solid –,** geometría del espacio.

geophysical | ˌdʒɪəʊ'fɪzɪkl | *adj.* geofísico.

geophysicist | ˌdʒɪəʊ'fɪzisɪst | *s.c.* geofísico, experto en geofísica.

geophysics | ˌdʒi:əʊ'fɪzɪks | *s.i.* geofísica (estudio de los fenómenos geológicos).

geopolitical | ˌdʒɪəʊpə'lɪtɪkl | *adj.* geopolítico.

geopolitics | 'dʒi:əʊ'pɔlɪtɪks | *s.sing.* geopolítica.

George | dʒɔ:dʒ | *s.* **1** Jorge. || *s.c.* **2** jorge (moneda británica del reinado de Enrique VIII).

georgette | dʒɔ:'dʒet | *s.i.* seda diáfana.

Georgian | 'dʒɔ:dʒjən | *adj.* **1** georgiano (natural de una de las dos Georgias: de la URSS o de EE.UU.). **2** ARQ. georgiano (estilo británico del período 1714-1830). **3** LIT. georgiano (estilo poético británico del período 1912-1922). || *s.c.* **4** georgiano (persona, lengua, estilo).

geranium | dʒɪ'renjəm | *s.c.* **1** BOT. geranio. **2** rojo fuerte (color).

geriatric(s) | ˌdʒerɪ'ætrɪk | *s.i.* **1** [– *v.sing.*] geriatría.

geriatric | ˌdʒerɪ'ætrɪk | *adj.* geriátrico.

geriatrician | ˌdʒerɪə'trɪʃn | *s c.* experto en geriatría, médico geriátrico.

germ | dʒə:m | *s.c.* **1** BIOL. germen. **2** (fig.) germen, comienzo. || **3 – carrier,** portador de gérmenes. **4 – cell,** célula embrionaria. **5 – plasm,** citoplasma del germen. **6 – warfare,** guerra biológica.

German | 'dʒə:mən | *s.c.* **1** alemán (persona). || *s.i.* **2** alemán (lengua). || *adj.* **3** alemán (nacionalidad). || **4 – measles,** MED. rubéola.

germane | dʒə:'meɪn | *adj.* **1** (p.u.) relacionado, conectado, relativo, oportuno, relevante. || **2 not –,** inoportuno.

Germanic | dʒə:'mænɪk | *adj* **1** germánico, alemán. || *s.i.* **2** germánico (familia de las lenguas indoeuropeas).

germanophile | dʒə:'mænəfaɪl | *s.c.* germanófilo.

germanophobe | dʒə:'mænəfəubl | *s.c.* germanófobo.

Germany | 'dʒə:mənɪ | *s.sing.* Alemania.

germicidal | ˌdʒə:mɪ'saɪdl | *adj.* germicida.

germicide | 'dʒə:mɪsaɪd | *s.c.* e *i.* germicida, bactericida.

germinal | 'dʒə:mɪnl | *adj.* germinal, en germen, en embrión.

germinate | 'dʒə:mɪneɪt | *v.t.* **1** germinar, brotar. **2** (fig.) germinar, aparecer (una idea). || *v.i.* **3** hacer germinar, hacer brotar.

germination | ˌdʒə:mɪ'neɪʃn | *s.i.* germinación.

germ-killer | ˌdʒə:'kɪlər | *s.i.* germicida, bactericida.

germproof | 'dʒə:pru:f | *adj.* a prueba de gérmenes.

gerontology | ˌdʒerɒn'tɒlədʒɪ | *s.i.* gerontología, estudio de la vejez.

gerrymander | 'dʒerɪmændər | | ˌdʒerɪ'mændar | *v.t.* e *i.* **1** (desp.) POL. alterar (un estado, una zona), dividir arbitrariamente distritos electorales (para conseguir ventaja en unas elecciones).

gerrymandering | ˌdʒerɪ'mændərɪŋ | *s.i.* POL. alteración de distritos fraudulenta. V. **gerrymander.**

gerund | 'dʒerənd | *s.c.* GRAM. gerundio.

gerundive | dʒɪ'rʌndɪv | *s.c.* gerundio, adjetivo verbal (expresa noción de necesidad).

Gestapo | ge'stɑ:pəʊ | *s.c.* [– + *v.sing.* o *pl.*] HIST. Gestapo (policía secreta del partido nazi en Alemania durante los años 1930-1940).

gestate | dʒe'steɪt | *v.t.* **1** BIOL. gestar, llevar en el útero. **2** (fig.) gestar, concebir, meditar (un plan, una idea).

gestation | dʒe'steɪʃn | *s.i.* **1** TEC. gestación. || **2 – period, a)** período de gestación. **b)** (fig.) elaboración, concepción (de un plan, una idea).

gesticulate | dʒe'stɪkjʊleɪt | *v.i.* **1** gesticular, manotear (al hablar). || *v.t.* **2** expresarse con gestos (de la cara, manos).

gesticulation | dʒe'stɪkjʊ'leɪʃn | *s.c.* e *i.* gesticulación, manoteo, ademán, seña.

gesture | 'dʒestʃər | *s.c.* e *i.* **1** gesto, ademán (especialmente de las manos). || *s.c.* **2** gesto, acto, muestra, detalle, demostración. || *v.i.* **3** [**to** – *adv./prep.*] gesticular, hacer señas. || *v.t.* **4** [**to** – + *adv./prep.*] señalar con un gesto, con un ademán.

get | get | *v.irr.pret.* **got,** *p.p.* (brit.) **got,** (EE.UU.) **gotten** *t.* **1** conseguir, obtener, lograr (permiso, resultado, objeto). **2** comprar, adquirir. **3** recibir, experimentar (emoción). **4** recibir (un regalo). **5** ganar, cobrar (dinero). **6** tener (vacaciones, la impresión). **7 [have got]** tener, poseer. **8** recibir, tener (una llamada telefónica, carta). **9** ser condenado (a prisión). **10** coger (un medio de locomoción, una enfermedad). **11** agarrar, asir. **12** recoger, traer, ir a buscar. **13** preparar, hacer (una comida). **14** oír bien, entender, comprender (algo dicho, un mensaje): *don't get me wrong = no me malinterpretes.* **15** conectar con, conseguir hablar con, poner con (por teléfono). **16** coger, contestar (al teléfono). **17** sintonizar, coger (una emisora). **18** emocionar, encantar, irle a uno (algo): *classic music really gets me = la música clásica verdaderamente me encanta.* **19** (fam.) molestar, irritar. **20** **[to – for]** pagar (por), castigar (por venganza): *I'll get you! = ¡me las pagarás!* **21** dar con, atrapar, coger, apresar. **22** golpear, dar en: *I got him right in his head = le di directamente en la cabeza.* **23** sorprender, asombrar, desconcertar. **24** memorizar, aprender de memoria. **25** sacar, conseguir, extraer (un material de otro). **26** reservar, conseguir (entradas, billetes, etc.). **27** hacerse (una reputación). **28** pasar por, pasar a través de. **29** DEP. eliminar, poner fuera de juego. **30** engendrar (usado para animales). **31** **[have got** *inf.***]** tener que, estar obligado a. **32** **[to –** *o. p.p.***]** hacerse, mandar (hacer algo): *she got her hair cut = se cortó el pelo (en la peluquería); I got my car repaired = me arreglaron el coche (en el taller).* **33** **[to –** *o. ger.***]** conseguir que, hacer que: *he got the clock working = consiguió hacer funcionar el reloj.* || *v.i.* **34** **[to –** *adj./p.p.***]** (fam.) ponerse, volverse, hacerse (gen. traducido según el *adj./p.p.* que le sigue): *get cold = ponerse frío; get lost = perderse; get well = mejorar.* **35** **[to –** *inf.***]** hacerse, llegar a (con el paso del tiempo): *when you get to know them = cuando se les conoce.* **36** (p.u. y fam.) salir inmediatamente, marcharse. **37** ganar, obtener (un beneficio). || **[to – +** *adv./prep.***]** **38** **to – about/around,** salir, viajar, andar por ahí. **39** **to – across,** hacerse entender (por), lograr comunicarse/entenderse (con), ser aceptado (por). **40** **to – after,** perseguir. **41** **to – ahead,** triunfar, hacer progresos. **42** **to – a kick out of,** pasárselo bien, divertirse, encantarle (algo a uno). **43** **to – along, a)** arreglárselas, ir tirando, avanzar; **b)** avanzar, ir hacia adelante (un trabajo). **44** **to – along with, a)** llevarse con (bien o mal), congeniar con; **b)** dársele a uno bien (algo). **45** **– along with you!,** ¡anda ya! no digas tonterías. **46** **to – a lot out of something,** sacar (partido a algo, pasárselo bien haciendo algo). **47** **to – around/round, a)** salir, viajar; **b)** evitar, evadir; **c)** solventar (un problema); **d)** extenderse, hacerse del dominio público (una noticia). **48** **to – around/round to,** encontrar tiempo para llegar a, ponerse a (hacer algo). **49** **to – at, a)** encontrar, descubrir; **b)** alcanzar, llegar a (un objeto lejano); **c)** (en forma progresiva) sugerir, dar a entender, insinuar; **d)** [*gen. pas.*] (fam. y brit.) sobornar; **e)** provocar, tomar el pelo. **50** **– away!,** ¡no digas bobadas! **51** **to – away, a)** conseguir marcharse, salir (de una situación, de un lugar): **b)** escaparse, huir, evadirse (de la justicia); **c)** romper (con una situación). **52** **to – away with,** cometer, hacer impunemente, salirse con la suya. **53** **to – away with murder,** salirse con la suya, hacer lo que uno quiere impunemente. **54** **to – back** (+ *in*), **a)** volver, regresar; **b)** volver al poder, volver a la política; **c)** retroceder, dar marcha atrás. **55** **to – back at somebody,** vengarse de alguien, desquitarse. **56** **to – back to somebody,** volver de nuevo con, estar de nuevo con (después de una interrupción). **57** **to – behind,** retrasarse (en el trabajo, en un pago). **58** **to – by, a)** ir tirando, arreglárselas, apañárselas; **b)** pasar, estar pasable (un trabajo); **c)** burlar, eludir (la ley). **59** **to – cracking,** V. **cracking.** **60** **to – down, a)** agacharse, bajarse; **b)** (fam. y brit.) dejar la mesa, levantarse de la mesa. **61** **to – down to,** abordar, prestar atención a, ponerse a (un trabajo). **62** **to – hold of someone,** encontrar, localizar a alguien. **63** **to – in, a)** subir (a un coche); **b)** llegar (a un lugar); **c)** ser admitido, ser aceptado; **d)** ser elegido (para un puesto político); **e)** hacer un hueco para, aceptar, encajar (un trabajo dentro de un período de fuerte actividad). **64** **to – in on,** participar. **65** **to – in the way,** V. **way.** **66** **to – into, a)** subir, montar (en un coche); **b)** ser admitido (en un centro escolar); **c)** pasársele (a uno algo raro) por la cabeza, (jerga) picarle (a uno) la mosca; **d)** ponerse nervioso, meterse en problemas; **e)** acostumbrarse a, aprender a; **f)** embarcarse en, meterse en (política). **67** **– knotted/lost/stuffed!,** ¡muérete! ¡piérdete! ¡vete al infierno! ¡fastídiate! **68** **to – no change,** V. **change.** **69** **to – nowhere,** no progresar, (fig.) no ir a ninguna parte. **70** **to – off, a)** bajarse, apearse (de un autobús, tren, etc.); **b)** quitar, sacar (manchas, tapaderas); **c)** quitarse (ropa); **d)** enviar (cartas, paquetes); **e)** escaparse de, librarse de (un castigo); **f)** conciliar el sueño, conseguir dormir; **g)** despegar (un avión); **h)** acabar, terminar, dejar (el trabajo diario); **i)** (fam.) tener un orgasmo; **j)** (fam. y juv.) colocarse (con drogas). **71** **to – off on,** (fam.) divertirse, entusiasmarse, encantar. **72** **to – off to,** empezar (algo bien o mal). **73** **to – on, a)** avanzar, progresar, continuar; **b)** (en forma progresiva) hacerse tarde (la hora); **c)** (en forma progresiva) hacerse viejo (una persona); **d)** arreglárselas; **e)** subir, montar (a un autobús, tren); **f)** ponerse (ropa). **75** **to – one's own back,** conseguir vengarse de. **76** **to – on for,** faltar poco para (una hora), rondar (una edad). **77** **to – on with,** mezclarse con, hacerse amigo de (por interés). **78** **to – on with,** continuar con (después de una interrupción). **79** **– on with it/you!,** ¡no lo creo! ¡tonterías!; ¡date prisa! ¡acaba ya! **80** **to – on with together,** congeniar con, llevarse con (bien o mal). **81** **to – onto, a)** ponerse en contacto con (por teléfono, carta); **b)** descubrir, tener una pista, caer en la cuenta de; **c)** ser elegido, ser nombrado; **d)** empezar (a hacer algo). **82** **to – out, a)** irse, salir (por propia voluntad); **b)** bajar, salir (de un coche); **c)** salir (a divertirse); **d)** publicar, hacer (un trabajo); **e)** hacerse público, filtrar (noticias); **f)** librar (a alguien de la cárcel); **g)** farfullar, titubear, hablar con dificultad; **h)** ser descubierto (un agente secreto); **i)** sacar, coger (algo de un sitio); **j)** quitar (manchas); **k)** dejar de (un hábito). **83** **to – out of, a)** bajar (de un coche); **b)** escaquearse, escabullirse, evitar (hacer algo fastidioso); **c)** sonsacar (la verdad), forzar a (hablar, pagar); **d)** ganar con, sacar de (una actividad no provechosa). **84** **to – out of the way,** V. **way.** **76** **to – over, a)** recuperarse, reponerse (de una enfermedad, una mala experiencia); **b)** superar, resolver, solucionar (dificultades, problemas); **c)** entenderse, dejar claro. **85** **to – over with,** terminar con (algo desagradable, pero necesario). **86** **to – round, a)** dar la vuelta; **b)** extender, divulgar (noticias); **c)** evitar, cumplir, soslayar (ley, regla); **d)** engatusar, convencer, persuadir. **87** **to – round to,** V. **– around to.** **88** **to – somebody down,** poner nervioso a alguien, deprimir, entristecer. **89** **to – somebody in,** traer a alguien, llamar a alguien (para un trabajo). **90** **to – someone's goat,** V. **goat.** **91** **to – something back,** devolver algo, conseguir algo de nuevo (gen. algo perdido). **92** **to – something down, a)** tragar (algo) con dificultad; **b)** anotar, tomar nota. **93** **to – something in, a)** recoger, recolectar (la cosecha); comprar algo en abundancia; **b)** repartir, entregar; **c)** (fam. y brit.) pagar una ronda; **d)** meter baza (en una conversación). **94** **to – somewhere,** progresar, llegar a algo (después de un estancamiento en una actividad). **95** **to – the message,** V. **message.** **96** **to – through, a)** pasar, aprobar (exámenes, leyes); **b)** soportar, aguantar, sobrellevar; **c)** terminar (una comida), gastar, malgastar (todo el dinero); **d)** (EE.UU.) terminar, acabar (el trabajo); **e)** **[to – to someone]** llegar a (un lugar), comunicar por teléfono con, hacerse entender, meterle a uno (algo) en la cabeza. **97** **to – together (with), a)** reunirse, hacer una fiesta; **b)** juntar, reunir (cosas, personas). **98** **to – up, a)** levantarse (de la cama), ponerse en pie; **b)** (brit.) empezar a soplar (el viento), avivarse (el fuego), embravecerse (el mar); **c)** (arc.) organizar (un grupo, un viaje); **d)** vestirse de, disfrazarse de. **99** **to – up to,** (fam.) hacer diabluras, hacer algo malo. || **100** **to – used to something,** V. **used.** **101** **to – weaving,** V. **weave.** **102** **how lucky/stupid can you –!,** ¡cómo se puede tener tanta suerte/ser tan estúpido! **103** **I can't/couldn't – over something!,** ¡si no lo veo, no lo creo! **104** **not – a look in,** V. **look-in.** **105**

to play hard to –, V. **play. 106 to tell someone where they can – off/where to – off,** cantarle a uno las cuarenta. **107 there's no getting away from,** admitamos que, hay que tener en cuenta que. **108 you've got me there!,** me has pillado en un renuncio.

OBS. **To get** se usa a menudo en lugar de **to be** como auxiliar de pasiva y también en lugar de «there is/are» = existe, hay, sucede.

getaway | 'getəweɪ | *s.c.* **1** huida, fuga, escapada. **2** salida, partida, despegue (carrera). || **3 the – car,** el coche para la huida, el medio de escape.

Gethsemane | geθ'semənɪ | *s.* **1** Getsemaní. **2** (fig.) calvario, sufrimiento.

get-together | 'gettə,gedər | *s.c.* **1** reunión, tertulia, fiesta (informal).

get-up | 'getʌp | *s.c.* **1** indumentaria, atavío. **2** maqueta, disposición (revista, libro).

geyser | 'gaɪzər | *s.c.* **1** GEOL. géiser. **2** (brit.) calentador de agua (de gas).

Ghana | 'gɑːnə | *s.* **1** Ghana (estado africano).

Ghanaian | gɑː'neɪən | *adj.* **1** de Ghana. || *s.c.* **2** ghaneano, natural de Ghana.

ghastliness | 'gɑːstlɪnɪs | *s.i.* **1** palidez extrema, palidez cadavérica. **2** brutalidad, enormidad (de un crimen o similar).

ghastly | 'gɑːstlɪ | *adj.* **1** desagradable, espantoso, terrible. **2** horrible, tremendo, horripilante, atroz (crimen, terror). **3** pálido, cadavérico.

gherkin | 'gəːkɪn | *s.c.* **1** BOT. pepinillo. **2** (Am.) tipo de vino.

ghetto | 'getəʊ | *s.c.* **1** ghetto, barrio pobre (donde vive una minoría étnica). **2** ghetto, judería. **3** (fig.) ghetto (grupo inaccesible, restrictivo). || **4 – blaster,** casete portátil grande.

ghettoize | 'getəʊaɪz | (también **ghettoise**) *v.t.* meter en la categoría de ghetto/barrio pobre.

ghettoization | ,getəʊaɪ'zeɪʃn | *s.i.* clasificación como barrio pobre.

ghost | gəʊst | *s.c.* **1** fantasma, espectro, aparición. **2** (arc.) alma. **3** (fig.) recuerdo, sombra, memoria. **4** TV sombra, imagen falsa. **5** negro (persona que escribe para otra). **6** demonio, espíritu maligno. **7** publicación fantasma (en una bibliografía). || *v.t.* e *i.* **8** (fam.) escribir para otro (anónimamente). || *v.t.* **9** rondar, vagar (como un fantasma). || **10 to give up the –,** dar el último suspiro, entregar el alma, (fig.) dejar de funcionar definitivamente (una máquina). **11 Holy Ghost,** Espíritu Santo. **12 not to have the – of a chance,** no tener la más mínima posibilidad. **13 – story,** cuento de fantasmas. **14 – town,** ciudad fantasma.

ghostly | 'gəʊstlɪ | *adj.* **1** siniestro, fantasmal, espectral. **2** espiritual.

ghostwrite | 'gəʊstraɪt | *v.i.* escribir para otro (que luego se apropia la fama).

ghostwriter | 'gəʊstraɪtər | *s.c.* escritor que trabaja para otro. V. **ghostwrite.**

ghostwriting | 'gəʊstraɪtɪŋ | *s.i.* trabajo de un escritor para otro. V. **ghostwrite.**

ghoul | guːl | *s.c.* **1** espíritu necrófago (de las leyendas musulmanas). **2** (fig.) persona de gustos repugnantes, inhumanos, persona morbosa. **3** ladrón, profanador de tumbas.

ghoulish | guːlɪʃ | *adj.* **1** desagradable, macabro, truculento. **2** sádico, cruel, morboso (personas).

giant | 'dʒaɪənt | *f.* **giantess.** *s.c.* **1** gigante. || *adj.* **2** gigantesco, enorme, gigante.

gibber | 'dʒɪbər | *v.i.* **1** farfullar, hablar atropelladamente. || *s.i.* **2** parloteo, guirigay.

gibberish | 'dʒɪbərɪʃ | *s.i.* guirigay, galimatías, monserga, sinsentido.

gibbet | 'dʒɪbɪt | *s.c.* (arc.) horca.

gibbon | 'gɪbən | *s.c.* ZOOL. gibón.

gibe | dʒaɪb | *s.c.* **1** burla, mofa, escarnio. || *v.t.* **2** burlarse, mofarse, escarnecer, ridiculizar. || *v.i.* **[to – about/at]** mofarse de, escarnecer a, burlarse de, ridiculizar.

giblets | 'dʒɪblɪts | *s.gen.pl.* menudillos (de ave).

Gibraltar | dʒɪ'brɔːltər | *s.* **1** Gibraltar. || **2 Straits of –,** GEOG. Estrecho de Gibraltar.

giddily | 'gɪdɪlɪ | *adv.* **1** aturdidamente, de modo tambaleante, con inseguridad, en el andar. **2** vertiginosamente. **3** (fam. y arc.) frívolamente, volublemente.

giddiness | 'gɪdɪnɪs | *s.i.* mareo, aturdimiento, vértigo.

giddy | 'gɪdɪ | *adj.* **1** mareado, aturdido, tambaleante. **2** vertiginoso. **3** (fam. y arc.) frívolo, ligero de cascos, voluble. || *v.t.* e *i.* **4** marearse, aturdirse, tener vértigo. || **5 – up!** ¡arre! (usado con animales).

gift | gɪft | *s.c.* **1** regalo, obsequio, presente. **2** dádiva, ofrenda. **3** (fig.) regalo. **4 [– for]** talento, dote, facultad (para). **5** (brit. y fam.) *gen.sing.* ganga. || **6 a – from the Gods,** (fig.) un regalo de los dioses, una suerte enorme. **7 – of the gab,** (fam.) poder de convicción, de persuasión, facilidad de palabra. **8 in some one's –/in the – of,** en manos de. **9 I wouldn't have it as a –,** no lo quiero ni regalado. **10 it's a –,** (fam.) ¡está tirado! (un examen, una pregunta). **11 never look a – horse in the mouth,** a caballo regalado no le mires el diente.

gifted | gɪftɪd | *adj.* **1** dotado, talentoso. **2** superdotado (niños).

gift-wrap | 'gɪftræp | *v.t.* envolver para regalo.

gift-wrapped | 'gɪftræpt | *adj.* envuelto como para regalo.

gift-wrapping | 'gɪftræpɪŋ | *s.i.* papel de regalo.

gig | gɪg | *s.c.* **1** (fam.) sesión musical, concierto (de jazz, música popular). **2** compromiso, contrato (para dar una sesión musical). **3** calesa. **4** arpón. **5** anzuelo múltiple. **6** canoa, lancha (de remos, a motor). **7** informe militar (por infracción menor). || *v.i.* **8** remar (en canoa). **9** pescar con anzuelo múltiple o con arpón. || *v.t.* **10** arponear. **11** castigar por infracción menor (en academia militar).

giga | 'gɪgə | *s.* INF. 1.000 millones.

gigahertz | 'gɪgə,hɜːts | *s.pl.* INF. 1.000 millones de ciclos por segundo.

gigantic | dʒaɪ'gæntɪk | *adj.* gigantesco, colosal, inmenso.

gigantically | dʒaɪ'gæntɪklɪ | *adv.* gigantescamente.

giggle | 'gɪgl | *s.c.* **1** risita, risa nerviosa, risa tonta. **2** (brit. y fam.) cachondeo, diversión. || *v.i.* **3** reírse tontamente, nerviosamente. || **4 to have got the giggles,** dar (a uno) la risa tonta, no poder parar de reírse.

giggly | 'gɪglɪ | *adj.* con facilidad para reír.

GIGO | 'gɪgəʊ | **garbage in/garbage out** INF. residuos dentro, residuos fuera.

gigolo | 'ʒɪgələʊ | *pl.* **gigolos.** *s.c.* gigolo, acompañante, amante pagado (por una mujer rica).

gild | gɪld | *v.t.irr.pret.p.p.* **gilded** o **gilt.** **1** dorar, dar una capa dorada. **2** dar brillo falso, sobredorar (metales). **3** (arc.) manchar, embadurnar de sangre. || **4 to – the lily,** (brit.) dorar la píldora.

gilder | 'gɪldər | *s.c.* dorador.

gilding | 'gɪldɪŋ | *s.i.* **1** dorado, doradura (arte). **2** pintura, capa de pintura dorada. **3** adorno, oropel.

gill | gɪl | *s.c.* **1** ZOOL. branquias, agallas. **2** papada, barba (reptiles, aves). **3** (fig.) *pl.* papada (en personas). **4** BOT. membrana (de los hongos). **5** | dʒɪl | 1/8 de litro (medida de volumen). || *v.t.* **6** limpiar (pescado), quitar las agallas. **7** pescar (con red especial). || **8 – green/white about the gills,** (fam. y hum.) pálido como un cadáver.

gillyflower | 'dʒɪlɪ,flauər | *s.c.* **1** BOT. alhelí amarillo. **2** BOT. gariofilea.

gilt | gɪlt | *v.pret.* y *p.p.* de **gild.** || *s.i.* **1** adorno. **2** brillo falso. | *adj.* **3** dorado, recubierto de oro. **4** (fig.) atractivo. || **5 to take the – off the gingerbread,** echar un jarro de agua fría, aguar la fiesta.

gilt-edged | ,gɪlt'edʒd | *adj.* **1** de cantos dorados. || **2 – securities/stocks/shares,** pagarés del Tesoro, valores de máxima seguridad (pero de bajo interés), (fig.) de la mejor calidad.

gimbals | 'dʒɪmblz | *s.pl.* MEC. balancines de brújula.

gimcrack | 'dʒɪmkræk | *adj.* (desp.) baratija, de baratija.

gimlet | 'gɪmlɪt | *s.c.* **1** barrena, taladro de mano. **2** (EE.UU.) cóctel de ginebra con zumo de lima. || *adj.* **3** penetrante (mirada).

gimmick | 'gɪmɪk | *s.c.* **1** (fam. y gen. desp.) truco, artimaña publicitaria. **2** dispositivo secreto (para amañar una ruleta). || *adj.* **3** artero, engañoso.

gimmickry | 'gɪmɪkrɪ | *s.i.* (desp.) artimañas, tretas, trampas.

gimmicky | 'gɪmɪkɪ | *adj.* (desp.) tramposo, con trampas, con artimañas.
gin | dʒɪn | *s.c.* e *i.* **1** ginebra. **2** (fam.) **– rummy,** juego de cartas. **3** MEC. polea, grúa. **4** MEC. (EE.UU.) máquina desmotadora de algodón. **5** trampa (para cazar). || *v.t.* **6** desmotar algodón. **7** cazar con trampa.
ginger | 'dʒɪndʒər | *s.i.* **1** BOT. jengibre. **2** jengibre (especial). **3** (fam.) brío, ánimo, energía. **4** color amarillento. || *v.t.* **5** sazonar con jengibre. **6** (fam.) animar, estimular. || **7 – ale,** gaseosa de jengibre (usada en combinados). **8 – beer,** cerveza de jengibre (ligeramente alcohólica).
gingerbread man | 'dʒɪndʒəbred mæn | [*pl.* **gingerbread men**] *s.c.* galleta de jengibre (con forma de hombrecillo).
gingerly | 'dʒɪndʒəlɪ | *adj.* **1** cuidadoso, cauteloso. || *adv.* **2** cuidadosamente, cautelosamente. **3** delicadamente, afectuosamente.
gingery | 'dʒɪndʒərɪ | *adj.* con color de jengibre.
gingham | 'gɪŋəm | *s.i.* guinga, zaraza (un tipo de tejido).
gingivitis | ˌdʒɪndʒɪ'vaɪtɪs | *s.i.* MED. gingivitis.
ginseng | 'dʒɪnseŋ | *s.i.* BOT. ginseng.
gipsy, gypsy | 'dʒɪpsɪ | *s.c.* **1** gitano. || *adj.* atr. **2** gitano.
giraffe | dʒɪ'rɑːf | [*pl.* **giraffes** o **giraffe**] *s.c.* jirafa.
gird | gəːd | *v.t.pret.* y *p.p.* **girded** o **girt.** **1** (arc.) rodear, apretar (con cinturón o banda). **2** ceñir, atar. **3** equipar, dotar. **4** **[to – oneself]** prepararse, disponerse (para la acción). || *v.t.* e *i.* **5** burlarse, mofarse, escarnecer. || *s.i.* **6** mofa, sarcasmo, burla. || **7 to – (up) one's loins,** (hum.) prepararse, disponerse (para algo difícil o peligroso).
girder | 'gəːdər | *s.c.* viga maestra.
girdle | 'gəːdl | *s.c.* **1** corsé, faja. **2** cinturón, ceñidor. **3** (fig. y lit.) anillo. **4** corte anular (en la corteza de los árboles). **5** borde de una gema (sujeto por el engarce). **6** ANAT. arco pectoral pelviano. || *v.t.* **7** (lit.) rodear, circundar. **8** atar, rodear (con cinturón, correa). **9** retirar, quitar una tira de corteza (a los árboles).
girl | gəːl | *s.c.* **1** chica, niña, muchacha. **2** hija (gen. joven). **3** (fam.) chica (término empleado para señoras de cualquier edad). **4** criada, chica. **5** (fam. y arc.) novia, amiga. (A veces puede ser un término ofensivo cuando se dirige a una mujer adulta). || **6 – scout,** chica exploradora, guía.
girlfriend | 'gəːlˌfrend | *s.c.* **1** novia. **2** amiga. **3** amante, amiguita.
girlhood | 'gəːlhʊd | *s.i.* niñez, juventud, mocedad (femenina).
girlish | 'gəːlɪʃ | *adj.* **1** aniñado, de niña. **2** afeminado.
girly, girlie | 'gəːlɪ | | gəːrlɪ | *adj.* (fam.) de desnudos femeninos: *a girly magazine = una revista de desnudos femeninos.*
giro | 'dʒaɪrəʊ | *s.c.* e *i.* **1** COM. giro, giro bancario. || *s.c.* **2** (brit.) giro (especialmente con el envío de pensiones).
Gironde | dʒɪ'rɒnd | *s.* Gironda (región francesa y partido político republicano del s. XVIII).
girt | gəːt | *pret.* y *p.p.* de **gird.**
girth | gəːθ | *s.c.* e *i.* **1** TEC. circunferencia (medida). **2** tamaño, volumen. || *s.c.* **3** cincha. || *v.t.* **4** medir la circunferencia. **5** rodear, ceñir.
gist | dʒɪst | *s.* **[the – of]** el quid de, la esencia de, el meollo de, la idea central de.
give | gɪv | *v.irr.pret.* **gave,** *p.p.* **given.** *t.* **1** dar, entregar (algo), (fig.) dar, entregar (el brazo). **2** dar, aceptar (una conferencia, entrevista). **3** dar (nombre, dirección, idea, impresión, prioridad, importancia, etc.). **4** dar, calcular (un precio, tiempo). **5** donar (órganos). **6** dar, donar, contribuir con (dinero). **7** regalar. **8** ofrecer (ayuda). **9** servir (bebidas). **10** subir (el sueldo). **11** dar, sacrificar (la vida). **12** dejar, dar (elección, tiempo). **13** hacer (un descuento). **14** producir, cansar, contagiar (una enfermedad). **15** producir, abrir, provocar (el apetito). **16** citar, revelar, hacer constar (detalles). **17** arrojar, dar (resultados). **18** administrar (medicamentos). **19** organizar, celebrar (una fiesta). **20** conferir (de autoridad). **21** otorgar, conferir (un derecho, un privilegio). **22** sentenciar, condenar (a prisión). **23** emitir (una señal). **24** entregar, consagrar, dedicar (a una persona, una cosa). **25** prestar (atención). **26** (fam.) admitir (la verdad). **27** excusar, disculpar. **28** brindar. || *i.* **29** hacer donaciones, regalos. **30** rendirse (a una presión, a una evidencia). **31** suceder, pasar: *what gives? = ¿qué pasa?* **32** entregarse (sexualmente). || *s.i.* **33** elasticidad, flexibilidad. || *v.* + *adv./prep.* **34 don't – me that!,** ¡no lo acepto! ¡imposible! **35 to – as good as one gets,** devolver golpe por golpe, devolvérselas, contestar adecuadamente (en pelea, discusión). **36 to – away, a)** dar, donar, regalar; **b)** (fig.) perder (posibilidad); **c)** entregar (a la novia); **d)** divulgar (un secreto); **e)** descubrir, revelar; **f)** entregar (premios oficialmente). **37 to – back (+ to),** devolver. **38 to – in,** rendirse, sucumbir. **39 to – it to someone** (straight), echar una regañina, reprender. **40 – me (something),** a mí que me den... **41 to – of something,** dar (sin esperar nada a cambio). **42 to – notice,** V. **notice. 43 to – off something,** emitir, despedir (calor, olor, líquido). **44 to – on/onto something,** dar a, tener vistas a (un lugar). **45 – or take,** más o menos (después de una cantidad), (minuto) arriba, (minuto) abajo. **46 to – out (to something), a)** repartir, distribuir; **b)** (fam.) dejar de funcionar, colapsar; **c)** producir (ruido); **d)** acabarse; **e)** dar a conocer, publicar. **47 to – over,** (gen. *imperativo)* (brit. y fam.) parar, dejar de (hacer algo). **48 to – over to, a)** asignar, dejar (algo) para; **b)** entregarse a, dedicarse a; **c)** dejar algo en manos de. **49 to – rise,** V. **rise. 50 to – rent,** V. **rent. 51 to – somebody up, a)** perder la esperanza; **b)** dejar de relacionarse con (alguien); **c)** delatar, descubrir, denunciar (a alguien, a la policía). **52 to – someone a ring,** V. **ring. 53 to – someone for dead,** (fam.) dar a alguien por muerto. **54 to – someone hell,** V. **hell. 55 to – something in,** entregar (un examen, un libro). **56 to – something up, a)** dejar de (hacer), abandonar (un hábito, esperanza); **b)** rendirse, desistir; **c)** rendir, entregar (algo al enemigo). || **57 to – the game away,** descubrir la jugada. **58 to – the sack,** V. **sack. 59 to – to believe/understand,** dar a entender, creer. **60 to – up on somebody,** (fam.) darse por vencido, rendirse (ante una situación, persona). **61 to – up the ghost,** V. **ghost. 62 to – way,** V. **way. 63 I don't/couldn't – a damn/hoot,** (fam.) me importa un rábano, un pepino. **64 I'll – that!,** ¡te lo admito! ¡te lo concedo! **65 I would – a lot/the world/anything/my right arm,** daría lo que fuera, cualquier cosa, todo el oro del mundo.
OBS. Este es uno de los verbos más utilizados en inglés y a menudo no tiene otro significado que el suyo propio, pero se traduce según la palabra que le sigue.
give-and-take | ˌgɪvən'teɪk | *s.i.* **1** toma y daca, concesiones mutuas.
giveaway | 'gɪvəweɪ | *s.c.* (fam.) **1** regalo; premio. **2** revelación involuntaria de un secreto.
giveaway | 'gɪvəweɪ | *s.* **1** (fam.) revelación, traición. **2** obsequio, regalo (que se da con un producto para animar a comprarlo). || **3 a – price,** un precio de saldo/ruina.
given | 'gɪvn | *p.p.* de **give.** || *adj.* **1** dado, determinado, específico: *at a given distance = a una distancia dada.* || *prep.* **2 [– s./that]** teniendo en cuenta (que), supuesto (que). || **3 to be – to** [*ger./s.*] ser propenso a, ser dado a, ser adicto a. || **4 any –** *s.* uno en particular.
giver | 'gɪvər | *s.c.* donante, donador.
gizzard | 'gɪzəd | *s.* molleja (de las aves).
glacial | 'gleɪsjəl | *adj.* **1** glacial, helado. **2** GEOL. glacial (período). **3** (fam. y fig.) glacial, helado, hostil.
glacially | 'gleɪsɪəlɪ | *adv.* heladamente, con un frío glacial.
glaciation | ˌglæsɪ'eɪʃn | *s.i.* GEOL. glaciación, congelación, helamiento.
glacier | 'glæsjər | *s.c.* glaciar, helero.
glad | 'glæd | *adj.* **1 [– about** *s./inf.*] contento, feliz, encantado. **2 [– of]** agradecido, encantado con. **3 [–** *inf.*] deseoso (de), encantado (de). **4** feliz, buena (noticia). || *v.t.* e *i.* **5** encantar, estar encantado. || **6 to be – for someone,** alegrarse por alguien. **7 – tidings,** buenas noticias.

gladden | 'glædn | *v.t.* alegrar, hacer feliz, ser feliz, regocijar.
glade | gleɪd | *s.c.* claro (en el bosque).
glad-hand | ˌglæd'hænd | *v.t.* (fam. y desp.) saludar efusiva pero falsamente.
gladiator | 'glædɪeɪtər | *s.c.* HIST. gladiador.
gladiolus | ˌglædɪ'əuləs | [*pl.* **gladioli, gladioluses**] *s.c.* BOT. gladiolo.
gladly | 'glædlɪ | *adv.* **1** gustosamente, con mucho gusto. **2** alegremente, con satisfacción.
gladness | 'glædnɪs | *s.i.* felicidad, alegría, regocijo, satisfacción.
glad-rags | 'glædrægz | *s.pl.* (fam.) traje de gala, ropa de los domingos.
gladsome | 'glædsəm | *adj.* (arc.) jubiloso, alegre.
gladiatorial | ˌglædɪə'tɔ:rɪəl | *adj.* de gladiadores.
glamorize | 'glæməraɪz | *v.t.* **1** hacer atractivo, embellecer. **2** ensalzar, alabar, presentar (algo) bajo un prisma favorable. **3** idealizar.
glamorous | 'glæmərəs | *adj.* glamoroso, atractivo, hechizante.
glamor, glamour | 'glæmər | *s.i.* **1** glamour, encanto, hechizo. **2** fascinación, admiración (gen. sexual). || **3 – girl,** una belleza (gen. opuesto a persona inteligente).
glamorously | 'glæmərəslɪ | *adv.* atractivamente, hechiceramente.
glance | glɑ:ns | *s.c.* **1** mirada, ojeada, vistazo. **2** GEOL. mineral brillante, lustroso. || *v.i.* **3 [to – *adv./prep.*]** mirar, lanzar una mirada. **4** (lit.) brillar, centellear (una superficie). || **5 at a –,** de una ojeada, de un vistazo. **6 at first –,** a primera vista. **7 to cast/look a quick –,** echar una ojeada rápida. **8 to – off something,** rebotar, chocar, desviarse con un bote.
glancing | glɑ:nsɪŋ | *adj.* indirecto, oblicuo (un golpe), sin fuerza.
gland | glænd | *s.c.* **1** ANAT. glándula. **2** MEC. collarín, prensa-estopas.
glandular | 'glændjulər | *adj.* **1** glandular. || **2 – fever,** MED. fiebre linfática, fiebre glandular.
glare | gleər | *v.i.* **1 [to – at]** mirar fieramente, echar chispas por los ojos. **2 [to – *adv./prep.*]** deslumbrar, fulgurar; (fig.) herir la vista. || **3** mostrar odio en la mirada. || *s.c.* **4** mirada fiera, de odio, feroz. **5** resplandor, fulgor, luz deslumbrante. || **6 in the – of publicity,** (fig.) en primer plano de la actualidad/en el ojo del huracán/en la cresta de la ola.
glaring | gleərɪŋ | *adj.* **1** deslumbrante, fulgurante, intenso (luz). **2** fuerte, chillón (color). **3** hiriente, notorio, que salta a la vista. **4** feroz, iracundo (mirada).
glaringly | 'gleərɪŋlɪ | *adv.* **1** deslumbrantemente, fulgurantemente, intensamente. **2** demasiado chillón (colores). **3** notoriamente, hirientemente, visiblemente. **4** ferozmente, iracundamente (mirada).
glasnot | 'glæznɒt | *s.i.* POL. apertura, transparencia (expresión rusa).
glass | glɑ:s | *s.i.* **1** cristal, vidrio (material). **2** cristalería, objetos de cristal. || *s.c.* **3** vaso, copa. **4 [a – of]** un vaso de, una copa de (licor, vino). **5** (brit. y fam.) espejo. **6** barómetro. **7** *pl.* gafas, lentes. **8** *pl.* gemelos. || *v.t.* **9** poner en recipiente de cristal, embotellar. **10 [to – in],** acristalar, cubrir con cristal. **11** vitrificar. **12** reflejarse en un espejo. || *v.i.* **13** vitrificarse. || *adj.atrib.* **14** de cristal, de vidrio. || **15 cut –,** cristal tallado. **16 dark glasses,** gafas oscuras. **17 ground –,** cristal esmerilado. **18 magnifying –,** V. **magnifying. 19 plate –,** V. **plate. 20 stained –,** V. **stained. 21 under –,** en invernadero, en vitrina.
glass-blower | 'glɑ:sbləuər | *s.c.* vidriero, soplador de vidrio, especialista en fabricación de vidrio (con la técnica de soplar).
glassful | 'glɑ:sful | *s.c.* vaso (el contenido).
glasshouse | 'glɑ:shaus | *s.c.* **1** (brit.) invernadero. **2** vidriera, fábrica de vidrio. **3 [the –]** (brit. y jerga) la prisión (gen. militar).
glassily | 'glɑ:sɪlɪ | *adv.* **1** transparentemente, cristalinamente. **2** acuosamente. **3** vidriosamente (mirada sin brillo).
glassiness | 'glɑ:sɪnɪs | *s.i.* **1** transparencia, (lo) cristalino. **2** acuosidad. **3** vidriosidad (de la mirada).
glassware | 'glɑ:sweər | *s.i.* cristalería, vajilla de cristal.
glassworks | 'glɑ:swə:ks | *s.pl.* [=N *v.sing./pl.*] fábrica de vidrio, vidriería.
glassy | 'glɑ:sɪ | | 'glæsɪ | *adj.* **1** cristalino, transparente (agua). **2** vítreo, acuoso (sustancia). **3** de cristal, de vidrio (objeto). **4** vidrioso, sin brillo, sin vida (mirada).
glassy-eyed | ˌglɑ:sɪ'aɪd | *adj.* con la mirada vidriosa, con la mirada sin vida.
glaucoma | glɔ:'kəumə | *s.i.* MED. glaucoma.
glaze | gleɪz | *v.t.* **1** barnizar, vidriar, lustrar. **2** glasear (alimentos). **3** acristalar, poner cristal. || *v.i.* **4 [to – over]** vidriarse (la mirada). || *s.c.* **5** mogate, vidriado. **6** barniz, lustre. **7** glaseado. **8** capa de barniz o de mogate (en alfarería). **9** mirada vidriosa.
glazed | gleɪzd | *adj.* **1** vidrioso, sin vida (mirada). **2** vidriado (material). **3** acristalado. **4** glaseado.
glazier | 'gleɪjər | *s.c.* cristalero, vidriero.
gleam | gli:m | *s.c.* **1** destello, centelleo, fulgor. **2** luz tenue. **3 [– of]** chispa de, viso de, vestigio de (interés, esperanza). || *v.i.* **4** destellar, fulgurar, centellear. **5** brillar tenuemente. **6 [to – *adj./prep.*]** mostrar, expresar (un sentimiento) tenue y fugazmente.
gleaming | gli:mɪŋ | *adj.* destellante, centelleante, fulgurante.
glean | gli:n | *v.t.* **1** entresacar, recoger (información poco a poco). || *v.t.* e *i.* **2** espigar.
gleaner | gli:nər | *s.c.* **1** investigador. **2** espigador.
gleanings | gli:nɪŋz | *s.pl.* **1** fragmentos de información. **2** espigas, rebusca (que quedan en el campo después de la cosecha).
glee | gli: | *s.i.* **1** satisfacción, júbilo, regocijo, placer. || *s.c.* **2** MUS. canción para 3 o 4 voces masculinas (sin acompañamiento). || **3 – club,** orfeón, coro.
gleeful | 'gli:fl | *adj.* jubiloso, alegre.
gleefully | 'gli:fulɪ | *adv.* con regocijo, alegremente, jubilosamente.
glen | glen | *s.c.* valle estrecho (en Escocia e Irlanda).
glib | glɪb | *adj.* **1** (desp.) de mucha verborrea, labia, locuaz, charlatán, poco sincero. **2** fácil, poco creíble, ligero: *a glib reply = una respuesta fácil.*
glibly | 'glɪbɪ | *adv.* **1** con ligereza, irreflexivamente. **2** elocuentemente, con desenvoltura.
glibness | 'glɪbnɪs | *s.i.* **1** elocuencia, verborrea, labia. **2** ligereza, falta de reflexión, falta de sinceridad.
glide | glaɪd | *v.i.* **1 [to – *adv./prep.*]** deslizarse. **2** moverse furtivamente. **3** escurrirse, irse silenciosamente. **4** AER. planear, volar sin motor. || *s.* **5** deslizamiento, escurrimiento. **6** planeo, vuelo sin motor. **7** MUS. ligadura. **8** FON. paso gradual de un sonido a otro (al pronunciar un diptongo). **9** FON. semivocal.
glider | 'glaɪdər | *s.c.* **1** AER. planeador (avión). **2** planeador (persona). **3** columpio.
gliding | 'glaɪdɪŋ | *s.i.* DEP. vuelo sin motor.
glimmer | 'glɪmər | *v.i.* **1** brillar con luz tenue e intermitente, cabrillear, reverberar, rielar, vislumbrar (una esperanza). || *s.c.* **2** luz trémula, tenue. **3** signo, rastro, noción vaga.
glimmering | 'glɪmərɪŋ | *s.c.* brillo vacilante, luz trémula.
glimpse | glɪmps | *v.t.* **1** vislumbrar, entrever, avistar. || *v.i.* **2** mirar fugazmente, echar una ojeada. || *s.c.* **3** ojeada, vislumbre, mirada rápida. **4** (arc.) breve destello, fulgor. || **5 to catch a – of,** vislumbrar, percibir vagamente.
glint | glɪnt | *v.t.* e *i.* **1** destellar, fulgurar, (fig.) brillar. || *s.c.* **2** destello, fulgor, centelleo.
glissade | glɪ'seɪd | EE.UU. | glɪ'sɑ:d | *s.c.* **1** descenso, deslizamiento (por la ladera de una montaña utilizando el piolet). **2** ART. paso suave de ballet. || *v.i.* **3** descender, deslizarse (por una ladera de montaña). **4** ART. dar un paso suave (en ballet).
glissando | glɪ'sændəu | [*pl.* **glissandi** o **glissandos**] *s.c.* MUS. glissando (arpegiar notas escala tras escala).
glisten | 'glɪsn | *v.i.* resplandecer, centellear, relucir, brillar (especialmente describiendo superficies espejadas).
glitter | 'glɪtər | *v.i.* **1** brillar, rutilar, relucir. **2** (fig.) brillar. || *s.i.* **3** brillo, resplandor. **4** glamour; atracción. **5** lentejuelas, brillo, purpurina o dorado

(usado en decoración). **6** (fig.) brillo, oropel. || **7 all that glitters is not gold,** no es oro todo lo que reluce.

glitterati | ˌglɪtə'rɑːtɪ | *s.pl.* (fam.) gente guapa, jet.

glittering | 'glɪtərɪŋ | *adj.* **1** reluciente, brillante, rutilante. **2** glamoroso, atractivo.

glittery | 'glɪtərɪ | *adj.* brillante, resplandeciente.

glitz | glɪts | *s.i.* (fam.) ostentación, mal gusto; horterada.

glitzy | 'glɪtsɪ | *adj.* (fam.) de relumbrón; hortera, cutre.

gloaming | 'gləʊmɪŋ | *s.sing.* (arc.) crepúsculo.

gloat | gləʊt | *v.i.* **1 [to – over]** (desp.) mirar o pensar maliciosamente, relamerse de gusto. **2** (desp.) recrearse, regocijarse (mirando o pensando). || *s.i.* **3** malicia, placer malsano.

glob | glɒb | *s.cuant.* **[a – of + *s.i.*] 1** gota, glóbulo. **2** grumo, montoncito, masa pequeña. **3** terrón.

global | 'gləʊbl | *adj.* **1** mundial. **2** global, total. **3** esférico. || **4 – entry,** COM. asiento global. **5 – profits,** COM. beneficios netos. **6 – sales,** COM. ventas globales.

globally | 'gləʊbəlɪ | *adv.* globalmente.

globe | gləʊb | *s.c.* **1** globo, esfera. **2** globo terráqueo. **3 [the –]** la tierra, el globo, el orbe. **4** orbe (emblema de soberanía). || *v.t.* e *i.* **5** (arc.) tomar forma de globo.

globe-trot | 'gləʊbtrɒt | *v.i.* (fam.) viajar por todas partes, viajar de un sitio a otro.

globe-trotter | 'gləʊbtrɒtər | *s.c.* (fam.) trotamundos.

globular | 'glɒbjulər | *adj.* esférico, redondo.

globule | 'glɒbjuːl | *s.cuant.* **1** glóbulo, gota. **2** ANAT. glóbulo.

gloom | gluːm | *s.sing.* **1** desesperanza, tristeza, desilusión, pesimismo. **2** (lit.) penumbra, oscuridad, tenebrosidad. **3** lugar tenebroso, en penumbra. || *v.i.* **4** oscurecerse, estar en penumbra. **5** entristecerse, desolarse. || *v.t.* **6** oscurecer. **7** desesperar, entristecer, desolarse. || **8 – and doom,** ruina y desesperación.

gloomily | 'gluːmɪlɪ | *adv.* **1** desesperadamente, melancólicamente, con pesimismo. **2** oscuramente, tenebrosamente.

gloominess | 'gluːmɪnɪs | *s.i.* **1** oscuridad, sombra (con aspecto lúgubre). **2** aspecto sombrío (del tiempo). **3** tristeza, melancolía, desdicha. **4** situación desesperada, aspecto desolador (de una situación).

gloomy | 'gluːmɪ | *adj.* **1** oscuro, sombrío (lugar). **2** cubierto. **3** triste, desdichado, abatido, melancólico (carácter). **4** desesperada, desalentadora (una situación).

glorification | ˌglɔːrɪfɪ'keɪʃn | *s.sing.* **1** glorificación. **2** bondad.

glorified | 'glɔːrɪfaɪd | *adj.* (desp.) exagerado; puesto por las nubes (cuando en realidad no es de buena calidad).

glorify | 'glɔːrɪfaɪ | *v.t.* **1** ensalzar, adular, alabar, (fig.) dar coba. **2** glorificar, alabar, dar gracias (a Dios). || *v.i.* **3** (fam.) tener pretensiones, ser algo con pretensiones.

glorious | 'glɔːrɪəs | *adj.* **1** glorioso, admirable, loable. **2** espléndido, maravilloso, celestial. **3** (fam.) magnífico, estupendo, delicioso, fantástico.

glory | 'glɔːrɪ | *s.i.* **1** gloria, fama, honor, admiración, prestigio. **2** esplendor, magnificencia. **3** gloria, honra (a Dios). || *v.i.* **4 [to – in something]** alegrarse con, gloriarse de/en. **5** (desp.) regodearse, refocilarse, relamerse. || **6 covered in/with –,** cubierto de gloria, con vanagloria. **7 in all its –,** en todo su esplendor.

gloriously | 'glɔːrɪəslɪ | *adv.* **1** gloriosamente, admirablemente, loablemente. **2** espléndidamente, maravillosamente, celestialmente. **3** (fam.) magníficamente, estupendamente, deliciosamente, fantásticamente.

glory-hole | 'glɔːrɪhəʊl | *s.c.* (brit. y fam.) cajón de sastre, cajón donde cabe todo (sin guardarlo en debido orden).

gloss | glɒs | *s.i.sing.* **1** brillo, lustre, pulimento (de una superficie), reflejo (del pelo). **2** (fig.) oropel, engaño, apariencia. **3** glosa, glosario, comentario, acotación. || *v.t.* **4** lustrar, pulir, pulimentar. **5** glosar, acotar, comentar. **6 [to – (over)]** encubrir, disimular, disculpar. || **7 – finish,** acabado brillante. **8 – paint,** pintura esmalte.

glossary | 'glɒsərɪ | *s.c.* glosario.

glossily | 'glɒsɪlɪ | *adv.* **1** lustrosamente, brillantemente (sobre el pelo). **2** satinadamente, brillantemente (con fotos). **3** (desp.) llamativamente, ostentosamente.

glossiness | 'glɒsɪnɪs | *s.i.* lustre, pulimento.

glossy | 'glɒsɪ | *adj.* **1** lustroso, brillante (el pelo), liso. **2** satinado, con brillo (el papel, fotografías). **3** (desp.) llamativo, ostentoso. || **4 – magazine,** revista de calidad, elegante.

glove | glʌv | *s.c.* **1** guante. **2** guante de boxeo, de béisbol. || *v.t.* **3** cubrir con guantes, poner guantes. || **4 to fit like a –,** quedar, sentar como un guante. **5 hand in –,** uña y carne, inseparables. **6 with gloves off,** sin miramientos, despiadadamente.

gloved | glʌvd | *adj.* enguantado.

glover | 'glʌvər | *s.c.* guantero (que hace o vende guantes).

glow | gləʊ | *v.i.* **1** estar incandescente, ponerse al rojo (por calor), arder (a causa del fuego). **2** brillar, resplandecer, fulgurar. **3 [to – with]** resplandecer de, rebosar de (orgullo, salud), enardecerse, enrojecer. || *s.c. gen.sing.* **4** resplandor, luz difusa. **5** brillo, luminosidad (de color), incandescencia. **6 [– (of)]** arrebol (en las mejillas). **7 [– (of)]** ardor, sensación de (placer, satisfacción).

glower | 'glaʊər | *v.i.* **1 [to – (at)]** mirar encolerizadamente, con ceño. **2** (fig.) amenazar. || *s.c.* **3** mirada colérica, ceñuda.

glowering | 'glaʊərɪŋ | *adj.* **1** ceñudo. **2** amenazador.

glowing | 'gləʊɪŋ | *adj.* **1** entusiasta, apasionado, ardoroso, extremadamente favorable. **2** radiante, resplandeciente, vivo, encendido.

glow-worm | 'gləʊwəːm | *s.c.* luciérnaga, gusano de luz.

glucose | 'gluːkəʊs | *s.i.* QUIM. glucosa.

glue | gluː | *s.i.* **1** cola, goma de pegar. || *v.t.* **2** encolar, pegar. **2 [– to]** (fig. y fam.) prestar mucha atención a, pegarse a, estar pegado a: *glued to him = sin perderse una coma = pegada a él (para no perder detalle).* || **3 glued to the spot,** pegado al suelo, sin moverse.

gluey | 'gluːɪ | *adj.* **1** pegajoso, viscoso. **2** cubierto de cola.

glum | glʌm | *adj.* melancólico, triste, abatido, apenado.

glut | glʌt | *s.c.gen.sing.* **1 [– (of)]** exceso, sobreabundancia. **2** (fig.) exceso, abuso. || *v.t.gen.pas.* **3** inundar, llenar en exceso. || *v.r.* **4 [– oneself with]** hartarse de, saciarse de.

gluten | 'gluːtən | *s.i.* gluten.

glutinous | 'gluːtɪnəs | *adj.* (lit.) glutinoso, pegajoso.

glutton | 'glʌtn | *s.c.* **1** (desp.) glotón, comilón, tragón. || **2 [– for]** (fam. y fig.) glotón, incansable, insaciable: *glutton for punishment = trabajador incansable.*

gluttonous | 'glʌtnəs | *adj.* (desp.) glotón, goloso, voraz.

gluttony | 'glʌtnɪ | *s.i.* (desp.) glotonería, voracidad.

glycerine | 'glɪsəriːn | *s.i.* QUIM. glicerina.

G-man | 'dʒiːmæn | *s.c.* [*pl.* **G-men**] **1** (EE.UU.) agente del FBI [de **G(overnment) man**].

gnarled | nɑːld | *adj.* **1** nudoso, retorcido. **2** nudosa, rugosa, encallecida (la piel, las manos). **3** curtido (una persona).

gnash næʃ | *v.t.* **1** hacer rechinar, crujir (los dientes). || *s.i.* **2** crujido (de dientes).

gnome | nəʊm | *s.c.* **1** gnomo. || **2 the gnomes of Zurich,** (fam.) los banqueros (gen. suizos).

gnu | nuː | *s.c.* ZOOL. ñu.

go | gəʊ | *v.irr.pret.* **went.** *p.p.* **gone.** *i.* **1** irse, marcharse, partir. **2** viajar, ir en (medio de locomoción). **3** (fig.) **[to – before]** ir, enviar, llevar ante (un tribunal, consejo). **4 [to – + *ger.*]** ir a (nadar), ir de: *go shopping = ir de compras.* **5** acabarse, consumirse, desaparecer. **6 [to – + *ger.*]** ir por ahí (haciendo, diciendo). **7 [to – + *adj.*]** volverse, ponerse, convertirse (loco, canoso, etc.). **8** llevarse (la mano al bolsillo). **9** ir a parar. **10** pasar a, ser heredado. **11 [to – + *adj./adv.*]** quedar (libre), permanecer, pasar (inadvertido). **12** temer (por la vida). **13** pasar (calamidades). **14** fallar, quebrarse, flaquear (la voz). **15** empezar (un trabajo, deporte). **16** funcionar, andar, marchar (un aparato). **17** estropearse, romperse, fastidiarse. **18** (fam.) decir, rezar, continuar (una historia). **19** sonar (el timbre, la campana). **20** **[to – +** *adv./prep.***]** llegar, llevar, ir (un camino de un lado a otro). **21** pasar (deprisa, despacio). **22** venir bien, sentar bien, caer bien (ropa). **23** hacer juego, ir bien, ser apropiado (los complementos, adornos). **24** **[to – +** *adv./prep.***]** ir (bien o mal), caber, entrar (algo en un espacio). **25** **[to –** *adv./prep.***]** tener éxito, marchar, desarrollarse (bien o mal). **26** venderse, conseguir un precio, tener venta. **27** pasar (a otro tema). **28** **[must /can/to have to –]** deshacerse de, descartarse, abolir. **29** **[to – far/further/beyond]** comprometerse, aventurar. **30** ser válido, ser terminante, aceptarse, (fam.) ir a misa (algo). **31** (lit.) morirse, agonizar. **32** *inf.* quedar, faltar (distancia, tiempo). **33** *inf.* llevar (a casa una comida de restaurante). **34** dar como resultado (de una división). **35** circular, pasar de uno a otro. **36** contribuir, ayudar. **37** ser, existir (por regla general): *not expensive, as clothes go = no es caro, para el precio que tiene la ropa.* **38** estar, haber disponible (trabajo). || *t.* **39** decir, continuar, rezar (una inscripción): *then he goes... = luego él dice...* **40** sonar, hacer dar (un ruido, la hora): *it went «boom» = hizo «bum».* || *s.c.* **41** (fam.) turno, vez. **42** (brit.) intento, tentativa, ensayo, esfuerzo. **43** *pl.* viajes, caminatas, marchas. || *s.i.* **44** (fam.) energía, vitalidad. **45** ganga, negocio redondo. **46** dosis, porción, trago, copa. **47** **[the –]** la moda. **48** (brit.) protesta, bronca. **49** éxito. || *adj.* **50** (fam.) preparado, dispuesto, listo (para la acción). || **[to –** *adv./prep.***]** **51** **to – about something, a)** empezar, emprender (algo): **b)** realizar, abordar, afrontar; **c)** virar, girar en redondo (barcos). **52** **to – after something/somebody,** ir detrás de, perseguir, intentar conseguir. **53** **to – against somebody/something, a)** ir en contra de, oponerse; **b)** estar en contra de; **c)** chocar con. **54** **to – ahead, a)** seguir, continuar; **b)** empezar, proceder a; **c)** avanzar. **55** **to – along,** continuar, proseguir. **56** **to – along with something/somebody,** concordar con, estar de acuerdo con, coincidir con. **57** **to – around/round,** extenderse, propagarse (una enfermedad, noticias). **58** **to – around/round with, a)** tener tratos con, asociarse con, tener relación con; **b)** bastar, alcanzar, dar para. **59** **to – at something,** (fam.) atacar, abalanzarse sobre. **60** **to – back, a)** regresar, volver; **b)** **[to – back +** *adv./prep.***]** ser originario de, tener su origen en, ser de (fecha). **61** **to – back on something/somebody,** romper, traicionar (una promesa, amigos). **62** **to – by, a)** pasar el tiempo; pasar por un lugar, (fig.) perder (una oportunidad); **b)** **[to – by something]** atenerse a, sujetarse a, guiarse por; **c)** juzgar por, decir por (un modo de actuar). **63** **to – down, a)** bajar, descender (de un lugar); **b)** bajar, descender (de posición), disminuir, caer (precios, calidad, nivel); **c)** hundirse (barcos); **d)** deshincharse; **e)** ser aceptado, tener buena acogida; **f)** tragar (comida); **g)** quedar grabado, registrado; **h)** bajar, llegar (hasta un lugar); **i)** (brit.) salir, irse, dejar (un centro de estudios para siempre o por vacaciones); **j)** (jerga) ir a prisión; **k)** ponerse (el sol). **64** **to – down with something,** (fam.) caer enfermo con, contraer, coger (una enfermedad infecciosa). **65** **to – for somebody/something, a)** atacar (físicamente o de palabra); **b)** intentar conseguir; **c)** escoger, elegir; **d)** (fam.) gustar, atraer; **e)** concernir, valer para, aplicarse a. **66** **to – in, a)** entrar (en un lugar); **b)** oscurecer, ocultarse (el sol, la luna); **c)** **[to – with]** unirse a/con, asociarse, juntarse. **67** **to – in for something, a)** participar, tomar parte en (concurso de habilidad, conocimientos); **b)** dedicarse a, interesarse por (un pasatiempo). **68** **to – into something, a)** meterse en, dedicarse a (una actividad profesional); **b)** ahondar, profundizar (en una materia); **c)** investigar. **69** **to – off, a)** explotar, estallar; **b)** dispararse, sonar (la alarma, timbre); **c)** apagarse, dejar de funcionar; **d)** discurrir, resultar (bien o mal); **e)** estropearse, pudrirse, agriarse (alimentos, comida); **f)** desaparecer; **g)** (fam.) perder el interés por, dejar de gustar; **h)** (brit. y fam.) disminuir, bajar, descender (interés, nivel o calidad). **70** **to – off with something/somebody,** (fam.) **a)** irse, largarse (con otro); **b)** coger, llevarse algo (sin permiso). **71** **to – on, a)** suceder, ocurrir, pasar, tener lugar, hacer (algo); **b)** empezar a funcionar; **c)** probar, basar; **d)** continuar, ir adelante, proseguir; **e)** pasar, avanzar (el tiempo); **f)** continuar, proseguir, durar (una actividad, un comportamiento); **g)** protestar, criticar; **h)** avanzar, desarrollarse; **i)** (fam.) hablar, charlar. **72** **to – on with,** ir tirando. **73** **to – out, a)** salir de casa (a divertirse); **b)** **[to – together/with],** salir juntos, tener relaciones con, ser novios; **c)** irse a vivir; **d)** hacerse público, difundirse (noticias); **e)** apagarse (luz, fuego), (fig.) apagarse (sentimiento), (fig.) dormirse; **f)** bajar (la marea); **g)** pasar de moda; **h)** (lit.) simpatizar, estar con; **i)** finalizar, terminar, pasar. **74** **to – over, a)** ver, visitar, examinar (un lugar); **b)** comprobar, repasar (un asunto); **c)** repetir; **d)** aceptarse, acogerse (bien o mal); **e)** **[to – to/from],** cambiarse de, pasarse de(a) (un partido, una religión); **f)** TV. conectar con (un lugar). **75** **to – round, a)** bastar, ser suficiente; **b)** extenderse, propagarse; **c)** estar presente, rondar la cabeza. **76** **to – slow,** (brit.) hacer huelga de brazos caídos. **77** **to – through, a)** sufrir, experimentar, soportar, sobrellevar; **b)** terminar, acabar; **c)** aprobar (una ley, plan); **d)** practicar, volver sobre (algo); **e)** examinar con cuidado, registrar (ropas, papeles). **78** **to – through with,** cumplir, llevar a cabo, continuar con (algo prometido). **79** **to – to, a)** pasar por, sufrir; **b)** empezar. **80** **to – together,** hacer fuego con, ir bien con, armonizar. **81** **to – under, a)** hundirse (un barco); **b)** fracasar, fallar, hundirse (un proyecto, un plan). **82** **to – up, a)** subir, incrementar, elevar (precios); **b)** construir, levantar (edificios); **c)** estallar (en llamas), destruirse; **d)** subir (el telón); **e)** (brit.) ir a la universidad; **f)** llegar hasta (una altura). **83** **to – with, a)** hacer juego con, ir bien con, armonizar con; **b)** tener que ver con, tener relación con, ser el resultado de; **c)** (fam.) salir con, tener relación con alguien (social o sexualmente). **84** **to – without,** pasarse sin, arreglárselas sin. || **85** **anything goes,** se acepta todo, cualquier cosa vale. **86** **as (something) goes,** comparado con la media, para lo que hay. **87** **to be going,** ir (en el futuro). **88** **to be going to,** tener intención de, ir a. **89** **from the word –,** desde el principio, desde el comienzo, desde el primer instante. **90** **– along with you!,** ¡qué tontería! ¡qué estupidez! **91** **to – as far as/so far as,** llegar hasta (un lugar). **92** **to – by the book,** hacer al pie de la letra. **93** **gone and done,** dicho y hecho, por fin lo hizo. **94** **to – far/a long way,** triunfar, ir lejos. **95** **to – for nothing,** perderse, irse por la borda (un trabajo). **96** **to – it,** actuar con desenfreno. **97** **to – it alone,** actuar independientemente, por sí mismo. **98** **to – into details,** entrar en detalles. **99** **– on!,** ¡no creo! ¡tonterías! **100** **to – on like a light,** quedarse dormido. **101** **to – one better,** hacerlo mejor que, ir más allá que. **102** **to – to great lengths,** tomarse muchas molestias. **103** **to – to pieces,** sufrir un ataque de nervios, quedarse hecho pedazos, desesperarse. **104** **to – to show,** probar, confirmar. **105** **to – with the crowd/the times/the stream,** ir con, seguir la corriente. **106** **it goes without saying,** ni que decir tiene. **107** **it's all –,** (brit. y fam.) hay exceso de trabajo. **108** **it's no –,** ni hablar, no hubo suerte. **109** **to have a –,** (fam.) intentarlo. **110** **to make a – of,** (fam.) tener éxito con. **111** **on the –,** en plena actividad.

goad | gəʊd | *v.t.* **1** **[to – (into/on)]** provocar, picar, enervar. **2** azuzar, incitar. **3** arrear (ganado) con aguijada. || *s.c.* **4** aguijada.

go-ahead | 'gəʊəhed | *s.sing.* **1** permiso, aprobación, visto bueno. || *adj.* **2** emprendedor, enérgico, progresista.

goal | gəʊl | *s.c.* **1** DEP. portería, meta. **2** DEP. tanto, gol. **3** objetivo, meta, finalidad. || **4** **– area,** (brit.) DEP. área. **5** **– keeper,** DEP. portero. **6** **– kick,** DEP. tiro libre. **7** **– line,** DEP. línea de gol. **8** **to score a –,** DEP. marcar un gol. **9** **to keep –,** DEP. jugar de portero.

goalie | gəʊlɪ | *s.c.* DEP. (fam.) portero.

goalpost | 'gəʊl,pəʊst | *s.c.* DEP. poste de la portería.

goat | gəʊt | *s.c.* **1** cabra, macho cabrío. **2** (fam. desp. y hum.) hombre lujurioso, casanova, donjuán. **3** capricornio. **4** chivo expiatorio, cabeza de turco. || **5 to get someone's –,** tomar el pelo, mofarse, irritar a alguien.

goatee | gəʊ'tiː | *s.c.* chiva, barba de chivo, barbas de mandarín.

goatherd | 'gəʊthəːd | *s.c.* cabrero, pastor de cabras.

goatskin | 'gəʊtskɪn | *s.c.* e *i.* **1** piel, cuero de cabra. **2** odre, bota de vino.

gob | gɒb | | gɑːb | *s.c.* **1** (vulg.) boca, bocaza. **2 [– (of)]** (jerga) grumo, burujo (de algo líquido y pegajoso): *gobs of spit = salivazo.* **3** (fam.) mogollón, cantidad (gen. de dinero).

gobble | 'gɒbl | *v.t.* e *i.* **1 [to – (up)]** (fam.) comer groseramente, engullir, devorar. **2** (fig.) tragar, devorar, arramblar con. || *v.i.* **3** graznar. || *s.* **4** graznido (del pavo).

gobbledygook, gobbledydegook | 'gɒbəldɪguːk | | 'gɑːbəldɪgʊk | *s.i.* (fam. y desp.) blablablá, jeri-gonza, discurso rimbombante y confuso (gen. político).

go-between | 'gəʊbɪˌtwiːn | *s.c.* **1** mensajero, mediador. **2** correveidile, alcahuete.

gobblet | 'gɒblɪt | *s.c.* (arc.) copa, ciborio, cáliz (de cristal o metal).

gobblin | 'gɒblɪn | *s.c.* duende, trasgo, gnomo.

go-by | 'gəʊbaɪ | *s.c.* **1** (fam.) esquinazo, menosprecio, rechazo. **2** ZOOL. gobio, cadoz. || **3 to give a place the –,** dejar de frecuentar un lugar.

go-cart | 'gəʊkɑːt | *s.c.* **1** tacatá, andaderas. **2** carretilla de mano. **3** carretón de niños.

god | gɒd | *s.c. m.* **1** dios, deidad. **2** ídolo. **3** (fig.) dios, lo más importante: *money was his god = el dinero era lo más importante para él.* **3** *pl.* paraíso (en el teatro). || **4 act of God,** V. **act. 5 for God's sake!,** ¡por Dios!, ¡por amor de Dios! **6 God alone knows,** sólo Dios lo sabe, sabe Dios. **7 God forbid!,** ¡pongo a Dios por testigo! ¡Dios no lo quiera! **8 God helps those who help themselves,** a Dios rogando y con el mazo dando. **9 God willing,** si Dios quiere, Dios mediante. **10 in the lap of the gods,** V. **lap. 11 Oh, God!/my God!/good God!,** ¡Dios mío! **12 thank God,** gracias a Dios. **13 tin –,** V. **tin.**

godchild | 'gɒdtʃaɪld | *pl.* **goodchildren,** *s.c.* **1** ahijado, ahijada.

gooddaughter | 'gɒdˌdɔːtər | *s.c.* ahijada.

goddess | 'gɒdɪs | *s.c. f.* **1** diosa, deidad. **2** ídolo (femenino). **3** (fig.) diosa, belleza.

godfather | 'gɒdˌfɑːðər | *s.c.* **1** padrino.

godfearing | 'gɒdˌfɪərɪŋ | *adj.* (arc.) devoto, piadoso, temeroso de Dios.

godforsaken | 'gɒdfəˌseɪkən | *adj.* **1** (desp.) remoto, desolado, abandonado de Dios (un lugar). **2** aburrido, monótono, repulsivo (un lugar).

godless | 'gɒdlɪs | *adj.* (form.) impío, ateo, descreído.

godly | 'gɒdlɪ | *adj.* (form.) santo, divino. **2** piadoso, devoto.

godmother | 'gɒdˌmʌðər | *s.c. f.* **1** madrina. || **2 fairy –,** hada madrina.

godparents | 'gɒdˌpeərənts | *s.pl.* padrinos.

godsend | 'gɒdsend | *s.c.* bendición, regalo de Dios, don del cielo.

godson | 'gɒdsʌn | *s.c.* ahijado.

goes | gəʊz | *3a. persona sing. presente de* **to go.** V. **go.**

go-getter | ˌgəʊ'getər | *s.c.* (fam.) ganador, triunfador.

goggle | 'gɒgl | *v.i.* **1 [to – (at)]** ponerse los ojos como platos, quedarse atónito, quedarse boquiabierto, salirse los ojos de las órbitas. || *s.pl.* **2** gafas protectoras (para el agua, el viento). **3** (fam.) gafas.

going | gəʊɪŋ | *ger.* de *to go.* || *s.i.* **1** marcha, partida, ida. **2** tiempo invertido (en una marcha, en una retirada). **3** estado, condición (del firme). **4** rumbo, orientación, posibilidad de movimiento. || *adj.* **5** disponible, obtenible (un trabajo). **6** actual, existente, corriente (un precio). **7** activo, en marcha, rentable (un negocio). **8** [*adj.sup.* + *s.* + –] existente, que existe, que hay: *the cheapest car going = el coche más barato en el mercado.* || **9 a – concern,** COM. un negocio en marcha, establecido. **10 comings and goings,** V. **coming. 11 heavy –,** (fig.) pesadez, peñazo, rollo. **12 to have a lot/plenty/nothing – for one,** tener muchas ventajas o cualidades,/no tener ventajas o cualidades. **13 while the – is good,** mientras se pueda.

going-over | 'gəʊɪŋ'əʊvər | *s.c.* **1** revisión, inspección. **2** paliza, tunda, somanta. **3** reprimenda, riña.

goings-on | gəʊɪŋz'ɒn | *s.pl.* (fam.) comportamientos, asuntos, historias (desagradables).

gold | gəʊld | *s.i.* **1** MIN. oro. **2** oro (joyas, monedas). **3** color oro, amarillo oro. **4** (fig.) riqueza. **5** DEP. medalla de oro. || *adj.* **6** de oro, dorado. || **7 as good as –,** muy bueno, muy educado, más bueno que el pan (de un niño). **8 to be worth one's weight in –,** valer lo que uno pesa. **9 – digger,** (jerga y desp.) buscador de oro; buscona. **10 – mine,** mina de oro; (fig.) mina, fuente (de información). **11 – standard,** COM. patrón oro. **12 rolled –,** chapado en oro.

goldbrick | 'gəʊldˌbrɪk | *s.i.* **1** bisutería, oro falso, oropel. **2** (EE.UU.) holgazán, vago, gandul (un soldado). || *v.i.* **3** holgazanear, haraganear, huir del trabajo. || *v.t.* **4** engañar, embaucar, timar, estafar.

Gold Coast | 'gəʊldkɒst | *s.* Costa de Oro (hoy Ghana).

golden | 'gəʊldən | *adj.* **1** (lit.) de oro. **2** (lit.) dorado, de color del oro. **3** excelente, valiosa, maravillosa (una oportunidad). **4** prometedor, próspero, exitoso. **5** radiante, espléndido. || **6 Golden Age,** Siglo de Oro; Edad de Oro. **7 – chance/opportunity,** oportunidad de oro, muy ventajosa. **8 – wedding anniversary,** bodas de oro.

goldenrod | 'gəʊldənˌrɒd | *s.c.* BOT. vara de San José.

goldfilled | 'gəʊldˌfɪld | *adj.* **1** TEC. chapado en oro, revestido de oro. **2** empastado de oro (un diente).

goldfinch | 'gəʊldfɪntʃ | *s.c.* ZOOL. jilguero, pintadillo, siete colores.

goldfish | 'gəʊldfɪʃ | *s.c.* **1** ZOOL. carpa dorada, pececillo dorado (para peceras). || **2 – bowl,** pecera (redonda). **3 in a – bowl,** expuesto al público, de cara al público (un actor, un político).

goldsmith | 'gəʊldʃmɪθ | *s.c.* joyero, orfebre.

golf | gɒlf | *s.i.* **1** DEP. golf. || *v.i.* **2** jugar al golf. || **3 – club,** palo de golf; club de golf. **4 – course,** campo de golf. **5 – links,** campo de golf (al lado del mar). **6 iron –,** V. **iron. 7 wood –,** V. **wood.**

golfer | 'gɒlfər | *s.c.* DEP. jugador de golf, golfista.

Goliath | gəʊ'laɪəθ | *s.* **1** Goliath. **2** (fig.) goliath, gigante, monstruo.

golly | 'gɒlɪ | | 'gɑːlɪ | *interj.* (arc. y fam.) ¡Dios!, ¡dioses! (expresa sorpresa).

golosh | gə'lɒʃ | *s.c.* **1** chanclo, catiusca. **2** (arc.) almadreñas, zuecos.

gonad | 'gəʊnæd | *s.c.* BIOL. gónada.

gondola | 'gɒndələ | *s.c.* **1** góndola. **2** (EE.UU.) batea, barca de fondo plano. **3** AER. barquilla (de aeronave, de globo). **4** teleférico. **5** góndola (camión).

gone | gɒn | *p.p.* de **to go,** V. **go.** || *adj.* **1** (fam.) ido, absorto, ausente, perdido (a causa del alcohol, las drogas). **2** embarazada: *4 months gone = embarazada de cuatro meses.* **5 [– (on)]** enamorado (de), loco (por). **6** pasado, transcurrido (tiempo, edad). **7** agonizante, desaparecido, muerto. **8** perdido, arruinado. **9** exhausto, agotado.

goner | 'gɒnər | *s.c.* **1** (arc. y jerga) condenado, desahuciado. **2** persona perdida, sin esperanza, arruinada.

gong | gɒŋ | *s.c.* **1** gong, campana. **2** (brit. y jerga) medalla.

gonorrhoea, gonorrhea | ˌgɒnə'rɪə | *s.i.* MED. gonorrea.

goo | guː | *s.i.* **1** (fam.) sustancia pegajosa. **2** (desp.) zalamería, halago, adulación, lisonja.

good | gʊd | *adj.* [*comp.* **better,** *super.* **best**] **1** bueno, abnegado, fiel. **2** útil, adecuado, apropiado, práctico. **3** agradable, divertido, estupendo. **4** apto, válido, en perfectas condiciones. **5** atractivo, espléndido (de apariencia). **6** bueno, beneficioso (para la salud). **7** inteligente, habilidoso. **8** virtuoso, justo, bueno, santo. **9 [– to/about]** amable con, servicial con, generoso con. **10** bien educado, dócil. **11** total, completo: *a good look = una ojeada completa.* **12** seguro, fiable, fijo. **13 [a –]** mucho, un montón (de tiempo); muchas (veces), gran (posibilidad); por lo menos: *we spent a good 2 days on it = nos llevó por lo menos dos días.* || *s.i.* **14** bien, beneficio, provecho, mejora. **15** bien, bondad, virtud. **16 [the –]** la buena gente, los buenos de espíritu, los justos. **17** *pl.* bienes de consumo, mercancías, existencias. **18** *pl.* COM. flete, carga, mercancía (por barco, avión, o carretera). **19** bienes muebles, propiedades muebles, riqueza. || *adv.* **20** bien. || **21 a – deal,** V. **deal. 22 a – few,** V. **few. 23 a – sailor,** V. **sailor. 24 all in – time/in one's own time,** (fam.) en el momento oportuno, cada cosa a su debido tiempo. **25 as – as,** casi, prácticamente. **26 as – as gold,** V. **gold. 27 as – as new,** perfecto, como nuevo. **28 to be as – as one's word,** mantener lo dicho, cumplir lo prometido. **29 to be in someone's – books,** V. **book. 30 to catch with the goods,** pillar con las manos en la masa. **31 to come to no –,** terminar mal. **32 to come up with/deliver the goods,** dar lo esperado, producir lo esperado. **33 to do someone –/the pover of –/the world of –,** venir bien, sentar bien. **34 for –,** definitivamente, para siempre. **35 for – measure,** V. **measure. 36 for your own –,** por tu propio bien. **37 – and,** completamente, totalmente, bien, muy. **38 – for,** suficiente para, probable. **39 – for you!,** ¡enhorabuena!, ¡hiciste bien! **40 – God/gracious/grief/heavens/Lord!,** ¡Dios mío! (expresa sorpresa). **41 – show!,** (brit. arc. y fam.) ¡me alegro! **42 – turn,** V. **turn. 43 to have a – mind to,** sentir inclinación por. **44 to have a – time,** divertirse, pasarlo bien. **45 to hold –,** valer por o para, tener validez. **46 in – faith,** V. **faith. 47 in – taste,** V. **taste. 48 in – time,** temprano, pronto. **49 it's a – thing/job,** afortunadamente, por suerte. **50 to make –,** tener éxito, hacerse rico. **51 to make – (something), a)** asumir, abonar (deudas, pérdidas); **b)** llevar a cabo, cumplir con, realizar con éxito; **c)** (brit.) reparar, arreglar (algo que uno ha estropeado). **52 more harm than –,** más mal que bien. **53 no –/not much –/not any –,** inútil, vano. **54 so far so –,** V. **far. 55 that's a – one!,** ¡buen chiste!, ¡qué mentira! **56 the – old days,** V. **day. 57 the goods,** (brit. y fam.) el no va más; expectativas, necesidades, requerimientos. **58 too much of a – thing,** lo bueno si breve dos veces bueno; lo poco agrada, lo mucho enfada. **59 to the –,** con un beneficio de, por encima de (lo calculado). **60 up to no –,** tramar algo malo, intentar algo ilegal o deshonesto, tener mala intención. **61 very –!,** (brit. y arc.) naturalmente, claro que sí. **62 what's the – of...?/what – is...?,** ¿qué sentido tiene...? **63 while the going is –,** V. **going.**

good-bye | ˌgʊdbaɪ | *interj.* adiós, hasta luego, hasta la vista.

good-for-nothing | 'gʊdfəˌnʌθɪŋ | *s.c.* vago, haragán, holgazán, inútil, gandul.

good-humored | ˌgʊd'hjuːməd | *adj.* encantador, con buen humor, jovial.

goodly | 'gʊdlɪ | *adj.* **1** (arc.) grande, gran, considerable. **2** agradable, atractivo, de buena apariencia.

good-natured | ˌgʊd'neɪtʃəd | *adj.* **1** de buen corazón, bondadoso, generoso, amable. **2** dócil.

goodness | 'gʊdnɪs | *s.i.* **1** bondad, amabilidad, generosidad. **2 [the –],** lo mejor, la esencia, las propiedades (de un alimento). || **3 my –!/– me!/for – sake!/I wish to –!,** ¡por Dios santo!, ¡Dios mío!, ¡ojalá! (expresan sorpresa).

good-tempered | ˌgʊd'tempəd | *adj.* afable, tranquilo, de buen carácter.

good-time | 'gʊdˌtaɪm | *adj.* **1** alegre, frívolo, despreocupado.

goody | 'gʊdɪ | *s.c.* **1** (fam.) *pl.* golosinas, dulces. **2** *pl.* atractivos, caprichos, cosas deseables. **3** (arc.) tía (seguido del apellido de mujeres casadas humildes). || *interj.* **4** guay, chupi, chachi (expresión infantil).

goodwill | ˌgʊd'wɪl | *s.i.* **1** buena voluntad. **2** COM. plusvalía; valor comercial (de un negocio al ser vendido).

gooey | 'guːɪ | *adj.* **1** (fam.) viscoso, pegajoso, empalagoso (los dulces). **2** (fig. y desp.) pegajoso, almibarado, sensiblero.

goofy | 'guːfɪ | *adj.* (fam.) ridículo, estúpido, bobo.

goon | guːn | *s.c.* **1** (fam.) imbécil, tonto, estúpido. **1** (EE.UU.) gorila, pistolero a sueldo.

goose | guːs | [*pl.* **geese**] [*m.* **gander**] *s.c.* **1** ganso, ánsar. **2** (fig.) ganso, tonto. || **3 can't/couldn't say boo to a –,** V. **boo. 4 to cook someone's –,** echarle a perder los planes a uno, fastidiarle los planes a uno. **5 too kill the – that lays the golden eggs,** (fig.) matar la gallina de los huevos de oro. **6 wild – chase,** V. **chase.**

gooseberry | 'gʊzbərɪ | *s.c.* **1** BOT. grosellero, uva espina. **2** grosella. || **3 to play –,** (brit. y fam.) hacer de carabina, estar de carabina.

gooseflesh | 'guːsfleʃ | *s.i.* carne de gallina (por frío, miedo).

goosepimples | 'guːsˌpɪmplz | (EE.UU.) **goosebumps,** *s.i.* **1** carne de gallina (por frío, miedo).

goose-step | 'guːsstep | *s.i.* **1** MIL. paso de la oca (desfilar sin doblar la rodilla). || *v.i.* **2** MIL. marchar al paso de la oca.

gopher | 'gəʊfər | *s.c.* ZOOL. **1** tuza (mamífero americano similar a la rata). **2** ardilla de tierra. **3** tortuga de tierra.

gore | gɔː | *v.t.* **1** acornar, embestir, coger, empitonar. **2** sesgar, nesgar, poner nesgas. || *s.i.* **3** (lit.) sangre coagulada, coágulo de sangre. || *s.c.* **4** nesga, cuchillo. **5** terreno en forma triangular.

gorge | gɔːdʒ | *s.c.* **1** desfiladero, garganta, paso entre montañas. **2** gola, entrada (a una fortificación). **3** garganta, gorja (de una persona). **4** atasco, masa que obstruye. || *v.t.* **5** atiborrar, llenar, hartar. **6** devorar, engullir. || *v.i.* **7 [to – oneself on/with]** (desp.) hartarse de, atiborrarse de, atracarse de. || **8 to make someone's – rise,** ponerse uno enfermo, dar a uno asco, ponerse uno fuera de sí.

gorgeous | 'gɔːdʒəs | *adj.* **1** (fam.) fantástico, maravilloso, precioso, delicioso. **2** bellísimo, magnífico, espléndido.

gorilla | gə'rɪlə | *s.c.* **1** ZOOL. gorila. **2** (fig.) gorila, bruto.

gormandize | 'gɔːməndaɪz | (brit. **gormandise**) *v.t.* e *i.* (form.) glotonear, comer con avidez, engullir glotonamente, comer por placer.

gorse | gɔːs | *s.i.* BOT. tojo, aulaga.

gory | 'gɔːrɪ | *adj.* **1** (fam.) sangriento, violento, desagradable. **2** (lit.) sanguinolento, cubierto de sangre.

gosh | gɒʃ | *interj.* (fam.) ¡dioses!, ¡ostras!, ¡Jesús!

gosling | 'gɒzlɪŋ | *s.c.* **1** ZOOL. gansito, cría de ganso. **2** (fig.) tontorrón, ingenuo, inexperto.

go-slow | ˌgəʊ'sləʊ | (EE.UU. **go-down**) *s.c.* **1** huelga de celo, huelga de mínimos, jornada a bajo rendimiento. || *v.i.* **2** trabajar a ritmo lento, hacer huelga de celo.

gospel | 'gɒspl | *s.i.* **1** evangelio. **2** verdad indiscutible, artículo de fe. **3** doctrina, credo. **4** MUS. música gospel (cantada por los cristianos negros). || **5 the Gospel,** REL. el Evangelio.

gossamer | 'gɒsəmər | *s.i.* **1** telaraña, hilo de telaraña (que flota en el aire, en arbustos). **2** gasa; (EE.UU.) tela delicada, tela finísima. **3** delicadeza, finura.

gossip | 'gɒsɪp | *s.c.* e *i.* **1** cotilleo, chismorreo, rumor. **2** trivialidad, frivolidad. || *s.c.* **3** cotilla, chismoso. **4** (arc.) amigo íntimo. **5** (arc.) padrino, madrina (de bautismo). || *v.i.* **6** cotillear, chismorrear, rumorear. || **7 – column,** columna de cotilleo (en un periódico).

gossiping | 'gɒsɪpɪŋ | *adj.* **1** chismoso, cotilla, murmurador. || *s.i.* **2** cotilleo, chismorreo, rumor.

gossipy | 'gɒsɪpɪ | *adj.* **1** (fam.) lleno de cotilleo, lleno de rumores. **2** chismoso, cotilla.

got | gɒt | *pret.* y *p.p.* de **to get.**

Goth | gɒθ | *s.c.* HIST. godo.

Gothic | 'gɒθɪk | *adj.* **1** ARQ. gótico. **2** LIT. gótico, de terror, de misterio. **3** gótica (la letra). **4** germánico, teutónico. **5** bárbaro, cruel. || *s.i.* **6** gótica (lengua). **7** ARQ. gótico. **8** letra gótica. **9** LIT. novela gótica.

gotten | gɒtn | (EE.UU.) *p.p.* de **to get.**

gouge | gaʊdʒ | *s.c.* **1** gubia, formón de media caña (para carpintería). **2** ranura, agujero. **3** estría, acanaladura. **4** (jerga) estafa, extorsión, engaño, fraude. || *v.t.* **5** estriar, acanalar. **6** cavar, mellar. **7** sacar, arrancar (los ojos). **8** (EE.UU. y fam.) extorsionar, estafar, engañar.

gourd | gʊəd | *s.c.* **1** calabaza, calabacín. **2** recipiente de calabaza.

gourmand | 'gʊəmənd | *s.c.* glotón, goloso (para la comida o la bebida).

gout | gaʊt | *s.i.* **1** MED. gota. **2** gota (de líquido).

govern | 'gʌvn | *v.t.* e *i.* **1** gobernar, dirigir, gestionar (un país). || *v.t.* **2** controlar, fijar, determinar (las leyes, los precios). **3** GRAM. regir.

governess | 'gʌvnɪs | *s.c.f.* institutriz, aya.

governing | 'gʌvnɪŋ | *adj.atr.* gobernante, dominante, regulador, regente.

government | 'gʌvəmənt | | 'gʌvənmənt | | 'gʌvərnmənt | *s.c.* **1** [– + *v.sing.* o *pl.*] gobierno, administración, poder ejecutivo, autoridad: *central government = gobierno central.* || *s.i.* **2** gobierno, administración (sistema). **3** gobierno, regulación, autoridad. **4** política administrativa (ciencia). **5** GRAM. concordancia. || **6 national –,** gobierno de concentración nacional (en guerra).

governmental | ˌgʌvn'mentl | *adj.* **1** gubernamental, ministerial, gubernativo, administrativo: *governmental control = control administrativo.* || **3 – policy,** política de gobierno, política administrativa.

governor | 'gʌvənər | *s.c.* **1** gobernador. **2** director, alcaide (de una prisión). **3** jefe, superior, patrón. **4** director, administrador. **5** tutor. **6** MEC. automático, regulador. **7** (brit. y fam.) señor (como título en direcciones).

Governor-General | ˌgʌvənə'dʒenərəl | [*pl* **Governors-General** o **GovernorGenerals**] *s.c.* **1** Gobernador General (representante de la Reina de Inglaterra en países de la Commonwealth no republicanos).

governorship | 'gʌvənəʃɪp | *s.i.* **1** gobierno, ministerio. **2** período de gobierno. **3** jurisdicción.

gown | gaʊn | *s.c.* **1** traje de noche, vestido de noche (femenino). **2** toga (de profesores, magistrados). **3** bata de casa. **4** sotana, traje talar. **5** (fig.) miembros de la universidad, cuerpo universitario. || *v.t.* **6** vestir de largo, llevar traje largo. **7** investir (de toga).

grab | græb | *v.t.* **1** agarrar, arrebatar, apropiarse de, robar. **2** (fam.) tomar apresuradamente, coger a la carrera (sin escrúpulos). **3** apresar, capturar, sujetar. **4** (fig.) agarrar, tomar (la suerte, una oportunidad). **5** (fam.) apetecer, interesar (una idea, un plan). **6** (jerga), captar, atraer (la atención). **7 [to – at]** echar mano a, tirarse a. || *s.i.* **8** tirón. **9 [– at/for something]** ansia de, ambición de, avidez de (fama, poder). || **10 to make a – at,** dar el tirón (un ladrón). **11 up for the grabs,** (fam.) disponible, a la vista, vacante.

grace | greɪs | *s.i.* **1** gracia, ángel, encanto, atractivo, elegancia. **2** gracia, benevolencia, favor, concesión, merced. **3** gracia, suspensión de una ejecución. **4** respiro, gracia (para realizar un pago). **5** bendición (de la mesa). **6** tacto, educación. **7** gracia, don, favor (de Dios). **8** gracia (estado del alma). **9** generosidad, benevolencia, amabilidad, buena voluntad. **10 [his/her/your Grace]** Su Alteza, Su Excelencia, Su Majestad, Vuecencia. **11** MUS. nota de adorno. **12** *pl.* buenos modos, buenas maneras. || *v.t.* **13 [to – with/by]** (hum. o lit.) *gen.pas.* favorecer con, honrar con, distinguir con. **14** adornar, decorar, embellecer. **15** MUS. poner notas de adorno. || **16 airs and graces, V. air. 17 to be in someone's good graces,** gozar de la estima de, gozar del favor de. **18 by the – of,** gracias a. **19 by the – of God,** por la gracia de Dios. **20 coup de –,** V. **coup. 21 to fall from –,** caer en desgracia; recaer en malas costumbres. **22 to have the – to,** tener la amabilidad de; tener la discreción de. **23 saving –,** V. **saving. 24 with good/bad –,** de buena o mala gana, de buen o mal talante.

graceful | 'greɪsfʊl | *adj.* **1** gracioso, atractivo, garboso, elegante. **2** amable, honorable, bien educado.

gracefully | 'greɪsfəlɪ | *adv.* **1** graciosamente, elegantemente, garbosamente. **2** honorablemente, amablemente, educadamente.

graceless | 'greɪslɪs | *adj.* **1** sin gracia, desgarbado. **2** mal educado, grosero, intratable.

gracious | 'greɪʃəs | *adj.* **1** amable, condescendiente, bondadoso, generoso (con personas de rango inferior). **2** placentero, ameno, elegante, lujosa (la forma de vida). **3** graciosa (en un título): *Her Gracious Majesty = Su graciosa Majestad.* || **4 good –!,** V. **good. 5 – me!,** (arc.) ¡Dios mío!

gradation | grə'deɪʃn | *s.c.* **1 [in (in/of)]** gradación, graduación, escalonamiento. **2** grado, fase, etapa. **3** progreso gradual. **4** apofonía.

grade | greɪd | *s.c.* **1** nivel, categoría, calidad (de un producto). **2** grado, nivel, categoría (profesional). **3** (EE.UU.) grado, año (escolar). **4** (EE.UU.) nota, calificación (escolar). **5** (EE.UU.) inclinación, declive. || *v.t.* **6** clasificar, graduar. **7** (EE.UU.) evaluar, calificar. **8** mejorar la raza, mejorar la sangre (de un animal). || *v.i.* **9** tener categoría, tener rango, tener posición. **10** progresar, cambiar gradualmente. || **11 – A,** sobresaliente (calificación). **12 – crossing,** (EE.UU.) paso a nivel. **13 – school,** (EE.UU.) escuela elemental. **14 to make the –,** (fig.) llegar a la cima, triunfar, tener éxito.

gradient | 'greɪdjənt | *s.c.* **1** pendiente, declive, cuesta. **2** nivel de inclinación, nivel de pendiente. **3** curva, nivel de crecimiento, tasa de crecimiento.

gradual | 'grædʒʊəl | *adj.* **1** gradual, progresivo, escalonado. || *s.c.* **2** REL. antífona. **3** REL. gradual (parte de la misa).

gradually | 'grædjʊəlɪ | *adv.* gradualmente, progresivamente, escalonadamente, paulatinamente.

graduate | 'grædjueɪt | *s.c.* **1** graduado, titulado (en la Universidad). **2** (EE.UU.) graduado, bachiller (en la escuela). **3** probeta, pipeta. || *adj.* (EE.UU.) graduado, titulado. **5** de graduado, para graduado. || *v.i.* **6** graduarse, titularse (en la Universidad). **7** (EE.UU.) graduarse, obtener el título de bachiller (en la escuela). **8** clasificarse, graduarse, dividirse en niveles. || *v.t.* **9** graduar, titular. **10** TEC. graduar, marcar con grados (un instrumento).

graduation | ˌgrædju'eɪʃn | *s.i.* **1** graduación, diplomatura (una ceremonia). || *s.c.* **2** graduación, marca (en un instrumento).

graft | grɑːft | *s.c.* **1** injerto. **2** MED. injerto, transplante. || *s.i.* **3** (EE.UU.) soborno, astilla (a un funcionario). **4** extorsión, mangoneo, chanchullo (ejercido por personas en puestos influyentes en propio beneficio). **5** (brit. y fam.) trabajo duro. || *v.t.* **6** injertar, aplicar un injerto. **7** MED. injertar, transplantar, implantar. || *v.i.* **8** injertarse. **9** añadirse, introducirse.

grahamflour | 'greɪəmˌflaʊər | *s.i.* harina de trigo entero.

Grail | greɪl | *s.* Grial.

grain | greɪn | *s.c.* **1** grano, semilla (de cereales). **2** grano, partícula (de arena, de sal). **3** grano (unidad de medida en farmacia). **4** ZOOL. cochinilla, quermes. || *s.i.* **5** mieses, cereales, grano. **6 [the –]** la fibra, la hebra (de la madera, de la carne). **7** veta, vena (de la roca). **8** hilo, fibra, granilla (de una tela). **9** flor (del cuero). **10** pizca, miaja, pellizco, poquito. **11** AER. masa propulsora. **12** gránulo, granulación. **13** superficie veteada, estampado, impresión (sobre tela o papel). **14** cristalización, coagulación. **15** (fig.) temperamento, disposición. **16** tinte rápido, tinte, color. **17** *pl.* masa (germinada). || *v.t.* **18** granular, motear. **19** vetear. **20** desgranar, sacar el grano. **21** pulir, quitar el pelo (a la piel). || *v.i.* **22** granularse, cristalizarse. || **23 to go against the –,** ir contra corriente, ir a contrapelo. **24 – elevator,** silo con elevador mecánico. **25 with a – of salt,** V. **salt.**

gram, grame | græm | *s.c.* gramo (unidad métrica). **2** BOT. variedad de garbanzo (de Asia tropical).

grammar | 'græmər | *s.i.* **1** gramática (ciencia). || *s.c.* **2** gramática (un texto). **3** principios, elementos (de una ciencia, de un arte).

grammarian | grə'meərɪən | *s.c.* gramático, lingüista.

grammatical | grə'mætɪkl | *adj.* **1** gramatical. **2** correcto, concordante.

grammatically | grə'mætɪkəlɪ | *adv.* gramaticalmente.

gramophone | 'græməfəʊn | *s.c.* **1** gramófono, fonógrafo: *gramophone record = disco para gramófono.*

granary | 'grænərɪ | | 'greɪnərɪ | *s.c.* **1** granero. **2** (fig.) granero (país productor de grano).

grand | grænd | *adj.* **1** impresionante, imponente, magnífico. **2** ilustre, distinguido, noble, importante (una persona). **3** (arc. y fam.) maravilloso, fascinante, encantador, agradabilísimo. **4** importante, ambicioso (un plan, una acción). **5** gran, principal, más importante (un momento, una actividad). **6** gran (ante nombres de edificios, hoteles). || *s.c.* **7** (jerga) 1000 dólares; 1000 libras. **8** piano de cola.

granddad, grandad | 'grændæd | *s.c.* **1** (fam.) abuelo, abuelito. **2** (desp.) abuelito.

grandchild | 'græntʃaɪld | [*pl.* **grandchildren**] *s.c.* nieto, nieta.

granddaughter | 'græn,dɔːtər | *s.c.* nieta.
grandeur | 'grændjər | *s.i.* **1** grandeza, grandiosidad, esplendor, magnificencia. || **2 delusions of –,** delirios de grandeza.
grandfather | 'grænd,fɑːðər | *s.c.* **1** abuelo. || **2 – clock,** reloj alto de pared.
grandiloquent | græn'dɪləkwənt | *adj.* **1** (lit. y desp.) grandilocuente, pomposo, rimbombante.
grandiose | 'grændɪəʊs | *adj.* **1** (gen. desp.) grandioso, magnífico. **2** afectado, pomposo.
grandma | 'grænmɑː | *s.c.* (fam.) abuela, abuelita.
grandmother | 'græn,mʌðər | *s.c.* abuela.
grandpa | 'grænpɑː | *s.c.* (fam.) abuelo, abuelito.
grandparents | 'græn,peərənt | *s.pl.* abuelos.
grandson | 'grænsʌn | *s.c.* nieto.
grandstand | 'grændstænd | *s.c.* **1** tribuna (en estadios, hipódromos). **2** espectadores de tribuna, público. || *v.i.* **3** actuar para la tribuna, tratar de impresionar.
granite | 'grænɪt | *s.i.* **1** granito. **2** dureza, resistencia.
granny, grannie | 'grænɪ | *s.c.* (brit. y fam.) abuelita.
grant | grɑːnt | *v.t.* **1** consentir, conceder, admitir, permitir. **2** (lit.) conferir, dispensar, otorgar, conceder (un favor, un privilegio). **3** admitir, aceptar, reconocer (la verdad). **4** subvencionar, asignar (dinero). || *s.c.* **5** subvención, dotación, beca. || **6 granted,** de acuerdo, claro, sí. **7 granted that,** suponiendo que (en una discusión). **8 to take someone for granted,** pasar de, no dar importancia a, no hacer caso de. **9 to take something,** dar por hecho, dar por sentado (fam.).
granulated | 'grænjʊleɪtid | *adj.* granulado, granular.
granule | 'grænjuːl | *s.c.* **1** gránulo, partícula, granito. **2** ASTR. grano, copo (en la fotosfera del sol).
grape | greɪp | *s.c.* **1** uva. **2** vid, parra. || *s.i.* **3** MIL. metralla. || **4 – harvest,** vendimia. **5 sour grapes,** V. **sour.**
grapefruit | 'greɪpfruːt | *s.c.* **1** BOT. pomelo, toronjo, toronjil (árbol). **2** pomelo, toronja (fruto).
grapejuice | 'greɪpfruːt | *s.i.* zumo de uva.
grapeshot | 'greɪpʃ't | *s.i.* MIL. metralla.
grapevine | 'greɪpvaɪn | *s.c.* **1** parra. **2** (fig.) mentidero, fuentes bien informadas, medios extraoficiales, rumoreo.
graph | græf | *s.c.* **1** gráfico, gráfica, diagrama. || *v.t.* **2** representar gráficamente, dibujar una gráfica. || **3 – paper,** papel milimetrado (para gráficos).
graphic | 'græfɪk | *adj.* **1** gráfica, detallada, vívida (una descripción). **2** gráficas (las artes). || *s.pl.* **3** representaciones gráficas, cálculos gráficos. || **4 – data processing,** INF. proceso de gráficos.
graphite | 'græfaɪt | *s.i.* **1** MIN. grafito. **2** lápiz de grafito.
graphology | græ'f'lədʒɪ | *s.i.* grafología.
grapnel | 'græpnl | *s.c.* **1** MAR. rezón, arpeo. **2** ancla pequeña (con varios garfios).
grapple | 'græpl | *v.t.* **1 [to – with]** agarrar con, asir con. **2** MAR. aferrar, asegurar, enganchar (con bichero, con rezón). || *v.i.* **3** agarrarse, aferrarse. **4** luchar cuerpo a cuerpo. **5** (fig.) luchar (consigo mismo, con la conciencia). **6** abordar, tratar de resolver (un problema). || *s.c.* **7** MAR. garfio, arpón, rezón, bichero. **8** lucha libre, lucha cuerpo a cuerpo. **9** concurso de lucha libre.
grappling iron | 'græplɪŋ,aɪən | *s.c.* MAR. arpeo, arpón, garfio.
grasp | grɑːsp | *v.t.* **1** asir, coger, sujetar (con las manos). **2** aferrar, atraer, arrastar (con garfio o arpón). **3** (fig.) tomar, coger, asir (una oportunidad). **4** comprender, entender (algo difícil). || *v.i.* **5 [to – (at)]** tratar de asir, tratar de coger, tratar de arrebatar. **6** (fig.) aceptar, tomar. || *s.sing.* **7** asimiento, aferramiento, sujeción. **8** apretón, abrazo. **9** comprensión, entendimiento. **10** (lit.) control, poder, dominio. **11** (fig.) garra, atractivo. **12** alcance, posibilidad. || **13 to – the nettle,** poner el cascabel al gato, tratar con firmeza (un asunto difícil).
grasping | 'grɑːspɪŋ | *adj.* (desp.) pesetero, avaricioso, codicioso.
grass | grɑːs | | græs | *s.i.* **1** hierba, pasto, heno. **2** césped, tapín, gallón. **3** (fam.) hierba, mariguana. **4** ELECTR. oscilación, variación (del oscilógrafo). || *s.pl.* **5** hierbas, hierbajos. **6** (jerga) chivato, soplón (que informa a la policía). || *v.t.* **7** sembrar hierba, cubrir con hierba. **8** apacentar, alimentar con pasto, con heno. || *v.i.* **9 [to – on]** cubrirse de hierba, llenarse de hierba. **10** pacer, pastar. **11 [to – on]** (jerga) delatar, dar el chivatazo (a la policía). || **12 to be put out to –/pasture,** (fam.) retirar, jubilar, dejar a un lado (a alguien por incapacidad). **13 – roots,** POL. movimiento de base, las bases; a nivel local, a nivel regional; (fig.) fuente, origen, fundamento. **14 not to let the – grow under one's feet,** no perder el tiempo, andarse listo. **15 the – is always greener on the other side of the fence,** siempre es mejor todo en casa del vecino.
grasshopper |'grɑːs,hɒpər| |'græs,hɑːpər| *s.c.* **1** ZOOL. saltamontes, langosta, cigarra. || **2 kneehigh to a –,** (fam. y hum.) enano, pequeñajo, diminuto (especialmente un niño).
grassland | 'grɑːslænd | *s.c.* e *i.* pastizal, prado, zona de pastoreo.
grassy | 'grɑːsɪ | *adj.* **1** cubierto de hierba, enyerbado, herboso. **2** del color de la hierba, verde hierba.
grate | greɪt | *s.c.* **1** morrillo, rejilla (cocina). **2** rejilla, reja, enrejado. **3** chimenea, hogar. **4** tamiz, cedazo, criba (de minerales). **5** chirrido. || *v.t.* **6** rallar. **7** hacer rechinar (los dientes). **8** raspar, chirriar. **9** irritarse, molestarse, exacerbarse. **10** (arc.) raspar, rozar. || *v.i.* **11 [to – on]** chirriar, rechinar. **12** (fig.) irritar, molestar, poner los nervios de punta.
grateful | 'greɪtfʊl | *adj.* **1** agradecido, reconocido. **2** agradable, amable, grato. || **3 to be – for,** agradecer.
gratefully | 'greɪtfəlɪ | *adv.* **1** agradecidamente, con agradecimiento, con gratitud.
grater | greɪtər | *s.c.* rallador, raspador.
gratification | ,grætɪfɪ'keɪʃn | *s.c.* e *i.* **1** gratificación, recompensa, premio. **2** gratificación, satisfacción, placer. **3** propina.
gratify | 'grætɪfaɪ | *v.t.* **1** (lit.) complacer, producir satisfacción, alegrar, satisfacer. **2** satisfacer (un deseo).
gratifying | 'grætɪfaɪɪŋ | *adj.* gratificante, grato, satisfactorio, loable.
grating | 'greɪtɪŋ | *s.c.* **1** reja, enrejado, verja. **2** rejilla. **3** FIS. red de difracción. **4** chirriante, áspero, desagradable (sonido).
gratis | greɪtɪs | *adv.* gratis, gratuito.
gratitude | 'grætɪtjuːd | *s.i.* gratitud, agradecimiento, reconocimiento.
gratuitous | grə'tjuːɪtəs | *adj.* **1** (desp.) gratuito, injustificado, innecesario, inmerecido. **2** (p.u.) gratuito, gracioso. **3** ECON. naturales (bienes que no provienen del trabajo).
gratuitously | grə'tjuːɪtəslɪ | *adv.* gratis, gratuitamente, sin coste.
gratuity | grə'tjuːɪtɪ | *s.c.* **1** propina, aguinaldo (gen. de dinero). **2** (brit.) gratificación, indemnización (por cese en el trabajo, especialmente a militares).
grave | greɪv | *s.c.* **1** sepultura, sepulcro, tumba. **2 [the –]** (lit.) la muerte. || *adj.* **3** grave, preocupante, serio (una situación, noticias, amenazas). **4** importante, trascendental, difícil (decisión). **5** solemne, respetable (ceremonia, saludo). **6** grave, peligrosa (enfermedad). **7** sombrío, oscuro, sobrio (color). | grɑːv | **8** grave (acento, tono). || *v.t.* **9** esculpir, grabar. **10** fijar, grabar (en la mente). **11** MAR. despalmar y calafatear (cascos de embarcaciones). || *adv.* **12** gravemente, solemnemente, despacio. || **13 to dig one's own –,** (fig.) cavar su propia fosa. **14 from the cradle to the –,** de toda la vida, desde siempre, desde el nacimiento a la tumba. **15 to have one foot in the –,** tener un pie en la tumba. **16 silent as the –,** V. **silent. 17 to turn in one's –,** (fig.) revolverse en la tumba.
gravedigger | ,greɪv'dɪgər | *s.c.* sepulturero.
gravel | grævl | *s.i.* **1** gravilla, grava, cascajo. **2** MED. arenilla, cálculo. || *v.t.* **3** cubrir de grava, de cascajo. **4** confundir, dejar perplejo, desconcertar. **5** (fam.) irritar, exacerbar.
gravelled, graveled | 'grævld | *adj.* cubierto de grava, de grava, de cascajo: *a gravelled lane = un camino de grava.*
gravelly | 'grævlɪ | *adj.* **1** arenoso, cascajoso, de grava. **2** áspera, grave, ronca (la voz).

gravely | 'greɪvlɪ | *adv.* **1** gravemente, preocupadamente, seriamente. **2** solemnemente.

graven | 'greɪvn | *adj.* **1** grabado, esculpido, tallado: *graven image = ídolo, fetiche.* **2** (fig.) grabado (en la memoria).

gravestone | 'greɪvstəʊn | *s.c.* lápida sepulcral.

graveyard | 'greɪvjɑːd | *s.c.* **1** cementerio, camposanto. || **2 – shift,** turno de noche, obreros del turno de noche.

graving dock | 'greɪvɪŋdɒk | *s.c.* dique de carenado, dique seco.

gravitate | 'grævɪteɪt | *v.i.* **1** gravitar. **2 [– to/towards]** tender hacia, estar orientado hacia. **3** (fig.) ir gradualmente hacia, dejarse atraer por.

gravitation | ˌgrævɪ'teɪʃn | *s.i.* **1** FIS. gravedad, gravitación. **2** (fig.) tendencia, propensión, inclinación, orientación.

gravitational | ˌgrævɪ'teɪʃnl | *adj.* FIS. gravitatorio, de gravedad: *the gravitational field = el campo de gravedad.*

gravity | 'grævətɪ | *s.i.* **1** FIS. gravedad, gravitación, peso. **2** (lit.) gravedad, seriedad, importancia, trascendencia. **3** solemnidad (de voz, de movimientos). || **4 centre of –,** centro de gravedad.

gravy | 'greɪvɪ | *s.i.* **1** salsa, jugo (de carne). **2** (EE.UU. y jerga) dinero fácil. **3** (jerga) ganga, chollo. || **4 – boat,** salsera. **5 the – train,** (fam. y EE.UU.) mina de oro, chollo, oportunidad de conseguir dinero fácil.

gray | greɪ | (brit.) **grey.** V. **grey.**

graze | greɪz | *v.t.* e *i.* **1** pacer, pastar. **2** apacentar, pastorear. || *v.t.* **3** rozar, desollar, raspar. **4** rozar, tocar ligeramente. || *s.sing.* **5** rozadura, desolladura, rasguño, arañazo. **6** abrasión, desgaste.

grease | griːs | *s.i.* **1** grasa, unto. **2** brillantina. **3** grasa, aceite lubricante. **4** juarda, suarda, churre (suciedad grasienta de la lana). **5** lana sucia, con juarda. || *v.t.* **6** engrasar, lubricar (una máquina). **7** untar, dar una capa de grasa; ponerse brillantina. || **8 – gun,** pistola o jeringa engrasadora, inyector de grasa. **9 to – someone's palm,** (fam.) sobornar, untar (con dinero).

greasepaint | 'griːspeɪnt | *s.i.* maquillaje teatral.

greaseproof | 'griːspruːf | *adj.* impermeable a la grasa, encerado: *greaseproof paper = papel de cera o antigraso.*

greasiness | 'griːzɪnɪs | *s.i.* **1** untuosidad, lo grasiento. **2** la mugre. **3** zalamería, adulación, coba.

greasy | 'griːzɪ | *adj.* **1** grasiento, untuoso. **2** resbaladizo. **3** (desp.) zalamero, adulador, cobista.

great | greɪt | *adj.* **1** gran, grande, enorme. **2** numeroso. **3** avanzado (edad). **4** importante, destacado, significativo. **5** famoso, eminente, distinguido. **6** (fam.) espléndido, fantástico, maravilloso. **7 [– at],** experto en, hábil en, fuerte en; aficionado a, interesado en. **8 [– *adj.*]** gran, muy: *a great friend = un amigo íntimo.* **9** principal (un ala, una escalera). **10** largo (tiempo, distancia). **11** noble. **12** poderoso, influyente. **13** (arc.) preñada, embarazada. **14** (fam.) entusiasta. **15** excelente, admirable, de primera categoría. **16** gran, grande, magno (ante nombres propios): *The Great War = la Gran Guerra* (la Primera Guerra Mundial); *Alexander the Great = Alejandro Magno.* || *s.pl.* **17** los grandes, los famosos, las estrellas. || *adv.* **18** (fam.) muy bien. || **19 all times greats,** estrellas más importantes de todos los tiempos. **20 to go – guns,** V. **gun. 21 Great Britain,** Gran Bretaña. **22 Great Lakes,** Los Grandes Lagos. **23 no – shakes,** (fam.) no muy bueno, no gran cosa, no muy efectivo.

great-aunt | ˌgreɪt'ɑːnt | *s.c.* tía abuela.

great-coat | 'greɪtkəʊt | *s.c.* gabán, sobretodo, tres cuartos (especialmente militar).

greater | greɪtər | *adj.comp.* de **great. 1** mayor. || **2 Greater London,** el Gran Londres (utilizado con nombres de ciudades para designar la ciudad y su área metropolitana).

greatest | 'greɪtɪst | *adj.super.* de **great. 1** el mayor, la mayor. **2** el mejor, el más grande. || **3 at its –,** cuanto más..., en lo más.

great-grandchild | ˌgreɪt'grænt∫aɪld | *s.c.pl. great-grandchildren,* biznieto, biznieta.

great-grandfather | ˌgreɪt'grændfɑːðər | *s.c.* bisabuelo.

great-grandmother | ˌgreɪt'grændmoːðər | *s.c.* bisabuela.

great-great-grandfather | ˌgreɪtˌgreɪt'grænfɑːðər | *s.c.* tatarabuelo.

great-great-grandson | ˌgreɪtˌgreɪt'grænsʌn | *s.c.* tataranieto.

great-hearted | ˌgreɪt'hɑːtɪd | *adj.* **1** noble, valiente, atrevido. **2** generoso, magnánimo.

gretly | 'greɪtlɪ | *adv.* muy, enormemente, en gran medida, sumamente.

greatness | greɪtnɪs | *s.i.* grandeza, magnificencia.

Grecian | 'griːʃn | *adj.* (lit.) griego, helénico (de aspecto, estilo).

Greece | griːs | *s.* Grecia.

greed | griːd | *s.i.* **1** (desp.) avaricia, codicia, avidez (de dinero, de poder). **2** gula, glotonería.

greedily | 'griːdɪlɪ | *adv.* **1** ávidamente, con avaricia. **2** glotonamente, con gula, vorazmente.

greedy | 'griːdɪ | *adj.* **1** (desp.) voraz, glotón, goloso. **2 [– (for)]** ávido, codicioso. || **3 greed – makes a hungry puppy,** la avaricia rompe el saco.

Greek | griːk | *adj.* **1** griego, de Grecia (nacionalidad, idioma). || *s.i.* **2** griego (idioma). **3** griego (habitante de Grecia). || **4 to be all – to someone,** (fam.) sonar a chino a alguien, ser chino (que no se entiende).

green | griːn | *adj.* **1** verde (color). **2** cubierto de hierba, verdoso, reverdecido. **3** verde, agrio, inmaduro. **4** crudo, no cocido (verduras). **5** no curada, verde (madera). **6** pálido, cetrino, verdoso (rostro). **7** joven, inexperto, cándido, novato. **8** (fam.) demudado, lívido, celoso (de envidia). **9** (lit.) fresco, juvenil, vigoroso. **10** suave, templado (clima). **11** completamente nuevo, reciente. **12** Verde (partido político, gen. mayúscula). **13** unidad monetaria de la CEE: *the green pound = el ecu.* || *s.c.* e *i.* **14** verde (color). || *s.c.* **15** césped, jardín. **16** DEP. pista, campo de juego. **17** *pl.* foliaje, follaje, hierbas. **18** *pl.* verduras, vegetales. || *v.t.* e *i.* **19** plantar verde, verdear, verdecer. || **20 – about the gills,** V. **gills.**

green-back | 'griːbæk | *s.c.* (EE.UU., arc. y fam.) billete de banco.

greenery | 'griːnərɪ | *s.i.* **1** follaje, verdor, verdura. **2** follaje, verde (para decoración). **3** invernadero, huerta, jardín.

green-eyed | 'griːnaɪd | *adj.* **1** de ojos verdes. **2** (lit. y hum.) celoso, envidioso.

greengrocer | 'griːnˌgrəʊsər | *s.c.* **1** verdulero, vendedor de verduras. || **2** greengrocer's, verdulería.

greenhorn | 'griːhɔːn | *s.c.* **1** recién llegado, inmigrante. **2** novato, inexperto, inmaduro. **3** crédulo, simplón.

greenhouse | 'griːnhaʊs | *s.c.* **1** invernadero, invernáculo. || **2 – effect,** efecto invernadero.

greenish | 'griːnɪʃ | *adj.* verdoso, ligeramente verde.

Greenland | 'griːnlənd | *s.* Groenlandia.

Greenlander | 'griːnləndər | *s.c.* groenlandés.

greenness | 'griːnnɪs | *s.i.* **1** verdor. **2** inexperiencia, inmadurez.

greenstuff | 'griːnstʌf | *s.i.* verduras, hortalizas.

greet | griːt | *v.t.* **1** saludar, dar la bienvenida (con gestos o palabras). **2** recibir (con una reacción específica). **3** *gen.pas.* (lit.) percibir por, sentirse, presentirse.

greeting | griːtɪŋ | *s.c.* **1** saludo, salutación. **2** *pl.* bienvenida. **3** *pl.* recuerdos, saludos (despedida de carta).

gregarious | grɪ'geərɪəs | *adj.* **1** sociable, gregario, comunicativo. **2** ZOOL. gregario. **3** BOT. arracimado, en colonias.

gremlin | 'gremlɪm | *s.c.* **1** *gen.pl.* (lit.) duende, duendecillo travieso (causante de daños en máquinas, según la leyenda).

grenade | grɪ'neɪd | *s.c.* **1** MIL. granada, bomba de mano. **2** cóctel molotov.

grenadine | ˌgrenə'diːn | | 'grenədiːn | *s.i.* **1** granadina, zumo de granada. **2** granadina (tela calada de seda, algodón o sintética).

grew | gruː | *pret.* de **to grow.**

grey | greɪ | *adj.* **1** gris. **2** gris, canoso, cano (pelo). **3** pálido, lívido (rostro). **4** (fig.) gris, triste, deprimente. **5** nuboso, plomizo. **6** (fig.) maduro, venerable, antiguo. **7** de dudosa moralidad (el carácter); semi-ilegal (propiedad). || *s.c.*

e *i.* **8** gris. **9** (EE.UU.) Ejército Confederado (en la guerra civil). **10** (EE.UU.) soldado confederado. || *v.t.* e *i.* **11** encanecer, ponerse canoso. || **12 Grey Code,** INF. Código de Grey (código de bloques binario).

grey-haired | ˌgreɪ'heəd | *adj.* cano, canoso, encanecido, gris (pelo).

grey-hound | 'greɪhaʊnd | *s.c.* **1** galgo, lebrel. **2** (EE.UU.) autobús de línea (entre ciudades).

greyish | 'greɪʃ | (EE.UU.) **grayish.** *adj.* **1** grisáceo, plomizo: *a greyish sky = un cielo plomizo.* **2** agrisado (un color). **3** entrecano.

grid | grɪd | *s.c.* **1** rejilla, reja. **2** parrilla (de cocina). **3** (brit.) ELEC. red. **4** cuadro, cuadrícula numerada (de un mapa). **5** DEP. parrilla de salida (en carreras de coches). **6** (EE.UU.) campo de fútbol. **7** ELECTR. reja de visualizadores fluorescentes. **8** red portaequipajes. **9** plancha de estereotipo (en imprenta).

gridiron | 'grɪdˌaɪən | *s.c.* **1** parrilla (de asar). **2** (EE.UU.) campo de fútbol. **3** telar (de teatro).

grief | griːf | *s.i.* **1** pena, dolor, aflicción, pesar. **2** desdicha, disgusto, castigo, desgracia. || **3 to come to –,** fracasar, frustrarse, venirse abajo; sufrir daño. **4 good –!,** V. **good.**

grievance | 'griːvns | *s.c.* e *i.* **1** motivo de queja, motivo de protesta. **2** injusticia, agravio. **3** resentimiento, indignación. **4** dolor. || **5 nursing a –,** dar vueltas a, pensar mucho en (un tema).

grieve | griːv | *v.i.* **1 [to – for/over]** llorar por, afligirse por, entristecerse por, apenarse por. || *v.t.* **2** (lit.) apenar, afligir, entristecer. **3** (arc.) hacer daño, causar daño, herir.

grievous | 'griːvəs | *adj.* **1** (lit.) grave, lamentable, craso (un error). **2** dolorosa (una pérdida). **3** fuerte, severo, intenso, agudo: *a grievous toothache = un intenso dolor de cabeza.* **4** atroz, espantoso, horrible (un crimen). **5** penosa: *a grievous task = una tarea penosa.*

griffin, griffon, griphon | 'grɪfɪn | *s.c.* LIT. grifo, grifón.

grill | grɪl | (EE.UU.) **broil.** *v.t.* e *i.* **1** asar a la parrilla. **2** (fig.) estar asado, estar muy acalorado. || *v.t.* **3** torturar sin piedad. **4** (fam.) interrogar, freír a preguntas (por la policía). **5** marcar a fuego. || *s.c.* **6** (EE.UU.) **broiler,** parrilla. **7** gratinador. || **8 mixed –,** carnes variadas a la parrilla.

grille | grɪl | *s.c.* **1** reja, rejilla (en ventanas). **2** verja. **3** rejilla (del coche). **4** TEC. reja de los visualizadores fluorescentes.

grilled | grɪld | *adj.* **1** a la parrilla, asado a la parrilla. **2** enrejado, con rejas.

grillroom | 'grɪlrʊm | *s.c.* restaurante especializado en asados a la parrilla, parrilla.

grim | grɪm | *adj.* **1** sombrío, torvo (gesto). **2** desagradable, repulsivo, siniestro. **3** deprimente, funesto, lúgubre (lugar). **4** implacable, inflexible, rígido, feroz, salvaje. || **6 [feel –]** muy enfermo. || **7 to hang on/hold on like – death,** agarrarse con determinación, fuertemente (a causa del miedo). **8 the – truth,** la verdad pura y simple.

grimace | grɪ'meɪs | | 'grɪməs | *v.i.* **1 [– (at/with)]** hacer muecas a. || *s.c.* **2** mueca, gesto.

grime | graɪm | *s.i.* mugre, tizne, suciedad.

grimly | 'graɪmlɪ | *adv.* **1** desagradablemente, tétricamente. **2** resueltamente, implacablemente, inflexiblemente, severamente. **3** ferozmente, encarnizadamente. || **4 to hang on –,** resistir con determinación.

grimy | 'graɪmɪ | *adj.* mugriento, tiznado, sucio.

grin | grɪn | *v.t.* e *i.* **1 [– (with/at)]** sonreír abiertamente. **2** sonreír irónicamente, de forma burlona. || *s.c.* **3** sonrisa abierta. **4** mueca burlona, irónica, forzada. || **5 to – and bear it,** sonreír y aguantar, poner al mal tiempo buena cara. **6 to – like a Cheshire cat.** V. **Cheshire cat. 7 take/wipe that – of your face!,** ¡quita esa sonrisa estúpida de tu cara!

grind | graɪnd | *v.irr.pret.* **ground,** *p.p.* **ground.** *t.* **1** moler, pulverizar. **2** rechinar (los dientes). **3** pulir (superficies) esmerilar (cristales). **4** afilar (cuchillos). **5 [– +** *o.* **+** *adv./prep.*] oprimir, aplastar, presionar, apretar. **6** tocar un organillo (con manubrio). **7** inculcar, enseñar, meter algo en la cabeza (por repetición). || *v.i.* **8** molerse, pulverizarse. **9** rechinar. **10** renquear, circular lenta y ruidosamente. **11** (EE.UU. y fam.) empollar, chapar, estudiar. **12** (jerga) menear las caderas (eróticamente). || *s.sing.* **13** trabajo pesado, rutinario. **14** paliza, zurra, cansancio. **15** (EE.UU. fam. y desp.) empollón, chapón. **16** molienda. **17** (jerga) meneo de caderas, contoneo de caderas, movimiento erótico. || **18 to – somebody down,** (fig.) tratar como esclavos, agobiar, oprimir; desgastar, pulverizar. **19 to – something out,** (desp.) repetir machaconamente, producir, crear algo como churros (gen. historias, música), repetir hasta la saciedad. **20 to – the faces of the poor,** explotar a uno, abusar, aprovecharse de. **21 to – to a halt, a)** parar lentamente (un vehículo); **b)** dejar de funcionar (la economía, un sistema).

grinder | 'graɪndər | *s.c.* **1** molinero. **2** afilador. **3** TEC. esmerilador, pulidor. **4** molino, molinillo. **5** máquina de afilar. **6** esmeril, máquina esmeriladora, pulidora. **7** picadora (de carne). **8** *pl.* (fam.) las muelas.

grindstone | 'graɪndstəʊn | *s.c.* **1** muela, piedra de afilar. || **2 to keep one's nose to the –,** (fam.) dar el callo, currárselo, batirse el cobre.

gringo | grɪŋgəʊ | *s.c.* (desp.) gringo (angloparlante, especialmente norteamericano, en Latinoamérica).

grip | grɪp | *v.t.* e *i.* **1** agarrar, coger fuertemente, asir, apretar (la mano, el brazo). **2** empuñar (una espada, bastón). || *v.t.* **3** atraer, absorber, conquistar, embelesar, tener en un puño. **4** afectar, embargar (por una enfermedad, sentimiento). || *s.c.* **5** agarrón, apretón, asimiento. **6** (fig.) control, poder, influencia, puño, garra. **7** facultad, capacidad (para una actividad). **8** forma de asir, de agarrar (un instrumento). **9** asa, asidero, agarradero, mango, empuñadura. **10** prendedor, sujetador, fijador. **11** maletín, bolso o saco de mano. **12** TV. ayudante de dirección; tramoyista (en un teatro). || **13 to come/get to grips with, a)** llegar al fondo de, abordar un asunto, un problema; **b)** luchar cuerpo a cuerpo, a brazo partido. **14 to get /keep a – on oneself,** controlarse, dominarse, mantener la calma.

gripe | grɪp | *v.i.* **1 [– (at/about)]** refunfuñar, rezongar, quejarse. **2** sentir retortijones, tener o padecer un cólico. || *v.t.* **3** causar retortijones, producir un cólico. **4** (fam.) irritar, molestar, fastidiar. **5** agarrar, asir. **6** (arc.) oprimir, afligir. || *s.c.* **7** *pl.* (arc. y fam.) retortijones, cólicos. **8** queja, lamentación, protesta. **9** asa, asidero, agarradero.

gripping | grɪpɪŋ | *adj.* atractivo, absorbente, emocionante, con garra.

grisly | 'grɪzlɪ | *adj.* repugnante, espeluznante, horripilante, macabro.

grist | grɪst | *s.i.* **1** grano, molienda. || **2 (all) – to/the/for one's mill,** todo sirve, todo vale (para una situación particular), a todo se le saca ventaja.

gristle | 'grɪsl | *s.i.* ternilla, cartílago.

gristly | grɪzlɪ | *adj.* ternilloso, cartilaginoso.

grit | grɪt | *s.i.* **1** gravilla, arena, arenilla. **2** (fam.) agallas, valor, aguante. **3** estructura, dureza de una muela (de moler). **4** GEOL. piedra de asperón, de sílice, de chispa. || *v.t.* **5** cubrir de gravilla, echar arena (a una carretera). **6** apretar los dientes. || *v.i.* **7** rechinar. || **8 to – one's teeth,** (fig.) apretar los dientes (ante una dificultad).

grizzle | 'grɪzl | *v.i.* **1** (brit. y fam.) lloriquear, hacer pucheros (gen. los niños). **2** quejarse autocompasivamente, hablar con voz lastimera. || *v.t.* e *i.* **3** agrisar, volver(se) gris, canoso. || *s.i.* **4** color grisáceo. **5** (arc.) pelo encanecido, entrecano.

grizzled | grɪzld | *adj* **1** grisáceo, pardusco, canoso. || **2 – bear,** oso pardo.

groan | grəʊn | *v.i.* **1** gemir, quejarse, gimotear. **2** gruñir. **3** crujir. || *v.t.* **4** expresarse con gemidos, proferir gemidos. || *s.c.* **5** gemido, gimoteo. **6** gruñido. **7** crujido.

groat | grəʊt | *s.c.* **1** HIST. (brit.) antigua moneda de cuatro peniques. **2** *pl.* farro, avena descascarillada y a medio moler.

grocer | 'grəʊsər | *s.c.* **1** tendero de ultramarinos, (Am.) bodeguero, almacenero. **2** dependiente de ultramarinos, de almacén. || **3 grocer's shop,** tienda de ultramarinos, (Am.) almacén, bodega, tienda de abarrotes.

groceries | 'grəusərɪz | *s.c.pl.* comestibles, ultramarinos, víveres, (Am.) abarrotes.
grocery | 'grəusərɪ | *s.c.* **1** tienda de ultramarinos, de comestibles, (Am.) almacén, bodega, tienda de abarrotes. || **2 – store,** almacén de ultramarinos.
grog | grɒg | *s.i.* **1** grog (bebida de marineros). **2** (fam.) bebida alcohólica.
groggy | 'grɒgɪ | *adj.* **1** (fam.) tambaleante, inseguro, débil, mareado. **2** aturdido, atontado. **3** aturdido.
groin | grɔɪn | *s.c.* **1** ANAT. ingle. **2** (euf.) órganos genitales externos. **3** ARQ. arista de encuentro (de dos bóvedas). || *v.t.* **4** ARQ. construir con aristas de encuentro.
groom | gruːm | *s.c.* **1** mozo de cuadra. **2** novio (el día de la boda). **3** (brit.) oficial, ayuda de cámara (de la casa real). **4** (arc.) criado. **5** (arc.) hombre. || *v.t.* **6** cuidar caballos, lavar, cepillar. **7 [to – (for)]** acicalar, asear, cuidar mucho el aspecto. **8** entrenar para, preparar para (una ocasión especial, un trabajo). || *v.t.* e *i.* **9** despiojarse, limpiarse (los animales).
groove | gruːv | *s.c.* **1** surco, ranura, estría, muesca, rodada. **2** (fig.) rutina, costumbre. **3** (jerga) deleite, placer, goce. || *v.t.* **4** hacer un surco, ranurar, estriar. || *v.i.* **5** (jerga) disfrutar, deleitarse, gozar, pasárselo bien; estar en onda.
grooved | gruːvd | *adj.* estriado, ranurado, acanalado.
grope | grəup | *v.i.* **1 [to – *adv./prep.* for]** buscar a tientas. **2** (fig.) vacilar, titubear, dudar: *groping for the right answer = buscando la respuesta adecuada con titubeos.* || *v.t.* **3 [to – + *o.* + *adv./prep.*]** andar a tientas (en la oscuridad). **4** (jerga) meter mano, magrear, tocar. || *s.c.* **5** duda, vacilación, titubeo. **6** manoseo, sobadura, magreo.
gross | grəus | *adj.* **1** *no comp.* total, completo, bruto (un beneficio, una ganancia). **2** (form.) inexcusable, injustificable, flagrante, craso (un error). **3** vulgar, burdo, tosco, descortés, falto de sensibilidad (hábitos, lenguaje). **4** (EE.UU. y fam.) soez, obsceno, grosero. **5** grueso, voluminoso, corpulento. **6** denso, espeso. **7** amplio, general. **8** MED. macroscópico, claramente visible. || *v.t.* **9** ganar en bruto, rendir en total. || *s.c.* **10** el total, el grueso. **11** gruesa (12 docenas). || **12 by the –,** al por mayor. **13 to – out,** (EE.UU.) dar náuseas. **14 in the –,** en total, en conjunto. **15 the – national product,** el producto interior bruto.
grossly | grəuslɪ | *adv.* **1** en total, al completo. **2** vulgarmente, toscamente, burdamente. **3** groseramente, soezmente. **4** en exceso, enormemente. **5** aproximadamente, poco más o menos.
grossness | grəusnɪs | *s.i.* **1** gordura, voluminosidad, corpulencia, pesadez. **2** densidad, espesor. **3** grosería, vulgaridad. **4** totalidad. **5** flagrancia, injustificación.
grotesque | grəu'tesk | *adj.* **1** grotesco, extravagante, ridículo. || *s.c.* **2 [the –]** lo grotesco, lo extravagante.
grotto | grɒtəu | [*pl.* **grottoes** o **grottos**] *s.c.* **1** gruta, cueva. **2** hornacina (para imágenes religiosas).
grouch | grautʃ | *s.c.* **1** sing. (fam.) gruñido, refunfuño. **2** gruñón, refunfuñón, quejica. **3** mal genio, mal humor. || *v.i.* **4** (fam.) gruñir, refunfuñar, renegar.
grouchy | grautʃɪ | *adj.* gruñón, refunfuñón, malhumorado.
ground | graund | (*pret.* y *p.p.* de **grind**) || *s.i.* **1** suelo, tierra, terreno. **2** suelo, piso (de una habitación). **3** *pl.* tierras, propiedades. **4** fondo (del mar). **5** campo, tema, tópico, área (de conocimiento). **6** *pl.* base, fundamento, justificación. **7** causa, motivo, razón. **8** posición, ventaja, terreno: *she was on safe ground = estaba en terreno seguro, conocía el tema.* || *s.c.* **9** terreno, lugar, área, emplazamiento. **10** campo, cancha (de juego, de batalla). **11** parque, jardín comunal. **12** área, campo, terreno (de desarrollo de ideas). **13** fondo (de una tela): *on a red ground = sobre un fondo rojo.* **14** baño, capa (de pintura). **15** *pl.* posos, sedimentos. **16** ELEC. tierra, toma de tierra. || *v.t.* e *i.* **17** varar, encallar (un barco). || *v.t.* **18** obligar a permanecer en tierra, impedir despegar: *he was grounded because of the weather = se le impidió volar a causa del tiempo.* **19** (EE.UU. y fam.) prohibir salir, castigar a quedarse en casa (a un niño). **20 [to – + *o.* + *adv./prep.* in/on]** basar, apoyar, fundar (una idea, una teoría). **21** poner en tierra, colocar en tierra, traer a tierra. **22** ELEC. conectar a tierra. **23** DEP. golpear el suelo (la pelota); enviar fuera (la pelota). || *adj.* **24** de tierra, terrestre. **25** a nivel del suelo, a ras del suelo. **26** fundamental, básico. **27** ELEC. de tierra, a tierra. || **28 to break fresch –, V. fresh. 29 to cut the – from under one's feet,** minar la moral, destruir los razonamientos (en una discusión). **30 down to the –,** totalmente, completamente. **31 to gain – on,** ganar terreno en, progresar en. **32 to get something off the –,** sacar adelante, sacar a flote, hacer funcionar (un plan). **33 to go to –,** esconderse, ocultarse. **34 to – in,** enseñar la base, los fundamentos (de una materia). **35 – colour,** primera capa, capa de fondo (de pintura). **36 – crew,** tripulación de tierra, personal de tierra. **37 – glass,** cristal esmerilado; vidrio en polvo. **38 – hog,** ZOOL. marmota americana. **39 – plan,** planta, distribución (de un edificio); proyecto base (de un trabajo). **40 to have/keep one's feet on the –,** V. **foot. 41 into the –,** en exceso, demasiado. **42 to loose –,** perder terreno, retroceder. **43 on grounds of,/on the grounds of/that,** por, a causa de. **44 on one's own –,** en su elemento, en su propio terreno. **45 to shift one's –,** cambiar de tema, cambiar de tercio. **46 to stand one's –,** enfrentarse con valor, mantenerse firme (ante un problema). **47 to suit someone down to the –,** sentarle bien a uno, quedarle bien, venirle bien (la ropa). **48 well grounded,** bien razonado. **49 well grounded in,** muy versado en.
grounding | 'graundɪŋ | *s.c.sing.* entrenamiento de base, curso básico, fundamentos, rudimentos.
groundless | 'graundlɪs | *adj.* sin fundamento, sin base, sin razón, infundado, insostenible.
groundsel | 'graunsl | *s.i.* BOT. hierba cana, hierba caballar.
groundsheet | 'graunʃiːt | *s.c.* tela impermeable, tela de plástico (para proteger de la humedad del suelo o de la lluvia).
groundswell | 'graundswel | *s.c.sing.* **1** (fig.) mar de fondo, corriente (de opinión). **2** MAR. marejada, marejadilla.
ground-to-air | graundtəeər | *adj.* **1** de tierra a aire: *a ground-to-air missile = un proyectil tierra-aire.*
groundwork | 'graunwəːk | *s.i.* trabajo de base, cimientos, trabajo previo.
group | gruːp | *s.c.* **1** [– *v.sing./pl.*] grupo, agrupación. **2** conjunto, grupo (musical). || *v.t.* e *i.* **3** agrupar(se), juntar(se), reunir(se). || **4 – calculation,** INF. cálculo por grupos. **5 – extension,** INF. ampliación por grupos. **6 – insurance,** seguro colectivo, seguro de grupo. **7 – mark,** INF. señal de final de registro. **8 – printing,** INF. tabulado. **9 – separator,** INF. código separador de grupos. **10 – sorting,** clasificación por grupos. **11 – theory,** MAT. teoría de grupos.
grouper | 'gruːpər | *s.c.* ZOOL. mero.
grouse | graus | [*pl.* **grouse** o **grouses**] *s.c.* **1** ZOOL. urogallo, gallo de monte. || *s.i.* **2** (fam.) queja, refunfuño, protesta. || *v.i.* **3 [to – (about)]** (fam.) refunfuñar, rezongar, quejarse. || **4 black –,** ZOOL. ave lira. **5 red –,** ZOOL. lagópodo escocés.
grout | graut | *s.i.* **1** lechada (pintura). **2** yeso fino (para tapar grietas). **3** *pl.* (brit.) sedimentos, posos. || *v.t.* **4** rellenar con yeso. **5** dar lechada, enlechar.
grovel | 'grɒvl | | 'gɑːvl | | 'grʌvl | [(brit.) **grovell**] *v.i.* **1 [to – (to)]** (desp.) humillarse (ante), comportarse servilmente (ante), arrastrarse (ante), envilecerse (ante). **2** arrastrarse, serpear (un perro, por temor).
grovelling | 'grɒvlɪŋ | *adj.* servil, abyecto, rastrero.
grow | grəu | *v.irr.pret.* **grew,** *p.p.* **grown.** *i.* **1** crecer, ganar estatura, medrar. **2** madurar, desarrollarse (mentalmente). **3** brotar, retoñar, crecer (las plantas). **4** darse, adecuarse (una planta en un lugar). **5** desarrollarse, expandirse, crecer, hacerse más importante (un lugar, una organización, una idea, un problema). **6 [to – *adj./p.p./inf.*]** (form. o lit.) aprender a, empezar a, convertirse en, volverse (gen. se traduce por el verbo que corresponde al significado del *adj./p.p./inf.* que le sigue): *to grow rich = enriquecerse; to grow accustomed = empezar a acostumbrarse a; to grow to enjoy literature = gustar la*

literatura cada vez más. || *v.t.* **7** cultivar, producir (hortalizas, flores). **8** dejar crecer (el pelo, la barba). || **[to – *adv./prep.*] 9 to – away from,** desligarse de, despegarse de, alejarse de (alguien íntimo). **10 to – into somebody/something,** convertirse en alguien, hacerse (un hombre, una mujer); ser suficientemente mayor para, crecer para, hacerse grande para (ponerse ropa o zapatos de otros mayores). **11 to – on somebody,** gustar alguien cada vez más, ir apoderándose de uno. **12 to – on trees,** darse como hongos, abundar. **13 to – out of something, a)** quedar algo pequeño, dejar algo pequeño (ropas, zapatos); **b)** perder un hábito, abandonar una costumbre (juvenil, infantil); **a)** (lit.) tener origen en, salir de. **14 to – up,** hacerse adulto, madurar. **15 – up!,** ¡no seas infantil!

grower | 'grəʊər | *s.c.* **1** cultivador, criador. **2** crecimiento (rápido o lento).

growing | 'grəʊɪŋ | *adj.* **1** crecedero, que está creciendo. || **2 – pains, a)** primeras dificultades, primeros obstáculos (de una actividad); **b)** males o dolores del crecimiento (en los niños).

growl | graʊl | *v.i.* **1** gruñir (los animales). **2** (fig.) aullar, ulular, bramar (el viento). **3** (lit.) bramar, refunfuñar, rezongar. || *v.t.* **4** decir refunfuñando, expresarse con gruñidos. || *s.c.* **4** gruñido, aullido.

grown | grəʊn | *p.p.* de **to grow.**

grown-up | 'grəʊnʌp | *adj.* **1** adulto, maduro, juicioso. || *s.c.* **2** adulto, persona mayor.

growth | grəʊθ | *s.i.* **1** desarrollo, crecimiento, evolución (de un proceso). **2** tamaño, amplitud. **3** madurez, plenitud (de una persona). **4 [– (in)]** desarrollo, expansión, incremento, aumento. **5** evolución. || *s.c.* **6** alargamiento, protuberancia, saliente, bulto. **7** MED. tumor. **8** media barba, barba de días. **9** producción. || *s.c.* e *i.* **10** vegetación, planta. || **11 full –,** crecimiento máximo, desarrollo completo; (fig.) madurez, plenitud. **12 – point,** polo de desarrollo.

grub | grʌb | *s.c.* **1** larva, gusano. **2** (jerga) comida, manduca: *grub's up! = ¡la comida está servida!* **3** esclavo, trabajador servil, persona ajetreada. || *v.i.* **4 [to – *adv./prep.*]** remover la tierra, cavar (para esconder algo). **5** buscar afanosamente, revolverlo todo (buscando algo). **6** trabajar como un esclavo, afanarse mucho. || *v.t.* **7** arrancar de raíz, desarraigar. **8** limpiar de hierbas, quitar la maleza. **9** (jerga) limpiar, birlar, afanar.

grubby | 'grʌbɪ | *adj.* **1** (fam.) mugriento, roñoso, sucio, desaseado. **2** infectado de gusanos. **3** despreciable, vil.

grudge | grʌdʒ | *v.t.* **1 [to – *ger.*]** resistirse a dar, escatimar, dar de mala gana. **2** admitir de mala gana, permitir con reparos. **3** envidiar. || *s.c.* **4** rencor, resentimiento, hostilidad. || **5 to bear a –/grudges,** guardar rencor, tener manía.

grudging | 'grʌdʒɪŋ | *adj.* poco generoso, envidioso, egoísta.

grudgingly | 'grʌdʒɪŋlɪ | *adv.* de mala gana.

gruel | grʊəl | *s.i.* **1** papilla de avena, gachas. **2** (brit.) castigo severo.

gruelling | grʊəlɪŋ | (EE.UU.) **grueling.** *adj.* **1** duro, agotador, extenuante, pesado (una actividad). **2** abrumador, agobiante. **3** reñido, disputado (un partido, una pelea).

gruesome | 'gru:səm | *adj.* **1** horripilante, aterrador, que pone los pelos de punta (una muerte, un sufrimiento): *gruesome crimes = crímenes horripilantes.*

gruff | grʌf | *adj.* **1** duro, áspero, bronco (el tono de voz). **2** brusco, malhumorado, rudo.

grumble | 'grʌmbl | *v.i.* **1** quejarse, protestar, rezongar. **2** rugir, retumbar (un trueno en la lejanía). || *s.c.* **3** queja, protesta. **4** estruendo, estrépito, trueno (lejano).

grumpy | 'grʌmpɪ | *adj.* (fam.) gruñón, malhumorado, quejica, protestón.

grunt | grʌnt | *v.i.* **1** gruñir (los cerdos). || *v.t.* e *i.* **2** refunfuñar, rezongar, gruñir (una persona). || *s.c.* **3** gruñido, refunfuño. **4** ZOOL. ronco. **5** (EE.UU. y jerga) infante de marina (en Vietnam). **6** (jerga) uno que hace trabajos rutinarios.

guarantee | gærən'ti: | *s.c.* **1** garantía (por escrito). **2** garantía, promesa firme. **3** fianza. **4** DER. garante, fiador. || *v.t.* **5** garantizar, prometer, asegurar. **6** avalar, responder por. || **7 under –,** en garantía.

guaranteed | ˌgærən'ti:d | *adj.* **1** garantizado, asegurado. **2** avalado.

guarantor | ˌgærən'tɔ:r | *s.c.* DER. garante, fiador, avalador.

guard | gɑ:d | *s.c.* guardián, guarda, guardia, centinela, vigilante. **2 [the – *v.sing./pl.*]** la guardia (grupo de soldados). **3** (gen. en combinación) protector: *sheen guards = rodilleras.* **4** maquinista, ferroviario. **5** DEP. defensa. **6** MEC. defensa, guarda. **7** ELECTR. dispositivo, cierre de seguridad. || *s.i.* **8** guardia, protección, vigilancia, custodia. **9** (en) guardia, alerta. **10** salvaguarda, protección. || *v.t.* **11** proteger, vigilar, custodiar, escoltar. **12** (fig.) guardar (un secreto). **13** controlar. **14** proteger con seguro o guarda, asegurar. || **15 changing of the –,** relevo, cambio de guardia. **16 to – against,** tomar precauciones contra, evitar. **17 – band,** banda de protección (en cintas de video, cassettes). **18 to keep – (over),** vigilar. **19 off –,** desprevenido, con la guardia bajada. **20 on (one's) –,** en guardia, vigilante, alerta. **21 to stand/mount –,** montar la guardia, vigilar. **22 under –,** a buen recaudo, en custodia.

guarded | 'gɑ:dɪd | *adj.* **1** cauteloso, prudente, mesurado, moderado. **2** protegido, vigilado, custodiado.

guardedly | 'gɑ:dɪdlɪ | *adv.* cautelosamente, prudentemente, mesuradamente, moderadamente.

guardhouse | 'gɑ:dhaʊs | [*pl.* **guardhouses**] *s.c.gen.sing.* **1** caseta, garita de vigilancia. **2** cuartelillo (para la guardia de vigilancia). **3** prisión militar (para pequeñas ofensas).

guardian | 'gɑ:djən | *s.c.* **1** (form. o lit.) guardián, protector, paladín. **2** DER. tutor. **3** superior franciscano. || *adj.* **4** guardián, custodio.

guardsman | 'gɑ:dzmən | [*pl.* **guardsmen**] *s.c.* MIL. centinela, guardia, vigilante.

Guatemala | ˌgwætɪ'mɑ:lə | *s.sing.* Guatemala.

Guatemalan | ˌgwætɪ'mɑ:lən | *adj.* **1** guatemalteco. || *s.c.* **2** guatemalteco.

guava | 'gwɑ:və | *s.c.* **1** BOT. guayabo (árbol). **2** guayaba (fruto).

Guayana | 'gaɪ'ɑ:nə | *s.sing.* Guayana.

gubernatorial | ˌgu:bənə'tɔ:rɪəl | *adj.* **1** (EE.UU.) gubernativo, de gobernador, a gobernador: *gubernatorial elections = elecciones a gobernador.*

guerrilla, guerila | gə'rɪlə | *s.c.* **1** guerrillero. **2** guerrilla. || **3 – warfare,** guerra de guerrillas.

guess | ges | *v.t.* **1** adivinar, suponer, imaginar, inferir, conjeturar: *guess who's coming! = ¡adivina quien viene!* **2 [to – (that)]** (EE.UU. y fam.) considerar probable, creer, pensar, sospechar: *I guess so = creo que sí.* || *v.i.* **3** hacer una conjetura. || *s.c.* **4** conjetura, suposición. **5** sospecha, teoría (sobre algo dudoso). || **6 anybody's –!,** ¡quién sabe! **7 to keep someone guessing,** mantener a uno intrigado, mantener a uno en suspenso. **8 your – is a good as mine,** vaya Vd. a saber.

guesswork | 'geswɜ:k | *s.i.* suposición, conjetura, adivinanza.

guest | gest | *s.c.* **1** huésped, invitado, visita, convidado. **2** TV. artista invitado, participante de honor. **3** huésped, cliente (de hotel, restaurante). **4** ZOOL. parásito (animal o vegetal). | *v.t.* e *i.* **5** hospedar, invitar a casa, convidar. **6** TV. tener como artista invitado. **7 [to – (on)]** asistir, intervenir, actuar como artista invitado. || **8 be my –!,** ¡claro!, ¡adelante! (como respuesta a una petición); ¡invito yo! **9 – house,** pensión, casa de huéspedes. **10 – room,** cuarto de invitados.

guffaw | gʌ'fɔ: | *v.i.* **1** reírse a carcajadas, dar risotadas, reírse vulgarmente. || *s.c.* **2** risotada, carcajada.

Guiana | gaɪ'ænə | *s.sing.* Guayana (francesa, holandesa).

guidance | 'gaɪdns | *s.i.* **1** asesoramiento, consejo (profesional, escolar). **2** teledirección (de un misil, cohete). || **3 – counselor,** asesor, consejero.

guidebook | 'gaɪdbʊk | *s.c.* guía de viaje (libro).

guide | gaɪd | *s.c.* **1** asesor, consejero. **2** guía turístico. **3** guía de viaje (libro). **4** manual informativo, guía informativa. **5** MIL. guía. **6** poste indicador, mojón, hito. **7** MEC. guía, montante, corredera, deslizadero. || *v.t.* **8 [to – *o. adv./prep.*]** guiar, señalar el camino, mostrar el camino, conducir. **9** aconsejar, asesorar, orientar. **10** conducir, pilotar, manejar (un aparato en movimiento). **11** *gen. pas.* ejercer control, influir. **12** teledirigir, dirigir (un misil). || *v.i.* **13** trabajar como guía. || **14 – girl,** exploradora. **15 – plate,** INF. placa guía.

guided | 'gaɪdɪd | *adj.* dirigido, teledirigido.

guidepost | 'gaɪdpəust | *s.c.* poste indicador, señalizador de carretera.

guild | gɪld | *s.c.* **1** gremio, hermandad, cofradía. **2** asociación, sociedad. **3** BOT. grupo ecológico de plantas parásitas.

guile | gaɪl | *s.i.* **1** astucia, maña, engaño. **2** ardid, truco, estratagema. || *v.t.* **3** (arc.) engañar, burlar.

guileful | 'gaɪlful | *adj.* astuto, artero, timado, engañoso.

guileless | 'gaɪllɪs | *adj.* ingenuo, cándido, inocente.

guilty | gɪltɪ | *adj.* **1** DER. culpable. **2 [– (of)]** responsable (de), culpable (de). **3 [– (about)]** cargado de culpa, de vergüenza, lleno de remordimiento. || **4 a – veredict,** DER. una sentencia de culpabilidad. **5 to find someone –,** DER. declarar culpable a uno. **7 to plead –,** DER. confesarse culpable.

Guinea | 'gɪnɪ | *s.sing.* Guinea.

guinea-pig | 'gɪnɪpɪg | *s.c.* **1** ZOOL. conejillo de Indias, cobaya, (Am.) cuí. **2** (fig.) conejillo de Indias, cobaya (persona objeto de experimento).

Guinevere | 'gwɪnɪ,vɪər | *s.* LIT. Ginebra (esposa del Rey Arturo).

guise | gaɪz | *s.c.* **1** guisa, manera, forma, aspecto, apariencia. **2** vestidura, disfraz, vestimenta. **3** (arc.) hábito, costumbre. || **4 in that –,** de ese modo. **5 under the – of,** so pretexto de.

guitar | gɪ'tɑːr | *s.c.* MUS. guitarra.

gulch | gʌtʃ | *s.c.* **1** (EE.UU.) barranco, cañada, quebrada.

gulf | gʌlf | *s.c.* **1** GEOG. golfo. **2** (lit.) abismo, precipicio, sima. **3** (fig.) diferencia, abismo (entre opiniones). **4** (EE.UU.) torbellino, remolino. || **5 Gulf Stream,** Corriente del Golfo (de Méjico).

gull | gʌl | *s.c.* **1** ZOOL. gaviota, golondrina de mar. **2** ingenuo, incauto, primo. || *v.t.* **3** (lit. y arc.) engañar, estafar, timar.

gullet | 'gʌlɪt | *s.c.* **1** ANAT. esófago. **2** (fam.) garganta, gorja, gaznate, gola. || **3 to stick in one's –,** atragantársele a uno, revolvérsele el estómago, resultar inaceptable (algo).

gullibility | ,gʌlə'bɪlɪtɪ | *s.i.* ingenuidad, candidez, inocencia.

gullible | 'gʌlibl | *adj.* ingenuo, cándido, inocentón, bobalicón.

gully | gʌlɪ | *s.c.* **1** barranco, torrentera, hondonada. **2** reguera, requero. **3** (brit.) faca, navaja larga. || *v.t.* **4** formar un barranco, una torrentera.

gulp | gʌlp | *v.t.* **1 [to – (down)]** tragar, engullir, devorar. **2** tragar saliva; sofocar, cortar (los sollozos). || *v.i.* **3** entrecortarse la voz, entrecortarse la respiración, no poder hablar. || *s.c.* **4** trago, tragantona. **5** INF. varios bytes (gen. dos). || **6 at one –,** de un trago. **7 to – something back,** (fig.) tragarse (las lágrimas, las palabras).

gum | gʌm | *s.i.* **1** goma, caucho. **2** goma, cola de pegar, pegamento. **3** chicle, goma de mascar. || *s.c.* **4** eucalipto, árbol que produce goma. **5** *gen.pl.* ANAT. encías. **6** caramelo de goma, pastilla de goma. || *v.t.* **7** pegar, engomar. **8** rellenar de cola, cubrir de cola. || *v.i.* **9** pegarse, ponerse pegajoso. **10** exudar goma. || **11 by –!,** (p.u.), ¡caramba!, ¡por favor!, ¡válgame Dios! **12 – tree,** eucalipto, árbol que produce goma. **13 to – up,** (fam.) fastidiar, estropear, echar a perder, inutilizar. **14 to – up the works,** (fam.) estropear todo, fastidiar el invento.

gumdrop | 'gʌmdrɒp | *s.c.* caramelo, pastilla de goma (bañado de azúcar).

gummy | 'gʌmɪ | *adj.* **1** pegajoso, viscoso. **2** gomoso, de goma. **3** cubierto de cola.

gumption | 'gʌmpʃn | *s.i.* **1** (brit. y fam.) sentido común, sentido práctico, perspicacia. **2** iniciativa, valentía, audacia, coraje.

gun | gʌn | *s.c.* **1** arma de fuego, pistola, revólver, fusil, escopeta, carabina, cañón. **2 [the =N *pl.*]** la artillería. **3** pistola inyectora, pistola de presión. **4** cañonazo, salva (de saludo). **5** (EE.UU. y fam.) pistolero. **6** cazador. **7** MEC. inyector, bomba de gasolina. **8** ELECTR. cañón (de luz). || *v.t.* **9** disparar a, tirar a. **10** acelerar el motor (de un coche). || *v.i.* **11** cazar, ir de caza (con arma de fuego). || **12 to go great guns,** progresar con rapidez, hacer grandes progresos. **13 – carriage,** MIL. armón de artillería, cureña. **14 – licence,** licencia de armas. **15 – turret,** torreta. **16 to – for somebody,** (brit. y fam.) perseguir, andar a la caza de alguien, ir a pillar a alguien. **17 to – somebody down,** (fam.) asesinar a tiros, herir a tiros. **18 to jump the –,** V. **jump. 19 to spike someone's guns,** V. **spike. 20 to stick to one's guns,** V. **stick.**

gunboat | 'gʌnbəut | *s.c.* MIL. lancha cañonera, cañonero.

gunfire | 'gʌn,faɪər | *s.i.* **1** MIL. fuego de artillería, cañoneo. **2** tiroteo, disparo (ruido).

gunman | 'gʌnmən | [*pl.* **gunmen**] *s.c.* **1** pistolero, asesino a sueldo, matón profesional, (Am.) baleador. **2** terrorista.

gunner | 'gʌnər | *s.c.* **1** MIL. soldado (de los tres ejércitos). **2** (brit.) MIL. cabo de artillería, artillero. **3** cazador (con arma de fuego).

gunnery | gʌnərɪ | *s.i.* **1** MIL. artillería. **2** uso de armas de fuego.

gunpowder | 'gʌn,paudər | *s.i.* pólvora.

gunrunner | 'gʌn,rʌnər | *s.c.* traficante de armas.

gunrunning | 'gʌn,rʌnɪŋ | *s.i.* tráfico de armas, contrabando de armas.

gunshot | 'gʌnʃ't | *s.c.* **1** disparo, tiro, balazo. || *s.i.* **2** tiro, alcance (de un arma de fuego). || **3 to be within –,** estar a tiro.

gunsmith | 'gʌnsmɪθ | *s.c.* armero.

gunwale | 'gʌnweɪl | *s.c.* MAR. borda, regala.

gurgle | 'gəːgl | *v.i.* **1** gorgotear, gorgojear, hacer gorgoritos (los niños pequeños). **2 [to – *adv./prep.*]** gorgotear, hacer gluglú (el agua). || *v.t.* **3** expresarse con gorgoritos. || *s.c.* **4** gorgoteo, gorgorito, gluglú.

gush | gʌʃ | *v.i.* **1 [to – *adv./prep.*]** salir a borbotones, salir a chorros, brotar, manar. **2 [to – (over)]** (desp.) hablar efusivamente, deshacerse en elogios (sobre), dorar la píldora. || *v.t.* **3** echar a borbotones, verter chorros, chorrear. || *s.sing.* **4** chorro, borbotón; estallido. **5** (fig.) estallido (de aplausos); derroche (de energía). **6** efusión, afecto.

gushing | 'gʌʃɪŋ | *adj.* efusivo, cordial, afectuoso.

gusset | 'gʌsɪt | *s.c.* cuchillo, nesga, escudete (en una prenda).

gust | gʌst | *s.c.* **1** ráfaga, racha (de aire, de lluvia). **2** explosión. **3** acceso, arrebato: *a gust of happiness = un arrebato de felicidad.* **4** (arc.) sazón, sabor, condimento. **5** gusto, apetencia. || *v.i.* **6** soplar a ráfagas.

gusto | 'gʌstəu | *s.i.* **1** gusto, placer, deleite. **2** entusiasmo, vitalidad. **3** (arc.) estilo artístico, gusto (estético, artístico).

gusty | 'gʌstɪ | *adj.* **1** borrascoso, chubascoso. **2** (jerga) impetuoso; valeroso, resuelto.

gut | gʌt | *s.c.* **1** ANAT. intestino. **2** pasaje, garganta, desfiladero. **3** MAR. estrecho. **4** *pl.* intestinos, entrañas, agallas (de animales, peces). **5** *pl.* (fig.) tripas, interiores (de un aparato); intríngulis (de un tema). **6** (fam.) glotón, comilón. **7** (fam.) panza, barrigón (de un bebedor). **8** subconsciente. || *s.i.* **9** cuerda (de tripa, para instrumentos musicales, raquetas, suturas quirúrgicas). **10** *pl.* (jerga) agallas, estómago, coraje. || *v.t.* **11** destripar, desentrañar (animales); limpiar (pescado). **12** destruir el interior (de una casa por el fuego). || *adj.* **13** visceral. **14** fácil, básico, fundamental. || **15 to hate someone's guts,** odiar a alguien a muerte, odiar intensamente. **16 to work/run/scream one's guts out,** trabajar, correr, gritar hasta extenuarse, hasta quedarse sin aliento, salírsele a uno el corazón por la boca (por un esfuerzo intenso).

gutter | 'gʌtər | *s.c.* **1** cuneta, zanja. **2** canalón, canal, gotera. **3** surco, cárcava, acanaladura. **4 [the –]** los suburbios, los barrios bajos; la escoria, la clase más depauperada. **5** canal, depresión (a ambos lados de una bolera). **6** margen interior (entre dos páginas de un libro). || *v.t.* **7** acanalar, estriar, formar zanjas. || *v.i.* **8** (lit.) parpadear, brillar con luz mortecina. **9** fluir, correr (un líquido). **10** fundirse, chorrear (una vela). || **11 the – press,** la prensa sensacionalista, prensa del corazón.

guttersnipe | 'gʌtəsnaɪp | *s.c.* **1** (desp.) golfillo, pilluelo, niño vagabundo, de la calle. **2** vago, maleante.
guttural | 'gʌtərəl | *adj.* **1** gutural (sonido). **2** FON. velar.
guy | gaɪ | *s.c.* **1** (fam.) tío, tipo, individuo. **2** *pl.* (EE.UU.) chicos y chicas. **3** (brit.) muñeco, monigote (que representa a Guy Fawkes). **4** (brit.) adefesio, fantoche, mamarracho. **5** viento, cuerda, cable (de una tienda de campaña). **6** MAR. obenque. || *v.t.* **7** (p.u.) ridiculizar, parodiar, burlarse, mofarse. || **8 wise –**, sabelotodo.
guzzle | 'gʌzl | *v.t.* e *i.* **1** tragar, engullir (comida, bebida).
gym | dʒɪm | *s.c.* **1** (fam.) gimnasio. || *s.i.* **2** gimnasia, educación física.
gymnasium | dʒɪm'neɪzʃəm | *s.c.* (form.) gimnasio.
gymnast | 'dʒɪmnæst | *s.c.* gimnasia.
gymnastic | dʒɪm'næstɪk | *adj.* **1** gimnástico. || *s.pl.* **2** gimnasia, educación física.
gynecologist | ˌgaɪnɪ'kɒlədʒɪst | *s.c.* ginecólogo.
gynecology | ˌgaɪnɪ'kɒlədʒɪ | *s.i.* ginecología.
gyp | dʒɪp | *s.i.* **1** (brit. y jerga) dolor agudo, pinchazo. **2** timo, estafa. **3** estafador, timador. **4** (brit.) timar, estafar, embaucar, defraudar. || **5 to give someone –**, echar a uno un rapapolvo, poner a uno a caldo, poner a uno como un trapo.
gypsum | 'dʒɪpsəm | *s.i.* yeso.
gypsy | 'dʒɪpsɪ | V. **gipsy.**
gyrate | 'dʒaɪərɪt | *v.i.* **1** (lit.) girar, rotar. || *adj.* **2** redondo, curvo.
gyration | ˌdʒaɪə'reɪʃn | *s.c.* e *i.* **1** (form.) giro, rotación.
gyratory | 'dʒaɪərətərɪ | *adj.* **1** (form.) giratorio, rotatorio.
gyrocompass | 'dʒaɪərəkʌmpəs | *s.c.* **1** FIS. girocompás, compás giroscópico.
gyroscope | 'dʒaɪərəskəup | *s.c.* **1** FIS. giroscopio, giróscopo.

h, H | eɪtʃ | *s.c.* **1** letra octava del abecedario. || **2 to drop one's h's,** no pronunciar las haches (signo de cierta clase social).

ha | hɑː | (también **hah**) *interj.* **1** ¡ah!(sorpresa, ironía, enfado, etc.). **2** (fam.) ¡ja!, ¡toma!, ¡venga! (expresando sorpresa o enfado). || **3 –,** sonido de risa.

habeas corpus | ˌheɪbɪəs'kɔːpəs | *s.i.* DER. hábeas corpus.

haberdasher | 'hæbədæʃər | *s.c.* **1** (brit.) mercero. **2** (EE.UU.) especialista en ropa de caballero.

haberdashery | 'hæbədæʃərɪ | *s.i.* **1** (brit.) productos de mercería. **2** (EE.UU.) artículos de caballero, ropa de caballero. || *s.c.* **3** mercería (tienda).

habit | 'hæbɪt | *s.c.* e *i.* **1** hábito, costumbre, uso (personal). || *s.c.* **2** vi cio (de drogas). **3** hábito (de un monje o similar). || **4 a creature of –,** persona de hábitos fijos. **5 a – of mind,** un hábito mental. **6 to be in the – of,** tener la costumbre de, tener el hábito de. **7 from force of –,** por puro hábito, por simple costumbre. **8 to make a – of/to make something a –,** adquirir la costumbre de/tener la costumbre de.

habitability | ˌhæbɪtə'bɪlɪtɪ | *s.i.* habitabilidad.

habitable | 'hæbɪtəbl | *adj.* habitable.

habitat | 'hæbɪtæt | *s.c.* BIOL. hábitat.

habitation | ˌhæbɪ'teɪʃn | *s.i.* **1** habitación, ocupación (de vivienda). || *s.c.* **2** (form.) vivienda, habitáculo, morada, residencia.

habit-forming | 'hæbɪtfɔːmɪŋ | *adj.* causante de adicción.

habitual | hə'bɪtʃʊəl | *adj.* habitual, regular, acostumbrado, usual.

habitually | hə'bɪtʃʊəlɪ | *adv.* habitualmente, regularmente, acostumbradamente, usualmente.

habituate | hə'bɪtʃʊeɪt | *v.t.* y *r.* (normalmente *pasiva.*) (form.) habituar, acostumbrar.

habitué | hə'bɪtʃʊeɪ | *s.c.* asiduo, parroquiano (de un lugar).

hack | hæk | *v.t.* **1** cortar, hacer tajos, tajar. **2** abrir camino, hacer una trocha (en un bosque o parecido). **3** toser con gran fuerza. **4** dar una patada fuerte, atizar una patada fuerte. || *s.c.* **5** caballo de alquiler. **6** monta de alquiler. **7** (fig.) viaje dificultoso, viaje por caminos de mulo. **8** (fam.) escritorzuelo. **9** (fam. y EE.UU.) taxi. || *v.i.* **10** (brit.) ir a caballo (especialmente por carreteras). **11** (fam. y EE.UU.) conducir un taxi. || *adj.* **12** (fam.) pesado, aburrido (trabajo). || **13 to – about,** cortar, recortar, arreglar (un texto). **14 to – at,** lanzar golpes cortantes a, dar golpes cortantes a; cortar a grandes tajos. **15 to – through, a)** abrirse camino con dificultad, abrir una senda. **b)** trabajar a gran velocidad sin prestar atención a la calidad. **16 to go hacking,** ir de paseo a caballo.

hacker | 'hækər | *s.c.* (fam.) fanático de los ordenadores, rata de ordenador.

hacking | 'hækɪŋ | *adj.* **1** seca y fuerte (tos). || **2 – jacket,** chaqueta de montar (a caballo).

hackles | 'hæklz*s.* | *pl.* **1** pelos del cuello, plumas del cuello (en perros, gatos, gallos, etc.). || **2 to make someone's – rise,** encolerizar a alguien, poner a alguien enfermo (de ira).

hackneyed | 'hæknɪd | *adj.* gastado, trillado, repetido hasta la saciedad (expresión, palabra, etc.).

hacksaw | 'hæksɔː | *s.c.* MEC. sierra para cortar metal.

had | hæd | (forma relajada | həd |) *pret.* y *p.p.irreg.* de **have.**

haddock | 'hædək*s.c.* e *i.* ZOOL. abadejo, bacalao.

hadji | 'hædʒɪ | (también **hajji**) *s.c.* REL. musulmán que ha estado en La Meca como peregrino.

hadn't | 'hædnt*contr.* de **had** y **not.**

haematologist | ˌhiːmə'tɒlədʒɪst | (EE.UU. **hematologist**) *s.c.* hematólogo.

haematology | ˌhiːmə'tɒlədʒɪ | (EE.UU. **hematology**) *s.i.* hematología.

haemoglobin | ˌhiːmə'gləubɪn| (EE.UU. **hemoglobin**) *s.i.* BIOL. hemoglobina.

haemophilia | ˌhiːmə'fɪlɪə | (EE.UU. **hemophilia**) *s.i.* MED. hemofilia.

haemophiliac | ˌhiːmə'fɪlɪæk | (EE.UU. **hemophiliac**) *s.c.* MED. hemofílico.

haemorrhage | 'hemərɪdʒ | (EE.UU. **hemorrhage**) *s.c.* e *i.* **1** hemorragia. || *v.i.* **2** sufrir una hemorragia, sangrar.

haemorrhoids | 'hemərɔɪdz | (EE.UU. **hemorrhoids**) *s.pl.* MED. hemorroides.

haft | hɑːft | (EE.UU.) | hæft*s.c.* mango, puño (de cuchillo, hacha, etc.).

hag | hæg*s.c.* (desp.) bruja, vieja bruja.

haggard | 'hægəd *adj.* ojeroso, demacrado (normalmente por falta de sueño).

haggle 'hægl*v.i.* **1** discutir, disputar (normalmente sobre el precio de algo). || *s.c.* **2** discusión, disputa (por el precio de algo).

hahV. ha.

hail | heɪl | *v.i.* **1** granizar. **2 [to – from]** (form.) ser originario de, ser de, venir de, proceder de (lugar, región, país, etc.). || *s.i.* **3** granizo. || *s.c.* **4** (normalmente *sing.*) (fig.) lluvia, torrente (de objetos o insultos): *a hail of criticism* = *un torrente de críticas.* _ *v.t.* **5** llamar, atraer la atención de (alguien). **6** llamar, parar (taxi o similar). **7** aclamar (persona o acontecimiento de gran importancia). || **8 –!,** (arc.) ¡salve! **9 to – down,** (fig.) llover (golpes, tiros, etc.). **10 within hailing distance (of),** al alcance de la voz, al alcance del oído.

hailstone | 'heɪlstəun | *s.c.* piedra de granizo, granizo.

hailstorm | 'heɪlstɔːm | *s.c.* tormenta de granizo, granizada.

hair | heər | *s.c.* e *i.* **1** pelo, cabello, vello; pelo de animal (para ropa o relleno). || *s.c.* **2** pelo, crin (de animal). || **3 a**

hair's breadth, un pelo, un tanto así, una pizca. **4 to get in one's –,** (fam.) tener a uno hasta la coronilla, poner a uno malo. **5 -haired,** de pelo (en compuestos): *short-haired = de pelo corto.* **6 – shirt,** cilicio. **7 keep your – on,** (fam.) cálmate, no te sulfures tanto. **8 to let one's – down,** (fam.) relajarse por completo, abandonar toda reserva. **9 to make one's – stand on end/rise,** (fam.) poner a uno los pelos de punta. **10 not a – out of place,** (fam.) ni el menor detalle incorrecto, absolutamente impecable (especialmente en el vestir). **11 not to turn a –,** (fam.) no inmutarse, ni pestañear. **12 to split hairs,** (desp. y fam.) hilar demasiado fino, pararse en minucias increíbles, prestar demasiada atención a nimiedades. **13 to tear one's – out,** (fam.) mesarse los cabellos de uno. **14 to touch/harm a – on someone's head,** tocar un pelo de alguien (hacerle daño).

hairbrush | 'heəbrʌʃ | *s.c.* cepillo para el pelo.

haircut | 'heəkʌt | *s.c.* corte de pelo, estilo de corte de pelo.

hairdo | 'heədu: | *s.c.* (form.) peinado, estilo de peinado (especialmente de una mujer).

hairdresser | 'heədresər | *s.c.* peluquero.

hairdressing | 'heədresɪŋ | *s.i.* peluquería (como oficio).

hairdryer | 'heədraɪər | (también **hairdrier**) *s.c.* secador para el pelo.

hair-grip | heəgrɪp | *s.c.* (brit.) horquilla (para el pelo).

hairiness | 'heərɪnɪs | *s.i.* abundancia de pelo, abundancia de cabello, vellosidad.

hairless | 'heəlɪs | *adj.* sin pelo, calvo.

hair-line | 'heəlaɪn | *s.c.* **1** (normalmente *sing.*) entradas, límite del pelo en la frente: *a receding hair-line = entradas pronunciadas.* _ *adj.* **2** (fig.) del tamaño de un pelo, mínimo.

hairnet | 'heənet | *s.c.* redecilla para el pelo.

hairpiece | 'heəpi:s | *s.c.* tupé, peluca.

hairpin | 'heəpɪn | *s.c.* **1** horquilla. || **2 – bend,** curva cerradísima.

hair-raising | 'heəreɪzɪŋ | *adj.* horripilante, que pone los pelos de punta.

hair-slide | 'heəslaɪd | *s.c.* (brit.) pasador.

hair-splitting | 'heəsplɪtɪŋ | (desp.) *s.i.* **1** detalles nimios, puntos de discusión desechables, puro sofisma. || *adj.* **2** nimio, de pura minucia.

hairstyle | 'heəstaɪl | *s.c.* peinado, estilo de peinado.

hairy | 'heərɪ | *adj.* **1** peludo, velludo, hirsuto. **2** (fam.) peligroso, enervante (situación).

hake | heɪk | [*pl.* **hake**] *s.c.* ZOOL. merluza.

halcyon | 'hælsɪən | *adj.* (form.) pacífico, próspero, apacible (estado mental).

hale | heɪl | *adj.* **1** (lit.) sano, robusto. || **2 – and hearty,** sano y lleno de vida.

half | hɑ:f | (EE.UU.) | hæf | [*pl.* **halves**] | s.c. **1** medio, mitad: *the first half of May = la primera mitad de Mayo.* **2** DEP. mitad, parte (de un partido). **3** media pinta (en medidas de bebida; equivalente aproximadamente a un cuarto). **4** billete de niño (mitad de precio). || *adj.* **5** medio: *a half chicken = medio pollo.* **6** medio, mitad: *half the audience left = la mitad de los espectadores se fueron.* _ *pron.* **7** la mitad: *half were Chinese and the rest Japanese = la mitad eran chinos y el resto japoneses.* _ *adv.* **8** medio: *this is half full = esto está medio lleno.* **9 [– past]** y media (en las horas). **10** (fam.) medio, casi: *I'm half dead = estoy medio muerto.* _ **11 a problem/meal/etc. and a –,** un problema de aúpa/vaya comida (puede ser positivo o negativo). **12 better/other –,** (hum.) costilla (esposa). **13 by –,** en un cincuenta por ciento. **14 to go off at – cock,** salir bien sólo a medias. **15 – a mind,** V. **mind. 16 – a minute/second,** (fam.) en seguida, inmediatamente, sin más tardar. **17 – an ear,** V. **ear. 18 – board,** media pensión (en hoteles). **19 – cock,** montado a la mitad, medio amartillado (arma de fuego). **20 – holiday,** medio día libre. **21 – measures,** a la mitad, a medio gas, a medias. **22 – moon,** media luna. **23 – the battle,** V. **battle. 24 in –,** en dos (partido). **25 not –,** (fam.) **a)** ya lo creo, por supuesto; **b)** ni mucho menos: *he didn't half love her = él no la amaba ni mucho menos.* **26 six of one and – a dozen of the other,** V. **six. 27 too ... by –,** demasiado... con mucho, pasarse de...: *he's too clever by half = él se pasa de listo.*

half-baked | hɑ:fbeɪkt | *adj.* disparatado, absurdo, a medio hacer (plan, proyecto, etc.).

half-brother | 'hɑ:fbrʌðər | *s.c.* hermanastro.

half-caste | 'hɑ:fkeɪst | *s.c.* **1** mestizo. || *adj.* **2** mestizo.

half-day | 'hɑ:fdeɪ | *s.c.* medio día de trabajo, medio día de descanso.

half-hearted | ˌhɑ:f'hɑ:tɪd | *adj.* indiferente, desanimado, poco entusiasta; apático.

half-heartedly | ˌhɑ:f'hɑ:tɪdlɪ | *adv.* indiferentemente, desanimadamente.

half-life | 'hɑ:flaɪf | *s.c.* FIS. período medio (de desintegración de un cuerpo con radioactividad).

half-mast | ˌhɑ:f'mɑ:st | **at –,** a media asta.

half-note | 'hɑ:fnəut | *s.c.* MUS. (EE.UU.) blanca.

halfpenny | 'heɪpnɪ | [*pl.* **halfpennies** o **halfpence**] *s.c.* **1** moneda de medio penique. || *s.sing.* **2 [a –]** una perra gorda (poco valor).

half-price | ˌhɑ:f'praɪs | *adj.* y *adv.* mitad de precio, a mitad de precio.

half-sister | 'hɑ:fsɪstər | *s.c.* hermanastra.

half-term | ˌhɑ:f'tɜ:m | *s.c.* e *i.* vacaciones de mitad de trimestre.

half-timbered | ˌhɑ:f'tɪmbəd | *adj.* ARQ. entramado.

half-time | ˌhɑ:f'taɪm | *s.i.* DEP. descanso.

halftone | 'hɑ:ftəun | *s.c.* **1** MUS. (EE.UU.) semitono. | *adj.* **2** PER. a media tinta (ilustración).

halfway | ˌhɑ:f'weɪ | *adv.* **1** a mitad de camino, en la mitad del camino, a mitad de trayecto. **2** en la mitad (de algún proceso temporal). **3** mínimamente, aceptablemente. || **4 to meet someone –,** hacer concesiones a alguien, encontrarse con alguien a la mitad del camino (en una negociación o similar).

half-wit | 'hɑ:fwɪt | *s.c.* (fam.) mentecato, tonto, imbécil.

half-witted | 'hɑ:fwɪtɪd | *adj.* (fam.) atontado, estúpido.

half-yearly | ˌhɑ:f'jəlɪ | *adj.* bianual.

halibut | 'hælɪbət | [*pl.* **halibut**] *s.c.* ZOOL. halibut (pez).

halitosis | ˌhælɪ'təusɪs | *s.i.* MED. halitosis.

hall | hɔ:l | *s.c.* **1** vestíbulo, entrada, recibidor (de una casa). **2** sala (de conciertos, congresos, etc.). **3** salón de actos. **4** (brit.) comedor (de una Universidad o similar). **5** (brit.) casa señorial, casa de campo señorial. || **6 – of residence,** residencia universitaria. **7 in –,** en la universidad (sitio donde se vive en la época universitaria).

hallelujah | hælɪ'lu:ja | (también **halleluiah** o **alleluia**) *interj.* REL. aleluya; aleluya (grito de alegría ante algo bueno).

hallmark | 'hɔ:lmɑ:k | *s.c.* **1** marca, sello (en metales preciosos asegurando su calidad). **2** (fig.) marca esencial, sello distintivo (de algo o alguien). || *v.t.* **3** poner una marca, poner un sello (a metales preciosos).

hallo V. hello.

hallowed | 'hæləud | *adj.* **1** REL. santo, consagrado (suelo, objeto, etc.). **2** (fig.) muy respetado, altamente reverenciado.

Halloween | ˌhæləu'i:n | (también **Hallowe'en**) *s.i.* víspera de Todos los Santos (especialmente en EE.UU. significa un acontecimiento social).

hallstand | 'hɔ:lstænd | *s.c.* perchero.

hallucinate | hə'lu:sɪneɪt | *v.i.* ver alucinaciones, alucinar (a causa de drogas o parecido).

hallucination | həˌlu:sɪ'neɪʃn | *s.c.* e *i.* alucinación.

hallucinatory | hə'lu:sɪnətrɪ | (EE.UU.) | hə'lu:sɪnətɔ:rɪ | *adj.* con alucinaciones, irreal.

hallucinogen | hə'lu:sɪnədʒen | *s.c.* alucinógeno.

hallucinogenic | həˌlu:sɪnə'dʒenɪk | *adj.* causante de alucinaciones (droga o similar).

hallway | 'hɔ:lweɪ | *s.c.* **1** entrada, vestíbulo, zaguán. **2** (EE.UU.) pasillo.

halo | 'heɪləu | [*pl.* **halos** o **haloes**] *s.c.* halo, aureola.

halt | hɔ:lt | *v.t.* e *i.* **1** parar(se), detener(se). **2** finalizar(se), interrumpir(se) (un proceso o actividad). || *s.c.* **3** alto, parada. **4** (brit.) apeadero (de tren). || **5 –!,** MIL. ¡alto! **6 to call a – (to),** parar, detener, interrumpir. **7 to come to a –,** pararse, detenerse, interrumpirse. **8 to a –,** hasta quedar interrumpido, hasta su final: *his fault brought the game to a halt = su falta hizo que el juego quedara interrumpido.*

halter | 'hɔːltər | *s.c.* ronzal.

halterneck | 'hɔːltənek | *adj.* sin hombreras (traje de señora).

halting | 'hɔːltɪŋ | *adj.* titubeante, vacilante.

haltingly | 'hɔːltɪŋlɪ | *adv.* con titubeos, con vacilación.

halve | hɑːv | (EE.UU.) | hæv | *v.t.* e *i.* **1** reducir(se) a la mitad. || *v.t.* **2** partir en dos, dividir en dos (físicamente).

halves | hɑːvz | (EE.UU.) | hævz*pl.* **1** de **half.** **2 to go – (with),** ir a medias (con), dividir los costes a medias (con). **3 never to do things by –,** no hacer nunca las cosas a medias.

ham | hæm | *s.i.* **1** jamón. || *s.c.* **2** jamón, pernil. **3** comicastro, actor fatal. **4** radioaficionado. || *adj.* **5** fatal, malísimo (actuación artística). || **6 to – it up,** exagerar, pasarse (en actuación de teatro o similar).

hamburger | 'hæmbəːgər | *s.c.* hamburguesa.

ham-fisted | ˌhæm'fɪstɪd | *adj.* (fam.) torpón, desmañado, manazas.

ham-handed | ˌhæm'hændɪd | V. **hamfisted.**

hamlet | 'hæmlɪt | *s.c.* aldea, villorrio.

hammer | 'hæmər | *s.c.* **1** martillo. **2** percusor, martillo (de arma de fuego). **3** MUS. macillo. **4** DEP. martillo. || *v.t.* **5** golpear con un martillo, martillar. **6** (fig.) golpear sin parar, dar golpes sin parar. **7 [to – + *o.* + into]** meter como sea, meter a martillazos (una idea, mensaje, etc.). **8** criticar, machacar. **9** (fam.) DEP. derrotar contundentemente. || *v.i.* **10 [to – at]** repetir insistentemente, decir machaconamente (una idea, mensaje, etc.). **11 [to – *prep.*]** golpear, martillear: *the rain was hammering down on the shelter = la lluvia estaba golpeando sobre el refugio.* **12 [to – at]** empollar, estudiar/trabajar sin parar. || *s.sing.* **13 [the –]** DEP. el martillo. || **14 to come under the –,** ser vendido en pública subasta, ser subastado. **15 – and tongs,** violentamente, con gran fuerza, con ahínco. **16 to – away (at),** trabajar con ahínco (en), estudiar con tenacidad. **17 to – out,** elaborar con trabajo (acuerdo o similar). **18 the – and sickle,** la hoz y el martillo.

hammock | 'hæmək | *s.c.* hamaca.

hamper | 'hæmpər | *s.c.* **1** cesto, canasta, capacho. **2** cesta (especialmente de Navidad). || *v.t.* **3** impedir, entorpecer, poner trabas a.

hamster | 'hæmstər | *s.c.* ZOOL. hámster.

hamstring | 'hæmstrɪŋ | *v.t.* [*pret.* y *p.p.* **hamstringed** o **hamstrung**] **1** incapacitar, paralizar. || *s.c.* **2** ANAT. tendón del corvejón.

hamstrung | 'hæmstrʌŋ | *pret.* y *p.p.* de **hamstring.**

hand | hænd | *s.c.* **1** mano. **2** operario, peón (especialmente agrario). **3** manilla (de reloj). **4** mano (en cartas). **5** palmo (para medir especialmente caballos). || *s.sing.* **6 [the – of]** la mano de (influencia): *I can see the hand of the Communists there = puedo ver la mano de los comunistas ahí.* **7 [a –]** aplauso. **8** (p.u.) mano (matrimonio): *I asked for her hand = pedí su mano.* **9 [a – (with)]** una ayuda, una ayudita, una mano. **10** (lit.) letra, estilo de caligrafía, caligrafía. || *v.t.* **11** dar, pasar, acercar (en la mano). || **12 a free –,** carta blanca (total libertad para hacer lo que sea). **13 all hands to the pump,** todos a ayudar, todos a poner su granito de arena. **14 at first/second/etc. –,** V. **first. 15 at –/near at –/close at –,** muy cerca, al lado, muy a mano, a mano. **16 at the hands of,** a manos de (con matiz desagradable). **17 to be a dab hand (at),** V. **dab. 18 to bite the – that feeds,** cría cuervos y te sacarán los ojos; ser un desagradecido. **18 by –, a)** a mano (no hecho con máquina); **b)** en la mano (entregado). **19 to change hands,** cambiar de poseedor, cambiar de propietario, cambiar de manos. **20 to eat out of somebody's –,** V. **eat. 21 to force someone's –,** obligar a alguien a actuar, forzar a alguien a actuar (abiertamente o prematuramente para ellos). **22 to get/lay/etc. one's hands on,** (fam.) echar/poner las manos encima, dar con (alguien o algo). **23 to get out of –,** desmadrarse, descontrolarse, salirse de madre. **24 to go – in – (with),** estar íntimamente relacionado (con), ir de la mano (con), ir acompañando (a): *politics goes hand in hand with stratagems, unfortunately = la política está íntimamente relacionada con las maniobras, desgraciadamente.* **25 – and foot,** de pies y manos (atado). **26 to – around/round,** repartir, ir dando uno a uno. **27 to – back,** devolver (un objeto, normalmente). **28 to – down,** pasar, transmitir (objetos, conocimientos, costumbres, etc.). **29 -handed,** de la mano, para... manos (en compuestos): *a left-handed guitar = una guitarra para la mano izquierda.* **30 to – in,** entregar (trabajo, documentación, carta de renuncia a un trabajo, etc.). **31 – in glove (with),** en estrecha relación (con). **32 – in –,** de la mano, cogiéndose de la mano. **33 to – on,** dejar, pasar (especialmente herencia a personas). **34 to – out, a)** distribuir, repartir (con equidad); **b)** dar (consejo o castigo). **35 to – over (to), a)** dar, regalar, entregar para siempre; **b)** entregar, ceder (un prisionero, responsabilidades, etc.). **36 – over –,** una mano tras otra (físicamente). **37 – over fist,** a toda velocidad, sin tregua; a manos llenas (ganando dinero especialmente). **38 hands off,** quítame las manos de encima, no me toques, esas manos. **39 hands up,** manos arriba, arriba las manos. **40 to have a – in,** estar metido en (cualquier actividad). **41 to have one's hands full,** no tener un minuto libre, estar hasta arriba de trabajo. **42 to have got to – it to,** (fam.) tener que reconocer la valía de, no tener más remedio que admitir la valía de: *you've got to hand it to her, she works very hard = tienes que reconocer su valía, trabaja muchísimo.* **43 to hold one's –,** (fam. y fig.) apoyar, ser un apoyo para. **44 to hold hands,** cogerse de la mano. **45 in –, a)** libre, de sobra (tiempo); **b)** entre manos, a llevar a cabo (tarea o similar); **c)** controlado, bajo control (situación). **46 in the hands of,** bajo el poder de, bajo la poderosa influencia de; controlado por. **47 to keep one's – in,** mantenerse al día, estar al tanto, no perder la práctica (en un hobby o destreza). **48 to know something like the back of one's –,** conocer algo como la palma de la mano. **49 to lend a –,** V. **lend. 50 to live from – to mouth,** pasarlo muy mal económicamente, no tener qué llevarse a la boca. **51 off –,** sin consultar nada, de corrido (manera de saber algo). **52 off one's hands,** fuera del control de uno, ya no bajo la responsabilidad de uno. **53 on –,** a mano, disponible (algo o alguien). **54 on one's hands,** bajo el control de uno, bajo la responsabilidad de uno. **55 on one's hands and knees,** a gatas, a cuatro patas. **56 on the one –,** por una parte. **57 on the other –,** por otra parte. **58 out of –,** instantáneamente, sin más. **59 to play right into someone's hands,** caer en la trampa de alguien, actuar de la manera que otra persona quiere, seguirle el juego a alguien. **60 to shake hands,** V. **shake. 61 to show one's –,** descubrir el juego de uno, revelar la intención de uno. **62 to take in –,** hacerse cargo (de algo o alguien). **63 to –,** disponible, a mano. **64 to try one's – at,** probar por primera vez, poner la mano por primera vez en. **65 to turn one's – to,** emprender por primera vez, iniciar por primera vez (un trabajo o similar). **66 to wait on someone – and foot,** V. **wait. 67 to wash one's hands of,** desentenderse de. **68 to win hands down,** V. **win. 69 with one's bare hands,** V. **bare.**

handbag | 'hændbæg | *s.c.* bolso (de señora).

handball | 'hændbɔːl | *s.c.* DEP. balonmano; pelota mano.

handbill | 'hændbɪl | *s.c.* hoja de propaganda, panfleto propagandístico.

handbook | 'hændbʊk | *s.c.* libro de instrucciones, cuaderno de instrucciones.

handbrake | 'hændbreɪk | *s.c.* freno de mano.

handcart | 'hændkɑːt | *s.c.* carretilla, carretilla de mano.

handclap | 'hændklæp | **a slow –,** (brit.) palmas de desencanto, palmas de abucheo.

handcuff | 'hændkʌf | *s.c.* **1** (normalmente *pl.*) esposa, manilla. || *v.t.* **2** esposar.

handful | 'hændfʊl | *s.c.* **1** puñado, manojo; pocos: *a handful of big students = unos pocos estudiantes grandotes.* **2** (normalmente *sing.*) (fam.) pillo, pillín, trasto (algo o alguien que es difícil de controlar).

handgun | 'hændgʌn | *s.c.* pistola, revólver.

handicap | 'hændɪkæp | [*ger.* **handicapping,** *pret.* y *p.p.* **handicapped**] *v.t.* **1** estorbar, perjudicar, poner trabas a, poner obstáculos a. || *s.c.* **2** MED. hándicap, minusvalía. **3** DEP. hándicap, lastre (en las carreras de caballos, golf y otros deportes). **4** impedimento, estorbo, obstáculo (de todo tipo).

handicapped | 'hændɪkæpt | *adj.* **1** MED. minusválido, de minusvalía. **2** DEP. con lastre, lastrado, handicapado. || **3 the –,** los minusválidos, las personas con minusvalía (física o mental).

handicraft | 'hændɪkrɑ:ft | (EE.UU.) | 'hændɪkræft | *s.c.* [normalmente *pl.*] **1** artesanía, oficios manuales. **2** objetos de artesanía.

handily | 'hændɪlɪ | *adv.* convenientemente, cómodamente.

handiness | 'hændɪnɪs | *s.i.* conveniencia, comodidad.

handiwork | 'hændɪwɜ:k | *s.i.* **1** trabajo manual, obra manual (normalmente de poca monta). **2** (p.u.) artesanía, oficios manuales.

handkerchief | 'hæŋkətʃi:f | 'hæŋkətʃɪf | [*pl.* **handkerchiefs** o **handkerchieves**] *s.c.* pañuelo.

handle | 'hændl | *v.t.* **1** manejar (objetos). **2** manosear, toquetear, tocar. **3** (fig.) controlar, resolver, manejar (una situación, problema, etc.). **4** llevar, gestionar (un aspecto empresarial, sección, etc.). **5** manejar, llevar, trabajar con (algún tipo de máquina). **6** manejar, usar (palabras, ideas, números, etc.). || *v.i.* **7** manejarse, llevarse, funcionar (cualquier tipo de máquina). || *s.c.* **8** manilla, manillar, manija, manivela, manubrio. **9** mango, asa (de una taza, escoba, bolsa, etc.). **10** (fam.) título nobiliario. || *s.sing.* **11 [– for]** (fig.) pretexto para. || **12 to fly off the –,** (fam.) perder los estribos, cogerse un enfado de campeonato.

handlebar | 'hændlbɑ:*r* | *s.c.* **1** manillar (de bicicleta). || **2 – moustache,** bigote en forma de manillar.

handler | 'hændlə*r* | *s.c.* **1** manipulador (de equipajes y otras cosas). **2** entrenador de animales (especialmente perros).

handling | 'hændlɪŋ | *s.i.* **[– of]** control de, manejo de, solución de (problemas o similar).

handmade | ˌhænd'meɪd | *adj.* hecho a mano, artesanal, de artesanía.

handmaiden | 'hændmeɪdən | (también **handmaid**) *s.c.* **1** (lit. o p.u.) criada, chica, doncella. **2 [– (of/to)]** auxiliar de/a, secundario de/para, subordinado de/para.

hand-me-down | 'hændmi:daʊn / *s.c.* (normalmente *pl.*) ropa vieja y usada, ropa de segunda mano.

handout | 'hændaʊt / *s.c.* **1** regalo, limosna. **2** folleto, impreso, octavilla (con propaganda, resumen de algún tema, etc.).

hand-pick | ˌhænd'pɪk | *v.t.* escoger con sumo cuidado, seleccionar cuidadosamente.

hand-picked | ˌhænd'pɪkt | *adj.* escogido con sumo cuidado, seleccionado cuidadosamente.

handrail | 'hændreɪl | *s.c.* pasamano, barandilla.

handshake | 'hændʃeɪk | *s.c.* apretón de manos.

handsome | 'hænsəm | *adj.* **1** bien parecido, guapo (hombre). **2** guapetona, guapa (con una cara que muestra carácter). **3** majo, elegante, bien puesto (lugar). **4** considerable, generosa (cantidad de dinero). **5** espléndido, gene-roso (acción sin reparar en gastos). || **6 – is as – does,** no hay que hacer caso de las apariencias sino de los hechos.

handsomely | 'hænsəmlɪ | *adv.* **1** elegantemente, agradablemente, con buen gusto (la manera de construir, adornar, etc. un lugar). **2** considerablemente, generosamente (en dinero). **3** espléndidamente, sin reparar en gastos, vistosamente.

handsomeness | 'hænsəmnɪs | *s.i.* **1** buen ver, atractivo físico. **2** elegancia, buen hacer (en un sitio). **3** generosidad (con dinero o similar).

handstand | 'hændstænd | *s.c.* posición de pino, pino.

hand-to-hand | ˌhændtə'hænd | *adj.* y *adv.* cuerpo a cuerpo (lucha).

hand-to-mouth | ˌhændtə'maʊθ | *adj.* y *adv.* precario, con ingresos mínimos, al día (forma de vivir sin medios).

handwriting | 'hændraɪtɪŋ | *s.i.* letra, caligrafía.

handwritten | 'hændrɪtn | *adj.* escrito a mano, escrito de su puño y letra.

handy | 'hændɪ | *adj.* **1** útil, práctico (objeto). **2** (fam.) mañoso, diestro, manitas. **3** (fam.) a mano, cercano, próximo (lugar). || **4 to come in –,** venir bien, resultar ser útil, ser práctico. **5 to keep/have something –,** tener algo a mano, tener algo en un lugar práctico/accesible.

handyman | 'hændɪmæn | [*pl.* **handymen**] *s.c.* persona mañosa, (fam.) manitas.

handymen | 'hændɪmən | *pl.* de **handyman.**

hang | hæŋ | *v.* [*pret.* y *p.p.irreg.* **hung**] *i.* **1** colgar, suspender: *there was a huge lamp hanging over them = había una lámpara enorme colgando sobre ellos.* **2** (fig.) flotar, estar suspendido (en el aire): *there was a lot of smoke hanging around the room = había mucho humo flotando por la habitación.* **3** flotar, colgar (ropa). **4** quedar curando, curarse (comida). **5 [to – over]** cernerse sobre (problemas, dudas, dificultades, etc.): *their threats hung over us = sus amenazas se cernían sobre nosotros.* _ *t.* **6** colgar, suspender: *I hung this big picture myself = yo solo colgué este cuadro enorme.* **7** dejar curar, curar (comida). || *s.sing.* **8 [the –]** la forma de colgar, la caída (de ropa o tejido). || **9 to be hung with,** estar adornado de (objetos que han sido colgados). **10 to get the – of,** (fam.) coger el tranquillo de, coger el tino de. **11 – ...!,** (fam.) ¡al carajo con...!, ¡a la porra con...! **12 to – about,** (fam.) **a)** no hacer nada, estar mano sobre mano, estar en plan vago; **b)** dejar momentáneamente (la tarea). **13 to – around,** (fam.) **a)** esperar sin hacer nada, estar sin hacer nada; **b)** frecuentar (lugar), ir a menudo con, estar siempre con (una persona). **14 to – back, a)** quedarse (en un sitio después de que todos los demás se han ido); **b)** titubear, no atreverse a (emprender una acción): *we all hung back when he took out the gun = todos titubeamos cuando sacó la pistola.* **15 to – by a thread,** V. **thread. 16 to – in the air,** quedar sin solucionar, quedar sin resolver. **17 to – loose,** (EE.UU. y fam.) mantenerse en calma, mantenerse bajo control, no perder los estribos. **18 to – on, a)** (fam.) esperar, aguardar: *hang on a minute = espera un minuto;* **b)** aguantar (una situación difícil); **c)** depender de: *everything hung on a difficult solution = todo dependía de una solución difícil.* **19 – on in there,** (EE.UU. y fam.) aguanta, aguanta fuerte, dale ahí (invitando a alguien a no dejar en su empeño). **20 to – one's head,** bajar la cabeza, inclinar la cabeza (como signo de timidez, vergüenza, etc.). **21 to – on someone's every word,** estar pendiente de lo que dice alguien, estar embobado con lo que dice alguien. **22 to – on/onto, a)** sujetar, agarrarse con fuerza a, apoyarse fuertemente en; **b)** (fig.) agarrarse a, aferrarse (a una situación favorable, a la vida, etc.). **23 to – onto, a)** sujetar con fuerza, agarrar con fuerza (enla mano); **b)** conservar, guardar (cosas). **24 to – out, a)** tender (la ropa lavada); **b)** (fam.) frecuentar (lugar). **25 to – together, a)** vivir juntos, estar juntos, aguantar juntos; **b)** tener sentido, corresponderse (dos historias, cifras, ideas, etc.). **26 to – up, a)** colgar (teléfono); **b)** estar colgado, estar suspendido; colgar (normalmente en un lugar alto: *I hung up my hat = colgué el sombrero;* **c)** guardar, no utilizar más, dejar en su sitio. **27 to – up on,** (fam.) colgar a, acabar una conversación telfónica con (alguien).**28 to let it all – out,** (EE.UU. y fam.) relajarse por com pleto olvidándose de todo, soltarse el pelo y olvidarse de las preocupaciones.

hang | hæŋ | (forma verbal regular) *v.t.* **1** ahorcar, colgar (a alguien). || **2 I**

am/will be hanged if..., (fam.) que me ahorquen si..., que me zurzan si... que me maten si... (normalmente indicando que uno no hará algo).
hangar | 'hæŋər | *s.c.* hangar.
hangdog | 'hæŋdɒg | *adj.* culpable, avergonzado (en la expresión de la cara).
hanger | 'hæŋər | *s.c.* percha (para ropa).
hanger-on | ˌhæŋgə'ɒn | [*pl.* **hangers-on**] *s.c.* (desp.) parásito, acompañante interesado (normalmente de alguien con fama o dinero).
hang-glider | 'hæŋglaɪdər | *s.c.* **1** ala delta. **2** deportista de ala delta.
hang-gliding | 'hæŋglaɪdɪŋ | *s.i.* DEP. práctica de ala delta.
hanging | 'hæŋɪŋ | *s.c.* e *i.* **1** ahorcamiento, ejecución en la horca. || *s.c.* **2** colgadura (tela de adorno en una pared, por ejemplo). || *adj.* **3** pendiente, sin decidir (asunto).
hangman | 'hæŋmən | [*pl.irreg.* **hangmen**] *s.c.* verdugo (de horca).
hangmen | 'hæŋmən | *pl.irreg.* de **hangman.**
hangout | 'hæŋəʊt | *s.c.* (fam.) lugar (favorito de alguien).
hangover | 'hæŋəʊvər | *s.c.* **1** resaca. **2** [**– from/of**] reliquia de, vestigio de, cosa antigua de: *kissing women's hands is a hangover from earlier times = besar a las mujeres en la mano es una cosa antigua de épocas pasadas.*
hang-up | 'hæŋʌp | *s.c.* (fam.) inhibición, complejo, corte.
hank | hæŋk | *s.c.* madeja.
hanker | 'hæŋkər | *v.i.* [**to – after/for**] anhelar, desear vivamente, añorar fuertemente.
hankering | 'hæŋkərɪŋ | *s.c.* [**– for**] anhelo por, deseo vivo de, añoranza de.
hanky | 'hæŋkɪ | (también **hankie**) *s.c.* (fam.) pañuelo.
hanky-panky | ˌhæŋkɪ'pæŋkɪ | *s.i.* (fam. y hum.) **1** magreo, filete (con personas del otro sexo). **2** trampas, trucos.
hansom | 'hænsəm | (también **hansom cab**) *s.c.* (p.u.) cabriolé (tipo de coche de caballos).
haphazard | hæp'hæzəd | *adj.* fortuito, casual, impensado.
haphazardly | hæp'hæzədlɪ | *adv.* fortuitamente, casualmente, impensadamente.
hapless | 'hæplɪs | *adj.* (lit.) desventurado, desafortunado, desgraciado.
happen | 'hæpən | *v.i.* **1** ocurrir, suceder, acontecer, tener lugar, acaecer: *what happened? he fell = ¿qué ocurrió? se cayó.* **2** [**to – to**] ocurrir a, pasar a (normalmente con sentido de daño): *what happened to your face? = ¿qué le pasó a tu cara?* **3** [**to –** *inf.*] dar la casualidad de (que), por casualidad (ocurrir algo): *I happened to meet him on the street = dio la casualidad de que me encontré con él en la calle.* || **4 accidents will –,** desgraciadamente hay accidentes, es inevitable que ocurran accidentes. **5 as it happens/happened,** por pura coincidencia, por casualidad, de casualidad. **6 to – on,** (lit. y p.u.) encontrarse por casualidad con (alguien).
happening | 'hæpənɪŋ | *s.c.* **1** suceso, acontecimiento. **2** ART. espectáculo improvisado, happening.
happily | 'hæpɪlɪ | *adv.* **1** felizmente, alegremente. **2** con mucho gusto, sin problemas: *I'll happily help you = te ayudaré con mucho gusto.* **3** afortunadamente, por suerte.
happiness | 'hæpɪnɪs | *s.i.* felicidad, alegría, contento, dicha.
happy | 'hæpɪ | *adj.* **1** feliz, alegre, contento (persona, lugar, expresión, etc.). **2** [**– about/with**] alegre con, contento de: *I'm happy about the exam = estoy contento del examen.* **3** [**–** *inf.*] dispuesto a (con alegría). **4** afortunada (coincidencia o similar). || **5 a – event,** (fig.) un feliz acontecimiento (nacimiento de un hijo). **6 as – as Larry,** más contento que unas pascuas, más contento que un niño con zapatos nuevos. **7 – ...!,** ¡feliz...!: *happy anniversary! = ¡feliz aniversario!* **8 many – returns,** V. **return. 9 to strike a – medium,** V. **medium.**
happy-go-lucky | ˌhæpɪgəʊ'lʌkɪ | *adj.* despreocupado, sin cuidados (en la actitud vital).
hara-kiri | ˌhærə'kɪrɪ | *s.i.* haraquiri, harakiri (costumbre japonesa).
harangue | hə'ræŋ | *s.c.* **1** (a veces desp.) arenga, perorata. || *v.t.* **2** arengar, lanzar una perorata.
harass | 'hærəs | (EE.UU.) | hə'ræs*v.t.* **1** acosar, hostigar, atormentar, vejar. **2** MIL. acosar, hostigar.
harassed | 'hærəst | (EE.UU.) | hə'ræst*adj.* acosado, hostigado, atormentado, vejado (por preocupaciones insistentes o similar).
harassing | 'hærəsɪŋ | (EE.UU.) | hə'ræsɪŋ*adj.* atormentante, preocupante.
harassment | 'hærəsmənt | (EE.UU.) | hə'ræsmənt*s.i.* **1** acoso, hostigamiento, vejamen. **2** MIL. hostigamiento. **3** preocupación excesiva, tormento continuo, irritación continua.
harbinger | 'hɑːbɪndʒər | *s.c.* [**– of**] (lit.) heraldo de, presagio de.
harbor | 'hɑːbər | (*brit.* **harbour**) *s.c.* **1** puerto. **2** (fig.) refugio, lugar protegido. || *v.t.* **3** proteger, encubrir (especialmente a alguien buscado por la policía). **4** albergar, abrigar (esperanzas, temores y otras emociones). || *v.i.* **5** encontrar puerto seguro (barco).
hard | hɑːd | *adj.* **1** duro, sólido, firme, compacto. **2** difícil, arduo (problema, vida, situación, etc.). **3** agotador, duro, penoso: *a hard day = un día agotador.* **4** duro, severo (cualidad personal). **5** fuerte, violento (movimiento físico, expresión verbal, etc.). **6** fría, dura (expresión o mirada). **7** frío, duro (tiempo o clima). **8** [**– on**] duro con, inflexible con, enérgico con (alguien). **9** [**– on**] duro con, difícil con; malo para: *this job is hard on someone = este empleo es duro con uno.* **10** desagradable, fuerte (color o sonido). **11** dura (agua). **12** concreto, sólido (hecho, evidencia, prueba, etc.). **13** dura (droga). **14** energético, vigoroso (cualidad para el trabajo o similar). **15** FON. duro (sonido consonántico). || *adv.* **16** duramente, fuertemente, intensamente (trabajar, intentar, entrenar, etc.). **17** fijamente (mirar); atentamente (oír); intensamente (pensar). **18** violentamente, fuertemente (una acción física). **19** mucho, en grandes cantidades, con gran fuerza (reír, llover, nevar, llorar y muchos otros verbos). **20** repentinamente, inesperadamente, pronunciadamente (movimiento direccional). **21** de cerca (en el espacio), inmediatamente, inmediatamente después (en el tiempo). **22** duramente, estrictamente, con fuerza (manera de comportarse con otros). || **23 a – nut to crack,** V. **nut. 24 as – as nails,** duro, resistente; despiadado, sin compasión. **25 to be – going,** ser difícil, ser difícil de entender, ser difícil de disfrutar (un viaje, libro, película, etc.). **26 to be – hit (by),** ser afectado fuertemente (por), ser golpeado severamente (por) (alguna desgracia o similar). **27 to be – put/pushed/pressed,** estar en un aprieto, tenerlo muy negro: *she was hard put to explain her attitude = estuvo en un aprieto para explicar su actitud.* **28 to drive a – bargain,** V. **bargain. 29 to follow – on the heels of,** V. **heel. 30 – and fast, a)** estricto, inflexible (regla, ordenanza, orden, etc.); **b)** concreta, real (información). **31 – at it,** dándole fuerte, pegándole duro (trabajando). **32 – by,** justo al lado de, muy cerca de, muy próximo a. **33 – cash,** dinero contante y sonante, dinero en metálico, (Am.) plata pura. **34 – copy,** INF. copia impresa (que se puede leer directamente). **35 – core,** núcleo duro, grupo intransigente (en un partido, asociación, etc.). **36 – court,** DEP. pista dura (tenis). **37 – cover,** tapas duras (de un libro). **38 – currency,** ECON. moneda segura, moneda estable. **39 – disk,** INF. disco duro. **40 – done by,** injustamente tratado (persona). **41 – drink,** bebida alcohólica. **42 – labour** (EE.UU. **labor**), DER. trabajos forzados. **43 – line,** línea dura (ideológica, por ejemplo). **44 – luck/– lines,** (fam.) mala suerte, mala pata. **45 – of hearing,** duro de oído. **46 – porn/– pornography,** pornografía dura. **47 – sell,** venta agresiva. **48 – shoulder,** arcén. **49 – top,** techo duro para el coche. **50 – up,** sin un centavo, sin un duro, en las últimas. **51 to play – to get,** V. **play. 52 to take something –,** tomar algo muy mal, tomar algo con la actitud equivocada, no aceptar algo, significar algo un golpe muy fuerte de

encajar. **53 (the) – left,** POL. la izquierda intransigente, la extrema izquierda. **54 (the) – right,** POL. la derecha montaraz, la derecha intransigente, la derecha autoritaria.

hardback | 'hɑːdbæk | *s.c.* **1** libro de tapas duras (más caro, consiguientemente). || **2 in –,** en formato duro (libro).

hard-bitten | 'hɑːdbɪtn | *adj.* tenaz, decidido.

hardboard | 'hɑːdbɔːd | *s.i.* chapa de madera dura.

hard-boiled | ˌhɑːd'bɔɪld | *adj.* **1** duro (huevo). **2** duro, insensible, de carácter endurecido.

hard-core | 'hɑːdkɔː | *adj.* básico, de un núcleo básico: *the hard-core activists = los activistas de un núcleo básico.*

hard-drinking | 'hɑːddrɪŋkɪŋ | *adj.* muy bebedor, medio alcoholizado.

harden | 'hɑːdn | *v.t.* e *i.* **1** endurecer(se), solidificar(se). **2** (fig.) endurecer(se) (ideas, actitudes, etc.). **3** (fig.) endurecer(se), hacer(se) duro (el carácter). || *v.i.* **4** ECON. estabilizarse (precios, situación económica, etc.). **5** hacerse más concreta, hacerse más segura (la evidencia, información, etc.).

hardened 'hɑːdnd | *adj.* empedernido, endurecido (criminal o similar).

hardening | 'hɑːdənɪŋ | *s.i.* endurecimiento (de posturas).

hard-headed | ˌhɑːd'hedɪd | *adj.* práctico, realista, astuto.

hard-hearted | ˌhɑːd'hɑːtɪd | *adj.* despiadado, frío, cruel, insensible.

hardiness | 'hɑːdɪnɪs | *s.i.* **1** dureza, robustez, resistencia (persona). **2** osadía, intrepidez.

hard-line | ˌhɑːd'laɪn | *adj.* intransigente, exagerado (en ideas).

hardliner | ˌhɑːd'laɪnər | *s.c.* POL. duro, político de la línea dura.

hardly | hɑːdlɪ | *adv.* **1** apenas: *I can hardly stand = apenas puedo tenerme en pie.* **2 [– (ever, any, etc.)]** casi: *do you go out? hardly ever = ¿sales por ahí? casi nunca.* **3** no, casi no (normalmente con cierto tono irónico): *it's hardly surprising she's angry = no es sorprendente que esté muy enfadada.*

hardness | 'hɑːdnɪs | *s.i.* **1** dureza, solidez. **2** dureza, severidad, insensibilidad (de alguien). **3** dureza, crueldad, rigor (de la vida, clima, etc.). **4** dureza (de oído).

hard-nosed | ˌhɑːd'nəuzd | *adj.* práctico, pragmático (con los pies en la tierra).

hard-pressed | ˌhɑːd'prest | *adj.* con dificultades económicas.

hardship | 'hɑːdʃɪp | *s.c.* e *i.* dificultad, apuro, privación (de medios económicos).

hardware | 'hɑːdweər | *s.i.* **1** artículos de ferretería. **2** INF. hardware. **3** MIL. armamento.

hard-wearing | hɑːd'weərɪŋ | *adj.* fuerte, duradero (ropa especialmente).

hardwood | 'hɑːdwʊd | .*c.* e *i.* madera dura, árbol de madera dura.

hardy | hɑːdɪ | *adj.* **1** duro, fuerte, robusto, resistente (persona). **2** intrépido, osado. **3** BOT. duro, resistente (planta).

hare | heə | *s.c.* e *i.* **1** liebre. || *v.i.* **2 [to – off/away]** irse a toda velocidad, irse rápidamente. || **3 mad as a March –,** más loco que una cabra. **4 to run with the – and hunt with the hounds,** ponerle una vela a Dios y otra al diablo. **5 to start/raise a –,** sacar un tema de conversación; cambiar de tercio en la conversación.

harebrained | 'heəbreɪnd | *adj.* desatinado, alocado (plan o similar).

harelip | 'heəlɪp | *s.c.* e *i.* labio leporino.

harem | 'hɑːriːm | (EE.UU.) | 'hærəm | *s.c.* harem (mujeres y lugar).

haricot | 'hærɪkəu | (también **haricot bean**) *s.c.* BOT. judía, alubia, habichuela.

hark | hɑːk | *v.i.* **1** (arc.) escuchar. || **2 to – back (to), a)** recordar, rememorar; **b)** recordar (parecer): *this style harks back to the 19th century = este estilo recuerda al siglo XIX;* **c)** volver, regresar (a un tema).

harlequin | hɑːlɔɪkwɪn | *s.c.* | **1** ART. arlequín. || *adj.* **2** de arlequín, colorido, de distintos colores (especialmente ropa).

harlot | 'hɑːlət | *s.c.* (lit. y desp.) ramera, meretriz.

harm | hɑːm | *s.i.* **1** daño, herida, perjuicio (físico o intangible): *he meant no harm = no tenía ninguna intención de causar daño.* || *v.t.* **2** dañar, herir, hacer daño (físicamente). **3** perjudicar, estropear (no físicamente): *her words harmed our relationship = sus palabras perjudicaron nuestra relación.* _ **4 to come to no –/no – (to) come,** no tener un resultado perjudicial, no recibir ningún prejuicio de ninguna clase, no salir perjudicado de ningún modo. **5 to do no/little –/there's no – in,** no haber ningún mal en, no causar ningún perjuicio. **6 to do someone no –,** no sentar mal a alguien, no ser motivo de perjuicio para alguien, no perjudicar a alguien: *the medicine will do you no harm = la medicina no te sentaría mal.* **7 no – done,** (fam.) no ha pasado nada, no ha sido nada. **8 out of harm's way, a)** a salvo, en lugar seguro, en sitio protegido, libre de peligro; **b)** a buen recaudo (donde no hará daño a nadie).

harmful | 'hɑːmfl | *adj.* dañino, perjudicial, nocivo (especialmente en temas de salud).

harmfully | 'hɑːmfəlɪ | *adv.* nocivamente, con grave perjuicio (especialmente para la salud).

harmless | 'hɑːmlɪs | *adj.* **1** seguro, que no causa daño alguno. **2** (fam.) inofensivo: *a harmless fellow = un tipo inofensivo.* **3** inocuo (algo).

harmlessly | 'hɑːmlɪslɪ | *adv.* **1** con toda seguridad, sin posibilidad de daño alguno. **2** (fam.) inofensivamente, inocentemente. **3** inocuamente (forma de reaccionar algo).

harmlessness | 'hɑːmlɪsnɪs | *s.i.* **1** ausencia de peligro, ausencia de posibilidad de daño. **2** (fam.) inocencia (de una persona). **3** inocuidad (de una sustancia o cosa).

harmonic | hɑː'mɒnɪk | MUS. *adj.* **1** de sonido armonioso, armónico. || *s.c.* **2** armónico (nota más alta en armonía con la primera). || *s.pl.* **3** armonía.

harmonica | hɑː'mɒnɪkə | *s.c.* MUS. armónica (instrumento).

harmonious | hɑː'məunɪəs | *adj.* **1** cordial, de buena vecindad (relaciones, discusiones, etc.). **2** MUS. armonioso, melódico, suave. **3** equilibrado, lleno de armonía (forma de ordenar o colocar algo).

harmoniously | hɑː'məunɪəslɪ | *adv.* **1** cordialmente, amigablemente. **2** armoniosamente, melódicamente, suavemente (sonido musical). **3** equilibradamente, con buen gusto (arreglo o colocación de algo).

harmonium | hɑː'məunɪəm | *s.c.* MUS. armonio (instrumento).

harmonize | 'hɑːmənaɪz | (también **harmonise**) *v.t.* e *i.* **1** MUS. armonizar, poner armonía a (una melodía); cantar en armonía, hacer armonías. || *v.i.* **2 [to – (with)]** ir bien juntos, armonizar (colores, estilos, formas, etc.). **3 [to – (with)]** estar en armonía, equilibrar (dos ideas, opiniones, etc.). **4** (form.) estar de acuerdo.

harmony | 'hɑːmənɪ | *s.i.* **1** armonía, concordia, unidad (de sentimientos o parecido). || *s.c.* e *i.* **2** MUS. armonía. **3** armonía, equilibrio, simetría (de formas, colores, estilos, etc.). || **4 in – (with),** en armonía (con), en concordancia (con): *her interests are in harmony with mine = sus intereses están en concordancia con los míos.*

harness | 'hɑːnɪs | *s.c.* e *i.* **1** arreos (de monturas). || *s.c.* **2** correaje, correa de sujección (de un paracaidista o niño pequeño). || *v.t.* **3 [to – + o. + (to)]** enjaezar, poner los arreos (a una montura, especialmente para que tire de un carro o similar). **4** aprovechar, utilizar, sacar partido de (elementos naturales): *to harness a waterfall = aprovechar una cascada natural.* _ **5 to die in –,** morir al pie del cañón, morir con las botas puestas. **6 in – (with),** en conjunción (con) (en un trabajo).

harp | hɑːp | *s.c.* **1** MUS. arpa. || **2 to – on,** no cesar de repetir, no parar de decir, insistir una y otra vez.

harpist | 'hɑːpɪst | *s.c.* MUS. arpista.

harpoon | hɑː'puːn | *s.c.* **1** arpón. || *v.t.* **2** arponear.

harpsichord | 'hɑːpsɪkɔːd | *s.c.* MUS. clavicordio.

harpy | 'hɑːpɪ | *s.c.* (lit.) arpía (mujer).
harried | 'hærɪd *adj.* atormentada, acosada (expresión).
harrow | 'hærəʊ | *s.c.* AGR. grada, rastra.
harrowing | 'hærəʊɪŋ | *adj.* horroroso, angustioso, horripilante, horrendo.
harry | 'hærɪ | *v.t.* **1** acosar, hostigar, molestar constantemente, dar la lata. **2** saquear, pillar (de manera constante).
harsh | hɑːʃ | *adj.* **1** severo, duro (persona o sus acciones). **2** áspero, duro (sonido). **3** chillón, áspero (color, luz, etc.). **4** duro, severo (forma de vida, tiempo, etc.).
harshly | 'hɑːʃlɪ | *adv.* **1** severamente, duramente (trato o similar). **2** ásperamente, con dureza, estridentemente (sonido).
harshness | 'hɑːʃnɪs | *s.i.* **1** dureza, severidad (cualidad personal). **2** dureza, rigor, severidad (de una forma de vivir, clima, etc.). **3** aspereza, estridencia (de un sonido).
hart | hɑːt | [*pl.* **hart** o **harts**] *s.c.* ZOOL. ciervo (macho).
harvest | 'hɑːvɪst | *s.c.* **1** AGR. cosecha, recolección; vendimia (uva). || *s.i.* **2** tiempo de la cosecha, tiempo de recolección. || *s.sing.* **3** **[the –]** AGR. la cosecha, la siega. || *v.t.* **4** AGR. cosechar, recolectar; vendimiar (uva). **5** (lit. y fig.) recoger (fruto de alguna acción o parecido). || **6 – festival,** REL. fiesta de acción de gracias por la cosecha. **7 – home,** (brit.) fiesta de la cosecha. **8 – moon,** luna otoñal (22 o 23 de Septiembre). **9 to reap the –,** (fig.) sacar buen partido, sacar ventaja, sacar beneficio (al trabajo de uno o de otros).
harvester | 'hɑːvɪstər | *s.c.* **1** MEC. cosechadora. **2** segador (persona).
has | hæz | (forma relajada | həz |) *tercera persona sing. pres.* de **have.**
has-been | 'hæzbiːn | *s.c.* (fam. y desp.) vieja gloria, reliquia del pasado.
hash | hæʃ *s.i.* **1** GAST. picadillo (de carne). **2** (fam.) hachís. || **3 to make a – of,** (fam.) embrollar, hacer un estropicio de (una situación, tarea, responsabilidad, etc.).
hashish | 'hæʃiːʃ | *s.i.* hachís.
hasn't | 'hæznt | *contr.* de **has** y **not.**
hasp | hɑːsp | (EE.UU.) | hæsp*s.c.* MEC. pasador (en puerta, ventana, etc.).
hassle | 'hæsl | (fam.) *s.c.* e *i.* **1** follón, molestia, incordio. **2** pelea, discusión, regañina. || *v.t.* **3** dar la lata, dar el té, fastidiar, encordiar.
hassock | 'hæsək | *s.c.* REL. cojín para arrodillarse.
haste | heɪst | *s.i.* **1** prisa; precipitación. || **2 in –,** con prisa, apresuradamente, precipitadamente. **3 to make –,** (p.u.) darse prisa, apresurarse.
hasten | 'heɪsn | *v.t.* **1** acelerar, apresurar (cualquier proceso o acción). **2 [to – *inf.*] apresurarse a, darse prisa en.** || *v.i.* **3** (lit.) dirigirse con prisa, apresurarse (a un lugar).
hastily | 'heɪstɪlɪ | *adv.* **1** apresuradamente, precipitadamente. **2** irreflexivamente, imprudentemente, inconsideradamente.
hastiness | 'heɪstɪnɪs | *s.i.* **1** apresuramiento, precipitación. **2** imprudencia, inconsideración, manera irreflexiva.
hasty | 'heɪstɪ | *adj.* **1** apresurado, precipitado (acción). **2** irreflexivo, imprudente, inconsiderado (persona o comportamiento).
hat | hæt | *s.c.* **1** sombrero. || *s.sing.* **2** (fam.) función profesional, capacidad oficial: *today I'm wearing my headmaster's hat = hoy estoy llevando a cabo mi función de director.* _ **3 at the drop of a –,** V. **drop. 4 to eat one's –,** (fam.) ser cura: *if he passes I'll eat my hat = si aprueba yo soy cura.* **5 to hang up one's –,** (fam.) arrojar la toalla (especialmente en el trabajo). **6 – trick,** DEP. tercer gol seguido, tercer golpe seguido (en distintos deportes). **7 to keep something under one's –,** (fam.) guardar un secreto, mantener algo secreto. **8 my –!,** (p.u.) ¡caramba! (expresando sorpresa). **9 old –,** (fam.) archisabido, archiconocido. **10 to pass the – round,** (fam.) pasar el sombrero (para recoger dinero). **11 to take off one's – to someone,** (fam.) quitarse el sombrero ante alguien. **12 to talk through one's –,** (fam.) decir chorradas, decir bobadas.
hatband | 'hætbænd | *s.c.* cinta de sombrero.
hatbox | 'hætbɒks | *s.c.* sombrerera, caja de los sombreros.
hatch | hætʃ | *s.c.* **1** MAR. escotilla, compuerta, escotillón de carga. **2** AER. puerta, escotilla. **3** ventanuco (entre habitaciones); ventanilla (en una puerta o similar). || *v.i.* **4** salir del cascarón, romper el cascarón. || *v.t.* **5** (fig.) tramar, proyectar, idear (plan). || **6 down the –,** (fam.) pa' dentro (al beber). **7 to – out,** salir del cascarón, acabar la incubación. **8 to – up,** planear, tramar (plan).
hatchback | 'hætʃbæk | *s.c.* **1** coche de cinco puertas. **2** puerta trasera (en un coche de cinco puertas).
hatchery | 'hætʃərɪ | *s.c.* vivero, criadero (especialmente de peces).
hatchet | 'hætʃɪt | *s.c.* **1** hacha pequeña. || **2 a – face,** una cara alargada, una cara afilada. **3 to bury the –,** reconciliarse, enterrar el hacha de guerra. **4 – job,** (fam.) faena de campeonato, ataque brutal (por escrito o de palabra). **5 – man,** (fam.) lacayo a sueldo, asesino a sueldo.
hatchway | 'hætʃweɪ | V. **hatch 1.**
hate | heɪt | *v.t.* **1** odiar, detestar. **2 [to – *o./inf./ger.*] no gustar en absoluto:** *I hated milk when I was five = no me gustaba en absoluto la leche cuando tenía cinco años.* || *s.c.* **3** odio, repugnancia, aborrecimiento. || **4 to – somebody's guts,** V. **gut. 5 I – to disturb/trouble/etc. you,** siento muchísimo molestarte, siento en lo más íntimo molestarte. **6 I – to say it,** siento mucho tener que decirlo.
hated | 'heɪtɪd | *adj.* odiado, detestado, aborrecido.
hateful | 'heɪtfl | *adj.* odioso, detestable, aborrecible.
hatefully | 'heɪtfəlɪ | *adv.* odiosamente, detestablemente, aborreciblemente.
hatefulness | 'heɪtflnɪs | *s.i.* (lo) odioso, (lo) detestable.
hatpin | 'hætpɪn | *s.c.* alfiler de sombrero.
hatred | 'heɪtrɪd | *s.i.* **[– (for/of/towards)]** odio, desprecio, aborrecimiento.
hatstand | 'hætstænd | *s.c.* percha para sombreros.
hatter | 'hætər | *s.c.* **1** fabricante de sombreros, sombrerero. || **2 as mad as a –,** más loco que una regadera.
haughtily | 'hɔːtɪlɪ | *adv.* arrogantemente, desdeñosamente.
haughtiness | 'hɔːtɪnɪs | *s.i.* arrogancia, desdén.
haughty | 'hɔːtɪ | *adj.* arrogante, desdeñoso, altivo.
haul | hɔːl | *v.t.* e *i.* **1** arrastrar, tirar con fuerza de, acarrear; transportar. || *v.r.* **2** ponerse, introducirse, meterse (en algún lugar). || *s.c.* **3** tirón, arrastre. **4** captura (de peces de una vez). **5** redada, botín (de algo robado). || **6 a/the long –,** un/el largo camino, una/la larga lucha (hasta conseguir un derecho, meta, etc.). **7 to – someone over the coals,** V. **coal. 8 to – up,** enviar a, llevar ante (un juez o persona con autoridad).
haulage | 'hɔːlɪdʒ | *s.i.* transporte en carretera.
hauler | 'hɔːlər | V. **haulier.**
haulier | hɔːlɪər | (EE.UU. **hauler**) *s.c.* transportista, contratista de transporte en carretera.
haunch | hɔːntʃ | *s.c.* (normalmente *pl.*) cuartos traseros, ancas, grupa (parte del cuerpo de una persona o animal).
haunt | hɔːnt | *v.t.* **1** embrujar (lugar o persona, por parte de fantasmas). **2** obsesionar (una idea, imagen, recuerdo, etc.). **3** frecuentar (lugar). **4** perseguir (problemas, dificultades, etc.): *I've been haunted by continuous economic problems = los problemas económicos me han perseguido.* _ *s.c.* **5** sitio favorito, lugar predilecto.
haunted | 'hɔːntɪd | *adj.* **1** embrujado (lugar o persona). **2** obsesionado, perturbado (expresión facial).
haunting | 'hɔːntɪŋ | *adj.* obsesionante, perturbador: *a haunting melody = una melodía obsesionante.*
hauntingly | 'hɔːntɪŋlɪ | *adv.* obsesionantemente, perturbadoramente.
hauteur | əʊ'təːr | *s.i.* (form.) desprecio, altivez, altanería.
have | hæv | (forma relajada | həv |) *v.t.* [*pret.* y *p.p.irreg.* **had**] **1 [to – (got)]** tener, poseer: *I have a big factory = tengo una fábrica enorme.* **2 [to – (got)]** sufrir de, tener (enfermedad). **3 [to – (got)]** experimentar, recibir, tener (duda, sospecha, experiencia, etc.). **4 [to –**

(got)] tener (como resultado): *we've got letters coming from everywhere = tenemos cartas que vienen de todos los sitios.* **5 [to – (got)]** tener, recibir (en casa de uno): *I'm having my parents next Christmas = tendré a mis padres las próximas Navidades.* **6 [to – (got)]** tener (postura del cuerpo), sujetar (en una parte del cuerpo); dar (parte del cuerpo): *why did you have your back to us at the table? = ¿por qué nos diste la espalda en la mesa?* **7 [to – (got)]** tener, mostrar (amabilidad, descaro, detalle o cualquier otra cualidad personal): *I didn't have the nerve to refuse = no tuve la valentía de negarme.* **8 [to – (got) +** *inf.***]** tener que, verse obligado a, deber: *I have to go at once = tengo que irme enseguida.* **9** dar a luz, tener (bebé). **10** causar, producir (una reacción, efecto, influencia, etc.). **11** recibir, tener (carta, mensaje, etc.). **12** tomar, ingerir, comer, beber (comida o bebida): *I had breakfast at 7 = tomé el desayuno a las 7.* **13** echarse (un cigarrillo). **14** pasar por, recibir (operación, tratamiento, etc.). **15 [to – +** *o.d.* **+** *p.p.***]** mandar que, encargar que, hacer que: *I had the carpet cleaned = encargué que limpiaran la alfombra.* **16 [to – +** *o.d.* **+** *p.p.***]** sufrir (una experiencia dura): *I had the whole manuscript scribbled on by the children = sufrí el horrible disgusto de que los niños me pintarrajearan el manuscrito.* **17 [to – +** *o.d.* **+** *inf.***]** ordenar, hacer mandar: *I'll have the children wash your car = haré a los niños lavarte el coche.* **18 [to –** *o./ger.***]** permitir, tolerar: *I won't have anybody shouting = no toleraré que nadie grite.* **19 [to –** *ger.***]** causar, tener (un cierto estadoen alguien): *she had us all dreaming about the wonderful future = ella nos tuvo a todos soñando sobre un futuro maravilloso.* **20** tener (invitados): *we're having the Smiths for dinner = tendremos a los Smiths a cenar.* **21** [normalmente *pas.*] (fam.) engañar, tomar el pelo: *I was had = me tomaron el pelo.* **22** (vulg.) poseer, tirarse, follarse, (Am) coger. **23** (fam.) ganar, vencer (en una discusión): *she certainly had you yesterday = ciertamente te ganó ayer (en la discusión).* || **24 to be had up for,** (fam.) ser llevado a juicio por, ser puesto en la picota por. **25 to give something all you –/to put everything you – into something,** (fam.) poner toda la carne en el asador, hacer un esfuerzo sobrehumano en algo. **26 to – a good/bad/fantastic/horrible/etc. time,** pasarlo en/mal/fantásticamente/fatal/etc. **27 to – had it,** (fam.) **a)** estar para el arrastre, estar hecho unos zorros; **b)** estropearse, changarse; **c)** haberla diñado, haberla fastidiado (ya no se puede arreglar una situación). **28 to – it,** (fam.) recordarlo, venir a la mente. **29 to – it in,** (fam.) tener, poseer (cualidades insospechadas); valer (personalmente): *I neverthought you had it in you = nunca pensé que tú valías.* **30 to – it in for,** (fam.) guardársela a, tenérsela jurada a. **31to – it off/away (with),** (fam. y brit.)pegarse el lote (con), darse un filete(con) (sexualmente). **32 to – it/themat-ter/the whole thing/etc. out (with),** (fam.) hablar a las claras (con), ajustar las cuentas hablando (con). **33 to – no time for,** V. **time. 34 to – on,** (fam.) **a)** llevar puesto (ropa o similar); **b)** tener encendido (aparato eléctrico). **35 to – somebody in,** tener a alguien trabajando en casa (pintores, fontaneros, etc.). **36 to – somebody on,** (fam.) burlarse de alguien, cachondearse de alguien. **36 to – something over with,** (fam.) acabar algo de una vez, dar algo por terminado definitivamente (y que se está deseando que acabe). **37 I/you/we/etc. –,** tengo, tienes/tenemos/etc. (como dando un ejemplo): *at the beginning of the century we have the working class striking everywhere = al comienzo del siglo tenemos a la clase obrera haciendo huelgas por todos los sitios.* **38 what – you,** V. **what.**

OBS. Este verbo tiene otros muchos usos que se explican a continuación.

39 haber (como verbo auxiliar en los tiempos que lo tienen): *I have read his novel = he leído su novela; I would have gone, but I couldn't = habría ido, pero no pude.* **40** (form.) si (en oraciones condicionales): *had there been time, I would have helped = si hubiera habido tiempo, habría ayudado.* **41** con muchísimos sustantivos tiene significados acordes con el sustantivo: *to have a holiday = tomarse/coger unas vacaciones; to have a meeting = celebrar una reunión; to have a general election = llevar a cabo unas elecciones nacionales.* **42** (fam.) con un verbo sustantivado por el artículo indeterminado coge el significado del verbo: *to have a look = echar un vistazo; to have a swim = darse un chapuzón; to have a try = intentar; to have a read = leer un rato.*

*En general, se puede decir que cuando este verbo tiene sentido de"tener" puede ser conjugado comoverbo auxiliar, y cuando no lo tienees un verbo normal que debe utilizar***do** y **did.**

En el inglés americano este verbo se utiliza de forma distinta. En general, los americanos no utilizan este verbo junto con la partícula got, para indicar posesión y siempre, en negativas e interrogativas, utilizan auxiliares.

haven | 'heɪvn | *s.c.* **1** lugar seguro, refugio. **2** (arc.) MAR. puerto.

have-nots | 'hævnɒts | *s.pl.* pobres, desposeídos.

haven't | 'hævnt | *contr.* de **have** y **not.**

haversack | 'hævəsæk*s.c.* mochila, macuto, morral.

haves | hævz | *s.pl.* ricos, acaudalados.

havoc | 'hævək | *s.i.* **1** desolación, destrucción total. || **2 to play – with,** hacer estragos en, estropear totalmente.

haw | hɔː | *s.c.* **1** BOT. marzoleta, marjoleta. || **2 –!,** ¡jo jo! (risa superior). **3 to hum and –,** V. **hum.**

hawk | hɔːk | *s.c.* **1** ZOOL. halcón. **2** (fig.) POL. halcón (que no quiere la paz). || *v.t.* **3** (frecuentemente desp.) vender en plan barato, pregonar de casa en casa/de calle en calle (los artículos en venta). || **4 to watch someone like a –,** no perder de vista a alguien, vigilar a alguien con todo detenimiento.

hawker | 'hɔːkər | *s.c.* vendedor ambulante, quincallero.

hawk-eyed | hɔːk'aɪd | *adj.* de vista de lince.

hawkish | 'hɔːkɪʃ | *adj.* POL. de la línea dura, intransigente (en el campo internacional).

hawser | 'hɔːzər | *s.c.* MAR. cable, estacha, guindaleza, maroma.

hawthorn | 'hɔːθɔːn | *s.c.* e *i.* BOT. espino, marzoleto, marjoleto.

hay | heɪ | *s.i.* **1** AGR. heno. || **2 a roll in the –,** (fam. de connotación sexual) pegarse un revolcón. **3 to hit the –,** (fam.) meterse en la cama, acostarse. **4 to make – while the sun shines,** hacer uso inteligente de las oportunidades mientras duran.

haycock | 'heɪkɒk | *s.c.* AGR. cono de heno (que se deja a secar).

hay-fever | 'heɪfiːvər | *s.i.* MED. fiebre del heno (alergia).

haystack | 'heɪstæk | *s.c.* **1** montón grande de heno, almiar. || **2 a needle in a –,** una aguja en un pajar.

haywire | 'heɪwaɪər | **to be/go –,** (fam.) estar embrollado, embrollarse ponerse difícil.

hazard | 'hæzəd | *s.c.* **1** riesgo, peligro. **2** DEP. obstáculo (en golf). || *v.t.* **3** (form.) poner en peligro, arriesgar (algo o a alguien). **4** arriesgar, aventurar (una hipótesis, sugerencia, etc.).

hazardous | 'hæzədəs | *adj.* peligroso, arriesgado, aventurado.

hazardously | 'hæzədəslɪ | *adv.* peligrosamente, arriesgadamente, aventuradamente.

haze | heɪz | *s.i.* **1** neblina, niebla fina, bruma. || *s.sing.* **2 [a –]** (fig.) una confusión, un desconcierto: *my mind's in a haze = mi mente está desconcertada.* **3** humo, como neblina (de cualquier sustancia).

hazel | 'heɪzl | *s.c.* e *i.* **1** BOT. avellano. || *adj.* **2** avellanado (ojos).

hazelnut | 'heɪzlnʌt | *s.c.* avellana.

hazily | 'heɪzɪlɪ | *adv.* confusamente, desconcertadamente.

haziness | 'heɪzɪnɪs | *s.i.* **1** (lo) neblinoso, (lo) brumoso. **2** (fig.) confusión, desconcierto.

hazy | 'heɪzɪ | *adj.* **1** neblinoso, brumoso. **2** (fig.) confuso, desconcertado. **3** (fig.) débil (después de enfermedad o borrachera). **4** desleído, pálido (color).

H-bomb | 'eɪtʃbɒm | *s.c.* QUIM. bomba de hidrógeno.

he | hi: | *pron.pers.* **1** él. **2** él (desconocido): *if somebody came, he'd know where we are = si alguien viniera, él sabría dónde estamos.*

head | hed | *s.c.* **1** cabeza. **2** (fig.) cabeza, mente, cerebro. **3** jefe, mandamás (en una organización). **4** cabecera, parte superior (de un objeto). **5** nacimiento (de un río). **6** director, directora (de colegio). **7** división, sección, parte. **8** ELECTR. cabezal (de magnetófono). **9** punta (de algunos objetos). **10** punta inflamada (de un grano o furúnculo). || *s.sing.* **11** parte de arriba, parte superior (de una página). **12** parte de delante, parte frontal (de una procesión, cola, etc.). **13** presión (del agua o vapor). **14** espuma (de cerveza). **15** (fam.) dolor de cabeza. **16** cabeza(s) (de ganado). **17** cabeza (de un caballo): *he won by a head = ganó por una cabeza.* _ *adj.* **18** principal, central: *head office.* _ *v.t.* **19** dirigir, controlar (empresa, organización, etc.). **20** encabezar (una manifestación, procesión, una lista, etc.). **21** dirigir (a alguien a un sitio). **22** titular, poner de título (de un libro o similar). **23** DEP. cabecear (el balón). || *v.i.* **24** dirigirse, dirigir los pasos hacia: *head south = dirígete al sur.* **25** acercarse a, llegar hasta (en una cantidad). || **26 above/over one's –,** por encima de mis posibilidades intelectuales, más allá de mis entendederas. **27 to bang one's – against the wall,** V. **bang. 28 to bite/snap someone's – off,** (fam.) maltratar de palabra a alguien, hablar violentamente a alguien. **29 to bring/come to a —,** traer a su punto culminante, llevar a un punto álgido (en el que hay que tomar una decisión). **30 to bury one's – in the sand,** ocultar la cabeza en la arena (como la avestruz). **31 from – to foot,** de los pies a la cabeza. **32 to get one's – round,** (fam.) entender, sacar en limpio, sacar en claro. **33 to get something into one's –,** caer en la cuenta de algo, darse cuenta de algo. **34 to get something into someone's –,** hacer entender algo a alguien, meter algo en la cabeza de alguien. **35 to give someone their –,** dar rienda suelta a alguien. **36 to go to one's –, a)** subirse a la cabeza (el alcohol); **b)** (desp. y fig.) subirse a la cabeza (el éxito o similar). **37 to have a good – of hair,** tener una magnífica melena. **38 to have a good – on one's shoulders,** tener sentido común, tener sentido práctico. **39 to have a swollen –,** estar hinchado de vanidad, estar lleno de estúpido orgullo. **40 to have one's – in the clouds,** V. **cloud. 41 – boy,** alumno jefe (el primero entre los delegados de curso). **42 – count,** recuento de personas presentes. **43 headed notepaper,** papel con membrete, papel con encabezamiento. **44 to – for,** dirigirse hacia, marchar en dirección a. **45 – girl,** alumna jefe. V. **38. 46 to – off,** ahuyentar, desviar (dirección o atención). **47 – over heels,** de cabeza, con la cabeza por delante. **48 – over heels in love,** locamente enamorado. **49 heads or tails,** cara o cruz. **50 heads will roll,** las cabezas van a rodar. **51 to hold one's – high,** mantener la cabeza bien alta. **52 in one's –,** en la memoria de uno, en la cabeza de uno. **53 to keep one's –,** mantener la cabeza, mantener la calma. **54 to keep one's – above water,** V. **water. 55 to laugh/cry/etc. one's – off,** (fam.) reírse/llorar/etc. a más no poder. **56 to lose one's –,** perder la cabeza, perder la calma, perder la serenidad. **57 to make – or tail of,** (fam.) sacar en claro, entender. **58 not right in the –,** V. **right. 59 off one's –,** (fam.) memo, ido, locatis. **60 off the top of one's –,** según se le ocurre a uno, a bote pronto. **61 on one's own –,** que caiga sobre la cabeza de uno (la consecuencia de una acción). **62 on your own – be it,** que sea bajo tu responsabilidad, que sepas pechar con las consecuencias. **63 over someone's –,** sin que alguien se entere, sin consultar con alguien (que está en posición de autoridad). **64 per/a –,** por barba, por cabeza. **65 to put one's – in the noose,** meterse en la trampa tontamente. **66 to put one's heads together,** tratar de resolver algo entre más de uno, colaborar en la solución de algún problema. **67 to put something into someone's –,** meter algo en la cabeza de alguien, sugerir algo a alguien, dar una idea a alguien. **68 to put something out of someone's –,** quitarle a alguien algo de la cabeza. **69 to stand on one's –,** (fam.) hacer algo con la gorra. **70 to stand/turn something on its –,** dar a algo la vuelta (especialmente en discusión). **71 to take into its – to, [- *inf.*]** metérsele a uno en la cabeza, darle a uno por. **72 to talk one's – off,** hablar por los codos. **73 to turn somebody's –,** envanecer a alguien: *his success has turned his head = su éxito le ha envanecido.* **74 two heads are better than one,** dos piensan mejor que uno.

headache | 'hedeɪk | *s.c.* **1** dolor de cabeza. **2** (fig.) fastidio, pesadez, dolor de cabeza.

headband | 'hedbænd | *s.c.* cinta (para sujetarse el pelo).

headboard | 'hedbɔ:d | *s.c.* cabezal, cabecera (de cama).

headdress | 'heddres | *s.c.* tocado (en la cabeza).

header | 'hedər | *s.c.* **1** DEP. cabezazo. || *s.sing.* **2 [a –]** un chapuzón de cabeza, un salto de cabeza.

head-first | ˌhed'fɜ:st | *adv.* **1** de cabeza, con la cabeza por delante. **2** (fig.) sin pensar, sin más, de cabeza (emprendiendo un proyecto).

headgear | 'hedgɪər | *s.i.* adorno en la cabeza, sombreros.

head-hunter | 'hedhʌntər | *s.c.* **1** buscador de talentos. **2** cazador de cabezas (de una tribu).

heading | 'hedɪŋ | *s.c.* encabezamiento (en un escrito).

headlamp | 'hedlæmp | V. **headlight.**

headland | 'hedlənd | *s.c.* GEOG. cabo, punta.

headless | 'hedlɪs | *adj.* descabezado, sin cabeza.

headlight | 'hedlaɪt | *s.c.* faro, luz delantera (de vehículo).

headline | 'hedlaɪn | PER. *s.c.* **1** titular, encabezamiento. || *s.pl.* **2** grandes titulares. || *v.t.* **3** titular, encabezar (noticia). || **4 to hit/make/reach the headlines,** aparecer en los periódicos, ser objeto de una gran noticia.

headlong | 'hedlɒŋ | *adj.* y *adv.* **1** derecho, directo (movimiento físico). || *adj.* **2** precipitado, temerario. || *adv.* **3** precipitadamente, temerariamente.

headman | 'hedmæn | [*pl.irreg.* **headmen**] *s.c.* jefe tribal, cacique.

headmaster | hed'mɑ:stər | *s.c.* director (de colegio).

headmen | 'hedmən | *pl.irreg.* de **headman.**

headmistress | hed'mɪstrɪs | *s.c.* directora (de colegio).

head-on | ˌhed'ɒn | *adj.* **1** frontal (choque). **2** (fig.) total, frontal, sin cuartel (conflicto o similar). || *adv.* **3** frontalmente (choque). **4** de lleno, de frente (forma de encarar algo).

headphone | 'hedfəun | *s.c.* [normalmente *pl.*] auricular, casco.

headquarters | ˌhed'kwɔ:təz | *s.pl.* **1** MIL. cuartel general. **2** sede, centro (donde se toman las decisiones directivas de empresa o similar).

headrest | 'hedrest | *s.c.* apoyo (para la cabeza), reposacabezas.

headroom | 'hedru:m | *s.i.* altura, espacio superior.

headscarf | 'hedskɑ:f | [*pl.irreg.* **headscarves**] *s.c.* pañuelo de cabeza.

headship | 'hedʃɪp | *s.c.* puesto de director, dirección (especialmente de escuelas).

head-shrinker | 'hedʃrɪŋkər | *s.c.* (fam.) psiquiatra.

headstand | 'hedstænd | *s.c.* pino, posición de pino.

head-start | ˌhed'stɑ:t | *s.c.* ventaja, posición ventajosa.

headstone | 'hedstəun | *s.c.* lápida.

headstrong | 'hedstrɒŋ | (EE.UU.) | 'hedstrɔ:ŋ | *adj.* obstinado, terco; voluntarioso.

headteacher | hed'ti:tʃər | *s.c.* director (de escuela primaria).

headway | 'hedweɪ | **to make –,** abrirse camino, avanzar, progresar.

headwind | 'hedwɪnd | *s.c.* viento contrario.

headword | 'hedwə:d | *s.c.* entrada (especialmente de un diccionario).

heady | 'hedɪ | *adj.* **1** embriagador (bebida, perfume, ambiente). **2** excitante, apasionante, extasiador (experiencia, idea, vida, etc.).

heal | hi:l | *v.t.* e *i.* **1** curar(se), sanar(se) (de una herida o enfermedad). || *v.t.* **2** (fig.) remediar, cicatrizar, curar: *time*

heals everything = el tiempo lo cura todo. _ **3 to – up,** cicatrizar(se), sanar(se) por completo.
healer | 'hiːlər | *s.c.* médico, curandero, sanador (cosa o persona).
health | helθ | *s.i.* **1** salud, buena salud. **2** (fig.) salud, buen estado, prosperidad (de una empresa o similar). || **3 to drink (to) someone's –,** beber a la salud de alguien, brindar por la salud de alguien. **4 – centre,** (brit.) centro de salud (local o municipal). **5 – food,** alimento natural, alimento integral. **6 – service,** servicio público de la sanidad, seguridad social. **7 – visitor,** (brit.) enfermera visitante (que va por las casas).
healthily | 'helθɪlɪ | *adv.* saludablemente, sanamente.
healthiness | 'helθɪnɪs | *s.i.* disfrute de buena salud.
healthy | 'helθɪ | *adj.* **1** sano, saludable. **2** (fig.) próspero, sano, fuerte (empresa o similar). **3** natural, beneficioso (actitud para con algo): *a healthy regard for one's parents = una admiración beneficiosa para los padres de uno.* **4** sustancial (cantidad).
heap | hiːp | *s.c.* **1** montón, pila (en desorden). **2** (fam.) montón, gran cantidad de (lo que sea): *heaps of money = montones de dinero.* _ *v.t.* **3** amontonar, apilar, poner en montones (desordenadamente). **4 [to – + o. + on/upon]** (fig.) prodigar (insultos, críticas, etc.) sobre; colmar de (alabanzas, favores, etc.). || **5 heaps,** (fam.) un montón, muchísimo: *this set is heaps better = este aparato es muchísimo mejor.* **6 to – up,** amontonar hasta arriba, apilar totalmente. **7 in a –,** como un fardo (caer). **8 the bottom/top of the –,** el escalón interior/superior de la sociedad, la parte baja/alta de la escala social.
heaped | hiːpt | *adj.* **[– (with)]** hasta arriba, abarrotado, lleno.
hear | hiər | *v.* [*pret.* y *p.p.irreg.* **heard**] *t.* **1** oír: *I heard you = te oí.* **2** escuchar, prestar atención a (un programa de radio, conferencia, etc.). **3** DER. ver, dar audiencia a (caso judicial). **4** escuchar (una oración, ruego, etc.). **5** saber, estar informado de, oír. || *i.* **6** oír, escuchar. **7 [to – (about/of)]** tener noticias, recibir noticias; oír hablar: *I have heard of him many times = he oído hablar de él muchas veces.* **8 [to – from]** escuchar a, recibir información de; tener noticias de: *I haven't heard from you for ages = no he tenido noticias tuyas durante muchísimo tiempo.* _ **9 can't/couldn't – oneself think,** no poder/pude concentrarse en lo que uno hace (por haber demasiado ruido). **10 do you – (me)?,** ¿me oyes?, ¿de acuerdo?, ¿está claro? **11 to have heard something before,** haber oído algo antes, estar al tanto de algo desde hace tiempo. **12 –,** sí señor, muy bien dicho, estupendo. **13 to – a pin drop,** poderse oír el vuelo de una mosca. **14 to – somebody out,** escuchar a alguien hasta que acabe de hablar. **15 won't – of,** negarse a, negarse a aceptar: *I won't hear of you paying for everything = me niego a aceptar que pagues todo.*
heard | hɜːd | *pret.* y *p.p.irreg.* de **hear.**
hearer | 'hɪərər | *s.c.* oyente (dentro de una audiencia).
hearing | 'hɪərɪŋ | *s.i.* **1** oído (uno de los sentidos corporales). || *s.c.* **2** audiencia, proceso, investigación oficial; vista. || **3 a (fair) –,** una oportunidad de expresar la opinión de uno: *OK I'll give you a fair hearing = de acuerdo te concederé una oportunidad de expresar tu opinión.* **4 hard of –,** V. **hard. 5 – aid,** audífono, prótesis auditiva. **6 in/within someone's –,** al alcance del oído.
hearsay | 'hɪəseɪ | *s.i.* rumores; habladurías.
hearse | hɜːs | *s.c.* coche fúnebre, coche mortuorio.
heart | hɑːt | *s.c.* **1** corazón. **2** pecho (parte más o menos cercana al corazón). **3** (fig.) corazón (sentimiento). **4** carta del palo de corazones. **5** cogollo (de verduras). **6** centro, corazón, parte más interior, cogollo (física o figurativamente): *the heart of the problem = el centro del problema.* **7** forma de corazón, corazón (forma física). || *s.i.* **8** coraje, valentía, arrojo: *I have not the heart to go = no tengo la valentía de irme.* _ *s.c.* e *i.* **9** (fig.) corazón, generosidad, compasión. || **10 a broken –,** un corazón roto (normalmente por desengaño amoroso). **11 a change of –,** cambio de opinión. **12 after one's own –,** que uno admira, que a uno le gusta mucho. **13 at –,** en el fondo, básicamente, en lo más íntimo. **14 to break one's –, a)** romperse el corazón de uno (especialmente por desengaño amoroso); **b)** dar a uno muchísima pena. **15 by –,** de memoria. **16 close/dear/near to one's –,** muy querido por uno, muy importante para uno. **17 to come from the –,** salir del corazón, ser genuino y natural (un sentimiento). **18 cross my – (and hope to die),** lo juro (dicho por niños). **19 to do one's – good,** animar a uno, reconfortar a uno. **20 everything the – can desire,** todo lo que el corazón pueda desear, todo lo que uno pueda imaginarse (como deseable). **21 from the –/from the bottom of one's –,** desde lo más profundo del corazón de uno, desde lo más íntimo de mi alma, con toda sinceridad. **22 to harden/steel one's – against,** endurecer el corazón contra, desengañarse de la buena voluntad de. **23 have a –,** (fam.) no me aprietes tanto, ten compasión de mí. **24 to have a – of gold,** V. **gold. 25 to have one's – in one's boots,** tener el ánimo por los suelos. **26 to have one's – in one's mouth,** tener el corazón en un puño. **27 to have one's – in the right place,** tener buen corazón. **28 – attack, a)** ataque al corazón; **b)** (fig.) ataque (de rabia, impotencia, cólera, etc.). **29 -hearted,** de corazón (en compuestos): *a kindhearted old lady = una anciana de corazón amable.* **30 – failure,** MED. insuficiencia coronaria, insuficiencia cardiaca. **31 hearts,** corazones (palo de la baraja). **32 in one's – of hearts,** en lo más íntimo del corazón de uno, en lo más íntimo del alma de uno. **33 to lose –,** desanimarse. **34 to lose one's – to,** (lit.) entregar el corazón por completo a (alguien, enamorándose de él). **35 one's heart's desire,** (p.u.) lo más querido por uno, el deseo más íntimo de uno. **36 one's – not to be in,** no poner el corazón en: *my heart is not in my work but in her = no pongo el corazón en mi trabajo sino en ella.* **37 one's – to leap,** darle a uno un vuelco el corazón. **38 one's – to sink,** caérsele el alma a uno a los pies. **39 to open one's – (to),** abrir el alma de uno (a), abrir el corazón de uno (a). **40 to pour out one's – (to),** mostrar los secretos/pensamientos más íntimos del alma de uno (a). **41 to set one's – on,** poner todas las esperanzas de uno en, poner todo la ilusión de uno en, poner toda el alma de uno en. **42 to take –,** cobrar ánimo, animarse. **43 to take something to –,** tomar algo a pecho. **44 the – of the matter,** la madre del cordero, el quid del tema. **45 to throw oneself – and soul into,** meterse de lleno de, meterse con todo el ánimo de uno en. **46 to one's heart's content,** a gusto de uno, a plena satisfacción de uno. **47 two hearts that beat as one,** dos personas que están muy unidas, dos personas que se encuentran íntimamente unidas. **48 to wear one's – on one's sleeve,** llevar el corazón de uno en la mano, manifestar los sentimientos de uno demasiado abiertamente. **49 to win someone's –,** enamorar a alguien (real y figuradamente). **50 with all one's –,** con todo el corazón de uno.
heartache | 'hɑːteɪk | *s.c.* e *i.* pena, tristeza, pesar.
heartbeat | 'hɑːtbiːt | *s.c.* e *i.* latido, latido del corazón.
heartbreak | 'hɑːtbreɪk | *s.c.* e *i.* angustia, dolor insoportable (especialmente después de la rotura de relaciones amorosas).
heartbreaking | 'hɑːtbreɪkɪŋ | *adj.* desgarrador, que parte el corazón.
heartbroken | 'hɑːtbrəʊkn | *adj.* destrozado, con el corazón destrozado.
heartburn | 'hɑːtbɜːn | *s.i.* MED. acidez gástrica (típica del embarazo).
hearten | 'hɑːtn | *v.t.* animar, dar ánimos, alentar.
heartening | 'hɑːtnɪŋ | *adj.* confortante, que infunde ánimo.
hearteningly | 'hɑːtnɪŋlɪ | *adv.* confortantemente.
heartfelt | 'hɑːtfelt | *adj.* sincero, ferviente.
hearth | hɑːθ | *s.c.* **1** chimenea, hogar. || *s.sing.* **2 [the –]** (form.) el hogar (la familia). || **3 – and home,** (fig.) el fuego del hogar.
hearthrug | 'hɑːθrʌg | *s.c.* alfombra (que se suele poner ante la chimenea).
heartily | 'hɑːtɪlɪ | *adv.* **1** cordialmente, con gran entusiasmo, enérgicamente. **2**

por completo, totalmente, verdaderamente: *I'm heartily pleased to see you = estoy verdaderamente contento de verte.*

heartiness | 'hɑːtɪnɪs | *s.i.* entusiasmo, energía; cordialidad.

heartland | 'hɑːtlænd | *s.c.* GEOG. zona central, centro (de un país).

heartless | 'hɑːtlɪs | *adj.* cruel, desalmado.

heartlessly | 'hɑːtlɪslɪ | *adv.* cruelmente, sin corazón.

heartlessness | 'hɑːtlɪsnɪs | *s.i.* crueldad, ausencia de sentimientos.

heartrending | 'hɑːtrendɪŋ | *adj.* desgarrador, angustioso.

heart-searching | 'hɑːtsəːtʃɪŋ | *s.i.* introspección, consideración cuidadosa, examen cuidadoso (de una situación).

heartstrings | 'hɑːtstɪŋz | **to tug at one's –,** tocar la fibra sensible de uno, llegar al alma de uno.

heartthrob | 'hɑːtərɒb | *s.c.* (fam.) tipo guaperas, (de quien se enamoran todas las mujeres).

heart-to-heart | ˌhɑːttə'hɑːt | *s.c.* **1** conversación íntima. || *adj.* **2** íntima (conversación).

heartwarming | 'hɑːtwɔːmɪŋ | *adj.* reconfortante, grato; animador.

hearty | 'hɑːtɪ | *adj.* **1** enérgico; alegre, campechano, entusiasta (persona). **2** franca (risa); vigoroso (golpe, movimiento, etc.). **3** copioso, abundante (especialmente comidas). **4** total, completo; verdadero: *a hearty dislike of apples = un odio total a las manzanas.* _ **5 a – eater,** un tragón, un comilón, una persona de buen saque.

heat | hiːt | *s.i.* **1** calor. **2** temperatura (cuando es alta): *blood heat = temperatura de la sangre.* **3** (fig.) pasión, vehemencia. || *s.sing.* **4** sofoco, calor, bochorno (del tiempo atmosférico). **5** calefacción, punto de calor (en una calefacción): *turn off the heat = quita la calefacción.* **6 [the – of]** el calor de, el acaloramiento de (una emoción). || *s.c.* **7** DEP. eliminatoria (carrera o partido). || *v.t.* **8** calentar. || **9 – rash,** MED. sarpullido de calor (cuando se bloquean las glándulas del sudor). **10 to – up, a)** calentarse, ponerse a una temperatura más alta; **b)** calentar, recalentar (especialmente comida anteriormente cocinada); **c)** (fig.) ponerse mal, calentarse (una situación). **11 in/on –,** en celo (animales). **12 in the – of the moment,** en el calor del momento. **13 the – of the day,** el momento de más calor del día.

heated | 'hiːtɪd | *adj.* **1** acalorada (discusión); pasional. **2** que funciona con calor artificial, que funciona con calor eléctrico.

heatedly | 'hiːtɪdlɪ | *adv.* acaloradamente, pasionalmente, vehementemente.

heater | 'hiːtər | *s.c.* MEC. calentador.

heath | hiːθ | *s.c.* BOT. brezal, tierra de brezos.

heathen | 'hiːðn | *s.c.* **1** pagano, infiel. **2** (fig.) vándalo, guerrero. || *adj.* **3** pagano, infiel.

heather | 'heðər | *s.i.* BOT. brezo.

heating | 'hiːtɪŋ | *s.i.* calefacción.

heat-stroke | 'hiːtstrəʊk | V. **sunstroke.**

heatwave | 'hiːtweɪv | *s.c.* ola de calor.

heave | hiːvv. [*pret.* y *p.p.* **heaved** o (lit.)/MAR. **hove**] *t.* **1** tirar de, levantar, mover (algo muy pesado). **2** tirar, arrojar (algo muy pesado). || *i.* **3** tirar, empujar, hacer un movimiento fuerte (con algo pesado). **4** vomitar fuertemente, vomitar violentamente. **5** subir y bajar (pechos, por ejemplo); palpitar. || *s.c.* **6** empellón, tirón, movimiento violento (para tirar, mover, etc. algo muy pesado). || **7 to – a sigh,** suspirar profundamente, dar un suspiro profundo. **8 to – in sight/into view,** (lit.) aparecer ante la vista, surgir ante la mirada. **9 to – to,** MAR. ponerse al pairo. **10 one's stomach to —,** tener náuseas fuertes.

heaven | 'hevn | *s.i.* **1** (fig. y fam.) paraíso, cielo: *this is heaven = esto es un paraíso.* _ *s.pl.* **2** (lit.) cielo, firmamento. || **3 for heaven's sake,** V. **sake. 4 good heavens/heavens!,** ¡cielos! ¡Dios mío! **5 Heaven,** REL. Cielo, Paraíso. **6 – forbid,** Dios no lo quiera. **7 – knows,** (fam.) **a)** Dios sabe: *heaven know I've fried = Dios sabe que lo he intentado;* **b)** vete tú a saber, quién sabe. **8 – help,** (fam.) Dios ayude (a alguien). **9 – on earth,** (fam.) paraíso terrestre, lugar maravilloso. **10 in heaven's name,** en nombre de Dios, por el amor de Dios: *where in heaven's name is the key? = por el amor de Dios, ¿dónde está la llave?* **11 to move – and earth,** mover cielo y tierra, hacer lo imposible, remover Roma con Santiago. **12 to smell/stink to high –,** (fam.) heder a más no poder, echar un olor inaguantable. **13 to thank –,** V. **thank. 14 the heavens open/opened, etc.,** ponerse/se puso a llover a mares.

heavenly | 'hevnlɪ | *adj.* **1** (fam.) maravilloso, divino. **2** ASTR. celestial, del cielo. || **3 – body,** ASTR. cuerpo celeste.

heaven-sent | ˌhevn'sent | *adj.* providencial, milagroso, venido del cielo.

heavenward | 'hevnwəd | (también **heavenwards**) *adv.* (lit.) hacia el cielo, en dirección al cielo.

heavily | 'hevɪlɪ | *adv.* **1** abundantemente, considerablemente, fuertemente (en intensidad, fuerza, cantidad, etc.). **2** fornidamente (físicamente formado). **3** laboriosamente, dificultosamente (respirando o similar). **4** pesadamente, torpemente, lentamente (de movimientos).

heaviness | 'hevɪnɪs | *s.i.* **1** pesadez (física). **2** corpulencia.

heavy | 'hevɪ | *adj.* **1** pesado (de mucho peso): *how heavy are you? = ¿cuánto pesas?* **2** abundante, considerable, fuerte (con gran intensidad, fuerza, cantidad, etc. de algo normalmente desagradable): *heavy rains = lluvias abundantes; heavy responsibility = responsabilidad considerable.* **3** denso, espeso (líquido o sustancia). **4** fornido, grandote (de cuerpo). **5** pesada (maquinaria o artillería). **6** pesado, torpe, lento (en movimientos). **7** ocupado, activo, apretado (tiempo de trabajo). **8** laboriosa (respiración o similar). **9** pesado, difícil, duro, penoso (trabajo). **10** triste, decaído: *with a heavy heart = con el ánimo decaído.* **11** (desp.) pesado, aburrido (libro, música, conferencia, etc.). **12** pesada, indigesta, que llena (comida). **13 [– with]** (lit.) cargado de (aire, ambiente, árboles, etc.): *the air was heavy with the spring scents = el aire estaba cargado de fragancias primaverales.* **14** (fam.) difícil, serio (problema, situación, etc.). **15** grueso (de apariencia). **16** encapotado (cielo). **17** opresivo, cargado (tiempo atmosférico o ambiente). **18** obvio, torpe (tipo de humor, broma, indirecta, etc.). **19** QUIM. pesada (agua). **20** empedernido (bebedor o fumador). **21** profundo (dormir). || *s.c.* **22** (fam.) matón, gorila. || **23 a – hand,** V. **hand. 24 to be – on,** (fam.) **a)** consumir mucho, gastar mucho: *this heater is too heavy on coal = este calentador consume demasiado carbón;* **b)** usar mucho, utilizar mucho (por parte de una persona): *don't be so heavy on the varnish = no uses tanta laca.* **25 – going,** terreno pesado; marcha difícil. **26 – industry,** industria pesada. **27 – metal,** MUS. heavy, duro. **28 to make – weather of,** V. **weather.**

heavy-duty | ˌhevɪ'djuːtɪ*adj.* duradero, fuerte, para trabajos pesados.

heavy-handed | ˌhevɪ'hændɪd | *adj.* **1** autoritario, duro, despótico. **2** torpe, desmañado.

heavy-handedly | ˌhevɪ'hændɪdlɪ | *adv.* **1** autoritariamente, duramente, despóticamente. **2** torpemente, desmañadamente.

heavy-handedness | ˌhevɪ'hændɪdnɪs | *s.i.* **1** autoritarismo, dureza, despotismo. **2** torpeza (con las manos).

heavy-set | ˌhevɪ'set | *adj.* (especialmente EE.UU.) corpulento, fornido.

heavyweight | 'hevɪweɪt | *adj.* **1** DEP. de los pesos pesados. **2** (fig.) importante, sustancial (persona o tema). || *s.c.* **3** DEP. peso pesado. **4** (fig.) grandullón, grandote.

Hebraic | hiː'breɪɪk | *adj.* hebraico.

Hebrew | 'hiːbruː | *s.i.* **1** hebreo (idioma). || *s.c.* **2** hebreo, judío (habitante). || *adj.* **3** hebreo, judío.

heck | hek | (vulg.) *interj.* **1** mierda, coño. || **2 a – of a,** pero que muy.

heckle | 'hekl | *v.t.* e *i.* interrumpir con abucheos.

heckler | 'heklər | *s.c.* abucheador; provocador (en reuniones públicas).

heckling | 'heklɪŋ | *s.i.* abucheos, interrupciones (en reuniones públicas).

hectare | 'hekteə | *s.c.* hectárea.

hectic | 'hektɪk | *adj.* agitado; frenética (actividad).

hectically | 'hektɪklɪ | *adv.* agitadamente; frenéticamente.

hector | 'hektər | *v.t.* e *i.* intimidar.

hectoring | 'hektərɪŋ | *adj.* intimidante, apabullante.

he'd | hiːd | *contr.* **1** de **he** y **had. 2** de **he** y **would.**

hedge | hedʒ | *s.c.* **1** seto. **2 [– against]** protección contra, seguro contra (de índole financiero). || *v.i.* **3 [to – against]** asegurarse contra, protegerse contra (mediante medios financieros, seguros, etc.). **4 [to – (on)]** no comprometerse; evadir la contestación (de preguntas): *the lecturer hedged on every issue = el conferenciante no se comprometió en ningún tema importante.* _ *v.t.* **5** poner un seto alrededor de (un espacio). **6** evadir, evitar (contestación). || **6 to be hedged about/around/in (with),** estar entorpecido (por), estar obstruido (por), estar limitado (por): *we are hedged in with too many petty rules = estamos limitados por demasiadas regulaciones minuciosas.* **7 to – one's bets,** dividir inteligentemente las apuestas de uno, equilibrar las apuestas de uno.

hedgehog | 'hedʒhɒg | (EE.UU.) | 'hedʒhɔːg*s.c.* ZOOL. erizo, puerco espín.

hedgerow | 'hedʒrəʊ | *s.c.* seto vivo.

hedonism | 'hiːdənɪzəm | *s.i.* (form.) hedonismo.

hedonist | 'hiːdənɪst | *s.c.* (form.) hedonista.

hedonistic | ˌhiːdə'nɪstɪk | *adj.* (form.) hedonista.

heed | hiːd | (form.) *v.t.* **1** prestar atención a, atender a. || **2 to take – of/to pay – to,** prestar atención a.

heedless | 'hiːdlɪs | *adj.* **[– (of)]** (form.) sin atención, desatento.

heedlessly | 'hiːdlɪslɪ | *adv.* (form.) descuidadamente, sin prestar atención a nada.

hee-haw | 'hiːhɔː | *s.c.* rebuzno (onomatopéyico).

heel | hiːl | *s.c.* **1** ANAT. talón. **2** tacón (de zapato). **3** parte del talón (de un calcetín, media, etc.). **4 [– of]** base del pulgar de (la mano). || *v.t.* **5** poner tacones (a zapatos). || **6 at someone's heels,** pisándole los talones a alguien; inmediatamente detrás de alguien. **7 to bring someone to –,** meter a alguien en cintura. **8 to click one's heels,** chocar los tacones de uno. **9 to dig one's heels in,** mantenerse en sus trece. **10 to drag one's heels,** arrastrar los pies; hacer algo sin ganas. **11 to follow hard on the heels of,** suceder inmediatamente después de, seguir inmediatamente después de (en el tiempo). **12 head over heels,** V. **head. 13 to – over,** ladearse, escorarse, inclinarse pronunciadamente. **14 to kick /cool one's heels,** (fam.) hacer antesala, esperar sin hacer nada. **15 to spin /turn/swing on one's –,** girar sobre los pasos de uno, dar media vuelta. **16 to take to one's heels,** (lit.) irse corriendo, escaparse, huir. **17 to tread hard on someone's heels/to be hot on someone's heels,** ir pisándole a alguien los talones. **18 under/beneath one's –,** bajo su poder, bajo su bota.

heftily | 'heftɪlɪ | (fam.) *adv.* **1** fuertemente, vigorosamente. **2** sustancialmente, considerablemente (en cantidad, peso o tamaño).

hefty | 'heftɪ | (fam.) *adj.* **1** fuerte, vigoroso; robusto. **2** sustancial, considerable (cantidad, peso o tamaño).

hegemony | hɪ'gmənɪ | (EE.UU.) | 'hedʒəməʊnɪ*s.c.* e *i.* (form.) hegemonía, preeminencia.

heifer | 'hefər | *s.c.* vaca joven, novilla.

height | haɪt | *s.c.* e *i.* *1* altura (de algo o alguien). **2** altura, elevación (sobre el suelo o el nivel del mar). || *s.i.* **3** talla, estatura, medidas (de altura de alguien). || *s.c.* **4** (normalmente *pl.*) altura, cerro, altozano. **5** [normalmente *pl.*] (fig.) apogeo, cumbre (de una profesión, por ejemplo). || *s.sing.* **6** punto más alto, punto más álgido: *the height of the hunting season = el punto más álgido de la época de caza.* **7 [the – of]** (form.) el colmo de. || **8 to draw oneself up to one's full –,** erguirse en toda la estatura de uno. **9 to gain –,** ganar altura, subir. **10 to lose –,** perder altura, descender.

heighten | 'haɪtn | *v.t.* e *i.* intensificar(se), aumentar (sentimiento o sensación).

heightened | 'haɪtnd | *adj.* intensificado, aumentado, fortalecido (sentimiento o sensación).

heinous | 'heɪnəs | *adj.* (form.) atroz, infame, horrendo (casi maléfico).

heinously | 'heɪnəslɪ | *adv.* (form.) atrozmente, infamemente, horrendamente.

heinousness | 'heɪnəsnɪs | *s.i.* (form.) atrocidad, infamia (casi maldad).

heir | eər | *s.c.* **1 [– (to)]** heredero. || **2 to be – to,** (fig.) ser heredero de, heredar (algo que otros han hecho no materialmente). **3 – apparent,** DER. heredero forzoso. **4 – presumptive,** DER. presunto heredero.

heiress | 'eərɪs | *s.c.* heredera.

heirloom | 'eəluːm | *s.c.* objeto preciado heredado, objeto de familia (que se hereda de generación en generación).

heist | haɪst | (EE.UU.) *s.c.* **1** robo a mano armada. || *v.t.* **2** robar a mano armada.

held | held | *pret.* y *p.p.irreg.* de **hold.**

helicopter | 'helɪkɒptər | *s.c.* helicóptero.

heliport | 'helɪpɔːt | *s.c.* helipuerto.

helium | 'hiːlɪəm | *s.i.* QUIM. helio.

hell | hel | *s.i.* **1** (fam.) un infierno, un tormento: *his home life is hell = su vida de hogar es un infierno.* _ *interj.* **2** mecachis, mierda, jolines. || **3 a – of a/one – of a,** (fam.) de aúpa, de campeonato, de primera clase: *a hell of a problem = un problema de campeonato.* **4 all – breaks/broke/etc. loose,** (fam.) se arma/armó/etc. un follón de espanto. **5 come – or high water,** (fam.) pase lo que pase, aunque se hunda el mundo. **6 for the – of it,** (fam.) porque sí, por gusto, por pura gracia: *they beat me for the hell of it = me dieron una paliza por gusto.* **7 to get the – out (of),** (fam. y EE.UU.) irse a la mierda fuera (de), irse a hacer puñetas fuera (de). **8 to give someone –/to make someone's life –,** (fam.) hacerle a alguien la vida imposible; ponérselo difícil a alguien. **9 go to –,** (fam.) vete a la mierda, vete a hacer puñetas. **10 Hell,** REL. Infierno. **11 – for leather,** a toda velocidad, como si le persiguiera a uno el diablo. **12 – on earth,** (fam.) tormento infernal, infierno en vida. **13 like a bat out of –,** (fam.) como alma que persigue el diablo. **14 like –,** (fam.) y una mierda (desacuerdo). **15 ... like –/... as –,** (fam.) ... como un negro, a toda mecha, con toda la intensidad que uno pueda (énfasis del verbo que sea): *work like hell = trabaja como un negro; run like hell = corre a toda mecha.* **16 not to have a hope in –,** V. **hope. 17 to play (merry) – with,** (fam.) destrozar, dejar destrozado, dejar hecho unos zorros, echar a perder. **17 to raise –,** (fam.) armar un escándalo, armar un follón. **18 the – out of,** (fam.) hasta la saciedad, hasta un grado increíble (como énfasis de verbos con algún matiz negativo): *they kicked the hell out of me = me dieron patadas hasta en el carnet de identidad; she scared the hell out of me = me dio un susto del demonio.* **19 there'll be – to pay,** (fam.) va a haber follón, va a haber problemas serios, va a haber tela marinera. **20 the road to – is paved with good intentions,** el camino al infierno está lleno de buenas intenciones. **21 to – with,** (fam.) al infierno con, a la mierda con. **22 what the –,** (fam.) y qué, y a mí qué (quitando importancia). **23 why/who/where/etc. the –...,** (fam.) por qué/quién/dónde/etc. demonios, coño... **24 to wish/hope to – (that),** (fam.) por lo que Dios más quiera (que), ojalá por lo que Dios más quiera (que).

he'll | heːl | *contr.* de **he** y **will.**

hell-bent | ˌhel'bent *adj.* **[– on]** resuelto por completo a, decidido firmemente a.

Hellenic | he'liːnɪk | *adj.* helénico.

hellish | 'helɪʃ | *adj.* (fam.) **1** infernal, diabólico. **2** V. **hellishly.**

hellishly | 'helɪʃlɪ | *adv.* (fam.) diabólicamente, infernalmente (énfasis de algo negativo): *hellishly difficult = infernalmente difícil.*

hello | 'heləʊ | (también **hallo** y **hullo**) *s.c.* **1** hola; saludo. | *interj.* **2** vaya, caramba (sorpresa). || **3 –, a)** hola, qué tal, qué hay; **b)** diga (por teléfono); **c)** ¿hay alguien aquí?, ¿hay alguien en casa?

helm | helm | *s.c.* **1** (normalmente *sing.*) timón. **2** (fig.) timón, mando, dirección (del gobierno, una empresa, etc.). || **3 at the –,** al mando, al timón (de una organización). **4 to take over the –,** hacerse cargo del mando, tomar la responsabilidad de dirigir.

helmet | 'helmɪt | *s.c.* casco (de todo tipo).

helmsman | 'helmzmən | [*pl.irreg.* **helmsmen**] *s.c.* MAR. timonel, piloto.

helmsmen | 'helmzmən | *pl.irreg.* de **helmsman.**

help | help | *v.t.* **1** ayudar, socorrer, auxiliar: *I helped to lift the case = ayudé a levantar la maleta.* **2** ayudar, asistir, ser útil para: *this photograph will help you to understand = esta fotografía te será útil para entender.* **3 [to – + *o.* + to]** servir (comida o bebida): *I'll help you to some more fish = te serviré más pescado.* **4** aliviar, ayudar, contribuir (a sentirse mejor o aguantar mejor): *an aspirin will help me = una aspirina me aliviará.* **5 [to – + *o.* + up/down + with]** ayudar a (alguien) a ponerse/quitarse (algo): *I helped the old man on with his coat = ayudé al viejo a ponerse el abrigo.* _ *v.r.* **7 [to – (to)]** servirse (comida o bebida). **8** coger uno mismo, tomar uno mismo (algo). **9** solucionar los problemas de uno: *modern societies must help themselves= las sociedades modernas deben solucionar sus propios problemas.* **10 [to – (to)]** (fig. y fam.) robar, coger sin permiso. || *s.i.* **11** ayuda, socorro, asistencia. **12** apoyo, consejo (especialmente psicológico). || *s.c.* **13** asistenta (persona). || **14 a –/a great –/a lot of –/etc.,** una gran ayuda (persona o cosa). **15 to be of –,** servir de gran ayuda, ser un magnífico apoyo. **16 can't – (but), [+ *o./ger.*] no poder evitar; no poder dejar de:** *I could not help wondering = no pude evitar hacerme preguntas comprometidas.* **17 –!,** ¡socorro!, ¡auxilio! **18 to – out, a)** ayudar con algo de dinero; **b)** ayudar a acabar el trabajo. **19 to – someone to their feet,** ayudar a alguien a ponerse en pie. **20 so – me God,** que Dios me ayude; y así lo prometo firmemente (a cumplir una promesa o juramento previamente mencionado). **21 there is no – for it,** no hay nada que hacer, no hay otra opción, no tenemos más remedio.

helper | 'helpər | *s.c.* ayudante, colaborador.

helpful | 'helpfl | *adj.* **1** útil, servicial, que sirve de ayuda (persona o consejo). **2** beneficioso, provechoso (que ayuda a soportar algo mejor).

helpfully | 'helpfəlɪ | *adv.* servicialmente, amablemente.

helpfulness | 'helpflnɪs | *s.i.* amabilidad (de una persona).

helping | 'helpɪŋ | *s.c.* **1** porción, ración (cantidad de comida). || **2 a – hand,** una mano, una ayuda.

helpless | 'helplɪs | *adj.* desvalido, impotente, desamparado, indefenso; vulnerable.

helplessly | 'helplɪslɪ | *adv.* impotentemente, sin posibilidad de defensa; vulnerablemente.

helplessness | 'helplɪsnɪs | *s.i.* impotencia, desamparo, indefensión; vulnerabilidad.

helter-skelter | ˌheltə'skeltər | *adv.* **1** atropelladamente, en desbandada; desorganizadamente, sin orden ni concierto. || *adj.* **2** atropellado, precipitado; desorganizado. || *s.c.* **3** tobogán gigante (con partes rectas y partes inclinadas).

hem | hem | [*ger.* **hemming,** *pret.* y *p.p.* **hemmed**] *v.t.* e *i.* **1** hacer el dobladillo en, hacer los bajos (ropa). || *s.c.* **2** dobladillo, bajo (de ropa). || *v.i.* **3** hacer ejem, decir ejem. || *interj.* **4** ejem. || **5 to – in,** cercar por completo; apretujar, apretar fuertemente (no dejando espacio).

he-man | 'hiːmæn | [*pl.irreg.* **he-men**] *s.c.* macho, machote, hombre hecho un macho.

he-men | 'hiːmən | *pl.irreg.* de **he-man.**

hematologist V. **haematologist.**

hematology V. **haematology.**

hemisphere | 'hemɪsfɪər | *s.c.* **1** GEOM. semiesfera. **2** ANAT. hemisferio (cerebral). **3** GEOG. hemisferio (terráqueo).

hemline | 'hemlaɪn | *s.c.* dobladillo, bajo, bastilla (de ropa).

hemlock | 'hemlɒk | *s.i.* **1** cicuta (veneno). || *s.c.* e *i.* **2** BOT. cicuta.

hemoglobin V. **haemoglobin.**

hemophilia V. **haemophilia.**

hemophiliac V. **haemophiliac.**

hemorrhage V. **haemorrhage.**

hemorrhoids V. **haemorrhoids.**

hemp | hemp | *s.i.* BOT. cáñamo.

hemstitch | 'hemstɪtʃ | *s.i.* vainica.

hen | hen | *s.c.* **1** gallina. **2** hembra (de muchas aves).

hence | hens | *adv.* (form.) **1** así, así pues, por lo tanto, por ello. **2** a partir de ahora, desde este momento. **3** (arc.) desde aquí, desde este sitio, desde este punto.

henceforth | ˌhens'fɔːθ | (también **henceforward**) *adv.* (form.) de ahora en adelante, en lo sucesivo.

henchman | 'hentʃmən | [*pl.irreg.* **henchmen**] *s.c.* (desp.) secuaz.

henchmen | 'hentʃmən | *pl.irreg.* de **henchman.**

henna | 'henə | *s.i.* alheña (tinte para teñir el pelo).

hennaed | 'henəd | *adj.* teñido con alheña (pelo).

hen-party | 'henpɑːtɪ | *s.c.* (fam.) despedida de soltera (fiesta de sólo mujeres).

henpecked | 'henpekt | *adj.* (fam.) calzonazos.

hepatitis | ˌhepə'taɪtɪs | *s.i.* MED. hepatitis.

heptagon | 'heptəgən | (EE.UU.) | 'heptəgɒn *s.c.* GEOM. heptágono.

heptagonal | hep'tægənl | *adj.* GEOM. heptagonal.

her | həːr | (pronunciación relajada | həːr |) *pron.o.* **1** le, la, a ella (persona, algunos animales hembra y coches, barcos o naciones). || *adj.pos.* **2** su (de ella): *Mary's tired, her boss makes her work too hard = Mary está cansada, su jefe le hace trabajar demasiado.*

herald | 'herəld | *v.t.* **1** anunciar, señalar el comienzo de, señalar la entrada de: *Mussolini's rise to power heralded Fascism = la ascensión al poder de Mussolini señaló el comienzo del fascismo.* **2** proclamar, anunciar (públicamente). || *s.c.* **3 [– of]** anuncio de, anunciador de, presagio de. **4** HIST. mensajero, heraldo. || **5 Herald,** PER. Heraldo (en nombres de periódicos): *New York Herald.*

heraldic | he'rældɪk | *adj.* heráldico.

heraldry | 'herəldrɪ | *s.i.* heráldica.

herb | həːb | *s.c.* hierba (de las que se usan en infusiones o similar).

herbaceous | həː'beɪʃəs | BOT. *adj.* **1** herbáceo. || **2 – border,** banco de flores (en un jardín).

herbal | 'həːbl | *adj.* herbario, de hierbas (para infusiones): *herbal tea = té de hierbas.*

herbalist | 'həːbəlɪst | *s.c.* herbolario, experto en hierbas.

herbicide | 'həːbɪsaɪd | *s.c.* e *i.* QUIM. herbicida.

herbivore | 'həːbɪvɔː | *s.c.* BIOL. herbívoro.

herbivorous | həː'bɪvərəs | *adj.* herbívoro.

herculean | ˌhəːkjʊ'liːən | (también **Herculean**) *adj.* (lit.) hercúleo.

herd | həːd | *s.c.* **1** rebaño, manada, piara (según la clase de animal). **2** (normalmente desp.) multitud, turba; montón (de personas). || *v.t.* **3** agrupar, reunir (personas o animales). || **4 to – up,** reunir en manada, reunir por completo.

herdsman | 'həːdzmən | [*pl.irreg.* **herdsmen**] *s.c.* vaquero (de ganado); pastor (de cabras).

herdsmen | 'həːdzmən | *pl.irreg.* de **herdsman.**

here | hɪər | *adv.* **1** aquí. **2** aquí, de aquí, junto a mí: *my friend here doesn't like Spanish wine = aquí, a mi amigo, no le gusta el vino español.* **3** en este punto, en este momento: *here I would like to introduce two more points = en este punto quisiera introducir dos reflexiones más.* **4** (fam.) que tengo aquí, de aquí: *this here prisoner is not English = este prisionero que tengo aquí no es inglés.* _ *interj.* **5** presente (contestación a la lectura de una lista). **6** oye, eh. || **7 –/– you are/here's ...,** toma, coge; dame, pásame (tanto al dar o al querer coger algo en la mano). **8 – and now, a)** aquí y ahora, en esta vida; **b)** en este mismo instante (como énfasis). **9 – and there,** aquí y allí, aquí y allá, por varios sitios, por varios puntos. **10 – comes/here's,** aquí llega, aquí viene: *here comes the train = aquí llega el tren.* **11 – I am/– we are,** ya hemos llegado. **12– it is/– we are,** ya lo he encontrado, aquí está, ya está (al encontrar algo que se estaba buscando). **13 here's/— is/— are,** aquí tenemos, aquí entra a colación, aquí se nos presenta (como fórmula de introducción de un artista, atracción de la atención, introducir un punto nuevo de conversación, etc.). **14 here's to,** a la salud de (al brindar). **15 – we are/– you are,** así pues, fíjate, fijémonos (detallando información sobre una persona): *here you are, my brother an engineer and his wife a maid = fíjate, mi hermano ingeniero y su mujer una criada.* **16 – we go/– we go again/– I go again,** (fam.) seguimos igual, otra vez igual, ya estamos otra vez en lo mismo.

hereabouts | ˌhɪərə'bauts | (también **hereabout**) *adv.* por aquí, en algún sitio de aquí, por esta zona.

hereafter | ˌhɪər'ɑːftər | (EE.UU.) | ˌhɪərӕftər | (form.) *adv.* **1** a partir de ahora, desde este momento; en el futuro. || *s.sing.* **2** futuro, otra vida, más allá, eternidad.

hereby | ˌhɪə'baɪ | *adv.* (form.) por esto, como resultado de esto, mediante esto.

hereditary | hɪ'redɪtrɪ | (EE.UU.) | hɪ'redɪtərɪ *adj.* hereditario (características genéticas, propiedades materiales, título, etc.).

heredity | hɪ'redɪtɪ | *s.i.* herencia (genética).

herein | ˌhɪər'ɪn | *adv.* (form.) en este punto, en este sitio, en esto; en este pasage (libro o documento).

hereinafter | hɪərɪn'ɑːftər | (EE.UU.) | ˌhɪərɪn'ӕftər | *adv.* (form.) DER. a partir de ahora, desde este punto, a partir de este momento.

heresy | 'herəsɪ | *s.c.* e *i.* herejía (especialmente la religiosa).

heretic | 'herətɪk | *s.c.* hereje (especialmente religioso).

heretical | hɪ'retɪkl | *adj.* herético.

heretofore | ˌhɪətuː'fɔː | *adv.* (form.) anteriormente, antes; previamente.

herewith | ˌhɪə'wɪð | *adv.* (form.) **1** incluido aquí (especialmente en una carta). **2** V. **hereby.**

heritage | 'herɪtɪdʒ | *s.sing.* herencia (cultural, histórica, etc.).

hermaphrodite | həː'mӕfrədaɪt | *s.c.* BIOL. hermafrodita.

hermetic | həː'metɪk | *adj.* (form.) hermético (especialmente, cerrado).

hermetically | həː'metɪklɪ | *adv.* (form.) herméticamente.

hermit | 'həːmɪt | *s.c.* **1** ermitaño (especialmente por razones religiosas). || **2 – crab,** ZOOL. cangrejo ermitaño.

hermitage | 'həːmɪtɪdʒ | *s.c.* REL. ermita; lugar retirado y solitario para ermitaños.

hernia | 'həːnɪə | *s.c.* e *i.* MED. hernia.

hero | 'hɪərəu | [*pl.* **heroes**] *s.c.* **1** héroe; valiente. **2** LIT. héroe, personaje principal. **3** héroe, persona admirada, persona idolatrada (por alguien).

heroic | hɪ'rəuɪk | *adj.* **1** heroico; valiente. **2** LIT. heroico. || *s.pl.* **3** altisonante, rimbombante (lenguaje, comportamiento, etc.). || **4 – verse/couplets,** LIT. verso heroico.

heroically | hɪ'rəuɪklɪ | *adv.* heroicamente; valientemente.

heroin | 'herəuɪn | *s.i.* QUIM. heroína.

heroine | 'herəuɪn | *s.c.* **1** heroína. **2** LIT. heroína, personaje principal.

heroism | 'herəuɪzəm | *s.i.* heroísmo.

heron | 'herən | *s.c.* ZOOL. garza, garza real (ave).

herpes | 'həːpiːz | MED. *s.i.* **1** herpes. || **2 – simplex,** herpes simple.

herring | 'herɪŋ | [*pl.* **herring** o **herrings**] ZOOL. *s.c.* **1** arenque. || **2 – gull,** gaviota argéntea.

herringbone | 'herɪŋbəun | *s.i.* espinapez (patrón de dibujo en las construcciones); punto de espina (costura).

hers | həːz | *pron.pos.* suyo, suya, suyos, suyas (de ella): *Pamela has the same car as mine, but hers is blue = Pamela tiene el mismo coche que yo, pero el suyo es azul.*

herself | həː'self | *pron.r.* **1** a ella misma, se... a sí misma: *she killed herself = ella se suicidó.* **2** ella sola, ella sin ayuda de nadie: *she did it herself = ella lo hizo sin ayuda de nadie.* **3** misma, mismita (enfáticamente).

hertz | həːtz | [*pl.* **hertz**] *s.c.* FIS. hercio.

he's | hiːz | *contr.* de **he** e **is** o **he** y **has.**

hesitancy | 'hezɪtənsɪ | (también **hesitance**) *s.i.* vacilación, indecisión, titubeo.

hesitant | 'hezɪtənt | *adj.* vacilante, indeciso, titubeante.

hesitantly | 'hezɪtəntlɪ | *adv.* con vacilación, de forma indecisa.

hesitate | 'hezɪteɪt | *v.i.* **1** vacilar, titubear, mostrarse indeciso. **2** [**to – +** *inf.*] **vacilar en, titubear en:** *I hesitated to ask him why = yo vacilé en preguntarle por qué.* _ **3 don't – to,** no dudes/dude en, no vaciles/vacile en: *don't hesitate to come when you like = no dudes en venir cuando te apetezca.*

hesitation | ˌhezɪ'teɪʃn | *s.c.* e *i.* **1** vacilación, indecisión, titubeo. **2** reticencia, indecisión. || **3 to have no – in,** no tener vacilación alguna sobre, no tener ninguna duda de. **4 without –,** sin vacilación alguna, decisivamente.

hessian | 'hesɪən | (EE.UU.) | 'heʃn *s.i.* arpillera (material normalmente para sacos).

heterodox | 'hetərədɒks | *adj.* (form.) heterodoxo.

heterodoxy | 'hetərədɒksɪ | *s.i.* (form.) heterodoxia.

heterogeneous | ˌhetərə'dʒiːnɪəs | *adj.* (form.) heterogéneo.

heterogeneously | ˌhetərə'dʒiːnɪəslɪ | *adv.* (form.) heterogéneamente.

heterosexual | ˌhetərə'sekʃuəl | *adj.* **1** heterosexual. || *s.c.* **2** heterosexual.

heterosexuality | ˌhetərəˌsekʃu'ӕlətɪ | *s.i.* heterosexualidad.

het up | 'hetʌp | *adj.* (fam.) sofocado, acalorado (por alguna emoción o enfado).

heuristic | hjuə'rɪstɪk | (form.) *adj.* **1** heurístico. || *s.i.* **2** FIL. heurística.

hew | hjuː | [*pret.* **hewed,** *p.p.* **hewed** o **hewn**] *v.t.* **1** [**to – +** *o.* **+ out**] hendir, partir (sin ningún cuidado). **2** [**to –** *o.* **+ out/from**] excavar (alguna obra pública considerable); tallar (con cierto objetivo cultural). **3** [**to —** *prep.*] abrirse camino a base de tajos (hacia cualquier dirección): *they hewed their way through the thick forest = se abrieron camino a machetazos a través del tupido bosque.*

hewn | hjuːn | *p.p.irreg.* de **hew.**

hexagon | 'heksəgən | (EE.UU.) | 'heksəgɒn | *s.c.* GEOM. hexágono.

hexagonal | heks'ӕgənl | *adj.* GEOM. hexagonal.

hey | heɪ | *interj.* (fam.) eh (sorpresa); oye (llamada).

heyday | 'heɪdeɪ | *s.sing.* auge, apogeo.

hi | haɪ | *interj.* (fam.) **1** hola, qué tal. **2** oye, escucha (atrayendo atención).

hiatus | haɪ'eɪtəs | *s.c.* (form.) pausa, interrupción, hiato.

hibernate | 'haɪbəneɪt | *v.i.* BIOL. **1** hibernar, invernar (animales). **2** (hum.) pasar el invierno acurrucado (junto al calor).

hibernation | ˌhaɪbə'neɪʃn | *s.i.* BIOL. hibernación: *to go into hibernation = entrar en hibernación.*

hibiscus | hɪ'bɪskəs | (EE.UU.) | haɪ'bɪskəs *s.c.* BOT. hibisco.

hiccup | hɪkʌp | (también **hiccough**) *s.c.* **1** [normalmente *pl.*] hipo. **2** (fam.) malfuncionamiento, dificultad. || *v.i.* **3** hipar, decir con hipo, dar hipos.

hick | hɪk | (fam., desp. y EE.UU.) *s.c.* **1** palurdo, paleto. || *adj.* **2** de palurdo, de paleto.

hickory | 'hɪkərɪ | *s.c.* BOT. nogal, nuez dura.

hid | hɪd | *pret.irreg.* de **hide.**

hidden | 'hɪdn | *p.p.irreg.* **1** de **hide.** _ *adj.* **2** oculto, escondido, secreto (lugar o significado).

hide | haɪd | *v.* [*pret.* **hid,** *p.p.* **hidden**] *t.* **1** esconder, ocultar. **2** disimular (sentimientos o similar). **3** ocultar (información). **4** cubrir (ocultando): *his beard hid his lips = la barba ocultaba los labios.* _ *i.* y *r.* **5** esconderse, ocultarse. || *s.c.* **6** piel (de animal más bien grande con la que se hace cuero posteriormente). **7** (hum.) pellejo (para personas). **8** puesto oculto, escondrijo (para la caza o la observación). || **9 I/you/etc. haven't seen – hide nor hair (of),** (fam.) no he/has/etc. visto el pelo (a) (alguien). **10 to tan some-one's –,** (p.u.) zurrarle labadana a alguien.

hide-and-seek | ˌhaɪdn'siːk | *s.i.* escondite (juego de niños).

hideaway | 'haɪdəweɪ | *s.c.* escondrijo, escondite; lugar de retiro.

hidebound | 'haɪdbaund | *adj.* aferrado al pasado, de miras estrechas, cerrado a lo nuevo.

hideous | 'hɪdɪəs | *adj.* espantoso, atroz, horripilante (algo).

hideously | 'hɪdɪəslɪ | *adv.* **1** espantosamente, atrozmente, horripilantemente. **2** horriblemente (enfático de algo negativo): *this is hideously expensive = esto es horriblemente caro.*

hideousness | 'hɪdɪəsnɪs | *s.i.* fealdad; (lo) espantoso, (lo) atroz.

hideout | 'haɪdaut | *s.c.* escondite, escondrijo (más bien para personas huyendo de la policía o parecido).

hiding | 'haɪdɪŋ | *s.c.* **1** (fam.) zurra, paliza. || **2 in/into/from/etc. –,** en un escondrijo/del escondrijo, en la clandestinidad/de la clandestinidad: *to go into hiding = meterse en un escondrijo.*

hiding-place | 'haɪdɪŋpleɪs | *s.c.* escondite, escondrijo, sitio secreto (para cosas o personas).
hierarchical | ˌhaɪə'rɑːkɪkl | *adj.* (form.) jerárquico.
hierarchy | 'haɪərɑːkɪ | *s.c.* (form.) **1** jerarquía, sistema jerárquico, ordenación jerárquica. **2** REL. jerarquía (los cardenales y obispos).
hieroglyph | 'haɪərəglɪf | *s.c.* FILOL. jeroglífico.
hieroplyphic | ˌhaɪərə'glɪfɪk | FILOL. *adj.* **1** jeroglífico. || *s.pl.* **2** sistema jeroglífico de escritura.
hi-fi | 'haɪfaɪ | *s.c.* e *i.* **1** ELECTR. aparato de alta fidelidad, cadena; alta fidelidad. || *adj.* **2** de alta fidelidad.
higgledy-piggledy | ˌhɪgldɪ'pɪgldɪ | *adj.* y *adv.* en total desorden, de cualquier manera, a la buena de Dios (desorden de cosas).
high | haɪ | *adj.* **1** alto, elevado (cosas). **2** de altura, de alto: *the house is seven storeys high = la casa tiene siete pisos de altura.* **3** alto, importante (en una empresa u organización). **4** elevado, grande (aprecio, admiración, etc.); buena (opinión). **5** excelente, de primera (en calidad): *a high standard of manufacturing = un nivel de fabricación de primera.* **6** elevado, agudo, alto (voz o sonido). **7** fuerte, intenso (viento). **8** avanzado, alto: *high finance = altas finanzas.* **8** exuberante, alegre (de ánimo). **9** **[– (on)]** (fam.) drogado, colocado. **10** elevado, alto (principio, ideal o similar). **11** un poco pasado, empezando a estropearse, dudoso (cualquier tipo de comida). **12** en su punto adecuado (sólo la carne). **13** crecido (río, marea, etc.). **14** intenso (aventura, drama, etc.): *moments of high tension = momentos de tensión intensa.* **15** alta (cambio de velocidad en un vehículo). || *adv.* **16** alto, elevado, a lo alto: *you missed because you aimed high = fallaste porque apuntaste alto.* **17** intensamente, con fuerza (del soplar del viento). **18** intensamente, acaloradamente, violentamente (de pasiones o emociones). || *s.c.* **19** punto álgido, punto culminante (cuantitativamente). **20** anticiclón, zona de altas presiones. **21** sentimiento de euforia, momento de euforia. **22** directa, marcha directa (en un vehículo). || **23 to be for the – jump,** (fam.) ser el objeto de una buena regañina, ser candidato a una buena bronca. **24 come hell or – water,** V. **hell. 25 to have a – old time,** (fam.) pasarlo como un enano, pasarlo fantásticamente. **26 -high,** de alto, a la altura de (en compuestos): *the snow was ankle-high = la nieve llegaba a la altura de los tobillos.* **27 – altar,** altar mayor. **28 – and dry,** (fam.) en la estacada, en un apuro. **29 – and low,** por todos los sitios, poniendo patas arriba todo (buscando algo). **30 – and mighty,** (desp. y fam.) en plan mandón, en plan engreído. **31 – church/High Church,** REL. la sección conservadora de la Iglesia Anglicana. **32 – colour,** color subido, color un poco demasiado fuerte (en una persona). **33 – command,** MIL. alto mando. **34 High Commission,** Embajada de otro país de la Commonwealth. **35 High Commissioner,** Embajador de otro país de la Commonwealth. **36 High Court,** DER. TribunalSupremo (en Inglaterra y Gales). **37 – explosive,** QUIM. explosivo de alta potencia. **38 – heels,** tacones altos. **39 – jinks,** (fam.) pipa, guay. **40 – jump,** DEP. salto de altura. **41 – life,** vida de la jet, vida por todo lo alto. **42 High Mass,** REL. misa mayor, misa solemne. **43 – noon,** (lit.) mediodía. **44 – point,** momento supremo, momento crucial (de un período de tiempo). **45 – school,** (EE.UU.) escuela secundaria, instituto de enseñanza media; (brit.) escuela secundaria (especialmente femenina). **46 – season,** temporada alta. **47 – spot,** punto crucial, sitio crucial, acontecimiento más llamativo (de un recorrido, excursión o similar). **48 – street,** calle mayor. **49 – summer,** mitad del verano. **50 – tea,** merienda (no como la española exactamente). **51 – tide,** marea alta, pleamar. **52 – treason,** alta tensión. **53 – water,** punto más alto del agua (en un río, lago, etc.). **54 in – dudgeon,** V. **dudgeon. 55 it is – time (that),** ya es hora (de que). **56 on –, a)** REL. de lo alto, del cielo. **b)** (fig. y hum.) de arriba, de los mandamases. **57 on the – seas,** V. **sea. 58 to – heaven,** V. **heaven.**
highborn | 'haɪbɔːn | *adj.* de alta cuna, de cuna noble.
highbrow | 'haɪbraʊ | (a veces desp.) *adj.* **1** pedante, sofisticado. || *s.c.* **2** intelectual, intelectualoide, pedante.
high-chair | ˌhaɪ'tʃeər | *s.c.* silla alta, silla para bebé.
high-class | ˌhaɪ'klɑːs | *adj.* de clase alta, de clase superior.
higher | 'haɪər | *adj.comp.* **1** de **high.** _ *adj.* **2** superior (cursillo, estudios, examen, etc.). **3** BIOL. superior (forma de vida). || **4 – education,** educación superior.
highfalutin | ˌhaɪfə'luːtn | *adj.* (fam.) presuntuoso; chuleta.
high-fidelity | ˌhaɪfɪ'delɪtɪ | *adj.* ELECTR. de alta fidelidad.
high-flown | ˌhaɪ'fləʊn | *adj.* (desp.) exagerado, pomposo, altisonante (lenguaje).
high-flyer | ˌhaɪ'flaɪər | (también **high-flier**) *s.c.* persona ambiciosa, persona deseosa de triunfar.
high-flying | ˌhaɪ'flaɪɪŋ | *adj.* ambicioso, deseoso de triunfar.
high-handed | ˌhaɪ'hændɪd | *adj.* (desp.) arbitrario; despótico.
high-handedly | ˌhaɪ'hændɪdlɪ | *adv.* (desp.) arbitrariamente; despóticamente.
high-handedness | ˌhaɪ'handɪdnɪs | *s.i.* (desp.) arbitrariedad; despotismo.
high-heeled | ˌhaɪ'hiːld | *adj.* de tacones altos.
highlands | 'haɪləndz | *s.pl.* tierras altas, zonas altas.
highlight | 'haɪlaɪt | *v.t.* **1** subrayar, destacar. **2** resaltar (escrito). || *s.c.* **3** momento más importante, momento crucial, momento culminante: *Tom Jones was the highlight of the evening = Tom Jones fue el momento culminante de la noche.* **4** FOT. realce de luz. || *s.pl.* **5** reflejos (en el pelo).
highly | 'haɪlɪ | *adv.* **1** altamente, elevadamente, en alto grado (situado, educado, etc.). **2** bien, favorablemente (hablar, pensar, etc.). **3** altamente, muy (como enfático): *highly interesting = muy interesante.*
highly-strung | ˌhaɪlɪ'strʌŋ | *adj.* muy nervioso.
high-minded | ˌhaɪ'maɪndɪd | *adj.* noble, magnánimo, altruista.
high-mindedly | ˌhaɪ'maɪndɪdlɪ | *adv.* noblemente, magnánimamente, de forma altruista.
high-mindedness | ˌhaɪ'maɪndɪdnɪs | *s.i.* nobleza, magnanimidad, altruismo.
Highness | 'haɪnɪs | **Your/His –,** su alteza (para miembros de la familia real menos el rey y la reina).
high-pitched | ˌhaɪ'pɪtʃt | *adj.* chillona, aguda, estridente (voz).
high-powered | ˌhaɪ'paʊəd | *adj.* **1** de gran potencia (maquinaria). **2** de nivel superior, de exigencia superior (actividad profesional especialmente). **3** dinámico, agresivo (persona)
high-rise | 'haɪraɪz | *adj.* de gran altura, gigante (edificio).
highroad | 'haɪrəʊd | *s.c.* **1** carretera principal. **2** **[– to]** camino más rápido a, camino más fácil a, camino mejor a: *the highroad to success is work = el camino más rápido al éxito es el trabajo.*
high-sounding | 'haɪsaʊndɪŋ | *adj.* (a veces desp.) rimbombante, grandioso (lenguaje).
high-spirited | ˌhaɪ'spɪrɪtɪd | *adj.* **1** brioso (caballo). **2** animoso, alegre (alguien).
high-technology | ˌhaɪtək'nɒlədʒɪ | *s.i.* alta tecnología, tecnología avanzada.
high-tension | ˌhaɪ'tenʃn | *adj.* ELEC. de alta tensión (cable).
high-up | 'haɪʌp | *s.c.* (fam.) alto personaje, mandamás, pez gordo.
high-water mark | ˌhaɪ'wɔːtəmɑːk | *s.c.* **1** nivel máximo (de un río o del mar). **2** momento más decisorio, momento más importante, estadio más esencial (de un proceso): *one of the high-water marks of our history was the "Reconquista" = uno de los momentos más decisorios de nuestra historia fue el de la Reconquista.*
highway | 'haɪweɪ | *s.c.* **1** (EE.UU.) carretera principal, autopista. **2** (fig.) camino más directo; método más directo (de lograr algo). || **3 Highway Code,** DER. Código de la Circulación.
highwayman | 'haɪweɪmən | [*pl.irreg.* **highwaymen**] *s.c.* HIST. salteador de caminos, bandido.
highwaymen | 'haɪweɪmən | *pl.irreg.* de **highwayman.**

high-wire | ˌhaɪ'waɪə | *s.c.* cuerda, cuerda floja (de funambulistas).

hijack | 'haɪdʒæk | *v.t.* secuestrar (especialmente un avión).

hijacker | 'haɪdʒækər | *s.c.* secuestrador, pirata aéreo.

hijacking | 'haɪdʒækɪŋ | *s.c.* e *i.* secuestro, secuestro aéreo.

hike | haɪk | *s.c.* **1** paseo largo, caminata (por algún paraje natural). **2**(fam.) subida, incremento (de dinero osimilar). || *v.i.* **3** dar largos paseos,dar largas caminatas (por parajes naturales). || **4 to – up,** subirse, tirarsehacia arriba de (calcetines, pantalones,etc.).

hiker | 'haɪkər | *s.c.* paseante, excursionista (por el campo).

hiking | 'haɪkɪŋ | *s.i.* excursionismo (a pie).

hilarious | hɪ'leərɪəs | *adj.* divertidísimo, regocijante.

hilariously | hɪ'leərɪəslɪ | *adv.* divertidísimamente, regocijantemente.

hilarity | hɪ'lærətɪ | *s.i.* regocijo, diversión impresionante.

hill | hɪl | *s.c.* **1** colina, cerro, altozano. || **2 as old as the hills,** más viejo que Matusalén.

hillbilly | 'hɪlbɪlɪ | *s.c.* paleto, habitante rural (del sureste de América).

hillock | 'hɪlək | *s.c.* otero, cerro pequeño.

hillside | 'hɪlsaɪd | *s.c.* ladera (de una colina).

hilltop | 'hɪltɒp | *s.c.* cumbre (de una colina).

hilly | 'hɪlɪ | *adj.* lleno de colinas, con fuertes cuestas, de montañas bajas.

hilt | hɪlt | *s.c.* **1** puño, empuñadura (de espada, cuchillo, etc.). || **2 (up) to the –,** (fam.) incondicionalmente, totalmente, desde el principio hasta el final (apoyo).

him | hɪm | (pronunciación relajada | həm |) *pron.o.* a él, le: *Jim! I hafe him = ¡Jim! le odio.*

himself | hɪm'self| *pron.r.* **1** él mismo, se: *my son hurt himself = mi hijo se hizo daño.* **2** él sólo, él sin ayuda de nadie. **3** mismo, mismito (como énfasis).

hind | haɪnd | *adj.* **1** trasera (pata de un animal). || *s.c.* [*pl.* **hind** o **hinds**]. **2** ZOOL. cierva. || **3 to talk the – legs off a donkey,** V. **donkey.**

hinder | 'haɪndər | *adj.* **1** trasera, posterior, de atrás (pata de un animal). || | 'hɪndə*v.t.* **2** dificultar, estorbar, impedir (el movimiento, el avance en la vida, el progreso, etc.).

Hindi | 'hɪndiː | *s.i.* hindú (idioma).

hindquarters | ˌhaɪnd'kwɔːtəz | *s.pl.* cuartos traseros (de un animal).

hindrance | 'hɪndrəns | *s.c.* e *i.* **[– (to)]** obstáculo, estorbo, dificultad: *you shouldn't be a hindrance to your dad's career = no deberías ser un obstáculo para la carrera de tu padre.*

hindsight | 'haɪndsaɪt | *s.i.* retrospectiva, visión retrospectiva.

Hindu | ˌhɪn'duː | (EE.UU.) | 'hɪnduː*s.c.* **1** hindú. || *adj.* **2** hindú.

Hinduism | 'hɪnduːɪzəm | *s.i.* REL. hinduismo.

Hindustani | ˌhɪndʊ'stænɪ | *s.i.* indostani (grupo de lenguas del norte de India).

hinge | hɪndʒ | *s.c.* **1** gozne, bisagra. || **2 to – on/upon,** depender de, girar sobre: *the whole plan hinged on James = todo el plan giraba sobre James.*

hinged | hɪndʒt | *adj.* con bisagra, con gozne (objeto).

hint | hɪnt | *v.i.* **1 [to – (at)]** insinuar, lanzar una indirecta, hacer alusión a. || *s.c.* **2** alusión, indirecta, insinuación. **3** sugerencia, consejo (normalmente sobre algo concreto). **4 [– of]** señal de, indicio de; posibilidad de: *there was no hint of anger in his voice = no había indicio de cólera en su voz.* _ **5 to drop a –,** soltar una indirecta, dejar caer una insinuación. **6 to take a –,** darse por aludido, darse cuenta de la indirecta (dirigida a uno).

hinterland | 'hɪntəlænd | *s.c.* interior (del país).

hip | hɪp | *s.c.* **1** ANAT. cadera (hueso o parte del cuerpo). **2** BOT. escaramujo. || *adj.* **3** (fam.) al día, moderno (ropa, ideas, etc.).

hip-bath | 'hɪpbɑːθ | *s.c.* baño de asiento (el agua sólo llega a la cintura).

hip-flask | 'hɪpflɑːsk | *s.c.* botellín de bolsillo.

hippie | 'hɪpɪ | (también **hippy**) *s.c.* hippy.

hippo | 'hɪpəʊ | *s.c.* (fam.) hipopótamo.

Hippocratic oath | ˌhɪpəkrætɪk'əʊθ | *s.c.* MED. juramento hipocrático.

hippopotamus | ˌhɪpə'pɒtəməs | [*pl.* **hippopotamuses** o **hippopotami**] *s.c.* ZOOL. hipopótamo.

hippopotami | ˌhɪpə'pɒtəmaɪ | *pl.irreg.* de **hippopotamus.**

hippy V. hippie.

hire | 'haɪər | *v.t.* **1** alquilar, contratar los servicios de (cosas o personas). || *s.i.* **2** alquiler, contratación temporal. || **3 for –,** en alquiler, se alquila (casa, oficina, etc.); libre (taxi). **4 to – out,** contratar en alquiler, alquilar (a alguien): *I hired out my boat to a Canadian = alquilé mi barca a un canadiense.*

hireling | 'haɪəlɪŋ | *s.c.* (desp.) mercenario (que se vende al mejor postor).

hire-purchase | ˌhaɪə'pɜːtʃəs | *s.i.* COM. compra a plazos.

hirsute | 'hɜːsjuːt | *adj.* (form. o lit.) hirsuto.

his | hɪz | *adj.pos.* **1** su (de él): *James has hir car outside = James tiene su coche fuera.* _ *pron.pos.* **2** suyo (de él).

Hispanic | hɪ'spænɪk | *adj.* español, de España; hispanoamericano.

hiss | hɪs | *v.i.* **1** sisear, silbar, hacer un ruido siseante. **2** soltar entre dientes (con ira). || *v.t.* e *i.* **3** abuchear (discurso, actuación, etc.). || *s.c.* **4** siseo, ruido siseante.

histamine | 'hɪstəmiːn | *s.i.* QUIM. histamina.

historian | hɪ'stɔːrɪən | *s.c.* historiador.

historic | hɪ'stɒrɪk | (EE.UU.) | hɪ'stɔːrɪk | *adj.* histórico (especialmente con acontecimientos o personas de gran importancia o trascendencia).

historical | hɪ'stɒrɪkl | (EE.UU.) | hɪ'stɔːrɪkl*adj.* histórico.

historically | hɪ'stɒrɪklɪ | (EE.UU.) | hɪ'stɔːrɪklɪ | *adv.* históricamente.

history | hɪstrɪ | *s.i.* **1** historia (especialidad de estudio). **2** (fig.) agua pasada, historia (que ya no tiene importancia para el presente). || *s.c.* **3** historia (concreta). **4** historia, historial (médico, disciplinario, etc.). **5 [– of]** pasado lleno de, historial de: *he has a history of heart disease = tiene un historial de problemas de corazón.* _ **6 to go down in –,** pasar a la historia. **7 to make –,** dejar marca en la historia, dejar huella en la historia; crear un precedente.

histrionic | ˌhɪstrɪ'ɒnɪk | *adj.* **1** histriónico; melodramático. **2** (form.) dramático, teatral. || *s.pl.* **3** comportamiento histriónico, comportamiento melodramático.

histrionically | ˌhɪstrɪ'ɒnɪklɪ | *adv.* de manera histriónica, de modo melodramático.

hit | hɪt | *v.* [*ger.* **hitting,** *pret.* y *p.p.irreg.* **hit**] *t.* **1** pegar, golpear, dar (con intención de hacer daño). **2** golpear, pegar, dar (con intención de hacer daño). **2** golpear, pegar, dar (normalmente con un vehículo de manera accidental). **3** (fam.) llegar a, alcanzar: *when you hit the road turn left = cuando llegues a la carretera gira a la izquierda.* **4** DEP. golpear (la pelota con algún instrumento en muchos deportes). **5** venir a la mente, pasar por la cabeza: *the thought hit me suddenly = el pensamiento me vino a la mente de repente.* **6** llegar a, alcanzar (una cantidad): *the jackpot hit 40.000 pounds = el bote llegó a 40.000 libras.* **7** azotar, afectar gravemente (fenómeno meteorológico, catástrofe económica, desgracia familiar, etc.). **8** estallar contra, dar (bomba). || *i.* **9** golpear con fuerza (una desgracia, catástrofe o similar). **10** DEP. golpear (la pelota). **11** estallar (bomba). || *s.c.* **12** éxito (película, libro, canción, etc.). **13 [– (at)]** indirecta (llena de veneno). **14** golpe (violento). **15** impacto directo (bomba o similar). **16** DEP. golpe, acierto (en el balón). || **7 to – a man when he's down,** (fam.) pegar fuerte al que está en una situación débil, hacer leña del árbol caído. **18 to – back (at),** devolver el golpe (contra) (física o figurativamente). **19 to – home,** acertar, dar en el blanco (con lo que uno dice). **20 to – it off (with),** hacer buenas migas (con). **21 – list,** lista de los que van a ser asesinados (por terroristas, gángsters, etc.). **22 – man,** pistolero, asesino a sueldo. **23 to – on/upon,** dar con (una idea). **24 to – out (at), a)** lanzar un golpe (a), intentar pegar (a); **b)** (fig.) atacar virulentamente (a), lanzar una crítica feroz (contra). **25 – parade,** lista de éxitos musicales. **26**

to – someone for six, dejar a alguien lelo, dejar a alguien estupefacto. **27 to – the bottle,** (fam.) darse a la bebida. **28 – the headlines,** llegar a los grandes titulares de los periódicos. **29 to – the nail on the head,** dar en el clavo; acertar con la frase adecuada. **30 to – the road,** (fam.) ponerse en camino. **31 to – the roof/ceiling,** (fam.) ponerse malo, cogerse un cabreo del demonio. **32 to – the sack/hay,** (fam.) irse a acostar, irse a la cama. **33 to make a – (with),** causar una profunda impresión (en) (una persona).

hit-and-miss | ˌhɪtn'mɪs | (también **hit-or-miss**) *adj.* al azar, a lo que salga, a la buena de Dios.

hit-and-run | ˌhɪtn'rʌn | *adj.* de los que causan un accidente y no se paran a ayudar: *a hit-and-run driver.*

hitch | hɪtʃ | *v.t.* **1** atar, enganchar (especialmente caballos a carros). || *v.t.* e *i.* **2** (fam.) hacer autostop; conseguir, ser llevados en (un viaje gratis): *we hitched a ride from London to Oxford = hicimos autostop desde Londres a Oxford.* _ *s.c.* **3** dificultad, problema. **4** tirón, empujón (físico). || **5 to get hitched,** (fam.) atarse la soga al cuello (casarse). **6 to – up,** arremangar, levantar, alzar (especialmente una prenda de vestir).

hitchhike | 'hɪtʃhaɪk | *v.i.* hacer autostop, viajar en autostop.

hitchhiker | 'hɪtʃhaɪkər | *s.c.* autostopista.

hi tech | ˌhaɪ'tek | *adj.* modernísimo, ultimísimo; de avanzada tecnología.

hither | 'hɪðər | *(lit. o p.u.) adv.* **1** aquí, acá. || **2 – and thither,** de aquí para allá, por todos los sitios.

hitherto | ˌhɪðə'tuː | *adv.* (form.) hasta ahora, anteriormente.

hit-or-miss | ˌhɪtɔː'mɪs | V. **hit-and-miss.**

hive | haɪv | *s.c.* **1** BIOL. colmena (de abejas). **2 [– of]** hervidero de: *my office is a hive of activity in the mornings = mi oficina es un hervidero de actividad durante la mañana.* _ **3 to – off,** FIN. vender una buena parte de un negocio por separado (especialmente en los casos de privatización de empresas públicas). **4 hives,** MED. urticaria.

ho | həʊ | *interj.* **1** (p.u.) eh (atrayendo la atención). || **2 –!,** ¡jo, jo! (imitando risa).

hoard | hɔːd | *v.t.* **1** amontonar, acaparar, acumular. || *s.c.* **2 [– (of)]** tesoro secreto; acumulación.

hoarding | 'hɔːdɪŋ | *s.c.* valla publicitaria, cartel gigante publicitario.

hoarse | hɔːs | *adj.* ronco (en la voz).

hoarsely | 'hɔːslɪ | *adv.* roncamente, con carraspera.

hoarseness | 'hɔːsnɪs | *s.i.* ronquera, carraspera fuerte.

hoariness | 'hɔːrɪnɪs | *s.i.* **1** canosidad (del pelo). **2** antigüedad.

hoary | 'hɔːrɪ | *adj.* **1** (lit.) plateado (el pelo por la edad). **2** antiquísimo, viejísimo.

hoax | həʊks | *s.c.* **1** burla, engaño; (fig.) cuento. || *v.t.* **2** burlarse de, engañar.

hob | hɒb | *s.c.* quemador (de una cocina).

hobble | 'hɒbl | *v.i.* **1** andar con dificultad, caminar como cojeando. || *v.t.* **2** manear (caballo); poner cadenas (a una persona, para que pueda dar pasos cortos solamente).

hobby | 'hɒbɪ | *s.c.* pasatiempo, entretenimiento, hobby.

hobby-horse | 'hɒbɪhɔːs | *s.c.* **1** caballo de juguete. **2** caballo de batalla, tema preferido (de conversación, discusión, etc.).

hobnail | 'hɒbneɪl | (también **hobnailed**) *s.c.* clavo, de clavo (botas).

hobnob | 'hɒbnɒb | *v.i.* **[to – with]** (fam.) codearse con, alternar con.

hobo | 'həʊbəʊ | [*pl.* **hobos** o **hoboes**] *s.c.* **1** vagabundo. **2** temporero, trabajador temporero.

Hobson's choice | ˌhɒbsnz'tʃɔɪs | *s.sing.* elección forzosa, situación de lo tomas o lo dejas; falsa elección (porque sólo existe una posibilidad real, aunque parezca que hay más).

hock | hɒk | *s.i.* **1** vino blanco alemán. **2** empeño (acción de empeñar objetos). || *s.c.* **3** ANAT. corvejón (de animales). || *v.t.* **4** (fam.) empeñar. || **5 in –,** (fam.) **a)** en la cárcel, en chirona; **b)** endeudado, con deudas; **c)** empeñado.

hockey | 'hɒkɪ | *s.i.* DEP. hockey.

hocus-pocus | ˌhəukəs'pəukəs | *s.i.* (desp.) treta de distracción, truco, verbal.

hod | hɒd | *s.c.* capacho (para ladrillos).

hodge-podge | ˌhɒdʒ'pɒdʒ | *s.sing. [– (of)]* (EE.UU.) mezcolanza.

hoe | həʊ | *s.c.* **1** azada, azadón. || *v.t.* e *i.* **2** remover el suelo con azada, azadonar.

hog | hɒg | (EE.UU.) | hɔːg | *s.c.* **1** ZOOL. cerdo capado; (Am.) chancho. **2** (fam.) puerco, cerdo, guarro (persona). || [*ger.* **hogging,** *pret.* y *p.p.* **hogged**] *v.t.* **3** acaparar, coger lo mejor de (cualquier cosa). || **4 to go the whole –,** (fam.) liarse la manta a la cabeza (en gastos, decisiones, etc.).

hogwash | hɒgwɑʃ | *s.i.* (fam.) estupideces, bazofia, chorradas (definiendo algo que alguien ha dicho).

hoi polloi | ˌhɔɪpə'lɔɪ | *s.pl.* **[the –]** (desp.) el vulgo, las masas.

hoist | hɔɪst | *v.t.* **1** enarbolar (bandera); izar (velas). **2** elevar, alzar (mediante grúa o aparato similar). **3** subir, elevar (utilizando las manos): *I hoisted the box onto the shelf = subí la caja a la estantería.* _ *s.c.* **4** montacargas, grúa, cabria. || **5 to – with one's own petard,** V. **petard.**

hoity-toity | ˌhɔɪtɪ'tɔɪtɪ | *adj.* (fam. y desp.) presumido, engreído, repipi.

hold | həʊld | *v.* [*pret.* y *p.p.irreg.* **held**] *t.* **1** sujetar, sostener, agarrar (en la mano). **2** abrazar, coger en los brazos. **3** agarrar, mantener inmóvil, inmovilizar. **4** detener, retener (prisionero). **5** coger, sujetar (una parte del cuerpo): *she held his head in her arms = cogió su cabeza en sus manos.* **6** mantener (una parte del cuerpo en una posición). **7** mantener, tener (una opinión, creencia, etc.). **8** aguantar, soportar (un peso notable). **9** contener, tener capacidad para (una cantidad). **10** defender (contra ataque militar o político). **11** mantener abierta (la comunicación telefónica). **12** considerar (culpable, responsable, etc.). **13** mantener (la atención o interés de alguien). **14** tener, retener (una posición, récord, etc.). **15** retener, retrasar (cualquier acontecimiento en el tiempo). **16** reservar, guardar (sitio, billete, etc.). **17** tener, tener la propiedad de. **18** saber aguantar (bebida alcohólica): *he holds his liquor impressively = él sabe aguantar la bebida de manera impresionante.* **19** coger (mensajes telefónicos). || *i.* **20 [to – on to/to]** sujetar, sostener, agarrar. **21 [to – to]** tener, mantener (opinión, creencia, etc.). **22** mantenerse pegado, mantenerse fijo, mantenerse sujeto. **23** durar, mantenerse agradable (tiempo): *we are lucky, so far the weather has held = tenemos suerte, hasta ahora el tiempo se ha mantenido bien.* **24** durar, mantenerse (la suerte). **25** estar en pie, seguir en pie (invitación u oferta). **26** sostenerse (un argumento, raciocinio, teoría, etc.). **27** valer, estar en vigencia (leyes o similar). **28** estar a la espera (en una llamada telefónica). || *s.c.* **29** apoyo, punto de apoyo (físico). **30** DEP. llave (en lucha libre). **31** compartimento de carga, bodega (en barco o avión). || *s.i.* **32** capacidad de agarrarse (ruedas): *because of the rain the tyres didn't have much hold on the old cobblestones = a causa de la lluvia los neumáticos no tenían mucha capacidad de agarrarse a las viejas piedras de la carretera.* _ *s.sing.* **33** asimiento, acción de agarrar, acción de sostener; manera de agarrar. **34 [– on/over]** poder sobre, control sobre, influencia sobre (otras personas). **35 [– over]** poder sobre, dominio sobre (porque se sabe algo que la otra persona quiere mantener secreto). || **36 to be held hostage,** V. **hostage. 37 to get/grab/take/seize – (of), a)** agarrar, sujetar (fuertemente); **b)** controlar, hacerse con el control (de). **38 to get – of, a)** conseguir, hacerse con (algo); **b)** descubrir (una información que se quería mantener secreta); **c)** contactar con (una persona); **d)** sacar (una impresión, idea, etc. que no es verdad); **e)** captar, entender. **39 to – against,** guardar en contra de, tener en cuenta: *I will hold your insults against you for ever = yo siempre tendré en cuenta tus insultos.* **40 to – back, a)** retener, retrasar: *I'm busy, don't hold me back = estoy ocupado, no me retengas;* **b)** reprimir (lágrimas o risa); **c)** mantener bajo control (precios, multitudes, etc.); **d)** mantener secreto, mantener reservado (secreto, información, etc.); **e)** mantener en reserva (algo). **41 to – court,** V. **court. 42 to – down, a)** controlar, sujetar (físicamente a alguien); **b)** mantener (un puesto de

trabajo); **c)** mantener reducido, mantener bajo (sueldos, precios, etc.). **43 – everything,** alto todo el mundo. **44 to – fast,** V. **fast. 45 to – forth,** hablar largo y tendido, disertar. **46 to – in,** reprimir, contener (emociones). **47 – it,** para, un momento. **48 to – off, a)** mantener a distancia, mantener alejado; **b)** no empezar a llover; **c)** retrasar (decisión). **49 to – on, a)** continuar con esfuerzo, aguantar con fuerza; b) esperar: *hold on a minute = espera un minuto.* **50 to – one's breath,** V. **breath. 51 to – one's ground,** V. **ground. 52 to – one's own,** mantenerse firme, mantenerse en su terreno. **53 to – one's peace,** V. **peace. 54 to – one's tongue,** V. **tongue. 55 to – on (to), a)** agarrar, sujetarse (a); **b)** no soltar (algo); **c)** guardar, quedarse (con); **d)** (fam.) guardar transitoriamente (algo de otra persona); **e)** mantener (las ideas, creencias, etc.). **56 to – out, a)** extender la mano (para coger algo o saludar); **b)** resistir, aguantar (una situación difícil); **c)** mantener (la esperanza o similar). **57 to – out (for),** exigir, no ceder en la exigencia (de) (derechos). **58 to – (out) hope,** V. **hope. 59 to – out (on),** (fam.) negarse a dar información (a). **60 to – over, a)** retrasar, dejar para más tarde, aplazar (asunto); **b)** dejar más tiempo en cartel (película o parecido). **61 to – someone to ransom,** V. **ransom. 62 to – something at bay,** V. **bay. 63 to – something in check,** V. **check. 64 to – still/steady,** mantenerse inmóvil, no moverse, quedarse quieto. **65 to – sway,** V. **sway. 66 to – the door (open) (for),** abrir la puerta (a) (alguien). **67 to – the fort,** V. **fort. 68 to – the road,** agarrarse bien al firme, agarrarse bien a la carretera (vehículo). **69 to – tight,** agarrarse fuerte, sujetarse con fuerza (intentando evitar caerse). **70 to – together, a)** aguantar, durar (un objeto): *I'm not sure if the car will hold together = no estoy seguro si el coche aguantará;* **b)** mantener cohesionado (un grupo o colectivo). **71 to – up, a)** levantar, elevar, alzar (una extremidad, objeto, etc.); **b)** soportar el peso de, mantener erguido (algo); **c)** detener, retrasar, atrasar; **d)** atracar, asaltar (para robar); **e)** presentar como modelo, ofrecer como modelo (conducta); **f)** mantener fuerza, mantener vigencia, ser válido (ideas, teorías, creencias, etc.); **g)** (fam.) aguantar, soportar (algún objeto un duro tratamiento): *these shoes held up very well = estos zapatos aguantaron muy bien.* **72 to – with,** aprobar, estar de acuerdo con, estar a favor de (cualquier actividad). **73 not to – a candle to someone,** V. **candle. 74 no holds barred,** V. **bar. 75 there's no holding someone,** no hay manera de pararle, no hay forma humana de que alguien deje (una actividad).
OBS. Este verbo tiene muy distintas traducciones que no se pueden abarcar en su totalidad. **76** según el sustantivo que le siga, adquiere un matiz acorde con el significado de ese sustantivo: *to hold a meeting = celebrar una reunión; to hold the power = tener el poder; to hold a university degree = estar en poder de un título universitario; the future holds countless promises = el futuro alberga promesas sin cuento.*

holdall | 'həuldɔːl | *s.c.* bolsa de viaje; neceser.

holder | 'həuldər | *s.c.* **1** persona que tiene (una opinión, creencia, teoría, etc.). **2** persona que lleva, persona que tiene; poseedor (de un objeto como pasaporte, billete, acción de bolsa, etc.). **3** boquilla (para cigarrillos). **4** soporte, agarradera, base (donde encaja otro objeto): *a lamp holder; a pen holder.*

holding | həuldɪŋ | *s.c.* **1** posesión de fincas, posesión de terreno; porcentaje de tierras (en propiedad o arrendamiento). **2** participación (en un negocio o empresa). **3** colección (de libros, cuadros, etc.). || *adj.* **4** de contención, controlador (de una situación de cierto peligro). || **5 – company,** FIN. holding de empresas.

hold-up | 'həuldʌp | *s.c.* **1** atasco (de tráfico, de trabajo, etc.). **2** atraco, robo.

hole | həul | *s.c.* **1** agujero, hoyo, boquete. **2** rotura, agujero, roto (como defecto). **3** agujero, madriguera (para animales). **4** (fig.) agujero, defecto, fallo (en una ley, plan, proyecto, etc.). **5** DEP. hoyo (sección o excavación en la tierra del golf). **6** (fam.) cuchitril, sitio de mala muerte (vivienda, oficina, etc.). **7** (fam.) apuro, aprieto, dificultad. || *v.t.* **8** hacer un agujero en (normalmente con disparos). || *v.t.* e *i.* **9** DEP. meter en el agujero, embocar (en golf). || **10 a – in one,** DEP. un acierto de un solo golpe (golf). **11 to – out,** DEP. acabar todos los hoyos, finalizar el recorrido (golf). **12 to – up,** (fam.) esconderse, refugiarse (para trabajar tranquilo o para huir de alguien). **13 in holes,** lleno de agujeros, lleno de rotos. **14 to make a – in,** (fam.) reducir gravemente, dejar temblando (sueldo, ahorros, etc.). **15 to pick holes in,** (fam.) encontrar fallos en, encontrar defectos en (una teoría, argumento, idea, etc.).

holiday | 'hɒlədeɪ | *s.c.* **1** vacaciones, vacación. || *s.c.* e *i.* **2** fiesta, descanso, vacación: *tomorrow is a holiday = mañana es fiesta.* _ *v.i.* **3** ir de vacaciones, estar de vacaciones. || **4 – camp,** colonia veraniega, centro veraniego (lugar especial con todo tipo de servicios para veraneantes). **5 on –/on holidays,** de vacaciones.

holidaymaker | 'hɒlədeɪmeɪkər | *s.c.* veraneante; turista.

holiness | 'həulɪnɪs | REL. *s.i.* **1** santidad. || **2 Your/His Holiness,** Su Santidad (forma de dirigirse o hablar del Papa).

Holland | 'hɒlənd | *s.sing.* Holanda.

holler | 'hɒlər | (fam.) *v.i.* **1** pegar gritos, lanzar chillidos, berrear. || *s.c.* **2** grito, chillido, berrido.

hollow | 'hɒləu | *adj.* **1** hueco: *a hollow wall = una pared hueca.* **2** hueco, cóncavo, ahuecado, hundido (cualquier superficie): *hollow eyes = ojos hundidos.* **3** hueco, vacío, pobre (idea, teoría, etc.). **4** hueco, sordo (sonido). **5** sepulcral, cavernosa (voz). **6** falsa (risa o similar). || *s.c.* **7** hueco, agujero: *a hollow in the tree-trunk = un agujero en el tronco de un árbol.* **8** cavidad, hondonada (del terreno). || *v.t.* **9** hacer un hueco en. **10** hundir ligeramente (una superficie). || **11 to beat someone –,** DEP. ganar a alguien con toda facilidad, dar a alguien una paliza de campeonato. **12 to have – legs,** (hum. y brit.) tener la tripa rota, comer como un hambriento. **13 to – out, a)** excavar un agujero en, hacer un agujero en; **b)** hundir (una superficie). **14 the – of one's hand,** el hueco de la mano de uno.

hollowly | 'hɒləulɪ | *adv.* **1** huecamente, sordamente (sonido). **2** falsamente (reír).

hollowness | 'hɒləunɪs | *s.i.* vaciedad, falsedad (de ideas, opiniones, etc.).

holly | 'hɒlɪ | *s.i.* BOT. acebo.

holocaust | 'hɒləkɔːst | *s.c.* e *i.* holocausto, desastre terrible.

hologram | 'hɒləgræm | *s.c.* FOT. holograma.

holograph | 'hɒləgrɑːf | (EE.UU.) | 'hɒləgræf*s.c.* (form.) escrito a mano, manuscrito.

hols | hɒlz | *s.pl.* **[the –]** (brit. y fam.) las vacaciones.

holster | 'həulstər | *s.c.* funda de pistola, pistolera.

holy | 'həulɪ | *adj.* **1** REL. santo, sagrado. || **2 holier than thou,** (desp.) santurrón, meapilas; farisaico. **3 Holy Communion,** REL. Sagrada Comunión. **4 – of holies,** (fam. y fig.) sanctasanctórum (despacho, oficina, etc. de una persona importante). **5 – water,** REL. agua bendita. **6 Holy Week,** REL. Semana Santa. **7 Holy Writ,** (p.u.) REL. Escritura Santa. **8 the Holy City,** Jerusalén. **9 the Holy Father,** REL. el Papa. **10 the Holy Ghost/Spirit,** REL. el Espíritu Santo. **11 the Holy Land,** Tierra Santa. **12 the Holy See,** REL. el Vaticano, la Santa Sede.

homage | 'hɒmɪdʒ | *s.i.* **1 [– (to)]** homenaje. || **2 to pay/do – (to),** rendir homenaje (a).

home | həum | *s.c.* e *i.* **1** hogar, casa. **2** patria; patria chica (nación o región de donde uno procede): *in summer I'm going home = en verano me iré a mi país.* _ *s.c.* **3** asilo, casa cuna (para personas o niños sin hogar). **4** (fam.) sitio (donde guardar algo). || *s.i.* **5** DEP. base, meta, casa (en algunos juegos y deportes). || *adj.* **6** donde nací, de nacimiento, natal: *my home town = mi ciudad natal.* **7** DEP. en casa (partido). **8** regional; nacional (según el contexto o enfoque): *our home market is not big enough = nuestro mercado nacional no es lo suficientemente grande.* **9** de casa, doméstico, en casa; artesanal (algunos productos naturales): *home-made bread = pan* *artesanal; home help = ayuda doméstica.* _ *s.sing.* **10** (fig.) cuna, lugar de origen: *Spain is the home of guerrilla wars = España es el lugar de origen de la guerra de guerrillas.* _ *adv.* **11** a casa. **12** en el blanco, con acierto: *I drove the point home = yo llevé el tema con acierto.* **13** en su sitio exacto: *I hammered the whole thing home = yo metí todo a martillazos en su sitio exacto.* _ **14 a – from –,** un hogar igual que la casa de uno, un hogar lejos del hogar. **15 at –, a)** en casa; **b)** en el país de uno, en la tierra natal; **c)** como en casa, cómodo, relajado, a gusto: *she's so kind I felt at home in two minutes = ella es tan amable que me sentí como en casa en dos minutos.* **16 at – in,** conocedor de, al tanto de, a gusto en (tema, especialidad, asunto, etc.). **17 to bring something closer to –,** ayudar a darse cuenta cabal de algo, hacer que algo tenga trascendencia (especialmente por primera vez): *the civil war brought the darker side in human nature closer to home for my family = la guerra civil ayudó a mi familia a darse cuenta cabal del lado peor de la naturaleza humana.* **18 to bring something =N to someone,** hacer que alguien se dé cuenta de algo, hacer que algo se haga patente para alguien. **19 – and dry,** (fam.) a salvo, a buen puerto. **20 – economics,** hogar (asignatura). **21 – ground,** DEP. campo propio, campo de casa (en algunos deportes, como el fútbol). **22 – help,** ayuda doméstica (especialmente aquella subvencionada por la Seguridad Social para personas mayores sin recursos o enfermos). **23 to – in (on),** MIL. ir derecho (al), dirigirse directamente (al) (objetivo de la bomba, misil, etc.). **24 – time,** (fam.) hora de irse a casa (utilizado por niños pequeños en la escuela). **25 – town,** ciudad natal. **26 – truth,** las cuarenta; verdades que no gustan (sobre el carácter de uno): *you'd better listen to some home truths now = ahora será mejor que escuches unas cuantas verdades de las que no gustan.* **27 Home Rule,** POL. Gobierno directo, Gobierno local, Gobierno regional, Gobierno autonómico (de una parte del Reino Unido o caso similar). **28 – run, a)** DEP. golpe que permite correr todas las bases de una vez (en béisbol); **b)** (fig.) última sección de un viaje (cuando uno se está acercando a casa). **29 to leave –,** irse de casa (especialmente gente joven). **30 to make one's – somewhere,** hacer el hogar de uno en algún sitio, levantar el hogar de uno en algún sitio. **31 make yourself at –,** ponte cómodo, siéntete como si estuvieras en tu casa. **32 nothing to write – about,** (fam.) nada de extraordinario, nada de particular, nada digno de mencionar. **33 on – ground, a)** en sitios conocidos cercanos a casa, en zona cercana a casa y conocida; **b)** (fig.) en temas de los que uno es experto, en asuntos de los que uno no es ignorante. **34 the Home Guard,** MIL. la milicia local (durante la Segunda Guerra Mundial). **35 the Home Office,** POL. el Ministerio del Interior inglés. **36 the Home Secretary,** POL. el Ministro del Interior inglés. **37 the – straight/stretch, a)** el final, la última parte, el último trecho (antes de llegar a la meta); **b)** el final, lo último, el último esfuerzo, el remate (en cualquier actividad, cuando se está a punto de acabar).

home-brew | ˌhəʊm'bruː | *s.i.* cerveza casera.

homecoming | ˌhəʊmkʌmɪŋ | *s.c.* e *i.* regreso a casa (especialmente después de una larga ausencia).

home-grown | ˌhəʊm'grəʊn | *adj.* de cosecha casera, de cosecha propia; del propio huerto.

homeland | 'həʊmlænd | *s.c.* **1** patria, solar patrio. || *s.pl.* **2** POL. regiones teóricamente independientes de población negra en Suráfrica.

homeless | 'həʊmlɪs | *adj.* **1** sin hogar, sin techo, sin casa. || **2 the –,** los que están sin hogar, los que están sin techo.

homelessness | 'həʊmlɪsnɪs | *s.i.* situación de estar sin casa, problema de no tener techo: *homelessness is a problem nowadays = la situación de estar sin un techo es un problema hoy en día.*

homeliness | 'həʊmlɪnɪs | *s.i.* **1** (brit.) sencillez, simplicidad (del carácter). **2** comodidad (de un ambiente). **3** (EE.UU. y desp.) poca atracción (física de una persona).

homely | 'həʊmlɪ | *adj.* **1** (brit.) sencillo, simple, llano. **2** hogareño, familiar; cómodo (ambiente). **3** (EE.UU. y desp.) feúcho, no muy agraciado.

home-made | ˌhəʊm'meɪd | *adj.* casero, hecho en casa; artesanal.

homeopath | 'həʊmɪəpæθ | (también **homoeopath**) *s.c.* MED. homeópata, médico homeópata.

homeopathic | ˌhəʊmɪə'pæθɪk | (también **homoeopathic**) *adj.* MED. homeopático.

homeopathy | ˌhəʊmɪ'ɒpəθɪ | (también **homoeopathy**) *s.i.* MED. homeopatía.

homeowner | ˌhəʊm'əʊnər | *s.c.* propietario, dueño (de una casa).

homesick | 'həʊmsɪk | *adj.* nostálgico, lleno de morriña.

homesickness | 'həʊmsɪknɪs | *s.i.* nostalgia, morriña.

homespun | 'həʊmspʌn | *s.i.* **1** paño casero. || *adj.* **2** sencillo, llano (en opiniones, creencias, virtudes, costumbres, etc.).

homestead | 'həʊmsted | *s.c.* AGR. granja (casa y tierras).

homeward | 'həʊmwəd | *adj.* **1** en dirección a casa. || *adv.* (también **homewards**). **2** de vuelta a casa, de regreso a casa, en dirección a casa.

homeward-bound | 'həʊmwədbaʊnd | *adj.* en dirección a casa.

homework | 'həʊmwɜːk | *s.i.* **1** deberes, tarea (de la escuela). **2** (fig.) preparación, documentación, trabajo preparatorio (especialmente antes de escribir un libro, dar una conferencia, etc.).

homey | 'həʊmɪ | (también **homy**) *adj.* (fam. y EE.UU.) cómodo, como en casa.

homicidal | ˌhɒmɪ'saɪdl | *adj.* homicida; (fig.) salvaje.

homicide | 'hɒmɪsaɪd | *s.c.* e *i.* **1** homicidio. || *s.c.* **2** homicida.

homily | 'hɒmɪlɪ | *s.c.* **1** REL. homilía. **2** (fig. y form.) sermón (normalmente aburrido y para regañar a alguien).

homing | 'həʊmɪŋ | *adj.* **1** MIL. direccional, con sistema de dirección (armas). **2** BIOL. con instinto direccional hacia el nido (algunas aves). || **3 – pigeon,** ZOOL. paloma mensajera.

homoeopath V. **homeopath.**

homoeopathic V. **homeopathic.**

homoeopathy V. **homeopathy.**

homogeneity | ˌhɒmədʒɪ'niːətɪ | *s.i.* homogeneidad.

homogeneous | ˌhɒmə'dʒiːnɪəs | *adj.* homogéneo.

homogenized | hə'mɒdʒənaɪzd | (también **homogenised**) *adj.* homogeneizada (leche).

homonym | 'hɒmənɪm | *s.c.* GRAM. homónimo.

homophone | 'hɒməfəʊn | *s.c.* FON. homófono.

homosexual | ˌhɒmə'sekʃʊəl | *adj.* **1** homosexual. || *s.c.* **2** homosexual.

homosexuality | ˌhɒməsekʃʊ'ælətɪ | *s.i.* homosexualidad.

Honduran | hɒn'djʊərən | *adj.* **1** hondureño. || *s.c.* **2** hondureño.

Honduras | hɒn'djʊərəs | *s.sing.* GEOG. Honduras.

hone | həʊn | *v.t.* **1** afilar (especialmente piedras). **2** (fig.) preparar, capacitar, entrenar (la mente, el cuerpo, un objeto para un propósito, etc.).

honest | 'ɒnɪst | *adj.* **1** honrado, sincero (que no engaña en ningún sentido). **2** franco, sincero, directo (opinión, palabra, etc.). **3** legal. || *adv.* **4** (fam.) de verdad, te lo juro. || **5 to be –,** de verdad, te lo aseguro, te lo juro. **6 – to God/goodness,** (p.u.) vaya por Dios, por el amor de Dios. **7 to make an – woman of,** (p.u. o hum.) ser decente y casarse con (una mujer a la que uno ha dejado embarazada).

honestly | 'ɒnɪstlɪ | *adv.* **1** de verdad, realmente, francamente (expresando énfasis, remachando que uno dice verdad, indicando impaciencia): *I don't understand you, honestly = francamente no te entiendo.* **2** sinceramente, honradamente. **3** francamente, sinceramente, directamente (sin ocultar nada). **4** legalmente: *I can't honestly change this foreign currency = no puedo cambiar legalmente esta moneda extranjera.*

honesty | 'ɒnɪstɪ | *s.i.* **1** honradez. **2** franqueza, sinceridad. **3** legalidad. **4** BOT. lunaria. || **5 in all –,** con toda franqueza, con toda honradez, con toda sinceridad.

honey | 'hʌnɪ | *s.i.* **1** miel (de abejas). || *s.c.* **2** (fam.) encanto, cielo **3** (EE.UU.) cariño, amor, querido.

honeybee | 'hʌnɪbiː | *s.c.* ZOOL. abeja (obrera).

honeycomb | 'hʌnɪkəʊm | *s.c.* e *i.* panal.

honeydew | 'hʌnɪdjuː | *s.i.* **1** BOT. secreción dulce (en algunas plantas). || **2 – melon,** melón dulce.

honeyed | 'hʌnɪd | *adj.* suave, meloso, apaciguante (palabras que calman).

honeymoon | 'hʌnɪmuːn | *s.c.* **1** luna de miel. **2** (fig.) luna de miel, período de gracia (especialmente en política). || *v.i.* **3** ir de luna de miel, viajar de luna de miel.

honeysuckle | 'hʌnɪsʌkl | *s.i.* BOT. madreselva.

honk | hɒŋk | *v.t.* **1** tocar (la bocina de un vehículo). || *v.i.* **2** tocar (la bocina). **3** graznar (especialmente los gansos). || *s.c.* **4** bocinazo. **5** graznido.

honor V. **honour.**

honorable V. **honourable.**

honorary | 'ɒnərərɪ | (EE.UU.) | 'ɒnərerɪ *adj.* honorario: *honorary consul = cónsul honorario.*

honorific | ˌɒnə'rɪfɪk | *adj.* **1** honorífico. || *s.c.* **2** GRAM. formas respetuosas de dirigirse a las personas, fórmulas de respeto.

honour | 'ɒnər | (EE.UU. **honor**) *s.i.* **1** honor, honra. **2** honor, señal de respeto; condecoración honorífica. || *s.sing.* **3 [an – to]** un honor para, una honra para (persona o cosa). **4** honor: *do me the honour of dancing with me = hágame el honor de bailar conmigo.* _ *v.t.* **5** respetar (un acuerdo o similar). **6** honrar, rendir honores a (alguien que se lo merece). **7** respetar, honrar (a una persona): *you should honour your parents = debes honrar a tus padres.* **8** (form.) hacer el honor de: *would you honour me and come to my house for dinner? = ¿me haría Vd. el honor de venir a mi casa a cenar?* _ **9 to do someone –,** honrar a alguien (mediante una buena acción): *what you did does you honour = lo que hiciste te honra.* **10 to do the honours,** hacer los honores (en una fiesta o parecido). **11 to have the – (of)/to be one's – to,** (form.) tener el honor (de), tener el privilegio (de). **12 honours,** matrícula, matrícula de honor (en educación). **13 honours list,** (brit.) lista de condecoraciones reales. **14 in – of,** en honor de. **15 in one's –,** en honor de uno. **16 your –,** señoría (forma de dirigirse a un juez).

honourable | 'ɒnərəbl | (EE.UU. **honorable**) *adj.* **1** digno, honroso (acción, actitud, etc.). **2** honorable (como título de algunos puestos). || **3 – member,** POL. señoría (del Parlamento). **4 – mention,** mención honorífica.

honourably | 'ɒnərəblɪ | *adv.* honorablemente, dignamente.

honoured | 'ɒnəd | *adj.* **1** honrado, reverenciado, respetado. **2** celebrado, homenajeado.

hooch | huːtʃ | *s.i.* (fam.) licor, bebida alcohólica.

hood | hʊd | *s.c.* **1** capucha (de una prenda de vestir). **2** capucha (para tapar la cara). **3** (brit.) capota, toldo (de coche, carrito, etc.). **4** (EE.UU.) capó.

hooded | hʊdɪd | *adj.* **1** con capucha (ropa). **2** de enormes pestañas (ojos).

hoodlum | huːdləm | *s.c.* (fam.) matón, gorila; gángster.

hoodwink | 'hʊdwɪŋk | *v.t.* burlar, engañar, poner una trampa a.

hooey | 'huːɪ | *s.i.* (fam.) bobadas, chorradas, memez.

hoof | huːf | [*pl.* **hoofs** o **hooves**] *s.c.* casco (de equino).

hook | hʊk | *s.c.* **1** gancho, garfio. **2** DEP. gancho (golpe en el boxeo). **3** DEP. golpe desviado a izquierda (en golf y críquet). || *v.t.* **4** enganchar, sujetar con un gancho. **5** pescar (con anzuelo de gancho). **6** (fig. y hum.) pescar (marido o mujer). **7** enganchar (un objeto arqueando un brazo, pie, pierna, etc.). || **8 by – and by crook,** (p.u.) por las buenas o las malas. **9 to get off the –,** escaparse de una buena, librarse de una buena, escapar del atolladero. **10 – and eye,** corchete. **11 to – up,** conectar, enganchar (una computadora u otro aparato a una central). **12 to let/get someone off the –,** sacar a alguien del atolladero, sacar a alguien de un apuro. **13 off the –,** descolgado (teléfono). **14 to sling one's –,** V. **sling.**

hookah | 'hʊkə | *s.c.* narguile, pipa de agua (para marihuana o tabaco).

hooked | hʊkt | *adj.* **1** en forma de gancho, en forma de garfio. **2** corvada, en gancho (nariz). || **3 – on,** (fam.) **a)** loco por, interesadísimo por; **b)** enganchado a (las drogas).

hooker | 'hʊkər | *s.c.* (fam.) puta.

hook-nosed | 'hʊknəʊzd | *adj.* de nariz aguileña, de nariz ganchuda.

hook-up | 'hʊkʌp | *s.c.* ELECTR. enganche (entre material sofisticado, como ordenadores, satélites, etc.).

hooky | 'hʊkɪ | **to play –,** (EE.UU.) hacer novillos.

hooligan | 'huːlɪgən | *s.c.* (desp.) gamberro (especialmente en el fútbol).

hooliganism | 'huːlɪgənɪzəm | *s.i.* (desp.) gamberrismo.

hoop | huːp | *s.c.* **1** aro (especialmente para juegos de niños). **2** arco, aro (en croquet). || **3 to go through the hoops/to put someone through the hoops,** pasar por las horcas caudinas, pasar las de Caín/hacerle a uno pasar mal.

hooped | huːpt | *adj.* en forma de aro.

hoop-la | 'huːplɑː | *s.c.* e *i.* juego de aros.

hooray | hʊ'reɪ | *interj.* hurra.

hoot | huːt | *v.i.* **1** dar un bocinazo. **2** abuchear, armar un griterío. **3** ulular (búho). || *v.t.* **4** dar (bocinazo). || *s.c.* **5** bocinazo. **6** grito ululato (de búho). **7** abucheo, griterío. || **8 to – down,** abuchear, acallar a base de abucheos. **9 to – off,** abuchear, echar a base de abucheos (de un escenario). **10 not to give a –/not to care two hoots,** importar un pepino, importar un pito.

hooter | 'huːtər | *s.c.* **1** bocina. **2** (brit. y fam.) narizotas.

hoover | 'huːvər | *s.c.* **1** aspirador (marca registrada). || *v.t.* e *i.* **2** pasar el aspirador.

hooves | huːvz | *pl.* de **hoof.**

hop | hɒp | [*ger.* **hopping,** *pret.* y *p.p.* **hopped**] *v.i.* **1** dar saltitos, saltar, brincar (personas o animales). **2 [to – *prep.*]** saltar, dar un salto (en distintas direcciones): *I hopped out of bed at 9 = salté de la cama a las 9.* _ *s.c.* **3** saltito, brinco. **4** baile concurrido. **5** (fam.) salto, viaje corto. **6** (normalmente *pl.*) BOT. lúpulo (para hacer cerveza). || **7 to catch someone on the –,** (fam.) coger a alguien desprevenido, coger a alguien en la luna de Valencia. **8 – it,** (fam.) lárgate, desaparece de mi vista. **9 hopping mad,** (fam.) loco de remate. **10 on the –,** (fam.) sin parar, ocupadísimo, desmelenado (con muchísimo trabajo).

hope | həʊp | *v.t.* **1 [to – that/*inf.*]** esperar, confiar: *I hope that you will pass = espero que apruebes.* _ *v.i.* **2 [to – (for)]** esperar, confiar: *I hope for a real improvement = espero una mejora real.* _ *s.i.* **3** esperanza (una virtud teologal). || *s.c.* **4** esperanza, deseo, aspiración, ilusión: *I have a baseless hope = tengo una ilusión sin base.* _ *s.sing.* **5** esperanza, posibilidad, salvación (cosa o persona): *you are my hope = eres mi esperanza.* _ **6 to be beyond –,** no tener posibilidad alguna (de triunfar, sobrevivir, etc.). **7 to – against –,** esperar contra toda esperanza, esperar a pesar de la imposibilidad de la esperanza. **8 – chest,** (EE.UU.) ajuar. **9 to – for the best,** esperar que ocurra lo mejor posible (especialmente de una manera pasiva). **10 to hold out –,** mantener esperanzas; dar seguridades. **11 I –,** confío, espero. **12 in the – (of),** con la esperanza (de), con la ilusión (de). **13 to live in –,** vivir esperanzado, no perder la esperanza. **14 not to have a – in hell,** (fam.) carecer de posibilidad alguna, no existir la menor posibilidad. **15 to raise one's hopes,** hacerse ilusiones (fundadas). **16 what a –/some –/not a –,** ninguna posibilidad, nada que hacer, no hay manera, ninguna esperanza en absoluto.

hopeful | 'həʊpfl | *adj.* **1** esperanzado, optimista, confiado: *I am very hopeful everything will turn out all right = estoy confiado de que todo saldrá bien.* **2** esperanzador, prometedor: *hopeful news = noticias esperanzadoras.* _ *s.c.* **3** aspirante, candidato, persona llena de ilusión (por un futuro trabajo, puesto político, etc.).

hopefully | 'həʊpfəlɪ | *adv.* **1** lleno de esperanza, esperanzadoramente. **2** es de esperar; con suerte: *hopefully, we'll pass = es de esperar que aprobemos.*

hopefulness | 'həʊpflnɪs | *s.i.* promesa, promisión; optimismo.

hopeless | 'həʊplɪs | *adj.* **1** imposible, inútil, sin solución: *that situation is hopeless = esa situación es imposible* *de solucionar.* **2** (fam.) inútil, un cero a la izquierda (en algo): *I am hopeless at music = soy un cero a la izquierda en música.*

hopelessly | 'həʊplɪslɪ | *adv.* inútilmente, desesperanzadoramente, irremediablemente, desesperadamente: *I am hopelessly in love = estoy desesperadamente enamorado.*

hopelessness | 'həʊplɪsnɪs | *s.i.* desesperanza, desesperación.

hopper | 'hɒpər | *s.c.* tolva (para almacenaje).

hopscotch | 'hɒpskɒtʃ | *s.i.* pata coja, castro (juego de niños).

horde | hɔːd*s.c.* horda.

horizon | hə'raɪzn | *s.c.* **1** horizonte (físico). **2** (normalmente *pl.*) (fig.) futuro, horizonte. || **3 on the –,** inminente, a punto de llegar. **4 over the –,** tras la esquina, acercándose peligrosamente.

horizontal | ˌhɒrɪ'zɒntl | (EE.UU.) | ˌhɔːrɪ'zɒntl | *adj.* **1** horizontal. || *s.sing.* **2 [the –]** la horizontal (posición).

horizontally | ˌhɒrɪ'zɒntəlɪ | (EE.UU.) ˌhɔːrɪ'zɒntəlɪ | *adv.* horizontalmente.

hormonal | hɔːməʊnl | *adj.* BIOQ. hormonal.

hormone | 'hɔːməʊn | *s.c.* BIOQ. hormona.

horn | hɔːn | *s.c.* **1** (normalmente *pl.*) cuerno, asta. **2** cuerno (órgano de similar apariencia en otros animales); antena (insectos); tentáculo (caracol). **3** MUS. cuerno, trompa. **4** cuerno, objeto parecido a un cuerno. **5** bocina, claxon. || *s.i.* **6** cuerno (sustancia). || **7 on the horns of a dilemma,** entre la espada y la pared. **8 to take the bulls by the horns,** coger al toro por los cuernos.

horned | hɔːnd | *adj.* con cuernos, con cornamenta (animales).

hornet | 'hɔːnɪt | *s.c.* **1** ZOOL. avispón. || **2 a hornet's nest,** (fam. y fig.) un avispero (situación muy difícil).

horn-rimmed | 'hɔːnrɪmd | *adj.* de concha (gafas).

horny | 'hɔːnɪ | *adj.* **1** duro, duro como un hueso. **2** callosa (mano). **3** (fam.) cachondo, caliente, salido.

horoscope | 'hɒrəskəʊp | (EE.UU.) | 'hɔːrəskəʊp | *s.c.* horóscopo.

horrendous | hɒ'rendəs | *adj.* (fam.) horroroso, horrendo, horrible.

horrendously | hɒ'rendəslɪ | *adv.* (fam.) horrorosamente, horrendamente, horriblemente.

horrible | 'hɒrɪbl | (EE.UU.) | 'hɒːrəbl | *adj.* **1** horrible, espantoso (asesinato, accidente, etc.). **2** (fam.) asqueroso, fatal, horrible, desagradable (califica una amplia gama de cosas negativas).

horribly | 'hɒrəblɪ | (EE.UU.) | 'hɔːrəblɪ | *adv.* **1** horriblemente, espantosamente. **2** (fam.) asquerosamente, fatalmente, horriblemente, desagradablemente.

horrid | 'hɒrɪd | (EE.UU.) | 'hɔːrɪd | *adj.* (fam.) **1** desagradable, horroroso, horrible (lo contrario de lo que es agradable): *a horrid taste = un sabor horroroso.* **2** bestia, maleducado, antipático (rasgo del carácter de una persona).

horridly | 'hɒrɪdlɪ | (EE.UU.) | 'hɔːrɪdlɪ | *adv.* **1** desagradablemente, horrorosamente, horriblemente. **2** de forma maleducada, antipáticamente.

horridness | 'hɒrɪdnɪs | (EE.UU.) | 'hɔːrɪdnɪs | *s.i.* **1** (lo) desagradable. **2** mala educación, antipatía.

horrific | hɒ'rɪfɪk | *adj.* **1** sobrecogedor, horroroso, espantoso. **2** (fam.) excesivo, de espanto, de susto (especialmente precios).

horrifically | hɒ'rɪfɪklɪ | *adv.* **1** sobrecogedoramente, horrorosamente, espantosamente. **2** (fam.) excesivamente (caro, especialmente).

horrify | 'hɒrɪfaɪ | (EE.UU.) | 'hɔːrɪfaɪ | *v.t.* horrorizar, aterrar; (fig.) dejar sorprendidísimo: *we were horrified by the news = la noticia nos dejó sorprendidísimos.*

horrifying | 'hɒrɪfaɪɪŋ | *adj.* horripilante, horroroso.

horrifyingly | 'hɒrɪfaɪɪŋlɪ | *adv.* horripilantemente, horrorosamente.

horror | 'hɒrər | (EE.UU.) | 'hɔːrər | *s.i.* **1** horror, pavor, miedo irracional. || *s.c.* **2** (normalmente *pl.*) experiencia horrorosa, hecho pavoroso, horror. **3** (fam.) adefesio, monstruo, cosa/persona horriblemente fea. **4** (fam.) trasto, desobediente (niño). || *s.sing.* **5 [a – of]** odio a, aversión a: *he has a horror of violence = tiene aversión a la violencia.* **6 [the – of]** el horror de, la horrible experiencia de, el golpe horroroso de. || *atr.* **7** de miedo, de terror (película, historia, etc.). || **8 to give someone the horrors,** (fam.) dar a alguien pavor, causar a alguien espanto: *talking in public gives me the horrors = hablar en público me da pavor.* **9 – of horrors,** (hum.) horror y pavor.

horror-stricken | 'hɒrəstrɪkn | (también **horror-struck**) *adj.* horrorizado, aterrorizado.

hors de combat | ˌɔːdə'kɒmbɑː | *adj.* (form. o lit.) fuera de combate (especialmente en la guerra o deporte).

hors d'oeuvre | ˌɔː'dəːvrə | (EE.UU.) | ˌɔː'dəːv | [*pl.* **hors d'oeuvre** o **hors d'oeuvres**] *s.c.* [normalmente *pl.*] GAST. entremés.

horse | hɔːs | *s.c.* **1** caballo. **2** DEP. potro (para saltar en gimnasia). || *s.i.* **3** (fam.) caballo; heroína. || **4 to – about/around,** (fam.) hacer el tonto, hacer el chorra, hacer el bobo. **5 – laugh,** carcajada, risotada. **6 to put the cart before the –,** V. **cart. 7 to straight from the horse's mouth,** V. **mouth. 8 the horses,** los caballos, las carreras de caballos.

horseback | 'hɔːsbæk | *adj.* y *adv.* **1** a caballo, de montar a caballo. || **2 on –,** a caballo.

horse-box | 'hɔːsbɒks | *s.c.* remolque de transporte de caballos.

horse-chestnut | ˌhɔːs'tʃesnʌt | *s.c.* BOT. **1** castaño de Indias. **2** castaña de Indias.

horse-drawn | 'hɔːsdrɔːn | *adj.* tirado por caballos.

horseflesh | 'hɔːsfleʃ | *s.c.* **1** (también **horsemeat**) carne de caballo, caballo (para comer). || **2 to be a bad/good judge of –,** saber poco/mucho de cabalos, ser mal/buen conocedor de caballos.

horsefly | 'hɔːsflaɪ | *s.c.* ZOOL. tábano.

horsehair | 'hɔːsheər | *s.i.* pelo de caballo (de la cola o crin).

horseman | 'hɔːsmən | [*pl.irreg.* **horsemen**] *s.c.* jinete.

horsemanship | 'hɔːsmənʃɪp | *s.i.* equitación, estilo de equitación, conocimiento de equitación.

horsemen | 'hɔːsmən | *pl.irreg.* de **horseman.**

horseplay | 'hɔːspleɪ | *s.i.* (p.u.) peleas de mentirijillas; payasadas.

horsepower | 'hɔːspəʊər | *s.i.* FIS. potencia, caballo.

horseracing | 'hɔːsreɪsɪŋ | *s.i.* carreras de caballos; hípica.

horseradish | 'hɔːsrædɪʃ | *s.i.* BOT. rábano.

horseriding | 'hɔːsraɪdɪŋ | *s.i.* montar a caballo; hípica.

horse-sense | 'hɔːssens | *s.i.* (fam. y p.u.) sentido común.

horseshoe | 'hɔːsʃuː | *s.c.* **1** herradura. **2** forma de herradura.

horse-show | 'hɔːsʃəʊ | *s.c.* concurso hípico.

horse-trading | 'hɔːstreɪdɪŋ | *s.i.* negociaciones de toma y daca, toma y daca, chalaneo.

horsewhip | 'hɔːswɪp | *s.c.* **1** fusta. || *v.t.* **2** dar con la fusta.

horsewoman | 'hɔːswʊmən | [*pl.irreg.* **horsewomen**] *s.c.* amazona.

horsewomen | 'hɔːswɪmɪn | *pl.irreg.* de **horsewoman.**

horsey | 'hɔːsɪ | (también **horsy**) *adj.* **1** aficionado a los caballos, interesado por los caballos. **2** de facciones equinas, de caballo (especialmente el rostro).

horticultural | ˌhɔːtɪ'kʌltʃərəl | *adj.* hortícola.

horticulturalist | ˌhɔːtɪ'kʌltʃərɪst | *s.c.* horticultor.

horticulture | 'hɔːtɪkʌltʃə | *s.i.* horticultura.

hose | həʊz | *s.c.* **1** manguera. **2** mango, manguito (de conducción de gases o líquidos). || *s.i.* **3** (arc.) calzas, calzones de pernera (para hombres). **4** medias, leotardos (para mujeres). || *v.t.* e *i.* **5** regar, echar agua (con manguera). || **6 to – down,** limpiar bien (con manguera). **7 to – out,** lavar el interior de.

hosiery | 'həʊzɪər | (EE.UU.) | 'həʊʒər | *s.i.* (form.) ropa interior.

hospice | 'hɒspɪs | *s.c.* **1** hospital de enfermos terminales. **2** casa de beneficencia. **3** (arc.) hospedería (especialmente la llevada por una orden religiosa).

hospitable | hɒ'spɪtəbl | | 'hɒspɪtəbl | *adj.* **1** hospitalario, amable con los extraños. **2** acogedor (lugar o persona); favorable (terreno): *this soil is very*

hospitable to tropical plants = este suelo es favorable para plantas tropicales.
hospitably | hɒ'spɪtəblɪ | 'hɒspɪtəblɪ | *adv.* acogedoramente, hospitalariamente.
hospital | 'hɒspɪtl | *s.c.* hospital.
hospitality | ˌhɒspɪ'tælɪtɪ | *s.i.* hospitalidad.
hospitalization | ˌhɒspɪtəlaɪ'zeɪʃn | (EE.UU.) | ˌhɒspɪtəlɪ'zeɪʃn | (también **hospitalisation**) *s.i.* hospitalización.
hospitalize | 'hɒspɪtəlaɪz | (también **hospitalise**) *v.t.* hospitalizar.
host | həʊst | *s.c.* **1** anfitrión. **2** país anfitrión. **3** TV. presentador, anfitrión (de un programa). **4** (arc.) patrón (de establecimiento); mesonero. **5** BIOL. huésped (animal o planta). **6** multitud, montón, sinnúmero: *a host of problems = un sinnúmero de problemas.* _ *v.t.* **7** TV. presentar (un programa). **8** hacer de anfitrión de, actuar de país anfitrión de. || **9 the Host,** REL. la Hostia.
hostage | 'hɒstɪdʒ | *s.c.* **1** rehén. || **2 to be taken/held –,** ser tomado como rehén.
hostel | 'hɒstl*s.c.* hostal, albergue, residencia (económica).
hostess | 'həʊstɪs | *s.c.* **1** anfitriona. **2** TV. presentadora, anfitriona (de un programa). **3** azafata. **4** acompañante de club nocturno. **5** (EE.UU.) camarera jefe.
hostile | 'hɒstaɪl | (EE.UU.) | 'hɒstl | *adj.* **1** hostil, poco amable (persona). **2** enemigo (especialmente en lo militar). **3** desfavorable, en contra (de una idea, proyecto, grupo de personas, etc.).
hostility | hɒ'stɪlɪtɪ | *s.i.* **1** hostilidad, antagonismo. || *s.pl.* **2** (form.) hostilidades (guerra). **3** sentimientos hostiles, sentimientos de enemistad, resentimiento.
hot | hɒt | [*comp.* **hotter,** *super.* **hottest**] *adj.* **1** caluroso, caliente (objeto, sustancia, tiempo atmosférico, etc.): *how hot is it here in summer? = ¿a qué temperatura se está aquí en verano?* **2** caliente, recién hecha (comida). **3** picante (comida). **4** (fam.) intenso, brutal, fiero (lucha, conflicto, etc.). **5** apasionado, pasional, vehemente (de temperamento). **6** (fam.) caliente, reciente, de actualidad (noticia, información, etc.). **7 [– on/at]** (fam.) puesto en, al tanto de, conocedor de, manitas en. **8 [– on/at]** (fam.) puntilloso, remilgado con, tiquismiquis en: *that teacher is very hot on pronunciation = ese profesor es muy tiquismiquis en la pronunciación.* **9** de moda, en boga (algo que todo el mundo quiere ver). **10** (fam.) peligroso, comprometido (asunto ilegal). **11** (fam.) caliente (en juegos de niños). || **12 to blow – and cold,** (fam.) decidir contradictoriamente, no tener un criterio fijo, ir de un lado para otro (en decisiones, juicios, etc.). **13 to drop something/someone like a – potato,** (fam.) dar de lado a algo/alguien, dejar a algo/alguien a un lado: *I dropped him like a hot potato when I learn he was a sadist = yo le dejé a un lado cuando me enteré de que era un sádico.* **14 to get into – water/to be in – water,** (fam.) meterse en un lío, meterse en una buena/estar metido en un lío, estar metido en una buena. **15 to go – and cold,** (fam.) darle a uno sudores fríos (al pensar el peligro de algo). **16 – air,** (fam. y desp.) promesas huecas, vaciedades. **17 hot-air balloon,** globo (para personas). **18 – and bothered,** (fam.) con un sofoco excesivo (preocupación). **19 – cross bun,** GAST. bollo (que se come en Cuaresma). **20 – dog,** perro caliente. **21 – flush,** sofoco (en la menopausia). **22 – line,** teléfono rojo. **23 – potato,** (fam.) asunto caliente, mal asunto, tema peligroso, tema comprometido. **24 – spot,** (fam.) **a)** lugar de moda, sitio de moda; **b)** punto conflictivo, lugar conflictivo (políticamente, militarmente, etc.). **25 – stuff,** (fam.) **a)** pasatiempo favorito, actividad de moda; **b)** (vulg.) tío bueno, tía buena (sexualmente). **26 to – up,** (fam.) **a)** intensificarse, ponerse trepidante, ponerse en un plan fantástico (una actividad, un lugar, etc.); **b)** aumentar la potencia de (un vehículo). **27 — water bottle,** bolsa de agua caliente. **28 in the – seat,** (fam.) con la responsabilidad sobre los hombros; en primera fila (al tomar decisiones).
hotbed | hɒtbed | *s.c.* **1** AGR. almajara, semillero. **2** (fig.) **[– of]** semillero de (ideas, intriga, crimen, etc.).
hot-blooded | ˌhɒt'blʌdɪd | *adj.* **1** apasionado, vehemente, pasional. **2** pasional (sexualmente).
hotchpotch | 'hɒtʃpɒtʃ | *s.sing.* (fam.) mezcolanza, batiburrillo, desorden.
hotel | həʊ'tel*s.c.* hotel.
hotelier | həʊ'telɪər | (EE.UU.) | ˌhəʊtel'jeɪ | *s.c.* hotelero.
hotfoot | ˌhɒt'fuːt | *adv.* (fam.) a toda prisa, a toda velocidad.
hothead | 'hɒthed | *s.c.* (desp.) alocado, arrebatado; extremista.
hot-headed | ˌhɒt'hedɪd | *adj.* (desp.) impulsivo, impetuoso (que no piensa en las consecuencias de sus actos).
hot-headedly | ˌhɒt'hedɪdlɪ | *adv.* (desp.) impulsivamente, impetuosamente.
hot-headedness | ˌhɒt'hedɪdnɪs | *s.i.* (desp.) arrebato, impetuosidad, falta de reflexión.
hothouse | 'hɒthəʊs | *s.c.* **1** invernadero. **2** hervidero de ideas (típico de intelectuales y artistas).
hotly | 'hɒtlɪ | *adv.* **1** con vehemencia, apasionadamente, acaloradamente. **2** de cerca, pisándole los talones (en persecución de alguien).
hot-plate | 'hɒtpleɪt | *s.c.* fuego, placa (en una cocina).
hotpot | 'hɒtpɒt | *s.c.* e *i.* GAST. estofado (de carne con verduras).
hound | haʊnd | *s.c.* **1** perro, sabueso (especialmente de caza). || *v.t.* **2** perseguir, no dejar en paz (con insultos, críticas, etc.). || **3 to – out,** obligar a irse, perseguir para que se vaya (a alguien).
hour | aʊər *s.c.* **1** hora (sesenta minutos). **2 [the –]** la hora: *the clock struck the hour = el reloj dio la hora.* **3** (lit.) hora, momento, tiempo (de hacer algo, de desgracia, de felicidad, etc.): *she helped me in my darkest hour = ella me socorrió en mi hora más negra.* *s.pl.* **4** horario (de trabajo, de vida, etc.): *we keep acceptable hours at the bank = en el banco, tenemos un horario aceptable.* **5** período, tiempo (en el que uno hace alguna actividad). **6** horas y horas, muchísimo tiempo. || **7 after hours,** pasado el límite legal (especialmente para beber alcohol). **8 at all hours,** continuamente, sin parar, a todas horas. **9 at this/that –,** a esta hora/a esa hora (expresando lo inusual de la hora). **10 – after –/for – after –,** hora tras hora, continuamente (durante mucho tiempo). **11 – hand,** la manilla pequeña (del reloj). **12 on the –,** en punto. **13 out of hours,** fuera del horario de trabajo, fuera del horario de actividad comercial. **14 the small hours,** la madrugada. **15 till all hours,** hasta tardísimo, hasta horas escandalosas.
hourglass | 'aʊəglɑːs | *s.c.* reloj de arena.
hourly | 'aʊəlɪ | *adj.* **1** de cada hora: *an hourly train service = un servicio de trenes cada hora.* _ *adv.* **2** por hora, por cada hora. **3** constantemente.
house | haʊs | [*pl.* **houses** | 'haʊzɪz |] *s.c.* **1** casa. **2** empresa, firma, casa: *publishing house = empresa editorial; a fashion house = casa de diseño.* **3** POL. cámara parlamentaria. **4** casa real, casa (de gran raigambre). **5** casa (de comidas, restaurante, etc.): *coffee house = café.* **6** (brit.) club (dentro de colegio): *our house won the prize = nuestro club ganó el premio.* _ *atr.* **7** de la casa (especialmente vino). | *v.t.* **8** albergar, contener (un edificio algo dentro de él). **9** alojar, proveer viviendas para (alguien): *nowadays everybody is better housed than 10 years ago = hoy en día todo el mundo está mejor provisto de vivienda que hace 10 años.* _ *s.sing.* **10 [the –]** la casa, la familia. **11** (form.) público, sala (en un debate o teatro). || **12 to bring the – down,** (fam.) hacer venirse abajo la sala (con los aplausos). **13 to eat somebody out of – and home,** (fam.) arruinar a alguien a base de gorronear en su casa. **14 to get on like a – on fire,** (fam.) llevarse maravillosamente bien, llevarse de miedo (dos personas). **15 – arrest,** DER. arresto domiciliario. **16 – guest,** invitado en casa. **17 – lights,** luces de la sala (en contraposición con las luces del escenario). **18 – martin,** ZOOL. avión común (ave). **19 – of God,** REL. casa de Dios. **20 to keep —,** hacer de ama de casa, llevar la casa. **21 on the –,** (fam.) paga la casa. **22 open –,** (fam.) casa abierta a todos (para una fiesta). **23 to put/set one's own – in order,** arreglar los asuntos personales de uno (más que ir dando consejos a otros). **24 to set up –,**

V. **set up. 25 the House,** la Cámara (Baja, Alta, etc.). **26 the House of Commons,** POL. la Cámara Baja. **27 the House of Lords,** POL. la Cámara de los Lores. **28 the House of Representatives,** (EE.UU.) POL. el Congreso. **29 the Houses of Parliament,** el Parlamento (inglés).
houseboat | 'hausbəut | *s.c.* casa flotante.
housebound | 'hausbaund | *adj.* que no puede moverse de casa.
houseboy | 'hausbɔɪ | *s.c.* (p.u.) criado, sirviente (especialmente en el mundo colonial).
housebreaker | 'hausbreɪkər | *s.c.* ladrón de casas.
housebreaking | 'hausbreɪkɪŋ | *s.i.* robo de casas.
housecoat | 'hauskəut | *s.c.* bata (especialmente de mujer para la casa).
housefather | 'hausfɑːðər | *s.c.* tutor, preceptor (en instituciones de atención a niños marginados).
houseful | 'hausful | *s.c.* casa llena (de gente, niños, etc.): *at birthdays I've got a houseful of children = en los cumpleaños tengo la casa llena de niños.*
household | 'haushəuld | *s.c.* **1** casa, familia (desde el punto de vista de las personas que viven juntas). || *s.sing.* **2** casa, hogar (como trabajo): *household chores = tareas del hogar.* _ *adj.* **3** conocido, familiar, conocido en todas las casas. || **4 Household,** MIL. de la casa real (con tipos de soldados conectados con la casa real).
householder | 'haushəuldər | *s.c.* cabeza de familia; arrendatario; propietario.
housekeeper | 'hauskiːpər | *s.c.* ama de llaves.
housekeeping | 'hauskiːpɪŋ | *s.i.* **1** dirección del hogar, gobierno de la casa. **2** dinero para los gastos de la casa. **3** gestión económica del hogar.
housemaid | 'hausmeɪd | *s.c.* criada.
houseman | 'hausmən | [*pl.irreg.* **housemen**] *s.c.* (brit.) médico interno (de hospital).
housemaster | 'hausmɑːstər | *s.c.* profesor encargado de una sección (de un internado).
housemen | 'hausmən | *pl.irreg.* de **houseman.**
housemistress | 'hausmɪstrɪs | *s.c.* profesora encargada de una sección (en un internado).
housemother | 'hausmʌðər | *s.c.* tutora, preceptora (en una institución de acogida de niños con problemas).
house-owner | 'hausəunər | *s.c.* propietario (de una casa).
house-party | 'hauspɑːtɪ | *s.c.* fiesta en una casa de campo (que suele durar varios días).
houseplant | 'hausplænt | *s.c.* BOT. planta de casa, planta interior.
houseproud | 'hauspraud | *adj.* exagerado en el cuidado de la casa.
houseroom | 'hausruːm | **would't give something –,** (fam.) no lo metería en mi casa (algo) por nada del mundo.
house-servant | 'haussəːvənt | *s.c.* criado, criada.
house-to-house | ˌhaustə'haus | *adj.* de casa en casa.
housetop | 'haustɒp | *s.c.* **1** tejado, terraza (en el tejado). || **2 to shout/proclaim something from the housetops,** (lit.) gritar/proclamar algo desde los tejados/terrados, pregonar algo a los cuatro vientos.
housetrain | 'haustreɪn | *v.t.* acostumbrar a vivir en casa (a un animal).
housetrained | 'haustreɪnd | *adj.* acostumbrado a vivir en casa.
house-warming | 'hauswɔːmɪŋ | *s.c.* fiesta de estreno de una casa.
housewife | 'hauswaɪf | [*pl.* **housewives**] *s.c.* ama de casa.
housework | 'hauswəːk | *s.i.* tareas de la casa, quehaceres domésticos.
housing | 'hauzɪŋ | *s.i.* **1** vivienda. || *s.c.* **2** MEC. caja, cubierta, tapa. || **3 – association,** cooperativa de viviendas. **4 – development,** urbanización. **5 – estate,** urbanización. **6 – project,** (EE.UU.) urbanización.
hove | həuv | *pret.* y *p.p.* de **heave.**
hovel | 'hɒvl | *s.c.* **1** casucha, choza. **2** (fig.) chabola, cuchitril.
hover | 'hɒvər | (EE.UU.) | 'hʌvər | *v.i.* **1** permanecer quieto en el aire. **2** titubear, dudar, no decidirse (en movimientos físicos o en decisiones de actuación).
hovercraft | 'hɒvəkrɑːft | [*pl.* **hovercraft**] *s.c.* hidrodeslizador, hovercraft.
how | hau | *adv.interr.* **1** cómo: *how are you? = ¿cómo estás?* **2** de qué manera, de qué modo: *how do you go about this? = ¿de qué manera se hace esto?* **3 [– *adj./adv.* (old, long, etc.)]** qué, cuánto, cuántos (para expresar edad, medidas, volúmenes, etc.): *how old are you? = ¿cuántos años tienes?; how often do you go out? = ¿con qué frecuencia sales?; how long are you going to be here? = ¿cuánto tiempo vas a estar aquí?* **4 [– *adj./adv.*]** qué (en formas exclamativas): *how pretty she is! = ¡qué guapa es!* _ *conj.* **5** (fam.) de la manera en que, del modo como: *this is how you do it = esta es tu manera de actuar, el modo de hacerlo tú.* _ **6 and –!,** (fam.) ¡ya lo creo que sí!, ¡y de qué manera! (contestando afirmativamente con énfasis). **7 – about...?,** ¿y...? (introduciendo un tema nuevo dirigiéndose a otra persona): *OK everybody likes beer, how about wine? = vale, a todo el mundo le gusta la cerveza, ¿y el vino?* **8 – about.../– would you.../how's about...?,** (fam.) ¿qué tal si...?, ¿qué te parece si...? **9 – about that/how's that?,** ¿qué te parece eso?, ¿qué te parece? (indicando sorpresa). **10 – about you?,** ¿y tú qué?, ¿y tú? **11 – come/so?,** ¿por qué?, ¿por qué razón?, ¿cómo es que...? **12 – do you do,** mucho gusto, encantado (tanto para iniciar como para responder a una presentación). **13 – do you mean?** ¿qué quieres decir?, ¿a qué te refieres? **14 – much/many?,** ¿cuánto?, ¿cuánta?/¿cuántos?, ¿cuántas? **15 how's that?, a)** ¿qué te parece?, ¿cómo lo ves?; **b)** (fam.) ¿cómo?, ¿qué dijiste? **16 how's that!.** (grito en el críquet que indica que el bateador ha fallado). **17 how's that for ...?,** ¿qué opinas de...?, ¿qué te parece...?
howdy | 'haudɪ | *interj.* (fam. y EE.UU.) ¿qué hay?, ¿qué tal?, ¿cómo vas?, ¿cómo estás?
however | hau'evər | *conj.* **1** sin embargo, no obstante. **2** del modo que, de la manera que: *I travel however I can = viajo del modo que puedo.* _ *adv.* **3 [– *adj./adv.*] por muy... que...:** *however hard you try you can't = por muy intensamente que lo intentes, no puedes.* _ *adv.interr.* **4** cómo, cómo es posible que: *however can you say that? = ¿cómo es posible que digas eso?*
howitzer | 'hauɪtsər | *s.c.* MIL. cañón sin retroceso; mortero.
howl | haul | *v.i.* **1** aullar (lobo o perro); aullar, dar un aullido, dar un alarido (personas): *he howled with pain = dio un aullido de dolor.* **2** aullar (viento). **3** (fam.) decir con una voz estentórea. || *s.c.* **4** aullido (animal); alarido, aullido (personas). || **5 to – down,** acallar con alaridos, no dejar hablar a base de chillidos (a alguien). **6 to – with laughter,** reírse a carcajadas, reírse como un energúmeno.
howler | 'haulər | *s.c.* **1** (fam.) gazapo, metedura de pata de campeonato. **2** persona que da aullidos, animal que da aullidos.
howling | 'həulɪŋ | *s.i.* **1** aullidos, alaridos (de personas o animales). **2** aullar (del viento). || *adj.* **3** clamoroso (fracaso o éxito).
hub | hʌb | *s.c.* **1 [– (of)]** cubo, eje (de una rueda). **2 [– of]** centro de (una actividad): *a hub of commerce = un centro de comercio.*
hubbub | 'hʌbʌb | *s.sing.* **1** barahúnda, follón (ruido). **2** pandemonio, gran confusión.
hubby | 'hʌbɪ | *s.c.* (fam.) marido, esposo.
hubcap | 'hʌbkæp | *s.c.* tapacubos (especialmente en vehículo).
hubris | 'hjuːbrɪs | *s.i.* (form. o lit.) hibris, soberbia desmedida.
huckster | 'hʌkstər | *s.c.* (p.u.) vendedor ambulante, buhonero.
huddle | 'hʌdl | *v.i.* **1** apretarse (unos contra otros). **2 [to – with]** reunirse con (con cierto matiz de secreto). **3** agazaparse, acurrucarse. || *s.c.* **4** grupo apelotonado, grupo amontonado (de cosas o personas).
huddled | 'hʌdld | *adj.* **1** acurrucado, agazapado. **2** apretado (uno con otro): *we sat huddled together = nos sentamos apretados unos contra otros.*
hue | hjuː | *s.c.* **1** (form.) color. || **2 a – and cry,** clamor, protesta encendida.
huff | hʌf | (fam.) *v.i.* **1** decir con mal humor, decir malhumoradamente. **2**

echar aliento. || **3 to – and puff, a)** estar indignado; **b)** soplar con fuerza; **c)** jadear. **4 in a –,** con una rabieta, malhumorado.

huffily | 'hʌfɪlɪ | *adv.* (fam.) con un gran pique, malhumoradamente, con un gran enfado, a cajas destempladas.

huffiness | 'hʌfɪnɪs | *s.i.* (form.) malhumor, pique.

huffy | 'hʌfɪ | *adj.* (fam.) enfadado, malhumorado.

hug | hʌg | [*ger.* **hugging,** *pret.* y *p.p.* **hugged**] *v.t.* e *i.* **1** abrazar, estrechar contra sí. || *v.t.* **2** coger con fuerza, abrazar contra sí, agarrar contra sí (un objeto, niño, etc.). **3** agarrarse con fuerza a, ceñirse a (la carretera, en el caso de un vehículo). || *s.c.* **4** abrazo.

huge | hjuːdʒ | *adj.* enorme, gigantesco, inmenso (en tamaño, cantidad, grado, etc.).

hugely | 'hjuːdʒlɪ | *adv.* enormemente, gigantescamente, inmensamente.

hugeness | 'hjuːdʒnɪs | *s.i.* inmensidad (en tamaño, cantidad, etc.).

huh | hʌ | *interj.* (fam.) **1** (EE.UU.) ¿no? **2** ¿eh?, ¿cómo? **3** bah, ¿y qué? (despreciativamente). **4** ¿para qué?

hulk | hʌlk | *s.c.* **1** MAR. barco viejo, cascarón. **2** mole (cualquier cosa grande).

hulking | 'hʌlkɪŋ | *adj.* gigantesco.

hull | hʌl | *s.c.* **1** armazón, casco (de un barco o tanque). **2** BOT. vaina (en flores o frutos). || *v.t.* **3** quitar la vaina a.

hullabaloo | ˌhʌləbə'luː | *s.c.* [normalmente *sing.*] (fam.) bronca, tumulto.

hullo V. **hello.**

hum | hʌm | *v.i.* **1** zumbar, hacer un ruido de zumbido (insectos, especialmente). **2** tararear, canturrear en voz baja. || *v.t.* **3** canturrear (canciones). || *s.c.* **4** zumbido, ruido de zumbidos. || *interj.* **5** ejem (indicando vacilación). || **6 to – and haw,** hablar entrecortadamente, hablar con grandes dificultades. **7 humming (with),** vibrando (de) (actividad energética).

human | 'hjuːmən | *adj.* **1** humano, del hombre, de hombre. **2** (fig.) humano, frágil: *he's only human = sólo es humano.* _ *s.c.* **3** humano, ser humano. || **4 – being,** ser humano, criatura. **4 – interest,** PER. interés humano, noticiable. **5 – nature,** naturaleza humana. **6 – rights,** derechos humanos. **7 the – race,** la raza humana, la humanidad.

humane | hjuː'meɪn | *adj.* **1** humano, compasivo, bondadoso. **2** humanizador (tipo de estudio o actividad).

humanely | hjuː'meɪnlɪ | *adv.* compasivamente, bondadosamente.

humaneness | hjuː'meɪnnɪs | *s.i.* compasión, humanidad.

humanise V. **humanize.**

humanism | 'hjuːmənɪzəm | *s.i.* FIL. humanismo.

humanist | 'hjuːmənɪst | *s.c.* humanista.

humanistic | ˌhjuːmə'nɪstɪk | *adj.* humanista, humanístico.

humanitarian | hjuːˌmænɪ'teərɪən | *adj.* **1** humanitario. || *s.c.* **2** humanitario, filántropo.

humanitarianism | hjuːˌmænɪ'teərɪənɪzəm | *s.i.* humanitarismo.

humanity | hjuː'mænɪtɪ | *s.i.* **1** humanidad (colectivo). **2** condición humana, humanidad. **3** humanidad, compasión. || *s.pl.* **4** humanidades, letras (tipo de estudio).

humanization | ˌhjuːmənaɪ'zeɪʃn | (EE.UU.) | ˌhjuːmənɪ'zɪʃn | (también **humanisation**) *s.i.* humanización.

humanize | 'hjuːmənaɪz | (también **humanise**) *v.t.* **1** humanizar. **2** humanizar, hacer muy parecido a humano (a un animal o máquina).

humankind | ˌhjuːmən'kaɪnd | *s.i.* género humano, raza humana.

humanly | 'hjuːmənlɪ | *adv.* **1** humanamente. || **2 to do all that is – possible,** hacer lo humanamente posible.

humanoid | 'hjuːmənɔɪd | *s.c.* **1** humanoide, robot. || *adj.* **2** de aspecto humano, casi como un hombre (una máquina o similar).

humble | 'hʌmbl | *adj.* **1** humilde. **2** humilde (de categoría). **3** insignificante, mínimo (cosas o personas): *I need a humble salary to start with = necesito un salario mínimo para comenzar.* _ *v.t.* **3** humillar. || **4 to eat – pie,** tragarse lo dicho anteriormente, reconocer que uno estaba equivocado. **5 my – opinion,** mi humilde opinión.

humbly | 'hʌmblɪ | *adv.* **1** humildemente. **2** modestamente (manera de expresar una opinión o parecido).

humbug | 'hʌmbʌg | *s.c.* **1** (brit.) caramelo de menta (previamente hervido). **2** farsante. || *s.i.* **3** embustes; farsa (ideas, palabras, comportamiento, etc.).

humdinger | ˌhʌm'dɪŋər | *s.c.* (fam.) auténtica maravilla, maravilla.

humdrum | 'hʌmdrʌm | *adj.* monótono, tedioso, vulgar, mediocre.

humeri | 'hjuːməraɪ | *pl.* de **humerus.**

humerus | 'hjuːmərəs | [*pl.* **humeruses** o **humeri**] *s.c.* ANAT. húmero (hueso).

humid | 'hjuːmɪd | *adj.* húmedo.

humidify | hjuː'mɪdɪfaɪ | *v.t.* humedecer.

humidity | hjuː'mɪdɪtɪ | *s.i.* humedad.

humiliate | hjuː'mɪlɪeɪt | *v.t.* humillar.

humiliated | hjuː'mɪlɪeɪtɪd | *adj.* humillado: *I felt humiliated = me sentí humillado.*

humiliating | hjuː'mɪlɪeɪtɪŋ | *adj.* humillante.

humiliatingly | hjuː'mɪlɪeɪtɪŋlɪ | *adv.* humillantemente.

humiliation | hjuː mɪlɪ'eɪʃn | *s.c.* e *i.* humillación.

humility | hjuː'mɪlɪtɪ | *s.i.* humilidad.

hummingbird | 'hʌmɪŋbɜːd | *s.c.* ZOOL. colibrí.

humor V. **humour.**

humorist | 'hjuːmərɪst | *s.c.* humorista.

humorous | 'hjuːmərəs | *adj.* gracioso, divertido, cómico.

humorously | 'hjuːmərəslɪ | *adv.* graciosamente, divertidamente, cómicamente.

humour | 'hjuːmər (EE.UU. **humor**) *s.i.* **1** humor. **2** gracia, elemento cómico (de una situación o similar). **4** humor, genio: *in excellent humour = con humor excelente.* _ *v.t.* **5** complacer (a alguien fastidioso).

humourless | 'hjuːməlɪs | *adj.* solemne, serio, adusto.

hump | hʌmp | *s.c.* **1** ANAT. joroba (persona); jiba (animal). **2** altozano, cerro, montículo. || *v.t.* **3** (fam.) llevar con dificultad, arrastrar (objeto pesado). **4 [to – + *o.* + (onto)]** elevar, levantar, tirar de (un objeto pesado).

humpback | 'hʌmpbæk | *s.c.* **1** (vulg.) jorobado, chepa. || *adj.* **2** de fuerte pendiente (puente).

humpbacked | 'hʌmpbækt | *adj.* **1** con jiba (animal). **2** de fuerte pendiente (puente).

hunch | hʌntʃ | *s.c.* **1** (fam.) corazonada, intuición. || *v.t.* **2** encoger (los hombros). || *v.i.* **3** encogerse (de hombros). encorvarse, doblarse (el cuerpo).

hunchback | 'hʌntʃbæk | *s.c.* (vulg.) chepa, jorobado.

hunched | 'hʌntʃt | *adj.* doblado, encorvado (posición corporal).

hundred | 'hʌndrəd | *num.card.* **1** cien, ciento. || **2 a – per cent/one – per cent,** totalmente, completamente: *he's one hundred per cent honest = es completamente honrado.* **3 hundreds,** cientos, montones.

hundredth | 'hʌndrədə | *num.ord.* **1** centésimo. || *s.c.* **2 [– of]** centésima parte de.

hundredweight | 'hʌndrədweɪt | *s.c.* quintal (unidad de medida).

hung | hʌŋ *pret.* y *p.p irreg.* **1** de **hang.** _ **2 – parliament,** POL. situación parlamentaria sin mayoría decisoria. **3 – up,** (fam. y desp.) obsesionado; acomplejado.

Hungarian | hʌŋ'geərɪən | *adj.* **1 húngaro.** || *s.c.* **2** húngaro. || *s.i.* **3** húngaro (idioma).

Hungary | 'hʌŋgərɪ | *s.sing.* Hungría.

hunger | 'hʌŋgər | *s.i.* **1** hambre. || *s.sing.* **2 [– (for)]** (form. o lit.) ansia, deseo vehemente, anhelo. || *v.i.* **3 [to – for/after]** ansiar, anhelar. || **4 – march,** marcha de parados. **5 – strike,** huelga de hambre. **6 – striker,** huelguista de hambre.

hungover | ˌhʌŋ'gəuvər | *adj.* (fam.) con una resaca fuerte.

hungrily | 'hʌŋgrɪlɪ | *adv.* **1** con hambre, con ansia (de hambre). **2** ávidamente, ansiosamente, anhelantemente.

hungry | 'hʌŋgrɪ | *adj.* **1** hambriento: *I'm hungry = tengo hambre.* **2 [– (for)]** (form. o lit.) deseoso, anhelante, ansioso. || **3 to go –,** pasar hambre. **4 – work,** trabajo de desgaste.

hunk | hʌŋk | *s.c.* **1** pedazo, trozo. **2** (fam.) hombrón, hombre muy macho (sexualmente).

hunt | hʌnt | *v.t.* e *i.* **1** cazar, ir de caza. **2** (brit.) cazar, ir de caza (sólo de zorros). || *v.i.* 3 **[to – for]** buscar afanosamente, buscar ansiosamente. || *v.t.* 4 dar caza, perseguir, perseguir con saña (a un criminal o similar). 5 [**to** – *prep.*] perseguir; echar (de un sitio): *the children hunted the dog out of the house = los chicos echaron al perro de la casa.* _ *s.c.* 6 caza (en general). 7 (brit.) caza (del zorro). 8 **[– for]** búsqueda afanosa de, búsqueda ansiosa de. || **9 to – down,** dar caza a, perseguir (a un criminal o similar). **10 to – out/up,** intentar encontrar afanosamente, dar con (entre muchos otros objetos o datos): *I simply must hunt that book out = sencillamente tengo que dar con ese libro.* **11 to run with the hare and – with the hounds,** V. **hare.**

hunter | 'hʌntər | *s.c.* 1 cazador (persona o animal): *that dog is a good hunter = ese perro es un buen cazador.* 2 personas a la caza (de oportunidades, objetos, libros extraños, etc.). 3 caballo para la caza (especialmente del zorro en el Reino Unido).

hunting | 'hʌntɪŋ | *s.i.* 1 caza: *to go hunting = ir de caza.* 2 (brit.) caza del zorro. 3 (fam.) búsqueda (de objetos, oportunidades, etc.). || **4 – ground,** lugar ideal, sitio típico de búsqueda (de algo).

huntsman | 'hʌntsmən | [*pl.irreg.* **huntsmen**] *s.c.* cazador (especialmente de zorros).

huntsmen | 'hʌntsmən | *pl.irreg.* de **huntsman.**

hurdle | 'hɜːdl | *s.c.* 1 DEP. obstáculo, valla (en carreras). 2 (fig.) obstáculo, problema, dificultad (no necesariamente física). || *s.pl.* 3 DEP. carrera de vallas, carrera de obstáculos. || *v.t.* 4 DEP. correr en una carrera de obstáculos, participar en una carrera de vallas.

hurdler | 'hɜːdlər | *s.c.* DEP. especialista en vallas.

hurl | hɜːl | *v.t.* 1 arrojar violentamente, tirar con gran fuerza (algo). 2 (fig.) llenar de, arrojar (insultos, críticas, etc.): *they hurled abuse at us = nos llenaron de insultos.* _ *v.r.* 3 arrojarse violentamente (contra alguien, dentro de un sitio, etc.).

hurly-burly | 'hɜːlɪbɜːlɪ | *s.sing.* **[the – (of)]** el follón, el tumulto, el montaje ruidoso: *the hurly-burly of publicity = el follón de la publicidad.*

hurrah | hʊ'rɑː | (también **hurray**) V. **hooray.**

hurricane | 'hʌrɪkən | *s.c.* 1 huracán. 2 (fig.) situación violenta, acontecimiento de gran intensidad. || **3 – lamp,** (también **storm lantern**) lámpara con protección de cristal.

hurried | 'hʌrɪd | *adj.* 1 apresurado (acción). 2 superficial, hecho con prisa (lectura, estudio, mirada, etc.). 3 apurado, apremiado (persona).

hurriedly | 'hʌrɪdlɪ | *adv.* 1 apresuradamente. 2 superficialmente, con demasiada prisa (lectura, mirada, etc.).

hurry | 'hʌrɪ | *v.i.* 1 darse prisa, apresurarse, moverse con prisa, andar de prisa. 2 **[to –** *inf.***] darse prisa en:** *I hurried to finish everything = me di prisa en acabar todo.* _ *v.t.* 3 apresurar, dar prisa (a alguien). || *s.i.* 4 prisa, apresuramiento; (Am.) apuro. || **5 to – on,** darse prisa en, apresurarse en añadir. **6 to – up,** darse mucha prisa, apresurarse mucho; apresurar (a alguien). **7 in a –,** con gran prisa, apresuradamente: *I'm in a hurry = tengo prisa.* **8 in no –/not in any –,** sin prisa alguna, sin ninguna urgencia (para hacer algo). **9 there's no –/no great –,** no existe urgencia alguna, no hay ninguna necesidad de apresurarse. **10 what's the –?,** ¿dónde está el incendio?, ¿a qué tanta prisa?

hurt | hɜːt | *v.* [*pret.* y *p.p.irreg.* **hurt**] *t.* 1 herir, hacer daño, lastimar (física o moralmente): *you're hurting me = me estás haciendo daño.* 2 dañar, perjudicar (intereses económicos, posibilidades, etc.). || *i.* 3 doler: *my back is hurting = me duele la espalda.* _ *adj.* 4 herido, lastimado (física o moralmente). || *s.c.* e *i.* 5 herida, daño (moral), ofensa. || **6 it won't – to/it never hurts to,** (fam.) no hace daño, no cuesta nada: *it never hurts to help other people = no cuesta nada ayudar a otras personas.*

hurtful | 'hɜːtfl | *adj.* hiriente (comentario, artículo escrito, etc.).

hurtfully | 'hɜːtfəlɪ | *adv.* de manera hiriente.

hurtfulness | 'hɜːtflnɪs | *s.i.* (lo) hiriente (de un comentario o similar).

hurtle | 'hɜːtl | *v.i.* **[to –** *prep.***] abalanzarse, arrojarse:** *we hurtled down the road = nos abalanzamos por la carretera.*

husband | 'hʌzbənd | *s.c.* 1 marido, esposo. || *v.t.* 2 conservar, economizar (algo valioso o necesario).

husbandry | 'hʌzbəndrɪ | *s.i.* (form.) 1 AGR. labranza, agricultura; cría (de animales). 2 conservación, economización (de existencias o energía).

hush | hʌʃ | *v.i.* 1 callarse, guardar silencio. || *v.t.* 2 acallar, hacer callar: *my mother finally hushed the baby to sleep = mi madre finalmente hizo callar al niño hasta que se durmió.* _ *interj.* 3 silencio. || *s.i.* 4 silencio, quietud. || **5 – money,** dinero por el silencio, dinero para hacer callar (una corruptela). **6 to – up,** (desp.) encubrir; tapar la boca a (alguien para que no hable).

hushed | hʌʃt | *adj.* en silencio, en calma: *the hushed forest = el bosque en silencio.*

hush-hush | ˌhʌʃ'hʌʃ | *adj.* (fam.) secreto, confidencial.

husk | hʌsk | *s.c.* BOT. cáscara, vaina (del grano, arroz, maíz, etc.). || *v.t.* 2 quitar la vaina a, descascarillar.

huskily | 'hʌskɪlɪ | *adv.* con voz ronca.

huskiness | 'hʌskɪnɪs | *s.i.* ronquera.

husky | 'hʌskɪ | *adj.* 1 ronca (voz). 2 (fam.) fornido, atractivo (especialmente un hombre). || *s.c.* 3 ZOOL. perro esquimal.

hussy | 'hʌsɪ | *s.c.* (p.u. y desp.) 1 desvergonzada, pícara. 2 libertina (sexualmente).

hustings | 'hʌstɪŋz | *s.pl.* (form.) POL. campaña electoral.

hustle | 'hʌsl | (fam.) *v.t.* 1 impeler, apresurar, empujar con prisas (molestando o aprovechándose de la fuerza de uno). 2 (fam. y EE.UU.) vender agresivamente (y normalmente con medios ilícitos). || *v.i.* 3 (vulg. y EE.UU.) hacer la calle (como prostituta). || *s.c.* 4 bullicio, actividad vibrante.

hustler | 'hʌslər | *s.c.* (EE.UU.) 1 (fam.) estafador, timador. 2 (vulg.) prostituta.

hut | hʌt | *s.c.* 1 cabaña, choza (por ejemplo, en poblados nativos). 2 barraca temporal (típica de trabajadores mientras hacen obras).

hutch | hʌtʃ | *s.c.* conejera (como jaula).

hyacinth | 'haɪəsɪnθ | *s.c.* BOT. jacinto.

hyaena, V. **hyena.**

hybrid | 'haɪbrɪd | *s.c.* 1 BIOL. híbrido (animal o planta). 2 (fig.) mezcla, híbrido. || *adj.* 3 híbrido (animal o planta). 4 (fig. y form.) mezclado, híbrido, compuesto (sistema, funcionamiento, etc.).

hydrant | 'haɪdrənt | *s.c.* boca de riego, boca de incendios.

hydrate | 'haɪdreɪt | *s.c.* QUIM. hidrato.

hydraulic | haɪ'drɔːlɪk | *adj.* 1 hidráulico. || *s.pl.* 2 FIS. hidráulica.

hydro- | ˌhaɪdrə | *prefijo* hidro, hídrico: *hydrochloric acid = ácido clorhídrico.*

hydrocarbon | ˌhaɪdrə'kɑːbən | *s.c.* QUIM. hidrocarburo.

hydro-electric | ˌhaɪdrəʊɪ'lektrɪk | *adj.* hidroeléctrico.

hydro-electricity | ˌhaɪdrəʊˌɪlek'trɪsətɪ | *s.i.* FIS. energía hidroeléctrica.

hydrofoil | 'haɪdrəfɔɪl | *s.c.* MAR. hidroala.

hydrogen | 'haɪdrədʒən | *s.i.* 1 QUIM. hidrógeno. || **2 – bomb,** FIS. bomba de hidrógeno. **3 – peroxide,** QUIM. peróxido de hidrógeno.

hydrophobia | 'haɪdrə'fəʊbɪə | *s.i.* MED. hidrofobia (especialmente como resultado de la rabia).

hydroplane | 'haɪdrəpleɪn | *s.c.* 1 hidroavión. || *v.i.* 2 elevarse por encima del agua (un barco cuando va a gran velocidad).

hydroponics | ˌhaɪdrə'pɒnɪks | *s.i.* AGR. acuicultura.

hydrotherapy | ˌhaɪdrəʊ'θerəpɪ | *s.i.* MED. hidroterapia.

hyena | haɪ'iːnə | (también **hyaena**) *s.c.* ZOOL. hiena.

hygiene | 'haɪdʒiːn | *s.i.* higiene.

hygienic | haɪ'dʒiːnɪk | *adj.* higiénico.

hymen | 'haɪmən | *s.c.* ANAT. himen.

hymn | hɪm | *s.c.* REL. himno.

hymnal | 'hɪmnəl | *s.c.* (form.) REL. libro de himnos, himnario.

hyper- | ˌhaɪpər | *prefijo* hiper: *hypercritical = hipercrítico.*

hyperactive | ˌhaɪpər'æktɪv | *adj.* hiperactivo.

hyperbola | haɪ'pɜːbələ | *s.c.* MAT. hipérbola.
hyperbole | haɪ'pɜːbəlɪ | *s.c.* GRAM. hipérbole.
hypermarket | 'haɪpəmɑːkɪt | *s.c.* hiper, hipermercado.
hypersensitive | ˌhaɪpə'sensətɪv | *adj.* **1** hipersensible (a agentes químicos, ambientales, etc.). **2** (desp.) hipersensible (a la crítica o similar).
hypertension | ˌhaɪpə'tenʃn | *s.i.* MED. hipertensión arterial.
hyphen | 'haɪfn | *s.c.* guión (signo de puntuación).
hyphenated | 'haɪfəneɪtɪd | *adj.* unido mediante guión.
hypnosis | hɪp'nəʊsɪs | *s.i.* hipnosis.
hypnotic | hɪp'nɒtɪk | *adj.* hipnótico.
hypnotise V. **hypnotize.**
hypnotism | 'hɪpnətɪzəm | *s.i.* hipnotismo.
hypnotist | 'hɪpnətɪst | *s.c.* hipnotista.
hypnotize | 'hɪpnətaɪz | (también **hypnotise**) *v.t.* **1** hipnotizar. **2** (fig.) dejar alelado, hipnotizar, atraer poderosamente la atención.
hypo | ˌhaɪpə | *prefijo* hipo: *hypothalamus= hipotálamo.*
hypochondria | ˌhaɪpə'kɒndrɪə | *s.i.* PSIQ. hipocondria.
hypochondriac | ˌhaɪpə'kɒndrɪæk | *s.c.* PSIQ. hipocondríaco.
hypocrisy | hɪ'pɒkrəsɪ | *s.c.* e *i.* (desp.) hipocresía.
hypocrite | 'hɪpəkrɪt | *s.c.* (desp.) hipócrita.
hypocritical | ˌhɪpə'krɪtɪkl | *adj.* (desp.) hipócrita.
hypodermic | ˌhaɪpə'dɜːmɪk | (también **hypodermic needle** o **hypodermic syringe**) *s.c.* inyección (todo el objeto).
hypotenuse | haɪ'pɒtənjuːz | (EE.UU.) | haɪ'pɒtənuːs*s.c.* GEOM. hipotenusa.
hypothermia | ˌhaɪpə'θɜːmɪə | *s.i.* MED. hipotermia.
hypotheses | haɪ'pɒθəsiːz | *pl.* de **hypothesis.**
hypothesis | haɪ'pɒθəsɪs | *s.c.* e *i.* (form.) hipótesis.
hypothetical | ˌhaɪpə'θetɪkl | *adj.* hipotético.
hypothetically | ˌhaɪpə'θetɪklɪ | *adv.* hipotéticamente.
hysterectomy | ˌhɪstə'rektəmɪ | *s.c.* MED. histerectomía.
hysteria | hɪ'stɪərɪə | *s.i.* **1** PSIQ. histeria. **2** (form. o lit. y fig.) histeria. **3** (form.) ataque de risa incontrolada.
hysterical | hɪ'sterɪkl | *adj.* **1** PSIQ. histérico. **2** (fig.) descontrolado (en sus emociones); histérico. **3** (fam.) descontrolada (risa). **4** (fam.) divertidísimo, para mondarse de risa.
hysterically | hɪ'sterɪklɪ | *adv.* **1** histéricamente, descontroladamente, en puro paroxismo. **2** (fam.) descontroladamente (reír). **3** (fam.) con gran regocijo, con gran diversión; a más no poder (de divertido).
hysterics | hɪ'sterɪks | *s.pl.* **1** PSIQ. histerismo, ataque de histeria. **2** (fam.) paroxismo (de miedo, excitación, etc.). **3** (fam.) ataque de risa incontrolable.

I | aɪ | *pl.* **I's, i's** o **Is, is.** novena letra del alfabeto inglés.

I | aɪ | *pron.* **1** yo (sujeto). **2** **[the –]** FIL. el ego. || *num.* **3** I (número romano). **4** QUIM. (I) símbolo del yodo.

ice | aɪs | *s.i.* **1** hielo. **2** hielo, cubitos de hielo (para bebidas). **3** (EE.UU.) joyas; diamantes. **4** (fam.) frialdad, indiferencia, reserva. || *s.c.* **5** (brit. y p.u.) helado, cono de helado. **6** sorbete, granizado. **7** capa de azúcar, glasé, escarcha, garapiña (en pastelería, coctelería). **8** (EE.UU.) DEP. pista de hielo. || *v.t.* **9** refrigerar, enfriar en refrigerador, helar. **10** glasear, escarchar, cubrir con una capa de azúcar (pasteles, cócteles). **11** congelar. **12** (EE.UU. y jerga) DEP. asegurar una victoria, afianzar (un resultado). || *v.t.* e *i.* **13** **[to – over/up]** *gen.pas.* cubrirse de hielo, helarse (una superficie). || **14** **black –,** V. **black.** **15** **to break the,** (fig.) romper el hielo, relajar el ambiente. **16** **to cut no –,** no convencer, no tener efecto especial, no importar nada. **17** **to put/keep a plan/project on –,** mantener un plan o un proyecto congelado, en suspenso, postergar un plan o un proyecto. **18** **to skate on thin –,** pisar terreno peligroso.

iceberg | 'aɪsbəːg | | 'aɪsbəːrg | *s.c.* **1** iceberg. **2** (fam.) témpano, hielo (una persona).

ice-blue | 'aɪsbluː | *adj.* azul celeste, azul pálido.

ice-box | 'aɪsbɒks | | 'aɪsbɑːks | *s.c.* **1** nevera portátil. **2** (EE.UU.) frigorífico, refrigerador.

icebucket | 'aɪs,bʌkɪt | *s.c.* cubitera (para enfriar bebidas).

icecap | 'aɪskæp | *s.c.* **1** casquete de hielo, casquete polar. **2** helero, capa de hielo.

ice-cold | ,aɪs'kəuld | *adj.* helado, gélido, glacial, tan frío como el hielo.

ice-cream | ,aɪs'kriːm | *s.c.* e *i.* helado (golosina, postre).

ice-cube | ,aɪs'kjuːb | *s.c.* cubito de hielo.

iced | aɪst | *adj.* **1** helado, refrigerado. **2** helado, cubierto de hielo. **3** glaseado, escarchado, garapiñado, cubierto por una capa dura de azúcar.

ice-floe | 'aɪs,fləu | *s.c.* **1** témpano flotante, masa de hielo flotante.

ice-hockey | 'aɪs,hɒkɪ | *s.i.* **1** DEP. hockey sobre hielo.

Iceland | 'aɪslənd | *s.sing.* **1** Islandia.

Icelander | 'aɪsləndər | *s.c.* **1** islandés.

Icelandic | aɪs'lændɪk | *adj.* **1** islandés (de origen). || *s.c.* **2** islandés (lengua).

ice-lolly | 'aɪs,lɒlɪ | *s.c.* **1** polo (golosina).

ice-rink | 'aɪsrɪnk | *s.c.* **1** pista de patinaje sobre hielo.

ice-skate | 'aɪsskeɪt | *v.i.* **1** patinar sobre hielo. || *s.c.* **2** patín para hielo.

ice-skating | 'aɪsskeɪtɪŋ | *s.i.* **1** DEP. patinaje sobre hielo.

icicle | 'aɪsɪkl | *s.c.* **1** carámbano, calamoco, pinganillo.

icing | 'aɪsɪŋ | *s.i.* **1** (brit.) glasé, alcorza, capa de azúcar glasé. || **2** **– sugar,** azúcar glasé. **3** **the – on the cake,** (fig. y desp.) fruslerías, detalles innecesarios.

icon, ikon | 'aɪkɒn | | 'aɪkɑːn | *s.c.* **1** REL. icono, imagen religiosa. **2** (fig.) símil, símbolo, ideal. **3** INF. icono.

iconoclast | aɪ'kɒnəuklæst | | aɪ'kɒnəu'klɑːst | *s.c.* **1** (arc.) iconoclasta, hereje. **2** iconoclasta, crítico.

iconoclastic | aɪ,kɒnəu'klæstɪk | | aɪ,kɒnəu'klɑːstɪk | *adj.* **1** iconoclasta.

icy | 'aɪsɪ | *adj.* **1** helado, glacial, gélido. **2** (fig.) glacial, fría (una mirada). **3** helado, cubierto de hielo.

icily | 'aɪsɪlɪ | *adv.* **1** gélidamente, glacialmente. **2** (fig.) fríamente, gélidamente.

iciness | 'aɪsɪnɪs | *s.i.* frialdad extrema, gelidez.

idea | aɪ'dɪə | *s.c.* **1** idea, ocurrencia, sugerencia. **2** idea, tema. **3** noción, punto de vista, concepto. **4** impresión, intuición. **5** plan, intención, propósito, objetivo. || *s.c.* e *i.* **6** idea, noción, conocimiento, concepción. || **7** **to get the –,** (fam.) entender, comprender, coger la idea. **8** **to put ideas into someone's head,** sugerir ideas, hacer concebir vanas esperanzas. **9** **that's the idea!** ¡eso es!, ¡esa es la idea! **10** **what's the idea?,** (fam.) ¿pero qué pretendes? (con enfado). **11** **what's the big –?,** (EE.UU.) ¿qué estás tramando? **12** **you've no –!,** ¡no tienes ni idea!, ¡no te haces idea!

ideal | aɪ'dɪəl | *adj.* **1** ideal, perfecto. **2** **[– for]** ideal para, adecuado para. **3** modélico, soñado. || *s.c.* **4** **ideals,** ideales, metas, fines. **5** ideal, modelo, ejemplo perfecto, sueño.

idealism | aɪ'dɪəlɪzəm | *s.i.* **1** idealismo. **2** ART. idealismo.

idealist | aɪ'dɪəlɪst | *s.c.* (desp.) idealista.

idealistic | aɪ,dɪə'lɪstɪk | *adj.* idealista, utópico.

idealization | aɪ,dɪəlaɪ'zeɪʃn | *s.c.* e *i.* idealización.

idealize | aɪ'dɪəlaɪz | (brit.) **idealise.** *v.t.* **1** idealizar. || *v.i.* **2** concebir un ideal.

idealized | aɪ'dɪəlaɪz | *adj.* idealizado.

ideally | aɪ'dɪəlɪ | *adv.* **1** idealmente, a la perfección. **2** idealmente, preferiblemente.

identical | aɪ'dentɪkl | *adj.* **1** idéntico, exacto, igual. **2** el mismo. || **3** **– twin,** *gen.pl.* mellizo, gemelo.

identically | aɪ'dentɪkəlɪ | *adv.* idénticamente, exactamente.

identifiable | aɪ'dentɪfaɪəbl | *adj.* identificable, reconocible, obvio.

identification | aɪ'dentɪfɪ'keɪʃn | *s.i.* **1** identificación, reconocimiento. **2** **[– with]** identificación con, entendimiento con, solidaridad con, empatía con (sentimientos, ideas, personas). || **3** **– parade,**

(brit.) rueda de reconocimiento (en comisaría).
identify | aɪ'dentɪfaɪ | *v.t.* **1** identificar, reconocer. **2** descubrir, identificar (un problema, una causa). **3** **[to – with]** identificarse con, solidarizarse con, empatizar con (una persona, un problema). **4** **[to – somebody with something]** identificar a alguien con algo.
identikit | aɪ'dentɪkɪt | *s.c.* **1** retrato robot. **2** (fig.) copia, imitación, remedo (una persona con respecto a otra).
identity | aɪ'dentɪtɪ | *s.c.* e *i.* **1** identidad. **2** exactitud, parecido exacto. || **3 – card,** carnet de identidad. **4 loss of –,** pérdida de identidad. **5 – crisis,** crisis de identidad.
ideological | ˌaɪdɪə'lɒdʒɪkl | *adj.* ideológico.
ideologically | ˌaɪdɪə'lɒdʒɪkəlɪ | *adv.* ideológicamente.
ideology | ˌaɪdɪ'ɒlədʒɪ | | ˌaɪdɪ'ɑːlədʒɪ | *s.c.* e *i.* ideología.
idiocy | 'ɪdɪəsɪ | *s.i.* **1** idiotez, imbecilidad. || *s.c.* **2** idiotez, tontería, estupidez.
idiom | 'ɪdɪəm | *s.c.* **1** modismo, frase hecha. **2** lenguaje, jerga, habla peculiar, estilo (de una comunidad, de un período, de una materia).
idiomatic | ˌɪdɪə'mætɪk | *adj.* idiomático.
idiosyncrasy | ˌɪdɪə'sɪŋkrəsɪ | *s.c.* **1** idiosincrasia, peculiaridad. **2** hipersensibilidad (a una droga).
idiosyncratic | ˌɪdɪəsɪŋkrætɪk | *adj.* idiosincrático, peculiar.
idiot | 'ɪdɪət | *s.c.* **1** idiota, imbécil, tonto, majadero. **2** PSIC. deficiente psíquico, deficiente mental.
idiotic | ˌɪdɪ'ɒtɪk | | ˌɪdɪ'ɑːtɪk | *adj.* idiota, imbécil, tonto.
idiotically | ˌɪdɪ'ɒtɪkəlɪ | *adv.* tontamente, estúpidamente, como un imbécil.
idle | 'aɪdl | *adj.* **1** ocioso, desocupado, inoperante. **2** inactivo, en paro. **3** holgazán, perezoso, haragán. **4** inútil, vago (una amenaza, un rumor). **5** infundado, frívolo (un comentario). **6** mera, simple (curiosidad). || *v.i.* **7** estar ocioso, estar inactivo, estar desocupado. **8** haraganear, holgazanear. **9** MEC. marchar en vacío. || *v.t.* **10** **[to – away]** desperdiciar el tiempo, pasar el rato.
idleness | 'aɪdlnɪs | *s.i.* **1** inactividad, ociosidad. **2** vagancia, holgazanería. **3** desempleo, desocupación, despido. **4** inutilidad. **5** frivolidad, futilidad.
idler | 'aɪdlər | *s.c.* **1** holgazán, haragán, vago. **2** ocioso, desocupado.
idling | 'aɪdlɪŋ | *adj.* MEC. en baja, en vacío (un motor).
idly | 'aɪdlɪ | *adv.* **1** ociosamente, inactivamente. **2** vanamente, fútilmente, frívolamente. **3** distraídamente.
idol | 'aɪdl | *s.c.* **1** ídolo, falso dios. **2** (fig.) ídolo, héroe. **3** (arc.) imagen.
idolatrous | aɪ'dɒlətrəs | | aɪ'dɑːlətrəs | *adj.* **1** idólatra, idolátrico. **2** (fig.) desmedido, desmesurado (un amor).
idolatry | aɪ'dɒlətrɪ | | aɪ'dɑːlətrɪ | *s.i.* **1** idolatría. **2** (fig.) idolatría, amor desmedido, afición desmedida.
idolize | 'aɪdəlaɪz | (brit.) **idolise.** *v.t.* idolatrar, adorar, admirar ciegamente.
idyl | 'ɪdɪl | | 'aɪdɪl | (brit.) **idyll.** *s.c.* idilio.
idyllyc | aɪ'dɪlɪk | | ɪ'dɪlɪk | *adj.* idílico, bucólico.
i.e. | ˌaɪ'iː | (**id est.**) es decir, por ejemplo.
if | ɪf | *conj.* **1** si, en caso de que, suponiendo que, supuesto que: *if she should come, ... = en caso de que ella viniera,...* **2** **[even –]** aunque, a pesar de que: *even if I can't = aunque no pueda.* **3** [*s./adj./adv.* – *s./adj./adv.*] si bien, aunque, aun aceptando que: *a nice party, if a little noisy = una fiesta agradable, si bien un poco ruidosa.* **4** **[to know/remember/wonder --,** o en preguntas indirectas] **si (o no):** *I wonder if he's at home = me pregunto si estará en casa (o no).* **5** **[sorry/don't care/mind –]** que: *I don't care if he cries = me importa un rábano que llore.* || *s.c.* **6** (generalmente *pl.*) duda, hipótesis, suposición. || **as –,** como si: *as if it were a problem! = ¡como si eso fuera un problema!* **8 – anything,** quizás, si acaso, hasta creo que. **9 – ever,** si alguna vez, si en algún momento. **10 – not,** si no, por no decir. **11 – only,** ¡ojalá!, si por lo menos; aunque solo fuera (para): *if only for a minute = aunque solo fuera durante un minuto.* **12 – you like,** si quieres, por decirlo de otro modo, por así decir. **13 ifs and buts,** dudas, reservas, pegas, disculpas. **14 it isn't as/it's not as –,** no es que sea, no es como si fuera: *Why does she marry him? It's not as if he were rich... = ¿por qué se casa con él? No es que sea rico...*
iffy | 'ɪfɪ | *adj.* (fam.) dudoso, inseguro, lleno de incertidumbre.
igloo | 'ɪgluː | *s.c.* iglú.
igneous | 'ɪgnɪəs | *adj.* **1** GEOL. ígneo, volcánico. **2** (fig.) apasionado, ardiente.
ignite | ɪg'naɪt | *v.t.* e *i.* (form.) encender, inflamarse, prender (un fuego).
ignition | ɪg'nɪʃn | *s.i.* **1** ignición. **2** MEC. encendido, contacto.
ignoble | ɪg'nəʊbl | *adj.* **1** (lit.) innoble, abyecto, deshonesto, despreciable, indigno. **2** plebeyo.
ignominous | ˌɪgnəʊ'mɪnɪəs | *adj.* ignominioso, deshonroso, vergonzoso.
ignominiously | ˌɪgnəʊ'mɪnɪəslɪ | *adv.* ignominiosamente, vergonzosamente.
ignominy | 'ɪgnəmɪnɪ | *s.i.* **1** ignominia, deshonra, deshonor, humillación. || *s.c.* **2** infamia, vergüenza, conducta ignominiosa.
ignoramus | ˌɪgnə'reɪməs | *s.c.* ignorante, inculto, analfabeto.
ignorance | 'ɪgnərəns | *s.i.* ignorancia, incultura, desconocimiento.
ignorant | 'ɪgnərənt | *adj.* ignorante, inculto, iletrado, indocumentado.
ignore | ɪg'nɔː | *v.t.* ignorar, no prestar atención, desatender, pasar por alto, cerrar los ojos a.
ikon | 'aɪkɒn | V. **icon.**
ilk | ɪlk | *s.sing.* clase, tipo, familia, raza.
ill | ɪl | *comp.* **worse,** *sup.* **worst.** *adj.* **1** enfermo, indispuesto, malo. **2** (brit.) herido, malherido. **3** aciago, funesto, malísimo, poco propicio (un día, la suerte). **4** penoso, adverso (un resultado). **5** nocivo, perjudicial (un efecto). **6** hostil, con mala intención. || *adv.* **[***gen.* – *p.p.***].** **7** cruelmente, desagradablemente, mal: *ill-treated = maltratado.* **8** apenas, pobremente, no suficientemente: *illresearched = apenas investigado.* **9** desfavorablemente. || *s.c. gen.pl.* **10** (arc.) enfermedades, males; desgracias, infortunios, desastres. || *s.i.* **11** (arc.) mal, pecado, maldad, daño. || **12 to augur/bode –,** (lit.) presagiar algo malo. **13 to be taken/fall –,** caer enfermo, ponerse enfermo, enfermar. **14 for good or –,** para bien o para mal. **15 to make somebody –,** poner malo a alguien, poner a alguien de los nervios. **16 to serve somebody –,** poner en desventaja a alguien. **17 to speak – of,** criticar, hablar mal de. **18 – at ease,** nervioso, incómodo, raro (ante una situación). **19 – will,** hostilidad, mala fe, rencor, mala voluntad. **20 it's an – wind that blows nobody any good,** nunca llueve a gusto de todos.
ill-advised | ˌɪləd'vaɪzd | *adj.* imprudente, insensato, necio, malaconsejado.
ill-assorted | ˌɪlə'sɔːtɪd | *adj.* mal combinado, mal mezclado (la ropa, los complementos).
ill-bred | ˌɪl'bred | *adj.* maleducado, malcriado, rudo, descortés.
ill-disposed | ˌɪldɪ'spəʊz | *adj.* contrario, hostil, maldispuesto, dispuesto en contra.
illegal | ɪ'liːgl | *adj.* **1** ilegal, ilícito, contra la ley (un acto). **2** ilegal, prohibido, fuera de la ley (una organización).
illegality | ˌɪliː'gælətɪ | *s.i.* **1** ilegalidad, ilicitud. || *s.c.* **2** ilegalidad, acto ilegal.
illegaly | ɪ'liːgəlɪ | *adv.* ilegalmente, ilícitamente.
illegible | ɪ'ledʒəbl | *adj.* ilegible, indescifrable, difícil de entender (la escritura).
illegitimacy | ˌɪlɪ'dʒɪtɪməsɪ | *s.i.* ilegitimidad.
illegitimate | ˌɪlɪ'dʒɪtɪmət | *adj.* **1** ilegítimo, bastardo. **2** ilícito, no permitido.
ill-equiped | ˌɪlɪ'kwɪpt | *adj.* mal equipado, mal preparado.
ill-fated | ɪl'feɪtɪd | *adj.* desafortunado, desdichado, trágico, desgraciado.
ill-founded | ɪl'faʊndɪd | *adj.* infundado, falso, sin fundamento (un rumor).
ill-gotten gains | ˌɪl'gɒtn'geinz | *s.pl.* (form.) ganancias adquiridas deshonestamente, beneficios deshonestos.
ill-health | 'ɪl'helθ | *s.i.* mala salud.
illiberal | ɪ'lɪbərəl | *adj.* **1** conservador. **2** intolerante, represor. **3** tacaño, poco generoso, mezquino.
illicit | ɪ'lɪsɪt | *adj.* ilícito, prohibido, ilegal.
illiteracy | ɪ'lɪtərəsɪ | *s.i.* analfabetismo, incultura.
illiterate | ɪ'lɪtərət | *s.c.* **1** analfabeto. **2** (fam.) inculto, iletrado, ignorante.

illness | 'ɪlnɪs | *s.c.* e *i.* **1** enfermedad, dolencia, afección, indisposición. **2** perversidad, maldad.
illogical | ɪ'lɒdʒɪkl | | ɪ'lɑːdʒkl | *adj.* **1** ilógico, poco razonable. **2** (fam.) irracional, disparatado.
illogically | ɪ'lɒdʒɪkəlɪ | *adv.* **1** ilógicamente, sin razón. **2** irracionalmente, disparatadamente.
ill-omened | ˌɪl'əumend | *adj.* desdichado, desgraciado, aciago.
ill-starred | ˌɪl'stɑːd | *adj.* (lit.) desdichado, malaventurado, malhadado.
ill-tempered | ˌɪl'tempəd | *adj.* **1** (form.) irritable, irascible, destemplado, regañón. **2** caprichoso, extravagante.
ill-timed | ˌɪl'taɪmd | *adj.* inoportuno, falto de tacto, a destiempo (un comentario).
ill-treat | ˌɪl'triːt | *v.t.* maltratar, abusar de, tratar con crueldad.
ill treatement | 'ɪl'triːtmənt | *s.c.* malos tratos.
illuminate | ɪ'luːmɪneɪt | | ɪ'luːmɪneɪt | *v.t.* **1** iluminar, alumbrar, encender (una habitación). **2** (fig.) iluminar, encender (la mirada). **3** iluminar, decorar (con luces de colores). **4** clarificar, esclarecer, explicar, arrojar luz. **5** (arc.) ilustrar (un libro con letras doradas, colores).
illuminated | ɪ'luːmɪneɪtɪd | *adj.* **1** iluminado, luminoso. **2** ilustrado (un libro con letras doradas, colores).
illuminating | ɪ'luːmɪneɪtɪŋ | | ɪ'luːmɪneɪtɪŋ | *adj.* esclarecedor, aclarativo, instructivo.
illumination | ɪ'luːmɪ'neɪʃn | | ɪˌluːmɪ'↓ neɪʃn | *s.i.* **1** iluminación, alumbrado, luz. || *s.c.* **2** (gen. *pl.*) (arc.) ilustración, grabado (en un libro). **3** (brit.) iluminación, decoración con luces de colores (gen. en Navidad).
illumine | ɪ'luːmɪn | *v.t.* **1** (lit.) iluminar, alumbrar. **2** (lit.) iluminar, decorar (con bombillas de colores). **3** clarificar, esclarecer, arrojar luz. **4** ilustrar (un libro con letras doradas, colores).
illusion | ɪ'luːʒn | *s.c.* e *i.* **1** ilusión, espejismo, fantasía. || *s.c.* **2** ilusión, fantasía, falsa impresión. **3** ilusionismo, truco de magia. **4** gasa, cendal. || **5 to be under an –,** tener la falsa impresión, pensar equivocadamente. **6 to have no illusions about,** no hacerse ilusiones de.
illusory, illusive | ɪ'luːsərɪ | | ɪ'luːsɪv | *adj.* ilusorio, imaginario, engañoso.
illustrate | 'ɪləstreɪt | *v.t.* **1** (gen. *pas.*) ilustrar (un libro, una conferencia con grabados, filminas). **2** ilustrar, ejemplificar, demostrar. **3** (arc.) iluminar, alumbrar, encender. || *v.i.* **4** clarificar, poner un ejemplo, explicar con un ejemplo.
illustration | ˌɪlə'streɪʃn | *s.c.* **1** ilustración, grabado, lámina, diagrama. **2** ilustración, ejemplo, aclaración, demostración. || *s.i.* **3** ilustración, clarificación. || **4 by way of –,** como ilustración, como ejemplo.
illustrative | 'ɪləstrətɪv | | 'ɪlʌstrətɪv | *adj.* ilustrativo, clarificador, aclaratorio, explicativo.

illustrator | 'ɪləstreɪtər | *s.c.* ilustrador.
illustrious | ɪ'lʌstrɪəs | *adj.* ilustre, distinguido, eminente, célebre, egregio, emérito, famoso.
image | 'ɪmɪdʒ | *s.c.* **1** OPT. imagen. **2** concepto, idea, noción. **3** imagen, reflejo. **4** imagen, opinión, reputación. **5 [the – of]** el reflejo de, el retrato de, la estampa de. **6** LIT. metáfora, símil, imagen poética. **7 to be the living/very – of,** ser el vivo retrato de. **8** (arc.) imagen, semejanza: *made in the – of = hecho a semejanza de.* **9 mirror –,** V. **mirror. 10 spitting –,** V. **spitting.**
imagery | 'ɪmɪdʒərɪ | *s.i.* LIT. imágenes, metáforas.
imaginable | ɪ'mædʒɪnəbl | *adj.* imaginable, posible, concebible.
imaginary | ɪ'mædʒɪnərɪ | *adj.* imaginario.
imagination | ɪˌmædʒɪ'neɪʃn | *s.c.* e *i.* **1** imaginación, inventiva, fantasía. **2** imaginación, mente. || *s.i.* **3** (fam.) imaginación, fantasía, ilusión. **4** imaginación, ingenio, creatividad.
imaginative | ɪ'mædʒɪnətɪv | *adj.* imaginativo, creativo, ingenioso, original.
imaginatively | ɪ'mædʒɪnətɪvlɪ | *adv.* imaginativamente, creativamente, ingeniosamente, de forma original, con creatividad.
imagine | ɪ'mædʒɪn | *v.t.* **1** imaginar, figurar, formarse una idea, visualizar. **3** fantasear, soñar, inventar. **3 [to – (that)/o.]** suponer, pensar, creer. || *v.i.* **4** usar la imaginación, ejercitar la imaginación. **5** hacer conjeturas, adivinar. || **6 just – (it/that),** ¡imagínate! (expresa sorpresa).
imaginings | ɪ'mædʒɪnɪŋz | *s.pl.* (lit.) imaginaciones, fantasías, ensoñaciones.
imbalance | ˌɪn'bæləns | *s.c.* e *i.* desigualdad, desequilibrio, desproporción.
imbecile | 'ɪmbəsiːl | *s.i.* **1** imbécil, idiota, tonto, estúpido. **2** (arc.) disminuido psíquico, deficiente mental.
imbecility | ˌɪmbə'sɪlɪtɪ | *s.i.* **1** imbecilidad, idiotez, estupidez. || *s.c.* **2** estupidez, disparate, locura.
imbibe | ɪm'baɪb | *v.t.* e *i.* **1** (hum. o form.) beber, absorber (alcohol). **2** (fig.) embeber, absorber, asimilar (ideas). **3** (arc.) saturar, empapar, embeber, absorber (agua, humedad).
imbroglio | ɪm'brəulɪəu | *pl.* **imbroglios.** *s.c.* **1** (lit.) embrollo, lío, enredo. **2** (lit.) malentendido, situación confusa, embrollo (en una obra de teatro).
imbue | ɪm'bjuː | *v.t.* (gen. *pas.*) **1** imbuir, impregnar (de sentimientos, ideas). **2** (EE.UU.) saturar, empapar. **3** (EE.UU.) teñir. **4** (EE.UU.) manchar.
imbued | ɪm'bjuːd | *adj.* **1** imbuido, impregnado. **2** (EE.UU.) saturado, empapado. **3** (EE.UU.) teñido. **4** (EE.UU.) manchado.
imitate | 'ɪmɪteɪt | *v.t.* **1** imitar, copiar, remedar. **2** plagiar. **3** imitar, tomar como ejemplo, tomar como modelo.
imitation | ˌɪmɪ'teɪʃn | *s.c.* e *i.* **1** imitación, remedo, copia. **2** plagio. **3** MUS. repetición melódica. || *s.c.* **4** imitación, reproducción. || *adj.* **5** de imitación, artificial, falso: *imitation flowers = flores artificiales.*
imitative | 'ɪmɪtətɪv | | 'ɪmɪteɪtɪv | *adj.* (gen. desp.) imitativo, imitador, que imita.
imitator | 'ɪmɪteɪtər | *s.c.* imitador.
immaculate | ɪ'mækjulət | *adj.* **1** inmaculado, limpísimo. **2** perfecto, impecable.
immaculately | ɪ'mækjulətlɪ | *adv.* inmaculadamente, impecablemente, perfectamente, sin tacha.
immaterial | ˌɪmə'tɪərɪəl | *adj.* **1** irrelevante, sin importancia, sin consecuencias. **2** indiferente. **3** inmaterial, incorpóreo.
immature | ˌɪmə'tjuər | *adj.* **1** inmaturo, verde, sin formar, poco hecho. **2** inmaturo, infantil, juvenil.
immaturity | ˌɪmə'tjuərɪtɪ | *s.i.* inmadurez, falta de madurez, infantilismo.
immeasurably | ɪ'meʒərəblɪ | *adv.* inconmensurablemente, enormemente, ilimitadamente.
immediacy, immediateness | ɪ'miːdɪəsɪ | | dɪətnɪs | *s.i.* **1** inmediatez, cercanía, proximidad. **2** urgencia, perentoriedad importancia.
immediate | ɪ'miːdɪət | *adj.* **1** inmediato, instantáneo, apremiante, urgente, sin retraso. **2** inmediato, próximo, a la vista. **3** cercano, directo (un familiar, una causa).
immediately | ɪ'miːdɪətlɪ | *adv.* **1** inmediatamente, sin demora, enseguida, al instante. **2** directamente, al lado mismo: *immediately in front of the house = al lado mismo de casa.* || *conj.* **3** (brit.) tan pronto como, así que, en cuanto.
immemorial | ˌɪmɪ'mɔːrɪəl | *adj.* **1** inmemorial, inmemorable. || **2 from/since –,** desde tiempo inmemorial, desde hace muchísimo.
immense | ɪ'mens | *adj.* **1** inmenso, enorme, infinito. **2** inconmensurable, vastísimo. **3** (jerga) espléndido, excelente.
immensely | ɪ'menslɪ | *adv.* **1** inmensamente, enormemente, infinitamente. **2** inconmensurablemente.
immensity, immensities | ɪ'mensətɪ | | ɪz | *s.i.* inmensidad, magnitud, vastedad.
immerse | ɪ'məːs | *v.t.* **1 [to – in]** sumergir en, hundir en. **2 [to – in]** estar inmerso en, enfrascarse en. **3** REL. bautizar por inmersión.
immersed | ɪ'məːst | *adj.* **1** BOT. sumergido. **2** absorto, inmerso, enfrascado.
immersion | ɪ'məːʃn | *s.i.* **1** inmersión (en agua). **2** bautismo por inmersión. **3** método de inmersión (para el aprendizaje de lenguas extranjeras). **4** ASTR. inmersión, eclipse. || **5 – heater,** (brit.) calentador eléctrico, calentador de inmersión.
immigrant | 'ɪmɪgrənt | *s.c.* inmigrante.
immigration | ˌɪmɪ'greɪʃn | *s.c.* e *i.* **1** inmigración. || **2 – control,** control de inmigración.

imminence, imminency | 'ɪmɪnəns | | nənsɪ | *s.i.* (form.) inminencia.

imminent | 'ɪmɪnənt | *adj.* inminente.

immobile | ɪ'məubaɪl | | ɪ'məubi:l | *adj.* inmóvil, inmovible, estático, fijo.

immobility | ˌɪməu'bɪlɪtɪ | *s.i.* inmovilidad.

immobilize | ɪ'məubɪlaɪz | (brit.) **immobilise.** *v.t.* **1** inmovilizar, paralizar. **2** (fig.) paralizar (el trabajo).

immoderate | ɪ'mɒdərət | | ɪ'mɑːdərət | *adj.* (form.) inmoderado, excesivo, ilimitado, extremo.

immoderately | ɪ'mɒdərətlɪ | *adv.* excesivamente, sin moderación, ilimitadamente.

immodest | ɪ'mɒdɪst | | ɪ'mɑːdɪst | *adj.* **1** (form.) inmodesto, vanidoso, presumido, jactancioso. **2** (form.) impúdico, indecente.

immodestly | ɪ'mɒdɪstlɪ | *adv.* **1** (form.) inmodestamente, vanidosamente, con presunción. **2** (form.) impúdicamente, indecentemente.

immodesty | ɪ'mɒdɪstɪ | *s.i.* **1** (form.) falta de modestia, vanidad, presunción, jactancia. **2** (form.) impudicia, indecencia.

immoral | ɪ'mɒrəl | *adj.* inmoral, deshonesto, ilícito.

immorality | ˌɪmə'rælɪtɪ | *s.i.* **1** inmoralidad, deshonestidad. || *s.c.* **2** (gen. *pl.*) inmoralidad, acto inmoral, acto ilícito.

immortal | ɪ'mɔːtl | | ɪ'mɔːrtl | *adj.* **1** inmortal, eterno, imperecedero. **2** inmortal, de fama eterna. || *s.c.* **3** inmortal (una deidad, un héroe).

immortality | ˌɪmɔː'tælɪtɪ | *s.i.* **1** inmortalidad. **2** fama inmortal, fama perdurable.

immortalize | ɪ'mɔːtəlaɪz | | ɪ'mɔːrtəlaɪz | (brit.) **immortalise.** *v.t.* inmortalizar, celebrar, perpetuar.

immovable | ɪ'muːvəbl | *adj.* **1** inamovible, inmóvil, firme, que no se puede mover. **2** inmutable, inalterable, inflexible. **3** inconmovible, impasible, imperturbable.

immovably | ɪ'muːvəblɪ | *adv.* **1** firmemente. **2** inmutablemente. **3** inalterablemente, impasiblemente, imperturbablemente.

immune | ɪ'mjuːn | *adj.* **1** MED. inmune. **2** inmune, invulnerable (a las críticas). **3** inmune, protegido (ante la ley). **4** exento, libre (de impuestos).

immunity | ɪ'mjuːnətɪ | *s.i.* **1** MED. inmunidad. **2** inmunidad, invulnerabilidad (diplomática, a las críticas). **3** protección (ante la ley). **4** exención (de impuestos).

immunize | 'ɪmjuːnaɪz | (brit.) **immunise.** *v.t.* MED. inmunizar.

immunization | ˌɪmjuːnaɪ'zeɪʃn | *s.c.* e *i.* MED. inmunización.

immutable | ɪ'mjuːtəbl | *adj.* (form.) inmutable, inalterable.

imp | ɪmp | *s.c.* **1** diablillo, duende. **2** (fig.) diablillo, travieso, trasto (un niño). **3** (arc.) injerto. || *v.t.* **4** injertar plumas, reforzar (las alas de un halcón para mejorar el vuelo).

impact | 'ɪmpækt | *s.c.* **1** impacto, choque, golpe, colisión. **2** impacto, impresión, efecto intenso. || *v.t.* e *i.* **3** (EE.UU.) tener impacto, tener repercusión. **4** fijar, incrustar.

impacted | ɪm'pæktɪd | *adj.* MED. impactado (un diente debajo de otro).

impair | ɪm'peər | *v.t.* debilitar, empeorar, deteriorar, perjudicar.

impaired | ɪm'peəd | *adj.* debilitado, deteriorado, perjudicado, dañado.

impale | ɪm'peɪl | *v.t.* empalar, atravesar, espetar.

impart | ɪm'pɑːt | *v.t.* **1** (form.) comunicar, transmitir (un sentimiento, una cualidad). **2** despedir (un olor). **3** impartir, transmitir, comunicar (formación, conocimientos).

impartial | ɪm'pɑːʃl | *adj.* imparcial, objetivo, neutral, justo, equitativo.

impartially | ɪm'pɑːʃəlɪ | *adv.* imparcialmente, objetivamente, neutralmente, equitativamente.

impartiality | 'ɪmˌpɑːʃɪ'ælɪtɪ | *s.i.* imparcialidad, objetividad, neutralidad, equidad.

impassable | ɪm'pɑːsəbl | | ɪm'pæsəbl | *adj.* intransitable, impracticable (una carretera).

impasse | æm'pɑːs | | 'ɪmpæs | *s.sing.* **1** callejón sin salida, punto muerto. **2** atolladero, parálisis; (Am.) impasse.

impassioned | ɪm'pæʃnd | *adj.* **1** apasionado, ardiente. **2** entusiasmado, exaltado.

impassive | ɪm'pæsɪv | *adj.* **1** impasible, imperturbable, impertérrito. **2** indiferente, insensible. **3** inmóvil, sereno, quieto.

impassively | ɪm'pæsɪvlɪ | *adv.* **1** impasiblemente, imperturbablemente. **2** indiferentemente, insensiblemente.

impatience | ɪm'peɪʃns | *s.i.* **1** impaciencia, nerviosismo. **2** exasperación. **3** intolerancia.

impatient | ɪm'peɪʃnt | *adj.* **1** impaciente, nervioso. **2** exasperado, irritado. **3** intolerante.

impaciently | ɪm'peɪʃntlɪ | *adv.* **1** impacientemente, con nerviosismo. **2** exasperadamente, con irritación. **3** de forma intolerante.

impeach | ɪm'piːtʃ | *v.t.* **1** (form.) censurar, poner en tela de juicio, poner en duda, atacar. **2** DER. inculpar, culpar, acusar (de un crimen de estado). **3** DER. (EE.UU.) procesar (a un funcionario por alta traición).

impeachable | ɪm'piːtʃəbl | *adj.* inculpable, acusable (de alta traición).

impeachement | ɪm'piːtʃmənt | *s.i.* **1** acusación, inculpación (de alta traición). **2** causa, proceso (por alta traición).

impeccable | ɪm'pekəbl | *adj.* impecable, intachable, inmaculado.

impeccably | ɪm'pekəblɪ | *adv.* impecablemente, inmaculadamente.

impecunious | ˌɪmpɪ'kjuːnjəs | *adj.* (form. y hum.) pobre, indigente, sin un duro (casi siempre).

impede | ɪm'piːd | *v.t.* impedir, entorpecer, estorbar, dificultar, obstaculizar.

impediment | ɪm'pedɪmənt | *s.c.* **1** impedimento, obstáculo, dificultad, estorbo, traba. **2** impedimento, defecto (físico).

impedimenta | ɪm'pedɪ'mentə | *s.pl.* **1** equipaje, parafernalia. **2** MIL. impedimenta. **3** (fig.) impedimenta, trastos, cachivaches.

impel | ɪm'pel | (brit.) **impell.** *v.t.* **1** impeler, impulsar. **2** incitar, instigar, obligar.

impending | ɪm'pendɪŋ | *adj.* inminente, próximo, cercano (algo desagradable).

impenetrable | ɪm'penɪtrəbl | *adj.* **1** impenetrable, inaccesible. **2** (fig.) indescifrable, enigmático, insondable.

impenetrability | ɪmˌpenɪtrə'bɪlɪtɪ | *s.i.* impenetrabilidad, inaccesibilidad.

impenetrably | ɪm'penɪtrəblɪ | *adv.* impenetrablemente, inaccesiblemente.

imperative | ɪm'perətɪv | *adj.* **1** imperioso, urgente, ineludible, vital. **2** impe[illegible]rativo, autoritario (el tono de voz). [illegible] GRAM. imperativo. || *s.c.* **4** GRAM. mo[illegible] imperativo. **5** (form.) imperativo, deb[illegible] prioridad, obligación.

imperceptible | ˌɪmpə'septɪbl | | ˌɪmpər'septəbl | *adj.* **imperceptible.**

imperceptibly | ˌɪmpə'septɪblɪ | *adv.* imperceptiblemente, sin notarlo, sin darse cuenta.

imperfect | ɪmˌ'pəːfɪkt | *adj.* **1** imperfecto, defectuoso, con fallos, con taras. [illegible] GRAM. imperfecto. || *s.sing.* **3** pretérito imperfecto.

imperfection | ˌimpə'fekʃn | *s.c.* e *i.* **1** imperfección, debilidad. **2** imperfección, defecto, fallo.

imperfectly | ɪm'pəːfɪktlɪ | *adv.* imperfectamente, defectuosamente.

imperial | ɪm'pɪərɪəl | *adj.* **1** imperial. **2** (brit.) imperial (el sistema de pesos y medidas). **3** (arc.) imperial, soberano, mayestático. **4** grandioso, magnífico. || *s.c.* **5** imperial (el techo del automóvil). **6** tamaño imperial (del papel).

imperialism | ɪm'pɪərɪəlɪzəm | *s.i.* **1** imperialismo. **2** (desp.) imperialismo, expansionismo (gobierno, autoridad, sistema de control).

imperialist | ɪm'pɪərɪəlɪst | *adj.* imperialista, expansionista.

imperil | ɪm'perɪl | (brit.) **imperill.** *v.t.* (form.) arriesgar, poner en peligro; estar en peligro.

imperious | ɪm'pɪərɪəs | *adj.* imperioso, autoritario, dominante, arrogante.

imperiously | ɪm'pɪərɪəslɪ | *adv.* imperiosamente, autoritariamente, arrogantemente.

imperisable | ɪm'perɪʃəbl | *adj.* imperecedero, indestructible.

impermanence | ɪm'pəːmənəns | *s.i.* temporalidad, transitoriedad.

impermanent | ɪm'pəːmənənt | *adj.* temporal, transitorio, variable, no permanente.

impermeable | ɪm'pəːmjəbl | | ɪm'pəːrmjəbl | *adj.* (form.) impermeable, impenetrable.

impersonal | ɪm'pɜːsnl | | ɪm'pɜːrsənl | *adj.* 1 impersonal, distante. 2 GRAM. impersonal; indefinido.

impersonally | ɪm'pɜːsənəlɪ | *adv.* impersonalmente, distantemente.

impersonate | ɪm'pɜːsəneɪt | | ɪm'pɜːrsəneɪt | *v.t.* 1 asumir la personalidad de, usurpar la personalidad de. 2 interpretar, imitar (en teatro). 3 (form.) fingir, hacerse el, simular.

impersonation | ɪm,pɜːsə'neɪʃn | *s.i.* 1 imitación, interpretación (teatral). 2 usurpación (de personalidad). || *s.c.* e *i.* 2 fingimiento, simulación.

impersonator | ɪm'pɜːsəneɪtər | *s.c.* imitador.

impertinence | ɪm'pɜːtɪnəns | *s.i.* impertinencia, insolencia, rudeza, descaro, inoportunidad.

impertinent | ɪm'pɜːtɪnənt | *adj.* impertinente, insolente, descarado, inoportuno, cara dura.

imperturbable | ,ɪmpə'tɜːbəbl | | ɪmpər'tɜːrbəbl | *adj.* imperturbable, impasible, tranquilo, sereno.

impervious | ɪm'pɜːvjəs | | ɪm'pɜːrvjəs | *adj.* 1 impermeable, impenetrable (al agua, al gas, al calor). 2 no influenciable, insensible, indiferente, sordo (a las críticas).

impetuosity | ɪm,petjʊ'ɒsɪtɪ | | ɪm,petʃʊ'ɑːsɪtɪ | *s.i.* impetuosidad, impulsividad, precipitación, vehemencia, irreflexión.

impetuous | ɪm'petjʊəs | *adj.* impetuoso, impulsivo, vehemente, irreflexivo, precipitado.

impetuously | ɪm'petjʊəslɪ | *adv.* impetuosamente, impulsivamente, vehementemente, irreflexivamente, precipitadamente.

impetus | 'ɪmpɪtəs | *s.i.* 1 ímpetu, fuerza, brío. 2 estímulo, impulso, acicate, incentivo.

impiety | ɪm'paɪətɪ | *s.i.* 1 (form.) irreverencia, impiedad, falta de respeto (a la religión). || *s.c.* 2 acto impío. 3 desobediencia.

impinge | ɪm'pɪndʒ | *v.t.* 1 **[to – on/upon]** afectar a, influir sobre, inmiscuirse en, interferir en. 2 golpear, chocar, colisionar.

impious | 'ɪmpɪəs | *adj.* 1 impío, irreverente. 2 desobediente.

impish | 'ɪmpʃ | *adj.* (desp.) travieso, revoltoso, diablillo, trasto.

implacable | ɪm'plækəbl | *adj.* implacable, inflexible, inexorable, severo.

implacably | ɪm'plækəblɪ | *adv.* implacablemente, inflexiblemente, inexorablemente.

implant | ɪm'plɑːnt | | ɪm'plænt | *v.t.* 1 implantar, infundir, inculcar. 2 introducir gradualmente. || | 'ɪmplɑːnt | *s.c.* 3 MED. implante, injerto.

implausible | ɪm'plɔːzəbl | *adj.* improbable, poco razonable, inverosímil, poco convincente.

implement | 'ɪmplɪmənt | *s.c.* 1 utensilio, herramienta, apero. 2 medio, instrumento, fórmula (para conseguir un fin). || *v.t.* 3 cumplir, ejecutar, llevar a cabo, hacer efectivo.

implementation | ,ɪmplɪmen'teɪʃn | *s.i.* cumplimiento, ejecución, realización.

implicate | 'ɪmplɪkəɪt | *v.t.* 1 DER. implicar, conectar. 2 comprometer, envolver (en un asunto). 3 implicar, entrañar, denotar, significar. 4 (arc.) entretejer, entrelazar, enmarañar, enredar.

implication | ,ɪmplɪ'keɪʃn | *s.c.* e *i.* 1 insinuación, deducción, inferencia. 2 implicación, trascendencia, significado. || *s.i.* 3 DER. implicación, conexión.

implicit | ɪm'plɪsɪt | *adj.* 1 implícito, tácito, sobreentendido. 2 inherente, esencial, inseparable. 3 completo, absoluto, incondicional, incuestionable (confianza).

implicitly | ɪm'plɪsɪtlɪ | *adv.* 1 implícitamente, tácitamente. 2 absolutamente, incondicionalmente, incuestionablemente.

implore | ɪm'plɔː | *v.t.* implorar, rogar, suplicar.

imploring | ɪm'plɔːrɪŋ | *adj.* implorante, suplicante.

imploringly | ɪm'plɔːrɪŋlɪ | *adv.* de forma implorante, a modo de súplica.

implied | ɪm'plaɪd | *adj.* implícito, tácito, insinuado, sobreentendido.

imply | ɪm'plaɪ | *v.t.* 1 insinuar, dar a entender, sugerir. 2 implicar, entrañar, llevar consigo, suponer, significar. 3 (arc.) entretejer, entrelazar, enredar.

impolite | ,ɪmpə'laɪt | *adj.* descortés, maleducado, indelicado, inatento, grosero.

impolitely | ,ɪmpə'laɪtlɪ | *adv.* descortésmente, ineducadamente, falto de delicadeza, groseramente.

impolitic | ɪm'p'lətɪk | *adj.* (form.) impolítico, inoportuno, imprudente, poco sabio.

imponderable | ɪm'p'ndərəbl | *adj.* 1 imponderable, incalculable, inestimable. || *s.c.* 2 (gen. *pl.*) imponderables.

import | 'ɪmpɔːt | *v.t.* 1 COM. importar. 2 introducir (ideas, valores). 3 importar, significar, afectar, interesar. || *s.c.* 4 (gen. *pl.*) COM. importaciones, mercancías de importación, productos importados. 5 préstamo lingüístico. 6 introducción, importación (de ideas, de valores). || *s.i.* 7 COM. importación. 8 **[the –]** (form.) significado, sentido. 9 importancia, valor, consecuencia.

importance | ɪm'pɔːtns | *s.i.* 1 importancia, valor, significado, alcance. 2 importancia, influencia, peso (social).

important | ɪm'pɔːtnt | *adj.* 1 importante, vital, esencial, significativo. 2 importante, valioso. 3 importante, influyente, de peso (social). 4 (arc.) insistente, apremiante.

importantly | ɪm'pɔːtnltɪ | *adv.* 1 esencialmente, significativamente, de forma vital. 2 pretenciosamente.

importation | ,ɪmpɔː'teɪʃn | *s.i.* 1 COM. importación. 2 importación, entrada (de ideas, valores). || *s.c.* 3 artículo importado, mercancía de importación.

importer | ɪm'pɔːtər | *s.c.* COM. importador.

importunate | ɪm'pɔːtjʊnət | | ,ɪmpɔːrtjʊnət | *adj.* 1 (form.) importuno, insistente, persistente, constante. 2 machacón, pesado.

importune | ɪm'pɔːtjuːn | | ɪmpər'tuːn | *v.t.* 1 (form.) importunar, insistir, persistir, urgir. 2 molestar, irritar, fastidiar, asediar. || *adj.* 3 insistente, persistente, machacón, molesto.

importunity | ,ɪmpɔː'tjuːnɪtɪ | | ,ɪmpər'tuːnɪtɪ | *s.c.* e *i.* (form.) importunidad, insistencia, persistencia, machaconería.

impose | ɪm'pəʊz | *v.t.* 1 imponer, gravar (oficialmente). 2 imponer, obligar a aceptar. 3 imponer, componer (en imprenta). || *v.i.* 4 **[to – upon]** abusar de, molestar a, aprovecharse de. || *v.r.* 5 **[to – oneself]** imponerse, hacerse notar.

imposing | ɪm'pəʊzɪŋ | *adj.* imponente, impresionante, grandioso.

imposition | ,ɪmpə'zɪʃn | *s.c.* e *i.* 1 imposición, gravamen, impuesto, carga, tributo. 2 imposición (de ideas, normas). 3 abuso, molestia. 4 imposición, composición (en imprenta).

impossibility | ɪm,p'sə'bɪlɪtɪ | | ɪm,pɑːsə'bɪlɪtɪ | *s.i.* 1 imposibilidad, dificultad enorme. 2 quimera, utopía.

impossible | ɪm'pɒsəbl | | ɪm'pɑːsəbl | *adj.* 1 imposible, irrealizable. 2 inconcebible, utópico. 3 imposible, insufrible, insoportable. || **4 to be asking/want the –,** pedir, querer lo imposible.

impossibly | ɪm'pɒsəblɪ | *adv.* 1 ridículamente, extravagantemente. 2 irremediablemente, desesperadamente. 3 intolerantemente.

impostor | ɪm'pɒstər | | ɪm'pɑːstər | (EE.UU.) imposter. *s.c.* impostor, embaucador.

imposture | ɪm'pɒstʃər | | ɪm'pɑːstʃər | *s.c.* e *i.* (form.) engaño, falsedad.

impotence | 'ɪmpətəns | *s.i.* 1 impotencia, incapacidad. 2 MED. impotencia, esterilidad.

impotent | 'ɪmpətənt | *adj.* 1 impotente, incapaz. 2 MED. impotente, estéril.

impound | ɪm'paʊnd | *v.t.* 1 (form.) DER. embargar. 2 aprisionar, acorralar, encerrar. 3 embalsar (agua).

impoverish | ɪm'pɒvərɪʃ | | ɪm'pɑːvərɪʃ | *v.t.* gen. pasiva 1 empobrecer, arruinar, depauperar. 2 (fig.) empobrecer (espiritualmente). 3 empobrecer, agotar, esquilmar (los recursos naturales).

impoverished | ɪm'pɒvərɪʃt | *adj.* 1 empobrecido, arruinado, depauperado. 2 (fig.) empobrecido (espiritualmente). 3 empobrecido, esquilmado, debilitado, agotado, reducido a la miseria (el suelo, una mina).

impoverishment | ɪm'pɒvərɪʃmənt | *s.i.* 1 empobrecimiento, ruina, depauperación. 2 agotamiento (de los recursos naturales).

impracticable | ɪm'præktɪkəbl | *adj.* 1 impracticable, imposible, irrealizable. 2 impracticable, intransitable. 3 (arc.)

inmanejable, ingobernable, intratable, indisciplinado.

impractical | ɪm'præktɪkəl | *adj.* **1** poco práctico, poco realista, falto de sentido. **2** desmañado, inútil, torpe, inhábil. **3** teórico.

imprecation | ˌɪmprɪ'keɪʃn | *s.c.* e *i.* (form.) imprecación, maldición.

impregnable | ɪm'pregnəbl | *adj.* **1** impenetrable, inextricable, inexpugnable. **2** firme, sólido, inconquistable, inatacable (las convicciones).

impregnate | 'ɪmpregneɪt | | ɪm'pregneɪt | *v.t.* **1** BIOL. (form.) fecundar, preñar, inseminar, dejar embarazada. **2** impregnar, empapar, saturar, empapar, calar.

impregnation | ˌɪmpreg'neɪʃn | *s.i.* **1** fecundación, inseminación. **2** impregnación, saturación.

impresario | ˌɪmprɪ'sɑːrɪəʊ | *pl.* **impresarios** *s.c.* empresario (teatral, de ópera).

impress | 'ɪmpres | *v.t.* **1** (gen. *pas.*) impresionar, causar impresión, asombrar. **2** afectar, influir. **3** **[to – on/upon +** *o.***]/[to – +** *o.* **+ with]** inculcar, imbuir, fijar (una idea). **4** imprimir, grabar, estampar. **5** presionar, ejercer presión. **6** reclutar, llamar a filas. **7** DER. confiscar, embargar, expropiar (propiedades). || *s.c.* **8** impresión, marca, huella. **9** sello, estampa. **10** reclutamiento, leva.

impression | ɪm'preʃn | *s.c.* **1** impresión, efecto, imagen, ilusión. **2** (gen. *sing.*) impresión, sensación, idea, noción, recuerdo vago. **3** impresión, marca, huella. **4** imitación, parodia (de una persona). **5** (gen. *sing.*) impresión, tirada, edición (de un libro). || *s.i.* **6** impresión. || **7 to be under the – (that),** tener la impresión de (que). **8 to make an –,** impresionar, causar una impresión.

impressionable | ɪm'preʃnəbl | *adj.* impresionable, influenciable, susceptible de cambio, crédulo.

impressionism | ɪm'preʃnɪzəm | *s.i.* ART. impresionismo.

impressionist | ɪm'preʃnɪst | *s.c.* **1** ART. impresionista. **2** imitador, parodiador, mimo (en teatro).

impressionistic | ɪmˌpreʃə'nɪstɪk | *adj.* aproximado, vago, basado en impresiones, incompleto: *an impressionistic description = una descripción vaga.*

impressive | ɪm'presɪv | *adj.* impresionante, enorme, grandioso, fantástico.

impressively | ɪm'presɪvlɪ | *adv.* impresionantemente, enormemente, fantásticamente.

impressiveness | ɪm'presɪvnɪs | *s.i.* magnificencia, grandiosidad, carácter impresionante.

imprint | ɪm'prɪnt | *v.t.* **1** imprimir, marcar, dejar una huella, grabar. **2** (fig.) dejar huella (en la memoria). || | 'ɪm↓prɪnt | *s.c.* **3** impresión, huella, marca, señal. **4** (fig.) influencia, huella, efecto (en la memoria). **5** sello, editorial, pie de impresión (en un libro).

imprison | ɪm'prɪzn | *v.t.* **1** encarcelar, recluir en prisión, arrestar. **2** reprimir, restringir (la libertad).

imprisonment | ɪm'prɪznmənt | *s.i.* **1** prisión, reclusión, encarcelamiento. || **2 life –,** cadena perpetua.

improbability | ɪmˌprɒbə'bɪlɪtɪ | *s.c.* e *i.* improbabilidad, inverosimilitud.

improbable | ɪm'prɒbəbl | *adj.* **1** improbable, inverosímil, increíble, dudoso. **2** fantástico, extraño, poco corriente.

improbably | ɪm'prɒbəblɪ | *adv.* improbablemente, increíblemente.

impromptu | ɪm'prɒmptjuː | | ɪm'↓prɑːmtuː | *adj.* **1** improvisado, espontáneo. **2** MUS. improvisación. || *adv.* **3** improvisadamente, espontáneamente, sobre la marcha.

improper | ɪm'prɒpər | | ɪm'prɑːpər | *adj.* **1** inapropiado, inadecuado, inoportuno, improcedente (un comportamiento). **2** incorrecto, desacertado, impropio, injusto, irregular (un uso). **3** indecoroso, indecente, deshonesto.

improperly | ɪm'prɒpəlɪ | *adv.* **1** inapropiadamente, inadecuadamente, improcedentemente. **2** incorrectamente, irregularmente. **3** indecentemente, indecorosamente.

impropriety | ˌɪmprə'praɪətɪ | *s.i.* **1** (form.) improcedencia, incorrección, irregularidad (de comportamiento, de lenguaje). **2** deshonestidad, indecoro. || *s.c.* **3** indecencia, acto indecoroso.

improve | ɪm'pruːv | *v.t.* **1** mejorar, perfeccionar (un área de conocimiento). **2** mejorar (una oferta, las condiciones). **3** aumentar, incrementar (el valor del suelo, la productividad). **4** abonar (la tierra). || *v.i.* **5** mejorar, sanar, recuperarse. **6** mejorar, progresar, enriquecerse (con el tiempo). || **7 to – on/ upon,** mejorar en, avanzar en, perfeccionar.

improved | ɪm'pruːvd | *adj.* **1** mejor. **2** perfeccionado. **3** elevado.

improvement | ɪm'pruːvmənt | *s.c.* e *i.* **1** progreso, perfeccionamiento, mejora. **2** reforma, ampliación. **3** enmienda. **4** mejoría. **5** aumento, subida.

improvidence | ɪm'prɒvɪdəns | *s.i.* **1** imprevisión, descuido, imprudencia.

improvident | ɪm'prɒvɪdənt | | ɪm'↓prɑːvɪdənt | *adj.* (form.) imprevisor, desprevenido, descuidado, imprudente.

improvisation | ˌɪmprəvaɪ'zeɪʃn | | ˌɪmprəvə'zeɪʃn | *s.c.* e *i.* improvisación.

improvise | 'ɪmprəvaɪz | *v.t.* e *i.* improvisar.

improvised | 'ɪmprəvaɪzd | *adj.* improvisado, provisional.

imprudent | ɪm'pruːdənt | *adj.* **1** imprudente, indiscreto, necio. **2** irreflexivo, atrevido, temerario.

impudence | 'ɪmpjuːdəns | *s.i.* insolencia, descaro, atrevimiento, caradura, desfachatez.

impudent | 'ɪmpjʊdənt | *adj.* **1** insolente, descarado, atrevido, caradura, irrespetuoso. **2** (arc.) inmodesto, jactancioso.

impudently | 'ɪmpjʊdəntlɪ | *adv.* insolentemente, descaradamente, irrespetuosamente.

impugn | ɪm'pjuːn | *v.t.* (form.) impugnar, rebatir, atacar, poner en tela de juicio, cuestionar.

impulse | 'ɪmpʌls | *s.c.* e *i.* **1** impulso, impulsividad. **2** impulso, instinto, corazonada. || *s.c.* **3** (form.) estímulo, acicate, determinación, inclinación. **4** ELEC. impulso. **5 – buy,** un capricho, un antojo. || **6 on –,** sin reflexionar, por un impulso.

impulsion | ɪm'pʌlʃn | *s.i.* **1** impulsión, impulso. || *s.c.* **2** impulso, estímulo, impulsividad.

impulsive | ɪm'pʌlsɪv | *adj.* impulsivamente, irreflexivamente, caprichosamente.

impulsiveness | ɪm'pʌlsɪvnɪs | *s.i.* impulsividad, impetuosidad.

impunity | ɪm'pjuːnɪtɪ | *s.i.* impunidad.

impure | ɪm'pjʊər | *adj.* **1** impuro, adulterado, mezclado. **2** contaminado. **3** impúdico, inmoral, obsceno. **4** impuro, compuesto (un color). **5** ecléctico, sincrético (un estilo artístico, ideas).

impurity | ɪm'pjʊərɪtɪ | *s.i.* **1** impurez deshonestidad, inmoralidad, pecado. *s.c.* **2** impureza, elemento contamina te. **3** polución. **4** adulteración.

impute | ɪm'pjuːt | *v.t.* **[to – to]** imputar a, achacar a, atribuir a (injustamente).

in | ɪn | *prep.* **1** en, dentro de (un lugar, profesión, actividad): *in a cage = en una jaula; she's in politics = está metido en política.* **2** en (una ciudad, un país, un mar): *she lives in Madrid = vive en Madrid.* **3** de, en: *a chapter in the book = un capítulo del libro.* **4** en, de (un modo de vestir): *the woman in red = la mujer de rojo.* **5** a, hacia, en, de (un lugar): *in the direction of Bristol = en dirección a Bristol.* **6** a, con, en (un instrumento, un color, una lengua): *in ink = a tinta; in Spanish = en español.* **7** en, durante, por, de, dentro de: *holidays are in a few weeks = las vacaciones son dentro de unas semanas; in winter = en el verano* **8** con, en (modo en que se hace algo): *looking at him in surprise = mirándole con sorpresa.* **9** en, en estado de: *they were in love = estaban enamorados.* **10** de... en... (división, planificación): *in groups of three = de tres en tres; cut it in two = córtalo por la mitad.* **11** por cada, en cada, sobre: *one person in four = una de cada cuatro personas.* **12** de, en, en cuanto a, por lo que respecta a: *equal in strength = igualado en cuanto a fuerza.* **13** en (una persona): *we had great help in her = encontramos una gran ayuda en ella.* **14** **[–** *ger.***]** al, cuando, mientras, durante: *he learnt a lot in visiting other countries = aprendió mucho durante sus visitas a otros países.* || *adv.* **15** dentro, adentro, en el interior, en casa: *come in = entra; we were in all evening = estuvimos en casa toda la tarde.* **16** hacia dentro, hacia el centro. **17** DEP. en su turno: *our team was in = tenía el turno nuestro equipo.* **18** DEP. dentro (de la portería, la línea). **19** de moda, popular: *suede is in at the moment = el ante* *está de moda en este momento.* **20** en su punto álgido, en lo más alto (la marea). **21** en el poder: *her party was in for 4 years = su partido gobernó durante cuatro años.* **22** en el mercado, a la venta (un producto). || *adj.* **23** interior, de adentro, interno: *the in pocket = el bolsillo interior.* **24** (fam.) de moda, moderno. **25** compartido por poca gente, para unos pocos elegidos. **26** encendido, ardiendo (el fuego). || *abreviatura* de **inch,** pulgada. || *prefijo* **27 in –,** in-, des- (se añade a *adj.* y *adv.* para formar opuestos): *inadvisable = desaconsejable.* || **28 to be – at,** estar presente en (un acontecimiento). **29 to be – for,** estar a punto de, estar expuesto a (conseguir algo, tener problemas). **30 to be – for it,** (fam.) estárselas buscando, estar a punto de armar la gorda. **31 to be/get – on,** (fam.) participar en, tomar parte en. **32 to be – with,** (fam.) tener amistades con, gozar del favor de (por interés). **33 to go/be – for,** tomar parte en, participar en, estar en lista de (una competición, un concurso). **34 to have (got) it – for someone,** (fam.) ir a por alguien, ir a hundir a alguien. **35 – all,** V. **all. 36 – and out (of),** entrando y saliendo (de), dentro y fuera (de). **37 – itself,** en sí mismo, por sí mismo. **38 ins and outs,** (fam.) detalles, pormenores, recovecos (de una situación difícil). **39 – so far as,** en tanto que. **40 – that,** porque, ya que, dado que.

inability | ˌɪnə'bɪlɪtɪ | *s.i.* **1 [– (to *inf.*)]** inhabilidad, incapacidad, ineptitud, impotencia.

inaccesibility | 'ɪnækˌsesə'bɪlɪtɪ | *s.i.* inaccesibilidad.

inaccesible | ˌɪnæk'sesəbl | *adj.* **1** inaccesible, inasequible, inalcanzable, remoto. **2** ininteligible, incomprensible, difícil.

inaccuracy | ɪn'ækjʊrəsɪ | *s.c.* (gen. *sing.*) e *i.* **1** inexactitud. **2** incorrección, error.

inaccurate | ɪn'ækjʊrət | *adj.* **1** inexacto. **2** incorrecto, erróneo.

inaction | ɪn'ækʃn | *s.i.* **1** inactividad, inacción, inercia. **2** ociosidad, pasividad, indolencia.

inactive | ɪn'æktɪv | *adj.* inactivo, pasivo, ocioso.

inactivity | ˌɪnæk'tɪvɪtɪ | *s.i.* inactividad, pasividad, ociosidad, indolencia.

inadequacy | ɪn'ædɪkwəsɪ | *s.i.* **1** falta de adecuación. **2** insuficiencia, incapacidad. || *s.c.* **3** debilidad, fallo, insuficiencia.

inadequate | ɪn'ædɪkwɪt | *adj.* **1** inadecuado, insuficiente, deficiente. **2** incompetente, inepto, inútil.

inadequately | ɪn'ædɪkwɪtlɪ | *adv.* inadecuadamente, deficientemente.

inadmissible | ˌɪnəd'mɪsəbl | *adj.* inadmisible, inaceptable, no permitido.

inadvertent | ˌɪnəd'vəːtənt | *adj.* **1** inadvertido, desapercibido. **2** involuntario, sin intención, accidental.

inadvertently | ˌɪnəd'vəːtəntlɪ | *adv.* **1** inadvertidamente, sin darse cuenta. **2** involuntariamente, accidentalmente, por equivocación.

inadvisable | ˌɪnəd'vaɪzəbl | *adj.* contraindicado, no aconsejable, inconveniente.

inalienable | ɪn'eiljənəbl | *adj.* (form.) inalienable, irrenunciable.

inane | ɪ'neɪn | *adj.* **1** estúpido, idiota, insustancial, fatuo, vacío (el comportamiento, una acción). || *s.i.* **2** vacío, nada.

inanely | ɪ'neɪnlɪ | *adv.* estúpidamente, insubstancialmente, tontamente, fatuamente.

inanity | ɪ'nænətɪ | *s.i.* estupidez, insustancialidad, fatuidad, vacío.

inanimate | ɪn'ænɪmət | *adj.* **1** inanimado, muerto. **2** desanimado, abatido, desalentado, apocado.

inapplicable | ɪn'æplɪkəbl | | ˌɪnə'plɪkəbl | *adj.* inaplicable, fuera de lugar, irrelevante.

inappropriate | ˌɪnə'prəuprɪət | *adj.* **1** inapropiado, inadecuado, inoportuno. **2** impropio.

inappropriately | ˌɪnə'prəuprɪətlɪ | *adv.* inadecuadamente, inoportunamente.

inapt | ɪn'æpt | *adj.* **1** (form.) inadecuado, inapropiado, inoportuno. **2** inepto, torpe.

inarticulate | ˌɪnɑː'tɪkjʊlət | | ˌɪnɑːr'tɪkjʊlət | *adj.* inarticulado, inconexo, incoherente, incomprensible.

inasmuch | ˌɪnəz'mʌtʃ | *adv.* (form.) **[– as]** debido a, ya que, puesto que, hasta el punto de que.

inattention | ˌɪnə'tenʃn | *s.i.* desatención, negligencia, descuido, distracción.

inattentive | ˌɪnə'tentɪv | *adj.* desatento, distraído, descuidado, negligente.

inaudible | ɪn'ɔːdəbl | *adj.* inaudible, imperceptible, que no se puede oír.

inaugural | ɪ'nɔːgjʊrəl | *adj.* **1** inaugural, de inauguración. **2** inaugural, inicial. || *s.c.* **3** (EE.UU.) discurso inaugural. **4** inauguración.

inaugurate | ɪ'nɔːgjʊreɪt | *v.t.* **1** inaugurar, iniciar (un edificio, un festival). **2** (gen. pasiva) investir, nombrar, dar posesión (de un cargo). **3** (form.) inaugurar, poner en marcha (un sistema, una ley).

inauguration | ɪˌnɔːgjʊ'reɪʃn | *s.c.* e *i.* **1** inauguración, iniciación. **2** estreno. **3** investidura, toma de posesión.

inauspicious | ˌɪnɔː'spɪʃəs | *adj.* (form.) adverso, poco propicio, perjudicial, desfavorable.

inborn | ˌɪn'bɔːn | | ˌɪn'bɔːrn | *adj.* innato, inherente, congénito, connatural, de nacimiento.

inbred | ˌɪn'bred | *adj.* **1** innato, consubstancial, inherente, intrínseco. **2** BIOL. endogámico, producido por endogamia, de padres consanguíneos.

imbreeding | ˌɪn'briːdɪŋ | *s.i.* endogamia, consanguinidad.

imbuilt | ˌɪn'bɪlt | *adj.* congénito, de origen.

incalculable | ɪn'kælkjʊləbl | *adj.* **1** incalculable, inmenso, inestimable. **2** voluble, imprevisible.

incandescende | ˌɪnkæn'desns | *s.i.* incandescencia.

incandescent | ˌɪnkæn'desnt | *adj.* incandescente, candente, al rojo.

incantation | ˌɪnkæn'teɪʃn | *s.c.* e *i.* conjuro, encantamiento, sortilegio.

incapable | ɪn'keɪpəbl | *adj.* **1** incapaz, incapacitado, inepto, incompetente. **2 [– of]** incapaz de (hacer algo malo). **3** inútil, vago, maleante. **4** DER. incapaz, sin cualificación legal; no elegible.

incapacitate | ˌɪnkə'pæsɪteɪt | *v.t.* **1** incapacitar, imposibilitar. **2** DER. inhabilitar.

incarcerate | ɪn'kɑːsəreɪt | *v.t.* **1** (form.) encarcelar, meter en prisión. **2** encerrar, confinar.

incarceration | ɪnˌkɑːsə'reɪʃn | *s.i.* **1** (form.) encarcelación, encarcelamiento, reclusión, prisión. **2** encierro, confinamiento.

incarnate | ɪn'kɑːnɪt | | ɪn'kɑːrneɪt | *adj.* **1** encarnado, personificado, en persona. **2** encarnado, de color carne. || *v.t.* **3** (gen. *pas.*) encarnar, dar forma (a una idea). **4** (gen. *pas.*) encarnar, personificar.

incarnation | ˌɪnkɑː'neɪʃn | | ˌɪnkɑːr'neɪʃn | *s.i.* **1** encarnación, personificación. || *s.c.* **2** reencarnación, encarnación (en otra vida). **3 [the – of]** la personificación de, la representación de, la encarnación de (una cualidad).

incautious | ɪn'kɔːʃəs | *adj.* **1** incauto, ingenuo. **2** imprudente, negligente.

incendiary | ɪn'sendjərɪ | | ɪn'sendɪerɪ | *adj.* **1** incendiario (un arma). **2** explosivo, subversivo, revolucionario (una persona, un discurso). || *s.c.* **3** bomba incendiaria. **4** agitador, revolucionario.

incense | 'ɪnsens | *s.i.* **1** incienso. **2** sustancia perfumada, perfume, aroma. || | ɪn'sens | *v.t.* **3** (gen. *pas.*) enfadar, enfurecer, irritar, encolerizar.

incensed | ɪn'senst | *adj.* **1** enfadado, enfurecido, irritado, encolerizado.

incentive | ɪn'sentɪv | *s.c.* **1** incentivo, aliciente, estímulo, acicate. || *s.i.* **2** incentivación, motivación. || *adj.* **3** motivador, estimulante, incitante.

inception | ɪn'sepʃn | *s.i. sing.* (form.) principio, inicio, comienzo.

incessant | ɪn'sesnt | *adj.* incesante, continuo, constante, ininterrumpido (algo desagradable).

incessantly | ɪn'sesntlɪ | *adv.* incesantemente, continuamente, constantemente, sin interrupción.

incest | 'ɪnsest | *s.i.* incesto.

incestuous | ɪn'sestjʊəs | *adj.* **1** incestuoso. **2** (desp.) cerrado, muy íntimo (un grupo de amigos).

inch | ɪntʃ | *s.c.* **1** pulgada (2.54 cm.). **2** (fig.) nimiedad, porción mínima, milímetro, centímetro, palmo, dedo: *not an inch left = no quedó ni un palmo.* || **3 [to – *adv./prep.*]** avanzar con dificultad, caminar lentamente, poco a poco. || *v.t.*

4 [to – *adv./prep.*] mover con dificultad, llevar con cuidado. || **5 by inches,** por los pelos, de milagro. **6 – by –,** palmo a palmo, milímetro a milímetro. **7 every –,** completamente, de arriba abajo; al dedillo. **8 give him an – and he'll take a yard,** le das un dedo y toma la mano.

inchoate | 'ɪnkəʊeɪt | *adj.* **1** (form.) incipiente, elemental, rudimentario. **2** incompleto, no acabado de formar, a medias.

incidence | 'ɪnsɪdəns | *s.sing.* **1** incidencia, frecuencia. **2** FIS. incidencia.

incident | ˌɪnsɪ'dent | *s.c.* **1** incidente, acontecimiento, episodio, caso. **2** incidente, suceso, episodio (violento). **3** DER. incidencia. || *adj.* **4** incidental, concomitante. **5** casual, fortuito.

incidental | ˌɪnsɪ'dentl | *adj.* **1** incidental, casual, fortuito. **2** suplementario, adicional: *incidental benefits = beneficios suplementarios.* || *s.c.* **3** incidencias, circunstancias concomitantes.

incidentally | ˌɪnsɪ'dentlɪ | *adv.* **1** a propósito, entre paréntesis. **2** casualmente, incidentalmente.

incinerate | ɪn'sɪnəreɪt | *v.t.* (gen. *pas.*) incinerar, quemar.

incinerator | ɪn'sɪnəreɪtər | *s.c.* incinerador (de basura).

incipient | ɪn'sɪpɪənt | *adj.* (form.) incipiente, inicial.

incise | ɪn'saɪz | *v.t.* **1** (gen. *pas.*) MED. incidir, hacer una incisión, cortar. **2** grabar, tallar.

incision | ɪn'sɪʒn | *s.c.* e *i.* **1** MED. incisión, cisura. **2** corte, rajadura.

incisive | ɪn'saɪsɪv | *adj.* **1** incisivo, cortante. **2** incisivo, agudo, mordaz, directo, efectivo (un discurso, un escrito).

incisor | ɪn'saɪzər | *s.c.* ANAT. incisivo (diente).

incite | ɪn'saɪt | *v.t.* **[to – (to)]** incitar, instigar, provocar, estimular.

inclement | ɪn'klemənt | *adj.* (form.) inclemente, riguroso (el tiempo atmosférico).

inclination | ˌɪnklɪ'neɪʃn | *s.c.* e *i.* **1** (gen. *pl.*) inclinación, afición, gusto, preferencia, disposición. || *s.c.* **2** (form.) tendencia, propensión. **3** (gen. *sing.*) GEOM. inclinación, ángulo inclinado. **4** inclinación, pendiente, rampa, cuesta. **5** inclinación, reverencia.

incline | ɪn'klaɪn | *v.t.* **1** inclinar, disponer, animar, influenciar. **2** inclinar, hacer una reverencia. || *v.i.* **3** inclinarse por, simpatizar con, tender a. **4** ser propenso a, tener tendencia a. || *v.t.* e *i.* **5** inclinar(se), ladear(se), poner oblicuamente. || *s.c.* **6** cuesta, pendiente, subida.

inclined | ɪn'klaɪnd | *adj.* **1** inclinado, tendente, propenso. **2** dispuesto, preparado. **3** inclinado, atraído (hacia una persona, materia). **4** GEOM. inclinado, oblicuo. **5** en cuesta, en pendiente.

include | ɪn'kluːd | *v.t.* **1** incluir, comprender, contener. **2** introducir en, poner en, formar parte de, ser parte de (un grupo).

included | ɪn'kluːdɪd | *adj.* incluido, comprendido.

including | ɪn'kluːdɪŋ | *prep.* incluso, inclusive, contando con, además de, hasta.

inclusion | ɪn'kluːʒn | *s.i.* **1** inclusión. || *s.c.* **2** inclusión, introducción. **3** GEOL. inclusión (en minerales, rocas).

inclusive | ɪn'kluːsɪv | *adj.* **1** inclusivo, completo, total. **2** [*s.* + –] (brit.) inclusive, incluyendo.

incoherence | ˌɪnkəʊ'hɪərəns | *s.i.* incoherencia, incongruencia, inconexión.

incoherent | ˌɪnkəʊ'hɪərənt | *adj.* **1** incoherente, inconexo, incongruente. **2** indescifrable, difícil de entender.

incoherently | ˌɪnkəʊ'hɪərəntlɪ | *adv.* incoherentemente, inconexamente, de forma indescifrable.

income | 'ɪŋkʌm | *s.c.* e *i.* **1** renta, ingresos, ganancias, entradas. **2** interés, rédito, ganancias de capital. || **3 – tax,** impuesto sobre la renta.

incoming | 'ɪnˌkʌmɪŋ | *adj.* entrante, que comienza, inmediato.

incomunicado | ˌɪnkəmjuːnɪ'kɑːdəʊ | *adv. incomunicado, aisladamente, sin conexión.*

incomparable | ɪn'kɒmpərəbl | | ɪn'kɑːmpərəbl | *adj.* incomparable, inigualable, inmejorable, sin par.

incomparably | ɪn'kɒmpərəblɪ | *adv.* incomparablemente, inigualablemente, inmejorablemente.

incompatibility | 'ɪnkəmˌpætə'bɪlɪtɪ | *s.i.* incompatibilidad.

incompatible | ˌɪnkəm'pætəbl | *adj.* **1** incompatible, opuesto, antagónico, inconciliable. || *s.c.* **2** (gen. *pl.*) incompatible (personas, objetos).

incompetence | ɪn'kɒmpɪtəns | *s.i.* incompetencia, ineptitud, incapacidad.

incompetent | ɪn'kɒmpɪtənt | *adj.* **1** incompetente, inepto, incapaz. || *s.c.* **2** incompetente, inepto.

incomplete | ˌɪnkəm'pliːt | *adj.* **1** incompleto, insuficiente, deficiente, defectuoso. **2** incompleto, parcial.

incompletely | ˌɪnkəm'pliːtlɪ | *adv.* **1** incompleto, insuficientemente, deficientemente. **2** parcialmente.

incomprehensible | ɪnˌkɒmprɪ'hensəbl | | ɪnˌkɑːmprɪ'hensəbl | *adj.* incomprensible, indescifrable.

incomprehension | ɪnˌkɒmprɪ'henʃn | | ɪnˌkɑːmprɪ'henʃn | *s.i.* incomprensión.

inconceivable | ˌɪnkən'siːvəbl | *adj.* inconcebible, increíble, inimaginable, impensable.

inconclusive | ˌɪnkən'kluːsɪv | *adj.* no concluyente, no decisivo, no definitivo.

incongruity, incongruousness | ˌɪnkɒŋ'gruːətɪ | *s.i.* **1** incongruencia, incoherencia. || *s.c.* **2** discrepancia, disconformidad, disensión.

incongruous | ɪn'kɒŋgruəs | *adj.* **1** incongruente, absurdo, discordante. **2** disonante, chocante, fuera de lugar.

incongruously | ɪn'kɒŋgruəslɪ | *adv.* incongruentemente, de forma disonante, discordantemente.

inconsequential | ˌɪnkɒnsɪ'kwenʃl | | ˌɪnkɑːnsɪ'kwenʃl | *adj.* insignificante, sin importancia, intranscendente.

inconsequently | ɪn'kɒnsɪkwəntlɪ | | ɪn'kɑːnsɪkwəntlɪ | *adv.* intranscendentemente, inconsecuentemente.

inconsiderable | ˌɪnkən'sɪdərəbl | *adj.* **1** insignificante, irrisorio, trivial. **2** vulgar.

inconsiderate | ˌɪnkən'sɪdərət | *adj.* (desp.) desconsiderado, desatento, irreflexivo.

inconsistency | ˌɪnkən'sɪstənsɪ | *s.c.* e *i.* (desp.) inconsistencia, contradicción, falta de lógica, incoherencia.

inconsistent | ˌɪnkən'sɪstənt | *adj.* **1** (desp.) inconsistente, contradictorio, falto de lógica, incoherente. **2** imprevisible, irregular, con altibajos. **3** incompatible.

inconsolable | ˌɪnkən'səʊləbl | *adj.* inconsolable, abatido, desconsolado.

inconsolably | ˌɪnkən'səʊləblɪ | *adv.* inconsolablemente, desconsoladamente.

inconspicuous | ˌɪnkən'spɪkjuəs | *adj.* irrelevante, poco visible, discreto, insignificante.

inconspicuously | ˌɪnkən'spɪkjuəslɪ | *adv.* irrelevantemente, discretamente, insignificantemente.

incontinence | ɪn'kɒntɪnəns | *s.i.* **1** MED. incontinencia. **2** (lit.) lascivia, lujuria, incontinencia sexual.

incontinent | ɪn'kɒntɪnənt | *adj.* **1** MED incontinente. **2** (lit.) lascivo, lujurioso, incontinente.

incontrovertible | ˌɪnkɒntrə'vɜːtəbl | | ˌɪnkɑːntrə'vɜːtəbl *adj.* (form.) incontrovertible, indisputable, innegable.

incontrovertibly | ˌɪnkɒntrə'vɜːtəblɪ | *adv.* incontrovertiblemente, innegablemente, indisputablemente.

inconvenience | ˌɪnkən'viːnjəns | *s.c.* e *i.* **1** inconveniencia, incomodidad, molestia, perjuicio. **2** problema, estorbo. || *v.t.* **3** incomodar, molestar, causar una inconveniencia, perjudicar. **4** estorbar.

inconvenient | ˌɪnkən'viːnjənt | *adj.* **1** inconveniente, incómodo, molesto, embarazoso, problemático. **2** inoportuno, a destiempo. **3** inapropiado, poco práctico.

inconveniently | ˌɪnkən'viːnjəntlɪ | *adv.* **1** inconvenientemente, perjudicialmente, incómodamente.

incorporate | ɪn'kɔːpərəɪt | | ɪn'kɔːrpərət | *v.t.* **1** incorporar, incluir, contener. **2** agregar, añadir. **3** admitir como miembro (de una compañía). **4** DER. constituir legalmente (una sociedad). || *v.i.* **5** incorporarse, sumarse, asociarse, agregarse. **6** DER. constituirse en sociedad.

incorrect | ˌɪnkə'rekt | *adj.* **1** incorrecto, erróneo, equivocado. **2** defectuoso, con fallos. **3** impropio, inapropiado.

incorrectly | ˌɪnkə'rektlɪ | *adv.* incorrectamente, erróneamente, equivocadamente.

incorrigible | ɪn'kɒrɪdʒəbl | | ɪn'kɑːrɪdʒəbl | *adj.* (desp.) incorregible, contumaz, obstinado.

incorrigibly | ɪn'kɒrɪdʒəblɪ | *adv.* incorregiblemente, contumazmente, obstinadamente.

incorruptible | ˌɪnkə'rʌptəbl | *adj.* 1 incorruptible, insobornable, íntegro. 2 indestructible.

increase | ɪn'kriːs | *v.t.* e *i.* 1 incrementar, crecer, aumentar. 2 incrementar, elevar, subir (una cantidad). 3 propagar, extender, multiplicar. || | 'ɪnkriːs | *s.c.* 4 incremento, aumento, desarrollo. 5 incremento, subida. 6 (arc.) propagación, reproducción. || 7 **on the –**, en aumento, multiplicándose, creciendo: *investments are on the increase = las inversiones van en aumento.*

increased | ɪn'kriːst | *adj.* creciente, elevado.

increasingly | ɪn'kriːsɪŋlɪ | *adv.* 1 cada vez más, más y más, de forma creciente. 2 cada vez más a menudo.

incredible | ɪn'kredəbl | *adj.* 1 increíble, inconcebible, extraño. 2 increíble, inmenso. 3 (fam.) maravilloso, fantástico, fabuloso, sorprendente.

incredibly | ɪn'kredəblɪ | *adv.* 1 increíblemente, inconcebiblemente. 2 extremadamente, inmensamente.

incredulity | ˌɪnkrɪ'djuːlɪtɪ | | ˌɪnkrɪ'duːlɪtɪ | *s.i.* incredulidad, escepticismo, desconfianza.

incredulous | ɪn'kredjʊləs | | ɪn'kredʒələs | *adj.* incrédulo, descreído, escéptico, desconfiado.

incredulously | ɪn'kredjʊləslɪ | *adv.* incrédulamente, escépticamente, con desconfianza.

increment | 'inkrəmənt | *s.c.* 1 incremento, aumento, crecimiento. 2 aumento, subida (de sueldo). 3 añadidura, añadido. 4 MAT. incremento (en una variable). || 5 **unearned –**, plusvalía.

incremental | ˌɪnkrə'mentl | *adj.* creciente, en aumento, en crecimiento.

incriminate | ɪn'krɪmɪneɪt | *v.t.* DER. incriminar, acriminar, imputar un delito.

incriminating | ɪnˌkrɪmɪ'neɪʃn | *adj.* DER. incriminador, acriminador, acusador.

incubate | 'ɪnkjʊbeɪt | *v.t.* e *i.* 1 incubar, empollar. 2 MED. incubar (una infección). 3 (fig.) tramar, madurar, meditar (una idea).

incubation | ˌɪnkjʊ'beɪʃn | *s.i.* 1 incubación, empolladura. 2 MED. incubación (de una bacteria).

incubator | 'ɪnkjʊbeɪtər | *s.c.* incubadora artificial.

inculcate | 'ɪnkʌlkeɪt | | ɪn'kʌlkeɪt | *v.t.* (form.) inculcar, infundir, imbuir.

incumbent | ɪn'kʌmbənt | *s.c.* 1 REL. ministro (de la iglesia Anglicana). 2 (form.) titular, funcionario. || *adj.* 3 obligatorio, necesario, incumbente. 4 titular, poseedor (de un cargo). 5 apoyado, reclinado.

incur | ɪn'kɜːr | *v.t.* 1 incurrir en, contribuir a, caer en, recaer en (una culpa). 2 contraer (una obligación).

incurable | ɪn'kjʊərebl | *adj.* 1 incurable, insanable. 2 (fig.) incurable, incorregible (un hábito).

incurably | ɪn'kjʊəreblɪ | *adv.* 1 incurablemente. 2 (fig.) incorregiblemente.

incurious | ɪn'kjʊərɪəs | *adj.* poco curioso, falto de interés, indiferente.

incuriously | ɪn'kjʊərɪəslɪ | *adv.* con indiferencia, sin curiosidad.

incursion | ɪn'kɜːʃn | | ɪn'kɜːrʒən | *s.c.* (gen. *sing.*) 1 (form.) MIL. incursión, invasión. 2 (fig.) invasión, entrada: *an incursion of foreign cars = una invasión de coches extranjeros.*

indebted | ɪn'detɪd | *adj.* 1 [– to] reconocido a, en deuda con, agradecidísimo a. 2 endeudado, empeñado (económicamente).

indebtedness | ɪn'detɪdnɪs | *s.i.* 1 agradecimiento, reconocimiento, deuda. 2 endeudamiento, deuda (económica).

indecency | ɪn'diːsnsɪ | *s.i.* indecencia, inmoralidad, obscenidad.

indecent | ɪn'diːsnt | *adj.* 1 indecente, inmoral, obsceno. 2 (fam.) inadecuado, inaceptable. 3 (fam.) sorprendente, enorme.

indecently | ɪn'diːsntlɪ | *adv.* 1 indecentemente, inmoralmente, obscenamente. 2 (fam.) inadecuadamente, inaceptablemente. 3 (fam.) sorprendentemente, enormemente.

indecipherable | ˌɪndɪ'saɪfərəbl | *adj.* indescifrable, incomprensible, ilegible (texto).

indecision | ˌɪndɪ'sɪʒn | *s.i.* indecisión, indeterminación, inseguridad.

indecisive | ˌɪndɪ'saɪsɪv | *adj.* 1 indeciso, indeterminado, inseguro, vacilante. 2 no decisivo, no concluyente, no definitivo.

indecisiveness | ˌɪndɪ'saɪsɪvnɪs | *s.i.* 1 indecisión, indeterminación, inseguridad, duda.

indefatigable | ˌɪndɪ'fætɪgəbl | *adj.* infatigable, incansable.

indefatigably | ˌɪndɪ'fætɪgəblɪ | *adv.* infatigablemente, incansablemente.

indefensible | ˌɪndɪ'fensəbl | *adj.* 1 injustificable, inaceptable. 2 indefinible, muy vulnerable, fácilmente atacable (un lugar).

indefinable | ˌɪndɪ'faɪnəbl | *adj.* indefinible, indescriptible.

indefinably | ˌɪndɪ'faɪnəblɪ | *adv.* indefiniblemente, indescriptiblemente.

indefinite | ɪn'defɪnət | *adj.* 1 indefinido, impreciso, vago, poco claro (un acto, un acontecimiento). 2 indefinido, indeterminado, ilimitado (un período de tiempo). 3 incierta, poco segura, no determinada (una fecha). || 4 **– article**, GRAM. artículo indefinido.

indefinitely | ɪn'defɪnətlɪ | *adv.* 1 indefinidamente, por tiempo indefinido. 2 vagamente, de forma imprecisa.

indelible | ɪn'deləbl | *adj.* 1 indeleble, imborrable, permanente. 2 (fig.) indeleble (un recuerdo).

indelibly | ɪn'deləblɪ | *adv.* indeleblemente, imborrablemente, permanentemente.

indelicate | ɪn'delɪkət | *adj.* 1 poco delicado, desconsiderado, vulgar, grosero, ordinario. 2 embarazoso, vergonzoso, chocante.

indemnity | ɪn'demnɪtɪ | *s.i.* 1 indemnidad, protección (por daños). 2 indemnización, reparación, compensación.

indent | 'ɪndent | *v.t.* 1 dentar, mellar, hacer muescas. 2 ensamblar, machihembrar, encajar. 3 sangrar (párrafos). 4 cortar en zigzag (un documento y copia para establecer más tarde su autenticidad). 5 extender por duplicado o triplicado (un documento). || *v.i.* 6 (brit.) COM. hacer un pedido por escrito, extender una orden de pedido. 7 requisar, incautarse. 8 formarse muescas. || *s.c.* 9 (brit.) COM. pedido, orden de envío (gen. al extranjero). 10 (brit.) orden de requisación. 11 muesca, mella. 12 ensamblaje, machihembrado. 13 documento cortado en zigzag (con su copia para establecer más tarde su autenticidad).

indentation | ˌɪnden'teɪʃn | *s.i.* 1 hendidura, mella, muesca. || *s.c.* 2 concavidad, hendidura, depresión, hoyo, entrante (en el terreno). 3 sangría (en un párrafo).

indented | ɪn'dentɪd | *adj.* 1 hendido, mellado, con muescas, dentado. 2 con desniveles, accidentado, con entrantes y salientes.

independence | ˌɪndɪ'pendəns | *s.i.* 1 independencia, libertad, autonomía. 2 (arc.) bienestar, solvencia, holgura (económica).

independent | ˌɪndɪ'pendənt | *adj.* 1 independiente, libre, emancipado. 2 acomodado, desahogado, autosuficiente (económicamente). 3 independiente, imparcial: *an independent opinion = una opinión imparcial.* 4 independiente, no subvencionado (una organización). || *s.c.* 5 independiente (políticamente). || 6 **of – means,** de posibles, con suficientes medios económicos, que se mantiene por sus propios medios.

independently | ˌɪndɪ'pendəntlɪ | *adv.* independientemente.

indescribable | ˌɪndɪ'skraɪbəbl | *adj.* indescriptible, inenarrable, increíble.

indescribably | ˌɪndɪ'kraɪbəblɪ | *adv.* indescriptiblemente, inenarrablemente, increíblemente.

indestructibility | ˌɪndɪˌstrʌktə'bɪlɪtɪ | *s.i.* indestructibilidad.

indestructible | ˌɪndɪˌstrʌktəbl | *adj.* indestructible, eterno, inquebrantable.

indeterminable | ˌɪndɪ'tɜːmɪnəbl | *adj.* indeterminable, impreciso, indefinido.

indeterminacy | ˌɪndɪ'tɜːmɪnəsɪ | *s.i.* indeterminación, imprecisión, vaguedad, indefinición.

indeterminate | ˌɪndɪ'tɜːmɪnət | *adj.* 1 indeterminado, impreciso, indefinido, vago. 2 BOT. racimado, racimoso.

index | 'ɪndeks | *pl.* **indexes** o **indices.** *s.c.* 1 (form.) índice, indicador, señal. 2 índice: *the cost of living index –, el índice del coste de vida.* 3 *pl.* **indexes**

índice (de un libro). || *v.t.* e *i.* **4** confeccionar un índice, poner índice. **5** catalogar, clasificar. || **6 – card,** fichero, catálogo. **7 – finger/forefinger,** dedo índice.
index-linked | 'ɪndeksˌlɪŋkt | *adj.* revalorizable, actualizable (en relación con el índice de precios al consumo): *an index-linked pension = una pensión revalorizable.*
Indian | 'ɪndɪən | *adj.* **1** indio, hindú. **2** indio, indiano, amerindio. || *s.c.* **3** hindú, indio. **4** indio, indiano, amerindio (de origen). **5** lengua india. || **6 – file,** fila india, uno tras otro. **7 – ink,** tinta china. **8 – summer,** veranillo de San Martín. **9 red –,** piel roja.
india rubber | ˌɪndɪə'rʌbər | *s.c.* e *i.* **1** goma de borrar. **2** caucho, goma.
indicate | 'ɪndɪkeɪt | *v.t.* **1** indicar, señalar, mostrar, apuntar hacia: *she indicated the school = apuntó hacia la escuela.* **2** explicar, aclarar. **3** MED. (gen. *pas.*) recetar. **4** recomendar, sugerir. || *v.t.* e *i.* **5** señalar la dirección, poner un intermitente (en un coche).
indication | ˌɪndɪ'keɪʃn | *s.c.* e *i.* **1** indicación, señal, muestra. **2** sugerencia, recomendación.
indicative | ɪn'dɪkətɪv | *adj.* **1** indicativo, sintomático. **2** sugerente, sugestivo. **3** GRAM. indicativo (modo). || *s.sing.* **4** GRAM. modo indicativo.
indicator | 'ɪndɪkeɪtər | *s.c.* **1** MEC. indicador, marcador, aguja indicadora (de temperatura, de gasolina). **2** intermitente (de un coche). **3** indicador, señal. **4** indicación, índice.
indices | 'ɪndɪsiːz | *pl.* de **index.** V. **index.**
indict | ɪn'daɪt | *v.t.* **1 [to – (for)]** DER. procesar. **2** DER. acusar, inculpar, incriminar, imputar.
indictable | ɪn'daɪtəbl | *adj.* DER. imputable, encausable, denunciable.
indictment | ɪn'daɪtmənt | *s.c.* e *i.* **1** acusación, denuncia. **2** DER. acusación, incriminación, inculpación.
indifference | ɪn'dɪfrəns | *s.i.* **[– (to/towards)]** indiferencia, apatía, falta de interés, impasibilidad.
indifferent | ɪn'dɪfrənt | *adj.* **1** indiferente, apático, falto de interés, impasible, distante. **2** mediocre, insignificante, de poca monta, pobre.
indifferently | ɪn'dɪfrəntlɪ | *adv.* indiferentemente, distraídamente, apáticamente, impasiblemente.
indigenous | ɪn'dɪdʒɪnəs | *adj.* **[– (to)]** (form.) indígena, originario, nativo, autóctono.
indigent | 'ɪndɪdʒənt | *adj.* (form.) indigente, menesteroso, necesitado, pobre.
indigestive | ˌɪndɪ'dʒestɪv | *adj.* **1** indigesto. **2** impenetrable, indescifrable (una idea, un acto).
indigestion | ˌɪndɪ'dʒestʃən | *s.i.* indigestión, empacho.
indignant | ɪn'dɪgnənt | *adj.* indignado, enfadado, enfurecido.
indignantly | ɪn'dɪgnəntlɪ | *adv.* indignantemente, enfurecidamente.
indignation | ˌɪndɪg'neɪʃn | *s.i.* indignación, enojo, enfado violento, enfurecimiento.
indignity | ɪn'dɪgnɪtɪ | *s.c.* e *i.* **1** indignidad, humillación, vejación, vergüenza, degradación. **2** afrenta, desprecio. **3** (arc.) deshonor, infamia, indignidad.
indigo | 'ɪndɪgəʊ | *adj.* **1** añil, índigo. || *s.i.* **2** color índigo. **3** BOT. índigo, añil.
indirect | ˌɪndɪ'rekt | *adj.* **1** indirecto. || **2 – speech,** GRAM. estilo indirecto. **3 – tax,** impuesto indirecto. **4 – taxation,** sistema de imposición indirecta.
indirectly | ˌɪndɪ'rektlɪ | *adv.* indirectamente.
indiscernible | ˌɪndɪsɜːnəbl | *adj.* indiscernible, imperceptible: *– indiscernible in the dark = apenas se ve en la oscuridad.*
indiscipline | ɪn'dɪsɪplɪn | *s.i.* indisciplina, insubordinación, desobediencia.
indiscreet | ˌɪndɪ'skriːt | *adj.* **1** indiscreto, imprudente, poco cauto, entrometido.
indiscretion | ˌɪndɪ'skreʃn | *s.c.* e *i.* **1** indiscreción, imprudencia, intromisión, metedura de pata. **2** (euf.) libertinaje, disipación (sexual).
indiscriminate | ˌɪndɪ'skrɪmɪnət | *adj.* indiscriminado, falto de criterio, sin distinción.
indiscriminately ˌɪndɪ'skrɪmɪnətlɪ | *adv.* indiscriminadamente, sin criterio.
indispensable | ˌɪndɪ'spensəbl | *adj.* indispensable, esencial, muy necesario, imprescindible.
indisposed | ˌɪndɪ'spəʊz | *adj.* **1** (form. y euf.) indispuesto, malucho. **2** no dispuesto, poco voluntarioso.
indisposition | ˌɪndɪspə'zɪʃn | *s.c.* e *i.* **1** indisposición, trastorno, arrechucho, malestar. || *s.i.* **2 [– to *inf.*]** falta de disposición para, falta de voluntad para, falta de inclinación para.
indisputable | ˌɪndɪ'spjuːtəbl | *adj.* indisputable, innegable, indiscutible, indudable.
indisputably | ˌɪndɪ'spjuːtəblɪ | *adv.* innegablemente, indiscutiblemente, indudablemente, sin disputa.
indissoluble | ˌɪndɪ'sɒljʊbl | | ˌɪndɪ'sɑːljʊbl | *adj.* **1** (form.) indisoluble, irrompible, inseparable, permanente.
indistinct | ˌɪndɪ'stɪŋkt | *adj.* indistinto, vago, confuso, oscuro, borroso (para la vista, para el oído, para la mente).
indistinctly | ˌɪndɪ'stɪŋktlɪ | *adv.* confusamente, borrosamente, indistintamente.
indistinguishable | ˌɪndɪ'stɪŋgwɪʃəbl | *adj.* indistinguible, imperceptible, poco claro.
individual | ˌɪndɪ'vɪdjʊəl | *adj.* **1** individual, particular, específico. **2** personal, propio, único, diferente, original: *an individual way of dressing = un estilo de vestir propio.* || *s.c.* **3** individuo, persona. **4** (fam.) espécimen, carácter, personaje.
individualism | ˌɪndɪ'vɪdjʊəlɪzəm | *s.i.* individualismo.
individualist | ˌɪndɪ'vɪdjʊəlɪst | *adj.* **1** individualista. || *s.c.* **2** independiente.
individualistic | 'ɪndɪˌvɪdjʊə'lɪstɪk | *adj.* individualista.
individuality | 'ɪndɪˌvɪdjʊ'ælɪtɪ | *s.i.* **1** individualidad, singularidad, característica, unicidad. **2** personalidad.
individualize | ˌɪndɪ'vɪdjʊəlaɪz | (brit.) **individualise.** *v.t.* **1** individualizar, caracterizar. **2** particularizar, considerar individualmente, tratar individualmente.
individually | ˌɪndɪ'vɪdjʊəlɪ | *adv.* **1** individualmente, separadamente, uno a uno, de forma individualizada. **2** personalmente, originalmente.
indivisible | ˌɪndɪ'vɪzəbl | *adj.* indivisible.
Indo- | 'ɪndəʊ | *prefijo.* indo (se antepone a adjetivos de nacionalidad): *indoeuropean languages = lenguas indoeuropeas.*
indoctrinate | ɪn'dɒktrɪneɪt | *v.t.* (desp.) indoctrinar, adoctrinar, lavar el cerebro
indoctrination | ɪnˌdɒktrɪ'neɪʃn | ɪnˌdɑːktrɪ'neɪʃn | *s.i.* adoctrinamiento, lavado de cerebro.
indolence | 'ɪndələns | *s.i.* indolencia, desidia, pereza, vagancia.
indolent | 'ɪndələnt | *adj.* (form.) indolente, perezoso, desidioso.
indomitable | ɪn'dɒmɪtəbl | | ɪn'dɑːmɪtəbl | *adj.* **1** (form.) indómito, indomable, rebelde. **2** invencible, inconquistable.
Indonesian | ˌɪndəʊ'niːzjən | | ˌɪndə'niːʒən | *adj.* **1** indonesio (nacionalidad). || *s.c.* **2** indonesio.
indoor | 'ɪndɔːr | *adj.* **1** interior, interno, de interior. **2** DEP. de salón, de sala, en pista cubierta, cubierta: *indoor swimming pool = piscina cubierta.*
indrawn | ˌɪn'drɔːn | *adj.* **1** acelerada, sofocada, sin resultado, de sorpresa (la respiración). **2** reservado, introspectivo.
indubitable | ɪn'djuːbɪtəbl | | ɪn'duːbɪtəbl | *adj.* (form.) indudable, incuestionable, indiscutible.
indubitably | ɪn'djuːbɪtəblɪ | *adv.* indudablemente, indiscutiblemente, incuestionablemente.
induce | ɪn'djuːs | *v.t.* **1 [to – + *o.* + to *inf.*]** (form.) inducir, incitar, impulsar, persuadir. **2** MED. provocar el parto, estimular el parto. **3** causar, producir. **4** FIL. inducir. **5** FIS. producir por inducción.
induced | ɪn'djuːst | *sufijo.* inducido, producido, causado.
OBS. **-induced** se combina con nombres para formar adjetivos que indican que un estado, una condición o enfermedad se produce por efecto de algo en particular: *work-induced illnesses = enfermedades profesionales.*
inducement | ɪn'djuːsmənt | | ɪn'duːsmənt | *s.c.* e *i.* **1** inducción, incitación, persuasión. **2** motivo, estímulo, incentivo, aliciente. **3** DER. informe, alegato (de la defensa).
induct | ɪn'dʌkt | *v.t.* **1** (gen. *pas.*) (form.) nombrar, dar posesión (de un

cargo). **2** consagrar (a un sacerdote). **3** (EE.UU. y form.) admitir, iniciar (en una organización). **4** (EE.UU.) MIL. reclutar, incorporar a filas.

induction | ɪn'dʌkʃn | *s.i.* **1** MED. estimulación, provocación (del parto). **2** FIS. inducción. || *s.c.* e *i.* **3** nombramiento, entrega de posesión (de un cargo oficial). **4** admisión, iniciación (en una sociedad). **5** FIL. proceso inductivo, inducción. **6** (arc.) preámbulo, prólogo. **7** MIL. incorporación a filas. || **8 – coil,** ELECTR. bobina de inducción, transformador. **9 – course,** cursillo de orientación (al incorporarse a un nuevo trabajo, centro de estudios).

inductive | ɪn'dʌktɪv | *adj.* **1** FIL. inductivo. **2** inductor, incitador, persuasivo. **3** introductorio. **4** ELECTR. inductor.

indulge | ɪn'dʌldʒ | *v.t.* **1** ser indulgente, mimar, consentir, dar rienda suelta. **2** **[to – (in)]** satisfacer, complacer, dar gusto. **3** conceder dispensa, conceder indulgencia. || *v.i.* **4** (form.) darse a la bebida. **5** permitirse el lujo, darse el gusto, entregarse a: *indulging in conversation = entregándonos a la conversación.*

indulgence | ɪn'dʌldʒəns | *s.i.* **1** indulgencia, complacencia, gusto, placer. **2** (fam.) desenfreno, falta de contención (en la bebida, la comida). **3** tolerancia, comprensión, clemencia. || *s.c.* **4** capricho, antojo. || *s.c.* e *i.* **5** REL. indulgencia. **6** COM. prórroga, aplazamiento, moratoria (para realizar un pago).

indulgent | ɪn'dʌldʒənt | *adj.* indulgente, complaciente, condescendiente, benevolente, amable.

indulgently | ɪn'dʌldʒəntlɪ | *adv.* indulgentemente, complacientemente, condescendientemente.

industrial | ɪn'dʌstrɪəl | *adj.* **1** industrial. || *s.c.* **2** trabajador de la industria. **3** (EE.UU.) empresa, sociedad industrial. **4** *pl.* (EE.UU.) acciones de una sociedad industrial. || **5 – action,** (brit.) presión de los trabajadores de la industria (huelgas, manifestaciones). **6 – state/** (EE.UU.) **– park,** polígono industrial. **7 – relations,** ECON. convenio de la industria (establecido por ley).

industrialism | ɪn'dʌstrɪəlɪzəm | *s.i.* industrialismo.

industrialist | ɪn'dʌstrɪəlɪst | *s.c.* empresario industrial, director de una industria.

industrialization | ɪnˌdʌstrɪəlaɪ'zeɪʃn | *s.i.* industrialización.

industrialize | ɪn'dʌstrɪəlaɪz | (brit.) **industrialise.** *v.t.* e *i.* industrializar.

industrialized | ɪn'dʌstrɪəlaɪzd | *adj.* industrializado.

industrious | ɪn'dʌstrɪəs | *adj.* **1** diligente, trabajador, industrioso, aplicado. **2** (arc.) experto, hábil.

industry | 'ɪndəstrɪ | *s.i.* **1** industria. **2** (form.) diligencia, industriosidad, aplicación, trabajo. || *s.c.* **3** industria, rama industrial, negocio: *the film industry = la industria cinematográfica.*

inebriate | ɪ'ni:brɪɪt | *v.t.* **1** *gen.pas.* (form.) embriagar, emborrachar. || *s.c.* **2** (form.) ebrio, beodo, borracho. || *adj.* **3** (form.) ebrio, beodo, embriagado, borracho.

inebriated | ɪ'ni:brɪəɪtɪd | *adj.* (form.) embriagado, ebrio, beodo, borracho.

inedible | ɪn'edɪbl | *adj.* incomestible, incomible.

ineffable | ɪn'efəbl | *adj.* **1** (form.) inefable, inolvidable, indescriptible. **2** (form.) inexpresable, indecible, tabú (el nombre de Dios en algunas religiones).

ineffably | ɪn'efəblɪ | *adv.* inefablemente, inolvidablemente, indescriptiblemente.

ineffective | ˌɪnɪ'fektɪv | *adj.* inefectivo, ineficaz, inútil, falto de eficacia: *the medicine proved ineffective = la medicina no surtió efecto.*

ineffectiveness | ˌɪnɪ'fektɪvnɪs | *s.i.* ineficacia, inutilidad.

ineffectual | ˌɪnɪ'fektʃʊəl | *adj.* **1** ineficaz, inútil: *an ineffectual person = un inútil.* **2** vano, fútil.

ineffectually | ˌɪnɪ'fektʃʊəlɪ | *adv.* ineficazmente, inútilmente, vanamente.

inefficiency | ˌɪnɪ'fɪʃnsɪ | *s.i.* ineficiencia, ineficacia, inoperancia, incompetencia, ineptitud.

inefficient | ˌɪnɪ'fɪʃnt | *adj.* ineficaz, inoperante, incapaz, incompetente, inepto.

inefficiently | ˌɪnɪ'fɪʃntlɪ | *adv.* ineficazmente, inoperantemente, incompetentemente.

inelegant | ɪn'elɪgənt | *adj.* poco elegante, de mal gusto, vulgar, ordinario, tosco.

inelegible | ɪn'elɪdʒəbl | *adj.* **1** no elegible, no apto. **2** **[to – to** *inf.***]** sin derecho a: *inelegible to vote = sin derecho a voto.*

ineluctable | ˌɪnɪ'lʌktəbl | *adj.* ineluctable, ineludible, inevitable.

inept | ɪ'nept | *adj.* **1** inepto, incapaz, incompetente. **2** torpe, desatinado. **3** inapropiado, absurdo.

ineptitude, ineptness | ɪ'neptɪtju:d | *s.i.* ineptitud, incapacidad, incompetencia.

inequality | ˌɪnɪ'kwɒlɪtɪ | | ˌɪnɪ'kwɑ:lɪtɪ | *s.c.* (gen. *pl.*) e *i.* **1** desigualdad, falta de equidad, injusticia (social). **2** desigualdad, discontinuidad, desnivel (en una superficie). **3** variabilidad, alteración, cambio (de carácter, del clima). **4** MAT. desigualdad.

inequitable | ɪn'ekwɪtəbl | *adj.* (form.) poco equitativo, injusto.

inequity | ɪn'ekwətɪ | *s.c.* e *i.* (form.) injusticia, falta de equidad, desigualdad.

ineradicable | ˌɪnɪ'rædɪkəbl | *adj.* (form.) inextirpable, inextinguible.

inert | ɪ'nɜ:t | | ɪ'nɜ:rt | *adj.* **1** inerte, inmóvil, inactivo. **2** apático, desidioso, perezoso. **3** QUIM. inerte, no reactivo (un gas).

inertia | ɪ'nɜ:ʃjə | | ɪ'nɜ:rʃjə | *s.i.* **1** FIS. inercia. **2** apatía, pereza, inactividad.

inescapable | ˌɪnɪ'skeɪpəbl | *adj.* inevitable, ineludible.

inessential | ˌɪnɪ'senʃl | *adj.* **1** no esencial, prescindible, sin importancia. || *s.pl.* **2** detalles innecesarios, cosas sin importancia.

inestimable | ɪn'estɪməbl | *adj.* **1** (form.) inestimable, incalculable. **2** inapreciable. **3** de gran valor, de valor incalculable.

inevitability | ɪnˌevɪtə'bɪlɪtɪ | *s.i.* inevitabilidad, certeza irremediable.

inevitable | ɪn'evɪtəbl | *adj.* **1** inevitable, irremediable, ineluctable, ineludible. **2** (fam.) obligado, forzoso. || *s.sing.* **3** **[the –]** lo inevitable, lo irremediable.

inevitably | ɪn'evɪtəblɪ | *adv.* inevitablemente, irremediablemente, ineludiblemente.

inexact | ˌɪnɪg'zækt | *adj.* inexacto, no preciso.

inexcusable | ˌɪnɪk'skju:zəbl | *adj.* inexcusable, imperdonable, intolerable, injustificable.

inexcusably | ˌɪnɪk'skju:zəblɪ | *adv.* inexcusablemente, injustificablemente.

inexhaustible | ˌɪnɪg'zɔ:stəbl | *adj.* **1** inagotable, infinito. **2** incansable, infatigable.

inexorable | ɪn'eksərəbl | *adj.* **1** inexorable, implacable. **2** (fam.) inflexible, inconmovible, firme.

inexorably | ɪn'eksərəblɪ | *adv.* inexorablemente, implacablemente.

inexpensive | ˌɪnɪk'spensɪv | *adj.* **1** (gen. euf.) de un precio razonable, barato.

inexperience | ˌɪnɪk'spɪərɪəns | *s.i.* **1** inexperiencia. **2** ignorancia.

inexperienced | ˌɪnɪk'spɪərɪənst | *adj.* **1** inexperto, falto de experiencia, principiante. **2** ignorante.

inexpert | ɪn'ekspɜ:t | *adj.* inexperto, falto de experiencia, inhábil.

inexplicable | ˌɪnɪk'splɪkəbl | | ɪn'eks↓plɪkəbl | *adj.* inexplicable, incomprensible, inconcebible, extraño, raro.

inexplicably | ˌɪnɪk'splɪkəblɪ | *adv.* inexplicablemente, incomprensiblemente, extrañamente.

inexpressible | ˌɪnɪk'spresəbl | *adj.* (form.) inexpresable, inenarrable, inefable.

inexpressive | ˌɪnɪk'spresɪv | *adj.* inexpresivo, hierático, hermético, distante (el rostro, la mirada).

in extremis | ɪnɪk'stri:mɪs | *adv.* (form.) in extremis, en el último momento, al borde de la muerte.

inextricable | ɪn'ekstrɪkəbl | *adj.* **1** (form.) inextricable, insoluble. **2** inseparable, indivisible, consubstancial.

inextricably | ɪn'ekstrɪkəblɪ | *adv.* inseparablemente, consubstancialmente, indivisiblemente.

infallibility | ɪnˌfælə'bɪlɪtɪ | *s.i.* infalibilidad.

infallible | ɪn'fæləbl | *adj.* infalible, indefectible (una persona, un remedio).

infamous | 'ɪnfəməs | *adj.* **1** (form.) infame, vil, canalla. **2** de mala reputación.

infamy | ’ɪnfəmɪ | *s.i.* **1** infamia, deshonor, ignominia. **2** mala reputación. || *s.c.* (gen. *pl.*) acto infame, acto ignominioso.

infancy | ’ɪnfənsɪ | *s.c.* e *i.* **1** infancia, niñez. **2** comienzo, principio, punto de partida. **3** DER. minoría de edad. || **4 to be in its –,** estar en pañales, estar en mantillas.

infant | ’ɪnfənt | *s.c.* **1** infante, criatura, niño pequeño. **2** DER. menor de edad. **3** cría (de un animal). || *adj.* **4** infantil, maternal. **5** naciente, en sus comienzos: *an infant organization = una organización naciente.* || **6 – school,** escuela de párvulos.

infanticide | ɪn’fæntɪsaɪd | *s.c.* e *i.* **1** (form.) infanticidio. || *s.c.* **2** infanticida.

infantile | ’ɪnfəntaɪl | *adj.* **1** (gen. desp.) infantil, pueril, ingenuo, irrazonable, estúpido. **2** infantil (una enfermedad).

infantry | ’ɪnfəntrɪ | *s.sing.* **[=N** *v.sing./pl.***]** MIL. infantería.

infantryman | ’ɪnfəntrɪmən | *pl.* **infantrymen.** *s.c.* MIL. soldado de infantería.

infatuated | ɪn’fætjueɪt | *adj.* **[– (with)]** (gen. desp.) loco (por), locamente enamorado (de), encaprichado (por) (una persona, una cosa).

infatuation | ɪnˌfætju’eɪʃn | *s.c.* e *i.* enamoramiento, infatuación, chifladura, encaprichamiento.

infect | ɪn’fekt | *v.t.* **1** MED. infectar, infestar, contagiar. **2** contaminar, corromper (el aire, los alimentos). **3** (fig.) contagiar, influir, extender: *her happiness infected us all = su felicidad nos contagió a todos.*

infected | ɪn’fektɪd | *adj.* MED. infectado, infestado, contagiado.

infection | ɪn’fekʃn | *s.c.* e *i.* **1** MED. infección, contagio. **2** MED. enfermedad infecciosa. **3** (fig.) contagio.

infectious | ɪn’fekʃəs | *adj.* **1** MED. infeccioso, contagioso. **2** (fig.) contagioso: *infectious giggles = risita contagiosa.*

infer | ɪn’fəːr | *v.t.* **1 [to – (form)]** inferir, deducir, desprenderse, concluir, colegir. || *v.i.* **2** sacar conclusiones.

inference | ’ɪnfərəns | *s.i.* **1** inferencia, deducción. || *s.c.* **2** deducción, conclusión.

inferior | ɪn’fɪərɪər | *adj.* **1** inferior, peor, de segunda categoría. **2** inferior, subordinado, subalterno, de rango inferior. || *s.c.* **3** (desp.) inferior, subordinado, subalterno. **4** BOT. ínfero.

inferiority | ɪnˌfɪərɪ’ɒrɪtɪ | | ɪnˌfɪərɪ’ɒːrɪtɪ | *s.i.* **1** inferioridad. || **2 – complex,** PSI. complejo de inferioridad.

infernal | ɪn’fəːnl | | ɪn’fəːrnl | *adj.* **1** (arc. y form.) infernal, desagradable, exasperante: *an infernal noise = un ruido infernal.* **2** terrible, cruel. **3** no **comp.** (lit.) infernal, endemoniado.

inferno | ɪn’fəːnəʊ | | ɪn’fəːrnəʊ | *pl.* **infernos** *s.c.* **1** (lit.) infierno, lugar, infernal. **2** infierno, hoguera.

infertile | ɪn’fəːtaɪl | | ɪn’fəːrtaɪl | *adj.* **1** no *comp.* estéril. **2** improductivo, infecundo, baldío (el terreno).

infertility | ˌɪnfəː’tɪlɪtɪ | | ˌɪnfəːr’tɪlɪtɪ | *s.i.* **1** esterilidad. **2** infecundidad, improductividad, aridez (del terreno).

infest | ɪn’fest | *v.t.* **1 [to – (with)]** infestar, plagar: *flees infested the place = las pulgas plagaron el lugar.*

infestation | ˌɪnfe’steɪʃn | *s.c.* e *i.* plaga.

infidel | ’ɪnfɪdəl | *s.c.* **1** (arc. y desp.) infiel, pagano, descreído. || *adj.* **2** infiel.

infidelity | ˌɪnfɪ’delɪtɪ | *s.c.* e *i.* **1** infidelidad, traición, deslealtad. **2** adulterio, infidelidad conyugal. **3** carencia de fe.

infighting | ’ɪnfaɪtɪŋ | *s.i.* **1** lucha interna, rivalidad. **2** contienda, disputa. **3** DEP. boxeo, lucha cuerpo a cuerpo.

infiltrate | ’ɪnfɪltreɪt | *v.t.* e *i.* **1** filtrar, infiltrarse en (una organización, un país). **2** infiltrar, calar. || *s.i.* **3** MED. infiltración, acumulación de sustancias (en los tejidos).

infiltration | ˌɪnfɪl’treɪʃn | *s.c.* e *i.* infiltración, penetración.

infinite | ’ɪnfɪnət | *adj.* **1** infinito, ilimitado, carente de límites, vasto. **2** enorme, muchísimo: *with infinite care = con enorme cuidado.* **3** MAT. infinito. || *s.i.* **4 [the –]** el Infinito, Dios.

infinitely | ’ɪnfɪnətlɪ | *adv.* **1** infinitamente, enormemente, sin límites.

infinitesimal | ˌɪnfɪnɪ’tesɪml | *adj.* **1** infinitesimal, mínimo, minúsculo. **2** MAT. infinitesimal. || *s.c.* **3** MAT. cantidad infinitesimal.

infinitive | ɪn’fɪnətɪv | *s.c.* GRAM. infinitivo.

infinity | ɪn’fɪnɪtɪ | *s.i.* **1** infinidad, lo infinito. **2** MAT. número infinito. **3** el infinito (punto en el espacio). **4** infinidad, inmensidad (de un área).

infirm | ɪn’fəːm | | ɪn’fəːrm | *adj.* **1** débil, achacoso, enfermizo (debido a la edad). **2** de carácter débil, vacilante, inseguro. || *s.pl.* **3 the –,** los ancianos.

infirmary | ɪn’fəːmərɪ | | ɪn’fəːrmərɪ | *s.c.* **1** hospital. **2** enfermería.

infirmity | ɪn’fəːmɪtɪ | | ɪn’fəːrmɪtɪ | *s.c.* (gen. *pl.*) e *i.* **1** achaque, dolencia, fragilidad: *infirmities typical from age = dolencias propias de la vejez.* **2** incapacidad (mental). **3** impedimento (físico).

inflame | ɪn’fleɪm | *v.t.* **1** enconar, enardecer, excitar (los ánimos). || *v.t.* e *i.* **2** enfurecer(se), encolerizar(se). **3** inflamar(se), prender(se) fuego, incendiar(se). **4** MED. inflamar(se), hinchar(se). **5** inflamar(se), incendiar(se).

inflamed | ɪn’fleɪmd | *adj.* MED. inflamado, hinchado.

inflammable | ɪn’flæməbl | (EE.UU.) **flammable** *adj.* **1** inflamable, combustible. **2** (fig.) explosivo (una situación). **3** irritable, violento, vivo de genio.

inflammation | ˌɪnflə’meɪʃn | *s.c.* e *i.* MED. inflamación, hinchazón, hinchamiento.

inflammatory | ɪn’flæmətərɪ | *adj.* **1** MED. inflamatorio. **2** explosivo, incendiario, violento.

inflatable | ɪn’fleɪtəbl | *adj.* hinchable, inflable.

inflate | ɪn’fleɪt | *v.t.* e *i.* **1** (form.) hinchar(se), inflar(se), llenar(se) de aire. **2** exagerar las bondades, elogiar en demasía, poner por las nubes. || *v.t.* **3** aumentar excesivamente, aumentar por la inflación (los precios), causar inflación.

inflated | ɪn’fleɪtɪd | *adj.* **1** exagerado, excesivo, elevadísimo, de inflación (un precio). **2** (desp.) desorbitada, exagerada, por las nubes (una idea, una opinión). **3** hinchado, inflado (de aire). **4** ampuloso, pretencioso, pomposo (un estilo, el modo de hablar).

inflation | ɪn’fleɪʃn | *s.i.* **1** ECON. inflación (de precios). **2** inflación (por aire).

inflationary | ɪn’fleɪʃnərɪ | | ɪn’fleɪʃənerɪ | *adj.* ECON. inflacionario, inflacionista.

inflect | ɪn’flekt | *v.t.* e *i.* **1** GRAM. inflexionar, alterar por inflexión, modificar. **2** modular (la voz). **3** doblar, torcer.

inflected | ɪn’flektɪd | *adj.* GRAM. fl[illegible] xional.

inflection | ɪn’flekʃn | (brit.) **inflexion** *s.i.* **1** GRAM. inflexión. || *s.c.* **2** GRAM. inflexión, parte que modifica (una palabra): *the «s» is the plural inflection = la «s» es la inflexión del plural.* **3** modulación, inflexión, entonación (de la voz).

inflexibility | ɪnˌfleksə’bɪlɪtɪ | *s.i.* inflexibilidad, rigidez.

inflexible | ɪn’fleksəbl | *adj.* **1** no flexible, rígido, duro. **2** (gen. desp.) inflexible, testarudo, cabezota, indómito.

inflexion | ɪn’flekʃn | V. **inflection.**

inflict | ɪn’flɪkt | *v.t.* **1 [to – (on/upon)]** infligir, imponer, obligar a (un castigo, ideas, a personas). **2** afligir, apenar, causar sufrimiento.

infliction | ɪn’flɪkʃn | *s.c.* e *i.* **1** imposición (de un castigo). **2** castigo, pena, molestia.

inflow, influx | ’ɪnfləʊ | *s.c.* e *i.* afluencia, flujo, entrada: *the inflow of foreign investments = la afluencia de inversiones extranjeras.*

influence | ’ɪnfluəns | *s.c.* e *i.* **1 [– (over/on/upon/with)]** influencia, influjo. **2 [– (for/on)]** influencia, ascendiente, predicamento. || *v.t.* **3** influir en, afectar a. **4** influenciar, manipular. || **5 to be under the influence of,** estar bajo la influencia de algo o de alguien, dejarse manipular por. **6 under the –,** (fam.) borracho, bebido.

influential | ˌɪnflu’enʃl | *adj.* **1** influyente, importante, poderoso, prestigioso.

influenza | ˌɪnflu’enzə | *s.i.* **1** (form.) MED. gripe.

influx | ’ɪnflʌks | *s.c.* (gen. *sing.*) V. **inflow.**

info | ’ɪnfəʊ | *s.i.* (fam. y jerga). V. **information.**

inform | ɪn’fɔːm | *v.t.* **1 [to – (of/about)]** (form.) informar, comunicar, exponer, hacer saber, notificar. **2** imbuir, animar, inspirar (una buena cualidad). **3** formar, conformar, instruir. || **4 to – against/on somebody,** (desp.) denunciar a alguien, delatar a alguien (a la policía).

informal | ɪn'fɔːml | | ɪn'fɔːrml | *adj.* **1** informal, extraoficial, sin protocolo: *informal talks about the project = conversaciones extraoficiales sobre el proyecto.* **2** informal, sin etiqueta (la ropa, una reunión). **3** informal, familiar, coloquial (el lenguaje). **4** informal, afable, desenvuelto (el comportamiento).

informality | ˌɪnfɔː'mæləti | *s.i.* **1** informalidad, ausencia de protocolo o ceremonia. **3** desenvoltura, afabilidad, familiaridad.

informally | ɪn'fɔːməlɪ | *adv.* **1** informalmente, sin protocolo, extraoficialmente. **2** con desenvoltura, afablemente, de modo informal.

informant | ɪn'fɔːmənt | | ɪn'fɔːrmənt | *s.c.* **1** (form.) delator, soplón, confidente. **2** informador, informante (de un investigador, especialmente a un lingüista).

information | ˌɪnfə'meɪʃn | *s.i.* **[– (on/ about)]** información, noticias. **2** información, datos, conocimientos. **3** DER. acusación (hecha por el fiscal). **4** denuncia, delación.

informative | ɪn'fɔːmətɪv | *adj.* **1** informativo, instructivo.

informed | ɪn'fɔːmd | *adj.* **1 [– (on/ about)]** informado, al corriente, sabedor. **3** aproximado, aproximativo: *an informed guess = una respuesta aproximada.*

informer | ɪn'fɔːmər | *s.c.* (desp.) informador, soplón, confidente.

infra dig | ˌɪnfrə'dɪg | *adj.* (brit. y fam.) degradante, deshonroso.

infra-red | ˌɪnfrə'red | *adj.* FIS. infrarrojos.

infrastructure | 'ɪnfrəˌstrʌktʃər | *s.c.* infraestructura, base.

infrequent | ɪn'friːkwənt | *adj.* (form.) infrecuente, raro, ocasional.

infrequently | ɪn'friːkwəntlɪ | *adv.* infrecuentemente, raramente, ocasionalmente.

infringe | ɪn'frɪndʒ | *v.t.* e *i.* **1** (form.) infringir, incumplir, quebrantar (la ley, un acuerdo). **2** violar, usurpar (un derecho). **3 [to – (on/upon)]** traspasar los límites, cometer intrusión. **4** (arc.) invalidar, anular.

infringement | ɪn'frɪndʒmənt | *s.c.* e *i.* **1** infracción, quebrantamiento, violación, incumplimiento (de una ley, de un acuerdo). **2** intrusión, abuso, usurpación (de derechos).

infuriate | ɪn'fjʊərɪeɪt | *v.t.* **1** enfurecer, encolerizar. || *adj.* **2** (arc.) furioso, encolerizado.

infuriating | ɪn'fjʊərɪeɪtɪŋ | *adj.* enloquecedor, irritante, exasperante.

infuriatingly | ɪn'fjʊərɪeɪtɪŋlɪ | *adv.* enloquecedoramente, irritantemente, exasperantemente.

infuse | ɪn'fjuːz | *v.t.* **1 [to – + *o.* + with]** infundir de, imbuir de (esperanzas, ánimos). **2** extender, introducir. || *v.t.* e *i.* **3** hacer o preparar una infusión.

infusion | ɪn'fjuːʒn | *s.c.* e *i.* **1** infusión, tisana, poción. **2** infusión, adición, inyección (de ideas, de capital).

ingenious | ɪn'dʒiːnjəs | *adj.* ingenioso, imaginativo, genial.

ingeniously | ɪn'dʒiːnjəslɪ | *adv.* ingeniosamente, imaginativamente, de forma genial.

ingenuity | ˌɪndʒɪ'njuːətɪ | | ˌɪndʒɪ'nuːətɪ | *s.i.* ingenio, genialidad, inventiva, imaginación.

ingenuous | ɪn'dʒenjʊəs | *adj.* **1** (gen. desp.) ingenuo, inocente, candoroso, inexperto. **2** franco, honesto.

ingenuously | ɪn'dʒenjʊəslɪ | *adv.* ingenuamente, inocentemente, candorosamente.

inglorious | ɪn'glɔːrɪəs | *adj.* **1** (lit.) vergonzoso, deshonroso, bochornoso. **2** (arc.) desconocido, sin fama.

ingloriously | ɪn'glɔːrɪəslɪ | *adv.* **1** vergonzosamente, bochornosamente, deshonrosamente. **2** (arc.) sin fama.

ingot | 'ɪŋgət | *s.c.* **1** lingote, barra. **2** molde de fundición.

ingrained | ˌɪn'greɪnd | *adj.* **1** incrustado, firmemente introducido, empotrado. **2** (fig.) arraigado, enraizado, innato (un sentimiento, una costumbre).

ingratiate | ɪn'greɪʃɪeɪt | *v.t.* **[to – (with)]** (desp.) congraciarse (con), ganarse (a), condescender (con), predisponer a favor.

ingratiating | ɪn'greɪʃɪeɪtɪŋ | *adj.* (desp.) adulador, zalamero, pelotillero.

ingratitude | ɪn'grætɪtjuːd | | ɪn'grætɪtuːd | *s.i.* ingratitud, desagradecimiento.

ingredient | ɪn'griːdjənt | *s.c.* **1** ingrediente, componente (de cocina). **2** (fig.) ingrediente, componente, factor: *the ingredient of the detective novel = los componentes de la novela negra.*

ingrowing, ingrown | 'ɪnˌgrəʊɪŋ | *adj.* **1** no *comp.* que crece hacia adentro: *a ingrowing toenail = uña del pie que crece hacia dentro.*

inhabit | ɪn'hæbɪt | *v.t.* **1** (form.) habitar, poblar, vivir. **2** residir, tener residencia en. **3** (fig.) abrigar, tener (en la mente). **4** estar presente en (un lugar).

inhabitant | ɪn'hæbɪtənt | *s.c.* habitante, residente, vecino, poblador.

inhale | ɪn'heɪl | *v.t.* e *i.* inspirar, aspirar, inhalar.

inherent | ɪn'hɪərənt | *adj.* inherente, innato, consubstancial, intrínseco.

inherently | ɪn'hɪərəntlɪ | *adv.* inherentemente, consubstancialmente, intrínsecamente.

inherit | ɪn'herɪt | *v.t.* e *i.* **1** heredar, recibir en herencia. **2** BIOL. heredar (una característica, una cualidad).

inheritance | ɪn'herɪtəns | *s.c.* (gen. *sing.*) **1** herencia, legado, patrimonio, donación. || *s.i.* **2** herencia, sucesión. **3** BIOL. herencia, transmisión (genética).

inheritor | ɪn'herɪtər | *s.c.* heredero.

inhibit | ɪn'hɪbɪt | *v.t.* **1** inhibir, impedir, contener, restringir. **2** frenar, moderar (el desarrollo). **3** inhibir, reprimir, refrenar. || **3 to – somebody from something,** impedir a alguien hacer algo.

inhibited | ɪn'hɪbɪtɪd | *adj.* **1** inhibido, reprimido, reservado, cohibido.

inhibition | ˌɪnhɪ'bɪʃn | *s.c.* e *i.* **1** inhibición, represión, reserva.

inhospitable | ɪn'hɒspɪtəbl | | ˌɪnhɑː's-pɪtəbl | *adj.* **1** (desp.) poco hospitalario, poco amistoso, frío (una persona). **2** inhóspito, inhabitable, desabrigado.

inhuman | ɪn'hjuːmən | *adj.* **1** inhumano, cruel, despiadado, falto de compasión. **2** frío, adusto, reservado. **3** monstruoso, no humano.

inhumane | ˌɪn'hjuː'meɪn | *adj.* **1** inhumano, cruel, despiadado.

inhumanity | ˌɪn'hjuː'mænətɪ | *s.c.* (gen. *pl.*) e *i.* inhumanidad, barbaridad, crueldad, falta de compasión.

inimical | ɪ'nɪmɪkl | *adj.* **1** (form.) hostil, adverso, perjudicial: *inimical circumstances = circunstancias adversas.* **2** poco amistoso, hostil.

inimitable | ɪ'nɪmɪtəbl | *adj.* inimitable, excepcional, único: *an inimitable style = un estilo inimitable.*

iniquitous | ɪ'nɪkwɪtəs | *adj.* (form.) inicuo, extremadamente injusto, perverso, malvado.

iniquity | ɪ'nɪkwəti | *s.c.* e *i.* iniquidad, injusticia, maldad, perversidad.

initial | ɪ'nɪʃl | *adj.* **1** no *comp.* inicial, primero, original, del principio. || *s.c.* **2** letra inicial. || *v.t.* **3** (brit.) **initiall** inicial, escribir las iniciales, firmar con iniciales.

initially | ɪ'nɪʃəlɪ | *adv.* inicialmente, al principio, originalmente.

initiate | ɪ'nɪʃɪəɪt | *v.t.* **1** iniciar, empezar, comenzar. **2 [to – (into)]** iniciar, introducir: *he was initiated into painting = se le inició en la pintura.* **3 [to – (into)]** (gen. *pas.*) admitir como miembro, introducir, presentar (a alguien en un club o asociación con ceremonia). **4** DER. entablar (un litigio). || | ɪ'nɪʃɪət | *s.c.* **5** iniciado.

initiation | ɪˌnɪʃɪ'eɪʃn | *s.c.* e *i.* **1 [– (into)]** iniciación, introducción, entrada: *his initiation into adulthood = su entrada en la edad adulta.* **2** iniciación, principio, comienzo, origen. **3** admisión.

initiative | ɪ'nɪʃɪətɪv | *s.c.* e *i.* **1** iniciativa, decisión, impulso. || **2 to do something on one's own –/to use one's –,** hacer algo por propia iniciativa, hacer algo independientemente.

inject | ɪn'dʒekt | *v.i.* **1 [to – (with /into)]** MED. inyectar, vacunar, inocular. **2** inyectar, introducir (con fuerza). **3** (fig.) inyectar, insuflar (entusiasmo, alegría). **4** ECON. inyectar (capital).

injection | ɪn'dʒekʃn | *s.c.* e *i.* **1** inyección, vacuna, inoculación. **2** ECON. inyección de capital.

injuditious | ˌɪndʒuː'dɪʃəs | *adj.* (form.) imprudente, alocado, poco juicioso, insensato.

injunction | ɪn'dʒʌŋkʃn | *s.c.* **1** DER. orden, requerimiento: interdicto. **2** advertencia, amonestación.

injure | 'ɪndʒər | *v.t.* **1** herir, lesionar. **2** (fig.) herir, ofender. **3** menoscabar, manchar (la reputación).

injured | 'ɪndʒəd | *adj.* **1** herido, lesionado. **2** (fig.) herido, ofendido. || *s.c.* **3** herido, lesionado. || **4 – party,** DER. víctima, parte agraviada.

injurious | ɪn'dʒʊərɪəs | *adj.* **1** (form.) perjudicial, lesivo, nocivo, pernicioso. **2** difamatorio, difamador, calumnioso.

injury | ɪndʒərɪ | *s.c.* e *i.* **1** daño, lesión, herida, accidente. **2** DER. ofensa, agravio. || **3 – time,** DEP. prórroga.

injustice | ɪn'dʒʌstɪs | *s.c.* e *i.* **1** injusticia, arbitrariedad, atropello. || **2 to do someone an –,** juzgar injustamente a alguien, juzgar mal a alguien.

ink | ɪŋk | *s.c.* e *i.* **1** tinta (de escribir, de los cefalópodos). || *v.t.* **2** entintar, poner tinta, embadurnar con tinta. || **3 to – something in,** pasar a tinta (un dibujo a lápiz).

inkling | 'ɪŋklɪŋ | *s.c.* **1** idea vaga, noción. **2** indicio, estimación, sospecha.

inkstand | 'ɪŋkstænd | *s.c.* escribanía, portatinteros.

inkwell | 'ɪŋkwel | *s.c.* tintero.

inky | 'ɪŋkɪ | *adj.* **1** entintado, manchado de tinta, embadurnado de tinta. **2** (fig.) oscuro, negro: *the inky blackness of the room = la negra oscuridad de la habitación.*

inlaid | ˌɪn'leɪd | [*pret.* y *p.p.* de **inlay.**] *adj. no comp.* [**– (in/into)**] incrustado, taraceado.

inland | ɪn'lænd | *adj. no comp.* **1** interior, del interior: *an inland region = una región del interior (no costera).* || *adv.* **2** tierra adentro.

in-laws | 'ɪnlɔː | *s.pl.* parientes políticos: *brother-in-law = cuñado.*

inlay | ˌɪnleɪ | *s.c.* e *i.* **1** incrustación, taracea. || *s.c.* **2** MED. empaste. || *v.t.* **3** incrustar, taracear, decorar con incrustaciones.

inlet | 'ɪnlet | | 'ɪnlət | *s.c.* **1** ría, cala, ensenada. **2** MEC. entrada, admisión.

inmate | 'ɪnmeɪt | *s.c.* **1** residente, habitante. **2** inquilino, huésped. **3** enfermo, paciente (de un hospital psiquiátrico). **4** preso, recluso.

inmost, innermost | 'ɪnməust | *adj.* **1** no *comp.* profundo, interior. **2** (fig.) recóndito, íntimo, secreto.

inn | ɪn | *s.c.* **1** posada, hostería, fonda (de estilo antiguo). **2** taberna, restaurante, bar. **3** (brit. y arc.) residencia de estudiantes.

innards | 'ɪnədz | *s.pl.* **1** entrañas, vísceras, tripas. **2** (fig.) tripas, interior, parte de dentro (de un aparato).

innate | ˌɪ'neɪt | *adj.* **1** innato, congénito. **2** inherente, natural, esencial.

innately | ˌɪ'neɪtlɪ | *adv.* **1** de forma innata, congénitamente. **2** inherentemente, naturalmente, esencialmente.

inner | 'ɪnər | *adj.* no *comp.* **1** interior, interno. **2** íntimo, secreto, interior (sentimientos, emociones). **3** profundo. **4** influyente, importante. || **5 – city,** casco antiguo de la ciudad. **6 – tube,** cámara (de una rueda).

innermost | 'ɪnəməust | *adj.* no *comp.* V. **inmost.**

inning | 'ɪnɪŋ | *s.c. pl.* [=N*v.sing./pl.*] **1** DEP. turno, entrada (en béisbol). **2** (fig.) oportunidad, turno. **3** (arc.) tierras ganadas al mar. || **4 to have had a good innings,** (brit. y fam.) haber tenido mucha suerte en la vida, haber tenido una vida plena.

innkeeper | 'ɪnˌkiːpər | *s.c.* (arc.) posadero, hostelero, mesonero.

innocence | 'ɪnəsəns | *s.i.* **1** inocencia, candor, ingenuidad. **2** DER. inocencia. **3** BOT. azulejo, anciano.

innocent | 'ɪnəsnt | *adj.* **1** DER. inocente, libre de culpa. **2** inocente, puro. **3** inofensivo, inocuo, falto de malicia: *innocent words = palabras sin malicia.* **4** (desp.) inocente, ignorante, inexperto, ingenuo. || *s.c.* **5** inocente. **6** simplón, ingenuo, ignorante.

innocently | 'ɪnəsntlɪ | *adv.* inocentemente, sin malicia, ingenuamente, cándidamente.

innocuous | ɪ'nɒkjʊəs | | ɪ'nɑːkjʊəs | *adj.* **1** inocuo, inofensivo. **2** insignificante, poco importante, sin impacto: *an innocuous speech = un discurso sin impacto.*

innovate | 'ɪnəuveɪt | *v.t.* e *i.* innovar, ser creativo, hacer cambio, introducir reformas.

innovation | ˌɪnəu'veɪʃn | *s.c.* e *i.* innovación, cambio, novedad.

innovative, innovatory | 'ɪnəˌveɪtɪv | *adj.* innovador, original, creativo, progresista.

innovator | 'ɪnəuveɪtər | *s.c.* innovador, creador, pionero.

innovatory | 'ɪnəvtərɪ | *adj.* V. **innovative.**

innuendo | ˌɪnju'endəu | *pl.* **innuendos** o **innuendoes.** *s.c.* **1** insinuación, indirecta. || *s.i.* **2** insinuación, insidia.

innumerable | ɪ'njuːmərəbl | | ɪ'nuːmərəbl | *adj.* innumerable, infinito, inmenso, incalculable, incontable.

inoculate | ɪ'nɒkjuleɪt | | ɪ'nɑːkjuleɪt | *v.t.* [**to – (with/against)**] MED. inocular, vacunar, inmunizar.

inoculation | ɪˌnɒkju'leɪʃn | | ɪˌnɑːkju'leɪʃn | *s.i.* **1** MED. inoculación, vacunación. || *s.c.* **2** MED. vacuna.

inoffensive | ˌɪnə'fensɪv | *adj.* **1** inofensivo, inocuo.

inoperable | ɪn'ɒpərəbl | | ɪn'ɑːpərəbl | *adj.* **1** MED. inoperable, intratable, impracticable. **2** (form.) impracticable, irrealizable, inútil.

inoperative | ɪn'ɒpərətɪv | | ɪn'ɑːpərətɪv | *adj.* **1** inoperante, ineficaz. **2** inaplicable (una ley, una regla).

inopportune | ɪn'ɒpətjuːn | | ˌɪnɒˌr'tuːn | *adj.* **1** (form.) inoportuno, inconveniente, a deshora. **2** desafortunado, fuera de tono, sin ton ni son.

inordinate | ɪ'nɔːdɪnət | | ɪ'nɔːrdənət | *adj.* **1** desproporcionado, desmesurado, inmenso, excesivo, inmoderado. **2** irregular, desordenado.

inordinately | ɪ'nɔːdɪnətlɪ | *adv.* desproporcionadamente, desmesuradamente, excesivamente, sin moderación.

inorganic | ˌɪnɔː'gænɪk | | ˌɪnɔːr'gænɪk | *adj.* **1** inorgánico. **2** artificial.

in-patient | 'ɪnˌpeɪʃnt | *s.c.* paciente, internado (en un hospital).

input | 'ɪnput | *s.c.* e *i.* **1** potencia, energía, consumo, gasto (que se consume). **2** inversión (de recursos financieros o de personal para que algo funcione). **3** INF. información (que se introduce en la máquina o en el cerebro humano o animal). || *v.t. pret.* y *p.p.* **inputted** o **input.** INF. introducir información.

inquest | 'ɪnkwest | *s.c.* **1** DER. investigación judicial, indagación judicial (en caso de muerte repentina por si hubiera posibilidad de crimen). **2** DER. jurado investigador. **3** (fig.) encuesta, indagación, análisis.

inquire | ɪn'kwaɪər | *v.t.* e *i.* **1** preguntar, inquirir, informarse de, consultar. **2** indagar, averiguar. || **3 to – after,** preguntar acerca de, pedir informes sobre. **4 to – into,** investigar, indagar, estudiar (un tema, un asunto). **5 to – something of somebody,** (form.) preguntar algo a alguien. **6 – within,** se da información, se dan informes.

inquirer | ɪn'kwaɪərər | *s.c.* **1** (form.) investigador, indagador, inquisidor.

inquiring, enquiring | ɪn'kwaɪərɪŋ | *adj.* **1** inquisitivo, penetrante, curiosa (una mirada, una expresión). **2** ávido de saber, de conocimientos.

inquiry | ɪn'kwaɪərɪ | | 'ɪŋkwərɪ | *s.c.* **1** [**– (into/about)**] indagación, interrogatorio, pesquisa, consulta. || *s.c.* **2** [**– (into)**] investigación: *an official inquiry into the accident = una investigación oficial sobre el accidente.* **3** *pl.* departamento de información, información: *could I get through inquiries? = ¿me pone con información?* || **4 to make inquiries,** pedir informes, hacer investigaciones.

inquisition | ˌɪnkwɪ'zɪʃn | *s.c.* **1** (desp.) investigación oficial, interrogatorio, inquisición (gen. violando los derechos de la persona). **2 Inquisition,** REL. inquisición.

inquisitive | ɪn'kwɪzətɪv | *adj.* (desp.) inquisitivo, curioso, preguntón, fisgón, entrometido, husmeador.

inquisitively | ɪn'kwɪzətɪvlɪ | *adv.* inquisitivamente, con curiosidad.

inquisitiveness | ɪn'kwɪzətɪvnɪs | *s.i.* curiosidad.

inquisitor | ɪn'kwɪzɪtər | *s.c.* **1** (desp.) inquisidor, investigador, interrogador. **2** REL. inquisidor.

inquisitorial | ɪnˌkwɪzɪ'tɔːrɪəl | *adj.* (form. y desp.) inquisitorial.

inroads, inroad | 'ɪnrəud | *s.* **1** ataque, avance, invasión, incursión, entrada. || **2 to make –,** hacer estragos, agotar, hacer mella.

insalubrious | ˌɪnsə'luːbrɪəs | *adj.* (form.) insalubre, insano, nocivo, malsano.

insane | ɪn'seɪn | *adj.* **1** (form.) demente, loco, enajenado. **2** (fig.) loco, ido, trastornado. || *s.c.* **3 [the –]** los enfermos mentales.
insanely | ɪn'seɪnlɪ | *adv.* locamente, absurdamente, terriblemente: *insanely in love = locamente enamorado.*
insanitary | ɪn'sænɪtərɪ | | ɪn'sænɪterɪ | *adj.* insalubre, nocivo, antihigiénico.
insanity | ɪn'sænətɪ | *s.i.* **1** locura, demencia, enajenación. **2** (fig.) locura, insensatez.
insatiable | ɪn'seɪʃjəbl | *adj.* **1 [– (for)]** insaciable, voraz. **2 [– (for)]** (fig.) insaciable: *an insatiable desire for knowledge = un deseo insaciable de saber.*
insatiably | ɪn'seɪʃjəblɪ | *adv.* insaciablemente, vorazmente.
inscribe | ɪn'skraɪb | *v.t.* **1** (form.) inscribir, grabar, marcar, impresionar (una superficie). **2** inscribir, alistar. **3** dedicar (un libro). **4** GEOM. inscribir: *an inscribed triangle = un triángulo inscrito.*
inscription | ɪn'skrɪpʃn | *s.c.* **1** inscripción, impresión, grabado, rótulo, letrero. **2** inscripción, alistamiento. **3** dedicatoria.
inscrutable | ɪn'skruːtəbl | *adj.* inescrutable, misterioso, impenetrable, indescifrable.
insect | 'ɪnsekt | *s.c.* **1** BIOL. insecto. **2** (fig.) bicho, miserable.
insecticide | ɪn'sektɪsaɪd | *s.c.* e *i.* insecticida.
insecure | ˌɪnsɪ'kjʊr | *adj.* **1** inseguro, inestable, en el aire. **2** inseguro, eventual (un trabajo). **3** inseguro, vacilante, dubitativo.
insecurity | ˌɪnsɪ'kjʊərɪtɪ | *s.i.* **1** inseguridad, incertidumbre. **2** inseguridad, peligro.
inseminate | ɪn'semɪneɪt | *v.t.* **1** inseminar (artificialmente). **2** sembrar, plantar.
insemination | ɪnˌsemɪ'neɪʃn | *s.i.* inseminación (artificial).
insensible | ɪn'sensəbl | *adj.* **1** (form.) inconsciente, sin conocimiento. **2** inconsciente, ignorante. **3** insensible, impasible (al dolor). **4** insensible, imperceptible, lento, gradual (un cambio).
insensitive | ɪn'sensətɪv | *adj.* **1** insensible, frío, indiferente. **2** insensible, sordo (a una petición). **3** insensible, inalterable: *insensitive to light = inalterable a la luz.*
insensitivity | ɪn'sensətɪvɪtɪ | *s.i.* **1** insensibilidad, indiferencia, frialdad. **2** insensibilidad (al dolor).
inseparable | ɪn'sepərəbl | *adj.* inseparable, indivisible, indisoluble: *inseparable friends = amigos íntimos, inseparables.*
inseparably | ɪn'sepərəblɪ | *adv.* inseparablemente, indivisiblemente, indisolublemente.
insert | 'ɪnsəːt | | 'ɪnsəːrt | *v.t.* **1** insertar, introducir, encajar, meter. **2** insertar, incluir, añadir, intercalar. || *s.c.* **3** inserción, añadido. **4** hoja suelta, lámina intercalada, material adicional (en un libro, revista).
insertion | ɪn'səːʃn | *s.i.* **1** inserción, introducción. || *s.c.* **2** inserción, anuncio, aviso. **3** material adicional, sección adicional (en un libro, revista).
inset | 'ɪnset | *s.c.* **1** mapa, grabado (insertado en un ángulo de otro mayor). **2** inserción de páginas (en un libro). **3** entredós (sobre una tela). **4** (EE.UU.) flujo (de agua). **5** (EE.UU.) canal.
inshore | ˌɪn'ʃɔː | *adv.* **1** a la orilla, cerca de la orilla. || *adj.* **2** *no comp.* cercano a la orilla, cercano a la costa.
inside | ˌɪn'saɪd | | 'ɪnsaɪd | *s.c.* **1 [the –]** el interior, la parte interior: *the inside of the building = el interior del edificio.* **2 [the –]** parte interna: *the inside of the arm = la parte interna del brazo.* **3** (form.) forro (de una prenda). **4 [the –]** el corazón (de una fruta). **5 [the –]** la izquierda o la derecha, (la parte más alejada del centro en una carretera, un camino): *fined for overtaking on the inside lane = multado por adelantar por la izquierda* (en Inglaterra). **6 [the –]** (fam.) los de confianza, los más próximos al poder (en una organización, una empresa). **7** *pl.* (argot) información confidencial, secretos, soplo. **8** *pl.* (fam.) ANAT. entrañas, tripas, vísceras. || | 'ɪnsaɪd | *adj.* **9** interior, interno. **10** central, de dentro. **11** derecho, izquierdo, cercano al arcén (carril de una carretera). **12** confidencial, secreto. || | ɪn'saɪd | *adv.* **13** adentro, dentro, en el interior. **14** (fig.) por dentro: *feeling terrified inside = sintiendo pánico por dentro.* **15** (brit. y jerga) en la cárcel, en prisión. **16** (brit.) piso de abajo, primer piso (de un autobús). || *prep.* **17** dentro de, en el interior de. **18** (fam.) en menos de, dentro de (un tiempo): *inside an hour = en menos de una hora.* || **19 to be on the –,** tener un puesto de confianza, tener influencia. **20 – of,** (fam.) dentro de (un lugar); en menos de (un período de tiempo). **21 – out,** del revés, lo de dentro hacia afuera. **22 to know – out,** conocer a fondo, muy bien. **23 to turn – out,** revolverlo todo, registrar de arriba abajo.
insider | ˌɪn'saɪdər | *s.c.* **1** persona de confianza, bien informada, con influencia (en una organización). **2** miembro, socio (de un grupo, de una empresa).
insidious | ɪn'sɪdɪəs | *adj.* **1** insidioso, malévolo, pérfido. **2** sutil, solapado, subrepticio, traicionero.
insidiously | ɪn'sɪdɪəslɪ | *adv.* insidiosamente, pérfidamente, subrepticiamente, solapadamente.
insight | 'ɪnsaɪt | *s.c.* e *i.* intuición, perspicacia, instinto, sutileza, discernimiento, clarividencia, entendimiento.
insignia | ɪn'sɪgnɪə | *s.c. sing.* y *pl.* **1** insignia, emblema, divisa. **2** distintivo, símbolo, signo.
insignificance | ˌɪnsɪg'nɪfɪkəns | *s.i.* insignificancia, pequeñez.
insignificant | ˌɪnsɪg'nɪfɪkənt | *adj.* insignificante, irrisorio, trivial, modesto.
insincere | ˌɪnsɪn'sɪər | *adj.* insincero, franco, hipócrita, falso.
insincerely | ˌɪnsɪn'sɪəlɪ | *adv.* hipócritamente, falsamente, de forma insincera.
insincerity | ˌɪnsɪn'serɪtɪ *s.i.* insinceridad, hipocresía, falsedad, doblez.
insinuate | ɪn'sɪnjʊeɪt | *v.t.* **1** insinuar, sugerir, dar a entender. **2** hacer insinuaciones. || **3 to – oneself into,** (fam.) introducirse subrepticiamente, ganarse la aceptación en. **4 to – something into,** colar algo de rondón, introducir algo como quien no quiere la cosa.
insinuation | ɪnˌsɪnjʊ'eɪʃn | *s.c.* e *i.* insinuación, sugerencia, indirecta, alusión.
insipid | ɪn'sɪpɪd | *adj.* **1** insípida, sosa (comida o bebida). **2** soso, insulso (el carácter).
insist | ɪn'sɪst | *v.i.* **1 [to – (on/upon)]** insistir en, hacer énfasis en, reiterar, hacer hincapié, porfiar. **2** reclamar, demandar, requerir, exigir. || *v.t.* **3 [to – (that)/o.]** hacer valer, sostener un derecho, reclamar con vehemencia.
insistence, insistency | ɪn'sɪstəns | *s.i.* insistencia, obstinación, énfasis, reiteración, empeño.
insistent | ɪn'sɪstənt | *adj.* **1** insistente, obstinado, porfiado. **2** urgente, apremiante.
insistently | ɪn'sɪstəntlɪ | *adv.* insistentemente, obstinadamente, porfiadamente.
in situ | ˌɪn'sɪtjuː | | ˌɪn'saɪtuː | *adv.* (latín) **1** en el mismo sitio, allí mismo. **2** MED. sin metástasis, sin afectar a partes próximas, en su estadío.
insofar, insofar as | ˌɪnsə'fɑːr | *adv.* V. **far.**
insole | 'ɪnsəʊl | *s.c.* plantilla (para zapatos, botas).
insolence | 'ɪnsələns | *s.i.* insolencia, audacia, arrogancia, atrevimiento, descaro, impertinencia.
insolent | 'ɪnsələnt | *adj.* insolente, audaz, arrogante, atrevido, descarado, impertinente.
insoluble | ɪn'sɒljʊbl | ɪn'sɑːljʊbl | *adj.* **1** insoluble, sin solución, inexplicable. **2** insoluble (en agua).
insolvency | ɪn'sɒlvənsɪ | *s.i.* insolvencia, carencia de liquidez.
insolvent | ɪn'sɒlvənt | *adj.* insolvente, en quiebra.
insomnia | ɪn'sɒmnɪə | | ɪn'sɑːmnɪə | *s.i.* insomnio.
insomniac | ɪn'sɒmnɪæk | | ɪn'sɑːmnɪæk | *adj.* **1** de insomnio, por insomnio, debido al insomnio. || *s.c.* **2** insomne.
insouciance | ɪn'suːsjəns | *s.i.* (form.) despreocupación, falta de cuidado, ligereza.
insouciant | ɪn'suːsjənt | *adj.* (form.) despreocupado, descuidado, indiferente, viva la Virgen.
inspect | ɪn'spekt | *v.t.* **1** inspeccionar, examinar, revisar, pasar revista. **2** MED. examinar, reconocer.
inspection | ɪn'spekʃn | *s.c.* e *i.* **1** inspección, examen, revisión, revista. **2** MED. reconocimiento, examen.

inspector | ɪn'spektər | *s.c.* **1** inspector, revisor, supervisor. **2** inspector de policía. || **3 customs –,** inspector de aduanas. **4 – of taxes,** inspector de hacienda.

inspectorate | ɪn'spektərət | *s.c.* **1** cuerpo de inspección, inspectorado. **2** distrito a cargo de un grupo de inspectores. **3** inspección, supervisión.

inspiration | ˌɪnspə'reɪʃn | *s.i.* **1** inspiración, iluminación, musa. || *s.c.* **2** inspiración, idea brillante. **3** inspiración, aspiración (del aire). **4 [– (for)]** inspiración, influencia, estímulo: *an inspiration for his students = un estímulo para sus alumnos (de él).*

inspirational | ˌɪnspə'reɪʃənl | *adj.* **1** inspirador, inspirante, iluminador. **2** inspirado.

inspire | ɪn'spaɪər | *v.t.* e *i.* **1** inspirar, estimular, influir, ser la musa. **2** respirar, inhalar, inspirar. || *v.t.* **3 [to – + *o.* + in/with]** inspirar, transmitir, infundir, despertar: *he inspired us with faith = nos infundió fe.*

inspired | ɪn'spaɪəd | *adj.* **1** inspirado, brillante. **2** acertado, certero, inteligente.

inspiring | ɪn'spaɪərɪŋ | *adj.* **1** inspirador, que inspira. **2** alentador.

instability | ˌɪnstə'bɪlɪtɪ | *s.i.* inestabilidad, inseguridad, vulnerabilidad.

install | ɪn'stɔːl | (EE.UU.) **instal.** *v.t.* **1** instalar, colocar. **2 [to – + *o.* + *adv./prep.*]** (fam.) instalarse, aposentarse, acomodarse: *I installed myself in the rear room = me instalé en la habitación trasera.* **3** nombrar, designar, dar posesión (de un cargo en una ceremonia).

installation | ˌɪnstə'leɪʃn | *s.i.* **1** instalación, colocación. || *s.c.* **2** instalación: *a new electric installation = una nueva instalación eléctrica.* **3** MIL. base, campamento. **4** ceremonia de nombramiento, toma de posesión.

instalment | ɪn'stɔːlmənt | (EE.UU.) **installment.** *s.c.* **1** LIT. fascículo, entrega. **2** TV. capítulo (de una serie). **3** COM. cuota, plazo, mensualidad (de un pago aplazado). || *s.i.* **4** instalación, colocación.

instance | 'ɪnstəns | *s.c.* **1** ejemplo, caso, antecedente. **2** DER. juicio, pleito, proceso, litigio. **3** instancia, solicitud, petición. || *v.t.* **4** (gen. y form.) citar como ejemplo, poner como ejemplo, poner por caso. || **5 at someone's –,** a instancias de alguien, a petición de alguien. **6 for –,** por ejemplo. **7 in the first –,** en primer lugar, en primer término.

instant | 'ɪnstənt | *s.c.* (gen. *sing.*) **1** instante, momento, periquete, santiamén. **2** el mes en curso: *the 16th instant = el 16 del mes en curso.* || *adj.* **3** inmediato, instantáneo, rápido (un resultado). **4** instantáneo: *instant coffee = café instantáneo.* **5** urgente, imperioso, perentorio. **6** presente, actual. || *adv.* **7** (EE.UU.) instantáneamente, al momento, inmediatamente. || **8 the next –,** a continuación, inmediatamente después. **9 this –,** inmediatamente, al momento.

instantly | 'ɪnstəntlɪ | *adv.* instantáneamente, al momento, inmediatamente.

instantaneous | ˌɪnstən'teɪnjəs | *adj.* instantáneo, inmediato, fulminante.

instantaneously | ˌɪnstən'teɪnjəslɪ | *adv.* instantáneamente, inmediatamente, fulminantemente.

instead | ɪn'sted | *adv.* **1** en lugar, en vez, en cambio, más bien. || **2 – of,** en lugar de, en vez de.

instep | 'ɪnstep | *s.c.* ANAT. empeine.

instigate | 'ɪnstɪgeɪt | *v.t.* **1** iniciar, fomentar, promover. **2 [to – + *o.* + *inf.*]** (form.) instigar, inducir, incitar.

instigation | ˌɪnstɪ'geɪʃn | *s.i.* instigación, incitación, sugerencia.

instigator | 'ɪnstɪgeɪtər | *s.c.* (desp.) instigador, incitador.

instil | ɪn'stɪl | (EE.UU.) **instill.** *v.t.* **1 [to – (in/into)]** inculcar, infundir, imbuir, implantar. **2** verter gota a gota.

instinct | 'ɪnstɪŋkt | *s.c.* e *i.* **1** instinto, inclinación, impulso natural. **2** intuición. || *adj.* **3** saturado, pleno, imbuido: *instinct with love = pleno de amor.*

instinctive | ɪn'stɪŋktɪv | *adj.* instintivo, espontáneo, no pensado, irracional.

instinctively | ɪn'stɪŋktɪvlɪ | *adv.* instintivamente, espontáneamente, irracionalmente.

instinctual | ˌɪns'tɪŋktjəl | *adj.* instintivo, espontáneo, irracional.

institute | 'ɪnstɪtjuːt | *s.c.* **1** instituto, sociedad, institución, organización, escuela (dedicado a la investigación): *the British Film Institute = Escuela Británica de Cinematografía.* **2** curso intensivo, cursillo, taller, seminario (de corta duración). **3** *pl.* DER. institución. || *v.t.* **4** (form.) instituir, establecer (una ley, un sistema). **5** organizar, planear (una acción). **6** DER. entablar, iniciar, abrir (acciones judiciales). **7** nombrar (para un cargo, puesto de trabajo).

institution | ˌɪnstɪ'tjuːʃn | | ˌɪnstɪtuːʃn | *s.c.* **1** DER. institución, práctica, costumbre. **2** (fam. y hum.) institución, personaje muy conocido. **3** institución, fundación, organización, instituto (un banco, una universidad, una iglesia). **4** (euf.) manicomio, hospital psiquiátrico. **5** (desp.) asilo de ancianos. **6** (desp.) hospicio. || *s.i.* **7** institución, establecimiento, puesta en marcha: *the institution of a new tax system = la puesta en marcha de un nuevo sistema de impuestos.*

institutional | ˌɪnstɪ'tjuːʃənl | *adj.* **1** institucional, de las instituciones. **2** institucional, consubstancial, (relativo a valores o cualidades de un grupo, sociedad).

institucionalize | ˌɪnstə'tjuːʃənəlaɪz | (brit.) institucionalise. *v.t.* **1** institucionalizar, establecer, instituir, estatuir. **2** (euf.) internar, confinar (en un asilo, en un manicomio, en un hospicio). **3** (gen. *pas.*) adaptar, acostumbrar (a un sistema de confinamiento).

instruct | ɪn'strʌkt | *v.t.* [to – + *o.* **+ to** *inf.*] ordenar, mandar, dar instrucciones. **2 [to – (in)]** instruir, enseñar, educar, documentar (sobre algo práctico). **3 [to – + *o.* + that]** DER. (gen. *pas.*) informar, notificar. **4** DER. designar, nombrar (abogado). || *v.i.* **5** actuar como instructor, servir como instructor.

instruction | ɪn'strʌkʃn | *s.c.* **1** (gen. *pl.*) instrucción, orden, mandato. **2** *pl.* instrucciones, consejos, información detallada (sobre el funcionamiento de máquinas, sobre un trabajo).

instructive | ɪn'strʌktɪv | *adj.* **1** instructivo, ilustrativo, aleccionador.

instructor | ɪn'strʌktər | *s.c.* **1** instructor, maestro, profesor (de prácticas). **2** (EE.UU.) instructor (grado inferior a profesor ayudante en universidades).

instrument | 'ɪnstrumənt | *s.c.* **1** instrumento, utensilio, herramienta. **2** MUS. instrumento. **3 [– (of)]** (lit.) instrumento, agente, medio: *an instrument of control = un instrumento de control.* **4** incauto, víctima de engaño, primo. **5** DER. documento público, escritura. || *v.t.* **6** equipar, dotar (de instrumentos). **7** DER. notificar, comunicar. || **8 – panel,** panel de instrumentos, salpicadero (en coches, aviones).

instrumental | ˌɪnstru'mentl | *adj.* **1** no *comp.* MUS. instrumental. **2** (form.) significativo, útil, de gran ayuda.

instrumentalist | ˌɪnstru'mentəlɪst | *s.c* **1** MUS. instrumentalista. **2** FIL. instrumentalista.

instrumentation | ˌɪnstrumen'teɪʃn | *s.i.* **1** MUS. instrumentación, orquestación. **2** instrumental, equipo de instrumentos (para el control de una máquina). **3** medio, conducto.

insubordinate | ˌɪnsəbɔːdnət | | ˌɪnsəbɔːrdnət | *adj.* (form. y desp.) insubordinado, rebelde, desobediente.

insubordination | 'ɪnsəˌbɔːdɪ'neɪʃn | *s.i.* insubordinación, rebelión, desobediencia.

insubstancial | ˌɪnsəb'stænʃl | *adj.* **1** insustancial, insignificante, anodino. **2** frágil, quebradizo, delicado, endeble.

insufferable | ɪn'sʌfərəbl | *adj.* insufrible, intolerable, inaguantable.

insufferably | ɪn'sʌfərəblɪ | *adv.* insufriblemente, intolerantemente, inaguantablemente.

insufficiency | ˌɪnsə'fɪʃnsɪ | *s.c.* e *i.* (form.) insuficiencia, deficiencia, escasez.

insufficient | ˌɪnsə'fɪʃnt | *adj.* insuficiente, deficiente, escaso.

insufficiently | ˌɪnsə'fɪʃntlɪ | *adv.* insuficientemente, deficientemente, escasamente.

insular | 'ɪnsjulər | *adj* **1** (desp.) insular, estrecho de miras, provinciano, intransigente. **2** aislado, desconectado, apartado. **3** no *comp.* isleño, insular. **4** MED. insular (un tejido).

insularity | 'ɪnsju'lærɪtɪ | ˌɪnsə'lærɪtɪ | *s.i.* **1** insularidad, aislamiento, incomunicación, separación. **2** estrechez de miras, provincianismo.

insulate | 'ɪnsjuleɪt | | 'ɪnsəleɪt | | 'ɪnʃəleɪt | *v.t.* **1 [to – (from/against)]** FIS.

aislar. **2** proteger, apartar, separar: *insulated from gossiping = protegidos contra el cotilleo.*
insulating | 'ɪnsjʊleɪtɪŋ | *adj.* aislante, protector: *insulating tape = cinta aislante.*
insulation | ˌɪnsjʊ'leɪʃn | | ˌɪnsə'leɪʃn | *s.i.* **1** FIS. aislamiento, protección. **2** capa aislante, material aislante: *wall insulation = aislante de paredes.*
insulator | 'ɪnsjʊleɪtər | | 'ɪnsəleɪtər | *s.c.* FIS. aislante.
insulin | 'ɪnsjʊlɪn | | 'ɪnsəlɪn | *s.i.* BIOQ. insulina.
insult | 'ɪnsʌlt | *v.t.* **1** insultar, injuriar, ofender, afrentar, agraviar. **2** (arc.) atacar, asaltar. || *v.i.* **3** comportarse con arrogancia, insolentarse. || *s.c.* **4** insulto, agravio, ofensa, afrenta. || **5 to add – to injury,** (fig.) echar leña al fuego, colmar el vaso, poner las cosas peor.
insulting | ɪn'sʌltɪŋ | *adj.* insultante, ofensivo, injuriante.
insultingly | ɪn'sʌltɪŋlɪ | *adv.* insultantemente, ofensivamente, injuriantemente.
insuperable | ɪn'sjuːpərəbl | | ɪn'suːpərəbl | *adj.* insuperable, insalvable, invencible, infranqueable.
insupportable | ˌɪnsə'pɔːtəbl | *adj.* **1** (form.) insoportable, inaguantable, insufrible, intolerable. **2** injustificable, indefendible.
insurance | ɪn'ʃʊərəns | *s.i.* **1** seguro, mutualidad (de vida, enfermedad, etc.). **2** COM. prima. **3** COM. indemnización (por accidente). **4** COM. seguros, compañía de seguros. **5** seguridad, protección. || *s.c.* **6 [– (against)]** seguro, garantía. || **7 – policy,** póliza de seguro.
insure | ɪn'ʃʊər | *v.t.* **1 [to – (against)]** asegurar, concertar un seguro (de vida, accidente, etc.). **2** (EE.UU.) asegurar, confirmar, verificar, aseverar. || *v.i.* **3** asegurarse. **4** comprar seguros, vender seguros.
insured | ɪn'ʃʊəd | | ɪn'ʃərd | *s.c.* **1** asegurado, persona asegurada. || *adj.* **2** asegurado: *insured jewels = joyas aseguradas.*
insurer | ɪn'ʃʊərər | *s.c.* asegurador, compañía aseguradora.
insurgent | ɪn'səːdʒənt | | ɪn'səːrdʒənt | *s.c.* **1** (gen. *pl.*) insurgente, rebelde, sublevado, insurrecto. || *adj.* **2** insurgente, rebelde, insurrecto, sublevado.
insurmountable | ˌɪnsə'maʊntəbl | | ˌɪnsər'maʊntəbl | *adj.* insuperable, irremontable, invencible.
insurrection | ˌɪnsə'rekʃn | *s.c.* e *i.* insurrección, sublevación, rebelión, levantamiento.
intact | ɪn'tækt | *adj.* **1** intacto, indemne, íntegro, impecable. **2** (fig.) intacta, incólume, indemne (la reputación).
intake | 'ɪnteɪk | *s.i.* **1** consumo, cantidad consumida (de alimentos, bebidas). **2** admisión, entrada, cantidad admitida (de gente en una organización, escuela). **3** respiración, inspiración, absorción (de aire). || *s.c.* **4** MEC. entrada, toma, conducto, válvula de admisión. || **5 – of breath,** inspiración, suspiro.
intangible | ɪn'tændʒəbl | *adj.* **1** intangible, etéreo, sutil, impalpable, difuso, imponderable, inmaterial. || *s.c.* **2** *pl.* bienes inmateriales.
integer | 'ɪntɪdʒər | *s.c.* **1** MAT. número entero. **2** unidad, entidad completa.
integral | 'ɪntɪgrəl | *adj.* **1** íntegro, completo. **2** intrínseco, esencial, necesario. **3** MAT. integral. || *s.c.* **4** MAT. integral. **5** unidad, conjunto.
integrate | 'ɪntɪgreɪt | *v.t.* e *i.* **1** integrar(se), unir(se), incorporar(se). **2** integrar(se), mezclar(se). **3** MAT. calcular una integral, integrar. || *v.t.* **4** (form.) integrar, combinar, introducir.
integrated | 'ɪntɪgreɪtɪd | *adj.* integrado, de integración: *an integrated school = una escuela de integración* (racial, religiosa).
integration | ˌɪntɪ'greɪʃn | *s.i.* integración (racial, religiosa, interestatal).
integrity | ɪn'tegrətɪ | *s.i.* **1** integridad, honestidad, honradez, firmeza de carácter. **2** (form.) integridad, unidad, indivisibilidad.
intellect | 'ɪntəlekt | *s.c.* e *i.* **1** intelecto, inteligencia, luces, entendimiento. || *s.c.* **2** persona inteligente, lumbrera, cerebro (aunque poco práctico). **3** (desp.) listo, astuto, avispado. **4** intelectual, erudito, docto.
intellectually | ˌɪntə'lektjʊəlɪ | *adv.* intelectualmente; teóricamente.
intelligence | ɪn'telɪdʒəns | *s.i.* **1** inteligencia, intelecto, razonamiento. **2 [– *v.sing./pl.*]** información secreta, informe secreto (del servicio de inteligencia). **3** servicio de inteligencia, espionaje.
intelligent | ɪn'telɪdʒənt | *adj.* **1** inteligente, despierto, espabilado, listo. **2** racional.
intelligently | ɪn'telɪdʒəntlɪ | *adv.* inteligentemente, con sensatez, razonablemente.
intelligentsia | ɪnˌtelɪ'dʒentsɪə | *s.sing.* **1 [the – *v.sing./pl.*]** la intelectualidad, los intelectuales.
intelligible | ɪn'telɪdʒəbl | *adj.* inteligible, comprensible, fácil de entender.
intemperate | ɪn'tempərət | *adj.* (form.) intemperante, inmoderado, desmedido, exagerado.
intend | ɪn'tend | *v.t.* **1** proponerse, planear, tener en mente. **2 [to – + to** *inf.* o *ger./o.* **+ to** *inf.*] pretender, tener intención de, tener el propósito de: *I intend to go there = tengo la intención de ir allí.* **3 [to – + *o.* + for/as]** ser para, destinar a, reservar a, dirigir a; tener la finalidad de: *the present was intended for him = el regalo era para él.* **4** llevar implícito, querer decir, dar a entender: *what do you intend by it? = ¿qué quieres decir con eso?*
intended | ɪn'tendɪd | *s.c.* **1** (gen. *sing.*) (arc. o hum.) prometido: *your intended is on the phone = tu prometido está al teléfono.* || *adj.* **2** pretendido, deseado, esperado: *her intended visit was postponed = su esperada visita fue pospuesta.*
intense | ɪn'tens | *adj.* **1** intenso, fuerte, impresionante. **2** violenta, dura, seria (una lucha). **3** intenso, profundo (un sentimiento). **4** exagerado, nervioso, vehemente (una persona). **5** fuerte, vivo, intenso (un color).
intensely | ɪn'tenslɪ | *adv.* **1** intensamente, enormemente, con fuerza. **2** profundamente.
intensification | ɪnˌtensɪfɪ'keɪʃn | *s.i.* intensificación, agravamiento, acrecentamiento.
intensified | ɪn'tensɪfaɪd | *adj.* intensificado, agravado, acrecentado.
intensifier | ɪn'tensɪfaɪər | *s.c.* **1** GRAM. intensificador (un adverbio). **2** FOT. reforzador, intensificador (de contraste).
intensify | ɪn'tensɪfaɪ | *v.t.* e *i.* **1** intensificar, acrecentar, aumentar. **2** FOT. reforzar.
intensity | ɪn'tensɪtɪ | *s.i.* **1** intensidad, fuerza. **2** FIS. potencia. **3** FOT. contraste.
intensive | ɪn'tensɪv | *adj.* **1** intensivo (un curso, un cultivo). **2** concentrado. || **3 – care unit,** MED. unidad de cuidados intensivos.
intensively | ɪn'tensɪvlɪ | *adv.* **1** intensamente, en profundidad.
intent | ɪn'tent | *s.i.* **1 [– (with)]** (form.) intención, propósito, objetivo. **2** DER. intencionalidad, propósito. **3** significado, sentido, tenor, connotación. || *adj.* **4** absorto, abstraído, absorbido. **5** determinado, resuelto, empeñado. || **6 loitering with –,** DER. merodear con malas intenciones, con intención criminal. **7 to all intents and purposes,** en realidad, a todos los efectos, en el fondo.
intention | ɪn'tenʃn | *s.c.* e *i.* **1** intención, propósito, objetivo. **2 intentions** *pl.* intenciones (para el matrimonio). **3** sentido, significado. **4** MED. intención.
intentional | ɪn'tenʃənl | *adj.* intencionado, a propósito, deliberado.
intentionally | ɪn'tenʃnəlɪ | *adv.* intencionadamente, deliberadamente.
intently | ɪn'tentlɪ | *adv.* fijamente, atentamente, absortamente.
intentness | ɪn'tentnɪs | *s.i.* **1** atención, fijeza, interés.
inter | ɪn'təːr | *v.t.* (form.) enterrar, sepultar.
inter- | 'ɪntər | *prefijo.* **1** inter, entre. **2** dentro de, en medio de. **3** mutuamente, recíprocamente: *interrelation = interrelación.*
interact | ˌɪntər'ækt | *v.i.* **1 [to – (with)]** obrar recíprocamente, afectarse mutuamente, reaccionar recíprocamente. **2** intercomunicarse, influirse.
interaction | ˌɪntər'ækʃn | *s.i.* **1** interacción, intercomunicación, influencia recíproca.
interactive | ˌɪntər'æktɪv | *adj.* **1** recíproco, mutuo. **2** INF. interactivo.
intercede | ˌɪntə'siːd | | ˌɪntər'siːd | *v.t.* e *i.* **1 [to – (with/for)]** interceder, mediar, abogar, hablar en favor de.
intercept | ˌɪntə'sept | | ˌɪntər'sept | *v.t.* **1** interceptar, detener; (arc.) atajar, impedir. **2** prevenir.

interception | ˌɪntə'sepʃn | *s.i.* **1** interceptación, interferencia.
interceptor | ˌɪntə'septər | | ˌɪntər'septər | *s.c.* **1** MIL. avión de caza. **2** interceptor.
intercession | ˌɪntə'seʃn | | ˌɪntər'seʃn | *s.i.* **1** intercesión, mediación. || *s.c.* e *i.* **2** REL. oración, intercesión.
interchange | ˌɪntə'tʃeɪndʒ | | ˌɪntər'tʃeɪndʒ | *v.t.* e *i.* **1 [to – (with)]** intercambiar, permutar. **2** canjear (prisioneros). || *s.c.* e *i.* **3** intercambio, cambio, permuta. || *s.c.* **4** cruce, paso elevado, salida (en autopistas, carreteras).
interchangeable | ˌɪntə'tʃeɪndʒəbl | | ˌɪntər'tʃeɪndʒəbl | *adj.* intercambiable, permutable.
interchangeably | ˌɪntə'tʃeɪndʒəblɪ | | ˌɪntər'tʃeɪndʒəblɪ | *adv.* de forma intercambiable, indistintamente.
intercom | 'ɪntəkɒm | | 'ɪntərkɑːm | *s.c.* sistema de megafonía.
interconnect | ˌɪntəkə'nekt | *v.t.* e *i.* interconectar, intercomunicar.
interconnected | ˌɪntəkə'nektɪd | *adj.* interconectado, intercomunicado.
interconnecting | ˌɪntəkə'nektɪŋ | *adj.* que interconecta, que comunica entre sí.
intercontinental | 'ɪntəˌk'ntɪ'nentl | | ɪntər'kɑːntɪnentl | *adj.* intercontinental.
intercourse | 'ɪntəkɔːs | | 'ɪntərkɔːs | *s.i.* **1** (form.) relación, comunicación, vínculo, lazo de unión. **2** (form.) coito, cópula.
interdependence | ˌɪntədɪ'pendəns | *s.i.* interdependencia, dependencia mutua.
interdependent | ˌɪntədɪ'pendənt | | ˌɪntərdɪ'pendənt | *adj.* interdependiente.
interdisciplinary | ˌɪntəˌdɪsə'plɪnərɪ | | ˌɪntər'dɪsəpləneri | *adj.* interdisciplinar.
interest | 'ɪntrɪst | *s.c.* e *i.* **1** interés, preocupación, afán. || *s.i.* **2** interés, atención, curiosidad. **3** COM. interés, rédito. || *s.c.* **4** interés, afición, pasatiempo. **5** interés, beneficio, provecho, favor. **6** COM. acción, participación, parte (en un negocio). **7** COM. sector, grupo de presión (financiero): *the industry interest = el sector industrial, los propietarios de la industria.* **8** *pl.* intereses, conexiones financieras: *politicians should declare their interests = los políticos deberían hacer declaración de intereses.* || *v.t.* **9** interesar, preocupar, tener curiosidad. **10 [to – in]** interesar en, llamar la atención sobre, persuadir de. || **11 to have someone's interests at heart,** tener un enorme interés por alguien, tener a alguien en mente, importar enormemente. **12 in the interests of,** en interés de, en beneficio. **13 vested –,** V. **vested.**
interested | 'ɪntrɪstɪd | *adj.* **1** interesado, preocupado. **2** interesado (por provecho propio).
interest-free | 'ɪntrɪstˌfriː | *adj.* **1** COM. libre de interés, sin interés. || *adv.* **2** sin interés.
interesting | 'ɪntrɪstɪŋ | *adj.* interesante, fascinante, seductor.
interestingly | 'ɪntrɪstɪŋlɪ | *adv.* interesantemente, curiosamente.
interface | 'ɪntəfeɪs | *s.c.* **1** (form.) zona de interconexión, frontera común. **2** INF. interfaz, interconexión, acoplamiento. || *v.t.* e *i.* **3** INF. interconectar, interactuar.
interfere | ˌɪntə'fɪər | *v.i.* **1 [to – (in/between)]** (desp.) interferir, interponerse, ingerirse, entrometerse. **2** interrumpir, entremeterse, intervenir (en una conversación). **3** tropezar, golpearse una pata con otra (los caballos). **4** ELECTR. interferir (las ondas). **5** DEP. bloquear, obstruir (ilegalmente). || **6 to – with, a)** estorbar, obstaculizar, obstruir; **b)** estar en contra de, chocar con (intereses); **c)** husmear, revolver, tocar (algo no permitido); **d)** practicar abusos deshonestos (a niños).
interference | ˌɪntə'fɪərəns | | ˌɪntər'fɪərəns | *s.i.* **1** interferencia, ingerencia, intromisión, intervención. **2** interrupción. **3** ELECTR. interferencia. **4** DEP. bloqueo, obstrucción.
interfering | ˌɪntə'fɪərɪŋ | *adj.* entrometido, curioso.
interim | 'ɪntərɪm | *adj.* **1** no *comp.* interino, provisional. **2** ínterin, intermedio, intervalo. || **3 in the –,** entre tanto, provisionalmente.
interior | ɪn'tɪərɪər | *s.c.* (gen. *sing.*) **1** interior. || *adj.* **2** interior, interno, tierra adentro. **3** (form.) interior, profundo, secreto (un pensamiento). || **4 – decorator,** diseñador de interiores.
interject | ˌɪntə'dʒekt | | ˌɪntər'dʒekt | *v.t.* e *i.* (form.) intercalar, interponer, insertar.
interjection | ˌɪntə'dʒekʃn | | ˌɪntər'dʒekʃn | *s.c.* e *i.* **1** observación, intervención, interrupción. || *s.c.* **2** GRAM. exclamación, interjección.
interlaced | ˌɪntə'leɪst | | ˌɪntər'leɪst | *adj.* entrelazado, entrecruzado, entremezclado.
interlink | ˌɪntə'lɪŋk | | ˌɪntər'lɪŋk | *v.t.* **[to – (with)]** interconectar, enlazar, unir, relacionar.
interlinked | ˌɪntə'lɪŋkt | *adj.* enlazado, interconectado, relacionado.
interlock | ˌɪntə'lɒk | | ˌɪntər'lɑːk | *v.t.* e *i.* **1** bloquear(se), trabar(se), entrelazar(se). **2** INF. interbloquear, trabar con intercierre. || *s.i.* **3** INF. interbloqueo.
interlocutor | ˌɪntə'lɒkjutər | | ˌɪntər'lɒːkjutər | *s.c.* (form.) interlocutor.
interloper | 'ɪntələupər | | 'ɪntərləupər | *s.c.* e *i.* **1** (desp.) intruso, entrometido. **2** COM. comerciante sin licencia.
interlude | 'ɪntəluːd | | 'ɪntərluːd | *s.c.* **1** intervalo, intermedio. **2** descanso, intermedio, entreacto (en el teatro, un concierto). **3** MUS. interludio. **4** entremés, farsa, sainete (que se representaba en el entreacto de obras teatrales en el s. XVI).
intermarriage | ˌɪntə'mærɪdʒ | | ˌɪntər'mærɪdʒ | *s.i.* **1** matrimonio entre clases sociales, razas o religiones diferentes. **2** matrimonio entre parientes.
intermarry | ˌɪntə'mærɪ | | ˌɪntər'mærɪ | *v.i.* **1** casarse con miembros de clases, razas o religiones diferentes. **2** casarse entre parientes.
intermediary | ˌɪntə'miːdjərɪ | | ˌɪntər'miːdɪerɪ | *s.c.* **1** intermediario, mediador. **2** intermedio, etapa intermedia.
intermediate | ˌɪntə'miːdjət | | ˌɪntər'miːdjət | *adj.* **1** no *comp.* intermedio. || *s.c.* **2** intermediario. **3** grado intermedio (de estudios). || *v.i.* **4** mediar, hacer de intermediario. **5** intervenir.
interment | ɪn'təːmənt | | ɪn'təːrmənt | *s.c.* e *i.* (form.) entierro, funeral, sepelio, enterramiento.
interminable | ɪn'təːmɪnəbl | | ɪn'təːrmɪnəbl | *adj.* (desp.) interminable, inacabable, eterno.
interminably | ɪn'təːmɪnəblɪ | *adv.* interminablemente, eternamente, de forma inacabable.
intermingle | ˌɪntə'mɪŋgl | | ˌɪntə[illegible]mɪŋgl | *v.i.* **[to – (with)]** mezclars[illegible] entremezclarse.
intermission | ˌɪntə'mɪʃn | | ˌɪntər'mɪʃn | (EE.UU.) **interval** *s.c.* intermedio, entreacto, descanso (en el teatro, el cine).
intermittent | ˌɪntə'mɪtənt | | ˌɪntər'mɪtənt | *adj.* intermitente, discontinuo ocasional.
intermittently | ˌɪntə'mɪtəntlɪ | *adv.* intermitentemente, a intervalos regulares, ocasionalmente.
intern | ɪn'təːn | | ɪn'təːrn | *v.t.* internar, recluir, confinar (a alguien peligroso en tiempo de guerra). || | 'ɪntəːn | *s.c.* **2** (EE.UU.) interno, médico residente. **3** (EE.UU.) profesor en prácticas. **4** interno, recluso.
internal | ɪn'təːnl | | ɪn'təːrnl | *adj.* **1** interno. **2** interior, nacional: *Minister of Internal Affairs = Ministro del Interior.* **3** intrínseco. **4** mental, subjetivo (ideas, imágenes). || **5 – combustion engine,** motor de combustión interna.
internally | ɪn'təːnəlɪ | | ɪn'təːrnəlɪ | *adv.* **1** interiormente, internamente. **2** mentalmente, subjetivamente, en el subconsciente.
internalize | ɪn'təːnəlaɪz | | ɪn'təːrnəlaɪz | (brit.) **internalise** *v.t.* **1** (form.) interiorizar, incorporar (experiencias, ideas).
internalization | ɪn'təːnəlaɪ'zeɪʃn | | ɪnˌtəːrnələ'zeɪʃn | *s.i.* interiorización, incorporación (de ideas, experiencias).
international | ˌɪntə'næʃənl | | ˌɪntər'næʃənl | *adj.* **1** internacional. || **2 – relations,** relaciones políticas internacionales.
internationally | ˌɪntə'næʃənəlɪ | *adv.* internacionalmente.
internacionalism | ˌɪntə'næʃnəlɪzəm | | ˌɪntər'næʃnəlɪzm | *s.i.* **1** internacionalismo.
internecine | ˌɪntə'niːsaɪn | | ˌɪntər'niːsaɪn | *adj.* (form.) mutuamente des-

tructivo, mutuamente aniquilador o mortífero (una lucha, un conflicto).

internee | ˌɪntɜːˈniː | | ˌɪntɜːrˈniː | *s.c.* interno, recluso, prisionero.

internment | ɪnˈtɜːnmənt | | ɪnˈtɜːrnmənt | *s.c.* **1** internamiento, reclusión, confinamiento, prisión. || *s.c.* **2** período de reclusión.

interpersonal | ˌɪntəˈpɜːsənəl | | ˌɪntərˈpɜːrsənəl | *adj.* interpersonal, entre personas.

interplay | ˌɪntəˈpleɪ | | ˌɪntərˈpleɪ | *s.i.* **[– (of/between)]** interacción, influencia mutua.

interpolate | ɪnˈtɜːpəuleɪt | | ɪnˈtɜːrpəleɪt | *v.t.* **1** (form.) interpolar, intercalar, añadir (una palabra). **2** alterar, insertar (material nuevo en un texto).

interpolation | ɪnˌtɜːpəuˈleɪʃn | | ɪnˌtɜːrpəˈleɪʃn | *s.c.* e *i.* (form.) interpolación, alteración, inserción (de material nuevo en un texto).

interpose | ˌɪntəˈpəuz | | ˌɪntərˈpəuz | *v.t.* e *i.* **1** **[to – (in)]** interponer(se), poner(se) en medio, meter(se) entre, mediar. **2** interpolar, intercalar, añadir, cortar (una conversación, un comentario). **3** interferir, tratar de influir.

interpret | ɪnˈtɜːpret | | ɪnˈtɜːrpret | *v.t.* **1** interpretar, tomar como, entender: *interpret the visit as an insult = interpretar la visita como un insulto.* **2** interpretar, representar (música, teatro). **3** interpretar, desentrañar, descifrar (un sueño, una obra artística). || *v.t.* e *i.* **4** traducir simultáneamente (de otra lengua).

interpretation | ɪnˌtɜːprɪˈteɪʃn | | ɪnˌtɜːrprɪˈteɪʃn | *s.c.* e *i.* **1** interpretación, explicación, significado, sentido. **2** interpretación, representación (de una obra teatral o musical).

interpretative, interpretive | ɪnˈtɜːprɪtətɪv | | ɪnˈtɜːrprəteɪtɪv | *adj.* interpretativo, explicativo.

interpreter | ɪnˈtɜːprɪtər | | ɪnˈtɜːrprɪtər | *s.c.* **1** intérprete, traductor. **2** intérprete, ejecutante (de una obra artística). **3** INF. intérprete, procesador de lenguaje; programa.

interregnum | ˌɪntəˈregnəm | *pl.* **interregnums** o **interregna** *s.c.* **1** interregno (monárquico, parlamentario). **2** intervalo, pausa, laguna.

interrelate | ˌɪntərɪˈleɪt | *v.t.* e *i.* interrelacionar, tener conexión entre sí, conectar.

interrelationship | ˌɪntərɪˈleɪʃnʃɪp | *s.c.* interrelación, conexión (entre cosas).

interrogate | ɪnˈterəugeɪt | *v.t.* **1** interrogar, preguntar, inquirir (a veces con violencia). **2** INF. interrogar, conseguir información, enviar señal (para que se inicie una respuesta).

interrogation | ɪnˌterəuˈgeɪʃn | *s.c.* e *i.* **1** interrogatorio (a veces con violencia). **2** GRAM. interrogación.

interrogative | ˌɪntəˈrɒgətɪv | | ˌɪntəˈrɑːgətɪv | *adj.* **1** GRAM. interrogativo. || *s.c.* **2** GRAM. interrogativa (una frase, una palabra).

interrogator | ɪnˈterəugeɪtər | *s.c.* interrogador.

interrupt | ˌɪntəˈrʌpt | *v.t.* **1** interrumpir, cortar. **2** molestar, perturbar, estorbar.

interruption | ˌɪntəˈrʌpʃn | *s.c.* e *i.* **1** interrupción. **2** molestia, perturbación.

intersect | ˌɪntəˈsekt | | ˌɪntərˈsekt | *v.t.* e *i.* intersectar, formar una intersección, cruzar, cortar transversalmente.

intersection | ˌɪntəˈsekʃn | | ˌɪntərˈsekʃn | *s.c.* **1** intersección, cruce (de calles, carreteras). || *s.i.* **2** intersección, unión.

intersperse | ˌɪntəˈspɜːs | | ˌɪntərˈspɜːrs | *v.t.* **1** **[to – (with/in)]** intercalar, esparcir, salpicar: *toys interspersed in the room = juguetes esparcidos por la habitación.*

interstate | ˌɪntəˈsteɪt | | ˌɪntərˈsteɪt | *adj.* **1** (EE.UU.) interestatal.

interstellar | ˌɪntəˈstelər | | ˌɪntərˈstelər | *adj.* interestelar.

interstice | ɪnˈtɜːstɪs | | ɪnˈtɜːrstɪs | *s.c.* (gen. *pl.*) (form.) intersticio, grieta, espacio, resquicio (entre objetos).

intertwine | ˌɪntəˈtwaɪn | | ɪntərˈtwaɪn | *v.t.* e *i.* **1** entretejer, entrelazar, entrecruzar. **2** (fig.) unir firmemente, entrelazar: *intertwined lives = vidas firmemente unidas.*

interval | ˈɪntəvl | | ˈɪntərvl | *s.c.* **1** intervalo, paréntesis, pausa, período intermedio. **2** (EE.UU.) intermisión, entreacto, intermedio (en el teatro). **3** MUS. intervalo. || **4 at intervals,** a intervalos, de vez en cuando, ocasionalmente. **5 at (weekly/monthly) intervals,** semanalmente, mensualmente. **6 at regular intervals,** regularmente. **7 at rare intervals,** de tarde en tarde.

intervene | ˌɪntəˈviːn | | ˌɪntərˈviːn | *v.i.* **1** **[to – (in)]** intervenir, mediar, interponerse (para evitar conflicto). **2** surgir, acontecer, sobrevenir, llegar: *but war intervened = pero sobrevino la guerra.* **3** intervenir, participar (en una conversación). **4** transcurrir, mediar (tiempo). **5** DER. interponer demanda de tercería.

intervening | ˌɪntəˈviːnɪŋ | | ˌɪntərˈviːnɪŋ | *adj.* intermedio: *those intervening years = esos años intermedios.*

intervention | ˌɪntəˈvenʃn | | ˌɪntərˈvenʃn | *s.c.* e *i.* **1** intervención, mediación, buenos oficios, participación (en un conflicto).

interview | ˈɪntərvjuː | | ˈɪntərvjuː | *s.c.* **1** entrevista, interviú, conferencia de prensa, audiencia. || *v.t.* e *i.* **2** entrevistar, tener una entrevista, conceder una entrevista.

interviewee | ˌɪntəvjuˈiː | | ˌɪntərvjuˈiː | *s.c.* entrevistado.

interviewer | ˈɪntəvjuːər | | ˈɪntərvjuːər | *s.c.* **1** entrevistador. **2** periodista.

interweave | ˌɪntəˈwiːv | | ˌɪntərˈwiːv | *v.t. irr. pret.* **interwove,** *p.p.* **interwoven. 1** entretejer, entremezclar. **2** (fig.) entrelazar, unir firmemente.

intestate | ɪnˈtesteɪt | *adj.* DER. intestado, sin testar: *he died intestate = murió sin testar.*

intestinal | ɪnˈtestɪnl | *adj.* intestinal.

intestine | ɪnˈtestɪn | *s.c.* **1** ANAT. intestino, tubo intestinal. || **2 large –,** ANAT. intestino grueso. **3 small –,** ANAT. intestino delgado.

intimacy | ˈɪntɪməsɪ | *s.i.* **1** intimidad, privacidad, confianza, familiaridad. **2** *pl.* (euf.) relaciones sexuales, relaciones íntimas. || *s.c.* **3** (gen. *pl.*) intimidad, secreto, interioridad: *talking about intimacies = charlando sobre intimidades.*

intimate | ˈɪntɪmət | *adj.* **1** íntimo, muy cercano, estrecho, familiar: *an intimate relationship = una relación estrecha.* **2** íntimo, cálido (un lugar). **3** (form.) detallado, profundo (un conocimiento). **4** íntimo, personal, privado (un pensamiento, una conversación). || *s.c.* **5** amigo íntimo, allegado. || | ˈɪntɪmət | *v.t.* **6** (form.) sugerir, insinuar, dar a entender, decir con una indirecta. **7** proclamar, anunciar, notificar. || **8 to be – with,** (euf.) hacer el amor con, tener relaciones sexuales con.

intimatelly | ˈɪntɪmətlɪ | *adv.* **1** íntimamente, estrechamente. **2** confidencialmente, privadamente. **3** a fondo, profundamente.

intimation | ˌɪntɪˈmeɪʃn | *s.c.* e *i.* **1** (form.) indicación, atisbo, sospecha. **2** sugerencia, indirecta, insinuación.

intimidate | ɪnˈtɪmɪdeɪt | *v.t.* **1** intimidar, atemorizar, acobardar, amilanar, amedrentrar. **2** (fig.) imponer respeto, quitar el aliento.

intimidated | ɪnˈtɪmɪdeɪtɪd | *adj.* intimidado, amedrentado, atemorizado, amilanado, acobardado.

intimidating | ɪnˈtɪmɪdeɪtɪŋ | *adj.* intimidador, atemorizador.

intimidation | ɪnˌtɪmɪˈdeɪʃn | *s.c.* e *i.* intimidación, atemorización, amilanamiento.

into | ˈɪntu | *prep.* **1** a, en: *to come into the kitchen = entrar en la cocina, to get into trouble = meterse en dificultades.* **2** hasta: *watching far into the night = velando hasta avanzada la noche.* **3** dentro, adentro. **4 -- the bargain,** por añadidura.

intolerable | ɪnˈtɒlərəbl | | ɪnˈtɑːlərəbl | *adj.* **1** intolerable, insoportable, insufrible, inaguantable. **2** inmoderado, extravagante, excesivo.

intolerably | ɪnˈtɒlərəblɪ | *adv.* intolerablemente, insoportablemente.

intolerance | ɪnˈtɒlərəns | *s.i.* intolerancia, intemperancia, intransigencia.

intolerant | ɪnˈtɒlərənt | | ɪnˈtɑːlərənt | *adj.* intolerante, intemperante, intransigente, iliberal.

intonation | ˌɪntəuˈneɪʃn | *s.c.* e *i.* FON. entonación, inflexión, modulación.

intone | ɪnˈtəun | *v.t.* e *i.* entonar, marcar el tono, cantar.

intoxicant | ɪnˈtɒksɪkənt | | ɪnˈtɑːksɪkənt | *s.c.* (form.) bebida intoxicante, bebida alcohólica.

intoxicated | ɪnˈtɒksɪkeɪtɪd | *adj.* **1** (form. y hum.) ebrio, beodo, borracho. **2** (fig.) embriagado, excitado, estimula-

do: *intoxicated with happiness = embriagado de felicidad.*
intoxicating | ɪn'tɒksɪkeɪtɪŋ | *adj.* **1** intoxicante, alcohólico, embriagante. **2** (fig.) estimulante, excitante, vivificante.
intoxication | ɪn'tɒksɪ'keɪʃn | | ɪn'tɑːksɪ'keɪʃn | *s.c.* e *i.* **1** intoxicación etílica, embriaguez. **2** (fig.) excitación, embriaguez.
intractable | ɪn'træktəbl | *adj.* **1** (form.) problemática, espinosa, difícil (una situación). **2** intratable, obstinado, terco, cabezota. **3** MED. intratable, incurable.
intransigence | ɪn'trænsɪdʒəns | *s.i.* intransigencia, intolerancia, obstinación.
intransitive | ɪn'trænsətɪv | *adj.* GRAM. intransitivo.
intravenous | ˌɪntrə'viːnəs | *adj.* MED. intravenoso.
intravenously | ˌɪntrə'viːnəslɪ | *adv.* por vía intravenosa.
in-tray | 'ɪntreɪ | *s.c.* bandeja de oficina (para colocar papeles que entran).
intrepid | ɪn'trepɪd | *adj.* (lit. y arc.) intrépido, atrevido, decidido, valiente.
intrepidly | ɪn'trepɪdlɪ | *adv.* (lit. y arc.) intrépidamente, decididamente, valientemente.
intricacy | 'ɪntrɪkəsɪ | *s.i.* **1** intricación, intrincamiento, complejidad. || *s.c.* **2** complicación, embrollo, enredo.
intricate | 'ɪntrɪkət | *adj.* intrincado, complejo, enrevesado, complicado.
intricatelly | 'ɪntrɪkətlɪ | *adv.* intricadamente, de forma complicada, de forma elaborada.
intrigue | ɪn'triːg | *v.t.* **1** intrigar, fascinar, despertar curiosidad, interesar. || *v.i.* **2 [to – (against)]** intrigar, maquinar, conspirar. || | 'ɪntriːg | *s.c.* e *i.* **3** intriga, conspiración, maquinación. **4** intriga amorosa, lío amoroso. **5** LIT. trama, intriga.
intrigued | ɪn'triːgd | *adj.* intrigado, interesado, fascinado.
intriguing | ɪn'triːgɪŋ | *adj.* intrigante, fascinante, interesante, seductor, curioso.
intriguingly | ɪn'triːgɪŋlɪ | *adv.* fascinantemente, curiosamente, seductoramente.
intrinsic | ɪn'trɪnsɪk | *adj.* intrínseco, inherente, natural, esencial.
intrinsically | ɪn'trɪnsɪkəlɪ | *adv.* intrínsecamente, inherentemente, esencialmente, de forma natural.
introduce | ˌɪntrə'djuːs | | ˌɪntrə'duːs | *v.t.* **1 [to – (to)]** presentar: *she introduced me to the audience = me presentó a la audiencia.* **2 [to – (to/into)]** introducir, poner de moda, implantar, lanzar (un producto). **3** introducir, proponer, establecer, implantar (una ley, un procedimiento). **4** introducir, dar entrada, dar comienzo. **5** mencionar, sacar a colación (un tema). **6** prologar, poner un prefacio (a un libro). **7** introducir, iniciar (a alguien en una materia nueva). || **8 to – (something) into,** introducir en, insertar en, inyectar en, meter en.
introduction | ˌɪntrə'dʌkʃn | *s.i.* **1** introducción, lanzamiento, presentación (de un producto). **2** introducción, inserción. **3** iniciación (en una materia nueva). || *s.c.* **4** (gen. *pl.*) presentación: *Sue made the introductions = Sue hizo las presentaciones.* **5** carta de presentación. **6** prólogo, prefacio (de un libro). **7** importación (de animales o plantas nuevas para un país): *tobacco is an introduction from America = el tabaco es una importación de América.*
introductory | ˌɪntrə'dʌktərɪ | *adj.* introductorio, preliminar.
introit | ˌɪntrɔɪt | *s.c.* introito.
introspection | ˌɪntrəʊ'spekʃn | *s.i.* introspección.
introspective | ˌɪntrəʊ'spektɪv | *adj.* introspectivo, contemplativo.
introvert | 'ɪntrəʊvəːt | | 'ɪntrəʊvəːrt | *s.c.* **1** introvertido. || *v.t.* **2** concentrarse en uno mismo.
introverted | ˌɪntrəʊ'vəːtɪd | | 'ɪntrəvəːrtɪd | *adj.* introvertido, introverso, introspectivo, concentrado en sí mismo.
intrude | ɪn'truːd | *v.i.* **1 [to – (into/on/upon)]** molestar, estorbar, inmiscuirse. **2** cometer intrusismo, transgredir los límites, entrar ilegalmente. || *v.t.* **3** (form.) interferir, influir. **4** interpolar, introducir. **5** MED. invaginar.
intruder | ɪn'truːdər | *s.c.* intruso, entrometido, transgresor.
intrusion | ɪn'truːʒn | *s.c.* e *i.* **1** intrusión, intrusismo, entrometimiento, invasión. **2** DER. allanamiento. **3** interrupción, molestia, distracción.
intrusive | ɪn'truːsɪv | *adj.* **1** intruso, entrometido. **2** añadido, insertado.
intuit | ɪn'tjuːɪt | *v.t.* e *i.* intuir, adquirir por intuición o por instinto.
intuition | ˌɪntjuː'ɪʃn | *s.c.* e *i.* intuición, instinto.
intuitive | ɪn'tjuːɪtɪv | | ɪn'tuːɪtɪv | *adj.* intuitivo, instintivo.
intuitively | ɪn'tjuːɪtɪvlɪ | *adv.* intuitivamente, instintivamente.
inundate | 'ɪnʌndeɪt | *v.t.* **1** (gen. *pas.*) inundar, cubrir de agua, anegar, encharcar. **2** (fig.) inundar, abrumar (con preguntas, regalos).
inure | ɪ'njʊər | *v.t.* **[to – to]** habituarse a, acostumbrarse a (cosas desagradables), endurecerse.
inured | ɪ'njʊəd | *adj.* habituado, acostumbrado, endurecido.
invade | ɪn'veɪd | *v.t.* e *i.* **1** invadir, ocupar, tomar, atacar (un país). **2** (fig.) invadir, infectar, entrar en gran número: *we invaded his office = invadimos su oficina.* || *v.t.* **3** (desp.) fastidiar, estropear, alterar, deteriorar, destruir (la paz, la intimidad).
invader | ɪn'veɪdər | *s.c.* invasor.
invading | ɪn'veɪdɪŋ | *adj.* invasor.
invalid | ɪn'vælɪd | *adj.* **1** DER. no válido, improcedente, falso, erróneo (una conclusión). **2** DER. inválido, nulo (un matrimonio, elecciones). || *s.c.* **3** inválido, impedido, imposibilitado. || | 'ɪnvəliːd | *v.t.* **4 to – somebody out,** (brit.) (gen. *pas.*) dar de baja por invalidez; MIL. licenciar por enfermedad.
invalidate | ɪn'vælɪdeɪt | *v.t.* DER. invalidar, anular (una ley, una conclusión, un matrimonio).
invalidity | ˌɪnvə'lɪdɪtɪ | *s.i.* **1** invalidez, nulidad. **2** invalidez, incapacidad (física).
invaluable | ɪn'væljʊəbl | *adj.* incalculable, inestimable, de gran valor, de incalculable utilidad.
invariable | ɪn'veərɪəbl | *adj.* **1** invariable, constante, inalterable, permanente, habitual: *invariable questions about the future = permanentes preguntas sobre el futuro.*
invariably | ɪn'veərɪəblɪ | *adv.* **1** invariablemente, permanentemente, habitualmente, siempre.
invasion | ɪn'veɪʒn | *s.c.* e *i.* **1** MIL. invasión. **2** intromisión, intrusión, irrupción. || **3 – of privacy,** (fig.) intromisión en la vida privada.
invective | ɪn'vektɪv | *s.c.* e *i.* (form.) improperio, insulto, ataque verbal.
inveigh | ɪn'veɪ | *v.t.* **1 [to – (against)]** (form.) condenar, reprobar, atacar, censurar.
inveigle | ɪn'veɪgl | *v.t.* **1** conseguir con lisonjas. **2 [to – someone into +** *ger.***]** (form.) engatusar, embaucar, seducir, persuadir con lisonjas.
invent | ɪn'vent | *s.i.* **1** invención. **2** inventiva, ingenio, fantasía. || *s.c.* **3** invención, invento. **4** mentira, falsedad, fantasía.
inventive | ɪn'ventɪv | *adj.* fantasioso, ingenioso, creativo.
inventiveness | ɪn'ventɪvnɪs | *s.i.* inventiva, ingenio, creatividad, talento.
inventor | 'ɪnvəntər | *s.c.* inventor, creador.
inventory | 'ɪnvəntrɪ | | 'ɪnvəntɔːrɪ | *s.c.* **1** inventario, lista. **2** existencias, artículos en existencia. || *v.t.* **3** inventariar, hacer inventario, incluir en inventario.
inverse | ˌɪn'vəːs | | ˌɪn'vəːrs | *s.sing.* **1** (form.) lo inverso, lo contrario, lo opuesto. || *adj.* **2** (form.) inverso, indirecto. **3** invertido, cambiado, del revés, lo de arriba hacia abajo.
inversion | ɪn'vəːʃn | | ɪn'vəːrən | *s.c.* e *i.* **1** inversión, alteración, transmutación. **2** inversión sexual, homosexualidad.
invert | ɪn'vəːt | | ɪn'vəːrt | *v.t.* **1** (form.) invertir, alterar, cambiar. **2** poner del revés, poner boca abajo.
inverted | ɪn'vəːtɪd | *adj.* **1** invertido, alterado, cambiado, boca abajo. || **2 – commas,** comillas. **3 – in commas,** (fig.) entre comillas, (por no decir lo contrario oralmente).
invertebrate | ɪn'vəːtɪbrət | | ɪn'vəːrtɪbreɪt | *s.c.* invertebr-ado. || *adj.* **1** invertebrado.
invest | ɪn'vest | *v.t.* e *i.* **1 [to – in]** invertir en, comprar (acciones, algo útil). **2** (fig.) invertir, dedicar (tiempo). || *v.t.* **3** (arc.) MIL. sitiar, cercar, rodear. || **4 to –**

somebody with, (gen. *pas.*) investir a alguien con, conferir a alguien (un poder, una medalla); (fig.) otorgar, conceder.

investigate | ɪn'vestɪgeɪt | *v.t.* e *i.* **1** investigar, indagar, hacer averiguaciones. **2** investigar, estudiar, observar, analizar.

investigation | ɪnˌvestɪ'geɪʃn | *s.c.* e *i.* **1** [– (into)] investigación, indagación, averiguación. **2** investigación, estudio, análisis, examen.

investigative | ɪn'vestɪgeɪtɪv | | ɪn'vestɪgətɪv | *adj.* **1** investigador. **2** de investigación: *investigative journalism = periodismo de investigación.*

investigator | ɪn'vestəgɪgeitər | *s.c.* investigador.

investiture | ɪn'vestɪtʃər | *s.c.* **1** investidura, ceremonia. **2** vestidura, ropaje, vestimenta.

investment | ɪn'vestmənt | *s.c.* e *i.* **1** inversión (de capital). **2** inversión, dedicación (de tiempo, esfuerzo). || *s.c.* **3** adquisición, compra. **4** investidura (ceremonia). **5** (arc.) vestimenta, ropaje, vestidura. **6** MIL. sitio, cerco.

investor | in'vestər | *s.c.* inversor, inversionista, accionista, comprador.

inveterate | ɪn'vetərət | *adj.* inveterado, empedernido, arraigado: *an inveterate smoker = un fumador empedernido.*

invidous | ɪn'vɪdɪəs | *adj.* **1** odioso, fastidioso (de actividades o empleos impopulares). **2** injusto. **3** discriminatorio. **4** (arc.) envidioso.

invigilate | ɪn'vɪdʒɪleit | *v.t.* e *i.* (brit.) vigilar un examen.

invigilator | ɪn'vɪdʒəɪleɪtər | *s.c.* (brit.) supervisor, celador.

invigorated | ɪn'vɪgəreɪtɪd | *adj.* revigorizado, revitalizado.

invigorating | ɪn'vɪgəreɪtɪŋ | *adj.* revigorizante, revitalizante, estimulante.

invincible | ɪn'vɪnsəbl | *adj.* **1** invencible, irreductible. **2** inexpugnable. **3** inamovible (creencias, actitudes, convicciones).

invincibly | ɪn'vɪnsiblɪ | *adv.* **1** de modo incuestionable. **2** de forma inamovible.

inviolability | ɪnˌvaɪələ'bɪlɪtɪ | *s.i.* inviolabilidad.

inviolable | ɪn'vəɪələbl | *adj.* (form.) inviolable (leyes, principios).

inviolate | ɪn'vəɪəlɪt | *adj.* (form.) intacto, inviolado.

invisibility | ɪnˌvɪzə'bɪlɪtɪ | *s.i.* invisibilidad.

invisible | ɪn'vɪzəbl | *adj.* **1** invisible, oculto. **2** imaginario. **3** FIN. invisible, no declarados (ganancias, exportaciones): *invisible assets = activos invisibles.* || **4 – ink,** tinta simpática.

invisibly | ɪn'vɪzəblɪ | *adv.* invisiblemente.

invitation | ɪnvɪ'teɪʃən | *s.c.* **1** invitación, convite: *invitation card = tarjeta de invitación.* **2** proposición, sugerencia. **3** estímulo, tentación. || **4 an open –,** un reclamo, una invitación: *an unlocked door is an open invitation to burglary = una puerta sin cerrar es una invitación al robo.*

invite | in'vəɪt | *v.t.* **1 [to – + *o.* + to/for]** invitar a, convidar a. **2** pedir, solicitar. **3** propiciar (la crítica). **4** provocar, estimular (problemas). || | 'ɪnvəɪt | *s.c.* **5** (fam.) invitación escrita.

inviting | ɪn'vɪŋ | *adj.* **1** atractivo, sugerente, provocativo, seductor. **2** apetitoso (un alimento).

invitingly | ɪn'vəɪtɪŋgli | *adv.* apetitosamente, tentadoramente, incitantemente.

invocation | ɪnvəu'keiʃən | *s.i.* **1** invocación. || *s.c.* **2** oración, invocación. **3** conjuro, encantamiento.

invoice | 'ɪnvɔɪs | *s.c.* **1** factura, cuenta. || *v.t.* **2** pasar factura, enviar factura.

invoke | ɪn'vəuk | *v.t.* **1** (form.) recurrir a, alegar, acogerse a (una ley). **2** invocar, apelar a (un principio). **3** invocar, orar (a Dios). **4** conjurar (a los espíritus). **5** provocar (sentimientos). **6** suplicar, implorar (ayuda). **7** evocar (recuerdos).

involuntarily | ɪn'vɔləntərɪlɪ | *adv.* involuntariamente, sin intención.

involuntary | ɪn'vələntərɪ | *adj.* **1** involuntario, espontáneo. **2** automático, sin control.

involve | ɪn'vɔlv | | ɪn'vəːlv | *v.t.* **1** implicar, involucrar, complicar: *involving us in her affairs = involucrándonos en sus asuntos.* **2** incluir, suponer, traer consigo, ocasionar (una situación, una actividad). **3** participar, tomar parte. **4** afectar, incluir (proyectos, planes). **5** absorber, abstraer, acaparar (la atención). **6** envolver, embalar. **7** MAT. elevar a una potencia.

involved | ɪn'vɔlvd | *adj.* **1** comprometido, complicado (en una actividad, situación). **2** liado, comprometido (sexualmente). **3** interesado, en juego: *the political parties involved = los partidos políticos en juego.* **4** complicado, complejo, enrevesado, confuso.

involvement | ɪn'vɔlvmənt | | ɪn'vəlvmənt | *s.i.* **1** participación, compromiso. || *s.c.* **2** (fam.) relación amorosa, lío amoroso.

invulnerability | ɪnˌvʌlnərə'bilɪti | *s.i.* invulnerabilidad.

invulnerable | ɪn'vʌlnərəbəl | *adj.* invulnerable.

inward | 'ɪnwəd | *adj.* **1** interior, interno. **2** privado, secreto, íntimo (un pensamiento, un sentimiento). **3** íntimo, familiar. || *adv.* **4** hacia dentro, hacia el interior.

inward-looking | 'ɪnwədlukiŋ | *adj.* **1** introspectivo. **2** introvertido.

inwardly | 'ɪnwədlɪ | *adv.* **1** interiormente. **2** para sus adentros, entre sí, para sí.

inwards | 'ɪnwədz | *adv.* V. **inward.** || *s.pl.* tripas, entrañas.

iodine | 'əiəudiːn | *s.i.* yodo.

ion | 'aiən | *s.c.* (gen. *pl.*) FIS. ión.

iota | ai'əutə | *s.c.* **1** pizca, ápice. **2** iota, novena letra del alfabeto griego.

IOU | 'aɪəu'juː | *s.c.* **owe you,** pagaré, vale: *an IOU for 300 = un pagaré por valor de 300 libras.*

IQ | aikjuː | *s.c.* **intelligence quotient,** cociente intelectual (CI).

Iran | ɪ'rɑːn | *s.* Irán.

Iranian | ɪ'reɪnjən | *adj.* **1** iraní. || *s.c.* e *i.* **2** iraní (habitante, lengua).

Iraq | ɪ'raːk | *s.* Irak, Iraq.

Iraqi | ɪ'rɑːki | *adj.* **1** iraquí. || *s.c.* e *i.* **2** iraquí (habitante, lengua).

irascible | ɪ'ræsɪbl | *adj.* irascible, irritable.

irate | əɪ'reɪt | *adj.* airado, indignado, furioso.

ire | 'aɪə | *s.i.* (lit.) ira, cólera.

Ireland | 'əɪələnd | *s.* Irlanda.

iridiscent | ɪrɪ'desnt | *adj.* iridiscente, tornasolado, irisado.

iris | 'əiərɪs | *s.c.* **1** ANAT. iris del ojo. **2** BOT. lirio.

Irish | 'aɪərɪs | *adj.* **1** irlandés. || *s.pl.* **2** **[the –]** los irlandeses. || *s.i.* **3** irlandés (lengua).

Irishman | 'aɪərɪʃmən | *pl.* **Irishmen.** *s.c.* irlandés.

Irishwoman | 'aɪərɪʃwuman | *pl.* **Irishwomen.** *s.c.* irlandesa.

irk | əːk | *v.t.* molestar, fastidiar, irritar.

irksome | 'əːksəm | *adj.* **1** molesto, pesado, fastidioso, irritante. **2** aburrido, tedioso.

iron | 'aɪən | *s.i.* **1** MIN. hierro. **2** (fig.) acero, hierro: *nerves of iron = nervios de acero.* || *s.c.* **3** plancha. || *v.t.* **4** planchar. || **5 to have many irons in the fire,** tener muchos asuntos entre manos. **6 to strike while the – is hot,** a hierro caliente, batir de repente.

iron-grey | 'aiən'greɪ | *adj.* gris oscuro.

ironic, ironical | aɪ'rɔnɪk | *adj.* **1** irónico. **2** paradójico.

ironically | ai'rɔnɪkəli | *adv.* **1** irónicamente. **2** paradójicamente.

ironing | 'əɪənɪŋ | *s.i.* **1 [the –]** el planchado de la ropa. **2** ropa planchada o por planchar.

ironing-board | 'aɪənɪŋbɔːd | *s.c.* tabla de planchar.

ironmonger | 'aɪənˌmʌŋgər | *s.c.* **1** ferretería (tienda). **2** (brit.) ferretero.

ironmongery | 'aɪənˌmʌŋgəri | *s.i.* (brit.) objetos de ferretería.

ironstone | 'aɪənstəun | *s.i.* MIN. mineral de hierro, siderita, oligisto.

ironwork | 'aɪənwəːk | *s.i.* obras de hierro (verjas, balcones).

irony | 'aiərəni | *s.i.* ironía, sarcasmo, burla.

irradiate | ɪ'reɪdɪeɪt | *v.t.* e *i.* **1** irradiar, emitir (luz, energía, radioactividad). **2** MED. tratar con rayos X. **3** exponer a radioactividad.

irradiation | ɪˌreɪdɪ'eɪʃən | *s.i.* **1** irradiación (nuclear). **2** MED. terapia de irradiación.

irrational | ɪ'ræʃənl | *adj.* **1** irracional (un sentimiento, una actitud). **2** ilógico, absurdo. || *s.c.* **3** MAT. número irracional.

irrationality | ɪˌræʃənælɪtɪ | *s.i.* irracionalidad.

irrationally | ɪ'ræʃnəlɪ | *adv.* irracionalmente.

irreconciliable | ɪ'rekənsəɪləbl | *adj.* **1** irreconciliable. **2** incompatible. || *s.c.* **3** inadaptado, persona intransigente.

irredeemable | ɪrɪ'dɪːməbl | *adj.* **1** (p.u.) incorregible, incurable. **2** COM. no amortizable. **3** inconvertible (papel moneda).

irredeemably | ˌɪrɪ'dɪːməbl | *adv.* sin remisión, sin arreglo.

irreducible | ˌɪrɪ'djuːsəbl | *adj.* irreducible, irreductible.

irrefutable | ɪ'refjutəbl | *adj.* irrefutable, irrebatible, indiscutible.

irregular | ɪ'regjulər | *adj.* **1** irregular, desigual (una superficie). **2** asimétrica (una cara). **3** irregular, atípico, ilegal (un comportamiento, una actitud). **4** GRAM. irregular. **5** a intervalos irregulares. || *s.pl.* **6** tropas que no pertenecen al ejército regular.

irregularity | ɪˌregju'læriti | *s.c.* **1** irregularidad, anomalía. **2** falta.

irregularly | ɪ'regjuləli | *adv.* irregularmente.

irrelevance | ɪ'relɪvəns | *s.c.* e *i.* **1** irrelevancia, improcedencia, inaplicabilidad. **2** inconexión.

irrelevancy | ɪ'relɪvənsɪ | *s.c.* e *i.* V. **irrelevance.**

irrelevant | ɪ'relɪvənt | *adj.* **1** irrelevante, no pertinente. **2** improcedente, inapropiado, inoportuno, inaplicable, fuera de propósito.

irrelevantly | ɪ'relɪvəntli | *adv.* **1** sin venir a cuento, fuera de propósito. **2** inoportunamente.

irreligious | ɪrɪ'lɪdʒəs | *adj.* irreligioso, impío.

irremediable | ɪrɪ'mɪdjəbl | *adj.* irremediable, irreparable, insubsanable.

irreparable | ɪ'repərəbl | *adj.* irreparable, irrecuperable.

irreplaceable | ɪrɪ'pleisəbl | *adj.* irreemplazable, insustituible.

irrepressible | ɪrɪ'presəbl | *adj.* **1** activo, enérgico, animoso. **2** indomable, irrefrenable.

irrepressibly | ɪrɪ'presəbli | *adv.* de modo irreprimible.

irreproachable | ɪrɪˌprəutʃəbl | *adj.* irreprochable, intachable (el carácter, los actos).

irresistible | ɪrɪ'zistəbl | *adj.* **1** irresistible (un deseo, una pasión). **2** fascinante, atrayente (una persona, una cosa). **3** inexorable.

irresistibly | ɪrɪ'zɪstəbli | *adv.* **1** irresistiblemente. **2** inexorablemente.

irresolute | ɪ'rezəluːt | *adj.* (form.) indeciso, vacilante, titubeante.

irrespective | iris'pektiv | *prep.* **[– of]** con independencia de, sin consideración a.

irresponsibility | 'ɪris,pənsəbilɪtɪ | *s.i.* irresponsabilidad.

irresponsible | ɪrɪs'pɔnsəbl | *adj.* **1** irresponsable, alocado, poco serio (una persona). **2** irresponsable, poco meditado (un acto).

irresponsibly | ɪris'pɔnsibli | *adv.* **1** de manera irresponsable, alocadamente. **2** sin pensarlo debidamente.

irretrievable | ɪrɪ'triːvəbl | *adj.* irreparable, irrecuperable, irremediable (un daño).

irretrievably | ɪrɪ'triːvəblɪ | *adv.* **1** irremediablemente, sin remisión. **2** de forma irrecuperable.

irreverence | ɪ'revərəns | *s.i.* irreverencia, falta de respeto.

irreverent | ɪ'revərənt | *adj.* **1** irreverente (en asuntos religiosos). **2** irrespetuoso, impertinente.

irreverently | ɪ'revərəntli | *adv.* **1** irrespetuosamente, de modo irreverente. **2** en plan de mofa.

irreversible | ɪrɪ'vəːsəbl | *adj.* **1** irreversible, irreparable (un daño). **2** irrevocable.

irreversibly | ɪrɪ'vəːsəbli | *adv.* de forma irreversible, de forma irreparable.

irrevocable | ɪ'revəkəbl | *adj.* irrevocable, inapelable, inalterable.

irrevocably | ɪ'revəkəbli | *adv.* irrevocablemente, sin remedio.

irrigate | 'ɪrɪgeɪt | *v.t.* **1** AGR. regar. **2** MED. irrigar.

irrigated | 'ɪrɪgeɪtid | *adj.* de regadío, regadas (tierras).

irrigation | ɪrɪ'geɪʃən | *s.i.* **1** AGR. riego. **2** MED. irrigación.

irritability | iritə'bɪlɪtɪ | *s.i.* irritabilidad, desasosiego.

irritable | 'ɪrɪtəbl | *adj.* **1** irritable, nervioso. **2** TEC. excitable.

irritably | 'ɪrɪtəbli | *adv.* con irritación, de mal humor.

irritant | 'ɪrɪtənt | *s.c.* **1** (form.) irritación, circunstancia irritante. **2** irritante (una sustancia).

irritate | 'ɪrɪteɪt | *v.t.* **1** irritar, fastidiar, molestar, exasperar, provocar. **2** MED. irritar (la piel, las mucosas). **3** TEC. excitar.

irritated | 'ɪrɪteɪtɪd | *adj.* **1** irritado, enfadado, molesto. **2** MED. irritada (la piel).

irritating | 'ɪrɪteɪtɪŋ | *adj.* irritante, molesto, fastidioso.

irritatingly | 'ɪrɪteɪtɪŋgli | *adv.* de forma molesta, de forma irritante.

irritation | ɪrɪ'teɪʃən | *s.i.* **1** irritación, enfado. || *s.c.* **2** molestia, pega. **3** MED. picor, irritación.

is | iz | *v.* **1** *3a. persona sing.* de **to be,** es, está. **2 Is.,** abreviatura de **Island, Islands, Isle** o **Isles,** isla, islas.

Islam | 'ɪzlaːm | *s.* **1** El Islam (religión). **2** El Islam, los países musulmanes.

Islamic | ɪz'læmɪk | *adj.* islámico, mahometano, musulmán.

island | 'aɪlənd | *s.c.* **1** isla. **2** isleta, isla (en calles, aeropuertos). **3** (fig.) oasis, lugar de descanso. **4** ANAT. isla.

islander | 'aɪləndər | *s.c.* isleño, insular.

isle | ail | *s.c.* (lit.) isla: *the British Isles = las Islas Británicas.*

islet | 'aɪlɪt | *s.c.* islote, isleta.

isolate | aɪsəuleɪt | *v.t.* **1** (gen. *pas.*) aislar, apartar, separar. **2** QUIM. aislar (una sustancia, un elemento). **3** MED. poner en cuarentena. **4** alejar, indisponerse con.

isolated | 'aɪsəuleɪt | *adj.* **1** aislado, apartado, solitario (un lugar). **2** único, aislado (un caso).

isolation | aɪsəu'leɪʃən | *s.i.* **1** aislamiento, incomunicación. **2** MED. aislamiento por cuarentena. || **3 in –,** independientemente, aislado, aparte, sin ayuda.

isolationism | aɪsəu'leɪʃnɪzəm | *s.i.* POL. aislacionismo.

isolationist | aɪsəu'leɪʃnist | *s.c.* **1** POL. aislacionista. || *adj.* **2** POL. aislacionista.

isometric | aɪsəu'metrɪk | *adj.* **1** isométrico. **2** MIN. cúbico. **3** perspectiva isométrica. || *s.pl.* **4** isométricos (ejercicios gimnásticos).

isotope | 'aɪsəutəup | *s.c.* FIS. isótopo.

Israel | 'ɪzreiəl | *s.* Israel.

Israeli | ɪz'reɪlɪ | *adj.* **1** israelí. || *s.c.* **2** israelí.

issue | 'ɪʃu | | 'ɪsjuː | *s.c.* **1** asunto, cuestión, problema, tema punto (de discusión). **2** edición, tirada (de una revista, libro). **3** emisión (de sellos, moneda). **4** número (de revista, periódico). **5** reparto, distribución, entrega. **6** desacuerdo, discusión. **7** (p.u. y form.) resultado, consecuencia. || *s.i.* **8** MED. flujo, pérdida, emisión. **9** publicación, edición. **10** DER. descendencia, sucesión. **11** salida, partida. **12** *pl.* ganancias. || *v.t.* **13** promulgar (un decreto). **14** entregar, dar, proveer (oficialmente). **15** emitir, poner en circulación (sellos, moneda). **16** publicar, editar. **17** distribuir, repartir. **18** expedir (documentos oficiales). **19** extender, librar (un cheque). **20** impartir (una orden). || *v.i.* **21** emerger, brotar, salir, fluir. **22 [to – from]** (fig.) proceder de, provenir de. **23 [to – in]** resultar en. || **24 at –,** asunto importante, cuestión a considerar; DER. causa para sentencia. **25 to cloud/confuse the –,** irse por las ramas, salirse por la tangente. **26 to duck/evade the –,** soslayar el problema, no querer abordar el tema. **27 to make an – of something,** crear un problema en torno a algo, machacar sobre el mismo tema. **28 to make an – with,** contradecir a, mostrar desacuerdo con, llevar la contraria a.

isthmus | 'ɪsməs | *s.c.* **1** GEOG. istmo. **2** ZOOL. istmo.

it | ɪt | *pron.* **1** [como *suj.* u *o.*] él, ella, ello; lo, la, le; eso, esa, esto, esta. || *s.i.* **2** el que se queda, el que la lleva (en el juego del escondite): *you're it! = ¡te quedas!* **3** (arc.) vermut italiano: *gin and it = ginebra con vermut.* **4** (argot) el momento más importante, la hora de la verdad. **5** (argot) sexo, coito; (arc.) atracción sexual, un no sé qué, tilín. **6** IT., *abreviatura* de **Information Technology,** INF. Tecnología de la información. || **7 catch –,** V. **catch. 8 to go – alone,** montárselo por su cuenta. **9 to have had –,** V. **have. 10 to have what – takes,** V. **take. 11 that's –,** eso es todo, y no hay más que decir; eso es, así es.

OBS.: Se utiliza: **12** para sustituir a una cosa, a una idea, o a un grupo anteriormente mencionado: *take the photograph and show it to her = coge la fotografía y enséñasela (a ella);* **13** para personas o animales cuyo sexo se desconoce o no es importante: *they had a baby! it was born yesterday = ¡tuvieron un niño! Nació ayer;* **14** como sujeto de un verbo impersonal (que se refiere al tiempo, distancia, hora): *it often rains in April = en abril llueve a menudo;* **15** para referirse a algo que no se menciona, pero se da por entendido: *he can't stand it = no lo puede soportar.* **16** como antecedente de un *suj.* u *o.* que va postergado: *it drives me crazy when he comes late = me pone enferma que llegue tarde; what's it like being in New York? = ¿qué tal te va en Nueva York?; it's sure that he'll be there = seguro que él estará allí;* **17** como *suj.* de **seem, appear, happen o look:** *it seems you've passed = parece que has aprobado; it looks as if she was angry = parece que está enfadada;* **18** para resaltar una parte de la oración: *it was him who sent it = fue él quien lo envió; it was yesterday when he sent it = fue ayer cuando lo envió;* **19** (fam.) como *o.* sin significado alguno de ciertos verbos: *the party was really it! = ¡la fiesta fue maravillosa!*

Italian | ɪ'tæljən | *adj.* **1** italiano. || *s.c.* e *i.* **2** italiano (habitante, lengua).

italic | ɪ'tælɪk | *s.pl.* **1** cursiva, bastardilla (la letra). || *adj.* **2** cursiva, bastardilla. **3** itálico (de Italia).

Italy | 'ɪtəli | | 'ɪtlɪ | *s.* Italia.

itch | ɪtʃ | *v.i.* **1** picar, sentir picor: *my back itches = siento picor en la espalda.* || **2 to – to do something,** tener ganas de hacer algo, estar impaciente por hacer algo. || *s.c.* **3** picor, picazón, prurito. **4 [the –]** la sarna. || *s.i.* **5** deseo imperioso.

itchy | 'ɪtʃɪ | *adj.* **1** (fam.) sensible al picor, que pica. **2** (fig.) ansioso, impaciente. || **to have – feet,** ser un culo inquieto, estar deseando moverse o emprender un viaje o cambiar de sitio.

item | 'aɪtəm | *s.c.* **1** cosa, artículo, objeto (de una serie). **2** vocablo, palabra. **3** asunto a tratar. **4** noticia, reportaje, artículo. **5** COM. partida. || *adv.* **6** (arc.) y, más, además, también.

itemize | 'aɪtəmaɪz | (brit.) **itemise.** *v.t.* pormenorizar los detalles, detallar, especificar.

itinerant | aɪ'tɪnərənt | *adj.* **1** ambulante, itinerante. || *s.c.* **2** (gen. *sing.*) viajero, viajante (por razón de trabajo).

itinerary | aɪ'tɪnərərɪ | *s.c.* **1** ruta, itinerario, plan de viaje. **2** guía de viaje.

its | ɪts | *adj. pos.* de 3.ª persona *sing.* **1** su, sus (de una cosa, de un animal, de un lugar o de un niño): *the dog lifted its head = el perro levantó su cabeza.* || *pron. pos.* **2** (el) suyo, (la) suya.

itself | ɪt'self | *pron. r.* y enfático de 3.ª persona *sing.* **1** mismo, él mismo, ella misma, ello mismo (una cosa, un animal, un lugar, un niño): *it turns itself = él mismo se da la vuelta.* **2** sí mismo, se: *the country must decide itself = el país debe decidir por sí mismo.* **3** solo, por sí, en sí mismo: *the story itself makes me laugh = la historia en sí me da la risa.* || **4 by –, a)** por sí solo, automáticamente; **b)** solo, solitario, aislado, separado: *the tree stands by itself in the garden = un solo árbol se eleva en el jardín.* **5 he is politiness/kindness, etc. –,** es la educación, la amabilidad en persona.

IUD | ˌaɪjuː'diː | *s.c.* **Intrauterine Device,** dispositivo intrauterino (DIU).

ivory | 'aɪvərɪ | *s.i.* **1** marfil. || *s.c.* **2** colmillo de elefante. **3** *pl.* teclas de piano. **4** (fam.) dientes. **5** bolas de billar. || *adj.* **6** de marfil, marfileño. || **7 – tower,** (fig.) torre de marfil, aislamiento total.

ivy | 'aɪvɪ | *s.i.* hiedra.

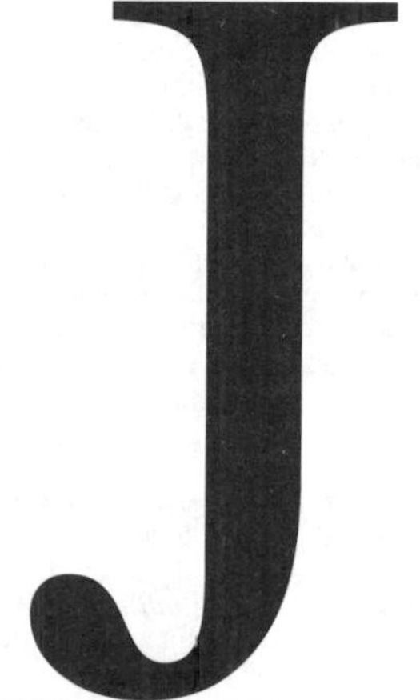

j, J | dʒeɪ | *s.c.* j, J (décima letra del alfabeto inglés).

jab | dʒæb | *v.t.* e *i. pret.* y *p.p.* **jabbed. 1** pinchar, clavar, punzar, herir con arma blanca. **2** golpear, presionar (con el dedo, o con algo punzante). || *s.c.* **3** pinchazo, punzada. **4** golpe brusco; presión (de algo punzante). **5** (fam. y brit.) inyección. || **6 to – at something,** golpear algo repetidamente, aporrear (con algo punzante): *jabbing at the computer keys = golpeando las teclas del ordenador.*

jabber | 'dʒæbər | *v.i.* **1 [to – (away)]** farfullar, hablar atropelladamente, parlotear. || *v.t.* **2 [to – (out)]** mascullar, decir atropelladamente. || *s.c.* **3** guirigay, bulla, jaleo, parloteo.

jack | dʒæk | *s.c.* **1** MEC. gato. **2** sacabotas. **3** sota, valet (en juegos de naipes). **4** DEP. bolo, bola, boliche. **5** jornalero; leñador. **6** marinero. **7** ZOOL. pollino, burro, borrico. **8** ZOOL. lucio. **9** ELEC. enchufe hembra. **10** MAR. bandera de proa. **11** (argot) pasta, plata, pelas. **12** aguardiente de manzana. || *v.t.* **13** pescar con farol o con antorcha. || **14 every man –,** todos y cada uno, absolutamente todos. **15 I'm all right, Jack,** (fam.) ¡paso de todo!, ¡y a mí que me importa! **16 to – in,** (brit.) dejar, abandonar (un trabajo, una actividad). **17 to – of,** (vulg. y argot) masturbarse. **18 to – up,** levantar, elevar (con gato); subir, elevar (los precios, la producción); apoyar, tener confianza en.

jackal | 'dʒækɔːl | | 'dʒækəl | *s.c.* **1** ZOOL. chacal. **2** cómplice, secuaz; mercenario. **3** sirviente, lacayo.

jackass | 'dʒækæs | *s.c.* **1** (arc.) imbécil, estúpido, cretino, necio. **2** ZOOL. burro, asno, pollino.

jackboot | 'dʒækbuːt | *s.c.* **1** bota militar (hasta la rodilla). || **2 under the –,** bajo la dictadura militar, bajo una política totalitaria, bajo la bota.

jackdaw | 'dʒækdɔː | *s.c.* ZOOL. corneja, grajo.

jacket | 'dʒækɪt | *s.c.* **1** americana, chaqueta de paño, saco; chaquetilla (de camarero). **2** patata asada con su piel; piel (de la patata asada). **3** forro, sobrecubierta (de un libro). **4** MEC. camisa, chaqueta (de un cilindro, de los pistones). **5** (EE.UU.) funda, cubierta (de un disco). **6** carpeta (de cartulina). **7** funda metálica (de una bala). || *v.t.* **8** envolver, cubrir, enfundar.

jack-in-the-box | 'dʒækɪnðəbks | *s.c.* caja sorpresa, caja con muñeco resorte (que salta al ser abierta).

jack-knife | 'dʒæknaɪf | *s.c.* **1** navaja. **2** DEP. salto de carpa (en natación). || *v.t.* e *i.* **3** desarticularse (un camión articulado al perder el control). || *v.t.* **4** dar un navajazo, cortar con navaja.

jack-of-all-trades | ˌdʒækəv'ɔːltreɪdz | *s.c.* hombre de muchos oficios (que no es experto en ninguno).

jackpot | 'dʒækpɒt | | 'dʒækpɑːt | *s.c.* **1** premio gordo, apuesta acumulada, bote. || **2 to hit the –,** acertar el gordo, ganar el bote; (fig.) tener una suerte loca, dar en el blanco.

jade | dʒeɪd | *s.i.* **1** MIN. jade. **2** color verde jade. || *s.c.* **3** (desp.) mujerzuela, fulana, pécora, lagartona, arrabalera. **4** rocín, jamelgo. || *v.t.* e *i.* **5** cansar, hartar, quedar exhausto.

jaded | dʒeɪdɪd | **adj. [– (with)]** cansado, harto, aburrido, falto de entusiasmo (por exceso de experiencia).

jagged, jaggy | dʒægɪd | *adj.* **1** dentado, mellado, desigual. **2** abrupto, escarpado, accidentado. **3** áspero, tosco, basto.

jaguar | 'dʒægjuər | | 'dʒægwɑːr | *s.c.* ZOOL. jaguar.

jail | dʒeɪl | (brit.) **gaol** *s.c.* e *i.* **1** prisión, cárcel, confinamiento. || *v.t.* **2** encarcelar, confinar, encerrar en prisión.

jailbird | 'dʒeɪlbɔːd | | 'dʒeɪlbɔːrd | (brit.) **gaolbird** *s.c.* (fam.) presidiario, convicto.

jailbreak | 'dʒeɪlbreɪk | (brit.) **gaolbreak** *s.c.* evasión, fuga.

jailer | 'dʒeɪlər | (brit.) **gaoler** *s.c.* (arc.) carcelero, guardián.

jalopy | dʒə'lɒpɪ | | dʒə'lɑːpɪ | *s.c.* (fam. y arc.) cacharro, coche destartalado, tartana.

jam | dʒæm | (EE.UU.) **jelly** *s.c.* **1** mermelada, configura de frutas. || *s.c.* **2** atasco, aglomeración, barullo, apelotonamiento (de cosas, de personas). **3** embotellamiento, atasco (de tráfico). **4** apuro, aprieto, embrollo: *a financial jam = una situación financiera difícil.* || *v.t.* e *i.* **5** apretar(se), apretujar(se), estrujar(se). || *v.t.* **6** apiñar, aglomerar, atestar (un lugar). **7** (generalmente pasiva) bloquear (el teléfono por exceso de llamadas). **8** obstruir, atascar (una tubería). **9** magullar, pillarse (un dedo, una mano). **10** introducir por la fuerza, meter a presión. **11** MUS. improvisar (en jazz). **12** RAD. interferir. || *v.i.* **13 [to – up]** atascarse, obstruirse, trabarse (una máquina). || **14 to get into a –,** meterse en un lío. **15 to – on the brakes,** dar un frenazo, frenar bruscamente. **16 a – session,** una sesión de jazz improvisado.

Jamaica | dʒə'meɪkə | *s.* Jamaica.

Jamaican | dʒə'meɪkən | *adj.* **1** jamaicano. || *s.c.* **2** jamaicano.

jamb | dʒæm | *s.c.* ARQ. jamba.

jamboree | ˌdʒæmbə'riː | *s.c.* **1** (fam.) juerga, jolgorio, fiesta, celebración. **2** congreso de niños exploradores y guías. **3** congreso, reunión, asamblea (profesional).

jam-full | 'dʒæm'ful | *adv.* de bote en bote.

jam-jar | 'dʒæmdʒɑːr | *s.c.* **1** (EE.UU.) tarro de mermelada.

jammed | dʒæmd | *adj.* congestionado, atascado, bloqueado.

jamming | 'dʒæmɪŋ | *s.i* RAD. interferencia.

jammy | 'dʒæmɪ | *adj.* **1** (brit. y argot) fácil, tirado, simple. **2** (brit. y argot) suertudo, que tiene mucha potra; de chorra. **3** viscoso, pegajoso.

jam-packed | ˌdʒæm'pækt | *adj.* **[– (with)]** (fam.) a tope, abarrotado, atestado.

jangle | 'dʒæŋgl | *v.t.* e *i.* **1** producir un ruido discordante, hacer un ruido metálico, tintinear, cencerrear. || *v.t.* **2** crispar, enervar, irritar. || *s.i.* **3** cencerreo, tintineo, esquilada, ruido metálico (desagradable).

janitor | 'dʒænɪtər | *s.c.* (EE.UU.) portero (de un edificio). **2** (arc.) conserje.

January | 'dʒænjʊərɪ | | 'dʒænjʊrɪ | | 'dʒænjʊerɪ | *s.c.* e *i.* Enero.

Japan | dʒə'pæn | *s.* el Japón.

Japanese | ˌdʒæpə'ni:z | *s.c.* e *i.pl.* **the –, 1** japonés (nacionalidad, lengua). || *adj.* **2** japonés (de origen).

jar | dʒɑ:r | *s.c.* **1** tarro, pote, bote, tinaja. **2** contenido de un tarro. **3** impacto, choque, sacudida, golpe. **4** chirrido, ruido discordante. || *v.i.* **5** irritar, sacar de quicio, crispar. **6 [to – (with)]** chocar, discrepar, no llevarse bien, no compaginar. **7 [to – (in)]** chirriar, rechinar, sonar estridentemente. **8** sacudirse, vibrar, estremecerse. || *v.t.* **9** sacudir, agitar, hacer vibrar. **10** sobresaltar, asustar, dar un susto.

jargon | 'dʒɑ:gən | | 'dʒɑ:rgən | *s.c.* e *i.* **1** (generalmente desp.) jerga, tecnicismo, lenguaje propio de un grupo o materia: *the jargon of computers = el lenguaje propio de los ordenadores.* **2** galimatías, jerigonza, cháchara incoherente.

jarring | 'dʒærɪŋ | *adj.* **1** molesto, irritante. **2** impactante, estremecedor; sorprendente, desagradable.

jasmine | 'dʒæsmɪn | *s.c.* e *i.* BOT. jazmín.

jaundice | 'dʒɔ:ndɪs | | 'dʒɑ:ndɪs | *s.i.* MED. ictericia.

jaundiced | 'dʒɔ:ndɪst | | 'dʒɑ:ndɪst | *adj.* **1** (desp.) envidioso, celoso, hostil. **2** amargado, decepcionado. **3** amarillento, macilento, cetrino. **4** MED. afectado por la ictericia.

jaunt | dʒɔ:nt | | dʒɑ:nt | *s.c.* e *i.* **1** viajecito, excursión corta; paseo. || *v.i.* **2** hacer un viaje corto, ir de excursión.

jauntily | 'dʒɔ:ntɪlɪ | *adv.* **1** con desenvoltura, con garbo. **2** alegremente.

jaunty | 'dʒɔ:ntɪ | *adj.* **1** elegante, airoso, garboso. **2** seguro de sí, desenvuelto. **3** alegre, enérgico, lleno de vida.

javelin | 'dʒævlɪn | *s.c.* **1** DEP. jabalina. **2** DEP. competición de jabalina.

jaw | dʒɔ: | *s.c.* **1** ANAT. mandíbula, quijada, maxilar inferior. **2** *pl.* ANAT. boca; fauces; pico. **3** *pl.* MEC. mordaza, telera, abrazadera. **4** *pl.* (fig.) garras: *the jaws of death = las garras de la muerte.* **5** embocadura, entrada (de un valle, de una caverna). || *s.c.* e *i.* **6** (fam. y desp.) cháchara, palique, charla vacía. || *v.i.* **7** (fam.) charlar, dar palique, hablar por los codos, hablar interminablemente. **8** vociferar, gritar, vocear.

jawbone | 'dʒɔ:bəʊn | *s.c.* **1** ANAT. hueso de la mandíbula, quijada, maxilar. || *v.t.* **2** presionar, persuadir con presiones.

jay | dʒeɪ | *s.c.* **1** ZOOL. grajo, arrendajo, ronzuela. **2** charlatán, hablador. **3** (argot) novato, neófito, recién llegado.

jaywalker | 'dʒeɪwɔ:kər | *s.c.* peatón imprudente, peatón atolondrado.

jaywalking | 'dʒeɪwɔ:kɪŋ | *s.i.* cruce de una calle imprudentemente, atolondradamente.

jazz | dʒæz | *s.i.* **1** MUS. jazz. **2** (EE.UU. y argot) palique, charla vacía, tonterías, exageración. **3** animación, entusiasmo. || *v.t.* **4** tocar jazz. || *v.t.* e *i.* **5** (argot) exagerar, tomar el pelo, mentir. || **6 to – up,** animar, activar, avivar: *jazzing it up with bright colours = dándole más vida con colores claros.* **6 and all that –,** (argot) y todo eso, y todo lo demás, y todas esas tonterías.

jazzed-up | 'dʒæzʌp | *adj.* (fam.) MUS. sincopada, al estilo del jazz, animada: *a jazzed-up version of Yesterday = una versión jazz de Yesterday.*

jazzy | dʒæzɪ | *adj.* **1** (fam.) chillón, de colores llamativos, chocante. **2** animado, jazzístico.

jealous | 'dʒeləs | *adj.* **1** (desp.) celoso, desconfiado en extremo, posesivo. **2** envidioso, resentido, celoso. **3** intolerante, despótico (con la infidelidad).

jealously | 'dʒeləslɪ | *adv.* **1** celosamente. **2** envidiosamente, con resentimiento.

jealousy | 'dʒeləsɪ | *s.c.* e *i.* **1** celos, recelo. **2** envidia, resentimiento.

jeans | dʒi:nz | *s.pl.* (EE.UU.) pantalones vaqueros, tejanos.

jeep | dʒi:p | *s.c.* jeep, coche todo terreno (usado por el ejército).

jeer | dʒɪər | *v.t.* e *i.* **1 [to – (at)]** mofarse, escarnecer, hablar irónicamente. || *v.t.* **2** insultar, abuchear. || *s.c.* **3** abucheo, insulto. **4** burla, mofa.

jeering | 'dʒɪərɪŋ | *adj.* **1** que abuchea, que insulta. **2** irónico, burlón.

jeeringly | 'dʒɪərɪŋlɪ | *adv.* **1** irónicamente, burlonamente. **2** con insultos, con abucheos.

jejune | dʒɪ'dʒu:n | *adj.* **1** (form.) infantil, inmaduro, pueril, ingenuo. **2** (formal y arc.) aburrido, insustancial, falto de interés (material escrito). **3** poco alimenticio.

jell, gel | dʒel | *s.c.* e *i.* **1** gel, brillantina (para el pelo). || *v.i.* **2** gelatinarse, solidificarse, cuajar, convertirse en gelatina. **3** enfocar el tema, aclararse, cuajar (una idea); ver con claridad (una forma).

jellied | 'dʒelɪd | *adj.* gelatinado, en gelatina, cuajado.

jelly | 'dʒelɪ | *s.c.* e *i.* **1** gelatina, pasta gelatinosa (para postres). **2** jalea. **3** jugo, gelatina (de la carne, del pescado). **4** (EE.UU.) mermelada. **5** (fig.) fosfatina: *hit to a jelly by a bomb = quedó hecho fosfatina a causa de una bomba.* || *v.t.* e *i.* **6** solidificar, cuajar, hacerse gelatina.

jellyfish | 'dʒelɪfɪʃ | *pl.* **jellyfish** o **jellyfishes** *s.c.* **1** ZOOL. medusa, (Am.) aguamala. **2** (argot) calzonazos, persona débil de carácter.

jemmy | 'dʒemɪ | (EE.UU.) **jimmy** *s.c.* **1** palanca, palanqueta, alzaprima (usada por los ladrones). || *v.t.* **2** abrir con palanqueta (puertas, cajones).

jeopardize | 'dʒepədaɪz | (brit.) **jeopardise** *v.t.* **1** exponer, arriesgar, poner en peligro.

jeopardy | 'dʒepədɪ | *s.i.* riesgo, peligro.

jerk | dʒə:k | *v.t.* **1** tirar bruscamente, sacar de un tirón, arrancar con fuerza. **2** quitar de un tirón. **3** arrojar bruscamente. **4** hablar con convulsiones, entrecortadamente. || *v.i.* **5** moverse a saltos, ir traqueteando. **6** moverse con espasmos. || *s.c.* **7** tirón, sacudida, movimiento brusco. **8** FISIOL. espasmo, convulsión. **9** (EE.UU. y argot) estúpido, torpe, ignorante. || **10 to – off,** (EE.UU. y argot) masturbarse.

jerkin | 'dʒə:kɪn | | 'dʒ:ərkɪn | *s.c.* jubón, (EE.UU.) chaleco de cuero.

jerkily | 'dʒə:kɪlɪ | *adv.* **1** a tirones, a sacudidas. **2** convulsamente, a saltos. **3** estúpidamente.

jerky | 'dʒə:kɪ | *adj.* **1** brusco, nervioso, espasmódico. **2** movido, con mucho traqueteo, a sacudidas (un viaje). **3** desigual, con baches (una carretera). **4** estúpido, ignorante.

jerry-build | 'dʒerɪˌbɪld | *v.t.* (desp.) construir deprisa y mal, hacer una chapuza.

jerry-built | 'dʒerɪbɪlt | *adj.* chapucero, chafallón, de pacotilla (una vivienda).

jersey | 'dʒə:zɪ | | 'dʒə:rzɪ | *s.c.* **1** jersey, (Am.) chompa. **2 Jersey,** Jersey (raza de vacas lecheras). || *s.i.* **3** tejido de lana, lana (para prendas femeninas).

jessamine | 'dʒesəmɪn | *s.c.* jazmín.

jest | dʒest | *v.i.* **1** (form.) bromear, hacer chistes, burlarse, mofarse. || *v.t.* **2** ridiculizar, escarnecer. || *s.c.* **3** broma, chiste, gracia. **4** mofa, befa, burla. || **5 in –,** en broma, de guasa.

jester | 'dʒestər | *s.c.* bufón (medieval).

Jesus | 'dʒi:zəs | *s.* **1** REL. Jesús. || *interj.* **2** (argot) ¡Jesús! (para expresar sorpresa, fastidio, utilizado por no católicos). || **3 – Christ,** Jesucristo.

jet | dʒet | *s.c.* **1** avión a reacción, reactor. **2** chorro, borbotón, borbollón. **3** mechero, quemador (de gas). || *s.c.* e *i.* **4** MIN. azabache. **5** color negro azabache, negro profundo. || *adj.* **6** de azabache, de color azabache. || *v.t.* e *i.* **7** salir a chorro, brotar. **8** lanzar a chorro, arrojar a borbollones. || *v.i.* **9 [to – *adv./prep.*]** (fam.) viajar en avión, volar. || **10 – engine,** motor a reacción.

jet-black | ˌdʒet'blæk | *adj.* negro azabache, como el azabache.

jet-lag | 'dʒetlæg | *s.i.* desarreglo psicofísico (ocasionado por los viajes transoceánicos en avión).

jet-propelled | ˌdʒetprə'peld | *adj.* AER. propulsado por motor a reacción, a reacción.

jetsam | 'dʒetsəm | *s.i.* **1** echazón (que los barcos arrojan al mar para liberar peso). **2** desperdicios, cachivaches, telares.

jet-set | 'dʒetset | *s.sing.* **1** alta sociedad, gente adinerada (que frecuenta los centros de vacaciones de moda).

jettison | 'dʒetɪsn | | 'dʒetɪzən | *v.t.* **1** echar, arrojar, deshacerse de (carga de un barco, objetos que no se necesitan). **2** abandonar, rechazar, descartar (ideas, posibilidades). || *s.i.* **3** echazón (que los barcos arrojan al mar).

jetty | 'dʒetɪ | *s.c.* **1** espigón, rompeolas, malecón, espaldón. **2** muelle, embarcadero. || *adj.* **4** de azabache, de color azabache.

Jew | dʒuː | *f.* **Jewess** *s.c.* judío, israelita, hebreo.

jewel | 'dʒuːəl | *s.c.* **1** piedra preciosa, gema. **2** (generalmente *pl.*) joyas, alhajas. **3** rubí (en relojería). **4** (fig.) joya, tesoro, perla, lo más preciado. || *v.t.* **5** adornar con joyas, enjoyar. **6** engastar (una joya).

jewelled | 'dʒuːəld | (EE.UU.) **jeweled** *adj.* enjoyado, adornado de joyas.

jeweller | 'dʒuːələr | (EE.UU.) **jeweler** *s.c.* joyero.

jewellery | 'dʒuːəlrɪ | (EE.UU.) **jewelery** *s.c.* **1** joyería. || *s.i.* **2** joyas, alhajas.

Jewess | 'dʒuːɪs | *m.* **Jew** *s.c.* (desp.) judía, hebrea.

Jewish | 'dʒuːɪʃ | *adj.* judío, hebreo, israelita.

Jewishness | 'dʒuːɪʃnɪʃ | *s.i.* judaísmo.

Jewry | 'dʒʊərɪ | *s.i.* (form.) judaísmo, pueblo judío, judería.

jib | dʒɪb | *s.c.* **1** MEC. brazo de una grúa mecánica. **2** MEC. aguilón, pescante (de grúa). **3** NAUT. foque, vela triangular. || *v.i.* **4** rehusar, avanzar, plantarse, resistirse a avanzar (un animal). **5 [to – at]** resistirse a, oponerse a, negarse a. || *v.t.* e *i.* **6** NAUT. cambiar la vela de amura (para virar).

jibe, gibe | dʒaɪb | *s.c.* y *v.* V. **gibe.**

jiffy | 'dʒɪfɪ | *s.c.* (fam.) momento, periquete, santiamén.

jig | dʒɪg | *s.c.* **1** giga (baile rápido). **2** (fig.) papel, comportamiento (que se desempeña). **3** chiste, gracia, truco. **4** MEC. plantilla, patrón, guía. **5** MIN. criba de vaivén, clasificadora hidráulica. || *v.t.* e *i.* **6** bailar o tocar una giga. **7** moverse a saltitos, a sacudidas. **8** pescar a cuchara. || *v.t.* **9** cribar o separar minerales con criba.

jiggery-pockery | ˌdʒɪgərɪ'pəʊkərɪ | *s.i.* (brit. y fam.) pucherazo, tongo, trampa, fraude, maquinación.

jiggle | 'dʒɪgl | *v.t.* e *i.* **1** (fam.) balancear(se), hacer oscilar, zangolotear(se). **2** mover(se) nerviosamente, con desasosiego. || *s.c.* **3** balanceo, zangoloteo.

jigsaw, jigsaw puzzle | 'dʒɪgsɔː | *s.c.* **1** rompecabezas, (de piezas irregulares y planas). **2** sierra de vaivén. **3** (fig.) rompecabezas, lío, situación complicada.

jilt | dʒɪlt | *v.t.* **1** (desp.) dar calabazas, dejar plantado, abandonar, rechazar (a un novio). || *s.c.* **2** mujer que da calabazas.

jilted | 'dʒɪltɪd | *adj.* abandonado, rechazado, plantado.

jimmy | 'dʒɪmɪ | (brit.). V. **jemmy.**

jingle | 'dʒɪŋgl | *s.sing.* **1** tintineo, tintín, cascabeleo. **2** soniquete, cancioncilla pegadiza, estribillo (de anuncio comercial). || *v.i.* **3** tintinear, cascabelear. || *v.t.* **4** hacer sonar.

jingling | 'dʒɪŋglɪŋ | *adj.* tintineante, cascabelero.

jingoism | 'dʒɪŋgəʊɪzəm | *s.i.* (desp.) jingoísmo, patrioterismo.

jingoistic | 'dʒɪŋgəʊɪstɪk | *adj.* (desp.) jingoísta, patriotero.

jink | dʒɪŋk | *v.i.* **1** correr en zigzag. || *s.c.* **2** movimiento en zigzag, regate. **3** *pl.* jugueteo, travesuras. || **4 high jinks,** V. **high.**

jinx | dʒɪŋks | *s.c.* **1 [– (on)]** mal de ojo, aojo, maldición. **2** gafe, cenizo. || *v.t.* **3** (fam.) estar maldito, tener gafe; echar mal de ojo.

jinxed | dʒɪŋkst | *adj.* maldito, gafado, hechizado, aojado.

jitters | 'dʒɪtəz | | 'dʒɪtərz | *s.pl.* **1 [the –]** ansiedad, inquietud, nervios, desasosiego, aprensión (antes de hacer algo importante).

jittery | 'dʒɪtərɪ | *adj.* **1** (fam.) nervioso, desasosegado, inquieto, aprensivo, (Am.) muñequeado. **2** de nerviosismo, de agitación: *a jittery moment = un momento de nerviosismo.*

jive | dʒaɪv | *s.i.* **1** MUS. música con mucho ritmo, sincopada, (entre jazz y rock). **2** baile frenético, con mucho ritmo. **3** (EE.UU. y argot) palabrería, cháchara, palique. || *v.i.* **4** bailar o tocar música de ritmo frenético. **5** bromear, tomar el pelo.

job | dʒɒb | *s.c.* **1** trabajo, empleo, puesto de trabajo, profesión. **2** trabajo, asignación, encargo, tarea. **3** labor, chapuza (manual). **4** problema, situación difícil: *it was a job to get it = fue un problema conseguirlo.* **5** deber, responsabilidad, cometido, función, papel: *it's not his job to serve the coffee = no es responsabilidad suya servir el café.* **6** (fam.) fracaso, desastre: *she had a job done on her hair = le dejaron el pelo hecho un desastre.* **7** maravilla, delicia, buen trabajo: *the design was a real job = el diseño era una verdadera maravilla.* **8** (fam.) operación de cirugía plástica. **9** (argot) robo. **10** INF. trabajo, ejecución del conjunto de programas. **11** (arc.) pinchazo, punzada. || *v.i.* **12** trabajar ocasionalmente, esporádicamente. **13** trabajar a destajo. || *v.t.* **14** especular, realizar transacciones deshonestas. || *v.t.* e *i.* **15** conseguir por influencia, explotar la posición (para beneficio propio). **16** trabajar como intermedio, subcontratar (comprando o vendiendo). **17** pinchar, punzar, aguijonear (con arma blanca). || **18 to be doing a god –,** estar haciendo un trabajo meritorio, un buen trabajo. **19 to do/make a bad –,** ser un desastre. **20 to do the –,** (fam.) conseguirlo, tener éxito, sacar algo adelante: *no matter how as it does the job = no importa cómo mientras se saque adelante.* **21 to give something/someone up as a bad –,** dejar algo o a alguien por imposible. **22 jobs for the boys,** (desp.) para los enchufados, para los amiguetes. **23 – lot,** lote, saldo, surtido. **24 – sharing,** trabajo compartido (por dos personas). **25 just the –,** lo adecuado, lo que se necesita; ¡estupendo! **26 to make the best of a bad –,** poner al mal tiempo buena cara. **27 on the –,** manos a la obra, a lo suyo, en su puesto, alerta. **28 the – in hand,** lo que tenemos entre manos. **29 it's a good –,** V. **good.**

Job | dʒəʊb | *s.* **1** Job. || **2 to have the patience of –,** tener más paciencia que Job. **3 Job's conforter,** persona que cuenta sus desgracias para animar a otro y le desanima más.

jobbing | dʒbɪŋ | *adj.* (brit.) ocasional, que hace chapuzas (un trabajador).

jobless | dʒblɪs | *adj.* **1** desempleado, en paro, desocupado. || *s.pl.* **2** los parados, los desempleados.

jockey | 'dʒɒkɪ | | 'dʒɑːkɪ | *s.c.* **1** jockey, yoquey, jinete profesional. **2** (EE.UU. y argot) conductor, operador (Am.) (de máquinas). | *v.t.* e *i.* **3 [to – *o.* (into)]** manipular, maniobrar, persuadir con mañas, con intrigas, disuadir con mañas. **4** engañar, hacer trampas. || *v.t.* **5** montar a caballo (profesionalmente). || **6 to – for a position,** maniobrar para conseguir ventajas (sobre un competidor).

jockstrap | 'dʒɒkstræp | | 'dʒɑːkstræp | *s.c.* suspensorio.

jocose | dʒə'kəʊs | | dʒəʊ'kəʊs | *adj.* (lit.) jocoso, humorístico, burlesco, guasón, zumbón.

jocosely | dʒə'kəʊslɪ | *adv.* (lit.) jocosamente, humorísticamente.

jocular | 'dʒkjʊlər | | 'dʒɑːkjʊlər | *adj.* (form.) jocoso, humorístico, gracioso, festivo.

jocularity | ˌdʒkjʊ'lærɪtɪ | | ˌdʒɑːkjʊ'lærɪtɪ | *s.i.* (form.) jocosidad, gracia, humor.

jocularly | 'dʒkjʊləlɪ | *adv.* (form.) jocosamente, humorísticamente, festivamente.

jodhpurs | 'dʒɒdpəz | *s.pl.* pantalones de montar, de equitación.

jog | dʒɒg | *v.t.* **1** empujar levemente, dar un empujoncito. **2** tocar ligeramente con el codo, dar un codazo. **3** estimular, avivar (la conciencia). || *v.i.* **4 [to – *adv./prep.*]** moverse lentamente, avanzar lentamente y dando tumbos. **5** hacer footing, correr a ritmo lento y regular. **6** (fig.) ir sin prisas, transcurrir sin sobresaltos (la vida). **7** (EE.UU.) virar, torcer repentinamente. || *s.sing.* **8** empujoncito, sacudida leve, codazo. **9** carrera lenta, trote corto, footing. **10** (EE.UU.) viraje, cambio repentino de dirección. **11** (EE.UU.) saliente, elevación, prominencia, elevamiento. || **12 to – one's memory,** refrescar a alguien la memoria.

jogger | dʒɒgər | *s.c.* corredor de carrera lenta (ejercicio).

jogging | 'dʒɒgɪŋ | *s.i.* footing, carrera lenta.

joggle | 'dʒɒgl | *v.t.* e *i.* **1** (fam.) sacudir ligeramente, balancear de arriba a abajo. **2** traquetear, ir dando tumbos. || *v.t.* **3** ensamblar, unir con espiga, empalmar. || *s.c.* **4** sacudida, traqueteo, balanceo de arriba abajo, pieza de unión, ensambladura, espiga, clavo.

join | dʒɔɪn | *v.t.* **1 [to – (to/together /up)]** unir, juntar, ensamblar, combinar, poner juntos. **2** conectar, unir (dos puntos). **3** reunirse con, unirse a, acompañar en (una diversión). **4** agregarse a, unirse a (una cola). **5** estar contiguo a, lindar con, colindar con. **6** tomar parte en, intervenir en, participar en (un debate). || *v.t.* e *i.* **7** confluir, juntarse (dos ríos, caminos). **8** hacerse socio, asociarse, formar parte de (un club). **9** ingresar en, afiliarse a (un partido). **10** MIL. incorporarse, alistarse. **11** abrazar (una religión). || *s.c.* **12** juntura, unión, conexión. **13** costura. || **14 to – battle,** (fam.) trabar combate, empezar los golpes. **15 to – hands with,** cogerse de las manos. **16 to – in,** tomar parte en, participar en (una actividad). **17 to – up,** (brit.) MIL. alistarse, enrolarse; unir, juntar. **18 to – forces,** V. **forces.**

joiner | dʒɔɪnər | *s.c.* **1** ebanista. **2** ensamblador. **3** (fam.) persona a la que gusta asociarse a organizaciones varias.

joinery | dʒɔɪnərɪ | *s.i.* **1** ebanistería.

joint | dʒɔɪnt | *s.c.* **1** ANAT. articulación, coyuntura; nudillo. **2** BOT. nudo. **3** unión, empalme, conexión, juntura, ensamblaje. **4** ARQ. junta. **5** GEOL. grieta. **6** (EE.UU.) **roast,** pieza de carne para asar; cuarto (de ave). **7** (argot) casa de juego, garito, club nocturno. **8** residencia, morada; fonda. **9** (argot) porro de mariguana. **10** (EE.UU. y argot) pene. || *adj.* **11** común, combinado (un esfuerzo, una aventura). **12** conjunta, indistinta (una cuenta bancaria). **13** mancomunada, compartida (una propiedad). **14** solidaria (una responsabilidad). **15** mixta (una comisión de estudio). || *v.t.* **16** combinar, unir, ensamblar, juntar. **17** articular, unir con articulación. **18** cortar, descuartizar, despiezar (animales). || **19 out of –,** descoyuntado, dislocado. **20 to put something out of –,** (fam.) desconcertar, desbaratar, desarreglar (una máquina, un ordenador). **21 to put someone's nose out of –,** (fam. y brit.) quitar protagonismo a alguien, robar a alguien la atención del público.

jointed | 'dʒɔɪntɪd | *adj.* **1** articulado, plegable. **2** descuartizado, en cuartos (un ave, para asar).

jointly | dʒɔɪntlɪ | *adv.* conjuntamente, en común, mancomunadamente, colectivamente.

joint-stock company | 'dʒɔɪntst'k'kʌmpənɪ | *s.c.* **1** DER. sociedad anónima, sociedad de capitales.

joist | dʒɔɪst | *s.c.* ARQ. viga, vigueta, cabrio (para fijar las tablas del suelo).

joke | dʒəʊk | *s.c.* **1** chiste, gracia, juego de palabras. **2** broma, chufla, burla, pitorreo. **3** escarnio, insulto, hazmerreír. || *v.t.* e *i.* **4** tomar el pelo, divertirse a costa de, gastar bromas. **5** hacer chistes, contar chistes. || **6 to be joking,** estar de guasa, tomar el pelo, bromear. **7 can't take a –,** no tener aguante, no saber tomar una broma. **8 to go beyond a –,** pasarse de la raya, ser el colmo. **9 it's no –,** no es broma, no tiene gracia. **10 the – is on someone,** (fam.) alguien fue a por lana y salió trasquilado (alguien que pretende reírse de otro y acaba él mismo siendo el ridículo). **11 joking apart/aside,** hablando en serio, bromas aparte. **12 to make a – of,** reírse de, tomar a broma (algo serio). **13 one must be joking/one has got to be joking,** debe estar de broma, no va en serio.

joker | dʒəʊkər | *s.c.* **1** chistoso, gracioso. **2** (fam.) bromista, guasón. **3** comodín (naipes). **4** DER. letra pequeña (de un documento). **5** (argot) tío, tipo, sujeto. **6** circunstancia imprevisible.

jokey | 'dʒəʊkɪ | *adj.* (fam.) chistoso, gracioso, divertido.

jokingly | 'dʒəʊkɪŋlɪ | *adv.* **1** humorísticamente, con gracia.

jollity, jolliness | 'dʒlətɪ | *s.i.* alegría, contento, gozo, regocijo.

jolly | 'dʒɒlɪ | | 'dʒɑːlɪ | *adj.* **1** alegre, animado, divertido, jovial (el carácter). **2** divertido, agradable, grato. **3** extraordinario, espléndido. || *adv.* **4** (fam.) muy, enormemente, extraordinariamente. || *v.t.* **5 [to – *o.* + into/out of]** (brit. y fam.) camelar, engatusar, convencer con zalamerías. || *s.pl.* **6** (brit. y argot) diversión, juerga. || **7 to – somebody along,** animar con carantoñas, con gracias a alguien. **8 to – something up,** (fam.) alegrar, animar (un lugar). **9 – well,** ¡estupendo!, ¡fantástico!

jolt | dʒəʊlt | *v.t.* e *i.* **1** traquetear (un vehículo). **2** sacudir, estremecer. **3** (fig.) desconcertar, estremecer, asustar, sobresaltar. || *s.c.* **4** sacudida, impacto. **5** estremecimiento, susto, sobresalto.

Jordan | 'dʒɔːdn | *s.* **1** Jordania. **2** Jordán (río).

Jordanian | dʒɔː'deɪnɪən | *adj.* **1** jordano, de Jordania. || *s.c.* **2** jordano.

joss stick | 'dʒɒsˌstɪk | | 'dʒɑːsˌstɪk | *s.c.* **1** pebete de incienso, varita perfumada.

jostle | 'dʒɒsl | | 'dʒɑːsl | *v.t.* e *i.* **1** empujar, dar empellones. **2** forcejear, pasar dando codazos. **3** chocar, colisionar. **4** estar lado a lado, estar uno al lado del otro. **5** competir, luchar unos contra otros. || *s.c.* **6** empujón, empellón, sacudida. **7** hacinamiento, amontonamiento.

jot | dʒɒt | | dʒɑɪt | *s.c.* **1 [to – *v. negativo*]** ápice, jota, pizca. || *v.t.* **2 [to – down]** tomar notas, anotar, apuntar, garabatear.

jotter | 'dʒɒtər | | 'dʒɑːtər | *s.c.* **1** taco para escribir notas.

jotting | 'dʒɒtɪŋ | | 'dʒɑːtɪŋ | *s.c.* (generalmente pl.) notas, apuntes.

joule | dʒuːl | *s.c.* FIS. julio.

journal | 'dʒəːnl | | 'dʒəːrnl | *s.c.* **1** revista, publicación: *the ELT journal = Revista de la Enseñanza de la Lengua Inglesa.* **2** periódico. **3** (lit.) diario (personal). **4** acta, registro. **5** NAUT. cuaderno de bitácora, diario de navegación. **6** MEC. muñón.

journalese | ˌdʒəːnə'liːz | | ˌdʒəːrnə'liːz | *s.i.* (desp.) lenguaje periodístico, estilo periodístico.

journalism | 'dʒəːnəlɪzəm | | 'dʒəːrnəlɪzəm | *s.i.* **1** periodismo. **2** prensa.

journalist | 'dʒəːnəlɪst | | 'dʒəːrnəlɪst | *s.c.* periodista.

journalistic | ˌdʒəːnə'lɪstɪk | | ˌdʒəːrnə'lɪstɪk | *adj.* periodístico.

journey | 'dʒəːnɪ | | 'dʒəːrnɪ | *s.c.* **1** viaje, jornada de viaje. **2** trayecto, camino. **3** (lit.) experiencia, viaje (vida). || *v.i.* **4 [to – *adv./prep.*]** viajar, ir de viaje. || **5 to break one's –,** hacer escala en un viaje (quedándose en una ciudad unos días).

journeyman | 'dʒəːnɪmən | | 'dʒəːrnɪmən | (*pl.* **journeymen**) *s.c.* aprendiz, oficial (al que se paga por días).

joust | dʒaʊst | *v.i.* **1 [to – (with)]** justar, tomar parte en un torneo. **2** (fig.) luchar, combatir, trabar combate. || *s.c.* **3** torneo, justa. **4** competición, combate (personal).

Jove | dʒəʊv | *s.* **1** Júpiter (dios mitológico). || *interj.* **2 By –,** ¡por Júpiter!

jovial | 'dʒəʊvjəl | *adj.* **1** jovial, alegre, bromista, divertido.

joviality | ˌdʒəʊvɪ'ælɪtɪ | *s.i.* **1** jovialidad, alegría.

jovially | 'dʒəʊvjəlɪ | *adv.* **1** jovialmente, alegremente.

jowl, jowls | dʒaʊl | *s.c.* **1** ANAT. papada, barbada, quijada. **2** ZOOL. carrillada, carrillera. || **3 cheek by –,** (fig.) uña y carne, amigos inseparables.

joy | dʒɔɪ | *s.i.* **1** alegría, júbilo, regocijo. **2** (brit. y fam.) éxito, fuerte posibilidad, motivo de alegría. || *s.c.* **3** (form.) placer, delicia, deleite, dicha, honor. || *v.t.* e *i.* **4 [to – (in)]** (lit.) alegrarse, regocijarse, deleitarse. **5** gozar de, disfrutar de.

joyful | 'dʒɔɪful | *adj.* (form.) alegre, feliz, jubiloso, gozoso, encantado.

joyfully | 'dʒɔɪfulɪ | *adv.* alegremente, jubilosamente, gozosamente, regocijadamente.

joyless | 'dʒɔɪlɪs | *adj.* **1** triste, sin alegría, compungido. **2** penoso, lúgubre (un acontecimiento).

joyous | 'dʒɔɪəs | *adj.* (lit.) alegre, lleno de entusiasmo, radiante de alegría, exultante.

joyously | 'dʒɔɪəslɪ | *adv.* (lit.) alegremente, gozosamente.

joyride | 'dʒɔɪraɪd | *s.c.* **1** (argot) paseo en coche (generalmente robado). || *v.i.* **2** ir a dar una vuelta en coche (robado).

joystick | 'dʒɔɪstɪk | *s.c.* **1** AER. palanca de mando. **2** palanca (de máquinas de juego).

jubilant | 'dʒuːbɪlənt | *adj.* jubiloso, alborozado (después de un éxito).

jubilation | ˌdʒuːbɪ'leɪʃn | *s.i.* júbilo, alborozo, regocijo.

jubilee | 'dʒuːbɪli | | ˌdʒuːbɪ'liː | *s.c.* **1** aniversario. **2** fiesta de aniversario. **3** júbilo, regocijo. **4** jubileo.

Judaic | dʒuː'deɪɪk | *adj.* judaico.

Judaism | 'dʒuːdeɪɪzəm | | 'dʒuːdəɪzəm | | 'dʒuːdɪzəm | *s.i.* judaísmo.

Judas | 'dʒu:dəs | *s.* **1** Judas (Iscariote). **2** (desp.) judas, traidor, desleal.
judder | 'dʒʌdər | *v.i.* (brit.) vibrar, estremecerse violentamente (un vehículo).
judge | dʒʌdʒ | *v.t.* **1** DER. juzgar. || *v.t.* e *i.* **2** arbitrar, juzgar (una competición). **3** opinar, pensar, decidir, formarse una opinión, considerar, determinar. **4** calcular, evaluar, estimar, conjeturar. || *s.c.* **5** DER. juez. **6** juez, árbitro, jurado (de un concurso, de una competición). **7** conocedor, experto, perito (en un tema). || **8 as far as can be judged/as far as you can judge,** en la medida en que puede ser apreciado. **9 I'll be the – of that/let me be the – of that,** deja que sea yo quien decida, eso lo decidiré yo (en respuesta a consejos que molestan).
judgement, judgment | 'dʒʌdʒmənt | *s.i.* **1** juicio, sensatez, perspicacia, criterio. || *s.c.* **2** opinión, juicio, parecer, criterio. **3** castigo. || *s.c.* e *i.* **4** DER. sentencia, veredicto, fallo, juicio. **5** crítica, enjuiciamiento. || **6 against one's better –,** en contra de la opinión de uno, contra el parecer de uno. **7 to pass –,** dar una opinión, hacer un comentario; DER. juzgar. **8 to reserve –,** reservarse la opinión (hasta tener más datos). **9 to sit in – on/over,** juzgar.
judicial | dʒu:'dɪʃl | *adj.* **1** DER. judicial, legal. **2** sensato, perspicaz.
judicially | dʒu:'dɪʃəlɪ | *adv.* **1** DER. judicialmente, legalmente. **2** perspicazmente.
judiciary | dʒu:'dɪʃɪərɪ | | dʒu:'dɪʃərɪ | *s.sing.* **[the – *v.sing./pl.*]** (form.) el poder judicial, la judicatura.
judicious | dʒu:'dɪʃəs | *adj.* **1** (form.) juicioso, sensato, prudente.
judiciously | dʒu:'dɪʃəslɪ | *adv.* **1** (form.) juiciosamente, sensatamente.
judo | 'dʒu:dəʊ | *s.i.* **1** DEP. judo.
jug | dʒʌg | (EE.UU.) **pitcher** *s.c.* **1** jarra, jaro, vasija, caneca. **2** contenido de una jarra. **3** (argot y arc.) chirona, talego, (Am.) cana. || *v.t.* **4** estofar (generalmente liebre). **5** (argot y arc.) enchironar, meter en el talego.
jugged hare | dʒʌgdheər | *s.i.* estofado de liebre.
juggernaut | 'dʒʌgənɔ:t | | 'dʒʌgərnɔ:t | *s.c.* **1** (brit., fam. y desp.) camión de gran tonelaje. **2** monstruo destructivo, fuerza destructiva. **3** creencia destructiva.
juggle | 'dʒʌgl | *v.t.* e *i.* **1** hacer juegos malabares, hacer malabarismo. **2 [to – (with)]** (fig.) hacer malabarismos, intercambiar, jugar con, barajar (posibilidades). **3** manipular, falsear. || *s.i.* **4** malabarismo, juegos malabares, prestidigitación. **5** engaño, truco, treta. || **6 to – with,** manosear, juguetear nerviosamente con; hacer trampas, falsificar, engañar.
juggler | 'dʒʌglər | *s.c.* **1** malabarista, prestidigitador. **2** impostor, defraudador, tramposo.
jugular | 'dʒʌgjʊlər | *s.c.* **1** ANAT. yugular. || *adj.* **2** yugular, del cuello, de la garganta. || **3 to go for the –,** (fam.) atacar sin piedad, sin miramientos (un argumento, un punto débil).
juice | dʒu:s | *s.i.* **1** zumo, jugo, extracto (de frutas, de carne). **2** (generalmente *pl.*) jugos (gástricos), secreciones. **3** (argot) corriente eléctrica; gasolina; aceite. **4** (argot) licor. **5** (EE.UU. y argot) meollo, miga. || *v.t.* **6** exprimir, sacar (zumos). || **7 to – up,** (EE.UU. y fam.) animar, divertir, suscitar interés, despertar interés. **8 to stew in one's own –,** V. **stew.**
juicy | 'dʒu:sɪ | *adj.* **1** jugoso. **2** (fam.) enjundioso, picante: *a juicy story = una historia picante.* **3** (fam.) apetecible, interesante, suculento, jugoso.
juju | 'dʒu:dʒu: | *s.c.* **1** talismán, amuleto, fetiche. || *s.i.* **2** magia, poder.
jukebox | 'dʒu:kbɒks | | 'dʒu:kbɑ:ks | *s.c.* máquina de discos tragaperras (en bares).
July | dʒu:'laɪ | (abreviatura **Jul**) *s.c.* e *i.* Julio (mes).
jumble | 'dʒʌmbl | *v.t.* **1 [to – (up/ together)]** (generalmente *pas.*) desordenar, mezclar, embarullar, revolver, amontonar en desorden: *the books were jumbled up = los libros estaban amontonados.* **2** embrollar, confundir. || *v.i.* **3** mezclarse, embarullarse, moverse en desorden. || *s.sing.* **4** embrollo, lío, desorden. || *s.i.* **5** (brit.) mezcolanza, revoltijo, montón. || **6 – sale,** (EE.UU.) **rummage sale,** venta de objetos usados, tómbola de caridad.
jumbo | 'dʒʌmbəʊ | *adj.* **1** (fam.) de tamaño gigante, más grande de lo normal (en publicidad): *a jumbo sized packet = un paquete tamaño gigante.* || *s.c.* **2** AER. avión jumbo.
jump | dʒʌmp | *v.i.* **1** dar saltos, brincar. **2** tirarse, arrojarse, saltar. **3** sobresaltarse, asustarse, pegar un bote. **4 [to – *adv./prep.*]** saltar, desviarse, pasarse (de un tema a otro). **5** subir como la espuma, dispararse (los precios, el nivel). **6** ascender de golpe (de posición). **7** coger al vuelo, coger con rapidez. **8** llegar (a una conclusión). || *v.t.* **9** saltar de un lado a otro, cruzar de un salto. **10** (fam.) escapar, fugarse, abandonar (ilegalmente un sitio). **11** (fam.) saltarse, pasarse (un semáforo, una cola). **12** (EE.UU. y fam.) viajar en, saltar a (un tren sin billete). **13** (fam.) atacar por sorpresa. **14** comer (una ficha en el juego de damas). **15** elevar una apuesta (en el bridge). **16** descarrilar, salirse (un tren). || *s.c.* **17** salto, brinco, bote. **18** valla, obstáculo, barrera. **19** salto, desviación (de tema). **20** subida, elevación (de precios, nivel). **21** paso, peldaño (para conseguir algo). **22** etapa, fase (de un viaje). || **23 to – at something,** apresurarse a aceptar algo. **24 to – down somebody's throat,** (fam.) estallar contra alguien, interrumpir a alguien con exabruptos. **25 to – for joy,** saltar de alegría, no caber en sí de gozo. **26 to – the gun,** (fam.) levantar la liebre. **27 to – in,** interrumpir (una conversación). **28 – jet,** avión de despegue vertical. **29 to – on,** (fam.) poner verde, criticar. **30 – leads,** cable auxiliar, cangrejos (para arrancar un vehículo sin batería). **31 – to it!,** ¡date prisa!, ¡muévete! **32 to – up and down,** dar botes (de alegría).
jumped-up | ˌdʒʌmpt'ʌp | *adj.* (brit., fam. y desp.) presuntuoso, pretencioso.
jumper | dʒʌmpər | *s.c.* **1** (brit.) jersey, suéter. **2** (EE.UU.) vestido pichi. **3** saltador.
jumping-off point, jumping-off place | ˌdʒʌmpɪŋ'ɔfˌpɔɪnt | *s.c.* **1** punto de partida. **2** lugar remoto, punto lejano.
jump-suit | 'dʒʌmpsu:t | | 'dʒʌmpsju:t | *s.c.* mono (de paracaidista, de mecánico).
jumpy | 'dʒʌmpɪ | *adj.* nervioso, inquieto, asustadizo.
junction | 'dʒʌŋkʃn | *s.c.* **1** cruce, confluencia (de carreteras). **2** empalme (de vías). **3** conexión, unión. **4** ELECTR. empalme.
juncture | 'dʒʌŋktʃər | *s.c.* **1** coyuntura, punto, momento, ocasión: *at this juncture = en esta coyuntura.* **2** unión, junta, articulación. **3** costura.
June | dʒu:n | *s.i.* Junio.
jungle | 'dʒʌŋgl | *s.c.* e *i.* **1** jungla, selva. **2** (fig.) selva, maraña, lío. || *s.c.* **3** laberinto, embrollo, jaleo. **4** (EE.UU. y argot) campamento, lugar de citas (de jóvenes desocupados).
junior | 'dʒu:njər | *s.c.* **1** menor, joven **2** subordinado, subalterno. **3** (brit.) alumno de primaria. **4** (EE.UU.) alumno de tercer año de secundaria o de Universidad. **5** (EE.UU.) juvenil (talla de ropa para adolescentes). **6** Junior, hijo. || *adj.* **7** menor, joven, juvenil. **8** (EE.UU.) **Junior,** hijo: *James Benn, Jr. = James Benn hijo.* **9** (EE.UU.) alumno de tercer año de secundaria o de Universidad. **10** subordinado, subalterno. || **11 – school,** (brit.) escuela primaria (de 7 a 11 años).
juniper | 'dʒu:nɪpər | *s.c.* e *i.* **1** BOT. enebro, junípero, grojo.
junk | dʒʌŋk | *s.i.* **1** (fam.) cachivaches, trastos viejos, basura. **2** (fam.) chatarra, vidrio o papel usado. **3** baratijas: *a junk shop = una tienda de baratijas.* **4** (argot) psicotrópico, narcótico, droga. **5** bobadas, tonterías, porquería. || *s.c.* **6** NAUT. junco (chino). **7** NAUT. cecina. || *v.t.* **8** deshacerse de trastos viejos, echar cachivaches a la basura. || **9 – food,** (fam.) comida rápida (de mala calidad, tratada químicamente). **10 – mail,** (desp.) correo publicitario (que se mete en buzones).
junket | 'dʒʌŋkɪt | *s.c.* **1** (fam. y desp.) viaje, visita (pagado con fondos públicos o políticos). || *s.i.* **2** cuajada, crema de queso (con frutas, azúcar). || *v.t.* e *i.* **3** hacer fiesta, tener un banquete. **4** agasajar, festejar.
junketing | 'dʒʌŋkətɪŋ | *s.c.* e *i.* **1** (fam.) fiesta, banquete, guateque. **2** diversión, agasajo.
junkie, junky | 'dʒʌŋkɪ | *s.c.* **1** (argot) adicto, colgado, drogata. **2** (fig.) adicto, adepto, devoto.

junta | ˈdʒʌntə | | ˈhuntə | *s.c.* **1** [– *v.sing./pl.*] (desp.) junta militar. **2** asamblea, consejo, cuerpo legislativo (en Centro y Sudamérica). **3** camarilla, facción (política).
jurisdiction | ˌdʒuərɪsˈdɪkʃn | *s.i.* **1** DER. jurisdicción.
jurisprudence | ˌdʒuərɪsˈpruːdəns | *s.i.* **1** (form.) DER. jurisprudencia, doctrina judicial.
jurist | ˈdʒuərɪst | *s.c.* **1** DER. jurista, legista.
juror, juryman | ˈdʒuərər | *f.* **jurywoman** *s.c.* **1** DER. jurado, miembro del jurado.
jury | ˈdʒuərɪ | *s.c.* **1** [– *v.sing./pl.*] DER. jurado (grupo de 12 personas). **2** tribunal examinador. || *adj.* **3** NAUT. provisional, temporal. || **4 – box,** DER. tribuna del jurado.
just | dʒʌst | *adv.* **1** exactamente, precisamente. **2** muy cerca, al lado: *just by the Museum = al lado del Museo.* **3** [– *pret.perfecto*] justamente, en este momento, recién: *he has just left = acaba de irse.* **4** ya, ahora mismo, enseguida: *I'm just coming = ya voy.* **5** simplemente, solamente, ni más ni menos, no más que: *it was just a joke = no era más que una broma.* **6** apenas, escasamente, no más de: *it takes just 2 hours = lleva escasamente dos horas.* **7** [– **may/might /could**] posiblemente, quizás: *just may go = posiblemente vaya.* **8** (fam.) francamente, verdaderamente, sencillamente: *just impossible = sencillamente imposible.* **9** [**can/could –**] fácilmente, sin problema: *I could just see her = la podría imaginar fácilmente.* || *adj.* **10** (form.) justo, imparcial, recto. **11** (form.) correcto, razonable. **12** merecido, adecuado, apropiado (un castigo, una recompensa). **13** legítimo, legal. **14** fundado, justificado, lógico. || **15 just a minute/moment/second!,** ¡espera!, ¡calma!, ¡un minuto! **16 – about,** aproximadamente, poco más o menos, casi. **17 – like/as/the same,** lo mismo, exactamente: *just as your mum told us = exactamente como nos lo dijo tu madre.* **18 – now,** hace un instante, en este momento, ahora mismo. **19 – one's luck,** siempre tiene uno la negra, la mala pata. **20 – so,** (brit. y form.) perfecto, de acuerdo, naturalmente; a gusto de uno, todo en su sitio, ordenadamente. **21 – then,** en aquel preciso momento, justo entonces.
justice | ˈdʒʌstɪs | *s.i.* **1** justicia, equidad, imparcialidad. **2** justicia, sistema legal. **3** legitimidad, rectitud (de una causa, de una reclamación). || *s.c.* **4** (EE.UU.) juez, magistrado. || **5 to bring to –,** llevar ante la ley, capturar y enjuiciar. **6 to do – to,** hacer justicia a, apreciar lo bueno de (una persona, una cosa). **7 to do oneself –,** rendir al máximo dar lo mejor de uno mismo, estar a la altura de las circunstancias.
justifiable | ˈdʒʌstɪfaɪəbl | *adj.* **1** justificable. || **2 – homicide,** DER. homicidio con causa de justificación.
justifiably | ˈdʒʌstɪfaɪəblɪ | *adv.* justificadamente.
justification | ˌdʒʌstɪfɪˈkeɪʃn | *s.i.* **1** justificación, razonamiento. **2** justificación, alineamiento (de márgenes de un escrito). || *s.c.* **3** disculpa, excusa, defensa. || **4 in – of,** en defensa de, como justificación de.
justified | ˈdʒʌstɪfaɪd | *adj.* **1** [– **(in)**] justificado, excusado, disculpado. **2** justificado, razonable, correcto. **3** justificado, alineado (un margen de un escrito).
justify | ˈdʒʌstɪfaɪ | *v.t.* **1** [**to –** *o.* **+** *ger.*] justificar, disculpar, razonar, explicar satisfactoriamente. **2** defender. **3** justificar, alinear (márgenes).
justly | dʒʌstlɪ | *adv.* **1** justamente, con justicia, con imparcialidad. **2** con razón, debidamente, merecidamente.
jut | dʒʌt | *v.i.* **1** [**to –** *adv./prep.*] sobresalir, proyectarse, resaltar. || *s.c.* **2** proyección, prominencia, saliente, vuelo.
jute | dʒuːt | *s.i.* BOT. yute, cáñamo.
jutting | dʒʌtɪŋ | *adj.* prominente, saliente, que sobresale.
juvenile ˈdʒuːvənaɪl | | ˈdʒuːvənəl | *adj.* **1** (no *comp.*) DER. de menores, menor. **2** juvenil, inmaduro. || *s.c.* **3** (form.) joven, menor. **4** cachorro. **5** galán (de cine, de teatro). **6** libro juvenil, libro infantil. || **7 – court,** DER. tribunal de menores. **8 – delinquency,** delincuencia juvenil. **9 – delinquent,** delincuente juvenil.
juxtapose | ˌdʒʌkstəˈpəuz | | ˈdʒʌkstəpəuz | *v.t.* (form.) yuxtaponer.
juxtaposition | ˌdʒʌkstəpəˈzɪʃn | *s.i.* yuxtaposición.

k, K | keɪ | *s.c.* **1** k, K (decimoprimera letra del alfabeto inglés). || *s.sing.* **2** (fam.) abreviatura de 1000; abreviatura de kilo.

kaftan V. **caftan.**

kale | keɪl | (también **kail**) *s.c.* e *i.* BOT. col rizada.

kaleidoscope | kə'ləɪdəskəʊp | *s.c.* caleidoscopio.

kaleidoscopic | kəˌləɪdəs'kɒpɪc | *adj.* caleidoscópico.

kamikaze | kæmɪ'kɑːzɪ | *adj.* kamikaze, suicida (acción): *it was a kamikaze mission = fue una misión suicida.*

kangaroo | 'kæŋgəˌruː | *s.c.* ZOOL. canguro. **2** (fam.) niñera. || **3 – court,** juicio no oficial a un miembro de alguna organización que haya roto las reglas de la misma.

kapok | 'keɪpɒk | *s.i.* capoc (fibra para rellenar cojines, edredones, etc.).

karate | kə'rɑːtɪ | *s.i.* DEP. karate.

karma | 'kɑːmə | *s.i.* (form.) destino.

kayak | 'kaɪæk | *s.c.* kayac (barco pequeño usado por los esquimales).

kebab | kə'bæb | *s.c.* GAST. kebab, pincho moruno.

kedgeree | 'kedʒəriː | *s.i.* GAST. plato de arroz, pescado y huevos.

keel | kiːl | *s.c.* **1** MAR. quilla. || **2 to be/keep on an even –,** (fam.) **a)** MAR. en iguales calados; **b)** (fig.) estabilizado, equilibrado: *it was difficult to keep the situation on an even keel = fue muy difícil mantener la situación equilibrada.* || **3 to – over, a)** zozobrar, dar de quilla; **b)** (fig.) volcarse, desplomarse (persona).

keen | kiːn | *adj.* **1** entusiasta. **2** afilado (filos de cuchillos, etc.). **3** penetrante, glacial (viento). **4** agudo (vista, oído). **5** agudo, perspicaz (comentario). **6** fijo, penetrante (mirada). **7** bajo, competitivo, económico (precios). **8** intenso, con fuerza (competición). **9** grande (interés). **10** intenso, hondo, vivo, pasional (emoción). **11** bueno (apetito). || **12 to be as – as mustard,** ser extraordinariamente entusiasta. **13 to be – on something/someone,** gustar, interesar. **14 to be – to** [*inf.*] tener un vivo deseo de, ansiar.

keenly | 'kiːnlɪ | *adv.* **1** profundamente, intensamente, con fuerza. **2** con entusiasmo (trabajar).

keenness | 'kiːnnɪs | *s.i.* **1** entusiasmo, afición, interés. **2** viveza, agudeza, penetración.

keep | kiːp | *v.* [*pret.* y *p.p. irreg.* **kept**] *t.* **1** guardar. **2** cumplir, guardar (promesa). **3** observar, atenerse (regla). **4** acudir (cita). **5** observar, celebrar, atender (fiesta religiosa). **6** mantener, imponer (orden). **7** tener (animales, servidumbre). **8** criar, ocuparse de la cría de (animales). **9** mantener económicamente. **10** tener, ser propietario de, dirigir (tienda, hotel, negocio). **11** escribir (diario). **12** llevar (cuentas, la casa). **13** poner aparte, reservar. **14** detener. **15** entretener (conversación). || *i.* **16** permanecer, seguir, continuar. || *s.c.* **17** torre del homenaje. **18** mantenimiento, comida, subsistencia. || **19 for keeps,** permanentemente. **20 to – at,** trabajar sin descanso. **21 – at it!,** ¡dale! **22 to – away from,** mantenerse alejado de, mantenerse a distancia; no acudir, no dejarse ver. **23 to – back, a)** hacerse a un lado; **b)** ocultar (información); **c)** contener, reprimir (emoción); **d)** no dejar avanzar (enemigo). **24 to – down, a)** controlar algo, poner medios para que no vaya a más; **b)** agacharse, acurrucarse, bajar la cabeza; **c)** oprimir; **d)** procurar mantener la comida en el estómago para no vomitar. **25 to – from** [+ *ger.*] abstenerse de, guardarse de [+ *inf.*] **26 to – someone from doing something,** impedir a uno hacer algo. **27 to – in,** mantener encerrado, no dejar salir (persona); mantener encendido (fuego); quedar castigado en la escuela. **28 to – in with,** mantener buenas relaciones con, cultivar la amistad de. **29 to – something clean,** conservar limpio. **30 to – off,** mantenerse alejado de; no aludir a un tema determinado. **31 to – on** [+ *ger.*] **a)** continuar; **b)** mantener a uno en un trabajo; **c)** seguir conservando algo; **d)** hablar continuamente. **32 to – one's end up,** defenderse bien. **33 to – one's eyes fixed on something,** tener los ojos puestos en algo. **34 to – one's hand in,** mantenerse en forma. **35 to – one's head,** conservar la sangre fría. **36 to – one's seat,** permanecer sentado, mantener el escaño (parlamentario). **37 to – out,** permanecer fuera. **38 to – out of,** no entrar en (sitio, organización, etc.); no meterse en (asunto); evitar (problema). **39 to – pace,** ir al mismo paso. **40 to – quiet,** no hacer ruido, no decir nada, permanecer callado, callarse. **41 to – to, a)** observar (ley, reglas); **b)** limitarse a algo; **c)** permanecer, guardar (cama). **42 to – oneself to oneself,** evitar el contacto con otros, aislarse. **43 to – under, a)** controlar algo o alguien; **b)** tener a alguien en estado de inconsciencia bajo los efectos de una droga. **44 to – track of,** no perder de vista; seguir la suerte de. **45 to – up,** no rezagarse, mantenerse a la altura. **46 to – up with the times,** mantenerse/estar al día, ir con los tiempos. **47 to – well,** estar bien de salud.

keeper | 'kiːpər | *s.c.* **1** guardián (zoo, campo de juego). **2** custodio (museo, galería de arte). **3** archivero (biblioteca). || **4 finders-keepers,** V. **finder. 5 to be someone's –,** responder por alguien: *I am not my sister's keeper = no respondo por mi hermana.* **6 goal –,** (fam.) portero, guardameta. **7 wicket –,** (fam.) en críquet, el que está situado en los palos. **8 keeper** se añade a algunos sustantivos contables para indicar la persona que está a cargo de algo: *shop-keeper = encargado de la tienda.*

keep-fit | kiːp'fɪt | *s.i.* ejercicio físico.

keeping | 'kiːpɪŋ | *s.i.* **1 to be in – with,** estar de acuerdo con, estar en armonía con. **2 to be in the – of someone,** estar bajo la custodia de alguien. **3 to be in safe –,** estar en lugar seguro, estar en buenas manos. **4 to be out of – with,** estar en desacuerdo con; estar fuera de lugar. **5 to give something to someone for safe –,** dar algo a alguien, para mayor seguridad.

keepsake | 'ki:pseɪk | *s.c.* recuerdo: *he gave me this keepsake so that I don't forget him = me dio este recuerdo para que no me olvide de él.*

keg | keg | *s.c.* **1** barrilete. || *s.i.* **2** cerveza de barril.

ken | ken | (arc.) **1 to be beyond one's –,** ser incomprensible para uno. **2 to be within one's –,** ser comprensible para uno.

kennel | 'kənəl | (también **kennels**) *s.c.* **1** perrera. **2** (fig.) cuchitril. **3** especie de residencia para perros; lugar donde los entrenan.

Kenya | 'kenjə | | 'ki:njə | *s.sing.* Kenia.

Kenyan | 'kenjən | | 'kənjən | *s.c.* keniata.

kept | kept | *pret.* y *p.p.irreg.* de **keep.** *adj.* mantenido: *he was the old woman's kept youth = era el joven mantenido de la anciana.*

kerb | kə:b | *s.c.* **1** bordillo. || **2 – crawling,** la conducción lenta a lo largo de la acera para hablar y alquilar a una prostituta.

kerchief | 'kə:tʃɪf | *s.c.* pañuelo, pañoleta.

kerfuffle | kə'fʌfl | *s.c.* (fam. y brit.) tumulto, confusión.

kernel | 'kə:nl | *s.c.* **1** BOT. almendra. **2** (fig.) meollo, esencia, parte más importante de una cuestión. || **3 a – of truth,** una parte de verdad.

kerosene | 'kerəsɪn | *s.i.* **1** queroseno. || **2 – lamp,** lámpara de petróleo.

kestrel | 'kestrəl | *s.c.* ZOOL. (vulg.) cernícalo.

ketch | ketʃ | *s.c.* MAR. queche (barco de vela de dos mástiles).

ketchup | 'ketʃəp | *s.i.* GAST. salsa de tomate.

kettle | 'ketl | *s.c.* **1** recipiente culinario; tetera. || **2** (fam.) **something is another – of fish/a different – of fish,** no tiene nada que ver; es completamente distinto: *English meals are a different kettle of fish from the Spanish = las comidas inglesas son completamente distintas de las españolas.* **3 a fine/pretty – of fish,** (situación), situación difícil, (vulg.) berenjenal.

kettledrum | 'ketlədrʌm | *s.c.* MUS. timbal.

key | ki: | *s.c.* **1** llave. **2** tecla (piano, máquina de escribir, ordenador, etc.). **3** ELEC. interruptor, llave. **4** TEC. chaveta, cuña. **5** clave (libros, mapas, situación). **6** MUS. tono, tonalidad. || *v.t.* **7** TEC. enchavetear, acuñar. **8** MUS. templar, afinar. || **9 to be all – ed up,** estar emocionadísimo, tener los nervios de punta. **10 to be in –,** estar a tono. **11 to – in,** INF. meter información en el ordenador; teclear el ordenador para obtener una información. **12 to – up,** emocionar. **13 to play off –,** desafinar. **14 under lock and –,** V. **lock.**

keyboard | 'ki:bɔ:d | *s.c.* teclado (en máquina de escribir, música y similares).

keyhole | 'ki:həul | *s.c.* ojo de la cerradura.

keynote | 'ki:nəut | *s.c.* **1** idea fundamental, idea clave. || **2 – speech,** discurso de apertura en que se sientan las bases de un programa político: *the keynote for Conservative policy was acting = la clave para el partido conservador era actuar.*

keyring | 'ki:rɪŋ | *s.c.* llavero.

keystone | 'ki:stəun | *s.c.* **1** piedra base, pilar principal (edificio). **2** (fig.) pilar, base de un proceso: *music was the keystone of his happiness = la música fue la base de su felicidad.*

kg *s.c.* abreviatura de kilogramo.

khaki | 'kɑ:kɪ | *s.i.* **1** tela fuerte de color amarillo marronáceo utilizada para uniformes militares. || *adj.* **2** color caqui.

kibbutz | kɪ'buts | [*pl.* **kibbutzes** o **kibbutzim**] *s.c.* comuna de origen judío instalada en territorio israelí.

kibbutzim | kɪ'butʒəm | *pl.irr.* de **kibbutz.**

kibosh | 'kaɪbɒʃ | **to put the – on something,** acabar con algo definitivamente, arruinar.

kick | kɪk | *s.c.* **1** puntapié, patada; coz (animal). **2** (fig.) reacción. || *v.t.* dar patadas, dar de coces (animal). || *v.i.* **4** dar coces, cocear; recular; (fig.) protestar, quejarse, reaccionar. || **5** (fam.) **to do something for kicks,** hacer algo sólo para divertirse. **6 a drink with a – to it,** una bebida muy fuerte. **7 to get a – out of,** entusiasmar, encontrar placer. **8 to – about,** (fam.) dejar algo abandonado. **9 to – against,** reaccionar violentamente. **10 to – around,** (fam.) **a)** considerar, discutir informalmente (ideas, sugerencias); **b)** abandonar. **11 to – a ball about,** divertirse dando patadas a un balón. **12 to – a ball away,** apartar el balón de una patada. **13 to – in,** romper algo de una patada. **14 to – a man when he's down,** dar a moro muerto gran lanzada. **15 to – off, a)** DEP. lanzar el balón desde el centro del campo al inicio de un partido de fútbol; **b)** (fam.) empezar una conversación, discusión, etc.; **c)** quitarse de una patada (los zapatos). **16 to – one's legs in the air,** agitar las piernas. **17 to – out,** echar, ordenar a alguien que se vaya. **18 to – out against,** reaccionar ante algo. **19 to – someone's bottom,** dar una patada en el culo. **20 to – someone downstairs,** echar a alguien escaleras abajo. **21 to – the bucket,** V. **bucket. 22 to – up, a)** con **fuss,** armar un lío, dar cuatro voces; **b)** levantar nubes (de polvo, arena, etc.).

kickback | 'kɪkbæk | *s.c.* suma de dinero recibida, normalmente de forma ilegal.

kick-off | 'kɪkəf | *s.c.* **1** principio de un partido de fútbol. **2** (brit. y fam.) la hora en la que empieza una fiesta o concierto. || **3 for a –,** para empezar...

kickstart | 'kɪkstərt | (también **kickstarter**) *s.c.* (brit.) palanca de arranque de una motocicleta.

kickstarter | 'kɪkstɑ:rtər | V. **kickstart.**

kid | kɪd | *s.c.* **1** (fam.) niño, chaval. **2** ZOOL. cabrito, chivo. **3** GAST. carne de cabrito. | *v.t.* **4** (fam.) tomar el pelo. || *v.i.* **5** bromear, no hablar en serio. || **6 to – oneself,** engañarse a sí mismo, vivir engañado. **7** (fam.) **I – you not,** sinceramente, honestamente. **8** (fam.) **no kidding,** ser sincero. || *adj.* **9** de piel de cabritillo usada para hacer guantes: *kid gloves = guantes de piel.* **10 to treat/to handle someone with – gloves,** tratar a alguien con sumo cuidado.

kiddie | 'kɪdɪ | *s.c.* (fam.) niño muy pequeño.

kidnap | 'kɪd,næp | *v.t.* secuestrar, raptar.

kidnapper | 'kɪd,næpər | *s.c.* secuestrador.

kidnapping | 'kɪdnæpɪŋ | *s.c.* secuestro, rapto.

kidney | 'kɪdnɪ | *s.c.* **1** FISIOL. riñón. **2** ZOOL. vísceras de los animales. || **3 – bean,** BOT. judía blanca. **4 – machine,** MED. riñón artificial.

kill | kɪl | *v.t.* **1** matar, dar muerte a, asesinar. **2** (fig.) acabar con (rumor, dolor, pena, engaño). **3** (fig.) acabar con (rumor, dolor, pena, engaño). **3** (fig.) destruir (sentimiento, esperanza). **4** (fig.) quitar (sabor, gusto). **5** (fig.) parar (máquina, motor, luz). || **6 to be dressed to –,** vestir con mucha elegancia para impresionar a alguien. **7 to be in at the –,** presenciar algo desagradable. **8 to come/move/close in for the –,** dar el golpe final, rematar, bien figuradamente, bien en el sentido de rematar a un animal. **9 something – or cure,** en una situación extrema, el hallazgo de alguna solución que puede resolverla, o acabar con ella definitivamente. **10 to – the goose that lays the golden eggs,** matar la gallina de los huevos de oro. **12 to – someone with kindness,** tratar a alguien con tanto cuidado, con tanta amabilidad que llega a molestar; (brit.) niños que están consentidos. **13 to – off,** matar, exterminar. **14 to – with laughter,** morirse de risa. **14 to – time,** matar el tiempo. **15 to – two birds with one stone,** matar dos pájaros de un tiro.

killer | 'kɪlər | *s.c.* **1** asesino. **2** cualquier sustancia, animal o situación destructora. || **3 – instinct,** instinto asesino. **4 – whale,** ZOOL. orca (ballena blanca y negra).

killing | 'kɪlɪŋ | *s.c.* **1** asesinato, matanza. || *adj.* **2** extremadamente gracioso, hilarante. || **3 to make a –,** tener un gran éxito financiero.

killingly | 'kɪlɪŋlɪ | *adv.* **1 – funny,** graciosísimo, divertidísimo. **2 to be – funny,** para morirse de risa.

killjoy | 'kɪldʒɔɪ | *s.c.* aguafiestas.

kiln | kɪln | *s.c.* horno.

kilo | 'ki:ləu | *s.c.* kilogramo, kilo.

kilogram | 'kɪləgrəm | *s.c.* kilogramo.

kilohertz | 'kɪləhə:tz | [*pl.* **kilohertz**] *s.c.* kilohercio.

kilometre | 'kɪləmi:tər | (EE.UU. **kilometer**) *s.c.* kilómetro.

kilowatt | 'kɪləwɒt | *s.c.* kilowatio.
kilt | kɪlt | *s.c.* **1** falda escocesa confeccionada con tartán. || **2 kilted regiment,** regimiento escocés en la armada británica, cuyo uniforme lleva incluido la típica falda escocesa.
kimono | kɪ'məunəu | *s.c.* quimono.
kin | kɪn | *s.c.* **1** familia, parentela, pariente. || **2 to be no – to,** no estar emparentado con. **3 kith and –,** (arc.) familiares y amigos. **4 next of –,** pariente más próximo.
kind | kaɪnd | *s.c.* **1** clase, género, especie, variedad. || *adj.* **2** amable, bondadoso, bueno. **3** buena (acción). **4** benigno (clima). **5** elogioso, comprensivo, favorable (crítica, apreciación, palabras). **6** cariñoso, dulce, tierno (tono de voz). **7** bueno, blando (tratamiento). || **8 all kinds of,** toda clase de. **9 and all that – of things,** y cosas por el estilo. **10 to be – enough, to** [+ *inf.*], tener la amabilidad de. **11 to be – to someone,** ser amable con alguien. **12 a – of,** uno a modo de, más o menos: *he's a kind of a doctor = es algo así como un médico.* **13 to do something in –,** responder del mismo modo: *I waved my hand to say goodbye, and my brother answered in kind = dije adiós con la mano y mi hermano respondió de igual forma.* **14 to pay in –,** pagar en especie; (fig.) pagar con la misma moneda.
kindergarten | 'kɪndəgɑːtən | *s.c.* jardín de infancia.
kind-hearted | 'kaɪnd,hɑːtɪd | *adj.* bondadoso, de buen corazón.
kind-heartedly | 'kaɪnd,hɑːtɪdlɪ | *adv.* bondadosamente.
kind-heartedness | 'kaɪnd'hɑːtɪdnɪs | *s.i.* bondad.
kindle | 'kɪndl | *v.t.* **1** encender (fuego). **2** inspirar, encender (emoción, sentimiento). || *v.i.* **3** encenderse.
kindliness | 'kaɪndlɪnɪs | *s.i.* bondad, benevolencia.
kindling | 'kaɪndlɪŋ | *s.c.* leña menuda, astillas.
kindly | 'kaɪndlɪ | *adj.* **1** bondadoso, benévolo. **2** benigno (clima). **3** elogioso, comprensivo (crítica, comentario, etc.). **4** cariñoso, dulce (tono de voz). || *adv.* **5** bondadosamente, amablemente. || **6 to ask someone to – do something,** pedírselo por favor, de buenas maneras, amablemente. **7 to look – on/upon,** aprobar, mirar con buenos ojos. **8 to think – of,** tener buena opinión de, gustar. **9 to take – to something,** aceptar de buen grado.
kindness | 'kaɪndnɪs | *s.i.* **1** amabilidad, bondad, benevolencia, atención, consideración. || *s.c.* **2** favor. || **3 to do someone a –,** hacer un favor a alguien.
kindred | 'kɪndrɪd | *s.i.* **1** parentesco, lazos familiares. || *adj.* **2** emparentado. **3** semejante, análogo, afín. || **4 – spirits,** espíritus afines.
kinetic | kɪ'netɪk | *adj.* **1** cinético. || **2 – art,** esculturas con partes móviles. **3 – energy,** FIS. energía cinética.
kinetically | kɪnə'tɪkəlɪ | *adv.* cinéticamente, con movimiento.
kinetics | kɪ'netɪks | *s.i.* FIS. cinética (parte de la física que estudia el movimiento).
king | kɪŋ | *s.c.* **1** rey. **2** rey (ajedrez, cartas). || **3 to describe someone as a –,** tratarle como al miembro más destacado de un grupo: *Elvis Presley is the king of rock and roll = Elvis Presley es el rey del rock and roll.* **4 to live like a –,** vivir a cuerpo de rey.
kingcup | 'kɪŋkʌp | *s.c.* BOT. botón de oro.
kingdom | 'kɪŋdəm | *s.c.* **1** reino. **2** (fig.) dominio, feudo de alguien o algún grupo concreto, partido, etc. || **3 animal –,** reino animal, mundo animal. **4 plant –,** reino, mundo vegetal.
kingfisher | 'kɪŋfɪʃər | *s.c.* ZOOL. martín pescador (pájaro).
kingly | 'kɪŋlɪ | *adj.* real, regio; digno de un rey.
kingpin | 'kɪŋpɪn | *s.c.* **1** TEC. perno, pinzote. **2** (fig.) piedra angular. **3** (fig.) personaje principal, cosa fundamental.
kingship | 'kɪŋʃɪp | *s.i.* dignidad real, monarquía.
king-size | 'kɪŋsaɪz | *adj.* de tamaño extra.
kink | kɪŋk | *s.c.* **1** coca, enroscadura (cuerda). **2** rizo (pelo). **3** arruga, pliegue (papel, tela, etc.). **4** (fig.) peculiaridad, manía. **5** perversión (sexual).
kinky | 'kɪŋkɪ | *adj.* **1** enroscado, rizado, ensortijado, arrugado. **2** (fig.) peculiar (personalidad). **3** pervertido (sexualmente).
kinship | 'kɪnʃɪp | *s.i.* **1** parentesco. **2** (fig.) afinidad, relación estrecha, relación íntima.
kinsman | 'kɪnzmən | [*pl.irreg.* **kinsmen**] *s.c.* (arc.) pariente.
kinsmen | 'kɪnzmən | *pl.irreg.* de **kinsman.**
kinswoman | 'kɪns,wumən | [*pl.irreg.* **kinswomen**] *s.c.* parienta.
kinswomen | 'kɪns,wɪmɪn | *pl.irreg.* de **kinswoman.**
kiosk | 'kiːɒsk | *s.c.* **1** quiosco. **2** (brit.) cabina de teléfono.
kip | kɪp | (fam.) *s.c.* **1** alojamiento, cama, sueño. || *v.i.* **2** dormir. || **3 to have a –,** dormir un rato. **4 to – down,** echarse a dormir.
kipper | 'kɪpər | *s.c.* ZOOL. arenque ahumado.
kirk | kəːk | *s.c.* **1** iglesia (Escocia). **2 the Kirk,** la Iglesia Presbiteriana escocesa.
kirsh | kɪəʃ | *s.i.* GAST. bebida alcohólica hecha de cereza y que suele servirse después de las comidas.
kiss | kɪs | *s.c.* **1** beso. **2** roce (toque ligero). || *v.t.* **3** besar. || *v.i.* **4** besarse. || **5 to blow someone a –,** tirar un beso. **6 to – and be friends,** hacer las paces. **7 to – hands,** (brit.) besamanos real cuando una figura gubernamental toma posesión de su cargo. **8 – of death,** (fig.) el beso de la muerte, acabar de estropear algo. **9 – of life,** respiración boca a boca; (fig.) impulso vital. **10 to – the book,** besar la Biblia en un juramento. **11 to – the rod,** aceptar un castigo sin rechistar. **12 to – the dust/ground,** aceptar un reto.
kisser | 'kɪsər | *s.c.* **1** persona que besa. **2** (fam.) boca.
kissproof | 'kiːspruːf | *adj.* indeleble.
kit | kɪt | *s.c.* **1** avíos, equipaje. **2** herramientas, instrumental. **3** botiquín (de primeros auxilios). **4** MIL. equipo. || **5 to – someone out,** equipar a uno.
kitbag | 'kɪtbæg | *s.c.* **1** saco de viaje. **2** MIL. saco, macuto.
kitchen | 'kɪtʃɪn | *s.c.* **1** cocina. || **2 – garden,** huerto. **3 – range,** cocina económica; fogón. **4 – sink,** fregadero. **5 – play,** obra ultrarrealista con los bajos fondos como tema. **6 to take something except/but the –,** coger muchas cosas, incluso las menos necesarias.
kitchenette | 'kɪtʃɪnet | *s.c.* **1** cocina pequeña. **2** parte de una habitación que se usa para cocinar.
kitchenware | ,kitʃɪn'weər | *s.c.* batería de cocina.
kite | kaɪt | *s.c.* **1** cometa (juguete). **2** ZOOL. milano real. || **3 to fly a –,** (fig.) lanzar una idea para sondear la opinión.
kith | kɪθ | (arc.) **– and kin,** parientes y amigos.
kitten | 'kɪtn | *s.c.* **1** gatito. || **2 to have kittens,** (brit.) estar muy nervioso.
kittenish | 'kɪtənɪʃ | *adj.* picaruelo, coquetón.
kittiwake | 'kɪtɪweɪk | *s.c.* gaviota tridáctila, gavina.
kitty | 'kɪtɪ | *s.c.* **1** colecta. **2** fondos de una apuesta. || **3 kitty,** apelativo cariñoso a un gato.
kiwi | 'kiːwɪ | *s.c.* **1** BOT. kiwi. || **2 kiwis,** (fam.) neozelandeses.
klaxon | 'klæksən | *s.c.* bocina, claxon.
Kleenex | 'kliːneks | *s.c.* [*pl.* **kleenex**] marca registrada de unos pañuelos de papel.
kleptomania | ,kleptə'meɪnɪə | *s.i.* cleptomanía.
kleptomaniac | ,kleptə'meɪnɪæk | *s.c.* cleptómano.
knack | næk | *s.i.* **1** talento, maña, destreza, truco. || **2 it's just a –,** es un truco que se aprende. **3 to get the – of doing something,** aprender el modo de hacer algo. **4 to have the – of doing something,** tener el don de hacer algo. **5 to have the right – of saying the right thing,** acertar siempre con la palabra exacta.
knacker | 'nækər | *s.c.* (brit.) **1** matarife de caballos. **2** persona que vende cosas usadas y de desecho.
knackered | 'nækəd | *adj.* (fam.) agotado, exhausto.
knapsack | 'næpsæk | *s.c.* mochila.
knave | neɪv | *s.c.* **1** bellaco, bribón. **2** valet, sota (cartas).
knavery | 'neɪvərɪ | *s.i.* bellaquería, bribonería.
knead | niːd | *v.t.* **1** amasar, sobar. **2** dar masajes.
knee | niː | *s.c.* **1** rodilla || *v.t.* **2** dar un rodillazo. || **3 on bended knees, on one's knees,** de rodillas. **4 to bow the – to,** humillarse ante, someterse a. **5 to bring someone to his knees,** someter a uno, humillar. **6 to fall on one's knees,** arrodi-

llarse, caer de rodillas. **7 to go down on one's knees to someone,** implorar a alguien de rodillas. **8 -- breeches,** calzón corto.

kneecap | ˌniːˌkæp | *s.c.* ANAT. **1** rótula. || **2 to – someone,** disparar a alguien en las rodillas para que tenga que arrastrarse.

kneedeep | 'niːˌdiːp | *adj.* **1** hasta las rodillas, al nivel de las rodillas. || **2 to be – in,** estar metido hasta las rodillas. **3 to go into the water –,** avanzar hasta que el agua llegue a las rodillas.

knee-high | ˌniː'haɪ | *adj.* que llega hasta las rodillas, hasta la altura de las rodillas de un adulto; levantar un palmo del suelo: *she could speak before she was knee-high = ya hablaba antes de levantar un palmo del suelo.*

kneel | niːl | *v.* [*pret.* y *p.p.irreg.* **knelt**] *i.* **1** arrodillarse, ponerse de rodillas, hincarse de rodillas. || **2 to – to,** hincar la rodilla ante. || **3** *adj.* **keeling,** arrodillado.

kneepad | 'niːpæd | *s.c.* rodillera.

knees-up | 'niːsʌp | [también **knees-ups**] *s.c.* (fam. y brit.) fiesta o celebración.

knell | nel | *s.c.* toque de difuntos.

knelt | nelt | *pret.* y *p.p.irreg.* de **kneel.**

knew | njuː | *pret.irreg.* de **know.**

knickerbockers | 'nɪkəbɒkəz | *s.pl.* pantalones cortos.

knickers | 'nɪkəz | *s.pl.* **1** bragas de señora. || **2 to be getting one's – in a twist,** (fam.) empezar a enfadarse, empezar a estar triste. **3 –!** (vulg.) exclamación de desacuerdo.

knick-knack | 'nɪknæk | *s.c.* chuchería, baratija.

knife | naɪf | [*pl.* **knives**] *s.c.* **1** cuchillo, navaja. **2** MEC. cuchilla. || *v.t.* acuchillar. || **4 before one can say –,** en un amén Jesús. **5 (to be) the knives out,** existir una tirantez manifiesta entre dos o más personas. **6 carving –,** trinchante. **7 flick –,** navaja automática. **8 to have one's – into someone,** tener inquina a uno. **9 jack –,** navaja. **10 – and fork,** cubierto (en la mesa). **11 palette –,** espátula. **12 pen –,** navaja. **13 paper –,** abrecartas. **14 pocket –,** navaja. **15 to twist/turn the – in the wound,** hurgar en la herida, en el sentido de recordar algo desagradable. **16 war to the –,** guerra a muerte.

knife-box | 'naɪfbɒks | *s.c.* portacubiertos.

knife-edge | 'naɪfedʒ | *s.c.* **1** filo (de un cuchillo). || **2 to be balanced on a –,** (fig.) estar pendiente de un hilo.

knife-grinder | 'naɪfˌgraɪndər | *s.c.* amolador, afilador.

knifing | 'naɪfɪŋ | *s.c.* puñalada, acuchillamiento.

knight | naɪf | *s.c.* **1** caballero. **2** caballo (ajedrez). || *v.t.* **3** HIST. armar caballero. **4** (brit.) dar el título de Sir a alguien.

knight-errant | ˌnaɪf'erənt | *s.c.* caballero andante.

knight-errantry | ˌnaɪt'erəntrɪ | *s.i.* caballería andante.

knighthood | 'naɪthʊd | *s.c.* **1** orden de caballería. **2** título de caballero. **3** (brit.) título de Sir.

knightly | 'naɪtlɪ | *adj.* caballeroso, caballeresco.

knit | nɪt | *v.t.* **1** hacer punto de aguja. **2** hacer calceta. **3** fruncir (el ceño). **4** soldarse (huesos). **5** (fig.) unirse. || **6 to – together,** juntar, unir. **7 to – up,** tejer algo en su totalidad.

knitted | 'nɪtɪd | *adj.* **1** de punto. || **2 – goods,** géneros de punto.

knitter | 'nɪtər | *s.c.* tejedora, persona que hace calceta.

knitting | 'nɪtɪŋ | *s.c.* **1** labor de punto. || **2 – machine,** máquina de tricotar. **3 – needle,** aguja de hacer punto. || **4 plain –,** punto de media.

knitwear | 'nɪtweər | *s.i.* géneros de punto.

knives | 'naɪvz | *pl.* de **knife.**

knob | nɒb | *s.c.* **1** protuberancia, bulto. **2** MEC. botón, interruptor. **3** tirador (puerta). **4** puño (bastón). || **5 – of sugar,** terrón de azúcar.

knobbly | 'nɒblɪ | *adj.* nudoso.

knobby | 'nɒbɪ | *adj.* (EE.UU.) nudoso.

knock | nɒk | *v.t.* **1** golpear. **2** chocar contra. **3** (fam.) criticar, denigrar, hablar mal de. **4** hacer publicidad en contra de algo. || *v.i.* **5** llamar a la puerta. **6** golpear, martillear. || *s.c.* **7** golpe. **8** choque (colisión). **9** llamada (puerta). || **10 to be knocking on,** (fam.) ir para (edad): *she is knocking on 40 = va para los cuarenta.* **11 to get a –,** recibir un golpe. **12 to get the –,** (vulg.) mosquearse, ofenderse, perder la paciencia, ponerse negro. **13 to – about/around, a)** vagabundear, andar vagando, rodar; **b)** ver mundo, vivir experiencias; **c)** ser amigo de, salir con; **d)** discutir, comentar (idea). **14 to – back, a)** (fam.) beberse de un trago; costar (precio). **15 to – against,** chocar contra, dar contra. **16 to – the bottom out of a box,** desfondar una caja. **17 to – down, a)** derribar, demoler, echar abajo (edificio); **b)** derribar (persona); **c)** atropellar (peatón); **d)** destruir (argumento); rebajar (precio). **18 to – a hole in something,** abrir a la fuerza un agujero en algo. **19 to – in, a)** hacer entrar a golpes; **b)** clavar (clavo). **20 to – into, a)** chocar contra; **b)** topar (persona). **21 to – off, a)** quitar de un golpe; **b)** hacer caer; **c)** (vulg.) birlar, limpiar, mangar; **d)** (vulg.) detener, arrestar; **e)** ejecutar prontamente, despachar (tarea); **f)** terminar, suspender, salir de (trabajo). **22 to – the price off,** rebajar el precio. **23 to – the smile off someone's face,** hacer que uno deje de sonreír a fuerza de golpes. **24 – it off!,** (fam.) ¡déjalo! **25 to – out, a)** dejar sin sentido, hacer perder el conocimiento (persona); **b)** poner fuera de combate (boxeo); **c)** romper (dientes); **d)** suprimir, quitar. **26 to – over, a)** volcar; **b)** atropellar (peatón). **27 to – together,** construir, componer deprisa. **28 to – up, a)** construir toscamente, deprisa (edificio); **b)** llamar, despertar; **c)** agotar; **d)** (vulg. y EE.UU.) dejar encinta; **e)** pelotear (tenis). **29 to – up against,** chocar contra; topar (persona).

knockabout | 'nɒkəbaʊt | *adj.* **1** bullicioso, tumultuoso, confuso. || **2 – comedy,** farsa bulliciosa; (fig.) payasada.

knockdown | 'nɒkdaʊn | *adj.* **1** baratísimo, de regalo (precio). **2** (fam.) poderoso, convincente (razonamiento, argumento).

knocker | 'nɒkər | *s.c.* **1** aldaba. **2** (fam.) detractor, crítico. || **3 woman's knockers,** (vulg.) senos de una mujer.

knocker-up | 'nɒkərˌʌp | *s.c.* (fam.) despertador.

knocking | 'nɒkɪŋ | *s.c.* **1** golpe. **2** llamada (puerta), golpeo. || **3 – copy,** anuncio destinado a denigrar un producto.

knock-kneed | ˌnɒk'niːd | *adj.* **1** patizambo. **2** (fig.) débil, irresoluto.

knock-knees | ˌnɒk'niːz | *s.pl.* piernas patizambas.

knock-on | 'nɒkən | *adj.* secundario (efecto, acción).

knockout | 'nɒkəʊt | *s.c.* **1** fuera de combate (boxeo). **2** concurso eliminatorio, eliminatoria (competición). **3 to be a –,** ser estupendo, atractivo. || **4 – blow,** golpe aplastante.

knock-up | 'nɒkʌp | *s.c.* peloteo (tenis, badminton, squash).

knoll | nəʊl | *s.c.* otero, montículo.

knot | nɒt | *s.c.* **1** nudo. **2** lazo (pajarita). **3** grupo, corrillo (gente). **4** MAR. nudo. || *v.t.* **5** anudar, atar; (fig.) tener un nudo en el estómago. || *v.i.* **6** anudarse. || **7 to get tied up in knots, a)** anudarse, enmarañarse; **b)** (fig.) crearse confusiones, armarse un lío. **8 get knoted!** (fam.) ¡fastidiate! **9 to tie a –,** hacer un nudo. **10 to travel, move, etc., at a rate of knots,** viajar, moverse, etc., muy deprisa.

knot-hole | 'nɒthəʊl | *s.c.* agujero que deja un nudo en la madera.

knotty | 'nɒtɪ | *adj.* **1** nudoso. **2** (fig.) difícil, complicado (pregunta, problema).

knout | nəʊt | *s.c.* knut (clase de látigo usado en Rusia para castigar a la gente).

know | nəʊ | *v.* [*pret.* **knew** y *p.p.irr.* **known**] *t.* e *i.* **1** saber, conocer. **2** reconocer. **3** hablar un idioma: *do you know French? = ¿hablas francés?* || **4 as far as I –,** tal como tengo entendido, por lo que yo sé. **5 as we – it,** tal como se sabe. **6 to be in the –,** estar enterado, conocer. **7 to get to – someone,** encontrar y conocer casualmente a alguien. **8 Heaven/God/Christ knows,** (vulg.) ¡Dios sabe! **9 how was I to –,** ¡cómo lo iba a saber! **10 I don't – about you,** no sé tú... **11 I'm blessed/damned if I –!,** ¡que me mate si lo sé! **12 to – best,** tener el máximo conocimiento gracias a la experiencia adquirida. **13 to – better than,** conocer mejor que, saber más que. **14 to – how to do something,** saber hacer algo gracias a un conocimiento y una práctica previa. **15 to – someone by sight,** conocer a alguien de vista. **16 to – someone by his walk,** conocer por la forma de andar. **17 you never –/one never knows,** nunca se sabe. **18 not that I – of,** forma enfática de negar. **19 you don't –,** no te imaginas:

you don't know how glad I am to see you = no te imaginas lo contento que estoy de verte. **20 you –,** (muletilla utilizada en conversación, y sin una traducción concreta) podría traducirse por: ¿sabes?, ¿me sigues?, ¿no?, etc. **21 you – what I mean,** sabes lo que quiero decir, sabes a lo que me refiero.
knowable | 'nəʊəbəl | *adj.* conocible.
know-all | nəʊɔːl | *s.c.* sabelotodo.
know-how | 'nəʊˌhəʊ | *s.i.* **1** habilidad, destreza. **2** experiencia. **3** pericia.
knowing | 'nəʊɪŋ | *adj.* **1** astuto, avispado. **2** malicioso (mirada). || **3 worth –,** digno de saberse.
knowingly | 'nəʊɪŋlɪ | *adv.* **1** a sabiendas, adrede. **2** maliciosamente, con malicia.
know-it-all | 'nəʊɪtɔːl | *s.c.* (EE.UU.) sabelotodo.
knowledge | 'nɒlɪdʒ | *s.i.* **1** información, conocimiento, saber. **2** erudición, ciencia. || **3 to have a working – of,** dominar los principios esenciales de. **4 to have a thorough – of,** conocer a fondo. **5 it is common – that,** se sabe con certeza que. **6 not to my –,** no que yo sepa. **7 to my –,** según mi leal entender y saber. **8 without my –,** sin saberlo yo.
knowledgeable | ˌnɒ'lɪ'dʒəbl | *adj.* entendido, erudito.
known | nəʊn | *p.p.* **1** de **know.** || *adj.* **2** conocido, reconocido. || **3 to be well –,** ser conocido en todas partes. **4 to become –,** llegar a saberse (hecho); llegar a ser conocido (persona). **5 to make something – to someone,** anunciar algo a alguien, hacer que uno se entere de algo.
knuckle | 'nʌkl | *s.c.* **1** nudillo (mano). || **2 to – down to something,** ponerse a hacer algo con ahínco, dedicarse a algo en serio. **3 near the –,** ser rudas, ofensivas (palabras, acciones). **4 to – under,** someterse. **5 to rap someone's knuckles/ to rap someone over the knuckles,** V. **rap.**
knuckleduster | 'nʌklˌdʌstər | *s.c.* puño de hierro.
knurl | nəːl | *s.c.* **1** nudo, protuberancia. **2** moleteado (moneda). || *v.t.* **3** moletear (moneda).
knurled | nəːld | *adj.* **1** nudoso. **2** moleteado (moneda).
KO | keɪəʊ | *s.c.* abreviatura de **knock out,** fuera de combate.
koala | kəʊ'ɑːlə | *s.c.* ZOOL. koala (tipo de oso australiano).
kohl | kəʊl | *s.i.* cosmético usado por las mujeres del Este para oscurecer los párpados.
Koran | kɒːr'ɑːn | *s.sing.* REL. El Corán (libro sagrado de los islámicos).
Koranic | kɒ'rænɪk | *adj.* coránico.
Korea | kəriːə | *s.sing.* Corea.
Korean | kə'riːən | *adj.* coreano.
kosher | 'kəʊʃər | *adj.* **1** autorizado por la ley judía. **2** (fam.) propio, correcto, honesto: *there's nothing kosher about it, don't worry = no hay nada deshonesto en ello, no te preocupes.*
kow-tow | ˌkaʊ'təʊ | *v.i.* saludar humildemente. || **2 to – to someone,** humillarse ante uno.
kraal | krɑːl | *s.c.* **1** tipo de pueblo en Africa formado por cabañas rodeadas de verjas. **2** en Sudáfrica, pedazo de tierra cercada para criar vacas, ovejas, etc.
Kremlin | 'kremlɪn | *s.c.* POL. Kremlin; organismo gubernamental soviético.
kris | krɪs | *s.c.* cuchillo con el filo curvado usado en Malasia e Indonesia como arma.
krona | 'krəʊnə | *s.c.* corona (moneda) danesa y noruega.
krugerrand | kruːgərænd | *s.c.* moneda de oro sudafricana que se compra como inversión.
kudos | 'kjuːdɒs | *s.i.* (esp. brit.) mérito, gloria, prestigio.
Ku Klux Klan | ˌkuːklʌks'klæn | *s.i.* (EE.UU.) organización política secreta racial.
kuk-ri | 'kukrɪ | *s.c.* tipo de cuchillo curvo usado en Nepal.
kumis | 'kuːmɪs | *s.i.* bebida alcohólica hecha de leche de yegua por los tártaros.
kümmel | 'kuməl | *s.i.* GAST. en Alemania, bebida alcohólica hecha de plantas y que se sirve después de las comidas.
kumquat | 'kʌmkwɒt | *s.c.* BOT. fruto pequeño parecido a la naranja.
Kung Fu | ˌkʌŋ'fuː | *s.i.* DEP. tipo de lucha china en la que sólo se usan pies y manos.
Kuwait | kʊ'weɪt | (EE.UU.) | kʊ'waɪt | *s.sing.* Kuwait.
Kuwaiti | kʊ'weɪtɪ |(EE.UU.)| kʊ'waɪtɪ | *s.c.* **1** kuwaití. || *adj.* **2** kuwaití.
kwashiorkor | ˌkwɒʃɪ'ɔːkər | *s.i.* MED. enfermedad tropical producida por la falta de alimentación.

l, L | el | *s.c.* l, L (duodécima letra del alfabeto inglés).
lab | læb | *s.c.* (fam.) laboratorio.
label | 'leɪbl | *s.c.* **1** etiqueta, rótulo. **2** sello discográfico. || *v.t.* **3** etiquetar. **4** **[to – as]** tachar de: *he was labelled as a demagogue = lo tacharon de demagogo.*
labia | 'leɪbɪə | *s.pl.* ANAT. labios (del aparato genital femenino).
labial | 'leɪbjəl | *adj.* FON. labial.
labiate | 'leɪbɪeɪt | *adj.* BOT. labiado.
labiodental | ˌleɪbɪəʊ'dentl | FON. *adj.* **1** labiodental. || *s.c.* **2** labiodental.
labionasal | ˌleɪbɪəʊ'neɪzl | FON. *adj.* **1** labionasal. || *s.c.* **2** labionasal.
labiovelar | ˌleɪbɪəʊ'viːlər | FON. *adj.* **1** labiovelar. || *s.c.* **2** labiovelar.
laboratory | lə'bɒrətərɪ | *s.c.* laboratorio.
laborious | lə'bɔːrɪəs | *adj.* laborioso, arduo, duro.
laboriously | lə'bɔːrɪəslɪ | *adv.* laboriosamente.
laboriousness | lə'bɔːrɪəsnɪs | *s.i.* diligencia, laboriosidad.
labour | 'leɪbər | (EE.UU. **labor**) *s.i.* **1** trabajo, tarea, labor, faena. || *v.i.* **2** trabajar con ahínco, esforzarse. **3** avanzar con dificultad, costar: *the old man laboured up the hill = al viejo le costaba subir la colina.* **4** **[to – under]** actuar bajo, tener (una falsa impresión, engaño): *he laboured under the misapprehension that... = tenía la falsa impresión de que...* **5** insistir, abundar en detalles. || **6 a – of love,** trabajo hecho con gusto. **7 to be in –,** estar de parto. **8 hard –,** trabajos forzados. **9 – force,** población en edad laboral, asalariados de una empresa. **10 – market,** ECON. mercado de trabajo. **11 – pains,** dolores de parto. **12 – union,** (EE.UU.) sindicato de trabajadores. **13 the Labor Party,** el partido laborista. **14 the labors of Hercules,** los trabajos de Hércules.
laboured | 'leɪbəd | *adj.* **1** dificultoso (respiración). **2** poco ágil (estilo literario).
labourer | 'leɪbərər | *s.c.* peón, bracero.
labour-intensive | 'leɪbərɪnˌtensɪv | *adj.* que emplea mucha mano de obra.
labour-saving | 'leɪbəˌseɪvɪŋ | *adj.* que ahorra trabajo o esfuerzo.
laburnum | lə'bɜːnəm | *s.c.* BOT. codeso.
labyrinth | 'læbərɪnθ | *s.c.* laberinto.
labyrinthine | læbə'rɪnθɪn | *adj.* laberíntico.
lace | leɪs | *s.c.* **1** cordón (de zapato). || *s.i.* **2** encaje, puntilla. || *v.t.* **3** atar (los cordones de los zapatos). **4** **[to – (with)]** añadir (licor a bebidas): *he always laces his coffee with brandy = siempre añade coñac al café.* || **5** **[to – up],** atar los cordones (de los zapatos, botas, etc.):*he laced up his shoes = se ató los zapatos.*
lacerate | 'læsəreɪt | *v.t.* **1** lacerar, magullar. **2** (fig.) herir (sentimientos).
laceration | læsə'reɪʃn | *s.c.* laceración, herida.
lace-ups | 'leɪsʌps | *s.pl.* (fam.) zapatos de cordón.
lachrymose | 'lækrɪməʊs | *adj.* (lit.) propenso a las lágrimas, llorón.
lack | læk | *s.i.* **1** carencia, falta, escasez, privación: *lack of money.* || *v.t.* **2** carecer: *the book lacks interest = el libro carece de interés.* || *v.i.* **3** **[to – in]** carecer de, faltar: *he lacks in courage = le falta valor.* || **4 for/through – of something,** debido a la falta de... **5 no – of something,** abundancia de algo.
lackadaisical | ˌlækə'deɪzɪkl | *adj.* falto de interés, indolente.
lackadaisically | ˌlækə'deɪzɪklɪ | *adv.* con falta de interés, con desgana, lánguidamente.
lackey | 'lækɪ | *s.c.* (desp.) lacayo.
lacking | 'lækɪŋ | *adj.* **1** **[to – in]** carente de. **2** (p.u.) torpe, corto.
lacklustre | 'læklʌstər | (EE.UU. **lackluster**) *adj.* apagado, carente de brillo.
laconic | lə'kɒnɪk | *adj.* lacónico, conciso, de pocas palabras.
laconically | lə'kɒnɪkəlɪ | *adv.* lacónicamente.
lacquer | 'lækər | *s.i.* **=f** laca. || *v.t.* **2** lacar.
lacquered | 'lækəd | *adj.* lacado.
lacrosse | lə'krɒs | *s.i.* DEP. juego de pelota de Canadá, en el que los contendientes recogen y lanzan la pelota con un palo provisto de una pequeña red.
lactation | læk'teɪʃn | *s.i.* secreción de leche, lactancia.
lactic acid | 'læktɪkˌæsɪd | *s.i.* QUIM. ácido láctico.
lactose | 'læktəʊs | *s.i.* azúcar láctea.
lacuna | lə'kjuːnə | [*pl.* **lacunae** o **lacunas**] *s.c.* (form.) omisión, laguna (en un manuscrito, libro, discurso, etc.).
lacy | 'leɪsɪ | *adj.* **1** de encaje: *a pretty lacy dress = un bonito vestido de encaje.* **2** (fig.) delicado (similar al encaje): *lacy white flowers = flores blancas delicadas.*
lad | læd | *s.c.* **1** (fam.) muchacho, chaval. || **2 lads** (fam.) muchachos (como grupo o equipo que comparte intereses): *the lads won = el equipo ganó.*
ladder | 'lædər | *s.c.* **=f** escalera de mano. **2** escala social. **3** carrera (en las medias). **4** ANTR. escala, estadio (en la cadena evolutiva). || *v.t.* **5** romper, hacerse carreras (en las medias).
laddie | 'lædɪ | *s.c.* (fam.) muchacho, chaval (Escocia).
laden | 'leɪdn | *adj.* **[– with]** lleno, repleto, cargado de: *laden with fruit.*
la-di-da | lɑːdɪ'dɑː | *adj.* **1** (desp.) afectado, pretencioso. || *adv.* **2** (desp.) afectadamente: *she speaks so la-di-da... = habla tan afectadamente...*
ladle | 'leɪdl | *s.c.* **1** cucharón, cacillo. || *v.t.* **2** servir (sopa).
lady | 'leɪdɪ | *s.c.* **1** señora, dama: *an American lady.* **2** (título nobiliario): *Lady Jane.* || **3 Ladies and Gentlemen,**

señoras y señores. **4 ladies' man,** mujeriego. **5 ladies' room/the ladies,** lavabo de señoras. **6 – friend,** (arc.) amiga, novia. **7 Lady Muck,** (desp.) mandona, engreída. **8 – novelist/doctor,** etc., una novelista, una doctora. **9 lady's maid,** (arc.) camarera, sirvienta. **10 Our Lady,** REL. Nuestra Señora, la Virgen. **11 young –,** señorita.
ladybird | 'leɪdɪbɜːd | *s.c.* ZOOL. mariquita.
lady-in-waiting | ˌleɪdɪɪn'weɪtɪŋ | *s.c.* dama de honor.
lady-killer | 'leɪdɪkɪlər | *s.c.* mujeriego, tenorio.
ladylike | 'leɪdɪlaɪk | *adj.* **1** fino, educado (referido a una mujer.): *she's got ladylike manners = posee finos modales.* **2** afeminado (referido a un hombre.).
ladyship | 'leɪdɪʃɪp | *s.c.* señoría (tratamiento de damas nobles).
lag | læg | *v.i.* **1 [to – behind]** quedarse atrás, rezagarse: *he lagged behind = se quedó atrás.* **2** descender (en producción). || *v.t.* **3** revestir, proteger (tuberías, depósitos, techos... para ahorrar energía). || *s.c.* **4** (fam.) presidiario reincidente. || **5 time –,** intervalo de tiempo.
lager | 'lɑːgər | *s.i.* cerveza (ligera y clara).
laggard | 'lægəd | *s.c.* (desp.) vago, remolón, perezoso.
lagging | 'lægɪŋ | *s.i.* aislante, revestimiento (tuberías, techos...).
lagoon | lə'guːn | *s.c.* laguna.
laid | leɪd | V. **lay.**
laid-back | 'leɪdbæk | *adj.* tranquilo, sosegado.
lain | leɪn | V. **lie.**
lair | leər | *s.c.* **1** cueva, madriguera, cubil. **2** (fig.) guarida, lugar de retiro: *he retreated to his lair to read = se retiró a su guarida para leer.*
laird | leəd | *s.c.* terrateniente, hacendado (Escocia).
laissez-faire | ˌleɪseɪ'feər | *s.i.* **1** política de libertades. || *adj.* **2** liberal.
laity | 'leɪɪtɪ | *s.i.* **1** REL. laicado. **2** legos (ajenos a una profesión).
lake | leɪk | *s.c.* lago.
lakeside | 'leɪksaɪd | *s.c.* orilla, ribera de un lago.
lam | læm | *v.t.* **1** golpear, pegar. || *v.i.* **2** (EE.UU.) (fam.) largarse, tomar las de Villadiego. || **3 on the –,** huido, escapado (especialmente de la policía).
lama | 'lɑːmə | *s.c.* lama (monje budista).
lamb | læm | *s.c.* **1** cordero. || *s.i.* **2** carne de cordero. || **3 – chops,** chuletas de cordero. **4 like a lamb,** dócil, sumiso, obediente.
lambing | 'læmɪŋ | *s.c.* época de parir las ovejas: *spring is the lambing season = la primavera es la estación en que paren las ovejas.*
lambskin | 'læmskɪn | *s.i.* piel de cordero.
lamb's-wool | 'læmzwul | *s.i.* lana de oveja.
lambaste | læm'beɪst | *v.t.* (fam.) **1** zurrar, dar una tunda. **2** reprender, regañar, cantar las cuarenta.
lambency | 'læmbənsɪ | *s.i.* brillo tenue, brillo suave (especialmente de las llamas).
lambent | 'læmbənt | (form.) *adj.* **1** de brillo suave (las llamas). **2** suavemente brillante (ojos, cielo, etc.). **3** suave, fácil (humor, carácter, estilo, etc.).
lame | leɪm | *adj.* **1** cojo. **2** débil, inconsistente (argumentación, excusa).
lamé | 'lɑːmeɪ | *s.i.* lamé.
lame-duck | 'leɪmˌdʌk | *s.c.* **1** incapaz, inútil. **2** (EE.UU.) cesante (funcionario). **3** diputado no reelegido.
lamely | 'leɪmlɪ | *adv.* débilmente, sin convicción.
lameness | 'leɪmnɪs | *s.i.* **1** cojera. **2** debilidad, inconsistencia (de una argumentación, excusa).
lament | lə'ment | *v.t.* e *i.* **1** lamentar, lamentarse. || *s.c.* **2** lamento, canto elegíaco.
lamentable | lə'mentəbl | *adj.* lamentable, deplorable.
lamentably | lə'mentəblɪ | *adv.* lamentablemente.
lamentation | 'læmenˌteɪʃn | *s.c.* lamentación.
lamented | lə'mentɪd | *adj.* llorado: *our lamented brother = nuestro llorado hermano.*
laminate | 'læmɪneɪt | *v.t.* **1** laminar. || | 'læmɪnət | *adj.* **2** laminado.
laminated | 'læmɪneɪtɪd | *adj.* laminado.
lamp | læmp | *s.c.* lámpara.
lamplight | 'læmplaɪt | *s.i.* luz (de lámpara).
lamplit | 'læmplɪt | *adj.* iluminado.
lampoon | læm'puːn | *s.c.* **1** sátira, libelo, invectiva. || *v.t.* **2** satirizar.
lamp-post | 'læmppəust | *s.c.* farola.
lamprey | 'læmprɪ | *s.c.* ZOOL. lamprea.
lampshade | 'læmpʃeɪd | *s.c.* pantalla (de lámpara).
lance | lɑːns | *v.t.* **1** MED. punzar (un absceso). || *s.c.* **2** lanza. **3** MED. lanceta. || **4 – corporal,** MIL. cabo interino.
lancer | 'lɑːnsər | *s.c.* MIL. lancero.
lancet | 'lɑːnsɪt | *s.c.* MED. bisturí.
land | lænd | *s.i.* **1** tierra (en contraste con mar). **2** tierra de labor. || *s.c.* **3** terreno, hacienda, solar. **4** (lit.) patria. **5** *v.i.* aterrizar, poner pie en tierra. || *v.t.* **6** (fam.) llevar (a una situación difícil): *that would land him in jail = eso le llevaría a la cárcel.* **7** (fam.) golpear, dar un puñetazo. || **8 – mass,** gran extensión de tierra, continente. **9 to – on one's feet,** caer de pie, tener suerte. **10 – reform,** reforma agraria, redistribución de la tierra. **11 – registry,** registro de propiedad rústica, catastro. **12 lands,** tierras de una zona o región. **13 to see how the – lies,** tantear el terreno.
land-agent | 'lændeɪdʒənt | *s.c.* (brit.) administrador (de fincas o similar).
land-breeze | 'lændbriːz | *s.sing.* terral, brisa (que sopla de la tierra al mar por la noche).
landau | 'lændɔː | *s.c.* landó.
landed | 'lændɪd | *adj.* **1** terrateniente, hacendado, que posee terrenos. || **2 – gentry,** terratenientes.
landfall | 'lændfɔːl | *s.c.* recalada, llegada a tierra.
land-holder | 'lændhəuldər | *s.c.* hacendado, propietario de tierras.
landing | 'lændɪŋ | *s.c.* **1** rellano. **2** aterrizaje. **3** plataforma de embarco o desembarco. **4** MIL. desembarco de tropas.
landing-craft | 'lændɪŋkræft | *s.c.* MAR. lancha de desembarco.
landing-stage | 'lændɪŋsteɪdʒ | *s.c.* embarcadero flotante.
landing-strip | 'lændɪŋstrɪp | *s.c.* pista de despegue o aterrizaje.
landlady | 'lændˌleɪdɪ | *s.c.* **1** patrona. **2** propietaria. **3** encargada.
landless | 'lændlɪs | *adj* desposeído, sin tierras.
landlessness | 'lændlɪsnɪs | *s.i.* carencia de tierras, de recursos.
landlocked | 'lændlɒkt | *adj.* cercado, rodeado de tierra, sin salida al mar.
landlord | 'lændlɔːd | *s.c.* **1** dueño. **2** propietario. **3** encargado.
landlubber | 'lændˌlʌbər | *s.c.* MAR. (fam.) marinero de agua dulce.
landmark | 'lændmɑːk | *s.c.* señal, mojón, punto de referencia, hito.
landmine | 'lændmaɪn | *s.c.* artefacto explosivo, mina.
landowner | 'lændˌəunər | *s.c.* terrateniente.
landowning | 'lændˌəunɪŋ | *adj.* terrateniente.
landscape | 'lænskeɪp *s.c.* **1** paisaje, vista. || *v.t.* **2** ajardinar. || **3 – architect,** arquitecto paisajista. **4 – gardener,** jardinero paisajista.
landscaping | 'lænsˌkeɪpɪŋ | *s.i.* área ajardinada.
landslide | 'lændslaɪd | *s.c.* **1** corrimiento de tierra, avalancha. **2** victoria electoral abrumadora.
landslip | 'lændslɪp | *s.c.* pequeña avalancha.
landsman | 'lændzmən | [*pl.* **landsmen**] *s.c.* persona de tierra firme (no marinero).
landward | 'lændwəd | *adj.* orientado a tierra, cercano a tierra.
lane | leɪn | *s.c.* **1** senda. **2** carril (de calzada). **3** calle (de piscina). **4** AER./MAR. ruta aérea o marítima.
language | 'læŋgwɪdʒ | *s.c.* **1** lengua, idioma. **2** lenguaje (el específico de una disciplina, de un grupo o el inarticulado). **3** INF. código, sistema de un lenguaje de máquina. || **4 – laboratory,** laboratorio de idiomas. **5 to talk/speak the same –,** tener las mismas ideas u opiniones.
languid | 'læŋgwɪd | *adj.* (lit.) lánguido, indolente, perezoso.
languidly | 'læŋgwɪdlɪ *adv.* (lit.) lánguidamente.
languish | 'læŋgwɪʃ | *v.i.* **1** languidecer, soportar (una situación adversa). **2 [to – (for)]** suspirar por.

languishing | 'læŋgwɪʃɪŋ | *adj.* lánguido, sentimental.
languor | 'læŋgər | *s.i.* (lit.) languidez, indolencia.
languorous | 'læŋgərəs | *adj.* (lit.) indolente, sentimental.
languorously | 'læŋgərəslɪ | *adv.* (lit.) indolentemente, sentimentalmente.
lank | læŋk | *adj.* **1** lacio (cabello). **2** alto y delgado.
lankiness | 'læŋkɪnɪs | *s.i.* delgadez suma.
lanky | 'læŋkɪ | *adj.* larguirucho, desgarbado.
lanolin | 'lænəlɪn | (también **lanoline**) *s.i.* lanolina.
lantern | 'læntən | *s.c.* **1** farol, linterna. || **2 – jaws,** cara chupada, quijada larga.
lanthanum | 'lænθənəm | *s.i.* QUIM. lantano.
lanyard | 'lænjəd | *s.c.* acollador.
Laos | 'lɑːɒs | *s.* Laos.
Laotian | 'lauʃɪən | *adj.* laosiano.
lap | læp | *s.c.* **1** regazo, seno. **2** doblez (de un vestido). **3** etapa. **4** DEP. vuelta (en un circuito). || *v.t.* **5** doblar, ganar una vuelta. **6** beber (como un gato). || *v.i.* **7 [to – (against)]** (lit.) chapotear contra, bañar, lamer: *the waves lapped against the shore = las olas chapoteaban contra la costa.* || **8 in the – of luxury,** nadar en la abundancia. **9 in the – of the gods,** sólo Dios lo sabe. **10 – of honour,** DEP. vuelta de honor. **11 to – up,** beber ávidamente, disfrutar, tragarse.
lap-dog | 'læpdɒg | *s.c.* perrito faldero.
lapel | lə'pel | *s.c.* solapa.
lapidary | 'læpɪdərɪ | (form.) *s.c.* **1** lapidario, cortador/pulidor de piedras. || *adj.* **2** lapidario; conciso.
lapis lazuli | ˌlæpɪs'læzjuli | *s.i.* lapislázuli.
lapping | 'læpɪŋ | *s.i.* chapotear suave (del mar).
lapse | læps | *s.c.* **1** error, lapsus, olvido momentáneo. **2** espacio temporal. **3** (fig.) desliz (de conducta). || *v.i.* **4 [to – (into)]** sumirse en, descender gradualmente en actividad: *he lapsed into silence = se sumió en el silencio.* **5** pasar, transcurrir (el tiempo). **6** (desp.) incurrir en falta. **7** DER. prescribir, caducar. **8** REL. abandonar (práctica religiosa).
lapsed | læpst | *adj.* **1** REL. no practicante. **2** DER. caducado, prescrito.
lapwing | 'læpwɪŋ | *s.c.* ZOOL. avefría.
larcenous | 'lɑːsənəs | *adj.* DER. de hurto: *a larcenous crime = un delito de hurto.*
larceny | 'lɑːsənɪ | *s.i.* DER. **1** hurto, robo. || **2 petty –,** pequeño robo.
larch | lɑːtʃ | *s.c.* BOT. alerce.
lard | lɑːd | *s.i.* **1** manteca (de cerdo). || *v.t.* **2** mechar. **3 [to – (with)]** (fig.) entreverar, salpicar de (un discurso o escrito).
larder | 'lɑːdər | *s.c.* **=f** despensa. || **2 to raid the –,** (fam.) asaltar la despensa.
large | lɑːdʒ | *adj.* **1** grande, voluminoso, abundante. **2** serio (problema). || **3 as – as life,** en persona. **4 at –,** libre, sin control, en general. **5 to be larger than life,** ser excesivo, exagerado. **6 by and –,** en términos generales.
largely | 'lɑːdʒlɪ | *adv.* principalmente.
largeness | 'lɑːdʒnɪs | *s.i.* **1** tamaño, grosor. **2** (fig.) amplitud (de mente).
large-scale | 'lɑːdʒˌskeɪl | *adj.* a gran escala, masivo.
largesse | lɑː'dʒes | *s.i.* generosidad, largueza.
largish | 'lɑːdʒɪʃ | *adj.* bastante grande.
largo | 'lɑːgəu | MUS. *s.c.* **1** largo. || *adj.* y *adv.* **2** largo.
lariat | 'lærɪət | *s.c.* (EE.UU.) lazo (para coger animales).
lark | lɑːk | *s.c.* **1** ZOOL. alondra. **2** (fam.) broma, travesura. **3** (fam.) juerga. || **4 to get up with the –,** levantarse con el alba.
larkspur | 'lɑːkspəːr | *s.c.* BOT. consólida real, espuela de caballero.
larva | 'lɑːvə | *s.c.* ZOOL. larva.
larval | 'lɑːvl | *adj.* **1** ZOOL. larval. **2** MED. larvado.
laryngitis | ˌlærɪn'dʒaɪtɪs | *s.i.* MED. laringitis.
larynx | 'lærɪŋks | [*pl.* **larynges**] *s.c.* ANAT. laringe.
lasagne | lə'zænjə | *s.i.* GAST. lasaña (un tipo de pasta fina italiana).
lascivious | lə'sɪvɪəs | *adj.* lascivo, lujurioso.
lasciviously | lə'sɪvɪəslɪ | *adv.* lascivamente.
lasciviousness | lə'sɪvɪəsnɪs | *s.i.* lascivia, lujuria.
laser | 'leɪzəər | *s.c.* láser: *laser beam = rayo láser.*
lash | læʃ | *s.c.* **1** látigo, tralla. **2** azote, latigazo. **3** coletazo. **4** golpe (de viento, mar). **5** (fig.) sarcasmo. **6** ANAT. pestaña. **7** MAR. amarra. || *v.t.* **8** azotar, dar latigazos. **9** atar. **10** (fig.) fustigar, reprender. **11** MAR. amarrar. || *v.i.* **12** sacudir, chocar (viento, olas...). **13 [to – down]** caer con fuerza (lluvia, granizo). **14 [to – out]** soltar coces.
lashing | 'læʃɪŋ | *s.c.* **1** flagelación, azotes. **2** atadura. **3** gran cantidad, montones: *lashings of... = montones de...*
lass | læs | *s.c.* (fam.) chica, muchacha, novia.
lassie | 'læsɪ | *s.c.* (fam.) chica, jovencita (Escocia).
lassitude | 'læsɪtjuːd | *s.i.* lasitud, abandono, pereza.
lasso | læ'suː | *s.c.* lazo (para atrapar animales).
last | lɑːst | *adj.* **1** último, final. **2** pasado: *last week = la semana pasada.* || *adv.* **3** en último lugar, el último: *he arrived last.* **4** por última vez: *I last saw her in London = la vi por última vez en Londres.* **5** finalmente, por último: *and last we went home = por último se fue a casa.* || *s.c.* **6** el último, el resto, lo último. **7** horma (de zapato). || *v.i.* **8** durar. **9** alcanzar, llegarle a uno. **10** resistir. || **11 at –,** por fin. **12 at long –,** al fin, al fin y al cabo. **13 at the –,** por fin. **14 to breath one's –,** expirar, exhalar el último suspiro. **15 every –,** todos y cada uno. **16 if it is the – thing one does,** por costoso que sea. **17 – but not least,** por último y no menos importante. **18 – but one,** penúltimo. **19 – in first out,** los últimos en entrar salen los primeros (en reajustes de plantilla). **20 – rites,** últimos sacramentos. **21 – thing,** lo último. **22 to leave someone or something till –,** dejarlo para el final. **23 to look one's –,** mirar por última vez. **24 not to have heard the – of,** se volverá a oír hablar de, trae cola. **25 to see the – of someone,** ver a alguien por última vez. **26 stick to your –,** ¡zapatero, a tus zapatos! **27 the – I/he/she... heard,** de acuerdo con la última información. **28 the – of the month,** el último día del mes. **29 the month/year before –,** hace dos meses/años. **30 to the –,** hasta el final. **31 to the – degree,** al máximo. **32 to the – man/detail...,** hasta el último hombre/detalle...
last-ditch | 'lɑːstˌdɪtʃ | *adj.* último, desesperado.
lasting | 'lɑːstɪŋ | *adj.* duradero, constante, profundo.
lastly | 'lɑːstlɪ | *adv.* finalmente, por último.
last-minute | 'lɑːstˌmɪnɪt | *adj.* de última hora, el más reciente.
latch | lætʃ | *s.c.* **1** picaporte, pestillo. || *v.t.* **2** cerrar con picaporte. || **3 on the –/off the –,** estar cerrado con/sin picaporte.
latchkey | 'lætʃkiː | *s.c.* **1** llave de picaporte. || **2 – child,** (arc.) niño que posee llave de casa (para entrar y salir mientras sus padres están fuera).
late | leɪt | *adj.* **1** tardío, retrasado. **2** de fines de. **3** reciente. **4** ex, antiguo: *the late Prime Minister = el ex primer Ministro.* **5** fallecido, difunto: *her late husband.* || *adv.* **6** tarde. **7** al final de. || **8 as – as,** todavía en. **9 – in the day,** tarde. **10 of –,** últimamente, recientemente.
latecomer | 'leɪtkʌmər | *s.c.* rezagado, recién llegado.
lately | 'leɪtlɪ | *adv.* recientemente, últimamente, hace poco.
late-night | 'leɪtˌnaɪt | *adj.* nocturno, de últimas horas de la noche.
latent | 'leɪtənt | *adj.* latente, escondido, implícito.
later | 'leɪtər | (*comp.* de **late**) *adj.* **=f** posterior. || *adv.* **2** más tarde, después.
lateral | 'lætərəl | *adj.* **1** lateral. || **2 – thinking,** proceso indirecto de pensamiento.
laterally | 'lætərəlɪ | *adv.* lateralmente.
laterite 'lætəraɪt | *s.i.* GEOL. laterita.
latest | 'leɪtɪst | (*super.* de **late**) *adj.* **1** último, el más reciente. || **2 at the –,** como muy tarde, no después.
latex | 'leɪteks | *s.i.* látex.
lath | lɑːθ | *s.i.* listón, soporte.
lathe | leɪθ | *s.c.* MEC. torno.
lather | 'lɑːθər | *s.c.* **=f** espuma, jabonadura. **2** sudor (de caballo). || *v.i.* **3** hacer espuma. || *v.t.* **4** enjabonar. || **5 to be in a –,** estar muy molesto y confuso.
Latin | 'lætɪn | *s.i.* **1** latín. || *s.c. adj.* **2** latino.

Latin American | 'lætɪn ə'merɪkən | *adj. s.c.* latinoamericano.
Latinist | 'lætɪnɪst | *s.c.* latinista.
latitude | 'lætɪtjuːd | *s.c.* **1** GEOG. latitud. || *s.i.* **2** libertad de acción.
latitudinal | ˌlætɪ'tjuːdɪnl | *adj.* latitudinal.
latitudinarian | ˌlætɪtjuːdɪ'neərɪən | *s.c.* (form.) latitudinario, amplio de miras.
latrine | lə'triːn | *s.c.* letrina.
latter | 'lætər | *adj.* =**f** posterior, más reciente. **2** segundo, último. || **3** *the former... the –, = aquél... éste.*
latter-day | 'lætəˌdeɪ | *adj.* moderno, de nuestros días.
latterly | 'lætəlɪ | *adv.* últimamente, recientemente.
lattice | 'lætɪs | *s.c.* **1** rejilla, celosía, estructura geométrica. || **2 – window,** ventana de cristales emplomados.
latticed | 'lætɪst | *adj.* enrejado, con celosías.
latticework | 'lætɪsˌwəːk | *s.i.* enrejado, celosía.
laud | lɔːd | *v.t.* (arc.) loar, alabar.
laudable | 'lɔːdəbl | *adj.* loable, encomiable, admirable.
laudably | 'lɔːdəblɪ | *adv.* admirablemente, encomiablemente.
laudanum | 'lɒdnəm | *s.i.* QUIM. láudano.
laudatory | 'lɔːdətərɪ | *adj.* elogioso, laudatorio, encomiástico.
laugh | lɑːf | *v.i.* **1** reír. **2 [to – (at)]** reírse de. || *s.c.* **3** risa, carcajada. || **4 a –/a good –/a bit of a –,** cosa de broma. **5 to be laughing,** mostrar regocijo. **6 to be laughing all the way to the bank,** estar haciéndose de oro. **7 to be laughing on the other side of one's face,** pasar de la risa al llanto. **8 for a –/for laughs,** para diversión. **9 to get/raise a –,** provocar risa, hilaridad. **10 to have a –,** tomar a broma. **11 to have the last –,** reír el último. **12 he who laughs last laughs longest,** el que ríe el último ríe mejor. **13 to – loud/to – out loud,** reírse a carcajadas. **14 to – one's head off,** partirse de risa. **15 to – up one's sleeve,** reírse para los adentros. **16 to make one –,** dar risa. **17 not to know whether to – or to cry,** no saber si reír o llorar. **18 you have (got) to –,** hay que tomarlo a risa.
laughable | 'lɑːfəbl | *adj.* divertido, regocijante.
laughing-gas | 'lɑːfɪŋˌgæs | *s.i.* QUIM. gas hilarante.
laughingly | 'lɑːfɪŋlɪ | *adv.* riendo, entre risas.
laughing-stock | 'lɑːfɪŋˌstɒk | *s.c.* hazmerreír.
laughter | 'lɑːftər | *s.c.* carcajada, risa, hilaridad.
launch | lɔːntʃ | *v.t.* **1** lanzar, enviar. **2** iniciar, emprender. **3** botar (un barco). || *v.i.* **4 [to – (out into)]** lanzarse a, aventurarse en. || *s.c.* **5** botadura (de un barco). **6** MAR. lancha, chalupa.
launching-pad | 'lɔːntʃɪŋˌpæd | *s.c.* plataforma de lanzamiento.
launder | 'lɔːndər | *v.t.* lavar y planchar.
launderette | ˌlɔːndə'rət | *s.c.* lavandería automática.
laundress | 'lɔːndrɪs | *s.c.* lavandera.
laundry | 'lɔːndrɪ | *s.c.* **1** lavandería. || *s.i.* **2** (fam.) ropa lavada o por lavar.
laurel | 'lɒrəl | *s.i.* **1** laurel. || **2 to be resting on one's laurels,** dormirse en los laureles. **3 laurels,** (fig.) laureles, honores, victoria.
lava | 'lɑːvə | *s.i.* lava.
lavatory | 'lævətərɪ | *s.c.* **1** lavabo, retrete, servicios. || **2 – paper,** papel higiénico.
lavender | 'lævəndər | *s.i.* =**f** BOT. espliego, lavanda. || *adj.* **2** azul, color de lavanda. || **3 – water,** agua de lavanda.
lavish | 'lævɪʃ | *adj.* **1** pródigo, generoso. **2** abundante, copioso. || *v.t.* **3** dar a manos llenas, malgastar, derrochar.
law | lɔː | *s.c.* **1** ley. **2** norma, regla, reglamento. || *s.i.* **3** derecho, jurisprudencia. || **4 a – onto oneself,** una ley a la medida de uno. **5 to go to –,** poner un pleito. **6 to have the – on,** pleitear contra. **7 – and order,** orden público. **8 to lay down the –,** hablar con autoridad por creerse en posesión de la verdad. **9 someone's word is –,** su palabra es ley. **10 to take the – into one's own hands,** tomarse la justicia por su mano.
law-abiding | 'lɔːəˌbaɪdɪŋ | *adj.* observante, cumplidor de la ley, probo.
law-breaker | 'lɔːˌbreɪkər | *s.c.* infractor de la ley.
law-breaking | 'lɔːˌbreɪkɪŋ | *s.i.* infracción de la ley.
law-court | 'lɔːˌkɔːt | *s.c.* juzgado, audiencia, tribunal de justicia.
law-enforcement | 'lɔːɪnˌfɔːsmənt | *s.i.* (EE.UU.) imperio, peso de la ley.
law-ful | 'lɔːful | *adj.* lícito, legal, legítimo, conforme a derecho.
lawfully | 'lɔːfəlɪ | *adv.* legalmente, legítimamente.
lawless | 'lɔːlɪs | *adj.* sin ley, incontrolado, ingobernable.
lawlessly | 'lɔːlɪslɪ | *adv.* ingobernablemente, incontroladamente, sin hacer caso caso a las leyes.
lawlessness | 'lɔːlɪsnɪs | *s.i.* ausencia de ley, anarquía, arbitrariedad.
lawmaker | 'lɔːmeɪkər | *s.c.* POL. legislador.
lawn | lɔːn | *s.i.* **1** césped. || **2 – tennis,** tenis sobre hierba.
lawnmower | 'lɔːnˌməuər | *s.c.* segadora de césped, cortacésped.
lawsuit | 'lɔːsuːt | *s.c.* DER. pleito, litigio, litis, proceso judicial.
lawyer | 'lɔːjər | *s.c.* abogado.
lax | læks | *adj.* **1** negligente, descuidado, laxo. **2** MED. descompuesto.
laxative | 'læksətɪv | *adj.* laxante.
laxity | 'læksɪtɪ | *s.i.* **1** negligencia, descuido, relajamiento. **2** MED. colitis, descomposición.
laxly | 'lækslɪ | *adv.* negligentemente, descuidadamente, de manera laxa.
lay | leɪ | v. **[laid, laid]** *t.* **1** poner, colocar, tender. **2** poner, disponer, preparar (la mesa, el fuego). **3** despejar, disipar, asentar (el polvo). **4** poner (huevos). **5 [to – (on)]** apostar dinero en. **6** reducir, llevar (a una situación anímica determinada). **7** formular (reclamación, acusación, juicio de valor...). **8** cargar (impuestos, obligaciones). **9** cubrir, recubrir (superficies). **10** colorear, poner pintura (en lienzo). **11** (vulg.) ligar, follar. **12** MIL. poner, sembrar de (minas). || *i.* **13** poner huevos (aves). || *s.c.* **14** posición. **15** balada. **16** (vulg.) ligue. || *adj.* **17** lego, profano. || **18 to – about,** atacar salvajemente: *he laid about the burglars with a club = atacó salvajemente a los ladrones con un garrote.* **19 to – a curse,** amenazar con castigos. **20 to – a finger on,** molestar, maltratar. **21 to – a ghost, a)** librarse de un fantasma. **b)** (fig.) calmar los ánimos. **22 to – aside, a)** reservar, ahorrar: *she laid aside a few pounds out of her wages = ahorró unas libras de su sueldo.* **b)** suspender (prácticas, planes...): *they had to lay aside their plans because of the rain = tuvieron que suspender los planes a causa de la lluvia.* **23 to – claim to,** formular una reclamación de propiedad. **24 to – down, a)** tirar, dejar caer (armas). **b)** poner (los cimientos de un edificio). **c)** declarar, afirmar expresamente: *it is laid down in the law = se afirma expresamente en la ley.* **25 to – emphasis on,** poner énfasis en. **26 to – eyes on,** ver, echar la vista a. **27 to – hold of,** agarrar. **28 to – in,** almacenar (provisiones): *the little ant laid in food supplies = la hormiguita almacenaba provisiones.* **29 to – into,** atacar (física, verbal o figuradamente): *he laid into the cake =* (fig.) *atacó la tarta.* **30 to – off, a)** despedir (empleados temporalmente). **b)** (fam.) dejar, quitarse de (malos hábitos o actitudes). **31 to – on, a)** proporcionar, agasajar: *they laid on a huge meal for the authorities = agasajaron con un banquete a las autoridades.* **b)** cargar, depositar (responsabilidad): *it was a lot to lay on one person = demasiada responsabilidad para cargar en una persona.* **c)** (fam.) exagerar, alabar en demasía. **32 to – oneself open to,** estar expuesto a. **33 to – open, a)** revelar, descubrir: *He laid the plan open = reveló el plan.* **b)** abrir una herida: *he got his head laid open = le abrieron una herida en la cabeza.* **34 to – one's hands on,** adueñarse de. **35 to – out, a)** extender: *she laid out the map.* **b)** proyectar, diseñar (edificios, ciudades...): *the house was laid out again = proyectaron de nuevo la casa.* **c)** amortajar (un cadáver). **d)** dejar inconsciente a golpes: *he was laid out with a blow to the head = lo dejaron inconsciente de un golpe en la cabeza.* **36 to – something at the door of,** cargar el mochuelo a alguien. **37 to – the blame,** acusar. **38 to – up, a)** guardar para el futuro. **b)** retener (en casa o cama): *the flu laid him up for a week = la gripe lo retuvo en cama una semana.* **c)** dejar de usar (algo que necesita reparación): *he laid up his car to have it checked = dejó el coche para que lo revisaran.*

layabout | ˈleɪəˌbaʊt | *s.c.* (fam.) vago, gandul, haragán.
layaway | ˈleɪəweɪ | *s.i.* (EE.UU.) compra en reserva (pagando sólo parte del precio).
lay-by | ˈleɪbaɪ | *s.c.* área de descanso (en carreteras, autopistas).
layer | ˈleɪər | *s.c.* **=f** capa, veta. **2** ponedora (gallina). **3** instalador, montador (de materiales, objetos). **4** GEOL. estrato. **5** AGR. acodo.
layered | ˈleɪəd | *adj.* veteado, a capas o estratos, estratificado.
layette | leɪˈet | *s.c.* canastilla, ajuar (de recién nacido).
layman | ˈleɪmən | *s.c.* **1** profano, no experto. **2** REL. lego.
layoff | ˈleɪof | *s.c.* despido (por escasez de trabajo).
layout | ˈleɪaʊt | *s.c.* **1** trazado, disposición. **2** formato, diseño.
lay-over | ˈleɪəʊvər | *s.c.* (EE.UU.) parada.
laze | leɪz | *v.i.* holgar, descansar, holgazanear.
lazily | ˈleɪzɪlɪ | *adv.* perezosamente.
laziness | ˈleɪzɪnɪs | *s.i.* pereza, indolencia, vagancia.
lazy | ˈleɪzɪ | *adj.* **1** perezoso, vago, indolente. **2** dedicado a ocio: *a lazy afternoon = una tarde dedicada al ocio.* **3** lento, pausado.
lazybones | ˈleɪzɪˌbəʊnz | *s.c.* (fam.) holgazán, vago.
lead | liːd | *s.c.* **1** guía, dirección, iniciativa, mando. **2 [to – (over)]** ventaja sobre. **3** papel de protagonista. **4** cadena, correa (para controlar un perro). **5** mano, salida (en juegos). **6** pista (de información). **7** ELEC. conductor eléctrico principal. || *adj.* **8** principal, destacado, sobresaliente. || *v.* **[led, led]** *t.* **9** guiar, conducir. **10** inducir. **11** llevar (un tipo de vida determinado). || *i.* **12** abrir camino, guiar. **13** capitanear, dirigir. **14** ser mano (juego de naipes). **15** DEP. ganar, llevar la delantera. || **16 in the –,** a la cabeza. **17 to – astray,** pervertir, llevar por mal camino. **18 to – off,** comenzar, arrancar: *they led off the show with a song = comenzaron el espectáculo con una canción.* **19 to – on,** inducir: *his older friends led the child on = sus amigos mayores indujeron al niño.* **20 to – someone by the nose,** (fam.) dominar a alguien completamente. **21 to – someone up the garden path,** (fam.) engañar a alguien, llevarlo al huerto. **22 to – the way,** ir delante. **23 to – up to,** llevar a, resultar, acabar en: *his speech led up to a request of money = su discurso acabó en una petición de dinero.* **24 one thing led to another,** una cosa llevó a la otra. **25 to take the –/a –, a)** tomar la iniciativa. **b)** dar ejemplo. **26 this leads me to,** esto me lleva a, me hace concluir que...
lead | led | *s.i.* **1** plomo. **2** mina (de lápiz). || **to swing the –,** (fam.) escabullirse, no ayudar inventando excusas, escurrir el bulto.
leaded | ˈledɪd | *adj.* emplomado, reforzado con plomo.
leaden | ˈledn | *adj.* **1** plúmbeo, de plomo. **2** gris plomizo. **3** (fig.) pesado, aburrido.
leader | ˈliːdər | *s.c.* **=f** líder, cabecilla, guía. **2** el primero, el que encabeza (una lista, clasificación o carrera). **3** editorial de un periódico. **4** MUS. primer violín, concertino. **5** BOT. guía, rama principal (de una planta).
leadership | ˈliːdəʃɪp | *s.i.* **1** liderazgo, dirección, primacía, iniciativa. **2** mando o conjunto de jefes (de una organización).
lead-free | ˈledˌfriː | *adj.* limpio de plomo, sin plomo.
lead-in | ˈliːdɪn | *s.c.* entrada, entradilla, introducción (en programas de radio, televisión).
leading | ˈliːdɪŋ | *adj.* **1** principal, prominente, destacado. || **2 – article,** artículo de fondo, editorial. **3 – light,** (fam.) persona cuyas ideas marcan camino. **4 – question,** pregunta que sugiere la respuesta.
leading | ˈledɪŋ | *s.i.* emplomado, emplomadura (de vidrieras, techos...).
lead-poisoning | ˌledˈpɔɪznɪŋ | *s.i.* MED. envenenamiento por plomo.
leaderless | ˈliːdəlɪs | *adj.* descabezado, sin líder.
leading-rein | ˈliːdɪŋreɪn | *s.c.* **1** cabestro, ramal (parte del freno de los caballos). **2** correas (para sujetar a un niño que está empezando a andar).
leaf | liːf | *s.c.* **1** hoja (de árbol, de libro). **2** lámina (de metal, especialmente de oro o plata). **3** hoja, ala, trampilla (de una puerta, mesa...). || *v.t.* **4 [to – through]** hojear (un libro). || **5 to come into –,** brotar, echar hojas. **6 in –,** cubierto de hojas. **7 to take leaves from someone's book,** seguir el ejemplo de alguien. **8 to turn over a new –,** iniciar una nueva etapa en la vida.
leafage | ˈliːfɪdʒ | *s.i.* follaje.
leafless | ˈliːflɪs | *adj.* sin hojas, deshojado.
leaflet | ˈliːflɪt | *s.c.* **1** folleto, octavilla. || *v.t.* **2** (brit.) distribuir, repartir (folletos, publicidad...).
leaf-mould | ˈliːfmaʊld | *s.i.* mantillo, follaje semipodrido.
leafy | ˈliːfɪ | *adj.* **1** cubierto de hojas, frondoso. **2** (lit.) arbolado, abundante en árboles.
league | liːg | *s.c.* **1** liga (de equipos). **2** alianza, asociación. **3** (fam.) nivel (de calidad). **4** (arc.) legua (5 km.). || *v.i.* **5** aliarse. || **6 in – with,** en connivencia con.
leak | liːk | *s.c.* **1** fisura, rotura. **2** gotera. **3** escape, fuga (de líquido, gas, etc.). **4** infiltración (de una noticia). || *v.i.* **5** escaparse, (líquido, gas, etc.). || *v.t.* **6** filtrar (noticias, información). || **7 to take a –/to go for a –,** (vulg.) echar una meada.
leakage | ˈliːkɪdʒ | *s.c.* **1** fuga, goteo, filtración. **2** ELEC. pérdida, fuga (de tensión eléctrica).
leaky | ˈliːkɪ | *adj.* rajado, desajustado, que pierde líquido, gas, etc.
lean | liːn | *v.* **[leant, leant** (EE.UU. **leaned)]** *i.* **1** inclinarse. **2 [to – (against, on)]** apoyarse sobre. || *t.* **3 [to – (against)]** apoyar, sostener contra: *to lean a ladder against a wall = apoyar una escalera contra una pared.* || *adj.* **4** flaco, enjuto, magro. **5** deficiente, de poco valor. || *s.i.* **6** magro, carne magra. || **7 to be leaning over backwards for,** (fig.) no escatimar esfuerzos por. **8 to – on/upon someone, a)** necesitar ayuda, depender de alguien: *he leans upon his friends' advice = depende del consejo de sus amigos.* **b)** presionar a alguien (incluso con amenazas): *he was leant on to pay his debts = lo presionaron para que pagara sus deudas.* **9 to – out,** asomarse: *she was leaning out of the window = estaba asomándose a la ventana.* **10 to – towards,** (fam.) inclinarse por, preferir: *she has always leaned towards Henry = siempre se ha inclinado por Enrique.*
leaning | ˈliːnɪŋ | *s.c.* **1** inclinación, tendencia, propensión. **2** predilección. || *adj.* **3** inclinado, agachado.
leanness ˈliːnnɪs | *s.i.* **1** delgadez, escasez de carnes. **2** escasez, pobreza.
leant | lent | V. **lean.**
lean-to | ˈliːntuː | *s.c.* cobertizo, colgadizo, anejo.
leap | liːp | *v.* **[leapt, lept** (EE.UU.) **leaped]** *i.* **1** saltar, brincar. **2** (fig.) apresurarse. || *t.* **3** (lit.) saltar, rebasar. || *s.c.* **4** salto, brinco, bote. **5** incremento súbito. **6** (fig.) esfuerzo mental. || **7 a – in the dark,** un salto en el vacío. **8 by leaps and bounds,** a pasos agigantados. **9 to – at,** aprovechar (una oferta u oportunidad): *she leapt at the chance of studying abroad = aprovechó la oportunidad de estudiar fuera.* **10 to – out at/to – off the page at,** llamar poderosamente la atención algo escrito. **11 to – to one's mind/to – into one's mind,** venir a la mente, ocurrírsele a uno. **12 – year,** año bisiesto. **13 to look before one leaps,** actuar con cautela. **14 one's heart leaps,** darle a uno un vuelco el corazón.
leapfrog | ˈliːpfrɒg | *s.i.* **1** juego de la pídola. || *v.t.* **2** saltar (puestos, categorías).
leaping | ˈliːpɪŋ | *adj.* variable, irregular.
leapt | lept | V. **leap.**
learn | lɜːn | V. [también **learnt**] *t.* **1** aprender. **2** saber, llegar a saber, darse cuenta. **3** memorizar, aprender de me moria. || *i.* **4 [to – (of/about)]** averiguar, informarse de. **5** (fam.) enterarse. || **6 to – by heart,** aprender de memoria. **7 to – from one's mistakes,** aprender de los errores propios. **8 to – the hard way,** aprender sin ayuda de nadie, por propia experiencia.
learned | ˈlɜːnɪd | *adj.* culto, docto, erudito, estudioso.
learnedly | ˈlɜːnɪdlɪ | *adv.* cultamente, doctamente, eruditamente, estudiosamente.
learner | ˈlɜːnər | *s.c.* **1** aprendiz, estudiante. **2 -- driver,** aprendiz de conductor.
learning | ˈlɜːnɪŋ | *s.i.* ciencia, sabiduría, cultura.

learnt | lɜːnt | V. **learn.**
lease | liːs | *s.c.* **1** arriendo. **2** COM. contrato de arriendo. || *v.t.* **3** arrendar, dar o recibir en arriendo. || **4 a new – of life,** recuperación de la energía e ilusión, cobro de nuevos bríos.
leasehold | 'liːshəuld | *adj.* arrendado, en arriendo.
leaseholder | 'liːshəuldər | *s.c.* arrendatario.
leash | liːʃ | *s.c.* correa, cadena (para controlar al perro).
least | liːst | [*super.* de **little**] *adv.* **1** menos, mínimamente. **2** mucho menos, de ningún modo. || *adj./pron.* **3** mínimo, menor, más pequeño. || **4 at –,** al menos. **5 it was the – I could do,** era lo menos que podía hacer, no tiene importancia. **6 – of all,** mucho menos. **7 not in the/the – bit,** en absoluto. **8 not –,** principalmente. **9 that is the – of it,** eso es lo de menos, nada comparado con. **10 the – that someone can do,** lo menos que uno puede hacer. **11 to say the –/to say the – of it,** sin exageración alguna.
leastways o **leastwise** | 'liːstweɪz | | 'liːstwaɪz | *adv.* (fam. y p.u.) por lo menos, al menos.
leather | 'leðər | *s.i.* piel, cuero, suela.
leatherette | ˌleðə'ret | *s.i.* piel imitación de cuero.
leather-jacket | 'leðadʒækɪt | *s.c.* chaqueta de cuero.
leathery | 'leðarɪ | *adj.* **1** (desp.) semejante, parecido a la piel o el cuero. **2** (fig.) duro y tieso: *leathery meat = carne dura como una suela.*
leave | liːv | *v.* **[left, left]** *i.* **1** partir, marcharse, irse. || *t.* **2** dejar, abandonar. **3** partir de, marcharse de, alejarse de. **4** dejar olvidado. **5** DER. legar, dejar en herencia. || *s.c.* **6** licencia, permiso (en algunas profesiones): *the captain was on leave = el capitán estaba de permiso.* || **7 to be left with,** quedarse con lo que nadie quiere. **8 to be something –,** quedar algo: *there is some food left = queda algo de comida.* **9 to have something left,** quedarle a alguien algo: *they still have ten minutes left = todavía les quedan diez minutos.* **10 to – it,** dar poder o responsabilidad. **11 – of absence,** permiso, ausencia autorizada. **12 to – off,** parar, detenerse: *if the rain left off... = si para de llover...* **13 to – out,** dejar fuera, omitir. **14 to – someone alone,** dejar a alguien en paz. **15 leaving aside,** dejando de lado, prescindiendo de. **16 take it or – it,** tómalo o déjalo, lo tomas o lo dejas. **17 to take – of/to take one's –,** decir adiós, despedirse.
leaven | 'levn | *s.c.* **1** levadura, fermento. **2** (lit.) influencia, causa (en el cambio del carácter de una persona). || *v.t.* **3** poner levadura, fermentar. **4** (lit.) influir, transformar.
leavened | 'levnd | *adj.* activado con levadura, fermentado.
leaves | liːvz | V. **leaf.**
leave-taking | 'liːvteɪkɪŋ | *s.c.* (form.) despedida.
leavings | 'liːvɪŋz | *s.c.* restos, sobras, desperdicios, despojos.
Lebanese | ˌlebə'niːz | *adj.* libanés, del Líbano.
Lebanon | 'lebənən | *s.* Líbano.
lecher | 'letʃər | *s.c.* (desp.) libertino, lascivo.
lecherous | 'letʃərəs | *adj.* (desp.) libidinoso, lascivo, lujurioso.
lecherously | 'letʃərəslɪ | *adv.* (desp.) libidinosamente, lascivamente, lujuriosamente.
lechery | 'letʃərɪ | *s.i.* lascivia, lujuria, libido.
lectern | 'lektɜːn | *s.c.* atril.
lecture | 'lektʃər | *s.c.* **1** conferencia, disertación, lección magistral. **2** (fig.) advertencia, reprimenda, sermón. || *v.t.* e *i.* **3** disertar, dar una conferencia. **4** (fig.) sermonear.
lecturer | 'lektʃərər | *s.c.* **=f** conferenciante. **2** profesor universitario (no estable, de rango inferior).
lectureship | 'lektʃəʃɪp | *s.i.* cargo o puesto de profesor universitario (de rango inferior).
led | led | V. **lead.**
ledge | ledʒ | *s.c.* **1** repisa, antepecho, alféizar. **2** GEOL. plataforma rocosa (que penetra en el mar).
ledger | 'ledʒər | *s.c.* **=f** COM. libro mayor. || **2 – line,** MUS. línea suplementaria (para añadir notas que caen fuera del pentagrama).
lee | liː | *s.c.* **1** socaire, abrigo, refugio. **2** MAR. sotavento.
leech | liːtʃ | *s.c.* **1** sanguijuela. **2** (fig.) gorrón. **3** (arc.) médico.
leek | liːk | *s.c.* BOT. puerro.
leer | lɪər | *s.c.* **=f** (desp.) mirada maliciosa, insinuante o lasciva. || *v.i.* **2 [to – (at)]** mirar maliciosa o lascivamente.
lees | liːz | *s.pl.* sedimentos, posos.
leery | 'lɪərɪ | *adj.* desconfiado, inseguro.
leeward | 'liːwəd | *adv.* a sotavento.
leeway | 'liːweɪ | *s.i.* **1** libertad de acción, margen de libertad. **2** (brit.) recuperación (por tiempo perdido). **3** MAR. movimiento descontrolado (de un barco).
left | left | V. **leave.**
left | left | *adj.* **1** izquierdo, zurdo (posición, dirección, referencia). **2** de izquierdas, izquierdista: *he is very left = es muy de izquierdas.* || *s.i.* **3** izquierda: *keep to the left = mantenerse a la izquierda.* **4** golpe de izquierda. **5** POL. la izquierda, las izquierdas. || *adv.* **6** a/hacia la izquierda: *turn left = girar a la izquierda.* || **7 on the –,** a la izquierda.
left-hand | 'lefthænd | *adj.* **1** izquierdo, de mano izquierda. **2** a la izquierda: *left hand bend = curva a la izquierda.* || **3 – drive car,** coche para circular por la izquierda, coche con volante a la derecha.
left-handed | ˌleft'hændɪd | *adj.* **1** zurdo, izquierdo: *a left-handed tennis-player = un tenista zurdo.* **2** producido con la mano izquierda, de izquierda: *a left-handed shot = un tiro de izquierda.* **3** para zurdos: *left-handed scissors = tijeras para zurdos.* **4** (fig.) ambiguo, irónico (comentario, proposición).
left-handedness | ˌleft'hændɪdnɪs | *s.i.* hecho de ser zurdo.
left-hander | ˌleft'hændər | *s.c.* zurdo, izquierdo.
leftie | 'leftɪ | *s.c.* **1** (brit.) (desp.) de izquierdas (política). **2** (EE.UU.) zurdo.
leftism | 'leftɪzm | *s.i.* POL. izquierdismo, la izquierda, las izquierdas.
leftist | 'leftɪst | *s.* y *adj.* POL. izquierdista, izquierdoso.
left-luggage office | ˌleft'lʌgɪdʒˌɒfɪs | *s.c.* consigna (aeropuertos, estaciones de ferrocarril...).
left-of-centre | 'leftəvˌsentər | *s.* y *adj.* POL. centroizquierda.
leftover | 'leftəuvər | *adj.* **=f** restante, sobrante. || **2 leftovers,** restos, sobras (de un día para otro).
leftward(s) | 'leftwədz | *adv.* hacia la izquierda.
left-wing | ˌleft'wɪŋ | *s.i.* **1** POL. izquierda, ala izquierda (dentro de un grupo o partido). || *adj.* **2** izquierdista, de izquierdas: *left-wing policy = política de izquierdas.*
left-winger | ˌleft'wɪŋər | *s.c.* POL. izquierdista, del ala izquierda (de un partido o grupo político).
leg | leg | *s.c.* **1** pierna. **2** pata. **3** pernera (de pantalón). **4** DEP. etapa. || *v.i.* **5** (arc.) correr, escapar. || **6 to give someone a –, a)** ayudar a alguien a subir. **b)** (fig.) echar una mano a alguien. **7 to – it,** poner pies en polvorosa. **8 on one last legs,** cerca de la muerte, en las últimas. **9 to pull someone's –,** tomar el pelo a alguien. **10 second – match,** DEP. partido de vuelta (en eliminatoria de fútbol a doble encuentro). **11 someone does not have a – to stand on,** (fig.) quedarse sin base argumental.
legacy | 'legəsɪ | *s.c.* **1** DER. herencia, legado. **2** (fig.) resultado, consecuencia.
legal | 'liːgl | *adj.* **1** legal, lícito, legítimo. || **2** DER. **– aid,** asistencia jurídica de oficio. **3 – tender,** curso legal, moneda de curso legal.
legalism | 'liːgəlɪzəm | *s.i.* (desp.) legalismo.
legatee | ˌlegə'tiː | *s.c.* DER. legatario, asignatario.
legalistic | ˌliːgə'lɪstɪk | *adj.* (desp.) legalista, demasiado pegado a la letra de la ley.
legalistically | ˌliːgə'lɪstɪklɪ | *adv.* (desp.) de manera legalista.
legality | liː'gælətɪ | *s.i.* legalidad.
legalization | ˌliːgəlaɪ'zeɪʃn | *s.c.* legalización.
legalize | 'liːgəlaɪz | *v.t.* legalizar.
legally | 'liːgəlɪ | *adv.* legalmente; según la ley.
legate | 'legɪt | *s.c.* legado, nuncio.
legation | lɪ'geɪʃn | *s.c.* legación, sede de una legación diplomática.
legend | 'ledʒənd | *s.c.* **1** leyenda. **2** celebridad, personaje famoso, leyenda. || *s.i.* **3** cuerpo de leyendas, mitología.

legendary | 'legəndərɪ | *adj.* **1** legendario. **2** famoso, célebre.
leger | 'ledʒər | (también **leger line/ledger /ledger line**) *s.c.* MUS. líneas adicionales al pentagrama.
legerdemain | ˌledʒədə'meɪn | *s.i.* (form.) **1** prestidigitación. **2** (fig.) labia, trapacería (en la discusión).
-legged | legd | | 'legɪd | *adj.* **1** compuesto del número señalado de patas: *four-legged animals = animales de cuatro patas.* **2** con las piernas en la posición señalada: *he sat cross-legged = se sentó con las piernas cruzadas.*
leggings | 'legɪŋz | *s.c.* polainas.
leggy | 'legɪ | *adj.* zanquilargo, zancudo.
legibility | ˌledʒɪ'bɪlɪtɪ | *s.i.* legibilidad.
legible | 'ledʒəbl | *adj.* legible.
legibly | 'ledʒəblɪ | *adv.* legiblemente.
legion | 'liːdʒən | *s.c.* **1** legión. **2** legiones, multitud. || *adj.* **3** legión: *his fans are legion = sus admiradoras son legión.*
legionary | 'liːdʒənərɪ | *s.c.* legionario.
legionnaire | ˌliːdʒə'neər | *s.c.* **1** legionario (de cualquier legión extranjera). || **2 legionnaire's disease,** enfermedad del legionario, legionela.
legislate | 'ledʒɪsleɪt | *v.i.* legislar.
legislation | ˌledʒɪs'leɪʃn | *s.i.* legislación.
legislative | 'ledʒɪslətɪv | *adj.* legislativo.
legislator | 'ledʒɪsleɪtər | *s.c.* legislador.
legislature | 'ledʒɪsleɪtʃər | *s.c.* legislatura, poder legislativo como cuerpo, como asamblea.
legitimacy | lɪ'dʒɪtɪməsɪ | *s.i.* legitimidad.
legitimate | lɪ'dʒɪtɪmɪt | *adj.* **1** legítimo, lícito, conforme a derecho. **2** legítimo (hijo). **3** razonable, sensato, justificable (acción, medida, actitud).
legitimately | lɪ'dʒɪtɪmɪtlɪ | *adv.* legítimamente.
legitimation | lɪˌdʒɪtɪ'meɪʃn | *s.c.* legitimación.
legitimization | lɪˌdʒɪtɪmaɪ'zeɪʃn | *s.c.* legitimación.
legitimize | lɪ'dʒɪtɪmaɪz | *v.t.* legitimar, justificar.
legless | 'leglɪs | *adj.* (fam.) (brit.) borracho perdido.
leg-room | 'legruːm | *s.i.* espacio (para estirar las piernas): *some cars have little leg-room in their back seats = algunos coches tienen poco espacio en sus asientos traseros.*
legume | 'legjuːm | | lɪ'gjuːm | *s.c.* e *i.* legumbre.
leguminous | lɪ'gjuːmɪnəs | *adj.* leguminoso.
leg-warmer | 'legˌwɔːmər | *s.c.* calientapiernas.
leisure | 'leʒər | *s.i.* **1** ocio, tiempo libre. || **2 at –,** desocupado. **3 at one's –,** cuando a uno le venga bien. || **4 – centre,** centro de actividades deportivas y culturales.
leisured | 'leʒəd | *adj.* **1** desocupado, ocioso. **2** pausado, tranquilo. **3** acomodado: *culture used to be for the leisured classes = la cultura era antes para las clases acomodadas.*
leisurely | 'leʒəlɪ | *adj.* **1** pausado, lento, parsimonioso. || *adv.* **2** (p.u.) pausadamente.
leitmotiv | 'laɪtməuˌtiːf | *s.sing.* **1** leitmotiv, patrón repetido (en obra de arte o conducta de una persona). **2** MUS. tema musical recurrente, leitmotiv.
lemming | 'lemɪŋ | *s.c.* **1** ZOOL. lemming, rata campestre de regiones árticas. **2** (fig.) seguidor seguro y fiel (de su líder).
lemon | 'lemən | *s.c.* **1** limón. **2** (fam.) fracaso, ruina: *that car is a real lemon = ese coche es una ruina.* **3** (brit.) (fam.) bobo. || *s.i.* **4** zumo de limón. **5** limón (color). || **6 – cheese/curd,** cuajada de limón. **7 – juice/squash,** zumo de limón. **8 – sole,** ZOOL. lenguado.
lemonade | ˌlemə'neɪd | *s.i.* **1** limonada, agua de limón. **2** (brit.) gaseosa con sabor de limón.
lemur | 'liːmər | *s.c.* ZOOL. lémur, mono de Madagascar.
lend | lend | *v.t.* [**lent, lent**] **1** dejar, ceder. **2** prestar. **3** conceder un crédito. **4** dar, conferir, añadir (calidad): *the Ambassador lent the meeting more dignity = el embajador dio a la reunión mayor dignidad.* || **5 to – an ear to,** prestar atención a. **6 lending library,** biblioteca con servicio de préstamo. **7 lending rate,** interés de un préstamo. **8 to – oneself to,** prestarse a. **9 to – one's name to,** consentir ser asociado públicamente con: *he lent his name to a campaign against nuclear energy = consintió que lo asociaran públicamente con una campaña contra la energía nuclear.* **10 to – someone a hand,** echar una mano a alguien.
lender | 'lendər | *s.c.* prestamista.
length | leŋθ | *s.i.* **1** longitud. **2** duración (espacio-temporal). || *s.c.* **3** trozo (de algunas materias para ser empleado en una situación concreta): **a – of string,** un trozo de cuerda. **4** DEP. largo (referido a la longitud por la que una embarcación o un caballo ganan en competiciones). || **5 along the – of/the – of,** todo a lo largo de/en toda su longitud: *they walked the length of the street = recorrieron la calle en toda su longitud.* **6 at full –,** todo lo largo que uno es: *he was lying at full length on the grass = estaba tumbado en la hierba todo lo largo que era.* **7 at –, a)** extensamente, detalladamente (discurso, disertación). **b)** (lit.) finalmente, al cabo. **8 to go to** *(adj.)* **lengths,** estar dispuesto/recurrir a cualquier cosa por costosa que sea: *he'll go to any lengths to get his job back = está dispuesto/recurrirá a cualquier cosa para recuperar su empleo.* **9 to keep someone at arm's –,** evitar excesiva familiaridad. **10 the – and breadth of,** a lo largo y a lo ancho: *he travels the length and breadth of the country every year = recorre el país a lo largo y ancho todos los años.*
length | leŋθ | *adj.* largo (determinado por la primera parte del compuesto, con la que el sufijo forma un *adj.*): *shoulder-length hair = pelo largo hasta el hombro; knee-length skirt = falda por la rodilla.*
lengthen | 'leŋθən | *v.t.* e *i.* alargar(se), prolongar(se).
lengthily | 'leŋθɪlɪ | *adv.* prolongadamente, dilatadamente, prolijamente.
lengthways | 'leŋθweɪz | *adv.* a lo largo, en sentido longitudinal.
lengthy | 'leŋθɪ | *adj.* largo, prolongado, difuso.
leniency | 'liːnjənsɪ | *s.i.* suavidad, lenidad, benignidad, indulgencia.
lenient | 'liːnjənt | *adj.* suave, benigno, indulgente, clemente.
leniently | 'liːnjəntlɪ | *adv.* suavemente, benignamente.
lens | lenz | *s.c.* **1** lente. **2** ANAT. cristalino. || **3 wide-angle –,** FOT. lente gran angular, lente de ángulo ancho.
lent | lent | V. **lend.**
lent | lent | *s.i.* Cuaresma.
lentil | 'lentl | *s.c.* lenteja.
lento | 'lentəu | *adj.* y *adv.* MUS. lento.
leonine | 'liːəunaɪn | *adj.* aleonado, leonino.
leopard | 'lepəd | *s.c.* ZOOL. leopardo.
leopardess | ˌlepə'des | *s.c.* ZOOL. leopardo hembra.
leotard | 'liːəutɑːd | *s.c.* mallas, maillot.
leper | 'lepər | *s.c.* **=f** leproso. **2** (fig.) indeseable (por razones morales o sociales).
leprosy | 'leprəsɪ | *s.i.* lepra.
lesbian | 'lezbɪən | *s./adj.* lesbiana.
lesbianism | 'lezbɪənɪzm | *s.i.* lesbianismo.
lesion | 'liːʒən | *s.c.* MED. **1** lesión. **2** disfunción (de algún órgano).
less | les | [*comp.* de **little**] *adv.* **1** menos: *you should try to shout less = deberías tratar de gritar menos.* || *adj.* **2** menos: *we eat less bread now = ya comemos menos pan.* || *prep.* **3** menos: *100 pounds a week less 10 for insurance contribution = 100 libras a la semana menos 10 para seguros.* || **4 – and –,** cada vez menos. **5 – of that/it,** ¡ya está bien! **6 – than** *(adj./adv.)*, (euf.) en absoluto, lejos de. **7 – than no time,** en menos de un abrir y cerrar de ojos. **8 no –,** nada menos. **9 no – than,** por lo menos, como mínimo. **10 still –/much –/even –,** mucho menos, menos todavía.
OBS. En inglés coloquial muchos hablantes emplean **less** con sustantivos plurales: *there are less cars in London on Sundays = hay menos coches en Londres los domingos.* Pero se considera incorrecto. **Fewer** es la forma gramaticalmente correcta en el ejemplo.
lessee | le'siː | *s.c.* DER. arrendatario, inquilino.
lessen | 'lesn | *v.t.* e *i.* **1** reducir, disminuir. **2** restar (importancia, valor).
lesser | 'lesər | *adj.* (lit.) menos, menor, inferior (tamaño, grado, valor): *the lesser of two evils = el menor entre dos males.*
lesson | 'lesn | *s.c.* **1** lección. **2** clase: *the English lesson is at 10 = la clase de*

inglés es a las 10. **3** lección, aviso, escarmiento: *the accident was a lesson to him = el accidente le sirvió de lección.* **4** pasaje bíblico (leído en el servicio religioso). || **5 to teach someone a –,** servirle a uno de escarmiento.

lessor | 'lesɔːr | *s.c.* DER. arrendador.

lest | lest | *conj.* **1** (lit.) para que no, no sea que, por miedo a que: *he ran away lest he should be seen = huyó para que no lo vieran.* **2** (lit.) que (determinado por idea de temor): *they were afraid lest she should lose her job = temían que perdiera su empleo.*

let | let | *v.t.* **[let, let]** 1 dejar, permitir: *let me buy you a drink = déjame invitarte.* **2** (brit.) arrendar, alquilar: *a flat to let = piso para alquilar.* **3** (lit.) deber: *let each man take his responsibility = cada uno debe asumir su responsabilidad.* **4** suponer, tomar como hipótesis (en planes, cálculos, etc.): *let line AD be as long as XY = supongamos que la línea AD es tan larga como XY.* || *s.c.* **5** (brit.) arrendamiento, alquiler. **6** casa, piso... en arriendo o alquiler. **7** DEP. repetición de servicio (en tenis). || *s.i.* **8** DER. impedimento. **9** – alone, cuánto menos: *he can't walk let alone run = no puede caminar, cuánto menos correr.* **10 to – by,** dejar pasar. **11 to – down, a)** alargar (ropa): *to let down an old dress = alargar un vestido viejo.* **b)** decepcionar, defraudar (expectativas): *I count on you, don't let me down = cuento contigo, no me defraudes.* **12 to – fall,** dejar caer (una pista, una insinuación, etc.). **13 to – fly (at),** golpear, disparar a. **14 – it go at that,** dejémoslo así. **15 – me see,** veamos. **16 to – on, a)** permitir subir (en un vehículo): *he wouldn't let me on the bus with the dog = no me permitía subir al autobús con el perro.* **b)** (fam.) decir, revelar (algo secreto): *don't let on who told you = no digas quién te lo dijo.* **17 to – one's hair down,** soltarse el pelo, relajarse. **18 to – out, a)** dejar salir: *he was let out of prison = le dejaron salir de prisión.* **b)** emitir, expresar violentamente: *he let out a cry of pain = emitió un grito de dolor.* **c)** sacar, agrandar (ropa): *he had to have all his trousers let out = tuvo que sacarse todos los pantalones.* **d)** dar a conocer: *news of the accident was let out yesterday = la noticia del accidente se dio a conocer ayer.* **e)** (EE.UU.) cerrar, terminar: *school lets out at 5 = el colegio cierra a las 5.* **f)** (brit.) arrendar, alquilar. **19 let's face it,** admitámoslo. **20 to – someone alone,** dejar a alguien en paz. **21 to – someone down lightly,** dar a alguien malas noticias con tacto. **22 to – someone go, a)** dejar a alguien libre. **b)** (euf.) despedir a alguien de su empleo. **23 to – someone in,** dejar a alguien entrar. **24 to – someone in for,** (fam.) meter a alguien, meterse (en una situación difícil): *he didn't know what he was letting himself in for = no sabía dónde se estaba metiendo.* **25 to – someone in on,** (fam.) hacer partícipe a alguien de un secreto. **26 to – someone into, a)** dejar entrar a alguien. **b)** dejar pertenecer: *they don't let women into their club = no dejan a las mujeres pertenecer a su club.* **c)** confiar un secreto. **27 to – someone know,** avisar a alguien. **28 to – someone off, a)** perdonar, dejar libre a alguien (de un deber o castigo): *she let the children off their homework = perdonó a los niños sus deberes.* **b)** permitir bajar (de un vehículo): *he wouldn't let me off the bus = no me dejaba bajar del autobús.* **29 to – someone off lightly,** rebajar un castigo: *he was let off slightly = le rebajaron el castigo.* **30 to – someone/something be,** dejarlo estar. **31 to – something drop,** dejar caer, decir, insinuar (a propósito o inadvertidamente): *he let the name of the lucky one drop = dejó caer el nombre del afortunado.* **32 to – something slip,** perder, dejar pasar (una oportunidad). **33 to – up,** ceder, acabar, pasar (algo negativo): *when will this bad weather let up? = ¡cuándo acabará este tiempo!* **34 to – up on someone,** tratar menos severamente, dejar de estar encima: *let up on him for a while = deja de estar encima de él un rato.* **35 to – well (enough) alone,** dejarlo como está.

letdown | letdaun | *s.c.* (fam.) decepción, desilusión.

lethal | 'liːθl | *adj.* **1** letal, mortal. **2** (fig.) subido de alcohol (una fiesta).

lethally | 'liːθəlɪ | *adv.* letalmente, mortalmente.

lethargic | lɪ'θɑːdʒɪk | *adj.* letárgico, aletargado.

lethargically | 'leθədʒɪklɪ | *adv.* letárgicamente, aletargadamente.

let's | lets | *contr.* de **let** y **us.**

lethargy | 'leθədʒɪ | *s.i.* **1** letargo, somnolencia, sueño. **2** (fig.) indolencia.

let-up | 'letʌp | *s.c.* pausa, interrupción.

letter | 'letər | *s.c.* **=f** letra: *a capital letter = una letra mayúscula.* **2** carta, epístola. || *s.i.* **3** letra, texto, redacción, literalidad (de un escrito, ley, acuerdo, etc.). || **4 to keep/stick to the – (of),** atenerse a la letra o literalidad de.

letter-bomb | 'letəˌbɒm | *s.c.* carta bomba.

letter-box | 'letəˌbɒks | *s.c.* **1** buzón (de correos). **2** (brit.) buzón, caja de correspondencia (en casas particulares).

lettered | 'letəd | *adj.* (arc.) culto, instruido, cultivado.

letterhead | 'letəhed | *s.c.* membrete de una carta.

lettering | 'letərɪŋ | *s.i.* inscripción, rotulación, diseño de letras.

letterpress | 'letəpres | *s.i.* impresión tipográfica.

letting | 'letɪŋ | *s.c.* (brit.) arrendamiento, casa arrendada, casa para arrendar.

lettuce | 'letɪs | *s.c.* e *i.* BOT. lechuga.

leucocyte | 'luːkəsaɪt | (EE.UU. **leukocyte**) *s.c.* BIOL. leucocito.

leukaemia | luː'kiːmɪə | *s.i.* MED. leucemia.

levee | 'levɪ | *s.c.* **1** (arc.) recepción (especialmente formal). **2** (EE.UU.) dique de contención.

level | 'levl | *adj.* **1** plano, llano, raso. **2** nivelado, a nivel, equilibrado, igualado. **3** fijo, penetrante: *a level look = una mirada fija.* **4** estable, uniforme: *a level temperature = una temperatura uniforme.* **5** ecuánime, ordenado: *a level life = una vida ordenada.* **6** tranquilo, sin emoción: *a level voice.* || *s.c.* **7** nivel. **8** plano, llanura, llano. **9** comprobador de nivel. **10** altura: *to come down to someone's level = ponerse a la altura de alguien.* **11** índice: *the alcohol level in the blood = índice de alcohol en la sangre.* **12** (brit.) grado (cualificación escolar): *he got A level Maths = alcanzó en matemáticas el grado A.* || *adv.* **13** a nivel, horizontalmente. || *v.t.* **14** nivelar, allanar, igualar. **15** arrasar, destruir: *the hurricane levelled the town = el huracán arrasó la ciudad.* **16 [to – (at)]** apuntar (un arma) a. || **17 to do one's – best,** hacer todo lo que uno puede (en situaciones difíciles). **18 to find one's own –,** encontrar su sitio en la sociedad. **19 to – against someone,** dirigir, formular (cargos, acusaciones): *serious accusations were levelled against him = le fueron dirigidas serias acusaciones.* **20 to – down,** rebajar al mismo nivel. **21 to – off/out, a)** estabilizarse: *inflation has levelled off at 5% = la inflación se ha estabilizado en el 5%.* **b)** allanar, terraplenar: *the ground was levelled out = se allanó el suelo.* **22 to – up,** elevar al mismo nivel. **23 to – with,** ser sincero con, decir la verdad: *I've always levelled with you = siempre he sido sincero contigo.* **24 on a – with,** al nivel de, a la misma altura que. **25 on the –,** (fam.) honrado, serio, en serio: *to tell something on the level = decir algo en serio.*

level-crossing | ˌlevl'krɒsɪŋ | *s.c.* (brit.) paso a nivel.

level-headed | ˌlevl'hedɪd | *adj.* sensato, juicioso, equilibrado.

levelly | 'levəlɪ | *adv.* tranquilamente, ordenadamente.

lever | 'liːvər | *s.c.* **=f** palanca. **2** MEC. mando, palanca (de velocidades). || *v.t.* **3** apalancar.

leverage | 'liːvərɪdʒ | *s.i.* **1** apalancamiento. **2** (fig.) influencia, fuerza.

leveret | 'levərɪt | *s.c.* ZOOL. lebrato, liebre joven.

leviathan | lɪ'vaɪəθn | *s.c.* leviatán.

levitate | 'levɪteɪt | *v.t.* e *i.* levitar, mantener en el aire.

levitation | ˌlevɪ'teɪʃn | *s.c.* e *i.* levitación.

levity | 'levɪtɪ | *s.i.* (lit.) ligereza, levedad, frivolidad, superficialidad, informalidad.

levy | 'levɪ | *s.c.* **1** exacción, recaudación, impuesto. **2** MIL. leva, alistamiento, reclutamiento (de soldados). ||*v.t.* **3** recaudar (impuestos).

lewd | luːd | *adj.* lascivo, lúbrico, obsceno, indecente.

lewdly | 'lju:dlɪ | *adv.* lascivamente, obscenamente, indecentemente.
lewdness | 'lu:dnɪs | *s.i.* lascivia, obscenidad.
lexical | 'leksɪkl | *adj.* FILOL. léxico.
lexically | 'leksɪklɪ | *adv.* en cuanto al léxico, léxicamente.
lexicographer | ˌleksɪ'kɒgrəfər | *s.c.* lexicógrafo.
lexicographical | ˌleksɪkə'græfɪkl | *adj.* lexicográfico.
lexicography | ˌleksɪ'kɒgrəfɪ | *s.i.* lexicografía.
lexicon | 'leksɪkən | *s.c.* FILOL. léxico, diccionario.
liability | ˌlaɪə'bɪlɪtɪ | *s.i.* **1** responsabilidad: *a child is its parents' liability = un niño es responsabilidad de sus padres.* **2** tendencia. **3** riesgo: *tobacco increases your liability to lung cancer = el tabaco aumenta el riesgo de cáncer de pulmón.* || *s.c.* **4** deuda, debe, débito, pasivo: *liabilities can lead to bankruptcy = las deudas pueden llevar a la bancarrota.* **5** carga, inconveniente: *big houses are often a real liability = las casas grandes son a menudo una auténtica carga.* || **6 to meet one's liabilities,** satisfacer sus deudas.
liable | 'laɪəbl | *adj.* **1 [– (to)]** expuesto, sujeto, propenso: *liable to floods = expuesto a inundaciones; liable to colds = propenso a catarros.* **2** DER. responsable, acreedor (de sanción): *liable to a fine for driving too fast = acreedor de sanción por conducir deprisa.*
liaise | lɪ'eɪz | *v.i.* **[to – (with)]** conectar, captar, contactar con.
liaison | li:'eɪzən | *s.i.* **1** conexión, relación, coordinación. || *s.c.* **2** lío, relación amorosa (extraconyugal).
liana | lɪ'ɑ:nə | *s.c.* BOT. liana.
liar | 'laɪər | *s.c.* mentiroso, embustero, cínico.
lib | lɪb | *s.i.* (fam.) movimiento de liberación (de la mujer, de homosexuales).
libation | laɪ'beɪʃn | *s.c.* **1** libación. **2** (p.u.) copa (bebida alcohólica).
libel | 'laɪbl | *s.c.* **1** libelo. **2** (fam.) calumnia, difamación, injuria. **3** DER. delito de libelo. || *v.t.* **4** difamar, desacreditar.
libellous | 'laɪbələs | *adj.* difamatorio, injurioso.
liberal | 'lɪbərəl | *adj.* **1** liberal, tolerante, generoso. **2** POL. liberal: *the Liberal Party = el partido liberal.* || *s.c.* **3** liberal: *the liberals supported the motion = los liberales apoyaron la moción.*
liberalism | 'lɪbərəlɪzəm | *s.i.* liberalismo.
liberality | ˌlɪbə'rælɪtɪ | *s.i.* **1** generosidad, liberalidad. **2** apertura mental, liberalidad.
liberalization | ˌlɪbərəlaɪ'zeɪʃn | *s.i.* liberalización.
liberalize | 'lɪbərəlaɪz | *v.t.* liberalizar.
liberally | 'lɪbərəlɪ | *adv.* liberalmente, generosamente, abundantemente.
liberate | 'lɪbəreɪt | *v.t.* liberar, poner en libertad, librar.
liberated | 'lɪbəreɪtɪd | *adj.* liberado, independiente.
liberation | ˌlɪbə'reɪʃn | *s.i.* liberación: *the women's liberation movement = movimiento de liberación de la mujer.*
liberator | 'lɪbəreɪtər | *s.c.* libertador.
Liberia | laɪ'bɪərɪə | *s.* Liberia.
Liberian | laɪ'bɪərɪən | *adj./s.c.* liberiano.
libertarian | ˌlɪbəteərɪən | *adj.* libertario.
libertine | 'lɪbəti:n | *atr.* libertino.
liberty | 'lɪbətɪ | *s.c.* e *i.* **1** (lit.) libertad (de acción o pensamiento). **2** (fam.) libertad, familiaridad, confianza, privilegio: *Sorry I took the liberty to answer the telephone = perdón por tomarme la confianza de contestar al teléfono.* **3** MAR. permiso, licencia: *liberty boat = barco que lleva a los marineros de permiso.* || **4 to be at – (to), a)** estar en libertad. **b)** estar libre, desocupado. **c)** (fam.) estar autorizado a, tener derecho a: *I'm not at liberty to say it = no estoy autorizado a decirlo.* **5 to take a –/liberties,** tomarse la libertad, libertades: *you shouldn't take liberties with chaps like him = no puede uno tomarse libertades con tipos como ése.*
libidinous | lɪ'bɪdɪnəs | *adj.* libidinoso, lujurioso.
libido | lɪ'bi:dəu | *s.i.* PSIC. libido (impulso sexual).
librarian | laɪ'breərɪən | *s.c.* bibliotecario.
library | 'laɪbrərɪ | *s.c.* **1** biblioteca. **2** colección de libros: *a library of modern masters = colección de maestros modernos.*
librettist | lɪ'bretɪst | *s.c.* libretista.
libretto | lɪ'bretəu | *s.c.* libreto.
Libya | 'lɪbɪə | *s.sing.* Libia.
Libyan | 'lɪbɪən | *adj./s.c.* libio.
lice | laɪs | V. **louse.**
licence | 'laɪsəns | (también EE.UU. **license**) *s.c.* **1** permiso, carnet: *driving licence = permiso de conducir.* **2** autorización, licencia: *licence to sell alcohol = autorización para vender bebidas alcohólicas.* || *s.i.* **3** libertad (de acción, palabra o pensamiento): *he took some licence in his translation = se tomó cierta libertad en su traducción.* **4** (desp.) libertinaje: *in favour of liberty but against licence = a favor de la libertad pero en contra del libertinaje.* **5** licencia, recurso (en la creación artística): *poetic licence = licencia poética.* **6** COM. patente (cedida o autorizada). || **7 – plate,** matrícula (de un coche). **8 under –,** con patente ajena autorizada: *they make cars under licence = fabrican coches con patente autorizada.*
license | 'laɪsəns | *v.t.* **1** permitir, autorizar (oficialmente): *to license the sale of alcohol = autorizar la venta de alcohol.* || **2 licensing hours,** (brit.) horario autorizado para vender bebidas alcohólicas. **3 licensing laws,** leyes que controlan la venta de alcohol.
licensed | 'laɪsənst | *adj.* autorizado (oficialmente): *a fully licensed restaurant = restaurante oficialmente autorizado para servir bebidas alcohólicas.*
licensee | ˌlaɪsən'si: | *s.c.* concesionario.
licentiate | laɪ'senʃɪət | *s.c.* (form.) licenciado.
licentious | laɪ'senʃəs | *adj.* licencioso, libertino.
licentiously | laɪ'senʃəslɪ | *adv.* licenciosamente, libertinamente.
licentiousness | laɪ'senʃəsnɪs | *s.i.* licenciosidad, libertinaje.
lichen | 'laɪkən | *s.i.* BOT. liquen.
lich-gate | 'lɪtʃgeɪt | V. **lychgate.**
lick | lɪk | *v.t.* **1** lamer. **2** beber (como un gato). **3** (fig.) bañar: *the waves lick the beach = las olas bañan la playa.* **4** (fam.) vencer, dar una paliza (en juego, deporte). **5** (fig.) superar (problemas, dificultades): *we licked it at last = lo superamos finalmente.* **6** atacar como a lengüetadas (las llamas de fuego): *the flames licked (against) the building = las llamas atacaban como a lengüetadas el edificio.* || *s.c.* **7** lamedura, lamido, lengüetada. **8** (fam.) mano (de pintura, barniz, etc.). **9** (brit.) (fam.) velocidad, rapidez, prisa: *he went donstairs at quite a lick = bajó a toda velocidad.* **10** (fam.) paliza: *to give someone a lick.* | **11 at a great/tremendous –,** a toda velocidad, a toda pastilla. **12 to – one's lips,** relamerse, hacerse la boca agua. **13 to – one's wounds,** curarse de las heridas para seguir en la brecha. **14 to – someone's boots, a)** obedecer sin rechistar, como un esclavo. **b)** hacer la pelota a alguien. **15 to – something into shape,** poner a punto: *it was quite a job to lick the house into shape = costó poner la casa a punto.* **16 to – something off,** limpiar a lametones: *the girl licked the jam off her lips = la niña se limpiaba la mermelada de sus labios a lametones.* **17 to – the dust,** caer al suelo derrotado, morder el polvo. **18 not to do a – of work,** no dar ni golpe.
licking | 'lɪkɪŋ | *s.c.* (p.u.) (fam.) paliza, derrota.
licorice | 'lɪkərɪs | V. **liquorice.**
lid | lɪd | *s.c.* **1** tapa, tapadera. **2 [eye –]** ANAT. párpado. || **3 to flip one's –,** volverse loco. **4 to put the (tin) – on,** (fam.) para colmo de males. **5 to take the – off,** manifestar el lado negativo.
lidded | 'lɪdɪd | *adj.* **1** cerrado, provisto de tapa. **2** de párpados (gruesos, finos, etc.): *a man with heavily lidded eyes = un hombre de párpados gruesos.*
lido | 'li:dəu | *s.c.* (brit.) **1** piscina (pública y al aire libre). **2** zona de baño (en playas, orillas de lagos, etc.).
lidless | 'lɪdlɪs | *adj.* sin tapa.
lie | laɪ | *v.* **[lay, lain]** *i.* **1** echarse, tumbarse. **2** estar, permanecer (en posición horizontal): *there was a book lying on the table = había un libro sobre la mesa.* **3** estar tendido: *he lay dead on the ground = estaba tendido sin vida en el suelo.* **4** estar echado, tumbado, acostado: *to lie in bed = estar acostado.* **5** yacer, reposar, estar enterrado: *here lies*

the hero = aquí yace el héroe. **6** hallarse, residir, estribar: *the difference lies in the fact that... = la diferencia estriba en el hecho de...* **7** situarse, estar situado o emplazado: *the town lies down the valley = la ciudad está situada en el valle.* **8 [to – with]** depender de: *the decision lies with the minister = la decisión depende del ministro.* **9 [to – (with)]** (arc.) yacer, copular con. **10** estar escondido, permanecer al acecho: *the thieves were lying in wait of their victims = los ladrones estaban escondidos en espera de sus víctimas.* **11** estar próximo, abrirse: *the future lies before us = el futuro se abre ante nosotros.* **12** cernirse, extenderse: *a cloud of pollution lay over the city = una nube de polución se cernía sobre la ciudad.* || *s.c.* **13** posición, situación, emplazamiento. **14** DEP. caída, situación de la pelota (golf). || **15 to let it –/to let things –,** dejar las cosas como están. **16 to – about/around, a)** (desp.) holgazanear. **b)** estar desordenado, desparramado. **17 to – back, a)** recostarse. **b)** dejarlo como está, despreocuparse. **18 to – behind,** estar detrás, esconderse: *what lies behind his words? ¿qué se esconde en sus palabras?* **19 to – by, a)** estar postergado, sin utilizar. **b)** estar a mano. **20 to – down,** echarse, acostarse. **21 to – down on the job,** trabajar en algo desagradable. **22 to – heavy/heavily on,** producir un efecto incómodo, pesar sobre: *it will lie heavily on his conscience = pesará sobre su conciencia.* **23 to – in,** (brit.) levantarse tarde. **24 to – in state,** estar a la vista del público (el cadáver de una personalidad), estar de cuerpo presente. **25 to – low,** esconderse. **26 to – off,** mantener cierta distancia (barcos): *the fleet lay off the coast = la flota se mantenía a cierta distancia de la costa.* **27 to – to,** MAR. aguantar con dificultades, estar al pairo (barcos). **28 to – up, a)** guardar cama (cierto tiempo). **b)** (brit.) escabullirse, huir de la notoriedad. **29 to take something lying down,** aguantar algo desagradable sin rechistar. **30 the – of the land/how the land lies, a)** caída del terreno. **b)** (fig.) estado general de la situación.

lie | laɪ | *v.i.* **1** *mentir*: *to lie out of a scrape = mentir para salir de un apuro.* **2** engañar: *the result can lie when the facts are misused = el resultado puede engañar cuando se manipulan los datos.* || *s.c.* **3** mentira, embuste. || **4 a pack of/a tissue of lies,** una sarta de mentiras. **5 to give the – to,** desmentir, demostrar la falsedad de. **6 – detector,** detector de mentiras. **7 one – makes many,** de una mentira nacen ciento. **8 to tell a –,** decir una mentira. **9 white –,** mentira piadosa.

lie-down | 'laɪdaʊn | *s.c.* (brit.) (fam.) breve descanso (en cama generalmente).

liege | liːdʒ | HIST. *adj.* **1** feudatario, feudal. || **2 – lord,** señor feudal.

liegeman | 'liːdʒmən | *s.c.* HIST. vasallo.

lie-in | 'laɪɪn | *s.c.* (fam.) permanencia en cama más de lo habitual: *to have a lie-in on Sunday morning = levantarse más tarde el domingo.*

lien | lɪən | *s.c.* **[– (on/upon)]** DER. embargo preventivo, derecho de embargo.

lieu | ljuː | *s.i.* **1** (lit.) lugar, puesto. ||**2 in – of,** en lugar de, en vez de, a cambio de: *to do this in lieu of that = hacer esto en lugar de aquello.*

lieutenancy | lef'tenənsɪ | (EE.UU. | luː'tenənsɪ |) *s.i.* MIL. rango de teniente, oficialato.

lieutenant | lef'tenənt | (EE.UU. | luː'tenənt |) *s.c.* **1** MIL. teniente. **2** MIL. teniente (más la categoría del compuesto): *a lieutenant colonel = teniente coronel.* **3** sustituto, lugarteniente.

life | laɪf | *s.i.* y *c.* **1** vida. **2** existencia humana: *life is full of surprises = la existencia humana está llena de sorpresas.* **3** vida, funcionamiento (de una máquina). **4** duración, vigencia (de una institución): *the life of the present parliament = la vigencia del parlamento actual.* **5** persona, hombre: *ten lives were lost = se perdieron diez vidas (personas).* **6** tipo concreto de vida: *country life = vida rural; married life = vida de casado; one's private life = la vida privada de uno; the sex life of a monkey = la vida sexual del mono.* **7** mundo, experiencia: *you'll see a lot of life if you move round the world = se ve mucho mundo viajando.* **8** actividad social: *there is not much life in a village = no hay mucha vida social en un pueblo.* **9** vigor, energía: *the kids are full of life today = los chicos están llenos de energía hoy.* **10** biografía: *Boswell's life of Dr. Johnson = la biografía del Dr. Johnson por Boswell.* **11** (fam.) cadena perpetua: *the terrorist got life = al terrorista le cayó cadena perpetua.* **12** realidad (como fuente artística): *from life not from photographs = de la realidad, no de fotografías.* || **13 to be the – (and soul) of,** ser el animador de. **14 to come/bring to –, a)** recuperar la consciencia. **b)** mostrar interés, entusiasmo. **15 for dear –,** con el mayor esfuerzo: *he grasped the branch for dear life = se agarró a la rama con todas sus fuerzas.* **16 for –,** de por vida, por el resto de su vida. **17 for the – of one,** a pesar de todos sus esfuerzos. **18 to have the time of one's –,** (fam.) pasarlo en grande. **19 "how's=N?",** (fam.) ¿qué tal? **20 – assurance,** seguro de vida. **21 – expectancy,** esperanza de vida. **22 – form,** forma de vida, cualquier viviente. **23 – imprisonment,** cadena perpetua. **24 – peer,** lord vitalicio (título no heredable por sus sucesores). **25 – science,** ciencia relacionada con la vida. **26 – sentence,** condena a cadena perpetua. **27 – -support system, a)** lo necesario para sobrevivir. **b)** equipo necesario (para circunstancias concretas). **28 –'s work, a)** trabajo de una vida. **b)** la obra más importante. **29 to live one's own –,** vivir su vida. **30 matter of – and death,** asunto de vida o muerte, de crucial importancia. **31 not on your –,** en absoluto. **32 to risk – and limb,** hacer algo muy arriesgado. **33 to run for one's –,** correr como alma que lleva el diablo. **34 to take one's – in one's (own) hands, a)** (fam.) poner la vida de uno en continuo peligro. **b)** llegar a controlar la propia vida. **35 to take one's own –,** quitarse la vida, suicidarse. **36 to take someone's –,** matar a alguien. **37 that's –,** así es la vida. **38 to the –,** copia exacta: *the portrait shows him to the life = el retrato es su copia.* **39 the – of Riley,** (fam.) la gran vida. **40 this is the –,** esto es vivir. **41 true to –,** la vida tal como es: *the film is true to life = la película muestra la vida tal como es.* **42 what a –!,** ¡qué vida ésta!

life-and-death | 'laɪfən'deθ | *adj.* **1** de vida o muerte, crítico, crucial. **2** encarnizado (lucha).

lifebelt | 'laɪfbelt | *s.c.* cinturón salvavidas.

lifeblood | 'laɪfblʌd | *s.i.* **1** alma, nervio, oxígeno: *expansion is the lifeblood of industry = la expansión es el alma de la industria.* **2** (lit.) sangre vital.

lifeboat | 'laɪfbəʊt | *s.c.* **1** barco salvavidas (para protección en costas). **2** bote salvavidas (de buques).

lifebuoy | 'laɪfbɒɪ | *s.c.* cinturón salvavidas.

life-cycle | 'laɪf,saɪkl | *s.c.* **1** ciclo biológico. **2** pasos, vicisitudes (de un proceso, teoría, etc.).

life-giving | ,laɪfgɪvɪŋ | *adj.* revitalizador, vivificante, vigorizante.

lifeguard | 'laɪfgɑːd | *s.c.* **1** salvavidas, guarda de playa. **2** MIL. guardia militar. || **3 Life-Guards,** (brit.) regimiento real de caballería.

life-insurance | 'laɪfɪn,ʃʊərəns | *s.i.* seguro de vida.

lifejacket | ɒlaɪfɪdʒɑekɪt | *s.c.* chaleco salvavidas.

lifeless | 'laɪflɪs | *adj.* **1** (lit.) muerto, sin vida. **2** (desp.) inerme, insípido, apagado, flojo, soso.

lifelike | 'laɪflaɪk | *adj.* fiel, parecido, similar, cercano a la realidad: *a lifelike portrait = un fiel retrato.*

lifeline | 'laɪflaɪn | *s.c.* **1** cuerda, lazo salvavidas, andarivel de salvamento. **2** cuerda de comunicación (de buceadores). **3** (fig.) medio de comunicación indispensable, cordón umbilical: *the telephone is his lifeline to the world = el teléfono es su cordón umbilical con el mundo.*

lifelong | 'laɪflɒŋ | *adj.* que dura toda la vida, para siempre: *a lifelong friend = un amigo de toda la vida.*

life-preserver | 'laɪfprɪzəːvər | *s.c.* (EE.UU.) chaleco salvavidas.

lifer | 'laɪfər | *s.c.* (fam.) condenado a cadena perpetua.

life-saver | 'laɪfseɪvər | *s.c.* algo que salva, salvación: *the new dishwasher* *was our life-saver = el lavaplatos nuevo fue nuestra salvación.*

life-size | ˌlaɪf'saɪz | *adj.* de tamaño natural.

life-sized | ˌlaɪf'saɪzd | V. **life-size.**

lifespan | 'laɪfspæn | *s.i.* vida, duración media (de vivientes o aparatos): *the lifespan of men = la vida media de los hombres.*

lifestyle | 'laɪfstaɪl | *s.c.* forma, talante, estilo de vida: *urban lifestyle = forma de vida urbana.*

lifetime | 'laɪftaɪm | *s.c.* **1** vida, duración de una vida: *in my lifetime = en toda mi vida.* || **2 of a – a)** de toda una vida. **b)** lo más importante de una vida: *the work of a lifetime = la obra más importante de toda una vida.*

life-work | ˌlaɪf'wɜːk | (también **life's work**) *s.c.* (normalmente *sing.*) trabajo de toda una vida.

lift | lɪft | *v.t.* **1** levantar, alzar, elevar (objetos, miembros del cuerpo, los ánimos, etc.). **2** transportar (por avión). **3** rescindir, invalidar, suprimir, levantar (hipotecas, leyes, embargos, etc.). **4 [to – (down)]** bajar, levantar y bajar: *she lifted the child down from the tree = bajó al niño del árbol.* **5** (fam.) copiar, plagiar (ideas, escritos): *to lift from someone else's work = plagiar la obra de otro.* **6** aliviar (problemas), quitar (peso de encima). **7** (fam.) robar (cosas de poca importancia). **8** arrancar, sacar (verduras, patatas, etc.). **9** (lit.) elevar la voz (al hablar o cantar). **10** mejorar (condiciones socioeconómicas). || *v.i.* **11** levantar, desaparecer (nubes, niebla, etc.): *the plane took off when the fog lifted = el avión despegó cuando la niebla levantó.* || *s.c.* **12** levantamiento, elevación. **13** (brit.) ascensor, montacargas. **14** transporte (gratuito y en coche particular): *he gave her a lift to the station = la llevó en su coche a la estación.* **15** empuje (hacia arriba), ascensión. **16** (fam.) energía, vigor, ánimo, exaltación: *on her arrival he felt a new lift = con la llegada de ella él sintió un nuevo vigor.* || **17 to – off,** despegar (un avión). **18 not to – a finger to,** no levantar un dedo por, no hacer esfuerzo alguno por: *he wouldn't lift a finger to help her = no haría esfuerzo alguno por ayudarla.*

lift-off | 'lɪftɒf | *s.c.* despegue (de avión).

ligament | 'lɪgəmənt | *s.c.* ANAT. ligamento.

ligature | 'lɪgətʃər | *s.c.* **1** (form.) ligadura, vendaje. **2** MUS. ligado.

light | laɪt | *s.i.* **1** luz (natural o artificial). **2** claridad, luz, espacio iluminado: *you're standing in my light = estás en medio, me quitas la luz.* **3** luz, viveza, brillo (en la expresión del rostro): *the light died out of her eyes = el brillo de sus ojos se desvaneció.* **4** (lit.) luz, conocimiento, información: *that will shed new light on the matter = eso arrojará nueva luz al asunto.* || *s.c.* **5** luz (cualquier medio de iluminación): *switch off the lights = apaga las luces.* **6** semáforo: *when you get to the lights, turn left = al llegar al semáforo, doble a la izquierda.* **7** fuego, lumbre, fósforo (para encender un cigarrillo, pipa, etc.): *can I have a light, please? = fuego, por favor.* **8** ventana, claraboya o abertura en la pared (por donde penetre la luz). **9** (lit.) aspecto, perspectiva: *to look upon the matter in other light = considerar el tema desde otro aspecto.* **10** lumbrera, eminencia: *one of the shining lights of his age = una de las lumbreras de su tiempo.* **11** claro (parte más iluminada de un cuadro): *light and shade = claro y oscuro.* || *v.* **[lit, lit (o lighted)]** *t.* **12** encender: *to light a cigarette.* **13** iluminar: *four spotlights lit the stage = cuatro focos iluminaban la escena.* **14** (arc.) alumbrar (el camino): *she lighted him in = le alumbró la entrada.* || *i.* **15** arder (el fuego): *the fire wouldn't light = el fuego se resistía a arder.* **16** (arc.) posarse (pájaros). **17** caer, llegar a tierra: *he fell and lit on his feet = cayó de pie.* || *adj.* **18** iluminado, claro, encendido. **19** claro, pálido (color): *a light-coloured dress = un vestido claro.* **20** ligero, liviano. **21** corto, reducido, disminuido, menguado: *a light crop of wheat = cosecha corta de trigo.* **22** llevadero, suave, benigno: *a light punishment = castigo benigno.* **23** frívolo, de pasatiempo: *a light reading.* **24** suave, moderado: *a light wind.* **25** ágil, grácil: *the light movements of a dancer.* **26** ligero, superficial (sueño). **27** frugal, ligero (comida). **28** moderado, sobrio (fumador, bebedor). **29** suave, de pocos grados (bebidas alcohólicas). **30** (lit.) alegre, feliz, despreocupado. **31** suelto, arenoso (terreno). || *adv.* **32** ligero (de equipaje): *to travel light = viajar ligero de equipaje.* || **33 according to one's own lights,** según el propio parecer. **34 against the –,** al contraluz. **35 as – as a feather,** ligero como una pluma. **36 to be – on one's feet,** ser ágil de movimientos. **37 to bring something to –,** descubrir, sacar a relucir algo. **38 by the – of nature,** por instinto. **39 to go out like a –,** (fam.) **a)** caer profundamente dormido. **b)** quedar inconsciente. **40 in a bad –,** en perspectiva desfavorable: *it showed his business in a bad light = ello mostró su negocio bajo una perspectiva desfavorable.* **41 in the – of/in – of,** teniendo en cuenta, considerando. **42 in this –,** desde este punto de vista. **43 – aircraft,** avioneta. **44 – at the end of the tunnel,** ver el final de algo desagradable. **45 – industry,** industria ligera. **46 to – out for,** (EE.UU.) (fam.) escapar, huir a: *fed up, he lit out for the West = harto, escapó hacia el Oeste.* **47 lights, a)** posibilidades, medios, recursos, luces: *do according to your lights = actúa según tus posibilidades.* **b)** (arc.) bofe, pulmones (de animales, como alimento). **48 to – up,** iluminar, iluminarse: *two candles lit up the room.* **49 to – upon/on something,** (arc.) encontrar o descubrir algo que produce satisfacción: *he lit upon a rare book = descubrió un libro raro.* **50 to make – of something,** infravalorar, menospreciar algo. **51 to see in a different –,** ver desde otro punto de vista. **52 to see the –, a)** (lit.) ver la luz, nacer. **b)** encontrar al fin la solución a algún problema. **53 to set – to,** prender fuego a. **54 to stand/be in someone's –, a)** quitar la luz a alguien. **b)** estorbar el éxito de alguien. **55 to throw/shed – on,** (lit.) arrojar luz sobre (algún problema o asunto). **56 traffic lights,** semáforo.

lightbulb | 'laɪtbʌlb | *s.c.* bombilla, lámpara.

lighted | 'laɪtɪd | *adj.* encendido, iluminado.

lighten | 'laɪtn | *v.t.* **1** iluminar, alumbrar, dar luz: *white paint lightens a room = la pintura blanca da más luz a una habitación.* **2** avivar (color). **3** aligerar, aliviar, agilizar: *to lighten workload = aligerar carga laboral.* **4** reducir carga, descargar (barcos). || *v.i.* **5** iluminarse, brillar, destellar, fulgurar. **6** clarear, aclararse, despejarse (el cielo). **7** aligerarse (de peso). **8** hacerse más alegre, alegrarse: *he lightens when she shows up = se alegra cuando ella aparece.*

lighter | 'laɪtər | *s.c.* =f encendedor, mechero. **2** MAR. gabarra, barcaza. || *adj.* **3** más ligero, más claro (*comp.* de **light**).

light-fingered | ˌlaɪt'fɪŋgəd | *adj.* **1** (fam.) ladronzuelo. **2** ágil de dedos (para tocar instrumentos musicales).

light-headed | ˌlaɪt'hedɪd | *adj.* **1** aturdido, mareado, torpe. **2** insensato, superficial, frívolo.

light-hearted | ˌlaɪt'hɑːtɪd | *adj.* **1** alegre, optimista, feliz. **2** desenfadado, festivo: *a light-hearted view of life = una visión desenfadada de la vida.*

lighthouse | 'laɪthaus | *s.c.* faro.

lighting | 'laɪtɪŋ | *s.i.* **1** iluminación, alumbrado, encendido (de habitaciones, edificios, calles, etc.). || **2 – -up time,** horario o duración del alumbrado.

lightly | 'laɪtlɪ | *adv.* ligeramente, suavemente, superficialmente.

lightness | 'laɪtnɪs | *s.i.* agilidad, rapidez, ligereza.

lightning | 'laɪtnɪŋ | *s.i.* **1** rayo, relámpago. || *adj.* **2** (fig.) fugaz, corto, rápido, relámpago: *a lightning visit = una visita relámpago.* || **3 a flash of –,** un relámpago. **4 as quick as –,** rápido como un rayo. **5 – conductor,** pararrayos. **6 – rod,** (EE.UU.) pararrayos. **7 – strike,** huelga repentina (realizada sin previo aviso).

lightship | 'laɪtʃɪp | *s.c.* barco-faro.

lightweight | 'laɪtweɪt | *adj.* **1** ligero, de poco peso. **2** (fig.) de poca entidad: *a lightweight politician = un político de poca entidad.* || *s.c.* **3** DEP. peso ligero.

light-year | 'laɪtjɪər | *s.c.* **1** ASTR. año-luz. || **2 light-years,** (fam.) enorme distancia, años-luz.

likable | 'laɪkəbl | V. **likeable.**

like | laɪk | *v.t.* **1** gustarle (a uno), gustar: *I like reading = me gusta leer.* **2** gustar, tener simpatía por: *she likes John = a ella le gusta John.* **3** parecerle (a uno), encontrar, opinar: *how do you like this dress? = ¿qué te parece este vestido?* **4** querer, desear: *what would you like to drink? = ¿qué quiere tomar?* **5** preferir: *I like this better = prefiero éste.* **6 not to like:** no estar dispuesto a: *I don't like to go now = no estoy dispuesto a ir ahora.* || *prep.* **7** como, igual que, del mismo modo que: *to fight like a man = luchar como un hombre.* **8** propio de, típico de: *it's not like her = no es propio de ella, no es su proceder habitual.* **9** como, por ejemplo: *all the people like the Smiths, the Shaws... = todo el mundo, como los Smith, los Shaw...* || *conj.* **10** (fam.) como, del mismo modo que: *do it like he does = hazlo como él lo hace.* || *adj.* **11** parecido, semejante, similar: *people of like tastes = gentes de gustos parecidos.* **12** igual, equivalente, análogo: *like poles = polos equivalentes.* || *adv.* **13** probablemente: *like as not, he won't be back till six = probablemente no volverá hasta las seis.* || *s.c.* **14** igual: *he is the like of Dickens = es el igual de Dickens.* **15** similar: *psychology, sociology and the like = psicología, sociología y similares.* || **16 and the likes,** y cosas por el estilo, etcétera. **17 as – as two peas (in a pod),** (fam.) como dos gotas de agua. **18 to be of – mind,** ser del mismo parecer. **19 I don't feel – it,** (fam.) no me apetece, no me da la gana. **20 I like that!ia,** (euf.) ¡qué desagradable! **21 – anything/–** (*adj.*), (fam.) como si tal cosa: *he nodded back like anything = asintió como si tal cosa.* **22 – as not/– enough,** probablemente. **23 – hell,** (fam.) muchísimo, extraordinariamente duro: *he's worked like hell all morning = ha trabajado muchísimo toda la mañana.* **24 – it or not/whether you – it or not,** te guste o no te guste. **25 – nothing on earth,** (fam.) como no hay cosa igual (de extraño o desagradable). **26 likes and dislikes,** simpatías y antipatías, gustos y fobias. **27 – this/that/so,** así: *do it like this = hazlo así.* **28 more –,** más bien, más cerca de, mejor: *you said fifty dollars, more like sixty = dijiste 50 dólares, más bien 60.* **29 nothing – it,** nada como, lo mejor: *nothing like keeping in bed for colds = nada como guardar cama para curar catarros.* **30 something –,** algo así como, aproximadamente. **31 that's more – it,** eso está mejor. **32 the – of someone/something,** (fam.) a su antojo: *I won't change my plans just for the like of him = no cambiaré mis planes a su antojo.* **33 the – of which/the likes of which,** (lit.) como nunca antes, sin parangón: *a slaughter the like of which man has never known = una matanza como el hombre nunca ha conocido.*

-like | laɪk | *adj.* del tipo de, a modo de, como de (según el significado del sustantivo al que va unido el sufijo para formar *adjs.*): *a landscape with a dream-like air = un paisaje de ensueño.*

likeable | 'laɪkəbl | *adj.* agradable, simpático, encantador.

likelihood | 'laɪklɪhud | *s.i.* **1** probabilidad, posibilidad: *little likelihood of success = pocas posibilidades de éxito.* || **2 in all –,** con toda probabilidad, muy probablemente.

likely | 'laɪklɪ | *adj.* **1** probable, verosímil, posible, esperado: *he's likely to arrive late = es probable que llegue tarde.* **2** realista, verosímil, sensato: *a likely suggestion = una sugerencia sensata.* **3** (brit.) (fam.) formal, prometedor: *likely lads = chicos prometedores.* || *adv.* **4** probablemente: *very likely nobody will come = muy probablemente nadie vendrá.* || **5 a – story/tale,** (fam.) información de poco crédito, un cuento. **6 as – as not,** (fam.) probablemente. **7 not –,** (fam.) seguro que no.

like-minded | ˌlaɪk'maɪndɪd | *adj.* de igual, parecido, similar (pensamiento, sentir, intereses): *like-minded people = gente de igual sentir.*

liken | 'laɪkən | *v.t.* (lit.) **[to – (to)]** comparar con: *life has been likened to a journey = se ha comparado a la vida con un viaje.*

likeness | 'laɪknɪs | *s.i.* y *c.* **1** parecido, semejanza, similitud. **2** (p.u.) retrato: *a good likeness of her = un buen retrato de ella.*

likewise | 'laɪkwɑɪz | *adv.* **1** de igual modo, igual, lo mismo. **2** también, asimismo, además. || **3 to do –,** hacer lo mismo, seguir el modelo.

liking | 'laɪkɪŋ | *s.c.* **1** afición, simpatía, cariño: *a liking to sports.* || **2 too (adj.) for someone's –,** demasiado (*adj.*) para el gusto de uno: *too sweet to my liking = demasiado dulce para mi gusto.* **3 to one's –,** a la medida de los gustos, deseos o esperanzas de uno.

lilac | 'laɪlək | *s.c.* **1** BOT. lila. || *adj.* **2** lila (color).

Lilliputian | ˌlɪlɪ'pjuːʃjən | (lit.) *s.c.* y *adj.* **1** liliputiense. || *adj.* **2** diminuto, muy pequeño, ínfimo.

lilo | 'laɪləu | *s.c.* (brit. y fam.) colchón de playa hinchable.

lilt | lɪlt | *s.c.* **1** ritmo, cadencia (en habla o canto). **2** (fig.) gracia, soltura (de movimiento).

lilting | 'lɪltɪŋ | *adj.* **1** rítmico, cadencioso (voz). **2** gracioso, rítmico (movimiento).

lily | 'lɪlɪ | *s.c.* **1** BOT. lirio. || **2 to gild the –,** tratar de mejorar obras de por sí perfectas. **3 – of the valley,** BOT. lirio de los valles. **4 water –,** BOT. nenúfar. **5 white –,** BOT. lirio blanco, azucena.

lily-livered | ˌlɪlɪ'lɪvəd | *adj.* (fam.) cobarde, miedoso, retraído.

limb | lɪm | *s.c.* **1** extremidad (pierna, brazo, pata, ala). **2** (lit.) rama (de árbol). || **3 in wind and –,** (lit.) en todo el cuerpo, totalmente: *to be sound in wind and limb = estar totalmente sano.* **4 out on a –,** (fam.) en situación precaria (por hechos o palabras). **5 to risk life and –,** poner la vida en grave peligro. **6 to tear someone – from –,** hacer trizas a alguien.

limbed | lɪmd | *adj.* de piernas y brazos (según especifique el *adj.* al que esta palabra va unida): *loose-limbed = de brazos y piernas ágiles y elásticos.*

limber | 'lɪmbər | *adj.* =**f** (lit.) ágil, flexible, elástico: *limber legs.* || *v.i.* **2 [to – up],** entrenar, ejercitar los músculos: *to limber up for a race = entrenar para una carrera.*

limbo | 'lɪmbəu | *s.c.* **1** incógnita, incertidumbre: *I'm in limbo about getting the job = estoy en la total incertidumbre sobre si conseguiré el empleo.* **2** limbo (danza india). **3** REL. limbo.

lime | laɪm | *s.c.* **1** lima (fruta). **2** BOT. limero (árbol). || *s.i.* **3** zumo de lima. **4** QUIM. cal. || *v.t.* **5** encalar, fertilizar (campos para regular su acidez). || **6 quick –,** cal viva. **7 slaked –,** cal apagada.

lime-green | 'laɪmgriːn | *adj.* verde amarillento.

lime-juice | 'laɪmdʒuːs | *s.i.* zumo de lima.

limelight | 'laɪmlaɪt | *s.i.* **1** luz, alumbrado (de carburo). **2** centro, foco (de atención). || **3 to be fond of –,** estar ávido de publicidad. **4 to be in the centre of –,** ser el centro de atención.

limerick | 'lɪmərɪk | *s.c.* quintilla absurda y humorística.

limestone | 'laɪmstəun | *s.i.* GEOL. piedra caliza.

limey | 'laɪmɪ | *s.c.* (EE.UU.) (desp.) británico.

limit | 'lɪmɪt | *s.c.* **1** límite, confín, término (geográfico, temporal, de la paciencia, de la seguridad, en apuestas, etc.). **2** colmo, lo último: *that was really the limit = aquello fue realmente el colmo.* || *v.t.* **3** limitar, restringir, reducir: *to limit one's spending = limitar los gastos.* || **4 to be the –,** ser el colmo. **5 off limits (of),** (EE.UU.) más allá de los límites, de lo permitido o autorizado. **6 the sky is the –,** sin restricciones, todo vale. **7 within limits, a)** dentro de los limites de lo razonable. **b)** hasta cierto punto.

limitation | ˌlɪmɪ'teɪʃn | *s.c.* limitación, restricción: *we all have our limitations = todos tenemos nuestras limitaciones.*

limited | 'lɪmɪtɪd | *adj.* **1** limitado, reducido, restringido: *limited resources = recursos limitados.* || **2 – edition,** edición de tirada limitada. **3 – liability company,** COM. sociedad de responsabilidad limitada. **4 – monarchy,** monarquía constitucional.

limiting | 'lɪmɪtɪŋ | *adj.* limitativo, restrictivo.

limitless | 'lɪmɪtlɪs | *adj.* ilimitado, sin límites.

limousine | 'lɪmuːziːn | *s.c.* limusina, coche de representación.

limp | lɪmp | *v.i.* **1** cojear, renquear. **2** ser irregular o desequilibrado (discurso, música, poesía, etc.) || *s.c.* **3** cojera. || *adj.* **4** flojo, fláccido, mustio, débil.

limpet | 'lɪmpɪt | *s.c.* **1** ZOOL. lapa. || **2 to cling like a –,** pegarse como una lapa.

limpid | 'lɪmpɪd | *adj.* (lit.) límpido, claro, transparente.

limpidity | lɪm'pɪdɪtɪ | *s.i.* (lit.) claridad, transparencia, diafanidad.

limply | 'lɪmplɪ | *adv.* débilmente, fláccidamente.

linchpin | 'lɪntʃpɪn | *s.c.* **1** (fig.) pieza clave, aglutinante: *the linchpin of the economic policy = la pieza clave de la política económica.* **2** MEC. pezonera.

linctus | 'lɪŋktəs | *s.i.* (brit.) jarabe anticatarral.

linden | 'lɪndən | *s.c.* BOT. tilo, limero.

line | laɪn | *s.c.* **1** línea. **2** línea de meta. **3** frontera, divisoria. **4** dirección, trayectoria: *a ball's line of flight = trayectoria de una pelota.* **5** fila: *the soldiers were standing in line = los soldados formaban en fila.* **6** generación, familia: *a long line of musicians = una larga generación de músicos.* **7** renglón, línea: *ten words to a line = diez palabras por línea.* **8** verso (de un poema). **9** arruga (de la piel): *a face covered with lines = una cara llena de arrugas.* **10** contorno, línea externa: *the fine lines of a sports ship = la bella línea de un barco deportivo.* **11** cuerda (de tender ropa). **12** sedal, hilo (de pescar). **13** tendido (telefónico o eléctrico): *the lines were damaged by a storm = el tendido quedó averiado por una tormenta.* **14** línea, comunicación (telefónica): *the line is engaged = la línea está ocupada.* **15** (fam.) carta, (unas) líneas: *drop us a line when you arrive = escríbenos unas líneas a la llegada.* **16** línea, medio de transporte (suministrado por una compañía): *a shipping line = línea de transporte por barco.* **17** cadena (de producción o montaje): *an assembly line = una cadena de montaje.* **18** vía, línea (de argumentación, información, investigación, etc.). **19** (fam.) área, línea (de interés o actividad): *what line of business does he work? = ¿qué área de negocios trabaja?* **20** diseño, línea: *a new line of handbags = una nueva línea de bolsos.* **21** (fig.) facilidad, gracia, destreza: *a good line in funny stories = facilidad para contar historias divertidas.* **22** (fam.) impresión, idea (falsa): *to give the line that... = dar la falsa impresión de...* **23** GEOG. ecuador. **24** MIL. frente, línea (que divide dos ejércitos): *behind the enemy lines = detrás del frente enemigo.* **25** MIL. (brit.) fuerza de infantería: *a line regiment = regimiento de infantería.* **26** MIL. (EE.UU.) fuerzas de combate (en conjunto). || *v.t.* **27** trazar líneas, rayar: *lined paper = papel rayado.* **28** marcar con líneas o arrugas, arrugar (el rostro): *the age had lined his face = la edad le había arrugado el rostro.* **29** alinearse, estar en línea: *the trees line the avenues = los árboles se alinean en las avenidas.* **30 [to – (with)]** revestir, forrar: *to line a coat with silk = forrar de seda una chaqueta.* **31** enriquecerse, llenarse (el bolsillo), atiborrarse, llenarse (el estómago). || **32 a – on,** información de buena fuente. **33 all along the –,** desde el principio. **34 to be in – for,** tener muchas posibilidades de (conseguir un empleo, promoción, etc.). **35 to be in – with, a)** estar al mismo nivel de. **b)** estar de acuerdo con. **36 to be on the right lines,** seguir un método acertado. **37 to bring someone into – with,** poner a alguien de acuerdo con. **38 down the lines,** (EE.UU.) (fam.) completamente, sin reservas: *they supported her down the lines = la apoyaron sin reservas.* **39 to draw the – (at),** fijar los límites. **40 to follow the party –,** seguir la política impuesta por el partido. **41 hard lines!,** ¡qué mala suerte! **42 hold in –,** no cuelgue (el teléfono). **43 in the – of duty/service,** como exigencia del cumplimiento del deber. **44 to lay down the broad lines,** trazar las grandes líneas. **45 to lay it on the –,** hablar con franqueza. **46 to keep someone in –,** mantener bajo control (a miembros de un grupo o partido). **47 – drawing,** dibujo lineal. **48 – of battle,** MIL. orden de combate. **49 – of sight/vision,** línea de visión. **50 to – one's pocket/purse,** (fam.) forrarse (con dinero no bien visto). **51 – printer,** INF. impresora de línea. **52 lines, a)** línea de ferrocarril, raíles, vías: *don't cross the lines = no crucen las vías.* **b)** papel, texto (de un actor): *the actor wasn't sure of his lines = el actor no se sabía bien su papel.* **53 to – someone/something up, a)** alinear, poner en fila. **b)** (fam.) organizar, montar (espectáculos). **c)** contratar (para un espectáculo ocasional): *they've lined up the best tenor = han contratado al mejor tenor.* **54 out of – (with someone/something), a)** estar fuera de línea. **b)** ser diferente (y menos competitivo). **55 to read between the lines,** leer entre líneas. **56 to shoot a –,** exagerar, fanfarronear. **57 to sign on the dotted –,** (fig.) aprobar a ciegas. **58 to stand in –,** hacer cola. **59 to step out of –,** escapar al control. **60 to take a tough/hard – with,** emplear mano dura con. **61 to toe the –,** acatar la disciplina (de un grupo o partido).

lineage | 'laɪnɪdʒ | *s.i.* número de líneas, extensión (de un escrito o texto).

lineage | 'lɪnɪɪdʒ | *s.c.* (lit.) linaje, ascendencia, dinastía, casta, alcurnia.

lineal | 'lɪnɪəl | *adj.* (lit.) lineal, en línea directa, hereditario.

lineally | 'lɪnɪəlɪ | *adv.* (lit.) linealmente, directamente (en la ascendencia o descendencia).

lineament | 'lɪnɪəmənt | *s.c.* (lit.) **1** corte, línea, configuración, rasgos (de la cara). **2** rasgos, cualidad específica.

linear | 'lɪnɪər | *adj.* **1** lineal, compuesto de líneas: *a linear design = un diseño lineal.* **2** de longitud, longitudinal: *linear measurements = medidas de longitud.* || **3 – equation,** MAT. ecuación de primer grado.

linearity | ˌlɪnɪ'ærɪtɪ | *s.i.* MAT. linealidad.

lined | laɪnd | *adj.* **1** arrugado (de cara). **2** pautado (papel).

linen | 'lɪnɪn | *s.i.* **1** lino, tejido de lino. **2** ropa doméstica: *bed linen = ropa de cama.* **3** (arc.) ropa interior. || **4 to wash one's dirty – in public, a)** ventilar asuntos privados en público. **b)** sacar a relucir los trapos sucios.

liner | 'laɪnər | *s.c.* **=f** transatlántico. **2** forro, revestimiento. **3** bolsa de plástico (para depositar la basura).

linesman | 'laɪnzmən | *s.c.* **1** cuidador, reparador del tendido (eléctrico o telefónico). **2** guardavía (del ferrocarril). **3** DEP. juez de línea, linier.

line-up | 'laɪnʌp | *s.c.* **1** (EE.UU.) cola, fila (de gente en espera). **2** rueda de sospechosos (para su identificación por testigos). **3** DEP. formación, selección, equipo.

ling | lɪŋ | *s.i.* **1** BOT. brezo común. || *s.c.* **2** ZOOL. molva (pez).

linger | 'lɪŋgər | *v.i.* **=f** persistir, subsistir, continuar (tradición, ideas, sentimientos, etc.). **2** quedarse, retrasarse, rezagarse. **3** alargar el tiempo (dedicado a una actividad). **4** prolongar (agonía).

lingerer | 'lɪŋgərər | *s.c.* rezagado.

lingerie | 'lænʒərɪ | *s.i.* ropa interior femenina, lencería.

lingering | 'lɪŋgərɪŋ | *adj.* lento, rezagado, persistente, último.

lingeringly | 'lɪŋgərɪŋlɪ | *adv.* rezagadamente, persistentemente.

lingo | 'lɪŋgəu | *s.c.* **1** (fam.) lengua, idioma (extranjero, extraño). **2** jerga.

lingua franca | ˌlɪŋgwə'fræŋkə | *s.c.* (lit.) lengua franca (empleada por hablantes de distintas lenguas para entenderse).

linguist | 'lɪŋgwɪst | *s.c.* lingüista.

linguistic | lɪŋ'gwɪstɪk | *adj.* lingüístico.

linguistically | lɪŋ'gwɪstɪkəlɪ | *adv.* lingüísticamente.

linguistics | lɪŋ'gwɪstɪks | *s.i.* lingüística.

liniment | 'lɪnɪmənt | *s.i.* linimento.

lining | 'laɪnɪŋ | *s.c.* forro, revestimiento, refuerzo.

link | lɪŋk | *s.c.* **1** eslabón. **2** conexión, enlace, vínculo. || *v.t.* **3** unir, enlazar, conectar. || *v.i.* **4 [to – (with)]** unirse, conectarse a. || **5 cuff links,** gemelos (de camisa). **6 links,** campo de golf. **7 to – up,** conectar, enlazar. **8 the missing –,** el eslabón perdido (en la cadena evolutiva entre el mono y el hombre).

linked | lɪŋkt | *adj.* conectado, enlazado, ligado, vinculado.

linkage | 'lɪŋkɪdʒ | *s.c.* **1** unión, conexión, relación. **2** compromiso, concierto (entre países o naciones).

linkman | 'lɪŋkmən | *s.c.* TV. enlace, introductor, presentador (de los distintos componentes de un programa de radio o televisión).

link-up | 'lɪŋkʌp | *s.c.* conexión, unión (entre cosas o partes alejadas): *a TV link-up between studios throughout the world = programa de TV con conexiones de todo el mundo.*

linnet | 'lɪnɪt | *s.c.* ZOOL. pardillo, jilguero.

lino | 'laɪnəʊ | *s.i.* (fam.) linóleo.
linoleum | lɪ'nəʊljəm | *s.i.* linóleo.
linseed | 'lɪnsiːd | *s.i.* **1** linaza. || **2 – oil,** aceite de linaza.
lint | lɪnt | *s.i.* **1** gasa, hilas (para cubrir heridas): *a link bandage = vendaje de gasa.* **2** pelusa, tamo.
lintel | 'lɪntl | *s.c.* dintel.
lion | 'laɪən | *s.c.* **1** ZOOL. león. **2** (fig.) famoso, bravo, valiente, celebrado: *a literary lion = escritor famoso.* || **3 to fight like a –,** luchar como un león, bravamente. **4 the lion's share,** la parte del león, la mejor o más importante.
lioness | 'laɪənɪs | *s.c.* ZOOL. leona.
lion-hearted | ˌlaɪən'hɑːtɪd | *adj.* valiente, de corazón valeroso.
lionize | 'laɪənaɪz | (también **lionise**) *v.t.* agasajar a las celebridades.
lip | lɪp | *s.c.* **1** labio. **2** borde, reborde, saliente (vasos, vasijas, etc.). **3** (fam.) insolencia, impertinencia, grosería: *no more lip from you = basta de impertinencias.* || **4 to bite one's –,** morderse los labios, guardarse la rabia o disgusto. **5 to keep a stiff upper –,** actuar con decisión. **6 my lips are sealed,** no diré una palabra, seré como una tumba. **7 on everyone's lips/on every –,** en boca de todos, todo el mundo habla de ello.
lipped | lɪpt | *adj.* de labios, con labios... (según el significado del *adj.* al que este sufijo adjetival va unido): *thin-lipped = de labios finos; tight-lipped = con los labios apretados.*
lip-read | 'lɪpˌriːd | *v.t.* e *i.* leer en los labios o por el movimiento de los labios (propio de sordos).
lip-reading | 'lɪpriːdɪŋ | *s.i.* lectura de los labios.
lip-service | 'lɪpˌsɜːvɪs | *s.i.* (desp.) palabras (sin intención de cumplir), hablar de boquilla: *don't trust him, he's paying lip-service = no le creas, está hablando de boquilla.*
lipstick | 'lɪpstɪk | *s.c.* **1** pintura de labios. **2** barra de labios.
liquefy | 'lɪkwɪfaɪ | *v.t.* e *i.* licuar, licuarse.
liquescent | lɪ'kwesnt | *adj.* que se hace líquido.
liqueur | lɪ'kjuər | *s.i.* licor.
liquid | 'lɪkwɪd | *s.i.* **1** líquido. || *s.c.* **2** FON. consonante líquida. || *adj.* **3** líquido: *liquid soap = jabón líquido.* **4** (lit.) claro, transparente, brillante (ojos): *she has liquid eyes = tiene ojos claros.* **5** claro, fluido (sonido). **6** ECON. líquido: *liquid cash = dinero líquido.* || **7 – assets,** ECON. activo (líquido). **8 – lunch,** (euf.) comida abundante en bebidas alcohólicas.
liquidate | 'lɪkwɪdeɪt | *v.t.* **1** liquidar, matar, eliminar, deshacerse de. **2** COM. cerrar (empresas o negocios). **3** COM. liquidar, saldar (deudas).
liquidation | ˌlɪkwɪ'deɪʃn | *s.c.* **1** eliminación, aplastamiento. **2** COM. liquidación.
liquidator | 'lɪkwɪdeɪtər | *s.c.* COM. liquidador.
liquidity | lɪ'kwɪdɪtɪ | *s.i.* ECON. liquidez.
liquidize | 'lɪkwɪdaɪz | (brit.) también **liquise.** *v.t.* licuar (frutas, verduras, etc.).
liquidizer | 'lɪkwɪˌɪdaɪər | *s.c.* licuadora.
liquor | 'lɪkər | *s.i.* **1** (brit.) licor (cualquier bebida alcohólica). **2** (EE.UU.) licor (bebida alcohólica de alta graduación). **3** (p.u.) jugo (de carne frita o asada).
liquorice | 'lɪkərɪs | (EE.UU. **licorice**) *s.i.* **1** regaliz. **2** BOT. orozuz, regaliz (planta).
lira | 'lɪərə | [*pl.* **lire** o **liras**] *s.c.* FIN. lira (moneda italiana).
lisle | laɪl | *s.i.* hilo de Escocia.
lisp | lɪsp | *s.c.* **1** ceceo. **2** balbuceo. || *v.t.* e *i.* **3** cecear. **4** balbucear.
lispingly | 'lɪspɪŋlɪ | *adv.* con un ceceo (en el habla).
lissom | 'lɪsəm | *adj.* ágil, ligero, grácil.
lissomness | 'lɪsəmnɪs | *s.i.* agilidad, ligereza, gracia (en los movimientos).
list | lɪst | *s.c.* **1** lista, relación, catálogo: *shopping list = lista de la compra.* **2** inclinación, posición inclinada. || *v.t.* **3** hacer una lista, poner en lista, inscribir, catalogar: *he listed the books = catalogó los libros.* || *v.i.* **4** inclinarse, escorarse, vencerse hacia un lado (especialmente barcos). **5** (arc.) desear. **6** (arc.) escuchar, oír. || **7 to enter the lists,** (lit.) ser admitido a una competición. **8 – price,** COM. precio de tarifa u oficial. **9 on the danger –,** (fam.) muy enfermo, cercano a la muerte.
listed | 'lɪstɪd | *adj.* **1** incluido en lista, catalogado, clasificado. || **2 a – building,** (brit.) edificio protegido (por su valor histórico o arquitectónico).
listen | 'lɪsn | *v.i.* **1** escuchar, atender, prestar atención: *listen to me = escúchenme.* **2** dejarse persuadir: *I never listen to publicity = nunca me dejo persuadir por la publicidad.* **3** enterarse, prestar oídos: *I told him but he wouldn't listen = se lo dije pero no quiso enterarse.* || *s.c.* **4** (fam.) atención, oído, audición: *have a listen to this new record = escucha este nuevo disco.* || **5 to – for some /something,** prestar atención, advertir: *listen for the change of the rhythm = advierte el cambio de ritmo.* **6 to – in (on/to), a)** escuchar por la radio: *to listen in to the news = escuchar las noticias por la radio.* **b)** espiar, controlar (conversaciones): *they are listening in on his phone calls = le están controlando las llamadas.* **7 to – out (for),** (fam.) estar al tanto (para oír algo imprevisto): *listen out for the phone while I'm in the bath = estáte al tanto del teléfono mientras estoy en el baño.*
listener | 'lɪsnər | *s.c.* oyente, radioyente.
listing | 'lɪstɪŋ | *s.c.* lista, listado.
listless | 'lɪstlɪs | *adj.* lánguido, decaído, apático, indiferente.
listlessly | 'lɪstlɪslɪ | *adv.* lánguidamente, débilmente, sin energía.
listlessness | 'lɪstlɪsnɪs | *s.i.* indiferencia, languidez, desgana.
lit | lɪt | V. **light.**
litany | 'lɪtənɪ | *s.c.* **1** (fig.) letanía, lista (larga y aburrida): *a litany of complaints = una letanía de quejas.* **2** REL. letanía, serie de oraciones.
literacy | 'lɪtərəsɪ | *s.i.* **1** capacidad de leer y escribir. || **2 – campaign,** campaña de alfabetización.
literal | 'lɪtərəl | *adj.* **1** literal: *literal sense of a word = sentido literal de una palabra.* **2** (desp.) literal, prosaico, carente de creatividad o imaginación: *a rather too literal interpretation = una interpretación carente de creatividad.*
literally | 'lɪtərəlɪ | *adv.* **1** literalmente, al pie de la letra: *most idioms are hard to translate literally = es difícil traducir las expresiones idiomáticas literalmente.* **2** (fam.) literalmente, materialmente, absolutamente: *it was literally impossible to work = era materialmente imposible trabajar.* || **3 to take something –,** tomar algo al pie de la letra.
literalness | 'lɪtərəlnɪs | *s.i.* literalidad, exactitud (en escritos).
literary | 'lɪtərərɪ | *adj.* literario: *a literary hero = un héroe literario.*
literate | 'lɪtərət | *adj.* **1** que sabe leer y escribir. **2** culto, instruido.
literati | ˌlɪtə'rɑːtiː | *s.c.* (lit.) literatos, personas de amplios conocimientos literarios.
literature | 'lɪtrətʃər | (EE.UU. | 'lɪtrəɪtʃʊər |) *s.i.* **1** literatura (escritos literarios). **2** documentación, literatura (sobre una disciplina o campo específico): *scientific literature = documentación científica.* **3** folletos, material escrito (de propaganda o publicidad).
lithe | laɪð | *adj.* ligero, grácil, elástico, flexible (persona o animal).
lithium | 'lɪθɪəm | *s.i.* QUIM. litio.
lithograph | 'lɪθəʊgrɑːf *s.c.* **1** litografía: *a lithograph of Dickens.* || *v.t.* **2** litografiar.
lithographic | ˌlɪθəʊ'græfɪk | *adj.* litográfico.
lithography | lɪɒθɒgrəfɪ | *s.i.* litografía (forma, proceso de impresión).
Lithuania | ˌlɪəjuː'eɪnjə | *s.i.* Lituania.
Lithuanian | ˌlɪəjuː'eɪnjən | *adj./s.c.* lituano.
litigant | 'lɪtɪgənt | *s.c.* DER. litigante.
litigation | ˌlɪtɪ'geɪʃn | *s.c.* e *i.* DER. litigio, pleito.
litigious | lɪ'tɪdʒəs | *adj.* DER. litigioso, pleitista.
litmus | 'lɪtməs | *s.i.* **1** tornasol. || **2 – paper,** papel de tornasol. **3 – test,** prueba simple y efectiva.
litre | 'liːtər | (EE.UU. **liter**) *s.c.* litro.
litter | 'lɪtər | *s.i.* **1** basura, desperdicios, papeles. **2** desorden, cosas desordenadas: *a litter of magazines = un desorden de revistas.* **3** cama, lecho de paja (de animales). || *s.c.* **4** camada. **5** camilla (para transporte de heridos). **6** (arc.) litera (para transporte de personas notables). || *v.t.* **7** ensuciar, desordenar, esparcir, tirar (basura o desperdicios): *to litter the streets = tirar basura a la calle.* **8** andar rodando, estar esparcido,

estar tirado: *books littered the room = los libros estaban tirados por la habitación.* **9** cubrir, llenar (de cosas desordenadas): *his desk was littered with papers = su mesa estaba cubierta de papeles.* **10** acostar (animales). || *v.i.* **11** parir (animales). || **12 – bin,** cubo de la basura, contenedor de basura. **13 – lout,** (Brit.) persona que ensucia lugares públicos.

litterburg | 'lɪtə,bʌg | *s.c.* (EE.UU.) persona que ensucia lugares públicos.

little | 'lɪtl | *adj.* **1** pequeño (con cierto matiz de afecto): *a little house in the country = una casita en el campo.* **2** corto, poco (tiempo), un rato: *he stayed for a little while = se quedó un rato.* **3** menor, más joven: *my little brother = mi hermano menor.* **4** pequeño, intrascendente, insignificante, trivial: *the little things of everyday life = las pequeñas cosas de la vida diaria.* **5** poco, insuficiente: *we have very little money left = nos queda muy poco dinero.* **6** un poco de, algo: *add a little sugar = añada un poco de azúcar.* || *pron.* **7** poco, no mucho, insuficiente: *they see very little of their children = ven muy poco a sus hijos.* **8** un poco, algo: *give me a little more = déme un poco más.* **9** un poco, un rato: *he came back after a little = regresó un poco después.* || *adv.* **10** poco: *the book is little known = el libro es poco conocido.* **11** (form.) poco, nada, en absoluto: *little did we know of his coming = no sabíamos nada de su llegada.* **12** poco, raramente: *they go out very little = salen muy raramente.* || **13 a – bit,** (fam.) un poco. **14 every – helps,** aun lo más pequeño tiene su importancia. **15 – by –,** poco a poco, gradualmente. **16 – finger,** dedo meñique. **17 – if any,** muy poco. **18 – or nothing,** entre poco y nada. **19 – people,** duendes, hadas. **20 to make – of, a)** restar importancia a. **b)** no alcanzar a entender.

OBS. Uno de los significados más frecuentes de **little** es "pequeño", con el matiz afectivo que en español queda expresado con las formas diminutivas de los sustantivos, como se indica en **l.**

littoral | 'lɪtərəl | *s./adj.* (lit.) litoral, costa.

liturgical | lɪ'tɜːdʒɪkl | *adj.* litúrgico.

liturgically | lɪ'tɜːdʒɪklɪ | *adv.* litúrgicamente.

liturgy | 'lɪtədʒɪ | *s.c.* e *i.* liturgia.

live | lɪv | *v.i.* **1** vivir, existir: *we need water to live = necesitamos el agua para vivir.* **2** vivir, persistir, perdurar: *his work will live = su obra perdurará.* **3** vivir, residir, morar: *where do you live?* **4 [to – by/on]** alimentarse de, vivir de: *sheep live on grass = la oveja se alimenta de hierba.* **5** vivir, llevar una vida determinada: *he lived alone all his life = vivió solo toda su vida.* **6** vivir, disfrutar de la vida: *he's never lived really = no ha disfrutado de la vida.* **7** (fig.) guardar, poner (una cosa en su lugar habitual): *where does this knife live? = ¿dónde se guarda este cuchillo?* || *v.t.* **8** vivir, revivir (experiencias): *the child lived the film = el niño vivía la película.* || | laɪv | *adj.* **9** vivo, viviente: *a live snake = una serpiente viva.* **10** en directo, en vivo (retransmisiones audiovisuales): *live pictures of man on the moon = imágenes en directo del hombre en la luna.* **11** en persona, en directo (espectáculos): *Pavarotti live in concert = concierto de Pavarotti en directo.* **12** candente, de interés, importante: *malnutrition is still a live issue = la desnutrición es todavía un tema candente.* **13** encendido, ardiendo: *a live match = un fósforo encendido.* **14** activado, cargado, sin explotar (munición). **15** conectado, con corriente (material electrónico). || | laɪv | *adv.* **16** en directo: *the speech was broadcast live on the radio = el discurso fue radiado en directo.* || **17 a – wire,** (fig.) persona viva y activa. **18 a real –,** de verdad: *a real live lion = un león de verdad.* **19 to – a lie,** vivir en la mentira. **20 to – and learn,** vivir para ver. **21 to – and let –,** vivir y dejar vivir. **22 to – beyond one's means,** vivir por encima de las posibilidades de uno. **23 to – by/on one's wits,** vivir de recursos dudosos. **24 to – by something, a)** vivir o alimentarse de algo. **b)** vivir conforme a (normas). **25 to – for,** vivir para, dedicarse por entero a: *he only lives for his work = sólo vive para su trabajo.* **26 to – from hand to mouth,** vivir al día. **27 to – in,** vivir interno (personal de servicio). **28 to – in sin,** (arc.) vivir amancebado. **29 to – it up,** (fam.) gozar de la vida al máximo. **30 to – like fighting cooks,** disfrutar los mejores manjares. **31 to – off/on the fat of the land,** disfrutar lo mejor de la vida. **32 to – off someone/something,** vivir de/a costa de: *he lives off his parents = vive de sus padres.* **33 to – off the land,** vivir de productos naturales. **34 to – on,** perdurar, sobrevivir: *his memory will live on = su recuerdo perdurará.* **35 to – on borrowed time,** continuar vivo más allá de los pronósticos. **36 to – out, a)** vivir hasta: *he won't surely live out of the week = seguro que no vive hasta el final de la semana.* **b)** vivir externo (personal doméstico). **37 to – out something,** hacer realidad (sueños, ambiciones). **38 to – rough,** vivir sin techo. **39 to – through,** sobrevivir, sobreponerse a: *he lived through the famine = sobrevivió al hambre.* **40 to – together,** vivir amancebado. **41 to – up to something,** estar a la altura de, responder a lo esperado. **42 to – within one's means,** vivir de acuerdo con las posibilidades de uno. **43 to – with someone/something, a)** vivir amancebado. **b)** soportar, aceptar (situaciones desagradables): *you have to live with it = hay que aceptarlo.*

liveable | 'lɪvəbl | (también **livable**) *adj.* sufrible, soportable.

liveable-in | 'lɪvəblɪn | (también **livable-in**) *adj.* habitable.

liveable-with | 'lɪvəblwɪθ | (también **livable-with**) *adj.* tratable, agradable (que se puede vivir con esa persona).

live-in | 'lɪvɪn | *adj.* (fam.) interno: *a live-in servant = sirviente interno.*

livelihood | 'laɪvlɪhud | *s.c.* vida, medio de vida, sustento.

liveliness | 'laɪvlɪnɪs | *s.i.* vida, viveza, vivacidad, energía, vigor.

livelong | 'laɪvlɔːŋ | (EE.UU. | 'llɔːŋ |) *adj.* (lit.) **1** todo, todo a lo largo (del día, de la noche). || **2 all the – day,** todo el santo día.

lively | 'laɪvlɪ | *adj.* **1** vivo, animado, vigoroso: *a lively girl = una chica animada.* **2** vivo, sorprendente: *a lively imagination = imaginación sorprendente.* **3** movido, alegre, divertido: *a lively party = una fiesta divertida.* **4** vivo, brillante (color). **5** enérgico, vigoroso (esfuerzo, discurso, campaña, etc.). **6** agitado, revuelto (el mar). || **7 to look –,** darse prisa, aligerar. **8 to make it/things – for someone,** (hum.) poner una trampa a alguien.

liven up | 'laɪvnʌp | *v.t.* e *i.* **1** animar(se), alegrar(se): *do liven up a bit = anímate un poco.* || **2 to liven someone /something up,** hacer que alguien o algo se anime.

liver | 'lɪvər | *s.c.* e *i.* **=f** ANAT. hígado. **2** hígado (como alimento). **3** persona (de un determinado modo de vida): *a quiet liver = persona de vida tranquila.* || **4 – sausage** (EE.UU. **liverwurst**), embutido de hígado.

liveried | 'lɪvərɪd | *adj.* uniformado, de librea.

liverish | 'lɪvərɪʃ | *adj.* **1** enfermo del hígado: *to feel liverish = sentirse enfermo del hígado.* **2** irritable, irascible.

livery | 'lɪvərɪ | *s.c.* e *i.* **1** uniforme, librea: *a servant in livery = sirviente uniformado.* **2** vestimenta (de los gremios de Londres). **3** (lit.) cubierto de hojas (árbol): *trees in their spring livery = árboles cubiertos de hojas nuevas.* || **4 – company,** gremio de Londres con su uniforme. **5 liveryman, a)** componente uniformado de un gremio. **b)** caballerizo, empleado de caballerizas de alquiler. **6 – stable,** caballeriza de alquiler.

lives | laɪvz | V. **life.**

livestock | 'laɪvstɒk | *s.i.* ganado, ganadería, cabaña.

livid | 'lɪvɪd | *adj.* **1** lívido, amoratado: *livid bruises = contusiones amoratadas.* **2** (fam.) furiosos, fuera de sí: *livid with rage = furioso de rabia.*

living | 'lɪvɪŋ | *adj.* **1** vivo, viviente: *the finest living tenor = el mejor tenor vivo.* **2** vivo, en uso, activo: *living languages = lenguas vivas.* || *s.c.* e *i.* **3** vida, medio de vida: *he earns his living from writing = se gana la vida escribiendo.* **4** forma de vida, vivir: *to understand the art of living = saber vivir.* **5** REL. beneficio, provisión de sustento (de clérigos). || **6 a – legend,** persona muy famosa en vida. **7 to be – proof of something,** ser la prueba viviente de algo. **8 in the land of the –,** (hum.) vivo. **9 – death,** muerte en vida, vida de continua miseria. **10 – image,** la viva imagen, exactamente igual. **11 – standard,** medio o tren de vida. **12 – wage,** salario de subsistencia. **13 to scrape a –,** ganarse la vida con dificultad. **14 the –,** los vivos. **15 within/in – memory,** que se recuerde, hasta donde alcanza el recuerdo de los vivos: *the coldest winter within living memory = el invierno más frío que se recuerde.*

living-room | 'lɪvɪŋrum | *s.c.* salón; cuarto o sala de estar.

lizard | 'lɪzəd | *s.c.* ZOOL. lagarto, lagartija.

llama | 'lɑːmə | *s.c.* ZOOL. llama.

lo | ləu | *interj.* **1** (arc.) ¡ojo!, ¡mira!, ¡atención! || **2 – and behold,** (fam.) hete aquí, mira por dónde.

load | ləud | *s.c.* **1** carga, peso: *the load of shopping = la carga de la compra.* **2** cantidad de carga (transportada por un vehículo). **3** carga, cantidad de trabajo (a realizar según un horario o programa): *teaching load = carga docente.* **4** peso, carga (a soportar por una estructura, puente, etc.). **5** (fig.) peso, responsabilidad, preocupación: *the heavy load of guilt = el gran peso de la culpa.* **6** FIS. fuerza (de una fuente de energía). || *v.i.* **7** cargar. **8** recibir carga: *the boat is still loading = el barco está aún recibiendo carga.* || *v.t.* **9 [to – (up) with]** cargar de: *to load a lorry (up) with bricks = cargar un camión de ladrillos.* **10 [to – (into)]** cargar (armas, cámaras de fotografías), poner (munición, carrete, etc.): *to load a new film into the camera = poner carrete nuevo en la cámara.* **11** INF. cargar, pasar, transferir (datos, un programa, etc. a la memoria de un ordenador). || **12 a –/loads of,** (fam.) gran cantidad de, montones de: *she's got loads of money = tiene montones de dinero.* **13 a – of (old) rubbish,** (fam.) una basura, no vale nada: *that book is a load of old rubbish = ese libro no vale nada.* **14 a – off someone's mind,** peso que uno se quita de encima. **15 get a – of this,** (fam.) mira, presta atención a esto. **16 -load,** cantidad de carga (determinada por la primera parte del compuesto): *two lorry-loads of sand = dos camiones de arena.* **17 to – someone down with,** agobiar a alguien con: *he was loaded down with all his worries = estaba agobiado con todas sus preocupaciones.* **18 to – someone with honours/presents, etc.,** colmar a alguien de honores, regalos, obsequios, etc.

loaded | 'ləudɪd | *adj.* **1** cargado: *a loaded gun = una escopeta cargada.* **2** reforzado, preparado (como arma contundente): *a loaded stick = bastón reforzado.* **3** (fam.) forrado (de dinero). || **4 a – question,** una pregunta capciosa. **5 the dice are – (against someone),** tener los hados en contra, tener mala suerte.

loading | 'ləudɪŋ | *s.c.* e *i.* COM. recargo, pago adicional (en pólizas de seguro por riesgo especial).

load-shedding | 'ləudˌʃedɪŋ | *s.i.* corte de energía eléctrica (por sobrecarga).

loadstar | 'ləudstɑːr | V. **lodestar.**

loadstone | 'ləudstəun | *s.c.* e *i.* **1** FIS. magnetita. **2** FIS. imán. **3** (fig.) imán, foco de atracción: *she's a loadstone for people in trouble = es un imán para la gente necesitada.*

loaf | ləuf | *s.c.* **1** barra, pistola, hogaza (de pan). || *v.i.* **2** (fam.) holgazanear, gandulear, haraganear. || **3 half a – is better than none/no bread,** (fam.) a falta de pan, buenas son tortas. **4 – sugar,** azúcar en terrones. **5 use your –,** (brit. y fam.) recapacita, usa la cabeza.

loafer | 'ləufər | *s.c.* **1** holgazán, vago, gandul, haragán. **2** (EE.UU.) zapato mocasín.

loam | ləum | *s.i.* GEOL. marga.

loamy | 'ləumɪ | *adj.* margoso (arcilloso y con plantas en descomposición).

loan | ləun | *s.c.* **1** préstamo (de dinero, principalmente): *a bank loan = un préstamo bancario.* **2** préstamo, permiso (para usar una cosa): *he asked his father for the loan of his car = pidió permiso a su padre para usar su coche.* || *v.t.* **3** (EE.UU.) prestar, dejar: *can you loan me your bike? = ¿me dejas tu bici?* **4** ceder, prestar (objetos de gran valor por tiempo determinado): *a painting loaned by the National Gallery = cuadro cedido por la National Gallery.* || **5 – shark,** (desp.) usurero. **6 – word,** FILOL. préstamo lingüístico. **7 on –,** en calidad de préstamo.

loan-collection | 'ləunkəlekʃn | *s.c.* ART. préstamo de obras (para una exhibición).

loath | ləuθ | (form.) *adj.* **1** reacio, contrario, retraído: *he seemed loath to speak = se mostraba reacio a hablar.* || **2 nothing –,** de buena gana, bien dispuesto.

loathe | ləuð | *v.t.* odiar, detestar, aborrecer.

loathing | 'ləuðɪŋ | *s.i.* odio, aversión, aborrecimiento, inquina.

loathsome | 'ləuðsəm | *adj.* ocioso, asqueroso, repugnante.

loaves | ləuvz | V. **loaf.**

lob | lɒb | DEP. *v.t.* e *i.* **1** lanzar un globo (en tenis). || *s.c.* **2** globo (golpe de pelota por encima del contrario, en tenis).

lobby | 'lɒbɪ | *s.c.* **1** vestíbulo, antesala (de un hotel, teatro, etc.). **2** antecámara del Parlamento británico (abierta al público y prensa). **3** camarilla, grupo de opinión (capaz de influir en las decisiones políticas). || *v.t.* e *i.* **4** cabildear, hacer política de pasillos, ejercer influencia o presión (en políticos). **5 [to – (through)]** aprobar o rechazar un proyecto de ley (mediante influencias o presiones).

lobbyist | 'lɒbɪɪst | *s.c.* cabildero, intrigante, que ejerce presiones, negociador (político).

lobe | ləub | *s.c.* ANAT. lóbulo (de la oreja, del cerebro o del pulmón).

lobed | ləubd | *adj.* lobado, lobulado, con lóbulos.

lobotomy | 'ləu'bɒtəmɪ | *s.c.* e *i.* MED. lobotomía.

lobster | 'lɒbstər | *s.c.* e *i.* **=f** ZOOL. langosta (crustáceo). || **2 – pot,** nasa, garlito, langostera.

local | 'ləukl | *adj.* **1** local, lugareño, de la localidad, del barrio. **2** de cercanías (tren, autobús, etc.). **3** MED. local, localizado, aislado: *is the pain local? = ¿está el dolor localizado?* || *s.c.* **4** (brit.) (fam.) bar, taberna (de la vecindad y frecuentada habitualmente): *what is your local? = ¿qué bar frecuentas?* **5** (EE.UU.) ramo, sección (de un sindicato). **6** (EE.UU.) tren o autobús local. || **7 – authority,** (brit.) los encargados de la administración local. **8 – colour,** detalles minuciosos y concretos (en la descripción de un lugar). **9 – time,** hora local.

locale | ləu'kɑːl | *s.c.* (form.) lugar o escenario natural, exteriores (para el rodaje de una película).

locality | ləu'kælɪtɪ | (form.) *s.c.* **1** posición, situación (de una cosa). **2** localidad, vecindad, zona: *all the locality is affected by the motorway = toda la zona está afectada por la autopista.*

localization | ˌləukəlaɪ'zeɪʃn | *s.i.* (form.) localización, ubicación (de focos de enfermedad, plaga, violencia, etc.).

localize | 'ləukəlaɪz | *v.t.* (form.) localizar, aislar (focos de enfermedad, plaga, violencia, etc.).

localized | 'ləukəlaɪzd | *adj.* (form.) localizado, aislado (foco de enfermedad, plaga, violencia, etc.).

locally | 'ləukəlɪ | *adv.* **1** localmente, en ciertas áreas: *there may be some rain locally = puede llover en ciertas áreas.* **2** cerca, en la vecindad: *I live locally, so I come on foot = vivo cerca, por lo que vengo andando.*

locate | ləu'keɪt | (EE.UU. | 'ləukeɪt |) (form.) *v.t.* **1** localizar, descubrir, encontrar, hallar: *to locate a town on a map = localizar una ciudad en un mapa.* **2** establecer, asentar, abrir: *a bank is to be located on this site = se va a abrir un banco en este local.* || *v.i.* **3** (EE.UU.) establecerse, asentarse: *the company finally located in Dallas = la compañía se estableció por fin en Dallas.*

location | ləu'keɪʃn | *s.c.* e *i.* **1** (form.) lugar, posición, situación: *a suitable location for a cinema = lugar adecuado para un cine.* **2** localización, hallazgo: *the location of a missing car = localización de un coche desaparecido.* **3** exteriores (para el rodaje de una película). **4** INF. unidad básica de memoria (capaz de almacenar un dato). || **5 on –,** en exteriores auténticos: *the film was shot on location in China = la película se rodó en exteriores auténticos en China.*

loch | lɒk | | lɒx | (Escocia) *s.c.* **1** lago: *Loch Ness.* **2** ría, brazo de mar.

lock | lɒk | *s.c.* **1** cerradura. **2** esclusa. **3** (brit.) ángulo de giro (de vehículos): *this car has a good lock = este coche* *tiene un buen ángulo de giro.* **4** mechón de cabello. **5** DEP. llave (en lucha libre). || *s.i.* **6** posición de bloqueo (en máquinas). || *v.t.* **7** cerrar (con llave): *to lock a door = cerrar una puerta con llave.* **8** guardar (bajo llave o en caja fuerte): *she locked her jewels in the safe = guardó sus joyas en la caja fuerte.* **9** agarrar, amarrar: *the fighters were locked together = los luchadores estaban agarrados.* || *v.i.* **10 [to – (into)]** (fig.) enzarzarse (en debates, disputas, etc.): *they locked into a senseless dispute = se enzarzaron en una disputa absurda.* **11** bloquearse, atascarse: *the wheels have locked = las ruedas se han bloqueado.* || **12 to – away,** guardar, cerrar bajo llave: *lock your valuables away before you go = guarda tus cosas de valor antes de irte.* **13 to – in,** encerrar (personas o animales): *they locked him in = lo encerraron.* **14 to – onto,** seguir la trayectoria correcta (misiles). **15 to – out (of), a)** quedarse fuera, no poder entrar: *I lost my key, so I was locked out = perdí la llave, por lo que me quedé fuera.* **b)** (desp.) impedir la entrada, dejar fuera (por cierre patronal): *the workers were locked out of the factory = se impidió la entrada a la fábrica a los trabajadores.* **16 locks,** (lit.) pelo, cabello: *he shook his black locks = se revolvió su negro pelo.* **17 –, stock and barrel,** totalmente, al completo: *they sold the firm lock, stock and barrel = vendieron la empresa totalmente.* **18 to – up, a)** dejar seguro un edificio (cerrado con llave). **b)** guardar bajo llave. **c)** tener seguro el dinero (invertido). **d)** (fam.) encerrar a alguien (en prisión, hospital, etc.). **19 under – and key,** bajo siete llaves.

lockable | ˈlɒkəbl | *adj.* que se puede cerrar, que se puede bloquear: *the car has a lockable steering-wheel = el coche tiene un volante que se puede bloquear.*

locker | ˈlɒkər | *s.c.* **=f** taquilla, armario individual, casillero (en centros escolares o militares, fábricas, etc.). || **2 to be in/go to Dary tones's locker,** (fam.) ahogarse en el mar.

locker-room | ˈlɒkərum | *s.c.* vestuario, sala (con taquillas, armarios individuales, etc.).

locket | ˈlɒkɪt | *s.c.* relicario (para colgar del cuello).

lock-gate | ˌlɒkˈgeɪt | *s.c.* compuerta, esclusa (especialmente en un canal).

lock-jaw | ˈlɒkdʒɔː | *s.i.* (fam.) MED. trismo.

lock-keeper | ˈlɒkˌkipər | *s.c.* esclusero.

lock-nut | ˈlɒknʌt | *s.c.* MEC. contratuerca, tuerca de seguridad.

lockout | ˈlɒkaut | *s.c.* (desp.) cierre patronal.

locksmith | ˈlɒksmɪθ | *s.c.* cerrajero.

lock-stitch | ˈlɒkstɪtʃ | *s.c.* doble pespunte (en corte y confección); punto de cadeneta.

lockup | ˈlɒkʌp | *s.c.* calabozo, prisión, cárcel.

loco | ˈləukəu | (fam.) *s.c.* **1** locomotora. || *adj.* **2** (EE.UU.) loco, majareta.

locomotion | ˌləukəˈməuʃn | *s.i.* (form.) locomoción.

locomotive | ˈləukəˌməutɪv | (form.) *s.c.* **1** locomotora. || *adj.* **2** motriz, locomotor: *locomotive power = energía motriz.*

locum | ˈləukəm | *s.c.* (brit.) suplente, interino (hospitales, parroquias, etc.).

locus | ˈləukəs | (form.) *s.c.* **1** lugar, sitio, situación, punto. || **2 – classicus,** cita clásica conocida.

locust | ˈləukəst | *s.c.* ZOOL. langosta (insecto).

locution | ləuˈkjuːʃn | (form.) *s.c.* **1** locución, forma de hablar, acento, habla. **2** expresión local o de un grupo concreto.

lode | ləud | *s.c.* MIN, filón, veta.

lodestar | ˈləudstɑːr | (lit.) *s.c.* **1** ASTR. estrella polar. **2** (fig.) norte, guía, ejemplo.

lodestone | ˈləudstəun | V. **loadstone.**

lodge | lɒdʒ | *s.c.* **1** cabina, cuarto, casa (de un vigilante, portero, etc.): *the porter's lodge = portería o conserjería.* **2** logia: *a Masonic lodge = logia masónica.* **3** cabaña, refugio (de cazadores, esquiadores, etc.). **4** cobertizo, anejo. **5** cubil, madriguera (de castor, principalmente). **6** tienda de campaña (tipo indio). || *v.t.* e *i.* **7** (form.) alojarse, hospedarse (a cambio de dinero). **8** alojar, acomodar, buscar hospedaje. **9** alojarse, quedarse sujeto o fijo: *the bullet lodged in his spine = la bala se alojó en su columna.* **10** presentar, interponer (recursos, quejas, etc., oficialmente). **11** poner, depositar (dinero): *he lodged his money in a bank = depositó su dinero en el banco.* **12** quedar, mantenerse, perdurar (recuerdos, sentimientos, etc.): *her face is still lodged in my mind = su cara se mantiene aún en mi mente.*

lodgement | ˈlɒdʒmənt | (form.) *s.i.* **1** hueco, espacio, acomodo, alojamiento. **2** COM. depósito (de dinero).

lodger | ˈlɒdʒər | *s.c.* huésped, inquilino.

lodging | ˈlɒdʒɪŋ | *s.c.* e *i.* **1** alojamiento, pensión: *a night's lodging = alojamiento durante la noche.* || **2 lodgings,** habitación amueblada alquilada. **3 to stay in lodgings/in digs,** vivir en una pensión o de patrona.

lodging-house | ˈlɒdʒɪŋhaus | *s.c.* casa de huéspedes, pensión.

loess | ˈləuɪs | *s.i.* GEOL. loes.

loft | lɒft | *s.c.* **1** ático, desván. **2** galería, triforio (en iglesias). **3** pajar. **4** DEP. golpe alto (en golf o críquet). || *v.t.* **5** DEP. golpear alto (en golf o críquet).

lofted | ˈlɒftɪd | *adj.* DEP. para golpear hacia lo alto (señalando la forma de un palo de golf).

loftily | ˈlɒftɪlɪ | *adv.* (desp.) altivamente, arrogantemente, con altanería.

loftiness | ˈlɒftɪnɪs | *s.i.* **1** (desp.) altivez, orgullo, altanería. **2** nobleza, elevación (de ideales, pensamientos, etc.). **3** distinción, eminencia (en un discurso, escrito, etc.).

lofty | ˈlɒftɪ | *adj.* **1** noble, elevado: *lofty ideals = nobles ideales.* **2** (desp.) altanero, altivo, arrogante: *lofty disdain = altanero desdén.* **3** (lit.) alto: *the lofty walls of the old town = las altas murallas de la vieja ciudad.* **4** elevado, afectado, elaborado (discurso o escrito).

log | lɒg | *s.c.* **1** tronco, leño. **2** AER., MAR. diario de a bordo, libro de navegación o de bitácora. || *v.t.* **3** escribir, anotar (en el diario de a bordo o libro de navegación). **4 [to – (up)]** viajar, navegar (largas distancias o muchas horas): *the plane has logged up hundreds of hours = el avión ha navegado cientos de horas.* || **5 to – in/on,** INF. iniciar acceso a una base de datos de línea. **6 to – off/out,** INF. cerrar acceso a una base de datos de línea. **7 to sleep like a –,** dormir como un tronco.

loganberry | ˈləugənbərɪ | *s.c.* e *i.* frambuesa norteamericana.

logarithm | ˈlɒgərɪðəm | *s.c.* MAT. logaritmo.

log-book | ˈlɒgbuk | *s.c.* **1** documentación de registro (de un vehículo a motor). **2** AER., MAR. diario de a bordo, libro de navegación o de bitácora, respectivamente.

loggerheads | ˈlɒgəhedz | *s.pl.* || **at – (with),** enfrentado, peleado: *he and his wife are always at loggerheads = él y su esposa están siempre peleados.*

loggia | ˈləudʒə | *s.c.* galería, mirador.

logging | ˈlɒgɪŋ | *s.c.* tala forestal.

logic | ˈlɒdʒɪk | *s.i.* **1** lógica (ciencia). **2** lógica (método de pensamiento). **3** lógica (línea de razonamiento): *the logic of an argument = la lógica de una argumentación.* **4** INF. base lógica (de un ordenador y sus circuitos).

logical | ˈlɒdʒɪkl | *adj.* **1** lógico, coherente. **2** capaz de razonar.

logically | ˈlɒdʒɪklɪ | *adv.* lógicamente, en buena lógica.

logician | ləuˈdʒɪʃn | *s.c.* lógico.

logistic | ləuˈdʒɪstɪk | *adj.* logístico.

logistically | ləuˈdʒɪstɪklɪ | *adv.* logísticamente.

logistics | ləuˈdʒɪstɪks | *s.i.* logística.

log-jam | ˈlɒgdzæm | *s.c.* (EE.UU.) obstrucción, bloqueo; estancamiento.

logo | ˈləugəu | *s.c.* logotipo.

log-rolling | ˈlɒgrəulɪŋ | *s.i.* (EE.UU. y desp.) intercambio de favores interesados, alabanza recíproca (normalmente entre escritores, políticos, etc.).

loin | lɔɪn | *s.c.* e *i.* **1** lomo (alimento). **2** ANAT. lomo. || **3 to gird (up) one's loins,** (hum.) aprestarse para la lucha. **4 loins, a)** (arc.) ijada. **b)** (euf.) órganos genitales.

loincloth | ˈlɔɪnklɒθ | *s.c.* taparrabos.

loiter | ˈlɔɪtər | *v.i.* **=f** merodear: *two boys are loitering on the corner = dos chicos merodean en la esquina.* **2** rezagarse, distraerse, entretenerse, despistarse: *don't loiter or you'll be late = no* *te entretengas o llegarás tarde.* || **3 loitering with intent,** DER. merodeando con fines delictivos.

logarithmic | ˌlɒgəˈrɪðmɪk | *adj.* MAT. logarítmico.

logarithmically | ˌlɒgəˈrɪðmɪklɪ | *adj.* MAT. logarítmicamente.

logicality | ˌlɒdʒɪˈkæləti | *s.i.* lógica (de una persona).

loiterer | ˈlɔɪtərər | *s.c.* holgazán, vagabundo; merodeador.

loll | lɒl | *v.t.* e *i.* **1 [to – (about)]** vaguear, estar relajado, tener pereza: *the boys lolled (about) in the grass = los muchachos vagueaban en la hierba.* **2** colgar, dejar caer, caerse: *he was sitting and his head was lolling = estaba sentado y se le caía la cabeza.*

lollipop | ˈlɒlɪpɒp | *s.c.* **1** pirulí, piruleta. **2** (brit.) polo (helado). || **3 – lady,** (brit. y fam.) mujer que ayuda a los niños en cruces peligrosos. **4 – man,** (brit. y fam.) hombre que ejerce la misma función.

lollop | ˈlɒləp | *v.i.* (fam.) moverse torpe y pesadamente.

lolly | ˈlɒlɪ | (brit. y fam.) *s.c.* **1** polo (helado). **2** pasta, parné, dinero.

lone | ləun | (lit.) *adj.* **1** solo, solitario, aislado, desierto. **2** solo, separado, independiente (y que cuida de sus hijos): *few lone mothers own their homes = pocas madres separadas son dueñas de sus casas.* || **3 a – wolf,** persona independiente y solitaria.

loneliness | ˈləunlɪnɪs | *s.i.* soledad, aislamiento.

lonely | ˈləunlɪ | *adj.* **1** solo, aislado, solitario. **2** solitario, desértico, desolado: *the lonely country roads = las desérticas carreteras rurales.* || **3 – hearts,** persona que busca pareja: *a lonely hearts club = club de personas que buscan pareja.*

loner | ˈləunər | *s.c.* solitario, independiente.

lonesome | ˈləunsəm | (EE.UU. y fam.) *adj.* **1** solo, solitario: *lonesome without her children = sola, sin sus hijos.* **2** solitario, desértico, desolado: *a lonesome valley = un valle desértico.* || **3 by/on one's lonesome,** solo, sin nadie.

long | lɒŋ | (EE.UU. | lɔːŋ |) *adj.* **1** largo (longitud, distancia, tiempo): *a long journey = un largo viaje.* **2** largo, dilatado: *the film is too long = la película es demasiado larga.* **3** largo, cansado, interminable: *I've had a very long day = he tenido un día muy largo.* **4** bueno, que llega muy lejos, largo (memoria): *he's got a long memory = tiene buena memoria.* **5** grande, mucho, numeroso (probabilidades en juego, apuestas, etc.): *the odds against him winning are long = son grandes las probabilidades de que pierda.* **6** fresco, ligero (bebida no alcohólica): *I'd love a nice long drink = me encantaría una buena bebida fresca.* **7** FON. largo (sonido vocálico). || *s.i.* **8** largo rato, mucho tiempo (poco tiempo, según los casos): *they came back before long = volvieron poco después.* | *adv.* **9** mucho, mucho tiempo: *were you in London long? = ¿estuviste mucho tiempo en Londres?* **10** hace tiempo, tiempo antes, tiempo después: *he came long ago = llegó hace tiempo.* **11** a lo largo, todo a lo largo: *I've waited for this my whole life long = lo he esperado todo a lo largo de mi vida.* || *v.i.* **12 [to – for]** estar deseoso de, desear, anhelar, suspirar por: *children long for their holidays = los niños anhelan las vacaciones.* || **13 a – face,** cara larga, expresión de tristeza. **14 a – haul,** ardua tarea. **15 a – shot,** intento desesperado. **16 as/so – as, a)** (brit.) siempre que, si: *as long as it doesn't rain we can play = siempre que no llueva, podremos jugar.* **b)** (EE.UU.) puesto que: *as long as it doesn't rain we can play = puesto que no llueve, podemos jugar.* **17 at the longest,** lo más tardar, como mucho: *he's only away for short, a couple of days at the longest = está ausente por poco tiempo, un par de días como mucho.* **18 be not – for this world,** no durará mucho vivo. **19 to cut a – story short,** ir al grano. **20 to go a – way, a)** tener éxito, llegar lejos. **b)** cundir mucho, dar mucho de sí (dinero, alimento): *she makes a little money go a long way = hace que el dinero cunda para mucho.* **c)** llegar al límite (de lo que se puede aguantar): *a little of his company goes a long way = un rato en su compañía te hace llegar al límite.* **21 go a – way towards doing something,** contribuir notablemente a algo: *his effort doesn't go a long way towards solving the problem = su esfuerzo contribuye poco a resolver el problema.* **22 happy as the day is –,** muy feliz. **23 to have a – arm,** tener mucha influencia, tener vara alta. **24 to have come a – way,** haber progresado mucho. **25 in – pants,** (EE.UU.) mayor, adulto: *look, we're already in long pants = mira, ya somos mayores.* **26 in the – run,** últimamente: *in the long run things are getting worse = las cosas están empeorando últimamente.* **27 in the –/short term,** a largo/corto plazo. **28 – in the tooth,** (hum.) bastante viejo: *he's getting a bit long in the tooth to... = se está haciendo bastante viejo como para...* **29 – johns,** (fam.) calzoncillos largos. **30 – jump,** DEP. salto de longitud. **31 – odds,** apuestas muy desequilibradas (como 50 a 1). **32 – time no see,** (fam.) ¡cuánto tiempo sin vernos! **33 not by a – chalk/shot,** en absoluto. **34 to take a – (cool/hard) look at something,** sopesar la situación. **35 to take the – view,** analizar todas las implicaciones. **36 the – and (the) short of it,** todo lo que hay que decir sobre el asunto.

long-awaited | ˌlɒŋəˈweɪtɪd | *adj.* largamente esperado, muy deseado.

longboat | ˈlɒŋbəut | *s.c.* MAR. lancha (normalmente de salvamento transportada en un barco).

longbow | ˈlɒŋbəu | *s.c.* arco (de grandes proporciones, para lanzar flechas).

long-distance | ˌlɒŋˈdɪstəns | *adj.* **1** de gran distancia o recorrido: *long-distance coach = autocar de largo recorrido.* **2** DEP. de fondo: *a long-distance runner = corredor de fondo o fondista.* || *adv.* **3** desde un punto lejano, desde lejos: *to phone long-distance = poner una conferencia.* || **4 a – call,** una conferencia telefónica.

long-drawn-out | ˌlɒŋdrɔːnˈaut | *adj.* larguísimo, prolongado, interminable.

longed-for | ˈlɒŋdfər | *adj.* anhelado, ansiado, soñado.

longevity | lɒnˈdʒevɪtɪ | *s.i.* **1** longevidad, larga vida. **2** vida, ciclo vital: *the longevity of the horse = la vida del caballo.*

longhand | ˈlɒŋhænd | *s.i.* escritura a mano (ordinaria).

longing | ˈlɒŋɪŋ | *s.c.* e *i.* **1** anhelo, ansia, vivo deseo. || *adj.* **2** anhelante, ansioso: *a longing look = una mirada anhelante.*

longingly | ˈlɒŋɪŋlɪ | *adv.* anhelantemente, ansiosamente.

longish | ˈlɒŋɪʃ | *adj.* (fam.) largo, tirando a largo, bastante largo.

longitude | ˈlɒndʒɪtjuːd | *s.c.* e *i.* GEOG. longitud.

longitudinal | ˌlɒndʒɪˈtjuːdɪnl | *adj.* longitudinal, a lo largo.

longitudinally | ˌlɒndʒɪˈtjuːdɪnlɪ | *adv.* longitudinalmente, a lo largo.

long-lasting | ˌlɒŋˈlɑːstɪŋ | *adj.* duradero, perdurable, largo.

long-life | ˌlɒŋˈlaɪf | *adj.* que se conserva mucho tiempo (productos de alimentación o consumo): *long-life milk.*

long-lived | ˌlɒŋˈlɪvd | (EE.UU. | ˌlɔːŋˈlvd) | *adj.* **1** longevo: *a long-lived family = una familia longeva.* **2** largo, duradero: *a long-lived friendship = una amistad duradera.*

long-lost | ˌlɒŋˈlɒst | *adj.* perdido hace tiempo, largo tiempo perdido.

long-playing | ˌlɒŋˈpleɪɪŋ | **1** de larga duración. || **2 – record,** disco de larga duración, álbum, LP.

long-range | ˌlɒŋˈreɪndʒ | *adj.* **1** de largo alcance: *long-range missiles = misiles de largo alcance.* **2** a largo plazo: *the long-range weather forecast = predicción del tiempo a largo plazo.*

long-running | ˌlɒŋˈrʌnɪŋ | *adj.* de largo tiempo en cartel, de éxito (teatro, televisión).

long-shoreman | ˈlɒŋʃɔːmən | *adj.* (EE.UU.) estibador.

long-sighted | ˌlɒŋˈsaɪtɪd | *adj.* que no ve bien de cerca, présbita.

long-standing | ˌlɒŋˈstændɪŋ | *adj.* largamente establecido o asentado, acreditado, histórico.

long-suffering | ˌlɒŋˈsʌfərɪŋ | *adj.* paciente, consentidor, condescendiente.

long-suit | ˌlɒŋˈsuːt | *s.c.* e *i.* el palo que uno domina (juego de naipes). **2** (fam.) virtud, punto fuerte (de una persona).

long-term | ˌlɒŋˈtəːm | *adj.* a largo plazo: *long-term planning = planificación a largo plazo.*

long-time | ˌlɒŋ'taɪm | *adj.* duradero, que viene de antiguo.
long-vacation | ˌlɒŋvə'keɪʃn | *s.i.* (brit.) vacaciones de verano (universidad inglesa).
long-wave | ˌlɒŋ'weɪv | *s.c.* e *i.* onda larga (más de mil metros de longitud).
long-winded | ˌlɒŋ'wɪndɪd | *adj.* largo, farragoso, difuso (persona, discurso o escrito).
long-windedness | ˌlɒŋ'waɪndɪdnɪs | *s.i.* prolijidad, verbosidad, farragosidad.
longways | 'lɒŋweɪz | (también **longwise**) V. **lengthways.**
loo | luː | *s.c.* (brit. y fam.) lavabo, retrete, servicio.
loofah | 'luːfər | *s.c.* esponja de baño.
look | luk | *v.t.* e *i.* mirar. **2 [to – (at)]** mirar, ver, prestar atención: *she's looking at the pictures = está viendo las fotos.* **3** observar, fijarse, notar: *look at the time! = ¡fíjate la hora que es!* **4** parecer, dar la apariencia de, tener aspecto de: *you look tired = pareces cansado.* **5 [to – like]** parecer, parecerse a, ser como: *it looks like sugar, but it's salt = parece azúcar pero es sal.* **6 [to – out on/onto/towards]** mirar a, dar a, estar orientado a (edificios, generalmente): *the house looks onto the park = la casa da al parque.* **7** dar la apariencia, aspecto o impresión adecuados: *you have to look your best in the interview = tienes que dar tu mejor impresión en la entrevista.* **8** (fam.) pensar, tener la intención de: *if you're looking to buy a new flat... = si piensas comprar un nuevo piso...* **9** expresar con los ojos, hablar con los ojos: *she said nothing but looked all interest = no dijo nada pero expresó con los ojos todo su interés.* || *s.c.* **10 [– (at)]** mirada, vistazo: *have a look at this picture = echa un vistazo a esta foto.* **11** mirada (según se especifique): *he gave me an angry look = me dirigió una mirada de enfado.* **12** apariencia, aspecto: *he's got the look of a winner = tiene el aspecto de un ganador.* **13** estilo, moda: *the broad-shouldered look is in this year = la moda de hombros anchos se lleva este año.* || *interj.* **14** ¡mira!: *look, I'm fed up! = mira, estoy harto.* || **15 to be looking to do something,** intentar llevar algo a efecto. **16 by the look(s) of it,** al parecer, probablemente. **17 to give/get a dirty –,** dirigir/recibir una mirada de desaprobación o disgusto. **18 to – after,** cuidar, ser responsable de: *her mother looks after the children = la madre de ella cuida de los niños.* **19 to – ahead,** prever, planificar el futuro. **20 to – alive/lively,** (fam.) actuar deprisa. **21 to – around/round (for),** buscar, andar buscando: *we're looking around for a nice place to eat = andamos buscando un sitio agradable para comer.* **22 to – at, a)** considerar, juzgar: *as a boss, she looks at the work in a different way = como jefe, considera el trabajo de forma distinta.* **b)** examinar, ver: *go to a doctor to have that cold looked at = ve al médico para que te examine ese catarro.* **c)** mirar, acordarse de, aprender de: *look at Jane: drugs killed her = acuérdate de Jane: la droga la mató.* **23 to – back (to/on), a)** recordar: *I look back on those days as my happiest = recuerdo esos días como los más felices.* **b)** (fam.) cambiar la suerte de uno: *after winning once, he never looked back = tras ganar una vez, ya no cambió su suerte.* **24 to – bad,** estar mal visto: *It looks bad leaving so early = está mal visto irse tan pronto.* **25 to – daggers at someone,** mirar muy enojado a alguien. **26 to – down on someone/something,** (fam.) mirar con superioridad, minusvalorar. **27 to – down one's nose at,** (desp.) mirar por encima del hombro, despreciar. **28 to – for, a)** buscar: *I'm looking for a new job = busco un nuevo trabajo.* **b)** (fam.) buscar, provocar, meterse (en problemas): *he's always looking for trouble = siempre está provocando.* **c)** (arc.) esperar: *we're looking for your improvement = estamos esperando que progreses.* **29 to – forward to, a)** esperar con ansiedad, estar deseando: *I look forward to seeing you again = estoy deseando volver a verte.* **b)** mantenerse a la espera (cartas comerciales): *we really look forward to your reply = nos mantenemos a la espera de su respuesta.* **30 to – good,** ser prometedor, progresar favorablemente: *the sales figures look good = las cifras de ventas son prometedoras.* **31 to – in (on),** (fam.) pasarse un rato por: *I'll look in on the party = me pasaré un rato por la fiesta.* **32 to – into,** investigar, examinar: *they're looking into the report = están examinando el informe.* **33 to – on/upon, a)** mirar, ser espectador: *they all looked on while the man was being beaten = todos miraban mientras golpeaban al hombre.* **b)** considerar, tener por: *I look upon him as a friend = le considero un amigo.* **34 to – on the bright side (of things),** ser optimista. **35 to – out (for), a)** ¡cuidado! (en imperativos): *look out, there's a car coming = cuidado, que viene un coche.* **b)** prestar atención (para ver): *look out for your brother coming out = presta atención a la salida de tu hermano.* **c)** (brit.) elegir: *to look out a dress for a party = elegir un vestido para una fiesta.* **36 to – over,** examinar por encima: *I only looked over the plans = sólo examiné por encima los planos.* **37 to – round,** ver, mirar, observar (en movimiento): *let's look round shops = vamos a mirar tiendas.* **38 to – sharp,** (brit. y fam.) **a)** darse prisa: *look sharp if you want to get there on time = date prisa si quieres llegar a tiempo.* **b)** tener cuidado. **39 looks,** aspecto de una persona: *she's got her father's good looks = tiene el mismo buen aspecto de su padre.* **40 to – small,** no ser tenido en cuenta, ser infravalorado. **41 to – someone in the eye/face,** mirar a los ojos (para descubrir la verdad): *look me in the eye and say you didn't steal it = mírame a los ojos y di que no lo robaste.* **42 to – someone up and down,** mirar a alguien de arriba abajo (en busca de algún defecto). **43 to – through something/someone, a)** examinar: *look through that report before you speak = examina ese informe antes de hablar.* **b)** mirar en la dirección de alguien (distraídamente): *he just looked through me when I tried to tell him = sólo me miró distraídamente cuando intenté decírselo.* **44 to – to one's laurels,** tratar de mantener una buena situación. **45 to – to someone/something (for), a)** depender de: *we look to you for support = dependemos de ti para conseguir apoyo.* **b)** (form.) cuidar, prestar atención: *you should look to your health = deberías cuidar tu salud.* **46 to – up, a)** (fam.) mejorar, recuperarse (una situación, negocios, etc.): *things are looking up = las cosas están mejorando.* **b)** buscar información (en un libro, generalmente): *look up the word in the dictionary.* **c)** (fam.) dar con, localizar y visitar a alguien: *I must look up an old friend who lives nearby = tengo que dar con un viejo amigo que vive por aquí.* **47 to – up to someone,** respetar, admirar a alguien: *she looks up to her father very much = admira mucho a su padre.* **48 to – well,** (form.) sentar bien: *the coat looks well on you = la chaqueta te sienta bien.*
look-alike | 'lukəˌlaɪk | *s.c.* (fam.) sosia, doble (de otra persona): *the Humphrey Bogart look-alike = el doble de Humphrey Bogart.*
looker | 'lukər | *s.c.* (fam.) mujer bella, belleza: *she's a real looker = es una auténtica belleza.*
looker-on | ˌlukər'ɒn | *s.c.* mirón, espectador, curioso.
look-in | 'lukɪn | *s.sing.* oportunidad, posibilidad (de participación o éxito): *he's a good player but he never gets a look-in = es un buen jugador pero no le dan una oportunidad.*
-looking | 'lukɪŋ | *adj.* de un determinado aspecto (definido por la primera parte del compuesto): *a strange-looking girl = chica de aspecto extraño.*
looking-glass | 'lukɪŋglɑːs | *s.c.* (arc.) espejo.
lookout | 'lukaut | *s.c.* e *i.* **1** atalaya, garita, puesto de vigilancia. **2** centinela, vigía, vigilante, guardián. **3** vigilancia, guardia. **4 [– (for)]** (fam.) perspectiva, futuro: *a bad lookout for the company = malas perspectivas para la empresa.* || **5 to keep a – for,** estar alerta para detectar algo. **6 one's –,** (fam.) asunto o responsabilidad de uno mismo, allá uno: *if you go out in this rain, that's your lookout = si sales, con lo que llueve, allá tú.* **7 on the –,** alerta, en guardia.
look-over | 'lukəuvər | *s.sing.* vistazo de comprobación.
look-through | 'lukəruː | *s.sing.* vistazo rápido.

loom | luːm | *s.c.* **1** telar. || *v.i.* **2** **[to – (up)]** surgir, aparecer, constituirse en amenaza: *a shape loomed (up) out of the mist = una figura surgió de la bruma.* || **3 to – large,** hacerse importante y grave, crecer, cernirse amenazante: *the prospect of war loomed large = un futuro de guerra se cernía amenazante.*

looming | 'luːmɪŋ | *adj.* **1** elevado, descollante: *the looming towers of Oxford Street = las elevadas torres de Oxford Street.* **2** futuro, inminente, inquietante: *the looming populations problems = los inminentes problemas de población.*

loony | 'luːnɪ | (fam.) *adj.* **1** loco, bobo, lunático. || **2 – bin,** (hum.) manicomio.

loop | luːp | *s.c.* **1** lazo, vuelta, bucle, lazada, cruce (de cuerda, cable, etc.). **2** trayectoria con giros cruzados, rizos: *the plane flew in wide loops = el avión seguía un vuelo a base de rizos.* **3** espiral o DIU (dispositivo anticonceptivo intrauterino). **4** ELECTR. circuito electrónico completo. **5** INF. bucle repetitivo. || *v.t.* e *i.* **6** **[to – (up)]** hacer lazos, bucles, lazadas, etc.: *to loop (up) a rope = hacer lazos con una cuerda.* **7** atar, sujetar (haciendo un lazo o lazada): *loop the curtains back = vuelve a sujetar las cortinas.* || **8 – line,** desvío o ramal de ferrocarril (que se separa momentáneamente de la línea principal). **9 to – the –,** volar en círculos verticales.

loophole | 'luːphəul | *s.c.* **1** aspillera, tronera. **2** escapatoria, pretexto, subterfugio legales: *a good lawyer can find a loophole = un buen abogado puede encontrar un subterfugio legal.*

loopy | 'luːpɪ | *adj.* (fam.) loco, sonado, descabellado: *a loopy idea = una idea descabellada.*

loose | luːs | *adj.* **1** flojo, inseguro, movedizo: *a loose connection of wires = conexión de cables floja.* **2** suelto, descontrolado: *he let the dogs loose = dejó a los perros sueltos.* **3** suelto, no envasado. **4** holgado, ancho (en prendas de vestir). **5** suelto, ralo, disperso: *a loose soil = tierra suelta.* **6** inexacto, impreciso, descontrolado: *a loose translation = traducción imprecisa.* **7** descuidado, irresponsable, imprudente: *she's got a loose tongue = es imprudente hablando.* **8** (arc.) de moral relajada. **9** flojo, ligero, suelto (de vientre). || *v.t.* **10** soltar, liberar, dejar suelto. **11** disparar (flechas, armas de fuego, etc.). || *adv.* **12** holgado, holgadamente: *I like wearing it loose = me gusta llevarlo holgado.* || **13 at a – end/**(EE.UU.) **at – ends,** no saber qué hacer, no tener nada que hacer. **14 to break –,** soltarse, escaparse, liberarse, apartarse: *to loose from tradition = apartarse de la tradición.* **15 to hang/keep/stay –,** (EE.UU.) (fam.) estar tranquilo y sin preocupaciones. **16 to have a screw –,** (fam.) faltarle a uno un tornillo. **17 – cover,** funda de mueble. **18 – ends,** cosas sueltas, partes sin quilatar, flecos: *there are still a few loose ends in the contract = quedan aún algunos flecos en el contrato.* **19 on the –, a)** huido de prisión: *a dangerous criminal on the loose = peligroso malhechor huido.* **b)** sin control, sin ataduras, desinhibido.

loose-fitting | ˌluːs'fɪtɪŋ | *adj.* holgado, ancho, que queda holgado o ancho.

loose-leaf | ˌluːs'liːf | *adj.* de hojas sueltas, de quita y pon, cambiables (las de un cuaderno de anillas).

loosely | 'luːslɪ | *adv.* holgadamente, libremente, aproximadamente, en general.

loosen | 'luːsn | *v.t.* e *i.* **1** aflojar: *to loosen one's tie = aflojarse la corbata.* **2** soltar, liberar: *a drink makes the tongue loosen = la bebida hace que la lengua se suelte.* || **3 to – someone's tongue,** hacer que alguien hable más libremente. **4 to –/tight the purse-strings,** aflojarse/apretarse el cinturón (aumentar/reducir gastos, respectivamente). **5 to – up, a)** relajar (los músculos). **b)** quedarse relajado y distendido.

looseness | 'luːsnɪs | *s.i.* soltura, holgura, relajación, imprecisión.

loot | luːt | *s.i.* **1** botín, ganancias (de guerra o de robo). **2** (fam.) dinero, riqueza, plata. || *v.t.* **3** saquear, realizar rapiña: *the mob looted the shops = las masas saquearon las tiendas.*

looter | 'luːtər | *s.c.* saqueador, que realiza pillaje.

looting | 'luːtɪŋ | *s.i.* rapiña, pillaje, desvalijamiento.

lop | lɒp | *v.t.* **1** mochar, desmochar, podar. || **2 to – something off/away, a)** cortar, cercenar (ramas de un árbol). **b)** (fig.) cortar (miembros del cuerpo). **c)** acortar, disminuir (carga, beneficios, etc.).

lope | ləup | *v.i.* **1** **[to – (off)]** correr a grandes zancadas (animales): *the giraffe started loping = la jirafa echó a correr.* || *s.sing.* **2** zancada veloz.

lop-eared | 'lɒpˌɪəd | *adj.* de orejas caídas: *a lop-eared rabbit = conejo de orejas caídas.*

lopsided | ˌlɒp'saɪdɪd | *adj.* desequilibrado, ladeado, caído de un lado.

loquacious | ləu'kweɪʃəs | *adj.* (form.) locuaz, hablador.

loquaciously | lə'kweɪʃəslɪ | *adv.* locuazmente.

loquacity | ləu'kæsətɪ | *s.i.* (form.) locuacidad, verbosidad.

loquat | 'ləukwt | *s.c.* BOT. níspero (tanto el árbol como el fruto).

lord | lɔːd | *s.c.* **1** señor, amo. **2** señor feudal. **3** lord (perteneciente a la nobleza): *dukes, earls and barons are all lords = los duques, los condes y los barones son todos lores.* **4** (brit.) miembro de la Cámara de los Lores. **5** (brit.) título de algunos altos cargos: *the Lord Mayor of London = el Lord Alcalde de Londres.* || *v.t.* **6** (fam.) esclavizar, tratar dominantemente. || **7 good Lord!** ¡santo cielo! **8 to live like a –,** llevar una vida fastuosa. **9 to – it over someone,** (fam.) esclavizar, tratar a alguien dominantemente. **10 Lord knows,** nadie lo sabe, sabe Dios. **11 lords spiritual,** (brit.) obispos y arzobispos de la Cámara de los Lores. **12 lords temporal,** (brit.) nobles de la Cámara de los Lores (con título heredado o vitalicio). **13 one's – and master,** (hum.) el propio marido. **14 our Lord.** REL. nuestro Señor, Cristo. **15 the Lord,** Dios, el Señor, Cristo. **16 the – of the manor,** señor feudal medieval. **17 the Lords,** los Lores, la Cámara de los Lores. **18 the Lord's Day,** el día del Señor, el domingo. **19 the Lord's Prayer,** REL. la oración del Señor, el padrenuestro.

lordly | 'lɔːdlɪ | *adj.* **1** (desp.) arrogante, dominante, mandón: *lordly manners = modales dominantes.* **2** (lit.) digno de un lord, selecto, distinguido: *a loordly party = una fiesta distinguida.*

Lordship | 'lɔːdʃɪp | *s.c.* **1** señoría. || *s.i.* **2 – (over)/**(form.) autoridad, mando.

lore | lɔː | *s.i.* conocimiento, cultura, tradiciones (de un grupo o tribu): *Celtic lore = cultura celta.*

lorgnette | lɔː'njet | *s.c.* (arc.) impertinentes, anteojos con mango.

lorn | lɔːn | *adj.* (arc.) (lit.) melancólico, triste, solo.

lorry | 'lɒrɪ | (EE.UU. | 'lɔːrɪ |) *s.c.* (brit.) camión.

lose | luːz | *v.* **[lost, lost]** *t.* **1** perder (por accidente, desgracia, vejez, muerte, etc.): *he lost his money = perdió el dinero.* **2** perder, dejar de tener, disminuir (calidad mental o moral): *to lose one's confidence = perder confianza.* **3** perder, disminuir, desaparecer, dejar escapar (calor, peso, sangre, etc.): *she lost a lot of weight = perdió mucho peso.* **4** perder, no encontrar: *I've lost my keys = he perdido las llaves.* **5** **[to – (on)]** perder significado, no entender, no hacer gracia: *I'm afraid his humour is lost on me = me temo que su humor no me hace gracia.* **6** perder, escapar de, eludir: *we've lost our pursuers = hemos eludido a nuestros perseguidores.* **7** causar, costar (la pérdida de algo): *his nervousness lost him the job = los nervios le costaron el empleo.* **8** perder (tiempo u oportunidades): *there's no time to lose = no hay tiempo que perder.* **9** **[to – (in)]** embeberse, entregarse totalmente: *he loses himself in his reading = se embebe en la lectura.* **10** perder el hilo, cortarse, confundirse, no recordar: *he lost himself in the speech = se cortó en el discurso.* || *v.i.* **11** perder, ser derrotado (en competiciones, disputas, pleitos, etc.): *the team has lost = el equipo ha perdido.* **12** perder, disminuir, empobrecerse: *poetry loses in translation = la poesía se empobrece con la traducción.* **13** retrasar(se), perder tiempo (el reloj): *my watch loses a little = mi reloj retrasa un poco.* || **14 to have nothing to –,** no tener nada que perder. **15 to – face,** ser humillado, perder imagen, crédito o reputación. **16 to – heart,** desanimarse.

17 to – one's cool/temper, ofuscarse por el enfado. **18 to – one's head/nerve,** asustarse y perder el control: *he lost his nerve and opened fire = se asustó y comenzó a disparar.* **19 to – one's heart (to),** enamorarse de. **20 to – one's shirt,** perder hasta la camisa. **21 to – one's touch,** perder las facultades que a uno le llevaron al éxito. **22 to – out (on something),** (fam.) perder terreno: *cinema has lost out to TV = el cine ha perdido terreno frente a la televisión.* **24 to – sight (of),** perder de vista, olvidar. **25 to – touch (with),** perder el contacto con alguien. **26 to – track,** perder la pista, no tener información.

loser | 'luːzər | *s.c.* **=f** perdedor. **2** (desp.) calamidad, fracaso, ruina (persona). || **3 a bad –,** un mal perdedor. **4 a born –,** un perdedor nato. **5 a good –,** un buen perdedor.

loss | lɒs | (EE.UU. | lɔːs |) *s.c.* e *i.* **1** pérdida (material, moral, afectiva, etc.): *his death was a great loss = su muerte fue una gran pérdida.* **2** bajas (personas o cosas perdidas en batalla). **3** dinero perdido (en negocios, transacciones, etc.): *to sell something at a loss = vender perdiendo dinero.* **4** pérdida, daño, contratiempo, desventaja: *a great loss to the team = una gran desventaja para el equipo.* || **5 at a –, a)** a precio ruinoso. **b)** sin saber qué hacer o decir: *it left me at a loss (for words) = me dejó sin saber qué decir.* **6 to cut one's losses,** cambiar, rectificar a tiempo los planes equivocados. **7 dead –,** (form.) inútil, sin valor: *it looked good but it turned out to be a dead loss = parecía bueno pero resultó inútil.*

loss-leader | ˌlɒs'liːdər | *s.c.* COM. artículo-reclamo (vendido a precio muy bajo para atraer clientes).

lost | lɒst | (EE.UU. | lɔːst |) **1** [*pret.* y *p.p.* de **lose.**] || *adj.* **2** perdido, desaparecido: *lost keys = llaves desaparecidas.* **3** (fig.) perdido, confundido, despistado: *I got rather lost in the city = me vi bastante despistado en la ciudad.* **4** perdido, malogrado, desperdiciado: *a lost chance = una oportunidad perdida.* **5** perdido, desaparecido, destruido, hundido, ahogado: *the boat and its men were lost = el barco y sus hombres fueron dados por desaparecidos.* **6 to be – in something,** estar absorbido en algo. **7 to be – on someone,** fracasar un efecto en alguien: *his mother's advice was lost on him = los consejos de su madre fracasaron con él.* **8 to be – (to someone/something),** dejar de existir: *when he watches TV, he's lost to the world = cuando ve la televisión, deja de existir.* **9 get –,** (fam.) vete a paseo, olvídame. **10 – cause,** causa perdida. **11 – property office/**(EE.UU.) **– -and-found (office),** oficina de objetos perdidos.

lot | lɒt | *s.c.* **1 [– (of)]** gran cantidad de, número elevado de, mucho, muchos: *she's got lots of money = tiene gran cantidad de dinero.* **2** todo, el conjunto, el total: *I'll take the lot = me llevaré todo.* **3** remesa, tanda, lote: *another lot of first aid = otra remesa de primeros auxilios.* **4** lote, conjunto, grupo (en subastas). **5** (EE.UU.) solar, terreno, aparcamiento de coches. **6** (lit.) suerte, fortuna, destino, vida (de una persona): *her lot was a hard one = el destino fue duro con ella.* **7** medio, método, objetos (de echar suertes): *they drew lots to decide the winner = echaron suertes para decidir el vencedor.* **8** suerte, azar, sorteo = *the winner was chosen by lot = el vencedor salió por sorteo.* **9** estudio cinematográfico (y espacio que lo rodea). || *adv.* (fam.) **10** bastante, considerablemente: *I'm feeling a lot better now = ahora me siento bastante mejor.* **11** mucho: *I care about you a lot = me preocupo mucho de ti.* **12** a menudo, con frecuencia: *I play chess quite a lot in the winter = en invierno juego a menudo al ajedrez.* || **13 a bad –/egg,** (arc.) (fam.) persona poco fiable. **14 a fat –,** (fam. y hum.) absolutamente nada: *a fat lot you care! = ¡mucho que te preocupa!* **15 a – (of),** (fam.) mucho, muchos. **16 to cast/draw lots (for something),** echar suertes, sortear: *they drew lots for the prize = se sortearon el premio.* **17 to fall to someone's – to do something,** (fam.) caerle a uno en suerte la responsabilidad de hacer algo. **18 lots** (fam.) mucho, muchos. **19 the –/all the –/the whole –,** todo, todos. **20 to throw in one's – with someone,** decidir unirse a alguien y compartir su suerte.

loth | ləuθ | V. **loath.**

lotion | 'ləuʃn | *s.c.* e *i.* loción.

lottery | 'lɒtərɪ | *s.c.* e *i.* **1** lotería. **2** (fig.) azar, suerte, lotería, incógnita: *life is a lottery = la vida es una lotería.*

lotto | 'lɒtəu | *s.i.* loto (juego similar al bingo en que los jugadores sacan sus propios números).

lotus | 'ləutəs | *s.c.* e *i.* **1** loto (fruta que provocaba indolencia y olvido en la mitología griega). **2** BOT. flor de loto. || **3 – position,** posición de loto (actitud meditativa).

lotus-eater | 'ləutəsˌiːtər | *s.c.* lotófago, persona indolente.

loud | laud | *adj.* **1** fuerte, elevado, alto (sonido). **2** ruidoso, gritón, chillón, bullanguero: *a loud customer refused to pay the bill = un cliente chillón no quería pagar.* **3** chillón, llamativo (de color): *a rather loud shirt = camisa de colores muy llamativos.* || **4 – and clear,** bien claro. **5 out –,** bien alto, nada de susurros.

loudhailer | ˌlaud'heɪlər | *s.c.* (brit.) megáfono.

loudly | 'laudlɪ | *adv.* ruidosamente, llamativamente, escandalosamente.

loudmouth | 'laudmauθ | *s.c.* (fam.) gritón, bocazas.

loud-mouthed | 'laudmauðd | *adj.* de voz chillona, gritona, destemplada.

loudness | 'laudnɪs | *s.i.* volumen (de sonido), ruido, vulgaridad, mal gusto.

loudspeaker | ˌlaud'spiːkər | *s.c.* altavoz.

lough | lɒk | , | lɒx | *s.c.* lago, brazo de mar (en Irlanda).

lounge | laundʒ | *s.c.* **1** sala de espera (en aeropuertos). **2** salón público (hoteles, clubs, etc.). **3** (brit.) salón, cuarto de estar (en casa particular). || *v.i.* **4** estar recostado perezosamente (de pie o sentado). || **5 – bar,** (brit.) bar reservado (más elegante y caro, en hoteles). **6 – suit,** (brit.) traje (de calle u oficina).

lounger | 'laundʒər | *s.c.* vago, gandul, haragán.

lour | 'lauər | *v.i.* **[to – (at/on)] 1** mirar amenazantemente, fruncir el ceño. **2** (fig.) oscurecerse, amenazar tormenta.

louse | laus | *s.c.* **1** ZOOL. piojo. **2** (fig.) (fam.) persona despreciable. || *v.t.* **3 [to – (up)]** (fam.) estropear, echar a perder, arruinar.

lousy | 'lauzɪ | *adj.* **1** piojoso. **2** (fam.) malo, malvado, desastroso: *lousy holidays = vacaciones desastrosas.* **3 [– (with)]** (fam.) abarrotado, infectado: *the place is lousy with tourists = el lugar está infectado de turistas.*

lout | laut | *s.c.* patán, gamberro.

loutish | 'lautɪʃ | *adj.* grosero, maleducado, incivil.

louvre | 'luːvər | (EE.UU. **louver**) *s.c.* **1** listón, tablilla, banda (de persiana). **2** persiana.

louvred | 'luːvəd | (EE.UU. **louvered**) *adj.* que es del tipo de una persiana, hace sus veces, etc.

lovable | 'lʌvəbl | *adj.* amable, bondadoso, simpático, cariñoso.

love | lʌv | *s.i.* **1** amor, cariño. **2** amor, pasión, deseo, atracción sexual: *their love has cooled = su amor se ha enfriado.* **3** amor, inclinación, interés, afición (por el arte, el deporte, la aventura, etc.): *a strong love of learning = un vivo interés por aprender.* **4** besos, saludos, recuerdos, etc. (en cartas o tarjetas): *give my love to your son = besos para tu hijo.* **5** (fam.) encanto, delicia, cielo: *what a love her daughter is! = ¡qué cielo de hija tiene!* **6** DEP. cero, nada (tenis). **7** REL. amor, caridad, misericordia (de Dios). || *s.c.* **8** amor, persona amada: *the great love of his life = el gran amor de su vida.* **9** (brit.) (fam.) amor, cielo, guapo, cariño (en vocativos; entre personas no enamoradas): *here you are, love = aquí tienes, guapa.* || *v.t.* **10** amar, querer. **11** amar, gustar, sentir debilidad, tener afición (por animales o cosas): *she's always loved cats = siempre ha sentido debilidad por los gatos.* **12** querer, gustar, apetecer: *I'd love a cup of tea = me apetecería un té.* || **13 to be in – (with),** estar enamorado de. **14 to fall in – (with),** enamorarse de. **15 for the – of God,** ¡por el amor de Dios! **16 to give/send someone one's –,** mandar besos, saludos, recuerdos (por carta, teléfono, etc.). **17 (just) for –/for the – of something,** sin retribución económica, por amor al arte. **18 – at first sight,** amor a primera vista, flechazo. **19 – -hate rela-**

tionship, relación de amor-odio. **20 – me, – my dog,** quien quiere a Beltrán quiere a su can. **21 to make – (to someone), a)** hacer el amor con alguien. **b)** (p.u.) cortejar a, ser especialmente atento y amable con alguien. **22 not for – or money,** de ninguna manera posible: *we couldn't find a room for love or money = no hubo manera de encontrar habitación.* **23 the – of someone's life,** el amor de su vida. **24 there's little/no – lost (between),** (fam.) poca o ninguna amistad hay (entre).

love-affair | 'lʌvəɪfeər | *s.c.* relación amorosa (no muy duradera).

love-bird | 'lʌvbɜːd | *s.c.* **1** periquito, tortolito (pájaro muy enamorado de su pareja). || **2 love-birds,** (fig.) (fam.) tortolitos, enamorados.

love-child | 'lʌvtʃaɪld | *s.c.* (euf.) hijo hijo del amor (nacido fuera del matrimonio).

loveless | 'lʌvlɪs | *adj.* sin amor, que no ama ni es amado: *a loveless marriage = matrimonio sin amor.*

love-letter | 'lʌvletər | *s.c.* carta de amor.

love-life | 'lʌvlaɪf | *s.c.* vida amorosa, vida sentimental.

loveliness | 'lʌvlɪnɪs | *s.i.* belleza, atractivo, encanto.

lovelorn | 'lʌvlɔːn | *adj.* triste, infeliz (por ausencia del amado).

lovely | 'lʌvlɪ | *adj.* **1** bello, atractivo, precioso (una mujer, un paisaje, el tiempo, etc.): *what a lovely girl = ¡qué chica tan preciosa!* **2** (fam.) agradable, maravilloso, estupendo: *a lovely dinner = una cena estupenda.* || *s.c.* **3** (fam.) belleza, mujer bella: *a couple of lovelies = un par de bellezas.*

OBS. No suele emplearse **lovely** para describir el aspecto físico de un hombre. Se emplea en su lugar **handsome** o **good-looking.**

love-making | 'lʌv,meɪkɪŋ | *s.i.* relación amorosa, acto sexual.

lover | 'lʌvər | *s.c.* =f amante: *she has had many lovers = ha tenido muchos amantes.* **2** amante, aficionado, entusiasta, interesado en (objetos o actividades): *they are music lovers = son amantes de la música.* || **3 lovers,** pareja de enamorados (haciendo vida marital): *they became lovers soon after they met = se hicieron amantes apenas conocerse.*

love-match | 'lʌvmætʃ | *s.c.* unión matrimonial por amor, matrimonio por amor.

love-potion | 'lʌvpəʊʃn | (también **love-philtre**) *s.c.* filtro de amor, poción de amor.

love-seat | 'lʌvsiːt | *s.c.* confidente (sofá para dos cuyos asientos se miran).

lovesick | 'lʌvsɪk | *adj.* enfermo de amor.

love-song | 'lʌvsɒŋ | *s.c.* canción de amor, balada amorosa, romance de amor.

love-story | 'lʌv,stɒrɪ | *s.c.* historia de amor (en películas y novelas, generalmente).

loving | 'lʌvɪŋ | *adj.* amante, amoroso, cariñoso, tierno: *a loving son = un hijo cariñoso.*

loving-cup | 'lʌvɪŋkʌp | *s.c.* copa de amistad (normalmente con dos asas, que se pasa de uno a otro).

loving-kindness | ,lʌvɪŋ'kaɪndnɪs | *s.i.* (arc.) bondad; compasión.

lovingly | 'lʌvɪŋlɪ | *adv.* amorosamente, tiernamente, cariñosamente.

low | ləu | *adj.* **1** bajo (estatura, alzada): *a low building = un edificio bajo.* **2** bajo (colocación en relación con el suelo): *the mirror is too low = el espejo está demasiado bajo.* **3** bajo, pequeño, reducido (en cantidad, grado, valor, etc.): *families on low incomes = familias de ingresos reducidos.* **4 [– (on)]** bajo, corto, escaso (de existencias o cantidad disponible): *we're getting low on petrol = vamos escasos de gasolina.* **5** negativo, desfavorable: *they have a low opinion of us = tienen una opinión negativa de nosotros.* **6 [– (in)]** bajo en, con poca cantidad de: *this milk is low in fat = esta leche es baja en grasa.* **7** bajo, suave (sonido): *let's keep our voices low = mantengamos la voz baja.* **8** bajo (en tesitura o tono musical): *too low for a tenor = demasiado bajo para un tenor.* **9** triste, deprimido, bajo: *to recover from low spirits = recobrarse de un bajo estado de ánimo.* **10** bajo, corto, lento (velocidad): *use a low gear to drive slowly = pon una velocidad corta para conducir despacio.* **11** bajo, rastrero, vulgar, malintencionado (acción, conducta): *that was a low trick = fue una treta rastrera.* **12** débil, mortecino, insuficiente (luz, alumbrado): *the lights in the corridor are too low = la luz del pasillo es insuficiente.* || *adv.* **13** bajo (nivel, situación, precio, etc.): *to buy low and sell high = comprar bajo (barato) y vender alto (caro).* **14** bajo (tono, voz): *to speak low = hablar bajo.* || *s.c.* e *i.* **15** nivel o valor bajo (de una moneda frente a otra). **16** área de baja presión barométrica. **17** velocidad corta. **18** mugido. || *v.i.* **19** (lit.) mugir. || **20 at a – ebb,** en un estado de depresión, en horas bajas: *her spirits are at a very low ebb = sus ánimos están muy bajos.* **21 at a record –/at an all-time –,** en los momentos más bajos, peores: *relations between them were at a record low = su relación atravesaba los peores momentos.* **22 to be brought –,** verse perjudicado (en salud, riqueza, posición, etc.). **23 in the – twenties/thirties...,** en los primeros veinte/treinta... **24 to lay someone –,** derrotar a alguien. **25 to lie –, a)** estar tumbado todo lo largo que uno es. **b)** estar callado o escondido: *the escaped prisoner lay low for months = el recluso fugado estuvo meses escondido.* **26 – season,** estación baja, temporada baja. **27 – tide, a)** marea baja. **b)** el tiempo en que ésta se produce. **28 – water,** nivel bajo de agua en un río, embalse, etc. **29 – water mark, a)** señal que marca el nivel más bajo del agua. **b)** el punto más bajo o desfavorable (en fama, fortuna, negocios, etc.).

low-born | 'ləubɔːn | *adj.* (lit.) de baja cuna, de origen humilde.

lowbrow | 'ləubrau | *adj.* **1** simple, superficial, ordinario, fácil de entender. || *s.c.* **2** (desp.) persona ignorante, inculta, poco interesada en la cultura.

low-class | ,ləu'klɑːs | *adj.* de clase baja.

low-cut | 'ləukʌt | *adj.* escotado (de prendas de vestir): *a low-cut dress = un vestido escotado.*

low-down | 'ləudaun | *s.sing.* **1** (fam.) la realidad, la verdad de los hechos, lo que hay que saber: *to know the low-down on the conflict = conocer la verdad de los hechos en conflicto.* || | ləu'daun | *adj.* **2** (fam.) bajo, vil, rastrero: *what a low-down trick = ¡qué treta tan vil!*

lower | 'ləuər | *adj.* =f más bajo (*comp. de* **low**). **2** bajo, inferior: *the lower deck of a bus = el piso inferior de un autobús (de dos pisos).* **3** bajo, segundo, menos importante (de dos sistemas, grupos, etc.): *the Speaker of the lower House = el Presidente de la Cámara Baja.* **4** bajo, parte baja, bajos: *he was wounded in the lower leg = le hirieron en la parte baja de la pierna.* **5** de bajo nivel o graduación (en una escala, cadena, etc.): *the lower military officers = oficiales de baja graduación.* || *v.t.* **6** bajar: *he lowered his arm = bajó el brazo.* **7** bajar, abaratar, reducir, disminuir (en cantidad, calidad, valor, etc.): *they've lowered the price of milk = han abaratado la leche.* **8** rebajarse (en negativas): *I don't lower myself by doing that = yo no me rebajo a hacer eso.* **9** bajar (los ojos): *she lowered her eyes.* **=f0** hablar bajo, bajar (la voz): *he lowered his voice.* || 'lauə | *v.i.* **11** oscurecerse, amenazar tormenta (el cielo). **12 [to – (at/on)]** mirar con enfado, fruncir el ceño. || **13 – class/classes,** clase baja, clase trabajadora. **14 Lower House,** Cámara Baja, Cámara de los Comunes (en el Parlamento inglés).

lower-case | ,ləuə'keɪs | *s.i.* caja baja, caracteres de imprenta pequeños, impresión de letra ordinaria o minúscula.

lowering | 'ləuərɪŋ | *s.i.* bajada, descenso: *the lowering of the sea level = la bajada de nivel de los mares.*

lowest common denominator | 'ləuɪst'-kɒməndi'nɒmɪ,neɪtər | *s.c.* **1** mínimo común denominador, intereses mayoritarios, intereses del sector más bajo (en un grupo, asociación, sindicato, etc.). **2** MAT. mínimo común denominador.

low-flying | ,ləu'flaɪɪŋ | *adj.* de vuelo bajo, que vuela más bajo de lo normal (aves, aviones, etc.): *warning of low-flying aircraft = alarma de un avión al volar demasiado bajo.*

low-key | ,ləu'kiː | *adj.* controlado, bajo de tono, contemporizador, conciliador: *a low-key speech = un discurso conciliador.*

lowlands | 'ləuləndz | *s.c.* tierras bajas.
lowliness | 'ləulınıs | *s.i.* modestia, humildad (en orígenes familiares o similar).
lowly | 'ləulı | *adj.* **1** bajo, modesto, humilde, discreto. || *adv.* **2** modestamente, humildemente, discretamente.
low-lying | ˌləu'laııŋ | *adj.* **1** bajo, al nivel o bajo el nivel del mar: *low-lying areas affected by the flood = zonas bajas afectadas por la inundación.* **2** más bajo de lo normal, muy bajo: *low-lying clouds = nubes muy bajas.*
low-minded | ˌləu'maındıd | *adj.* vulgar, chabacano, tabernario, procaz.
low-necked | ˌləu'nekt | *adj.* escotado, despechugado (prendas de vestir).
low-paid | ˌləu'peıd | *adj.* **1** de remuneración baja, mal pagado: *low-paid workers = trabajadores mal pagados.* || **2 the –,** los que tienen baja retribución.
low-pitched | ˌləu'pıtʃt | *adj.* **1** bajo, profundo (sonido). **2** suave, tranquilo (voz). **3** de poca inclinación o pendiente (tejado).
low-spirited | ˌləu'spırıtıd | *adj.* bajo de ánimos, deprimido, triste, infeliz.
lox | lɒks | , | lɑ:ks | (EE.UU. **salmon**) *s.i.* salmón (ahumado).
loyal | 'lɔıəl | *adj.* **[– (to)]** leal, fiel, consecuente: *loyal to one's principles = fiel a los propios principios.*
loyalist | 'lɔıəlıst | *s.c.* **1** persona fiel, leal (a un régimen o gobernante en época de revolución, principalmente). || *adj.* **2** fiel, leal.
loyally | 'lɔıəlı | *adv.* fielmente, lealmente.
loyalty | 'lɔıəltı | *s.c.* e *i.* **1 [– (to)]** lealtad, fidelidad. || **2 loyalties,** lealtades: *a case of divided loyalties = conflicto de lealtades.*
lozenge | 'lɒzındʒ | *s.c.* **1** pastilla, gragea, tableta (medicinal): *a throat lozenge = una pastilla para la garganta.* **2** losange, figura romboidal (en heráldica).
LP | ˌel'pi: | (abreviatura de **long-playing record**) *s.c.* LP, disco grande, o de larga duración (33 revoluciones por minuto).
L-plate | 'elpleıt | *s.c.* (brit.) placa con la letra, signo de conductor novato.
LSD | ˌeles'di: | *s.i.* **1** LSD, ácido lisérgico. **2** (brit.) (p.u.) dinero.
lubber | 'lʌbər | *s.c.* (p.u.) palurdo, patán.
lubberly | 'lʌbəlı | *adj.* (p.u.) palurdo.
lubricant | 'lu:brıkənt | *s.c.* e *i.* lubricante.
lubricate | 'lu:brıkeıt | *v.t.* **1** lubricar, engrasar: *to lubricate the bearings = engrasar los cojinetes.* **2** (fig.) hacer que se suelte la lengua, hacer hablar: *a drink will lubricate him = una copa le soltará la lengua.*
lubrication | ˌlu:brı'keıʃn | *s.c.* e *i.* lubricación, engrase.
lubricious | lu:'brıʃəs | *adj.* (form.) libidinoso, lúbrico, lujurioso, lascivo.
lucerne | lu:'sə:n | (EE.UU. **alfalfa**) *s.i.* alfalfa.
lucid | 'lu:sıd | *adj.* **1** lúcido, claro, fácil (de entender): *a lucid explanation = una explicación clara.* **2** lúcido, consciente, cabal, sano (mental): *lucid intervals = ratos de lucidez mental.*
lucidity | lu:'sıdıtı | *s.i.* lucidez, coordinación (mental).
lucidly | 'lu:sıdlı | *adv.* lúcidamente, conscientemente, en sus cabales.
luck | lʌk | *s.i.* **1** suerte, fortuna, azar. **2** buena suerte, buena fortuna, buenaventura: *any luck with the job? = ¿hubo (buena) suerte con el empleo?* || **3 any –?,** ¿hubo suerte? **4 as (good/ill) – would have it,** por suerte/por desgracia. **5 a stroke of –,** una suerte, un golpe de fortuna. **6 to be bad/hard/tough – (on someone),** tener mala suerte, ser mala suerte: *it was hard luck (on you) to get ill on your holiday = ya fue mala suerte que enfermaras en vacaciones.* **7 to be down on one's –,** (fam.) tener la suerte en contra, atravesar una racha de mala suerte. **8 to be in/out of –,** estar de suerte/mala suerte: *we're in luck; the train hasn't left yet = estamos de suerte; el tren no ha salido todavía.* **9 better – next time,** que haya más suerte la próxima vez. **10 good/best of – (to someone),** suerte, que haya suerte: *good luck in your exams! = suerte en tus exámenes.* **11 just one's –,** la misma suerte de siempre, sigue la mala racha. **12 to – out,** (EE.UU.) (fam.) tener suerte, ser afortunado. **13 no such –,** desgraciadamente no, no caerá esa breva. **14 one's – is in,** se tiene la suerte a favor, se tiene una buena racha. **15 to push one's –,** (fam.) tentar a la suerte. **16 the devil's own –,** (fam.) pura chiripa. **17 the – of the draw,** ¡las cosas del azar! **18 the – of the game,** efecto del azar (no del mérito o el esfuerzo). **19 to try one's – (at something),** probar suerte, poner la suerte a prueba: *I'll try my luck at roulette = pondré mi suerte a prueba en la ruleta.* **20 worse –,** mala suerte, qué se le va a hacer.
luckily | 'lʌkılı | *adv.* afortunadamente, por fortuna, por suerte.
luckless | 'lʌklıs | *adj.* desafortunado, desgraciado, desdichado.
lucky | 'lʌkı | *adj.* **1** afortunado, de suerte (en la vida, en general): *he's a lucky man = es un hombre de suerte.* **2** afortunado, agraciado (en una situación concreta): *the lucky winner = el afortunado ganador.* **3** por suerte, por casualidad: *it's lucky I'm here = por suerte estoy aquí.* **4** que da suerte, de la suerte, de buena suerte: *a lucky rabbit's foot = pata de conejo de buena suerte.* || **5 – devil/– you,** (fam.) los hay con suerte. **6 – dip(s),** (brit.) tómbola. **7 to strike (it) –,** (fam.) tener suerte (en una situación concreta): *we certainly struck it lucky with the weather = tuvimos verdadera suerte con el tiempo.* **8 to thanks one's – stars,** reconocer, agradecer la buena suerte: *thank your lucky stars you don't have to take orders = agradece que no tengas que obedecer órdenes.* **9 third time –,** a la tercera va la vencida. **10 you'll be lucky/you should be so –,** (hum.) ¡vas a necesitar suerte!
lucrative 'lu:krətıv | *adj.* lucrativo, rentable (negocio, empleo, actividad).
lucratively | 'lu:krətıvlı | *adv.* lucrativamente, rentablemente.
lucrativeness | 'lu:krətıvnıs | *s.i.* rentabilidad.
lucre | 'lu:kər | *s.i.* **1** (p.u.) lucro, ganancia, negocio, provecho económico (por medios no muy legales, generalmente). || **2 filthy –,** vil metal.
Luddite | 'lʌdaıt | *s.c.* (form.) reaccionario, retrógrado, enemigo de innovaciones (en la industria, por la destrucción de empleo que pueden traer).
ludicrous | 'lu:dıkrəs | *adj.* ridículo, hilarante, absurdo, descabellado.
ludicrously | 'lu:dıkrəslı | *adv.* ridículamente, absurdamente.
ludicrousness | 'lu:dıkrəsnıs | *s.i.* ridiculez, absurdo.
ludo | 'lu:dəu | *s.i.* (brit.) parchís.
luff | lʌf | *v.i.* MAR. orzar, barloventear.
lug | lʌg | *v.t.* **1** (fam.) arrastrar, llevar con dificultad: *she was lugging the suitcase = arrastraba la maleta.* || *s.c.* **2** mango, saliente, asa.
luggage | 'lʌgıdʒ | (EE.UU. **baggage**) *s.i.* **1** equipaje, maletas: *five pieces of luggage = cinco bultos de equipaje.* || **2 – boot,** maletero, portaequipajes (en automóviles). **3 – rack,** portaequipajes, baca, redecilla. **4 – trolley,** carro, carre tilla, portamaletas. **5 – van,** furgón de equipaje.
lugger | 'lʌgər | *s.c.* MAR. lugre (tipo de embarcación).
lughole | 'lʌghəul | *s.c.* (brit. y hum.) oído.
lugsail | 'lʌgseıl | *s.c.* MAR. vela al tercio.
lugubrious | lu:'gu:brıəs | *adj.* (lit.) lúgubre, sombrío, triste, tétrico.
lugubriously | lu:'gu:brıəslı | *adv.* (lit.) lúgubremente, sombríamente, tristemente.
lugubriousness | lə'gu:brıəsnıs | *s.i.* (lit.) tristeza, melancolía.
lugworm | 'lʌgwə:m | *s.c.* gusano (que se encuentra en la arena de la playa y sirve de cebo para pescar).
lukewarm | 'lu:kwɔ:m | *adj.* **1** tibio, templado (líquidos): *that water is only luckewarm = ese agua está sólo tibia.* **2** (fig.) poco entusiasta, frío, desinteresado: *his plan got a lukewarm reception = su plan recibió una fría acogida.*
lull | lʌl | *s.c.* **1** pausa, calma, momento de inactividad: *after a lull of weeks = tras una pausa de semanas.* || *v.t.* **2** calmar, sosegar, adormecer: *the motion of the train lulled us = el movimiento del tren nos adormeció.* **3** dar (falsa impresión): *it lulled him a false sense of security = le dio una falsa impresión de seguridad.* || **4 – before the storm,** calma antes de la tempestad, se prevén tormentas.
lullaby 'lʌləbaı | *s.c.* nana, canción de cuna.

lumbago | lʌm'beɪgəʊ | *s.i.* lumbago.

lumbar | 'lʌmbər | *adj.* **1** ANAT. lumbar: *the lumbar region of the spine = la región lumbar de la columna.* || **2 – puncture,** MED. punción en la columna.

lumber | 'lʌmbər | *s.i.* **=f** (brit.) trastos, cosas inservibles. **2** (EE.UU.) madera: *piles of lumber = montones de madera.* || *v.i.* **3** moverse con dificultad, avanzar pesadamente: *the truck lumbered up the hill = el camión subía la cuesta pesadamente.* **4** (EE.UU.) cortar árboles, hacer madera. || **5 to – someone with,** (fam.) pasar, dejar a alguien una carga no deseada: *women are lumbered with the housework = se deja a las mujeres las tareas de la casa.*

lumbering | 'lʌmbərɪŋ | *adj.* pesado, patoso, lento, torpe: *a lumbering trot = un trote pesado.*

lumberjack | 'lʌmbədʒæk | *s.c.* (EE.UU.) leñador.

lumber-jacket | 'lʌmbədʒækɪt | *s.c.* cazadora de leñador (típicamente a cuadros y corta).

lumberman | 'lʌmbəmən | *s.c.* (EE.UU.) leñador, maderero.

lumber-room | 'lʌmbərum | *s.c.* (brit.) trastero.

lumberyard | 'lʌmbəjɑːd | *s.c.* almacén de madera.

luminary | 'luːmɪnərɪ | *s.c.* (lit.) lumbrera, figura descollante, persona famosa.

luminiscence | ˌluːmɪ'nesəns | *s.i.* (lit.) luminiscencia, resplandor.

luminosity | ˌluːmɪ'nɒsɪtɪ | *s.i.* (lit.) luminosidad.

luminous | 'luːmɪnəs | *adj.* luminoso, resplandeciente: *the luminous hands of a watch = las luminosas manecillas de un reloj.*

luminously | 'luːmɪnəslɪ | *adv.* resplandecientemente, luminosamente.

lump | lʌmp | *s.c.* **1** trozo, pedazo, bloque (de materia sólida): *a lump of coal = un trozo de carbón.* **2** grumo, trozo sin disolver: *lumps in the soup = grumos en la sopa.* **3** bulto, protuberancia, dureza (en el cuerpo humano): *to examine one's breast for lumps = examinarse el pecho en prevención de durezas.* **4** terrón (de azúcar): *a lump of sugar = un terrón de azúcar.* **5** cantidad, masa, conjunto, total (de dinero hecho en un solo pago): *a lump donation to a charity cause = donación en un solo pago a una causa benéfica.* **6** (brit. y fam.) conjunto de trabajadores eventuales (de la construcción, especialmente). **7** (fig.) pelmazo, imbécil. || *v.t.* **8** tratar de forma conjunta, amontonar, agrupar, globalizar: *don't lump them all together = no los amontones.* **9** aceptar, soportar (algo impuesto). || **10 to have a – in one's throat,** sentirse embargado por la emoción, hacerse un nudo en la garganta. **11 to – it/to have to – it,** tener que aceptar una situación impuesta, tener que tragar: *he said so, and I had to lump it = eso dijo y yo tuve que aceptarlo.* **12 – sum,** entrega de dinero (en un solo pago): *choose between a lump sum or a pension = elija entre recibir todo en un pago o una pensión.* **13 to – together,** tratar de forma conjunta, agrupar, globalizar: *we lump the two trips together = globalizamos los dos viajes.*

lumpish | 'lʌmpɪʃ | *adj.* patoso, torpe, pesado, bobo.

lumpy | 'lʌmpɪ | *adj.* abultado, apelmazado, grumoso, aterronado.

lunacy | 'luːnəsɪ | *s.i.* **1** locura, enajenación mental. **2** (arc.) conducta paranoica. || **3 sheer –,** disparate en toda regla.

lunar | 'luːnər | *adj.* (form.) **1** lunar: *a lunar eclipse = un eclipse lunar.* || **2 – month,** mes lunar.

lunatic | 'luːnətɪk | *s.c.* **1** (fam.) lunático, loco: *he's a bloody lunatic = es un lunático perdido.* **2** (p.u.) enfermo mental. **3** descabellado, erróneo: *the new budget is lunatic = el nuevo presupuesto es descabellado.* **4** confuso, descontrolado (una situación): *the lunatic atmo sphere of the place = la confusa atmósfera del lugar.* || **5 – asylum,** (arc.) manicomio. **6 – fringe,** extremistas, fanáticos, radicales (de un grupo, movimiento, etc.).

lunch | lʌntʃ | *s.c.* **1** almuerzo, comida (de mediodía). **2** hora del almuerzo, mediodía: *they met from breakfast till lunch = estuvieron reunidos desde el desayuno hasta el mediodía.* **3** almuerzo, banquete (como homenaje o acontecimiento señalado): *the minister is giving a lunch = el ministro va a ofrecer un banquete.* **4** (EE.UU.) piscolabis, tentempié, colación (a cualquier hora): *we'll have a lunch after the show = tomaremos un piscolabis tras el espectáculo.* || *v.i.* **5** (form.) almorzar (en restaurante, generalmente). || *v.t.* **6** agasajar, divertir a alguien (invitándole a comer).

luncheon | 'lʌntʃən | *s.c.* **1** (form.) almuerzo, banquete (como celebración especial): *they had a literary luncheon = celebraron un almuerzo literario.* **2** (arc.) almuerzo, comida de mediodía. || **3 – meat,** carne enlatada (mezcla de cerdo y cereal, generalmente). **4 – voucher,** (brit.) bono de comida (concedido a sus empleados por algunas empresas).

luncheonette | ˌlʌntʃə'net | *s.c.* (EE.UU.) pequeño restaurante (que suele servir comidas muy sencillas).

lunch-hour | 'lʌntʃauər | *s.c.* tiempo dedicado al almuerzo (al mediodía e interrumpiendo el trabajo).

lunch-room | 'lʌntʃrum | *s.c.* (EE.UU.) snack bar, restaurante (que sirve comidas ligeras).

lunchtime | 'lʌntʃtaɪm | *s.c.* e *i.* hora del almuerzo.

lung | lʌŋ | *s.c.* **1** ANAT. pulmón. || **2 to have good lungs, a)** tener buenos pulmones. **b)** tener voz potente.

lunge | lʌndʒ | *v.i.* **1 [to – (at/towards)]** abalanzarse, lanzarse, arremeter, atacar: *he lunged at me with a club = arremetió contra mí con un palo.* || *s.c.* **2** ataque, embestida, arremetida. **3** DEP. directo (boxeo).

lung-power | 'lʌŋpaʊər | *s.i.* capacidad de pulmón, fuelle (para cantar, gritar, etc. con fuerza).

lupin | 'luːpɪn | (EE.UU. **lupine**) *s.c.* BOT. lupino, altramuz.

lurch | ləːtʃ | *v.i.* **1** dar bandazos, tambalearse, desequilibrarse: *he lurched and fell = dio un bandazo y se cayó.* **2** (fig.) variar, cambiar (de opinión, actitud o conducta): *he lurched away from the party = cambió de ideas y de partido.* || *s.c.* **3** bandazo, sacudida: *with a lurch he fell over me = dando un bandazo cayó sobre mí.* **4** cambio, variación (de opinión, actitud o conducta). || **5 to leave someone in the –,** (fam.) dejar a alguien en la estacada.

lure | ljuər | , | luə | *v.t.* **1** atraer, tentar, fascinar, sugerir, engañar: *low prices lure people = los bajos precios atraen al público.* || *s.c.* **2** atractivo, fascinación, gancho, señuelo, aliciente: *the lure of adventure = la fascinación de la aventura.* **3** cebo, señuelo (para atraer animales salvajes).

lurgy | 'ləːgɪ | *s.sing.* (brit. y fam.) enfermedad leve.

lurid | 'ljuərɪd | *adj.* **1** coloreado, d[illegible] color vivo, brillante, llamativo, chilló[illegible] *a lurid sunset = una brillante puesta* [illegible] *sol.* **2** violento, fuerte, pintoresco, co[illegible]rista, terrorífico, sobrecogedor: *th*[illegible] *lurid details of the murder = los terroríficos detalles del crimen.*

luridly | 'ljuərɪdlɪ | *adv.* brillantemente, llamativamente, violentamente, horriblemente.

lurk | ləːk | *v.i.* **1** estar escondido, acechar, estar al acecho: *someone was lurking in the shadows = alguien acechaba en las tinieblas.* **2** existir (sin ser percibido), estar latente, ocultarse: *danger lurks in that quiet lake = el peligro se oculta en la quietud del lago.* **3** surgir (veladamente), insinuarse (especialmente en la mente): *a lurking suspicion = la insinuación de una sospecha (una insinuante sospecha).*

luscious | 'lʌʃəs | *adj.* **1** delicioso, apetitoso, suculento, exquisito: *the luscious taste of a ripe peach = el apetitoso sabor de un melocotón maduro.* **2** rico, sugerente, sensual (en manifestaciones artísticas): *the luscious colour of the picture = el sugerente colorido del cuadro.* **3** (fam.) voluptuoso, sensual, apetitoso, atractivo (sexualmente): *a luscious blonde = una rubia sensual.*

lusciously | 'lʌʃəslɪ | *adv.* deliciosamente, sugerentemente, sensualmente.

lusciousness | 'lʌʃəsnɪs | *s.i.* **1** suculencia, sabor suculento, exquisitez. **2** voluptuosidad, sensualidad.

lush | lʌʃ | *adj.* **1** exuberante, lozano, lujuriante (plantas, hierbas, etc.): *lush vegetation = vegetación exuberante.* **2** (fam.) lujoso, de lujo, selecto: *a lush atmosphere = un ambiente de lujo.* ||

s.c. **3** (EE.UU. y fam.) borracho, bebido.

lushness | 'lʌʃnɪs | *s.i.* exuberancia, lozanía, lujo.

lust | lʌst | *s.c.* e *i.* **1** lujuria, lascivia, libido: *to curb one's lust = reprimirse la lujuria.* **2 [– (for/of)]** codicia, afán, ansia, deseo vehemente: *a lust for power = afán de poder.* || *v.i.* **3 [to – (after/for)]** desear (sexualmente), codiciar, ansiar: *he lusts for money = codicia el dinero.*

lustful | 'lʌstful | *adj.* lujurioso, libidinoso, lascivo.

lustfully | 'lʌstfulɪ | *adv.* lujuriosamente, lascivamente.

lustre | 'lʌstər | (EE.UU. **luster**) *s.c.* e *i.* **1** lustre, brillo, esplendor. **2** (fig.) lustre, brillo, toque, distinción: *travelling gave his image a new lustre = los viajes añadieron un nuevo brillo a su imagen.*

lustrous | 'lʌstrəs | *adj.* (lit.) lustroso, brillante: *lustrous eyes = ojos brillantes.*

lustrously | 'lʌstrəslɪ | *adv.* (lit.) lustrosamente, brillantemente.

lustily | 'lʌstɪlɪ | *adv.* vigorosamente, fuertemente, vitalmente.

lusty | 'lʌstɪ | *adj.* vigoroso, vital, sano, robusto, lozano.

lute | lu:t | *s.c.* **1** MUS. laúd. || *s.i.* **2** zulaque.

lutenist | 'lu:tənɪst | (también **lutanist**) *s.c.* tocador de laúd, laudista.

Lutheran | 'lu:θərən | REL. *s.c.* **1** luterano. || *adj.* **2** luterano.

luv | lʌv | (grafía regional de **love**) *s.c.* e *i.* (brit. y p.u.) amor.

luxuriance | lʌg'zjuərɪəns | *s.i.* exuberancia, vigor, lozanía, vicio (vegetación).

luxuriant | lʌg'zjuərɪənt | *adj.* **1** exuberante, lozano, vigoroso, lujuriante. **2** recargado, artificioso (en decoración).

luxuriantly | lʌg'zjuərɪəntlɪ | *adv.* exuberantemente, lozanamente, vigorosamente.

luxuriate | lʌg'zjuərɪeɪt | *v.i.* **[to – (in)]** disfrutar, deleitarse: *to luxuriate in one's hot bath = deleitarse con un baño de agua caliente.*

luxurious | lʌg'zjuərɪəs | *adj.* **1** lujoso, de lujo, fastuoso, caro: *a luxurious flat = un piso de lujo.* **2** voluptuoso, sensual, placentero, relajante: *she took a luxurious long hot bath = se tomó un largo y placentero baño de agua caliente.*

luxuriously | lʌg'zjuərɪəslɪ | *adv.* voluptuosamente, sensualmente, placenteramente.

luxury | 'lʌkʃərɪ | *s.c.* e *i.* **1** lujo, confort (sin considerar el coste): *they live in great luxury = llevan una vida de gran lujo.* **2** lujo (bienes superfluos y caros): *clothes, food and little luxuries = vestido, comida y pequeños lujos.* || *atr.* **3** de lujo, lujoso, caro, fastuoso: *luxury hotels = hoteles de lujo.* || **4 – goods,** bienes superfluos.

LV | ˌel'vɪ: | (abreviatura de **luncheon voucher**) V. **luncheon.**

LW | ˌel'dʌblju: | (abreviatura de **long wave**) V. **wave.**

lychee | 'laɪtʃi: | *s.c.* e *i.* lichi (fruta china parecida a la nuez y de carne blanca y dulce).

lychgate | 'litʃgeɪt | *s.c.* portada, portadillo, soportal (en cementerios e iglesias).

lye | laɪ | *s.i.* QUIM. lejía.

lying | 'laɪɪŋ | [*p.pres.* de **lie**] V. **lie.**

lying-in | ˌlaɪɪŋ'ɪn | *s.sing.* **1** (arc.) período en cama (de parturienta antes del parto). **2** (fam.) período en cama en plan perezoso después de despertar.

lymph | lɪmf | *s.i.* ANAT. **1** linfa. **2** MED. linfa animal (para vacuna). || **3 – gland,** ANAT. glándula linfática.

lymphatic | lɪm'fætɪk | *adj.* **1** linfático: *lymphatic vessels = vasos linfáticos.* **2** (fig. y form.) lento, perezoso, inerte.

lynch | lɪntʃ | *v.t.* **1** linchar. || **2 – law,** procedimiento legal seguido en caso de linchamiento.

lynx | lɪŋks | *s.c.* ZOOL. lince.

lynx-eyed | ˌlɪŋks'aɪd | *adj.* con vista de lince.

lyre | 'laɪər | *s.c.* lira.

lyre-bird | 'laɪəbə:d | *s.c.* ZOOL. ave lira (Australia).

lyric | 'lɪrɪk | *adj.* **1** lírico: *a lyric poet = un poeta lírico.* **2** para ser cantado. || *s.c.* **3** poema lírico. || **4 lyrics,** letra de canción.

lyrical | 'lɪrɪkl | *adj.* **1** lírico. **2** jovial, muy entusiasta: *she waxed lyrical about natural food = se hizo muy entusiasta de los alimentos naturales.*

lyrically | 'lɪrɪkəlɪ | *adv.* líricamente, jovialmente, con mucho entusiasmo.

lyricism | 'lɪrɪsɪzəm | *s.c.* e *i.* **1** lirismo. **2** expresión de gran emoción o entusiasmo.

lyricist | 'lɪrɪsɪst | *s.c.* escritor de canciones (de su letra o texto).

lyrics | 'lɪrɪks | *s.pl.* letra, texto de canción (en espectáculos musicales).

lysergic | 'lɪ'sə:dʒɪk | *adj.* lisérgico.

m, M | em | *s.c.* m, M (decimotercera letra del alfabeto inglés). **2** abreviatura de **metre, million, minute, male, masculine y married.** **3** 1000, número romano. **4** contracción de am: *I'm = yo soy.*

ma | mɑː | *s.c.* (fam.) mamá, mami.

ma'am | mɑːm | | mæm | | məm | *(contracción* de **madam)** *s.c.* señora (tratamiento respetuoso para una mujer).

mac | mæk | *s.c.* **1** (brit. y fam.) impermeable. **2** (EE.UU. y argot) Mac (para dirigirse a un hombre cuyo nombre se desconoce).

macabre | mə'kɑːbr | | mə'kɑːbər | *adj.* macabro, truculento, espantoso, siniestro.

macadam | mə'kædəm | *s.i.* macadán (en la construcción de carreteras).

macadamise V. **macadamize.**

macadamize | mə'kædəmaɪz | *v.t.* echar macadán (en una carretera).

macaroni | ˌmækə'rəʊnɪ | *s.i.* **1** macarrones. || **2 – cheese,** GAST. macarrones gratinados.

macaroon | ˌmækə'ruːn | *s.c.* galleta de coco y almendra, mostachón.

mace | meɪs | *s.c.* **1** bastón de mando, maza cer emonial. **2** maza, porra. || *s.i.* **3** macís (especia de la corteza de la nuez moscada).

macerate | 'mæsəreɪt | *v.t.* (form.) ablandar, macerar.

maceration | ˌmæsə'reɪʃn | *s.i.* (form.) ablandamiento, maceración.

Mach | mæk | | mɑːk | *s.i.* Mach (cociente entre la velocidad de un avión y el sonido).

machete | mə'ʃeɪtɪ | | mə'tʃeɪtɪ | *s.c.* machete.

Machiavellian | ˌmækɪə'velɪən | (también **machiavellian**) *adj.* (lit. y desp.) maquiavélico.

machinations | ˌmækɪ'neɪʃn | *s.pl.* maquinaciones, intrigas, complot.

machine | mə'ʃiːn | *s.c.* **1** máquina, aparato. **2** (fig.) máquina, autómata. **3** computadora, ordenador. **4** (fam.) coche, automóvil, (Am.) carro; motocicleta; avión. **5** (fig.) aparato, maquinaria (política, logística). || *v.t.* **6** producir a máquina, trabajar a máquina; cortar o coser a máquina. **7** troquelar, fresar, tornear. || **8 – code,** INF. código de máquina, código de operación. **9 – language,** V. **– code.**

machine-gun | mə'ʃiːngʌn | *s.c.* **1** MIL. ametralladora. || *v.t.* **2** ametrallar.

machine-made | məˌʃiːn'meɪd | *adj.* fabricado, hecho en fábrica.

machine-readable | məˌʃiːn'riːdəbl | *adj.* INF. procesable por el ordenador, comprensible por el ordenador.

machinery | mə'ʃiːnərɪ | *s.i.* **1** maquinaria, equipo. **2** mecanismo. **3** aparato, organización, sistema.

machine-tool | mə'ʃiːntuːl | *s.c.* herramienta eléctrica, sierra eléctrica.

machinist | mə'ʃiːnɪst | *s.c.* **1** maquinista, mecánico, operario. **2** costurera a máquina. **3** (arc.) tramoyista.

machismo | mə'tʃɪzməʊ | | mə'kɪzməʊ | | mɑː'tʃɪzməʊ | *s.i.* (desp.) machismo.

macho | 'mætʃəʊ | | 'mɑːtʃəʊ | *adj.* **1** (desp.) machista, macho. || *[pl.* **machos]** *s.c.* **2** machista. **3** machismo.

mackerel | 'mækrəl | *[pl.* **mackerel** o **mackerels]** *s.c.* e *i.* **1** ZOOL. caballa, escombro, sarda. || **2 – sky,** cielo con nubes como jirones.

mackintosh, macintosh | 'mækɪntɒʃ | *s.c.* **1** (brit.) impermeable. || *s.i.* **2** material impermeable, tela impermeabilizada.

macro- | ˌmækrəʊ | *prefijo.* macro: *macroeconomy = macroeconomía.*

macrobiotic | ˌmækrəʊbaɪ'ɒtɪk | *adj.* macrobiótico.

macrobiotics | ˌmækrəʊbaɪ'ɒtɪks | | ˌmækrəʊbɑː'ɒtɪk | *s.i.* macrobiótica.

macrocosm | 'mækrəʊkɒzəm | | 'mækrəʊkɑːzəm | *s.c.* **1 [the –]** el universo. **2** macrocosmos.

mad | mæd | *adj.* **1** loco, demente, enfermo mental. **2** (fig.) loco, enloquecido, furioso, frenético. **3** insensato, ilógico, disparatado, descabellado. **4 [– about]** (fam.) loco por (algo o alguien). **5** (EE.UU.) furioso, enfurecido, resentido. **6** incontrolado, desenfrenado, desordenado (una carrera). **7** hilarante, divertidísimo. **8** rabioso, afectado por la rabia (un animal). || **9 to drive somebody –,** enfurecer a alguien, volver loco a alguien. **10 to go –,** enloquecer, volverse loco (mentalmente, de alegría). **11 like –,** como loco, intensamente, enloquecidamente. **12 – as a hatter/a March hare,** como una cabra, como una regadera, loco de atar. **13 – keen,** (brit. y fam.) entusiasmado, como loco.

madam | 'mædəm | *s.c.* **1** señora (tratamiento respetuoso para una mujer): *good morning, madam = buenos días, señora.* **2** (brit. y desp.) consentida, caprichosa, mandona (una niña). **3** (arc.) madam, dueña de un prostíbulo.

madcap | 'mædkæp | *adj.* **1** (fam.) alocado, tarambana, atolondrado, impulsivo (una persona). **2** insensato (un plan). || *s.c.* **3** calavera, locuelo, tarambana.

madden | 'mædn | *v.t.* e *i.* **1** (gen. pasiva) enfurecer, volver loco, perder el juicio, encolerizarse. || *v.t.* **2** enloquecer, volver loco (mental).

maddened | 'mædnd | *adj.* enloquecido, furioso, encolerizado.

maddening | 'mædnɪŋ | *adj.* **1** desesperante, enloquecedor, exasperante (un dolor). **2** (fam.) irritante, insufrible, inaguantable (una persona).

maddeningly | 'mædnɪŋlɪ | *adv.* de modo exasperante, enloquecedoramente, insufriblemente.

made | meɪd | *pret.* y *p.p.* V. **make.** || *adj.* **1 [– from/of]** hecho de, formado por, compuesto de, confeccionado con. **2 [– for]** hecho para, adecuado para: *really made for him = lo más adecuado para él.* || **3 to be – for life/to have it –,** (fam.) tener el éxito asegurado.

made-to-measure | ˌmeɪdtə'meʒər | *adj.* a la medida, hecho a medida.
made-up | 'meɪdʌp | *adj.* **1** maquillado. **2** falso, inventado, ficticio. **3** preparado. **4** asfaltado.
madhouse | 'mædhaus | *s.c.* **1** (fam. y arc.) manicomio, psiquiátrico. **2** (fig.) casa de locos, guirigay.
madly | 'mædlɪ | *adv.* **1** enloquecidamente, alocadamente, como loco. **2** furiosamente, salvajemente. **3** (fam.) muchísimo, enormemente. || **4 – in love,** marcadamente enamorado, perdidamente enamorado.
madman | 'mædmən | *[pl.* **madmen.**] *s.c.* loco, demente, lunático.
madness | mædnɪs | *s.i.* **1** locura, demencia. **2** (fig.) locura, estupidez, insensatez. **3** furia, rabia.
Madonna | mə'dɒnə | | mə'dɒːnə | *s.* **1** Madona, la Virgen María. || *s.c.* **2** ART. madona. **3** señora (tratamiento para mujeres italianas casadas).
madras | mə'drɑːs | *s.i.* **1** madrás, algodón de Madrás. **2** pañuelo de colores luminosos (usado como turbante).
madrigal | 'mædrɪgl | *s.c.* MUS. y LIT. madrigal.
madwoman | 'mædˌwumən | *[pl.* **madwomen**] *s.c.* loca, demente, lunática.
maelstrom | 'meɪlstrɒm | *s.sing.* **1** (lit.) remolino. **2** (fig.) torbellino, vorágine, vórtice: *the maelstrom of war = la vorágine de la guerra.*
maestri | 'maɪstrɪ | *pl.* de **maestro.**
maestro | mɑː'estrəu | *[pl.* **maestros** o **maestri**] *s.c.* MUS. maestro, profesor, compositor, director de orquesta.
Mafia | 'mæfɪə | | 'mɑːfɪə | *s.sing.* **1** **[the – +** *v.sing./pl.***]** la Mafia, la Camorra, la sociedad del crimen organizado. **2** (desp.) mafia, organización (profesional).
Mafiosi | ˌmæfɪ'əusiː | *pl.* de **Mafioso.**
Mafioso | ˌmæfɪ'əusəu | [*pl.* **Mafiosi**] *s.c.* mafioso, miembro de la Mafia.
mag | mæg | *s.c.* (fam.) revista.
magazine | ˌmægə'ziːn | | 'mægəziːn | *s.c.* **1** revista. **2** TV. magazine, programa de noticias cortas. **3** recámara, cargador (de un arma). **4** FOT. cámara, cartucho. **5** MIL. polvorín, almacén de armas, depósito (de armas, explosivos). **6** MIL. armas, pertrechos.
magenta | mə'dʒentə | *adj.* **1** magenta, rojo, púrpura. || *s.c.* **1** color magenta, color rojo púrpura.
maggot | 'mægət | *s.c.* **1** larva, gusano. **2** capricho, extravagancia.
maggoty | 'mægətɪ | *adj.* lleno de gusanos, cubierto de gusanos.
Magi | 'meɪdʒaɪ | *s.pl.* **[the –]** los Reyes Magos.
magic | 'mædʒɪk | *s.i.* **1** magia, encantamiento. **2** juegos de magia. **3** (fig.) magia, encanto, misterio: *the magic of electronics = la magia de la electrónica.* || *adj.* **4** mágico, encantado. **5** (fig.) mágico, misterioso, clave. **6** (brit. y argot) maravilloso, encantador. || **7 as if by –,** como por arte de magia, como por ensalmo. **8 – carpet,** LIT. alfombra mágica. **9 – lantern,** OPT. linterna mágica.
magical | 'mædʒɪkl | *adj.* **1** mágico, encantador, misterioso. **2** mágico, sobrenatural (un poder).
magically | 'mædʒɪkəlɪ | *adv.* mágicamente, misteriosamente.
magician | mə'dʒɪʃn | *s.c.* **1** mago, hechicero, brujo. **2** mago, prestidigitador, nigromante.
magisterial | ˌmædʒɪ'stɪərɪəl | *adj.* **1** (form.) magistral. **2** autoritario, dominante, dogmático. **3** de magistrado.
magisterially | ˌmædʒɪ'stɪərɪəlɪ | *adv.* magistralmente, autoritariamente.
magistracy | 'mædʒɪstrəsɪ | DER. *s.c.* **1** posición de magistrado. || **2 the magistracy,** la magistratura (el colectivo).
magistrate | 'mædʒɪstreɪt | *s.c.* DER. magistrado; juez (local, municipal).
magma | 'mægmə | *s.i.* GEOL. magma.
magnanimity | ˌmægnə'nɪmɪtɪ | *s.i.* **1** (form.) magnanimidad, generosidad, indulgencia. **2** acto magnánimo.
magnanimous | mæg'nænɪməs | *adj.* (form.) magnánimo, generoso, indulgente.
magnanimously | mæg'nænɪməslɪ | *adv.* (form.) magnánimamente, generosamente.
magnate | 'mægneɪt | *s.c.* magnate, potentado.
magnesia | mæg'niːʃə | *s.i.* QUIM. magnesia, magnesio (para tomar como medicina).
magnesium | mæg'niːzjəm | *s.i.* MIN. magnesio.
magnet | 'mægnɪt | *s.c.* **1** imán. **2** (fig.) imán, atracción.
magnetic | mæg'netɪk | *adj.* **1** magnético, imantado. **2** (fig.) magnética, atractiva (la personalidad). || **3 – field,** FIS. campo magnético. **4 – north,** norte magnético (de la brújula). **5 – tape,** cinta de magnetófono.
magnetically | mæg'netɪkəlɪ | *adv.* magnéticamente.
magnetism | 'mægnɪtɪzəm | *s.i.* **1** magnetismo. **2** (fig.) atracción, atractivo.
magnetize | 'mægnɪtaɪz | (brit.) **magnetise** *v.t.* **1** magnetizar, imantar. **2** (fig.) atraer, fascinar, encantar.
magneto | mæg'niːtəu | *s.c.* ELEC. magneto.
Magnificat | mæg'nɪfɪkæt | *s.sing.* REL. Magnificat (canto de la Virgen).
magnification | ˌmægnɪfɪ'keɪʃn | *s.i.* **1** magnificación, engrandecimiento. || *s.c.* **2** aumento, amplificación, agrandamiento.
magnificence | mæg'nɪfɪsns | *s.i.* magnificencia, esplendor.
magnificent | mæg'nɪfɪsnt | *adj.* **1** magnífico, maravilloso, espléndido, soberbio. **2** generoso.
magnificently | mæg'nɪfɪsntlɪ | *adv.* magníficamente, espléndidamente.
magnifier | 'mægnɪfaɪər | *s.c.* FOT. amplificadora.
magnify | 'mægnɪfaɪ | *v.t.* **1** OPT. aumentar, ampliar, agrandar. **2** (fig.) magnificar, exagerar. **3** (arc.) magnificar, ensalzar (a Dios).
magnifying glass | 'mægnɪfaɪɪŋglɑːs | *s.c.* OPT. lupa, lente de aumento.
magniloquence | mæg'nɪləkwəns | *s.i.* (form.) grandilocuencia, pomposidad.
magniloquent | mæg'nɪləkwənt | *adj.* (form.) grandilocuente, pomposo.
magniloquently | mæg'nɪləkwəntlɪ | *adv.* (form.) grandilocuentemente, pomposamente.
magnitude | 'mægnɪtjuːd | | 'mægnɪtuːd | *s.i.* **1** (form.) magnitud, envergadura, grandeza. **2** magnitud, importancia. || *s.c.* **3** ASTR. magnitud.
magnolia | mæg'nəuljə *s.c.* **1** BOT. magnolio, magnolia. || *s.i.* **2** color rosa pálido, color magnolia.
magnum | 'mægnəm | *s.c.* **1** botella de 1.5 litros (de vino). || **2 – opus,** ART. obra maestra.
magpie | 'mægpaɪ | *s.c.* **1** ZOOL. urraca. **2** (fig.) cotorra, charlatán, parlanchín. **3** (fig. y fam.) coleccionista de objetos sin valor.
maharaja | ˌmɑːhə'rɑːdʒə | (también **maharajah**) *s.c.* maharajá, príncipe hindú.
maharani | ˌmɑːhə'rɑːniː | (también **maharanee**) *s.c.* maharani, princesa hindú.
mahatma | mə'hɑːtmə | | mə'hætmə | *s.c.* mahatma, gran maestro (en la India título de autoridad espiritual, religiosa).
mah-jong | mɑː'dʒɒŋ | | mɑː'dʒaːˌh | *s.i.* mah-jong (juego chino de mesa parecido al dominó).
mahogany | mə'hɒgənɪ | | mə'hɑːgənɪ | *s.c.* **1** BOT. caoba, árbol de la caoba. || *s.i.* **2** madera de caoba. **3** color caoba.
maid | meɪd | *s.c.* **1** doncella, criada, sirvienta, (Am.) mucama, fámula. **2** (lit. y arc.) doncella, virgen, soltera. || **3 – of honor,** (EE.UU.) dama de honor (en una boda); doncella (de la reina); pastelito, tartita.
maiden | 'meɪdn | *s.c.* **1** (lit.) joven, doncella, soltera. **2** DEP. caballo no ganador. **3** guillotina (escocesa). || *adj.* **4** primero, inaugural (un viaje, una travesía). **5** soltera, virgen. || **6** (arc.) tía solterona. **7 – name,** nombre de soltera. **8 – ove,** DEP. juego sin carreras (en críquet). **9 – speech,** discurso inaugural (de un miembro del Parlamento). **10 – voyage,** viaje inaugural, primer viaje (especialmente de un barco).
maidenhair | 'meɪdnheər | *s.i.* BOT. cilandrillo.
maidenhead | 'meɪdnhed | (arc.) *s.c.* **1** himen. || *s.i.* **2** virginidad.
maidenhood | 'meɪdnhud | *s.i.* (form.) **1** virginidad, estado virginal. **2** período de virginidad.
maidenly | 'meɪdnlɪ | *adj.* pudoroso, púdico, modesto.
mail | meɪl | *s.i.* **1** **[the –]** (EE.UU.) correo (sistema). **2** correspondencia, correo, cartas; paquetes. || *s.i.* **3** cota de malla, armadura. **4** caparazón (de animales). || *v.t.* **5** (EE.UU.) enviar por

correo. **6** proteger con cota de malla. || *v.i.* **7** enviar cartas.

mailbag | 'meɪlbæg | *s.c.* **1** valija, saca de correos. **2** (EE.UU.) bolsa del cartero.

mailbox | 'meɪlbɒks | *s.c.* (EE.UU.) buzón (en una vivienda).

mailing list | 'meɪlɪŋ lɪst | *s.c.* lista de direcciones (para enviar información, propaganda).

mailman | 'meɪlmæn | *[pl.* **mailmen**] *s.c.* (EE.UU.) cartero.

mailshot | 'meɪlʃɒt | *s.i.* "mailing", envío de correo de propaganda.

mail-order | 'meɪl,ɔːdər | *s.i.* pedido por correo, venta por catálogo.

maim | meɪm | *v.t.* **1** mutilar, tullir, lisiar. **2** estropear, desfigurar, deformar.

main | meɪn | *adj.* no *comp.* **1** principal, más importante, esencial. **2** ARQ. maestra (una viga). **3** fundamental, exclusiva. **4** MAR. mayor (una vela). **5** primero, principal, bajo (un piso). **6** central (una oficina). || *s.c.* **7** *pl.* cañerías principales, tubería general. **8** ELEC. línea principal, conductor principal. **9** fuerza física. **10** tierra firme. **11** océano, mar abierta. **12** MAR. vela mayor; palo mayor, mástil. || **13 to have an eye to the – chance,** (brit.) estar a la que salta, estar atento a la más mínima oportunidad (de obtener ganancias). **14 in the –,** en general, principalmente, en su mayoría. **15 – clause,** GRAM. oración principal. **16 – drag,** (EE.UU. y fam.) calle mayor, calle principal. **17 – line,** línea principal (ferroviaria); (argot) vena (para inyectarse narcóticos). **18 – road,** carretera principal, carretera nacional.

mainframe | 'meɪnfreɪm | *s.c.* INF. superordenador.

mainland | 'meɪnlənd | *s.sing.* **1 [the –]** el continente, el interior, tierra firme. || *adj.* **2** interior, continental, de tierra adentro: *the mainland Spain = la España continental.*

mainline | 'meɪnlaɪn | *v.t.* e *i.* **1** (argot) inyectarse en vena, chutarse, picarse (narcóticos). || *adj.* **2** de la línea principal: *a mainline station = una estación de la línea principal.*

mainly | meɪnlɪ | *adv.* no *comp.* principalmente, en la mayoría de los casos, en mayor grado.

mainspring | 'meɪnsprɪŋ | *s.c. sing.* **1** muelle real (de un reloj). **2** móvil, causa, razón, motivo.

mainstay | 'meɪnsteɪ | *s.c. (gen.sing.)* **1** punto clave, pilas, sostén, soporte. **2** MAR. estay mayor.

mainstream | 'meɪnstriːm | *s.sing.* **1 [the –]** la corriente principal, la tendencia principal, la línea convencional. || *adj.* **2** corriente, ordinario, en la línea convencional, de la corriente principal.

maintain | meɪn'teɪn | *v.t.* **1** mantener, conservar (algo en buenas condiciones, un puesto de trabajo). **2** mantener, sostener, afirmar, asegurar. **3** mantener, sostener, alimentar. **4** conservar (la vida). || *v.i.* **5** (EE.UU. y fam.) mantenerse, conservarse (joven).

maintenance | 'meɪntənəns | *s.i.* **1** mantenimiento, conservación, reparación; limpieza. **2** (brit.) manutención, pensión, provisión de víveres. **3** mantenimiento, conservación (de leyes, costumbres). || **4 – order,** DER. orden judicial de pensión alimenticia.

maisonette | ,meɪzə'net | *s.c.* (brit.) apartamento dúplex.

maize | meɪz | (EE.UU. **corn**) *s.i.* **1** BOT. maíz. **2** color amarillo anaranjado, color maíz.

majestic | mə'dʒestɪk | *adj.* majestuoso, solemne, sublime, imponente.

majestically | mə'dʒestɪkəlɪ | *adv.* majestuosamente, solemnemente.

majesty | 'mædʒəstɪ | *s.i.* **1** majestad, grandeza, solemnidad, esplendor. **2** majestad, soberanía. || *s.c.* **3 Majesty,** Majestad (título).

major | 'meɪdʒər | *adj.* **1** mayor, máximo, más significativo, más importante, principal. **2** MUS. mayor: *in a major key = en clave mayor.* **3** [*s.* + ;ms] (brit.) mayor (para nombrar a un chico con el mismo apellido que otro en clase): *Robinson major = Robinson el mayor.* **4** grave, seria (una enfermedad). **5** DER. mayor de edad. **6** de especialización, de la especialidad (universitaria). || *s.c.* **7** MIL. comandante, mayor. **8** especialidad, especialización (universitaria). **9** (EE.UU.) estudiante que está especializándose. **10** DER. mayor de edad. || **11 – premise,** FIL. premisa.

majordomo | ,meɪdʒə'dəuməu | *s.c.* mayordomo.

majorette | ,meɪdʒə'ret | *s.c.* (EE.UU.) "majorette", chica que desfila con uniforme y bastón delante de una banda de músicos.

major-general | ,meɪdʒə'dʒenərəl | *s.c.* MIL. general de división.

majority | mə'dʒɒrɪtɪ | *s.sing.* **1 [the – +** *v.sing./pl.***]** la mayoría, la mayor parte. || *s.c.* **2** (gen.*sing.)* mayoría, margen (de votos). || *s.i.* **3** DER. mayoría de edad. **4** MIL. comandancia. || **5 in a –/in the –,** en la mayoría. || **6 – verdict,** DER. veredicto mayoritario (de un jurado).

make | meɪk | *v.irr. [pret.* y *p.p.* **made**] *t.* **1** hacer, fabricar, manufacturar, construir, elaborar, confeccionar, crear (un objeto, un vestido, etc.). **2** hacer, preparar, aderezar (una comida, una bebida). **3 [to – +** *s.***]** hacer (un esfuerzo, un descubrimiento, un comentario). **4** traer, proporcionar (problemas). **5** componer, escribir, crear (una obra). **6** pronunciar (un discurso). **7** cometer (errores). **8** instituir, establecer (una ley). **9** redactar (un testamento, un documento). **10 [to – +** *o.* **+** *adj.***]** poner, hacer, volver: *it makes me crazy = me vuelve loco.* **11** hacer, nombrar, proponer (para un puesto). **12** convertir, hacer: *they made him a man there = le convirtieron en un hombre allí.* **13 [to – +** *o.* **+ (to)** *inf.***]** obligar a, inducir a, forzar a, causar, motivar: *you made me do it = me obligaste a hacerlo.* **14 [to – +** *o.* **+ (to)** *inf.***]** representar, hacer parecer, suponer: *the story is made place to take in India = se supone que la historia tiene lugar en la India.* **15** (fam.) llegar a, alcanzar (un lugar, un tren). **16** triunfar, conseguir. **17** ganar, obtener (dinero); adquirir (fama); hacerse, valerse (enemigos). **18** calcular, considerar, deducir, sacar una conclusión, suponer, entender: *what do you make by it? = ¿qué supones que es esto?* **19** citarse, quedar (con alguien). **20** hacer, sumar. **21** ofrecer, servir de, constituir: *that will make a good table = eso servirá de mesa estupendamente.* **22** llegar a ser, convertirse en, comportarse como: *you'll make a fantastic clown = llegarás a ser payaso fantástico.* **23** (fam.) hacer, formar, completar (un grupo, un círculo). **24** hacer, arreglar (la cama). **25** (arc.) hacer, recorrer, cubrir (una distancia). **26** (lit. y arc.) estar a punto de, disponerse a. **27** conceder, donar (dinero). **28** formar parte de, conseguir un puesto en (un equipo). **29** DEP. obtener, marcar, conseguir (un tanto). **30** hacer prosperar, significar el éxito de: *he can make or break it = él puede convertirlo en un éxito o arruinarlo.* **31** (fam. y vulg.) seducir, llevar al huerto, conseguir acostarse con. **32** MAR. avistar (tierra); llegar a puerto, arribar. || *v.i.* **33** comportarse, actuar. **34** disponerse a, empezar a: *he made as if to talk = se disponía a hablar.* **35** ir, dirigirse, encaminarse. **36** afectar, producir un efecto. **37** formarse, crecer. || *s.c.* **38** marca, modelo; fabricación, producto. **39** fabricación, manufactura, creación. **40** hechura, estilo, figura. **41** tipo, índole. || **to – +** *adv./prep.* **42 to – away with something /someone,** robar algo, llevarse algo; suicidar(se), matar(se). **43 to – for something,** dirigirse a, encaminarse a, ir hacia; contribuir a, servir para, resultar. **44 to – into,** convertir en. **45 to – something of, a)** sacar de, entender por, pensar de; **b)** dar importancia a, hacer un mundo de; **c)** querer guerra (en una discusión). **46 to – off,** marcharse deprisa, escapar de estampida, largarse. **47 to – off with,** (fam.) llevarse, arrebatar, llorar. **48 to – out, a)** extender, hacer, rellenar (una solicitud, un cheque); **b)** (fam.) distinguir, vislumbrar, entender, descifrar; **c)** (fam.) mantener, sostener, alegar; **d)** justificar, probar; **e)** ir, salir, marchar (algo bien o mal); **f)** aparentar, dar a entender, fingir, simular. **g) 49 to – out with,** (fam.) hacer el amor con. **50 to -- something over, a)** transferir, ceder, traspasar (una propiedad a otra persona); **b)** (EE.UU.) rehacer, volver a hacer, renovar. **51 to – towards,** (fam.) ir hacia, entrar en dirección a. **52 to – up, a)** inventar, tramar (una historia); **b)** maquillar(se), pintar(se); **c)** preparar, arreglar (una cama); **d)** juntar, recopilar, reunir; **e)** formar, constituir, integrar; **f)** confeccionar, realizar, transformar; **g)** conseguir, reunir (una cantidad, una puntuación); **h)** devolver (dinero); **i)**

reconciliarse, hacer las paces; **j)** subsanar (un error, una opinión); **k)** cubrir (un déficit); **l)** indemnizar, compensar; **m)** componer, maquetar (una página). **53 to – up for,** compensar, subsanar, reparar; recuperar. **54 to – up to,** (desp.) adular, halagar, hacer la pelota; recompensar, compensar, devolver el favor. **55 to – with,** (EE.UU. y argot) traer, poner, sacar (algo de comer). || **56 to – a day/evening/night of it,** pasar un día/ tarde/noche fantásticos, de maravilla. **57 to – do,** (fam.) conformarse con, arreglarse con. **58 to – like,** (fam.) hacer de, actuar de. **59 to – one's day,** ser toda una experiencia, ser muy satisfactorio. **60 to – one's way,** (form.) progresar, avanzar, abrirse camino. **61 on the –,** decidido a triunfar, a sacar partido (social o económicamente). **62 to – up one's mind,** V. **mind.**

make-believe | 'meɪkbɪˌliːv | *s.i.* **1** ficción, simulación, ensueño, engaño, falsedad, pretensión. || *adj.* **2** falso, de mentira, fingido.

maker | meɪkər | *s.c.* **1** fabricante, elaborador, productor, constructor. **2** director (de cine). **3** (gen.*pl.*) firma creadora, fábrica, fabricante: *send it to the makers = envíalo a fábrica.* **4** (euf.) Dios, Hacedor, Creador. **5** DER. librador (de una letra). **6** (arc.) poeta.

makeshift | 'meɪkʃɪft | *adj.* **1** improvisado, provisional, temporal. || *s.i.* **2** improvisación, invento, arreglo provisional.

make-up | 'meɪkʌp | *s.i.* **1** maquillaje, cosmético, afeite. **2** composición, estructura, construcción (de un objeto). **3** modo de ser, temperamento, naturaleza, disposición. **4** composición, maquetación (de una página). **5** examen de repesca, examen de recuperación.

make-weight | 'meɪkweɪt | *s.c.* **1** contrapeso (de una balanza). **2** (fig.) suplente, sustituto.

making | meɪkɪŋ | *s.i.* **1** (gen. en combinación) fabricación, creación, elaboración, producción, construcción, confección: *the dressmaking and shoemaking industries = la industria del vestido y del calzado.* **2 [the – of]** el talento de, la formación de: *the making of a great painter = el talento de un gran pintor.* **3** [*pl.*] cualidades, facultades, ingredientes, elementos necesarios. **4** [*pl.*] (EE.UU. y argot) papel y tabaco (para liar cigarrillos). || **5 to be the – of,** ser la causa de, ser el motivo de, ser la razón de. **6 in the –,** en vías de formación, en marcha, en potencia. **7 of one's own –,** de su incumbencia, de la propia responsabilidad de uno, debido a los propios actos de uno.

mal- | mæl | *prefijo* mal-, des-: *maladminister = maladministrar.*

OBS. Se usa para formar palabras que se refieren a cosas mal o equivocadamente hechas o que son poco normales.

malachite | 'mæləkaɪt | *s.i.* MIN. malaquita.

maladministration | ˌmælədˌmɪnɪ's-treɪʃn | *s.i.* (form.) administración fraudulenta.

maladjusted | ˌmælə'dʒʌstɪd | *adj.* **1** PSIC. inadaptado, desequilibrado, mal adaptado. **2** desajustado, mal ajustado (un tornillo).

maladjustement | ˌmælə'dʒʌstmənt | *s.c.* e *i.* **1** PSIC. inadaptación, desequilibrio. **2** MEC. desajuste. **3** desequilibrio (regional).

maladroit | ˌmælə'drɔɪt | *adj.* (form.) torpe, sin tacto, desacertado, inhábil.

maladroitly | ˌmælə'drɔɪtlɪ | *adv.* (form.) torpemente, desacertadamente.

maladroitness | ˌmælə'drɔɪtnɪs | *s.i.* (form.) torpeza, desacierto, falta de tacto.

malady | 'mælədɪ | *s.c.* **1** (lit.) mal, defecto (de un sistema). **2** (lit.) enfermedad, dolencia, trastorno.

malaise | mə'leɪz | *s.i.* **1** malestar, indisposición, desazón. **2** preocupación, intranquilidad, insatisfacción, depresión.

malaria | mə'leərɪə | *s.i.* **1** MED. malaria, paludismo. **2** (arc.) aire malsano, miasma.

malarial | mə'leərɪəl | *adj.* palúdico.

Malay | mə'leɪ | | 'meɪleɪ | *adj.* **1** malayo, de Malasia (de origen). **2** malaya (lengua). || *s.i.* **3** malayo (lengua). || *s.c.* **4** malayo (habitante). **5** ZOOL. especie de gallo de plumaje rojo y negro.

Malaysia | mə'leɪzɪə | *s.sing.* Malaysia.

Malaysian | mə'leɪzɪən | *adj.* malayo, de Malaysia.

malcontent | 'mælkənˌtent | | ˌmælkən'tent | (form.) *s.c.* **1** descontento, rebelde, agitador, revoltoso. || *adj.* **2** perturbador, revoltoso, descontento.

male | meɪl | *adj.* **1** BIOL. masculino, varón: *a male child = un hijo varón.* **2** ZOOL. macho. **3** machista. **4** masculino, viril, varonil. **5** BOT. masculino. **6** ELEC. macho. || *s.c.* **7** varón. **8** ZOOL. macho. **9** BOT. planta masculina. || *s.i.* **10** lo masculino. || **11 – chauvinism,** (desp.) machismo, sexismo, misoginia. **12 – chauvinist,** (desp.) machista, chauvinista. **13 – chauvinist pig,** (desp.) cerdo machista (insulto a un hombre). **14 – voice choir,** coro masculino.

malediction | ˌmælɪ'dɪkʃn | *s.c.* (form.) maldición, maleficio.

malefactor | 'mælɪfæktər | *s.c.* **1** (form.) malhechor, criminal. **2** malvado, canalla, perverso.

maleficence | mə'lefɪsns | *s.i.* (form.) maldad, acción maléfica.

maleficent | mə'lefɪsnt | *adj.* (form.) maléfico.

maleness | 'meɪlnɪs | *s.i.* masculinidad.

malevolence | mə'levələns | *s.i.* (form.) malevolencia, maldad, perversidad.

malevolent | mə'levələnt | *adj.* (lit.) malévolo, perverso, maligno.

malevolently | mə'levələntlɪ | *adv.* (lit.) con malevolencia, con malicia, perversamente.

malformation | ˌmælfɔː'meɪʃn | *s.i.* **1** malformación, deformidad. || *s.c.* **2** deformidad, deformación.

malformed | ˌmæl'fɔːmd | *adj.* malformado, deforme, contrahecho.

malfunction | ˌmæl'fʌŋkʃn | *s.c.* **1** (form.) funcionamiento defectuoso (de una máquina). || *v.i.* **2** funcionar mal, funcionar defectuosamente.

malice | 'mælɪs | *s.i.* **1** malicia, malevolencia, despecho, rencor. || **2 with – afore thought,** DER. con premeditación.

malicious | mə'lɪʃəs | *adj.* malicioso, maléfico, malévolo.

maliciously | mə'lɪʃəslɪ | *adv.* maliciosamente, malévolamente.

malign | mə'laɪn | *v.t.* **1** difamar, calumniar, desacreditar, tratar injustamente. || *adj.* **2** (desp. y lit.) maligno, pernicioso, nocivo, funesto.

malignancy | mə'lɪgnənsɪ | *s.i.* **1** malignidad, malevolencia, rencor. || *s.c.* e *i.* **2** MED. tumor maligno.

malignant | mə'lɪgnənt | *adj.* **1** maligno, malévolo, rencoroso. **2** injurioso, perverso, pernicioso. **3** MED. maligno; virulento.

malignantly | mə'lɪgnəntlɪ | *adv.* malignamente, con malevolencia.

malignity | mə'lɪgnɪtɪ | *s.i.* (desp. y lit.) malignidad, malevolencia, rencor.

malinger | mə'lɪŋgər | *v.i.* fingirse enfermo, simular una enfermedad (para no ir al trabajo).

malingerer | mə'lɪŋgərər | *s.c.* persona que simula una enfermedad (para no ir al trabajo).

mall | mɔːl | | mæl | *s.c.* **1** (EE.UU.) galerías comerciales, centro comercial en zona peatonal. **2** alameda, paseo (arbolado). **3** mediana (de una autopista).

mallard | 'mælɑːd | | 'mæləd | [*pl.* **mallard** o **mallards**] *s.c.* pato salvaje, ánade real.

malleability | ˌmælɪə'bɪlɪtɪ | *s.i.* **1** maleabilidad (metales). **2** (fig.) maleabilidad (persona).

malleable | 'mælɪəbl | *adj.* **1** maleable (metales). **2** (fig.) moldeable, influenciable, dócil (una persona).

mallet | 'mælɪt | *s.c.* **1** mazo, maza, cachiporra. **2** DEP. mazo, mallete (de crocket).

mallow | 'mæləʊ | *s.c.* BOT. malva.

malnourished | ˌmæl'nʌrɪʃt | | ˌmæl'nːːrɪʃt | *adj.* desnutrido.

malnutrition | ˌmælnjuː'trɪʃn | | ˌmælnjʊ'trɪʃn | *s.i.* desnutrición.

malodorous | mæl'əʊdərəs | *adj.* maloliente, fétido.

malpractice | ˌmæl'præktɪs | *s.c.* e *i.* negligencia, incompetencia; falta de ética profesional.

malt | mɔːlt | *s.i.* **1** malta. **2** bebida malteada (alcohólica). **3** leche malteada (combinación refrescante). || *v.t.* e *i.* **4** maltear(se), convertir(se) en malta.

Malta | 'mɔːltə | *s.sing.* Malta.

Maltese | ˌmɔːl'tiːz | *adj.* **1** maltés, de Malta (la lengua, los habitantes). || *s.c.*

2 maltés (habitante). || *s.i.* **3** maltés (idioma).

maltreat | ˌmælˈtriːt | *v.t.* **1** maltratar, abusar. **2** herir, humillar.

maltreatment | mælˈtriːtmənt | *s.i.* **1** maltrato, abuso. **2** humillación.

mam | mæm | *s.c.* (brit.) mamá.

mama, momma | mɑːmə | | məˈmɑː | *s.c.* (EE.UU. y fam.) mamá, mama.

mamba | ˈmæmbə | | mɑːmbə | *s.c.* ZOOL. cobra africana.

mamma | məˈmɑː | *s.c.* (fam.) mamá.

mammal | ˈmæml | *s.c.* ZOOL. mamífero.

mammalian | mæˈmeɪljə | *adj.* ZOOL. mamífero.

mammary | ˈmæmərɪ | *adj.* ZOOL. mamario: *mammary glands = glándulas mamarias.*

mammon | ˈmæmən | (también **Mammon**) *s.i.* (desp.) Mammón, la riqueza (ídolo de la riqueza). **2** (fig.) avaricia, codicia.

mammoth | ˈmæməθ | *s.c.* **1** ZOOL. mamut. || *adj.* **2** enorme, de gigante, gigantesco: *a mammoth task = una tarea gigantesca.* **3** de tamaño extra.

mammy | ˈmæmɪ | *s.c.* **1** (EE.UU.) mamá, mami (usado por los niños). **2** (EE.UU. y desp.) ama de cría (de color para niños blancos).

man | mæn | [*pl.* **men**] *s.c.* **1** hombre, varón. **2** el ser humano, el hombre, la especie humana. **3** empleado, obrero, trabajador; (arc.) sirviente, criado; [*pl.*] personal, empleados. **4** MIL. soldado raso. **5** DEP. jugador. **6** (fam.) hombre, marido, amante. **7** (fam.) hombre, amigo, tío, chaval (en exclamaciones): *hey you, man! = ¡eh tú, tío!* **8** pieza, ficha (de ajedrez, damas). **10** NAUT. barco (en combinación con otra palabra): *a man-of-war = un barco de guerra.* **11** (EE.UU. y argot) policía, madero. || *s.i.* **12** la raza humana, la humanidad. || *v.t.* **13** tripular, manejar (un barco, un avión). **14** manejar, estar a cargo de (una máquina). **15** disponer para, dotar de personal, ocupar un puesto. **16** MIL. guarnecer, disponer para (la defensa). || **17 a – about town,** un hombre de moda, un personaje mundano. **18 a man's –,** un hombre popular entre hombres. **19 as one –,** como un solo hombre, todos a una, unánimemente. **20 to be – enough,** ser muy hombre, ser muy valiente. **21 to be one's own –,** ser dueño de sus propios actos, ser independiente. **22 to make a – out of,** hacer un hombre de, convertir en un hombre a (un muchacho). **23 – to –,** de hombre a hombre. **24 my –/my good –,** amigo mío, buen hombre. **25 to separate/sort the men from the boys,** dar la cara (frente a una situación difícil). **26 the – in the street,** el hombre de la calle, los de a pie. **27 to a –,** sin excepción.

manacle | ˈmænəkl | *s.c.* [gen. *pl.*] **1** esposa, grillete, manilla. **2** (fig.) freno, traba. || *v.t.* **3** esposar, encadenar, engrilletar. **4** (fig.) restringir, atar.

manage | ˈmænɪdʒ | *v.t.* **1** administrar, dirigir, llevar, encargarse de (un negocio). **2** controlar, dominar, manejar, gobernar (una máquina). **3** hacer, conseguir, lograr (tiempo). || *v.t.* e *i.* **4** **[can/could –]** (fam.) tomarse, atreverse con (una comida, bebida): *I couldn't manage one cup = no podría tomarme ni una taza.* **5** permitirse (vacaciones, tiempo libre). **6** llevar, transportar, poder con (un peso). **7** arreglárselas, ingeniárselas, ir tirando. **8** manejar, controlar (a una persona).

manageable | ˈmænɪdʒəbl | *adj.* **1** manejable, dócil, controlable (una persona). **2** razonable, manejable (un objeto).

management | ˈmænɪdʒmənt | *s.i.* **1** supervisión, administración, gerencia. **2** manejo, control. || *s.c.* e *i.* **3** **[– + *v.sing./pl.*]** junta directiva, dirección, administración, patronal, empresa.

manager | ˈmænɪdʒər | [*f.* **manageress**] *s.c.* **1** gerente, director, administrador, supervisor: sales maneger = director de ventas. **2** empresario (de teatro); representante (de un cantante). **3** DEP. director de equipo, seleccionador. **4** ahorrador, administrador, gestor.

manageress | ˌmænɪdʒəˈres | | ˈmænɪdʒərəs | [*m.* **manager**] *s.c.* administradora, gerente, directora.

managerial | ˌmænəˈdʒɪərɪəl | *adj.* administrativo, directivo, gerencial, patronal.

managing director | ˈmænɪdʒɪŋˌdɪˈrektər | *s.c.* director gerente.

mandarin | ˈmændərɪn | *s.c.* **1** mandarina (fruta). **2** mandarín (dignatario chino). **3** (fig.) mandarín, persona influyente (un político, un intelectual). **4** (brit. y fam.) funcionario, burócrata. || *s.i.* **5** mandarín (lengua).

mandate | ˈmændeɪt | *s.c.* **1** mandato, encargo (a un gobierno electo); comisión. **2** (form.) mandato, orden, tarea, encargo. **3** DER. mandato, mandamiento. **4** POL. mandato (otorgado por la ONU sobre un territorio); territorio bajo mandato. || *v.t.* **6** (gen. *pas.*) otorgar mandato, administrar (un territorio) bajo mandato. **5** otorgar mandato (a un gobierno por elecciones).

mandatory | ˈmændətərɪ | *adj.* **1** (form.) obligatorio, forzoso. **2** por mandato, bajo mandato (un territorio). **3** mandatario, mandante.

mandible | ˈmændɪbl | *s.c.* ANAT. mandíbula, maxilar inferior; quijada; pico; pinza (de insectos, cangrejos).

mandolin | ˈmændəlɪn | *s.c.* MUS. mandolina.

mandragora | mænˈdrægərə | V. **mandrake.**

mandrake | ˈmændreɪk | *s.c.* (también **mandragora**) BOT. mandrágora.

mandrill | ˈmændrɪl | *s.c.* ZOOL. mandril.

mane | meɪn | *s.c.* **1** crin (de caballo); melena (de león); penacho (de pichón). **2** (fig.) melena (de una persona).

man-eater | ˈmænˌiːtər | *s.c.* **1** caníbal, antropófago; animal carnívoro. **2** (desp. y hum.) devoradora de hombres.

man-eating | ˈmænˌiːtɪŋ | *adj.* carnívoro.

maneuver V. **manoeuvre.** (también V. otros derivados de **manoeuvre**).

manfully | ˈmænfəlɪ | *adv.* (hum.) valientemente, con determinación, resueltamente.

manganese | ˈmæŋgəniːz | *s.i.* QUIM. manganeso.

mange | meɪndʒ | *s.i* MED. sarna animal.

manger | ˈmeɪndʒər | *s.c.* pesebre, comedero.

mangle | ˈmæŋgl | *v.t.* (gen. *pas.*) **1** destrozar, despedazar, mutilar. **2** (fig.) destrozar, deformar, mutilar (un texto, una noticia). **3** escurrir con rodillo, pasar por escurridora de rodillo (ropa). || *s.c.* **4** (brit.) máquina escurridora de rodillo (para la ropa); planchadora de rodillo.

mango | ˈmæŋgəʊ | [*pl.* **mangoes** o **mango**] *s.c.* BOT. mango.

mangrove | ˈmæŋgreʊv | *s.c.* BOT. mangle.

mangy | ˈmeɪndʒɪ | *adj.* **1** sarnoso. **2** (fam.) roñosa, pelada, con calvas (una alfombra, un abrigo de piel).

manhandle | ˈmænˌhændl | *v.t.* **1** arrastrar, mover a mano, cargar con. **2** (desp.) tratar a baquetazo, zarandear.

manhole | ˈmænhəʊl | *s.c.* boca de alcantarilla, registro.

manhood | ˈmænhʊd | *s.i.* **1** edad adulta, edad viril. **2** (form.) hombres. **3** (euf.) virilidad, hombría.

man-hour | ˈmænˈaʊər | *s.c.* [gen. *pl.*] hora-hombre (medida industrial de producción).

manhunt | ˈmænhʌnt | *s.c.* persecución, búsqueda, caza del hombre (gen. de un criminal).

mania | ˈmeɪnɪə | *s.c.* e *i.* **1** PSIQ. manía. **2** (fam.) manía, obsesión, idea fija.

maniac | ˈmeɪnɪæk | *s.c.* **1** PSIQ. maníaco. **2** maniático, obsesivo. **3** (fam. y desp.) loco, entusiasta, maniático. || *adj.* **4** maniático, lunático, loco. || **5 like a –,** como un loco.

maniacal | məˈnaɪəkl | *adj.* maníaco, violento, agresivo.

maniacally | məˈnaɪəkəlɪ | *adv.* violentamente, agresivamente, de forma frenética.

manic | ˈmænɪk | *adj.* **1** PSIQ. maníaco. **2** frenético, enloquecido.

manic-depressive | ˌmænɪkdɪˈpresɪv | *s.c.* **1** PSIQ. maníaco-depresivo. || *adj.* **2** maníaco-depresivo.

manicure | ˈmænɪˌkjʊər | *s.c.* e *i.* **1** manicura. || *v.t.* **2** hacer la manicura. **3** (fig.) recortar, podar (plantas).

manicurist | ˈmænɪˌkjʊərɪst | *s.c.* manicura, manicuro.

manifest | ˈmænɪfest *adj.* **1** (form.) manifiesto, patente, claro, evidente. || *v.t.* **2** manifestar, revelar, mostrar. **3** probar, demostrar, evidenciar. **4** MAR. registrar en un manifiesto de carga. || *s.c.* **5** MAR. manifiesto de carga; lista de pasajeros; lista de coches (en un tren).

manifestation | ˌmænɪfeˈsteɪʃn | | ˌmænɪfəˈsteɪʃn | *s.c.* e *i.* **1** (form.) manifestación, evidencia, demostración, prueba. || *s.c.* **3** manifestación, aparición (de un espíritu).
manifestly | ˈmænɪfestlɪ | *adv.* manifiestamente, claramente, evidentemente.
manifesto | ˌmænɪˈfestəʊ | [*pl.* **manifestoes** o **manifestos**] *s.c.* manifiesto, programa, plataforma, declaración pública (de un partido, un sindicato).
manifold | ˈmænɪfəʊld | *adj.* **1** (form.) múltiple, variado, diverso. || *s.c.* **2** MEC. tubo colector de escape, tubo colector de gases. **3** MAT. variedad.
manikin V. **mannequin.**
manila | məˈnɪlə | *s.i.* **1** papel manila. **2** cuerda de cáñamo. **3** color amarillento. **4** BOT. abacá.
manioc | ˈmænɪɒk | *s.i.* BOT. mandioca.
manipulate | məˈnɪpjʊleɪt | *v.t.* **1** (desp.) manipular, manejar, controlar (a la gente, la opinión). **2** MED. manipular, colocar en su sitio (un hueso), dar masajes. **4** falsificar (libros de cuentas, informes).
manipulation | məˌnɪpjʊˈleɪʃn | *s.c.* e *i.* **1** manipulación, manejo, control. **2** falseamiento, falsificación (de documentos, cuentas). **3** MED. manipulación, masaje.
manipulative | məˈnɪpjʊlətɪv | | məˈnɪŋjʊleɪtɪv | *adj.* (form.) manipulador, que maneja (una situación).
manipulator | məˈnɪpjʊleɪtər | *s.c.* manipulador.
mankind | mænˈkaɪnd | *s.i.* **1** [;ms + *v.sing./pl.*] humanidad, el género humano, la especie humana. **2** los hombres, el hombre (por oposición a la mujer).
man-like | ˈmænlaɪk | *adj.* como de hombre, como un hombre, de hombre.
manliness | ˈmænlɪnɪs | *s.i.* hombría, virilidad, masculinidad.
manly | ˈmænlɪ | *adj.* **1** masculino, viril, varonil, fuerte. **2** valiente, resuelto. || *adv.* **3** varonilmente, virilmente. **4** valientemente, con resolución.
man-made | ˌmænmeɪd | *adj.* **1** hecho por el hombre. **2** artificial, sintético (un material).
manna | ˈmænə | *s.i.* **1** maná. **2** (fig.) maná, regalo del cielo. **3** BOT. maná (ausencia gomosa del fresno florido). || **4 like –/like – from heaven,** como caído del cielo, milagrosamente.
manned | ˈmænd | *adj.* pilotado, tripulado (un satélite).
mannequin, manikin | ˈmænɪkɪn | *s.c.* **1** maniquí (de escaparate). **2** (arc.) maniquí, modelo.
manner | ˈmænər | *s.c.* **1** (gen. *sing.)* (form.) modo, estilo, forma, método. **2** [normalmente *sing.*] (form.) hábito, costumbre. **3** conducta, proceder, educación, comportamiento. **4** tono (de voz). **5 [– of]** (arc.) tipo de, clase de: *what manner of student is she? = ¿qué tipo de alumna es?* || **6 all – of,** todo tipo de, todo género de. **7 by any – of means,** de todas formas, de todos modos. **8 in a –,** al estilo, a la manera, al modo. **9 in a – of speaking,** por así decirlo, como si dijéramos.
mannered | ˈmænəd | | ˈmænərd | *adj.* **1** (form.) afectado, amanerado, artificial. **2** de (ciertos) modales: *ill-mannered = de malos modales.*
mannerism | ˈmænərɪzəm | *s.c.* **1** hábito, característica, gesto. **2** (desp.) amaneramiento, afectación. || *s.i.* **3** ART. manierismo.
mannish | ˈmænɪʃ | *adj.* (desp.) hombruna, masculina, varonil (una mujer).
mannishly | ˈmænɪʃlɪ | *adv.* varonilmente, de forma masculina.
mannishness | ˈmænɪʃnɪs | *s.i.* (desp.) masculinidad (de una mujer).
manoeuvrable | məˈnuːvrəbl | (EE.UU. **maneuverable**) *adj.* maniobrable, manejable, movible.
manoeuvre | məˈnuːvər | (EE.UU. **maneuver**) *s.c.* **1** (gen. *pl.)* MIL. maniobras, ejercicios tácticos. **2** maniobra, manejo, táctica, truco. || *v.t.* **3** maniobrar, mover hábilmente, controlar, manejar (una máquina). **4** (fig.) maniobrar, manipular (a una persona). || **5 room for –,** posibilidad de maniobra, margen de movimiento.
manoeuvering | məˈnuːvərɪŋ | (EE.UU. **maneuvering**) *s.c.* e *i.* **1** maniobra, manipulación.
manometer | məˈnɒmɪtər | *s.c.* MEC. manómetro.
manor | ˈmænər | *s.c.* **1** finca, terreno, propiedad, señorío. **2** HIST. feudo. **3** (brit.) distrito, zona, área. || **4 – house,** mansión, casa solariega.
manorial | məˈnɔːrɪəl | *dj.* **1** feudal. **2** señorial, solariego.
manpower | ˈmænˌpaʊər | *s.i.* mano de obra.
manqué | ˈmɑːŋkeɪ | | ˈmɒŋkeɪ | *adj.* [*s.* + ;ms] frustrado, fracasado, insatisfecho.
mansard | ˈmænsɑːd | ARQ. *s.i.* **1** en mansarda, en buhardilla. || **2 – roof,** tejado en mansarda, tejado abuhardillado.
manse | mæns | *s.c.* **1** casa parroquial, rectoría, casa del cura (gen. protestante). **2** (arc.) mansión.
manservant | ˈmænˌsɜːvənt | *s.c.* (arc.) sirviente, criado, (Am.) mucamo.
mansion | ˈmænʃn | *s.c.* **1** mansión, palacete, casa solariega. **2** [*S.* + **Mansions**] (brit.) Edificio: *Carlile Mansions = Edificio Carlile.* **3** (arc.) morada, residencia, domicilio. **4** ASTR. casa.
manslaughter | ˈmænˌslɔːtər | *s.i.* DER. homicidio.
mantel | ˈmæntl | *s.c.* (arc.) repisa de la chimenea.
mantelpiece | ˈmæntlpiːs | *s.c.* (arc.) repisa de la chimenea.
mantelshelf, mantleshelf | ˈmæntlʃelf | [*pl.* **mantelshelves**] *s.c.* (arc.) repisa de la chimenea.
mantis | ˈmæntɪs | *s.c.* (también **praying mantis**) ZOOL. mantis, mantis religiosa.
mantle | ˈmæntl | *s.c.* (gen. *sing.*) **1** manto, capa. **2** (lit.) manto, capa (de nieve, de vegetación). **3** valía, responsabilidad (profesional). **4** mecha (de una lámpara de gas). **5** ANAT. corteza cerebral. **6** ZOOL. manto, membrana (de moluscos). **7** camisa exterior (de un alto horno). || *v.t.* **8** (lit.) cubrir, envolver, ocultar. || *v.i.* **9** esparcirse, extenderse (sobre una superficie líquida). **10** cubrirse (una superficie líquida de espuma, de impurezas). **11** ponerse rojo, ruborizarse.
man-to-man | ˌmæntəˈmæn | *adj.* **1** (fam.) franco, sin formalismos, de tú a tú, de hombre a hombre. **2** DEP. hombre a hombre (defensa).
manual | ˈmænjʊəl | *adj.* **1** manual. || *s.c.* **2** manual, libro. **3** MUS. teclado (de un órgano). **4** MIL. ejercicio de armas.
manually | ˈmænjʊəlɪ | *adv.* manualmente, a mano.
manufacture | ˌmænjuˈfæktʃər | *v.t.* **1** manufacturar, fabricar, producir, elaborar. **2** (fig.) inventar, urdir, tramar, sacarse de la manga (una mentira). || *s.i.* **3** manufactura, fabricación, elaboración, producción. || *s.c.* **4** artículo, producto, manufactura. **5** industria, manufactura.
manufacturer | ˌmæbnjʊˈfæktʃərər | *s.c.* fabricante, industrial.
manufacturing | ˌmænjʊˈfæktərɪŋ | *s.i.* **1** manufactura, fabricación. || *adj.* **2** manufacturero, fabril, industrial.
manure | məˈnjʊər | | məˈnʊər | *s.i.* **1** estiércol, abono, fertilizante (natural). || *v.t.* **2** abonar, estercolar.
manuscript | ˈmænjʊskrɪpt | *s.c.* **1** manuscrito, original, copia (de una obra literaria). **2** manuscrito, pergamino. || *adj.* **3** manuscrito, escrito a mano. || **4 in –,** sin publicar; en forma de manuscrito.
Manx | mæŋks | *adj.* **1** de la isla de Man. || *s.i.* **2** dialecto de la isla de Man. || **3 – cat,** gato de Man (sin cola).
many | ˈmenɪ | pron. y *adj.* [*comp.* **more,** *super.* **most**] **1** muchos, numerosos, varios. **2** [**so –**] tantos. **3** [**too –**] demasiados. || *s.pl.* **3** [;ms + *v.pl.*] muchos, gran número, la mayoría. || **4 a good/ great –,** muchísimos, un número bastante elevado. **5 as – as,** tantos como, no menos de. **6 – a,** muchas, mas de: *many a time I called him = lo telefoneé más de una vez.* **7 many's the time/the day,** más de una vez, más de un día. **8 the –,** la mayoría, las masas.
many-sided | ˌmenɪˈsaɪdɪd | *adj.* **1** multilateral, de múltiples lados. **2** polifacético. **3** complejo, complicado.
map | mæŋ | *s.c.* **1** mapa, plano, carta. **2** diagrama. || *v.t.* **3** dibujar un mapa de, trazar un mapa de. **4** explorar con fines cartográficos. || **5 to – out,** delinear, trazar al detalle, planificar (un itinerario de vacaciones). **6 to put (a place) on the –,** dar a conocer un lugar, subrayar la importancia de un lugar, hacer famoso un lugar.
maple | ˈmeɪpl | *s.c.* **1** BOT. arce. || *s.i.* **2** (madera de) arce.

map-reader | 'mæpri:dər | *s.c.* lector de mapa: *you lead and I'll be the map-reader = tú ve primero y yo seré el lector de mapa.*

maquis | 'mæki: | | 'mɑ:ki: | (también **Maquis**) *s.sing.* **[the –]** HIST. la resistencia (de los franceses durante la II Guerra Mundial).

mar | mɑ:r | *v.t.* **1** (lit.) dañar, perjudicar, estropear, echar a perder, desfigurar. **2** aguar, fastidiar. || *s.c.* **3** mancha, marca, imperfección. || **4 to make or –,** sacar adelante o hacer fracasar.

marabou | 'mærəbu: | *s.c.* **1** ZOOL. marabú (un pájaro). || *s.i.* **2** de marabú (especialmente las plumas).

marathon | 'mærə,θn | | 'mærə,θan | *s.c.* **1** maratón (carrera olímpica). **2** (fig.) maratón, prueba de resistencia: *a film marathon = una maratón de cine.* || *adj.* **3** interminable, enormemente largo: *a marathon play = una obra interminable.*

marauder | mə'rɔ:dər | *s.c.* **1** merodeador, ladrón, saqueador. **2** ZOOL. depredador.

marauding | mə'rɔ:dɪŋ | *adj.* **1** merodeador, ladrón, saqueador. **2** ZOOL. predador.

marble | 'mɑ:bl | *s.i.* **1** mármol. **2** moteado, jaspeado. || *s.c.* **3** canica, bola de cristal. **4** escultura de mármol. || *adj.* **5** marmóreo, de mármol, como el mármol. || *v.t.* **6** vetear, jaspear, motear. || **7 to lose one's marbles,** (argot) volverse loco, perder el juicio. **8 marbles,** canicas (juego de chicos).

marbled | 'mɑ:bld | *adj.* veteado, jaspeado, moteado.

marcasite | 'mɑ:kəsaɪt | *s.c.* e *i.* MIN. marcasita.

march | mɑ:tʃ | *v.i.* **1** marchar, desfilar. **2** manifestarse, ir en manifestación. **3** (fig.) proseguir, avanzar (el tiempo). **4** irse, largarse. || *v.t.* **5** marchar, recorrer marchando (una distancia). **6** obligar a andar, llevar sin contemplaciones, por la fuerza: *she marched me out of the room = me sacó de la habitación sin contemplaciones.* || *s.c.* e *i.* **7** marcha, caminata; desfile. **8** marcha, progreso, avance. **9 March,** marzo (mes). **10** frontera, línea fronteriza, zona fronteriza; HIST. marca. || *s.c.* **11** MUS. marcha. **10** manifestación. || **12 a day's –,** un día de camino (para medir la distancia). **13 marching orders/** (EE.UU.) **walking papers,** (fam.) orden de despido, despido; MIL. orden de movilización. **14 on the –,** MIL. avanzado; mejorando, progresando. **15 to steal a – on someone,** tomar la delantera.

marcher | mɑ:tʃər | *s.c.* **1** caminante. **2** manifestante.

marching | mɑ:tʃɪŋ | *s.i.* **1** marcha. || *adj.* **2** de marcha.

marchioness | 'mɑ:ʃənɪs | [*m.* **marquis**] *s.c.* **1** marquesa.

mare | meər | *s.c.* **1** yegua; burra; cebra hembra. **2** [*pl.*] ASTR. mar, región oscura (de la Luna o de Marte).

margarine | ,mɑ:dʒə'ri:n | | ,mɑ:gə'ri:n | | 'mɑ:rdʒərɪn | *s.i.* margarina.

marge | mɑ:dʒ | *s.i.* (brit. y fam.) margarina.

margin | 'mɑ:dʒɪn | *s.c.* **1** margen (de página). **2** (fig.) margen, diferencia. **3** (lit.) margen, límite, borde, extremo. || *s.c.* e *i.* **4** margen, reserva. **5** COM. ganancia, margen. **6** ECON. garantía, fianza (dinero depositado para avalar pérdidas en el mercado de valores). || *v.t.* **7** poner margen, dejar margen. **8** bordear, rodear, ribetear. **9** anotar al margen. **10** ECON. depositar fianza, depositar garantía.

marginal | 'mɑ:dʒɪnl | *adj.* **1** [no *comp.*] marginal, periférico. **2** fronterizo, lindante. **3** insignificante, pequeño. **4** (brit.) rico. **2** fronterizo, lindante. **3** insignificante, pequeño. **4** (brit.) incierto, dudoso (un escaño parlamentario a causa del escaso margen de votos). **5** poco fértil, improductiva, de escaso valor agrícola (la tierra). **6** marginal (la economía, un escritor). || **7 marginals,** dudosos, inciertos (un escaño parlamentario).

marginally | 'mɑ:dʒɪnəlɪ | *adv.* marginalmente, al margen.

marguerite | ,mɑ:gə'ri:t | *s.c.* BOT. margarita.

marigold | 'mærɪgəuld | *s.c.* BOT. caléndula, maravilla.

marijuana, marihuana | ,mærɪ'jwɑ:nə | *s.i.* BOT. marihuana, marijuana, cáñamo, cannabis.

marimba | mə'rɪmbə | *s.c.* MUS. marimba (instrumento parecido al xilofón).

marina | mə'ri:nə | *s.c.* puerto deportivo, dársena.

marinade | ,mærɪ'neɪd | *s.c.* e *i.* **1** escabeche, mezcla para macerar; maceración (para carnes y pescados). || *v.t.* **2** escabechar, macerar, marinar.

marinate | 'mærɪneɪt | *v.t.* escabechar, macerar, marinar.

marinated | 'mærɪneɪtɪd | *adj.* escabechado, marinado, macerado.

marine | mə'ri:n | *adj.* **1** marino, marítimo (el medio, el derecho, el transporte). **2** náutico. **3** MIL. de marina. || *s.c.* **4** MIL. infante de marina. **5** flota mercante, flota naval. **6** Ministerio de Marina. **7** ART. marina. || **8 the Marines,** MIL. los Marines.

mariner | 'mærɪnər | *s.c.* (lit.) marinero, marino.

marionette | ,mærɪə'net | *s.c.* marioneta, títere.

marital | 'mærɪtl | *adj.* **1** marital, conyugal. || **2 – status,** estado civil.

maritime | 'mærɪtaɪm | *adj.* marítimo.

marjoram | 'mɑ:dʒərəm | *s.i.* BOT. mejorana, orégano, amáraco.

mark | mɑ:k | *s.c.* **1** marca, mancha, señal, garabato. **2** marca, huella, indicio. **3** (fig.) marca, huella, estigma, efecto, sello. **4** etiqueta, marca, sello (de fábrica); marca (en el ganado). **5** *sing.* signo, prueba, muestra (de educación, de fuerza). **6** (brit.) calificación, puntuación, nota; apreciación, opinión. **7** objetivo, meta, propósito; blanco. **8 [the –]** (brit.) estándar, nivel, altura, punto de referencia; señal, letrero, mojón. **9** marca, cruz, señal (para firmar quien no sabe escribir). **10** MAR. señal de flotación, nudo; línea de carga. **11** atención, importancia, distinción. **12** (argot) tonto, primo. **13** DEP. marca, récord. **14** frontera, límite. **15** marco (moneda alemana, finlandesa, etc...). || *s.c.* e *i.* **16** modelo, versión, tipo (de máquina, de coche). || *v.t.* **17** marcar, señalar, desfigurar. **18** marcar, indicar, señalar. **19** caracterizar, distinguir. **20** marcar, registrar. **21** (brit.) DEP. marcar (a un jugador). **22 [to – + *o.* /what]** (arc.) escuchar, prestar atención, observar, tomar nota. **23** COM. marcar, poner precios. || *v.i.* **24** hacer marcas. **25** rayarse. **26** prestar atención, darse cuenta, notar. || *v.t.* e *i.* **27** DEP. marcar, anotar (tantos). **28** calificar, puntuar. || **29 to leave a –/one's –,** dejar huella, dejar impronta. **30 to make a –/one's –,** tener éxito, distinguirse. **31 to – down, a)** anotar, escribir, tomar nota; **b)** rebajar, reducir (los precios); **c)** considerar, suponer, imaginar; **d)** calificar bajo, puntuar algo. **32 – my words,** piensa en lo que te digo, fíjate en lo que te digo. **33 to – off, a)** cerrar, vallar, tapiar (un terreno); **b)** tachar, quitar (nombres o fechas de una lista); **c)** distinguir, separar (una persona o cosa de otra). **34 to – out, a)** trazar, delinear; **b)** distinguir, destacar; **c)** destinar a, escoger a (una persona para un puesto). **35 to – time, a)** MIL. marchar sobre el propio terreno; **b)** hacer tiempo. **36 to – up,** elevar los precios. **37 – you,** entiéndeme, si entiendes lo que te digo: *she's not very nice, mark you! = ella no es muy agradable, si entiendes lo que te digo.* **38 off the –,** incorrecto. **39 on the –,** totalmente correcto. **40 on your marks!,** ¡preparados! (al empezar una carrera). **41 quick off the –,** (fam.) muy inteligente, muy listo. **42 slow off the –,** (fam.) duro de mollera, poco inteligente. **43 up to the –,** a la altura de las circunstancias, al nivel esperado; (fig.) no muy bien (de salud). **44 wide of the –,** poco acertado, lejos del blanco.

mark-down | 'mɑ:kdaun | *s.c.* reducción, rebaja (de precios).

marked | mɑ:kt | *adj.* **1** marcado, significativo, elevado, notable, manifiesto. **2** condenado, en peligro. **3** marcado, señalado.

markedly | mɑ:kɪdlɪ | *adv.* marcadamente, notablemente, significativamente.

marker | mɑ:kər | *s.c.* **1** rotulador. **2** marcador, señal; mojón. **3** calificador, puntuador. **4** bosquejo, línea, orientación, perfil (de un trabajo). **5** DEP. marcador. **6** anotador, apuntador. **7** (jerga) pagaré.

market | 'mɑ:kɪt | *s.c.* **1** mercado, plaza de abastos, mercadillo. **2** mercado, comercio (interior, exterior). **3** bolsa, mercado de valores. **4** mercado (de trabajo). || *s.i.* **5** demanda, mercado. || *v.t.* **6** vender, poner en venta, tener en venta. || *v.i.* **7** (EE.UU.) mercar, comprar, hacer la compra. || **8 a buyer's –,** mercado favorable al comprador. **9 a seller's –,** mercado favorable al vendedor. **10 to be in the – (for),** estar dispuesto a comprar, estar impaciente por comprar, estar a la caza (de). **11 to bring something onto the –,** sacar algo a la venta, poner algo a la venta. **12 to come onto the –,** salir al mercado, ponerse a la venta. **13 – garden,** huerta, huerto de hortalizas (para llevar a la plaza). **14 – gardener,** hortelano. **15 – gardening,** horticultura, cultivo de hortalizas. **16 – research,** investigación de mercado. **17 on the –,** a la venta, en el mercado. **18 on the open –,** fácilmente asequible al público, a la venta.

marketable | 'mɑːkɪtəbl | *adj.* vendible, de valor comercial, de venta fácil.

market-day | 'mɑːkɪtdeɪ | *s.c.* día de mercado.

marketing | 'mɑːkɪtɪŋ | *s.i.* **1** comercialización, distribución. **2** publicidad, técnica de venta.

marketplace | 'mɑːkɪtpleɪs | *s.c.* **1** mercado, plaza del mercado. **2** comercio, negocio, mundo mercantil.

marking | 'mɑːkɪŋ | *s.sing.* e *i.* **1** marca, mancha, coloración (en animales, plantas). **2** corrección (de un trabajo escolar). || **3 – ink,** tinta indeleble.

marksman | 'mɑːksmən | [*pl.* **marksmen,** *f.* **markswoman**] *s.c.* DEP. tirador (al blanco, al plato).

marksmanship | 'mɑːksmənʃɪp | *s.i.* puntería, tino.

markup | 'mɑːk ʌp | *s.c.* COM. margen de ganancia, diferencia de precio (que se añade al precio de costo).

marl | mɑːl | *s.i.* marga (un tipo de fertilizante con barro).

marlin | 'mɑːlɪn | [*pl.* **marlin**] *s.c.* pez aguja.

marmalade | 'mɑːməleɪd | *s.i.* **1** mermelada (de cítricos). || *adj.* **2** color naranja oscuro.

marmoreal | mɑː'mɔːrɪəl | *adj.* (form.) marmóreo, semejante al mármol, blanco como el mármol.

maroon | mə'ruːn | *v.t.* **1** abandonar a la suerte, abandonar en un lugar desierto, dejar a la aventura. **2** (gen. *pas.*) dejar abandonado, dejar solo, aislar, no prestar atención. || *adj.* **3** rojo oscuro, rojo marronáceo. || *s.c.* **4** bengala (que lanzan los barcos en petición de ayuda). **5** persona abandonada (en un lugar desierto). **6** (Am.) cimarrón (esclavo fugitivo o sus descendientes).

marooned | mə'ruːnd | *adj.* **1** abandonado (en un lugar desierto). **2** aislado, dejado en la estacada, apartado.

marquee | mɑː'kiː | *s.c.* **1** dosel, entoldado, tienda de campaña (de grandes dimensiones). **2** toldo, marquesina.

marquis, marquess | 'mɑːkwɪs | [*f.* **marchioness**] *s.c.* marqués.

marriage | 'mærɪdʒ | *s.c.* e *i.* **1** boda, casamiento, ceremonia de matrimonio. **2** matrimonio, vida matrimonial. **3** vínculo matrimonial, lazos matrimoniales. **4** (fig.) unión, vínculo. **5 – certificate,** certificado de matrimonio, partida de matrimonio. **6 – guidance,** orientación matrimonial, ayuda matrimonial, servicio de ayuda matrimonial. **7 – licence,** licencia matrimonial. **8 – lines,** (brit. y fam.) licencia matrimonial. **8 – of convenience,** matrimonio de conveniencia.

marriageable | 'mærɪdʒəbl | *adj.* (form.) casadera, en edad de casarse (una mujer).

married | mærɪd | *adj.* **1** casado, unido en matrimonio. **2** matrimonial, conyugal. || *s.c.* **3** casado, persona casada. || **4 to be – to,** estar casado con. **5 to get – to,** casarse con.

marrow | 'mærəʊ | *s.i.* **1** ANAT. médula espinal, tuétano. **2** (fig.) médula, meollo, esencia. **3** vitalidad, energía, fuerza, vigor. || *s.c.* **4** calabacín (de color verde oscuro). || **5 – bone,** hueso de caña (con mucho tuétano). **6 to the –,** (fig.) hasta la médula, hasta el tuétano.

marry | 'mærɪ | *v.t.* e *i.* **1** casar(se), unir(se) en matrimonio, contraer matrimonio. **2** conseguir por matrimonio. **3** MAR. unir cabos, ajustar cabos. **4** (fig.) casar, juntar. || *v.t.* **5** unir en matrimonio, casar (un juez, un sacerdote). **6** casar, dar en matrimonio. || **7 to – into,** emparentar con (una familia). **8 to – somebody off,** casar a alguien con, dar a alguien en matrimonio.

Mars | mɑːz | *s.sing.* **1** ASTR. Marte (planeta). **2** Marte (dios del Olimpo).

marsh | mɑːʃ | *s.c.* e *i.* **1** pantano, marisma, ciénaga. || **2 – gas,** gas metano, gas de los pantanos.

marshal | 'mɑːʃl | *s.c.* **1** MIL. mariscal. **2** maestro de ceremonias. **3** DEP. organizador (de carreras). **4** (EE.UU.) DER. alguacil, oficial. **5** (EE.UU.) jefe de policía; jefe de bomberos (de un área, de un departamento). **6** consejero militar (de un rey). || (brit. **marshall**) *v.t.* **7** ordenar, clasificar, poner en orden. **8** reunir, conseguir, juntar. **9** guiar, dirigir, conducir.

marshland | 'mɑːʃlænd | *s.c.* e *i.* zona pantanosa, cenagal.

marshmallow | ˌmɑːʃ'mæləʊ | | 'mɑːrʃmeləʊ | *s.c.* **1** BOT. malvavisco, altea. **2** pastilla de merengue seco, caramelos de altea. **3** (EE.UU. y argot) cobarde, tímido.

marshy | 'mɑːʃɪ | *adj.* pantanoso, cenagoso.

marsupial | mɑː'suːpjəl | *s.c.* ZOOL. marsupial.

mart | mɑːt | *s.c.* **1** mercado, mercadillo (para coleccionistas). **2** centro comercial, emporio comercial. **3** (arc.) feria.

marten | 'mɑːtɪn | *s.c.* ZOOL. marta.

martial | 'mɑːʃl | *adj.* **1** marcial, castrense, militar. || **2 – art,** DEP. artes marciales. **3 – law,** MIL. ley marcial, estado de sitio.

Martian | 'mɑːʃɪən | *s.c.* **1** marciano. || *adj.* **2** marciano, de Marte.

martin | 'mɑːtɪn | *s.c.* ZOOL. vencejo, avión.

martinet | ˌmɑːtɪ'net | *s.c.* **1** (desp. y form.) legalista, formalista. **2** tirano, ordenancista.

martyr | 'mɑːtər | *s.c.* **1** mártir. **2** (fig.) mártir, víctima. || *v.t.* **3** martirizar, torturar. || **4 to be a – to,** ser víctima de, sufrir a causa de: *he's a victim to awful headaches = sufre fuertes dolores de cabeza.*

martyrdom | 'mɑːtədəm | *s.i.* **1** martirio, tortura. **2** (fig. y desp.) martirio, sufrimiento.

martyred | 'mɑːtəd | *adj.* martirizado, patético, de sufrimiento (un gesto).

marvel | 'mɑːvl | *s.c.* **1** maravilla, portento, prodigio, milagro. **2** asombro, sorpresa. || (brit. **marvell**) *v.t.* e *i.* **3** (form.) maravillarse, admirarse. || **4 marvels,** maravillas: *to perform marvels = hacer maravillas.*

marvellous | 'mɑːvələs | (EE.UU. **marvelous**) *adj.* **1** maravilloso, portentoso, prodigioso. **2** milagroso, sobrenatural. **3** espléndido, magnífico, qué bien: *isn't it marvellous? = ¡qué bien!.*

marvellously | 'mɑːvələslɪ | *adv.* maravillosamente, de maravilla.

Marxism | 'mɑːksɪzəm | *s.i.* POL. marxismo.

Marxism-Leninism | 'mɑːksɪzəm'lenɪnɪzəm | *s.i.* POL. marxismo-leninismo.

Marxist | 'mɑːksɪst | *s.c.* **1** marxista. || *adj.* **2** marxista.

Marxist-Leninist | 'mɑːksɪst'lenɪnɪst | *s.c.* marxista-leninista.

marzipan | ˌmɑːzɪ'pæn | *s.i.* mazapán, pasta de almendras.

mascara | mæ'skɑːrə | | mæ'skærə | **1** *s.i.* rímel, cosmético para los ojos || *v.t.* **2** aplicar rímel.

mascaraed | mæ'skɑːrəd | | mæ'skærəd | *adj.* maquillado con rímel.

mascot 'mæskət | | 'mæskɑːt | *s.c.* mascota, emblema, talismán, amuleto.

masculine | 'mæskjʊlɪn | *adj.* **1** masculino, varonil. **2** (desp.) hombruna, masculina (una mujer). **3** GRAM. masculino. || *s.c.* **4** GRAM. género masculino. **5** hombre, varón.

masculinity | ˌmæskjʊ'lɪnɪtɪ | *s.i.* masculinidad.

mash | mæʃ | *v.t.* **1 [to – (up)]** aplastar, hacer puré, despachurrar, hacer una pasta. **2** majar, moler. **3** (argot) flirtear, coquetear (agresivamente). || *s.i.* **4** (brit. y fam.) puré de patata. **5** malta remojada (para hacer cerveza). || *s.c.* e *i.* **6** pienso hervido, mezcla de granos molidos (para animales). **7** masa, mezcla. **8** mezcolanza, batiburrillo.

mashed | mæʃt | *adj.* en puré, hecho puré: *mashed potatoes = puré de patata.*

mask | mɑːsk | | mæsk | *s.c.* **1** máscara, careta, antifaz. **2** MED. mascarilla. **3** máscara (para protegerse en esgrima, de gas). **4** (fig.) máscara, disfraz, careta. **5** ARQ. mascarón. **6** mascarilla cosmética. **7** MIL. camuflaje. || *v.t.* **8** enmascarar,

encubrir, ocultar, esconder. **9** MIL. camuflar. **10** FOT. velar.
masked | mɑːskt | | mæskt | *adj.* **1** enmascarado, cubierto, oculto, camuflado. **2** disfrazado, enmascarado, disimulado. **3** MED. latente (una enfermedad). || **4 – ball,** baile de disfraces, baile de máscaras.
masking tape | 'mɑːskɪŋˌteɪp | *s.i.* cinta adhesiva (para proteger los bordes o esquinas al pintar).
masochism | 'mæsəʊkɪzəm | *s.i.* masoquismo.
masochist | 'mæsəʊkɪst | *s.c.* masoquista.
masochistic | ˌmæsəʊ'kɪstɪk | *adj.* masoquista.
masochistically | ˌmæsəʊ'kɪstɪkəlɪ | *adv.* de forma masoquista.
mason | 'meɪsn | *s.c.* **1** albañil, cantero. **2** Mason, masón, francmasón.
masonic | mə'sɒnɪk | | mə'sɑːnɪk | *adj.* masónico.
masonry | 'meɪsnrɪ | *s.i.* **1** albañilería. **2** mampostería. **3** masonería, francmasonería.
masquerade | ˌmæskə'reɪd | *s.c.* **1** mascarada, simulación, fingimiento, farsa, hipocresía. **2** baile de máscaras. || *v.i.* **3** enmascarar, disfrazar, simular, ocultar.
mass | mæs | *s.c.* **1** masa, montón, mole, bulto. **2** [*pl.*] (fam.) un gran número, cantidades ingentes. **3** masas, muchedumbre, mayoría: *the mass of people = la mayoría de la gente.* || *s.i.* **4** FIS. masa. **5** MUS. misa. || *v.i.* **6** masificarse, concentrarse, juntarse en masa. || *adj.* **7** *no comp.* en masa, en gran número. **8** de masas, para las masas. **9** masivo, en serie (la fabricación). **10** popular, público. || **11 Mass,** REL. misa. **12 – media,** medios de comunicación de masas. **13 – noun,** GRAM. nombre incontable (a veces con *v.sing.* o *pl.*).
massacre | 'mæsəkər | *s.c.* e *i.* **1** masacre, matanza, carnicería, degüello. || *s.c.* **2** (fam.) sarracina, tunda, vapuleo (a un partido en elecciones). || *v.t.* **3** hacer una carnicería, degollar, matar en masa, matar ferozmente. **4** (fam.) machacar, aplastar, infligir una severa derrota.
massage | 'mæsɑːʒ | | mə'sɑːʒ | *s.c.* e *i.* **1** masaje. || *v.t.* **2** dar masaje, masajear, dar fricciones. **3** falsear, manipular, alterar (cifras).
massed | mæst | *adj.* **1** denso, tupido, espeso (follaje, plantas). **2** apiñado, concentrado (un grupo de personas). **3** colectivo, congregado.
masseur | mæ'səːr | | mə'səːr | [*f.* **masseuse**] *s.c.* masajista.
masseuse | mæ'səːz | | mə'səːz | [*m.* **masseur**] *s.c.* masajista.
massif | 'mæsiːf | | mæ'siːf | *s.c.* GEOG. macizo.
massive | 'mæsɪv | *adj.* **1** macizo, sólido. **2** pesado. **3** imponente, sobrehumano, extraordinario, inmenso, abultado. **4** MED. masivo, más de lo normal; extendida (una enfermedad). **5** enérgico, fuerte, en gran escala.
massively | 'mæsɪvlɪ | *adv.* **1** sólidamente, macizamente. **2** imponentemente. **3** enérgicamente.
massiveness | 'mæsɪvnɪs | *s.i.* **1** enormidad, grandeza. **2** solidez (de un objeto, edificio, etc.).
mass-produce | 'mæsprəˌdjuːs | *v.t.* producir en masa, fabricar en serie.
mass-produced | 'mæsprəˌdjuːst | *adj.* fabricado en serie.
mass-production | ˌmæsprə'dʌkʃn | *s.i.* producción en serie, fabricación en serie.
mast | mɑːst | | mæst | *s.c.* **1** MAR. mástil, palo. **2** TV. antena, torre. **3** BOT. bellota, hayuco. || **4 before the –,** (lit.) como marinero, de marinero. **5 to nail one's colours to the –,** pronunciarse a favor de, dejar claro lo que se piensa de.
mastectomy | mæ'stektəmɪ | *s.c.* MED. mastectomía.
master | 'mɑːstər | *s.c.* **1** amo, dueño, patrono. **2** (brit.) tutor, maestro, profesor, instructor. **3 Master,** Rector, Director (de un Colegio Universitario). **4** doctor (universitario). **5** doctorado (universitario). **6** ART. maestro, artista (del pasado). **7** maestro, experto (en artesanía). **8 The Master,** El Maestro, Jesucristo. **9** MAR. capitán, patrón. **10** maestre. **11** vencedor, triunfador. **12** copia original (de un disco, cinta magnetofónica). **13** (arc.) Señor (como título ante un nombre). || *s.i.* **14** dueño (de una situación). || *adj.* **15** [no *comp.*] experto. **16** original, primera (una copia). **17** principal, más importante; jefe. || *v.t.* **18** conocer a fondo, dominar (una materia). **19** dominar, vencer, superar, salvar (un sentimiento, un obstáculo). || **20 – bedroom,** dormitorio principal. **21 – key,** llave maestra. **22 Master of Arts,** Doctor en Filosofía, en Humanidades. **23 Master of ceremonies,** Maestro de ceremonias. **24 Master of Science,** Doctor en Ciencias. **25 – plan,** plan maestro, plan guía. **26 – switch,** ELECT. conmutador, interruptor principal.
masterful | 'mɑːstəful | | 'mæstərfəl | *adj.* **1** (lit.) magistral, hábil, experto. **2** autoritario, mandón, dominante, imperioso. **3** maestra (una técnica).
masterfully | 'mɑːstəfəlɪ | *adv.* **1** (lit.) magistralmente, con gran habilidad. **2** autoritariamente, imperiosamente.
masterly | 'mɑːstəlɪ | | 'mæstəlɪ | *adj.* magistral, brillante, genial, excelente.
mastermind | 'mɑːstəmaɪnd | | 'mæstərmaɪnd | *s.c.* **1** cerebro, genio, organizador. **2** cerebro, mente despierta, persona genial. || *v.t.* **3** (fam.) planificar inteligentemente, dirigir hábilmente, organizar brillantemente.
masterpiece | 'mɑːstəpiːs | *s.c.* obra maestra, obra de arte.
masterstroke | 'mɑːstəstrəuk | *s.c.* golpe maestro.
mastery | 'mɑːstərɪ | | 'mæstərɪ | *s.i.* **1** [**– (over/of)**] dominio, autoridad, poder. **2** competencia, maestría, destreza. **3** dominio, conocimiento (de una materia).
masthead | 'mɑːsthed | *s.c.* **1** MAR. celces, tope, espiga. **2** PER. cabecera, rótulo, carátula (de un periódico).
masticate | 'mæstɪkeɪt | *v.t.* e *i.* (form.) masticar, mascar.
mastication | ˌmæstɪ'keɪʃn | *s.i.* (form.) masticación.
mastiff | 'mæstɪf | *s.c.* **1** mastín, alano.
mastitis | mæ'staɪtɪs *s.i.* MED. mastitis.
mastodon | mæstədən | s.c. mastodonte.
masturbate | 'mæstəbeɪt | *v.t.* e *i.* masturbar(se).
masturbation | ˌmæstə'beɪʃən | *s.i.* masturbación.
mat | mæt | *s.c.* **1** estera, esterilla, felpudo, alfombrilla. **2** salvamanteles, mantelito individual. **3** tapete; posavasos. **4** DEP. colchoneta, estera. **5** orla, borde, reborde, marco. **6** matriz (en imprenta). || *s.i.* **7** (fig.) mata, maraña (de pelo). || *adj.* **8** mate, sin brillo. || *v.t.* **9** alfombrar, cubrir con estera. **11** enmarcar, poner orla, poner reborde (a una fotografía). || *v.t.* e *i.* **12** enmarañar, enredar.
matador | 'mætədɔːr | *s.c.* matador, torero, diestro.
match | mætʃ | *s.c.* **1** DEP. partido, competición, encuentro, juego, asalto, carrera. **2** [**– (for)**] contendiente, rival, competidor. **3** [**– (for)**] combinación, conjunto (ropas, zapatos): *shoes and bag were a nice match = los zapatos y el bolso combinaban muy bien.* **4** (gen. *sing.)* (arc.) partido (para casarse). **5** matrimonio, pareja; casamiento, boda. **6** cerilla, fósforo. **7** mecha. || *v.t.* e *i.* **8** hacer juego, coordinar, conjuntar, armonizar, ir a tono, hacer buena pareja. || *v.t.* **9** ser igual, corresponder, valer tanto como, ser tan bueno como. **10** casar, emparejar. **11** DEP. competir, rivalizar. **12** comparar, establecer comparación. **13** jugar a las chapas (con monedas). || **14 to be/make a good –,** hacer buena pareja. **15 to be no – for,** no poder competir con, no llegar a la altura de. **16 to – against,** competir contra, batirse contra, enfrentarse a. **17 – point,** DEP. tanto crítico, punto decisivo (para ganar un partido). **18 to – up to/with,** comparar con, ser tanto como. **19 to meet one's –,** (fig.) encontrarse con la horma de su propio zapato.
matchbox | 'mætʃbɒks | | 'mætʃbɑːks | *s.c.* caja de cerillas, caja de fósforos.
matched | mætʃt | *adj.* **1** acorde, coincidente, bien avenido, armonioso (una relación, una pareja). **2** equiparados, igualados, parejos (equipos, fuerzas).
matching | 'mætʃɪŋ | *adj.* a juego, conjuntado, combinado, coordinado.
matchless | 'mætʃlɪs | *adj.* (lit.) sin par, incomparable, sin rival.
matchmaker | 'mætʃˌmeɪkər | *s.c.* **1** casamentero. **2** DEP. organizador, promotor.

matchmaking | 'mætʃˌmeɪkɪŋ | *s.i.* **1** actividad de casamentero. **2** DEP. promoción, organización (de pruebas deportivas).
matchstick | 'mætʃˌstɪk | *s.c.* **1** cerilla, fósforo (usado).
matchwood | 'mætʃwʊd | *s.i.* **1** astilla, fragmento, añicos. **2** madera para fabricar cerillas.
mate | meɪt | *s.c.* **1** (fam.) amigo, compañero, camarada. **2** pareja, hembra, macho (entre animales). **3** esposo, cónyuge. **4** MAR. segundo de a bordo, primer oficial. **5** (brit. y fam.) amigo, tío, chaval, hombre (para dirigirse a un hombre). **6** ayudante, peón. **7** mate (en ajedrez). || *v.t.* e *i.* **8** cruzar, aparear (animales). **9** casar, unir en matrimonio. **10** dar mate, recibir mate.
material | mə'tɪərɪəl | *adj.* **1** material. **2** físico, corporal. **3** sustancial, relevante, notable; pertinente, oportuno, adecuado. || *s.c.* e *i.* **4** material, materia. **5** tela, tejido, género. || *s.i.* **6** **[– (for)]** material, ideas, datos, información. **7** *[pl.]* instrumentos, material, útiles, efectos, herramientas. **8** (fig.) madera, potencial (de una persona para desempeñar un trabajo).
materialise V. **materialize.**
materialization | məˌtɪərɪəlaɪ'zeɪʃn | (también **materialisation**) *s.i.* materialización.
materially | mə'tɪərɪəlɪ | *adv.* **1** materialmente. **2** esencialmente, notablemente, sensiblemente.
materialism | mə'tɪərɪəlɪzəm | *s.i.* **1** (desp.) materialismo. **2** FIL. materialismo.
materialist | mə'tɪərɪəlɪst | *s.c.* **1** FIL. materialista. || *adj.* **2** materialista.
materialistic | məˌtɪərɪə'lɪstɪk | *adj.* materialista.
materialize | mə'tɪərɪəlaɪz | (brit.) **materialise.** *v.t.* e *i.* **1** materializar(se), hacer aparecer, tomar forma. **2** (fig.) aparecer, llegar (alguien a un lugar). || *v.i.* **3** hacerse realidad, suceder, producirse.
maternal | mə'tɜːnl | | mə'tɜːrnl | *adj.* **1** maternal (un sentimiento). **2** materno (un familiar, un rasgo).
maternally | mə'tɜːnəlɪ | *adv.* maternalmente.
maternity | mə'tɜːnɪtɪ | | mə'tɜːrnɪtɪ | *s.i.* **1** (form.) maternidad. || *s.c.* **2** maternidad, hospital materno-infantil, casa de maternidad.
matey | 'meɪtɪ | *adj.* (brit. y fam.) amistoso, simpático, afable, sociable.
math | mæɵ | *s.i.* (EE.UU.) matemáticas.
mathematical | ˌmæɵə'mætɪkl | *adj.* **1** matemática (una fórmula). **2** matemático, preciso, científico.
mathematically | ˌmæɵə'mætɪkəlɪ | *adv.* matemáticamente.
mathematician | ˌmæɵəmə'tɪʃn | *s.c.* matemático.
mathematics | ˌmæɵə'mætɪks | *s.i.* matemáticas.
maths | mæɵs | *s.i.* (brit. y fam.) matemáticas.
matinee | 'mætɪneɪ | *s.c.* función de tarde, (Am.) matinée (de cine, teatro).
mating | meɪtɪŋ | *s.i.* **1** apareamiento, cruce (de animales). || *adj.* **2** de apareamiento, de celo: *mating season = época de celo.*
matins, mattins | 'mætɪnz | *s.i.* [;ms + *v.sing./pl.*] REL. maitines.
matriarch | 'meɪtrɪɑːk | | 'meɪtrɪɑːrk | *s.c.* matriarca.
matriarchal | ˌmeɪtrɪ'ɑːkl | | meɪtrɪ'ɑːrkl | *adj.* matriarcal.
matriarchy | 'meɪtrɪɑːkɪ | | 'meɪtrɪɑːrkɪ | *s.c.* e *i.* matriarcado.
matrices | 'meɪtrɪsiːz | *pl.* de **matrix.**
matricide | 'mætrɪsaɪd | *s.c.* e *i.* **1** matricidio. || *s.c.* **2** matricida.
matriculate | mə'trɪkjʊleɪt | *v.i.* matricularse (en la Universidad).
matriculation | məˌtrɪkjʊ'leɪʃn | *s.i.* matrícula, matriculación (en la Universidad).
matrimonial | ˌmætrɪ'məʊnɪəl | *adj.* (form.) matrimonial, marital, conyugal.
matrimony | 'mætrɪmənɪ | *s.i.* (form.) matrimonio, nupcias; vida conyugal.
matrix | 'meɪtrɪks | *[pl.* **matrices** o **matrixes]** *s.c.* **1** MAT. matriz. **2** ANAT. matriz, útero. **3** matriz, molde. **4** GEOL. roca madre, matriz. **5** matriz (de la uña).
matron | 'meɪtrən | *s.c.* **1** (brit.) matrona, jefa de enfermeras (en un hospital). **2** (brit.) supervisora, ama de llaves (en un internado). **3** (EE.UU.) matrona (en cárceles, comisarías). **4** (lit. y arc.) matrona, mujer casada (de mediana edad). || **5 – of honour,** (EE.UU.) madrina de boda.
matronly | 'meɪtrənlɪ | *adj.* (euf.) como una matrona, de matrona, de aspecto bonachón.
matt, mat | mæt | (EE.UU.) **matte** *adj.* mate, sin brillo.
matted | mætɪd | *adj.* enmarañado, apelotonado, enredado (el pelo, raíces).
matter | 'mætər | *s.c.* **1** tema, asunto, cuestión. **2 [the – (with)]** el problema, el motivo, la causa. **3** *[pl.]* las cosas: *that simplifies matters = eso simplifica las cosas.* || *s.i.* **4** FIS. materia. **5** sustancia, materia: *a pinkish matter = una sustancia rosácea.* **6** contenido, tópico, tema (de una charla, de una novela). **7** material impreso, material. || *v.i.* **8** importar, tener importancia. || **9 a – of,** una cuestión de, aproximadamente, más o menos. **10 a – of opinion,** cuestión de gustos, cuestión de opiniones, algo discutible. **11 a – of time/weeks,** cuestión de tiempo; cosa de semanas. **12 another/a different –,** otro asunto, cuestión diferente. **13 as a – of,** debido a, a causa de, por. **14 as a – of course,** automáticamente, porque sí, por rutina. **15 as a – of fact,** en realidad, de hecho. **16 but that is another –,** eso es otro cantar, eso es harina de otro costal. **17 for that –,** si vamos a eso, si es que se puede decir. **18 is anything the –?,** ¿algo va mal? **19 it doesn't –,** no importa, da igual. **20 to make matters worse,** para colmo de males, para empeorar las cosas. **21 no easy –,** no es asunto fácil. **22 no laughing –,** en serio, no es cosa de broma. **23 no –,** no importa, qué importa. **24 no – what,** a pesar de todo, pase lo que pase, de todos modos. **25 that's the end of the –/that's an end to the –,** punto final, y punto, asunto zanjado, es todo lo que tengo que decir. **26 the fact/truth of the –,** la verdad es, el hecho es. **27 what's the –?,** ¿qué pasa?, ¿qué hay?
matter-of-fact | ˌmætərəʊ'fækt | *adj.* práctico, pragmático, realista, prosaico, desapasionado.
matter-of-factly | ˌmætərəʊ'fæktlɪ | *adv.* de forma realista, desapasionadamente.
matter-of-factness | ˌmætərəʊ'fæktnɪs | *s.i.* desapasionamiento, pragmatismo, prosaísmo.
matting | 'mætɪŋ | *s.i.* **1** estera, esterilla, alfombra. **2** superficie mate, acabado mate, sin brillo. **3** cartulina, fieltro (utilizado como fondo alrededor de cuadros, fotografías enmarcadas).
mattins V. **matins.**
mattock | 'mætək | *s.c.* azadón, piqueta.
mattress | 'mætrɪs | *s.c.* **1** colchón. **2** defensa de alambre y ramaje entretejidos (contra la erosión en embarcaderos).
maturation | ˌmætjʊ'reɪʃn | *s.i.* maduración.
mature | mə'tjʊər | *adj.* **1** maduro, adulto, sensato. **2** maduro, en sazón. **3** (fam.) madurado, bien pensado (un plan). **4** COM. pagadero, vencido. **5** GEOL. erosionado. || *v.t.* e *i.* **6** madurar(se). **7** COM. vencer, ser pagadero. || **8 – student,** estudiante universitario que empieza a los 25 años.
maturely | mə'tjʊəlɪ | *adv.* con madurez, con sensatez.
maturity | mə'tjʊrətɪ | *s.i.* **1** madurez, desarrollo. **2** madurez, sabiduría, sagacidad, cordura. **3** COM. vencimiento.
maudlin | mɔːdlɪn | *adj.* sensiblero, sentimental, lacrimoso, llorón (por efecto del alcohol).
maul | mɔːl | *v.t.* **1** herir, destrozar, magullar, lacerar. **2** manosear, sobar (a una persona). **3** (fig.) destrozar, poner los suelos, hundir, pegar el palo (por la crítica). || *s.c.* **4** (EE.UU.) mazo, maza, moleta.
maunder | 'mɔːndər | *v.i.* (fam.) **1** hablar sin sentido, chapurrear. **2 [to – (about)]** andar sin rumbo fijo, estar sin hacer nada.
Mauritian | mə'rɪʃən | *adj.* **1** de Isla Mauricio (nacionalidad, origen, lengua). || *s.c.* **2** persona natural de Isla Mauricio.
Mauritius | mə'rɪʃəs | *s.* Isla Mauricio.
mausoleum | ˌmɔːsə'lɪəm | *s.c.* **1** mausoleo, sepulcro monumental. **2** (fig.) lugar tétrico, deprimente.
mauve | məʊv | *adj.* **1** de color malva, malva. || *s.i.* **2** color malva.
maverick | 'mævərɪk | *s.c.* **1** (desp.) independiente, disidente (un político);

inconformista, rebelde. **2** (EE.UU.) res sin marca. || *adj.* **3** independiente, disidente, inconformista.

maw | mɔː | *s.c.* **1** estómago, cuajar, fauces, buche, molleja. **2** (fig.) fauces.

mawkish | 'mɔːkɪʃ | *adj.* **1** empalagoso, sensiblero, sentimental, efusivo en extremo. **2** insípido, soso, insulso.

mawkishly | 'mɔːkɪʃlɪ | *adv.* **1** empalagosamente, sensibleramente. **2** insípidamente, sosamente, insulsamente.

mawkishness | 'mɔːkɪʃnɪs | *s.i.* **1** sensiblería, sentimentalismo, efusividad extrema. **2** insipidez, insulsez, sosería.

maxim | 'mæksɪm | *s.c.* máxima, dicho, lema, proverbio.

maximal | 'mæksɪml | *adj.* máximo posible: *maximal returns = máximos beneficios.*

maximise V. **maximize.**

maximization | ˌmæksəmaɪ'zeɪʃən | | ˌmæksəmə'zeɪʃən | *s.i.* incremento máximo, aumento máximo, multiplicación.

maximize | 'mæksəmaɪz | (brit. **maximise**) *v.t.* **1** incrementar al máximo, aumentar exageradamente, multiplicar (las ganancias). **2** dar la máxima importancia.

maximum | 'mæksɪməm | [*pl.* **máxima** o **máximums**] *s.c.* **1** máximo, máximum. || *adj.* **2** máximo, mayor. || **3 at the –,** como máximo, a lo sumo, como mucho. **4 over the –,** más de lo permitido, por encima de lo normal. **5 to the –,** al máximo.

may | meɪ | *v.t.irr.* [*pret.* **might.**] **1** poder, ser posible: *he may come soon = puede que venga pronto.* **2** (form.) poder, estar permitido, tener permiso para. **3** [;ms + *suj.*] (form.) ¡ojalá!, ¡Dios lo quiera! (para introducir un deseo): *may you live long! = ¡Dios quiera que viva Vd. muchos años!* **4** DER. deber, tener obligación de (en documentos, estatutos). || *s.i.* **5 May,** mayo (mes). **6** (brit.) flor de espino, flor del marjoleto. **7** (fig.) juventud, primavera, flor de la vida. || **8 May Day,** Primero de Mayo, Día del Trabajo.

OBS. **May** es un *v.* defectivo que sólo tiene *presente* y *pret.* y siempre va con un infinitivo sin **to.**

maybe | 'meɪbiː | *adv.* quizá, posiblemente, tal vez.

mayday | 'meɪdeɪ | *s.c.* llamada de socorro (utilizada en radiotelegrafía internacional desde barcos o aviones en peligro).

mayfly | 'meɪflaɪ | *s.c.* ZOOL. efímera, cachipolla, mosca de un día.

mayhem | 'meɪhem | *s.i.* **1** caos, pánico, confusión, desorden. **2** DER. mutilación criminal. **3** destrucción, daño (injustificable y cruel).

mayn't | meɪnt | (brit.) *contr.* de **may not.**

mayonnaise | ˌmeɪə'neɪz | | 'meɪəneɪz | *s.i.* mayonesa, mahonesa (salsa).

mayor | meər | | meɪər | *s.c.m.* alcalde.

mayoral | 'meərəl | | 'meɪərəl | *adj.* del alcalde.

mayoress | meərɪs | | meɪərɪs | *s.c.f.* **1** alcaldesa. **2** mujer del alcalde.

may've | meɪəv | *contr.* de **may have.**

maze | meɪz | *s.c.* **1** laberinto. **2** (fig.) laberinto, maraña, embrollo, confusión. || *v.t.* **3** dejar perplejo, confundir, azorar. **4** aturdir, atontar, ofuscar.

mazurka | mə'zəːkə | *s c.* MUS. mazurca.

McCarthyism | mə'kɑːθɪɪzəm | *s.i.* macartismo (caza de brujas anticomunista de los años 50 en Estados Unidos).

McCoy, the real McCoy | məkɔɪ | *s.c.* (argot) el auténtico, el genuino, el verdadero.

me | miː | | mɪ | *pron. o.* 1a. persona. **1** me, mi, a mí. || **2 it's –,** (fam.) soy yo. **3 with –,** conmigo.

mead | miːd | *s.i.* **1** (brit.) aguamiel, hidromiel. || *s.c.* **2** (lit.) prado, pradera, vega.

meadow | 'medəu | *s.c.* **1** prado, pradera, vega. || **2 – lark,** ZOOL. sabanero (pájaro).

meagre | 'miːgər | (EE.UU. **meager**) *adj.* **1** escaso, exiguo, miserable. **2** flaco, esmirriado, delgaducho. **3** infecunda, estéril, infructuosa (la tierra).

meal | miːl | *s.c.* **1** comida: *three meals a day = tres comidas al día.* || *s.i.* **2** harina. || **3 to make a – of something,** (fam. y desp.) dedicar más tiempo del necesario a algo, dar a algo más importancia de la que tiene. **4 – ticket,** (EE.UU.) bono intercambiable por una comida; (brit.) sustento, fuente de ingresos.

meals-on-wheels | miːlsənwiːls | *s.pl.* servicio de comidas a domicilio para enfermos o ancianos (como servicio social).

mealtime | 'miːltaɪm | *s.c.* e *i.* hora de comer.

mealy | 'miːlɪ | *adj.* **1** enharinado, cubierto de harina. **2** harinoso, farináceo.

mealy-mouthed | 'miːlɪmauʃd | *adj.* (desp.) hipócrita, engañoso, falso, que no habla claro.

mean | miːn | *adj.* **1** tacaño, cicatero, roñoso, ruin. **2** cruel, poco amable, mezquino, detestable. **3** (EE.UU.) arisco, peligroso, malo (un animal). **4** perverso, violento, ruin, malvado. **5** (lit. y arc.) humilde, pobre. **6** (lit.) oscuro, miserable, zarrapastroso (un lugar). **7** (EE.UU. y argot) maravilloso, fantástico, estupendo. **8** medio, de término medio, por término medio. || *v.t. irr. [pret.* y *p.p.* **meant]** **9** significar, querer decir. **10** denotar, representar, simbolizar: *flower means youth here = aquí, la flor simboliza la juventud.* **11** referirse a, ir dirigido a: *that means you too! = ¡eso también va para ti!* **12** pretender, tener intención de, intentar, querer. **13** ser muy importante, tener importancia, importar. **14** decir en serio, hablar en serio, no bromear, no exagerar. **15** planear, querer (ser): *the photograph is meant to be her = la fotografía quiere ser ella.* **16** ir dirigido a, ser para (una persona). **17** estar destinado para (un edificio); estar predestinado, nacer para (una persona). || *s.pl.* **18** medio, instrumento, método. **19** medios, recursos, renta. || *s.sing.* **20** punto medio, promedio. || **21 a means to an end,** un medio para conseguir un fin. **22 by all means,** por favor, naturalmente, claro que sí. **23 by means of,** por medio de, mediante. **24 by no means/by no manner of means/not by any means,** de ningún modo, en absoluto. **25 I –,** o sea, es decir; perdón, lo siento (al corregir un error cometido al hablar). **26 to know what it means,** saber de que va, saber lo que conlleva, saber de que se trata. **27 to live beyond one's means,** vivir por encima de sus posibilidades económicas, gastar más de lo que uno gana. **28 to live within one's means,** vivir de acuerdo con los propios medios económicos, vivir de acuerdo a sus ingresos. **29 to – something to,** recordarle algo a, sonarle algo a (alguien). **30 means test,** averiguación de recursos económicos (cuando se pide una ayuda pública). **31 to – well,** tener buenas intenciones. **32 no – ...,** nada despreciable..., ... cualquiera, no... corriente: *he's no mean painter = no es un pintor cualquiera.* **33 not to – anything/any harm,** sin querer, sin mala intención. **34 you mean?,** ¿no?, ¿verdad? (al final de una pregunta para pedir más detalles.

meander | mɪ'ændər | *v.i.* **1** serpentear, serpear, zigzaguear, deslizarse por un curso tortuoso (un río, una carretera). **2** vagar, andar sin rumbo fijo, andar sin un propósito. **3** (fig.) hablar vagamente, hablar desordenadamente. || *s.c.* **4** meandro. **5** camino tortuoso. **6** ARQ. meandro.

meandering | mɪ'ændərɪŋ | *adj.* **1** serpenteante, zigzagueante (un río, una carretera). **2** desordenado, vago, poco claro (un discurso).

meanderingly | mɪ'ændrɪŋlɪ | *adv.* **1** serpenteantemente, en zigzag. **2** desordenadamente, con poca claridad (un discurso o similar).

meanie | 'miːnɪ | *s.c.* (brit. y fam.) bruto, bestia, persona abominable.

meaning | 'miːnɪŋ | *s.c.* e *i.* **1** significado, acepción, sentido. **2** significado, importancia, valor. **3** objetivo, propósito, intención. || *adj.* **4** significativo, expresivo, elocuente. **5** intencionado, con propósito. || **6 to get someone's –,** captar el significado, entender, comprender. **7 not to know the – of the word,** no saber lo que se dice, no tener ni idea. **8 what's the – of this?,** ¿qué sentido tiene esto? (de algo que se desaprueba).

meaningful | 'miːnɪŋfəl | *adj.* **1** significativo, con sentido. **2** comprensible, claro. **3** significativo, elocuente, expresivo. **4** profunda, importante (una relación).

meaningfully | 'miːnɪŋfəlɪ | *adv.* **1** comprensiblemente, claramente. **2** significativamente, elocuentemente. **3** de forma útil.

meaningless | 'miːnɪŋlɪs | *adj.* **1** sin sentido, falto de significado. **2** sin valor, inútil, sin importancia, fútil.
meanly | miːnlɪ | *adv.* detestablemente, cruelmente, vilmente.
meanness | miːnɪs | *s.i.* **1** tacañería, cicatería, ruindad. **2** vileza, bajeza, crueldad.
means-test | 'miːnztest | *s.c.* investigación sobre recursos económicos (antes de conceder a alguien una subvención).
means-tested | 'miːns,testɪd | *adj.* investigado en cuanto a recursos económicos (antes de conceder una subvención).
meant | ment | *pret.* y *p.p.* de **mean.**
meantime | ,miːn'taɪm | *s.sing.* **1** ínterin, intervalo. || *adv.* **2** entre tanto, mientras tanto, en el ínterin. || **3 for the –,** por el momento. **4 in the –,** entretanto, mientras tanto.
meanwhile | ,miːn'waɪl | *adv.* **1** entre tanto, mientras tanto. **2** por otra parte. || **3 in the –,** entre tanto, mientras tanto.
measles | 'miːzlz | *s.i.* **1** MED. sarampión. || **2 German –,** MED. rubéola.
measly | 'miːzlɪ | *adv.* **1** (fam. y desp.) miserable, de poquísimo valor, magro. **2** con sarampión, infectado de sarampión.
measurable | 'meʒərəbl | *adj.* **1** mensurable, que se puede medir. **2** significativo, perceptible.
measurably | 'meʒərəblɪ | *adv.* significativamente, perceptiblemente.
measure | 'meʒər | *v.t.* e *i.* **1** medir, tomar medidas. **2** valorar, tasar, estimar. || *v.t.* **3** medir, marcar, registrar, señalar (la hora, la temperatura). **4** medir, sopesar, elegir cuidadosamente (las palabras). **5** (arc.) hacer, recorrer (una distancia). || *s.c.* **6** *pl.* medidas, acciones, disposiciones. **7 [– (of)]** medida, unidad de medida, medición. **8** porción, cantidad, medida (en cocina). **9** (arc.) MUS. medida, compás, ritmo. || *s.i.* **10** (form.) grado, categoría, extensión, importancia. **11** moderación. **12** LIT. métrica, metro, medida. || **13 beyond –** (lit.) excesivo. **14 for good –,** además, por añadidura, para completar. **15 to get/take someone's –,** (fig.) juzgar lo que alguien vale, tomarle la medida a alguien, evaluar a alguien. **16 in some/large –,** (form.) de algún modo, hasta cierto punto; en buena medida, en gran parte. **17 to – against,** medir con, comparar con (la fuerza, la calidad). **18 to – off /out,** medir, sacar (metros, gramos, etc... de una cantidad mayor): *measure 3 yards more = mide 3 yardas más.* **19 to – up (to),** estar a la altura de, satisfacer las expectativas.
measured | 'meʒəd | *adj.* **1** mesurado, comedido, moderado, prudente. **2** calculado, preciso, exacto, deliberado. **3** medido. **4** LIT. métrico. **5** regular, rítmico. **6** limitado.
measureless | 'meʒəlɪs | *adj.* sin medida, sin límite (que no se puede medir físicamente).
measurement | 'meʒəmənt | *s.i.* **1** medida, cálculo. || *s.c.* **2** (gen. *pl.*) medidas (de una persona). **3** medición.
measuring | 'meʒərɪŋ | *adj.* medidor: *a measuring spoon = una cuchara medidora.*
measuring-tape | 'meʒərɪŋ teɪp | V. **tape-measure.**
meat | miːt | *s.i.* **1** carne (de animales, pescado, fruta). **2** (fig.) ideas, sustancia, meollo, materia (de reflexión). **3** punto fuerte, fuerte. **4** (arc.) comida. || **5 to be – and drink,** no poder vivir sin, ser muy importante para, producir gran satisfacción.
meatball | 'miːtbɔːl | *s.c.* GAST. albóndigas (o similar).
meaty | miːtɪ | *adj.* **1** carnoso, rollizo, metido en carnes. **2** (fam. y fig.) sustancioso, lleno de ideas.
mecca | 'mekə | *s.c.* **1** (gen. *sing.*) (fig.) meca, centro de interés, centro de reunión. **2 Mecca,** La Meca (en Arabia Saudí).
mechanic | mɪ'kænɪk | *s.c.* **1** mecánico.
mechanical | mɪ'kænɪkl | *adj.* **1** no *comp.* mecánico, automático. **2** (fig. y desp.) mecánico, maquinal, rutinario. **3** mecánico (conocedor de las máquinas).
mechanically | mɪ'kænɪkəlɪ | *adv.* **1** mecánicamente, automáticamente. **2** rutinariamente, maquinalmente, como un autómata.
mechanics | mɪ'kænɪks | *s.i.* **1** FIS. mecánica. || **2 the – of,** el mecanismo de, la forma de funcionar de, el funcionamiento de.
mechanise V. **mechanize.**
mechanism | 'mekənɪzəm | *s.c.* **1** mecanismo. **2** (fig.) mecanismo, procedimiento. **3** PSI. mecanismo (de defensa).
mechanistic | ,mekə'nɪstɪk | *adj.* **1** FIL. mecanicista. **2** mecánico, maquinal.
mechanization | ,mekənaɪ'zeɪʃn | *s.i.* **1** mecanización, automatización.
mechanize | 'mekənaɪz | (brit. **mechanise**) *v.t.* mecanizar, automatizar.
mechanized | 'mekənaɪzd | *adj.* mecanizado, automatizado.
medal | 'medl | *s.c.* **1** medalla, condecoración, insignia. **2** medalla (religiosa).
medallion | mɪ'dælɪən | *s.c.* medallón.
medallist | 'medlɪst | (EE.UU. **medalist**) *s.c.* **1** ganador de una medalla, deportista premiado con medallas.
meddle | 'medl | *v.i.* **1** entrometerse, interferir, ingerir. **2** manipular indebidamente, estropear, manosear.
meddler | 'medlər | *s.c.* (desp.) entrometido.
meddlesome | 'medlsəm | *adj.* entrometido, impertinente, que interfiere.
media | 'miːdɪə | *s.sing.* **1 [– + *v.sing./pl.*]** (form.) medios de comunicación (radio, TV, prensa). **2** *[pl.]* de **medium.**
mediaeval V. **medieval.**
median | 'miːdɪən | *s.sing.* **1** GEOM. mediana. **2** media, valor medio, punto medio. **3** (EE.UU.) mediana (de una autopista). || *adj.* no *comp.* **4** medio, intermedio, corriente. **5** ANAT. medial, del medio.
mediate | 'miːdɪəɪt | *v.i.* **1 [to – (between/in)]** mediar, actuar como mediador, intervenir (en un conflicto). || *v.t.* **2** resolver, arbitrar, dirimir. **3** *pas.* (lit.) modificar, cambiar.
mediation | ,miːdɪ'eɪʃn | *s.i.* **1** mediación, arbitraje, intervención. **2** DER. tercería.
mediator | 'miːdɪeɪtər | *s.c.* **1** mediador, árbitro. **2** DER. tercero.
medic | 'medɪk | *s.c.* (fam.) médico; estudiante de medicina.
medical | 'medɪkl | *adj.* **1** médico, facultativo, clínico. **2** de medicina. || *s.c.* **3** (fam.) reconocimiento médico, examen facultativo.
medically | 'medɪkəlɪ | *adv.* médicamente, facultativamente.
medicament | me'dɪkəmənt | | mɪ'dɪkəmənt | *s.c.* (gen. *pl.*) (form.) medicamento, medicina.
medicated | 'medɪkeɪtɪd | *adj.* medicado, con medicina (un producto).
medication | medɪ'keɪʃn | *s.c.* e *i.* **1** (EE.UU.) medicamento, medicina. **2** tratamiento, medicación.
medicinal | me'dɪsɪnl | *adj.* medicinal, curativo.
medicinally | me'dɪsɪnəlɪ | *adv.* medicinalmente.
medicine | me'dɪsɪn | *s.c.* e *i.* **1** medicina, medicamento. **2** (fig.) remedio, medicina. || *s.i.* **3** ciencia médica, medicina. || **4 to give someone a taste/dose of their own –,** (fam.) dar a alguien su merecido, castigar a alguien con sus propias armas. **5 to take one's –,** sufrir las consecuencias, recibir su merecido.
medico | 'medɪkeu | V. **medic.**
medieval | ,medɪ'iːvl | | ,miːdɪ'iːvl | *adj.* medieval.
mediocre | ,miːdɪ'əukər | *adj.* mediocre, corriente, pobre, mediano.
mediocrity | ,miːdɪ'ɒkrɪtɪ | *s.c.* e *i.* mediocridad, medianía.
meditate | 'medɪteɪt | *v.t.* e *i.* **1 [to – (on/upon)]** meditar, pensar, reflexionar, considerar. || *v.i.* **2** REL. meditar, sumirse en estado contemplativo.
meditation | ,medɪteɪʃn | *s.i.* **1** mediación, contemplación. || *s.c.* e *i.* **2** meditación, pensamiento, reflexión, cavilación.
meditative | 'medɪtətɪv | | 'medɪteɪtɪv | *adj.* meditabundo, contemplativo.
meditatively | 'medɪtətɪvlɪ | *adv.* meditativamente.
Mediterranean | ,medɪtə'reɪnjən | *adj.* **1** mediterráneo. || *s.* **2 Mediterranean,** Mediterráneo, mar Mediterráneo.
medium | 'miːdɪəm | [*pl.* **media** o **mediums**] *adj.* **1** mediano, medio, media, intermedio (de tamaño, color, valor...). || *s.c.* **2** medio, forma, instrumento. **3** medio, ambiente. **4** [*pl.*] mediums, medio, medium (espiritista). **5** posición intermedia, medio. || **6 – term,** medio plazo. **7 – wave,** onda media. **8 to strike a happy –,** llegar a un término

medio, encontrar el punto óptimo, encontrar el punto de equilibrio.

medium-dry | 'mi:dɪəmdraɪ | *adj.* semiseco (el vino, el jerez).

medlar | 'medlər | *s.c.* BOT. níspero (la fruta y el árbol).

medley | 'medlɪ | *s.c.* **1** mezcla, variedad, mezcolanza. **2** MUS. popurrí. **3** DEP. prueba de relevos, prueba de estilos (en natación).

meek | mi:k | *adj.* **1** dulce, dócil, tímido, apacible, humilde. **2** sumiso, obediente.

meekly | 'mi:kɪ | *adv.* **1** dócilmente, tímidamente, dócilmente. **2** sumisamente, obedientemente.

meekness | 'mi:knɪs | *s.i.* **1** dulzura, timidez, docilidad, paciencia. **2** sumisión, mansedumbre, obediencia.

meet | mi:t | *[v.irr.pret.* y *p.p.* **met]** *t.* e *i.* **1** encontrarse con, reunirse con, quedar con, darse cita con, verse con. **2** presentar(se), conocer(se). **3** DEP. jugar contra, enfrentarse a, batirse con, luchar contra. || *t.* **4** ir a buscar a, ir a esperar a, ir al encuentro de, esperar la llegada de; tener correspondencia (un tren, un autobús con otro). **5** hallar, topar con, tropezar con. **6 [to – (with)]** recibir, responder, contestar: *the propos al was met with a refusal = la propuesta fue recibida con una negativa.* **7** satisfacer, cubrir, atender (una demanda, una necesidad). **8** pagar, cubrir, satisfacer, correr con (deudas, gastos). **9** enfrentarse a, arreglárselas con, salir adelante con (un problema). || *i.* **10** reunirse, congregarse (en asamblea), convocar (una reunión). **11** confluir, unirse, empalmar (calles, ríos). **12** tocar, encontrarse, rozar. || *s.c.* **13** (EE.UU.) DEP. encuentro, competición, torneo; (brit.) cacería, partida de caza. || *adj.* **14 [– (for)]** (arc.) adecuado, correcto, apropiado, conveniente. || **15 to – one's/a violent death,** encontrar la muerte, tener una muerte violenta. **16 to – one's eyes, a)** toparse con, presentársele a uno a la vista (algo que impresiona); **b)** sostener la mirada a alguien. **17 to – someone's eyes/gaze,** cruzarse las miradas, encontrarse con la mirada de alguien. **18 to – someone halfway,** llegar a un acuerdo, hacer concesiones mutuas. **19 to – up (with),** (fam.) encontrarse, quedar citados, reunirse. **20 to – with, a)** (form.) toparse con, tropezar con (una persona, una dificultad, un accidente); **b)** experimentar, sufrir (un trato); **c)** (EE.UU.) reunirse con, tener una reunión con. **21 there's more to this than meets the eye,** esto no es tan simple como parece, aquí hay gato encerrado.

meeting | 'mi:tɪŋ | *s.c.* **1** mitin, asamblea, congreso, sesión, junta. **2 [the – +** *v.sing./pl.***]** los asistentes, la concurrencia, el público, la asamblea; REL. la congregación. **3** *sing.* reunión, encuentro, cita, entrevista. **4** DEP. encuentro, competición, concurso. **5** confluencia (de ríos).

meeting-house | 'mi:tɪŋhaus | *s.c.* iglesia, capilla, templo (cuáquero).

meeting-place | 'mi:tɪŋpleɪs | *s.c.* punto de encuentro, lugar de cita.

megacycle | 'megəsaɪkl | V. **megahertz.**

megahertz | 'megəhə:ts | *s.c.* RAD. megahercio, megaciclo.

megalith | 'megəlɪθ | *s.c.* HIST. megalito.

megalomania | ˌmegələu'meɪnjə | *s.i.* megalomanía.

megalomaniac | ˌmegələu'meɪnɪæk | *adj.* megalómano.

megaphone, loudhailer | 'megəfəun | (EE.UU.) **bullhorn** *s.c.* megáfono.

megaton | 'megətʌn | *s.c.* megatón (medida de fuerza explosiva).

melancholia | ˌmelən'kəuljə | *s.i.* (arc. y form.) PSIQ. melancolía, depresión.

melancholic | ˌmelən'kɒlɪk | | ˌmelən'ka:lɪk | *adj.* (form.) melancólico, triste, lánguido.

melancholy | 'melənkəlɪ | | 'melənka:lɪ | *s.i.* **1** (form.) melancolía, tristeza, languidez, abatimiento. **2** bilis negra. || *adj.* **3** (form.) melancólico, triste. **4** entristecedor, deprimente, funesto. **5** pensativo, meditabundo.

mélange | meɪ'lɑ:nʒ | *s.sing.* mezcla, mezcolanza, colección.

melanin | 'melənɪn | *s.i.* BIOL. melanina.

mêlée | 'meleɪ | *s.c.* **1** barullo, confusión, tumulto. **2** refriega, pelea.

mellifluous | me'lɪfluəs | *adj.* (form.) melifluo, melodioso, dulce.

mellifluously | me'lɪfluəslɪ | *adv.* (form.) melodiosamente, dulcemente (sonidos, música, etc.).

mellow | 'meləu | *adj.* **1** maduro, dulce, jugoso (una fruta). **2** cálido, suave (un color). **3** dulce, melosa, suave, aterciopelada (la voz). **4** tranquilo, apacible, dulcificado (por el paso del tiempo). **5** (fam.) relajado, tranquilo; achispado, alegre (por el alcohol). **6** margosa, húmeda (la tierra). || *v.t.* e *i.* **7** suavizar(se), dulcificar(se), ablandar(se) (un color, el carácter). **8** madurar. **9** relajarse, ponerse alegre (con el alcohol).

mellowly | 'meləulɪ | *adv.* **1** dulcemente, jugosamente (sabor). **2** cálidamente, suavemente (color). **3** dulcemente, melosamente, aterciopeladamente (sonido). **4** tranquilamente, apaciblemente (en la actitud vital). **5** (fam.) relajadamente, tranquilamente (a causa del alcohol, por ejemplo).

mellowness | 'meləunɪs | *s.i.* **1** dulzura, jugosidad (sabor). **2** suavidad, condición cálida (color). **3** dulzura, melosidad, aterciopelamiento (sonido). **4** tranquilidad (vital). **5** (fam.) relajación.

melodic | mɪ'lɒdɪk | | mɪ'lɑ:dɪk | *adj.* MUS. melódico, melodioso.

melodious | mɪ'ləudjəs | *adj.* melodioso, dulce, armonioso.

melodiously | mɪ'ləudɪəslɪ | *adv.* melodiosamente, armoniosamente.

melodiousness | mɪ'ləudɪəsnɪs | *s.i.* melodiosidad, armonía.

melodrama | 'meləuˌdrɑ:mə | *s.c.* e *i.* melodrama.

melodramatic | ˌmeləudrə'mætɪk | *adj.* melodramático.

melodramatically | ˌmeləudrə'mætɪkəlɪ | *adv.* melodramáticamente.

melody | 'melədɪ | *s.c.* **1** melodía, canción. || *s.i.* **2** melodía.

melon | 'melən | *s.c* BOT. melón.

melt | melt | *v.t.* e *i.* **1** derretir(se), licuar(se), fundir(se), disolver(se). **2** (fig.) ablandar(se), enternecer(se), aplacar(se). || *v.i.* **3 [to – (away)]** esfumarse, desvanecerse, desaparecer. **4 [to – (into)]** perderse, transformarse, mezclarse (un sonido, un color con otro); esfumarse, confundirse, desaparecer (entre la multitud). || *s.i.* **5** derretimiento, licuefacción. || **7 to – down,** fundir (un metal).

melting | meltɪŋ | *s.i.* **1** licuefacción, disolución, derretimiento. || *adj.* **2** agradable, suave, tierna, dulce (la voz). || **3 in the – pot,** en formación, en discusión, sujeto a cambios. **4 – point,** punto de fusión. **5 – pot,** crisol (fig.) amalgama, confluencia (de distintas razas, nacionalidades).

member | 'membər | *s.c.* **1** miembro, socio, militante. **2** parlamentario, diputado. **3** asistente, integrante. **4** (form.) ANAT. miembro, extremidad; (lit. y euf.) pene. || **5 Member of Parliament,** parlamentario, diputado.

membership | 'membəʃɪp | | 'membərʃɪŋ | *s.i.* **1** pertenencia, calidad de socio. || *s.c.* **2 [– +** *v.sing./pl.***]** número de socios o militantes, personal afiliado.

membrane | 'membreɪn | *s.c.* e *i.* MED. membrana, tejido.

memento | mɪ'mentəu | *s.c.* recuerdo, reliquia.

memo | 'meməu | *s.c.* (fam.) V. **memorandum.**

memoir | 'memwɑ:r | *s.c.* **1** (form.) memoria, diario, recuento. **2** *[pl.]* memorias, autobiografía (de un personaje importante).

memorabilia | ˌmemərə'bɪlɪə | *s.pl.* objetos de recuerdo, recuerdos.

memorable | 'memərəbl | *adj.* memorable.

memorably | 'memərəblɪ | *adv.* memorablemente.

memoranda | ˌmemə'rændə | *pl.* de **memorandum.**

memorandum | ˌmemə'rændəm | *[pl.* **memoranda** o **memorandums**] *s.c.* **1** (form.) memorándum, nota oficial, comunicado; nota diplomática. **2** recordatorio, nota, apunte, minuta. **3** DER. contrato.

memorial | mɪ'mɔ:rɪəl | *s.c.* **1** memorial, monumento conmemorativo, rememoración. **2** petición oficial. || *adj.* **3** conmemorativo, rememorativo.

memorise V. **memorize.**

memorize | mɪ'məraɪz | (brit. **memorise**) *v.t.* memorizar, retener en la memoria, aprender de memoria.

memory | 'memərɪ | *s.c.* **1** memoria, retentiva. **2** recuerdo, reminiscencia, remembranza. 3 INF. memoria, capacidad. || **4 to commit something to –,** memorizar algo, aprender algo de memoria. **5 from –,** de memoria. **6 in – of,** en memoria de, en recuerdo de (alguien fallecido). **7 to loose one's –,** perder la memoria, no tener memoria para. **8 within living –,** que se recuerda, de que tengamos recuerdo, que recordemos los de esta generación. **9 within one's –,** que uno recuerde: *my first salary within my memory = mi primer salario que yo recuerde.*

memsahib | 'mem,sɑːhɪb | | 'mem,sɑːb | *s.c.* (arc.) señora, título de respeto que se aplicaba a la mujer blanca europea en la India.

men | men | *s.* **1** *[pl.* de **man]** || **2 men's room,** retrete de caballeros, servicio de caballeros.

menace | 'menɪs | *s.c.* e *i.* **1** amenaza, intimidación. || *s.c.* **2** (fam.) latoso, pesado, fastidioso (una persona). **3** molestia, estorbo, fastidio.

menacing | 'menɪsɪŋ | *adj.* amenazador, amenazante, intimidatorio.

menacingly | 'menɪsɪŋlɪ | *adv.* amenazadoramente, de forma intimidatoria.

ménage | me'nɑːʒ | | 'meɪnɑːʒ | *s.c.* **1 [– +** *v.sing./pl.***]** menaje del hogar, casa; familia. || **2 – a trois,** (lit.) triángulo amoroso, amor en triángulo.

menagerie | mɪ'nædʒərɪ | *s.c.* parque zoológico, colección de animales salvajes para exhibición.

mend | mend | *v.t.* **1** reparar, arreglar, componer. **2** remendar, zurcir, repasar. || *v.i.* **3** (fam.) recuperarse, reponerse, curarse, mejorar, sanar. || *s.c.* **4** remiendo, zurcido. **5** reparación, mejora. || **6 to – one's ways,** enmendarse, reformarse. **7 on the –,** (fam.) recuperándose, reponiéndose, mejorando (de salud, en los negocios).

mendacious | men'deɪʃəs | *adj.* (form.) mendaz, mentiroso, embustero, falso.

mendaciously | men'deɪʃəslɪ | *adv.* (form.) mendazmente, mentirosamente, falsamente.

mendacity | men'dæsɪtɪ | *s.i.* (form.) mendacidad, falsedad, embuste, mentira.

mending | mendɪŋ | *s.i.* **1** ropas para remendar, zurcir o reparar. **2** zurcido, arreglo (de ropas).

menfolk | 'menfəuk | *s.pl.* los hombres (de la familia), familiares masculinos.

menial | 'miːnɪəl | *adj.* **1** doméstico, modesto, bajo, servil (un trabajo). **2** de criados, de sirvientes. || *s.c.* **3** (desp.) criado, sirviente.

meningitis | ,menɪn'dʒaɪtɪs | *s.i.* MED. meningitis.

menopause | 'menəupɔːz | *s.i.* FISIOL. menopausia.

menstrual | 'menstruəl | *adj.* **1** FISIOL. menstrual. **2** mensual.

menstruate | 'menstrueɪt | *v.i.* FISIOL. menstruar.

menstruation | ,menstru'eɪʃn | *s.c.* e *i.* FISIOL. menstruación.

menswear | menswεər | *s.i.* ropa de caballero, artículos de caballero.

mental | 'mentl | *adj.* **1** mental, psíquico. **2** mental, intelectual. **3** MED. mental, psiquiátrico. **4** (argot) loco, anormal, estúpido. || **5 to make a – note of,** hacer un esfuerzo por memorizar. **6 – age,** edad mental. **7 – hospital,** hospital psiquiátrico. **8 – patient,** enfermo mental.

mentality | men'tælɪtɪ | *s.i.* **1** capacidad intelectual o mental. || *s.c.* **2** mentalidad, personalidad, carácter, forma de pensar.

mentally | 'mentəlɪ | *adv.* **1** mentalmente, intelectualmente. **2** psicológicamente.

menthol | 'menθɒl | | 'menθɔːl | | 'menθɑːl | *s.i.* QUIM. mentol.

mentholated | 'menθəleɪtəd | *adj.* mentolado, de menta.

mention | menʃn | *v.t.* **1** mencionar, hablar de, aludir, tocar, mentar, referirse a, citar a, nombrar (un tema, una persona). || *s.c.* **2** mención, alusión, referencia, cita. || **3 don't – it,** de nada, no hay de qué (para contestar al dar las gracias). **4 not to –,** además de, amén de, sin olvidar.

mentor | 'mentɔːr | *s.c.* (form.) mentor, consejero, maestro.

menu | 'menjuː | *s.c.* **1** menú, carta, lista de platos. **2** INF. menú, lista de opciones.

mercantile | məːkəntaɪl | | 'məːrkəntiːl | *adj.* **1** (form.) mercantil, comercial. || **2 – marine,** marina mercante.

mercenary | 'məːsɪnərɪ | *adj.* **1** (desp.) mercenario, pesetero, interesado. || *s.c.* **2** MIL. mercenario.

merchandise | 'məːtʃəndaɪz | *s.i.* **1** mercancía, género. || *v.t.* **2** comerciar con, comerciar en, promover la venta de, comercializar, vender.

merchant | 'məːtʃənt | *s.c.* **1** comerciante, negociante, traficante, mercader. || *adj.* **2** mercante. **3** comercial. || **4 – bank,** COM. banco comercial, banco de negocios. **5 – sailor,** marino mercante. **6 – ship,** buque mercante.

merciful | 'məːsɪfʊl | *adj.* **1** misericordioso, indulgente, compasivo, clemente, humano. **2** afortunado, venturoso, placentero.

mercifully | 'məːsɪfʊlɪ | *adv.* **1** afortunadamente, por ventura. **2** compasivamente, indulgentemente, misericordiosamente.

merciless | 'məːsɪlɪs | *adj.* despiadado, inhumano, cruel, implacable.

mercilessly | 'məːsɪlɪslɪ | *adv.* despiadadamente, de modo inhumano, implacablemente, cruelmente.

mercurial | məː'kjʊərɪəl | *adj.* **1** (lit.) imprevisible, veleidoso, variable, explosivo (una persona, el carácter). **2** hábil, sagaz, astuto. **3** mercurial, de Mercurio.

mercury | 'məːkjurɪ | *s.i.* **1** QUIM. mercurio. **2** (EE.UU.) temperatura. || *s.c.* **3 Mercury,** Mercurio (planeta, dios mensajero). **4** BOT. mercurial, malcoraje.

mercy | 'məːsɪ | *s.i.* **1** misericordia, compasión, clemencia. **2** (fam.) suerte, bendición, consuelo. || **3 at the – of,** a merced de. **4 to be left to the mercies/the tender mercies of,** (hum.) verse abandonado a las piadosas manos de. **5 in one's –,** gracias a su generosidad. **6 – killing,** eutanasia, muerte piadosa. **7 to throw oneself upon someone's –,** suplicar de rodillas a alguien, pedir clemencia a alguien.

mere | mɪər | *adj.* **1** no *comp.* mero, solo, simple, único, puro. **2** no más de, no más que: *a mere 2% = no más de un 2%, un 2% pelado.* || *s.c.* **3** (brit.) lago, laguna (generalmente en combinación con otro nombre): *Windermere.* **4** (arc.) frontera.

merely | mɪəlɪ | *adv.* **1** meramente, simplemente, solamente, únicamente. || **2 not –,** no solo.

meretricious | ,merɪ'trɪʃəs | *adj.* (form.) falso, engañoso, de relumbrón, de oropel, de apariencia.

meretriciously | ,merɪ'trɪʃəslɪ | *adv.* (form.) falsamente, engañosamente.

meretriciousness | ,merɪ'trɪʃəsnɪs | *s.i.* (form.) falsedad, engaño.

merge | məːdʒ | *v.t.* e *i.* **1** fundir(se), mezclar(se), confundir(se). **2** COM. fusionar(se).

merger | 'məːdʒər | *s.c.* **1** COM. fusión, unión, incorporación. **2** DER. fusión, absorción (de una ley por otra).

meridian | mə'rɪdɪən | *s.c.* **1** GEOG. meridiano. **2 [the –]** (form.) el punto, el auge, el culmen, la apoteosis, el súmmum.

meridional | mə'rɪdɪənl | *adj.* GEOG. meridional.

meringue | mə'ræŋ | *s.c.* e *i.* merengue.

merit | 'merɪt | *s.i.* **1** mérito, gratificación, valor. || *s.c.* **2** *pl.* excelencias, cualidades, ventajas. || *v.t.* **3** (form.) merecer, ser digno de. || *v.i.* **4** hacer méritos. || **5 to have the – of being,** tener el mérito de ser. **6 on one's –,** por sus propios méritos, según las circunstancias.

meritocracy | ,merɪ'tɒkrəsɪ | | ,merɪ'↓ tɑːkrəsɪ | *s.c.* **1** meritocracia. **2 [the – +** *v.sing./pl.***]** la élite (intelectual, social).

meritorious | ,merɪ'tɔːrɪəs | *adj.* (form.) meritorio, loable, digno, sobresaliente.

meritoriously | ,merɪ'tɔːrɪəslɪ | *adv.* (form.) meritoriamente, loablemente, dignamente.

merlin | 'məːlɪn | *s.c.* ZOOL. azor (pájaro).

mermaid | 'məːmeɪd | *m.* **(merman)**, *s.c.* sirena.

merrily | 'merɪlɪ | *adv.* alegremente, con alborozo.

merriment | 'merɪmənt | *s.i.* **1** hilaridad, diversión. **2** regocijo, alegría, alborozo, juerga, jarana.

merry | 'merɪ | *adj.* **1** alegre, feliz, contento, jovial, festivo. **2** divertido, gracioso, simpático. **3** (brit. y fam.) achispado, contento (por el alcohol). || **4 to make –,** (fam. y lit.) divertirse, pasarlo bien (comiendo, bebiendo). **5 Merry Christmas,** Felices Navidades.

merry-go-round | 'merɪgəʊˌraʊnd | *s.c.* carrusel, tiovivo, caballitos.

merry-making | 'merɪˌmeɪkɪŋ | *s.i.* (lit.) jolgorio, jarana, juerga.

mesh | meʃ | *s.c.* e *i.* **1** malla, trama. **2** malla, poro, anilla (en un tejido de red). **3** (fig.) trama, trampa. **4** MEC. engranaje. || *v.i.* **5** **[to – (with)]** MEC. engranar, encajar. **6** concordar, encajar, cuadrar. || *v.t.* e *i.* **7** enredar(se), entretejer(se).

mesmerize | 'mezmərаɪz | (brit. **mesmerise**) *v.t.* **1** fascinar, hechizar, deslumbrar. **2** (arc.) hipnotizar.

mesmerizing | 'mezmərаɪzɪŋ | *adj.* fascinante, deslumbrante, hechizante.

mess | mes | *s.i.* **1** desorden, revoltijo, caos, suciedad. **2** (fam.) confusión, embrollo, lío, problema. || *s.c.* **3** [*sing.*] (fam.) persona desarreglada, persona desaliñada; desastre, horror (una cosa): *this painting is a mess = este cuadro es un desastre.* **4** MIL. comedor de cuartel. **5** plato, ración; MIL. rancho. || *s.c.* e *i.* **6** basura, porquería; heces (de animales). || *v.i.* **7** MIL. tomar el rancho, hacer el rancho. || **8 in a –,** hecho un lío, revuelto, desordenado. **9 to – about/** (EE.UU.) **around,** (fam.) **a)** perder el tiempo en tonterías, entretenerse en tonterías; **b)** decir tonterías, hacer el tonto; **c)** liar, confundir, fastidiar (a alguien). **10 to – about with,** pasar el tiempo con, entretener el ocio con, experimentar con. **11 to – up,** (fam.) desordenar, revolver, manchar, armar el lío (en un lugar). **12 to – with,** mezclarse, relacionarse, involucrarse (en algo peligroso). **13 no messing,** (brit. y fam.) no miento, es la pura verdad.

message | 'mesɪdʒ | *s.c.* **1** mensaje, nota, encargo, recado, aviso. **2** mensaje, sentido, tema. || **3 to get the –,** captar la insinuación, entender, comprender, darse cuenta, darse por enterado.

messenger | 'mesɪndʒər | *s.c.* **1** mensajero, recadero, correo. **2** profeta, precursor. **3** (arc.) heraldo. **4** MAR. virador, calabrote. || **5 – boy,** chico de los recados, mensajero.

messiah | mɪ'saɪə | *s.sing.* **1** REL. **Messiah,** Mesías. || *s.c.* **2** (fig.) mesías, profeta.

messianic | ˌmesɪ'ænɪk | *adj.* (form.) mesiánico.

messily | 'mesɪlɪ | *adv.* **1** desordenadamente, desaliñadamente. **2** confusamente.

Messrs | 'mesəz | | 'mesərz | *s.pl.* de **Mr.** Señores (gen. ante 2 o más apellidos en nombres de empresas, firmas).

mess-up | 'mesʌp | *s.c.* **1** (fam.) lío, embrollo, enredo. **2** fracaso, error.

messy | 'mesɪ | *adj.* **1** desordenado, descuidado, desaliñado, sucio, caótico (un lugar, una persona). **2** confuso, complicado, poco claro (un asunto).

met | met | **1** *[pret.* y *p.p.* de **meet]** || **2** *abreviatura* de **meteorological, metaphore, metropolitan** y **metaphisic.**

metabolic | ˌmetə'bɒlɪk | *adj.* FISIOL. metabólico.

metabolise V. **metabolize.**

metabolism | mə'tæbəlɪzəm | *s.c.* e *i.* FISIOL. metabolismo.

metabolize | mə'tæbəlaɪz | (también **metabolise**) *v.t.* metabolizar.

metal | 'metl | *s.c.* e *i.* **1** metal. **2** (fig.) temple, brío, fortaleza. **3** (brit.) gravilla, grava, cascajo. **4** vidrio fundido. **5** hierro fundido. **6** caracteres de imprenta. **7** [*pl.*] (brit.) raíles. || (brit.) **metall** *v.t.* **8** (arc.) cubrir con grava, con cascajo. || *adj.* **9** de metal, metálico.

metalled | 'metld | *adj.* cubierto de gravilla, de cascajo.

metallic | mɪ'tælɪk | *adj.* **1** metálico, de metal. **2** metalizado (un color). **3** (fig.) metálica, desagradable, bronca (la voz). **4** acre, amargo, avinagrado, fermentado (un sabor, un alimento).

metallurgist | me'tælədʒɪst | *s.c.* metalúrgico.

metallurgy | me'tælədʒɪ | *s.i.* metalurgia.

metalwork | 'metlwɜːk | | 'metlwəːrk | *s.i.* **1** artesanía del metal, metalistería. **2** metal, parte metálica (de un objeto).

metamorphose | ˌmetə'mɔːfəʊz | | ˌme-tə'mɔːrfəʊz | *v.t.* e *i.* **[to – (from /into)]** metamorfosear(se), transfigurar(se), transformar(se).

metamorphoses | ˌmetə'mɔːfəsiːz | *pl.* de **metamorphosis.**

metamorphosis | ˌmetə'mɔːfəsɪs | [*pl.* **metamorphoses**] *s.c.* e *i.* (form.) metamorfosis, transformación.

metaphor | 'metəfər | *s.c.* e *i.* **1** LIT. metáfora. || **2 to mix one's metaphors,** salirle a uno una frase disparatada, decir un disparate (por la mezcla de dos palabras, dos frases).

metaphorical | ˌmetə'fɒrɪkl | | ˌmetə'fɔːrɪkl | | ˌmetə'fɑːrɪkl | *adj.* metafórico.

metaphorically | ˌmetə'fɒrɪklɪ | *adv.* metafóricamente.

metaphysical | ˌmetə'fɪzɪkl | *adj.* **1** *no comp.* FIL. metafísico. **2** (form.) metafísico, abstracto. **3** (brit.) LIT. metafísico (movimiento poético del siglo XVII).

metaphysics | ˌmetə'fɪzɪks | *s.i.* FIL. metafísica.

mete | miːt | *v.t.* **1** **[to – out]** imponer, sancionar con, condenar a. **2** (arc.) medir, mensurar. || *s.c.* **3** límite, frontera.

meteor | 'miːtɪər | *s.c.* ASTR. meteoro, meteorito, bólido.

meteoric | ˌmiːtɪ'ɒrɪk | *adj.* **1** meteórico. **2** (fig.) rápido, deslumbrante.

meteorite | 'miːtjəraɪt | *s.c.* meteorito, bólido.

meteorological | ˌmiːtɪərə'lɒdʒɪkl | *adj.* meteorológico.

meteorologist | ˌmiːtɪə'rɒlədʒɪst | *s.c.* meteorólogo.

meteorology | ˌmiːtɪə'rɒlədʒɪ | *s.i.* meteorología.

meter | 'miːtər | *s.c.* **1** contador, medidor (de gas, electricidad); taxímetro; parquímetro. **2** (EE.UU.) metro (unidad de medida). || *v.t.* **3** medir con contador, taxímetro o parquímetro.

methadone | 'meθədəʊn | *s.i.* QUIM. metadona.

methane | 'miːθeɪn | | 'meθeɪn | *s.i.* QUIM. metano.

method | 'meθəd | *s.c.* **1** método, procedimiento, técnica, sistema. || *s.i.* **2** método, metodología, línea: *no clear scientific method = un método no muy científico.* || **3 there's – in someone's madness,** hay método en su locura, no está tan loco como parece por su modo de actuar.

methodical | mɪ'θɒdɪkl | | ˌmɪ'θɑːdɪkl | *adj.* metódico, sistemático, ordenado, cuidadoso.

methodically | mɪ'θɒdɪkəlɪ | *adv.* metódicamente, sistemáticamente, ordenadamente.

Methodism | 'meθədɪzəm | *s.i.* REL. Metodismo.

Methodist | 'meθədɪst | *s.c.* REL. metodista.

methodology | ˌmeθə'dɒlədʒɪ | | ˌmeθə'dɑːlədʒɪ | *s.c.* e *i.* metodología.

meths, methylated spirit | meθs | *s.i.* (brit.) alcohol desnaturalizado, alcohol metílico.

meticulous | mɪ'tɪkjʊləs | *adj.* meticuloso, minucioso, quisquilloso, exigente, preciso.

meticulously | mɪ'tɪkjʊləslɪ | *adv.* meticulosamente, minuciosamente, de forma precisa, con exigencia.

meticulousness | mɪ'tɪkjʊləsnɪs | *s.i.* meticulosidad, minuciosidad, precisión.

metier | 'metɪeɪ | | 'meɪtɪeɪ | | me'tjeɪ | *s.c.* trabajo, profesión, oficio.

metre | 'miːtər | (EE.UU. **meter**) *s.c.* **1** metro (unidad de medida). || *s.c.* e *i.* **2** LIT. metro, medida.

metric | 'metrɪk | *adj.* **1** métrico. || **2 – system,** sistema métrico. **3 – ton,** tonelada métrica.

metrication | ˌmetrɪ'keɪʃn | *s.i.* proceso de cambio del sistema imperial al métrico.

metro | 'metrəʊ | *s.c.* [gen. *sing.*] metro, metropolitano.

metronome | 'metrənəʊm | *s.c.* MUS. metrónomo.

metropolis | mɪ'trɒpəlɪs | mɪ'trɑːpəlɪs | *s.c.* (form.) metrópolis, capital.

metropolitan | ˌmetrə'pɒlɪtən | | ˌmetrə'pɑːlɪtən | *adj.* **1** metropolitano. || *s.c.* **2** REL. obispo metropolitano (de la iglesia ortodoxa). || **3 Metropolitan Police,** Policía Metropolitana (de Londres).

mettle | 'metl | *s.i.* **1** (form.) coraje, temple, valor, brío. || **2 on one's –,** (arc.) dispuesto a mostrar lo que uno vale, dispuesto a mostrar lo que uno es capaz de hacer. **3 to show/prove one's –,** dar pruebas de su valor.

mew | mjuː | *v.i.* **1** maullar, mallar. **2** mudar la pluma, cambiar la pluma (un halcón). **3** encerrar en jaula (a un halcón cuando cambia de pluma). || *s.c.* **4** maullido. **5** [*pl.*] callejón trasero, callejón de garajes, (arc.) callejuela de caballerizas (en la parte trasera de las casas). **6** escondite, lugar secreto, guari-

da. **7** jaula para halcones (cuando cambian de pluma).
Mexican | 'meksɪkən | *adj.* **1** mejicano, de Méjico. || *s.c.* **2** mejicano.
Mexico | 'meksɪkəʊ | *s.sing.* Méjico.
mezzanine | 'metsəniːn | | 'mezəniːn | *s.c.* entresuelo.
mezzo | ˌmedzəʊ | *s.c.* e *i.* **1** (fam.) MUS. mezzo-soprano, contralto. || *adv.* **2** MUS. mezzo, bastante, no demasiado.
mezzo-soprano | ˌmedzəʊsə'prɑːnəʊ | *s.c.* e *i.* mezzo, contralto.
miaow | miː'aʊ | (EE.UU.) **mew.** *v.i.* maullar, mayar.
miasma | mɪ'æzmə | *s.c.* e *i.* **1** (lit.) miasma, hedor, hediondez, olor fétido, emanación nociva. **2** influencia demoniaca, influencia nociva.
mica | 'maɪkə | *s.i.* MIN. mica.
mice | maɪs | *pl.* de **mouse.**
mickey | 'mɪkɪ | (EE.UU. **mickey Finn**) *s.i.* **1** bebida alcohólica a la que se ha añadido droga (para dejar inconsciente a alguien). || **2 to take the – out of someone,** (fam.) tomar el pelo a alguien.
micro | 'maɪkrəʊ | *s.c.* **1** (fam.) INF. microordenador, ordenador personal. || *prefijo* **2** micro, pequeñísimo: *microbiology = microbiología.*
microbe | 'maɪkəʊb | *s.c.* microbio, microorganismo.
microbiological | ˌmaɪkrəʊbaɪə'lɒdʒɪkl | | ˌmaɪkrəʊbaɪə'lɑːdʒɪkl | *adj.* microbiológico.
microbiologist | ˌmaɪkrəʊbaɪ'ɒlədʒɪst | | ˌmaɪkrəʊbaɪ'ɑːlɒdʒɪst | *s.c.* microbiólogo.
microbiology | ˌmaɪkrəʊbaɪ'ɒlədʒɪ | | ˌmaɪkrəʊbaɪ'ɑːlədʒɪ | *s.i.* microbiología.
microchip | 'maɪkrəʊˌtʃɪp | *s.c.* INF. microchip.
microcomputer | ˌmaɪkrəʊkəm'pjuːtər | *s.c.* microordenador, ordenador personal.
microcosm | 'maɪkrəʊkɒzəm | *s.c.* microcosmo.
microelectronics | 'maɪkrəʊˌɪlək'trɒnɪks | *s.i.* microelectrónica.
microfiche | 'maɪkrəʊfiːʃ | *s.c.* e *i.* microficha.
microfilm | 'maɪkrəʊfɪlm | *s.c.* e *i.* **1** microfilm. || *v.t.* **2** microfilmar, hacer un microfilm.
micro-organism | ˌmaɪkrəʊ'ɔːgənɪzəm | | ˌmaɪkrəʊ'ɔːrgənɪzəm | *s.c.* BIOL. microorganismo, microbio.
microphone | 'maɪkrəfəʊn | *s.c.* micrófono.
microprocessor | ˌmaɪkrəʊ'prəʊsesər | *s.c.* microprocesador.
microscopic | ˌmaɪkrə'skɒpɪk | | ˌmaɪkrə'skɑːpɪk | *adj.* **1** microscópico, a través de microscopio. **2** microscópico, extremadamente pequeño. **3** detallado, minucioso.
microscopically | ˌmaɪkrə'skɒpɪkəlɪ | *adv.* **1** microscópicamente. **2** minuciosamente, detalladamente.
microsecond | ˌmaɪkrəʊ'sekənd | *s.c.* microsegundo.
microwave | 'maɪkrəweɪv | *s.c.* **1** RAD. microonda. **2** microondas, horno de microondas.
mid- | mɪd | *prefijo* **1** medio, en medio de, a mediados de. **2** pleno: *in midwinter = en pleno invierno.* || *adj.* **3** medio, central.
mid-air | ˌmɪd'eər | *s.i.* punto en el aire, región aérea: *in mid-air = en el aire.*
midday | 'mɪddeɪ | *s.i.* mediodía.
middle | 'mɪdl | *s.c.* [gen. *sing.*] **1** medio, parte central, mitad, núcleo. **2** (fam.) cintura, talle. || *adj.* **3** medio, de en medio, intermedio, central. || *v.t.* **4** DEP. centrar la pelota. **5** MAR. plegar velas. || **6 down the –,** justo por la mitad, por el centro (al cortar o partir algo). **7 in the – of,** cuando, a mitad de (un proceso, de una tarea). **8 in the – of nowhere,** donde Cristo dio las tres voces.
middle-age | ˌmɪdˌl'eɪdʒ | *s.i.* **1** mediana edad, edad madura. || **2 – spread,** (fam. y hum.) michelines, grasa alrededor de la cintura.
middle-aged | ˌmɪdˌl'eɪdʒd | *adj.* de mediana edad, cuarentón.
middle-brow | 'mɪdlbraʊ | *adj.* apto para el gran público, sin pretensiones, poco intelectual, de divulgación (un libro, música, pintura).
middle-class | ˌmɪdl'klɑːs | *s.c.* **1** clase media, burguesía. || *adj.* **2** de clase media, burgués.
middle-distance | ˌmidl'dɪstəns | *s.sing.* **1** segundo plano. **2** DEP. carrera de medio fondo.
middle-name | ˌmɪdlneɪm | *s.c.* segundo nombre.
middle-school | 'mɪdlskuːl | *s.c.* (brit.) escuela de ciclo medio (de 9 a 13 años).
middleman | 'mɪdlmæn | *s.c.* COM. intermediario.
middle-of-the-road | ˌmɪdləvðə'rəʊd | *adj.* **1** moderado, de centro (un gobierno, un político). **2** indeciso, vacilante, fluctuante. **3** música popular.
middling | 'mɪdlɪŋ | *adj.* **1** regular, mediano, mediocre, del montón. || *adv.* **2** (fam.) regular: *"How is your dad?" "Well, middling" = "¿Cómo está tu papá?" "Tirando".* **3** bastante, medianamente.
midge | mɪdʒ | *s.c.* mosquito.
midget | 'mɪdʒit | *s.c.* **1** enano, pequeño (una persona). **2** miniatura. || *adj.* **3** en miniatura, diminuto, muy pequeño.
midnight | 'mɪdnaɪt | *s.i.* **1** media noche. || *adj.* **2** de media noche. || **3 to burn the middle – oil,** quedarse trabajando o estudiando hasta muy tarde, (fig.) quemarse las cejas trabajando.
midpoint | 'mɪdpɔɪnt | *s.c.* e *i.* punto medio, centro, mitad.
midriff | 'mɪdrif | *s.c.* **1** ANAT. diafragma. **2** (fig.) estómago.
midships | 'mɪdʃɪps | V. **amidships.**
midst | mɪdst | *prep.* LIT. **1** en medio de. || **2 in the – of,** en pleno, en medio de. **3 in our –/in our very –,** entre nosotros.
midstream | ˌmɪd'striːm | *s.i.* **1** medio de la corriente, centro de la corriente (de un río). || **2 to stop/pause in –,** hacer una pausa, parar de hablar.
midsummer | 'mɪdˌsʌmər | *s.i.* **1** pleno verano. **2** solsticio de verano. || **3 – day,** 24 de junio (fiesta del verano). **4 – madness,** locura total.
midway | ˌmɪd'weɪ | *adv.* **1** a medio camino (entre dos puntos). **2** hacia la mitad (de un período de tiempo). || *adj.* **3** intermedio, situado a medio camino.
midweek | ˌmɪd'wiːk | *adv.* **1** a media semana, entre semana. || *adj.* **2** de entre semana.
midwife | 'mɪdwaɪʃ | *s.c.* comadrona.
midwifery | 'mɪdwɪfərɪ | *s.i.* MED. obstetricia, partería.
midwinter | ˌmɪd'wɪntər | *s.i.* **1** pleno invierno. **2** solsticio de invierno.
mien | miːn | *s.i.* semblante; expresión, apariencia, aire (de la cara).
miffed | mɪft | *adj.* **[– (at/by)]** (fam.) ofendido, enfadado.
might | mait | *v.t.* **1** ser posible, tener posibilidad, quizá (indica posibilidad o probabilidad): *I might see her again = quizá la vea otra vez.* **2** *[pret.* de **may***]* poder, ser posible: *I thought he might say so = pensé que él podía decir eso.* **3** (brit. y form.) poder, tener permiso (más amablemente que con **may**). **4** deber, ser necesario o conveniente (similar a **should** o a **ought to**): *you might have helped her = deberías haberla ayudado.* || *s.i.* **5** (form.) poder, fuerza, energía, vigor, influencia. || **6 with all one's –/with all one's – and main,** con todas sus fuerzas, a más no poder.
OBS. **might** lo mismo que **may** va seguido por un infinitivo sin **to** y no lleva **s** en la 3a. persona del *sing.* Habitualmente expresa una posibilidad más remota e incierta que **may.** Algunas veces se utiliza en lugar del auxiliar en preguntas: *who might you be? = ¿quién es usted?; what might that mean? = ¿qué significa eso?*
mightily | 'maɪtɪlɪ | *adv.* **1** (lit.) con fuerza, poderosamente. **2** (brit. y p.u.) muy, extremadamente.
mightn't | 'maɪtnt | contracción de **might not.**
might've | 'maɪtəv | contracción de **might have.**
mighty | 'maɪtɪ | *adj.* (lit.) **1** poderoso, fuerte. **2** grandioso, inmenso. || *adv.* **3** (EE.UU. fam.) muy, extremadamente: *mighty difficult = extremadamente difícil.*
migraine | 'miːgreɪn | *s.i.* MED. migraña, jaqueca, dolor de cabeza.
migrant | 'maɪgrənt | *s.c.* **1** temporero, trabajador ambulante. **2** animal migratorio. || *adj.* **3** migratorio.
migrate | maɪ'greɪt | *v.i.* **1** migrar, emigrar, trasladarse (personas). **2** ZOOL. trashumar, migrar.
migration | maɪ'greɪʃn | *s.i.* **1** migración, trashumancia. **2** QUIM. migración (de átomos).
migratory | 'maɪgrətərɪ | *adj.* ZOOL. migratorio.

mike | maɪk | *s.c.* (fam.) micro, micrófono.
milch | mɪltʃ | *adj.* lechera, que da leche (una vaca, una cabra).
mild | maɪld | *adj.* agradable, dulce, sereno, cariñoso, apacible, de buen carácter. **2** suave, templado, benigno, bonancible (el tiempo). **3** suave, ligera (una comida, una bebida). **4** blando, leve (un castigo, una riña). **5** MED. leve. **6** (brit.) suave (un tipo de cerveza). || **7 – steel,** MET. acero maleable.
mildew | 'mɪldjuː | *s.i.* **1** moho. **2** AGR. mildiu de la vid, añublo del trigo. || *v.t.* e *i.* **3** enmohecer(se).
mildewed | 'mɪldjuːd | *adj.* enmohecido, atacado por el moho.
mildly | maɪldlɪ | *adv.* **1** suavemente, apaciblemente, dulcemente. **2** ligeramente. || **3 to put it –,** por decirlo de alguna manera, por no decir más, por no decir una grosería.
mild-mannered | 'maɪldmænəd | *adj.* amable, cortés, delicado.
mildness | 'maɪldnɪs | *s.i.* **1** suavidad, dulzura, mansedumbre. **2** levedad, ligereza.
mile | maɪl | *s.c.* **1** milla (1.609 metros). **2** [*pl.*] (fam.) mucho, un montón, a años luz, a cien leguas. || **3 to be miles away,** estar en las nubes, estar en Babia, írsele a uno el santo al cielo. **4 to run a –,** (fam.) correr como alma que lleva el diablo (ante un trabajo, algo que asusta). **5 to see/recognize a – off,** ver o reconocer a la legua, darse cuenta en seguida. **6 to stick/stand out a –,** (fam.) sobresalir por encima de, estar a millas de distancia.
mileage | 'maɪlɪdʒ | *s.c.* [gen. *sing.*] **1** distancia recorrida en millas, kilometraje. **2** gastos de desplazamiento. **3** (fam.) ventaja, partido, rendimiento, utilidad, tajada.
milepost | 'maɪlpəust | *s.c.* **1** poste, mojón. **2** (fig.) hito.
miler | 'maɪlər | *s.c.* (fam) DEP. corredor especialista en la milla.
milestone | 'maɪlstəun | *s.c.* **1** mojón, señal. **2** (fig.) hito, logro, acontecimiento importante (histórico, para una persona).
milieu | 'miːljəː | *s.c.* (form.) medio social, entorno, ambiente, medio.
militancy | 'mɪlɪtənsi | *s.i.* **1** militancia, activismo (político, social). **2** combatividad, beligerancia.
militant | 'mɪlɪtənt | *s.c.* **1** militante, activista, luchador. || *adj.* **2** agresivo, hostil, beligerante, combativo.
militantly | 'mɪlɪtəntlɪ | *adv.* **1** enérgicamente, activamente. **2** agresivamente.
militarily | 'mɪlɪtərɪlɪ | *adv.* militarmente.
militarism | 'mɪlɪtərɪzəm | *s.i.* militarismo.
militarist | 'mɪlɪtərɪst | *s.c.* **1** militarista. || *adj.* **2** militarista.
militaristic | mɪlɪtə'rɪstɪk | *adj.* militarista, armamentista.
militarized | 'mɪlɪtəraɪzd | (brit.) **militarised.** *adj.* militarizado, organizado militarmente.
military | 'mɪlɪtərɪ | *adj.* **1** militar, relativo a las fuerzas armadas. || *s.pl.* **2 [the –]** las fuerzas armadas, los militares. || **3 – police,** policía militar. **4 – policeman,** miembro de la policía militar.
militate | 'mɪlɪteɪt | *v.t.* **[to – (against)] 1** (form.) debilitar, obstaculizar, servir como razón. **2** militar.
militia | mɪ'lɪʃə | *s.c.* e *i.* milicia.
militiaman | mɪ'lɪʃəmən | *s.c.* miliciano, miembro de la milicia.
milk | milk | *s.i.* **1** leche. **2** producto lácteo. **3** jugo de coco. || *v.t.* **4** ordeñar. **5** (desp.) explotar, aprovecharse de, chupar (dinero). **6** presionar, exprimir, sacar. || *v.i.* **7** dar leche, proporcionar leche, suministrar leche. **8** añadir leche. || **9 to cry over spilt –,** lamentar lo que ya no tiene remedio. **10 – float,** (brit. y fam.) camioneta del repartidor de leche. **11 – tooth,** diente de leche.
milker | 'mɪlkər | *s.c.* (fam.) animal que da mucha leche.
milkiness | 'mɪlkɪnɪs | *s.i.* lechosidad (en textura).
milking | mɪlkɪŋ | *s.i.* tarea de ordeñar, ordeño.
milking-machine | 'mɪlkɪŋməʃiːn | *s.c.* máquina automática de ordeño.
milkmaid | 'mɪlkmeɪd | *s.c.* lechera, mujer que ordeña las vacas.
milkman | 'mɪlkmən | *s.c.* lechero, repartidor de leche.
milkshake | 'mɪlkʃeɪk | *s.c.* **1** (brit.) batido (con leche como base). **2** (EE.UU.) leche malteada.
milksop | 'mɪlksɒp | *s.c.* (desp.) llorica (especialmente con chicos).
milk-white | ˌmɪlk'waɪt | *adj.* lechoso (color).
milky | 'mɪlki | *adj.* **1** pálido, lechoso, blanquecino. **2** con leche: *milky coffee = café con leche (con mucha leche).* **3** (fig.) tierno, suave, dulce. || **4 Milky Way,** Vía Láctea.
milord | mɪ'lɔːd | *s.c.* señor (forma de llamar a nobles).
mill | mɪl | *s.c.* **1** molino, aceña, molinejo. **2** molinillo de cocina. **3** fábrica, taller (de tejidos, acero). **4** MEC. fresadora, laminadora. **5** prensa para acuñar moneda. || *v.t.* **6** moler, triturar. **7** acordonar (moneda). **8** MEC. fresar, laminar. **9** batir. **10** abatanar el paño. || **11 to put someone through the –,** hacérselas pasar moradas a alguien, hacer pasar muchos sufrimientos a alguien.
mill-dam | 'mɪldæm | *s.c.* presa de molino.
millennium | mɪ'lenɪəm | *s.c.* **1** milenio, milenario. **2** (fig.) período de paz y prosperidad.
miller | 'mɪlər | *s.c.* **1** molinero. **2** ZOOL. polilla, mariposa nocturna.
millet | 'mɪlɪt | *s.i.* BOT. mijo, semilla de mijo.
milligram | 'mɪlɪgrem | *s.c.* miligramo.
millilitre | 'mɪlɪliːtər | *s.c.* mililitro.
millimetre | 'mɪlɪˌmiːtər | *s.c.* milímetro.
milliner | 'mɪlɪnər | *s.c.* sombrerero (de sombreros de señora).
millinery | 'mɪlɪnərɪ | *s.i.* sombrerería, artículos de sombrerería.
milling | 'mɪlɪŋ | *s.i.* **1** molienda. **2** cordoncillo (de la moneda). **3** fresado (del metal). || *adj.* **4** errabundo, errático, incierto.
million | 'mɪljən | *s.c.num.* **1** millón. || **2 millions,** (fig.) millones, una gran cantidad.
millionaire | ˌmɪljə'neər | *s.c.* millonario.
millionth | 'mɪljənθ | *s.c.ord.* **1** millonésimo. **2** millonésima parte (fracción). || *adj.ord.* **3** millonésimo.
millipede | 'mɪlɪpiːd | *s.c.* ZOOL. milpiés, miriápodo, cochinilla.
millstone | 'mɪlstəun | *s.c.* **1** muela, rueda de molino. **2** (fig.) lastre. || **3 a – round one's neck,** losa que uno lleva encima, grave problema que uno tiene que afrontar.
mime | maɪm | *s.i.* **1** mímica, gesticulación, expresión por gestos. **2** pantomima, mimo. **3** actor de mimo. || *v.t.* **4** representar con mímica, expresar con gestos. || *v.i.* **5** actuar como mimo, ser actor de mímica.
mimeograph | 'mɪmɪəgrɑːf | *s.c.* **1** mimógrafo. **2** mimeografía, copia mimeográfica. || *v.i.* **3** reproducir copias en el mimógrafo.
mimetic | mɪ'metɪk | *adj.* (form.) mimético, imitativo.
mimic | 'mɪmɪk | *v.t.* **1** imitar, parodiar, remedar (voces, acentos, expresiones). **2** fingir, simular (que uno es otra persona). || *s.c.* **3** imitador, parodiador. || *adj.* **4** simulado, fingido. **5** BIOL. mimético.
mimicry | 'mɪmɪkrɪ | *s.i.* **1** imitación, simulación, remedo. **2** BOT. mimetismo.
minaret | 'mɪnəret | *s.c.* ARQ. minarete, alminar.
minatory | 'mɪnətərɪ | *adj.* (form.) amenazante, amenazador.
mince | mɪns | *s.i.* **1** (brit.) carne picada. || *v.t.* **2** hacer picadillo, picar carne. **3** hablar afectadamente, amaneradamente. || *v.i.* **4** andar de manera afeminada. || **5 not to – one's words,** no andarse con rodeos, no tener pelos en la lengua.
minced | mɪnst | *adj.* (brit.) picada (carne de buey o vaca).
mincemeat | 'mɪnsmiːt | *s.i.* **1** masa o pasta a base de fruta y frutos secos triturados (para hacer pastelitos de Navidad). **2** (EE.UU.) carne picada. || **3 to make – of someone,** (fam. y fig.) hacer picadillo a alguien, hacer pedazos a alguien (en una discusión).
mince-pie | ˌmins'paɪ | *s.c.* pastel relleno de fruta y frutos secos (típico de Navidad).
mincer | mɪnsər | *s.c.* máquina de picar, picadora.
mincing | mɪnsɪŋ | *adj.* afectado, amanerado, afeminado (al andar, al hablar).

mincingly | 'mɪnsɪŋlɪ | *adv.* de forma amanerada, con afectación.
mind | maɪnd | *s.c.* e *i.* **1** mente, cabeza, pensamiento. **2** deseo, intención, voluntad, cabeza. || *s.c.* **3** [gen. *sing.*] inteligencia, poder mental, intelecto, cerebro, entendimiento. **4** atención, esmero, interés. **5** opinión, juicio, parecer. **6** cerebro, persona, sabio, portento, inteligente. **7** mentalidad. || *s.i.* **8** memoria, retentiva. **9** espíritu, mente (opuesto al cuerpo). **10** inclinación. || *v.t.* **11** cuidar, atender, vigilar, estar al cuidado de. **12** preocuparse por, considerar, hacer caso de. **13** sentirse molesto por, oponerse a, tener inconveniente en: *do you mind the music? = ¿te molesta la música?* **14** acordarse de, no olvidar hacer algo. **15** fijarse, prestar atención, tener cuidado con/en: *mind the step = ten cuidado con el escalón.* || *v.i.* **16** preocuparse, importarle a uno, oponerse, objetar. || **17 a closed –,** retrógrado, conservador, persona de mente cerrada. **18 a load/weight off one's –,** quitarse un peso de encima. **19 an open –,** abierto, progresista, de mente amplia, sin ideas preconcebidas. **20 at the back of one's –,** recordar vagamente, tener recuerdos imprecisos. **21 to bear/keep in –,** tener presente, tener en cuenta. **22 bored/ stoned out of one's –,** (fam.) mortalmente aburrido; colgado, ido (a causa de drogas). **23 to bring/call to –,** traer a la memoria, recordar algo. **24 to change one's –,** cambiar de opinión, cambiar de parecer. **25 to change someone's –,** convencer a alguien de, persuadir a alguien, hacer que alguien cambie de opinión, de decisión. **26 don't – me,** no os preocupéis por mí, continuad con lo que estábais haciendo. **27 to get one's – round something,** llegar a comprender algo complicado. **28 to give someone a piece of one's –,** (fam.) cantarle a uno las cuarenta, echar en cara algo a alguien, decirle a alguien cuatro frescas. **29 to go over something in one's –/to turn it over in one's –,** darle vueltas a algo (un problema). **30 to have a good – to,** tener ganas de, tener la firme intención de. **31 to have a – to,** estar en disposición de, estar pensando en, querer (hacer algo). **32 to have half a – to,** estar dispuesto a, desear (llevar algo a cabo pero sin tomar la decisión). **33 to have in –,** tener pensado, tener en mente. **34 to have it in – to,** tener intención de, tener algo en mente. **35 to have one's – on/someone's – is/was etc. on,** preocuparse de, estar preocupado por. **36 I don't –,** no me importa, me es igual, me da lo mismo; (fam.) sí, por favor, sí, vale (para aceptar algo). **37 I don't – if I do,** bueno, no digo que no (para aceptar comida, bebida). **38 If you don't –,** si no te importa, si no te molesta. **39 if you don't – me/my saying so,** permíteme que te diga. **40 in one's mind's eye,** en la imaginación. **41 in one's right –,** en su sano juicio, en sus cabales. **42 in two minds,** indeciso, dudoso. **43 I/he/you etc. wouldn't –,** me gustaría, me apetecería, no me importaría. **44 to know one's own –,** tener ideas claras, saber lo que uno quiere, no ser fácilmente influenciable. **45 to loose one's –,** perder el juicio, volverse loco. **46 to make up one's –/to make one's – up,** tomar una decisión, decidir, tomar partido. **47 – how you go,** (fam.) cuídate (en despedidas). **48 – out!,** (brit.) ¡cuidado! **49 – over matter,** el poder de la mente, el triunfo de la mente. **50 to – one's language/manners,** cuidar lo que uno dice o como se comporta. **51 to – one's P's and Q's,** tener mucho cuidado con lo que uno dice o hace. **52 – reader,** adivino, persona que adivina el pensamiento. **53 – you,** fíjate bien (para poner énfasis en lo que uno va a decir); te advierto que... **54 never –,** no importa, no se preocupe, no haga caso (al aceptar disculpas por algo carente de importancia, o para consolar a alguien). **55 never you –,** (fam.) no es asunto tuyo, no te metas en esto. **56 of one –/of like –/of the same –,** de la misma opinión. **57 on one's –,** tener en la cabeza, no poder quitarse de la cabeza, no poder dejar de pensar en. **58 out of one's –,** loco, fuera de sí. **59 out of sight, out of –,** ojos que no ven, corazón que no siente. **60 to put one in – of,** recordar a alguien (por asociación, por parecido): *she puts me in mind of another person = ella me recuerda a otra persona.* **61 to put one's – to,** dedicarse a algo con interés. **62 to read someone's –,** adivinar lo que alguien está pensando. **63 to set/put someone's – at rest,** dar confianza a alguien, tranquilizar a alguien. **64 to slip one's –/to go out of one's –,** olvidar, escapársele a uno, no recordar (hacer algo). **65 someone's – is/was etc. made up,** tener totalmente decidido (sin pensar cambiar de opinión). **66 to speak one's –,** hablar claro, decir lo que uno piensa, no andarse por las ramas. **67 state of –,** estado de ánimo. **68 to stick in one's –,** quedársele a uno grabado en la memoria. **69 to take one's – off,** hacer olvidar los problemas por un rato, distraer a uno de sus problemas. **70 to my –,** en mi opinión. **71 with something/someone in –,** pensando en algo o alguien (como estímulo).
mind-bending | 'maɪndbendɪŋ | *adj.* (fam.) de solución problemática.
mind-blowing | 'maɪndˌbləuɪŋ | *adj.* **1** (fam.) alucinante, alucinógena (una droga). **2** asombroso, sorprendente, emocionante, chocante.
mind-boggling | 'maɪndˌbɒglɪŋ | *adj.* (fam.) alarmante, abrumador, extraordinario (por enorme o complicado).
minded | 'maɪndɪd | *adj.* **1** [– + *inf.*] (form.) dispuesto, inclinado. **2** [*adj.* + ;ms] de mente, de mentalidad, de carácter: *open-minded = progresista, sin prejuicios.* **3** [*adv.* + ;ms] dedicado a, interesado por: *technically minded = interesado por la técnica.* **4** [*s.* ;ms] inclinado a, orientado hacia: *marriage-minded = inclinado al matrimonio.*
minder | 'maɪndər | *s.c.* **1** (brit.) guardaespaldas. **2** cuidador, celador, vigilante.
mindful | 'maɪndful | *adj.* **1** atento, cortés, fino, educado. **2** cuidadoso, consciente, responsable.
mindless | 'maɪndlɪs | *adj.* **1** (desp.) tedioso, estúpido, sin sentido (un trabajo). **2** descuidado, negligente, ominoso.
mindlessly | 'maɪndlɪslɪ | *adv.* **1** (desp.) tediosamente, estúpidamente (que no tiene sentido). **2** descuidadamente, negligentemente.
mindlessness | 'maɪndlɪsnɪs | *s.i.* **1** (desp.) sin sentido, tedio. **2** descuido, negligencia.
mine | maɪn | *[pron.pos.* la. persona.] **1** mío, míos: *the fault was mine = fue un error mío.* || *adj.pos.* (arc.) **2** mi (ante palabras que comienzan por h o vocal): *mine aunt = mi tía.* || *s.c.* **3** mina, yacimiento, filón. **4** MIL. mina. **5** (arc.) MIL. túnel, galería, pasaje (bajo posiciones enemigas). || *v.t.* e *i.* **6** trabajar en una mina, dedicarse a la minería. || *v.t.* **7** extraer de la mina, explotar una mina. **8** [gen. *pas.*] MIL. minar, sembrar de minas. **9** [gen. *pas.*] destruir con minas. **10** (arc.) minar, socavar (con galerías o túneles). || **11 a – of information,** gran fuente de información, abundante fuente de datos.
minefield | 'maɪnfi:ld | *s.c.* **1** campo de minas, zona minada (en tierra o mar). **2** (fig.) patata caliente, asunto pleno de problemas o dificultades.
miner | 'maɪnər | *s.c.* **1** minero. **2** MIL. minador, zapador.
mineral | 'mɪnərəl | *s.c.* e *i.* **1** mineral, mena. || *s.c.* **2** [gen. *pl.*] (brit.) aguas minerales, soda. || *adj.* **3** mineral. || **4 – water,** agua mineral.
mineralogist | ˌmɪnə'rælədʒɪst | *s.c.* mineralogista.
mineralogy | ˌmɪnə'rælədʒɪ | *s.i.* mineralogía.
minestrone | ˌmɪnɪ'strəunɪ | *s.i.* sopa minestrone, sopa de verduras y pasta.
minesweeper | 'maɪnˌswi:pər | *s.c.* MAR. dragaminas.
mineworker | 'maɪnwə:kər | *s.c.* minero, trabajador de mina.
mingle | 'mɪŋgl | *v.t.* e *i.* **1** mezclar, entremezclar, unir, juntar, fusionar, combinar. || *v.i.* **2 [to – (with/together)]** mezclarse, juntarse (con otra gente).
mingy | 'mɪndʒɪ | *adj.* (brit. y fam.) **1** tacaño, poco generoso, cicatero (una persona). **2** miserable, mínimo, mísero (una porción).
mini | 'mɪnɪ | *s.c.* **1 Mini,** Mini (un coche). **2** (fam.) minifalda. || *prefijo* **3** mini, micro, a pequeña escala: *a minigolf = un minigolf.*
miniature | 'mɪnətʃə | | 'mɪnɪətʃə | | 'mɪnɪətʃuər | *s.c.* **1** ART. miniatura. **2** modelo en miniatura, copia en miniatura. || *s.i.* **3** arte de la miniatura, diminuto. || *adj.* **4** en miniatura. || **5 in –,** en miniatura.
miniaturise V. **miniaturize.**

miniaturization ǀ 'mɪnətʃəraɪzeɪʃn ǀ *s.i.* miniaturización, producción en miniatura.

miniaturize ǀ ˌmɪnɪtʃə'raɪz ǀ (brit. **miniaturise**) *v.t.* construir en miniatura, reducir a miniatura, planificar a escala.

miniaturized ǀ ˌmɪnɪtʃə'raɪzt ǀ *adj.* en miniatura.

minibus ǀ 'mɪnɪbʌs ǀ *s.c.* microbús.

minicab ǀ 'mɪnɪkæb ǀ *s.c.* (brit.) microtaxi (pedido con anticipación).

minim ǀ 'mɪnɪm ǀ (EE.UU. **half note**) *s.c.* **1** MUS. mínima. **2** ápice, pizca, porción insignificante. **3** trazo (caligráfico).

minima ǀ 'mɪnɪmə ǀ *pl.* de **minimum.**

minimal ǀ 'mɪnɪml ǀ *adj.* (form.) mínimo, diminuto, insignificante.

minimally ǀ 'mɪnɪməlɪ ǀ *adv.* mínimamente, insignificantemente.

minimise V. **minimize.**

minimize ǀ 'mɪnɪmaɪz ǀ (brit.) **minimise.** *v.t.* **1** reducir al mínimo, minimizar, empequeñecer, disminuir. **2** subestimar, menospreciar, restar importancia.

minimum ǀ 'mɪnɪməm ǀ *adj.* **1** mínimo, diminuto, muy bajo, inferior. ‖ [*pl.* **minima** o **minimums**] *s.c.* **2** mínimo, minimum. ‖ **3 at the –,** al mínimo, como mínimo, por lo menos. **4 to keep/ reduce something to a –,** mantener o reducir algo al mínimo. **5 – wage,** salario mínimo.

mining ǀ 'maɪnɪŋ ǀ *s.i.* **1** minería, extracción de minerales. **2** MIL. minado, siembra de minas.

minion ǀ 'mɪnjən ǀ *s.c.* **1** (form. y desp.) subalterno, subordinado, servidor, ayudante; (fig.) esbirro. **2** valido, favorito. **3** adulador, parásito.

mini-skirt ǀ 'mɪnɪskɜːt ǀ *s.c.* minifalda.

minister ǀ 'mɪnɪstə*r* ǀ *s.c.* **1** POL. ministro. **2** REL. ministro, pastor. **3** POL. ministro plenipotenciario, enviado extraordinario. **4** agente, enviado. ‖ *v.t.* e *i.* **5 [to – to]** (lit.) atender a, ayudar a, auxiliar a. ‖ *v.t.* **6** administrar, dispensar (un sacramento).

ministerial ǀ ˌmɪnɪ'stɪərɪəl ǀ *adj.* **1** POL. ministerial, de gobierno, administrativo. **2** REL. ministerial, pastoral. **3** instrumental, útil, coadyutorio.

ministerially ǀ ˌmɪnɪ'stɪərɪəlɪ ǀ *adv.* gubernamentalmente, administrativamente; de ministro.

ministration ǀ ˌmɪnɪ'streɪʃn ǀ *s.i.* [gen. *pl.*] **1** (form.) ayuda, dedicación, servicio, atención. **2** REL. ministerio, servicio religioso.

ministry ǀ 'mɪnɪstrɪ ǀ *s.c.* **1** POL. ministerio, gabinete ministerial. **2 [the – +** *v.sing./pl.*] clero, sacerdocio. **3** mediación, intercesión.

mink ǀ mɪŋk ǀ *s.c.* **1** ZOOL. visón. ‖ *s.i.* **2** piel de visón.

minnow ǀ 'mɪnəʊ ǀ *s.c.* ZOOL. pececillo de agua dulce (plateado, de la familia de la carpa).

minor ǀ 'maɪnə*r* ǀ *adj.* **1** menor, mínimo, secundario, inferior, leve, sin importancia. **2** MUS. menor: *in F minor = en Do menor.* **3** [*s.* + ;ms] (brit. y arc.) el pequeño (se usa en la escuela para distinguir a dos alumnos del mismo nombre y apellido): *Smith minor = Smith el pequeño.* ‖ *s.c.* **4** DER. menor de edad. **5** (EE.UU.) asignatura secundaria (en la Universidad).

minority ǀ maɪ'nɒrɪtɪ ǀ ǀ mɪ'nɔːrətɪ ǀ ǀ mɪ'nɑːrətɪ ǀ *s.c.* **1 [the – +** *v.sing./pl.*] la minoría, la mínima parte. **2** minoría (étnica, religiosa). ‖ *s.i.* **3** DER. minoría de edad. ‖ *adj.* **4** de la minoría, de minorías, minoritario. ‖ **5 in a/the –,** en minoría, dentro de la minoría. **6 – government,** POL. gobierno minoritario, gobierno en minoría.

minstrel ǀ 'mɪnstrəl ǀ *s.c.* **1** HIST. juglar, trovador, bardo. **2** cómico, cantor, bailarín (que se maquilla de negro y toca y canta música de negros).

minstrelsy ǀ 'mɪnstrəlsɪ ǀ *s.i.* LIT. juglaría.

mint ǀ mɪnt ǀ *s.i.* **1** BOT. menta, hierbabuena. ‖ *s.c.* **2** pastilla de menta, caramelo de menta. **3** casa de la moneda, fábrica de moneda. **4** (fam. y fig.) fortuna, dineral, mina de oro. ‖ *v.t.* **5** acuñar, fabricar, troquelar (moneda, medallas). **6** (fig.) acuñar, inventar, fabricar (frases, palabras). ‖ **7 in – condition,** en perfecto estado, sin usar, intacto. **8 – sauce,** salsa de menta (para la carne de cordero).

minuet ǀ ˌmɪnjʊ'et ǀ *s.c.* MUS. minueto.

minus ǀ 'maɪnəs ǀ *prep.* **1** menos: *7 minus 3 equals 4 = 7 menos 3 es igual a 4.* **2** bajo, por debajo de: *minus 2 degrees = 2 grados bajo cero.* **3** (fam.) sin, de menos, desprovisto de. ‖ [*pl.* **minusses**] *s.c.* **4** signo menos. **5** desventaja, inconveniente, problema. ‖ *adj.* **6** menos. **7** negativo, en contra. **8** bajo (en calificaciones escolares): *a B minus = un notable bajo.* ‖ **9 – sign,** signo menos, signo negativo.

minuscule, miniscule ǀ 'mɪnəskjuːl ǀ *adj.* **1** minúsculo, insignificante, muy pequeño. ‖ *s.c.* **2** (EE.UU.) letra minúscula, minúscula, letra de caja baja.

minute ǀ 'mɪnɪt ǀ *s.c.* **1** minuto. **2** (fam.) momento, minuto, segundo, periquete, instante. **3** GEOM. minuto (de grado). **4** minuta, memorándum, nota. **5** [*pl.*] actas (de una reunión). ‖ *v.t.* **6** escribir en acta, levantar un acta, constar en acta. **7** anotar, apuntar. ‖ ǀ maɪ'njuːt ǀ *adj.* **8** diminuto, minúsculo, muy pequeño. **9** (form.) minucioso, exacto, meticuloso. ‖ **10 at any –,** en cualquier momento. **11 at the last –,** en el último momento. **12 at this –,** en este mismo instante, ahora mismo. **13 the – that,** en el momento en que, tan pronto como. **14 this –,** al momento, al instante, ahora mismo. **15 wait/just a –,** espera un instante. **16 within minutes,** en minutos, segundos más tarde.

minute-book ǀ 'mɪnɪtbʊk ǀ *s.c.* libro de actas.

minute-hand ǀ 'mɪnɪthænd ǀ *s.c.* manilla para los minutos (en un reloj).

minutely ǀ maɪ'njuːtlɪ ǀ *adv.* (form.) **1** minuciosamente, meticulosamente, con precisión. **2** ligeramente, a intervalos (un movimiento). **3** primorosamente, sutilmente.

minute-man ǀ 'mɪnɪtmæn ǀ [*pl.* **minutemen**] *s.c.* (EE.UU.) HIST. miliciano (en época de la Revolución Americana).

minuteness ǀ maɪ'njuːtnɪs ǀ *s.i.* **1** minuciosidad, meticulosidad. **2** pequeñez extrema.

minutiae ǀ maɪ'njuːʃiː ǀ ǀ mɪnuːʃɪaɪ ǀ *s.pl.* minucias, detalles minuciosos, nimiedades, pequeñeces.

minx ǀ mɪŋks ǀ *s.c.* (desp. o hum.) coquetona; desvergonzada.

miracle ǀ 'mɪrəkl ǀ *s.c.* **1** milagro. **2** (fam. y fig.) milagro, maravilla, prodigio. **3 [– of]** obra maestra de. **4** LIT. auto sacramental. ‖ **5 to do/work miracles,** (fam. y fig.) hacer milagros.

miraculous ǀ mɪ'rækjʊləs ǀ *adj.* **1** milagroso. **2** sorprendente, extraordinario, inesperado.

miraculously ǀ mɪ'rækjʊləslɪ ǀ *adv.* **1** milagrosamente. **2** increíblemente, inesperadamente.

mirage ǀ 'mɪrɑːʒ ǀ ǀ mərɑːʒ ǀ *s.c.* **1** espejismo, ilusión óptica. **2** (fig.) ilusión, esperanza, deseo, sueño imposible.

mire ǀ 'maɪə*r* ǀ *s.i.* (lit.) **1** lodazal, fango, cieno. **2** (fig.) cieno, lodo. ‖ *v.t.* (p.u.) **3** enfangar, enlodar. **4** atrapar, enredar, enmarañar.

mirror ǀ 'mɪrə*r* ǀ *s.c.* **1** espejo. **2** (fig.) espejo, modelo, reflejo. ‖ *v.t.* **3** reflejar, reflectar. **4** (fig.) reflejar, ser la viva imagen, ser copia exacta.

mirror-image ǀ 'mɪrəˌɪmɪdʒ ǀ *s.c.* **1** OPT. imagen refleja, imagen reflexa. **2** réplica, copia.

mirth ǀ mɜːθ ǀ *s.i.* (lit.) alegría, júbilo, regocijo, hilaridad.

mirthful ǀ 'mɜːθfl ǀ *adj.* (form.) alegre, jubiloso.

mirthless ǀ mɜːθlɪs ǀ *adj.* (lit.) triste, abatido, melancólico, alicaído, falto de alegría.

mirthlessly ǀ mɜːθlɪslɪ *adv.* (lit.) tristemente, sin alegría, melancólicamente.

misadventure ǀ ˌmɪsəd'ventʃə ǀ *s.c.* e *i.* **1** desventura, desgracia, desastre, accidente, percance, contratiempo. ‖ **2 death by –,** DER. muerte accidental.

misalliance ǀ ˌmɪsə'laɪəns ǀ *s.c.* unión desgraciada (especialmente matrimonial).

misanthrope, misanthropist ǀ 'mɪzənθrəʊp ǀ *s.c.* (form. y desp.) misántropo.

misanthropic ǀ ˌmɪzən'θrɒpɪk ǀ ǀ ˌmɪsən'θrɑːŋɪk ǀ *adj.* (form. y desp.) misantrópico.

misanthropy ǀ ˌmɪ'zænθrəpɪ ǀ *s.i.* (form. y desp.) misantropía.

misapplication ǀ 'mɪsˌæplɪ'keɪʃn ǀ *s.c.* e *i.* mala aplicación, abuso.

misapply ǀ ˌmɪsə'plaɪ ǀ *v.t.* aplicar mal, abusar de, usar con malos propósitos.

misapprehend ǀ 'mɪsˌæprɪ'hend ǀ *v.t.* (form.) mal entender, comprender mal.

misapprehension ǀ 'mɪs æprɪ'henʃn ǀ *s.c.* e *i.* (form.) malentendido, equívoco, equivocación, interpretación equivocada.

misappropriate | ˌmɪsə'prəuprɪeɪt | *v.t.* (form.) apropiarse indebidamente, desfalcar, malversar (dinero, fondos).

misappropiation | 'mɪsəˌprəuprɪ'eɪʃn | *s.c.* e *i.* (form.) apropiación indebida, desfalco, malversación (de fondos, dinero).

misbegotten | ˌmɪsbɪ'gɒtn | *adj.* espurio, ilegítimo.

misbehave | mɪsbɪ'heɪv | *v.t.* e *i.* comportarse mal, portarse mal; ser malo, hacer travesuras (un niño).

misbehaviour | ˌmɪsbɪ'heɪvjər | (EE.UU. **misbehavior**) *s.i.* mala conducta, mal comportamiento.

miscalculate | ˌmɪs'kælkjʊleɪt | *v.t.* e *i.* **1** calcular mal, equivocarse en los cálculos. **2** juzgar mal, formarse un juicio equivocado.

miscalculation | 'mɪsˌkælkjʊ'leɪʃn | *s.c.* e *i.* **1** error de cálculo, equivocación, mal cálculo. **2** (fig.) error, desacierto.

miscarriage | ˌmɪs'kærɪdʒ | *s.c.* e *i.* **1** aborto involuntario, malparto. **2** COM. extravío, pérdida (de bienes, fletes, cartas). || **3 – of justice,** DER. error judicial.

miscarry | ˌmɪs'kærɪ | *v.i.* **1** abortar involuntariamente. **2** (form.) fallar, fracasar, frustrarse (un plan, una intención). **3** COM. perderse, extraviarse (fletes, cartas).

miscast | ˌmɪs'kɑːst | | ˌmɪs'kæst | *v.i.irr.* [pret. y *p.p.* **miscast**] 1 dar un mal papel, dar un papel inapropiado (a un actor).

miscellaneous | ˌmɪsɪ'leɪnjəs | *adj.* misceláneo, heterogéneo, diverso, variado.

miscellany | mɪ'selənɪ | | 'mɪsəleɪnɪ | *s.c.* miscelánea, variedad, mezcla, colección.

mischance | ˌmɪs'tʃɑːns | | ˌmɪs'tʃæns | *s.c.* e *i.* (form.) desgracia, mala suerte, infortunio.

mischief | 'mɪstʃɪf | *s.i.* **1** travesura, diablura, mala conducta. **2** malicia, picardía. **3** (form.) mal, daño, deterioro, destrucción, avería. || *s.c.* **4** (fam. y arc.) diablillo, duende, trasto (un niño). || **5 to do someone/yourself a –,** causar a alguien o a sí mismo una mala faena, hacer daño a alguien o a uno mismo.

mischief-maker | 'mɪstʃɪˌmeɪkər | *s.c.* revoltoso, intrigante, buscapleitos, alborotador, provocador.

mischievous | 'mɪstʃɪvəs | *adj.* **1** travieso, juguetón, diablejo, trasto, revoltoso. **2** malicioso, pícaro. **3** dañino, malévolo. **4** irritante, problemático.

mischievously | 'mɪstʃɪvəslɪ | *adv.* malévolamente, pícaramente.

misconceived | ˌmɪskən'siːvt | *adj.* mal entendido, mal interpretado, equivocado.

misconception | ˌmɪskən'sepʃn | *s.c.* e *i.* equívoco, equivocación, mala interpretación.

misconduct | ˌmɪs'kɒndʌkt | | ˌmɪs'kɑːndʌkt | *s.c.* e *i.* **1** (form.) mala conducta, inmoralidad, deshonestidad. **2** malversación, descontrol (en negocios).

misconstruction | ˌmɪskən'strʌkʃn | *s.c.* e *i.* (form.) **1** mala interpretación. **2** mala construcción, mala traducción, orden equivocado (de una frase).

misconstrue | ˌmɪskən'struː | *v.t.* (form.) mal interpretar, mal entender, tergiversar (algo que se ha dicho o hecho).

miscreant | 'mɪskrɪənt | *s.c.* (p.u.) bribón, villano.

misdate | ˌmɪs'deɪt | *v.t.* poner la fecha errónea.

misdeal | ˌmɪs'diːl | *v.* [*pret.* y *p.p.* **misdealt**] *i.* **1** dar mal (las cartas). || *s.c.* **2** equivocación (al dar las cartas).

misdealt | ˌmɪs'delt | *pret.* y *p.p.* de **misdeal.**

misdeed | ˌmɪs'diːd | *s.c.* (form.) delito, ofensa, falta, infracción, acción ilegal.

misdemeanour | ˌmɪsdɪ'miːnər | (EE.UU. **misdemeanor**) *s.c.* e *i.* **1** DER. delito, ofensa, infracción. **2** (form.) fechoría, canallada.

misdirect | ˌmɪsdɪ'rekt | *v.t.* **1** poner mal una dirección, escribir mal las señas; dar una dirección errónea, informar mal. **2** [gen. *pas.*] (form.) usar mal, manejar mal, abusar; descaminar, equivocar. **3** DER. inducir a error de derecho, dar información errónea (al jurado).

misdirected | ˌmɪsdɪ'rektɪd | *adj.* desacertado, descaminado, desorientado, erróneo, equivocado.

miser | maɪzər | *s.c.* (desp.) **1** avaro, avariento, cicatero, (Amer.) amarrete. **2** avaricioso, goloso, glotón.

miserable | 'mɪzərəbl | *adj.* **1** triste, desdichado, deprimido, infeliz (una persona). **2** deprimente, desagradable, pobre, triste (un lugar, el tiempo). **3** (gen. desp.) miserable, vil, indecente, despreciable. **4** inferior, ínfimo, pésimo, de mala calidad. **5** mezquino, raquítico, humillante, decepcionante (de tamaño o calidad).

miserably | 'mɪzərəblɪ | *adv.* **1** tristemente. **2** miserablemente.

miserliness | 'maɪzəlɪnɪs | *s.i.* **1** (desp.) avaricia, tacañería, cicatería. **2** mezquindad (en tamaño o calidad).

miserly | 'maɪzərlɪ | *adj.* **1** (desp.) avariento, tacaño, cicatero. **2** raquítico, mezquino (de tamaño o calidad).

misery | 'mɪzərɪ | *s.i.* **1** desdicha, desgracia, tristeza, depresión. **2** miseria, privación, pobreza, calamidad, mugre. || *s.c.* **3** (brit., fam. y desp.) quejica, llorica, refunfuñón, gimoteador. || **4 to make one's life a –,** amargar la vida a alguien. **5 to put an animal out of its –,** acortar la agonía a un animal, matar a un animal que sufre. **6 to put someone out of their –,** (fam. y fig.) sacar de dudas a alguien, satisfacer la curiosidad de alguien.

misfire | ˌmɪs'faɪər | *v.i.* **1** errar el tiro, fallar el disparo. **2** fallar el encendido, no arrancar correctamente (un vehículo). **3** fallar, fracasar, frustrarse (un plan).

misfit | 'mɪsfɪt | *s.c.* **1** inadaptado, desplazado. **2** que no encaja, que no cae bien (una prenda).

misfortune | mɪs'fɔːtʃən | *s.c.* e *i.* **1** desventura, desgracia, infortunio, mala suerte. **2** percance, revés, adversidad.

misgiving | mɪs'gɪvɪŋ | *s.c.* e *i.* duda, desconfianza, suspicacia, recelo, prevención.

misguided | ˌmɪs'gaɪdɪd | *adj.* engañado, mal informado, descaminado, equivocado.

mishandle | ˌmɪs'hændl | *v.t.* **1** manejar mal, llevar mal, tratar torpemente (un asunto). **2** maltratar, tratar con mala educación.

mishap | 'mɪshæp | *s.c.* e *i.* percance, contratiempo, accidente, desgracia, novedad.

mishear | ˌmɪs'hɪər | *v.t.* e *i. irr.* [*pret.* y *p.p.* **misheard**] entreoír, mal entender, oír mal.

misinform | ˌmɪsɪn'fɔːm | *v.t.* (gen.*pas.*) (form.) dar información errónea o falsa, informar mal, engañar, despistar.

misinformed | ˌmɪsɪn'fɔːmd | *adj.* mal informado, engañado, despistado, mal aconsejado.

misinformation | ˌmɪsɪnfə'meɪʃən | *s.i.* (euf.) información errónea o falsa.

misinterpret | ˌmɪsɪn'təːprɪt | *v.t.* **1** interpretar mal, tergiversar; leer mal. **2** explicar mal, sacar una conclusión equivocada.

misinterpretation | 'mɪsɪnˌtəːprɪ'teɪʃn | *s.i.* mala interpretación, interpretación errónea, tergiversación.

misjudge | ˌmɪs'dʒʌdʒ | *v.t.* juzgar equivocadamente o injustamente a, formarse una mala opinión de, equivocarse con.

misjudgment, misjudgement | ˌmɪs'dʒʌdʒmənt | *s.c.* e *i.* **[– (of)]** juicio erróneo, interpretación equivocada, opinión injusta, mal cálculo.

mislay | ˌmɪs'leɪ | *v.t.irr.* [*pret.* y *p.p.* **mislaid**] (gen. euf.) traspapelar, extraviar, colocar en un lugar olvidado.

mislead | ˌmɪs'liːd | *v.t.irr.* [*pret.* y *p.p.* **misled**] (gen. euf.) equivocar, engañar, descaminar, despistar.

misleading | ˌmɪs'liːdɪŋ | *adj.* engañoso, ilusorio, falso, erróneo.

misleadingly | ˌmɪs'liːdɪŋlɪ | *adv.* engañosamente, falsamente, erróneamente.

misled | ˌmɪs'led | *pret.* y *p.p.* de **mislead.**

mismanage | ˌmɪs'mænɪdʒ | *v.t.* administrar mal, gobernar mal, llevar mal, organizar mal, manejar mal (un negocio, un asunto).

mismanagement | ˌmɪs'mænɪdʒmənt | *s.i.* mala administración, desgobierno.

misnamed | ˌmɪs'neɪmd | *adj.* mal llamado, de nombre equivocado.

misnomer | ˌmɪs'nəumər | *s.c.* nombre inapropiado, término erróneo, desatino, estupidez: *calling it a book is a misnomer = llamarle libro es una estupidez.*

misogynist | mɪ'sɒdʒɪnɪst | | mɪ'sɑːdʒɪnɪst | *s.c.* misógino.

misplaced | ˌmɪs'pleɪst | *adj.* **1** inapropiado, inoportuno, fuera de lugar. **2** descolocado, mal colocado, equivocado.

misprint | 'mɪsprɪnt | *s.c.* **1** errata, error de imprenta, fallo de impresión. || *v.t.* **2** imprimir con erratas, imprimir mal.
mispronounce | mɪsprə'naʊns | *v.t.* pronunciar incorrectamente, pronunciar mal.
mispronunciation | 'mɪsprə,nʌnsɪ'eɪʃn | *s.c.* e *i.* mala pronunciación, pronunciación incorrecta.
misquote | ,mɪs'kwəʊt | *v.t.* citar incorrectamente, reproducir inexactamente las palabras, mal interpretar.
misread | ,mɪs'ri:d | *v.t.irr.* [*pret.* y *p.p.* **misread**] | ,mɪs'red | **1** leer mal, equivocarse al leer. **2** juzgar mal, interpretar mal.
misreading | ,mɪs'ri:dɪŋ | *s.c.* lectura errónea (por ejemplo, de un contador).
misrepresent | 'mɪs,reprɪ'zent | *v.t.gen.pas.* **1** describir engañosamente, distorsionar, tergiversar (personas, palabras, hechos). **2** representar mal (a una persona).
misrepresentation | 'mɪs,reprɪzen'teɪʃn | *s.c.* e *i.* **1** tergiversación, falsificación, distorsión. **2** mala representación (de una persona).
misrule | ,mɪs'ru:l | *s.i.* **1** desgobierno, mal gobierno (de un país). **2** (lit.) confusión, desorden. || *v.t.* **3** gobernar mal, desgobernar.
miss | mɪs | *v.t.* e *i.* **1** errar el objetivo, fallar, fracasar. **2** pasar por alto, escapársele a uno, pasar desapercibido. **3** no encontrar, no dar con (una persona). **4** perder, no poder asistir a (una reunión, al trabajo). **5** no comprender, no captar, escapársele, no acertar (el mensaje, las palabras). **6** perder, no llegar a, llegar con retraso (al tren, una oportunidad). **7** no dar con, equivocar(se) (el camino). || *v.t.* **8** evitar, escaparse de. **9** añorar, echar de menos, extrañar, echar en falta. **10** descubrir la falta de, descubrir la pérdida de. || *s.c.* **11** fracaso, fallo, tiro errado. **12** señorita (tratamiento para mujeres solteras ante el apellido). **13** jovencita, señorita. **14** miss, representante (en un concurso de belleza). **15** (brit.) señorita (forma respetuosa para dirigirse a una profesora). **16** (hum. y arc.) descarada, picarona, atrevida (una mujer). || **17 to give something a –,** (brit. y fam.) evitar hacer algo, pasar de algo. **18 to – the boat/bus,** (fig.) perder el tren, perder una oportunidad de oro, llegar tarde. **19 to – the mark,** errar el tiro, malograr(se). **20 to – out, a)** saltarse, omitir (hechos, personas en una lista); **b)** perderse algo agradable. **21 to never – a trick,** (fam. y desp.) no perderse un detalle, estar a la que salta, no dejar pasar nada por alto (de lo que concierne a uno mismo o a otros).
missal | 'mɪsl | *s.c.* REL. misal.
misshapen | ,mɪs'ʃeɪpən | | ,mɪʃeɪpən | *adj.* deformado, deforme, desfigurado.
missile | 'mɪsaɪl | | 'mɪsəl | *s.c.* **1** MIL. misil, proyectil teledirigido. **2** (form.) arma arrojadiza.
missing | 'mɪsɪŋ | *adj.* **1** desaparecido, perdido, extraviado, ausente, que falta. || **2 – in action,** MIL. desaparecido en combate, desaparecido en acto de servicio. **3 – link,** eslabón perdido, pieza que falta en el engranaje.
mission | 'mɪʃn | *s.c.* **1** MIL. misión, tarea, objetivo. **2** misión, vocación (en la vida). **3 [– +** *v.sing./pl.*] misión diplomática, comisión negociadora, representación diplomática. **4** misión, casa misionera (de tipo religioso, caritativo). **5** legación diplomática, representación diplomática (una oficina, un edificio). || *v.t.* **6** MIL. enviar en una misión. **7** comisionar, enviar en representación diplomática. **8** trabajar como misionero, ir a misiones.
missionary | 'mɪʃənrɪ | | 'mɪʃənerɪ | *s.c.* **1** REL. misionero, evangelizador. **2** propagandista, proselitista. || *adj* **3** misional, misionero.
missis V. **missus.**
missive | 'mɪsɪv | *s.c.* misiva, carta, mensaje, nota.
misspell | ,mɪs'spel | *v.t.* e *i.irr.* [*pret.* y *p.p.* **misspelt** o **misspelled.**] deletrear mal, cometer errores ortográficos.
misspelt | ,mɪs'spelt | *pret.* y *p.p.* de **misspell.**
misspend | ,mɪs'spend | *v.t.irr.* [*pret.* y *p.p.* **misspent.**] malgastar, despilfarrar, desperdiciar, perder, dilapidar (la vida, el dinero).
misspent | ,mɪs'spent | *pret.* y *p.p.* de **misspend.**
missus, missis | 'mɪsəz | *s.sing.* **1** (fam. y hum.) señora, esposa, mujer. **2** (brit. y fam.) señora (fórmula de cortesía para llamar la atención de una mujer).
missy | 'mɪsɪ | *s.c.* (p.u. y fam.) señorita, damita.
mist | mɪst | *s.c.* e *i.* **1** neblina, bruma, calina, calígine. **2** (fig.) bruma, velo, nube. || *s.i.* **3** velo (de lágrimas). **4** vaho, vapor, empañamiento. || *v.t.* e *i.* **5 [to – over]** nublar(se), oscurecer(se), empañar(se). || *v.i.* **6** caer una fina lluvia.
mistake | mɪ'steɪk | *v.t.irr.* [*pret.* **mistook,** *p.p.* **mistaken**] **1** entender mal, comprender mal, mal interpretar, juzgar erróneamente. **2** confundir, equivocar. **3 [to – for]** confundir con, tomar por (otra persona). || *s.c.* e *i.* **4** error, errata. **5** error, equivocación, desacierto. || **6 by –,** por error, por descuido. **7 there's no mistaking,** no hay duda posible, no hay ni la más mínima duda.
mistaken | mɪ'steɪkən | *adj.* **1** equivocado, confundido, mal entendido. **2** incorrecta, errónea (una creencia, una idea).
mistakenly | mɪ'steɪkənlɪ | *adv.* equivocadamente, erróneamente.
mister | 'mɪstər | *s.* **1** señor, caballero (para atraer la atención). **2** V. **Mr.**
mistime | ,mɪs'taɪm | *v.t.* anunciar inoportunamente, decir a destiempo, decir a deshora.
mistletoe | 'mɪsltəʊ | *s.i.* BOT. muérdago.
mistook | mɪ'stʊk | *pret.* de **mistake.**
mistreat | mɪs'tri:t | *v.t.* maltratar, tratar desconsideradamente.
mistreatment | ,mɪs'tri:tmənt | *s.c.* e *i.* maltrato.
mistress | 'mɪstrɪs | *s.c.* **1** dueña, ama, señora. **2** (fig.) dueña (de una situación). **3** amante, querida. **4** LIT. amada, amor. **5** (brit.) profesora, maestra. **6** reina de, experta en, la mejor en. || **7 to be one's own –,** ser dueña de una misma, ser totalmente independiente.
mistrial | ,mɪs'traɪəl | *s.c.* DER. **1** juicio nulo. **2** (EE.UU.) juicio en que no se pone de acuerdo el jurado.
mistrust | ,mɪs'trʌst | *v.t.* **1** desconfiar, recelar, dudar. || *s.i.* **2** desconfianza, recelo, duda, sospecha.
mistrustful | ,mɪs'trʌstful | *adj.* desconfiado, receloso, sospechoso.
mistrustfully | ,mɪs'trʌstfəlɪ | *adv.* desconfiadamente, recelosamente.
misty | 'mɪstɪ | *adj.* **1** brumoso, caliginoso. **2** (fig.) nebuloso, vago, confuso, incierto. **3** pálido, deslucido (un color).
misunderstand | ,mɪsʌndə'stænd | | ,mɪsʌndər'stænd | *v.t.* e *i.irr.* [*pret.* y *p.p.* **misunderstood**] entender mal, comprender mal, interpretar mal, no coger el sentido correcto (de palabras).
misunderstanding | ,mɪsʌndə'stændɪŋ | | ,mɪsʌndər'stændɪŋ | *s.c.* e *i.* **1** malentendido, mala interpretación, equívoco, error, equivocación. || *s.c.* **2 [– (with)]** (gen. euf.) disensión, desavenencia, discrepancia, divergencia, disputa.
misunderstood | ,mɪs,ʌndə'stʊd | *pret.* y *p.p.* de **misunderstand.**
misuse | ,mɪs'ju:s | *v.t.* **1** malgastar, derrochar, perder (el tiempo). **2** (form.) maltratar, tratar sin consideración (a una persona); estropear.
mite | maɪt | *s.c.* **1** garrapata, ácaro, coloradilla. **2** (fig.) angelito, desdichado, desgraciado, infeliz (de un niño). **3** (arc. y form.) pizca, ápice, poquito. **4** óbolo, contribución, pequeña cantidad (de dinero). || **5 a –,** (fam.) ligeramente, un tanto: *a mite tall = ligeramente alto.*
mitigate | 'mɪtɪgeɪt | *v.t.* mitigar, aliviar, calmar, templar, suavizar (un dolor, un daño).
mitigating | 'mɪtɪgeɪtɪŋ | *adj.* DER. atenuante.
mitigation | ,mɪtɪ'geɪʃn | *s.i.* **1** mitigación, alivio. || **2 in –,** DER. como atenuante.
mitre | 'maɪtə | (EE.UU. **miter**) *s.c.* **1** mitra, tiara (de obispos). **2** inglete, escuadra (para unir piezas de madera en ángulo). || *v.t.* **3** conferir la mitra, investir como obispo. **4** unir con inglete, con escuadra (piezas de madera en ángulo).
mitt | mɪt | *s.c.* **1** mitón, manopla. **2** DEP. guante (de béisbol, de boxeo). **3** (jerga y hum.) manazas, zarpa.
mitten | 'mɪtn | *s.c.* mitón, manopla.
mix | mɪks | *v.t.* e *i.* **1** mezclar, ligar, amalgamar, unir, diluir. **2** combinar, ir bien (dos colores). **3** aderezar. **4** amasar. || *v.t.* **5** mezclar, servir, preparar (un

combinado). 6 RAD. hacer mezclas, mezclar (sonidos). || *v.i.* 7 ser sociable, hacer migas, llevarse bien. || *s.c.* e *i.* 8 mezcla, masa, mixtura, amalgama, pasta, disolución. 9 combinación (de bebidas). || **10 to – in,** mezclar, combinar (ingredientes de cocina). **11 to – up,** confundir, mezclar, desordenar.

mixed | mɪkst | *adj.* 1 variados, diversos, conflictivos (sentimientos). 2 [no *comp.*] mixto (un centro escolar). || **3 a – bag,** (fam.) un surtido, una mezcolanza, un poco de todo. **4 in – company,** ante las damas, delante de una señora. **5 – ability,** heterogéneo, de diferentes niveles (un grupo de alumnos). **6 – blessing,** bueno y malo a la vez, contradictorio, ambivalente. **7 – doubles,** DEP. partido de doble (en tenis). **8 – economy,** economía mixta. **9 – farming,** agricultura mixta. **10 – grill,** parrillada (de carnes).

mixed-up | 'mɪkstʌp | *adj.* 1 **[– in]** mezclado en, involucrado en, metido en. 2 **[– with]** en contacto con, relacionado con, implicado en, comprometido con. 3 confuso, confundido, atolondrado.

mixer | 'mɪksər | *s.c.* 1 batidora, licuadora; hormigonera, mezcladora. 2 combinado, combinación. 3 RAD. mezclador (de sonido). || **4 a good/bad –,** persona muy o poco sociable, persona de trato fácil o difícil.

mixing bowl | 'mɪksɪŋ'bəul | *s.c.* cuenco, escudilla, bol, fuente honda (para mezclar ingredientes de cocina).

mixture | 'mɪkstʃər | *s.c.* 1 mezcla, combinación, surtido, mezcolanza. || *s.i.* 2 jarabe, medicina, mixtura. 3 (form.) mezcla, combinación, acción de mezclar. || **4 the – as before,** lo mismo de siempre, sin variación.

mix-up | 'mɪksʌp | *s.c.* (fam.) 1 lío, confusión. 2 pelotera, riña, pelea.

mnemonic | niː'mɒnɪk | | nɪ'mɑːnɪk | *adj.* 1 mnemotécnico, mnemónico. || *s.c.* 2 regla nemotécnica, fórmula, mnemónica.

mnemonics | nɪ'mɒnɪks | *s.pl.* nemotecnia.

mo | məu | *s.sing.* 1 (brit. y fam.) momento, segundo, instante. 2 | ˌem'əu | **MO** (brit.) médico militar. 3 **MO,** abreviatura de **modus operandi.**

moan | məun | *s.c.* 1 gemido, lamento, quejido. 2 (fig.) bramido, ulular, silbido, rugido (del viento). 3 (fam. y desp.) queja, protesta, reproche, lloriqueo. || *v.i.* 4 gemir, lamentarse, quejarse. 5 (fig.) ulular, bramar, silbar (el viento). || *v.t.* e *i.* 6 protestar, quejarse, hacer reproches, lloriquear.

moaner | məunər | *s.c.* (fam. y desp.) quejica, llorón, protestón.

moat | məut | *s.c.* 1 foso (de una fortificación). || *v.t.* 2 rodear con foso, cavar un foso.

mob | mɒb | | mɑːb | *s.c.* [;ms + *v.sing./pl.*] 1 (gen. desp.) masa, gentío, turba, tropel de gente. 2 pandilla, grupo de amigotes. 3 gentuza, canalla, chusma. 4 (arc.) sindicato del crimen, organización mafiosa. || *v.t.* 5 rodear, atropellar, acosar, apiñarse alrededor, aglomerarse alrededor (una multitud).

mob-cap | 'mɒbkæp | *s.c.* gorro de casa (que llevaban las mujeres en el siglo XVIII).

mobile | 'məubaɪl | | 'məubəl | | 'məubiːl | *adj.* 1 móvil, movible, versátil, cambiante, variable. 2 (no *comp.*) móvil, ambulante. || *s.c.* 3 móvil (decorativo). || **4 – home,** casa remolque, caravana, "roulotte." **5 – library,** (EE.UU. **bookmobile**), biblioteca ambulante.

mobilise V. **mobilize.**

mobility | məu'bɪlɪtɪ | *s.i.* 1 movilidad. 2 versatilidad. || **3 – allowance,** subvención a los disminuidos físicos (como ayuda para transporte).

mobilize | 'məubɪlaɪz | (brit. **mobilise**) *v.t.* 1 movilizar, reunir (gente, apoyos). || *v.i.* 2 MIL. movilizar, enrolar, llamar a filas, alistar.

mobilization | ˌməubɪlaɪ'zeɪʃn | *s.i.* 1 movilización, organización, reunión (de gente, apoyo). 2 MIL. movilización, enrolamiento, alistamiento.

mobster | 'mɒbstər | | 'mɑːbstə | *s.c.* gángster, mafioso.

moccasin | 'mɒkəsɪn | | 'mɑːkəsɪn | *s.c.* 1 mocasín, zapato indio. 2 ZOOL. serpiente mocasín, serpiente de agua.

mock | mɒk | | mɑːk | *v.t.* e *i.* 1 (form.) mofar(se), burlar(se), reír(se). || *v.t.* 2 ridiculizar, imitar, parodiar, remedar. 3 (form.) desbaratar, frustrar, estropear, echar por la borda (planes). || *adj.* 4 fingido, simulado, falso. || *s.pl.* 5 (brit. y fam.) ensayo de exámenes, exámenes simulados (antes de los que son enviados a la Universidad). 6 burla, mofa, escarnio. 7 hazmerreír. 8 simulacro, remedo, imitación.

mockers | mɒkəz | *s.pl.* 1 ruina, fracaso. || **2 to put the – on,** (fam.) echar al traste, fastidiar.

mockery | 'mɒkərɪ | *s.i.* 1 irrisión, burla, mofa, escarnio. 2 farsa, comedia, parodia, engaño. || **3 to make a – of,** poner en ridículo.

mocking | mɒkɪŋ | *adj.* 1 burlón, despectivo, desdeñoso, altanero. || *s.c.* 2 burla, mofa.

mockingly | mɒkɪŋlɪ | *adv.* burlonamente, con sorna.

mock-up | 'mɒkʌp | *s.c.* maqueta, modelo a escala.

mod | mɒd | | mɑːd | *s.c.* 1 (brit. y argot) mod, abreviatura de **modern** (miembro de tribu urbana en auge en los años 60). 2 **MoD,** abreviatura de **Ministry of Defense.** || **3 – cons,** (brit. y fam.) abreviatura de **modern conveniencies,** servicios, comodidades del hogar (utilizado en publicidad).

modal | 'məudl | *adj.* 1 GRAM. modal, de modo. 2 MUS. modal, de tono, en escala, en clave. || *s.c.* 3 GRAM. defectivo, verbo auxiliar de modo: *may and can are modals = may y can son defectivos.*

mode | məud | *s.c.* 1 (form.) modo, estilo, forma, manera. 2 MUS. modo, tono, escala, clave. 3 **[the –]** la moda, el estilo, la manera. 4 posición, disposición (en que se encuentra una tecla de una máquina).

model | 'mɒdl | *s.c.* 1 copia, réplica, maqueta, imitación, representación. 2 modelo (de pasarela, que posa para un artista). 3 modelo, marco, ilustración; imagen, ejemplo, ideal, patrón (a copiar). 4 patrón, figurín. 5 pauta, norma (a seguir). 6 modelo, versión, prototipo, muestra (de fábrica). 7 (brit. y euf.) modelo, (como reclamo en periódicos, revistas). || *v.t.* (EE.UU. **modell**). 8 modelar, dar forma. 9 exhibir, presentar, llevar puesto (un modelo en un desfile de moda). 10 ilustrar, tomar como ejemplo. || *v.i.* 11 trabajar como modelo. || *adj.* 12 modélico, excelente, ejemplar. 13 modelo, piloto (un centro). || **14 to – on/upon,** copiar, imitar, basar en (un sistema, un comportamiento).

modelling | 'mɒdlɪŋ | *s.i.* pase de modelos, profesión de modelo.

moderate | 'mɒdərət | | 'mɑːdərət | *adj.* 1 moderado, medio, razonable, normal, regular, módico. 2 POL. moderado. 3 mediocre, normal (de calidad). 4 ligero, moderado (un cambio). || | mɒdə'reɪt | *v.t.* e *i.* 5 (form.) moderar, templar, atenuar, suavizar, calmar, reducir. | *s.c.* 6 POL. moderado.

moderately | 'mɒdərətlɪ | | 'mɑːdərətlɪ | *adv.* 1 moderadamente, ligeramente.

moderating | 'mɒdəreɪtɪŋ | *adj.* moderado, mitigado, discreto, atenuante.

moderation | ˌmɒdə'reɪʃn | | ˌmɑːdə'reɪʃn | *s.i.* 1 moderación, prudencia, contención, prudencia, autocontrol. 2 **[– (in)]** (form.) moderación, atenuación, disminución (de fuerza, de grado). || **3 in –,** con moderación, dentro de un límite.

moderator | 'mɒdəreɪtər | *s.c.* mediador, moderador (en una disputa).

modern | 'mɒdən | | 'mɑːdərn | *adj.* 1 (no *comp.*) moderno, contemporáneo, actual, nuevo. 2 progresista, avanzado. || **3 – languages,** lenguas modernas (denominación escolar).

modern-day | 'mɒdənˌdeɪ | *adj.* de hoy en día, de nuestro tiempo.

modernise V. **modernize.**

modernism | 'mɒdənɪzəm | | 'mɑːdərnɪzəm | *s.i.* ART. modernismo.

modernist | 'mɒdənɪst | | 'mɑːdərnɪst | *s.c.* 1 ART. modernista. || *adj.* 2 modernista.

modernistic | ˌmɒdə'nɪstɪk | | ˌmɑːdə'nɪsˌtɪk | *adj.* modernista, vanguardista.

modernity | mɒ'dəːnɪtɪ | | mə'dəːrnɪtɪ | *s.i.* modernidad, vanguardia, innovación.

modernization | ˌmɒdənaɪ'zeɪʃn | | ˌmɑːdərnə'zeɪʃn | *s.c.* e *i.* modernización, innovación.

modernize | 'mɒdənaɪz | | 'mɑːdərnaɪz | (brit. **modernise**) *v.t.* e *i.* modernizar(se), actualizar(se), poner(se) al día.

modest | 'mɒdɪst | | 'mɑːdɪst | *adj.* **1** modesto, discreto, humilde. **2** limitado, módico, moderado, razonable (de precio, de tamaño). **3** (arc.) vergonzosa, pudorosa, recatada (una mujer, su ropa).

modestly | 'mɒdɪstlɪ | *adv.* modestamente, moderadamente, discretamente.

modesty | 'mɒdɪstɪ | *s.i.* **1** modestia, discreción, humildad. **2** recato, pudor, compostura, timidez.

modicum | 'mɒdɪkəm | | 'mɑːdɪkəm | *s.sing.* [;ms + *v.sing./pl.*] mínimo, ápice, pizca.

modification | ˌmɒdɪfɪ'keɪʃn | *s.i.* **1** modificación, transformación, cambio, alteración. || *s.c.* e *i.* **2** revisión, ajuste.

modifier | 'mɒdɪfaɪər | | 'mɑːdɪfaɪə | *s.c.* GRAM. modificador, modificante, calificativo.

modify | 'mɒdɪfaɪ | *v.t.* **1** modificar, moderar, suavizar, alterar, variar. **2** GRAM. modificar.

modish | 'məʊdɪʃ | *adj.* (a veces desp.) en boga, ultimísimo (en moda).

modishly | 'məʊdɪʃlɪ | *adv.* (a veces desp.) en boga, a la última (moda).

modular | 'mɒdjʊlər | | 'mɑːdʒələr | *adj.* modular, por módulos, de módulos.

modulation | ˌmɒdjʊ'leɪʃn | | ˌmɑːdʒəleɪʃn | *s.c.* e *i.* modulación (de sonido, de frecuencia).

modulate | 'mɒdjʊleɪt | | 'mɑːdʒəleɪt | *v.t.* **1** modular, ajustar, regular. **2** RAD. modular (la frecuencia). **3** moderar, atemperar. || *v.i.* **4** MUS. modular, cambiar de tono.

modulated | 'mɒdjʊleɪtɪd | | 'mɑːdʒəleɪtɪd | *adj.* modulado (la voz, el tono).

module | 'mɒdjuːl | | 'mɑːdʒuːl | *s.c.* **1** módulo, elemento, componente, unidad. **2** TEC. módulo (lunar, espacial). **3** módulo (educativo).

modus operandi | ˌmɒdəsˌɒpə'rændɪ | | ˌmɒdəsˌɑːŋə'rændɪ | *s.sing.* (form.) modus operandi, método, procedimiento.

modus vivendi | məudəsvi'vəndi | *s.sing.* (form.) **1** modus vivendi, compromiso, acuerdo (entre dos partes). **2** modus vivendi, forma de vida.

mog | mɒg | V. **moggy.**

moggy, mog | 'mɒgɪ | | 'mɑːgɪ | | 'mɔːgɪ | *s.c.* (brit., fam. y hum.) gato.

mogul | 'məʊgʌl | *s.c.* **1** potentado, magnate, poderoso, persona acaudalada. **2** HIST. mogol, mongol (en la India).

mohair | 'məʊheər | *s.i.* moer, mohair, tejido o lana de Angora.

Mohammedan | məʊ'hæmɪdən | *adj.* **1** (arc.) mahometano, musulmán. || *s.c.* **2** mahometano, musulmán.

Mohammedanism | məʊ'hæmɪdənɪzəm | *s.i.* REL. mahometanismo.

moist | mɔɪst | *adj.* **1** húmedo, mojado, empapado. **2** llorosos, acuosos (los ojos).

moisten | 'mɔɪsn | *v.t.* e *i.* **1** humedecer(se), mojar(se), empapar(se). **2** tener (los ojos) llorosos.

moisture | 'mɔɪstʃə | *s.i.* humedad.

moisturize | 'mɔɪstʃəraɪz | (también **moisturise**) *v.t.* hidratar, humedecer (la piel con cremas de belleza).

moisturizer | 'mɔɪstʃəraɪzər | (también **moisturiser**) *s.c.* crema hidratante, crema humedecedora (de la piel).

moke | məʊk | *s.c.* (brit., fam. y hum.) burrito, jumento.

molar | 'məʊlər | *s.c.* **1** ANAT. molar, muela. || *adj.* **2** ANAT. molar. || **3** QUIM. molar.

molasses | məʊ'læsɪz | (EE.UU. **treacle**) *s.i.* melaza.

mold V. **mould** (y derivados).

mole | məʊl | *s.c.* **1** ZOOL. topo. **2** (fam. y fig.) topo, espía. **3** lunar (en la piel). **4** MAR. malecón, espigón, rompeolas; muelle, embarcadero. **5** MED. tumor uterino. **6** QUIM. mol, molécula. || *s.i.* **7** piel de topo. **8** color gris oscuro.

molecular | məʊ'lekjʊlər | *adj.* FIS. molecular.

molecule | 'mɒlɪkjuːl | | 'mɑːlɪkjuːl | *s.c.* **1** QUIM. molécula, mol. **2** (fig.) molécula, ápice, pizca.

molehill | 'məʊlhɪl | *s.c.* **1** topera, topinera. || **2 to make a mountain out of a –,** hacer una montaña de un grano de arena, exagerar.

molest | məʊ'lest | *v.t.* **1** (desp.) atacar, arremeter, agredir, meterse con, emprenderla con. **2** (form. y euf.) abusar sexualmente, acosar sexualmente. **3** (EE.UU.) molestar, fastidiar, incomodar, importunar.

molestation | ˌməʊle'steɪʃn | *s.i.* **1** molestia, fastidio, incomodo. **2** abuso sexual, acoso sexual.

molester | məʊ'lestər | *s.c.* **1** persona que comete abusos deshonestos.

moll | mɒl | | mɑːl | *s.c.* **1** (EE.UU. y jerga) amante de un gangster. **2** mujer de vida alegre, golfa.

mollifier | 'mɒlɪfaɪər | | mɑːlɪfaɪər | *s.c.* apaciguador, pacificador, reconciliador, conciliador.

mollify | 'mɒlɪfaɪ | | 'mɑːlɪfaɪ | *v.t.* **1** apaciguar, aplacar, calmar, pacificar, atemperar. **2** suavizar, ablandar (a una persona).

mollusc | 'mɒləsk | | 'mɑːləsk | (EE.UU. **mollusk**) *s.c.* ZOOL. molusco.

mollycoddle | 'mɒlɪˌkɒdl | | 'mɑːlɪˌkɑːdl | *v.t.* **1** (fam. y desp.) mimar, proteger en exceso, consentir. || *s.c.* **2** mimado, protegido (un niño, un hombre).

molt V. **moult.**

molten | 'məʊltən | *adj.* **1** fundido, derretido. **2** resplandeciente, fulgurante.

mom | mɒm | (EE.UU. **mum**) *s.c.* (fam.) mamá.

moment | 'məʊmənt | *s.c.* **1** momento, rato, instante. **2** momento, punto (en el tiempo). **3** [gen. *sing.*] momento, ocasión, hora, período (para realizar algo): *do it the moment you want = hazlo en el momento que prefieras.* **4** [gen. *sing.*] MEC. momento. || *s.i.* **5** **[of –]** (form.) de importancia, de peso. || **6 at the last –,** en el último momento, a última hora. **7 at the –/at the present –/at this – in time,** en este preciso momento, ahora mismo, de momento, por ahora. **8 at this –,** ahora mismo, en este mismo instante. **9 for a/one –,** ni por un momento, ni por asomo, en absoluto. **10 for the –,** por ahora, por el momento. **11 to have one's moments,** (fam.) tener sus momentos, tener sus ratos. **12 in a –,** enseguida, dentro de un instante. **13 just this –,** hace un instante. **14 – of truth,** momento de la verdad. **15 of great –,** (form.) de gran importancia. **16 of the –,** del momento, de actualidad. **17 the –,** en el momento en que, en cuanto, tan pronto como. **18 on the spur of the –,** V. **spur.**

momentarily | 'məʊməntərɪlɪ | | ˌməʊmən'tərəlɪ | *adv.* **1** momentáneamente, temporalmente. **2** (EE.UU.) al instante, en un momento.

momentary | 'məʊməntərɪ | | 'məʊmənterɪ | *adj.* **1** momentáneo, pasajero, breve, temporal, transitorio. **2** (EE.UU.) pronto, inmediato.

momentous | məʊ'mentəs | | mə'mentəs | *adj.* importante, crítico, trascendental, decisivo.

momentum | məʊ'mentəm | | mə'mentəm | *pl.* **momenta** o **momentums**] *s.c.* e *i.* **1** fuerza, ímpetu, velocidad: *to gather momentum = adquirir velocidad.* || *s.i.* **2** FIS. momento.

momma | 'mɒmə | | 'mɑːmə | *s.c.* (EE.UU. y fam.) mamá.

monarch | 'mɒnək | | 'mɑːnərk | *s.c.* **1** monarca, soberano. **2** ZOOL. gran mariposa de alas de color naranja y negro.

monarchical | mɒ'nɑːkɪkl | | mə'nɑːrkɪkl | *adj.* monárquico, de monarca.

monarchist | 'mɒnəkɪst | | 'mɑːnərkɪst | *adj.* monárquico, realista.

monarchy | 'mɒnəkɪ | | 'mɑːnərkɪ | *s.c.* e *i.* monarquía.

monastery | 'mɒnəstərɪ | | 'mɑːnəstərɪ | *s.c.* monasterio, convento, claustro.

monastic | mə'næstɪk | *adj.* monástico (una comunidad, una vida).

Monday | 'mʌndɪ | *s.c.* e *i.* lunes.

monetarism | 'mʌnɪtərɪzəm | | 'mɑːnɪtərɪzəm | *s.i.* ECON. monetarismo.

monetarist | 'mʌnɪtərɪst | | 'mɑːnɪtərɪst | *adj.* **1** ECON. monetarista. || *adj.* **2** ECON. monetarista.

monetary | 'mʌnɪtərɪ | | 'mɑːnɪtərɪ | *adj.* (form.) monetario, financiero.

money | 'mʌnɪ | *s.i.* **1** dinero, moneda. **2** riqueza, capital, fortuna, peculio, (fig.) plata. || *s.pl.* **3** fondos, finanzas, caudales. || **4 to be in the –,** nadar en la abundancia, ser acaudalado. **5 for my –,** en mi opinión. **6 to get one's – worth,** comprar bien, estar contento con lo adquirido, sacar el valor de lo que se paga. **7 to have – to burn,** (desp.) quemar el dinero, malgastar el dinero. **8 to make –,** hacer dinero, ganar dinero. **9 – for old rope/jam,** (brit. y fam.) dinero fácil, dinero sin esfuerzo. **10 – market,** ECON. mercado de valores, mercado monetario. **11 to put one's – where one's mouth**

is, (fam. y hum.) predicar con el ejemplo.
money-bags | 'mʌnɪbægz | [*pl.* **money-bags**] *s.c.* (fam. y desp.) ricachón.
moneybox | 'mʌnɪbɒks | | 'mʌnɪbɑːks | *s.c.* hucha.
money-changer | 'mʌnɪtʃeɪndʒər | *s.c.* COM. cambista (de moneda).
money-grubber | 'mʌnɪgrʌbər | *s.c.* codicioso, avaro.
money-grubbing | 'mʌnɪgrʌbɪŋ | *s.i.* codicia, avaricia.
moneylender | 'mʌnɪˌlendər | *s.c.* **1** (arc.) prestamista. **2** (fig. y desp.) estafador.
moneymaker | 'mʌnɪˌmeɪkər | *s.c.* **1** negocio redondo, éxito económico, negocio lucrativo. **2** (desp.) experto en ganar dinero, experto en hacer negocios.
money-making | 'mʌnɪmeɪkɪŋ | *adj.* que da beneficios.
money-spinner | 'mʌnɪspɪnər | *s.c.* (brit. y fam.) negocio redondo.
Mongol | 'mɒŋgɒl | | 'mɑːŋgəl | *s.c.* **1** mongol, mogol, de Mongolia. **2 mongol,** (desp.) mongólico, persona con el síndrome de Down. || *adj.* **3** de mongolia, mongol, mogol.
Mongolia | mɒŋ'gəʊljə | *s.sing.* Mongolia.
Mongolian | mɒŋ'gəʊljən | *s.i.* **1** mongol, mogol (la lengua). || *s.c.* **2** mongol, mogol (habitante de Mongolia). || *adj.* **3** mongol, mogol, de Mongolia.
mongolism | 'mɒŋgəlɪzəm | | 'mɑːŋgəlɪzəm | *s.i.* (desp.) mongolismo, síndrome de Down.
mongoose | 'mɒŋguːs | | 'mɑːŋguːs | *s.c.* ZOOL. mangosta.
mongrel | 'mʌŋgrəl | | 'mɑːŋgrəl | *s.c.* **1** cruce, sin pedigrí, callejero. **2** (fam. y fig.) híbrido, mezcla.
monied | 'mʌnɪd | *adj.* (arc.) acaudalado, rico, adinerado.
monitor | 'mɒnɪtər | | 'mɑːnɪtə | *s.c.* **1** TV. monitor, receptor de imagen. **2** INF. monitor, pantalla. **3** monitor (alumno que ayuda a un profesor en tareas de clase). **4** RAD. escucha (persona encargada de oír noticias y mensajes de radios extranjeras). **5** consejero, amonestador. **6** MED. monitor: *a heart monitor = monitor cardiaco.* || *v.t.* **7** controlar, revisar, comprobar, verificar (sistemáticamente). **8** RAD. escuchar (transmisiones de radio para ser analizadas). **9** supervisar, vigilar (un examen). **10** MED. monitorizar (partes corporales).
monk | mʌŋk | *s.c.* monje, fraile.
monkey | 'mʌŋkɪ | *s.c.* **1** ZOOL. mono, primate. **2** (fam.) diablillo, trasto, bribón (un niño). **3** (brit. y argot) billete de 500 libras o 500 dólares. **4** maza, mazo (de martinete). || *v.i.* **5 [to – about/around]** (fam.) hacer el tonto, hacer payasadas. || *v.t.* **6 [to – with]** (fam.) jugar con, tratar irresponsablemente (algo peligroso, delicado). || **7 to have a – on one's back,** (EE.UU. y argot) estar con el mono, estar colgado, ser un toxicómano. **8 to make a – out of someone,** (fam.) embaucar a uno, engañar a uno, poner a uno en ridículo. **9 – business,** (brit. y fam.) trampas, trapisondas, juego sucio.
monkey-nut | 'mʌŋkɪnʌt | *s.c.* (fam.) cacahuete, cacahué, cacahuet.
mono | 'mɒnəʊ | | mɑːnəʊ | *adj.* **1** mono, mono aural (un aparato de música). || *s.c.* **2** sonido mono aural. **3** MED. mononucleosis. || *prefijo.* **4** mono.
monochrome | 'mɒnəkrəʊm | | 'mɑːnəkrəʊm | *adj.* **1** TV. monocromo, en blanco y negro. **2** FOT. monocromo, en un solo color. **3** (fig.) monótono, uniforme, aburrido.
monocle | 'mɒnəkl | | 'mɑːnəkl | *s.c.* monóculo.
monogamous | mɒ'nɒgəməs | *adj.* monógamo.
monogamy | mɒ'nɒgəmɪ | | mə'nɑːgəmɪ | *s.i.* monogamia.
monogram | 'mɒnəgræm | | 'mænəgræm | *s.c.* monograma, enlace (bordado o decorado con iniciales).
monogrammed | 'mɒnəgræmd | *adj.* decorado con monograma, con las iniciales grabadas.
monograph | 'mɒnəgrɑːf | | 'mɑːnəgræf | *s.c.* monografía, tratado sobre un tema.
monolingual | ˌmɒnə'lɪŋgwəl | *adj.* de un solo idioma.
monolith | 'mɒnəʊlɪθ | | 'mɑːnəʊlɪθ | *s.c.* monolito.
monolithic | ˌmɒnəʊ'lɪθɪk | | ˌmɑːnəʊ'lɪθɪk | *adj.* **1** monolítico, colosal, monumental. **2** (desp.) monolítico, sin fisuras, autoritario, no plural (un sistema).
monologue | 'mɒnəlɒg | | 'mɑːnəl (EE.UU. **monolog**) *s.c.* e *i.* monólogo, soliloquio.
monopolise V. **monopolize.**
monopolistic | məˌnɒpə'lɪstɪk | | məˌnɑːpə'lɪstɪk | *adj.* (form.) monopolizador, monopolista, de monopolio.
monopolization | məˌnɒpəlaɪ'zeɪʃn | | məˌnɑːŋələ'zeɪʃən | *s.i.* monopolización.
monopolize | mə'nɒpəlaɪz | | mə'nɑːŋəlaɪz | (brit. **monopolise**) *v.t.* monopolizar.
monopoly | mə'nɒpəlɪ | | mə'nɑːŋəlɪ | *s.c.* **1** monopolio. **2 [– of]** monopolio de, control sobre, propiedad de. || *s.i.* **3** monopoly (juego de mesa).
monorail | 'mɒnəʊreɪl | | 'mɑːnəʊreɪl | *s.c.* tren monorail, tren monoviga.
monosyllabic | ˌmɒnəʊsɪ'læbɪk | | ˌmɑːnəsɪ'læbɪk | *adj.* **1** GRAM. monosilábico, de una sola sílaba. **2** monosilábica, corta (una respuesta).
monosyllabically | ˌmɒnəsɪ'læbɪklɪ | *adv.* monosilábicamente.
monosyllable | 'mɒnəˌsɪləbl | | 'mɑːnəˌsɪləbl | *s.c.* monosílabo.
monotheism | 'mɒnəʊθiːɪzəm | *s.i.* REL. monoteísmo.
monotheist | 'mɒnəʊθiːɪst | *s.c.* REL. monoteísta.
monotheistic | ˌmɒnəʊθiː'ɪstɪk | *adj.* REL. monoteísta.
monotone | 'mɒnətəʊn | | 'mɑːnətəʊn | *s.c.* **1** monotono, monotonía, uniformidad. || *adj.* **2** monótono, aburrido, uniforme.
monotonous | mə'nɒtnəs | | mə'nɑːtənəs | *adj.* monótono, repetitivo, uniforme, aburrido.
monotonously | mə'nɒtnəslɪ | *adv.* monótonamente, uniformemente.
monotony, monotonousness | mə'nɒtənəsnɪs | | mə'nɑːtənəsnɪs | *s.i.* monotonía, repetición, falta de variedad.
Monsignor | mɒn'siːnjər | | mɑːn'siːnjər | *s.c.* REL. Monseñor (en la Iglesia Católica).
monsoon | mɒn'suːn | | mɑːn'suːn | *s.c.* **1 [the –]** monzón. **2** (fam.) chaparrón, aguacero.
monster | 'mɒnstər | | 'mɑːnstər | *s.c.* **1** monstruo, engendro. **2** monstruo, malvado, fiera, loco. **3** (fam.) monstruo, gigante (un objeto, un edificio). || *adj.* **4** monstruo, gigante, enorme.
monstrosity | mɒn'strɒsɪtɪ | | mɑːn'strɑːsɪtɪ | *s.c.* (fam.) monstruosidad, engendro.
monstrous | 'mɒnstrəs | | 'mɑːnstrəs | *adj.* **1** monstruoso, inmoral, vergonzoso, ignominioso. **2** monstruoso, enorme; deforme, grotesco.
monstrously | 'mɒnstrəslɪ | *adv.* monstruosamente, vergonzosamente, ignominiosamente.
montage | 'mɒntɑːʒ | | mɑːn'tɑːʒ | *s.c.* e *i.* FOT. montaje.
month | mʌnθ | *s.c.* **1** mes, período de cuatro semanas. || **2 a – of Sundays,** (fam.) una eternidad, siglos. **3 – after –,** continuamente, mes tras mes. **4 – by –,** todos los meses, cada mes. **5 – in, – out,** con regularidad, un mes sí y otro también.
monthly | mʌnθlɪ | *adj.* **1** mensual. || *adv.* **2** mensualmente. || *s.c.* **3** revista mensual.
monument | 'mɒnjʊmənt | | 'mɑːnjʊmənt | *s.c.* **1** monumento (conmemorativo, histórico). **2 [– (to/of)]** (fig.) monumento, ejemplo, modelo. **3** hito, mojón, lindero. **4** documento escrito, documento legal.
monumental | ˌmɒnjʊ'mentl | | ˌmnjʊ'mentl | *adj.* **1** monumental, inmortal. **2** enorme, grandioso. **3** (fam.) monumental, tremendo, garrafal, terrible. **4** (fam.) fantástico, estupendo.
monumentally | ˌmɒnjʊ'mentəlɪ | | ˌmɑːnjʊ'mentəlɪ | *adv.* inmensamente, enormemente.
moo | muː | *v.i.* **1** mugir. || *s.c.* **2** mugido. **3** (brit. y argot), pánfila, zote (una mujer).
mooch | muːtʃ | *v.t.* **1** (EE.UU. y argot) gorronear, aprovecharse de, sablear, vivir de gorra. || *v.i.* **2 [to – about/around]** (fam.) deambular, vagar sin objetivo alguno.

mood | muːd | *s.c.* **1** humor, estado de ánimo, talante, genio, temple. **2** [gen. *pl.*] mal humor. **3** *sing.* atmósfera, ambiente. **4** inclinación, disposición. **5** GRAM. modo. || **6 in no – for,** no tener ganas de, no estar de humor para. **7 in the – for,** apetecer, tener ganas de, querer.

moodily | 'muːdlɪ | *adv.* **1** malhumoradamente, displicentemente. **2** melancólicamente.

moodiness | 'muːdɪnɪs | *s.i.* **1** inclinación a cambios de humor caprichosos. **2** mal humor; tristeza, melancolía, depresión.

moody | 'muːdɪ | *adj.* **1** dado a cambios repentinos de humor, caprichoso. **2** malhumorado; melancólico, triste, deprimido.

moon | muːn | *s.sing.* **1** luna. || *s.c.* **2** [gen. *pl.*] (lit.) meses, lunas. || *v.i.* **3 [to – about/around]** (fam.) soñar despierto, estar en la luna, mirar a las musarañas; vagar, andar sin objetivo, deambular. || *v.t.* **4 [to – over]** (fam.) soñar, fantasear. || **5 once in a blue –,** de Pascuas a Ramos, muy de vez en cuando, en rarísimas ocasiones. **6 over the –,** (fam.) pedir o querer la luna, pedir peras al olmo, pedir lo imposible.

moonbeam | 'muːnˌbiːm | *s.c.* rayo de luna.

moon-faced | 'muːnˌfeɪst | *adj.* carirredondo, de cara como un pan, mofletudo.

moonless | 'muːnlɪs | *adj.* sin luna, oscura (la noche).

moonlight | 'muːnlaɪt | *s.i.* **1** luz de luna. || *v.i.* **2** pluriemplearse, tener dos trabajos (gen. uno nocturno y sin declarar).

moonlit | 'muːnlɪt | *adj.* iluminado por la luna, de luna.

moonshine | 'muːnʃaɪn | *s.i.* **1** (fam.) tontería, patochada, pamplina, sinsentido. **2** (EE.UU.) licor destilado ilegalmente. **3** luz de luna, claro de luna. || *v.t.* e *i.* **4** (EE.UU.) destilar licor ilegalmente.

moony | 'muːnɪ | *adj.* **1** (fam.) soñador, despistado, ido. **2** semejante a la luna (en tamaño, color).

moor | muər | *s.c.* **1** (brit.) páramo, brezal. || *v.t.* e *i.* **2** MAR. anclar, echar anclas, amarrar, echar amarras. || **3 the Moors,** los moros.

moorhen | 'muəhen | | 'muərhen | *s.c.* (brit.) ZOOL. polla de agua.

mooring | 'muərɪŋ | *s.c.* **1** MAR. amarras, guindaste, proís. **2** amarradero, argolla. **3** amarradura, amarra; (fig.) amarras, lazos, ataduras.

Moorish | 'muərɪʃ | *adj.* moro, morisco.

moorland | 'muələnd | | 'muərlənd | *s.i.* (brit.) páramo, paramera.

moose | muːs | *s.c.* [*sing.* y *pl.* **moose**] ZOOL. alce, ante.

mooted | 'muːtɪd | *adj.* (form. y arc.) sugerido, insinuado, dado a entender.

moot point | 'muːtˌpɔɪnt | *s.c.* [generalmente *sing.*] interrogante, cuestión discutible, punto de debate.

mop | mɒp | *s.c.* **1** mopa, fregona. **2** (fam.) greña, mata (de pelo sucio). || *v.t.* **3** limpiar con mopa, fregar con fregona (suelos). **4 [to – (with)]** secar, enjugar, retirar, absorber, limpiar (un líquido con un paño). || **5 to – up, a)** enjugar, secar, absorber; **b)** MIL. acabar con, limpiar (un territorio de enemigos).

mope | məup | *v.i.* **1** (desp.) estar deprimido, languidecer, estar taciturno, consumirse. || **2 to – about/around,** (desp.) andar alicaído, vagar lánguidamente.

moped | məupəd | *s.c.* moto, motocicleta, ciclomotor.

moral | 'mɒrəl | | 'mɔːrəl | *adj.* **1** (no *comp.*) moral, ético. **2** moral (una responsabilidad, una obligación). **3** intachable, íntegro, casto, honrado. || *s.c.* **4** moral, moraleja, lección, mensaje. **5** [*pl.*] moralidad, principios, valores. || **6 a – victory,** una victoria moral. **7 – support,** apoyo moral.

morale | 'mɒ'rɑːl | | mə'ræl | *s.i.* moral, alto estado de ánimo, confianza, optimismo.

moralist | 'mɒrəlɪst | | 'mɔːrəlɪst | *s.c.* **1** FIL. moralista, profesor de ética. **2** (desp.) moralista, moralizador, puritano.

moralistic | ˌmɒrə'lɪstɪk | | ˌmɔːrə'lɪstɪk | *adj.* (desp.) moralizador, moralista, puritano.

morality | mə'rælɪtɪ | *s.i.* **1** moralidad, virtud, honradez, decencia, principios, integridad. || *s.c.* **2** moralidad, sistema de valores. || **3 – play,** LIT. auto (representación alegórica de las virtudes por humanos).

moralize | 'mɒrəlaɪz | | 'mɔːrəlaɪz | (brit. **moralise**) *v.t.* e *i.* **[to – (about/on)]** (desp.) moralizar, dar lecciones morales.

morally | 'mɒrəlɪ | | 'mɔːrəlɪ | *adv.* **1** moralmente, éticamente. **2** virtuosamente, honradamente, de forma íntegra, de forma aceptable. **3** (form.) probablemente, con toda seguridad.

morass | mə'ræs | *s.c.* **1** (lit.) marisma, ciénaga, terreno pantanoso. **2** (fig.) laberinto, enredo, maraña, embrollo, mar (de dificultades, de problemas).

moratoria | ˌmɒrə'tɔːrɪə | *pl.* de **moratorium.**

moratorium | ˌmɒrə'tɔːrɪəm | | ˌmɔːrə'tɔːrɪəm | [*pl.* **moratoria**] *s.c.* moratoria, período de suspensión (oficial).

morbid | 'mɔːbɪd | | 'mɔːrbɪd | *adj.* **1** (desp.) morboso, malsano, enfermizo. **2** horrible, horroroso, horripilante, espantoso, espeluznante. **3** MED. mórbido; patológico.

morbidity | mɔː'bɪdɪtɪ | *s.i.* (desp.) morbosidad.

morbidly | 'mɔːbɪdlɪ | *adv.* morbosamente.

mordant | 'mɔːdənt | | 'mɔːrdənt | *adj.* (lit.) mordaz, cruel, sarcástico, agudo, crítico.

more | mɔːr | *adv.comp.* **1** más, en mayor extensión, en mayor grado. **2** ya, en este momento, otra vez. || *pron.* **3** más, mayor número, mejor: *more was told about him = se decía lo mejor sobre él.* **4** más, otro, adicional: *one more biscuit? = ¿otra galleta?* || *s.i.* **5** mayoría, mayor parte, mayor cantidad, cantidad adicional. || **6 no – than,/not – than,** no más de, no por encima de. **7 not any –,/no –,** nunca más, ya no: *I saw her no more = no la volví a ver.* **8 no – than,/nothing – than,/not much – than,** no más allá de, escasamente, meramente, apenas. **9 – and –,** cada vez más, más y más. **10 – or less,** más o menos. **11 – than,** ampliamente, por encima de. **12 – ... than,** más... que: *more tall than short = más alto que bajo.* **13 once –,/twice –, etc.,** una vez más, dos veces más, etc. **14 what is –,/what's –,** y lo que es más, y además de todo eso.

OBS. El *adv.* **more** se usa para formar el comparativo de la mayoría de los *adj.* y *adv.* de más de dos sílabas y de muchos de dos, además de ser el *comp.* de **much** y **many.**

moreover | mɔː'rəuvər | *adv.* además, por otra parte.

mores | 'mɔːriːz | *s.pl.* (form.) costumbres, tradiciones, convenciones, hábitos, usos.

morgue | mɔːg | | mɔːrg | *s.c.* **1** morgue, depósito de cadáveres. **2** (desp. y fig.) cementerio, lugar aburrido. **3** hemeroteca.

moribund | 'mɒrɪbʌnd | | 'mɔːrɪbʌnd | | 'mɑːrɪbʌnd | *adj.* **1** (form.) moribundo, agonizante. **2** obsoleto, caduco, anticuado (un sistema).

Mormon | 'mɔːmən | *s.c.* **1** REL. mormón. || *adj.* **2** REL. mormón, mormónico.

morn | mɔːn | *s.c.* e *i.* (lit.) alborada, alba, amanecer, aurora.

morning | 'mɔːnɪŋ | *s.c.* e *i.* **1** mañana, madrugada, alba, amanecer. || *adj.* **2** de mañana, matutino, mañanero, de la mañana. || **3 in the –,** por la mañana. **4 – coat,** chaqué, levita. **5 – dress,** traje de chaqué, traje de ceremonia; (EE.UU.) bata de casa, delantal. **6 – sickness,** náuseas, vómitos (producidos por el embarazo).

morning-room | 'mɔːnɪŋrum | *s.c.* (arc.) sala de estar, cuarto de estar (en la parte más soleada por la mañana).

Moroccan | mə'rɒkən | | mə'rɑːkən | *adj.* **1** marroquí, de Marruecos. || *s.c.* **2** marroquí.

Morocco | mə'rɒkəu | | mə'rɑːkəu | *s.* **1** Marruecos. || **2 morocco,** tafilete, marroquín.

moron | 'mɔːrɒn | | 'mɔːrɑːn | *s.c.* **1** (desp. y fam.) imbécil, bruto, idiota. **2** PSIQ. deficiente mental, minusválido psíquico, discapacitado psíquico.

moronic | mə'rɒnɪk | *adj.* **1** (fam. y desp.) imbécil, bruto, idiota. **2** deficiente.

morose | mə'rəus | *adj.* (desp.) arisco, hosco, malhumorado.

morosely | mə'rəuslɪ | *adv.* (desp.) de forma arisca, malhumoradamente.

moroseness | mə'rəusnɪs | *s.i.* (desp.) mal humor, displicencia.
morpheme | 'mɔːfiːm | *s.c.* FILOL. morfema.
morphia | 'mɔːfjə | *s.i.* (arc.) QUIM. morfina.
morphine | 'mɔːfiːn | *s.i.* QUIM. morfina.
morphology | mɔː'fɒlədʒɪ | *s.i.* GRAM. morfología.
morphological | ˌmɔːfə'lɒdʒɪkl | *adj.* GRAM. morfológico.
morris dancer | ˌmɒrɪs'dɑːnsər | *s.c.* (brit.) bailarín de danzas populares.
morris dancing | ˌmɒrɪs'dɑːnsɪŋ | | 'mɔːrɪsdænsɪŋ | | 'mɑːrɪsdænsɪŋ | *s.i.* (brit.) bailes populares, danzas populares.
morrow | 'mɒrəu | | 'mɑːrəu | *s.sing.* **[the –]** (arc. y lit.) el día siguiente, mañana; el futuro, el porvenir.
morse, morse code | mɔːs | *s.i.* código morse, alfabeto morse, morse.
morsel | 'mɔːsl | | mɔːrsəl | *s.i.* **1** porción, pedazo, trozo, fragmento. **2** (fam.) bocado exquisito, "bocato di cardinale", golosina.
mortal | 'mɔːtl | | 'mɔːrtl | *adj.* **1** mortal, perecedero. **2** mortal, humano, de humanos. **3** mortal, implacable (el odio, un enemigo). **4** mortal, letal, de muerte, fatal, mortífero (un ataque, un accidente). **5** inmenso, enorme, aburrido, terrible. **6** concebible. || *s.pl.* **7** (lit.) mortal, ser humano. || *adv.* **8** extremadamente, muy. || **9 – sin,** REL. pecado mortal.
mortality | mɔː'tælɪtɪ | | mɔːr'tælɪtɪ | *s.i.* **1** mortalidad, mortandad (tasa, promedio). **2** mortalidad (condición de mortal).
mortally | 'mɔːtəlɪ | | 'mɔːrtəlɪ | *adv.* **1** mortalmente, fatalmente. **2** enormemente, profundamente, extremadamente.
mortar | 'mɔːtər | | 'mɔːrtər | *s.i.* **1** mortero, argamasa. || *s.c.* **2** mortero, almirez. **3** MIL. mortero.
mortardboard | 'mɔːtəbɔːd | | 'mɔːrtəbɔːrd | *s.c.* **1** birrete (de profesor en escuelas británicas). **2** llana (de albañil).
mortgage | 'mɔːgɪdʒ | | 'mɔːrgɪdʒ | *s.c.* **1** hipoteca, crédito hipotecario, préstamo hipotecario. **2** interés (de un crédito). || *v.t.* **3** hipotecar, empeñar.
mortician | mɔː'tɪʃən | (brit. **undertaker**) *s.c.* (EE.UU.) empresario de pompas fúnebres.
mortification | ˌmɔːtɪfɪ'keɪʃn | | ˌmɔːrtɪfɪ'keɪʃən | *s.i.* **1** mortificación, humillación, vergüenza, orgullo herido. **2** MED. gangrena.
mortify | 'mɔːtɪfaɪ | *v.t.* **1** (gen. *pas.*) mortificar, avergonzar, humillar, ofender. **2** controlar, mortificar (pasiones, apetitos).
mortifying | 'mɔːtɪfaɪɪŋ | *adj.* mortificante, humillante, hiriente.
mortise | 'mɔːtɪs | | 'mɔːrtɪs | *s.c.* **1** muesca, mortaja, entalladura, cavidad rectangular (en madera o piedra). || **2 – lock,** cerradura embutida.
mortuary | 'mɔːtjuərɪ | *s.c.* **1** morgue, depósito de cadáveres. **2** tanatorio. || *adj.* **3** mortuorio, funerario.
mosaic | məu'zeɪɪk | *s.c.* e *i.* **1** mosaico. || *s.c.* **2** (fig.) mosaico, mezcla, variedad. **3** TV. fotosensor (de una cámara). || *v.t.* **4** decorar con mosaico. || *adj.* **5 Mosaic,** mosaico, de Moisés.
mosey | 'məuzɪ | *v.i.* **1 [to – +** *adv./pre.***]** (EE.UU. y fam.) vagar, deambular, andar sin prisa. **2** irse, marcharse.
mosque | mɒsk | *s.c.* mezquita.
mosquito | mə'skiːtəu | [*pl.* **mosquitones** o **mosquitos**] *s.c.* **1** mosquito. || **2 – net,** mosquitero.
moss | mɒs | | mɔːs | *s.i.* **1** BOT. musgo, moho. || **2 a rolling stone gathers no –,** V. **gather.**
mossy | mɒsɪ | | mɔːsɪ | *adj.* **1** musgoso, cubierto de musgo. **2** de color verde musgo.
most | məust | [*super.* de **many** y de **much**] *adv.* **1** más, en mayor grado. **2** (form.) muy, enormemente, sumamente. **3** (EE.UU.) casi: *most every day = casi todos los días.* || *pron.* **4** casi todos, en su mayoría. **5** el mayor, el máximo (en número, en cantidad). || *adj.* **6** más, mayor (en número, en cantidad). || *sufijo* **-most,** más: *southernmost = más al sur.* || **8 at –/at the –,** a lo más, a lo sumo, como máximo. **9 for the – part,** en su mayor parte, en la mayoría de los casos, principalmente. **10 to make the – of,** sacar el mayor partido de, sacar el mayor provecho de.
OBS. El *adv.* **most** forma el *super.* de *adj.* y *adv.* de más de dos sílabas y de muchos de dos sílabas.
mostly | məustlɪ | *adv.* **1** principalmente, en su mayor parte, en general, en la mayoría de los casos.
motel | məu'tel | (EE.UU.) **motor lodge** *s.c.* motel, hotel de carretera.
moth | mɒθ | | mɔːθ | *s.c.* **1** ZOOL. polilla, mariposa nocturna. **2 [the –]** la polilla (que ataca las ropas).
mothball | 'mɒθbɔːl | | 'mɔːθbɔːl | *s.*gen.pl. **1** bolas de alcanfor, naftalina. || **2 in mothballs,** almacenado, guardado, en reserva.
moth-eaten | 'mɒθˌiːtn | *adj.* apolillado, raído, en mal estado.
mother | 'mʌðər | *s.c.* **1** madre. **2 [the – of]** (lit.) la causa de, el origen de, la fuente de. **3 Mother,** Madre (tratamiento para religiosas). **4** (fam.) madre, tía (tratamiento respetuoso para una anciana). **5** madre, sedimento (del vino). **6** amor maternal. || *v.t.* **7** (gen., desp.) mimar, proteger (como una madre). **8** parir, dar a luz. **9** crear, producir. || *adj.* **10** materno, matriz. **11** nativo, patrio. || **12 – country,** país de origen, madre patria. **13 Mothering Sunday,** (brit. y form.) Día de la Madre. **14 Mother Nature,** Madre Naturaleza. **15 Mother of God,** REL. Madre de Dios. **16 Mother's Day,** Día de la Madre. **17 – ship,** MAR. buque nodriza. **18 Mother Superior,** Madre Superiora (de un convento).
mother-figure | 'mʌðəˌfɪgər | *s.c.* (fig.) madre, figura materna, consejera.
motherhood | 'mʌðəhud | | 'mʌðərhud | *s.i.* maternidad.
mother-in-law | 'mʌðərɪnlɔː | [*pl.* **mothers-in-law**] *s.c.* suegra, madre política.
motherland | 'mʌðəlænd | *s.c.* patria, país de origen.
motherless | 'mʌðəlɪs | *adj.* huérfano de madre, sin madre.
motherly | 'mʌðəlɪ | | 'mʌðərlɪ | *adj.* maternal, como una madre, de madre.
mother-of-pearl, nacre | ˌmʌðərəu'pɜːl | *s.i.* **1** nácar, madreperla. || *adj.* **2** nacarado.
mother-to-be | ˌmʌðətə'biː | [*pl.* **mothers-to-be**] *s.c.* embarazada, futura madre.
mother-tongue | ˌmʌðə'tʌŋ | [*pl.* **mother-tongues**] *s.c.* **1** lengua materna. **2** lengua madre (de la que otras se derivan).
motif | məu'tiːf | *s.c.* **1** ART. motivo. **2** motivo, adorno. **3** MUS. tema, motivo.
motion | 'məuʃn | *s.i.* **1** movimiento, ritmo, marcha, acción. || *s.c.* **2** movimiento, gesto, ademán, señal. **3** moción, sugerencia, preposición, propuesta, petición. **4** (brit. y form.) defecación, movimiento del vientre. **5** impulso, inclinación. **6** MUS. modulación. **7** DER. recurso, solicitud, petición. || *v.i.* **8 [to – +** *inf./adv./prep.***]** hacer señas, hacer un ademán, hacer un gesto (con la mano). || **10 to go through the motions,** (fam.) hacer algo por puro formulismo, hacer lo que mandan los cánones (pero sin interés). **11 in –,** en marcha, en movimiento. **12 to set something in –/to put the wheels in –,** poner algo en marcha, empezar algo.
motionless | 'məuʃnlɪs | *adj.* inmóvil, firme, paralizado, quieto, estático.
motion-picture | ˌməuʃn'pɪktʃə | *s.c.* (EE.UU. y form.) película, filme.
motivate | 'məutɪveɪt | *v.t.* **1** motivar, inspirar, estimular, impulsar, mover, incitar. **2** (gen. *pas.*) ser el motivo, ser la causa.
motivated | 'məutɪveɪtɪd | *adj.* motivado, inspirado, impulsado, causado.
motivation | ˌməutɪ'veɪʃn | *s.i.* **1** motivación, estímulo, impulso, fuerza, vigor. || *s.c.* e *i.* **2** motivación, incentivo. **3** finalidad, necesidad.
motive | 'məutɪv | *s.c.* **1** motivo, inspiración, estímulo, móvil. **2** ART. motivo, tema. || *adj.* **3** (form.) motriz, motivador, inspirador, impulsor. || *v.t.* **4** motivar, impulsar, inspirar.
motley | 'mɒtlɪ | | 'mɑːtlɪ | *adj.* **1** (desp.) heterogéneo, variopinto, variado. **2** (lit.) multicolor, policromo, abigarrado. || *s.i.* **3** (lit.) botarga, traje de colores, traje de payaso. **4** mezcla multicolor, mezcla heterogénea de colores.
motiveless | 'məutɪvlɪs | *adj.* sin motivo, sin motivo aparente.
motor | 'məutər | *s.c.* **1** motor (de un vehículo, de una máquina). **2** (brit. y fam.) vehículo, automóvil. || *adj.* **3** a

motor, de motor. **4** automovilístico, del motor. **5** ANAT. motor. **6** motriz, motor. || *v.i.* **7 [to – + *adv./prep.*]** (brit. y p.u.) dar una vuelta en coche, pasear en coche.

motorbike | 'məʊtəbaɪk | | 'məʊtər baɪk | *s.c.* **1** (brit. y fam.) motocicleta, ciclomotor. **2** (EE.UU.) moto.

motorboat | 'məʊtəbəʊt | | 'məʊtər bəʊt | *s.c.* lancha motora.

motorcade | 'məʊtəkeɪd | *s.c.* caravana de automóviles, desfile de automóviles.

motorcar | 'məʊtəkɑːr | *s.c.* (brit. y form.) vehículo, automóvil, coche.

motorcycle | 'məʊtəˌsaɪkl | *s.c.* ciclomotor, motocicleta (ligera).

motorcyclist | 'məʊtəsaɪklɪst | *s.c.* motociclista.

motoring | 'məʊtərɪŋ | *adj.* automovilístico, del automóvil.

motorist | 'məʊtərɪst | *s.c.* automovilista, conductor, motorista.

motorized | 'məʊtəraɪzt | (brit.) **motorised** *adj.* motorizado.

motorway | 'məʊtəweɪ | (EE.UU.) **expressway, freeway** *s.c.* autopista.

mottled | 'mɒtld | | 'mɑːtld | *adj.* moteado, jaspeado, con manchas, multicolor.

motto | 'mɒtəʊ | | 'mɑːtəʊ | [*pl.* **mottoes** o **mottos**] *s.c.* **1** lema, consigna, máxima, divisa. **2** (brit.) chiste sorpresa, mensaje sorpresa, versos sorpresa (dentro de un pastel, de un objeto). **3** cita (al comienzo de un libro).

mould | məʊld | (EE.UU. **mold**) *s.i.* **1** moho, cardenillo. **2** mantillo, tierra vegetal. || *s.c.* **3** molde, matriz, plantilla. **4** (lit.) carácter, temple, naturaleza. **5** forma, configuración. || *v.t.* **6** moldear, vaciar, dar forma. **7** (fig.) moldear, amoldar (el carácter). **8** amoldar, ajustarse a, ir pegado a (las ropas al cuerpo).

moulder | 'məʊldər | (EE.UU. **molder**) *v.i.* (lit.) descomponerse, desmoronarse, decaer, deshacerse, convertirse en polvo.

moulding | 'məʊldɪŋ | (EE.UU. **molding**) *s.c.* e *i.* **1** moldura, junquillo, listón. **2** ARQ. cornisa, moldura. || *s.c.* **3** moldura, pieza de vaciado.

mouldy | 'məʊldɪ | (EE.UU. **moldy**) *adj.* **1** mohoso, enmohecido. **2** (brit. y argot) miserable, infame, cochino. **3** (brit. y argot) pasado de moda, anticuado.

moult | məʊlt | (EE.UU. **molt**) *v.t.* e *i.* **1** mudar, cambiar (la pluma, el pelo un animal). || *s.c.* e *i.* **2** muda, cambio (de pluma, de pelo).

mound | maʊnd | *s.c.* **1** túmulo (funerario). **2** montículo, terraplén. **3** montón, pila (de objetos).

mount | maʊnt | *v.t.* e *i.* **1** (form.) montar, subirse (a caballo, en bicicleta). **2** subir, remontar (una altura, una escalera). || *v.t.* **3 [to – (on)]** proveer de montura, poner a caballo. **4** lanzar, emprender, iniciar (un ataque, una campaña). **5** montar, poner en marcha (un negocio, una exposición). **6** engastar, montar (una joya). **7** enmarcar (un cuadro, una foto). **8** disecar. **9** montar (un animal a otro para la cría). || *v.i.* **10** subir, aumentar, crecer, elevarse, incrementar (un precio, una deuda). || *s.c.* **11** engaste, montadura (de una joya). **12** base, soporte, montaje. **13** montura, cabalgadura; vehículo. **14 Mount,** monte, montaña, colina: *Mount Everest = Monte Everest.* || **15 to – a guard over,** MIL. apostar la guardia, emplazar la guardia, poner vigilancia. **16 to – the throne,** subir al trono, acceder al trono.

mountain | 'maʊntɪn | *s.c.* **1** montaña, monte. **2** (gen. *pl.*) montón, pila, pilada. **3** (fam.) cúmulo, cantidad enorme, sinnúmero. || *adj.* **4** montañero, montañés, de montaña. || **5 – range/range of mountains,** cordillera, cadena de montañas.

mountaneer | ˌmaʊntɪ'nɪər | *s.c.* **1** DEP. montañero, alpinista, escalador. **2** montañés, serrano. || *v.i.* **3** DEP. escalar, hacer alpinismo, hacer montañismo.

mountaneering | ˌmaʊntɪ'nɪərɪŋ | *s.i.* DEP. montañismo, alpinismo.

mountainous | 'maʊntɪnəs | *adj.* **1** montañoso. **2** enorme, inmenso, colosal, impresionante.

mountainside | 'maʊntɪnsaɪd | *s.c.* (gen. *sing.*) ladera de una montaña, falda de una montaña.

mountebank | 'maʊntɪbæŋk | (lit. y desp.) *s.c.* **1** charlatán de feria, embaucador, farsante. || *v.i.* **2** actuar como charlatán de feria, embaucar, engañar.

mounted | 'maʊntɪd | *adj.* **1** montado, a caballo. **2** montada (un arma).

mounting | 'maʊntɪŋ | *adj.* **1** ascendente, que sube, progresivo. || *s.c.* **2** engaste, montadura (de una joya). **3** base, soporte.

mourn | mɔːn | *v.t.* e *i.* **1** lamentar(se), afligir(se), entristecer(se), gemir. **2** plañir, llorar la muerte de.

mourner | 'mɔːnər | *s.c.* **1** deudo, asistente a un funeral, plañidera. **2** quejica, llorón.

mournful | 'mɔːnfl | *adj.* (gen. desp.) **1** triste, apesadumbrado, afligido, melancólico (una persona). **2** triste, lastimero, lúgubre (el tono de voz).

mournfully | 'mɔːnfəlɪ | *adv.* tristemente, melancólicamente.

mournfulness | 'mɔːnflnɪs | *s.i.* tristeza, melancolía.

mourning | 'mɔːnɪŋ | *s.i.* **1** duelo, luto, dolor, aflicción. **2** luto (ropas). **3** lamento, gemido. || **4 in –,** de luto.

mouse | maʊs | [*pl.* **mice**] *s.c.* **1** ratón, roedor. **2** (fam.) cobarde, apocado, asustadizo (especialmente una mujer). **3** INF. ratón. **4** moretón, cardenal. || *v.i.* **5** cazar ratones. **6** andar al acecho, merodear, buscar furtivamente.

mousetrap | 'maʊstræp | *s.c.* ratonera, trampa para ratones.

moussaka | muː'sɑːkə | *s.i.* moussaka, pastel de berenjena, carne y queso (plato griego).

mousse | muːs | *s.c.* e *i.* crema, mousse (de chocolate, etc.).

moustache | mə'stɑːʃ | | 'mʌstæʃ | (EE.UU.) **mustache** *s.c.* bigote, mostacho.

mousy | 'maʊsɪ | *adj.* **1** (gen. desp.) pardusco, grisáceo (el pelo). **2** (desp.) tímida, poquita cosa, callada, sin personalidad (una mujer). **3** (fam.) ratonil, ratonero, de ratón.

mouth | maʊθ | *s.c.* **1** ANAT. boca, labios. **2** (fam.) bocazas, charlatán, vocero. **3** embocadura, boca, entrada, boquilla (de una cueva, de un instrumento). **4** desembocadura (de un río). **5** boca, cuello (de botella, de jarra). **6** mueca, gesto. **7** (fig.) lengua, lenguaje, palabras: *watch your mouth = cuida tus palabras.* **8** portavoz. || *v.t.* **9** recitar silenciosamente, esbozar con los labios. **10** proferir, mascullar, vocear. **11** llevar a la boca, tomar con la boca, mover en la boca. || *v.i.* **12** declamar afectadamente. **13** gesticular con la boca, hacer muecas. || **14 down in the –,** (fam.) triste, deprimido, alicaído. **15 from the horse's –,** de primera mano, de fuentes solventes, de gente muy enterada. **16 to keep one's – shut,** mantener la boca cerrada, estar como un muerto, mantener un secreto. **17 to make one's – water,** hacérsele a uno la boca agua. **18 to – off,** (fam. y desp.) criticar a voces, protestar a voces, quejarse ruidosamente. **19 – organ,** (fam.) MUS. armónica. **20 mouths to feed,** (fig.) bocas que alimentar, personas a cargo de uno. **21 not to open one's –,** no decir ni una palabra, no abrir la boca. **22 from hand to –,** V. **hand. 23 by word of –,** V. **word. 24 to put/take out words into/out of someone's –,** V. **word.**

mouthful | 'maʊθfʊl | *s.c.* **1** bocado. **2** (fam. y hum.) trabalenguas, palabra kilométrica. **3** (EE.UU. y fam.) gran verdad, declaración importante, observación perspicaz.

mouthpiece | 'maʊθpiːs | *s.c.* **1** embocadura, boquilla (de un instrumento musical, de una pipa). **2** bocina, micrófono (del teléfono). **3** (gen. desp.) portavoz, órgano de expresión. **4** DEP. protector dental (en boxeo). **5** (argot) abogado defensor.

mouthwash | 'maʊθwɒʃ | | 'maʊθwɔːʃ | | 'maʊθwɑːʃ | *s.c.* e *i.* enjuague, colutorio, enjuagadientes.

mouth-watering | 'maʊθˌwɔːtərɪŋ | *adj.* apetitoso, que hace la boca agua.

movable moveable | 'muːvəbl | *adj.* **1** móvil, articulado. **2** movible, cambiable. **3** DER. bienes muebles, posesiones muebles. **4** mobiliario, muebles.

move | muːv | *v.t.* e *i.* **1** mover(se), desplazar(se), avanzar. **2** sacudir(se), agitar(se). **3** pasar(se), cambiar(se), trasladar(se), transferir. **4** (fam.) correr, ir deprisa, rodar a gran velocidad (un vehículo). **5** mover, cambiar de posición (una pieza, una ficha). **6** presentar como moción, proponer una resolución, recomendar, (Am.) mocionar. **7** vender, promocionar una venta, tener una salida. || *v.t.* **8 [to – (to)]** (form.) conmover, entristecer, emocionar, enternecer, impresionar; encolerizar. **9** (form.) persuadir, motivar, inducir, impulsar, hacer cambiar de opinión. **10** sacar, quitar, remover (una mancha). || *v.i.* **11** avanzar, progresar, hacer progresos. **12** mudarse, trasladarse, cambiar de casa. **13 [to – +** *adv./prep.*] avanzar, moverse (una ficha, una pieza). **14 [to – (on)]** tomar medidas, hacer gestiones, entrar en acción. **15 [to – +** *adv./prep.* **among/in]** frecuentar, alternar, moverse en (un ambiente). || *s.c.* **16** movimiento, sacudida. **17** mudanza, traslado, cambio (de casa, de trabajo). **18** jugada, movimiento (de una ficha). **19** paso, maniobra, gestión: *a bad move = un mal paso.* **20** avance, progreso, marcha. || **21 to get a – on,** darse prisa, moverse, caminar. **22 to get moving,** ponerse en marcha, ponerse en movimiento; avanzar, hacer progresos, estar en marcha. **23 to get something moving,** poner algo en marcha, poner algo en funcionamiento. **24 to make a –, a)** (fam.) moverse, hacer un ademán, dar un paso; **b)** tomar medidas; **c)** jugar, realizar una jugada. **25 to – along,** avanzar, ir hacia delante, pasar hacia delante. **26 to – heaven and earth,** remover cielo y tierra, hacer lo imposible. **27 to – in,** tomar posesión de, instalarse en; (desp.) invadir, tomar el control (del mercado). **28 to – off,** irse, marcharse, salir. **29 to – on, a)** cambiar de tema, pasar a otro tema; **b)** avanzar, progresar; **c)** trasladarse, cambiarse, mudarse; **d)** largar, echar de un lugar (a alguien); **e)** pasar, transcurrir (el tiempo). **30 to – one's vowels/one's vowels –,** mover el vientre, desocupar el vientre, defecar, evacuar. **31 to – over,** pasar a, cambiar a, moverse hacia (otro sistema, otro trabajo); dejar sitio, hacer sitio, correrse hacia otro lado; a) dejar sitio, hacer sitio, correrse hacia otro lado. **32 to – up, a)** dejar sitio, hacer sitio, correrse hacia otro lado; **b)** subir, ascender, pasar (de nivel); **c)** MIL. movilizar. **33 to – with the times,** ir con los tiempos, progresar de acuerdo con los tiempos. **34 on the –,** en movimiento, en marcha, de viaje, de un lado a otro.

moved | ʼmuːvd | *adj.* emocionado, conmovido, enternecido, impresionado, afectado.

moveable V. **movable.**

movement | ʼmuːvmənt | *s.c.* e *i.* **1** movimiento, agitación, sacudida. **2** cambio, alteración, perturbación. **3** cambio, desplazamiento, movimiento. **4** tendencia, giro, inclinación. || *s.c.* **5 [– +** *v.sing./pl.*] movimiento, organización (sindical, político). **6** MUS. movimiento. **7** MEC. mecanismo, movimiento. **8** MED. (form.) movimiento de vientre, defecación, evacuación. **9** MIL. maniobra, movimiento. **10** [*pl.*] movimientos, actividades, planes. **11** LIT. progresión, desarrollo, ritmo, tiempo.

mover | muːvər | *s.c.* **1** proponente, promovedor, instigador (de una moción). **2** [*adj.* + –] persona que se mueve: *a slow mover = persona de ritmo lento.* **3** (fam.) éxito, triunfo, logro (una persona, una cosa): *one of the best movers = uno de los mayores éxitos.* **4** (EE.UU.) transportista de mudanzas, empleado de mudanzas.

movie | ʼmuːvɪ | *s.c.* (EE.UU. y fam.) **1** película cinematográfica, filme. **2 [the movies]** cine, sala de cine, sala de proyección cinematográfica. **3** [*pl.*] industria cinematográfica, el cine.

moviegoer | muːvɪʼgəʊər | *s.c.* (EE.UU.) cinéfilo, aficionado al cine.

moving | muːvɪŋ | *adj.* **1** conmovedor, enternecedor, emocionante, impresionante. **2** [no *comp.*] motor, motriz. **3** que se mueve, articulado. **4** de mudanza, de traslado. || **5 – picture** (arc.) película cinematográfica, filme. **6 the – spirit/the – force,** la inspiración, el motor, el espíritu que mueve (una actividad, una aventura).

movingly | ʼmuːvɪŋlɪ | *adv.* conmovedoramente, enternecedoramente, emocionantemente.

mow | məʊ | *v.t.* e *i.* [*irr.pret.* **mowed** *p.p.* **mowed** o **mown**] **1** segar, cortar (el césped). || **2 to – down,** abatir, sesgar la vida, destruir, arrasar.

mower | məʊər | *s.c.* **1** segadora mecánica, cortacésped. **2** segador.

MP | ˌemʼpiː | *s.c.* **1** *abreviatura* de **Member of Parliament,** parlamentario, diputado, miembro del parlamento. **2** (fam.) *abreviatura* de **Military Police,** policía militar.

Mr | ʼmɪstər | *s. abreviatura* de **Mister,** *Sr., señor (ante apellidos de hombres, puestos oficiales masculinos): Mr. President = Sr. Presidente.*

Mrs | ʼmɪsɪz | *s. abreviatura* de **Mistress,** Sra., señora (ante apellidos de señoras casadas).

Ms | mɪz | | məz | *s.* abreviatura ante el apellido de una mujer (que se aplica por igual para casadas o solteras).

much | mʌtʃ | *adv.* **1** mucho, con mucho. **2** enormemente, considerablemente, muy. **3** casi, virtualmente. || *adj.* **4 [– +** *s.i.*] mucho, abundante, enorme, gran. || *s.sing.* **5** mucho, gran cantidad, gran parte. **6** importante, notable. **7 [How –]** cuánto (en interrogativas). || **8 as – as one could do,** todo cuanto se pudo hacer, apenas se pudo hacer algo. **9 I thought as –,** (desp.) me lo suponía, me lo figuraba. **10 – as,** a pesar de que, aunque. **11 – of a muchness,** (brit. y fam.) iguales en todos los sentidos, no muy diferentes, bastante similares (dos cosas). **12 nothing –,** no mucho más, apenas nada, nada más. **13 not – of a,** no muy bueno, de poca calidad. **14 not – of a one for,** no gustar, no estar muy interesado en. **15 not so – ... as,** no tanto... como (para expresar contraste). **16 not to hear – of,** no tener noticias de, no saber nada de. **17 not to see – of,** no verse con frecuencia, verse poco. **18 so – as,** siquiera, apenas. **19 so – for,** se acabó, basta de (un tema). **20 so – the better,** tanto mejor. **21 too –,** demasiado. **22 too – for,** demasiado para.

muck | mʌk | *s.i.* (fam.) **1** suciedad, porquería, mierda, inmundicia. **2** barro, lodo, cieno, fango. **3** estiércol, bosta, abono. **4** mantillo, humos. **5** (fig.) basura, bazofia, porquería. || *v.t.* **6** (fam.) estercolar, abonar. || **7 to make a – of,** (brit. y fam.) estropear, fastidiar, dejar hecho un asco. **8 to – about/arround,** (brit. y fam.) hacer el tonto, perder el tiempo; desorientar, despistar, tratar con desconsideración. **9 to – in,** (brit. y fam.) unir fuerzas, juntarse para trabajar, unirse para realizar una actividad. **10 to – out,** desestercolar, limpiar (una cuadra, animales). **11 to – up,** (brit. y fam.) manchar, ensuciar, poner hecho un asco; estropear, fastidiar (un plan) hacer mal (un examen).

muckraker | ʼmʌkreɪkər | *s.c.* periodista o político buscador de corrupciones o escándalos con fines políticos o comerciales.

muckraking | ʼmʌkreɪkɪŋ | *s.i.* búsqueda y revelación de escándalos o corrupción (con fines políticos o comerciales).

mucky | ʼmʌkɪ | *adj.* (fam.) **1** sucio, embadurnado, asqueroso, inmundo. **2** (brit.) horrible, desapacible, riguroso (en tiempo). **3** sucio, pornográfico (un libro, una película).

mucous ʼmjukəs | *adj.* **1** mucoso. || **2 – membrane,** ANAT. membrana mucosa, mucosa.

mucus | ʼmjuːkəs | *s.i.* moco, mucosidad, mucus.

mud | mʌd | *s.i.* **1** barro, lodo, fango, cieno. || **2 someone's name is –,** el nombre de alguien está por los suelos, alguien tiene muy mala reputación.

muddiness | ʼmʌdɪnɪs | *s.i.* **1** fangosidad. **2** turbulencia; suciedad (en el agua).

muddle | ʼmʌdl | *s.c.* (gen. *sing.*) **1** confusión, desorden, barullo, embrollo. **2** dilema, aprieto, apuro, confusión mental. || *v.t.* **3 [to – (up)]** desordenar, revolver, mezclar. **4** confundir, aturdir, azorar, aturullar, embarullar, atontar, entontecer. **5** estropear, hacer una chapuza, fastidiar. **6** mezclar, revolver (una bebida suavemente). || **7 to – along,** vivir a la buena de Dios, no tener planes claros, ir tirando, ir al tuntún. **8 to – through,** arreglárselas, apañárselas, salir del paso.

muddled | ʼmʌdld | *adj.* **1** embarullado, mezclado, desordenado. **2** confuso, turbado, aturdido, atontado.

muddled-headed | ʼmʌdlˌhedɪd | *adj.* **1** confuso, impreciso, poco claro. **2** atontado, tonto, estúpido.

muddy | ʼmʌdɪ | *adj.* **1** enlodado, fangoso, lleno de barro. **2** pardusco, descolorido, turbio. **3** confuso, poco claro, vago, impreciso, oscuro. || *v.t.* **4** enlodar, enfangar, embarrar. **5** nublar, oscurecer. **6** confundir, embrollar.

mudflat | 'mʌdflæt | *s.c.* (gen. *pl.*) marismas, tierras bajas.
mudguard | 'mʌdgɑːd | | 'mʌdgɑːrd | *s.c.* guardabarros, (Am.) guardafango.
mudslinging | 'mʌdslɪŋgɪŋ | *s.i.* (desp.) difamación: *there is too much mudslinging in the newspapers today = hay demasiada difamación en los periódicos hoy.*
muesli | 'mjuːzlɪ | (EE.UU.) **granola** *s.i.* mezcla de frutos secos y cereales que se toma con leche para desayunar.
muezzin | muː'ezɪn | | 'mwezɪn | *s.c.* REL. muezín, almuecín, almuédano.
muff | mʌf | *s.c.* **1** manguito (para proteger las manos). **2** torpeza, error, fallo. || *v.t.* **3** DEP. fallar, errar el tiro, no lograr coger, dejar escapar (la pelota). **4 [to – (up)]** (fam.) desperdiciar, estropear, echar a perder, equivocarse, obrar con torpeza.
muffin | 'mʌfɪn | *s.c.* (brit.) bollito, pastelito (que se toma caliente con mantequilla).
muffle | 'mʌfl | *v.t.* (gen. *pas.*) **1** atenuar, amortiguar, apagar (un sonido). **2 [to – (up)]** embozarse, taparse, envolverse. **3** enfundar (una máquina para evitar ruidos). **4** moderar, suavizar, aplacar, templar (un sentimiento, una emoción). **5** oscurecer el significado, decir de forma imprecisa. || *s.c.* **6** amortiguador. **7** horno para porcelana. **8** hocico, nariz (de un animal).
muffled | 'mʌfld | *adj.* apagado, débil, tenue (un sonido).
muffler | 'mʌflər | *s.c.* **1** (arc.) bufanda, chalina, embozo. **2** (EE.UU.) MEC. silenciador.
mug | mʌg | *s.c.* **1** taza alta, pichel (sin platillo). **2** (brit. y fam.) primo, incauto, bobo, tonto. **3** (jerga) jeta, hocico, boca. **4** gesto, mueca, ademán. **5** rufián, matón, malhechor, ladrón. **6** fotografía, retrato (para archivos policiales). || *v.t.* **7** asaltar, atacar, robar con violencia. **8** fotografiar, retratar (a un criminal en comisaría). || *v.i.* **9** gesticular, hacer muecas, hacer gestos. || **10 a mug's game,** (brit. y fam.) trabajo poco provechoso. **11 – shot,** (argot) fotografía de identificación (de un criminal); fotografía de carnet. **12 to – up,** (brit. y fam.) empollar, estudiar duramente.
mugger | 'mʌgər | *s.c.* asaltante, ladrón, rufián.
muggin | 'mʌgɪn | *s.c.* e *i.* asalto, robo con violencia.
muggins | 'mʌgɪnz | *s.c.sing.* (brit. y fam.) tonto, bobalicón, simplón, incauto, primo.
muggy | 'mʌgɪ | *adj.* (fam.) bochornoso, sofocante y húmedo (el tiempo).
mulberry | 'mʌlbərɪ | | 'mʌlberɪ | *s.c.* **1** BOT. morera, moral. **2** BOT. mora. **3** color morado.
mulch | mʌltʃ | *s.i.* **1** mezcla de paja y hojas, compost (de protección a las plantas). || *v.t.* **2** cubrir con paja y hojas, proteger con compost (una planta).
mule | mjuːl | *s.c.* **1** mula, macho. **2** máquina de hilar intermitente, selfactina. **3** (gen. *pl.*) pantufla, chinela.
mulish | 'mjuːlɪʃ | *adj.* testarudo, cabezota, como una mula, terco, obstinado.
mull | mʌl | *v.t.* **1** calentar (vino o cerveza con azúcar y especias). || *s.c.* **2** promontorio sobre el mar. **3** muselina. || **4 to – over,** meditar, reflexionar, ponderar.
mullah | 'mʌlə | *s.c.* intérprete o profesor de derecho y religión musulmanes.
mulled | mʌld | *adj.* azucarado, especiado y caliente (vino, cerveza).
mullet | 'mʌlɪt | *s.c.* ZOOL. mújol, salmonete.
multi- | 'mʌltɪ | *prefijo* multi-: *multistorey = de muchos pisos.*
multicoloured | ˌmʌltɪ'kʌləd | *adj.* multicolor.
multifarious | ˌmʌltɪ'feərɪəs | *adj.* múltiple, diverso, variado, plural.
multilateral | ˌmʌltɪ'lætərəl | *adj.* **1** multilateral (un tratado, un acuerdo). **2** GEOM. multilátero.
multilingual | ˌmʌltɪ'lɪŋgwəl | *adj.* **1** multilingüe, en muchas lenguas (escrito o dicho). **2** políglota.
multimillonaire | ˌmʌltɪˌmɪljə'neər | *s.c.* multimillonario.
multinational | ˌmʌltɪ'næʃənəl | *adj.* **1** multinacional, internacional. || *s.c.* **2** multinacional.
multiple | 'mʌtɪpl | *adj.* **1** [no *comp.*] múltiple, diverso, variado. || *s.c.* **2** MAT. múltiplo. || **3 – sclerosis,** MED. esclerosis múltiple.
multiple-choice | 'mʌtɪplˌtʃɔɪs | *adj.* con varias posibilidades, de elección múltiple, con varias respuestas (pero sólo una es válida).
multiplex | 'mʌtɪpleks | *adj.* **1** múltiple, complejo. **2** RAD. multiplex. || *v.t.* **3** RAD. transmitir por sistema multiplex.
multiplication | ˌmʌltɪplɪ'keɪʃn | *s.i.* **1** MAT. multiplicación. **2** aumento, incremento, amplificación, multiplicación. || **3 – table,** MAT. tabla de multiplicar.
multiplicity | ˌmʌltɪ'plɪsɪtɪ | *s.i.* **[– (of)]** multiplicidad, variedad, sinnúmero.
multiply | 'mʌltɪplaɪ | *v.t.* e *i.* **1** MAT. multiplicar. **2** incrementar, aumentar, multiplicar. || *v.i.* **3** reproducirse, propagarse (los animales).
multiracial | ˌmʌltɪ'reɪʃəl | *adj.* multiracial, de diversas razas.
multistorey | ˌmʌltɪ'stɔːrɪ | *adj.* de muchos pisos, de varios pisos.
multitude | 'mʌltɪtjuːd | | 'mʌltɪtuːd | *s.c.* **1 [–** *v.sing./pl.*] multitud, sinnúmero, montón. **2 [the –/multitudes]** (arc.) la multitud, la muchedumbre, la población, la plebe, las masas. || **3 to cover/hide a – of sins,** ser una excusa útil, ser una disculpa corriente.
mum | mʌm | (EE.UU.) **mom** *s.c.* **1** (fam.) mamá, mami, mamaíta. **2** (fam.) BOT. crisantemo. || *adj.* **3** silencioso, callado. || *v.i.* **4** actuar en una pantomima, tomar parte en una fiesta de disfraces. || **5 to keep –,** (fam.) guardar secreto, mantener en secreto, guardar silencio. **6 mum's the word,** chitón, punto en boca.
mumble | 'mʌmbl | *v.t.* e *i.* **1** mascullar, decir entre dientes, farfullar, barbotear, balbucir. || *v.t.* **2** masticar con dificultad. || *s.c.* **3** murmullo, balbuceo, barboteo.
mumbo-jumbo | ˌmʌmbəʊ'dʒʌmbəʊ | *s.i.* (desp.) **1** (fam.) galimatías, monserga, sinsentido, tonterías. **2** fetiche. **3** conjuro, ritual.
mummer | 'mʌmər | *s.c.* ART. actor de mimo.
mummified | 'mʌmɪfaɪd | *adj.* momificado.
mummify | 'mʌmɪfaɪ | *v.t.* **1** momificar. || *v.t.* e *i.* **2** disecar(se), secar(se), marchitar(se).
mumming | 'mʌmɪŋ | *s.i.* ART. mimo.
mummy | 'mʌmɪ | (EE.UU.) **mommy, momma** *s.c.* **1** (fam.) mamá, mami, mamaíta. **2** momia.
mumps | mʌmps | *s.i.* MED. paperas, parotiditis.
munch | mʌntʃ | *v.t.* e *i.* ronchar, ronzar, masticar ruidosamente (algo crujiente).
mundane | ˌmʌn'deɪn | *adj.* **1** mundano, banal, trivial, prosaico, vulgar. **2** mundano, terrenal.
municipal | mjuː'nɪsɪpl | | mjʊ'nɪsɪŋl | *adj.* **1** municipal. **2** interno.
municipality | mjuːˌnɪsɪ'pælɪtɪ | | mjʊˌnɪsɪ'ŋælətɪ | *s.c.* **1** municipio, ayuntamiento. **2 [–** *v.sing./pl.*] municipalidad, gobierno municipal.
munificence | mjuː'nɪfɪsns | *s.i.* (form.) munificencia.
munificent | mjuː'nɪfɪsnt | | mjʊ'nɪfɪsnt | *adj.* (form.) munificente, munífico, extremadamente generoso.
munificently | mjuː'nɪfɪsntlɪ | *adv.* (form.) munificentemente, con gran generosidad (especialmente en el dinero).
munitions | mjuː'nɪsnz | | mjʊ'nɪʃnz | *s.pl.* municiones, armas.
mural | 'mjʊərəl | *s.c.* **1** ART. mural, fresco. || *adj.* **2** mural.
murder | 'məːdər | | 'məːrdər | *s.c.* e *i.* **1** asesinato, homicidio, crimen. || *s.c.* **2** (fam.) horror, complicación atroz. || *v.t.* **3** asesinar, matar. **4** (fam.) destrozar, estropear, fastidiar, acabar con (una obra musical, literaria). **5** (argot) vapulear, derrotar abrumadoramente. || **6 to be –,** (fam.) ser muy peligroso, ser horrible, ser una atrocidad. **7 to scream blue –/to shout bloody –,** (fam.) berrear, protestar ruidosamente, poner el grito en el cielo. **8 to get away with –,** V. **get.**
murderer | 'məːdərər | *s.c.m.* asesino, homicida.
murderess | 'məːdərɪs | *s.c.f.* asesina, homicida.
murderous | 'məːdərəs | *adj.* asiento, homicida, sanguinario, criminal.
murderously | 'məːdərəslɪ | *adv.* criminalmente, sanguinariamente.
murk | 'məːk | *s.i.* **1** (lit.) oscuridad, penumbra, tenebrosidad. || *adj.* **2** (arc.) oscuro, en penumbra, lóbrego, tenebroso.

murkily | ’mɜːkɪlɪ | *adv.* **1** tenebrosamente, lóbregamente. **2** oscuramente, turbiamente (el pasado de una persona). **3** nebulosamente, calinosamente. **4** confusamente, vagamente, imprecisamente.

murky | ’mɜːkɪ | *adj.* **1** sombrío, en penumbra, tenebroso, lóbrego, desagradable. **2** oscuro, turbio, sucio (un líquido, el pasado de una persona). **3** nebuloso, brumoso, calinoso. **4** confuso, vago, impreciso, oscuro.

murmur | ’mɜːmər | *s.c.* **1** murmullo, susurro, rumor. **2** queja, lamento, protesta. || *s.c.* e *i.* **3** MED. soplo cardiaco. || *v.t.* e *i.* **4** murmurar, susurrar, hablar en voz baja. || *v.i.* **5** protestar, refunfuñar, rezongar.

muscle | ’mʌsl | *s.c.* e *i.* **1** ANAT. músculo, tejido muscular, musculatura. || *s.i.* **2** fuerza muscular, vigor. **3** poder, influencia, autoridad (política). || *v.i.* **4 [to – in/into]** entrar por la fuerza en, abrirse paso a empujones; meterse en lo que no importa, inmiscuirse. || **5 not to move a –,** no mover un músculo, quedarse impertérrito.

muscular | ’mʌskjʊlər | *adj.* **1** muscular. **2** musculoso, fuerte, fornido. || **3 – dystrophy,** MED. distrofia muscular.

muse | mjuːz | *v.i.* **1 [to – (over/(up)on)]** meditar, reflexionar, cavilar, especular, ponderar. || *s.c.* **2 [the Muse]** la Musa (diosa del arte). **3** musa, inspiración. || *s.i.* **4** reflexión, meditación, cavilación.

museum | mjuː’zɪəm | | mjʊ’zɪəm | *s.c.* **1** museo. || **2 – piece,** antigüedad, pieza de museo, pieza artística; (fig. y hum.) antigualla, carcamal (una persona, un objeto).

mush | mʌʃ | *s.i.* **1** (fam.) pasta, masa, sustancia pegajosa. **2** (EE.UU.) papilla, gachas de maíz. **3** (fam.) sentimentalismo, sensiblería, zalamería, lisonja. **4** marcha en trineo, viaje en trineo (arrastrado por perros). || *v.i.* **5** viajar en trineo (de perros).

mushroom | ’mʌʃrʊm | | ’mʌʃruːm | *s.c.* **1** BOT. seta, champiñón, hongo. **2** (forma de) hongo: *a nuclear mushroom = un hongo nuclear.* || *v.i.* **3** multiplicarse, propagarse, crecer como hongos, crecer de la noche a la mañana, expandirse con rapidez. **4 [to – + *adv./prep.*]** tomar forma de hongo.

mushy | ’mʌʃɪ | *adj.* **1** blando, pastoso, pulposo, cremoso. **2** sensiblero, sentimental.

music | ’mjuːzɪk | *s.i.* **1** música, sonido musical, harmonía. **2** música, composición musical, arte musical. || **3 – to one's ears,** música celestial. **4 to face the –,** encarar la realidad, enfrentarse al problema.

musical | ’mjuːzɪkl | *adj.* **1** [no *comp.*] musical, músico. **2** amante de la música, aficionado a la música, de músicos. **3** armonioso, melodioso, musical (el tono de voz). || *s.c.* **4** comedia musical. **5** (arc.) velada musical. || **6 – box,** (EE.UU.) músic box, cajita de música. **7 – chairs,** juego de la silla vacía. **8 – instrument,** instrumento musical.

musically | ’mjuːzɪkəlɪ | *adv.* **1** armoniosamente, melodiosamente, musicalmente.

music-hall | ’mjuːzɪkhɔːl | (EE.UU.) **vaudeville** *s.c.* e *i.* **1** (brit.) variedades; teatro de variedades. || *s.c.* **2** (EE.UU.) auditorio, sala de conciertos.

musician | mjuː’zɪʃn | | mjʊ’zɪʃn | *s.c.* músico (instrumentista, compositor).

musicianship | mjuː’zɪʃənʃɪp | | mjʊ’zɪʃənʃɪp | *s.i.* maestría musical, talento musical, habilidad musical.

music-stand | ’mjuːzɪkstænd | *s.c.* atril.

musk | mʌsk | *s.i.* **1** almizcle. **2** olor de almizcle, perfume de almizcle. **3** ZOOL. almizclero, cervatillo almizclero. **4** *BOT* almizcleña.

musket | ’mʌskɪt | *s.c.* MIL. mosquete.

musky | ’mʌskɪ | *adj.* almizclado, a almizcle (un olor).

Muslim, Moslem | ’mʊslɪm | *s.c.* **1** musulmán, mahometano. || *adj.* **2** musulmán, mahometano.

muslin | ’mʌzlɪn | *s.i.* muselina.

mussel | ’mʌsl | *s.c.* ZOOL. mejillón.

must | mʌst | | məst | *v.t.* [*pret.* **had to** o **must**] **1** deber, ser preciso, ser obligatorio (obligación impuesta por ley, moralidad o costumbre). **2** requerir, necesitar (físicamente). **3** deber, ser probable: *you must be thirsty after the walk = debes tener sed después del paseo.* **4** tener que, estar determinado a (realizar algo). **5** deber, tener seguridad, tener la certeza. **6** deber, tener que (como invitación, consejo, orden): *you must read it = tienes que leerlo.* || *s.sing.* **7** (fam.) deber, necesidad, obligación; algo indispensable, algo que uno debe tener; algo que no se debe uno perder: *a microwave is a must today = un microondas es algo indispensable hoy día.* **8** mosto. **9** almizcle. **10** enranciamiento, enmohecimiento, olor a moho. || **11 if I –,** si no tengo más remedio, si es que tengo que hacerlo. **12 if you –,** si te empeñas, si es absolutamente necesario. **13 if you – know,** si quieres saberlo, si quieres saber la verdad.

OBS. **Must** es un verbo defectivo que solamente tiene esta forma. La mayoría de las veces funciona como *pres.* y en ocasiones como *pret.* No añade *s* en la tercera pers. del *pres.* y va seguido de *inf.* sin **to.**

mustard | ’mʌstəd | *s.i.* **1** mostaza (salsa, polvo). **2** BOT. mostaza. || **3 as keen as –,** (brit. y fam.) como un lince, listo como un conejo.

muster | ’mʌstər | *v.t.* e *i.* **1** (form.) congregar(se), reunir(se), agrupar(se), convocar. || *s.c.* **2** reunión, asamblea. **3** NAUT. rol, lista de dotación. || **4 to – in,** MIL. alistar. **5 to – out,** MIL. licenciar, dar de baja. **6 to – up,** reunir, cobrar, tomar (ánimo, fuerza). **7 to pass –,** ser aceptado, ser adecuado.

mustn't | ’mʌsnt | *contracción* de **must not.**

must've | ’mʌstv | *contracción* de **must have.**

musty | ’mʌstɪ | *adj.* **1** mohoso, húmedo, rancio (un olor, un sabor). **2** anticuado, pasado de moda. **3** trillado, gastado.

mutant | ’mjuːtənt | *s.c.* BIOL. **1** mutante, mutación. || *adj.* **2** mutante.

mutate | mjuː’teɪt | *v.t.* e *i.* BIOL. mutar(se), transformar(se), mudar(se), alterar(se).

mutation | mjuː’teɪʃn | *s.c.* e *i.* **1** BIOL. mutación, mutante. **2** alteración, transformación (vocálica).

mute | mjuːt | *adj.* **1** mudo, silencioso, callado. **2** FON. oclusiva, muda. || *s.c.* **3** mudo. **4** FON. oclusiva, muda. **5** MUS. sordina. || *v.t.* **6** atenuar, amortiguar, poner sordina. **7** aplacar, silenciar, reprimir (un sentimiento). **8** suavizar, apagar (un color). || *v.i.* **9** defecar, evacuar (un pájaro).

muted | mjuːtɪd | *adj.* **1** amortiguado, de poca intensidad (un sonido). **2** mudo, reprimido, controlado (un sentimiento, una actividad).

mutilate | ’mjuːtɪleɪt | *v.t.* (gen. *pas.*) **1** mutilar, lisiar. **2** desfigurar, destrozar (un objeto), adulterar, cambiar, alterar (un texto).

mutilation | ˌmjuːtɪ’leɪʃn | *s.c.* e *i.* mutilación, tara, daño físico.

mutineer | ˌmjuːtɪ’nɪər | | ˌmjuːtə’nɪər | *s.c.* amotinado, rebelde, sedicioso, insurrecto.

mutinous | ’mjuːtɪnəs | | ’mjuːtənəs | *adj.* **1** amotinado, rebelde, sedicioso, insurrecto. **2** desobediente, rebelde, ingobernable. **3** incontrolable, turbulenta (una pasión).

mutiny | ’mjuːtɪnɪ | | ’mjuːtənɪ | *s.c.* e *i.* **1** motín, rebelión, sedición, insurrección, revuelta. || *v.i.* **2** amotinarse, sublevarse, rebelarse.

mutt | mʌt | *s.c.* **1** (fam.) incompetente, estúpido, tonto, bobo. **2** perro callejero, perro de raza no definida, cruce canino.

mutter | ’mʌtər | *v.t.* e *i.* **1** murmurar, bisbisear, hablar entre dientes, decir en voz baja. || *v.i.* **2** refunfuñar, rezongar. **3** retumbar en la lejanía, rugir a lo lejos (una tormenta). || *s.c.* **4** (gen. *sing.*) rumor, murmullo, bisbiseo. **5** refunfuño.

muttering | ’mʌtərɪŋ | *s.c.* e *i.* murmullo, bisbiseo, protesta, refunfuño.

mutton | ’mʌtn | *s.i.* **1** carne de cordero mayor. || **2 – dressed as lamb,** (fam.) mujer madura que viste de jovencita.

mutual | ’mjuːtʃʊəl | *adj.* **1** mutuo, recíproco (un sentimiento). **2** común, compartido (un interés, un gusto).

mutually | mjuːtʃʊəlɪ | *adv.* **1** mutuamente, recíprocamente. || **2 – exclusive /contradictory,** incompatibles, contradictorios, el uno excluye al otro.

muzzle | ’mʌzl | *s.c.* **1** hocico, morro. **2** bozal, badal, acial, frenillo. **3** boca, orificio (de un arma de fuego). **4** mordaza. || *v.t.* **5** poner bozal, abozalar. **6** (fig. y desp.) amordazar, hacer callar.

muzzy | 'mʌzɪ | *adj.* **1** confuso, borroso, indistinto, poco claro. **2** atontado, confuso (por el alcohol).
my | maɪ | *adj.pos.* **1** mí. **2** [;ms + *s.*] mío: *my darling = querido mío.* || *interj.* **3** ¡oh!, ¡caramba!, ¡Dios mío!
myopia | maɪ'əupjə | *s.i.* (form.) MED. miopía.
myopic | maɪ'ɒpɪk | | maɪ'ɑːpɪk | *adj.* **1** MED. miope. **2** (fig.) miope, ciego.
myriad | 'mɪrɪəd | *adj.* (lit.) **1** innumerable, en gran cantidad. || *s.* **2** miríada, ejército, cantidad ingente, sinnúmero. **3** (arc.) diez mil.
myself | maɪ'self | [*pl.* **myselves**] *pron.* **1** me, mí. **2** mí mismo, yo mismo (para enfatizar). **3** (fam.) el mismo, yo mismo: *I wasn't quite myself = yo no era el mismo.* || **4 all by –,** completamente solo. **5 to –,** para mi propio uso, privado, no compartido.
mysterious | mɪ'stɪərɪəs | *adj.* **1** incomprensible, sorprendente, curioso, inexplicable. **2** misterioso, enigmático.
mysteriously | mɪ'stɪərɪəslɪ | *adv.* **1** inexplicablemente, sorprendentemente. **2** misteriosamente, enigmáticamente.
mystery | 'mɪstərɪ | *s.c.* **1** misterio, enigma. **2** (gen. *pl.*) REL. misterio. **3** LIT. novela negra, novela policiaca; auto sacramental. | *s.i.* **4** misterio, magia, secreto. || *adj.* **5** misterioso, enigmático.
mystic | 'mɪstɪk | *s.c.* **1** místico. || *adj.* **2** místico, contemplativo, espiritual.
mystical | 'mɪstɪkl | *adj.* **1** místico, contemplativo, espiritual. **2** esotérico, taumatúrgico, mágico.
mysticism | 'mɪstɪsɪzəm | *s.i.* misticismo, contemplación.
mystification | ˌmɪstɪfɪ'keɪʃn | *s.i.* **1** mistificación, misterio, engaño. **2** confusión, perplejidad, desconcierto.
mystified | 'mɪstɪfaɪd | *adj.* desconcertado, perplejo, confuso.
mystifying | 'mɪstɪfaɪɪŋ | *adj.* desconcertante, turbador.
mystify | 'mɪstɪfaɪ | *v.t.* **1** confundir, desconcertar, dejar perplejo, estar perplejo. **2** mistificar.
mystique | mɪ'stiːk | *s.sing.* **1** (form.) mística, misterio, secretismo. **2** capacidad, idoneidad (para una actividad).
myth | mɪθ | *s.c.* e *i.* **1** mito. || *s.c.* **2** mito, fábula, leyenda, ficción.
mythic | 'mɪθɪk | *adj.* mítico, imaginario, ficticio.
mythical | 'mɪθɪkl | *adj.* V. **mythic.**
mythological | ˌmɪθə'lɒdʒɪkl | | ˌmɪθə'lɑːdʒɪkl | *adj.* **1** mitológico. **2** fabuloso, imaginario.
mythology | mɪ'θɒlədʒɪ | | mɪ'θɑːlədʒɪ | *s.c.* e *i.* mitología.

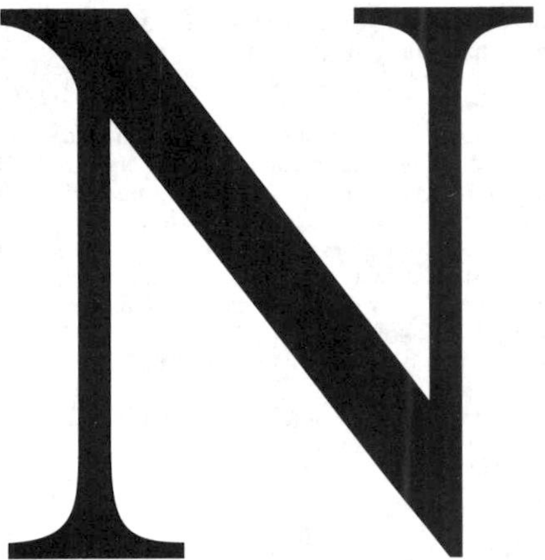

n, N | en | *s.c.* n, N **1** (decimocuarta letra del alfabeto inglés). OBS. **2** Se usa como abreviatura de palabras que empiezan por n: *north, noun, nitrogen...* **3 'n** representa a **and:** *fish'n chips.*

nab | næb | *v.t.* **[nabbing, nabbed]**. **1** atrapar, detener y tener bajo custodia, echar el guante. **2** arrebatar, sustraer. V. **nap.**

nacelle | næ'sel | *s.c.* AER. barquilla, góndola.

nacre | neɪkər | *s.i.* nácar.

nacreous | neɪkrɪəs | *adj.* nacarino, nacarado, de nácar.

nadir | neɪdɪər | *s.sing.* **1** ASTR. nadir (punto celeste verticalmente debajo del observador, opuesto a **zenith**). **2** punto bajo, en que se toca fondo, peor momento en la vida de alguien o de algo: *that century was the nadir of the human mind in Europe = en aquel siglo tocó fondo en Europa la mente humana.*

naff | næf | (fam. y brit.) *adj.* **1** cutre, pasado. || **2 to – off,** [normalmente *imp.*] irse a la mierda, irse a tomar por saco.

nag | næg | *v.i.* **[nagging, nagged]** **1** quejarse de modo continuo, importunar, regañar, reprender, reprochar: *it's no good my mother nagging at me = no sirve de nada que mi madre me regañe continuamente.* || *s.c.* **2** jaco, jamelgo, penco, rocín.

nagging | nægɪŋ | *adj.* **1** gruñón, regañón, quejica, quera. **2** continuo, persistente (un dolor...): *a nagging headache = un dolor de cabeza continuo.*

naiad | 'naɪæd | *s.c.* LIT. náyade.

nail | neɪl | *s.c.* **1** clavo. **2** ANAT. uña. V. **fingernail.** || *v.t.* **3 [to – (up/down)]** clavar, fijar, asegurar, sujetar. **4** descubrir, destapar, detectar, dejar en claro. || **5 to hit the – on the head,** dar en el clavo, acertar. **6 to – a lie,** desenmascarar, demostrar una mentira.

nailbrush | neɪlbrʌʃ | *s.c.* cepillo de uñas.

nailfile | neɪlfaɪl | *s.c.* lima de uñas.

nailpolish | neɪlpɒlɪʃ | *s.i.* **1** esmalte de uñas. **2 – enamel,** esmalte de uñas. **3 – remover,** quitaesmalte.

nail-scissors | neɪlˌsɪzəz | *s.pl.* tijera de uñas.

nail-varnish | neɪlvaːniʃ | *s.i.* **1** laca de uñas. **2 – remover,** quitalaca.

naive | neɪv | *adj.* inocente, ingenuo, infeliz, simple.

naively | neɪvˌlɪ | *adv.* inocentemente, ingenuamente.

naivety | naɪ'iːvtɪ | *s.i.* inocencia, ingenuidad, candidez.

naked | 'neɪkɪd | *adj.* **1** desnudo, expuesto, al descubierto. **2** obvio, claro, distinto: *naked emotions = emociones que saltan a la vista.* **3** insolente, descarado, agresivo: *naked racism = racismo descarado.* **4 – eye,** a simple vista. **5 the – truth,** la pura verdad.

nakedly | 'neɪkɪdlɪ | *adv.* completamente, abiertamente, descarnadamente, profundamente: *the scene was so nakedly revolting, that she fainted = la escena era tan sumamente repugnante que se desmayó.*

nakedness | 'neɪkɪdnɪs | *s.i.* desnudez, desabrigo, indefensión.

namby-pamby | 'næmbɪ'pæmbɪ | *adj.* remilgado, sensiblero, blando, insulso, insípido: *she was a namby-pamby wishy-washy affected creature = era una criatura remilgada, insípida y artificial.*

name | 'neɪm | *s.c.* **1** nombre: *first name/Christian name = nombre de pila, family name/second name = apellido.* **2** reputación, fama, un famoso. || *v.t.* **3** nombrar, llamar, denominar, dar o poner nombre. || **4 – s.o. after/for,** poner a alguien el nombre de alguien o de algo. **5 to be a –,** ser alguien (conocido o famoso). **6 by –,** de nombre, por nombre. **7 by the – of...** que responde al nombre de... **8 to call someone names/a –,** insultar, motejar. **9 in all but –,** de hecho, para todos los efectos, aunque no de derecho. **10 in – only,** en apariencia, sólo de nombre, nominalmente. **11 in the – of...,** en nombre de..., por el poder conferido por... **12 to make a – for oneself,** crearse un nombre, hacerse famoso. **13 the – of the game,** lo que cuenta en una situación, la clave del asunto.

named | 'neɪmd | *adj.* **1** llamado, que se llama: *a man named horse = un hombre llamado caballo.* **2** un tal... *I'm looking for a man named Tom = estoy buscando a un tal Tom.*

name-day | 'neɪmdeɪ | *s.c.* día del santo.

name-drop | 'neɪmdrɒp | *v.i.* dejar caer nombres, mentar, soltar nombres (de gente famosa como si fueran conocidos con el fin de impresionar).

name-dropping | 'neɪmdrɒpɪŋ | *s.i.* dejar caer nombres, mentar, soltar nombres, (mencionar gente famosa por su nombre de pila como si fueran amigos, con el objeto de impresionar).

nameless | 'neɪmlɪs | *adj.* **1** sin nombre, anónimo, desconocido. **2** inconfesable, indescriptible, innombrable: *nameless feelings = sentimientos indescriptibles.* **3** sin clasificar: *he had a new and nameless disease = él tuvo una enfermedad nueva y sin clasificar.*

namely | 'neɪmlɪ | *adv.* a saber, es decir.

name-part | 'neɪmpɑːt | *s.c.* papel principal (de una obra de teatro, película, etc.).

name-plate | 'neɪmpleɪt | *s.c.* placa (plancha con el nombre que se coloca en la puerta para darse a conocer).

namesake | 'neɪmseɪk | *s.i.* tocayo, homónimo, colombroño.

name-tape | 'neɪmteɪp | *s.c.* etiqueta nominal, etiqueta con el nombre (que se cose en la ropa para no confundirla con la de otras personas).

Namibia | nə'mɪbɪə | *s.sing.* Namibia.

Namibian | nə'mɪbɪən | *adj.* **1** de Namibia. || *s.c.* **2** ciudadano de Namibia.
nanny | 'nænɪ | *s.c.* niñera, ama seca. V. **nurse.**
nannygoat | 'nænɪgəut | *s.c.* cabra, V. **billy-goat.**
nap | næp | *s.c.* **1** siesta, cabezada, sueñecito. **2** lanilla, pelo de un tejido, superficie suave. **3** juego de cartas. || *v.i.* [**napping, napped**] **4** echar una cabezada, dormitar, dormir la siesta, cabecear. **5** (vulg.) coger, atrapar, arrestar, retener. V. **kidnap. 6** (vulg.) robar. V. **nab. 7** (fam.) PER. predecir el ganador en una carrera de caballos. **8 to be caught napping,** coger a alguien desprevenido, coger en fallo.
napalm | 'neɪpɑːm | *s.i.* **1** napalm (gelatina de petróleo usada como explosivo). || *v.t.* **2** atacar con napalm.
nape | neɪp | *s.i.* nuca, cogote, cerviz: *the nape of the neck = la nuca.*
naphtha | 'næfθə | *s.i.* QUIM. nafta.
naphthalene | 'næfθəliːn | *s.i.* QUIM. naftalina.
napkin | 'næpkn | *s.c.* **1** servilleta. **2 – ring,** servilletero.
nappy | 'næpɪ | *s.c.* **1** (brit.) pañal. **2** (EE.UU.) V. **diaper.**
nark | nɑːk | (brit. y fam.) *s.c.* **1** soplón (de la policía). || *v.t.* **2** molestar, incordiar: *I was narked about your attitude = estaba molesto por tu actitud.*
narcissism | 'nɑːsɪsɪzəm | *s.i.* PSIQ. narcisismo, egotismo.
narcissistic | ˌnɑːsɪsɪstɪk | *adj.* PSIQ. narcisista.
narcissistically | ˌnɑːsɪsɪs'tɪkalɪ | *adv.* narcisistamente.
narcissus | nɑː'sɪsəs | *s.c.* [*pl.* **narcissi** | 'aɪ |] BOT. narciso.
narcotic | nɑː'kɒtɪk | *s.c.* **1** narcótico, analgésico, anestésico, droga, estupefaciente. || *adj.* **2** narcótico, estupefactivo, dormitivo.
narrate | nə'reɪt | *v.t.* **1** narrar, contar, referir, relatar, describir (sucesos, experiencias...). **2** novelar, fabular, glosar, comentar.
narration | nə'reɪʃən | *s.c.* **1** relato, narración, historia. || **2** *s.i.* descripción, comentario, explicación, glosa, reseña.
narrative | 'nærətɪv | *s.i.* **1** LIT. narrativa. || *s.c.* **2** narración, cuento, historia. || *adj.* **3** narrativo: *a narrative poem = un poema narrativo.*
narrator | nə'reɪtər | *s.c.* narrador, comentarista, cronista.
narrow | 'nærəu | *adj.* **1** estrecho, angosto: *a narrow street = una calle estrecha.* **2** restringido, estrecho (de miras), cerrado. **3** escaso, pequeño, conseguido por los pelos (margen en una votación, competición): *a narrow triumph = una victoria por los pelos.* **4** atento, cuidadoso, preciso: *a narrow examination = un examen atento.* || *v.t.* **5** estrechar, encoger, reducir, restringir, entrecerrar (los ojos). || *v.i.* **6** estrecharse, reducirse. || **7 to – something down,** precisar, centrar, concentrar, reducir: *the options were narrowed down to just a few = las opciones quedaron reducidas a unas pocas.* || **8 a – squeak,** una situación apurada.
narrowing | 'nærəuɪŋ | *s.i.* limitación, estrechamiento (del campo de actuación): *the narrowing of human rights in certain countries = las limitaciones de los derechos humanos en ciertos países.*
narrowly | 'nærəuli | *adv.* **1** estrechamente, por poco, con escaso margen. **2** de modo atento, cuidadosamente.
narrow-minded | 'nærəu'maɪndɪd | *adj.* corto de miras, cerrado de mente, intolerante, torpe.
narrow-mindedness | 'nærəu'maɪndnɪs | intolerancia, cerrazón, estrechez de miras, obstinación.
narrow-mindedly | ˌnærəu'maɪndɪdlɪ | *adv.* con cortedad de miras, con cerrazón mental, intolerantemente, torpemente.
narrowness | 'nærəunɪs | *s.i.* estrechez, cortedad.
narrows | 'nærəuz | *s.pl.* GEOG. estrechos, pasos estrechos, pasajes angostos.
narwhal | 'nɑːwəl | *s.c.* ZOOL. narval.
nasalise V. **nasalize.**
nasal | 'neɪzəl | *s.c.* **1** FON. nasal. || *adj.* **2** nasal, gangoso.
nasalize | 'neɪzəlaɪz | (también **nasalise**) *v.t.* nasalizar, dar un tono nasal, hablar con voz gangosa.
nasally | 'neɪzəli | *adv.* nasalmente, gangosamente.
nascent | 'næsənt | *adj.* naciente, floreciente.
nasturtium | ne'stəːʃəm | *s.c.* BOT. capuchina.
nastily | 'nɑːstɪlɪ | *adv.* de modo desagradable, groseramente, de mala manera: *he interrupted nastily = interrumpió de mala manera.*
nastiness | 'nɑːstɪnɪs | *s.i.* malicia, grosería.
nasty | 'naːstɪ | *adj.* **1** desagradable, obsceno. **2** peligroso (un lugar), de mal aspecto (una herida). || **3 a – piece of work,** (fam.) un tipo que no es de fiar.
nation | 'neɪʃən | *s.c.* nación, estado, población, pueblo.
national | 'næʃənəl | *adj.* **1** nacional. || **2 – anthem,** himno nacional. **3 – government,** gobierno de concentración. **4 – insurance,** seguridad social. **5 – park,** parque nacional. **6 – service,** servicio militar.
nation-wide | ˌneɪʃn'waɪd | *adj.* por toda la nación, en toda la nación.
nationally | 'næʃənəli | *adv.* a nivel nacional, nacionalmente.
nationalism | 'næʃənəlɪzəm | *s.i.* nacionalismo.
nationalist | 'næʃənəlɪst | *adj.* **1** nacionalista (grupos, partidos...). || *s.c.* **2** nacionalista (persona).
nationalistic | ˌnæʃən'lɪstɪk | *adj.* nacionalista.
nationality | ˌnæʃə'nælɪtɪ | *s.i.* nacionalidad.
nationalization | ˌnæʃənəlaɪ'zeɪʃən | *s.i.* nacionalización.
nationalize | 'næʃənəlaɪz | *v.t.* nacionalizar.
nationalized | 'næʃənəlaɪzd | *adj.* nacionalizado.
nation-state | 'næʃən'steɪt | *s.c.* estado nacional, país.
nationwide | ˌneɪʃən'waɪd | *adj.* a escala nacional, por todo el país.
native | 'neɪtɪv | *s.c.* **1** nativo, natural de un país, oriundo. **2** indígena, aborigen. || *adj.* **3** natal, nativo, de nacimiento, del lugar, autóctono, materno (idioma), originario. || **4 to go –,** vivir según las costumbres (de un país extranjero en el que se reside), adoptar las costumbres, adaptarse. **5 – speaker,** hablante nativo.
Nativity | nə'tɪvɪtɪ | *s.sing.* **1** Natividad, nacimiento de Cristo. || **2 – play,** auto del nacimiento. **3 – scene,** escena navideña, belén.
natter | 'nætər | *v.i.* **1** charlar, charrar. || *s.sing.* **2** charla, plática, cháchara. || **3 to have a – (with),** echar una parrafada (con).
nattily | 'nætɪlɪ | *adv.* (normalmente desp.) peripuestamente, acicaladamente, primorosamente (especialmente en ropa).
natty | 'nætɪ | *adj.* **1** elegante, peripuesto, acicalado. **2** ingenioso (objeto): *a natty little gadget = un ingenioso y diminuto cachivache.*
natural | 'nætʃərəl | *adj.* **1** natural, instintivo, sin afectación, nato. **2** natural, no artificial, sin componentes químicos. || *s.i.* **3** MUS. nota natural, tecla blanca (piano). || *s.c.* **4** superdotado, genio: *he is a very good painter, a natural = es un pintor muy bueno, un superdotado.* **5** (arc.) simple, idiota: *she is not quite a natural, that is, not an absolute idiot = no es exactamente una simple, quiero decir, no es una idiota total.* || **6 – causes,** causas naturales. **7 – childbirth,** parto natural. **8 – gas,** gas natural. **9 – history,** historia natural. **10 – resources,** recursos naturales. **11 – selection,** selección natural.
naturalism | 'nætʃrəlɪzəm | *s.i.* FIL. LIT. naturalismo.
naturalist | 'nætʃərəlɪst | *s.c.* naturalista, que estudia la naturaleza.
naturalistic | ˌnætʃərə'lɪstɪk | *adj.* FIL., LIT. naturalista, que sigue la corriente del naturalismo.
naturalization | ˌnætʃərəlaɪ'zeɪʃn | *s.i.* **1** naturalización. || **2 – papers,** DER. documentos de naturalización, papeles de naturalización (cambio de nacionalidad).
naturalize | 'nætʃərəlaɪz | *v.i.* **1** naturalizarse, nacionalizarse. || *v.t.* **2** naturalizar, aclimatar, adoptar (una palabra en otro idioma).
naturally | 'nætʃərəlɪ | *adv.* **1** naturalmente, de modo natural, con naturalidad. **2** ¡naturalmente!, ¡desde luego! || **3 to come –,** aprender con facilidad, resul-

tar fácil: *languages come naturally to him = los idiomas le resultan fáciles a él.*
naturalness | 'nætʃərəlnɪs | *s.i.* naturalidad, estado natural.
nature | 'neɪtʃər | *s.i.* **1** la Naturaleza, naturaleza. **2** esencia, forma de ser, carácter. || **3 back to –,** regreso a la naturaleza, vuelta a una forma de vida menos compleja. **4 better –,** buenos sentimientos. **5 by –,** por naturaleza. **6 by its (very) –,** por propia naturaleza. **7 call of –,** necesidad de evacuar orina o excrementos. **8 in one's –,** propio de la forma de ser de alguien. **9 in the – of,** algo así como, comparable a. **10 in the – of things,** es natural, lógico. **11 – study,** estudio de la naturaleza por simple observación. **12 – trail,** circuito señalizado para el estudio de la naturaleza de una zona. **13 or something of that –,** o algo por el estilo. **14 second –,** algo completamente natural.
naturism | 'neɪtʃərɪzəm | *s.i.* naturismo, nudismo.
naturist | 'neɪtʃərɪst | *s.c.* naturista, nudista.
naturopath | 'neɪtʃərəpæθ | *s.c.* naturópata, naturista.
naturopathic | ˌneɪtʃərə'pæθɪk | *adj.* propio de naturista.
naturopathically | ˌneɪtʃərə'pæθɪklɪ | *adv.* a la manera de los naturistas.
naturopathy | ˌneɪtʃə'rɒpəθɪ | *s.i.* naturismo.
naught | nɔːt | V. **nought.**
naughtily | 'nɔːtɪlɪ | *adv.* **1** con travesura; desobedientemente. **2** con obscenidad, con picardía, inmoralmente, escabrosamente.
naughtiness | 'nɔːtɪnɪs | *s.i.* **1** mala conducta, travesuras, desobediencia. **2** picardía, inmoralidad, escabrosidad: *adult naughtiness = picardía de adultos.*
naughty | 'nɔːtɪ | *adj.* **1** travieso, desobediente, malo. **2** obsceno, inmoral, escabroso, verde: *a naughty joke = un chiste escabroso.*
nausea | 'nɔːzɪə | *s.i.* náusea, deseo de vomitar.
nauseate | 'nɔːzɪeɪt | *v.t.* dar náuseas, producir asco, repugnancia.
nauseating | 'nɔːzɪeɪtɪŋ | *adj.* repugnante, asqueroso.
nauseatingly | 'nɔːsɪeɪtɪŋlɪ | *adv.* repugnantemente, asquerosamente.
nauseous | 'nɔːzɪəs | *adj.* nauseabundo, repulsivo.
nautical | 'nɔːtɪkəl | *adj.* **1** náutica, marítima. **2 – mile,** milla marina.
nautilus | 'nɔːtɪləs | *s.c.* ZOOL. nautilus (animal marítimo).
naval | 'neɪvəl | *adj.* naval, de la marina (de guerra), marítimo.
nave | neɪv | *s.c.* ARQ. nave.
navel | 'neɪvəl | *s.c.* **1** ombligo. || **2 – orange,** naranja grande.
navigability | ˌnævɪgə'bɪlətɪ | *s.i.* navegabilidad.
navigable | 'nævɪgəbəl | *adj.* navegable.
navigate | 'nævɪgeɪt | *v.i.* **1** navegar, marear, gobernar. **2** ir por, viajar de un extremo a otro (de un trayecto difícil): *the number of vehicles which navigate the streets is increasing = está aumentando el número de vehículos que van por las calles.*
navigation | ˌnævɪ'geɪʃən | *s.i.* navegación, arte náutica.
navigational | ˌnævɪ'geɪʃənəl | *adj.* de navegación.
navigator | 'nævɪgeɪtər | *s.c.* AER., MAR. navegante.
navvy | 'nævɪ | *s.c.* peón, bracero.
navy | 'neɪvɪ | *s.c.* **1** la Armada, la flota de guerra. **2 – blue,** azul oscuro, azul marino.
nay | neɪ | *adv.* (arc.) **1** no, mejor dicho. || *s.c.* **2** negativa, voto negativo: *the nays have it = ganan los noes.*
Nazi | 'nɑːtsɪ | POL. *s.c.* **1** nazi, nazista. || *adj.* **2** nazi, nazista.
Nazism | 'nɑːtsɪzəm | *s.i.* POL. nazismo.
Neanderthal | niː'ændətɑːl | *adj.* HIST. de Neandertal.
neap | niːp | (también **neap-tide**) *s.sing.* marea muerta, marea de cuadratura.
Neapolitan | nɪə'pɒlɪtən | *adj.* **1** napolitano (de Nápoles). || **2 neapolitan ice cream,** napolitano (helado a base de capas de distintos sabores).
neap-tide | 'niːptaɪd | V. **neap.**
near | nɪər | *prep.* **1** cerca de, próximo a, al borde de, a punto de, en torno a, alrededor de. || *adv.* **2** cerca. **3 to come/to draw/to pull –,** acercar(se), aproximar(se), atraer hacia. || *adj.* **4** cercano, próximo. || **5 a – thing,** casi, por muy poco, por un pelo. **6 in the – future,** en un futuro próximo, dentro de poco. **7 – enough/as – as makes no difference/as – as no matter,** es casi lo mismo, la diferencia es mínima, no es significativo. **8 nearest and dearest,** los íntimos, los seres queridos. **9 nowhere –/not anywhere –,** en modo alguno, en ningún caso, ni con mucho. **10 the nearest thing to,** lo más parecido a.
nearby | nɪə'baɪ | *prep.* **1** cerca de, próximo a. || *adv.* **2** cercano, en las proximidades, por aquí cerca.
nearly | 'nɪəlɪ | *adv.* **1** casi, aproximadamente, en torno a. || **2 not –,** ni con mucho, en modo alguno.
near-miss | ˌnɪə'mɪs | *s.c.* **1** no acertar por poco, fallar por un pelo. **2** salvarse por poco, de milagro.
nearness | 'nɪənɪs | *s.i.* cercanía, proximidad, intimidad.
nearside | 'nɪəsaɪd | *s.sing.* lado interior, (costado del vehículo próximo al límite de la vía de circulación). V. **Offside. nearsighted** | ˌnɪə'saɪtɪd | *adj.* corto de vista, miope.
nearsightedness | ˌnɪə'saɪtɪdnɪs | *s.i.* miopía.
neat | niːt | *adj.* **1** pulcro, limpio, elegante. **2** claro, preciso: *he was neat and methodical in all small matters = él era preciso y metódico en todas las cosas pequeñas.* **3** puro, sin mezcla.
neatly | 'niːtli | *adv.* cuidadosamente, con precisión: *the line is neatly drawn between joy and sorrow = entre la alegría y la tristeza existe una línea trazada con precisión.*
neatness | 'niːtnɪs | *s.i.* pulcritud, limpieza, elegancia, precisión.
nebula | 'nebjʊlə | [*pl.* **nebulas** o **nebulae**] *s.c.* ASTR. nebulosa.
nebulae | 'nebjʊliː | V. **nebula.**
nebular | 'nebjʊlər | *adj.* ASTR. de nebulosa.
nebulous | 'nebjʊləs | *adj.* vago, impreciso, nebuloso.
necessaries | 'nesəsərɪz | *s.pl.* cosas necesarias (en la vida).
necessarily | 'nesɪsərɪlɪ | *adv.* necesariamente, inevitablemente. *adj.* **1** necesario, importante. || **2 to do the –,** hacer lo que hay que hacer.
necessitate | nɪ'sesɪteɪt | *v.t.* necesitar, ser necesario, exigir.
necessitous | nɪ'sesɪtəs | *adj.* (form.) necesitado, indigente.
necessity | nɪ'sesɪtɪ | *s.i.* **1** necesidad. **2** indigencia. **3** artículo o cosa necesaria, de primera necesidad. || **4 of –,** por necesidad, inevitablemente, necesariamente. **5 the necessities of life,** las cosas básicas, esenciales, indispensables, de primera necesidad.
neck | nek | *s.c.* **1** ANAT. cuello, garganta, cerviz, pescuezo, morrillo (en todos los sentidos: de persona, animal, de botella, de prenda de vestir...), escote, gollete, istmo, mástil de un instrumento. || *v.t.* **2** besarse, acariciarse, besuquearse, abrazarse. || **3 around one's –/hanging around one's –,** responsabilidades acuciantes. **4 to break/wring someone's –,** romper o retorcer el pescuezo a alguien (dicho en sentido figurado y como muestra de enfado). **5 breathing down one's –,** vigilar estrechamente, estar pegado a los talones de alguien. **6 down one's –,** bajar o escurrirse algo por el cuello y la espalda. **7 to get it in the –,** recibir una crítica, una reprimenda, cargársela. **8 – and –,** ir a la par, hombro con hombro. **9 to risk one's –,** arriesgarse; jugarse el cuello, el pellejo. **10 to stick one's – out,** exponerse a la crítica, o al ataque personal al expresar una opinión. **11 up to one's –,** metido hasta el cuello. **12 to win by a –,** ganar por escaso margen.
neckband | 'nekbænd | *s.c.* tira del cuello (en ropa).
neckerchief | 'nekətʃɪf | *s.c.* pañuelo de cuello.
necklace | 'neklɪs | *s.c.* collar (de joyería).
necklet | 'neklɪt | *s.c.* piel de cuello; adorno del cuello (en ropa).
neckline | 'neklaɪn | *s.c.* escote.
necktie | 'nektaɪ | *s.c.* corbata.
neckwear | 'nekweər | *s.i.* adornos para el cuello, prendas para el cuello, complementos (bufandas, corbatas, etc.).
necromancer | 'nekrəumænsər | *s.c.* nigromante; brujo.

necropoles | nɪ'krɒpəliːz | V. **necropolis.**
necromancy | 'nekrəmænsɪ | *s.i.* nigromancia, magia negra.
necropolis | nɪ'krɒpəlɪs | [*pl.* **necropoles**] *s.c.* ART. necrópolis.
nectar | 'nektər | *s.i.* néctar.
nectarine | 'nektəriːn | *s.c.* nectarina.
née | neɪ | *prep.* nombre de soltera, apellido de la familia: *Madame de Staël, née Necker.*
need | niːd | *s.c.* **1** necesidad, lo necesario, deber, obligación. || *s.i.* **2** carencia, indigencia, estado de necesidad, pobreza. || *v.t.* **3** necesitar, ser necesario, tener la necesidad. **4** exigir, requerir, hacer falta a: *one needs to have a visa to go to the U.S.A. = se necesita tener visado para ir a EE.UU.* **5** tener que, deber, ser preciso. || (*auxiliar negativo*) **6** no ser necesario que, no hacer falta que, no tener por qué: *he needn't stay if he doesn't want to = no hace falta que se quede si no quiere; you needn't have bought all that food = no era necesario que comprases toda esa comida* (significa que la compró realmente); *you didn't need to buy all that food = no necesitabas comprar toda esa comida* (no sabemos si la compró o no). || **7 to have no – of,** no necesitar algo, poder pasar sin. **8 I – hardly say/– I say,** no hace falta que diga, no es necesario decir. **9 if – be/if needs be,** si es necesario, llegado el caso. **10 in – of,** verdaderamente necesitado de. **11 no –/there is no –,** no haber necesidad de, no valer la pena. **12 who needs...?,** ¿quién necesita...?, ¿a quién le hacen falta...? **13 without the –,** sin la necesidad de, sin que sea necesario.
OBS. Morfológicamente funciona tanto como verbo modal, necesidad inmediata, como léxico, en sentido más general; siendo esta segunda mucho más frecuente. **Needn't** es la forma modal más común, que se usa como forma de expresar ausencia de obligación. V. **must.** La idea de pasado se construye con infinitivo de perfecto o con **didn't** + ;ms + *inf.*, produciéndose un cambio de significación. V. **6** arriba.
needful | 'niːdfvl | *adj.* **1** necesario. || **2 to do the –,** hacer lo que es necesario.
needfully | 'niːdfəlɪ | *adv.* necesariamente.
needle | 'niːdl | *s.c.* **1** aguja (en todos los sentidos: de coser, de hacer punto, de jeringuilla, de tocadiscos, de contador, ...) || *v.t.* **2** pinchar, molestar, provocar.
needlecraft | 'niːdlkrɑːft | *s.i.* la técnica de la costura, el arte de la costura.
needless | 'niːdləs | *adj.* **1** innecesario. || **2 – to say,** excusado es el decir, es obvio que.
needlessly | 'niːdlɪsli | *adv.* innecesariamente, sin necesidad.
needlewoman | 'niːdl,wʊmən | *s.c.* costurera, hábil con las agujas.
needlework | 'niːdlwɜːk | *s.i.* la costura, el punto, la labor.
needs | niːdz | (arc.) *adv.* **1** **[must –]** tener que, tener la manía de (expresando disgusto): *she must needs say the last word = ella tiene que decir la última palabra.* || **2 – must when the devil drives,** uno se ve obligado a hacer cosas que no quiere.
needy | 'niːdi | *adj.* necesitado, indigente.
ne'er | neər | *adv.* (arc.) nunca.
ne'er-do-well | 'neəduːwel | *s.c.* bala perdida, vago, inútil.
nefarious | nɪ'feərɪəs | *adj.* (form.) injusto, inmoral, vil.
nefariously | nɪ'feərɪəslɪ | *adv.* (form.) injustamente, inmoralmente, vilmente.
nefariousness | nɪ'feərɪəsnɪs | *s.i.* (form.) inmoralidad, vileza.
negate | nɪ'geɪt | *v.t.* negar, invalidar, refutar.
negation | nɪ'geɪʃən | *s.i.* negación, rechazo.
negative | 'negətɪv | *s.c.* **1** negativa. **2** FOT. negativo. | *adj.* **3** negativo, que deniega. **4** negativo (actitud, sentimiento...). **5 in the –,** en negativa, conteniendo una negación.
negatively | 'negətɪvlɪ | *adv.* negativamente, en sentido negativo, con actitud negativa.
neglect | nɪ'glekt | *s.i.* **1** abandono, descuido, negligencia. || *v.t.* **2** olvidar, desatender, descuidar, dejar de hacer, ignorar.
neglected | nɪ'glektɪd | *adj.* abandonado, descuidado.
neglectful | nɪ'glektfvl | *adj.* negligente, descuidado.
neglectfully | nɪ'glektfəlɪ | *adv.* negligentemente, descuidadamente.
neglectfulness | nɪ'glektfəlnɪs | *s.i.* negligencia, descuido.
negligee | 'neglɪʒeɪ | *s.c.* salto de cama, bata.
negligence | 'neglɪdʒens | *s.i.* negligencia.
negligent | 'neglɪdʒent | *adj.* negligente, descuidado.
negligently | 'neglɪdʒentlɪ | *adv.* de modo descuidado, negligente.
negligible | 'neglɪdʒəbəl | *adj.* carente de importancia, insignificante.
negotiable | nɪ'gəʊʃɪəbəl | *adj.* **1** negociable, sujeto a acuerdos; transferible: *the funds and other negotiable securities = los fondos y otros activos transferibles.* **2** transitable: *the path was easily negotiable = el camino era fácilmente transitable.*
negotiate | nɪ'gəʊʃɪeɪt | *v.t.* **1** negociar, gestionar, intentar alcanzar acuerdos. **2** atravesar una zona de difícil tránsito, vérselas con. || *v.i.* **3 – for,** negociar para obtener. **4 – with,** negociar con alguien. || **5 the negotiating table,** la mesa de negociación.
negotiation | nɪgəʊʃɪ'eɪʃən | *s.c.* negociación (política, comercial...).
negotiator | nɪ'gəʊʃɪeɪtər | *s.c.* negociador.
Negress | 'niːgrəs | *s.c.* negra africana, o de origen africano.
Negro | 'niːgrəʊ | *s.c.* negro africano, o de origen africano.
Negroid | 'niːgrɔɪd | *adj.* negroide, de rasgos negroides.
neigh | neɪ | *s.c.* **1** relincho. || *v.i.* **2** relinchar.
neighbour | 'neɪbər | *s.c.* **1** vecino, persona que vive al lado de uno; que está o se sienta al lado de uno; país fronterizo. **2** prójimo: *love thy neighbour = ama a tu prójimo.*
neighbourhood | 'neɪbəhʊd | *s.c.* **1** vecindario, vecindad, barrio. **2 friendly –,** vecindario amable, bien dispuesto. **3 in the –, a)** en las proximidades de, en las cercanías de. **b)** en torno a, aproximadamente: *he was paid in the neighbourhood of £600 for his old car = se le pagó en torno a 600 libras por su coche viejo.*
neighbouring | 'neɪbərɪŋ | *adj.* vecino, próximo, de las proximidades.
neighbourliness | 'neɪbəlɪnɪs | (EE.UU. **neighborliness**) *s.i.* sentimiento de buena vecindad, buena disposición (a ayudar).
neighbourly | 'neɪbəlɪ | *adj.* amistoso, amigable, servicial, bien dispuesto: *farmers as, a rule, are neighbourly = los agricultores son por lo general serviciales.*
neither | 'naɪðər | | 'niːðər | *pron.* **1** ninguno, ninguno de los dos, ni el uno ni el otro: *neither of them knew = ninguno de los dos lo sabía.* || *conj.* **2 – ... nor,** ni... ni: *neither my father nor my mother smokes = ni mi padre ni mi madre fuman.* || *adv.* **3 – am, is, have, has, do, does, ..., I, he, ...,** yo, el..., tampoco. || **4 – here nor there,** no hace al caso, no tiene nada que ver con, es irrelevante.
OBS. **Neither** y **nor** se usan al principio de la oración con el significado de *tampoco,* y con inversión de sujeto y verbo, siendo este último un auxiliar: *"I didn't go to the cinema last night". "Neither did I" = "yo no fui al cine ayer noche". "Yo tampoco".*
nelly | 'nelɪ | **not on your –,** (brit. y fam.) en absoluto, ni soñarlo, y un jamón.
nem con | ,nem'kɒn | *adv.* (form.) con unanimidad, unánimemente (del latín **nemine contradicente**).
nemesis | 'nemɪsɪs | *s.sing.* justo castigo, justicia retributiva.
neo- | 'niːəʊ | *prefijo* neo-, nuevo.
neoclassical | 'niːəʊ'klæsɪkəl | *adj.* ARQ. neoclásico.
neoclassicism | 'kiːəʊ'nlæsɪsɪzəm | *s.i.* neoclasicismo.
neo-colonialism | ,niːəʊkə'ləunɪəlɪzəm | *s.i.* neocolonialismo.
neolithic | ,niːə'lɪθɪk | *adj.* HIST. neolítico, edad de la piedra pulimentada.
neologism | niː'ɒlədʒɪzəm | *s.c.* neologismo.
neon | 'niːɒn | *s.i.* **1** gas neón. **2** lámpara de neón.
neophyte | 'nɪəfaɪt | *s.c.* neófito, novicio.
Nepal | nɪ'pɔːl | *s.sing.* Nepal.
Nepalese | ,nepəliːz | *adj.* **1** nepalés (cultura, costumbres, etc.). | *s.c.* **2** nepa-

lés (de nacionalidad). || *s.i.* **3** nepalés (idioma).
nephew | 'nevjuː | *s.c.* sobrino.
nephritis | nɪ'fraɪtɪs | *s.i.* MED. nefritis.
nepotism | 'nepətɪzəm | *s.i.* nepotismo, favoritismo.
Neptune | 'neptjuːn | *s.sing.* **1** Neptuno (dios de la mitología griega). **2** ASTR. Neptuno (uno de los planetas).
nerve | nəːv | *s.c.* **1** ANAT. nervio. || *s.i.* **2** nervio, valor, coraje. || *v.t.r.* **3** infundir(se) valor, armar(se) de valor, dar(se) ánimo: *the student nerved himself to talk to the headmaster = el estudiante se armó de valor para hablar con el director.* || **4 to be living on one's nerves,** vivir en tensión. **5 to get on one's –,** atacar, crispar los nervios, irritar, molestar mucho. **6 to have a/the –,** tener el valor, la presencia de ánimo. **7 to lose one's nerve,** perder el control, desmoronarse. **8 – centre,** cuartel general, centro neurálgico. **9** MIL. **– gas,** gas paralizante. **10 to strain every –,** esforzarse al máximo, intentarlo con todas las fuerzas. **11 to touch a raw –,** decir algo inconveniente, herir la sensibilidad de alguien.
nerve-cell | 'nəːvsel | *s.c.* ANAT. célula del sistema nervioso, neurona.
nerveless | 'nəːvləɪ | *adj.* **1** débil, sin fuerza: *his hand lay nerveless, dead = su mano estaba sin fuerza, muerta.* **2** valiente, sin miedo, frío.
nervelessly | 'nəːvlɪslɪ | *adv.* **1** débilmente, impotentemente (sin fuerza). **2** valientemente; fríamente.
nerve-racking | 'nəːvˌrækɪŋ | *adj.* agobiante, angustioso, inquietante: *his time in power was a nerve-racking period for him = su período de tiempo en el poder fue angustioso para él.*
nervous | 'nəːvəs | *adj.* **1** nervioso, ansioso, tenso, agitado, inquieto. **2** asustado, preocupado, intranquilo. || **3 – breakdown,** crisis nerviosa, ataque de nervios, agotamiento nervioso. **4 – system,** sistema nervioso. **5 – wreck,** deshecho de los nervios, desquiciado, fuera de sí, histérico.
nervously | 'nəːvəslɪ | *adv.* nerviosamente, con nerviosismo.
nervousness | 'nəːvəsnɪs | *s.i.* nerviosismo, agitación, inquietud.
nervy | 'nəːvɪ | *adj.* **1** (Brit.) tenso, nervioso, ansioso, irritable. **2** (EE.UU.) rudo, áspero.
nest | nest | *s.c.* **1** nido (de pájaros, de arañas...). **2** nido, lugar acogedor. **3** (mesa, cama, etc.) nido. || *v.i.* **4** anidar, encajar. || **5 machine-gun –,** nido de ametralladoras.
nest-egg | 'nesteg | *s.c.* ahorros, dinero que se guarda para algún propósito concreto: *a nest-egg of five hundred pounds in the bank = unos ahorros de 500 libras en el banco.*
nesting | 'nestɪŋ | *adj.* **1** anidamiento. || *s.* **2** búsqueda de nidos para coger huevos.
nestle | 'nesəl | *v.* **1** acurrucarse, acomodarse, arrimarse. **2** yacer o estar situado al abrigo o al cobijo de algo o alguien. V. **nuzzle.**
nestling | 'nestlɪŋ | *s.c.* cría de ave.
net | net | *s.i.* **1** red (en todos los sentidos), tejido, redecilla, enrejado. || *adj.* **2** neto (beneficio, peso...) || *v.t.* **3** adquirir, conseguir, capturar, atrapar. **4** cubrir con una red. **5** ganar dinero neto, en limpio. || **6 to cast one's – wider,** ampliar el campo de análisis o de acción. **7 to slip through the –,** escapar, lograr escurrirse. **8 the nets,** DEP. unas redes de práctica (en el críquet).
netball | 'netbɔːl | *s.i.* nétbol.
OBS. Juego de equipo, formado por siete jugadores, en el que se puntúa pasando el balón por dos aros situados en lo alto de dos postes, que se encuentran en los extremos de la pista.
nether | 'neðər | *adj.* (p.u.) **1** inferior, de abajo: *nether lip = labio inferior.* || **2 the – regions/world,** (arc.) el mundo de los muertos.
nethermost | 'neðəməust | *adj.* (arc.) el más inferior.
nett V. **net.**
netting | 'netɪŋ | *s.i.* malla, red (tejido).
nettle | 'netl | *s.c.* **1** ortiga. || *v.t.* **2** molestar, irritar. || **to grasp the –,** actuar con decisión, coger el toro por los cuernos.
nettled | 'netld | *adj.* irritado, molesto, ofendido.
nettle-rash | 'netlræʃ | *s.i.* urticaria, erupción de manchas rojizas producida por el roce con ortigas.
network | 'netwəːk | *s.c.* **1** (fig.) red, sistema (de calles, de tuberías...). **2** organización (servicio organizado a gran escala e interconectado): *radio or television network = la organización de la radio o televisión.* || *v.t.* **3** interconectar, transmitir en conexión.
neural | 'njuərəl | *adj.* MED. neural, nervioso.
neuralgia | nju'rældʒə | *s.i.* MED. neuralgia.
neuralgic | njuə'rældʒɪk | *adj.* MED. neurálgico.
neurasthenia | ˌnjuərəs'θiːnɪə | *s.i.* PSIQ. neurastenia.
neurasthenic | ˌnjuərəs'θenɪk | *adj.* PSIQ. neurasténico.
neuritis | njuə'raɪtɪs | *s.i.* MED. neuritis.
neurological | nju'rɒlədʒɪkəl | *adj.* MED. neurológico.
neurologist | nju'rɒlədʒɪst | *s.c.* MED. neurólogo.
neurology | nju'rɒlədʒɪ | *s.i.* MED. neurología.
neuron | 'njurən | *s.c.* BIOL. neurona.
neurone | 'njurəun | *s.c.* V. **neuron.**
neurosis | nju'rəusɪs | *s.i.c.* [*pl.* **-ses**] **1** PSIQ. neurosis. **2** (fig.) neurosis, manía, fobia.
neurotic | nju'rɒtɪk | *s.c.* **1** neurótico. || *adj.* **2** neurótico, maniático: *she is becoming neurotic about the school problems = se está poniendo neurótica con los problemas de la escuela.*
neurotically | njuə'rɒtɪklɪ | *adv.* neuróticamente.
neuter | 'njuːtər | *adj.* **1** GRAM. neutro (género). **2** sin sexo. || *s.c.* **3** GRAM. neutro. || *v.t.* **4** castrar, capar.
neutral | 'njuːtrəl | *adj.* **1** neutral (un país, una persona...), no alineado, ecuánime. **2** neutral (actitud, opinión...), imparcial, equilibrado. **3** neutral (emociones, sentimientos...), desapasionado, frío, sereno: *a neutral voice = una voz serena.* **4** neutral, sin matices, grisáceo, indeterminado, indefinido: *the sky was a neutral colour = el cielo era de un color grisáceo.* **5** ELEC., FIS., QUIM., neutro, sin carga, ni ácido ni alcalino. || *s.i.* **6** MEC. punto muerto.
neutralism | 'njuːtrəlɪzəm | *s.i.* neutralismo. neutrality | njuː'trælɪtɪ | *s.i.* neutralidad, imparcialidad.
neutralization | ˌnjuːtrəlaɪ'zeɪʃən | *s.i.* neutralización, eliminación.
neutralize | 'njuːtrəlaɪz | *v.t.* neutralizar, bloquear, contrarrestar, incapacitar: *they just want to neutralize any course of action = quieren precisamente bloquear cualquier tipo de acción.*
neutrally | 'njuːtrəlɪ | *adv.* **1** neutralmente, ecuánimemente, imparcialmente, equilibradamente. **2** desapasionadamente, fríamente, serenamente (en emociones, sentimientos, etc.). **3** de forma gris, indeterminadamente, indefinidamente.
neutron | 'njuːtrɒn | *s.c.* **1** QUIM. neutrón, partícula atómica. || **2 – bomb,** bomba de neutrones.
never | 'nevər | *adv.* **1** nunca, nunca antes, en ningún caso, bajo ninguna circunstancia: *you've never been here before = nunca has estado aquí antes.* **2 – ever,** nunca más, nunca jamás. **3 – mind,** no te preocupes, no importa. **4 well, I –,** ¡nunca lo hubiera imaginado!, ¡nunca he visto/oído cosa semejante! **5 will – do/would – do,** no va a valer, no va a servir, o funcionar.
never-ending | 'nevərendɪŋ | *adj.* interminable, inacabable.
nevermore | ˌnevə'mɔːr | *adv.* (arc.) nunca más.
never-never | ˌnevə'nevər | *s.i.* **1** a plazos, a crédito. || **2 to buy on the –,** comprar a plazos. **3 – land,** el país de nunca jamás, jauja.
nevertheless | ˌnevəðə'les | *adv.* sin embargo, no obstante, aun con todo: *though he is seriously ill, he is nevertheless in a good humour = aunque está gravemente enfermo, sin embargo está de buen humor.*
new | njuː | | nuː | *adj.* **1** nuevo, moderno, reciente. **2** nuevo, fresco, temprano: *new potatoes = patatas nuevas.* **3** nuevo, novato, recién llegado: *the new students = los nuevos estudiantes.* **4** novedoso, original, nuevo, desconocido, extraño, no familiar: *this part of the country is new to me = esta parte del país es desconocida para mí.* **5** un nuevo, otro: *the school had a new headmaster, when the former one was promoted = la escuela recibió otro direc-*

tor después de que el anterior fuera ascendido. || **6 as good as –,** como nuevo, en perfectas condiciones de uso. **7 – moon,** luna nueva, novilunio. V. **full moon. 8 – Testament,** Nuevo Testamento. V. **Old Testament. 9** GEOG. **– town,** ciudad satélite de nueva planta. **10** ART. **– wave,** nueva ola. **11 – World,** el Nuevo Mundo, América del Norte, Central, y del Sur. V. **Old World 12 – Year,** Año Nuevo. **13 – Year's Day,** el día de Año Nuevo. **14 – Year's Eve,** Nochevieja, víspera de Año Nuevo.

newborn | 'nju:bɔ:n | *adj.* recién nacido.

newcomer | 'nju:kʌmər | *s.c.* recién llegado.

newel | 'nju:əl | *s.c.* **1** pilar de escalera que soporta el pasamanos. **2** pilar en el centro de una escalera de caracol.

new-fangled | ˌnju:fæŋgəld | *adj.* (desp.) nuevo, moderno: *a new fangled machine = un ultra-moderno cachivache.*

new-found | nju:faund | *adj.* reciente, recién descubierto.

new-laid | 'nju:leɪd | *adj.* fresco, recién puesto: *new-laid eggs = huevos frescos.*

newly | 'nju:li | *adv.* **1** recién, reciente. **2** de una nueva manera, de modo novedoso.

newly-weds | 'nju:liweds | *s.pl.* recién casados.

newness | 'nju:nɪs | *s.i.* novedad.

news | nju:z | | nu:z | *s.i.* **1** noticias: *here is the news = ahora vienen las noticias.* **2 a piece of –,** una noticia. **3 the –,** las noticias, el noticiario: *news is at ten on T.V. = a las diez dan las noticias por la televisión.* **4 to be –,** ser noticia. **5 bad –,** (fam.) gente problemática. **6 good –,** (fam.) buena gente. **7 – agency,** agencia de noticias. **8 – conference,** (EE.UU.) conferencia de prensa. V. **press conference. 9 no – is good –,** si no hay noticias es buena noticia. **10 that's – to me,** eso es nuevo para mí, es la primera noticia que tengo, no tenía noticia.

newsagent | nju:zˌeɪdʒent | *s.c.* **1** vendedor de periódicos. **2 news dealer** (EE.UU.), vendedor de periódicos, **3 newsagent's,** tienda de periódicos.

newscast | 'nju:zkɑ:st | *s.c.* TV. telediario.

newscaster | 'nju:zkɑ:stər | *s.c.* locutor de noticias en radio o televisión.

newsflash | 'nju:flæʃ | *s.c.* noticia de última hora.

newsletter | 'nju:zˌletər | *s.c.* hoja informativa.

newsman | 'nju:man | *s.c.* periodista, reportero.

newsmonger | 'nju:zmʌŋgər | *s.c.* (desp.) sembrador de rumores, cotilla.

newspaper | 'nju:zˌpeipər | *s.c.* **1** periódico, diario. **2** editora de periódicos. || *s.i.* **3** papel de periódico: *he wrapped it up in newspaper = lo envolvió en papel de periódico.*

newspapermen | 'nju:zˌpeipəmən | *s.c.* periodista, reportero.

newsprint | 'nju:zˌprɪnt | *s.i.* **1** TEC. papel de impresión o de imprimir, de periódico, papel offset. || *s.c.* **2** texto impreso.

newsreader | 'nju:zri:dər | V. **newscaster.**

newsreel | 'nju:zri:l | *s.c.* noticiario, documental.

newsroom | 'nju:zrum | *s.c.* **1** redacción, sala de prensa. **2** sala de lectura de periódicos (en una biblioteca).

news-sheet | 'nju:zʃi:t | *s.c.* hoja informativa, gaceta.

news-stand | 'nju:zstænd | *s.c.* quiosco de periódicos.

news-vendor | 'nju:zvendər | *s.c.* (EE.UU.) vendedor de periódicos.

newsworthy | 'nju:zwə:ðɪ | *adj.* noticiable, que es noticia: *a year book covering the newsworthy events of... = un anuario que incluye las cosas que fueron noticia de...*

newsy | 'nju:zi | *adj.* (fam.) lleno de noticias, plagado de noticias.

newt | nju:t | | nu:t | *s.c.* tritón.

New Zealand | nju:'zi:lənd | *s.c.* Nueva Zelanda.

New Zealander | nju:'zɪ:ləndər | *s.c.* neozelandés.

next | nekst | *adj.* **1** el siguiente, el próximo, el que viene: *next Friday, the next train, the next street on the left = el viernes que viene, el próximo tren, la siguiente calle a la izquierda.* || *adv.* **2** a continuación, después, de al lado: *when I met her next, she... = cuando me encontré con ella después, ella...* || *prep.* **3** junto a, al lado de, casi: *they live next to me, next to nothing = viven al lado, casi nada.* || **4 as the –,** como otro cualquiera, como los demás. **5 – door,** de al lado, en vecindad, junto a. **6 – of kin,** familiar más próximo. **7 – thing/the – thing I knew,** lo siguiente que recuerdo, sólo sé que a continuación: *next thing I was in an ambulance = lo siguiente que recuerdo es que iba en una ambulancia.* **8 the week (month, year...) after –,** dentro de dos semanas, meses, años...; la que viene no, la siguiente.

nexus | 'neksəs | *s.c.* (plu.=sing.). nexo, unión, vínculo.

niacin | 'naɪəsɪn | *s.i.* QUIM. niacina (vitamina).

nib | nɪb | *s.c.* plumilla.

nibble | 'nɪbəl | *s.c.* **1** bocado, mordisco, picoteo, tentempié, refrigerio: *I'm not hungry, I'll just have a nibble = no tengo hambre, tomaré sólo un bocado.* || *v.t.* e *i.* (con **at**) **2** mordisquear, roer, picar (un pez), mermar (el dinero): *small debts nibbled away their savings = las pequeñas deudas mermaron sus ahorros.* || **3 – at,** (fig.) mostrar interés, considerar: *she nibbied at the offer of a new job = mostró interés por la oferta de un nuevo empleo.*

nibs | nɪbz | **his –,** (Brit., hum. y fam.) su excelencia (burlándose de un hombre que se cree muy importante).

nice | naɪs | *adj.* **1** (personas) simpático, agradable, amable, ameno, encantador: *she is an extremely nice woman = es un encanto de mujer.* **2** (actos) amable, buenos, de agradecer, un detalle, *nice manners = buenos modales, it's nice of you = muy amable por su parte, es todo un detalle, es de agradecer.* **3** (saludos) encantado, es un placer: *nice to meet you = encantado, es un placer conocerle.* **4** (objetos, tiempo) interesante, agradable, ameno, atractivo, buen, bien: *it was a nice film; have a nice time = pásalo bien; nice day, isn't it? = buen día, ¿eh?* **5** fino, sutil, culto: *the nicer shades of meaning = los significados más sutiles.* **6** (fam., desp.) ¡vaya!, ¡valiente!, ¡bonito!, ¡muy bien me parece!: *what a nice friend you are! = ¡vaya/valiente amigo estás tú hecho! So you broke it, that's very nice! = ¡lo has roto! ¡muy bonito!* || *(adv.)* **7** agradablemente: *it was a nice long letter = era una carta agradablemente larga.* || **8 to be – (to),** ser agradable con, portarse bien con alguien. **9** (fam.) **– and,** bien, bastante, muy, tan, -ito (diminutivo): *it's nice and warm in here = se está tan calentito aquí. You'll be nice and ill in the morning = estarás muy enfermo.* **10** (fam.) **a – one,** ¡muy buena!, ¡buena la has hecho!

nice-looking | 'naɪslukɪŋ | *adj.* atractivo, guapo.

nicely | 'naɪslɪ | *adv.* **1** amablemente, correctamente, cortésmente: *he behaved very nicely = se comportó muy amablemente.* **2** inteligentemente, sutilmente. **3** bastante bien, bueno: *it's working very nicely = está funcionando bastante bien.* **4 to be doing very –/to be doing very – for oneself,** prosperar.

niceness | 'naɪsnɪs | *s.i.* amabilidad, simpatía, sutileza.

nicety | 'naɪsɪtɪ | *s.i.* **1** detalles, sutilezas: *theological niceties.* **2** placeres, ventajas: *the niceties of country life = los placeres de la vida campestre.* **3** claridad, exactitud, precisión. **4 to a –,** hasta el mínimo detalle, con toda precisión.

niche | nɪtʃ | *s.c.* **1** hornacina, nicho (en una pared). **2** colocación, puesto de trabajo: *to find a niche = abrirse paso en la vida.*

nick | nɪk | *s.c.* **1** muesca, marca, corte, entalladura. || *s.sing.* **2** (argot) prisión, trena, chirona. || *v.t.* y *r.* **3** hacer(se) un corte, hacer una muesca, muescar. **4** (argot) robar, birlar. **5** (argot) arrestar, trincar. **6** (vulg. EE.UU.) cobrar (abusivamente). **7 in good/bad –,** en buenas/malas condiciones. **8 in the – of time,** en el último momento, justo a tiempo, en el momento oportuno.

nickel | 'nɪkəl | *s.i.* **1** níquel. || *s.c.* **2 a)** (EE.UU.) níquel (moneda de cinco centavos). **b)** poco dinero, cuatro perras: *it's worth a nickel = vale cuatro perras.*

nick-nack V. **knick-knack.**

nickname | 'nickneɪm | *s.c.* **1** apodo, mote, alias, sobrenombre, mal nombre.

|| *v.t.* **2** apodar, llamar: *they nicknamed him Little John = le apodaron Pequeño John.*
nicotine | 'nɪkətiːn | *s.i.* nicotina.
niece | niːs | *s.c.* sobrina.
niff | nɪf | *s.i.* (brit. y argot) olor, tufo.
niffy | 'nɪfɪ | *adj.* (brit. y argot) maloliente.
nifty | nɪfti | *adj.* (fam.) agradable, elegante, bien hecho.
Nigeria | naɪ'dʒɪərɪə | *s.c.* Nigeria.
Nigerian | naɪ'dʒɪərɪən | *adj.* y *s.c.* nigeriano.
niggardliness | 'nɪgədlɪnɪs | *s.i.* avaricia, mezquindad, tacañería.
niggardly | 'nɪgədli | *adj.* avariento, tacaño, miserable.
nigger | 'nɪgər | *s.c.* (desp.) negro.
niggle | 'nɪgəl | *v.t.* e *i.* **1** inquietar, molestar, preocupar. **2** criticar, quejarse, murmurar de.
niggling | 'nɪgəlɪŋ | *adj.* **1** delicado, melindroso, mezquino, de miras estrechas. **2** nimio, insignificante, de poca monta.
nigh | naɪ | *adv.* **1** (lit., p.u.) cerca, cercano, próximo. || **2 – on,** casi, próximo a, cerca de. **3 well –,** prácticamente, virtualmente.
night | naɪt | *s.c.* e *i.* **1** noche. || *adj.* **2** nocturno. || **3 at –,** de, por la noche. **4 day and –/ =N and day,** noche y día, continuamente. **5 to have a bad –,** dormir mal, pasar mala noche. **6 to have an early –,** acostarse pronto. **7 to have a late –,** acostarse tarde. **8 to make a – of it,** echar la noche, pasar la noche de juerga. **9 – owl,** trasnochador, nocherniego. **10 – porter,** recepcionista, portero de noche. || **– safe,** cajero nocturno.
night-bird | 'naɪtbəːd | *s.c.* **1** ZOOL. ave nocturna. **2** (fig. y fam.) trasnochador.
night-blindness | ˌnaɪt'blaɪndnɪs | *s.i.* ceguera nocturna.
nightcap | 'naɪtkæp | *s.c.* **1** gorro de noche, de dormir. **2** la espuela, (la última copa que toma un bebedor antes de acostarse).
nightclothes | 'naɪtkləʊðz | *s.pl.* ropa de dormir, camisón, pijama.
nightclub | 'naɪtklʌb | *s.c.* cabaret, club nocturno, sala de fiestas.
nightdress | 'naɪtdres | *s.c.* camisón.
nightfall | 'naɪtfɔːl | *s.i.* anochecer, crepúsculo.
nightgown | 'naɪtgaʊn | *s.c.* camisón.
nightie | 'naɪtɪ | *s.c.* (fam.) camisón.
nightingale | 'naɪtɪŋgeɪl | *s.c.* ruiseñor.
nightjar | 'naɪtdʒɑːr | *s.c.* ZOOL. chotacabras (pájaro nocturno).
nightlife | 'naɪtlaɪf | *s.i.* vida nocturna.
nightlight | 'naɪtlaɪt | *s.c.* luz nocturna, lamparilla, piloto.
night-line | 'naɪtlaɪn | *s.c.* caña de pescar dejada durante toda la noche.
night-long | 'naɪtlɒŋ | *adj.* y *adv.* durante toda la noche, durante la noche, de toda la noche.
nightly | 'naɪtlɪ | *adj.* **1** de la noche, de cada noche: *the nightly television news = las noticias de la noche de la televisión.* || *adv.* **2** cada noche, todas las noches: *watch it nightly = contémplalo todas las noches.*
nightmare | 'naɪtmeər | *s.c.* **1** sueño angustioso, mal sueño, pesadilla. **2** (fig.) de pesadilla, terrible (situación, experiencia).
nightmarish | naɪtmeərɪʃ | *adj.* aterrador, de pesadilla.
nights | naɪts | *adv.* (EE.UU.) por la noche, durante la noche.
night-school | 'naɪtskʊl | *s.i.* y *c.* escuela nocturna.
nightshade | 'naɪtʃeɪd | *s.c.* e *i.* BOT. solano; dulcamara.
night-shift | 'naɪtʃɪft | *s.c.* e *i.* turno de noche.
nightshirt | 'naɪtʃəːt | *s.c.* camisón, camisa de dormir.
night-soil | 'naɪtsɔɪl | *s.i.* (euf.) excremento humano (especialmente el recogido durante la noche).
nightstick | 'naɪtˌstɪk | *s.c.* (EE.UU.) cachiporra, porra.
night-time | 'naɪttaɪm | *s.i.* noche, las horas de la noche.
night-watch | ˌnaɪt'wɒtʃ | *s.i.* **[– + *v.sing./v.pl.*]** vigilancia nocturna, vigilantes nocturnos, ronda nocturna.
nightwatchman | ˌnəɪt'wɒtʃmən | *s.c.* vigilante nocturno.
nightwear | 'naɪtweər | *s.i.* (form.) ropa de dormir, camisón o pijama.
nihilism | 'naɪɪlɪzəm | *s.i.* FIL. nihilismo.
nihilist | 'naɪɪlɪst | *s.c.* nihilista.
nihilistic | ˌnaɪɪ'lɪstɪk | | ˌnɪhɪ'lɪstɪk | *adj.* nihilista.
nil | nɪl | *s.i.* **1** nada, nulo: *costs can be reduced to nil = los costes pueden quedar reducidos a nada.* **2** (brit.) DEP. a cero: *our team was beaten five points to nil = nuestro equipo fue derrotado 5 a 0.* V. **nought.**
nimble | 'nɪmbəl | *adj.* **1** ágil, rápido de movimientos, diestro: *a nimble penny is worth a slow sixpence.* **2** listo, vivo, ágil, rápido de mente: *a nimble dialectician.* || *s.pl.* **3** (vulg.) los dedos.
nimbleness | 'nɪmblnɪs | *s.i.* **1** agilidad, destreza (física). **2** viveza, agilidad (mental).
nimbly | 'nɪmblɪ | *adv.* ágilmente, con destreza, con elegancia.
nimbus | 'nɪmbəs | *s.c.* [*pl.* **nimbuses** o **nimbi**] **1** GEOG. nimbo. **2** REL. halo, aureola.
nincompoop | 'nɪŋkəmpuːp | *s.c.* (fam.) loco, estúpido, tonto.
nine | naɪn | *num.* **1** nueve. || **2 to dress onself up to the – -s,** ponerse las mejores ropas, vestirse de gala, de domingo. **3 – times out of ten,** (fam.) casi siempre.
nineteen | ˌnaɪn'tiːn | *num.* **1** diecinueve. **2 to talk – to the dozen,** (fam.) hablar atropelladamente, muy deprisa.
nineteenth | ˌnaɪn'tɪːnɵ | *ord.* **1** decimonoveno, decimonono. **2** diecinueveavo. **3** diecinueve: *the nineteenth century = el siglo diecinueve.*
ninetieth | 'naɪntɪɪɵ | *ord.* **1** nonagésimo. **2** noventavo.
ninety | 'naɪntɪ | *num.* **1** noventa. || **2 ninety-nine times out of a hundred,** casi siempre.
ninny | 'nɪnɪ | *s.c.* (fam. y desp.) bobo, memo, tonto.
ninth | naɪnɵ | *ord.* nono, noveno.
ninthly | 'naɪnɵlɪ | *adv.* en noveno lugar.
nip | nɪp | *v.* **[nipping, nipped]** *tr.* **1** pellizcar, atrapar, coger (entre dos cosas, o superficies), mordisquear: *the dog nipped the man on the leg = el perro mordisqueó al hombre en la pierna.* || *v.i.* **2 [=N off, in, out, up, down]** salir o entrar rápido, darse prisa, ir en una corrida: *"nip in, sir", said the driver = "Entre, señor": dijo el conductor; please, nip down to the shop round the corner and get some coffee = baja en un momento a la tienda de la esquina y compra café.* **3** arrancar, cortar: *nip off a feather = arranca una pluma.* || *s.c.* **4** pellizco, mordisco. **5** (fam.) un trago, un sorbo (de bebida alcohólica), un latigazo. **6 a – in the air,** (fam.) frío, viento fresco. **7 Nip,** (desp.) nipón. **8 – in the bud,** cortar de raíz.
nipper | 'nɪpər | *s.c.* **1** (fam.) chico, muchacho, pibe, zagal. **2 nippers,** alicates, tenacillas, tenazas.
nipple | 'nɪpəl | *s.c.* **1** pezón, tetilla. **2** boquilla de biberón, tetina.
nippy | 'nɪpɪ | *adj.* **1** ágil, rápido, listo. **2** frío: *a A nippy wind = un viento frío.*
nirvana | nɪə'vɑːnə | *s.i.* **1** nirvana. **2** (fig.) paraíso, estado de felicidad.
Nissen hut | 'nɪsnhʌt | *s.c.* barraca prefabricada (normalmente militar).
niter V. **nitre.**
nit | nɪt | *s.i.* **1** liendre, parásito. **2** (desp.) imbécil, idiota. **3 to be picking nits,** criticar, razonar sobre trivialidades, trivializar, perderse en cuestiones de detalle, en nimiedades.
nitpicking | 'nɪtˌpɪkɪŋ | *s.i.* sofismas, sutilezas, nimiedades, objeciones de poca monta: *her arguments were mere nitpicking = sus argumentos eran meras objeciones de poca monta.*
nitrate | 'naɪtreɪt | *s.c.* e *i.* QUIM. nitrato.
nitre | 'naɪtər | (EE.UU. **niter**) *s.i.* QUIM. nitro, nitrato potásico.
nitric 'naɪtrɪk | QUIM. *adj.* **1** nítrico. || **2 – acid,** ácido nítrico, agua fuerte.
nitrogen | 'naɪtrədʒən | *s.i.* nitrógeno.
nitrogenous | naɪ'trɒdʒɪnəs | *adj.* QUIM. de nitrógeno.
nitty-gritty | ˌnɪtɪ'grɪtɪ | *s.sing.* (fam.) el núcleo, el grano, lo básico, lo fundamental (en un tema): *let's get down to the nitty-gritty of the matter = vayamos a lo fundamental del tema.*
nitwit | 'nɪtwɪt | *s.c.* estúpido, tonto.
nitwitted | ˌnɪt'wɪtɪd | *adj.* estúpido, lelo, imbécil.
nix | nɪks | *s.i.* (argot) nada, ni pún.
no | nəʊ | *adv.* [pl. **noes,** o **no's**] **1** no: *do you want it? No, I don't = ¿lo quieres? No.* **2** ¡no!, ¡vale!, ¡basta!: *no! stop it!* **3** no, no sin, sin (con *adj.* para dar el sig-

nificado opuesto): *the no small admiration = la no poca admiración; no-coloured = sin color.* **4** no, ya no, no por más tiempo (con comparativo). *They no longer enjoyed... = ya no siguieron disfrutando...* **5** no (disyuntivo): *whether or no = sí o no.* || **6** nada de, ningún, no: *there's no wine left = no queda vino.* **7** no, prohibido (en avisos públicos): *No smoking.* **8** en poco, casi nada: *we'll be there in no time = estaremos allí en poco tiempo.* || *s.* **9** un no, noes: *she gave a clear no to my request; the noes and the ayes in Parliament = ella me dio un claro no a mi petición; los noes y los síes en el parlamento.* **10 – ball,** DEP. lanzamiento incorrecto (en críquet). **11 not to take a – for an answer,** no aceptar un no por respuesta. **12 there's –,** no es posible, no hay forma de: *there's no knowing what'll be the end of the affair = no hay forma de saber cuál será el final del asunto.* V. **nought.**

nob | nɒb | *s.c.* **1** (vulg.) cabeza. **2** (hum. o desp.) rico, pez gordo. || *v.t.* **3** (vulg.) golpear en la cabeza.

nobble | 'nɒbl | *v.t.* (vulg.) **1** atraer la atención, persuadir. **2** presionar, chantajear. **3** drogar, narcotizar (a un caballo).

nobility | nəʊ'bɪlɪtɪ | *s.i.* **1** dignidad, nobleza, rango. **2 the –,** la aristocracia, la nobleza.

noble | 'nəʊbl | *adj.* **1** noble, admirable, valioso: *whether 'tis nobler in the mind to suffer = si es más noble sufrir.* **2** noble, aristocrático. *Noble birth.* **3** agradable, bello, distinguido, superior: *a noble-looking man = un hombre de aspecto distinguido.* **4** QUIM. noble (metales como el oro, la plata...). || *s.c.* **5** noble, aristócrata. || **6 Nobel Prize,** Premio Nobel.

nobleman | 'nəʊblmən | *s.c.* noble, aristócrata.

noblewoman | 'nəʊblwumən | *s.c.* drama noble, aristócrata.

noblesse oblige | nəʊˌblesə'bliːʒ | *interj.* nobleza obliga (proverbio francés).

nobly | 'nəʊbli | *adv.* **1** noblemente, con nobleza, generosamente. **2** espléndidamente, magnificentemente. **3 – born,** de noble cuna: *better to be nobly remembered than nobly born = es mejor ser recordado noblemente que ser de noble cuna.*

nobody | 'nəʊbədɪ | *pron.ind.* **1** nadie. || *s.c.* **2** don nadie, nulidad, cero a la izquierda.

nocturnal | nɒk'tɜːnl | *adj.* nocturno, nocturnal, noctívago.

nocturnally | nɒk'tɜːnəlɪ | *adv.* nocturnalmente.

nocturne | 'nɒktɜːn | *s.c.* MUS. nocturno, serenata nocturna.

nod | nɒd | *s.c.* **[nodding, nodded]. 1** cabezada. **2** movimiento, indicación, señal, orden o saludo (hecho con la cabeza): *a nod is as good as a wink = un saludo hecho con la cabeza es tan útil como un guiño.* || *v.i.* **3** asentir, indicar, señalar, invitar, saludar..., con la cabeza. **4** cabecear, dar cabezadas, dormitar: *even Homer sometimes nods = incluso Homero a veces dormita.* || *v.r.* **5** inclinarse, moverse: *the trees nodded in the wind = los árboles se inclinaban al viento.* **6 to give the –, to give someone the –,** dar permiso, mostrar acuerdo. **7 – off,** quedarse dormido, echar una cabezada. **8 on nodding terms,** conocerse de vista y saludarse. **10 on the –, a)** con facilidad, fácilmente, ponerse de acuerdo rápidamente. **b)** a crédito.

noddle | 'nɒdl | *s.c.* (fam.) la cabeza.

node | nəud | *s.c.* **1** ASTR., BIOL. nodo. **2** BOT. nudo.

nodular | 'nɒdjuːlər | *adj.* nodular.

nodule | 'nɒdjuːl | *s.c.* **1** concreción, dureza, nódulo, protuberancia. **2** GEOL. núcleo, nódulo, gabarro.

Noel | nəʊ'el | *s.* Navidad.

noggin | 'nɒgɪn | *s.c.* **1** (vulg.) la cabeza. **2** un trago, vaso, vasito, caña. **3** medida de capacidad (a **dram,** a **gill**).

no-go area | nəʊ'gəueɪrɪə | *s.c.* zona prohibida, peligrosa. V. **area.**

nohow | 'nəʊhau | *adv.* (fam.) de ninguna manera.

noise | nɔɪz | *s.c.* **1** ruido. **2** escándalo: *the novel made quite a noise when published = la novela causó bastante escándalo cuando se publicó.* || *s.i.* **3** ruido, ruidos molestos, jaleo, estrépito, clamor, interferencias: *preferring quiet and solitude to the noise of a great town = prefiriendo la tranquilidad y la soledad al ruido de una gran ciudad.* **4 big –,** personaje, pez gordo. **5 to make a – about,** hacer notar, meter ruido, quejarse. **6 to make noises,** expresar sentimientos, referirse a, manifestarse, hacer notar. **7 to make the right noises/to make all the right noises,** mostrar entusiasmo, hacer el paripé, cumplir. **8 to – about/abroad,** divulgar, hacer correr un rumor.

noiseless | 'nɔɪzlɪs | *adj.* silencioso, sin ruido, silente, sosegado, tranquilo: *the noiseless foot of time = el paso sosegado del tiempo.*

noilessly | 'nɔɪzˌlɪsli | *adv.* silenciosamente.

noiselessness | 'nɔɪzlɪsnɪs | *s.i.* paz, tranquilidad, sosiego.

noisily | 'nɔɪzɪlɪ | *adv.* ruidosamente, estrepitosamente.

noisiness | 'nɔɪzɪnɪs | *s.i.* ruido, estrépito.

noisome | 'nɔɪsəm | *adj.* (form.) **1** nocivo, dañoso. **2** desagradable, molesto, ofensivo. **3** maloliente, hediondo.

noisy | 'nɔɪzi | *adj.* ruidoso, estrepitoso.

nomad | 'nəʊmæd | *s.c.* nómada, errante.

nomadic | nəʊ'mædɪk | *adj.* nómada.

no man's land V. **land.**

nom de plume | ˌnɒmdə'pluːm | *s.c.* pseudónimo (forma francesa).

nomenclature | nə'menklətʃər | *s.i.* clasificación, nomenclatura.

nominal | 'nɒmɪnl | *adj.* **1** nominal, aparente, teórico, cabeza visible. **2** nominal, relación nominal. **3** nominal, nominativo, a nombre de. **4** GRAM. nominal, perteneciente al nombre. **5** simbólico (precio).

nominally | 'nɒmɪnəli | *adv.* nominalmente, teóricamente.

nominate | 'nɒmɪneɪt | *v.t.* **1** nombrar, nominar, llamar, poner un nombre. **2** elegir, nombrar, proponer. **3** nombrar, asignar, designar (para un puesto de trabajo).

nomination | ˌnɒmɪ'neɪʃn | *s.c.* **1** seleccionado, clasificado, propuesto. || *s.i.* **2** nombramiento, propuesta, candidatura. **3** elección, asignación, nombramiento. || **3 to place someone's name in – for,** proponer a alguien para un cargo.

nominative | 'nɒmɪnətɪv | *adj.* **1** GRAM. nominativo (caso del sujeto): *a nominative pronoun = un pronombre nominativo.* || *s.c.* **2** nominativo (caso), palabra en ese caso: *the nominative is rosa; there are three nominatives = el nominativo es rosa; hay tres nominativos.*

nominee | ˌnɒmɪ'niː | *s.c.* candidato, aspirante, pretendiente (a un puesto), persona o cosa propuesta (para un premio, beca, etc...).

non- | nɒn | *prefijo* no-, in-, que no puede ser, sin. *non-attendance = inasistencia; non-absorbable = que no puede ser absorbido.*

nonage | 'nəʊnɪdʒ | *s.i.* (form.) minoría de edad.

nonagenarian | ˌnɒnədʒɪ'neərɪən | *s.c.* **1** nonagenario. || *adj.* **2** nonagenario.

non-aggression | ˌnɒnə'greʃn | *s.i.* no agresión: *non-agression treaty = tratado de no agresión.*

non-alcoholic | ˌnɒnˌælkə'hɒlɪk | *adj.* no alcohólico, sin alcohol.

non-aligned | ˌnɒnə'laɪnd | *adj.* no alineado, neutral.

non-alignment | ˌnɒnə'laɪnment | *s.i.* no alineamiento, neutralidad.

nonce | nɒns | **for the –,** (arc.) por esta vez; por el momento.

nonce-word | 'nɒnswɜːd *s.c.* palabra ad hoc (creada solamente para una ocasión).

nonchalance | 'nɒnʃələns | *s.i.* **1** indiferencia, falta de entusiasmo, despreocupación, falta de interés. **2** frialdad, tranquilidad.

nonchalant | 'nɒnʃələnt | *adj.* indiferente, despreocupado, frío.

nonchalantly | 'nɒnʃələntlɪ | *adv.* despreocupadamente, indiferentemente, negligentemente.

non-combatant | ˌnɒn'kɒmbətən | *s.c.* no combatiente.

non-commissioned officer V. **officer.**

noncommittal | ˌnɒnkə'mɪtl *adj.* vago, evasivo, sin definir, no comprometido: *he was noncommittal on that matter = no se definió sobre ese asunto.*

noncommittally | ˌnɒnkə'mɪtəli | *adv.* vagamente, evasivamente, sin comprometerse, cautelosamente: *he answered*

noncommittally = él contestó evasivamente.
non-compliance | ˌnɒnkəm'plaɪəns | *s.i.* incumplimiento (de una ley o similar).
non compos mentis | ˌnɒnˌkɒmpəs'mentɪs | *adj.* DER. enajenación mental.
non-conductor | ˌnɒnkən'dʌktər | *s.i.* ELEC. no conductor (hilo, cable, etc.).
nonsuch V. **none such.**
nonconformist | ˌnɒnkən'fɔːmɪst | *s.c.* **1** inconformista, rebelde, individualista, disidente. **2** no conformista. || *adj.* **3** inconformista, disconforme: *nonconformist party; nonconformist conscience = partido inconformista; conciencia disconforme.*
OBS. Miembro de un grupo religioso separado de la Iglesia de Inglaterra. **Protestant Dissenter,** disidente protestante. **Free Churchman.**
nonconformity | ˌnɒnkən'fɔːmɪti | *s.i.* **[=N to/with]** inconformismo, disidencia: *the problems caused by the nonconformity to the laws of life = los problemas causados por el inconformismo con respecto a las leyes de la vida.*
non-contributory | ˌnɒnkən'trɪbjʊtəri | *adj.* sin cotización, sin participación.
OBS. plan de cotización de pensión o jubilación en el que los derechos pasivos los abona únicamente el empresario.
non-cooperation | ˌnɒnkəʊˌɒpə'reɪʃn | *s.i.* no cooperación, pasividad: *a policy of non-cooperation = una política de no cooperación.*
nondescript | 'nɒndɪskrɪpt | *adj.* sin carácter, sin personalidad, mediocre, normal, indeterminado: *he was wearing some nondescript clothes = llevaba puesta ropa sin personalidad.*
none | nʌn | *pron.* **1** nadie, ninguno. *none of them; none can tell = ninguno de ellos; nadie puede decir.* **2** nada, ninguno: *there are none left = no queda ninguno.* **3** no, ya no, no... tal cosa, no... de eso: *I used to have, but now I have none = solía tener, pero ahora no tengo nada de eso.* **4 – but,** (form.) solo, únicamente, no o nada más que, ni más ni menos que: *none but the best = únicamente lo mejor.* **5 to have – of,** (fam.) no aceptar, no tolerar: *I won't have none of that any more = no aceptaré más eso.* **6 – other than,** no otra cosa que, ni más ni menos que, el mismísimo: *It was none other than the king = era el mismísimo rey.* **7 – the,** (form.) no, no más, de ninguna manera, en modo alguno: *they were none the better off after all = no habían mejorado en modo alguno.* **8 – too,** (form.) no muy, no demasiado, de ningún modo: *it was none too easy = no era de ningún modo fácil.* V.
nought nonentity | nɒ'nəntɪti | *s.c.* **1** nulidad, cero a la izquierda, don nadie, insignificante. || *s.i.* **2** insignificancia, anonimato.
non-essential | nɒnɪ'senʃl | *adj.* innecesario, no esencial, superfluo.
nonesuch | 'nʌnsʌtʃ | (también nonsuch) *s.sing.* (form.) dechado, modelo, persona sin par.
nonetheless | ˌnʌnðə'lɪs | *adv.* sin embargo, no obstante, con todo.
non-event | nɒnɪ'vent | *s.c.* decepción, algo carente de interés: *the debate we had expected so much turned out to be a real non-event = el debate que habíamos esperado tanto resultó ser una decepción.*
non-existence | nɒnɪg'zɪstəns | *s.i.* inexistencia, ausencia (de algo).
non-existent | nɒnɪg'zɪstənt | *adj.* inexistente.
non-fiction | ˌnɒn'fɪkʃn | *s.i.* no ficción.
non-flammable | ˌnɒn'flæməbl | *adj.* no inflamable, ininflamable, resistente al fuego, incombustible, no combustible, **non-inflammable.**
non-human | ˌnɒn'hjuːmən | *adj.* no humano, animal.
non-interference | ˌnɒnɪntə'fɪərəns | V. **non-intervention.**
non-intervention | ˌnɒnɪntə'venʃn | *s.i.* no intervención (política de).
non-iron | ˌnon'aɪən | *adj.* que no necesita plancha (ropa).
non-member | nɒn'membər | *s.c.* no miembro, no afiliado, visitante.
no-no | nəʊnəʊ | *s.sing.* (fam.) algo prohibido, inaceptable.
non-nuclear | nɒn'njuːklɪər | *adj.* no nuclear, desnuclearizado.
non-observance | ˌnɒnəb'zəːvəns | *s.i.* (form.) falta de observancia, no observancia, incumplimiento (de una ley, tratado, etc.).
no-nonsense | ˌnəʊ'nɒnsns | *adj.* directo, eficaz, claro, preciso: *the no-nonsense set of instructions made everything clear = el conjunto de instrucciones precisas aclaró todo.*
nonpareil | ˌnɒnpə'reɪl | V. **nonesuch.**
non-payment | ˌnɒn'peɪment | *s.i.* falta de pago, impago.
nonplussed | ˌnɒn'plʌst | *adj.* **1** confundido, perplejo, perdido, desconcertado, sorprendido, desorientado, turbado: *he was nonplussed by their questions, and didn't know what to say = quedó confundido por sus preguntas, y no sabía qué decir.* **2** superado, desbordado, vencido (por una situación...): *I'm nonplussed! Anyone who can, go further! = ¡No puedo más! ¡Que siga quien pueda!*
non-profit-making | nɒn'prɒfɪtmeɪkɪŋ | *adj.* **1** no lucrativo, benéfico, altruista, caritativo. **2** ruinoso, que no produce ganancias.
non-proliferation | ˌnɒnprəlɪfə'reɪʃn | *s.i.* **1** no proliferación, restricción, limitación (referido a armas nucleares). **2** no reproducción, no multiplicación, no generación (acción de limitar la expansión de algo).
non-resident | ˌnɒn'rezɪdənt | *s.c.* no residente, transeúnte, huésped de paso: *the hotel parking is not open to non-residents = el aparcamiento del hotel no está abierto a no residentes.*
nonsense | 'nɒnsns | *s.i.* **1** disparate, sinsentido, tontería, tontada, desatino, despropósito, estupidez: *he is always talking nonsense = siempre está diciendo disparates.* || **2 to make a – of/to make – of,** estropear, echar a perder, desbaratar.
nonsensical | nɒn'sensɪkl | *adj.* estúpido, disparatado, ridículo, absurdo, falso: *nobody believed his nonsensical speech = nadie se creyó su discurso disparatado.*
nonsensically | nɒn'sensɪklɪ | *adv.* estúpidamente, disparatadamente, ridículamente, absurdamente.
non sequitur | ˌnɒn'sekwɪtər | *s.c.* (form.) falso razonamiento, falsa conclusión, que no se sigue de las premisas: *that is a non sequitor from your own arguments = no es eso lo que se sigue de tus propios argumentos.*
non-skid | ˌnɒn'skɪd | *adj.* antideslizante (neumáticos).
non-shrink | ˌnɒn'ʃrɪŋk | *adj.* inencogible, que no encoge.
non-smoker | ˌnɒn'sməʊkər | *s.c.* no fumador.
non-smoking | ˌnɒn'sməʊkɪŋ | *adj.* de no fumador: *non-smoking area = zona en la que está prohibido fumar.*
non-standard | ˌnɒn'stændərd | *adj.* no normalizado, no estándar, no tipificado, familiar, llano, vulgar, inelegante.
non-starter | ˌnɒn'stɑːtər | *s.c.* **1** imposible, impracticable, irrealizable: *it was a good idea, but an obvious non-starter = la idea era buena, pero irrealizable.* **2** no iniciado, que no se inicia: *he was a non-starter in the team = no llegó a jugar como miembro del equipo.*
non-stick | ˌnɒn'stɪk | *adj.* antiadherente: *a non-stick fryingpan = una sartén antiadherente.*
non-stop | ˌnɒn'stɒp | *adj.* **1** continuo, ininterrumpido, constante, seguido: *a twenty four hour non-stop folk music concert = un concierto de música folk de 24 horas ininterrumpidas.* **2** directo: *a non-stop train.*
non-U | ˌnɒn'juː | *adj.* (brit.) vulgar, de clase baja, inferior, impropio de la clase alta **(Upper class).** V. **U.**
non-union | ˌnɒn'juːnɪən | *adj.* **1** no afiliado, no sindicado, independiente. **2** que emplea a trabajadores no sindicados: *a Non-union factory.*
non-unionized | ˌnɒn'juːnɪənaɪzd | *adj.* V. **non-union.**
non-verbal | ˌnɒn'vəːbl | *adj.* no verbal, no oral, no elocutivo, sin palabras: *nonverbal communication, reasoning = comunicación sin palabras, razonamiento sin palabras.*
non-violence | ˌnɒn'vaɪələns | *s.i.* no violencia, pacifismo, resistencia pasiva.
non-violent | ˌnɒn'vaɪələnt | *adj.* no violento, pacífico.
non-white | ˌnɒn'waɪt | *adj.* de color, que no es de raza blanca.
noodles | nuːdl | *s.pl.* tallarines.
nook | nʊk | *s.c.* **1** rincón, rinconcito, refugio, lugar, retiro, escondrijo, cobi-

jo. || **2 every – and cranny,** todos los rincones, por todas partes: *we looked for it into every nook and cranny = lo buscamos por todos los rincones.*
noon | nuːn | *s.c.* **1** mediodía, las doce de la mañana. || *adj.* **2** del mediodía, de la mañana: *try to finish it before noon break = intenta acabarlo antes del descanso del mediodía.* || **3 the – of night,** medianoche. **4 – light,** luz del mediodía.
noonday | nuːndeɪ | *s.i.* (p.u.) **1** mediodía, la mitad del día. || *adj.* **2** del mediodía: *the noonday press.*
no-one | 'nəuwʌn | *pron.* V. **nobody.**
noose | nuːs | *s.c.* **1** nudo corredizo, lazo. || *v.t.* **2** asegurar con un nudo, ahorcar, lazar, capturar con lazo. V. **ensnare.**
nope | nəup | *adv.* (fam.) no.
nor | nɔːr | *conj.* **1** ni. V. **neither.**
OBS. **2** se usa al principio de oraciones, con inversión del orden de sujeto y verbo, para añadir información coincidente: *"I didn't go out yesterday" "Nor did I" = "no salí ayer", "Ni yo".* **3** Se usa para introducir una segunda alternativa negativa: *neither Tom nor John smokes = ni Tom ni John fuman.* **4** En enumeraciones negativas: *she didn't bring her book, nor her pen, nor her notebook = no trajo su libro, ni su pluma, ni su cuaderno.*
Nordic | 'nɔːdɪk | *adj.* **1** nórdico, del norte de Europa, germánico. **2** nórdico, de los países escandinavos. **3** de aspecto nórdico: *she looked nordic, she was tall, slender and white-blonde haired = tenía aspecto de nórdica, era alta, esbelta y rubia.*
norm | nɔːm | *s.c.* **1** norma, conducta habitual, pauta, norma social. **2** norma, normas legales, requisitos, disposiciones: *it had been built according to the government norms = había sido construido según las normas legales gubernamentales.* || **3 the –,** lo típico, la media.
normal | 'nɔːml | *adj.* **1** normal, acostumbrado, corriente: *normal temperatures = temperaturas normales.* **2** natural, sano, sin defectos, de carácter normal. **3** TEC. perpendicular. **4** QUIM. solución normal.
normalcy | 'nɔːmlsi | *s.i.* (p.u.) V. **normality.**
normality | nɔː'mælɪtɪ | *s.i.* normalidad, situación normal.
normalization | ˌnɔːməlaɪ'zeɪʃn | *s.i.* normalización.
normalize | 'nɔːməlaɪz | *v.t.* normalizar, regularizar, poner en regla.
normally | 'nɔːməlɪ | *adv.* **1** normalmente, con normalidad, bien: *he's already sleeping normally = ya duerme bien.* **2** normalmente, frecuentemente, como norma, hábito: *I normally have coffee after lunch = suelo tomar café después de comer.*
Norman | 'nɔːmən | *s.c.* **1** normando, natural de Normandía. || *adj.* **2** normando, referido al período normando: *there is a Norman castle there = hay un castillo normando allí.*
normative | 'nɔːmətɪv | *adj.* normativo, que sirve de norma.
Norse | nɔːs | *s.i.* **1** escandinavo (idioma antiguo). || *adj.* **2** escandinavo.
north | nɔːθ | *s.sing.* **1** GEOL. norte, septentrión. **2** el norte, la zona norte: *he lives in the nort of Spain = vive en el norte de España.* || *adj.* **3** norteño, del norte, septentrional, boreal: *north wind = bóreo, aquilón.* || *adv.* **4** hacia el norte, en el norte: *they were heading due north = se dirigían hacia el norte.* || **5 the North Pole,** GEOG. el Polo Norte.
northbound | ˌnɔːθ'bəund | *adj.* en dirección norte, que se dirige al norte.
north-east | ˌnɔːθiːst | *s.sing.* **1** GEOG. nordeste. **2** el nordeste, la zona nordeste: *the north-east is highly populated = la zona nordeste está muy poblada.* || *adj.* **3** nordestal, del nordeste. || *adv.* **4** hacia el nordeste, en el nordeste.
north-easterly | ˌnɔːθ'iːstəli | *adj.* **1** en dirección nordeste. **2** del nordeste, nordestal, provenientes del nordeste (viento).
north-eastern | ˌnɔːθ'iːstən | *adj.* del nordeste, nordestal.
northerly | 'nɔːðəlɪ | *adj.* norte, en el norte, del norte.
northerner | 'nɔːðənər | *s.c.* habitante del norte, norteño, nortino.
northernmost | 'nɔːðənməust | *adj.* más al norte, más septentrional, extremo norte de: *north Cape is regarded as the northermost point in Europe = el cabo del norte se ve como el punto más septentrional de Europa.*
northward | ˌnɔːθwəd | (EE.UU.) **northwards,** *adv.* y *adj.* hacia el norte: *the plane was flying northward; there was a northward migration = el avión estaba volando hacia el norte; hubo una emigración hacia el norte.*
Norway | 'nɔːweɪ | *s.sing.* Noruega.
north-west | ˌnɔːθwest | *s.sing.* **1** GEOG. noroeste, norueste. **2** el noroeste, la zona noroeste. || *adj.* **3** del noroeste, noroccidental. || *adv.* **4** en o hacia el noroeste.
north-westerly | ˌnɔːθ'westəli | *adv.* **1** en dirección noroeste, hacia el noroeste. **2** noroeste, noroccidental, proveniente del noroeste (viento).
north-western | ˌnɔːθ'westən | *adj.* en el noroeste, del noroeste.
Norwegian | nɔː'wiːdʒən | *s.c.* **1** noruego, habitante de Noruega. || *s.i.* **2** noruego, idioma de Noruega. || *adj.* **3** noruego, relativo a Noruega.
nose | nəuz | *s.c.* **1** ANAT. nariz, narices. **2** hocico, morro, trompa. **3** morro, proa, parte delantera de un vehículo, un arma. **4** olfato, intuición: *he's got a good nose for business = tiene un buen olfato para los negocios.* || *v.t.* **5** empujar con la nariz: *the cat nosed the cage door open = el gato abrió la puerta de la jaula empujando con la nariz.* || *v.i.* **6** deslizarse, desplazarse lentamente, con cuidado: *they nosed towards the house silently = se deslizaron hacia la casa silenciosamente.* || **7 to cut off one's – to spite someone's face,** causarse un daño para perjudicar a otro, no comer rancho para fastidiar al jefe. **8 to follow one's –,** obedecer, seguir la propia intuición o instinto; dejarse guiar por el olfato. **9 to get up one's –,** hartarse, estar hasta las narices: *they get up to my nose = estoy hasta las narices de ellos.* **10 to have a – for,** tener olfato, intuición, instinto para. **11 to have one's – in a book,** estar embebido en la lectura de un libro, estar enfrascado en la lectura. **12 to keep one's – clean,** mantenerse al margen, no comprometerse, no ser indiscreto. **13 to keep one's – out,** no meter las narices donde no le llaman, no ingerirse, no meterse en vidas ajenas. **14 to keep one's – to the grindstone,** estar metido a fondo en el trabajo, batir el cobre. **15 to lead someone by the –,** dominar, controlar, tener a alguien sometido. **16 to look down one's –,** despreciar, tratar con desdén, mirar con superioridad, mirar a alguien por encima del hombro. **17 to – about,** curiosear, fisgonear, husmear, fisgar. **18 to – out,** descubrir, detectar, destapar. **19 to pay through the – for,** pagar sin tasa por, a espuertas por, ser sangrado con: *I'm paying through the nose for the flat = me están sangrando con el piso.* **20 to poke/stick one's – into,** meter las narices en, inmiscuirse, entrometerse. **21 to powder one's –,** empolvarse la nariz, maquillarse, pintarse, arreglarse, acicalarse. **22 to rub someone's – in,** pasar, refrotar, refregar una cosa a alguien por las narices. **23 to see no further than one's –,** no ver más allá de sus narices. **24 to thumb one's – at,** ignorar, no hacer caso de, no prestar atención a, mostrar indiferencia hacia, encogerse de hombros. **25 to turn up one's – at,** volverle la cara a alguien o a algo, volverle la espalda a alguien o a algo, despreciar. **26 under someone's –,** delante de, en las propias narices. **27 with one's – in the air,** mostrando superioridad con aires de superioridad, creyéndose por encima de los demás.
nosebag | 'nəuzbəg | *s.c.* morral, cebadera.
nosebleed | 'nəuuzbliːd | *s.c.* hemorragia por la nariz, epistaxis.
nose-cone | 'nəuzkəun | *s.c.* cono de proa (de un cohete o similar).
nosedive | 'nəudaɪv | *s.c.* **1** AER. caída, bajada en picado. **2** caída repentina, descenso brusco, bajada en picado de los precios. || *v.i.* **3** AER. picar, entrar, descender un avión en picado, hacer un picado. **4** caer, bajar los precios en picado.
nosegay | 'nəuzgeɪ | *s.c.* ramillete de flores, ramo de novia.
nosering | 'nəuzrɪŋ | *s.c.* aro de nariz (para animales especialmente).
nose-wheel | 'nəuzwiːl | *s.c.* AER. rueda de proa, rueda delantera.
nosey-parker | ˌnəuzɪ'pɑːkər | [**nosy-parker**] *s.c.* (desp.) fisgón, cotilla, metomentodo, entrometido.

nosh | nɒʃ | *s.i.* **1** (vulg.) papeo, pitanza, manduca. **2** bocado, tentempié: *shall we have a nosh now? = ¿comemos un bocado?* || *v.t.* e *i.* **3** tragar, zampar, comer.

nosh-up | 'nɒʃʌp | *s.c.* (brit. y argot) comilona.

nosily | 'nəʊzɪlɪ | *adv.* curiosamente, indiscretamente, entrometidamente.

nosiness | 'nəʊzɪnɪs | *s.i.* curiosidad, indiscreción, entrometimiento.

nostalgia | nɒ'stældʒə | *s.i.* nostalgia, añoranza, remembranza.

nostalgic | nɒ'stældʒik | *adj.* nostálgico, evocativo, sentimental.

nostalgically | nɒ'stældʒɪklɪ | *adv.* nostálgicamente, con nostalgia.

nostril | 'nɒstrəl | *s.c.* **1** ventana de la nariz. **2** aletas de la nariz.

nostrum | 'nɒstrəm | *s.c.* (p.u.) **1** panacea, curalotodo, remedio de curandero, potingue, mejunje. **2** panacea, teoría particular, proyecto favorito: *another party's nostrum is more schools, more teachers = otro proyecto favorito del partido son más escuelas, más profesores.*

nosy | 'nəʊzɪ | *adj.* [**nosey**] inquisitivo, fisgón, metomentodo, curioso, entrometido. V. **nosey-parker.**

not | nɒt | *adv.* [**n't**] **1** no (con verbos): *he's not here = él no está aquí.* **2** no (con otras palabras): *not everybody was there = no todos estaban allí.* **3** ni a, no más de (con expresiones de distancia, tiempo y cantidad): *he was not a couple of meters away = no estaba a más de un par de metros.* **4** no tanto: *we did so, not because he wanted but because it was the only way = lo hicimos no porque él quisiera, sino porque era la única solución.* **5** no es que, no quiero decir que: *not that I mind, but I should have been told = no es que me importe, pero lo deberían haber dicho.* **6** que no (con ciertos verbos): *I hope not, I'm afraid not = espero que no, me temo que no.* || **7 – a,** ni un: *not a minute was wasted = no se perdió ni un minuto.* **8 – always,** no siempre. **9 – at all,** en absoluto, de ninguna manera, de nada. **10 – but what,** aunque. **11 – even,** ni siquiera, ni tan siquiera. **12 – only/– just/– simply... (but also),** no sólo, no únicamente, no simplemente... (sino también). **13 – to say,** por no decir.

OBS. **N't** se usa en las **question tags,** y en formas interrogativo-negativas; es frecuente, en todo caso, en registro oral; pero no en registro escrito formal, o si se quiere enfatizar la negación. **Shall + not = shan't will + not = won't.** Con verbos tales como **think, want,** la negativa recae sobre la subordinada. *I thought you weren't coming = pensé que no venías.* **Not any = no.**

notability | ˌnəʊtə'bɪlɪtɪ | *s.c.* personaje, notable, persona importante.

notable | 'nəʊtəbl | *s.c.* **1** notable, persona importante o principal, V.I.P. || *adj.* **2** importante, interesante, notable, famoso.

notably | 'nəʊtəblɪ | *adv.* **1** notablemente, considerablemente, de modo no común. **2** notablemente, particularmente, especialmente.

notary | 'nəʊtərɪ | *s.c.* notario. V. **solicitor.**

notation | nəʊ'teɪʃn | *s.i.* **1** notación (matemática, química, musical...), sistema de signos. || *s.c.* **2** signo o signos de una notación.

notch | nɒtʃ | *s.c.* **1** muesca, entalladura, incisión, melladura, escotadura, hendidura. **2** puntos, diferencia, distancia, por encima, por debajo: *his performance was a few notches above the other's = su actuación estuvo por encima de la de los otros.* || *v.t.* **3** hacer una muesca, mellar. **4** anotarse, apuntarse (una victoria), marcar un hito, reservarse (un puesto en los anales).

note | nəʊt | *s.c.* **1** nota, mensaje: *she sent me a note with the details = me envió una nota con los detalles.* **2** nota, anotación, apunte: *I made a note in order to remember it = tomé un apunte para acordarme.* **3** nota, aclaración, información adicional: *read the footnote = lea la nota a pie de página.* **4** nota, circular, certificación: *a diplomatic note.* **5** billete de banco, papel moneda: *a bank note.* **6** nota musical, nota (su representación gráfica). **7** tecla, llave, registro (de un instrumento musical con teclado). **8** sonido, ruido. **9** tono de voz: *there was a note of bitterness in his voice = había una nota de amargura en su voz.* **10** advertencia, punto. || *v.t.* **11** notar, observar, fijarse, reparar, darse cuenta. **12** anotar, registrar, llevar cuenta. **13** hacer notar, manifestar, citar. || **14 to compare notes,** discutir, intercambiar opiniones. **15 to make/have/keep a mental – of,** tomar nota mentalmente. **16 to – down,** anotar, tomar nota. **17 of –,** importante, de ser notado, digno de mención. **18 to take –,** tomar nota, fijarse.

notebook | 'nəʊtbʊk | *s.c.* libro de notas, cuaderno de clase, libreta.

notecase | 'nəʊtkeɪs | *s.c.* billetera.

noted | nəʊtɪd | *adj.* conocido, famoso, notable, notorio.

notepad | 'nəʊtpæd | *s.c.* bloc, taco de papel.

notepaper | 'nəʊtpeɪpər | *s.i.* papel de cartas.

noteworthy | 'nəʊtwəːðɪ | *adj.* notable, significativo, digno de mención.

nothing | 'nʌθɪŋ | *pron.* **1** nada, naderia, trivialidad: *they were talking about nothing = hablaban de trivialidades. It cost me nothing = me costó muy poco, casi nada. There's nothing like home = no hay cosa alguna como el hogar.* || *adv.* **2** en modo alguno, nada de eso, ni mucho menos, nada por el estilo: *"£ 300!" "No, nothing near!" = "¡300 libras!", "No, en modo alguno te acercas".* || *s.c.* **3** nada, nulidad, nadie, don nadie: *he's a perfect nothing = él es una nulidad.* || **4 all or –,** o todo o nada. **5 for –, a)** innecesariamente, por nada, para nada. **b)** gratis. **6 it's –,** no es nada, no pasa nada. **7 not for –,** no por nada, no en vano. **8 – but,** simplemente de, no otra cosa que, nada más que, sólo: *I've had nothing but bread and butter since yesterday = no he tomado nada más que pan y mantequilla desde ayer.* **9** (vulg.) **– doing,** nada que hacer. **10 – if not,** muy, extremadamente, por encima de todo. **11 – in it/to it,** es falso, no es nada, no hay nada de eso, no hay tal cosa. **12 – less than,** ni más ni menos que, no otra cosa que, nada menos que. **13 – more than,** nada más que de, simplemente de. **14 – of the sort,** nada por el estilo, de ninguna manera, de eso nada. **15 – to it,** es fácil, no tiene nada, eso no es nada, no tiene ciencia. **16 something for –/money for –,** todo por nada, gratuitamente, gratisdato, de balde. **17** (brit.) **there is – for it,** no haber otra cosa que hacer más que, no quedar más remedio que.

nothingness | 'nʌθɪŋnɪs | *s.i.* la nada, el vacío.

notice | 'nəʊtɪs | *s.i.* **1** aviso, notificación, comunicación, cartel. **2** despido, dimisión. **3** PER. anuncio, nota, reseña, recensión, crítica, noticia crítica, suelto. **4** reconocimiento, consideración, atención, interés. || *v.t.* **5** notar, percibir, fijarse, prestar atención, darse cuenta, reconocer. **6** escribir una nota, una reseña, reseñar, escribir una crítica. || **7 at a moment's –/at five minutes' –,** en un momento, en cinco minutos, en el plazo de cinco minutos, en el término de cinco minutos. **8 at short –,** inmediatamente, de repente, con poco tiempo, en muy breve plazo, sin previo aviso. **9 to bring to someone's –,** hacer saber, dar a conocer, comunicar algo a alguien, dar cuenta. **10 to come to one's –,** darse cuenta, llegar a saber, caer en la cuenta. **11 to escape one's –,** no darse cuenta, pasarse por alto. **12 to give –,** avisar el despido, dar la cuenta. **13 to hand in one's –,** dimitir. **14 to serve –,** revelar, manifestar, avisar, hacer un comunicado. **15 to take –,** prestar atención, tomar nota. **16 to take no –,** no prestar atención, no reparar, no hacer caso. **17 until further –,** hasta nuevo aviso.

noticeable | 'nəʊtɪsəbl | *adj.* **1** notable, obvio, evidente, perceptible, muy visible. **2** notable, conspicuo, sobresaliente.

noticeably | 'nəʊtɪsəblɪ | *adv.* notablemente, perceptiblemente, evidentemente, visiblemente, obviamente.

noticeboard | 'nəʊtɪsbɔrd | *s.c.* (brit.) tablón de anuncios, tablero, tablilla. V. **bulletin board** (EE.UU.).

notifiable | 'nəʊtɪfaɪəbl | *adj.* (brit.) DER. notificable, que debe ser notificado obligatoriamente a la autoridad, de lo que debe darse parte oficial.

notification | ˌnəʊtɪfɪ'keɪʃn | *s.i.* notificación, comunicación, aviso oficial.

notify | 'nəʊtɪfaɪ | *v.t.* **1** notificar, comunicar, avisar. **2** denunciar, informar. **3** hacer saber, publicar, proclamar.

notion | 'nəuʃn | *s.c.* **1** noción, concepto, categoría. **2** idea, creencia, opinión, teoría, concepción. **3** deseo, intención: *I have no notion of dying of hunger = no tengo intención de morirme de hambre.* **4** (pl.) **a)** invenciones, imaginaciones, ingenios. **b)** COM. (EE.UU.) complementos; artículos de mercería. V. **haberdashery.**

notional | 'nəuʃənl | *adj.* **1** hipotético, especulativo, abstracto, teórico, imaginario. **2** GRAM. con significado propio.

notoriety | ˌnəutə'raɪətɪ | *s.i.* notoriedad, fama.

notorious | nəu'tɔːrɪəs | *adj.* (desp.) notorio, famoso, conocido por, célebre, de mala fama: *his notorious untruths render him contemptible = sus famosas mentiras le hacen incompatible.*

notoriously | nəu'tɔːrɪəslɪ | *adv.* notoriamente, notablemente, especialmente: *a notoriously bad year for crops = un año especialmente malo para la cosecha.*

notwithstanding | ˌnɒtwɪθ'stændɪŋ | *prep.* **1** (form.) a pesar de, no obstante: *notwithstanding the rise in prices, everything has been sold = a pesar del incremento de los precios, se ha vendido todo.* || *adv.* **2** sin embargo, todavía, aún, a pesar de todo: *he did his best but he lost notwithstanding = hizo lo que pudo pero perdió a pesar de todo.* || *conj.* **3** aunque, a pesar de que: *notwithstanding that the weather was good, we stayed in all day = a pesar de que el tiempo era bueno, nos quedamos en casa todo el día.*

nougat | 'nuːgɑː | *s.i.* turrón, guirlache.

nought | nɔːt | *num.* **1** (brit.) cero. V. **naught/nil/O/zero/love.** || **2 noughts and crosses,** (brit.) tres en raya (jugado con papel y lápiz usando los símbolos "O" y "+").

OBS. En uso general se suele sustituir por el determinante **no,** o el pronombre **none**: *no survivors were found = no se encontraron supervivientes.*

noun | naun | *s.c.* nombre, sustantivo (marcados en este diccionario con *s.c.* contable o *s.i.* incontable).

nourish | 'nʌrɪʃ | *v.t.* **1** alimentar, dar de comer, nutrir, sustentar, mantener. **2 [to -- on]** alimentarse, nutrirse, sustentarse, mantenerse de, con. **3** alimentar, mantener vivo, alentar, favorecer, acariciar: *she nourished an implacable hate against rapists = ella mantenía vivo un odio implacable contra los violadores.*

nourished | 'nʌrɪʃd | *adj.* alimentado, nutrido, lucido.

nourishing | 'nʌrɪʃɪŋ | *adj.* nutritivo, nutricio, de valor alimenticio.

nourishment | 'nʌrɪʃmənt | *s.i.* **1** alimento, nutrimento, sustento, comida. **2** alimentación, nutrición, dieta alimenticia.

nous | nəus | *s.i.* (brit., p.u. y fam.) **1** inteligencia, sentido común, seso. **2 – box,** la cabeza, el coco, la sesera.

nouveau-rich | ˌnuːvəu'riːʃ | *s.c.* nuevo rico.

nova | 'nəuvə | [*pl.* **novae** o **novas**] *s.c.* ASTR. nova.

novae | 'nəuviː | V. **nova.**

novel | 'nɒvl | *s.c.* **1** LIT. novela. || *adj.* **2** novedad, innovación, nuevo, original, novedoso: *a decoration more novel than elegant = una decoración más novedosa que elegante.*

novellette | ˌnɒvə'let | *s.c.* novela corta, historia, cuento, folletín.

novelist | 'nɒvəlɪst | *s.c.* novelista, escritor.

novelty | 'nɒvltɪ | *s.i.* **1** nuevo, diferente, inusual, novedad, novedoso. || *s.c.* **2** novedad, invención.

November | nəu'vembər | *s.i.* noviembre.

novice | 'nɒvɪs | *s.c.* **1** novato, principiante, aprendiz, inexperto. **2** REL. novicio, neófito.

noviciate | nə'vɪʃɪɪt | (también **novitiate**) *s.i.* noviciado, período de noviciado.

novitiate V. **noviciate.**

now | nau | *adv.* **1 a)** ahora, en este momento, ahora mismo, inmediatamente: *come here right now! = ¡ven aquí ahora mismo!* **b)** bajo las presentes circunstancias, a la vista de los hechos, visto lo visto: *now I can believe anything = a la vista de los hechos puedo creerme cualquier cosa.* **2** hasta ahora, hace ahora: *it's an hour now since I came = hace ahora una hora que llegué.* **3** en aquel momento, por aquel entonces, ya: *they had arrived by now = ya habían llegado.* **4** pues bien, hete aquí que: *now then, the old man called his three sons = pues bien, el viejo llamó a sus tres hijos.* **5** ahora bien, en caso de que, sin embargo: *I don't know, now we can ask him = no sé, sin embargo podemos preguntarle.* || **6 – and again,** una y otra vez, cada dos por tres. **7 any day –/any moment –/any time –,** en cualquier momento, cualquier día de estos, al llegar, al caer: *they should come round any moment now = deben de estar al caer.* **8 every – and then,** de vez en cuando, ocasionalmente, de cuando en cuando. **9 here and –,** aquí y ahora. **10 it's – or never,** ahora o nunca, este es el momento. **11 just –,** ahora mismo, hace un momento, recientemente: *he's come just now = ha venido hace un momento.* **12 – and then,** de vez en cuando, algunas veces, ocasionalmente. **13 – for,** y ahora por lo que se refiere a. **14 – –,** ¡venga, hombre, vamos!, ¡ánimo!: *now, now, take it easy, that's nothing = ánimo, tómatelo con calma, no es nada.* **15 – that,** ahora que, ya que, puesto que: *now that you've bought it, make good use of it = ahora que lo has comprado, úsalo bien.* **16 – then,** entonces pues, así pues: *now then, what's up? = Bueno, vamos a ver ¿qué pasa?* **17 there –,** bueno, pues ya está: *there now, it is working at last = vale pues, ¡ya funciona, por fin!*

nowadays | 'nauədeɪz | *adv.* hoy en día, en nuestros días, hoy, ahora, actualmente: *I don't like the fashions nowadays = actualmente no me gustan las modas.*

nowhere | 'nəuweər | *adv.* (fam., EE.UU.) **1** ningún sitio, sitio alguno, no (hay) donde: *there's nowhere to go = no hay donde ir.* **2** no sirve de nada, a ningún sitio, a ninguna parte: *that behaviour will get you nowhere = esa conducta no conduce a nada.* || **3 to be –/to be getting –,** fracasar, no tener éxito, no alcanzar resultados, no llegar a nada: *so many years of hard work, and we are nowhere = tantos años de trabajo duro y no hemos llegado a nada.* **4 from –/out of –,** de ningún sitio, de ninguna parte, de la nada, como llovido del cielo. V. **out of the blue. 5 in the middle of –,** en mitad de ningún sitio, un lugar perdido, un lugar dejado de la mano de Dios, que no está en el mapa. **6 – near,** en modo alguno, de ninguna manera, ni con mucho, ni mucho menos tan.

noxious | 'nɒkʃəs | *adj.* **1** nocivo, dañino, venenoso. **2** desagradable, repugnante, sucio, asqueroso, viciado.

noxiously | 'nɒkʃəslɪ | *adv.* **1** nocivamente, dañinamente, venenosamente. **2** desagradablemente, repugnantemente, asquerosamente, viciadamente.

noxiousness | 'nɒkʃəsnɪs | *s.i.* **1** nocividad. **2** repugnancia, asquerosidad, vicio.

nozzle | 'nɒzl | *s.c.* **1** tobera, inyector, lanza de manga de riego, tubo, boquilla, caño, cánula, pulverizador, dispersor. **2** (vulg.) la nariz.

nth | enθ | *adj.* **1** enésimo: *the nth degree = el enésimo grado; the nth power = la enésima potencia.* **2** (fig.) enésima vez, una vez más: *I'm telling you for the nth time to do it = te estoy diciendo una vez más que lo hagas.* || **3 to the –/– plus one,** mil veces.

nuance | 'njuːɑːns | *s.i.* **1** sutileza, matiz, tono. || *s.c.* **2** matiz, característica. || **3 to give nuances to,** matizar, dar matices, expresión.

nub | nʌb | *s.sing.* **1** el núcleo, lo crucial, el quid, lo esencial, el grano, el corazón de un asunto: *the nub of the matter = el quid del tema.* || *s.c.* **2** tocón, colilla, cabo, muñón. **3** terrón, trozo, pedazo: *a nub of coal = un pedazo de carbón.* || **4** (vulg.) cuello.

nubile | 'njuːbaɪl | *adj.* núbil, en edad de merecer, casadera.

nuclear | 'njuːklɪər | *adj.* **1** FIS. nuclear, atómico: *nuclear power = energía atómica.* **2** nuclear, del núcleo, la parte central de, lo más importante. || **3 – family,** familia nuclear (considerando sólo al núcleo familiar, es decir, los padres y sus hijos). **4 – reactor,** reactor nuclear, reactor atómico, pila atómica, generador atómico.

nuclear-free | ˌnjuːklɪə'friː | *adj.* desnuclearizado, libre de energía nuclear.

nucleic acid | njuːˌkliːɪk'æsɪd | *s.i.* QUIM. ácido nucleico.

nucleus | 'njuːklɪəs | *s.c.* **1** FIS. núcleo del átomo. **2** BIO. núcleo celular. **3**

núcleo, conjunto, base, centro: *they were the nucleus of the colony = ellos eran el centro de la colonia.*

nude | nju:d | *s.c.* **1** ART. desnudo. || *adj.* **3** desnudo, destapado, sin ropas. V. **naked.** || **3 in the –,** desnudo, en cueros vivos.

nudge | nʌdʒ | *v.t.* **1** tocar o dar con el codo, avisar. || *v.i.* **2** abrirse camino, empujar a algo o a alguien, apartar. **4** convencer, incitar, impulsar, empujar a alguien a hacer algo. **5** aproximarse, acercarse, rozar. || *s.c.* **6** golpe con el codo, toque de aviso.

nudism | nju:dɪzəm | *s.i.* desnudismo.

nudist | nju:dɪst | *s.c.* desnudista.

nudity | nju:dɪtɪ | *s.i.* desnudez.

nugatory | 'nju:gətərɪ | *adj.* (form.) vano, fútil.

nugget | 'nʌgɪt | *s.c.* **1** pepita, palacra, palacrana, trozo de metal (en estado natural): *gold nugget = trozo de metal de oro.* **2** información valiosa, noticia, chisme.

nuisance | 'njusns | *s.c.* **1** molestia, problema, fastidio, inconveniente. **2** (fam.) pelma, pesado, impertinente, plomo. || **3 to make a – of oneself,** resultar molesto, pesado, cargante, pasarse, convertirse en una molestia.

nuke | nu:k | *s.c.* (fam., EE.UU.) **1** armas nucleares. || *v.t.* **2** atacar, bombardear con armas nucleares.

null | nʌl | *adj.* **1** nulo, no válido. **2 – and void,** nulo de pleno derecho, sin efecto, inválido: *the election was declared null and void = la elección fue declarada nula de pleno derecho.*

nullification | ˌnʌlɪfɪ'keɪʃn | *s.i.* anulación, invalidación.

nullify | 'nʌlɪfaɪ | *v.t.* **1** DER. anular, invalidar, declarar legalmente nulo, dejar legalmente sin efecto. **2** cancelar, neutralizar, frustrar, negar: *their opposition nullified all our attempts = la oposición de ellos frustró todos nuestros intentos.*

nullity | 'nʌlɪtɪ | *s.i.* **1** nulidad: *a petition of nullity of marriage = una petición de nulidad matrimonial.* **2** sin sentido, nada: *such a mere nullity is life = la vida es tal sin sentido.* || *s.c.* **3** nulidad, inútil (persona).

numb | nʌm | *adj.* **1** aterido, insensible por el frío, adormecido, dormido, entumecido. **2** aturdido, anonadado, pasmado, paralizado: *numb with fear, he couldn't move = paralizado por el miedo, no podía moverse.* || *v.t.* **3** adormecer, entumecer, aterir: *winter numbs the labouring hand = el invierno entumece la mano laboriosa.* **4** calmar, apaciguar: *to numb the pain = calmar el dolor.*

numbed | nʌmd | *adj.* entumecido, insensibilizado, que no se siente, adormecido, aterido: *hands numbed with cold = las manos ateridas por el frío.*

number | 'nʌmbər | *s.c.* **1** número, cifra, guarismo: *odd number = número impar; even number = número par; phone number = número de teléfono.* **2** cierto número, cierta cantidad: *a number of students didn't sit for the exam = cierto número de estudiantes no hizo el examen.* **3** grupo: *I'd like to be in the number, when the saints go marching in = me gustaría estar en el grupo, cuando los santos entren desfilando.* **4** número, ejemplar, copia: *a back number of "Time" magazine = un ejemplar atrasado de la revista "Time".* **5** número, actuación: *a musical number = un número musical.* **6** prenda de vestir. **7** chica. **8** GRAM. número. || *v.i.* **9** numerar, contar. **10** sumar un total de, llegar a, alcanzar el número de: *the school numbers 212 students = la escuela suma un total de 212 estudiantes.* **11** contar, incluir, encontrarse entre: *he's numbered among the best painters in the country = él se encuentra entre los mejores pintores del país.* || **12 a – of,** varios, unos cuantos. **13 any – of,** un montón de, muchos. **14 beyond –/without –,** incontables, innumerables. **15 by –,** numerado, por números. **16 by numbers/by the numbers,** ordenadamente, punto por punto. **17 – one, a)** el primero, el número uno, el mejor, el jefe, el principal. **b)** uno mismo. **18 one of someone's –,** uno del grupo, uno de los (nuestros). **19 – plate,** (brit.) matrícula de un vehículo. **20 safety in –,** más ven cuatro ojos que dos, la unión hace la fuerza. **21 someone's – comes up,** tocar el turno, llegar la hora, tocar pasar por algo. **22 someone's days are numbered,** tener los días contados, acabarse el tiempo de. **23 someone's – is up,** llegar la hora, estar en las últimas, acabarse todo. **24 to have someone's –,** tenerlos cogidos, saberlo todo de alguien. **25 to look out for/after – one/to take care of – one,** creerse el único, pensar sólo en uno mismo, cuidarse a sí mismo: *if a man doesn't take care of no. 1, he will soon have 0 to take care of = si un hombre no se cuida a sí mismo, pronto no tendrá a quien cuidar.*

numberless | 'nʌmbəlɪs | *adj.* incontable, innumerable, sin número.

numbly | 'nʌmlɪ | *adv.* **1** ateridamente, entumecidamente. **2** aturdidamente, anonadadamente.

numbness | 'nʌmnɪs | *s.i.* **1** insensibilidad, adormecimiento. **2** anonadamiento, pasmo.

numeracy | 'nju:mərəsi | *s.i.* capacidad para la aritmética.

numeral | 'nju:mərəl | *s.c.* números, sistema numérico. *Arabic numerals = números árabigos.*

numerate | 'nju:mərɪt | *adj.* bueno con los números.

numeration | ˌnju:mə'reɪʃn | *s.i.* **1** numeración, ordenación numérica. **2** MAT. numeración, expresión numérica.

numerator | 'nju:məreɪtər | *s.c.* MAT. numerador.

numerical | 'nju:'merɪkl | *adj.* numérico.

numerically | 'nju:merɪklɪ | *adv.* numéricamente.

numerous | 'nju:mərəs | *adj.* numeroso, muchos.

numinous | 'nju:mɪnəs | *adj.* (form.) divino, divinal, deífico, santo.

numismatics | ˌnju:mɪz'mætɪks | *s.pl.* [– + *v.sing.*] numismática.

numismatist | nju:'mɪzmətɪst | *s.c.* coleccionista de monedas.

numskull | 'nʌmskʌl | *s.c.* (p.u. y fam.) estúpido, tonto, zote.

nun | nʌn | *s.c.* monja, religiosa.

nuncio | 'nʌnsɪəu | *s.c.* POL. nuncio.

nunnery | 'nʌnəri | *s.c.* convento de religiosas. V. **convent.**

nuptial | 'nʌpsl | *adj.* (form.) nupcial, de (la) boda: *the nuptial day = el día de la boda.*

nuptials | 'nʌpʃlz | *s.pl.* boda, nupcias, ceremonia del casamiento, celebración del matrimonio.

nurse | nə:s | *s.c.* **1** MED. enfermera. **2** niñera. V. **nanny.** || *v.t.* e *i.* **3** actuar de enfermera, cuidar, atender, ayudar, asistir. **2** cuidar, reposar, curarse: *go to bed, and nurse that cold = acuéstate y cuida ese resfriado.* **3** amamantar, dar el pecho. **4** acariciar (un deseo), conservar, mantener, alimentar (un sentimiento). **5** saborear, hacer durar: *to nurse a drink = saborear una bebida.* **6** fomentar, promover (un negocio, una candidatura). || **7 to – one's pride,** lamerse las heridas, restañar el orgullo, las heridas. **8 wet –,** nodriza, ama de cría, de leche.

nursemaid | 'nə:smeɪd | *s.c.* niñera.

nursery | 'nə:sərɪ | *s.c.* **1** guardería, habitación para juegos: *nursery education = educación preescolar.* **2** invernadero, plantel, semillero. || **3 – nurse,** puericultora. **4 – rhyme/Mother Goose rhyme,** canción infantil. **5 – school,** jardín de infancia, escuela de preescolar. **6 – slopes,** pistas de esquí para principiantes.

nurseryman | 'nə:sərɪmən | [*pl.* **nurserymen**] *s.c.* cuidador de viveros, experto en semilleros, experto en viveros.

nursing | 'nə:sɪŋ | *s.i.* **1** profesión de enfermera, atención sanitaria: *go into nursing = hacerse enfermera.* **2** período de lactancia. || **3 – home, a)** asilo, hogar de ancianos, residencia para la tercera edad. **b)** (brit.) hospital privado, clínica de reposo. **c)** casa de maternidad particular. **4 – mother,** madre que está amamantando (debido al nacimiento de un bebé).

nurture | 'nə:tʃər | *s.i.* **1** educación, crianza, formación, nutrición, atención, cuidado. || *v.t.* **2** nutrir, cuidar, proteger el desarrollo de alguien o de algo. **3** cultivar, animar, hacer prosperar. **4** alimentar, nutrir, conservar, desarrollar (un sentimiento, una emoción...).

nut | nʌt | *s.c.* **1** BOT. fruto seco, nuez: *wallnut = nuez; chestnut = castaña; hazelnut = avellana.* **2** tuerca: *wing nut = palomilla.* **3** loco, lunático. **4** admirador, fanático: *he's nuts about chess = es* *fanático del ajedrez.* **5** (vulg.) el coco, el tarro, la cabeza. **6** MUS. puente. **7** (vulg.) cojones, testículos. || **8 a hard – to crack/a tough – to crack,** un hueso duro de roer, tarea o asunto difícil. **9 a tough –,** un tipo duro, un tipo difícil. **10 nuts and bolts, a)** lo básico, lo esencial, los detalles prácticos, el meollo, lo que cuenta. V. **nitty-gritty. b)** los mecanismos, las tripas (de una máquina). **11 to be nuts,** estar loco. **12 to do one's –, a)** echar el resto. **b)** estar furioso, muy enfadado; estar preocupado, darle a la cabeza.

nut-brown | ˌnʌtbraʊn | *adj.* color avellana, marrón rojizo oscuro.

nutcase | 'nʌtkeɪs | *s.c.* (vulg.) loco, lunático, majareta.

nutcracker | 'nʌtˌkrækər | *s.c.* cascanueces.

nuthouse | 'nʌthaus | *s.c.* (vulg.) manicomio, casa de locos.

nutmeg | 'nʌtmeg | *s.c.* **1** BOT. mirística, otoba. **2** nuez moscada (fruto de la mirística). || *s.i.* **3** nuez moscada (especia). V. **mace.**

nutrient | 'nju:trient | *adj.* TEC. **1** alimenticio, nutricio, nutritivo. || *s.c.* **2** nutriente, nutrimento, alimento (químico o natural).

nutriment | 'nju:trɪment | *s.c.* e *i.* alimento, nutrimento, nutriente.

nutrition | nju:'trɪʃn | *s.i.* **1** nutrición, alimentación, dieta alimenticia. **2** nutrientes, valor nutritivo, sustancias nutritivas.

nutritional | nju:'trɪʃənl | *adj.* nutrimental, nutritivo, de la nutrición.

nutritionally | nju:'trɪʃənəlɪ | *adv.* nutritivamente, desde el punto de vista de la nutrición.

nutritionist | nju:'trɪʃənɪst | *s.c.* experto en nutrición.

nutritious | nju:'trɪʃəs | *adj.* nutricio, nutritivo, nutriz.

nutritive | 'nju:trətɪv | *adj.* nutritivo, nutricio, que nutre.

nutshell | 'nʌtʃel | *s.c.* **1** cáscara. **2 in a –,** en pocas palabras, en resumidas cuentas, en resumen.

nutter | 'nʌtər | *s.c.* (vulg.) loco, chiflado, grillado, majareta.

nutty | 'nʌtɪ | *adj.* **1** sabor a nuez, hecho con nuez. **2** sabroso, agradable: *life goes on nutty and nice = la vida sigue sabrosa y estupenda.* **3** colado por, loco por: *he was so nutty upon her = estaba tan colado por ella.* **4** (vulg.) loco, chiflado, majareta: *what a nutty idea! = ¡qué idea más loca!* || **5 – as a fruitcake,** (fam.) chalado, majareta.

nuzzle | 'nʌzl | *v.t.* **[to =N against] 1** rozar, tocar, acariciar con la nariz. || *v.i.* **2** acomodarse, arrebujarse (contra).

nylon | 'naɪlɒn | *s.i.* **1** nilón, fibra sintética. || *adj.* **2** de nilón. || **3 a pair of nylons,** (p.u.) medias de nilón.

nymph | nɪmf | *s.c.* **1** ninfa, semidiosa o divinidad menor. **2** chica, muchacha, doncella. **3** ZOOL. crisálida.

nymphet | nɪm'fet | *s.c.* (hum. y fam.) ninfa, moza hermosa.

nympho | 'nɪmfəʊ | *s.c.* (fam.) ninfómana.

nymphomania | ˌnɪmfə'meɪnɪə | *s.i.* PSIQ. ninfomanía.

nymphomaniac | ˌnɪmfə'meɪnɪæk | *s.c.* ninfómana.

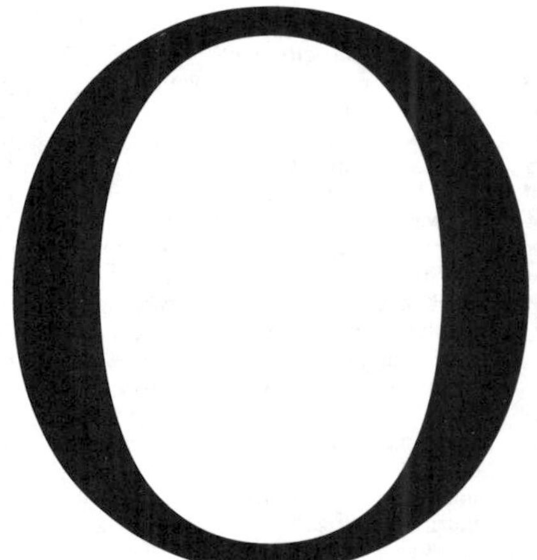

o, O | əʊ | *s.c.* **1** o, O (decimosexta letra del alfabeto inglés). || *num.* **2** cero (principalmente en números de teléfono). || *interj.* **3** ¡oh! || **4 O level,** calificación de asignaturas utilizada en las escuelas secundarias de Inglaterra, Gales e Irlanda del Norte.

oaf | əʊf | *s.c.* [*pl.* **oafs** u **oaves**] idiota, bruto, patán.

oafish | 'əʊfɪʃ | *adj.* torpe, tosco, rudo.

oak | əʊk | *s.c.* **1** BOT. roble. || *adj.* **2** de roble: *an oak door = una puerta de roble.* || **3 to sport one's oaks,** (fig.) cerrar (para que no entren visitas).

oaken | 'əʊkən | *adj.* (lit.) de roble.

oar | ɔːr | *s.c.* **1** remo. || *v.i.* **2** remar. || **3 to get/put/shove/stick one's – in,** (fam.) interferir, entrometerse, meter baza. **4 to rest on one's oars,** dormirse en los laureles.

oasis | əʊ'eɪsɪs | *s.c.* [*pl.* **oases**] **1** oasis. **2** (fig.) refugio, remanso: *an oasis of peace = un oasis de paz.*

oat | əʊt | *s.pl.* **1** avena, granos de avena. || **2 to be off one's oats,** (fam.) estar inapetente, estarse indispuesto. **3 to feel one's oats,** (fam.) estar en forma; sentirse importante. **4 to get one's oats,** (brit. y fam.) tener relaciones sexuales con frecuencia. **5 to sow one's wild oats,** (fam.) ir de parranda, andar de picos pardos.

oath | əʊθ | *s.c.* **1** juramento. **2** insulto, taco, blasfemia. || **3 on/under –,** bajo juramento: *the witness spoke on oath = el testigo habló bajo juramento.*

oatmeal | 'əʊtmiːl | *s.i.* **1** harina de avena. || *adj.* **2** color beige-grisáceo.

obduracy | 'ɒbdjʊrəsɪ | (form.) *s.i.* **1** obstinación, tozudez, obcecación. **2** dureza, inflexibilidad.

obdurate | 'ɒbdjʊrɪt | *adj.* **1** obstinado, tozudo. **2** tenaz, inflexible, duro.

obdurately | 'ɒbdjʊrətlɪ | *adv.* obstinadamente.

obedience | ə'biːdɪəns | *s.i.* **1** obediencia. || **2 in – to,** de conformidad con.

obedient | ə'biːdɪənt | *adj.* **1** obediente; sumiso. || **2 your – servant,** (lit.) fórmula convencional para finalizar cartas.

obediently | ə'biːdɪəntlɪ | *adv.* **1** obedientemente. || **2 yours –,** COM. a su entera disposición.

obeisance | əʊ'beɪsəns | *s.i.* **1** (lit.) reverencia, profundo respeto. || *s.c.* **2** reverencia, saludo (gesto). || **3 to do/make/play – to,** rendir homenaje a.

obelisk | 'ɒbəlɪsk | *s.c.* ARQ. obelisco.

obese | əʊ'biːs | *adj.* (form.) obeso, gordo, corpulento.

obesity | əʊ'biːsɪtɪ | *s.i.* obesidad, gordura, corpulencia.

obey | ə'beɪ | *v.t.* **1** obedecer (una persona, una orden). **2** acatar, cumplir, respetar (una orden, la ley). **3** seguir (reglamentos, instrucciones): *he obeyed the instructions perfectly = siguió las instrucciones al pie de la letra.* || *v.i.* **4** obedecer.

obfuscate | 'ɒbfʌskeɪt | *v.t.* e *i.* (lit.) ofuscar, confundir, desorientar.

obfuscation | ˌɒbfʌ'skeɪʃn | *s.i.* (lit.) ofuscación, confusión.

obituary | ə'bɪtʃʊərɪ | *s.c.* nota de defunción, obituario.

object | 'ɒbdʒɪkt | *s.c.* **1** objeto, cosa. **2** **[– (of)]** objetivo, finalidad, propósito, intención: *the object of my journey = el propósito de mi viaje.* **3** GRAM. complemento (del verbo). || | 'ɒb'dʒekt | *v.i.* **4** **[– (to)]** oponerse, tener inconveniente, desaprobar: *who objects to my decision? = ¿quién se opone a mi decisión?* || *v.t.* **5** objetar, protestar. || **6 to be no –,** no importar: *money is no object = el dinero no importa.* **7 – lesson,** lección práctica, demostración. **8 objet d'art,** pequeño objeto artístico.

objection | əb'dʒekʃn | *s.c.* **[– + (to)]** objeción, reparo, inconveniente, dificultad.

objectionable | əb'dʒekʃnəbl | *adj.* **1** inadmisible, reprobable, censurable, inaceptable. **2** desagradable, molesto.

objective | əb'dʒektɪv | *s.c.* **1** objetivo, meta. || *adj.* **2** objetivo, imparcial (una persona, una opinión). **3** real, basado en hechos (un dato, una información). || **4 – case,** GRAM. dativo; acusativo.

objectively | əb'dʒektɪvlɪ | *adv.* **1** objetivamente, imparcialmente. **2** verdaderamente.

objectivity | ˌɒbdʒek'tɪvɪtɪ | *s.i.* objetividad, imparcialidad.

objector | əb'dʒektər | *s.c.* **1** objetor. || **2 conscientious –,** objetor de conciencia.

obligated | 'ɒblɪgeɪtɪd | *adj.* (form.) obligado, comprometido: *he felt obligated to be present = se sintió obligado a asistir.*

obligation | ˌɒblɪgeɪʃn | *s.c.* e *i.* **1** obligación, deber. **2** compromiso. || **3 to be under (an) – to,** deber favores a, estar muy agradecido a.

obligatory | ə'blɪgətərɪ | *adj.* obligatorio; necesario.

oblige | ə'blaɪdʒ | *v.t.* **1** **[to – to + (to)]** obligar, compeler: *they obliged us to go out = nos obligaron a salir.* **2** ayudar, hacer un favor; complacer. || **3 much obliged/I am obliged to you,** (lit.) muy agradecido. **4 would be obliged,** (lit.) le agradecería.

obliging | ə'blaɪdʒɪŋ | *adj.* **1** servicial, solícito, condescendiente. **2** cortés, considerado, atento.

obligingly | ə'blaɪdʒɪŋlɪ | *adv.* atentamente.

oblique | ə'bliːk | *adj.* **1** oblicuo; inclinado. **2** (fig.) indirecto (afirmación, comentario). **3** (fig.) evasivo, no sincero (personas, comportamiento). || *s.c.* **4** MAT. oblicua (línea).

obliquely | ə'bliːklɪ | *adv.* oblicuamente, diagonalmente.

obliterate | ə'blɪtəreɪt | *v.t.* **1** arrasar, devastar (un sitio). **2** destruir (un objeto, un sitio). **3** (lit.) borrar, hacer desaparecer (un recuerdo, un pensamiento). **4** matasellar.

obliteration | əˌblɪtə'reɪʃn | *s.i.* eliminación, aniquilación, destrucción.

oblivion | ə'blɪvɪən | *s.i.* **1** inconsciencia. **2** olvido: *rescued from oblivion =*

rescatado del olvido. || **3 to fall into –,** caer en el olvido.

oblivious | ə'blɪvɪəs | *adj.* **1** **[– of/to]** inconsciente, abstraído: *oblivious of danger, she lit a cigarette = inconsciente del peligro, encendió un cigarrillo.* **2** olvidadizo, desmemoriado.

oblong | 'ɒblɒŋ | *s.c.* **1** GEOM. rectángulo. || *adj.* **2** GEOM. oblongo.

obnoxious | əb'nɒkʃəs | *adj.* **1** desagradable, repugnante (personas, comportamientos). **2** odioso, aborrecible. **3** ofensivo.

obnoxiously | əb'nɒkʃəslɪ | *adv.* ofensivamente.

oboe | 'əubəu | *s.c.* MUS. oboe.

oboist | 'əubəuɪst | *s.c.* MUS. oboísta.

obscene | əb'siːn | *adj.* **1** obsceno, indecente. **2** (fam.) repugnante, asqueroso, repulsivo. **3** grosero.

obscenity | əb'senɪtɪ | *s.i.* **1** obscenidad, indecencia. || *s.c.* **2** (fig.) barbaridad, atrocidad: *holding those children hostage was an obscenity = tener a esos niños como rehenes fue una barbaridad.* || **3 obscenities,** obscenidades, groserías (palabras groseras): *don't tell obscenities = no digas groserías.*

obscurantism | ˌɒbskjʊ'ræntɪzəm | *s.i.* oscurantismo, obscurantismo.

obscurantist | ˌɒbskjʊ'ræntɪst | *adj.* oscurantista, obscurantista.

obscure | əb'skjuər | *adj.* **1** poco conocido: *an obscure play.* **2** incomprensible, ininteligible: *an obscure manuscript.* **3** confuso, indistinto: *an obscure shape.* **4** oscuro: *an obscure room.* **5** escondido, recóndito (lugares). || *v.t.* **6** esconder, ocultar. **7** oscurecer. **8** (fig.) ocultar, encubrir (la verdad). **9** (fig.) complicar, confundir. **10** (fig.) eclipsar: *nothing could obscure her beauty = nada podía eclipsar su belleza.*

obscurity | əb'skjuərətɪ | *s.i.* **1** penumbra, oscuridad. **2** complejidad, dificultad. **3** (fig.) oscuridad, desconocimiento: *he lived in obscurity = pocos lo conocían.*

obsequious | əb'siːkwɪəs | *adj.* servil, adulador, zalamero.

obsequiously | əb'siːkwɪəslɪ | *adv.* servilmente.

obsequiousness | əb'siːkwɪəsnɪs | *s.i.* adulación, servilismo.

observable | əb'zəːvəbl | *adj.* **1** visible, observable: *it is observable from the earth = es visible desde la tierra.* **2** perceptible, notable. **3** claro, evidente.

observably | əb'zəːvəblɪ | *adv.* visiblemente.

observance | əb'zəːvns | *s.i.* **1** obediencia, cumplimiento (leyes, normas). **2** fidelidad, observación (costumbres). || **3 observances,** REL. rito, ceremonia, práctica: *religious observances: prácticas religiosas.*

observant | əb'zəːvnt | *adj.* **1** observador, atento. **2** agudo, perspicaz. **3** cumplidor, observador, obediente (de una regla, de una ley). **4** REL. observante.

observation | ˌɒbzə'veɪʃn | *s.i.* **1** observación, examen, estudio. **2** observación, percepción. || *s.c.* **3** observación, indicación, aclaración: *he made some observances = hizo algunas aclaraciones.* **4** descubrimiento, hallazgo: *scientific observations : descubrimientos científicos.* || **5 under –,** en observación; bajo vigilancia.

observational | ˌɒbzə'veɪʃənl | (form.) *adj.* **1** relativo a la capacidad de observación: *observational faculties : capacidad de observación.* **2** experimental.

observatory | əb'zəːvətrɪ | *s.c.* **1** ASTR. observatorio. **2** mirador, atalaya.

observe | əb'zəːv | *v.t.* e *i.* **1** observar, examinar. || *v.t.* **2** cumplir, acatar (una regla, una ley). **3** respetar; celebrar (las fiestas). **4** guardar (silencio). **5** (form.) advertir, notar. || *v.i.* **6** (form.) decir, hacer una observación.

observer | əb'zəːvər | *s.c.* observador.

obsess | əb'ses | *v.t.* obsesionar, causar obsesión.

obsession | əb'seʃn | *s.c.* PSIC. obsesión, idea fija.

obsessional | əb'seʃənəl | *adj.* PSIC. obsesivo.

obsessionally | əb'seʃənəlɪ | *adv.* obsesivamente.

obsessive | əb'sesɪv | *adj.* PSIC. obsesivo.

obsessively | əb'sesɪvlɪ | *adv.* obsesivamente.

obsolescence | ˌɒbsəu'lesns | *s.i.* caída en desuso, obsolescencia.

obsolescent | ˌɒbsəu'lesnt | *adj.* que se vuelve anticuado, que cae en desuso, obsolescente.

obsolete | 'ɒbsəliːt | *adj.* **1** anticuado, caído en desuso, obsoleto; pasado de moda. **2** BIOL. atrofiado.

obstacle | 'ɒbstəkl | *s.c.* **1** obstáculo. **2** (fig.) obstáculo, impedimento, traba: *bureaucratic obstacles : obstáculos burocráticos.* **3 – race,** DEP. carrera de obstáculos.

obstetric | ɒb'stetrɪk | *adj.* MED. obstétrico.

obstetrician | ˌɒbstə'trɪʃn | *s.c.* MED. tocólogo.

obstetrics | ɒb'stetrɪks | *s.i.* MED. tocología, obstetricia.

obstinacy | 'ɒbstɪnəsɪ | *s.i.* **1** obstinación, terquedad, tozudez. **2** MED. persistencia (de una enfermedad).

obstinate | 'ɒbstɪnɪt | *adj.* **1** obstinado, terco, cabezota. **2** obstinado, tenaz (comportamiento). **3** (fig.) persistente: *an obstinate drought scourged the country = una persistente sequía azotaba el país.* **4** MED. rebelde (a tratamiento).

obstinately | 'ɒbstɪnɪtlɪ | *adv.* **1** obstinadamente; tenazmente. **2** persistentemente.

obstreperous | əb'strepərəs | *adj.* **1** ruidoso, turbulento. **2** rebelde, protestón: *an obstreperous child = un niño protestón .*

obstruct | əb'strʌkt | *v.t.* **1** obstruir, atascar, bloquear. **2** obstaculizar, estorbar: *it is obstructing the traffic = obstruye el tráfico.* **3** (fig.) impedir, dificultar, entorpecer (el desarrollo de algo).

obstruction | əb'strʌkʃn | *s.c.* **1** obstrucción, bloqueo, atasco. **2** estorbo, obstáculo. **3** MED. oclusión. || *s.i.* **4** DER. obstrucción: *obstruction of justice.*

obstructionism | əb'strʌkʃənɪzəm | *s.i.* DER. obstruccionismo.

obstructive | əb'strʌktɪv | *adj.* que obstruye.

obstructiveness | əb'strʌktɪvnɪs | *s.i.* calidad de lo que obstruye.

obtain | əb'teɪn | *v.t.* **1** obtener, lograr, conseguir. **2** sacar: *it can be obtained from the library = puede sacarse de la biblioteca.* || *v.i.* **3** (form.) ser, existir (costumbres, situaciones). **4** prevalecer; estar en vigor: *some old customs still obtain here = todavía prevalecen aquí algunas antiguas costumbres.*

obtainable | əb'teɪnəbl | *adj.* asequible, obtenible.

obtrude | əb'truːd | *v.t.* e *i.* **1** (lit.) imponer: *he always obtruded his opinion = siempre imponía su opinión.* **2** (lit.) manifestar, dejar entrever (a su pesar). **3** entrometerse, inmiscuirse. || *v.i.* **4** asomar, sobresalir (un objeto).

obtrusive | əb'truːsɪv | *adj.* **1** molesto, fastidioso. **2** intruso, entrometido. **3** visible, evidente, obvio. **4** penetrante (olor).

obtrusively | əb'truːsɪvlɪ | *adv.* manifiestamente, con toda evidencia.

obtuse | əb'tjuːs | *adj.* **1** (form.) torpe, obtuso. **2** (fig.) sordo (dolor). **3** MAT. obtuso (ángulo). **4** (fig.) embotado (sentidos).

obtuseness | əb'tjuːsnɪs | (fig.) *s.i.* **1** torpeza. **2** embotamiento.

obverse | 'ɒbvəːs | *s.sing.* **1** **[the =N(of)]** lo contrario, lo opuesto (de una opinión, situación o argumento). **2** anverso (de una moneda, de una medalla). || *adj.* **3** del anverso.

obviate | 'ɒbvɪeɪt | *v.t.* **1** prevenir, evitar (un peligro, un inconveniente). **2** (form.) apartar, alejar. **3** allanar (obstáculos, dificultades).

obvious | 'ɒbvɪəs | *adj.* **1** obvio, evidente, innegable, claro. **2** elemental, de cajón. || **3 to state the –,** decir algo que es innecesario porque ya se sabe.

obviously | 'ɒbvɪəslɪ | *adv.* **1** obviamente, con toda evidencia; claramente. **2** claro, por supuesto (en respuestas).

obviousness | 'ɒbvɪəsnɪs | *s.i.* evidencia.

occasion | ə'keɪʒn | *s.c.* **1** ocasión, momento, circunstancia: *on one occasion = en una ocasión.* **2** ocasión, acontecimiento: *a great occasion = una gran ocasión.* **3** ceremonia. **4** oportunidad: *if you give me an occasion = si me das una oportunidad.* **5** (form.) causa, motivo: *by occasion of his illness = a causa de su enfermedad.* || *v.t.* **6** (form.) causar, ocasionar, producir. || **7 on/upon –,** de vez en cuando, ocasionalmente. **8 to be equal to the –,** estar a la altura de las circunstancias. **9 to rise to the –,** ponerse a la altura de las circunstancias.

occasional | ə'keɪʒənl | *adj.* **1** ocasional, infrecuente, excepcional. **2** fortuito, esporádico. **3** alguno que otro.

occasionally | ə'keɪʒnəlɪ | *adv.* a veces, de vez en cuando, ocasionalmente.
occidental | ˌɒksɪ'dentl | *adj.* (form.) occidental.
occult | ɒ'kʌlt | *s.sing.* **1** ocultismo. || *adj.* **2** oculto, esotérico, misterioso. || *v.t.* **3** ASTR. ocultar.
occupancy | 'ɒkjʊpənsɪ | *s.i.* (form.) ocupación, posesión (de un lugar, de un puesto).
occupant | 'ɒkjʊpənt | *s.c.* **1** ocupante (de un vehículo, asiento, etc.). **2** inquilino (de una casa).
occupation | ˌɒkjʊ'peɪʃn | *s.c.* e *i.* **1** ocupación, trabajo, profesión. || *s.c.* **2** quehacer. **3** pasatiempo. || *s.i.* **4** MIL. ocupación, invasión: *the German occupation = la ocupación alemana.* **5** ocupación (de una casa, de un edificio).
occupational | ˌɒkjuː'peɪʃənl | *adj.* **1** profesional: *occupational options = alternativas profesionales.* || **2 – hazard/–hazards,** gajes del oficio. **3 – therapy,** terapia ocupacional.
occupationally | ˌɒkjuː'peɪʃənlɪ | *adv.* profesionalmente.
occupied | 'ɒkjʊpaɪd | *adj.* **1** ocupado: *the toilet is occupied = el lavabo está ocupado.* **2** invadido, ocupado (por la fuerza).
occupier | 'ɒkjʊpaɪər | *s.c.* ocupante; inquilino.
occupy | 'ɒkjʊpaɪ | *v.t.* **1** ocupar, habitar. **2** ocupar (llenar un espacio): *it occupied the whole room = ocupaba toda la habitación.* **3** ocupar, invadir, tomar por la fuerza (un sitio, país). **4** ocupar (un puesto). **5** desempeñar (una función). **6 [to – + *o.* + in/with]** emplear, utilizar. **7** ocupar (dar en qué trabajar): *he needs something to occupy his hands = necesita en qué ocupar sus manos.* **8** durar: *it occupied many years = duró muchos años.*
occur | ə'kɜːr | *v.i.* **1** ocurrir, suceder; tener lugar. **2** producirse, verificarse: *a sudden change occurred = se produjo un cambio repentino.* **3** hallarse, encontrarse: *this species only occurs in Australia = esta especie solamente se halla en Australia.* **4** ocurrirse, venir a la mente (un pensamiento, una idea): *it occured to me that... = se me ocurrió que...*
occurrence | ə'kʌrəns | (form.) *s.c.* **1** acontecimiento, incidente. || *s.i.* **2** incidencia, existencia: *the occurrence of juvenile deliquency = la incidencia de la delincuencia juvenil.*
ocean | 'əʊʃn | *s.c.* **1** océano: *the five oceans.* || *s.sing.* **2** (lit. y fig.) mar, océano: *a creature from the ocean.* **3** (lit. y fig.) gran cantidad, mar: *an ocean of sand = un mar de arena.* || **4 oceans of,** (fam.) montones de: *oceans of butter.*
ocean-going | ˌəʊʃn'gəʊɪŋ | *adj.* MAR. transatlántico.
oceanic | ˌəʊʃɪ'ænɪk | *adj.* MAR. oceánico.
oceanographer | ˌəʊʃə'nɒgrəfər | *s.c.* MAR. oceanógrafo.
oceanographic | ˌəʊʃjənəʊ'græfɪk | *adj.* MAR. oceanográfico.
oceanography | ˌəʊʃə'nɒgrəfɪ | *s.i.* MAR. oceanografía.
ochre | 'əʊkər | (EE.UU. **ocher**) *s.i.* **1** ocre (tierra arcillosa utilizada en pintura). || *adj.* **2** ocre (color).
o'clock | ə'klɒk | *adv.* **1** se utiliza después de los números 1 a 12, para expresar las horas: *it is three o'clock = son las tres.* || *s.sing.* **2** (fam.) se refiere a un vehículo que llega o parte a determinada hora: *he is coming on the one o'clock = viene en el de la una.*
octagon | 'ɒktəgən | *s.c.* GEOM. octágono, octógono.
octagonal | ɒk'tægənl | *adj.* GEOM. octagonal, octogonal.
octane | 'ɒkteɪn | *s.i.* **[– + *s.*]** QUIM. octano: *octane value = índice de octano.*
octave | 'ɒktɪv | *s.c.* MUS. octava.
October | ɒk'təʊbər | *s.i.* octubre.
octogenarian | ˌɒktəʊdʒɪ'neərɪən | *s.c.* y *adj.* octogenario.
octopus | 'ɒktəpəs | *s.c.* [*pl.* **octopus** u **octopuses**] ZOOL. pulpo.
oculist | 'ɒkjʊlɪst | *s.c.* (EE.UU.) OPT. oculista, oftalmólogo.
odd | ɒd | *adj.* **1** raro, extraño. **2** impar, non (número). **3** desparejado, suelto: *an odd sock.* **4** variado: *odd jobs.* **5** libre, de ocio: *odd moments.* **6** suelto: *odd coins = monedas sueltas.* **7** ocasional: *odd job = trabajo ocasional.* || *adv.* **8 [*num.* – *s.pl.*]** aproximadamente, y pico: *thirty odd years = treinta y tantos años.* **9 [the/an – *s.*]** alguno, alguno que otro. || **10 against all the odds/in the face of ... odds,** contra todo pronóstico. **11 to be at odds, [– (with)]** estar enemistado. **12 it makes no odds,** (fam.) da lo mismo. **13 – man out/– woman out/– one out,** de más, sobrante. **14 odds,** posibilidades, probabilidades; ventaja (en el juego). **15 odds and ends,** (fam.) cosas sueltas. **16 the odds are...,** (fam.) es probable que... **17 the odds are against,** la suerte es contraria. **18 the odds are in favour,** las posibilidades son a favor.
oddball | 'ɒdbɔːl | *s.c.* (fam.) persona excéntrica.
oddity | 'ɒdɪtɪ | *s.c.* **1** rareza, cosa rara. **2** peculiaridad: *her personal oddities = sus peculiaridades personales.* || *s.i.* **3** rareza, extrañeza.
odd-job man | 'ɒdʒɒbmən | *s.c.* hombre al que se paga para que haga pequeños trabajos.
odd-looking | ˌɒd'lʊkɪŋ | *adj.* de aspecto extraño.
oddly | 'ɒdlɪ | *adv.* **1** extrañamente. || **2 – enough,** por extraño que parezca.
oddments | 'ɒdmənts | *s.pl.* cosas sueltas.
oddness | 'ɒdnɪs | *s.i.* singularidad, peculiaridad.
odds-on | ˌɒdz'ɒn | *adj.* **1** (fam.) probable. || **2 – favourite,** DEP. caballo favorito.
ode | əʊd | *s.c.* LIT. oda.
odious | 'əʊdɪəs | *adj.* odioso, aborrecible.
odium | 'əʊdɪəm | *s.i.* (form.) odio.
odorous | 'əʊdərəs | *adj.* (lit.) oloroso, fragante.
odour | 'əʊdər | (EE.UU. **odor**) *s.c.* **1** olor. **2** aroma, fragancia. || **3 to be in good/bad – with,** estar bien/mal visto por, tener buena/mala fama entre.
odourless | 'əʊdəlɪs | *adj.* inodoro.
odyssey | 'ɒdɪsɪ | *s.c.* odisea.
o'er | əʊər | *prep.* (p.u.) LIT. contracción de **over,** utilizada en poesía.
oesophagus | ɪ'sɒfəgəs | *s.c.* [*pl.* **oesophagi** u **oesophaguses**] ANAT. esófago.
oestrogen | 'iːstrəʊdʒən | (también **estrogen**) *s.i.* MED. estrógeno.
of | ɒv | *prep.* **1 [*s.* + –]** de: *a cup of tea = una taza de té.* **2 [– + *num.*]** de: *a girl of sixteen = una chica de dieciséis años.* **3**[*num./cuant.* + –] de: *one of my brothers = uno de mis hermanos.* **4** [*adj.* + – + ***pr.***] de parte de: *it was kind of him = fue amable de su parte.* **5** [*s.* + – + *s.*] de: *the village of Springfield = la localidad de Springfield.* **6** de, acerca de: *let's talk of it = hablemos de ello.* **7** de, que tiene: *a man of courage = un hombre de valor.* **8** [*s.* + – + a/an + *s.*] de: *a ruin of a house = una ruina de casa.* **9** (EE.UU.) menos (en horas): *a quarter of five = las cinco menos cuarto.* **10** en: *doctor of medicine = doctor en medicina.* **11** a: *love of nature = amor a la naturaleza.* **12** entre: *she of all women = ella entre todas.* || **13 – an evening,** (fam.) por la tarde. **14 – course,** por supuesto, claro. **15 – late,** últimamente. **16 – old,** (lit.) de antaño. **17 – someone,** por uno mismo.
OBS. La preposición **of** tiene distintas traducciones según el verbo que la acompañe; así, por ejemplo: pensar en = **to think of**; soñar con = **to dream of,** etc., por lo que hay que consultar los distintos verbos para encontrar la traducción correspondiente.
off | ɒf | *adv.* **1** de distancia, a una distancia de: *it is ten miles off = está a diez millas de distancia.* **2** de descuento: *twenty per cent off = veinte por ciento de descuento.* **3 [to be =N + *prep./ger.*]** lejos; fuera: *they are off in Washington = están fuera, en Washington.*
OBS. **Off** posee varios usos adverbiales: **4** idea de despegarse o desprenderse: *the wallpaper is peeling off = el papel de la pared se está despegando.* **5** idea de alejarse o marcharse: *he went off = se marchó.* **6** idea de apagar o desconectar: *switch off the light = apaga la luz.* **7** idea de ausencia: *he is off work = no trabaja, está ausente del trabajo.* || *prep.* **8** fuera de; lejos de: *keep off the grass = no pisar el césped.* **9** cerca de (una carretera): *a restaurant off the main road = un restaurante cerca de la carretera principal.* **10** MAR. frente a (una costa): *two miles off Long Island = dos millas frente a Long Island.* **11** de: *she fell off a tree = se cayó de un árbol.* **12** en: *he eats off silver plate = come en vajilla de plata.* **13** con: *it works off two batteries = funciona con dos pilas.* **14** de, a expensas de: *they live off the State = viven del Estado.*
OBS. **Off** posee además otros usos preposicionales: **15** idea de estar fuera o

libre de una actividad: *take a week off work = tómate una semana de vacaciones.* **16** (fam.) idea de dejar, abandonar o perder el gusto por algo: *I am off tobacco = he dejado de fumar.* || *adj.* **17** apagado (luz, aparatos eléctricos): *the lights are off = las luces están apagadas.* **18** cancelado, suspendido: *the wedding is off = se ha suspendido la boda.* **19** remoto, lejano: *off chance = posibilidad remota.* **20** malo, estropeado (comida): *the fish is off = el pescado está malo.* **21** cortada (leche). **22** no disponible (en un menú): *veal is off = no queda ternera.* **23** malo: *an off year = un año malo.* **24** libre, sin compromisos: *I am off today = hoy es mi día libre.* **25** quitado: *with my hat off = con el sombrero quitado.* **26** equivocado: *you are off in your accounts = estás equivocado en tus cuentas.* **27** cortado (gas, agua). **28** lateral, adyacente (calle). || **29 a bit –,** (fam.) inaceptable (comportamiento): *that's a bit off = no hay derecho.* **30 to be badly –,** andar mal de dinero. **31 to be having it – with,** (fam.) hacer el amor con. **32 to be –,** irse: *he is off to London = se va a Londres.* **33 to be right – it,** (fam.) estar completamente equivocado. **34 to be well –,** andar bien de dinero. **35 to fell –,** sentirse algo indispuesto. **36 how to be – for,** (fam.) qué tal se está de: *how are you off money? = ¿qué tal estás de dinero?* **37 on the – chance,** por si acaso: *he came on the off chance of finding her = vino por si acaso la encontraba.* **38 – and on,** de vez en cuando. **39 – guard,** desprevenido. **40 – side,** DEP. fuera de juego. **41 – the track,** (fam.) despistado. **42 – the wind,** MAR. viento en popa. **43 they're –,** DEP. acaban de tomar la salida.

OBS. Puesto que el sentido de muchos verbos se modifica al ir acompañados de **off,** hay que consultar los verbos para su correspondiente traducción.

offal | 'ɒfl | *s.i.* **1** GAST. menudos, menudillos. **2** desechos, despojos (de carnicería).

off-balance | ˌɒf'bæləns | *adj.* **1** inestable, sin equilibrio. **2** desprevenido: *they caught us off-balance = nos cogieron desprevenidos.*

offbeat | ˌɒf'biːt | (también **off-beat**) *adj.* (fam.) poco ortodoxo; original.

off-centre | ˌɒf'sentər | *adj.* descentrado.

off-colour | ˌɒf'kʌlər | (EE.UU. **off-color**) *adj.* **1** indispuesto, malo: *I am feeling a bit off-colour = me siento algo indispuesto.* **2** verde, atrevido; de mal gusto: *an off-colour joke = una broma de mal gusto.* **3** desteñido: *an off-colour shirt = una camisa desteñida.*

off-day | ˌɒf'deɪ | *s.c.* (fam.) día malo.

off-duty | ˌɒf'djuːtɪ | *adj.* libre (que no está de turno): *she is off-duty on Mondays = libra los lunes.*

offence | ə'fens | (EE.UU. **offense**) *s.c.* **1** DER. delito, infracción. || *s.c.* e *i.* **2** ofensa, agravio. || **3 to cause/give – (to),** ofender. **4 no –,** sin intención de ofender. **5 to take – (at),** ofenderse.

offend | ə'fend | *v.t.* **1** ofender, insultar; escandalizar: *his words offended her = sus palabras la ofendieron.* **2** (form.) **[– (against)]** ir en contra de, infringir, transgredir (una ley): *it offends every law = va en contra de todas las leyes.* || *v.i.* **3** delinquir. **4** REL. pecar.

offended | ə'fendɪd | *adj.* ofendido, insultado.

offender | ə'fendər | *s.c.* **1** (form.) delincuente, transgresor, infractor. **2** culpable. **3** REL. pecador.

offensive | ə'fensɪv | *adj.* **1** ofensivo, insultante: *offensive words = palabras ofensivas.* **2** desagradable: *an offensive smell = un olor desagradable.* **3** MIL. ofensivo: *offensive weapon = arma ofensiva.* || *s.c.* **4** MIL. ofensiva: *the enemy took the offensive = el enemigo tomó la ofensiva.* || **5 to go on the –/go over to the –/take the –,** (fig.) pasar al ataque.

offensively | ə'fensɪvlɪ | *adv.* ofensivamente, insultantemente.

offer | 'ɒfər | *v.t.* **1 [to – + *o.* + (to)]** ofrecer. **2** dar; brindar. **3** proponer (un proyecto, un servicio). **4** presentar, ofrecer: *it offers many advantages = ofrece muchas ventajas.* **5** mostrar: *he offered his driving licence to the policeman = mostró al policía su carnet de conducir.* **6** REL. ofrecer, ofrendar. || *v.i.* **7** ofrecerse: *they offered to help us = se ofrecieron para ayudarnos.* || *s.c.* **8** oferta, ofrecimiento. **9** rebaja, oferta (en el precio). **10** propuesta: *offer of marriage = propuesta de matrimonio.* || **11 on –,** en venta; de oferta. **12 open to offers,** dispuesto a negociar.

offering | 'ɒfərɪŋ | *s.c.* **1** oferta (algo para vender). **2** REL. ofrenda, sacrificio (a Dios).

off-guard | ˌɒf'gɑːd | (también **off guard**) *adj.* desprevenido, por sorpresa: *it caught me off-guard = me cogió desprevenido.*

off-hand | ˌɒf'hænd | (también **off hand**) *adj.* **1** indiferente; displicente (comportamiento). **2** brusco. **3** improvisado, impensado: *off-hand speech = discurso improvisado.* **4** desenvuelto, natural (comportamiento). || *adv.* **5** de improviso, sin pensar: *I can't tell you off-hand = no te lo puedo decir así de improviso.*

office | 'ɒfɪs | *s.c.* **1** oficina, despacho: *a big office = un despacho grande.* **2** oficina (establecimiento público): *post office = oficina de correos.* **3** bufete. **4** departamento. **5** POL. ministerio: *Foreign Office = Ministerio de Asuntos Exteriores.* **6** (EE.UU.) consultorio (de un médico, de un dentista). || *s.i.* **7** funciones, ejercicio; cargo. || **8 good offices,** (form.) mediación, apoyo (diligencias en favor): *he got it through the good offices of his uncle = lo consiguió por mediación de su tío.* **9 head –,** oficina central. **10 Holy –,** Inquisición. **11 in –,** POL. en el poder. **12 – for the dead/last offices,** REL. oficio de difuntos. **13 – hours,** horas de oficina. **14 out of –,** POL. fuera del poder. **15 to take –,** POL. entrar en funciones.

office-boy | 'ɒfɪsbɔɪ | (también **office boy**) *s.c.* (p.u.) botones de oficina, recadero.

office-holder | ˌɒfɪs'həuldər | *s.c.* (form.) funcionario.

officer | 'ɒfɪsər | *s.c.* **1** MIL. oficial. **2** funcionario, alto empleado, secretario (principalmente cargo público). **3** oficial, agente de policía; alguacil. || *v.t.* **4** MIL. comandar (como oficial). **5** MIL. proveer de oficiales.

official | ə'fɪʃl | *adj.* **1** oficial: *official document = documento oficial* **2** (hum.) aducido, alegado, pretendido (un motivo). || *s.c.* **3** empleado, funcionario (del gobierno). **4** REL. provisor, juez eclesiástico.

officialdom | ə'fɪʃldəm | *s.i.* **1** burocracia. **2** funcionariado.

officially | ə'fɪʃəlɪ | *adv.* **1** oficialmente. **2** supuestamente, en teoría.

officiate | ə'fɪʃɪeɪt | *v.i.* **[– (at)]** REL. oficiar.

officious | ə'fɪʃəs | *adj.* **1** entrometido, importuno.

offing | 'ɒfɪŋ | *s.sing.* **1** MAR. alta mar. || **2 in the –,** (fig.) inminente, en perspectiva.

off-key | ˌɒf'kiː | *adj.* MUS. desentonado.

off-licence | 'ɒfˌlaɪsns | (también **off licence**) *s.c.* (brit.) taberna, tasca.

off-limits | 'ɒfˌlɪmɪts | (también **off limits**) *adj.* **[– (to)]** (EE.UU.) prohibido (un lugar).

offload | 'ɒfˌləud | *v.t.* **1 [– (onto)]** (fam.) deshacerse de algo que no se quiere dándoselo a otro: *he offloaded his work onto me = me cargó con su trabajo.*

off-peak | 'ɒfpiːk | *adj.* **1** de horas de menor consumo (de gas, electricidad). **2** de menor afluencia (de personas, de tráfico): *an offpeak bus = un autobús de poca afluencia.*

off-putting | ˌɒf'putɪŋ | *adj.* antipático.

off-season | ˌɒf'siːzn | *s.sing.* temporada baja.

offset | 'ɒfset | *v.t.* **1 [– (against)]** compensar, contrarrestar. **2** TEC. imprimir por offset. || *s.c.* **3** AGR. acodo. **4** TEC. offset (proceso de impresión).

offshoot | 'ɒfʃuːt | *s.c.* **1** rama, ramificación. **2** (fig.) retoño, vástago.

offshore | ˌɒf'ʃɔː | *adj.* **1** MAR. que está a cierta distancia de la costa: *offshore islands = islas a cierta distancia de la costa.* || *adv.* **2** mar adentro, a vista de la costa: *a boat sailing offshore = un barco que navega mar adentro.*

offside | ˌɒf'saɪd | *s.sing.* **1** (brit.) lado del automóvil opuesto al que se conduce. **2** DEP. fuera de juego.

offspring | 'ɒfsprɪŋ | *s inv.* **1** (form. y hum.) prole, descendencia, hijos. **2** crías (de animales). **3** (fig.) resultado, producto.

off-stage | ˌɒf'steɪdʒ | (también **off stage**) *adj.* **1** TEAT. de entre bastidores: *off-stage sounds = ruidos entre bastidores.* || *adv.* **2** entre bastidores; fuera del escenario.

off-the-cuff | ˌɒfðə'kʌf | *adj.* **1** espontáneo. || *adv.* **2** de improviso.
off-the-peg | ˌɒfðə'peg | *adj.* **1** confeccionado (ropa). || *adv.* **2** de confección.
off-the-record | ˌɒfðə'rekəd | *adj.* **1** confidencial, oficioso. || *adv.* **2** confidencialmente, oficiosamente.
off-white | 'ɒfˌwaɪt | *adj.* blanquecino, blancuzco.
oft | ɒft | *adv.* (lit.) a menudo, muchas veces.
often | 'ɒfn | *adv.* **1** a menudo, con frecuencia, muchas veces. || **2 as – as not,** casi siempre; la mitad de las veces. **3 every so –,** cada poco, de cuando en cuando. **4 how –?,** ¿con qué frecuencia?, ¿cuántas veces? **5 more – than not,** la mayoría de las veces, por lo general.
ogle | 'əugl | *v.t.* **1** (hum.) echar el ojo: comer con los ojos (a alguien). || *s.c.* **2** mirada provocativa.
ogre | 'əugər | *s.c.* [*f.* **ogress**] **1** LIT. ogro. **2** (fig.) monstruo.
oh | əu | *interj.* **1** ¡ah!: **¡Oh yes! = ¡Ah sí!** **2** ¡oh! (para indicar admiración, asombro, alegría, pena o dolor).
ohm | əum | *s.c.* FIS. ohm, ohmio.
oil | ɔɪl | *s.i.* **1** MIN. petróleo. **2** TEC. fuel. **3** aceite: *olive oil = aceite de oliva.* || *s.c.* **4** ART. óleo. || *v.t.* **5** engrasar, lubrificar. **6** aceitar, untar con aceite. || **7 – paint/– paintings,** ART. pintura al óleo. **8 to – the wheels,** (fig.) preparar el terreno.
oilcan | 'ɔɪlkæn | (también **oil-can**) *s.c.* **1** aceitera, alcuza. **2** bidón de aceite.
oilcloth | 'ɔɪlklɒθ | *s.i.* tela de hule.
oilfield | 'ɔɪlfiːld | (también **oil field**) *s.c.* MIN. yacimiento petrolífero.
oil-fired | ˌɔɪl'faɪəd | *adj.* TEC. alimentado con fuel (calefacciones, radiadores).
oilman | 'ɔɪlmən | *s.c.* [*pl.* **oilmen**] **1** dueño de una compañía petrolífera. **2** trabajador de una compañía petrolífera.
oilrig | 'ɔɪlrɪg | (también **oil rig**) *s.c.* TEC. plataforma de perforación.
oilskin | 'ɔɪlskɪn | *s.c.* prenda de vestir impermeable.
oil-slick | 'ɔɪlslɪk | (también **oil slick**) *s.c.* capa de aceite (en el agua).
oil-tanker | ˌɔɪl'tæŋkər | (también **oil tanker**) *s.c.* **1** MAR. buque petrolero. **2** petrolero (vehículo que transporta petróleo).
oil-well | 'ɔɪlwel | (también **oil well**) *s.c.* TEC. pozo de petróleo.
oily | 'ɔɪlɪ | *adj.* **1** aceitoso. **2** grasiento, grasoso. **3** (fig.) cobista, zalamero.
ointment | 'ɔɪntmənt | *s.i.* **1** MED. ungüento, bálsamo. || **2 a fly in the –,** (fig.) pega, inconveniente.
okay | ˌəu'keɪ | (también **OK** = ¿estás bien?) *adj.* **1** (fam.) bueno, correcto, adecuado. **2** bien, perfectamente (en perfecto estado): *are you OK? = ¿estás bien?*|| *adv.* **3** muy bien. || *interj.* **4** ¡bien!, ¡vale! || *v.t.* **5** aprobar, dar el visto bueno. || **6 to do –,** ir bien (especialmente de dinero). **7 to give the –,** dar el visto bueno.
okra | 'əukrə | *s.i.* BOT. quimbombó.
old | əuld | *adj.* **1** viejo: *an old man, old clothes = un anciano, ropa vieja.* **2** antiguo: *Old English, an old painting = el inglés antiguo, una pintura antigua.* **3** antiguo (anterior): *an old pupil, her old job = un antiguo alumno, su antiguo trabajo.* **4** de edad: *he's twenty years old.* **5** antiguo, viejo (de muchos años): *an old friend, an old habit = un viejo amigo, una vieja costumbre.* **6** familiar: *an old face = una cara familiar.* **7** añejo: *old wine = vino añejo.*|| *s.pl.* **8 the –,** los ancianos.
OBS [num. + **year –**] s.c. se utiliza para indicar una determinada edad: *a five year old child = un crío de cinco años.* || **9 any –,** (fam.) cualquier: *any old thing = cualquier cosa.* **10 in the – days/in the olden days,** antaño, antiguamente. **11 of –,** de antaño: *days of old = antaño.* **12 – age pensioner,** pensionista. **13 – boy,** (brit.) antiguo alumno de un colegio; (fam. y p.u.) hombre mayor. **14 – boy network,** (brit.) intercambio de influencias entre antiguos alumnos. **15 – flame,** antiguo amor. **16 – girl,** (brit.) antigua alumna (fam., y p.u.) mujer mayor. **17 – guard, [the – +** *v.sing./pl.*] vieja guardia. **18 – hand,** veterano, experto. **19 – hat,** algo que ha perdido interés. **20 – maid,** (desp.) solterona. **21 – man,** (fam.) padre: my old man = mi padre; mi marido. **22 – master,** ART. maestro de la pintura. **23 – school,** vieja escuela. **24 – school tie,** (brit.) intercambio de influencias entre antiguos alumnos. **25 Old Testament,** Antiguo Testamento. **26 – wives' tale,** cuento de viejas; supersticiones. **27 – woman,** (fam.) madre; parienta, mujer. **28 to be – enough,** tener suficiente edad.
olde | əuld | *adj.* viejo, antiguo (en nombres de sitios y en publicidad).
old-fashioned | ˌəuld'fæʃnd | *adj.* **1** pasado de moda, anticuado. **2** chapado a la antigua.
old-timer | 'əuldtaɪmər | *s.c.* **1** (EE.UU. y fam.) veterano (en un trabajo). **2** antiguo residente. **3** viejo, anciano.
ole | əul | *adj.* LIT. viejo (en inglés escrito; representa la palabra **old** pronunciada de ese modo).
oleander | ˌəulɪ'ændər | *s.c.* BOT. adelfa.
olfactory | ɒl'fæktərɪ | *adj.* MED. olfativo.
oligarchy | 'ɒlɪgɑːkɪ | *s.c.* e *i.* oligarquía.
olive | 'ɒlɪv | *s.c.* **1** BOT. aceituna. **2** BOT. olivo. || *adj.* **3** verde oliva. || **4 – green,** verde oliva. **5 – grove,** BOT. olivar.
olive-branch | 'ɒlɪvbrɑːntʃ | (también **olive branch**) *s.c.* **1** ramo de olivo. || *s.sing.* **2** (fig.) ofrecimiento de paz, de amistad.
olive-oil | ˌɒlɪv'ɔɪl | (también **olive oil**) *s.i.* aceite de oliva.
Olympian | əu'lɪmpɪən | *adj.* (lit.) fenomenal, enorme, tremendo.
olympic | əu'lɪmpɪk | *adj.* **1** DEP. olímpico (relativo a los Juegos Olímpicos). || *s.pl.* **2 – Games,** DEP. Juegos Olímpicos, Olimpiadas. **3 The Olympics,** DEP. Olimpiadas, Juegos Olímpicos.
ombudsman | 'ɒmbudzmən | *s.c.* intermediario del gobierno.
omega | 'əumɪgə | *s.i.* omega.
omelette | 'ɒmlɪt | (EE.UU. **omelet**) **1** tortilla. || **2 You can't make an – without breaking eggs,** quien algo quiere algo le cuesta.
omen | 'əumen | *s.c.* **1** presagio, augurio. || *v.t.* **2** presagiar.
ominous | 'ɒmɪnəs | *adj.* siniestro; amenazador, inquietante.
ominously | 'ɒmɪnəslɪ | *adv.* de modo inquietante; amenazadoramente.
omission | ə'mɪʃn | *s.c.* **1** descuido, olvido: *it was an omission on his part = fue un descuido suyo.* || *s.i.* **2** omisión.
omit | ə'mɪt | *v.t.* **1** omitir. **2 [– to + *inf.*]** (form.) dejar de (deliberadamente); olvidar (accidentalmente): *he omitted to mention it = olvidó mencionarlo.*
omnibus | 'ɒmnɪbəs | *s.sing.* **1** LIT. antología. **2** RAD. y TV. recopilación (de programas). || *s.c.* **3** autobús.
omnipotence | ɒm'nɪpətəns | *s.i.* (form.) omnipotencia.
omnipotent | ɒm'nɪpətənt | *adj.* (form.) omnipotente, todopoderoso.
omnipresent | ˌɒmnɪ'preznt | *adj.* (form.) omnipresente.
omniscient | ɒm'nɪsɪənt | *adj.* (form.) omnisciente.
omnivorous | ɒm'nɪvərəs | *adj.* **1** BIOL. omnívoro. **2** (fig.) infatigable, que se entrega con ganas a una determinada actividad: *omnivorous reader = lector infatigable.*
on | ɒn | *prep.* **1** en: *it's on the floor = está en el suelo.* **2** sobre, encima de: *on the table = encima de la mesa.* **3** sobre, acerca de: *a book on art.* **4** a costa de: *he lives on his wife = vive a costa de su mujer.* **5** a: *on foot = a pie.* **6** de: *on holiday = de vacaciones.* **7 [– + *ger.*]** (lit.) al: *on arriving... = al llegar...* **8** con: *it* works on batteries = funciona con pilas. **9** por (radio, televisión): *we heard it on the radio = lo oímos por la radio.* **10** por, en: *on the road = en la carretera.* **11** por: *he swore on his honour = juró por su honor.* **12** contra: *attacks on the president = ataques contra el presidente.* **13** bajo: *on his word = bajo su palabra.* **14** junto a (un río, lago, mar, etc.).
OBS. Se utiliza **on** antes de una fecha o día determinado: *on May 15th = el 15 de mayo.* || *adv.* **15** encima, puesto (prendas de vestir): *he had his hat on = tenía el sombrero puesto.*
OBS. **On** posee además otros usos adverbiales: **16** idea de seguir, continuar: *he went on talking = siguió hablando.* **17** [*comp.* + –] enfatiza el sentido de un comparativo: *later on = más tarde.* **18** idea de encender (un interruptor, una luz): *switch on the lights = enciende las luces.* || *adj.* **19** enchufado, conectado (aparatos eléctricos, luz): *the washing machine is on = la lavadora está enchufada.* **20** puesto: *his coat is on = lleva puesto el abrigo.* **21** empezado: *the show is on = ha comenzado el espectáculo.* **22** abierto (grifo). || **23 and so –,** y así sucesivamente. **24 to be (just)**

not –, (fam.) estar mal; no ser satisfactorio: *that's not on = eso está mal, eso no se hace.* **25 from now –/from this time –/from this moment –/etc.,** de ahora en adelante, a partir de ahora. **26 to have a lot –,** (fam.) tener mucho que hacer. **27 – about,** (fam.) hablando sobre (un tema o una persona de forma aburrida o reiterativa). **28 – (an) average,** por término medio. **29 – and off,** de vez en cuando. **30 – and –,** continuamente, sin parar. **31 – at,** tenerla tomada con: *you are always on at me = la tienes tomada conmigo.* **32 – purpose,** adrede, a propósito. **33 – sale,** en venta. **34 – time,** puntualmente, a la hora. **35 – the sly/quiet,** a escondidas, a hurtadillas.

OBS. La partícula **on** modifica el sentido de muchos verbos; consultar cada verbo para la correspondiente traducción.

once | wʌns | *adv.* **1** una vez: *he called me once = me llamó una vez.* **2 [– a + s.]** una vez: *once a year = una vez al año.* **3** en otro tiempo: *it was once a beautiful house = en otro tiempo fue una casa hermosa.* || *conj.* **4** cuando, una vez que, en cuanto: *once they finished the exam, they left = en cuanto terminaron el examen, se fueron.* || **5 all at –,** de repente; simultáneamente, al mismo tiempo. **6 at –,** en seguida, en el acto; simultáneamente, al mismo tiempo. **7 for –,** por una vez. **8 not –,** ni siquiera una vez. **9 – again/– more,** de nuevo, una vez más. **10 – and for all,** de una vez por todas, definitivamente. **11 – every...,** una vez cada...: *Halley's comet comes once every seventy-five years = el cometa Halley viene una vez cada setenta y cinco años.* **12 – in a while,** de vez en cuando. **13 – or twice,** un par de veces. **14 – upon a time,** érase una vez; en otro tiempo.

once-over | 'wʌns,əuvər | *s.c.* (fam.) vistazo, mirada, ojeada.

oncoming | 'ɒn,kʌmɪŋ | *adj.* **1** que se aproxima: *the oncoming hurricane = el huracán que se aproxima.* **2** próximo: *the oncoming decade = la próxima década.* || *s.sing.* **3** proximidad: *the oncoming of spring = la proximidad de la primavera.*

one | wʌn | *num.* **1** uno: *one book.* || *adj.* **2 [– + *sing.*]** único: *he was the one person who understood her = fue la única persona que la entendió.* **3** (form.) un tal: *one Mr. Smith = un tal señor Smith.* **4** primero: *chapter one = primer capítulo.* **5** mismo: *of one height = de la misma altura.* || *pron.* **6** (form.) uno: *one can get lost here = uno se puede perder aquí.* **7** uno: *one of your friends = uno de tus amigos.* || *s.c.* **8** uno (número uno). || *s.sing.* **9** la una (hora): *it's one o'clock = es la una.* || **10 a hundred and –/a thousand and –/etc.,** muchísimos, gran cantidad de. **11 all –,** indiferente: *it's all one to me = me es indiferente, me da lo mismo.* **12 a quick –,** (fam.) un trago. **13 as –,** (form.) a la vez. **14 at –,** (p.u.) en armonía, de acuerdo. **15 to be a –,** (fam.) ser único: *you're a one! = ¡eres único!* **16 to be – for,** ser aficionado a: *my friend is a real one for basketball = mi amigo es aficionado al basketball.* **17 for –,** desde luego: *I for one don't like it = a mí, desde luego, no me gusta.* **18 in ones and twos,** en pequeños grupos. **19 not –, [– to + *inf.*]** no ser de la clase de persona que: *he's not one to give up = no es la clase de persona que se da por vencida.* **20 – after another,** uno tras otro: *one excuse after another = disculpa tras disculpa.* **21 – after the other,** uno tras otro (en sucesión): *I saw four films, one after the other = vi cuatro películas, una tras otra.* **22 – and all,** todo el mundo, todos. **23 – and only,** (fam.) único e inimitable (para presentar cantantes o personajes famosos): *they help one another = se ayudan unos a otros.* **25 – at a time,** uno de cada vez. **26 – by –,** uno por uno. **27 – eyed,** tuerto. **28 – in a million/– in a thousand/etc.,** singular, poco común. **29 – for the road,** (fam.) la última copa, la espuela (antes de irse). **30 – or two,** unos pocos. **31 – up on,** (fam.) tener ventaja sobre: *they were one upon us = tenían ventaja sobre nosotros.* **32 the – who,** el que: *I'm the one who telephoned = soy el que llamó por teléfono.* **33 two in –/three in –/all in –,** dos/tres/todo a la vez. **34 with – accord,** de común acuerdo. **35 you've got it in –,** (fam.) acertaste.

one-armed bandit | ,wʌn'ɑːmd'bændɪt | *s.c.* máquina tragaperras.

one-horse | ,wʌn'hɔːs | *adj.* **1** de un caballo: *a one-horse sledge = un trineo de un caballo.* || **2 – horse town,** ciudad de poca importancia, poblacho.

one-liner | ,wʌn'laɪnər | *s.c.* (fam.) golpe (de ingenio).

one-man | 'wʌnmən | *adj.* **1** de un solo hombre: *a one-man television programme = un programa de televisión realizado por un solo hombre.* **2** individual, para una sola persona: *a one-man vehicle = un vehiculo para una sola persona.* || **3 – band,** hombre orquesta. **4 – woman,** (p.u.) mujer de un solo hombre.

one-night stand | ,wʌnaɪt'stænd | *s.c.* **1** asunto amoroso, lío. **2** (fam.) única representación de una obra.

one-off | ,wʌn'ɒf | *s.c.* **1** único ejemplar. || *adj.* **2** único.

one-parent family | ,wʌnpeərənt'fæməlɪ | *s.c.* familia formada por uno solo de los padres y sus hijos.

one-piece | ,wʌn'piːs | *adj.* de una sola pieza (principalmente ropa).

onerous | 'ɒnərəs | *adj.* **1** (form.) pesado, fastidioso. **2** caro, costoso.

oneself | wʌn'self | *pron.ref.* **1** uno mismo, sí mismo: *to speak to oneself = hablar consigo mismo.* **2** se: *to cut oneself = cortarse.* **3** (form.) solo, sin ayuda: *to do it oneself = hacerlo solo.* || **4 by –,** solo; por sí solo.

one-sided | ,wʌn'saɪdɪd | *adj.* **1** unilateral: *one-sided agreement = acuerdo unilateral.* **2** parcial: *a one-sided author = un autor parcial.* **3** desigual, injusto. **4** de un solo lado: *a one-side street = calle con casas en un solo lado.*

one-time | ,wʌn'taɪm | (también **onetime**) *adj.* **1** ex (que fue): *a one-time actor = un ex actor.* **2** antiguo; anterior.

one-to-one | ,wʌntə'wʌn | *adj.* **1** individual (de una persona a otra): *these patients need one-to-one attention = estos pacientes necesitan atención individual.* **2** exacto: *a one-to-one correspondence = correspondencia exacta.*

one-track mind | ,wʌntræk'maɪnd | *adj.* capaz de pensar en una sola cosa: *he has a one-track mind = sólo piensa en una cosa.*

one-upmanship | ,wʌn'ʌpmənʃɪp | *s.i.* afán de estar por encima de los demás.

one-way | ,wʌn'weɪ | *adj.* **1** de sentido único: *a one-way street = una calle de sentido único.* **2** de ida (un billete, un viaje). **3** unilateral. || **4 – mirror,** espejo en el que sólo se ve por un lado.

one-woman | ,wʌn'wʊmən | *adj.* **1** de una sola mujer: *a one-woman show = espectáculo realizado por una sola mujer.* || **2 – man,** (p.u.) hombre de una sola mujer.

ongoing | 'ɒn,gəuɪŋ | *adj.* **1** actual (que está ocurriendo): *the ongoing energy crisis = la actual crisis de energía.* **2** continuo (en progreso) *an ongoing increase in the number of unemployed = un continuo incremento en el número de parados.*

onion | 'ʌnjən | *s.c.* e *i.* **1** BOT. cebolla. || **2 to be off one's –,** (fam.) estar loco. **3 to know one's onions,** (fam.) saber mucho de la materia.

onlooker | 'ɒn,lʊkər | *s.c.* **1** espectador. **2** mirón.

only | 'əunlɪ | *adv.* **1** sólo, solamente: *it was only a joke = sólo era un chiste.* **2** únicamente. || *adj.* **3** único: *his only hope = su única esperanza.* || *conj.* **4 [– (if)]** sólo: *I'll buy it only if you lend me the money = sólo lo compraré si me prestas el dinero.* **5** (fam.) pero: *I wanted to go, only I couldn't = quería ir, pero no pude.* || **6 not –,** no sólo: *she not only sings but composes her songs = no sólo canta sino que también compone sus canciones.* **7 – just,** apenas: *it has only just begun = apenas ha empezado, acaba de empezar.* **8 only too,** demasiado (más de lo que se quisiera): *I remember it only too clearly = lo recuerdo demasiado bien.*

onomatopoeia | ,ɒnəumætəu'piːə | *s.i.* onomatopeya.

onomatopoeic | ,ɒnəumætəu'piːɪk | *adj.* onomatopéyico.

onrush | 'ɒn,rʌʃ | *s.sing.* **1** embestida, arremetida. **2** (form. y fig.) oleada, avalancha.

onset | 'ɒn,set | *s.sing.* **1** principio (normalmente de algo desagradable). **2** ataque, embestida.

onshore | 'ɒn,ʃɔː | *adj.* o *adv.* **1** que viene hacia tierra: *onshore wind = viento hacia tierra.* **2** en tierra.

onslaught | ’ɒnˌslɔːt | *s.c.* **1** ataque violento. **2** (fig.) crítica, ataque.
on-the-spot | ˌɒnðə’spɒt | *adj.* que está en el lugar (donde ha ocurrido o está ocurriendo algo).
onto | ’ɒntʊ | (también **on to**) *prep.* hacia; sobre (V. **on.**)
onus | ’əʊnəs | *s.sing.* (form.) responsabilidad: *the onus is on the government = es responsabilidad del gobierno.*
onward | ’ɒnwəd | *adj.* **1** que avanza hacia adelante. **2** (fig.) que progresa, que cobra importancia.
onwards | ’ɒnwədz | *adv.* **1** (brit.) hacia adelante. || **2 from then –/from 1980 –, etc.,** desde entonces, a partir de 1980, etc.
onyx | ’ɒnɪks | *s.i.* GEOL. ónice, ónix.
oodles | ’uːdəlz | *s.pl.* (fam.) montones, cantidad: *oodles of money = cantidad de dinero.*
ooh | uː | (también **o**) *interj.* ¡oh!
oomph | ʊmf | (fam.) *s.i.* **1** vigor, energía, vitalidad. **2** atractivo (especialmente sexual). **3** encanto personal, magnetismo.
oops | ʊps | | uːps | *interj.* ¡uy!
ooze | uːz | *v.t.* e *i.* **1** rezumar(se), manar, fluir, gotear (un líquido). || *v.t.* **2** sudar. **3** (fig.) rebosar: *he oozed with pride = rebosaba de orgullo.* || *s.i.* **4** fango, lodo, cieno.
op | ɒp | (fam.) *s.c.* **1** operación, intervención (quirúrgica). **2** operación militar.
opacity | əʊ’pæsɪtɪ | *s.i.* **1** (fam.) opacidad. **2** (fig.) complejidad, falta de claridad: *Nietzsche's opacity = la complejidad de Nietzsche.* **3** torpeza (de mente).
opal | ’əʊpl | *s.c.* e *i.* GEOL. ópalo.
opalescent | ˌəʊpə’lesnt | *adj.* opalescente.
opaque | əʊ’peɪk | *adj.* **1** (form. o lit.) opaco. **2** (fig.) ininteligible. **3** torpe, obtuso.
open | ’əʊpən | *v.t.* **1** abrir: *open the window = abre la ventana.* **2** inaugurar, poner (una tienda, un negocio). **3** inaugurar, empezar (una exhibición). **4** empezar (una maniobra militar). **5** emprender, iniciar (un negocio). **6** inaugurar (un edificio, una plaza, etc.). **7** abrir, iniciar (un debate). **8** entablar (una conversación). || *v.i.* **9** abrirse: *the door opened = la puerta se abrió.* **10** estrenarse (una obra, una película). **11** empezar, comenzar: *the story opens with a discription = la historia empieza con una descripción.* || *adj.* **12** abierto: *an open book = un libro abierto.* **13** franco, abierto: *an open smile = una sonrisa franca.* **14** abierto, receptivo: *open to suggestions = abierto a las sugerencias.* **15** expuesto: *open to criticisms = expuesto a las críticas.* **16** descubierto: *open carriage = coche descubierto.* **17** destapado: *an open bottle = una botella destapada.* **18** despejado. **19** manifiesto, evidente (actitud, situación). **20** abierto a todos (una reunión, una competición). **21** abierto, desabrochado: *an open jacket = una chaqueta desabrochada.* **22** sin resolver: *an open question = una cuestión sin resolver.* **23** disponible, vacante (un empleo, un puesto). **24** libre (sin obstáculos). **25** sin nieve: *open winter = un invierno sin nieve.* || **26 to have/keep one's ears –,** afinar el oído. **27 to have/keep one's eyes –,** estar atento. **28 in the –, into the –,** revelado, sacado a la luz (una actitud, una situación). **29 – book,** (fig.) persona fácil de entender. **30 – day,** día en que una institución está abierta al público. **31 to – fire,** abrir fuego. **32 – house,** casa abierta (a amigos o visitantes). **33 to – into/on/upon /toward,** comunicarse con, tener paso a, dar a, mirar a, salir a. **34 to – its borders/frontiers,** abrir sus fronteras. **35 – letter,** carta abierta. **36 – market,** mercado libre. **37 to – one's eyes/to – someone's eyes,** (fig.) abrir los ojos, desengañar. **38 to – one's heart,** sincerarse. **39 to – out to someone,** confiarse a alguien. **40 – secret,** secreto a voces. **41 to – the door/to – doors,** (fig.) abrir puertas (hacer algo posible). **42 Open University,** (brit.) universidad que enseña por medio de emisiones de radio o televisión. **43 to – up, a)** hablar francamente; **b)** abrir fuego; **c)** abrir (un local); **d)** conquistar (tierras, mercados); **e)** crear (oportunidades). **44 the clouds/the heavens/the skies –,** (lit.) empieza a llover. **45 with – arms,** con los brazos abiertos, con entusiasmo.
open-air | ˌəʊpn’eər | *s.sing.* al aire libre.
open-and-shut | ˌəʊpnən’ʃʌt | *adj.* claro, evidente.
open-cast | ’əʊpənkɑːst | (también **opencast**) *adj.* MIN. a cielo abierto (mina).
open-ended | ˌəʊpn’endɪd | *s.c.* **1** indefinido (sin límites determinados).
opener | əʊpənər | *s.c.* **1** abrelatas. **2** abridor (de cartas, de botellas). **3 for openers,** (fam.) para principiantes.
opening | ’əʊpnɪŋ | *s.i.* **1** abertura. || *s.c.* **2** abertura, hendidura, grieta. **3** principio, comienzo: *the opening of the book = el principio de un libro.* **4** apertura (en ajedrez). **5** apertura (de un acto). **6** oportunidad. **7** inauguración. **8** puesto vacante. **9** (EE.UU.) claro (en un bosque). || *adj.* **10** primero: *the opening scene = la primera escena.* || **11 – hours,** horas de comercio. **12 – night,** noche de estreno (de una obra, de una ópera). **13 – time,** hora de comercio.
openly | əʊpnlɪ | *adv.* abiertamente, francamente.
open-minded | ˌəʊpn’maɪndɪd | *adj.* **1** receptivo. **2** liberal, sin prejuicios.
open-mindedness | əʊpn’maɪndɪdnɪs | *s.i.* liberalidad, amplitud de miras.
open-mouthed | ˌəʊpn’maʊðd | *adj.* boquiabierto.
open-necked | ˌəʊpn’nekt | *adj.* con el cuello desabrochado: *an open-necked shirt = una camisa con el cuello desabrochado.*
openness | ’əʊpnɪs | *s.i.* sinceridad, franqueza.
open-plan | ˌəʊpn’plæn | *adj.* ARQ. sin paredes interiores: *an open-plan house = una casa sin paredes interiores.*
opera | ’ɒpərə | *s.c.* **1** MUS. ópera: *a Verdi opera = una ópera de Verdi.* || *s.i.* **2** MUS. ópera (género). || *s.sing.* **3** compañía de ópera: *the English National Opera.* || **4 comic –,** ópera cómica, zarzuela. **5 light –,** opereta. **6 – glasses,** prismáticos de teatro. **7 – house,** ópera, teatro de la ópera.
operate | ’ɒpəreɪt | *v.t.* e *i.* **1** operar, actuar, funcionar. **2** manejar, hacer funcionar, funcionar (una máquina, un aparato). || *v.t.* **3** realizar, llevar a cabo (un plan, un proyecto). || *v.i.* **4** MED. operar, intervenir. **5** obrar, actuar, producir efecto. **6** MIL. operar, efectuar una maniobra militar.
operatic | ˌɒpə’rætɪk | *adj.* MUS. operístico.
operating | ’ɒpəreɪtɪŋ | *adj.* **1** que opera. || **2 – room/teatre,** MED. quirófano, sala de operaciones. **3 – table,** MED. mesa de operaciones.
operation | ˌɒpə’reɪʃn | *s.c.* **1** operación, actuación. **2** maniobra. **3** MIL. operación, maniobra: *military operations = maniobras militares.* **4** COM. empresa, actividad. **5** MED. operación, intervención. || *s.i.* **6** funcionamiento. **7** manejo || **8 to come into –/to put something into –,** poner en funcionamiento; entrar en vigor (una ley). **9 in –,** en funcionamiento, en vigor. **10 to undergo an –,** someterse a una operación.
operational | ˌɒpə’reɪʃənl | *adj.* **1** apto para su función (una máquina, un aparato). **2** coyuntural: *operational difficulties = dificultades coyunturales.* **3** operacional.
operative | ’ɒpərətɪv | *adj.* **1** operante, operativo. **2** MED. operatorio. || *s.c.* **3** (form.) operario; artesano. **4** (EE.UU.) agente secreto, detective privado. || **5 the – word,** la palabra (palabra de especial relevancia en un contexto; se utiliza normalmente en sentido humorístico).
operator | ’ɒpəreɪtər | *s.c.* **1** telefonista. **2** operador (encargado de hacer funcionar una máquina o aparato). **3** (EE.UU.) especulador (en la Bolsa). **4** explotador (empresario): *mine operator = explotador de minas.* **5** (fam.) embaucador, timador. **6** INF. operador: *computer operator.* **7** MAT. operador.
operetta | ˌɒpə’retə | *s.c.* e *i.* MUS. opereta; zarzuela.
ophthalmic | ɒf’θælmɪk | *adj.* MED. (form.) oftálmico.
opiate | ’əʊpɪət | *s.c.* **1** (form.) narcótico. **2** (fig.) droga.
opine | əʊ’paɪn | *v.t.* e *i.* **1** (form. y p.u.) opinar.
opinion | ə’pɪnjən | *s.c.* **1** opinión; parecer, modo de ver: *nobody asked his opinion = nadie pidió su opinión.* **2** dictamen (de un experto). | *s.sing.* **3** opinión, juicio, concepto (referente a personas): *I have a good opinion of him = tengo una buena opinión de él.* || *s.i.* **4** opi-

nión, criterio: *a difference of opinion = diferencia de criterio.* **5** opinión (parecer general): *public opinion = opinión pública.* || **6 to be of the – that,** ser de la opinión que. **7 in one's –,** según la opinión de uno. **8 – poll,** sondeo de opinión, encuesta.

opinionated | ə'pɪnjəneɪtɪd | *adj.* testarudo, terco, obstinado.

opium | 'əupjəm | *s.i.* opio.

opossum | ə'pɒsəm | *s.c.* ZOOL. zarigüeya, oposum.

opponent | ə'pəunənt | *s.c.* **1** adversario, oponente: *political opponent = adversario político.* **2** contrincante, competidor, antagonista. **3 [– (of)]** enemigo, contrario (que se opone a algo): *opponent of the arms race = contrario a la carrera armamentista.* || *adj.* **4** opuesto. || **5 – muscle,** ANAT. oponente.

opportune | 'ɒpətju:n | (form.) *adj.* **1** oportuno: *opportune moment = momento oportuno.* **2** providencial. **3** conveniente.

opportunism | 'opətju:nɪzəm | *s.i.* (form.) oportunismo: *commercial opportunism = oportunismo comercial.*

opportunist | 'ɒpətju:nɪst | *s.c.* **1** (form.) oportunista. || *adj.* **2** oportunista, egoísta.

opportunistic | 'ɒpətju:nɪstɪk | *adj.* (form.) oportunista, sin escrúpulos.

opportunity | ˌɒpə'tju:nɪtɪ | *s.c.* e *i.* **1** oportunidad, ocasión. || **2 at every –,** siempre que sea posible. **3 at the earliest/first –,** a la primera oportunidad. **4 to take the –,** aprovechar la ocasión.

oppose | ə'peuz | *v.t.* **1** (form.) oponerse a, mostrarse contrario a: *he opposed my plan = se opuso a mi proyecto.* **2 [to – + o. + (to)],** contrastar, comparar. **3** oponer (poner frente a frente): *to oppose two forces = oponer dos fuerzas.* || **4 as opposed to,** en contraste con, en comparación con. **5 to be opposed to,** estar/ir en contra de: *it is opposed to my principles = va en contra de mis principios.* **6 to – oneself to,** (form.) oponerse a: *I opposed myself to it with all my power = me opuse con todas mis fuerzas.*

opposed | ə'pəuzd | *adj.* **1 [– (to)]** opuesto: *black is opposed to white = el negro es opuesto al blanco.* **2** contradictorio, opuesto: *two opposed versions = dos versiones opuestas.*

opposing | ə'pəuzɪŋ | *adj.* contrario, opuesto: *the opposing team = el equipo contrario.*

opposite | 'ɒpəzɪt | *prep.* **1** enfrente de, frente a: *my house is opposite the school = mi casa está enfrente del colegio.* || *adv.* **2** enfrente: *the school is opposite = el colegio está enfrente.* || *adj.* **3** opuesto, de enfrente: *the opposite door = la puerta de enfrente.* **4** contrario, opuesto: *the opposite effect = el efecto contrario.* **5 [– (to/from)]** completamente diferente, opuesto: *your tastes are opposite to mine = tus gustos son opuestos a los míos.* || *s.c.* **6 [the –]** lo opuesto, lo contrario: *that's the opposite of what you told me = eso es lo contrario de lo que me contaste.* || **7 – number,** colega. **8 the – sex,** el sexo contrario.

opposition | ˌɒpə'zɪʃn | *s.i.* **1** oposición, disconformidad, resistencia. || *s.sing.:* **[– + *v.sing.*** o *pl.*] **2** POL. oposición (partido de la oposición): *the leader of the Opposition = el líder de la oposición.* **3** oposición (grupo de personas que se oponen a algo). **4** DEP. persona o equipo contrario. || **5 in – to,** en desacuerdo con.

oppress | ə'pres | *v.t.* **1** oprimir, sojuzgar; tiranizar. **2** agobiar, angustiar: *that flat oppressed me = aquel piso me agobiaba.*

oppressed | ə'prest | *adj.* **1** oprimido, tiranizado: *oppressed peoples = los pueblos oprimidos.* || **2 the oppressed,** los oprimidos.

oppression | ə'preʃn | *s.c.* e *i.* **1** opresión. || *s.c.* **2** tiranía, abuso. || *s.i.* **3** agobio, angustia; desánimo.

oppressive | ə'presɪv | *adj.* **1** sofocante, bochornoso (tiempo, atmósfera). **2** agobiante, abrumador: *an oppressive situation = una situación agobiante.* **3** opresor, opresivo, injusto, tiránico: *an oppressive law = una ley opresiva.*

oppressively | ə'presɪvlɪ | *adv.* opresivamente, agobiantemente.

oppressor | ə'presər | *s.c.* opresor, tirano.

opprobrious | ə'prəubrɪəs | *adj.* (form.) infamante, ultrajante, ignominioso.

opprobrium | ə'prəubrɪəm | *s.i.* (form.) oprobio, infamia; deshonra.

opt | ɒpt | *v.i.* **1 [to – + for]** optar por, elegir (algo). **2 [to – + to + *inf.*]** optar (por hacer algo). || **3 to – out,** [– (of)] optar por no participar.

optic | 'ɒptɪk | *adj.* **1** OPT. óptico. **2** (hum.) ojo.

optical | 'ɒptɪkl | *adj.* **1** OPT. óptico: *optical microscope = microscopio óptico.* **2** visual, óptico: *optical art = arte visual.* || **3 — illusion,** ilusión óptica.

optician | ɒp'tɪʃn | *s.c.* OPT. óptico.

optics | 'ɒptɪks | *s.i.* óptica (ciencia).

optimism | 'ɒptɪmɪzəm | *s.i.* optimismo, confianza.

optimist | 'ɒptɪmɪst | *s.c.* optimista.

optimistic | ˌɒptɪmɪstɪk | *adj.* optimista; animoso.

optimistically | ˌɒptɪmɪstɪkəlɪ | *adv.* con optimismo.

optimum | 'ɒptɪməm | (form.) *adj.* **1** óptimo: *optimum temperature = temperatura óptima.* || *s.sing.* **2** grado óptimo.

option | 'ɒpʃn | *s.c.* **1** opción, alternativa: *I have two options = tengo dos opciones.* **2** asignatura opcional. || *s.sing.* **3** derecho a elegir, elección, alternativa: *we had no option = no teníamos elección.* || **4 to have no – but,** no tener más remedio que. **5 to keep/leave one's options open,** no comprometerse. **6 to make one's – between,** elegir entre.

optional | 'ɒpʃənl *adj.* opcional, facultativo; discrecional.

opulence | 'ɒpjuləns | *s.i.* (form.) opulencia, riqueza.

opulent | 'ɒpjulənt (form.) *adj.* **1** opulento, rico, acaudalado. **2** abundante. **3** suntuoso, fastuoso.

opus | 'əupəs | [*pl.* **opuses** u **opera**] *s.c.* **1 [– + *num.*]** MUS. opus (cada una de las obras de un compositor).

or | ɔ: | *conj.* **1** o; u: *tea or coffee? = ¿té o café?* **2 [not ... =N]** ni: *she doesn't work or study = no trabaja ni estudia.* || **3 – else,** sino, de otro modo. **4 – no,** con o sin: *you'll have to study, noise or no noise = tendrás que estudiar, con ruido o sin él.* **5 – so,** o poco más o menos.

oracle | 'ɒrəkl | *s.c.* **1** oráculo: *Delphic oracle = oráculo de Delfos.* **2** oráculo, predicción (respuesta de una pitonisa).

oracular | ɒ'rækjulər | (form.) *adj.* **1** relativo al oráculo. **2** misterioso, ambiguo. **3** profético.

oral | 'ɔ:rəl | *adj.* **1** oral, verbal: *oral tradition = la tradición oral.* **2** oral, bucal (que se toma por vía oral): *oral contraceptive = anticonceptivo oral.* || *s.c.* **3** (fam.) oral, examen oral.

orally | 'ɔ:rəlɪ | *adv.* **1** oralmente, verbalmente. **2** por vía oral.

orange | 'ɒrɪndʒ | *s.c.* **1** BOT. naranja. || *adj.* **2** naranja, color naranja. || *s.i.* bebida de naranja (natural o artificial). || **4 – blossom,** BOT. azahar.

orangeade | ˌɒrɪndʒ'eɪd | *s.i.* naranjada (natural o artificial).

orangery | 'ɒrɪndʒərɪ | *s.c.* BOT. naranjal.

orangey | 'ɒrɪndʒɪ | *adj.* anaranjado (color).

orang-outang | ɔ:ˌræŋu:'tæŋ | (también **orang-utan**) *s.c.* ZOOL. orangután.

oration | ɔ:'reɪʃn | *s.c.* **1** discurso; arenga. || **2 funeral –,** oración fúnebre.

orator | 'ɒrətər | *s.c.* orador.

oratorical | ˌɒrə'tɒrɪkl | *adj.* (form.) oratorio (relativo al discurso).

oratorio | ˌɒrə'tɔ:rɪəu | *s.c.* MUS. oratorio (drama musical de tema religioso).

oratory | 'ɒrətərɪ | *s.i.* **1** (form.) RET. oratoria. || *s.c.* **2** REL. capilla, oratorio.

orb | ɔ:b | *s.c.* **1** esfera, globo. **2** (lit.) orbe; cuerpo celeste. **3** (lit.) ojo.

orbit | 'ɔ:bɪt | *s.c.* **1 [in/into –]** ASTR. órbita: *a satellite into orbit = un satélite en órbita.* **2** ANAT. órbita ocular. || *v.t.* **3** girar alrededor de. **4** poner en órbita (un satélite). || *v.i.* **5** moverse en órbita, girar. || *s.sing.* **6** (fig.) órbita, ámbito, esfera: *out of the family orbit = fuera de la órbita familiar.*

orbital | 'ɔ:bɪtl | *adj.* **1** que rodea una gran ciudad (una carretera). **2** ASTR. orbital: *orbital flight = vuelo orbital.*

orchard | 'ɔ:tʃəd | *s.c.* **1** AGR. huerto, pomar.

orchestra | 'ɔ:kɪstrə | *s.c.* **1** MUS. orquesta. **2** (EE.UU.) platea, patio de butacas. || **3 – pit,** foso (piso inferior del escenario donde se coloca la orquesta).

orchestral | ɔ:'kestrəl | *adj.* MUS. orquestal.

orchestrate | 'ɔ:kɪstreɪt | *v.t.* **1** MUS. orquestar, instrumentar para orquesta (una partitura). **2** (fig.) orquestar, organizar, dirigir.

orchestrated | 'ɔːkɪstreɪtɪd | *adj.* **1** MUS. orquestado. **2** (fig.) organizado, dirigido.
orchestration | ˌɔːke'streɪʃn | *s.i.* **1** MUS. orquestación. **2** (fig.) organización, dirección.
orchid | 'ɔːkɪd | *s.c.* BOT. orquídea.
ordain | ɔː'deɪn | *v.t.* **1** REL. ordenar: *he was ordained priest = fue ordenado sacerdote.* **2** (form.) decretar; mandar, ordenar (una autoridad). **3** (form.) destinar, establecer (Dios, el destino, etc.).
ordained | ɔː'deɪnd | *adj.* REL. ordenado.
ordeal | ɔː'diːl | *s.c.* experiencia muy dura, situación penosa.
order | 'ɔːdər | *conj.* **1 [in – to/that]** para (que), a fin de (que): *he came here in order to see you = vino para verte.* || *s.c.* **2** orden, instrucción: *to obey the orders = obedecer las órdenes.* **3** COM. pedido, encargo: *an order for books = un pedido de libros.* **4** DER. orden, mandato. **5** giro postal. **6** REL. orden (comunidad religiosa): *the Franciscan order = la orden franciscana.* **7** orden (civil o militar): *order of knigthood = orden de caballería.* **8** BIOL. orden, clase: *order of arthropoda = orden de los artrópodos.* || *s.c.* e *i.* **9** orden: *in alfabethical order = por orden alfabético.* || *s.c.* **10** orden, tranquilidad: *to restore order = restablecer el orden.* || *s.sing.* **11** orden, sistema (forma de organización): *a new moral order = un nuevo orden moral.* **12** (form.) tipo, categoría, índole: *problems of another order = problemas de otro tipo.* || *v.t.* **13 [to – + *o.* + (to)]** ordenar: *they ordered me to go out = me ordenó que saliese.* **14 [to – + *o.* + *prep.*]** ordenar, mandar: *he ordered me in = me mandó entrar.* **15** pedir (en un bar, restaurante, etc.): *he ordered a beer = pidió una cerveza.* **16** COM. encargar, hacer un pedido. **17** organizar, ordenar, poner en orden: *I have to order my life = tengo que organizar mi vida.* **18** BIOL. clasificar (animales, plantas). || **19 in good –/in perfect –, etc.,** en buen estado, en perfecto estado. **20 in –,** en regla, en orden; por (su) orden (en correcta sucesión); correcto. **21 in –/in working –,** en buen estado, en funcionamiento (una máquina, un vehículo). **22 in/of/on the – of,** aproximadamente, del orden de. **23 to keep –/to keep someone in/into –,** mantener el orden, controlar. **24 law and –,** orden público. **25 on –,** pedido, encargado. **26 to – about/around,** traer de acá para allá, dominar. **27 out of –, a)** en desorden; **b)** estropeado (máquina, aparato, vehículo); **c)** fuera de lugar (persona, comportamiento); **d)** descompuesto (vientre). **28 the – of the day,** imperante; de moda. **29 to –,** siempre que se requiera; a petición. **30 to take orders,** REL. ordenarse. **31 under orders,** bajo órdenes.
ordered | 'ɔːdəd | *adj.* ordenado, organizado; controlado.
order-form | 'ɔːdəfɔːm | *s.c.* COM. orden de pedido.
orderliness | 'ɔːdəlɪnɪs | *s.i.* **1** orden, método, disciplina. **2** orden, pulcritud.
orderly | 'ɔːdəlɪ | *adj.* **1** ordenado, organizado. **2** disciplinado, obediente. || *s.c.* **3** asistente de hospital. **4** MIL. ordenanza.
ordinal | 'ɔːdɪnl | *adj.* y *s.c.* **1** ordinal, número ordinal. || **2 – number,** número ordinal.
ordinance | 'ɔːdɪnəns | *s.c.* **1** (form.) ordenanza, decreto, ley. **2** REL. rito religioso.
ordinand | 'ɔːdɪnænd | *s.c.* REL. ordenando.
ordinarily | 'ɔːdnrɪlɪ | *adv.* de ordinario, normalmente, comúnmente.
ordinary | 'ɔːdnrɪ | *adj.* **1** común, corriente: *an ordinary ball-pen = un bolígrafo corriente.* **2** (desp.) mediocre, ordinario, vulgar: *an ordinary person = una persona vulgar.* **3** habitual: *in his ordinary manner of talking = con su habitual modo de hablar.* || **4 in the – way,** en circunstancias normales. **5 out of the –,** fuera de lo común, especial.
ordination | ˌɔːdɪ'neɪʃn | *s.c.* **1** REL. ordenación. **2** ley, ordenanza. || *s.i.* **3** ordenación, disposición, arreglo. **4** REL. ordenación.
ordnance | 'ɔːdnəns | *s.i.* **1** MIL. suministros de guerra (especialmente armas); artillería. || **2 – survey,** (brit.) servicio oficial de topografía y cartografía.
ordure | 'ɔːˌdjuər | (form.) *s.i.* **1** excrementos, porquería, suciedad. **2** estiércol. **3** lenguaje obsceno.
ore | ɔː | *s.inv.* **1** MIN. mineral, mena: *iron ore = mineral de hierro.* **2** (lit.) metal (especialmente oro).
oregano | ˌɒriː'gɑːnəʊ | *s.i.* GAST. orégano.
organ | 'ɔːgən | *s.c.* **1** ANAT. órgano: *vital organs = órganos vitales.* **2** MUS. órgano. **3** órgano (compañía, periódico o revista portavoz de un grupo, causa u opinión): *government organ = órgano del gobierno.*
organdie | 'ɔːgəndɪ | (EE.UU. **organdy**) *s.i.* organdí.
organ-grinder | 'ɔːgənˌgraɪndər | *s.c.* MUS. organillero.
organic | ɔː'gænɪk | *adj.* **1** FISIOL. orgánico: *organic life = vida orgánica.* **2** (form.) orgánico, constitucional, fundamental (una estructura, una entidad, una ley). **3** (form.) sistemático, coordinado (desarrollo, cambio). **4** MED. orgánico (enfermedad). || **5 – chemistry,** química orgánica.
organically | ɔː'gænɪkəlɪ | *adv.* sistemáticamente, de forma coordinada.
organism | 'ɔːgənɪzəm | *s.c.* **1** BIOL. organismo (ser vivo). **2** FISIOL. organismo (conjunto de órganos y funciones): *the human organism = el organismo humano.* **3** (fig.) organismo (cuerpo o institución).
organist | 'ɔːgənɪst | *s.c.* MUS. organista.
organization | ˌɔːgənaɪ'zeɪʃn | (también **organisation**) *s.c.* **1** organización (organismo, entidad): *World Health Organization = Organización Mundial de la Salud.* || *s.i.* **2** organización, preparación: *the organization of the feast = la preparación del banquete.* **3** organización, estructura (de una sociedad, institución o entidad). **4** organización, planificación, ordenación.
organizational | ˌɔːgənaɪ'zeɪʃnəl | (también **organisational**) *adj.* **1** organizativo, organizador. **2** relativo a un organismo, sistema o entidad.
organize | 'ɔːgənaɪz | (también **organise**) *v.t.* **1** organizar, preparar: *they organized the party = ellos organizaron la fiesta.* **2** ordenar, poner en orden: *who organized these papers? = ¿quién ordenó estos papeles?* || *v.i.* **3** organizarse (formar una sociedad, un sindicato, etc.). **4 to – oneself,** organizarse.
organized | 'ɔːgənaɪzd | (también **organised**) *adj.* organizado, ordenado. **2** planificado, estructurado.
organizer | 'ɔːgənaɪzər | (también **organiser**) *s.c.* **1** organizador.
orgasm | 'ɔːgæzəm | *s.c.* **1** orgasmo. **2** (form.) exaltación, frenesí.
orgasmic | 'ɔːgæzmɪk | *adj.* **1** MED. relativo al orgasmo. **2** (fam.) culminante.
orgiastic | ˌɔːdʒɪ'æstɪk | *adj.* orgiástico, desenfrenado.
orgy | 'ɔːdʒɪ | *s.c.* **1** orgía. **2** (fig.) exceso, abuso.
orient | 'ɔːrɪənt | *v.t.* **1** (form.) adaptarse, aclimatarse (a una nueva situación). **2** orientar. || *adj.* **3** brillante (perlas, piedras preciosas). || **4 to be oriented (to/towards),** (form.) inclinarse, interesarse (por algo, por alguien). **5 the Orient,** (lit.) Oriente. **6 to – oneself,** orientarse.
oriental | ˌɔːrɪ'entl | *adj.* y *s.c.* oriental.
orientate | 'ɔːrɪenteɪt | *v.t.* e *i.* **1** orientar(se). **2** (fig.) adaptarse, aclimatarse. || **3 to be oriented (to/towards),** (fig.) inclinarse (por); dirigir su mirada (hacia). **4 to – oneself,** orientarse.
orientated | 'ɔːrɪenteɪtɪd | *adj.* **[*adv./s.* + –]** orientado (que tiende hacia algo): *politically orientated = orientado hacia la política.*
orientation | ˌɔːrɪen'teɪʃn | *s.c.* **1** orientación, tendencia, inclinación. **2** orientación, situación, posición. || *s.i.* **3** orientación: *orientation course = curso de orientación.*
oriented | 'ɔːrɪentɪd | *adj.* [*adv./s.* + –] orientado (que tiende hacia algo): *politically orientated = orientado hacia la política.*
orifice | 'ɒrɪfɪs | (form.) *s.c.* **1** (hum.) orificio (principalmente del cuerpo). **2** orificio, abertura, agujero.
origin | 'ɒrɪdʒɪn | *s.c.* e *i.* **1** origen, principio: *the origin of the universe = el origen del universo.* **2** origen, causa, motivo: *the origin of this dispute = el origen de esta disputa.* **3** origen, procedencia: *of Spanish origin = de procedencia española.* **4** origen, ascendencia (clase social de la que se procede): *of humble origin = de origen humilde.*
original | ə'rɪdʒɪnl | *adj.* **1** original, inicial: *the original idea = la idea inicial.* **2** primero, primitivo: *the original inha-*

bitants = los primeros habitantes. **3** auténtico, genuino (que no es copia): *the original picture.* **4** nuevo, inédito (un texto, una partitura, etc.): *an original story = una historia inédita.* **5** original, poco común: *a very original programme = un programa muy original.* **6** creativo, original: *an original mind = una mente creativa.* || *s.c.* **7** original (de un documento, de una obra de arte): *where is the original? = ¿dónde está el original?* **8** persona excéntrica. || **9 in the –,** en el (idioma) original. **10 – sin,** pecado original.

originality | əˌrɪdʒə'nælɪtɪ | *s.i.* originalidad.

originally | ə'rɪdʒənəlɪ | *adv.* **1** inicialmente, en un principio.

originate | ə'rɪdʒəneɪt | (form.) *v.t.* **1** originar, dar origen, iniciar, provocar: *his negligence originated the fire = su descuido provocó el incendio.* || *v.i.* **2** originarse, tener su origen (en), surgir: *football originated in England = el fútbol tuvo su origen en Inglaterra.* || **3 to – from/in,** tener su origen en: *Romanesque originated in the Middle Ages = el arte románico tuvo su origen en la Edad Media.* **4 to – with/from,** surgir de (alguien): *the idea originated with her = la idea surgió de ella.*

originator | ə'rɪdʒəneɪtər | *s.c.* **[– + (of)]** (form.) creador; autor; inventor.

ornament | 'ɔːnəmənt | *s.c.* **1** adorno. **2** (p.u.) honra, orgullo (persona de la que se está orgulloso): *he is an ornament to his country = es un orgullo para su país.* **3** REL. ornamento. || *s.i.* **4** adorno. **5** adornos, arabescos. **6** MUS. florituras. || *v.t.* **7** adornar, decorar; embellecer.

ornamental | ˌɔːnə'mentl | *adj.* ornamental, decorativo, de adorno.

ornamentation | ˌɔːnəmen'teɪʃn | *s.i.* decoración, ornamentación, adorno.

ornate | ɔː'neɪt | *adj.* **1** excesivamente adornado, recargado (un objeto, un estilo). **2** adornado, florido; rebuscado (lenguaje).

ornatelly | ɔː'neɪtlɪ | *adv.* cuidadosamente (con todo detalle).

ornery | 'ɔːnərɪ | (EE.UU. y fam.) *adj.* **1** terco, testarudo. **2** malhumorado, intratable; grosero.

ornithological | ˌɔːnɪθə'lɒdʒɪkl | *adj.* ZOOL. ornitológico.

ornithologist | ˌɔːnɪ'θɒlədʒɪst | *s.c.* TEC. ornitólogo.

ornithology | ˌɔːnɪ'θɒlədʒɪ | *s.i.* ZOOL. ornitología.

orphan | 'ɔːfn | *s.c.* y *adj.* **1** huérfano: *an orphan boy = un niño huérfano.* **2** (fig.) (persona) privada de algo. || **3 to be orphaned,** quedar huérfano.

orphanage | 'ɔːfənɪdʒ | *s.c.* **1** orfanato, orfelinato. || *s.i.* **2** orfandad. **3** (fig.) desamparo.

orphaned | 'ɔːfnd | *adj.* huérfano.

orthodox | 'ɔːθədɒks | *adj.* **1** ortodoxo, convencional: *orthodox medicine = medicina convencional.* **2** ortodoxo, tradicional: *Orthodox Jews = judíos ortodoxos.* || **3** REL. **– Church,** iglesia ortodoxa.

orthodoxy | 'ɔːθədɒksɪ | *s.c.* e *i.* (form.) ortodoxia.

orthography | ɔː'θɒgrəfɪ | *s.i.* (form.) GRAM. ortografía.

orthopaedic | ˌɔːθəʊ'piːdɪk | (EE.UU. **orthopedic**) *adj.* MED. ortopédico.

oscillate | 'ɒsɪleɪt | (form.) *v.i.* **1** oscilar. **2 [to – (between)]:** vacilar, estar indeciso, titubear. **3** oscilar, variar, fluctuar.

oscillation | ˌɒsɪ'leɪʃn | *s.c.* **1** fluctuación, variación, cambio.

osier | 'əʊzɪər | *s.c.* e *i.* BOT. mimbre.

osmosis | ɒz'məʊsɪs | *s.i.* **1** BIOL. ósmosis. **2** (fig.) ósmosis (influencia recíproca).

ossification | ˌɒsɪfɪ'keɪʃn | *s.i.* **1** (fig.) estancamiento (falta de evolución). **2** osificación.

ossified | 'ɒsɪfaɪd | *adj.* **1** osificado. **2** (fig.) estancado, fosilizado.

ossify | 'ɒsɪfaɪ | (form.) *v.t.* e *i.* **1** osificar(se). **2** (fig.) estancar(se), fosilizar(se), (no evolucionar).

ossuary | 'ɒsjʊərɪ | *s.c.* osario.

ostensible | ɒ'stensəbl | *adj.* (form.) aparente: *the ostensible reason = la causa aparente.*

ostensibly | ɒ'stensəblɪ | *adv.* al parecer, aparentemente.

ostentation | ˌɒsten'teɪʃn | *s.i.* (form.) ostentación, alarde.

ostentatious | ˌɒsten'teɪʃəs | *adj.* **1** ostentoso, lujoso: *an ostentatious car = un coche ostentoso.* **2** ostentoso, extravagante (una persona). **3** claro, manifiesto; aparatoso (acción, comportamiento).

ostentatiously | ˌɒsten'teɪʃəslɪ | *adv.* **1** con ostentación, extravagantemente: *ostentatiously dressed = vestido extravagantemente.* **2** manifiestamente; aparatosamente.

osteopath | 'ɒstɪəpæθ | *s.c.* MED. osteópata.

ostracism | 'ɒstrəsɪzəm | *s.i.* (form.) ostracismo.

ostracize | 'ɒstrəsaɪz | (también **ostracise**) *v.t.* (form.) condenar al ostracismo, tratar con frialdad.

ostrich | 'ɒstrɪtʃ | *s.c.* **1** ZOOL. avestruz. **2** (fig.) persona que se niega a aceptar los hechos.

other | 'ʌðər | *adj.* **1** otro: *do you know the other girl? = ¿conoces a la otra chica?* **2** demás: *the other people = la demás gente.* || *pron.* **3** otro: *this box and the other = esta caja y la otra.* || *s.pl.* **4** otros, demás: *I don't care what the others think = no me importa lo que piensen los demás.* || **5 to be – than,** ser distinto a: *she is other than she seems = ella es distinta de lo que parece.* **6 every –,** cada dos: *every other day = cada dos días.* **7 none/no – than,** nada menos que: *it was none other than his father = era nada menos que su padre.* **8 no/nothing – than,** nada más que, otra cosa que (lo único posible). **9 one after the –,** uno tras otro. **10 one or –,** uno de, cualquiera de: *one or other of us = cualquiera de nosotros.* **11 on the –,** por otra parte, por otro lado (cuando la oración va introducida por "on the one hand"): *on the one hand I would like to go, on the other I know it is dangerous = por una parte me gustaría ir, por otra sé que es peligroso.* **12 on the – hand,** por otra parte. **13 – than,** excepto, a parte de: *there wasn't anyone there other than yourself = no había nadie allí excepto tú.* **14 some or –/something or –/somehow or –, etc.,** (principalmente en inglés hablado) uno u otro; de uno u otro (modo); por una u otra (razón), etc. **15 the – day/evening/etc.,** el otro día, la otra tarde, etc.

otherness | 'ʌðənɪs | *s.i.* calidad de lo que es extraño, nuevo o diferente de lo que se conoce: *the otherness of India = lo exótico de la India.*

otherwise | 'ʌðəwaɪz | *adv.* **1** de otro modo: *I would have acted otherwise = yo hubiera actuado de otro modo.* **2** por lo demás: *she is a little absentminded, but otherwise a good student = es un poco distraída, pero por lo demás buena estudiante.* **3** de lo contrario, o si no: *hurry up, otherwise you will miss the bus = apresúrate o de lo contrario perderás el autobús.* || *adj.* **4** otro; diferente, distinto: *it couldn't be otherwise = no podía ser diferente.* || **5 and/or –,** o no; o de otro tipo; o lo contrario (de lo que se ha dicho). **6 – called,** alias.

other-worldly | ˌʌðə'wɜːldlɪ | *adj.* alejado de lo mundano, espiritual.

otter | 'ɒtər | *s.c.* **1** ZOOL. nutria. **2** piel de nutria.

ouch | autʃ | *interj.* ¡ay! (para expresar dolor).

ought | ɔːt | *v.mod.* **1** deber, tener que: *I think you ought to sit down = creo que deberías sentarte.* **2** deber, tener que (implica una obligación moral): *you ought to help them = deberías ayudarlos, debes ayudarlos.* **3** deber (implica una obligación pasada): *you ought to have done it = deberías haberlo hecho.* **4** deber (expresa una posibilidad): *they ought to be there = deben estar allí, debieran estar allí.*

oughtn't | 'ɔːtnt | *v.mod.* (fam.) contracción de **ought not,** (utilizada habitualmente en inglés hablado).

ounce | auns | *s.c.* **1** onza (medida de peso). **2** ZOOL. onza. || *s.sing.* **3** (fig. y fam.) pizca: *an ounce of common sense = una pizca de sentido común.*

our | 'aʊər | *adj.pos.* nuestro: *our parents = nuestros padres.*

ours | 'aʊəz | *pron.pos.* (el) nuestro: *it is better than ours = es mejor que el nuestro.*

ourselves | ˌaʊə'selvz | *pron.* **1** nosotros mismos (enfatiza el sujeto): *we ourselves will do it = nosotros mismos lo haremos.* **2** nos, a nosotros (reflexivo): *we shall harm ourselves = nos haremos daño.* **3** por nosotros mismos, solos, sin ayuda: *we want to do it ourselves = queremos hacerlo solos.* **4** nosotros (normalmente después de *prep.*; tiene sentido enfático): *for ourselves = para nosotros.*

oust | aust | (form.) *v.t.* **[to – + *o.* + (from)]** **1** echar, despedir (de un trabajo): *they are going to oust her from her job = la van a echar del trabajo.* **2** echar (de un sitio), desalojar. **3** expulsar. **4** destituir.

out | aut | *adv.* **1** fuera: *he always eats out = siempre come fuera.* **2** afuera: *she was out in the terrace = estaba afuera en la terraza.*

OBS. **Out** posee varios usos adverbiales: **3** idea de estar de viaje: *he is out in America.* **4 [– (of)]** idea de salir: *he went out of the house = salió de la casa.* **5** idea de estar fuera (de casa o del trabajo): *Mrs. Jones is out.* **6** idea de sacar: *he brought some coins out of his pocket = se sacó unas monedas del bolsillo.* **7** idea de echar o mantener alejado: *keep him out = mantenlo alejado.* **8** idea de haberse descubierto (algo secreto): *the secret is out = se ha revelado el secreto.* **9** idea de que un libro, etc., salió a la venta o ha sido publicado: *when will your new book come out? = ¿cuándo saldrá su próximo libro?* **10** idea de apagar(se): *your cigarette is out = tu cigarrillo está apagado.* **11** idea de acabarse: *the coffee is out = se ha acabado el café.* **12** idea de desaparecer, extinguirse: *many species are in danger of dying out = muchas especies están en peligro de extinción.* **13** idea de estar dislocado: *he put his arm out = se dislocó el brazo.* **14** idea de no estar de moda: *goatees are out = las perillas están pasadas de moda.* **15** idea de agotarse: *the edition sold out = la edición se agotó.* **16** idea de estar dormido o inconsciente: *I was out for five minutes = estuve inconsciente durante cinco minutos.* **17** idea de estar descartado (un plan, una idea, una posibilidad): *that idea is out = esta idea queda descartada.* **18** ideas de distribuir: *they gave out food to the children = repartieron comida entre los niños.* **19** idea de despedir (un olor, una luz, etc.). **20** idea de llegar hasta el final: *he heard me out = me escuchó hasta el final.* **21** (arc.) idea de ser presentado en sociedad (una joven). || *adj.* **22** en huelga: *the miners are out = los mineros están en huelga.* **23** equivocado: *you were not out in your calculations = no te equivocabas en tus cálculos.* **24** abierta, en flor (una planta, una flor): *the roses are out = las rosas están abiertas.*

OBS. Como adjetivo **out** posee otros significados: **25** idea de que se termina un período de tiempo determinado: *before the week is out = antes de que termine la semana.* **26 [– (for)]** idea de querer, buscar o intentar obtener algo: *they are out for money = intentan conseguir dinero.* **27 [– (to)]** idea de tener la intención de hacer algo: *they are out to win = están decididos a vencer.* || *prep.* **[– of]** **28** fuera de: *out of the building = fuera del edificio.* **29** por, movido por (una razón, un sentimiento, etc.): *I asked out of curiosity = pregunté por curiosidad.* *30* de: *he made it out of wood = lo hizo de madera.* **31** de cada: *two children out of ten = dos de cada diez niños.* **32** entre: *she must choose out of these five options = debe escoger entre estas cinco opciones.* **33** sin: *out of breath = sin aliento.* **34** sacado de (un libro, una película): *out of a Fellini film = sacado de una película de Fellini.* **35** de (indicando origen): *a scene of a play = una escena de una obra.*

OBS. **Out** tiene además otros usos preposicionales: **36** idea de quedarse sin: *I'm out of money = me he quedado sin dinero.* **37** idea de conseguir algún beneficio de algo: *did you get any profit out of it? = ¿sacaste algún provecho de ello?* **38** idea de que se ha perdido un hábito: *he has got out the habit of smoking = ha perdido el hábito de fumar.* **39** idea de estar a cierta distancia de un sitio: *it is five miles out of London = está a cinco millas de Londres.* **40** idea de sacarle algo a alguien: *I got some money out of him = le saqué algún dinero.* || **41 – and about,** haciendo vida normal (después de una enfermedad). **42 – loud,** en voz alta. **43 – tray,** bandeja para cartas o documentos (de una oficina). **44 – with it,** suéltalo, desembucha. **45 the ins and outs,** los pormenores, los detalles.

OBS. La partícula **out** acompaña a muchos verbos modificándoles el significado. Consultar los distintos verbos para conocer su correspondiente traducción.

out-and-out | autnd'aut | *adj.* **1** empedernido: *he's an out-and-out romantic = es un romántico empedernido.* **2** perfecto, completo: *an out-and-out idiot = un perfecto idiota.* **3** rotundo, categórico: *an out-and-out refusal = una negativa rotunda.* **4** acérrimo: *an out-and-out supporter = un acérrimo partidario.*

outback | 'autbæk | *s.sing.* el interior (se dice de las remotas zonas interiores y casi despobladas de Australia).

outbid | ˌaut'bɪd | *v.t.* [*pret.* y *p.p.* **outbid** u **outbidded**] pujar más alto que, mejorar la oferta de.

outboard | 'autbɔːd | MAR. *adj.* **1** cercano al borde de una embarcación. || **2 – motor,** motor fuera borda.

outbreak | 'autbreɪk | *s.c.* **1** comienzo (de algo desagradable). **2** estallido (de una guerra). **3** aparición, brote (de una epidemia). **4** erupción (de un volcán). **5** estallido (de violencia, de rabia); arrebato (de cólera, de ira). **6** motín, tumulto, insurrección.

outbuilding | 'autˌbɪldɪŋ | *s.c.* construcción anexa a otra mayor del mismo propietario.

outburst | 'autbəːst | *s.c.* **1** explosión (de algo repentino, normalmente de un sentimiento). **2** arranque, arrebato (de ira, de cólera, de pasión, etc.). **3** ataque (de risa).

outcast | 'autkɑːst | *s.c.* y *adj.* proscrito; paria.

outclass | ˌaut'klɑːs | *v.t.* **1** superar con mucho a, aventajar a, eclipsar a: *she outclassed all her rivals = aventajaba a todas sus rivales.*

outcome | 'autkʌm | *s.c.* **1** resultado: *the outcome of the elections = el resultado de las elecciones.* **2** consecuencias: *the outcome of the event = las consecuencias del suceso.*

outcrop | 'autkrɒp | *s.c.* **1** GEOL. afloramiento. || *v.i.* **2** GEOL. aflorar. **3** (fig.) aparecer, surgir, manifestarse.

outcry | 'autkraɪ | *s.c.* **1** protesta pública. **2** tumulto, alboroto. **3** clamor, griterío.

outdated | 'autˌdeɪtɪd | *adj.* **1** anticuado, obsoleto; pasado de moda: *outdated ideas = ideas anticuadas.*

outdid | ˌaut'dɪd | *pret.* de **outdo.**

outdistance | ˌaut'dɪstəns | *v.t.* **1** dejar atrás (en una carrera). **2** (fig.) superar, dejar atrás (en una actividad).

outdo | ˌaut'duː | *v.t.* [*pret.* **outdid**; *p.p.* **outdone**] **1** superar, aventajar: *nobody outdoes him in his job = nadie le supera en su trabajo.*

outdoor | 'autdɔːr | *adj.* **1** al aire libre: *outdoor sports = deportes al aire libre.* **2** de calle (ropa). **3** persona a la que le gusta estar al aire libre. || **4 outdoors, a)** al aire libre: *it's too cold to sleep outdoors = hace demasiado frío para dormir al aire libre;* **b)** afuera: *it's hot outdoors = hace calor afuera.*

outer | 'autər | *adj.* **1** externo, exterior: *the outer part = la parte externa.* || **2 – space,** ASTR. espacio exterior.

outermost | 'autəməust | *adj.* **1** más alejado: *the outermost districts = los barrios más alejados.* **2** más exterior.

outfit | 'autfɪt | *s.c.* **1** ropa (equipo, conjunto de ropas): *winter outfit = ropa de invierno.* **2** (fam.) equipo (grupo de personas que hacen un mismo trabajo). **3** equipo, herramientas, útiles de trabajo: *a plumber's outfit = las herramientas de un fontanero.* **5** equipo, pertrechos: *a camping outfit = pertrechos de camping.* **6** uniforme: *a schoolboy's outfit = el uniforme de un colegial.* || *v.t.* **7** equipar.

outfitter | 'autfɪtər | *s.c.* (p.u.) **1** vendedor de ropa, especialmente masculina. **2** tienda de ropa masculina.

outflank | ˌaut'flæŋk | *v.t.* **1** MIL. rebasar el flanco enemigo. **2** (fig.) colocarse en posición ventajosa.

outflow | 'autfləu | *s.c.* **1** salida de agua u otro líquido; flujo. **2** desagüe. **3** (fig.) flujo: *an outflow of dirty words = un flujo de palabras soeces.*

outfox | 'autˌfɒks | *v.t.* (fam.) burlar; ser más listo que.

outgoing | ˌaut'gəuɪŋ | *adj.* **1** saliente, que se va (que deja un lugar, puesto o empleo): *the outgoing government = el gobierno saliente; the outgoing ship = el barco que se va.* **2** extrovertido (persona, carácter). **3** descendiente (marea). || **4 outgoings,** gastos: *more outgoings*

than incomings = más gastos que ingresos.
outgrow | 'aʊtgrəʊ | *v.t.* [*pret.* **outgrew**; *p.p.* **outgrown**] **1** crecer más que: *he has outgrown his friends = ha crecido más que sus amigos.* **2** dejar atrás, perder (hábitos, opiniones, gustos, etc.) al hacerse mayor: *he will outgrow his impudence = perderá su descaro con la edad.* **3** crecer o engordar demasiado para ponerse una prenda: *he has outgrown his shirts = ya no le valen las camisas.*
outgrowth | 'aʊtgrəʊθ | *s.sing.* resultado, producto, consecuencia natural.
outhouse | 'aʊthaʊs | *s.c.* **1** edificio pequeño anexo a otro mayor. **2** (EE.UU.) servicio, retrete que está fuera de la casa.
outing | 'aʊtɪŋ | *s.c.* **1** excursión, viaje de placer: *an outing to the seaside = una excursión a la costa.* **2** vuelta, caminata, paseo.
outlandish | aʊt'lændɪʃ | *adj.* **1** estrafalario: *outlandish dress = vestimenta estrafalaria.* **2** extraño, raro. **3** extravagante (comportamiento). **4** grosero, tosco.
outlast | ˌaʊt'lɑːst | *v.t.* sobrevivir a (una persona); durar más que.
outlaw | 'aʊtlɔː | *v.t.* **1** declarar ilegal, prohibir: *the use of those pills was outlawed = se prohibió el uso de esas píldoras.* **2** declarar fuera de la ley, proscribir (a alguien). || *s.c.* **3** (p.u.) proscrito; forajido; bandido.
outlay | 'aʊtleɪ | *s.c.* gasto, inversión.
outlet | 'aʊtlet | *s.c.* **1 [– + (for)]** (fig.) vía de escape (de sentimientos, emociones, energía, etc.). **2** COM. salida, mercado (para un producto). **3** COM. punto de venta. **4** desagüe. **5** conducto (por donde sale gas, aire, etc.).
outline | 'aʊtlaɪn | *v.t.* **1** esbozar, trazar las líneas generales (un plan, un proyecto, etc.). **2** perfilar: *the light outlined her silhouete = la luz perfilaba su silueta.* **3** resumir. || *s.sing.* **4** visión general: *an outline of American Literature = una visión general de la literatura americana.* **5** silueta, contorno, perfil: *you could see the outline of the mountains against the sky = se podía ver el contorno de las montañas contra el cielo.* **6** esquema (de un proyecto, de un discurso). **7** bosquejo (de una situación). **8** ART. boceto, esbozo (dibujo).
outlive | ˌaʊt'lɪv | *v.t.* **1** sobrevivir a, vivir más que: *she outlived her husband = vivió más que su marido.* **2** durar más que. || **3 to – one's usefulness,** perder su razón de ser.
outlook | 'aʊtlʊk | *s.c.* **1** actitud, punto de vista: *pessimistic outlook = actitud pesimista.* **2** vista, panorama: *a lovely outlook from the hill = una agradable vista desde la colina.* **3** mirador, atalaya. || *s.sing.* **4** expectativas, perspectivas: *good economic outlook = buenas perspectivas económicas.* **5** predicción (meteorológica): *the outlook for the next three days = la predicción meteorológica para los próximos tres días.*
outlying | 'aʊtˌlaɪɪŋ | *adj.* **1** distante, remoto; aislado: *outlying villages = pueblos aislados.* **2** alejado del centro (de una ciudad): *New York's outlying areas = zonas alejadas del centro de Nueva York.*
outmanoeuvre | ˌaʊtmə'nuːvər | (EE.UU. **outmaneuver**) *v.t.* ganar a, superar a (utilizando una estrategia): *I haven't found the way to outmanoeuvre him = no he encontrado la manera de ganarle.*
outmoded | ˌaʊt'məʊdɪd | *adj.* pasado de moda, anticuado.
outnumber | ˌaʊt'nʌmbər | *v.t.* exceder en número a, ser más numeroso que: *Catholics outnumber Protestants = los católicos son más numerosos que los protestantes.*
out-of-date | ˌaʊtəv'deɪt | (también **out of date** cuando no antecede a un *s.*) *adj.* **1** pasado de moda, anticuado. **2** desfasado: *an out-of-date dictionary = un diccionario desfasado.*
out-of-doors | ˌaʊtəv'dɔːz | (también **out of doors**) *adv.* **1** al aire libre; afuera. || *s.pl.* **2** el exterior.
out-of-the-way | ˌaʊtəvðə'weɪ | *adj.* **1** aislado, apartado, remoto (lejos de una ciudad): *an out-of-the-way hamlet = una aldea remota.* **2** (fig.) no muy conocido, poco corriente.
out-of-work | ˌəʊtəv'wəːk | (también **out of work** cuando no antecede a un *s.*) *adj.* sin trabajo, en paro: *an out-of-work doctor = un médico en paro.*
out-patient | 'aʊtˌpeɪʃnt | (también **outpatient**) *s.c.* MED. paciente de consulta externa, paciente no hospitalizado.
outpost | 'aʊtpəʊst | *s.c.* **1** MIL. avanzada (partida de soldados). **2** puesto fronterizo.
outpouring | 'aʊtˌpɔːrɪŋ | *s.c.* **1 [– (of)]** torrente, flujo, chorro: *an outpouring of insults = un torrente de injurias.* || **2 outpourings,** efusión, manifestación de un sentimiento; desahogo.
output | 'aʊtpʊt | *s.i.* **1** producción: *the output of a factory = la producción de una fábrica; literary output = producción literaria.* || *s.c.* e *i.* **2** INF. salida de información. **3** ELECTR. producción total de energía; circuito de salida de energía. || *v.t.* **4** INF. producir información (una computadora).
outrage | 'aʊtreɪdʒ | *v.t.* **1** escandalizar. **2** ultrajar, ofender. **3** violar. **4** ir en contra de (la ley, la moralidad, etc.). || *s.c.* **5** ataque, atentado: *an outrage against mankind = un atentado contra la humanidad.* **6** atropello, agravio. **7** atrocidad. || *s.i.* **8** indignación, enojo.
outraged | 'aʊtreɪdʒd | *adj.* furioso, indignado.
outrageous | aʊt'reɪdʒəs | *adj.* **1** chocante, extravagante. **2** escandaloso, inmoral (que ofende la opinión pública): *an outrageous behaviour = una conducta inmoral.* **3** atroz, monstruoso. **4** ofensivo, ultrajante, desaforado. **5** escandaloso, exorbitante: *an outrageous price = un precio exorbitante.*
outrageously | aʊt'reɪdʒəslɪ | *adv.* de forma escandalosa.
outran | ˌaʊt'ræn | *pret.* de **outrun.**
outré | 'uːtreɪ | *adj.* (form.) estrafalario, extravagante.
outrider | 'aʊtˌraɪdər | *s.c.* persona que escolta a un vehículo, a caballo o en moto.
outright | 'aʊtraɪt | *adj.* **1** claro, inequívoco: *an outright reply = una respuesta inequívoca.* **2** franco, directo: *outright hostility = franca hostilidad.* **3** absoluto, total: *outright certainty = certeza absoluta.* || *adv.* **4** abiertamente, francamente, sin reserva: *I'm going to tell you outright what I think of you = te voy a decir francamente lo que pienso de ti.* **5** de una vez, al contado: *he bought the car outright = compró el coche al contado.* **6** completamente, en su totalidad. || **7 to be killed –,** morir en el acto.
outrun | ˌaʊt'rʌn | *v.t.* [*pret.* **outran**; *p.p.* **outrun**] **1** correr más que, adelantar: *he outran me and won the prize = él me adelantó y se llevó el premio.* **2** (fig.) sobrepasar, ir más allá de: *it outruns any hopes = va más allá de cualquier expectativa.*
outsell | ˌaʊt'sel | *v.t* [*pret.* y *p.p.* **outsold**] **1** venderse más, más caro o más de prisa que (otro producto): *small cars are outselling big ones = los coches pequeños se están vendiendo más que los grandes.*
outset | 'aʊtset | *s.sing.* **1** principio, comienzo. || **2 at the –,** al principio. **3 from the –,** desde el principio.
outshine | ˌaʊt'ʃaɪn | *v.t.* [*pret.* y *p.p.* **outshone**] **1** brillar más que. **2** (fig.) superar, ser mejor que.
outside | ˌaʊt'saɪd | *s.c.* **1** parte exterior, exterior: *the outside of the cathedral = el exterior de la catedral.* **2** aspecto exterior, apariencia externa: *you shouldn't give so much importance to the outside = no deberías conceder tanta importancia a la apariencia externa.* || *adj.* **3** exterior (que da para afuera): *outside room = habitación exterior.* **4** exterior (ajeno a lo que se está acostumbrado): *the outside world = el mundo exterior.* **5** externo (que viene de fuera): *outside help = ayuda externa.* || *adv.* **6** fuera, afuera: *wait for me outside = espérame fuera.* **7** en la calle; al aire libre. || *prep.* **8** fuera de: *outside the house = fuera de la casa.* **9** al otro lado de (una puerta, una pared, etc.). **10** más allá de: *it is outside morality = está más allá de la moralidad.* **11** aparte de, excepto: *I have no entertainement outside my books = no tengo ninguna distracción excepto mis libros.* || **12 at the –,** a lo sumo, como mucho: *there were twenty people at the outside = había como mucho veinte personas.* **13 – broadcast,** RAD. y TV. emisión fuera del estudio, en exteriores.

outsider | ˌaut'saɪdər | *s.c.* **1** extraño, persona de fuera (que no pertenece al grupo). **2** intruso. **3** DEP. caballo que no está entre los favoritos en una carrera.
outsize | 'autsaɪz | *adj.* **1** más grande de lo normal; muy grande. **2** talla muy grande (en prendas de vestir).
outsized | 'autsaɪzd | *adj.* más grande de lo normal: *an outsized encyclopedia = una enciclopedia más grande de lo normal.*
outskirts | 'autskəːts | *s.pl.* afueras, alrededores, cercanías: *the outskirts of London = las afueras de Londres.*
outsmart | ˌaut'smɑːt | *v.t.* ser más astuto que, burlar: *they outsmarted the police = burlaron a la policía.*
outspoken | ˌaut'spəukən | *adj.* franco, sincero: *an outspoken remark = una observación sincera.*
outspokenness | ˌaut'spəukənnɪs | *s.i.* franqueza, sinceridad.
outspread | ˌaut'spred | *adj.* desplegado: *an outspread newspaper = un periódico desplegado.*
outstanding | ˌaut'stændɪŋ | *adj.* **1** notable, excepcional, sobresaliente: *an outstanding lawyer = un abogado notable; an outstanding work = un trabajo excepcional.* **2** notable, digno de tener en cuenta: *an outstanding success = un éxito notable.* **3** sin cobrar (dinero, deudas, etc.). **4** pendiente (un trabajo, un asunto, un problema).
outstandingly | ˌaut'stændɪŋlɪ | *adv.* excepcionalmente, notablemente.
outstay | ˌaut'steɪ | *v.t.* **1** quedarse más tiempo que (otros). || **2 to – one's welcome,** quedarse demasiado tiempo (más de lo conveniente).
outstretched | ˌaut'stretʃt | *adj.* estirado, extendido: *outstretched hands = manos extendidas.*
outstrip | ˌaut'strɪp | *v.t.* **1** superar (en habilidad, en importancia, etc.). **2** dejar atrás, sobrepasar (en una carrera).
outvote | ˌaut'vəut | *v.t.* **1** ganar en una votación. || **2 to be outvoted,** ser derrotado en una votación.
outward | ˌautwəd | *adj.* **1** de ida: *the outward voyage = el viaje de ida.* **2** externo: *outward signs = signos externos.* || *adv.* **3** hacia fuera: *fold it outwards = dóblalo hacia fuera.* || **4 to be – bound for/from,** salir hacia/de (un barco, un viajero): *they are outward bound for Africa = salen hacia África.*
outwardly | 'autwədlɪ | *adv.* **1** aparentemente: *he is outwardly calm = aparentemente está tranquilo.* **2** por fuera, exteriormente.
outweigh | ˌaut'weɪ | *v.t.* (form.) superar, tener más importancia que: *the advantages outweigh the disadvantages = las ventajas superan a las desventajas.*
outwit | ˌaut'wɪt | *v.t.* burlar con astucia, ser más astuto que: *you can't outwit this detective = no puedes burlar a este detective.*
outworn | 'autwɔːn | *adj.* **1** anticuado, antiguo (prácticas, creencias, costumbres, etc.). **2** demasiado usado, trillado: *outworn quotations = citas demasiado trilladas.*
oval | 'əuvl | *s.c.* **1** óvalo. || *adj.* **2** ovalado, oval: *an oval face = una cara ovalada.*
ovary | 'əuvərɪ | *s.c.* BIOL. ovario.
ovation | əu'veɪʃn | *s.c.* **1** (form.) ovación. || **2 a standing –,** una ovación para la cual el público se ha puesto de pie.
oven | 'ʌvn | *s.c.* horno.
ovenproof | 'ʌvnpruːf | *adj.* refractario (fuente de horno).
over | 'əuvər | *prep.* **1** sobre, por encima de: *a plane is flying over the ocean = un avión vuela sobre el océano.* **2** sobre: *her fringe hung over her eyes = le caía el flequillo sobre los ojos.* **3** por encima de: *throw it over the gate = lánzalo por encima de la verja.* **4** sobre, encima de: *he always wears a waistcoat over his shirt = siempre lleva un chaleco encima de la camisa.* **5** más de: *she is over thirty = ella tiene más de treinta años.* **6** (fig.) por encima de: *there is nobody over him in the firm = no hay nadie por encima de él en la empresa.* **7** al otro lado de: *over the road = al otro lado de la carretera.* **8** (fig.) sobre: *he has no control over his son = no tiene control sobre su hijo.* **9** junto a: *over the fire = junto al fuego.* **10** por (radio, teléfono, televisión, etc.): *did you hear it over the radio? = ¿lo oíste por la radio?* **11** por (un precipicio, un acantilado, etc.). **12** por, a causa de: *they quarreled over a woman = discutían por una mujer.* **13** hasta: *I'm sorry, I can't stay over your birthday = lo siento, pero no puedo quedarme hasta tu cumpleaños.* **14** a lo largo de: *it has evolved over many centuries = ha evolucionado a lo largo de muchos siglos.* **15** durante: *I met him over Christmas = lo conocí durante las navidades.*
OBS. **Over** posee además otros usos preposicionales: **16** idea de hacer algo a la vez que se está haciendo otra cosa: *let's talk over a cup of tea = hablemos mientras tomamos una taza de té.* **17** idea de recobrarse, recuperarse (de una enfermedad, de una mala experiencia): *I'll get over it = se me pasará, me recuperaré.* **18** idea de cruzar (una calle, una carretera): *help him over the road = ayúdale a cruzar la carretera.* **19** para indicar división en matemáticas: *fifty hundred and three over twenty one = quinientos tres dividido por veintiuno.* || *adv.* **20** hasta el final: *I read it over = lo leí hasta el final.* **21** otra vez, de nuevo: *count them over = cuéntalos de nuevo.* **22** más: *two metres and a bit over = dos metros y algo más.*
OBS. **Over** posee varios usos adverbiales: **23** indica movimiento hacia abajo, a menudo violento: *he fell over on the ground = se cayó al suelo.* **24** idea de que algo pasa por encima: *there is a plane going over = hay un avión pasando por encima.* **25** se utiliza para enfatizar el hecho de estar mirando hacia una dirección, hacia algo o alguien: *she looked over at him with horror = lo miró con horror.* **26** idea de movimiento (de un lugar a otro): *she is going over to the other room = se va a la otra habitación.* **27** idea de cruzar (unos límites, una calle, un río, etc.). **28** idea de moverse o deslizarse sobre una superficie: *the sledge slid over the ice = el trineo se deslizaba por el hielo.* **29** idea de cambiar de grupo, partido, opinión, etc.: *they passed over to the opposition = se pasaron a la oposición.* **30** idea de pasar algo a otra persona: *hand it over to me = entrégamelo.* **31** idea de sobrar: *I have ten pounds over = me sobran diez libras.* **32** idea de darse la vuelta (estando tumbado): *he turned over in bed = se dio la vuelta en la cama.* **33** idea de dar la vuelta (a un objeto): *turn the page over = vuelve la página.* **34** idea de desaparecer, disiparse: *the cause of the dispute blew over = desapareció el motivo de la disputa.* **35** idea de hablar, discutir o pensar en algo con detenimiento: *they talked over what they had seen = hablaron detenidamente sobre lo que habían visto.* **36** se utiliza para referirse a toda la extensión de un determinado sitio: *she is famous all the world over = es famosa por todo el mundo.* **37** idea de salirse o rebosar (un líquido al hervir): *the milk boiled over = se salió la leche.* || **38 all –, a)** por todo: *all over the city = por toda la ciudad;* **b)** (fam.) demasiado atento con: *he is all over her = es demasiado atento con ella;* **c)** del todo, cien por cien: *he is English all over = es inglés cien por cien.* **39 – again/all – again,** de nuevo, una vez más (algo desagradable, que se repite): *I couldn't do it all over again = no podría hacerlo de nuevo.* **40 to be –/to be all –,** haberse terminado: *the work is over = se terminó el trabajo; it is all over = se ha acabado.* **41 – and above,** además de. **42 – and out,** RAD. cambio y corto. **43 – and – (again),** repetidas veces, muchas veces: *he saw the film over and over again = vio la película repetidas veces.* **44 – to,** le toca el turno a: *over to you = le toca el turno a usted.* **45 twice –/three times –, etc.,** dos veces seguidas, tres veces seguidas, etc. **46 that's him/her/you all –,** etc., (fam.) eso es muy propio de él, de ella, de ti, etc.
OBS. La partícula **over** acompaña a muchos verbos modificando su sentido, por lo que es necesario consultar el verbo para conocer su correspondiente traducción.
overact | ˌəuvər'ækt | *v.t.* e *i.* exagerar (emociones, gestos, etc., principalmente representando un papel).
overall | 'əuvərɔːl | *adj.* **1** total: *the overall length = la largura total.* **2** global, general: *the overall impression = la impresión general.* || *adv.* **3** en general,

en términos generales. **4** en todas partes. || *s.c.* **5** bata, guardapolvo, baby. **6** **overalls,** mono de trabajo.

overarm | 'əʊvərɑːm | *adj.* y *adv.* DEP. de brazo, por encima del brazo.

overawe | ˌəʊvər'ɔː | *v.t.* intimidar; impresionar: *all of us are overawed by his knowledge = todos estamos impresionados por sus conocimientos.*

overbalance | ˌəʊvə'bæləns | *v.i.* **1** perder el equilibrio: *he overbalanced and fell from the horse = perdió el equilibrio y se cayó del caballo.* || *v.t.* **2** hacer perder el equilibrio. **3** hacer volcar (una embarcación). **4** (lit.) preponderar.

overbearing | ˌəʊvə'beərɪŋ | *adj.* dominante, autoritario: *she has an overbearing father = tiene un padre autoritario.*

overboard | 'əʊvəbɔːd | *adv.* **1** por la borda. || **2 to go –,** (fam.) pasarse de la raya. **3 to go – for,** (fam.) estar loco por (alguien). **4** MAR. **man –!,** ¡hombre al agua! **5 to throw somebody –,** (fam.) librarse de (alguien). **6 to throw something –,** (fam.) descartar, abandonar (un proyecto, un plan, una idea).

overburdened | ˌəʊvə'bɜːdnd | *adj.* **[– (with)]** sobrecargado (de trabajo, de problemas).

overcame | ˌəʊvə'keɪm | *pret.* de **overcome.**

overcast | 'əʊvəkɑːst | *adj.* **1** nublado, encapotado (el cielo, el tiempo). **2** cubierto (el cielo). **3** (fig.) triste, sombrío. || *v.t.* [*pret.* y *p.p.* **overcast**] **4** nublar, encapotar. **5** (fig.) entristecer. **6** sobrehilar. || *v.i.* **7** nublarse.

overcharge | ˌəʊvə'tʃɑːdʒ | *v.t.* e *i.* cobrar de más, cobrar demasiado: *she was overcharged for the fish = le cobraron demasiado por el pescado.*

overcoat | 'əʊvəkəʊt | *s.c.* abrigo.

overcome | ˌəʊvə'kʌm | *v.t.* [*pret.* **overcame**; *p.p.* **overcome**] **1** superar (un problema, una dificultad). **2** vencer: *to overcome the enemy = vencer al enemigo.* **3** resistir (a la tentación). **4** salvar (un obstáculo). || **5 to be – (by/with),** estar/sentirse agobiado (generalmente por un sentimiento).

overcrowded | ˌəʊvə'kraʊdɪd | *adj.* **1** superpoblado (una ciudad, un país). **2** lleno, abarrotado (de gente, de cosas): *an overcrowded bus = un autobús abarrotado de gente.*

overcrowding | ˌəʊvə'kraʊdɪŋ | *s.i.* superpoblación.

overdo | ˌəʊvə'duː | *v.t.* [*pret.* **overdid**; *p.p.* **overdone**] **1** excederse en: *you have overdone the punishment = te has excedido en el castigo.* **2 [– it]** exagerar: *don't overdo it = no exageres.*

overdone | ˌəʊvə'dʌn | *adj.* demasiado hecho, demasiado cocido (comidas).

overdose | 'əʊvədəʊs | *s.c.* dosis excesiva, sobredosis: *an overdose of heroin = una sobredosis de heroína.*

overdraft | 'əʊvədrɑːft | *s.c.* descubierto (en una cuenta bancaria).

overdrawn | ˌəʊvə'drɔːn | *adj.* **1** en descubierto, en números rojos: *an overdrawn account = una cuenta en descubierto.*

overdressed | ˌəʊvə'drest | *adj.* demasiado vestido (con mucha ropa); demasiado bien vestido (más de lo que requiere la ocasión).

overdue | ˌəʊvə'djuː | *adj.* **1** atrasado, retrasado: *the bus is overdue = el autobús lleva retraso.* **2** atrasado (un pago, una renta, etc.). **3** requerido (una reforma, un cambio, etc.).

overeat | ˌəʊvər'iːt | *v.i.* [*pret.* **overate**; *p.p.* **overeaten**] comer demasiado.

overeating | ˌəʊvər'iːtɪŋ | *s.i.* excesiva comida.

overemphasize | ˌəʊvər'emfəsaɪz | (también **overemphasise**) *v.t.* dar demasiada importancia.

overestimate | ˌəʊvər'estɪmeɪt | *v.t.* sobreestimar.

overflow | 'əʊvəfləʊ | *v.t.* e *i.* **1** rebosar (un líquido de un recipiente). **2** desbordarse (un río, un lago, etc.). **3** (fig.) inundar, llenar por completo: *the crowd overflowed the stadium = la multitud llenaba por completo el estadio.* || *v.i.* **4** **[– (with)]** rebosar, desbordarse (por estar muy lleno). || *s.c.* **5** salida (de un líquido); desagüe. **6** excelente. || **7 to be overflowing with,** estar rebosante de: *they were overflowing with happiness = estaban rebosantes de felicidad.* **8 to overflowing,** hasta los topes: *full to overflowing = lleno hasta los topes.*

overgrown | ˌəʊvə'grəʊn | *adj.* **1** cubierto de plantas, hierbas, etc. (por falta de cuidado): *an overgrown garden = un jardín cubierto de hierbas.* **2** que ha crecido demasiado deprisa (una persona).

overhang | 'əʊvəhæŋ | *v.* [*pret.* y *p.p.* **overhung**] *t.* **1** pender sobre, colgar por encima de: *her balcony overhung the brushwood = su balcón pendía sobre el matorral.* **2** (fig.) cernerse sobre, amenazar (un peligro, un desastre). || *i.* **3** pender, colgar; sobresalir. || *s.c.* **4** saliente, parte que sobresale: *the overhang of a roof = el saliente de un tejado.*

overhaul | 'əʊvəhɔːl | *v.t.* **1** revisar (una máquina, un aparato). **2** revisar, someter a un nuevo examen (con objeto de corregir o mejorar algo): *they are overhauling their old techniques = están revisando sus viejas técnicas.* **3** alcanzar (a una persona, a un vehículo). || *s.c.* **4** examen, revisión.

overhead | ˌəʊvə'hed | *adv.* **1** arriba, en lo alto; por lo alto: *it passed overhead = pasó por lo alto (por encima de nuestras cabezas).* || *adj.* **2** de arriba; situado en sitio elevado. || **3 overheads,** gastos generales (de un negocio, de una empresa).

overhear | ˌəʊvə'hɪər | *v.t.* e *i.* [*pret.* y *p.p.* **overheard**] acertar a oír (por casualidad o intencionadamente).

overheat | ˌəʊvə'hiːt | *v.t.* e *i.* sobrecalentar(se).

overheated | ˌəʊvə'hiːtɪd | *adj.* acalorado (una persona, una discusión, etc.).

overheating | ˌəʊvə'hiːtɪŋ | *s.i.* sobrecalentamiento.

overhung | ˌəʊvə'hʌŋ | *pret.* y *p.p.* de **overhang.**

overjoyed | ˌəʊvə'dʒɔɪd | *adj.* **1 [– (at)]** encantado: *I am overjoyed at the lessons = estoy encantado con las clases.*

overkill | 'əʊvəkɪl | *s.i.* poder de destrucción que excede al necesario para destruir al enemigo.

overland | 'əʊvəlænd | *adj.* o *adv.* por tierra (un viaje, una ruta): *to travel overland = viajar por tierra.*

overlap | 'əʊvəlæp | *v.t.* e *i.* **1** cubrir (una cosa a otra, tapándose parcialmente). **2** (fig.) coincidir (dos cosas a la vez): *their meetings overlapped = sus reuniones coincidieron.* || *s.c.* e *i.* **3** coincidencia.

overlay | 'əʊvəleɪ | *v.t.* [*pret.* y *p.p.* **overlaid**] **1 [– (with)]** recubrir, cubrir con una capa: *it is overlaid with silver = está recubierto de plata.* || *s.sing.* **2** capa, revestimiento.

overleaf | ˌəʊvə'liːf | *adv.* en la otra página, al dorso de la página.

overload | 'əʊvələʊd | *v.t.* **1** sobrecargar. **2** (fig.) sobrecargar, abrumar (con trabajo, preocupaciones, etc.). || *s.c.* **3** sobrecarga.

overlook | ˌəʊvə'lʊk | *v.t.* **1** mirar a, dar a: *my window overlooked the garden = mi ventana daba al jardín.* **2** pasar por alto, ignorar (sin querer o deliberadamente). **3** perdonar (un error, una falta). **4** supervisar.

overlord | 'əʊvəlɔːd | *s.c.* HIST. señor feudal.

overly | 'əʊvəlɪ | *adv.* (form.) demasiado.

overmanned | ˌəʊvə'mænd | *adj.* con exceso de personal (un trabajo, una empresa).

overmanning | ˌəʊvə'mænɪŋ | *s.i.* exceso de personal (en una empresa, en un trabajo).

overmuch | ˌəʊvə'mʌtʃ | (form.) *adv.* **1** demasiado, excesivamente. || *adj.* **2** demasiado, excesivo.

overnight | ˌəʊvə'naɪt | *adv.* **1** durante la noche. **2** (fig.) de la noche a la mañana: *he can't change overnight = no puede cambiar de la noche a la mañana.* || *adj.* **3** de una noche: *overnight trip = viaje de una noche.* **4** para la noche (ropa, etc. para pasar la noche fuera).

overpaid | ˌəʊvə'peɪd | *adj.* demasiado bien pagado (una persona, un trabajo).

overpass | ˌəʊvə'pɑːs | *s.c.* (EE.UU.) viaducto.

overplay | ˌəʊvə'pleɪ | *v.t.* **1** dar demasiada importancia a, exagerar. || **2 to – one's hand,** darse demasiada importancia.

overpopulated | ˌəʊvə'pɒpjʊleɪtɪd | *adj.* superpoblado.

overpopulation | 'əʊvəˌpɒpjʊ'leɪʃn | *s.i.* superpoblación.

overpower | ˌəʊvə'paʊər | *v.t.* **1** dominar, subyugar, vencer. **2** (fig.) abrumar (un olor, una sensación, una emoción): *they were overpowered by worry = estaban abrumados por la preocupación.*

overpowering | ˌəuvə'pauərɪŋ | *adj.* **1** irresistible, arrollador (una emoción, una sensación). **2** muy intenso (un perfume).
overpriced | ˌəuvə'praɪs | *adj.* demasiado caro.
overran | ˌəuvə'ræn | *pret.* de **overrun.**
overrate | 'əuvəreɪt | *v.t.* supervalorar.
overreach | 'əuvəriːtʃ | *v.t.* **1** engañar, embaucar. **2** pasar, llegar más allá de. || **3 to – oneself,** extralimitarse, pasarse de listo, propasarse.
overreact | ˌəuvərɪ'ækt | *v.i.* reaccionar fuertemente.
override | ˌəuvə'raɪd | *v.t.* [*pret.* **over rode**; *p.p.* **overriden**] **1** sustituir, reemplazar. **2** hacer caso omiso de (una orden, una objeción). **3** agotar, fatigar (a un caballo). **4** anular, invalidar. **5** (fig.) pisotear (a alguien).
overriding | ˌəuvə'raɪdɪŋ | *adj.* primordial, principal, más importante.
overrule | ˌəuvə'ruːl | *v.t.* **1** rechazar (una objeción, un argumento, una propuesta). **2** anular, invalidar (una decisión). **3** DER. denegar. **4** DER. rescindir.
overrun | ˌəuvə'rʌn | *v.t.* [*pret.* **overran**; *p.p.* **overrun**] **1** extenderse por; invadir, infectar (malas hierbas, insectos, etc.). **2** MIL. invadir (un país). **3** rebasar, sobrepasar (un límite). **4** inundar. || *v.i.* excederse (en tiempo).
overseas | ˌəuvə'siːz | *adj.* **1** de ultramar. **2** COM. exterior: *overseas market = mercado exterior.* **3** extranjero (persona). || *adv.* **4** allende los mares, en ultramar. **4** en el extranjero.
oversee | ˌəuvə'siː | *v.t.* [*pret.* **oversaw; p.p. overseen**] **1** supervisar, dirigir (un trabajo). **2** (form.) controlar, vigilar (a una persona).
overseer | 'əuvəsɪər | *s.c.* **1** supervisor. **2** capataz (de una construcción, de una finca).
oversell | ˌəuvə'sel | *v.t.* [*pret.* y *p.p.* **oversold**] sobrevalorar, valorar en exceso (méritos o habilidades).
oversexed | ˌəuvə'sekst | *adj.* demasiado interesado por el sexo.
overshadow | ˌəuvə'ʃædəu | *v.t.* dominar (estar en una posición más alta): *the mountains that overshadow the city = las montañas que dominan la ciudad.* **2** (fig.) eclipsar: *she overshadows her sister in every way = eclipsa a su hermana en todos los aspectos.* **3** (fig.) ensombrecer, entristecer (una situación, un acontecimiento). **4** deslucir.
overshoe | 'əuvəʃuː | *s.c.* chanclo.
overshoot | ˌəuvə'ʃuːt | *v.t.* e *i.* [*pret.* y *p.p.* **overshot**] **1** pasarse (de), ir más allá (de) (el sitio a/por donde se quiere ir): *you overshot the diversion again = te pasaste de nuevo el desvío.* **2 to – the mark,** (fig.) pasarse de listo, ir demasiado lejos.
oversight | 'əuvəsaɪt | *s.c.* e *i.* **1** descuido, negligencia. **2** vigilancia.
oversimplify | 'əuvəˌsɪmplɪfaɪ | *v.t.* e *i.* simplificar demasiado.
oversize | ˌəuvə'saɪz | *adj.* demasiado grande, extragrande (una prenda, una talla).
oversized | ˌəuvə'saɪzd | *adj.* V. **oversize.**
oversleep | ˌəuvə'sliːp | *v.i.* [*pret.* y *p.p.* **overslept**] quedarse dormido (más de la cuenta).
overspill | 'əuvəspɪl | *s.i.* TEC. arreglo por el cual sectores de la población dejan una ciudad superpoblada para ir a vivir a otra más pequeña.
overstaffed | ˌəuvə'stɑːft | *adj.* con demasiado personal (trabajando): *an overstaffed restaurant = un restaurante con demasiado personal.*
overstate | ˌəuvə'steɪt | *v.t.* exagerar.
overstatement | ˌəuvə'steɪtmənt | *s.c.* e *i.* exageración.
overstay | ˌəuvə'steɪ | *v.t.* **1** quedarse demasiado. || **2 to – one's time/ welcome,** quedarse más tiempo del conveniente.
overstep | ˌəuvə'step | *v.t.* **1** propasar, ir más allá de (unos límites convenientes): *she overstepped the bounds of decency = fue más allá de los límites de la decencia.* || **2 to – the mark,** (fig.) pasarse de la raya, ir demasiado lejos.
overt | 'əuvəːt | *adj.* **1** claro, evidente, manifiesto: *overt injustice = injusticia manifiesta.*
overtly | 'əuvəːtlɪ | *adv.* abiertamente, claramente, manifiestamente.
overtake | ˌəuvə'teɪk | *v.t.* e *i.* [*pret.* **overtook**; *p.p.* **overtaken**] **1** adelantar (en una carretera, en un camino): *I couldn't overtake that car = no pude adelantar ese coche.* **2** sorprender (algo que ocurre inesperadamente): *a storm overtook us = nos sorprendió una tormenta.* **3** (lit.) apoderarse de: *fear overtook them = el miedo se apoderó de ellos.* || **4 to be overtaken by,** ser reemplazado por.
overtax | ˌəuvə'tæks | *v.t.* **1** abrumar con impuestos. || **2 to – oneself,** exigirse demasiado. **3 to be overtaxed,** estar física o mentalmente agotado.
overthrow | 'əuvəθrəu | *v.t.* [*pret.* **overthrew**; *p.p.* **overtrown**] **1** derribar, derrocar (un gobierno, un régimen). **2** derribar (un líder). **3** deponer (un rey). || *s.c.* **4** derrocamiento (de un gobierno, de un régimen, de un líder). || **5 to be overthrown,** ser sustituido.
overtime | 'əuvətaɪm | *s.i.* **1** horas extras. || *s.c.* **2** (EE.UU.) DEP. prórroga (en un partido). || *adv.* **3** en horas extraordinarias. || **4 to work –,** (fam.) hacer horas extras.
overtone | 'əuvətəun | *s.c.* **1** MUS. armónico. **2** (fig.) indicio: *overtones of madness = indicios de locura.* **3** insinuación, alusión: *political overtones = alusiones políticas.* **4** sugerencia.
overtook | ˌəuvə'tuk | *pret.* de **overtake.**
overture | 'əuvəˌtjuər | *s.c.* **1** MUS. obertura. **2** preludio: *the overture to a war = el preludio de una guerra.* **3** proposición, oferta: *overtures of friendship = proposiciones de amistad.* **4** propuesta (amorosa).
overturn | 'əuvətəːn | *v.t.* e *i.* **1** volcar(se): *the car overturned = el coche volcó.* || *v.t.* **2** DER. invalidar, anular (una decisión legal). **3** derrocar (un gobierno, un régimen).
overvalue | əuvə'væljuː | *v.t.* supervalorar, dar demasiada importancia a.
overview | 'əuvəvjuː | *s.c.* **[– + (of)]** visión general.
overweening | ˌəuvə'wiːnɪŋ | *adj.* (form.) **1** desmesurado, desmedido: *overweening ambition = ambición desmesurada.* **2** arrogante, presuntuoso.
overweight 'əuvəweɪt | *adj.* **1** obeso. **2** que pesa más de lo permitido (un equipaje). || *s.i.* **3** exceso de peso (en un equipaje). || *v.t.* **4** cargar excesivamente.
overwhelm | ˌəuvə'welm | *v.t.* **1** abrumar, confundir: *your reasoning overwhelms me = tu razonamiento me abruma.* **2** abrumar, dejar atónito: *the news overwhelmed us = las noticias nos dejaron atónitos.* **3 [– (with)]** abrumar, agobiar (con trabajo, preocupaciones, etc.). **4 [– (with)]** abrumar, molestar (con un exceso de algo): *I was overwhelmed with questions = me abrumaron con preguntas.* **5** colmar (de atenciones, de honores, etc.). **6** arrollar, confundir (en una discusión). **7** MIL. arrollar, derrotar (al enemigo).
overwhelming | ˌəuvə'welmɪŋ | *adj.* **1** abrumador, agobiante: *an overwhelming task = una tarea abrumadora.* **2** abrumador, aplastante, arrollador (una victoria, una mayoría). **3** irresistible (un deseo, un dolor).
overwhelmingly | ˌəuvə'welmɪŋlɪ | *adv.* predominantemente.
overwork | 'əuvəwəːk | *v.t.* **1** abrumar con excesivo trabajo, hacer trabajar demasiado. **2** (fam. y fig.) utilizar demasiado, abusar de, emplear mucho. || *v.i.* **3** trabajar demasiado. || *s.i.* **4** exceso de trabajo.
overwrought | ˌəuvə'rɔːt | *adj.* **1** sobreexcitado, con los nervios de punta. **2** exhausto, rendido, extenuado (por el trabajo). **3** demasiado trabajado (un estilo, un objeto, etc.).
ovulate | 'ɒvjəˌleɪt | *v.i.* FISIOL. ovular.
ovulation | ˌɒvju'leɪʃn | *s.i.* FISIOL. ovulación.
ovum | 'əuvəm | [*pl.* **ova**] *s.c.* BIOL. óvulo.
ow | au | *interj.* ¡ay! (denota dolor repentino).
owe | əu | *v.t.* **1** deber (dinero): *he owes me some money = me debe algún dinero.* **2 [– + *o.* + (to)]** deber (una cualidad, una habilidad, un logro, etc. a alguien o a algo): *I owe my success to my father = mi éxito se lo debo a mi padre.* **3** deber (respeto, lealtad). **4** deber, tener que dar: *you owe me an explanation = me debes una explicación.* || **5 to – someone a living,** tener la obligación de atender o apoyar. **6 owing to,** debido a: *owing to the circumstances = debido a las circunstancias.*
owl | aul | *s.c.* ZOOL. **1** búho. **2** lechuza. || **3 little –,** mochuelo.
owlish | 'aulɪʃ | *adj.* (fig.) serio, austero, grave (con un semblante que recuerda a un búho).
owlishly | 'aulɪʃlɪ | *adv.* con seriedad.

own | əun | *adj.* **1** propio (para enfatizar el poseedor): *with my own eyes = con mis propios ojos.* **2** propio, característico: *her own style = su estilo característico.* **3** propio, natural: *his own hair = su pelo natural.* **4** propio (con sentido enfático): *she makes her own decisions = toma sus propias decisiones.* || *pron.* **5** [*adj.pos.* + –] los míos, los tuyos, los suyos, etc. (parientes o personas relacionadas con uno). **6** [*adj.pos.* + –] (el) mío, (el) tuyo, (el) suyo, etc.: *this is your own = esto es suyo.* || *v.t.* **7** poseer, tener, ser dueño de: *he owns a mansion = posee una mansión.* **8** (p.u.) reconocer: *I own my defects = reconozco mis defectos.* **9** confesar, admitir: *I own I was afraid = confieso que tenía miedo.* || *v.i.* **10** **[to – + (to + *ger.*)]** reconocer, confesar, admitir: *he owned to having done it = reconoció haberlo hecho.* || **11 each to one's –,** cada uno a lo suyo, cada uno tiene su gusto. **12 for my –,** para mí solo. **13 to get one's – back,** (fam.) tomar revancha, desquitarse. **14 to hold one's –,** mantenerse firme (no abandonar). **15 like/as if to – the place,** (fam.) como Pedro por su casa. **16 to make something one's –,** hacer algo suyo, apoderarse de algo (como si no pudiera ser de nadie más). **17 of one's –,** suyo, de su propiedad: *money of my own = dinero mío.* **18 of one's –/all of one's –,** muy suyo, muy peculiar: *it has a value all its own = tiene un valor muy peculiar.* **19 on one's –,** por su cuenta, solo: *I work on my own = trabajo por mi cuenta.* **20 to – up (to),** admitir, confesar.

owner | 'əunər | *s.c.* propietario, dueño, amo.

owner-occupier | ˌəunər'ɒkjupaɪər | *s.c.* propietario de la casa en la que vive.

ownership | 'əunəʃɪp | *s.i.* propiedad, posesión.

ox | ɒks | [*pl.* **oxen**] *s.c.* ZOOL. buey.

oxcart | 'ɒkskɑːt | *s.c.* carreta de bueyes.

oxidation | ˌɒksɪ'deɪʃn | *s.i.* TEC. oxidación.

oxide | 'ɒksaɪd | *s.c.* e *i.* QUIM. óxido.

oxidize | 'ɒksɪdaɪz | *v.t.* e *i.* QUIM. oxidar(se).

oxtail | 'ɒksteɪl | *s.i.* GAST. rabo de buey: *oxtail soup = sopa de rabo de buey.*

oxyacetylene | ˌɒksɪə'setɪliːn | *s.i.* **1** QUIM. oxiacetileno. | *adj.* **2** TEC. oxiacetilénico: *oxyacetylene welding = soldadura oxiacetilénica.*

oxygen | 'ɒksɪdʒən | *s.i.* **1** QUIM. oxígeno. || **2 – mask,** máscara de oxígeno. **3 – tent,** cámara de oxígeno.

oxygenate | ɒksɪdʒəneɪt | *v.t.* QUIM. oxigenar.

oxygenated | ɒksɪdʒəneɪtɪd | *adj.* QUIM. oxigenado: *oxygenated water = agua oxigenada.*

oyster | 'ɔɪstər | *s.c.* **1** ZOOL. ostra. || **2 – bed,** criadero de ostras. **3 the world is someone's –,** el mundo está al alcance de sus manos.

ozone | 'əuzəun | *s.i.* **1** QUIM. ozono: *ozone layer = capa de ozono.* **2** (fam.) aire saludable de la costa.

p, P | piː | *s.c.* **1** p, P (decimosexta letra del alfabeto inglés.) || **2** (brit. y fam.) *abreviatura* de **penny** o **pence**: *it costs 50p = cuesta 50 peniques.* **3** *abreviatura* de **page, participle, population.** **4** MUS. piano, suave (en partituras). **5** *abreviatura* de **parking, police.** **6** *abreviatura* de **Phosphorus.** || **6 to mind your p's and q's,** V. **mind.**

pa | pɑː | *s.sing.* (fam. y p.u.) papá, papi, papaíto.

pace | peɪs | *s.i.* **1** paso, velocidad, ritmo, marcha: *at a slow pace = a ritmo lento.* || *s.c.* **2** aire, caminar, forma de andar: *a jaunty pace = un caminar garboso.* **3** paso (de distancia, de velocidad). || *v.t.* e *i.* **4** caminar de un lado a otro, pasear (a ritmo regular). || *v.t.* **5 [to – (out)]** medir a pasos. **6** controlar el ritmo, fijar el ritmo: *she paced my exercices = controlaba el ritmo de mis ejercicios.* || | 'peɪsiː | | 'pɑːkeɪ | *prep.* **7** (form.) en contra de, a pesar de (para contradecir). || **8 at one's own –,** a su propio ritmo, a su propio paso. **9 to go through one's paces/to show one's paces,** mostrar lo que uno vale, mostrar las cualidades que uno tiene. **10 to keep –,** mantener el ritmo, ir al mismo paso, avanzar al mismo ritmo. **11 to put one through one's –,** poner a uno a prueba. **12 to set the –,** marcar el ritmo, imponer la velocidad, establecer el paso. **13 to stand the –,** soportar el ritmo.

pacemaker | 'peɪsˌmeɪkər | (EE.UU. **pacesetter**) *s.c.* **1** el que marca el paso, el que impone el ritmo (una persona, un animal). **2** ejemplo, modelo, inspirador. **3** MED. marcapasos.

pachiderm | 'pækɪdəːm | *s.c.* ZOOL. paquidermo.

pacific | pə'sɪfɪk | *adj.* **1** pacífico, conciliador, apaciguador, tranquilo. || **2 Pacific,** GEOG. del Pacífico: *Pacific islands = islas del Pacífico.* **3 the Pacific Ocean,** GEOG. el Océano Pacífico.

pacification | ˌpæsɪfɪ'keɪʃn | *s.i.* pacificación, conciliación, apaciguamiento.

pacifier | 'pæsɪfaɪər | *s.c.* **1** pacificador, conciliador. **2** (EE.UU.) chupete, chupeta, (Am.) chupón.

pacifism | 'pæsɪfɪzəm | *s.i.* pacifismo.

pacifist | 'pæsɪfɪst | POL. *s.c.* **1** pacifista. || *adj.* **2** pacifista: *the pacifist movement = el movimiento pacifista.*

pacify | 'pæsɪfaɪ | *v.t.* **1** calmar, tranquilizar, apaciguar, aplacar. **2** pacificar, llevar la paz (a un territorio).

pack | pæk | *s.c.* **1** fardo, lío, envoltorio, atadijo. **2** mochila, morral; alforja. **3** (EE.UU.) cajetilla, paquete. **4** caja, envase. **5 [–** *v.sing./pl.***]** manada, hato (de animales salvajes). **6** jauría (de perros de caza). **7** baraja, naipes, cartas. **8** DEP. delanteros, grupo de ataque (en rugby). **9** grupo, partida: *a pack of scouts = un grupo de chicos boy scouts.* **10** (desp.) pandilla, cuadrilla, banda. **11** MED. gasa, compresa. **12** mascarilla cosmética. || *v.t.* e *i.* **13** empaquetar, empacar, embalar. **14** atestar, llenar de bote en bote. **15** amontonar, aglomerar, apilar, hacinar, formar una masa compacta. || *v.t.* **16** empacar, hacer el equipaje, hacer las maletas. **17** proteger con, embalar entre, envolver en (algo, un objeto frágil): *pack the jersey round the vase = protege el jarrón con el jersey.* **18** envasar, enlatar. **19** (desp.) elegir con fraude, nombrar con fraude. **20** (EE.UU. y fam.) ir regularmente armado. || *v.i.* **21** salir a toda prisa, irse de estampida. || **22 a – of lies,** un montón de mentiras. **23 – animal,** animal de carga. **24 – ice,** témpanos flotantes. **25 to – off,** (fam.) quitar(se) de en medio a, deshacerse de: *she packed him off on a holiday = se lo quitó de en medio mandándole de vacaciones.* **26 to – something in,** (fam.) dejar algo de una vez, abandonar algo definitivamente. **27 to – them in,** (fam.) ser un exitazo, tener lleno continuo (un espectáculo). **28 to – up,** (fam.) **a)** acabar de trabajar, abandonar la tarea: *I packed at 6 = acabé el trabajo a las seis*; **b)** (brit. y fam.) estropearse, apagarse, dejar de funcionar (una máquina); **c)** dejar de: *I packed smoking = dejé de fumar.* **29 to send someone packing,** (fam.) despedir a alguien con cajas destempladas, echar a alguien sin miramientos.

package | 'pækɪdʒ | *s.c.* **1** paquete, bulto, lío. **2** (EE.UU.) cajetilla, paquete. **3** caja, envase. **4** paquete, proposición, oferta: *a package of economic measures = un paquete de medidas económicas.* || *v.t.* **5 [to – (up)]** empaquetar, embalar, hacer un paquete. **6** envasar, enlatar. || **7 – deal,** (fam.) convenio, acuerdo (con concesiones mutuas); COM. lote de productos vendidos en conjunto. **8 – holiday,** vacaciones organizadas, vacaciones programadas.

packaging | 'pækɪdʒɪŋ | *s.i.* embalaje, envase, empaquetado, envoltura.

packed | pækt | *adj.* **1** atestado, abarrotado, colmado, lleno hasta los topes, repleto, hasta el borde. **2** con las maletas hechas, con el equipaje preparado: *I was already packed = ya tenía las maletas preparadas.* || **3 – lunch,** almuerzo, merienda, bocadillo (para comer fuera de casa al mediodía). **4 – out,** (brit. y fam.) abarrotado, hasta la bandera.

packer | 'pækər | *s.c.* **1** empaquetador, embalador, envasador. **2** empleado de una empresa de mudanzas.

packet | 'pækɪt | (EE.UU. **pack**) *s.c.* **1** paquete, cajetilla. **2** envase, caja, sobre: *a packet of plasters = un paquete de tiritas.* **3** (generalmente *sing.*) (argot) fortuna, dineral, pastón. **4** MAR. paquebote. || **5 to catch/cop/get/stop a –,** (brit. y argot) tener un enorme disgusto, meterse en problemas graves; ser castigado con rigor, resultar herido de gravedad.

packing | 'pækɪŋ | *s.i.* **1** equipaje, maletas: *I'll do my packing = haré mi equipaje.* **2** embalaje, empaquetado, envoltura: *with a nice packing = con una envoltura agradable.* **3** MED. aplicación de compresas o gasas (a una herida). || **4 – case,** caja de embalaje.

pact | pækt | *s.c.* pacto, acuerdo, compromiso, trato.

pad | pæd | *s.c.* **1** almohadilla, cojinete, hombrera, relleno, postizo (para dar forma). **2** bayeta, bola (de algodón, etc. para limpiar). **3** DEP. peto, plastrón protector. **4** taco de papel, bloc de notas. **5**

tampón, almohadilla de entintar. **6** almohadilla, carnosidad (en las patas de los gatos). **7** yemas (de los dedos). **8** BOT. hoja de planta acuática, hoja de nenúfar. **9** plataforma de lanzamiento, pista de despegue (para cohetes, helicópteros). **10** (argot) casa, nido, vivienda. **11** ruido de pisadas; golpe sordo. **12** caballo al paso (sonido). || *v.t.* **13** rellenar, almohadillar, acolchar, forrar. **14** **[to – (out)]** meter mucha paja, alargar, hinchar con material innecesario (un discurso, un escrito); poner postizos, meter relleno (a una prenda). || *v.i.* **15** [**to** – *adv./prep.*] ir al paso, andar sin hacer ruido.

padded | 'pædɪd | *adj.* **1** forrado, relleno, almohadillado. **2** gordo, grueso, con una capa de grasa. || **3 – cell,** celda acolchada (en un manicomio).

padding | 'pædɪŋ | *s.i.* **1** relleno, almohadilla, borra, miraguano. **2** (fig.) paja, material innecesario.

paddle | 'pædl | *s.c.* **1** remo, canalete, zagual. **2** paleta, espátula (de cocina). **3** paleta, pala (para revolver, sacudir). **4** MEC. paleta de hélice. **5** (EE.UU.) DEP. raqueta de ping-pong; bate plano (de críquet). **6** chapoteo. || *v.t.* e *i.* **7** remar, impulsar con remo o canalete. || *v.t.* **8** (EE.UU. y argot) dar un sopapo, dar una torta, pegar con la mano abierta; dar de paletazos, pegar con paleta. **9** remover con paleta, revolver con espátula. || *v.i.* **10** nadar como un pato, nadar como un perro. **11** chapotear, golpear el agua (con manos y pies). || **12 – boat/steamer,** vapor de ruedas. **13 to paddle one's own canoe,** aguantar cada uno su vela, arreglárselas uno mismo, bastarse a sí mismo. **14 paddling pool,** estanque con juegos, estanque de recreo.

paddock | 'pædək | *s.c.* **1** prado, corral, cercado (al lado de los establos). **2** DEP. paddock, corral de ensilladura.

paddy, paddy field, rice paddy | 'pædɪ | *s.c.* **1** arrozal. **2** (brit. y fam.) rabieta, pataleo. || *s.i.* **3** arroz con cáscara. || **4 in a –,** enrabietado, con una pataleta. **5 Paddy,** (fam. y hum.) irlandés típico (forma familiar del nombre Patrick). **6** (argot) policía.

padlock | 'pædlɒk | *s.c.* **1** candado. || *v.t.* **2** cerrar con candado.

padre | 'pɑːdrɪ | | 'pɑːdeɪ | *s.c.* **1** (fam.) padre, capellán. **2** MIL. cura castrense, capellán castrense.

paean | 'piːən | *s.c.* **1** (lit.) himno, encomio, apología, alabanza: *a paean to terrorism = una apología del terrorismo.* **2** canto de alabanza, acción de gracias.

paediatrician | ˌpiːdɪə'trɪʃn | (EE.UU. **pediatrician**) *s.c.* MED. pediatra, médico puericultor.

paediatrics | ˌpiːdɪ'ætrɪks | (EE.UU. **pediatrics**) *s.i.* MED. pediatría.

paella | paɪ'elə | | pɑː'elə | *s.i.* paella (plato español a base de arroz, carne o pescado y verduras).

pagan | 'peɪgən | *s.c.* **1** (desp.) pagano, infiel, impío. **2** HIST. pagano, gentil. **3** hedonista. || *adj.* **4** pagano, infiel, impío; idólatra.

paganism | 'peɪgənɪzəm | *s.i.* paganismo.

page | peɪdʒ | *s.c.* **1** página, plana, cuartilla, folio, hoja. **2** (lit.) página, (acontecimiento histórico). **3** chico de los recados, botones (de hotel). **4** acomodador. **5** (EE.UU.) ujier, ordenanza. **6** paje (en una boda). **7** HIST. paje, escudero. || *v.t.* **8** hacer llamar, buscar por medio de un botones, llamar por altavoz (en hoteles, aeropuertos): *I heard my name paged = oí mi nombre por el altavoz.* **9** servir como paje. **10** trabajar como botones, acomodador u ordenanza. **11** paginar, numerar las páginas. || *v.i.* **12** pasar páginas.

pageant | 'pædʒənt | *s.c.* **1** exhibición al aire libre, espectáculo teatral al aire libre, fiestas públicas. **2** desfile, cortejo, procesión. || *s.i.* **3** pompa, exhibición, ostentación, esplendor, boato.

pageantry | 'pædʒəntrɪ | *s.i.* pompa, boato, esplendor, ostentación, vistosidad: *the pageantry of the ceremony = el esplendor de la ceremonia.*

pageboy | 'peɪdʒbɔɪ | *s.c.* **1** paje (en una ceremonia). **2** corte de pelo a lo paje.

pagination | ˌpædʒɪ'neɪʃn | *s.i.* (form.) paginación, foliación, numeración de páginas.

pagoda | pə'gəʊdə | *s.c.* pagoda, templo oriental.

pah | pɑː | *exclamación* (arc.) bah (expresa disgusto).

paid | peɪd | **1** *pret.* y *p.p.* de **pay.** || *adj.* **2** remunerado, retribuido, pagado. || **3 to put – to,** dar al traste con, acabar con (las esperanzas, una posibilidad).

paid-up | ˌpeɪd'ʌp | *adj.* **1** que pagan cuotas, con las cuotas pagadas: *many are paid-up members of the club = muchos son socios de cuota del club.* **2** comprometido, vinculado (a un grupo político).

pail | peɪl | *s.c.* e *i.* cubo, tina, pozal, balde (instrumento, cantidad).

pain | peɪn | *s.i.* **1** dolor, malestar, sufrimiento. **2** angustia, disgusto, dolor. || *s.c.* **3** dolor, punzada, retortijón: *a pain in the stomach = un dolor de estómago.* **4** (fam.) aburrimiento, fastidio (una persona o cosa). || *v.t.* **5** (lit.) dar pena, dar lástima, angustiar, disgustar, causar dolor (mental): *it pained me to leave = me daba pena irme.* **6** (form.) doler, hacer daño. || **7 a – in the arse/backside,** (argot y vulg.) una persona o cosa insoportable, como una patada en el estómago. **8 a – in the neck,** (argot) un tostonazo, una persona o cosa inaguantable, que da cien patadas. **9 to be at pains,** esmerarse, afanarse, tomárselo con interés. **10 for one's pains,** por el esfuerzo hecho, por el trabajo realizado: *not much for my pains = no mucho por el trabajo que hice.* **11 to go to great pains/to take pains,** esmerarse, molestarse, afanarse, tomarse un trabajo enorme. **12 pains,** dolores de parto. **13 under/on -- of,** (form.) so pena de, bajo pena de.

pained | peɪnd | *adj.* **1** herido, ofendido, disgustado; de reproche: *a pained look = una mirada de reproche.* **2** afligido, apenado, dolorido.

painful | 'peɪnfʊl | *adj.* **1** doloroso, penoso, dolorido (físicamente). **2** penoso, embarazoso, difícil, traumático, desagradable: *a painful solution = una solución desagradable.* **3** laborioso, arduo, difícil (una actividad). **4** (arc.) diligente, esmerado, cuidadoso.

painfully | 'peɪnfəlɪ | *adv.* **1** dolorosamente, penosamente. **2** desagradablemente, de forma embarazosa. **3** laboriosamente, con dificultad.

painkiller | 'peɪnˌkɪlər | *s.c.* analgésico, calmante.

painless | 'peɪnlɪs | *adj.* **1** indoloro, que no causa dolor. **2** (fam.) que no exige esfuerzo, fácil, hacedero, elemental, libre de complicación.

painlessly | 'peɪnlɪslɪ | *adv.* **1** sin dolor. **2** fácilmente, sin esfuerzo.

painstaking | 'peɪnzˌteɪkɪŋ | *adj.* esmerado, cuidadoso, laborioso, concienzudo, escrupuloso.

painstakingly | 'peɪnzˌteɪkɪŋlɪ | *adv.* esmeradamente, cuidadosamente, concienzudamente, escrupulosamente.

paint | peɪnt | *s.i.* **1** pintura, tinte, coloración. **2** (arc.) maquillaje, cosmético, afeite, colorete. **3** (EE.UU.) caballo pinto con manchas. | *v.t.* e *i.* **4** pintar, decorar, aplicar pintura (a una superficie). **5** pintar (un cuadro). || *t.* **6** (desp. y arc.) maquillar, pintar (el rostro). **7** MED. limpiar con algodón, aplicar con algodón. || **8 to – a gloomy/vivid, etc. picture,** pintar una escena desalentadora, con todo lujo de detalles, etc. **9 to – over,** tapar con pintura, cubrir con pintura. **10 – stripper,** decapante, quitapintura. **11 to – the town red,** (fam.) irse de juerga, salir de copas (para celebrar algo).

paintbox | 'peɪntbɒks | *s.c.* estuche de pinturas, caja de colores.

paint-brush | 'peɪntbrʌʃ | *s.c.* brocha, pincel.

painted | 'peɪntɪd | *adj.* **1** pintado, decorado. **2** maquillado.

painter | 'peɪntər | *s.c.* **1** pintor, decorador. **2** pintor, artista. **3** MAR. amarra, cabo. **4** (EE.UU.) ZOOL. puma.

painting | 'peɪntɪŋ | *s.i.* **1** pintura, decoración: *we've just done the painting = acabamos de pintar.* || *s.c.* **2** cuadro, pintura: *a painting by Miró = un cuadro de Miró.*

paintwork | 'peɪntwɜːk | *s.i.* pintura, capa de pintura, superficie: *it damaged the paintwork = estropeó la pintura.*

pair | peər | *s.c.* **1** [**– of**] par: *a pair of shoes = un par de zapatos.* **2** [– *v.sing./pl.*] pareja: *in pairs = por parejas.* **3** yunta (de animales). **4** dos miembros de un tribunal que se abstienen de votar por diferir exageradamente. || *v.t.* e *i.* **5** **[to – off]** emparejarse, casarse. **6** aparear(se), cruzar(se) (los animales). **7** **[to – up]** emparejar(se), formar pareja, hacer pareja (para un juego, un trabajo).

paisly | 'peɪzlɪ | *s.i.* tejido de lana de vistosos colores mezclados en formas curvilíneas.

Pakistan | ˌpɑːkɪ'stɑːn | *s.sing.* Pakistán.

Pakistani | ˌpɑːkɪ'stɑːnɪ | | ˌpɑːkɪ's-tænɪ | *adj.* **1** pakistaní, de Pakistán. || *s.c.* **2** paquistaní.

pal | pæl | *s.c.* 1 (fam.) amigo, camarada, compañero, compinche. || *v.i.* 2 **[to – (up/with)]** (brit. y fam.) hacerse amigos.

palace | 'pælɪs | *s.c.* 1 palacio, mansión. || *s.sing.* 2 **[the –]** la gente de palacio.

palatable | 'pælətəbl | *adj.* 1 sabroso, delicioso, apetitoso, suculento. 2 (fig.) agradable, aceptable, admisible: *a palatable solution = una solución aceptable.*

palate | 'pælət | *s.c.* 1 ANAT. paladar. || *s.c.* e *i.* 2 **[– (for)]** paladar, gusto: *a fine palate for wine = un paladar exquisito para el vino.*

palatial | pə'leɪʃl | *adj.* 1 grandioso, suntuoso, espléndido. 2 palaciego, de palacio.

palaver | pə'lɑːvər | | pə'lævər | *s.i.* 1 (fam.) palabrería, cháchara, tonterías, banalidades. 2 (fam.) incomodidad, molestia, engorro, lío. || *s.c.* 3 (p.u.) debate, conferencia, parlamento (entre dos opositores).

pale | peɪl | *adj.* 1 pálido, blanquecino, descolorido. 2 claro, pálido, apagado (un color). 3 tenue, débil: *a pale light = una luz tenue.* 4 estaca. 5 empalizada, vallado. || *v.i.* 6 palidecer, ponerse pálido. 7 **[to – (before/beside)]** (fig.) palidecer, perder importancia: *she pailed beside her sister = ella perdía importancia frente a su hermana.* || *v.t.* 8 cercar, empalizar, vallar. || 9 **beyond the –,** totalmente inaceptable, que pasa de la raya, irrazonablemente.

paleness | 'peɪlnɪs | *s.i.* palidez, blancura.

Palestine | 'pæləstaɪn | *s.sing.* Palestina.

Palestinian | ˌpælə'stɪnɪən | *adj.* 1 palestino, de Palestina. || *s.c.* 2 palestino.

palette | 'pælɪt | *s.c.* 1 paleta, tabloza (del pintor). 2 paleta, gama de colores, cualidades: *a limited palette = una gama de colores limitada.* || 3 **– knife,** espátula.

palindrome | 'pælɪndrəum | *s.c.* palíndromo (frase o palabra que se lee igual de derecha a izquierda que viceversa).

palings | 'peɪlɪŋz | *s.pl.* empalizada, valla, vallado, cerca.

palisade | ˌpælɪ'seɪd | *s.c.* 1 empalizada, estacada (de defensa). || 2 **palisades,** (EE.UU.) acantilado.

pall | pɔːl | *v.t.* e *i.* 1 **[to – (on/upon)]** dejar de gustar, cansar, aburrir, hastiar, empalagar, dejar de interesar: *acid music palls me = la música acid me aburre.* || *s.sing.* 2 nube, capa, manto: *a pall of silence = un manto de silencio.* || *s.c.* 3 paño mortuorio, mortaja. 4 (EE.UU.) ataúd, féretro.

pallbearer | 'pɔːlˌbeərər | *s.c.* persona que lleva el féretro, miembro de la comitiva fúnebre.

pallet | 'pælɪt | *s.c.* 1 MEC. palet, plataforma de carga (de una carretilla elevadora). 2 jergón, camastro, colchoneta de paja. 3 paleta, base del torno (de ceramista). 4 paleta (de pintor). 5 MEC. trinquete.

palliative | 'pælɪətɪv | *s.c.* 1 (form.) paliativo, aminorativo, atenuante. 2 calmante, sedante.

pallid | 'pælɪd | *adj.* 1 pálido, enfermizo, macilento, descolorido. 2 (fig.) soso, insípido, sin interés.

pallor | 'pælər | *s.i.* palidez.

pally, palsy walsy | 'pælɪ | *adj.* **[– (with)]** (fam.) amistoso, amigo.

palm, palm tree | pɑːm | *s.c.* 1 BOT. palmera, palma. 2 palma (de la mano, de un guante). 3 palmo (medida). 4 pala (de remo). 5 palma, triunfo, victoria. || *v.t.* 6 esconder en la mano, hacer desaparecer en la mano: *he palmed the scarf = hizo desaparecer el pañuelo dentro del puño.* || 7 **to bear the –,** llevarse la palma. 8 **to cross one's –/to cross one's – with silver,** (fig.) untarle a uno la mano, comprar a uno (para obtener información). 9 **to grease one's –,** V. **grease.** 10 **to have/hold someone in the – of one's hand,** tener a uno en el bolsillo, tener a uno totalmente controlado, hacer de uno lo que se quiere. 11 **to – off (with)/(on/onto),** colar, endosar, deshacerse de (algo que no merece la pena); engañar, distraer, disuadir: *he tried to palm me off with his old car = trató de colarme su viejo coche.* 12 **– oil,** aceite de palma. 13 **Palm Sunday,** REL. Domingo de Ramos.

palmistry | 'pɑːmɪstrɪ | *s.i.* quiromancia.

palomino | ˌpælə'miːnəu | *s.c.* caballo alazán, caballo pardo con crin y cola blancas.

palpable | 'pælpəbl | *adj.* (form.) 1 perceptible, obvio, notorio, evidente, manifiesto. 2 palpable, tangible.

palpably | 'pælpəblɪ | *adv.* 1 perceptivamente, obviamente, manifiestamente, evidentemente. 2 palpablemente, al tacto.

palpitate | 'pælpɪteɪt | *v.i.* 1 palpitar. 2 **[to – (with)]** (form.) temblar, vibrar: *palpitate with emotion = temblar de emoción.*

palpitation | ˌpælpɪ'teɪʃn | *s.c.* e *i.* palpitación.

palsied | 'pɔːlzɪd | *adj.* (arc.) paralítico, debilitado, paralizado.

palsy | 'pɔːlzɪ | *s.i.* 1 MED. (arc.) parálisis, perlesía. 2 MED. debilitamiento muscular, pérdida de control muscular. 3 (fig.) impotencia, incapacidad (de acción). || *v.t.* 4 paralizar.

paltry | 'pɔːltrɪ | *adj.* 1 insignificante, miserable, mezquino, misérrimo, magro: *a paltry rise = una subida miserable.* 2 despreciable, bajo, vil, ruin (una actitud).

pampas | 'pæmpəs | *s.sing.* 1 pampa, llanura (de Argentina). || 2 **– grass,** BOT. cortadera argentina.

pamper | 'pæmpər | *v.t.* 1 mimar, consentir. 2 (fig.) mimar, regalar, tratar bien: *I pampered myself with a new coat = me regalé un abrigo nuevo.*

pamphlet | 'pæmflɪt | *s.c.* panfleto, folleto.

pamphleteer | ˌpæmflɪ'tɪər | *s.c.* 1 panfletista, folletista. || *v.i.* 2 escribir panfletos.

pan | pæn | *s.c.* 1 cazuela, cacerola, perol, sartén, cazo. 2 plato (de la balanza). 3 (brit.) taza (del retrete). 4 batea, criba (para separar metales preciosos). 5 charco, hoyo, fangal (con agua). 6 salina, mina de sal. 7 MIL. cazoleta (de un arma de fuego). 8 (argot) cara, jeta, rostro, semblante. 9 (fam.) palo, vapuleo (de la crítica). 10 hoja de betel, hoja de betel rellena de nueces y lima (que se mastica en Oriente). || *v.t.* e *i.* 11 lavar en batea, separar con la batea, cribar en batea (un metal precioso). 12 tomar panorámicas (con cámara de cine). || *v.i.* 13 girar para tomar panorámicas (la cámara de cine). || *v.t.* 14 (fam.) dar el palo, poner por los suelos, vapulear, censurar, criticar con severidad. 15 cocinar en cazuela. || *prefijo.* 16 pan: *pan-American = panamericano.* || 17 **to – out,** (fam.) funcionar bien, desarrollarse adecuadamente, tener éxito, dar resultado.

panacea | ˌpænə'sɪə | *s.c.* 1 (generalmente desp.) panacea, remedio. 2 medicina, elixir.

panache | pæ'næʃ | (EE.UU.) | pə'næʃ | *s.i.* 1 desenvoltura, garbo, brío, donaire, estilo, elegancia, talento. 2 penacho (en un casco).

Panama | ˌpænə'mɑː | *s.sing.* Panamá.

panama hat, panama | ˌpænə'mɑː'hæt | *s.c.* sombrero panamá, sombrero jipijapa.

Panamanian | ˌpænə'meɪnjən | *adj.* 1 panameño, de Panamá. || *s.c.* 2 panameño.

panatella | ˌpænə'telə | *s.c.* panatela (purito).

pancake | 'pænkeɪk | (EE.UU. **crepe**) *s.c.* 1 hojuela, tortilla fina, crepe, (Am.) panqueque (generalmente relleno). || *v.t.* e *i.* 2 aterrizar verticalmente, aterrizar de plano. || 3 **Pancake Day,** Martes de Carnaval. 4 **– landing,** aterrizaje de emergencia, aterrizaje en vertical. 5 **– roll,** GAST. rollo de primavera (plato chino).

pancreas | 'pæŋkrɪəs | *s.c.* ANAT. páncreas.

panda | 'pændə | *s.c.* 1 ZOOL. panda. || 2 **– car,** (brit.) coche patrulla, coche policial.

pandemic | pæn'demɪk | *adj.* 1 MED. pandémico. || *s.c.* 2 MED. pandemia, plaga.

pandemonium | ˌpændɪ'məunjəm | *s.i.* pandemonio, caos, griterío, bullicio, desorden, estruendo infernal.

pander | 'pændər | *v.t.* **[to – to]** (desp.) satisfacer a, complacer a, mimar a, dar gusto a, condescender con: *pandering to the public love in sex scandals = condescendiendo con el gusto del público por los escándalos.*

pandit | 'pʌndɪt | *s.c.* pandit (título que se da en la India a un hombre prudente).

pane | peɪn | *s.c.* 1 hoja de vidrio, cristal (de una ventana). 2 panel, tablero, entrepaño (de una puerta, de una pared). 3 cara, lado (de tuerca).

panegyric | ˌpænɪ'dʒɪrɪk | *s.c.* **[– (on/upon)]** (form.) panegírico, elogio, encomio, alabanza.

panel | 'pænl | *s.c.* 1 panel, tablero, entrepaño (de puerta, de ventana, de pared). 2 artesón (del techo). 3 tablero, panel, cuadro (de control, de mando):

all the switches on the control panel = todas las llaves del tablero de control. **4** paño (de tela). **5** ART. tabla. **6** [– *v.sing./pl.*] TV. panel, equipo (de gente): *a panel of writers in the program = un equipo de escritores en el programa.* **7** grupo, equipo (de expertos). **8** jurado. || *v.t.* **9** poner paneles, decorar con paneles, con artesonado: *the ceiling, panelled with wood = el techo, decorado con artesonado de madera.* **10** seleccionar jurado, elegir jurado. || **11 – pin,** punta, clavo fino de cabeza pequeña.

panelled | 'pænld | (EE.UU. **paneled**) *adj.* decorado con paneles, artesonado.

panelling | 'pænəlɪŋ | (EE.UU. **paneling**) *s.i.* paneles, artesonado, empanelado.

panellist | 'pænəlɪst | (EE.UU. **panelist**) *s.c.* TV. miembro de un equipo, miembro de un jurado (de un concurso).

pang | pæŋ | *s.c.* dolor agudo, espasmo, punzada, pinchazo: *a pang of remorse = remordimiento.*

panic | 'pænɪk | *s.c.* e *i.* **1** pánico, terror, pavor, horror. **2** (EE.UU. y fam.) persona o cosa hilarante, desternillante, que causa mucha risa. **3** (brit. y fam.) prisa, urgencia, precipitación, apuro: *there's no panic = no hay prisa.* || *v.t.* e *i.* **4** aterrar, tener pánico, ser presa del pánico. **5** dar pánico, aterrar, infundir terror. || **6 to push the – button,** actuar presa de pánico, actuar llevado por el pánico.

panicky | 'pænɪkɪ | *adj.* aterrado, dominado por el pánico, presa del terror.

panic-stricken | 'pænɪk,strɪkən | *adj.* aterrorizado, aterrado, muerto de miedo, sobrecogido de terror.

pannier | 'pænɪər | *s.c.* **1** cesta, cesto, canasta, cuévano. **2** alforja, angarillas, árguenas. **3** cartera, bolsa (en las bicicletas, motocicletas). **4** miriñaque, guardainfantes.

panoply | 'pænəplɪ | *s.i.* (form.) panoplia, esplendor, pompa, boato, ceremonial, lujo.

panorama | ,pænə'rɑːmə | *s.c.* **1** panorama, vista panorámica. **2** panorama, visión de conjunto: *a panorama of Spanish painting = un panorama de la pintura española.*

panoramic | ,pænə'ræmɪk | *adj.* panorámico, de conjunto.

panpipes | 'pænpaɪps | *s.pl.* zampoña, siringa, flauta.

pansy | 'pænzɪ | *s.c.* **1** BOT. pensamiento. **2** (fam. y desp.) marica, mariquita, afeminado, homosexual.

pant | pænt | *v.i.* **1** jadear, resollar, respirar fatigadamente, resoplar. **2 [to – (for)]** (lit.) suspirar, anhelar, ansiar, desear vehementemente. || *v.t.* **3** hablar entrecortadamente, jadeando. || *s.c.* **4** jadeo, resuello, resoplido. || **5 to bore the pants off somebody,** aburrir mortalmente a alguien. **6 by the seat of one's pants,** instintivamente, guiándose por la experiencia de uno mismo. **7 to catch someone with their pants down,** pillar a uno por sorpresa, sorprender a alguien con la guardia baja, coger a alguien en un renuncio. **8 pants,** (brit.) calzoncillos, bragas; (EE.UU.) pantalones.

pantaloons | ,pæntə'luːn | *s.pl.* **1** HIST. calzones, pantalones, pantalones bombachos. || **2 Pantaloon,** LIT. Pantalón, Arlequín (en la Comedia del Arte); bufón, gracioso.

pantechnicon | pæn'teknɪkən | *s.c.* **1** camión de mudanzas, capitoné. **2** depósito de muebles, almacén de muebles.

pantheism | 'pænθiːɪzəm | *s.i.* panteísmo.

pantheist | 'pænθiːɪst | *s.c.* panteísta, adepto al panteísmo.

pantheistic | ,pænθiː'ɪstɪk | *adj.* panteísta, panteístico.

pantheon | 'pænθɪən | (EE.UU.) | 'pænθɪɒn | *s.c.* **1** panteón, conjunto de dioses; (fig.) flor y nata, firmamento, conjunto estelar, grupo principal: *the pantheon of painters = el grupo principal de pintores.* **2** panteón (monumento funerario, templo).

panther | 'pænθər | *s.c.* ZOOL. pantera, leopardo.

panties | 'pæntɪz | (brit. **pants**) *s.pl.* bragas, (Am.) bombacha.

panto | 'pæntəʊ | *s.c.* (fam.) pantomima, imitación, parodia.

pantomime | 'pæntəmaɪm | *s.c.* e *i.* **1** pantomima. || *s.i.* **2** mimo. **3** (fig.). || *s.c.* **4** pantomima, farsa, parodia, patraña, engaño.

pantry | 'pæntrɪ | *s.c.* despensa.

pantyhose | 'pæntɪhəʊz | *s.pl.* (EE.UU.) medias hasta la cintura, pantis.

pap | pæp | *s.i.* (generalmente desp.). **1** papilla, papas, (Am.) gachas. **2** (EE.UU.) cultura basura, información poco valiosa. **3** (jerga) sinecura, prebendas (políticas): *a newspaper seeking pap = un periódico en busca de prebendas políticas.* **4** (arc.) pezón.

papa, poppa | pə'pɑː | *s.c.* (EE.UU. y fam., o brit. y arc.) papá, papaíto, papi.

papacy | 'peɪpəsɪ | *s.sing.* (form.) papado, pontificado.

papal | 'peɪpl | *adj.* papal, pontificio.

papaya, papaw | pə'paɪə | *s.c.* e *i.* BOT. **1** papaya (fruta). **2** papayo (árbol).

paper | 'peɪpər | *s.i.* **1** papel, hoja de papel, trozo de papel. **2** papel pintado, papel decorado. | *s.c.* **3** periódico, rotativo, diario, gaceta, revista. **4** (form.) cuestionario de examen, examen, ejercicio: *an easy English paper = un ejercicio de inglés fácil.* **5** disertación, ponencia, conferencia, discurso, artículo, lección magistral. **6** [– *s.*] título, credenciales; documento escrito: *paper evidence = testimonio escrito.* **7** COM. valor, letra de cambio, pagaré, vale. **8** (argot) pase (para el teatro). || *v.t.* **9** empapelar, decorar con papel (una pared). **10 [to – (over/up)]** tapar, esconder, disimular, ocultar, encubrir. **11** envolver, cubrir con papel, forrar. **12** (argot) regalar pases (para el teatro). || *adj.* **13** de papel, como el papel: *paper thin = delgado como el papel.* **14** (fig. y gen. desp.) de papel, teórico, imaginario, de mentira, de boquilla: *paper threats = amenazas de boquilla.* || **15 not to be worth the – it's written on,** no tener valor alguno, ser completamente inservible, ser nulo. **16 on –,** por escrito, sobre el papel; teóricamente, a juzgar por las estadísticas. **17 – money,** billetes de banco, papel moneda. **18 – round,** ruta de reparto de periódicos por las casas. **19 – shop,** quiosco de prensa. **20 papers,** documentación, credenciales, papeles, carnet de identidad; diario, colección de cartas, escritos. **21 – tiger,** (fig.) tigre de papel (persona, institución, país). **22 to put pen to –,** empezar a escribir.

paperback | 'peɪpəbæk | *s.c.* libro de bolsillo, libro en rústica.

paperboy | 'peɪpəbɔɪ | *s.c.* repartidor de periódicos.

paperclip | 'peɪpəklɪp | *s.c.* clip, sujetapapeles.

paper-knife | 'peɪpənaɪf | *s.c.* abrecartas, cortapapel, plegadera.

paperweight | 'peɪpəweɪt | *s.c.* pisapapeles.

paperwork | 'peɪpəwɜːk | *s.i.* papeleo, burocracia, trámites burocráticos, trabajo de oficina, trabajo administrativo; aspecto teórico.

papery | 'peɪpərɪ | *adj.* de papel, delgado como el papel, fino como el papel.

papier-mâché | ,pæpɪeɪ'mæʃeɪ | *s.i.* **1** cartón piedra. || *adj.* **2** de cartón piedra.

paprika | 'pæprɪkə | *s.i.* pimienta roja, pimentón.

papyri | 'pæpɪraɪ | V. **papyrus.**

papyrus | 'pəpaɪərəs | [*pl.* **papyruses** o **papyri**] *s.c.* **1** BOT. papiro. **2** papiro, documento sobre papiro. || *s.i.* **3** papel de papiro.

par | pɑːr | *s.sing.* **1** par, semejanza, nivel. **2** ECON. paridad, patrón, par. || *s.i.* **3** DEP. par, número de golpes necesarios para un hoyo (en golf). || *v.t.* **4** DEP. marcar un par (en golf). || *adj.* **5** normal, corriente, común. **6** ECON. nominal. || **7 below/under/not up to –,** sentirse mal, sentirse indispuesto; estar agotado, sentirse cansado; inferior a la calidad normal, por debajo de la media, insatisfactorio. **8 on a –,** a la par, al mismo nivel. **9 – for the course,** lo normal, lo que se supone, lo esperado.

para | 'pɑːrə | *s.c.* **1** (fam.) MIL. paracaidista. **2** *abreviatura* de **paragraph.**

parable | 'pærəbl | *s.c.* parábola, alegoría, moraleja.

parabola | pə'ræbələ | *s.c.* GEOM. parábola, curva, arco.

parabolic | ,pærə'bɒlɪk | | ,pærə'bɑːlɪk | *adj.* **1** parabólico, curvilíneo. **2** parabólico, alegórico.

parachute | 'pærəʃuːt | *s.c.* **1** paracaídas. **2** ZOOL. patagio, membrana alar. || *v.t.* e *i.* **3** arrojar(se) en paracaídas, lanzar(se) en paracaídas.

parachutist | 'pærəʃuːtɪst | *s.c.* paracaidista.

parade | pə'reɪd | *s.c.* **1** desfile, marcha, procesión. **2** MIL. desfile, parada. **3** exhibición, ostentación, alarde. **4** (brit.) fila de tiendas. **5** sucesión, serie, secuencia: *a parade of changes = una serie de* *cambios*. **6** plaza pública, paseo. || *v.i.* **7** **[to** – *adv./prep.*] desfilar, marchar, ir en procesión. || *v.t.* e *i.* **8** MIL. formar, reunir para pasar revista. **9** (generalmente desp.) exhibir(se), alardear, hacer ostentación, lucir(se), hacer gala de. || **10 to be on –,** MIL. desfilar, marchar. **11 – ground,** MIL. patio de armas, plaza de armas.

paradigm | 'pærədaɪm | *s.c.* **1 [– (of)]** paradigma, ejemplo, modelo. **2** GRAM. paradigma.

paradise | 'pærədaɪs | *s.i.* **1** paraíso, cielo. **2** (fig.) paraíso, delicia, gloria, maravilla, Jauja: *being on my own was paradise = quedarme a solas fue una maravilla.* || **3 a shopper's/swimmer's –,** un paraíso para el comprador, para el nadador.

paradox | 'pærədɒks | *s.c.* paradoja, contradicción, antítesis.

paradoxical | ˌpærə'dɒksɪkl | | ˌpærə'dɑːksɪkl | *adj.* paradójico, contradictorio, antitético.

paradoxically | ˌpærə'dɒksɪklɪ | | ˌpærə'dɑːksɪklɪ | *adv.* paradójicamente, contradictoriamente.

paraffin | 'pærəfɪn | (EE.UU. **kerosene**) *s.i.* **1** parafina. || *v.t.* **2** parafinar, impregnar de parafina. || **3 – wax,** parafina sólida, parafina en cera.

paragon | 'pærəgən | (EE.UU.) | 'pærəgɒn | *s.c.* **1 [– (of)]** parangón, dechado, ideal, modelo: *a paragon of virtue = un dechado de virtud.* **2** diamante de 100 kilates. **3** perla esférica enorme. || *v.t.* **4** parangonar, comparar, confrontar, equiparar.

paragraph | 'pærəgrɑːf | (EE.UU.) | 'pærəgræf | *s.c.* **1** párrafo. **2 new paragraph,** punto y aparte. **3** PER. artículo breve, noticia, anuncio.

parakeet | 'pærəkiːt | *s.c.* ZOOL. periquito.

parallel | 'pærəlel | *adj.* **1** GEOM. paralelo. **2 [– (to/with)]** en paralelo, lado a lado, en línea paralela. **3 [– (to)]** paralelo, análogo, semejante, correspondiente, parejo, en la misma dirección: *a parallel case = un caso semejante.* || *s.c.* **4** GEOM. línea paralela, paralela. **5 [– (between/with)]** semejanza, afinidad, parentesco, analogía, similitud, equivalencia. **6** GEOG. paralelo. || *s.c.* e *i.* **7 [– (to/with)]** paralelo, igual, equivalente (persona o cosa): *it has no parallel in real life = no tiene equivalente en la vida real.* || *v.t.* **8** poner en paralelo; extenderse en paralelo, estar en paralelo. **9** ser paralelo a, ser análogo a, ser similar a, correr parejas con, ser comparable con. **10** (form.) igualar, equiparar. || **11 in –,** ELEC. en paralelo.

parallelogram | ˌpærə'leləʊgræm | *s.c.* GEOM. paralelogramo.

paralyse | 'pærəlaɪz | (EE.UU. **paralyze**) *v.t.* **1** paralizar, inmovilizar. **2** (fig.) paralizar, petrificar: *paralysed by terror = paralizado de terror.* **3** paralizar, parar, suspender, entorpecer (una actividad).

paralysed | 'pærəlaɪzd | *adj.* **1** paralizado, inmovilizado: *paralysed after the accident = inmovilizado después del accidente.* **2** paralizado, petrificado (por el miedo).

paralysing | 'pærəlaɪzɪŋ | *adj.* paralizante, obstaculizador, entumecedor.

paralysis | pə'rælɪsiːz | *s.c.* e *i.* **1** MED. parálisis. **2** (fig.) parálisis, entorpecimiento, inmovilización, obstaculización.

paralytic | ˌpærə'lɪtɪk | *adj.* **1** MED. paralítico. **2** (brit. y fam.) muy borracho, totalmente ebrio (que se cae). || *s.c.* **3** MED. paralítico.

paramedic | ˌpærə'medɪk | *s.c.* auxiliar de médico (enfermero, auxiliar de clínica, conductor de ambulancia).

parameter | pə'ræmɪtər | *s.c.* (generalmente *pl.*) parámetro, límite establecido.

paramilitary | ˌpærə'mɪlɪtrɪ | *adj.* **1** paramilitar. || *s.c.* **2** paramilitar, miembro de banda paramilitar.

paramount | 'pærəmaʊnt | *adj.* **1** (form.) máximo, supremo, primero, primordial, capital: *of paramount importance = de capital importancia.* **2** principal, más importante, de rango superior (una persona). || *s.c.* **3** soberano, autoridad, gobernador.

paranoia | ˌpærə'nɔɪə | *s.i.* **1** MED. paranoia. **2** (fam.) paranoia, suspicacia, desconfianza, sospecha.

paranoiac, paranoic | ˌpærə'nɔɪæk | *adj.* MED. **1** paranoico. || *s.c.* **2** paranoico.

paranoid | 'pærənɔɪd | *adj.* **1** paranoico, paranoide, neurótico (una persona). **2** obsesivo (una idea, un sentimiento). || *s.c.* **3** MED. paranoico.

paranormal | ˌpærə'nɔːml | *adj.* paranormal, sobrenatural.

parapet | 'pærəpɪt | *s.c.* **1** parapeto, brocal. **2** MIL. parapeto.

paraphernalia | ˌpærəfə'neɪlɪə | *s.i.* **1** pertrechos, objetos personales, chismes, cachivaches, cosas: *all my paraphernalia = todos mis cachivaches.* **2** (brit. y fam.) parafernalia, burocracia, molestias. **3** DER. dote (de una mujer casada).

paraphrase | 'pærəfreɪz | *s.c.* **1** paráfrasis, explicación, interpretación, versión. || *v.t.* e *i.* **2** parafrasear.

paraplegia | ˌpærə'pliːdʒə | *s.i.* MED. paraplejía.

paraplegic | ˌpærə'pliːdʒɪk | *s.c.* MED. **1** parapléjico. || *adj.* **2** parapléjico.

parapsychology | ˌpærəsaɪ'kɒlədʒɪ | | ˌpærəsaɪ'kɑːlədʒɪ | *s.i.* parasicología.

parasite | 'pærəsaɪt | *s.c.* **1** BIOL. parásito. **2** (desp.) parásito, gorrón, oportunista.

parasitic, parasitical | ˌpærə'sɪtɪk | *adj.* parásito, parasitario: *a parasitic animal = un animal parásito.*

parasol | 'pærəsɒl | (EE.UU.) | 'pærəsɔːl | *s.c.* sombrilla, parasol, quitasol.

paratrooper | 'pærətruːpər | *s.c.* MIL. soldado paracaidista.

paratroops | 'pærətruːpz | *s.pl.* MIL. tropas paracaidistas.

parboil | 'pɑːbɔɪl | *v.t.* **1** sancochar, cocer parcialmente, cocer a medias. **2** (fig.) hacer sudar, someter a calor intenso.

parcel | 'pɑːsl | (EE.UU.) **package.** *s.c.* **1** paquete, bulto, envoltorio, lío, fardo. **2** DER. parcela, lote, porción (de tierra). **3** lote, partida (de mercancía). || *s.c.* e *i.* **4** montón, partida, grupo, conjunto, número: *a parcel of people = un montón de gente.* || *v.t.* **5 [to – out]** parcelar, dividir, fraccionar. **6 [to – up]** empaquetar, embalar, envolver. **7** MAR. precintar cabos.

parch | pɑːtʃ | *v.t.* e *i.* **1** tostar, torrar, asar. **2** secar, resecar, deshidratar, quemar, agostar: *plants were parched = las plantas estaban resecas.*

parched | 'pɑːtʃt | *adj.* **1** deshidratado, sediento. **2** reseco, seco, agostado.

parchment 'pɑːtʃmənt | *s.i.* **1** pergamino. || *s.c.* **2** escrito en pergamino. || *s.c.* e *i.* **3** papel pergamino.

pardon | 'pɑːdn | *s.c.* **1** DER. perdón, indulto, amnistía, gracia. **2** REL. indulgencia. || *s.c.* e *i.* **3 [– (for)]** (form. y arc.) perdón, excusas. || *v.t.* **4** perdonar, excusar, dispensar. || **5 to beg someone's –,** pedir perdón a alguien. **6 I beg your/his, etc. –/I do beg your –/–/– me,** lo siento, excúseme, perdone (al cometer un error al hablar, al pisar o empujar, etc.). **7 if you'll – the expresion,** (fam.) si me disculpa (al decir alguna rudeza). **8 pardon?/I beg your –?,** ¿cómo ha dicho? ¿cómo? (si no se ha entendido algo, o es sorprendente u ofensivo). **9 – me/I beg your –,** perdone que disienta, perdone que le contradiga. **10 – me for existing, etc.,** (fam.) gracias por dejarme vivir, etc. (en tono sarcástico). **11 – me for interrupting, etc./– me/– me interrupting,** perdone que le interrumpa. **12 – me/– my bluntness,** perdone, perdone mi brusquedad.

pardonable | 'pɑːdnəbl | *adj.* perdonable, excusable.

pare | peər | *v.t.* **1 [to – (down)]** cortar, recortar, rebajar: *she had her hair pared = se cortó un poco el pelo.* **2 [to – (down)]** reducir, recortar, rebajar (gastos). **3 [to – (away/off)]** pelar, mondar: quitar la corteza (de una fruta, del queso).

parent | 'peərənt | *s.c.* **1** padre, madre. **2** progenitor, ancestro. **3** (fig.) matriz, principal. **4** guardián, protector. **5** causa, origen.

parent-teacher association | ˌpeərənt'-tiːtʃəəsaʊˌsɪ'eiʃn | *s.c.* asociación de padres de alumnos y profesores (en cada escuela).

parentage | 'peərəntɪdʒ | *s.i.* **1** paternidad, origen, ascendencia, linaje. **2** origen, procedencia, derivación.

parental | pə'rentl | *adj.* paterno o materno, de los padres.

parentheses | pə'renθɪsiːz | V. **parenthesis.**

parenthesis | pə'renθɪsɪs | [*pl.* **parentheses**] *s.c.* **1** (brit. y form.) (generalmente *pl.*) corchete, llave. **2** paréntesis, intervalo.

parenthetical, parenthetic | ˌpærən'θetɪkl | *adj.* parentético, explicativo, aclarativo, entre paréntesis.

parenthetically | ˌpærən'θetɪkəlɪ | *adv.* entre paréntesis, a modo de aclaración, a modo de explicación.

parenthood | 'peərənthʊd | *s.i.* paternidad o maternidad.
parenting | 'peərəntɪŋ | *s.i.* cuidado de los hijos.
par excellence | ˌpɑːr'eksəlɑːns | *adj.* por excelencia, más típico.
pariah | 'pærɪə | | pə'raɪə | *s.c.* (form. y desp.) paria, desposeído.
paring | 'peərɪŋ | *s.c.* (generalmente *pl.*) peladura, mondadura, piel, desperdicio, cáscara, recorte.
parish | 'pærɪʃ | *s.c.* **1** REL. parroquia. **2** (brit.) parroquia, ayuntamiento, concejo: *the parish has 400 inhabitants = el ayuntamiento tiene 400 habitantes.* **3** parroquia, feligresía, comunidad. **4** (EE.UU.) condado (sólo en Luisiana).
parishioner | pə'rɪʃənər | *s.c.* feligrés, parroquiano.
Parisian | pə'rɪzjən | *s.c.* **1** parisino, parisién, parisiense. || *adj.* **2** parisino, parisiense.
parity | 'pærɪtɪ | *s.i.* paridad, igualdad, equivalencia.
park | pɑːk | *s.c.* **1** parque, jardines. **2** **[(the) –]** (brit. y argot) DEP. campo de fútbol, campo de deportes, estadio. **3** polígono, zona, parte: *industrial park = polígono industrial.* **4** (brit.) jardines, bosques, pastos (pertenecientes a una gran casa de campo). **5** MIL. parque (armamentístico). || *v.t.* e *i.* **6** aparcar, estacionar(se), (Am.) parquear (un vehículo). || *v.t.* **7** **[to – *o.* + *adv./prep.*]** aparcar, dejar, depositar, colocar: *park your books anywhere = deja los libros en cualquier parte.*
parka | pɑːkə | *s.c.* chaquetón largo acolchado con capucha, chaquetón esquimal.
parking | pɑːkɪŋ | *s.i.* **1** aparcamiento, estacionamiento (de un vehículo): *not much parking place = poco sitio para aparcar.* || **2 – lot,** (EE.UU.) zona de estacionamiento, aparcamiento. **3 – meter,** parquímetro, reloj de aparcamiento. **4 – ticket,** multa de aparcamiento.
Parkinson's disease | 'pɑːkɪnsndɪˌziːz | *s.i.* MED. enfermedad de Parkinson.
Parkinson's law | 'pɑːkɪnsnˌlɔː | *s.i.* (hum.) ley de Parkinson (la idea de que el trabajo se alarga para llenar el tiempo de que se dispone).
parkway | 'pɑːkweɪ | *s.c.* (EE.UU.) autopista, carretera (con plantas o árboles en el centro y los lados).
parky | pɑːkɪ | *adj.* (brit. y fam.) frío, helado, glacial.
parlance | 'pɑːləns | *s.i.* **1** (form.) lenguaje, jerga, forma de hablar, palabrería, terminología: *legal parlance = jerga legal.* || **2 in medical –,** según la terminología médica.
parley | 'pɑːlɪ | *s.c.* e *i.* **1** conversaciones, charlas, conferencia, parlamento (para llegar a un acuerdo dos grupos opuestos). || *v.i.* **2** parlamentar, conferenciar, discutir, mantener conversaciones.
parliament | 'pɑːləmənt | *s.c.* **1** parlamento (cuerpo legislativo, edificios). **2** período de tiempo parlamentario: *within this Parliament = en este período parlamentario.*
parliamentarian | ˌpɑːləmen'teərɪən | *s.c.* **1** parlamentario, miembro del Parlamento, diputado. **2** (brit.) HIST. partidario del Parlamento, oponente de Carlos I en la Guerra Civil. || *adj.* **3** parlamentario.
parliamentary | ˌpɑːlə'mentərɪ | *adj.* parlamentario.
parlour | 'pɑːlər | (EE.UU. **parlor**) *s.c.* **1** (EE.UU.) tienda, salón, sala, casa: *a beauty parlour = salón de belleza.* **2** (arc.) sala de estar, salón recibidor, sala de visitas (en una vivienda, un centro oficial). || **3 – game,** juego de salón, juego de mesa.
parlourmaid | 'pɑːləmeɪd | (EE.UU. **parlormaid**) *s.c.* camarera, doncella.
parlous | 'pɑːləs | *adj.* (form. o hum.) tambaleante, peligroso, lamentable, deplorable, atroz, crítico.
Parmesan | ˌpɑːmɪ'zæn | *s.i.* **1** queso parmesano. || *adj.* **2** parmesano, de Parma. || **3 – cheese,** queso parmesano.
parochial | pə'rəʊkɪəl | *adj.* **1** parroquial. **2** (desp.) provinciano, estrecho de miras, atrasado, ridículo.
parochialism | pə'rəʊkɪəlɪzəm | *s.i.* (desp.) provincianismo, estrechez de miras, atraso.
parodist | 'pærədɪst | *s.c.* parodista, humorista.
parody | 'pærədɪ | *s.c.* e *i.* **1** parodia. || *v.t.* **2** parodiar, imitar.
parole | pə'rəʊl | *s.i.* **1** DER. libertad bajo palabra, libertad condicional. **2** MIL. santo y seña. **3** palabra de honor, promesa. || *v.t.* **4** dar libertad bajo palabra, dar libertad condicional. || *adj.* **5** bajo palabra, condicional. || **6 to be on –,** estar en libertad bajo palabra.
paroxysm | 'pærəksɪzəm | *s.c.* **1** paroxismo, ataque, frenesí, arrebato. **2** MED. paroxismo.
parquet | 'pɑːkeɪ | (EE.UU.) | pɑːr'keɪ | *s.i.* **1** parquet, tarima, entarimado. || *s.c.* **2** platea (en un teatro). || *v.t.* **3** poner parquet, entarimar.
parricide | 'pærɪsaɪd | *s.i.* **1** parricidio. || *s.c.* **2** parricida.
parrot | 'pærət | *s.c.* **1** ZOOL. loro, papagayo, cotorra. **2** (fig. y desp.) loro, papagayo. || *v.t.* **3** (desp.) repetir como un papagayo, imitar como un loro, decir sin sentido. || **4 – fashion,** (desp.) mecánicamente, como un loro.
parry | 'pærɪ | *v.t.* **1** esquivar, parar, rechazar, evitar (un golpe, un ataque). **2** (fig.) rehuir, eludir, soslayar, evadir, evitar con habilidad (una respuesta). || *s.c.* **3** quite, parada. **4** evasiva, evasión.
parse | pɑːz | *v.t.* e *i.* **1** GRAM. analizar(se) (oraciones).
parsimonious | ˌpɑːsɪ'məʊnjəs | *adj.* (form. y desp.) ahorrativo, mesurado, cicatero, frugal, parco, sobrio.
parsimony | 'pɑːsɪmənɪ | *s.i.* (form. y desp.) ahorro, mesura, cicatería, frugalidad, sobriedad, parquedad.
parsley | 'pɑːslɪ | *s.i.* BOT. perejil.
parsnip | 'pɑːsnɪp | *s.c.* e *i.* chirivía.
parson | 'pɑːsn | *s.c.* **1** ministro, párroco, pastor (de la iglesia protestante). **2** (fam.) sacerdote, cura, párroco, vicario. || **3 parson's nose,** (EE.UU.) **pope's nose,** mitra, rabadilla, obispillo (de las aves).
parsonage | 'pɑːsnɪdʒ | *s.c.* (arc.) casa parroquial, casa del cura.
part | pɑːt | *s.c.* e *i.* **1** **[– (of)]** parte, pedazo, trozo, fragmento, segmento: *the last part of the book = la última parte del libro.* || *s.c.* **2** entrega, episodio, parte, capítulo, folletín: *a serial in three parts = un serial en tres capítulos.* **3** fascículo, número. **4** MEC. pieza, elemento. **5** parte, porción, medida (en recetas). **6** papel, rol: *he played the part of an old lady = hace el papel de una vieja dama.* **7** (EE.UU.) raya (del pelo). || *s.i.* **8** **[– (in)]** parte, participación, contribución, colaboración, intervención, responsabilidad: *he had great part in it = tuvo una gran responsabilidad en ello.* **9** lado, parte, partido (en una discusión). **10** DER. parte, parte litigante. **11** MUS. parte: *the mezzosoprano part = la parte de la mezzosoprano.* || *v.t.* e *i.* **12** (form.) separar(se), despedir(se), partir, abandonar: *they parted as friends = se separaron como amigos.* **13** separar, apartar (las cortinas), dividir, fragmentar, fraccionar. **14** disolver, disgregar, dispersar; hacerse a un lado (una multitud). || *v.t.* **15** peinarse con raya, hacerse la raya. **16** marchar, partir, salir. **17** morir, fallecer. || *adv.* **18** parcialmente, en parte. || *adj.* **19** parcial. || *prefijo.* **20** **[– *adj./s./v.*]** co-: *part-owner = copropietario.* || **21 a good /large – of,** una gran parte de, una buena parte de. **22 to do one's –,** cumplir con sus obligaciones, hacer lo que le toca a uno. **23 for one's –,** en lo que a uno respecta, por lo que a uno concierne. **24 for the most –,** por lo general, mayoritariamente, en su mayor parte; en la mayoría de los sitios. **25 in large –,** principalmente, mayormente. **26 in –,** parcialmente, hasta cierto punto, en parte. **27 in/round this parts/those parts,** (fam.) por aquí/allí, por estos/aquellos pagos, por esta/aquella parte del mundo. **28 more/greater than the sum of its parts,** más efectivo que la suma de sus partes. **29 on the – of,** (form.) de parte de, por parte de. **30 – and parcel,** parte esencial, elemento básico, parte integral. **31 to – company,** separarse, distanciarse; estar en desacuerdo, romper relaciones. **32 – of it is...,** en parte es..., parte de ello es... **33 – of speech,** GRAM. parte de la oración. **34 parts,** región, territorio, paraje, distrito; partes, genitales (externos). **35 to – with,** desprenderse de, deshacerse de, renunciar a, ceder, privarse de. **36 to play a –,** tomar parte, participar, contribuir. **37 to play a –/to play/act the – of,** (fig.) actuar como, desempeñar un papel, hacer el papel, fingir. **37 to take – in,** participar en, tomar parte en. **38 to take somebody's –,** ponerse del lado de alguien, tomar partido por alguien, apoyar a alguien, defender a alguien. **39 to take something in good –,** no ofenderse por algo, tomar algo a bien: *he took the criticism in good part = no se ofendió por la crítica.* **40 the best – of/the better – of, the gre-**

ater – of, la mayor parte de, casi todo: *for the best part of this year = casi todo este año.* **41 to want no – of/in,** no querer tener parte de/en, rechazar.

partake | pɑː'teɪk | *v.* [*irr.pret.* **partook,** *p.p.* **partaken**] *t.* e *i.* (arc.) **1 [to – (in)]** participar, tomar parte (en una actividad). || *v.i.* **2 [to – (of)]** (hum.) beber, comer, tomar, consumir. **3** tener algo de, tener rasgos de (una cualidad).

partial | 'pɑːʃl | *adj.* **1** parcial, incompleto, insuficiente, no total. **2** (desp.) parcial, sin objetividad. **3 [– to]** (fam.) aficionado a, con gusto por, con predilección por: *she is very partial to ice-cream = es muy aficionada a los helados.* || *s.i.* **4** MUS. tono parcial. **5** MAT. diferencial parcial.

partiality | ˌpɑːʃɪ'ælɪtɪ | *s.i.* **1** (desp.) parcialidad, falta de objetividad, partidismo. **2 [– for]** predilección por, inclinación hacia, afición por, gusto por: *her partiality for antiques = su afición a las antigüedades.*

partially | 'pɑːʃəlɪ | *adv.* **1** parcialmente, en parte. **2** con parcialidad, de forma partidista.

participant | pɑː'tɪsɪpənt | *s.c.* **1** participante, concursante. || *adj.* **2** participante, partícipe.

participate | pɑː'tɪsɪpeɪt | *v.i.* **1 [to – (in)]** (form.) participar, tomar parte, intervenir, unirse. || *v.t.* **2** tomar, beber, comer, consumir.

participation | pɑːˌtɪsɪ'peɪʃn | *s.i.* **[– (in)]** participación, intervención.

participatory | pɑːˌtɪsɪ'peɪtərɪ | *adj.* participativo, participante, partícipe.

participial | ˌpɑːtɪ'sɪpɪəl | *adj.* GRAM. participial.

participle | 'pɑːtɪsɪpl | *s.c.* GRAM. participio.

particle | 'pɑːtɪkl | *s.c.* **1** partícula, gránulo, brizna. **2** (fig.) pizca, ápice, parte, traza: *not a particle of doubt = ni un ápice de duda.* **3** GRAM. partícula. **4** REL. partícula (consagrada). **5** (arc.) cláusula, artículo (de un documento).

particular | pə'tɪkjʊlər | *adj.* **1** [no *comp.*] particular, especial, singular, peculiar, raro, excepcional. **2** [no *comp.*] particular, individual, determinado, específico, concreto, diferenciador. **3 [– (about/ over)]** exigente, fastidioso, quisquilloso, extravagante, raro, delicado. **4** minucioso, detallado, exacto, cuidadoso, escrupuloso. **5** FIL. particular, privativo. || *s.c.* **6** (generalmente *pl.*) particular, detalle, parte, pormenor. **7** FIL. proposición particular. || **8 anything/anyone in –,** algo o alguien en particular, algo o alguien en especial. **9 in –,** en particular, particularmente, especialmente. **10 nothing/nobody in –,** nada o nadie en particular, nada o nadie importante.

particularize | pə'tɪkjʊləraɪz | (brit. **particularise**) *v.t.* e *i.* (form.) particularizar, pormenorizar, detallar, especificar, concretar.

particularly | pə'tɪkjʊləlɪ | *adv.* en particular, particularmente, especialmente, expresamente.

parting | 'pɑːtɪŋ | *s.c.* e *i.* **1** división, separación, distribución, segmentación, repartición. **2** despedida, partida. || *s.c.* **3** (brit.) raya (del pelo). || *adj.* **4** de despedida, final: *a parting present = un regalo de despedida.* || **5 a – of the ways,** el momento de la separación, el momento de las despedidas. **6 – shot,** corte, punto y final (en una discusión, una conversación).

partisan | ˌpɑːtɪ'zæn | | 'pɑːrtəzən | (EE.UU.) | 'pɑːrtɪzn | *adj.* **1** (desp.) partidista, parcial (una opinión, una actitud). **2** de partisanos, de guerrilleros. || *s.c.* **3** MIL. partisano, guerrillero. **4** militante, partidario, afecto.

partition | pɑː'tɪʃn | *s.c.* **1** tabique, pared, mampara. **2** parte, sección, compartimento. || *s.i.* **3 [– (into)]** partición, división, fragmentación, distribución, reparto. **4** FIL. partición, división. || *v.t.* **5 [to – (into)]** dividir, fragmentar, demarcar, seccionar. **6 [to – off]** dividir, separar, poner tabiques.

partitive | 'pɑːtɪtɪv | *s.c.* **1** GRAM. partitivo. || *adj.* **2** partitivo.

partly | 'pɑːtlɪ | *adv.* parcialmente, en parte, en cierto modo, hasta cierto punto.

partner | 'pɑːtnər | *s.c.* **1** compañero, pareja (de juegos, de baile). **2** COM. socio, accionista, asociado. **3** compañero, cónyuge, esposo, consorte. **4** cómplice, compinche. **5** (EE.UU. y fam.) amigo, camarada (para dirigirse amistosamente a alguien). || *v.t.* **6** acompañar. **7** emparejar. || *v.i.* **8 [to – (up/with)]** formar pareja, emparejarse.

partnership | 'pɑːtnəʃɪp | *s.i.* **1** asociación, sociedad, consorcio. || *s.c.* COM. sociedad.

partook | pɑː'tʊk | *pret.* de **partake.**

partridge | 'pɑːtrɪdʒ | [*pl.* **partridges** o **partridge**] *s.c.* ZOOL. perdiz.

part-singing | 'pɑːtˌsɪŋɪŋ | *s.i.* MUS. canto a varias voces, canto coral.

part-time | 'pɑːtˌtaɪm | *adj.* **1** a tiempo parcial, por horas, de media jornada (una actividad). || *adv.* **2** a tiempo parcial, por horas, de media jornada: *I work part-time = trabajo por horas.*

part-timer | 'pɑːtˌtaɪmər | *s.c.* trabajador por horas.

partway | 'pɑːtˌweɪ | *adv.* (fam.) parcialmente, hasta un punto, a medias.

party | 'pɑːtɪ | *s.c.* **1** fiesta, celebración, guateque, reunión, velada. **2** [– *v.sing./pl.*] grupo, partida, banda, cuadrilla: *a rescue party = un grupo de rescate.* **3** MIL. pelotón, destacamento. **4** [– *v.sing./pl.*] POL. partido, grupo. **5** DER. parte, interesado, tercero. **6** (fam.) persona, individuo, sujeto, tipo: *a nice party = un tipo estupendo.* **7** (argot) coito, cópula. **8** (argot) orgía, desenfreno. || *v.i.* **9** (EE.UU. y fam.) hacer una fiesta, hacer un guateque, celebrar una fiesta, divertirse en una fiesta. || *adj.* **10** de fiesta, de gala. **11** de partido. || **12 to be a – to/to be – to,** tener parte en, mezclarse en; DER. ser cómplice de; firmar (un acuerdo). **13 – line,** línea oficial del partido, línea ideológica; linea telefónica colectiva (para varios abonados). **14 – piece,** (fam. y hum.) gracia, representación de costumbre (chiste, poema, canción que alguien siempre hace en una fiesta). **15 – political broadcast,** TV. minutos de propaganda electoral (en período electoral). **16 – politics,** (desp.) actividades electoralistas de partido, politiqueo, partidismo (para conseguir más votos). **17 – wall,** pared medianera, pared común, pared divisoria (entre dos viviendas).

parvenu | 'pɑːvənjuː | *s.c.* (gen. desp.) nuevo rico, arribista, advenedizo.

pas de deux | pɑːdədəː | *s.c.* paso de dos, variación (en ballet).

pass | pɑːs | (EE.UU.) | pæs | *v.t.* e *i.* **1 [to – (by)]** pasar por delante, circular por; cruzarse. **2** mover(se), circular, pasar. **3** convertir(se), pasar a ser. **4** (fig.) intercambiar (palabras). **5** pasar, cruzar, atravesar, traspasar (fronteras, límites). **6** DEP. pasar, hacer un pase. **7** aceptar, aprobar, pasar (una ley, un examen). **8** pasar, transcurrir (el tiempo). **9** pasar, gastar (el tiempo). **10** DER. pronunciar sentencia, dictar sentencia. || *v.t.* **11 [to – (to)]** pasar, dar, entregar. **12** pasar por, atravesar, transcurrir (un río, una carretera). **13** poner en circulación, pasar (dinero generalmente falso). **14 [to – (on/upon)]** expresar, exponer, dar (una opinión). **15** pasar por alto, dejar de lado. **16** (form.) evacuar, segregar (del cuerpo). **17** exceder, ir más allá, sobrepasar. || *v.i.* **18 [to – +** *adv./prep.* **(from/to/to)]** pasar a ser, convertirse en, cambiar a. **19 [to – +** *adv./prep.* **(to/into)]** pasar, ir a parar, ser transferido: *the property passed to his daughter = la propiedad pasó a su hija.* **20** pasar (en juegos de cartas). **21** morir, fallecer, expirar, dejar de existir. || *s.c.* **22** pase, pasada; MIL. vuelo rasante (sobre un objetivo). **23** certificado, papeleta (de notas). **24** aprobado. **25** DEP. pase (de pelota); pase, finta (en boxeo, esgrima). **26** desfiladero, paso de montaña. **27** (fam.) situación crítica, estado de penuria, aprieto. **28** paso, fase: *the first pass was easy = el primer paso fue fácil.* **29** salvoconducto, pase; MIL. permiso, autorización; entrada de favor; carnet de admisión. **30** pase (en juegos de cartas). || **31 to come to –,** (arc.) suceder, ocurrir, acontecer. **32 to let something –,** dejar pasar algo, no hacer caso de algo, pasar algo por alto. **33 to make a –,** echar un tiento, hacer proposiciones amorosas. **34 –/I –,** paso (en juegos de cartas). **35 to – as/for somebody,** pasar por alguien, ser considerado como, ser aceptado como. **36 to – away/on,** (euf.) morir, fallecer, expirar, terminar. **37 to – the buck,** V. **buck. 38 to – by/over,** dejar de lado, olvidarse de, no hacer caso de; pasar de largo. **39 to – down/on,** pasar, transmitir (de uno a otro). **40 to – judgement,** V. **judgement. 41 to – muster,** V. **muster. 42 to – off,** transcurrir, terminar (un acto); hacerse pasar por, fingir ser. **43 to – on, a)** (euf.) morir, expirar, terminar; **b)** transmitir, pasar (de uno a otro); **c)** cambiar, pasar (a otro tema). **44 to –**

out, a) (fam.) desmayarse, perder el conocimiento; **b)** (brit.) graduarse, terminar un curso, finalizar un curso (en una escuela militar); **c)** distribuir, repartir, pasar. **45 to – over,** dejar de lado, olvidarse de, postergar. **46 to – up,** perder, dejar pasar (una oportunidad). **47 to – water,** (form.) orinar, evacuar. **48 to – word,** V. **word.**

passable | 'pɑːsəbl | *adj.* **1** pasable, aceptable, tolerable, adecuado. **2** transitable; vadeable: *a passable road = una carretera transitable.* **3** corriente, admitido, autorizado (dinero).

passably | 'pɑːsəblɪ | *adv.* adecuadamente, pasaderamente, medianamente.

passage | 'pæsɪdʒ | *s.c.* **1** pasillo, galería, corredor, pasaje, pasadizo, callejón. **2** MED. conducto, tubo, canal: *nasal passage = tubo nasal.* **3 [– (through)]** paso, camino (entre la gente). **4 [– (from/to)]** pasaje (precio de viaje); travesía, viaje, trayecto (en avión, en barco). **5** LIT. pasaje, episodio, parte. || *s.i.* **6 [– (of)]** (form.) tránsito, circulación, tráfico, cruce, paso; acceso, permiso de paso. **7** promulgación, aprobación (de una ley). **8** paso, transcurso (del tiempo). **9** (arc.) muerte, fallecimiento. **10** intercambio (de palabras, saludos). **11** incidente, lance (de armas). **12** MED. evacuación, defecación, deposición. || **13 to work one's –,** conseguir pasaje a cambio de trabajo en el barco.

passageway | 'pæsɪdʒˌweɪ | *s.c.* pasillo, galería, corredor, pasaje, pasadizo, callejón.

passé | 'pæːseɪ | (EE.UU.) | pæ'seɪ | *adj.* **1** (desp.) pasado de moda, anticuado. **2** en decadencia, marchito (una persona).

passenger | 'pæsɪndʒər | *s.c.* **1** pasajero, viajero. **2** (brit. y desp.) parásito, aprovechado, caradura: *several passengers in the team = varios caraduras en el equipo.*

passerby | ˌpɑːsə'baɪ | *s.c.* peatón, viandante, transeúnte.

passim | 'pæsɪm | *adv.* frecuentemente, en varios lugares (en índices de libros).

passing | 'pɑːsɪŋ | , (EE.UU.) | 'pæsɪŋ | *s.i.* **1** paso, transcurso, el pasar: *the passing of the time = el paso del tiempo.* **2** desaparición, supresión. **3** (euf.) muerte, desaparición, fallecimiento. || *adj.* **4** que pasa, que circula. **5** breve, efímero, corto, fugaz, pasajero, transitorio. || **6 in –,** de pasada, de paso. **7 with each – day/with every – week,** conforme pasan los días o las semanas, a cada día o semana que pasa, andando los días o las semanas. || *adv.* **8** (arc.) muy, sobremanera, sumamente.

passion | 'pæʃn | *s.c.* e *i.* **1** pasión, ardor, delirio, frenesí, amor, fervor. **2** pasión, deseo, lujuria. **3** cólera, ira, furia, indignación. **4** *sing.* ataque de cólera, arranque de furia. **5** *s.sing.* **[– for]** (fam.) pasión por, amor por, entusiasmo por (algo): *his passion for music = su amor por la música.* || **6 (the) Passion,** REL. (la) Pasión. **7 – fruit,** granadilla. **8 – play,** REL. drama de la Pasión de Cristo.

passionate | 'pæʃənət | *adj.* **1** apasionado, ferviente, ardiente, amoroso. **2** vehemente, entusiasta, enardecido: *passionate words = palabras entusiastas.* **3** intenso, grande, profundo. **4** colérico, airado, irascible.

passionately | 'pæʃənətlɪ | *adv.* **1** apasionadamente, ardientemente, con frenesí. **2** apasionadamente, vehementemente.

passive | 'pæsɪv | *adj.* **1** (generalmente desp.) pasivo, paciente, resignado. **2** inerte, inactivo. **3** pasiva, no activa (resistencia). **4** [no *comp.*] GRAM. pasivo. **5** COM. pasivo, que no devenga intereses. || *s.i.* **6 [the –]** GRAM. la voz pasiva, la pasiva.

passively | 'pæsɪvlɪ | *adv.* pasivamente, pacientemente, resignadamente.

passiveness | 'pæsɪvnɪs | V. **passivity.**

passivity | pæ'sɪvɪtɪ | *s.i.* (generalmente desp.) pasividad, inactividad, inmovilidad, inercia.

passivize | 'pæsɪvaɪz | (brit. **passivise**) *v.t.* e *i.* GRAM. convertir en voz pasiva, pasar a pasiva.

Passover | 'pɑːsˌəuvər | *s.i.* REL. Pascua judía.

passport | 'pɑːspɔːt | (EE.UU.) | 'pæspɔːt | *s.c.* **1** pasaporte; salvoconducto. **2 [– (to)]** (fig.) pasaporte, catapulta: *beauty as a passport to fame = la belleza como pasaporte a la fama.*

password | 'pɑːswɔːd | (EE.UU.) | 'pæswɔːrd | *s.c.* **1** MIL. santo, seña y contraseña. **2** INF. contraseña, clave, código de entrada.

past | pɑːst | (EE.UU.) | pæst | *adj.* **1** pasado, anterior, antiguo, último: *in past months = en estos últimos meses.* **2** pasado, transcurrido, finalizado, concluido: *problems were now past = los problemas habían terminado.* **3** anterior, ex, previo, precedente: *his past wife = su anterior esposa.* **4** GRAM. pasado, pretérito. || *prep.* **5** más allá de, una vez pasado: *past the bank = más allá del banco.* **6** más de, más allá de: *she's past 45 = tiene más de 45 años.* **7** y, después de, más de (con las horas): *quarter past seven = las siete y cuarto.* **8** más de, más allá de, sin: *past my understanding = incomprensible.* || *s.c.* **9 [(the) –]** (el) pasado, otros tiempos, historia: *in the past = en el pasado, antiguamente.* **10 [(the) –]** GRAM. pasado, pretérito. **11** (arc. y desp.) pasado, antecedentes, historia: *he had a strange past = tenía un extraño pasado.* || *adv.* **12** más allá, por delante, de un lado a otro: *they went past runing = se adelantaron corriendo.* || **13 to be – it,** (fam.) ya no está para eso, ya no puede, ya se le ha pasado la edad. **14 not to put it – someone,** creer a alguien capaz hasta de eso, no poner la mano en el fuego por alguien. **15 – master,** experto, gran conocedor, maestro. **16 – participle,** GRAM. participio pasado. **17 – perfect,** GRAM. pretérito pluscuamperfecto. **18 – tense,** GRAM. tiempo pasado.

pasta | 'pæstə | (EE.UU.) | 'pɑːstə | *s.i.* pasta (macarrones, tallarines).

paste | peɪst | *s.c.* e *i.* **1** pasta, masa. **2** engrudo, goma. **3** pasta, crema, puré: *salmon paste = crema de salmón.* **4** vidrio para fabricar bisutería. **5** (argot) puñetazo, bofetada. || *v.t.* **6 [to – *adv./prep.*]** pegar, engomar, encolar. **7** (argot) abofetear, pegar un puñetazo, pegar un guantazo.

pastel | 'pæstel | (EE.UU.) | pæ'stel | *s.c.* e *i.* **1** pastel, clarioncillo. || *s.c.* **2** pintura al pastel, dibujo al pastel. **3** color pastel. **4** bosquejo literario, trabajo breve en prosa. || *adj.* **5** al pastel. **6** de color pastel.

pasteurization | ˌpɑːstʃəraɪ'zeɪʃn | (EE.UU.) | ˌpæstʃərɪ'zeɪʃn | *s.i.* pasteurización.

pasteurize | 'pæːstʃəraɪz | (EE.UU.) | 'pæstʃəraɪz | (brit. **pasteurise**) *v.t.* pasteurizar.

pasteurized | 'pæːstʃəraɪzd | (EE.UU.) | 'pæstʃəraɪzd | *adj.* pasteurizado.

pastiche | pæ'stiːʃ | *s.c.* e *i.* MUS. pastiche, imitación, parodia, remedo.

pastille | 'pæstɪl | *s.c.* pastilla, tableta (generalmente medicinal).

pastime | 'pɑːstaɪm | (EE.UU.) | 'pæstaɪm | *s.c.* pasatiempo, interés, afición.

pasting | 'peɪstɪŋ | *s.sing.* (fam.) **1** paliza, rapapolvo, repaso, palo: *they gave him quite a pasting = le echaron un buen rapapolvo.* **2** DEP. paliza, zurra.

pastor | 'pɑːstər | (EE.UU.) | 'pæstə | *s.c.* **1** REL. pastor protestante, párroco, cura, sacerdote. **2** (p.u.) pastor, ovejero, zagal.

pastoral | 'pɑːstərəl | (EE.UU.) | 'pæstərəl | *adj.* **1** REL. pastoral, sacerdotal. **2** (lit.) pastoril, bucólico. **3** de pasto, con pasto (una tierra). **4** campestre, rústico, rural. || *s.c.* **5 – letter,** carta pastoral, pastoral.

pastrami | pæ'strɑːmɪ | *s.i.* (EE.UU.) buey ahumado y muy sazonado (plato judío-rumano).

pastry | 'peɪstrɪ | *s.i.* **1** pasta, masa. || *s.c.* **2** pasta, pastel, tartaleta, empanada.

pasture | 'pɑːstʃər | (EE.UU.) | 'pæstʃər | *s.c.* e *i.* **1** pasto, hierba, forraje; prado, dehesa, pastizal. || *v.t.* **2** apacentar, pastorear, llevar a pacer, llevar a pastar. || *v.i.* **3 [to – (on)]** pastar, pacer. || **4 out to –,** a pacer, al prado. **5 pastures new,/greener/lusher pastures,** nuevas experiencias, nuevos horizontes, aires más frescos. **6 to put someone out to –,** (fam.) retirarse, jubilarse (forzosamente).

pastureland | 'pɑːstʃəlænd | (EE.UU.) | 'pæstʃərlænd | *s.i.* pastizal, prado, dehesa.

pasty | 'peɪstɪ | *s.c.* **1** empanadilla. || | 'peɪstɪ | *adj.* **2** pálido, paliducho, anémico, cadavérico, descolorido (la cara).

pat | pæt | *s.c.* **1** golpecito, palmadita, palmada. **2** [normalmente *sing.*] ruido de palmadas, ruido de pasos. **3 [– (for)]** bola, nuez, pedacito, trocito (de mantequilla). || *v.t.* **4** dar una palmadita, golpear ligeramente, acariciar, pasar la mano: *patting the cat = acariciando al gato.* **5** aplastar con golpecitos, moldear con la palma: *she patted the pastry = moldeó la masa con la palma de la mano.* || *adv.* **6** (generalmente desp.) sin vacilación, rotundamente, con prontitud, al instante. || *adj.* **7** (generalmente desp.) rápido, rotundo, pronto, oportuno. || **8 a – on the back,** (fam.) una palmadita en la espalda, una felicitación, un elogio. **9 to have/know something off –,** saberse algo al dedillo, saberse algo de memoria. **10 to – somebody on the back,** (fam.) elogiar a alguien, felicitar a alguien, alabar a alguien.

patch | 'pætʃ | *s.c.* **1** mancha, lunar, trozo, parte, porción. **2** parche, remiendo, plastrón. **3** parcela, cuadro, sembrado (de un producto). **4** parche de ojo. **5** (brit. y fam.) zona, distrito, área, territorio (policial). **6** fragmento, pasaje, trozo. || *v.t.* **7** parchear, remendar. || **8 a bad/sticky –,** (brit.) un mal momento, un período de mala suerte. **9 in patches,** por parte, a trozos. **10 not to be a – on,** no estar a la altura de, no poderse comparar con. **11 to – together,** recomponer, formar. **12 to – up,** hacer las paces; poner un parche, remendar, componer, arreglar; (fig.) MED. curar.

patchwork | 'pætʃwɜːk | *s.c.* e *i.* **1** labor hecha a base de retazos de distintos colores. **2** (fig.) mezcolanza, batiburrillo, combinación.

patchy | 'pætʃɪ | *adj.* **1** desigual, irregular, a trozos. **2** (generalmente desp.) incompleto, defectuoso, insuficiente. **3** remendado, de remiendos.

pate | peɪt | *s.i.* (arc. y fam.) **1** coronilla, cráneo. **2** cerebro, mollera, sesera.

pâté | 'pæteɪ | (EE.UU.) | pɑː'teɪ | *s.i.* paté, pastel de hígado; pasta de pescado.

patella | pə'telə | *s.c.* ANAT. rótula.

paten | 'pætən | *s.c.* patena.

patent | 'peɪtənt | | 'pætənt | (EE.UU.) | 'pætnt | *adj.* **1** (form.) patente, obvio, evidente, manifiesto. **2** COM. potentado, de patente, con marca registrada; de patentes: *patent law = ley de patentes.* **3** (fam.) ingenioso, hábil, genial. || *s.c.* **4** COM. patente, marca registrada. **5** título de propiedad (de una tierra). || *v.t.* **6** patentar. || **7 – medicine,** medicamento de patente; elixir, curatodo, medicina de curanderos.

patented | 'peɪtəntɪd | *adj.* patentado, registrado.

patentee | ɪpeɪtən'tɪ | *s.c.* poseedor de una patente.

patently | 'peɪtəntlɪ | *adv.* patentemente, claramente, manifiestamente, obviamente.

paterfamilias | ˌpeɪtəfə'mɪlɪæs | (EE.UU.) | ˌpætəfə'mɪlɪæs | *s.c.* (form.) paterfamilias, patriarca.

paternal | pə'tɜːnl | *adj.* **1** paternal, paterno. **2** (desp.) paternalista, paternal.

paternalism | pə'tɜːnəlɪzəm | *s.i.* (desp.) paternalismo.

paternalist | pə'tɜːnəlɪst | *s.c.* **1** (desp.) paternalista. || *adj.* **2** paternalista.

paternalistic | pə'tɜːnəlɪstɪk | *adj.* (desp.) paternalista.

paternally | pə'tɜːnəlɪ | *adv.* paternalmente.

paternity | pə'tɜːnɪtɪ | *s.i.* DER. **1** paternidad: *paternity test = prueba de paternidad.* **2** (form.) paternidad, condición paterna, ascendencia paterna. **3** (fig.) autoría, origen, paternidad (de una obra). || **4 – leave,** licencia de paternidad. **5 – suit,** DER. investigación de paternidad.

paternoster | ˌpætə'nɒstər | *s.c.* **1** REL. padrenuestro, paternóster. **2** undécima cuenta del rosario. **3** jaculatoria, ruego; hechizo, conjuro. **4** ascensor, elevador, montacargas (de varios compartimentos que suben y bajan lentamente).

path | pɑːθ | (EE.UU.) | pæθ | *s.c.* **1** camino, sendero, senda, vereda. **2** (fig.) camino, trayectoria, senda, vía: *the path of success = el camino del éxito.* **3 [– (of)]** curso, trayectoria, ruta (de un proyectil, de un huracán). || **4** *abreviatura* de **pathological, patho-;** *a neuropath = neurólogo.* || **5 to cross someone's –/one's paths cross,** tropezar con alguien, cruzarse con alguien.

pathetic | pə'θetɪk | *adj.* **1** patético, conmovedor, impresionante, lastimoso. **2** (desp.) inútil, inservible, ineficaz, inadecuado: *pathetic efforts = esfuerzos inútiles.*

pathetically | pə'θetɪkɪlɪ | *adv.* patéticamente, lastimosamente, de forma conmovedora.

pathfinder | 'pɑːθˌfaɪndər | *s.c.* **1** explorador, guía. **2** descubridor, inventor.

pathological | ˌpæθə'lɒdʒɪkl | *adj.* **1** MED. patológico, patógeno, morboso. **2** (fam.) patológico, compulsivo, irracional.

pathologist | pə'θɒlɒdʒɪst | *s.c.* MED. patólogo.

pathology | pə'θɒlədʒɪ | *s.i.* MED. patología.

pathos | 'peɪθɒs | *s.i.* (lit.) pathos, patetismo, lo patético.

pathway | 'pɑːθweɪ | *s.c.* sendero, camino, vereda, senda.

patience | 'peɪʃns | *s.i.* **1** paciencia, perseverancia, aguante. **2** resignación, entereza, calma, tolerancia. **3** solitario (juego de cartas). || **4 to try someone's –,** acabar con la paciencia de alguien, impacientar a alguien.

patient | 'peɪʃnt | *adj.* **1** paciente, tolerante, sufrido. **2** paciente, comprensivo, tranquilo, sosegado: *a patient waiting = una espera paciente.* **3** perseverante, constante: *a patient worker = un trabajador constante.* || *s.c.* **4** MED. paciente, enfermo.

patiently | 'peɪʃntlɪ | *adv.* **1** pacientemente, de forma tolerante, perseverantemente. **2** pacientemente, tranquilamente, con calma.

patina | 'pætɪnə | *s.i.* **1** pátina, brillo, lustre. **2** (fig.) pátina, capa, lustre.

patio | 'pætɪəʊ | [*pl.* **patios**] *s.c.* **1** patio (zona no verde, sino enlosada, de un jardín). || **2 – doors,** puertas acristaladas.

patisserie | pə'tiːsərɪ | *s.c.* e *i.* pastelería de estilo francés.

patois | 'pætwɑː | [*pl.* **patois**] | 'pætwɑːz | *s.c.* e *i.* dialecto.

patriarch | 'peɪtrɪɑːk | *s.c.* **1** patriarca, anciano venerable. **2** REL. (arc.) obispo; patriarca.

patriarchal | ˌpeɪtrɪ'ɑːkl | *adj.* **1** patriarcal, gobernado por hombres: *a patriarchal society = una sociedad patriarcal.* **2** patriarcal, venerable.

patriarchy | 'peɪtrɪɑːkɪ | *s.c.* e *i.* patriarcado.

patrician | pə'trɪʃn | *s.c.* **1** HIST. patricio. **2** (generalmente desp.) patricio, aristócrata, noble. || *adj.* **3** HIST. patricio. **4** (generalmente desp.) aristocrático, noble.

patricide | 'pætrɪsaɪd | *s.i.* **1** DER. parricidio. || *s.c.* **2** parricida.

patrimony | 'pætrɪmənɪ | (EE.UU.) | 'pætrɪməʊnɪ | *s.i.* (form.) patrimonio, herencia, posesiones.

patriot | 'pætrɪət | (EE.UU.) | 'pe ɪtrɪət | *s.c.* patriota.

patriotic | ˌpætrɪ'ɒtɪk | (EE.UU.) | ˌpe ɪtrɪ'ɒtɪk | *adj.* patriótico.

patriotically | ˌpætrɪ'ɒtɪklɪ | *adv.* patrióticamente.

patriotism | 'pætrɪətɪzəm | *s.i.* patriotismo, lealtad a la patria.

patrol | pə'trəʊl | *s.i.* **1** patrulla, vigilancia, ronda. | *s.c.* **2 [–** *v.sing./pl.***]** patrulla de vigilancia. **3 [–** *v.sing./pl.***]** grupo de exploradores, grupo de guías. || *v.t.* e *i.* **4** patrullar, vigilar, defender. || **5 – car,** coche patrulla (de policía).

patrolman | pə'trəʊlmæn | [*pl.* **patrolmen**] *s.c.* **1** (EE.UU.) agente de policía, agente de seguridad. **2** (brit.) empleado de una asociación de ayuda en carretera.

patron | 'peɪtrən | [*f.* **patroness**] *s.c.* **1 [– (of)]** benefactor, protector, defensor: *a patron of the arts = un protector del arte.* **2** patrocinador, mecenas. **3** (form.) cliente, comprador, consumidor, parroquiano. **4** patrón, dueño: *the patron of the restaurant = el dueño del restaurante.* || **5 – saint,** patrono, santo patrón.

patronage | 'pætrənɪdʒ | *s.i.* **1** patrocinio, patronazgo, mecenazgo, protección. **2** defensa, apoyo, protección. **3** influencia política, enchufe, prebendas. **4** clientela, parroquianos, consumidores.

patroness | 'peɪtrənɪs | V. **patron.**

patronize | 'pætrənaɪz | (EE.UU.) | 'peɪtrənaɪz | (brit. **patronise**) *v.t.* **1** (desp.) tratar con aire protector, tratar condescendientemente, hablar con altivez, tratar como a un inferior. **2** (form.) frecuentar, ser cliente de, comprar en. **3** patrocinar, apoyar, ayudar, beneficiar.

patronizing | 'pætrənaɪzɪŋ | (brit. **patronising**) *adj.* **1** (desp.) condescendiente, protector.

patronizingly | 'pætrənaɪzɪŋlɪ | (brit. **patronisingly**) *adv.* condescendientemente, con aire protector.

patsy | 'pætsɪ | *s.c.* (argot) simplón, tonto, poco espabilado, panoli.

patter | 'pætər | *v.i.* **1 [to –** *adv./prep.***]** golpear, golpetear, repiquetear, tamborilear: *the rain pattered on the roof = la lluvia golpeteaba sobre el tejado.* **2** andar con ruido ligero, andar a pasitos con ruido sordo: *a cat pattering = el ruido del gato al corretear.* || *v.t.* e *i.* **3** parlotear, borbollar, parlar. **4** rezar mecánicamente, musitar oraciones de forma autómata. || *s.sing.* **5 [– (of)]** tamborileo, repiqueteo, golpeteo. || *s.i.* **6** parloteo, cháchara, palique. **7** jerga, lenguaje, habla: *doctor's patter = jerga médica.* || **8 the – of tiny feet,** (hum.) sonidos infantiles, pasitos infantiles.

pattern | 'pætən | *s.c.* e *i.* **1** dibujo, estampado, motivo. **2** diseño, configuración, esquema: *gramatical pattern = esquema gramatical.* || *s.c.* **3** pauta, regla, línea, norma: *patterns of behaviour = pautas de comportamiento.* **4** modelo, muestra, molde, diagrama, plano. **5** patrón (de costura). **6** (EE.UU.) corte de tela. || *v.t.* **7 [to – (with)]** estampar, dibujar, decorar, adornar. **8 [to –** *adv./prep.* **after/on/upon]** (form.) imitar, hacer a imagen y semejanza de, copiar de, basar en.

patterned | 'pætənd | *adj.* estampado, decorado, con dibujos.

patterning | 'pætənɪŋ | *s.i.* **1** (form.) formación de pautas de comportamiento, adiestramiento, habituación. **2** marcas, manchas (en la piel de un animal).

patty | 'pætɪ | *s.c.* **1** (EE.UU.) empanadilla, pastelito de carne. **2** hamburguesa, filete ruso. **3** pastilla, caramelo.

paucity | 'pɔːsətɪ | *s.sing.* (form.) escasez, falta, carencia, penuria, insuficiencia: *paucity of resources = escasez de recursos.*

paunch | pɔːntʃ | *s.c.* (desp.) panza, barriga, tripa.

paunchy | 'pɔːntʃɪ | *adj.* (desp.) panzudo, barrigudo, tripudo.

pauper | 'pɔːpər | *s.c.* (arc.) pobre, mendigo, indigente.

pauperism | 'pɔːpərɪzəm | *s.i.* pobreza, indigencia, mendicidad, pauperismo.

pauperize | 'pɔːpəraɪz | *v.t.* depauperar, empobrecer, arruinar, reducir a la miseria.

pause | pɔːz | *s.c.* **1** pausa, alto, parada (en el trabajo). **2** pausa, silencio, vacilación, titubeo, incertidumbre: *a pause in her speech = un silencio en su discurso.* **3** MUS. pausa. **4** LIT. pausa, cesura. || *v.i.* **5** hacer una pausa, callar, parar. **6** pararse, detenerse, suspender (una actividad). || **7 to give one –,** (form.) dar que pensar a uno, hacer dudar a uno, hacer vacilar a uno.

pave | peɪv | *v.t.* **1 [to – (with)]** pavimentar, asfaltar, losar, empedrar. || **2 to – the way,** (fig.) preparar el terreno, allanar el camino. **3 paved with gold,** (un camino) empedrado de oro (facilidad para enriquecerse).

paved | peɪvd | *adj.* pavimentado, asfaltado, losado, empedrado.

pavement | 'peɪvmənt | *s.c.* **1** (brit.) acera. || *s.c.* e *i.* **2** (EE.UU.) calzada. **3** pavimento, asfalto, pavimentación. || **4 – artist,** pintor de aceras, artista callejero.

pavilion | pə'vɪlɪən | *s.c.* **1** DEP. caseta, vestuario. **2** pabellón, tienda de campaña, dosel (en fiestas y ferias, como protección o para exhibición). **3** pabellón, anexo, ala (de un edificio). **4** quiosco, cenador (en un parque, en una casa de campo).

paving | 'peɪvɪŋ | *s.i.* **1** pavimentación, pavimento, asfalto, adoquinado, losado. || **2 – stone,** losa, baldosa, adoquín.

paw | pɔː | *s.c.* **1** garra, zarpa, pata. **2** (fam. y hum.) mano, manaza, puño: *his big paw = su manaza.* || *v.t.* e *i.* **3** escarbar, arañar, dar zarpazos (con las patas). **4** (fam.) meter mano, manosear, toquetear (a una persona).

pawn | pɔːn | *v.t.* **1** empeñar, dejar en prenda, pignorar. **2** arriesgar, exponer, aventurar, comprometer. || *s.i.* **3** depósito, prenda, garantía. || *s.c.* **4** peón (de ajedrez). **5 [– (in)]** (fig.) peón, muñeco, instrumento. || **6 – shop,** casa de empeños, monte de piedad.

pawnbroker | 'pɔːnˌbrəukər | *s.c.* prestamista, usurero, dueño de una casa de empeños.

pawpaw | 'pɔːpɔː | *s.c.* (brit.) BOT. papaya.

pax | pæks | *s.* **1** REL. paz. **2** ¡me rindo! (convencionalismo que utilizan los niños para finalizar una pelea).

pay | peɪ | *v.* [*irr. pret.* y *p.p.* **paid**] *t.* e *i.* **1** pagar, abonar, remunerar. **2** producir, hacer rentable, rendir, dar; compensar, merecer la pena: *a business that pays = un negocio rentable.* || *t.* **3** pagar, saldar, liquidar, satisfacer (una deuda). **4 [to – (in/into)]** ingresar, depositar (un cheque). **5** ofrecer, presentar: *pay respects = presentar respetos.* **6** prestar, poner: *pay attention = prestar atención.* **7** hacer: *pay a visit = hacer una visita.* **8** rendir (homenaje). || *s.i.* **9** sueldo, salario, honorarios, remuneración, retribución, paga, jornal. **10** recompensa, premio. **11** castigo, sanción. || *s.c.* **12** pagador (bueno o malo). || **13 to be in the – of,** (desp.) estar a sueldo de, estar al servicio de, estar pagado por. **14 to – back,** devolver, retornar, reembolsar, restituir. **15 to – for,** pagar por, recibir su merecido por (algo mal hecho). **16 to – off, a)** terminar de pagar, saldar, redimir, amortizar (una deuda, un crédito); **b)** pagar y despedir (a un trabajador); **c)** tapar la boca con dinero, pagar por mantener la boca cerrada; **d)** tener éxito, dar resultado. **17 to – one's way,** costearse uno sus propios gastos, contribuir a los gastos. **18 to – out, a)** pagar, desembolsar (una gran cantidad); **b)** MAR. arriar; **c)** (brit. y arc.) devolver, reembolsar, restituir. **19 to – the piper,** aguantar las consecuencias, pagar por lo hecho. **20 to – up,** devolver, restituir, cancelar (una deuda de mal grado).

payable | 'peɪəbl | *adj.* **1** COM. pagadero, pagable, por pagar. **2 [– (to)]** al portador.

pay-bed | 'peɪbed | *s.c.* (brit.) cama de pago (en hospitales públicos).

payday | 'peɪdeɪ | *s.i.* día de paga, día de cobro.

paydesk | 'peɪdesk | *s.c.* caja.

payee | peɪ'iː | *s.c.* COM. portador, tenedor, beneficiario, portador (de un cheque).

payer | peɪər | *s.c.* pagador.

paying guest | 'peɪɪŋgest | *s.c.* inquilino, huésped de pago.

paying-in book | 'peɪɪŋɪnˌbuk | *s.c.* talonario (de impresos).

paying-in slip | 'peɪɪŋɪnˌslɪp | *s.c.* impreso, formulario.

payload | 'peɪləud | *s.c.* e *i.* **1** carga útil, cargamento (de un vehículo). **2** pasaje, carga aérea. || *s.c.* **3** MIL. carga explosiva (en la cabeza de un cohete). **4** AER. tripulación y equipo (en una nave espacial, en un avión, en un cohete).

paymaster | 'peɪˌmɑːstər | *s.c.* pagador, habilitado, cajero, tesorero.

payment | peɪmənt | *s.i.* **1** pago, retribución, remuneración. **2** (fig.) agradecimiento, premio, pago, recompensa: *in payment for my efforts = en pago de mis esfuerzos.* || *s.c.* **3** pago, plazo; cobro: *yearly payments = pagos anuales.*

payoff | 'peɪɒf | *s.c.* (inf.). **1** paga, retribución, remuneración. **2** soborno, dádiva, propina. **3** recompensa, resultado; castigo, venganza. **4** desenlace, momento decisivo, resultado final (de una historia).

pay-packet | 'peɪˌpækɪt | (EE.UU. **pay-envelope**) *s.c.* **1** (brit.) sobre de la paga. **2** salario, paga.

pay-phone | 'peɪfəun | *s.c.* teléfono público.

payroll | 'peɪrəul | *s.c.* **1** nómina: *he had 12 workers on the payroll = tenía 12 trabajadores en nómina.* **2** dinero para pagar la nómina.

payslip | 'peɪslɪp | *s.c.* nómina (que un trabajador recibe a fin de mes).

PE | ˌpiː'iː | *s.c.* (**Physical Education**) educación física, gimnasia (asignatura).

pea | piː | *s.c.* **1** BOT. (generalmente *pl.*) guisante; guisante de olor. || **2 like two peas in a pod,** (fam.) como dos gotas de agua.

peace | piːs | *s.i.* **1** paz, concordia. **2 [the –]** la paz, el orden, la tranquilidad: *don't disturb their peace = no interrumpas su tranquilidad.* **3** acuerdo, pacto, tratado de paz. **4** armonía, conformidad: *peace in the group = armonía dentro del grupo.* **5** calma, sosiego, serenidad (interior). || *interj.* **6** ¡paz! ¡silencio! ¡tranquilidad! || **7 to be at –,** estar en paz (un país, una persona fallecida). **8 to hold/keep one's –,** guardar silencio, mantenerse callado. **9 in –,** como amigos, como gente de paz. **10 to keep the –,** (form.) mantener la paz, mantener el orden. **11 to make – with/to make one's – with,** hacer las paces con, pedir perdón a. **12 may someone rest in –,** que descanse en paz, que Dios tenga en la gloria. **13 rest in –,** descanse en paz (escrito sobre una lápida).

peaceable | 'piːsəbl | *adj.* pacífico, apacible, tranquilo, sosegado.

peacibly | 'piːsəblɪ | *adv.* pacíficamente.

peaceful | 'piːsful | *adj.* **1** apacible, sereno, tranquilo, sosegado, en calma: *a peaceful street = una calle tranquila.* **2 pacífico, sin violencia:** *a peaceful coexistence = coexistencia pacífica.*

peacefully | 'piːsfəlɪ | *adv.* **1** apaciblemente, serenamente, tranquilamente. **2** pacíficamente: *they demonstrated peacefully = se manifestaron pacíficamente.*

peace-keeping | 'piːsˌkiːpɪŋ | *adj.* pacificador, de pacificación: *peace-keeping troops = fuerzas de pacificación.*

peace-loving | 'piːsˌlʌvɪŋ | *adj.* apacible, amante de la paz.

peacemaker | 'pi:s,meɪkər | *s.c.* mediador, conciliador, pacificador, apaciguador, árbitro.
peace-offering | 'pi:s,ɒfərɪŋ | *s.c.* oferta de paz, regalo de conciliación, sacrificio propiciatorio: *a box of chocolates as a peace-offering = una caja de bombones como regalo de conciliación.*
peacetime | 'pi:staɪm | *s.i.* tiempos de paz, período de paz.
peach | pi:tʃ | *s.c.* **1** melocotón. **2** BOT. melocotonero. || *s.i.* **3** color de melocotón. || *s.sing.* **4** (fam.) belleza, monada, encanto, bombón. || *adj.* **5** de color melocotón. || *v.t.* e *i.* **6** (argot) delatar, denunciar, incriminar, traicionar; soplar. || **7 – melba,** melocotón con helado y zumo de frambuesas (postre).
peacock | 'pi:kɒk | *s.c.* **1** ZOOL. pavo real, pavón. **2** dandi, petimetre. || *adj.* **3** verde azulado (color). || *v.i.* **4** pavonearse, presumir, contonearse, exhibirse.
pea-green | ,pi:'gri:n | *adj.* verde claro.
peahen | ,pi:'hen | *s.c.* ZOOL. hembra de pavo real, pava real.
peak | pi:k | *s.c.* **1** pico, picacho, cima, cumbre. **2** pico, cresta, (de una ola). **3** punto culminante, apogeo, cumbre, punto más alto: *at the peak of his career = en la cumbre de su carrera.* **4** visera. **5** NAUT. rasel, racel, delgado. || *v.i.* **6** alcanzar la cumbre, llegar al máximo (del valor, la intensidad, el desarrollo). **7** llevar a punto de nieve, formar picos: *the egg whites piked = las claras de huevo a punto de nieve.* || *v.t.* **8** MAR. embicar; orzar. **9** hacer culminar, llevar al máximo. || *adj.* **10** punta, de máximo tráfico: *peak hour = hora punta.* **11** máximo, óptimo, más elevado: *peak conditions = condiciones óptimas.*
peaked | 'pi:kt | *adj.* **1** visera, con visera; puntiagudo, en pico: *a peaked cap = una gorra con visera.* **2** demacrado, pálido, consumido.
peaky | 'pi:kɪ | *adj.* (brit. y fam.) demacrado, pálido, enfermizo.
peal | pi:l | *s.c.* **1** estruendo, ruido, fragor: *peals of laughter = carcajadas; peals of thunder = truenos.* **2** repiqueteo, tañido, repique (de campanas). **3** MUS. melodía, son, sonsonete. || *v.t.* e *i.* **4** repicar, tañer, resonar, tocar a vuelo.
peanut | 'pi:nʌt | *s.c.* **1** cacahuete. || **2 – butter,** mantequilla de cacahuete.
pear | peər | *s.c.* e *i.* **1** pera. **2** BOT. peral.
pearl | pɜ:l | *s.c.* e *i.* **1** perla. || *s.i.* **2** color gris perla. **3** nácar, madreperla. **4** (fig.) perla, joya. || *v.t.* **5** adornar con perlas, cubrir de perlas. **6** formar perlas, dar forma de perla. || *v.i.* **7** pescar perlas. **8** formarse en perlas. || *adj.* **9** de color gris perla; en forma de perla, perlado. **10** de perlas: *a pearl necklace = un collar de perlas.* || **11 to cast pearls before swine,** echar margaritas a los cerdos.
pearl-grey | 'pɜ:l,greɪ | *adj.* gris perla.
pearly | 'pɜ:lɪ | *adj.* **1** perlado, nacarado, color perla. **2** adornado con perlas, cubierto de perlas, de perlas, de madreperla.
peasant | 'peznt | *s.c.* **1** campesino, labrador, labriego. **2** (fam. y desp.) palurdo, pueblerino, rústico, gañán, patán. || *adj.* **3** pueblerino, rústico, paleto.
peasantry | 'pezntrɪ | *s.sing.* **[the – v.sing./pl.]** el campesinado, los campesinos, la gente del campo.
pease pudding | 'pi:z'pʊdɪŋ | *s.i.* (brit. y arc.) puré de guisantes, pasta de guisantes.
peashooter | 'pi:,ʃu:tər | *s.c.* cerbatana, canuto, bodoquera, tiratacos (juguete).
peasouper | ,pi:'su:pər | *s.c.* (brit. y fam.) niebla densa y sucia, dorondón.
peat | pi:t | *s.c.* e *i.* turba: *they were burning peat = estaban quemando turba.*
peaty | 'pi:tɪ | *adj.* con turba.
pebble | 'pebl | *s.c.* **1** guijarro, china, guija, piedrecita, canto rodado. || **2 the only – on the beach,** la única persona en el mundo.
pebbledash | 'pebldæʃ | (EE.UU. **rock dash**) *s.i.* (brit.) mezcla de cemento con guijarros, cascajo (para recubrir paredes exteriores).
pebbly | 'peblɪ | *adj.* de cantos rodados, guijarroso: *a pebbly beach = una playa de cantos rodados.*
pecan | pɪ'kæn | | pi:'kæn, | (EE.UU.) | pɪ'kɑ:n | *s.c.* **1** pacana, nuez lisa. **2** BOT. nogal pacanero.
peccadillo | ,pekə'dɪləʊ | [*pl.* **peccadillos** o **peccadilloes**] *s.c.* (arc.) pecadillo, falta leve, ofensa poco importante, peccata minuta.
peck | pek | *v.t.* e *i.* **1** picar, picotear (un ave). **2** pinchar, punzar. **3** mordisquear, picar, comer a bocaditos, comer con desgana. || *v.t.* **4 [to – (on)]** (fam.) besar con desgana, besar apresuradamente. || *v.i.* **5** censurar, criticar, rezongar. || *s.c.* **6** picotazo, picotada. **7 [– (on)]** (fam.) beso apresurado, beso rápido. **8** medida de áridos (equivalente a 9,087 litros). **9** (fam.) montón, cantidad, mar: *a peck of problems = la mar de problemas.*
pecker | pekər | *s.c.* **1** picoteador. **2** rezungón, criticón. **3** (brit. y argot) coraje, ánimo, valor, resolución. **4** (EE.UU., vulg.) verga (pene). || **5 to keep one's – up,** (brit. y fam.) animarse, tener valor.
pecking order | 'pekɪŋ,ɔ:dər | *s.c.* **[the –] 1** la jerarquía, el orden jerárquico. **2** BIOL. orden en que picotean las gallinas. **3** (fig.) la ley del más fuerte.
peckish | 'pekɪʃ | *adj.* (brit. y fam.) ligeramente hambriento, con el gusanillo: *I felt rather peckish = necesitaba matar el gusanillo.*
pectin | 'pektɪn | *s.i.* BIOQ. pectina.
pectoral | 'pektərəl | *adj.* **1** ANAT. pectoral. **2** pectoral, del pecho: *a pectoral cross = pectoral* (de un obispo). || *s.c.* **3** ANAT. pectoral, músculo pectoral. **4** adorno para el pecho. **5** ungüento pectoral, medicina para el pecho. || **6 – fin,** ZOOL. aleta pectoral.
peculiar | pɪ'kju:ljər | *adj.* **1** extraño, raro, grotesco. **2 [– (to)]** peculiar, propio, típico, característico. **3** (euf.) extravagante, excéntrico. **4** (fam.) débil, mal, delicado, enfermo: *I'm feeling peculiar = me siento mal.* || *s.c.* **5** privilegio, propiedad. **6** (brit.) parroquia no dependiente de la diócesis en que se encuentra.
peculiarity | pɪ,kju:lɪ'ærɪtɪ | *s.i.* **1** peculiaridad, particularidad, cualidad. || *s.c.* **2** rasgo distintivo, característica, cualidad: *a peculiarity of the country = una característica del país.* **3** excentricidad, idiosincrasia, rareza, extravagancia.
peculiarly | pɪ'kju:lɪəlɪ | *adv.* **1** peculiarmente, particularmente, especialmente. **2** extrañamente, de forma rara, extravagantemente.
pecuniary | pɪ'kju:nɪərɪ | (EE.UU.) | pɪ'kju:nɪerɪ | *adj.* (form.) pecuniario, financiero, monetario.
pedagogic, pedagogical | ,pedə'gɒdʒɪk | *adj.* pedagógico.
pedagogically | ,pedə'gɒdʒɪklɪ | *adv.* pedagógicamente.
pedagogue | 'pedəgɒg | *s.c.* **1** pedagogo, educador. **2** pedante, engolado, sabihondo.
pedagogy | 'pedəgɒdʒɪ | *s.i.* (form.) pedagogía.
pedal | 'pedl | *s.c.* **1** pedal (de una máquina, de un vehículo, de un piano). || (brit. **pedall**) *v.t.* e *i.* **2** pedalear, impulsar a pedal (una máquina, etc.). **3** [**to –** *o.* + *adv./prep.*] pedalear, ir en bicicleta. || *adj.* **4** de pedal, a pedal. **5** del pie: *pedal extremities = los pies.* **6 – bin,** cubo de basura con pedal.
pedant | 'pedənt | *s.c.* **1** (desp.) formalista. **2** pedante, exhibicionista, ostentador. **3** (arc.) maestro de escuela.
pedantic | pɪ'dæntɪk | *adj.* (desp.) pedante, ostentoso, redicho, sabelotodo, formalista.
pedantry | 'pedəntrɪ | *s.c.* e *i.* (desp.) pedantería.
peddle | 'pedl | *v.t.* e *i.* (generalmente desp.) **1** vender de puerta en puerta, vender por las calles, vender como buhonero. || *v.t.* **2** extender, hacer correr, difundir (rumores). **3** (argot) hacer de camello, pasar (drogas). || *v.i.* **4** dedicarse a fruslerías, ocuparse de bagatelas.
peddler | 'pedlər | *s.c.* **1** camello, traficante (de drogas). **2** (EE.UU.) buhonero, mercachifle.
pedestal | 'pedɪstl | *s.c.* **1** pedestal, basamento, soporte, pie. **2** (fig.) pedestal. || **3 to put someone on a –,** poner a alguien en un pedestal, idolatrar a alguien. **4 to knock someone off the –/one's –,** desenmascarar a alguien, tirar a alguien de su pedestal.
pedestrian | pɪ'destrɪən | *s.c.* **1** peatón. || *adj.* **2** (desp.) pedestre, ramplón, ordinario, vulgar, mediocre. **3** peatonal, de peatones, para peatones. || **4 – crossing,** paso de cebra, paso de peatones. **5 – precinct,** zona peatonal, calle peatonal.
pedestrianize | pɪ'destrɪənaɪz | (brit. **pedestrianise**) *v.t.* peatonalizar, cerrar al tráfico (una zona, una calle).
pedestrianized | pɪ'destrɪənaɪzd | *adj.* peatonalizado, de peatones, para peatones.
pedicure | 'pedɪ,kjʊər | *s.i.* **1** pedicura, quiropedia. || *s.c.* **2** pedicuro, callista. || *v.t.* **3** hacer la pedicura, ejercer la quiropedia.
pedigree | 'pedɪgri: | *s.c.* **1** pedigree, pura raza. **2** genealogía, árbol familiar. || *adj.* **2** de pedigree, de pura raza, de casta.

pediment | 'pedɪmənt | *s.c.* ARQ. frontón.
pedlar | 'pedlər | (EE.UU. **peddler**) *s.c.* (brit.) buhonero, mercachifle, vendedor ambulante.
pee | piː | *v.i.* (fam. y vulg.) **1** mear, orinar. || *s.c.* **2** meada. **3** pe (letra). || *s.i.* **4** orina, urea.
peek | piːk | *v.i.* **1** (fam.) fisgar, atisbar, acechar, mirar a hurtadillas. || *s.c.* **2** **[– (at)]** ojeada, mirada rápida, mirada furtiva, atisbo.
peekaboo, peepbo | ˌpiːkə'buː | *s.i.* **1** juego en que repetidamente uno se oculta y aparece de súbito para divertir a los niños. || *interj.* **2** ¡cucú! (grito que se da al aparecer súbitamente frente a un niño en este juego).
peel | piːl | *v.t.* e *i.* **1** pelar, mondar, quitar la piel, descortezar(se), descascarar(se), despegar(se) (la fruta, un papel). || *v.i.* **2** desconcharse, desprenderse, despegarse, quitarse: *the wall paper was peeling = el papel de la pared se estaba despegando.* **3** pelarse (la piel con el sol). || *s.i.* **4** monda, peladura, cáscara, corteza, hollejo, pellejo, piel. || *s.c.* **5** pala de horno (para sacar el pan). **6** colgador (en imprenta). || **7 to keep your eyes peeled,** V. **eye. 8 to – off, a)** salirse de la formación (un avión para atacar, aterrizar); **b)** separarse, hacerse a un lado, abrirse: *people peeled off to let her enter = la gente se hizo a un lado para dejarla entrar;* **c)** desvestirse, desnudarse, despojarse (de las ropas); **d)** pelar, mondar, quitar la piel.
peeler | 'piːlər | *s.c.* **1** peladora (de patatas, de frutas). **2** (argot) bailarina de strip-ttease, (Am.) desnudista, calatista. **3** (brit. y argot) policía.
peelings | piːlɪŋz | *s.i.* peladuras, raspas, mondaduras, pieles, hollejo.
peep | piːp | *v.i.* **1** fisgar, atisbar furtivamente, mirar a hurtadillas, mirar por rendijas y cerraduras. **2** piar (un pájaro). || *v.t.* e *i.* **3** **[to – *adv./prep.*]** asomarse, empezar a salir, aparecer gradualmente: *the moon was peeping = estaba saliendo la luna.* || *s.c.* **4** **[– (at)]** ojeada, mirada, atisbo. **5** pío, piada. **6** (fam.) pío, palabra, ruido, sonido: *not a peep out of your mouth = no digas ni pío.* **7** (fam.) pi, (sonido que usan los niños para imitar el claxon).
peepbo | 'piːpbəʊ | V. **peekaboo.**
peephole | 'piːphəʊl | *s.c.* mirilla, agujero, atisbadero.
Peeping Tom | ˌpiːpɪŋ'tɒm | *s.c.* (desp.) mirón, voyeur.
peepshow | 'piːpʃəʊ | *s.c.* **1** espectáculo pornográfico, película pornográfica corta (que se puede ver en una máquina de monedas). **2** titirimundi (de feria).
peer | pɪər | *s.c.* **1** (brit.) par, noble (título). **2** (form.) semejante, análogo, par, igual. **3** (arc.) compañero, amigo. || *v.i.* **4** **[to – *adv./prep.*]** mirar con ojos de miope, mirar con dificultad, mirar con los ojos fijos: *she peered at me = me miraba con ojos fijos.* **5** asomarse, aparecer poco a poco. || **6 – group,** grupo de la misma edad, clase social, intereses, etc... **7 – of the realm,** par del reino, miembro de la Casa de los Lores.
peerage | 'pɪərɪdʒ | *s.c.* **1** rango de par, título de nobleza. **2** guía de la nobleza (libro). || *s.sing.* **3** **[the – *v.sing./pl.*]** nobleza, aristocracia, cuerpo de pares.
peeress | 'pɪərɪs | *s.c.f.* **1** paresa, mujer de la nobleza. **2** esposa de un par.
peerless | 'pɪəlɪs | *adj.* (form.) sin par, sin igual, incomparable.
peeve | piːv | *v.t.* (generalmente pasiva) **1** (fam.) enfadar, enojar, irritar, estar resentido, ofender. || *s.c.* **2** vejación, ofensa. **3** resentimiento, rencor.
peeved | piːvd | *adj.* resentido, ofendido.
peevish | 'piːvɪʃ | *adj.* **1** irritado, enfadado, de mal humor, quejumbroso, descontento, impaciente. **2** terco, rebelde, díscolo.
peevishly | 'piːvɪʃlɪ | *adv.* **1** quejumbrosamente, malhumoradamente, impacientemente. **2** tercamente, de forma díscola.
peewit | 'piːwɪt | *s.c.* ZOOL. avefría.
peg | peg | *s.c.* **1** gancho, percha, perchero, colgador, colgadero: *the coats hang on pegs = los abrigos están colgados en perchas.* **2** (brit.) pinza de la ropa. **3** clavija, estaca, espiga, perno: *camping tent pegs = clavijas de la tienda de campaña.* **4** MUS. clavija. **5** (brit. y p.u.) traguito, pequeña cantidad (de alcohol). **6** garfio, gancho. **7** (fam.) grado, escala, nivel (en estimación, jerarquía). **8** (fig.) pretexto, disculpa, ocasión, oportunidad, pie: *a peg for complaints = un motivo de queja.* **9** (fam.) pie o pierna de madera. **10** DEP. tiro corto y bajo (en béisbol). || *v.t.* **11** asegurar con clavijas, fijar con estacas. **12** (brit.) colgar con pinzas, sujetar con pinzas, tender. **13** **[to – out]** delimitar con estacas, demarcar con estacas, jalonar. **14** fijar, estabilizar (precios). **15** (fam.) clasificar, categorizar, jerarquizar. **16** (fam.) arrojar, tirar. || *v.i.* **17** **[to – away]** insistir, persistir, afanarse, trabajar con ahínco. **18** **[to – out]** (brit. y fam.) morir, estirar la pata. || **19 to be brought down a – or two,** bajarle un poco los humos a uno. **20 – on which to hang something,** pretexto en que basar algo, pie para algo. **21 square – in a round hole,** como pez fuera del agua, fuera de su ambiente.
peg-leg | 'pegleg | *s.c.* (fam.) pierna artificial, pierna de madera.
pejorative | 'piːdʒɒrɪtɪv | (EE.UU.) | pɪ'dʒɔːrətɪv | *adj.* **1** (form.) peyorativo, despectivo. || *s.c.* **2** palabra despectiva.
pekinese | ˌpiːkɪ'niːz | *s.c.* pequinés.
pelican | 'pelɪkən | *s.c.* **1** ZOOL. pelícano. || **2 – crossing,** (brit.) paso de peatones (donde el peatón pone en marcha un semáforo presionando un botón).
pellagra | pə'lægrə | *s.i.* MED. pelagra.
pellet | 'pelɪt | *s.c.* **1** pelotilla, bolita (de algo suave): *wax pellets = bolitas de cera.* **2** bala, perdigón, proyectil. **3** proyectil de piedra (para una catapulta).
pell-mell | ˌpel'mel | *adv.* (arc.) desordenadamente, atropelladamente, confusamente.
pellucid | pe'ljuːsɪd | *adj.* (lit.) límpido, diáfano, transparente, terso, claro.
pelmet | 'pelmɪt | (EE.UU. **valance**) *s.c.* galería (para ocultar la barra de las cortinas en ventanas).
pelt | pelt | *v.t.* **1** **[to – (with)]** atacar, arremeter, arrojar, tirar, lanzar: *pelting him with dishes = arrojándole platos.* **2** (fig.) bombardear con, hacer (preguntas). || *v.i.* **3** **[to – (down/with)]** llover a cántaros, diluviar, llover a mares. **4** **[to – *adv./prep.*]** (fam.) pasar como un rayo, correr a gran velocidad. || *s.c.* **5** golpe, empellón. **6** piel, pellejo (de animales). || **7 at full –,** a toda velocidad, como un rayo.
pelvic | 'pelvɪk | *adj.* ANAT. pelviano, pélvico.
pelvis | 'pelvɪs | *s.c.* ANAT. pelvis.
pen | pen | *s.c.* **1** pluma, bolígrafo, rotulador. **2** (fig.) escritor, autor: *he worked as a pen = trabajó como escritor.* **3** (fig.) pluma, estilo, forma, modo (de escritura). **4** ZOOL. pluma, concha (del calamar). **5** (generalmente en combinación) redil, corral, aprisco, toril. **6** corralito, parque (para niños). **7** dique de reparación (para submarinos). **8** ZOOL. hembra de cisne. **9** (EE.UU. y argot) chirona, prisión. || *v.t.* **10** (form.) escribir, redactar. **11** encerrar en redil, acorralar (animales). **12** recluir, confinar (personas en un espacio pequeño). || **13 a slip of the –,** error de escritura. **14 – pal,** (EE.UU. y fam.) amigo por correspondencia, amigo epistolar. **15 to put – to paper,** (lit.) escribir algo.
penal | 'piːnl | *adj.* **1** penal (un castigo, un establecimiento). **2** muy severo, muy gravoso, muy desagradable. || **3 – code,** DER. código penal. **4 – servitude,** trabajos forzados.
penalize | 'piːnəlaɪz | (brit.) **penalise.** *v.t.* **[to – (for)]** penalizar, perjudicar, castigar, sancionar.
penalty | 'penltɪ | *s.c.* **1** **[– (for)]** pena, sanción, multa, castigo. **2** precio, desventaja, inconveniente: *the penalties of fame = el precio de la fama.* **3** DEP. penalty, castigo; ventaja. || **4 – area,** DEP. área de castigo, área de penalty. **5 – box,** DEP. **a)** área de penalty, área de castigo; **b)** área de castigo (en hockey lugar en que se sienta un jugador penalizado). **6 – clause,** DER. cláusula penal.
penance | 'penəns | *s.c.* e *i.* penitencia.
pen-and-ink | ˌpenənd'ɪŋk | *adj.* a pluma, a tinta (un dibujo).
pence | pens | *s.pl.* de **penny. 1** peniques. || **2 -pence,** de... peniques, por valor de... peniques: *a 12-pence stamp = un sello de 12 peniques.*
penchant | 'pɑːnʃɑːn | (EE.UU.) | 'pentʃənt | *s.sing.* **[– (for)]** (form.) inclinación, afición, tendencia, propensión, apego, pasión.
pencil | 'pensl | *s.c.* **1** lapicero, lápiz. **2** lápiz de ojos. **3** (arc.) pincel, brocha. **4** (fig.) pincel, estilo pictórico. **5** haz, rayo (de luz). || *v.t.* **6** escribir a lápiz, anotar a lápiz. **7** dibujar a lápiz, esbozar a lápiz. || **8 in –,** a lápiz. **9 to – in,** añadir a lápiz, incluir a lápiz (algo que se puede borrar más tarde).
pencilled | 'pensld | *adj.* a lápiz, con lápiz.

pendant, pendent | 'pendənt | *s.c.* **1** medallón, pendiente, colgante. **2** lámpara de techo, araña, candelabro que cuelga. **3** complemento, pareja. || *adj.* (lit.) **4** colgante, pendiente, suspendido, que pende. **5** que se proyecta, que sobresale.

pending | 'pendɪŋ | *prep.* **1** (form.) mentiras, hasta que: *pending her arrival = hasta que llegara.* || *adj.* **2** (form.) pendiente, no decidido, en trámite, a la espera: *a pending decision = una decisión pendiente.* **3** inminente, cercano.

pendulous | 'pendjʊləs | (EE.UU.) | 'pendʒʊləs | *adj.* **1** (form.) colgante, oscilante, bamboleante. **2** pendular, indeciso, titubeante, vacilante.

pendulum | 'pendjʊləm | *s.c.* **1** péndulo, péndola. **2 [the – (of)]** (fig.) péndulo: *the pendulum of public opinion = el movimiento pendular de la opinión pública.*

penetrate | 'penɪtreɪt | *v.t.* e *i.* **1** penetrar, traspasar, atravesar, entrar. **2** (fig.) infiltrar(se). **3** (fam.) comprender, entender, darse cuenta de. || *v.t.* **4** (generalmente pasiva) afectar profundamente, conmover, invadir: *terror penetrated me = el terror me invadió.* **5** penetrar, ahondar, llegar al fondo de, ver a través de: *penetrating the mystery = llegando al fondo del misterio.* **6** calar, difundir, afectar profundamente.

penetrating | 'penɪtreɪtɪŋ | *adj.* **1** penetrante, profundo, agudo, que taladra (una mirada, un sonido). **2** (fig.) penetrante, agudo, sagaz (una persona, la mente). **3** creciente, que se extiende: *penetrating rumours = rumores crecientes.*

penetration | ˌpenɪ'treɪʃn | *s.c.* e *i.* **1** penetración, introducción: *penetration of products in the market = penetración de productos en el mercado.* **2** infiltración: *penetration of spies = infiltración de espías.* **3** perspicacia, sagacidad, agudeza, comprensión.

penfriend | 'penfrend | *s.c.* (brit.) amigo epistolar, amigo por correspondencia.

penguin | 'peŋgwɪn | *s.c.* ZOOL. pingüino, pájaro bobo.

penicillin | ˌpenɪ'sɪlɪn | *s.i.* MED. penicilina.

penile | 'piːnaɪl | *adj.* (form.) del pene, relativo al pene.

peninsula | pɪ'nɪnsjʊlə | *s.c.* GEOG. península.

penis | 'piːnɪs | *s.c.* ANAT. pene.

penitence | 'penɪtəns | *s.i.* arrepentimiento, contrición, remordimiento.

penitent | 'penɪtənt | *adj.* **1** (form.) penitente, arrepentido, compungido. || *s.c.* **2** penitente.

penitential | ˌpenɪ'tenʃl | *adj.* **1** penitencial, de penitencia. || *s.c.* **2** libro de penitencias, manual de penitencias. **3** penitente.

penitentiary | ˌpenɪ'tenʃərɪ | *s.c.* **1** (EE.UU.) penitenciaría, cárcel, presidio. || *adj.* **2** penitenciario, carcelario. **3** penal. **4** penitencial, de penitencia.

penknife | 'pennaɪf | *s.c.* navaja.

penmanship | 'penmənʃɪp | *s.i.* (form.) caligrafía, escritura.

pen-name | 'penneɪm | *s.c.* seudónimo.

pennant | 'penənt | *s.c.* **1** DEP. banderín, banderola. **2** MAR. gallardete, pendón; bandera de señales.

pennies | 'penɪz | *pl.irreg.* de **penny.**

penniless | 'penɪlɪs | *adj.* pobre, paupérrimo, indigente, sin un penique.

penny | 'penɪ | [*pl.* **pennies** o **pence**] *s.c.* **1** (brit.) penique; (EE.UU.) centavo. **2** (fig. y en frases negativas) centavo, perra, céntimo, duro: *not a penny worth = no vale un duro.* || **3 a – for your thoughts,** ¿en qué piensas? **4 a pretty –,** una fortuna, un dineral, un ojo de la cara. **5 in for a – in for a pound,** (brit.) de perdidos al río, preso por mil, preso por mil quinientos. **6 not to have a – to one's name,** no tener un centavo, no tener un duro, no tener donde caerse muerto. **7 not to have two pennies to rub together,** (brit.) no tener donde caerse muerto, ser más pobre que una rata. **8 – whistle,** silbato, pito. **9 to spend a –,** (brit. y arc.) ir al retrete. **10 take care of the pennies and the pounds will take care of themselves,** toda economía es buena por pequeña que esta sea. **11 the – dropped,** (brit. y fam.) sonó la flauta, se dio cuenta, comprendió. **12 to turn up like a bad –,** aparecer como la falsa moneda, aparecer en el momento menos oportuno. **13 two/ten a –,** (fam.) fácil de encontrar, baratísimo, a patadas: *books like this are ten a penny = libros como ese los hay a patadas.*

penny-farthing | ˌpenɪ'fɑːðɪŋ | *s.c.* (brit.) velocípedo.

penny-pinching | 'penɪˌpɪntʃɪŋ | *s.i.* **1** tacañería, escasez, penuria. || *adj.* **2** cicatero, tacaño, mezquino, miserable.

pennyworth | 'penɪwəθ | *s.sing.* **1** valor de un penique, lo que se compra con un penique: *it was a pennyworth = costó un penique.* **2** poco, pizca, nadería. **3** ganga, chollo.

penpusher | 'penˌpʊʃər | *s.c.* (desp. y hum.) chupatintas, cagatintas, empleadillo, escribiente.

pension | 'penʃn | *s.c.* **1** pensión, jubilación, subsidio de vejez, retiro. | 'pɑːŋsɪɔːŋ | **2** pensión, hospedaje, hotelito (generalmente en Europa): *we stayed at a pension in Rome = en Roma nos hospedamos en una pensión.* || *v.t.* **3 [to – off]** jubilar, conceder una pensión de jubilación, dar el subsidio de vejez. **4** (fig.) jubilar, retirar de la circulación (algo viejo). || **5 – book,** (brit.) libreta de la Seguridad Social con los bonos canjeables por la pensión. **6 – scheme,** plan de jubilación.

pensionable | 'penʃənəbl | *adj.* con derecho a jubilación, con derecho a pensión.

pensioned | 'penʃnd | *adj.* pensionado, que recibe pensión: *pensioned teachers = profesores que reciben pensión.*

pensioner | 'penʃənər | *s.c.* **1** pensionista, jubilado, retirado. **2** pariente, inválido (dependiente de otra persona). **3** mercenario.

pensive | 'pensɪv | *adj.* **1** pensativo, meditabundo. **2** melancólico, triste, soñador.

pensively | 'pensɪvlɪ | *adj.* **1** pensativamente, meditabundamente. **2** melancólicamente, soñadoramente.

pentagon | 'pentəgən | *s.c.* **1** GEOM. pentágono. || **2 the Pentagon,** (EE.UU.) el Pentágono (ministerio de Defensa).

pentamenter | pen'tæmɪtər | *s.c.* e *i.* LIT. pentámetro.

pentathlon | pen'tæθlɒn | *s.c.* DEP. pentatlón, competición que consta de cinco pruebas de atletismo.

Pentecost | 'pentɪkɒst | *s.i.* Pentecostés.

penthouse | 'penthaʊs | *s.c.* **1** ático (generalmente de lujo). **2** cobertizo, caseta.

pent-up | ˌpent'ʌp | *adj.* **1** reprimido, contenido: *pent-up emotions = emociones reprimidas.* **2** encerrado, enjaulado, enclaustrado, recluido.

penultimate | pe'nʌltɪmət | *adj.* penúltimo.

penurious | pɪ'njʊərɪəs | *adj.* (form.) **1** de penuria, pobrísimo, indigente, mísero. **2** tacaño, cicatero. **3** pobre, árido (un terreno).

penury | 'penjʊrɪ | *s.i.* (form.) penuria, miseria, pobreza, escasez, carencia.

peony | 'pɪənɪ | *s.c.* BOT. peonía.

people | 'piːpl | *s.pl.* **1** gente, personas: *many people come = viene mucha gente.* **2** los humanos, la raza humana. **3** pueblo, ciudadanos: *a man of the people = un hombre del pueblo.* **4 [the –]** (desp.) la plebe, las masas, el populacho. **5** antepasados, parientes; (fam.) padres, familia, gente: *my people come from the North = mi familia es del norte.* || *s.c.* **6 [– v.sing./pl.]** nación, país, pueblo, habitantes: *the Spanish people = el pueblo español.* || *v.t.* (generalmente pasiva) **7** habitar, poblar. **8 [to – (with)]** (lit. y desp.) llenar, abarrotar: *peopled with narrow-minded writers = abarrotado de escritores de miras estrechas.*

pep | pep | *s.i.* (fam.) **1** energía, dinamismo, empuje, fuerza, vigor. || *v.t.* **2 [to – up]** animar, alentar, reanimar, estimular. || **3 – pill,** (fam.) píldora estimulante (como la anfetamina). **4 – talk,** (fam.) discurso para elevar los ánimos, exhortación, arenga.

pepper | 'pepər | *s.i.* **1** pimienta (condimento). || *s.c.* **2** pimiento, ají. **3** BOT. planta de pimiento. || *v.t.* **4 [to – (with)]** (fam.) acribillar (a tiros). **5 [to – (with)]** salpicar, motear: *peppered with questions = salpicado de preguntas.* **6** salpimentar, sazonar.

pepper-and-salt | ˌpepərən'sɔːlt | *adj.* **1** mezclado de blanco y negro (ambos por igual): *a pepper-and-salt dress = un vestido en blanco y negro.* **2** entrecano (el pelo).

peppercorn | 'pepəkkɔːn | *s.c.* **1** grano de pimienta. **2** pequeñez, insignificancia, bagatela.

peppered | 'pepəd | *adj.* **1** sazonado con pimienta. **2** lleno, abarrotado, salpicado:

peppered with stars = abarrotado de estrellas.

peppermint | ’pepəmɪnt | *s.i.* **1** menta (planta, sabor). || *s.c.* **2** caramelo de menta, pastilla de menta.

pepperpot | ’pepəpɒt | (EE.UU. **pepperbox**) *s.c.* **1** pimentero. || *s.i.* **2** sopa de legumbres con carne y callos sazonada con pimienta.

peppery | ’pepərɪ | *adj.* **1** picante, con sabor a pimienta. **2** irritable, malhumorado, áspero, de malas pulgas.

peptic ulcer | ’peptɪk’ʌlsər | *s.c.* MED. úlcera péptica.

per | pəːr | *prep.* **1** por, a: *50 miles per hour = 50 millas por hora.* **2** durante, a: *4 pages per day = 4 páginas al día.* || **3 as –,** (fam.) según, de acuerdo con: *as per instructions = según las instrucciones.* **4 as – usual,** (fam.) como de costumbre, como siempre. **5 – annum,** al año, por año. **6 – capita/head,** por persona, por cabeza. **7 – cent,** por ciento. **8 – se,** de por sí.

perambulate | pə’ræmbjuleɪt | *v.t.* e *i.* **1** (form.) deambular, vagar, pasear, errar. || *v.t.* **2** recorrer andando, visitar (para inspeccionar).

perambulation | pəˌræmbju’leɪʃn | *s.c.* e *i.* **1** paseo. **2** visita de inspección.

perambulator | pə’ræmbjuleɪtər | *s.c.* (brit. y form.) cochecito de niño.

perceive | pə’siːv | *v.t.* (form.) **1** percibir, darse cuenta de, percatarse de, notar, observar. **2** comprender, entender, percibir.

percentage | pə’sentɪdʒ | *s.c.* **1** porcentaje, tanto por ciento, parte, porción. **2** (fam.) porcentaje, ganancia, tajada, comisión.

perceptible | pə’septəbl | *adj.* perceptible, apreciable, discernible.

perceptibly | pə’septɪblɪ | *adv.* perceptiblemente, apreciablemente, de modo discernible.

perception | pə’sepʃn | *s.i.* (form.) **1** percepción, apreciación, discernimiento, conciencia. **2** percepción, sagacidad, penetración, agudeza.

perceptive | pə’septɪv | *adj.* **1** perceptivo. **2** sagaz, agudo, penetrante.

perceptively | pə’septɪvlɪ | *adv.* sensiblemente, sagazmente, agudamente.

perceptiveness | pə’septɪvnɪs | *s.i.* capacidad de percepción, sagacidad, agudeza, penetración.

perch | pəːtʃ | *s.c.* **1** percha, varal, rama, cetro (para los pájaros). **2** (fam.) posición elevada; (fig.) pedestal. **3** asiento, lugar de descanso. **4** (brit.) medida de longitud (equivalente a 5,029 m). **5** ZOOL. perca. || *v.i.* **6** posarse (un pájaro). || *v.t.* e *i.* **7** (fam.) asentar(se) en una posición elevada, colocar(se) en lugar alto; subir(se) a un lugar peligroso, colgar(se), sentar(se) al borde: *a village perching on the mountain = un pueblo colgado en la montaña.*

perchance | pə’tʃɑːns | *adv.* (arc. y lit.) **1** quizá, acaso, por ventura, tal vez. **2 [if/lest –]** por casualidad.

perched | pəːtʃt | *adj.* al borde, sentado al borde, colocado al borde.

percipient | pə’sɪpɪənt | *adj.* (form.) perceptivo, agudo, sagaz, penetrante, observador.

percolate | ’pəːkəleɪt | *v.t.* e *i.* **1 [to – adv./prep.]** colar, filtrar; preparar con filtro (café). **2** (fig.) infiltrar(se), extender(se) llegar hasta (ideas, noticias).

percolator | ’pəːkəleɪtər | *s.c.* cafetera con filtro, percolador.

percussion | pə’kʌʃn | *s.i.* **1 [the – v.sing./pl.]** MUS. la percusión, instrumentos de percusión. || *adj.atr.* **2** MUS. de percusión. || **3 – cap,** cápsula fulminante (de un arma, de un juguete).

percussionist | pə’kʌʃənɪst | *s.c.* MUS. percusionista, músico que toca instrumentos de percusión.

perdition | pə’dɪʃn | *s.i.* (form.) **1** infierno, perdición, condena, castigo (tras la muerte). **2** destrucción, perdición.

peregrination | ˌperɪgrɪ’neɪʃn | *s.c.* **1** (lit.) peregrinación. **2** (fig.) vagabundeo, viaje, periplo.

peregrine (falcon) | ’perɪgrɪn ’fɔːlkən | | ’perɪgrɪn ’fɑːlkən | *s.c.* ZOOL. halcón peregrino.

peremptorily | pə’remptərɪlɪ | *adv.* perentoriamente, autoritariamente, imperiosamente, terminantemente.

peremptory | pə’remptərɪ | (EE.UU.) | ’perəmptɔːrɪ | *adj.* (form.) **1** (desp.) perentorio, autoritario, imperativo, terminante, dogmático: *a peremptory person = una persona autoritaria.* **2** indiscutible, incuestionable (una orden). **3** urgente, perentorio: *in a peremptory tone = en tono perentorio.*

perennial | pə’renɪəl | *adj.* **1** perenne, eterno, constante, permanente: *perennial conflicts = conflictos constantes.* **2** no *comp.* BOT. perenne, vivaz.

perennially | pə’renɪəlɪ | *adv.* perennemente, eternamente, constantemente, permanentemente.

perfect | ’pəːfɪkt | *adj.* **1** perfecto, ideal, intachable, completo, preciso: *a perfect artist = un artista perfecto.* **2** perfecto, magistral, correcto; preciso, exacto. **3 [– (for)]** perfecto, adecuado, apropiado, apto. **4** perfecto, excelente, maravilloso, fantástico: *a perfect party = una fiesta fantástica.* **5** completo, entero, íntegro: *in perfect conditions = en excelentes condiciones.* **6** puro, sin mezcla (un color). **7** integral, redomado, total, absoluto: *a perfect idiot = un idiota redomado.* **8** GRAM. perfecto. || *v.t.* **9** perfeccionar, mejorar, pulir. || *s.c.* **10 [the –]** GRAM. el perfecto, el pretérito perfecto. || **11 – pitch,** MUS. afinación perfecta. **12 practice makes –,** la práctica nos hace perfectos.

perfection | pə’fekʃn | *s.i.* **1** perfección, excelencia. **2** perfeccionamiento, mejora, progreso. **3** maravilla, prodigio: *she is perfection playing the violin = es una maravilla tocando el violín.* || **4 to –,** a la perfección, perfectamente.

perfectionism | pə’fekʃnɪsm | *s.i.* perfeccionismo.

perfectionist | pə’fekʃnɪst | *s.c.* (a veces desp.) perfeccionista.

perfectly | pə’fektlɪ | *adv.* **1** perfectamente, correctamente, magistralmente. **2** muy, completamente, absolutamente, totalmente: *perfectly stupid = completamente estúpido.*

perfidious | pə’fɪdɪəs | *adj.* (form. y lit.) pérfido, falso, desleal, traidor, infiel.

perfidy | ’pəːfɪdɪ | *s.c.* e *i.* (form. y lit.) perfidia, deslealtad, traición.

perforate | ’pəːfəreɪt | *v.t.* perforar, taladrar, agujerear; trepar (para cortar fácilmente).

perforation | ˌpəːfə’reɪʃn | *s.c.* **1** (generalmente *pl.*) perforación, agujero, orificio; trepado. || *s.i.* **2** perforación, trepado.

perforce | pə’fɔːs | *adv.* (arc. y form.) forzosamente, por fuerza, inevitablemente, necesariamente.

perform | pə’fɔːm | *v.t.* **1** llevar a cabo, realizar, efectuar, hacer (una tarea complicada). **2** cumplir, desempeñar, ejercer (un trabajo, una función). || *v.t.* e *i.* **3** interpretar, representar, hacer un papel, actuar, dar (en teatro). **4** MUS. interpretar, ejecutar, tocar, cantar. || *v.i.* **5** MEC. funcionar, marchar, andar, comportarse: *the clock is performing all right = el reloj funciona perfectamente.* **6** (fam.) funcionar, trabajar bien, hacer un buen papel (una persona, un equipo).

performance | pə’fɔːməns | *s.c.* **1** interpretación, actuación, ejecución (teatral, musical). **2** función, sesión (teatral, cinematográfica). **3** actuación, papel, comportamiento, realización: *her performance in the negotiations = su papel en las negociaciones.* **4** funcionamiento, rendimiento (de una máquina). **5** DEP. performance. **6** (brit. y fam.) trabajo, esfuerzo, aburrimiento, lío: *what a performance just for a soup! = ¡qué lío solo para hacer una sopa!*

performer | pə’fɔːmər | *s.c.* **1** artista, actor, actriz, bailarín, acróbata. **2** músico, intérprete, ejecutante, cantante.

performing arts | pə’fɔːmɪŋˌɑːts | *s.pl.* artes escénicas (teatro, danza, música, etc...).

perfume | ’pəːfjuːm | (EE.UU.) | pər’fjuːm | (brit. **scent**) *s.c.* e *i.* **1** perfume, aroma, fragancia, olor agradable. **2** perfume, esencia: *he gave her a bottle of perfum = (él) le regaló un frasco de perfume (a ella).* || | pə’fjuːm | *v.t.* **2 [to – (with)]** (form.) perfumar, aromatizar, impregnar de aroma.

perfumed | ’pəːfjuːmd | *adj.* perfumado, aromatizado, impregnado de aroma.

perfunctorily | pə’fʌŋktərɪlɪ | *adv.* superficialmente, descuidadamente, negligentemente, a la ligera, mecánicamente, con desgana: *she greeted perfunctorily = saludó mecánicamente.*

perfunctory | pə’fʌŋktərɪ | *adj.* superficial, negligente, mecánico, desganado.

pergola | ’pəːgələ | *s.c.* pérgola.

perhaps | pə’hæps | | præs | *adv.* quizá(s), tal vez, acaso, posiblemente, puede ser, puede.

peril | ’perɪl | *s.i.* **1** (form. y lit.) peligro: *he was in great peril = estaba en grave peligro.* || *s.c.* **2** peligro, riesgo, trance:

the perils of mountain climbing = los peligros del alpinismo. || *v.t.* **3** poner en peligro, arriesgar. || **4 at one's –,** por cuenta y riesgo de uno: *he did it at his peril = lo hizo por su cuenta y riesgo.*
perilous | 'perɪləs | *adj.* (lit.) peligroso, arriesgado, aventurado, expuesto.
perilously | 'perɪləslɪ | *adv.* peligrosamente, arriesgadamente, aventuradamente.
perimeter | pə'rɪmɪtər | *s.c.* e *i.* **1** GEOM. perímetro. **2** perímetro, contorno, límite.
period | pɪərɪəd | *s.c.* **1** período, etapa, ciclo, fase, temporada. **2** racha: *winds and rainy periods = vientos y rachas de lluvia.* **3** período, sesión: *training periods = sesiones de entrenamiento.* **4** HIST. era, época, edad. **5** hora, clase: *I teach four periods today = hoy doy cuatro clases.* **6** MED. regla, período. **7** GRAM. punto (ortográfico). **8** DEP. tiempo. **9** MUS. frase musical.
periodic, periodical | ˌpɪərɪ'ɒdɪk | *adj.* **1** periódico, regular. || **2 – table,** QUIM. tabla periódica.
periodical | ˌpɪərɪ'ɒdɪkl | *s.c.* **1** periódico, publicación periódica, revista. || *adj.* **2** periódico, regular.
periodically | ˌpɪərɪ'ɒdɪklɪ | *adv.* periódicamente, regularmente, a intervalos regulares, de vez en cuando.
peripatetic | ˌperɪpə'tetɪk | *adj.* **1** (form.) itinerante, ambulante, sin residencia fija. **2** FIL. peripatético.
peripheral | pə'rɪfərəl | *adj.* (form.) **1** menor, escaso, insignificante, limitado: *of peripheral importance = de escasa importancia.* **2** periférico, exterior. || *s.c.* **3** INF. dispositivo periférico (que se conecta a un ordenador).
periphery | pə'rɪfərɪ | *s.c.* (form.) **1** periferia, afueras, parte exterior: *situated on the periphery = situado en las afueras.* **2** (fig.) extremo, margen: *on the periphery of politics = al margen de la política.* **3** MED. periferia. **4** MAT. perímetro.
periscope | 'perɪskəup | *s.c.* periscopio.
perish | 'perɪʃ | *v.i.* **1** PER. perecer, fallecer, morir, sucumbir. || *v.t.* e *i.* **2** (brit.) estropear(se), dañar(se), perjudicar, deteriorar(se), echar(se) a perder, pudrir(se) (la comida, un material). || **3 – the thought,** (fam.) ni pensarlo, Dios me valga, Dios no lo permita.
perishable | 'perɪʃəbl | *adj.* perecedero, que se estropea fácilmente, deteriorable (un alimento).
perisher | 'perɪʃər | *s.c.* (arc. y fam.) diablo, tunante, golfo, destrozón (se dice de un niño).
perishing | 'perɪʃɪŋ | *adj.* **1** helado, congelado, tieso (una persona). **2** glacial, extremadamente frío, helador, que pela: *it's perishing cold = hace un frío que pela.* **3** (brit. y arc.) insoportable, molesto, pesado, fastidioso, cargante, maldito.
peritonitis | ˌperɪtəu'naɪtɪs | *s.i.* MED. peritonitis.
periwinkle | 'perɪˌwɪŋkl | *s.c.* **1** BOT. vincapervinca, hierba doncella. **2** ZOOL. bígaro, caracolillo, litorina.
perjure | 'pəːdər | *v.t.* **1 [to – oneself]** perjurar, perjurarse.
perjured | 'pəːdʒəd | *adj.* falso.
perjury | 'pəːdʒərɪ | *s.c.* e *i.* DER. perjurio, falso testimonio, falsedad, mentira.
perk | pəːk | *s.c.* (generalmente *pl.*) (form.) **perquisite. 1** (fam.) ventajas, extras, sobresueldo, plus, salario en especie, paga extra (de un trabajo). || *v.t.* e *i.* **[to – up] 1** (fam.) animar(se), alegrar(se), reanimar(se). **2** (fam.) mover, levantar (la cola, las orejas un perro). **3** emperifollarse, engalanarse. **4** (fam.) colar, hacer (café).
perky | 'pəːkɪ | *adj.* **1** (fam.) animado, alegre, contento, jovial, vivaz. **2** impetuoso, descarado, insolente.
perm, permanent wave | pəːm | (EE.UU. **permanent**) *s.c.* **1** (fam.) permanente, moldeado. || *v.t.* **2** (fam.) hacer la permanente, moldear. **3 [to – (from)]** (brit. y fam.) hacer combinaciones, barajar (nombres de equipos al hacer quinielas).
permafrost | 'pəːməfrɒst | (EE.UU.) | 'pəːməfrɔːst | *s.i.* GEOL. permafrost, permagel.
permanence, permanency | 'pəːmənəns | *s.i.* permanencia, continuidad, constancia.
permanency | 'pəːmənənsɪ | *s.c.* **1** cosa permanente; ocupación fija, puesto fijo: *she got a permanency = consiguió un puesto fijo.* || *s.i.* **2** permanencia, continuidad, constancia.
permanent | 'pəːmənənt | *adj.* **1** permanente, constante, duradero, de por vida. **2** fijo, definitivo, estable: *a permanent job = un trabajo fijo.* || *s.c.* **3** (EE.UU.) permanente, moldeado.
permanently | 'pəːmənəntlɪ | *adv.* permanentemente, constantemente, continuamente.
permeable | 'pəːmjəbl | *adj.* (form.) permeable, absorbente, filtrable.
permeate | 'pəːmɪeɪt | *v.t.* e *i.* impregnar, saturar, penetrar, infiltrar(se), pasar.
permissible | pə'mɪsəbl | *adj.* (form.) permisible, permitido, lícito.
permission | pə'mɪʃn | *s.i.* permiso, consentimiento, autorización, licencia.
permissive | pə'mɪsɪv | *adj.* **1** (generalmente desp.) permisivo: *a permissive society = una sociedad permisiva.* **2** permitido, consentido, lícito. **3** tolerante, condescendiente, indulgente. **4** opcional, alternativo, facultativo.
permissiveness | pə'mɪsɪvnɪs | *s.i.* permisividad.
permit | 'pə'mɪt | *v.t.* (form.) **1 [to –** *o.i.* + *o.d./ger./o.* + *inf.***]** permitir, autorizar, consentir. **2** permitir, conceder: *permit me to tell you... = permítame decirle...* **3 [to –** *o.* + *adv./prep.***]** permitir, tolerar, consentir, aguantar: *I won't permit him in = no consentiré que pase.* **4** [no pasiva] admitir, aceptar: *his leaving permits no other explanation = su marcha no admite otra explicación.* || *v.i.* **5** permitir, hacer posible, dar lugar a: *if time permits = si el tiempo lo permite.* || | 'pəːmɪt | *s.c.* **6** permiso, autorización, pase, licencia (por escrito).
permutation | ˌpəːmjuː'teɪʃn | *s.c.* (form.) permutación, permuta, cambio, alteración, variación.
pernicious | pə'nɪʃəs | *adj.* **1** (form.) pernicioso, nocivo, mortal, perjudicial, dañino, peligroso, nefasto, destructivo, ruinoso. **2** (arc.) maligno, malvado, demoníaco.
pernickety | pə'nɪkɪtɪ | (EE.UU. **persnickety**) *adj.* (fam. y desp.) **1** quisquilloso, maniático, escrupuloso, fastidioso. **2** minucioso, delicado, meticuloso (un trabajo).
peroration | ˌperə'reɪʃn | *s.c.* **1** peroración. **2** (form. y desp.) perorata, rollo.
peroxide | pə'rɒksaɪd | *s.i.* **1** QUIM. peróxido, peróxido de hidrógeno, agua oxigenada. || *v.t.* **2** tratar con agua oxigenada, aplicar agua oxigenada. **3** teñir con agua oxigenada. || **4 – blonde,** rubia oxigenada, rubia teñida.
perpendicular | ˌpəːpən'dɪkjulər | *adj.* **1** perpendicular, vertical. **2** (fam.) derecho, en pie, de pie: *drunk sailors who couldn't stand perpendicular = marineros borrachos que no se tenían en pie.* **3** GEOM. perpendicular. **4** ARQ. perpendicular (estilo gótico). || *s.c.* e *i.* **5** línea perpendicular, posición vertical.
perpetrate | 'pəːpɪtreɪt | *v.t.* (form.) perpetrar, cometer, llevar a cabo, consumar (un crimen).
perpetrator | 'pəːpɪtreɪtər | *s.c.* (form.) perpetrador, autor.
perpetual | pə'petʃuəl | *adj.* **1** (generalmente desp.) perpetuo, continuo, incesante, constante. **2** perpetuo, perenne, imperecedero: *perpetual snows = nieves perpetuas.*
perpetually | pə'petʃuəlɪ | *adv.* perpetuamente, constantemente, incesantemente, continuamente.
perpetuate | pə'petʃueɪt | *v.t.* (form.) perpetuar, preservar, inmortalizar: *perpetuating sex inequality = perpetuando la desigualdad de los sexos.*
perpetuation | pəˌpetʃu'eɪʃn | *s.i.* perpetuación, inmortalización.
perpetuity | ˌpəːpɪ'tjuːətɪ | (EE.UU.) | ˌpəːpɪ'tuːətɪ | *s.i.* **1** perpetuidad, eternidad. **2** anualidad perpetua, renta perpetua. || **3 in –,** a perpetuidad, para siempre.
perplex | pə'pleks | *v.t.* (form.) dejar perplejo, desconcertar, desorientar, confundir.
perplexed | pə'plekst | *adj.* **1** (form.) perplejo, desconcertado, confuso, desorientado. **2** complicado, enredado, confuso.
perplexing | pə'pleksɪŋ | *adj.* (form.) que deja perplejo, confuso, desconcertante.
perplexity | pə'pleksətɪ | *s.i.* perplejidad, desconcierto, desorientación, confusión, incertidumbre.
perquisite | 'pəːkwɪzɪt | V. **perk.**
persecute | 'pəːsɪkjuːt | *v.t.* **1** perseguir, hostigar, maltratar, oprimir. **2** molestar, vejar, atormentar.
persecution | ˌpəːsɪ'juːʃn | *s.c.* e *i.* persecución, hostigamiento, opresión.

persecutor | ’pəːsɪkjuːtər | *s.c.* perseguidor, torturador.

perseverance | ˌpəːsɪ’vɪərəns | *s.c.* perseverancia, constancia, tenacidad, persistencia, tesón.

persevere | ˌpəːsɪ’vɪər | *v.i.* **[to – (at/in /with)]** perseverar, insistir, persistir, continuar con tenacidad, no abandonar.

persevering | ˌpəːsɪ’vɪərɪŋ | *adj.* perseverante, tenaz, insistente, persistente.

Persia | ’pəːʃə | *s.sing.* Persia, (hoy Irán).

Persian | ’pəːʃən | *adj.* **1** (arc.) persa, de Persia (lengua, nacionalidad, etc.). || *s.i.* **2** persa (la lengua).

persimmon | pəː’sɪmən | *s.c.* BOT. caqui, placaminero.

persist | pə’sɪst | *v.i.* **1** **[to – (in/with)]** persistir, insistir, obstinarse, obcecarse, empeñarse. **2** persistir, continuar, seguir: *if rain persists we'll stay home = si sigue lloviendo nos quedaremos en casa.*

persistence | pə’sɪstəns | *s.i.* **1** persistencia, insistencia, continuidad. **2** persistencia, perseverancia, tenacidad.

persistent | pə’sɪstənt | *adj.* (generalmente desp.) **1** persistente, pertinaz, continuo. **2** persistente, permanente: *a persistent sore throat = un dolor de garganta persistente.*

persistently | pə’sɪstəntlɪ | *adv.* **1** persistentemente, constantemente, permanentemente, repetidamente. **2** tenazmente, con tesón, con determinación, con firmeza.

person | ’pəːsn | *s.c.* **1** [*pl.* **people**] persona, individuo, ser humano. **2** [*pl.* **persons**] DER. persona: *missing persons = desaparecidos.* **3** (generalmente *sing.*) [*pl.* **persons**] (arc.) persona, ropas, cuerpo: *they searched her person = la registraron.* **4** personalidad, carácter, tipo, personaje: *the religious person in me = mi personalidad religiosa.* || *s.c.* e *i.* **5** [*pl.* **persons**] GRAM. persona. || **6 in –,** en persona, personalmente. **7 in the – of,** (form.) en, en la persona de: *we have an admirer in the person of Peter = tenemos un admirador en Peter.*

OBS. **-person,** funciona como sufijo en palabras como **chairperson, spokesperson,** en lugar de **man** o **woman,** e indica que una persona realiza un trabajo determinado sin prejuzgar el sexo de la persona que lo desempeña.

persona | pəːˌsəʊnə | *s.c.* **1** (form.) persona, personaje, imagen, carácter. || **2 – non grata,** persona no grata.

personable | ’pəːsnəbl | *adj.* presentable, agradable, atractivo, bien parecido.

personage | ’pəːsnɪdʒ | *s.c.* **1** (form.) personaje, persona famosa. **2** personaje, carácter (dramático).

personal | ’pəːsnl | *adj.* **1** [no *comp.*] personal, privado, particular. **2** [no *comp.*] personal, en persona: *a personal visit = una visita en persona.* **3** personal, íntimo, maleducado, rudo, grosero (una observación, una persona). **4** [no *comp.*] (form.) íntimo, de uso privado, corporal (la higiene). **5** DER. personal, privado: *personal possessions = propiedades privadas.* **6** GRAM. personal. || *s.c.* **7** (EE.UU.) anuncio personal, nota personal (en un periódico). || **8 – assistant,** secretario particular. **9 – column,** PER. columna de anuncios personales. **10 – computer,** INF. ordenador personal. **11 – pronoun,** GRAM. pronombre personal.

personality | ˌpəːsə’nælɪtɪ | *s.c.* e *i.* **1** personalidad, carácter, naturaleza. || *s.c.* **2** personalidad, celebridad. || **3 personalities,** ataques personales, personalismos.

personalization | ’pəːsənəlaɪ’zeɪʃn | *s.i.* personalización.

personalize | ’pəːsnəlaɪz | (brit. **personalise**) *v.t.* **1** personalizar, poner nombre o apellidos, poner (membrete), marcar, grabar (con iniciales sobres, ropa, etc.). **2** (desp.) personalizar, tomar personalmente, dar carácter individual: *don't personalize the subject = no personalices el tema.*

personalized | ’pəːsnəlaɪzd | *adj.* **1** grabado con nombre, marcado con iniciales, con nombre: *personalized envelopes = sobres con el nombre.* **2** personalizado, particularizado, individual: *personalized teaching = enseñanza personalizada.*

personally | ’pəːsnəlɪ | *adv.* **1** personalmente, directamente, en persona. **2** personalmente, particularmente: *Personally, I think... = yo personalmente pienso...* **3** personalmente, como persona, como individuo. **4** (desp.) personalmente, de forma personal: *she shouldn't take it so personally = no se lo debería tomar de forma tan personal.* **5** en privado, en particular.

personification | pəːˌsɒnɪfɪ’keɪʃn | *s.c.* e *i.* personificación, representación, símbolo, encarnación.

personify | pəː’sɒnɪfaɪ | *v.t.* personificar, representar, encarnar, simbolizar.

personnel | ˌpəːsə’nel | *s.pl.* **1** personal, plantilla, dotación. || *s.i.* **2** [– *v.sing./pl.*] personal (departamento en una organización, fábrica): *she used to work in personnel = solía trabajar en personal.*

perspective | pə’spektɪv | *s.i.* **1** ART. perspectiva. **2** perspectiva, objetividad. || *s.c.* e *i.* **3** perspectiva, punto de vista, panorama. || **4 in/into –, a)** en perspectiva, con sensibilidad; **b)** ART. en perspectiva, de tamaño y posición correctas. **5 out of –,** ART. sin perspectiva, sin el debido tamaño o posición: *the horse was out of perspective = al caballo le faltaba la perspectiva.*

perspicacious | ˌpəːspɪ’keɪʃəs | *adj.* (form.) perspicaz, astuto, sagaz, agudo.

perspicacity | ˌpəːspɪ’kæsətɪ | *s.i.* (form.) perspicacia, sagacidad, astucia, agudeza.

perspiration | ˌpəːspə’reɪʃn | *s.i.* (euf.) transpiración, sudor.

perspire | pə’spaɪə | *v.i.* (euf.) transpirar, sudar.

persuade | pə’sweɪd | *v.t.* **1** **[to – (in to/out of)]** persuadir, inducir, instar, disuadir. **2** **[to – (into/out of)]** forzar, introducir gradualmente, obligar a entrar (un elemento en otro). **3** **[to – (of)]** (form.) convencer, persuadir, hacer creer: *he persuaded his father he was sincere = hizo creer a su padre que era sincero.*

persuaded | pə’sweɪdɪd | *adj.* persuadido, convencido.

persuasion | pə’sweɪʒn | *s.i.* **1** persuasión, convicción: *her powers of persuasion = su poder de persuasión.* || *s.c.* **2** (form.) creencia, credo, convicción, grupo, secta (política, filosófica). **3** (form.) escuela, moda, estilo, carácter, género, clase. **4** opinión, juicio, criterio: *it was her persuasion that ... = fue su opinión que ...* || **5 of ... –,** de la escuela ...: *of the minimal persuasion = de la escuela minimalista.*

persuasive | pə’sweɪsɪv | *adj.* persuasivo, convincente.

persuasively | pə’sweɪsɪvlɪ | *adv.* persuasivamente, convincentemente.

pert | pəːt | *adj.* **1** fresca, descarada, atrevida, insolente (una niña, una joven). **2** gracioso, encantador, simpático, coquetón, con mucho estilo (una cosa): *a pert little dress = un vestido coquetón.*

pertain | pəː’teɪn | *v.t.* **[to – (to)]** (form.) pertenecer, corresponder, atañer, incumbir, tener que ver, tener relación: *all questions pertaining to the National Health = todas las preguntas relacionadas con la Seguridad Social.*

pertinacious | ˌpəːtɪ’neɪʃəs | *adj.* (form.) pertinaz, tenaz, obstinado, terco, persistente.

pertinent | ’pəːtɪnənt | *adj.* **[– (to)]** (form.) pertinente, relevante, oportuno, relacionado, conectado.

perturb | pə’təːb | *v.t.* (form.) perturbar, alterar, inquietar, turbar, trastornar, agitar.

perturbation | ˌpəːtə’beɪʃn | *s.i.* perturbación, alteración, inquietud, trastorno, agitación.

perturbed | pə’təːbd | *adj.* alarmado, inquieto, trastornado, agitado, alterado.

Peru | pə’ruː | *s.sing.* Perú.

perusal | pə’ruːzl | *s.i.* (form.) lectura cuidadosa; examen detenido.

peruse | pə’ruːz | *v.t.* **1** (form.) leer cuidadosamente, leer con atención; examinar a fondo. **2** (fig.) leer, estudiar, inspeccionar.

Peruvian | pə’ruːvjən | *adj.* **1** peruano (nacionalidad, origen). || *s.c.* **2** peruano.

pervade | pə’veɪd | *v.t.* (form.) extenderse por, saturar, impregnar, llenar: *an awful smell pervading the house = un olor horrible que impregnaba la casa.*

pervasive | pə’veɪsɪv | *adj.* penetrante, extendido, que satura, que impregna, omnipresente.

perverse | pə’vəːs | *adj.* **1** perverso, excesivo, exagerado, poco razonable, inaceptable: *a perverse pleasure in irritating people = un placer perverso en irritar a la gente.* **2** terco, contumaz. **3** díscolo, desobediente, rebelde: *a perverse child = un niño díscolo.*

perversely | pə’vəːslɪ | *adv.* tercamente, contumazmente.

perversion | pə'vɜːʃn | (EE.UU.) | pə'vɜːʒn | *s.c.* **1** distorsión, alteración, falseamiento. || *s.c.* **2** perversión (sexual). || *s.i.* **3** perversión, corrupción.

perversity, perverseness | pə'vɜːsɪtɪ | *s.i.* **1** perversidad, depravación. **2** terquedad, contumacia.

pervert | pə'vɜːt | *v.t.* **1** pervertir, corromper, viciar, depravar. **2** emplear mal, utilizar con malos propósitos. **3** distorsionar, alterar, falsear, adulterar. || | 'pɜːvɜːt | *s.c.* **4** (desp.) pervertido, depravado (sexual).

perverted | pə'vɜːtɪd | *adj.* **1** pervertido, depravado, vicioso, corrompido. **2** malsano, enfermizo, perverso.

pesky | 'peskɪ | *adj.* (EE.UU. y fam.) irritante, cargante, molesto, fastidioso.

pessary | 'pesərɪ | *s.c.* MED. **1** pesario, dispositivo intrauterino. **2** pesario (anticonceptivo).

pessimism | 'pesɪmɪzəm | *s.i.* pesimismo.

pessimist | 'pesɪmɪst | *s.c.* pesimista.

pessimistic | ˌpesɪ'mɪstɪk | *adj.* pesimista, melancólico, triste.

pessimistically | ˌpesɪ'mɪstɪkəlɪ | *adv.* con pesimismo, con tristeza.

pest | pest | *s.c.* **1** peste, plaga, insecto o animal dañino. **2** (fam.) pelmazo, latazo, pesado, molestia. **3** peste, pestilencia.

pester | 'pestər | *v.t.* **[to – (for/with)]** molestar, importunar, acosar, no dejar en paz.

pesticide | 'pestɪsaɪd | *s.i.* QUIM. pesticida, insecticida.

pestilence | 'pestɪləns | *s.c.* e *i.* (lit.) pestilencia, peste, (especialmente) peste bubónica.

pestle | 'pesl | *s.c.* mano de mortero, mano de almirez.

pet | pet | *s.c.* **1** animal de compañía, animal doméstico, mascota. **2** (a veces desp.) niño mimado, favorito, preferido, predilecto. **3** *sing.* (fam.) cariño, amor, cielo, encanto: *come here, pet = ven aquí, cariño.* **4** (arc.) mal humor, enfado, enojo (pasajero). || *v.t.* **5** acariciar, mimar (a una persona, a un animal). || *v.t.* e *i.* **6** (fam.) acariciar(se), besuquear(se), sobar(se). || **7 – name,** apelativo cariñoso.

petal | 'petl | *s.c.* BOT. pétalo.

petard | pe'tɑːd | *s.c.* **1** petardo. || **2 to be hoist with one's own –,** salirle a uno el tiro por la culata.

peter | 'piːtər | *v.i.* **[to – out]** agotarse, acabarse, desaparecer (gradualmente): *my interest on the matter petered out = mi interés por la materia desapareció poco a poco.*

petite | pə'tiːt | *adj.* pequeña, chiquita, menuda (una mujer).

petitfour | ˌpetɪ'fʊər | *s.c.* pastelito, mazapán, galletita.

petition | pɪ'tɪʃn | *s.c.* **1 [– (for/against)]** petición, solicitud, instancia. **2** DER. demanda, recurso. **3** ruego, súplica. **4** oración, petición. || *v.t.* e *i.* **5 [to – (for /against)]** solicitar, requerir, pedir, demandar, suplicar.

petitioner | pɪ'tɪʃənər | *s.c.* **1** solicitante, firmante de una solicitud o instancia. **2** DER. demandante, solicitante (de divorcio).

petrification | ˌpetrɪfɪ'keɪʃn | *s.i.* **1** petrificación, fosilización. **2** (form. y fig.) fosilización, estancamiento, paralización (de una institución).

petrified | 'petrɪfaɪd | *adj.* **1** petrificado, aterrado, horrorizado. **2** petrificado, fosilizado.

petrify | 'petrɪfaɪ | *v.t.* **1** petrificar, paralizar, aterrar, horrorizar, atemorizar. || *v.t.* e *i.* **2** petrificar(se), fosilizar(se).

petrochemical | 'petrəʊ'kemɪkəl | *s.c.* petroquímica (substancia, planta).

petrol | 'petrəl | (EE.UU.) **gasoline, gas.** *s.i.* **1** (brit.) gasolina. || **2 – bomb,** cóctel molotov, bomba de gasolina. **3 – station,** gasolinera.

petroleum | pɪ'trəʊlɪəm | *s.i.* **1** petróleo. || **2 – jelly**/(EE.UU.) **petrolatum,** MED. petrolato.

petticoat | 'petɪkəʊt | *s.c.* **1** enaguas, combinación, falda, (Am.) fustán. **2** (argot) chica, muchacha, mujer. || *adj.* **3** hembra, femenina. **4** de mujeres, por las mujeres: *a petticoat government = un gabinete de mujeres.*

pettifogging | 'petɪfɒgɪŋ | *adj.* **1** (arc.) quisquilloso, puntilloso, meticuloso. **2** insignificante, baladí, trivial.

pettiness | 'petɪnɪs | *s.i.* **1** mezquindad, estrechez de miras, cicatería, ruindad. **2** insignificancia, trivialidad, nimiedad, pequeñez.

pettish | 'petɪʃ | *adj.* (desp.) pesado, irritante, malhumorado, quisquilloso, petulante.

petty | 'petɪ | *adj.* **1** insignificante, nimio, de poca monta, trivial, menor: *petty problems = problemas insignificantes.* **2** (desp.) mezquino, cicatero, ruin, poco comprensivo, intolerante: *don't be so petty = no seas tan mezquino.* || **3 – cash,** dinero para gastos menores (en una oficina). **4 – larceny,** DER. hurto menor, ratería. **5 – officer,** MAR. suboficial de marina.

petulance | 'petjʊləns | *s.i.* mal humor, enfurruñamiento, resentimiento.

petulant | 'petjʊlənt | *adj.* malhumorado, enfurruñado, de malas pulgas, de mal genio, irritable.

petulantly | 'petjʊləntlɪ | *adv.* malhumoradamente, con malas pulgas, con mal genio.

petunia | pɪ'tjuːnɪə | *s.c.* BOT. petunia.

pew | pjuː | *s.c.* **1** banco (de iglesia). || **2 to take a –,** (brit. y fam.) tomar asiento, sentarse.

pewter | 'pjuːtər | *s.i.* **1** peltre. || *adj.* **2** de peltre. || **3 – ware,** utensilios de peltre (tazas, platos).

phalanx | 'fælæŋks | [*pl.* **phalanxes** o **phalanges**] *s.c.* **1** [– *v.sing./pl.*] (form.) falange: *a phalanx of soldiers = una falange de soldados.* **2** ANAT. falange.

phallic | 'fælɪk | *adj.* fálico.

phallus | 'fæləs | *s.c.* (form.) falo, pene.

phantasmagoria | ˌfæntæzmə'gɒrɪə | (EE.UU.) | ˌfæntæzmə'gɔːrɪə | *s.c.* fantasmagoría.

phantom | 'fæntəm | *s.c.* **1** fantasma, aparecido, espectro. **2** (fig.) fantasma, ilusión, quimera. || *adj.* **3** fantasma, fantasmal; imaginario, irreal: *phantom shadows = sombras fantasmales.*

pharaoh | 'feərəʊ | *s.c.* faraón.

Pharisee | 'færɪsiː | *s.c.* **1** HIST. fariseo. || **2 pharisee,** (form. y desp.) fariseo, hipócrita.

pharmaceutical | ˌfɑːmə'sjuːtɪkl | *adj.* **1** farmacéutico. || **2 pharmaceuticals,** productos farmacéuticos.

pharmacist | 'fɑːməsɪst | *s.c.* farmacéutico, boticario, (Am.) químico farmacéutico.

pharmacologist | ˌfɑːmə'kɒlədʒɪst | *s.c.* farmacólogo.

pharmacology | ˌfɑːmə'kɒlədʒɪ | *s.i.* farmacología.

pharmacy | 'fɑːməsɪ | *s.c.* **1** (form.) farmacia, botica. || *s.i.* **2** farmacia (ciencia).

phase | feɪz | *s.c.* **1 [(in/of) –]** fase, período, etapa. **2 [– (of)]** ASTR. fase. **3** parte, aspecto (de una operación). || *v.t.* **4** realizar en fases, proyectar por etapas, organizar en fases: *the course is phased = el curso está organizado en fases.* || **5 to – in,** introducir gradualmente, implantar por etapas: *the new education law will be phased = se implantará gradualmente la nueva ley de educación.* **6 to – out,** retirar gradualmente, eliminar por etapas. **7 in –,** sincronizado, correlacionado, en fase. **8 out of –,** desincronizado, sin correlación, fuera de fase.

pheasant | 'feznt | *s.c.* [*pl.* **pheasant**] ZOOL. faisán.

phenomena | fɪ'nɒmɪnə | *s.pl.* de **phenomenom.**

phenomenal | fɪ'nɒmɪnəl | *adj.* **1** fenomenal, enorme, increíble, extraordinario. **2** [no *comp.*] FIL. fenoménico, percibido por los sentidos.

phenomenally | fɪ'nɒmɪnəlɪ | *adv.* extremadamente, increíblemente, extraordinariamente.

phenomenon | fɪ'nɒmɪnən | [*pl.* **phenomena**] *s.c.* **1** FIL. fenómeno. **2** fenómeno, prodigio, portento.

phew | fjuː | *interj.* ¡puf!, ¡fiu! (sonido silbante que expresa sorpresa, cansancio).

phial, vial | 'faɪəl | *s.c.* frasco, ampolla.

philanderer | fɪ'lændər | *s.c.* (arc. y desp.) mujeriego, tenorio, conquistador.

philanthropic | ˌfɪlən'θrɒpɪk | *adj.* filantrópico, caritativo.

philanthropist | fɪ'lænθrəpɪst | *s.c.* filántropo, benefactor.

philanthropy | fɪ'lænθrəpɪ | *s.i.* **1** filantropía, caridad. || *s.c.* **2** acción o institución filantrópica.

philatelist | fɪ'lætəlɪst | *s.c.* filatelista, coleccionista de sellos.

philately | fɪ'lætəlɪ | *s.i.* filatelia.

Philippine | 'fɪlɪpiːn | *adj.* **1** filipino (nacionalidad). || *s.c.* **2** filipino (de origen).

Philippines | 'fɪlɪpiːns | *s.sing.* Filipinas.

philistine | 'fɪlɪstaɪn | *s.c.* **1** (desp.) persona inculta, ignorante, persona sin inquietudes intelectuales (que se vanagloria de ello). || *adj.* **2** ignorante, inculto.

philistinism | 'fɪlɪstɪnɪzəm | *s.i.* ignorancia, incultura, falta de inquietud intelectual.

philologist | fɪ'lɒlədʒɪst | *s.c.* filólogo.

philology | fɪ'lɒlədʒɪ | *s.i.* filología.

philosopher | fɪ'lɒsəfər | *s.c.* **1** filósofo. **2** (fig.) filósofo, pensador.

philosophic, philosophical | ˌfɪlə'sɒfɪkl | *adj.* **1** filosófico: *a philosophical essay = un ensayo filosófico.* **2** (fig.) filosófico, estoico, comprensivo, tranquilo, calmado.

philosophically | fɪ'lɒsəfɪkəlɪ | *adv.* **1** filosóficamente. **2** (fig.) filosóficamente, estoicamente, con calma.

philosophize | fɪ'lɒsəfaɪz | (brit. **philosophise**) *v.i.* **[to – (about)]** filosofar, especular.

philosophy | fɪ'lɒsəfɪ | *s.i.* filosofía.

phlegm | flem | *s.i.* **1** flema, moco, mucosidad, esputo. **2** (form.) flema, calma, cuajo, cachaza, pachorra.

phlegmatic | fleg'mætɪk | *adj.* (form.) flemático, cachazudo.

phobia | 'fəubjə | *s.c.* **[– (about)]** fobia, aversión, antipatía, asco.

phobic | 'fəubɪk | *adj.* fóbico.

phoenix | 'fiːnɪks | *s.c.* **1** fénix, ave fénix. **2** ASTR. constelación fénix. || **3 to rise like a – from the ashes,** resurgir de las cenizas como el ave fénix.

phoenix-like | 'fiːnɪksˌlaɪk | *adj.* como ave fénix.

phone | fəun | *s.c.* e *i.* **1** teléfono. **2** (EE.UU.) audífono. **3** FON. fonema. || *v.t.* e *i.* **4 [to – (up)]** telefonear, llamar por teléfono. || **5 to be on the –, a)** estar hablando por teléfono; **b)** tener teléfono, estar abonado al teléfono: *she wasn't on the phone = no tenía teléfono.* **6 – book,** guía telefónica. **7 to – in,** llamar por teléfono al centro de trabajo (para justificar una ausencia, recibir instrucciones).

phone-booth | 'fəunˌbuːð | *s.c.* **1** locutorio telefónico. **2** (EE.UU.) cabina telefónica.

phone-box | 'fəunˌbɒks | *s.c.* cabina telefónica.

phone-in | 'fəunˌɪn | *s.c.* RAD. programa con llamadas telefónicas de oyentes.

phoneme | 'fəuniːm | *s.c.* fonema.

phonetic | fəu'netɪk | *adj.* fonético.

phonetically | fəu'netɪkəlɪ | *adv.* fonéticamente.

phonetics | fəu'netɪks | *s.i.* fonética.

phoney | 'fəunɪ | (EE.UU. **phony**) *adj.* **1** (fam. y desp.) falso, falsificado, simulado, falaz: *a phoney accent = un acento falso.* **2** insincero, pretencioso, hipócrita (una persona). || *s.c.* **3** fraude, engaño, estafa (una persona, una cosa).

phonograph | 'fəunəgrɑːf | *s.c.* (EE.UU. y brit. arc.) gramófono, fonógrafo, tocadiscos.

phonological | ˌfəunə'lɒdʒɪkl | *adj.* fonológico.

phonology | fəu'nɒlədʒɪ | *s.i.* fonología.

phong V. **phoneg.**

phooey | 'fuːɪ | *interj.* (fam.) ¡puff!, ¡bueno!, ¡tonterías! (expresa desprecio, decepción o irritación).

phosphate | 'fɒsfeɪt | *s.c.* e *i.* **1** QUIM. fosfato. **2** fertilizante (para plantas). **3** bebida efervescente, agua gasificada (con ácido fosfórico).

phosphorescence | ˌfɒsfə'resns | *s.i.* fosforescencia, luminiscencia.

phosphorescent | ˌfɒsfə'resnt | *adj.* fosforescente, luminiscente.

phosphorus | 'fɒsfərəs | *s.i.* fósforo.

photo | 'fəutəu | *s.c.* [*pl.* **photos**] **1** (fam.) foto, fotografía. || *v.t.* e *i.* **2** fotografiar(se), tomar fotografías. || *prefijo* **3** foto: *fotoelectric = fotoeléctrico.* || **4 – finish,** resultado comprobado por fotocontrol (en una carrera); (fig.) final muy reñido, competición muy reñida: *a photo finish contest = un concurso con final muy reñido.*

photocopier | 'fəutəuˌkɒpɪər | *s.c.* fotocopiadora.

photocopy | 'fəutəuˌkɒpɪ | *s.c.* **1** fotocopia. || *v.t.* **2** fotocopiar.

Photofit | 'fəutəufɪt | *adj.* (retrato) robot (es marca registrada y forma compuesto con un nombre): *a Photofit picture = un retrato robot.*

photogenic | ˌfəutəu'dʒenɪk | *adj.* **1** fotogénico. **2** BIOL. fotógeno, fosforescente. **3** FIS. fotogénico, causado por la luz.

photograph | 'fəutəgrɑːf | (EE.UU.) | 'fəutəgræf | *s.c.* **1** fotografía. || *v.t.* **2** fotografiar, hacer fotografías, sacar fotografías. || *v.i.* **3 [to –** *adv.***]** ser fotogénico, salir bien en las fotos, quedar bien en fotografía: *models usually photograph well = las modelos son muy fotogénicas.* || **4 to take a –,** sacar una foto.

photographer | fə'tɒgrəfər | *s.c.* fotógrafo.

photographic | ˌfəutə'græfɪk | *adj.* **1** fotográfico. **2** fotográfica, portentosa, privilegiada (la memoria).

photography | fə'tɒgrəfɪ | *s.i.* fotografía.

photostat | 'fəutəustæt | *s.c.* **1** fotostato, copia fotostática (es marca registrada). || *v.t.* **2** fotocopiar con fotostato, hacer una copia fotostática.

phrasal verb | ˌfreɪzl'vɜːb | *s.c.* GRAM. verbo con partícula (*prep.* o *adv.*): *"to look after" is a phrasal verb = "to look after" es un verbo con partícula.*

phrase | freɪz | *s.c.* **1** frase, locución: *"singing in the rain" is a phrase not a sentence = "cantando bajo la lluvia" es una locución, no una oración.* **2** expresión, giro, dicho. **3** MUS. frase. || *v.t.* **4 [to –** *o.* + *adv./prep.***]** frasear, formular, expresar (oralmente o por escrito): *she phrased her ideas one by one = formuló sus ideas una a una.* **5** MUS. dividir en frases. || **6 in ... –/to use ... –** en palabras de ..., según ... **7 – book,** libro de frases hechas. **8 to turn a –,** expresarse de forma original, expresarse con ingenio. **9 turn of –,** forma de expresarse: *an intelligent turn of phrase = una inteligente forma de expresarse.*

phraseology | ˌfreɪzɪ'ɒlədʒɪ | *s.i.* fraseología.

phrasing | freɪzɪŋ | *s.i.* **1** fraseología, estilo, modo de expresarse, términos; redacción. **2** MUS. fraseo.

phrenologist | frɪ'nɒlədʒɪst | *s.c.* frenólogo.

phrenology | frɪ'nɒlədʒɪ | *s.i.* frenología.

phut | fʌt | (brit. y fam.) *interj.* **1** puf, pof (sonido de una máquina que deja de funcionar, de algo que estalla). || **2 to go –,** estropearse, averiarse, hacer puf.

physical | 'fɪzɪkl | *adj.* **1** físico, corporal: *physical strength = fuerza física.* **2** físico, material. **3** físico, científico, de la física. **4** GEOG. física. **5** (euf.) violento, brutal, brusco (especialmente en deporte). **6** (fam.) sobón, tocón, pulpo. **7** real (un hecho). | *s.c.* **8** MED. reconocimiento médico, chequeo médico. || **9 – education,** educación física, deporte, gimnasia. **10 – jerks,** (arc. y hum.) ejercicios físicos, gimnasia (para estar en forma). **11 – science/sciences,** ciencia(s) físicas. **12 – training,** (arc.) educación física, deporte, entrenamiento.

physically | 'fɪzɪkəlɪ | *adv.* **1** físicamente, corporalmente. **2** materialmente, realmente. **3** (fam.) físicamente, completamente, totalmente: *it's physically impossible = es totalmente imposible.*

physician | fɪ'zɪʃn | *s.c.* **1** (arc.) médico, doctor. **2** (EE.UU.) curandero.

physicist | 'fɪzɪsɪst | *s.c.* físico, especialista en ciencias físicas.

physics | 'fɪzɪks | *s.i.* **1** física. **2** propiedades físicas, leyes físicas.

physio | 'fɪzɪəu | *s.c.* **1** (fam.) fisioterapeuta. || *s.i.* **2** fisioterapia. || *prefijo.* **3** fisio: *physiological = fisiológico.*

physiognomy | ˌfɪzɪ'ɒnəmɪ | *s.c.* **1** (form.) fisionomía, fisonomía. **2** fisonomía, aspecto, características geográficas (de un país).

physiological, physiologic | ˌfɪzɪə'lɒdʒɪkl | *adj.* fisiológico.

physiologist | ˌfɪzɪ'ɒlədʒɪst | *s.c.* fisiólogo.

physiology | ˌfɪzɪ'ɒlədʒɪ | *s.i.* fisiología.

physiotherapist | ˌfɪzɪəu'θerəpɪst | *s.c.* MED. fisioterapeuta.

physiotherapy | ˌfɪzɪəu'θerəpɪ | *s.i.* MED. fisioterapia.

physique | fɪ'ziːk | *s.c.* e *i.* físico, aspecto físico, planta, presencia, apariencia: *an attractive physique = un físico atractivo.*

pi | paɪ | *num.* **1** GEOM. pi, 3.14159. **2** decimosexta letra del alfabeto griego. **3** mezcla de tipos, pastel, encaballado (en imprenta). || *v.t.* e *i.* **4** mezclar(se), encaballar(se), empastelar(se) (los caracteres, los renglones en imprenta).

pianissimo | pjæ'nɪsɪməu | *adv.* MUS. **1** pianísimo. || *adj.* **2** pianísimo.

pianist | 'pɪənɪst | *s.c.* pianista.

piano | pj'ɑːnəu | *s.c.* e *i.* MUS. **1** piano. || *adv.* **2** piano, suavemente.

pianoforte | ˌpjænəu'fɔːtɪ | *s.c.* e *i.* (form. y arc.) MUS. piano.

piazza | pɪ'ætsə | *s.c.* **1** plaza (en ciudades italianas). **2** pórtico, galería, columnata; soportales. **3** (EE.UU.) porche, terraza.

picaresque | ˌpɪkəˈresk | *adj.* LIT. picaresco (un género).
picalilli | ˈpɪkəlɪlɪ | *s.i.* salsa picante a base de verduras en vinagre (que se toma con la carne).
piccolo | ˈpɪkələʊ | [*pl.* **piccolos**] *s.c.* MUS. flautín.
pick | pɪk | *v.t.* **1** elegir, escoger, seleccionar, optar por. **2** coger, recoger, recolectar: *they were picking fruit = estaban recogiendo la fruta.* **3** **[to – (from/out of)]** picar, picotear; mordisquear, roer; deshuesar: *pick meat from a bone = roer un hueso.* **4** hurgar (la nariz). **5** mondarse, limpiarse, escarbarse (los dientes). **6** provocar, causar intencionadamente: *picking a fight = provocando una riña.* **7** ratear, robar (pequeñas cantidades). **8** forzar, abrir con ganzúa, abrir ilegalmente. **9** (EE.UU.) desplumar (un ave). **10** picar, cavar, perforar, hacer (un agujero). **11** buscar las vueltas, encontrar los puntos flojos (de un argumento). **12** lanzar (la lanzadera al tejer). **13** tirar, lanzar, arrojar. || *s.i.* **14** elección, opción, selección. **15** **[the – of]** lo mejor, la crema, lo más escogido: *the pick of the month = lo mejor del mes.* **16** recolección, cosecha. || *s.c.* **17** pico, piqueta. **18** MUS. púa. **19** hilo de la trama (de un tejido). **20** golpe de lanzadera (al tejer). || **21 to have a bone to – with someone,** V. **bone. 22 to have one's –,** escoger lo que a uno le gusta, elegir a gusto de uno. **23 to – and choose,** (fam.) escoger con cuidado, tardar en decidirse al elegir. **24 to – at, a)** picar, picotear, comer sin ganas (la comida); **b)** arrancar, tirar de, desplumar (un animal a otro); **c)** (fam.) regañar, irritar, picar. **25 to – holes in,** (fam.) sacar las faltas, encontrar los puntos débiles (de un argumento). **26 to – one's way,** andar con tiento, caminar con cuidado. **27 to – off, a)** matar a tiros sucesivos, tirotear (uno a uno); **b)** levantarse lentamente (después de una caída); **c)** (EE.UU.) DEP. eliminar de un golpe, poner fuera de juego con un golpe (en béisbol); **d)** (EE.UU.) DEP. interceptar un pase (en fútbol). **28 to – on, a)** (fam.) criticar, coger manía a, meterse con, perseguir, tomarla con; **b)** escoger, elegir. **29 to – out, a)** elegir con cuidado, escoger con esmero, entresacar; **b)** distinguir, reconocer, discernir, identificar; **c)** (generalmente pasiva) resaltar, destacar (en un cuadro): *the trees were picked out in an intense green = los árboles se destacaban en un color verde intenso.* **d)** MUS. tocar de oído (una melodía). **30 to – over,** tomar y examinar con cuidado, escoger (generalmente fruta). **31 to – someone's brains,** robar parte del tiempo a alguien, pedir ayuda sobre una materia: *can I pick your brain about this exercise? = ¿puedo robarle un poco de su tiempo para ayudarme con este ejercicio?* **32 to – someone's pocket,** robarle a uno lo que lleva en el bolsillo, quitarle a uno la cartera. **33 to – up, a)** recoger, levantar (del suelo); **b)** levantar(se) del suelo, recuperar(se), recobrarse (después de un error, un susto, una enfermedad); **c)** juntar, recoger, acumular (objetos); **d)** retomar, continuar, tomar el hilo de (una conversación); **e)** conseguir, lograr, aprender (ideas, hábitos); obtener, comprar, adquirir: *where did you pick up this cupboard? = ¿dónde compraste este armario?;* comprender, entender: *you'll pick the problem up easily = entenderás el problema fácilmente;* coger (una enfermedad); **f)** ir a buscar, ir a recoger; **g)** (fam.) coger, recoger (a un autostopista); **h)** (fam.) ligar, enrollar, trabar conversación (con un desconocido); **i)** detener, arrestar (a un criminal); **j)** captar, recibir, escuchar; interceptar (un mensaje, la radio); **k)** ECON. mejorar, recuperarse, reflotar. **34 to – up speed,** acelerar, tomar velocidad. **35 to – up the pieces,** (fig.) recoger los pedazos (después de un desastre). **36 to – up the tab,** (fam.) pagar la cuenta, correr con los gastos. **37 to take one's –,** escoger, elegir (lo que uno quiera).
pickax V. | | **pickaxe**.
pickaxe | ˈpɪkæks | (EE.UU. **pickax**) *s.c.* **1** pico, piqueta, azadón. || *v.t.* **2** picar con azadón, con piqueta.
picked | pɪkt | *adj.* escogido, elegido, selecto.
picker | ˈpɪkər | *s.c.* recogedor, recolector.
picket | ˈpɪkɪt | *s.c.* **1** piquete de vigilancia (de huelga). **2** MIL. piquete. **3** estaca puntiaguda, piquete. || *v.t.* e *i.* **4** actuar como piquete, rodear con piquetes (en huelga). || *v.t.* **5** [**to** – *o.* + *adv./prep.*] MIL. vigilar por piquetes, guardar por piquetes, colocar piquetes.
picketing | ˈpɪkɪtɪŋ | *s.i.* actuación de piquetes, vigilancia de piquetes.
picket-line | ˈpɪkɪtˌlaɪn | *s.c.* línea de piquetes de huelga, grupo de vigilancia de huelguistas.
pickings | ˈpɪkɪŋz | *s.pl.* **1** ganancias extra, comisiones adicionales, sobresueldo (ganados deshonestamente en ciertas empresas o actividades). **2** sobras, desperdicios.
pickle | ˈpɪkl | *s.i.* **1** escabeche, adobo, salmuera. **2** (brit.) encurtido (de verduras); (EE.UU.) encurtido de pepino. **3** (fam.) lío, dificultad, aprieto, apuro; desorden. **4** ácido para limpiar metales oxidados. || *s.c.* **5** (brit. y fam.) diablo, pilluelo. || *v.t.* **6** encurtir, escabechar, conservar en vinagre. **7** limpiar con ácido, dar un baño químico (a un metal).
pickled | ˈpɪkld | *adj.* **1** en vinagre, en escabeche, en salmuera. **2** (fam.) borracho, enchispado, mamado, (Am.) chupado.
pick-me-up | ˈpɪkmiːʌp | *s.c.* **1** (fam.) estimulante, reconstituyente, tónico (para animarse, para ponerse fuerte). **2** tentempié, refrigerio.
pickpocket | ˈpɪkˌpɒkɪt | *s.c.* carterista, ratero, (Am.) pericote.
pick-up | ˈpɪkʌp | *s.c.* **1** ELECTR. brazo (de tocadiscos). **2** camioneta, furgoneta de reparto. **3** reparto, distribución. **4** (fam.) ligue, rollo, conquista (especialmente una mujer). **5** recogida, encuentro (un punto). **6** DEP. recogida (de pelota). **7** (argot) arresto, detención. **8** pasajero, viajero. **9** (fam.) autostopista. **10** ELECTR. fonocaptor. **11** RAD. dispositivo de captación (de ondas). || *s.i.* **12** (EE.UU.) aceleración, aceleramiento (de un automóvil). || **13 – truck,** camioneta de reparto, furgoneta de reparto.
picky | ˈpɪkɪ | *adj.* (EE.UU., fam. y desp.) escogido, quisquilloso, melindroso.
picnic | ˈpɪknɪk | *s.c.* **1** merienda campestre, comida campestre. **2** (fam.) tarea fácil, asunto agradable, asunto placentero. **3** jamón curado. || *v.i. pret.* y *p.p.* **picnicked. 4** merendar en el campo, ir de merienda al campo. || **5 to be no –,** no ser tarea fácil, no tener nada de agradable.
picnicker | ˈpɪknɪkər | *s.c.* excursionista, participante en una merienda campestre.
pictorial | pɪkˈtɔːrɪəl | *adj.* **1** pictórico. **2** ilustrado, gráfico: *a pictorial magazine = una revista ilustrada.*
picture | ˈpɪktʃər | *s.c.* **1** pintura, cuadro, dibujo, lámina, ilustración. **2** [– **(of)**] fotografía, retrato. **3** TV. imagen. **4** (fig.) descripción, imagen, visión, retrato, cuadro: *an awful picture of her future = una horrible descripción de su futuro.* **5** situación, etapa, circunstancia. **6** cuadro, maravilla, belleza, encanto, hermosura: *the mountains are a picture with the snow = las montañas son muy hermosas con nieve.* **7** película, filme. || *v.t.* **8** imaginar, representar. **9** [**to** – *o.* + *adv./prep.*] pintar, representar, retratar. **10** (fig.) describir, ilustrar, ofrecer una visión: *he pictured her with love words = la describió con amorosas palabras.* || **11 a – of health/misery, etc. ...,** la salud, la miseria, etc. ... personificada, la viva imagen de la salud, de la miseria, etc. ... **12 to get the –,** (fam.) entender la situación, coger el mensaje. **13 the pictures,** (brit.) el cine; la industria del cine. **14 to put someone in the –,** (fam.) informar a alguien, poner a alguien sobre aviso, poner a alguien al tanto.
picture-book | ˈpɪktʃəbʊk | *s.c.* libro infantil ilustrado.
picture-rail | ˈpɪktʃəreɪl | *s.c.* moldura (situada en la pared, bajo el techo para colgar cuadros).
picturesque | ˌpɪktʃəˈresk | *adj.* **1** pintoresco, llamativo, encantador, atractivo (un lugar). **2** pintoresco, extraño, raro (una persona, sus ropas). **3** (euf.) expresivo, descriptivo, colorista (el lenguaje).
picturesquely | ˌpɪktʃəˈresklɪ | *adv.* pintorescamente.
piddle | ˈpɪdl | *v.i.* (fam.) **1** mear, hacer pis. **2** malgastar, perder (tiempo). || *s.i.* **3** pis, orina, meados.
piddling | ˈpɪdlɪŋ | *adj.* (fam. y desp.) sin importancia, insignificante, trivial, de poca monta.
pidgin | ˈpɪdʒɪn | *s.c.* e *i.* lengua franca (mezcla de dos o más idiomas, generalmente usada en los negocios).
pie | paɪ | *s.c.* e *i.* **1** empanada, pastel (de carne, fruta). **2** tarta, bizcocho relle-

no. 3 ZOOL. urraca. || **4 a finger in every –,** V. **finger. 5 as easy as –,** V. **easy. 6 to eat humble –,** V. **humble. 7 – in the sky,** (fam.) la luna, el no va más: *they promised pie in the sky = prometieron la luna.*

piebald | 'paɪbɔːld | *adj.* pío; de dos colores, moteado (un animal).

piece | piːs | *s.c.* **1 [– (of)]** trozo, pedazo, porción, fracción, fragmento, parte. **2** ART. composición, obra, pieza, trabajo, fragmento (musical, literario, etc.). **3** pieza, prenda, artículo (de vestir). **4** ficha, pieza, figura (de juego). **5** PER. artículo, noticia. **6** moneda, pieza: *10 pieces of gold = 10 monedas de oro.* **7** trabajo a destajo: *pay by the piece = pagar por trabajo a destajo.* **8** MIL. rifle, fusil, metralleta. **9** un acto de, un ejemplo de: *a piece of folly = una locura.* **10** (argot y vulg.) tía buena, maciza, persona sexualmente atractiva. || *v.t.* **11** remendar, echar una pieza a. **12 [to – together]** pegar las partes, unir los fragmentos. **13 [to – together]** (fig.) atar cabos. || *sufijo.* **14 -piece,** de... piezas, de... elementos: *a 15-piece coffee set = un juego de café de 15 piezas.* || **15 a – of cake,** V. **cake. 16 all of a –,** de una sola pieza, uniforme. **17 bits and pieces,** V. **bit. 18 to give someone a – of one's mind,** V. **mind. 19 to go to pieces,** desmoronarse, venirse abajo, desmoralizarse (una persona). **20 in one –,** entero, de una pieza, en perfecto estado (una persona). **21 in pieces,** hecho pedazos, acabado, roto (un plan, un sistema). **22 of a –** (form.) del mismo tipo, de la misma clase. **23 to pick up the pieces,** V. **pick up. 24 – by –,** uno a uno, trozo a trozo. **25 to say one's –,** expresar su opinión, decir todo lo que hay que decir. **26 to tear/pull to pieces,** (fam.) hacer pedazos, destrozar (un objeto, una teoría). **27 to pieces,** en pedazos, roto, deshecho, destrozado.

piecemeal | 'piːsmiːl | *adj.* **1** gradual, fragmentado, a intervalos, lento. || *adv.* **2** gradualmente, poco a poco, por etapas. **3** por fragmentos, por trozos.

piecework | 'piːswəːk | *s.i.* trabajo a destajo.

pie-eyed | ˌpaɪ'aɪd | *adj.* (fam. y hum.) jumado, achispado.

pier | pɪər | *s.c.* **1** espigón, malecón (con restaurantes, diversiones). **2** embarcadero, muelle. **3** ARQ. pilar, machón, pilastra; entrepaño, muro entre ventanas.

pierce | pɪəs | *v.t.* (form.) **1** agujerear, perforar, atravesar, pinchar. **2** cortar, apuñalar. **3** (fig.) penetrar, atravesar, abrirse paso, desgarrar, herir (la luz, el sonido, un dolor): *the pain was piercing my shoulder = el dolor me atravesaba el hombro.* **4** comprender, penetrar: *she pierced the real meaning = comprendió el verdadero significado.* **5** afectar, conmover, paralizar: *pierced by terror = paralizado por el terror.*

pierced | 'pɪəst | *adj.* agujereado, perforado, horadado.

piercing | 'pɪəsɪŋ | *adj.* **1** cortante, helado (el viento). **2** estremecedor, desgarrador, agudo; chillón (un sonido). **3** penetrante, agudo, punzante (un dolor, una mirada). **4** inquisitivo, inquisitorio.

piercingly | pɪəsɪŋlɪ | *adv.* **1** estremecedoramente, desgarradoramente. **2** penetrantemente, agudamente, punzantemente. **3** inquisitivamente.

pierrette | 'pɪərət | V. **pierrot.**

pierrot | 'pɪərəu | *f.* **pierrette.** *s.c.* pierrot.

piety, piousness | paɪətɪ | *s.i.* (form.) piedad, devoción, fervor religioso.

piffle | 'pɪfl | *s.i.* (fam.) tonterías, disparates, chorradas.

piffling | 'pɪflɪŋ | *adj.* (fam.) ridículo, insignificante, trivial, inútil, sin sentido.

pig | pɪg | (EE.UU. **hog**) *s.c.* **1** ZOOL. puerco, cerdo, gorrino, cochino, marrano, (Am.) chancho. **2** carne de cerdo. **3** (fam. y fig.) cerdo, marrano, cochino, maleducado. **4** (brit. y fam.) difícil, desagradable, molesto, embrollado (un asunto, un problema). **5** (fam. y desp.) policía. **6** lingote (de metal); molde de lingote. || *v.i.* **7** parir (una cerda). **8 [to – (out/on)]** vivir como un cerdo. || **9 to make a – of oneself,** (brit. y fam.) ponerse como un cerdo, darse un atracón. **10 to make a pig's ear of,** (brit. y fam.) estropear, fastidiar, salir (algo) mal. **11 – in a poke,** trato a ciegas, gato por liebre. **12 to –,** (brit.) vivir como cerdos. **13 pigs might fly,** (fam. y hum.) imposible, y qué más, claro, como que los cerdos vuelan (ante algo que no se cree). **14 –/piggy in the middle,** (brit.) balón prisionero, bureo, buré (juego infantil de pelota); (nadar) entre dos aguas, (estar) entre dos fuegos.

pigeon | 'pɪdʒən | [*pl.* **pigeon** o **pigeons**] *s.c.* **1** ZOOL. pichón, paloma, palomo. **2** primo, incauto. || **3 to be someone's –,** (fam.) ser responsabilidad de alguien, ser asunto de alguien. **4 to set/put the cat among the pigeons,** mentar la bicha, mentar el diablo, armar el follón (al decir o hacer algo inesperado que causa disgusto).

pigeon-hole | 'pɪdʒənhəul | *s.c.* **1** casilla, casillero (para cartas, papeles). || **2** (fam.) compartimento, categoría, clase, papel. || *v.t.* **3** almacenar, reservar, archivar, dar carpetazo a (un asunto). **4** encasillar, etiquetar, clasificar, meter en compartimentos (algo o a alguien).

piggery | 'pɪgərɪ | *s.c.* **1** granja de cerdos. **2** pocilga, cochiquera, zahúrda. || *s.i.* **3** (desp.) cerdada, guarrería, indecencia.

piggy | 'pɪgɪ | *s.c.* (fam.) **1** cerdito, lechón, cochinillo, (Am.) chanchito. || *adj.* **2** (desp.) glotón, goloso, tragón (un niño). **3** de cerdo: *piggy face = cara de cerdo.*

piggyback | ˌpɪgɪ'bæk | *s.c.* **1** carrera a cuestas, paseo sobre los hombros (a un niño). || *adv.* **2** a cuestas, a caballo, sobre los hombros: *I carried her piggyback = la llevé a cuestas.*

piggybank | ˌpɪgɪ'bæŋk | *s.c.* hucha (en forma de cerdito).

pigheaded | ˌpɪg'hedɪd | *adj.* (fam. y desp.) terco, cabezota, obstinado, testarudo.

piglet | 'pɪglɪt | *s.c.* cerdito, lechón, cochinillo.

pigment | 'pɪgmənt | *s.c.* e *i.* **1** (form.) pigmento, colorante. || *s.i.* **2** BIOL. pigmento.

pigmentation | ˌpɪgmen'teɪʃn | *s.i.* pigmentación, coloración.

pigpen | 'pɪgen | *s.c.* (EE.UU.) pocilga, cochiquera, zahúrda.

pigskin | ˌpɪgskɪn | *s.i.* **1** piel de cerdo. **2** (fam.) pelota de fútbol. **3** (fam.) silla de montar.

pigsty | ˌpɪgstaɪ | *s.c.* **1** pocilga, cochiquera, zahúrda. **2** (fig. y fam.) pocilga, desorden, suciedad: *their house was a real pigsty = la casa era una verdadera pocilga.*

pigtail | ˌpɪgteɪl | *s.c.* **1** trenza, coleta. **2** hoja de tabaco enrollado.

pike | paɪk | [*pl.* **pike** o **pikes**] *s.c.* **1** ZOOL. lucio. **2** MIL. punta de lanza, pica. **3** (EE.UU.) carretera de peaje. **4** peaje (barrera o dinero). || *v.t.* **5** matar con lanza, herir con pica. || *v.i.* **6** irse deprisa, marchar rápidamente.

pikestaff | ˌpaɪkstɑːf | *s.c.* **1** asta de lanza, asta de pica. || **2 as plain as a –,** (arc.) claro como la luz del día, más claro agua.

pilaf | ˌpɪlæf | *s.i.* V. **pilau.**

pilau, pilaf | pɪ'lau | *s.c.* e *i.* plato oriental a base de arroz con verdura, carne, o pescado y especias.

pilchard | ˌpɪltʃəd | *s.c.* ZOOL. sardina, arenque.

pile | paɪl | *s.c.* **1 [– (of)]** montón, pila, pilada, cúmulo, montaña. **2** pira funeraria, hoguera. **3** (fam.) montón, abundancia, cantidad, sinnúmero: *piles of problems = cantidad de problemas.* **4** (generalmente *sing.*) (fam.) fortuna, dineral. **5** conjunto grandioso, complejo imponente, mole (de edificios). **6** FIS. reactor nuclear, reactor atómico. **7** ELEC. pila, batería. **8** poste, pilar, pilote. **9** HIST. pilo, jabalina romana. || *s.c.* e *i.* **10** pelo, pelillo, lana, lanilla (de un tejido, de una alfombra). || *v.t.* e *i.* **11 [to – (on/up)]** amontonar(se), apilar(se), acumular(se), hacer un montón. **12 [to – (onto/with)]** cargar, llenar. || *v.i.* **13** entrar o salir en tropel, entrar o salir desordenadamente: *people piled off the building = la gente salió del edificio en tropel.* || **14 at the bottom of the –,** (brit. y fam.) de la escoria de la sociedad; poco pudiente, poco influyente. **15 at the top of the –,** con influencias; con dinero, de lo mejor. **16 to make a –,** hacer una fortuna, hacer el agosto. **17 piles,** MED. hemorroides, almorranas. **18 to – on,** (fam.) exagerar, pasarse. **19 to – up, a)** amontonar(se), apilar(se), acumular(se); **b)** colisionar, chocar (varios vehículos).

pileup | ˌpaɪlʌp | *s.c.* colisión múltiple, accidente múltiple (de vehículos).

pilfer | ˌpɪlfər | *v.t.* e *i.* ratear, sisar, robar (en pequeñas cantidades).

pilfering | ˌpɪlfərɪŋ | *s.i.* ratería, hurto, sisa.

pilgrim | ˌpɪlgrɪm | *s.c.* peregrino, romero.

pilgrimage | ˌpɪlgrɪmɪdʒ | *s.c.* e *i.* peregrinaje, peregrinación, romería.
pill | pɪl | *s.c.* **1** píldora, tableta, cápsula, pastilla. **2 [the –]** (fam.) píldora anticonceptiva, anticonceptivo. **3** (argot) pelota, bola de billar, bala de cañón. **4** disgusto, sinsabor. **5** bobalicón, papanatas, insustancial, soso. || *v.t.* **6** recetar píldoras, dar pastillas. **7** (argot) boicotear, rechazar, votar en contra de. **8** (arc.) extorsionar, chantajear. || *v.i.* **9** formar bolas, hacer bolas (un tejido). **10** (brit.) desprenderse en escamas, desprenderse en copos. || **11 a bitter –/a bitter – to swallow,** una píldora amarga, un duro trago. **12 to be on the –,** tomar la píldora anticonceptiva. **13 to sugar/ sweeten the –,** suavizar el mal trago, endulzar la píldora.
pillage | ˌpɪlðdʒ | *s.i.* (arc.) **1** pillaje, saqueo, rapiña. **2** botín, despojos. || *v.t.* e *i.* **3** pillar, saquear, despojar.
pillar | ˌpɪlər | *s.c.* **1** pilar, pilastra, poste. **2** columna, estatua, pedestal (monumento). **3 [– (of)]** columna (de humo). **4 [– (of)]** (fig.) pilar, soporte, sostén, puntal. || *v.t.* **5** sostener con pilares, sujetar con postes. || **6 from – to post,** de la Ceca a la Meca.
pillar-box | ˌpɪləbɒks | *s.c.* (brit.) buzón.
pillared | ˌpɪləd | *adj.* de pilares, de columnas, posteado.
pillbox | ˌpɪlbɒks | *s.c.* **1** cajita para píldoras. **2** MIL. búnker, fortín (en la costa). **3** sombrero pequeño de ala corta (de señora).
pillion | ˌpɪljən | *s.c.* **1** asiento trasero, asiento de pasajero (en motos). || **2 to ride –,** ir de paquete, ir en el asiento trasero.
pillory | ˌpɪlərɪ | *s.c.* **1** cepo, picota (como castigo público). || *v.t.* **2** (fig.) poner en la picota, poner en ridículo. **3** castigar en la picota.
pillow | ˌpɪləʊ | *s.c.* **1** almohada, cojín. **2** mundillo, almohadilla de bolillos. || *v.t.* **3 [to – *o.* + *adv./prep.*]** apoyar, recostar, descansar (sobre una almohada, sobre un hombro). || **4 – talk,** (fam.) charla de alcoba, conversación íntima.
pillowcase | ˌpɪləʊkeɪs | *s.c.* almohadón, funda de almohada.
pillowslip | ˌpɪləʊslɪp | *s.c.* almohadón, funda de almohada.
pilot | ˌpaɪlət | *s.c.* **1** AER. piloto, aviador. **2** MAR. práctico. **3** MAR. timonel. **4** guía, director, orientador, consejero. **5** MEC. pieza guía. **6** ELEC. piloto. **7** TV. programa piloto. || *adj.* **8** piloto, experimental: *a pilot scheme = un plan piloto.* || *v.t.* **9** pilotar, llevar (un avión). **10 [to – *o.* + *adv./prep.* (through)]** guiar, mostrar el camino, conducir, dirigir. **11** (fig.) conducir, llevar a buen término, dirigir (un asunto, una negociación). || **12 – light,** luz indicadora; piloto de un calentador (de gas).
pimento | pɪ'mentəʊ | *s.c.* **1** BOT. pimiento morrón. || *s.i.* **2** pimienta.
pimp | pɪmp | *s.c.* **1** proxeneta, chulo. || *v.i.* **2 [to – (for)]** ser un proxeneta, ser un chulo.
pimple | ˌpɪmpl | *s.c.* **1** grano, pústula, barro. || **2 goose pimples,** V. **goose.**
pimply | ˌpɪmplɪ | *adj.* lleno de granos, cubierto de granos, granuloso.
pin | pɪn | *s.c.* **1** alfiler. **2** (generalmente en combinación) alfiler, pasador: *a tie pin = un alfiler de corbata.* **3** (EE.UU.) broche, prendedor, insignia, escudo, emblema. **4** espiga, clavija, clavo, ensambladura, chaveta. **5** pinza, gancho (de ropa, de dentista). **6** paletón (de la llave). **7** (fam.) pierna. **8** MIL. clavija (de granada). **9** (fam.) comino, pepino; *I don't care a pin = me importa un pepino.* **10** MAR. cabilla, cabillero. **11** MUS. clavija. **12** DEP. asta del banderín (en golf). **13** DEP. bolo (parte alargada). || *v.t.* **[pinned, pinning]. 14 [to – *o.* + *adv./prep.*]** prender con alfileres, sujetar con alfiler. **15** sujetar, apretar, aprisionar, inmovilizar (con un peso). || **16 for two pins,** (fam.) por poco, por menos de nada, casi: *she goes to pieces for two pins = por menos de nada se desmorona.* **17 to – back one's ears/lugholes,** (brit. y fam.) escuchar atentamente, prestar atención. **18 to – down, a)** precisar, delimitar, determinar, concretar, especificar; **b)** forzar, obligar (a tomar una decisión). **19 – money,** dinero para caprichos, dinero para imprevistos. **20 to – on/upon,** echar la culpa a, acusar falsamente, imputar. **21 to – one's hopes on someone,** poner las esperanzas en alguien.
pinafore | ˌpɪnəfɔːr | *s.c.* **1** delantal, mandil. || **2 – dress,** vestido pichi (para llevar con blusa debajo).
pinball | ˌpɪnbɔːl | *s.i.* **1** juego de máquinas recreativas. || **2 – machine,** (EE.UU.) máquina recreativa, máquina de bolas.
pince-nez | ˌpəns'neɪ | *s.c.* [*sing.* y *pl.*] quevedos.
pincer | ˌpɪnsər | *s.c.* (generalmente *pl.*) **1** ZOOL. pinza (de crustáceos). || **2 – movement,** MIL. movimiento de pinza. **3 pincers,** tenazas, pinzas.
pinch | pɪntʃ | *v.t.* e *i.* **1** pellizcar. **2** apretar, comprimir, oprimir, aplastar: *the rock pinched my finger = la roca me aplastó el dedo.* || *v.t.* **3** (brit. y fam.) afanar, guindar, quitar, birlar, robar. **4 [to – (with)** y generalmente *pas.*] causar dolor, acongojar, angustiar, consumir: *he was pinched with grief = estaba consumido por la pena.* **5** [**to – (for)** y generalmente pasiva] (fam.) pescar, pillar, arrestar, detener: *he got pinched for shoplifting = le pescaron robando en una tienda.* **6** reducir, constreñir, reducir (a un país). **7** MEC. mover con palanca. **8** MAR. flamear la vela, navegar ciñendo el viento. || *v.i.* **9** escatimar, economizar, ser tacaño. || *s.c.* **10** pellizco: *I gave him a pinch = le di un pellizco.* **11 [– (of)]** pellizco, pizca, grano: *a pinch of pepper = una pizca de pimienta.* **12** apuro, aprieto, mal momento, dificultad. **13** (fam.) robo, hurto. **14** (fam.) arresto, detención. || **15 at a –,** para un apuro, en caso de necesidad, si es absolutamente necesario. **16 to feel the –,** pasar apuros, saber lo que significa (una carencia): *shipyards are feeling the pinch of the crisis = los astilleros se empiezan a dar cuenta de la crisis.* **17 to – and scrape /save,** hacer economías, economizar gastos, pasar privaciones. **18 to take something with a – of salt,** V. **salt.**
pinched | pɪntʃt | *adj.* **1 [– (for)]** falto, corto, escaso, en apuros (de dinero). **2** consumido, angustiado, pálido.
pincushion | ˌpɪnˌkʊʃn | *s.c.* acerico.
pine, pinetree | paɪn | *s.c.* **1** BOT. pino. || *s.i.* **2** madera de pino. || *v.i.* **3 [to – (away)]** languidecer, consumirse: *after she left he pined away = cuando ella se fue él languideció.* **4 [to – (for)]** suspirar por, llorar por, consumirse pensando en: *pining for her mum = suspirando por su mamá.*
pineapple | ˌpaɪnˌæpl | *s.c.* e *i.* **1** BOT. piña, ananás. || *s.c.* **2** (argot) MIL. granada de mano.
pinecone | ˌpaɪnˌkəʊn | *s.c.* BOT. piña.
pine-needle | ˌpaɪnˌniːdl | *s.c.* BOT. aguja de pino.
pine-tree | ˌpaɪntriː | *s.c.* V. **pine.**
pinewood | ˌpaɪnwʊd | *s.c.* **1** pinar. || *s.i.* **2** madera de pino.
ping | pɪŋ | *s.c.* **1** (fam.) tintineo, tintín (de cristales); zumbido, silbido, sonido agudo (de bala). || *v.i.* **2** (fam.) tintinear; producir un sonido agudo, silbar, zumbar.
ping-pong | ˌpɪŋpɒŋ | *s.i.* ping-pong, tenis de mesa.
pinhead | ˌpɪnhed | *s.c.* **1** cabeza de alfiler. **2** (fam. y desp.) cabeza de chorlito, bobalicón, estúpido. **3** pizca, insignificancia, nadería.
pinion | ˌpɪnjən | *v.t.* (form.) **1** sujetar, aprisionar, amarrar, maniatar. **2** atar las alas, atar las patas (a un animal). || *s.c.* **3** MEC. piñón. **4** LIT. ala (de un pájaro). **5** ZOOL. extremo del ala, punta del ala.
pink | pɪŋk | *adj.* **1** rosa, rosado (color). **2** ruborizado. **3** (desp.) POL. izquierdoso, rojillo, de ideas socialistas. || *s.c.* e *i.* **4** color rosa. || *s.c.* **5** BOT. clavel, clavelina. **6** MAR. pingue. || (EE.UU. **pring**) *v.i.* **7** picar, zumbar, hacer un ruido metálico (un motor). **8** picar, cortar en ondas, perforar (una tela para que no deshile). **9** pinchar, herir ligeramente, picar (con un arma). || **10 to be tickled –,** V. **tickled. 11 in the –,** rebosante de salud.
pinkie | ˌpɪŋkɪ | *s.c.* **1** (EE.UU. y fam.) dedo meñique. **2** MAR. pingue.
pinking shears | ˌpɪŋkɪŋˌʃɪəz | *s.pl.* tijeras de corte ondulado (usadas en costura).
pinkish | ˌpɪŋkɪʃ | *adj.* ligeramente rosado, que tira a rosado.
pinnacle | ˌpɪnəkl | *s.c.* **1 [– (of)]** apogeo, auge, cumbre, cúspide: *the pinnacle of success = la cumbre del éxito.* **2** ARQ. pináculo. **3** punta, pico (de una roca).
pinny | ˌpɪnɪ | *s.c.* (fam.) mandil, delantal.
pinpoint | ˌpɪnpɔɪnt | *v.t.* **1** detectar, identificar, determinar, establecer (una causa). **2** localizar, encontrar (un punto). **3** atravesar, punzar. **4** apuntar con precisión (a un objetivo). || *s.c.* **5 [–**

(of)] partícula, punto diminuto. || *adj.* **6** exacto, preciso, matemático. **7** de precisión, diminuto, minúsculo.

pinprick | ˌpɪnprɪk | *s.c.* **1** pinchazo, picotazo de alfiler. **2** molestia menor, pinchazo.

pins and needles | ˌpɪnzən'niːdlz | *s.pl.* (fam.) **1** hormiguillo, hormigueo. || **2 on –,** (EE.UU.) en ascuas, lleno de ansiedad.

pinstripe | ˌpɪnstraɪp | *s.c.* **1** raya (en un tejido). || **2 pinstripes/pinstripes suit,** traje a rayas.

pint | paɪnt | *s.c.* **1** pinta (medida del sistema imperial = 0,57 litros). **2** (brit. y fam.) pinta, jarra de cerveza (de esta medida).

pin-table | ˌpɪnˌteɪbl | *s.c.* (brit.) máquina recreativa, máquina de bolas.

pint-size, pint-sized | ˌpaɪntˌsaɪz | *adj.* (desp.) insignificante, minúsculo, diminuto.

pinup | ˌpɪnʌp | *s.c.* **1** fotografía de chica o chico atractivo (que se pone en la pared). **2** muchacha sexualmente atractiva. || *adj.* **3** para poner en la pared.

pioneer | ˌpaɪə'nɪər | *s.c.* **1** pionero, colonizador, explorador. **2 [– (of)]** pionero, innovador, iniciador, promotor: *a pioneer in the computer field = un pionero en el campo de los ordenadores.* **3** MIL. zapador. || *adj.* **4** pionero, de colonización, colonizador. **5** experimental, innovador. || *v.t.* **6** establecer, iniciar, promover, poner los cimientos. **7** innovar, ensayar, experimentar. **8** explorar, colonizar (una región).

pioneering | ˌpaɪə'nɪərɪŋ | *adj.* pionero, innovador, iniciador, experimental.

pious | ˌpaɪəs | *adj.* **1** pío, piadoso, devoto. **2** (desp.) hipócrita, fariseo, gazmoño, mojigato. **3** improbable, difícil de llevar a cabo. **4** recomendable, que merece la pena.

piousness | ˌpaɪəsnɪs | *s.i.* V. **piety.**

pip | pɪp | (EE.UU. **seed**) *s.c.* **1** pepita, semilla (de una fruta). **2** (fam.) maravilla, prodigio, preciosidad. **3** RAD. pitido, silbido (al dar las horas). **4** señal (de teléfono). **5** mancha, mota. **6** (fam.) punto (de naipes, de dados). **7** (brit.) estrella en trajes militares. **8** BOT. rizoma, bulbo (del lirio). **9** señal de radar. **10** MED. moquillo, pepita (de las aves). **11** (fam.) disgusto, fastidio, contrariedad, malestar. || *v.t.* **[pipped, pipping]**. 12 (brit. y fam.) superar, derrotar; suspender (por décimas): *she pipped Maths = suspendió las matemáticas por décimas.* **13** (brit. y argot) herir, lesionar. || **13 to give someone the –,** fastidiar enormemente, irritar enormemente, disgustar mucho, ser una contrariedad. **15 to – someone at the post,** derrotar por un margen mínimo, perder en el último momento.

pipe | paɪp | *s.c.* **1** tubería, cañería, caño, tubo, conducto (de gas, agua). **2** pipa, cachimba (de fumar). **3** MUS. flauta, flautín, caramillo. **4** MUS. tubo, cañón (de órgano); canuto (de gaita). **5** silbido, voz atiplada. **6** MAR. silbato, pito (para llamar a los marineros). **7** BIOL. vaso, tubo, conducto. **8** pipa, barrica (de vino). **9** (argot) tarea fácil, exitazo (escolar). || *v.t.* **10 [to – (in/on)]** conducir por tubería, llevar por tubos, entubar. **11** poner tuberías, conectar con tuberías. **12 [to – *o.* + *adv./prep.*]** MAR. recibir al son del silbato, despedir al son del silbato; llamar con silbato. **13 [to – (with)]** ribetear, adornar con galones (un vestido); decorar (una tarta). || *v.t.* e *i.* **14** LIT. cantar, silbar (un pájaro). **15** hablar o cantar con voz atiplada. **16** tocar la flauta, la gaita o el caramillo. || **17 – cleaner,** limpiador de pipas (de fumar). **18 to – down,** (fam.) callar, bajar la voz; dejar de hacer ruido. **19 pipes,** (brit. y fam.) MUS. gaita escocesa. **20 to – up,** (fam.) comenzar a cantar o hablar inesperadamente y con voz de pito.

piped music | ˌpaɪpt'mjuːzɪk | *s.i.* hilo musical, música enlatada (que suena sin parar en hoteles, restaurantes).

pipe-dream | ˌpaɪpdriːm | *s.c.* sueño imposible, castillos en el aire, ilusión, anhelo.

pipeline | ˌpaɪplaɪn | *s.c.* **1** oleoducto, gasoducto. **2** tubería, conducto, cañería (de distribución). **3** fuente confidencial, canal de información. **4** línea, conducto, canal (de distribución). || **5 in the –,** a punto de suceder, en camino, en trámite.

piper | ˌpaɪpər | *s.c.* **1** MUS. gaitero, flautista. **2** fontanero, instalador de tuberías. || **3 he who plays the – calls the tune,** el que paga manda. **4 to play the –,** pagar el pato, cargar con los gastos.

pipette | pɪ'pet | | paɪ'pet | *s.c.* QUIM. pipeta, probeta, tubo de ensayo.

piping | ˌpaɪpɪŋ | *s.i.* **1** sistema de tuberías, cañerías. **2** vivo, ribete, cordoncillo (en costura). **3** adorno, figura (de una tarta). **4** MUS. música de gaita, de flauta. **5** silbido, pitido. || *adj.* **6** agudo, silbante, aflautado (un sonido). || **7 – hot,** quemando, extremadamente caliente.

pipsqueak | ˌpɪpskwiːk | *s.c.* (desp.) insignificancia, poquita cosa, nulidad.

piquancy | ˌpiːkənsɪ | *s.i.* **1** sabor picante, interés, provocación, excitación (de una situación). **2** sabor picante, sabor a especias.

piquant | ˌpiːkənt | *adj.* **1** agradablemente picante, especiado (de sabor). **2** (fig.) picante, excitante, cautivador. **3** (arc.) irritante, fastidioso.

pique | piːk | *s.i.* **1** pique, resentimiento, despecho, rencor. || *v.t.* (generalmente pasiva) **2** ofender, herir, agraviar, incomodar, irritar. **3** provocar, picar, despertar (la curiosidad). **4** enorgullecerse de. || **5 in a fit of –,** en un ataque de despecho, motivado por el rencor.

piqued | piːkt | *adj.* picado, resentido, despechado, rencoroso.

piracy | ˌpaɪərəsɪ | *s.i.* **1** piratería. **2** piratería, publicación no autorizada (literaria, musical, etc.). || *s.c.* **3** acto de piratería, ataque de piratas. **4** publicación pirata, grabación pirata.

piranha | pɪ'rɑːnjə | *s.c.* ZOOL. piraña.

pirate | ˌpaɪərɪt | *s.c.* **1** pirata, corsario, bucanero; barco pirata. **2** pirata, reproductor, copista (de música, literatura, programas). || *v.t.* **3** piratear, copiar, reproducir o editar sin permiso. || *v.t.* e *i.* **4** atacar, robar, actuar como pirata. || **5 – radio,** RAD. emisora pirata, emisora clandestina.

pirouette | ˌpɪru'et | *s.c.* **1** pirueta, cabriola (en baile). || *v.i.* **2** hacer piruetas, hacer cabriolas.

piss | pɪs | (argot y vulg.) *v.i.* **1** mear, hacer pis, orinar. **2 [to – (down)]** (brit.) llover a cántaros. || *v.r.* **3 [to – oneself]** mearse de risa, partirse de risa, no poder parar de reír. || *s.i.* **4** meados, pis, orina. || *s.c.* **5** meada, pis. || **6 to – about/around,** perder el tiempo, hacer el tonto. **7 to – off, a)** (generalmente pasiva) aburrirse, perder el interés; **b)** irritar, molestar, fastidiar. **8 – off!,** ¡lárgate!, ¡vete al cuerno! **9 to take the – out of,** (brit.) burlarse de, reírse de.

pissed | 'pɪst | (argot y vulg.) *adj.* **1** (brit.) borracho, curda, trompa. **2** (EE.UU.) irritado, enfadado, hasta la coronilla. || **3 – as a newt/– out of one's head/– out of one's mind,** completamente borracho, borracho como una cuba.

pistol | ˌpɪstl | *s.c.* **1** pistola, revólver. || *v.t.* **2** (form.) disparar con pistola.

piston | 'pɪstən | *s.c.* **1** MEC. pistón. **2** MUS. pistón, llave.

pit | pɪt | *s.c.* **1** hoyo, fosa, agujero, trampa, sumidero. **2** mina, pozo, cantera. **3 [the –]** el foso de la orquesta (de un teatro). **4 [the –]** (brit.) la platea, la parte posterior del patio de butacas (de un teatro). **5** cicatriz, hoyo (de viruela, natural). **6** (brit. y hum.) cama. **7** abismo, sima, precipicio, depresión. **8 [the –]** REL. el infierno. **9** cancha, reñidero (para peleas de gallos, perros). **10** (EE.UU.) bolsa (parte donde se produce el intercambio). **11** (EE.UU.) BOT. hueso, tito (de fruta). || *v.t.* **(pitted, pitting). 12** hacer hoyos, hacer marcas, agujerear. **13** poner en contra, oponerse a, luchar contra. **14** deshuesar, quitar el tito (a la fruta). **15** DEP. parar en los boxes (durante una carrera de coches). || **16 to – against,** competir con, habérselas con, oponerse a. **17 to – one's wits against,** medir la inteligencia de uno con. **18 the – of one's stomach,** la boca del estómago. **19 the pits, a)** DEP. los boxes (en carreras de coches); **b)** la escoria de la sociedad, lo peor que uno pueda imaginarse: *some of them were the pits = alguno de ellos era la escoria de la sociedad.*

pit-a-pat, pitter-patter | ˌpɪtə'pæt | *adv.* **1** con latidos rápidos, con un rápido tictac (el corazón). **2** con un trotecito rápido, a pasitos. || *s.c.* **3** latido rápido, tic-tac. **4** pasitos rápidos. || *v.t.* **5** latir violentamente. **6** trotar, golpetear.

pitch | pɪtʃ | *v.t.* **1** montar, armar, preparar, disponer (una tienda, un campamento). **2** clavar, fijar (una estaca). **3 [to – *o.* + *adv./prep.*]** MUS. graduar, ajustar (un sonido, una nota). **4 [to – *o.* + *adv./prep.*]** expresar en forma clara, ajustar (un discurso). **5** **[to – *o.* + *adv./prep.*]** arrojar, lanzar, tirar. **6** DEP. dejar (la pelota), golpear el suelo (en críquet). **7** (argot) bregar, pelear, trabajar con fuerte presión. || *v.i.* **8** cabecear, arfar, levantarse de proa y de popa (un barco, un avión). **9** DEP. golpear el suelo (la pelota en críquet, golf). **10** **[to – *adv./prep.*]** inclinarse, caer en declive. **11** tambalearse, bambolearse. **12** tomar una decisión rápida, precipitarse. || *v.t.* e *i.* **13** precipitar(se), caer(se) (hacia delante, de cabeza). **14** DEP. lanzar, jugar de lanzador (en críquet). || *s.c.* **15** (brit.) DEP. campo, terreno: *a football pitch = un campo de fútbol.* **16** DEP. lanzamiento, tiro. **17** MUS. tono, altura; diapasón (de voz). **18** puesto callejero, zona (de ventas, de un mimo, de un músico). **19** cabeceo, balanceo (de un barco, avión). **20** (fam.) dotes de convicción, propaganda (comercial). **21** MEC. paso, avance (en la rosca de un tornillo). || *s.sing.* **22** **[– (of)]** grado, nivel, tono, extremo, punto: *voices rising to a pitch of anger = voces que alcanzaron un tono de ira.* **23** inclinación, desnivel, declive, pendiente. **24** ARQ. ángulo de inclinación, grado de inclinación (de un tejado, de una escalera). || *s.i.* **25** galipote, brea, pez (para calafatear). || **26 to – in,** echar una mano, ayudar, ponerse a ello, contribuir a. **27 to – into,** arremeter contra, atacar, reñir, criticar. **28 to queer the – for,** (fam.) estropear los planes a.

pitch-black | ˌpɪtʃ'blæk | *adj.* extremadamente oscuro, negro como la noche, negro como boca de lobo.

pitch blackness | ˌpɪtʃ'blæknɪs | *s.i.* oscuridad total.

pitched | pɪtʃt | *adj.* **1** inclinado (un techo). || **2 – battle,** batalla campal.

pitcher | ˌpɪtʃər | *s.c.* **1** (brit.) cántaro, jarro (grande). **2** (EE.UU.) jarra. **3** DEP. lanzador (en béisbol). **4** DEP. palo de hierro con cabeza ligeramente inclinada (en golf).

pitchfork | ˌpɪtʃfɔːk | *s.c.* **1** horca, horquilla, bieldo. || *v.t.* **2** tirar con horca, recoger con horca (el heno). **3 [to – *o.* + *adv./prep.*]** impeler, lanzar, forzar (a una situación inesperada).

piteous | ˌpɪtɪəs | *adj.* (lit.) lastimero, lastimoso.

piteously | ˌpɪtɪəslɪ | *adv.* (lit.) de forma lastimera, lastimosamente.

pitfall | ˌpɪtfɔːl | *s.c.* problema, peligro, trampa, escollo.

pith | pɪθ | *s.i.* **1** BOT. médula. **2** pan (de la naranja). **3** (fig.) meollo, esencia, jugo (de una idea).

pithead | ˌpɪthed | *s.c.* bocamina.

pithy | ˌpɪθɪ | *adj.* **1** conciso, sustancioso, jugoso, expresivo. **2** meduloso, medular.

pitiable | ˌpɪtɪəbl | *adj.* (form.) lastimoso, deplorable, digno de compasión.

pitiably | ˌpɪtɪəblɪ | *adv.* lastimosamente, deplorablemente.

pitiful | ˌpɪtɪful | *adj.* **1** lastimoso, digno de compasión, conmovedor, patético. **2** (desp.) despreciable, deplorable. **2** (arc.) compasivo.

pitifully | ˌpɪtɪfulɪ | *adv.* **1** lastimosamente, conmovedoramente, patéticamente. **2** lamentablemente, deplorablemente.

pitiless | ˌpɪtɪlɪs | *adj.* **1** despiadado, inhumano, cruel, desalmado, implacable. **2** (fig.) severo, sin señales de cambio (el tiempo).

pitilessly | ˌpɪtɪlɪslɪ | *adv.* despiadadamente, cruelmente, de forma inhumana.

pittance | ˌpɪtəns | *s.sing.* miseria, renta mísera, sueldo de hambre.

pitted | ˌpɪtɪd | *adj.* **1** picado de viruelas, lleno de cicatrices, lleno de hoyos. **2** deshuesado, sin hueso (una fruta).

pitter-patter | ˌpɪtəpætər | *s.sing.* V. **pit-a-pat.**

pituitary | pɪ'tjuɪtə'rɪ | *s.c.* **1** ANAT. pituitaria. **2** mucus pituitario. || *adj.* **3** pituitario. || **4 – gland,** ANAT. glándula pituitaria.

pity | pɪtɪ | *s.i.* **1** lástima, pena, piedad, compasión. **2** clemencia, compasión. || *v.t.* **3** apiadarse de, compadecer a, dar lástima. || **4 a thousand pities,** muy lamentable, una verdadera lástima. **5 for pity's sake!,** ¡por el amor de Dios! **6 more's the –,** tanto peor, por desgracia. **7 to take – on,** apiadarse de, compadecerse de.

pitying | ˌpɪtɪɪŋ | *adj.* compasivo, de lástima (una mirada).

pityingly | ˌpɪtɪŋlɪ | *adv.* compasivamente, con lástima.

pivot | ˌpɪvət | *s.c.* **1** pivote, fulcro, eje. **2** (fig.) factor esencial, punto crucial, eje central. || *v.i.* **3 [to – (on)]** girar sobre un eje, dar vueltas sobre un pivote, rotar. || *v.t.* **4** montar con pivote, fijar con eje. || **5 to – on,** (fig.) depender de: *the job pivoted on an interview = el trabajo dependía de una entrevista.*

pivotal | ˌpɪvətl | *adj.* **1** de pivote. **2** central, más importante, crucial: *the pivotal scene = la escena crucial.*

pixie | ˌpɪksɪ | *s.c.* **1** duende, trasgo. || *adj.* **2** duende, travieso (un niño). || **3 – hat,** gorro en punta, caperuza.

pizza | ˌpiːtsə | *s.c.* e *i.* pizza (plato italiano).

pizzaz | ˌpɪtsæz | *s.i.* (EE.UU. y argot) atractivo, carisma, elegancia, gusto, gracia.

pizzicato | ˌpɪtsɪ'kɑːtəu | *adv.* **1** MUS. pizzicato, con los dedos. || *adj.* **2** MUS. pizzicato, pulsada con el dedo (una cuerda de violín).

placard | ˌplækɑːd | *s.c.* **1** pancarta, cartel, anuncio, rótulo. || *v.t.* **2** poner pancartas, cubrir con carteles, llenar de anuncios.

placate | plə'keɪt | (EE.UU.) | 'pleɪkeɪt | *v.t.* aplacar, calmar, sosegar, apaciguar.

placating | plə'keɪtɪŋ | *adj.* conciliador, apaciguador.

placatory | plə'keɪtərɪ | (EE.UU.) | 'pleɪkətɔːrɪ | *adj.* conciliatorio, apaciguador.

place | pleɪs | *s.c.* **1** lugar, sitio, paraje, zona, parte, punto. **2** (fig.) lugar, cabida, espacio, puesto, papel: *he has no place in the system = no tiene cabida en el sistema; a good place in the committee = un buen puesto en el comité.* **3** turno, posición, vez (en una cola). **4** pasaje, parte, página, línea: *I closed the book and missed my place = cerré el libro y perdí la página.* **5** lugar, localidad, ciudad, pueblo, región; casa, piso, habitación: *they've got a place in the country = tienen una casa en el campo; they come from a small place = son de un pueblo pequeño.* **6** (brit.) plaza: *Stansfeld Place = Plaza Stansfeld.* **7** (generalmente *sing.*) localidad, asiento, sitio, plaza (en un hotel, teatro, etc...); plato, cubierto (lugar a la mesa). **8** plaza, puesto (escolar, de trabajo). **9** ocasión, momento, circunstancia, lugar (apropiada para algo). **10** posición, puesto, lugar, calificación (en una competición, una carrera, un examen). **11** posición, rango, condición (social). **12** MAT. puesto (decimal). **13** deber, incumbencia, cometido, responsabilidad. **14** DEP. primera, segunda o tercera posición (en carreras de caballos). || *v.t.* **15 [to – *o.* + *adv./prep.*]** (form.) situar, colocar, ubicar, instalar, disponer, emplazar. **16** imponer, asignar (una responsabilidad, restricción). **17** COM. hacer, colocar (un pedido). **18** poner, colocar (un anuncio, llamada telefónica). **19 [to – *o.* + *adj./adv./prep.*; generalmente pasiva]** DEP. colocar, llegar, tener (en una posición): *she was placed second = se colocó en segunda posición.* **20** recordar, acordarse de, identificar: *I can't really place this face = no recuerdo donde he visto esta cara.* **21** colocar, emplear, dar un trabajo. || *v.i.* **22** DEP. llegar entre los tres primeros (en una carrera de caballos). **23** (EE.UU.) DEP. llegar en segunda posición. || **24 all over the –, a)** por todas partes, en muchos sitios; **b)** en completo desorden. **25 to be going places,** estar en camino del éxito. **26 to fall/click/fit into –,** tener sentido, cuadrar, encajar, ser claro: *everything started falling into place when I saw her = todo empezó a cuadrar cuando la vi.* **27 to change places with,** intercambiarse por, intercambiar los papeles con. **28 to go places,** (EE.UU.) salir a divertirse, salir de excursión. **29 in a high –/in high places,** en un puesto de influencia, en las altas esferas. **30 in one's –,** en su lugar, en lugar de uno: *in his place I wouldn't go = yo en su lugar no iría.* **31 in/into –,** en su sitio, en el lugar adecuado. **32 in – of,** en lugar de, reemplazando a. **33 in places,** a veces, en algunos sitios, en algunas zonas: *the road has bends in places = la carrera tiene curvas en algunas zonas.* **34 in the first –,** al principio; en primer lugar. **35 not to be one's –,** no ser de incumbencia de uno. **36 out of –,** fuera de lugar, poco apropiado. **37 – setting,** cubierto completo, servicio de mesa (para una persona). **38 to put into –,** poner en su sitio, poner en el lugar donde debe estar. **39 to put someone in their place,** bajar los humos a alguien, poner a alguien en su sitio. **40 to scre-**

am/howl /etc... the – down, no parar de gritar como un loco. **41 to take one's –,** ir a su sitio, tomar asiento. **42 to take –,** ocurrir, suceder, tener lugar. **43 to take the – of,** sustituir a, reemplazar a. **44 the other/another –,** la otra Cámara (los Comunes o los Lores se nombran así recíprocamente).

placebo | plə'siːbəu | *s.c.* 1 MED. placebo. 2 (fig.) palabra de ánimo; regalo, capricho (para animar a alguien).

placement | ˌpleɪsmənt | *s.c.* e *i.* 1 colocación, empleo. 2 emplazamiento, colocación.

placenta | plə'sentə | *s.c.* ANAT. placenta.

placid | ˌplæsɪd | *adj.* plácido, apacible, sereno, sosegado, tranquilo (lugar, persona).

placidity | plæ'sɪdɪtɪ | *s.i.* placidez, serenidad, sosiego, tranquilidad, calma.

placidly | ˌpləsɪdlɪ | *adv.* plácidamente, serenamente, sosegadamente, con tranquilidad, con calma.

plagiarise V. **plagiarize.**

plagiarism | ˌpleɪdʒjərɪzəm | *s.i.* plagio, piratería.

plagiarist | ˌpleɪdʒjərɪst | *s.c.* plagiario.

plagiarize | ˌpleɪdʒjəraɪz | (brit. **plagiarise**) *v.t.* e *i.* plagiar, copiar, piratear.

plague | pleɪg | *s.c.* 1 MED. peste, plaga, epidemia. 2 **[– (of)]** (fig.) plaga de, invasión de, una epidemia de. 3 azote, maldición, engorro. || *s.i.* 4 **[the –]** la peste bubónica. || *v.t.* 5 sufrir, afectar, pasar, afligir (una enfermedad). 6 plagar, infectar. 7 importunar, fastidiar, molestar. || **8 a – on ...!,** ¡maldito sea...! **9 to avoid someone or something like the –,** huir de alguien o de algo como de la peste.

plaice | pleɪs | [*pl.* **plaice**] *s.c.* e *i.* ZOOL. platija, platuja, acedía.

plaid | plæd | *s.i.* 1 tela a cuadros, tartán escocés. || *s.c.* 2 manta escocesa.

plain | pleɪn | *adj.* 1 sencillo, simple, normal, sin complicación. 2 simple, claro, llano, evidente (hecho, lenguaje). 3 franco, directo, honesto. 4 de un solo color, sin dibujos, sin líneas, sin adornos, sencillo (tela, papel). 5 liso, de media (punto). 6 (euf.) fea, sin atractivo, corriente (chica). 7 completa, pura (verdad). || *s.c.* 8 GEOG. llanura, llano, planicie, pradera. || *adv.* 9 (fam.) completamente, totalmente, claramente. || **10 as – as day/as the nose in your face,** tan claro como la luz del día. **11 in – clothes,** de paisano, de calle, no uniformado. **12 – chocolate,** chocolate sin leche. **13 – flour,** harina pura, sin aditivos.

plain-clothes | ˌpleɪn'kləuðz | *adj.* de paisano, de calle, no uniformado (policía, militar).

plainly | ˌpleɪnlɪ | *adv.* 1 claramente, perfectamente, evidentemente. 2 manifiestamente, obviamente.

plainness | ˌpleɪnnɪs | *s.i.* 1 sencillez, simplicidad, llaneza. 2 claridad, evidencia. 3 franqueza, sinceridad. 4 fealdad, falta de atractivo.

plainsong | ˌpleɪnsɒŋ | *s.i.* MUS. canto gregoriano, canto llano.

plainspoken | ˌpleɪn'spəukən | *adj.* franco, directo, llano, sincero.

plaint | pleɪnt | *s.c.* 1 (lit.) queja, lamento. 2 DER. querella; demanda.

plaintiff | ˌpleɪntɪf | *s.c.* DER. demandante, querellante.

plaintive | ˌpleɪntɪv | *adj.* 1 lastimero, desconsolado, dolorido, quejumbroso. 2 triste, melancólico (canción).

plaintively | ˌpleɪntɪvlɪ | *adv.* lastimeramente, desconsoladamente, en forma quejumbrosa.

plait | plæt | (EE.UU. **braid**) *s.c.* 1 trenza, coleta. 2 tabla, plisado, fruncido. || *v.t.* 3 trenzar, entretejer. 4 fruncir, plisar.

plan | plæn | *s.c.* 1 **[– (for/of)]** plan, estrategia, proyecto. 2 plan, intención, programa. 3 plano, mapa, esquema, diagrama, diseño. 4 ARQ. plano, proyecto. || *v.t.* e *i.* **[planned, planning]** 5 planear, planificar, preparar, idear, proyectar, pensar. || *v.t.* 6 ARQ. hacer un plano de, hacer un proyecto de, diseñar. || **7 according to –,** como estaba previsto, de acuerdo con lo planeado. **8 to – for,** prever, tener previsto. **9 – of action /campaign,** plan de campaña. **10 to – on, a)** proponerse, tener intención; **b)** esperar, sospechar, creer, suponer (que algo va a suceder de otro modo). **11 to – out,** planificar al detalle.

plane | pleɪn | *s.c.* 1 AER. avión, aeroplano, hidroplano; plano, ala (de avión). 2 plano, nivel (de desarrollo). 3 GEOM. plano, superficie plana. 4 garlopa, cepillo (de carpintero). 5 BOT. plátano. || *adj.* 6 plano, liso, nivelado. 7 GEOM. plano. || *v.t.* 8 cepillar, alisar (con galopa). || *v.i.* 9 AER. planear 10 (EE.UU.) viajar en avión. || **11 – tree,** BOT. plátano.

planet | ˌplænɪt | *s.c.* ASTR. planeta.

planetarium | ˌplænɪ'teərɪəm | [*pl.* **planetariums** o **planetaria**] *s.c.* planetario.

planetaria | ˌplænɪ'teərɪə | *p.irr.* de **planetarium.**

planetary | ˌplænɪtərɪ | *adj.* 1 planetario, de los planetas. 2 terrestre, mundial. 3 errante. 4 MEC. planetario (engranaje).

plangent | ˌplændʒənt | *adj.* (lit.) 1 lastimero, quejumbroso (tono). 2 vibrante, reverberante (sonido).

plank | plæŋk | *s.c.* 1 tablón, tabla. 2 POL. punto del programa, plataforma (de un partido). || *s.i.* 3 tablazón, tarima, entarimado. || *v.t.* 4 entarimar, tablar, poner tablas. 5 cocinar y servir en tabla. 6 (fam.) pagar en el acto, apoquinar deprisa. 7 tirar violentamente, arrojar con fuerza. || **8 to walk the –,** caminar sobre la tabla (como castigo de pirata).

planking | ˌplæŋkɪŋ | *s.i.* tarima, tablazón, tablado.

plankton | ˌplæŋktən | *s.i.* BIOL. plancton.

planned | plænd | *adj.* 1 planeado, premeditado. 2 planificado, proyectado. 3 dirigida (economía).

planner | plænər | *s.c.* 1 urbanista, planificador. 2 persona metódica, persona minuciosa.

planning | plænɪŋ | *s.i.* 1 planificación, control. 2 urbanismo, trazado urbanístico. || **3 – permission,** licencia de edificación.

plant | plɑːnt | (EE.UU.) | plænt | *s.c.* 1 BOT. planta, vegetal. 2 planta, instalación, fábrica: *new nuclear plants* = *nuevas instalaciones nucleares.* 3 (argot) infiltrado, informador, espía (en una organización). 4 (fam.) pista falsa, prueba falsa, trampa, engaño, estratagema (para inculpar a un inocente). || *s.i.* 5 maquinaria, equipo, instalación. || *v.t.* 6 plantar, cultivar. 7 **[to – (with)]** sembrar (un campo, jardín). 8 (fig.) introducir, esparcir, inculcar, implantar (ideas). 9 cultivar, criar (ostras, truchas). 10 establecer, fundar (una colonia). 11 **[to – (on)]** (fam.) ocultar, esconder, colocar (una prueba falsa para inculpar a alguien): *they planted the drugs on her house* = *colocaron las drogas en su casa para inculparla.* 12 **[to – *o.* + *adv./prep.*]** (fam.) infiltrar, camuflar, disimular, esconder (un micrófono, un policía). 13 **[to – *o.* + *adv./prep.*]** (fam.) plantar, fijar, clavar: *he planted himself in front of her* = *se plantó delante de ella.* || **14 – pot,** tiesto, maceta. **15 to – out,** trasplantar (de una maceta al exterior).

plantain | ˌplæntɪn | *s.c.* e *i.* BOT. 1 plátano, bananero. 2 llantén, arta.

plantation | plæn'teɪʃn | | plɑːn'teɪʃn | *s.c.* 1 plantación (de té, de algodón). 2 plantío, arboleda. 3 hacienda, granja. 4 colonia.

planter | plɑːntər | *s.c.* 1 dueño de una plantación, hacendado. 2 máquina sembradora. 3 (EE.UU.) jardinera, maceta, tiesto (decorativo). 4 colonizador.

planting | plɑːntɪŋ | *s.i.* siembra, cultivo.

plaque | plɑːk | *s.c.* 1 placa (conmemorativa, decorativa). 2 insignia, medalla (de una asociación). | *s.i.* 3 placa (bacteriana).

plasma | ˌplæzmə | *s.i.* 1 FISIOL. plasma, suero. 2 BIOL. protoplasma, citoplasma. 3 suero (de la leche). 4 FIS. gas (presente en el sol y estrellas).

plaster | ˌplɑːstər | (EE.UU.) | 'plæstər | *s.i.* 1 yeso, escayola, argamasa, enlucido. || *s.c.* e *i.* 2 (brit.) tirita, parche. 3 emplasto, cataplasma. || *v.t.* 4 enyesar, poner escayola, enlucir, revocar (una pared). 5 (fig.) ocultar, callar, tapar, encubrir, disimular. 6 cubrir totalmente, llenar hasta arriba (de carteles, de suciedad). 7 **[to – *o.* + *adv./prep.*]** fijar, engominar, aplastar (el cabello). 8 poner tiritas, cubrir con esparadrapo. 9 (fam.) dar una paliza, pegar fuerte. || **10 in –,** enyesado, escayolado. **11 – of Paris,** escayola, yeso mate, sulfato de cal.

plaster-board | ˌplɑːstəbɔːd | *s.i.* cartón de yeso, plancha de yeso.

plaster-cast | ˌplɑːstəˌkɑːst | *s.c.* 1 escultura vaciada en escayola, vaciado. 2 MED. vendaje de yeso, vendaje de escayola.

plastered | ˌplɑːstəd | *adj.* 1 engominado, fijado (cabello). 2 cubierto, lleno (de una sustancia pegajosa). 3 extendido de arriba abajo, colocado muy a la vista. **4** (argot) borracho como una cuba, curda, jumado.

plasterer | ˌplɑːstərər | *s.c.* enyesador, enlucidor, revocador.

plastering | ˌplɑːstərɪŋ | *s.i.* enlucido, escayola, enyesado, revoque.

plastic | ˌplæstɪk | *s.c.* e *i.* **1** plástico. || *adj.* **2** plástico, dúctil, flexible, manejable, moldeable. **3** (fam. y desp.) artificial, sintético (comida, forma de vida). **4** BIOL. plástico, formativo. || **5 – bomb,** bomba de plástico. **6 – explosive,** explosivo plástico. **7 – money,** dinero de plástico, tarjeta de crédito. **8 – surgery,** MED. cirugía plástica.

plasticity | plæ'stɪsɪtɪ | *s.i.* plasticidad, ductilidad, flexibilidad.

plat du jour | ˌplɑːdʊ'ʒʊə | *s.c.* plato del día (del francés).

plate | pleɪt | *s.c.* **1** (EE.UU. **dish**) plato (de comida). **2 [the –]** platillo de colectas (en la iglesia). **3** placa, lámina, plancha, chapa; blindaje. **4** rótulo, placa, letrero (de metal). **5** lámina, ilustración, grabado (en un libro). **6** FOT. placa, diapositiva. **7** base de una dentadura postiza (de metal o plástico). **8** matrícula, placa de matrícula (en un coche). **9** placa, estereotipo, electrotipo (en imprenta). **10** DEP. base del bateador (en béisbol). **11** DEP. copa, bandeja (de premio en competiciones). **12** ELEC. electrodo; placa de ánodo. || *s.i.* **13** orfebrería, plata, objetos de valor (en una casa, una iglesia). **14** metal chapado (en oro o plata): *gold plate = oro chapado.* **15** falda (de vaca). || *v.t.* **16** chapar, platear, dorar, niquelar. **17** blindar, chapear, cubrir con placas metálicas. **18** satinar (el papel). **19** hacer un estereotipo (en imprenta). || **20 to clean/empty one's --,** rebañar el plato, acabar todo lo del plato. **21 to hand on a –,** (fam.) entregar en bandeja de plata, servir en bandeja. **22 to have a lot on one's –,** (fam.) tener mucho que hacer, estar muy ocupado, tener muchos asuntos entre manos.

plateau | ˌplætəʊ | (EE.UU.) | plæ'təʊ | *s.c.* **1** meseta, altiplanicie, altiplano. **2** estabilización, estancamiento: *prices are reaching a plateau = los precios se están estabilizando.*

plateful | ˌpleɪtfʊl | *s.c.* plato (lleno de comida): *a plateful of soup = un plato de sopa.*

plate-glass | ˌpleɪt'glɑːs | *s.i.* vidrio cilindrado, luna (de escaparates).

platform | ˌplætfɔːm | *s.c.* **1** andén, plataforma. **2** plataforma, tribuna, estrado. **3** plataforma, andamio (petrolífera, de construcción). **4** (fig.) plataforma, tribuna, oportunidad: *a good platform for spreading his ideas = una buena tribuna para extender sus ideas.* **5** (brit.) plataforma de autobús. **6** manifiesto, programa electoral (de un partido). || *adj.* **7** de plataforma (zapatos). || **8 to appear on the same – as/to share a – with,** aparecer en el mismo mitin electoral que.

plating | pleɪtɪŋ | *s.i.* **1** chapado, plateado, dorado, niquelado. **2** blindaje.

platinum | ˌplætɪnəm | *s.i.* **1** QUIM. platino. || *adj.* **2** platino: *a platinum blonde = una rubia platino.*

platitude | ˌplætɪtjuːd | *s.c.* (desp.) **1** tópico, trivialidad, banalidad, perogrullada. **2** falta de originalidad.

platitudinous | ˌplætɪ'tjuːdɪnəs | *adj.* lleno de tópicos, trivial, banal, de perogrullada.

Platonic | plə'tɒnɪk | *adj.* **1** platónico, amistoso, ideal (un sentimiento). **2 platonic,** FIL. platónico, de Platón. **3 platonic,** especulativo, teórico.

platoon | plə'tuːn | *s.c.* [– *v.sing./pl.*] MIL. pelotón, compañía, sección.

platter | ˌplætər | *s.c.* **1** (EE.UU.) fuente, (Am.) azafata. **2** (brit. y arc.) bandeja de madera. **3** (EE.UU. y fam.) disco de gramófono.

plaudits | ˌplɔːdɪts | *s.pl.* (form.) aplausos, alabanzas, aclamaciones.

plausibility | ˌplɔːzə'bɪlɪtɪ | *s.i.* credibilidad, verosimilitud.

plausible | ˌplɔːzəbl | *adj.* **1** (desp.) plausible, razonable, verosímil, creíble (explicación). **2** que convence, a quien se puede creer, de argumentos convincentes (persona).

plausibly | ˌplɔːzəblɪ | *adv.* convincentemente, razonablemente, verosímilmente.

play | pleɪ | *s.i.* **1** juego, diversión, entretenimiento, pasatiempo. **2** DEP. juego: *fair play = juego limpio.* **3** (form.) juego, acción, movimiento: *all her influence was into play = toda su influencia estaba en juego.* **4** juego, movimiento libre, holgura: *the chain allowed little play = la cadena no dejaba libertad de movimiento.* **5** (fig.) libertad, rienda suelta (a un sentimiento). **6** juego, reflejo, movimiento (de luz, color). || *s.c.* **7** obra de teatro, obra dramática, comedia. **8** función, representación (de teatro). **9** turno, vez, jugada. **10** apuesta, juego (por dinero). **11** broma, burla, chanza. || *v.i.* **12** jugar, divertirse, entretenerse, juguetear. **13 [to – *adv./prep.*]** (lit.) reflejarse (en), dar (en), rielar (sobre el agua), caer (sobre), bambolearse, flotar (una tela); brotar, manar (agua): *the light played on the water = la luz se reflejaba en el agua; the fountain was playing noisily = la fuente manaba ruidosamente.* || *v.t.* **14 [to – (on)]** jugar (una mala pasada), gastar (una broma). **15 [to – *o.* + *adv./prep.*]** DEP. lanzar, arrojar, enviar, golpear (una pelota). **16 [to – *o.* + *adv./prep.*]** dirigir (hacia, sobre), enviar (hacia); *he played the torch on me = me enfocó con la linterna.* **17 [to – *adv./prep.*]** (fam.) manejar, llevar, tratar (un asunto). **18** echar, jugar (una carta); mover (una ficha). **19** apostar, jugar (dinero). **20** DEP. incluir, meter, utilizar (a un jugador en un equipo). **21** agotar, cansar (a un pez en el anzuelo). || *v.t.* e *i.* **22** sonar, tocar (alto, bajo); poner (discos, música): *we were playing records = estuvimos poniendo discos.* **23** tocar, ejecutar (un instrumento, una pieza musical): *he plays the violin = toca el violín.* **24** DEP. jugar, enfrentarse (contra equipo), jugar (para un equipo), participar (en un deporte), practicar (un deporte), jugar de (portero, defensa). **25** representar, hacer un papel: *he plays Romeo = hace el papel de Romeo.* **26** pasar, poner, dar (una obra, una película): *"Distant Voices" is playing at the Rosi = ponen "Voces Distantes" en el cine Rosi.* **27** (fig.) jugar, hacer (un papel): *she played an important role in my life = jugó un papel importante en mi vida.* **28** fingir(se), hacer(se) pasar por, jugar a: *he usually plays the fool = generalmente se hace el loco.* **29** comportarse, conducirse, actuar (fríamente, seriamente). || **30 a smile plays on/over someone's lips,** una sonrisa brota en los labios de alguien, alguien esboza una sonrisa, una sonrisa se dibuja en labios de alguien. **31 at –,** estar jugando. **32 to come/to be brought/to be called into –,** (form.) entrar en juego, hacer entrar en juego, introducir, ser puesto sobre el tapete. **33 to give/allow full – to,** dar rienda suelta a. **34 to give no – to,** contener, frenar (la imaginación, un sentimiento). **35 to have (time/money) to – with,** (fam.) tener (tiempo o dinero) para gastar, para perder. **36 in –,** DEP. en juego. **37 to make a – for/to make one's –,** (fam.) hacer un intento, hacer su jugada. **38 out of –,** DEP. fuera de juego. **39 to – a part/role,** jugar un papel. **40 to – about/around,** pasárselo bien, divertirse. **41 to – about/around with,** coquetear, flirtear, tontear. **42 to – along with,** fingir estar de acuerdo con, continuar con (por miedo, para obtener ventajas). **43 to – somebody along,** engañar con falsas promesas. **44 to – around with, a)** jugar con distintas posibilidades de, hacer juegos malabares con; **b)** jugar con, tratar irresponsablemente; **c)** considerar, pensar en, jugar con (una idea); **d)** juguetear nerviosamente (con un objeto). **45 to – at, a)** jugar a; **b)** fingir, jugar a (ser algo). **46 to – something back,** volver a poner, repetir (un disco, una canción). **47 to – ball,** (fam.) cooperar, aceptar hacer algo. **48 to – something down,** quitar importancia a algo, restar importancia a algo. **49 to – for time,** tratar de ganar tiempo. **50 to – in, a)** DEP. hacer ejercicios de precalentamiento; **b)** (fig.) adaptarse, acostumbrarse (a un trabajo). **51 to – hard to get,** (fam.) hacerse el duro, hacerse el difícil (ante una enamorada). **52 to – into someone's hands,** ceder la ventaja al contrario, hacer el juego a alguien. **53 to – it by ear,** actuar de acuerdo según las circunstancias. **54 to – it cool,** (fam.) mantener la calma (en una situación de peligro). **55 to – it safe,** (fam.) curarse en salud, tomar la precaución. **56 to – off,** DEP. jugar el desquite, jugar un partido adicional (para decidir el desempate en una competición). **57 to – off against,** poner en contra, enfrentar (a dos personas para sacar provecho). **58 to – on/upon,** jugar con, utilizar, aprovecharse de (los sentimientos de otros, con ideas, palabras). **59 –**

on words, juego de palabras. **60 to – one's cards close to one's chest,** (fig.) saber tener sus cartas guardadas, mantener sus planes en secreto. **61 to – one's cards right/properly,** (fam. y fig.) jugar bien las cartas que uno tiene, montárselo uno bien. **62 to – out, a)** continuar hasta el final, seguir hasta el final, consumir (un juego, una pelea, el tiempo); **b)** representar, hacer (una escena). **63 to – the devil with,** perjudicar, hacer mucho daño. **64 to – the field,** (EE.UU. y fam.) citarse con más de un chico o chica, salir con varios novios, dejarse ver con distintos ligues. **65 to – the game,** (fam.) ser honesto, ser justo. **66 to – the market,** ECON. jugar en bolsa. **67 to – to the gallery,** (fig.) actuar para la galería. **68 to – up, a)** exagerar, dar mucha importancia, dar énfasis (a un hecho); **b)** (fam.) causar problemas, funcionar mal; **c)** (fam.) portarse mal, dar guerra. **69 to – up to,** (desp.) hacer la pelota. **70 to – with, a)** jugar con, dar vueltas a, juguetear con (una idea, un objeto); **b)** disponible: *not much money to play with = no mucho dinero disponible.* **71 to – with oneself,** (euf.) masturbarse. **72 state of –,** el estado de la cuestión, las cosas, la situación. **73 what someone is playing at,** (fam.) a que juega alguien (para indicar que alguien se equivoca).

play-act ǀ ˌpleɪˌækt ǀ *v.i.* **1** (desp.) fingir, hacer la comedia. **2** actuar, representar un papel (en el teatro).

playback ǀ ˌpleɪbæk ǀ *s.i.* previo (grabación del sonido antes de impresionar la imagen en cine).

playbill ǀ ˌpleɪbɪl ǀ *s.c.* cartel, anuncio, programa (de teatro).

playboy ǀ ˌpleɪbɔɪ ǀ *s.c.* vividor, hombre de mundo.

player ǀ ˌpleɪər ǀ *s.c.* **1** DEP. jugador. **2** MUS. músico. **3** (form.) actor (de teatro).

playful ǀ ˌpleɪfʊl ǀ *adj.* **1** juguetón, retozón, travieso, alegre, vivaracho. **2** en broma, de guasa, humorístico.

playfully ǀ ˌpleɪfəlɪ ǀ *adv.* en broma, jugando, humorísticamente.

playground ǀ ˌpleɪgraʊnd ǀ *s.c.* **1** (EE.UU. **recreation ground**) patio de recreo, campo de deportes. **2** zona recreativa (en un parque). **3** (fig.) dominio, imperio: *the South coast was the playground of gangsters = la costa sur era del dominio de los gángsters.*

playgroup ǀ ˌpleɪgruːp ǀ *s.c.* e *i.* (brit.) guardería, jardín de infancia.

playhouse ǀ ˌpleɪhaʊs ǀ [*pl.* **playhouses** ǀ ˌpleɪhaʊzɪz ǀ] *s.c.* **1** teatro, sala de teatro. **2** casa de muñecas; cabaña en miniatura (para jugar).

playing ǀ ˌpleɪɪŋ ǀ *s.i.* **1** MUS. modo de tocar, estilo de tocar. ǁ **2 – card,** naipe, carta.

playing-field ǀ ˌpleɪɪŋfiːld ǀ *s.c.* DEP. campo de deporte (generalmente en escuelas, universidades).

playlet ǀ ˌpleɪlɪt ǀ *s.c.* comedia corta, obra de teatro corta.

playmate ǀ ˌpleɪmeɪt ǀ *s.c.* compañero de juegos.

playoff ǀ ˌpleɪɒf ǀ *s.c.* DEP. partido de desempate, partido decisivo (en una competición).

playpen ǀ ˌpleɪpen ǀ *s.c.* corralito, parque (de niños).

playroom ǀ ˌpleɪrʊm ǀ *s.c.* cuarto de juegos.

plaything ǀ ˌpleɪθɪŋ ǀ *s.c.* **1** (form.) juguete. **2** (lit. y fig.) juguete, muñeco, títere: *a plaything of fate = un juguete del destino.*

playtime ǀ ˌpleɪtaɪm ǀ *s.i.* hora del recreo, recreo (en la escuela).

playwright ǀ ˌpleɪraɪt ǀ *s.c.* dramaturgo, autor dramático.

plaza ǀ ˌplɑːzə ǀ (EE.UU.) ǀ ˌplæzə ǀ *s.c.* **1** plaza (en ciudades españolas o latinoamericanas). **2** (EE.UU.) centro comercial, zona comercial.

plea ǀ pliː ǀ *s.c.* **1 [– (for)]** (form.) petición, ruego, súplica. **2 [– (of)]** DER. alegato, defensa; apelación, petición (de clemencia). **3** (p.u. y form.) excusa, pretexto, disculpa, justificación. ǁ **4 – bargaining,** DER. declaración de culpabilidad en un crimen menor (para no ser acusado de otro mayor).

pleached ǀ ˌpliːtʃt ǀ *adj.* trenzado, entretejido, entrelazado (las ramas de un árbol).

plead ǀ pliːd ǀ *v.* [*pret.* y *p.p.* **pleaded,** (EE.UU.) **pled**] *i.* **1** DER. abogar por, defender, pedir clemencia para, interceder por: *no one to plead his cause = nadie que defendiera su causa.* ǁ *t.* **2** rogar, pedir, suplicar, implorar. **3** DER. alegar, aducir (algo como excusa): *he pleaded insanity = alegó locura.* ǁ *t.* e *i.* **4** rogar, suplicar, implorar, pedir. **5** DER. declarar(se), confesar(se) (inocente, culpable): *do you plead guilty? = ¿se declara culpable?*

pleading ǀ ˌpliːdɪŋ ǀ *adj.* **1** suplicante, implorante. ǁ *s.pl.* o *i.* **2** ruego, súplica, intercesión. **3** DER. alegato, defensa.

pleadingly ǀ ˌpliːdɪŋlɪ ǀ *adv.* suplicantemente, en tono implorante.

pleasant ǀ ˌpleznt ǀ *adj.* **1** agradable, estupendo, grato, placentero, atractivo, encantador. **2** simpático, afable, amable, atento, educado, amistoso (una persona).

pleasantly ǀ ˌplezntlɪ ǀ *adv.* **1** agradablemente, gratamente, placenteramente. **2** afablemente, amablemente, educadamente, atentamente.

pleasantry ǀ ˌplezntrɪ ǀ *s.c.* (form.) cumplido, galantería, gentileza, ocurrencia.

please ǀ pliːz ǀ *v.t.* e *i.* **1** agradar, complacer, contentar, dar gusto, satisfacer: *certain people are difficult to please = es difícil agradar a ciertas personas.* ǁ *v.i.* **2 [to – *adv./prep.* en *oraciones subordinadas*]** gustar, desear, apetecer, preferir, elegir: *do whatever you please = haz lo que te apetezca.* ǁ *interj.* **3** por favor, si hace el favor (para pedir algo amablemente, para expresar un deseo, indignación): *coffee, please = café, si hace el favor; Clare, please! = ¡Clara, por favor!* **4** gracias, sí, gracias (para aceptar algo): *"milk"? "Please" = "¿leche"? "Sí, gracias".* **5** por favor, oiga, discúlpeme (para llamar la atención). ǁ **6 if you –, a)** (form.) si le parece, si hace el favor (para reforzar una petición); **b)** (arc.) ¡créetelo!, ¡imagínate!, ¡fíjate!: *she wanted me to pay for it, if you please! = quería que yo se lo pagara, ¡imagínate!* **7 – God,** (form.) Dios lo quiera, así lo espero, confío. **8 – yourself,** ¡como quieras!, ¡como se te antoje!

pleased ǀ pliːzd ǀ *adj.* **1 [– (with/about)]** encantado, satisfecho, complacido, feliz, dichoso. ǁ **2 – to meet you/etc...,** (form.) encantado de conocerle.

pleasing ǀ pliːzɪŋ ǀ *adj.* (form.) **[– (to)] 1** agradable, grato, placentero. **2** satisfactorio, favorable.

pleasurable ǀ ˌpleʒərəbl ǀ *adj.* (form.) agradable, placentero, grato.

pleasurably ǀ ˌpleʒərəblɪ ǀ *adv.* (form.) agradablemente, placenteramente, gratamente.

pleasure ǀ ˌpleʒər ǀ *s.i.* **1** placer, deleite, gozo, gusto, satisfacción. **2** placer, recreo, diversión: *a pleasure trip = un viaje de placer.* ǁ *s.c.* **3** placer, delicia, lujo: *pleasures difficult to get = placeres de difícil consecución.* **4** (form.) placer, honor: *it's a pleasure to join you = es un honor poder acompañaros.* ǁ **5 at someone's –,** (form.) a la voluntad de uno, como a uno le plazca. **6 during the king's/queen's –,** DER. a voluntad del rey o de la reina (una condena sin límite preciso). **7 it was a –/my –/a –,** ha sido un placer, de nada, no hay de que (al contestar a quien da las gracias). **8 to take – in (doing),** complacerse en (hacer). **9 with –,** con mucho gusto.

pleat ǀ pliːt ǀ *s.c.* **1** pliegue, tabla, frunce, doblez. ǁ *v.t.* **2** plisar, tablear, fruncir, hacer dobleces.

pleated ǀ pliːtɪd ǀ *adj* plisado, tableado, fruncido, con pliegues.

pleb ǀ pleb ǀ *s.c.* (fam. y desp.) plebeyo.

plebeian ǀ plɪ'biːən ǀ *s.c.* **1** (desp.) plebeyo, persona de clase baja. ǁ *adj.* **2** plebeyo, ordinario, de clase baja.

plectrum ǀ ˌplektrəm ǀ (también **pick**) [*pl.* **plectrums** o **plectra**] *s.c.* MUS. plectro, púa.

plectra ǀ ˌplektrə ǀ *pl.irr.* de **plectrum.**

pled ǀ pled ǀ (EE.UU.) *pret.* y *p.p.* de **plead.**

pledge ǀ pledʒ ǀ *s.c.* **1** promesa formal, garantía, compromiso (del gobierno, de un político, en la prensa): *the pledge to stop producing nuclear weapons = la promesa formal de detener la producción de armamento nuclear.* **2 [– (of)]** prenda, señal, prueba, garantía (de amor, amistad). **3** fianza, garantía, señal. **4** brindis. ǁ *v.t.* **5** prometer formalmente, jurar, garantizar. **6 [to – (to)]** (form.) hacer prometer; comprometerse a, dedicarse a: *I pledged myself to help them = me comprometí a ayudarles.* **7** empeñar, dejar en prenda, pignorar. ǁ *v.i.* **8** brindar. ǁ **9 to – one's word,** empeñar uno la palabra, dar uno su palabra. **10 to sign /take the –,** (arc.) prometer dejar de beber alcohol.

plenary ǀ ˌpliːnərɪ ǀ *adj.* [no comp.] (form.) **1** plenaria (una asamblea, una

sesión). **2** plenario, completo, ilimitado (un poder).
plenipotenciary | ˌplenɪpəʊ'tenʃərɪ | *s.c.* **1** (form.) plenipotenciario. || *adj.* **2** plenipotenciario, con todos los poderes (ministro).
plentiful | ˌplentɪfʊl | *adj.* abundante, copioso.
plentifully | ˌplentɪfəlɪ | *adv.* abundantemente, copiosamente.
plenty | ˌplentɪ | *pron.* **1** abundante, mucho, muchísimo, bastante, suficiente: *we've got plenty of work = tenemos muchísimo trabajo.* || *s.i.* **2** (form.) abundancia, copiosidad, prosperidad, exceso, opulencia. || *adv.* **3** bastante, excesivamente, mucho, muy: *she's plenty fat enough = está muy gorda.* || **4 in –,** en abundancia, bastante. **5 to see – of,** ver a menudo, ver con frecuencia.
plethora | ˌpleθərə | *s.sing.* (form.) **1** plétora, exceso, superabundancia. **2** MED. plétora, exceso de sangre.
pleurisy | ˌplʊərɪsɪ | *s.i.* MED. pleuresía.
pliable | ˌplaɪəbl | *adj.* **1** flexible, dúctil, moldeable (metal). **2** adaptable, flexible (persona). **3** (desp.) dócil, manejable, influenciable.
pliant | ˌplaɪənt | *adj.* **1** (desp.) influenciable, impresionable, maleable. **2** adaptable, flexible (una persona). **3** flexible, dúctil (metal).
pliers | ˌplaɪəz | *s.pl.* alicate, tenacilla.
plight | plaɪt | *s.sing.* **1** adversidad, situación, condición. || *v.t.* **2** prometer, jurar, dar palabra de. || **3 to – one's troth,** (arc.) prometerse en matrimonio, dar palabra de casamiento.
plimsoll | ˌplɪmsəl | (EE.UU. **sneaker**) *s.c.* **1** (brit.) zapatilla playera, zapatilla con suela de goma, zapatilla de gimnasia. || **2 Plimsoll line/mark,** MAR. línea de flotación.
plinth | plɪnθ | *s.c.* **1** peana. **2** ARQ. plinto, basamento.
plod | plɒd | [**plodded, plodding**]. *v.i.* **1** [**to – *adv./prep.***] caminar cansina y penosamente, andar pesadamente. **2** [**to – *adv./prep.* (away/on)**] trabajar con perseverancia, trabajar laboriosamente. || *s.i.* **3** trabajo o camino lento y pesado.
plodder | plɒdər | *s.c.* (desp.) **1** trabajador perseverante pero poco entusiasta, persona trabajadora pero falta de talento. **2** empollón, chapón, (Am.) chancón.
plonk | plɒŋk | | plɑːŋk | | plɔːŋk | (EE.UU. **plunk**) *s.c.* **1** golpe seco, sonido seco, ruido seco. **2** (brit. y fam.) vino barato. **3** MUS. rasgueo, punteo (de guitarra). || *v.t.* **4** [**to – *o.* + *adv./prep.***] (fam.) dejar caer con ruido seco, arrojar pesadamente, caer pesadamente. **5** MUS. rasguear, puntear (una guitarra).
plop | plɒp | | plɑːp | *s.c.* **1** (fam.) plaf, plof, catapún (ruido al caer el agua). || *adv.* **2** plaf, plof, catapum: *he fell plop into the water = cayó haciendo plof en agua.* || *v.i.* [**plopped, plopping**]. [**to – *adv./prep.* (into)**] caer haciendo plaf.
plot | plɒt | | plɑːt | *s.c.* **1** LIT. argumento, trama, enredo, intriga (de una obra). **2** complot, conspiración, maquinación, conjura, confabulación. **3** parcela, solar, terreno. **4** (EE.UU.) plano de un terreno, diagrama (para construir). || *v.i.* [**plotted, plotting**]. **5** [**to – (against)**] conspirar, maquinar, urdir, tramar, conjurarse. || *v.t.* **6** AER. trazar, marcar, calcular (la posición en un mapa, con radar). **7** delinear, dibujar, realizar (un gráfico). **8** [**to – (out)**] urdir la trama, urdir el argumento (de una novela).
plotter | plɒtər | *s.c.* **1** conspirador, conjurado, maquinador. **2** localizador de coordenadas, persona o instrumento que marca posiciones (en un mapa).
plough | plaʊ | (EE.UU. **plow**) *s.c.* **1** arado. || *v.t.* e *i.* **2** [**to – (up/in)**] arar, hacer surcos, roturar, labrar; cubrir arando, enterrar arando. **3** (argot) catear, cargar, suspender. **4** abrirse camino con dificultad, abrirse paso a la fuerza, destrozar a su paso: *the lorry ploughed the house walls = el camión destrozó las paredes de la casa.* || *v.i.* **5** [**to – *adv./prep.***] surcar (las aguas). **6** (fig.) terminar con dificultad, conseguir acabar (una lectura). || *v.t.* **7** acanalar, hacer ranuras. || **8 to go under the –,** roturar (un terreno para siempre). **9 to – back, (into),** reinvertir (ganancias). **10 The Plough/** (EE.UU.) **The Big Dipper,** ASTR. la Osa Mayor.
ploughed | plaʊd | *adj.* arado, roturado.
ploughman | ˌplaʊmən | [*pl.* **ploughmen**] *s.c.* **1** campesino, labrador, arador. || **2 ploughman's lunch,** (brit.) bocadillo de queso con encurtidos vegetales que se toma en bares como almuerzo.
ploughmen | ˌplaʊmən | *pl.irr.* de **ploughman.**
ploughshare | ˌplaʊʃeər | *s.c.* **1** reja de arado. || **2 to turn swords into ploughshares,** hacer las paces (después de una pelea).
plover | ˌplʌvər | *s.c.* ZOOL. chorlito, charadrio.
ploy | ˌplɔɪ | *s.c.* táctica, estratagema, truco, maniobra.
pluck | plʌk | *v.t.* **1** desplumar, pelar (un ave). **2** [**to – (out/from/of)**] depilar (las cejas). **3** [**to – (out/from/of)**] arrancar, extraer, quitar de un tirón, coger de un tirón. **4** (lit.) cortar, coger (una flor). **5** (fig.) sacar, rescatar (de una situación de peligro, desagradable). || *v.t.* e *i.* **6** MUS. pulsar, tocar, puntear (las cuerdas de un instrumento). || *s.i.* **7** (fam.) coraje, valor, determinación, fuerza. || *s.c.* **8** tirón. **9** asadura (de un animal). || **10 to – at,** tirar de, dar tirones a: *plucking at his mother's skirt = tirando de la falda de su madre.* **11 to – something out of the air,** sacarse algo de la manga, decir algo sin pensarlo bien. **12 to – up the courage,** hacer de tripas corazón, armarse de valor, cobrar ánimos.
pluckily | ˌplʌkɪlɪ | *adv.* valientemente, intrépidamente, con resolución.
plucky | ˌplʌkɪ | *adj.* valiente, valeroso, atrevido, intrépido, resuelto.
plug | plʌg | *s.c.* **1** tapón (para obstruir, contra ruidos): *bath plug = tapón de la bañera; ear plugs = tapones de cera para los oídos.* **2** taco (de madera, de plástico). **3** MED. tampón. **4** ELEC. enchufe, clavija; toma de corriente. **5** (fam.) opinión favorable, publicidad solapada (desde un medio de difusión): *he kept giving his new book plugs = estuvo todo el rato haciendo publicidad solapada de su nuevo libro.* **6** (fam.) bujía (de automóvil). **7** porción de tabaco, pastilla de tabaco (de mascar). **8** GEOL. obturación ígnea (de un volcán). **9** (argot), penco, jamelgo. **10** balazo, tiro. **11** (argot), chistera, sombrero de copa. || *v.t.* [**plugged, plugging**]. **12** [**to – (up)**] tapar, cerrar, bloquear, taponar, obstruir, obturar. **13** MED. empastar (un diente). **14** (fam.) hacer publicidad solapada, anunciar insistentemente. **15** (EE.UU. y argot) pegar un tiro, (Am.) balear, abalear. **16** (EE.UU. y argot) dar un puñetazo, pegar un puñetazo. || **17 to – away at,** (fam.) trabajar con perseverancia (en algo aburrido). **18 to – in/into,** ELEC. enchufar, conectar. **19 to – into, a)** (EE.UU. y fam.) conectar con, sintonizar con (ideas, gente); **b)** conectar con, utilizar, engancharse a (un sistema bancario a través de computadora). **20 to pull the – on,** (fam.) abandonar, renunciar a, dejar (un proyecto).
plugged | plʌgd | *adj.* obstruido, obturado, bloqueado.
plughole | plʌghəʊl | *s.c.* **1** (brit.) desagüe, tubo de salida (de una bañera, de un fregadero). || **2 down the –,** al traste.
plum | plʌm | *s.c.* **1** BOT. ciruela, pruna. **2** (fam.) chollo, bicoca, ganga, (Am.) pichincha. || *adj.* **3** (lit.) morado, rojizo, rojo oscuro. || **4 – pudding,** pudín de Navidad, pastel de ciruelas.
plumage | ˌpluːmɪdʒ | *s.i.* **1** plumaje. **2** (hum.) ropaje, ropas (de gran colorido, raras).
plumb | plʌm | *v.t.* **1** (fig.) sondear, examinar en profundidad, estudiar a fondo, profundizar, desentrañar. **2** sondar, sondear, verificar la profundidad. **3** aplomar, comprobar la verticalidad o el ángulo. || *adv.* (fam.) **4** [**– *adv./prep.***] exactamente, directamente, de lleno: *plumb in the middle = de lleno en el centro.* **5** (EE.UU.) completamente, absolutamente, totalmente: *they are plumb fool = están completamente locos.* || *adj.* **6** vertical, recto, a plomo, perpendicular. **7** (fam.) completo, total, absoluto. || *s.c.* **8** plomada, plomo. || **9 to – in,** (brit.) instalar, conectar (un aparato, un tubo a la red de agua): *the dishwasher was plumbed in seconds = instalaron el lavavajillas en un momento.* **10 to – the depths (of),** alcanzar al grado más absoluto (de), ser el súmmum (de).
plumber | ˌplʌmər | *s.c.* fontanero.
plumbing | ˌplʌmɪŋ | *s.i.* tuberías, cañerías, fontanería: *he did all the plumbing himself = él mismo se instaló toda la fontanería.*
plumb-line | ˌplʌmlaɪn | *s.c.* cuerda de plomada.
plume | pluːm | *s.c.* **1** pluma, plumaje, penacho (de adorno). **2** pluma (de ave). **3** [**– (of)**] penacho, nubecilla, voluta (de humo). **4** condecoración, premio, laurel.

|| *v.t.* **5** limpiar el plumaje, arreglar las plumas (un pájaro). **6** adornar con plumas, decorar con plumas. || **7 to – oneself in,** enorgullecerse, felicitarse (por una victoria).
plumed | plu:md | *adj.* (lit.) **1** adornado con plumas, con penacho. **2** en forma de pluma.
plummet | ˌplʌmɪt | *v.i.* **1** caer en picado, caer a plomo. || *s.c.* **2** peso, carga, opresión. **3** plomada.
plummy | ˌplʌmɪ | *adj.* (fam.) **1** (desp.) empalagosa, afectada, pastosa (la voz). **2** deseable, envidiable, fabuloso. **3** (lit.) rojizo, rojo oscuro, morado.
plump | plʌmp | *adj.* **1** (euf.) regordete, gordinflón, rechoncho, rollizo, llenito. **2** abundante, amplio, generoso. **3** brusco, de lleno (un golpe). || *s.c.* **4** caída pesada, porrazo, golpazo. || *adv.* **5** a plomo, directamente, de lleno. **6** bruscamente, contundentemente, sin miramientos. || *v.t.* e *i.* **7 [to – (up)]** mullir, sacudir (un cojín, una almohada). || **8 to – down,** (fam.) caer como un peso muerto, dejarse caer como un fardo. **9 to – for,** (brit. y fam.) optar por, decidirse por, elegir.
plumply | ˌplʌmplɪ | *adv.* firmemente, decidididademte.
plumpness | ˌplʌmpnɪs | *s.i.* gordura, rechonchez, corpulencia.
plunder | ˌplʌndər | *v.t.* e *i.* **1** saquear, someter al pillaje, rapiñar. **2** robar, expoliar. || *s.i.* **3** botín, despojo. **4** saqueo, pillaje, rapiña.
plunge | plʌndʒ | *v.t.* e *i.* **1** salir disparado, precipitar(se). **2** zambullir(se), sumergir(se), arrojar(se), lanzar(se). **3** (fig.) caer en picado, venirse abajo (los precios). || *v.i.* **4** cabecear (un barco). **5** tener mucho escote, ser muy escotado (un vestido). **6** (fig.) sumergirse, meterse, engancharse (en un trabajo). **7** hundirse (en un estado, condición). **8** (fam.) apostar arriesgadamente, arriesgar mucho dinero, especular. || *s.c.* **9** salto, zambullida, inmersión, baño, remojón. **10** caída, hundimiento (de precios). **11** piscina, estanque. || **12 to take the –,** arriesgarse, dar el paso decisivo, decidirse a.
plunger | plʌndʒər | *s.c.* **1** desatascador, bomba de desatascar. **2** MEC. brazo móvil, émbolo. **3** nadador, uno que se zambulle.
plunging | plʌndʒɪŋ | *adj.* de escote en pico muy pronunciado (un vestido).
plunk | plʌŋk | *s.c.* (EE.UU. y fam.) V. **plonk.**
pluperfect | ˌplu:'pɜ:fɪkt | GRAM. *s.sing.* **1 [the –]** el pluscuamperfecto. || *adj.* **2** pluscuamperfecto.
plural | ˌpluərəl | *adj.* **1** GRAM. plural. || *adj.* **2** GRAM. plural. **3** plural, diverso, variado: *a plural society = una sociedad plural.*
pluralism | ˌpluərəlɪzəm | *s.i.* **1** pluralismo, pluralidad, diversidad. **2** (desp.) pluriempleo (especialmente eclesiástico).
pluralist | ˌpluərəlɪst | *adj.* **1** pluralista, diverso, plural. || *s.c.* **2** pluralista, partidario del pluralismo.
pluralistic | ˌpluərəlɪstɪk | *adj.* pluralista, pluralístico.
plurality | pluə'rælɪtɪ | *s.i.* **1** GRAM. pluralidad. **2** pluralidad, multiplicidad. || *s.c.* **3 [– (of)]** POL. mayoría, pluralidad.
plus | plʌs | *prep.* **1** más: *3 plus 3 is 6 = 3 más 3 son seis.* **2** (fam.) además de, y además: *this includes lessons plus accomodation = esto incluye las clases además del alojamiento.* || *s.c.* [*pl.* **pluses,** o **pluses**]. **3** (también **plus sign**) más, signo más, positivo. **4** (fam.) ventaja, bonificación, suma positiva: *she gets a plus apart from her salary = aparte del sueldo le dan una bonificación.* | *adj.* **5** más de, por encima de: *he earns $1,500 plus = gana más de 1.500 dólares.* **6** adicional, extra, de más. **7** positivo, de signo positivo. || **8 – sign,** signo más, signo positivo.
plush | plʌʃ | (también **plushy**). *adj.* **1** (fam.) elegante, caro, de lujo. **2** de felpa, afelpado. || *s.i.* **3** felpa.
plushy | plʌʃɪ | *adj.* lujoso, de lujo, elegante, caro.
plutocracy | plu:'tɒkrəsɪ | *s.c.* e *i.* **1** (form.) plutocracia, gobierno de los ricos. **2** plutocracia, élite financiera.
plutocrat | ˌplu:təʊkræt | *s.c.* **1** plutócrata. **2** (fam. y desp.) ricachón, ricacho.
plutonium | plu:'təʊnjəm | *s.i.* QUIM. plutonio.
ply | plaɪ | *s.i.* **1** cabo, hilo, cordón, capa (para medir el grosor de la lana, cuerda, tela): *three-ply wool = lana de tres cabos.* **2** chapa, capa (de la madera contrachapada). **3** inclinación, propensión, tendencia, predisposición. || *v.i.* **4 [to – *adv./prep.*]** estar de servicio, ofrecerse para alquilar, buscar pasajeros (especialmente un taxista). || *v.t.* e *i.* **5** hacer el trayecto, hacer el servicio regular, volar, navegar (entre ciudades, aeropuertos, puertos, etc...). || *v.t.* **6** (lit. y arc.) realizar, ejercer, aplicarse a, emplearse diligentemente en (un trabajo). **7** manejar, usar, utilizar (una herramienta). || **8 to – somebody with, a)** atiborrar a uno de, empachar a uno con, emborrachar a uno de (comida, bebida); **b)** importunar a uno con, atosigar a uno con (preguntas).
plywood | ˌplaɪwʊd | *s.i.* madera contrachapada, (Am.) triplex.
p.m., P.M. | ˌpi:'em | *abreviatura* de **1 post meridiem,** después del mediodía, pasado el meridiano: *2.30 p.m. = 2 y media de la tarde.* **2 Prime Minister,** (brit.) Primer Ministro. **3 Pay Master,** habilitado, pagador. **4 Police Magistrate,** DER. juez de instrucción.
pneumatic | nju:'mætɪk | *adj.* **1** neumático. **2** FIL. espiritual.
pneumonia | nju:'məʊnɪə | *s.i.* MED. neumonía, pulmonía.
PO | ˌpi:'əʊ | *abreviatura* de **1 Post Office,** Correos, Oficina Central de Correos. **2 Postal Order,** giro postal. **3 Petty Officer,** MAR. suboficial. || **4 PO box,** apartado de correos.
poach | pəʊtʃ | *v.t.* **1** escalfar (huevos). || *v.t.* e *i.* **2** cazar furtivamente, pescar en zona vedada, entrar en propiedad ajena a cazar o pescar. **3 [to – (from /on)]** pisar, robar, apropiarse de, conseguir con medios poco honestos (ideas o empleados una compañía a otra). **4** pisotear, pisar, hollar, estropear (un terreno).
poacher | pəʊtʃər *s.c.* cazador furtivo.
pock | pɒk | | pɑ:k | *s.c.* **1** pústula, grano. **2** cicatriz de viruela o grano, hoyo de viruela. || *v.t.* **3** marcar (la viruela); dejar hoyos la viruela.
pocked | pɒkt | | pɑ:kt | *adj.* picado de viruela.
pocket | pɒkɪt | | pɑ:kɪt | *s.c.* **1** bolsillo, bolso (en una prenda). **2** bolsa, monedero. **3** saco, saca, bolsa. **4** (fam.) bolsillo, cuenta, medios, dinero: *he paid the bill out of his pocket = pagó la factura de su bolsillo.* **5** bolsa, red, receptáculo, cavidad (en una maleta, en un asiento, en la puerta de un coche). **6** bolsa, bache; área, zona (de aire, de niebla). **7** GEOL. bolsa. **8** grupúsculo, foco (de resistencia). **9** tronera (de billar). **10** DEP. encajonamiento, posición encajonada (en una carrera). || *v.t.* **11** meter al bolsillo, guardar en el bolso. **12** embolsarse, guardarse, quedarse con, apropiarse de (dinero de otros). **13** entronear (en el billar). **14** tolerar, aguantar (un insulto). **15** tragarse (el orgullo). **16** (EE.UU.) POL. retener sin firmar una ley hasta después de la clausura del Congreso (el presidente). **17** DEP. encajonar, arrinconar, cerrar el paso (a un corredor, un caballo). || *adj.* **18** de bolsillo. **19** en pequeño, en miniatura, minúsculo. || **20 to have someone in one's –,** tener a uno metido en el bolsillo, tener a uno en el bote. **21 in –,** (brit.) con beneficios, con ganancias (después de hacer un negocio). **22 to line one's pockets,** ponerse las botas (deshonestamente). **23 to live in each other's pockets,** (desp.) ser uña y carne, ser inseparables. **24 out of –,** (brit.) con pérdidas, sin beneficios (después de realizar un negocio). **25 to pick someone's –,** robarle a uno (un carterista), vaciarle a uno los bolsillos. **26 – calculator, calculadora de bolsillo. 27 – handkerchief,** pañuelo de bolsillo. **28 to put one's hand in/into one's –,** rascarse el bolso, gastar.
pocketbook | ˌpɒkɪtbʊk | *s.c.* **1** libreta de notas; libro de bolsillo. **2** (EE.UU. y arc.) cartera, monedero, bolso de mano. **3** cartera portafolios, carpeta. **4** (EE.UU.) recursos financieros, dinero.
pocketful | ˌpɒkɪtful | *s.c.* **1** bolso, bolsillo (cantidad que en él cabe): *a pocketful of pebbles = un bolsillo de guijarros.* **2** (fam.) montón, pellizco (de dinero).
pocket-knife | ˌpɒkɪtnaɪf | | ˌpɑ:kɪtnaɪf | [*pl.* **pocket-knives**] *s.c.* navaja.
pocket-money | ˌpɒkɪtˌmʌnɪ | *s.i.* **1** propina. **2** dinero para gastos personales, dinero para caprichos.
pocket-sized | ˌpɒkɪtˌsaɪzd | *adj.* de bolsillo, diminuto, muy pequeño.
pockmark | ˌpɒkmɑ:k | ˌpɑ:kmɑ:rk | *s.c.* cicatriz de viruelas, hoyos de viruelas.

pockemarked | ˌpɒkmɑːkt | *adj.* **1** lleno de hoyos de viruelas, lleno de cicatrices de viruelas. **2** (fig.) lleno de hoyos (un terreno).

pod | pɒd | | pɑːd | *s.c.* **1** BOT. vaina (de legumbres). **2** depósito, receptáculo (en aviones bajo las alas, para gasolina, armas). **3** AER. cabina de pasajeros y material (en una nave espacial). **4** manada, bandada (de ballenas, de focas). **5** MEC. portabroca (de taladro, de berbiquí). || *v.t.* [**podded, podding**]. quitar vainas (a las legumbres). || *v.i.* **7** producir vainas. **8** engordar, abultarse, hincharse.

podgy | ˌpɒdʒɪ | | ˌpɑːdʒɪ | (también **pudgy**) *adj.* (desp.) regordete, rechoncho, gordito, gordinflón.

podia | ˌpəudɪə | *pl.irr.* de **podium.**

podium | ˌpəudɪəm | [*pl.* **podiums** o **podia**] *s.c.* podio, estrado, plataforma, templete.

poem | ˌpəuɪm | *s.c.* LIT. poema, poesía.

poet | ˌpəuɪt | *s.c.* **1** poeta. **2** persona dotada de gran imaginación y sensibilidad. || **3 – laureate,** poeta laureado.

poetic | pəu'etɪk | *adj.* **1** poético, lírico. **2** bello, emotivo, expresivo, imaginativo, con gran sensibilidad. || **3 – justice,** totalmente merecido, justa retribución. **4 – licence,** licencia poética.

poetically | pəu'etɪkəlɪ | *adv.* poéticamente, líricamente.

poetry | ˌpəuɪtrɪ | *s.i.* **1** poesía, verso, poemas. **2** poesía, lírica (como arte). **3** (fig.) poesía, belleza, sensibilidad: *the poetry of his paintings = la belleza de sus cuadros.*

pogo stick | ˌpəugəu stɪk | *s.c.* saltador, pogo saltarín (juguete consistente en una barra con muelles para saltar).

pogrom | ˌpɒgrəm | | pə'grɑːm | *s.c.* pogromo, persecución, masacre, matanza (de un grupo social y animada desde el poder).

poignancy | ˌpɔɪnjənsɪ | *s.i.* (form.) **1** patetismo, sentimentalismo, emoción, profundidad de sentimientos. **2** mordacidad, sarcasmo, acritud.

poignant | ˌpɔɪjənt | *adj.* (form.) **1** patético, conmovedor, emocionante. **2** profundo, hondo, intenso, agudo (un dolor, una pena). **3** incisivo, mordaz, punzante. **4** importante, relevante, al día (información). **5** picante; agrio, ácido, fuerte (olor, sabor).

poignantly | ˌpɔɪnjənjlɪ | *adv.* (form.) **1** patéticamente, de forma conmovedora, emocionantemente. **2** profundamente, intensamente, agudamente. **3** incisivamente, mordazmente.

poinsettia | pɔɪn'setɪə | *s.c.* BOT. poinsetia, flor de Pascua.

point | pɔɪnt | *s.c.* **1** punta, pico (de aguja, de herramienta). **2** punto, lugar, sitio. **3** punto, característica, cualidad, habilidad: *his strong point was English = su punto fuerte era el inglés.* **4** DEP. punto, tanto. **5** punto, tema, idea, detalle, hecho: *a few interesting points in his speech = algunas ideas interesantes en su discurso.* **6** [**the –**] lo importante, lo significativo, el objetivo, la gracia, el sentido (de un asunto). **7** (también decimal point). MAT. punto decimal, coma. **8** (EE.UU.) punto (ortográfico, vocálico). **9** ECON. punto, entero: *the pound has gained 2 points = la libra ha subido dos puntos.* **10** [**– (of)**] punto, foco, partícula (de luz). **11** MAR. cuarta (de la rosa náutica). **12** GEOG. punta, cabo. **13** (también **power –**), (brit.) ELECT. toma, conexión. **14** clavija, borne. **15** punzón, buril. **16** MUS. melodía corta, frase corta. **17** HIST. cordón de corpiño. || *s.c.* e *i.* **18** punto, grado; momento, instante, ocasión. || *s.i.* **19** [**– (in/of)**] sentido, ventaja, utilidad, beneficio, provecho: *there's no point in telling her = no merece la pena decírselo a ella.* **20** encaje de bolillos; punto de cruz. || *v.i.* **21** [**to (at/to)**] apuntar, señalar con el dedo, indicar con el dedo. **22** [**to –** *adv./prep.*] apuntar, señalar, marcar, mostrar (una dirección). || *v.t.* e *i.* **23** DEP. pararse y mostrar la caza (un perro). || **24** MAR. barloventear, navegar de bolina, avanzar contra el viento. || *v.t.* **25** [**to – (at /towards)**] apuntar, dirigir (un arma). **26** rellenar, rejuntar, resanar (grietas). **27** afilar, sacar punta. **28** puntuar, separar por punto; separar con punto decimal. || **29 at this – in time,** (fam.) ahora, en este momento. **30 beside the –,** que no viene a cuento, que no viene al caso, irrelevante. **31 case in –,** V. **case. 32 to come/get to the –,** entrar en harina, ir al grano. **33 finer points,** sutilezas, aspectos más complicados. **34 from the – of view of/from a/the ... – of view,** desde el (un) punto de vista de. **35 to get the –,** entender, comprender. **36 to have its points,** tener algunas cualidades, tener algunos puntos favorables. **37 high –,** el punto álgido, el apogeo, el mejor momento. **38 in – of fact,** V. **fact. 39 I take your –,** lo admito, lo acepto. **40 low –,** punto bajo, peor momento. **41 to make/prove one's –,** convencer los argumentos de uno, persuadir las palabras de uno, establecer su punto de vista. **42 not to put too fine a – on it,** hablando claro, sin tapujos, en román paladino. **43 on the – of,** a punto de. **44 – of no return,** V. **return. 45 – of order,** (form.) cuestión de orden, cuestión de procedimiento. **46 – of reference,** punto de referencia. **47 – of view,** punto de vista. **48 to – out, a)** señalar, indicar, mostrar; **b)** [**to – out (that)**] hacer notar, observar, advertir. **49** points, **a)** (EE.UU. **switches**) agujas (de ferrocarril); **b)** puntas (de los pies en ballet); **c)** DEP. puntos (en boxeo). **50 to – someone in the direction,** (fam.) indicar a alguien la dirección (de un lugar). **51 – taken,** lo admito, excepto el punto de vista. **52 to – the finger at,** V. **finger. 53 to – the way,** indicar el modo, señalar la forma. **54 to – to/towards,** apuntar hacia, señalar a. **55 to – up,** (form.) destacar, poner de relieve. **56 saturation –,** V. **saturation. 57 to score points,** V. **score. 58 to see someone's –,** comprender los puntos de vista de uno. **59 sore –,** V. **sore. 60 to stretch a –,** hacer una concesión. **61 to the – of,** casi, rayando en: *to the point of stupidity = rayando en la estupidez.* **62 up to a –,** hasta cierto punto.

point-blank | ˌpɔɪnt'blæŋk | *adv.* **1** a quemarropa, a bocajarro, muy de cerca. **2** directamente, sin ambages. || *adj.* **3** a quemarropa, a bocajarro. **4** directo, franco, sin ambages.

pointed | ˌpɔɪntɪd | *adj.* **1** puntiagudo, afilado, en punta. **2** directo, evidente, claro. **3** sarcástico, mordaz, cortante, agudo (un comentario).

pointedly | ˌpɔɪntɪdlɪ | *adv.* mordazmente, cortantemente, sarcásticamente.

pointer | ˌpɔɪntər | *s.c.* **1** aguja, manecilla, indicador, fiel. **2** puntero. **3** pista, dato, indicación, información, consejo. **4** ZOOL. pointer, perro perdiguero, perro de muestra.

pointing | ˌpɔɪntɪŋ | *s.i.* **1** trabajo de restauración de fachadas de ladrillo o piedra. **2** cemento (entre los ladrillos o las piedras de un edificio).

pointless | ˌpɔɪntlɪs | *adj.* (generalmente desp.) **1** sin razón, inmotivado. **2** sin sentido, inútil, inefectivo: *talking to her was pointless = fue inútil hablar con ella.*

pointlessly | ˌpɔɪntlɪslɪ | *adv.* inútilmente, sin motivo.

pointlessness | ˌpɔɪntlɪsnɪs | *s.i.* inutilidad, falta de sentido, falta de motivo.

poise | pɔɪz | *s.i.* **1** aplomo, serenidad, calma, confianza en sí mismo, autocontrol. **2** elegancia, donaire, porte, gracia. **3** estabilidad, equilibrio. || *v.t.* **4** [**to –** *adv./prep.*] colocar equilibradamente, llevar equilibradamente. || *v.i.* **5** cernerse, mantenerse en el aire (un ave). **6** flotar en el aire, estar en suspenso, pender en el aire.

poised | ˌpɔɪzd | *adj.* **1** [**– between**] suspendido entre: *poised between life and death = entre la vida y la muerte.* **2** [**– for + to** *inf.*] preparado para, listo para, dispuesto para, presto a. **3** [**–** *adv./prep.*] flotante, en suspenso, en equilibrio. **4** sereno, ecuánime, tranquilo, en calma, confiado en sí mismo.

poison | ˌpɔɪzn | *s.c.* e *i.* **1** veneno. **2** (fig.) veneno, ponzoña. || *s.i.* **3** (argot) bebida alcohólica, matarratas: *what's your poison? = ¿qué te tomas?* || *v.t.* **4** envenenar, matar con veneno. **5** corromper, contaminar, viciar, emponzoñar. **6** (fig.) estropear, corromper, envenenar (a una persona, una situación). **7** (brit.) infectar, infestar (una herida). **8** QUIM. inhibir, retardar (una reacción). || **9 to be –,** (arc.) ser un veneno, ser muy desagradable (una persona). **10 to hate somebody like –,** odiar a alguien a muerte, odiar enormemente a alguien. 11 – gas, gas tóxico. **12 poison-pen letter,** anónimo injuriante. **13 to – someone's mind,** poner a uno en contra, envenenarle a alguien la cabeza (en contra de otra persona).

poisoner | ˌpɔɪznər | *s.c.* envenenador.

poisoning | ˌpɔɪznɪŋ | *s.i.* envenenamiento, intoxicación.

poisonous | ˌpɔɪznəs | *adj.* **1** venenoso, tóxico. **2** (fig.) perniciosa, perjudicial, dañina, peligrosa (una influencia, una persona). **3** (desp.) desagradable, perverso, detestable, malintencionado.

poke | pəʊk | *v.t.* e *i.* **1 [to – *o.* + *adv./prep.*]** asomar, sobresalir, proyectarse. **2 [to – (in/with)]** pinchar, clavar, punzar, aguijonear, introducir, insertar. || *v.t.* **3** (fig.) abrirse camino a través de, atravesar, pasar a través de. **4 [to – (at)]** atizar, remover, escarbar (el fuego). || *v.i.* **5** (fig.) entrometerse, inmiscuirse. **6** perder el tiempo, haraganear. || *s.c.* **7** pinchazo, codazo, empujón, golpe, puñetazo. **8** holgazán, haragán. || **9 pig in a –,** V. **pig. 10 to – fun at,** V. **fun. 11 to – about/around,** fisgonear, andar, husmear. **12 to – one's nose into,** (fam.) meter las narices en.

poker | pəʊkər | *s.c.* **1** badila, atizador. || *s.i.* **2** póquer (juego de cartas). || **3 – face,** (fam.) expresión impasible, (Am.) cara de palo.

poker-faced | pəʊkəfeɪst | *adj.* (fam.) impasible, inmutable, sin expresión.

poky | ˌpəʊkɪ | (también **pokey**). *adj.* [*comp.* **pokier,** *super.* **pokiest**] **1** (brit., fam. y desp.) pequeño, estrecho, apretado (una habitación). **2** lento, perezoso. **3** desaliñado, andrajoso, raído.

polar | ˌpəʊlər | *adj.* **1** polar. **2** (form.) totalmente opuesto, contrario. || **3 – bear,** oso polar, oso blanco.

polarise V. **polarize.**

polarity | pəʊ'lærɪtɪ | *s.c.* e *i.* (form.) polaridad.

polarization | ˌpəʊləraɪ'zeɪʃn | | ˌpəʊlərə' | | zeɪʃn | *s.i.* polarización.

polarize | ˌpəʊləraɪz | (brit. **polarise**) *v.t.* e *i.* **[to – (into)]** polarizar(se), dividir(se).

pole | pəʊl | *s.c.* **1** poste, palo, estaca, vara, mástil. **2** DEP. pértiga, percha. **3** GEOG. polo. **4** (fig. y lit.) polo, extremo, punta: *from pole to pole = de punta a punta.* **5** FIS. polo. || **6 Pole,** polaco (nacionalidad). **7 – star,** ASTR. estrella polar. **8 – vault,** DEP. salto con pértiga. **9 poles apart,** totalmente contrarios, en mundos completamente diferentes.

poleaxe | ˌpəʊlæks | *v.t.* **1** derribar de un golpe, (Am.) noquear. **2** descabellar, desnucar (a un animal). || *s.c.* **3** hacha de matadero.

poleaxed | ˌpəʊlækst | *adj.* (fam.) **1** patitieso, estupefacto, extremadamente sorprendido, incapaz de reaccionar. **2** completamente borracho, trompa, mamado, curda.

polecat | ˌpəʊlkæt | *s.c.* ZOOL. **1** turón. **2** (EE.UU.) mofeta.

polemic | pɒ'lemɪk | *s.c.* e *i.* (form.) **1** polémica, debate, controversia. || *adj.* **2** polémico, controvertible. || **3 polemics,** arte de polemizar, polémica.

polemical | pɒ'lemɪkl | *adj.* polémico, controvertible.

polemicist | pɒ'lemɪsɪst | *s.c.* polemista.

police | pə'liːs | *s.pl.* **1 [(the) –]** policía, cuerpo de policía. **2** policías (hombres o mujeres). **3** (EE.UU.) MIL. limpieza, cuidado, aseo (de cuarteles). **4** (EE.UU.) MIL. pelotón de limpieza, brigada de limpieza. || *v.t.* **5** patrullar, vigilar las calles, mantener el orden público (la policía, el ejército). **6** controlar, supervisar, vigilar. **7** MIL. mantener la limpieza (en un cuartel). || **8 – constable,** (brit.) policía, guardia. **9 – force,** fuerza policial. **10 – officer,** oficial de policía, guardia. **11 – state,** (desp.) estado policiaco. **12 – station,** comisaría de policía.

policeman | pə'liːsmən | [*pl.* **policemen,** *m*]. *s.c.* policía, guardia.

policewoman | pə'liːˌwʊmən | [*pl.* **policewomen,** *f.*] *s.c.* policía, guardia.

policewomen | pə'liːˌwɪmɪn | *pl.* de **policewoman.**

policy | ˌpɒləsɪ | | ˌpɑːləsɪ | *s.c.* e *i.* **1** plan de acción, política, régimen, asunto: *they'll have to change their policy = tendrán que cambiar de política.* **2** sagacidad, prudencia, precaución. || *s.c.* **3** póliza (de seguros).

polio | ˌpəʊlɪəʊ | (también **poliomyelitis**) *s.i.* (fam.) MED. poliomielitis, polio.

poliomyelitis | ˌpəʊlɪəʊmaɪə'laɪtɪs | *s.i.* V. **polio.**

polish | ˌpɒlɪʃ | | ˌpɑːlɪʃ | *v.t.* **1 [to – (up)]** lustrar, abrillantar, pulimentar, bruñir. **2** refinar, educar, pulir (a una persona). || *s.i.* **3** cera, betún, líquido abrillantador. **4** lustre, brillo. **5** brillantez, elegancia, gracia. **6** refinamiento, finura, urbanidad. **7** polaco (idioma). || *s.c.* **8** limpieza, pulido, lustre, bruñido: *he gave the table a good polish = sacó brillo a la mesa.* **9** polaco (de origen). || *adj.* **10** polaco, de Polonia. || **11 to – off,** (fam.) terminar rápidamente, dar cuenta de (especialmente comida). **12 to – up,** perfeccionar, mejorar (con la práctica).

polished | ˌpɒlɪʃt | *adj.* **1** perfecto, correcto, impecable. **2** refinado, elegante, culto, fino. **3** bruñido, pulido, brillante.

polisher | ˌpɒlɪʃər | *s.c.* máquina enceradora.

Politburo | ˌpɒlɪtˌbjʊərəʊ | *s.c.* Buró Político, Politburó (en países comunistas).

polite | pə'laɪt | *adj.* **1** cortés, educado, atento, considerado, fino, correcto. **2** (arc.) refinado, elegante. **3** de cortesía, de cumplido: *a polite smile = una sonrisa de cortesía.*

politely | pə'laɪtlɪ | *adv.* cortésmente, atentamente, correctamente.

politeness | pə'laɪtnɪs | *s.i.* cortesía, corrección, finura, educación, urbanidad.

politic | ˌpɒlɪtɪk | | ˌpɑːlɪtɪk | *adj.* (form.) **1** prudente, sensato, juicioso, útil. **2** ingenioso, hábil, astuto, artero.

politics | ˌpɒlɪtɪks | *s.i.* política.

political | pə'lɪtɪkl | *adj.* **1** [no *comp.*] político. **2** politizado. || **3 – asylum,** asilo político. **4 – economy,** economía política. **5 – prisoner,** prisionero político. **6 – science,** Políticas, ciencia política. **7 – scientist,** experto en ciencias políticas.

politically | pə'lɪtɪkəlɪ | *adv.* políticamente.

politician | ˌpɒlɪ'tɪʃn | *s.c.* **1** político, estadista. **2** (fig.) diplomático, político.

politicization | ˌpɒlɪtɪsaɪzeɪʃn | *s.i.* politización.

politicize | pə'lɪtɪsaɪz | (brit. **politicise**) *v.t.* (generalmente desp.). **1** politizar, dar carácter político. **2** politizar, concienciar políticamente, introducir política en. || *v.i.* **3** politizarse, meterse en política; discutir de política.

politicking | pɒlɪtɪkɪŋ | *s.i.* (desp.) politiqueo, manejos electorales, electorerismo.

politico | pə'lɪtɪkəʊ | [*pl.* **politicoes** o **politicos**] *s.c.* **1** (desp.) politiquero, politicastro. || **2 politico-, [– *adj.*]** político-: *a politico-social problem = un problema político-social.*

polity | ˌpɒlɪtɪ | [*pl.* **polities**] *s.c.* e *i.* (form.) **1** organización política, gobierno, estado, forma de gobierno. **2** administración, gobierno (eclesiástico).

polka | ˌpɒlkə | *s.c.* **1** polca (baile). || **2 – dot,** estampado de lunares: *wearing a polka dot dress = llevaba un vestido de lunares.*

poll | pəʊl | *s.c.* **1** (también **opinion poll**) encuesta, muestreo de opinión, sondeo de opinión. **2** votos, porcentaje de votos, número de votos. **3** cuero cabelludo, cogote, nuca. **4** cotillo, cabeza (de un martillo). || *v.t.* **5** encuestar, realizar un muestreo. **6** conseguir, obtener, recibir (votos). **7** descornar, cortar el extremo de los cuernos (al ganado). **8** desmochar, podar (árboles). **9** esquilar, trasquilar. **10** cortar a tijera, recortar (el pelo). || *v.i.* **11** votar, emitir un voto. || **12 – tax,** impuesto de capitación (impuesto obligatorio para ciudadanos en edad de votar). **13 polls,** POL. elecciones, votación electoral.

pollarded | ˌpɒlədɪd | *adj.* **1** podado, desmochado, recortado (un árbol). **2** descornado, mocho (un animal).

pollen | ˌpɒlən | | ˌpɑːlən | *s.i.* **1** BOT. polen. || **2 – count,** medida de la concentración de polen en el aire.

pollinate | ˌpɒlɪneɪt | | ˌpɑːləneɪt | *v.t.* BOT. polinizar.

pollination | ˌpɒlɪ'neɪʃn | | ˌpɑːlɪ'neɪʃn | *s.i.* BOT. polinización.

polling | pəʊlɪŋ | *s.i.* POL. **1** votación, elecciones. **2** porcentaje de votantes, número de votos: *polling was very low = el porcentaje de votantes fue muy bajo.* || **3 – day,** día de elecciones. **4 – station,** colegio electoral.

pollutant | pə'luːtənt | *s.c.* e *i.* agente contaminante, sustancia química contaminante.

polluted | pə'luːtɪd | *adj.* contaminado, sucio.

pollution | pə'luːʃn | *s.i.* polución, contaminación.

polo | ˌpəʊləʊ | *s.i.* DEP. polo.

polo-necked | ˌpəʊləʊnek | (también **polo-neck**) *adj.* de cuello alto (jersey).

poltergeist | ˌpɒltəgaɪst | *s.c.* espíritu, duende, fantasma (que hace ruidos, mueve objetos, muebles).

poly | ˌpɒlɪ | | ˌpɑːlɪ | *s.c.* **1** (brit. y fam.) politécnico, escuela politécnica. || *prefijo.* **2** poli: *polychromatic = policromático.*

polyandry | ˌpɒlɪændrɪ | | ˌpɒlɪ'ændrɪ | *s.i.* poliandria.

polyester | ˌpɒlɪ'estər | , (EE.UU.) | ˌpɒliːestər | *s.i.* QUIM. poliéster.
polyethylene | ˌpɒlɪ'eθɪliːn | | ˌpɑːlɪ'eθɪliːn | (brit. **polythene**). *s.i.* QUIM. polietileno.
polygamy | pə'lɪgəmɪ | *s.i.* poligamia.
polyglot | ˌpɒlɪglɒt | | ˌpɑːlɪglɑːt | *adj.* **1** políglota, multilingüe. || *s.c.* **2** políglota.
polygon | ˌpɒlɪgən | | ˌpɑːlɪgɑːn | *s.c.* GEOM. polígono.
polymath | ˌpɒlɪmæθ | | ˌpɑːlɪmæθ | *s.c.* (form.) polifacético.
polymer | ˌpɒlɪmər | *s.c.* QUIM. polímero.
Polynesia | ˌpɒlɪ'niːzɪə | *s.* Polinesia.
Polynesian | ˌpɒlɪ'niːzɪən | *adj.* **1** polinesio, de la Polinesia. || *s.c.* **2** polinesio, persona natural de la Polinesia.
polyp | ˌpɒlɪp | | ˌpɑːlɪp | *s.c.* e *i.* **1** ZOOL. pólipo. || *s.c.* **2** MED. pólipo.
polyphony | pə'lɪfənɪ | *s.i.* MUS. polifonía.
polystyrene | ˌpɒlɪ'staɪriːn | *s.i.* QUIM. poliestireno.
polysyllable | ˌpɒlɪsɪləbl | *s.c.* GRAM. palabra polisílaba.
polytechnic | ˌpɒlɪ'teknɪk | *s.c.* (brit.) politécnico, escuela politécnica.
polythene | ˌpɒlɪθiːn | *s.i.* QUIM. polietileno.
polyunsaturated | ˌpɒlɪʌn'sætʃəreɪtɪd | *adj.* QUIM. poliinsaturado.
polyurethane | ˌpɒlɪ'juərɪθeɪn | *s.i.* QUIM. poliuretano.
pom | pɒm | *s.c.* (fam.) V. **pommy.**
pomegranate | ˌpɒmɪˌgrænɪt | | ˌpʌmgrænɪt | *s.c.* BOT. **1** granado. **2** granada (fruto).
pommel | ˌpʌml | *s.c.* **1** perilla (de la montura). **2** pomo (de la empuñadura de una espada). || *v.t.* **3** (EE.UU.) dar puñetazos, golpear con los puños, aporrear.
pommy | ˌpɒmɪ | (también **pomie**) *s.c.* (desp.) inglés (apelativo para inmigrantes en Nueva Zelanda, Australia).
pomp | pɒmp | | pɑːmp | *s.i.* pompa, ostentación, fausto, boato.
pom-pom | ˌpɒmpɒm | *s.c.* **1** pompón (de adorno). **2** MIL. cañón antiaéreo automático.
pomposity | pɒm'pɒsɪtɪ | | pɑːm'pɑːsɪtɪ | *s.i.* (form.) pomposidad, ostentación.
pompous | ˌpɒmpəs | | ˌpɑːmpəs | *adj.* (desp.) **1** pomposo, ostentoso, ceremonioso. **2** pomposo, grandioso, magnífico (un edificio, una ceremonia). **3** ampuloso, rimbombante.
pompously | pɒmpəslɪ | *adv.* **1** pomposamente, ostentosamente, ceremoniosamente. **2** ampulosamente, de forma rimbombante.
ponce | pɒns | | pɑːns | *s.c.* (brit.) **1** (desp. y vulg.) afeminado, marica, homosexual. **2** proxeneta, chulo. || *v.i.* **3** **[to -- about/around]** (brit. y desp.) moverse amaneradamente, actuar de forma afeminada. *4* perder el tiempo, haraganear.
poncho | 'pɒntʃəu | | 'pɑːntʃəu | *s.c.* poncho.
pond | pɒnd | | pɒːnd | *s.c.* charca, laguna, estanque.
ponder | 'pɒndər | | 'pɒːndər | *v.t.* e *i.* (lit.) ponderar, reflexionar (sobre), considerar, meditar (sobre), madurar: *we'll have to ponder the situation = tendremos que considerar la situación.*
ponderous | 'pɒndərəs | | 'pɒːndərəs | *adj.* (form.) **1** pesado voluminoso, masivo. **2** sin gracia, torpe, lento. **3** aburrido, pesado, poco fluido (un discurso).
ponderously | 'pɒndərəslɪ | *adv.* pesadamente, lentamente, tediosamente.
pong | pɒŋ | | pɒːŋ | *s.c.* (brit., fam. y desp.). **1** peste, pestilencia, tufo, hediondez. || *v.i.* **2** apestar, desprender mal olor.
pontiff | 'pɒntɪf | | 'pɒːntɪf | *s.* (form.) REL. pontífice, Sumo Pontífice.
pontifical | 'pɒntɪfɪkl | *adj.* **1** pontificio, papal, obispal, episcopal. **2** (form.) pontifical, dogmático, autoritario.
pontificate | 'pɒntɪfɪkɪt | | pɒːntɪfɪkeɪt | *v.i.* **1** **[to -- (about/on)]** (desp.) pontificar, dogmatizar. || *s.c.* **2** pontificado.
pontoon | pɒn'tuːn | | pɒːn'tuːn | *s.c.* **1** pontón, plataforma flotante (para sujetar un puente). **2** AER. flotador. || *s.i.* **3** (brit.) veintiuno (juego de cartas).
pony | 'pəunɪ | *s.c.* **1** poney, caballito, jaca. **2** (fam.) caballo de carrera. **3** (EE.UU. y fam.) chuleta (para un examen). **4** (brit. y argot) 25 libras esterlinas. || *v.t.* **5** utilizar chuletas, hacer chuletas (para un examen). || **6 on Shanks's –/mare,** V. **shank. 7 to – up,** (argot) pagar deudas, apoquinar.
ponytail | ˌpəunɪ'teɪl | *s.c.* cola de caballo (como peinado).
poodle | ˌpuːdl | *s.c.* **1** caniche, perro de lanas. || **2 to be someone's –,** (brit., hum. y desp.) ser el perrillo faldero de uno.
poof | puf | (también **pouf** y **poofter**). [*pl.* **poofs** o **pooves**]. *s.c.* (brit., argot y desp.) marica, afeminado.
poofter | ˌpuftər | *s.c.* V. **poof.**
pooh | puː | *interj.* (fam.) **1** ¡uf! (expresa desagrado, mal olor). **2** ¡bah!, ¡qué va! (expresa desdén, desaprobación). || *s.i.* **3** (brit.) caca (usado por los niños).
pooh-pooh | ˌpuː'puː | *v.t.* (fam.) desdeñar, desechar, menospreciar, burlarse de, restar importancia a.
pool | puːl | *s.c.* **1** poza, balsa, remanso (en un río). **2** laguna, charca, alberca, estanque. **3** charco (de cualquier líquido). **4** piscina. **5** COM. consorcio, mancomunidad, fusión (entre empresas, utilizando en común trabajadores, maquinaria, etc...). **6** apuesta, pozo (en juegos de cartas). || *s.i.* **7** (EE.UU.) billar americano. || *v.t.* **8** combinar, mancomunar, aunar (recursos, ideas). || **9 pools,** DEP. quinielas.
poop | puːp | *s.c.* MAR. **1** popa. **2** (también – **deck**) castillo de popa, toldilla. || *v.t.* **3** (argot) cansar, agotar, dejar sin resuello.
pooped | ˌpuːpt | *adj.* (EE.UU. y argot) exhausto, agotado, acabado, sin resuello.
poor | puər | | pɔːr | *adj.* **1** pobre, indigente, menesteroso, necesitado. **2** (form.) malo, deficiente, de baja calidad, inferior, inadecuado: *poor attendance = atención deficiente.* **3** (form.) escaso, exiguo, insuficiente, modesto, humilde: *she gets quite a poor salary = gana un salario bastante modesto.* **4** (form.) débil, endeble, enfermizo, malo. **5** (desp.) desagradable, envidioso, mal (perdedor). **6** pobre, desgraciado, infortunado. **7** árido, yermo, infecundo, estéril (el suelo). **8** desnutrido, flaco. **9** trivial, insignificante, poco valioso. || *sufijo.* **10** [*s.* **poor-**] pobre en, pobre de, falto de: *poor-spirited = mezquino, pobre de espíritu.* || **11 – girl/boy, etc., ...,** pobrecito, pobrecita. **12 – relation,** (fig.) pariente pobre. **13 the –,** los pobres.
poorhouse | ˌpuəhaus | [*pl.* **poorhouses**]. *s.c.* asilo, institución de beneficencia.
poorhouses | ˌpuəhauzɪz | *pl.* de **poorhouse.**
poorly | ˌpuəlɪ | *adv.* (form.) **1** pobremente, humildemente, modestamente. **2** mal, desastrosamente, insatisfactoriamente. || *adj.* **3** (brit. y fam.) enfermo, malo, indispuesto. || **4 to think – of,** tener una mala opinión de.
pop | pɒp | [**popped, popping**]. *v.t.* e *i.* **1** estallar, reventar, saltar (con un ruido seco): *as he shook the bottle the cork popped = al agitar la botella saltó el corcho.* **2** disparar, dar un pistoletazo, tirar. || *v.i.* **3** [**to** – *adv./prep.*] (fam.) saltar, salirse (los ojos de las órbitas). **4** [**to** – *adv./prep.*] entrar de sopetón, llegar por sorpresa. **5** [**to** – *adv./prep.*] marchar repentinamente, largarse de sopetón. || *v.t.* **6** [**to** – *o.* + *adv./prep.*] (fam.) asomar, meter (la cabeza, algo en un sitio), poner (durante breves instantes): *I'll pop it in the fridge to chill = lo meteré en el frigorífico a enfriar.* **7** (brit., arc. y argot) empeñar, pignorar. **8** pegar, golpear. **9** (EE.UU. y argot) ingerir, tomar (drogas por vía oral). **10** (argot) echar, tomar (un trago). || *s.c.* **11** ruido seco, chasquido, estallido; taponazo. **12** detonación, pistoletazo. **13** (EE.UU. y fam.) papá. **14** (argot) trago, bebida alcohólica. || *s.i.* **15** (EE.UU. soda, fam. y arc.) gaseosa, soda. **16** MUS. música pop, pop. || **17** *abreviatura de* **population,** población. || *adv.* **18** deprisa, inesperadamente. **19** ruidosamente, estrepitosamente. || **20 – art,** ART. arte pop. **21 to – off, a)** (brit. y fam.) morir repentinamente; **b)** largarse, irse de repente; **c)** vociferar, gritar. **22 to – on, a)** (fam.) ponerse (un vestido); **b)** (fam.) enchufar, poner. **23 to – the question,** V. **question. 24 to – up,** aparecer de repente, inesperadamente.
popadam | ˌpɒpədəm | *s.c.* V. **poppadum.**
popcorn | pɒpkɔːn | *s.i.* palomitas de maíz.
Pope | pəup | *s.* REL. **1** Papa. **2** pope (sacerdote ortodoxo). **3** (fig.) pope, autoridad.
popery | ˌpəupərɪ | *s.i.* (desp. y arc.) papismo.

pop-eyed | ˌpɒp'aɪd | *adj.* (fam.) de ojos saltones, con los ojos desorbitados (por la sorpresa): *she looked at me pop-eyed = me miró con ojos desorbitados.*
popish | ˌpəʊpɪʃ | *adj.* (desp. y arc.) papista.
poplar | ˌpɒplər | *s.c.* e *i.* BOT. chopo, álamo.
poplin | ˌpɒplɪn | *s.i.* popelín.
poppa | ˌpɒpə | | ˌpɑːpə | *s.c.* (EE.UU. y fam.) papá, padre.
poppadum | ˌpɒpədəm | | ˌpɑːpədəm | (también **papadom, papadum, popadam**) *s.c.* papadom (pan redondo, fino y crujiente que se toma con la comida india).
popper | ˌpɒpər | | ˌpɑːpər | (EE.UU. **press-stud**). *s.c.* **1** (brit. y fam.) corchete, botón de presión. **2** utensilio para tostar maíz. **3** QUIM. frasco de popas, ampolla de nitrato de amilo (que se toma ilícitamente como estimulante).
poppet | ˌpɒpɪt | | ˌpɑːpɪt | *s.c.* **1** (brit. y fam.) amor, cariño, chiquitín, cielo, encanto (se le dice a un niño o a un animal como expresión de cariño). **2** MAR. escálamo, tolete.
poppy | ˌpɒpɪ | | ˌpɑːpɪ | *s.c.* **1** BOT. amapola; adormidera. || *s.i.* **2** QUIM. opio. **3** color rojo amapola, rojo vivo. || **4 Poppy Day,** (fam.) Día de la Amapola (día de Noviembre en que los británicos recuerdan a los muertos de las dos guerras mundiales, adornándose con una amapola artificial).
poppycock | ˌpɒpɪkɒk | | ˌpɑːpɪkɑːk | *s.i.* (arc. y fam.) tonterías, estupideces, basura, memeces.
populace | ˌpɒpjʊlɪs | | ˌpɑːpjʊləs | *s.sing.* [**the** – *v.sing./pl.*] (form.) el pueblo, la plebe, el vulgo, el populacho, las masas.
popular | ˌpɒpjʊlər | | ˌpɑːpjʊlər | *adj.* **1** [**– (with)**] popular, querido, respetado. **2** generalizado, corriente, extendido: *it's quite a popular belief = es una creencia bastante extendida.* **3** popular, de vulgarización (una obra); sensacionalista, amarilla (la prensa). **4** [no *comp.*] popular, de masas: *a popular sport = un deporte de masas.*
popularity | ˌpɒpjʊ'lærɪtɪ | | ˌpɑːpjʊ'lærɪtɪ | *s.i.* popularidad, renombre, fama.
popularize | ˌpɒpjʊləraɪz | | 'pɑːpjʊləraɪz | (brit. **popularise**). *v.t.* **1** popularizar, divulgar, extender, propalar, difundir. **2** vulgarizar (una obra difícil).
popularly | ˌpɒpjʊləlɪ | | ˌpɑːpjʊləlɪ | *adv.* popularmente, corrientemente, vulgarmente, por regla general.
populate | ˌpɒpjʊleɪt | | ˌpɑːpjʊleɪt | *v.t.* (generalmente pasiva) poblar, habitar.
populated | ˌpɒpjʊleɪtɪd | | ˌpɑːpjʊleɪtɪd | *adj.* poblado, habitado.
population | ˌpɒpjʊ'leɪʃn | | ˌpɑːpjʊ'leɪʃn | *s.sing.* **1** población, habitantes, vecinos. **2** población, demografía. **3** poblamiento, asentamiento (de pobladores en una zona). **4** ECOL. colonia de organismos.
populism | ˌpɒpjʊlɪzəm | *s.i.* (form.) POL. populismo.
populist | ˌpɒpjʊlɪst | *s.c.* (desp.) POL. **1** populista. || *adj.* **2** populista.
populous | ˌpɒpjʊləs | *adj.* populoso, muy poblado.
pop-up | ˌpɒpʌp | *adj.* **1** con mecanismo de expulsión, automático: *a pop-up toaster = un tostador automático.* **2** (cuento infantil) que lleva escenas en relieve al abrirse sus páginas.
porcelain | ˌpɔːslɪn | *s.i.* porcelana.
porch | pɔːtʃ | *s.c.* **1** porche, pórtico. **2** (EE.UU.) terraza cubierta. **3** (EE.UU.) soportales, paseo cubierto.
porcine | ˌpɔːsaɪn | *adj.* (lit. y desp.) porcino, como un cerdo.
porcupine | ˌpɔːkjʊpaɪn | *s.c.* ZOOL. puerco espín.
pore | pɔːr | *s.c.* **1** poro (en la piel, suelo, etc...). || *v.t.* **2** [**to – over**] examinar, inspeccionar, analizar, investigar, escrutar, estudiar atentamente. **3** observar absorto, clavar la mirada. **4** meditar, ponderar, reflexionar, considerar.
pork | pɔːk | *s.i.* **1** carne de cerdo. || **2 – pie, a)** (brit.) empanada de cerdo, pastel de cerdo; **b)** sombrero de hombre de ala ancha y copa baja y plana.
porn | pɔːn | *s.i.* (fam.) **1** porno, pornografía. || *adj.* **2** pornográfico.
pornographic | ˌpɔːnəʊ'græfɪk | *adj.* (desp.) pornográfico, obsceno.
pornography | pɔː'nɒgrəfɪ | | pɔː'nɑːgrəfɪ | *s.i.* **1** (desp.) pornografía, tratamiento pornográfico. **2** material pornográfico (revistas, fotos, etc...).
porous | ˌpɔːrəs | *adj.* poroso, permeable.
porphyry | ˌpɔːfɪrɪ | *s.i.* MIN. pórfido.
porpoise | ˌpɔːpəs | *s.c.* ZOOL. marsopa.
porridge | ˌpɒrɪdʒ | *s.i.* **1** papilla de avena cocida con leche, gachas de avena (que se toma para desayunar). || **2 to do –,** (brit. y fam.) pasar un tiempo a la sombra, en la cárcel.
port | pɔːt | *s.c.* e *i.* **1** MAR. puerto. **2** puerto de mar, ciudad portuaria. **3** INF. puerta, vía de acceso, terminal. **4** MAR. portilla, lumbrera. **5** MAR. ojo de buey. **6** MIL. tronera, cañonera. **7** puerta, entrada (a una ciudad, en Escocia). || *s.i.* **8** MAR. babor. **9** oporto, vino de Oporto. || *adj.* **10** portuario, de puerto. || *v.t.* **11** MIL. presentar, colocar terciado (el fusil): *port arms! = ¡presenten armas!* || *v.t.* e *i.* **12** poner a babor, virar a babor. || **13 any – in a storm,** en el peligro cualquier refugio es bueno, estando en peligro se agarra uno a un clavo ardiendo. **14 – of call,** MAR. escala, puerto de escala.
portability | ˌpɔːtə'bɪlɪtɪ | *s.i.* portabilidad, transportabilidad.
portable | ˌpɔːtəbl | *adj.* **1** portátil, transportable. **2** (arc.) soportable, tolerable, llevadero. || *s.c.* **3** máquina de escribir portátil; objeto portátil.
portal | ˌpɔːtl | *s.c.* **1** (form.) pórtico, portada, atrio, entrada. **2** (fig.) umbral, puerta. **3** ANAT. vena porta.
portcullis | ˌpɔːt'kʌlɪs | *s.c.* rastrillo (de una fortificación, de un castillo).
portend | pɔː'tend | *v.t.* (lit.) presagiar, augurar, anunciar, pronosticar (generalmente algo malo).
portent | ˌpɔtent | *s.c.* (form.) **1** [**– (of)**] presagio, augurio, premonición. || *s.i.* **2** carácter profético, significado premonitorio, sentido amenazador. **3** portento, prodigio, maravilla.
portentous | pɔː'tentəs | *adj.* (lit.) **1** (desp.) pomposo, petulante, pretencioso. **2** premonitorio, amenazador, siniestro, de mal agüero. **3** portentoso, prodigioso, maravilloso.
portentously | pɔː'tentəslɪ | *adv.* (form.) **1** petulantemente, de forma pretenciosa, con pomposidad. **2** ominosamente, amenazadoramente, siniestramente. **3** portentosamente.
porter | 'pɔːtər | *s.c.* **1** mozo de estación, mozo de cuerda, maletero. **2** porteador, descargador. **3** (brit.) portero, conserje (de hotel, escuela, etc...). **4** (EE.UU.) mozo, camarero (de trenes). || *s.i.* **5** cerveza negra (fuerte).
portfolio | ˌpɔːt'fəʊlɪəʊ | *s.c.* **1** portafolios, cartera de ejecutivo. **2** muestra, serie, muestrario (especialmente del trabajo de un artista): *he sent a portfolio of his drawings = envió una muestra de sus dibujos.* **3** COM. cartera de valores. **4** POL. cartera, ministerio. || **5 minister without –,** ministro sin cartera.
porthole | ˌpɔːthəʊl | *s.c.* **1** MAR. ojo de buey, portilla, lumbrera. **2** MIL. tronera, cañonera, saetera.
portico | ˌpɔːtɪkəʊ | [*pl.* **porticoes** o **porticos**]. *s.c.* ARQ. pórtico, atrio, portada.
portion | ˌpɔʃn | *s.c.* **1** [**– (of)**] parte, sección, zona, área, región. **2** parte, porcentaje, cuota: *a portion of the responsability = una parte de la responsabilidad.* **3** porción, ración, trozo, pedazo. **4** dote. **5** (lit.) destino, sino, fortuna, suerte. || *v.t.* **6** [**to – out**] repartir, dividir en porciones. **7** legar bienes, dotar.
portly | ˌpɔːtlɪ | *adj.* (euf. o hum.) **1** corpulento, fuerte, gordo. **2** (arc.) majestuoso, solemne, imponente.
portmanteau | ˌpɔːt'mæntəʊ | [*pl.* **portmanteaus** o **portmanteaux**]. *s.c.* **1** (arc.) baúl de viaje, valija. || *adj.* **2** combinado, mixto, mezclado: *"smog" is a portmanteau word = "smog" es una palabra mixta* (viene de **smoke** y **fog**).
portrait | ˌpɔːtrɪt | *s.c.* **1** ART. retrato. **2** (fig.) retrato, descripción vivida.
portraiture | ˌpɔːtrɪtʃər | *s.i.* **1** ART. retrato, pintura del retrato. || *s.c.* **2** retrato.
portray | pɔː'treɪ | *v.t.* **1** retratar a, pintar un retrato de, dibujar un retrato de. **2** [**– (as)**] describir, retratar gráficamente o verbalmente. **3** representar, hacer de, actuar de (en teatro).
portrayal | pɔː'treɪəl | *s.c.* e *i.* **1** representación (teatral): *his portrayal of Richard V = su representación de Ricardo V.* **2** ART. retrato. **3** (fig.) retrato, descripción: *her portrayal of life in India is excelent = su descripción de la vida en la India es excelente.*
Portugal | ˌpɔːtʃʊgl | *s.sing.* Portugal.
Portuguese | ˌpɔːtʃʊ'giːz | *adj.* **1** portugués, de Portugal (de nacionalidad). || *s.c.* **2** portugués. || *s.i.* **3** portugués, lengua portuguesa.

pose | pəʊz | *v.t.* e *i.* **1** posar, colocar(se), (para una fotografía, un cuadro). || *v.t.* **2** presentar, plantear (un problema, una pregunta). || *v.i.* **3** (desp.) darse tono, pavonearse, hacerse el importante. || *s.c.* **4** postura, pose, posición. **5** (desp.) pose, imagen, afectación, pavoneo.

poser | ˌpəʊzər | *s.c.* (fam.) **1** enigma, problema, misterio, rompecabezas. **2** persona afectada, jactancioso, presuntuoso.

poseur | pəʊ'zɜːr | *s.c.* persona afectada, jactancioso, presuntuoso.

posh | pɒʃ | *adj.* (brit. y fam.). **1** de lujo, caro, elegante, a la moda. **2** refinado, de clase alta, afectado, cursi (gente, un acento). || **3 to talk –,** hablar con afectación.

posit | ˌpɒzɪt | *v.t.* (form.) **1** postular, proponer, aseverar, asumir. **2** situar, colocar.

position | pə'zɪʃn | *s.c.* **1** posición, situación, lugar, sitio, emplazamiento: *the house was in a good position = la casa estaba en un buen lugar.* **2** posición, postura: *in a horizontal position = en posición horizontal.* **3 [– (in)]** DEP. posición, puesto, lugar. **4 [– (in)]** categoría, rango (en una organización, social). **5** [generalmente *sing.*] situación, estado, condición: *in his present position, he can't do anything = no puede hacer nada en su actual situación.* **6 [– (on)]** opinión, política, actitud, punto de vista: *what's your position on this matter? = ¿cuál es tu opinión sobre este asunto?* **7 [– (with/in)]** (form.) empleo, colocación, puesto de trabajo: *to apply for a position = solicitar un empleo.* **8** postulado, aserto, propuesta. || *v.t.* **9 [to – *o.* + *adv./prep.*]** situar, colocar, disponer, poner, ubicar. **10** MIL. localizar la posición, marcar el emplazamiento. || **11 in a – to,** estar en condiciones de. **12 in no – to,** no estar en condiciones de. **13 in/into –,** en posición correcta, en su lugar. **14 out of –,** desplazado, fuera de su sitio. **15 – paper,** POL. documento de base ideológica.

positional | pə'zɪʃənl | *adj.* de posición, de puesto.

positive | ˌpɒzɪtɪv | | 'pɑːzətɪv | *adj.* **1 [– (about/of)]** seguro, convencido, persuadido: *he's absolutely positive about it = está totalmente seguro de ello.* **2** positivo, constructivo, práctico. **3** positiva, optimista, confiada, de esperanza (una actitud). **4** definitivo, seguro, cierto, firme: *a positive proof = una prueba definitiva.* **5** [no *comp.*] GRAM. positivo (el grado), afirmativa. **6** [no *comp.*] MAT., MED. etc... positivo. **7** [no *comp.*] ELEC. positivo, electropositivo. **8** [no *comp.*] absoluto, enorme, sumo: *a positive pleasure = un placer absoluto.* **9** MEC. de acción directa. || *s.c.* **10** GRAM. grado positivo (de la comparación). **11** FOT. positiva. || **12 – discrimination/reverse discrimination,** discriminación positiva, compensación. **13 – vetting,** (brit. y form.) investigación (relativa a una persona que va a disponer de información secreta).

positively | ˌpɒzətɪvlɪ | *adv.* **1** con toda seguridad, definitivamente. **2** (fam.) absolutamente, realmente. **3** positivamente, afirmativamente. **4** ELEC. positivamente, con carga positiva.

positivism | ˌpɒzɪtɪvɪzəm | *s.i.* FIL. positivismo.

positivist | ˌpɒzɪtɪvɪst | *s.c.* FIL. positivista.

posse | ˌpɒsɪ | *s.c.* **[– (of)] 1** partida, pelotón, somatén (bajo el mando del sheriff para ayudar a la captura de un criminal). **2** (fig.) recua, tropel (de gente).

possess | pə'zes | *v.t.* **1** (form.) poseer, tener. **2** (generalmente pasiva) poseer, dominar, influir: *he's possessed by a strange idea = está dominado por una idea extraña.* || **3 to be possessed of,** (lit.) disfrutar de, estar en posesión de. **4 what possessed someone to ...?,** ¿cómo pudo alguien?: *what possessed him to do that? = ¿cómo pudo él hacer eso?*

possession | pə'zeʃn | *s.i.* **1** posesión. **2** (form.) posesión, conocimiento: *I had a few details in my possession = tenía conocimiento de algunos detalles.* **3 [– (of)]** DER. posesión, tenencia. **4** posesión, endemoniamiento, hechizamiento. || *s.c.* **5** [generalmente *pl.*] posesión, propiedad, bienes. **6** posesión, territorio, colonia, protectorado. || **7 to be in – of,** (form.) estar en posesión de.

possessive | pə'zesɪv | *adj.* **1** posesivo, absorbente, dominante, egoísta. **2** GRAM. posesivo. || *s.c.* **3** GRAM. posesivo.

possessively | ˌpə'zesɪvlɪ | *adv.* posesivamente, absorbentemente, dominantemente, egoístamente.

possessiveness | ˌpə'zesɪvnɪs | *s.i.* posesividad, egoísmo, carácter absorbente.

possessor | pə'zesər | *s.sing.* (form.) posesor, dueño (de una cualidad).

possibility | ˌpɒsə'bɪlɪtɪ | *s.c.* e *i.* **1** posibilidad, perspectiva, probabilidad. || **2 possibilities,** posibilidades, potencial, condiciones.

possible | ˌpɒsəbl | *adj.* **1** posible, factible, realizable: *it's not possible to cure cancer today = hoy no es posible curar el cáncer.* **2 posible, probable, plausible:** *it's possible that she went without permission = es probable que se haya ido sin permiso.* **3** razonable, aceptable, admisible: *a possible solution = una solución razonable.* || *s.c.* **4 [the –]** lo posible, lo factible, lo realizable. **5** candidato, aspirante, pretendiente: *two of them could be possibles = dos de ellos podrían ser candidatos.* || **6 as much as –,** en lo posible. **7 as soon as –,** cuanto antes, lo antes posible. **8 if –/if at all –/etc...,** de ser posible, si es posible. **9 the best/biggest –,** lo mejor que hay, lo más grande que existe, etc... **10 where /wherever/whenever, etc... –,** si es posible, en cualquier momento, si hay posibilidad.

possibly | ˌpɒsəblɪ | *adv.* **1** posiblemente, razonablemente, concebiblemente. **2** probablemente, quizás, tal vez.

possum | ˌpɒsəm | (brit. **opossum**) *s.c.* **1** (fam.) ZOOL. zarigüeya, (Am.) carachupa, churcha. || **2 to play –,** fingirse dormido, hacerse el muerto.

post | pəʊst | *s.c.* **1** poste, pilar, columna, estaca. **2 [the –]** DEP. la meta, el poste de llegada. **3** (también **goalpost**) DEP. portería, puerta, marco, meta. **4** (fam.) puesto, empleo, cargo, colocación. **5** MIL. puesto (de vigilancia); fuerte, guarnición. **6** factoría, establecimiento comercial. || *s.i.* (EE.UU. **mail**). **7 [the –]** correos, servicio de correos. **8 [the –]** correo, correspondencia; entrega, recogida (de correspondencia). **9 [the –]** oficina de correos, buzón, estafeta de correos. **10** (brit.) MIL. retreta, toque de retreta. || *prefijo.* **11** pos, post: *post-industrial = postindustrial.* || *v.t.* **12 [to – (off/to)]** (EE.UU. **mail**) echar al correo, enviar por correo, mandar por correo. **13** contabilizar, asentar (en el libro de contabilidad). **14** INF. registrar, actualizar (ficheros). **15 [to – (up)]** apostar, situar, colocar (centinelas, policías). **16 [to – *o.* + *adv./prep.*]** (brit.) anunciar, informar, comunicar, avisar, hacer saber (por medio de carteles). **17** fijar, pegar, poner (carteles). **18** denunciar públicamente, delatar (a un ladrón). **19** publicar en una lista, anotar en una lista (un nombre). **20** destinar, nombrar, asignar (a un puesto), delegar (el mando, para un cargo). || *v.i.* **21** viajar en posta, viajar por etapas.|| *adv.* **22** en posta, por etapas. **23** a toda prisa, a toda velocidad, rápidamente. || **24 to catch the –,** alcanzar el correo, llegar al correo. **25 first past the –,** POL. sistema mayoritario (en elecciones). **26 in the –,** en el correo, enviado al correo. **27 to keep someone posted,** mantener a uno informado, tener a uno al día. **28 – office,** correos, oficina de correos, estafeta de correos.

postage | ˌpəʊstɪdʒ | *s.i.* **1** franqueo, gastos de correo, porte. || **2 – stamp,** (form.) sello de correos.

postal | ˌpəʊstəl | *adj.* **1** postal, de correos. || *s.c.* **2** (EE.UU.) tarjeta postal. || **3 – order,** (brit.) giro postal.

postbag | ˌpəʊstbæg | *s.c.* **1** (EE.UU. **mailbag**) cartera de cartero. **2** (fam.) correo, correspondencia, cartas (especialmente las recibidas por un periódico, TV., etc...): *they always recive a big postbag = siempre reciben mucha correspondencia.*

post-box | ˌpəʊstbɒks | (EE.UU. **mailbox**) *s.c.* buzón.

post-card | ˌpəʊstkɑːd | *s.c.* tarjeta postal.

postcode | ˌpəʊstkəʊd | (EE.UU. **zip code**) *s.c.* código postal.

postdate | ˌpəʊst'deɪt | *v.t.* **1** fechar con posterioridad, poner fecha adelantada, extender con fecha posterior (un cheque). **2** HIST. ocurrir después de, suceder con posterioridad a, venir después de.

poster | ˌpəʊstər | *s.c.* **1** cartel, anuncio, aviso, rótulo. || **2 – paint/colour,** pintura al temple.

poste restante | ˌpəʊst'restɑːnt | | ˌpəʊst'restɒnt | (EE.UU. **general delivery**). *s.i.* **1** lista de correos. || *adv.* **2** a lista de correos: *the letter was sent post* *restante = la carta se envió a lista de correos.*

posterior | pɒ'stɪərɪər | | pɑː'stɪərɪər | *adj.* [no *comp.*]. **1** **[– to]** (form.) posterior, ulterior, subsecuente, siguiente. **2** BIOL. posterior, trasero. || *s.c.* **3** (form. o hum.) trasero, nalgas, culo.

posterity | pɒ'sterɪtɪ | | pɑː'sterɪtɪ | *s.i.* (form.) posteridad.

postgraduate | ˌpəust'grædjuət | | ˌpəust'grædʒuət | (EE.UU. **graduate**). *s.c.* **1** postgraduado. || *adj.* **2** postgraduado, para postgraduados, de postgrado.

posthumous | ˌpɒstjuməs | | ˌpɑːst-ʃəməs | *adj.* póstumo.

posthumously | ˌpɒstjuməslɪ | | ˌpɑːst-ʃə-məslɪ | *adv.* después de la muerte.

post-industrial | ˌpəustɪn'dʌstrɪəl | *adj.* postindustrial.

posting | ˌpəustɪŋ | *s.c.* (brit.) destino, traslado (generalmente otra ciudad, otro país).

postman | ˌpəustmən | [*pl.* **postmen**]. (EE.UU. **mailman**). *s.c.* cartero.

postmark | 'pəustmɑːk | | 'pəustmɑːrk | *s.c.* **1** matasellos. || *v.t.* **2** (generalmente pasiva) matar, timbrar (el sello).

postmaster | ˌpəustmɑːstər | | ˌpəust | mæstər | *f.* **postmistress.** *s.c.* **1** administrador de correos. **2** administrador de una estación para viajeros, el que suministraba caballos de posta.

postmen | pəustmən | *pl.* de **postman.**

postmistress | ˌpəustˌmɪstrɪs | *m.* **postmaster.** *s.c.* administradora de correos.

post-mortem | ˌpəust'mɔːtem | | ˌpəust' | | mɔːrtem | (también **post-mortem examination**). *s.c.* **1** autopsia. **2** (fig.) investigación, estudio, análisis: *a postmortem on the firm's failure = una investigación sobre el fracaso de la firma.*

post-natal | ˌpəust'neɪtl | *adj.* postnatal, después del nacimiento.

postpone | ˌpəust'pəun | *v.t.* **[to – (to/until)]** posponer, aplazar, retrasar, postergar.

postponement | ˌpəust'pəunmənt | *s.c.* e *i.* aplazamiento.

postscript | ˌpəusskrɪpt | (también **P.S.**). *s.c.* postdata, posdata.

postulate | ˌpɒstjulyɪt | | pɑːstʃəleɪt | *v.t.* **1** (form.) postular, argüir, invocar, aducir, presuponer, dar por sentado. **2** solicitar, reivindicar, demandar, reclamar. || | ˌpɒstjulət | | ˌpɑːstʃələt | *s.c.* **3** (form.) postulado, hipótesis, planteamiento.

posture | ˌpɒstʃər | | ˌpɑːstʃər | *s.c.* e *i.* **1** postura, posición, pose. || *s.c.* **2** **[– (on)]** postura, actitud, disposición. **3** tendencia, inclinación, preferencia. || *v.i.* **4** (generalmente desp.) adoptar una postura, asumir una actitud, actuar con afectación. || *v.t.* **5** posar, colocarse en una postura.

post-war | ˌpəust'wɔːr | *adj.* **1** de posguerra. || *adv.* **2** de posguerra.

posy | ˌpəuzɪ | *s.c.* **1** (lit.) ramillete de flores. **2** lema, inscripción.

pot | pɒt | (EE.UU.) | pɑːt | *s.c.* **1** tiesto, maceta. **2** tarro, frasco, bote, recipiente. **3** pote, olla, marmita, puchero (el cacharro y el contenido). **4** jarra, copa, vaso (y su contenido). **5** **[– (of)]** (también **potful**) cafetera, tetera: *she brought a pot of tea for two = trajo té para dos.* **6** (fam.) fuente, plato. **7** orinal, bacinilla. **8** apuesta, banca, pozo (cantidad total apostada en juegos de cartas). **9** (brit.) carambola (en billar). **10** (fam.) disparo a mansalva, tiro al azar. **11** nasa (para la pesca de crustáceos). **12** escote, fondo común (de dinero para gastos entre varios). || *s.i.* **13** (argot) marihuana, yerba. || *v.* **[potted, potting]** *t.* e *i.* **14** cazar, disparar, abatir, matar: *potting at partridge = cazando perdices.* || *v.t.* **15** **[to – (up)]** plantar, poner (flores en tiestos). **16** (brit.) hacer carambola, entronerar. **17** conservar, poner en conserva, envasar (alimentos). **18** cocinar en olla, hacer en marmita. || **19 gone to –,** (fam.) deteriorado, estropeado, echado a perder. **20 to keep the – boiling,** mantener las cosas en marcha, mantener el interés. **21 – belly,** panza, tripa, barrigaza. **22 – luck,** (compartir) lo que haya, (tomar) comida normal (cuando se invita a casa a alguien sin planearlo antes): *come tonight and we'll take pot luck = ven esta noche y compartiremos lo que haya de cena.* **23 – plant,** planta ornamental, planta de interior. **24 pots,** (fam.) montones, cantidades ingentes (de dinero). **25 potting compost,** mantillo (para macetas). **26 potting shed,** cobertizo para utensilios de jardinería. **27 to take a – at,** (fam.) disparar a mansalva a, disparar al azar. **28 the – calling the kettle back,** el puchero dijo a la sartén "apártate de mí que me tiznas".

potash | ˌpɒtæʃ | | ˌpɑːtæʃ | *s.i.* QUIM. potasa.

potassium | pə'tæsɪəm | *s.i.* QUIM. potasio.

potato | pə'teɪtəu | [*pl.* **potatoes**] *s.c.* e *i.* **1** BOT. patata, (Am.) papa. || **2 a hot –,** (fig.) una patata caliente, un asunto molesto.

potatoes | pə'teɪtəuz | *pl.* de **potato.**

pot-bellied | ˌpɒtˌbelɪd | *adj.* tripudo, panzudo, barrigudo.

pot-boiler | ˌpɒtˌbɔɪlər | | ˌpɑːtˌbɔɪlər | *s.c.* obra artística mediocre producida para obtener dinero.

pot-bound | ˌpɒtˌbaund | | ˌpɑːtˌbaund | *adj.* sin espacio para el crecimiento de las raíces (una planta).

potency | ˌpəutənsɪ | *s.i.* **1** fuerza, poder, acción, influencia. **2** potencia (sexual).

potent | ˌpəutənt | *adj.* **1** fuerte, eficaz, efectiva (una bebida, una medicina). **2** efectivo, convincente, persuasivo (un argumento). **3** (lit.) potente, poderoso. **4** potente, viril.

potentate | ˌpəutənteɪt | *s.c.* potentado, señor feudal, soberano.

potential | pəu'tenʃl | *adj.* **1** [no *comp.*] potencial, en potencia, posible, latente. **2** GRAM. potencial. || *s.i.* **3** **[– (for)]** potencial, potencialidad, futuro, perspectivas, posibilidades. **4** ELEC. potencia, voltaje, tensión. **5** GRAM. modo potencial.

potentiality | pəuˌtenʃɪ'ælɪtɪ | *s.c.* e *i.* **1** [generalmente *pl.*] (form.) potencialidad, poderes ocultos. **2** potencialidad, posibilidad, futuro, perspectivas.

potentially | pəu'tenʃlɪ | *adv.* potencialmente, virtualmente, presumiblemente.

potently | ˌpəutəntlɪ | *adv.* potentemente.

pot-herb | ˌpɒthɜːb | *s.c.* hierba aromática (para condimentar).

pothole | ˌpɒthəul | *s.c.* **1** poza, pozo, hoyo (en terrenos calizos). **2** bache (en carretera).

potholer | ˌpɒthəulər | *s.c.* DEP. espeleólogo.

potholing | ˌpɒthəulɪŋ | *s.i.* DEP. espeleología.

potion | ˌpəuʃn | *s.c.* (lit.) poción, pócima, brebaje.

potpourry | ˌpəu'puriː | *s.c.* **1** mezcla de flores secas (para perfumar una habitación). **2** **[– (of)]** MUS. popurrí. **3** LIT. antología, colección, miscelánea. **4** mezcolanza, batiburrillo.

pot-roast | ˌpɒtˌrəust | *s.c.* e *i.* GAST. trozo de carne de vaca que se dora y cuece a fuego lento en marmita.

pot-shot | ˌpɒt 'ʃɒt | | ˌpɑːtʃɑːt | *s.c.* **1** **[– (at)]** (fam.) disparo al azar, tiro al azar. **2** (fig.) crítica irresponsable.

potted | pɒtɪd | *adj.* **1** en conserva, de bote, de lata. **2** plantado en tiesto, de maceta. **3** (brit. y desp.) simplificado, condensado, resumido. **4** (argot) intoxicado, achispado, bebido; pasado, flipado (con psicotrópicos).

potter | ˌpɒtər | | ˌpɑːtər | *s.c.* **1** alfarero, ceramista. || (EE.UU. **putter**). *v.i.* **2** **[to – *adv./prep.*]** (brit. y fam.) andar con desgana, vagar, deambular. **3** (brit. y fam.) pasar el rato, perder el tiempo, ocuparse de cosas sin importancia, en fruslenás. **4 potter's wheel,** torno de alfarero.

pottery | ˌpɒtərɪ | *s.i.* **1** alfarería, cerámica, artesanía del barro. **2** cacharros de cerámica, piezas de barro, loza. || *s.c.* **3** alfar, taller de alfarería, fábrica de cerámica.

potty | ˌpɒtɪ | | ˌpɑːtɪ | *adj.* (brit. y fam.). **1** chiflado, loco, extravagante, alocado. **2** insignificante, trivial, poco importante. || *s.c.* **3** orinal, bacinilla (para niños). || **4 to be – about,** estar loco por, encantar, gustar mucho (una persona, una actividad).

potty-trained | ˌpɒtɪtreɪnd | (también **toilet-trained**). *adj.* (brit.) acostumbrado a hacer sus necesidades controladamente (un niño).

potty-training | ˌpɒtɪtreɪnɪŋ | *s.i.* (brit.) período en que el niño aprende a hacer sus necesidades controladamente.

pouch | pautʃ | *s.c.* **1** bolsillo, saquito, faltriquera, taleguilla, zurrón (para dinero, objetos, etc...). **2** tabaquera, petaca. **3** valija (de correos, diplomática). **4** ZOOL. bolsa (de los marsupiales). **5** bolsa (bajo los ojos). **6** ZOOL. abazón (de ciertos animales). || *v.t.* **7** embolsar, meter en el bolsillo. **8** tragar, comer, ingerir (ciertos animales). || *v.t.* e *i.* **9** abolsar(se), formar(se) en una bolsa.

pouf | puːf | *s.c.* V. **poof.**
pouffe | puːf | *s.c.* puf (asiento).
poultice | ˌpəʊltɪs | *s.c.* **1** cataplasma, emplaste. || *v.t.* **2** aplicar una cataplasma, poner un emplaste.
poultry | ˌpəʊltrɪ | *s.i.* **1** carne de aves de corral, volatería. || *s.pl.* **2** aves de corral.
pounce | paʊns | *v.i.* **1 [to – (on)]** saltar (sobre), arrojarse (sobre), atacar (a), precipitarse (sobre). || *v.t.* **2** empolvar, secar con polvo de sandáraca. || *s.sing.* **3** ataque, salto (sobre una presa). **4** zarpa, garra (de un ave de presa). || *s.i.* **5** polvo de sandáraca, grasilla, arenilla, polvo secante. **6** carbón en polvo. || **7 to – on, a)** (fig.) coger al vuelo, aceptar sin pensarlo dos veces (un ofrecimiento); **b)** abalanzarse sobre, echarse encima (de alguien a causa de un error).
pound | paʊnd | *s.c.* **1** (*abreviatura* **lb**) libra (unidad de peso equivalente a 0.454 kg): *half a pound of sugar = media libra de azúcar.* **2** libra (unidad monetaria). **3** perrera municipal, refugio de animales (perdidos). **4** depósito municipal de automóviles. || *v.t.* **5 [to – (up)]** triturar, machacar, majar, moler, pulverizar. || *v.i.* **6 [to – *adv./prep.*]** moverse estrepitosamente, caminar ruidosamente: *girls pounding down the High Street = chicas que bajaban taconeando por la Calle Mayor.* || *v.t.* e *i.* **7** latir con fuerza, palpitar con violencia (el corazón). **8** aporrear, golpear, martillear: *pounding on the wall in despair = aporreando la pared con desesperación.* || **9 to have someone's – of flesh,** exigir lo que es de uno pese a quien pese.
pounded | paʊndɪd | *adj.* triturado, molido, en polvo.
pounding | paʊndɪŋ | *s.c.* e *i.* **1** latido, palpitación. **2** martilleo, golpeteo, aporreamiento. || *s.c.* **3** (fam.) DEP. paliza, derrota. **4** apaleamiento, paliza.
pour | pɔːr | *v.t.* **1 [to – *o.* + *adv./prep.*]** escanciar, servir, derramar, verter (un líquido). **2** (fig.) invertir mucho dinero, subvencionar con abundantes fondos. || *v.i.* **3 [to – *adv./prep.*]** manar, fluir, salir, brotar, salir a raudales. **4** (fam.) servir, llenar (una copa, una taza). **5 [to – *adv.*]** dejar salir, derramar mal (un líquido): *the jug pours sideways = la cafetera derrama por los lados.* **6 [to – (down)]** diluviar, llover torrencialmente, llover a cántaros: *it's pouring with rain = está lloviendo a cántaros.* || **7 to – cold water on,** echar un jarro de agua fría, desanimar, desalentar. **8 to – oil on troubled waters,** V. **water. 9 to – out,** desahogarse, **a)** abrir el corazón, revelar, contar atropelladamente (problemas, noticias, historias); **b)** servir, escanciar. **10 to – scorn on,** reírse de, mofarse de, hablar despectivamente de.
pout | paʊt | *v.t.* e *i.* **1** hacer pucheros, poner mala cara. **2** hacer gestos provocativos, poner morritos (con los labios). || *s.c.* **3** pucheros, mala cara: *a sensual pout = morritos sensuales.*
poverty | ˌpɒvətɪ | *s.i.* **1** pobreza, miseria, indigencia, escasez, penuria. **2 [– (of)]** (form. y desp.) pobreza, escasez, falta, carencia.
poverty-stricken | ˌpɒvətɪˌstrɪkən | *adj.* extremadamente pobre, menesteroso, indigente.
pow | paʊ | *interj.* (fam.) ¡paf!, ¡zas!
POW | ˌpiːəʊ'dʌbljuː | *s.c.* **(prisoner of war),** prisionero de guerra.
powder | 'paʊdər | *s.c.* e *i.* **1** polvo. || *s.i.* **2** polvos de maquillaje. **3** pólvora. || *s.c.* **4** (arc.) medicina en polvo. || *v.t.* **5** empolvar, polvorear, poner polvos. **6** pulverizar, triturar. **7** (argot) hacer polvo, dar una paliza, derrotar completamente. || **8 to – one's nose,** (euf.) ir al tocador, ir al lavabo, ir al retrete (una mujer). **9 to take a –,** tomar las de Villadiego, poner pies en polvorosa.
powdered | ˌpaʊdəd | *adj.* **1** en polvo. **2** cubierto de polvo, lleno de polvo.
powder-puff | ˌpaʊdəpʌf | *s.c.* borla (para empolvarse).
powder-room | ˌpaʊdəruːm | *s.c.* (euf.) tocador de señoras, lavabo de señoras (en hoteles).
powdery | ˌpaʊdərɪ | *adj.* **1** quebradizo, quebrajoso, friable, frágil, delicado. **2** polvoriento, empolvado. **3** en polvo, polvoroso.
power | ˌpaʊər | *s.i.* **1** poder, autoridad, influencia, control: *it wasn't in my power to do it = no estaba en mis manos hacerlo.* **2** POL. poder, gobierno, mandato: *the Labour Party are in power = gobiernan los laboristas.* **3 [– (of)]** facultad, habilidad, capacidad. **4** fuerza, empuje, impulso, poderío. **5** MEC. potencia, energía, fuerza motriz. **6** ELEC. electricidad, luz, energía, fluido. **7** OPT. potencia. || **8** potencia, nación influyente; autoridad, persona influyente: *Japan is an industrial power = Japón es una potencia industrial.* **9** MAT. potencia, exponente. **10 [– (of)]** (fam.) montón, cantidad, multitud. || *s.c.* e *i.* **11** poder, derecho, facultad, mandato, autoridad: *the power of veto = el derecho de veto.* || *v.t.* **12** (generalmente pasiva) impulsar, mover, accionar, funcionar (un vehículo, una máquina): *the car is powered by petrol = el coche funciona con gasolina.* || *v.i.* **13 [to – *adv./prep.*]** (fam.) ir a gran velocidad, pasar volando (un vehículo). || *adj.* **14** eléctrico, mecánico: *a power saw = una sierra eléctrica.* || **15 at the high of one's powers,** (lit.) en el momento cumbre de su vida, en lo mejor de su carrera. **16 to do someone a – of good,** hacerle a uno mucho bien, sentarle (algo) a uno estupendamente: *the holidays did her a power of good = las vacaciones le sentaron estupendamente.* **17 everything in one's –,** todo lo posible, todo lo que esté en mis manos. **18 in –,** POL. en el poder, gobernando. **19 in someone's –,** bajo control de alguien, en poder de alguien, bajo su férula. **20 in/within someone's –,** dentro de las posibilidades de uno, en manos de uno. **21 -powered,** *sufijo,* impulsado por, que funciona con, mecánico: *electrically-powered tools = herramientas eléctricas.* **22 – failure,** apagón, corte de luz. **23 – game,** lucha por el poder. **24 – line,** ELEC. línea de conducción eléctrica. **25 – plant, a)** (brit.) ELEC. central eléctrica; **b)** AER. grupo electrógeno, grupo motor. **26 – point,** (brit.) ELEC. enchufe. **27 – station,** (brit.) ELEC. central eléctrica. **28 – worker,** empleado de una central eléctrica. **29 the powers that be,** los poderes establecidos, los poderes fácticos.
power-boat | ˌpaʊəbəʊt | *s.c.* lancha motora.
power-cut | ˌpaʊəkʌt | *s.c.* corte de luz, apagón.
powerful | ˌpaʊəfʊl | *adj.* **1** fuerte, robusto, fornido, vigoroso: *his powerful arms = sus brazos robustos.* **2** fuerte, potente, agudo: *a powerful voice = una voz potente.* **3** eficaz, eficiente: *a powerful pill = una pastilla eficaz.* **4** fuerte, intenso (un olor, una emoción). **5** poderoso, influyente, pujante (una persona, un país). **6** enérgico, contundente (un argumento). || *adv.* **7** muy, enormemente: *powerful hot = muy caluroso.*
powerhouse | ˌpaʊəhaʊs | [*pl.* **powerhouses** | ˌpaʊəhaʊzɪz |] *s.c.* **1** (fam.) persona enérgica, persona fuerte. **2** fuente de saber, foco influyente. **3** central eléctrica.
powerless | ˌpaʊəlɪs | *adj.* **1** impotente, incapaz, ineficaz. **2** sin autoridad, sin poder, sin influencia.
powerlessness | ˌpaʊəlɪsnɪs | *s.i.* impotencia, incapacidad, ineficacia.
power-sharing | ˌpaʊəʃɪərɪŋ | *s.i.* participación en el poder, autogestión, cogestión.
pox | pɒks | *s.sing.* **1** MED. (fam.) sífilis. || *s.i.* **2** (arc.) viruela. || **3 a – on...!,** (arc.) maldito sea...
practicability | ˌpræktɪkə'bɪlɪtɪ | *s.i.* viabilidad, factibilidad.
practicable | ˌpræktɪkəbl | *adj.* (form.) **1** practicable, posible, realizable, factible. **2** práctico, adecuado, útil (una cosa).
practical | ˌpræktɪkl | *adj.* **1** práctico: *she gave us advice of practical use = nos dio consejos de uso práctico.* **2** práctico, conveniente, efectivo, útil, funcional. **3** práctico, pragmático, sensato. **4** practicable, viable, posible, factible. **5** virtual. || *s.c.* **6** (fam.) examen práctico. || **7 for all – purposes,** en realidad, de hecho. **8 – joke,** broma pesada.
practicality | ˌpræktɪ'kælɪtɪ | *s.c.* e *i.* **1** uso práctico, viabilidad, factibilidad. **2** sentido práctico, espíritu práctico.
practically | ˌpræktɪklɪ | *adv.* **1** prácticamente, virtualmente, casi, en efecto. **2** de modo práctico, de modo útil.
practice | ˌpræktɪs | (EE.UU. **practise**) *s.c.* e *i.* **1** práctica, entrenamiento, adiestramiento, ejercicio. **2** práctica, costumbre, hábito, procedimiento. || *s.c.* **3** clientela (de un médico, de un abogado). **4** consulta (médica). **5** bufete, despacho (de abogado). || **6 in –, a)** en la práctica; **b)** en forma, entrenado. **7 out of –,** en baja forma, desentrenado. **8 – makes perfect,** la práctica hace maestro.

9 to put something into –, poner algo en práctica.

practise | ˌpræktɪs | (EE.UU. **practice**) *v.t.* e *i.* **1** practicar, entrenar, hacer ejercicios (de), ejercitarse (en), ensayar. **2 [to – (as)]** ejercer de, practicar la profesión de (médico, abogado). || *v.t.* **3** practicar, ejercitar, predicar, observar (una religión, la paciencia, una creencia). **4** (form.) efectuar, hacer, realizar. || **5 to – what one preaches,** predicar con el ejemplo.

practised | ˌpræktɪst | (EE.UU. **practiced**) *adj.* **1 [– (in)]** experimentado, experto, avezado, diestro. **2** (generalmente desp.) estudiado, aprendido, poco natural.

practising | ˌpræktɪsɪŋ | *adj.* **1** en ejercicio, en activo, que ejerce (una profesión). **2** REL. practicante.

practitioner | præk'tɪʃnər | *s.c.* (form.) **1** médico. **2** abogado. **3** (a veces desp.) profesional, practicante.

praesidium | prɪ'sɪdɪəm | *s.c.* V. **presidium.**

praetorian guard | priː'tɔːrɪəngɑːd | *s.c.* clan, cohorte (de gente ambiciosa alrededor de un político, banquero, etc...).

pragmatic | præg'mætɪk | *adj.* **1** pragmático, práctico, realista. || *s.c.* **2** HIST. sanción pragmática. **3** entrometido, chismoso. || **4 pragmatics,** FIL. pragmatismo.

pragmatically | præg'mætɪkəlɪ | *adv.* pragmáticamente, prácticamente.

pragmatism | ˌprægmətɪzəm | *s.i.* pragmatismo.

pragmatist | ˌprægmətɪst | *s.c.* pragmático, realista.

prairie | ˌpreərɪ | *s.c.* e *i.* pradera, llanura, (Am.) pampa, sabana.

praise | preɪz | *v.t.* **1 [– (for)]** alabar, elogiar, ensalzar, exaltar, encomiar: *praising him for his results = elogiándole por sus resultados.* **2** (lit.) glorificar, loar, ensalzar (a Dios). || *s.i.* **3** alabanza, elogio, encomio, aplauso, admiración. **4** (lit.) gloria, loa. **5** (arc.) mérito, estimación, valía. || **6 – be!/– be to God!/– God!,** (arc.) ¡gracias a Dios!, ¡menos mal! **7 to – someone/something to the skies,** poner a uno por las nubes, elogiar a uno efusivamente. **8 to sing one's own praises,** ponerse a sí mismo por las nubes, hacer alarde de uno mismo, fanfarronear. **9 to sing someone's praises,** cantar las alabanzas de alguien, elogiar a uno con efusión.

praiseworthy | ˌpreɪzˌwəːðɪ | *adj.* digno de alabanza, digno de elogio, loable, meritorio, plausible.

pram | præm | (también arc. y brit. **perambulator,** EE.UU. **baby buggy, baby carriage**) *s.c.* cochecito de niño.

prance | prɑːns | (EE.UU.) | præns | *v.i.* **[to – *adv./prep.*]. 1** encabritarse, empinarse (un caballo). **2** (a veces desp.) pavonearse, contonearse, moverse con afectación.

prancing | prɑːnsɪŋ | *adj.* ostentoso, con pavoneo, con afectación.

prank | præŋk | *s.c.* **1** travesura, broma, jugarreta. || *v.t.* e *i.* **2** acicalar(se), engalanar(se), vestir(se) llamativamente. || *v.i.* **3** hacer ostentación, jactarse, pavonearse.

prankster | præŋkstər | *s.c.* (arc. y fam.) bromista.

prat | præt | *s.c.* **1** (brit., desp. y argot) bobo, idiota, necio, lerdo, payaso. **2** (argot) trasero, nalgas.

prattle | ˌprætl | *v.i.* (fam. y desp.) **1 [to – (about/on)]** parlotear, balbucear, chacharear (como los niños). || *s.i.* **2** parloteo, balbuceo, cháchara (de niños).

prawn | prɔːn | *s.c.* **1** gamba, langostino. || **2 – cocktail,** GAST. cóctel de gambas.

pray | preɪ | *v.t.* e *i.* **1** rezar, orar, rogar, implorar. **2** (fig.) esperar, hacer votos (para), rogar (que): *I pray he doesn't come now = espero fervientemente que no venga ahora.* || *v.t.* **3** (lit.) rogar fervientemente, suplicar, implorar: *I pray you not to go! = ¡te suplico que no vayas!* || *adv.* **4** (lit.) por favor, haga el favor, se lo ruego: *pray come in! = ¡entre, por favor!.*

prayer | ˌpreɪər | *s.c.* **1** oración, plegaria. **2** ruego, súplica, esperanza. **3** DER. petición. || *s.i.* **4** oración, devoción: *she was kneeling there in prayer = estaba allí arrodillada orando.* || **5 evening prayers,** vísperas. **6 morning prayers,** maitines. **7 not to have got a –,** (fam.) no tener ni la más mínima posibilidad de sacar (algo) adelante. **8 – book,** misal, devocionario, libro de oraciones. **9 prayers,** servicio religioso, oraciones, rezos (que un grupo celebra diariamente).

preach | priːtʃ | *v.t.* e *i.* **1** predicar, sermonear, exhortar. || *v.t.* **2** (generalmente desp.) predicar, aconsejar, alentar, defender, apoyar (ideas, creencias). || *v.i.* **3 [to – (at/about/to)]** (fig.) dar lecciones, moralizar, sermonear. || **4 to practise what one preaches,** predicar con el ejemplo.

preacher | priːtʃər | *s.c.* predicador.

preamble | priː'æmbl | | 'priːæmbl | *s.c.* e *i.* (form.) preámbulo, prefacio, prólogo, introducción.

prearranged | ˌpriːə'reɪndʒt | *adj.* planeado de antemano, dispuesto de antemano.

precarious | prɪ'keərɪəs | *adj.* (form.) **1** precario, inseguro, peligroso, arriesgado. **2** incierto, improbable, dudoso.

precariously | prɪ'keərɪəslɪ | *adv.* precariamente.

precaution | prɪ'kɔːʃn | *s.c.* precaución, cautela, cuidado, prudencia.

precautionary | prɪ'kɔːʃnərɪ | *adj.* (form.) precautorio, cautelar, preventivo.

precede | ˌprɪː'siːd | *v.t.* **1** (form.) preceder, anteceder. **2 [to – *o.* + *adv./prep.*]** prologar, hacer una introducción, empezar con.

precedence | ˌpreː'siːdəns | *s.i.* **1** (form.) precedencia, prioridad, preferencia, primacía. || **2 to take – over,** tener prioridad sobre, primar sobre.

precedent | ˌpresɪdənt | *s.c.* e *i.* (form.) precedente, antecedente.

preceding | ˌpriː'siːdɪŋ | *adj.* (form.) precedente, anterior, previo.

precept | ˌpriːsept | *s.c.* precepto, regla, pauta, mandato, norma.

precinct | ˌpriːsɪŋkt | *s.c.* **1** (brit.) zona comercial peatonal. **2** (EE.UU.) distrito, circunscripción (electoral, policial). || **3 precincts, a)** recinto, alrededores, límites, contorno; **b)** (p.u.) vecindad, vecindario.

precious | ˌpreʃəs | *adj.* **1** preciado, costoso, caro. **2** apreciado, querido, valioso. **3** (desp.) preciosista, amanerado, afectado, rebuscado. **4** (fam. y desp.) estúpido, despreciable, inservible; querido, amado (indica desprecio): *you may as well go with your precious friend! = ¡puedes largarte con tu querido amigo!* || *adv.* **5** (fam.) muy: *precious little = poquísimo.* || *s.c.* **6** (fam. y p.u.) querido, amor, encanto: *my precious! = ¡querido!* || **7 – metal,** metal precioso. **8 – stone,** piedra preciosa.

precipice | ˌpresɪpɪs | *s.c.* **1** precipicio, abismo, despeñadero, sima. **2** (fig.) abismo, desastre, fracaso, ruina.

precipitate | prɪ'sɪpɪtɪt | *v.t.* **1** (form.) precipitar, acelerar, provocar (un acontecimiento). **2 [to – (into)]** (form.) precipitar, arrojar, lanzar, despeñar. **3** motivar, provocar, producir, causar (problemas). || *v.t.* e *i.* **4 [to – (out)]** QUIM. precipitar. || *s.c.* e *i.* **5** QUIM. precipitado. || *adj.* (también **precipitous**) **6** (form.) precipitado, apresurado, alocado, impulsivo, atropellado.

precipitately | prɪ'sɪpɪtətlɪ | *adv.* precipitadamente, apresuradamente.

precipitation | prɪˌsɪpɪ'teɪʃn | *s.i.* **1** (form.) precipitación, apresuramiento, prisa, atropellamiento. **2** precipitación (atmosférica). **3** QUIM. precipitado.

precipitous | prɪ'sɪpɪtəs | *adj.* (form.) **1** escarpado, pendiente, empinado. **2** precipitado, alocado, precipitoso.

précis | ˌpreɪsiː | | preɪ'siː | *s.c.sing.* y *pl.* **1** resumen, sumario. || *v.t.* **2** resumir, compendiar, sintetizar.

precise | prɪ'saɪs | *adj.* **1** preciso, exacto, riguroso, matemático. **2** preciso, mismo, exacto (momento). **3** (a veces desp.) meticuloso, claro, escrupuloso. || **4 to be –,** para ser exacto, en rigor.

precisely | prɪ'saɪslɪ | *adv.* **1** con precisión, puntualmente, en punto. **2** exactamente, claro que sí, eso es, perfectamente. **3** claramente, meticulosamente, escrupulosamente.

preciseness | prɪ'saɪsnɪs | *s.i.* V. **precision.**

precision | prɪ'sɪʒn | (también **preciseness**). *s.i.* **1** precisión, exactitud, claridad. **2** puntualidad. **3** meticulosidad, escrúpulo. || *adj.* **4** de precisión. **5** exacto, matemático.

preclude | prɪ'kluːd | *v.t.* (form.) **[to – (from)]** excluir, descartar, eliminar, imposibilitar, evitar, impedir.

precocious | prɪ'kəʊʃəs | *adj.* (generalmente desp.) precoz, adelantado.

precociously | prɪ'kəʊʃəslɪ | *adv.* precozmente.

precociousness | ˌprɪ'kəʊʃəsnɪs | (también **precocity**). *s.i.* precocidad.

precocity | prɪ'kɒsɪtɪ | *s.i.* V. **precociousness.**

preconceived | ˌpriːkən'siːvd | *adj.* preconcebido, prejuzgado, premeditado (una opinión, una idea).
preconception | ˌpriːkən'sepʃn | *s.c.* **[– (about)]** preconcepción, prejuicio, idea preconcebida.
precondition | ˌpriːkən'dɪʃn | *s.c.* **[– (for /of)]** condición previa, prerequisito, formalidad previa.
pre-cooked | priː'kʊkt | *adj.* precocinado.
precursor | ˌpriː'kɜːsər | *s.c.* **[– (of/to)]** (form.) precursor, predecesor.
predaceous, predacious | prɪ'deɪʃəs | *adj.* V. **predatory.**
predate | prɪ'deɪt | *v.t.* **[to – (by)] (form.) preceder, anteceder, ser anterior a.**
predator | ˌpredətər | *s.c.* **1** ZOOL. predador, animal de rapiña. **2** (fig.) persona ambiciosa, aprovechado, buitre, carroñero, oportunista, abusón.
predatory | ˌpredətərɪ | *adj.* **1** (también **predaceous** o **predacious**) ZOOL. de presa, de rapiña, rapaz, depredador. **2** (fig.) aprovechado, buitre, ladrón, voraz, oportunista.
predecessor | ˌpriːdɪsesər | *s.c.* **1** predecesor, antecesor. **2** antepasado, precursor.
predestination | priːˌdestɪ'neɪʃn | | prɪˌdes | | tɪ'neɪʃn | *s.i.* predestinación, destino.
predestined | ˌpriː'destɪnd | *adj.* predestinado.
predetermined | ˌpriːdɪ'tɜːmɪnd | *adj.* predeterminado.
predeterminer | ˌpriːdɪ'tɜːmɪnər | *s.c.* GRAM. determinante agrupado: *"all", "half" and "both" may be predeterminers = "todos", "medio" y "ambos" pueden ser determinantes agrupados.*
predicament | prɪ'dɪkəmənt | *s.c.* **1** (form.) dilema, apuro, aprieto, situación difícil, situación embarazosa. **2** LOG. predicamento.
predicate | ˌpredɪkət | *s.c.* **1** GRAM. predicado. || *v.t.* (form.) **2 [to – (on),** generalmente pasiva**]** basar, apoyar, fundar: *arguments predicated on several facts = argumentos que se basan en varios hechos.* **3 [to – (of)]** predicar, proclamar, declarar, divulgar. **4** dar a entender, denotar, entrañar. **5** LOG. predicar, formar el predicado (de una proposición).
predicative | prɪ'dɪkətɪv | *adj.* GRAM. predicativo.
predict | prɪ'dɪkt | *v.t.* predecir, profetizar, anticipar, pronosticar.
predictability | prɪ'dɪktəbɪlɪtɪ | *s.i.* pronosticabilidad, posibilidad de predecir.
predictable | prɪ'dɪktəbl | *adj.* **1** predecible, pronosticable, profetizable. **2** (desp.) fácil de predecir, esperado, conocido (un hecho). **3** de reacciones predecibles, falto de imaginación (una persona).
predictably | prɪ'dɪktəblɪ | *adv.* de manera que se puede pronosticar.
prediction | prɪ'dɪkʃn | *s.c.* e *i.* predicción, profecía, pronóstico.
predictive | prɪ'dɪktɪv | *adj.* profético, que vale como predicción, que pronostica.
pre-digested | ˌpriːdaɪ'dʒestɪd | *adj.* **1** (desp. y fam.) simplificada, fácil, sintetizada (información). **2** digerido de antemano.
predilection | ˌpriːdɪ'lekʃn | | ˌpredl 'ekʃn | *s.c.* **[– (for)]** (form.) predilección, inclinación, preferencia, propensión.
predispose | ˌpriːdɪ'spəuz | *v.t.* **[to –** *o.* **+** *adv./prep.* **+ to** *inf.***]** (form.) predisponer, inclinar.
predisposed | ˌpriːdɪ'spəuzd | *adj.* predispuesto, inclinado, propenso.
predisposition | ˌpriːˌdɪspə'zɪʃn | *s.c.* predisposición, inclinación, propensión.
predominance | prɪ'dɒmɪnəns | *s.i.* **[– (of)]** (form.) predominio, preponderancia, dominación.
predominant | prɪ'dɒmɪnənt | *adj.* **[– (over)]** (form.) predominante, preponderante.
predominantly | prɪ'dɒmɪnəntlɪ | *adv.* predominantemente, principalmente.
predominate | prɪ'dɒmɪneɪt | *v.i.* **[to – (over)]** (form.) **1** predominar, ser preponderante. **2** prevalecer, influir, dominar.
pre-eminence | ˌpriː'emɪnəns | *s.i.* preeminencia, superioridad.
pre-eminent | ˌpriː'emɪnənt | *adj.* **[– (among/at/in)]** (form.) preeminente, superior, que sobresale.
pre-eminently | ˌpriː'emɪnəntlɪ | *adv.* preeminentemente, predominantemente, sobre todo.
pre-empt | ˌpriː'empt | *v.t.* **1** (generalmente pasiva) frustrar, malograr, estropear. **2** apropiarse de, adquirir por derecho de prioridad. **3** preceder, darse con prioridad a. **4** tomar la delantera, ganar un lugar preferencial.
pre-emptive | ˌpriːemptɪv | *adj.* prioritario, por derecho de prioridad.
preen | priːn | *v.t.* e *i.* **1** limpiar, arreglar con el pico (las plumas un pájaro). **2** (fig. y desp.) acicalarse, componerse, aderezarse, atildarse. || **3 to – oneself on/upon,** (desp. y p.u.) jactarse de, enorgullecerse de, mostrarse pagado de sí mismo, pavonearse de.
prefab | ˌpriːfæb | | ˌpriː'fæb | *s.c.* (brit. y fam.) casita prefabricada, estructura prefabricada.
prefabricated | ˌpriː'fæbrɪkeɪtəd | *adj.* prefabricado.
preface | ˌprefɪs | *s.c.* **1** prólogo, introducción. **2** REL. prefacio. **3** fase preliminar. || *v.t.* (form.) **4** prologar, servir como introducción. **5 [to –** *o.* **+** *adv./prep.* (generalmente **with**)**]** preceder, anunciar.
prefect | ˌpriːfekt | *s.c.* **1** (brit.) prefecto, tutor, monitor (en escuelas). **2** prefecto (de policía).
prefer | prɪ'fɜːr | **[preferred, preferring]** *v.t.* **1** preferir. **2 [to – (to)]** (form.) ascender, nombrar, promover (especialmente por la iglesia). **3** DER. dar prioridad, dar preferencia. || **4 to – charges,** DER. presentar cargos, acusar formalmente; formular una reclamación.
preferable | ˌprefərəbl | *adj.* **[– (to)]** preferible.
preferably | ˌprefərəblɪ | *adv.* preferiblemente, preferentemente.
preference | ˌprefərəns | *s.c.* e *i.* **1 [– (for/to)]** preferencia. **2 [– (over/to)]** preferencia, prioridad, favoritismo.
preferential | ˌprefə'renʃl | *adj.* preferencial, preferente, de favor.
preferentially | ˌprefə'renʃəlɪ | *adv.* preferencialmente, preferentemente, con favoritismo.
preferment | ˌprɪ'fɜːmənt | *s.i.* **[– (to)]** ascenso, promoción, nombramiento (especialmente dentro de la iglesia).
preferred | prɪ'fɜːd | *adj.* preferido.
prefigure | priː'fɪgər | *v.t.* (form.) prefigurar; presagiar, anunciar.
prefix | ˌpriː'fɪks | *s.c.* **1** GRAM. prefijo. **2** título: *"Dr" is a prefix = "Dr" es un título.* || *v.t.* **3** anteponer un prefijo, colocar un prefijo. **4** anteponer, colocar al principio: *he prefixed a few lines on theory = antepuso unas líneas de teoría.* **5** (arc.) prefijar, fijar de antemano.
pregnancy | ˌpregnənsɪ | *s.c.* e *i.* **1** embarazo. || **2 – test,** prueba del embarazo.
pregnant | ˌpregnənt | *adj.* **1** embarazada, preñada, encinta. **2** (lit.) significativo, importante, característico. **3** creativo, inventivo. **4 [– (with)]** fructífero, fecundo, abundante, pleno, profuso, rico.
preheat | ˌpriː'hiːt | *v.t.* precalentar, calentar de antemano.
prehensile | prɪ'hensaɪl | | prɪ'hensəl | *adj.* prensil: *a prehensile tail = una cola prensil.*
prehistoric | ˌpriːhɪ'stɒrɪk | *adj.* **1** prehistórico. **2** (fig.) prehistórico, anticuado.
prehistory | ˌpriːhɪ'stərɪ | *s.i.* prehistoria.
preignition | ˌpriːɪg'nɪʃən | *s.i.* preignición.
pre-industrial | ˌpriːin'dʌstrɪəl | *adj.* preindustrial.
prejudge | ˌpriː'dʒʌdʒ | *v.t.* (desp.) prejuzgar, juzgar de antemano.
prejudice | ˌpredʒʊdɪs | *s.c.* e *i.* **1 [– (against/in favour of)]** prejuicio, parcialidad, prevención, discriminación: *racial prejudices = prejuicios raciales.* **2** perjuicio, detrimento, deterioro, menoscabo. || *v.t.* **3 [to – (against/in favour of)** y generalmente pasiva**]** predisponer, inclinar, mostrar prejuicios, prevenir (contra). **4** perjudicar, vulnerar, dañar, menoscabar. || **5 without – to,** DER. sin detrimento de, sin perjuicio de.
prejudiced | ˌpredʒʊdɪst | *adj.* (desp.) con prejuicios, parcial, injusto, arbitrario.
prejudicial | ˌpredʒʊ'dɪʃl | *adj.* (form.) perjudicial, lesivo, dañino, pernicioso.
prelate ˌprelɪt | *s.c.* prelado, obispo, abad.
preliminary | prɪ'lɪmɪnərɪ | (EE.UU.) | prɪ'lɪmɪnerɪ | *adj.* **1** preliminar, primero, preparatorio. || *s.c.* **2** (generalmente *pl.*) medida preliminar, preparativo.
prelude | ˌprelju:d | *s.c.* **1** preludio, principio, preámbulo. **2** MUS. preludio.

premarital | ˌpriː'mærɪtl | *adj.* premarital, prematrimonial, prenupcial.
premature | ˌpremətjʊər | (EE.UU.) | ˌpriːmə'tʊər | *adj.* **1** prematuro, temprano, anticipado (un hecho). **2** precoz. **3** prematuro (un niño). **4** (desp.) prematuro, inapropiado, pronto: *her judgement was a bit premature = su juicio fue un poco prematuro.*
prematurely | ˌpreməˌtjʊəlɪ | *adv.* prematuramente, antes de tiempo.
premeditated | ˌpriː'medɪteɪtɪd | *adj.* premeditado, deliberado.
premeditation | priːˌmedɪ'teɪʃn | *s.i.* premeditación.
premier | ˌpremɪər | (EE.UU.) | ˌpriːmɪər | *s.c.* **1** PER. primer ministro, presidente. || *adj.* **2** principal, primordial, vital, capital: *Spain's premier interests = los intereses primordiales de España.*
premiere | ˌpremɪər | (EE.UU.) | prɪ'mɪər | *s.c.* **1** estreno (teatral, cinematográfico). || *v.t.* **2** (generalmente pasiva) estrenar.
premiership | ˌpremjəʃɪp | *s.i.* presidencia, cargo de primer ministro.
premise | prɪ'maɪz | *s.c.* **1** (form.) premisa, aseveración, aserto. **2** LOG. premisa. || *v.t.* **3** (form.) basar, fundar, apoyar, asentar (una teoría). || **4 premises,** establecimiento, local, edificio, propiedad.
premium | ˌpriːmɪəm | *s.c.* **1** prima, pago (de seguro). **2** prima, bonificación, gratificación, premio. || *adj.* **3** mayor, más alto (un precio). || **4 at a –,** COM. **a)** sobre la par, a más de su valor nominal (debido a la escasez); **b)** muy solicitado, difícil de conseguir. **5 – bond,** bonos del Estado (que participan en sorteos mensuales). **6 to put/place a high –,** dar mucha importancia, sobrevalorar.
premonition | ˌpriːmə'nɪʃn | | ˌpremə'nɪʃn | *s.c.* premonición, presentimiento, corazonada.
premonitory | prɪ'mɒnɪtərɪ | (EE.UU.) *adj.* premonitorio.
prenatal | ˌpriː'neɪtl | *adj.* prenatal.
preoccupation | priːˌɒkjʊ'peɪʃn | *s.i.* **1** [– (with)] preocupación, inquietud, obsesión. || *s.c.* **2** preocupación, problema, tribulación, desvelo.
preoccupied | ˌpriː'ɒkjʊpaɪd | *adj.* preocupado, intranquilo, atribulado, inquieto.
preoccupy | ˌpriː'ɒkjʊpaɪ | *v.t.* preocupar, inquietar, intranquilizar, desvelar.
preordained | ˌpriːɔː'deɪn | *adj.* (form.) predestinado, preordinado.
pre-packed | priː'pækt | *adj.* preempaquetado, empaquetado de antemano.
prepaid | ˌpriː'peɪd | *adj.* pagado por adelantado.
preparation | ˌprepə'reɪʃn | *s.i.* **1** [– (for /of)] preparación, preparamiento. **2** (form.) deberes, estudio, trabajo escolar (que se hace en casa para un examen). || *s.c.* **3** [– (for) generalmente *pl.*] preparativo, plan. **4** QUIM. preparado.
preparatory | prɪ'pærətrɪ | (EE.UU.) | prɪ'pærətɔːrɪ | *adj.* **1** preparatorio, introductorio, preliminar. || **2 – school /prep school, a)** (brit.) escuela preparatoria privada (de los 7 a los 13 años); escuela primaria; **b)** (EE.UU.) curso preparatorio (para entrar en la Universidad). **3 – to,** con miras a, antes de.
prepare | prɪ'peər | *v.t.* **[to – (for)] 1** preparar, disponer, aprestar. **2** preparar, organizar, arreglar (un asunto, una comida). || *v.t.* e *i.* **3** planificar, hacer preparativos. **4** preparar(se) (para una situación nueva): *prepare yourself for what's coming next = prepárate para lo que viene ahora.*
prepared | prɪ'peəd | *adj.* **1** preparado, hecho de antemano. **2 [– to** *inf.***]** preparado, dispuesto: *I was prepared to do anything = estaba preparado para cualquier cosa.* **3 [– for]** preparado, acostumbrado, prevenido.
preparedness | prɪ'peədnɪs | | prɪ'peə | rɪdnɪs | *s.i.* estado de preparación, preparación, apresto.
preponderance | prɪ'pɒndərəns | *s.i.* (form.) preponderancia, predominio, superioridad.
preponderant | prɪ'pɒndərənt | *adj.* (form.) preponderante, predominante, superior.
preponderantly | prɪ'pɒndərəntlɪ | *adv.* predominantemente, principalmente, en su mayoría.
preposition | ˌprepə'zɪʃn | *s.c.* GRAM. preposición.
prepossessing | ˌpriːpə'zesɪŋ | *adj.* (form.) encantador, atractivo, agradable, encantador, seductor (de apariencia, modales).
preposterous | prɪ'pɒstərəs | *adj.* (form.) **1** absurdo, ilógico, descabellado. **2** ridículo, grotesco, cómico.
preposterously | prɪ'pɒstərəslɪ | *adv.* (form.) **1** absurdamente, ilógicamente, descabelladamente. **2** ridículamente.
prep school | ˌprepskuːl | *s.c.* e *i.* (fam.) **1** (brit.) escuela preparatoria privada, escuela primaria privada. **2** (EE.UU.) curso preparatorio (para entrar en la Universidad).
prepubescent | ˌpriːpjʊ'besənt | *adj.* (form.) prepúber, prepubescente.
pre-Raphaelite | ˌpriː'ræfəlaɪt | | ˌpriː'ræ | | fɪəlaɪt | *s.c.* ART. **1** prerrafaelista. || *adj.* **2** prerrafaelista.
pre-recorded | ˌpriːrɪ'kɔːd | *adj.* pregrabado, grabado de antemano.
prerequisite | ˌpriː'rekwɪzɪt | **[– (for /of/to)]** (form.) *s.c.* **1** requisito previo, condición previa. || *adj.* **2** necesario de antemano, esencial.
prerogative | prɪ'rɒgətɪv | *s.c.* (generalmente *sing.*) prerrogativa, ventaja, privilegio.
presage | ˌpresɪdʒ | | prɪ'seɪdʒ | *v.t.* **1** (lit.) presagiar, predecir, pronosticar, anunciar. || *s.c.* **2 [– (of)]** (lit.) presagio, premonición, augurio.
presbytery | ˌprezbɪtrɪ | (EE.UU.) | ˌprezbɪtərɪ | *s.c.* **1** tribunal eclesiástico presbiteriano. **2** parroquia, rectoría. **3** presbiterio.
pre-school | ˌpriː'skuːl | *adj.* **1** preescolar: *pre-school age = edad preescolar.* || *s.c.* **2** preescolar, jardín de infancia.
prescience | ˌpresɪəns | *s.i.* (form.) presciencia.
prescient | ˌpresɪənt | *adj.* (form.) presciente.
prescribe | prɪ'skraɪb | *v.t.* e *i.* **1** prescribir, recetar (un medicamento). **2** (form.) prescribir, ordenar, dictar, preceptuar (la ley).
prescribed | prɪ'skraɪbd | *adj.* prescrito, determinado, fijado, establecido.
prescription | ˌprɪ'skrɪpʃn | *s.c.* **1 [– (for)]** prescripción médica, receta. **2** (fig.) prescripción, consejo, sugerencia. **3** DER. precepto, regla. || **4 on –,** con receta.
prescriptive | prɪ'skrɪptɪv | *adj.* (form.) prescriptivo, preceptivo, legal, sancionado por la ley, estricto.
presence | ˌprezns | *s.i.* **1** presencia, existencia. **2** presencia, cooperación, ayuda (militar, policial). **3** personalidad, carácter: *a person of enormous presence = una persona de gran personalidad.* || *s.c.* **4** (generalmente *sing.*) presencia, influencia, entidad: *a mysterious presence = una presencia misteriosa.* || **5 in someone's –,** en presencia de alguien. **6 to make one's – felt,** hacerse valer, hacer que se den cuenta de lo que uno vale. **7 – of mind,** presencia de ánimo, sangre fría.
present | ˌpreznt | *s.c.* **1** presente, regalo, obsequio. **2 [the –]** el presente, la actualidad. **3** GRAM. presente. || | prɪ'zent | *v.t.* **4** presentar, plantear, representar, mostrar (problemas, dificultades). **7 [to – (to)]** presentar, exponer, poner a consideración (un trabajo, un informe). **8** presentar, retratar, mostrar, exhibir (un aspecto). **9** representar, exhibir, poner (un espectáculo). **10** TV. presentar, tomar parte en (un programa). **11** presentar, ofrecer (excusas, respetos). **12** MIL. presentar (armas). || *v.r.* **13** presentarse: *if the opportunity presents itself = si se presenta la oportunidad.* || *adj.* **14** presente, asistente: *many were present = muchos estaban allí.* **15** actual, presente, vigente, existente: *the present government = el gobierno actual.* **16** GRAM. presente (tiempo verbal). **17** presente, que se recuerda, que se siente: *an accident still present in her mind = un accidente que aún recuerda.* **18** (arc.) inmediato, instantáneo, asequible. || **19 at –/at the – time,** en este momento, ahora, en la actualidad. **20 by these presents,** DER. por este documento. **21 for the –,** por lo presente, por el momento, por ahora. **22 – company excepted/excepting – company,** exceptuando a los presentes (al hacer una crítica). **23 – participle,** GRAM. gerundio, participio de presente. **24 – perfect,** GRAM. pretérito perfecto. **25 – tense,** GRAM. tiempo presente. **26 the – day,** la actualidad, hoy en día, hoy.
presentable | prɪ'zentəbl | *adj.* **1** presentable, adecuado, aceptable. || **2 to make oneself –,** arreglarse, vestirse.
presentably | prɪ'zentəblɪ | *adv.* presentablemente, adecuadamente.

presentation | ˌprezən'teɪʃn | (EE.UU.) | ˌpriːzen'teɪʃn | *s.c.* e *i.* **1** presentación, representación, ceremonia. **2** MED. presentación, colocación (de un niño en el vientre de su madre). || *s.i.* **3 [– (of)]** presentación, apariencia. || *s.c.* **4 [– (on)]** presentación, exposición, introducción (de un tema).
present-day | ˌpreznt ˌdeɪ | *adj.* [no *comp.*] actual, moderno, de hoy en día.
presenter | prɪ'zentər | *s.c.* TV. presentador.
presentiment | prɪ'zentɪmənt | *s.c.* (form.) presentimiento, premonición, presagio.
presently | ˌprezntlɪ | *adv.* **1** pronto, en un momento, dentro de poco. **2** (EE.UU.) actualmente, en este momento, ahora.
preservation | ˌprezə'veɪʃn | *s.i.* **1** preservación, conservación, mantenimiento, custodia, defensa.
preservative | prɪ'zəːvətɪv | *s.c.* e *i.* **1** conservante, preservativo, antiséptico (para alimentos, madera, metal). || *adj.* **2** conservante, preservativo, antiséptico.
preserve | prɪ'zəːv | *v.t.* **1 [to – (from)]** preservar, proteger, amparar, defender. **2 [to – (from)]** (hum.) guardar, librar: *God preserve us from this kind of prophets = Dios nos libre de esa clase de profetas.* **3** preservar, mantener, salvaguardar (la paz, la independencia). **4 [to – (in)]** poner en conserva, hacer conserva de, confitar, curar. || *s.c.* **5** coto, zona vedada, reserva. **6** dominio, propiedad exclusiva: *nursing has remained a woman preserve = la mujer sigue dominando el campo de la enfermería.* || **7 preserves,** conservas en vinagre; mermelada, confitura.
preserved | prɪ'zəːvd | *adj.* **1** conservado, cuidado (un lugar, un mueble). **2** en conserva (un alimento).
preserver | prɪ'zəːvər | *s.c.* preservador, conservador.
pre-set | ˌpriː'set | [*pret.* y *p.p.* **preset,** *ger.* **presetting**] *v.t.* programar, prefijar: *preset the video before you leave = programa el vídeo antes de irte.*
preside | prɪ'zaɪd | *v.i.* **1 [to – (at/over)]** (form.) presidir, dirigir. **2 [to – (over)]** (form.) presidir, dominar, destacar.
presidency | ˌprezɪdənsɪ | *s.c.* e *i.* presidencia.
president | ˌprezɪdənt | *s.c.* **1** POL. presidente. **2** presidente, rector, decano (de una sociedad, de Universidad). **3** (EE.UU.) COM. presidente, director.
president-elect | 'prezɪdəntɪ'lekt | *s.c.* POL. presidente electo.
presidential | ˌprezɪdenʃl | *adj.* presidencial.
presidia | prɪ'sɪdɪə | *pl.* de **presidium.**
presidium | prɪ'sɪdɪəm | (también **praesidium**) [*pl.* **presidiums** o **presidia**] *s.c.* presidium, comité administrativo y gubernamental en países comunistas.
press | pres | *v.t.* **1** presionar, apretar, empujar, pulsar: *press the switch = aprieta el interruptor.* **2** prensar, exprimir, estrujar. **3** planchar. **4** apretar (la mano), abrazar. **5 [to – *o.* + to *inf.*]** obligar, exigir, forzar, urgir: *she pressed me to accompany her = me forzó a acompañarla.* **6** insistir en, porfiar en, persistir en. **7** hacer una copia de la matriz (de un disco). || *v.i.* **8** (fam.) ejercer presión, presionar, apremiar, acuciar, pesar: *time presses! = ¡el tiempo apremia!* **9** hacer presión, apretarse, apiñarse (la gente). || *s.i.* **10 [the – *v.sing./pl.*]** la prensa; el periodismo, los periodistas. || *s.c.* **11** prensa, imprenta, impresión. **12** editorial: *Ullswater Press = Editorial Ullswater.* **13** presión, apretón. **14** (fam.) planchazo, planchada (a una prenda). **15** prensa, compresor, prensador (para una raqueta, para hacer vino). || **16 to get a bood/bad/etc... –,** tener buena, mala, etc... prensa. **17 to go to –,** PER. entrar en prensa, entrar en máquinas. **18 to – ahead/forward/on,** seguir adelante (a pesar de las dificultades). **19 – box,** tribuna de la prensa. **20 – conference,** rueda de prensa, conferencia de prensa. **21 – corps,** (EE.UU.) plantilla de periodistas. **22 – cutting,** (EE.UU.) **– clipping,** recorte de prensa. **23 – home, a)** aprovechar al máximo, sacar el máximo rendimiento; **b)** presionar, atacar. **24 to – for,** pedir con urgencia, insistir en. **25 to – into service,** utilizar temporalmente, utilizar por necesidad. **26 – officer,** jefe de prensa, portavoz (de un grupo, de un partido político). **27 to – one's advantage/to – an advantage,** (lit.) aprovecharse al máximo de una ventaja. **28 – release,** comunicado de prensa.
pressed | prest | *adj.* en apuros, escaso (de tiempo, de dinero).
pressgang | ˌpresgæŋ | *s.c.* **1** HIS. patrulla de reclutamiento, ronda de enganche. || **2 to be pressganged into,** estar forzado a, verse obligado a.
pressing | ˌpresɪŋ | *adj.* **1** apremiante, urgente, imperioso, acuciante. **2** insistente, pesado: *pressing demands = peticiones insistentes.* || *s.c.* **3** copia (de la matriz de un disco). **4** planchado: *the skirt needed a quick pressing = la falda necesitaba un planchado rápido.*
pressman | ˌpresmæn | [*pl.* **pressmen**] *s.c.* **1** (brit. y fam.) periodista, reportero. **2** impresor.
pressmen | ˌpresmən | *pl.* de **pressman.**
press-up | ˌpresʌp | (EE.UU. **push-up**). *s.c.* (generalmente *pl.*) flexión (ejercicio): *he did 10 press-ups and fell down = hizo 10 flexiones y cayó.*
pressure | ˌpreʃər | *s.i.* **1** presión, prensadura, compresión. **2** presión, influencia, persuasión. **3** urgencia, apremio, prisa. || *s.c.* e *i.* **4** presión, fuerza, peso: *he stopped to check the tyre pressure = paró a comprobar la presión de las ruedas.* **5** tensión, fatiga, cansancio, agotamiento. || *v.t.* **6 [to – (into)]** (EE.UU.) ejercer presión, forzar, obligar. || **7 to bring – to bear,** ejercer presión sobre, hacer presión (para que alguien haga algo). **8 – group,** POL. grupo de presión. **9 under –,** bajo presión, presionado, forzado, obligado.
pressure-cooker | ˌpreʃəˌkukər | *s.c.* olla a presión.
pressurize | ˌpreʃəraɪz | (brit. **pressurise**) *v.t.* **1** (EE.UU.) presionar, obligar, forzar. **2** AER. presurizar, comprobar la presión.
pressurized | ˌpreʃəraɪzd | (EE.UU. **pressurised**) *adj.* a presión, presurizado, altimático.
prestige | pre'stiːʒ | *s.i.* **1** prestigio, fama, reputación, renombre. || *adj.* **2** (desp.) de prestigio, prestigioso, de renombre.
prestigious | pre'stɪdʒəs | *adj.* prestigioso, afamado, reputado.
prestressed concrete | ˌpriːstrest'kɒŋˌkriːt | *s.i.* V. **concrete.**
presumably | prɪ'zjuːməblɪ | *adv.* presumiblemente, probablemente.
presume | prɪ'zjuːm | *v.t.* **1** presumir, suponer, dar por sentado: *I presume she'll be here soon = supongo que llegará pronto.* **2** DER. presumir: *he was presumed innocent = se le presumía inocente.* **3** (form.) presuponer, suponer: *getting the job presumes asking for it = conseguir el trabajo presupone solicitarlo.* || *v.i.* **4** (form.) atreverse, ser un atrevido, tomarse la libertad, permitirse la confianza de: *he presumed to tell me how to mark an exam = se atrevió a decirme como debía calificar un examen.* || **5 I –,** presumiblemente, según creo, tengo entendido: *you are coming, I presume = tengo entendido que vienes.* **6 to – on/upon,** pedir demasiado, pasarse de la raya, abusar.
presumption | prɪ'zʌmpʃn | *s.c.* e *i.* **1** DER. presunción. **2** presunción, suposición, conjetura. || *s.i.* **3** (form. y desp.) atrevimiento, falta de respeto, insolencia.
presumptive | prɪ'zʌmptɪv | *adj.* (form.) DER. presunto, probable.
presumptuous | prɪ'zʌmptjuəs | *adj.* (desp.) presuntuoso, atrevido, insolente, vanidoso, presumido.
presumptuously | prɪ'zʌmptjuəslɪ | *adv.* presuntuosamente, con atrevimiento, insolentemente.
presumptuousness | prɪ'zʌmptjuəsnɪs | *s.i.* presuntuosidad, presunción, insolencia, vanidad.
presuppose | ˌpriːsə'pəuz | *v.t.* (form.) presuponer, asumir, dar por sentado, suponer.
presupposition | ˌpriːsʌpə'zɪʃn | *s.c.* e *i.* (form.) presuposición.
pretence | prɪ'tens | | 'priːtens | (EE.UU. **pretense**). *s.c.* e *i.* **1** simulación, farsa, fingimiento. || *s.i.* **2 [– to]** pretensión, vanidad. || **3 under false –,** con engaño, fraudulentamente, bajo apariencia engañosa.
pretend | prɪ'tend | *v.t.* e *i.* **1** fingir, simular, aparentar: *she was just pretending she was angry = sólo fingía que estaba enfadada.* **2** imaginar, hacer (de mentirijillas), suponer (en juegos): *let's pretend we are the parents = nosotros hacemos de padres.* || *v.t.* **3** pretender, tener la pretensión de, afirmar: *I don't pretend you to give it to me = no pretendo que me lo des.* || *adj.* **4** (fam.) imaginario, de mentirijillas (usado en juegos de niños).

pretender | prɪ'tendər | *s.c.* pretendiente (al trono, a un puesto).

pretension | prɪ'tenʃn | *s.c.* 1 **[– (to)]** pretensión, demanda, reclamación, aspiración. 2 pretexto, alegación. || *s.i.* 3 presunción, ostentación, pretenciosidad, suntuosidad.

pretentious | prɪ'tenʃəs | *adj.* 1 pretencioso, ambicioso. 2 pretencioso, ostentoso, jactancioso, cursi.

pretentiousness | prɪ'tenʃəsnɪs | *s.i.* pretenciosidad, presunción, cursilería.

preternatural | ˌpriːtə'nætʃrəl | *adj.* (form.) 1 preternatural, inexplicable, increíble. 2 preternatural, extraño, insólito.

preternaturally | ˌpriːtə'nætʃrəlɪ | *adv.* inexplicablemente, increíblemente.

pretext | ˌpriːtekst | *s.c.* **[– (for/of)]** pretexto, disculpa, evasiva, excusa.

prettify | ˌprɪtɪfaɪ | *v.t.* (generalmente desp.) adornar extravagantemente, embellecer, acicalar.

prettily | ˌprɪtɪlɪ | *adv.* hermosamente, bellamente, atractivamente, con gracia, con donaire.

prettiness | ˌprɪtɪnɪs | *s.i.* hermosura, belleza, encanto, atractivo, gracia, donaire.

pretty | ˌprɪtɪ | *adj.* 1 bonito, precioso, gracioso, encantador, atractivo (un niño, una mujer, un lugar). 2 elegante, mono, fino (un vestido, un objeto). 3 (desp.) afeminado. 4 (desp. y arc.) bonito, desagradable, lamentable: *the pretty state of affairs = el lamentable estado del asunto.* 5 excelente, bueno, fantástico. 6 enorme, considerable, importante: *a pretty fortune = una considerable fortuna.* || *adv.* (fam.) 7 bastante, moderadamente, un poco, hasta cierto punto; muy, considerablemente: *a pretty hot day = un día bastante caluroso.* || **8 a – pass,** (arc.) una situación límite, tal extremo. **9 to cost a – penny,** costar un ojo de la cara, ser muy caro. **10 to lead someone a – dance,** V. **dance. 11 not a – sight,** (fam.) poco agradable de ver, poco atractivo a la vista. **12 – fair,** astuto, adecuado, magnífico. **13 – much /nearly,** (fam.) bastante, casi, aproximadamente: *she's pretty much the same as him = ella es más o menos lo mismo que él.* **14 – well,** medianamente, regular: *she's doing pretty well at school = va regular en los estudios.* **15 to sit –,** (fam.) estar bien situado, estar en circunstancias favorables.

pretzel | ˌpretsl | *s.c.* rosquilla espolvoreada con sal (generalmente en forma de ocho, que se toma con la cerveza).

prevail | prɪ'veɪl | *v.i.* (form.) 1 **[to – (among/in)]** prevalecer, ser corriente, imperar, regir, predominar, estar extendido: *some oldfashioned ideas still prevail = aún prevalecen algunas viejas ideas.* 2 **[to – (against/over)]** prevalecer, vencer, triunfar, imponerse: *they prevailed over the enemy = vencieron al enemigo.* || **3 to – on/upon,** (form.) persuadir, convencer.

prevailing | prɪ'veɪlɪŋ | *adj.* 1 predominante, reinante: *prevailing winds from the north = vientos predominantes del norte.* 2 (form.) existente, actual, corriente: *the prevailing point of view = el punto de vista actual.*

prevalence | ˌprevələns | *s.i.* predominio, preponderancia, frecuencia: *the prevalence of anti-semitic sentiments = el predominio de sentimientos antisemitas.*

prevalent | ˌprevələnt | *adj.* (form.) **[– (among/in)]** 1 existente, predominante, frecuente, corriente, generalizado. 2 de moda, en boga, actual.

prevaricate | prɪ'værɪkeɪt | *v.i.* (form.) 1 tergiversar, equivocar, contestar con evasivas. 2 (euf.) mentir, engañar. 3 DER. prevaricar.

prevarication | prɪ'værɪkeɪʃn | *s.c.* e *i.* 1 tergiversación, equívoco, engaño, evasiva. 2 DER. prevaricación.

prevaricator | prɪ'værɪkeɪtər | *s.c.* 1 tergiversador, liante, mentiroso. 2 DER. prevaricador.

prevent | prɪ'vent | *v.t.* **[to – (from)]** 1 prevenir, precaver, evitar, impedir, eludir, obstruir: *to prevent him from doing a silly thing = para impedirle que hiciera una tontería.* 2 anticipar, prever. 3 (arc.) preceder, anteceder.

preventable | prɪ'ventəbl | (también **preventible**). *adj.* inevitable: *preventable deseases = enfermedades que se pueden prevenir.*

preventative | prɪ'ventətɪv | *adj.* V. **preventive.**

prevention | prɪ'venʃn | *s.i.* 1 prevención. || *s.i.* 2 obstáculo, impedimento.

preventive | prɪ'ventɪv | *adj.* 1 preventivo, de precaución, impeditivo: *preventive measures = medidas de precaución.* 2 MED. profiláctico, preventivo. || *s.c.* 3 obstáculo, impedimento.

preverbal | ˌpriː'vɜːbl | *adj.* (form.) preverbal (estadio infantil).

preview | ˌpriːvjuː | (también **prevue**). *s.c.* 1 preestreno (de una película). 2 vista anticipada, muestra anticipada, pase privado: *we had a preview of the exhibition = logramos un pase privado de la exposición.* 3 avance, resumen (de un libro, de una película): *I heard a preview of the book on the radio = oí de qué trataba el libro por la radio.* || *v.t.* 4 preestrenar, presentar previamente. 5 dar un avance, hacer una presentación preliminar (de un libro, una obra, etc...).

previous | ˌpriːvɪəs | *adj.* 1 previo, anterior, precedente: *her previous husband = su anterior marido.* 2 (fam. y arc.) prematuro, apresurado, anticipado: *he was too previous acting like that = fue demasiado apresurado al actuar así.*

previously | ˌpriːvɪəslɪ | *adv.* 1 previamente, anteriormente, con anterioridad. 2 antes: *he had been there two months previously = había estado allí dos meses antes.*

pre-war | ˌpriː'wɔːr | *adj.* de preguerra, de antes de la guerra (especialmente la Segunda Guerra Mundial).

prey | preɪ | *s.i.* 1 presa, despojos: *an eagle looking for prey = un águila buscando despojos.* 2 rapiña, caza: *a bird of prey = un ave de rapiña.* || *v.i.* 3 cazar, rapiñar. || **4 to be – to,** ser víctima de, ser presa de: *she was prey to fear = fue presa del terror.* **5 to fall – to,** (desp.) caer víctima de, estar atormentado por. **6 to – on/upon, a)** atacar, devorar, comer (un animal); **b)** aprovecharse, abusar. **7 to – on one's mind,** preocupar, atormentar, atosigar, abrumar, agobiar, afectar profundamente.

price | praɪs | *s.c.* 1 precio, importe, valor, tarifa, cuantía. 2 diferencia (entre el dinero apostado y el que se gana en el juego): *I am offering 5 to 1 = ofrezco 5 a 1.* 3 recompensa, precio (por la captura de alguien). || *v.t.* 4 **[to – *o.* + *adv./prep.*]** (generalmente pasiva) tasar, valorar, preciar: *the watch was priced at $150 = el reloj estaba valorado en 150 dólares.* 5 (fam.) establecer el precio, poner precio, fijar precio, tasar: *he used to price paintings = era tasador de cuadros.* || **6 at any –,** (fig.) **a)** a toda costa, cueste lo que cueste, a cualquier precio; **b)** de ningún modo. **7 at a –,** al precio: *she bought it at a price of $ 60 = lo compró al precio de 60 dólares.* **8 to – oneself out of the market,** subir (un artículo) exageradamente hasta que resulte imposible de vender, alcanzar un precio que excluye (un artículo) del mercado. **9 the – to pay/that you –,** (fig.) el precio que hay que pagar, el coste que supone, el castigo que hay que pagar: *there was a high price to pay for democracy = la democracia se pagó a alto precio.* **10 to set a – on someone's head,** poner precio a la cabeza de uno. **11 what – ...,** de qué vale, de qué sirve, y qué me dicen de.

priceless | ˌpraɪslɪs | *adj.* 1 que no tiene precio, inestimable, inapreciable. 2 (arc. y fam.) divertido, cómico, para morirse de risa.

pricey | ˌpraɪsɪ | *adj.* (brit., fam. y desp.) caro, costoso.

prick | prɪk | *s.c.* 1 pinchazo, punzada, picotazo. 2 (fig.) remordimiento, escrúpulo (de conciencia). 3 aguijón, púa, espino, espina, punzón. 4 (desp. y vulg.) pito, polla, pene. 5 (argot, vulg. y desp.) gilipollas, soplapollas, estúpido. 6 rastro, pisadas (de liebre). || *v.t.* 7 **[to – (with /on)]** pinchar, punzar, picar, agujerear. 8 incitar, animar, aguijonear. 9 marcar con agujeritos, dibujar con agujeritos. || *v.t.* e *i.* 10 causar escozor, picar, tener picazón. 11 (fig.) tener escrúpulos, remorder (la conciencia). || *v.i.* 12 galopar, ir a galope. || **13 to – out,** trasplantar, plantar. **14 to – up one's ears/someone's ears – up, a)** aguzar el oído, escuchar con atención; **b)** levantar las orejas (un animal).

pricking | ˌprɪkɪŋ | *adj.* 1 agudo, punzante, penetrante (un dolor). || *s.c.* 2 punzada, pinchazo, picotazo. 3 picazón, escozor: *feeling a pricking in his eyes = sintiendo escozor en sus ojos.* || **4 prickings,** remordimientos, escrúpulos.

prickle | ˌprɪkl | *s.c.* 1 BOT. espina, espino, pincho. 2 ZOOL. púa, aguijón. 3

[(the) –] picazón, escozor. || *v.t.* e *i.* **4** picar, causar picazón: *pure wool makes my skin prickle = la pura lana me causa picazón.* **5** sentir picazón. **6** (fig.) sentir hormigueo.

prickly | ˌprɪklɪ | *adj.* **1** espinoso, lleno de espinas. **2** lleno de púas. **3** que pica, que causa picor (la lana). **4** (fam.) malhumorado, difícil, avinagrado, destemplado (de carácter). || **5 – heat,** MED. sarpullido causado por el sol o por el calor. **6 – pear,** BOT. **a)** higo chumbo, higo de pala; **b)** chumbera, higuera de pala.

pride | praɪd | *s.i.* **1** (desp.) orgullo, altanería, arrogancia, soberbia. **2** orgullo, amor propio, dignidad. **3** orgullo, satisfacción. **4** flor y nata, lo mejor. **5** REL. orgullo (pecado). **6** temperamento (de un caballo). || *s.c.* **7 [– *v.sing./pl.*]** manada de leones. || *v.t.* **8 [to – on/ upon]** enorgullecerse de, ufanarse de, jactarse de. || **9 to have/take –,** enorgullecerse de, deleitarse en, sentirse orgulloso de. **10 to nurse one's –,** recuperar el amor propio, recuperar la dignidad perdida. **11 – and joy,** la niña de los ojos de uno, la joya más preciada, el mayor tesoro. **12 – of place,** el puesto más importante, el lugar de honor. **13 to swallow one's –,** tragarse el orgullo de uno, hacer de tripas corazón, tragarse la afrenta.

priest | priːst | *s.c.m.* sacerdote, cura, clérigo, religioso.

priestess | ˌpriːstɪs | *s.c.f.* sacerdotisa (en religiones no cristianas).

priesthood | ˌpriːsthʊd | *s.sing.* **[the –]** el sacerdocio, el clero.

priestly | ˌpriːstlɪ | *adj.* (form.) sacerdotal, pastoral, clerical: *priestly duties = deberes sacerdotales.*

prig | prɪg | *s.c.* (desp.) **1** melindroso, mojigato, gazmoño. **2** presumido, pedante, engreído (de su religiosidad y superioridad moral).

priggish | ˌprɪgɪʃ | *adj.* (desp.) **1** melindroso, mojigato, gazmoño: *a prigish old lady = una anciana mojigata.* **2** presumido, engreído, pedante.

priggishness | ˌprɪgɪʃnɪs | *s.i.* **1** mojigatería, gazmoñería. **2** presunción, engreimiento, pedantería.

prim | prɪm | *adj.* **1** (desp.) remilgado, pudibundo, excesivamente sensato, gazmoño, melindroso. **2** formalista, decoroso. **3** primoroso, pulido, pulcro, arreglado.

prima ballerina | ˌprɪmə bælə'riːnə | *s.c.* primera bailarina (en ballet).

primacy | ˌpraɪməsɪ | *s.i.* **1 [– (of/over)]** (form.) primacía, superioridad, supremacía, preeminencia. **2** REL. primacía, posición de primado.

prima donna | ˌpriːmə'dɒnə | *s.c.* **1** MUS. prima donna, primera cantante. **2** (desp.) diva, persona caprichosa, persona de carácter cambiante.

primaeval | praɪmiːvəl | *adj.* (brit.) V. **primeval.**

prima facie | ˌpraɪmə'feɪʃiː | *adj.* DER. **1** prima facie, suficiente a primera vista, suficiente para justificar la presunción de un hecho, presunto: *prima facie evidence = prueba suficiente a primera vista.* || *adv.* **2** a primera vista, presuntamente.

primal | ˌpraɪml | *adj.* (form.) **1** original, inicial, primitivo. **2** primario, primero, elemental, básico, fundamental: *primal needs = necesidades básicas.*

primarily | ˌpraɪmərɪlɪ | *adv.* (form.) **1** primordialmente, principalmente, esencialmente, ante todo. **2** primitivamente, originalmente, al principio.

primary | ˌpraɪmərɪ | (EE.UU.) | ˌpraɪ↓merɪ | *adj.* **1** primero, principal, fundamental, vital, primordial, cardinal: *a case of primary importance = un caso de vital importancia.* **2** de educación primaria (un curso, un profesor). **3** primario, original, elemental, primitivo. **4** GEOL. primario. || *s.c.* **5** (EE.UU.) POL. primarias, elección preliminar. **6** lo fundamental, lo primordial, lo principal. || **7 – colour,** color primario, color simple. **8 – education,** educación primaria. **9 – school,** (brit.) escuela primaria; (EE.UU.) escuela elemental.

primate | ˌpraɪmeɪt | *s.c.* **1** ZOOL. primate. **2** REL. primado.

prime | praɪm | *s.sing.* **1 [(the) –]** juventud, plenitud, (lo) mejor, (la) flor (de la vida): *she's 50 but still in her prime = tiene 50 años pero aún se conserva joven.* **2** REL. hora prima, primera hora del día. **3** amanecer, aurora, alba. **4** primavera. **5 [the –]** la flor y nata, lo más valioso, lo escogido. **6** DEP. primera (en esgrima). || *s.c.* **7** MAT. número primo. || *v.t.* **8** imprimar, preparar (una pared, un objeto), dar una primera mano de pintura. **9 [to – (with)]** preparar, dar instrucciones, aleccionar, informar: *she was well primed to say what I wanted = estaba bien aleccionada para decir lo que yo quería.* **10** cebar (un arma de fuego antigua). **11 [to – (with)]** cargar, llenar (una máquina de gasolina, de aceite). **12** (fig.) cargado, borracho. || **13 in the – of life,** en la flor de la vida. **14 Prime Minister,** POL. Primer Ministro. **15 – mover, a)** inspirador, instigador, incitador (de un plan, de una idea); **b)** móvil, motivo, fundamento (de una causa); **c)** fuerza motriz, fuente de energía (de una máquina); **d)** generador, motor; **e)** remolcador, tractor. **16 – number,** MAT. número primo. **17 to – the pump,** (fam.) animar el crecimiento, insuflar ánimos; invertir, meter una inyección de capital (a un negocio en baja).

primer | ˌpraɪmər | *s.c.* e *i.* **1** imprimación (para pintar). || *s.c.* **2** cartucho, carga; detonador (de una bomba). **3** (arc.) catón, silabario, cartilla, libro de texto elemental. **4** manual, compendio (de una materia).

primeval | praɪ'miːvl | (brit.) **primaeval** *adj.* primitivo, primario.

primitive | ˌprɪmɪtɪv | *adj.* **1** HIST. primitivo. **2** rudimentario, elemental. **3** (desp.) primitivo, pasado de moda, miserable, espantoso: *primitive living conditions = condiciones de vida miserables.* || *s.c.* **4** ART. primitivo (anterior al Renacimiento, o que lo imita).

primly | prɪmlɪ | *adv.* decorosamente, remilgadamente.

primordial praɪ'mɔːdɪəl | *adj.* (form.) primordial.

primrose | ˌprɪmrəuz | *s.c.* **1** BOT. prímula, primavera. || **2 – yellow,** amarillo pálido.

primula | ˌprɪmjulə | *s.c.* BOT. prímula.

prince | prɪns | *s.c.* **1** príncipe. **2 [– (among/of)]** (lit.) epítome, príncipe; persona importante, personaje influyente, poderoso: *a prince among poets = el más importante de los poetas.* || **3 Prince Charming,** (fam. y hum.) Príncipe encantador (que esperan las jovencitas). **4 Prince of Wales,** Príncipe de Gales.

princely | ˌprɪmslɪ | *adj.* **1** principesco, regio. **2** (fam.) espléndido, magnífico, muy generoso: *a princely present = un regalo magnífico.* || **3 a – sum,** una bonita suma.

princess | prɪn'ses | *s.c.f.* princesa.

principal | ˌprɪnsəpl | *adj.* **1** principal, primordial, esencial, capital, mayor. || *s.c.* **2** director, rector (de escuela, de Universidad). **3** FIN. principal, capital. **4** protagonista, actor principal. **5** MUS. cantante solista, músico solista. **6** (form.) principal, representado, jefe. **7** DER. cómplice, criminal. **8** ARQ. cimbra, cercha; jácena, viga maestra.

principality | ˌprɪnsɪ'pælɪtɪ | *s.c.* **1** principado. || **2 principalities,** REL. principado (uno de los nueve coros de ángeles).

principally | ˌprɪnsəplɪ | *adv.* principalmente, en su mayor parte.

principle | ˌprɪnsəpl | *s.c.* e *i.* **1** principio, norma, pauta, precepto. || *s.c.* **2 principio, regla, ley:** *the principle of geometry = las reglas geométricas.* **3** principio, dogma, doctrina: *based on the last economic principles = basado en las últimas doctrinas de economía.* || **4 a matter of principle,** cuestión de principios. **5 in –,** en teoría; en principio. **6 on –,** por principio, por norma.

principled | ˌprɪnsəpld | *adj.* (generalmente en combinación) de principios, basado en principios: *low-principled behaviour = comportamiento de bajos principios.*

print | prɪnt | *s.i.* **1** letra impresa. || *s.c.* **2** (en combinación) huella, marca, señal: *a footprint = una pisada.* **3** (fam.) huella digital. **4** FOT. copia, positivo. **5** grabado, estampa, dibujo, diseño. **6** sello, molde. || *s.c.* e *i.* **7** estampado (en tejido). || *v.t.* e *i.* **8** imprimir, grabar, ilustrar. **9** imprimir, editar, tirar. **10** escribir en letras de molde, escribir con letra de imprenta. || *v.t.* **11** FOT. sacar una copia. **12** publicar, sacar (en la prensa). **13** estampar (un tejido). **14** grabar, marcar, hacer marcas: *she printed her name in the sand = grabó su nombre en la arena.* || **14 in –,** publicado, impreso. **15 into –,** en la prensa, en los periódicos. **16 out of –,** agotado (un libro). **17 to – money,** (desp.) darle a la máquina del dinero. **18 to – out,** INF. imprimir, editar. **19 small/fine –,** letra pequeña, letra menuda. **20 the printed word,** la letra impresa, la información.

printable | ˌprɪntəbl | *adj.* publicable, editable, imprimible.
printer | ˌprɪntər | *s.c.* **1** impresor, trabajador gráfico; editor. **2** fotocopiadora. **3** INF. impresora.
printing | ˌprɪntɪŋ | *s.i.* **1** imprenta, tipografía. **2** escritura (a mano). || *s.c.* **3** tirada, impresión: *the book had 4 printings in a year = se sacaron 4 tiradas del libro en un año.* || **4 – press,** prensa, máquina impresora.
printout | ˌprɪntaut | *s.c.* e *i.* INF. impresión de salida.
prior | ˌpraɪər | *adj.* **1** previo, anterior, precedente: *a prior appointment = una cita previa.* **2** prioritario, más importante. || *s.c.* **3** REL. prior. || **4 – to,** (form.) antes de, previamente.
priority | praɪ'ɒrɪtɪ | *s.i.* **1 [– (over)]** prioridad, anterioridad, precedencia. **2** preferencia: *vehicles entering the roundabout have priority = los vehículos que entran en la plaza tienen prioridad.* || *s.c.* **3** prioridad, inquietud, preocupación, finalidad: *the main priority was to get the tickets = la principal preocupación era conseguir los billetes.* || **4 to give –,** dar prioridad. **5 to take/have –,** tener prioridad.
priory | ˌpraɪərɪ | *s.c.* REL. priorato.
prise | praɪz | (EE.UU. **prize**) *v.t.* **1** abrir por la fuerza, abrir con palanca; abrir una tapa con palanca. || **2 to – out,** sonsacar, conseguir con maña, obtener con halagos (información).
prism | ˌprɪzəm | *s.c.* GEOM., OPT. prisma.
prismatic | prɪz'mætɪk | *adj.* (form.) **1** prismático, en forma de prisma. **2** brillante, claro, centelleante, luminoso (un color).
prison | ˌprɪzn | *s.c.* e *i.* **1** prisión, cárcel, presidio. || *s.i.* **2** prisión, reclusión, cautiverio, encarcelamiento. **3** (fig.) prisión, cautiverio, jaula: *the house became a prison = la casa se convirtió en una prisión.* || *v.t.* **4** encarcelar, recluir, meter en presidio. || **5 – camp,** campamento de prisioneros (de guerra).
prisoner | ˌprɪzjnər | *s.c.* **1** preso, recluso, convicto, detenido. **2** prisionero, cautivo. || **3 to hold someone –,** mantener a uno preso, tener en prisión a uno. **4 – of war,** prisionero de guerra. **5 to take someone –,** hacer prisionero a uno, apresar a uno.
prissy | ˌprɪsɪ | *adj.* (form. y desp.) escrupuloso, remilgado, afectado, melindroso.
pristine | ˌprɪstaɪn | *adj.* (form.) prístino, inmaculado, primero, original, primigenio, puro.
privacy | ˌprɪvəsɪ | *s.i.* **1** privacidad, intimidad, soledad. **2** secreto, ocultación, reserva.
private | ˌpraɪvɪt | *adj.* **1** privado, íntimo, confidencial, personal, secreto: *private documents = documentos privados.* **2** privado, particular, propio: *private property = propiedad particular.* **3** privado, independiente, no estatal, particular (una industria, la educación, un banco, etc...): *she gets some private lessons = le dan unas clases particulares.* **4** privado, personal, extraoficial: *a private visit = una visita no oficial.* **5** privado, solitario, retirado, aislado (un lugar). **6** callado, reservado, solitario, casero (una persona). || *s.c.* **7** MIL. soldado raso. || **8 to be –,** estar a solas. **9 in –,** en privado, en secreto. **10 – detective,** detective privado, investigador privado. **11 – enterprise,** empresa privada. **12 – eye,** (EE.UU. y fam.) detective privado, investigador privado. **13 – member's bill,** POL. proposición de ley particular. **14 – parts/privates,** (euf.) genitales, partes pudendas. **15 – school,** escuela privada, colegio privado. **16 – sector,** ECON. sector privado.
privately | ˌpraɪvɪtlɪ | *adv.* **1** privadamente, en privado, en secreto, a puerta cerrada: *the talks were held privately = las conversaciones se tuvieron a puerta cerrada.* **2** personalmente, en particular: *I privately thought it wasn't a good idea = personalmente pensé que no era una buena idea.* **3** íntimamente, en la intimidad. **4** extraoficialmente.
privation | praɪ'veɪʃn | *s.c.* e *i.* (form.) privación, estrechez.
privatization | ˌpraɪvɪtaɪ'zeɪʃn | *s.i.* ECON. privatización (de industrias, servicios gubernamentales).
privatize | ˌpraɪvɪtaɪz | (brit. **privatise**) *v.t.* ECON. privatizar (industrias, servicios gubernamentales).
privatized | ˌpraɪvɪtaɪzd | (brit. **privatised**) *adj.* ECON. privatizado.
privet | ˌprɪvɪt | *s.i.* BOT. ligustro, aligustre, alheña.
privilege | ˌprɪvɪlɪdʒ | *s.c.* e *i.* **1** privilegio, prerrogativa, ventaja, gracia. || *s.c.* **2** privilegio, honor, oportunidad, favor especial: *working with her was a privilege = fue un privilegio trabajar con ella.* || *v.t.* **3** privilegiar, conceder privilegios. **4** liberar, eximir.
privileged | ˌprɪvɪlɪdʒd | *adj.* **1** privilegiado, afortunado: *only some privileged people could go = sólo algunos afortunados pudieron ir.* **2** (desp.) con privilegios, que gozan de privilegios: *some privileged students = algunos alumnos que gozan de privilegios.*
privy | ˌprɪvɪ | *adj.* **1 [– to]** informado de, enterado de, al tanto de: *he was privy to all the details = estaba informado de todos los detalles.* **2** (arc.) secreto, privado, reservado, oculto. || *s.c.* **3** (arc.) retrete, servicio. || **4 Privy Council,** (brit.) Consejo Privado del rey o la reina.
prize | praɪz | *s.c.* **1** premio, galardón. **2** (fig.) recompensa, retribución. **3** HIST. buque apresado, botín. **4** presa, víctima: *the lion was eating up the prize = el león devoraba a su presa.* || *adj.* **5** premiado, galardonado: *the prize book = el libro premiado.* **6** de premio, ofrecido como premio: *the prize medal was real gold = la medalla del premio era de oro.* **7** perfecto, clásico, de primera clase: *a prize example = un ejemplo clásico.* **8** (fam.) completo, de remate: *he's a prize fool = está loco de remate.* || *v.t.* **9** apreciar, estimar, valorar: *this material is most prized = este tejido es muy apreciado.* **10** (brit.) **prise [to – *o.* + *adv./prep.*]** levantar con palanca, mover a palanca, palanquear, abrir por la fuerza: *prizing the lid off the tin with a knife = forzando la tapa del bote con un cuchillo.* || **11 no prizes for guessing,** (fam.) extremadamente fácil de adivinar. **12 to – out (of),** conseguir por la fuerza, sacar con engaño (información).
prize-fighter | ˌpraɪzfaɪtər | *s.c.* boxeador profesional.
prize-giving | ˌpraɪzgɪvɪŋ | *s.c.* e *i.* ceremonia de entrega de premios (en la escuela).
pro | prəu | [*pl.* **pros**] *s.c.* **1** (fam.) profesional. **2** (brit., fam. y arc.) prostituta. || *prep.* **3** pro, a favor de, partidario de: *are you pro or anti abortion? = ¿estás a favor o en contra del aborto?* || prefijo. **4 [pro- *adj./s.*]** pro, a favor de: *pro-American = proamericano; pro-English = anglófilo.* **5** en lugar de, en sustitución de: *pronoun = pronombre.* || **6 – rata,** prorrata, en proporción. **7 – tem,** (fam.) temporalmente, por el momento, de forma interina. **8 the pros and cons,** los pros y los contras.
probability | ˌprɒbə'bɪlɪtɪ | *s.c.* e *i.* **1 [– (of)]** probabilidad, posibilidad. || **2 in all –,** muy probablemente, sin duda.
probable | ˌprɒbəbl | *adj.* probable, verosímil, posible.
probably | ˌprɒbəblɪ | *adv.* probablemente, posiblemente, sin duda, a lo mejor: *he's probably thinking he's going to pass = a lo mejor piensa que va a aprobar.*
probation | prə'beɪʃn | (EE.UU.) | prəu'beɪʃn | *s.i.* **1** período de prueba, prueba (antes de dar un contrato laboral). **2** DER. libertad provisional, libertad vigilada. || **3 on –,** a prueba, en período de prueba: en libertad condicional. **4 – officer,** agente judicial de vigilancia (para alguien en libertad condicional).
probationary | prə'beɪʃnrɪ | (EE.UU.) | prəu'beɪʃənerɪ | (también **probational**) *adj.* probatorio, de prueba (un período de tiempo).
probationer | prə'beɪʃnər | *s.c.* **1** enfermera en período de prueba. **2** persona en libertad condicional, delincuente en libertad vigilada.
probe | prəub | *s.c.* **1** MED. sonda; cala, tienta; excavador. **2** BOT. antena, tentáculo. **3** (también **space –**) sonda espacial, nave de exploración espacial. **4 [– (into)]** PER. investigación, indagación, averiguación, interrogatorio. || *v.t.* e *i.* **5** tentar, explorar, registrar, examinar: *probing all through the garden with a torch = examinando todo el jardín con una linterna.* **6** MED. sondar, explorar. **7 [to – (into)]** (fig.) indagar, investigar, averiguar.
probing | prəubɪŋ | *s.i.* investigación, indagación.
probity | ˌprəubɪtɪ | *s.i.* (form.) probidad, honestidad, rectitud, honradez, integridad.

problem | ˌprɒbləm | *s.c.* **1** problema, dificultad. **2** MAT. problema. || *adj.* **3** difícil, que da problemas (un niño). || **4 no –,** (fam.) seguro, no hay problema.
problematic | prɒblɪ'mætɪk | (también **problematical**) *adj.* **1** problemático, complicado, lleno de problemas, lleno de dificultades. **2** dudoso, incierto, discutible.
problematical | prɒblə'mætɪkl | *adj.* V. **problematic.**
proboscis | prəʊ'bɒsɪs | **1** (form.) ZOOL. probóscide, trompa. **2** (fam.) trompa, nariz prominente.
procedural | prə'siːdjʊrəl | *adj.* **1** DER. procesal, de procedimiento.
procedure | prə'siːdʒər | *s.c.* e *i.* procedimiento, fórmula, trámite.
proceed | prə'siːd | *v.i.* (form.) **1 [to – (to/with)]** proceder, ir, continuar, seguir su curso, seguir adelante (con una acción, un proceso): *can we proceed with the plan? = ¿puedo seguir adelante con el plan?* **2 [to –** *adv./prep.***]** proceder, avanzar, trasladarse, proseguir: *we proceeded north = avanzamos hacia el norte.* || **3 to – against,** DER. procesar a, proceder contra. **4 to – from,** (form.) proceder de, originarse en. **5 proceeds,** ganancias, ingresos (de una venta).
proceeding | prə'siːdɪŋ | *s.c.* (generalmente *pl.*) **1** procedimiento, medida, trámite. **2** (form.) acto, función, práctica. || **3 proceedings, a)** actas de sesiones (de un club, asociación); **b)** DER. procedimientos, acciones legales, trámites.
process | ˌprəʊses | (EE.UU.) | 'prɒses | *s.c.* **1** proceso, avance, desarrollo, progresión. **2** procedimiento, sistema, técnica, método. **3** ANAT. protuberancia, bulto, excrecencia. **4** DER. proceso, causa, expediente. **5** fotograbado, fotomecánica (en imprenta). || *v.t.* **6** tratar, procesar, elaborar. **7** FOT. procesar, elaborar (una película). **8** someter a examen, estudiar (una petición). **9** INF. procesar (textos). || *v.i.* **10** ir en procesión, desfilar. || *adj.* **11** procesado, elaborado con procedimientos especiales. **12** FOT. fotograbado fotomecánico. || **13 to be in the – of,** estar en proceso de, estar en: *the tower is in the process of construction = la torre está en construcción.* **14 in the –,** al mismo tiempo, mientras tanto, durante el proceso.
processed | prə'sest | *adj.* elaborado, tratado, preparado: *processed materials = materiales elaborados.*
processing | prə'sesɪŋ | *s.i.* elaboración, tratamiento, preparación.
procession | prə'seʃn | *s.c.* **1** desfile, cabalgata, parada; cortejo, comitiva. **2** (fig.) procesión, ir y venir. || *s.c.* e *i.* **3** procesión, movimiento. **4** sucesión, avance: *the procession of the years = el paso de los años.*
processional | prə'seʃənl | *adj.* **1** procesional. || *s.c.* **2** procesionario (libro). **3** himno procesionario, música de procesión.
proclaim | prə'kleɪm | *v.t.* **1** (form.) proclamar, anunciar, declarar oficialmente, divulgar. **2** (lit.) proclamar, ser signo de, mostrar, indicar: *her way of dressing proclaimed that she was Asian = su forma de vestir indicaba que provenía de Asia.* **3** elogiar, ensalzar.
proclamation | ˌprɒklə'meɪʃn | *s.c.* **1** proclamación, declaración. **2** proclama, anuncio, edicto.
proclivity | prə'klɪvɪtɪ | *s.c.* propensión, tendencia, inclinación, predisposición.
procrastinate | prəʊ'kræstɪneɪt | *v.i.* (form. y desp.) aplazar, retrasar, demorar, retardar, diferir (un asunto, una decisión).
procrastination | prəʊˌkræstɪ'neɪʃn | *s.i.* (form. y desp.) aplazamiento, retraso, demora, dilación.
procreate | ˌprəʊkrɪeɪt | *v.t.* e *i.* (form.) procrear, reproducir, engendrar.
procreation | prəʊkrɪ'eɪʃn | *s.i.* (form.) procreación, reproducción.
procurator | ˌprɒkjʊəreɪtər | *s.c.* DER. **1** procurador. **2** HIST. procurador. || **3 – fiscal,** fiscal (especialmente en Escocia).
procure | prə'kjʊər | | prəʊ'kjʊə | *v.t.* **1 [to – (for)]** (form.) procurar, obtener, adquirir, conseguir, lograr (con esfuerzo). **2** (p.u.) causar, motivar, ocasionar. || *v.t.* e *i.* **3** (desp. y lit.) proporcionar una prostituta a otro, hacer de alcahuete, presentar una prostituta a un cliente.
procurement | prə'kjʊəmənt | *s.i.* adquisición, obtención, consecución.
procurer | prə'kjʊərər | *s.c.m.* **1** (desp.) alcahuete. **2** proveedor (de bienes para una organización).
procuress | prə'kjʊərɪs | *s.c.f.* (desp.) alcahueta, madama.
prod | prɒd | [*pret.* y *p.p.* **prodded**] *v.t.* e *i.* **1 [to – (at)]** pinchar, picar, aguijonear. **2 [to – (at)]** empujar con el dedo, señalar con el dedo; dar un codazo. || *v.t.* **3 [to – (into)]** (fig.) estimular, urgir, apremiar, acuciar, meter prisa: *sometimes they need to be prodded = a veces necesitan que se les meta prisa.* || *s.c.* **4** pinchazo, picotazo. **5** (fig.) empujón, estímulo; recordatorio, advertencia. **6** aguijada, pincho.
prodding | prɒdɪŋ | *s.i.* aviso, recordatorio, estímulo.
prodigal | ˌprɒdɪgl | *adj.* **1** (desp.) pródigo, derrochador, gastador, despilfarrador: *when she's got money she's quite prodigal = cuando tiene dinero es bastante derrochadora.* **2 [– (of)]** (form.) pródigo, exuberante, abundante, profuso: *trees prodigal of fruit = árboles con abundante fruta.* || *s.c.* **3** (form. y hum.) pródigo, despilfarrador, derrochador, gastador.
prodigious | prə'dɪdʒəs | *adj.* (lit.) **1** prodigioso, colosal, impresionante, tremendo. **2** extraordinario, excepcional, maravilloso. **3** portentoso.
prodigiously | prə'dɪdʒəslɪ | *adv.* (lit.) **1** prodigiosamente, colosalmente, de forma impresionante. **2** extraordinariamente, excepcionalmente. **3** portentosamente.
prodigy | ˌprɒdɪdʒɪ | *s.c.* **1** prodigio, portento: *a child prodigy = un niño prodigio.* **2** maravilla, prodigio (de la naturaleza).
produce | prə'djuːs | *v.t.* **1** producir, dar (un fruto, una sustancia). **2** producir, elaborar, hacer, crear, inventar. **3** producir, parir (un animal). **4** sacar, mostrar, presentar, exhibir: *he produced some sweets from his pocket = sacó unos caramelos del bolsillo.* **5** aducir, presentar (una prueba). **6** presentar al público (una obra, un libro). **7** ocasionar, producir, causar, originar: *the food produced spots in his skin = la comida le produjo granos en la piel.* **8** GEOM. prolongar, alargar, extender (una línea). || *v.t.* e *i.* **9** manufacturar, fabricar: *it produces 100 items per hour = fabrica 100 elementos por hora.* || | ˌprɒdjuːs | | ˌprəʊduːs | *s.i.* **10** producto, producción.
producer | prə'djuːsər | *s.c.* **1** productor, fabricante, proveedor (un país, una compañía, una persona). **2** productor (de cine, de teatro).
product | ˌprɒdʌkt | *s.c.* **1** producto, fruto. **2** (fig.) producto, resultado, consecuencia: *unemployement as a product of the crisis = desempleo como producto de la crisis.* **3 [– (of)]** MAT. producto.
production | prə'dʌkʃn | *s.i.* **1** presentación, exhibición. **2** producción, elaboración, fabricación: *the production of vehicles has decreased = la producción de vehículos ha descendido.* || *s.c.* **3** producción, obra, producto. || **4 to make a – out of,** (fam.) montar una película a causa de, montar un número por. **5 – line,** línea de montaje, cadena de producción.
productive | prə'dʌktɪv | *adj.* **1** productivo, prolífico: *a very productive film director = un director de cine muy prolífico.* **2** fértil, fructífero, provechoso, útil: *a productive experience = una experiencia fructífera.* **3** productivo, lucrativo. **4** (form.) productor, causante, resultante: *productive of dispute = causante de disputas.*
productively | prə'dʌktɪvlɪ | *adv.* productivamente, provechosamente.
productivity | prɒdʌk'tɪvɪtɪ | *s.i.* productividad, rendimiento.
prof | prɒf | *s.c.* (juv. y hum.) profe, profesor.
profane | prə'feɪn | *adj.* **1** profano, irreverente, sacrílego, irrespetuoso (un acto). **2** blasfemo, fuerte, obsceno (el lenguaje). **3** (form.) profano, no religioso (arte). || *v.t.* **4** profanar.
profanity | prə'fænɪtɪ | *s.c.* e *i.* irreverencia, blasfemia, obscenidad, sacrilegio (en el lenguaje).
profess | prə'fes | *v.t.* (form.) **1** confesar, alegar, reconocer, admitir (generalmente con falsedad): *she professed to know nothing about computers = confesó no tener ni idea de informática.* **2** profesar, declarar, manifestar (una creencia, sentimiento). **3** profesar (una religión).
profession | prə'feʃn | *s.c.* **1** profesión, carrera, trabajo, oficio. **2 [the –** *v.sing./pl.***]** profesionales, cuerpo: *the legal profession = la abogacía, los profesionales de la abogacía.* **3 [– (of)]**

(form.) profesión, declaración, aserción.
professional | prəˈfeʃənl | *adj.* **1** [no *comp.*] profesional, de carrera: *a professional actor = un actor profesional.* **2** de profesional, de experto: *a very professional job = un trabajo de experto.* **3** [no *comp.*] (euf.) DEP. intencionada (una falta). || (también **pro**) *s.c.* **4** profesional, experto, perito. **5** DEP. jugador profesional.
professionalism | prəˈfeʃnəlɪzəm | *s.i.* profesionalismo.
professionally | prəˈfeʃnəlɪ | *adv.* **1** profesionalmente, como profesional. **2** expertamente, con pericia, con gran habilidad.
professor | prəˈfesər | *s.c.* **1** (brit.) catedrático (de Universidad). **2** (EE.UU.) profesor, instructor.
professorial | ˌprɒfɪˈsɔːrɪəl | *adj.* (form.) profesoral, de profesor.
professorship | prɒˈfesəʃɪp | *s.c.* cátedra, puesto profesoral.
proffer | ˌprɒˈfər | *v.t.* **[to – (to)]** (form.) **1** ofrecer, brindar, tender: *he proffered his hand to me = me ofreció su mano.* **2** (fig.) ofrecer, proponer, brindar, dar (consejos, amistad). || *s.c.* **3** oferta, proposición, propuesta.
proficiency | prəˈfɪʃnsɪ | *s.i.* **1 [– (at/in)]** habilidad, pericia, destreza. **2** rendimiento, aprovechamiento: *a proficiency test = un examen de rendimiento.*
proficient | prəˈfɪʃnt | *adj.* **1 [– (at/in)]** experto, versado, experimentado, competente. || *s.c.* **2** perito, conocedor.
profile | ˌprəʊfaɪl | *s.c.* **1** perfil, silueta: *she has a nice profile = tiene un perfil agradable.* **2** atractivo, característica. **3** PER. perfil, biografía, descripción: *a profile of British romantic painters = un perfil de los pintores británicos románticos.* **4** gráfico. || *v.t.* **5** PER. perfilar, hacer una breve biografía, describir. || **6 in –,** de perfil. **7 to keep a low –,** mantenerse en segundo plano, actuar con discreción.
profit | ˌprɒfɪt | *s.c.* e *i.* **1** beneficio, ganancia, rendimiento, rentabilidad. || *s.i.* **2** (form.) utilidad, provecho, aprovechamiento. || *v.t.* **3 [to –** *o. (indirecto) + o. (directo)***]** (form.) beneficiar, ser de provecho, tener utilidad. || **4 to – by /from,** sacar provecho de, beneficiarse de.
profitability | ˌprɒfɪtəˈbɪlɪtɪ | *s.i.* rentabilidad, rendimiento, beneficios.
profitable | ˌprɒfɪtəbl | *adj.* **1** rentable, productivo, lucrativo, ventajoso. **2** útil, valioso, provechoso: *a profitable course = un curso provechoso.*
profitably | ˌprɒfɪtəblɪ | *adv.* **1** rentablemente, ventajosamente, de forma lucrativa. **2** útilmente, provechosamente.
profiteer | ˌprɒfɪˈtɪər | *s.c.* (desp.) **1** buitre, acaparador (de bienes para sacarles rendimiento en períodos de escasez). || *v.i.* **2** acaparar (bienes), vender a precios abusivos (en períodos de escasez).
profiteering | ˌprɒfɪˈtɪərɪŋ | *s.i.* acaparamiento, ganancias abusivas (al vender en períodos de escasez).
profit-making | ˌprɒfɪtˌmeɪkɪŋ | *s.i.* **1** rentabilidad, ganancias, beneficios. || *adj.* **2** rentable, lucrativo (un negocio).
profit-sharing | ˌprɒfɪtˌʃeərɪŋ | *s.i.* participación en beneficios, reparto de beneficios.
profligacy | ˌprɒflɪgəsɪ | *s.i.* **1** prodigalidad, derroche, despilfarro. **2** (form.) libertinaje, licencia, relajación.
profligate | ˌprɒflɪgɪt | *adj.* **1** pródigo, derrochador, despilfarrador. **2** (form.) libertino, inmoral, licencioso. || *s.c.* **3** (form.) pródigo, derrochador, despilfarrador. **4** libertino, inmoral, licencioso.
profound | prəˈfaʊnd | *adj.* **1** profundo, intenso, extremo, vehemente, agudo, marcado: *a profound dislike = una marcada aversión.* **2** profundo, serio, inteligente, sabio. **3** (lit.) profundo, hondo: *a profound well = un pozo profundo.* **4** profundo, completo, total: *he's a profound imbecile = un completo imbécil.*
profoundly | prəˈfaʊndlɪ | *adv.* **1** profundamente, intensamente, vehementemente. **2** profundamente, completamente, totalmente.
profundity | prəˈfʌndɪtɪ | *s.i.* (form.) **1** profundidad, seriedad, erudición, inteligencia. **2** profundidad, grandeza (de un sentimiento). || **3 profundities,** ideas profundas, pensamientos profundos.
profuse | prəˈfjuːs | *adj.* **1** profuso, copioso, cuantioso, abundante: *profuse tears = abundantes lágrimas.* **2** pródigo, generoso.
profusely | prəˈfjuːslɪ | *adv.* profusamente, copiosamente, abundantemente.
profusion | prəˈfjuːʒn | *s.i.* (form.) profusión, abundancia, copiosidad, exceso, prodigalidad.
progenitor | prəʊˈdʒenɪtər | *s.c.* (form.) **1** progenitor, antepasado, ancestro. **2** precursor.
progeny | ˌprɒdʒɪnɪ | *s.i.* [– *v.sing./pl.*] **1** (form.) progenie, descendientes. **2** (hum.) prole.
prognoses | prɒgˈnəʊsiːz | [*pl.*] V. **prognosis.**
prognosis | prɒgˈnəʊsɪs | [*pl.* **prognoses**] *s.c.* (form.) **1** MED. pronóstico. **2** pronóstico, prognosis, predicción.
prognostication | prəgˌnɒstɪˈkeɪʃn | *s.c.* e *i.* (form.) pronosticación, pronóstico.
program | ˌprəʊgræm | *s.c.* **1** INF. programa. **2** (EE.UU.) programa, proyecto, plan. **3** TV. programa, espacio. **4** programa (de actividades, de teatro, etc...). || *v.* [*pret.* y *p.p.* **programmed** o **programed**] *t.* **5** INF. introducir un programa, programar.
programme | ˌprəʊgræm | (brit. **program**) *s.c.* **1** programa (de teatro, actividades, etc...). **2** TV. programa, espacio. **3** programa, proyecto, plan. || *v.t.* **4** programar: *the alarm clock is programmed for 6.00 = el despertador está programado para las 6.*
programmer, programer | ˌprəʊgræmər | *s.c.* INF. programador.
programming | ˌprəʊgræmɪŋ | *s.i.* INF. programación.
progress | ˌprəʊgres | | ˈprɑːgres | *s.i.* **1** progreso, avance, movimiento hacia delante, marcha. **2** progreso, desarrollo, mejora. || *s.c.* **3** (arc.) viaje oficial (de reyes). || | prəʊˈgres | *v.i.* **4** progresar, avanzar, marchar hacia delante. **5** progresar, hacer progresos, mejorar. **6** viajar. || **7 in –,** en proceso de realización, en vías de realización.
progression | prəˈgreʃn | *s.i.* **1** progresión, secuenciación. || *s.c.* **2** MAT. progresión. **3** MUS. sucesión, secuencia (de acordes).
progressive | prəˈgresɪv | *adj.* **1** [no *comp.*] progresivo, gradual (un movimiento). **2** POL. progresista, radical, de ideas avanzadas. **3** [no *comp.*] progresivo (un impuesto). **4** [no *comp.*] GRAM. progresivo, continuo (un tiempo verbal). || *s.c.* **5** POL. progresista, radical.
progressively | prəˈgresɪvlɪ | *adv.* progresivamente, cada vez (más, mejor, etc...).
prohibit | prəˈhɪbɪt | | prəʊˈhɪbɪt | *v.t.* **1 [to – (from)]** (form.) prohibir, vedar, restringir: *smoking is prohibited in the classrooms = prohibido fumar en las clases.* **2** impedir, entorpecer, dificultar: *her illness prohibits her from moving = su enfermedad le impide moverse.*
prohibition | ˌprəʊɪˈbɪʃn | *s.c.* e *i.* **1** prohibición, restricción. **2** (EE.UU.) prohibicionismo.
prohibitionist | ˌprəʊɪˈbɪʃnɪst | *s.c.* prohibicionista.
prohibitive | prəˈhɪbɪtɪv | | prəʊˈhɪbɪtɪv | *adj.* prohibitivo, excesivo (un precio).
prohibitively | prəˈhɪbɪtɪvlɪ | *adv.* prohibitivamente.
project | ˌprɒdʒekt | *s.c.* **1** proyecto, investigación. **2** plan, esquema. | prəˈdʒekt | *v.t.* e *i.* **3** proyectar(se), sobresalir, resaltar. **4** vender, ofrecer, hacer propaganda de (ciertas cualidades para obtener una ventaja). **5 [to – (on/onto)]** proyectar(se), cargar (los malos sentimientos propios sobre otros). || *v.t.* **6** (generalmente pasiva) proyectar, planear, programar (una acción). **7** calcular, estimar, prever (crecimiento, ventas, etc...). **8 [to – (into/onto)]** proyectar, pasar (una película, diapositivas). **9** proyectar, emitir, difundir (un sonido, una luz).
projectile | prəʊˈdʒektaɪl | | prəʊˈdʒektl | *s.c.* **1** (form.) proyectil. || *adj.* **2** arrojadizo. **3** ZOOL. que sobresale, protuberante, abultado.
projection | prəˈdʒekʃn | *s.c.* **1** saliente, protuberancia. **2** planificación, plan, cálculo, suposición. **3** proyección (imagen, sonido). || *s.i.* **4** proyección (de imagen, sonido). **5** PSIC. proyección (de sentimientos, deseos).
projectionist | prəˈdʒekʃənɪst | *s.c.* operador de cabina.
projector | prəˈdʒektər | *s.c.* **1** proyector (máquina, de luz). **2** planificado, proyectista.
proletarian | ˌprəʊlɪˈteərɪən | *adj.* (generalmente desp.) **1** proletario. || *s.c.* **2** proletario.

proletariat | ˌprəʊlɪ'teərɪət | *s.sing.* **[the** – *v.sing./pl.*] el proletariado, la clase trabajadora.
proliferate | prəʊ'lɪfəreɪt | *v.i.* proliferar, multiplicarse, extenderse, abundar.
proliferating | prəʊ'lɪfəreɪtɪŋ | *adj.* que prolifera, que se multiplica, que abunda: *proliferating shops anywhere = tiendas que proliferan por todas partes.*
proliferation | prəʊˌlɪfə'reɪʃn | *s.i.* **1** proliferación, multiplicación, abundancia. || *s.c.* **2** BIOL. multiplicación.
prolific | prəʊ'lɪfɪk | *adj.* prolífico, fértil, productivo, fecundo.
prolix | ˌprəʊlɪks | | prəʊ'lɪks | *adj.* (form.) prolijo, detallado, tedioso, pesado, extenso (discurso, escritor, texto).
prologue | ˌprəʊlɒg | (EE.UU.) | ˌprəʊlɔːg | (EE.UU. **prolog**). *s.c.* **1** LIT. prólogo, prefacio. **2 [– (to)]** preludio, introducción: *her speech was a prologue to protests = su discurso fue el preludio de las protestas.*
prolong | prə'lɒŋ | | prə'lɔːŋ | *v.t.* prolongar, dilatar, retardar, alargar, extender.
prolongued | prə'lɒŋd | *adj.* prolongado, dilatado, extenso.
prom | prɒm | *s.c.* **1** (brit. y fam.) concierto con localidades de pie; concierto al aire libre. **2** (brit. y fam.) paseo, alameda (al lado del mar). **3** (EE.UU.) baile de etiqueta (en colegios y Universidades).
promenade | ˌprɒmə'nɑːd | (EE.UU.) | prɒmə'neɪd | *s.c.* **1** (brit. **prom**) paseo, alameda (al lado del mar). **2** (form.) paseo, caminata, vuelta. || *v.t.* e *i.* **3** (form. y arc.) pasear, salir de paseo, dar una vuelta. || *v.t.* **4** (desp.) pasear, llevar a dar una vuelta (a alguien para presumir). || **5 – concert,** concierto con localidades de pie.
prominence | ˌprɒmɪnəns | *s.i.* **1** preeminencia, importancia, notabilidad, distinción. || *s.c.* **2** (form.) prominencia, protuberancia, abultamiento.
prominent | ˌprɒmɪnənt | *adj.* **1** prominente, protuberante, sobresaliente. **2** destacado, visible, perceptible (un lugar). **3** notable, sobresaliente, eminente, famoso, significativo.
prominently | ˌprɒmɪnəntlɪ | *adv.* **1** destacadamente, visiblemente, de forma perceptible. **2** notablemente, significativamente.
promiscuity | ˌprɒmɪ'skjuːɪtɪ | *s.i.* **1** (desp.) promiscuidad, libertinaje (sexual). **2** (form.) promiscuidad, mezcolanza, confusión, desorden. **3** (form.) indiscriminación.
promiscuous | ˌprə'mɪskjʊəs | *adj.* **1** (desp.) promiscuo, libertino (sexual). **2** (form.) confuso, mezclado, desordenado. **3** (form.) indiscriminado.
promiscuously | prə'mɪskjʊəslɪ | *adv.* promiscuamente.
promise | ˌprɒ'mɪs | *s.c.* **[– (of)] 1** promesa, palabra, compromiso. || *s.i.* **2** promesa, expectativa, esperanza: *some writers of promise = algunos escritores que prometen.* || *v.t.* e *i.* **3** prometer, dar palabra, comprometerse. || *v.t.* **4** prometer, pronosticar, presagiar: *her good humor promised a nice evening = su buen humor prometía una tarde agradable.* || **5 to – someone the moon/ the earth,** (fam.) prometer la luna a alguien.
promising | ˌprɒmɪsɪŋ | *adj.* prometedor, halagüeño, que promete: *a promising painter = un pintor que promete.*
promissory note | ˌprɒmɪsərɪ 'nəʊt | *s.c.* V. **note.**
promontory | ˌprɒməntrɪ | | ˌprɑːməntɔːrɪ | *s.c.* promontorio, acantilado.
promote | prə'məʊt | *v.t.* **1** ascender, promover, subir (de rango, de posición): *she has just been promoted = acaban de ascenderla.* **2** adelantar, pasar de curso (escolar). **3** promover, alentar, apoyar: *he's promoting a new show = es el promotor del nuevo espectáculo.* **4** presentar (una ley). **5** anunciar, hacer propaganda de, hacer publicidad de: *promoting a new product = hacer propaganda de un producto nuevo.* **6** (form.) favorecer, fomentar: *promoting peace = fomentando la paz.*
promoter | prə'məʊtər | *s.c.* **1** promotor, agente, empresario. **2** promotor, motor (de una causa).
promotion | ˌprə'məʊʃn | *s.c.* e *i.* **1** promoción, ascenso. **2** promoción, fomento, propaganda (de ventas). || *s.c.* **3** campaña de promoción, campaña publicitaria.
promotional | ˌprə'məʊʃənəl | *adj.* de promoción: *a promotional campaign = una campaña de promoción.*
prompt | prɒmpt | *v.t.* **1** inspirar, evocar, sugerir, traer a la memoria, hacer pensar. **2** impulsar, mover, alentar, instigar, ocasionar. **3** recordar, insinuar (algo a alguien). || *v.t.* e *i.* **4** apuntar (en teatro). || *adj.* **5** pronto, rápido, inmediato. **6** puntual, diligente, rápido (una persona). || *adv.* **7** puntualmente, a la hora en punto. || *s.c.* **8** aviso, toque, recordatorio. **9** (también **prompter**) apuntador (de teatro).
prompter | ˌprɒmptər | *s.c.* apuntador (de teatro).
prompting | ˌprɒmptɪŋ | *s.c.* e *i.* aviso, ayuda, recordatorio.
promptly | prɒmptlɪ | *adv.* puntualmente, a la hora en punto.
promptness | prɒmptnɪs | *s.i.* prontitud, puntualidad, rapidez.
promulgate | prɒmlgeɪt | *v.t.* (form.) **1** promulgar (una ley). **2** promulgar, divulgar, propagar (una idea, una creencia).
prone | prəʊn | *adj.* **1** propenso, con tendencia, susceptible, inclinado: *prone to infection = propenso a la infección.* **2** (form.) tendido boca abajo, postrado boca abajo.
prong | prɒŋ | | prɔːŋ | *s.c.* púa, diente, punta.
-pronged | prɒŋd | *sufijo.* **1** de... púas, de... dientes: *a three-pronged fork = un tenedor de tres puntas.* **2** (fig.) en... flancos, en... direcciones: *a two-pronged attack = un ataque en dos direcciones.*
pronominal | prəʊ'nɒmɪnl | *adj.* GRAM. pronominal.
pronoun | ˌprəʊnaʊn | *s.c.* GRAM. pronombre.
pronounce | prə'naʊns | *v.t.* **1** pronunciar, articular, emitir (sonidos). **2 [to – *o.* + *adj./s.*]** declarar, proclamar, anunciar: *the judge pronounced them free = el juez los declaró libres.* || *v.i.* **3 [to – *prep.*]** DER. pronunciarse, expresar una opinión: *she pronounced against the trip = se pronunció contra el viaje.*
pronounced | prə'naʊnst | *adj.* **1** pronunciado, obvio, marcado, notable: *a very pronounced accent = un acento muy marcado.* **2** tajante, decidido, terminante, resuelto (un punto de vista, una opinión).
pronouncement | prə'naʊnsmənt | *s.c.* (form.) pronunciamiento, declaración solemne.
pronto | ˌprɒntəʊ | *adv.* (fam.) pronto, al momento, en seguida, presto.
pronunciation | prəˌnʌnsɪ'eɪʃn | *s.c.* e *i.* pronunciación.
proof | pruːf | *s.c.* e *i.* **1 [– (of)]** prueba, comprobación, evidencia. || *s.c.* **2** prueba, demostración, examen. **3** prueba, galerada (de imprenta). **4** MAT. prueba, demostración. || *s.i.* **5** graduación (del alcohol). || *adj.* **6 [– (against)]** a prueba de, protegido contra, resistente a: *proof against robbers = a prueba de ladrones.* **7** de graduación, de grado (alcohólico). || *v.t.* **8 [to – (against)]** impermeabilizar, someter a prueba de (especialmente agua). || *sufijo* **-proof 9** a prueba de, resistente a: *water-proof = impermeabilizado.* || **10 the – of the pudding is in the eating,** el movimiento se demuestra andando.
proof-read | ˌpruːfˌriːd | *v.t.* e *i.* [*pret.* y *p.p.* **proof-read**] corregir pruebas, corregir galeradas (en imprenta).
proof-reader | ˌpruːfˌriːdər | *s.c.* corrector de pruebas, corrector de galeradas.
prop | prɒp | *s.c.* **1** puntal, poste, entibo, horquilla, rodrigón. **2** (fig.) sostén, soporte: *the prop in his old age = el sostén de su vejez.* **3** (también **property**) (fam.) atrezzo escenográfico, accesorios de escena (en teatro). **4** (también **propeller**) (fam.) AER. hélice. || *v.t.* [*pret.* y *p.p.* **propped**] **5 [to – *o.* + *adv./prep.*]** sostener, sujetar, apoyar: *she propped the ladder against the wall = apoyó la escalera contra la pared.* **6** apuntalar, postear, entibar (un edificio, un árbol). || **7 to – something up,** (desp.) sostener, apoyar, mantener (económicamente).
propaganda | ˌprɒpə'gændə | *s.i.* (desp.) propaganda (generalmente oficial).
propagandist | ˌprɒpə'gændɪst | *s.c.* **1** (desp.) propagandista. || *adj.* **2** propagandístico.
propagandize | ˌprɒpə'gændaɪz | (brit. **propagandise**) *v.t.* e *i.* (desp.) hacer propaganda de, adoctrinar a.
propagate | ˌprɒpəgeɪt | *v.t.* e *i.* **1** propagar(se), multiplicar(se). || *v.t.* **2** (form.) propagar, difundir, divulgar, extender, diseminar (ideas, información).

propagation | ˌprɒpə'geɪʃn | *s.i.* **1** propagación, multiplicación, generación, procreación. **2** propagación, difusión, divulgación, diseminación.
propane | ˌprəupeɪn | *s.i.* QUIM. propano.
propel | prə'pel | *v.t.* [*pret.* y *p.p.* **propelled**] **1** propulsar, impulsar, impeler, empujar. || **2 propelling pencil,** lapicera, lapicero portaminas.
propellant | prə'pelənt | (también **propellent**) *s.c.* e *i.* **1** carga de proyección, explosivo. **2** propulsor (gas). || *adj.* **3** propulsor, impelente.
propeller | prə'pelər | *s.c.* hélice (de barco, de avión).
propensity | prə'pensɪtɪ | *s.c.* **[– (for /to/towards)]** (form.) propensión, tendencia, inclinación, disposición.
proper | ˌprɒpər | *adj.* **1** [no *comp.*] correcto, adecuado, apropiado: *proper baby food = alimento adecuado para bebés.* **2** (desp.) respetable, decente, oportuno, conveniente (vestido, comportamiento). 3 (fam.) verdadero, de verdad, real, auténtico, genuino: *she's only had a proper holiday once = sólo una vez ha disfrutado de unas verdaderas vacaciones.* **4** [*s.* **+ –**] propiamente dicho, mismo, exacto: *she's just started the course proper = acaba de empezar el curso propiamente dicho.* **5** [no *comp.*] (brit. y fam.) total, completo, absoluto, verdadero: *a proper cleaning = una limpieza en condiciones.* **6 [– to]** (form.) propio de, natural de, perteneciente a: *proper to liquids = propio de los líquidos.* || *adv.* **7** (fam.) realmente, completamente, totalmente, muy. || **8 – noun,** GRAM. nombre propio.
properly | ˌprɒpəlɪ | *adv.* **1** correctamente, adecuadamente, apropiadamente. **2** realmente, en realidad, exactamente, propiamente: *properly speaking, she's not one of the family = en realidad no es un miembro de la familia.* **3** (brit. y fam.) completamente, totalmente, verdaderamente, absolutamente: *she seemed properly bored = parecía absolutamente aburrida.*
propertied | ˌprɒpətɪd | *adj.* (form.) acomodado, adinerado, acaudalado, propietario.
property | ˌprɒpətɪ | *s.i.* **1** propiedad, posesión, pertenencia: *personal property = objetos personales.* **2** propiedad, hacienda: *property in the centre is going up = el suelo en el centro está subiendo.* || *s.c.* **3** propiedad, finca, casa, bienes muebles: *she owns several properties = posee varias fincas.* **4** propiedad, cualidad, atributo, característica: *healing properties = propiedades curativas.* **5** [generalmente *pl.*] (form.) atrezzo escenográfico, accesorios de escena (en teatro).
prophecy | ˌprɒfɪsɪ | *s.c.* e *i.* profecía, predicción.
prophesy | ˌprɒfɪsaɪ | *v.t.* e *i.* profetizar, predecir, vaticinar.
prophet | ˌprɒfɪt | | ˌprɑːfɪt | *s.c.m.* **1** REL. profeta. **2** (fig.) profeta, difusor, abogado (de una causa). **3** profeta, vaticinador.
prophetess | ˌprɒfɪtɪs | *s.c.f.* profetisa, vaticinadora.
prophetic | prə'fetɪk | (también **prophetical**) *adj.* profético.
prophetically | prə'fetɪkəlɪ | *adv.* proféticamente.
prophylactic | prɒfɪ'læktɪk | *adj.* (form.) MED. **1** profiláctico, preventivo. || *s.c.* **2** profiláctico.
prophylaxis | ˌprɒfɪ'læksɪs | [*pl.* **prophylaxes**] *s.i.* (form.) MED. profilaxis, tratamiento preventivo.
propinquity | prə'pɪŋkwɪtɪ | *s.i.* **[– (of/to)]** (form.) **1** propincuidad, cercanía, proximidad. **2** consanguinidad, parentesco.
propitiate | prə'pɪʃɪeɪt | *v.t.* (form.) sosegar, apaciguar, aplacar, calmar.
propitiation | prəˌpɪʃɪ'eɪʃn | *s.i.* **[– (for)]** apaciguamiento, aplacamiento, sosiego.
propitiatory | prə'pɪʃɪətərɪ | | prə'pɪʃɪətɔːrɪ | *adj.* (form.) propiciatorio, expiatorio, conciliatorio.
propitious | prə'pɪʃəs | *adj.* **[– (for/to /towards)]** (form.) propicio, ventajoso, favorable, oportuno: *a propitious time = un momento propicio.*
proponent | prə'pəunənt | *s.c.* defensor, partidario, abogado: *an active nature proponent = un activo defensor de la naturaleza.*
proportion | prə'pɔʃn | *s.i.* **1** proporción, simetría. **2** MAT. proporción. || *s.c.* e *i.* **3 [– (of)]** parte, fracción, porción, porcentaje, número: *a large proportion of them were left-handed = un gran porcentaje de ellos eran zurdos.* || *v.t.* **4 [to – (to)]** (form.) adecuar, adaptar, ajustar a proporción, proporcionar. || **5 a sense of –,** un sentido de la medida, un sentido de la proporción. **6 to get something out of –,** sacar las cosas de quicio. **7 in –,** en proporción, en relación. **8 in – to /with,** en proporción a, en relación con. **9 out of all –,** totalmente desproporcionado, muy exagerado. **10 -proportioned,** proporcionado: *well-proportioned = bien proporcionado.* **11 proportions,** dimensiones, medidas.
proportional | prə'pɔːʃənl | *adj.* **1 [– (to)]** proporcional, en proporción. **2** proporcionado, a medida. **3** MAT. proporcional. || **4 – representation,** POL. representación proporcional del electorado.
proportionally | prə'pɔːʃnəlɪ | *adv.* proporcionalmente, en proporción.
proportionate | prə'pɔːʃnət | *adj.* **1 [– (to)]** proporcionado, en la debida proporción: *a rise proportionate to the age = una subida en proporción a la edad.* || *v.t.* **2** adecuar, adaptar, hacer proporcional.
proportionately | prə'pɔːʃnɪtlɪ | *adv.* proporcionadamente.
proposal | prə'pəuzl | *s.c.* e *i.* **1** proposición, propuesta, oferta, sugerencia. || *s.c.* **2** propuesta matrimonial, declaración de amor.
propose | prə'pəuz | *v.t.* **1** proponer, sugerir, plantear, ofrecer (un candidato, una idea, un plan). **2** (form.) tener en mente, tener intención de, planear, pensar: *I propose a break next week = tengo intención de tomar un descanso la semana que viene.* **3** (form.) brindar, ofrecer un brindis: *he proposed a toast to our trip = brindó por nuestro viaje.* || *v.t.* e *i.* **4 [to – (to)]** proponer matrimonio, pedir la mano, declararse.
proposed | prə'pəuzd | *adj.* planeado, pensado, intencionado.
proposer | prə'pəuzər | *s.c.* proponente.
proposition | ˌprɒpə'zɪʃn | *s.c.* **1** proposición, materia, tesis. **2** propuesta, oferta, plan, sugerencia: *his proposition wasn't accepted = su sugerencia no fue aceptada.* **3** (fam.) asunto, proyecto, empresa, problema: *a difficult proposition = un asunto difícil.* **4** (euf.) proposición (amorosa, sexual). **5** LOG. proposición. **6** MAT. proposición, teorema. || *v.t.* **7** (fam.) hacer una proposición (amorosa, sexual).
propound | prə'paund | *v.t.* (form.) proponer, plantear, presentar, exponer (un asunto, un problema).
proprietary | prə'praɪətərɪ | (EE.UU.) | prə'praɪəterɪ | *adj.* **1** patentado: *a proprietary cleaning material = un producto de limpieza patentado.* **2** de propietario, de dueño: *proprietary air = aire de propietario.* **3** privado, exclusivo. || *s.c.* **4** propietario, dueño. **5** (EE.UU.) HIST. propietario, dueño (de una colonia). **6** medicina patentada, fórmula patentada. || *s.i* **7** propiedad, derecho de propiedad, posesión.
proprietor | prə'praɪətər | *s.c.m.* propietario, dueño (de un negocio, de una patente).
proprietorial | prəˌpraɪə'tɔːrɪəl | *adj.* (form.) **1** de propietario, de propiedad: *proprietorial rights = derechos que poseen los propietarios.* **2** típico de propietario, de dueño, de amo: *proprietorial manners = comportamientos típicos de propietario.*
proprietorship | prə'praɪətəʃɪp | *s.i.* derecho de propiedad, posesión.
proprietress | prə'praɪətrɪs | *s.c.f.* propietaria, dueña (de un negocio, de una patente).
propriety | prə'praɪətɪ | *s.i.* **1** corrección, educación, modales, compostura, decoro. **2** conveniencia, adecuación, interés, utilidad: *I doubt the propriety of the plan = dudo de la conveniencia del plan.* || **3 proprieties,** las convenciones, los cánones sociales.
propulsion | prə'pʌlʃn | *s.i.* propulsión.
prosaic | prəu'zeɪɪk | *adj.* **1** prosaico, aburrido, falto de interés. **2** prosaico, vulgar, ordinario, poco imaginativo.
prosaically | prəu'zeɪɪkəlɪ | *adv.* prosaicamente, vulgarmente.
proscenium | prəu'siːnɪəm | | prə'siːnjəm | *s.c.* proscenio (de un teatro).
proscribe | prəu'skraɪb | *v.t.* **1** (form.) proscribir, prohibir (por ley). **2** denunciar, condenar. **3** (arc.) proscribir, publicar el nombre de un proscrito.
proscription | prəu'skrɪpʃn | | prə'skrɪpʃn | *s.c.* e *i.* **1** proscripción, prohibición. **2** proscripción, condición de proscrito.

prose | prəuz | *s.i.* 1 LIT. prosa. || *s.c.* 2 (brit.) ejercicio de traducción (a una lengua extranjera): *have you finished your English prose? = ¿has acabado tu ejercicio de inglés?* 3 REL. himno (que se canta después del gradual).

prosecute | ˌprɒsɪkjuːt | *v.t.* e *i.* 1 **[to – (for)]** DER. procesar, demandar, proceder legalmente contra: *trespassers will be prosecuted = se procederá legalmente contra los intrusos.* || *v.i.* 2 DER. acusar, querellarse. || *v.t.* 3 (form.) proseguir, continuar, seguir adelante con.

prosecution | ˌprɒsɪ'kjuːʃn | *s.c.* e *i.* DER. 1 procesamiento, proceso, demanda. 2 **[the –** *v.sing./pl.***]** acusación, parte acusadora. || *s.i.* 3 prosecución, continuación, proseguimiento (de una acción).

prosecutor | ˌprɒsɪkjuːtər | *s.c.* DER. acusador, querellante, demandante.

proselytize | ˌprɒsɪlɪtaɪz | (brit. **proselytise**) *v.t.* e *i.* (form. y desp.) hacer proselitismo, ganar adeptos, convertir.

prospect | ˌprɒspekt | *s.c.* e *i.* 1 **[– (of)]** esperanza, confianza, expectativa. || *s.i.* 2 **[– (of)]** perspectiva, probabilidad, posibilidad: *little prospect of reducing the military service = posibilidad remota de reducir el servicio militar.* || *s.c.* 3 vista, panorama, perspectiva: *a fantastic prospect of the town = una fantástica vista de la ciudad.* 4 posible candidato, posible cliente, comprador en perspectiva. || *v.t.* e *i.* 5 **[to – (for)]** realizar una prospección, explorar, buscar (oro, petróleo). || 6 **prospects,** probabilidades de éxito, expectativas de futuro, posibilidades de promoción.

prospective | prə'spektiv | *adj.* 1 probable, posible, presunto, supuesto: *a prospective client = un posible cliente.* 2 inminente, esperado: *a prospective closing of shipyards = un inminente cierre de astilleros.*

prospector | prə'spektər | *s.c.* prospector, buscador (de oro, petróleo).

prospectus | prə'spektəs | *s.c.* prospecto, programa, folleto informativo.

prosper | ˌprɒspər | *v.i.* 1 prosperar, florecer, progresar, triunfar (financieramente). 2 mejorar, crecer sano. || *v.t.* 3 (arc.) favorecer, proteger, hacer triunfar, hacer progresar.

prosperity | prɒ'sperɪtɪ | *s.i.* prosperidad, buena fortuna, éxito, bienestar.

prosperous | ˌprɒspərəs | *adj.* próspero, floreciente.

prostate | ˌprɒsteɪt | (también **prostate gland**) *s.c.* ANAT. próstata, glándula prostática.

prostitute | 'prɒstɪtjuːt | (EE.UU.) | 'prɒstɪtuːt | *s.c.f.* 1 prostituta, ramera. || *v.t.* (form.). 2 (fig.) prostituir, vender (el talento). || *v.r.* 3 prostituir(se) (una mujer).

prostitution | ˌprɒstɪ'tjuːʃn | (EE.UU.) | ˌprɒstɪ'tuːʃn | *s.i.* prostitución.

prostrate | ˌprɒstreɪt | | prɒ'streɪt | *v.r.* 3 postrarse, arrodillarse. || *v.t.* 4 (generalmente pasiva) postrar, humillar, abatir.

prostration | prɒ'streɪʃn | *s.i.* 1 postración. 2 postración, humillación, abatimiento.

prosy | ˌpreuzɪ | *adj.* prosaico, pesado, aburrido, tedioso (un discurso, un escrito).

protagonist | prəu'tægənɪst | *s.c.* 1 protagonista, mentor, defensor, dirigente (de una idea). 2 LIT. protagonista, héroe, carácter principal. 3 DEP. campeón.

protean | prəu'tiːən | | prəu'tɪən | *adj.* (lit.) proteico, versátil, inconstante.

protect | prə'tekt | *v.t.* 1 **[to – (against /from)]** proteger, defender, amparar, custodiar. 2 ECON. proteger arancelariamente, favorecer, ayudar (la industria, el comercio). 3 **[to – (against)]** FIN. asegurar (contra pérdida, desastre).

protection | prə'tekʃn | *s.i.* 1 protección, custodia, defensa, amparo: *protection of the army = la protección del ejército.* 2 (también **protection money**) (fam. y euf.) canon de protección, dinero de extorsión (que se paga a una organización criminal). 3 ECON. proteccionismo, protección (a la industria, al comercio). || *s.c.* 4 protección, elemento protector: *she was wearing gloves as a protection for her hands = llevaba guantes para proteger sus manos.* 5 pase, salvoconducto, pasaporte.

protectionism | prə'tekʃənɪzəm | *s.i.* (generalmente desp.) ECON. proteccionismo.

protectionist | prə'tekʃənɪst | *s.c.* ECON. 1 proteccionista. || *adj.* 2 proteccionista.

protective | prə'tektɪv | *adj.* 1 [no *comp.*] protector, defensor, de protección: *protective paint = pintura de protección.* 2 **[– (towards)]** protector, deseoso de proteger: *protective towards her friends = deseosa de proteger a sus amigos.* 3 preventivo.

protectively | prə'tektɪvlɪ | *adv.* protectoramente, de modo protector.

protectiveness | prə'tektɪvnɪs | *s.i.* protección, proteccionismo.

protector | prə'tektər | *s.c.* 1 protector, defensor, guardián. 2 protector, defensa: *knee protectors = protectores para las rodillas.* 3 (arc.) HIST. regente (príncipe o noble en lugar del rey).

protectorate | prə'tektərət | *s.c.* protectorado.

protégé | ˌprɒteʒeɪ | (EE.UU.) | ˌprəutɪ'ʒeɪ | *s.c.m.* (*f.* **protégée**) protegido, favorito (por un personaje influyente).

protein | ˌprəutiːn | *s.c.* e *i.* BIOQ. proteína.

protest | ˌprəutest | *s.c.* e *i.* 1 protesta, queja, objeción, disconformidad, desacuerdo. || *s.c.* 2 DER. protesta. 3 COM. protesto. || | prə'test | *v.i.* 4 **[to – (about/against/at)]** protestar, quejarse, indignarse, abuchear. || *v.t.* 5 protestar, declarar, asegurar, afirmar: *he protested that he was wrong = aseguró que él estaba equivocado.* 6 (EE.UU.) manifestarse contra, realizar una protesta contra. 7 DER. recusar, rechazar. || 8 **under –,** contra su voluntad.

protestant | ˌprɒtɪstənt | *s.c.* 1 REL. protestante. || *adj.* 2 REL. protestante.

Protestantism | ˌprɒtɪstəntɪzəm | *s.i.* REL. protestantismo.

protestation | ˌprəute'steɪʃn | | ˌprɒte's | | teɪʃn | *s.c.* 1 (form.) declaración, afirmación (solemne, enérgica): *protestations of innocence = declaración de inocencia.* || *s.i.* 2 protesta, queja, objeción.

protester | prə'testər | *s.c.* manifestante.

protocol | ˌprəutəkɒl | *s.c.* e *i.* protocolo.

proton | ˌprəutɒn | *s.c.* FIS. protón.

protoplasm | ˌprəutəuplæzəm | *s.i.* BIOL. protoplasma.

prototype | ˌprəutəutaɪp | *s.c.* prototipo, original.

protract | prə'trækt | (EE.UU.) | prəu'trækt | *v.t.* 1 (desp.) prolongar, alargar, dilatar: *he protracted the discussion = alargó la discusión.* 2 trazar con transportador (en dibujo). 3 ANAT. extender, sobresalir.

protracted | prə'træktɪd | (EE.UU.) | prəu'træktɪd | *adj.* extenso, prolongado, dilatado.

protractor | prə'træktər | (EE.UU.) | prəu'træktər | *s.c.* 1 transportador (instrumento de dibujo). 2 ANAT. músculo tensor.

protrude | prə'truːd | (EE.UU.) | prəu'truːd | *v.i.* 1 **[to – (from)]** (form.) sacar fuera, sobresalir, destacarse, resaltar: *his head protruding from the window = su cabeza que sobresalía por la ventana.* || *v.t.* 2 (form.) empujar hacia afuera, hacer salir.

protruding | prə'truːdɪŋ | (EE.UU.) | prəu'truːdɪŋ | *adj.* sobresaliente, prominente, saltón.

protrusion | prə'truːʒn | (EE.UU.) | prəu'truːʒn | *s.c.* 1 prominencia, protuberancia, saliente, bulto, proyección. || *s.i.* 2 prominencia, relieve.

protuberance | prə'tjuːbərəns | (EE.UU.) | prəu'tuːbərəns | *s.c.* protuberancia, prominencia, bulto, chichón.

protuberant | prə'tjuːbərənt | (EE.UU.) | prəu'tuːbərənt | *adj.* 1 (form.) prominente, sobresaliente, abultado. 2 saltón.

proud | praud | *adj.* [*comp.* **prouder,** *super.* **proudest**] 1 orgulloso, digno: *they're poor but proud = son pobres pero orgullosos.* 2 (desp.) orgulloso, altanero, engreído, soberbio, vano. 3 **[– (of)]** orgulloso, satisfecho, contento, encantado: *he's proud of her daughter = está orgulloso de su hija.* 4 gratificante, glorioso, memorable: *a proud day = un día glorioso.* 5 magnífico, espléndido, imponente. 6 (brit.) sobresaliente, prominente, en proyección, saliente, que resalta. || 7 **to do someone –,** (fam.) tratar a alguien espléndidamente, ser muy hospitalario con alguien, dar buena vida a alguien. 8 **– as a peacock,** engreído como un pavo real. 9 **someone's proudest possession,** la más preciada posesión de alguien.

proudly | ˌpraudly | *adv.* 1 orgullosamente, con orgullo, con dignidad. 2 altivamente, arrogantemente, con engreimiento, soberbiamente.

provable | ˌpruːvəbl | *adj.* comprobable, verificable, demostrable (una teoría).
prove | pruːv | *v.t.* [*pret.* y *p.p.* **proved,** (EE.UU.) *p.p.* **proven**] **1** probar, demostrar, hacer ver: *the documents proves him innocent = los documentos prueban que es inocente.* **2** confirmar, verificar. **3** DER. verificar, autentificar (un testamento). **4** experimentar, sufrir. || *v.i.* **5** resultar, venir a ser, salir, comprobarse: *it proved easier than I thought = resultó más fácil de lo que pensaba.* || **6 the exception proves the rule,** la excepción confirma la regla.
proven | pruːvən | (brit. **proved**). *adj.* **1** comprobado, verificado, demostrado. || **2 not –,** DER. no probado, sin pruebas (en Escocia).
provenance | ˌprɒvɪnəns | *s.i.* (form.) procedencia, origen.
provender | ˌprɒvɪndər | *s.i.* **1** (arc.) pienso, forraje. **2** (fam. y hum.) provisiones, comida.
proverb | ˌprɒvəːb | *s.c.* proverbio, refrán.
proverbial | prəˈvəːbjəl | *adj.* **1** proverbial. **2** relativo al dicho, al refrán (popular).
proverbially | prəˈvəːbjəlɪ | *adv.* proverbialmente.
provide | prəˈvaɪd | *v.t.* **1 [to – (for /with)]** suministrar, proporcionar, facilitar, dar: *it provides shelter = proporciona cobijo.* **2 [to – that]** (form.) disponer que, ordenar que, estipular que (una ley, un acuerdo): *the law provides for pensions = la ley estipula pensiones.* || **3 to – against, a)** tomar precauciones contra, tomar medidas contra; **b)** prohibir, impedir. **4 to – for, a)** mantener, alimentar, sustentar; **b)** prever, prepararse para. **c)** estipular, disponer.
provided | prəˈvaɪdɪd | (también **provided that, providing, providing that**). *conj.* si, con tal que, siempre que, siempre y cuando, a condición de que: solo sí: *come, provided (that) you get the money = ven, siempre y cuando consigas el dinero.*
providence | ˌprɒvɪdəns | *s.i.* **1** providencia, destino. **2** (arc.) prevención, previsión, vista. **3** prudencia, economía.
providential | prɒvɪˈdenʃl | *adj.* (form.) providencial, milagroso, afortunado.
providentially | ˌprɒvɪˈdenʃəlɪ | *adv.* providencialmente, milagrosamente, afortunadamente.
provider | prəˈvaɪdər | *s.c.* proveedor, suministrador, abastecedor.
providing | prəˈvaɪdɪŋ | *conj.* V. **provided.**
province | ˌprɒvɪns | | ˌprɑːvɪns | *s.c.* **1** HIST. provincia, departamento (romanos). **2** rama, campo, especialidad: *a topic outside my province = un tema que no es de mi especialidad.* **3** competencia, incumbencia, jurisdicción. **4** REL. diócesis. || **5 provinces,** provincias.
provincial | prəˈvɪnʃl | *adj.* **1** [no *comp.*] provincial, de provincia. **2** (desp.) provinciano, rústico, de pueblo, paleto. || *s.c.* **3** provinciano. **4** REL. arzobispo; padre provincial.
provincialism prəˈvɪnʃəlɪzəm | *s.c.* e *i.* (desp.) provincianismo.
provision | prəˈvɪʒn | *s.i.* **1 [– (of)]** provisión, abastecimiento, suministro. **2 [– (against/for)]** previsión, prevención: *provision against fire = prevención contra el fuego.* || *s.c.* **3** disposición, estipulación, cláusula (en un contrato). || *v.t.* **4 [to – (for)]** aprovisionar, abastecer, surtir, equipar: *provisioned for a long siege = aprovisionados para un largo asedio.* || *adj.* **5** de aprovisionamiento, de abastecimiento (un barco). | **6 to make – for,** proveerse de, prepararse para, asegurarse el porvenir. **7 provisions,** alimentos, provisiones.
provisional | prəˈvɪʒənl | *adj.* provisional, transitorio, temporal, interino, potencial.
provisionally | prəˈvɪʒnəlɪ | *adv.* provisionalmente, transitoriamente, temporalmente.
proviso | prəˈvaɪzəʊ | [*pl.* **provisos**] *s.c.* cláusula, disposición, estipulación, condición.
provocation | ˌprɒvəˈkeɪʃn | *s.i.* **1** provocación, incitación. || *s.c.* **2** reto, desafío, estímulo.
provocative | prəˈvɒkətɪv | *adj.* **1** provocativo, erótico, sugestivo. **2** provocador, incitador.
provocatively | prəˈvɒkətɪvlɪ | *adv.* **1** provocativamente, sugestivamente. **2** provocadoramente.
provoke | prəˈvəʊk | *v.t.* **1 [to – (in to/to)]** provocar, irritar, excitar, poner nervioso. **2** provocar, suscitar, causar, motivar, producir: *his behaviour provoked a violent reaction = su comportamiento provocó una reacción violenta.*
provost | ˌprɒvəst | , (EE.UU.) | ˌprəʊvəst | *s.c.* **1** (brit.) director, rector (de un colegio universitario). **2** alcalde, jefe de la corporación municipal (en ciudades escocesas). **3** REL. prepósito, superior. **4** director de prisión, guardián de prisión.
prow | praʊ | *s.c.* (lit.) MAR. proa.
prowess | ˌpraʊɪs | *s.c.f.* (lit.) **[– (as/ at/in)] 1** destreza, aptitud, habilidad. **2** valentía, valor, coraje.
prowl | praʊl | *v.t.* e *i.* **1** merodear, acechar, rondar (animales, ladrones). **2** vagar, rondar, ir de un lado a otro. || *s.c.* **3** ronda, acecho, merodeo. || **4 on the –,** al acecho. **5 – car,** (EE.UU.) coche patrulla, (Am.) radiopatrulla.
prowler | ˌpraʊlər | *s.c.* (fam.) merodeador, hombre que ronda en busca de mujeres.
proximity | prɒkˈsɪmɪtɪ | *s.i.* **[– (of/to)]** (form.) proximidad, cercanía.
proxy | ˌprɒksɪ | *s.i.* **1** poder, procuración, representación, delegación. || *s.c.* **2** apoderado, representante, delegado, sustituto. || **3 by –,** por poderes, mediante sustituto (un matrimonio, una votación).
prude | pruːd | *s.c.* (desp.) puritano, mojigato, remilgado.
prudence | ˌpruːdns | *s.i.* (form.) prudencia, discreción, sensatez, seriedad, juicio.
prudent | ˌpruːdnt | *adj.* (form.) prudente, discreto, juicioso, sensato, serio, cauto.
prudently | ˌpruːdnlɪ | *adv.* prudentemente, con discreción, con sensatez, juiciosamente, con cautela.
prudery | ˌpruːdərɪ | (también **prudishness**). *s.i.* (desp.) puritanismo, mojigatería, remilgo.
prudish | ˌpruːdɪʃ | *adj.* (desp.) puritano, mojigato, gazmoño, remilgado.
prudishness | ˌpruːdɪʃnɪs | *s.i.* V. **prudery.**
prune | pruːn | *v.t.* **1** podar, desramar, mochar, cortar. **2 [to – (away/down)]** recortar, reducir, cortar (un discurso, gastos). || *s.c.* **3** ciruela pasa, pruna.
pruning | pruːnɪŋ | *s.i.* **1** poda, desrame. || **2 – hook,** podadera.
prurience | ˌprʊərɪəns | *s.i.* sensualidad, lascivia, salacidad, libido.
prurient | ˌprʊərɪənt | *adj.* (form.) lascivo, salaz, sensual, libidinoso.
pry | praɪ | *v.i.* **[to – (into)]** (desp.) entrometerse, fisgonear (en las vidas de otros). || *v.t.* **2** (EE.UU. **prise**) abrir con palanca, forzar, levantar por la fuerza (una caja, una tapadera).
PS | ˌpiːˈes | (**postscript**) postdata.
psalm | sɑːm | | sɑːlm | *s.c.* salmo, cántico religioso.
psephology | seˈfɒlədʒɪ | (EE.UU.) | siːˈfɑːlədʒɪ | *s.i.* psefología, tratado del voto.
pseud | sjuːd | | suːd | *s.c.* (brit., fam. y desp.) seudoentendido (en arte, literatura).
pseudonym | ˈsjuːdənɪm | (EE.UU.) | ˈsuːdənɪm | *s.c.* seudónimo.
psych | saɪk | *v.t.* **1 [to – out]** (EE.UU. y argot) alterar, poner nervioso, conturbar, minar la confianza (mentalmente a un oponente). **2 [to – out]** conocer por intuición, intuir: *I psych her out immediately = intuí cómo era en seguida.* || *v.r.* **3 [to – up]** (EE.UU. y argot) prepararse mentalmente, mentalizarse, concentrarse (para una competición). || *s.i.* **4** psicología. || **5 psyched up,** concentrado, mentalizado.
psyche | ˈsaɪkɪ | *s.sing.* PSIC. psique, alma.
psychedelic | ˌsaɪkɪˈdelɪk | *adj.* **1** psicodélico, alucinógeno. **2** ART. psicodélico.
psychiatric | ˌsaɪkɪˈætrɪk | *adj.* psiquiátrico.
psychiatrist | ˌsaɪkaɪətrɪst | *s.c.* psiquiatra.
psychiatry | saɪˈkaɪətrɪ | *s.i.* MED. psiquiatría.
psychic | ˈsaɪkɪk | (también **psychical**) *adj.* **1** adivino, con poderes psíquicos (persona). **2** [no *comp.*] psíquico, mental. || *s.c.* **3** médium, vidente (espiritista).
psychical | ˈsaɪkɪkl | *adj.* V. **psychic.**
psycho | ˈsaɪkəʊ | *s.c.* **1** (fam.) psicópata. || *prefijo* **2** psico: *psycholinguistics = psicolingüística.*
psychoanalyse | ˌsaɪkəʊˈænəlaɪz | (EE.UU. psychoanalyze). *v.t.* psicoanalizar.

psychanalysis | ˌsaɪkəʊəˈnæləsɪs | *s.i.* psicoanálisis.

psychoanalyst | ˌsaɪkəʊˈænəlɪst | *s.c.* psicoanalista.

psychoanalytic | ˌsaɪkəʊˈænəlɪtɪk | *adj.* psicoanalítico.

psychological | ˌsaɪkəˈlɒdʒɪkl | *adj.* **1** psicológico, mental. || **2 – warfare,** guerra psicológica. **3 the – moment,** (fam.) el momento oportuno, el momento idóneo.

psychologically | saɪkəˈlɒdʒɪkəlɪ | *adv.* psicológicamente.

psychologist | saɪˈkɒlədʒɪst | *s.c.* psicólogo.

psychology | saɪˈkɒlədʒɪ | *s.i.* psicología.

psychopath | ˈsaɪkəʊpæθ | *s.c.* psicópata.

psychopathic | ˌsaɪkəʊˈpæθɪk | *adj.* psicopático, psicópata.

psychosis | saɪˈkəʊsɪs | [*pl.* **psychoses**] *s.c.* e *i.* psicosis.

psychosomatic | ˌsaɪkəʊsəʊˈmætɪk | | ˌsaɪkəsəˈmætɪk | *adj.* psicosomático.

psychotherapist | ˌsaɪkəʊˈθerəpɪst | *s.c.* psicoterapeuta.

psychotherapy | ˌsaɪkəʊˈθerəpɪ | *s.i.* MED. psicoterapia.

psychotic | saɪˈkɒtɪk | *adj.* **1** psicótico, psicópata. || *s.c.* **2** psicópata.

PT | ˌpiːˈtiː | *s.i.* **1** *abreviatura* de **physical training,** educación física, gimnasia. **2** *abreviatura* de **Pacific Time,** hora del Pacífico.

PTA | ˌpiːtiːˈeɪ | *s.c.* **1** *abreviatura* de **Parent Teacher Asociation,** Asociación de Padres y Profesores.

pterodactyl | ˌterəʊˈdæktɪl | *s.c.* ZOOL. pterodáctilo.

pub | pʌb | (también **public house**). *s.c.* **1** (brit.) bar, taberna, tasca, cantina. || **2 – crowl,** (fam.) de bar en bar, (ir de) bares: *we all went on a pub crowl after the meeting = después de la reunión nos fuimos todos de bares.*

puberty | ˌpjuːbətɪ | *s.i.* pubertad, adolescencia.

pubescent | pjuːˈbesnt | *adj.* púber, pubescente, adolescente.

pubic | ˌpjuːbɪk | *adj.* ANAT. púbico, pubiano.

public | ˌpʌblɪk | *adj.* **1** [no *comp.*] público, general. **2** público, estatal (servicios). **3** público, conocido, sabido. || *s.sing.* **4** [**the** *v.sing./pl.*] el público, la gente. **5** [**the** *v.sing./pl.*] el público, la concurrencia, los aficionados, los espectadores; los lectores. || **6 from the – eye,** (desaparecer) de la vida cotidiana, (quitarse) de en medio. **7 to go –,** ECON. entrar en Bolsa, empezar a cotizar en Bolsa (las acciones de una empresa). **8 in –,** en público, públicamente, abiertamente. **9 in the – eye,** en el ojo del huracán, muy popular. **10 – address system,** sistema de megafonía, sistema de amplificación. **11 – bar,** (brit.) reservado de bar, de tasca, de cantina, de taberna (donde la bebida es más barata). **12 – company,** ECON. empresa que cotiza en Bolsa. **13 – convenience,** retrete público (en la calle, en estaciones). **14 – enterprise,** ECON. empresa pública, empresa estatal. **15 – house,** (brit. y form.) bar, tasca, taberna, cantina. **16 – nuisance, a)** DER. desorden público; **b)** molestia, estorbo (una persona). **17 – opinion,** opinión pública. **18 – relations,** relaciones públicas. **19 – relations officer,** encargado de las relaciones públicas (en una organización, en una compañía). **20 – school,** (brit.) escuela privada; (EE.UU.) escuela pública. **21 – sector,** ECON. sector público, sector estatal. **22 – works,** obras públicas (carreteras, edificios).

publican | ˌpʌblɪkən | *s.c.* (brit. y arc.) cantinero, tabernero, dueño de bar.

publication | ˌpʌblɪˈkeɪʃn | *s.i.* **1** publicación, divulgación (de una noticia). **2** publicación, impresión, edición, lanzamiento (de un libro, revista). || *s.c.* **3** publicación, libro, revista.

publicist | ˌpʌblɪsɪst | *s.c.* publicista.

publicity | pʌbˈlɪsɪtɪ | *s.i.* **1** publicidad, propaganda. **2** publicidad, atención, notoriedad: *he was just seeking publicity = el sólo buscaba notoriedad.* || **3 – agent,** agente publicitario.

publicize | ˌpʌblɪsaɪz | (brit. **publicise**) *v.t.* dar publicidad, dar a conocer, hacer campaña publicitaria de, divulgar.

public-spirited | ˌpʌblɪkˈspɪrɪtɪd | *adj.* cívico, modelo, ejemplar, consciente: *a public-spirited citizen = un ciudadano consciente.*

publish | ˌpʌblɪʃ | *v.t.* e *i.* **1** publicar, editar. || *v.t.* **2** (generalmente pasiva) publicar, divulgar, dar a conocer, revelar: *all the information will soon be published = pronto se dará a conocer toda la información.*

publisher | ˌpʌblɪʃər | *s.c.* editor.

publishing | ˌpʌblɪʃɪŋ | *s.i.* **1** publicación, edición. || **2 – house,** editorial, empresa editora.

puce | pjuːs | *adj.* de color castaño rojizo.

puck | pʌk | *s.c.* **1** DEP. disco de goma (en hockey). || **2 Puck,** duende, trasgo.

pucker | ˌpʌkər | *v.t.* e *i.* **1** enfurruñar(se), fruncir, arrugar (el ceño, la cara al empezar a llorar): *puckering her lips as if to cry = haciendo pucheros como si fuera a llorar.* **2** arrugar(se), fruncir(se) (una tela). || *s.c.* **3** arruga, frunce, pliegue.

puckered | ˌpʌkəd | *adj.* arrugado, lleno de arrugas, fruncido.

puckish | ˌpʌkɪʃ | *adj.* (lit. y arc.) travieso, juguetón, malicioso.

pud | pʊd | *s.c.* e *i.* (fam.) pudín, budín.

pudding | ˌpʊdɪŋ | *s.c.* e *i.* **1** pudín, budín (postre). **2** (brit. y fam.) postre, dulces. || **3 Christmas –,** V. **Christmas –. 4 plum –,** V. **plum –. 5 the proof of the – is in the eating,** V. **proof. 6 – basin,** bol para el pudín, fuente honda (para mezclar los ingredientes del pudín). **7 Yorkshire –,** V. **Yorkshire –.**

puddle | ˌpʌdl | *s.c.* **1** charco, poza. **2** mezcla de grava y arcilla, argamasa (para impermeabilizar). || *v.t.* **3** enlodar, embarrar. **4** mezclar arcilla y arena, hacer argamasa (para impermeabilizar). **5** pudelar (metales impuros).

puerile | ˌpjʊəraɪl | *adj.* (form.) pueril, infantil, inmaduro, ingenuo, tonto.

puff | pʌf | *v.i.* **1** resoplar, resollar, respirar agitadamente. || *v.t.* e *i.* **2** [**to –** *adv./prep.*] aspirar, absorber, inhalar (humo); fumar, dar caladas, chupar: *puffing a cigarette = dando caladas al cigarro.* **3** [**to –** *adv./prep.*] echar humo, lanzar humo, salir humo a bocanadas (de un vehículo). **4** hinchar(se), ufanarse (de orgullo); alabar exageradamente, magnificar, dar(se) bombo: *he kept puffing his new novel = seguía dando bombo a su nueva novela.* || *s.c.* **5** bocanada, soplido, resoplido. **6** calada, chupada (al cigarro). **7** ráfaga, soplo (de aire). **8** racha, nubecilla (de humo). **9** bullón; borla (adorno). **10** borla (de polvera). **11** buñuelo, pastelito de crema. **12** (fam.) elogio exagerado, bombo. **13** (argot) marica, homosexual. || *s.i.* **14** aliento, respiración, jadeo, resuello. || **15 huff and –,** V. **huff. 16 out of –,** sin resuello, sin aliento. **17 to – and blow/to – and pant, a)** jadear, respirar con dificultad (después de un esfuerzo); **b)** echar chispas, ponerse como una fiera. **18 – pastry,** hojaldre fino. **19 to – out,** hinchar, expandir, abullonar: *puffing his chest = hinchando el pecho.* **20 to – up,** hinchar(se), inflamarse, inflar(se) (una herida, de orgullo).

puffball | ˌpʌfbɔːl | *s.c.* BOT. bejín, pedo de lobo (hongo esférico).

puffed | pʌft | *adj.* **1** hinchado, inflamado. **2** [**– (out)**] sin resuello, sin aliento, extenuado. || **3 – sleeve,** manga abullonada. **4 – up,** engreído, henchido de orgullo, presuntuoso, jactancioso.

puffin | ˌpʌfɪn | *s.c.* ZOOL. frailecillo.

puffy | ˌpʌfɪ | *adj.* hinchado, inflamado, abultado.

pug | pʌg | *s.c.* **1** ZOOL. doguillo, dogo faldero. **2** máquina para batir arcilla. **3** huella, pisada (de animal). **4** (jerga) púgil, boxeador. || *s.i.* **5** arcilla batida. | *v.t.* [*pret.* y *p.p.* **pugged**] **6** mezclar, amasar (arcilla). **7** rellenar de arcilla, tapar con argamasa. **8** impermeabilizar (con argamasa, con arcilla). || **9 – nose,** nariz respingona, nariz chata.

pugnacious | pʌgˈneɪʃəs | *adj.* (form.) beligerante, belicoso, guerrero, agresivo.

puke | pjuːk | *v.t.* e *i.* **1** [**to – (up)**] (argot) vomitar, devolver. || *s.i.* **2** (argot) vómito.

pull | pʊl | *v.t.* e *i.* **1** tirar de, arrastrar, empujar, remolcar. **2** DEP. golpear oblicuamente, tirar (la pelota) con efecto (en béisbol, en golf). **3** remar, tirar de los remos. **4** virar, desviar, torcer (a la derecha, o a la izquierda). || *v.t.* **5** apretar, presionar (el gatillo de un arma). **6** [**to – (out/up)**] extraer, sacar, quitar, arrancar (un diente, hierbas). **7** correr, extender (una cortina). **8** dislocar, forzar, causar un tirón (a un músculo). **9** atraer, ganar (apoyo, espectadores). **10** (fig.) conquistar, seducir, enamorar: *dressed like that just to pull the girls = vestido de ese modo sólo para seducir a las chicas.* **11** [**to – (on)**] sacar, desenvainar (un arma). **12** (brit.) tirar (una cerveza de barril). **13** (EE.UU. y argot) cometer, realizar, llevar a cabo con éxito (un crimen, un robo). **14** frenar, sujetar (a un caballo para impedir que gane). **15** DEP. suavizar el golpe, golpear con poca fuerza, contener el golpe (en boxeo, para evitar la victoria). **16** imprimir, tirar (una prueba de imprenta). ‖ *v.i.* **17** tirar, dar un tirón (de la brida, un caballo). **18 [to – (at/on)]** dar una calada, chupar (un cigarro). ‖ *s.c.* e *i.* **19** tirón, estirón, golpe. **20** cuesta, pendiente, repecho, subida (con esfuerzo): *a long pull up to the top = una buena subida hasta la cima.* **21** calada, bocanada, chupada (de cigarro). **22** trago. **23** (generalmente en combinación) aldaba, llamador, tirador, cuerda: *the bellpull = el llamador.* **24** DEP. tiro desviado (en golf). ‖ *s.i.* **25** (fam.) atracción, atractivo, magnetismo, tirón: *an actress with a strong pull = una actriz con gran magnetismo.* **26** influencia, fuerza, poder, peso, cuña: *he has pull with the headmaster = tiene influencia en el director.* ‖ *v.r.* **27** arrastrarse, salir arrastrándose. ‖ **28 to be pulled off/out of,** (fam.) retirar de (la circulación), quitar de (en medio) (un objeto, una persona). **29 to – ahead (of),** adelantar velozmente (a), pasar por delante (de). **30 to – apart/to pieces, a)** separar, desunir, romper en dos; **b)** criticar severamente, destrozar (un trabajo). **31 to – at, a)** dar tirones a, tirar de (repetidamente); **b)** (arc.) dar caladas, dar chupadas (a un cigarro); **c)** (arc.) dar un buen trago, beber un buen trago. **32 to – away (from),** alejarse, marchar, salir (un vehículo, el conductor). **33 to – back, a)** MIL. retirarse; **b)** no actuar, dejar, retirarse. **34 to – down, a)** derribar, demoler, derruir, tirar (un edificio); **b)** debilitar (la salud); **c)** (fig.) hacer fracasar, hacer caer, debilitar (a una persona, a un gobierno). **35 to – a face,** V. **face. 36 to – a fast one,** V. **fast. 37 to – one's finger out,** V. **finger. 38 to – in, a)** llegar a la estación, llegar al andén (un tren); **b)** parar junto a la acera, aparcar (un vehículo); **c)** (brit. y fam.) arrestar, detener; **d)** (fam.) ganar, hacer (dinero); **e)** atraer, ganar (público). **39 to – someone's leg,** V. **leg. 40 to – off, a)** parar, aparcar (un vehículo); **b)** salir, arrancar, alejarse (un vehículo después de estar estacionado); **c)** lograr, conseguir, terminar con éxito; **d)** arrancar, quitar de un tirón, quitarse deprisa (las ropas). **41 to – out, a)** salir, marchar, arrancar (un vehículo después de estar estacionado, un tren); **b)** salir, retirar(se), apartar(se) (de una actividad poco interesante, de una situación de peligro); **c)** extraer, sacar (información). **42 to – something out of the bag,** V. **bag. 43 to – over,** estacionar(se), aparcar, echarse a un lado de la carretera (un vehículo). **44 to – out all the stops,** V. **stop. 45 to – punches,** V. **punch. 46 to – rank,** V. **rank. 47 to – round,** volver en sí (de un desmayo), recuperarse de una enfermedad. **48 to – the rug out from under,** V. **rug. 49 to – your socks up,** V. **sock. 50 to – strings,** V. **strings. 51 to – through,** recuperarse de, superar, salir de (una enfermedad, un problema, un apuro). **52 to – together, a)** trabajar en equipo, aunar esfuerzos; **b)** organizar, ordenar, coordinar, poner en orden. **53 to – oneself together,** animarse, sobreponerse, dominarse, controlarse. **54 to – up, a)** parar(se), detener(se), refrenar(se) (un vehículo, una persona); **b)** nivelar(se), ganar terreno (en una carrera, en una competición); **c)** reprender, reñir, regañar (por errores); **d)** mejorar, ayudar a mejorar (en una materia); **e)** bajar el ritmo de trabajo, tomarse las cosas con calma; **f)** arrancar, extraer, quitar, sacar. **55 to – up short/with a jerk,** detenerse a pensar, pararse y pensar. **56 to – your weight,** V. **weight. 57 to – the wool over one's eyes,** V. **wool.**

pullet | ˌpʊlɪt | *s.c.* ZOOL. pollo (de menos de un año).

pulley | ˌpʊlɪ | *s.c.* MEC. polea, garrucha.

pull-in | ˌpʊlɪn | *s.c.* (brit. y fam.) bar de carretera, restaurante de carretera.

Pullman | ˌpʊlmən | *s.c.* **1** coche pullman, coche-cama, vagón de primera. ‖ **2 Pullman train,** tren pullman, tren de lujo.

pull-out | ˌpʊlaʊt | *s.c.* **1** separata, parte despegable (de una revista). **2** MIL. evacuación, retirada. **3** AER. nivelado, restablecimiento (después de un picado).

pullover | ˌpʊlˌəʊvər | *s.c.* jersey.

pulmonary | ˌpʌlmənərɪ | | pʊlmənerɪ | *adj.* pulmonar.

pulp | pʌlp | *s.i.* **1** BOT. pulpa, carne (de una fruta, de un vegetal). **2** pulpa, masa, puré (de fruta, de vegetales). **3** pasta de madera. **4** ANAT. pulpa dentaria. **5** (EE.UU. y jerga) revista sensacionalista, basura informativa. ‖ *v.t.* e *i.* **6** reducir(se) a pulpa, hacer(se) pulpa. ‖ *adj.* **7** (desp.) sensacionalista, de mala calidad (un libro, una revista). ‖ **8 to beat/mash someone to a –,** darle una paliza a uno. **9 to reduce someone to a –,** asustar a uno, intimidar a uno.

pulpit | ˌpʊlpɪt | *s.c.* **1** púlpito. **2 [the –]** (form.) los predicadores.

pulpy | ˌpʌlpɪ | *adj.* **1** pulposo, carnoso. **2** de mala calidad, sensacionalista (una revista, un libro).

pulsate | pʌl'seɪt | | ˌpʌlseɪt | *v.i.* **1 [to – (with)]** vibrar, temblar, agitarse. **2** palpitar, latir.

pulsation | pʌl'seɪʃn | *s.c.* **1** latido, palpitación. ‖ *s.i.* **2** pulsación, palpitación.

pulse | pʌls | *s.c.* **1** ANAT. pulso, latido. **2** ritmo, cadencia. **3** RAD. impulso. **4** ELEC. pulsación. ‖ *v.i.* **5 [to – (through /with)]** latir, palpitar. **6** temblar, agitarse. **7** enviar señales a intervalos regulares. ‖ **8 to have/keep one's finger on the –,** estar a la última, conocer las últimas tendencias. **9 pulses,** BOT. legumbres, leguminosas. **10 to take someone's pulse,** tomar el pulso a alguien.

pulverize | ˌpʌlvəraɪz | (brit. **pulverise**) *v.t.* **1** moler, reducir a polvo, triturar, machacar. **2** (fam. y fig.) pulverizar, hacer polvo, destrozar, aniquilar, anonadar, cascar.

puma | ˌpju:mə | *s.c.* ZOOL. puma.

pumice | ˌpʌmɪs | (también **pumice stone**). *s.i.* **1** pómez, piedra pómez. ‖ *v.t.* **2** limpiar o suavizar o pulir con piedra pómez.

pummel | ˌpʌml | (también **pommel,** brit. **pummell**). *v.t.* golpear con los puños, dar puñetazos (repetidos): *she pummelled the table shouting = daba puñetazos sobre la mesa gritando.*

pump | pʌmp | *s.c.* **1** bomba: *a water pump = una bomba de agua.* **2** bomba, bombín, inflador (de aire). ‖ *s.sing.* **3** bombeo, extracción; inflamiento (de agua, de aire). ‖ *v.t.* **4 [to – *adv./prep.*]** inflar, llenar de aire. **5 [to – *adv./prep.*]** sacar con bomba, extraer, bombear (agua, aire). **6** mover de arriba hacia abajo: *pumping my arm up and down = moviéndome el brazo de arriba hacia abajo.* **7** (fam.) sonsacar, interrogar sin tregua. ‖ *v.i.* **8 [to – (away)]** accionar una bomba, mover una bomba (de agua, de aire). **9 [to – (away)]** latir con fuerza, palpitar violentamente. **10 [to – *adv./prep.*]** salir a borbotones, manar, brotar (un líquido). ‖ **11 petrol –,** surtidor de gasolina. **12 to prime the –,** V. **prime. 13 to – out,** (fam.) producir en enormes cantidades, abrumar continuamente. **14 to – out someone full of bullets,** llenarle a uno el cuerpo de balas. **15 to – out rounds,** disparar ráfagas (de metralleta). **16 pumps,** zapatillas de lona.

pumpernickel | ˌpʊmpənɪkl | *s.i.* pan de centeno.

pumpkin | ˌpʌmpkɪn | *s.c.* e *i.* BOT. calabaza, (Am.) zapallo (el fruto y la planta).

pun | pʌn | *s.c.* **1** retruécano, juego de palabras. ‖ *v.i.* [*pret.* y *p.p.* **punned**] **2 [to – (on/upon)]** hacer juegos de palabras, hacer retruécanos.

punch | pʌntʃ | *v.t.* **1 [to – (in/on)]** dar puñetazos, golpear con los puños. **2** picar, perforar, taladrar, horadar, agujerear. **3** INF. apretar, presionar (una tecla). ‖ *s.c.* **4 [– (in/on)]** puñetazo, golpe, trompazo. **5** punzón, taladro, perforadora. ‖ *s.i.* **6** fuerza, energía, empuje, gancho, atractivo. **7** ponche (bebida). ‖ **8 not to pull one's punches,** morderse la lengua, contenerse. **9 to pull punches, a)** contener el golpe, no emplear toda la fuerza de que uno es capaz (en una pelea); **b)** no andarse con rodeos, decir las cosas claras. **10 Punch and Judy show,** teatrillo de títeres, de marionetas. **11 to – in,** (EE.UU.) fichar a la entrada (del trabajo). **12 to – out,** (EE.UU.) fichar a la salida (del trabajo). **13 to – up,** (brit. y fam.) dar puñetazos, golpear con los puños repetidamente. **14 punching bag,** saco de arena (para entrenarse en boxeo).

punchbag | ˌpʌntʃbæg | *s.c.* DEP. saco de arena (para entrenarse en boxeo).

punchball | ˌpʌntʃbɒl | *s.c.* DEP. balón (de entrenamiento en boxeo).

punchbowl | ˌpʌntʃbəʊl | *s.c.* ponchera.
punch-drunk | ˌpʌntʃ'drʌnk | *adj.* **1** aturdido, tocado (por los golpes en boxeo). **2** (fam.) confuso, aturdido (por el trabajo, por la desgracia).
punch-line | ˌpʌntʃlaɪn | *s.c.* **1** gracia, esencia, final (de un chiste). **2** parte más ingeniosa, parte humorística (de una historia).
punch-up | ˌpʌntʃʌp | *s.c.* (brit. y fam.) riña, pelea, batalla, lucha.
punchy | ˌpʌntʃɪ | *adj.* **1** (fam.) incisivo, agudo, mordaz, ingenioso (un escrito). **2** (fam.) aturdido, tocado (por los golpes).
punctilious | pʌŋk'tɪlɪəs | *adj.* (form.) puntilloso, meticuloso, escrupuloso.
punctiliously | pʌŋk'tɪlɪəslɪ | *adv.* puntillosamente, meticulosamente, escrupulosamente.
punctual | ˌpʌŋktjʊəl | *adj.* puntual, preciso, exacto.
punctuality | ˌpʌnktjʊ'ælɪtɪ | *s.i.* puntualidad, precisión, exactitud.
punctually | ˌpʌŋktjʊəlɪ | *adv.* puntualmente, con precisión, de manera exacta.
punctuate | ˌpʌŋktjʊeɪt | *v.t.* **1** GRAM. puntuar, poner puntuación. **2** **[to – (with),** generalmente pasiva] interrumpir, cortar: *her talk was punctuated by the doorbell = su charla fue interrumpida por el timbre.*
punctuation | ˌpʌŋktjʊ'eɪʃn | *s.i.* **1** GRAM. puntuación (sistema, signos). || **2 – mark,** signo de puntuación.
puncture | ˌpʌŋktʃər | *s.c.* **1** pinchazo, perforación, picadura (especialmente en un neumático). **2** MED. punción. || *v.t.* e *i.* **3** pinchar, picar, perforar. || *v.t.* **4** (fig.) deshinchar, desinflar, demoler, dejar por los suelos, mermar (la confianza, el orgullo): *remarks that punctured her ego = comentarios que dejaron su ego por los suelos.*
punctured | ˌpʌŋktʃəd | *adj.* pinchado, picado, perforado.
pundit | ˌpʌndɪt | *s.c.* **1** (hum.) experto, erudito, sabio, maestro, autoridad: *a pundit on mind illnesses = una autoridad en enfermedades mentales.* **2** pandit, brahmán erudito.
pungency | ˌpʌndʒənsɪ | *s.i.* **1** sabor picante; olor fuerte. **2** (form.) mordacidad, incisión, sarcasmo, causticidad (en el lenguaje, la escritura).
pungent | ˌpʌndʒənt | *adj.* **1** fuerte, picante, agrio (un sabor, un olor). **2** mordaz, incisivo, sarcástico, cáustico (el lenguaje).
punish | ˌpʌnɪʃ | *v.t.* **1 [to – (for)]** castigar, penalizar, penar; multar, encarcelar. **2** (fam. y fig.) castigar, maltratar, golpear, debilitar, agotar: *he punished his oponent severely = golpeó duramente a su oponente.* **3** (fam.) devorar, agotar, reducir (reservas).
punishable | ˌpʌnɪʃəbl | *adj.* castigable, punible, penalizable, penable.
punishing | ˌpʌnɪʃɪŋ | *adj.* **1** severo, duro, agotador, debilitador. || *s.sing.* **2** (fam.) castigo, paliza, desgaste, destrozo: *I've taken a good punishing this morning = me he dado una buena paliza esta mañana.*
punishment | ˌpʌnɪʃmənt | *s.i.* **1** castigo, pena, penalización, multa, encarcelamiento: *they won't scape punishment = no escaparán al castigo.* **2** (fam.) maltrato, paliza, desgaste, destrozo. || *s.c.* **3 [– (for)]** castigo, sanción, correctivo: *an unjust punishment = un castigo injusto.*
punitive | pju:nɪtɪv | *adj.* **1** (form.) punitivo, de castigo. **2** exagerado, severo, duro, fuerte: *punitive prices = precios exagerados.*
Punjab | ˌpʌn'dʒɑ:b | *s.sing.* Punjab (estado de la India).
Punjabi | ˌpʌn'dʒɑ:bi: | *s.i.* **1** penjabi (lengua). || *s.c.* **2** penjabo (habitante de Punjab). || *adj.* **3** del Punjab, penjabo.
punk | pʌŋk | *adj.* **1** (juv.) punk (estilo de ropa, arte o diseño de esta tribu urbana). **2** (EE.UU., argot y p.u.) enfermizo, delicado, débil. **3** (EE.UU.) malo, de baja calidad, inferior. || *s.c.* **4** (también **punk rocker**) (juv.) rockero punk. **5** (EE.UU., argot y desp.) gamberro, macarra, joven antisocial. || **6 – rock,** (juv.) rock punk. **7 – rocker,** (juv.) rockero punk.
punnet | ˌpʌnɪt | *s.c.* (brit.) cesta, canasta, caja (en que se vende la fruta).
punt | pʌnt | *s.c.* **1** batea, barquita de fondo plano. **2** DEP. puntapié, patada dejando la pelota caer de las manos (en fútbol). || *v.t.* e *i.* **3** llevar en batea, transportar en batea. **4** DEP. dar un puntapié, dar una patada (sin que la pelota toque el suelo en fútbol). || *v.t.* **5** navegar en batea, impulsar la batea con percha. || *v.i.* **6** jugar contra la banca (en la ruleta). **7** (brit.) apostar (a los caballos).
punter | ˌpʌntər | *s.c.* (brit.) **1** bateador. **2** (fam.) jugador de apuestas (de caballos). **3** (fam.) consumidor, cliente (de un servicio, de un producto). **4** (vulg.) putero, putañero.
puny | ˌpju:nɪ | *adj.* (desp.) **1** débil, canijo, insignificante. **2** insignificante, pequeño.
pup | pʌp | *s.c.* **1** cría (de foca). **2** cachorro, perrito. **3** joven inexperto, novel. || *v.i.* [*pret.* y *p.p.* **pupped** *ger.* **pupping**] **4** parir cachorros. || **5 to sell someone a –,** V. **sell.**
pupa | ˌpju:pə | [*pl.* **pupas** o **pupae**] *s.c.* ZOOL. crisálida.
pupil | ˌpju:pl | *s.c.* **1** alumno, estudiante, discípulo. **2** DER. pupilo. **3** ANAT. pupila.
puppet | ˌpʌpɪt | *s.c.* **1** títere, marioneta. **2** muñeca. **3** (fig.) títere, marioneta: *a puppet manipulated by her boss = una marioneta en manos de su jefe.*
puppeteer | ˌpʌpə'tɪər | *s.c.* titiritero, marionetista.
puppy | ˌpʌpɪ | *s.c.* **1** cachorro, perrito. **2** (arc.) petimetre, lechuguino, pisaverde. || **3 – fat,** (brit. y fam.) mollas, mollete (en los bebés). **4 –/calf love,** amor de adolescente, amor juvenil.
purchase | ˌpɜ:tʃəs | *v.t.* (form.) **1** comprar, mercar, adquirir. **2** ganar, alcanzar, lograr, conquistar, conseguir (con esfuerzo). **3** elevar con palanca, subir mecánicamente. || *s.i.* **4** (form.) compra, adquisición. **5** punto de apoyo, soporte, punto de agarre (en una roca). || *s.c.* **6** (form.) compra, artículo: *she made several purchases = compró varios artículos.* **7** MEC. palanca, cabrestante, gato. || **8 – tax,** (brit.) impuesto de venta. **9 – power,** poder adquisitivo, poder de compra; valor adquisitivo (de una moneda).
purchaser | ˌpɜ:tʃəsər | *s.c.* (form.) comprador, cliente.
purdah | ˌpɜ:dɑ: | *s.i.* **1** sistema indio de reclusión y ocultamiento de la mujer. **2** cortina, biombo. || **3 in –,** en reclusión, oculto, tras el velo.
pure | pjʊər | *adj.* **1** puro, sin mezcla (un material, el sonido, el color). **2** puro, limpio, sin contaminar: *pure air = un aire puro.* **3** potable (el agua). **4** (lit.) puro, casto, virtuoso. **5** [no *comp.*] (fam.) puro, completo, mero, simple: *pure coincidence = mera coincidencia.* **6** ART. puro. **7** pura, teórica, no aplicada (una ciencia). || **8 – and,** simple, sencillamente, exclusivamente, pura y simplemente.
pure-bread | ˌpjʊəbred | *adj.* **1** de raza, de pura raza, de pura sangre. || *s.c.* **2** animal de pura sangre, animal de raza.
puree | ˌpjʊəreɪ | | pjʊ'reɪ | *s.c.* e *i.* **1** puré. || *v.t.* **2** hacer en puré.
purely | pjʊəlɪ | *adv.* **1** puramente, solamente, exclusivamente, completamente, simplemente. || **2 – and simply,** pura y simplemente, exclusivamente, sencillamente.
purgative | ˌpɜ:gətɪv | *s.c.* **1** MED. purgante, laxante. || *adj.* **2** MED. purgante, laxante, purgativo.
purgatory | ˌpɜ:gətərɪ | *s.i.* **1** purgatorio. **2** (hum.) purgatorio, sufrimiento.
purge | pɜ:dʒ | *v.t.* **1 [to – (of/from)]** POL. purgar, depurar, deshacerse de. **2 [to – (of/from)]** (lit.) purgar, purificar. **3** DER. cumplir, purgar (una sentencia), expiar (una culpa). **4** MED. purgar, evacuar. || *s.c.* **5** purga, depuración, eliminación. **6** MED. purgante, purgativo, laxante.
purification | ˌpjʊərɪfɪ'keɪʃn | *s.i.* purificación.
purify | ˌpjʊərɪfaɪ | *v.t.* **1 [to – (of)]** purificar, refinar (la sal); acrisolar (un metal); depurar, potabilizar (agua). **2** purificar, limpiar de culpa, librar de pecado. **3** POL. depurar.
purist | ˌpjʊərɪst | *s.c.* purista.
puritan | ˌpjʊərɪtən | *adj.* **1** (desp.) puritano, gazmoño, mojigato. **2** HIST. puritano. || *s.c.* **3** puritano, austero, mojigato. **4** HIST. puritano.
puritanical | ˌpjʊərɪ'tænɪkl | *adj.* (desp.) puritano, austero, riguroso.
puritanism | ˌpjʊərɪtənɪzəm | *s.i.* **1** puritanismo, rigor, austeridad. **2** HIST. puritanismo.
purity | ˌpjʊərɪtɪ | *s.i.* pureza, castidad, virginidad.
purl | pɜ:l | *s.i.* **1** punto del revés, punto invertido. **2** remate bordado o de encaje, cenefa bordada o de encaje. **3** hilo de plata o de oro (para bordar). **4** murmu-

llo, susurro (del agua). || *v.t.* e *i.* 5 TEC. tejer del revés, hacer (puntos) del revés. 6 rematar con encaje o con bordado. || *v.i.* 7 (lit.) susurrar, murmurar (el agua).

purlieus | ˌpəːljuːz | | ˌpəːrluːz | *s.pl.* 1 **[– (of)]** alrededores, cercanías, contornos, inmediaciones, afueras: *the purlieus of the town = las afueras de la ciudad.* 2 lugar frecuentado.

purloin | pəː'lɔɪn | *v.t.* (form.) hurtar, ratear, substraer.

purple | ˌpəːpl | *adj.* 1 de color púrpura, purpúreo, morado. 2 real, imperial. 3 elaborado, barroco, artificioso (el estilo). || *s.i.* 4 color púrpura, color morado. 5 púrpura (mano real). 6 rango imperial, poder real. 7 cardenalato; obispado (rango). || 8 **– hart,** (EE.UU.) medalla al valor (para soldados heridos en combate).

purplish | ˌpəːplɪʃ | *adj.* ligeramente purpúreo, purpurino, de tono morado.

purport | ˌpəːpət | *v.t.* 1 **[to – to** *v./o.***]** (form.) pretender, dar a entender, aparentar, manifestar: *it purported to finish with corruption = pretendía el fin de la corrupción.* 2 proponer, proyectar. || *s.i.* 3 **[– (of)]** (form.) significado, sentido, contenido, intención: *I didn't understand the purport of the letter = no comprendí el sentido de la carta.*

purpose | ˌpəːpəs | *s.c.* 1 propósito, intención, objetivo, razón, finalidad: *the purpose of the trip = la finalidad del viaje.* 2 uso, utilidad, fin. || *s.i.* 3 determinación, resolución, fuerza de voluntad. || *v.t.* 4 (form.) proponerse, tener intención de, proyectar, planear. || 5 **for all practical purposes,** prácticamente, en el fondo. 6 **on –,** deliberadamente, intencionadamente, a posta. 7 **to serve a –,** servir para el caso, ser de utilidad; venir al caso. 8 **to all intents and purposes,** V. **intent.** 9 **to good –,** con buenos resultados, provechosamente. 10 **to no –,** inútilmente, en vano. 11 **to the –,** (form.) pertinente, procedente, conveniente.

purpose-built | ˌpəːpəs'bɪt | *adj.* (brit.) hecho con el propósito de ser, construido expresamente para: *purpose-built AIDS hospital = un hospital construido especialmente para enfermos de SIDA.*

purposeful | ˌpəːpəsfʊl | *adj.* determinado, resuelto, intencionado: *she said it in a purposeful way = lo dijo con determinación.*

purposefully | ˌpəːpəsflɪ | *adv.* determinadamente, resueltamente.

purposeless | ˌpəːpəslɪs | *adj.* sin propósito, sin finalidad, sin objetivo concreto.

purposely | ˌpəːpəslɪ | *adv.* intencionalmente, deliberadamente, adrede, aposta.

purposive | ˌpəːpəsɪv | *adj.* (form.) intencionado, deliberado.

purr | pəːr | *v.i.* 1 ronronear (un gato). 2 (fig.) ronronear, zumbar (un motor). || *v.t.* e *i.* 3 murmurar, susurrar, musitar (una persona). || *s.sing.* 4 ronroneo. 5 zumbido (de un motor).

purring | ˌpəːrɪŋ | *s.i.* 1 ronroneo (de un gato). 2 zumbido, ronroneo (de un motor).

purse | pəːs | *s.c.* 1 (brit.) monedero, billetera. 2 (EE.UU.) bolso de mano. 3 premio (en metálico en una competición). || *s.sing.* 4 (form.) bolsillo, finanzas, gastos, recursos. || *v.t.* 5 **[to – (up)]** fruncir (los labios, la frente).

purser | ˌpəːsər | *s.c.* MAR. sobrecargo.

purse-strings | ˌpəːsstrɪŋz | *s.pl.* 1 finanzas, recursos. || 2 **to hold the –,** controlar las finanzas, disponer del dinero, tener la llave de la caja.

pursuance | pə'sjuːəns | (EE.UU.) | pə'suːəns | *s.i.* 1 prosecución, cumplimiento, ejecución. || 2 **in the – of,** en cumplimiento de, en el curso de.

pursue | pə'sjuː | (EE.UU.) | pə'suː | *v.t.* 1 perseguir, acosar, asediar, seguir la pista de, dar caza a: *pursued by ricksaw driver = acosados por conductores de ricksaw.* 2 proseguir, continuar, seguir (estudios, un plan). 3 desempeñar, dedicarse, ejercer (una profesión).

pursuer | pə'sjuːər | (EE.UU.) | pə'suːər | *s.c.* perseguidor.

pursuit | pə'sjuːt | (EE.UU.) | pə'suːt | *s.i.* 1 persecución, seguimiento, busca. 2 (fig.) prosecución, búsqueda, afán: *the pursuit of happiness = la búsqueda de la felicidad.* || *s.c.* 3 (form.) ocupación, actividad, pasatiempo, profesión: *dedicated to literary pursuits = dedicado a actividades literarias.* || 4 **in hot –,** pisando los talones, siguiendo muy de cerca.

purvey | pə'veɪ | *v.t.* (form.) 1 proveer, abastecer, suministrar. 2 propagar, divulgar, transmitir (información).

purveyor | pə'veɪər | *s.c.* (form.) 1 proveedor, abastecedor, suministrador. 2 propagador, divulgador, transmisor (de noticias).

pus | pʌs | *s.i.* pus.

push | pʊʃ | *v.t.* e *i.* 1 empujar, dar empujones, mover, impeler: *we were pushed inside = entramos a empujones.* 2 pulsar, presionar, apretar: *push the button = aprieta el botón.* 3 abrirse paso a empujones, pasar dando empujones: *pushing her way out = abriéndose paso a empujones hasta la salida.* || *v.t.* 4 **[to – (into)]** presionar, forzar, urgir, apremiar, obligar, incitar, animar: *don't push me into doing it = no me obligues a hacerlo.* 5 (fam.) promover, divulgar, hacer propaganda de: *they were pushing a new product = estaban promoviendo un producto nuevo.* 6 **[to – (forward)]** poner en el candelero, hacer notar, colocar en primer término (un asunto, una persona). 7 (fam.) vender, pasar (drogas ilegales). 8 explotar, aprovechar, utilizar (una oportunidad, una ventaja). 9 INF. apilar, cargar. || *v.i.* 10 **[to – (into)]** MIL. avanzar, atacar. 11 (lit.) extenderse, proyectarse, ir hacia, seguir: *the road pushes north = la carretera sigue hacia el norte.* || *s.c.* 12 empujón, empellón, envite. 13 ofensiva, acometida, embestida. 14 estímulo, esfuerzo. || *s.i.* 15 (fam.) empuje, energía, brío, fuerza, nervio: *he's got push = tiene brío.* || 16 **at a –,** (brit. y fam.) si es necesario, en un apuro. 17 **to be pushing,** estar cerca de, tener casi (unos años). 18 **to give someone the –/to get the –,** (fam.) **a)** despedir a alguien, ser despedido (de un trabajo); **b)** dejar a alguien, cortar una relación con alguien (amorosa). 19 **to – about/around,** dar órdenes, mandonear, intimidar, maltratar, dirigir. 20 **to – ahead/forward/on,** continuar, avanzar, seguir (un viaje, una actividad, un plan). 21 **to – along,** (fam.) marcharse, irse, largarse. 22 **to – around,** V. **to – about.** 23 **to – aside,** dejar de lado, poner a un lado, arrinconar, no prestar atención. 24 **– bike,** (fam.) bici, bicicleta. 25 **to – for,** (p.u.) presionar, ejercer presión, forzar, urgir. 26 **to – forward,** (generalmente desp.) atraer la atención, llamar la atención (sobre uno mismo). 27 **to – in,** dar empujones, entrar a la fuerza. 28 **to – off, a)** (generalmente *imperativo*) (fam. y vulg.) largarse, irse, marcharse; **b)** MAR. alejarse del muelle, desatracar. 29 **to – on,** V. **to – ahead.** 30 **to – one's luck,** V. **luck.** 31 **to – out, a)** (generalmente pasiva) despedir, deshacerse de, destituir (de un puesto); **b)** producir en cantidad; enviar en cantidad. 32 **to – over,** tirar al suelo, hacer caer. 33 **to – through, a)** hacer aprobar, hacer aceptar (a una persona), conseguir llevar a cabo (un plan, un asunto): *they pushed the law through Parliament = consiguieron que la ley se aprobara en el Parlamento;* **b)** nacer, aparecer (las plantas). 34 **to – up,** elevar en exceso, poner por las nubes (un precio). 35 **to – up the daisies,** (hum.) estar muerto y enterrado, estar alimentando a los gusanos.

push-button | ˌpʊʃˌbʌtn | *adj.* accionado por botones, pulsadores, de botón, de llave: *it wasn't a push-button radio = no era una radio de pulsadores.*

push-cart | ˌpʊʃkɑːt | *s.c.* (EE.UU.) carretilla de mano, carrito de mano.

pushchair | ˌpʊʃtʃeər | (EE.UU.) stroller. *s.c.* sillita de ruedas, cochecito de niño.

pushed | pʊʃt | *adj.* (fam.) 1 **[– (for)]** apurado, falto (de tiempo, de dinero): *she was pushed for time = tenía mucha prisa.* 2 ocupado, atareado, con mucho que hacer. || 3 **to be hard –/to be –,** encontrar muy difícil (un asunto, una idea).

pusher | ˌpʊʃər | *s.c.* (desp.) 1 (argot) camello, traficante (de drogas). 2 (fam.) impulsor, emprendedor, brioso, persona con empuje. 3 (brit.) empujador (que usan los niños para colocar la comida en la cuchara).

pushing | ˌpʊʃɪŋ | *prep.* 1 (fam.) cerca de, casi con, llegando a (una edad determinada). || *adj.* 2 emprendedor, agresivo, enérgico, ambicioso, lleno de empuje.

pushover | ˌpʊʃˌəʊvər | *s.c.* (fam.) 1 chollo, ganga, cosa fácil. 2 **[– (for)]** incauto, inocente, persona fácil de engañar.

push-up | ˌpʊʃʌp | *s.c.* (EE.UU.) V. **press-up.**

pushy | ˌpʊʃɪ | (también **pushing**) *adj.* (desp.) emprendedor, agresivo, ambicioso.

pusillanimity | ˌpjuːsɪlə'nɪmɪtɪ | *s.i.* (form.) pusilanimidad, cobardía, timidez.
pusillanimous | ˌpjuːsɪ'lænɪməs | *adj.* (form. y desp.) pusilánime, cobarde, tímido.
puss | pʊs | *s.c.* **1** (fam.) gato, gatito, minino, micifú. **2** (fig.) chica, chavala, moza. **3** (argot) morro, hocico. **4** (argot) jeta, cara, rostro.
pussy | ˌpʊsɪ | *s.c.* **1** (brit. y fam.) gatito, minino, micifú. **2** (argot y vulg.) coño, vulva (órgano sexual femenino). **3** (fig.) gatita, nena. **4** (fam.) amento (del sauce). || *adj.* **5** lleno de pus.
pussyfoot | ˌpʊsɪfʊt | *v.i.* **[to – (about, around)]** (fam. y desp.) andar con mucho tiento, ser muy cauteloso, ser poco directo, andar con rodeos, andar con contemplaciones.
pussy-willow | ˌpʊsɪˌwɪləʊ | *s.c.* e *i.* BOT. sauce.
pustule | ˌpʌstjuːl | (EE.UU.) | ˌpʌs-tʃuːl | *s.c.* MED. pústula.
put | pʊt | *v.* [*pret.* y *p.p.irreg.* **put** *ger.* **putting**] *t.* **1** [**to –** *o.* + *adv./prep.*] poner, colocar, situar, ubicar, introducir, meter. **2** poner, echar, añadir, usar: *she put too much sugar = echó demasiado azúcar.* **3** [**to –** *o.* + *adv./prep.*] poner, colocar (en un estado o condición): *he put me in an awful position = me puso en una terrible posición; the children put her in a bad mood = los niños la pusieron de mal humor.* **4** [**to –** *o.* + *adv./prep.*] echar (la culpa), ejercer (presión), poner (fin), poner (la cabeza), concentrarse en: *she put her mind to the problem = se concentró en el problema.* **5** [**to –** *o.* + *adv./prep.*] invertir, colocar (dinero), comprar (acciones). **6** [**to –** *o.* + *adv./prep.*] expresar, exponer, decir: *to put it simply = por decirlo de un modo más simple.* **7** [**to – (to/before)**] formular, hacer (preguntas), presentar, exponer (una sugerencia). **8** [**to –** *o.* + *adv./prep.*] escribir, poner, trazar: *put a line underneath = traza una línea debajo.* **9** [**to –** *o.* + *adv./prep.* **(into)**] pasar a, traducir a, adaptar (un texto, una pieza musical): *put the text into French = traduce el texto al francés; put prose into verse = versificar un texto en prosa.* **10** [**to –** *o.* + *adv./prep.*] ocupar, emplear, destinar (a un trabajo): *they were put to work = se les puso a trabajar.* **11** [**to –** *o.* + *adv./prep.*] dirigir, conducir, encaminar, guiar (un caballo, un barco). **12** DEP. arrojar, lanzar (la jabalina). **13** clasificar, colocar: *where would you put his book? = ¿cómo clasificarías su libro?* **14** [**to – above/before/over**] anteponer, dar mayor importancia a: *he often puts his family before work = a menudo antepone la familia al trabajo.* **15** [**to –** + *o.* + **(on)**] poner, imponer (un impuesto). **16** [**to –** *o.* + **(on)**] apostar: *put 5 pounds on that horse = apuesta 5 libras a ese caballo.* || *i.* [**to –** *adv./prep.*] **17** dirigirse, encaminarse, empezar a moverse. || **18 as somebody – it,** como alguien dijo, como ya dijo alguien. **19 to be hard – to do,** V. **hard. 20 not to know where to – oneself,** no saber dónde meterse uno, estar totalmente abochornado. **21 to – about, a)** (fam.) extender, divulgar, propagar, hacer correr (rumores); **b)** MAR. virar, cambiar de rumbo, cambiar de bordada. **22 to – across/ over, a)** comunicar, lograr explicar, hacer entender, dejar claro (ideas, sentimientos); **b)** (brit. y fam.) engañar, embaucar, hacer creer. **23 to – aside, a)** dejar a un lado (un trabajo), ahorrar (dinero); **b)** hacer caso omiso de, desatender, no prestar atención; **c)** desechar, rechazar. **24 to – at,** calcular, estimar, suponer: *he put the time at 2.30 = calculó que eran las 2.30.* **25 to – away, a)** guardar, devolver a su sitio, colocar en su lugar; **b)** guardar dinero, poner aparte un dinero (para una ocasión); **c)** (fam.) comer exageradamente, ponerse como un pepe; **d)** (euf.) encarcelar, poner a la sombra; **e)** (euf.) internar en un manicomio; **f)** (arc.) DER. repudiar (a una mujer). **26 to – back, a)** retrasar, demorar, posponer, aplazar; **b)** retrasar, atrasar (un reloj); **c)** MAR. volver, regresar, retornar (a puerto); **d)** (fam.) beber muy deprisa (alcohol). **27 to – by,** V. **to – aside. 28 to – down, a)** sofocar, reprimir, aplastar (una rebelión); **b)** (fam.) humillar, bajar los humos; **c)** (euf.) matar, sacrificar (a un animal viejo); **d)** escribir, anotar, tomar nota de; **e)** (brit.) dejar apearse, poner en tierra, dejar (a un pasajero): *you can put me down at the corner = déjame en la esquina;* **f)** hacer un desembolso inicial, pagar una entrada (de una deuda); **g)** AER. aterrizar, llevar a tierra; **h)** dejar, posar, poner en el suelo (un objeto); **i)** dejar, abandonar (una actividad interesante): *I* couldn't put the novel down = me era imposible dejar la novela. **29 to – down as,** considerar, calificar como, creer que es. **30 to – down for,** inscribir para, apuntar para (una competición, una donación). **31 to – down roots,** echar raíces, establecer la residencia en. **32 to – down to,** atribuir (un estado) a, achacar (una causa) a. **33 to – forth,** (form.) **a)** BOT. echar (hojas, brotes); **b)** publicar, dar a conocer (una idea, una teoría); **c)** V. **to – forward. 34 to – forward, a)** sugerir, exponer, proponer (un plan, un candidato); **b)** adelantar, anticipar (un asunto); **c)** adelantar (el reloj); **d)** llamar la atención sobre, dar a conocer a, presentar a (una persona). **35 to – in, a)** MAR. entrar en puerto, hacer escala, atracar; **b)** presentar, enviar (una reclamación, una solicitud); **c)** pasar, echar, emplear (tiempo en una actividad); **d)** interrumpir, intercalar, añadir, insertar; **e)** votar a, elegir a (un gobierno, una persona); **f)** instalar, colocar; plantar. **36 to – in for,** solicitar formalmente, hacer una petición formal. **37 to – in a good word for,** V. **word. 38 to – in mind,** recordar. **39 to – into,** MAR. atracar, hacer escala. **40 to – it to someone (that),** sugerir, invitar a considerar. **41 to – off, a)** retrasar, aplazar, posponer; **b)** deshacerse de, desembarazarse de, dar largas, dar una disculpa; **c)** desanimar, disuadir, apartar de su propósito, distraer, desconcentrar; **d)** apartar, alejar, hacer repeler, quitar las ganas (de algo o de alguien); **e)** dejar en tierra, apear (de un vehículo). **42 to – on, a)** ponerse, vestirse, calzarse (ropa, zapatos, gafas); **b)** encender, enchufar, poner (la radio, la luz); **c)** engordar, aumentar (de peso); **d)** aumentar, elevar (un precio); **e)** calcular, suponer, estimar; **f)** apostar, arriesgar; **g)** adoptar, representar (una actitud); **h)** poner en escena, representar (una obra); **i)** (EE.UU. y fam.) tomar el pelo, bromear, engañar. **43 to – on a brave/good face,** V. **face. 44 to – one's back into,** V. **back. 44 to – one's finger on,** señalar con el dedo, identificar. **45 to – one's foot down,** plantarse, ponerse en actitud muy firme. **46 to – one's foot in one's mouth,** meter la pata, decir algo inconveniente, decir algo sin tacto alguno. **47 to – one's house in order,** organizar los asuntos de uno. **48 to – one's shirt on something,** V. **shirt. 49 to – on the dog,** (fam.) darse aires de suficiencia. **50 to – onto,** (fam.) poner al corriente, hablar de, recomendar. **51 to – out, a)** apagar, extinguir (un fuego); **b)** disgustar, enfadar, irritar, molestar; **c)** publicar, extender, divulgar; **d)** MED. dislocar, descoyuntar; **e)** MAR. salir de puerto, iniciar la navegación, echarse a la mar; **f)** MED. anestesiar; **g)** (EE.UU. y argot) desear irse a la cama con alguien; **h)** sacar, alargar (la lengua, un brazo); **i)** DEP. expulsar, eliminar (a un jugador). **52 to – over,** V. **to – across. 53 to – over on,** (fam.) engañar, embaucar. **54 to – someone off their stroke,** V. **stroke. 55 to – someone out of his/her/ their misery,** quitarle a uno la intriga, satisfacer la curiosidad de uno (contando algo que deseaba saber). **56 to – someone's mind at rest,** V. **mind. 57 to – someone through it/the mill,** (fam.) probar a uno hasta límites insospechados, someter a una severa prueba. **58 to – someone through their paces,** V. **pace. 59 to – someone to death,** V. **death. 60 to – the clock back,** V. **clock. 61 to – through, a)** conectar, poner con (al teléfono); **b)** llevar a cabo, completar con éxito, concluir. **62 to – the arm/bite on,** (argot) pedir dinero, pedir pelas. **63 to – the finger on,** (jerga) delatar, informar, soplonear (a la policía). **64 to – the screws to/on someone,** apretarle los tornillos a alguien, presionar a alguien. **65 to – to, a)** proponer, sugerir, hacer (una pregunta); **b)** someter a, someter a (votación, consideración). **66 to – to sea,** salir al mar, navegar. **67 to – together, a)** componer, reunir, juntar; **b)** combinar, coordinar. **68 to – two and two together,** sacar la conclusión correcta, cuadrar los hechos. **69 to – up, a)** construir, montar, levantar, colocar en alto, alzar; **b)** poner, fijar, pegar, colgar (en sitio visible); **c)** elevar, incrementar (los precios); **d)** alojar, acomodar, hospedar, albergar; **e)** oponer, mostrar, ofrecer (resistencia); **f)** poner, ofrecer (a la venta); **g)** financiar, contribuir con, colaborar con, cooperar con (dinero);

h) recomendar, encomendar, proponer (para un puesto); **i)** TEC. levantar (la caza); **j)** enlatar, poner en conserva; **k)** nombrar, nominar, ser candidato (en unas elecciones). **70 to – up a fight,** V. **fight. 71 to – up a good show,** V. **show. 72 to – upon,** (brit.) causar molestias, abusar de la amabilidad, incomodar. **73 to – up to,** incitar, animar, alentar (a hacer algo malo). **74 to – up with,** (fam.) soportar, aguantar, tolerar (algo o alguien molesto).

putative | ˌpjuːtətɪv | *adj.* **1** (form.) supuesto. **2** DER. putativo.

put-down | ˌputdaun | *s.c.* (fam.) humillación, desaire, desprecio, rechazo.

putrefaction | ˌpjuːtrɪ'fækʃn | *s.i.* putrefacción, corrupción, descomposición.

putrefy | ˌpjuːtrɪfaɪ | *v.t.* e *i.* **1** (form.) corromper(se), pudrir(se), descomponer(se). **2** MED. gangrenar(se).

putrescent | ˌpjuː'tresnt | *adj.* (form.) putrescente, en estado de descomposición.

prutrid | ˌpjuːtrɪd | *adj.* **1** pútrido, putrefacto, podrido, descompuesto. **2** corrupto, depravado, malsano. **3** (fam.) malísimo, espantoso, horrible, terrible: *what a putrid book! = ¡qué libro tan espantoso!*

putsch | putʃ | *s.c.* golpe de estado.

putt | pʌt | *s.c.* **1** DEP. golpe suave, golpe corto (en golf). || *v.t.* e *i.* **2** DEP. dar un golpe corto, golpear suavemente (en golf).

putter | ˌpʌtər | *s.c.* DEP. **1** palo de golf para golpes cortos. **2** putter, jugador de golpe corto (en golf). || *v.t.* e *i.* **3** (EE.UU.) perder el tiempo, zascandilear, pasar el rato ocupado en tonterías.

putting-green | ˌpʌtɪŋgriːn | *s.c.* DEP. campo de minigolf, campo de golf en miniatura.

putty | ˌpʌtɪ | *s.i.* **1** masilla. **2** emplaste, mastique, almáciga. **3** color pardusco, color amarillento. || *v.t.* **4** rellenar, emplastecer, enmasillar. || **5 to be like – in someone's hands,** ser muy influenciable por alguien.

put-up | ˌput'ʌp | *adj.* (fam.) tramado, planeado, proyectado de antemano, urdido: *a put-up job = un trabajo tramado de antemano.*

put-upon | ˌputˌʌpɒn | *adj.* utilizado, engañado, explotado (una persona).

puzzle | ˌpʌzl | *v.t.* **1** (generalmente pasiva) confundir, dejar perplejo, asombrar, extrañar. || *v.i.* **2 [to – adv./prep.]** tratar de descifrar, darle vueltas, desenmarañar, volverse loco tratando de entender: *puzzling over the loss of my watch = dándole vueltas a la pérdida del reloj.* || *s.c.* **3** rompecabezas (juego). **4** crucigrama. **5** acertijo, adivinanza. **6** enigma, misterio. || **7 to – out,** resolver, descifrar. **8 to – over,** devanarse los sesos acerca de.

puzzled | ˌpʌzld | *adj.* **1** perplejo, confuso, desorientado, desconcertado. **2** misterioso, enigmático, oscuro, inexplicable.

puzzlement | ˌpʌzəlmənt | *s.i.* perplejidad, confusión, desconcierto.

puzzling | ˌpʌzlɪŋ | *adj.* misterioso, enigmático, oscuro, inexplicable, incomprensible.

PVC | ˌpiːviː'siː | *s.i.* (**polyvinyl chloride**) PVC (material plástico).

pygmy | ˌpɪgmɪ | *s.c.* **1** pigmeo. || *adj.* **2** enano, diminuto, minúsculo. **3** (fig.) insignificante, sin importancia.

pyjamas | pə'dʒɑːməz | (EE.UU. **pajamas**) *s.pl.* pijama.

pylon | ˌpaɪlən | (EE.UU.) | ˌpaɪlɒn | *s.c.* **1** ELEC. poste, torre metálica. **2** AER. torre marcadora, poste marcador. **3** ARQ. pilón, pilono (de un templo egipcio).

pyramid | ˌpɪrəmɪd | *s.c.* **1** GEOM. pirámide. **2** ARQ. pirámide.

pyramidal | pɪ'ræmɪdl | *adj.* piramidal.

pyre | ˌpaɪər | *s.c.* pira, hoguera (funeraria).

pyrotechnics | ˌpaɪrəu'teknɪks | | paɪərə' | | teknɪks | *s.i.* **1** pirotecnia. **2** espectáculo de fuegos artificiales. **3** (fig. y a veces desp.) elocuencia, retórica, brillantez, ingenio.

Pyrrhic victory | ˌpɪrɪk'vɪktərɪ | *s.c.* V. **victory.**

python | ˌpaɪθn | (EE.UU.) | ˌpaɪθɒn | *s.c.* ZOOL. pitón, serpiente pitón.

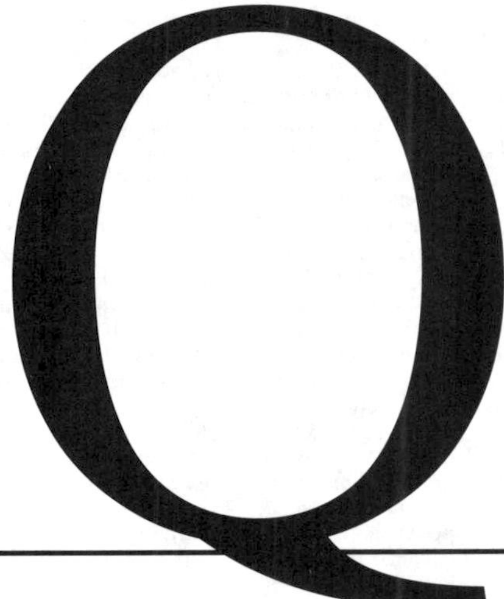

q, Q | kjuː | **1** q (décimo-séptima letra del alfabeto inglés). || *abreviatura* (también Q) **2** de **question** o **Queen.** || **3 to mind one's p's and q's,** V. **p.**

QC | ˌkjuː 'siː | *siglas* (brit.) DER. **(Queen's Counsel)** abogado emérito (título que suele seguir al nombre).

QED | ˌkjuː iː 'diː | *siglas* (del latín quod erat demonstrandum) **1** (fam.) ahí está la respuesta. **2** MAT. queda demostrado.

qua | kweɪ | | kwː | *prep.* (form.) qua, en cuanto, en tanto que, como.

quack | kwæk | *s.c.* **1** graznido (de pato). **2** (desp.) charlatán, curandero, matasanos. || *v.i.* **3** graznar (el pato).

quad | kwɒd | *s.c.* **1** cuatrillizo. **2** (brit.) patio (de centro docente).

Quadragesima | ˌkwɒdrə'dʒesɪmə | *s.sing. primer domingo de cuaresma.*

quadrangle | 'kwɒdræŋgl | *s.c.* **1** patio (rodeado de edificios). **2** GEOM. cuadrángulo.

quadrangular | kwɒ'dræŋgjʊlər | *adj.* cuadrangular.

quadrant | 'kwɒdrənt | *s.c.* **1** GEOM. cuadrante. **2** ASTR. cuadrante.

quadraphonic | ˌkwɒdrə'fɒnɪk | *adj.* cuadrafónico.

quadrilateral | ˌkwɒdrɪ'lætərəl | *s.c.* GEOM. cuadrilátero.

quadrille | kwə'drɪl | *s.c.* contradanza.

quadruped | 'kwɒdrʊped | *s.c.* (form.) cuadrúpedo.

quadruple | 'kwɒdrʊpl | | kwɒ'druːpl | *adj.* **1** cuádruple. || *v.t.* **2** cuadruplicar.

quadruplet | 'kwɒdrʊplet | | kwɒ'↓ druːplit | *s.c.* cuatrillizo.

quaff | kwɑːf | *v.t.* (arc.) beber de un trago.

quagmire | 'kwægmaɪə | *s.c.* **1** tremedal, cenegal. **2** atolladero, apuro.

quail | kweɪl | *s.c.* **1** ZOOL. codorniz. || *v.i.* **2 [to – (at/before)]** acobardarse, amedrentarse, intimidarse.

quaint | kweɪnt | *adj.* curioso, original, típico, pintoresco.

quaintly | 'kweɪntlɪ | *adv.* curiosamente, típicamente.

quaintness | 'kweɪntnɪs | *s.i.* curiosidad, originalidad, tipismo.

quake | kweɪk | *v.i.* **1** temblar, estremecerse. **2** temblar (la tierra). || *s.c.* **3** (fam.) terremoto.

Quaker | kweɪkər | *s.c.* cuáquero.

qualification | ˌkwɒlɪfɪ'keɪʃn | *s.c.* **1** calificación: *good academic qualifications = buenas calificaciones académicas.* **2** cualificación, aptitud, capacidad, habilitación (para desempeñar un puesto o trabajo). **3** reserva, puntualización, restricción, salvedad: *we agreed with certain qualifications = estuvimos de acuerdo, con algunas reservas.* || *s.i.* **4** calificación, cualificación.

qualified | 'kwɒlɪfaɪd | *adj.* **1** cualificado, capacitado, habilitado, apto, competente (para desempeñar un puesto o trabajo). **2** limitado, con reservas, matizado (acuerdo, aprobación, alabanza, etc.).

qualifier | 'kwɒlɪfaɪər | *s.c.* **1** clasificado, persona que supera una prueba. **2** GRAM. calificativo.

qualify | 'kwɒlɪfaɪ | *v.t.* e *i.* **1** capacitar(se), habilitar(se) (para desempeñar un oficio). **2** matizar, especificar, limitar, restringir (una afirmación o juicio general). **3 [to – (for)]** tener derecho, tener acceso, optar, conseguir. **4 [to – (as)]** calificar, describir, considerar. **5** pasar, clasificarse (para la siguiente prueba).

qualitative | 'kwɒlɪtətɪv | (EE.UU.) | 'kwɒlɪteɪtɪv | *adj.* cualitativo.

qualitatively | 'kwɒlɪtətɪvlɪ | *adv.* cualitativamente.

quality | 'kwɒlɪtɪ | *s.i.* **1** calidad, clase, categoría. || *s.c.* **2** características, atributos, virtudes (personales). **3** propiedades, características (positivas de objetos). **4** carácter, espíritu, sabor (que guardan un objeto o lugar). || *atr.* **5** serio, de calidad (periódicos). || *s.pl.* **6** periódico serio: *a story in one of the qualities = noticia de uno de los periódicos serios.* || **7 – control,** control de calidad.

qualm | kwɑːm | *s.c.* duda, reparo, escrúpulo.

quandary | 'kwɒndərɪ | *s.c.* dilema, aprieto, apuro, perplejidad.

quanta | 'kwɒntə | *pl.irreg.* de **quantum.**

quantifiable | 'kwɒntɪfaɪəbl | *adj.* cuantificable.

quantification | ˌkwɒntɪfɪ'keɪʃn | *s.i.* cuantificación.

quantify | 'kwɒntɪfaɪ | *v.t.* cuantificar.

quantitative | 'kwɒntɪtətɪv | (EE.UU.) | 'kwɒntɪteɪtɪv | *adj.* cuantitativo.

quantity | 'kwɒntɪtɪ | *s.c.* e *i.* **1** cantidad, volumen. || **2 to be an unknown –,** ser un misterio, una incógnita. **3 – surveyor,** aparejador.

quantum | 'kwɒntəm | *s.c.* [*pl.irreg.* **quanta**] **1** (form.) cantidad (pequeña), cantidad requerida. **2** FIS. cuanta. || **3 – leap/jump,** paso de gigante.

quarantine | 'kwɒrəntiːn | *s.sing.* **1** cuarentena. || *v.t.* **2** poner en cuarentena.

quarrel | 'kwɒrəl | *s.c.* **1** disputa, riña, pelea, bronca, reyerta, pendencia, (Am.) zafacoca, follisca. **2** razón, causa (de pelea). || *v.i.* **3 [to – (about/over/with)]** disputar, reñir, pelear. **4** objetar, estar en desacuerdo (con un juicio, frase, etc.).

quarrelling | 'kwɒrəlɪŋ | (EE.UU. **quarreling**) *s.i.* disputa, riña, altercado.

quarrelsome | 'kwɒrəlsəm | *adj.* pendenciero, provocador, peleador, (Am.) rechelero.

quarry | 'kwɒrɪ | (EE.UU.) | 'kwɔːrɪ | *s.c.* **1** presa, caza. **2** cantera, mina. || *v.t.* **3** extraer, sacar, cortar (piedra). || *v.i.* **4** investigar, seguir el rastro (de un tema o de una información).

quart | kwɔːt | *s.c.* cuarto de galón (1,136 litros).

quarter | 'kwɔːtər | *s.c.* e *i.* **1** cuarto, cuarta parte. **2 [– (to/of)]** (menos) cuarto (hora). **3 [– (past/after)]** (y) cuarto (unidad de peso equivalente a cuatro onzas). **4** parte, dirección (del viento): *the wind blew from all quarters = el viento soplaba de todas partes.* **5** barrio, distrito. **6** sector, parte, grupo, mundo: *a warning from the scientific quarters = un toque de alarma del sector científico.* **7** (arc.) cuartel, piedad. **8** cuarto, fase (lunar). || *v.t.* **9** cuartear; dividir, partir (en cuatro partes). **10** reducir a un cuarto (la cantidad, el precio, etc. originales). **11** acomodar, alojar, dar cobijo (durante un cierto tiempo). || **12 at close quarters,** de cerca. **13 quarters,** alojamiento (prestado a soldados, principalmente).

OBS. La frase *it's a quarter to five = son las cinco menos cuarto* puede convertirse en *it's a quarter of five,* en inglés americano; del mismo modo que *it's a quarter past five* encuentra su correspondencia en *it's a quarter after five = son las cinco y cuarto.*

quarterdeck | 'kwɔːtədek | *s.c.* MAR. alcázar.

quarterfinal | ˌkwɔːtə'faɪnl | *s.c.* **1** cuartos de final (en competiciones deportivas). || **2 quarterfinals,** partido de cuartos de final.

quarterly | 'kwɔːtəlɪ | *adv.* **1** trimestralmente, cuatro veces al año. || *adj.* **2** trimestral: *a new quarterly journal = una nueva publicación trimestral.* || *s.c.* **3** publicación trimestral.

quartermaster | 'kwɔːtəˌmaːtər | *s.c.* MIL. intendente, comisario, furriel.

quartet | kwɔː'tet | *s.c.* **1** cuarteto, conjunto de cuatro (personas o cosas). **2** MUS. cuarteto (grupo de intérpretes, pieza musical).

quarto | 'kwɔːtəʊ | *s.i.* **1** cuarto (hoja de papel de 20 x 26 cm aproximadamente). || *s.c.* **2** libro en cuarto.

quartz | kwɔːts | *s.i.* **1** MIN. cuarzo. || *atr.* **2** de cuarzo.

quasar | 'kweɪzɑːr | *s.c.* ASTR. quasar.

quash | kwɒʃ | *v.t.* **1** anular, invalidar, revocar (decisiones, juicios, etc.). **2** reprimir (personas, emociones, deseos, etc.).

quasi- | 'kweizaɪ | *prefijo* cuasi- (en compuestos de sustantivos o adjetivos): *a quasi-republic = una cuasi-república; a quasi-official body = un cuerpo cuasioficial.*

quatrain | 'kwɒtreɪn | *s.c.* cuarteto, estrofa de cuatro versos.

quaver | 'kweɪvər | *v.i.* **1** temblar, vibrar (la voz o sonido musical). **2 [to – (out)]** decir o cantar con voz temblorosa. || *s.sing.* **3** temblor, vibración (de la voz). || *s.c.* **4** MUS. (brit.) corchea.

quavering | 'kweɪvərɪŋ | *adj.* tembloroso, trémulo.

quay | kiː | *s.c.* muelle, desembarcadero.

quayside | 'kiːsaɪd | *s.sing.* plataforma del muelle.

queasiness | 'kwiːzɪnɪs | *s.i.* indisposición, náuseas, incomodidad.

queasy | 'kwiːzɪ | *adj.* **1** indispuesto, mareado. **2** delicado, revuelto (estómago). **3** incómodo, preocupado, escrupuloso.

queen | kwiːn | *s.c.* **1** reina, reina consorte. **2** reina, figura (famosa, sobresaliente en un campo): *a great movie queen = una gran reina del cine.* **3** reina (elegida en una competición, para presidir un festival, etc.). **4** reina (abeja, avispa, etc.). **5** reina (en ajedrez, en juegos de cartas). **6** (fam.) mariquita. || *v.t.* **7** coronar peón, meter reina (ajedrez). || **8 to be a – bee,** creerse una reina. **9 to – it (over someone),** ser demasiado mandona (una mujer). **10 – mother,** reina madre (madre de rey o reina).

queenly | 'kwiːnlɪ | *adj.* regio, de reina.

queer | kwɪər | *adj.* **1** extraño, raro, peculiar, inesperado, excéntrico. **2** indispuesto, enfermo. **3** (fam.) loco, chalado, irracional, desequilibrado. **4** (fam.) amariconado. || *s.c.* **5** (fam.) maricón. || **6 to be in Queer Street,** (Brit. y fam.) atravesar malos momentos (económicos). **7 to – someone's pitch,** V. **pitch.**

queerly | 'kwɪəlɪ | *adv.* extrañamente, raramente.

quell | kwel | *v.t.* **1** suprimir, reprimir, sofocar, eliminar (conducta violenta, rebelión, oposición, etc.). **2** vencer, superar, reprimir (temor, dolor, etc.).

quench | kwentʃ | *v.t.* **1** calmar, apagar (la sed). **2** dominar, sofocar, apagar (fuego). **3** enfriar en agua (objetos candentes). **4** poner fin, reprimir (sentimientos).

querulous | 'kwerʊləs | *adj.* **1** quejoso, quejumbroso, irritable. **2** impaciente, exigente (niño).

querulously | 'kwerʊləslɪ | *adv.* quejosamente, impacientemente.

query | 'kwɪərɪ | *s.c.* **1** pregunta, duda, cuestión, interrogante. || *v.t.* **2** poner en duda, cuestionar. **3** (EE.UU.) preguntar, indagar, inquirir.

quest | kwest | (lit.) *s.c.* **1 [– (for)]** busca, búsqueda. || *v.i.* **2 [to – (for)]** buscar (objetos de gran aprecio). || **3 in – of something,** a la busca de algo.

question | 'kwestʃən | *s.c.* **1** pregunta, interrogante. **2** problema, cuestión, asunto. || *s.i.* **3** duda, incertidumbre. || *v.t.* **4** interrogar, hacer preguntas. **5** cuestionar, poner en duda. || **6 to beg the –,** dejar sin resolver el asunto en discusión: *your proposal begs the question whether ... = su propuesta deja sin resolver si...* **7 beyond –,** fuera de toda duda. **8 to bring something/come into –, hacer que algo sea considerado como problema. 9 to call something into –,** manifestar serias dudas sobre algo, poner en entredicho. **10 in –, a)** en cuestión, ya aludido; **b)** en cuestión, en duda. **11 open to –,** abierto a discusión, debatible. **12 out of the –,** imposible, no merece la pena discutirlo. **13 to pop the –,** (fam.) declararse. **14 – mark, a)** el signo de interrogación; **b)** interrogante, incertidumbre (que pesa sobre alguien o algo). **15 – tag,** coletilla o breve pregunta de confirmación (que sigue a un enunciado). **16 – time,** (brit.) tiempo dedicado a plantear cuestiones a los ministros (en la Cámara de los Comunes).

questionable | 'kwestʃənəbl | *adj.* cuestionable, discutible, dudoso.

questioner | 'kwestʃənər | *s.c.* preguntador, interrogador (en concursos o entrevistas).

questioning | 'kwestʃənɪŋ | *s.i.* **1** interrogatorio: *taken to the police station for questioning = llevado a comisaría para interrogatorio.* || *adj.* **2** interrogante, inquisitivo: *a questioning expression = expresión interrogante.*

questioningly | 'kwestʃənɪŋlɪ | *adv.* interrogantemente, inquisitivamente.

question-master | 'kwestʃənˌmɑːstər | *s.c.* presentador de un programa-concurso.

questionnaire | ˌkwestɪə'neər | *s.c.* cuestionario.

queue | kjuː | (brit.) *s.c.* **1** cola, fila (de gente, coches, etc. esperando). || *v.i.* **2** hacer cola. || **3 to – up,** hacer cola.

quibble | 'kwɪbl | *v.i.* **1** argumentar con sutilezas, hablar de detalles sin importancia. || *s.c.* **2** objeción menor, menudencia, sutileza, detalle sin importancia.

quiche | kiːʃ | *s.c.* quiche.

quick | kwɪk | *adj.* **1** rápido, veloz, ligero. **2** rápido, presto (que lleva poco tiempo). **3** inteligente, brillante, despierto. **4** sensible, fino (de oído), agudo (de vista). **5** fácilmente irritable. || *s.sing.* **6** carne viva, carne de la uña. || *adv.* **7** rápido, pronto: *he wants to get rich quick = quiere hacerse rico pronto.* || **8 to cut someone to the –,** pincharle a uno donde le duele. **9 quick-,** de rápido... (según el adjetivo con el que forma un compuesto): *quick-growing plants = plantas de crecimiento rápido.* **10 – as a flash,** V. **flash. 11 – march,** MIL. paso ordinario. **12 – off the mark,** V. **mark. 13 – one,** (fam.) trago rápido, copa rápida (antes de marchar). **14 – on the uptake,** V. **uptake. 15 the – and the dead,** (arc.) todos, los vivos y los muertos.

quicken | 'kwɪkən | *v.t.* e *i.* **1** acelerar, avivar, aligerar, apresurar. **2** avivar, aumentar (el interés, la atención, etc.).

quickie | 'kwɪkɪ | *s.c.* (fam.) una rápida (copa, pregunta, etc., cuando no hay tiempo para más).

quicklime | 'kwɪklaɪm | *s.i.* QUIM. cal viva.

quickly | 'kwɪklɪ | *adv.* rápidamente, velozmente, deprisa, pronto.

quickness | 'kwɪknɪs | *s.i.* velocidad, rapidez, inteligencia, agudeza.

quicksand | 'kwɪksænd | *s.c.* e *i.* arena movediza.

quicksilver | 'kwɪkˌsɪlvər | *s.i.* (arc.) QUIM. mercurio.

quid | kwɪd | *s.c.* [*pl.* **quid**] (brit. y fam.) **1** libra (esterlina). || **2 to be quids in,** forrarse.

quid pro quo | ˌkwid prəʊ'kwəʊ | *s.c.* (form.) quid pro quo, compensación, recompensa.
quiescent | kwaɪ'esnt | *adj.* (form.) inactivo, quieto, pasivo, apaciguado.
quiet | 'kwaɪət | *adj.* **1** callado, silencioso, de poco ruido. **2** suave, bajo (voz): *a quiet voice = voz suave.* **3** tranquilo, sosegado, apacible, sin sobresaltos: *a quiet life = una vida tranquila.* **4** suave, discreto, callado (actitud): *a lady of quiet disposition = una señora de porte discreto.* **5** apagado, suave (color). **6** tranquilo, inactivo, de poco movimiento (negocio, ciudad, institución, etc.). **7** reservado, secreto, confidencial. || *v.t.* e *i.* **8** (EE.UU.) calmar, callar, acallar, tranquilizar, apaciguar. || *s.i.* **9** tranquilidad, descanso. || **10 to do something on the –,** hacer algo en secreto. **11 to keep – about something/to keep something –,** mantener algo en secreto. **12 to – down,** (EE.UU.) calmar, callar, tranquilizar, apaciguar.
quieten | 'kwaiətn | *v.t.* **1** calmar, tranquilizar, apaciguar, acallar, hacer callar. || *v.i.* **2** calmarse, tranquilizarse, sosegarse, callarse. || **3 to – down,** (brit.) calmar, callar, apaciguar.
quietism | 'kwaɪɪtɪzəm | *s.i.* (form.) quietismo.
quietist | 'kwaɪɪtɪst | *s.c.* (form.) quietista.
quietly | 'kwaɪətlɪ | *adv.* calladamente, en silencio; tranquilamente, sosegadamente, mansamente; discretamente.
quietness | 'kwaɪətnɪs | *s.i.* silencio, calma, tranquilidad, sosiego, quietud, discreción.
quiff | kwɪf | *s.c.* copete.
quill | kwɪl | *s.c.* **1** pluma (grande: de la cola o ala de un ave). **2** pluma (de ganso: para escritura). **3** púa. || **4 – pen,** pluma (de ganso: de escritura).
quilt | kwɪlt | *s.c.* edredón, colcha.
quilted | 'kwɪltɪd | *adj.* acolchado.
quin | kwɪn | V. **quintuplet.**
quince | kwɪns | *s.c.* membrillo (árbol, fruta).
quinine | kwɪ'niːn | *s.i.* quinina.
Quinquagesima | ˌkwɪŋkwə'dʒesɪmə | *s.sing.* domingo de quincuagésima.
quint | kwɪnt | (EE.UU.) V. **quintuplet.**
quintessence | kwɪn'tesns | *s.sing.* (form.) quintaesencia.
quintessential | ˌkwɪntɪ'senʃl | *adj.* quintaesencial, genuino, prototípico.
quintet | kwɪn'tet | *s.c.* quinteto.
quintuplet | 'kwɪntjʊplet | *s.c.* quintillizo.
quip | kwɪp | (arc.) *s.c.* **1** ingeniosidad, gracia, agudeza, chiste, pulla. || *v.i.* **2** hacer o decir una gracia, apuntillar, ironizar.
quirk | kwəːk | *s.c.* **1** rareza, originalidad, excentricidad, manía. **2** casualidad, accidente. **3** capricho, quiebro (del destino, suerte o fortuna).
quirkily | 'kwəːkɪlɪ | *adv.* raramente, casualmente.
quirky | 'kwəːkɪ | *adj.* raro, original, extraño.
quisling | 'kwɪzlɪ | *s.c.* (arc.) colaboracionista, traidor.
quit | kwɪt | (fam.) *v.t.* e *i.* **[quit, quit;** (brit.) **quitted]** **1** dejar, abandonar (hábitos, trabajos, lugares, etc.). **2** irse, marcharse. **3** cesar, dimitir, desistir. || *adj.* **4** (p.u.) libre, liberado, descargado. || **5 to be quits,** estar en paz, quedar en paz (no deber nada). **6 to call it quits,** acabar la discusión, quedar en paz.
quite | kwaɪt | *adv.* **1** bastante, relativamente, hasta cierto punto: *he was quite young = era bastante joven.* **2** completamente, totalmente, del todo: *I'm not quite sure = no estoy seguro del todo.* **3** (EE.UU.) muy, realmente: *the meal was quite good = la comida fue muy buena.* **4** (brit.) ciertamente, así es, de acuerdo (como respuesta): *it's impossible to do it faster. – Quite = no se puede hacer más rápido. – Así es.* || **5 to be – something,** (fam.) tener su importancia, ser algo a tener en cuenta. **6 (not) – the (done) thing,** no ser costumbre, no estar bien visto. **7 – a/– some,** (EE.UU.) excepcional, fuera de serie (persona o cosa): *it must be quite some car = debe de ser un coche fuera de serie.* **8 – so,** así es, ciertamente, de acuerdo. **9 – the fashion/rage/etc.,** (estar) muy de moda, (hacer) furor.
quittance | 'kwɪtəns | *s.c.* DER. diligencia de exoneración (de deuda, obligación, etc.).
quitter | 'kwɪtər | *s.c.* (fam.) inconstante, remolón, perezoso.
quiver | 'kwɪvər | *v.i.* **1** temblar, estremecerse. || *s.c.* **2** temblor, estremecimiento. **3** aljaba, carcaj.
quixotic | kwɪk'sɒtɪk | *adj.* (form.) quijotesco, idealista, romántico.
quixotically | kwɪk'sɒtɪkəlɪ | *adv.* quijotescamente, de manera idealista.
quiz | kwɪz | *s.c.* [*pl.* **quizzes**] **1** concurso, competición. **2** (EE.UU.) examen, prueba rápida (de conocimientos). || *v.t.* **3 [to – (about)]** (p.u.) interrogar.
quizmaster | 'kwɪzˌmɑːtər | *s.c.* presentador (de un programa concurso).
quizzical | 'kwɪzɪkl | *adj.* burlón, irónico, intencionado.
quizzically 'kwɪzɪkəlɪ | *adv.* burlonamente, irónicamente, con intención.
quod | kwɒd | *s.i.* (brit. y argot.) chirona, trena, talego, (Am.) chichera.
quoit | kɔit | *s.i.* **1** juego de aros, juego de tejo. || *s.c.* **2** aro, tejo.
quorum | 'kwɔːrəm | *s.sing.* quórum.
quota | 'kwəʊtə | *s.c.* **1** cuota, cupo. **2** ración, parte (que corresponde dar o recibir).
quotable | 'kwəʊtəbl | *adj.* **1** citable, digno de mención. **2** FIN. cotizable.
quotation | kwəʊ'teɪʃn | *s.c.* **1** cita (textual). **2** precio, presupuesto (de un trabajo). **3** FIN. cotización (de valores). || **4 – marks,** comillas.
quote | kwəʊt | *v.t.* e *i.* **1** citar; decir, expresar (con las mismas palabras). **2** presupuestar, señalar precio (a un trabajo). **3** citar, mencionar (como ejemplo o prueba de autoridad). **4 [to – (at)]** FIN. cotizar (en mercado de valores). || *s.c.* **5** cita (textual). **6** precio, presupuesto (de un trabajo). || **7 quotes,** (fam.) comillas. **8 –/unquote,** abrir/cerrar comillas (lenguaje hablado).
quoth | kwəʊθ | *v.i.* (arc.) dijo.
quotidian | kwɒ'tidiən | *adj.* (form.) cotidiano, diario, habitual.
quotient | 'kwəʊʃnt | *s.sing.* **1** cociente, grado, nivel: *intelligence quotient = cociente intelectual.* || *s.c.* **2** MAT. cociente.
Quran | kɔː'rɑːn | (también **Koran**) *s.sing.* Corán.
Quranic | kə'ræniк | (también **Koranic**) *adj.* coránico.
qv | ˌkjuː 'viː | *abreviatura* (del latín quod vide) (form.) véase.
qwerty | 'kwəːtɪ | *adj.* INF. (brit.) qwerty, ordinario (teclado): *qwerty system = sistema qwerty.*

r, R | ɑː | *s.c.* **1** r, R (decimoctava letra del alfabeto inglés). || **2 the three R's,** lectura, escritura y aritmética.

rabbi | 'ræbaɪ | *s.c.* REL. rabino; rabí (cuando precede a un nombre).

rabbit | 'ræbɪt | *s.c.* **1** ZOOL. conejo. **2** (fam.) mal jugador (principalmente en tenis y golf). || *s.i.* **3** conejo (su carne; su piel). || **4 to go rabbiting,** cazar conejos. **5 Welsh –,** GAST. tostada con queso fundido.

rabble | 'ræbl | *s.sing.* **1** multitud, muchedumbre, gentío. **2** [**the** –] (desp.) populacho, gentuza, plebe, chusma.

rabble-rouser | 'ræbl,rauzər | *s.c.* POL. agitador (provocador de conflictos sociales); demagogo.

rabble-rousing | 'ræbl,rauzɪŋ | POL. *s.i.* **1** incitación, instigación. || **2** *adj.* demagógico, que provoca agitación: *a rabble-rousing speech = un discurso demagógico.*

rabid | 'ræbɪd | *adj.* **1** exaltado, ferviente. **2** fanático. **3** violento, furioso. **4** rabioso (que padece rabia): *a rabid dog.*

rabies | 'reɪbiːz | *s.i.* MED. rabia.

raccoon | rə'kuːn | *s.c.* ZOOL. mapache.

race | reɪs | *s.c.* **1** DEP. carrera, competición de velocidad: *horse race = carrera de caballos.* **2** DEP. regata. || *s.c.* e *i.* **3** raza: *the human race = la raza humana.* **4** estirpe, familia, linaje. || *s.sing.* **5** carrera (lucha por lograr algo antes que el adversario): *arms race = carrera armamentista.* || *v.t.* **6** [**– (against)**] competir en una carrera: *he has to race against the best runners in the world = tiene que competir con los mejores corredores del mundo.* **7** DEP. hacer correr, presentar a una carrera (un vehículo o animal). **8** acelerar al máximo (un motor). **9** (fam.) echar una carrera (a alguien): *I'll race you = te echo una carrera.* || *v.i.* **10** correr, ir corriendo a toda velocidad. **11** DEP. correr, competir en una carrera o regata: *they won't race tomorrow = no correrán mañana.* **12** latir apresuradamente (el corazón, el pulso). || **13 to – against time,** ir contra reloj. **14 – relations,** relaciones de convivencia entre distintas razas. **15 the races,** DEP. carreras (de caballos).

racecourse | 'reɪskɔːs | (también **race-course** o **race course**). *s.c.* (brit.) DEP. hipódromo.

racehorse | 'reɪshɔːs | *s.c.* DEP. caballo de carreras.

race-meeting | 'reɪs,miːtɪŋ | (también **race meeting**) *s.c.* concurso hípico.

racer | 'reɪsər | *s.c.* **1** vehículo de carreras (coche, bicicleta, moto, etc.). **2** caballo de carreras.

racetrack | 'reɪstræk | *s.c.* **1** pista de carreras. **2** (EE.UU.) hipódromo.

racial | 'reɪʃl | *adj.* racial: *racial conflicts = conflictos raciales.*

racialism | 'reɪʃəlɪzəm | *s.i.* (brit. y p.u.) racismo.

racialist | 'reɪʃəlɪst | *adj.* y *s.c.* (brit. y p.u.) racista.

racing | 'reɪsɪŋ | *s.i.* **1** DEP. carreras (de caballos, de coches, etc.). || *adj.* **2** de carreras: *a racing car.* || **3 – world,** hipismo, deporte hípico.

racism | 'reɪsɪzəm | *s.i.* racismo.

racist | 'reɪsɪst | *adj.* y *s.c.* racista.

rack | ræk | *s.c.* **1** percha, perchero. **2** escurreplatos. **3** estante. **4** rejilla, portaequipajes (en un vehículo). **5** potro de tortura. **6** soporte. || *v.t.* (EE.UU. también **wrack**) **7** (lit.) torturar, atormentar: *he was racked by those memories = esos recuerdos le atormentaban.* **8** pedir demasiada renta (a un inquilino). || **9 to go to – and ruin,** venirse abajo, echarse a perder. **10 on the –,** (fig.) atormentado. **11 to – one's brains (for),** (fam.) devanarse los sesos.

racket | 'rækɪt | *s.sing.* **1** jaleo, alboroto, bullicio: *those boys are making a racket = aquellos niños están armando jaleo.* || *s.c.* **2** (fam.) estafa, timo, fraude organizado. **3** chantaje. **4** negocio sucio, actividad ilegal: *the drug racket = el negocio de la droga.* **5** (hum.) actividad, negocio: *the buying and selling racket = el negocio de la compraventa.* **6** (también **racquet**) raqueta: *tennis racket.* || *v.i.* **7** (lit.) alborotar, armar jaleo. || **8 to knick up/make a –,** armar jaleo, alborotar. **9 to – about,** armar jaleo, alborotar. **10 rackets,** (también **racquets**) DEP. juego parecido a la pelota vasca o al frontón. **11 to stand the –, a)** superar una prueba; **b)** pagar el pato, sufrir las consecuencias.

racketeer | ,rækə'tɪər | *s.c.* **1** timador, estafador. **2** chantajista.

racketeering | ,rækə'tɪərɪŋ | *s.i.* crimen organizado.

racking | 'rækɪŋ | *adj.* **1** terrible (dolor): *a racking headache = un terrible dolor de cabeza.* **2** muy fuerte (emoción).

raconteur | ,rækɒn'təː | *s.c.* persona con facilidad para contar chistes o anécdotas con gracia o ingenio.

racily | 'reɪsɪlɪ | *adv.* de forma graciosa; con salero.

racy | 'reɪsɪ | *adj.* **1** gracioso, saleroso (persona, comportamiento). **2** picante, gracioso (chiste). **3** vigoroso (estilo). **4** (fig.) fuerte, picante (un sabor).

radar | 'reɪdɑːr | *s.i.* radar.

radar-trap | 'reɪdɑː træp | (también **radar trap**) *s.c.* radar utilizado por la policía para detectar el exceso de velocidad.

radial | 'reɪdjəl | *adj.* **1** radial: *radial road = carretera radial.* || *s.c.* **2** neumático radial.

radiance | 'reɪdɪəns | *s.i.* **1** resplandor. **2** (fig.) esplendor, brillo (de una persona, de una cara).

radiant | 'reɪdɪənt | *adj.* **1** radiante (de alegría, satisfacción, etc.): *a radiant face = un rostro radiante.* **2** esplendoroso, hermoso. **3** (lit.) brillante, resplandeciente: *the radiant sun = el sol brillante.* **4** FIS. radiante (transmitido por radiación): *radiant heat = calor radiante.*

radiantly | 'reɪdɪəntlɪ | *adv.* **1** esplendorosamente. **2** con alegría. **3** con brillo, con resplandor.

radiate | 'reɪdɪeɪt | *v.i.* **1 [– (from)]** extenderse (desde un punto central), salir (de un punto central): *streets that radiate from the main square = las calles que salen de la plaza mayor.* **2** FIS. irradiar, emitir radiaciones. || *v.t.* e *i.* **3 [– (from)]** irradiar, despedir, emitir (luz, rayos, calor). **4 [– (from)]** (fig.) irradiar, transmitir (una emoción, un sentimiento): *she radiated happiness = irradiaba felicidad.*

radiation | ˌreɪdɪ'eɪʃn | *s.c.* e *i.* **1** FIS. radiación. || **2 – sickness,** MED. enfermedad causada por la exposición a la radiación.

radiator | 'reɪdɪeɪtər | *s.c.* **1** radiador (aparato de calefacción). **2** MEC. radiador.

radical | 'rædɪkl | *adj.* **1** radical, extremista: *a radical politician = un político radical.* **2** radical, fundamental, básico: *a radical error = un error fundamental.* **3** radical, absoluto, total: *a radical change = un cambio radical.* || *s.c.* **4** POL. radical (persona con ideas radicales). **5** FILOL. radical. || **6 – Party,** POL. partido Radical. **7 – sign,** MAT. radical.

radicalise V. **radicalize.**

radicalism | 'rædɪkəlɪzəm | *s.i.* radicalismo.

radicalize | 'rædɪkəlaɪz | (también **radicalise**) *v.t.* (form.) radicalizar, volver radical.

radically | 'rædɪkəlɪ | *adv.* radicalmente, fundamentalmente.

radio | 'reɪdɪəʊ | *s.i.* **1** radio: *the message was sent by radio = se envió el mensaje por radio.* || *s.c.* **2** radio (aparato de radio), receptor de radio radiorreceptor. || *v.t.* e *i.* **3** radiar, radiodifundir, transmitir por la radio. || *adj.* **4** radiofónico, de radio: *radio programme = programa de radio.* || **5 on the/by –,** por radio.

radiactive | ˌreɪdɪəʊ'æktɪv | *adj.* FIS. radiactivo.

radii | 'reɪdɪaɪ | *pl.* de **radius.**

radioactivity | ˌreɪdɪəʊæk'tɪvɪtɪ | *s.i.* FIS. radiactividad.

radiocarbon | ˌreɪdɪəʊ'kɑːbən | *s.i.* QUIM. carbono 14, radiocarbono.

radio-controlled | ˌreɪdɪəʊkən'trəʊld | *adj.* teledirigido, radiodirigido.

radiogram | 'reɪdɪəʊgræm | *s.c.* (brit.) radiogramola.

radiograph | 'reɪdɪəʊgrɑːf | *s.c.* **1** (p.u.) MED. radiografía. || *v.t.* **2** MED. radiografiar.

radiographer | ˌreɪdɪ'ɒgrəfər | *s.c.* MED. persona que hace radiografías.

radiography | ˌreɪdɪ'ɒgrəfɪ | *s.i.* MED. radiografía (proceso).

radiologist | ˌreɪdɪ'ɒlədʒɪst | *s.c.* MED. radiólogo.

radiology | ˌreɪdɪ'ɒlədʒɪ | *s.i.* MED. radiología.

radio-telephone | ˌreɪdɪəʊ'telɪfəʊn | *s.c.* TEC. radioteléfono.

radio-telescope | ˌreɪdɪəʊ'telɪskəʊp | (también **radio telescope**) *s.c.* ASTR. radiotelescopio.

radiotherapist | ˌreɪdɪəʊ'θerəpɪst | *s.c.* MED. radioterapeuta.

radiotherapy | ˌreɪdɪəʊ'θerəpɪ | *s.i.* MED. radioterapia.

radish | 'rædɪʃ | *s.c.* BOT. rábano.

radium | 'reɪdɪəm | *s.i.* QUIM. radio.

radius | reɪdɪəs | *s.c.* [*pl.* **radii** o **radiuses**]. **1** MAT. radio (de una circunferencia). **2** (fig.) radio: *within a radius of 50 miles = en un radio de 50 millas, 50 millas a la redonda.*

raffia | 'ræfɪə | *s.i.* BOT. rafia.

raffish | 'ræfɪʃ | (lit.) *adj.* **1** de mala reputación (una persona, un lugar). **2** chulo.

raffishness | 'ræfɪʃnɪs | *s.i.* (lit.) chulería.

raffle | 'ræfl | *s.c.* **1** rifa, sorteo: *a ticket for a raffle = un boleto para una rifa.* || *v.t.* **2** rifar, sortear.

raft | rɑːft | *s.c.* **1** balsa, plataforma flotante. **2** colchón hinchable, colchoneta. || **3 a – of,** (EE.UU. y fam.) un montón de, gran cantidad de.

rafter | 'rɑːftər | *s.c.* ARQ. viga.

rag | ræg | *s.c.* e *i.* **1** trapo, paño (para limpiar). **2** trapo, harapo. **3** trozo de tela. **4** (fam.) periodicucho. **5** (fam.) festividad anual estudiantil organizada con fines benéficos. **6** broma. **7** canción con ritmo de jazz. || *v.t.* **8** (p.u.) tomar el pelo a. || **9 to be in rags and tatters,** ir hecho un desastre. **10 a red – to a bull,** (brit. y fam.) una provocación (lo que más enfurece a alguien). **11 – and bone man,** (brit.) trapero. **12 – doll,** muñeca de trapo. **13 rags,** harapos, andrajos. **14 rags to riches,** (fam.) de la pobreza a la riqueza o al éxito. **15 – trade,** (brit. y fam.) negocio consistente en diseñar, confeccionar y vender ropa femenina. **16 – week,** (brit.) semana en que se celebra una fiesta estudiantil anual, con fines benéficos.

ragamuffin | 'rægəˌmʌfɪn | (p.u.) *s.c.* **1** golfillo, pilluelo, granuja. **2** pelagatos.

ragbag | 'rægbæg | (también **rag-bag**) *s.c.* **1** (fig. y fam.) mezcolanza, revoltijo, cajón de sastre. **2** bolsa para guardar trapos. **3** (fam.) persona andrajosa.

rage | reɪdʒ | *s.c.* e *i.* **1** ira, rabia: *a fit of a rage = un arrebato de ira.* **2** (fig.) furia: *the rage of the wind = la furia del viento.* || *s.sing.* **3 [– (for)]** (fam.) manía, pasión: *his rage for old cars = su pasión por los coches antiguos.* || *v.i.* **4 [– (about/at/against)]** rabiar, encolerizarse, estar enfurecido (una persona). **5** seguir con gran violencia, hacer estragos (una pasión, una catástrofe, un dolor, una enfermedad, una batalla, etc.). || **6 to be (all) the –,** (fam.) estar muy de moda, hacer furor: *this record was all the rage that summer = este disco hizo furor aquel verano.* **7 to be in/to fly into a –,** ponerse hecho una furia.

ragged | 'rægɪd | *adj.* **1** andrajoso, harapiento: *a ragged old man = un viejo andrajoso.* **2** roto, raído, desaliñado (ropa): *a ragged jacket.* **3** desaseado, desaliñado, descuidado (persona, aspecto). **4** desarreglado: *a ragged beard = una barba desarreglada.* **5** desigual (una superficie). **6** descuidado (un estilo). **7** imperfecto: *a ragged work = un trabajo imperfecto.* **8** mellado (un borde). **9** desordenado: *a ragged line = una fila desordenada.* || **10 to be at the – edge,** (EE.UU.) estar muy nervioso. **11 to run someone –,** (fam.) agotar.

raggedly | 'rægɪdlɪ | *adv.* **1** de forma andrajosa: *he was raggedly dressed = vestía de forma andrajosa.* **2** desordenadamente.

raggedy | 'rægɪdɪ | (fam.) *adj.* **1** desgastado (por los bordes). **2** raído. **3** deshilachado.

raging | 'reɪdʒɪŋ | *adj.* **1** violento (un sentimiento, un deseo): *raging passions = pasiones violentas.* **2** furioso (viento, tempestad). **3** feroz, terrible (hambre). **4** (fig.) embravecido, encrespado (el mar). **5** terrible (sed, dolor, deseo).

raglan | 'ræglən | *adj.* **1** raglán (manga). **2** de manga raglán: *a raglan sweater = un jersey de manga raglán.* || *s.c.* **3** abrigo de manga raglán.

ragtag | 'rægtæg | (también **rag-tag**) *adj.* **1** (fam.) desorganizado, alborotado: *a ragtag house.* **2** poco respetable (personas). || **3 – and bobtail,** (fam.) gente poco respetable, gentuza, chusma.

ragtime | 'rægtaɪm | *s.i.* MUS. estilo de música jazz de origen negro americano.

raid | reɪd | *s.c.* **1 [– (on)]** MIL. incursión, invasión repentina. **2** batida policial, redada. **3** asalto, atraco: *a raid on a bank = un atraco a un banco.* || *v.t.* **4** MIL. invadir, tomar por asalto. **5** hacer una redada, registrar (la policía). **6** asaltar, atracar. **7** (fig.) invadir, asaltar: *the children raided the larder last night = anoche los niños asaltaron la despensa.* || **8 air –,** MIL. ataque aéreo.

raider | reɪdər | *s.c.* **1** MIL. invasor. **2** agente de policía que hace una redada. **3** asaltante, atracador.

raiding | reɪdɪŋ | *adj.* invasor.

rail | reɪl | *s.c.* **1** verja. **2** cerca, vallado. **3** barra (para colgar). **4** barandilla (de un barco). **5** raíl, carril (de una vía férrea). **6** DEP. barrera. **7** baranda, barandilla, pasamano. || *v.i.* **8 [to – (against/at)]** (p.u.) protestar, quejarse amargamente. || **9 by –,** por vía férrea, por ferrocarril. **10 to go off the rails,** (fig. y fam.) descarriarse. **11 to – in,** cercar, poner cerco (a personas, a animales). **12 to – off,** cercar, vallar (una zona, un terreno).

railcard | 'reɪlkɑːd | *s.c.* (brit.) tarjeta con la cual se obtienen descuentos en las tarifas ferroviarias.

railing | reɪlɪŋ | *s.c.* **1** verja. **2** baranda, barandilla. **3** pasamanos, barandilla (en una escalera). **4** barrera. || **5 railings,** verja, cerca.

raillery | 'reɪlərɪ | *s.i.* (lit.) guasa, broma, burla.
railroad | 'reɪlrəud | (EE.UU.) *s.c.* **1** ferrocarril. **2** vía férrea. || **3 – car,** vagón ferroviario. **4 – crossing,** paso a nivel. **5 – track,** vía férrea.
railway | 'reɪlweɪ | (brit.) *s.c.* **1** ferrocarril. **2** vía férrea. **3** línea ferroviaria. || **4 – car,** (EE.UU.) vagón ferroviario. **5 – crossing, a)** paso a nivel; **b)** cruce de vías. **6 – line,** (brit.) **a)** línea ferroviaria; **b)** carriles ferroviarios. **7 – station,** estación de ferrocarril. **8 – track,** (brit.) vía férrea.
railwayman | 'reɪlweɪmən | *s.c.* [*pl.irreg.* **railwaymen**] (brit.) ferroviario.
railwaymen | 'reɪlweɪmən | *pl.* de **railwayman.**
raiment | 'reɪmənt | *s.i.* (lit.) vestimentas, ropaje.
rain | reɪn | *s.i.* **1** lluvia. || *s.sing.* **2 [a –]** (lit. o fig.) lluvia (gran cantidad): *a rain of kisses = una lluvia de besos.* || *v.imp.* **3** llover: *it is raining = está lloviendo.* || *v.i.* **4 [– on/upon]** (fig.) llover, caer como lluvia: *rice rained upon the newlyweds = el arroz llovió sobre los novios.* **5 [– on/upon]** (fig.) caer: *misfortune rained upon him = la desgracia cayó sobre él.* **6** caer (del cielo, de las nubes, etc.). || *v.t.* **7** colmar, enviar en grandes cantidades: *they rained gifts upon us = nos colmaron de regalos.* || **8 as right as –,** (fam.) perfectamente; como una rosa. **9 to be rained off,** DEP. ser suspendido a causa de la lluvia (un partido). **10 come – or shine,** (fam.) llueva o no llueva; pase lo que pase. **11 it never rains but it pours,** las desgracias nunca vienen solas. **12 to – cats and dogs,** (fam.) llover a cántaros, caer chuzos de punta. **13 rains, [the –]** estación de las lluvias, temporada de lluvias. **14 to take a – check, [– (on)]** (EE.UU. y fam.) **a)** DEP. coger una entrada para poder presenciar un partido que se había interrumpido a causa de la lluvia; **b)** (fig.) tomar en consideración más adelante (un ofrecimiento, una sugerencia).
rainbow | 'reɪnbəu | *s.c.* **1** arco iris. || **2 at the end of the –,** (fig.) inalcanzable.
raincoat | 'reɪnkəut | *s.c.* impermeable, chubasquero.
raindrop | 'reɪndrɒp | *s.c.* gota de lluvia.
rainfall | 'reɪnfɔːl | *s.i.* lluvia (cantidad de lluvia que ha caído en un determinado sitio en un espacio de tiempo determinado).
rainforest | 'reɪnfɒrɪst | (también **rain forest**). *s.c.* ECOL. bosque tropical.
rainstorm | 'reɪnstɔːm | *s.c.* chaparrón, aguacero.
rainwater | 'reɪnˌwɔːtər | *s.i.* agua de lluvia.
rainy | 'reɪnɪ | *adj.* **1** lluvioso: *a rainy day = un día lluvioso.* || **2 for a – day,** (fig.) para tiempos difíciles, para cuando se pueda necesitar.
raise | reɪz | *v.t.* **1** levantar, alzar: *he raised his hand = alzó la mano.* **2** aumentar, subir (sueldos, precios, etc.): *they raised his salary = aumentaron su sueldo.* **3** levantar, construir: *they raised a wall = levantaron una pared.* **4** subir, alzar, elevar (la voz, el tono, etc.). **5** levantar, elevar (un peso). **6** erigir, construir, levantar (un monumento, un edificio). **7** levantar, reclutar (un ejército). **8** sacar a flote (un barco hundido). **9** levantar (polvo). **10** conseguir, reunir (dinero, fondos). **11** mejorar, subir (una apuesta, una puja). **12** mejorar (el nivel de algo). **13** levantar (una prohibición, protestas). **14** provocar (risa, sonrisa, controversia). **15** (fig.) ascender, poner en un cargo más elevado (a alguien). **16** educar (a un niño). **17** cultivar (una planta). **18** criar (un animal). **19** plantear (un tema, una pregunta). **20** causar (perjuicios, problemas). **21** suscitar (falsas esperanzas, controversias, dudas). **22** poner (objecciones). **23** contactar con (por la radio o teléfono). **24** traer (recuerdos). **25** armar (un alboroto). **26** MAT. elevar (a una potencia). || *v.r.* **27** (lit.) levantarse: *she raised herself = se levantó.* || *s.c.* **28** (EE.UU.) aumento de sueldo. || **29 to – one's eyebrows,** alzar las cejas (para mostrar sorpresa).
raised | reɪzd | *adj.* **1** abultado: *a raised scar = una cicatriz abultada.* **2** en relieve.
raisin | 'reɪzn | *s.c.* pasa, uva pasa.
raison d'etre | ˌreɪzɔːn'deɪtrə | *s.c.* (form.) razón de ser.
rake | reɪk | *s.c.* **1** AGR. rastrillo, rastro. **2** (p.u.) libertino. || *s.sing.* **3** inclinación (de una superficie, de un objeto). | *v.t.* **4** AGR. rastrillar, rastrear. **5** AGR. barrer con el rastrillo, rastrillar: *to rake the weeds = rastrillar las hierbas.* **6** atizar (el fuego). **7 [– (around/through/over)]** rebuscar, escudriñar: *to rake through old documents = rebuscar en viejos documentos.* **8** (fig.) recorrer (un área, con una luz o un arma): *the light raked the open field from one side to the other = la luz recorrió el descampado de parte a parte.* || **9 to – in,** (fam.) ganar mucho (dinero); amasar (una fortuna). **10 to – over,** (fig.) hurgar (en la memoria, en algo ya pasado). **11 to – up, a)** reunir (con dificultad); **b)** sacar a relucir (algo que es preferible olvidar): *they raked up her past = sacaron a relucir su pasado.*
raked | reɪkt | *adj.* inclinado.
rake-off | 'reɪkˌɔf | *s.sing.* (vulg.) comisión (ilegal); tajada.
rakish | 'reɪkɪʃ | *adj.* **1** (p.u.) disoluto, libertino (una persona, un modo de vida). **2** garboso: *a rakish appearance = un aspecto garboso.* || **3 at a – angle,** (un sombrero) ladeado, inclinado hacia un lado (con garbo).
rakishly | 'reɪkɪʃlɪ | *adv.* **1** de forma disoluta. **2** (ladeado) con garbo, con gracia: *his hat was rakishly tilted = su sombrero estaba ladeado con garbo.*
rally | 'rælɪ | *s.c.* **1** POL. mitin, manifestación: *a peace rally = una manifestación en pro de la paz.* **2** recuperación (financiera, de fuerzas, de salud). **3** DEP. rally. **4** DEP. peloteo (en tenis, badminton, etc.). || *v.t.* **5** reunir: *he rallied his men = reunió a sus hombres.* **6** MIL. rehacer, concentrar: *the enemy rallied his trops = el enemigo concentró sus tropas.* **7** recuperar (fuerzas, ánimos). **8** burlarse de, tomar el pelo a. || *v.i.* **9** reunirse. **10** MIL. rehacerse, organizarse (tropas, fuerzas, etc.). **11** MED. reponerse (de una enfermedad). **12** ECON. recuperarse (las finanzas, el mercado, etc.). || **13 to – round,** reunirse (en apoyo de algo o alguien): *they rallied round their leader = se reunieron en torno a su líder.*
rallying | 'rælɪɪŋ | *adj.* **1** de adhesión: *a rallying call = una llamada de adhesión.* || **2 – point,** punto de encuentro, punto de reunión.
ram | ræm | *s.c.* **1** ZOOL. carnero. **2** TEC. maza; pisón. **3 [the –]** ASTR. Aries (constelación). **3** TEC. ariete. || *v.t.* **4** colisionar (un vehículo, un barco). **5 [– (against/at/on/into)]** chocar fuertemente contra: *it rammed against the wall = chocó fuertemente contra la pared.* **6** apisonar. **7** (fam.) meter apretadamente: *she rammed her clothes into the suitcase = metió sus ropas apretadamente en la maleta.* || **8 to – something down someone's throat,** (fig.) enseñar o hacer creer algo a alguien a fuerza de repetírselo. **9 to – something home,** consolidar, dar firmeza.
Ramadan | ˌræmə'dæn | *s.i.* REL. Ramadán.
ramble | 'ræmbl | *s.c.* **1** caminata, paseo: *he went for a ramble = fue a dar un paseo.* || *v.i.* **2** pasear, caminar sin rumbo fijo. **3** (fig.) divagar, perder el hilo (en una conversación). **4** trepar (una enredadera).
rambler | 'ræmblər | *s.c.* **1** caminante, paseante. || **2** BOT. **rose –,** rosal trepador.
rambling | 'ræmblɪŋ | *adj.* **1** que se extiende de forma irregular; sin límites establecidos (un edificio, una calle, una ciudad). **2** (fig.) inconexo, confuso, incoherente (un discurso, un escrito, etc.): *a rambling essay = una redacción incoherente.* **3** BOT. trepador (una planta). || *s.i.* **4** acción de pasear por el campo.
ramification | ˌræmɪfɪ'keɪʃn | *s.c.* (form.) implicación: *they don't know all the ramifications of their decision = no conocen todas las implicaciones de su decisión.*
ramp | ræmp | *s.c.* **1** rampa. **2** desnivel en una carretera debido a obras. **3** topes puestos en la carretera para que los coches reduzcan la velocidad. **4** (vulg.) estafa. || **5 to – about,** (hum.) ponerse hecho una furia.
rampage | ræm'peɪdʒ | *v.i.* **1** correr de un lado a otro haciendo estragos (personas, animales). || **2 to be/go on the –,** alborotarse (causando estragos).
rampant | 'ræmpənt | *adj.* **1** incontrolado (males sociales, enfermedades, etc.): *rampant violence = violencia incontrolada.* **2** BOT. exhuberante (vegetación). **3**

rampante: *rampant lion = león rampante.*
rampart | 'ræmpɑːt | *s.c.* **1** muralla: *the ramparts of Avila = las murallas de µvila.* **2** (fig.) defensa, protección.
ramrod | 'ræmrɒd | *s.c.* **1** baqueta. || *adj.* **2** rígido, tieso, erguido. || **3 as stiff/straight as a –,** (fig.) más tieso que el palo de una escoba.
ramshackle | 'ræmˌʃækl | *adj.* **1** ruinoso, a punto de caerse: *a ramshackle building = un edificio ruinoso.* **2** destartalado, desvencijado (un vehículo). **3** (fig.) decadente: *a ramshackle empire = un imperio decadente.*
ran | ræn | *pret.* de **run.**
ranch | rɑːntʃ | *s.c.* **1** hacienda, finca, rancho (especialmente en EE.UU. y Canadá). **2** (EE.UU.) granja.
rancher | rɑːntʃər | *s.c.* (EE.UU.) ranchero.
rancid | 'rænsɪd | *adj.* rancio: *rancid butter = mantequilla rancia.*
rancor V. **rancour.**
rancorous | 'ræŋkərəs | *adj.* (form.) rencoroso.
rancour | 'ræŋkər | (EE.UU. **rancor**) *s.i.* (form.) rencor.
random | 'rændəm | *adj.* **1** hecho al azar: *a random shot = un disparo hecho al azar.* **2** tomado al azar: *a random sample = una muestra tomada al azar.* **3** fortuito, hecho al azar: *random remarks = comentarios fortuitos.* **4** casual, accidental. || **5 at –,** al azar.
randomly | 'rændəmlɪ | *adv.* al azar.
randy | 'rændɪ | *adj.* (vulg.) cachondo (excitado sexualmente).
rang | ræŋ | *pret.* de **ring.**
range | reɪndʒ | *s.c.* **1 [– (of)]** alcance (de una radio, de un telescopio, etc.). **2** alcance, radio de acción (de un arma). **3** (fig.) alcance, importancia (de una actividad). **4** (fig.) esfera (de influencias). **5** (fig.) incumbencia. **6** surtido, variedad, gama: *a wide range of colours = una amplia gama de colores.* **7** (fig.) alcance: *this author is outside my range = este autor no está a mi alcance (no lo entiendo).* **8** escala, gama (de precios, etc.). **9** FIS. escala (de un termómetro, barómetro, etc.). **10** dehesa. **11** hilera, fila (de casas, edificios, árboles). **12** cadena (de montañas). **13** MIL. campo de tiro. **14** cocina económica. **15** (EE.UU.) campo de pasto. || *s.i.* **16** alcance: *it is out of range = está fuera del alcance.* || *s.sing.* **17** autonomía (de un vehículo). **18** MUS. registro (vocal). || *v.t.* **19** poner en fila, alinear (personas, cosas): *the teacher ranged his pupils = el profesor puso a sus alumnos en fila.* **20** (lit.) recorrer, rondar (un sitio): *they ranged the forests = rondaban los bosques.* || *v.i.* **21** extenderse: *his properties ranged from the river to the mountains = sus propiedades se extendían desde el río a las montañas.* **22 [– (from... to/between... and)]** oscilar: *temperatures here range from 15 to 25 degrees = aquí las temperaturas oscilan entre los 15 y los 25 grados.* **23** alcanzar (un arma): *this gun ranges ten miles = este arma tiene un alcance de diez millas.* **24 [– (through/over/along)]** (lit.) recorrer: *they ranged over the village = recorrieron el pueblo.* **25 [– (through/over)]** (fig.) abarcar: *his research ranged the whole of Europe = su investigación abarcó toda Europa.* || **26 at point-blank –,** a quemarropa.
rangefinder | 'reɪndʒˌfaɪndər | (también **range-finder**) *s.c.* TEC. telémetro.
ranger | 'reɪndʒər | *s.c.* **1** guardabosques. **2** (EE.UU.) miembro de la policía montada.
rank | ræŋk | *s.c.* e *i.* **1** categoría, clase: *a teacher of the first rank = un profesor de primera categoría.* **2** MIL. graduación: *what rank is that officer? = ¿qué graduación tiene aquel oficial?* **3** (p.u.) rango, posición social: *a man of high rank = un hombre de alto rango.* || *s.c.* **4** fila, hilera. **5** MIL. fila (de soldados). **6** parada de taxis. || *adj.* **7** completo, absoluto; auténtico: *it's a rank nonsense = es una completa tontería.* **8** (form.) maloliente; acre. **9** (form.) de mal sabor; acre. **10** (form.) BOT. exuberante (vegetación). || *v.t.* **11** clasificar, situar: *nobody knows where to rank this author = nadie sabe dónde clasificar a este autor.* **12** MIL. alinear (soldados). || *v.i.* **13** figurar, encontrarse: *he ranks among the best athletes in the world = se encuentra entre los mejores atletas del mundo.* || **14 to break ranks, a)** MIL. romper filas; **b)** (fig.) desertar. **15 to close ranks,** apoyarse. **16 to pull –,** utilizar influencias. **17 – and file, a)** MIL. tropa; **b)** gente corriente; **c)** base (de un partido o empresa). **18 ranks**, filas (de un partido, sindicato o agrupación).
ranking | ræŋkɪŋ | *s.c.* **1** clasificación, categoría. || *adj.* **2** (EE.UU.) de más categoría, de mayor graduación.
rankle | 'ræŋkl | *v.i.* **[– (with)]** doler, apenar: *your insults still rankles with me = sus insultos todavía me duelen.*
ransack | 'rænsæk | *v.t.* **1** registrar de arriba abajo, revolver (para buscar algo): *to ransack a drawer = revolver un cajón.* **2** saquear: *they killed the owner and ransacked his house = mataron al propietario y saquearon la casa.*
ransom | 'rænsəm | *s.c.* **1** rescate. || *v.t.* **2** rescatar (mediante pago). || **3 to hold someone to –, a)** pedir rescate por alguien; **b)** (fig.) chantajear, poner entre la espada y la pared.
rant | rænt | *v.i.* **1** vociferar, gritar necedades. **2** desvariar. **3** hablar ampulosamente (en tono teatral). || **4 to – and rave,** vociferar; despotricar; desvariar.
ranting | ræntɪŋ | *s.c.* desvaríos, necedades: *nobody listened to his rantings = nadie escucha sus desvaríos.*
rap | ræp | *v.t.* e *i.* **1 [– (at)]** golpear, dar golpes: *someone rapped (at) the door = alguien daba golpes en la puerta.* || *v.i.* **2** (EE.UU. y fam.) charlar. || *s.c.* **3** golpe seco. **4** reprimenda, crítica. || **5 to care a –,** importar un comino: *I don't care a rap = no me importa un comino.* **6 a – on/over the knuckles,** llamada al orden, reprimenda. **7 to – something out,** soltar, decir algo de golpe. **8 to take the –,** (fam.) pagar el pato.
rapacious | rə'peɪʃəs | *adj.* (form.) codicioso, avaricioso: *a rapacious person = una persona codiciosa.*
rapacity | rə'pæsɪtɪ | *s.c.* (form.) codicia, avaricia.
rape | reɪp | *v.t.* **1** violar, forzar (sexualmente) **2** (lit. y fig.) tomar por la fuerza. || *s.c.* e *i.* **3** violación, estupro. || *s.c.* **4** (lit.) rapto. || *s.sing.* **5 [– (of)]** (form.) ECOL. destrucción, ruina (de un paisaje, bosque, etc.). || *s.i.* **6** BOT. colza.
rapid | 'ræpɪd | *adj.* **1** rápido: *a rapid victory = una victoria rápida.* **2** veloz: *a rapid messenger = un mensajero veloz.* || **3 rapids,** rápidos (de un río).
rapidity | rə'pɪdɪtɪ | *s.i.* rapidez; velocidad.
rapidly | 'ræpɪdlɪ | *adv.* rápidamente; velozmente.
rapier | 'reɪpɪər | *s.c.* (form. y p.u.) estoque.
rapist | 'reɪpɪst | *s.c.* violador.
rapport | ræ'pɔː | *s.i.* **[– (between/with)]** compenetración, entendimiento mutuo.
rapprochement | ræ'prɒʃmɑːŋ | *s.sing.* **[– (between/of/with)]** (form.) reconciliación, restablecimiento de las relaciones.
rapt | ræpt | *adj.* **1** absorto, ensimismado: *he was rapt in his work = estaba absorto en su trabajo.* **2** extasiado, embelesado. **3** profundo: *rapt attention = profunda atención.*
rapture | 'ræptʃər | *s.i.* **1** (lit.) éxtasis. || **2 to be/go into raptures, [– (over/about)]** extasiarse, quedarse extasiado: *he went into raptures over the pictures I showed him = se quedó extasiado ante los cuadros que le enseñé.*
raptourous | 'ræptʃərəs | *adj.* (lit.) entusiasta.
rare | reər | *adj.* **1** raro, poco frecuente: *a rare event = un suceso poco frecuente.* **2** raro, singular, poco corriente: *a rare book = un libro poco corriente.* **3** extraordinario, poco común: *a rare beauty = una belleza extraordinaria.* **4** poco hecho (carne). **5** enrarecido (aire). **6** extraordinario, fenomenal, estupendo.
rarebit | 'reəbɪt | *s.i.* GAST. tostada con queso fundido.
rarefied | 'reərɪfaɪd | (también **rarified**) *adj.* **1** (fig.) refinado (ambiente). **2** (fig.) enrarecido (atmósfera, ambiente). **3** enrarecido (aire).
rarely | reəlɪ | *adv.* raramente, apenas, rara vez.
rarified V. **rarefied.**
raring | reərɪŋ | *adj.* **1** [– + *inf.*] deseoso: *he is raring to try it = está deseoso de probarlo.* || **2 – to go,** (fam.) deseando empezar.
rarity | 'reərətɪ | *s.c.* **1** rareza (cosa poco frecuente). || *s.i.* **2** rareza, escasez: *its rarity makes it so valuable = su escasez lo hace tan valioso.*

rascal | 'rɑːskəl | *s.c.* **1** bribón, pillo, travieso (un niño). **2** (desp. y p.u.) granuja, canalla.
rascally | 'rɑːskəlɪ | *adj.* bribón, pillo.
rase V. **raze.**
rash | ræʃ | *adj.* **1** impetuoso, irreflexivo: *a rash boy = un chico impetuoso.* **2** temerario, imprudente, precipitado: *a rash act = un acto temerario.* || *s.c.* **3** MED. sarpullido. || *s.sing.* **4** (fig.) abundancia repentina, oleada: *a rash of strikes = una oleada de huelgas.*
rasher | 'ræʃər | *s.c.* loncha: *a rasher of ham = una loncha de jamón.*
rashly | ræʃlɪ | *adv.* precipitadamente, sin reflexionar.
rashness | ræʃnɪs | *s.i.* imprudencia, temeridad.
rasp | rɑːsp | *s.sing.* **1** chirrido, sonido estridente. || *s.c.* **2** TEC. escofina. || *v.i.* **3** chirriar. || *v.t.* **4** raspar. **5** (fig.) crispar, irritar: *it rasps my nerves = me crispa los nervios.* **6** pronunciar con voz áspera (una orden, un insulto).
raspberry | 'rɑːzbərɪ | *s.c.* **1** BOT. frambuesa. **2** BOT. frambueso. **3** (fam.) pedorreta (sonido grosero hecho con la lengua y los labios para ofender o burlarse de alguien).
rasping | 'rɑːspɪŋ | *adj.* áspero, irritante, desagradable (un sonido): *a rasping voice = una voz áspera.*
Rasta | 'ræstə | *s.c.* y *adj.* (fam.) REL. rastafari.
Rastafarian | ˌræstə'fɪərɪən | *s.c.* y *adj.* REL. rastafari.
rat | ræt | *s.c.* **1** ZOOL. rata. **2** (fig. y fam.) canalla, miserable. **3** (fig.) traidor, delator. **4** POL. esquirol. **5** (EE.UU.) postizo (para el pelo). || *v.i.* **6** **[– (on)]** (fam.) chivarse. **7** **[– (on)]** desertar. **8** **[– (on)]** (fam.) romper (un trato, una promesa). || **9 like a drowned –,** calado hasta los huesos. **10 rats!,** ¡mecachis!
ratchet | 'rætʃɪt | *s.c.* TEC. trinquete.
rate | reɪt | *s.c.* **1** razón: *they pay us at the rate of two hundred dollars a week = nos pagan a razón de doscientos dólares a la semana.* **2** índice, tasa: *birth rate = índice de natalidad.* **3** tipo, porcentaje (de interés, de cambio, de descuento): *rate of interest = tipo de interés.* **4** velocidad: *the car is travelling at a great rate = el coche circula a gran velocidad.* **5** tarifa, precio: *reduced rate = tarifa reducida.* **6** ritmo: *the rate of work is too slow = el ritmo de trabajo es demasiado lento.* || *v.t.* **7** **[– (as)]** considerar: *he is rated as the best = se le considera el mejor.* **8** **[– (at)]** valorar, tasar: *it was rated at =p 50 = fue valorado en 50 libras.* **9** (fam.) estimar, apreciar: *everybody rates him = todos le tienen aprecio.* **10** (EE.UU.) merecer: *he rates whatever he gets = merece todo lo que le ocurra.* **11** DEP. clasificar. **12** regañar, echar una bronca. **13** FIN. gravar (con un tributo). || *v.i.* **14** **[– (as)]** ser considerado (como): *he rates as the best = es considerado el mejor.* || **15 at any –, a)** en todo caso, de todos modos; **b)** para ser más exactos. **16 at this –,** a este paso (si las cosas siguen así). **17 rates,** (brit.) FIN. contribución municipal, impuesto municipal.
rateable value | 'reɪtəbl'væljuː | *s.c.* (brit.) ECON. valor catastral.
ratepayer | 'reɪtˌpeɪər | *s.c.* (también **rate-payer**) FIN. (brit.) contribuyente.
rather | 'rɑːðər | *adv.* **1** algo, ligeramente: *I feel rather better today = me siento algo mejor hoy.* **2** **[– than]** más bien (que): *it's rather big than small = es más bien grande que pequeño.* **3** bastante: *the show was rather good = el espectáculo era bastante bueno.* **4** **[or –]** mejor dicho: *that man, or rather, that boy... = ese hombre, o mejor dicho, ese chico...* **5** por el contrario: *it was not a matter of money, but rather a matter of time = no era cuestión de dinero sino, por el contrario, de tiempo.* || *prep.* o *conj.* **6** **[– than]** antes que, en vez de: *he remained silent rather than say a nonsense = se calló antes que decir una tontería.* || *interj.* **7** (brit. y p.u.) ¡sin duda!, ¡por supuesto! || **8 – you than me/– her than me,** no te envidio/no la envidio, etc. OBS. **9** **[would/had – (than)]** se utiliza para expresar preferencias: *he would rather die than go = preferiría morirse antes que ir.* **10** se utiliza para hacer más suave una afirmación o una crítica: *I rather think she has made a mistake = me parece, me inclino a creer que se ha equivocado.*
ratification | ˌrætɪfɪ'keɪʃn | *s.i.* (form.) ratificación.
ratify | 'rætɪfaɪ | *v.t.* (form.) ratificar: *they ratified the treaty = ratificaron el tratado.*
rating | 'reɪtɪŋ | *s.c.* **1** categoría, clase, rango. **2** puntuación. **3** FIN. gravamen. **4** MAR. marinero. **5** (fam.) reprensión, bronca. || *s.i.* **6** valoración, tasación (de una propiedad). || **7 ratings,** TV. índice de audiencia.
ratio | 'reɪʃɪəʊ | *s.c.* **1** MAT. proporción, razón, relación: *they are in the ratio of 3 to 1 = están en la proporción de 3 a 1.* || **2 in direct – to,** en relación directa con.
ration | 'ræʃn | *s.c.* **1** ración (porción de algo escaso que se reparte a alguien): *two rations of bread a day = dos raciones de pan al día.* **2** (fig.) porción: *her ration of proud = su porción de orgullo.* || *v.t.* **3** racionar (algo que escasea): *to ration sugar = racionar el azúcar.* **4** **[– (to)]** (fig.) restringir, limitar el consumo de algo a una cantidad determinada: *his doctor rationed him to a couple of cigarettes a day = su médico le limitó a un par de cigarrillos al día.* || **5 – book/card,** MIL. cartilla de racionamiento. **6 to – out,** MIL. racionar. **7 rations,** víveres, provisiones.
rational | 'ræʃənl | *adj.* **1** racional: *a rational being = un ser racional.* **2** sensato, razonable: *a rational behaviour = una conducta razonable.*
rationale | ˌræʃə'nɑːl | *s.sing.* **[– (for/of)]** (form.) fundamento, base lógica.
rationalise V. **rationalize.**
rationalism | 'ræʃnəlɪzəm | *s.i.* FIL. racionalismo.
rationalist | 'ræʃnəlɪst | *s.c.* y *adj.* FIL. racionalista.
rationalistic | ˌræʃnə'lɪstɪk | V. **rationalist.**
rationality | ˌræʃə'nælɪtɪ | *s.i.* racionalidad, lógica, sensatez: *it lacks rationality = carece de lógica.*
rationalization | ˌræʃnəlaɪ'zeɪʃn | *s.c.* e *i.* **1** justificación, disculpa. || *s.i.* **2** racionalización, organización sistemática.
rationalize | 'ræʃnəlaɪz | (también **rationalise**) *v.t.* e *i.* **1** (fam.) justificar, buscar excusas: *she had to rationalize her misbehaviour = tenía que justificar su mala conducta.* || *v.t.* **2** razonar, analizar por medio de la razón: *try to rationalize your fears = trata de razonar tus temores.* **3** racionalizar (una industria, un sistema, etc.). **4** MAT. extraer raíces.
rationally | 'ræʃnəlɪ | *adv.* razonablemente.
rationing | 'ræʃnɪŋ | *s.c.* racionamiento.
rat-race | 'rætreɪs | (también **rat race**) *s.sing.* (fig.) competición, lucha constante (en busca del éxito).
rattiness | 'rætɪnɪs | *s.i.* mal genio, mal humor.
rattle | 'rætl | *v.t.* e *i.* **1** golpear (haciendo ruido); sacudir ruidosamente: *the wind rattled the blinds = el viento sacudió las persianas.* || *v.t.* **2** desconcertar, turbar, desorientar: *her presence rattled him = su presencia le turbaba.* || *v.i.* **3** traquetear: *a bus that rattles = un autobús que traquetea.* **4** sonar, hacer ruido. || *s.c.* **5** ruido. **6** traqueteo. **7** sonajero. **8** carraca. **9** golpeteo: *the rattle of a door = el golpeteo de una puerta.* **10** MED. estertor. || **11 to – away/on/along, [– (about)]** (fam.) (estar de cháchara.) **12 to – off, a)** decir de corrido; **b)** despachar. **13 to – through,** despachar (terminar rápidamente).
rattler | 'rætlər | *s.c.* (EE.UU. y fam.) ZOOL. cascabel (serpiente).
rattlesnake | 'rætlsneɪk | *s.c.* ZOOL. serpiente de cascabel, crótalo.
rattling | 'rætlɪŋ | *adv.* **[– + *adj./adv.*]** (fam. y p.u.) realmente, muy: *it is rattling good = es realmente bueno.*
ratty | 'rætɪ | *adj.* (brit. y fam.) malhumorado, irritable.
raucous | 'rɔːkəs | *adj.* **1** ronco, bronco (un sonido). **2** áspero (voz). **3** estentóreo, estridente, sonoro: *a raucous laughter = una risa sonora.* **4** (fig.) ruidoso: *a raucous morning = una mañana ruidosa.*
raucously | 'rɔːkəslɪ | *adv.* **1** de forma ruidosa. **2** ásperamente.
raunchy | 'rɔːntʃɪ | *adj.* (fam.) lascivo, erótico, provocativo: *a raunchy look = un aspecto provocativo.*
ravage | 'rævɪdʒ | (form.) *v.t.* **1** devastar, arrasar, estropear: *the fire has ravaged the crops = el incendio ha arrasado las cosechas.* **2** destruir, asolar (una enfermedad, una epidemia, una desgra-

cia): *civilizations ravaged by war = civilizaciones asoladas por la guerra.* **3** saquear. || *s.i.* **4** destrucción, destrozo. || **5 ravages,** estragos: *the ravages of war = los estragos de la guerra.*

rave | reɪv | *v.i.* **1** desvariar, desatinar, delirar: *the patient is raving = el enfermo está delirando.* **2 [– (against/about/at)]** (fam.) echar pestes, despotricar: *he began to rave at me = empezó a despotricar contra mí.* **3 [– (about/of/over)]** deshacerse en elogios, hablar con entusiasmo: *they raved about her new novel = hablaron con entusiasmo de su nueva novela.* || *s.c.* **4** (fam.) reseña elogiosa (sobre un libro, obra de arte, etc.). **5** (juv.) fiesta muy animada. || *adj.* **6** (juv.) de moda: *a rave place = un sitio de moda.* || **7 to – it up,** (fam. y p.u.) estar de juerga. **8 the latest –,** (juv.) el último grito, lo último.

raven | 'reɪvn | *s.c.* **1** ZOOL. cuervo. || *adj.* **2** (lit.) negro como el azabache (pelo). || *v.t.* (p.u.) devorar.

ravenous | 'rævənəs | *adj.* **1** (fam.) muerto de hambre, hambriento: *I'm ravenous = estoy muerto de hambre.* **2** voraz: *a ravenous appetite = un apetito voraz.* **3 [– (for)]** (fig.) ansioso, ávido: *he is ravenous for money = está ansioso de dinero.*

ravenously | 'rævənəslɪ | *adv.* vorazmente; con ansia.

raver | 'reɪvər | *s.c.* (brit. y fam.) juerguista.

rave-up | 'reɪvʌp | *s.c.* (brit. y fam.) guateque, fiesta.

ravine | rə'viːn | *s.c.* GEOG. barranco, garganta, desfiladero.

raving | 'reɪvɪŋ | *adj.* **1** (fam.) chalado. || **2 – mad,** loco perdido. **3 ravings,** desvaríos.

ravioli | ˌrævɪ'əulɪ | *s.i.* GAST. ravioles, raviolis.

ravish | 'rævɪʃ | *v.t.* **1** (form. y lit.) deleitar, encantar, fascinar: *I was ravished with her beauty = me quedé fascinado con su belleza.* **2** (p.u.) violar (a una persona). **3** (arc.) arrebatar. **4** MIL. saquear (una ciudad). **5** (arc.) llevarse a la fuerza.

ravishing | 'rævɪʃɪŋ | *adj.* **1** encantador. **2** (fam.) arrebatador, imponente: *a ravishing brunette = una morena imponente.*

ravishingly | 'rævɪʃɪŋlɪ | *adv.* sorprendentemente, asombrosamente.

raw | rɔː | *adj.* **1** crudo (sin cocer): *raw fish = pescado crudo.* **2** crudo, sin elaborar (una sustancia, un material): *raw silk = seda cruda.* **3** sin clasificar (datos). **4** bruto, sin refinar: *raw sugar = azúcar sin refinar.* **5** puro, sin mezcla: *raw spirit = alcohol puro.* **6** natural (una cualidad). **7** en carne viva (una parte del cuerpo, una herida). **8** riguroso, crudo (clima). **9** frío y húmedo: *a raw morning = una mañana fría y húmeda.* **10** sin pulir (un estilo). **11** franco, directo (un escrito, un informe). **12** (EE.UU.) inexperto, novato. **13** sin coser (un dobladillo). **14** basto, ordinario (una persona). || **15 a – deal,** (fam.) un trato injusto. **16 in the –, a)** (fam.) desnudo, en cueros vivos; **b)** en su estado natural. **17 – cotton,** algodón en rama. **18 – material,** materia prima. **19 to touch a – nerve/to touch someone on the –,** (fig.) herir a alguien donde más le duele, herir en lo más vivo.

raw-boned | 'rɔːbəund | *adj.* flaco, esquelético, en los huesos: *a raw-boned girl = una chica esquelética.*

rawhide | 'rɔːhaɪd | (EE.UU.) *s.i.* **1** cuero crudo, sin curtir. || *s.c.* **2** látigo de cuero.

ray | reɪ | *s.c.* **1** rayo: *a ray of sunshine = un rayo de sol.* **2** ZOOL. raya. || *s.sing.* **3** (fig.) pizca, poquito: *a ray of truth = una pizca de verdad.* **4** MUS. re.

rayon | 'reɪɒn | *s.i.* rayón.

raze | reɪz | (también **rase**) *v.t.* **1 [– (to)]** arrasar, destruir (un edificio, una ciudad). **2** (fig.) borrar (de la memoria). || **3 to – to the ground,** arrasar.

razor | 'reɪzər | *s.c.* **1** maquinilla de afeitar. **2** navaja de afeitar. **3** máquina de afeitar (eléctrica). || **4 – blade,** cuchilla.

razor-sharp | 'reɪzəˌʃɑːp | *adj.* **1** afilado. **2** (fig.) agudo, perspicaz.

razzle | 'ræzl | *s.i.* **1** animación, juerga, parranda. || **2 to go on the –,** (fam.) ir de juerga.

re | riː | *prep.* **1** (form.) con respecto a, en cuanto a (para iniciar cartas comerciales o documentos legales). || *s.sing.* **2** MUS. re.

reach | riːtʃ | *v.t.* **1** llegar a: *we reached his house by seven = llegamos a su casa sobre las siete.* **2** alcanzar, pasar, acercar: *reach me that shirt from the wardrobe = alcánzame esa camisa del armario.* **3** alcanzar, llegar hasta: *the child can't reach the window = el crío no puede alcanzar la ventana.* **4** ponerse en contacto con: *I was unable to reach him by telephone = no pude ponerme en contacto con él por teléfono.* **5** (fig.) llegar a, alcanzar: *I couldn't reach the end of the book = no pude llegar al final del libro.* **6** (fig.) ascender a: *the number of compet itors reached 500 = el número de participantes ascendió a 500.* **7** alcanzar, conseguir, lograr (un objetivo). **8** llegar a (un acuerdo, un arreglo, una conclusión). **9 [to – out (for)]** alargar, extender (la mano, para coger algo): *she reached out her hand for her glass = extendió la mano para coger su vaso.* **10** extenderse a, llegar a: *the fire reached the roof = el fuego se extendió al tejado.* || *v.i.* **11 [– (to)]** extenderse: *his lands reach to the mountains = sus tierras se extienden hasta las montañas.* **12** llegar: *this ladder won't reach = esta escalera no llega.* || *s.i.* **13** alcance: *it's out of their reach = está fuera de su alcance.* || **14 beyond one's –,** fuera del alcance de uno. **15 reaches, [– (of)] a)** tramos, extensiones (de terreno); **b)** cuenca (de un río). **16 within (easy) –,** a corta distancia, muy cerca. **17 within one's –,** al alcance de uno.

reach-me-downs | ˌriːtʃmɪ'daun | *s.pl.* (vulg.) ropa usada, ropa de segunda mano.

react | rɪ'ækt | *v.i.* **1 [– (to)]** reaccionar (ante un estímulo): *how did he react to your question? = ¿cómo reaccionó ante tu pregunta?* **2 [– (against)]** reaccionar, rebelarse: *some day he will react against their methods = algún día se rebelará contra sus métodos.* **3 [– (with)]** QUIM. producirse una reacción. **4 [– (on/ upon)]** producir un efecto (sobre).

reaction | rɪ'ækʃn | *s.c.* e *i.* **1** reacción: *an unexpected reaction = una reacción inesperada.* || *s.c.* **2 [– (against)]** reacción: *a reaction against Romanticism = una reacción contra el Romanticismo.* **3** QUIM. reacción: *chain reaction = reacción en cadena.* **4 [– (to)]** MED. reacción: *a reaction to antibiotics = una reacción a los antibióticos.* **5** MIL. contraataque. || *s.i.* **6** POL. conservadurismo, oposición al progreso: *their reaction made changes difficult = su conservadurismo dificultaba los cambios.* || *s.sing.* **7 [– (against)]** reacción, rechazo: *a reaction against divorce = una reacción en contra del divorcio.* || **8 reactions,** reflejos (reacciones rápidas y automáticas).

reactionary | rɪ'ækʃnərɪ | *adj.* y *s.c.* POL. reaccionario.

reactivate | rɪ'æktɪveɪt | *v.t.* reactivar.

reactivation | rɪæktɪ'veɪʃn | *s.i.* reactivación.

reactive | rɪ'æktɪv | *adj.* QUIM. reactivo: *reactive compounds = compuestos reactivos.*

reactiveness | rɪæktɪvnɪs | *s.i.* reactividad.

reactor | rɪ'æktər | *s.c.* **1** FIS. reactor nuclear. **2** QUIM. reactor.

read | riːd | *v.* [*pret.* y *p.p.* **read**] *t.* e *i.* **1** leer: *to read the newspaper = leer el periódico.* || *t.* **2** leer (en voz alta): *she read me the letter twice = me leyó la carta dos veces.* **3** descifrar: *he can read hieroglyphics = sabe descifrar jeroglíficos.* **4** comprender, entender: *I must confess that I don't read her = tengo que confesar que no la entiendo.* **5** indicar, señalar, marcar (un instrumento): *the thermometer reads 14º = el termómetro señala 14º.* **6** leer, consultar (un instrumento): *to read the meter = leer el contador.* **7** interpretar: *it was read as cowardice = fue interpretado como cobardía.* **8** RAD. oír (recibir la transmisión). **9** estudiar (una asignatura universitaria): *she is reading a degree in chem istry = está estudiando para licenciarse en química.* **10** adivinar (un acertijo, el pensamiento, el porvenir). **11** interpretar (un sueño, un presagio). **12** (fig.) leer (el pensamiento, la palma de la mano, en la cara, en la mirada). **13** PER. corregir: *to read proofs = corregir pruebas.* || *i.* **14** leerse: *it reads easily = se lee fácilmente.* **15** leer: *this child can't read = este niño no sabe leer.* **16**

decir: *the text reads thus = el texto dice así.* || *s.sing.* **17 [a –]** lectura (tiempo dedicado a leer). || **18 a good/excellent/etc. –**, una buena/excelente lectura. **19 to have a reading knowledge of,** tener un conocimiento académico (de un idioma). **20 to – between the lines,** (fig.) leer entre líneas. **21 to – into,** ver (más de lo que hay en realidad). **22 to – out,** leer en voz alta. **23 to – over/through, a)** volver a leer, repasar; **b)** leer por encima. **24 to – up, a)** estudiar, empollar; **b) [– on]** documentarse (sobre).

read | red | *pret.* y *p.p.* de **read.**

readable | 'riːdəbl | *adj.* **1** que vale la pena leer: *a readable novel.* **2** legible, que se puede leer.

reader | 'riːdər | *s.c.* **1** lector (persona aficionada a la lectura). **2** lector (de manuscritos, en una editorial). **3** corrector (de pruebas tipográficas). **4** RAD. lector, locutor. **5** LIT. libro de texto. **6** INF. dispositivo para leer microfilms. **7** INF. lector, dispositivo informático capaz de leer textos. **8** (brit.) profesor adjunto (en una universidad).

readership | 'riːdəʃɪp | *s.sing.* **1** número de lectores de una publicación. || *s.c.* **2** puesto de profesor adjunto.

readily | 'redɪlɪ | *adv.* **1** de buena gana, con gusto: *I readily accepted his invitation = acepté con gusto su invitación.* **2** pronto, con presteza, rápidamente. **3** fácilmente, sin dificultad: *he understood it readily = lo comprendió sin dificultad.*

readiness | 'redɪnɪs | *s.i.* **1** prontitud, presteza. **2** buena disposición (para hacer o aceptar algo). **3** rapidez, celeridad. **4** agudeza (de ingenio). **5** facilidad. || **6 to be in – (for),** estar preparado (para).

reading | riːdɪŋ | *s.i.* **1** lectura. **2** cultura, erudición, conocimientos: *a man of vast reading = un hombre con amplios conocimientos.* || *s.c.* **3** lectura (texto que se lee). **4** FILOL. versión (de un texto). **5** (fig.) interpretación, visión, versión: *my reading of the facts = mi visión de los hechos.* **6** lectura, indicación (de un instrumento). **7** recital (de poesía). **8** DER. (brit.) lectura (de un proyecto de ley en el parlamento).

reading-lamp | 'riːdɪŋlæmp | (también **reading lamp**) *s.c.* lámpara portátil, flexo.

reading-room | 'riːdɪŋrum | (también **reading room**) *s.c.* sala de lectura.

readjust | ˌrɪə'dʒʌst | *v.t.* e *i.* **1 [– (to)]** readaptar(se): *we have to readjust (ourselves) to this way of life = tenemos que readaptarnos a este modo de vida.* || *v.t.* **2** reajustar, volver a ajustar.

readjustment | ˌrɪə'dʒʌstmənt | *s.i.* **1** readaptación: *they need a period of readjustment = necesitan un período de readaptación.* || *s.c.* e *i.* **2** reajuste: *readjustment of salaries = reajuste de sueldos.*

ready | 'redɪ | *adj.* **1 [– (for/to)]** listo, preparado: *is everything ready? = ¿está todo listo?* **2** dispuesto: *we are ready to help you = estamos dispuestos a ayudarte.* **3 [– (for/to)]** preparado (para algo): *he's not ready to face the facts = no está preparado para afrontar los hechos.* **4** rápido, pronto: *a ready answer = una respuesta rápida.* **5** efectivo, dinero contante: *ready cash = dinero efectivo.* **6** agudo (el ingenio). || *v.t.* **7 [– (for)]** preparar, disponer. **8** [– + *pron.r.* + **(for/to)**] (form.) prepararse: *they are readying themselves for the race = se están preparando para la carrera.* || **9 at the –,** MIL. listo para disparar (un fusil). **10 to get/make something –,** preparar algo. **11 to have a – tongue,** (fig.) no tener pelos en la lengua. **12 readies,** (fam.) dinero contante; pasta. **13 – and wait ing,** a punto, preparado. **14 – when you are,** (fam.) cuando quieras.

ready-made | ˌredɪ'meɪd | *adj.* **1** hecho, confeccionado, de confección : *ready-made clothes = ropa de confección.* **2** prefabricado. **3** precocinado: *ready-made food = comida precocinada.* **4** (fig.) preconcebido: *ready-made ideas = ideas preconcebidas, tópicos.*

reaffirm | ˌriːfəːm | *v.t.* reafirmar: *he reaffirmed his loyalty to our cause = reafirmó su fidelidad a nuestra causa.*

real | rɪəl | *adj.* **1** real, verdadero (no ficticio): *a real story = una historia verdadera.* **2** auténtico, legítimo: *a real diamond = un brillante auténtico.* **3** verdadero: *the real reason = la verdadera razón.* **4** verdadero, de verdad: *a real friend = un amigo de verdad.* **5** genuino, verdadero, auténtico: *a real case of war psychosis = un auténtico caso de psicosis de guerra.* **6** efectivo, real: *real aid = ayuda efectiva.* **7** real, total: *the real cost = el coste real.* || *adv.* **8** (EE.UU.) muy, realmente: *it's real good = es realmente bueno.* || **9 for –,** de veras. **10 – estate,** [también **– estate** cuando precede a un *s.*] **a)** DER. bienes inmuebles, bienes raíces; **b)** (EE.UU.) inmobiliario: *real estate agent = agente inmobiliario.* **11 – time,** [también **– world** cuando precede a un *s.*] la realidad, el mundo real. **12 the – thing,** la realidad; lo verdadero.

realign | ˌriːə'laɪn | (form.) *v.t.* **1** reorganizar, reestructurar. **2** reagrupar. || *v.i.* **3** POL. aliarse, coligarse, unirse (partidos políticos).

realignment | ˌriːə'laɪnmənt | *s.i.* (form.) reestructuración, reorganización.

realise V. **realize.**

realism | 'rɪəlɪzəm | *s.i.* **1** realismo, pragmatismo, sentido común. **2** realismo, verosimilitud. **3** autenticidad. **4** ART. realismo.

realist | 'rɪəlɪst | *s.c.* realista (persona partidaria del realismo).

realistic | ˌrɪə'lɪstɪk | *adj.* **1** realista, pragmático: *a realistic politician = un político realista.* **2** ART. realista.

reallistically | ˌrɪə'lɪstɪkəlɪ | *adv.* de un modo realista, con realismo.

reality | rɪ'ælɪtɪ | *s.i.* **1** realidad: *painful reality = lamentable realidad.* **2** realismo: *it was reproduced with reality = estaba reproducido con realismo.* || *s.c.* e *i.* **3** verdad, realidad: *her dreams have become reality = sus sueños se han hecho realidad.* || **4 in –, a)** en realidad, de hecho; **b)** en la realidad (no en la ficción).

realizable | 'rɪəlaɪzəbəl | *adj.* **1** realizable, viable, factible: *your proyect is not realizable = su proyecto no es factible.* **2** FIN. convertible (bienes, inversiones, etc.).

realization | ˌrɪəlaɪ'zeɪʃn | , (EE.UU.) | ˌrɪəlɪ'zeɪʃn | *s.sing.* **1** comprensión, reconocimiento; descubrimiento (de un hecho). **2** realización (de un plan, de una ambición, etc.). **3** FIN. convertibilidad (de bienes, inversiones, etc.).

realize | 'rɪəlaɪz | (también **realise**) *v.t.* **1** darse cuenta de, comprender: *he didn't realize what was happening there = el no se dio cuenta de lo que estaba ocurriendo allí.* **2** (form.) realizar, hacer realidad (un proyecto, una aspiración, un deseo). **3** (form.) llevar a cabo (un proyecto, un plan). **4** (form.) realizarse (uno mismo, sus posibilidades). **5 [– (on)]** FIN. sacar, obtener (por): *to realize a profit = obtener un beneficio.* **6** FIN. convertir en dinero (acciones, bienes, etc.). || **7 my/your/etc. worst fears were –,** se confirmaron mis temores.

realized | 'rɪəlaɪzd | *adj.* realizado, hecho realidad.

really | 'rɪəlɪ | *adv.* **1** (fam.) verdaderamente, realmente: *it is really good = es realmente bueno.* **2** de veras: *I'm really sorry = lo siento de veras.* **3** en realidad: *I don't really want to go = en realidad no quiero ir.*

OBS. **Really** también se utiliza como *interj.* para expresar sorpresa, interés, censura, enfado, duda o incredulidad, según el contexto, variando en cada caso su entonación.

realm | relm | (form.) *s.c.* **1** (fig.) reino, campo, terreno, esfera: *in the realm of poetry = en el terreno de la poesía.* **2** reino (país gobernado por un rey o reina).

realtor | 'rɪəltɔːr | *s.c.* (EE.UU.) COM. agente inmobiliario.

reams | riːmz | *s.pl.* (fam.) gran cantidad de, montones de (algo escrito): *he wrote reams of verse = escribió montones de versos.*

reap | riːp | *v.t.* e *i.* **1** AGR. cosechar. **2** AGR. segar. || *v.t.* **3** (fig.) cosechar, recoger (el fruto de algo). **4** (fig.) obtener (ganancias, provecho). **5** (fig.) cosechar, ganar: *they reaped quite a lot of awards = cosechó numerosos galardones.*

reaper | riːpər | AGR. *s.c.* **1** cosechadora (máquina). **2** segadora (máquina). **3** cosechero. **4** segador.

reaping | riːpɪŋ | AGR. *s.i.* **1** siega. || **2 – machine,** segadora.

reappear | ˌriːə'pɪər | *v.i.* reaparecer.

reappearance | ˌriːə'pɪərəns | *s.c.* reaparición.

reappraisal | ˌriːə'preɪzəl | *s.c.* e *i.* (form.) nueva valoración, nueva estimación, nuevo examen: *he wants a reappraisal of the situations = quiere un nuevo examen de la situación.*
reappraise | ˌriːə'preɪz | *v.t.* (form.) reconsiderar.
rear | rɪər | *s.sing.* **1 [the – (of)]** la parte de atrás, la parte posterior: *the rear of the house = la parte de atrás de la casa.* **2** (fam.) water, retrete. **3** MIL. retaguardia. || *adj.* **4** trasero, de atrás, posterior: *rear entrance = entrada trasera.* || *v.t.* **5** criar, educar (a un niño). **6** criar (animales). **7** cultivar (vegetales). **8** erguir, levantar: *it reared its head = irguió la cabeza.* **9** alzar, levantar (la voz, la mano). **10** erigir, levantar, alzar (un monumento). || *v.t.* e *i.* **11** erguir(se), levantar(se), empinar(se). || *v.i.* **12 [– (over)]** alzarse, erguirse (un edificio, una montaña). || **13 to bring up the –/to take up the –, a)** quedarse en la retaguardia; **b)** MIL. cubrir la retaguardia. **14 to – its ugly head,** (fig.) empezar a asomar (algo desagradable). **15 to – up, a)** erguirse, empinarse (una persona, un animal); **b)** encabritarse (un caballo). **16 – view mirror,** espejo retrovisor.
rearguard | 'rɪəgɑːd | *s.sing.* **1** MIL. retaguardia. || **2 to fight a – action,** (fig.) mantener una lucha sin esperanza.
rearm | ˌriː'ɑːm | *v.t.* e *i.* MIL. rearmar(se).
rearmament | rɪ'ɑːməmənt | *s.i.* MIL. rearme.
rearmost | rɪəməust | *adj.* último (en una fila): *the rearmost taxi.*
rearrange | ˌriːə'reɪndʒ | *v.t.* **1** ordenar de otro modo, disponer de distinta forma: *who rearranged my books? = ¿quién dispuso mis libros de distinta forma?* **2** volver a concertar (una cita).
rearrangement | ˌriːə'reɪndʒmənt | *s.c.* e *i.* **1** reordenación, nueva disposición. **2** cambio (en la hora o en la fecha de una cita).
reason | 'riːzn | *s.c.* e *i.* **1 [– (for/to)]** razón, motivo: *there is no reason to be worried = no hay razón para estar preocupado.* **2** porqué, causa: *he wants to know the reason for everything = él quiere saber el porqué de todas las cosas.* || *s.i.* **3** razón, raciocinio: *animals lack reason = los animales carecen de razón.* **4** razón, sentido común, juicio. || *v.i.* **5** razonar, raciocinar. **6** pensar, discurrir. **7** argumentar, alegar. **8** reflexionar. || **9 all the more –, [– for/to]** razón de más (para). **10 to bring somebody to –,** hacer que alguien entre en razón. **11 by – of,** (form.) con motivo de, a causa de, en virtud de. **12 for reasons best known to himself/herself, etc.,** por los motivos que él/ella, etc. sabrá. **13 for some –,** por alguna razón (desconocida): *for some reason I remembered her = por alguna razón me acordé de ella.* **14 to listen to/hear –,** avenirse a razones. **15 to lose one's –,** perder el juicio, volverse loco. **16 to – out,** resolver por medio del razonamiento (un problema, una cuestión). **17 to – with somebody,** discutir con alguien (alegando razones). **18 to see –,** entrar en razón. **19 to stand to –,** ser lógico, ser razonable. **20 within –,** dentro de lo razonable.
reasonable | 'riːznəbl | *adj.* **1** razonable, sensato: *be reasonable, you can't see him now = sé razonable, no le puedes ver ahora.* **2** razonable, lógico: *a reasonable explanation = una explicación razonable.* **3** razonable, módico (un precio, una suma, etc.). **4** justo, razonable: *reasonable complaints = quejas razonables.* **5** razonable, aceptable, moderado: *it's a reasonable offer, you shouldn't decline it = es una oferta razonable, no deberías rechazarla.*
reasonableness | 'riːznəblnɪs | *s.i.* sentido común, sensatez, juicio, moderación.
reasonably | 'riːznəblɪ | *adv.* **1** razonablemente, moderadamente, bastante: *reasonably good salaries = sueldos bastante buenos.* **2** razonablemente, con sensatez, con moderación.
reasoned | 'riːznd | *adj.* razonado, basado en la razón.
reasoning | 'riːznɪŋ | *s.i.* razonamiento, argumentos, raciocinio: *I don't understand your reasoning = no entiendo tu razonamiento.*
reassemble | ˌriːə'sembl | *v.t.* e *i.* **1** reagrupar(se), volver(se) a reunir: *his family will reassemble to talk about the question = su familia se volverá a reunir para discutir el asunto.* || *v.t.* **2** TEC. volver a montar (una máquina, un aparato).
reassembly | ˌriːə'semblɪ | *s.i.* **1** reagrupación, nueva reunión. **2** TEC. montaje (de una máquina, de un aparato).
reassert | ˌriːə'sɜːt | *v.t.* **1** reafirmar (posición, autoridad, etc.). **2** *r.* reafirmar(se) (una idea, un principio, un hábito, etc.).
reassess | ˌriːə'ses | *v.t.* **1** reconsiderar, volver a analizar: *to reassess the situation = reconsiderar la situación.* **2** volver a tasar.
reassessment | ˌriːə'sesmənt | *s.c.* e *i.* **1** reconsideración. **2** nuevo análisis. **3** nueva valoración.
reassurance | ˌriːə'ʃʊərəns | *s.i.* **1** confianza, tranquilidad. **2** apoyo. || *s.c.* **3** reconfortante (palabra, noticia, acción, etc.).
reassure | ˌriːə'ʃʊər | *v.t.* **1** reconfortar, tranquilizar (a una persona, diciéndole algo). **2** alentar, dar ánimos.
reassuring | ˌriːə'ʃʊərɪŋ | *adj.* reconfortante, tranquilizador; alentador.
reassuringly | ˌriːə'ʃʊərɪŋlɪ | *adv.* de modo reconfortante, de modo tranquilizador.
rebate | 'riːbeɪt | *s.c.* **1** FIN. devolución, desembolso. **2** COM. descuento, rebaja. **3** COM. reintegro.
rebel | 'rebl | *s.c.* **1** rebelde, inconformista: *my son is a rebel = mi hijo es un rebelde.* **2** MIL. rebelde, insurrecto: *the rebels attacked at dawn = los rebeldes atacaron al alba.* || *adj.* **3** rebelde: *the rebel forces = las fuerzas rebeldes.* || | rɪ'bel | *v.i.* **4 [– (against)]** rebelarse, sublevarse: *they rebelled against the governement = se rebelaron contra el gobierno.* **5** negarse a obedecer; rebelarse. **6** (fig.) rebelarse, no aguantar (el cuerpo, una parte del cuerpo): *he ran until his legs rebelled = corrió hasta que sus piernas no aguantaron.*
rebellion | rɪ'beljən | *s.c.* e *i.* **1** MIL. rebelión, revuelta, sublevación, levantamiento: *a rebellion against the governement = una sublevación contra el gobierno.* **2** rebeldía. **3** POL. oposición, resistencia.
rebellious | rɪ'beljəs | *adj.* **1** rebelde, incontrolable, revoltoso: *a rebellious child = un niño rebelde.* **2** MIL. rebelde, sedicioso.
rebelliously | rɪ'beljəslɪ | *adv.* sediciosamente.
rebelliousness | rɪ'beljəslnɪs | *s.i.* rebeldía.
rebirth | ˌriː'bɜːθ | *s.i.* **1** renacimiento. **2** renovación. **3** resurgimiento. **4** despertar.
rebound | rɪ'baʊnd | *v.i.* **1 [– (from)]** rebotar: *the ball rebounded from the ground = la pelota rebotó en el suelo.* **2 [– (on/upon)]** (fig.) recaer (sobre), tener repercusiones (en): *his bad acts will rebound on himself = sus malas acciones recaerán sobre él.* | 'riːbaʊnd | *s.c.* **3** rebote. || **4 on the –, a)** DEP. al rebote; **b)** (fig.) bajo efecto de un rechazo en una relación anterior: *she married John on the rebound = se casó con John al ser rechazada por otro.*
rebuff | rɪ'bʌf | *v.t.* **1** despreciar, desairar, rechazar con desdén (una oferta, una sugerencia, una propuesta): *they rebuffed his offer = rechazaron su oferta.* || *s.c.* **2** desaire, desdén. **3** negativa.
rebuild | ˌriː'bɪld | *v.* [*pret.* y *p.p.* **rebuilt**] *t.* e *i.* **1** reconstruir: *after the storm they began to rebuild the huts = después de la tormenta empezaron a reconstruir las cabañas.* **2** reedificar. **3** repasar, arreglar (una máquina, un aparato). **4** restablecer (un negocio, una organización).
rebuilt | ˌriː'bɪlt | *pret.* y *p.p.* de **rebuild.**
rebuke | rɪ'bjuːk | *v.t.* **1 [– (of)]** reprender, regañar: *his mother rebuked him for hitting his sister = su madre le regañó por pegar a su hermana.* **2** censurar, criticar, reprochar. || *s.c.* e *i.* **3** reprimenda, reprensión. **4** censura, reproche.
rebut | rɪ'bʌt | *v.t.* (form.) refutar, rebatir; impugnar.
rebuttal | rɪ'bʌtl | *s.c.* (form.) refutación; impugnación.
recalcitrance | rɪ'kælsɪtrəns | *s.c.* (form.) obstinación.
recalcitrant | rɪ'kælsɪtrənt | *adj.* (form.) recalcitrante, obstinado, terco; reacio.
recall | rɪ'kɔːl | *v.t.* **1** recordar, acordarse de: *I can't recall when I did it = no*

puedo recordar cuándo lo hice. **2** [– + *o.* + **(from/to)**] hacer volver (a su país, después de trabajar en el extranjero). **3** retirar (a un diplomático, a un embajador). **4** revocar, anular (una decisión, una orden). **5** traer a la memoria, recordar: *this street recalls my schooldays = esta calle me trae a la memoria mis días de escuela.* **6** MIL. llamar (a filas). **7** aceptar la devolución de (una compra, un regalo). || *s.i.* **8** recuerdo; memoria. **9** aviso, llamada (para hacer que alguien vuelva). **10** retirada (de un diplomático, de un embajador). **11** MIL. llamada (a filas). **12** revocación, anulación (de una orden, de una decisión). || *s.c.* **13** MIL. toque de llamada. || **14 to be beyond/past –, a)** ser irrevocable (una decisión, una orden); **b)** pertenecer al pasado, ser imposible de recordar.

recant | rɪ'kænt | (form.) *v.t.* e *i.* **1** retractar(se): *they recanted their statements = se retractaron de sus declaraciones.* || *v.t.* **2** renunciar a (creencias): *he recanted his religion = renunció a su religión.*

recap | riː'kæp | (fam.) *v.t.* e *i.* **1** resumir, recapitular. **2** (EE.UU.) recauchutar. || *s.c.* **3** resumen, sumario, recapitulación.

recapitulate | ˌriːkə'pɪtjuleɪt | *v.t.* e *i.* resumir, recapitular.

recapitulation | 'riːkəˌpɪtju'leɪʃn | *s.c.* e *i.* resumen, recapitulación, sumario.

recapture | ˌriː'kæptʃər | *v.t.* **1** recuperar, recobrar: *try to recapture your good mood = trata de recobrar tu buen humor.* **2** volver a capturar, volver a apresar. **3** (fig.) recordar, traer de vuelta (el pasado). **4** MIL. recuperar, reconquistar, volver a tomar (una ciudad, una tierra, etc.). || *s.sing.* **5** **[the – (of)]** MIL. recuperación (de una ciudad, tierra, etc.).

recast | ˌriː'kɑːst | *v.* [*pret.* y *p.p.* **recast**] *t.* **1** reestructurar, remodelar: *they are recasting the system = están reestructurando el sistema.* **2** volver a escribir: *I had to recast two paragraphs = tuve que volver a escribir dos párrafos.* **3** refundir (una obra literaria). **4** cambiar el reparto de (una obra de teatro).

recede | rɪ'siːd | *v.i.* **1** **[– (from)]** alejarse, retroceder (hasta desaparecer): *the shore receded as we moved away towards the open sea = la costa se alejaba según nos acercábamos a mar abierto.* **2** (fig.) descender, bajar (los precios, la marea). **3** (fig.) perder pelo, quedarse calvo: *he is receding = se está quedando calvo.* **4** (fig.) caerse, ir a menos (el pelo). **5** **[– (from)]** (fig.) desvanecerse, disiparse, desaparecer gradualmente (un sentimiento, un recuerdo). **6** **[– (from)]** desvanecerse, esfumarse (un color).

receding | rɪ'siːdɪŋ | *adj.* **1** que se aleja, que retrocede. **2** que desaparece gradualmente, que se desvanece. **3** (fig.) que se inclina hacia atrás o hacia adentro: *he has a receding forehead = tiene la frente hacia adentro.*

receipt | rɪ'siːt | *s.c.* **1** COM. recibo. || *s.i.* **2** **[– (of)]** (form.) recibo, recepción: *you have to acknowledge receipt of the books = tiene que acusar recibo de los libros.* || *s.pl.* **3** ingresos, entrada, recaudación. || *v.t.* **4** dar un recibo por. || **5 on – of,** (form.) al recibo de, al recibir. **6 – book,** talonario de recibos.

receive | rɪ'siːv | *v.t.* **1** recibir: *I received your letter yesterday = recibí tu carta ayer.* **2** recibir (ser objeto de): *he received many insults = recibió muchos insultos.* **3** recibir, salir al encuentro: *she came out to receive me = salió a recibirme.* **4** **[– (into)]** admitir, aceptar (como miembro de un grupo, organización, etc.): *she wasn't received into the club = no fue admitida en el club.* **5** recibir, acoger: *the actress was received with applause = la actriz fue recibida con aplausos.* **6** (form.) recibir, contener: *the barrels are prepared to receive the wine = los barriles están preparados para recibir el vino.* **7** aceptar: *I'm not going to receive his gift = no voy a aceptar su regalo.* **8** DEP. restar (el saque, la pelota). **9** REL. recibir (un sacramento). || *v.t.* e *i.* **10** DER. ocultar, guardar (objetos robados). **11** RAD. y TV. recibir, captar (imágenes, sonidos). **12** recibir, dar la bienvenida. || **13 to be at/on the receiving end, [– (of)]** soportar lo más recio (de algo desagradable).

received | rɪ'siːvd | *adj.* **1** admitido por la mayoría, que se da por bueno (un texto, una versión, una opinión). || **2** **Received Pronunciation,** (brit.) FILOL. forma de pronunciación inglesa admitida como modelo académico.

receiver | 'rɪ'siːvər | *s.c.* **1** auricular (del teléfono). **2** TEC. aparato receptor (de televisión, de radio, etc.). **3** encubridor de objetos robados. **4** (brit.) ECON. síndico. **5** QUIM. recipiente.

receivership | ˌrɪ'siːvəʃɪp | *s.i.* ECON. quiebra.

recent | 'riːsnt | *adj.* **1** reciente: *a recent accident = un accidente reciente.* **2** último, reciente: *recent news = últimas noticias.*

recently | 'riːsntlɪ | *adv.* **1** recientemente. **2** últimamente.

receptacle | rɪ'septəkl | *s.c.* (form.) receptáculo, recipiente.

reception | rɪ'sepʃn | *s.i.* **1** recepción (de un hotel, hospital, etc.). **2** RAD. y TV. recepción, captación (de una emisión). || *s.c.* **3** recibimiento, acogida: *his novel had a good reception = su novela tuvo buena acogida.* **4** recepción (ceremonia oficial). **5** recepción, gran fiesta (en una boda, etc.). || *s.sing.* **6** (form.) recibimiento (de invitados). || **7 – center,** centro de acogida (de personas refugiadas, evacuadas, etc.). **8 – class,** (form.) primera clase a la que van los párvulos. **9 – room,** recibidor.

receptionist | rɪ'sepʃənɪst | *s.c.* recepcionista.

receptive | rɪ'septɪv | *adj.* **[– (to/of)]** receptivo, abierto: *a receptive mind = una mente abierta.*

receptiveness | rɪ'septɪvnɪs | *s.i.* receptividad.

receptivity | ˌresep'tɪvətɪ | *s.c.* **[– (to)]** receptividad.

recess | rɪ'ses | *s.c.* e *i.* **1** descanso, pausa (en el trabajo). **2** intermedio, período de suspensión (del Parlamento). **3** (EE.UU.) recreo (en una escuela). || *s.c.* **4** ARQ. hueco, nicho (en la pared de una habitación). || *v.t.* **5** suspender (el trabajo, la sesión). || *v.i.* **6** (EE.UU.) levantar la sesión. || **7 recesses, a)** lugar remoto o secreto; **b)** (fig.) lo más hondo, lo más recóndito: *in the recesses of my mind = en lo más recóndito de mi mente.*

recessed | 'riːsest | *adj.* colocado en un hueco de la pared: *a recessed door.*

recession | rɪ'seʃn | *s.c.* e *i.* **1** ECON. recesión económica. **2** retroceso.

recharge | ˌriː'tʃɑːdʒ | *v.t.* **1** recargar (una batería). || **2 to – one's batteries,** (fig.) tomarse un período de descanso para recuperarse.

rechargeable | ˌriː'tʃɑːdʒəbəl | *adj.* recargable (una batería).

recherché | rə'ʃeəʃeɪ | *adj.* rebuscado: *a recherché article = un artículo rebuscado.*

recidivist | rɪ'sɪdɪvɪst | *s.c.* DER. reincidente.

recipe | 'resɪpɪ | *s.c.* **1** **[– (for)]** GAST. receta: *a recipe for a pie = una receta de un pastel.* **2** MED. receta. **3** (fig.) fórmula, receta: *a recipe for making money = una fórmula para ganar dinero.* || **4 to be a – for,** (fig.) ser la fórmula para conseguir algo: *this isn't the recipe for sucess = ésta no es la fórmula para conseguir éxito.*

recipient | rɪ'sɪpɪənt | *s.c.* **[– (of)]** (form.) persona que recibe algo; destinatario.

reciprocal | rɪ'sɪprəkl | *adj.* recíproco, mutuo: *reciprocal love = amor recíproco.*

reciprocate | rɪ'sɪprəkeɪt | *v.t.* e *i.* **1** (form.) corresponder: *he is very kind to her but she doesn't reciprocate = él es muy amable con ella pero ella no le corresponde.* **2** intercambiar: *they reciprocated good wishes = se intercambiaron votos de felicidad.*

reciprocity | ˌresɪ'prɒsɪtɪ | *s.i.* reciprocidad, correspondencia mutua.

recital | rɪ'saɪtl | *s.c.* **1** ART. recital: *a piano recital = un recital de piano.* **2** narración, relación, relato: *a long and boring recital = un largo y aburrido relato.*

recitation | ˌresɪ'teɪʃn | *s.c.* e *i.* **1** recitación, declamación. **2** relación, enumeración: *the recitation of his talents = la enumeración de sus habilidades.* || *s.c.* **3** poema o texto que se recita.

recite | rɪ'saɪt | *v.t.* e *i.* **1** recitar, declamar (un poema, un texto). **2** (EE.UU.) decir la lección (de memoria). || *v.t.* **3** enumerar.

reckless | 'reklıs | *adj.* **1** temerario, imprudente: *reckless driving = conducción temeraria.* **2** irreflexivo. **3** desconsiderado. **4** alocado: *a reckless youth = un joven alocado.* || **5 to be – with one's money,** ser derrochador.
recklessly | 'reklıslı | *adv.* imprudentemente; de forma temeraria.
recklessness | 'reklıslınıs | *s.i.* **1** temeridad, imprudencia. **2** irreflexión.
reckon | 'rekən | *v.t.* e *i.* **1** (fam.) creer, pensar: *I reckon that they will come = creo que vendrán.* **2** considerar: *he is reckoned the cleverest boy in the class = se le considera el chico más listo de la clase.* **3** juzgar, estimar. **4** calcular: *did you reckon the costs of the trip? = ¿calculaste los gastos del viaje?* **5** contar: *I reckon him among my friends = le cuento entre mis amigos.* **6 [– to + *inf.*]** calcular: *we reckon to arrive there by ten = calculamos que llegaremos sobre las diez.* || **7 to – in,** incluir. **8 to – on one's fingers,** contar con los dedos. **9 to – on/upon,** contar con: *I reckon on your help = cuento con tu ayuda.* **10 to – up,** (p.u.) calcular (el total). **11 to – with, a)** tener en cuenta, contar con: *he didn't reckon with this = él no contaba con esto;* **b)** tratar con, ajustar las cuentas (con alguien). **12 to – without,** (fam.) no tener en cuenta.
reckoning | 'rekənıŋ | *s.c.* e *i.* **1** cálculo. || *s.c.* **2** cuenta, factura. **3** ajuste de cuentas. || **4 to be out in one's –,** equivocarse en los cálculos. **5 the day of –,** (fig.) el momento del ajuste de cuentas.
reclaim | rı'kleım | *v.t.* **1** reclamar (para recobrar algo): *he reclaimed his money = reclamó su dinero.* **2** aprovechar, recuperar (tierras baldías para cultivar o edificar). **3 [– (from)]** (p.u.) enmendar, regenerar (a una persona): *to reclaim a juvenile delinquent = enmendar a un joven delincuente.* **4** regenerar (materiales usados). || **5 to be past/beyond –,** no tener remedio.
reclaimed | rı'kleımd | *adj.* **1** recuperado (tierra). **2** regenerado, enmendado (persona). **3** regenerado (material).
reclamation | ˌreklə'meıʃn | *s.i.* **1** recuperación, aprovechamiento (de tierras baldías, para cultivar o edificar). **2** regeneración, recuperación (de materiales). **3** regeneración, recuperación moral.
recline | rı'klaın | *v.t.* e *i.* **1** recostar(se), reclinar(se): *a reclining seat = un asiento reclinable.* **2 [– (on)]** apoyar(se): *she reclined her arms on the table = apoyó sus brazos sobre la mesa.*
recluse | rı'kluːs | *s.c.* solitario, recluso, ermitaño.
reclusive | rı'kluːsıv | *adj.* (form.) solitario, huraño.
recognisable V. **recognizable.**
recognise V. **recognize.**
recognised V. **reconized.**
recognition | ˌrekəg'nıʃn | *s.i.* **1** acción de reconocer (a una persona, una cosa). **2** identificación (de un objeto). **3** reconocimiento, aceptación: *the recognition of their mistakes = el reconocimiento de sus equivocaciones.* **4** reconocimiento, aceptación oficial (de un nuevo estado, administración, gobierno, etc.). **5** reconocimiento (de un hijo). || **6 beyond/out/of (all) –,** hasta hacerse irreconocible: *it has changed beyond recognition = ha cambiado hasta hacerse irreconocible.* **7 in – of,** en reconocimiento de.
recognizable | 'rekəgnaızəbl | (también **recognisable**) *adj.* **1** reconocible. **2** identificable.
recognizably | 'rekəgnaızəblı | *adv.* sensiblemente.
recognize | 'rekəgnaız | (también **recognise**) *v.t.* **1 [– (as)]** reconocer, identificar (una persona, un objeto): *nobody recognized him = nadie le reconoció.* **2** reconocer, admitir, aceptar: *he recognized his mistakes = admitió sus errores.* **3** reconocer oficialmente (un gobierno, un título, unos servicios prestados, etc.). **4** reconocer (a un hijo).
recognized | 'rekəgnaızd | (también **recognised**) *adj.* reconocido como tal: *a recognized authority = una autoridad reconocida como tal.*
recoil | rı'kɔıl | *v.i.* **1 [– (at/from)]** retroceder, echarse atrás: *he recoiled in fear = retrocedió atemorizado.* **2 [– (on/upon)]** (form.) repercutir (desfavorablemente): *his impudence may recoil on his sons = su desvergÅenza puede repercutir en sus hijos.* **3** retroceder (un arma de fuego). || | 'riːkɔıl | *s.i.* **4** culatazo, retroceso (de un arma de fuego). **5** (fig.) retroceso (acción de retroceder, de dolor o miedo).
recollect | ˌrekə'lekt | *v.t.* (form.) recordar: *he couldn't recollect where he had left it = no pudo recordar dónde lo había dejado.*
recollection | ˌrekə'lekʃn | *s.c.* **1** recuerdo: *an unpleasant recollection = un recuerdo desagradable.* || *s.i.* **2** memoria, recuerdo. || **3 to the best of my recol lect,** que yo recuerde.
recommend | ˌrekə'mend | *v.t.* **1 [– (as/for/to)]** recomendar: *I don't recommend her as an assistant = no la recomiendo como ayudante.* **2 [– (to)]** recomendar, aconsejar: *I recommend you to take your umbrella = le aconsejo que coja su paraguas.* **3** hablar en favor de: *the way he acts doesn't recommend him = la forma en que actúa no habla en su favor.* **4** (arc.) encomendar, confiar a la protección de: *I recommend my son to you = os encomiendo a mi hijo.*
recommendation | ˌrekəmen'deıʃn | *s.c.* e *i.* recomendación: *I bought it on the recommendation of a friend = lo compré por recomendación de un amigo.*
recompense | 'rekəmpens | *v.t.* **1 [– (for)]** recompensar, premiar: *they recompensed her for her job = la recompensaron por su trabajo.* **2 [– (for)]** compensar, indemnizar (por una pérdida). || *s.c.* e *i.* **3 [– (for)]** recompensa, premio: *they gave me a little recompense for my help = me dieron una pequeña recompensa por mi ayuda.* **4** compensación, indemnización.
reconcile | 'rekənsaıl | *v.t.* **1 [– (to/with)]** conciliar, avenir, hacer compatibles (dos cosas opuestas). **2 [– (to/ with)]** reconciliarse (con alguien). || *v.r.* **3 [– to]** resignarse a; amoldarse, avenirse: *she will have to reconcile herself to a life of poverty = tendrá que amoldarse a una vida de pobreza.*
reconciled | 'rekənsaıld | *adj.* **1 [– (to)]** adaptado. || **2 to become – to,** resignarse a; avenirse, amoldarse. **3 to become – with,** reconciliarse con.
reconciliation | ˌrekənsılı'eıʃn | *s.c.* e *i.* **1 [– (between/of/with)]** reconciliación. || *s.c.* **2 [– (between/of/with)]** conciliación; avenimiento, acuerdo.
recondite | 'rekəndaıt | *adj.* (form.) abstruso, oscuro, difícil de comprender.
recondition | ˌriːkən'dıʃən | *v.t.* **1** arreglar, reparar (una máquina, un aparato). **2** revisar: *to recondition an engine = revisar una máquina.* **3** volver a equipar.
recondicioned | ˌriːkən'dıʃənd | *adj.* revisado (una máquina, un aparato): *a reconditioned car = un coche revisado.*
reconnaissance | rı'kɒnısəns | *s.i.* MIL. reconocimiento: *reconnaissance flights = vuelos de reconocimiento.*
reconnoitre | ˌrekə'nɔıtər | (EE.UU. **reconnoiter**) *v.t.* e *i.* MIL. reconocer, explorar; hacer un reconocimiento.
reconsider | ˌriːkən'sıdər | *v.t.* e *i.* reconsiderar; volver a examinar.
reconsideration | 'riːkənˌsıdə'reıʃn | *s.i.* revisión; nuevo examen.
reconstitute | ˌriː'kɒnstıtjuːt | *v.t.* **1** reconstituir, reorganizar, volver a tomar: *to reconstitute a political party = reconstituir un partido político.* **2** reconstituir (hechos pasados). **3** GAST. reconstituir (un alimento deshidratado).
reconstituted | ˌriː'kɒnstıtjuːtıd | *adj.* reconstituido, reorganizado.
reconstruct | ˌriːkən'strʌkt | *v.t.* **1** reconstruir, reedificar: *are you going to reconstruct this old barn? = ¿vas a reconstruir este viejo granero?* **2** reconstituir, reorganizar: *to reconstruct a system = reconstituir un sistema.* **3** reconstruir, reproducir: *the police reconstructed the crime = la policía reconstruyó el crimen.*
reconstructed | ˌriːkən'strʌktıd | *adj.* reconstruido, restaurado.
reconstruction | ˌriːkən'strʌkʃn | *s.i.* **1** reconstrucción, reedificación. **2** reorganización, reconstitución (de un sistema u organización). **3** reconstrucción (de hechos pasados). || *s.c.* **4** reproducción, copia (de algo que ya no existe): *a reconstruction of a Spanish caravel = una reproducción de una carabela española.*
record | 'rekɔːd | *s.c.* **1** registro. **2** acta (de una reunión, tribunal, etc.). **3** antecedentes (personales): *criminal records = antecedentes penales.* **4** DEP. marca,

récord. **5** hoja de servicio (de un empleado, de un funcionario). **6** currículum vitae; historial profesional. **7** expediente académico. **8** nota, calificación (de un alumno). **9** MUS. disco. **10** MUS. grabación. || *adj.* **11** récord: *a record time = un tiempo récord.* **12** sin precedentes; inigualable. || | rɪ'kɔːd | *v.t.* **13** registrar. **14** anotar, apuntar: *to record an order = apuntar un pedido.* **15** grabar (en una cinta magnetofónica o de vídeo): *this phone call is being recorded = esta llamada está siendo grabada.* **16** hacer constar (una opinión). **17** indicar, marcar (una medida, un valor, etc.): *the thermometer records 25º = el termómetro marca 25º.* **18** consignar, poner por escrito; citar. || *v.t.* e *i.* **19** MUS. grabar. || **20 a matter of –,** un hecho constatado, un hecho indiscutible. **21 to beat/break the –,** batir el récord. **22 for the –,** públicamente, oficialmente. **23 to go/to be on –,** [**– as** + *ger.*] declarar públicamente. **24 off the –,** (fam.) confidencial, hecho en confianza. **25 on –, a)** [*super.* –] jamás alcanzado, jamás registrado: *the best score on record = la mejor puntuación jamás registrada;* **b)** archivado. **26 – library,** MUS. fonoteca. **27 records, a)** archivos; **b)** evidencias, muestras: *records of ancient civilizations = evidencias de antiguas civilizaciones.* **28 to set/put/get/keep the – straight,** deshacer un malentendido.

record-breaker | 'rekɔːd'breɪkər | *s.c.* DEP. plusmarquista.

record-breaking | 'rekɔːd'breɪkɪŋ | *adj.* **1** extraordinario, excepcional. **2** DEP. que ha batido todos los récords: *a record-breaking team = un equipo que ha batido todos los récords.*

recorded | rɪ'kɔːdɪd | *adj.* **1** grabado: *a recorded programme = un programa grabado.* **2** constatado: *a recorded fact = un hecho constatado.* || **3 – delivery,** (brit.) por correo certificado: *I sent the letters recorded delivery = envié las cartas por correo certificado.*

recorder | rɪ'kɔːdər | *s.c.* **1** MUS. flauta. **2** TEC. indicador, contador. **3** TEC. registrador. **4** (brit.) DER. juez municipal. **5** magnetófono. || **6 tape –,** magnetófono.

recording | rɪ'kɔːdɪŋ | *s.c.* **1** grabación: *a recording of her voice = una grabación de su voz.* || *s.i.* **2** de grabación: *record ing session = una sesión de grabación.* || **3 – tape,** cinta magnetofónica.

record-player | 'rekɔːd,pleɪər | (también **record player**) *s.c.* MUS. tocadiscos.

recount | rɪ'kaunt | *v.t.* **1** (form.) relatar (un suceso, un cuento). || | 'riːkaunt | *s.c.* **2** recuento (de votos).

recoup | rɪ'kuːp | *v.t.* **1** recuperar (una suma de dinero). **2** recuperarse de, resarcirse de (una pérdida). **3** [**– (for)**] compensar, indemnizar (por una pérdida).

recourse | rɪ'kɔːs | (form.) *s.i.* **1** recurso, medio: *his only recourse was violence = su único recurso era la violencia.* || **2 to have – to,** recurrir a: *I advised her to have recourse to her parents = le aconsejó que recurriera a sus padres.*

recover | rɪ'kʌvər | *v.i.* **1** [**– (from)**] recuperarse, reponerse. **2** [**– (from)**] recuperarse (la economía). **3** recobrar: *he recovered his good humour = recobró su buen humor.* || *v.t.* **4** [**– (from)**] recobrar, recuperar: *did you recover your money? = ¿recuperaste tu dinero?* **5** [**– (from)**] rescatar, recuperar: *the police will recover the prisoner = la policía rescatará al prisionero.* **6** | ,riː'kʌvə | tapizar: *to recover a chair = tapizar una silla.* **7** revestir.

recoverable | rɪ'kʌvərəbl | *adj.* **1** recuperable. **2** DER. reivindicable.

recovered | rɪ'kʌvəd | *adj.* recuperado.

recovery | rɪ'kʌvərɪ | *s.c.* e *i.* **1** [**– (from)**] restablecimiento, recuperación: *a quick recovery from an ilness = una rápida recuperación de una enfermedad.* **2** ECON. mejora, reactivación. || *s.i.* **3** rescate, recuperación. **4** ECON. reembolso.

recreate | ,riːkrɪ'eɪt | *v.t.* **1** recrear, crear de nuevo (algo ya pasado). || *v.t.* e *i.* **2** recrear(se), entretener(se).

recreation | ,rekrɪ'eɪʃn | *s.c.* e *i.* **1** distracción, entretenimiento; ocio. || | ,riːkrɪ'eɪʃn | *s.i.* **2** [**– (of)**] recreación (de algo que ya no existe). || **3 – ground,** parque recreativo.

recreational | ,rekrɪ'eɪʃnəl | *adj.* recreativo, de recreo.

recriminate | rɪ'krɪmɪneɪt | *v.i.* recriminar.

recrimination rɪ,krɪmɪ'neɪʃn | *s.pl.* y *s.i.* **1** recriminación. || **2 to make a – (against),** recriminar (a).

recriminatory | rɪ'krɪmɪnətərɪ | *adj.* recriminatorio.

recruit | rɪ'kruːt | *s.c.* **1** MIL. recluta. **2** nuevo miembro (de una organización, institución, etc.). || **3** MIL. reclutar, alistar (reclutas voluntarios). **4** (fig.) reclutar (trabajadores, ayudantes). **5** reponer: *to recruit supplies = reponer provisiones.* || *v.i.* **6** MIL. reclutar, alistar. **7** (arc.) recuperarse, reponerse (de salud).

recruiting | rɪ'kruːtɪŋ | V. **recruitment.**

recta | 'rektə | *pl.* de **rectum.**

rectangle | 'rek,tæŋgl | *s.c.* GEOM. rectángulo.

rectangular | rek'tæŋgjulər | *adj.* GEOM. rectangular.

rectification | ,rektɪfɪ'keɪʃn | *s.i.* (form.) rectificación.

rectify | 'rektɪfaɪ | *v.t.* **1** (form.) rectificar, enmendar, corregir: *she could not rectify her mistakes = no pudo rectificar sus errores.* **2** ELEC. rectificar (transformar corriente alterna en continua). **3** QUIM. rectificar, purificar (una bebida alcohólica).

rectilineal | ,rektɪ'lɪnɪəl | V. **rectilinear.**

rectilinear | ,rektɪ'lɪnɪər | *adj.* GEOM. rectilíneo.

rectitude | 'rektɪtjuːd | *s.i.* (form. o lit.) rectitud, probidad, honradez.

rector | 'rektər | *s.c.* **1** REL. vicario, cura párroco. **2** (brit.) rector, superior de una universidad.

rectory | 'rektərɪ | *s.c.* REL. casa parroquial.

rectum | 'rektəm | *s.c.* [*pl.* **rectums** o **recta**] ANAT. recto.

recumbent | rɪ'kʌmbənt | *adj.* (lit.) tendido, yacente.

recuperate | rɪ'kuːpəreɪt | *v.i.* **1** [**– (from)**] (form.) recuperarse, restablecerse, reponerse (de una enfermedad, de una conmoción, etc.). || *v.t.* **2** recuperar, recobrar.

recuperation | rɪ,kuːpə'reɪʃn | *s.i.* (form.) recuperación, restablecimiento.

recuperative | rɪ'kjuːpərətɪv | *adj.* (form.) recuperador.

recur | rɪ'kɜːr | *v.i* **1** repetirse: *the same dream recurred periodically = el mismo sueño se repetía frecuentemente.* **2** [**– (to)**] volver: *recurring to that matter = volviendo a ese asunto.* **3** volver a la mente.

recurrence | rɪ'kʌrəns | (form.) *s.c.* e *i.* **1** repetición, reaparición. **2** MED. recaída.

recurrent | rɪ'kʌrənt | *adj.* **1** que se repite, que reaparece periódicamente: *a recurrent theme = un tema que se repite.* **2** MED. recurrente: *recurrent nerves = nervios recurrentes.* || **3 – decimals,** MAT. fracciones decimales periódicas.

recurring | rɪ'kɜːrɪŋ | V. **recurrent.**

recycle | ,riː'saɪkl | *v.t.* TEC. reciclar (transformar un material ya utilizado para que sea aprovechado).

recycled | ,riː'saɪkld | *adj.* TEC. que ha sido reciclado (un material).

red | red | *adj.* **1** rojo, colorado, encarnado: *a red carnation = un clavel rojo.* **2** (fig.) encendido, muy colorado: *a red face = una cara encendida.* **3** (fam. y desp.) POL. rojo, comunista, izquierdista. **4** enrojecido, rojo: *red eyes = ojos enrojecidos.* || *s.c.* e *i.* **5** rojo, color rojo: *the reds and blues of the picture = los rojos y azules del cuadro.* || *s.inv.* **6** vino tinto. || *s.c.* **7** (fam. y desp.) POL. rojo, comunista, izquierdista. || **8 as – as a beetroot/peony/lobster/tomato,** (fam.) **a)** colorado como un tomate (por el rubor); **b)** rojo como un cangrejo (por el sol). **9 in the –,** ECON. en números rojos, al descubierto: *my bank account is in the red = mi cuenta bancaria está al descubierto.* **10 in –,** de rojo (vestido de rojo): *the girl in red = la chica de rojo.* **11 – alert,** alerta roja. **12 – carpet,** tratamiento privilegiado que recibe un visitante importante. **13 – cell/corpuscle,** ANAT. glóbulo rojo, eritrocito. **14 Red Crescent,** organización de los países musulmanes, correspondiente a la Cruz Roja. **15 Red Cross,** Cruz Roja. **16 – ensign,** MAR. bandera de la marina mercante británica. **17 – herring, a)** (fam.) pretexto para desviar la atención; **b)** GAST. arenque ahumado. **18 Red Indian,** (desp.) piel roja. **19 – light, a)** disco rojo, luz roja (señal de tráfico); **b)** (fig.) señal de peligro. **20 – light district,** barrio chino (de prostitución). **21 – meat,** GAST. carne roja. **22 – pepper,** GAST, **a)** pimiento rojo;

b) pimentón. **23 – tape,** (fig.) papeleo, trámites burocráticos. **24 – wine,** vino tinto. **25 to see –,** enfurecerse, salirse de sus casillas.

red-blooded | ˌred'blʌdɪd | *adj.* **1** (fam.) enérgico, vigoroso, fuerte: *a red-blooded youth = un joven vigoroso.*

redbrick | 'redbrɪk | (también **red-brick**) *adj.* **1** de ladrillo rojo (una construcción). **2** (brit.) adjetivo que se aplica a las Universidades inglesas fundadas con posterioridad a las de Oxford y Cambridge.

redcurrant | ˌred'kʌrənt | BOT. *s.c.* **1** grosella roja. **2** grosellero.

redden | 'redn | *v.t.* e *i.* **1** enrojecer(se): *his face reddened = su cara enrojeció.* **2** ruborizarse, ponerse rojo (una persona). || *v.t.* **3** teñir de rojo.

reddish | 'redɪʃ | *adj.* rojizo.

redecorate | ˌriː'dekəreɪt | *v.t.* volver a decorar; renovar (un edificio, una habitación, etc.).

redecoration | ˌriːdekə'reɪʃən | *s.i.* nueva decoración; renovación.

redeem | rɪ'diːm | (form.) *v.t.* **1** (fig.) salvar (una situación desagradable). **2** **[– (from)]** (fig.) compensar (un defecto, una característica desagradable). **3** dejar libre (algo empeñado o hipotecado). **4** cumplir (una promesa, una obligación). **5** cancelar (una deuda, una hipoteca, etc.). **6** recuperar (honor, posición, derechos). **7** salvar, rescatar (a un esclavo, a un cautivo). **8** REL. redimir, salvar.

redeemable | rɪ'diːməbl | *adj.* COM. amortizable.

redeemer | rɪ'diːmər | *s.sing.* **1** **[the –]** REL. el Salvador, el Redentor. || *s.c.* **2** (p.u.) salvador: *the redeemer of our country = el salvador de nuestra patria.*

redeeming | rɪ'diːmɪŋ | *adj.* **1** compensatorio (aplicado a una característica o cualidad que compensa un defecto): *a dreadful film with no redeeming features = una película malísima sin ninguna característica compensatoria.*

redemption | rɪ'dempʃn | (form.) *s.i.* **1** REL. redención, salvación. **2** cumplimiento (de una promesa). || **3 past/beyond –,** irremediable.

redemptive | rɪ'demptɪv | *adj.* (form.) REL. redentor.

redeploy | ˌriːdɪ'plɔɪ | *v.t.* redistribuir, reorganizar: *to redeploy the workers = reorganizar a los trabajadores.*

redeployment | ˌriːdɪ'plɔɪmənt | *s.i.* redistribución: *redeployment of labour = redistribución del trabajo.*

redevelop | ˌriːdɪ'veləp | *v.t.* reconstruir, replanificar (una zona de una ciudad, un barrio, etc.).

redevelopment | ˌriːdɪ'veləpmənt | *s.c.* e *i.* reconstrucción, replanificación (de una zona de una ciudad, un barrio, etc.).

red-faced | ˌred'feɪst | *adj.* de rostro encendido, que tiene la cara colorada (por el sonrojo o por la bebida).

redhead | 'redhed | *s.c.* pelirrojo.

redheaded | ˌred'hedɪd | *adj.* pelirrojo: *a redheaded boy = un chico pelirrojo.*

red-hot | ˌred'hɒt | *adj.* **1** candente, al rojo vivo (un metal). **2** al rojo, demasiado caliente (un objeto). **3** (fig.) ardiente, apasionado, vehemente: *a red-hot speech = un discurso vehemente.* **4** de máxima importancia o actualidad.

redirect | ˌriːdɪ'rekt | *v.t.* **1** reencauzar, volver a orientar. **2** desviar: *to redirect traffic = desviar el tráfico.* **3** volver a enviar, volver a expedir (por correo).

redistribute | ˌriːdɪ'strɪbjuːt | *v.t.* redistribuir.

redistribution | 'riːˌdɪstrɪ'bjuːʃn | *s.i.* redistribución.

redness | 'rednɪs | *s.i.* rojez.

redo | ˌriː'duː | [*pret.* **redid;** *p.p.* **redone**] *v.t.* rehacer, volver a hacer.

redolent | 'redələnt | (lit.) *adj.* **1** **[– of]** (fig.) evocador de, que recuerda, que hace pensar en: *it is a film redolent of the epoch of silent films = es una película que recuerda la época del cine mudo.* **2** **[– of]** que huele a, que tiene la fragancia de: *sheets redolent of jasmine = sábanas que huelen a jazmín.*

redouble | ˌriː'dʌbl | *v.t.* **1** redoblar, intensificar, aumentar: *I redoubled my efforts = redoblé mis esfuerzos.* **2** redoblar (en el bridge).

redoubt | rɪ'daʊt | (form.) *s.c.* **1** MIL. reducto. **2** (fig.) refugio.

redoubtable | rɪ'daʊtəbl | *adj.* (form. o lit.) temible: *a redoubtable opponent = un adversario temible.*

redress | rɪ'dres | (form.) *v.t.* **1** desagraviar, reparar: *to redress the wrong I have done = reparar el daño que he hecho.* **2** rectificar, corregir, enmendar (un error). || *s.i.* **3** desagravio, reparación. **4** compensación. || **5 to – the balance/imbalance, [– (between)]** equilibrar la balanza, devolver la igualdad.

redskin | 'redskɪn | *s.c.* (desp.) piel roja.

reduce | rɪ'djuːs | *v.t.* **1** **[– (from/to)]** reducir, disminuir, mermar: *I'll reduce my expenses = reduciré mis gastos.* **2** **[– (to)]** reducir, convertir: *his house was reduced to ashes = su casa quedó reducida a cenizas.* **3** COM. rebajar (un precio, un sueldo). **4** reducir, someter: *they reduced the rebels = sometieron a los rebeldes.* **5** **[– (to)]** llevar: *it reduced her to despair = ello la llevó a la desesperación.* **6** obligar, reducir: *to reduce to silence = reducir al silencio.* **7** QUIM. reducir (separar el oxígeno). || *v.t.* e *i.* **8** (fam.) bajar peso. **9** **[– (to)]** reducir(se), concentrar(se) (un líquido, una solución).

reduced | rɪ'djuːst | *adj.* **1** reducido, mermado. || **2 to be –, [– to +** *ger.*] verse obligado a: *she was reduced to begging = se vio obligado a pedir limosna.*

reduction | rɪ'dʌkʃn | *s.i.* **1** **[– (in/of)]** reducción, aminoración: *reduction of prices = reducción de los precios.* || *s.c.* **2** **[– (in)]** COM. rebaja, descuento. **3** reducción, copia reducida (de un mapa, cuadro, escultura, etc.). || *s.sing.* **4** **[– of]** simplificación.

redundancy | rɪ'dʌndənsɪ | *s.c.* **1** despido por reducción de plantilla. || *s.i.* **2** desempleo por reducción de plantilla || **3 – payment,** paga de despido, liquidación por despido.

redundant | rɪ'dʌndənt | *adj.* **1** redundante, superfluo, innecesario, sobrante. **2** sin empleo (por reducción de plantilla). **3** GRAM. redundante, pleonástico.

redwood | 'redwʊd | BOT. *s.c.* e *i.* **1** secoya. **2** madera de la secoya.

reed | riːd | *s.c.* e *i.* **1** BOT. caña, carrizo. || *s.c.* **2** MUS. lengÅeta (de un instrumento de viento). **3** MUS. caramillo, flautilla de caña. || **4 broken –,** (fig.) persona o cosa de poco fiar. **5 reeds,** MUS. instrumentos de lengÅeta.

reedy | 'riːdɪ | *adj.* **1** BOT. lleno de cañas o carrizos. **2** agudo, estridente, aflautado (un sonido, una voz).

reef | riːf | MAR. *s.c.* **1** arrecife, banco: *coral reef = arrecife de coral, banco de coral.* **2** escollo. **3** rizo. || *v.t.* **4** tomar rizos. || **5 – knot,** MAR. nudo de rizo. **6 to take in a –,** (lit. o fig.) proceder con cautela.

reefer | 'riːfər | *s.c.* **1** chaqueta gruesa ajustada (utilizada a menudo por los marineros). **2** (argot y p.u.) porro de marihuana. **3** (p.u.) MAR. guardiamarina. || **4 – jacket,** chaqueta gruesa ajustada (utilizada a menudo por los marineros).

reek | riːk | *v.i.* **1** **[– (of/with)]** apestar (a): *the whole house reeked of fish = toda la casa apestaba a pescado.* **2** **[– (with)]** rebosar (de), estar atestado (de), rezumar: *that lake reeked with fish = aquel lago estaba atestado de peces.* **3** **[– (of)]** (fig.) oler a, apestar a: *it reeked of corruption = olía a corrupción.* **4** exhalar. || *s.sing.* **5** **[– (of)]** peste, hedor, tufo. **6** (lit.) exhalación.

reel | riːl | *s.c.* **1** bobina, carrete (de hilo). **2** rollo, carrete (de película). **3** carrete, carretel (de caña de pescar). **4** baile escocés. || *v.i.* **5** tambalear(se): *the drunkard reeled to and fro = el borracho se tambaleaba de un lado para otro.* **6** **[– (from)]** aturdir(se), atolondrarse. **7** (fig.) dar vueltas: *her head was reeling = la cabeza le daba vueltas.* || *v.t.* **8** devanar. || **9 off the –,** (fam.) de un tirón, sin parar. **10 to – in,** sacar con el carrete (un pez el agua). **11 to – off,** decir de un tirón.

re-elect | ˌriːɪ'lekt | *v.t.* POL. reelegir: *to re-elect a member of parliament = reelegir a un diputado.*

re-election | ˌriːɪ'lekʃn | *s.i.* POL. reelección.

re-enact | ˌriːɪ'nækt | *v.t.* **1** volver a representar (un papel, una obra, una escena). **2** POL. volver a promulgar (una ley).

re-entry | riː'entrɪ | *s.i.* reentrada; reingreso.

re-examination | 'riːɪgˌzæmɪ'neɪʃn | *s.c.* e *i.* **[– (of)]** revisión, nuevo examen.

re-examine | ˌriːɪg'zæmɪn | *v.t.* **1** revisar, reconsiderar. **2** DER. revisar (un testimonio).

ref | ref | *s.c.* (fam.) DEP. árbitro.
refectory | rɪ'fektərɪ | *s.c.* (form.) refectorio, comedor (de un convento, monasterio o universidad).
refer | rɪ'fɜːr | *v.i.* **[– (to)] 1** referirse (a): *I am not referring to that girl = no me refiero a esa chica.* **2** remitirse: *I refer to the facts = me remito a los hechos.* **3** consultar, acudir, recurrir (a una fuente de información): *he translated the text without referring to a dictionary = tradujo el texto sin acudir a un diccionario.* || *v.t.* **[– (to)] 4** aludir, mencionar, hacer referencia a: *he has never referred to that subject = nunca ha aludido a ese tema.* **5** remitir, enviar: *the author refers us to the first page = el autor nos remite a la primera página.* **6** relacionar; achacar, atribuir: *he refers his headaches to estrés = atribuye sus dolores de cabeza al stress.* **7** enviar (a un especialista, a un hospital, etc.). **8** remitir: *the judge referred the matter to the High Court = el juez remitió el asunto al Tribunal Supremo.* || **9 to – to something/someone as,** calificar de: *the critics referred to the book as pornographic = los críticos calificaron el libro de pornográfico.*
referee | ˌrefə'riː | *s.c.* **1** DEP. árbitro. **2** DER. mediador, intermediario. **3** fiador, garante. || *v.t.* e *i.* **4** DEP. arbitrar.
reference | 'refrəns | *s.i.* **1 [– (to)]** referencia, mención, alusión. **2 [– (to)]** consulta: *works of reference = obras de consulta.* **3 [– (to)]** relación: *it has not reference to the subject = no tiene relación con el tema.* || *s.c.* **4** FILOL. remisión, llamada (en un libro): *a dictionary full of references = un diccionario lleno de remisiones.* **5** informe, referencia, recomendación. **6 [– (to)]** alusión, mención: *biblical references = alusiones bíblicas.* **7** fiador, garante. **8** nota, referencia: *a reference in the margin of a book = una nota al margen de un libro.* || **9 for future –,** para utilización futura (una información). **10 – book,** FILOL. libro de consulta. **11 – mark,** FILOL. llamada. **12 with – to,** con referencia a.
referendum | ˌrefə'rendəm | *s.c.* [*pl.* **referenda** o **referemdums**] POL. referéndum.
refill | 'riːfɪl | *v.t.* **1** volver a llenar: *he refilled my glass = él volvió a llenar mi vaso.* **2** cargar (un bolígrafo, pluma, etc.). || *s.c.* **3** recambio, carga (de bolígrafo, de pluma, etc.).
refine | rɪ'faɪn | *v.t.* **1** refinar, librar de impurezas (una sustancia): *to refine sugar = refinar azúcar.* **2** (fig.) depurar, perfeccionar: *she is refining her style = está perfeccionando su estilo.* || *v.i.* **3** refinarse.
refined | rɪ'faɪnd | *adj.* **1** refinado: *refined sugar = azúcar refinado.* **2** (fig.) refinado, distinguido, cultivado (una persona). **3** perfeccionado, sofisticado: *a very refined machine = una máquina muy perfeccionada.* **4** refinado, pulido, primoroso: *a refined language = un lenguaje refinado.*
refinement | rɪ'faɪnmənt | *s.c.* e *i.* **1** modificación, alteración (hecha para perfeccionar algo). || *s.i.* **2** refinamiento, buen gusto, distinción: *a man of refinement = un hombre de buen gusto.* **3** esmero, refinamiento. **4** finura, cortesía; elegancia. || *s.c.* **5** sutileza: *refinements of meaning = sutilezas de significado.*
refinery | rɪ'faɪnərɪ | *s.c.* refinería: *oil refinery = refinería de petróleo.*
refit | ˌriː'fɪt | *v.t.* e *i.* MAR. volver a equipar, arreglar (un barco).
reflate | ˌriː'fleɪt | *v.t.* ECON. reactivar: *to reflate the economy = reactivar la economía.*
reflation | riː'fleɪʃn | *s.i.* ECON. inflación.
reflationary | ˌriː'fleɪʃənərɪ | *adj.* ECON. inflacionario; inflacionista.
reflect | rɪ'flekt | *v.t.* **1** reflejar: *her expression reflected her feelings = su expresión reflejaba sus sentimientos.* || *v.t.* e *i.* **2** reflejar(se), reflectar(se). || *v.i.* **3 [– (on/over/upon)]** meditar, reflexionar: *I have to reflect about the matter = tengo que reflexionar sobre el asunto.* **4 [– (on/upon)]** repercutir (desfavorablemente). **5** desacreditar, desprestigiar.
reflection | rɪ'flekʃn | *s.c.* **1 [– (of)]** reflejo: *a reflection of reality = un reflejo de la realidad.* **2** reflejo, imagen: *a reflection in a mirror = una imagen en un espejo.* **3** reflexión: *moral reflections = reflexiones morales.* || *s.c.* e *i.* **4** meditación, reflexión. || *s.i.* **5** FIS. reflexión (de la luz o sonido). || *s.sing.* **6 [– (on/upon)]** comentario (que trae descrédito), crítica, reproche. || **7 on –,** pensándolo bien.
reflective | rɪ'flektɪv | *adj.* **1** pensativo, meditabundo. **2** reflexivo (que obra con reflexión). **3 [– (of)]** (form.) indicativo: *his words are reflective of his mood = sus palabras son indicativas de su estado de ánimo.* **4** reflectante.
reflectively | rɪ'flektɪvlɪ | *adv.* pensativamente.
reflector | rɪ'flektər | *s.c.* **1** reflector, priyector.
reflex | 'riːfleks | *s.c.* **1** reflejo (movimiento involuntario). || *adj.* **2** reflejo: *a reflex movement = un movimiento reflejo.* || **3 reflexes,** reflejos (reacción rápida y automática ante un estímulo): *quick reflexes = reflejos rápidos.*
reflexive | rɪ'fleksɪv | *adj.* **1** reflejo: *a reflexive move = un movimiento reflejo.* || **2 – pronoun,** GRAM. pronombre reflexivo. **3 – verb,** GRAM. verbo reflexivo.
reflexively | rɪ'fleksɪvlɪ | *adv.* irreflexivamente, de una manera refleja.
reforest | ˌriː'fɒrɪst | *v.t.* ECOL. repoblar (de árboles).
reforestation | ˌriːfɒrɪ'steɪʃən | *s.i.* ECOL. repoblación forestal.
reform | rɪ'fɔːm | *s.c.* e *i.* **1** reforma: *the reform of our administrative system = la reforma de nuestro sistema administrativo.* || *s.i.* **2** regeneración, recuperación (moral). || *v.t.* e *i.* **3** corregir(se), enmendar(se), reformar(se): *a sinner who wants to reform = un pecador que quiere reformarse.* || *v.t.* **4** reformar, modificar: *to reform a law = modificar una ley.*
re-form | riː'fɔːm | *v.t.* e *i.* **1** volver(se) a formar: *the party re-formed two years later = el partido se volvió a formar dos años más tarde.* **2** MIL. volver(se) a poner en filas, volver(se) a formar: *the soldiers re-formed = los soldados volvieron a formar.*
reformation | ˌrefə'meɪʃn | *s.i.* **1** reforma, modificación; cambio radical. || **2 The Reformation,** REL. la Reforma.
reformed | rɪ'fɔːmd | *adj.* reformado: *a reformed delinquent = un delincuente reformado.*
reformer | rɪ'fɔːmər | *s.c.* reformador: *a social reformer = un reformador social.*
reformist | rɪ'fɔːmɪst | *adj.* y *s.c.* POL. reformista.
refract | rɪ'frækt | *v.t.* e *i.* FIS. refractar.
refraction | rɪ'frækʃn | *s.i.* FIS. refracción.
refractory | rɪ'fræktərɪ | *adj.* **1** (form.) terco, obstinado. **2** (form.) rebelde, difícil de tratar (una persona, una enfermedad). **3** (form.) refractario (una persona). **4** FIS. refractario (una sustancia, un material).
refrain | rɪ'freɪn | *v.i.* **1 [– (from)]** (form.) abstenerse: *he refrained from drinking = se abstuvo de beber.* **2 [– (from)]** contener(se), reprimir(se): *I couldn't refrain from laughing = no pude contener la risa.* || *v.t.* **3** (arc.) contener, reprimir: *she couldn't refrain her tears = no pudo reprimir sus lágrimas.* || *s.c.* **4** MUS. estribillo. **5** (fig.) cantinela, canción.
refresh | rɪ'freʃ | *v.t.* **1** refrescar. **2 [– *r.*]** reanimarse: *we refreshed ourselves with a nice cup of hot coffee = nos reanimamos con una agradable taza de café caliente.* **3** (lit.) renovar. || **4 to – one's memory,** (fig.) refrescar la memoria, recordar.
refresher | rɪ'freʃər | *s.c.* **1** (fam.) refresco. || **2 – course,** curso de actualización.
refreshing | rɪ'freʃɪŋ | *adj.* **1** refrescante: *a refreshing shower = una ducha refrescante.* **2** reparador: *refreshing sleep = un sueño reparador.* **3** placentero, agradable: *a refreshing change = un cambio placentero.* **4** estimulante.
refreshingly | rɪ'freʃɪŋlɪ | *adv.* agradablemente.
refreshment | rɪ'freʃmənt | *s.i.* **1** refresco, refrigerio. **2** (lit.) alimento. || **3 refreshments,** refrescos, refrigerio.
refrigerate | rɪ'frɪdʒəreɪt | *v.t.* refrigerar (un alimento).
refrigeration | rɪˌfrɪdʒə'reɪʃn | *s.i.* refrigeración.
refrigerator | rɪ'frɪdʒəreɪtər | *s.c.* nevera, frigorífico.
refuel | ˌriː'fjuəl | *v.t.* e *i.* **1** repostar, reabastecer, reponer combustible (principalmente un avión o un buque). **2** (fig.) reforzar (un sentimiento, una emoción).

refuge | 'refju:dʒ | *s.i.* **1** (fig.) refugio, cobijo, amparo: *he seeks refuge in books = busca refugio en los libros.* || *s.c.* **2** refugio, cobijo: *a refuge from the rain = un refugio contra la lluvia.* **3** refugio (de montaña). **4** albergue. **5** asilo (para mujeres maltratadas). || **6 to take –,** refugiarse.

refugee | ˌrefju'dʒi: | *s.c.* POL. refugiado: *a refugee camp = un campo de refugiados.*

refund | 'ri:fʌnd | *s.c.* **1** COM. reembolso, reintegro, devolución. || *v.t.* **1 [– (to)]** COM. reembolsar, devolver: *the company refunded him his money = la compañía le devolvió su dinero.*

refurbish | ˌri:'fɜ:bɪʃ | *v.t.* (form.) renovar (un edificio, un local, una habitación).

refusal | rɪ'fju:zl | *s.i.* **1 [– (to)]** negativa: *her refusal surprised him = su negativa le sorprendió.* **2 [– (of)]** desaire (al rechazar una oferta). || **3 blank/flat –,** negativa rotunda. **4 (the) first –,** COM. la primera opción (la oportunidad de elegir primero).

refuse | rɪ'fju:s | *v.i.* **1 [– (to)]** rehusar, negarse: *they refuse to do it = se niegan a hacerlo.* || *v.t.* **2** negar, denegar: *the bank refused me a loan = el banco me negó un préstamo.* **3** rechazar: *he refused my offer = rechazó mi oferta.* || | 'refju:s | *s.i.* **4** desperdicios, desechos, basura.

refutation | ˌrefju:'teɪʃn | *s.c.* e *i.* **[– (of)]** (form.) refutación.

refute | rɪ'fju:t | (form.) *v.t.* **1** refutar, rebatir, impugnar: *they refuted my arguments = refutaron mis argumentos.* **2** contradecir (con argumentos).

regain | rɪ'geɪn | *v.t.* **1** recobrar, recuperar: *he regained his strength = recuperó su fuerza.* **2** (form.) volver a (un sitio, después de haber estado perdido o en peligro).

regal | 'ri:gl | *adj.* real, regio: *regal power = poder real.*

regale | rɪ'geɪl | *v.t.* **[– (with/on)]** (hum.) deleitar; entretener.

regalia | rɪ'geɪlɪə | *s.i.* (form.) insignias emblemas reales (cetro, corona, orbe, etc.).

regard | rɪ'gɑ:d | *v.t.* **1 [– (as)]** considerar: *they regard her as a heroine = la consideran una heroína.* **2 [– (with)]** mirar, considerar: *he is regarded with respect = se le mira con respeto.* **3** (form.) referirse a, concernir, afectar. **4** tener en cuenta, tomar en consideración: *you never regard my wishes = nunca tienes en cuenta mis deseos.* **5** (arc. o lit.) mirar, contemplar. || *s.i.* **6 [– (for)]** consideración, respeto, estima: *I have a high regard for them = les tengo un gran respeto.* **7** (arc. o lit.) mirada (fija o significativa). || **8 as regards,** en cuanto a, por lo que respecta a. **9 to hold someone/something in high –,** tener en gran estima. **10 to hold someone/something in low –,** no tener ninguna consideración por. **11 in this/that –,** (form.) con respecto a esto, con respecto a eso. **12 regards,** (fam.) recuerdos, saludos: *give my regards to your parents = dale recuerdos a tus padres.* **13 with/in – to,** (form.) por lo que se refiere a, en lo tocante a.

regarded | rɪ'gɑ:dɪd | *adj.* **1** considerado, apreciado. **2** respetado.

regarding | rɪ'gɑ:dɪŋ | *prep.* referente a, concerniente a.

regardless | rɪ'gɑ:dlɪs | *adv.* **1** a pesar de todo: *she went on regardless = siguió a pesar de todo.* || **2 – of,** a pesar de, sin preocuparse por, sin tener en cuenta: *regardless of the consequences = sin tener en cuenta las consecuencias.*

regatta | rɪ'gætə | *s.c.* DEP. regata.

regency | 'ri:dʒənsɪ | *s.c.* **1** regencia. || **2 Regency,** ART. de estilo Regencia: *a Regency dress = un vestido de estilo Regencia.*

regenerate | rɪ'dʒenərɪt | (form.) *v.t.* **1** regenerar, renovar (moralmente, espiritualmente). **2** renovar (un lugar). **3** reactivar, revitalizar: *to regenerate the economy = reactivar la economía.* **4** MED. regenerar, reconstituir (un órgano, un tejido orgánico). **5** transformar (para mejor). || *v.i.* **6** regenerarse. **7** renovarse. || *adj.* **8** renovado, transformado (espiritualmente).

regeneration | rɪˌdʒenə'reɪʃn | *s.i.* **1** regeneración, renovación. **2** reactivación. **3** transformación (para mejor). **4** revitalización.

regenerative | rɪdʒenərətɪv | *adj.* (form.) regenerador; revitalizador.

regent | 'ri:dʒənt | (también **Regent**) *s.c.* **1** POL. regente. **2** (EE.UU.) superior de una universidad estatal. || *adj.* **3** [*s.* –] regente: *Queen Regent = reina regente.*

reggae | 'regeɪ | *s.i.* MUS. música de origen jamaicano.

regicide | 'redʒɪsaɪd | (form.) *s.c.* **1** regicida. || *s.i.* **2** regicidio.

regime | reɪ'ʒi:m | (también **régime**) *s.c.* **1** POL. régimen: *political regimen = régimen político.* **2** (desp.) gobierno: *a corrupt regime = un gobierno corrupto.* **3** (form.) MED. régimen.

regimen | 'redʒɪmen | *s.c.* (form.) MED. régimen. **2** GRAM. régimen (relación sintáctica entre palabras). **3** (arc.) sistema de gobierno.

regiment | 'redʒɪmənt | (form.) *s.c.* **1** MIL. regimiento: *an artillery regiment = un regimiento de artillería.* || *v.t.* **2** MIL. agrupar en regimientos. **3** (fig.) organizar, reglamentar. || **4 (whole) – of,** (fig.) (todo) un ejército de, gran cantidad de: *a whole regiment of ants = todo un ejército de hormigas.*

regimental | ˌredʒɪ'mentl | MIL. *adj.* **1** del regimiento. || **2 regimentals,** uniforme (del regimiento, militar).

regimentation | ˌredʒɪmen'teɪʃn | *s.i.* reglamentación, organización (bajo estricto control). **2** POL. control disciplinario.

regimented | 'redʒɪmentɪd | *adj.* reglamentado; estrictamente controlado.

region | 'ri:dʒən | *s.c.* **1** GEOG. región, zona: *a fertile region = una región fértil.* **2** (fig.) esfera, terreno: *the region of psychoanalysis = el terreno del psicoanálisis.* **3** ANAT. región, zona: *abdominal region = región abdominal.* || **4 in the – of,** alrededor de, aproximadamente. **5 regions,** GEOG. comarcas, regiones. **6 the lower regions,** (fig.) el infierno.

regional | 'ri:dʒənl | *adj.* **1** regional: *regional delegation = delegación regional.*

regionalism | 'ri:dʒənəlɪzəm | *s.i.* (form.) regionalismo.

register | 'redʒɪstər | *s.c.* **1** registro (libro de registro): *parish register = registro parroquial.* **2** lista: *electoral register = lista de electores.* **3** (EE.UU.) registrador: *cash register = caja registradora.* || *s.c.* e *i.* **4** FILOL. nivel (lingÅística). || *s.sing.* **5** MUS. registro (de la voz, de un instrumento). || *v.t.* **6** registrar (anotar en un registro): *to register a birth = registrar un nacimiento.* **7** manifestar: *he registered his opposition = manifestó su oposición.* **8** mostrar, expresar: *her face showed disbelief = su rostro mostraba incredulidad.* **9** certificar (una carta, un envío postal). **10** (form. o lit.) registrar, conseguir (un éxito, una victoria, etc.): *they registered a new triumph = consiguieron un nuevo triunfo.* **11** matricular: *to register a car = matricular un coche.* **12** inscribir, matricular (en un centro de enseñanza). **13** marcar, indicar, señalar: *the thermometer registers 20º = el termómetro indica 20º.* **14** facturar (el equipaje). **15** acusar, experimentar: *he registered an improvement = acusó una mejoría.* || *v.i.* **16** registrarse (en un libro de registro). **17** inscribirse, matricularse (en un centro de enseñanza). **18** quedar registrado, quedar grabado (en un registro, en un instrumento). **19 [– (with)]** (fam.) quedar grabado (en la mente): *my name didn't register with her = mi nombre no le quedó grabado (ella no lo recordará).* || **20 – office,** V. **registry office.**

registered | 'redʒɪstəd | *adj.* **1** registrado: *registered trade mark = marca registrada.* **2** certificado: *registered package = paquete certificado.* **3** acreditado (oficialmente): *registered nurse = enfermera acreditada.* **4** matriculado (una persona, un coche). **5** facturado (un equipaje).

registrar | ˌredʒɪ'strɑ:r | *s.c.* **1** registrador (funcionario encargado del registro). **2** secretario general (de una Universidad). **3** MED. doctor de un hospital (que hace una especialidad).

registration | ˌredʒɪ'streɪʃn | *s.i.* **1** registro. **2** matriculación (de un coche, de un barco). **3** matrícula, inscripción (en un centro de enseñanza). **4** facturación (de equipaje). **5** certificación (de una carta, de un envío postal). || **6 – number /mark,** número de matrícula (en un vehículo).

registry | 'redʒɪstrɪ | *s.c.* **1** registro. **2** oficina de registro. || **3 – office,** registro civil.

regress | 'ri:gres | (form.) *v.i.* **1 [– (to)]** retroceder, volver (a un estado anterior o más primitivo).

regression | rɪ'greʃn | (form.) *s.i.* 1 vuelta, retorno (a un estado anterior o más primitivo): *regression to puritanism = retorno al puritanismo.* 2 regresión: *an epidemic in regression = una epidemia en regresión.*
regressive | rɪ'gresɪv | (form.) *adj.* regresivo; retrógrado.
regret | rɪ'gret | *v.t.* 1 arrepentirse de: *I regret what I have done = me arrepiento de lo que he hecho.* 2 **[– (to)]** lamentar, sentir: *I regret not having seen her = lamento no haberla visto.* 3 llorar (una pérdida). || *s.i.* 4 pesar, pena, dolor: *we heard with great regret that he had died = oímos con mucho dolor que él había muerto.* 5 arrepentimiento, pesar. || **6 to express one's regrets (for/to),** disculparse (por/con). 7 **regrets, a)** pesar, dolor; **b)** disculpas, excusas (por rechazar una invitación): *accept my regrets = acepte mis disculpas;* **c)** arrepentimiento.
regretfull | rɪ'gretfʊl | *adj.* 1 apenado, pesaroso. 2 triste. 3 arrepentido.
regretfully | rɪ'gretfʊlɪ | *adv.* 1 con pesar. 2 con arrepentimiento. 3 con tristeza.
regrettable | rɪ'gretəbl | *adj.* deplorable, lamentable: *a regrettable failure = un fracaso lamentable.*
regrettably | rɪ'gretəblɪ | *adv.* 1 lamentablemente. 2 desafortunadamente, desgraciadamente.
regroup | ˌriː'gruːp | *v.t.* e *i.* reagrupar(se).
regular | 'regjʊlər | *adj.* 1 regular, uniforme: *regular rhythm = ritmo regular.* 2 normal, corriente: *regular size = tamaño normal.* 3 habitual: *a regular customer = un cliente habitual.* 4 regular, fijo: *regular habits = hábitos regulares.* 5 metódico, ordenado: *a regular life = una vida ordenada.* 6 regular, simétrico, armonioso: *regular features = facciones armoniosas.* 7 (fam.) regular (que menstrúa o evacúa a intervalos regulares). 8 correcto, convencional: *a regular attitude = una actitud correcta.* 9 GRAM. regular: *regular verb = verbo regular.* 10 acostumbrado: *regular bedtime = hora acostumbrada de acostarse.* 11 MIL. regular: *regular army = ejército regular.* 12 REL. regular: *regular clergy = clero regular.* 13 (fam.) verdadero, completo: *a regular fool = un completo imbécil.* 14 permanente, fijo, estable: *a regular salary = un sueldo fijo.* 15 (fam.) estupendo, agradable: *a regular fellow = un tipo agradable.* || *s.c.* 16 (fam.) cliente habitual. 17 MIL. soldado regular. 18 trabajador fijo.
regularise V. **regularize.**
regularity | ˌregjʊ'lærɪtɪ | *s.c.* e *i.* regularidad.
regularize | 'regjʊləraɪz | (también **regularise**) *v.t.* regularizar, poner un orden: *to regularize a situation = regularizar una situación.*
regularly | 'regjʊləlɪ | *adv.* 1 regularmente, de modo regular. 2 uniformemente. 3 con regularidad. 4 normalmente. 5 habitualmente.
regulate | 'regjʊleɪt | *v.t.* 1 regular, controlar: *to regulate the traffic = regular la circulación.* 2 regular, ajustar, poner a punto (un mecanismo, un aparato). 3 reglamentar. 4 regular (la velocidad).
regulated | 'regjʊleɪtɪd | *adj.* controlado; ordenado.
regulation | ˌregjʊ'leɪʃn | *s.c.* 1 reglamento, regla: *I'm contrary to regulations = soy contrario a los reglamentos.* || *s.i.* 2 reglamentación. 3 regulación, reajuste; control. || *adj.* 4 reglamentario: *regulation uniform = uniforme reglamentario.* 5 normal, estándar: *regulation size = tamaño normal.*
regulator | 'regjʊleɪtər | *s.c.* TEC. regulador.
regurgitate | rɪ'gəːdʒɪrtert | *v.t.* e *i.* 1 regurgitar; vomitar sin esfuerzo, devolver. || *v.t.* 2 (fig.) repetir de forma mecánica (algo que se ha aprendido).
rehabilitate | ˌriːə'bɪlɪteɪt | *v.t.* 1 rehabilitar (a un delincuente, a un enfermo). 2 POL. rehabilitar, reintegrar (restablecer en sus derechos o situación). 3 restaurar, arreglar: *to rehabilitate an old church = restaurar una antigua iglesia.*
rehabilitation 'riːəˌbɪlɪ'teɪʃn | *s.i.* 1 rehabilitación: *rehabilitation center = centro de rehabilitación.* 2 restauración (de edificios, calles, etc.).
rehash | ˌriː'hæʃ | *s.c.* 1 **[– (of)]** copia, reproducción, imitación (a la que se han hecho cambios superficiales para que parezca original): *his last work is a rehash of his first one = su último trabajo es una copia del primero.* 2 **[– (of)]** refundición (de una obra literaria). || *v.t.* 3 rehacer, recomponer (con ligeros cambios para que parezca original).
rehearsal | rɪ'həːsl | *s.c.* e *i.* 1 ART. ensayo (de una obra, concierto, etc.). || 2 **dress –,** ensayo general.
rehearse | rɪ'həːs | *v.t.* e *i.* 1 ensayar: *I have to rehearse my part = tengo que ensayar mi papel.* || *v.t.* 2 (form.) repetir, enumerar. 3 (fig.) ensayar, probar (repetir mentalmente).
rehouse | ˌriː'haʊz | *v.t.* proporcionar una nueva vivienda a: *the governement will have to rehouse them = el gobierno tendrá que proporcionarles una nueva vivienda.*
reign | reɪn | *v.i.* 1 **[– (over)]** reinar (un rey, una reina). 2 (fig.) reinar, prevalecer, imperar: *an atmosphere of anxiety reigned everywhere = reinaba por todas partes una atmósfera de desasosiego.* || *s.c.* 3 reinado (gobierno de un rey o reina). || *s.sing.* 4 **[– (of)]** (form.) reinado, imperio, dominio: *the reign of democracy = el imperio de la democracia.* || **5 – of terror,** régimen de terror.
reigning | reɪnɪŋ | 1 reinante, actual: *the reigning champion = el campeón actual.* 2 (fig.) dominante, que prevalece: *the reigning tendency = la tendencia dominante.*
reimburse | ˌriːɪm'bəːs | *v.t.* 1 **[– (to)]** reembolsar: *they reimbursed her expenses = le reembolsaron los gastos.* 3 **[– (for)]** indemnizar (por): *who will reimburse me for it? = ¿quién me indemnizará por ello?*
reimbursement | ˌriːɪm'bəːsmənt | *s.i.* 1 reembolso, reintegro. 2 indemnización.
rein | reɪn | *s.c.* o *s.pl.* 1 riendas (de una caballería). 2 andadores (para sostener a un niño que aprende a andar). 3 **[the – (of)]** (fig.) riendas (control): *the reins of power = las riendas del poder.* || **4 to give a free – to,** (fig.) **a)** dar rienda suelta: *he gave a free rein to his imagination = dio rienda suelta a su imaginación;* **b)** dar plena libertad, dar carta blanca. **5 to hold/take the reins,** (fig.) tomar las riendas, controlar. **6 to keep a tight – on,** (fig.) mantener estricto control sobre. **7 to – in,** refrenar (un caballo).
OBS. **Rein** se utiliza a menudo en *pl.* con el mismo significado que en *sing.*
reincarnate | ˌriːɪn'kɑːneɪt | *v.t.* REL. reencarnar.
reincarnated | ˌriːɪnkɑː'neɪtɪd | *adj.* REL. reencarnado.
reincarnation | ˌriːɪnkɑː'neɪʃn | REL. *s.i.* 1 reencarnación. || *s.c.* 2 metempsicosis, espíritu reencarnado.
reindeer | 'reɪnˌdɪər | *s.inv.* ZOOL. reno.
reinforce | ˌriːɪn'fɔːs | *v.t.* 1 reforzar, aumentar, intensificar: *it reinforces his guilt feelings = ello aumenta su sentimiento de culpabilidad.* 2 confirmar, ratificar: *this reinforces what I said = esto confirma lo que dije.* 3 **[– (with)]** reforzar: *to reinforce a wall = reforzar una pared.* 4 afianzar. 5 MIL. reforzar. || **6 reinforced concrete.** V. **concrete.**
reinforcement | ˌriːɪn'fɔːsmənt | *s.c.* e *i.* 1 aumento, intensificación. 2 esfuerzo (algo que se añade a un objeto para fortalecerlo). || 3 **reinforcements,** MIL. refuerzos.
reinstate | ˌriːɪn'steɪt | (form.) *v.t.* 1 rehabilitar (en un puesto). 2 reincorporar, reinstalar. 3 recobrar.
reinstatement | ˌriːɪn'steɪtmənt | (form.) *s.i.* 1 rehabilitación (en un puesto). 2 reincorporación.
reissue | ˌriː'ɪʃuː | *s.c.* 1 reedición, nueva edición (de un libro). 2 nueva emisión (de un sello). || *v.t.* 3 reeditar. 4 volver a emitir.
reiterate | riː'ɪtəreɪt | (form.) *v.t.* reiterar, repetir: *to reiterate a statement = reiterar una afirmación.*
reiteration | riːˌɪtə'reɪʃn | (form.) *s.c.* e *i.* reiteración, repetición.
reject | rɪ'dʒekt | *v.t.* 1 rechazar, rehusar, denegar: *he rejected my offer = rechazó mi oferta.* 2 rechazar, desairar, despedir: *to reject a suitor = rechazar un pretendiente.* 3 repudiar: *his parents rejected him = sus padres le repudiaron.* 4 despreciar, desestimar: *to reject a claim = desestimar una petición.* 5 descartar: *they rejected the plan = descartaron el plan.* 6 MED. rechazar (no aceptar un injerto o un transplante). || | 'riːdʒekt | *s.c.* 7 desecho (cosa que se desecha).
rejection | rɪ'dʒekʃn | *s.c.* e *i.* rechazo, negativa. 2 MED. rechazo. || *s.i.* 3 desprecio, desestimación. 4 repulsa.

rejoice | rɪ'dʒɔɪs | (form. y lit.) *v.t.* e *i.* **1 [– (in/at/over/to)]** regocijar(se), alegrar(se), causar alegría (a): *his success rejoiced his parents = su éxito alegró a sus padres.* || **2 to – in the name of/in the tittle of,** (hum.) tener el honor de llamarse.
rejoicing | rɪ'dʒɔɪsɪŋ | *s.i.* (lit.) **1** júbilo, alegría, regocijo. || **2 rejoicings,** fiestas, celebraciones, diversión.
rejoin | ˌriː'dʒɔɪn | *v.t.* **1** reunirse con: *he'll rejoin them at six = se reunirá con ellos a las seis.* **2** reincorporarse a: *he must rejoin his regiment = debe reincorporarse a su regimiento.* || | rɪ'dʒɔɪn | *v.i.* **3** (form.) replicar, responder.
rejoinder | rɪ'dʒɔɪndər | *s.c.* (form. o lit.) réplica, contestación.
rejuvenate | rɪ'dʒuːvəneɪt | (form.) *v.t.* e *i.* **1** rejuvenecer: *this haircut rejuvenates you = este corte de pelo te rejuvenece.* || *v.t.* **2** (fig.) renovar, modernizar (una organización, un sistema).
rejuvenating | rɪ'dʒuːvəneɪtɪŋ | (form.) *adj.* **1** rejuvenecedor. **2** renovador.
rejuvenation | rɪˌdʒuːvə'neɪʃn | (form.) *s.i.* **1** rejuvenecimiento. **2** (fig.) renovación, modernización.
rekindle | ˌriː'kɪndl | *v.t.* e *i.* **1** volver a encender: *to rekindle a fire = volver a encender un fuego.* || **2** (lit. o fig.) reavivar, despertar (un sentimiento).
relaid | ˌriː'leɪd | *pret.* y *p.p.* de **relay.**
relapse | rɪ'læps | (form. o lit.) *v.i.* **1 [– (into)]** reincidir, volver a caer (en un vicio, en un error). **2** recaer, volver a (un estado anterior). **3** MED. recaer. || | rɪːlæps | [ri,l%ps *s.c.* **4 [– (into)]** recaída, vuelta (a un vicio, error, etc.). **5** reincidencia. **6** MED. recaída.
relate | rɪ'leɪt | *v.t.* e *i.* **1 [– (to/with)]** relacionar(se), poner en relación (una cosa con otra): *it's impossible to relate one fact to another = es imposible relacionar un hecho con otro.* || *v.i.* **2 [– (to)]** relacionarse, tener que ver, referirse: *my question refers to what you said yesterday = mi pregunta se refiere a lo que dijiste ayer.* **3 [– (to)]** relacionarse, mantener relaciones (con otras personas). **4** (form.) relatar, contar, narrar: *he is always relating strange stories = siempre está contando historias extrañas.* || **5 strange to –,** (form.) por extraño que parezca.
related | rɪ'leɪtɪd | *adj.* **1 [– (to)]** de la misma familia: *we are not related = no somos de la misma familia.* **2 [– (to)]** emparentado (que ha contraído parentesco por vía matrimonial). **3** vinculado, relacionado. **4** afín: *related languages = idiomas afines.*
relating | rɪ'leɪtɪŋ | *prep.* **[– to]** acerca de, en relación con, referente a, concerniente a: *questions relating to her private life = preguntas en relación con su vida privada.*
relation | rɪ'leɪʃn | *s.i.* **1 [– (of/to)]** relación, conexión: *the film bears no relation to the book = la película no guarda relación con el libro.* **2** (form.) narración, relato. || *s.c.* **3 [– (between/with)]** relación: *the relation between us is that of father and son = nuestra relación es la de un padre y un hijo.* **4** pariente: *is he a relation of yours? = ¿es pariente tuyo?* || **5 in/with – to,** en relación con, en comparación con. **6 relations, a)** relaciones (trato entre personas): *friendly relations = relaciones amistosas;* **b)** (form.) relaciones sexuales.
relationship | rɪ'leɪʃnʃɪp | *s.c.* **1 [– (between/with)]** relaciones: *the relationship between Spain and Portugal = las relaciones entre España y Portugal.* **2 [– (between/with)]** relación amorosa. **3 [– (between/to/of/with)]** relación, conexión. || *s.sing.* **4** relación: *the relationship between Paul and his boss = la relación entre Pablo y su jefe.* **5** parentesco.
relative | 'relətɪv | *adj.* **1** relativo (verdadero hasta cierto punto): *relative success = éxito relativo.* **2** respectivo: *the relative advantages of the two systems = las respectivas ventajas de los dos sistemas.* **3** FIL. relativo (no absoluto). **4** GRAM. relativo: *relative pronoun = pronombre relativo.* || *s.c.* **5** pariente. || **6 – to,** (form.) **a)** en relación con, referente a; **b)** en comparación con.
relatively | 'relətɪvlɪ | *adv.* relativamente: *the exam was relatively easy = el examen fue relativamente fácil.*
relativity | ˌrelə'tɪvɪtɪ | *s.i.* **1** FIS. relatividad: *theory of relativity = teoría de la relatividad.* **2** FIL. relatividad, calidad de relativo.
relax | rɪ'læks | *v.t.* **1** relajar, aflojar: *he relaxed his muscles = relajó sus músculos.* **2** relajar, hacer menos riguroso, aflojar: *to relax severity = aflojar la severidad.* **3** reducir, disminuir: *I didn't relax my efforts = no disminuí mis esfuerzos.* || *v.i.* **4** relajarse, descansar, reposar. **5** aflojarse: *his muscles relaxed = sus músculos se aflojaron.* || **6 to – the bowels,** hacer de vientre.
relaxation | ˌriːlæk'seɪʃn | *s.i.* esparcimiento, recreo. **2** relajación, aflojamiento: *relaxation of discipline = relajación de la disciplina.* **3** reducción, disminución. **4** relajación, disminución de la tensión. || *s.c.* **5** distracción, pasatiempo: *reading is my favourite relaxation = la lectura es mi pasatiempo favorito.*
relaxed | rɪ'lækst | *adj.* **1** relajado, tranquilo, sosegado. **2** distendido: *a relaxed atmosphere = un ambiente distendido.* || **3 – throat,** MED. garganta dolorida.
relaxing | rɪlæksɪŋ | *adj.* **1** relajante. || **2 – climate,** clima que causa amodorramiento.
relay | 'riːleɪ | *s.c.* **1** relevo: *relay race = carrera de relevos.* **2** (fam.) DEP. carrera de relevos. **3** ELECTR. relé, repetidor (de radio o televisión). || | riː'leɪ | *v.t.* **4 [– (to)]** transmitir: *I relayed the message to him = le transmití el mensaje.* **5** RAD. y TV. retransmitir. **6** [*pret.* y *p.p.* **relaid**] | ˌriː'leɪ | volver a tender; volver a colocar, volver a poner. || **7 in relays,** por turnos. **8 – station,** RAD. y TV. repetidor (estación retransmisora).
release | rɪ'liːs | *v.t.* **1 [– (from)]** soltar, poner en libertad: *they released the prisoner = soltaron al prisionero.* **2 [– (from)]** (form.) librar, liberar, eximir (de una carga u obligación). **3** soltar: *don't release the brakes = no sueltes los frenos.* **4** lanzar (una bomba, un mísil). **5** desprender, despedir, emitir (calor, energía, radiactividad, etc.). **6** disparar (apretar el disparador de un mecanismo). **7** estrenar (una película). **8** lanzar, poner en venta (un disco). **9** (form.) entregar, dar. **10** divulgar, dar a conocer, hacer público: *to release a piece of news = divulgar una noticia.* **11** (form.) desahogar, dar libre curso (a un sentimiento). || *s.c.* e *i.* **12** liberación, puesta en libertad. | *s.c.* **13** anuncio, comunicado (para ser publicado o emitido). **14** producción (película, disco, etc. que se da a conocer al público). || *s.i.* **15 [– (from)]** alivio: *a feeling of release = un sentimiento de alivio.* **16** exención (de una carga u obligación). **17** lanzamiento (de un mísil, de una bomba). **18** estreno (de una película). **19** emisión (de energía, de calor, etc.). **20** (fig.) estallido, arrebato (de un sentimiento): *a release of joy = un estallido de alegría.* || **21 on (general) –,** en exhibición (una película de cine).
relegate | 'relɪgeɪt | *v.t.* **1 [– (to)]** relegar (enviar a una posición o situación inferior). **2 [– (to)]** desterrar. **3 [– (to)]** remitir, confiar (un asunto a alguien). || **4 to be relegated [– (to)]** DEP. descender (a una división inferior): *his team is relegated to the second division = su equipo desciende a segunda división.*
relegation | ˌrelɪ'geɪʃn | *s.i.* DEP. descenso (de un equipo a una división inferior).
relent | rɪ'lent | (form.) *v.i.* ceder, ablandarse, apenarse: *at last her father relented and let her go with him = al final su padre cedió y la dejó ir con él.*
relentless | rɪ'lentlɪs | (lit.) **1** implacable, inexorable, despiadado: *relentless persecution = persecución implacable.* **2** (fig.) incesante: *this relentless noise is driving me mad = este ruido incesante me está volviendo loco.*
relentlessly | rɪ'lentlɪsnɪs | *adv.* **1** implacablemente, inexorablemente, de forma despiadada. **2** incesantemente.
relevance | 'reləvəns | *s.i.* **1 [– (to)]** pertinencia, conexión. **2 [– (to)]** relevancia, importancia: *the relevance of these documents = la importancia de estos documentos.*
relevant | 'reləvənt | *adj.* **1 [– (to)]** pertinente, oportuno: *a relevant answer = una respuesta pertinente.* **2 [– (to)]** relativo, concerniente, referente: *documentation relevant to the case = documentación relativa al caso.* **3** adecuado, apropiado (para un propósito determinado).
reliability | rɪˌlaɪə'bɪlɪtɪ | *s.i.* fiabilidad, seguridad (de una máquina, de un dispositivo).

reliable | rɪ'laɪəbl | *adj.* 1 fiable, de confianza, digno de confianza (una persona). 2 fiable, seguro (una máquina, un dispositivo). 3 fiable, serio: *a reliable company = una empresa seria.* 4 fidedigna: *reliable sources = fuentes fidedignas.* 5 fehaciente: *a reliable document = un documento fehaciente.*

reliably | rɪ'laɪəblɪ | *adv.* de fuente fidedigna.

reliance | rɪ'laɪəns | *s.i.* 1 **[– (on/upon)]** confianza: *he has no reliance on doctors = no tiene confianza en los médicos.* 2 dependencia: *his reliance on his parents = su dependencia de sus padres.*

reliant | rɪ'laɪənt | *adj.* 1 **[– (on/upon)]** necesitado, dependiente. || **2 to be -- (on), a)** depender (de); **b)** confiar (en).

relic | 'relɪk | *s.c.* 1 reliquia, restos, vestigios: *relics of old traditions = vestigios de antiguas tradiciones.* 2 reliquia (objeto). 3 REL. reliquia (de un santo). || **4 old –,** antigualla. **5 relics, a)** restos mortales; **b)** ruinas; **c)** restos, residuos.

relief | rɪ'liːf | *s.i.* o *s.sing.* 1 alivio: *she heaved a sigh of relief = dio un suspiro de alivio.* 2 descanso, consuelo, alivio: *it was a relief for her = fue un consuelo para ella.* || *s.i.* 3 ayuda (social). 4 relieve: *a profile in relief = una silueta en relieve.* 5 DER. reparar, remediar. || *s.c.* 6 ART. relieve (escultura). 7 relevo (persona o grupo de personas que releva). || *s.sing.* **8 [the – (of)]** MIL. relevo, refuerzo (para una ciudad sitiada). || **9 to be on –,** recibir ayuda social, vivir de la beneficencia. **10 light/comic –,** ART. diversión, distracción. **11 low/high –,** ART. bajo/alto relieve. **12 – map,** mapa en relieve. **13 to stand out in bold/sharp /clear – (against), a)** resaltar (sobre); **b)** contrastar (con).

relieve | rɪ'liːv | *v.t.* 1 aliviar, mitigar: *this medicine will relieve the pain = esta medicina aliviará el dolor.* 2 aliviar (una pena). 3 **[– (of)]** librar de (una preocupación, un deber, una dificultad o un sentimiento desagradable). 4 ayudar, socorrer: *to relieve the poor = ayudar a los pobres.* 5 relevar, tomar el relevo de. 6 MIL. liberar (una ciudad o plaza fuerte sitiada). 7 MIL. relevar (tropas). 8 aligerar (una carga). || **9 to – oneself/nature,** (p.u.) orinar; hacer sus necesidades. **10 to – one's feelings,** desahogarse. **11 to – someone of something,** (form.) **a)** cogerle algo a alguien (para ayudarle): *let me relieve you of your cases = déjame que coja tus maletas;* **b)** (hum.) quitar, robar algo a alguien: *somebody relieved him of his wallet = alguien le robó su cartera.* **12 to – someone of their duties /post,** (form.) echar (del trabajo); destituir.

relieved | rɪ'liːvd | *adj.* aliviado: *all of us felt relieved = todos nos sentimos aliviados.*

religion | rɪ'lɪdʒən | *s.i.* 1 REL. religión. 2 (fig.) religión: *he made a religion of sport = hizo del deporte una religión.* || *s.c.* 3 REL. religión, doctrina, fe: *Muslim religion = religión musulmana.* || **4 freedom of –,** DER. libertad de culto.

religious | rɪ'lɪdʒəs | *adj.* 1 REL. religioso: *religious beliefs = creencias religiosas.* 2 REL. religioso, devoto, piadoso, creyente. 3 (fig.) concienzudo, escrupuloso. || *s.inv.* 4 religioso (persona perteneciente a una orden religiosa).

religiously | rɪ'lɪdʒəslɪ | *adv.* 1 religiosamente, puntualmente, exactamente, fielmente. 2 concienzudamente, escrupulosamente.

relinquish | rɪ'lɪŋkwɪʃ | (form.) *v.t.* 1 abandonar (una esperanza, un plan, un hábito, una creencia). 2 renunciar a: *he relinquished his rights = renunció a sus derechos.* 3 dejar (un trabajo).

reliquary | 'relɪkwərɪ | *s.c.* TEC. relicario.

relish | 'relɪʃ | *v.t.* 1 (form. o lit.) gustar, apetecer, agradar: *he didn't relish the idea of sleeping outside = no le gustó la idea de dormir fuera.* 2 disfrutar con, apreciar: *I relish a good book = disfruto con un buen libro.* 3 saborear (una comida o bebida). || *s.i.* **4 [– (for)]** gusto, entusiasmo: *he read it with relish = lo llevó con entusiasmo.* 5 apetencia. **6 [– (of)]** atractivo (cualidad atractiva). || *s.inv.* 7 GAST. condimento, aderezo. || **8 to – of,** saber a.

relive | ˌriː'lɪv | *v.t.* 1 revivir, recordar: *to relieve the old days = revivir los viejos tiempos.* 2 revivir, volver a pasar por (una experiencia). 3 (fig.) resucitar: *the wine revived me = el vino me resucitó.* || *v.i.* 4 (arc.) volver a la vida, resucitar.

reload | ˌriː'ləʊd | *v.t.* e *i.* volver a cargar (un arma).

relocate | ˌriːləʊ'keɪt | (form.) *v.t.* e *i.* trasladar(se) a otro sitio, establecer(se) en otro sitio.

relocation | ˌriːləʊ'keɪʃən | (form.) *s.i.* traslado; cambio de residencia.

reluctance | rɪ'lʌktəns | *s.i.* 1 **[– (to)]** reluctancia, oposición, resistencia. 2 **[– (to)]** desgana; repugnancia.

reluctant | rɪ'lʌktənt | *adj.* 1 **[– (to)]** desganado, poco entusiasta, poco dispuesto. 2 reticente, reacio: *he is reluctant to wear ties = es reacio a ponerse corbata.*

reluctantly | rɪ'lʌktəntlɪ | *adv.* 1 con desgana, sin entusiasmo. 2 a regañadientes, de mala gana.

rely | rɪ'laɪ | *v.i.* 1 **[– (on/upon)]** confiar en, contar con: *you can rely on me = puedes contar conmigo.* 2 **[– (on/upon)]** (fig.) fiarse de: *one can't rely on trains = uno no se puede fiar de los trenes.*

remain | rɪ'meɪn | *v.i.* 1 permanecer, quedar(se): *he remained motionless = permaneció inmóvil.* 2 seguir, continuar: *he remained sitting = siguió sentado.* 3 quedar, sobrar: *nothing remained of his house = no quedó nada de su casa.* 4 quedar, restar, faltar: *many things remain to be done = quedan muchas cosas por hacer.* || **5 remains, a) [– (of)]** restos, sobras: *the remains of the dinner = las sobras de la cena;* **b)** restos (mortales); **c)** ruinas: *Roman remains = ruinas romanas;* **d)** restos, vestigios: *the remains of an old civilization = los vestigios de una antigua civilización.* **6 to – to be seen,** estar por ver, estar por descubrir.

remainder | rɪ'meɪndər | *s.sing.* 1 **[the – (of)]** el resto, lo restante: *the remainder of my fortune = el resto de mi fortuna.* 2 **[the –]** el resto, los demás: *two of them went out and the remainder stayed at home = dos de ellos salieron y los demás se quedaron en casa.* 3 MAT. resto. || *v.t.* 4 saldar, liquidar (libros). || **5 remainders,** restos de edición de libros que van a ser saldados.

remaining | rɪ'meɪnɪŋ | *adj.* 1 sobrante, restante. 2 que queda: *my remaining relatives = los parientes que me quedan.*

remake | ˌriː'meɪk | *v.* [*pret.* y *p.p.* **remade**] *t.* 1 rehacer, hacer de nuevo; reconstruir. || | 'riːmeɪk | *s.c.* 2 nueva versión (cinematográfica): *a remake of "Tarzan" = una nueva versión de "Tarzán".*

remand | rɪ'mɑːnd | DER. *v.t.* 1 volver a enviar a la cárcel (hasta nuevo aviso, en espera de juicio). || *s.i.* 2 reencarcelamiento (en espera de juicio). || **3 to be remanded in custody,** mantenerse bajo custodia. **4 to be remanded on bail,** liberar bajo fianza. **5 on –,** detenido (en espera de juicio). **6 – centre/home,** reformatorio de menores.

remark | rɪ'mɑːk | *v.i.* 1 **[– (on/upon)]** comentar: *"she won't marry him", he remarked = "ella no se casará con él", comentó.* 2 **[– (on/upon)]** hacer una observación sobre; aludir a. || *v.t.* 3 (p.u.) ver, advertir, notar, observar. || *s.c.* 4 comentario, observación: *he made some remarks about it = hizo algunos comentarios sobre ello.* || **5 to pass remarks on/about someone,** (fam.) criticar a alguien. **6 worthy of –,** notable, digno de mención.

remarkable | rɪ'mɑːkəbl | *adj.* 1 notable, extraordinario. 2 digno de mención. 3 excepcional, fuera de lo común.

remarkably | rɪ'mɑːkəblɪ | *adv.* 1 extraordinariamente. 2 extremadamente. 3 notablemente.

remarriage | ˌriː'mærɪdʒ | *s.i.* segundas nupcias.

remarry | ˌriː'mærɪ | *v.t.* e *i.* volver a casarse (con).

remedial | rɪ'miːdɪəl | (form.) *adj.* 1 terapéutico, curativo: *remedial measures = medidas terapéuticas.* 2 de recuperación: *remedial class = clase de recuperación.* 3 correctivo, corrector: *remedial exercises = ejercicios correctivos.*

remedy | 'remədɪ | (form.) *s.c.* 1 **[– (for)]** remedio: *a household remedy for colds = un remedio casero para los catarros.* 2 **[– (for)]** remedio, solución: *there is no remedy for your problem = no hay solución para su problema.* 3 DER. recurso. || *v.t.* 4 remediar, curar (un mal). 5 remediar, reparar (un daño). 6 corregir, arreglar. 7 rectificar (un error).

remember | rɪ'membər | *v.t.* 1 recordar, acordarse de: *I don't remember his address = no recuerdo su dirección.* 2

recordar, tener presente, no olvidar: *remember that he is the boss = no olvides que él es el jefe.* **3** recordar, no olvidar de dar una propina a: *remember the waiter = no olvides de darle una propina al camarero.* **4** [– *o.* + **to**] dar recuerdos a: *remember me to him = dale recuerdos de mi parte.* || *v.i.* **5** recordar, acordarse: *if I remember rightly = si mal no recuerdo.* || **6 to – someone in one's will,** dejar una herencia a alguien (mencionarlo en su testamento). **7 you –,** como sabes: *her husband, you remember, was a famous actor = su marido, como sabes, fue un actor famoso.*

remembrance | rɪ'membrəns | *s.c.* **1** (form.) recuerdo: *an unpleasant remembrance = un recuerdo desagradable.* **2** (form.) recuerdo (objeto que se guarda como recuerdo). || *s.i.* **3** recuerdo, memoria: *a plaque in remembrance of the boys who died = una placa en memoria de los chicos que murieron.* || **4 Remembrance Day/Sunday,** (brit.) día en que se conmemora el fin de las dos guerras mundiales. **5 remembrances,** saludos, recuerdos: *give my remembrances to your mother = dale mis recuerdos a tu madre.*

remind | rɪ'maɪnd | *v.t.* **1** [– **(of /about/to)**] recordar (algo a alguien): *please remind me to lock the doors = por favor recuérdame que cierre las puertas.* **2** [– **(of)**] recordar a, parecerse a, hacer pensar en: *this boy reminds me of his father = ese chico me recuerda a su padre.*

reminder | rɪ'maɪndər | *s.c.* **1** recordatorio (algo que hace recordar). **2** advertencia. **3** notificación.

reminisce | ˌremɪ'nɪs | *v.i.* [– **(about)**] (form. o lit.) pensar o hablar acerca del pasado.

reminiscence | ˌremɪ'nɪsns | (form. o lit.) *s.i.* **1** memoria, recuerdo. || *s.c.* **2** recuerdo: *an unpleasant reminiscence = un recuerdo desagradable.* **3** reminiscencia; algo que recuerda a (alguna otra cosa o persona): *there is a reminiscence of Bach in this simphony = hay algo que recuerda a Bach en esta sinfonía.* || **4 reminiscences, a)** memorias; **b)** recuerdos.

reminiscent | ˌremɪ'nɪsnt | (form. o lit.) *adj.* **1** [– **(of)**] evocador: *old photographs reminiscent of our youth = viejas fotos que evocan nuestra juventud.* **2** que habla del pasado; que recuerda el pasado; nostálgico. **3** lleno de recuerdos. || **4 to be – of,** recordar a: *his voice is reminiscent of his father's = su voz recuerda a la de su padre.*

remiss | rɪ'mɪs | *adj.* (form.) descuidado, negligente.

remission | rɪ'mɪʃn | *s.i.* **1** DER. reducción de una pena de prisión (por buena conducta, etc.). **2** (form.) REL. remisión, perdón: *the remission of sins = la remisión de los pecados.* **3** MED. remisión (de unos síntomas, de una enfermedad, de un dolor).

remit | rɪ'mɪt | (form.) *v.t.* e *i.* **1** remitir (dinero, cheques, etc., por carta). **2** aplacar(se): *remit your anger = aplaca tu ira.* **3** [– **(to)**] DER. remitir. || *v.t.* **4** remitir, perdonar: *to remit sins = remitir los pecados.* **5** condonar (una deuda, una pena). **6** remitir (un castigo, un deber). || *v.i.* **7** remitir, disminuir su intensidad: *the fever has remitted = la fiebre ha remitido.*

remittance | rɪ'mɪtəns | *s.c.* **1** (form.) remesa, envío (de dinero). || **2 – man,** emigrante que sobrevive con el dinero que le envían de su patria.

remnant | 'remnənt | *s.c.* **1** [– **(of)**] resto: *remnants of a meal = restos de una comida.* **2** resto, vestigio: *remnants of her former beauty = vestigios de su antigua belleza.* **3** retal, retazo (de una tela). || **4 remnants,** remanente.

remodel | ˌriː'mɒdl | *v.t.* **1** remodelar, transformar, rehacer (una casa, una habitación, etc.).

remonstrance | rɪ'mɒnstrəns | *s.i.* (form.) protesta, reconvención.

remonstrate | 'remənstreɪt | (form.) *v.i.* **1** [– **(with/against)**] protestar: *he remonstrated against any kind of violence = él protestó contra cualquier tipo de violencia.* **2** [– **(with)**] reprender, censurar. **3** [– **(about)**] objetar a.

remorse | rɪ'mɔːs | *s.i.* (form.) remordimiento: *a twinge of remorse = un remordimiento.*

remorseful | rɪ'mɔːsfʊl | (form.) *adj.* **1** lleno de remordimiento; arrepentido. **2** compungido.

remorsefully | rɪ'mɔːsfəlɪ | *adv.* (form.) con remordimiento; con arrepentimiento.

remorseless | rɪ'mɔːslɪs | *adj.* (form.) despiadado, cruel; implacable.

remorselessly | rɪ'mɔːslɪslɪ | *adv.* (form.) despiadadamente, cruelmente; implacablemente.

remote | rɪ'məʊt | *adj.* **1** remoto, lejano, distante: *remote lands = tierras lejanas; in the remote future = en un futuro remoto.* **2** apartado, aislado: *a remote village = un pueblo apartado.* **3** [– **(from)**] (fig.) alejado, apartado, ajeno: *remote from the subject = ajeno al tema.* **4** [– **(from)**] reservado, distante (una persona). **5** lejano (un pariente). **6** remoto, ligero: *a remote possibility = una ligera posibilidad.* || **7 not to have the remotest chance,** no tener la más remota posibilidad. **8 not to have the remotest idea/notion,** no tener la más remota idea. **9 – control,** TEC. mando a distancia.

remote-controlled | rɪ'məʊtkən'trəʊld | *adj.* TEC. teledirigido, controlado por control remoto.

remotely | rɪ'məʊtlɪ | *adv.* **1** en un lugar remoto. **2** remotamente: *I know it is not even remotely possible = sé que no es ni remotamente posible.* || **3 to be – related,** ser parientes lejanos.

remoteness | rɪməʊtnɪs | *s.i.* **1** distancia, lejanía. **2** alejamiento. **3** aislamiento. **4** reserva (de carácter).

remould | 'riːməʊld | *s.c.* **1** neumático recauchutado. || | ˌriː'məʊld | *v.t.* **2** (form.) cambiar, reestructurar (basándose en diferentes principios): *she remoulded her way of thinking = cambió su forma de pensar.* **3** (p.u.) recauchutar.

remount | 'riːmaʊnt | *v.t.* e *i.* **1** volver a montar(se): *he remounted his bike = se volvió a montar en su bici.* **2** volver a subir(se). || *v.t.* **3** MIL. remontar (proveer de caballos). **4** volver a enmarcar (un cuadro, una foto). || *v.i.* **5** [– **(to)**] (p.u.) remontarse (a una determinada fecha, época, etc.). || *s.c.* e *i.* **6** MIL. remonta.

removable | rɪ'muːvəbl | *adj.* **1** trasladable (una cosa, una persona en un cargo). **2** amovible. **3** separable, desmontable, de quita y pon: *a removable hood = una capucha de quita y pon.*

removal | rɪ'muːvl | *s.i.* **1** traslado. **2** cambio de residencia, mudanza. **3** supresión, eliminación. || *s.c.* **4** traslado de muebles. || **5 – from office/from one's post,** deposición, destitución (de un cargo, de un empleo). **6 – van,** camión de mudanzas.

remove | rɪ'muːv | *v.t.* **1** [– **(from/to)**] retirar, llevarse: *they removed the cutlery from the table = retiraron los cubiertos de la mesa.* **2** quitar: *he removed his coat = se quitó el abrigo.* **3** [– **(from)**] quitar, eliminar (una mancha). **4** [– **(from)**] expulsar, echar (a alguien de un sitio). **5** [– **(from)**] retirar, quitar, apartar: *she removed her hand from my shoulder = apartó su mano de mi hombro.* **6** suprimir: *the government removed some taxes = el gobierno suprimió algunos impuestos.* **7** llevarse, robar: *someone removed my watch = alguien robó mi reloj.* **8** destituir, deponer (de un cargo, de un empleo). **9** quitar de en medio (un obstáculo). **10** MED. extirpar: *to remove a tumour = extirpar un tumor.* **11** [– **(from)**] apartar, alejar: *an illness removed him from football = una enfermedad le apartó del fútbol.* **12** hacer desaparecer (una duda, un temor, una sospecha, etc.). || *v.i.* **13** [– **(to)**] mudarse, cambiarse, trasladarse: *I am removing from Madrid to Barcelona = me traslado de Madrid a Barcelona.* || **14 to be at many removes from,** (form.) apartarse bastante, distar mucho de. **15 to be at one – from,** (form.) estar muy cercano a.

removed | rɪ'muːvd | *adj.* **1** [– **(from)**] distante, remoto, lejano.

OBS. **Once/twice/three times, etc. removed** indica un grado de parentesco: *first cousin once removed = sobrino en segundo grado; tío en segundo grado.*

remover | rɪ'muːvər | *s.c.* **1** agente de mudanzas.

OBS. **Remover** es también cualquier sustancia que se utiliza para eliminar algo; va normalmente con otro *s.* formando compuestos: **2 makeup –,** desmaquillador. **3 stain –,** quitamanchas. **4 superfluous hair –,** depilatorio del vello superfluo.

remunerate | rɪ'mjuːnəreɪt | *v.t.* (form.) [– **(for)**] remunerar.

remuneration | rɪˌmju:nə'reɪʃn | *s.c.* e *i.* (form.) remuneración, retribución.
remunerative | rɪ'mju:nərətɪv | *adj.* (form.) rentable, remunerador.
renaissance | rə'neɪsəns | *s.sing.* **1** renacimiento: *literary renaissance = renacimiento literario.* || *adj.* **2** HIST. renacentista: *Renaissance style = estilo renacentista.* || **3 the Renaissance,** HIST. el Renacimiento.
renal | 'ri:nl | *adj.* MED. renal.
rename | ˌri:'neɪm | *v.t.* cambiar de nombre, poner nuevo nombre a.
rend | rend | (lit.) *v.* [*pret.* y *p.p.* **rent**] *t.* **1** desgarrar, rasgar: *she rent her dress = desgarró su vestido.* **2** (fig.) desgarrar: *my cough rent my chest = la tos me desgarraba el pecho.* **3** (fig.) partir en dos, dividir: *a war that rent the country = una guerra que dividió el país.* **4** (fig.) rajar, hender, desgarrar: *a cry rent the air = un grito hendió el aire.* **5** arrancar (violentamente).
render | 'rendər | (form.) *v.t.* **1** volver, hacer: *to render useless = volver inútil.* **2** dejar (en un estado): *the accident rendered her paralysed from the neck down = el accidente la dejó paralizada del cuello para abajo.* **3** proporcionar, prestar (ayuda, asistencia, servicios, etc.). **4** rendir (honores, un homenaje). **5** dar, rendir: *she rended thanks to God = ella rindió gracias a Dios.* **6** COM. presentar, pasar (una factura). **7** mostrar, rendir (obediencia). **8** devolver: *to render good for evil = devolver bien por mal.* **9** MUS. interpretar, ejecutar (una pieza musical). **10** hacer (justicia). **11** ART. representar, interpretar (un papel). **12** retratar, reproducir: *no picture could render the scene = ningún cuadro podría reproducir la escena.* **13 [– (into/from)]** traducir: *how would you render this idiom into English? = ¿cómo traducirías este modismo al inglés?* **14** cubrir con una capa de cemento o yeso (una pared). **15** GAST. derretir (grasa). || **16 to – an account of,** (fig.) dar cuenta de, rendir cuentas de. **17 to – an account of oneself,** (fig.) justificarse.
rendering | 'rendərɪŋ | *s.c.* **1** ART. representación, función (de una obra teatral). **2** MUS. interpretación, ejecución (de una pieza musical). **3** ART. interpretación (de un poema). **4** traducción, versión: *a rendering of the Bible = una versión de la Biblia.*
rendezvous | 'rɒndɪvu: | (form.) *s.c.* **1** cita. **2** lugar donde se tiene una cita. **3** punto de encuentro: *his house is a rendezvous for writers = su casa es un punto de encuentro de escritores.* || *v.i.* **4 [– (with)]** encontrarse (con alguien con quien se ha concertado una cita previa).
OBS. La pronunciación del *pl.* y de la tercera persona de *sing.* del *v.* es | 'rɒn↓dɪvu:z | .
rendition | ren'dɪʃn | *s.c.* **1** ART. representación, función (de una obra teatral). **2** MUS. interpretación, ejecución (de una pieza musical). **3** ART. interpretación (de un poema, de una canción). **4** traducción.
renegade | 'renɪgeɪd | *s.c.* y *adj.* renegado.
renege | rɪ'ni:g | *v.i.* **1 [– (on)]** (form.) volverse atrás (en una promesa, un acuerdo, etc.). **2** renunciar (en un juego de naipes).
renew | rɪ'nju: | *v.t.* **1** renovar, reanudar: *they renewed their friendship = reanudaron su amistad.* **2** renovar (prolongar su validez): *to renew a contract = renovar un contrato.* **3** renovar, cambiar (por algo nuevo): *to renew the furniture = renovar el mobiliario.* **4** reponer (suministros). **5** recuperar (la fuerza, la juventud, etc.). **6** sustituir, cambiar (una pieza estropeada). || **7 to be renewed,** renovarse, transformarse.
renewable | rɪnju:əbl | *adj.* **1** transformable. **2** renovable: *a renewable contract = un contrato renovable.*
renewal | rɪ'nju:əl | *s.i.* **1 [– (of)]** reanudación: *renewal of our relations = reanudación de nuestras relaciones.* **2** ARQ. renovación, reestructuración: *urban renewal = reestructuración urbana.* **3** REL. renovación: *spiritual renewal = renovación espiritual.* || *s.c.* e *i.* **4** renovación (de un documento oficial o legal).
renewed | rɪ'nju:d | *adj.* renovado, nuevo: *with renewed enthusiasm = con renovado entusiasmo.*
rennet | 'renɪt | *s.i.* GAST. cuajo.
renounce | rɪ'naʊns | (form.) *v.t.* **1** renunciar a, renegar de, abjurar: *he renounced his faith = renegó de su fe.* **2** renunciar a: *they renounced their rights = renunciaron a sus derechos.* **3** (p.u.) rechazar, repudiar: *she renounced his son = ella repudió a su hijo.* || *v.i.* **4** renunciar, hacer renuncio (en un juego de naipes). || *s.i.* **5** renuncio (en naipes). || **6 to – the world,** apartarse del mundo, hacer una vida de recogimiento.
renovate | 'renəʊveɪt | *v.t.* **1** restaurar (un edificio viejo, un cuadro antiguo). **2** reparar (una máquina). **3** renovar (algo en mal estado).
renovation | ˌrenəʊ'veɪʃn | *s.c.* e *i.* **1** renovación. **2** restauración. **3** reparación.
renown | rɪ'naʊn | (form. o lit.) *s.i.* renombre, fama: *a painter of international renown = un pintor de renombre internacional.*
renowned | rɪ'naʊnd | (form. o lit.) *adj.* **[– (for)]** famoso, célebre: *he is renowned for his researches = es famoso por sus investigaciones.*
rent | rent | *v.* [*pret.* y *p.p.* **rent**] *t.* **1** alquilar, arrendar: *to rent a flat = alquilar un piso.* || *i.* **2** alquilarse, arrendarse: *this house rents at ú30 a month = esta casa se alquila por 30 libras al mes.* || *s.c.* e *i.* **3** renta, alquiler: *the rent for the flat = la renta del piso.* || *s.c.* **4** rasgadura, desgarrón. **5** grieta, raja, hendidura. **6** (fig.) división: *a rent in the party = una división en el partido.* || **7 for –, a)** (EE.UU.) se alquila; **b)** de alquiler: *cars for rent = coches de alquiler.* **8 – book,** libro donde se registran los pagos por alquiler. **9 to – out,** alquilar: *I'll rent out this room to a student = alquilaré esta habitación a un estudiante.*
rental | 'rentl | *adj.* **1** de alquiler. || *s.c.* **2** renta, alquiler: *quarterly rental = alquiler trimestral.* **3** (EE.UU.) inmueble alquilado.
rented | rentɪd | *adj.* alquilado: *a rented house = una casa alquilada.*
rent-free | ˌrent'fri: | *adj.* **1** exento de alquiler. || *adv.* **2** gratuitamente (sin pagar renta).
renunciation | rɪˌnʌnsɪəeɪʃn | (form.) **[– (of)]** renuncia.
reopen | ˌri:'əʊpən | *v.t.* e *i.* **1** volver a abrir(se) (un establecimiento, después de haber estado cerrado durante algún tiempo). **2** DER. reabrir(se) (un caso). **3** reanudar(se) (una conversación, una discusión). **4** volver a empezar: *school reopens on Monday = la escuela vuelve a empezar el lunes.* **5** MED. volver a abrir(se) (una herida). || *v.t.* **6** volver a abrir (una frontera, una ruta).
reopening | ˌri:'əʊpənɪŋ | *s.c.* reapertura.
reorganisation V. **reorganization.**
reorganise V. **reorganize.**
reorganization | 'ri:ˌɔ:gənaɪ'zeɪʃn | (también **reorganisation**) *s.c.* e *i.* reorganización.
reorganize | ˌri:'ɔ:gənaɪz | (también **reorganise**) *v.t.* e *i.* reorganizar.
rep | rep | (fam.) *s.c.* **1** COM. representante; viajante. **2** representante (de una colectividad). **3** (vulg.) persona inmoral. || *s.i.* **4** reps (tejido). **5** (vulg.) reputación. || **6 in –,** en un teatro o compañía de repertorio.
OBS. Con la grafía **Rep.: 7** (EE.UU.) POL. representante, diputado (abreviatura). **8** republicano; república (abreviatura).
repaid | ri:'peɪd | *pret.* y *p.p.* de **repay.**
repair | rɪ'peər | *s.c.* e *i.* **1** reparación: *this house needs some repairs = esta casa necesita algunas reparaciones.* **2** reforma: *closed for repairs = cerrado por reformas.* || *v.t.* **3** reparar, arreglar: *he is repairing my bicycle = él está arreglando mi bicicleta.* **4** remendar (ropas, zapatos). **5** (form.) reparar, corregir: *he repaired his error = corrigió su error.* || *v.i.* **6 [to – to]** (form.) dirigirse a; ir a, acudir a. **7 beyond –,** irreparable. **8 in good/bad –,** (form.) en buen/mal estado. **9 – shop,** taller de reparaciones.
reparation | ˌrepə'reɪʃn | *s.i.* **1** (form.) reparación, satisfacción (de un daño o agravio). || *s.c.* **2** (generalmente en *pl.*) indemnización (por daños de guerra).
repartee | ˌrepɑ:'ti: | *s.c.* **1** réplica ingeniosa. || *s.i.* **2** charla ingeniosa, sucesión de réplicas ingeniosas.
repast | rɪ'pɑ:st | *s.c.* (lit.) comida: *a slight repast = una comida ligera.*
repatriate | ri:'pætrɪeɪt | (form.) *v.t.* **1** repatriar (a una persona). **2** COM. enviar a su patria (beneficios, ganancias, conseguidos en otro país). || *s.c.* **3** repatriado.

repatriation | ˌriːpætrɪ'eɪʃn | *s.i.* repatriación.
repay | riː'peɪ | *v.* [*pret.* y *p.p.* **repaid**] *t.* **1** [**– (to)**] devolver (dinero). **2** [**– (for)**] pagar: *he repaid me with ingratitude = me pagó con ingratitud.* **3** corresponder a: *she didn't repay his kindness = ella no correspondió a su amabilidad.* **4** (form.) requerir, merecer: *it rewards investigation = requiere una investigación.* **5** recompensar, resacir, compensar: *how can I repay you? = ¿cómo puedo recompensarle?*
repayable | riː'peɪəbl | *adj.* reintegrable, reembolsable.
repayment | riː'peɪmənt | *s.c.* **1** (generalmente en *pl.*) pago: *loan repayments = pagos de un crédito.* || *s.i.* **2** reintegro, reembolso. **3** devolución.
repeal | rɪ'piːl | DER. *v.t.* **1** revocar, anular, derogar (una ley). || *s.i.* **2** [**– (of)**] revocación, anulación, derogación (de una ley).
repeat | rɪ'piːt | *v.t.* e *i.* **1** repetir: *repeat it, please = repítelo, por favor.* || *v.t.* **2** contar (algo confidencial): *don't repeat it to anybody = no se lo cuentes a nadie.* **3** recitar: *to repeat a poem = recitar un poema.* **4** repetir, reiterar: *to repeat a statement = reiterar una afirmación.* || *v.i.* **5** [**– (on)**] (brit. y fam.) repetir (comidas): *sardines repeat on me = las sardinas me repiten.* **6** (EE.UU.) votar más de una vez. || *s.c.* **7** repetición. **8** RAD. y TV. reposición, repetición (de un programa). || **9 to – oneself,** repetirse: *History repeats itself = la Historia se repite.*
repeated | rɪ'piːtɪd | *adj.* **1** repetido, reiterado: *repeated absences = repetidas ausencias.* || **2 to be repeated,** RAD. y TV. repetirse, reponerse (un programa).
repeatedly | rɪ'piːtɪdlɪ | *adv.* repetidamente, reiteradamente, una y otra vez.
repeater | rɪ'piːtər | *s.c.* **1** arma de repetición. **2** reloj de repetición. **3** TEC. repetidor.
repeating | rɪ'piːtɪŋ | *adj.* **1** de repetición: *repeating rifle = rifle de repetición.* **2** GAST. que repite: *repeating food = comida que repite.* || **3 – decimal,** MAT. fracción decimal periódica.
repel | rɪ'pel | *v.t.* **1** repeler, repugnar: *that idea repels me = esa idea me repugna.* **2** repeler, repugnar, dar asco: *snakes repel him = las serpientes le dan asco.* **3** rechazar: *he repelled my offer = rechazó mi ofrecimiento.* **4** (form.) rechazar (obligar a retroceder): *they repelled their assailants = rechazaron a sus atacantes.* **5** (form.) resistir a: *he repelled temptation = resistió a la tentación.* **6** (fig.) repeler: *this material repels water = esta tela repele el agua.* || *v.t.* e *i.* **7** FIS. repeler(se) (polos magnéticos opuestos).
repellent | rɪ'pelənt | *adj.* **1** [**– (to)**] (form.) repelente, repugnante, desagradable, repulsivo. || *s.inv.* **2** QUIM. repelente (sustancia): *mosquito repellent = sustancia que repele a los mosquitos.*
repent | rɪ'pent | *v.t.* e *i.* [**– (of/for)**] (form.) arrepentirse (de): *she repented of having bought it = se arrepintió de haberlo comprado.*
repentance | rɪ'pentəns | *s.i.* (form.) arrepentimiento.
repentant | rɪ'pentənt | *adj.* (form.) arrepentido: *a repentant sinner = un pecador arrepentido.*
repercussion | ˌriːpə'kʌʃn | (form.) *s.c.* e *i.* **1** repercusión, eco, resonancia. || *s.c.* **2** (normalmente en *pl.*) repercusión, consecuencia, resonancia: *it had great political repercussions = tuvo grandes repercusiones políticas.*
repertoire | 'repətwɑː | *s.sing.* (form.) ART. repertorio: *a wide repertoire of songs = un amplio repertorio de canciones.*
repertory | 'repətərɪ | *s.sing.* **1** (form.) repertorio. || *s.i.* **2** ART. repertorio: *repertory theatre = teatro de repertorio.*|| **3 in –,** ART. en un teatro o compañía de repertorio.
repetition | ˌrepɪ'tɪʃn | *s.c.* e *i.* **1** repetición. || *s.c.* **2** recitado. **3** copia, réplica.
repetitious | ˌrepɪ'tɪʃəs | (form.) *adj.* **1** repetitivo, monótono. **2** reiterativo.
repetitive | rɪ'petɪtɪv | *adj.* **1** repetitivo, monótono: *a repetitive work = un trabajo monótono.* **2** reiterativo.
rephrase | ˌriː'freɪz | *v.t.* expresar de otro modo, decir con otras palabras.
replace | rɪ'pleɪs | *v.t.* **1** [**– (with/by)**] sustituir: *it will taste nice if you replace vinegar with lemon juice = estará sabroso si sustituyes el vinagre por limón.* **2** reemplazar, sustituir: *nothing can replace a mother's care = nada puede sustituir el cuidado de una madre.* **3** volver a colocar (en un sitio): *he replaced the book on the shelf = volvió a colocar el libro en la estantería.* **4** volver a colgar (el auricular del teléfono). **5** restituir, reponer: *he had to replace the money he had stolen = tuvo que reponer el dinero que había robado.*
replaceable | rɪ'pleɪsəbl | *adj.* reemplazable, sustituible.
replacement | rɪ'pleɪsmənt | *s.i.* **1** sustitución, cambio. **2** restitución, reposición. || *s.c.* **3** sustituto, suplente. **4** repuesto, pieza de recambio. **5** MIL. reemplazo.
replay | 'riːpleɪ | *s.c.* **1** DEP. partido de desempate. **2** repetición (de una grabación). || *v.t.* **3** DEP. volver a jugar (un partido). **4** volver a poner (una grabación).
replenish | rɪ'plenɪʃ | (form.) *v.t.* **1** [**– (with)**] rellenar, volver a llenar: *he replenished my glass = volvió a llenar mi vaso.* **2** reponer (existencias). **3** [**– (with)**] reabastecer; volver a aprovisionar.
replete | rɪ'pliːt | (form. y p.u.) *adj.* **1** [**– (with)**] repleto, lleno, ahíto (saciado de comida y bebida). **2** [**– (with)**] repleto, totalmente lleno, atiborrado: *a drawer replete with clothes = un cajón repleto de ropa.*
replica | 'replɪkə | *s.c.* **1** [**– (of)**] réplica, copia, reproducción. **2** [**– (of)**] ART. reproducción (de una obra de arte). **3** [**– (of)**] copia exacta, doble (de una persona).
replicate | 'replɪkeɪt | *v.t.* (form.) reproducir, duplicar.
reply | rɪ'plaɪ | *v.i.* **1** [**– (to)**] replicar, contestar, responder: *he didn't reply to my question = no contestó a mi pregunta.* **2** [**– (to)**] responder (con una acción): *the enemy didn't reply to our attack = el enemigo no respondió a nuestro ataque.* || *s.c.* **3** [**– (to)**] réplica, contestación, respuesta. || **4 in – (to),** como respuesta, en respuesta, como contestación (a algo que se ha dicho o hecho): *he said nothing in reply = no dijo nada como contestación; in reply to your letter = en respuesta a su atenta.*
repoint | ˌriː'pɔɪnt | *v.t.* TEC. volver a cementar.
report | rɪ'pɔːt | *v.t.* **1** relatar, contar (un suceso). **2** informar: *they reported that everything was going well = informaron que todo iba bien.* **3** [**– (on/upon)**] informar, presentar un informe: *who is going to report on the situation? = ¿quién va a informar de la situación?* **4** [**– (to)**] denunciar: *I reported the theft to the police = denuncié el robo a la policía.* **5** [**– (to)**] dar cuenta de, informar (de un suceso, a una autoridad): *did they report his death to the police? = ¿informaron a la policía de su muerte?* **6** comunicar: *the results of his investigations have been reported = se han comunicado los resultados de sus investigaciones.* **7** [**– (on)**] PER. informar. || *v.i.* **8** [**– (to/for)**] presentarse: *he had to report to headquarters = tuvo que presentarse en el cuartel.* **9** [**– (on/upon)**] presentar un informe, informar. **10** [**– (to)**] (form.) rendir cuentas (a alguien). **11** PER. trabajar como reportero: *he reported for the "Daily News" for 10 years = trabajó como reportero para el "Daily News" durante 10 años.* || *s.c.* e *i.* **12** rumor, voz: *the report goes that she is pregnant = corre el rumor de que está embarazada.* || *s.i.* **13** (form.) reputación, fama: *a man of evil report = un hombre de mala reputación.* || *s.c.* **14** informe: *I need a complete report of the situation = necesito un informe completo de la situación.* **15** parte, informe, boletín: *weather report = parte meteorológico.* **16** (form.) estallido, estampido (de un disparo, de una explosión). **17** PER. reportaje: *illustrated report = reportaje gráfico.* **18** memoria, informe: *annual report = memoria anual.* **19** relación, relato. **20** reseña (de un libro, de un periódico). **21** (brit.) boletín (de un alumno). **22** DER. ponencia, informe. **23** noticia: *the report of his father's death upset him greatly = la noticia de la muerte de su padre le afectó mucho.* || **24 it is reported (that),** se dice, se rumorea. **25 to – back, a)** [**– (to/on)**] dar cuenta de, comunicar; **b)** [**– (to)**] presentarse de vuelta. **26 to – fit,** darse de alta (después de haber estado de baja por enfermedad). **27 to – sick,**

darse de baja por enfermedad. **28 reported speech,** V. **speech.**

reportage | ˌrepɔːˈtɑːʒ | *s.i.* PER. técnica o estilo de informar de las noticias.

reportedly | rɪˈpɔːtɪdlɪ | *adv.* (form.) supuestamente.

reporter | rɪˈpɔːtər | *s.c.* **1** PER. reportero. **2** DER. ponente.

reporting | rɪˈpɔːtɪŋ | *s.i.* PER. información: *sports reporting = información deportiva.*

repose | rɪˈpəuz | (form.) *s.i.* **1** reposo, descanso. **2** tranquilidad, sosiego, calma. || *v.i.* **3** reposar, descansar. **4** (fig.) reposar (estar): *her coat reposed on the floor = su abrigo reposaba en el suelo.* **5** (fig.) descansar, yacer (un muerto). **6** recostar: *she reposed her head on the pillow = recostó su cabeza en la almohada.* **7 [– (on)]** (fig.) basarse: *his system reposes on new theories = su sistema se basa en nuevas teorías.* || *v.t.* **8 [– (in)]** depositar: *she reposed her trust on me = ella depositó en mí su confianza.*

repository | rɪˈpɒzɪtərɪ | (form.) *s.c.* **1 [– (of)]** depositario: *they are repositories of a secret = son depositarios de un secreto.* **2** almacén, depósito. **3** panteón.

repossess | ˌriːpəˈzes | *v.t.* (form.) recobrar, volver a tomar posesión de (bienes confiscados).

repot | ˌriːˈpɒt | *v.t.* trasplantar, cambiar de maceta (una planta).

reprehensible | ˌreprɪˈhensɪbl | *adj.* (form.) reprensible, reprochable, censurable: *a reprehensible conduct.*

represent | ˌreprɪˈzent | *v.t.* **1** representar: *he was represented by his wife = estaba representado por su esposa.* **2** (form.) representar: *this drawing represents a horse = este dibujo representa un caballo.* **3** (form.) significar, equivaler a: *this house represents five years'-work = esta casa equivale a cinco años de trabajo.* **4** simbolizar: *this yellow spot represents the sun = esta mancha amarilla simboliza el sol.* **5** describir: *they are not what you represented them to be = no son como los describiste.* **6** ART. representar (en un escenario). || **7 to be well/strongly/etc. represented,** estar ampliamente representado: *Spanish painters were strongly represented at the exhibition = los pintores españoles estaban ampliamente representados en la exposición.*

representation | ˌreprɪzenˈteɪʃn | *s.i.* **1** representación. || *s.c.* **2 [– (of)]** ART. representación. || **3 representations,** (form.) protestas, quejas (hechas a una autoridad u organismo oficial).

representational | ˌreprɪzenˈteɪʃənəl | *adj.* ART. (form.) figurativo (arte).

representative | ˌreprɪˈzentətɪv | *s.c.* **1** representante: *they didn't come but they sent some representatives = no vinieron pero enviaron a algunos representantes.* **2** (form.) COM. representante, agente: *commercial representative = agente comercial.* **3** apoderado. **4** POL. diputado. **5** COM. delegado (de una sucursal). || *adj.* **6 [– (of)]** representativo, típico, característico: *this play is representative of modern Japanese theatre = esta obra es representativa del teatro japonés moderno.* **7** POL. representativo: *representative assembly = asamblea representativa.*

repress | rɪˈpres | *v.t.* **1** contener, reprimir: *she couldn't repress her laughter = no pudo contener la risa.* **2** refrenar (las pasiones). **3** PSIC. reprimir. **4** oprimir, subyugar, dominar por la fuerza.

repressed | rɪˈprest | *adj.* PSIC. reprimido (una persona).

repression | rɪˈpreʃn | *s.i.* **1** MIL. represión: *the government's brutal repression = la brutal represión del gobierno.* **3** PSIC. represión: *sexual repression.*

repressive | rɪˈpresɪv | *adj.* POL. represivo: *represive measures = medidas represivas.*

reprieve | rɪˈpriːv | *v.t.* **1** DER. indultar (a un condenado a muerte). **2** (fig.) dar un respiro (aliviar temporalmente). || *s.c.* **3** DER. indulto (de un reo). **4** DER. suspensión temporal de una pena de muerte. **5** (fig.) respiro, alivio.

reprimand | ˈreprɪmɑːnd | *v.t.* **1** amonestar, reprender. || *s.c.* e *i.* **2** reprimenda, reprensión, amonestación.

reprint | ˌriːˈprɪnt | *v.t.* **1** reimprimir (una publicación). || | ˌriːˈprɪnt | *s.c.* **2** reimpresión, nueva edición (de una publicación).

reprisal | rɪˈpraɪzl | *s.i.* **1** (form.) venganza, represalia. || **2 reprisals,** represalias: *the military forces took violent reprisals against the students = las fuerzas militares tomaron violentas represalias contra los estudiantes.*

reproach | rɪˈprəutʃ | (form.) *s.i.* **1** reproche, censura: *a look of reproach = una mirada de reproche.* **2** reproche, crítica, reprimenda. **3 [– (to)]** vergÅenza, deshonra: *these roads are a reproach to our country = estas carreteras son una vergÅenza para nuestro país.* || *v.t.* **4 [– (for/with)]** reprochar, censurar, criticar: *she reproached me with my behaviour = me censuró por mi comportamiento.* **5** [– *pron.r.* **(for/with)**] reprocharse, culparse: *they have nothing to reproach themselves with = no tienen nada que reprocharse.*

reproachful | rɪˈprəutʃful | *adj.* reprobador, recriminatorio, de reproche: *a reproachful look = una mirada de reproche.*

reproachfully | rɪˈprəutʃfulɪ | *adv.* con reproche.

reprobate | ˈreprəubeɪt | (p.u.) *s.c.* **1** réprobo. || *adj.* **2** depravado, inmoral. || *v.t.* **3** reprobar, condenar.

reproduce | ˌriːprəˈdjuːs | *v.t.* **1** reproducir, repetir: *the tape reproduced our voices perfectly = la cinta reprodujo nuestras voces a la perfección.* **2** imitar. **3** copiar. **4** BIOL. regenerar (una parte del cuerpo). || *v.i.* **5** BIOL. reproducirse, multiplicarse.

reproduction | ˌriːprəˈdʌkʃn | *s.i.* **1** reproducción. **2** BIOL. reproducción, procreación. || *s.c.* **3** ART. reproducción, copia (de un cuadro, de un objeto antiguo, etc.).

reproductive | ˌriːprəˈdʌktɪv | *adj.* BIOL. reproductor: *reproductive organs = órganos reproductores.*

reproof | riˈpruːf | (form.) *s.i.* **1** reproche, censura, reprensión. || *s.c.* **2** reprimenda, reproche.

reprove | rɪˈpruːv | *v.t.* (form.) **[– (for)]** reprender, regañar.

reproving | rɪˈpruːvɪŋ | *adj.* (form.) recriminatorio, de reprobación, de reproche: *reproving words = palabras de reproche.*

reptile | ˈreptaɪl | *s.c.* **1** ZOOL. reptil. || *adj.* **2** (fig.) rastrero, vil, ruin.

reptilian | repˈtɪlɪən | *adj.* **1** ZOOL. de reptil. **2** (fig.) rastrero, vil, ruin.

republic | rɪˈpʌblɪk | POL. *s.i.* **1** república (sistema de gobierno). || *s.c.* **2** república (país cuyo sistema de gobierno es la república).

OBS. Se utiliza en los nombres de algunas repúblicas: *the Argentine Republic = la República Argentina.*

republican | rɪˈpʌblɪkən | *s.c.* y *adj.* POL. republicano: *Republican Party = partido Republicano.*

republicanism | rɪˈpʌblɪkənɪzəm | *s.i.* POL. republicanismo.

repudiate | rɪˈpjuːdɪeɪt | (form.) *v.t.* **1** repudiar (a una persona). **2** negar, rechazar, negarse a reconocer: *he repudiated the charge = negó la acusación.* **3** negarse a aceptar. **4** negarse a pagar (una deuda). **5** negarse a cumplir (un compromiso, un contrato, etc.).

repudiation | rɪˌpjuːdɪˈeɪʃn | *s.i.* rechazo, repudio.

repugnance | rɪˈpʌgnəns | *s.i.* **1** repugnancia, repulsión, asco, aversión: *she felt repugnance towards them = ella sentía repugnancia hacia ellos.* **2** (fig.) repugnancia, aversión: *his repugnance to work = su aversión al trabajo.* **3 [– (of/with)]** incompatibilidad (de ideas, temperamentos, etc.).

repugnant | rɪˈpʌgnənt | *adj.* **1 [– (to)]** repugnante, repulsivo. **2 [– (to)]** desagradable. **3 [– (with)]** incompatible.

repulse | rɪˈpʌls | *v.t.* **1** repeler, rechazar: *to repulse an attack = rechazar un ataque.* **2** repeler, asquear. || *s.c.* **3** desaire: *she suffered a repulse = sufrió un desaire.*

repulsion | rɪˈpʌlʃn | *s.i.* **1** repulsión, aversión, asco: *I felt repulsion for him = sentía asco de él.* **2** FIS. repulsión.

repulsive | rɪˈpʌlsɪv | *adj.* repulsivo, repugnante, asqueroso: *a repulsive appearance = un aspecto repulsivo.* **2** repelente: *a repulsive child = un crío repelente.* **3** FIS. opuesto, que se rechaza: *repulsive forces = fuerzas opuestas.*

repulsively | rɪˈpʌlsɪvlɪ | *adv.* asquerosamente: *repulsively dirty = asquerosamente sucio.*

reputable | ˈrepjutəbl | *adj.* **1** de buena reputación, acreditado, de confianza: *a reputable make = una marca de con-*

fianza. **2** respetable: *a reputable business = un negocio respetable.*

reputably | 'repjʊtəblɪ | *adv.* respetablemente.

reputation | ˌrepjʊ'teɪʃn | *s.c.* e *i.* reputación, fama.

repute | rɪ'pjuːt | (form.) *s.i.* **1** reputacion, fama: *a place of ill repute = un sitio de mala reputación.* || **2 by –,** de oídas: *I know her by repute = la conozco de oídas (por su reputación).* **3 to hold someone in (high) –,** tener a alguien en alta estima. **4 of –,** de buena reputación, prestigioso: *a lawyer of repute = un prestigioso abogado.*

reputed | rɪ'pjuːtɪd | *adj.* **1** supuesto: *the reputed father of the baby = el supuesto padre del bebé.* **2** reputado, considerado. || **3 to be – (as/to be),** tener fama de: *they reputed to be very rich = tienen fama de ser muy ricos.* **4 it is –,** se supone; se rumorea.

reputedly | rɪ'pjuːtɪdlɪ | *adv.* supuestamente, según se cree.

request | rɪ'kwest | (form.) *v.t.* **1** solicitar: *I requested his presence = solicité su presencia.* **2** rogar, pedir: *he requested me not to smoke = me rogó que no fumara.* || *s.c.* **3** petición; súplica, ruego. **4** instancia, solicitud: *they turned down my request = rechazaron mi solicitud.* **5** RAD. petición (de un radioyente). || **6 at someone's –/at the – of someone,** a petición de; a instancia de. **7 by –,** RAD. a petición (de un oyente). **8 on –,** a solicitud. **9 – stop,** parada discrecional.

requiem | 'rekwɪəm | *s.c.* **1** REL. réquiem. **2** MUS. réquiem, canto fúnebre: *Mozart's Requiem = el Réquiem de Mozart.* || **3 – mass,** REL. misa de réquiem.

require | rɪ'kwaɪər | (form.) *v.t.* **1** requerir, exigir: *this job requires imagination = este trabajo requiere imaginación.* **2** necesitar: *they require another glass = necesitan otro vaso.* **3** desear: *do you require coffee? = ¿desea usted café?* || **4 to be required,** requerirse, necesitarse; exigirse: *what is required to enter the university? = ¿qué se requiere para ingresar en la Universidad?*

required | rɪ'kwaɪəd | *adj.* **1** requerido, necesario: *it hasn't the required qualities = no tiene las cualidades necesarias.* **2** obligatorio.

requirement | rɪ'kwaɪəmənt | *s.c.* **1** requisito, condición: *it fulfils all the requirements = cumple con todos los requisitos.* **2** necesidad: *his requirements are few = sus necesidades son pocas.* **3** exigencias: *requirements of the law = exigencias de la ley.*

requisite | 'rekwɪzɪt | (form.) *adj.* **1** [– (for)] requerido, necesario. || *s.c.* **2** requisito.

requisition | ˌrekwɪ'zɪʃn | *v.t.* **1** MIL. requisar (por orden militar). **2** requerir: *they requisitioned our services = requirieron nuestros servicios.* || *s.c.* **3** MIL. [– (for)] requisa, orden, demanda. || *s.i.* **4** MIL. requisición.

requite | rɪ'kwaɪt | (form.) *v.t.* **1** corresponder: *she didn't requite his love = ella no correspondió a su amor.* **2** recompensar, pagar.

re-route | ˌriː'ruːt | *v.t.* **1** desviar (el tráfico, un tren, etc.).

re-run | ˌriːrʌn | *s.c.* **1** reposición (de una película, obra teatral, etc.). || | ˌriː'rʌn | *v.* [*pret.* **re-ran**; *p.p.* **re-runt**] *t.* **2** reponer (una película, una obra teatral, etc.).

rescind | rɪ'sɪnd | (form.) *v.t.* **1** rescindir, cancelar, anular. **2** DER. derogar (una ley). **3** revocar (una orden, una ley).

rescue | 'reskjuː | *v.t.* **1** rescatar, salvar, librar (de un peligro). **2** (fig.) rescatar, sacar (del olvido). || *s.i.* **3** rescate, liberación. || *s.c.* **4** salvamento. || **5 to go /come to the – (of),** acudir en ayuda (de), ir a salvar (a). **6 – work,** trabajos de rescate.

rescuer | 'reskjuər | *s.c.* salvador, rescatador.

research | rɪ'sɜːtʃ | *s.i.* **1** investigación: *scientific research = investigación científica.* || *v.t.* e *i.* **2** investigar (sobre un tema). || **3 to do =N (on),** investigar (un científico). **4 researches,** investigaciones (sobre un tema).

researcher | rɪ'sɜːtʃər | *s.c.* investigador (científico).

reseat | ˌriː'siːt | (form.) *v.t.* **1** poner un nuevo asiento; poner nuevos asientos. **2** [– + *pron.r.*] volver a sentarse. **3** volver a ajustar (una válvula).

resell | ˌriː'sel | *v.* [*pret.* **resold;** *p.p.* **resold**] *t.* e *i.* revender.

resemblance | rɪ'zembləns | *s.sing.* o *s.i.* **1** [– (to/between)] parecido; semejanza: *family resemblance = parecido de familia.* || **2 to bear a – to,** tener parecido con; tener semejanza con.

resemble | rɪ'zembl | *v.t.* **1** asemejarse a; parecerse a: *she resembles her mother = se parece a su madre.*

resent | rɪ'zent | *v.t.* **1** ofenderse por. **2** estar resentido por.

resentful | rɪ'zentfʊl | *adj.* **1** resentido. **2** ofendido; indignado. **3** rencoroso.

resentfully | rɪ'zentfəlɪ | *adv.* **1** con resentimiento. **2** con rencor.

resentment | rɪ'zentmənt | *s.c.* e *i.* **1** resentimiento. **2** rencor: *I bear no resentment against you = no te guardo rencor.* || *s.i.* **3** indignación.

reservation | ˌrezə'veɪʃn | *s.c.* **1** reserva, salvedad. **2** limitación. **3** reserva (de un asiento, localidad, habitación, etc.). **4** (EE.UU.) reserva, territorio reservado: *Indian reservation = reserva de indios.* || *s.i.* **5** REL. Reserva. || **6 without –,** sin reservas, sin condiciones. **7 with –/ reservations,** con reservas.

reserve | rɪ'zɜːv | *v.t.* **1** reservar, guardar: *they are reserved for you = están reservadas para ti.* **2** reservar (un asiento, localidad, habitación, etc.). || *s.c.* **3** reserva: *food reserves = reservas de comida.* **4** DEP. reserva, suplente (jugador). **5** ECOL. reserva: *forest reserve = reserva forestal.* **6** (brit.) precio mínimo. || *s.sing.* **7 [the –]** MIL. reserva. || *s.i.* **8** reserva, comedimiento. **9** cautela. **10** introversión, timidez. || **11 in –,** de reserva. **12 – price,** (brit.) precio mínimo. **13 Reserves,** MIL. reserva. **14 to – the right,** reservarse el derecho.

reserved | rɪ'zɜːvd | *adj.* **1** reservado, introvertido, circunspecto. **2** reservado (una localidad, habitación, asiento, etc.).

reservist | rɪ'zɜːvɪst | *s.c.* MIL. reservista.

reservoir | 'rezəvwɑːr | *s.c.* **1** embalse, presa de contención. **2** depósito. **3** [– (of)] (fig.) mina: *a reservoir of knowledge = una mina de conocimientos.*

reset | ˌriː'set | *v.* [*pret.* y *p.p.* **reset**] *t.* **1** reajustar (una máquina, un aparato). **2** volver a montar (una joya). **2** ANAT. volver a encajar (hueso). **4** volver a afilar. **5** recomponer (caracteres de imprenta).

resettle | ˌriː'setəl | *v.i.* **1** volver a instalarse, volver a establecerse (en un nuevo lugar de residencia). || *v.t.* **2** ayudar a establecerse (en un nuevo lugar de residencia). **3** volver a colonizar, volver a poblar.

resettlement | ˌriː'setəlmənt | *s.i.* **1** nuevo establecimiento (de personas, en un nuevo lugar de residencia). **2** nueva colonización.

reshuffle | ˌriː'ʃʌfl | *s.c.* **1** POL. reorganización (de un gabinete político). **2** nueva mezcla (de naipes). || *v.t.* **3** reorganizar(se). **4** volver a barajar (naipes).

reside | rɪ'zaɪd | (form.) *v.i.* **1** residir, morar. **2** [– (in)] (fig.) residir: *the power resides in the King = el poder reside en el rey.*

residence | 'rezɪdəns | (form.) *s.c.* **1** residencia, domicilio, vivienda. || *s.i.* **2** residencia: *residence permit = permiso de residencia.* **3** permanencia, estancia. || **4 in –,** residente. **5 to take up –,** establecer su residencia, instalarse.

resident | 'rezɪdənt | *s.c.* **1** residente, habitante. **2** vecino. **3** ZOOL. no migratorio. || *adj.* **4** [– (in)] residente (habitante o morador permanente de un sitio). **5** residente, interno (que vive donde trabaja). **6** residente (un especialista): *resident doctor = médico residente.* || **7 resident's association,** asociación de vecinos.

residential | ˌrezɪ'denʃl | *adj.* **1** residencial: *residential area = zona residencial.* **2** residencial (un trabajo, un empleo, un curso). **3** interno (que tiene su residencia donde estudia o trabaja).

residual | rɪ'zɪdjʊəl | (form.) residual.

residue | 'rezɪdjuː | (form.) *s.c.* **1** residuo, sobra, desecho. **2** DER. bienes residuales. **3** (fig.) resto (lo que queda de un sentimiento).

resign | rɪ'zaɪn | *v.t.* e *i.* **1** [– (from/as)] dimitir (de), renunciar a: *he resigned his post = dimitió de su cargo.* || *v.t.* **2** [– + *pron.r.* + (to)] resignarse, conformarse: *she must resign herself to a modest life = debe resignarse a vivir modestamente.*

resignation | ˌrezɪg'neɪʃn | *s.c.* e *i.* **1** dimisión, renuncia: *I offered my resig-*

nation = presenté mi dimisión. || *s.i.* **2** resignación: *she accepted her misfortune with resignation = aceptó su desgracia con resignación.*

resigned | rɪ'zaɪnd | *adj.* **[– (to)]** resignado.

resignedly | rɪ'zaɪnɪdlɪ | *adv.* con resignación.

resilience | rɪ'zɪlɪəns | *s.i.* **1** elasticidad. **2** (fig.) resistencia. **3** (fig.) capacidad de recuperación. **4** (fig.) animación, fuerza moral.

resilient | rɪ'zɪlɪənt | *adj.* **1** elástico. **2** (fig.) resistente, fuerte. **3** (fig.) que se recobra fácilmente (de una desgracia, de una enfermedad).

resin | 'rezɪn | *s.i.* **1** BOT. resina. **2** QUIM. resina sintética.

resinous | 'rezɪnəs | *adj.* resinoso.

resist | rɪ'zɪst | *v.t.* **1** resistir: *he couldn't resist temptation = no pudo resistir la tentación.* **2** oponerse a: *they resisted the changes = se opusieron a los cambios.* **3** resistirse a: *did they resist the attack? = ¿resistieron el ataque?* **4** (form.) resistir, aguantar: *this kind of glass does not resist heat = este tipo de vidrio no resiste al calor.* || *v.i.* **5** resistirse, ofrecer resistencia.

resistance | rɪ'zɪstəns | *s.i.* **1 [– (to)]** resistencia, oposición: *my plan met fierce resistence = mi plan encontró fuerte oposición.* **2** POL. resistencia. **3 [– (to)]** MED. resistencia, capacidad de defensa (del organismo). **4 [– (to)]** FIS. resistencia. || **5 to take the line of least –,** (fig.) tomar el camino más fácil; seguir la ley del mínimo esfuerzo.

resistant | rɪ'zɪstənt | *adj.* **1 [– (to)]** contrario: *I am resistant to the disciplinary measures = soy contrario a las medidas disciplinarias.* **2 [– (to)]** resistente, inmune: *many pests are resistant to insecticides = muchos insectos son resistentes a los insecticidas.*

OBS. *s.* + **-resistant** significa resistente a + *s.*: *water-resistant suntan oil = aceite bronceador resistente al agua.*

resistor | rɪ'zɪstər | *s.c.* ELECTR. reostato.

resold | ˌriː'səʊld | *pret.* y *p.p.* de **resell.**

resolute | 'rezəluːt | (form.) **1** resuelto, decidido, determinado: *a resolute man = un hombre decidido.* **2** firme, inflexible: *a resolute attitude = una postura inflexible.*

resolutely | 'rezəluːtlɪ | *adv.* decididamente, con determinación.

resolution | ˌrezə'luːʃn | *s.i.* **1** resolución, determinación, firmeza, decisión. || *s.c.* **2 [– (to)]** propósito: *good resolutions = buenos propósitos.* **3** POL. resolución, acuerdo. || *s.sing.* **4** (form.) resolución (de un problema, de una dificultad). **5** FIS. descomposición. || **6 to make a –,** tomar una determinación.

resolve | rɪ'zɒlv | (form.) *v.i.* **1 [– (to)]** resolver, decidir: *she resolved to stay = decidió quedarse.* **2 [– (to)]** proponerse. || *v.t.* **3** resolver, solucionar (un problema, una dificultad). **4** FIS. descomponer. || *s.c.* e *i.* **5** propósito. **6** resolución, decisión.

resolved | rɪ'zɒlvd | *adj.* **[– (to)]** resuelto, decidido: *he was resolved to leave = estaba decidido a marcharse.*

resonance | 'rezənəns | (form.) *s.i.* **1** resonancia. || *s.c.* e *i.* **2** vibración (por resonancia).

resonant | 'rezənənt | (form.) *adj.* **1** resonante, sonoro: *a resonant voice = una voz sonora.* **2** que produce resonancia (un sitio). || *s.c.* **3** FON. fonema sonoro.

resonate | 'rezəneɪt | (form.) *v.i.* **1** resonar. **2 [– (with)]** retumbar.

resort | rɪ'zɔːt | *v.i.* **[– (to)]** recurrir, acudir (a algo o alguien): *they resorted to weapons = recurrieron a las armas.* **2 [– (to)]** acudir frecuentemente (a un sitio). || *s.c.* **3** lugar (al que se acude): *summer resort = lugar de veraneo.* **4** recurso: *the only resort = el único recurso.* **5** punto de encuentro, lugar de reunión. **6** refugio. || *s.i.* **7** recurso (acción de recurrir). **8** concurrencia. || **9 as a last –,** como último recurso. **10 in the last –,** en último caso. **11 without – to,** sin recurrir a.

resound | rɪ'zaʊnd | *v.i.* **1** resonar. **2 [– (with)]** retumbar. **3** repercutir (el sonido). **4** (form. y fig.) tener repercusiones, tener resonancia: *his fame resounded through all Europe = su fama tuvo resonancia en toda Europa.*

resounding | rɪ'zaʊndɪŋ | *adj.* **1** sonoro: *a resounding voice = una voz sonora.* **2** clamoroso, sonado: *a resounding success = un éxito clamoroso.*

resoundingly | rɪzaʊndɪŋlɪ | *adv.* sonoramente.

resource | rɪ'sɔːs | *s.c.* **1** recurso, medio: *economic resources = recursos económicos.* || *s.i.* **2** inventiva, ingenio. || **3 resources,** FIN. recursos.

resourceful | rɪ'sɔːsful | *adj.* ingenioso, mañoso.

resourcefulness | rɪ'sɔːsfulnɪs | *s.i.* inventiva, ingenio.

respect | rɪ'spekt | *v.t.* **1** respetar: *you must respect your parents = debes respetar a tus padres.* **2** respetar, acatar, cumplir: *he didn't respect the law = no cumplió la ley.* **3** respetar, valorar, tomar en consideración: *I respect their opinion = valoró su opinión.* || *s.i.* **4 [– (for)]** respeto: *they inspire respect = infunden respeto.* **5 [– (for)]** respeto, estima, consideración: *he has litle respect for me = me tiene poco respeto.* || **6 as respects,** por lo que respecta a. **7 in all respects,** en todos los sentidos. **8 in this –,** en cuanto a esto, a este respecto. **9 in may respects,** en cierto modo; desde muchos puntos de vista. **10 respects,** (form.) respetos, saludos: *she sends you her respects = te envía sus saludos.* **11 to pay one's respects,** (form.) **a)** presentar sus respetos (haciendo una visita, etc.); **b)** dirigir sus saludos respetuosos. **12 to pay one's last respects,** presentar sus últimos respetos (a un fallecido). **13 to treat with –,** (fig.) tratar con respeto; manejar con cuidado (algo peligroso). **14 with (all) due –,** (form.) con el debido respeto. **15 with – to/in – of,** con relación a, con respecto a.

respectability | rɪˌspektə'bɪlɪtɪ | *s.i.* respetabilidad; dignidad; reputación.

respectable | rɪ'spektəbl | *adj.* **1** respetable, decente: *a respectable home = un hogar respetable; a respectable woman = una mujer decente.* **2** (fam.) respetable, digno, aceptable: *a respectable wage = un sueldo aceptable.*

respectably | rɪ'spektəblɪ | *adv.* de forma respetable, dignamente, decentemente: *respectably dressed = vestido dignamente.*

respected | rɪ'spektɪd | *adj.* respetado, considerado, estimado.

respecter | rɪ'spektər | *adj.* **1** que respeta (una creencia, una idea, etc.). **2 to be no – of persons,** no hacer distinción de personas.

respectful | rɪ'spektful | *adj.* **[– (to)]** respetuoso: *a respectful behaviour = un comportamiento respetuoso.*

respectfully | rɪ'spektfəlɪ | *adv.* respetuosamente.

respective | rɪ'spektɪv | *adj.* respectivo: *we went to our respective rooms = nos fuimos a nuestras respectivas habitaciones.*

respectively | rɪ'spektɪvlɪ | *adv.* respectivamente.

respiration | ˌrespə'reɪʃn | (form.) *s.i.* **1** respiración. || **2 mouth-to-mouth –,** MED. respiración boca a boca.

respirator | 'respəreɪtər | *s.c.* **1** MED. respirador (para respiración artificial). **2** careta antigás.

respiratory | rɪ'spaɪərətərɪ | *adj.* MED. respiratorio: *respiratory disease = enfermedad respiratoria.*

respire | rɪ'spaɪər | *v.i.* (form. y p.u.) respirar.

respite | 'respaɪt | (form.) *s.i.* **1** respiro, tregua, descanso: *they worked without respite = trabajaron sin descanso.* **2** aplazamiento, prórroga. **3** alivio. || *s.c.* **4** DER. suspensión (de una pena).

resplendence | rɪ'splendəns | *s.i.* (lit.) resplandor, esplendor.

resplendent | rɪ'splendənt | *adj.* **[– (in)]** (lit.) resplandeciente, radiante, espléndido, esplendoroso.

resplendently | rɪ'splendəntlɪ | *adv.* (lit.) esplendorosamente; con resplandor.

respond | rɪ'spɒnd | *v.i.* **1 [– (to /with/by)]** responder, contestar: *he insulted her and she responded with a slap = él la insultó y ella respondió con una bofetada.* **2** (form.) replicar, contestar. **3 [– (to)]** reaccionar, responder: *she is responding to treatment = está reaccionando al tratamiento.* **4 [– (to)]** corresponder, ser sensible: *she responded to his attentions = correspondió a sus atenciones.* **5 [– (to)]** obedecer (a un tratamiento).

respondent | rɪ'spɒndənt | *s.c.* **1** encuestado. **2** DER. demandado (especialmente en un caso de divorcio).

response | rɪ'spɒns | *s.c.* **1** (form.) respuesta, contestación. **2** REL. responsorio. || *s.c.* e *i.* **3** reacción: *the reaction was favourable = la reacción fue favorable.* **4 [– (to)]** acogida. || **5 in – to,** como respuesta a.

responsibility | rɪˌspɒnsə'bɪlɪtɪ | *s.i.* **1 [– (for)]** responsabilidad: *on my responsibility = bajo mi responsabilidad.* **2** formalidad, seriedad, sentido de responsabilidad. || *s.c.* **3** responsabilidad, obligación: *I know my responsabilities = conozco mis obligaciones.*

responsible | rɪ'spɒnsəbl | *adj.* **1 [– (for/to)]** responsable: *he is not responsible for his acts = no es responsable de sus actos.* **2** responsable, formal, digno de confianza: *a responsible man = un hombre responsable.* **3** de responsabilidad: *a responsible post = un cargo de responsabilidad.*

responsibly | rɪ'spɒnsəblɪ | *adv.* responsablemente; con seriedad.

responsive | rɪ'spɒnsɪv | *adj.* **1 [– (to)]** sensible: *they are responsive to affect = son sensibles al afecto.* **2** fácil de conmover, impresionable. **3** que responde (a una acción).

responsiveness | rɪ'spɒnsɪvnɪs | *s.i.* **1** interés. **2** sensibilidad.

rest | rest | *s.i.* **1** descanso, reposo: *a moment's rest = un rato de descanso.* **2** MUS. pausa. **3** tregua, pausa. || *s.c.* **4** apoyo, soporte. **5** posada. **6** MUS. pausa (signo). **7** FILOL. cesura, pausa (en poesía). || *s.sing.* **8 [the – (of)]** resto: *the rest of the year = el resto del año.* **9 [the – (of)]** demás: *the rest of the people = la demás gente.* || *v.t.* e *i.* **10** apoyar(se): *don't rest your elbows on the table = no apoyes los codos sobre la mesa.* || *v.t.* **11** descansar, dejar descansar, relajar: *rest your muscles = relaje sus músculos.* **12** descansar (la vista). || *v.i.* **13** descansar, reposar: *he is resting = está descansando.* **14 [– (with)]** residir: *the authority rests with the President = la autoridad reside en el Presidente.* **15 [– (on)/(upon)]** apoyarse, basarse: *my arguments rests on reality = mi argumento se basa en la realidad.* **16 [– (on/upon)]** (lit.) posarse (los ojos, la mirada). **17** (p.u.) permanecer: *the situation rests serious = la situación permanece grave.* **18 [– (with)]** depender: *it rests with you = depende de ti.* || **19 and the –/and all the – of it,** (fam.) y todo lo demás. **20 at –, a)** en reposo, descansando (una persona); **b)** parado (un objeto); **c)** (euf.) muerto. **21 to come to –,** (form.) pararse (un objeto). **22 for the –,** por lo demás. **23 to give something a –,** (fam.) dar un descanso, dejar temporalmente (una actividad). **24 I – my case,** DER. terminé la presentación de mi argumento. **25 to lay/put to –,** (fig.) enterrar (una idea). **26 to lay someone to –,** (euf.) enterrar (a un muerto). **27 to let something –,** dejar (un tema). **28 to put/set someone's mind at –,** tranquilizar a alguien. **29 – assured that,** tenga la seguridad de que. **30 to – in peace,** V. **peace. 31 to – on one's laurels,** V. **laurel.**

restate | ˌriː'steɪt | *v.t.* (form.) **1** reafirmar, reiterar. **2** volver a expresar. **3** repetir.

restatement | ˌriː'steɪtmənt | *s.c.* e *i.* **1** reafirmación, reiteración. **2** nuevo planteamiento. **3** repetición.

restaurant | 'restərɒnt | *s.c.* restaurante.

restaurateur | ˌrestɒrə'təːr | *s.c.* (form.) propietario de un restaurante.

rested | restɪd | *adj.* descansado, tranquilo: *are you rested now? = ¿ahora estás descansado?*

restful | 'restful | *adj.* **1** tranquilo, apacible, sosegado: *a restful place = un sitio tranquilo.* **2** tranquilizador, reparador.

rest-home | 'resthəʊm | *s.c.* casa de reposo (para enfermos o ancianos).

resting-place | 'restɪŋpleɪs | (también **resting place**) *s.c.* **1** lugar de descanso. **2** última morada.

restitution | ˌrestɪ'tjuːʃn | (form.) *s.i.* **1** restitución, devolución. **2** indemnización.

restive | 'restɪv | *adj.* **1** impaciente; intranquilo, agitado: *the audience was restive = el público estaba impaciente.* **2** desobediente, ingobernable, inquieto (un caballo).

restiveness | 'restɪvnɪs | *s.i.* impaciencia, agitación, inquietud.

restless | 'restlɪs | *adj.* **1** inquieto, movido: *a restless person = una persona inquieta.* **2** impaciente: *a restless audience = un público impaciente.* **3** intranquilo, revoltoso: *a restless child = un crío revoltoso.* **4** (fig.) agitado: *a restless night = una noche agitada.*

restlessly | 'restlɪslɪ | *adv.* **1** con impaciencia. **2** nerviosamente; con inquietud.

restlessness | 'restlɪsnɪs | *s.i.* **1** impaciencia. **2** agitación, nervios. **3** desasosiego, inquietud, intranquilidad.

restock | ˌriː'stɒk | *v.t.* reabastecer, reaprovisionar. **2** ECOL. repoblar (un río, un lago, etc.). || *v.i.* **3** reponer existencias.

restoration | ˌrestə'reɪʃn | *s.i.* **1 [– (of)]** restauración, restablecimiento: *the restoration of the monarchy = el restablecimiento de la monarquía.* **2** recuperación (de algo perdido). **3** devolución, restitución. **4** renovación, restauración: *restoration of ancient monuments = restauración de monumentos históricos.* || *adj.* **5** ART. de la Restauración: *a Restoration drama = un drama de la Restauración.* || **6 the Restoration,** HIST. la Restauración.

restorative | rɪ'stɔrətɪv | *adj.* **1** reconstituyente; tonificante. || *s.c.* **2** (hum.) estimulante, reconstituyente (bebida, especialmente alcohólica).

restore | rɪ'stɔː | *v.t.* **1 [– (to)]** devolver, restituir: *it was restored to its owner = fue devuelto a su dueño.* **2** restaurar: *the church will be restored = la iglesia será restaurada.* **3** restablecer: *order was restored = se restableció el orden.* **4 [– (to)]** restituir, devolver (a un estado o condición anterior). **5** reconstruir (un texto).

restorer | rɪ'stɔːrər | *s.c.* **1** ART. restaurador. || **2 hair –,** tónico capilar.

restrain | rɪ'streɪn | *v.t.* **1 [– (from)]** reprimir, contener: *I couldn't restrain from laughing = no puede contener la risa.* **2 [– (from)]** moderar, reducir: *they restrained the spending of energy = redujeron el gasto de energía.* **3 [– (from)]** frenar, restringir; refrenar. **4 [– (from)]** impedir: *the rain restrained him from going out = la lluvia le impidió salir.* **5** cohibir: *your presence restrains me = su presencia me cohíbe.* **6** recluir (en un manicomio).

restrained | rɪ'streɪnd | *adj.* controlado, comedido, moderado.

restraint | rɪ'streɪnt | *s.c.* e *i.* **1** restitución, limitación. || *s.i.* **2** moderación, control, comedimiento. **3** reclusión, confinamiento (en un manicomio).

restrict | rɪ'strɪkt | *v.t.* **1 [– (to)]** restringir; limitar: *I restrict myself to five cigarettes a day = me limito a cinco cigarrillos diarios.*

restricted | rɪ'strɪktɪd | *adj.* **1** restringido, limitado. **2** reducido. **3** reservado, secreto (un documento). || **4 – area, a)** zona de velocidad limitada; **b)** MIL. zona prohibida. **5 – place,** zona restringida.

restriction | rɪ'strɪkʃn | *s.c.* **1 [– (of/on)]** restricción: *restrictions on the sale of stimulants = restricciones en la venta de estimulantes.* **2** limitación: *the restrictions of poverty = las limitaciones de la pobreza.* || *s.i.* **3** restricción; limitación.

restrictive | rɪ'strɪktɪv | *adj.* restrictivo: *restrictive practice = práctica restrictiva.*

rest-room | 'restruːm | (también **rest room**) *s.c.* (EE.UU.) retrete, lavabo (en un sitio público).

restructure | ˌriː'strʌktʃər | *v.t.* reestructurar, reconstruir.

result | rɪ'zʌlt | *s.c.* e *i.* **1** resultado, consecuencia: *it had satisfactory results = tuvo resultados satisfactorios.* || *s.c.* **2** MAT. resultado, solución (de un problema). || *v.i.* **3 [– (in)]** motivar, producir, causar: *the accident resulted in his death = el accidente causó su muerte.* **4** resultar: *it resulted in a failure = resultó un fracaso.* **5 [– (from)]** resultar, derivarse, ser consecuencia: *this situation results from the fact that some people are too careless = esta situación se deriva del hecho de que algunas personas son demasiado descuidadas.* || **6 as a –,** como resultado, como consecuencia. **7 results,** resultados (de una elección, examen, partido, etc.).

resultant | rɪ'zʌltənt | *adj.* **1 (from)** resultante, consiguiente. || *s.c.* **2** FIS. resultante.

resume | rɪ'zjuːm | *v.t.* e *i.* **1** reanudar, proseguir: *the trade unions resumed their activities = los sindicatos reanudaron sus actividades.* || *v.t.* **2** volver a tomar: *he resumed the thread of the story = volvió a tomar el hilo de la narración.* **3** volver a ocupar (un asiento, un territorio). **4** recuperar: *she resumed her liberty = recuperó su libertad.* **5** reasumir: *he resumed his duties =*

reasumió sus funciones. || *v.i.* **6** recomenzar, volver a empezar.

résumé | 'rezju:meɪ | (también **resumé**) *s.c.* **1** resumen, sumario. **2** (EE.UU.) curriculum vitae.

resumption | rɪ'zʌmpʃn | *s.i.* **1** reanudación, resurgimiento: *the resumption of diplomatic relations = la reanudación de las relaciones diplomáticas.* **2** reasunción. **3** prosecución, continuación.

resurface | ˌri:'sɜ:fɪs | *v.t.* **1** poner nueva superficie a; revestir. **2** poner nuevo firme a (una carretera). || *v.i.* **3** salir a la superficie (un submarino). **4** (fam.) reaparecer (después de haber estado alejado de la vida social).

resurgence | rɪˌ'sɜ:dʒəns | *s.i.* **[– (of)]** (lit.) reaparición, resurgimiento: *the resurgence of nationalism = el resurgimiento del nacionalismo.*

resurgent | rɪsɜ:dʒənt | *adj.* (lit.) renaciente.

resurrect | ˌrezə'rekt | *v.t.* **1** (fig.) resucitar, hacer revivir: *they want to resurrect some old customs = quieren resucitar algunas viejas costumbres.* **2** (fam.) desenterrar (un objeto). **3** desenterrar (un cadáver). || *v.t.* e *i.* **4** (p.u.) resucitar.

resurrection | ˌrezə'rekʃn | **1** (fig.) resurgimiento, reaparición. || **2 The Resurrection,** REL. la Resurrección.

resuscitate | rɪ'sʌsɪteɪt | *v.t.* e *i.* MED. revivir, reanimar, resucitar.

resuscitation | rɪˌsʌsɪ'teɪʃn | *s.i.* MED. reanimación.

retail | 'ri:teɪl | *s.i.* **1** COM. venta al por menor. || *adv.* **2** COM. al por menor. || *adj.* **3** COM. al por menor: *retail price = precio al por menor.* || *v.t.* **4** COM. vender al por menor. **5 [– (to)]** (form. y p.u.) detallar, contar con detalles. || *v.i.* **6** COM. **[– (at)]** venderse al por menor. || **7 at/by –,** COM. al por menor. **8 – price index,** (brit.) ECON. índice de precios al consumo.

retailer | ri:'teɪlər | *s.c.* COM. minorista, detallista.

retain | rɪ'teɪn | *v.t.* **1** conservar, mantener: *I want to retain my independence = quiero conservar mi independencia.* **2** retener, conservar: *it retains heat = retiene el calor.* **3** guardar, conservar: *I retain pleasant memories of my stay in Madrid = guardo buenos recuerdos de mi estancia en Madrid.* **4** detener, retener, guardar (en la memoria). **5** mantener (en su sitio). **6** DER. contratar (a un abogado).

retainer | rɪ'teɪnər | *s.c.* **1** anticipo: *a lawyer's retainer = el anticipo de un abogado.* **2** (p.u.) criado, sirviente. **3** HIST. secuaz.

retake | ˌri:'teɪk | *v.* [*pret.* **retook;** *p.p.* **retaken**] *t.* **1** MIL. reconquistar, volver a tomar: *the soldiers retook the building = los soldados volvieron a tomar el edificio.* **2** volver a capturar. **3** ART. volver a tomar (una escena, una foto). **4** repetir (un examen). || *s.c.* **5** ART. repetición (de una escena, de una toma). **6** nuevo examen.

retaken | ˌri:'teɪkən | *p.p.* de **retake.**

retaliate | rɪ'tælɪeɪt | *v.i.* **[– (against/on/upon)]** vengarse, desquitarse, tomar represalias: *they will retaliate against us = tomaron represalias contra nosotros.*

retaliation | rɪ'tælɪ'eɪʃn | *s.i.* **1** venganza, revancha, represalia. || **2 in – (for),** en desquite, como venganza.

retaliatory | rɪ'tælɪətərɪ | *adj.* **1** de desquite. || **2 to take – measures,** tomar represalias.

retard | rɪ'tɑ:d | *v.t.* **1** retrasar, retardar (el progreso o desarrollo de algo). **2** atrasar. **3** demorar.

retardation | ˌri:tɑ:'deɪʃn | *s.i.* (form.) retraso, atraso: *economic retardation = retraso económico.*

retarded | rɪ'tɑ:dɪd | *adj.* **1** PSIQ. retrasado, atrasado: *a retarded child = un niño retrasado.* || **2 the --** PSIQ. los retrasados mentales.

retch | retʃ | *v.i.* **1** tener arcadas, tener náuseas. || *s.c.* **2** arcada, náusea.

retell | ˌri:'tel | *v.* [*pret.* y *p.p.* de **retold**] *t.* volver a contar (un cuento, una historia, etc.).

retention | rɪ'tenʃn | *s.i.* **1** conservación: *the retention of democracy = la conservación de la democracia.* **2** retención, conservación: *they will fight for the retention of their lands = lucharán por la conservación de sus tierras.* **3** MED. retención: *retention of urine = retención de orina.*

retentive | rɪ'tentɪv | *adj.* retentivo: *retentive memory = memoria retentiva.*

rethink | ˌri:'θɪŋk | *v.* [*pret.* y *p.p.* **rethought**] *t.* e *i.* reconsiderar.

rethought | ˌri:'θɔ:t | *pret.* y *p.p.* de **rethink.**

reticence | 'retɪsəns | *s.c.* e *i.* **1** (form.) reticencia. || *s.i.* **2** (form.) reserva, taciturnidad.

reticent | 'retɪsənt | *adj.* **1 [– (about /on)]** reservado. **2** callado, taciturno.

reticule | 'retɪkju:l | *s.c.* (arc.) bolso pequeño de mujer.

retina | 'retɪnə | *s.c.* [*pl.* **retinae** o **retinas**] ANAT. retina.

retinae | 'retɪni: | *pl.* de **retina.**

retinal | 'retɪnəl | OPT. de retina; referente a la retina.

retinue | 'retɪnju: | *s.c.* **[– (of)]** séquito (de una persona): *the retinue of the king = el séquito del rey.*

retire | rɪ'taɪər *v.i.* **1** retirarse, jubilarse: *my father retired last year = mi padre se jubiló el año pasado.* **2** (form.) retirarse, marcharse: *she retired to her room = se retiró a su habitación.* **3** (form.) retirarse, recogerse, acostarse. **4** MIL. retirarse, replegarse. || *v.t.* **5** retirar anticipadamente, obligar a jubilarse. **6** DEP. abandonar (una carrera). **7** FIN. retirar, quitar de la circulación (un billete, moneda, etc.). || *s.sing.* **8** MIL. retirada, retreta (toque militar). || **9 to – from the world,** (fig.) apartarse del mundo. **10 to – into oneself,** (fig.) encerrarse en sí mismo.

retired | rɪ'taɪəd | *adj.* **1** retirado, jubilado. **2** solitario, retirado: *a retired life = una vida retirada.* **3** apartado, retirado, alejado: *a retired place = un lugar apartado.* || **4 – list,** MIL. lista de oficiales retirados. **5 – pay,** FIN. pensión de jubilación. **6 – person,** jubilado.

retirement | rɪ'taɪəmənt | *s.i.* **1** retiro, jubilación. **2** MIL. retirada, repliegue. **3** retirada: *the retirement of a bullfighter = la retirada de un torero.* **4** abandono: *the retirement a cyclist = el abandono de un ciclista.* || **5 to go into –,** jubilarse, retirarse. **6** pensión de jubilación.

retiring | rɪ'taɪərɪŋ | *adj.* **1** (form.) reservado, retraído: *a retiring boy = un chico reservado.* **2** saliente, que abandona sus funciones: *the retiring mayor = el alcalde saliente.*

retold | ˌri:'təʊld | *pret.* y *p.p.* de **retell.**

retook | ˌri:'tʊk | *pret.* de **retake.**

retort | rɪ'tɔ:t | *v.i.* **1** replicar. **2** (p.u.) devolver (una ofensa, un insulto, etc.). || *s.c.* **3** réplica, contestación. **4** QUIM. retorta (recipiente de laboratorio).

retouch | ˌri:'tʌtʃ | *v.t.* ART. retocar (una foto, una pintura, etc.).

retrace | rɪ'treɪs | *v.t.* **1** repasar mentalmente, evocar, recordar. || **2 to – one's steps/way,** volver sobre sus pasos, desandar el camino.

retract | rɪ'trækt | *v.t.* e *i.* **1** (form.) retirar, retractar(se): *he retracted what he had said = retiró lo que había dicho.* **2** retraer(se), encoger(se) (garras, cuernos, etc.): *the cat retracted its claws = el gato retrajo sus garras.* **3** replegar(se): *the undercarriage retracted = el tren de aterrizaje se replegó.* || *v.t.* **4** abandonar (un movimiento de ajedrez).

retractable | rɪ'træktəbl | *adj.* replegable, retráctil (un aparato).

retractile | rɪ'træktaɪl | *adj.* retráctil, contráctil: *retractile claws = garras retráctiles.*

retraction | rɪ'trækʃn | *s.c.* e *i.* **1** retractación: *public retraction = retractación pública.* **2** MED. retracción.

retrain | ˌri:'treɪn | *v.t.* readaptar (trabajadores).

retraining | ˌri:'treɪnɪŋ | *s.i.* readaptación (de trabajadores).

retread | 'ri:tred | *s.c.* **1** neumático recauchutado. || *v.t.* **2** recauchutar (un neumático).

retreat | rɪ'tri:t | *v.i.* **1 [– (to)]** retirarse, apartarse. **2** MIL. retroceder, batirse en retirada. **3 [– (from)]** volverse atrás. **4** (form. y fig.) **[– (into)]** refugiarse (en una actitud, etc.). || *s.c.* e *i.* **5** MIL. retirada. **6** (form. y fig.) **[– (into)]** refugio (en una actitud, etc.). **7 [– (from)]** apartamiento, alejamiento. || *s.i.* **8** (form.) retiro (espiritual). || *s.c.* **9** (form.) retirada. **10** retiro: *a country retreat = un retiro campestre.* **11** MIL. retreta. || **12 to beat a -- ** (fig. y form.) batirse en retirada.

retrench | rɪ'trentʃ | (p.u.) *v.t.* **1** reducir (gastos). || **2** economizar, ahorrar.

retrenchment | rɪ'trentʃmənt | (form.) *s.c.* e *i.* **1** reducción (de gastos). **2** ahorro, economía.

retrial | ˌriːˈtraɪəl | *s.c.* DER. nuevo proceso, nuevo juicio.
retribution | ˌretrɪˈbjuːʃn | *s.i.* (form.) REL. castigo, pena: *divine retribution = castigo divino.*
retributive | rɪˈtrɪbjʊtɪv | *adj.* (form.) de castigo, de venganza.
retrieval | rɪˈtriːvl | *s.i.* **1** recuperación (de un objeto). **2** DEP. cobra (del perro de caza). **3** reparación. **4** INF. recuperación (de información). || **5 beyond/past –,** irrecuperable.
retrieve | rɪˈtriːv | (form.) *v.t.* **1** recuperar, recobrar. **2** salvar (una situación). **3** reparar (un error, una pérdida). **4 [– (from)]** (fig.) rescatar, salvar: *he retrieved me from ruin = me salvó de la ruina.* **5** INF. recuperar (información). || *v.t.* e *i.* **6** DEP. cobrar (la caza). || *s.i.* **7** recuperación. || **8 beyond/past –,** irrecuperable.
retriever | rɪˈtriːvər | *s.c.* DEP. perro cobrador.
retroactive | ˌretrəʊˈæktɪv | *adj.* **1 [– (to)]** (form.) retroactivo. || **2 – law,** DER. ley con efectos retroactivos.
retrograde | ˈretrəʊgreɪd | *adj.* **1** (form.) retrógrado, hacia atrás: *retrograde motion = movimiento retrógrado.* || *v.i.* **2** (fig.) ir hacia atrás, empeorar, decaer.
retrogress | ˌretrəʊˈgres | (form.) *v.i.* **[– (to)]** retroceder. **2 [– (to)]** (fig.) degenerar, empeorar.
retrogression | ˌretrəʊˈgreʃn | (form.) *s.i.* **1** retroceso. **2** empeoramiento; decaimiento. **3** ASTR. retrogradación.
retrogressive | ˌretrəʊˈgresɪv | *adj.* (form.) retrógrado.
retrospect | ˈretrəʊspekt | *s.sing.* **1** mirada retrospectiva, examen retrospectivo. || **2 in –,** mirando hacia atrás; retrospectivamente.
retrospective | ˌretrəʊˈspektɪv | *s.c.* **1** ART. retrospectiva (exposición). || *adj.* **2** retrospectivo. **3** DER. con efecto retroactivo: *a retrospective law = una ley con efecto retroactivo.*
retrospectively | ˌretrəʊˈspektɪvlɪ | *adv.* retrospectivamente.
return | rɪˈtɜːn | *v.i.* **1** volver, regresar: *they never returned = nunca regresaron.* **2 [– (to)]** volver (a un tema). **3 [– (to)]** volver a, reanudar (una actividad que se había interrumpido). **4** MED. volver, reaparecer (un dolor, un síntoma). **5** (p.u.) replicar, contestar. || *v.t.* **6 [– (to)]** devolver: *he didn't return me the book I lent him = no me devolvió el libro que le presté.* **7 [– (to)]** devolver (a un sitio), volver a colocar (en su sitio). **8** devolver, corresponder a (un saludo, una mirada, etc.). **9** DEP. devolver; restar (la pelota). **10** (brit.) POL. elegir (en una votación). **11** DER. pronunciar (una sentencia). **12** dar (las gracias). **13** declarar (oficialmente): *he was returned guilty = fue declarado culpable.* **14** ECON. producir (lucro, beneficios, intereses, etc.). || *s.i.* **15** vuelta, regreso, retorno: *we are celebrating his return = estamos celebrando su regreso.* **16** ECON. devolución (de una mercancía). **17** devolución, restitución (de algo prestado). **18** reaparición (de un síntoma, de un dolor). **19** retroceso (de una máquina de escribir). **20** regreso, vuelta (a algo anterior). || *s.c.* e *i.* **21** ECON. beneficio; rédito, interés. || *s.c.* **22** DEP. resto, devolución (de la pelota). **23** FIN. informe, declaración: *official returns = informes oficiales.* **24** billete de ida y vuelta. || *s.sing.* **25 [– (to)]** retorno, vuelta: *return to dictatorship = vuelta a la dictadura.* || **26 by –/by – mail/by – of post,** a vuelta de correo. **27 in – (for),** a cambio (de); en recompensa (por). **28 law of diminishing returns,** ECON. ley de rendimientos decrecientes. **29 many happy returns (of the day),** feliz cumpleaños. **30 point of no –,** (fig.) punto sin retorno (sin opción a volverse atrás). **31 – address,** señas del remitente. **32 to – fire,** MIL. responder al ataque del enemigo. **33 returning officer,** (brit.) POL. escrutador. **34 to – like for like,** pagar con la misma moneda. **35 – match,** DEP. partido de revancha. **36 returns,** POL. resultados (de un escrutinio). **37 – ticket,** billete de ida y vuelta. **38 – trip/journey,** viaje de regreso.
returnable | rɪˈtɜːnəbl | *adj.* **1** en depósito, a devolver (envases, botellas, cascos, etc.). **2** restituible.
reunion | ˌriːˈjuːnjən | *s.i.* **1** reunión. || *s.c.* **2** reunión, reencuentro.
reunite | ˌriːjuːˈnaɪt | *v.t.* e *i.* **1 [– (with)]** reunir(se). **2 [– (with)]** reconciliar(se): *he reunited with his family = se reconcilió con su familia.* **3** reunificar.
re-use | ˌriːˈjuːs | (también **reuse**) *s.c.* **1** aprovechamiento (de un material). || | ˌriːˈjuːz | *v.t.* **2** aprovechar, volver a emplear (un material).
rev | rev | (fam.) *v.t.* e *i.* **1** acelerar(se) (un coche, un motor). || **2 revs,** revoluciones (de un motor). **3 to – up,** acelerar(se). OBS. **Rev.** se utiliza: **a)** (form.) abreviatura de reverendo (en lenguaje escrito); **b)** (fam.) reverendo (en lenguaje coloquial).
revaluation | ˌriːvæljuˈeɪʃən | *s.i.* revalorización, revaluación: *the revaluation of the peseta = la revalorización de la peseta.*
revalue | ˌriːˈvæljuː | *v.t.* **1** revalorizar. **2** volver a valorar.
revamp | ˌriːˈvæmp | (fam.) *v.t.* **1** (fig.) remendar, corregir. **2** renovar, rehacer.
revamped | ˌriːˈvæmpt | *adj.* (fam.) remendado; renovado.
revamping | ˌriːˈvæmpɪŋ | *s.sing.* (fam.) renovación, arreglo.
reveal | rɪˈviːl | *v.t.* **1** revelar, dar a conocer: *she revealed her secret = ella reveló su secreto.* **2** dejar al descubierto, mostrar. **3** revelar, manifestar: *you never revealed your feelings = nunca manifestaste tus sentimientos.* **4** (fig.) reflejar: *his face shows goodness = su cara refleja bondad.*
revealing | rɪˈviːlɪŋ | *adj.* revelador: *a revealing talk = una conversación reveladora.*
revealingly | rɪˈviːlɪŋlɪ | *adv.* de forma reveladora.
reveille | rɪˈvælɪ | *s.i.* MIL. toque de diana.
revel | ˈrevl | *v.i.* **1 [– (in)]** gozar, disfrutar: *she revels in gossip = ella disfruta con el cotilleo.* **2** divertirse, pasarlo bomba. || *v.t.* **3** gastar en diversiones (tiempo, dinero). || *s.c.* e *i.* **4** (normalmente en *pl.*) (p.u.) juerga, jolgorio, diversión.
revelation | ˌrevəˈleɪʃn | *s.c.* e *i.* **1 [– (of)]** revelación (de un hecho). **2** REL. revelación (divina). || *s.sing.* **3 [– (to)]** revelación, descubrimiento: *that news was a revelation for them = esa noticia fue una revelación para ellos.* || **4 Revelation(s),** REL. Apocalipsis: *the Book of Revelation = el libro del Apocalipsis.*
reveler V. **reveller.**
reveller | ˈrevələr | (EE.UU. **reveler**) *s.c.* (p.u.) juerguista.
revelry | ˈrevlrɪ | *s.i.* **1** juerga, jaleo, jolgorio. || **2 revelries,** fiestas, diversiones.
revenge | rɪˈvendʒ | *s.i.* **1** venganza: to be full of revenge = arder en deseos de venganza. **2** DEP. revancha. || *v.t.* **3 [– (on)]** (form.) vengar: *he will revenge his brother = vengará a su hermano.* || *v.i.* **4** vengarse.
revengeful | rɪˈvendʒful | *adj.* vengativo.
revengefully | rɪˈvendəfulɪ | *adv.* vengativamente.
revenue | ˈrevənjuː | FIN. *s.i.* o *s.pl.* **1** renta: *national revenue = renta pública.* **2** ingresos (de Estado). **3** rentas públicas. || **4 – cutter,** (brit.) guardacostas. **5 – officer, a)** agente de aduanas; **b)** agente fiscal. **6 – stamps,** timbre (fiscal).
reverberate | rɪˈvɜːbəreɪt | (form. o lit.) *v.i.* **1** retumbar, repercutir, resonar: *her scream reverberated through the wood = su grito retumbó en el bosque.* **2 [– (with)]** retumbar: *the walls reverberated with their shouts = las paredes retumbaban con sus gritos.* **3** (fig.) resonar, tener repercusiones. **4** FIS. reverberar.
reverberation | rɪˌvɜːbəˈreɪʃn | (normalmente *pl.*) (form. o lit.) **1** *s.c.* **1** repercusión (de un hecho). || *s.c.* e *i.* **2** eco, resonancia.
revere | rɪˈvɪər | *v.t.* (form.) reverenciar, venerar; mostrar profundo respeto.
revered | rɪˈvɪəd | *adj.* (form.) venerado, respetado.
reverence | ˈrevərəns | *s.i.* **1** reverencia, profundo respeto: *they feel reverence for their elders = sienten profundo respeto por sus mayores.* || *s.c.* **2** (arc.) reverencia (gesto). || *v.t.* **3** reverenciar, venerar, respetar profundamente.
reverend | ˈrevərənd | *s.inv.* **1** REL. reverendo. || *s.c.* **2** (fam.) REL. padre (católico); pastor (protestante). | *adj.* **3** (p.u.) venerable.
reverent | ˈrevərənt | *adj.* (form.) reverente, respetuoso.
reverently | ˈrevərəntlɪ | *adj.* (form.) respetuosamente.
reverential | ˌrevəˈrenʃl | *adj.* (form.) reverencial.

reverie | 'revərɪ | *s.c.* e *i.* (form.) ensueño, ensoñación.
reversal | rɪ'vɜːsl | *s.c.* **1** (form.) inversión, cambio de papeles. **2** cambio radical, transformación.
reverse | rɪ'vɜːs | *v.t.* **1** invertir: *they reversed the procedure = invirtieron el procedimiento.* **2** DER. revocar, anular (una decisión, una ley, una sentencia, etc.). **3** invertir, dar la vuelta (a un objeto). **4** intercambiar, trocar. **5** cambiar radicalmente (de política, de opinión). || *v.t.* e *i.* **6** dar marcha atrás (a un vehículo). || *v.i.* **7** moverse en sentido contrario. || *s.i.* **8** marcha atrás. || *s.c.* **9** revés, contratiempo: *the reverses of the fortune = los reveses de la fortuna.* **10** MIL. derrota. || *s.sing.* **11** reverso (de una moneda, medalla, etc.). **12** dorso (de un escrito). **13** revés (de la ropa). **14 [the –]** lo contrario, lo opuesto. || *adj.* **15** inverso: *in reverse order = en orden inverso.* **16** opuesto, contrario: *they run in reverse directions = corrían en direcciones opuestas.* || **17 to – arms,** MIL. llevar las armas a la funerala. **18 in /into –,** al revés; marcha atrás. **19 quite the –,** todo lo contrario. **20 – charge,** llamada a cobro revertido. **21 – gear,** marcha atrás. **22 to – oneself,** (EE.UU.) cambiar de opinión. **23 to – the charges,** (brit.) llamar a cobro revertido. **24 reversing light,** luz de marcha atrás.
reversible | rɪ'vɜːsəbl | *adj.* **1** reversible: *a reversible raincoat = un chubasquero reversible; a reversible process = un proceso reversible.* **2** revocable: *a reversible decision = una decisión revocable.*
reversion | rɪ'vɜːʃn | *s.c.* **1 [– (to)]** (form.) regreso, vuelta (a un estado o condición anterior). **2 [– (to)]** BIOL. regresión, salto atrás (en la evolución). **3** DER. reversión.
revert | rɪ'vɜːt | *v.i.* **1 [– (to)]** (form.) regresar, volver: *they are reverting to former ways = están volviendo a procedimientos antiguos.* **2** BIOL. sufrir una regresión, retroceder (en la evolución). **3 [– (to)]** (form.) volver (a algo que se ha dicho anteriormente). **4** PSIQ. sufrir una regresión (un enfermo mental). **5 [– (to)]** DER. revertir: *his properties will revert to his descendants = sus bienes revertirán a sus descendientes.*
review | rɪ'vjuː | *s.c.* **1** crítica, reseña (de un libro, obra teatral, etc.). **2** artículo: *stage review = artículo teatral.* **3** revista: *literary review = revista literaria.* || *s.c.* e *i.* **4** nuevo examen, revisión: *a periodic review = una revisión periódica.* **5** análisis, examen: *a reviews of the situation = un análisis de la situación.* **6** repaso, revisión: *a review of the lesson = un repaso de la lección.* **7** DER. revisión (de un caso, sentencia, etc.). **8** MIL. revista. || *v.t.* **9** hacer una crítica de (una obra, un libro, etc., en un medio de comunicación). **10** volver a examinar, revisar; analizar. **11** repasar, revisar: *let us review the lesson = repasemos la lección.* **12** MIL. pasar revista a. **13** DER. revisar (un caso, una sentencia, etc.). || **14 to come up for –,** estar preparados para revisión. **15 under –,** en estudio.
reviewer | rɪ'vjuːər | *s.c.* ART. crítico.
revile | rɪ'vaɪl | *v.t.* (form.) insultar, injuriar, denigrar.
revise | rɪ'vaɪz | *v.t.* **1** revisar; volver a examinar. **2** modificar, reconsiderar: *you should revise your attitude = deberías modificar tu actitud.* **3** revisar, corregir (un texto, una traducción, etc.). || *v.t.* e *i.* **4** repasar; estudiar, empollar.
revised | rɪ'vaɪzd | *adj.* **1** rectificado. **2** corregido: *a revised version = una versión corregida.*
revision | rɪ'vɪʒn | *s.c.* e *i.* **1 [– (of)]** revisión, corrección. **2** modificación. || *s.i.* **3** repaso (de una lección, tema, etc.).
revisionism | rɪ'vɪʒənɪzəm | *s.i.* FIL. revisionismo.
revisionist | rɪ'vɪʒənɪst | *adj.* y *s.c.* FIL. revisionista.
revisit | ˌriː'vɪzɪt | *v.t.* e *i.* volver a visitar.
revitalise V. **revitalize.**
revitalize | ˌriː'vaɪtəlaɪz | (también **revitalise**) *v.t.* revivificar, reavivar, infundir nueva fuerza a.
revival | rɪ'vaɪvl | *s.c.* e *i.* **1** resurgimiento, reaparición: *the revival of old customs = el resurgimiento de antiguas costumbres.* **2** REL. despertar (religioso). || *s.sing.* **3** reanimación, renovación. **4** (fig.) renacimiento: *revival of art = renacimiento del arte.* || *s.c.* **5** ART. reposición, reestreno.
revivalism | rɪ'vaɪvəlɪzəm | *s.i.* REL. movimiento dedicado a propagar una determinada religión.
revivalist | rɪ'vaɪvəlɪst | REL. *s.c.* **1** predicador. || *adj.* **2** dedicado a propagar una determinada fe o doctrina religiosa.
revive | rɪ'vaɪv | *v.t.* e *i.* **1** reactivar(se), impulsar(se): *to revive foreign trade = reactivar el comercio exterior.* **2** (fig.) renacer, recobrar fuerzas: *her interest in music revived = renació su interés por la música.* **3** MED. reanimar. **4** revivir, despertar, volver en sí. **5** (fig.) reanimar, infundir ánimos: *a glass of wine will revive you = un vaso de vino te reanimará.* **6** (fig.) resucitar (un recuerdo). || *v.t.* ART. reponer, reestrenar.
revivify | riː'vɪvɪfaɪ | *v.t.* (form.) revivificar, reavivar; reanimar.
revocation | ˌrevə'keɪʃn | *s.i.* DER. revocación, anulación.
revoke | rɪ'vəʊk | *v.t.* **1** DER. revocar: *to revoke a law = revocar una ley.* **2** anular, cancelar. **3** renunciar (en juego de naipes). || *s.c.* **4** renuncio (en juegos de naipes).
revolt | rɪ'vəʊlt | *s.c.* e *i.* **1** revuelta, rebelión. **2** sublevación, insurrección. || *s.i.* **3** rebeldía. || *v.i.* **4 [– (against)]** rebelarse, sublevarse: *they revolted against the government = se rebelaron contra el gobierno.* || *v.t.* **5** repugnar, repeler: *it revolts me = me repugna.* **6** indignar; escandalizar. || **7 to be in –,** estar en rebeldía.
revolting | rɪ'vəʊltɪŋ | *adj.* **1** repugnante, asqueroso. **2** odioso, detestable.
revoltingly | rɪ'vəʊltɪŋlɪ | *adv.* de forma repugnante; asquerosamente.
revolution | ˌrevə'luːʃn | *s.c.* e *i.* **1** POL. revolución: *the French Revolution = la Revolución Francesa.* || *s.c.* **2** (fig.) revolución, cambio: *it entails a revolution in our lifestyle = ello supone una revolución en nuestro estilo de vida.* **3** TEC. revolución, vuelta: *thirty revolutions a minute = treinta revoluciones por minuto.* **4** revolución, giro, vuelta: *the revolutions of the moon round the earth = las vueltas de la luna alrededor de la tierra.*
revolutionary | ˌrevə'luːʃnərɪ | *adj.* **1** POL. revolucionario. || **2** (fig.) innovador, revolucionario: *a revolutionary idea = una idea revolucionaria.* || *s.c.* **3** revolucionario.
revolutionise V. **revolutionize.**
revolutionize | ˌrevə'luːʃnaɪz | *v.t.* revolucionar, transformar totalmente: *microwave ovens are revolutionizing cookery = los hornos microondas están revolucionando el arte culinario.*
revolutionising V. **revolutionizing.**
revolutionizing | ˌrevə'luːʃənaɪzɪŋ | *adj.* transformador, innovador.
revolve | rɪ'vɒlv | *v.i.* **1 [– (around /round)]** girar, dar vueltas: *the earth revolves round the sun = la tierra gira alrededor del sol.* **2 [– (around/round)]** (fig.) girar, centrarse: *the conversation revolved around football = la conversación giró en torno al fútbol.*
revolver | rɪ'vɒlvər | *s.c.* revólver.
revolving | rɪ'vɒlvɪŋ | *adj.* giratorio.
revue | rɪ'vjuː | *s.c.* ART. revista (espectáculo).
revulsion | rɪ'vʌlʃn | *s.i.* **1** repulsa. **2** repugnancia, asco.
reward | rɪ'wɔːd | *s.c.* e *i.* **1** recompensa, premio, gratificación. || *s.c.* **2** recompensa, gratificación: *they offered a reward of two hundred dollars = ofrecieron una recompensa de doscientos dólares.* **3** galardón. || *v.t.* **4** recompensar, premiar. **5** (form.) merecer: *the matter rewarded my attention = el asunto merecía mi atención.* || **6 as a/in – for,** en recompensa por.
rewarding | rɪ'wɔːdɪŋ | *adj.* **1** que merece la pena: *a rewarding film = una película que merece la pena.* **2** gratificante: *a rewarding task = una tarea gratificante.* **3** provechoso: *a rewarding reading = una lectura provechosa.*
rewind | ˌriː'waɪnd | *v.* [*pret.* y *p.p.* **rewound**] *t.* **1** rebobinar (una cinta). **2** dar cuerda a (un reloj).
rewire | ˌriː'waɪər | *v.t* ELECTR. cambiar la instalación eléctrica a.
rewound | ˌriː'waʊnd | *pret.* y *p.p.* de **rewind.**
rework | ˌriː'wɜːk | *v.t.* poner al día.
rewrite | ˌriː'raɪt | *v.* [*pret.* **rewrote;** *p.p.* **rewritten**] *t.* **1** modificar, volver a redactar (un escrito). || | | *s.c.* **2** (fam.) corrección, modificación (en un texto).
rewritten | ˌriː'rɪtn | *p.p.* de **rewrite.**
rewrote | ˌriː'rəʊt | *pret.* de **rewrite.**

rhapsodic | ræp'sɒdɪk | *adj.* entusiasta, elogioso.
rhapsodise V. **rhapsodize.**
rhapsodize | 'ræpsədaɪz | *v.i.* **[– (about /on/over)]** (form.) elogiar, hablar con entusiasmo.
rhapsody | 'ræpsədɪ | *s.c.* **1** ART. rapsodia. || **2 to go into rhapsodies,** entusiasmarse.
rheostat | 'rɪəustæt | *s.c.* ELECTR. reostato.
rhesus | 'ri:səs | *s.c.* **1** ZOOL. macaco de la India. || **2 – factor,** BIOL. factor Rh.
rhetoric | 'retərɪk | *s.i.* **1** (desp.) palabrería, retórica. **2** ART. retórica, oratoria.
rhetorical | rɪ'tɒrɪkl | *adj.* **1** (fig.) retórico, afectado, exagerado. **2** ART. retórico. || **3 – question,** pregunta retórica.
rhetorically | rɪ'tɒrɪkəlɪ | *adv.* de forma retórica.
rhetorician | ˌretə'rɪʃn | *s.c.* **1** HIST. retórico. **2** orador.
rheumatic | ru:'mætɪk | MED. *adj.* o *s.c.* **1** reumático. || **2 – fever,** fiebre reumática. **3 rheumatics,** (fam.) reúma, reumatismo.
rheumatism | 'ru:mətɪzəm | *s.i.* MED. reumatismo, reúma.
rheumy | ru:mɪ | *adj.* (lit.) legañoso; acuoso (ojos).
rhinestone | 'raɪnstəun | *s.c.* diamante falso.
rhino | 'raɪnəu | *s.c.* ZOOL. (fam.) rinoceronte.
rhinoceros | raɪ'nɒsərəs | *s.c.* ZOOL. rinoceronte.
rhododendron | ˌrəudə'dendrən | *s.c.* BOT. rododendro.
rhombi | rɒm'baɪ | *pl.* de **rhombus.**
rhombus | 'rɒmbəs | [*pl.* **rhombuses** o **rhombi**] *s.c.* GEOM. rombo.
rhubarb | 'ru:bɑ:b | *s.i.* **1** BOT. ruibarbo. **2** (EE.UU.) discusión acalorada. **3** (fam.) bla-bla-bla.
rhyme | raɪm | *v.i.* **1 [– (with)]** LIT. rimar. || *s.c.* e *i.* **2** LIT. rima. || *s.c.* **3** LIT. rima, composición en verso. || **4 in –,** LIT. en verso. **5 without – or reason,** (fig.) sin ton ni son.
rhymed | raɪmd | *adj.* LIT. rimado: *rhymed verse = verso rimado.*
rhyming | raɪmɪŋ | *adj.* **1** que rima. || **2 – dictionary,** diccionario de rimas. **3 – slang,** jerga que en vez de utilizar una palabra normal la cambia por otra que rime con ella.
rhythm | 'rɪðəm | *s.c.* e *i.* **1** ritmo, cadencia. || **2 – and blues,** MUS. estilo de música jazz. **3 – method,** MED. método contraceptivo de abstinencia periódica (Ogino).
rhythmic | 'rɪðmɪk | *adj.* rítmico, cadencioso.
rhythmical | 'rɪðmɪkl | V. **rhythmic.**
rhythmically | 'rɪðmɪkəlɪ | *adv.* rítmicamente, de forma rítmica.
rib | rɪb | *s.c.* **1** ANAT. costilla. **2** varilla (de un abanico, de un paraguas, de una cometa, etc.). **3** BOT. nervio. **4** ARQ. cercha, cimbra. **5** MAR. cuaderna. || *s.i.* **6** cordoncillo (labor). || *v.t.* **7** (fam.) tomar el pelo.
ribald | 'rɪbəld | *adj.* (p.u.) obsceno, grosero: *a ribald jest = una broma grosera.*
ribaldry | 'rɪbəldrɪ | *s.i.* (p.u.) humor grosero u obsceno.
riband | 'rɪbənd | (también **ribband**) *s.c.* (arc.) lazo, cinta.
ribband V. **riband.**
ribbed | rɪbd | *adj.* **1** BOT. con nervadura. **2** acanalado: *a ribbed sock = un calcetín acanalado.*
ribbing | rɪbɪŋ | *s.i.* punto acanalado.
ribbon | 'rɪbən | *s.c.* e *i.* **1** cinta (de adorno). **2** cinta (de máquina de escribir). || *s.c.* **3** MIL. banda, condecoración. || **4 cut/torn/slashed to ribbons,** hecho jirones, hecho trizas.
rib-cage | 'rɪbkeɪdʒ | (también **rib cage**) *s.c.* ANAT. caja torácica.
rib-tickler | ˌrɪb'tɪklər | *s.c.* (arc.) historia o chiste divertido.
rice | raɪs | *s.i.* **1** BOT. arroz. || **2 – field,** BOT. arrozal. **3 – paper,** papel de arroz. **4 – pudding,** GAST. arroz con leche.
rich | rɪtʃ | *adj.* **1** rico: *a rich man.* **2 [– (in/with)]** rico, abundante: *rich in minerals = rico en minerales.* **3** fértil, rico (suelo). **4** costoso, suntuoso: *rich furniture = mobiliario suntuoso.* **5** melodioso (una voz). **6** vivo (un color). **7** copioso, opíparo (una comida). **8** pesado, fuerte (una comida). **9** (p.u.) divertido, gracioso: *a rich joke = un chiste divertido.* **10** fuerte (una fragancia, un perfume). **11** abundante: *a rich harvest = una cosecha abundante.* || **12 natural riches,** ECOL. riquezas naturales. **13 riches,** riqueza, riquezas. **14 the –,** los ricos. OBS. **-rich** forma *adj.* en combinación con algunos *s.: protein-rich food = alimento rico en proteínas.*
richly | rɪtʃlɪ | *adv.* **1** generosamente: *they rewarded me richly = me recompensaron generosamente.* **2** ampliamente. **3** abundantemente. **4** magníficamente, espléndidamente: *he was richly dressed = estaba espléndidamente vestido.* **5** suntuosamente, ostentosamente.
richness | rɪtʃnɪs | *s.i.* **1** riqueza. **2** fertilidad (del suelo). **3** viveza (de un color). **4** suntuosidad.
Richter scale | 'rɪktər skeɪl | V. **scale.**
rick | rɪk | *s.c.* **1** montón de paja o heno. **2** (fam.) tirón. || *v.t.* **3** (fam.) torcer, darse un tirón en: *he ricked his back = se dio un tirón en la espalda.* **4** amontonar (la paja, el heno).
rickets | 'rɪkɪts | *s.i.* MED. raquitismo.
rickety | 'rɪkətɪ | *adj.* **1** desvencijado, destartalado: *a rickety car = un coche desvencijado.* **2** tambaleante, inestable: *a rickety chair = una silla tambaleante.* **3** MED. raquítico.
rickshaw | 'rɪkʃɔ: | *s.c.* carreta oriental tirada por un hombre.
ricochet | 'rɪkəʃeɪ | *v.i.* **1** rebotar (una bala, una piedra). || *s.c.* **2** rebote (de una bala, de una piedra).
rid | rɪd | *v.* [*pret.* **rid** o **ridded;** *p.p.* **rid** o **ridded**] *t.* **1 [– (of)]** librar: *they rid their country of terrorists = libraron a su país de terroristas.* || *adj.* **2 [– (of)]** libre: *we are rid of her = estamos libres de ella.* || **3 to get – of, a)** librarse de (alguien); **b)** deshacerse de, desembarazarse de (algo); **c)** (fig.) librarse (de un sentimiento, un pensamiento, una situación, etc.); **d)** (fam.) vender.
riddance | 'rɪdəns | *s.i.* **1** acción de desembarazarse de algo o de alguien. || **2 good –/good – to bad rabbish,** vete con viento fresco.
ridden | 'rɪdn | *p.p.* de **ride.**
riddle | 'rɪdl | *s.c.* **1** adivinanza, acertijo. **2** enigma, misterio. **3** criba, tamiz. || *v.t.* **4 [– (with)]** acribillar. **5** (fig.) acribillar a preguntas. **6** refutar (un argumento). **7** pasar por la criba, tamizar. || **8 to – with bullets,** acribillar a balazos. **9 to speak/talk in riddles,** hablar en clave.
riddled | 'rɪdld | *adj.* **1 [– (with)]** acribillado. **2 [– (with)]** (fig.) plagado, infestado: *riddled with smugs = plagado de vanidosos.* **3 [– (with)]** lleno, plagado: *riddled with puzzles = lleno de misterios.* || **4 to be – like a sieve,** (fig.) estar como una criba.
ride | raɪd | *v.* [*pret.* **rode;** *p.p.* **ridden**] *t.* e *i.* **1 [– (on)]** montar: *to ride a bicycle = montar en bicicleta.* **2 [– (on)]** cabalgar, montar. **3** conducir: *to ride a motorcycle = conducir una motocicleta.* **4** (fig.) dominar (a alguien). **5** recorrer (una distancia). **6** DEP. correr (en una carrera). || *v.i.* **7 [– in]** ir en, viajar en (un vehículo): *to ride in a car = ir en un coche.* **8 [– (on)]** flotar (en el aire, en el agua). **9** montar a hombros. || *s.c.* **10** viaje; paseo, vuelta (a caballo, en un vehículo). **11** cabalgata. **12** camino (sin asfaltar). || **13 to give someone a –,** llevar a alguien en coche (en autostop). **14 to let something –,** (fig.) dejar que algo siga su curso. **15 to – at anchor,** MAR. estar anclado. **16 to – bareback,** montar a pelo. **17 to – horseback,** montar a caballo. **18 to – out,** (fig.) salir de, librarse de (un peligro, una dificultad, etc.). **19 to – out the storm,** (fig.) capear el temporal. **20 to – up,** subirse (una falda, un jersey, etc.). **21 to take someone for a –,** (fam.) engañar, embaucar, dar gato por liebre.
rider | 'raɪdər | *s.c.* **1** jinete. **2** ciclista. **3** motociclista, motorista. **4** (form.) añadidura. **5** DER. cláusula adicional.
ridge | rɪdʒ | *s.c.* **1** GEOG. loma, colina, cerro. **2** GEOG. contrafuerte, estribación. **3** AGR. lomo, caballón, caballete. **4** ARQ. caballete, lomo (de un tejado). **5** ANAT. caballete (de la nariz). **6 [– (of)]** TEC. zona (en meteorología): *a ridge of high pressure = una zona de altas presiones.* **7** ondulación (en una superficie). **8** cordoncillo (en una tela).
ridicule | 'rɪdɪkju:l | *s.i.* ridículo, irrisión. || *v.t.* **2** ridiculizar, burlarse de, poner en ridículo. || **3 to hold someone up to –,** mofarse de alguien, ridiculizar a alguien. **4 to lay oneself open to –,** exponerse al ridículo.
ridiculous | rɪ'dɪkjuləs | *adj.* **1** ridículo, grotesco, digno de risa. **2** absurdo, ridí-

culo: *a ridiculous idea = una idea ridícula.* **3** (fig.) ridículo, escaso: *a ridiculous profit = una ganancia ridícula.*

ridiculously | rɪ'dɪkjʊləslɪ | *adv.* ridículamente.

riding | 'raɪdɪŋ | *s.i.* **1** DEP. equitación. || *adj.* **2** DEP. de montar, de equitación. || **3 – habit,** DEP. traje de montar. **4 – light/lamp,** MAR. luz de posición (de un barco). **5 – master,** DEP. maestro de equitación.

rife | raɪf | (form.) *adj.* **1** corriente, frecuente: *corruption is rife in this country = la corrupción es frecuente en este país.* **2 [– (with)]** plagado, lleno.

riffle | 'rɪfəl | *v.t.* e *i.* **[– (through)]** hojear, mirar por encima: *I was riffling through a magazine = estaba hojeando una revista.*

riffraff | 'rɪfræf | (también **riff-raff**) *s.i.* gentuza, chusma.

rifle | 'raɪfl | *s.c.* **1** rifle, fusil. || *v.i.* **2 [– (through)]** hojear, mirar por encima. || *v.t.* **3** vaciar, limpiar (para robar); desvalijar.

rifleman | 'raɪflmən | *s.c.* [*pl.* **riflemen**] MIL. fusilero.

rifle-range | 'raɪflreɪndʒ | (también **rifle range**) *s.c.* **1** campo de tiro. || *s.i.* **2** alcance (de una bala de rifle).

rift | rɪft | *s.c.* **1 [– (between/in)]** desacuerdo, desavenencia, discrepancia. **2** (fig.) ruptura (de una amistad, de una relación). **3** grieta, abertura, hendidura. **4** claro (en una nube).

rig | rɪg | *v.t.* **1** amañar, arreglar (unas elecciones, un combate, una carrera, etc.). **2** trucar: *he rigged the dice = trucó los dados.* **3** improvisar: *we will have to rig a table = tendremos que improvisar una mesa.* **4** MAR. equipar, aparejar (un barco). || *s.c.* **5** MAR. aparejo, equipo. **6** TEC. plataforma: *drilling rig = plataforma de perforación.* || *s.i.* **7** (fam. y arc.) atuendo, atavío, indumentaria. || **8 to – oneself out/up,** (fam.) ataviarse. **9 to – up,** improvisar.

rigging | 'rɪgɪŋ | *s.c.* MAR. aparejo.

right | raɪt | *adj.* **1** correcto: *the right way = el camino correcto.* **2** justo, exacto: *the right time = la hora exacta.* **3** justo, debido: *the right price = el precio debido.* **4** apropiado, adecuado: *the right place = el sitio adecuado.* **5** derecho: *right foot = pie derecho.* **6** justo: *it is not right = no es justo.* **7** (fam.) bien: *are you right? = ¿está usted bien?* **8** verdadero: *a right idiot = un verdadero idiota.* **9** respetable: *right people = gente respetable.* **10** oportuno: *the right moment = el momento oportuno.* || *adv.* **11** bien, correctamente. **12** a la derecha: *turn right = gire a la derecha.* **13** justo, exactamente: *it is right behind you = está justo detrás de ti.* **14** muy: *right hungry = muy hambriento.* **15** (fam.) inmediatamente: *I'll be right back = estaré de vuelta inmediatamente.* **16** directamente. **17** completamente. **18** de lleno: *he hit me right in the eye = me dio de lleno en el ojo.* || *s.c.* **19 [– (to)]** derecho: *he has the right to complain = tiene derecho a quejarse.* **20** DEP. derechazo (en boxeo). || *s.i.* **21** bien: *right and wrong = el bien y el mal (lo que está bien y lo que está mal).* **22** derecho: *his right to the throne = su derecho al trono.* || *s.sing.* **23** derecha (lado derecho): *on the right = a la derecha.* **24 [the –]** POL. la derecha. || *v.t.* **25** enderezar: *the boat righted herself = la barca se enderezó sola.* **26** enderezar, arreglar (una situación). **27** deshacer (un entuerto). **28** corregir, rectificar (una falta, un error). || **29 as – as rain,** (fam.) perfectamente bien. **30 at – angles (to),** perpendicular. **31 at somebody's – hand,** al lado de alguien (para ayudarle o aconsejarle). **32 to be in one's – mind,** estar en sus cabales. **33 to be –,** tener razón: *you are right = tienes razón.* **34 by rights,** por derecho; en justicia. **35 to give one's – arm,** (fig.) dar su brazo derecho (por conseguir algo). **36 to go –,** salir bien: *the plan went right = el plan salió bien.* **37 in one's own –,** por derecho propio. **38 in the –,** del lado de la razón. **39 not – in the head,** (fam.) un poco mal de la cabeza. **40 on the – side of,** V. **side. 41 to put/set something –,** poner en orden, arreglar. **42 to reserve the – to,** V. **reserve. 43 – along,** sin cesar. **44 – and left,** a diestro y siniestro. **45 – angle,** GEOM. ángulo recto. **46 – away,** enseguida, inmediatamente. **47 – now,** (fam.) ahora mismo, en este momento. **48 – of way, a)** prioridad de paso, preferencia (de un vehículo); **b)** derecho de paso (por una propiedad privada). **49 – reverend,** REL. reverendísimo. **50 rights,** derechos: *human rights = derechos humanos.* **51 – side,** derecho (de un tejido, traje, etc.). **52 to serve someone –,** V. **serve. 53 when the time is –,** en el momento apropiado. **54 within one's rights,** en su derecho.

right-about turn | 'raɪtəbaut tɜːn | *s.c.* media vuelta.

right-angled | 'raɪtæŋgl | *adj.* **1** GEOM. rectangular; rectángulo: *a right-angled triangle = un triángulo rectángulo.* **2** en ángulo recto.

righteous | 'raɪtʃəs | *adj.* **1** virtuoso, honrado (una persona). **2** justo, justificado (un sentimiento).

righteousness | 'raɪtʃəsnɪs | *s.i.* **1** honradez, virtud. **2** justicia.

rightful | 'raɪtful | (form.) *adj.* **1** legítimo: *rightful heir = heredero legítimo.* **2** justo; justificable.

rightfully | 'raɪtfəlɪ | *adv.* legítimamente.

right-hand | 'raɪthænd | *adj.* **1** de la derecha; derecho. || **2 — drive,** con volante a la derecha (un vehículo). **3 – man,** (fig.) brazo derecho: *he is my right-hand man = es mi brazo derecho.*

right-handed | ˌraɪt'hændɪd | *adj.* diestro.

right-hander | ˌraɪt'hændər | *s.c.* persona diestra.

rightism | 'raɪtɪzm | *s.i.* POL. conservadurismo.

rightist | 'raɪtɪst | POL. *s.c.* **1** conservador. || *adj.* **2** de derechas, conservador: *a rightist politician = un político de derechas.*

rightly | raɪtlɪ | *adv.* **1** convenientemente, adecuadamente. **2** con razón, acertadamente. **3** correctamente, debidamente. **4** exactamente.

right-minded | ˌraɪt'maɪndɪd | *adj.* **1** honrado, virtuoso. **2** razonable, sensato.

righto | ˌraɪt'əʊ | (también **right-ho**) *interj.* (fam.) vale, de acuerdo.

right-of-centre | ˌraːtɔv'sentə | *adj.* POL. de centro derecha.

right-thinking | ˌraɪt'θɪŋkɪŋ | V. **right-minded.**

right-wing | ˌraɪt'wɪŋ | (también **right-wing**) POL. *adj.* **1** de derechas: *a right-wing governement = un gobierno de derechas.* || *s.c.* **2** derecha más radical, extrema derecha.

right-winger | ˌraɪt'wɪŋər | *s.c.* POL. persona de derechas.

rigid | 'rɪdʒɪd | *adj.* estricto, riguroso: *rigid principles = principios rigurosos.* **2** severo, riguroso, inflexible (una persona). **3** rígido, inflexible (un objeto, un material). || **4 to go –,** quedarse rígido (un cadáver). **5 to shake someone –,** (fig. y fam.) dejar tieso a alguien.

rigidity | rɪ'dʒɪdɪtɪ | *s.i.* **1** rigidez, firmeza. || *s.c.* e *i.* **2** inflexibilidad. **3** austeridad.

rigidly | 'rɪdʒɪdlɪ | *adv.* **1** rígidamente. **2** firmemente, inflexiblemente. **3** estrictamente, rigurosamente.

rigmarole | 'rɪgmərəul | (fam.) *s.c.* **1** galimatías, confusión. **2** (arc.) disparate, incoherencia.

rigor V. **rigour.**

rigorous | 'rɪgərəs | *adj.* **1** riguroso, estricto, severo: *rigorous discipline = disciplina rigurosa.* **2** escrupuloso, meticuloso. **3** riguroso, duro (clima).

rigorously | 'rɪgərəslɪ | *adv.* **1** rigurosamente, estrictamente. **2** escrupulosamente, cuidadosamente.

rigour | 'rɪgər | (EE.UU. **rigor**) *s.pl.* **1 [the – of]** (form.) rigores (condiciones duras): *the rigours of the winter = los rigores del invierno.* || *s.i.* **2** (brit. y form.) severidad, rigor, inflexibilidad, rigidez.

rig-out | 'rɪgaut | *s.c.* (arc. y fam.) atavío, indumentaria.

rile | raɪl | *v.t.* (fam.) enfadar, sacar de quicio, irritar.

rim | rɪm | *s.c.* **1** borde; orilla: *the rim of a glass = el borde de un vaso.* **2** llanta (de una rueda). **3** aro, montura (de gafas). **4 [– (of)]** cerco.

rimless | rɪmlɪs | *adj.* sin montura (gafas).

rimmed | rɪmd | *adj.* **1 [– (with)]** (lit.) bordeado: *a glass rimmed with silver = un vaso bordeado de plata.* **2 [– (with)]** con montura (gafas).

OBS. **-rimmed** se añade un *s.* o *adj.* formando otro *adj.*: *gold-rimmed glasses = gafas con montura de oro.*

rind | raɪnd | *s.c.* e *i.* **1** cáscara, corteza (de naranja, limón). **2** corteza (de queso, de tocino).

ring | rɪŋ | *v.* [*pret.* **rang**; *p.p.* **rung**] *t.* **1** llamar por teléfono a: *ring him later =*

llámale más tarde. **2** tocar: *did you ring the bell? = ¿tocaste el timbre?* **3** repicar, tañer, tocar (una campana). **4 [– (for)]** anunciar (con un timbre, una campana, etc.).
OBS. **Ring** tiene forma regular en los siguientes significados: **5 [– (with/by)]** rodear: *they are ringed with policemen = están rodeados de policías.* **6** encerrar, rodear (el ganado). **7** poner una anilla a (un animal). **8** rodear con un círculo. || *i.* **9** sonar: *the telephone is ringing = suena el teléfono.* **10** repicar, tañer, tocar (una campana). **11** llamar por teléfono. **12 [– (with)]** (lit.) resonar. **13** zumbar (los oídos). **14** llamar: *they rang at the door = llamaron a la puerta.* **15 [– (for)]** llamar (para pedir algo). || *s.c.* **16** llamada: *a ring at the door = una llamada a la puerta.* **17** timbre, timbrazo. **18** telefonazo. **19** tañido, repique. **20** anillo, sortija. **21 [– (of)]** corro, cerco (de personas). **22** argolla, aro. **23** DEP. ruedo, arena. **24** cerco (de una mancha). **25** halo. **26** aureola. **27** DEP. cuadrilátero (en boxeo). **28** anilla. **29** hornillo. **30** ojera. **31** banda, pandilla (que opera en algo ilegal). **32** pista (de circo). || *s.sing.* **33** (fig.) tono, retintín: *sarcastic ring = tono sarcástico, retintín.* **34** timbre, sonido metálico. || **35 to give someone a –,** (fam.) dar un telefonazo. **36 key –,** llavero. **37 to – a bell,** (fam.) sonar, ser familiar. **38 to – around/round,** hacer varias llamadas telefónicas. **39 to – back,** volver a llamar. **40 – binder,** cuaderno de anillas. **41 – finger,** dedo anular. **42 to – in the New Year/to – out the Old Year,** recibir el Año Nuevo/despedir el Año Viejo. **43 to – off,** colgar (el teléfono). **44 to – out,** oírse. **45 rings,** DEP. anillas. **46 to – true/false, etc.,** sonar verdadero/falso, etc. **47 to – up,** (fam.) llamar por teléfono. **48 to run rings round somebody,** (fig.) dar cien vueltas a alguien.
ringer | 'rɪŋər | *s.c.* **1** campanillero. || **2 to be a dead – (for),** (fam.) ser la viva imagen de.
ringing | 'rɪŋɪŋ | *s.i.* **1** timbre (sonido). **2** campanilleo, tintineo. **3** zumbido. || *adj.* **4** sonoro: *a ringing laugh = una risa sonora.*
ringleader | 'rɪŋ,liːdər | *s.c.* cabecilla.
ringlet | 'rɪŋlɪt | *s.c.* **1** bucle, tirabuzón, rizo. **2** (arc.) pequeña sortija.
ringmaster | 'rɪŋ,mɑːstər | *s.c.* director de pista (de un circo).
ring-road | 'rɪŋrəʊd | (también **ring road**) *s.c.* carretera de circunvalación.
ringside | 'rɪŋsaɪd | *s.sing.* **1** primera fila. || *adj.* **2** de primera fila, en primera fila: *a ringside seat = un asiento en primera fila.*
ringway | 'rɪŋweɪ | V. **ring-road.**
ringworm | 'rɪŋwəːm | *s.i.* MED. tiña.
rink | rɪŋk | *s.c.* **1** DEP. pista de patinaje.
rinse | rɪns | *v.t.* **1** aclarar, enjuagar (la ropa, los platos, el pelo, etc.). **2** enjuagar (la boca). **3** dar reflejos (al pelo). || *s.c.* **4** aclarado: *I gave my hair a good rinse = le di un buen aclarado a mi pelo.* **5** reflejo: *she gave her hair a red rinse = le dio reflejo rojizo a su pelo.* || **6 to – out,** aclarar, enjuagar.
riot | 'raɪət | *s.c.* **1** motín: *student riots = motines estudiantiles.* **2** disturbio, alboroto. || *s.sing.* **3 [– (of)]** (fig.) explosión, orgía (de colores). **4** (fig.) derroche. **5 [a –]** (fam.) éxito: *the party was a riot = la fiesta fue un éxito.* || *v.i.* **6** amotinarse, alborotarse. || **7 to read the – act,** (fam. y fig.) leer la cartilla, reprender. **8 to run –, a)** desmandarse, alborotarse; **b)** (fig.) volar (la imaginación).
rioter | 'raɪətər | *s.c.* alborotador, amotinado.
rioting | 'raɪətɪŋ | *s.i.* motín; tumulto, alboroto.
riotous | 'raɪətəs | *adj.* **1** desenfrenado: *a riotous crowd = una multitud desenfrenada.* **2** disoluto: *a riotous life = una vida disoluta.* **3** ruidoso, bullicioso.
rip | rɪp | *v.t.* e *i.* **1** rasgar(se), romper(se): *she ripped the seams = rompió las costuras.* || *v.t.* **2** arrancar: *he ripped the poster from the wall = arrancó el cartel de la pared.* || *s.c.* **3** rasgadura, rasgón, desgarrón. **4** descosido. || **5 let it –/let her –,** (fam.) ¡acelera!, ¡más rápido! **6 to – off, a)** (fam.) timar, estafar; **b)** arrancar, quitar; robar. **7 to – open,** abrir desgarrando o rompiendo. **8 to – through,** extenderse por. **9 to – up, a)** arrancar, desgarrar; **b)** destrozar, romper.
ripcord | 'rɪpkɔːd | *s.c.* cuerda de abertura (de un paracaídas).
ripe | raɪp | *adj.* **1** maduro: *ripe fruit = fruta madura.* **2** en su punto. **3** (fam.) acre, fuerte (olor). **4** (fam.) basto, grosero: *ripe language = lenguaje grosero.* **5 [– (for)]** listo, preparado. || **6 – old age (of),** la avanzada edad (de). **7 the time is – (for/to),** es el momento propicio.
ripen | 'raɪpən | *v.t.* e *i.* **1** madurar: *the sun is ripening the crops = el sol está madurando las cosechas.* **2** (form. y fig.) madurar (un sentimiento, una relación). **3** MED. madurar.
ripeness | raɪpnɪs | *s.i.* madurez, sazón.
rip-off | 'rɪpɒf | (también **ripoff**) *s.c.* (fam.) timo, estafa.
riposte | rɪ'pɒst | (lit.) *s.c.* **1** réplica ingeniosa, contestación aguda. || *v.i.* **2** contestar con ingenio.
ripper | 'rɪpər | *s.c.* (fam.) destripador.
ripple | 'rɪpl | *s.c.* **1** ondulación, rizo (en el agua). **2** onda (en el pelo). **3** pliegue (en un tejido). || *s.sing.* **4 [– (of)]** murmullo (de voces, de risas, de conversación, etc.). || *v.t.* e *i.* **5** ondear; rizar, ondular. || *v.i.* **6** agitarse; estremecerse. **7** murmurar.
rise | raɪz | *v.* [*pret.* **rose;** *p.p.* **risen**] *i.* **1** subir, ascender: *it rose into the air = ascendió por los aires.* **2** subir, aumentar (los precios, la temperatura). **3** salir (el sol, la luna). **4** GASTR. subir (una masa). **5** MIL. ascender (a un rango superior). **6** (form.) levantarse, ponerse de pie. **7** (form.) levantarse (de la cama). **8 [– (against)]** MIL. alzarse, sublevarse, rebelarse. **9** ascender (a una posición o nivel superior). **10** aumentar, incrementarse. **11** alcanzar (un nivel). **12** elevarse (la voz, un sonido). **13** DER. suspender la sesión. **14** elevarse, alzarse (una montaña, un edificio, etc.). **15** surgir, aparecer. **16 [– (from)]** proceder, originarse. **17** levantarse, aumentar (el viento). **18** (fig.) crecer (un río, un sentimiento). **19** elevarse (un objeto, del suelo). **20** subir (la marea). **21** emerger. **22 [– (to)]** replicar, contestar. **23** REL. resucitar: *Christ rose from the dead = Cristo resucitó de entre los muertos.* **24** nacer (un río). || *s.c.* **25** pendiente, cuesta. **26** (fam.) aumento de sueldo. **27 [– (in)]** subida, aumento, alza. || *s.i.* **28** subida, ascenso. || *s.sing.* **29** nacimiento (de un río). **30 [– (of)]** aumento. || **31 to give – to,** dar origen a. **32 on the –,** en aumento. **33 to – above,** sobreponerse a (una dificultad, un problema). **34 to – the occasion,** V. **occasion. 35 to – up, a)** (fig.) crecer (un sentimiento, una emoción); **b)** MIL. rebelarse, sublevarse, alzarse.
risen | 'rɪzn | *p.p.* de **rise.**
riser | 'raɪzər | *s.c.* **1** TEC. contrahuella. || **2 early –,** madrugador. **3 late –,** dormilón.
risible | 'rɪzəbl | *adj.* (form.) risible, cómico.
rising | 'raɪzɪŋ | *s.c.* **1** MIL. levantamiento, rebelión, revuelta. || *s.i.* **2** salida: *the rising of the sun = la salida del sol.* || *adj.* **3** creciente. **4** ascendente. **5** elevado, en pendiente. **6** prometedor, de porvenir. || **7 – damp,** humedad (en un edificio).
risk | rɪsk | *s.c.* e *i.* **1** riesgo; peligro. || *v.t.* **2** arriesgar, aventurar, poner en peligro: *he risked his life = arriesgó su vida.* **3** correr el riesgo de, exponerse a: *he risked failure = se expuso al fracaso.* || **4 at one's own –,** por su cuenta y riesgo. **5 at –,** en peligro. **6 at the – of,** a riesgo de. **7 calculated –,** V. **calculated. 8 to take a –,** correr el riesgo. **9 to run the – (of),** correr el riesgo (de); exponerse (a).
risky | rɪskɪ | *adj.* arriesgado, aventurado, peligroso.
risotto | rɪ'zɒtəʊ | *s.sing.* GAST. plato italiano de arroz.
risqué | 'riːskeɪ | *adj.* escabroso, al borde de lo obsceno, subido de tono (un relato, un chiste).
rissole | 'rɪsəʊl | *s.c.* GAST. croqueta.
rite | raɪt | *s.c.* REL. rito, ceremonia.
ritual | 'rɪtʃʊəl | *s.c.* e *i.* **1** REL. ritual, ceremonial. **2** (fig.) costumbre. || *adj.* **3** REL. ritual: *ritual murder = sacrificio ritual.*
ritualism | 'rɪtʃʊəlɪzəm | *s.i.* REL. ritualidad; ritualismo.
ritualistic | ,rɪtʃʊə'lɪstɪk | *adj.* **1** REL. ritual: *ritualistic words = palabras rituales.* **2** ritualista.
ritually | 'rɪtʃʊəlɪ | *adv.* según el ritual, de forma ritual.
rival | 'raɪvl | *s.c.* y *adj.* **1** rival, competidor: *rival teams = equipos rivales.* || *v.t.* **2 [to – +** *o.* **+ (in)]** rivalizar con, compararse con, competir con: *she can't rival Mary in beauty = no puede competir con María en belleza.*

rivalry | 'raɪvlrɪ | *s.c.* e *i.* **1** rivalidad, competencia: *rivalry between companies = rivalidad entre empresas.*
riven | 'rɪvən | *adj.* (form. y p.u.) partido, dividido, desgarrado.
river | 'rɪvər | *s.c.* **1** río: *a large river = un río caudaloso.* **2** (lit. y fig.) río, gran abundancia de: *a river of blood = un río de sangre.* || *adj.* **3** fluvial: *river traffic = tráfico fluvial.* || **4 to sell someone down the –,** V. **sell.**
river-bank | 'rɪvəbæŋk | (también **river bank**) *s.c.* orilla, margen, ribera.
river-bed | 'rɪvəbed | (también **river bed**) *s.c.* lecho, cauce (de un río).
riverside | 'rɪvəsaɪd | *s.sing.* **1** ribera. || *adj.* **2** ribereño.
rivet | 'rɪvɪt | *v.t.* **1** (normalmente en pasiva) absorber, cautivar. **2** atraer (la atención): *it riveted my attention = atrajo mi atención.* **3 [– (on)]** (fig.) clavar (la mirada, los ojos, etc.). **4** TEC. remachar. || *s.c.* **5** TEC. remache.
riveted | 'rɪvɪtɪd | *adj.* (fig.) clavado: *my eyes were riveted on the scene = mis ojos estaban clavados en la escena.*
riveting | 'rɪvɪtɪŋ | *adj.* **1** cautivador, atrayente, absorbente. || *s.i.* **2** TEC. remachado.
rivulet | 'rɪvjʊlɪt | *s.c.* (form.) riachuelo, arroyo.
roach | rəʊtʃ | *s.inv.* **1** ZOOL. gobio. || *s.c.* **2** (fam.) ZOOL. cucaracha.
road | rəʊd | *s.c.* **1** carretera: *main road = carretera principal.* **2** vía: *Roman road = vía romana.* **3** camino: *local road = camino vecinal.* **4** calle (en una ciudad). **5** calzada. **6 [– (to)]** (fig.) camino: *the road to world peace = el camino a la paz mundial.* **7** carretera de: *Madrid road = carretera de Madrid (que va a Madrid).* || *adj.* **8** de carretera: *road accidents = accidentes de carretera.* **9** vial: *road safety = seguridad vial.* || **10 one for the –,** (fam.) la última copa. **11 on the –, a)** en la carretera (de viaje); **b)** en circulación (un vehículo); **c)** de gira (una compañía de teatro, un circo, etc.); **d) [– (to)]** (fig.) camino de: *they are on the road to ruin = van camino de la ruina.* **12 roads,** MAR. rada, ensenada. **13 – sense,** habilidad para desenvolverse entre el tráfico. **14 the end of the –,** (fig.) el final (de algo que ha fracasado).
roadblock | 'rəʊdblɒk | *s.c.* control de carretera.
roadhog | 'rəʊhɒg | *s.c.* (fam.) conductor desconsiderado.
roadhouse | 'rəʊdhaʊs | *s.c.* (p.u.) restaurante de carretera.
roadside | 'rəʊdsaɪd | *s.c.* **1** borde del camino. || *adj.* **2** de carretera: *a roadside inn = un albergue de carretera.*
roadster | 'rəʊdstər | *s.c.* (p.u.) coche deportivo descapotable.
roadway | 'rəʊdweɪ | *s.c.* calzada; carretera.
road-works | 'rəʊdwəːks | (también **road works**) *s.pl.* obras de carretera.
roadworthy | 'rəʊd,wəːðɪ | *adj.* en buenas condiciones (un coche).
roam | rəʊm | *v.t.* e *i.* vagar, andar errante: *he is roaming about the world = vaga por el mundo.*
roan | rəʊn | *s.c.* ZOOL. roano (caballo o yegua).
roar | rɔːr | *v.i.* **1** bramar (el mar, el viento). **2** rugir (un animal). **3** (fig.) bramar, vociferar (una persona). **4 [– (with)]** aullar, gritar: *she roared with pain = aulló de dolor.* || *s.c.* **5** bramido, rugido. **6** estruendo: *the roar of engines = el estruendo de los motores.* || **7 – of laughter,** carcajada. **8 to – with laughter,** reír a carcajadas.
roaring | rɔːrɪŋ | *adj.* **1** ruidoso. **2** tempestuoso: *a roaring night = una noche tempestuosa.* **3** (fam.) clamoroso, estrepitoso: *a roaring success = un éxito clamoroso.* **4** magnífico (fuego). || **5 to be – drunk,** (fam.) completamente borracho. **6 to do a – trade,** (fam.) hacer un buen negocio.
roast | rəʊst | *v.t.* e *i.* **1** GAST. asar(se). || *v.t.* **2** GAST. tostar (café, granos). || *v.i.* **3** (fig.) asarse, achicharrarse, morirse de calor. **4** (EE.UU.) criticar duramente; ridiculizar. || *adj.* **5** asado: *roast sucking pig = cochinillo asado.* || *s.c.* e *i.* **6** GAST. asado, carne asada.
roasted | rəʊstɪd | *adj.* tostado (café).
roaster | rəʊstər | *s.c.* **1** tostador (de café). **2** GAST. alimento listo para asar.
roasting | rəʊstɪŋ | *s.c.* **1** (fam.) bronca, rapapolvo. || *s.i.* **2** tostado (del café).
rob | rɒb | *v.t.* **1 [– (of)]** robar: *I was robbed of my money = me robaron mi dinero.* **2** robar; asaltar, atracar. **3 [– (of)]** privar: *I don't want to rob you of her company = no quiero privarte de su compañía.* || **4 to – Peter to pay Paul,** (fig.) desnudar a un santo para vestir a otro.
robber | rɒbər | *s.c.* ladrón, atracador, asaltante.
robbery | 'rɒbərɪ | *s.c.* e *i.* robo, atraco, asalto.
robe | rəʊb | *s.c.* **1** bata. **2** (form.) toga (de un magistrado). **3** (form.) manto, túnica. **4** (form.) faldón (de bebé). || *v.t.* e *i.* **5 [– (in)]** (form.) vestir(se). || **6 robes,** (form.) ropajes.
robin | 'rɒbɪn | *s.c.* ZOOL. petirrojo.
robot | 'rəʊbɒt | *s.c.* **1** TEC. robot. **2** autómata; androide. **3** (fig.) autómata.
robotic | rəʊ'bɒtɪk | *adj.* (fig.) mecánico: *robotic movements = movimientos mecánicos.*
robotics | rəʊ'bɒtɪks | *s.i.* TEC. robótica.
robust | rəʊ'bʌst | *adj.* **1** robusto, fuerte: *a robust boy = un chico robusto.* **2** saludable. **3** duro (una actividad). **4** vigoroso. **5** firme (una afirmación, un discurso, etc.).
robustly | rəʊ'bʌstlɪ | *adv.* con fuerza; firmemente.
robustness | rəʊ'bʌstnɪs | *s.i.* robustez, fuerza, vigor.
rock | rɒk | *s.i.* **1** roca. **2** MUS. rock. **3** (brit.) GAST. golosina de forma cilíndrica. || *s.c.* **4** GEOG. peña. **5** GEOG. peñón: *the Rock of Gibraltar = el Peñón de Gibraltar.* **6** roca, piedra. **7** (EE.UU.) guijarro, canto. **8** (vulg.) diamante; piedra preciosa. || *v.t.* e *i.* **9** balancear(se). **10** mecer(se): *she was rocking her baby = estaba meciendo a su bebé.* **11** sacudir(se), (hacer) temblar: *an earthquake rocked the building = un terremoto hizo temblar el edificio.* || *v.t.* **12** (fig.) sacudir, conmocionar, estremecer: *a crime wave rocked the country = una ola de crímenes conmocionó al país.* || **13 on the rocks, a)** con cubitos de hielo (una bebida alcohólica); **b)** a punto de romperse, en peligro (una relación, un matrimonio); **c)** (fam.) sin blanca, arruinado; **d)** (fam.) en bancarrota (un negocio); **e)** MAR. encallado, varado (un barco). **14 – and roll, [– -and-roll** cuando precede a un *s.*] MUS. rock and roll. **15 – bun,** V. **bun. 16 – cake,** GAST. pastel que tiene una superficie dura. **17 – climbing,** DEP. alpinismo, escalada. **18 – music,** MUS. música rock. **19 – plant,** BOT. planta rupestre. **20 rocks,** (EE.UU. y vulg.) dinero. **21 – salt,** sal gema. **22 to – the boat,** (fig. y fam.) causar problemas. **23 to – with laughter,** partirse de risa.
rock-bottom | ,rɒk'bɒtəm | *adj.* **1** mínimo, muy bajo: *rock-bottom level = nivel muy bajo.*
rock-climber | ,rɒ'klaɪmər | (también **rock climber**) DEP. alpinista, escalador.
rocker | rɒkər | *s.c.* **1** mecedora, balancín. **2** arco (de una mecedora, de una cuna). **3** MUS. rockero. || **4 to be off one's –,** (fam.) estar chalado.
rockery | 'rɒkərɪ | *s.c.* BOT. jardincillo de roca.
rocket | 'rɒkɪt | *s.c.* **1** TEC. cohete: *space rocket = cohete espacial.* **2** cohete (fuego artificial). || *s.sing.* **3** (fam.) rapapolvo, reprimenda: *he gave me a rocket = me echó un rapapolvo.* || *v.i.* **4** (fam.) subir vertiginosamente (precios, beneficios, ventas, etc.). || **5 – launcher,** lanzacohetes.
rock-garden | 'rɒk,gɑːdn | (también **rock garden**) *s.c.* BOT. jardín rocoso.
rock-hard | rɒkhɑːd | *adj.* durísimo.
rocking-chair | 'rɒkɪŋtʃeər | (también **rocking chair**) *s.c.* mecedora.
rocking-horse | 'rɒkɪŋhɔːs | (también **rocking horse**) *s.c.* caballo de balancín.
rock-like | 'rɒklaɪk | *adj.* firme como una roca.
rock'n'roll | ,rɒkən'rəʊl | V. **rock and roll.**
rock-pool | 'rɒkpuːl | (también **rock pool**) MAR. charca entre rocas.
rocky | 'rɒkɪ | *adj.* **1** rocoso, pedregoso. **2** (fam.) inestable: *a rocky government = un gobierno inestable.* **3** (fam.) tambaleante: *a rocky chair = una silla tambaleante.*
rococo | rəʊ'kəʊkəʊ (también **Rococo**) *adj.* ART. rococó.
rod | rɒd | *s.c.* **1** varilla. **2** barra. **3** vara. **4** caña: *fishing rod = caña de pescar.* **5** (EE.UU. y vulg.) pistola. **6** medida de longitud de 5,03 metros.
rode | rəʊd | *pret.* de **ride.**

rodent | ’rəudənt | *s.c.* ZOOL. roedor.
rodeo | rəu’deɪəu | *s.c.* rodeo (fiesta de rancheros norteamericanos).
roe | rəu | ZOOL. *s.i.* hueva (de pescado). || *s.c.* o *inv.* **2** corzo.
rogue | rəug | *s.c.* **1** tunante, bribón, granuja. **2** canalla, sinvergÅenza. || *adj.* **3** solitario (un animal salvaje). **4** (fig.) solitario (persona que posee su propio sistema de trabajo). || **5 rogue's gallery, a)** (hum.) pandilla de indeseables; **b)** colección de fotografías de conocidos delincuentes.
roguery | ’rəugərɪ | (p.u.) *s.i.* **1** desvergÅenza, sinvergÅencería. **2** picaresca.
roguish | ’rəugɪʃ | *adj.* **1** pícaro, picaruelo, burlón: *a roguish smile = una sonrisa picaruela.* **2** malicioso. **3** travieso.
roguishly | ’rəugɪʃlɪ | *adv.* con picardía, con malicia, burlonamente.
role | rəul | (form.) (también **rôle**) *s.c.* **1** ART. papel (en una obra, película, etc.). **2** (fig.) papel, función: *the role of women in the business world = el papel de la mujer en el mundo de los negocios.* || **3 to play/take a –, a)** desempeñar un papel; **b)** ART. representar un papel.
role-playing | ’rəulpleɪɪŋ | *s.i.* ART. representación (de un papel).
roll | rəul | *v.t.* **1** hacer rodar: *he rolled the ball down = hizo rodar la pelota hacia abajo.* **2** doblar (una prenda). **3** liar (un cigarrillo). **4** enrollar: *he rolled the carpet = enrolló la alfombra.* **5** laminar (un metal). **6** allanar, aplanar, alisar. **7** alisar con un rodillo (una masa). **8** (lit.) mover en círculo; poner en blanco (los ojos). **9** balancear. || *v.i.* **10** rodar: *the coin rolled and fell into the hole = la moneda rodó y se cayó al agujero.* **11** balancearse, bambolearse (un barco, un avión). **12** retumbar (el trueno, un cañón). **13** redoblar (un tambor). **14** revolverse, revolcarse: *they were rolling on the ground = se revolcaban por el suelo.* **15** moverse, rodar (un vehículo). **16** funcionar (una máquina). **17 [– (down)]** correr (lágrimas, sudor, etc.). **18** ondular. || *s.c.* **19** rollo: *rolls of paper = rollos de papel.* **20** rollo, carrete (de película). **21** GAST. bollo, panecillo, rosco. **22** registro; lista (de nombres): *did the call the roll? = ¿pasó lista?* **23** estruendo, ruido (del trueno, de un cañón). **24** redoble (de un tambor). **25** rodete, rosca (de pelo). **26** (EE.UU.) fajo (de billetes). || *s.sing.* **27** balanceo (de un barco, de un avión). || **28 to – about/around,** revolcarse, revolverse. **29 to – down, a)** desenrollar (una persiana, etc.); **b)** desdoblar (una manga, una pernera, etc.). **30 to – in,** (fam.) llegar a raudales. **31 to – in money/in it,** (fig. y fam.) nadar en dinero. **32 to – in the aisles,** (fam.) revolcarse de risa (el público). **33 – of fat,** (fam.) michelín, protuberancia de grasa (del cuerpo). **34 – of honour,** lista de los que murieron por la patria. **35 to – on, a)** (fam.) que llegue pronto: *roll on one o'clock = que llegue pronto la una; b)* pasar (el tiempo). **36 to – on one's r's,** pronunciar exageradamente las erres. **37 to – over,** volverse, darse la vuelta. **38 to – up, a)** enrollar(se): *roll up the carpet = enrollar la alfombra;* **b)** arremangar; **c)** venir, acudir (en grandes grupos); **d)** envolver: *he rolled himself up in a blanket = se envolvió en una manta.*
roll-call | ’rəulkɔːl | (también **roll call**) *s.c.* lista.
rolled | rəuld | *adj.* **1** enrollado. **2** TEC. laminado: *rolled steel = acero laminado.* || **3 – into one,** en una sola pieza.
rolled-up | ˌrəuld’ʌp | *adj.* **1** enrollado: *a rolled up map = un mapa enrollado.* **2** arremangado.
roller | rəulər | *s.c.* **1** TEC. rodillo; cilindro. **2** rulo (para el pelo). || **3 road –,** TEC. apisonadora.
roller-coaster | ’rəuləˌkəustər | *s.c.* montaña rusa.
roller-skate | ’rəuləskeɪt | (también **roller skate**) *s.c.* **1** patín de ruedas. || *v.i.* **2** patinar (sobre ruedas).
rolling | ’rəulɪŋ | *s.i.* **1** balanceo (de un barco). **2** TEC. laminado. || *adj.* **3** bamboleante. **4** ondulado (una superficie). **5** rodante. || **6 – stone,** (fig.) culo de mal asiento.
rolling-pin | ’rəulɪŋpɪn | (también **rolling pin**) *s.c.* rollo de cocina, rodillo.
rolling-stock | ’rəulɪŋstɒk | (también **rolling stock**) *s.c.* material rodante.
roly-poly | ˌrəulɪ’pəulɪ | *adj.* (fam.) regordete, rechoncho.
Roman | ’rəumən | *adj.* **1** romano. || *s.c.* **2** romano. **3** redonda (tipo de letra). || **4 – alphabet,** FILOL. alfabeto romano. **5 – Catholic,** REL. católico. **6 – Cathol icism,** REL. catolicismo. **7 – law,** DER. derecho romano. **8 – nose,** ANAT. nariz aguileña. **9 – numeral,** número romano.
romance | rəu’mæns | *s.c.* e *i.* **1** romance, idilio, aventura amorosa. || *s.i.* **2** fantasía romántica. **3** lo romántico, lo poético. **4** LIT. literatura fantástica medieval. || *s.c.* **5** LIT. novela de amor. **6** LIT. libro de caballerías. || *adj.* **7** FILOL. romance, románico: *romance language = lengua románica.* || *v.i.* **8 [– (about)]** fantasear.
Romanesque | ˌrəumə’nesk | *adj.* ART. románico.
Romania | ruː’meɪnɪə | *s.sing.* GEOG. Rumanía.
Romanian | ruː’meɪnɪən | (también **Roumanian**) *adj., s.c.* e *i.* rumano.
romantic | rəu’mæntɪk | *adj.* **1** romántico, idealista. **2** poco realista. **3** romántico, amoroso: *a romantic scene = una escena amorosa.* **4** romántico, sugerente: *a romantic landscape = un paisaje romántico.* **5** ART. romántico: romantic poets. **6** romanticón. || *s.c.* **7** idealista.
romantically | rəu’mæntɪkəlɪ | *adv.* románticamente.
romanticism | rəu’mæntɪsɪzəm | *s.i.* **1** romanticismo, idealismo. **2** ART. romanticismo.
romanticise V. **romanticize.**
romanticize | rə’mæntɪsaɪz | (también **romanticise**) *v.t.* idealizar: *he romanticized her = él la idealizó.*
Romany | ’rɒmənɪ | *s.c.* y *adj.* **1** gitano. || *s.i.* **2** lenguaje gitano; caló.
romp | rɒmp | *v.i.* **1** juguetear, divertirse. || *s.sing.* **2** jugueteo, diversión.
rompers | ’rɒmpəz | *s.pl.* pelele (traje).
rondo | ’rɒndəu | *s.c.* MUS. rondó.
roof | ruːf | *s.c.* **1** tejado. **2** techo (de un coche, de una mina, de una cueva). **3** techumbre. **4** cielo (de la boca). **5** (fig.) techo, hogar. || *v.t.* **6 [to – + *o.* + (in/over)]** techar. || **7 to be going through the –,** (fam.) subir por las nubes (el precio de algo). **8 flat –,** azotea. **9 to go through the –,** (fam.) salirse de sus casillas. **10 to hit the –,** (fam.) poner el grito en el cielo. **11 to raise/lift the –,** (fig.) echar el techo abajo. **12 -roofed,** con techo de: *a wood-roofed hut = una caseta con techo de madera.* **13 – over one's head,** (fig.) techo, hogar. **14 to take somebody under one's –,** (fig.) acoger a uno bajo su techo. **15 under one –/ under the same –,** bajo el mismo techo, en la misma casa. **16 under one's –,** bajo su techo, en su casa.
roofed | ruːft | *adj.* **[– (with)]** techado.
roofing | ruːfɪŋ | *s.i.* techumbre, techado.
roofless | ’ruːflɪs | *adj.* **1** sin tejado; sin techo. **2** (fig.) sin hogar, sin abrigo.
roof-rack | ’ruːfræk | (también **roofrack**) *s.c.* baca (en un vehículo).
rooftop | ’ruːftɒp | (también **roof-top**) *s.c.* **1** tejado. || **2 to shout/proclaim from the rooftops,** (fig.) proclamar a los cuatro vientos.
rook | ruk | *s.c.* **1** ZOOL. grajo. **2** torre (pieza de ajedrez). || *v.t.* **3** (fam. y p.u.) timar, estafar.
rookery | ’rukərɪ | *s.c.* **1** colonia de grajos. **2** colonia de pingÅinos. **3** colonia de focas.
rookie | ’rukɪ | (fam.) *s.c.* **1** MIL. bisoño. **2** novato.
room | ruːm | *s.c.* **1** habitación: *a big room = una habitación grande.* **2** dormitorio. **3** despacho. **4** cuarto. **5** sala. **6** alojamiento. || *s.i.* **7** espacio: *it takes too much room = ocupa demasiado espacio.* **8 [– (for)]** sitio, cabida: *there is not room here for cowards = aquí no hay sitio para los cobardes.* || *v.i.* **9 [– (with/together)]** (EE.UU.) vivir, compartir habitación. **10 [– (with)]** alojarse, hospedarse. || **11 to give something houseroom,** V. **houseroom. 12 – for manoeuvre,** V. **manoeuvre. 13 rooms,** aposentos. **14 – temperature,** temperatura ambiente.
-roomed ruːmd | *adj.* de... habitaciones: *a five-roomed flat = un piso de cinco habitaciones.*
roomful | ’ruːmful | *s.i.* **[– (of)]** habitación llena de: *a roomful of women = una habitación llena de mujeres.*
rooming-house | ’ruːmɪŋˌhaus | (también **rooming house**) *s.c.* (EE.UU.) casa de huéspedes.
roomate | ’ruːmmeɪt | (también **roommate**) *s.c.* compañero de habitación.

room-service | 'ruːmˌsəːvɪs | (también **room service**) *s.i.* servicio de habitaciones (de un hotel).
roomy | 'ruːmɪ | *adj.* espacioso, amplio (un lugar). **2** amplio, holgado (una prenda de vestir).
roost | ruːst | *s.c.* **1** percha, vara (para pájaros). **2** gallinero. || *v.i.* **3** acurrucarse para dormir (un ave, en una percha). **4** (fig.) pasar la noche. || **5 to come home to –/one's chickens have come home to –,** (fam.) volverse en contra de uno (acciones pasadas). **6 to rule the –,** (fam.) llevar la voz cantante.
rooster | ruːstər | *s.c.* (EE.UU.) ZOOL. gallo.
root | ruːt | *s.c.* **1** BOT. raíz. **2** ANAT. raíz (del pelo, de un diente). **3** MAT. raíz: *square root = raíz cuadrada.* **4** FILOL. raíz; radical. **5** (fig.) fondo, base: *the root of the problem = el fondo del problema.* **6** (fig.) causa, origen: *his yearning for power is the root of his misfortune = su ansia de poder es la causa de su desgracia.* || *adj.* **7** básico, fundamental. || *v.i.* **8** BOT. prender, arraigar. **9** ZOOL. husmear, hozar. **10 [– (through/among)]** (fig.) husmear, fisgonear. || *v.t.* **11** BOT. fijar en la tierra (para que prenda) (una planta, un esqueje). || **12 to put down roots,** (fig.) echar raíces, establecerse. **13 to – about/around,** fisgonear. **14 – and branch,** (form.) de raíz, del todo, completamente. **15 – crop,** BOT. tubérculo. **16 to – for,** (EE.UU. y fam.) animar; vitorear, aclamar. **17 to – out,** (fig.) **a)** acabar con; **b)** sacar a la fuerza (a alguien de un sitio). **18 roots,** (fig.) raíces, orígenes (de una persona). **19 to – up,** BOT. arrancar, extraer de raíz (una planta). **20 to take –, a)** BOT. prender, echar raíces; **b)** (fig.) arraigar (ideas, costumbres, etc.).
rooted | ruːtɪd | *adj.* **1** arraigado: *a rooted sentiment = un sentimiento arraigado.* **2 [– (in)]** basado, fundamentado. || **3 to be/stand –,** (fig.) quedarse helado (de miedo, de sorpresa). **4 – to the spot,** (fig.) inmovilizado, helado (por el miedo, por la sorpresa).
rootless | ruːtlɪs | *adj.* desarraigado (una persona).
rope | rəʊp | *s.c.* e *i.* cuerda. **2** soga. **3** lazo. **4** MAR. maroma. || *v.t.* **5 [– (to /together)]** amarrar, atar (con una cuerda). **6** DEP. encordar (en alpinismo). || **7 to give someone plenty of –/enough –,** dar a alguien libertad de acción. **8 to know/learn the ropes,** (fig.) conocer el tema, estar al día en el asunto. **9 money for old –,** dinero fácil. **10 on the ropes,** en una situación desesperada. **11 to – in,** (fam.) embaucar, liar, persuadir. **12 to – off,** cercar con cuerdas; acordelar. **13 ropes,** DEP. cuerdas (en boxeo, lucha libre, etc.). **14 to show/teach someone the ropes,** poner a alguien al día en algo.
rope-ladder | 'rəʊpˌlædər | (también **rope ladder**) *s.c.* escalera de cuerdas.
ropey | rəʊpɪ | (vulg.) (también **ropy**) *adj.* **1** malo, de mala calidad: *a ropey food = una comida mala.* **2** malo, enfermo.
ropy V. **ropey.**
rosary | 'rəʊzərɪ | *s.c.* REL. rosario. **2** rosaleda.
rose | rəʊz | *pret.* de **rise.**
rose | rəʊz | *s.c.* BOT. rosa: *a red rose = una rosa roja.* **2** rosal. **3** alcachofa (de regadera, manguera, etc). || *adj.* **4** color de rosa. || **5 a bed of roses/all roses,** (fig.) camino de rosas. **6 to put the roses back in someone's cheeks,** (fig.) devolver el color a sus mejillas. **7 rambling –,** BOT. rosal trepador. **8 – garden,** BOT. rosaleda. **9 – window,** ARQ. rosetón. **10 to see things through – -coloured spectacles/– -tinted spectacles,** (fig.) verlo todo de color de rosa, ver el lado bueno de las cosas.
rosé | rəʊzeɪ | *s.i.* GAST. rosado (vino).
roseate | 'rəʊzɪɪt | *adj.* (form.) rosado (color).
rosebud | 'rəʊzbʌd | *s.c.* BOT. pimpollo, capullo de rosa.
rosebush | 'rəʊzbʊʃ | *s.c.* BOT. rosal.
rose-hip | 'rəʊzhɪp | (también **rose hip**) *s.c.* BOT. escaramujo.
rosemary | 'rəʊzmərɪ | *s.i.* BOT. romero.
rosette | rəʊ'zet | *s.c.* **1** escarapela (insignia). **2** roseta, rosetón (adorno).
rosewood | 'rəʊzwʊd | *s.i.* BOT. palisandro.
roster | 'rɒstər | *s.c.* lista (de personas que van a realizar un trabajo).
rostra | 'rɒstrə | *pl.* de **rostrum.**
rostrum | 'rɒstrəm | *s.c.* [*pl.* **rostrums** o **rostra**] **1** tribuna (de un orador). **2** (form.) ZOOL. pico.
rosy | 'rəʊzɪ | *adj.* **1** rosado, rosáceo (color). **2** sonrosado: *a rosy face = un rostro sonrosado.* **3** (fig.) prometedor, halagÅeño: *a rosy future = un futuro prometedor.*
rot | rɒt | *v.i.* **1** pudrirse: *the apples rotted = las manzanas se pudrieron.* **2** (fig.) pudrirse: *he will rot in jail = se pudrirá en la cárcel.* || *v.t.* **3** pudrir. **4** corromper (la madera). || *s.i.* **5** podredumbre, putrefacción. **6** (fig.) tonterías, estupideces: *don't talk rot = no digas tonterías.* || **7 to – away,** descomponerse, corromperse; pudrirse. **8 the – set in,** (fig.) ha empezado la decadencia.
rota | 'rəʊtə | *s.c.* (brit.) lista (de personas que van a realizar un trabajo).
rotary | 'rəʊtərɪ | *adj.* **1** rotativo, giratorio. || *s.c.* **2** (EE.UU.) glorieta. || **3 – press,** TEC. rotativa.
rotate | rəʊ'teɪt | *v.t.* **1** hacer rodar, hacer girar. **2** AGR. alternar (cosechas). **3** distribuir por turno, alternar (el trabajo). || *v.i.* **4** girar, rodar: *the wheels rotate = las ruedas giran.*
rotation | rəʊ'teɪʃn | *s.c.* e *i.* **1** rotación: *crop rotation = rotación de cultivos.* || *s.c.* **2** giro, vuelta; revolución. || *s.i.* **3** rotación: *the rotation of the earth = la rotación de la tierra.* **4** alternancia. || **5 in –,** en secuencia, por orden.
rote | rəʊt | *adj.* **1** maquinal. || **2 by –,** por rutina, maquinalmente: *he did it by rote = lo hizo por rutina.*
rotor | 'rəʊtər | *s.c.* **1** TEC. rotor. | **2 – blades,** palas giratorias (de un helicóptero).
rotten | 'rɒtn | *adj.* podrido (alimentos, madera). **2** (fam.) malísimo, de mala calidad: *a rotten book = un libro malísimo.* **3** (fam.) lamentable, desagradable: *a rotten situation = una situación lamentable.* **4** cariado (un diente, una muela). **5** (fam.) sucio, asqueroso: *rotten bastard = sucio bastardo.* **6** (fam.) malo, pachucho. **7** (fig.) corrompido. **8** malo, pésimo: *a rotten day = un día pésimo.* **9** (fam.) maldito: *a rotten dollar = un maldito dólar.* || **10 to smell –,** (fig.) oler a podrido.
rotter | 'rɒtər | *s.c.* (p.u. y fam.) grosero, canalla.
rotund | rəʊ'tʌnd | (form.) *adj.* rechoncho, gordo, redondo.
rotunda | rəʊ'tʌndə | *s.c.* ARQ. rotonda.
roué | 'ruːeɪ | *s.c.* (arc.) libertino, calavera.
rouge | ruːʒ | *s.c.* **1** colorete. || *v.t.* e *i.* **2** poner(se) colorete.
rough | rʌf | *adj.* **1** áspero, rugoso: *rough hands = manos ásperas.* **2** basto: *a rough material = una tela basta.* **3** escabroso, desigual (un terreno). **4** burdo, basto, tosco: *rough manners = modales toscos.* **5** alborotado, revuelto (el tiempo, el mar, el pelo). **6** DEP. violento: *a rough action = una acción violenta.* **7 [– (on)]** (fam.) duro, difícil: *a rough time = una época difícil.* **8** aproximado: *rough calculation = cálculo aproximado.* **9** severo, rudo: *he was rough with her = fue rudo con ella.* **10** grosero, basto (una persona). **11** fuerte, violento (el viento). **12** brutal, brusco, violento (una acción). **13** grueso (el mar). **14** imprecisa, por encima (una descripción, una traducción). **15** chapucero, mal acabado: *a rough work = un trabajo chapucero.* **16** duro (una travesía, un viaje). **17** baldío (terreno). **18** afilada (lengua). **19** sórdido (una zona de una ciudad). **20** (fam.) discordante (un sonido). **21** áspera (una voz). || **22 to cut up –,** (fam.) irritarse, enfadarse. **23 in –,** en sucio. **24 – and ready, a)** mal acabado, tosco; **b)** provisional. **25 – and tumble, a)** pelea; **b)** agitación, movimiento. **26 – diamond,** diamante en bruto. **27 – draft,** borrador, bosquejo. **28 to – it,** pasar dificultades. **29 – justice,** castigo merecido. **30 to – out,** bosquejar, esbozar. **31 to – someone up,** (fam.) dar una paliza a alguien. **32 to – somethings up,** (fam.) alborotar, revolver. **33 to sleep –,** dormir fuera (al aire libre). **34 to take the – with the smooth,** (fig.) estar a las duras y a las maduras.
roughage | 'rʌfɪdʒ | *s.i.* QUIM. fibra, restos celulósicos (de los alimentos).
roughcast | 'rʌfkɑːst | *s.i.* mezcla gruesa.
roughen | 'rʌfən | *v.t.* e *i.* **1** poner(se) áspero. **2** agrietar(se) (la piel).
rough-hewn | ˌrʌf'hjuːn | *adj.* **1** sin desbastar (un trozo de madera, una piedra). **2** labrado toscamente.

roughly | 'rʌflɪ | *adv.* **1** bruscamente; violentamente, brutalmente. **2** duramente, severamente. **3** aproximadamente, más o menos. **4** groseramente. **5** por encima, superficialmente. **6** toscamente.

roughness | 'rʌfnɪs | *s.i.* **1** aspereza. **2** rudeza, brusquedad. **3** grosería. **4** inclemencia (del tiempo). **5** agitación: *the roughness of the sea = la agitación del mar.* **6** violencia.

roughshod | 'rʌfʃɒd | *adj.* **1** herrado con ramplones (un caballo). || **2 to ride – over,** hacer caso omiso de, hacer oídos sordos a.

roulette | ruː'let | *s.i.* ruleta (juego).

Roumanian V. **Romanian.**

round | raʊnd | *adj.* **1** redondo, circular: *a round bath = una bañera redonda.* **2** muy abiertos (ojos). **3** esférico: *the earth is round = la tierra es esférica.* **4** rotundo, categórico (una afirmación, una negativa). **5** redondo, regordete: *round cheeks = mejillas regordetas.* **6** clara; suave (una voz). **7** completo: *a round dozen = una docena completa.* || *prep.* **8** alrededor de; en torno a: *she had a collar round her neck = tenía un collar alrededor del cuello.* **9** a la vuelta de: *round the corner = a la vuelta de la esquina.* **10** sobre, a eso de: *they will arrive round three o'clock = llegarán a eso de las tres.* **11** por, por todo (una ciudad, un país, etc.): *we travelled round the world = viajamos por todo el mundo.* **12** cerca de, por: *there were many people round the building = había mucha gente cerca del edificio.* **13** aproximadamente: *he owned round forty acres = poseía aproximadamente cuarenta acres.* **14** (fig.) en torno a: *she wrote a book round the murder = escribió un libro en torno al asesinato.*

OBS. **Round** como *prep.* se puede sustituir por **around,** excepto en algunas expresiones idiomáticas. || *adv.* **15** alrededor: *the house had a wall all round = la casa tenía un muro todo alrededor.* **16** de circunferencia: *the tree was twenty feet round = el árbol tenía veinte pies de circunferencia.* **17** a la redonda: *two miles round = dos millas a la redonda.* **18** de un lado para otro: *they walked round = caminaban de un lado para otro.*

OBS. **Round** como *adv.* posee además otros significados: **19** idea de que algo está por todas partes: *there are people all round = hay gente por todas partes.* **20** idea de dar(se) la vuelta: *he turned round and looked at me = se volvió y me miró.* **21** idea de pasar de mano en mano o de distribuir: *the tape passed round = la cinta pasó de mano en mano.* **22** idea de acercarse por casa de alguien (de visita): *come round tonight = acércate por mi casa esta noche.* **23** idea de volver: *summer will soon come round = pronto volverá en verano.* **24** idea de duración: *all the year round = durante todo el año.* **25** idea de dar un rodeo: *we had to go five miles round = tuvimos que dar un rodeo de cinco millas.*

OBS. **Round** como *adv.* se puede sustituir por **around,** excepto en algunas expresiones idiomáticas. || *s.c.* **26** serie, sucesión. **27** visita (comercial o médica). **28** DEP. recorrido (en golf, equitación, etc.). **29** ronda (de un juego de cartas). **30** DEP. asalto (de boxeo o lucha libre). **31** DEP. vuelta, ronda. **32** MUS. canon. **33** ronda (de bebidas). **34** recorrido (de un cartero, lechero, etc.). **35** ronda (de un vigilante, de un médico, de negociaciones). **36** tanda, salva (de aplausos). **37** POL. ronda, vuelta (electoral). **38** tiro, disparo; descarga. **39** ciclo: *yearly round = ciclo anual.* **40** rodaja: *a round of beef = una rodaja de carne.* **41** ART. danza en corro. || *v.t.* **42** (form.) rodear: *we rounded the mountain = rodeamos la montaña.* **43** redondear: *she rounded her lips = ella redondeó los labios.* **44** (fig.) doblar (una esquina). || **45 a way –,** una forma de esquivar (un problema, dificultad, etc.). **46 to do the rounds/to make the rounds, a)** hacer las visitas obligadas; **b)** recorrer las ofertas de trabajo. **47 to go the rounds, a)** ir de boca en boca; **b)** pasar de una persona a otra. **48 to move something –,** cambiar de sitio. **49 – about, a)** cerca; **b)** más o menos, aproximadamente. **50 – and –,** de un lado a otro (haciendo círculos). **51 – and – in one's head,** (fig.) dar vueltas en la cabeza. **52 – number/figure,** número redondo. **53 to – something off,** (fam.) terminar algo, rematar algo (satisfactoriamente). **54 to – on,** (fam.) agredir (física o moralmente). **55 – up, a)** juntar, reunir (personas, animales); **b)** redondear (una cifra, un precio). **56 – sum,** cuenta redonda. **57 the other way –,** al revés.

OBS. La partícula **round** acompaña a muchos verbos modificándoles el significado. Hay que buscar los verbos para su correspondiente traducción.

roundabout | 'raʊndəbaʊt | (brit.) *s.c.* **1** tiovivo. **2** glorieta. || *adj.* **3** indirecto (con rodeos): *he spoke in a roundabout way = habló de forma indirecta (dando rodeos).*

rounded | 'raʊndɪd | *adj.* redondeado.

rounders | 'raʊndəz | *s.i.* DEP. juego muy parecido al béisbol.

round-eyed | 'raʊndaɪd | *adj.* con los ojos desorbitados (por el miedo o la sorpresa): *he looked at her round-eyed = la miró con los ojos desorbitados.*

roundly | 'raʊndlɪ | (form.) **1** severamente: *he was roundly criticized = fue severamente criticado.* **2** categóricamente, terminantemente. **3** sin rodeos, con franqueza: *I told him roundly that I would not go = le dije sin rodeos que yo no iría.*

roundness | 'raʊndnɪs | *s.i.* redondez.

round-shouldered | ˌraʊnd'ʃəʊldəd | *adj.* encorvado, cargado de espaldas.

round-the-clock | 'raʊndðəklɒk | (también **round the clock**) *adj.* **1** permanente, que dura 24 horas. || **2 to sleep /work/etc. – the clock,** dormir/trabajar /etc. día y noche.

round-trip | 'raʊndtrɪp | (también **round trip**) *s.c.* **1** viaje de ida y vuelta. **2** gira.

roundup | 'raʊndʌp | (también **round-up**) *s.c.* **1** resumen: *a news roundup = un resumen informativo.* **2** rodeo (del ganado). **3** (fig.) redada (policial).

rouse | raʊz | *v.t.* e *i.* **1** (form.) despertar(se): *everybody was roused by the noise = el ruido despertó a todos.* || *v.t.* **2 [– (to)]** incitar, animar: *his words roused me to action = sus palabras me animaron a la acción.* **3 [– (to)]** provocar: *she is terrible when roused = ella es terrible cuando se la provoca.* **4** suscitar, provocar, despertar (sentimientos, pasiones, deseos). || **5 to – oneself, a)** animarse (a hacer algo); **b)** levantarse (para hacer algo).

rousing | raʊzɪŋ | *adj.* **1** conmovedor: *a rousing scene = una escena conmovedora.* **2** incitante. **3** animado. **4** caluroso: *a rousing welcome = una calurosa acogida.* **5** resplandeciente (fuego).

rout | raʊt | *v.t.* **1** derrotar fácilmente (a un enemigo, a un oponente). **2** MIL. poner en fuga. || *s.c.* e *i.* **3** derrota completa. **4** MIL. desbandada. || **5 to – out, a)** sacar, hacer salir: *he was routed out of bed at three o'clock in the morning = fue sacado de la cama a las tres de la mañana; b)* descubrir, encontrar.

route | ruːt | *s.c.* **1** ruta, camino. **2** itinerario, recorrido, trayecto: *the procession route = el trayecto de la procesión.* **3** rumbo (de un barco o avión). **4** (fig.) vía, camino. || *v.t.* **5** (normalmente en pasiva): enviar (por una determinada ruta); encaminar. || **6 sea –,** MAR. vía marítima.

OBS. **Route** se utiliza en EE.UU. seguido de un *num.* para indicar las carreteras generales entre las ciudades más importantes.

route-march | 'ruːtmɑːtʃ | (también **route march**) *s.c.* MIL. marcha de entrenamiento.

routine | ruː'tiːn | *adj.* **1** rutinario, de rutina: *routine procedure = procedimiento rutinario.* || *s.c.* e *i.* **2** rutina: *daily routine = rutina diaria.* || *s.sing.* **3** (fam.) farsa, montaje.

routinely | ruː'tiːnlɪ | *adv.* rutinariamente.

rove | rəʊv | (lit.) *v.t.* e *i.* **1** vagar (por), errar (por): *they rove the streets = vagan por las calles.* || *v.t.* **2** recorrer (con la mirada): *her eyes roved over the room = sus ojos recorrieron la habitación.* || *v.i.* **3** mirar en todas direcciones (los ojos).

rover | rəʊvər | *s.c.* **1** (lit.) vagabundo; trotamundos. **2** (arc.) MAR. pirata.

roving | rəʊvɪŋ | (lit.) *adj.* **1** errante. **2** itinerante. || **3 to have a – eye,** (fig.) irse los ojos detrás de (las mujeres, la propiedad ajena, etc.).

row | rəʊ | *s.inv.* **1** hilera: *a row of trees = una hilera de árboles.* || *s.c.* **2** fila (en un teatro, cine, etc.): *he was sitting in the front row = él estaba sentado en primera fila.* **3** (fam.) bronca, pelotera, riña. **4** (fam.) debate, disputa, discusión: *a political row = una discusión política.* **5** (fam.) escándalo, alboroto, ruido. || *v.i.* **6** remar: *we rowed against the current = remábamos contra corriente.* **7 [– (with)]** (fam.) pelear, discutir. || *v.t.* **8** hacer avanzar a remo. **9** llevar en barca de remo. || **10 to go for a –,** ir a remar, ir a dar un paseo en bote. **11 in a –, a)** seguidos: *five days in a row = cinco días seguidos;* **b)** en fila. **12 to make/kick up a –,** armar un escándalo, armar camorra. OBS. En los significados **3, 4, 5, 7** y **12** la pronunciación es | rau | .

rowboat | 'rəubəut | *s.c.* (EE.UU.) bote de remos.

rowdiness | 'raudɪnɪs | *s.i.* **1** carácter peleón, gamberrismo. **2** alboroto.

rowdies | 'raudɪz | *s.c.* [normalmente en *pl.*] gamberros, golfos, camorristas.

rowdy | 'raudɪ | *adj.* **1** camorrista, alborotador: *rowdy children = niños alborotadores.* **2** ruidoso: *a rowdy party = una fiesta ruidosa.*

rower | 'rəuər | *s.c.* remero.

rowing | 'rəuɪŋ | *s.i.* DEP. remo.

rowing-boat | 'rəuɪŋbəut | (también **rowing boat**) *s.c.* (brit.) bote de remos.

rowlock | 'rɒlək | *s.c.* MAR. escálamo.

royal | 'rɔɪəl | *adj.* **1** real: *royal palace = palacio real.* **2** (fig.) regio, magnífico, espléndido: *a royal entertainment = una diversión magnífica.* || **3 Royal,** real: *the Royal Academy = la Real Academia.* **4 Royal Assent,** V. **assent. 5 – blue,** azul oscuro. **6 – eagle,** ZOOL. águila real. **7 – family,** familia real. **8 Royal Highness,** Alteza Real. **9 royals,** (fam.) realeza, miembros de la familia real.

royalist | 'rɔɪəlɪst | *s.c.* y *adj.* monárquico.

royally | 'rɔɪəlɪ | *adv.* (fig.) magníficamente, fantásticamente, espléndidamente.

royalty | 'rɔɪəltɪ | *s.i.* **1** realeza. || **2** royalties, **a)** derechos de autor; **b)** derechos que se pagan al que posee una patente.

rub | rʌb | *v.t.* **1 [– (together)]** frotar(se): *he rubbed his hands = se frotó las manos.* **2** friccionar. **3** rozar. **4** sacar brillo a. **5** fregar, limpiar frotando. || *v.i.* **6** rozar: *I rubbed against the wire = me rocé con el alambre.* **7** frotarse, friccionarse. || *s.sing.* **8** (p.u. y lit.) dificultad, pega, impedimento. || *s.c.* **9** friega, restregón. **10** roce, rozadura. || **11 not to have two pennies to – together,** V. **penny. 12 to – along,** (fam.) **a)** llevarse bien, hacer buenas migas; **b)** ir tirando. **13 to – down, a)** lijar; **b)** secar (frotando con una toalla, balleta, etc.). **14 to – hard,** restregar, frotar. **15 to – in, a)** (fam.) recordar: *don't rub it in! = ¡no me lo recuerdes!; b)* machacar, insistir; **c)** frotar (una superficie con una sustancia). **16 to – off, a)** quitar frotando; **b)** (fig. y fam.) pegársele a uno (hábitos, etc., de otra persona). **17 to – out, a)** borrar; **b)** (EE.UU. y vulg.) matar, liquidar. **18 to – salt into someone's wounds,** V. **salt. 19 to – shoulders with,** V. **shoulder. 20 to – up,** pulir, sacar brillo a. **21 to – up the wrong way,** contrariar, irritar.

rubber | 'rʌbər | *s.i.* **1** goma, caucho: *rubber industry = industria del caucho.* || *s.c.* **2** goma de borrar. **3** (vulg.) goma, condón. **4** partida decisiva (en algunos juegos de naipes). || *adj.* **5** de goma: *rubber soles = suelas de goma.* || **6 – band,** goma elástica (para sujetar objetos o fajos). **7 – plant,** BOT. caucho, gomero. **8 rubbers,** chanclas.

rubber-stamp | ˌrʌbə'stæmp | (también **rubber stamp** cuando es *s.c.*) *s.c.* **1** estampilla. || *v.t.* **2** estampillar. **3** (fig.) aprobar de modo oficial. **4** (fig.) aprobar a ciegas.

rubbery | 'rʌbərɪ | *adj.* **1** parecido a la goma; que se estira o se dobla como la goma.

rubbing | rʌbɪŋ | *s.sing.* **1** roce (de los zapatos, de la ropa, etc.). || *s.c.* **2** fricción, friega. **3** dibujo hecho frotando con tiza, carboncillo, etc. sobre un relieve.

rubbish | 'rʌbɪʃ | *s.i.* **1** basura, desperdicios: *rubbish bin = cubo de basura.* **2** (fig.) basura, porquería: *this magazine in rubbish = esta revista es una porquería (no tiene calidad).* **3** (fam.) tonterías, sandeces, bobadas. || *v.t.* **4** (fam.) censurar, criticar.

rubbishy | 'rʌbɪʃɪ | *adj.* (fam.) malo, de mala calidad: *a rubbishy film.*

rubble | 'rʌbl | *s.i.* **1** escombros: *their house was reduced to rubble = su casa quedó reducida a escombros.* **2** ripio, escombros de albañilería, cascotes.

rubella | ru'belə | *s.i.* MED. rubéola.

rubicund | 'ruːbɪkənd | *adj.* (arc. y lit.) rubicundo.

rubric | 'ruːbrɪk | (form.) *s.c.* **1** rúbrica. **2** advertencia (en un documento oficial).

ruby | 'ruːbɪ | *s.c.* **1** rubí. || *adj.* **2** del color del rubí.

ruck | rʌk | *s.c.* **1** (p.u.) DEP. pelotón (en una carrera). **2** (p.u.) TEC. grupo que forman los jugadores de rugby. **3** arruga, pliegue, frunce (en la ropa). || *s.sing.* **4** (fig.) el vulgo, la gente corriente. || **5 to – up,** arrugarse, fruncirse.

rucksack | 'rʌksæk | *s.c.* mochila.

ruction | 'rʌkʃn | *s.c.* (fam.) follón, jaleo, lío.

rudder | 'rʌdər | *s.c.* TEC. timón (de un barco o avión).

ruddy | 'rʌdɪ | *adj.* **1** rubicundo (una persona). **2** colorado, encendido (un rostro, unas mejillas). **3** (lit.) rojizo. **4** (vulg.) maldito, puñetero.

rude | ruːd | *adj.* **1** rudo, descortés, mal educado. **2** grosero, indecente: *a rude joke = un chiste indecente.* **3** (lit.) brusco, inesperado, repentino. **4** (lit.) rudimentario: *rude methods = métodos rudimentarios.* **5** tosco, basto, sin refinar. **6** (fig.) violento: *rude passions = pasiones violentas.* || **7 in – health,** con una salud estupenda.

rudely | ruːdlɪ | *adv.* **1** de forma descortés, groseramente. **2** bruscamente, repentinamente. **3** toscamente. **4** rudimentariamente.

rudeness | ruːdnɪs | *s.i.* **1** descortesía, falta de educación. **2** tosquedad. **3** brusquedad. **4** grosería. **5** (fig.) violencia.

rudimentary | ˌruːdɪ'mentərɪ | (form.) *adj.* rudimentario, primitivo. **2** elemental, muy sencillo (conocimientos).

rudiments | ˌruːdɪ'ments | *s.pl.* rudimentos, nociones elementales: *rudiments of astronomy = rudimentos de astronomía.*

rue | ruː | *v.t.* **1** (lit.) lamentar, sentir, arrepentirse de: *you shall rue it = lo lamentarás.* || *s.c.* **2** (arc.) compasión, lástima. **3** BOT. ruda.

rueful | 'ruːful | (lit.) *adj.* **1** triste, lastimoso. **2** arrepentido.

ruefully | 'ruːfulɪ | *adv.* (lit.) tristemente.

ruff | rʌf | *s.c.* **1** gola, gorguera, lechuguilla. **2** ZOOL. collar (de plumas o de pelos). **3** fallo (en un juego de cartas). || *v.t.* e *i.* **4** fallar (en un juego de cartas).

ruffian | 'rʌfɪən | *s.c.* (p.u.) matón, rufián, canalla.

ruffle | 'rʌfl | *v.t.* **1** depeñar, desgreñar, alborotar (el pelo). **2** pasar rápidamente (las páginas, las hojas). **3** encrespar, erizar. **4** (lit.) agitar (una superficie). **5** perturbar, molestar. **6** rizar, fruncir, arrugar. || *v.i.* **7** despeinarse (el pelo). **8** encresparse. **9** agitarse. **10** rizarse. **11** incomodarse, molestarse. **12** arrugarse. || *s.c.* **13** frunce, pliegue; volante. **14** gola, lechuguilla. || *s.i.* **15** agitación. **16** enojo.

ruffled | 'rʌfld | *adj.* **1** agitado, nervioso, alterado. **2** molesto. **3** turbado, confundido. **4** desaliñado, alborotado. **5** agitado (una superficie). **6** fruncido: *a ruffled dress = un vestido fruncido.*

rug | rʌg | *s.c.* **1** alfombrilla, tapete. **2** (brit.) manta de viaje. || **3 to sweep something under the –,** V. **sweep.**

rugby | 'rʌgbɪ | *s.i.* DEP. rugby.

rugged | 'rʌgɪd | (lit.) *adj.* **1** accidentado, escabroso; rocoso (un terreno). **2** abrupto (una roca). **3** áspero (una superficie). **4** fuerte, recio: *a rugged man = un hombre recio.* **5** austero, duro: *a rugged life = una vida dura.* **6** tosco, basto: *rugged manners = modales toscos.* **7** fuerte, resistente (una máquina).

rugger | 'rʌgər | *s.i.* (p.u.) DEP. rugby.

ruin | 'ruɪn | *v.t.* **1** arruinar, estropear, echar a perder: *tobacco ruined his health = el tabaco arruinó su salud.* **2** destruir, asolar (un sitio). **3** estropear: *you ruined my umbrella = estropeaste mi paraguas.* **4** arruinar (económicamente): *gambling debts ruined me = las deudas de juego me arruinaron.* || *s.i.* **5** ruina, destrucción. **6** ruina, miseria, bancarrota. **7** (fig.) ruina, perdición. || *s.c.* **8** (normalmente el *pl.*) ruina, resto: *the ruins of a city = las ruinas de una ciudad.* || **9 to go to rack and –,** V. **rack. 10 in ruins,** en ruinas: *a building in ruins = un edificio en ruinas.*

ruination | ruɪ'neɪʃn | *s.i.* **1** ruina, destrucción. **2** perdición.

ruined | 'ruɪnd | *adj.* **1** arruinado, destruido, echado a perder. **2** arruinado (económicamente). **3** en ruinas: *a ruined building = un edificio en ruinas.* **4** estropeado.
ruinous | 'ruɪnəs | *adj.* **1** ruinoso: *ruinous expenses = gastos ruinosos.* **2** desastroso. **3** en ruinas, ruinoso: *a ruinous old factory = una vieja fábrica en ruinas.*
ruinously | 'ruɪnəslɪ | *adv.* de modo ruinoso.
rule | ruːl | *s.c.* **1** regla, norma. **2** reglamento. **3** pauta. **4** precepto. **5** regla (objeto). || *s.sing.* **6** **[the –]** lo normal, la regla general: *sunny weather is the rule here = el tiempo soleado es lo normal aquí.* || *s.i.* **7** control, mando: *under the rule of Mussolini = bajo el mando de Mussolini.* **8** dominio, imperio: *under British rule = bajo dominio británico.* **9** (fig.) gobierno: *the rule of the people = el gobierno del pueblo.* || *v.t.* **10** **[– (over)]** gobernar, regir: *who ruled the country? = ¿quién gobernaba el país?* **11** **[– (over)]** controlar; dominar: *computers will rule the world = las computadoras dominarán el mundo.* **12** (normalmente en pasiva) influenciar: *her words were ruled by hate = sus palabras estaban influenciadas por el odio.* **13** trazar (con una regla). **14** dirigir, regir: *my father rules the company = mi padre dirige la compañía.* || *v.i.* **15** gobernar. **16** (fig.) imperar, reinar: *violence ruled there = allí imperaba la violencia.* **17** DER. decidir, sentenciar. **18** mantenerse (los precios). || **19 as a –/as a general –,** por regla general. **20 to bend/stretch the rules,** pasar por alto el reglamento. **21 by the – book,** (fam.) como Dios manda, según las reglas. **22 to make a –/to make it a –,** tomar por costumbre. **23 – book,** libro de reglamento. **24 to – off,** trazar una línea de división (en un párrafo, sección, etc.). **25 – of law, [the –]** (form.) el imperio de la ley. **26 – of thumb,** V. **thumb. 27 to – out, a)** excluir, descartar; **b)** imposibilitar. **28 ... rules OK, etc.,** (vulg.)... es el mejor. **29 to – the roost,** V. **roost.**
ruled | ruːld | *adj.* rayado (papel).
ruler | ruːlər | *s.c.* **1** gobernantes, dirigentes. **2** regla (objeto).
ruling | ruːlɪŋ | *adj.* **1** gobernante, dirigente: *the ruling class = la clase dirigente.* **2** predominante, principal (sentimiento, ideas). **3** actual (precio). || *s.c.* **3** DER. fallo, sentencia, decisión.
rum | rʌm | *s.inv.* **1** ron. || *adj.* **2** (brit. y fam.) extraño: *a rum fellow = un tipo extraño.*
Rumanian V. **Romanian.**
rumble | 'rʌmbl | *s.c.* **1** rumor, murmullo: *rumble of voices = murmullo de voces.* **2** estruendo: *rumble of thunder = estruendo del trueno.* || *v.t.* **3** (fam.) calar, descubrir, darse cuenta de. || *v.i.* **4** sonar, hacer ruidos (el estómago). **5** retumbar. **6** pasar haciendo un ruido sordo (un vehículo). **7** hablar con voz sorda.
rumbling | 'rʌmblɪŋ | *s.c.* **1** rumor, murmullo. **2** estruendo. || **3 rumblings,** señales, muestras (de que ocurre algo desagradable).
ruminate | 'ruːmɪneɪt | *v.i.* **1** (form.) reflexionar, meditar, cavilar. **2** ZOOL. rumiar.
rumination | ˌruːmɪ'neɪʃn | *s.c.* (lit.) reflexión, cavilación.
ruminative | 'ruːmɪnətɪv | *adj.* (lit.) pensativo, meditabundo.
ruminatively | 'ruːmɪnətɪvlɪ | *adv.* (lit.) pensativamente.
rummage | 'rʌmɪdʒ | *v.i.* **1** **[– (among /in/through)]** revolver, rebuscar: *he rummaged in the drawer = rebuscó en el cajón.* || *v.t.* **2** **[– (through)]** registrar a fondo. || *s.i.* **3** (EE.UU.) prendas usadas: *rummage sale = venta de prendas usadas (con fines benéficos).* || *s.sing.* **4** registro desordenado (revolviéndolo todo).
rummy | 'rʌmɪ | *s.i.* juego de cartas.
rumour | 'ruːmər | (EE.UU. **rumor**) *s.c.* e *i.* **1** rumor, habladuría: *it was only a rumour = sólo era un rumor.* || **2 to be romoured,** rumorearse, correr el rumor: *she is rumoured to be pregnant = se rumorea que está embarazada.* **3 – has it that,** se rumorea que, se dice que.
rump | rʌmp | *s.c.* **1** (hum.) trasero, culo. **2** ZOOL. anca. **3** ZOOL. rabadilla. || *s.i.* **4** grupo remanente (de una organización, especialmente un partido). || **5 – steak,** GAST. cuarto trasero, cadera.
rumple | 'rʌmpl | (fam.) *v.t.* **1** arrugar. **2** desgreñar, despeinar. **3** chafar, estrujar.
rumpled | 'rʌmpld | (fam.) *adj.* **1** arrugado. **2** desgreñado, despeinado.
rumpus | 'rʌmpəs | (fam.) **1** barullo, jaleo, revuelo. || **2 to have a – with someone,** tener una pelea con alguien.
run | rʌn | *v.* [*pret.* **ran;** *p.p.* **run**] *i.* **1** **[– (to)]** correr: *why is he running? = ¿por qué corre?* **2** correr, competir (en una carrera). **3** escapar, huir. **4** **[– (to)]** acudir (a alguien). **5** POL. presentarse (como candidato en unas elecciones): *he ran for the presidency = se presentó a la presidencia.* **6** nadar río arriba (los salmones). **7** funcionar (una máquina, un aparato). **8** ir a dar una vuelta (en un coche). **9** circular (trenes, autobuses). **10** rodar: *that car runs well = ese coche rueda bien.* **11** fluir, correr: *the river flows through the trees = el río corre entre los árboles.* **12** moquear (la nariz). **13** desteñirse (una tela, un color). **14** derretirse (mantequilla, helado, etc.). **15** deslizarse: *it ran through his fingers = se deslizó entre sus dedos.* **16** desembocar (un río, una calle, etc.). **17** correr, deslizarse (un cajón, una puerta corredera, etc.). **18** manar, fluir. **19** chorrear: *I am running with sweat = estoy chorreando sudor.* **20** extenderse (una planta, una raíz). **21** recorrer: *a shiver ran through my body = un estremecimiento recorrió mi cuerpo.* **22** supurar (una herida). **23** tratar, girar (una conversación). **24** estar en cartel (una obra de teatro, una ópera). **25** correrse (pintura, tinta, etc.). **26** **[– (to/in)]** concentrarse (los pensamientos). **27** decir, rezar: *the document runs as follows = el documento dice lo siguiente.* **28** extenderse: *the road runs along the coast = la carretera se extiende a lo largo de la playa.* **29** **[– to/into]** alcanzar: *this magazine has run to four editions = esta revista ha alcanzado tres ediciones.* **30** durar: *the talk ran for two hours = la charla duró dos horas.* **31** extenderse (una noticia). **32** transcurrir: *life ran smootly = la vida transcurría tranquilamente.* **33** darse con frecuencia (en la familia): *green eyes run in the family = los ojos verdes se dan con frecuencia en la familia.* **34** encontrarse (una característica, un defecto). **35** hacerse una carrera (en una media). **36** estar vigente (un contrato, un documento legal). **37** MAR. navegar: *the ship ran before the wind = el barco navegaba viento en popa.* || *t.* **38** DEP. participar en, tomar parte en (una carrera). **39** presentar en una carrera (un caballo, un perro). **40** pasar ilegalmente (contrabando, personas). **41** pasar, deslizar: *he ran his fingers through her hair = deslizó sus dedos por su pelo.* **42** dirigir (una empresa, una organización, una escuela). **43** llevar (un negocio, una casa, un asunto). **44** establecer (un servicio). **45** manejar (una máquina). **46** llevar a cabo (un experimento, un proceso). **47** INF. ejecutar (un programa). **48** tener, poseer: *his son runs his own computer = su hijo tiene su propio ordenador.* **49** llevar en coche (a alguien). **50** poner, meter; llevar (un vehículo): *he ran the car into the garage = metió su coche en el garaje.* **51** llevar (mensajes, recados). **52** hacer fluir (un líquido de un grifo, manguera, etc.). **53** llenar (una bañera). **54** PER. publicar: *the magazine ran your article = la revista publicó tu artículo.* **55** (fig.) manejar (a alguien). **56** POL. proponer, presentar (a un candidato). **57** correr, perseguir, acosar (a un animal). **58** apacentar (al ganado). **59** **[– (at)]** (form.) ascender a (una cantidad). **60** MIL. romper (un bloqueo). **61** organizar (una campaña). **62** introducir, meter: *she ran a splinter into her finger = se metió una astilla en el dedo.* || *s.sing.* **63** carrera (acción de correr). **64** **[– (for)]** (fig.) carrera, lucha (por alcanzar un objetivo): *his run for power = su lucha por el poder.* **65** **[– (on)]** demanda extraordinaria (de fondos bancarios, de un artículo). **66** desarrollo (de un partido, etc.). **67** hilo (de un discurso, de una conversación). || *s.c.* **68** carrera, corrida. **69** vuelta, paseo (en coche). **70** carrera (en una media). **71** DEP. carrera de fondo. **72** DEP. recorrido, pista (de esquí). **73** viaje, recorrido: *a long run = un largo recorrido.* **74** trayecto (de un autobús, coche, etc.). **75** MIL. vuelo de bombardeo. **76** racha: *a run of good luck = una racha de buena suerte.* **77**

ART. período de representación (de una obra teatral, de una ópera). **78** PER. tirada. **79** cantidad de producción (de una fábrica). **80** MUS. escala. **81** permiso para disponer libremente: *he gave me the run of his house = me dio permiso para disponer libremente de su casa.* **82** DEP. punto (en críquet y béisbol). **83** ZOOL. banco (de peces en movimiento). **84** AGR. terreno de pasto. **85** corral (para animales de granja). || **86 at a –,** a la carrera, corriendo. **87 average/usual /common – of,** (fam.) el común de: *the common run of mankind = el común de las gentes.* **88 to cut and –,** V. **rut. 89 day's –,** MAR. singladura, recorrido. **90 to give someone a – for their money,** poner a uno las cosas difíciles; hacer que uno se esfuerce por lograr algo. **91 to go on the –,** fugarse, escaparse. **92 have a good – for one's money,** dar buena cuenta de sí. **93 in the long –,** a la larga, a largo plazo. **94 in the short –,** a corto plazo. **95 to make a – for it/to – for it,** escapar corriendo (de un sitio, de una situación). **96 to make one's blood – cold,** V. **blood. 97 on the –, a)** fugado, evadido; **b)** (fam.) de acá para allá, en constante ajetreo; **c)** en desventaja, perdiendo: **d)** MIL. en fuga. **98 to – about,** andar de un lado para otro (en busca de algo o alguien). **99 to – across,** encontrarse, topar, tropezar (con alguien). **100 to – after, a)** perseguir (un objetivo, etc.); **b)** (fam. y fig.) andar detrás de (alguien). **101 – along,** (fam.) márchate, lárgate. **102 to – a mile** (fig.) echar a correr. **103 to – amok,** V. **amok. 104 to – an errand,** V. **errand. 105 to – around, a)** andar de un lado para otro (en busca de algo o alguien); **b) [– (with/together)]** juntarse, alternar, asociarse. **106 to – a shore,** MAR. encallar, varar (un barco). **107 to – a temperature/fever,** tener fiebre. **108 to – away, a)** escapar, huir: *she ran away from home = se escapó de casa;* **b)** evadirse, escapar (un prisionero); **c) [– (from)]** eludir (una responsabilidad, un compromiso); **d)** librarse (de algo desagradable); **e)** (normalmente imperativo) (fam.) marcharse, largarse: *run away, children = marcháos niños.* **109 to – away with, a)** ganar fácilmente (un premio, una competición, etc.); **b)** dejarse llevar (por una idea, por una opinión); **c)** dominar (un sentimiento muy fuerte): *don't let your emotions run away with you = no dejes que tus emociones te dominen.* **110 to – cold,** helarse (la sangre). **111 to – down, a)** criticar, hablar mal de; **b)** pararse (un reloj, un mecanismo); **c)** descargarse (una batería); **d)** atropellar (con un vehículo); **e)** encontrar, dar con; **f)** coger, capturar (a un fugitivo, a un criminal, etc.); **g)** MAR. colisionar (una embarcación); **h)** enumerar rápidamente. **112 to – dry, a)** secarse (un río, pozo, etc.); **b)** (fig.) terminarse. **113 to – in,** (fam.) detenido, arrestado. **114 to – into, a)** enfrentarse con; tropezar con (alguien); **c)** elevarse a, llegar a (una cantidad determinada); **d)** chocarse con (un vehículo); **e)** clavar, meter. **115 to – into debt,** adeudarse. **116 to – its course,** V. **course. 117 to – off, a)** huir, fugarse; **b)** (fam.) imprimir, sacar (copias); **c)** (fam.) marcharse, largarse; **d)** dejar salir (un líquido); **e)** DEP. decidirse (una eliminatoria). **118 to – on, a)** (fam.) enrollarse, hablar sin parar; **b)** alargarse, prolongarse. **119 to – one's eye over something,** V. **eye. 120 to – out, a) [– (of)]** quedarse sin: *they ran out of petrol = se quedaron sin gasolina; b)* agotarse, acabarse: *my patience has run out = se me agotó la paciencia;* **c)** vencer, caducar (un documento); **d)** expirar (un contrato); **e) [– (on)]** dejar, abandonar: *his wife has ran out on him = su esposa le ha abandonado.* **121 to – out of steam,** V. **steam. 122 to – over, a)** atropellar, pillar (con un vehículo); **b)** derramarse (un líquido); **c)** rebosar, desbordarse: *the vessel is running over = el recipiente está rebosando; d)* repasar, echar un vistazo; **e)** ensayar, practicar. **123 to – riot,** V. **riot. 124 runs, [the –]** (vulg.) diarrea. **125 to – short,** V. **short. 126 to – the gamut of,** V. **gamut. 127 to – the risk,** V. **risk. 128 to – through, a)** extenderse (una noticia, una emoción, etc., entre un grupo de personas); **b)** estar presente en; **c)** practicar, ensayar; **d)** enumerar rápidamente; **e)** dilapidar, despilfarrar; **f)** hojear, leer por encima. **g)** (arc.) atravesar, traspasar (con una espada, con una bala, etc.). **129 to – to, a)** alcanzar, ascender a (una cantidad); **b)** tender hacia, inclinarse por (un gusto): *her tastes run to love stories = sus gustos se inclinan por las novelas de amor; c)* alcanzar para (un sueldo): *my salary doesn't run to a flat = mi sueldo no alcanza para un piso; d)* poder permitirse (comprar algo): *she doesn't run to a car = ella no puede permitirse un coche.* **130 to – to earth,** V. **earth. 131 to – to ground,** V. **ground. 132 to – up, a)** permitir que suba (una cuenta); **b)** acumular (deudas); **c)** coser rápidamente; **d)** DEP. tomar impulso. **133 to – up against,** enfrentarse con, tropezar con (problemas, dificultades). **134 to – wild,** V. **wild. 135 to take a –,** DEP. tomar carrerilla, tomar impulso (para saltar).

runabout | 'rʌnəbaut | *s.c.* utilitario, coche pequeño.

runaway | 'rʌnəweɪ | *s.c.* y *adj.* **1** fugitivo. || *adj.* **2** desbocado (un caballo). **3** incontrolado (un vehículo). **4** secreto, clandestino: *a runaway marriage = un matrimonio clandestino.* **5** inmediato, rápido: *a runaway success = un éxito inmediato.* || *s.c.* **6** caballo desbocado. **7** huida, fuga.

run-down | 'rʌndaun | (también **run down**) *adj.* **1** (fam.) agotado. **2** ruinoso (un edificio). **3** en decadencia: *a run-down industry = una industria en decadencia.* || *s.sing.* **4** declive, decadencia (de una industria, compañía, etc.). || *s.c.* **5 [– (on)]** informe.

rung | rʌŋ | *s.c.* **1** escalón, peldaño, barrote (de escalera de mano). **2 [the – (of)]** (fig.) escalón, grado (en una escala de importancia).

rung | rʌŋ | *p.p.* de **ring.**

run-in | 'rʌnɪn | *s c.* **1** (fam.) riña, discusión. **2** ART. ensayo general.

runner | 'rʌnər | *s.c.* **1** DEP. corredor: *long distance runner = corredor de fondo.* **2** recadero. **3** contrabandista. **4** tapete (de mesa). **5** corredera (en un mueble, ventana, etc.). **6** patín (de un trineo). **7** alfombra (para pasillo o escaleras). **8** caballo de carrera. **9** BOT. estolón. || **10 – bean,** BOT. alubia roja.

runner-up | ˌrʌnə'ʌp | [*pl.* **runners-up**] *s.c.* **1** DEP. subcampeón.

running | rʌnɪŋ | *s.i.* **1** DEP. carrera. **2** dirección, manejo (de una organización, de un negocio). **3** marcha, funcionamiento; manejo (de una máquina). || *adj.* **4** consecutivo, seguido: *for three months running = durante tres meses seguidos.* **5** corriente: *running water = agua corriente.* **6** con mocos (la nariz). **7** supurante (una herida). **8** corredizo (un nudo). **9** corrida (letra hecha a mano). || **10 to be in the – (for),** tener posibilidades de ganar (o de conseguir algo). **11 to be out of the – (for), a)** tener muy poca (o ninguna) posibilidad de ganar (o de conseguir algo): **b)** estar fuera de combate. **12 to come –,** (fig.) venir enseguida (dispuesto a obedecer). **13 in – order,** en buen estado. **14 to make the –,** ir por delante, ir a la cabeza. **15 record –/long –,** récord de permanencia (en cartel, en emisión): *a long-running television serial.* **16 – about,** correteo. **17 – board,** estribo (de un vehículo). **18 – commentary,** RAD. y TV. comentario en directo. **19 – fire,** MIL. fuego ininterrumpido. **20 – in,** rodaje (de un vehículo). **21 – mate,** (EE.UU.) POL. candidato a la vicepresidencia.

runny | 'rʌnɪ | (fam.) *adj.* **1** demasiado aguado, demasiado líquido (especialmente un alimento). **2** que moquea (nariz). **3** lloroso (ojos).

run-off | 'rʌnɒf | *s.c.* DEP. carrera de desempate.

run-off-the-mill | ˌrʌnəvðə'mɪl | *adj.* nada extraordinario, corriente y moliente: *a run-of-the-mill lawyer = un abogado corriente y moliente.*

runt | rʌnt | *s.sing.* **1 [the –]** el más pequeño de una camada de animales. || *s.c.* **2** (fam.) hombrecillo; enano.

run-through | 'rʌnθru: | *s.c.* ensayo, prueba.

run-up | 'rʌnʌp | *s.sing.* **1 [the – (to)]** tiempo anterior a (un acontecimiento): *during the run-up to the trial = durante el tiempo anterior al juicio.* || *s.c.* **2** DEP. impulso, carrerilla.

runway | 'rʌnweɪ | *s.c.* pista de aterrizaje.

rupture | 'rʌptʃər | *s.c.* **1** (form.) ruptura (de una relación). **2** MED. hernia. **3** MED. rotura. || *v.t.* **4** (form.) romper (una relación). || *v.r.* **5** herniarse.

ruptured | 'rʌptʃəd | *adj.* MED. herniado.
rural | 'rʊərəl | *adj.* rural.
ruse | ruːz | *s.c.* e *i.* (form.) estratagema, ardid.
rush | rʌʃ | *v.t.* **1** hacer deprisa, despachar con prisa: *she rushed her homework = hizo deprisa sus deberes.* **2** meter prisa, apresurar. **3** lanzarse sobre: *they rushed the stage = se lanzaron sobre el escenario.* **4** MIL. tomar por asalto. **5** llevar rápidamente: *rush him to hospital = llévenle rápidamente al hospital.* **6** (vulg.) sacar (a alguien una cantidad exagerada de dinero por algo). **7** enviar sin demora. || *v.i.* **8** darse prisa: *she rushed to open her present = se dio prisa en abrir su regalo.* **9** precipitarse, lanzarse: *they rushed towards the exit = se precipitaron hacia la salida.* **10 [– (at)]** abalanzarse: *he rushed at her = se abalanzó sobre ella.* **11** apresurarse; ir a gran velocidad. || *s.sing.* **12** prisa: *are you in a rush? = ¿llevas prisa?* **13** momento de mayor actividad. **14 [– (for/on)]** gran demanda: *a rush for imported goods = una gran demanda de bienes de importación.* **15** bullicio, ajetreo: *what a rush! = ¡qué ajetreo!* **16** arranque, arrebato (de una emoción, de un sentimiento). **17** torrente (de agua, de palabras). **18** afluencia, tropel. **19** ímpetu: *the rush of the ocean current = el ímpetu de la corriente marina.* **20** MIL. acometida. || *s.c.* **21** BOT. junco. || **22 in a –,** deprisa, con prisas. **23 rushes,** TEC. primeras pruebas (de una película). **24 to – in,** meterse en (un asunto o compromiso, sin meditarlo). **25 to – out,** lanzar a toda prisa (un producto al mercado). **26 to – through,** despachar con prontitud. **27 the blood rushes to one's head/to have a – of blood to the head,** (fig.) perder el control sobre sí mismo.
rushed | rʌʃt | *adj.* **1** ajetreado, ocupado. **2** hecho a toda prisa: *a rushed job = un trabajo hecho a toda prisa.* || **3 to be – off one's feet,** estar muy ajetreado.
rush-hour | 'rʌʃˌaʊər | *s.c.* hora punta, hora de mayor afluencia de tráfico.
rusk | rʌsk | *s.c.* especie de galleta crujiente.
russet | 'rʌsɪt | *adj.* (lit.) rojizo.
Russia | 'rʌʃə | *s.sing.* GEOG. Rusia.
Russian | 'rʌʃən | *adj.* **1** ruso. || *s.c.* **2** ruso, soviético. || *s.i.* **3** ruso (idioma).
rust | rʌst | *s.i.* **1** herrumbre, orín. **2** oxidación. || *adj.* **3** (lit.) rojizo. || *v.i.* **4** oxidarse. || **5 to – away,** oxidarse.
rusted | 'rʌstɪd | *adj.* oxidado.
rustic | 'rʌstɪk | *adj.* **1** rústico, sencillo, sin afectaciones. **2** (desp.) tosco, basto, paleto. **3** rústico: *a rustic chair = una silla rústica.* || *s.c.* **4** paleto, palurdo.
rustle | 'rʌsl | *v.t.* e *i.* **1** susurrar (las hojas). **2** crujir (tejido, hojas secas, papel, etc.). || *v.t.* **3** (EE.UU.) robar (ganado, caballos). || *s.c.* e *i.* **4** susurro. **5** crujido. || **6 to – up,** (fam.) improvisar, preparar rápidamente (una comida).
rustling | 'rʌslɪŋ | *s.c.* susurro; crujido.
rusty | 'rʌstɪ | *adj.* **1** oxidado. **2** rojizo. **3** (fig.) falto de uso, falto de práctica. **4** (fig.) desentrenado.
rut | rʌt | *s.c.* **1** rodada (señal que deja la rueda de un vehículo). **2** (fig.) rutina: *you have to get out of the rut = tienes que salir de la rutina.* || *s.sing.* **3** celo (de un animal macho).
ruthless | 'ruːθlɪs | *adj.* despiadado, cruel; implacable.
ruthlessly | 'ruːθlɪslɪ | *adv.* implacablemente; de forma despiadada.
ruthlessness | 'ruːθlɪsnɪs | *s.i.* **1** crueldad. **2** fiereza.
rutted | 'rʌtɪd | *adj.* lleno de baches: *a rutted road = una carretera llena de baches.*
rye | raɪ | *s.i.* **1** BOT. centeno. || **2 – bread,** GAST. pan de centeno. **3 – whiskey,** whisky de centeno.
ryegrass | raɪgrɑːs | (también **rye grass**) *s.i.* BOT. especie de hierba para pasto.

s, S | es | *s.c.* s, S (decimonovena letra del alfabeto inglés).

Sabbath | 'sæbəθ | *s.sing.* **[the –]** REL. el Sábado, el día del Señor.

sabbatical | sə'bætɪkl | *adj.* **1** (form.) REL. sabatino. **2** sabático (período de tiempo libre para la investigación). || *s.c.* **3** permiso sabático (de duración distinta). || **4 on –,** de período sabático.

saber V. **sabre.**

sable | 'seɪbl | [*pl.* **sables** o **sable**] *s.c.* e *i.* ZOOL. marta (animal o piel). || *adj.* **2** (form.) lúgubre, oscuro, tenebroso.

sabotage | 'sæbətɑːʒ | *s.i.* **1** sabotaje. || *v.t.* **2** sabotear (reunión o construcciones como puentes, ferrocarriles, etc.).

saboteur | ˌsæbə'tɜː*r* | *s.c.* saboteador.

sabre | 'seɪbə*r* | (EE.UU. **saber**) *s.c.* **1** sable. **2** DEP. espada ligera (en la esgrima).

sac | sæk | *s.c.* BIOL. saco, bolsa (parte anatómica de animales o plantas).

saccharine | 'sækəriːn | *s.i.* **1** (también **saccharin**) QUIM. sacarina. || *adj.* **2** (desp. y fig.) empalagoso, sentimentaloide (historia, película, etc.).

sachet | 'sæʃeɪ | *s.c.* **1** (brit.) sobre (con medicina); saquito, bolsita. **2** perfumador, ambientador (puesto en un saquito).

sack | sæk | *s.c.* **1** saco, costal, talego. || *s.sing.* **2** saqueo (después de una derrota). **3 [the –]** (fam. y EE.UU.) la cama. || *v.t.* **4** despedir (del trabajo). **5** saquear. || **6 to get the –,** ser despedido (del trabajo). **7 to give the –,** (fam.) despedir, echar (del trabajo).

sackcloth | sækkɒθ | *s.i.* **1** arpillera, tela de saco. || **2 – and ashes,** (p.u.) penitencia pública, penitencia exterior pública (con vestido de tela de saco y cenizas en la cabeza).

sacking | 'sækɪŋ | *s.i.* **1** arpillera (tejido o material). || *s.c.* **2** despido (del trabajo). **3** saqueo (de una ciudad).

sackload | 'sækləʊd | *s.c.* saco (contenido).

sacrament | 'sækrəmənt | REL. *s.c.* **1** sacramento. || **2 the Blessed/Holy Sacrament,** el sacramento de la Comunión.

sacred | 'seɪkrɪd | *adj.* **1** REL. sagrado, consagrado. **2** (fig.) sagrado, solemne. || **3 a – cow,** (desp.) tema intocable, persona intocable.

sacredly | 'seɪkrɪdlɪ | *adj.* **1** REL. sagradamente. **2** (fig.) solemnemente.

sacredness | 'seɪcrɪdnɪs | *s.i.* **1** REL. santidad, carácter sagrado. **2** (fig.) solemnidad; inviolabilidad.

sacrifice | 'sækrɪfaɪs | *s.c.* e *i.* **1** sacrificio, inmolación. **2** (fig.) renuncia, sacrificio. || *v.t.* **3** sacrificar, inmolar (animal, víctima propiciatoria, etc.). **4** (fig.) renunciar, sacrificar: *her parents sacrificed everything to give her a career = sus padres renunciaron a todo para darle una carrera.*

sacrificial | ˌsækrɪ'fɪʃl | *adj.* de sacrificio, inmolatorio, sacrificatorio.

sacrilege | 'sækrɪlɪdʒ | *s.i.* sacrilegio, profanación.

sacrilegious | ˌsækrɪ'lɪdʒəs | *adj.* sacrílego; irreverente.

sacrilegiously | ˌsækrɪ'lɪdʒəslɪ | *adv.* sacrílegamente.

sacristy | 'sækrɪstɪ | *s.c.* (normalmente *sing.*) REL. sacristía.

sacrosanct | 'sækrəʊsæŋkt | *adj.* sacrosanto, inviolable.

sad | sæd | [*comp.* **sadder,** *super.* **saddest**] *adj.* **1** triste, abatido. **2** deplorable, lamentable (estado, condición, situación, etc.): *this once prosperous town is now in a sad state = esta ciudad antaño próspera está ahora en un estado lamentable.* **3** desgraciado, desdichado (historia, suceso, noticia, etc.). || **4 – to say,** desgraciadamente, la triste verdad es que (especialmente al principio de una frase). **5 sadder but wiser,** más triste pero con más experiencia (después de una desgracia o similar).

sadden | 'sædn | *v.t.* entristecer, afligir, apenar.

saddened | 'sædnd | *adj.* entristecido, afligido, apenado.

saddening | 'sædənɪŋ | *adj.* triste, doloroso, acongojante.

saddle | 'sædl | *s.c.* **1** silla de montar, montura. **2** sillín, asiento (de bicicleta o moto). **3** GEOL. puerto, paso (entre dos montañas). || *s.c.* e *i.* **4 [– of]** lomo, cuarto trasero (de un animal, para comer). || *v.t.* **5** ensillar (caballo). **6 [to –** *o.* **+ with]** cargar con (un problema, responsabilidad, obligación, etc.): *he saddled me with the whole thing = él me cargó con todo el asunto.* || **7 in the –, a)** a caballo, montado, en la silla; **b)** (fig.) en el poder, en situación de control, en el puesto de mando. **8 to – up,** ensillar, poner la montura a.

saddlebag | 'sædlbæg | *s.c.* alforja, maletín de grupa.

saddler | 'sædlə*r* | *s.c.* talabartero, sillero, especialista en monturas.

sadism | 'seɪdɪzəm | *s.i.* PSIC. sadismo.

sadist | 'seɪdɪst | *s.c.* sadista.

sadistic | sə'dɪstɪk | *adj.* sádico, depravado; perverso.

sadistically | sə'dɪstɪklɪ | *adv.* sádicamente, depravadamente; perversamente.

sadly | 'sædlɪ | *adv.* **1** tristemente, abatidamente. **2** deplorablemente, lamentablemente.

sadness | 'sædnɪs | *s.i.* **1** tristeza, abatimiento. **2** desdicha, desgracia (suceso triste).

safari | sə'fɑːrɪ | *s.c.* **1** safari. || **2 on –,** de safari. **3 – park,** parque de animales, "safari park".

safe | seɪf | *adj.* **1 [– (from)]** a salvo, seguro, fuera de peligro, exento de daño: *thank God everybody is safe = gracias a Dios todos están a salvo.* **2** inofensivo, inocuo (algo). **3** ileso, indemne: *she arrived back safe from her trip = llegó ilesa del viaje.* **4 [– (with)]** a salvo, seguro (un secreto): *don't worry, your story is safe with me = no te preocupes, tu historia está segura conmigo.* **5** prudente, cauteloso (forma de comportarse): *a safe way to deal with a gangster = una forma prudente de tratar con un gangster.* **6** sin daños; adecuado (entrega de algún producto). **7** seguro, digno de credibilidad (comentario). || *s.c.* **8** caja fuerte; (Am.) caja de fierro. || **9 a – seat,** (brit.) POL. un escaño seguro. **10 to be on the – side,** para mayor seguridad. **11 in – hands,** en manos seguras. **12 to play (it) –,** (fam.) actuar con precaución. **13 – and sound,** totalmente a salvo, sano y salvo. **14 – deposit,** cámara de seguridad (normalmente en un banco). **15 – house,** casa refugio (especialmente para criminales que escapan de la justicia).

safe-conduct | ˌseɪf'kɒndəkt | *s.c.* e *i.* salvoconducto.
safeguard | 'seɪfgɑːd | *s.c.* **1 [– (against)]** salvaguardia, protección, garantía (regla, ley, etc.). || *v.t.* **2** salvaguardar, proteger, garantizar.
safekeeping | 'seɪfkiːpɪŋ | *s.i.* custodia, protección.
safely | 'seɪflɪ | *adv.* **1** sin ningún daño, sin percances: *they arrived safely = llegaron sin percances.* **2** sin desperfectos, sin ningún obstáculo (envío de productos). **3** con seguridad, con total seguridad, totalmente a salvo: *my money is safely kept = mi dinero está guardado con total seguridad.* **4** sin posibilidad de error (comentario). **5** inocuamente, sin peligro, inofensivamente (especialmente para la salud). **6** irremediablemente, definitivamente (expresando la irreversibilidad de una situación).
safety | 'seɪftɪ | *s.i.* **1** seguridad (estado). **2** asilo, refugio, abrigo (lugar). **3** inocuidad, cualidad de inofensivo (de un producto). **4** de seguridad (sistema, medidas, aspectos, etc.). || **5 – curtain,** cortina de seguridad, telón de seguridad, cortina a prueba de fuego. **6 – glass,** cristal de seguridad. **7 – lamp,** lámpara de seguridad (en minería). **8 – match,** cerilla de seguridad. **9 – razor,** cuchilla de seguridad.
safety-belt | 'seɪftɪbelt | *s.c.* cinturón de seguridad.
safety-catch | 'seɪftɪkætʃ | *s.c.* **1** seguro (de un arma). **2** dispositivo de seguridad (en una ventana, puerta, etc.).
safety-net | 'seɪftɪnet | *s.c.* **1** red de seguridad. **2** (fig.) protección, garantía, red.
safety-pin | 'seɪftɪpɪn | *s.c.* **1** imperdible. **2** anilla (de una granada).
safety-valve | 'seɪftɪvælv | *s.c.* **1** válvula de seguridad, válvula de escape (en una máquina o similar). **2** (fig.) escape (de sentimientos, pasiones, etc.).
saffron | 'sæfrən | *s.i.* **1** BOT. azafrán. || *adj.* **2** azafranado, amarillo, color azafrán.
sag | sæg | [*ger.* **sagging,** *pret.* y *p.p.* **sagged**] *v.i.* **1** combarse, hundirse. **2** flaquear, aflojarse, ceder (ánimo, precio, etc.). || *s.c.* **3** hundimiento, comba (físicamente).
saga | 'sɑːgə | *s.c.* **1** LIT. saga (nórdica), epopeya. **2** (fig.) saga, historia interminable.
sagacious | sə'geɪʃəs | *adj.* (form.) sagaz, astuto, perspicaz.
sagaciously | sə'geɪʃəslɪ | *adv.* (form.) sagazmente, astutamente, perspicazmente.
sagacity | sə'gæsətɪ | *s.i.* (form.) sagacidad, astucia, perspicacia.
sage | seɪdʒ | *s.c.* **1** (lit.) sabio (hombre). || *adj.* **2** (lit.) sabio. || *s.c.* **3** BOT. salvia.
sagely | 'seɪdʒlɪ | *adv.* sabiamente.
sago | 'seɪgəʊ | *s.i.* BOT. sagú.
sahib | sɑːhɪb | *s.c.* sahib, señor (título reverencial de la India).
said | sed | *pret.* y *p.p.irreg.* de **say.**
sail | seɪl | *s.c.* **1** MAR. vela (de barco). **2** aspa (de un molino). || *s.sing.* **3** viaje en barco, paseo en barco. || *v.t.* e *i.* **4** viajar en barco, viajar por el mar, navegar por. || *v.i.* **5** navegar, viajar (por el mar). **6** deslizarse, moverse suavemente, desplazarse. || **7 to – close to the wind,** V. **wind. 8 to – through,** hacer algo sin dificultad alguna: *the interview for the job was difficult, but she sailed through it = la entrevista para el trabajo era difícil, pero ella lo hizo sin dificultad alguna.* **9 to set –,** MAR. zarpar. **10 to take the wind out of someone's sails,** V. **wind. 11 under –,** en barco con velas, a vela.
sailcloth | 'seɪlklɒθ | *s.i.* **1** lona (de tiendas de campaña, velas, etc.). **2** lona ligera (para ropa).
sailing | 'seɪlɪŋ | *s.c.* **1** viaje en barco, travesía. || *s.i.* **2** DEP. vela, navegación a vela. || **3 plain –,** coser y cantar, facilísimo.
sailing-boat | 'seɪlɪŋbəʊt | *s.c.* MAR. barco de vela.
sailing-ship | 'seɪlɪŋʃɪp | *s.c.* MAR. velero, buque de vela.
sailor | 'seɪlər | *s.c.* **1** marinero. || **2 a good/bad –,** (fig.) persona que no se marea/persona que se marea. **3 – hat,** sombrero de marinero. **4 – suit,** traje de marinero (de niños).
saint | seɪnt | *s.c.* **1** REL. santo. **2** (fig.) santo, persona pacientísima, bendito.
sainted | 'seɪntɪd | *adj.* (p.u. o hum.) santo, bendito.
sainthood | 'seɪnthʊd | *s.i.* santidad.
saintliness | 'seɪntlɪnɪs | *s.i.* santidad (como virtud).
saintly | 'seɪntlɪ | *adj.* piadoso; virtuoso.
sake | seɪk | **1 for God's/heaven's –,** por el amor de Dios, por lo que más quieras, por Dios. **2 for its own –,** por su valor en sí mismo, porque sí. **3 for someone's –,** a causa de alguien, por el interés de alguien, para beneficio de alguien, para mejora de alguien. **4 for the – of,** por motivo de, por el bien de.
salaam | sə'lɑːm | *s.c.* **1** reverencia (típica del mundo musulmán). || *v.i.* **2** hacer reverencias. || *interj.* **3** la paz contigo, paz.
salable V. **saleable.**
salacious | sə'leɪʃəs | *adj.* (desp.) salaz, obsceno, escabroso, indecente.
salaciously | sə'leɪʃəslɪ | *adv.* (desp.) escabrosamente, indecentemente.
salaciousness | sə'leɪʃəsnɪs | *s.i.* (desp.) obscenidad, escabrosidad, indecencia.
salad | 'sæləd | *s.c.* e *i.* **1** ensalada; lechuga. **2** GAST. comida fría a base de ensalada. || **3 one's – days,** (lit.) juventud inexperta, período de inexperiencia juvenil. **4 – dressing,** GAST. aliño para ensaladas.
salamander | 'sæləmændər | *s.c.* ZOOL. salamandra.
salami | sə'lɑːmɪ | *s.i.* GAST. embutido, salami.
salaried | 'sælərɪd | *adj.* asalariado, con salario.
salary | 'sælərɪ | *adj.* asalariado, con salario.
salary | 'sælərɪ | *s.c.* e *i.* salario (mensual).
sale | seɪl | *s.c.* **1** venta. **2** rebajas, liquidación, venta de oportunidades. **3** subasta. || *s.pl.* **4** COM. volumen de ventas. **5** COM. ventas, sección de ventas (en una empresa). || **6 for –/up for –,** en venta, a la venta. **7 –,** a la venta (en tiendas). **8 sales talk,** argumento de venta, palabrería de ventas, animación típica de una venta.
saleable | 'seɪləbl | *adj.* fácil de vender, vendible.
sale-room | 'seɪlruːm | *s.c.* sala de subastas.
sales-clerk | 'seɪlsklɑːk | *s.c.* (EE.UU.) vendedor, dependiente.
salesgirl | 'seɪlsgɜːl | *s.c.* dependienta.
salesman | 'seɪlsmən | [*pl.irreg.* **salesmen**] *s.c.* vendedor (especialmente viajante).
salesmanship | 'seɪlsmənʃɪp | *s.i.* arte de la venta, arte de vender.
salesmen | 'seɪlsmən | *pl.irreg.* de **salesman.**
salesperson | 'seɪlspəːsn | [*pl.* **salespersons** o **salespeople**] *s.c.* vendedor (como dependiente o viajante).
saleswoman | 'seɪlswʊmən | [*pl.irreg.* **saleswomen**] *s.c.* dependienta, vendedora (especialmente en una tienda).
saleswomen | 'seɪlswɪmɪn | *pl.irreg.* de **saleswoman.**
salient | 'seɪlɪənt | (form.) *adj.* **1** sobresaliente, destacado, notable. || *s.c.* **2** ARQ. saliente.
saline | 'seɪlaɪn | (EE.UU.) | 'seɪliːn | *adj.* (form.) salino.
salinity | sə'lɪnɪtɪ | *s.i.* (form.) salinidad.
saliva | sə'laɪvə | *s.i.* saliva.
salivary | 'sælɪvərɪ | (EE.UU.) | 'sæləverɪ | *adj.* **1** de la saliva. || **2 – gland,** ANAT. glándula salival.
salivate | 'sælɪveɪt | *v.i.* (form.) salivar, producir saliva.
sallow | 'sæləʊ | *adj.* **1** amarillento, pálido, descolorido (de apariencia). || *s.c.* **2** BOT. sauce cabruno.
sallowness | 'sæləʊnɪs | *s.i.* palidez, amarillez.
sally | 'sælɪ | *s.c.* **1** (p.u.) MIL. salida, salida sorpresa (ataque). **2** (lit.) chiste, gracia. || **3 to – forth/out,** (p.u.) salir decididamente, salir energéticamente: *we sallied forth into the cold night = salimos decididamente en la fría noche.*
salmon | 'sæmən | [*pl.* **salmon**] *s.c.* e *i.* ZOOL. salmón.
salmonella | ˌsælmə'nelə | *s.i.* MED. salmonela.
salon | 'sælɒn | (EE.UU.) | sə'lɒn | *s.c.* **1** salón (de belleza, peluquería, etc.). **2** tienda, boutique (especialmente de ropa de última moda). **3** salón (en una casa señorial). **4** HIST. reunión literaria, tertulia literaria.
saloon | sə'luːn | *s.c.* **1** turismo. **2** MAR. bar, salón. **3** (EE.UU.) bar. || **4 – bar,** (brit.) bar (parte de un "pub" muy cómoda y cuidada).
salt | sɔːlt | *s.i.* **1** sal. || *adj.* **2** salino. || *v.t.* **3** GAST. salar. **4** echar sal (en las carreteras, contra la nieve). || *s.pl.* **5** sales (medicinales). || **6 to rub – into someone's wounds,** echar sal en la herida de alguien, poner sal en las llagas de alguien; empeorar la situación de alguien. **7 to – away,** (fam.) atesorar, acumular en secreto (dinero). **8 to take something with a pinch/grain of –,** (fam.) aceptar algo con muchas reservas; tener fuertes dudas sobre algo. **9 the – of the earth,** (fig.) la sal de la tierra, los mejores.
salted | 'sɔːltɪd | *adj.* salado, con sal.
salt-cellar | 'sɔːlt ˌselər | *s.c.* salero.
saltiness | 'sɔːltɪnɪs | *s.i.* sabor a sal, salinidad, salobridad.
saltpetre | sɔːlt'piːtər | (EE.UU. **saltpeter**) *s.i.* salitre.
saltwater | 'sɔːltwɔːtər | *s.i.* **1** agua salada, agua de mar. || *adj.* **2** de mar (especialmente referido a animales).
salty | 'sɔːltɪ | *adj.* salado, salobre.
salubrious | sə'luːbrɪəs | *adj.* (form.) sano, saludable, salubre (especialmente el clima).

salubriousness | sə'luːbrɪəsnɪs | *s.i.* (form.) salubridad (especialmente el clima).

salutary | 'sæljʊtrɪ | (EE.UU.) | 'sæljuterɪ | *adj.* beneficioso, provechoso; saludable: *salutary exercise = ejercicio saludable.*

salutation | ˌsæljuː'teɪʃn | (form. o p.u.) *s.c.* e *i.* **1** saludo (acción o palabra). || *s.c.* **2** saludo introductorio, saludo de encabezamiento (de una carta).

salute | sə'luːt | *s.c.* **1** MIL. saludo. **2 [– to]** (form.) tributo a, homenaje a; elogio de. || *v.t.* e *i.* **3** MIL. saludar. || *v.t.* **4** tributar un homenaje, homenajear; elogiar. || **5 to take the –,** pasar revista, presidir un desfile militar.

salvage | 'sælvɪdʒ | *v.t.* **1** rescatar, recuperar, salvar (cosas o situaciones). || *s.i.* **2** salvamento, rescate (de cosas). **3** objetos salvados, objetos recuperados; material reutilizable (de un desastre).

salvation | sæl'veɪʃn | *s.i.* **1** REL. salvación. **2** salvación, rescate: *you are my salvation = eres mi salvación.* || **3 Salvation Army,** REL. Ejército de Salvación (organización cristiana de ayuda a los pobres).

salve | sælv | (EE.UU.) | sæv | *s.i.* **1** ungüento, pomada, bálsamo. || **2 to – one's conscience,** (form.) tranquilizar la conciencia de uno, apaciguar la conciencia de uno.

salver | 'sælvər | *s.c.* bandeja (normalmente de plata y utilizada para traer cartas, mensajes, bebidas, etc.).

salvo | 'sælvəʊ | *s.c.* **1** MIL. salva. **2 [– of]** (fig.) salva de, estallido de (risas, aplausos, etc.).

Samaritan | sə'mærɪtən | *s.c.* samaritano, persona compasiva.

samba | 'sæmbə | *s.c.* MUS. samba.

same | seɪm | *adj.* **1 [the – (as)]** el mismo, la misma, los mismos, las mismas: *the same face as her mother = la misma cara que su madre.* || *pron.* **2 [the – (as)]** el mismo, la misma, lo mismo, los mismos, las mismas: *I'll do the same = yo haré lo mismo.* **3** (form.) el mismo, lo mismo, la misma, los mismos, las mismas: *painting of the doors and polishing of same, 50 $ = pintar las puertas y una capa de abrillantador en las mismas, 50 $.* || **4 all the –/just the –,** a pesar de todo, no obstante, con todo. **5 at the – time,** V. **time. 6 by the – token,** V. **token. 7 in the – boat,** V. **boat. 8 in the – breath,** V. **breath. 9 in the – way,** V. **way. 10 it's all the – to me,** (fam.) a mí me da lo mismo, me da igual, no tengo una especial preferencia. **11 not to be the – (as),** no ser lo mismo (que), no ser igual (a): *frozen food is not the same as food cooked at home = la comida congelada no es lo mismo que la comida hecha en casa.* **12 one and the –,** exactamente el mismo, exactamente lo mismo: *the person you and I are talking about is one and the same = la persona de la que estamos los dos hablando es exactamente la misma.* **13 – again,** (fam.) lo mismo (repitiendo la consumición). **14 – difference,** (fam.) qué más da, es igual, no significa ninguna diferencia (después de haber sido corregido en una conversación). **15 – here,** (fam.) yo digo lo mismo, pienso igual, lo mismo digo. **16 – to you,** (fam.) y tú igual, y tú más (contestando a un insulto). **17 thanks all the –,** gracias de todas formas, gracias de todos modos. **18 the –/the very –,** (form.) el mismo, la misma (confirmando la identidad sobre una persona): *is she the famous writer? the very same = ¿es ella la famosa escritora? la misma.* **19 the – old story,** V. **story. 20 the – as,** (fam.) igual que, lo mismo que: *Spain is having financial troubles the same as England is finding it difficult to repay debts = España está sufriendo problemas financieros igual que Inglaterra está viendo difícil poder hacer frente a las deudas.*

sameness | 'seɪmnɪs | *s.i.* (desp.) monotonía, igualdad repetitiva.

samovar | 'sæməʊvɑːr | *s.c.* samovar (instrumento para hacer té en Rusia).

sampan | 'sæmpæn | *s.c.* MAR. sampán (barco chino).

sample | 'sɑːmpl | (EE.UU.) | 'sæmpl | *s.c.* **1** muestra, ejemplar, espécimen; modelo. **2** muestreo (entre personas, para estadísticas). || *v.t.* **3** catar (comida o bebida). **4** probar, comprobar (un lugar, situación, etc.): *my students need to sample life in Anglosaxon country = mis estudiantes necesitan probar la vida real en un país anglosajón.*

sampler | 'sɑːmplər | (EE.UU.) | 'sæmplə | *s.c.* dechado en labores.

samurai | 'sæmʊraɪ | [*pl.* **samurai**] *s.c.* samurai.

sanatoria | ˌsænə'tɔːrɪə | *pl.* de **sanatorium.**

sanatorium | ˌsænə'tɔːrɪəm | (EE.UU. **sanitarium**) [*pl.* **sanatoriums** o **sanatoria**] *s.c.* sanatorio.

sanctify | 'sæŋktɪfaɪ | *v.t.* **1** santificar; declarar santo, declarar sagrado. **2** (fig.) sancionar, aprobar totalmente (una práctica, costumbre, etc.).

sanctimonious | ˌsæŋktɪ'məʊ | | nɪəs | *adj.* (desp.) beato, santurrón, mojigato.

sanctimoniously | ˌsæŋktɪ'məʊnɪəslɪ | *adv.* (desp.) a la manera de un santurrón, de un beato, con mojitería.

sanctimoniousness | ˌsæŋktɪ'məʊnɪəs | | nɪs | *s.i.* (desp.) beatería, santurronería.

sanction | 'sæŋkʃn | *v.t.* **1** sancionar, autorizar, aprobar (especialmente cuando ocurre de manera oficial). || *s.c.* **2** medida, remedio, arma (de castigo): *is beating the best sanction against indiscipline? = ¿es una paliza la mejor medida contra la indisciplina?* || *s.i.* **3** autorización, sanción, aprobación (especialmente oficial). || *s.pl.* **4 [– (on/against)]** sanciones, medidas disuasorias.

sanctity | 'sæŋktɪtɪ | *s.i.* **[– (of)]** inviolabilidad; santidad: *the sanctity of human life = la inviolabilidad de la vida humana.*

sanctuary | 'sæŋktʃʊərɪ | (EE.UU.) | 'sæŋktʃuerɪ | *s.c.* **1** santuario, refugio sagrado, refugio seguro. **2** BIOL. santuario, área de protección animal. || *s.i.* **3** asilo, santuario, refugio.

sand | sænd | *s.i.* **1** arena. || *s.pl.* **2** arenal. || *v.t.* **3** lijar. || **4 – castle,** castillo de arena (en la playa especialmente). **5 to – down,** lijar totalmente, dejar liso a base de lijar.

sandal | 'sændl | *s.c.* sandalia.

sandalwood | 'sændlwʊd | *s.i.* sándalo.

sandbag | 'sændbæg | *s.c.* **1** saco de arena (especialmente como defensa militar). || *v.t.* **2** proteger con sacos de arena.

sandbank | 'sændbæŋk | *s.c.* GEOL. banco de arena.

sander | 'sændər | *s.c.* lijadora (aparato).

sandiness | 'sændɪnɪs | *s.i.* arenosidad.

sandpaper | 'sændpeɪpər | *s.i.* **1** lija, papel de lija. || *v.t.* **2** lijar con papel lija.

sandpit | 'sændpɪt | *s.c.* (brit.) pozo de arena para jugar los niños.

sandstone | 'sændstəʊn | *s.i.* GEOL. piedra arenisca.

sandstorm | 'sændstɔːm | *s.c.* tormenta de arena.

sandwich | 'sænwɪdʒ | (EE.UU.) | 'sænwɪtʃ | *s.c.* **1** bocadillo, sandwich. **2 [– of]** (fig.) capa pequeña de, tira de, panel mínimo de (entre dos cosas). || *v.t.* **3** meter en medio, insertar, intercalar. **4** apretujar, aplastar (entre dos elementos): *I was sandwiched between two fat girls = quedé aplastado entre dos chicas gordas.* || **5 – board,** cartelón doble, anuncio de dos tablones. **6 – course,** curso de combinación de prácticas con el estudio, curso de clases y prácticas consecutivas. **7 – man,** hombre anuncio.

sandy | 'sændɪ | *adj.* **1** arenoso, lleno de arena. **2** rojizo (color del pelo).

sane | seɪn | *adj.* **1** cuerdo, en su sano juicio. **2** sensato, razonable.

sanely | 'seɪnlɪ | *adv.* **1** cuerdamente. **2** sensatamente, razonablemente.

sang | sæŋ | *pret.irreg.* de **sing.**

sang-froid | ˌsɒŋ'frwɑː | *s.i.* (form.) sangre fría, serenidad, autodominio.

sanguinary | 'sæŋgwɪnərɪ | (EE.UU.) | 'sæŋgwɪnerɪ | *adj.* (form. y p.u.) **1** sanguinario (persona). **2** sangriento (hecho).

sanguine | 'sæŋgwɪn | *adj.* (form.) **1** optimista, entusiasta, lleno de esperanza. **2** rojo, colorado (en la cara).

sanguinely | 'sæŋgwɪnlɪ | *adv.* (form.) de forma optimista, entusiástica.

sanguineness | 'sæŋgwɪnnɪs | *s.i.* (form.) **1** optimismo, entusiasmo. **2** apariencia rojiza (de la cara).

sanitarium | ˌsænə'teərɪəm | V. **sanatorium.**

sanitary | 'sænɪtrɪ | (EE.UU.) | 'sænɪtərɪ | *adj.* **1** sanitario, higiénico. **2** sanitario, de la salud, de la sanidad. || **3 – napkin,** (EE.UU.) compresa. **4 – towel/pad,** compresa.

sanitation | ˌsænɪ'teɪʃn | *s.i.* higiene, sanidad, sanidad pública.

sanity | 'sænɪtɪ | *s.i.* **1** cordura, sanidad mental. **2** sensatez, moderación, buen juicio.

sank | sæŋk | *pret.irreg.* de **sink.**

Sanskrit | 'sænskrɪt | *s.i.* sánscrito (idioma clásico de la India).

Santa Claus | 'sæntəklɔːz | *s.sing.* Santa Claus, Papá Noel.

sap | sæp | [*ger.* **sapping,** *pret.* y *p.p.* **sapped**] *v.t.* **1** agotar, consumir, debilitar, socavar, minar (fuerzas, energías, confianza, seguridad, etc.). || *s.i.* **2** BOT. savia. || *s.c.* **3** MIL. zapa.

sapling | 'sæplɪŋ | *s.c.* BOT. árbol joven.

sapphire | 'sæfaɪər | *s.c.* **1** MIN. zafiro. || *s.i.* **2** color zafiro.

sarcasm | 'sɑːkæzəm | *s.i.* sarcasmo.

sarcastic | sɑː'kæstɪk | *adj.* sarcástico.

sarcastically | sɑː'kæstɪklɪ | *adv.* sarcásticamente.

sarcophagi | sɑː'kɒfəgaɪ | *pl.* de **sarcophagus.**

sarcophagus | sɑː'kɒfəgəs | [*pl.* **sarcophaguses** o **sarcophagi**] *s.c.* sarcófago.

sardine | sɑː'diːn | *s.c.* **1** ZOOL. sardina. || **2 packed like sardines,** (fam.) apretujados como sardinas.

sardonic | sɑː'dɒnɪk | *adj.* burlón, sarcástico, irónico (con desprecio).

sardonically | sɑː'dɒnɪklɪ | *adv.* burlonamente, sarcásticamente, irónicamente (con cierto desprecio).

sartorial | sɑː'tɔːrɪəl | *adj.* (form.) elegante (especialmente hombres).

sartorially | sɑː'tɔːrɪəlɪ | *adv.* (form.) con elegancia.

sash | sæʃ | *s.c.* **1** fajín, faja (especialmente militar). **2** marco (de ventana de guillotina). || **3 – cord,** cuerda de contrapeso de ventana (de guillotina). **4 – window,** ventana de guillotina.

sat | sæt | *pret.* y *p.p.irreg.* de **sit.**

Satan | 'seɪtn | *s.sing.* REL. Satanás.

satanic | sə'tænɪk | (EE.UU.) | seɪ'tænɪk | *adj.* **1** REL. satánico. **2** diabólico, lleno de maldad.

satchel | 'sætʃəl | *s.c.* cartera (del colegio).

sated | seɪtɪd | *adj.* (form.) saciado, lleno, harto (de comida, placer, etc.).

satellite | 'sætəlaɪt | *s.c.* **1** ASTR. satélite. **2** ELECTR. satélite. **3** POL. satélite, país satélite. || **4 by –,** vía satélite, mediante satélite.

satiate | 'seɪʃɪeɪt | *v.t.* (form.) saciar, hartar, hastiar, saturar.

satiety | sə'taɪətɪ | *s.i.* (form.) saciedad, hartura.

satin | 'sætɪn | (EE.UU.) | 'sætn | *s.i.* **1** satén, raso. || *adj.* **2** de satén, de raso.

satire | 'sætaɪər | *s.i.* **1** LIT. sátira. **2** sátira.

satirical | sə'tɪrɪkl | *adj.* satírico.

satirically | sə'tɪrɪklɪ | *adv.* satíricamente.

satirist | 'sætərɪst | *s.c.* escritor satírico.

satirize | 'sætəraɪz | (también **satirise**) *v.t.* satirizar.

satisfaction | ˌsætɪs'fækʃn | *s.i.* **1** satisfacción, contento. **2** compensación económica, indemnización (por alguna injusticia). || **3 to someone's –,** a gusto de alguien, para contento de alguien: *the maid didn't do everything to my satisfaction = la criada no lo hizo todo a mi gusto.*

satisfactorily | ˌsætɪs'fæktərɪlɪ | *adv.* satisfactoriamente, adecuadamente, de modo satisfactorio.

satisfactory | ˌsætɪs'fæktərɪ | *adj.* satisfactorio, adecuado.

satisfied | 'sætɪsfaɪd | *adj.* **1** satisfecho, contento. **2** convencido: *I'm satisfied that you've done your best = estoy convencido de que has hecho todo lo posible.*

satisfy | 'sætɪsfaɪ | *v.t.* **1** satisfacer, llenar (comida, diversión, etc.). **2** convencer; complacer: *what you've explained satisfies me = lo que has explicado me convence.* **3** llenar, cumplir (requisitos). || *v.r.* **4** convencerse; quedar convencido.

satisfying | 'sætɪsfaɪɪŋ | *adj.* satisfactorio, que satisface.

satisfyingly | 'sætɪsfaɪɪŋlɪ | *adv.* satisfactoriamente.

saturate | 'sætʃəreɪt | *v.t.* **1** llenar hasta arriba, colmar, saturar. **2** (normalmente *pas.*) saturar, empapar (con líquido). **3** QUIM. disolver.

saturation | ˌsætʃə'reɪʃn | *s.i.* **1** saturación. **2** QUIM. disolución. **3** MIL. saturación (forma de bombardear). || **4 – point,** punto de saturación.

Saturday | 'sætədɪ | *s.c.* e *i.* sábado.

saturnine | 'sætənaɪn | *adj.* (form.) triste, melancólico.

satyr | 'sætər | *s.c.* (lit.) sátiro.

sauce | sɔːs | *s.i.* **1** salsa (culinaria). || *s.sing.* **2** (fam.) caradura, frescura: *he had the sauce to insult me = tuvo la cara dura de insultarme.*

sauce-boat | 'sɔːsbəut | *s.c.* salsera.

saucepan | 'sɔːspən | (EE.UU.) | 'sɔːspæn | *s.c.* cacerola, cazuela, cazo.

saucer | 'sɔːsər | *s.c.* **1** platillo (acompañante de taza). **2** TV. platillo (cualquier objeto con esa forma).

saucily | 'sɔːsɪlɪ | *adv.* (fam.) descaradamente, insolentemente, impertinentemente, con frescura.

sauciness | 'sɔːsɪnɪs | *s.i.* (fam.) descaro, insolencia, frescura, impertinencia.

saucy | 'sɔːsɪ | *adj.* (fam.) descarado, insolente, fresco, impertinente.

Saudi | 'saudɪ | *s.c.* **1** saudí, saudita. || *adj.* **2** saudí, saudita.

Saudi Arabia | ˌsaudɪə'reɪbɪə | *s.sing.* Arabia Saudita.

Saudi Arabian | ˌsaudɪə'reɪbɪən | *s.c.* **1** saudí, saudita. || *adj.* **2** saudí, saudita.

sauerkraut | 'sauəkraut | *s.i.* GAST. chucrut, col en salmuera.

sauna | 'sɔːnə | *s.c.* sauna (la acción y el baño).

saunter | 'sɔːntər | *v.i.* **1** pasear tranquilamente, pasear despacio. || *s.c.* **2** paseo tranquilo, paseo relajado.

sausage | 'sɒsɪdʒ | (EE.UU.) | 'sɔːsɪdʒ | *s.c.* e *i.* **1** salchicha. || **2 – dog,** (fam.) perro salchicha, perro tejonero. **3 – roll,** GAST. empanada de salchicha.

sauté | 'səuteɪ | (EE.UU.) | səu'teɪ | *v.t.* GAST. saltear.

sautéed | 'səuteɪd | *adj.* GAST. salteado: *sautéed potatoes.*

savage | 'sævɪdʒ | *s.c.* **1** salvaje, bruto. **2** salvaje, primitivo. || *adj.* **3** salvaje, brutal, violento. **4** salvaje, fiero (animal). || *v.t.* **5** atacar mortalmente, herir seriamente. **6** criticar salvajemente.

savagely | 'sævɪdʒlɪ | *adv.* salvajemente, brutalmente, violentamente.

savagery | 'sævɪdʒrɪ | *s.i.* salvajismo, violencia.

savannah | sə'vænə | (también **savanna**) *s.c.* e *i.* GEOG. sabana.

save | seɪv | *v.t.* **1** salvar, rescatar: *to save from death = salvar de la muerte.* **2** guardar, conservar, reservar (cosas): *save some beer for later = guarda algo de cerveza para más tarde.* **3** ahorrar (trabajo a alguien). || *v.t.* e *i.* **4** ahorrar (dinero, energía, tiempo, etc.). **5** REL. salvar. **6** DEP. parar, hacer una parada (el portero). || *v.i.* **7 [to – on]** ahorrar, economizar: *we must save on petrol = debemos ahorrar gasolina.* || *s.c.* **8** DEP. parada. || *prep.* **9** (form.) salvo, menos, con la excepción de, excepto. || **10 – for,** con la excepción de. **11 to – one's life,** (fam.) ni aunque tuviera que hacerlo para salvar la vida de uno, aunque le pusieran a uno una pistola en la sien: *he can't play chess to save his life = no sabe jugar al ajedrez ni aunque tuviera que hacerlo para salvar su vida.* **12 to – up,** ahorrar mucho, hacer grandes economías.

saver | 'seɪvər | *s.c.* **1** ahorrador. || **2 -saver,** que ahorra (en compuestos): *a petrol-saver device = un mecanismo que ahorra gasolina.*

saving | 'seɪvɪŋ | *s.c.* ahorro, economización. || *s.pl.* **2** ahorros (de dinero). || **3 -saving,** ahorro de (en compuestos): *energy-saving = ahorro de energía.* **4 – grace,** virtud, valor (de algo negativo): *the only saving grace in the novel is the style = la única virtud de la novela es el estilo.*

saviour | 'seɪvjər | *s.c.* **1** salvador. || **2 Saviour,** REL. Salvador (título dado a Jesucristo).

savoir-faire | ˌsævwɑː'feər | *s.i.* (form.) saber estar (en sociedad).

savour | 'seɪvər | (EE.UU. **savor**) *v.t.* **1** paladear, saborear. **2** (fig.) saborear (una experiencia placentera). || *s.c.* e *i.* **3** sabor, gusto. || **4 to – of,** tener un regusto de, tener resabios de, oler a (algo negativo).

savoury | 'seɪvərɪ | (EE.UU. **savory**) *adj.* **1** sabroso, apetitoso. **2** [con negativa] moral, decente. || *s.pl.* **3** platitos salados.

saw | sɔː | *pret.irreg.* **1** de **see.** || *s.c.* **2** sierra. **3** (arc.) proverbio, adagio, refrán, dicho. || *v.* [*pret.* **sawed,** *p.p.irreg.* **sawn**] *t.* **4** serrar, aserrar, cortar con sierra. || *i.* **5** cortar con sierra. **6 [to – away]** mover repetidamente, mover continuamente (el brazo en un movimiento sistemático, como el de tocar el violín, por ejemplo). || **7 to – off,** cortar con sierra (un trozo de algo). **8 to – up,** cortar en trozos con una sierra.

sawdust | 'sɔːdʌst | *s.i.* serrín.

sawmill | 'sɔːmɪl | *s.c.* aserradero.

sawn | sɔːn | *p.p.irreg.* **1** de **saw.** || **2 sawn-off shotgun,** escopeta con los cañones recortados.

sax | sæks | *s.c.* (fam.) MUS. saxo.

Saxon | 'sæksn | *adj.* HIST. sajón.

saxophone | 'sæksəfəun | *s.c.* MUS. saxofón.

saxophonist | sæk'sɒfənɪst | *s.c.* MUS. saxofonista.

say | seɪ | *v.t.* [*pret.* y *p.p.irreg.* **said**] **1** decir: *he said that he was going to London soon = dijo que iba a Londres pronto; he said: "shut up!" = él dijo: "¡cállate!".* **2** expresar, señalar, decir: *I want to say that I am thankful for everything = quiero señalar que estoy agradecido por todo.* **3** recitar, decir (de una manera un poco mecánica): *say your prayers = recitad vuestras oraciones.* **4** afirmar, admitir: *I must say I'm tired = debo admitir que estoy cansado.* **5** hablar, decir, expresar (palabras o sonidos): *I couldn't think what to say = no podía pensar qué decir.* **6** decir (una carta, cartel, letrero, etc.). **7** expresar (un sentimiento o similar mediante la expresión de la cara). **8** decir, expresar, comunicar (mediante el arte). || *interj.* **9** (EE.UU.) oye, oiga, eh (llamando la atención). || *s.sing.* **10 [– (in)]** capacidad de intervención, capacidad de decisión; parecer: *I didn't have a say in anything = no tuve capacidad de decisión en nada.* || **11 enough said/– no more,** (fam.) vale, basta, no hace falta decir más. **12 to have a lot to be said for it,** tener todas las ventajas, tener mucho a su favor. **13 to have one's –,** tener derecho a la opinión de uno. **14 to have something to – for oneself,** tener que explicar algo, tener que justificar algo. **15 it goes without saying,** ni que decir tiene, huelga decir, es obvio. **16 I will – this for him/her/etc.,** debo reconocer esto a su favor, debo decir a su favor (algo). **17 I wouldn't – no,** (fam.) no rechazaría, no diría que no a (tomar, sugerir, etc., algo). **18 needless to –,** por supuesto, ni que decir tiene. **19 not to –,** por no decir: *I'll call him stupid, not to say moron = le llamaré estúpido por no decir subnormal.* **20 –, a)** por ejemplo, como ejemplo; **b)** más o menos, aproximadamente. **21 to – a lot about/to – something about,** decir mucho de: *her forlorn look says a lot about her = su aspecto melancólico dice mucho sobre ella.* **22 to – a lot for,** estar a favor de, decir mucho a favor de. **23 to – nothing of,** por no decir, y no digamos, sin mencionar. **24 to – something to oneself,** decir algo a uno mismo, decir para sí mismo. **25 to – the least,** por no decir más; siendo conservadores en el cálculo. **26 – the word,** sólo tienes que decirlo, sólo tienes que pedirlo. **27 – what you like,** dirás que no, vas a decir que no. **28 that is to =N,** es decir. **29 there is no saying,** no hay manera de saber, no hay forma de saber. **30 well said,** bien dicho, muy bien. **31 what would you – to a cup of tea?/etc.,** (fam.) ¿qué te parece la idea de tomar una taza de té?/etc. **32 you can – that again!/you said it!,** (fam.) ¡ya lo creo que es así!, ¡sí señor! (expresando acuerdo total). **33 you don't –,** (fam.) no me digas (expresando sorpresa, normalmente sarcástica).

saying | 'seɪɪŋ | *s.c.* dicho, refrán, comentario común.

say-so | 'seɪsəʊ | *s.sing.* (fam.) permiso, autorización: *nothing can be done here without Jim's say-so = aquí no se puede hacer nada sin el permiso de Jim.*

scab | skæb | *s.c.* **1** costra (de una herida). **2** (desp.) esquirol.

scabbard | 'skæbəd | *s.c.* vaina (de espada).

scabby | 'skæbɪ | *adj.* lleno de costras.

scabies | 'skeɪbiːz | *s.i.* MED. sarna.

scads | skædz | *s.pl.* (fam. y EE.UU.) montones, porrones (de algo).

scaffold | 'skæfəuld | *s.c.* **1** (normalmente *sing.*) patíbulo, cadalso. **2** andamio.

scaffolding | 'skæfəldɪŋ | *s.i.* andamiaje.

scald | skɔːld | *v.t.* **1** quemar, escaldar (con líquido o vapor). **2** escaldar, calentar hasta el punto de ebullición (especialmente en recetas). **3** meter en agua /vapor hirviendo (para limpiar o esterilizar). || **4** quemadura (causada por líquido o vapor).

scalding | 'skɔːldɪŋ | *adj.* **1** hirviendo. || **2 – hot,** ardiendo, extremadamente caliente, hirviendo.

scale | 'skeɪl | *s.sing.* **1** escala, dimensión: *the scale of modern change = la dimensión del cambio moderno.* **2** escalafón, jerarquía: *the social scale = la jerarquía social.* || *s.c.* **3** escala, gradación (numérica). **4** escala salarial. **5** MUS. escala. **6** (normalmente *pl.*) escama (de pez o reptil). **7** platillo (de la balanza). || *s.pl.* **8** balanza, báscula: *a pair of scales = una balanza.* || *s.i.* **9** capa de óxido (que se forma en cacerolas o similar). **10** sarro (en los dientes). || *s.c.* e *i.* **11** escala, proporción (en mapas, maquetas, etc.). || *v.t.* **12** escalar, subir, trepar (montañas). || *adj.* **13** a escala (mapas, maquetas, etc.). || **14 on large –/large in –/etc.,** a gran escala. **15 out of –,** sin proporción, sin escala adecuada. **16 to – down,** disminuir la fuerza, disminuir, debilitar: *we have to scale down the military operations before it's too late = tenemos que disminuir la fuerza de las operaciones militares antes de que sea demasiado tarde.* **17 to –,** según escala, siguiendo unas dimensiones exactas.

scallop | 'skɒləp | *s.c.* **1** (normalmente *pl.*) festón (de adorno en la ropa). **2** (normalmente *pl.*) ZOOL. venera (molusco).

scalloped | 'skɒləpt | *adj.* festoneado (en ropa).

scallywag | 'skælɪwæg | *s.c.* (fam.) tunante, bribón, pillo.

scalp | skælp | *s.c.* **1** ANAT. cuero cabelludo. **2** cabellera (cortada). || *v.t.* **3** cortar la cabellera (práctica de los indios).

scalpel | 'skælpəl | *s.c.* bisturí, escalpelo.

scaly | 'skeɪlɪ | *adj.* escamoso (piel).

scamp | skæmp | *s.c.* (fam.) tunante, diablillo, pícaro (niño).

scamper | 'skæmpər | *v.i.* correr a toda prisa, corretear desenfrenadamente.

scampi | 'skæmpɪ | *s.i.* (brit.) GAST. langostinos rebozados.

scan | skæn | [*ger.* **scanning,** *pret.* y *p.p.* **scanned**] *v.t.* e *i.* **1** examinar, escudriñar, mirar con gran atención y cuidado. **2** echar un vistazo general (a algo escrito). **3** LIT. medir, escandir (poemas). || *v.t.* **4** leer a gran velocidad (mediante un láser, normalmente). **5** explorar, registrar (un radar). || *s.c.* **6** (normalmente *sing.*) exploración, registro (de radar).

scandal | 'skændl | *s.c.* **1** escándalo. || *s.i.* **2** murmuración escandalosa, cotilleo, habladurías. || *s.sing.* **3 [a –]** un escándalo, una desgracia nacional, una pena: *the concert was a scandal = el concierto fue una pena.*

scandalize | 'skændəlaɪz | (también **scandalise**) *v.t.* escandalizar, indignar.

scandalmonger | 'skændlmʌŋgər | *s.c.* (desp.) chismoso, murmurador, propagador de habladurías.

scandalous | 'skændələs | *adj.* **1** escandaloso, inmoral, indignante. **2** vergonzoso, ignominioso: *it's scandalous to have that situation in your own city = es vergonzoso tener una situación tal en tu propia ciudad.*

scandalously | 'skændələslɪ | *adv.* **1** escandalosamente, inmoralmente, indignantemente. **2** vergonzosamente, ignominiosamente.

Scandinavian | ˌskændɪ'neɪvɪən | *adj.* **1** escandinavo. || *s.c.* **2** escandinavo.

scanner | 'skænər | *s.c.* **1** MED. escáner. **2** ELECTR. antena direccional giratoria, antena de exploración.

scant | skænt | *adj.* escaso, exiguo.

scantily | 'skæntɪlɪ | *adv.* escasamente, insuficientemente.

scantiness | 'skæntɪnɪs | *s.i.* escasez, insuficiencia.

scanty | 'skæntɪ | *adj.* escaso, insuficiente.

scapegoat | 'skeɪpgəʊt | *s.c.* cabeza de turco.

scapula | 'skæpjʊlə | *s.c.* ANAT. escápula (hueso).

scar | skɑːr | *s.c.* **1** cicatriz (en el cuerpo). **2** señal, señal de destrucción (en cosas). **3** (fig.) cicatriz mental, herida en el alma. || *v.t.* **4** dejar una cicatriz, dejar señal (en el cuerpo). **5** dejar huellas de un desperfecto, dejar una señal (en una cosa). **6** (fig.) dejar una herida mental, dejar una cicatriz en el alma, marcar. || **7 to be scarred,** tener una cicatriz: *his chin is scarred = tiene una cicatriz en la barbilla.*

scarce | skeəs | *adj.* **1** raro, escaso, poco frecuente. || **2 to make oneself –,** (fam.) esfumarse, desaparecer, darse el piro.

scarcely | 'skeəslɪ | *adv.* **1** apenas, casi no: *there was scarcely any time left = apenas quedaba tiempo.* **2** probablemente no, casi seguro que no: *I need scarcely add that I love you = probablemente no necesito añadir que te quiero.*

scarcity | 'skeəsətɪ | *s.i.* escasez, falta: *the scarcity of food = la escasez de alimentos.*

scare | skeər | *v.t.* **1** asustar, espantar. || *v.i.* **2** [**to – +** *adv.*] asustarse, amilanarse, amedrentarse. || *s.c.* **3** (normalmente *sing.*) susto, espanto; sobresalto. **4** alarma, pánico (especialmente generalizado). || **5 to – away/off,** alejar, ahuyentar (físicamente). **6 – story,** rumores de historias alarmistas, historia alarmista. **7 to – the life/hell/etc. out of somebody,** aterrar a alguien, aterrorizar a alguien, dar un susto de muerte a alguien.

scarecrow | 'skeəkrəʊ | *s.c.* espantapájaros.

scared | skeəd | *adj.* **1** [– (*inf.*/**of**)] asustado, atemorizado: *I'm scared to look at the screen = estoy atemorizado de mirar a la pantalla.* **2 [– (of)]** inquieto, nervioso, con aprensión. || **3 – to death/stiff,** (fam.) muerto de miedo.

scaremonger | 'skeəmʌŋgər | *s.c.* alarmista.

scarf | skɑːf | [*pl.* **scarfs** o **scarves**] *s.c.* bufanda.

scarlatina | ˌskɑːlə'tiːnə | *s.i.* MED. escarlatina.

scarlet | 'skɑːlɪt | *adj.* **1** escarlata. || *s.c.* **2** escarlata (color). || **3 – fever,** MED. escarlatina.

scarper | 'skɑːpər | *v.i.* (brit. y fam.) salir corriendo, salir pitando.

scarves | skɑːvz | *pl.* de **scarf.**

scary | 'skeərɪ | *adj.* (fam.) que da miedo; espantoso, pavoroso.

scathing | 'skeɪðɪŋ | *adj.* mordaz, cáustico; agresivo.

scathingly | 'skeɪðɪŋlɪ | *adv.* mordazmente, cáusticamente; agresivamente.

scatter | 'skætər | *v.t.* **1** esparcir, desparramar. **2** dispersar, desperdigar (personas). || *v.i.* **3** dispersarse, desperdigarse (personas). || *s.sing.* **4** grupo esparcido, montón esparcido: *there was a scatter of country houses on the hill = había un montón de casas de campo esparcidas por la colina.*

scatterbrain | 'skætəbreɪn | *s.c.* (fam.) cabeza de chorlito, casquivano.

scatterbrained | 'skætəbreɪnd | *adj.* (fam.) olvidadizo, atolondrado.

scattered | 'skætəd | *adj.* **1** disperso, esparcido, desparramado: *lots of scatte-*

red boulders = montones de cantos rodados dispersos. **2** aislado, apartado (física y figurativamente). **3 [– (with)]** cubierto, sembrado (de manera profusa): *hair scattered with cherries = pelo cubierto de cerezas.*
scattering | 'skætərɪŋ | *s.c.* puñado, manojo, salpicadura: *a scattering of small trees = un puñado de pequeños árboles.*
scattily | 'skætɪlɪ | *adv.* (brit. y fam.) atontadamente, con gran despiste.
scattiness | 'skætɪnɪs | *s.i.* (brit. y fam.) atontamiento, despiste.
scatty | 'skætɪ | *adj.* (brit. y fam.) atontado, despistado.
scavenge | 'skævɪndʒ | *v.t.* e *i.* **1 [to – (for)]** rebuscar para comer, buscar entre la basura. **2 [to – (for)]** buscar carroña (animales).
scavenger | 'skævɪndʒər | *s.c.* **1** ZOOL. animal carroñero. **2** persona que rebusca entre la basura.
scenario | sɪ'nɑːrɪəʊ | *s.c.* **1** argumento, trama (de un libro, película, etc.). **2** (form.) escenario, serie de acontecimientos: *we can see a very interesting scenario developing in the middle east = podemos ver una serie de acontecimientos muy interesantes desarrollándose en Oriente Medio.*
scene | siːn | *s.c.* **1** escena (de película, teatro, etc.). **2** decorado. **3** lugar, sitio, escena: *the scene of the incident = el lugar del incidente.* **4** vista, perspectiva, paisaje. **5** escenario, marco (para una película o similar). **6** escándalo, escena, arrebato: *what a scene he made = vaya escándalo armó.* || *s.sing.* **7 [the –]** la escena, la situación, el panorama (político, social, etc.). || *s.c.* e *i.* **8** escena, ambiente: *a change of scene = un cambio de ambiente.* || **9 behind the scenes, a)** detrás del telón, entre bastidores; **b)** (fig.) secretamente, entre bastidores. **10 from the –,** de escena, de delante (desaparecer). **11 not to be one's –,** (fam.) no ser el ambiente de uno, no ser el mundo de uno. **12 on the –,** en escena. **13 to set the – (for), a)** crear el ambiente (para), crear el escenario (para); **b)** describir la situación (a) (alguien).
scenery | 'siːnərɪ | *s.i.* **1** paisaje, vista. **2** escenario, tramoya, decorado (en un teatro).
scene-shifter | 'siːnʃɪftər | *s.c.* tramoyista.
scenic | 'siːnɪk | *adj.* **1** escénico, de la escena (teatral). **2** paisajístico; pintoresco.
scent | sent | *s.c.* **1** fragancia, aroma, olor agradable. **2** rastro, pista. || *s.i.* **3** perfume. || *s.c.* e *i.* **4** rastro, olor (que deja un animal). || *v.t.* **5** olfatear, oler (animales o personas). **6** sospechar, tener sospecha de (algo): *to scent a crime = tener sospecha de un crimen.*
scented | 'sentɪd | *adj.* perfumado.
scepter V. **sceptre.**
sceptic | 'skeptɪk | (EE.UU. **skeptic**) *s.c.* escéptico.
sceptical | 'skeptɪkl | (EE.UU. **skeptical**) *adj.* escéptico, incrédulo.
sceptically | 'skeptɪklɪ | (EE.UU. **skeptically**) *adv.* escépticamente, incrédulamente.
scepticism | 'skeptɪsɪzəm | (EE.UU. **skepticism**) *s.i.* escepticismo.
sceptre | 'septər | (EE.UU. **scepter**) *s.c.* cetro.
schedule | 'ʃedjuːl | (EE.UU.) | 'skedʒʊl | *s.c.* **1** programa, plan. **2** horario: *train schedule.* **3** inventario, lista, relación. || **4 ahead of –,** con anterioridad, por delante del horario previsto. **5 behind –,** retrasado, más tarde de lo previsto. **6 to be scheduled,** [+ *inf.*/**for**] estar previsto, tener previsto, estar ya planeado, tener proyectado: *the President is scheduled to arrive at 5 = está previsto que el Presidente llegue a las 5.* **7 on –,** a su hora, en el momento previsto. **8 to –/according to –,** según lo previsto, según el horario previsto, de acuerdo con el programa previsto.
schema | 'skiːmə | [*pl.* **schemata**] *s.c.* (form.) esquema, proyecto, plan, diagrama.
schemata | 'skiːmətə | *pl.* de **schema.**
schematic | skiː'mætɪk | *adj.* (form.) esquemático, de diagrama.
schematically | skiː'mætɪklɪ | *adv.* (form.) esquemáticamente, en forma de diagrama.
scheme | skiːm | *s.c.* **1** plan, proyecto (especialmente a gran escala): *the present pension scheme = el plan de jubilación actual.* **2** (a veces desp.) estratagema, ardid, plan. || *v.i.* **3** (desp.) urdir, tramar. || **4 somebody's – of things,** el plan de alguien, el proyecto de alguien. **5 the – of things,** la situación general, la organización de las cosas.
schemer | 'skiːmər | *s.c.* (desp.) maquinador, conspirador.
scheming | 'skiːmɪŋ | (desp.) *s.i.* **1** intrigas. || *adj.* **2** intrigante, astuto.
schism | 'sɪzəm | *s.c.* e *i.* cisma, ruptura, escisión (especialmente de carácter ideológico).
schizophrenia | ˌskɪtsəʊ'friːnɪə | *s.i.* **1** PSIQ. esquizofrenia. **2** (fig.) incoherencia, inconsistencia, inconsecuencia.
schizophrenic | ˌskɪtsəʊ'frenɪk | *adj.* **1** PSIQ. esquizofrénico. **2** (fig.) incoherente, inconsistente, inconsecuente. || *s.c.* **3** PSIQ. esquizofrénico (persona que sufre de esquizofrenia).
scholar | 'skɒlər | *s.c.* **1** erudito, experto (intelectual). **2** becado. **3** (p.u.) alumno, estudiante.
scholarly | 'skɒləlɪ | *adj.* **1** erudito, docto. **2** académico, intelectual (discusión, asunto, actividad, etc.).
scholarship | 'skɒləʃɪp | *s.c.* **1 [– (to)]** beca. || *s.i.* **2** erudición, saber, cultura.
scholastic | skə'læstɪk | *adj.* (form.) **1** académico, escolar. **2** intelectual, escolástico.
school | skuːl | *s.c.* e *i.* **1** escuela, colegio. **2** escuela superior, facultad. || *s.c.* **3** escuela, corriente (de una misma opinión): *the Velazquez school = la escuela de Velázquez.* **4** BIOL. banco (de peces). **5** cursillo para adultos. || *s.i.* **6** (EE.UU. y fam.) Universidad, estudios superiores. || **7 to be schooled in,** estar versado en, estar instruido en, estar entrenado en. **8 of the old –,** de vieja escuela, chapado a la antigua. **9 – age,** edad escolar. **10 the old – tie,** (desp.) los enchufes entre alumnos de las mismas escuelas privadas (cuando están en el mundo profesional).
schoolbook | 'skuːlbuk | *s.c.* libro de texto.
schoolboy | 'skuːlbɔɪ | *s.c.* **1** alumno, colegial. || *adj.* **2** (desp.) de colegial, infantil (comportamiento).
schoolchild | 'skuːltʃaɪld | *s.c.* colegial, alumno pequeño.
schooldays | 'skuːldeɪz | *s.pl.* años escolares, años de escuela.
schoolfriend | 'skuːlfrend | *s.c.* compañero de escuela.
schoolgirl | 'skuːlgəːl | *s.c.* alumna, colegiala.
schoolhouse | 'skuːlhaʊs | *s.c.* escuela (especialmente pequeña).
schooling | 'skuːlɪŋ | *s.i.* educación, formación escolar.
school-leaver | 'skuːlliːvər | *s.c.* joven que finaliza los estudios obligatorios.
schoolmaster | 'skuːlmɑːstər | *s.c.* maestro (especialmente de colegio privado).
schoolmate | 'skuːlmeɪt | *s.c.* compañero de escuela, compañero de clase.
schoolmistress | 'skuːlmɪstrɪs | *s.c.* maestra (especialmente de colegio privado).
schoolroom | 'skuːlruːm | *s.c.* clase (especialmente pequeña).
schoolteacher | 'skuːltiːtʃər | *s.c.* profesor, maestro.
schoolteaching | 'skuːltiːtʃɪŋ | *s.i.* enseñanza, magisterio.
schoolwork | 'skuːlwəːk | *s.i.* tarea escolar, trabajo escolar (del alumno).
schooner | 'skuːnər | *s.c.* **1** MAR. goleta. **2** (brit.) vaso de jerez.
sciatica | saɪ'ætɪkə | *s.i.* MED. ciática.
science | 'saɪəns | *s.i.* **1** ciencia (en general). || *s.c.* e *i.* **2** ciencia, especialidad científica. || **3 – fiction,** LIT. ciencia ficción.
scientific | ˌsaɪən'tɪfɪk | *adj.* **1** científico, de la ciencia. **2** metódico, serio, científico, sistemático (manera).
scientifically | ˌsaɪən'tɪfɪklɪ | *adv.* **1** científicamente. **2** metódicamente, seriamente, sistemáticamente (manera de hacer).
scientist | 'saɪəntɪst | *s.c.* científico.
sci-fi | 'saɪfaɪ | *s.i.* (fam.) ciencia ficción.
scimitar | 'sɪmɪtər | *s.c.* cimitarra.
scintillating | 'sɪntɪleɪtɪŋ | *adj.* ingenioso, brillante (conversación o humor).
scion | 'saɪən | *s.c.* (lit.) **[– of]** vástago de, descendiente de.
scissors | 'sɪzəz | *s.pl.* tijeras: *a pair of scissors = unas tijeras.*
sclerosis | sklə'rəʊsɪs | *s.i.* MED. esclerosis.
scoff | skɒf | (EE.UU.) | skɔːf | *v.i.* **1 [to – (at)]** mofarse, burlarse; decir con befa. || *v.t.* **2** (brit. y fam.) devorar, arramblar con (comida).
scold | skəʊld | *v.t.* e *i.* regañar, reprender; decir en tono de reprimenda.
scolding | 'skəʊldɪŋ | *s.c.* regañina, reprimenda.
scone | skɒn | (EE.UU.) | skəʊn | *s.c.* GAST. bollo.
scoop | skuːp | *s.c.* **1** cazo, cucharón (especialmente para el grano). **2** MEC. pala, paleta. **3** PER. exclusiva, notición, primicia informativa. || *v.t.* **4** adelantarse en una exclusiva periodística a (otros periódicos). **5** coger con un cazo. **6** coger con las dos manos: *scoop a few handfuls of sand into the bucket = coge con las dos manos varios montones de arena y mételos en el cubo.* || **7 to – out,** quitar lo de enmedio (de un volumen, dejándolo hueco). **8 to – up,** coger con las dos manos, recoger a manos llenas.

scoopful | 'sku:pfʊl | *s.c.* cazo (cantidad que cabe en él).
scoot | sku:t | *v.i.* (fam.) escabullirse, largarse.
scooter | 'sku:tər | *s.c.* **1** motocicleta. **2** patinete (de niños).
scope | skəʊp | *s.i.* **1** campo, espacio (como oportunidad para hacer algo): *there's a lot of scope for new ideas here = hay mucho campo para ideas nuevas aquí.* **2** alcance, ámbito: *whithin the scope of my film = dentro del ámbito de mi película.*
scorch | skɔ:tʃ | *v.t.* **1** quemar un poco, chamuscar. **2** quemar, abrasar (el sol). **3** agostar || *v.i.* **4** (brit. y fam.) ir a toda velocidad, ir a toda pastilla. || *s.c.* **5** quemadura (de una plancha). || **6 scorched-earth policy,** MIL. política militar de abrasar la tierra totalmente. **7 – mark,** chamuscado, quemadura (especialmente de plancha).
scorcher | 'skɔ:tʃər | *s.c.* (fam.) día abrasador, día sofocante.
scorching | 'skɔ:tʃɪŋ | *adj.* (fam.) abrasador, sofocante.
score | skɔ: | *v.t.* e *i.* **1** DEP. marcar, hacer un gol, ganar un punto. **2** ganar, lograr (éxito, victoria, puntuación, etc.): *the government scored a few points in the education debate = el gobierno ganó unos puntos en el debate sobre educación.* || *v.t.* **3** DEP. hacer, conseguir (tantos, puntuación, etc.). **4** MUS. instrumentar, orquestar. **5** hacer una muesca a, hacer una marca en. || *v.i.* **6** DEP. llevar el tanteo, llevar la puntuación (de un encuentro). **7** (argot) comprar droga. || *s.c.* **8** (normalmente *sing.*) DEP. tanteo, marcador. **9** puntuación (de examen). **10** MUS. partitura. **11** marca, muesca. **12** (p.u.) veintena. || **13 by the –,** en gran número. **14 to know the –,** conocer el percal, estar al tanto de la situación. **15 on this/that –,** por esta/esa razón, por ello. **16 to – off,** responder con la misma moneda, responder igualmente. **17 to – off/out/through,** tachar, borrar. **18 scores of,** montones de, muchísimos. **19 to settle a –/to settle old scores,** ajustar una cuenta/ajustar cuentas.
scoreboard | 'skɔ:bɔ:d | *s.c.* DEP. marcador, tablero de puntuación.
scorecard | 'skɔ:kɑ:d | *s.c.* DEP. tarjeta (especialmente en golf).
scorer | 'skɔ:rər | *s.c.* **1** DEP. goleador, tanteador. **2** encargado del marcador, encargado del tablero del marcador.
scorn | skɔ:n | *s.i.* **1** desprecio, desdén, menosprecio. || *v.t.* **2** despreciar, menospreciar. **3** (form.) negarse a. || **4 to heap/pour – on,** vituperar, llenar de insultos. **5 to laugh to –,** ridiculizar, poner en ridículo total.
scornful | 'skɔ:nfl | *adj.* desdeñoso, menospreciativo, despectivo.
scornfully | 'skɔ:nfəlɪ | *adv.* desdeñosamente, despectivamente.
scorpion | 'skɔ:pɪən | *s.c.* ZOOL. escorpión.
Scot | skɒt | *s.c.* escocés.
scotch | skɒtʃ | *v.t.* **1** frustrar, anular (plan); desmentir (rumor). || **2 Scotch, a)** whisky escocés; **b)** escocés. **3 Scotch broth,** (brit.) GAST. sopa escocesa. **4 Scotch egg,** (brit.) GAST. huevo al estilo escocés. **5 Scotch tape,** (EE.UU.) cinta adhesiva (marca registrada). **6 Scotch whisky,** whisky escocés.
scot-free | ˌskɒt'fri: | *adj.* impune, sin castigo.
Scotland | 'skɒtlənd | *s.sing.* Escocia.
Scots | skɒts | *s.i.* **1** escocés (dialecto). || *adj.* **2** escocés.
Scotsman | 'skɒtsmən | [*pl.irreg.* **Scotsmen**] *s.c.* escocés.
Scotsmen | 'skɒtsmən | *pl.irreg.* de **Scotsman.**
Scotswoman | 'skɒtswʊmən | [*pl.irreg.* **Scotswomen**] *s.c.* escocesa.
Scotswomen | 'skɒtswɪmɪn | *pl.irreg.* de **Scotswoman.**
Scotticism | 'skɒtɪsɪzəm | *s.c.* expresión en dialecto escocés.
Scottish | 'skɒtɪʃ | *adj.* **1** escocés. || **2 the –,** los escoceses.
scoundrel | 'skaʊndrəl | *s.c.* canalla, sinvergüenza, truhán.
scour | 'skaʊər | *v.t.* **1** buscar por todos los sitios, batir en busca de, rebuscar (en una zona, libro, documento, etc.): *I have scoured all the library, but I haven't found it = he buscado en toda la biblioteca, pero no lo he encontrado.* **2** restregar, limpiar a base de restregones, fregotear. **3 [to – (away)]** GEOL. derrubiar. || *s.sing.* **4 [a –]** un buen restregón, una limpieza a fondo. || **5 scouring powder,** limpiador en polvo.
scourer | 'skəʊərər | *s.c.* estropajo.
scourge | skɜ:dʒ | *v.t.* **1** azotar, flagelar. **2** (fig.) hostigar, azotar (una calamidad o similar). || *s.c.* **3** flagelo. || *s.sing.* **4 [– (of)]** (fig.) azote, flagelo.
scout | 'skaʊt | *s.c.* **1** muchacho explorador, "boy scout". **2** MIL. explorador; aparato de reconocimiento. || *v.t.* e *i.* **3** MIL. reconocer, explorar; reconocer el terreno, hacer una incursión de reconocimiento. || **4 boy –,** muchacho explorador, "boy scout". **5 to – around (for),** buscar con afán, dar vueltas buscando: *I spent the morning scouting around for a good film = me pasé la mañana dando vueltas buscando una buena película.*
scoutmaster | 'skaʊtmɑ:stər | *s.c.* jefe de chicos exploradores, capitán de muchachos exploradores.
scowl | skaʊl | *v.i.* **1 [to – (at)]** fruncir el ceño, poner mala cara, mirar con aspecto amenazante. || *s.c.* **2** mirada amenazadora, gesto poco amigable.
scrabble | 'skræbl | *v.i.* **1 [to – (at/against)]** escarbar; rascar (con manos o pies). **2 [to – (round/around)]** rebuscar, buscar nerviosamente (sin poder ver muy bien). || **3 Scrabble,** juego de palabras (marca registrada).
scragginess | 'skrægɪnɪs | *s.i.* flaqueza extrema.
scraggy | 'skrægɪ | *adj.* flacucho, esquelético.
scram | skræm | *v.i.* (fam.) darse el bote, largarse a toda pastilla, poner pies en polvorosa.
scramble | 'skræmbl | *v.i.* **1** gatear, trepar, moverse a gatas (especialmente a gran velocidad). **2 [to – + *prep.*]** moverse de prisa; cambiar de posición a gran velocidad: *they all scrambled to their feet = todos se pusieron en pie de prisa.* **3 [to – for/*inf.*]** pelearse por (algo): *all the students scrambled for the best seats = todos los estudiantes se pelearon por los mejores asientos.* || *v.t.* **4** GAST. revolver (especialmente huevos). **5** RAD. desmodular (mensaje, conversación telefónica, etc.). || *v.t.* e *i.* **6** MIL. despegar por una emergencia; tener una emergencia aérea. || *s.c.* **7** subida a gatas, movimiento a gatas. **8** movimiento a gran velocidad (normalmente por tener prisa): *I hate the typical scrambles to get out of the house in the morning = no me gustan nada las típicas prisas para salir de casa por las mañanas.* **9** DEP. carrera de motocross. **10 [– (for)]** pelea, lucha. || **11 scrambled egg/eggs,** GAST. huevos revueltos.
scrambler | 'skræmbər | *s.c.* RAD. desmodulador.
scrambling | 'skræmblɪŋ | *s.i.* DEP. motocross.
scrap | skræp | *s.c.* **1 [– (of)]** trozo, fragmento, pedazo (de tela, papel, metal, etc.). **2** (fam.) pelea, bronca, riña (especialmente cuando no es muy seria o violenta). || *s.pl.* **3** sobras, desperdicios, migajas (de comida). || *s.i.* **4** chatarra. || *v.t.* **5** (fam.) desechar, descartar (plan, proyecto, etc.). **6** convertir en chatarra, desguazar para chatarra. || *v.i.* **7** (fam.) pelearse, tener una bronca (especialmente no muy seria). || **8 not a –,** ni una pizca, ni un trocito, ni un mísero pedazo. **9 – metal,** MET. chatarra.
scrapbook | 'skræpbʊk | *s.c.* álbum de recortes, colección de recortes.
scrape | 'skreɪp | *v.t.* **1** raspar, limpiar raspando, quitar la corteza raspando (con un cuchillo o similar). **2** rozar, raspar (haciéndose daño). || *v.i.* **3** ahorrar muchísimo, hacer unas economías impresionantes. **4** restregarse, rozarse (haciendo un ruido desagradable). **5** rozarse, rasparse, hacerse una raspadura (herida). || *s.sing.* **6** rozamiento, ruido de raspamiento. || **7 to bow and –,** (desp.) comportarse como un despreciable pelota (con alguien). **8 in/into a –,** (p.u.) en una buena, en un follón, en un lío. **9 to – the bottom of the barrel,** V. **barrel. 10 to – through,** aprobar muy justo, aprobar por los pelos. **11 to – together/up,** hacerse con la cantidad justa, conseguir por los pelos un mínimo de (de dinero, amigos, objetos, etc.).
scrap-heap | 'skræphi:p | *s.c.* **1** montón de chatarra. || **2 on the –,** (fig.) en el montón de chatarra, en el montón de desperdicios, en el montón de basura.
scraping | 'skreɪpɪŋ | *s.i.* **1** ruido desagradable de rozamiento. || *s.pl.* **2** desperdicios, restos (de comida).
scrappily | 'skræpɪlɪ | *adv.* **1** incompletamente, desorganizadamente; deslavazadamente.
scrappiness | 'skræpɪnɪs | *s.i.* **1** desorganización; estructura incompleta, estructura deslavazada.
scrappy | 'skræpɪ | *adj.* **1** incompleto, a trozos, desorganizado; deslavazado: *a scrappy film = una película deslavazada.* **2** (fam. y EE.UU.) camorrista.
scratch | skrætʃ | *v.t.* **1** arrascar, arrascarse (cuerpo). **2** rayar, marcar (un objeto). **3** escarbar (animales, normalmente en el suelo). **4** hacer un rasguño, hacer una pequeña herida: *the wire scratched my skin = el alambre me hizo un rasguño en la piel.* || *v.i.* y *r.* **5** arrascarse (cuerpo). || *s.c.* **6** arañazo; rasguño. **7** raya, marca (en un objeto). || **8 to**

be up to/to come up to –, estar en un buen estado, tener buena calidad. **9 from –,** desde cero, desde el principio; desde la primera lección. **10 to – one's head,** (fig.) quedarse perplejo, no saber a qué carta quedarse, estar totalmente desconcertado. **11 to – the surface,** (desp. y fig.) quedarse en la superficie de las cosas, no penetrar, no profundizar nada (un libro, proyecto, conferencia, artículo, etc.). **12 you – my back and I'll – yours,** favor con favor se paga.

scrawl | skrɔːl | *v.t.* e *i.* **1** pintarrajear, garabatear; hacer garabatos. || *s.c.* **2** garabato.

scrawny | skrɔːnɪ | *adj.* (desp.) escuchimizado, esquelético, descarnado, escuálido.

scream | skriːm | *v.i.* **1** chillar, gritar desaforadamente (persona). **2** hacer un ruido horripilante, emitir un sonido fuerte y agudo. **3** (fig.) ser demasiado llamativo (cualquier cosa). || *v.t.* **4** lanzar, arrojar (chillido); decir chillando: *he screamed the order at the soldiers = lanzó la orden con un chillido a los soldados.* **5** (fig.) lanzar demasiado llamativamente, señalar chillonamente. || *s.c.* **6** chillido, grito desaforado. **7** ruido fuerte y agudo, ruido horripilante. || *s.sing.* **8** (fam.) persona que te provoca un estallido de risa, incidente que hace morir de risa.

scree | skriː | *s.c.* e *i.* GEOL. montón de guijarros en la ladera de una montaña.

screech | skriːtʃ | *v.i.* **1** chillar, lanzar chillidos. **2** chirriar (neumáticos). || *v.t.* **3** decir a gritos, decir chillando. || *s.c.* **4** (normalmente *sing.*) chillido, grito. || *s.i.* **5** chirrido (típico de ruedas).

screen | skriːn | *s.c.* **1** TV. pantalla. **2** biombo, panel de separación (de habitaciones). **3** red metálica, tamiz, criba (para distintos usos). **4** FOT. retícula. **5** (fig.) protección, pantalla de protección: *use the towels as a screen against the sun = utiliza las toallas como pantalla contra el sol.* || *s.sing.* **6 [the –]** la pantalla, las películas, el mundo de la pantalla. || *v.t.* **7** (normalmente pasiva) echar, poner, exhibir (película). **8** hacer de pantalla para, proteger físicamente (a alguien). **9** cribar, pasar por la criba; investigar (a personas por razones de seguridad). **10** hacer una comprobación de (personas, por si padecen ciertas enfermedades). || **11 to – off,** tapar; hacer un pequeño cubículo (dentro de una habitación). **12 – test,** prueba cinematográfica (para comprobar si alguien es buen actor).

screening | 'skriːnɪŋ | *s.c.* e *i.* **1** exhibición, proyección (de película). **2** criba; investigación (por razones de seguridad). **3** comprobación, chequeo (para ver si una persona tiene una determinada enfermedad).

screenplay | 'skriːnpleɪ | *s.c.* guión cinematográfico.

screenwriter | 'skriːnraɪtər | *s.c.* guionista cinematográfico.

screw | skruː | *s.c.* **1** MEC. tornillo de rosca, clavo de rosca. **2** (fam.) funcionario de prisiones, guarda de prisión. || *v.t.* e *i.* **3** atornillar(se), unir(se) mediante tornillos, sujetar(se) con tornillos. **4** enroscar(se) (cualquier objeto con una tapa o mecanismo que se ajusta dando vueltas). **5** (vulg.) joder, follar; echar un polvo. || *v.t.* **6** estrujar (objeto); distorsionar (cara); casi cerrar (ojos), apretar (cambiando la forma de lo que se aprieta): *she screwed her eyes because of the glare = casi cerró los ojos por causa del resplandor.* **7** (fam.) engañar; sacar (dinero de otra persona engañándola). || **8 to have a – loose,** (fam.) faltarle un tornillo. **9 to have one's head screwed on,** (fam.) tener la cabeza sobre los hombros. **10 to put the screws on someone,** (fam.) apretarle las clavijas a alguien. **11 to – up, a)** estrujar, distorsionar, apretar (un objeto o partes del cuerpo cambiando su forma); **b)** (fam.) estropear; (vulg. y argot) joder, hacer cisco, hacer polvo (algo); **c)** (fam.) dejar desencajado, estropear los nervios (de alguien). **12 to – up one's courage,** armarse de valor.

screwdriver | 'skruːdraɪvər | *s.c.* MEC. destornillador.

screwed-up | ˌskruːd'ʌp | *adj.* **1** apretado (parte del cuerpo); hecho una bola, apretujado (papel o similar). **2** mal de los nervios, hecho un manojo de nervios.

screwtop | 'skruːtɒp | *adj.* **1** con tapa de rosca. || *s.c.* **2** tapa de rosca.

screwy | 'skruːɪ | *adj.* (fam.) chiflado, medio loco, chalado; descabellado.

scribble | 'skrɪbl | *v.t.* e *i.* **1** garabatear, hacer garabatos. || *v.i.* **2** pintarrajear, garabatear (haciendo figuras fantásticas). || *s.c.* e *i.* **3** garabato; escritura ilegible, escritura incomprensible.

scribe | skraɪb | *s.c.* **1** HIST. copista, amanuense (de la época cuando no había imprenta). **2** REL. escriba.

scrimmage | 'skrɪmɪdʒ | *s.c.* pelea, melé.

scrimp | skrɪmp | *v.i.* **[to – (on)]** economizar muchísimo; vivir como un monje, gastar poquísimo dinero.

script | skrɪpt | *s.c.* **1** guión (las palabras que se dicen en una película o similar). **2** (brit.) examen (entregado por un alumno). || *s.c.* e *i.* **3** sistema de escritura, escritura (de un idioma). || *s.i.* **4** manuscrito. **5** letra, forma de escribir (de una persona).

scripted | 'skrɪptɪd | *adj.* con ayuda de un escrito (discurso, programa, etc.).

scriptural | 'skrɪptʃərəl | *adj.* REL. escriturístico; bíblico.

scripture | 'skrɪptʃər | REL. *s.c.* e *i.* **1** escritura, libro religioso (de cualquier religión). || **2 Scripture,** Religión (como asignatura). **3 the Scripture/Scripture,** las Escrituras.

scriptwriter | 'skrɪptraɪtər | *s.c.* guionista (de películas, televisión, etc.).

scroll | skrəul | *s.c.* **1** HIST. pergamino, rollo de pergamino. **2** ARQ. voluta (como adorno).

scrota | 'skrəutə | *pl.* de **scrotum.**

scrotum | 'skrəutəm | [*pl.* **scrotums** o **scrota**] *s.c.* ANAT. escroto.

scrounge | 'skraundʒ | (fam.) *v.t.* e *i.* **1** gorronear, ir de gorra por la vida. || **2 on the –,** de gorra, de balde.

scrounger | 'skraundʒər | *s.c.* (fam. y desp.) gorrón.

scrub | skrʌb | [*ger.* **scrubbing,** *pret.* y *p.p.* **scrubbed**] *v.t.* e *i.* **1** fregar, fregotear, limpiar a base de fregoteo. || *v.t.* **2** quitar a base de fregar (una mancha o parecido). **3** cancelar (plan, proyecto, etc.). || *s.sing.* **4 [a –]** un buen fregoteo, una sesión de limpieza a base de fregar. || *s.i.* **5** BOT. matorral.

scrubby | 'skrʌbɪ | *adj.* lleno de matorrales.

scrubland | 'skrʌblnd | *s.i.* GEOG. área de matorrales, tierra de matorrales.

scruff | skrʌf | **by the – of the/one's neck,** por el pescuezo (normalmente forma de agarrar).

scruffily | 'skrʌfɪlɪ | *adv.* (fam.) desaliñadamente, con vestidos sucios; roñoso.

scruffiness | 'skrʌfɪnɪs | *s.i.* (fam.) desaliño; roña.

scruffy | 'skrʌfɪ | *adj.* (fam.) desaliñado, mal vestido, desharrapado.

scrum | skrʌm | *s.c.* DEP. melé (del rugby).

scrumptious | 'skrʌmpʃəs | *adj.* (fam.) de rechupete (comida).

scrunch | skrʌntʃ | *v.t.* e *i.* **1** estrujar(se); hacer un ruido como de apretujar papel. || *s.c.* **2** ruido de estrujar, ruido de apretujar, ruido de crujido (papel, arena, etc.). || **3 to – up,** estrujar por completo, hacer una bola aplastada.

scruple | 'skruːpl | *s.c.* (normalmente *pl.*) escrúpulo.

scrupulous | 'skruːpjuləs | *adj.* **1** escrupuloso. **2** detallista, minucioso, puntilloso.

scrupulously | 'skruːpjuləslɪ | *adv.* **1** escrupulosamente. **2** con gran minuciosidad/detalle, minuciosamente, puntillosamente.

scrutinize | 'skruːtɪnaɪz | (EE.UU.) | 'skruːtənaɪz | (también **scrutinise**) *v.t.* mirar con gran atención, observar cuidadosamente, examinar con detalle.

scrutiny | 'skruːtɪnɪ | (EE.UU.) | 'skruːtənɪ | *s.i.* **1** observación atenta, examen cuidadoso, mirada atenta. || **2 under –,** bajo observación cuidadosa, bajo la mirada atenta (de un guardián, periodista, etc.).

scuba | 'skuːbə | *s.c.* **1** equipo de buceo. || **2 – diving,** DEP. submarino, pesca submarina.

scud | skʌd | [*ger.* **scudding,** *pret.* y *p.p.* **scudded**] *v.i.* (lit.) moverse, deslizarse (especialmente las nubes).

scuff | skʌf | *v.t.* **1** arrastrar (los pies al andar). **2** desgastar, hacer rozadura (especialmente en los zapatos).

scuffed | skʌft | *adj.* desgastado, lleno de rozaduras (especialmente zapatos).

scuffle | 'skʌfl | *s.c.* **1** reyerta, refriega (normalmente corta). || *v.i.* **2** enzarzarse en una pelea, meterse en una reyerta. || *v.t.* e *i.* **3** hacer un ruido de rozamiento, hacer ruido continuado de rozamiento.

scuffling | 'skʌflɪŋ | *s.i.* ruido de rozamiento continuado.

scull | skʌl | *s.c.* **1** espadilla, remo corto. || *v.t.* e *i.* **2** remar con espadilla.

scullery | 'skʌlərɪ | *s.c.* fregadero, office (habitación junto a la cocina).

sculpt | skʌlpt | *v.t.* ART. esculpir.

sculptor | 'skʌlptʃər | *s.c.* escultor.

sculptural | 'skʌlptʃərəl | *adj.* de la escultura, escultural.

sculpture | 'skʌlptʃər | *s.c.* **1** ART. escultura. || *s.i.* **2** ART. escultura (como arte). || *v.t.* **3** ART. esculpir. **4** (fig.) hacer con gran detalle, fabricar con sumo cuidado (como si se tratase de una escultura artística).

scum | skʌm | *s.c.* e *i.* **1** espuma sucia, telilla, capa de suciedad (sobre la superficie de líquidos). || *s.pl.* **2** (fam.) desechos, heces, escoria (refiriéndose a gente): *the scum of our society = la escoria de nuestra sociedad.*
scupper | 'skʌpər | *s.c.* **1** (normalmente *pl.*) MAR. imbornal. || *v.t.* **2** (fam. y brit.) meter en una buena; fastidiar (un plan o similar).
scurrility | skə'rɪlɪtɪ | *s.i.* (lit.) procacidad, grosería; infamia.
scurrilous | 'skʌrɪləs | *adj.* procaz, grosero; infame.
scurrilously | 'skʌrɪləslɪ | *adv.* procazmente, groseramente; infamemente.
scurry | 'skʌrɪ | *v.i.* **1** correr a toda prisa, ir a toda prisa; escabullirse rápidamente. || *s.sing.* **2** movimiento/acción de correr a toda prisa; huida veloz.
scurvy | 'skə:vɪ | *s.i.* MED. escorbuto.
scuttle | 'skʌtl | *v.i.* **1** correr a pasos cortos; escabullirse. || *v.t.* **2** MAR. barrenar, echar a pique. || *s.c.* **3** cubo para carbón.
scythe | saɪð | *s.c.* **1** guadaña. || *v.t.* e *i.* **2** cortar con guadaña. || *v.i.* **3** (fig.) hacer un movimiento parabólico: *the stone scythed into the garden = la piedra cayó al jardín haciendo un movimiento parabólico.*
sea | si: | *s.c.* **1** mar. **2** GEOG. mar (concreto). || *s.sing.* **3** **[the –]** el mar, la costa: *a holiday by the sea = unas vacaciones junto al mar.* **4** **[the –]** el mar (como trabajo de un marinero). **5** **[– of]** mar de (gente); montón de (cosas). || *atr.* **6** marino, marítimo, del mar: *sea travel = viaje por mar.* || **7 at –, a)** en el mar, en alta mar; **b)** en el mar, en los barcos (vida profesional); **c)** desconcertado, sin saber qué hacer. **8 by –,** por mar, por vía marítima (viaje, envío, etc.). **9 to get/find one's – legs,** hacerse al movimiento del barco; no marearse ya más. **10 on the high seas,** en alta mar. **11 out to –,** hacia mar, mar adentro. **12 – anemone,** ZOOL. anémona de mar. **13 – breeze,** brisa marina. **14 – lane,** pasadizo marítimo, ruta marítima. **15 – level,** nivel del mar. **16 – power, a)** MIL. poderío naval; **b)** POL. potencia naval. **17 – urchin,** ZOOL. erizo de mar. **18 – water,** agua salada, agua de mar.
sea-air | ˌsi:'eə | *s.i.* brisa marina, aire de mar.
seabed | 'si:bed | *s.sing.* **[the –]** GEOL. lecho marino.
seabird | 'si:bə:d | *s.c.* pájaro marino, ave marina.
seaboard | si:bɔ:d | *s.c.* (normalmente *sing.*) GEOG. litoral, costa.
seaborne | 'si:bɔ:n | *adj.* transportado por mar.
seadog | 'si:dɒg | *s.c.* (a veces hum.) lobo de mar.
seafaring | 'si:feərɪŋ | *adj.* marítimo, marinero, que transcurre en el mar (especialmente profesional): *a seafaring life = una vida en el mar.*
seafood | 'si:fu:d | *s.i.* marisco.
seafront | 'si:frʌnt | *s.c.* paseo marítimo.
sea-going | 'si:gəuɪŋ | *adj.* de altura (tipo de embarcación).
seagull | 'si:gʌl | *s.c.* ZOOL. gaviota.
seahorse | 'si:hɔ:s | *s.c.* ZOOL. caballito de mar.
seal | si:l | *s.c.* **1** sello, precinto. **2** sello (objeto). **3** sello (en cartas). **4** MEC. cierre hermético (para gases, líquidos, etc.). **5** ZOOL. foca. || *v.t.* **6** sellar (carta, paquete, caja, etc.). **7** sellar, cerrar (conductos). || **8 to give something one's – of approval,** dar a algo la aprobación oficial. **9 my lips are sealed,** soy una tumba, mis labios están cerrados totalmente. **10 to put/set the – on,** sellar definitivamente (una amistad, relación, período de tiempo, etc.). **11 to – in,** cerrar herméticamente, sellar herméticamente (especialmente líquidos). **12 to – off,** separar, aislar (un espacio). **13 to – one's fate/doom,** sellar el destino de uno; poner la puntilla a uno.
sealing | 'si:lɪŋ | *s.i.* caza de focas.
sealing-wax | 'si:lɪŋwæks | *s.i.* lacre.
sealion | 'si:laɪən | *s.c.* ZOOL. león marino.
sealskin | 'si:lskɪn | *s.i.* piel de foca.
seam | si:m | *s.c.* **1** costura (de la ropa). **2** juntura (entre dos cosas). **3** GEOL. filón, veta. || **4 to burst/bulge at the seams,** ser demasiados; no caber, sobrepasar la capacidad. **5 to come/fall apart at the seams,** deshacerse, desintegrarse (objeto, relación personal, etc.).
seaman | si:mən | [*pl.irreg.* **seamen**] *s.c.* marinero, hombre de mar.
seamanship | 'si:mənʃɪp | *s.i.* náutica, navegación.
seamed | si:md | *adj.* lleno de costuras (ropa); lleno de arrugas (cara); veteado (terreno).
seamen | 'si:mən | *pl.irreg.* de **seaman.**
seamless | 'si:mlɪs | *adj.* **1** sin costuras (ropa). **2** (fig.) uniforme, sin divisiones visibles.
seamstress | 'semstrɪs | (brit. también **sempstress**) *s.c.* costurera, modista.
seamy | 'si:mɪ | *adj.* sórdido, miserable, vil (forma de vivir): *seamy hotels = hoteles sórdidos.*
seánce | 'seɪɑ:ns | (también **seance**) *s.c.* sesión de espiritismo.
seaplane | 'si:pleɪn | *s.c.* AER. hidroavión.
seaport | 'si:pɔ:t | *s.c.* puerto de mar.
sear | sɪər | *v.t.* **1** quemar, chamuscar (parte del cuerpo u objeto). **2** MED. cauterizar. **3** GAST. freír a fuego intenso brevemente.
search | sə:tʃ | *v.t.* e *i.* **1** **[to – (for)]** buscar: *I searched for the gun = busqué la pistola.* **2** explorar, rebuscar, examinar (en la mente): *I searched my mind for an answer = rebusqué en mi mente para hallar una respuesta.* || *v.t.* **3** registrar, cachear. || *s.c.* **4** **[– (for)]** búsqueda, busca. **5** registro. | **6 in – of,** en búsqueda de, a la búsqueda de. **7 – me,** ni idea, y yo qué sé. **8 to – out,** descubrir después de una larga búsqueda.
searching | 'sə:tʃɪŋ | *adj.* penetrante, interrogante (mirada, gesto, pregunta, etc.).
searchingly | 'sə:tʃɪŋlɪ | *adv.* penetrantemente, con una interrogación (en la mirada, gesto, etc.).
searchlight | 'sə:tʃlaɪt | *s.c.* reflector.
search-party | 'sə:tʃpɑ:tɪ | *s.c.* grupo de rescate, grupo de salvamento.
search-warrant | 'sə:tʃwɒrənt | *s.c.* DER. mandamiento de registro domiciliario.
searing | 'sɪərɪŋ | *adj.* **1** abrasador, ardiente, punzante (dolor, calor, etc.). **2** demoledor (crítica, artículo, etc.).
seascape | 'si:skeɪp | *s.c.* ART. escena marítima, marina.
seashell | 'si:ʃel | *s.c.* concha marina, caracol marino.
seashore | 'si:ʃɔ: | *s.c.* **1** litoral, costa, playa. **2** DER. zona costera (entre la pleamar y la bajamar).
seasick | 'si:sɪk | *adj.* mareado.
seasickness | 'si:sɪknɪs | *s.i.* mareo.
seaside | 'si:saɪd | *s.sing.* **1** playa, costa (especialmente desde el punto de vista de las vacaciones). || *adj.* **2** costero.
season | 'si:zn | *s.c.* **1** estación (del año). **2** temporada (de vacaciones, deporte, caza, etc.): *this is the low season = esta es la temporada baja.* **3** AGR. época, temporada (de algún tipo de planta). || *v.t.* **4** sazonar, condimentar (comida). **5** curar (madera). || **6 in –, a)** en sazón (frutos); **b)** con la veda abierta; **c)** en su temporada álgida; **d)** en celo. **7 out of –, a)** fuera de temporada (frutos); **b)** en temporada baja; **c)** en veda. **8 – ticket,** abono.
seasonable | 'si:znəbl | *adj.* **1** oportuno (tiempo). **2** normal, normal para la época del año (tiempo atmosférico).
seasonal | 'si:zənl | *adj.* de temporada, estacional (especialmente trabajo).
seasonally | 'si:zənəlɪ | *adv.* temporalmente, por temporada.
seasoned | 'si:znd | *adj.* experimentado, veterano, aguerrido.
seasoning | 'si:zənɪŋ | *s.c.* e *i.* GAST. condimento.
seat | si:t | *s.c.* **1** asiento: *take a seat = toma asiento.* **2** fondo, sillín (parte donde se sienta uno). **3** POL. escaño. **4** sede (de una organización); casa solariega (de una familia de abolengo). || *s.sing.* **5** **[the – of]** el fondillo de, el trasero de (ropa). || *v.r.* **6** sentarse. || *v.t.* **7** tener cabida para, tener aforo para. || **8 by the – of one's pants,** de oído, por intuición. **9 to take a back –,** tomar una posición secundaria, dejar el primer plano (para otros).
seat-belt | 'si:tbelt | *s.c.* cinturón de seguridad.
seated | 'si:tɪd | *adj.* **1** sentado. || **2 be –,** (form.) siéntese.
-seater | 'si:tər | *sufijo* de ...asientos, de ...plazas: *my aeroplane is a two-seater = mi avioneta es de dos plazas.*
seating | 'si:tɪŋ | *s.i.* **1** asientos, acomodo. **2** arreglo de asientos, distribución de asientos (en un acto social, por ejemplo).
seawards | 'si:wədz | (también **seaward**) *adj.* y *adv.* hacia el mar, en dirección al mar, del mar.
seaweed | 'si:wi:d | *s.c.* e *i.* BIOL. alga marina.
sec | sek | *s.c.* (fam.) momento, segundo.
secateurs | 'sekətə:z | ˌsekə'tə:z | *s.pl.* tijeras de podar: *a pair of secateurs = unas tijeras de podar.*
secede | sɪ'si:d | *v.i.* **[to – (from)]** (form.) separarse, secesionarse (especialmente una parte de una nación); darse de baja (en una organización).
secession | sɪ'seʃn | *s.c.* e *i.* **[– (from)]** secesión; baja.
seclude | sɪ'klu:d | *v.t.* y *r.* (form.) retirar(se), apartar(se), aislar(se).
secluded | sɪ'klu:dɪd | *adj.* apartado, retirado, aislado (lugar).
seclusion | sɪ'klu:ʒn | *s.i.* aislamiento, retiro (normalmente una casa): *I love the seclusion of my life = me encanta el aislamiento de mi vida.*

second | 'sekənd | *s.c.* **1** segundo. **2** momento, momentito, segundo. **3** (normalmente *pl.*) artículos de mediana calidad: resto (en una tienda). **4** MUS. intervalo de segunda. **5** padrino (en un duelo). **6** (brit.) notable (nota en la universidad). || *num.ord.* **7** segundo; dos (en fechas). || *adj.* **8** segundo. || *adv.* **9** en segundo lugar. || *s.pl.* **10** (fam.) postre; segunda porción (del mismo plato). || *v.t.* **11** secundar, apoyar (protesta, sugerencia, etc.). **12** (fam.) decir (lo mismo), estar de acuerdo con. || **13 at – hand,** de segunda mano (una experiencia o información). **14 to have – thoughts (about),** tener dudas (sobre) (una decisión ya tomada). **15 on – thoughts,** pensándolo otra vez, al pensarlo otra vez. **16 – childhood,** segunda infancia (una persona mayor). **17 – cousin,** primo segundo. **18 – hand,** manilla de los segundos, segundero. **19 – language,** segundo idioma. **20 – lieutenant,** MIL. alférez. **21 – nature,** hábito muy arraigado. **22 – only to,** solamente es inferior a, sólo es menos que, sólo puede compararse con: *Barcelona is only second to Madrid in Spain = en toda España, sólo Barcelona puede compararse con Madrid.* **23 – person,** GRAM. segunda persona. **24 – sight,** clarividencia. **25 – thought,** atención más cuidadosa, otro pensamiento: *I didn't give him a second thought = no le dediqué otro pensamiento.* **26 – to none,** no inferior a nadie, no a la zaga de nadie: *as a teacher Mary is second to none = como profesora, Mary no va a la zaga de nadie.* **27 – wind,** un segundo impulso, una segunda fuerza, una segunda infusión de energía.

second | sɪ'kɒnd | *v.t.* (brit.) trasladar, asignar temporalmente (especialmente en el mundo educativo).

secondary | 'sekəndrɪ | (EE.UU.) | 'sekənderɪ | *adj.* **1 [– (to)]** secundario (menos importante). **2** secundario (efecto). **3** secundario (nivel de enseñanza). || *s.c.* **4** escuela secundaria. || **5 – modern,** formación profesional. **6 – school,** escuela secundaria.

second-best | ˌsekənd'best | *adj.* **1** de segunda (dentro de una relativa calidad, pero no la más alta): *the car was only second-best but I had to buy it = el coche era sólo de segunda pero lo tuve que comprar.* || *s.sing.* **2** segunda clase.

second-class | ˌsekənd'klɑːs | *adj.* **1** de segunda clase. **2** de segunda clase (sello de correos). || *adv.* **3** de segunda clase. || *s.i.* **4** de segunda clase (billete de transporte). || *s.c.* **5** (normalmente *sing.*) notable (nota universitaria). || **6 – degree,** título de notable.

seconder | 'sekəndər | *s.c.* persona que apoya (propuesta, moción, etc.).

second-hand | ˌsekənd'hænd | *adj.* y *adv.* de segunda mano (tienda, noticias).

second-in-command | ˌsekəndɪnkə'mɑːnd | *s.c.* segundo de a bordo, segundo en el mando (especialmente en lo militar).

secondly | 'sekəndlɪ | *adv.* en segundo lugar.

secondment | sɪ'kɒndmənt | *s.c.* e *i.* (brit.) traslado temporal.

second-rate | ˌsekənd'reɪt | *adj.* mediocre, inferior, de segunda categoría.

secrecy | 'siːkrəsɪ | *s.i.* secreto, discreción.

secret | 'siːkrɪt | *adj.* **1** secreto. **2** secreto, encubierto, oculto (bebedor, admirador, etc.). || *s.c.* **3** secreto. **4** (normalmente *pl.*) secreto, misterio: *the secrets of womanhood = los misterios de la condición femenina.* || *s.sing.* **5 [the -- (of)]** el secreto, la clave, la solución. || **6 in --,** en secreto. **7 to keep a --,** mantener un secreto, guardar un secreto. **8 -- agent,** agente secreto. **9 -- police,** policía secreta. **10 -- service,** servicio secreto, servicio de espionaje.

secretarial | ˌsekrə'teərɪəl | *adj.* de oficinista, de secretariado.

secretariat | ˌsekrə'teərɪət | *s.c.* secretariado (de una organización).

secretary | 'sekrətrɪ | (EE.UU.) | 'sekrəterɪ | *s.c.* **1** secretario, oficinista. **2** secretario (de una organización o asociación). **3** (brit.) POL. secretario de Estado, jefe de Departamento. **4** (EE.UU.) POL. ministro. || **5 Secretary of State, a)** (brit.) secretario de Estado (para algún Departamento); **b)** (EE.UU.) secretario de Estado (equivalente a ministro de Asuntos Exteriores).

secretary-general | ˌsekrətrɪ'dʒenrəl | *s.c.* secretario general (de una organización internacional).

secrete | sɪ'kriːt | *v.t.* (form.) **1** BIOL. secretar, segregar (glándulas, plantas, etc.). **2** ocultar, guardar.

secretion | sɪ'kriːʃn | (form.) *s.c.* **1** BIOL. secreción, segregación. || *s.i.* **2** sustancia secretoria.

secretive | 'siːkrətɪv | *adj.* reservado, callado.

secretively | 'siːkrətɪvlɪ | *adv.* reservadamente, calladamente.

secretly | 'siːkrɪtlɪ | *adv.* **1** secretamente. **2** confidencialmente, ocultamente.

sect | sekt | *s.c.* REL. secta.

sectarian | sek'teərɪən | *adj.* (form.) sectario.

sectarianism | sek'teərɪənɪzəm | *s.i.* (form.) sectarismo.

section | 'sekʃn | *s.c.* **1** sección. **2** DER. sección (de una ley). **3** GEOM. sección, corte.

sectional | 'sekʃənl | *adj.* seccional, minoritario (intereses, objetivos, etc.).

sector | 'sektər | *s.c.* **1** sector (de la economía). **2** sector, parte (de un todo). **3** sector, zona (en el espacio). **4** MAT. sector.

secular | 'sekjʊlər | *ajd.* **1** secular, laico (no religioso). **2** REL. secular (clero).

secularism | sekjʊlərɪzəm | *s.i.* laicismo.

secularize | 'sekjʊləraɪz | (también **secularise**) *v.t.* secularizar.

secure | sɪ'kjʊər | *adj.* **1** seguro, fijo; estable: *a secure position = un puesto seguro.* **2** seguro, estable (casa). **3** sujeto, fijo (no suelto). **4** seguro, a salvo, confiado. **5** sólido, seguro: *a secure foundation = un fundamento sólido.* || *v.t.* **6** asegurar, proteger (contra algo). **7** sujetar, fijar (físicamente). **8** obtener, conseguir, asegurarse.

securely | sɪ'kjʊəlɪ | *adv.* **1** seguramente, fijamente; establemente. **2** fijamente, con sujeción.

security | sɪ'kjʊərətɪ | *s.i.* **1** seguridad (nacional). **2** seguridad, estabilidad (en empleo, vida, etc.). **3** seguridad, confianza (sin preocupaciones). || *s.c.* e *i.* **4** FIN. garantía, fianza (para un préstamo o similar). || *s.c.* **5** título, valor, obligación. || **6 – guard,** guarda jurado, guarda de seguridad. **7 – risk,** persona no de confianza, persona no confiable.

sedan | sɪ'dæn | *s.c.* **1** sedán, turismo. || **2 – chair,** HIST. silla de manos.

sedate | sɪ'deɪt | *adj.* **1** tranquilo, sosegado (persona). **2** tranquilo (paso). || *v.t.* **3** sedar, administrar un sedante a.

sedately | sɪ'deɪtlɪ | *adv.* tranquilamente, sosegadamente.

sedateness | sɪ'deɪtnɪs | *s.i.* tranquilidad, sosiego.

sedation | sɪ'deɪʃn | *s.i.* MED. tratamiento con calmantes, tratamiento con sedantes.

sedative | 'sedətɪv | *s.c.* **1** MED. sedante, calmante. || *adj.* **2** sedante, calmante.

sedentary | 'sedntrɪ | (EE.UU.) | 'sednterɪ | *adj.* sedentario (trabajo, ocupación, persona, etc.).

sedge | sedʒ | *s.c.* BOT. juncia.

sediment | 'sedɪmənt | *s.c.* e *i.* **1** poso (en cualquier líquido). **2** GEOL. sedimento.

sedimentary | ˌsedɪ'mentrɪ | *adj.* GEOL. sedimentario.

sedition | sɪ'dɪʃn | *s.i.* sedición.

seditious | sɪ'dɪʃəs | *adj.* sedicioso.

seduce | sɪ'djuːs | *v.t.* **1** inducir, tentar, seducir. **2** seducir (sexualmente).

seduction | sɪ'dʌkʃn | *s.c.* e *i.* **1** seducción (sexual). || *s.c.* **2** (normalmente *pl.*) tentación, seducción: *the seductions of the high society = las tentaciones de la alta sociedad.*

seductive | sɪ'dʌktɪv | *adj.* **1** tentador, seductor. **2** seductor (persona).

seductively | sɪ'dʌktɪvlɪ | *adv.* **1** tentadoramente, seductoramente. **2** seductoramente (connotación sexual).

seductiveness | sɪ'dʌktɪvnɪs | *s.i.* atractivo, capacidad de seducción.

see | siː | *v.* [*pret.* **saw,** *p.p.* **seen**] *i.* **1** ver (en sentido general): *I can hardly see because of the glare of the sun = apenas puedo ver por el resplandor del sol.* **2** darse cuenta, ver, ser capaz de ver, captar: *I could see she was worried = pude captar que estaba preocupada.* **3** entender, comprender. || *t.* **4** ver (algo). **5** acompañar, llevar: *after the film I saw her home = después de la película la acompañé a casa.* **6** detectar, ver, darse cuenta (visualmente): *I saw the chance when he stooped = me di cuenta de mi oportunidad cuando se agachó.* **7** ser testigo de: *we'll see great changes in the future = seremos testigos de grandes cambios en el futuro.* **8** imaginar, ver en la mente de uno; visualizar: *can you see James as the future headmaster? = ¿puedes imaginarte a James de director en el futuro?* **9** comprobar: *I'll see that the job is done properly = comprobaré que el trabajo se haga adecuadamente.* **10** asegurarse de: *see that the doors are locked = asegúrate de que las puertas estén bien cerradas.* **11** considerar: *I saw it was my duty to help = consideré que era mi deber ayudar.* **12** cubrir la apuesta, seguir la apuesta (especialmente en cartas). **13** tener una relación de noviazgo con, tener una relación amorosa con: *Mary is seeing an American man = Mary* *está teniendo una relación amorosa con un hombre americano.* || *r.* **14** verse, imaginarse: *I can't see myself going out with her = no puedo imaginarme saliendo con ella.* || *s.c.* **15** (form.) REL. sede (de un obispado). || **16 to be seeing things,** estar viendo visiones. **17 to be seen dead,** V. **dead. 18 I'll –/we'll –,** ya veré, ya veremos, quizás. **19 I –, a)** ya veo, entiendo, comprendo; **b)** ya veo (expresando insatisfacción o desencanto). **20 it remains to be** V. **remain. 21 let me –/let's –,** veamos (comprobando algo). **22 –?,** ¿de acuerdo?, ¿no ves? (con cierto matiz de agresividad). **23 to – about,** acordar, ponerse de acuerdo sobre; preparar, atender: *I want to see about the transfer = quiero atender al tema del traslado.* **24 to – eye to eye,** V. **eye. 25 to – fit,** V. **fit. 26 to – if,** comprobar si, ver si. **27 seeing as/that,** dado que, en vista de que. **28 to – off,** despedir, decir adiós, acompañar para despedir (a alguien). **29 to – red,** V. **red. 30 to – life,** V. **life. 31 to – the light,** V. **light. 32 to – the light of day,** V. **light. 33 to – the Old Year out/the New Year in,** recibir al año nuevo, dar la bienvenida al nuevo año, despedir el año. **34 to – through, a)** (fam.) calar (a alguien), darse cuenta de las ocultas intenciones de (alguien); **b)** sacar de apuros, echar una mano (normalmente con dinero). **35 to – to,** ocuparse de, atender, encargarse: *I'll see to the whole matter = me ocuparé de todo el tema.* **36 to – to it,** asegurarse de que (algo) se hace. **37 to – what one can do/what can be done,** ver lo que uno puede hacer/se puede hacer. **38 – you/– later/be seeing you,** (fam.) hasta luego, hasta más ver, hasta la vista. **39 to wait and –,** V. **wait. 40 we'll – about that,** ya veremos si te atreves (amenazante). **41 you'll –,** ya lo verás, ya lo comprobarás en el futuro, ya verás (que tengo razón). **41 you –, a)** mira, intenta entender, fíjate; **b)** se ven, existen: *you see plenty of blacks in Colombia = se ven bastantes negros en Colombia.*

seed | si:d | *s.c.* **1** AGR. semilla. **2** DEP. tenista clasificado/considerado/evaluado según un determinado criterio; cabeza de serie (tenis): *he's the number three seed = él es el tenista considerado número 3 en el "ranking".* || *s.i.* **3** AGR. simiente. **4** (form. y p.u.) descendencia (persona). || *v.t.* **5 [to – +** *o.* **+ (with)]** sembrar con semilla. **6** DEP. catalogar /clasificar/evaluar a un tenista según un determinado criterio; poner de cabeza de serie. || **7 to go/run to –,** granar, dar en grana. **8 to go to –,** (fam.) ir a menos, perder facultades (físicas o mentales). **9 to plant/sow the seeds of,** (fig.) sembrar, poner el germen de, sembrar el germen de: *he sowed the seeds of fear in her heart = él sembró el germen del miedo en su corazón.*

seedbed | 'si:dbed | *s.c.* **1** AGR. semillero. **2** (fig.) semillero, terreno abonado: *this place has been a seedbed of revolutionary ideas = este lugar ha sido un terreno abonado para las ideas revolucionarias.*

seedcake | 'si:dkeɪk | *s.c.* e *i.* GAST. torta de alcaravea, torta de semillas.

seediness | 'si:dɪnɪs | *s.i.* estado desaseado (personal); estado destartalado; sordidez (lugar).

seedless | 'si:dlɪs | *adj.* sin pepitas (fruta).

seedling | 'si:dlɪŋ | *s.c.* BOT. plantón, plántula.

seedy | 'si:dɪ | *adj.* **1** desaseado (persona), destartalado; sórdido (lugar). **2** (p.u.) pachucho, indispuesto. **3** lleno de pepitas (fruta).

seek | si:k | (form.) *v.* [*pret.* y *p.p.irreg.* **sought**] *t.* **1** buscar (algo). **2** buscar, querer (venganza, paz, contestación, solución, etc.). **3** solicitar, pedir (consejo, ayuda, etc.). **4 [to – +** *inf.*] intentar, procurar, tratar de. || *i.* **5 [to – for]** buscar. **6 [to – for]** solicitar, pedir (consejo, ayuda, etc.). | **7 to – one's fortune,** (p.u.) buscar fortuna, ir en busca de fortuna. **8 to – out,** buscar afanosamente, perseguir (a alguien).

seem | si:m | *v.i.* **1 [to – +** *adj./adv./inf.*] parecer: *he seems to be fed-up = parece que está harto; it seems essential to start now = parece importantísimo empezar ahora.* **2 [to – +** *inf.*] parecer (que): *you seem to forget everything he did = pareces olvidar todo lo que hizo.* || **3 can't/couldn't – to,** no parecer posible que (alguien) pueda/pudiera: *I can't seem to be able to pass that exam = no parece posible que yo sea capaz de aprobar ese examen.*

seeming | 'si:mɪŋ | *adj.* (form.) aparente, supuesto: *his seeming willingness to cooperate = su aparente disponibilidad a ayudar.*

seemingly | 'si:mɪŋlɪ | *adv.* **1** aparentemente, supuestamente. **2** al parecer, por lo que se ve.

seemliness | 'si:mlɪnɪs | *s.i.* (p.u. o form.) decoro, decencia, corrección (en el comportamiento, forma de vestir, etc.).

seemly | 'si:mlɪ | *adj.* (p.u. o form.) decoroso, apropiado (conducta, estilo, forma de vestir, etc.).

seen | si:n | *p.p.irreg.* de **see.**

seep | si:p | *v.i.* **1** filtrarse, fluir poco a poco, fluir muy gradualmente, rezumar: *the rain seeped through the ceiling = la lluvia se filtró a través del techo.* **2** penetrar poco a poco, filtrarse (humo, gas, etc.). **3** (fig.) filtrarse (una noticia, fuera de un lugar).

seer | 'sɪə | *s.c.* (p.u. o lit.) vidente, profeta, visionario.

seesaw | 'si:sɔ: | *s.c.* **1** columpio de sube y baja. || *v.i.* **2** hacer un vaivén, hacer un movimiento de sube y baja. **3** (fig.) fluctuar (precios, por ejemplo).

seethe | si:ð | *v.i.* **1** hervir, bullir, borbotar (líquidos). **2** estar agitado, estar colérico, estar furioso (sin mostrarlo). **3 [to – with]** ser un hervidero de, estar lleno de (gente, animales o cosas).

see-through | 'si:θru: | *adj.* transparente, que se ve lo de debajo (ropa).

segment | 'segmənt | *s.c.* **1** sección, parte, segmento (de un todo). **2** gajo (de fruta). **3** GEOM. segmento.

segmentation | ˌsegmen'teɪʃn | *s.i.* BIOL. segmentación, división (de células).

segmented | seg'mentɪd | *adj.* segmentado, dividido.

segregate | 'segrɪgeɪt | *v.t.* separar (especialmente razas).

segregated | 'segrɪgeɪtɪd | *adj.* de un único, de un solo (sexo, religión o raza).

segregation | ˌsegrɪ'geɪʃn | *s.i.* segregación, separación (especialmente racial).

seismic | 'saɪzmɪk | *adj.* GEOL. sísmico.

seismograph | 'saɪzməgrɑ:f | (EE.UU.) | 'saɪzməgræf | *s.c.* MEC. sismógrafo.

seismology | saɪz'mɒlədʒɪ | *s.i.* sismología.

seize | si:z | *v.t.* **1** agarrar, sujetar con fuerza, coger fuertemente: *the postman seized the thief as he ran by = el cartero agarró al ladrón al pasar corriendo a su lado.* **2** tomar (el poder en un país), dominar (una parte del mundo), capturar (terreno o personas). **3** embargar (propiedades); incautarse de (productos de contrabando). **4** (normalmente pasiva) detener, apoderarse de (personas). **5** coger, no dejar escapar (una oportunidad). **6** (normalmente pasiva) embargar, apoderarse de (un sentimiento fuerte): *panic seized me when I saw the frightening situation = el pánico se apoderó de mí al ver la horrible situación.* || **7 to – on/upon,** aprovechar al máximo, no dejar escapar, valerse de (una oportunidad, una posibilidad de mejora, etc.). **8 to – up,** pararse completamente, agarrotarse, atascarse (un músculo, vehículo, etc.).

seizure | 'si:ʒər | *s.i.* **1** MED. ataque (normalmente de corazón), convulsión, crisis. || *s.c.* e *i.* **2 [– of]** captura de, toma de, incautación (poder, lugar, contrabando, etc.): *seizures of drug are on the increase = las incautaciones de droga están aumentando.*

seldom | 'seldəm | *adv.* rara vez, raras veces, con poca frecuencia.

select | sɪ'lekt | *v.t.* **1** seleccionar, escoger, elegir. || *adj.* **2** selecto, escogido. **3** exclusivista, para la flor y nata (club, zona de viviendas, etc.). || **4 – committee,** (brit.) POL. comisión parlamentaria.

selected | sɪ'lektɪd | *adj.* seleccionado, escogido: *a carefully selected shop = una tienda cuidadosamente seleccionada.*

selection | sɪ'lekʃn | *s.i.* **1** selección. || *s.c.* **2** COM. surtido, gama (de productos). **3** selección (de literatura, música, etc.). || **4 – committee,** jurado, comité de selección (de personas o cosas).

selective | sɪ'lektɪv | *adj.* **1** selectivo (proceso o característica personal). || **2 – service,** (EE.UU.) servicio militar obligatorio, reclutamiento obligatorio.

selectively | sɪ'lektɪvlɪ | *adv.* selectivamente.

selector | sɪ'lektər | *s.c.* **1** DEP. seleccionador. **2** ELECTR. selector (en televisión, radio, etc.).

self | self | [*pl.* **selves**] *s.c.* **1** (form.) uno mismo (desde un punto de vista psicológico, filosófico, etc.). **2** personalidad, ser: *my whole self shakes at the idea = todo mi ser tiembla ante la idea.* || *s.i.* **3** uno mismo (desde el punto de vista egoísta). || **4 self-,** auto, en uno mismo (en compuestos): *selfgiving = generosidad (dar uno de sí mismo).*

self-absorbed | ˌselfəb'sɔ:bd | *adj.* absorto en uno mismo.

self-addressed | ˌselfə'drest | *adj.* dirigido a uno mismo (especialmente en un sobre incluido en otro mayor).

self-adhesive | ˌselfəd'hi:sɪv | *adj.* adhesivo.

self-appointed | ˌselfə'pɔɪntɪd | *adj.* autoproclamado, autonombrado, que se nombra a sí mismo: *a self-appointed saviour = un salvador que se nombra a sí mismo.*

self-assertion | ˌselfəˈsɜːʃn | *s.i.* energía, convencimiento, vigor (en la defensa de las propias ideas, creencias, opiniones, etc.).

self-assertive | ˌselfəˈsɜːtɪv | *adj.* enérgico, convencido, vigoroso (en las propias ideas, creencias, opiniones, etc.); autoritario.

self-assurance | ˌselfəˈʃɔːrəns | (EE.UU.) | ˌselfəˈʃʊərəns | *s.i.* confianza en uno mismo, seguridad en uno mismo.

self-assured | ˌselfəˈʃʊəd | (EE.UU.) | ˌselfəˈʃʊərd | *adj.* seguro en uno mismo, confiado en las fuerzas de uno mismo.

self-catering | ˌselfˈkeɪtərɪŋ | *s.i.* donde uno tiene que o puede hacerse su propia comida (apartamento, piso, aparthotel, etc.).

self-centred | ˌselfˈsentəd | (EE.UU. **self-centered**) *adj.* egoísta, egocéntrico, que piensa sólo en uno mismo.

self-confessed | ˌselfkənˈfest | *adj.* confeso, reconocido por uno mismo, admitido.

self-confidence | ˌselfˈkɒnfɪdəns | *s.i.* confianza en uno mismo, seguridad en uno mismo.

self-confident | ˌselfˈkɒnfɪdənt | *adj.* que confía en sus propias fuerzas, que está seguro de uno mismo.

self-congratulation | ˌselfkənˌgræ | | tʃʊˈleɪʃn | *s.i.* autocomplacencia.

self-conscious | ˌselfˈkɒnʃəs | *adj.* **1** cohibido, tímido, inseguro (al tener que hablar, relacionarse, etc. con otros). **2** con gran conciencia de la identidad de uno mismo.

self-consciously | ˌselfˈkɒnʃəslɪ | *adv.* tímidamente, cohibidamente, con inseguridad en uno mismo.

self-consciousness | ˌselfˈkɒnʃəsnɪs | *s.i.* timidez, inseguridad, encogimiento; falta de naturalidad.

self-contained | ˌselfkənˈteɪnd | *adj.* **1** autosuficiente, que cuenta con sus propios recursos. **2** independiente, autosuficiente (piso que no comparte cocina o baño con otro piso).

self-contradictory | ˌselfˌkɒntrəˈdɪktərɪ | *adj.* que lleva implícita una contradicción, contradictorio.

self-control | ˌselfkənˈtrəʊl | *s.i.* autocontrol, serenidad, autodominio.

self-controlled | ˌselfkənˈtrəʊld | *adj.* sereno, autocontrolado.

self-defeating | ˌselfdɪˈfiːtɪŋ | *adj.* contraproducente.

self-defence | ˌselfdɪˈfens | (EE.UU. **self-defense**) *s.i.* **1** autodefensa, defensa propia. || **2 in –,** en defensa propia.

self-denial | ˌselfdɪˈnaɪəl | *s.i.* autonegación, olvido de uno mismo, abnegación.

self-determination | ˌselfdɪtɜːmɪˈneɪʃn | *s.i.* **1** POL. autodeterminación. **2** independencia personal.

self-discipline | selfˈdɪsɪplɪn | *s.i.* autodisciplina, autodominio.

self-drive | ˌselfˈdraɪv | *adj.* sin chófer (alquiler de coches).

self-educated | ˌselfˈedʒʊkeɪtɪd | *adj.* autodidacta.

self-effacing | ˌselfɪˈfeɪsɪŋ | *adj.* modesto, humilde.

self-employed | ˌselfɪmˈplɔɪd | *adj.* autónomo, que trabaja por cuenta propia.

self-esteem | ˌselfɪˈstiːm | *s.i.* amor propio, autoestima.

self-evident | ˌselfˈevɪdənt | *adj.* patente, clarísimo, evidente.

self-evidently | ˌselfˈevɪdəntlɪ | *adv.* patentemente, clarísimamente, evidentemente.

self-examination | ˌselfɪgzæmɪˈneɪʃn | *s.i.* autoexamen, introspección, examen de uno mismo (en cuanto a acciones y forma de pensar de uno).

self-explanatory | ˌselfɪkˈsplænɪtrɪ | *adj.* que se explica por sí mismo, obvio.

self-expression | ˌselfɪkˈspreʃn | *s.i.* autoexpresión.

self-governing | ˌselfˈgʌvənɪŋ | *adj.* autónomo, independiente (organización, país, etc.).

self-government | ˌselfˈgʌvənmənt | *s.i.* autonomía, independencia.

self-help | ˌselfˈhelp | *s.i.* ayuda propia, esfuerzo propio: *a self-help group = un grupo que sólo se basa en su propio esfuerzo.*

self-importance | ˌselfɪmˈpɔːtəns | *s.i.* presunción, engreimiento, vanidad.

self-important | ˌselfɪmˈpɔːtənt | *adj.* presumido, engreído, vanidoso.

self-imposed | ˌselfɪmˈpəʊzd | *adj.* autoimpuesto, voluntario.

self-indulgence | ˌselfɪnˈdʌldʒəns | *s.i.* satisfacción excesiva de los propios apetitos o deseos; sibaritismo.

self-indulgent | ˌselfɪnˈdʌldʒənt | *adj.* comodón, sibarita.

self-inflicted | ˌselfɪnˈflɪktɪd | *adj.* que uno mismo se inflige (herida).

self-interest | ˌselfˈɪntrɪst | *s.i.* interés propio, egoísmo.

self-interested | ˌselfˈɪntrɪstɪd | *adj.* de interés propio, egoísta.

selfish | ˈselfɪʃ | *adj.* egoísta, interesado.

selfishly | ˈselfɪʃlɪ | *adv.* de forma egoísta, interesadamente.

selfishness | ˈselfɪʃnɪs | *s.i.* egoísmo, interés en lo propio de uno.

selfless | ˈselflɪs | *adj.* desinteresado, desprendido.

selflessly | ˈselflɪslɪ | *adv.* desinteresadamente, desprendidamente.

selflessness | ˈselflɪsnɪs | *s.i.* desinterés, desprendimiento.

self-made | ˌselfˈmeɪd | *adj.* que se ha hecho a uno mismo.

self-opinionated | ˌselfəˈpɪnjəneɪtɪd | *adj.* terco.

self-pity | ˌselfˈpɪtɪ | *s.i.* compasión de uno mismo, lástima de uno mismo.

self-portrait | ˌselfˈpɔːtreɪt | *s.c.* ART. autorretrato.

self-possessed | ˌselfpəˈzest | *adj.* sereno, dueño de uno mismo.

self-possession | ˌselfpəˈzeʃn | *s.i.* serenidad, dominio de uno mismo, aplomo.

self-preservation | ˌselfprezəˈveɪʃn | *s.i.* autoconservación (instinto).

self-raising flour | ˌselfreɪzɪŋˈflaʊər | (EE.UU. **self-rising flour**) *s.i.* harina para levadura.

self-reliance | ˌselfrɪˈlaɪəns | *s.i.* independencia, confianza en uno mismo.

self-reliant | ˌselfrɪˈlaɪənt | *adj.* independiente, confiado en uno mismo.

self-respect | ˌselfrɪˈspekt | *s.i.* amor propio, autorespeto, dignidad.

self-respecting | ˌselfrɪˈspektɪŋ | *adj.* **1** digno, digno de respeto, consciente de la dignidad personal. **2** digno del nombre, que se precie: *any self-respecting library should have a copy = toda biblioteca que se precie debe tener un ejemplar.*

self-righteous | ˌselfˈraɪtʃəs | *adj.* farisaico, santurrón.

self-righteously | ˌselfˈraɪtʃəslɪ | *adv.* farisaicamente, santurronamente.

self-righteousness | ˌselfˈraɪtʃəsnɪs | *s.i.* fariseísmo, santurronería.

self-rising flour | ˌselfraɪsɪŋˈflaʊər | V. **self-raising flour.**

self-sacrifice | ˌselfˈsækrɪfaɪs | *s.i.* abnegación, sacrificio de los gustos de uno.

self-sacrificing | ˌselfˈsækrɪfaɪsɪŋ | *adj.* abnegado, sacrificado.

self-same | ˈselfseɪm | *adj.* mismo, mismísimo.

self-satisfaction | ˌselfˌsætɪsˈfækʃn | *s.i.* autosatisfacción, suficiencia, complacencia.

self-satisfied | ˌselfˈsætɪsfaɪd | *adj.* autosatisfecho, suficiente, complaciente.

self-seeking | ˌselfˈsiːkɪŋ | *adj.* **1** egoísta. || *s.i.* **2** egoísmo.

self-service | ˌselfˈsɜːvɪs | *s.i.* **1** autoservicio. || *adj.* **2** de autoservicio.

self-starter | ˌselfˈstɑːtər | *s.c.* **1** MEC. motor de arranque. **2** persona con ideas propias para progresar en su vida.

self-styled | ˌselfˈstaɪld | *adj.* supuesto.

self-sufficiency | ˌselfsəˈfɪʃənsɪ | *s.i.* autarquía, autosuficiencia.

self-sufficient | ˌselfsəˈfɪʃənt | *adj.* **1 [– (in)]** autárquico, autosuficiente (especialmente un país en economía). **2** autónomo (persona).

self-supporting | ˌselfsəˈpɔːtɪŋ | *adj.* con los propios recursos.

self-taught | ˌselfˈtɔːt | *adj.* autodidacta.

self-willed | ˌselfˈwɪld | *adj.* (desp.) terco, cabezota.

sell | sel | *v.* [*pret.* y *p.p.irreg.* **sold**] *t.* **1** vender. **2** (fam.) convencer de: *did he sell you that stupid idea? = ¿te convenció de esa idea tonta?* **3** vender, traicionar (principio, valores, honor, etc.). || *i.* **4** vender, hacer ventas, venderse. **5** venderse, tener atractivo, ser aceptable (para el público). || *r.* **6** (fam.) comunicar bien, presentar una atrayente personalidad (para conseguir un trabajo, ser votado, etc.). || **7 to – off,** liquidar (existencias). **8 to – oneself short,** hacerse uno de menos, subestimarse. **9 to – out, a)** quedarse sin existencias (de algún producto); **b)** quedarse sin billetes (para un espectáculo). **10 to – out (to),** (fam.) venderse (a), entregarse (a): *he's sold out to the party = se ha entregado al partido.* **11 to – someone down the river,** (fam.) traicionar. **12 to – up,** venderlo todo, quedarse sin nada.

seller | ˈselər | *s.c.* **1** vendedor. **2** producto, producto que vende...: *this thing is a very poor seller = esto es un producto que se vende mal.*

selling | ˈselɪŋ | *s.i.* **1** venta. || **2 – point,** punto a su favor, aspecto ventajoso. **3 – price,** precio de venta.

Sellotape | ˈseləʊteɪp | (marca registrada) *s.i.* **1** celo, cinta adhesiva. || *v.t.* **2** pegar con celo.

sell-out | ˈselaʊt | *s.c.* **1** (normalmente *sing.*) éxito de taquilla. **2** (fam.) traición.

selves | selvz | *pl.* de **self.**
semantic | sɪ'mæntɪk | *adj.* FILOL. semántico.
semantics | sɪ'mæntɪks | *s.i.* semántica.
semaphore | 'seməfɔː | *s.i.* comunicación por banderines.
semblance | 'sembləns | *s.sing.* **[– of]** señal mínima de, mínima apariencia de: *he spoke without a semblance of truth = habló sin la más mínima apariencia de verdad.*
semen | 'siːmen | *s.i.* BIOL. semen.
semester | sɪ'mestər | *s.c.* (EE.UU.) semestre (división del período universitario).
semi | 'semɪ | *s.c.* **1** (brit. y fam.) chalet adosado. || **2 semi-**, semi (en compuestos): *semi-darkness = semioscuridad.*
semibreve | 'semɪbriːv | *s.c.* (brit.) MUS. semibreve.
semicircle | 'semɪsəːkl | *s.c.* GEOM. semicírculo.
semicircular | ˌsemɪ'səːkjulər | *adj.* semicircular.
semi-colon | ˌsemɪ'kəulən | *s.c.* punto y coma.
semiconductor | ˌsemɪkən'dʌktər | *s.c.* ELECTR. semiconductor.
semi-conscious | ˌsemɪ'kɒnʃəs | *adj.* semiconsciente.
semi-detached | ˌsemɪdɪ'tætʃt | *adj.* **1** ARQ. adosado, semiseparado. || *s.c.* **2** chalet adosado.
semifinal | ˌsemɪ'faɪnl | DEP. *s.c.* **1** semifinal. || *s.pl.* **2 [the –]** las semifinales.
semifinalist | ˌsemɪ'faɪnəlɪst | *s.c.* DEP. semifinalista.
seminal | 'semɪnl | *adj.* (form.) fundamental, básico, importantísimo (trabajo, novela, etc.).
seminar | 'semɪnɑːr | *s.c.* seminario, clase de discusión, clase práctica (en una universidad).
seminary | 'semɪnərɪ | (EE.UU.) | 'semɪnerɪ | *s.c.* REL. seminario.
semiotics | ˌsemɪ'ɒtɪks | *s.i.* semiótica.
semiprecious | ˌsemɪ'preʃəs | *adj.* semipreciosa (joya).
semiquaver | ˌsemɪkweɪvər | *s.c.* (brit.) MUS. semicorchea.
Semitic | sɪ'mɪtɪk | *adj.* **1** semítico. **2** judío.
semitone | 'semɪtəun | *s.c.* MUS. semitono.
semolina | ˌsemə'liːnə | *s.i.* sémola.
Senate | 'senɪt | *s.sing.* **1 [the –]** POL. el Senado, la Cámara Alta. **2 [the –]** la Junta Directiva (órgano directivo en algunas universidades).
senator | 'senətər | *s.c.* POL. senador.
senatorial | ˌsenətɔːrɪəl | *adj.* (form.) senatorial.
send | send | *v.t.* [*pret.* y *p.p.irreg.* **sent**] **1** enviar, mandar, despachar. **2** transmitir, enviar (por radio). **3** poner (en un estado); hacer (llegar a un estado): *his way of talking sends me to sleep = su forma de hablar me hace dormirme.* **4** expulsar, lanzar: *the grenade sent everybody running in all directions = la granada hizo que todo el mundo se lanzara a correr en todas las direcciones.* || **5 to – down,** (brit.) expulsar (de una universidad). **6 to – for, a)** hacer llamar, hacer venir, llamar; **b)** pedir, hacer un pedido de. **7 to – forth,** producir; echar (olor, hojas,etc.). **8 to – in, a)** presentar (documento, solicitud, etc.); **b)** enviar (tropas o policía, especialmente). **9 to – off, a)** DEP. expulsar (del juego); **b)** enviar por correo. **10 to – on,** hacer seguir, enviar a nueva dirección (desde la antigua). **11 to – someone packing,** (fam.) mandar a alguien a freír espárragos, mandar a alguien a hacer puñetas. **12 to – up,** (fam.) parodiar, imitar satíricamente. **13 to – word,** enviar aviso, enviar recado.
sender | 'sendər | *s.c.* remitente.
send-off | 'sendɒf | *s.c.* (fam.) despedida.
send-up | 'sendʌp | *s.c.* (fam.) parodia, imitación sarcástica.
Senegal | ˌsenɪ'gɔːl | *s.sing.* Senegal.
Senegalese | ˌsenɪgə'liːz | [*pl.* **Senegalese**] *s.c.* **1** senegalés. || *adj.* **2** senegalés.
senile | 'siːnaɪl | *adj.* senil.
senility | sɪ'nɪlɪtɪ | *s.i.* senilidad.
senior | 'siːnɪər | *adj.* **1** de mayor categoría, de categoría más alta (en un trabajo, organización, etc.). **2 [– (to)]** mejor, mayor, superior (en experiencia, rango, etc.). || *s.sing.* **3** [*adj.pos* –] mayor (en edad): *I'm four years his senior = soy cuatro años mayor que él.* || *s.c.* **4** alumno mayor, chico mayor (en la escuela). **5** (EE.UU.) alumno de COU, alumno del curso preuniversitario. || **6 – citizen,** (euf.) jubilado, persona de la tercera edad.
seniority | ˌsiːnɪ'ɒrɪtɪ | (EE.UU.) | ˌsiːnɪ'ɔːrətɪ | *s.i.* **1** antigüedad (en el trabajo, especialmente). **2** mayor categoría; mayor edad.
sensation | sen'seɪʃn | *s.i.* **1** sensación, sensación física; tacto. || *s.c.* **2** sensación física (concreta). **3** sensación (anímica): *I had the strange sensation of being spied on = tuve la extraña sensación de estar siendo espiado.* **4** sensación, clamor; escándalo. || *s.sing.* **5** bomba: *what a sensation! = ¡vaya bomba!*
sensational | sen'seɪʃənl | *adj.* **1** sensacional, clamoroso. **2** (desp.) sensacionalista. **3** (fam.) sensacional, magnífico, insuperable.
sensationalism sen'seɪʃənəlɪzəm | *s.i.* (desp.) sensacionalismo (especialmente periodístico).
sensationalist | sen'seɪʃənəlɪst | (desp.) *s.c.* **1** sensacionalista. || *adj.* **2** sensacionalista.
sensationally | sen'seɪʃənəlɪ | *adv.* **1** sensacionalmente, clamorosamente. **2** (desp.) con grandes dosis de sensacionalismo. **3** (fam.) sensacionalmente, magníficamente, insuperablemente.
sense | sens | *s.c.* **1** sentido: *the five senses = los cinco sentidos.* **2 [– of]** significado, sentido (de una palabra). || *s.sing.* **3** sentido (del deber, de la justicia, de lo bueno y lo malo, etc.). **4** talento, instinto, aptitud (para negocios, el humor, la oportunidad de una acción, etc.). **5 [– of]** sensación de (algo inmaterial): *a wonderful sense of freedom = una sensación maravillosa de libertad.* **6 [the – (of)]** lo fundamental, lo sustancial, lo básico; la impresión general: *I could understand the sense of what he said = pude entender lo sustancial de lo que dijo.* || *s.i.* **7** inteligencia, sentido común, capacidad mental, capacidad de razonamiento. || *v.t.* **8** percibir, captar, barruntar (casi inconscientemente). || **9 to come/to be brought to one's senses,** entrar en razón, recobrar el buen sentido, recobrar el juicio. **10 in a –,** hasta cierto punto, hasta cierto grado. **11 in a very real –,** de una manera muy real, de modo evidente (enfatizando la verdad de algo). **12 in no –,** de ninguna manera, de ninguna forma, en ningún sentido (enfatizando la falsedad de algo). **13 to make –, a)** tener sentido, tener lógica; ser comprensible, ser natural; **b)** decir cosas sensatas, hablar con sensatez; **c)** parecer razonable, parecer bien (un proceso, actividad, etc.). **14 to make – (of),** sacar en claro (de), entender, comprender el sentido (de). **15 no/little –,** ningún sentido, ninguna lógica. **16 – of direction,** V. **direction. 17 to take leave of one's senses,** perder el juicio, perder la capacidad de razonar; volverse loco. **18 to talk –,** hablar con lógica, hablar razonablemente.
senseless | 'senslɪs | *adj.* **1** sin sentido, inconsciente: *after the blow he was senseless for half an hour = después del golpe estuvo sin sentido durante media hora.* **2** (desp.) insensato, inconsciente, necio.
senselessly | 'senslɪslɪ | *adv.* (desp.) insensatamente, inconscientemente, neciamente.
senselessness | 'senslɪsnɪs | *s.i.* (desp.) insensatez, inconsciencia, falta de seriedad.
sensibility | ˌsensə'bɪlɪtɪ | *s.i.* **1** sensibilidad (artística, literaria, etc.). **2** sensibilidad, susceptibilidad (a lo que otros opinen de nosotros).
sensible | 'sensəbl | *adj.* **1** sensato, juicioso, prudente. **2** práctico, funcional (manera de vestir).
sensibly | 'sensəblɪ | *adv.* con gran sensatez, con buen juicio, prudentemente.
sensitise V. **sensitize.**
sensitive | 'sensɪtɪv | *adj.* **1 [– (to)]** sensible, delicado (normalmente una parte del cuerpo). **2** delicado, difícil (asunto, cuestión, conflicto, etc.). **3 [– (to)]** sensible (para lo artístico, los problemas de otros, etc.). **4** sensible (aparato). **5 [– (about/to)]** susceptible: *he's too sensitive to criticism = es demasiado susceptible ante la crítica.*
sensitively | 'sensətɪvlɪ | *adv.* con susceptibilidad.
sensitivity | ˌsensə'tɪvɪtɪ | *s.c.* e *i.* **1** susceptibilidad. **2** sensibilidad (artística, literaria, etc.). || *s.i.* **3** precisión (de aparatos). **4** sensibilidad, (lo) delicado (normalmente de una parte del cuerpo). **5** dificultad, (lo) delicado (de un problema, asunto, conflicto, etc.).
sensitize | 'sensɪtaɪz | (también **sensitise**) *v.t.* **1** sensibilizar (material fotográfico o similar). **2** (form.) sensibilizar (a personas ante un problema).
sensor | 'sensər | *s.c.* MEC. sensor.
sensory | 'sensərɪ | *adj.* (form.) sensorio, sensorial.
sensual | 'senʃuəl | *adj.* sensual.
sensuality | ˌsenʃu'ælɪtɪ | *s.i.* sensualidad.
sensually | 'senʃuəlɪ | *adv.* sensualmente.
sensuous | 'senʃuəs | *adj.* sensual, placentero.
sensuously | 'senʃuəslɪ | *adv.* sensualmente, placenteramente.
sensuousness | 'senʃuəsnɪs | *s.i.* sensualidad, placer.

sent | sent | *pret.* y *p.p.irreg.* de **send.**
sentence | 'sentəns | *s.c.* **1** GRAM. oración. || *s.c.* e *i.* **2** DER. sentencia, fallo. || *v.t.* **3** DER. sentenciar, condenar. **4** (fig.) condenar, destinar: *it's incredible there are so many millions of people sentenced to a life of solitude = es increíble que haya tantos millones de personas destinados a una vida de soledad.* || **5 – adverb,** GRAM. oración adverbial.
sententious | sen'tenʃəs | *adj.* (form.) sentencioso, ampuloso (especialmente en el lenguaje).
sententiously | sen'tenʃəslɪ | *adv.* (form.) sentenciosamente, ampulosamente.
sententiousness | sen'tenʃəsnɪs | *s.i.* (form.) estilo sentencioso, ampulosidad.
sentient | 'senʃnt | *adj.* (form.) sensible, sensitivo (físicamente): *a sentient being = un ser sensible.*
sentiment | 'sentɪmənt | *s.i.* **1** (normalmente desp.) sentimiento. || *s.c.* **2** opinión, sentir.
sentimental | ˌsentɪ'mentl | *adj.* **1** (normalmente desp.) sentimental, sentimentaloide, sensiblero. **2** emocional, sentimental; romántico.
sentimentality | ˌsentɪmen'tælɪtɪ | *s.i.* (desp.) sensiblería.
sentimentally | ˌsentɪ'mentəlɪ | *adv.* **1** (normalmente desp.) sentimentalmente, sensibleramente. **2** emocionalmente, sentimentalmente; románticamente.
sentimentalize | ˌsentɪ'mentəlaɪz | (también **sentimentalise**) *v.t.* e *i.* (form.) sentimentalizar, hablar demasiado emocionalmente.
sentinel | 'sentɪnl | *s.c.* (p.u.) centinela.
sentry | 'sentrɪ | MIL. *s.c.* **1** centinela. || **2 – box,** garita (de centinela).
separable | 'sepərəbl | *adj.* separable, divisible.
separably | 'sepərəblɪ | *adv.* separablemente, divisiblemente.
separate | 'seprɪt | *v.t.* **1** separar, dividir (física y figurativamente). **2** [**to – +** *o.* **+ from**] distinguir de, diferenciar de. **3** separar la clara de la yema (de un huevo). || *v.i.* **4** [**to – (from)**] separarse (una pareja). **5** separarse, alejarse; despedirse (momentáneamente). **6** cortarse; hacerse grumos (leche, mayonesa, etc.). || | 'sepəreɪt | *adj.* **7** [**– (from)**] separado, desunido (físicamente). **8** distinto, diferente, diferenciado, suelto (que se nota individualmente). || *s.pl.* **9** ropas sueltas, prendas sueltas. || **10 to go one's – ways,** separarse, ir cada uno por su lado.
separated | 'sepəreɪtɪd | *adj.* **1** separado (como pareja). || **2 the –,** los separados, las personas separadas.
separately | 'seprɪtlɪ | *adv.* **1** separadamente, por separado. **2** de manera suelta, diferentemente, distintamente.
separateness | 'seprətnɪs | *s.i.* estado de separación.
separation | ˌsepə'reɪʃn | *s.i.* **1** separación de: *the separation of Westerners from Asians is evident = la separación de los occidentales de los asiáticos es evidente.* || *s.c.* **2** separación, división, pared. || *s.c.* e *i.* **3** separación (de la pareja). **4** separación, tiempo de separación. **5** separación, distinción, diferenciación.
separatism | 'sepərətɪzəm | *s.i.* POL. separatismo.
separatist | 'sepərətɪst | POL. *s.c.* **1** separatista. || *atr.* **2** separatista.
sepia | 'siːpɪə | *adj.* **1** de sepia (color). || *s.i.* **2** sepia. **3** QUIM. sepia.
September | sep'tembər | *s.i.* septiembre.
septic | 'septɪk | *adj.* **1** MED. infectado, con infección: *a septic throat = una garganta con infección.* || **2 – tank,** pozo séptico.
septuagenarian | ˌseptjuədʒɪ'neərɪən | *s.c.* (form.) septuagenario.
sepulchral | sɪ'pʌlkrəl | *adj.* (lit.) sepulcral, fúnebre, tétrico, funesto.
sepulchre | 'seplkər | (EE.UU. **sepulcher**) *s.c.* (lit.) sepulcro.
sequel | 'siːkwəl | *s.c.* **1** [**– (to)**] continuación (de una novela, película, etc.). **2** [**– (to)**] consecuencia, resultado posterior, desenlace.
sequence | 'siːkwəns | *s.c.* **1** secuencia (de película). **2** [**– of**] secuencia de, serie de, sucesión de. **3** secuencia temporal. || **4 in/out of –,** en/sin secuencia, en/sin secuencia temporal. **5 – of tenses,** GRAM. secuencia temporal, secuencia de tiempos verbales.
sequential | sɪ'kwenʃl | *adj.* (form.) secuencial, serial.
sequentially | sɪ'kwenʃəlɪ | *adv.* (form.) secuencialmente.
sequester | sɪ'kwestər | *v.t.* DER. secuestrar, confiscar (propiedad).
sequestered | sɪ'kwestəd | *adj.* (lit.) aislado, remoto (lugar).
sequestrate | 'siːkwestreɪt | *v.t.* DER. secuestrar, confiscar (propiedad).
sequestration | ˌsiːkwe'streɪʃn | *s.i.* DER. secuestro, confiscación.
sequin | 'siːkwɪn | *s.c.* lentejuela (para adorno en la ropa).
sequinned | 'siːkwɪnd | (EE.UU. **sequined**) *adj.* con lentejuelas.
seraph | 'serəf | [*pl.* **seraphim** o **seraphs**] *s.c.* REL. serafín.
seraphim | 'serəfɪm | *pl.* de **seraph.**
Serbo-Croat | ˌsɜːbəʊ'krəʊæt | *s.i.* serbocroata (idioma).
serenade | ˌserə'neɪd | MUS. *s.c.* **1** serenata. **2** pieza para pequeña orquesta. || *v.t.* **3** dar una serenata.
serendipity | ˌserən'dɪpɪtɪ | *s.i.* (form.) hallazgo afortunado.
serene | sɪ'riːn | *adj.* sereno, tranquilo, compuesto.
serenely | sɪ'riːnlɪ | *adv.* serenamente, tranquilamente.
serenity | sɪ'renɪtɪ | *s.i.* serenidad, tranquilidad.
serf | sɜːf | *s.c.* HIST. siervo (medieval).
serfdom | 'sɜːfdəm | *s.i.* **1** HIST. sistema de siervos de la gleba. **2** (fig.) servidumbre.
serge | sɜːdʒ | *s.i.* estameña, sarga (tipo de tejido).
sergeant | 'sɑːdʒənt | *s.c.* MIL. sargento.
sergeant-major | ˌsɑːdʒənt'meɪdʒər | *s.c.* MIL. sargento mayor.
serial | 'sɪərɪəl | *adj.* **1** serial, en serie; consecutivo. || *s.c.* **2** serial (novela, programa, etc.).
serialization | ˌsɪərɪəlaɪ'zeɪʃn | (EE.UU.) | ˌsɪərɪəlɪ'zeɪʃn | (también **serialisation**) *s.c.* e *i.* serialización.
serialize | 'sɪərɪəlaɪz | (también **serialise**) *v.t.* publicación como serial, filmar como serial.
series | 'sɪəriːz | [*pl.* **series**] *s.sing.* **1** [**– (of)**] serie, sucesión. || *s.c.* **2** serie, ciclo (de conferencias, libros, etc.). **3** TV. serie. || **4 in –,** ELEC. en serie.
serious | 'sɪərɪəs | *adj.* **1** serio (carácter y comportamiento). **2** serio, difícil, comprometido, grave (asunto, situación, etc.). **3** grave (enfermedad).
seriously | 'sɪərɪəslɪ | *adv.* **1** seriamente. **2** seriamente, difícilmente, comprometidamente, gravemente. **3** gravemente (enfermo). **4** en serio, de verdad, no en broma. || **5 to take =N,** tomar en serio.
seriousness | 'sɪərɪəsnɪs | *s.i.* **1** seriedad (de carácter o comportamiento). **2** seriedad, gravedad, dificultad (de una situación). **3** gravedad (de una enfermedad).
sermon | 'sɜːmən | *s.c.* **1** REL. sermón. **2** (desp.) sermón, rollo.
sermonize | 'sɜːmənaɪz | (también **sermonise**) *v.t.* (desp.) dar un sermón, soltar un rollo, sermonear.
sermonizing | 'sɜːmənaɪzɪŋ | (también **sermonising**) (desp.) *adj.* **1** sermoneante. || *s.i.* **2** sermoneo.
serpent | 'sɜːpənt | *s.c.* (p.u. o lit.) serpiente.
serpentine | 'sɜːpəntaɪn | *adj.* (lit.) serpentino, sinuoso.
serrated | sɪ'reɪtɪd | (EE.UU.) | 'sereɪtɪd | *adj.* serrado, dentellado, dentado (objeto).
serried | 'serɪd | *adj.* (lit.) apretado, pegado (unos contra otros).
serum | 'sɪərəm | *s.i.* **1** FISIOL. suero (de la sangre). | *s.c.* e *i.* **2** QUIM. suero (para vacunas).
servant | 'sɜːvənt | *s.c.* **1** criado, sirviente. **2** (fig.) servidor: *the Pope is the servant of all Catholics = el Papa es el servidor de todos los católicos.*
serve | sɜːv | *v.t.* e *i.* **1** servir (comida o bebida). **2** DEP. sacar, tener el saque (tenis, bádminton, etc.). **3** servir, atender (especialmente a un cliente en una tienda). || *v.t.* **4** servir (al país, familia, comunidad, etc.). **5** suministrar, dar; haber (un servicio): *all this region used to be served by free buses = en toda esta zona solía haber un servicio gratis de autobuses.* **6** GAST. ser suficiente para, tener... porciones (en las recetas). **7** [**to – +** *o.* **+ with/on**] DER. entregar (notificación judicial). **8** cumplir (sentencia de cárcel), servir un tiempo de (aprendiz). || *v.i.* **9** servir (en el ejército o administración pública). **10** [**to – as/for**/*inf.*] servir de/para, hacer la función de, hacer el servicio de, valer para: *this serves as a knife and tin-opener = esto sirve de cuchillo y abridor de latas.* || *s.sing.* **11** DEP. servicio, saque. || **12 to – a purpose,** servir para un propósito, servir para el caso. **13 to – out/up,** servir, ir por las mesas sirviendo (comida). **14 to – someone right,** tenerlo merecido, merecerlo. **15 to – time,** (fam.) cumplir una condena.
server | 'sɜːvər | *s.c.* **1** DEP. jugador con el servicio. **2** pala, bandeja (para servir ciertos platos).
service | 'sɜːvɪs | *s.c.* **1** servicio (de correos, de información, de transportes, etc.). **2** servicio (como trabajo): *the library doesn't charge anything for this service = la biblioteca no cobra nada por este servicio.* **3** MIL. servicio, (fig.) ejército: *I spent twenty years in the service = pasé veinte años en el ejército.* **4**

REL. culto, oficio, misa. **5** mantenimiento, revisión (de un vehículo o máquina). **6** vajilla, juego, servicio de mesa: *a lovely dinner service = una vajilla preciosa.* || *s.i.* **7** servicio doméstico, trabajo doméstico. **8** tiempo de servicio (tiempo de trabajo). **9** funcionamiento (cualquier tipo de maquinaria): *in service = en funcionamiento.* **10** servicio, atención (al cliente). **11** MIL. batalla, acción de guerra. || *s.sing.* **12** DEP. servicio, servicio de saque (tenis o juego similar). **13** tiempo de servicio (tiempo de trabajo). || *s.pl.* **14** servicios (trabajo): *am I to understand my services are no longer needed? = ¿debo entender que mis servicios ya no son necesarios?* **15** ECON. servicios, sector de servicios, sector terciario. **16** servicios (especialmente públicos). || *adj.* **17** de servicio, para empleados sólo (no para el público): *service doors = puertas de servicio.* || *v.t.* **18** revisar, hacer el mantenimiento de (maquinaria). **19** dar un servicio a, prestar un servicio a (especialmente en infraestructura y cosas necesarias para el mantenimiento). **20** FIN. hacer frente a los intereses, pagar intereses (de una deuda). || **21 at the – of,** a disposición de, al servicio de. **22 at your –,** a su disposición, a su servicio (ofreciéndose a otra persona). **23 to do someone a –,** prestar un servicio a alguien; hacer un favor a alguien. **24 of –,** útil, de utilidad. **25 to press into –,** echar mano de; hacer prestar un servicio, obligar a tener una cierta utilidad. **26 – area,** zona de descanso, zona de servicios (junto a carretera). **27 – charge,** servicio, recargo de servicio (en restaurante o similar). **28 – flat,** (brit.) piso que incluye en su renta los servicios de jardinero, portero, etc. **29 – road,** camino de acceso (a una casa, bloque de oficinas, etc.). **30 – station,** estación de gasolina. **31 the services,** MIL. los tres ejércitos.

serviceable | 'sɜːvɪsəbl | *adj.* **1** útil, práctico. **2** servible, en funcionamiento, utilizable.

serviceman | 'sɜːvɪsmən | [*pl.irreg.* **servicemen**] *s.c.* soldado, militar (de cualquier ejército).

servicemen | 'sɜːvɪsmən | *pl.irreg.* de **serviceman.**

serviette | ˌsɜːvɪ'et | *s.c.* (brit.) servilleta.

servile | 'sɜːvaɪl | (EE.UU.) | 'sɜːvl | *adj.* (desp.) servil, de lacayo; rastrero.

servility | sɜː'vɪlɪtɪ | *s.i.* (desp.) servilismo.

serving | 'sɜːvɪŋ | *s.c.* **1** ración. || *adj.* **2** de servir (cuchara, plato, etc.).

servitude | 'sɜːvɪtjuːd | *s.i.* servidumbre, esclavitud, vasallaje.

sesame | sesəmɪ | *s.i.* BOT. ajonjolí, sésamo. || **2 open –,** (fig.) abrepuertas, especie de santo y seña.

session | 'seʃn | *s.c.* **1** sesión, período de sesiones (de cualquier organismo). **2** sesión (como período de tiempo): *a drinking session = una sesión de beber.* **3** año académico; período académico (en Universidades americanas y escocesas). || **4 in –,** en sesión.

set | set | *v.* [*pret.* y *p.p.irreg.* **set;** *ger.* **setting**] *t.* **1** poner, colocar. **2** estar asentado, estar situado, estar colocado: *the house is set quite far from any other human habitation = la casa está situada bastante lejos de cualquier otro habitáculo humano.* **3** poner (la mesa, una trampa, etc.). **4** fijar, señalar, determinar (un precio, un tiempo, un mínimo, etc.). **5** poner en hora (reloj), ajustar (cualquier máquina). **6** sentar la tendencia; poner como ejemplo: *he set the women's fashion in the 60's = él sentó la tendencia de la moda femenina en los años sesenta.* **7** marcar (pelo). **8** MED. asentar, colocar (un hueso roto). **9** sentar (precedente); dar (ejemplo). **10** dar (importancia, valor, etc., a algo). **11** poner (música a un poema o similar). **12** ambientar (una novela, película, etc.). **13** apretar (los dientes, especialmente demostrando gran determinación). **14** montar, encasar (una joya en un jarrón, una ventana en una pared, etc.). **15** asignar, poner (una tarea, examen, obligación, etc.). **16** establecer, fijar, poner (un objetivo). **17** ponerse, tener (una expresión facial). **18** [**to – +** *ger.*] hacer, causar: *his opinions set me thinking = sus opiniones me hicieron pensar.* || *i.* **19** ponerse, ocultarse (el sol). **20** solidificarse, endurecerse, cuajar (cualquier sustancia). **21** MED. asentarse, colocarse (hueso). || *r.* **22** [**to – +** *inf.*] decidirse firmemente, ponerse a... con firmeza: *I set myself to earn money to fulfil my dreams = me decidí firmemente a ganar dinero para hacer realidad mis sueños.* || *s.c.* **23** juego, colección, serie (de llaves, libros, ropa, etc.). **24** MAT. conjunto. **25** aparato (de radio o televisión). **26** DEP. set (tenis). **27** decorado (de teatro, cine, etc.). **28** MUS. serie de piezas, repertorio. || *s.sing.* **29** marcado (del pelo). **30** [**the – of**] la postura de, la forma de, la apariencia de, la expresión de, el porte de (la cara o el cuerpo). **31** (a veces desp.) pandilla, cuadrilla: *the jet set.* || *adj.* **32** fijo, determinado, fijado, establecido: *a set fee = unos honorarios fijos.* **33** del día (menú). **34** obligatorio, establecido (programa de lecturas, trabajo escolar, etc.). **35** [**– on**] decidido a, resuelto a. **36** [– + *inf.*/**for**] preparado para, dispuesto a. **37** invariable, inmovible, establecido: *a set timetable = un horario invariable.* **38** forzado, rígido (expresión o postura). || **39 to be – in one's ways,** tener costumbres muy arraigadas, ser una persona de hábitos fijos. **40 on –,** en el plató, en escena. **41 to – about,** [+ *inf.*] ponerse a, comenzar a (hacer algo). **42 to – against, a)** contrastar, comparar; **b)** contrarrestar (impuestos); **c)** lanzar contra, enemistar (especialmente a personas que son amigas). **43 to – apart,** reservar, guardar (para algo especial). **44 to – apart (from),** distinguir (de), diferenciar (de): *his kindness sets him apart from the rest of the staff = su amabilidad le diferencia del resto del personal.* **45 to – aside, a)** poner a un lado, dejar en reserva, guardar; **b)** DER. anular, declarar nulo; **c)** rechazar, apartar (un sentimiento, principio, valor moral, etc.). **46 to – back, a)** (fam.) retrasar, retardar (proyecto, plan, etc.); **b)** (fam.) pegar un susto (en el sentido económico); costar un pico. **47 to – down, a)** dejar (un vehículo a una persona en algún sitio); **b)** poner por escrito. **48 to – eyes on,** V. **eye. 49 to – fire to,** V. **fire. 50 to – foot,** V. **foot. 51 to – forth, a)** (form.) exponer (ideas, teorías, etc.); **b)** (lit.) ponerse en camino, partir. **52 to – great store by,** V. **store. 53 to – in,** comenzar (algo malo): *in October the bad weather set in = en Octubre comenzó el mal tiempo.* **54 to – off, a)** ponerse en camino, partir, empezar un viaje; **b)** hacer estallar, hacer explotar; **c)** hacer resaltar, hacer sobresalir (por fuerte contraste de color u otro); **d)** causar, hacer empezar: *his attack set off a wave of angry reactions = su ataque causó una cadena de reacciones airadas.* **55 to – off (on),** hacer (a alguien) hablar (sobre). **56 to – on/upon,** atacar, echarse encima (animales o personas contra personas). **57 to – one's face against,** V. **face. 58 to – one's heart on,** V. **heart. 59 to – one's mind on,** V. **mind. 60 to – out, a)** partir, ponerse en camino; **b)** ordenar, arreglar, disponer con cierto gusto; **c)** presentar, exponer (en un discurso, libro, debate, etc.); **d)** [+ *inf.*] intentar, tratar de; planear (hacer algo). **61 – piece, a)** movimiento estudiado (en el mundo del deporte o de la guerra); **b)** escena estudiada, escena precisa (en teatro, cine, etc.). **62 to – sail,** V. **sail. 63 – square,** escuadra. **64 – theory,** MAT. teoría de conjuntos. **65 to – the stage for,** V. **stage. 66 to – to,** ponerse a ello resueltamente, fajarse y empezar, aplicarse con vigor. **67 to – to work,** ponerse a trabajar con ahínco. **68 to – up, a)** colocar, erigir, levantar (algún tipo de estructura); **b)** establecer, crear (una empresa o similar); **c)** poner en marcha, hacer funcionar (aparato); **d)** desatar (una reacción): *the medicine set up an allergic reaction = la medicina desató una reacción alérgica;* **e)** (fam.) engañar, tomar el pelo; **f)** poner bien, dejar en buen estado (de salud, económico, etc.); **g)** establecerse, hacer vida por su cuenta; **h)** producir, causar: *our coming set up a tremendous racket = nuestra llegada produjo un ruido tremendo.* **69 to – up home/house,** montar casa, poner casa (propia). **70 to – up shop,** establecerse por su cuenta (con el propio negocio).

OBS. Este verbo aparece en muchas expresiones que expresan lo siguiente; **71** causación de algún estado o situación: *they set me free = me pusieron en libertad; he set the whole idea in motion = puso en marcha la idea completa; some youngsters set the buses alight = algunos jóvenes prendieron fuego a los autobuses.*

setback | 'setbæk | *s.c.* contratiempo, revés.

settee | se'tiː | *s.c.* sofá.

setter | 'setər | *s.c.* ZOOL. perro inglés, setter.

setting | 'setɪŋ | *s.c.* **1** escena, escenario, marco, decorado (de una historia). **2** cubierto (de vajilla). **3** composición, situación, ambiente: *the setting at the university is good = el ambiente en la universidad es bueno.* **4** graduación, ajuste (de una máquina). **5** MUS. arreglo, versión. **6** (normalmente *sing.*) ocaso, puesta (del sol). **7** engaste (de una joya). || **8 the – up of,** el establecimiento de, la creación de (una empresa, cuerpo especial, comité de investigación, etc.).

settle | 'setl | *v.t.* e *i.* **1** colocar(se), asentar(se), poner(se): *he settled the book* *on his knee = colocó el libro sobre la rodilla.* **2** posar(se) (la mirada). || *v.t.* **3** resolver, solucionar, poner en orden (problema, asunto, etc.). **4** (normalmente pasiva) dejar sentado, dejar acordado, quedar acordado: *fine, everything is settled = estupendo, todo ha quedado acordado.* **5** colonizar, asentarse en: *the Germans originally settled these regions = en un principio los alemanes se asentaron en estas tierras.* **6** pagar, liquidar, saldar: *to settle a bill = pagar una factura.* **7** **[to – +** *o.* **+ on]** (form.) dejar en herencia a (especialmente dinero). **8** (normalmente pasiva) asentarse, hacerse a (una nueva casa): *come and see us when we are settled = ven a vernos cuando estemos hechos a la nueva casa.* || *v.i.* **9** ponerse cómodo, relajarse. **10** quedarse en un sitio fijo, asentarse, establecerse. **11** descender sobre (un sentimiento, por ejemplo, sobre unas personas o un sitio). **12** llegar a un arreglo, alcanzar un acuerdo. **13** reposarse; digerirse (comida). **14** hundirse, posarse, asentarse (polvo, arena o parecido). **15** posarse (desde una posición superior a una inferior). **16** **[to – (with)]** echar las cuentas (de dinero). **17** **[to – on]** descender sobre, aparecer en (la cara una expresión): *a strange smile slowly settled on her face = una extraña sonrisa apareció lentamente en su rostro.* || *v.r.* **18** relajarse, ponerse cómodo. **19** descender, aposentarse, asentarse (una expresión sobre un rostro). || *s.c.* **20** banco (parecido a un sofá). || **21 to allow the dust to –,** V. **dust. 22 to – a score/account,** ajustar las cuentas. **23 to – down, a)** calmarse, apaciguarse; relajarse; **b)** sentar la cabeza. **24 to – down (to),** prepararse cuidadosamente, concentrarse bien (ante una tarea, pasatiempo, actividad, etc.). **25 to – for,** conformarse con. **26 to – in,** adaptarse, hacerse (a un nuevo lugar). **27 to – on,** aceptar, decidirse por: *we all settled on the first proposal = todos nos decidimos por la primera propuesta.* **28 to – somebody's hash,** (fam.) dar a alguien para el pelo, cansarse de alguien y decirle todo lo que le sale a uno. **29 to – up,** hacer las cuentas definitivas (de dinero).

settled | 'setld | *adj.* **1** HIST. sedentario. **2** establecido, asentado, fijo (físicamente). **3** asentado (en una casa o un sitio).

settlement | 'setlmənt | *s.c.* **1** asentamiento (donde viven personas). **2** acuerdo, arreglo, ajuste, satisfacción, solución (de un problema, deuda, etc., especialmente cuando se lleva a cabo amigablemente, sin ir a juicio). || *s.i.* **3** pago (de una deuda). **4** colonización (de tierras). || *s.c.* e *i.* **5** DER. contrato, convenio (oficial). || **6 in – (of),** como pago (de).

settler | 'setlər | *s.c.* colonizador, colono.

set-to | ˌset'tuː | *s.c.* pelea, lucha, bronca.

set-up | 'setʌp | *s.c.* **1** (normalmente *sing.*) montaje, tinglado. || **2 well –,** (p.u.) fornido, bien plantado (hombre).

seven | 'sevn | *num.card.* siete.

seventeen | sevn'tiːn | *num.card.* diecisiete.

seventeenth | sevn'tiːnθ | *num.ord.* décimoséptimo.

seventh | 'sevnθ | *num.ord.* **1** séptimo. || *s.c.* **2** **[– of]** séptima parte de. **3** MUS. séptima, intervalo de séptima.

seventieth | 'sevntɪɪθ | *num.ord.* septuagésimo.

seventy | 'sevntɪ | *num.card.* setenta.

sever | 'sevər | *v.t.* (form.) **1** cortar, partir, dividir (por completo): *the machine severed the tree's trunk = la máquina cortó el tronco del árbol.* **2** (fig.) romper (una relación o similar).

several | 'sevrəl | *adj.* y *pron.indef.* varios, unos cuantos, diversos, algunos: *several friends came = vinieron varios amigos.*

severance | 'sevərəns | *s.i.* **1** **[– (of /from)]** ruptura, rompimiento (de relaciones o similar). || **2 – pay,** indemnización por cese, compensación por despido.

severe | sɪ'vɪər | *adj.* **1** severo, adusto (de carácter). **2** austero (de apariencia, estilo, etc.). **3** grave, serio (problema, accidente, etc.).

severely | sɪ'vɪəlɪ | *adv.* **1** severamente, adustamente (comportarse). **2** austeramente (vivir). **3** gravemente, seriamente (con problemas).

severity | sɪ'verɪtɪ | *s.i.* **1** severidad, (de carácter). **2** austeridad (de estilo de vida). **3** gravedad, seriedad (de un problema, accidente, etc.).

sew | səʊ | *v.t.* e *i.* [*pret.* **sewed,** *p.p.irreg.* **sewn**] **1** coser. || **2 to – up, a)** coser, unir mediante costura; **b)** (fam.) arreglar, amañar (asunto).

sewage | 'sjuːɪdʒ | (EE.UU.) | 'suːɪdʒ | *s.i.* **1** aguas residuales, aguas negras. || **2 – farm,** estación depuradora de aguas.

sewee | 'suːə | *s.c.* cloaca, alcantarilla.

sewerage | sjuːərɪdʒ | (EE.UU.) | 'suːərɪdʒ | *s.i.* alcantarillado.

sewing | 'səʊɪŋ | *s.i.* **1** labor, costura (habilidad manual). **2** labor (ropa para coser).

sewing-machine | 'səʊɪŋməʃiːn | *s.c.* máquina de coser.

sewn | səʊn | *p.p.irreg.* de **sew.**

sex | seks | *s.i.* **1** sexo: *there's only sex in modern films = sólo hay sexo en las películas modernas.* || *s.c.* **2** sexo (masculino o femenino): *both sexes = ambos sexos.* || *v.t.* **3** BIOL. encontrar el sexo de (un animal). || **4 to have – (with),** irse a la cama (con). **5 – act,** acto sexual. **6 – appeal,** atracción sexual. **7 – education,** educación sexual. **8 – life,** vida sexual. **9 – object,** objeto sexual. **10 – shop,** tienda de objetos sexuales.

sexiness | 'seksɪnɪs | *s.i.* atractivo sexual.

sexism | 'seksɪzəm | *s.i.* (desp.) sexismo.

sexist | 'seksɪst | (desp.) *s.c.* **1** sexista. || *adj.* **2** sexista.

sexless | 'sekslɪs | *adj.* **1** asexuado, sin sexo. **2** sin atractivo sexual (una persona).

sextant | 'sekstənt | *s.c.* MEC. sextante.

sextet | seks'tet | *s.c.* MUS. sexteto.

sexton | 'sekstən | *s.c.* REL. sacristán; sepulturero (del camposanto de una iglesia).

sexual | 'sekʃʊəl | *adj.* **1** sexual. || **2 – intercourse,** coito, contacto sexual.

sexuality | ˌsekʃʊ'ælɪtɪ | *s.i.* sexualidad.

sexually | 'sekʃʊəlɪ | *adv.* sexualmente.

sexy | 'seksɪ | *adj.* **1** atractivo sexualmente. **2** con deseos de contacto sexual.

sh | ʃ | *interj.* chiss, chsss (para que alguien se calle).

shabbily | 'ʃæbɪlɪ | *adv.* **1** miserablemente, pobrísimamente (de un lugar). **2** andrajosamente, con harapos (vestimenta). **3** (fig.) vilmente, ruinmente, mezquinamente.

shabbiness | 'ʃæbɪnɪs | *s.i.* **1** estado empobrecido, condición miserable (de un lugar). **2** forma de vestir zarrapastrosa. **3** (fig.) vileza, mezquindad.

shabby | 'ʃæbɪ | *adj.* **1** miserable, en un estado muy deteriorado (lugar). **2** zarrapastroso, andrajoso, harapiento. **3** (fig.) vil, ruin, mezquino.

shack | ʃæk | *s.c.* **1** chabola (hecha con trozos de cartón, metal, etc.). || **2 to – up (with/together),** (fam.) vivir juntos; vivir con (alguien sin casarse).

shackle | 'ʃækl | *v.t.* **1** poner grilletes, encadenar con grilletes, sujetar con grilletes. **2** (fig.) impedir, estorbar, poner trabas (especialmente en casos en que la convención social tradicional estorba a uno). || *s.pl.* **3** grilletes, argollas: *a pair of shackles = unas argollas.* **4** (fig.) trabas, impedimentos, obstáculos (de tipo convencional o social): *the shackles of tradition = las trabas de la tradición.*

shade | ʃeɪd | *s.i.* **1** sombra, umbría. **2** ART. parte oscura, sombra (de una pintura). || *s.sing.* **3** **[the –]** la sombra, la zona de sombra (donde no da el sol). || *s.c.* **4** pantalla (de una lámpara). **5** matiz (de significado, ideología, etc.). **6** (lit.) espíritu, espectro. **7** (EE.UU.) persiana, celosía. **8** tono, tonalidad (de color). || *s.pl.* **9** (fam.) gafas de sol. || *v.t.* **10** (normalmente pasiva) dar sombra, proveer de sombra. **11** sombrear (en pintura). || *v.i.* **12** **[to – into]** mezclarse con, difuminarse en: *in 1970 Communism and Capitalism seemed to be very near to shading into one another = en 1970 el comunismo y el capitalismo parecían estar muy cerca de difuminarse entre ellos mismos.* **13** **[to – in]** sombrear (en pintura). || **14 a –,** (fam.) una pizca, un poquito: *a shade too bright = una pizca demasiado brillante.* **15 to put in the –,** eclipsar, hacer sombra (a algo o alguien). **16 to – one's eyes,** protegerse los ojos con la mano, hacer visera con las manos. **17 shades of,** me recuerda a, se parece a; justo igual que. **18 window –,** (EE.UU.) persiana, celosía.

shadily | 'ʃeɪdɪlɪ | *adv.* sospechosamente, dudosamente (hablando de una persona o actividad).

shading | 'ʃeɪdɪŋ | *s.i.* **1** ART. sombreado (en pintura). || *s.c.* **2** (normalmente *pl.*) matiz, matiz de color; escala sutil (en la sociedad, por ejemplo).

shadiness | 'ʃeɪdɪnɪs | *s.i.* actividad sospechosa, carácter dudoso (de actividad o persona).

shadow | 'ʃædəʊ | *s.c.* **1** sombra (que proyecta algo o alguien). **2** (hum.) sombra (niño que no se aparta nunca de su madre o guardián). **3** (fig.) sombra, persona que sigue (a alguien) a todas horas. || *s.i.* **4** sombra, oscuridad: *the place was in shadow = el lugar estaba en la oscuridad.* || *s.sing.* **5** [neg. + – **of]** sombra de, indicio de, huella de (duda, sospecha, etc.). || *adj.* **6** (brit.) POL. de la oposición (mencionando la persona que probablemente ocuparía tal o cual ministerio de ganar las elecciones): *the shadow cabinet = el gobierno (probable) de la oposición.* || *v.t.* **7** seguir muy de cerca, ir tras los pasos de. **8** (lit.)

sombrear, dar sombra (a un lugar). || **9 to be afraid/frightened of one's own –,** tener miedo de la propia sombra de uno. **10 to be a – of one's former self,** ser uno la sombra de uno mismo, ser uno la sombra de lo que era; haber quedado mal (especialmente después de operación, enfermedad, etc.).

shadowy | 'ʃædəʊɪ | *adj.* **1** sombreado, oscuro (lugar). **2** apenas visible, vago, indefinido (figura o forma). **3** misteriosa, oscura (actividad o persona).

shady | 'ʃeɪdɪ | *adj.* **1** lleno de sombra, sombreado, protegido (del sol). **2** que dan sombra (árboles). **3** sospechosa, dudosa (actividad o persona).

shaft | ʃa:ft | (EE.UU.) | ʃæft | *s.c.* **1** fuste, asta (de cualquier objeto). **2** pozo (de mina, ascensor, luz, etc.). **3** MEC. eje, árbol. **4 [– (of)]** haz (de luz). **5** (normalmente *pl.*) lanza (de un carro). **6 [– (of)]** (lit.) destello, dardo (de ingenio, ironía, etc.). **7** ARQ. fuste, caña (de una columna).

shag | ʃæg | [*ger.* **shagging** *pret.* y *p.p.* **shagged**] *v.t.* **1** (vulg.) follar, joder. || *interj.* **2** (vulg.) a la mierda con: *shag the pigs = a la mierda con los cerdos.* || *s.c.* **3** ZOOL. cormorán (ave). || *s.i.* **4** tabaco picado, caldo. || *adj.* **5** de felpa (alfombras o similar).

shagged | ʃægd | (también **shagged out**) *adj.* (vulg.) jodido, machacado (de cansancio).

shaggily | 'ʃægɪlɪ | *adv.* lleno de pelos (persona o cosa).

shagginess | 'ʃægɪnɪs | *s.i.* vellosidad.

shaggy | 'ʃægɪ | *adj.* **1** desgreñado; peludo. **2** con pelos (abrigo, tejido, etc.). || **3 – dog story,** chiste de nunca acabar, anécdota de nunca acabar (especialmente cuando no tiene gracia).

shah | ʃa: | *s.c.* Sha (de Persia).

shake | ʃeɪk | *v.* [*pret.irreg.* **shook;** *p.p.irreg.* **shaken**] *t.* **1** agitar, sacudir: *shake the reeds to frighten the frogs = agita los juncos para asustar a las ranas.* **2** [**to – +** *prep.*] quitar/desprender/etc. mediante sacudidas o movimiento de agitar: *he shook the snow off his shoes = se quitó la nieve de los zapatos a base de sacudirlos.* **3** sacudir, agitar (alfombras, ropas, etc., para limpiarlas de polvo o suciedad). **4** conmover, chocar (a causa de algo negativo). **5** debilitar, disminuir, hacer flaquear (creencias, ideas, etc.). || *i.* **6** agitar, sacudir: *shake before use = agítese antes de usarlo.* **7** temblar (la voz, el cuerpo, etc., por el miedo, frío, etc.). **8** temblar, menearse (movimiento físico). || *s.c.* **9 [a –]** una sacudida, un golpe, un meneo. || *s.sing.* **10** temblor, tremor (en la voz). || **11 to be no great shakes,** (fam.) no ser gran cosa, no ser nada del otro mundo. **12 to get/have the shakes,** ponerse nervioso; darle a uno los temblores (especialmente por el alcohol). **13 in a couple of shakes/in two shakes,** (fam.) en un abrir y cerrar los ojos, en menos que canta un gallo. **14 to – a leg,** (fam.) moverse, ponerse en marcha. **15 to – down,** (fam.) quedarse a dormir transitoriamente, dormir en cualquier sitio. **16 to – hands (with)/to – someone's hand/to – someone by the hand,** dar la mano (a), darse la mano (con). **17 to – off,** quitarse, deshacerse de (algo o alguien). **18 to – on,** acordar mediante un apretón de manos. **19 to – one's fist,** agitar el puño de uno amenazadoramente, amenazar con el puño. **20 to – one's head,** negar con la cabeza, mover la cabeza negando. **21 to – out,** sacudir, agitar (tejidos, alfombras, paraguas, etc.). **22 to – up, a)** agitar bien; remover todo, remover bien; **b)** perturbar; desconcertar, dejar sin saber qué hacer: *the news shook him up = la noticia le dejó sin habla.*

shaken | 'ʃeɪkən | *p.p.irreg.* **1** de **shake.** || *adj.* **2** conmocionado, desconcertado; perturbado (emocionalmente).

shaker | 'ʃeɪkər | *s.c.* **1** coctelera. **2** bote con agujeros, contenedor con agujeros (para, mediante sacudidas, expulsar su contenido).

shake-up | 'ʃeɪkʌp | (también **shake-out**) *s.c.* conmoción; reorganización completa (en algún grupo social o profesional); infusión de nuevas ilusiones (en la vida personal).

shakily | 'ʃeɪkɪlɪ | *adv.* **1** temblorosamente. **2** inciertamente, dudosamente, precariamente.

shakiness | 'ʃeɪkɪnɪs | *s.i.* **1** estado tembloroso, condición temblorosa. **2** incertidumbre, duda; precariedad.

shaky | 'ʃeɪkɪ | *adj.* **1** tembloroso. **2** incierto, dudoso; precario: *your arguments are shaky = tus argumentos son precarios.*

shale | ʃeɪl | *s.i.* GEOL. esquisto, pizarra.

shall | ʃæl | (forma relajada | ʃəl |) *v.i.* **1** [solamente *interr.*] qué te parece si, te parece que (en sugerencias): *shall we go to the cinema? = ¿qué te parece si nos vamos al cine?*

OBS. Este es un verbo auxiliar, que, principalmente, se utiliza para los siguientes significados de índole gramatical: **2** futuro: *I shall go tomorrow = me iré mañana.* **3** futuro con gran dosis de énfasis: *they shall not pass = no pasarán.*

Normalmente este verbo auxiliar sirve para el futuro de las primeras personas, menos en el punto **3** en que específicamente se debe solamente utilizar con la segunda y terceras personas.

shallot | ʃə'lɒt | *s.c.* BOT. chalote, escalona.

shallow | 'ʃæləʊ | *adj.* **1** poco profundo (zona de agua). **2** superficial, frívolo (idea, argumento, teoría, etc.). **3** poco profunda (respiración). || *s.pl.* **4** bajíos, aguas poco profundas.

shallowly | 'ʃæləʊlɪ | *adv.* **1** superficialmente, frívolamente (para hablar de ideas, argumentos, teorías, etc.). **2** con poca profundidad, sin casi fuerzas (respirar).

shallowness | 'ʃæləʊnɪs | *s.i.* **1** poca profundidad (de agua, en un río, lago, mar, etc.). **2** superficialidad, frivolidad (en ideas o similar). **3** poca profundidad, poca fuerza (en la respiración).

sham | ʃæm | *s.c.* **1** (desp.) impostor, farsante. **2** farsa, imitación, falsificación. || *adj.* **3** postizo, fingido. || *v.t.* **4** fingir, simular, aparentar.

shamble | 'ʃæmbl | *v.i.* andar arrastrando los pies.

shambles | 'ʃæmblz | *s.sing.* (fam.) follón, caos, confusión (escena).

shame | ʃeɪm | *s.i.* **1** vergüenza, deshonra. || *s.sing.* **2 [a –]** una lástima, una pena: *what a shame! = ¡qué lástima!* || *v.t.* **3** avergonzar; deshonrar. **4 [to – +** *o.* **+ into/out of]** obligar a (actuar) por vergüenza: *she shamed us into contributing to the fight against poverty = ella nos obligó a contribuir a la lucha contra la pobreza.* | **5 to put to –,** dejar chico, dejar pequeño; superar con mucho. **6 – on you,** debería darte vergüenza, qué vergüenza para ti. **7 to one's –,** para vergüenza de uno. **8 to the – of,** para vergüenza de.

shamefaced | ʃem'feɪst | *adj.* avergonzado, vergonzoso (con sentimiento de vergüenza).

shamefacedly | ʃeɪm'feɪstlɪ | *adv.* avergonzadamente, vergonzosamente, con mucha vergüenza.

shameful | 'ʃeɪmfl | *adj.* (desp.) vergonzoso; escandaloso, indecoroso.

shamefully | 'ʃeɪmfəlɪ | *adv.* (desp.) vergonzosamente; escandalosamente, indecorosamente.

shamefulness | 'ʃeɪmflnɪs | *s.i.* (desp.) descaro; escándalo, falta de decoro.

shameless | 'ʃeɪmlɪs | *adj.* (desp.) desvergonzado; impudente, insolente.

shamelessly | 'ʃeɪmlɪslɪ | *adv.* (desp.) desvergonzadamente; impudentemente, insolentemente.

shamelessness | 'ʃeɪmlɪsnɪs | *s.i.* (desp.) desvergüenza; impudencia, insolencia.

shampoo | ʃæm'pu: | *s.c.* e *i.* champú. **2** limpiador de alfombras. || *s.c.* **3** lavado con champú (en peluquería). || *v.t.* **4** lavar con champú (el pelo). **5** limpiar (la alfombra).

shamrock | 'ʃæmrɒk | *s.c.* BOT. trébol.

shandy | 'ʃændɪ | *s.c.* e *i.* clara (cerveza con gaseosa).

shank | ʃæŋk | *s.c.* **1** astil (de objetos). **2** enfranque (de zapato a tacón). **3** presilla (para botones). || *s.pl.* **4** pantorrillas (parte baja de la pierna).

shan't | ʃa:nt | *contr.* de **shall** y **not.**

shanty | 'ʃæntɪ | *s.c.* **1** chabola; (Am.) bohío. **2** MUS. canción de trabajo del mar, saloma. || **3 – town,** suburbio de chabolas, barrio de chabolas.

shape | ʃeɪp | *s.c.* e *i.* **1** forma, figura. || *s.c.* **2** silueta, forma borrosa (de persona u objeto). || *s.sing.* **3** estructura interna, forma organizativa (de un plan, proyecto, asociación, etc.). || *v.t.* **4** moldear, dar forma (física). **5** configurar, determinar (una situación). || **6 to come in all shapes and sizes,** haber de todos los tipos, existir de todos los tipos imaginables. **7 in any – or form,** en cualquier forma; de ningún modo. **8 in good/bad/etc. –,** en buen/mal/etc., estado, en buena/mala, etc., forma. **9 in –,** en forma, en buena forma física. **10 in the – of,** en forma de: *her mental disturbance showed itself in the shape of attacks of hysteria = su desarreglo mental apareció en forma de ataques de histeria.* **11 to lick/knock into –,** (fam.) llevar a (alguien) por donde uno quiere. **12 out of –,** desentrenado, con falta de forma física. **13 to – up,** (fam.) **a)** salir, resultar, perfilarse (de manera positiva); **b)** afinar, ponerse a funcionar, ponerse en serio. **14 to take –,** tomar forma, definirse. **15 the – of things to come,** la posibilidad futura, la posible configuración del futuro.

shaped | ʃeɪpt | *adj.* **1** con la forma de. || **2 -shaped,** con forma de (en palabras

compuestas): *a fish-shaped statute = una estatua con forma de pez.*
shapeless | 'ʃeɪplɪs | *adj.* **1** informe, sin forma (física y visible). **2** impreciso, informe, indefinido (emoción, pasión, plan, etc.).
shapelessly | 'ʃeɪplɪslɪ | *adv.* **1** demanera informe (física y visible). **2** imprecisamente, indefinidamente (en emociones, planes, etc.).
shapelessness | 'ʃeɪplɪsnɪs | *s.i.* **1** falta de forma física definida. **2** imprecisión, indefinición (en emociones, pasiones, planes, etc.).
shapeliness | 'ʃeɪplɪnɪs | *s.i.* belleza en formas físicas (del cuerpo).
shapely | 'ʃeɪplɪ | *adj.* bien formado, de bellas proporciones (persona, objeto, etc.).
shard | ʃa:d | *s.c.* (form.) fragmento (de cristal, metal, porcelana, etc.).
share | ʃeər | *v.t.* **1 [to – +** *o.* **+ with]** compartir con. **2** repartir (tareas, trabajos, etc.). **3** compartir, comunicar (ideas, creencias, etc.). **4** repartir, compartir (regalos, caramelos, etc.). || *v.i.* **5** compartir (como síntoma de generosidad). **6 [to – in]** repartirse (tareas). **7 [to – in]** participar en, poner la aportación de uno en. **8** repartir, compartir (cosas). || *s.c.* **9** FIN. acción (de una empresa). || *s.sing.* **10 [– (in/of)]** porción, parte: *I'm doing my share = estoy haciendo mi parte.* **11 [– (in/of)]** proporción, parte proporcional. || **12 to have one's – of,** tocarle a uno en parte (algo); tener la parte de uno: *my family has had its share of tragedy = mi familia ha tenido su parte de tragedia.* **13 – and – alike,** participemos a partes iguales, todo a partes iguales. **14 to – out,** distribuir a cada uno una parte, repartir a partes iguales.
shareholder | 'ʃeəhəʊldər | *s.c.* FIN. accionista.
share-out | 'ʃeəraʊt | *s.c.* **[– (of)]** repartición, reparto, distribución.
shark | ʃa:k | *s.c.* **1** ZOOL. tiburón. **2** (desp.) estafador (especialmente de altos vuelos).
sharp | ʃa:p | *adj.* **1** afilado: *a sharp knife = un cuchillo afilado.* **2** puntiagudo, con punta. **3** vivo, penetrante, agudo (de pensamiento). **4** definido, claro, marcado (con las líneas precisas en un objeto). **5** rápido, inmediato (cambio, fluctuación, etc.). **6** pronunciada (curva en la carretera). **7** tajante, cortante (forma de actuar o hablar). **8** [*num.* **+** –] en punto, exactamente. **9** agudo (sonido o ruido). **10** agudo, penetrante (dolor, frío, etc.). **11** anguloso (en rasgos faciales). **12** fuerte, picante, pungente (sabor). **13** vehemente, violento (golpe o acción enérgica). **14** (desp.) sin escrúpulos (especialmente en los negocios). **15** (fam.) elegantón, bien puesto (en forma de vestir). || *adv.* **16** pronunciadamente; abruptamente (movimiento físico). **17** con tono agudo, con voz estridente. || *s.c.* **18** MUS. sostenido. || **19 to look –,** darse prisa, moverse más rápidamente. **20 – as a needle,** más listo que el hambre; más avispado que nadie. **21 – practice,** forma de actuar poco honesta (especialmente en los negocios).
sharpen | 'ʃa:pən | *v.t.* **1** afilar, sacar filo; sacar punta. || **2 to – up,** sacar buena punta; hacer un buen filo.
sharpener | 'ʃa:pnər | *s.c.* sacapuntas; afiladora.
sharp-eyed | ʃa:p'aɪd | *adj.* con vista; de vista aguda.
sharpish | 'ʃa:pɪʃ | *adj.* (fam.) rápidamente, inmediatamente, a todo meter.
sharply | 'ʃa:plɪ | *adv.* **1** agudamente, con mucha punta; con mucho filo. **2** con gran interés; penetrantemente, agudamente (en pensamiento). **3** con gran definición; claramente, marcadamente (en su forma, silueta, figura, etc.). **4** vehementemente, violentamente (forma de golpear o actuar). **5** tajantemente, cortantemente (forma de hablar). **6** pronunciadamente (forma de tomar las curvas). **7** rápidamente, inmediatamente (forma de cambiar o fluctuar).
sharpness | 'ʃa:pnɪs | *s.i.* **1** agudeza, filo, condición afilada. **2** agudeza, astucia, viveza (de ingenio). **3** acritud, pungencia (de olor o sabor). **4** angulosidad (de los rasgos faciales).
shat | ʃæt | *pret.* y *p.p.irreg.* de **shit.**
shatter | 'ʃætər | *v.t.* e *i.* **1** hacer(se) añicos, romper(se), destrozar(se). **2** destrozar(se), destruir(se) (esperanzas, creencias, etc.). || *v.t.* **3** (fam.) agotar, dejar muerto (de cansancio). || **4 to be shattered,** quedar destrozado mentalmente, estar destrozado anímicamente.
shattering | 'ʃætərɪŋ | *adj.* **1** agotador, que agota. **2** demoledor (tragedia o similar).
shave | ʃeɪv | *v.t.* e *i.* **1** afeitar(se). || *v.t.* **2** afeitar. **3** cortar por completo, afeitar (todo el pelo de una parte del cuerpo). **4** reducir, recortar: *the company shaved my margin = la empresa recortó mi margen.* **5** cortar una capa fina de (madera u otro material). || *s.c.* **6** afeitado. || **7 a close –,** (fam.) un accidente/incidente del que uno escapa por los pelos.
OBS. En casi todos los significados verbales de este verbo también puede utilizarse la preposición off: *to shave my beard off = rasurarme por completo la barba.*
shaven | 'ʃeɪvn | *adj.* afeitado, rasurado (alguna parte del cuerpo).
shaver | 'ʃeɪvər | *s.c.* afeitadora, rasuradora (normalmente maquinilla eléctrica).
shaving | 'ʃeɪvɪŋ | *atr.* **1** de afeitar (crema, loción, etc.). || *s.pl.* **2** virutas.
shawl | ʃɔ:l | *s.c.* chal, mantón.
she | ʃi: | *pron.pers.* **1** ella (persona del sexo femenino). **2 =N who,** la que, aquella que, quien. || *s.sing.* **3** hembra: *the dog is not a he, but a she = el perro no es un macho sino una hembra.* || **4 she-,** hembra (en compuestos, especialmente para animales): *a she-wolf = una loba.*
sheaf | ʃi:f | [*pl.* **sheaves**] *s.c.* **1** haz, fajo (de papel). **2** manojo, gavilla (de alguna clase de cereal).
shear | ʃɪər | *v.t.* [*pret.* **sheared;** *p.p.irreg.* **shorn**] **1** trasquilar (ovejas). **2** (lit.) cortar (el pelo de una persona). || *s.pl.* **3** tijeras de trasquilar (ovejas). **4** tijeras de jardinería: *a pair of shears = unas tijeras de jardinería.* || **5 to – off,** cortarse (especialmente el metal).
sheath | ʃi:θ | *s.c.* **1** vaina (de cuchillo). **2** funda (de diversos objetos). **3** preservativo. || *s.sing.* **4 [the –]** el método de contracepción mediante preservativo. || **5 – knife,** cuchillo grande con vaina.
sheathe | ʃi:ð | *v.t.* **1** envainar (cuchillo). **2** meter en su funda (cualquier objeto).
sheaves | ʃi:vz | *pl.* de **sheaf.**
shed | ʃed | *v.t.* [*pret.* y *p.p.irreg.* **shed;** *ger.* **shedding**] **1** desprenderse de, despojarse de (ropa, especialmente). **2** mudar (piel, por parte de un animal). **3** derramar (lágrimas). **4** derramar, desprender (un líquido, poco a poco). || *s.c.* **5** cobertizo, nave. **6** cobertizo de protección (para bicicletas). **7** barracón (de posibles distintos usos). || **8 to – blood,** derramar sangre. **9 to – its load,** dejar caer su carga (un camión). **10 to – light on,** iluminar, alumbrar, prestar luz.
she'd | ʃi:d | *contr.* **1** de **she** y **had. 2** de **she** y **would.**
sheen | ʃi:n | *s.c.* lustre, brillo; resplandor.
sheep | ʃi:p | [*pl.* **sheep**] *s.c.* **1** oveja. || **2 a wolf in sheep's clothing,** V. **wolf. 3 like –,** como ovejas, como corderos (haciendo todos lo mismo). **4 to make sheep's eyes (at),** mirar con ojos de carnero (a), mirar con adoración (a), mirar amorosamente (a). **5 to separate the – from the goats,** separar a las ovejas de los cabritos.
sheepdip | 'ʃi:pdɪp | *s.i.* **1** desinfectante para ovejas. || *s.c.* **2** baño desinfectante para ovejas.
sheepdog | 'ʃi:pdɒg | *s.c.* ZOOL. perro pastor, perro ovejero.
sheepfold | 'ʃi:pfəʊld | *s.c.* redil, aprisco, corral de ovejas.
sheepish | 'ʃi:pɪʃ | *adj.* tímido, vergonzoso, pusilánime.
sheepishly | 'ʃi:pɪʃlɪ | *adv.* tímidamente, vergonzosamente, pusilánimemente.
sheepishness | 'ʃi:pɪʃnɪs | *s.i.* timidez, vergüenza, pusilanimidad.
sheepskin | 'ʃi:pskɪn | *s.c.* e *i.* piel de oveja.
sheer | ʃɪər | *adj.* **1** absoluto, puro, verdadero (siempre como énfasis): *this is sheer madness = esto es pura locura.* **2** fino, transparente, diáfano (telas, especialmente la seda). **3** abrupto, casi vertical, escarpado (precipicio, paso de montaña, etc.). || *adv.* **4** abruptamente, casi verticalmente, escarpadamente. || *v.i.* **5** desviarse, irse a un lado, cambiar de dirección abruptamente (físicamente, hablando o similar).
sheet | ʃi:t | *s.c.* **1** sábana (de cama). **2** lámina (de algún material). **3** hoja, lámina (de papel). **4** extensión, capa (de agua, hielo o fuego): *a sheet of flame = una gran extensión de llamas.* **5** hoja, panfleto (de algún tema informativo). **6** pliego (de sellos). **7** MAR. escota. || **8 – anchor, a)** MAR. ancla de la esperanza; **b)** último recurso, última posibilidad, áncora. **9 to – down,** llover a mares. **10 – ice,** capa de hielo resbaladiza (especialmente en carreteras). **11 – lightning,** relámpago. **12 – metal,** MET. metal laminado. **13 – music,** MUS. música en partituras sueltas.
sheeting | 'ʃi:tɪŋ | *s.i.* **1** lencería de sábanas. **2** material laminado (metal, plásticos, etc.).
sheikh | ʃeɪk | (también **sheik**) *s.c.* jeque (árabe).

sheikhdom | 'ʃeɪkdəm | (también **sheikdom**) *s.c.* dominio del jeque, zona bajo la influencia de un jeque, nación encabezada por un jeque.
shekels | 'ʃeklz | *s.pl.* (fam. y hum.) pasta, parné.
shelf | ʃelf | [*pl.* **shelves**] *s.c.* **1** estante, balda, repisa, anaquel. **2** GEOL. plataforma, zócalo submarino, plataforma submarina, plataforma continental. || **3 to be left on the –,** (p.u.) quedarse para vestir santos (soltera). **4 to leave on the –,** archivar, no atender, dejar para más tarde. **5 off the –,** directamente en la tienda, al otro lado del mostrador (producto que se puede comprar en la tienda aunque parezca un poco complicado o sofisticado).
shelf-life | 'ʃelflaɪf | *s.sing.* durabilidad, tiempo antes de caducar (de un producto).
shell | ʃel | *s.c.* e *i.* **1** cáscara, cascarón (de muchos tipos de frutos secos o de huevos). **2** concha (de moluscos o similar). **3** caparazón (de tortugas o similar). || *s.c.* **4** estructura desnuda, parte exterior (de un edificio, coche, etc., especialmente después de haber quedado medio destrozado). **5** MIL. proyectil, obús, bomba. || *v.t.* **6** quitar la cáscara. **7** MIL. bombardear. || **8 to come /crawl/be brought out of one's –,** salir del cascarón; abrirse a la gente, abrirse al mundo que rodea a uno. **9 to retire /crawl into one's –,** meterse en su cascarón, cerrarse al mundo que rodea a uno. **9 to – out,** (fam.) soltar, acoquinar, aflojar (dinero). **10 – shock,** MED. estado nervioso grave debido a la continuidad bajo fuego enemigo.
she'll | ʃiːl | *contr.* de **she** y **will.**
shellfish | 'ʃelfɪʃ | [*pl.* **shellfish**] *s.c.* e *i.* marisco.
shelling | 'ʃelɪŋ | *s.i.* MIL. bombardeo.
shell-shocked | 'ʃelʃɒkt | *adj.* **1** MED. en un estado nervioso grave debido a la continuidad bajo fuego enemigo. **2** (fig.) exhausto, destrozado (especialmente después de algo de cierta trascendencia y dificultad).
shelter | 'ʃeltər | *s.c.* **1** refugio (antiaéreo, contra la lluvia, de montaña, etc.). || *s.i.* **2** refugio, asilo, protección: *these poor people are looking for shelter = esta pobre gente está buscando protección.* **3** (fig.) techo (vivienda como necesidad básica). || *v.t.* **4** proteger, refugiar (a algo o alguien). **5** dar asilo, dar refugio (a personas huyendo de la policía o casos parecidos). || **6** refugiarse, buscar protección (de una tormenta, peligro, etc.).
sheltered | 'ʃeltəd | *adj.* **1** protegido (lugar). **2** superprotegida (vida de una persona). **3** vigilada (residencia); con acomodo especial (trabajo, en el caso de personas con alguna minusvalía).
shelve | ʃelv | *v.t.* **1** archivar, dejar a un lado, aparcar, aplazar indefinidamente (plan, proyecto, etc.). || *v.i.* **2** hacer declive, estar en cuesta; bajar suavemente.
shelves | 'ʃelvz | *pl.* de **shelf.**
shelving | 'ʃelvɪŋ | *s.i.* estanterías.
shepherd | 'ʃepəd | *s.c.* **1** pastor. || *v.t.* **2** conducir, guiar, ayudar de manera solícita (especialmente a alguien que no puede arreglárselas solo). || **3 shepherd's pie,** GAST. patatas con carne picada.
shepherdess | 'ʃepədɪs | *s.c.* pastora.
sherbet | ʃɜːbət | *s.i.* **1** polvos de pica-pica (dulce). || *s.c.* e *i.* **2** (EE.UU.) sorbete, helado.
sheriff | 'ʃerɪf | *s.c.* **1** (EE.UU.) jefe de policía del condado. **2** oficial mayor (para ceremonias) de Inglaterra y Gales. **3** juez de condado (en Escocia).
sherry | 'ʃerɪ | *s.c.* e *i.* jerez.
she's | ʃiːz | *contr.* **1** de **she** e **is. 2** de **she** y **has.**
shibboleth | 'ʃɪbələθ | *s.c.* (form.) palabra grandiosa, lema anticuado, doctrina pasada de moda.
shield | ʃiːld | *s.c.* **1** escudo. **2** escudo (como trofeo, en general, deportivo). **3** [**– (against)**] escudo, protección, defensa. || *v.t.* **4** proteger, servir de escudo para, defender.
shift | ʃɪft | *v.t.* e *i.* **1** mover(se), cambiar(se) de sitio. **2** cambiar(se), variar(se) (de idea, actitud, creencia, etc.): *she slowly shifted towards my point of view = ella varió lentamente hacia mi punto de vista.* **3** (EE.UU.) cambiar (de marcha en un vehículo). **4** quitar(se), desaparecer (mancha). || *v.t.* **5** transferir, echar (la culpa, responsabilidad, etc. a otra parte). || *s.c.* **6** cambio, variación, desplazamiento, movimiento (de una persona o cosa). **7** cambio de opinión, cambio de postura (mental). **8** [+ *v.sing./pl.*] tanda, turno (de trabajo). **9** turno (como período de tiempo). **10** (arc.) camisa (de mujer). **11** FILOL. cambio, variación (en vocales o consonantes). || **12 – key,** tecla de mayúsculas.
shiftily | 'ʃɪftɪlɪ | *adv.* con trampa, furtivamente, taimadamente; evasivamente.
shiftiness | 'ʃɪftɪnɪs | *s.i.* trampa, carácter furtivo, carácter taimado; condición evasiva (alguien).
shifting | 'ʃɪftɪŋ | *adj.* cambiante, en movimiento continuo, en cambio continuo: *the shifting crowds downtown = las multitudes en movimiento continuo en el centro de la ciudad.*
shiftless | 'ʃɪftlɪs | *adj.* (desp.) vago, ocioso, pasivo; inútil.
shiftlessness | 'ʃɪftlɪsnɪs | *s.i.* (desp.) vaguería, ociosidad, pasividad; inutilidad (como persona).
shifty | 'ʃɪftɪ | *adj.* tramposo, furtivo, taimado; evasivo (carácter personal).
shilling | 'ʃɪlɪŋ | *s.c.* **1** chelín (moneda inglesa que se dejó de utilizar en 1971, equivalente a 5 peniques de hoy). **2** chelín (moneda de países como Tanzania, Kenia, Uganda).
shilly-shally | 'ʃɪlɪʃælɪ | *v.i.* (fam.) titubear, vacilar, no decidirse, no saber qué hacer.
shimmer | 'ʃɪmər | *v.i.* **1** rielar, brillar tenuemente. || *s.sing.* **2** luz trémula, resplandor tenue, reflejo débil.
shin | ʃɪn | *s.c.* **1** ANAT. espinilla. **2** jarrete (de animales, especialmente para alimentación humana). || **3 to – up,** trepar, encaramarse (especialmente utilizando las rodillas vigorosamente).
shindig | 'ʃɪndɪg | *s.c.* (fam.) jarana, algazara, guateque.
shine | ʃaɪn | *v.* [*pret.* y *p.p.irreg.* **shone**] *i.* **1** brillar, dar luz, despedir luz, resplandecer: *the sun isn't going to shine any more = el sol no va a brillar nunca más.* **2** brillar, resplandecer (los ojos, la cara, objetos diversos, etc.). **3 [to – (at)]** brillar, ser excelente, destacar (en alguna habilidad o actividad). **4** traslucirse (un sentimiento o virtud personal, especialmente en la expresión facial de una persona). || *t.* **5** iluminar, dirigir la luz: *shine the torch on the floor = ilumina el suelo con la linterna.* || *s.sing.* **6** brillo, resplandor; lustre. || **7 to take a – to,** (fam.) caer fenomenalmente, tener una enorme simpatía hacia (una persona).
shine | ʃaɪn | *v.t.* **1** sacar brillo, hacer relucir, limpiar hasta que brille (un objeto). || *s.sing.* **2 [a –]** un lustre notable, una buena limpieza, un brillo magnífico.
shiner | 'ʃaɪnər | *s.c.* (fam.) un ojo a la funerala, un ojo a la turuleta.
shingle | 'ʃɪŋgl | *s.i.* **1** guijarros (junto al agua). || *s.c.* **2** ARQ. ripia. **3** (fam. y EE.UU.) rótulo, placa (de una oficina o similar). || *s.pl.* **4** MED. herpes.
shining | 'ʃaɪnɪŋ | *adj.* **1** brillante, reluciente. **2** (fig.) sobresaliente, extraordinario, magnífico (logro, victoria, virtud, etc.).
shiny | 'ʃaɪnɪ | *adj.* brillante, reluciente (después de limpiar o pulir).
ship | ʃɪp | *s.c.* **1** MAR. barco, buque, navío (grande). || *v.t.* **2** enviar por barco, remitir por transporte marítimo. || **3 by –,** por barco, por transporte marítimo, en barco.
shipboard | 'ʃɪpbɔːd | *adj.* **1** típico de barco, normal en un barco (tarea o similar). || **2 on –, a** bordo.
shipbuilder | 'ʃɪpbɪldər | *s.c.* constructor de buques; astilleros (empresa).
shipbuilding | 'ʃɪpbɪldɪŋ | *s.i.* construcción de buques, construcción naval.
shipmate | 'ʃɪpmeɪt | *s.c.* compañero de barco, camarada de la misma tripulación.
shipment | 'ʃɪpmənt | *s.c.* e *i.* transporte, envío (en cualquier medio de transporte).
shipping | 'ʃɪpɪŋ | *s.i.* **1** transporte marítimo. **2** flota, conjunto de la flota (de un país, organización internacional, etc.).
shipshape | 'ʃɪpʃeɪp | *adj.* en regla, en orden (un lugar, por ejemplo).
shipwreck | 'ʃɪprek | *s.c.* e *i.* **1** naufragio. || *s.c.* **2** MAR. barco naufragado. || **3 to be shipwrecked,** naufragar.
shipwrecked | 'ʃiprekt | *adj.* naufragado, que ha naufragado.
shipyard | 'ʃɪpjaːd | *s.c.* astillero (lugar).
shire | 'ʃaɪər | *s.c.* **1** HIST. condado, feudo, provincia (antigua división provincial de Gran Bretaña). || **2 – horse,** caballo de carga, caballo de tiro. **3 the shires/the shire counties,** GEOG. parte central, región central de Inglaterra.
shirk | ʃɜːk | *v.t.* e *i.* (desp.) equivaler, eludir, rehuir (trabajo, responsabilidad, obligación, etc.); hacer el vago.
shirt | ʃɜːt | *s.c.* **1** camisa (especialmente de caballero). || **2 to put one's – on something,** (fam.) arriesgar todo en algo (sea dinero, sea reputación, etc.).
shirtfront | 'ʃɜːtfrʌnt | *s.c.* pechera (de una camisa, especialmente de un traje muy formal).
shirtsleeve | 'ʃɜːtsliːv | *s.c.* **1** manga de camisa. || **2 in one's shirt-sleeves,** en mangas de camisa.
shirttail | 'ʃɜːtteɪl | *s.c.* (normalmente *pl.*) faldón (parte de la camisa que cubren los pantalones).

shirty | 'ʃɜːtɪ | *adj.* (fam.) molesto, enfadado.
shish kebab V. **kebab.**
shit | ʃɪt | *v.i.* [*pret.* y *p.p.irreg.* **shat;** también **shitted;** *ger.* **shitting**] (vulg.) **1** cagar. || *s.sing.* **2** cagada (acción). || *s.c.* **3** mierda, asco (insulto personal). || *s.i.* **4** mierda, heces, caca. **5** mierda, caca (algo que uno considera de mala calidad o negativamente). || *interj.* **6** joder, mierda. || **7 to beat/kick/knock the – out of someone,** dar una paliza de miedo a alguien, dejar a alguien machacado/jodido de una paliza. **8 in the –,** en un asunto muy jodido, en un problema muy serio. **9 not to give a – (about),** importar un pepino, importar un bledo. **10 to – oneself,** cagarse de miedo, acojonarse de miedo. **11 the shits,** diarrea. **12 tough –,** mala suerte, no hay más remedio que apechar con ello.
shitty | 'ʃɪtɪ | *adj.* (vulg.) de mierda, una mierda de: *a shitty friend = un amigo de mierda.*
shiver | 'ʃɪvər | *v.i.* **1** temblar, estremecerse (de miedo); tiritar (de frío). || *s.c.* **2** estremecimiento, escalofrío, temblor (de miedo o frío). || **3 to give someone the shivers,** (fam.) dar a alguien escalofríos, dar a alguien dentera (de miedo).
shivery | 'ʃɪvərɪ | *adj.* (fam.) tembloroso, temblando (de miedo o frío).
shoal | ʃəʊl | *s.c.* **1** BIOL. banco (de peces). **2** (fig.) montón, multitud (de personas).
shock | ʃɒk | *s.i.* **1** MED. trauma, choc, conmoción. || *s.c.* **2** conmoción, disgusto, choque (mental): *I got a shock when I heard of her death = me dio un disgusto cuando supe de su muerte.* **3** (fam.) calambre (eléctrico). **4** choque, golpetazo, colisión (físico): *a sudden shock = un golpetazo repentino.* || *s.c.* e *i.* **5** masa (de pelo en una persona). || *v.t.* e *i.* **6** escandalizar, disgustar, ofender (por su estilo, contenido, etc.). || *v.t.* **7** conmover, causar un choc, sobresaltar. || **8 – absorber,** MEC. amortiguador. **9 – tactics,** táctica de golpes sorpresa (especialmente en un contexto de guerra). **10 – therapy/treatment,** PSIQ. tratamiento por electroshock. **11 – troops,** MIL. tropas de choque.
shocked | ʃɒkt | *adj.* **1** escandalizado, ofendido, disgustado (por el contenido, estilo, etc.). **2** conmovido, sobresaltado, conmocionado (física o mentalmente).
shocker | 'ʃɒkər | *s.c.* (fam. y hum.) cosa que sobresalta, tema que asombra, acontecimiento que causa un fuerte sobresalto.
shocking | 'ʃɒkɪŋ | *adj.* **1** espantoso, escandaloso, ofensivo, vergonzoso. **2** (fam.) horrible, malísimo, fatal. || **3 – pink,** de un rosa chillón.
shockingly | 'ʃɒkɪŋlɪ | *adv.* **1** espantosamente, escandalosamente, ofensivamente, vergonzosamente. **2** (fam.) horriblemente, malísimamente, fatalmente.
shockproof | 'ʃɒkpruːf | *adj.* a prueba de golpes.
shock-wave | 'ʃɒkweɪv | *s.c.* **1** onda expansiva, onda de choque (de una explosión, objeto a gran velocidad, etc.). **2** (fig.) consecuencia, resultado (de un acontecimiento, cambio social, etc.).
shod | ʃɒd | *pret.* y *p.p.irreg.* **1** de **shoe.** || *adj.* **2** (form.) vestido, ataviado.
shoddily | 'ʃɒdɪlɪ | *adv.* (desp.) burdamente, con mala calidad, chapuceramente.
shoddiness | 'ʃɒdɪnɪs | *s.i.* (desp.) mala calidad, chapuza, mala fabricación.
shoddy | 'ʃɒdɪ | *adj.* (desp.) de mala calidad, burdo, de pura chapuza.
shoe | ʃuː | *s.c.* **1** zapato. **2** herradura. || [*pret.* y *p.p.irreg.* **shod**] *v.t.* **3** herrar (a un caballo). || **4 to fill someone's shoes/step into someone's shoes,** ocupar el puesto de alguien, ocupar el sitio de alguien (especialmente en un contexto profesional). **5 in someone's shoes,** en los zapatos de alguien, en el lugar de alguien.
shoehorn | 'ʃuːhɔːn | *s.c.* calzador.
shoelace | 'ʃuːleɪs | *s.c.* (normalmente *pl.*) (brit.) cordón (de zapato).
shoemaker | 'ʃuːmeɪkər | *s.c.* zapatero.
shoestring | 'ʃuːstrɪŋ | *s.c.* **1** (normalmente *pl.*) (EE.UU.) cordón (de zapato). || *adj.* **2** reducido, corto, restrictivo (presupuesto financiero). || **3 on a –,** (fam.) con gran cortedad de medios, con poquísimo dinero.
shoetree | 'ʃuːtriː | *s.c.* horma (de madera, plástico o metal).
shone | ʃɒn | (EE.UU.) | ʃəʊn | *pret.* y *p.p.irreg.* de **shine.**
shoo | ʃuː | *v.t.* **1** ahuyentar, alejar, asustar (animales o niños con movimiento de brazos y gritos). || *interj.* **2** fuera, fuera de aquí.
shook | ʃʊk | *pret.irreg.* de **shake.**
shoot | ʃuːt | *v.* [*pret.* y *p.p.irreg.* **shot**] *i.* **1 [to – (at)]** disparar, hacer fuego. **2** (brit.) cazar, ir de caza. **3** DEP. chutar, disparar a gol. **4** rodar, llevar a cabo el rodaje (de una película). **5** ir a gran velocidad, ir corriendo a gran velocidad, lanzarse a gran velocidad. **6** BOT. brotar (capullo o parecido). || *t.* **7** disparar; matar, herir: *he was shot in the leg = le hirieron en la pierna.* **8** (brit.) cazar, dar caza. **9** disparar, lanzar, soltar (una flecha). **10** rodar, filmar (una película). **11 [to – + *prep.*]** lanzar, enviar a gran velocidad, arrojar con fuerza: *the blow shot him through the window = el golpe le lanzó por la ventana.* **12** echar, lanzar (una mirada). || *s.c.* **13** BOT. brote (vegetal). **14** (brit.) caza. || **15 to – down, a)** derribar (avión); **b)** matar, matar sin misericordia (especialmente a alguien desarmado); **c)** (fam.) rechazar, rebatir (argumento). **16 to – one's mouth off,** (fam.) hablar demasiado, pasarse de la cuenta hablando. **17 to – the lights,** saltarse un semáforo a toda velocidad. **18 to – up,** crecer muchísimo, subir muchísimo.
shooting | 'ʃuːtɪŋ | *s.c.* e *i.* **1** tiroteo; (Am.) balacera. || *s.i.* **2** (brit.) caza. || **3 – gallery,** galería de tiro al blanco. **4 – star,** estrella fugaz. **5 – stick,** bastón taburete.
shoot-out | 'ʃuːtaʊt | *s.c.* tiroteo, tiroteo a muerte.
shop | ʃɒp | *s.c.* **1** tienda. **2** taller: *repair shop = taller de reparaciones.* || *v.i.* **3** hacer compras, comprar. || *v.t.* **4** (fam.) engañar, traicionar. || **5 all over the –,** (fam.) de cualquier modo, por cualquier sitio (en desorden). **6 to set up –,** establecer un negocio, establecer su propio negocio. **7 to =N around, a)** ir de tienda en tienda, dar vueltas de tienda en tienda; **b)** buscar al mejor postor, buscar la mejor oferta, buscar la mejor oportunidad. **8 – assistant,** dependiente. **9 – steward,** vocal sindical, representante sindical. **10 to shut up –,** cerrar, dejar la tarea (en tienda, oficina, etc.). **11 to talk –,** hablar de temas del trabajo (personas que trabajan en un mismo sitio).
shop-floor | ʃɒp'flɔːr | *s.sing.* **[the –]** los obreros, los trabajadores de base.
shop-front | 'ʃɒpfrʌnt | *s.c.* delantera de la tienda, fachada de la tienda (incluyendo puerta y escaparates).
shopkeeper | 'ʃɒpkiːpər | *s.c.* tendero, gerente de una tienda.
shoplifter | 'ʃɒplɪftər | *s.c.* ratero de tiendas, ladrón de tiendas (escondiendo lo robado en un bolso).
shoplifting | 'ʃɒplɪftɪŋ | *s.i.* robo en tiendas, ratería en tiendas.
shopper | 'ʃɒpər | *s.c.* comprador.
shopping | 'ʃɒpɪŋ | *s.i.* **1** compras. || *s.sing.* **2 [the –]** los recados, las compras, lo comprado. || **3 – centre,** centro comercial. **4 – list,** lista de compras.
shop-soiled | 'ʃɒpsɔɪld | *adj.* sucio por haber estado en el escaparate.
shopworn | 'ʃɒpwɔːn | *adj.* (EE.UU.) sucio por haber estado en el escaparate.
shore | ʃɔː | *s.c.* **1** orilla, ribera. || *s.pl.* **2** (lit.) tierras, confines (de un país). || **3 on –,** en tierra (lo contrario de a bordo). **4 to – up,** reforzar (física y figurativamente).
shoreline | 'ʃɔːlaɪn | *s.c.* costa, orilla.
shorn | ʃɔːn | *p.p.irreg.* **1** de **shear.** || *adj.* **2** cortado al cero (pelo); pelado, muy cortado (terreno). || **3 – of,** desprovisto de, despojado de: *shorn of her legitimate powers = despojada de sus poderes legítimos.*
short | ʃɔːt | *adj.* **1** corto, breve (tiempo). **2** bajo (de estatura). **3** corto, pequeño, diminuto. **4** abrupto, brusco, seco (movimiento o sonido). **5** corta, pequeña (distancia). **6** brusco, seco (de carácter): *he has a very short temper = tiene un genio muy brusco.* **7 [– with]** impaciente con, brusco con, hosco con. **8 [– (of)]** falto, carente (algo, como dinero o similar). **9** GAST. quebradizo (hasta para cocinar). || *s.c.* **10** corto, cortometraje. **11** (fam.) cortocircuito eléctrico. **12** copa (de licor). || *s.pl.* **13** pantalones cortos. **14** (EE.UU.) calzoncillos. || **15 a – word/a few – words,** unas palabras, una breve conversación, un diálogo breve. **16 at – notice,** con poco tiempo de aviso, con un corto preaviso. **17 to be – for,** ser diminutivo de, ser forma acortada de (un nombre). **18 to be taken –/caught –,** (fam.) tener unas ganas horrendas de orinar, sentir fuertes deseos de ir al baño (especialmente cuando no hay baño cerca). **19 to bring/pull up –,** dejar parado, interrumpir, parar (lo que se esté haciendo). **20 to cut a long story –,** V. **story. 21 to cut –,** interrumpir, cortar, dejar a la mitad: *the war cut short his promising career as a journalist = la guerra interrumpió su carrera prometedora de periodista.* **22 to draw/get the – straw,** V. **straw. 23 for –,** como diminutivo, como forma corta de su nombre. **24 to give someone – weight,** vender a alguien productos con peso insuficiente, engañar a alguien en el peso. **25 to go – (of),** empezar a pasarse (sin), no

tener lo suficiente (de), ir quedándose (sin). **26 in –,** en una palabra, en pocas palabras, dicho brevemente. **27 in – order,** prontamente, sin ninguna demora, sin pararse a nada. **28 in – supply,** escaso, sin existencias de ello. **29 in the – term,** V. **term. 30 little – of /nothing – of,** nada menos que, nada que no sea, ninguna otra cosa que: *he would accept nothing short of a total surrender = no quería aceptar nada que no fuera una rendición total.* **31 to make – work of,** (fam.) despachar en un minuto (asunto); consumir en menos que canta un gallo (algo). **32 to run – of,** agotarse, quedarse sin (algo, muy gradualmente): *we are running short of money = nos estamos quedando sin dinero.* **33 – and sweet,** corto y al tema, breve y al grano (normalmente una conversación). **34 – back-and-sides,** muy corto atrás y a los lados (tipo de corte de pelo especialmente militar). **35 – of, a)** casi, muy cerca de (normalmente con cantidades); **b)** dejando de lado, con la excepción de, excepto, menos: *short of killing him, what can I do? = ¿con la excepción de darle muerte, qué puedo hacer?* **36 – of breath,** sin aliento, con falta de aire, ahogado. **37 – on,** con poco, con falta de (una emoción o virtud). **38 – shrift,** V. **shrift. 39 – story,** LIT. historia corta, novela corta. **40 to stop –,** quedarse clavado, parar repentinamente. **41 to stop – of, a)** casi, estar en un tris de, casi llegar a: *I just stopped short of calling her a whore = estuve en un tris de llamarla puta;* **b)** casi llegar, casi alcanzar (cierto nivel de algo). **42 the long and the – of it,** V. **long.**

shortage | 'ʃɔːtɪdʒ | *s.c.* falta, escasez, insuficiencia (de algo).

shortbread | 'ʃɔːtbred | (también **shortake**) *s.i.* GAST. torta dulce con mantequilla.

shortcake | 'ʃɔːtkeɪk | V. **shortbread.**

short-change | ʃɔːt'tʃeɪndʒ | *v.t.* **1** dar mal el cambio, dar de menos en el cambio. **2** (fam.) engañar, tomar el pelo.

short-circuit | ʃɔːt'sɜːkɪt | *s.c.* **1** ELEC. cortocircuito. || *v.t.* e *i.* **2** haber un cortocircuito; causar un cortocircuito en. || *v.t.* **3** estropear en sus inicios, frustrar (plan o similar). **4** pasar por alto, tirar por el atajo, evitar (partes aburridas de un proceso).

shortcoming | 'ʃɔːtkʌmɪŋ | *s.c.* (normalmente *pl.*) deficiencia, defecto, imperfección, fallo (especialmente en el carácter de alguien).

shortcrust | 'ʃɔːtkrʌst | *adj.* GAST. quebradizo, de pasta quebradiza.

short-cut | 'ʃɔːtkʌt | *s.c.* **1** atajo (camino). **2** (fig.) atajo, vía rápida, forma expeditiva (de hacer algo más rápidamente).

shorten | 'ʃɔːtn | *v.t.* e *i.* acortar(se), abreviar(se).

shortening | 'ʃɔːtnɪŋ | *s.i.* (EE.UU.) GAST. manteca (de cocinar).

shortfall | 'ʃɔːtfɔːl | *s.c.* déficit: *a shortfall of teachers of Russian = un déficit de profesores de ruso.*

shorthand | 'ʃɔːthænd | *s.i.* **1** taquigrafía. **2** forma rápida, forma taquigráfica (de hablar o expresar algo). || **3 – typist,** secretario, taquígrafo.

short-handed | ʃɔːt'hændɪd | *adj.* con falta de personal, falto de mano de obra.

short-haul | 'ʃɔːthɔːl | *adj.* de corto recorrido (transporte).

shortie | 'ʃɔːtɪ | (también **shorty**) *s.c.* (fam.) bajito, pequeñín.

shortish | 'ʃɔːtɪʃ | *adj.* tirando a bajo, bajito, más bien bajo.

short-list | 'ʃɔːtlɪst | *s.c.* **1** (normalmente *sing.*) preselección, lista de los aspirantes favoritos. || *v.t.* **2** preseleccionar, poner en la lista de candidatos con más posibilidades.

short-lived | ʃɔːt'lɪvd | (EE.UU.) | ʃɔːt'laɪvd | *adj.* efímero, poco duradero.

shortly | 'ʃɔːtlɪ | *adv.* **1** en poco tiempo, inmediatamente, prontamente. **2** bruscamente, hoscamente, con mala educación (forma de hablar o dirigirse a otra persona).

short-range | ʃɔːt'reɪndʒ | *adj.* de cerca, de corto alcance, de radio pequeño (aparato, arma, etc.).

short-sighted | ʃɔːt'saɪtɪd | *adj.* **1** miope, corto de vista. **2** (desp.) de poca vista, de poca inteligencia, (fig.) miope.

short-sightedness | ʃɔːt'saɪtɪdnɪs | *s.i.* MED. miopía.

short-staffed | ʃɔːt'staːft | V. **shorthanded.**

short-tempered | ʃɔːt'tempəd | *adj.* de mal genio, de mal carácter.

short-term | ʃɔːt'tɜːm | *adj.* **1** de corto plazo, inmediato. || *adv.* **2** a corto plazo.

short-wave | ʃɔːt'weɪv | *adj.* RAD. de onda corta.

short-weight | ʃɔːt'weɪt | *v.t.* pesar mal, pesar de menos.

shorty V. **shortie.**

shot | ʃɒt | *pret.* y *p.p.irreg.* **1** de shot. || *s.c.* **2** disparo. **3** DEP. disparo, tiro a gol. **4** [*adj.* –] tirador: *a magnificent shot = un tirador muy bueno.* **5** DEP. peso (objeto). **6** FOT. fotografía, foto. **7** lanzamiento (de un cohete espacial). **8** escena (en una película). **9** inyección. **10 [– (at)]** intento, prueba, tentativa: *I had a shot at the camera = hice una tentativa de utilizar la cámara.* **11** (fam.) copazo (de bebida fuertemente alcohólica). || *s.i.* **12** perdigones, balines. || *adj.* **13** tornasolado (especialmente la seda). **14 [– through/with]** saturado de, cargado de: *the air is shot with light = el aire está saturado de luz.* || **15 a long –,** probabilidad remota, posibilidad remota. **16 a – in the arm,** un buen empujón, un estímulo potente, una dosis de energía. **17 a – in the dark,** una conjetura, una suposición totalmente al azar. **18 to get – of,** (fam.) quitarse de encima, deshacerse de, librarse de (algo que uno no quiere). **19 like a –,** (fam.) como un relámpago, a toda velocidad, como una bala. **20 – put,** DEP. lanzamiento de peso. **21 – putter,** DEP. lanzador de peso.

shotgun | 'ʃɒtgʌn | *s.c.* escopeta (de caza).

should | ʃʊd | (forma relajada | ʃəd |) *v.i.* **1** debería, deber (moral, de consejo, de instrucción, de recomendación, etc.): *I should go now, it's very late = me debo ir ahora, es demasiado tarde.* || **2 I –,** (fam.) yo que tu... (dando un consejo): *I should put all that money in a bank, not in your safe = yo que tú pondría todo ese dinero en un banco, no en la caja fuerte.* **3 you –,** tenías que (expresando sorpresa, extrañeza, etc.): *you should have heard him shouting when I insulted Tom, his beloved friend = tenías que haberle oído gritar cuando insulté a Tom, su queridísimo amigo.*

OBS. Este verbo es en gran medida un verbo auxiliar que no tiene un significado semántico, sino gramatical en los siguientes casos: **4** funciona como auxiliar de condicional con matiz (form.) y sólo para las primeras personas: *I should say it is a touchy issue = yo diría que es un tema difícil.* **5** en oraciones condicionales (form.) indica una posibilidad remota: *should you see him, tell him about it = si por un casual lo vieras, cuéntaselo.* **6** señala sorpresa enfática: *when I got on the bus, who should I see but Mary sitting on my seat = cuando subí al autobús, a quién me iba a encontrar sino a Mary sentada en mi asiento.* **7** aparece en oraciones completivas con un significado subjuntivo: *it's been suggested that you should step down = se ha sugerido que tú abandones tu puesto.*

shoulder | 'ʃəʊldər | *s.c.* **1** ANAT. hombro. **2** hombrera (de una prenda de vestir). **3** cuarto delantero, espalda (carne de animal para consumo). **4** lomo (de una colina o similar). **5** (EE.UU.) arcén, bordillo. || *s.pl.* **6** espaldas, hombros (donde recaen problemas, responsabilidades, cargas, etc.). || *v.t.* **7** golpear con el hombro, dar un codazo. **8** llevar sobre los hombros, cargar sobre la espalda. **9** acarrear, aguantar, sufrir, soportar (responsabilidad o similar). || **10 a – to cry on,** un hombro sobre el que llorar, un consuelo. **11 head and shoulders (above), a)** mucho más alto (que); **b)** muy por encima (de), muchísimo mejor (que). **12 over one's –,** hacia atrás por encima del hombro (mirada). **13 to put one's – to the wheel,** arrimar el hombro. **14 to rub shoulders with,** (fam.) codearse con, tener contacto con. **15 to – one's way,** abrirse camino a base de codazos, abrirse camino a empellones. **16 – to –, a)** hombro con hombro, juntos (físicamente); **b)** juntos, cooperando juntos.

shoulder-bag | 'ʃəʊldəbæg | *s.c.* bolso de bandolera.

shoulder-blade | 'ʃəʊldəbleɪd | *s.c.* ANAT. omóplato.

shoulder-high | 'ʃəʊldəhaɪ | *adj.* y *adv.* a la altura de los hombros.

shoulder-length | 'ʃəʊldəleŋθ | *adj.* hasta los hombros.

shoulder-strap | 'ʃəʊldəstræp | *s.c.* **1** bandolera, cinta (para llevar objetos colgando). **2** tirante (de vestido).

shouldn't | 'ʃʊdnt | (forma relajada | 'ʃədnt |) *contr.* de **should** y **not.**

should've | 'ʃʊdəv | (forma relajada | 'ʃədəv |) *contr.* de **should** y **have.**

shout | ʃaʊt | *v.i.* **1** gritar, chillar. **2 [to – (at)]** hablar en voz demasiado alta. || *v.t.* **3** decir a gritos, decir a voces. || *s.c.* **4** grito, chillido. || *s.sing.* **5** (fam.) turno (de invitar una ronda). || **6 all over bar the shouting,** se puede dar por terminado, el tema está prácticamente acabado. **7 to – down,** acallar a voces, no dejar hablar a base de gritar más. **8 to – oneself hoarse,** quedarse ronco de tanto gritar. **9 to – out,** pegar un grito fuerte, dar un fuerte grito.

shove | ʃʌv | *v.t.* **1** empujar, apartar de un empujón, dar un empellón. **2** meter, poner, colocar (rápida y descuidadamente): *I shoved the bank-notes into the box = metí los billetes dentro de la caja.* || *v.i.* **3** empujar, empellar. || *s.c.* **4** (normalmente *sing.*) empujón, empellón. || **5 to – off,** (fam.) irse al quinto pino, largarse a freír monas.
shovel | 'ʃʌvl | *s.c.* **1** pala; (Am.) palana. **2** MEC. pala, pala mecánica. || *v.t.* **3** cavar con una pala. **4** meter a montones en: *the baby was shovelling fruit into his mouth = el crío se estaba metiendo la fruta a montones en la boca.*
shovelful | 'ʃʌvlfʊl | *s.c.* palada.
show | ʃəʊ | *v.* [*pret.* **showed,** *p.p.irreg.* **shown**] *t.* **1** mostrar, enseñar, exhibir, exponer: *I showed her my books = le enseñé mis libros.* **2** indicar (un instrumento, una medida). **3** demostrar: *this shows he's a criminal = esto demuestra que es un criminal.* **4** poner (película o programa). **5** mostrar, evidenciar (una característica o rasgo): *small children show a dislike of order = los niños pequeños evidencian una aversión al orden.* **6** mostrar, enseñar, revelar (sentimiento, deseo, objetivo, etc.). **7** descubrir, destapar (para que se vea): *show your back to me = descúbrase la espalda.* **8** acompañar, llevar a: *will you show this gentleman to the door, Joan? = ¿quiere hacer el favor de acompañar a este caballero a la puerta, Joan?* **9** [**to – +** *o.* **+ how**] enseñar (para que otra persona aprenda): *show me how to play "mus" = enséñame a jugar al mus.* **10** comportarse con, mostrar (respeto, admiración, etc., hacia otro). **11** COM. arrojar (déficit, pérdidas, etc. por parte de una empresa). **12** dejar ver fácilmente (suciedad, unos zapatos o tela). || *i.* **13** verse, notarse (un sentimiento, realidad, etc.). **14** descubrirse, destaparse. **15** señalar (una preferencia en una votación). **16** (EE.UU.) aparecer, presentarse, llegar (una persona a algún acontecimiento social). || *r.* **17** dejarse ver (saliendo de la oscuridad, por ejemplo). **18** mostrarse (poseedor de una determinada característica): *she showed herself too shy to speak = ella se mostró demasiado tímida para hablar.* || *s.c.* **19** ostentación, espectáculo: *he put on the show for the Minister = organizó un espectáculo para el ministro.* **20** programa (de televisión o radio). **21** espectáculo (artístico). **22** exposición (de cualquier tema artístico o habilidoso, e incluso comercial). || *s.sing.* **23** (fam.) asunto, cosa, organización: *don't ask me, it's your show = no me preguntes, es cosa tuya.* || **24 a – of hands,** a mano alzada (forma de votación). **25 for –,** por boato, por ostentación. **26 good –/jolly good –,** (p.u.) estupendo, magnífico. **27 to have something to – for,** sacar algo de, sacar algún beneficio de, sacar algún resultado positivo de. **28 I'll – you,** ya te enseñaré yo, ya te haré ver. **29 it just goes to –/it just shows,** esto muestra rotundamente, esto es buena prueba de. **30 let's get this – on the road,** vamos a poner manos a la obra, vamos a ponernos a ello. **31 on –,** expuesto, en exposición. **32 to put up a good/poor –,** hacer un buen/mal papel. **33 to – around/round,** enseñar los sitios que merece la pena ver, enseñar las cosas decentes que hay alrededor. **34 to – off, a)** (desp.) hacer alarde, jactarse; **b)** hacer resaltar, destacar (algo en contraste con otra cosa); **c)** enseñar orgullosamente, lucir. **35 to – one's face,** V. **face. 36 to – one's hand,** V. **hand. 37 to – some one the ropes,** V. **rope. 38 to – up, a)** (fam.) aparecer, llegar, acudir, presentarse; **b)** avergonzar (por el mal comportamiento); **c)** revelar, hacer aparecer, resaltar, destacar: *the light suddenly showed up her damaged face = la luz repentinamente reveló su cara dañada;* **d)** aparecer, notarse, hacerse patente. **39 to steal the –,** llevarse los aplausos, hacerse con el centro de la atención.
showbiz | 'ʃəʊbɪz | *s.i.* (fam.) mundo del espectáculo.
show-business | 'ʃəʊbɪznɪs | *s.i.* mundo del espectáculo.
showcase | 'ʃəʊkeɪs | *s.c.* **1** vitrina (de exposición de objetos). **2** (fig.) escaparate: *this project is one of the most important showcases of European efficiency = este proyecto es uno de los más importantes escaparates de la eficacia europea.*
showdown | 'ʃəʊdaʊn | *s.c.* (normalmente *sing.*) confrontación, enfrentamiento.
shower | 'ʃaʊər | *s.c.* **1** ducha (objeto). **2** ducha (acción). **3** chubasco, aguacero. **4** (fig.) torrente, cascada: *a shower of cards = un torrente de tarjetas postales.* || *v.i.* **5** darse una ducha. || *v.t.* **6** [**to – +** *o.* **+ with**] colmar de, llenar de: *they showered him with all sorts of presents = le colmaron de todo tipo de regalos.* **7** tirar, desparramar (cosas sobre alguien).
showerproof | 'ʃaʊəpru:f | *adj.* a prueba de chaparrones (impermeable u otra vestimenta).
showery | 'ʃaʊərɪ | *adj.* de frecuentes chaparrones, de frecuentes chubascos; intermitentemente lluvioso.
showing | 'ʃəʊɪŋ | *s.c.* proyección (de una película).
show-jumping | 'ʃəʊdʒʌmpɪŋ | *s.i.* DEP. hípica, modalidad de saltos.
showman | 'ʃəʊmən | [*pl.irreg.* **showmen**] *s.c.* **1** empresario de espectáculos. **2** "showman", comediante, hombre del espectáculo.
showmanship | 'ʃəʊmənʃɪp | *s.i.* brillantez para el espectáculo, talento para el espectáculo.
showmen | 'ʃəʊmən | *pl.irreg.* de **showman.**
shown | ʃəʊn | *p.p.irreg.* de **show.**
show-off | 'ʃəʊɒf | *s.c.* (fam. y desp.) chulo, fantoche, farolero.
showpiece | 'ʃəʊpi:s | *s.c.* ejemplo sobresaliente, objeto de gran valor.
showplace | 'ʃəʊpleɪs | *s.c.* lugar sobresaliente, lugar de gran interés.
showroom | 'ʃəʊrʊm | *s.c.* salón de demostraciones (especialmente de coches).
showy | 'ʃəʊɪ | *adj.* (a menudo desp.) llamativo, vistoso, ostentoso.
showily | 'ʃəʊɪlɪ | *adv.* (a menudo desp.) llamativamente, vistosamente, ostentosamente.
showiness | 'ʃəʊɪnɪs | *s.i.* (a menudo desp.) vistosidad, ostentación.
shrank | ʃræŋk | *pret.irreg.* de **shrink.**
shrapnel | 'ʃræpnəl | *s.i.* MIL. metralla.
shred | ʃred | [*ger.* **shredding,** *pret.* y *p.p.* **shredded**] *v.t.* **1** desmenuzar, fragmentar, triturar, hacer pedacitos. || *s.c.* **2** (normalmente *pl.*) pedacito, fragmento, tira (especialmente de papel). **3** (fig.) pizca, fragmento, trocito (indicando pequeñez de algo): *there is not a shred of truth in his declaration = no hay un fragmento de verdad en su declaración.*
shredder | 'ʃredər | *s.c.* trituradora de papel.
shrew | ʃru: | *s.c.* **1** ZOOL. musaraña. **2** (desp.) fiera, fierecilla, bravía (mujer).
shrewd | ʃru:d | *adj.* astuto, sagaz, perspicaz, penetrante.
shrewdly | 'ʃru:dlɪ | *adv.* astutamente, sagazmente, perspicazmente; penetrantemente.
shrewdness | 'ʃru:dnɪs | *s.i.* astucia, sagacidad, perspicacia; penetración (de pensamiento).
shrewish | 'ʃru:ɪʃ | *adj.* fierecilla, valentona, indomable (mujer de carácter fuerte).
shriek | ʃri:k | *v.i.* **1** chillar, aullar (de dolor, pavor o similar). || *v.t.* **2** decir chillando, decir aullando. || *s.c.* **3** [**– of**] chillido, aullido, grito destemplado.
shrift | ʃrɪft | **to give someone/something short –,** prestar poca atención a alguien /algo, no hacer caso alguno a alguien /algo, hacer caso omiso de alguien /algo.
shrill | ʃrɪl | *adj.* **1** chillón, estridente, agudo (sonido). **2** destemplada, exagerada, estridente (protesta, petición, etc.). || *v.i.* **3** emitir un sonido desagradable, emitir un sonido estridente. || *v.t.* **4** decir con voz aguda, decir con voz estridente.
shrilly | 'ʃrɪlɪ | *adv.* **1** chillonamente, estridentemente, con demasiada agudeza (de sonido). **2** destempladamente, exageradamente, estridentemente (forma de protestar, demandar servicios, exigir derechos, etc.).
shrillness | 'ʃrɪlnɪs | *s.i.* **1** estridencia, agudeza excesiva (de sonido). **2** estridencia, exageración (de una protesta, petición, etc.).
shrimp | ʃrɪmp | *s.c.* **1** ZOOL. gamba. **2** (fig.) flaco, esmirriado.
shrimping | 'ʃrɪmpɪŋ | *s.c.* pesca de gambas.
shrine | ʃraɪn | *s.c.* **1** santuario, lugar sagrado. **2** relicario. **3** sepulcro, tumba (de un santo importante). **4** (fig.) santuario, lugar más importante (de un hecho histórico, personalidad artística o similar).
shrink | ʃrɪŋk | [*pret.irreg.* **shrank,** *p.p.irreg.* **shrunk**] *v.t.* e *i.* **1** encoger(se). **2** disminuir de tamaño, hacer(se) más pequeño. || *v.i.* **3** retroceder, apartarse, alejarse. **4** [**to – from**] acobardarse ante (una tarea o responsabilidad). || *s.c.* **5** (fam.) psiquiatra.
shrinkage | 'ʃrɪŋkɪdʒ | *s.i.* encogimiento (especialmente en prendas de vestir); reducción, disminución (en peso, medida, etc.).
shrivel | 'ʃrɪvl | *v.t.* e *i.* (también **shrivel up**) arrugarse, resecarse.

shrivelled | 'ʃrɪvld | (EE.UU. **shriveled**) *adj.* arrugado, reseco.
shroud | ʃraud | *s.c.* **1** mortaja. **2 [– of]** (fig.) velos (de misterio o similar). || *v.t.* **3** (normalmente pasiva) ocultar, cubrir, envolver (en algo tangible o intangible): *the valley was shrouded in thick fog = el valle estaba cubierto de una niebla espesa.*
shrub | ʃrʌb | *s.c.* BOT. arbusto.
shrubbery | 'ʃrʌbərɪ | *s.c.* e *i.* BOT. zona de arbustos, maleza.
shrug | ʃrʌg | [*ger.* **shrugging,** *pret.* y *p.p.* **shrugged**] *v.t.* e *i.* **1** encogerse (de hombros); encoger (los hombros). || *s.c.* **2** (normalmente *sing.*) encogimiento de hombros, gesto de encoger los hombros. || **3 to – off,** quitar importancia (a algo, con ese gesto característico de encogerse de hombros).
shrunk | ʃrʌŋk | *p.p.irreg.* de **shrink.**
shrunken | 'ʃrʌŋkən | *adj.* encogido, disminuido, empequeñecido (de tamaño, peso, medida, etc.).
shucks | ʃʌks | *interj.* (EE.UU.) caramba, vaya (expresando enfado, vergüenza o desilusión).
shudder | 'ʃʌdər | *v.i.* **1** temblar, estremecerse, tener un escalofrío (de miedo, horror, asco, etc.). **2** estremecerse, hacer un movimiento repentino (físicamente). || *s.c.* **3** (normalmente *sing.*) estremecimiento, escalofrío, temblor (de miedo o similar). **4** (normalmente *sing.*) movimiento súbito, movimiento repentino. || **5 to give someone the shudders,** (fam.) dar a alguien escalofríos (de miedo). **6 to – to think,** temblar al pensar, temblar al pasársele a uno por la cabeza (algo).
shuffle | 'ʃʌfl | *v.i.* **1** andar con los pies a rastras, caminar arrastrando los pies. || *v.t.* e *i.* **2** barajar (las cartas). **3** mover los pies nerviosamente, no estarse quieto en un sitio (moviendo los pies o cambiando de postura sentado). || *v.t.* **4** desordenar, entremezclar, poner patas arriba. || *s.sing.* **5 [a –]** una acción de barajar. **6** forma de andar arrastrando los pies. || **7 to – off,** evadir, dar rodeos (a un tema). **8 to – out/out of,** salirse de, rechazar (una tarea desagradable).
shun | ʃʌn | [*ger.* **shunning,** *pret.* y *p.p.* **shunned**] *v.t.* esquivar, rehuir (a alguien o algo).
shunt | ʃʌnt | *v.t.* **1** llevar, mover, trasladar, trajinar (cosas de un sitio a otro o personas). || *v.t.* e *i.* **2** hacer maniobras, maniobrar, cambiar de vía (ferrocarril).
shush | ʃuʃ | *interj.* **1** calla, chsss. || *v.t.* e *i.* **2** hacer callar, callar.
shut | ʃʌt | *v.* [*pret.* y *p.p.irreg.* **shut**] *t.* e *i.* **1** cerrar(se) (objeto o establecimiento). || *t.* **2** cerrar (la boca, los ojos, etc.). || *adj.* **3** cerrado (objeto, establecimiento, ojos, boca, etc.). || **4 to keep one's mouth/trap/etc. –,** mantener la boca/boquita/etc., cerrada. **5 to – away,** guardar, guardar bajo llave, guardar en un sitio apartado. **6 to – down,** cerrar (negocio o similar). **7 to – in,** encerrar (en prisión). **8 to – off, a)** cortar el suministro de, interrumpir el envío de; **b)** apagar, parar (máquina o similar); **c)** tapar (la visión). **9 to – oneself in,** encerrarse, aislarse (en una habitación). **10 to – one's eyes (to),** (desp.) cerrar los ojos de uno (ante) (la evidencia o realidad). **11 to – one's mouth/face/etc.,** callarse, cerrar la boca, dejar de hablar. **12 to – out, a)** excluir, no dejar entrar, no dejar participar (a algo o alguien); **b)** rechazar, no dar cabida (a un pensamiento, sentimiento, etc.). **13 to – up, a)** (fam.) callarse, cerrar la boca; **b)** (fam.) silenciar, dejar sin posibilidad de decir nada; **c)** encerrar, confinar (en manicomio, prisión, etc.).
shutdown | 'ʃʌtdaun | *s.c.* cierre (de negocio).
shut-eye | 'ʃʌtaɪ | *s.i.* (fam.) sueñecito (dormir): *you'd better get some shut-eye, you're too tired = será mejor que te eches un sueñecito, estás demasiado cansado.*
shutter | 'ʃʌtər | *s.c.* **1** (normalmente *pl.*) contraventana. **2** FOT. obturador. **3** cerrador, cierre (de objeto o mecanismo).
shuttered | 'ʃʌtəd | *adj.* **1** con contraventanas (casa). **2** con las contraventanas cerradas.
shuttle | 'ʃʌtl | *s.c.* **1** puente, enlace (normalmente aéreo). **2** avión que hace el puente aéreo, puente aéreo. **3** lanzadera (de un telar). **4** lanzadera, jugadera (en máquinas de coser). **5** pelota de bádminton. || *v.t.* **6** transportar, enlazar, enviar en transporte continuo, enviar en transporte de enlace: *the troops were shuttled to the Gulf = las tropas fueron transportadas continuamente al Golfo.* || *v.i.* **7** viajar a modo de puente o enlace (de manera continuada), hacer el trayecto de ida y vuelta casi sin parar. || **8 – diplomacy,** POL. diplomacia de puente aéreo (entre dos países). **9 – service,** servicio de puente aéreo, servicio de enlace continuo.
shuttlecock | 'ʃʌtlkɒk | *s.c.* pelota de bádminton.
shy | ʃaɪ | *adj.* **1** tímido, retraído, vergonzoso, huraño. **2** asustadizo (animal). **3 [– of]** miedo de, temeroso de, con prevención contra: *she was shy of telling everything to the police = ella tenía miedo de contárselo todo a la policía.* || *v.i.* **4** espantarse (caballo) || *v.t.* **5** (p.u.) tirar, lanzar (piedras o una pelota). || *s.c.* **6** (normalmente *sing.*) (p.u.) tirada (de piedra o pelota). || **7 to – away from,** alejarse de; apartar de sí, rechazar hacer (por falta de confianza en uno mismo).
Siamese | ˌsaɪə'miːz | [*pl.* **Siamese**] *s.c.* **1** (arc.) tailandés. **2** (fam.) gato siamés. || *adj.* **3** (p.u.) tailandés. || **4 – cat,** gato siamés. **5 – twins,** hermanos siameses, gemelos siameses.
sibilant | 'sɪbɪlənt | *adj.* **1** silbante, sibilante (sonido). || *s.c.* **2** FON. silbante, sibilante.
sibling | 'sɪblɪŋ | *s.c.* (form.) hermano, hermana.
sic | sɪk | *adv.* fórmula latina que indica que se está citando textualmente, a pesar de que se repita un error gráfico o de significado o construcción gramatical (siempre va entre paréntesis).
sick | sɪk | *adj.* **1** enfermo. **2** mareado, con náuseas (como a punto de devolver). **3** triste, entristecido; (fig.) enfermo, malo (ante algo injusto o parecido). **4** (desp.) mórbido, morboso (película, historia, chiste, etc.). **5 [– of]** harto de, hasta las narices de, insatisfecho de: *I am sick of him = estoy harto de él.* || *s.i.* **6** (brit. y fam.) vómito. || **7 to be –,** vomitar, devolver, arrojar. **8 to fall –,** (lit.) caer en cama, caer enfermo. **9 to make someone –,** poner a alguien malo, poner a alguien enfermo, sacar a alguien de sus casillas, enfermar a alguien: *his macho attitude makes me sick = su actitud machista me pone enferma.* **10 off –,** con la baja, con permiso por enfermedad. **11 – and tired (of),** hasta la coronilla (de), hasta las narices (de), con un hartazgo (de). **12 – bay,** enfermería (especialmente en un buque). **13 – leave,** permiso por enfermedad. **14 the –,** los enfermos. **15 worried –,** (fam.) enfermo de preocupación, preocupadísimo, que no vive de preocupación.
sickbed | 'sɪkbed | *s.c.* (normalmente *sing.*) lecho de enfermo, lecho de enfermedad.
sicken | 'sɪkən | *v.t.* **1** enfermar, sacar de quicio, enfadar, poner malo. || *v.i.* **2** (p.u.) enfermar, caer enfermo.
sickening | 'sɪkənɪŋ | *adj.* **1** desagradable, nauseabundo, repugnante. **2** (fam.) cabreante, que pone malo, que pone furioso: *a sickening attitude = una actitud que pone malo a cualquiera.*
sickeningly | 'sɪkənɪŋlɪ | *adv.* **1** desagradablemente, nauseabundamente, repugnantemente. **2** (fam.) cabreantemente, asquerosamente (que causa enfado).
sickle | 'sɪkl | *s.c.* hoz.
sickly | 'sɪklɪ | *adj.* **1** enfermizo, enclenque. **2** pálido, demacrado, descolorido (rostro). **3** nauseabundo, asqueroso, repugnante (olor o vista). || *adv.* **4** demacradamente, descoloridamente (sobre la forma del rostro).
sickness | 'sɪknɪs *s.i.* **1** enfermedad, dolencia. **2** mareo, náusea. || *s.c.* e *i.* **3** enfermedad (concreta). || **4 – benefit,** (brit.) subsidio de enfermedad.
sickroom | 'sɪkrum | *s.c.* (normalmente *sing.*) cuarto de enfermo, habitación del enfermo.
side | saɪd | *s.c.* **1** lado, parte (posición): *the left side of the house = el lado derecho de la casa.* **2** lado, costado (del cuerpo). **3** lado, cara (de un objeto). **4** lado, posición ideológica (en una discusión o parecido). **5** lado, borde (de un espacio). **6** lado, carril (de una carretera). **7** orilla (de un lago o río). **8** ladera (de montaña). **9 [– of]** mitad de (carne). **10** lado, equipo (en cualquier clase de competición). **11** parte, grupo (de un acuerdo comercial, especialmente). **12** lado, aspecto, enfoque (de un asunto, personalidad de alguien, etc.). **13** lado, parte, línea (de familia). **14** lado, vera (de alguien): *I want to spend all my life by your side = quiero pasar mi vida a tu vera.* **15** arcén (de carretera, especialmente cuando tiene hierba). || *adj.* **16** secundaria (calle o carretera). **17** lateral (puerta, entrada, etc.). || **18 to be on the safe =N ,** V. **safe. 19 to be on the – of the angels,** V. **angel. 20 to err on the – of something,** V. **err. 21 to get out of bed on the wrong –,** V. **bed. 22 from – to –,** de derecha a izquierda, de lado a lado. **23 to know which – one's bread is buttered on,** V. **bread. 24 leaving to one –,** dejando a un lado, sin hacer caso de, olvidando, sin mencionar para nada. **25 to let the – down,** desacreditar a la propia familia, avergonzar a la propia familia. **26 to**

look on the bright –, V. **bright. 27 on every –/on all sides,** por todas las partes, por todos los lados, por todo alrededor. **28 on one's –,** de parte de uno, del lado de uno: *everything but money is on our side = todo menos el dinero está de nuestra parte.* **29 on someone's –,** de parte de alguien, del lado de alguien, apoyando a alguien: *I am on the American's side = yo estoy de parte de los americanos.* **30 on the large/small/etc. –,** un poco demasiado grande, un poco demasiado pequeño, etc. **31 on the right – of,** (fig.) en plan simpático con, de manera amigable con, en plan complaciente con. **32 on the –, a)** de manera adicional, para negocio extra, aparte de la ocupación principal; **b)** como negocio añadido, como actividad secreta e ilegal extra. **33 on the – of,** a favor de, en apoyo de, del lado de. **34 on the wrong – of,** en plan problemático con, de manera poco amigable con, en plan peligroso con: *don't get on the wrong side of him, he can be very nasty = no te enzarzes de manera poco amigable con él, puede ser muy desagradable.* **35 to – against,** agruparse contra, unirse todos contra, acordar ir todos contra (alguien). **36 – by –, a)** hombro con hombro, pegados, juntos (físicamente); **b)** conjuntamente, codo con codo (trabajando, colaborando, etc.); **c)** al mismo tiempo, simultáneamente (dos acontecimientos). **37 – issue,** tema secundario, asunto de menor importancia. **38 – order,** (EE.UU.) plato adicional, plato de relleno (de la comida principal). **39 – to –,** en un constante balanceo, con un constante balanceo. **40 to – with,** ponerse del lado de, apoyar el lado de, tomar partido por. **41 somebody's – of the story/picture,** lo que cuenta uno de algún tema, el lado de quien cuenta la feria según le va en ella. **42 to take sides/to take someone's –,** tomar partido, tomar partido por alguien. **43 to take someone on one –,** coger a alguien aparte, hablar con alguien privadamente. **44 the other – of,** al otro extremo de, al otro lado de, más allá de (la ciudad, nación, mundo, etc.). **45 the other – of the coin,** V. **coin. 46 the wrong – of,** pasar de, ser ya mayor de (con edad). **47 this – of,** (fam.) antes de, antes de que llegue (un tiempo): *this side of Easter = antes de que llegue la Semana Santa.* **48 to one –,** a un lado (empujar, moverse, etc.). **49 to one –/on one –,** aparte, para más tarde (dejar). **50 to one – (of)/on one – (of),** a un lado (de), de lado (de).

sideboard | 'saɪdbɔːd | *s.c.* **1** aparador. || *s.pl.* **2** patillas (de pelo).

sidecar | 'saɪdkaːr | *s.c.* sidecar.

side-effect | 'saɪdɪfekt | *s.c.* **1** (normalmente *pl.*) efecto secundario. **2 [– (of)]** consecuencia, resultado, resultado secundario.

sidekick | 'saɪdkɪk | *s.c.* (fam.) compañero de trabajo (especialmente de categoría inferior)

sidelight | 'saɪdlaɪt | *s.c.* luz de posición.

sideline | 'saɪdlaɪn | *s.c.* **1** trabajo extra, empleo suplementario. **2** (normalmente *pl.*) línea de demarcación, línea lateral, línea de banda (en muchos deportes marcando los límites del campo). || **3 on the sidelines, a)** desde la barrera, sin comprometerse; **b)** en los laterales (esperando tomar parte).

sidelong | 'saɪdlɒŋ | *adj.* y *adv.* de soslayo (mirada); oblicuo, oblicuamente.

side-saddle | 'saɪdsædl | *adj. y adv.* a sentadillas, a estilo amazona.

sideshow | 'saɪdʃəʊ | *s.c.* barraca de feria.

side-splitting | 'saɪdsplɪtɪŋ | *adj.* (fam.) de partirse de risa.

sidestep | 'saɪdstep | *v.t.* e *i.* **1** evadir, soslayar (tema, asunto, etc.). **2** dar un paso a un lado, echarse a un lado.

sidestepping | 'saɪdstepɪŋ | *s.i.* evitación, evasión, soslayo (de un tema o similar).

sideswipe | 'saɪdswaɪp | *s.c.* golpe de refilón, puñetazo de refilón.

sidetrack | 'saɪdtræk | *v.t.* apartar de su finalidad, distraer de su cometido.

sidewalk | 'saɪdwɔːk | *s.c.* (EE.UU.) acera.

sideways | 'saɪdweɪz | *adj.* y *adv.* **1** de lado, hacia un lado, al lado. **2** sin progresar, con la marcha del cangrejo (en una actividad o similar). || **3 to knock someone –,** (fam.) dejar a alguien estupefacto, dejar a alguien con la boca abierta.

siding | 'saɪdɪŋ | *s.c.* apartadero; línea muerta (de ferrocarril).

sidle | 'saɪdl | *v.i.* moverse cautelosamente, andar furtivamente, acercarse sigilosamente.

siege | siːdʒ | *s.c.* e *i.* **1** MIL. sitio, cerco, asedio. **2** bloqueo, asedio (policial o similar). || **3 to lay – (to),** poner sitio (a), sitiar, asediar, cercar.

siesta | sɪ'estə | *s.c.* e *i.* siesta.

sieve | sɪv | *s.c.* **1** tamiz, colador. || *v.t.* **2** tamizar, cribar, pasar por un colador.

sift | sɪft | *v.t.* **1** tamizar, cribar. **2** examinar, escudriñar. || *v.i.* **3 [to – through]** examinar, repasar: *I have to sift through all these papers = tengo que examinar todos estos papeles.*

sigh | saɪ | *v.t.* e *i.* **1** suspirar. || *v.i.* **2** susurrar, quejarse (el viento). || *s.c.* **3** suspiro. || **4 to heave a –,** dar un suspiro, lanzar un suspiro, suspirar.

sight | saɪt | *s.i.* **1** vista (potencia física). || *s.c.* **2** vista, escena, paisaje. || *s.sing.* **3 [– (of)]** vista, visión (concreta): *he cried at the sight of his dead mother = lloró al ver a su madre muerta.* **4 [a –],** un espectáculo, un espantajo (negativo): *what a sight! = ¡vaya espectáculo!* || *s.pl.* **5** las vistas, las cosas dignas de ver (en una ciudad). **6** mira (de un fusil o aparato). || *v.t.* **7** ver momentáneamente, localizar, ver brevemente: *the missing child was sighted yesterday in Liverpool = la niña perdida fue localizada ayer en Liverpool.* || **8 a –,** (fam.) muchísimo, un montón, un potosí: *that's a sight better than what you did yesterday = eso es muchísimo mejor que lo que hiciste ayer.* **9 at first –,** a primera vista. **10 to catch – of,** ver, vislumbrar, avistar. **11 in –,** visible, a la vista. **12 in –/within –, a)** a la vista, que se puede ver; **b)** (fig.) a la vista, acercándose, a la mano (un resultado). **13 to know someone by –,** conocer a alguien de vista. **14 to lose – of,** perder de vista, no tener presente el hecho de. **15 on –,** sin más, a primera vista (disparar, por ejemplo). **16 out of –,** fuera de vista. **17 to set one's sights on,** decidirse por, decidir adquirir, desear adquirir. **18 – unseen,** sin ver, sin examinar (por ejemplo, comprar algo).

sighted | 'saɪtɪd | *adj.* que tiene vista, que puede ver (no ciego).

sighting | 'saɪtɪŋ | *s.c.* ocasión de observación, observación.

sightless | 'saɪtlɪs | *adj.* sin visión, sin vista, ciego.

sight-read | 'saɪtriːd | *v.t.* e *i.* MUS. repentizar.

sightseeing | 'saɪtsiːɪŋ | *s.i.* visita a lugares de interés.

sightseer | 'saɪtsiːər | *s.c.* turista, persona que visita lugares de interés turístico.

sign | saɪn | *s.c.* **1** signo, símbolo (con un significado concreto). **2** señal, gesto (con alguna parte del cuerpo). **3** señal, indicación (de algo que va a ocurrir). **4** señal, letrero. **5** signo (del zodíaco). **6** señal, prueba, muestra, manifestación (de algo): *she showed no signs of being tired = ella no dio muestras de estar cansada.* || *v.t.* e *i.* **7** firmar. || **8 a – of the times,** un signo de los tiempos, una señal de los tiempos. **9 to make the – of the cross,** REL. santiguarse, hacer la señal de la cruz. **10 no – of,** ni señal de, ningún indicio de (alguien). **11 to – away,** ceder, entregar (algo mediante firma). **12 signed and sealed,** firmado y sellado, firmado y lacrado (documentos oficiales). **13 to – for, a)** aceptar, acordar (mediante documento firmado); **b)** firmar (la recepción). **14 to – in, a)** firmar la entrada, registrarse (en un hotel); **b)** invitar (a una persona a un club o similar del que uno es miembro). **15 – language,** lenguaje por señas, lenguaje mímico. **16 to – off,** finalizar, acabar (carta). **17 to – on, a)** apuntarse, inscribirse (en un cursillo); firmar el contrato de trabajo; **b)** registrarse (en algún organismo oficial para tener derecho a lo que sea). **18 to – out, a)** salir (de un hotel, club, asociación, etc.); **b)** sacar (un libro de una biblioteca). **19 to – over,** firmar la cesión de, ceder oficialmente (una propiedad o similar). **20 to – up, a)** firmar un contrato por; inscribirse, apuntarse; **b)** reclutar (a alguien para un trabajo o puesto militar).

signal | 'sɪgnəl | *s.c.* **1** señal, seña; contraseña. **2** señal, aviso, indicación. **3** TV. señal (de emisión). **4** señal (aparato como semáforo del ferrocarril). || *v.t.* **5** hacer una señal, hacer señas: *he signalled me to stop = me hizo señas para que parara.* **6** indicar, señalizar (algo que puede ocurrir). || *adj.* **7** señalado, notable, insigne, memorable.

signal-box | 'sɪgnəlbɒks | *s.c.* garita de señales (de ferrocarril).

signally | 'sɪgnəlɪ | *adv.* señaladamente, notablemente, insignemente, memorablemente.

signalman | 'sɪgnəlmən | [*pl.irreg.* **signalmen**] *s.c.* **1** guardavía (de ferrocarril). **2** MIL. soldado del cuerpo de señales.

signalmen | 'sɪgnəlmən | *pl.irreg.* de **signalman.**

signatory | 'sɪgnətrɪ | (EE.UU.) | 'sɪgnətɔːrɪ | *s.c.* signatario, firmante (persona, país, etc.).

signature | 'sɪgnətʃər | *s.c.* e *i.* **1** firma, rúbrica: *the papers are ready for your signature = los papeles están listos*

para su firma. || *s.c.* **2** (fig.) marca, característica (de una persona o animal). || **3 to put one's – to,** firmar, estampar la firma de uno en. **4 – tune,** sintonía (de un programa).
signboard | 'saɪnbɔːd | *s.c.* letrero, tablero de anuncio.
signet | 'sɪgnɪt | *s.c.* **1** sello, sello personal. || **2 – ring,** anillo de sello.
significance | sɪg'nɪfɪkəns | *s.i.* **1** significación, importancia, trascendencia. **2** significado, implicación, sentido.
significant | sɪg'nɪfɪkənt | *adj.* **1** significante, importante, trascendente. **2** significativo, lleno de significado, lleno de sentido propio. **3** apreciable, marcado, importante (por su tamaño o cantidad): *a significant rise = una subida apreciable.*
significantly | sɪg'nɪfɪkəntlɪ | *adv.* **1** de gran significación, de suma importancia, trascendentemente. **2** significativamente, con gran sentido propio. **3** apreciablemente, marcadamente (en su cantidad o tamaño).
signify | 'sɪgnɪfaɪ | *v.t.* **1** significar, indicar (algo). || *v.i.* **2** (form.) tener importancia, importar.
signpost | 'saɪnpəust | *s.c.* **1** poste indicador. **2** (fig.) guía, faro, señal (normalmente de algo futuro). || *v.t.* **3** (fig. y lit.) ser guía de, servir de faro para.
signposted | 'səɪnpəustɪd | *adj.* señalizada (carretera).
Sikh | siːk | REL. *s.c.* **1** sij. || *adj.* **2** sij.
Sikhism | 'siːkɪzəm | *s.i.* REL. la religión sij.
silage | 'saɪlɪdʒ | *s.i.* AGR. ensilaje.
silence | 'saɪləns | *s.c.* e *i.* **1** silencio. || *s.i.* **2** silencio, quietud. **3** el hecho de que alguien se calle, silencio (de alguien sobre un tema): *his silence surprised the police = su silencio sorprendió a la policía.* || *v.t.* **4** hacer callar, acallar. || **5 – is golden,** el silencio es oro.
silencer | 'saɪlənsər | *s.c.* MEC. **1** silenciador. **2** (brit.) silenciador (de coche).
silent | 'saɪlənt | *adj.* **1** silencioso, callado (estado). **2** taciturno, callado (carácter personal). **3** mudo, que no dice nada: *the police are silent about the crime = la policía no dice nada sobre el crimen.* **4** FON. que no se pronuncia, muda (letra). **5** muda (película). **6** sin palabras, sin expresión verbal (oración, sentimiento, pensamiento, etc). || **7 the – majority,** POL. la mayoría silenciosa.
silently | 'saɪləntlɪ | *adv.* **1** silenciosamente, calladamente. **2** sin expresar nada, sin decir nada, sin que se oiga: *he was praying silently = estaba rezando sin que se oyera.*
silhovette | 'sɪluːˌet | *s.c.* **1** silueta, figura, forma. || **2 in =N, en perfil.**
silhouetted | ˌsɪluː'etɪd | *adj.* **[– against]** destacado sobre, señalado (un fondo).
silica | 'sɪlɪkə | *s.i.* MIN. sílice.
silicon | 'sɪlɪkən | *s.i.* **1** QUIM. silicio. || **2 – chip,** INF. chip de silicio.
silicone | 'sɪlɪkəun | *s.i.* QUIM. silicona.
silk | sɪlk | *s.c.* e *i.* **1** seda. || *s.i.* **2** BIOL. seda natural. || *s.pl.* **3** (p.u.) ropa de seda, prendas de seda.
silken | 'sɪlkən | *adj.* **1** de seda. **2** (fig.) sedoso, como seda.
silkiness | 'sɪlkɪnɪs | *s.i.* suavidad, calidad como de seda.
silk-screen | ˌsɪlk'skriːn | *adj.* **1** de serigrafía. || **2 – printing,** serigrafía.
silkworm | 'sɪlkwəːm | *s.c.* ZOOL. gusano de seda.
silky | 'sɪlkɪ | *adj.* suave, sedoso, como de seda.
sill | sɪl | *s.c.* **1** alféizar (de ventana); umbral (de puerta).
silliness | 'sɪlɪnɪs | *s.i.* ridiculez, bobada, tontería.
silly | 'sɪlɪ | *adj.* **1** tonto, bobo, ridículo. || **2 to drink/laugh oneself –,** (fam.) beber/reír hasta parecer tonto, beber/reír hasta no poder más.
silo | 'saɪləu | *s.c.* **1** AGR. silo. **2** MIT. silo (de armas atómicas).
silt | sɪlt | *s.i.* **1** GEOL. sedimento, aluvión. || **2 to – up,** bloquearse con sedimentos, obstruirse por la acumulación de sedimentos (río).
silting | 'sɪltɪŋ | *s.i.* obstrucción por sedimentos, bloqueo por excesiva sedimentación (río).
silver | 'sɪlvər | *s.i.* **1** MIN. plata. **2** monedas de plata; dinero en metálico. **3** cubertería de plata; cubertería. || *s.c.* e *i.* **4** color de la plata. || *adj.* **5** de plata. **6** de color de la plata, plateado. **7** como de plata, brillante, refulgente. || **8 to be born with a – spoon in one's mouth,** nacer de familia de rancio abolengo, nacer con sangre azul. **9 – birch,** BOT. abedul. **10 – jubilee,** vigésimo quinto aniversario (de algún acontecimiento importante). **11 – lining,** toque de valor, resquicio de esperanza (dentro de una situación comprometida). **12 – medal,** medalla de plata (especialmente en el deporte). **13 – paper,** papel de plata, papel de estaño. **14 – wedding,** bodas de plata. **15 the –,** la cubertería; la cubertería de plata.
silvered | 'sɪlvəd | *adj.* (lit.) plateado.
silverfish | 'sɪlvəfɪʃ | [*pl.* **silverfish**] *s.c.* ZOOL. pez plateado, lepisma.
silver-plated | sɪlvə'pleɪtɪd | *adj.* chapado en plata.
silversmith | 'sɪlvəsmɪθ | *s.c.* platero.
silverware | 'sɪlvəweər | *s.i.* vajilla de plata; (Am.) platería.
silvery | 'sɪlvərɪ | *adj.* **1** plateado, como de plata (pelo, vestimenta, etc.). **2** argentino (sonido).
simian | 'sɪmɪən | *adj.* **1** BIOL. característico de los simios, símico. **2** (fig.) de mono, como un mono (aspecto o similar).
similar | 'sɪmɪlər | *adj.* **1 [– (to)]** similar, parecido, semejante. **2** GEOM. semejante.
similarity | ˌsɪmɪ'lærɪtɪ | *s.i.* **1** semejanza, parecido, similitud. || *s.c.* **2** cosa parecida, rasgo semejante, parecido: *there are many similarities between Urdu and Hindi = hay muchos rasgos semejantes entre el Urdu y el Hindú.*
similarly | 'sɪmɪləlɪ | *adv.* **1** de manera parecida, de modo semejante. **2** igualmente, del mismo modo, asimismo.
simile | 'sɪmɪlɪ | *s.c.* LIT. símil.
simmer | 'sɪmər | *v.t.* e *i.* **1** GAST. cocer a fuego lento. || *v.i.* **2** hervir, estar a punto de estallar (la violencia). **3** (fam.) cocerse (de calor). || **4 to – down,** (fam.) calmarse, tranquilizarse.
simper | 'sɪmpər | *v.i.* **1** sonreír con expresión bobalicona, sonreír tontamente. || *s.c.* **2** sonrisa bobalicona, sonrisa tonta.
simpering | 'sɪmpərɪŋ | *adj.* con expresión tonta en la sonrisa, sonriente de un modo bobalicón.
simple | 'sɪmpl | *adj.* **1** sencillo, fácil, nada complicado. **2** sencillo, simple, natural (que no es elaborado). **3** sencillo, natural, inocente (carácter). **4** algo simple, cándido; un poquito retrasado mental. **5** sencillo, puro; nada más que un (como énfasis): *that's a simple fact = eso no es más que un hecho.* || **6 pure and –,** puro y simple (como énfasis). **7 – interest,** FIN. interés simple.
simple-minded | ˌsɪmpl'maɪndɪd | *adj.* (desp.) inocentón, ingenuo, mentecato.
simple-mindedness | ˌsɪmpl'maɪn | | dɪdnɪs | *s.i.* (desp.) inocencia excesiva, ingenuidad, embobamiento.
simpleton | 'sɪmpltən | *s.c.* (p.u.) inocentón, simplón.
simplicity | sɪm'plɪsɪtɪ | *s.i.* **1** simplicidad, sencillez. **2** sencillez, llaneza, naturalidad (en el comportamiento, vestir, etc.). || *s.c.* **3** (normalmente *pl.*) (lit.) simplicidad, cosa fácil. || **4 to be – itself,** ser la cosa más sencilla del mundo, ser de lo más sencillo.
simplification | ˌsɪmplɪfɪ'keɪʃn | *s.c.* e *i.* simplificación.
simplified | 'sɪmplɪfaɪd | *adj.* simplificado.
simplify | 'sɪmplɪfaɪ | *v.t.* simplificar.
simplistic | sɪm'plɪstɪk | *adj.* (desp.) simplista.
simply | 'sɪmplɪ | *adv.* **1** sólo, únicamente, exclusivamente: *it's simply a question of hard work = es exclusivamente una cuestión de trabajar duro.* **2** sencillamente, fácilmente. **3** (también **quite** –), sin duda alguna, sin más. **4** sólo, sin más (con abreviaturas de nombres): *they called him simply Ed = le llamaban Ed, sin más.* **5** sencillamente (como énfasis): *you simply must finish = sencillamente tienes que acabar.* **6** con sencillez, sencillamente; sin grandes medios, con pocos recursos (económicos).
simulate | 'sɪmjuleɪt | *v.t.* **1** fingir, simular. **2** querer sugerir, querer indicar: *those paintings simulate human forms = esas pinturas quieren indicar formas humanas.* **3** TEC. reproducir las condiciones lo mejor posible (en distintos tipos de experimentos).
simulated | 'sɪmjuleɪtɪd | *adj.* **1** fingido, simulado. **2** de imitación (material, sonido, etc.).
simulation | ˌsɪmju'leɪʃn | *s.c.* e *i.* **1** fingimiento, simulación. **2** TEC. creación /reproducción de las condiciones (reales o teóricas para un experimento).
simulator | 'sɪmjuleɪtər | *s.c.* MEC. simulador (especialmente con pilotos o astronautas).
simultaneous | ˌsɪml'teɪnɪəs | (EE.UU.) | ˌsaɪml'teɪnɪəs | *adj.* **[– (with)]** simultáneo.
simultaneously | ˌsɪml'teɪnɪəslɪ | (EE.UU.) | ˌsaɪml'teɪnɪəslɪ | *adv.* simultáneamente.
sin | sɪn | *s.c.* e *i.* **1** REL. pecado. || *s.c.* **2** (fig.) mal, pecado. || [*ger.* **sinning,** *pret.* y *p.p.* **sinned**] *v.i.* **3 [to – (against)]** pecar, cometer pecado. || **4 to cover/hide a multitude of sins,** V. **multitude. 5 to live in –,** (p.u. o hum.) vivir en pecado (una pareja, sin casarse).
since | sɪns | *prep.* **1** desde: *I have lived here since last spring = vivo aquí desde la primavera pasada.* || *conj.* **2** desde

que: *you haven't done anything since I told you = no has hecho nada desde que te lo mandé.* **3** ya que, puesto que, dado que: *since you're here, help me = puesto que estás aquí, ayúdame.* || *adv.* **4** subsiguientemente, desde entonces, desde ese momento: *she had a lovely girl in 1980 and she has since had two more children = tuvo una niña preciosa en 1980 y desde entonces ha tenido dos niños más.* || **5 ever –,** desde entonces, desde aquel momento. **6 long –,** desde hace mucho tiempo, desde hace largo tiempo.

sincere | sɪn'sɪər | *adj.* sincero, franco, veraz.

sincerely | sɪn'sɪəlɪ | *adv.* **1** sinceramente, francamente. **2** verdaderamente, en verdad. || **3 –/yours –/yours very –,** atentamente (despedida de carta formal).

sincerity | sɪn'serɪtɪ | *s.i.* sinceridad, franqueza, veracidad.

sinecure | 'saɪnɪkjʊər | | 'sɪnɪkjʊə | *s.c.* canonjía, sinecura (trabajo poco exigente).

sine qua non | ˌsɪneɪkwɑː'nəʊn | *s.sing.* (form.) sine qua non.

sinew | 'sɪnjuː | *s.c.* **1** ANAT. tendón. || *s.i.* **2** (lit.) nervio, fibra (energía o fuerza física). || **3 the sinews of war,** (fig.) los medios materiales para la guerra, los elementos necesarios para la guerra.

sinewy | 'sɪnjuːɪ | *adj.* musculoso; vigoroso (corporalmente).

sinful | 'sɪnfl | *adj.* pecaminoso, malo, inmoral.

sing | sɪŋ | *v.* [*pret.irreg.* **sang,** *p.p.irreg.* **sung**] *t.* e *i.* **1** cantar. **2** cantar (animales); trinar, gorjear (pájaros). || *t.* **3** cantar (ópera, rock, etc.). || *i.* **4 [to – (of)]** (p.u. o lit.) cantar, recitar (canturreando un poema). **5** silbar (balas, tetera, el viento, etc.). **6** zumbar (oídos). || **7 to – someone's praises,** alabar a alguien, poner a alguien por las nubes. **8 to – someone to sleep,** adormecer a alguien, cantándole. **9 to – someone's worries /problems/etc. away,** quitarle a alguien las preocupaciones/problemas/etc., cantándole. **10 to – up,** cantar más alto, cantar con más fuerza.

Singapore | ˌsɪŋə'pɔː | *s.sing.* Singapur.

Singaporean | ˌsɪŋə'pɔːrɪən | *s.c.* **1** habitante de Singapur. || *adj.* **2** de Singapur.

singe | sɪndʒ | [*ger.* **singeing**] *v.t.* e *i.* **1** chamuscar(se), quemar(se) ligeramente. || *s.c.* **2** quemadura leve (especialmente en pelo o ropa).

singer | 'sɪŋər | *s.c.* **1** cantante. **2** cantador, cantarín (animal).

Singhalese V. **Sinhalese.**

singing | 'sɪŋɪŋ | *s.i.* **1** canto (como un arte o profesión). **2** canturreo, canto (de animales), gorgojeo (de pájaros). **3** canciones, canto (en general). || *s.sing.* **4** zumbido (en el oído). || *adj.* **5** para cantar (voz): *he has a lovely singing voice = tiene una preciosa voz para cantar.*

single | 'sɪŋgl | *adj.* **1** único, solo: *there wasn't a single face I recognized = no había un solo rostro que yo reconociera.* **2** soltero (no casado). **3** concreto, individual: *give me a single example of it = dame un ejemplo concreto de eso.* **4** sencilla, individual (cama, habitación, etc.). **5** sólo de ida (billete). || *s.c.* **6** MUS. sencillo, disco sencillo. **7** billete de ida, billete sencillo. **8** habitación individual. **9** DEP. un solo golpe (en el críquet). || *s.pl.* **10** DEP. partidos individuales (tenis). || **11 in – figures,** no más de diez, en cifras de menos de dos dígitos. **12 in – file,** en fila india, en fila de a uno. **13 – combat,** combate singular. **14 – cream,** (brit.) GAST. nata líquida (con poca grasa). **15 – honours,** estudio de una sola asignatura. **16 to – out,** singularizar, escoger (entre muchos). **17 – parent,** de un solo progenitor, con un solo progenitor: *single parent families = familias donde sólo está uno de los progenitores.* **18 singles bar,** (EE.UU.) bar para solteros y solteras únicamente.

single-breasted | ˌsɪŋgl'brestɪd | *adj.* normal, sin cruzar (chaqueta).

single-decker | ˌsɪŋgl'dekər | *s.c.* autobús de un solo piso, autobús normal.

single-handed | ˌsɪŋgl'hændɪd | *adj.* y *adv.* sin ayuda de nadie, sólo.

single-handedly | ˌsɪŋgl'hændɪdl | *adv.* sin ayuda de nadie.

single-minded | ˌsɪŋgl'maɪndɪd | *adj.* resuelto, con un solo propósito, firme.

single-mindedly | ˌsɪŋgl'maɪndɪdlɪ | *adv.* resueltamente, decididamente, sin otro objetivo en la mente.

single-mindedness | ˌsɪŋgl'maɪndɪdnɪs | *s.i.* resolución, decisión, firmeza (en llevar a cabo un objetivo y no otro).

singlet | 'sɪŋglɪt | *s.c.* (brit.) **1** camiseta. **2** camiseta sin mangas.

singly | 'sɪŋglɪ | *adv.* individualmente, separadamente.

sing-song | 'sɪŋsɒŋ | *adj.* **1** monótono, uniforme (sonido de la voz). || *s.c.* **2** reunión con canciones, ocasión social donde se canta.

singular | 'sɪŋgjʊlər | *adj.* **1** GRAM. singular. **2** (form.) único, extraordinario, sobresaliente. **3** (form.) raro, extraño, peculiar. || *s.sing.* **4** GRAM. forma singular, singular.

singularity | ˌsɪŋgjʊ'lærɪtɪ | *s.i.* (form.) **1** (lo) extraordinario, (lo) sobresaliente. **2** extrañeza, peculiaridad, rareza.

singularly | 'sɪŋgjʊləlɪ | *adv.* (form.) extraordinariamente, de manera sobresaliente.

Sinhalese | ˌsɪnhə'liːz | (también **Singhalese**) *adj.* **1** cingalés, ceilanés (de Sri Lanka). || *s.i.* **2** cingalés (idioma).

sinister | 'sɪnɪstər | *adj.* siniestro, avieso, aciago.

sink | sɪŋk | *v.* [*pret.irreg.* **sank,** *p.p.irreg.* **sunk**] *i.* **1** hundirse (bajo el agua). **2** hundirse, descender (movimiento físico). **3** dejarse caer (especialmente por agotamiento). **4** descender, bajar (el tono de la voz). **5** decaer, debilitarse a ojos vistas (en la salud, normalmente presagiando un desenlace fatal). **6** deprimirse, entristecerse; caer a los suelos (el animo). **7 [to – into]** caer en (un estado negativo): *every day he sank deeper into debt = cada día que pasaba se endeudaba más y más.* || *t.* **8** hundir (barco). **9** DEP. meter (la bola en un agujero, en golf o billar). **10** excavar, hacer (pozos, minas o similar). **11 [to – + *o.* + into]** hincar en, clavar en: *she sank her feeth into my thigh = ella me clavó sus dientes en el muslo.* **12 [to – + *o.* + in/into]** meter (dinero) a raudales en, invertir mucho en. **13** (fam. y brit.) hacer desaparecer, tragarse, beber. || *s.c.* **14** pila, fregadero (en la cocina). **15** lavabo. || **16 to be sunk,** (fam.) ir dado, estar en una buena: *get that money or you are sunk = consigue ese dinero o estás en una buena.* **17 to – in,** caer, darse cuenta, entender; hacer mella, surtir efecto: *what you told him sank in = lo que dijiste surtió efecto.* **18 to – or swim,** quedar abandonado a la suerte de uno, tener que arreglárselas uno por sí solo.

sinker | 'sɪŋkər | *s.c.* plomo, plomada (en la caña de pescar).

sinking | 'sɪŋkɪŋ | *adj.* **1** que se hunde, hundiéndose. || *s.i.* **2** hundimiento. || **3 – fund,** COM. fondo de amortización (de deudas). **4 that – feeling,** ese sentimiento de que todo se hunde, esa sensación de que todo se va a pique.

sinner | 'sɪnər | *s.c.* pecador.

sinuous | 'sɪnjʊəs | *adj.* sinuoso, ondulado; tortuoso.

sinus | 'saɪnəs | *s.c.* ANAT. seno (nasal).

sip | sɪp | [*ger.* **sipping,** *pret.* y *p.p.* **sipped**] *v.t.* e *i.* **1** beber a sorbos, beber dando sorbitos. || *s.c.* **2** sorbo, sorbito.

siphon | 'saɪfn | (también **syphon**) *s.c.* **1** tubo, tubo de sifón. **2** botella de sifón, sifón. || *v.t.* (también **siphon off**). **3** sacar mediante sifón (un líquido). **4** malversar, defraudar, desviar (dinero hacia objetivos para los que no estaba destinado).

sir | sɜːr | *s.c.* **1** señor (también para los militares). || **2 Sir, Sir** (título nobiliario).

sire | saɪər | *v.t.* **1** (p.u.) engendrar (un hijo). **2** ser el padre de (con animales). || *s.c.* **3** (arc.) padre. **4** BIOL. padre (de un animal).

siren | 'saɪərən | *s.c.* **1** sirena, bocina, alarma. **2** sirena (mujer pez). **3** (fig.) mujer fatal, mujer atractiva pero peligrosa, seductora. **4** (fig.) hechizo, encantamiento (lugar u objeto). || **5 – call/song,** canto de sirena: *he was not deaf to the siren call of the jet-set = él no estaba sordo ante el canto de sirena de la alta sociedad.*

sirloin | 'sɜːlɔɪn | *s.c.* e *i.* solomillo.

sisal | 'saɪsl | *s.i.* BOT. sisal, pita.

sissy | 'sɪsɪ | (también **cissy**) *s.c.* (fam. y desp.) **1** cobarde, gallina. **2** marica, mariquita.

sister | 'sɪstər | *s.c.* **1** hermana. **2** REL. sor, hermana. **3** (brit.) enfermera jefe. **4** (fig.) hermana, compañera (especialmente en una misma causa). **5** (fam. y EE.UU.) amiga, compañera, tía. **6** hermano, hermana (sitio, casa, máquina, etc. muy similar al que se hace referencia): *this university is much better than its sister = esta universidad es mucho mejor que su hermana (otra universidad similar).* || *adj.* **7** hermano, hermana (V. **6**). || **8 big –,** hermana mayor. **9 little –,** hermana pequeña.

sisterhood | 'sɪstəhʊd | *s.i.* hermandad, compañerismo (entre mujeres).

sister-in-law | 'sɪstəɪnlɔː | [*pl.* **sisters-in-law**] *s.c.* cuñada.

sisterly | 'sɪstəlɪ | *adj.* de hermana (sentimientos, trato, etc.).

sit | sɪt | [*pret.* y *p.p.irreg.* **sat;** *ger.* **sitting**] *i.* **1** sentarse, tomar asiento. **2** sentarse, acurrucarse, descansar (animales). **3 [to – for]** hacer de modelo para, posar para. **4 [to – on/in]** ser miembro de (un comité, comisión, etc.). **5** (form.) estar en sesión, celebrar sesión (Corte,

Parlamento u otro organismo oficial). **6** (lit.) encontrarse, asentarse (un edificio en un sitio). **7 [to – on]** encubar, empollar (los huevos por parte de un ave). || *t.* **8** sentar, hacer sentar (a alguien). **9** (brit.) participar, hacer, tomar parte (en un examen). || **10 to be sitting and,** estar sentado y (hacer algo que no se supone que uno deba hacer): *you should be sitting and playing cards now = no deberías estar sentado y jugando a las cartas en este momento.* **11 to – around/about,** (fam.) estar sentado sin hacer nada, estar sentado por ahí sin hacer nada. **12 to – back,** (fam.) relajarse, cruzarse de brazos, sentarse cómodamente. **13 to – by,** estar sin tomar partido, dejar que ocurra lo que ocurra (especialmente cuando es una actividad ilegal). **14 to – down, a)** sentarse, tomar asiento; sentar (a alguien); **b)** tomarse todo el tiempo, sentarse tranquilamente sin prisas. **15 to – in on,** asistir, tomar parte en (reunión, discusión, etc.). **16 to – on,** (fam. y desp.) no dar curso a, no hacer ninguna gestión sobre, retrasar aposta. **17 to – on the fence,** V. **fence. 18 to – out,** aguantar, aguantar hasta el final (una charla aburrida, por ejemplo). **19 to – through,** quedarse hasta el final (especialmente cuando no es muy interesante). **20 to – tight,** no arriesgarse para nada, sentarse y esperar (a ver el posterior curso de los acontecimientos). **21 to – up, a)** incorporarse, ponerse en una posición vertical (sentado); **b)** quedarse levantado, no acostarse; **c)** prestar atención súbita (impresionado por algo): *we want to make people sit up and notice = queremos que la gente preste atención y mire.*

sitar | 'sɪtɑːr | *s.c.* MUS. sitar (instrumento hindú).

sitcom | 'sɪtkɒm | *s.c.* TV. serie cómica (sobre asuntos de todos los días).

sit-down | 'sɪtdaʊn | *s.sing.* **1 [a –]** una sentada. || *adj.* **2** de sentarse, sentados (comida). || **3 – strike,** huelga con sentadas.

site | saɪt | *s.c.* **1** solar (para viviendas); sitio, zona (que se puede dedicar a distintas finalidades). **2** lugar, escena, sitio (en que algo importante tuvo lugar). **3** yacimiento (arqueológico). || *v.t.* **4** (normalmente *pasiva*) situar, poner, localizar.

sit-in | 'sɪtɪn | *s.c.* encierro (protesta).

sitter | 'sɪtər | *s.c.* (fam.) chica canguro.

sitting | 'sɪtɪŋ | *adj.* **1** sentado (postura). **2** actual, en funciones (miembro de algún organismo o institución). || *s.i.* **3** sesión (de un juzgado, Parlamento, etc.). **4** turno (de comida). || **5 a – duck,** una presa fácil, un blanco fácil. **6 at one –,** de una sentada, de una sola sentada. **7 – pretty,** (fam.) posición ventajosa. **8 – tenant,** inquilino que ocupa una casa.

sitting-room | 'sɪtɪŋruːm | *s.c.* cuarto de estar.

situate | 'sɪtjueɪt | (EE.UU.) | 'sɪtʃueɪt | *v.t.* (form.) colocar, situar.

situated | 'sɪtjueɪtɪd | (EE.UU.) | 'sɪtʃueɪtɪd | *adj.* (form.) situado: *a pleasantly situated house = una casa situada en un sitio agradable.*

situation | ˌsɪtʃu'eɪʃn | *s.c.* **1** situación, circunstancias. **2** (form.) posición, situación (física). **3** crisis, situación problemática: *what a situation! = ¡qué crisis!* **4** (p.u. o form.) empleo en el servicio doméstico. || **5 – comedy,** comedia en serie. **6 Situations Vacant,** ofertas de empleo.

six | sɪks | *num.card.* **1** seis. || *s.c.* **2** DEP. seis (seis carreras en críquet). || **3 at sixes and sevens,** (fam.) **a)** patas arriba, en un total desorden; **b)** confuso, desorganizado (de pensamiento). **4 – of one and half a dozen of the other,** (fam.) da lo mismo.

sixpence | 'sɪkspəns | *s.c.* seis peniques, moneda de seis peniques.

sixteen | sɪk'stiːn | *num.card.* dieciséis.

sixteenth | sɪk'stiːnθ | *num.ord.* **1** decimosexto. || **2 – note,** (EE.UU.) MUS. semicorchea.

sixth | sɪksθ | *num.ord.* **1** sexto. || *s.c.* **2 [– (of)]** sexto de, sexta parte de. || **3 a – sense,** un sexto sentido. **4 – form,** (brit.) curso de preuniversitario. **5 – former,** (brit.) alumno de preuniversitario.

sixtieth | 'sɪkstɪəθ | *num.ord.* sexagésimo.

sixty | 'sɪkstɪ | *num.card.* sesenta.

sizable V. **sizeable.**

size | saɪz | *s.i.* **1** tamaño, magnitud, dimensiones. || *s.c.* **2** talla, número (de zapatos, ropa, etc.). || **3 to cut someone down to –,** poner a alguien en su sitio, bajarle a alguien los humos. **4 for –,** para comprobar si le sienta bien. **5 -size/sized,** de tamaño (en palabras compuestas): *a fair-sized dinner = una comida de un tamaño adecuado.* **6 to – up,** medir intuitivamente, evaluar (a algo o alguien a simple vista). **7 to –,** a un tamaño adecuado, a una medida idónea.

sizeable | 'saɪzəbl | (también **sizable**) *adj.* considerable, importante (tamaño o cantidad).

sizzle | 'sɪzl | *v.i.* crepitar, churruscar, chisporrotear.

skate | skeɪt | *s.c.* **1** patín (de ruedas o para hielo). **2** ZOOL. raya (pez). || *v.i.* **2** patinar (sobre patines o hielo). || **3 to get one's skates on,** (fam.) darse prisa, apurarse. **4 to – around/round/over,** evitar, esquivar (problema, asunto, etc.).

skateboard | 'skeɪtbɔːd | *s.c.* monopatín.

skateboarding | 'skeɪtbɔːdɪŋ | *s.i.* práctica en monopatín.

skater | 'skeɪtər | *s.c.* patinador.

skein | skeɪn | *s.c.* **1** madeja. **2** bandada (de gansos).

skeletal | 'skelɪtl | *adj.* **1** del esqueleto, esquelético. **2** delgadísimo, esquelético. **3** (form.) en esqueleto, en su estructura básica.

skeleton | 'skelɪtn | *s.c.* **1** ANAT. esqueleto. **2** (fig.) tipo delgadísimo, esqueleto. **3** esqueleto, estructura básica (de un edificio). **4** esqueleto, líneas maestras (de un escrito, ensayo, etc.). || *atr.* **5** mínimo (personal, infraestructura, etc.). || **6 a – in the cupboard/closet,** un cadáver en el armario, secreto vergonzoso de familia. **7 – key,** llave maestra.

skeptic V. **sceptic.**

skeptical V. **sceptical.**

skeptically V. **sceptically.**

sketch | sketʃ | *s.c.* **1** bosquejo, esbozo, boceto (dibujo). **2** sketch (pieza corta cómica). **3** (normalmente *sing.*) resumen, esbozo (de un tema). || *v.t.* e *i.* **4** hacer un bosquejo, esbozar (dibujo). || *v.t.* **5** esbozar, trazar las grandes líneas (de un tema). || **6 to – in,** añadir detalles, añadir información supletoria. **7 to – out,** dar los grandes trazos de (un tema).

sketchbook | 'sketʃbuk | (también **sketchpad**) *s.c.* bloc de bosquejos.

sketchily | 'sketʃɪlɪ | *adv.* a grandes rasgos, incompletamente.

sketchiness | 'sketʃɪnɪs | *s.i.* estilo a grandes rasgos, forma incompleta (de esbozar algo).

sketchpad | 'sketʃpæd | V. **sketchbook.**

sketchy | 'sketʃɪ | *adj.* incompleto, impreciso.

skew | skjuː | *v.i.* **1** torcerse, desviarse; ponerse al sesgo. || *adj.* **2** sesgado, torcido. || *adv.* **3** sesgadamente, torcidamente.

skewed | skjuːd | *adj.* **1** torcido, sesgado (físicamente). **2** torcido, sesgado (de pensamiento).

skewer | skjuːər | *s.c.* **1** brocheta, broqueta (de cocina). || *v.t.* **2** poner en brocheta, poner en un pincho.

skew-whiff | ˌskjuː'wɪf | *adj.* (fam.) torcido, mal puesto.

ski | skiː | *v.i.* **1** DEP. esquiar. || *s.c.* **2** esquí. || *atr.* **3** de esquiar (equipo, lugar, etc.). || **4 – jump,** DEP. salto de esquí. **5 – lift,** telesilla.

skid | skɪd | [*ger.* **skidding,** *pret.* y *p.p.* **skidded**] *v.i.* **1** derrapar, patinar. || *s.c.* **2** patinazo, derrape. || **3 – row,** (fam. y EE.UU.) barrio de mala muerte, barrio de mala vida.

skier | 'skiːər | *s.c.* esquiador.

skiff | skɪf | *s.c.* MAR. esquife.

skilful | 'skɪlfl | (EE.UU. **skillful**) *adj.* habilidoso, hábil, diestro (manual e intelectualmente).

skilfully | 'skɪlfəlɪ | (EE.UU. **skillfully**) *adv.* habilidosamente, hábilmente, diestramente.

skill | skɪl | *s.i.* **1** habilidad, destreza. || *s.c.* **2** técnica, arte manual.

skilled | skɪld | *adj.* **1** experto, cualificado. **2** especialista (obrero, trabajo, etc.).

skillet | 'skɪlɪt | *s.c.* sartén plana.

skillful V. **skilful.**

skim | skɪm | [*ger.* **skimming,** *pret.* y *p.p.* **skimmed**] *v.t.* **1** rozar, pasar rozando (una superficie). **2** desnatar (de la parte superior de la superficie). **3** echar un vistazo, hacer un rápido recorrido visual, hojear. **4** tirar (piedras) rozando la superficie del agua, tirar (piedras) haciendo el salto de la rana. || *v.i.* **5 [to – through]** hojear, echar un rápido vistazo. || **6 skimmed milk,** leche desnatada.

skimp | skɪmp | *v.t.* **1** ahorrar muchísimo, escatimar, economizar mucho. || *v.i.* **2 [to – on]** hacer grandes ahorros en, escatimar.

skimpily | 'skɪmpɪlɪ | *adv.* escasamente, limitadamente; con gran pequeñez.

skimpiness | 'skɪmpɪnɪs | *s.i.* escasez, limitación; pequeñez.

skimpy | 'skɪmpɪ | *adj.* escaso, limitado; pequeño.

skin | skɪn | *s.c.* e *i.* **1** piel, cutis. **2** piel, pellejo (de animal). **3** piel, cáscara (de fruta). **4** capa espesa, nata (sobre líquidos). || *v.t.* **5** rozarse (la piel haciéndose una herida). **6** despellejar, quitar la piel (a un animal). || **7 by the – of one's teeth,** a duras penas, por los pelos, por poco. **8 to get under one's –,** (fam.) irritar, poner malo, sacar de quicio. **9 it's no –**

off my nose, (fam.) a mí no me afecta para nada, no es asunto mío en absoluto. **10 to jump/leap out of one's –,** sufrir un susto tremendo, llevarse un susto del demonio. **11 to save/protect one's own –,** salvar el pellejo de uno. **12 – and bone/– and bones,** en los puros huesos, en los mismísimos huesos. **13 -skinned,** de piel (en palabras compuestas): *white-skinned = de piel blanca.*

skin-deep | ˌskɪn'diːp | *adj.* superficial, epidérmico.

skin-diver | 'skɪndaɪvər | *s.c.* buceador (sin equipo sofisticado).

skin-diving | 'skɪndaɪvɪŋ | *s.i.* DEP. submarinismo (natural).

skinflint | 'skɪnflɪnt | *s.c.* (fam.) avaro, agarrado, cicatero.

skinhead | 'skɪnhed | *s.c.* (juv.) cabeza rapada.

skinny | 'skɪnɪ | *adj.* (fam. y desp.) delgaducho, flacucho, en los huesos.

skint | skɪnt | *adj.* (fam.) sin blanca, sin una perra, sin un céntimo.

skin-tight | ˌskɪn'taɪt | *adj.* muy apretado, ajustado, ceñido.

skip | skɪp | [*ger.* **skipping**, *pret.* y *p.p.* **skipped**] *v.i.* **1** dar saltitos, moverse a base de saltitos. **2** saltar, saltar a la comba. **3** no centrarse, ir de tema en tema (sin parar en ninguno). || *v.t.* **4** omitir, saltar (en la lectura). **5** (fam.) saltarse, fumarse, no hacer, no tomar: *I am going to skip tomorrow's class = me voy a fumar la clase de mañana.* || *s.c.* **6** saltito, salto, brinco. **7** (brit.) contenedor (especialmente para escombros o similar).

skipper | 'skɪpər | *s.c.* (fam.) **1** MAR. capitán. **2** DEP. capitán.

skipping-rope | 'skɪpɪŋrəup | *s.c.* cuerda de saltar, comba.

skirmish | 'skəːmɪʃ | *v.i.* **1** MIL. pelear en escaramuzas. **2** (fig.) entrar en una refriega, pelearse (verbalmente). || *s.c.* **3** MIL. escaramuza. **4** (fig.) pelea, refriega (verbal).

skirt | skəːt | *s.c.* **1** falda; (Am.) pollera. **2** falda (de vestido). **3** cubierta, cubierta de protección (que se pone en ciertas máquinas). || *s.i.* **4** (vulg.) plan, filete, tías (en sentido sexual). || *v.t.* **5** rodear, ir alrededor de (una zona). **6** evitar, dar rodeos a (un tema o un obstáculo). || *v.i.* **7 [to – around/round]** evitar, dar rodeos a (tema o físicamente a un obstáculo).

skirting | 'skəːtɪŋ | (también **skirting board**) *s.c.* e *i.* (brit.) rodapié.

skit | skɪt | *s.c.* LIT. sátira, parodia (teatral).

skitter | 'skɪtər | *v.i.* dar rápidos saltos, dar brincos, deslizarse a saltitos.

skittish | 'skɪtɪʃ | *adj.* **1** caprichoso; juguetón. **2** nervioso, juguetón (animal).

skittishly | 'skɪtɪʃlɪ | *adv.* caprichosamente; juguetonamente.

skittishness | 'skɪtɪʃnɪs | *s.i.* capricho; carácter juguetón.

skittle | 'skɪtl | *s.c.* **1** bolo. || *s.pl.* **2** bolos (juego).

skive | skaɪv | *v.i.* (fam. y brit.) racanear, gandulear.

skulduggery | skʌl'dʌgərɪ | *s.i.* (p.u.) embustes, trampas, tretas, artimañas.

skulk | skʌlk | *v.i.* acechar, moverse furtivamente.

skull | skʌl | *s.c.* **1** ANAT. cráneo. **2** cabeza, cabecita (inteligencia). || **3 – and crossbones,** calavera (símbolo de la piratería).

skullcap | 'skʌlkæp | *s.c.* casquete, solideo (típico de obispos).

skunk | skʌŋk | *s.c.* **1** ZOOL. mofeta; (Am.) zorrillo. **2** (desp.) canalla.

sky | skaɪ | *s.sing.* **1 [the –]** el cielo, el firmamento. || **2 pie in the –,** V. **pie. 3 to praise someone to the skies,** poner a alguien por las nubes, alabar a alguien como si fuera divino.

sky-blue | ˌskaɪ'bluː | *adj.* azul celeste.

skydiver | 'skaɪdaɪvər | *s.c.* paracaidista de caída libre.

skydiving | 'skaɪdaɪvɪŋ | *s.i.* paracaidismo de caída libre.

sky-high | ˌskaɪ'haɪ | *adj.* **1** de gran altitud, de gran altura (edificio). **2** hasta arriba, por las nubes (precios, salarios, etc.). || **3 to blow something –,** destrozar por completo, hacer añicos, enviar por los aires.

skylark | 'skaɪlɑːk | *s.c.* ZOOL. alondra (ave).

skylight | 'skaɪlaɪt | *s.c.* tragaluz, claraboya.

skyline | 'skaɪlaɪn | *s.c.* horizonte, línea del horizonte.

skyscraper | 'skaɪskreɪpər | *s.c.* rascacielos.

skywards | 'skaɪwədz | (también **skyward**) *adj.* y *adv.* (lit.) hacia el cielo.

slab | slæb | *s.c.* losa, bloque.

slack | slæk | *adj.* **1** flojo (algo): *a slack rope = una cuerda floja.* **2** flojo, inactivo (negocio). **3** flojo, vago, perezoso (característica personal). **4** descuidado, negligente (en su trabajo). || *s.i.* **5** flojedad. **6** recesión, período flojo (en los negocios). || *s.pl.* **7** pantalones de sport. || **8 to take up the –, a)** tensar (cuerda); **b)** avivar, reanimar, reactivar (la economía).

slacken | 'slækən | *v.t.* **1** disminuir, aflojar (velocidad). **2** aflojar(se) (fuerza).

slacker | 'slækər | *s.c.* (fam.) vago, gandul, rácano.

slackness | 'slæknɪs | *s.i.* **1** flojedad (física). **2** inactividad, flojeza (en el movimiento comercial). **3** descuido, negligencia (en el trabajo). **4** pereza (característica personal).

slag | slæg | *s.i.* **1** escoria. || **2 basic –,** escoria básica. **3 -- heap,** escombrera, escorial. **4 to – off,** (fam.) criticar, hablar mal de alguien.

slain | sleɪn | *p.p.irreg.* de **slay.**

slake | sleɪk | *v.t.* apagar (sed).

slam | slæm | *v.t.* **1** golpear, cerrar de un golpe, hacer golpear. || *v.i.* **2** cerrarse de golpe (puerta). || *s.c.* **3** golpe. **4** portazo. || **5 to close the door with a –,** dar un portazo. **6 to – the door,** dar un portazo. **7 to – something down on something,** arrojar violentamente algo sobre algo.

slammer | 'slæmər | *s.c.* (fam.) cárcel, prisión.

slander | 'slɑːndər | *s.c.* **1** calumnia, difamación. || *v.t.* **2** calumniar, difamar. **3** hablar mal de. || **4 to sue someone for –,** demandar a uno por calumnias.

slanderer | 'slɑːndərər | *s.c.* calumniador, difamador.

slanderous | 'slɑːndərəs | *adj.* calumnioso, difamatorio.

slanderously | 'slɑːndərəslɪ | *adv.* calumniosamente, difamatoriamente.

slang | slæŋ | *s.i.* **1** argot, jerga. || *adj.* **2** palabra del argot, vulgarismo. || *v.t.* **3** llenar de insultos. **4** criticar duramente, poner como un trapo, emprenderla con. || **5 – word,** palabra muy coloquial.

slangly | 'slæŋlɪ | *adv.* vulgarmente.

slangy | 'slæŋgɪ | *adj.* **1** lleno de vulgarismos. **2** que emplea muchos vulgarismos, que habla en argot.

slant | slænt | *v.t.* **1** inclinar, sesgar. || *v.i.* **2** inclinarse, sesgarse. || *s.c.* **3** inclinación, sesgo. **4** (fig.) punto de vista, modo de ver una cosa, modo de enfocar un problema. || **5 to be on the –,** estar inclinado. **6 to get a – on the topic,** pedir parecer sobre un asunto. **7 to – a report,** escribir un informe parcial, escribir un informe desde un punto de vista determinado.

slant-eyed | ˌslɑːnt'aɪd | *adj.* de ojos almendrados.

slanting | 'slɑːntɪŋ | *adj.* inclinado, oblicuo, sesgado.

slantwise | 'slɑːntwaɪz | *adj.* oblicuamente, al sesgo.

slap | slæp | *v.t.* **1** dar una palmada a. **2** pegar, golpear. || *s.c.* **3** palmada, manotada. || *adv.* **4** de lleno, de plano. **5** directamente. || *interj.* **6** ¡zas! || **7 to fell – in the middle,** caer exactamente en el centro. **8 to run – into something,** dar de lleno contra algo. **9 to – someone around,** golpear varias veces a alguien. **10 – in the face, a)** bofetada; **b)** (fig.) palmetazo, golpe duro, desaire. **11 – on the back,** espaldarazo. **12 to – someone down, a)** derribar de una bofetada; **b)** (fig.) aplastar, apabullar a alguien. **13 to – someone's face, to – someone on the face,** dar una bofetada, pegar un tortazo a uno. **14 to – someone on the back,** dar un espaldarazo a alguien. **15 to – one's knees,** palmotearse las rodillas. **16 to – something on something,** arrojar violentamente sobre; añadir, aumentar.

slap-bang | 'slæpbæŋ | *adv.* **1** ruidosamente, violentamente. **2** directamente, exactamente.

slapdash | 'slæpdæʃ | *adj.* **1** descuidado, despreocupado (persona). **2** chapucero (trabajo).

slap-happy | 'slæp'hæpɪ | *adj.* **1** alegre y despreocupado. **2** totalmente inconsciente.

slapstick | 'slæpstɪk | *s.i.* **1** payasadas. **2** pequeña comedia llena de payasadas.

slap-up | 'slæpʌp | *adj.* (fam.) banquetazo, comilona.

slash | slæʃ | *v.t.* **1** acuchillar. **2** rasgar. **3** azotar. **4** machacar, quemar. **5** atacar, criticar severamente. **6** reducir radicalmente (estimación). **7** abreviar sensiblemente (texto, charla). || *s.c.* **8** cuchillada, latigazo. || **9 to go to the –,** (vulg.) ir al lavabo. **10 to – at someone,** tirar tajos a uno, tratar de acuchillar a alguien.

slashing | 'slæʃɪŋ | *adj.* fulminante.

slat | slæt | *s.c.* tablilla, hoja.

slate | sleɪt | *s.i.* **1** pizarra. || *s.c.* **2** trozos de pizarra. **3** pizarras (usadas por los niños antiguamente para escribir en la escuela). **4** (EE.UU.) lista de candidatos. || *v.t.* **5** cubrir de pizarras. **6** (brit.) censurar, criticar severamente. || *adj.* **7** de pizarra. **8** color pizarra. || **9** (EE.UU.) **to be slated** estar programado. **10** (brit.) **to be put on the –,** comprado a plazos. **11 to start with a clean –,** empezar de nuevo intentando que otros olviden el pasado.

12 to wipe the – clean, borrón y cuenta nueva.
slate-blue | 'sleɪt'bluː | *adj.* color azul pizarra.
slate-coloured | 'sleɪt,kʌləd | *adj.* color pizarra.
slatepencil | 'sleɪt'pensl | *s.c.* pizarrín.
slate quarry | 'sleɪt,kwɒrɪ | *s.c.* pizarral.
slater | 'sleɪtər | *s.c.* pizarrero.
slattern | 'slætən | *s.c.* mujer dejada, mujer sucia.
slatternly | 'slætənlɪ | *adj.* sucio, puerco, desaseado.
slaty | 'sleɪtɪ | *adj.* **1** parecido a la pizarra. **2** color pizarra.
slaughter | 'slɔːtər | *v.t.* **1** matar, sacrificar en gran número. **2** hacer una carnicería de. **3** (fam. y fig.) engañar. || *s.i.* **4** matanza, sacrificio, masacre. **5** mortandad. || **6 like a lamb to the –,** como un cordero al sacrificio.
slaughterer | 'slɔːtərər | *s.c.* jifero, matarife.
slaughterhouse | 'slɔːtəhaus | *s.c.* matadero.
Slav | slɑːv | *s.c.* **1** eslavo. || *adj.* **2** eslavo.
slave | sleɪv | *s.c.* **1** esclavo. || *v.i.* **2** trabajar como un esclavo. **3** sudar tinta. || **4 to be a – to,** ser esclavo de: *I'm a slave to tobacco = soy un esclavo del tabaco.* **5 to – away,** trabajar como un negro. **6 white –,** esclava blanca, prostituta.
slave-driver | 'sleɪv,draɪvər | *s.c.* **1** negrero. **2** (fig.) amo severo, jefe despótico.
slave-labor | 'sleɪv,leɪbər | V. **slave labour.**
slave-labour | 'sleɪv,leɪbər | (EE.UU. **slave labor**) *s.i.* **1** trabajo de esclavos. *s.pl.* **2** trabajadores forzados.
slaver | sleɪvər | *s.c.* **1** negrero. **2** barco negrero.
slaver | slævər | *v.i.* **1** babear. || *s.i.* **2** baba.
slavery | sleɪvrɪ | *s.i.* **1** esclavitud. || **2 to sell someone into –,** vender a uno como esclavo.
slave-trade | ,sleɪv'treɪd | *s.sing.* **1** comercio de esclavos, tráfico de esclavos. || **2 white –,** trata de blancas.
slave-trader | ,sleɪv'treɪdər | *s.c.* traficante de esclavos, negrero.
slavey | 'sleɪvɪ | *s.c.* fregona.
Slavic | 'slævɪc | *s.c.* **1** eslavo. || *adj.* **2** eslavo.
slavish | sleɪvɪʃ | *adj.* servil.
slavishly | 'sleɪvɪʃlɪ | *adv.* servilmente.
slavishness | 'sleɪvɪʃnɪs | *s.i.* servilismo.
Slavonic | slə'vɒnɪk | *adj.* **1** eslavo. || *s.c.* **2** eslavo.
slaw | slɔː | *s.c.* (EE.UU.) ensalada de col.
slay | sleɪ | *v.* [*pret.irreg.* **slew** y *p.p.irreg.* **slain**] *t.* **1** matar, asesinar. **2** (fam.) hacer morir de risa.
slayer | 'slɔːɪər | *s.c.* asesino.
sleazy | 'sliːzɪ | *adj.* **1** desaseado, desaliñado. **2** asqueroso, de mala fama (lugar).
sled | sled | V. **sledge.**
sledge | sledʒ | (EE.UU. **sled**) *s.c.* **1** trineo. || *v.t.* **2** transportar por trineo, llevar en trineo. || *v.i.* **3** ir en trineo. || **4 – hammer,** mazo.
sleek | sliːk | *adj.* **1** liso y brillante, lustroso. **2** pulcro, muy aseado (apariencia). **3** gordo y de buen aspecto (animal). || *v.t.* **4** alisar, pulir. || **5 to – one's hair down,** alisar y arreglarse el pelo.
sleekness | 'sliːknɪs | *s.i.* **1** lisura y brillantez, lustre. **2** pulcritud, aseo (apariencia). **3** gordura (animal).
sleep | sliːp | *s.i.* **1** sueño. || *v.* [*pret.* y *p.p.irreg.* **slept**] *i.* y *t.* **2** dormir. || **3 deep –, heavy –,** sueño profundo. **4 to drop off to –, to go to –,** dormirse, quedarse dormido. **5 to have a –,** dormir; descabezar un sueño (brevemente). **6 to get to –,** conciliar el sueño. **7 to have a good night's –,** dormir bien durante la noche. **8 to put someone to –,** acostar a uno, adormecer a uno. **9 to put an animal to –,** sacrificar a un animal. **10 to send someone to –,** dormir a uno. **11 to – around,** acostarse con todo el mundo, acostarse con cualquiera. **12 to – the hours away,** pasar las horas durmiendo. **13 to – in,** dormir tarde, seguir durmiendo. **14 to – in house,** dormir en casa. **15 to – heavily, to – soundly,** dormir profundamente. **16 to – like a log, to – like a top,** dormir profundamente. **17 to – it off, to – off a hanghover,** dormir la mona. **18 to – on,** dormir tarde, seguir durmiendo. **19 to – on something,** (fig.) consultar algo con la almohada. **20 to – out,** dormir fuera de casa. **21 to – out in the open air,** dormir al aire libre, pasar la noche al sereno. **22 to – the – of the just,** dormir a pierna suelta, dormir con la conciencia tranquila. **23 to – with someone,** acostarse con uno. **24 to walk in one's –,** ser sonámbulo, pasearse dormido.
sleeper | 'sliːpər | *s.c.* **1** durmiente, persona dormida. **2** traviesa (raíl). **3** cochecama (tren). || **4 to be a heavy –,** tener el sueño pesado. **5 to be a light –,** tener el sueño ligero.
sleepily | 'sliːpɪlɪ | *adv.* soñolientamente.
sleepiness | 'sliːpnɪs | *s.i.* **1** somnolencia. **2** (fig.) letargo, carácter soporífero.
sleeping | 'sliːpɪŋ | *adj.* **1** durmiente, dormido. **2** para dormir (pastillas, etc.). || *s.i.* **3** sueño, el dormir. || **4 between – and walking,** entre duerme y vela. **5 Sleeping Beauty,** la Bella Durmiente.
sleeping-bag | 'sliːpɪŋbæg | (también **sleeping bag**) *s.c.* **1** saco de dormir. **2** camiseta de dormir (bebé).
sleeping-car | 'sliːpɪŋkɑːr | *s.c.* cochecama.
sleeping-draught | 'sliːpɪŋdrɑːft | *s.c.* soporífero.
sleeping-partner | 'sliːpɪŋpɑːnər | *s.c.* (brit.) accionista pasivo de un negocio, aquel que aporta un capital, pero que no toma parte activa en el mismo.
sleeping-pill | 'sliːpɪŋpɪl | *s.c.* somnífero, comprimido para dormir.
sleeping-quarters | 'sliːpɪŋ,kwɔːtəz | *s.pl.* dormitorio, espacio para dormir.
sleeping-sickness | 'sliːpɪŋ,sɪknɪs | *s.c.* enfermedad del sueño, encefalitis letárgica.
sleeping-tablet | 'sliːpɪŋ,tæblɪt | *s.c.* somnífero.
sleepless | sliːplɪs | *adj.* **1** insomne, desvelado. **2** pasada en vela, sin dormir (noche).
sleeplessness | 'sliːplɪsnɪs | *s.i.* insomnio.
sleepwalker | 'sliːpwɔːkər | *s.c.* sonámbulo.
sleepwalking | 'sliːp,wɔːkɪŋ | *s.i.* sonambulismo.
sleepy | sliːpɪ | *adj.* **1** soñoliento. **2** soporífero (lugar). **3** agotado, fofo. **4 to be –,** tener sueño. **5 to feel –,** empezar a tener sueño.
sleepyhead | sliːpɪhed | *s.c.* dormilón.
sleet | sliːt | *s.i.* **1** nevisca, aguanieve. || **2 to be sleeting,** caer aguanieve.
sleeve | sliːv | *s.c.* **1** manga. **2** MEC. manguito, enchufe. || **3 to have something up one's –,** guardar algo en reserva, tener en secreto. **4 to laugh up one's –,** reírse con disimulo.
sleeved | sliːvd | *adj.* **1** con mangas. || **2 long-sleeved,** con mangas largas.
sleevless | 'sliːvlɪs | *adj.* sin mangas.
sleeve links | 'sliːvlɪŋks | *s.pl.* gemelos (camisas).
sleigh | sleɪ | V. **sledge.**
sleight | slaɪt | *s.i.* **1 – of hand,** escamoteo, prestidigitación. **2** destreza. **3 by – of hand,** (fig.) con maña, mañosamente.
slender | 'slendər | *adj.* **1** delgado, tenue. **2** esbelto (figura). **3** escaso, limitado, reducido (fuentes, recursos). **4** pequeño, escaso (oportunidad). **5** poco convicente (excusa).
slenderize | 'slendəraɪz | *v.t.* (EE.UU.) adelgazar.
slenderly | 'slendəlɪ | *adv.* **1 – built,** delgado, de talle esbelto. **2 – made,** de construcción delicada.
slenderness | 'slendənɪs | *s.i.* **1** delgadez, tenuidad. **2** esbeltez. **3** lo limitado, lo reducido (recurso). **4** lo remoto (posibilidad).
slept | slept | *pret.* y *p.p.irreg.* de **sleep.**
sleuth | sluːθ | *s.c.* (fam.) detective.
slew | sluː | *v.t.* **1** torcer. || *v.i.* **2** torcerse. **3** *pret.* de **slay.**
slice | slaɪs | *s.c.* **1** trozo. **2** rebanada. **3** tajada. **4** rodaja. **5** parte, porción. **6** pala, estrelladera. || *v.t.* **7** cortar, tajar. **8** cortar en rodajas. **9** rebanar (pan). **10** torcer. || **11 a – of life,** un trozo de vida tal y como es. **12 to – in two,** cortar en dos. **13 to – off,** cercenar.
slicer | 'slaɪsər | *s.c.* rebanadora, máquina de cortar.
slick | slɪk | *adj.* **1** hábil, diestro. **2** rápido. **3** astuto, mañoso (peyorativo). **4** meloso, zalamero. || *s.i.* **5** extensión, masa flotante. || *v.t.* **6** V. **sleek.**
slicker | 'slɪkər | *s.c.* (EE.UU.) **1** embaucador, trampcso. || **2 city –,** hombre urbano y astuto.
slickly | 'slɪkɪlɪ | *adv.* **1** hábilmente, diestramente. **2** rápidamente. **3** astutamente, mañosamente.
slickness | slɪknɪs | *s.i.* **1** habilidad, destreza. **2** rapidez, maña. **3** melosidad, zalamería.
slid | slɪd | *pret.* y *p.p.* de **slide.**
slide | slaɪd | *v.* [*pret.* y *p.p.irreg.* **slid**] *t.* **1** correr, pasar. **2** deslizar. || *v.i.* **3** resbalar, deslizarse. || *s.c.* **4** resbaladero, deslizadero. **5** tobogán. **6** resbalón. **7** desprendimiento (terreno). **8** diapositiva. || **9 colour –,** diapositiva en color. **10 to let things –,** no ocuparse de las cosas. **11 to – down,** bajar deslizando. **12 the – in share prices,** bajar las cotizaciones. **13 the – in temperature,** el descenso de las temperaturas. **14 to – into a habit,** caer en un hábito (sin darse cuenta). **15 to – the top on,** poner la tapa.
slide-holder | 'slaɪdhəuldər | *s.c.* portadiapositivas.
slide-projector | 'sləɪdprə,dʒektər | *s.c.* proyector de diapositivas.

slide-rule | 'slaɪdruːl | *s.c.* regla de cálculo.
sliding | 'slaɪdɪŋ | *adj.* **1** corredizo. **2** de corredera. || **3 – scale,** escala móvil.
slight | slaɪt | *adj.* **1** delgado, fino. **2** pequeño, bajo (estatura). **3** débil, frágil, delicado (apariencia). **4** leve, insignificante, de poca importancia. || *s.c.* **5** desaire, insulto. || *v.t.* **6** desairar, ofender, insultar. **7 to a – extent,** de escasa importancia.
slighting | 'slaɪtɪŋ | *adj.* despreciativo, menospreciativo, despectivo.
slightingly | 'slaɪtɪŋlɪ | *adv.* con desprecio, despectivamente.
slightly | 'slaɪtlɪ | *adv.* **1** un poco. || **2 --built,** de talle delgado.
slightness | 'slaɪtnɪs | *s.i.* **1** delgadez, finura. **2** pequeñez. **3** fragilidad. **4** insignificancia, poca importancia.
slim | slɪm | *adj.* **1** delgado, esbelto. **2** escaso, insuficiente (recurso). || *v.i.* **3** adelgazar. || **4 to get –,** adelgazar.
slime | slaɪm | *s.i.* **1** limo, légamo, cieno, lodo. **2** baba (caracol).
slimeness | slaɪmnɪs | *s.i.* **1** lo limoso. **2** lo baboso. **3** lo rastrero, zalamería.
slimming | slaɪmɪŋ | *s.i.* **1** adelgazamiento. || **2 to be on a – diet,** seguir un régimen para adelgazar.
slimness | 'slɪmnɪs | *s.i.* delgadez.
sling | slɪŋ | *v.* [*pret.* y *p.p.irreg.* **slung**] *t.* **1** lanzar, tirar, arrojar. **2** colgar, suspender. **3** alzar. **4** MAR. eslingar. || *s.c.* **5** honda. **6** portafusil. **7** MED. cabestrillo. **8** MAR. eslinga. **9 to have one's arm in a –,** llevar un brazo en cabestrillo. **10 to – something away,** tirar algo. **11 to – something over to someone,** tirar algo a alguien, pasar algo a alguien.
slingshot | 'slɪŋʃɒt | *s.c.* **1** honda, tirador. **2** hondazo.
slink | slɪŋk | *v.i.* [*pret.* y *p.p.irreg.* **slunk**] **1** esconderse, ir sin ser visto. || **2 to – along,** andar furtivamente. **3 to – away, to – off,** largarse, irse cabizbajo.
slinky | 'slɪŋkɪ | *adj.* (fam.) seductor, provocativo.
slip | slɪp | *v.t.* **1** deslizar. **2** eludir, escaparse de. || *v.i.* **3** declinar, caer. **4** irse, moverse. || *s.c.* **5** resbalón. **6** traspié, tropezón. **7** caída corriente. **8** GEOL. dislocación. **9** estaca, plantón. **10** falta, error, equivocación. **11** desliz (moral). **12** ficha. **13** funda (almohada). **14** combinación (ropa interior). || **15 to let it –,** revelar inadvertidamente. **16 to let a secret –,** revelar un secreto. **17 to let a chance –,** perder una oportunidad. **18 to – away, to – off,** marcharse pasando desapercibido, largarse, escabullirse. **19 to – something across to someone,** pasar algo a alguien. **20 to – an arm round someone's waist,** pasar el brazo por la cintura de alguien. **21 to – back,** regresar con sigilo. **22 to – a bone,** dislocarse un hueso. **23 to – by,** pasar inadvertido. **24 to – a cable,** MAR. soltar amarras. **25 to – a coin into a slot,** introducir una moneda en una ranura. **26 to – something in,** introducir suavemente. **27 to – into bed,** meterse en la cama. **28 to – off,** quitarse (rápidamente). **29 to – on,** ponerse (rápidamente). **30 to – one over, on someone,** jugar una mala pasada a uno, ganar por la mano a uno. **31 to – out for a moment,** salirse por un momento. **32 to – something out,** escaparse algo, decirlo sin querer. **33 to – trough,** colarse por. **34 to – up,** (fig.) equivocarse, cometer un error.
slipcase | 'slɪpkeɪs | *s.c.* estuche.
slipcover | 'slɪpkɔːvər | *s.c.* (EE.UU.) funda.
slipknot | 'slɪpnɒt | *s.c.* nudo corredizo.
slip-on | 'slɪpɒn | *adj.* sin cordones ni botones (ropa y zapatos).
slipover | 'slɪpəuvər | *s.c.* chaleco (de lana).
slipped disc | 'slɪptdɪsk | *s.c.* ANAT. disco de la columna que está movido.
slipper | 'slɪpər | *s.c.* zapatilla, babucha.
slippery | 'slɪpərɪ | *adj.* **1** resbaladizo. **2** viscoso. **3** astuto, escurridizo, evasivo (persona). **4** nada confiable, informal (peyorativo). || **5 to be as – as an eel, to be as – as they come,** ser de lo más informal.
slippy | 'slɪpɪ | *adv.* (fam.) **1 to be –, to look – about it,** darse prisa.
slip road | 'slɪprəud | *s.c.* (brit.) carretera de acceso y/o de abandono de una autopista.
slipshod | 'slɪpʃɒd | *adj.* **1** descuidado, poco correcto. **2** (fam.) metepatas.
slipstream | 'slɪpstriːm | *s.i.* AER. viento de la hélice.
slip-up | 'slɪpʌp | | 'slɪp'ʌp | *s.c.* **1** (fam.) **1** falta, error, equivocación. **2** desliz (moral). **3** descuido.
slipway | 'slɪpweɪ | *s.c.* MAR. grada, gradas.
slit | slɪt | *v.t.* [*pret.* y *p.p.irreg.* **slit**] **1** hender, rajar. || *s.c.* **2** hendedura, raja, resquicio, corte largo. **3 to make a – in something,** hacer un corte a algo. **4 to – one's eyes,** cerrar los ojos justo para ver (de igual modo que hacen los miopes para poder ver bien cuando no llevan gafas). **5 to – a sack open,** abrir un saco cortándolo con un cuchillo. **6 to – someone's throat,** degollar a alguien.
slither | 'slɪðər | *v.i.* **1** deslizarse (por una cuerda). **2** ir rodando (por una pendiente). || **3 to – about on ice,** ir resbalando sobre el hielo.
sliver | 'slɪvər | *s.c.* **1** raja. **2** astilla (madera, etc.).
slob | slɒb | *s.c.* **1** perezoso. **2** desordenado. **3** (fig.) odioso, detestable. || **3** (fam.) **you –!,** ¡bestia!
slobber | 'slɒbər | *v.i.* **1** babear. || *s.i.* **2** baba. || **3 to – over something,** extremar el sentimentalismo, entusiasmarse de un modo ridículo por algo.
slobbery | 'slɒbərɪ | *adj.* baboso.
sloe | sləu | *s.c.* **1** BOT. endrina (fruta). **2** endrino (árbol).
slog | slɒg | *v.i.* **1** afanarse, sudar tinta. **2** caminar penosamente. || *v.t.* **3** golpear sin arte (balón). || *s.i.* **4** trabajo duro. || **5 it was a –,** me costó mucho trabajo. **6 it's a hard – to the top,** cuesta mucho trabajo llegar a la cumbre. **7 to – away at something,** afanarse por hacer algo, trabajar como un negro para terminar algo. **8 to – it out,** dejar que alguien siga luchando.
slogan | 'sləugan | *s.c.* eslogan.
sloop | sluːp | *s.c.* MAR. balandra, corbeta.
slop | slɒp | *v.t.* **1** derramar, verter. || *v.i.* **2** derramarse, desbordarse. || *s.c.* **3** parte extremadamente sentimental o romántica de una obra teatral o película. || *s.i.* **4** líquido de desecho con sobras de comida para alimentar a los animales. || **5 to – about in the mud,** chapotear en el lodo. **6 to – over,** derramarse. **7 the water was sloping about in the bucket,** el agua chapoteaba en el cubo.
slop-basin | 'slɒp,beɪsn | *s.c.* **1** recipiente para agua sucia. **2** taza para las hojas de té utilizadas.
slope | sləup | *s.c.* **1** inclinación. **2** cuesta, pendiente (hacia arriba). **3** declive (hacia abajo). **4** falda, vertiente, ladera de la montaña. || *v.t.* **5** inclinar, sesgar. || *v.i.* **6** inclinarse, estar inclinado. **7** declinar, estar en declive. || **8 – arms!,** ¡armas al hombro! **9 to – down,** estar en declive, bajar: *the swimmingpool slops down to the sea = la piscina baja hacia el mar.* **10 to – forwards,** estar inclinado hacia delante. **11** (fam.) **to – off,** largarse. **12 to – up,** estar en pendiente.
sloping | 'sləupɪŋ | *adj.* **1** inclinado. || **2 – up,** en pendiente. **3 – down,** en declive.
slop-pail | 'slɒppeɪl | *s.c.* cubeta para agua sucia.
sloppily | 'slɒpɪlɪ | *adv.* **1** descuidadamente, sin sistema, desinteresadamente. **2** de manera sentimentaloide, sensiblemente. || **3 to dress –,** vestir con poca elegancia.
sloppiness | 'slɒpɪnɪs | *s.i.* **1** descuido, lo descuidado. **2** la falta de sistema, de organización. **3** falta de elegancia, desaseo. **4** sentimentalismo, sensiblería.
sloppy | 'slɒpɪ | *adj.* **1** descuidado, poco sistemático. **2** desaliñado (vestido). **3** nada elegante, desaseado (apariencia). **4** sentimental, sensiblero. **5** poco sólido, casi líquido. **6** lleno de charcos, lleno de barro (carretera).
slops | slɒps | *s.pl.* **1** GAST. gachas. **2** agua sucia.
slop-shop | 'slɒpʃɒp | *s.c.* (EE.UU. y vulg.) bazar de ropa barata, tienda de pacotilla.
slosh | slɒʃ | *v.i.* **1** derramarse, salirse de un recipiente. || *v.t.* **2** (fam.) pegar a alguien. || **3 to – about,** (fam.) derramar, chapotear. **4 to – some water over something,** echar agua sobre algo.
sloshed | slɒʃt | *adj.* (fam.) borracho, bebido.
slot | slɒt | *s.c.* **1** muesca, ranura. **2** hueco, espacio (horario, programación): *I only have two timetabled slots in the week for sporting = sólo tengo dos huecos en el horario a la semana para hacer deporte* || *v.t.* **3** introducir, meter. || **4 to – a part into another part,** encajar una pieza en la ranura de otra.
sloth | sləuθ | *s.c.* **1** pereza. **2** ZOOL. perezoso.
slothful | 'sləuθful | *adj.* perezoso.
slothfully | 'sləuθfəlɪ | *adv.* perezosamente.
slotmachine | ,slɒtmə'ʃiːn | *s.c.* **1** máquina automática de vender. **2** máquina tragaperras.
slouch | slautʃ | *v.i.* **1** andar desgarbadamente. **2** tumbarse a la bartola. || **3 to – about/along,** caminar arrastrando los pies. **4** (fig.) **to – about,** gandulear, golfear. **5 to – off,** irse cabizbajo, alejarse con las orejas gachas. **6 to walk with a –,** andar con aire gacho, andar arrastrando los pies.
slouch hat | 'slautʃ,hæt | *s.c.* sombrero de plato.
slough | slau | *s.c.* **1** fangal, cenagal. **2** abismo, abatimiento. **3** ZOOL. camisa, piel vieja que muda la serpiente. **4** MED.

escara. || | slʌf | *v.t.* **5** mudar, echar de sí. || *v.i.* **6** desprenderse, caerse. || **7 to – off,** deshacerse de, desechar, desprenderse, caerse.

Slovak | 'sləʊvæk | *adj.* **1** eslovaco. || *s.c.* **2** eslovaco.

Slovakia | sləʊv'ækɪə | *s.c.* Eslovaquia.

Slovakian | sləʊ'vækɪən | *adj.* eslovaco.

sloven | 'slʌnv | *s.c.* **1** persona desgarbada, desaseada. **2** vago (trabajo).

Slovene | 'sləʊviːn | *adj.* **1** esloveno. || *s.c.* **2** eslovenio.

Slovenia | 'sləʊviːnɪə | *s.c.* Eslovenia.

slovenliness | 'slʌvnlɪnɪs | *s.c.* desaseo, despreocupación, dejadez, descuido, chapucería.

slovenly | 'slʌvnlɪ | *adj.* **1** desgarbado, desaseado (apariencia). **2** despreocupado, dejado, descuidado (persona). **3** chapucero, descuidado (trabajo).

slow | sləʊ | *adj.* **1** lento, pausado. **2** atrasado (reloj). **3** flemático, torpe, lerdo (carácter). **4** aburrido. **5** poco elástico (superficie, pitido). || *adv.* **6** despacio, lentamente. || *v.t.* **7** retardar. **8** reducir la velocidad (máquina, motor). || *v.i.* **9** ir más despacio, aflojar el paso (caminando, etc.). **10** moderar la marcha, reducir la velocidad. || **11 to be – to do something,** tardar en hacer algo. **12 to be – to anger,** tener mucho aguante. **13 business is very –,** el negocio está flojo. **14 to go –,** ir despacio, trabajar a ritmo lento. **15 to – down/up,** ir más despacio, reducir la velocidad; entorpecer: *that car slows up the traffic = ese coche entorpece la circulación.* **16 – but sure,** lento pero seguro.

slow-burning | ˌsləʊ'bɜːnɪŋ | *adj.* que se quema lentamente.

slowcoach | ˌsləʊ'kəʊtʃ | *s.c.* (fam. y brit.) perezoso, vago, torpe.

slowdown | 'sləʊdaʊn | (EE.UU.) *s.c.* reducción en actividad o velocidad.

slowly | 'sləʊlɪ | *adv.* **1** despacio, lentamente, poco a poco.

slow-match | 'sləʊmætʃ | *s.c.* mecha tardía.

slow-motion | ˌsləʊməʊʃən | (también **slow motion**) *s.i.* cámara lenta.

slowness | 'sləʊnɪs | *s.i.* **1** lentitud, flema, torpeza. **2** aburrimiento. **3** falta de elasticidad.

slowpoke | 'sləʊpəʊk | *s.c.* (fam. y EE.UU.) perezoso, torpe, vago.

slow-witted | ˌsləʊ'wɪtɪd | *adj.* torpe, lerdo.

slow worm | 'sləʊəːm | *s.c.* culebra.

sludge | slʌdʒ | *s.i.* **1** lodo, fango. **2** sedimento fangoso. **3** aguas residuales.

slug | slʌg | *s.c.* **1** ZOOL. babosa. **2** (fam. y EE.UU.) posta. **3** lingotazo (bebida). || *v.t.* **4** (vulg.) pegar, aporrear.

sluggard | 'slʌgəd | *s.c.* haragán.

sluggish | 'slʌgɪʃ | *adj.* **1** perezoso, lento. **2** inactivo, inerte. **3** flojo (negocio). **4** flemático (temperamento).

sluggishly | 'slʌgɪʃlɪ | *adv.* **1** perezosamente, lentamente. **2** inactivamente. **3** flojamente. **4** con flema.

sluggisness | 'slʌgɪʃnɪs | *s.i.* **1** pereza, lentitud. **2** inactividad, inercia. **3** flojedad. **4** flema.

sluice | sluːs | *s.c.* **1** compuerta, exclusa, dique de contención. || *v.t.* **2 to – something down,** echar agua sobre algo. || *v.i.* **3 to – out,** salir a borbotones. || **4 to give something a – down,** echar agua sobre algo para lavarlo. **5 to – someone down,** dar una ducha a alguien.

sluice gate | 'sluːsgeɪt | *s.c.* compuerta.

sluiceway | 'sluːsweɪ | *s.c.* canal.

slum | slʌm | *s.c.* **1** barrio bajo, barrio pobre. **2** casucha, tugurio. || *v.i.* **3** visitar los barrios pobres, investigar los bajos fondos, conocer los lugares de los estratos sociales bajos.

slumber | 'slʌmbər | *s.i.* y *s.pl.* LIT. sueño profundo. **2** (fig.) inactividad, inercia. || *v.i.* **3** dormir, estar profundamente dormido. **4** (fig.) permanecer inactivo, estar inerte.

slumberous | 'slʌmbərəs | (también **slumbrous**) *adj.* **1** soñoliento. **2** (fig.) inactivo, inerte.

slumbrous | 'slʌmbrəs | V. **slumberous.**

slummy | 'slʌmɪ | *adj.* pobre, en malas condiciones (área de una ciudad).

slump | slʌmp | *v.i.* **1** hundirse, bajar repentinamente (precio). **2** bajar estrepitosamente (producción). **3** sufrir un bajón (moral). **4** desplomarse, dejarse caer pesadamente (sobre una silla, sillón, etc.). || *s.c.* **5** depresión, declive económico, retroceso.

slung | slʌŋ | *pret.* y *p.p.irreg.* de **sling.**

slunk | slʌŋk | *pret.* y *p.p.irreg.* de **slink.**

slur | sləːr | *s.c.* **1** calumnia, infamia. **2** borrón, mancha. **3** MUS. ligadura. || *v.t.* y *v.i.* **4** pasar por alto, omitir, suprimir, ocultar. **5** pronunciar con poca corrección (palabra). **6** comerse (sílaba). **7** MUS. ligar. || **8 to cast – on someone,** calumniar a alguien.

slurred | sləːd | *adj.* indistinto, poco correcto, poco claro (pronunciación).

slurp | sləːp | *v.t.* y *v.i.* **1** beber haciendo mucho ruido. || *s.c.* **2** ruido que se hace al beber.

slurry | slʌrɪ | *s.i.* barro, barrizal.

slush | 'slʌʃ | *s.i.* **1** nieve a medio derretir. **2** fango, lodo. **3** (fam.) cursilería, sentimentalismo excesivo.

slushy | 'slʌʃɪ | *adj.* **1** a medio derretir (nieve). **2** casi líquido. **3** fangoso. **4** (fam.) cursi, sentimental.

slut | slʌt | *s.c.* (insulto). **1** marrana, poco aseada. **2** ramera, puta.

sluttish | slʌtɪʃ | *adj.* puerco, desaliñado.

sly | slaɪ | *adj.* **1** disimulado, furtivo, sigiloso. **2** astuto, taimado. **3** malicioso, guasón, intencionado. || **4 on the –,** a hurtadillas; disimuladamente, sigilosamente.

slyly | 'slaɪlɪ | *adv.* **1** astutamente, furtivamente. **2** disimuladamente. **3** maliciosamente, con intención.

slyness | 'slaɪnɪs | *s.i.* **1** astucia. **2** disimulo, sigilo. **3** malicia, guasa, intención.

smack | smæk | *v.t.* **1** dar un manotazo, pegar con la mano. || *v.i.* **2** tener un sabor un poco raro; saber mal. || *s.c.* **3** tortazo, manotazo. **4** palmada. **5** ruido de un golpe, chasquido. **6** MAR. queche, barco de pesca. **7** (fam.) heroína (droga). || **8** *adv.* exactamente, en el lugar exacto. || **9 to – one's lips,** relamerse, chuparse los dedos. **10 to – a kiss,** dar un beso sonoro.

smacker | 'smækər | *s.c.* (fam.) **1** beso sonado. **2** golpe ruidoso. **3** (EE.UU.) dólar.

smacking | 'smækɪŋ | *s.c.* **1** zurra, paliza. || *adj.* **2** (fam.) dar pasos cortos, andar muy deprisa.

small | smɔːl | *adj.* **1** pequeño, chico. **2** bajo, pequeño (persona). **3** escaso, corto, exiguo. **4** menor. **5** insignificante (importancia). **6** minúsculo, menudo (letra impresa). **7** humilde (voz). || *s.pl.* **8** (arc. y brit.) paños menores. || **9 to be a – eater,** comer poco. **10 to feel –,** sentirse humillado, tener vergüenza. **11 it makes me feel pretty –,** me da vergüenza. **12 to make someone look –,** dar vergüenza a alguien. **13 to make oneself –,** agacharse. **14 – of the back,** parte más estrecha de la espalda. **15 hurs,** altas horas. **16 – wonder,** sorprendente: *It is no small wonder that he has come so slate = no es sorprendente que haya venido tan tarde.*

small-ad | 'smɔːləd | (también **small-ads**) *s.c.* anuncios por palabras (periódico).

small-arms | 'smɔːlˌɑːmz | *s.pl.* armas cortas.

small-change | ˌsmɔːl'tʃeɪndʒ | *s.i.* cambio en monedas de bajo valor.

small-fry | ˌsmɔːl'fraɪ | *s.c.* don nadie, persona de poco peso social.

smallholder | 'smɔːlhəʊldər | *s.c.* minifundista, parcelero, pequeño granjero.

smallholding | 'smɔːlhəʊldɪŋ | *s.c.* minifundio, parcela, granja pequeña.

smallish | 'smɔːlɪʃ | *adj.* más bien pequeño.

small-minded | 'smɔːlmaɪndɪd | *adj.* de miras estrechas, intolerante.

small-mindedness | 'smɔːlmaɪndɪdnɪs | *s.i.* estrechez de miras, intolerancia.

smallness | 'smɔːlnɪs | *s.i.* **1** pequeñez. **2** tamaño reducido. **3** escasez. **4** insignificancia.

smallpox | 'smɔːlpɒks | *s.i.* viruela.

small-scale | ˌsmɔːl'skeɪl | *adj.* en pequeña escala.

small-screen | ˌsmɔːlskriːn | *s.c.* pequeña pantalla, televisión.

small talk | 'smɔːltɔːk | *s.i.* **1** banalidades, vulgaridades, cotilleos. || **2 to swap – with someone,** intercambiar cotilleos, banalidades, etc., con alguien.

small-time | 'smɔːltaɪm | *adj.* **1** de escasa importancia. **2** en pequeña escala. **3** de poca monta.

small-town | 'smɔːltaʊn | *adj.* pueblerino.

smarm | smɑːm | *v.t.* **to – one's hair down,** alisarse el pelo.

smarmy | 'smɑːmɪ | *adj.* (fam.) pelota, cobista.

smart | smɑːt | *adj.* **1** elegante, pulcro, distinguido. **2** aseado. **3** de buen tono, elegante (sociedad). **4** (fig.) listo, vivo, inteligente. **5** ladino, astuto, cuco (sentido peyorativo). **6** pronto, rápido (paso, movimiento). **7** repentino (ataque). || *s.i.* **8** escozor. **9** (fig.) resentimiento, dolor. **10** MED. escocer, picar. || **11 to look – about it,** darse prisa. **12 to – under/to – with,** sufrir bajo, resentirse de. **13 to – under criticism,** resentirse de una crítica. **14 you shall – for this!,** ¡me las pagarás!

smarten | smɑːtn | *v.t.* **1** arreglar, mejorar el aspecto de. || *v.r.* **2 to =N oneself up,** arreglarse, mejorarse el aspecto, acicalarse.

smartly | 'smɑːtlɪ | *adv.* **1** elegantemente, pulcramente, de modo distinguido. **2** (fig.) inteligentemente. **3** astutamente (peyorativo). **4** prontamente, rápidamente. **5** repentinamente.

smartness | 'smɑːtnɪs | *s.i.* **1** elegancia, pulcritud, distinción. **2** aseo. **3** buen tono. **4** (fig.) viveza, inteligencia. **5** astucia (peyorativo). **6** rapidez, prontitud.

smarty | 'smɑːtɪ | *s.c.* (fam.) sabelotodo.

smash | smæʃ | *v.t.* **1** romper (haciendo el ruido del cristal al romperse). **2** hacer pedazos. **3** destruir. **4** golpear violentamente. **5** estallar (contra algo). **6** aplastar (oponente). || *v.i.* **7** romperse. **8** hacerse pedazos. **9** chocar (contra). **10** estrellarse. **11** quebrar (finanzas). || *s.c.* **12** choque, colisión. **13** encontronazo. **14** accidente. **15** rotura. **16** quiebra, depresión, crisis económica (finanzas). **17** golpe violento (tenis). || **18 – down,** tirar abajo (puerta). **19 to – one's fist into someone's face,** partir la cara a alguien. **20 to – up,** destruir completamente.

smash-and-grab raid | 'smæʃən'græbˌreɪd | *s.c.* robo relámpago (en joyería, etc.).

smashed | 'smæʃt | *adj.* **1** (fam.) bebido, borracho. **2** (fam.) drogado (hachís, marihuana). **3** roto en mil pedazos (objeto).

smasher | 'smæʃər | *s.c.* **1** (fam.) muy atractivo, bombón.

smashing | 'smæʃɪŋ | *adj.* (fam.) imponente, bárbaro, estupendo: *we have a smashing record player = tenemos un tocadiscos estupendo.*

smash-up | 'smæʃʌp | *s.c.* (fam.) accidente grave, colisión violenta.

smattering | 'smætərɪŋ | *s.c.* conocimientos elementales, nociones elementales.

smear | smɪər | *s.c.* **1** mancha. **2** (fig.) calumnia, difamación. **3** MED. frotis. || *v.t.* **4** manchar, untar. **5** (fig.) calumniar, difamar. || **6 – campaign,** campaña difamatoria. **7 to – someone because of,** tachar a alguien de.

smeary | 'smɪərɪ | *adj.* manchado.

smell | smel | *s.c.* **1** olor. || *s.i.* **2** olfato (sentido del). || *v.* [*pret.* y *p.p.irreg.* de **smelt**] *t.* y *v.i.* **3** oler, olfatear. || **4 to have a keen sense of –,** tener buen olfato. **5 to – out,** olfatear, husmear.

smelling-bottle | 'smelɪŋˌbɒtl | *s.c.* frasco de sales.

smelling-salts | 'smelɪŋsɔːts | *s.pl.* sales aromáticas.

smelly | 'smelɪ | *adj.* que huele mal, de mal olor, hediondo.

smelt | smelt | **1** *pret.* y *p.p.* de **smell.** || *v.t.* **2** fundir. **3** ZOOL. esperlano.

smelter | 'smeltər | (también **smelting-furnace**) *s.c.* horno de fundición.

smelting | 'smeltɪŋ | *s.c.* fundición.

smelting furnace | 'smeltɪŋˌfəːnɪs | V. **smelter.**

smile | smaɪl | *s.c.* **1** sonrisa. || *v.i.* **2** sonreír, sonreírse. || *v.t.* **3** expresar con una sonrisa. || **4 to be all –s,** ser feliz. **5 fortune – on someone,** favorecer la fortuna. **6 to give someone a –,** sonreír a uno. **7 to knock the – off someone's face,** hacer que uno deje de sonreír a fuerza de golpes. **8 to raise a –,** forzar una sonrisa. **9 to – a bitter,** sonreír amargamente. **10 to – at danger,** reírse del peligro. **11 to – on someone,** mirar con buenos ojos.

smiling | 'smaɪlɪŋ | *adj.* sonriente, risueño.

smilingly | 'smaɪlɪŋlɪ | *adv.* sonriendo, con cara risueña, con una sonrisa.

smirch | sməːɒtʃ | *v.t.* LIT. mancillar, desdorar.

smirk | sməːk | *v.i.* **1** sonreírse satisfecho, sonreírse afectadamente. || *s.c.* **2** sonrisa de satisfacción, afectada.

smirkingly | sməːkɪŋlɪ | *adv.* con una sonrisa afectada.

smite | smaɪt | *v.* [*pret.irreg.* **smote,** *p.p.irreg.* **smitten**] *t.* **1** golpear. **2** castigar. **3** doler, afligir. **4** herir. || **5 my conscience smites me,** me remuerde la conciencia. **6 an idea smites me,** se me ocurre una idea.

smith | smɪθ | *s.c.* herrero.

smithereens | 'smɪðəriːnz | *s.pl.* **1 to smash something to –,** hacer añicos. **2 it was in –,** estaba hecho añicos.

smithy | 'smɪðɪ | *s.c.* herrería.

smitten | 'smɪtɪn | *p.p.* de **smite.** *adj.* **1** cautivado, entusiasmado. || **2 to be – with,** entusiasmarse, estar cautivado por. **3 to be – by the urge to** [+ *inf.*], entrar deseos vehementes de.

smock | smɒk | *s.c.* **1** guardapolvo corto (especie de blusón). **2** delantal. **3** bata corta. || *v.t.* fruncir, adornar con frunces.

smocking | 'smɒkɪŋ | *s.c.* adorno de frunces.

smog | smɒg | *s.i.* niebla espesa con humo (sólo en ciudades industriales).

smoke | sməuk | *s.i.* **1** humo. **2** (fam.) cigarrillo, pitillo. || *v.t.* **3** fumar (tabaco). **4** ahumar. || *v.i.* **5** humear, echar humo (la chimenea). || **6 holy –!,** ¡caramba! **7 to go up in –, a)** quedar destruido en un incendio, quemarse; **b)** (fam.) subirse por las paredes. **8 to have a –,** echar un pitillo, fumar un cigarrillo. **9 there's no – without fire,** cuando el río suena, agua lleva; lo que hace humo es porque está ardiendo. **10 to – like a chimney,** fumar como un carretero.

smoke bomb | 'sməukbɒm | *s.c.* bomba de humo.

smoked | sməukt | *adj.* ahumado.

smoke-dried | 'sməukdraɪd | *adj.* ahumado, curado al humo.

smokeless | 'sməuklɪs | *adj.* **1** sin humo. || **2 – fuel,** combustible sin humo. **3 – zone,** zona libre de humo.

smoker | 'sməukər | *s.c.* **1** fumador. **2** vagón para fumadores (tren).

smokeroom | 'sməukrum | *s.c.* sala de fumadores.

smokescreen | 'sməukskriːn | *s.c.* **1** cortina de humo. || **2 to put up a –,** (fig.) ennegrecer un asunto, enmarañar un asunto para despistar.

smoke signal | 'sməukˌsɪgnl | *s.c.* señal de humo.

smokestack | 'sməukˌstæk | *s.c.* chimenea de una fábrica.

smoking | 'sməukɪŋ | *s.i.* **1** el hábito de fumar. || *adj.* **2** humeante, que humea. **3** de fumar; de, para fumador.

smoking-compartment | 'sməukɪŋkəmˌpɑːtmənt | *s.c.* **1** departamento de fumadores (tren). || **2** (EE.UU.) **– car,** vagón de fumadores (tren).

smoking-jacket | 'sməukɪŋˌdʒækɪt | *s.c.* chaqueta de andar por casa, especie de batín.

smoking-room | 'sməukɪŋˌrum | *s.c.* salón de fumar.

smoky | 'sməukɪ | *adj.* **1** humeante, que humea (chimenea, fuego). **2** lleno de humo (habitación). **3** ahumado. **4** sucio, sobado (en el sentido de no estar limpio). **5** medio gris, de un color no muy definido entre el azul y el gris.

smolder | 'sməuldər | V. **smoulder.**

smooch | smuːtʃ | *v.i.* **1** (vulg.) acariciarse, abrazarse amorosamente. || *s.c.* **2** (vulg.) abrazo amoroso.

smoochy | smuːtʃɪ | *adj.* (vulg.) romántico.

smooth | smuːð | *adj.* **1** liso, llano, uniforme, suave (superficie). **2** terso, suave (piel). **3** sin arrugas (ceño). **4** tranquilo, en calma (mar). **5** suave (voz). **6** fluido (estilo). **7** tranquilo, sin novedad (viaje). **8** afable (persona). **9** meloso, zalamero (peyorativo). || *v.t.* **10** alisar, allanar, igualar (superficie). **11** arreglar (vestido). **12** devastar (bosque). **13** suavizar (estilo). || **14 to – the way for someone,** allanar el camino para alguien. **15 to – away, to – over difficulties,** allanar dificultades, limar asperezas. **16 to – someone down,** calmar a uno.

smooth-chinned | 'smuːðˌtʃɪnd | *adj.* barbilampiño.

smooth-faced | 'smuːðˌfeɪst | *adj.* bien afeitado.

smoothie | 'smuːðɪ | (también **smoothy**) *s.c.* (fam.) afectado, persona que no pierde la compostura (peyorativo).

smoothing iron | 'smuːðɪŋˌarən | *s.c.* plancha.

smoothly | 'smuːðlɪ | *adv.* **1** lisamente. **2** suavemente. **3** de modo uniforme. **4** tranquilamente. **5** afablemente. || **6 everything went –,** todo fue sobre ruedas.

smoothness | 'smuːðnɪs | *s.c.* **1** lisura, suavidad, igualdad , uniformidad. **2** tranquilidad, calma. **3** fluidez. **4** afabilidad. **5** zalamería (peyorativo).

smooth-running | 'smuːðˌrʌnɪŋ | *adj.* que funciona suavemente.

smooth-spoken | 'smuːðˌspəukn | *adj.* **1** afable. **2** zalamero, meloso (peyorativo).

smooth-talking | 'smuːðˌtɔːkɪŋ | V. **smooth-spoken.**

smooth-tonged | 'smuð'tʌngd | *adj.* zalamero, meloso (peyorativo).

smoothy V. **smoothie.**

smote | sməut | *pret.irreg.* de **smite.**

smother | 'smʌðər | *v.t.* **1** ahogar, asfixiar, sofocar. **2** apagar (fuego). **3** contener (bostezo). **4** suprimir, desterrar (duda). || *v.i.* **5** ahogarse, sofocarse. || **6 fruit smothered in cream,** fruta cubierta de crema. **7 a book smothered in dust,** un libro cubierto de polvo.

smoulther | 'sməuldər | (EE.UU. **smolder**) *v.i.* **1** arder sin llama, arder lentamente. **2** (fig.) estar latente, estar sin apagarse: *her love for him still smoulders after fifty years = todavía está latente su amor por él después de cincuenta años.*

smoulding | 'sməuldɪŋ | (EE.UU. **smoldering**) *adj.* **1** que arde lentamente. **2** (fig.) latente.

smudge | 'smʌdʒ | *s.c.* **1** mancha, tizón. || *v.i.* **2** mancharse.

smudgy | 'smʌdʒɪ | *adj.* **1** manchado, lleno de manchas. **2** borroso (contorno, etc.).

smug | smʌg | *adj.* **1** orgulloso de sí mismo, autosuficiente. **2** presumido, creído. || **3 to be –,** presumir.

smuggle | 'smʌgl | *v.t.* **1** pasar de contrabando. || *v.i.* **2** hacer contrabando, dedicarse a pasar cosas de contrabando. || **3 to – goods in,** introducir artículos de contrabando. **4 to – something past/through the customs,** pasar algo por la aduana sin declararlo. **5 to – someone out in disguise,** hacer que uno pase inadvertido gracias a su disfraz.

smuggled | 'smʌgld | *adj.* de contrabando.

smuggler | 'smʌglər | *s.c.* contrabandista.

smuggling | 'smʌglɪŋ | *s.i.* contrabando.

smugly | 'smʌ'glɪ | *adv.* **1** con aire satisfecho, de suficiencia. **2** presunción.

smugness | 'smʌgnɪs | *s.i.* **1** satisfacción de uno mismo, autosuficiencia. **2** presunción.

smut | smʌt | *s.c.* **1** tizne, mancha. **2** mota de carbonilla (ojo). **3** tiznón (papel). **4** BOT. tizón. **5** (fig.) obscenidades. || **6 to talk –,** contar obscenidades.

smuttiness | 'smʌtɪnɪs | *s.pl.* (fig.) obscenidades.

smutty | 'smʌtɪ | *adj.* **1** tiznado, manchado. **2** (fig.) obsceno.

Smyrna | 'smə:nə | Esmirna.

snack | snæk | *s.c.* **1** bocadillo, tentempié, piscolabis. || **2 to have a –,** tomar un aperitivo, picar algo.

snack bar | 'snækbɑ:r | *s.c.* cafetería, bar.

snaffle | 'snæfl | *s.c.* **1** bribón. || *v.t.* **2** (vulg.) afanar.

snafu | 'snæˌfu: | *adj.* (EE.UU.) **1** confuso, complicadísimo. **2** arruinado, estropeado. || *s.c.* **3** equivocación grande. **4** confusionismo. **5** situación confusa. **6** asunto enmarañado, lío.

snag | snæg | *s.c.* **1** obstáculo, dificultad, estorbo. **2** nudo (madera). **3** tocón (árbol). **4** raigón (diente). || *v.t.* **5** rasgar (vestido). || **6 to be a –,** haber una dificultad. **7 to hit/to run into a –,** encontrar un pero, tropezar con una dificultad.

snail | sneɪl | *s.c.* **1** ZOOL. caracol. || **2 edible –,** caracol comestible. **3 at a snail's pace,** a paso de tortuga.

snake | sneɪk | *s.c.* **1** ZOOL. serpiente, culebra. || **2 to be the – in the grass,** ser el traidor, el peligro oculto. **3 a hand snaked out,** se extendió de repente una mano. **4 to – about, to – along,** serpentear.

snakebite | 'sneɪkˌbaɪt | *s.c.* mordedura de serpiente (también **snak-bite**).

snake-charmer | 'sneɪkˌtʃɑ:mər | *s.c.* encantador de serpientes.

snaky | sneɪkɪ | *adj.* serpentino, tortuoso.

snap | snæp | *v.t.* **1** chasquear, castañear. **2** romper, quebrar, hacer saltar. || *s.c.* **3** chasquido, castañeo (dedos). **4** estallido (noticia). **5** golpe, ruido seco. **6** rotura. **7** (fam.) vigor, energía. **8** cierre (cremallera). **9** foto instantánea. || *adj.* **10** repentino. **11** *adv.* crac (con exclamación). || **12 cold –,** ola de frío. **13 to go –,** hacer crac. **14 to put some – into it,** menearse. **15 to – at someone, a)** querer morder a alguien (perro); **b)** contestar bruscamente a uno. **16 to – something into place,** meter algo en su lugar con un golpe seco. **17 to – into something,** (fig.) emprender algo con entusiasmo. **18 to – someone,** tirar una foto a alguien. **19 to – someone's head off,** echar un rapapolvo a alguien. **20 to – off,** romper, separar con los dientes. **21 to – out of something,** (fig.) dejarse algo, quitarse algo de encima. **22 to – up a bargain,** comprar con avidez.

snapdragon | 'snæpdrægn | *s.c.* BOT. cabeza de dragón.

snap-fastener | 'snæpfɑ:stnər | *s.c.* corchete de presión.

snapish | 'snæpɪʃ | *adj.* brusco, abrupto, irritable.

snapishness | 'snæpɪʃnɪs | *s.c.* brusquedad, irritabilidad.

snappy | 'snæpɪ | *adj.* **1** que viste a la última. **2** (fam.) rápido, enérgico, vigoroso. || **3 to be – about something,** hacer algo con toda rapidez. **4 and be – about it!,** ¡y date prisa! **5 make it –!,** ¡rápido!

snapshot | 'snæpʃɒt | *s.c.* foto instantánea.

snare | snəər | *s.c.* **1** lazo, trampa. **2** (fig.) trampa, engaño. **3** *v.t.* coger con trampas. **4** (fig.) hacer caer en la trampa. || **5 it's a – and delusion,** es una trampa.

snarl | snɑ:l | *v.t.* **1** gruñir. **2** (fig.) gruñir (persona enfadada). || **3** *s.c.* gruñido. || **4 to – at s.o.,** decir algo gruñendo. **5 to – up,** enmarañar, enredar; enmarañarse, enredarse.

snatch | snætʃ | *v.t.* **1** asir, coger, agarrar. **2** arrebatar. **3** coger al vuelo. **4** (fam.) robar, secuestrar. || *s.c.* **5** arrebatamiento. **6** (fam.) robo, secuestro. **7** MUS. trocito, estrofa. || **8 to – a meal,** comer algo a toda prisa. **9 to – an opportunity,** aprovechar una oportunidad. **10 to – an hour of happiness,** procurarse (a pesar de todo) una hora de felicidad. **11 to – up,** asir. **12 to =N up a child,** coger a un niño en brazos. **13 to whistle snatches of...,** silbar trocitos de (canción, compositor).

snazzy | 'snæzɪ | *adj.* (vulg.) de lo más elegante.

sneak | sni:k | *v.t.* **1** moverse con sumo cuidado. **2** *(fam.)*robar a hurtadillas, afanar, birlar. || *s.c.* **3** soplón. || **4 to – about,** ir a hurtadillas, moverse furtivamente. **5 to – away, to – off,** escabullirse. **6 to – in,** entrar a hurtadillas, entrar sin ser visto. **7 to – on someone,** soplarse de uno, chivarse de uno. **8 to – off with something,** alzarse con algo.

sneakers | 'sni:kəz | *s.pl.* (fam.) zapatos ligeros de goma.

sneaking | 'sni:kɪŋ | *adj.* **1** furtivo, sigiloso. || **2 to have a – regard for someone,** respetar a uno a pesar de todo, respetar a alguien sin querer confesarlo abiertamente.

sneak preview | 'sni:kprəvju | *s.c.* tener acceso a alguna publicación, etc., de forma oficiosa.

sneak thief | 'sni:kθi:f | *s.c.* ratero.

sneaky | 'sni:kɪ | *adj.* **1** furtivo, sigiloso. **2** soplón.

sneer | snɪər | *v.i.* **1** hacer una expresión de burla y desprecio. || *s.c.* **2** expresión de burla y desprecio, sonrisa de desprecio. **3** burla, mofa (comentario). || **4 to – at s.o.,** mofarse de uno, hablar con desprecio de uno.

sneerer | 'snɪərər | *s.c.* socarrón.

sneering | 'snɪərɪŋ | *adj.* burlador y despreciativo, lleno de desprecio.

sneeringly | 'snɪərɪŋglɪ | *adv.* **1** en tono burlador y despreciativo. **2** con una sonrisa de desprecio.

sneeze | sni:z | *v.i.* **1** estornudar. || *s.c.* **2** estornudo. || **3 an offer not to be sneezed at,** una oferta que no es de despreciar.

snick | snɪk | *v.t.* **1** cortar (un poco). **2** desviar ligeramente (balón). || *s.c.* **3** corte, tijeretazo. **4 to – something off,** cortar algo con un movimiento rápido.

snicker | 'snɪkər | *v.i.* **1** reírse con disimulo. || *s.c.* **2** risa disimulada.

snide | snaɪd *adj.* despreciativo, sarcástico.

sniff | snɪf | *v.t.* **1** olfatear, esnifar, sorber por las narices. **2** husmear, olfatear (perro, etc.). || *s.c.* **3** olfateo, sorbo por las narices (para indicar que alguien está diciendo algo con aire superior). || **4 to go out for a – of air,** salir a tomar el fresco. **5 to – at,** oler. **6 to – at something,** (fig.) despreciar, tratar algo con desprecio. **7 an offer not to be sniffed at,** una oferta que no es de despreciar.

sniffle | 'snɪfl | *v.i.* **1** respirar con ruido, hacer ruido con la nariz (como cuando se llora o se tiene un resfriado). **2** gangosear (hablando). || *s.c.* **3** ruido de la nariz. **4** gangueo. || **5 to have got the –,** (fam.) tener un ligero resfriado.

snifly | 'snɪflɪ | *adj.* (fam.) estirado, desdeñoso.

snifter | 'snɪftər | *s.c.* **1** (vulg.) trago (bebida alcohólica). **2** (EE.UU.) copa para el coñac. || **3 to have a –,** echarse un trago.

snigger | 'snɪgər *v.i.* **1** reírse con disimulo. || *s.c.* **2** risa disimulada.

snip | snɪp | *v.t.* y *v.i.* **1** tijeretear. || *s.c.* **2** tijeretazo. **3** recorte. **4** (vulg.) ganga. || **5 to – off,** recortar.

snipe | snaɪp | *v.t.* **1** criticar, atacar verbalmente (sobre todo cuando la persona atacada no puede defenderse). || *s.c.* **2** ZOOL. agachadiza. || **3 to – at someone,** disparar desde un escondite a alguien.

sniper | 'snɪpər | *s.c.* francotirador.

snippet | 'snɪpɪt | *s.c.* **1** retazo, trozo. **2** retal (tela). **3** noticias breves (información).

snitch | snɪtʃ | *v.i.* (fam.) **1** acusarse, soplarse. || *s.c.* **2** napias.

snivel | 'snɪvl | *v.i.* **1** (EE.UU.) lloriquear. || *s.c.* **2** lloriqueo.

snivelling | 'snɪvlɪŋ | *adj.* llorón.

snob | snɒb | *s.c* esnob (aquel que se esfuerza por imitar la conducta de la alta sociedad o por seguir siempre la moda llamativa para darse importancia), pretencioso.

snobbery | 'snɒbərɪ | *s.i.* esnobismo.

snobbish | 'snɒbɪʃ | *adj.* esnob.

snobbishness | 'snɒbɪsnɪs | *s.i.* esnobismo.

snog | snɒg | *v.i.* **1** (fam.) abrazarse y besarse (especialmente entre adolescentes). || *s.c.* **2** abrazo y beso.

snood | snu:d | *s.c* **1** cintillo. **2** redecilla.

snook | snu:k | *s.c.* **1** (fam.) **to cock a – at someone,** sacar la lengua a uno, hacer una señal grosera a uno.

snooker | snu:kər *s.c.* **1** billar. || *v.t.* **2 to – someone,** poner en un aprieto.

snoop | snu:p | *v.i.* **1** curiosear, fisgonear. || *s.c.* **2** fisgón.

snooper | 'snu:pər | *s.c.* investigador encubierto, inspector que no anuncia públicamente sus visitas.

snooty | 'snu:tɪ | *adj.* **1** (fam.) fachendoso, presumido. **2 there's no call to be – about it,** usted no tiene motivo para presumir.

snooze | snu:z | *s.c.* **1** cabezada, siestecita, sueñecito. || *v.i.* **2 to have a –,** dormitar, echar una siestecita.

snore | snɔː | *v.i.* **1** roncar. || *s.c.* **2** ronquido.

snoring | snɔːrɪŋ | *s.pl.* ronquidos.

snorkel | 'snɔːkl | *s.c.* **1** tubo de respiración. || *v.i.* **2** bucear con un tubo.

snort | snɔːt | *v.i.* **1** bufar. || *s.c.* **2** bufido. || **3 with a – of rage,** con un bufido de enojo.

snorter | 'snɔːtər | *s.c.* (vulg.) estupendo, maravilloso.

snot | snɒt | *s.c.* (vulg.) moco.

snotty | 'snɒtɪ | *adj.* **1** (fam.) mocoso. **2** (fig.) fachendoso, presumido. **3** enojado.

snout | snaʊt | *s.c.* hocico, morro (animal).

snow | snəʊ | *s.i.* **1** nieve. **2** (vulg.) cocaína. || *v.i.* **3** nevar. || **4 to be – ed in, to be – ed up,** encerrado, aprisionado por la nieve. **5 to be –ed under,** (fig.) estar inundado.

snowball | 'snəʊbɔːl | *s.c.* **1** bola de nieve. || *v.t.* **2** lanzar bolas de nieve. || *v.i.* **3** (fig.) aumentar progresivamente, aumentar rápidamente.

snow-blind | 'snəʊblaɪnd | *adj.* cegado por los reflejos de la nieve.

snow blindness | 'snəʊˌblaɪndnɪs | *s.i.* ceguera causada por la nieve.

snow bound | 'snəʊbaʊnd | *adj.* aprisionado por la nieve.

snow-capped | 'snəʊkæpt | *adj.* coronado de nieve.

snow-covered | 'snəʊkʌvəd | *adj.* cubierto de nieve, nevado.

snowdrift | 'snəʊdrɪft | *s.c.* **1** ventisca de nieve. **2** montón de nieve, nieve amontonada.

snowdrop | 'snəʊdrɒp | *s.c.* BOT. campanilla de febrero, campanilla blanca.

snowfall | 'snaʊfɔːl | *s.c.* **1** nevada. || *s.i.* **2** cantidad de nieve registrada en un período determinado.

snow fence | 'snəʊfens | *s.c.* valla paranieves.

snowfield | 'snəʊfiːld | *s.c.* campo de nieve.

snowflake | 'snəʊfleɪk | *s.c.* capa de nieve.

snow line | 'snəʊlaɪn | *s.c.* límite de las nieves perpetuas.

snowman | 'snəʊmæn | *s.c.* muñeco de nieve.

snowplough | 'snəʊplaʊ | (EE.UU. **snowplow**) *s.c.* quitanieves.

snowplow V. **snowplough.**

snowshoe | 'snəʊʃuː | *s.c.* raqueta para la nieve.

snowslide | 'snəʊslaɪd | *s.c.* (EE.UU.) alud de nieve.

snowstorm | 'snəʊstɔːm | *s.c.* tormenta de nieve.

Snow-White | 'snəʊwaɪt | **1** Blancanieves. || **2 "– and the Seven Dwarfs",** "Blancanieves y los siete enanitos".

snow-white | 'snəʊwaɪt | *adj.* **1** blanco como la nieve. **2** níveo, cándido.

snowy | 'snəʊɪ | *adj.* **1** que tiene mucha nieve, de mucha nieve. **2** cubierto de nieve. **3** blanco como la nieve. **4** níveo, cándido. || **5 – day,** día de nieves. **6 – season,** estación de las nieves.

snub | snʌb | *v.t.* **1** desairar, ofender, repulsar. **2** rechazar con desdén (oferta). || *s.c.* **3** desaire, repulsa.

snub-nosed | 'snʌb'nəʊzd | *adj.* chato.

snuff | snʌf | *s.i.* **1** rapé, tabaco en polvo. || *v.t.* **2** aspirar, sorber por la nariz. || **3 to take –,** tomar rapé. **4 to – out,** apagar; (fig.) extinguir. **5 to – it,** (fam.) estirar la pata.

snuffbox | 'snʌfbɒks | *s.c.* tabaquera.

snuffers | 'snʌfəz | *s.pl.* despabiladeras.

snuffle | 'snʌfl | *v.i.* **1** respirar con ruido, hacer ruido con la nariz. **2** ganguear (hablando). || *s.c.* **3** ruido de la nariz. **4** gangueo.

snug | snʌg | *adj.* **1** cómodo y bien caliente. **2** abrigado, al abrigo. **3** ajustado (vestido). **4** respetable, nada despreciable (ingresos).

snuggery | 'snʌgərɪ | *s.c.* cuarto cómodo, despacho particular.

snuggle | 'snʌgl | *v.i.* **1** acomodarse. || **2 to – up to someone,** arrimarse a alguien, apretarse contra alguien.

snuggly | 'snʌglɪ | *adj.* **1** cómodamente, al abrigo de. || **2 it fits –,** se ajusta perfectamente.

so | səʊ | *adv.* **1** [– + *adj./adv.*] tan, hasta tal punto, tanto, de tal manera: *don't be so stupid = no seas tan estúpido;* **2** así, de esta manera, de este modo: *why do you do it so? = ¿por qué lo haces así?* **3** [– + **be/have/do/will/can/should** + *suj.*] también, otro tanto, igualmente: *she goes there often and so do I = ella va allí a menudo y yo también.* **4** por lo tanto, por consiguiente, consecuentemente, aparentemente (para comprobar que algo está claro): *so it wasn't him who phoned? = por lo tanto, ¿no fue él quien telefoneó?* **5** [– **there**/*pron.suj.* + **be/have/do/will/can/should**] sí, claro que sí, naturalmente, ciertamente: *"I saw the children in the garden." "So you did" = "vi a los niños en el jardín." "Claro".* **6** (form.) muy, mucho, tan: *I'm so glad you arrived! = ¡me alegro mucho de que hayas venido!* **7** aproximadamente, más o menos: *10p or so = 10 peniques aproximadamente.* || *conj.* **8** por tanto, como resultado, en consecuencia: *she didn't tell me anything, so I couldn't go = ella no me dijo nada, por tanto no pude ir.* **9** de modo que, así que: *I'm in a hurry, so I'll speak with you tomorrow = tengo prisa, así que hablaré contigo mañana.* **10** conque, así que: *so you've been here since then! = ¡conque has estado aquí desde entonces!* **11** y qué sí, que importa que: *so, I didn't go yesterday! = ¡qué importa que no haya ido ayer!* || *s.i.* **12** MUS. sol. || **13 and – on/forth,** etcétera, y así sucesivamente. **14 ever –,** V. **ever. 15 every – often,** V. **often. 16 in – far as/– far as,** V. **far. 17 just –,** V. **just. 18 not in – many words,** V. **word. 19 not –,** eso no es cierto, eso no es así. **20 not – much,** no tanto por, exclusivamente, solamente, únicamente: *it's not the time it takes so much, it's the work = no es únicamente el tiempo que lleva, es el trabajo.* **21 not – much ... as, a)** no... sino más bien: *he isn't so much intelligent as lazy = no es que no sea inteligente sino más bien vago; b)* ni siquiera, ni incluso: *I didn't have so much as the time for a shower = ni siquiera tuve tiempo para ducharme.* **22 Oh –?** (lit.) tan, hasta tal punto, hasta tal extremo. **23 or –,** aproximadamente, más o menos. **24 –?/– what?** ¿y qué? **25 –/– that,** por lo tanto, de modo que. **26 – far – good,** V. **far. 27 – help me,** V. **help. 28 – long,** V. **long. 29 – long as,** V. **long. 30 – many,** tantos. **31 – much, a)** tanto; **b)** hasta este punto, hasta aquí. **32 – much for,** V. **much. 33 – much the better,** V. **better. 34 – as (to)/that, a)** para qué, a fin de que, de suerte que; **b)** tan... que. **35 – there,** V. **there. 36 – to speak,** V. **speak.**

soak | səʊk | *v.t.* e *i.* **1 [to – (in)]** remojar, poner a remojo, sumergir (algo en líquido). **2** calar(se), empapar(se), saturar; penetrar, mojar(se): *It was soaked in water = estaba calado de agua.* **3** (argot) emborrachar(se), beber en exceso. || *v.t.* **4 [to – +** *o.* **+** *adv./prep.*] absorber, empapar, embeber, impregnar, secar. **5** (fam. y desp.) clavar, cobrar en exceso, desplumar: *they soaked them at the hotel = les clavaron en el hotel.* **6 [to – (in)]** (fam.) tener efecto, hacer mella (un comentario). || *s.c.* **7** remojo, remojón. **8** mojadura, caladura, empapadura. **9** líquido para remojo, para empapar. **10** (argot) borrachín, borrachuzo. || **11 to – up, a)** absorber, empapar, embeber (un líquido); **b)** (fig.) absorber, empaparse de (información, de sol).

soaked | səʊkt | *adj.* **1 [– (through)]** calado, empapado, mojado. **2 [– (in/with)]** versado, empapado, documentado (en una materia); lleno, saturado, repleto: *soaked in memories = lleno de recuerdos.* || **3 – to the skin,** calado hasta los huesos, como una sopa.

soaking | 'səʊkɪŋ | *adj.* **1** calado, empapado, mojado. || **2 – wet,** totalmente calado, hecho una sopa, calado hasta los huesos.

so-and-so | 'səʊənsəʊ | *s.i.* **1** (fam.) fulano de tal, mengano, uno, cualquiera: *and Mr. so-and-so asking silly questions = y don fulano de tal haciendo preguntas tontas.* **2** esto y lo otro, cualquier cosa: *many ideas about so-and-so = muchas ideas sobre esto y lo otro.* **3** (euf.) pelmazo, latoso, fastidioso, cargante.

soap | səʊp | *s.i.* **1** jabón. **2** (EE.UU. y argot) dinero (para soborno). || *s.c.* **3** (fam.) TV. serial, telenovela. || *v.t.* **4** enjabonar, jabonar, dar jabón. || **5 – flakes,** escamas de jabón. **6 – opera,** TV. serial, telenovela. **7 – bubble,** pompa de jabón.

soapbox | 'səʊpbɒks | | 'səʊpbɑːks | *s.c.* **1** caja vacía usada como plataforma, plataforma improvisada, tribuna improvisada. **2** caja vacía (para embalar jabón). || **3 to get on one's –,** (fig.) ponerse a hablar largo y tendido. **4 to get off one's –,** (fig.) dejar el tema, cambiar de opinión.

soapiness | 'səʊpɪnɪs | *s.i.* **1** consistencia jabonosa. **2** (fam. y desp.) untuosidad, viscosidad, asquerosidad.

soapsuds | 'səʊpsʌds | *s.pl.* burbujas, espuma de jabón.

soapy | 'səʊpɪ | *adj.* **1** jabonoso, lleno de jabón: *soapy water = agua jabonosa.* **2** (desp.) jabonoso, parecido al jabón (un sabor). **3** (fam. y desp.) zalamero, congraciador, cobista.

soar | sɔː | *v.i.* **1** remontarse, cernerse, volar muy alto, elevarse (un ave). **2** AER. planear. **3** (fig.) subir vertiginosamente,

elevarse (la temperatura, el tono de voz, la música). 4 dispararse, ponerse por las nubes (un precio). 5 elevarse, encumbrarse, remontarse, descollar (un edificio). 6 animarse, reanimarse.
soaring | sɔːrɪŋ | *adj.* 1 altísimo, elevadísimo (un edificio). 2 por las nubes, exagerado, altísimo (un precio). || *s.i.* 3 AER. planeo.
sob | sɒb | [*pret.* y *p.p.* **sobbed,** *ger.* **sobbing**] *v.t.* e *i.* 1 [**to** – + *o.* + *adv./prep.*] sollozar. || *v.t.* 2 [**to – (out)**] decir sollozando. || *s.c.* 3 sollozo. || **4 to – one's heart out,** (fam.) llorar a mares, deshacerse en llanto. **5 – story,** historia lacrimosa, historia sensiblera.
sobbing | sɒbɪŋ | *s.i.* sollozos.
sobbingly | sɒbɪŋglɪ | *adv.* con voz sollozante, con la voz entrecortada por los sollozos.
sober | 'səubər | *adj.* 1 sobrio, sereno, no embriagado. 2 abstemio, templado (en la bebida). 3 (form.) serio, moderado, sensato, juicioso, solemne. 4 (form.) sobrio, sencillo, discreto. || *v.t.* e *i.* **5 [to – (down)]** volverse serio, sentar la cabeza, calmarse, sosegarse. || **6 as – as a judge,** completamente sereno. **7 to – up,** pasársele a uno la borrachera, despejarse, espabilar la borrachera.
sobering | 'səubərɪŋ | *adj.* serio, juicioso, sensato.
soberly | 'səubəlɪ | *adv.* 1 sobriamente, juiciosamente, sensatamente, moderadamente. 2 sobriamente, discretamente, con sencillez.
sobriety | səu'braɪətɪ | *s.i.* (form.) seriedad, sensatez, cordura, juicio, discreción.
Soc | sɒk | *abreviatura* de **1 Socialist,** socialista. **2 society,** sociedad.
so-called | ˌsəu'kɔːld | *adj.* (generalmente desp.) 1 denominado, supuesto, presunto, así llamado: *her so-called friends = sus supuestos amigos.* 2 mal llamado, falsamente denominado.
soccer | 'sɒkər | (también **football**) *s.i.* DEP. fútbol.
sociable | 'səuʃəbl | *adj.* 1 sociable, afable, tratable, amistoso, agradable. || *s.c.* 2 (EE.UU.) reunión informal, velada, fiesta (en un club).
sociability | ˌsəuʃə'bɪlɪtɪ | *s.i.* sociabilidad, afabilidad, amistad, cordialidad.
social | 'səuʃl | *adj.* 1 social, de la sociedad, comunal. 2 ZOOL. gregario. 3 social (clase, estamento, club). 4 (fam.) sociable, amistoso, afable. || *s.c.* 5 (arc.) reunión informal, fiesta, velada, tertulia (en un club, en una institución). || **6 – climber,** (desp.) advenedizo, trepador. **7 – democracy,** POL. doctrina socialdemócrata; social-democracia (un país con ese sistema de gobierno). **8 – democrat,** POL. social-demócrata. **9 – democratic party,** POL. partido socialdemócrata. **10 – drinker,** persona que sólo bebe en reuniones sociales. **11 – drinking,** práctica de la bebida sólo en reuniones sociales. **12 – life,** vida social. **13 – order,** POL. orden social, régimen. **14 – science/studies,** sociología; ciencias sociales (antropología, economía, política). **15 – scientist,** sociólogo, especialista en ciencias sociales. **16 – security,** (brit.) seguridad social, previsión social, dinero del paro. **17 – services,** servicios sociales, asistencia social. **18 – studies,** (brit.) estudios sociales (asignatura escolar que incluye sociología, economía y política). **19 – work,** asistencia social, servicio social. **20 – worker,** asistente social.
socialism | 'səuʃəlɪzəm | *s.i.* socialismo.
socialist | 'səuʃəlɪst | *s.c.* 1 socialista. || *adj.* 2 socialista.
socialistic | ˌsəuʃə'lɪstɪk | *adj.* socialista.
socialite | 'səuʃəlaɪt | *s.c.* (desp.) persona de alta sociedad, persona mundana, persona muy conocida en los círculos sociales.
socialization | ˌsəuʃəlaɪ'zeɪʃn | (EE.UU.) | ˌsəuʃəlɪ'zeɪʃn | *s.i.* TEC. 1 socialización, adaptación al medio social. 2 socialización (de los medios de producción).
socialize | 'səuʃəlaɪz | (brit. **socialise**) *v.i.* **1 [to – (with)]** socializar, mezclarse, hacer amistades. 2 (generalmente pasiva) adaptar al medio. 3 (generalmente pasiva) TEC. socializar (los medios de producción).
socializing | 'səuʃəlaɪzɪŋ | (brit. **socialising**) *s.i.* reuniones sociales.
socially | 'səuʃəlɪ | *adv.* 1 socialmente, a la sociedad (orientado). 2 socialmente, sociablemente, de modo amistoso, en reuniones sociales: *they meet socially once or twice a month = hacen reuniones sociales una o dos veces al mes.*
society | sə'saɪətɪ | *s.i.* 1 sociedad, comunidad, población. 2 alta sociedad, vida social, vida elegante. 3 (form.) compañía, presencia: *she was in the society of someone I didn't know = estaba en compañía de alguien a quien yo no conocía.* || *s.c.* 4 sociedad, asociación, club; gremio, consorcio: *cooperative society = sociedad cooperativa; the local Drama Society = el Club de Teatro local.* || *s.c.* e *i.* 5 sociedad: *multiracial societies = las sociedades multiraciales.*
socio- | 'səusɪəu | *prefijo* [– + *adj./s.*] socio-, social: *socio-economic = socioeconómico.*
sociological | ˌsəusɪə'lɒdʒɪkl | *adj.* sociológico.
sociologically | ˌsəusɪə'lɒdʒɪklɪ | *adv.* sociológicamente.
sociologist | ˌsəusɪ'ɒlədʒɪst | *s.c.* sociólogo.
sociology | ˌsəusɪ'ɒlədʒɪ | *s.i.* sociología.
sock | sɒk | *s.c.* 1 calcetín, media corta. 2 **[– (on)]** (fam.) puñetazo, tortazo, golpe. 3 coturno (en las comedias griegas). 4 comedia. 5 manga de tela indicadora de la existencia y dirección del viento. || *v.t.* 6 (fam.) **[to – (on)]** golpear, pegar, pegar un puñetazo. 7 poner calcetines. || **8 to pull one's socks up,** (brit. y fam.) esforzarse más, hacer un esfuerzo, tratar de mejorar. **9 to put a – in it,** (brit. y hum.) callarse la boca, cerrar el pico. **10 to – away,** (fam. y fig.) guardar dinero en el calcetín, almacenar (dinero) en el calcetín. **11 to – in,** cerrar al tráfico aéreo. **12 to – it to someone,** (arc., fam. y fig.) atacar con fuerza, expresarse con dureza, poner de vuelta y media.
socket | 'sɒkɪt | *s.c.* 1 ELEC. enchufe hembra. 2 ANAT. cuenca, órbita (del ojo). 3 ANAT. fosa, cavidad (ósea). 4 ANAT. alveolo (dental). 5 MEC. encaje, manguito, casquillo.
socking | 'sɒkɪŋ | *adv.* (brit. y fam.) extremadamente, enormemente.
sod | sɒd | *s.c.* 1 (brit. y vulg.) cabrón, bestia, bruto; maricón, sodomita. 2 infeliz, desgraciado, estúpido (para mostrar simpatía hacia un hombre). 3 cabronada, pesadez: *a sod of a job = un trabajo pesadísimo.* || *s.i.* 4 (lit.) césped, tepe, suelo herboso. | *v.t.* **[sodded, sodding]** 5 cubrir de hierba, cubrir de césped. || **6 not to give/care a –,** no importar un comino, no importar en absoluto. **7 – all,** de nada (para mostrar enfado). **8 – it,** (brit. y vulg.) maldita sea. **9 to – off,** (brit., vulg. y argot) largarse, irse al diablo: *she told him to sod off = le dijo que se fuera al diablo.*
soda | 'səudə | *s.c.* e *i.* 1 soda, agua de soda, agua de seltz, sifón. || *s.i.* 2 (EE.UU.) bebida gaseosa (de naranja, de limón). 3 QUIM. sosa. || *s.c.* 4 (EE.UU.) refresco (a base de agua de soda y helado). || **5 – fountain,** (EE.UU.) bar de helados y bebidas no alcohólicas (generalmente en una tienda). **6 – siphon/syphon,** sifón, botella de agua de seltz. **7 – water,** soda, agua de seltz.
sodden | 'sɒdn | *adj.* empapado, saturado de agua, mojado, calado.
sodding | 'sɒdɪŋ | *adj.* (brit., vulg. y argot) maldito, maricón, endemoniado: *the sodding horse wouldn't walk = el maricón del caballo no se movía.*
sodium | 'səudɪəm | *s.i.* 1 QUIM. sodio. || **2 – bicarbonate,** QUIM. bicarbonato sódico. **3 – chloride,** QUIM. cloruro de sodio. **4 – hydroxide,** QUIM. hidróxido de sodio.
sodomite | 'sɒdəmaɪt | *s.c.* (form.) sodomita.
sodomy | 'sɒdəmɪ | *s.i.* sodomía.
sofa | 'səufə | *s.c.* 1 sofá. || **2 – bed,** sofá cama.
soft | sɒft | *adj.* 1 blando, suave, fláccido, muelle (un objeto, una materia): *a soft cushion = un cojín blando.* 2 dúctil (un metal). 3 suave, delicada, tersa (la piel). 4 suave, silencioso, tranquilo, sosegado, dulce: *soft music = música suave.* 5 tenue, suave (una luz, un color). 6 de trazo suave, de contorno delicado. 7 ligero, leve, suave, dulce, sin fuerza (un movimiento, el viento): *a soft breeze = una suave brisa.* 8 (fam. y desp.) fácil, sencillo, suave, sin problemas (un trabajo). 9 **[– (with)]** (fam. y desp.) débil, blandengue, falto de carácter, poco severo: *they are too soft with the kids = son poco severos con los críos.* **10 [– (on)]** conciliador, negociador, indulgente, tolerante, compasivo. 11 débil, flojo, fofo, sin fuerza. 12 (fam.) social, de las ideas (una ciencia). 13 blanda (una droga, pornografía). 14 no alcohólica (una bebida). 15 FON. suave, silbante (un sonido). 16 blanda, suave (el agua). 17 (fam.) tonto, loco, estúpido. || *s.c.* 18 parte suave o blanda. 19 objeto blando. || *adv.* 20 suavemente, delicadamente. || **21 to be – on someone, a)** (fam.) sentirse atraído por alguien, estar enamorado de alguien; **b)** ser muy tolerante con alguien, ser muy indulgente con alguien. **22 to have a – spot for someone,** (fam.) tener especial predilección por alguien, querer mucho a

alguien. **23 – currency,** ECON. moneda no convertible. **24 – drink,** bebida no alcohólica. **25 – focus,** FOT. borroso, desenfocado. **26 – fruit,** fruta blanda (sin hueso). **27 – furnishings,** (brit.) telas decorativas (para cortinajes, cojines y edredones). **28 – in the head,** (fam.) tocado, mal de la cabeza, tonto. **29 – palate,** ANAT. velo del paladar. **30 – porn,** pornografía blanda. **31 – sciences,** ciencias sociales (psicología, sociología). **32 – sell,** arte de vender persuadiendo con sutileza. **33 – soap, a)** jabón líquido; **b)** (fig.) jabón, halago, adulación, lisonja. **34 – touch,** (fam.) incauto, persona que se deja convencer fácilmente (especialmente para prestar dinero).

softball | 'sɒftbɔ:l | *s.i.* **1** DEP. variedad de béisbol (con pelota más blanda). || *s.c.* **2** pelota blanda de béisbol.

soft-boiled | 'sɒftbɔɪld | *adj.* pasado por agua (un huevo).

soften | 'sɒfn | (EE.UU.) | sɔ:fn | *v.t.* e *i.* **1** deshacer(se), ablandar(se), reblandecer(se). **2** suavizar(se), dulcificar(se). **3** debilitar(se), ablandar(se) (una actitud). **4** mitigar, aliviar, templar (un golpe, un disgusto). **5** suavizar, poner tersa (la piel). || **6 to – up, a)** MIL. debilitar las posiciones, debilitar la resistencia; **b)** (fam.) comer el coco, ablandar (a una persona para convencerla).

softener | 'sɒfnər | *s.c.* suavizante, suavizador (para la ropa).

soft-headed | 'sɒft,hedɪd | *adj.* poco juicioso, estúpido, tonto, de pocas luces.

soft-hearted | ,sɒft'hɑ:tɪd | *adj.* bondadoso, de buen corazón, compasivo, tierno.

softie V. **softy.**

softly | 'sɔ:ftlɪ | *adv.* **1** suavemente, delicadamente. **2** suavemente, tenuemente. **3** con dulzura, con ternura.

softly-softly | 'sɔ:ftlɪsɒftlɪ | *adj.* cauto, cauteloso, precavido, reservado, cuidadoso.

softness | 'sɒftnɪs | *s.i.* **1** blandura, suavidad. **2** suavidad, delicadeza, finura. **3** dulzura, ternura. **4** ductilidad. **5** indulgencia, tolerancia.

soft-pedal | ,sɒft'pedl | [(brit. **soft-pedalled, soft-pedalling**), (EE.UU. **soft-pedaled, soft-pedaling**)] *v.t.* restar importancia, no dar demasiado énfasis, dejar de lado.

soft-soap | 'sɒft,səup | *v.t.* (fam.) dar jabón, adular, halagar, lisonjear, dorar la píldora.

soft-spoken | 'sɒft,spəukən | *adj.* de voz dulce, de tono suave, de voz agradable.

software | 'sɒftweər | | sɑ:ftwɔ: | *s.i.* INF. soporte lógico informático, logicial, programas.

softwood | 'sɒftwud | | 'sɑ:ftwud | *s.i.* **1** madera blanda. || *s.c.* **2** árbol de madera blanda.

softy | 'sɒftɪ | (EE.UU.) | 'sɔ:ftɪ | (también **softie**) *s.c.* **1** sentimental, sensiblero, persona de corazón blando. **2** llorica, blandengue. **3** alfeñique, melindre, poca cosa.

soggy | 'sɒgɪ | *adj.* mojado, empapado, saturado de agua.

soil | sɔɪl | *s.c.* e *i.* **1** tierra, suelo. **2 [the –]** (lit.) campo, tierra: *a man of the soil = un hombre del campo.* || *s.i.* **3** país, suelo patrio, tierra, patria: *when she arrived in her native soil = cuando llegó a su patria.* || *v.t.* e *i.* **4** (form.) manchar(se), ensuciar(se), embadurnar(se). **5 [to – (on/with)]** (fig.) manchar(se), corromper(se), rebajar(se): *is she going to soil herself on that dirty job? = ¿va a hacer ese trabajo sucio?*

soiled | 'sɔɪld | *adj.* sucio, manchado.

soiree, soirée | 'swɑ:reɪ | (EE.UU.) | swɑ:'reɪ | *s.c.* (form.) velada, reunión social.

sojourn | 'sɒdʒən | (EE.UU.) | səu'dʒə:rn | *s.c.* **1** (lit.) estancia temporal, permanencia, temporada: *a sojourn by the sea = una temporada en la playa.* || *v.i.* **2 [to – + adv./prep.]** (lit.) pasar una temporada, permanecer, morar, residir temporalmente.

sol | sɒl | | sɑ:l | *s.i.* MUS. sol.

solace | 'sɒlɪs | *s.c.* e *i.* **1** (form.) desahogo, alivio, consuelo, confortamiento. || *v.t.* **2** (lit.) reconfortar, confortar, consolar, aliviar.

solar | 'səulər | *adj.* **1** solar (del sistema). **2** de energía solar: *solar panels = paneles de energía solar.* || **3 – cell,** ASTR. célula de energía solar. **4 – plexus,** ANAT. plexo solar. **5 – system,** ASTR. sistema solar.

solaria | səu'leərɪə | *pl.* de **solarium.**

solarium | səu'leərɪəm | [*pl.* **solaria** o **solariums**] *s.c.* solario, solana.

sold | səuld | *pret.* y *p.p.* de **sell.**

solder | 'sɒldər | (EE.UU.) | 'sɒdər | *s.i.* **1** soldadura. || *v.t.* **2** soldar.

soldering iron | 'sɒldərɪŋ,aɪən | *s.c.* soldador.

soldier | 'səuldʒər | *s.c.* **1** soldado, militar. || *v.i.* **2** servir como soldado, ser militar. || **3 – of fortune,** (arc.) mercenario, soldado de fortuna; aventurero. **4 to – on,** (brit.) continuar a pesar de las dificultades, seguir bregando.

soldierly | 'səuldʒəlɪ | *adj.* militar, marcial, de soldado.

sole | səul | *s.c.* **1** suela, piso. **2** ANAT. planta (del pie). || *s.c.* e *i.* **3** ZOOL. lenguado; suela. || *v.t.* **4** (generalmente pasiva) poner suelas, echar suelas (al calzado). || *adj.* **5** solo, único: *the sole person = la única persona.* **6** exclusivo, no compartido: *the sole right of the product = la exclusiva del producto.*

solecism | 'sɒlɪsɪzəm | *s.c.* **1** GRAM. solecismo, error de dicción. **2** error, incongruencia, despropósito. **3** falta de educación, incorrección (social).

-soled | səuld | *sufijo* de suela, de piso: *high-soled shoes = zapatos de suela alta.*

solely | səullɪ | *adv.* solamente, únicamente, exclusivamente.

solemn | 'sɒləm | *adj.* **1** solemne, formal (una promesa). **2** solemne, serio, grave. **3** solemne, suntuoso, grandioso.

solemnity | sə'lemnɪtɪ | *s.i.* **1** solemnidad, formalidad, seriedad. || *s.c.* **2** solemnidad, fiesta solemne, ceremonia.

solemnly | 'sɒləmlɪ | *adv.* solemnemente.

solicit | sə'lɪsɪt | *v.t.* e *i.* **1 [to – (for)]** (form.) solicitar, pedir, requerir, demandar. || *v.i.* **2** DER. incitar a la prostitución, dedicarse a la prostitución (abordando a la gente en la calle).

soliciting | sə'lɪsɪtɪŋ | *s.i.* incitación a la prostitución.

solicitor | sə'lɪsɪtər | *s.c.* **1** (brit.) DER. abogado defensor, procurador (en tribunales locales). || **2 Solicitor General, a)** (brit.) Subfiscal de la Corona; **b)** (EE.UU.) subsecretario de Justicia; procurador general del Estado.

solicitous | sə'lɪsɪtəs | *adj.* **[– (about /for/of)] 1** solícito, atento, preocupado. **2** meticuloso, esmerado, cuidadoso.

solicitously | sə'lɪsɪtəslɪ | *adv.* solícitamente, atentamente.

solicitude | sə'lɪsɪtju:d | *s.i.* (form.) solicitud, preocupación, ansiedad.

solid | 'sɒlɪd | *adj.* **1** sólido, consistente. **2** macizo (un metal, una rueda). **3** compacto, duro, denso. **4** resistente, firme, fuerte: *solid walls = paredes resistentes.* **5** firme, sólido, bien fundado (un argumento). **6** TEC. tridimensional, cúbico. **7** firme, seguro, serio, formal, de fiar: *a solid person = una persona de fiar.* **8 [– (against/for)]** unánime, acorde, general, total: *they gave us solid support = nos apoyaron unánimemente.* **9** (fam.) continuo, seguido, completo, entero, ininterrumpido, inseparable (una línea, un período de tiempo, una palabra). **10** densa, apiñada (una multitud). || *s.c.* **11** sólido, materia sólida, substancia sólida. **12** GEOM. cuerpo, sólido. || **13 to be/go – for,** apoyar unánimemente a. **14 solids, a)** alimentos sólidos; **b)** QUIM. sólidos. **15 – fuel,** combustible pirotécnico.

solidarity | ,sɒlɪ'dærɪtɪ | *s.i.* **[– (with)]** solidaridad, adhesión.

solidify | sə'lɪdɪfaɪ | *v.t.* e *i.* **1** solidificar(se), cristalizar(se), convertirse en sólido. **2** (fig. y form.) consolidar(se), afianzar(se), afirmar(se), fortalecer(se) (un sistema, una opinión).

solidity | sə'lɪdɪtɪ | (también **solidness**). *s.i.* **1** solidez, consistencia, resistencia, fortaleza, firmeza. **2** fiabilidad, dignidad, respetabilidad (moral). **3** solidez, cohesión (de un argumento, de una idea).

solidly | 'sɒlɪdlɪ | *adv.* **1** sólidamente, firmemente, consistentemente. **2** ininterrumpidamente, sin parar. **3** respetablemente, de fiar. **4** unánimemente, firmemente: *they were solidly behind her = estaban unánimemente con ella.*

solidness V. **solidity.**

solid-state | 'sɒlɪd,steɪt | *adj.* FIS. transistorizado, de estado sólido.

soliloquy | sə'lɪləkwɪ | *s.c.* e *i.* soliloquio, monólogo.

solitaire | ,sɒlɪ'teər | (EE.UU.) | 'sɒlɪteər | *s.c.* **1** solitario (anillo). || *s.i.* **2** (EE.UU.) solitario, (juego de naipes).

solitariness | 'sɒlɪtərɪnɪs | *s.i.* soledad.

solitarily | 'sɒlɪtrəlɪ | (EE.UU.) | ,sɒlɪ'terəlɪ | *adv.* solitariamente.

solitary | 'sɒlɪtrɪ | (EE.UU.) | 'sɒlɪterɪ | *adj.* **1** solitario, sin compañía, solo, retirado (por elección). **2** (lit.) solitario, solo: *a solitary tree by the river = un árbol solitario al lado del río.* **3** solitario, deshabitado, remoto, apartado (un lugar). **4** [en frases *interrogativas* y *negativas*] solo, único, exclusivo: *he didn't give me a solitary look = no me dirigió una sola mirada.* || *s.i.* **5** (argot) incomunicación, aislamiento penal. || *s.c.* **6** (lit.) solitario, ermitaño, eremita, anacoreta. || **7 – confinement,** incomunicación carcelaria, aislamiento penal.

solitude | 'sɒlɪtjuːd | (EE.UU.) | 'sɒlɪtuːd | *s.i.* (form.) soledad, aislamiento, apartamiento, retiro.
solo | 'səʊləʊ | *s.c.* **1** MUS. solo. **2** AER. vuelo en solitario, vuelo de un solo aviador. || *s.i.* **3** solo, solitario (juego de naipes). || *adj.* **4** solo, sin compañía. **5** MUS. para solista, para un solo. || *adv.* **6** a solas, solo.
soloist | 'səʊləʊɪst | *s.c.* MUS. solista.
solstice | 'sɒlstɪs | *s.c.* ASTR. solsticio: *winter solstice = solsticio de invierno.*
soluble | 'sɒljʊbl | *adj.* **1 [– (in)]** soluble: *soluble in water = soluble en agua.* **2** (form.) soluble, fácil de resolver (un problema).
solution | sə'luːʃn | *s.c.* **1 [– (to)]** solución, remedio, respuesta, explicación (a un problema, a una pregunta). **2** MAT. solución, resolución. || *s.c.* e *i.* **3** QUIM. solución. || *s.i.* **4 [(in) –]** solución: *bicarbonate in solution in water = bicarbonato disuelto en agua.*
solvable | sɒlvəbl | *adj.* soluble, resoluble, fácil de resolver.
solve | sɒlv | | sɔːlv | *v.t.* **1** resolver, solucionar, aclarar, explicar (un asunto, un problema). **2** descifrar, adivinar, aclarar: *he couldn't solve the mystery = no pudo aclarar el misterio.*
solvency | 'sɒlvənsɪ | *s.i.* (form.) solvencia.
solvent | 'sɒlvənt | | 'sɔːlvənt | *adj.* (form.) **1** solvente. **2** QUIM. soluble, disolvente. || *s.c.* e *i.* **3** QUIM. disolvente. || **4 – abuse,** (form.) acción de inhalar pegamento.
Somali | səʊ'mɑːlɪ | *adj.* **1** somalí. || *s.c.* **2** somalí.
sombre | 'sɒmbər | (EE.UU. **somber**) *adj.* **1** sombrío, grave, pesimista, melancólico, triste (una persona, un punto de vista). **2** sombrío, oscuro, lúgubre, lóbrego (un lugar, un color).
sombrely | 'sɒmbəlɪ | *adv.* sombríamente, de forma pesimista, gravemente.
sombreness | 'sɒmbənɪs | (EE.UU. **somberness**) *s.i.* **1** aspecto sombrío, gravedad, pesimismo, melancolía, tristeza. **2** lobreguez, oscuridad.
sombrero | sɒm'breərəʊ | *s.c.* sombrero (mejicano).
some | sʌm | *adj.* **1** alguno, algún, un poco de, unos: *some people came = algunos vinieron; have you got some money? = ¿tienes algo de dinero?* **2** algún, cierto: *some lady phoned = cierta dama llamó.* **3** algún, mucho, bastante, en gran parte; unos cuantos, varios (días): *for some time she keept calling me Sue = durante mucho tiempo seguía llamándome Sue.* **4** (fam.) [– + *s.*] valiente, vaya, en absoluto (para mostrar irritación, sarcasmo): *some friend he is! = ¡vaya amigo que tienes!* **5** (fam.) gran, todo un, notable, importante, de calidad (para intensificar): *that was some speech! = ¡fue todo un discurso!* || *pron.* **6** un poco, algo, algunos, unos pocos: *you'll see some in Madrid = verás algunos en Madrid.* **7 [– (of)]** algunos, ciertos, una parte: *some of her friends were quite rich = algunos de sus amigos eran bastante ricos.* || *adv.* **8** aproximadamente, cerca de, más o menos: *in some 2 hours = dentro de 2 horas aproximadamente.* **9** (EE.UU. y fam.) bastante, un poco, algo, hasta cierto punto, en cierto modo: *I think of him some = pienso bastante en él.* || **10 and then –,** (EE.UU. y fam.) y algunos más. **11 – day,** en el futuro, algún día, alguna vez. **12 – little/few,** bastante, mucho: *I hope it doesn't hurt for some little time = espero que no me duela durante bastante tiempo.* **13 – ... or (an)other,** algún ... que otro: *some friends or other = algún amigo que otro.*
OBS. **Some** no se utiliza generalmente en frases *negativas.*
somebody | 'sʌmbədɪ | | 'sʌmbɒdɪ | V. **someone.**
somehow | 'sʌmhaʊ | *adv.* **1** de algún modo, de alguna manera, por algún medio: *I'd bring him here somehow = de algún modo lo traeré hasta aquí.* **2** por alguna razón: *I knew, I'd get the job somehow = por alguna razón sabía que conseguiría el trabajo.*
someone | 'sʌmwʌn | (también **somebody**) *pron.ind.* **1** alguien, alguno, alguna persona: *someone informed me about it = alguien me informó de ello.* **2** alguien importante, un personaje: *he thinks himself a someone = se cree un personaje.* || *s.c.* **3** personaje, alguien importante. || **4 or –,** o alguien de ese tipo.
someplace | 'sʌmpleɪs | *adv.* (EE.UU. y fam.) en alguna parte, a otra parte.
somersault | 'sʌməsɔːlt | *s.c.* **1** voltereta, vuelta de campana, salto mortal. **2** (fig.) cambio de actitud, cambio de chaqueta. || *v.i.* **3** dar una voltereta, dar una vuelta de campana, dar un salto mortal.
something | 'sʌmθɪŋ | *pron.* **1** algo, alguna cosa: *I've got something for you = tengo algo para ti.* || *adv.* **2** algo, casi, un poco, hasta cierto punto: *she looks something like her mother = se parece un poco a su madre.* **3** (fam.) muy, extremadamente, sumamente: *she behaves something fanatical = se comporta muy fanáticamente.* **4** aproximadamente, más o menos, cerca de, casi: *it was something like $300 = valía cerca de 300 dólares.* || **5 to be –/really –,** (fam.) ser de importancia, ser mucho, ser demasiado (para mostrar sorpresa): *what she said was really something! = ¡lo que dijo ya es mucho!* **6 to have got – there,** decir algo interesante, decir algo de importancia. **7 to have – to do with,** tener que ver con, tener cierta conexión con, estar relacionado con. **8 or –,** (fam.) o algo así, o algo por el estilo: *I'd like it pink or something = lo quiero en rosa o algo por el estilo.* **9 – for nothing,** V. **nothing. 10 – like,** V. **like. 11 – of a/an,** medio, un poco, casi, en cierto modo: *he's something of a poet = es un poco poeta.* **12 there is – in,** hay algo de verdad en.
OBS. **Something** no suele ir en frases *negativas.*
sometime | 'sʌmtaɪm | *adv.* **1** algún día, alguna vez, en alguna ocasión (en el pasado o en el futuro): *ring me sometime next week = llámame por teléfono algún día de la semana que viene.* **2** (arc.) anteriormente, en otros tiempos, antiguamente. || *adj.* **3** (form.) anterior, ex: *the sometime headmaster of our school = el ex director de nuestra escuela.*
sometimes | 'sʌmtaɪmz | *adv.* **1** a veces, algunas veces, de vez en cuando. **2** (arc.) en otros tiempos, antiguamente.
somewhat | 'sʌmwɒt | (EE.UU.) | 'sʌmhwɒt | *adv.* **1** (form.) algo, un tanto, un poco, en cierto modo: *they were somewhat tired = estaban algo cansados.* || **2 more than –,** (form.) en extremo, extremadamente. **3 – of,** (form.) bastante, en gran medida.
somewhere | 'sʌmweər | (EE.UU.) | 'sʌmhweər | (EE.UU.) **someplace** *adv.* **1** en algún lugar, en alguna parte, a alguna parte. **2** aproximadamente, más o menos: *somewhere about 20 miles = aproximadamente 20 millas.* || *s.c.* **3** lugar, sitio (sin determinar). || **4 to be getting –,** estar progresando, hacer progresos, estar avanzando. **5 or –,** o algún sitio por el estilo, o algún otro lugar.
somnambulist | sɒm'næmbjʊlɪst | *s.c.* (form.) somnámbulo, sonámbulo.
somnolent | 'sɒmnələnt | *adj.* **1** soñoliento. **2** soporífico.
son | sʌn | *s.c.* **1** hijo, vástago. **2** (generalmente *pl.*) hijo, descendiente. **3** hijo (apelativo cariñoso para un joven). || **4 like father like *son,*** de tal palo tal astilla. **5 – et lumière,** luz y sonido (espectáculo). **6 – of a bitch,** (EE.UU. y vulg.) hijo de puta. **7 – of a gun,** (euf. y vulg.) hijo de puta. **8 the Son,** el Hijo de Dios, Cristo. **9 the Son of God/Man,** el Hijo de Dios, el Hijo del Hombre, Jesucristo.
sonar | 'səʊnɑːr | *s.i.* sonar, sonda de ultrasonido.
sonata | sə'nɑːtə | *s.c.* MUS. sonata.
song | sɒŋ | *s.c.* **1** canción, cantar. || *s.i.* **2** canto, cántico, canción (el arte, un festival). || *s.c.* e *i.* **3** canto, trino (de los pájaros). || **4 for a –,** (fam.) por cuatro perras, por una nimiedad, baratísimo, medio regalado. **5 to make a – and dance,** (fam.) armar la marimorena, poner el grito en el cielo. **6 to sing a different –/tune,** V. **sing. 7 – and dance,** espectáculo de música y danza. **8 wine, women and –,** V. **wine.**
songbird | 'sɒŋbɜːrd | *s.c.* pájaro cantor, ave cantora.
songbook | 'sɒŋbʊk | *s.c.* cancionero, libro de canciones, colección de canciones.
songwriter | 'sɒŋraɪtər | *s.c.* letrista, compositor de letras para canciones.
sonic | sɒnɪk | *adj.* **1** sónico. || **2 – barrier,** barrera del sonido. **3 – boom,** AER. explosión sónica.
son-in-law | 'sʌnɪnlɔː | [*pl.* **sons-in-law**] *s.c.* yerno, hijo político.
sonnet | 'sɒnɪt | *s.c.* LIT. soneto.
sonny | 'sʌnɪ | *s.c.* (fam. y arc.) hijito, hijo.
sonority | sə'nɒrɪtɪ | *s.i.* sonoridad.
sonorous | sə'nɔːrəs | | 'sɒnərəs | *adj.* (form.) **1** sonoro, vibrante. **2** sonoro, imponente, impresionante (la voz, el lenguaje).
soon | suːn | *adv.* **1** pronto, dentro de poco, en seguida, en breve. **2** pronto, antes, temprano, rápidamente: *come back soon = vuelve pronto; Sunday is too soon = el domingo es muy pronto.* || **3 as – as,** tan pronto como, en cuanto, así que: *as soon as I arrive I'll write = en cuanto llegue te llamo.* **4 as – as possible/as you/he, etc... can,** tan pronto como sea posible, lo antes posible, cuanto

antes, en cuanto puedas/pueda, etc... **5 I/you, etc... would just as –,** (fam.) preferiría, sería preferible, me/se quedaría más a gusto si: *I'd just as soon not go = preferiría no ir.*

sooner | suːnər | *adv.comp.* **1** más pronto, mucho antes. || **2 I/you/etc... would – (do),** prefiero (hacer) algo, antes (haría) algo: *I'd sooner do it myself = preferiría hacerlo yo misma.* **3 no – ... than,** apenas ... cuando, inmediatamente después de: *no sooner had he finished, than he collapsed = apenas hubo terminado, cuando se derrumbó.* **4 no – said than done,** dicho y hecho. **5 – or later,** tarde o temprano, algún día. **6 the – the better,** cuanto antes mejor.

soot | sʊt | *s.i.* **1** hollín, carbonilla, tizne. || *v.t.* **2 [to – up]** manchar de hollín, cubrir de carbonilla, tiznar.

soothe | suːð | *v.t.* **1 [to – (down)]** calmar, serenar, tranquilizar, sosegar, aplacar (a una persona). **2** calmar, aliviar, mitigar.

soothing | 'suːðɪŋ | *adj.* **1** tranquilizador, conciliador. **2** calmante, mitigante, sedante (de un dolor).

soothingly | 'suːðɪŋlɪ | *adv.* tranquilizadoramente, en tono conciliador, dulcemente.

sooty | sʊtɪ | *adj.* lleno, manchado de hollín, tiznado.

sop | sɒp | *s.c.* **1** (desp.) regalo, obsequio, dádiva, soborno, compensación, contrapartida (para ganarse a alguien). **2** sopa (de pan). || *v.t.* [*pret.* y *p.p.* **sopped,** *ger.* **sopping**] **3 [to – up]** (fam.) absorber, empapar. || *v.i.* **4** empaparse, remojarse, saturarse.

sophisticated | sə'fɪstɪkeɪtɪd | *adj.* **1** sofisticado, refinado, elegante, mundano, de gusto exquisito, a la última. **2** sofisticado, complejo, avanzado: *sophisticated machinery = aparatos sofisticados.*

sophistication | səˌfɪstɪ'keɪʃn | *s.i.* **1** sofisticación, refinamiento, elegancia. **2** complejidad.

sophistry | 'sɒfɪstrɪ | *s.i.* (desp.) sofismo, sofistería.

sophomore | 'sɒfəmɔː | *s.c.* (EE.UU.) estudiante de segundo año (de secundaria o de Universidad).

soporific | ˌsɒpə'rɪfɪk | *adj.* **1** soporífico, soporífero, inductor del sueño. **2** soporífero, tedioso, aburrido.

sopping | 'sɒpɪŋ | *adj.* (fam.) empapado, calado, como una sopa.

soppy | 'sɒpɪ | *adj.* (brit., desp. y fam.) **1** sentimentaloide, sensiblero, empalagoso. **2 [– (about)]** tonto, loco: *soppy about cats = loco por los gatos.* **3** venado, loco, enloquecido, estúpido. **4** húmedo, lluvioso. **5** empapado, mojado, hecho una sopa.

soprano | sə'prɑːnəʊ | (EE.UU.) | sə'prænəʊ | *s.c.* MUS. **1** soprano, tiple. || *adj.* **2** de soprano, para soprano. || *adv.* **3** con voz de soprano.

sorbet | 'sɔːrbɪt | | 'sɔːbeɪ | (EE.UU. **sherbet**) *s.c.* e *i.* sorbete.

sorcerer | 'sɔːsərər | *s.c.m.* brujo, hechicero, mago.

sorceress | 'sɔːsəres | *s.c.f.* bruja, hechicera.

sorcery | 'sɔːsərɪ | *s.i.* brujería, hechicería.

sordid | 'sɔːdɪd | *adj.* **1** sórdido, despreciable, canalla, miserable, vil, egoísta. **2** sórdido, inmundo, asqueroso, deprimente, desagradable.

sore | sɔː | *adj.* **1** dolorido, inflamado, hinchado, que escuece: *sore legs = piernas hinchadas.* **2** (fam.) doloroso, penoso, serio, grave, delicado. **3** (EE.UU. y fam.) disgustado, ofendido, herido, enfadado, picado, resentido, enconado. **4** mucho, enorme, gran, serio: *they were in sore worry = tenían gran preocupación.* || *s.c.* **5** herida, llaga, úlcera. || **6 a – point,** un asunto delicado. **7 like a bear with a – head,** V. **bear. 8 sight for – eyes,** V. **sight. 9 to stick out like a – thumb,** (fam.) llamar mucho la atención, dar el cante.

sorely | 'sɔːlɪ | *adv.* (form.) **1** enormemente, muchísimo, en extremo, indeciblemente. **2** gravemente, seriamente: *sorely hurt = gravemente herido.*

sorrel | 'sɒrəl | *s.i.* **1** BOT. acedera. **2** ZOOL. caballo alazán. **3** color alazán.

sorrow | 'sɒrəʊ | | 'sɔːrəʊ | *s.c.* e *i.* **1 [– (at/for/over)]** pena, aflicción, sufrimiento, tristeza, pesar. || *v.i.* **2 [to – (at/for/over)]** (lit.) apenarse, afligirse, sufrir, entristecerse, apesadumbrarse. || **3 to drown your/his/etc... sorrows,** (fam.) ahogar las penas en alcohol, emborracharse para olvidar las penas.

sorrowful | 'sɒrəʊfʊl | *adj.* apenado, afligido, triste, pesaroso: *a sorrowful expression = una expresión pesarosa.*

sorrowfully | 'sɒrəʊfʊlɪ | *adv.* con pena, con pesar, con aflicción, tristemente.

sorry | 'sɒrɪ | | 'sɔːrɪ | *adj.* **1 [– (about /for)]** apenado, triste, afligido: *he looked extremely sorry = parecía enormemente apenado.* **2 [– (about/for)]** avergonzado, arrepentido: *she was sorry for what she'd done = estaba arrepentida de lo que había hecho.* **3** lastimoso, penoso, espantoso, ridículo, terrible: *after the fight he was in a sorry state = después de la pelea estaba en un estado lastimoso.* **4** miserable, mezquino, poco convincente, despreciable, indigno: *a sorry excuse = una excusa poco convincente.* || **5 to be /feel – for,** sentir por, dar lástima de, compadecerse de; arrepentirse por. **6 better safe than –,** V. **better. 7 to cut a – figure,** V. **figure. 8 I'm –,** lo siento. **9 I'm – to say,** me temo, lo siento, lo lamento (para expresar decepción, desaprobación). **10 I really am –/I'm –/–,** lo siento mucho, lo siento muchísimo (para pedir disculpas ante algo que ha disgustado a otra persona). **11 –, a)** (brit.) perdón, perdone no he comprendido (para que repitan algo que no se ha oído); **b)** perdón, lo siento (expresa desacuerdo de forma educada): *sorry but you can't leave now = lo siento pero no puedes irte ahora;* **c)** quiero decir, digo (para corregirse uno mismo): *it's on the right, sorry, on the left of the road = está a la derecha, digo, a la izquierda de la carretera.*

sort | sɔːt | *s.c.* **1 [– (of)]** tipo, clase, especie, género, variedad: *he prefers this sort of friends = prefiere ese tipo de amigos.* **2** forma, modo, manera. **3** (generalmente *sing.*) (fam.) persona, tipo: *he's an honest sort = es una persona honesta.* **4** carácter, temperamento, naturaleza, índole. **5** tipo (en imprenta). || *v.t.* e *i.* **6 [to – (out/through)]** clasificar, ordenar, organizar: *sorting all the bills = clasificando las facturas.* || *v.t.* **7** arreglar, reparar, ajustar. || **8 all sorts of,** todo tipo de, gran número de. **9 it takes all sorts (to make a world),** hay de todo en la viña del Señor, tiene que haber de todo en este mundo. **10 nothing of the –/kind,** V. **nothing. 11 of sorts,/a –,** una especie de, algo así como, algo parecido a (pero de clase inferior): *it was food of sorts = era algo parecido a comida.* **12 out of sorts,** (fam.) molesto, enfadado, de mal humor. **13 – of,** (fam.) más bien, algo así, más o menos, en parte, en cierto modo, en cierta medida: *the boy is sort of fair = el chico es más bien rubio.* **14 to – out, (from), a)** separar, apartar, escoger, seleccionar: *we can sort the good ones out = podemos separar las buenas* (de las malas): **b)** arreglar, organizar, limpiar (un lugar). **15 to – out the men from the boys,** V. **man. 16 to – somebody out,** (argot) ajustar las cuentas a alguien. **17 to – something/oneself out,** encontrar una solución.

sortie | sɔːtiː | *s.c.* **1** MIL. salida, misión, ataque. **2** MIL. vuelo en misión de combate. **3** (fam.) salida, excursión, viaje (a un lugar desconocido).

sorting office | 'sɔːtɪŋˌɒfɪs | *s.c.* oficina de clasificación y distribución del correo.

sort-out | 'sɔːtaʊt | *s.c.* (brit. y fam.) limpieza, arreglo (de una casa, de una habitación).

SOS | ˌesəʊ'es | *s.sing.* **1** RAD. S.O.S. (llamada internacional de socorro en código morse). **2** (fig.) llamada de socorro, llamada de auxilio.

so-so | 'səʊsəʊ | *adj.* **1** (fam.) normal, corriente, del montón, así así, no demasiado bueno. || *adv.* **2** así así, regular, no muy bien.

sot | sɒt | *s.c.* (lit.) borracho.

sotto voce | ˌsɒtəʊ'vəʊtʃɪ | *adj.* **1** en voz baja. || *adv.* **2** en voz baja, por lo bajo.

souffle, soufflé | 'suːfleɪ | (EE.UU.) | suː'fleɪ | *s.c.* e *i.* suflé, "soufflé".

sough | saʊ | (EE.UU.) | saʊ | *v.i.* **1** (lit.) susurrar. || *s.c.* **2** susurro, murmullo.

sought | sɔːt | *pret.* y *p.p.* de **seek.**

sought-after | 'sɔːtˌɑːftər | *adj.* solicitado, demandado, buscado, codiciado: *a sought-after painter = un pintor solicitado.*

soul | səʊl | *s.c.* **1** alma, espíritu. **2** (arc. o lit.) alma, persona, criatura, ser humano: *about 2.000 souls in that place = unas 2.000 almas en aquel lugar.* **3** ánima, espíritu (de los muertos). **4 [– (of)]** esencia, naturaleza, eje central (de un movimiento, de un grupo). || *s.i.* **5** alma, sentimiento, emoción; moralidad, decencia, honestidad; vitalidad, energía: *a piece of music lacking soul = una pieza musical falta de sentimiento.* **6** MUS. música soul, música popular negra. **7** (EE.UU. y fam.) orgullo de pertenecer a la cultura negra americana con características raciales africanas. || *adj.* **8** (EE.UU.) propio de los negros, característico de la cultura negra. || **9 to bare one's –,** desnudar el alma, confesar los más íntimos sentimientos de uno. **10 to be the – of,** ser la personificación de, ser la imagen de. **11**

to keep body and – together, tener suficiente para vivir, arreglárselas uno mismo económicamente. **12 to sell one's soul,** V. **sell. 13 – music,** MUS. música con influencia de las canciones religiosas de los negros. **14 souls,** (form.) almas, habitantes. **15 the life and – of the party,** V. **life. 16 upon my –!,** (arc.) ¡Dios mío!, ¡Dios me valga!, ¡caramba!

soul-destroying | səuldɪ'strɔɪɪŋ | *adj.* (desp.) muy aburrido, totalmente tedioso, poco interesante (una actividad).

soulful | 'səulfʊl | *adj.* lleno de sentimiento, conmovedor, sentimental.

soulless | 'səullɪs | *adj.* **1** (desp.) sin alma, desalmado, falto de sentimientos (una persona). **2** sin interés, aburrido, monótono, tedioso, mecánico (un trabajo, una vida).

soul-searching | 'səul,sɜːtʃɪŋ | *s.i.* deliberación, análisis, examen profundo, examen de conciencia.

sound | saʊnd | *s.c.* e *i.* **1** sonido, son. **2** ruido, zumbido, alboroto. **3** impresión, implicación: *I don't like the sound of the news = las noticias no me dan muy buena espina.* **4** GEOG. brazo de mar, estrecho. **5** GEOG. ensenada, rada. **6** vejiga natatoria (de los peces). || *s.i.* **7** TV. sonido. **8** sonido, volumen (de un aparato). **9** sonda. || *v.i.* **10** sonar, parecer, dar la impresión: *his voice sounded angry = por la voz parecía estar enfadado.* **11** sumergirse (especialmente una ballena). || *v.t.* e *i.* **12** sonar, resonar, tocar, tañer: *the bells sounded at three = las campanas tañeron a las tres.* **13** sondar, comprobar la profundidad. || *v.t.* **14** hacer sonar, tocar, anunciar, avisar, comunicar: *they sounded retreat = tocar a retirada.* **15** celebrar, dar a conocer. **16** (form.) pronunciar, articular (un sonido). **17** MED. auscultar. **18** (fig.) sondear, tantear. || *adj.* **19** firme, sólido, seguro, resistente, fuerte (un edificio). **20** sano, fuerte, saludable, robusto. **21** sensato, razonable, prudente, juicioso, correcto (un consejo, un argumento). **22** segura, fiable, buena (una inversión, un negocio). **23** completo, total, sólido, acertado: *a sound training = una preparación sólida.* **24** fuerte, severo (castigo): *a sound beating = una severa paliza.* **25** profundo (el sueño). **26** conservador (de ideas). **27** DER. legal, válido. || *adv.* **28** profundamente, completamente. || **29 as – as a bell,** completamente sano, en perfecto estado de salud. **30 of – mind,** en su sano juicio, mentalmente sano. **31 safe and –,** V. **safe. 32 – asleep,** profundamente dormido. **33 – barrier,** barrera del sonido. **34 – effects,** TV. efectos de sonido. **35 – wave,** onda acústica. **36 to – off, a)** (fam. y desp.) protestar, refunfuñar, quejarse; **b)** MIL. gritar un, dos, un dos... (en un desfile). **37 to – out,** indagar, comprobar, averiguar, enterarse.

sounding | saʊndɪŋ | *s.sing.* **1** sonido, tañido: *the sounding of the horn = el sonido del claxon.* || *s.c.* **2** (generalmente *pl.*) GEOL. sondeo, sondaje. **3** (generalmente *pl.*) sondeo, indagación, comprobación, investigación. || *sufijo* **4 -sounding,** de tono, en tono, de resonancia: *loud-sounding music = música ensordecedora.* || **5 – board, a)** MUS. caja de resonancia; **b)** portavoz; **c)** (fig.) caja de resonancia, comprobante, prueba, reacción.

soundless 'saʊndlɪs | *adj.* insonoro, silencioso, sin ruido, sigiloso, mudo: *soundless movements = movimientos sigilosos.*

soundlessly | 'saʊndlɪslɪ | *adv.* silenciosamente, sigilosamente, sin ruido.

soundly | 'saʊndlɪ | *adv.* **1** totalmente, completamente, severamente: *soundly punished = severamente castigados.* **2** profundamente, completamente.

soundproof | 'saʊnpruːf | *adj.* **1** insonorizado, a prueba de ruidos: *a soundproof room = una habitación insonorizada.* || *v.t.* **2** insonorizar.

soundtrack | 'saʊndtræk | *s.c.* banda sonora.

soup | suːp *s.c.* e *i.* **1** sopa, caldo, consomé. || *v.t.* **2 [to – up]** (argot) aumentar la potencia, sobrealimentar (un motor). || **3 from – to nuts,** (EE.UU. y fam.) de principio a fin, completo y en detalle. **4 in the –,** (fam.) en apuros, en un aprieto. **5 – kitchen,** comedor de los pobres, auxilio social (para los necesitados).

souped-up | 'suːptʌp | *adj.* **1** preparado, sobrealimentado (un motor). **2** (fam. y desp.) corregido y aumentado: *a souped-up version = una versión corregida y aumentada.*

soupçon | 'suːpsɒn | (EE.UU.) | suːp'sɒn | *s.sing.* pizca, pellizco, poquito, pelín: *a soupçon of sage = una pizca de salvia.*

sour | 'saʊər | *adj.* **1** agrio, ácido, avinagrado, acre: *sour apples = manzanas agrias.* **2** agria, cortada, fermentada (la leche). **3** agrio, malhumorado, desabrido, desagradable (el carácter). || *v.t.* **4** agriar(se), amargar(se) (la vida); cortar(se), agriar(se), volver(se) ácido, avinagrar(se). || *s.i.* **5** (EE.UU.) cóctel a base de limón o lima con alcohol. || **6 to go/turn –,** ir mal, fastidiarse, agriarse (un asunto). **7 – cream,** crema ácida, leche cortada (usada en cocina). **8 – grapes,** celos, envidia.

source | sɔːs | *s.c.* **1 [– (of)]** fuente, medio de abastecimiento, suministro. **2** causa, razón, motivo, foco: *the source of the infection was unknown = se desconocía el foco de la infección.* **3** fuente, manantial, venero. **4** fuente, origen, procedencia (de información). || **5 at –,** en origen, desde el principio.

sourly | 'saʊəlɪ | *adv.* agriamente, amargamente, de modo acre.

south | saʊθ | *s.sing.* o *i.* **1 [the –]** el sur, el mediodía (dirección, parte de un país). || *adj.* **2** meridional, del sur, sureño. || *adv.* **3** hacia el sur, al sur, desde el sur. || **4 down –,** (fam.) hacia el sur, en el sur. **5 South Africa,** Sudáfrica, Africa del sur. **6 South America,** Sudamérica, América del Sur. **7 South Pole,** GEOG. Polo Sur. **8 The South, a)** (EE.UU.) los Estados del Sur; **b)** el Tercer Mundo, los países subdesarrollados.

southbound | 'saʊθ,baʊnd | *adj.* hacia el sur, con rumbo al sur: *south-bound trains = trenes con rumbo al sur.*

south-east | ,saʊθ'iːst | *s.sing.* o *i.* **1 [the –]** el sudeste. | *adj.* **2** del sudeste, al sudeste. || *adv.* **3** hacia el sudeste.

south-easterly | ,saʊθ'iːtəlɪ | *adj.* hacia el sudeste, con rumbo al sudeste, del sudeste.

south-eastern | ,saʊθ'iːstən | *adj.* del sudeste, sudeste.

southerly | 'sʌðəlɪ | *adj.* meridional, austral, del sur.

southern | 'sʌðən | *adj.* [no *comp.*] meridional, austral, sureño, del sur.

southerner | 'sʌðənər | *s.c.* habitante del sur, sureño.

southernmost | 'sʌðənməust | *adj.* al extremo sur, más meridional, situado en el extremo sur.

southward | 'saʊθwəd | *adj.* **1** hacia el sur, al sur. || *adv.* (también **southwards**). **2** hacia el sur, en dirección al sur.

south-west | ,saʊθ'west | *s.sing.* o *i.* **1 [the –]** el sudoeste, el suroeste (dirección, parte de un país). || *adj.* **2** del sudoeste, del suroeste. || *adv.* **3** hacia el suroeste.

south-westerly | ,saʊθ'westəlɪ | *adj.* hacia el suroeste, en el suroeste, del suroeste.

south-western | ,saʊθ'westən | *adj.* suroeste, en el suroeste, del sudoeste.

souvenir | ,suːvə'nɪər | (EE.UU.) | 'suːvənɪər | *s.c.* recuerdo, objeto de recuerdo.

sou'wester | ,saʊ'westər | *s.c.* **1** sueste, sombrero impermeable de marinero. **2** viento suroeste; tormenta del suroeste.

sovereign | 'sɒvrɪn | *s.c.* **1** (form.) soberano, monarca, rey. **2** soberano (moneda británica antigua). || *adj.* **3** soberano, sin límite, supremo, sumo (el poder). **4** soberano, libre, independiente, emancipado (un país). **5** (arc.) efectivo, eficaz, excelente: *a sovereign remedy = un remedio eficaz.*

sovereignty | 'sɒvrəntɪ | *s.i.* **1** (form.) soberanía, poder soberano. **2** soberanía, independencia.

Soviet | 'səuvɪət | *s.c.* **1** ciudadano soviético. || *adj.* **2** soviético, de la Unión Soviética. || **3 soviet,** soviet (consejo de gobierno en países comunistas).

sow | saʊ | *v.t.* e *i.* [*irr.pret.* **sowed,** *p.p.* **sown** o **sowed**] **1** sembrar, plantar. **2** (fig.) sembrar, esparcir, diseminar, propagar (sospechas, sentimientos). || *s.c.* **3** ZOOL. cerda, puerca, marrana. || **4 to – one's wild oats,** correrse muchas juergas de joven. **5 to – the seeds of,** (fig.) sembrar la semilla de, comenzar el proceso de.

sown | səun | *p.p.irreg.* de **sow.**

soy | sɔɪ | (también **soya**) *s.i.* **1** BOT. soja. || **2 – sauce,** salsa de soja.

soya, soy | 'sɔɪə | *s.i.* **1** soja. || **2 – bean,** BOT. soja, semilla de soja.

soybean | sɔɪbiːn | *s.c.* (EE.UU.) soja, semilla de soja.

sozzled | 'sɒzld | *adj.* (brit. y hum.) borracho, trompa, como una cuba.

spa | spɑː | (también **watering place**) *s.c.* balneario.

space | speɪs | *s.i.* **1** espacio, sitio, extensión, capacidad: *enough space to put an armchair = espacio suficiente para poner un sillón.* **2** espacio, distancia, infinito, vacío. **3** espacio, universo (cósmico). **4** GEOM. espacio. || *s.c.* **5** espacio, hueco (entre palabras, letras): *in the blank spaces = en los espacios en blanco.* || *s.c.* e *i.* **6** espacio, zona, área (verde, cerrado, vacío). **7** espacio, período, intervalo: *in a space of hours = en un intervalo de horas.* **8** rato, instante, momento: *for a space = durante un rato.* **9** RAD. espacio para publicidad.

10 MUS. espacio (entre las líneas del pentagrama). || *v.t.* **11** [**to – +** *o.* **+** *adv./prep.* **(out)**; generalmente *pas.*] espaciar, separar, distanciar: *the chairs were quite spaced = las sillas estaban bastante separadas.* || **12 into –,** al infinito, al vacío: *looking into space = mirando al infinito.* **13 to make – for,** hacer un hueco para, hacer sitio para. **14 – age, a)** era espacial; **b)** futurista, de la era espacial. **15 – capsule,** cápsula espacial. **16 Space Invaders,** máquinas de marcianos (en bares, salas de juego), juegos de marcianos (para ordenador). **17 – probe,** sonda espacial. **18 – shuttle,** nave espacial (de pasajeros, suministros). **19 – station,** estación espacial.

spacecraft | 'speɪskrɑːft | *s.c.* nave espacial, astronave.

-spaced | speɪst | *sufijo* espaciado, separado: *the lines were closely spaced = las líneas estaban muy juntas.*

spaced out | 'speɪstaʊt | *adj.* (fam.) ido, colgado, semiconsciente (por efecto de una droga).

spaceman | 'speɪsmæn | [*pl.irreg.* **spacemen**] *s.c.* astronauta, cosmonauta, piloto espacial.

spacemen | speɪsmən | *pl.irreg.* de **spaceman.**

spaceship | 'speɪʃʃɪp | *s.c.* nave espacial, astronave.

spacesuit | 'speɪssuːt | *s.c.* traje espacial, escafandra espacial.

spacing | speɪsɪŋ | *s.i.* espaciado, espacio, separación (interlinear).

spacious | 'speɪʃəs | *adj.* espacioso, holgado, amplio, grande.

spade | speɪd | *s.c.* **1** pala, laya. **2** [**– (of)**] palada, pala. **3** (arc., jerga y desp.) negro. || *s.c.* e *i.* **4** espada, palo de espadas (en juegos de naipes). || **5 to call a – a –,** llamar al pan pan y al vino vino, hablar con franqueza.

spadework | 'speɪdwəːk | *s.i.* (fig.) trabajo preliminar, trabajo preparatorio.

spaghetti | spə'getɪ | *s.i.* **1** espaguetis, tallarines, fideos largos. **2** ELEC. macarrón, tubo aislante. || **3 – western,** película del oeste hecha en Europa con director italiano.

Spain | speɪn | *s.sing.* España.

spake | speɪk | (arc. y hum.) *pret.irreg.* de **speak.**

span | spæn | **1** *pret.irreg.* de **spin.** || *s.c.* **2** período, espacio, lapso, intervalo (de tiempo). **2** ARQ. ojo, luz, tramo, arco: *a bridge in a single span = un puente de un solo ojo.* **3** palmo, cuarta (medida). **4** vano (de un tejado). **5** AER. envergadura (entre las alas). || *v.t.* [*pret.* y *p.p.* **spanned,** *ger.* **spanning**] **6** cruzar, pasar sobre, conectar, extenderse sobre: *the river is spanned by a single bridge = un solo puente cruza el río.* **7** abarcar, cubrir, incluir (un tiempo, un espacio): *it spans the last part of the war = abarca la parte final de la guerra.* || *adj.* **8** V. **spick-and-span.**

spangle | 'spæŋgl | *s.c.* **1** lentejuela, adorno brillante. || *v.t.* **2** [**to – (with)**] decorar, cubrir, sembrar (de lentejuelas, de adornos brillantes): *the sky spangled with stars = el cielo sembrado de estrellas.* || *v.i.* **3** brillar, centellear, relucir.

spangled | 'spæŋgld | *adj.* decorado, sembrado, cubierto (de adornos brillantes): *a glitter-spangled T-shirt = una camiseta decorada con polvo de purpurina.*

Spaniard | 'spænjəd | *s.c.* español.

spaniel | 'spænjəl | *s.c.* **1** ZOOL. spaniel, perro de aguas. **2** persona servil, persona dócil.

Spanish | 'spænɪʃ | *adj.* **1** español, hispano (nacionalidad). **2** español, castellano (la lengua). || *s.pl.* **3** [**the –**] los españoles.

spank | spæŋk | *v.t.* **1** dar una azotaina, zurrar, dar una zurra. || *v.i.* **2** [**to – +** *adv./prep.* **(along)**] caminar con garbo, ir muy deprisa, ir volando. || *s.c.* **3** azotaina, zurra, paliza.

spanking | spæŋkɪŋ | *adj.* **1** rápido, garboso (el paso). **2** fresca, fuerte (la brisa). **3** (fam.) asombroso, fenomenal, excelente. || *adv.* **4** (fam.) muy, completamente, totalmente: *a spanking clean dress = un vestido limpísimo.* || *s.i.* **5** azotaina, zurra, paliza.

spanner | 'spænər | (EE.UU. **wrench**) *s.c.* **1** MEC. llave de tuercas, llave inglesa. **2** ZOOL. variedad de oruga. || **3 to throw a – in the works,** (brit. y fam.) fastidiar un plan, meter un palo en la rueda, sabotear un plan.

spar | spɑːr | *s.c.* **1** MAR. palo, mástil, verga. **2** AER. viga, larguero. **3** pelea de gallos con espolones. **4** DEP. boxeo (un partido, ejercicios). || *s.i.* **5** MIN. espato. || *v.i.* **6** DEP. hacer prácticas de boxeo. **7** disputar, reñir, discutir. **8** pelear con espolones (los gallos). || *v.t.* **9** MAR. equipar con palos, poner mástiles. **10** (arc.) apretar con tuercas.

spare | speər | *v.t.* **1** [**to – (for)**] prescindir de, prestar, dejar, permitir, tener (tiempo, dinero): *can you spare 5 minutes? = ¿tienes 5 minutos?* **2** [en frases *negativas* e *interrogativas*] escatimar, economizar, cicatear: *they didn't spare time to do it = no escatimaron tiempo para hacerlo.* **3** [**to – +** *o.*] evitar, ahorrar, pasar de (una mala noticia, una necesidad, un problema): *he spared her the details = le ahorró los detalles.* **4** (lit.) salvar, perdonar, eximir (la vida, un castigo). || *v.i.* **5** ser frugal, escatimar. **6** ser misericordioso, tener piedad. || *adj.* **7** de repuesto, de recambio, de sobra, suplementario, de más. **8** libre, sobrante, disponible, de ocio (tiempo). **9** enjuto, seco, delgado. **10** frugal, pobre, escaso, parco. || *s.c.* **11** pieza de repuesto. **12** rueda de recambio, neumático de repuesto. || **13 to drive someone –,** enfadar mucho a alguien, encolerizar a alguien. **14 to go –,** (brit. y jerga) encolerizarse, poner el grito en el cielo. **15 to have a – tyre,** (brit. y hum.) tener michelines. **16 to – no expense,** no reparar en gastos. **16 – part,** pieza de repuesto, pieza de recambio. **17 – ribs,** costilla de cerdo (con poca carne). **18 – room,** habitación de invitados. **19 to – the rod and spoil the child,** niño mimado, niño malcriado. **20 to – someone's blushes,** V. **blush. 21 – time,** tiempo libre. **22 – tyre/wheel,** rueda de recambio.

sparing | speərɪŋ | *adj.* **1** frugal, prudente, ahorrativo, mesurado, moderado, parco. **2** poco generoso, tacaño.

spark | spɑːk | *s.c.* **1** chispa, chispazo, centella. **2** (fig.) chispa, factor activador: *the spark of rebellion = la chispa que inicia la rebelión.* **3** destello, resplandor, fulgor. **4** [**– (of)**] chispa, pizca, gota, átomo: *a spark of honesty = una pizca de honestidad.* **5** ELEC. chispazo, descarga eléctrica. **6** lechuguino, petimetre. **7** enamorado, cortejador, pretendiente. || *v.i.* **8** echar chispas, chispear. || *v.t.* **9** [**to – (off)**] hacer estallar, activar, desatar, desencadenar: *the incident sparked off the demonstrations = el incidente desencadenó las manifestaciones.* **10** (EE.UU.) estimular, animar, alentar, incitar: *the book sparked her enthusiasm about the trip = el libro estimuló su entusiasmo por el viaje.* **11** cortejar, galantear, pretender, hacer la corte. || **12 bright –,** V. **bright –. 13 – plug,** (EE.UU.) MEC. bujía. **14 sparks, a)** (fam.) radiotelegrafista (de barco); **b)** electricista; **c)** MEC. encendido de bujías. **15 the sparks fly,** reñir acaloradamente, ponerse como fieras. **16 to strike sparks off each other,** ayudarse, estimularse mental y mutuamente (dos personas).

sparking plug | 'spɑːkɪŋplʌg | *s.c.* (brit.) MEC. bujía.

sparkle | spɑːkl | *v.i.* **1** centellear, brillar, rutilar, destellar, relucir. **2** (fig.) estar animado, ser muy divertido, ser muy movido. **3** (fig.) brillar, ser ingenioso. **4** hacer burbujas, ser efervescente. || *s.c.* e *i.* **5** centelleo, brillo, destello, chispa. **6** (fig.) brillantez, esplendor, interés: *a ceremony lacking spakle = una ceremonia sin esplendor.*

sparkler | 'spɑːklər | *s.c.* bengala.

sparkling | 'spɑːklɪŋ | *adj.* **1** centelleante, brillante, reluciente, resplandeciente. **2** (fig.) ingenioso, chispeante, brillante. **3** (fig.) animado, movido, vivaz. **4** espumoso, burbujeante, efervescente (una bebida). || **5 – wine,** vino espumoso.

sparring match | 'spɑːrɪŋmætʃ | *s.c.* pelea en broma.

sparring partner | 'spɑːrɪŋpɑːtnər | *s.c.* **1** DEP. pareja de entrenamiento (en boxeo). **2** (fig.) compañero de discusiones (distendidas y humorísticas).

sparrow | 'spærəʊ | *s.c.* ZOOL. gorrión.

sparse | spɑːs | *adj.* escaso, exiguo, disperso, poco denso, ralo: *sparse black hair = pelo negro ralo.*

sparsely | spɑːslɪ | *adv.* escasamente, de forma rala, de forma dispersa.

spartan | 'spɑːtən | *adj.* espartano, austero, adusto, estricto.

spasm | 'spæzəm | *s.c.* e *i.* **1** espasmo, convulsión, contracción (muscular). **2** [**– (of)**] acceso, ataque, arrebato, explosión (de ira, de dolor).

spasmodic | spæz'mɒdɪk | *adj.* **1** intermitente, discontinuo, ocasional, irregular, inconstante. **2** espasmódico, convulso.

spasmodically | spæz'mɒdɪkəlɪ | *adv.* **1** intermitentemente, discontinuamente, ocasionalmente, irregularmente. **2** espasmódicamente, convulsamente.

spastic | 'spæstɪk | *s.c.* **1** MED. espástico, persona con parálisis espástica. **2** (desp. y jerga) retrasado mental, débil mental, manazas.

spat | spæt | **1** *pret.* y *p.p.* de **spit.** || *s.c.* **2** polaina corta, botín. **3** (fam.) riña, disputa (intranscendente). **4** (fam.) bofetada, sopapo. **5** ZOOL. freza, larva de ostra, ostra joven. || *v.i.* **6** ZOOL. desovar, frezar (los moluscos). **7** abofetear, dar

un sopapo. **8** discutir, reñir, disputar (por cosas intranscendentes).
spate | speɪt | *s.sing.* **1 [– (of)]** (brit.) serie, montón, exceso: *a spate of new books = un exceso de libros nuevos.* || **2 in –,** crecido (un río). **3 in full –,** (fig.) sin parar de hablar, como una cotorra.
spatial | 'speɪʃl | *adj.* (form.) espacial, del espacio.
spatter | 'spætər | *v.t.* **1** salpicar, rociar, manchar (un líquido). **2** (fig.) difamar, manchar la reputación. || *v.i.* **2 [to – (on)]** gotear, salpicar, caer: *the blood spattered on the wall = la sangre salpicó la pared.* || *s.sing.* **3** salpicadura, mancha. **4** lluvia, rociada: *a spatter of rain = unas gotas de lluvia.*
spattered | 'spætəd | *adj.* manchado, salpicado, rociado.
spatula | 'spætjʊlə | | 'spætʃələ | *s.c.* espátula.
spawn | spɔːn | *v.t.* e *i.* **1** ZOOL. frezar, desovar, depositar los huevos (peces, ranas). || *v.t.* **2** (fam.) producir, crear, engendrar (hijos, objetos): *the new administration has spawned lots of new departments = la nueva administración ha creado cientos de departamentos nuevos.* || *s.i.* **4** ZOOL. freza, hueva (de peces, ranas). **5** cría, prole, vástago, descendencia. **6** engendro. **7** producto, fruto, resultado. **8** BOT. micelio del hongo.
spay | speɪ | *v.t.* quitar los ovarios, esterilizar (a un animal hembra).
spaying | 'speɪɪŋ | *s.i.* esterilización (de animales).
speak | spiːk | *v.* [*pret.irreg.* **spoke,** *p.p.irreg.* **spoken**] *i.* **1 [to – (about/to /with)]** hablar: *speak slowly, please = hábleme despacio, por favor.* **2 [to – (about/on/to)]** dirigirse, hablar, pronunciar un discurso. **3 [to – (of)]** hablar (de), indicar, llevar (implícito) un mensaje, mostrar, decir mucho, dar a entender: *her visit speaks of reconciliation = su visita da a entender que se han reconciliado.* **4** hablarse, estar en buenos términos. **5** sonar, producir un sonido: *the cannons spoke = sonaron los cañones.* || *t.* **6** decir, articular, recitar, expresar: *he just spoke a few words = sólo articuló unas palabras.* **7** hablar, saber, conocer: *do you speak Chinese? = ¿habla Vd. chino?* **8** revelar, mostrar, demostrar (una evidencia). **9** MAR. ponerse al habla con (otro barco). || *sufijo* **10** [se añade al final de un *s.*] (fam. y desp.) lenguaje característico de, jerga (una persona, una ciencia, etc...): *computer speak = jerga informática.* || **11 actions – louder than words,** obras son amores y no buenas razones, del dicho al hecho va un trecho. **12 to be speaking to,/to be on speaking terms with,** llevarse con, estar en buenas relaciones con. **13 to be spoken for,** estar reservado para, estar apalabrado para (un objeto). **14 the facts – for themselves,** V. **fact. 15 nobody/nothing to – of,** nadie/nada digno de mención, nadie/nada de importancia. **16 not to – a word,** no decir ni pío, no decir una palabra, no decir ni mu. **17 not to – of,** sin mencionar a, y no digamos, ni que decir tiene: *she was very happy, not to speak of her parents = ella estaba encantada, y no digamos sus padres.* **18 so to –,** como quien dice, por así decirlo, metafóricamente hablando. **19 to – for, a)** hablar en nombre de, representar a; **b)** dar una idea de, hablar acerca de. **20 to – for itself,** ser evidente, hablar por sí mismo. **21 to – for oneself,** hablar por sí mismo, hablar en nombre de uno mismo. **22 to –/talk of the devil,** V. **devil. 23 to – one's mind,** hablar con franqueza, hablar en plata, decir lo que se piensa, expresar sus opiniones. **24 to – out,** hablar claro, atreverse a hablar de, hablar con valentía de. **25 to – the truth,** decir la verdad. **26 to – the same language as,** (fam.) tener los mismos gustos que, entenderse muy bien con. **27 to – to,** (fam. y euf.) hablar seriamente con, reñir a. **28 to – up, a)** hablar más alto, levantar la voz; **b)** hablar claro, atreverse a hablar de, hablar con valentía de. **29 to – volumes,** (fam.) ser muy significativo, ser muy sugerente.
speaker | 'spiːkər | *s.c.* **1** orador, conferenciante. **2 [– (of)]** hablante (de una lengua): *a Spanish speaker = hispanohablante.* **3** RAD. altavoz, pantalla acústica. || **4 Speaker,** POL. Presidente (del Parlamento).
speaking | 'spiːkɪŋ | *adj.* **1** hablante, parlante: *a speaking machine = una máquina parlante.* **2** expresivo, elocuente. **3** vivo, exacto, fiel: *a speaking likeness = un vivo parecido.* || *s.c.* e *i.* **4** discurso, charla, conferencia. || *sufijo* **5** [se añade a nombres de lenguas] de habla, hablante: *a French-speaking country = un país de habla francesa.* || **6 to be within – distance,** estar al habla. **7 broadly –,** V. **broadly. 8 in a manner of –,** V. **manner. 9 –!,** al habla (al teléfono).
spear | spɪər | *s.c.* **1** lanza, pica, arpón, venablo. **2** BOT. hoja (puntiaguda de hierba); brote, tallo (de espárrago, de bróculi). || *v.t.* **3** pinchar, atravesar, punzar. **4** cazar con lanza, herir con lanza, arponear, pescar con arpón.
spearhead | spɪəhed | *s.sing.* **1 [– (of)]** (fig.) punta de lanza, vanguardia, fuerza de choque. **2** punta de lanza, extremo de pica. || *v.t.* **3** lanzar, iniciar (un ataque). **4** dirigir, encabezar (una campaña).
spearmint | 'spɪəmɪnt | *s.i.* **1** BOT. menta verde. || *s.c.* **2** caramelo de menta, pastilla de menta.
spec | spek | *s.pl.* **1** (fam.) gafas: *she was wearing specs = llevaba gafas.* || **2 on –,** (brit. y fam.) **a)** para especular, como especulación; **b)** por probar suerte, a ver que pasa: *she went there on spec, although she didn't have much chance = fue allí por probar suerte, aunque no tenía muchas posibilidades.*
special | 'speʃl | *adj.* **1** especial, excepcional, único: *a special offer = una oferta especial.* **2** (también **especial**) (form.) especial, estimado, íntimo, más cercano (un amigo). **3** especial, enorme, mucho: *he took special care = puso mucho cuidado.* **4** especial, específico, único: *you need a special permission to enter = necesitas un permiso especial para entrar.* **5** urgente (correo). **6** principal, fundamental, esencial, único: *her special interest was painting = su interés principal era la pintura.* **7** especial, adicional, extra: *a special train = un tren especial.* **8** especial, especializado (una institución, un centro). || *s.c.* **9** programa especial, edición especial, número extraordinario. **10** tren especial. **11** (EE.UU. y fam.) ganga, oferta especial. **12** (EE.UU.) plato del día. || **13 to be on –,** estar de oferta. **14 (the) Special Branch,** (brit.) (el) Cuerpo de Seguridad del Estado. **15 – delivery,** correo urgente. **16 – effects,** efectos especiales (en el cine).
specialise V. **specialize.**
specialism | 'speʃəlɪzəm | *s.c.* **1** especialidad. || *s.i.* **2** especialización, limitación, restricción.
specialist | 'speʃəlɪst | *s.c.* **1** especialista, técnico, experto. **2** MED. especialista. || *adj.* **3** especializado: *a specialist teacher of Physics = un profesor especializado en Física.*
speciality | ˌspeʃɪ'ælɪtɪ | (EE.UU. **specialty**) *s.c.* **1** especialidad, especialización, campo de trabajo. **2** especialidad, producto especial, plato especial.
specialization | ˌspeʃəlaɪ'zeɪʃn | (EE.UU.) | ˌspeʃəlɪ'zeɪʃn | *s.c.* e *i.* especialización.
specialize | 'speʃəlaɪz | (brit. **specialise**) *v.i.* **1 [to – (in)]** especializarse, dedicarse, concentrarse. || *v.t.* **2** particularizar, mencionar en particular.
specialized | 'speʃəlaɪzd | (brit.) **specialised** *adj.* especializado.
specially | 'speʃəlɪ | *adv.* **1** especialmente. **2** particularmente, sobre todo, principalmente.
specialty | speʃltɪ | *s.c.* V. **speciality.**
species | 'spiːʃiːz | *s.c.sing.* y *pl.* **1** BOT. especie, variedad, género, clase, familia. **2 [– (of)]** (fam.) clase, tipo, modelo. **3** (arc.) metálico, efectivo.
specific | spɪ'sɪfɪk | *adj.* **1** específico, claro, explícito, preciso. **2** específico, determinado. **3 [– to]** específico de, limitado a, que se encuentra especialmente en: *smallpox is specific to men = la viruela es específica del hombre.* || *s.c.* **4** MED. tratamiento específico. || **5 – gravity,** FIS. peso específico. **6 specifics,** datos específicos, detalles específicos.
specifically | spɪ'sɪfɪkəlɪ | *adv.* **1** específicamente, particularmente, expresamente. **2** específicamente, taxativamente, exactamente. **3** en especial, para ser más exactos.
specification | ˌspesɪfɪ'keɪʃn | *s.i.* **1** especificación; requisito. || **2 specifications, a)** descripción detallada, características, normas, instrucciones (para una máquina, un edificio); **b)** presupuesto detallado.
specify | 'spesɪfaɪ | *v.t.* especificar, detallar, precisar, explicar, mencionar: *I specified that they came in formal clothes = precisé que vinieran de etiqueta.*
specimen | 'spesɪmɪn | *s.c.* **1 [– (of)]** espécimen, ejemplar, modelo. **2** muestra (para analizar). **3** (fam. y desp.) espécimen, individuo, tipo: *a strange specimen = un tipo raro.*
specious | 'spiːʃəs | *adj.* (form. y desp.) engañoso, aparente, ilusorio, falaz: *a specious argument = un argumento engañoso.*
speck | spek | *s.c.* **[– (of)] 1** mota, partícula. **2** manchita, marca. **3** (fig.) punto (en el horizonte). **4** pizca, poquito, ápice, vestigio: *a speck of truth = un ápice de verdad.*

speckle | 'spekl | *s.c.* **1** punto, salpicadura, mancha, mota, marca. || *v.t.* **2** motear, salpicar.
speckled | 'spekld | *adj.* moteado, pinto, salpicado, manchado: *a spekled hen = una gallina pinta.*
spectacle | 'spektəkl | *s.c.* **1** espectáculo, exhibición. **2 [– (of)]** (fig.) espectáculo, situación lamentable, ridículo: *an awful spectacle that was = eso fue un espectáculo lamentable.* || *s.c.* e *i.* **3** espectáculo, vista, panorama. || **4 to make a – of oneself,** dar el espectáculo, hacer el ridículo. **5 spectacles,** (form.) gafas, lentes, anteojos.
spectacular | spek'tækjulər | *adj.* **1** espectacular, impresionante, grandioso. || *s.c.* **2** espectáculo, obra espectacular, exhibición impresionante (musical, teatral, etc...).
spectacularly | spek'tækjuləlɪ | *adv.* espectacularmente, de forma impresionante, con grandiosidad.
spectator | spek'teɪtər | (EE.UU.) | 'spekteɪtər | *s.c.* espectador, asistente, concurrente.
spectra | 'spektrə | *pl.* de **spectrum.**
spectral | 'spektrəl | *adj.* **1** (lit.) espectral, fantasmal. **2** FIS. espectral.
spectre | 'spektər | (EE.UU. **specter**) *s.c.* **1** espectro, fantasma, aparición. **2** (fig.) fantasma, amenaza: *the spectre of a nuclear war = el fantasma de una guerra nuclear.*
spectrum | spektrəm | [*pl.* **spectra**] *s.sing.* **1** espectro, gama. **2** FIS. espectro.
speculate | 'spekjuleɪt | *v.t.* e *i.* **1** especular, hacer conjeturas, pensar, reflexionar: *speculating on the truth of the case = especulando sobre la verdad del asunto.* **2** COM. especular, negociar, comerciar: *she kept speculating in Texaco shares = continuaba especulando con acciones de Texaco.*
speculation | ˌspekju'leɪʃn | *s.c.* e *i.* **1** especulación, conjetura, reflexión, teoría. **2** COM. especulación.
speculative | 'spekjulətɪv | *adj.* **1** especulativo, contemplativo, pensativo, meditativo. **2** [no *comp.*] teórico, basado en la razón. **3** COM. especulativo, arriesgado.
speculatively | 'spekjulətɪvlɪ | *adv.* especulativamente, interrogativamente, inquisitivamente.
speculator | 'spekjuleɪtər | *s.c.* COM. especulador.
sped | sped | *pret.* y *p.p.irreg.* de **speed.**
speech | spiːtʃ | *s.i.* **1** habla, palabra: *the faculty of speech = la facultad de hablar.* **2** lenguaje, lengua, idioma, dialecto, habla (de un grupo, de una región). || *s.c.* **3 [– (to)]** discurso, conferencia, disertación, alocución. **4** parlamento, recitado (en el teatro). || **5 to give/make/deliver a –,** pronunciar un discurso, dar una conferencia. **6 – day,** acto de fin de curso, día de la entrega de premios (en la escuela). **7 – therapist,** MED. logopeda. **8 – therapy,** MED. logopedia.
speechless | spiːtʃlis | *adj.* **[– (with)]** mudo, enmudecido, sin habla, estupefacto, atónito.
speed | spiːd | *s.c.* e *i.* **1** FIS. velocidad: *at a speed of 90 Km an hour = a una velocidad de 90 por hora.* || *s.i.* **2** velocidad, ligereza, presteza, rapidez, prisa. **3** (jerga) anfetamina, estimulante. || *s.c.* **4** FOT. velocidad de obturación; sensibilidad (de la película). || *v.* [*pret.* y *p.p.* **speeded** or **speed**] *t.* e *i.* **5** pasar a gran velocidad, ir(se) de prisa, apresurar(se), correr a toda velocidad. || *v.i.* **6** correr mucho, conducir deprisa. || *sufijo* **7** de velocidades, de marchas: *a five-speed car = un coche de 5 velocidades.* || **8 a turn of –,** V. **turn. 9 at –,** deprisa, rápidamente. **10 at full –,** a toda velocidad, a velocidad máxima. **11 to be speeding,** exceder el límite de velocidad. **12 more-haste, less –,** V. **haste. 13 to pick up/gather –,** acelerar, cobrar velocidad. **14 – limit,** límite de velocidad. **15 to – someone on their way,** despedir a uno, desear un feliz viaje. **16 – trap,** zona de control policial de velocidad. **17 to – up,** darse prisa, ir más deprisa, acelerar (un proceso, la marcha). **18 with all –/haste,** tan pronto como sea posible. **19 with lightning –,** V. **lightning.**
speedboat | 'spiːdbəut | *s.c.* motora, lancha rápida.
speeding | 'spiːdɪŋ | *s.i.* exceso de velocidad.
speedometer | spiː'dɒmɪtər | *s.c.* velocímetro, cuentakilómetros.
speedway | 'spiːdweɪ | *s.i.* **1** DEP. carrera de motocicletas. || *s.c.* **2** pista de carreras (para motocicletas). **3** (EE.UU.) autopista.
speedwell | 'spiːdwel | *s.c.* BOT. verónica.
speedy | 'spiːdɪ | *adj.* **1** rápido, veloz. **2** presta, pronta (una respuesta). **3** (jerga) estimulante, anfetamínico.
speedily | 'spiːdɪlɪ | *adv.* rápidamente, velozmente.
speleologist | ˌspelɪ'ɒlədʒɪst | *s.c.* espeleólogo.
speleology, spelaeology | ˌspelɪ'ɒlədʒɪ | *s.i.* espeleología (ciencia, deporte).
spell | spel | *v.irr.* (brit.) *pret.* y *p.p.* **spelt,** (EE.UU.) **spelled.** *t.* e *i.* **1** escribir correctamente, tener buena ortografía. || *v.t.* **2** [no pasiva] deletrear, formar, componer (palabras). **3** (fam.) querer decir, significar, traer consigo, presagiar: *that spelt bad news = eso presagiaba malas noticias.* **4** sustituir, reemplazar, relevar. || *s.c.* **5** período, momento, racha, fase, rato, temporada: *a short spell of cold weather = una corta temporada de frío.* **6** ataque, acceso: *a flu spell = un acceso de gripe.* **7** relevo, sustitución. **8** turno, tanda. **9** encantamiento, conjuro, palabras mágicas. || *s.sing.* **10** encanto, hechizo (fig.) encanto, fascinación. **11** trance. || **12 to – out, a)** deletrear; **b)** explicar detalladamente, definir claramente. **13 under someone's –,** cautivado por alguien, fascinado por alguien.
spellbinding | 'spelbaɪndɪŋ | *adj.* fascinante, cautivador, encantador.
spellbound | 'spelbaund | *adj.* fascinado, encantado, hechizado, cautivado, embelesado.
speller | 'spelər | *s.c.* **1 to be a bad =N,** tener mala ortografía. **2** (EE.UU.) abecedario, silabario.
spelling | spelɪŋ | *s.i.* **1** deletreo, escritura. || *s.c.* **2** ortografía.
spelt | spelt | *pret.* y *p.p.* de **spell.**
spend | spend | *v.* [*irr.pret.* y *p.p.* **spent**] *t.* e *i.* **1 [to – (on)]** gastar, invertir, dedicar (dinero). || *v.t.* **2 [to – +** *o.* **+** *ger./adv./prep.*] pasar, utilizar, emplear (tiempo). **3** (lit.) extinguir, consumir, agotar, desgastar (la fuerza). **4** despilfarrar, derrochar, malgastar. **5** sacrificar, arriesgar. || **6 to – a penny,** V. **penny. 7 to – the night with,** pasar la noche con, acostarse con.
spender | 'spendər | *s.c.* gastador, derrochador: *he's a big spender = es un derrochador.*
spending | 'spendɪŋ | *s.i.* **1** gasto, dispendio, desembolso. || **2 – money,** dinero para gastos personales.
spendthrift | 'spendərɪft | *s.c.* **1** (desp.) gastador, derrochador, despilfarrador, manirroto. || *adj.* **2** derrochador, de despilfarro.
spent | spent | **1** *pret.* y *p.p.* de **spend.** || *adj.* **2** gastado, consumido, agotado, terminado. **3** viejo, pasado. **4** viciado (el aire). || **5 a – force,** algo pasado de moda; una vieja gloria. **6 to be –,** (lit.) estar exhausto, estar agotado.
sperm | spəːm | [*pl.* **sperm** o **sperms**] *s.c.* BIOL. **1** esperma, espermatozoo. || *s.i.* **2** semen. || **3 – whale,** ZOOL. cachalote.
spermatozoa | ˌspəːmətəu'zəuə | *pl.* de **spermatozoon.**
spermatozoon | ˌspəːmətəu'zəuɒn | [*pl.* **spermatozoa**] *s.i.* BIOL. espermatozoo.
spew | spjuː | *v.t.* e *i.* **1** fluir, brotar, salir. **2** lanzar, arrojar, echar: *a volcano spewing lava = un volcán arrojando lava.* **3 [to – (up)]** (jerga) vomitar, devolver.
sphere | sfɪər | *s.c.* **1** GEOM. esfera. **2** bola, globo. **3** planeta, orbe, globo. **4** (lit.) cielo, esfera celeste. **5** (fig.) esfera, área, competencia, dominio, campo (de conocimiento, de acción). **6** esfera, clase, círculo, posición (social). || **7 – of influence,** POL. área de influencia.
spherical | 'sferɪkl | *adj.* esférico, redondo.
sphinx | sfɪŋks | *s.c.* **1** esfinge. **2** (fig.) esfinge, persona enigmática.
spice | spaɪs | *s.c.* e *i.* **1** especia. || *s.i.* **2** interés, sabor picante, sabor; placer, deleite. || *v.t.* **3 [to – (up/with)]** adornar, añadir (interés, humor), dar cierto sabor picante (a una historia): *she spiced it with humor = le añadió humor.* **4 [to – (with)]** (generalmente pasiva) sazonar, condimentar, poner especias: *spice in with coriander = sazónalo con cilantro.* || **5 variety is the – of life,** en la variedad está el gusto, la variedad es la sal de la vida.
spiced | spaɪst | *adj.* especiado, sazonado, condimentado.
spick-and-span | 'spɪkˌəns'pæn | *adj.* impecable, limpísimo, reluciente, como un jaspe, hecho un primor (una habitación, una casa).
spicy | 'spaɪsɪ | *adj.* **1** especiado, picante, aromático, fuerte (un sabor, un olor). **2** picante, sabroso, audaz, satírico, atrevido: *spicy details = detalles sabrosos.*
spider | 'spaɪdər | *s.c.* **1** ZOOL. araña. **2** trébedes. **3** trípode.
spidery | 'spaɪdərɪ | *adj.* **1** fina, semejante a las patas de araña, alargada y angular (la letra). **2** lleno de arañas.
spiel | ʃpiːl | (EE.UU.) | spiːl | *s.c.* e *i.* (argot y desp.) perorata, palabrería, discurso, disertación (para convencer a alguien).

spike | spaɪk | *s.c.* **1** pincho, púa, punta, flecha, barrote rematado en punta. **2** DEP. clavo, tachuela (de una bota). **3** TEC. vértice, cúspide, subida pronunciada (de un gráfico). **4** BOT. espiga. **5** clavo largo, escarpia, punta. **6** ZOOL. cuerno, asta (no ramificado). **7** caballa joven. || *v.t.* **8** clavar un pincho, atravesar con un pincho, empalar, perforar. **9** **[to – (with)]** (EE.UU. y fam.) añadir alcohol: *she spiked my coffee with rum = añadió ron a mi café.* **10** impedir, bloquear, frenar, parar (los rumores, una publicación). || **11 to – someone's guns,** (fam.) frustrar los planes de alguien, anular los proyectos de alguien.

spiked | spaɪkt | *adj.* **1** con púas. **2** con tachuelas, claveteada (una bota).

spiky | 'spaɪkɪ | *adj.* **1** en punta, puntiagudo, erizado, espigado: *spiky hair = pelo en punta.* **2** (fam. y fig.) irritable, irascible, malhumorado.

spill | spɪl | *v.irr.* (brit.) *pret.* y *p.p.* **spilt,** (EE.UU.) **spilled.** *t.* e *i.* **1** derramar, verter, volcar. || *v.i.* **2** **[to – + *adv./prep.* (over)]** extenderse, desbordar (una multitud). || *v.t.* **3** hacer caer, arrojar (a un jinete). **4** MAR. quitar viento (a la vela). || *s.c.* **5** (también **spillage**) vuelco, derrame, vertido (de líquido). **6** (fam.) caída, accidente (de caballo, de bicicleta). **7** mecha, astilla (para encender un fuego, un cigarrillo). || **8 to cry over spilt milk,** V. **milk.** **9 to – out,** divulgar, difundir, extender, revelar (un secreto). **10 to – the beans,** V. **bean.** **11 to – someone's blood,** (lit.) matar a alguien, derramar la sangre de alguien. **12 thrills and spills,** V. **thrill.**

spillage | 'spɪlɪdʒ | *s.c.* e *i.* vertido, derramamiento, descarga (de petróleo de un barco en el mar).

spilt | spɪlt | *pret.* y *p.p.* de **spill.**

spin | spɪn | *v.* [*irr.pret.* **span** o **spun,** *p.p.* **spun,** *ger.* **spinning**] *t.* e *i.* **1** girar, rotar, dar vueltas, hacer girar: *I spun round to better observe her = giré para verla mejor.* **2** echar a cara o cruz. **3** rodar, bailar. **4** (fig.) dar vueltas (la cabeza). **5** hacer bailar, bailar (la peonza). **6** hilar. || *v.t.* **7** tejer, producir en forma de hilo (una araña, un gusano). **8** centrifugar (en la lavadora, en la secadora). **9** AER. descender en barrena. || *v.i.* **10** **[to – + *adv./prep.*]** (fam.) rodar velozmente, ir muy deprisa (en un vehículo). || *s.c.* **11** vuelta, giro, rotación. **12** (fam.) vuelta, paseo, salida, excursión. **13** AER. barrena. || *s.sing.* **14** rotación, movimiento giratorio. **15** centrifugado (de ropa). **16** DEP. rotación lateral, torcimiento, efecto (en tenis, en billar). **17** AER. barrena, caída en espiral. **18** (fam.) caída súbita, caída en picado. **19** (fam.) pánico, estado de ansiedad, nerviosismo. || **20 to be in a –/in a flat –,** estar completamente aturdido, estar muy confuso, estar totalmente despistado. **21 to – a story/yarn,** contar un cuento, narrar una aventura. **22 – drier,** centrifugadora. **23 to – off, a)** producir un resultado secundario, producir un derivado; **b)** (EE.UU.) derivar, segregar (una compañía). **24 to – out, a)** (brit. y desp.) alargar, extender, prolongar (una actividad); **b)** hacer durar (el dinero).

spina bifida | ˌspaɪnə'bɪfɪdə | *s.i.* MED. espina bífida.

spinach | 'spɪnɪdʒ | *s.i.* BOT. espinaca.

spinal | 'spaɪnl | *adj.* **1** ANAT. espinal. || **2 – column,** (form.) ANAT. columna vertebral, espina dorsal. **3 – cord,** ANAT. médula espinal.

spindle | 'spɪndl | *s.c.* **1** MEC. perno, eje. **2** huso.

spindly | 'spɪndlɪ | *adj.* (fam. y desp.) larguirucho, delgaducho: *spindly legs = piernas delgaduchas.*

spin-dry | ˌspɪn'draɪ | *v.t.* centrifugar (la ropa).

spin-drier | ˌspɪn'draɪər | *s.c.* centrifugadora, secadora por centrifugación.

spine | spaɪn | *s.c.* **1** (también **backbone, spinal column**) ANAT. columna vertebral, espina dorsal, espinazo. **2** BOT. espina, pincho. **3** ZOOL. púa, aguijón. **4** lomo (de un libro).

spine-chilling | 'spaɪnˌtʃɪlɪŋ | *adj.* de terror, de miedo: *a spine-chilling film = una película de terror.*

spineless | 'spaɪnlɪs | *adj.* **1** (fig. y desp.) cobarde, miedoso, blando, débil, falto de coraje, falto de voluntad, sin temple (una persona). **2** invertebrado, sin columna vertebral (un animal). **3** sin espinas, sin púas.

spinelessly | 'spaɪnlɪslɪ | *adv.* cobardemente, débilmente, con miedo.

spinelessness | spaɪnlɪsnɪs | *s.i.* cobardía, falta de voluntad, debilidad, miedo.

spinet | spɪ'net | *s.c.* MUS. espineta.

spinner | 'spɪnər | *s.c.* **1** hilandero, hilador. **2** DEP. bola con efecto (en críquet). **3** DEP. jugador que envía la bola con efecto (de críquet). **4** cebo artificial giratorio (para pescar). **5** aguja giratoria (en juegos de azar). **6** AER. ojiva, como (de la hélice).

spinney | 'spɪnɪ | *s.c.* (brit.) matorral, maleza, bosquecillo.

spinning | 'spɪnɪŋ | *s.i.* **1** hila, hilado, arte de hilar, hilanza. || *adj.* **2** de hilar. || **3 – jenny,** MEC. hiladora con varios husos. **4 – mill,** hilandería. **5 – wheel,** rueca, torno de hilar.

spin-off | 'spɪnɒf | *s.c.* e *i.* **1** subproducto, producto secundario, derivado. **2** consecuencia, secuela. **3** segunda parte, película, libro o serie de televisión derivada de otra, a partir de un personaje o varios: *the Colby is a spin-off from Dinasty = los Colby es la segunda parte de Dinastía.*

spinster | 'spɪnstər | *s.c.* **1** (form. y arc.) soltera, solterona. **2** hilandera.

spinsterhood | 'spɪnstəhʊd | *s.i.* soltería (de una mujer).

spiny | 'spaɪnɪ | *adj.* **1** espinoso, puntiagudo. **2** con púas, erizado de púas.

spiral | spaɪərəl | *adj.* **1** espiral, helicoidal, en espiral. **2** de caracol (una escalera). || *s.c.* **3** espiral, hélice. **4** (fig.) espiral, aceleración creciente o decreciente: *a spiral of inflaction = una espiral inflacionista.* || *v.i.* [(brit.) **spiralled, spiralling,** (EE.UU.) **spiraled, spiraling**]. **5** **[to – + *adv./prep.*]** moverse en espiral, dar vueltas en espiral: *the paper spiralled to the street = el papel cayó en espiral hacia la calle.* **6** subir vertiginosamente (los precios). || **7 to – downwards,** caer en picado, bajar vertiginosamente (los precios).

spire | 'spaɪər | *s.c.* **1** ARQ. aguja, chapitel: *the numerous church spires of Oxford = los numerosos chapiteles de las iglesias de Oxford.* **2** BOT. brizna. **3** cúspide, pináculo, cima.

spirit | 'spɪrɪt | *s.c.* **1** espíritu, alma, mente. **2** ser, persona, individuo: *a brave spirit = una persona valiente.* **3** ánima, fantasma, aparecido; hada. || *s.i.* **4** energía, determinación, brío, temple, ánimo, valor, coraje. **5** espíritu, tendencia: *he's got team spirit = tiene espíritu de equipo.* || *s.sing.* **6** **[– (of)]** espíritu, carácter, esencia, significado, propósito (de una ley, de un acuerdo). **7** **[– (of)]** espíritu, estado de ánimo, humor; alegría, animación. **8** actitud, gesto, postura, aire, disposición. || *v.t.* **9** **[to – + *o.* + *adv./prep.*]** llevarse deprisa y en secreto, llevarse misteriosamente: *the singer was spirited through the back door = el cantante fue sacado en secreto por la puerta trasera.* **10** animar, alentar, reanimar. || **11 to enter into the – of,** divertirse, pasarlo bien, meterse de lleno en. **12 high spirits,** V. **high.** **13 in –,** en espíritu: *we'll be there in spirit = estaremos allí en espíritu.* **14 kindred –,** V. **kindred.** **15 – level,** nivel de burbuja, nivel de aire. **16 spirits, a)** estado de ánimo, humor, temple; **b)** bebida alcohólica, licor fuerte: *brandy is a spirit = el coñac es una bebida alcohólica;* **c)** QUIM. alcohol; gasolina. **17 that's the –!,** ¡ánimo!, ¡anímate! **18 the – of the age /time,** el espíritu de los tiempos, de la época.

spirited | 'spɪrɪtɪd | *adj.* **1** animoso, voluntarioso, brioso, determinado. **2** fogoso, enérgico (una pelea, un animal).

spiritless | 'spɪrɪtlɪs | *adj.* **1** apocado, débil, falto de ánimo, falto de espíritu. **2** deprimido, triste, afligido, melancólico.

spiritual | 'spɪrɪtjʊəl | *adj.* **1** espiritual, anímico, psíquico, mental. **2** espiritual, religioso: *a spiritual adviser = un consejero espiritual.* **3** (form.) eclesiástico. **4** incorpóreo, sobrenatural. || *s.c.* **5** MUS. espiritual, canción religiosa (de los negros). || **6 – home,** patria espiritual, patria de adopción.

spiritualism | 'spɪrɪtjʊəlɪzəm | *s.i.* **1** espiritismo. **2** FIL. espiritualismo.

spiritualist | 'spɪrɪtjʊəlɪst | *s.c.* **1** espiritista. **2** FIL. espiritualista.

spirituality | ˌspɪrɪtjʊ'ælɪtɪ | *s.i.* espiritualidad.

spiritually | 'spɪrɪtjʊəlɪ | *adv.* espiritualmente.

spit | spɪt | *v.* [*irr.pret.* y *p.p.* **spat,** (EE.UU.) **spit,** *ger.* **spitting**] *t.* e *i.* **1** escupir, esputar, expectorar. || *v.t.* **2** **[to – (out)]** (fig.) escupir, arrojar, bufar, desembuchar (una respuesta). **3** espetar, pinchar, clavar (carne para asar). || *v.i.* **4** **[it + v. (with)]** lloviznar, caer unas gotas: *it's spitting with rain = están cayendo unas gotas.* **5** chisporrotear, (el fuego, una fritura). || *s.i.* **6** saliva, escupitajo, esputo. **7** **[the – (of)]** imagen, estampa, figura: *she's the spit of her mother = es la imagen de su madre.* || *s.c.* **8** espetón, asador, pincho, barilla (para asar carne). **9** GEOG. punta de tierra, lengua de tierra; banco de arena. || **10 – it out!,** (fam.) ¡desembucha!, ¡dilo de una vez!, ¡escupe lo que tengas que decir! **11 – and polish,** (fam.) arreglo, limpieza profunda, buena pasada (de una casa). **12 the spitting image of,/the – and image,/the**

dead – of, la viva imagen de, el vivo retrato de, la misma estampa que. **13 within spitting distance,** (fam.) muy cerca, a tiro de piedra.

spite | spaɪt | *s.i.* **1** rencor, despecho, ojeriza, resentimiento. || *v.t.* **2** fastidiar, molestar, incomodar, herir, mortificar: *she did that just to spite me = lo hizo sólo para molestarme.* || **3 to cut off one's nose to – one's face,** vengarse de alguien a costa de uno mismo, fastidiar a alguien a pesar del daño que uno mismo se hace. **4 in – of,** a pesar de, no obstante.

spiteful | 'spaɪtfʊl | *adj.* rencoroso, despechado, resentido, malévolo, vengativo.

spitefully | 'spaɪtfəlɪ | *adv.* rencorosamente, maliciosamente, con despecho, con resentimiento, vengativamente.

spitfire | 'spɪtˌfaɪər | *s.c.* fiera, salvaje, cascarrabias (una mujer).

spittle | 'spɪtl | *s.i.* saliva, salivazo, baba.

spittoon | 'spɪ'tu:n | (EE.UU. **cuspitor**) *s.c.* escupidera.

splash | splæʃ | *v.t.* e *i.* **1** caer ruidosamente, tirar ruidosamente, golpetear (agua, barro): *the waves splashed against the window = las olas golpeteaban contra la ventana.* **2 [to – (out/on)]** (fam. y brit.) derrochar, malgastar (dinero). || *v.t.* **3 [to – (with)]** esparcir, rociar, salpicar, manchar (con agua): *falling down he splashed us with water = al caer nos salpicó de agua.* **4** (fam.) dar mucha importancia, publicar con grandes titulares (una noticia). || *v.i.* **5** chapotear, chapalear (en el agua, en el barro): *splashing through the street puddles = chapoteando en los charcos de la calle.* || *s.c.* **6** chapoteo, chapaleo, ruido sordo (al caer en el agua): *she fell with a splash = cayó produciendo un ruido sordo en el agua.* **7** mancha, manchón, salpicadura, rociada: *a splash of milk on the floor = una mancha de leche en la alfombra.* **8** (fam.) impresión, efecto, sensación, éxito. **9** (brit.) gota, chorrito, poquito: *just a splash of milk in my tea = sólo un chorrito de leche en mi té.* || *adv.* **10** [– + *prep.*] con un chapoteo, con enorme ruido: *and the book fell splash into the water = y el libro cayó con un enorme ruido al agua.* || **11 to be splashed with colour/light,** tener zonas coloridas, tener manchas de luz. **12 to make a –,** causar sensación, asombrar, impresionar. **13 to – down,** AER. amarar, amerizar, posarse en el mar. **14 to – out,** (fam.) derrochar (dinero).

splashdown | 'splæʃdaʊn | *s.c.* e *i.* AER. amaraje, amerizaje, descenso en el mar (de una cápsula espacial).

splat | splæt | *s.sing.* **1** (fam.) ruido sordo, chapoteo (de algo húmedo). || *v.t.* e *i.* [*pret.* y *p.p.* **splatted,** *ger.* **splatting**] **2 [to – (against)]** (fam.) golpear sordamente, caer con ruido sordo (como de algo húmedo): *the egg splatted against the wall = los tomates golpearon la pared con ruido sordo.*

splatter | 'splætər | *v.t.* e *i.* **1** salpicar, rociar, manchar. || *s.c.* **2** salpicadura, chapoteo (ruido): *the splatter of the rain against the roof = el chapoteo de la lluvia contra el tejado.*

splay | spleɪ | *v.t.* e *i.* **1** derrumbar(se), despatarrar(se), caer(se) (sin gracia). **2** abrir(se), separar(se), partir(se) (al medio). **3** achaflanar, biselar. **4** dislocar(se) (un hueso un animal). || *adj.* **5** abierto, extendido, desplegado. **6** despatarrado, desmañado, derrumbado. || *s.i.* **7** extensión, expansión. **8** bisel, chaflán.

spleen | spli:n | *s.c.* **1** ANAT. bazo. || *s.i.* **2** (lit.) mal humor, bilis. || **3 to vent one's –,** (fig.) descargar la bilis.

splendid | 'splendɪd | *adj.* **1** espléndido, soberbio, suntuoso, impresionante, magnífico, vistoso, grandioso: *splendid jewels = joyas impresionantes.* **2** excelente, estupendo, maravilloso, fantástico, muy bueno: *a splendid day = un día maravilloso.*

splendidly | 'splendɪdlɪ | *adv.* **1** espléndidamente, suntuosamente, soberbiamente, esplendorosamente. **2** excelentemente, estupendamente, maravillosamente, fantásticamente.

splendiferous | splen'dɪfərəs | *adj.* (brit., fam. y hum.) espléndido, magnífico, maravilloso, grandioso.

splendour | 'splendər | (EE.UU. **splendor**) *s.i.* **1** esplendor, vistosidad, magnificencia, grandiosidad. || *s.sing.* **2** grandeza, esplendor, pompa.

splenetik | splɪ'netɪk | *adj.* **1** (form.) irritable, malhumorado, destemplado, enfadadizo, hosco, gruñón. **2** del bazo, cercano al bazo.

splice | splaɪs | *v.t.* **1 [to – (to/onto/together)]** empalmar, unir, juntar, pegar (una cinta, una película, una cuerda). || *s.c.* **2** empalme, unión. || **3 to get spliced,** (brit. y fam.) unirse en matrimonio, casarse.

splint | splɪnt | *s.c.* **1** tablilla (para impedir el movimiento): *the bird had a splint on its wing = el pájaro tenía una tablilla en el ala.* **2** varilla (para el entramado de un cesto). **3** ZOOL. sobrehueso (de un caballo). || *v.t.* **4** entablillar (un hueso roto).

splinter | 'splɪntər | *s.c.* **1** astilla, esquirla (de madera, cristal, hueso). || *v.t.* e *i.* **2** astillar(se), hacer(se) astillas, romper(se) en esquirlas. || *v.i.* **3 [to – (off)]** separarse, dividirse, disociarse (de una organización). || **4 – group,** facción o grupúsculo disidente (de una organización, de un partido).

splintery | 'splɪntərɪ | *adj.* astilloso, que se puede astillar: *a splintery surface = una superficie astillosa.*

split | splɪt | *v.* [*irr.pret.* y *p.p.* **split,** *ger.* **splitting**] *t.* e *i.* **1** partir(se), romper(se), rasgar(se), quebrar(se), rajar(se). **2 [to – (up/into)]** dividir(se), fraccionar(se), escindir(se), disgregar(se) (en grupos, partes): *the team split into two groups = el equipo se dividió en dos grupos.* || *v.t.* **3** dividir, repartir, distribuir: *they split the money = repartieron el dinero.* **4** DEP. ganar la mitad de los partidos. || *v.i.* **5 [to – up/with]** separarse, desunirse, romper relaciones (amorosas): *they split up last year = se separaron el año pasado.* **6 [to – on]** (brit. y fam.) chivarse, contar secretos, soplar. **7** (arc. y jerga) largarse, marcharse, irse. || *s.c.* **8 [– (in)]** grieta, raja, hendidura, fisura, ranura, rendija, brecha. **9 [– (in)]** escisión, división, cisma. **10** ruptura, separación (entre personas). **11** astilla, esquirla, fragmento. **12** tiras de mimbre (para cestería). **13** división, partición, parcelación, repartición. **14** copa de frutas cortadas en dos con helado (postre). **15** media botella, media jarra, media porción (de una bebida). || *adj.* **16** dividido, separado, fragmentado, cuarteado, rajado. || **17 to – hairs,** (desp.) pararse en los más nimios detalles, ser muy puntilloso, ser muy pejiguero. **18 – infinitive,** GRAM. infinitivo con una o más palabras interpuestas entre **to** y el verbo: *to easily win = ganar fácilmente.* **19 to – off, a)** resquebrajarse, separarse, desprenderse; **b)** escindirse, separarse (de un grupo). **20 to – one's sides,** (fam.) partirse de risa, desencajarse de risa. **21 – pea,** arveja seca (dividida en mitades). **22 – personality,** PSIQ. doble personalidad. **23 – second,** fracción de segundo, abrir y cerrar de ojos. **24 splits,** DEP. **a)** tijera, despatarrada (postura acrobática, en que se abren las piernas en línea recta); **b)** posición de bolos (en que es imposible derribarlos todos). **25 to – the difference,** (fam.) partir la diferencia.

split-level | 'splɪtˌlevl | *adj.* a desnivel, construida sobre dos niveles (una casa, generalmente construida sobre un terreno inclinado).

split-screen | 'splɪtˌskri:n | *adj.* **1** TV. mezcla, proceso por el que dos tomas se muestran al mismo tiempo, una a la derecha y otra a la izquierda. **2** INF. pantalla dividida, pantalla partida.

splitting | 'splɪtɪŋ | *adj.* muy fuerte, enloquecedor, terrible, agudo: *a splitting headache = un dolor de cabeza muy fuerte.*

splodge | splɒdʒ | (EE.UU. **splotch**) *s.c.* **1 [– (of)]** (fam.) manchón, borrón. || *v.t.* **2** manchar, llenar de borrones.

splodgy | 'splɒdʒɪ | *adj.* manchado, emborronado: *a splodgy paper = un papel emborronado.*

splotch | splɒtʃ | *s.c.* (EE.UU.) V. **splodge.**

splurge | splə:dʒ | *v.t.* e *i.* **1 [to – (on)]** (fam.) gastar en exceso, gastar más de lo que se gana. || *s.c.* **2** ostentación, exceso,lujo.

splutter | 'splʌtər | *s.c.* **1** chisporroteo, crepitación (del fuego). || *v.t.* e *i.* **2** tartamudear, farfullar, balbucear. || *v.i.* **3** chisporrotear, crepitar (el fuego).

spoil | spɔɪl | *v.t.* [*irr.pret.* y *p.p.* **spoiled** o **spoilt**] **1** estropear, echar a perder, arruinar, destrozar: *spoiling our holidays = estropeando nuestras vacaciones.* **2** dañar, deteriorar, perjudicar. **3** mimar, consentir, malcriar, ser indulgente, ser complaciente. **4** POL. rellenar mal, estropear (una papeleta de voto para inutilizarla). **5** despojar, empobrecer, arrebatar. || *v.i.* **6** pudrirse, deteriorarse, ponerse mal (una comida). || **7 to be spoiling for a fight,** tener ganas de pelea, estar buscando pelea. **8 to be spoilt for choice,** ser muy difícil elegir (entre tantas cosas). **9 to spare the rod and – the child,** V. **spare. 10 spoils,** (lit.) despojos, botín; recompensa, trofeos. **11 too many cooks – the broth,** V. **cook.**

spoilage | 'spɔɪlɪdʒ | *s.i.* (form.) desperdicio, desecho, residuos.

spoiled, spoilt | spɔɪləd | *adj.* mimado, malcriado, consentido.

spoilsport | 'spɔɪlspɔ:t | *s.c.* (fam.) aguafiestas, espantagustos, amargado.

spoilt | spɔɪlt | *pret.* y *p.p.irreg.* de **spoil.**

spoke | spəʊk | 1 *pret.* de **speak.** || *s.c.* 2 radio (de una rueda). 3 MAR. cabilla (del timón). 4 peldaño, barra (de una escalera de mano). || **5 to put a – in someone's wheel,** (fam.) ponerle la zancadilla a alguien, poner obstáculos a alguien, poner trabas a alguien.

spoken | spəʊkən | 1 *p.p.* de **speak.** || *adj.* 2 hablado, oral: *spoken English = inglés hablado.* || *sufijo* 3 [*adv.* + –] hablado: *badly-spoken = malhablado.* || **4 – for,** (fam.) **a)** reservado, vendido; **b)** comprometido, prometido (una persona).

spokesman | 'spəʊksmən | *s.c.m.* portavoz (de un grupo, de una organización).

spokesperson | 'spəʊkspɜːsn | *s.c.* portavoz (no indica si es femenino o masculino).

spokeswoman | 'spəʊks,wʊmən | *s.c.f.* portavoz.

sponge | spʌndʒ | *s.c.* 1 ZOOL. esponja. 2 gorrón, parásito (una persona). || *s.c.* e *i.* 3 esponja, material esponjoso: *a make-up sponge = una esponja para retirar el maquillaje.* 4 (brit.) bizcocho. 5 (jerga) borracho, gran bebedor; glotón. || *v.t.* 6 **[to – (down/off/out)]** limpiar con esponja, lavar con paño húmedo. 7 **[to – (up)]** absorber con esponja, quitar (una mancha) con esponja. || **8 – cake,** bizcocho. **9 to – off/on/from,** (desp.) vivir de gorra, vivir a costa de, gorronear, dar sablazos. **10 to throw in the –,** rendirse, darse por vencido.

spongebag | 'spʌndʒbæg | *s.c.* (brit.) bolsa de aseo, neceser.

sponger | 'spʌndʒər | *s.c.* (fam. y desp.) gorrón, parásito, sablista, sanguijuela.

spongy | 'spʌndʒɪ | *adj.* esponjoso, absorbente, mullido, poroso.

sponsor | 'spɒnsər | *s.c.* 1 patrocinador, promotor. 2 financiador, promotor. 3 padrino, madrina (de bautismo, de confirmación). 4 FIN. fiador, gerente. || *v.t.* 5 patrocinar, costear, financiar: *the concert was sponsored by Coca-Cola = Coca-Cola patrocinó el concierto.* 6 promover, fomentar, apoyar, auspiciar (un programa, una actividad, un plan). 7 apadrinar, actuar como padrino, actuar como madrina.

sponsorship | 'spɒnsəʃɪp | *s.i.* patrocinio, patronazgo.

spontaneity | ,spɒntə'neɪɪtɪ | (también **spontaneousness**). *s.i.* espontaneidad.

spontaneous | spɒn'teɪnɪəs | *adj.* 1 espontáneo, natural. 2 espontáneo, instintivo, no premeditado. 3 BOT. espontáneo.

spontaneously | spɒn'teɪnɪəslɪ | *adv.* espontáneamente, de forma natural.

spoof | spuːf | *s.c.* 1 **[– (of/on)]** (fam.) parodia, engaño, copia burda: *a spoof of Victorian way of life = una parodia de la época victoriana.* 2 truco, tomadura de pelo, broma. || *v.t.* e *i.* 3 tomar el pelo, burlarse de, engañar, bromear.

spook | spuːk | *s.c.* 1 (fam.) fantasma, espectro, aparecido. 2 (EE.UU. y fam.) espía, agente secreto. || *v.t.* 3 (EE.UU. y fam.) meter miedo, atemorizar, aterrar, espantar: *she liked spooking people at night = le gustaba meter miedo a la gente por la noche.*

spooky | spuːkɪ | *adj.* (fam.) 1 aterrador, fantasmal, espectral, misterioso. 2 inquieto, agitado, alterado, nervioso.

spool | spuːl | *s.c.* 1 carrete (de película, de una cámara). 2 (EE.UU.) canilla, bobina (de hilo). || *v.t.* 3 enrollar en carrete, hacer una canilla (una película, hilo).

spoon | spuːn | *s.c.* 1 cuchara. 2 **[– (of)]** cucharada: *one spoon of tea leaves = una cucharada de hojas de té.* 3 DEP. cucharilla, anzuelo de cuchara (para pescar). 4 MAR. remo de punta curva. 5 DEP. palo de golf de madera (para dar elevación a la pelota). || *v.t.* 6 [**to – +** *o.* + *adv./prep.*] recoger con cuchara, sacar con cuchara, servir (con cuchara): *spooning the gravy onto the plates = al servir la salsa en los platos.* || **7 to be born with a silver – in one's mouth,** ser de familia rica, haber nacido en buena cuna.

spoonerism | 'spuːnərɪzəm | *s.c.* retruécano, juego de palabras, trastocamiento de letras, de sonidos o de palabras (que producen un efecto gracioso como en "I'll sew you to a sheet" en lugar de "I'll show you to a seat").

spoon-feed | 'spuːnfiːd | *v.* [*irr.pret.* y *p.p.* **spoon-fed**] *t.* 1 alimentar con cuchara (a un bebé, a un enfermo). 2 (desp.) dar masticado, facilitar las cosas en exceso, tratar como a un niño: *you shouldn't spoon-feed the students = no deberías tratar a los alumnos como si fueran niños.*

spoonful | 'spuːnful | [*pl.* **spoonfuls** o **spoonsful**] *s.i.* **[– (of)]** cucharada (cantidad).

spoor | spʊər | *s.sing.* rastro, huella, pista, pisadas (de un animal).

sporadic | spə'rædɪk | *adj.* esporádico, ocasional, intermitente: *sporadic visits = visitas esporádicas.*

sporadically | spə'rædɪkəlɪ | *adv.* esporádicamente, ocasionalmente, intermitentemente.

spore | spɔː | *s.c.* 1 BIOL. espora. || *v.i.* 2 producir esporas, formar esporas.

sporran | 'spɒrən | *s.c.* faltriquera, escarcela (que llevan los escoceses a la cintura).

sport | spɔːt | *s.c.* e *i.* 1 deporte, ejercicio, juego, competición: *I'm not very fond of winter sports = los deportes de invierno no me atraen mucho.* || *s.c.* 2 (fam.) buen perdedor, persona generosa, buena persona, persona optimista: *she's a good sport = es una buena chica.* 3 BIOL. mutación. || *s.i.* 4 (form.) diversión, broma, chanza. || *v.t.* 5 hacer alarde de, vestir con ostentación, exhibir ostentosamente, lucir ostentosamente (ropa, joyas): *she was sporting a new diamong ring = lucía ostentosamente un nuevo anillo de diamantes.* || *v.i.* 6 (lit.) juguetear, retozar. || **7 to make – of someone,** ridiculizar a alguien, mofarse de alguien, burlarse de alguien. **8 sports car,** coche deportivo. **9 sports day,** día escolar del deporte. **10 sports jacket,** chaqueta deportiva, chaqueta de sport (de caballero).

sporting | 'spɔːtɪŋ | *adj.* 1 deportivo, caballeroso, amable (en el juego). 2 generoso, justo, equitativo (un gesto, una posibilidad, una oferta). 3 [no *comp.*] deportivo, para el deporte, del deporte, dedicado al deporte: *a sporting evening = una tarde dedicada al deporte.* || **4 a – chance,** una posibilidad de éxito.

sportsman | 'spɔːtsmən | [*pl.irreg.* **sportsmen**] *s.c.m.* 1 deportista. 2 buen perdedor, caballero.

sportsmanlike | 'spɔːtsmənlaɪk | *adj.* deportivo, caballeroso, honrado, decente, noble (el comportamiento).

sportsmanship | 'spɔːtsmənʃɪp | *s.i.* deportividad, caballerosidad, honradez, decencia, nobleza.

sportsmen | 'spɔːtsmən | *pl.irreg.* de **sportsman.**

sportswear | 'spɔːtsweər | *s.i.* ropa de deporte.

sportswoman | 'spɔːts,wʊmən | [*pl.irreg.* **sportswomen**] *s.c.f.* deportista.

sportswomen | 'spɔːtswɪmɪn | *pl.irreg.* de **sportswoman.**

sporty | 'spɔːtɪ | *adj.* (fam.) 1 (brit.) deportista, aficionado al deporte. 2 deportiva, informal, vistosa, colorida (especialmente la ropa). 3 alegre, despreocupado. 4 rápido, veloz (un coche).

spot | spɒt | *s.c.* 1 **[– (of)]** lunar, pinta, mancha: *a blouse with spots = una blusa de lunares; wipe the spots of egg, please = limpia las manchas de huevo, por favor.* 2 MED. grano, mancha, lunar, peca (en la piel). 3 (fig.) mancha, tacha, mancilla (en la reputación). 4 lugar, sitio, parte: *a nice holiday spot = un agradable lugar de vacaciones.* 5 aspecto, característica, rasgo. 6 (fam.) aprieto, apuro, situación difícil. 7 RAD. espacio, programa. 8 (fam.) posición, categoría, rango (en una organización). 9 (fam.) punto de luz, foco. || *s.sing.* 10 punto, talón de Aquiles, tema: *John's weak spot = el punto flaco de John.* 11 **[– (of)]** (brit. y fam.) poquitín, poquito, pequeña cantidad, algo: *a spot of dinner = algo de cenar.* || *s.i.* 12 gota (de lluvia). || *v.t.* [**spotted, spotting**] 13 ver, descubrir, detectar, avistar, encontrar: *we spotted a few strange objects = descubrimos algunos objetos extraños.* 14 **[to – (with)]** (generalmente *pasiva)* manchar, motear, salpicar. 15 decorar, estampar: *a piece of material spotted with blue = un trozo de tela con lunares azules.* 16 [**to – +** *o. indirecto* + *o.directo.*] (EE.UU. y fam.) dar ventaja, dejar la delantera (en el juego). || *v.i.* 17 [**it =N** + *v.*] (brit.) lloviznar, chispear, llover, gotear. || *adj.* 18 COM. al contado, de pago inmediato, contante y sonante (el dinero). 19 COM. de entrega inmediata (género). 20 al instante, en el momento (realizado, fabricado). 21 TV. publicitario, de publicidad: *a spot announcement = un anuncio publicitario.* || *adv.* 22 [– + *prep.*] (brit. y fam.) exactamente, precisamente. || **23 to change one's spots,** V. **change. 24 to have a soft – for someone,** V. **soft. 25 in a (tight) –,** entre la espada y la pared. **26 to knock spots off,** (brit. y fam.) ser infinitamente mejor que, darle cien vueltas a. **27 on the –, a)** en el sitio preciso, allí mismo; **b)** en ese preciso instante, en el momento, en el acto inmediatamente; **c)** en apuros, en un aprieto, entre la espada y la pared. **28 rooted to the –,** V. **rooted. 29 – check,** comprobación, reconocimiento.

spotless | 'spɒtlɪs | *adj.* **1** como un jaspe, sin mancha, inmaculado. **2** intachable (la reputación).

spotlessly | 'spɒtlɪslɪ | *adv.* inmaculadamente.

spotlight | 'spɒtlaɪt | *s.c.* **1** foco, reflector, lámpara. **2** **[the –]** atención, publicidad, notoriedad, prominencia. || *v.t.irr.pret.* y *p.p.* **spotlighted** o **spotlit.** **3** llamar la atención sobre, destacar, subrayar. || **4** **to be in the –,** estar en el candelero.

spotlit | 'spɒtlɪt | *adj.* iluminado.

spot-on | 'spɒtɒn | *adj.* (brit. y fam.) **1** totalmente correcto, muy cabal, totalmente exacto: *a spot-on analysis = un análisis correcto.* || *adv.* **2** correctísimamente, muy cabalmente, con total exactitud.

spotted | 'spɒtɪd | *adj.* **1** de lunares, estampado. **2** **[– (with)]** manchado, salpicado.

spotter | 'spɒtər | *s.c.* **1** localizador, descubridor, observador. **2** (fam.) persona cuyo trabajo consiste en detectar actos deshonestos (en un banco). **3** MIL. vigilante, centinela, observador. **4** RAD. locutor de deportes (que identifica fielmente a los jugadores en el campo). **5** DEP. vigilante (de prácticas deportivas). **6** empleado de tintorería (que se encarga de quitar manchas en las prendas). || *adj.* **7** MIL. de vigilancia, de observación.

spotty | 'spɒtɪ | *adj.* (generalmente desp.) **1** (brit. y fam.) lleno de granos, cubierto de pecas, cubierto de manchas (en la piel). **2** (EE.UU.) irregular, desigual: *a spotty show = un espectáculo irregular.* **3** estampado, de lunares.

spouse | spaʊz | *s.c.* (form.) **1** esposo, cónyuge, consorte. || *v.t.* **2** (arc.) desposar, casarse con.

spout | spaʊt | *v.t.* e *i.* **1** **[to – (out)]** salir a borbotones, echar a chorro (líquido). **2** llamear, salir a llamaradas. || *v.t.* **3** (fam. y desp.) hablar incansablemente, recitar sin descanso, hablar tediosamente. **4** (brit. y jerga) empeñar, entregar en prenda. || *v.i.* **5** lanzar agua a chorro, expulsar agua en forma de surtidor (las ballenas). || *s.c.* **6** espita, canilla. **7** pico, pitorro (de una jarra, de una cafetera). **8** surtidor, chorro (de agua). **9** (brit. y fam.) casa de empeño. || **10** **up the –,** (fam.) **a)** equivocado, erróneo, falso, incorrecto; **b)** (brit. y fam.) echado a perder, a hacer puñetas, acabado, perdido: *the plan has gone up the spout = el plan se ha ido a hacer puñetas.*

sprain | spreɪn | *v.t.* MED. **1** dislocar, torcer (un tobillo). || *s.c.* **2** torcedura, esguince, dislocación.

sprang | spræŋ | *pret.irreg.* de **spring.**

sprat | spræt | *s.c.* ZOOL. sardineta, arenque pequeño.

sprawl | sprɔːl | *v.t.* e *i.* **1** repantingarse, repanchingarse, arrellanarse: *sprawled out in an armchair = repanchingado en un sillón.* **2** desmadejarse, despatarrarse, caer a lo largo: *I lost balance and fell sprawling = perdí el equilibrio y caí cuan larga era.* || *v.i.* **3** **[to + *adv./prep.*]** (dep.) desparramarse de forma irregular, extenderse de manera desordenada (una ciudad, una casa). || *s.sing.* **4** postura desgarbada. **5** desparramamiento, extensión poco uniforme (de una ciudad, no planificado).

sprawled | sprɔːld | *adj.* repantigado, repanchingado, desmadejado, despatarrado, tumbado.

sprawling | sprɔːlɪŋ | *adj.* **1** desparramada irregularmente, extendida de forma desordenada (una casa, una ciudad). **2** irregular y grande (la letra).

spray | spreɪ | *v.i.* **1** [**to – +** *adv./prep.*] salir, esparcirse (un líquido). || *v.t.* **2** pulverizar, rociar, atomizar. **3** pintar con pistola pulverizadora. **4** diseminar, esparcir (objetos). || *s.i.* **5** rociada, pulverización, aspersión. **6** espuma (de mar). || *s.c.* **7** pulverizador, atomizador. **8** ramo, ramaje (de flores, una joya con ese diseño): *a spray of flowers = una ramo de flores.* || **9** **– can,** pulverizador, atomizador.

sprayer | 'spreɪər | *s.c.* pulverizador, atomizador (persona o aparato).

spread | spred | *v.* [*irr.pret.* y *p.p.* **spread**] *t.* e *i.* **1** extender(se), expandir(se), dispersar(se), desarrollar(se). **2** desplegar, extender, estirar, alargar. **3** extender(se), diseminar(se), propagar(se) (la alarma, una enfermedad). **4** **[to – (around)]** difundir, divulgar, propalar (noticias, rumores). **5** untar(se), extender(se), esparcir(se) (una crema, la mantequilla). || *v.i.* **6** [**to – +** *adv./prep.*] extenderse, cubrir (un tiempo, un área): *the village spreads as far as the mill = el pueblo se extiende hasta el molino.* || *v.t.* **7** **[to – (over/among)]** distribuir, dividir, espaciar (el coste, el trabajo). **8** compartir, repartir (un riesgo). **9** (arc.) poner, preparar (la mesa). || *s.sing.* **10** **[(the) – (of)]** diseminación, propagación, expansión, proliferación, difusión. **11** extensión, espacio (de tiempo). || *s.c.* **12** extensión, anchura, envergadura, expansión. **13** gama, rango, escala: *a wide spread of subjects = una amplia gama de materias.* **14** doble página; anuncio a doble página (en una revista, en un periódico); despliegue a toda página: *she paid for a double-page spread = pagó por un anuncio a doble página.* **15** (fam.) comilona, banquetazo, merendola. **16** (EE.UU.) rancho, granja (generalmente de gran tamaño). || *s.i.* **17** crema (queso, mermelada o paté para untar). || *s.c.* e *i.* **18** gordura, michelines (típicos de la mediana edad). || **19** **to – like wildfire,** (fig.) extenderse como el fuego, propagarse con rapidez. **20** **to – one's net,** (fig.) tender las redes para cazar a alguien, extender toda su influencia para pescar a alguien. **21** **to – one's wings,** coger alas, quitar el miedo. **22** **to – oneself, a)** ponerse cómodo, ponerse a sus anchas; **b)** explayarse, hablar mucho. **23** **to – out,** separarse, esparcirse, distanciarse, aislarse.

spread-eagled | ˌspred'iːgld | *adj.* extendido, derrumbado.

spree | spriː | *s.c.* **1** juerga, parranda, jolgorio. **2** período de gran actividad; gasto excesivo: *once they got the money they went on a shopping spree = en cuanto consiguieron el dinero fueron de compras a gastárselo todo.*

sprig | sprɪg | *s.c.* **1** **[– (of)]** ramillete, ramo (para cocinar, como decoración). **2** joven, retoño, chaval. **3** punta sin cabeza, clavo sin cabeza.

sprightliness | 'spraɪtlɪnɪs | *s.i.* animación, alegría, vivacidad, energía (en personas de edad).

sprightly | 'spraɪtlɪ | *adj.* animado, alegre, lleno de vida, enérgico (especialmente una persona de edad).

spring | sprɪŋ | *v.irr.pret.* **sprang** o **sprung,** *p.p.* **sprung.** *v.i.* **1** [**to – +** *adv./prep.*] saltar, brincar. **2** saltar con pértiga, saltar con garrocha, saltar por encima. **3** [**to – +** *adv./prep.*] levantarse, alzarse (el viento). **4** surgir, desarrollarse, nacer (una ciudad, una idea). **5** brotar (las lágrimas). **6** (fam.) aparecer, salir: *where did you spring from? = ¿de dónde sales?* **7** combarse, torcerse; resquebrajarse, rajarse (la madera). **8** saltar, salir despedido (como por resorte). || *v.t.* **9** abrirse o cerrarse con fuerza, saltar, soltar (un resorte). **10** **[to – (on)]** revelar, comunicar, divulgar (una noticia). **11** (fam.) ayudar a escapar (de prisión). || *s.c.* e *i.* **12** primavera. || *s.c.* **13** manantial, fuente. **14** resorte, muelle, espiral, ballesta. **15** salto, brinco. || *s.i.* **16** elasticidad, rebote. **17** vigor, energía, fuerza. || **18** **to – a leak,** empezar a hacer agua, abrirse una vía de agua, picarse (en un barco, una vasija). **19** **– chicken, a)** pollo tomatero; **b)** jovencito, pollo. **20** **to – from,** resultar de, producirse a partir de, tener su origen en. **21** **– onion,** (EE.UU.) **scallion,** cebolleta, cebolla de primavera. **22** **– roll,** rollito de primavera (se toma en restaurantes chinos). **23** **to – up,** surgir, aparecer repentinamente. **24** **with a – in one's step,** con alegría, con ganas, con entusiasmo.

springboard | 'sprɪŋbɔːd | *s.c.* **1** trampolín. || **2** **– for/to,** (fig.) trampolín para (el éxito).

springbok | 'sprɪŋbɒk | *s.c.* ZOOL. gacela, especie de antílope de Africa del Sur.

spring-clean | 'sprɪŋkliːn | *v.t.* e *i.* limpiar a fondo, hacer limpieza general (en casa).

spring-cleaning | 'sprɪŋkliːnɪŋ | *s.sing.* limpieza general, limpieza a fondo (de la casa).

springtime | 'sprɪŋtaɪm | *s.i.* primavera.

springy | 'sprɪŋɪ | *adj.* **1** elástico, muelle, flexible, adaptable: *a springy mattress = un colchón elástico.* **2** lleno de manantiales, con abundantes manantiales.

sprinkle | 'sprɪnkl | *v.t.* **1** rociar, salpicar, asperjar, esparcir, espolvorear (líquido, arena). **2** (fig.) sembrar, llenar, salpicar: *the book is sprinkled with examples = el libro está lleno de ejemplos.* || *v.i.* **3** [**it =N +** *v.*] lloviznar. || *s.sing.* **4** llovizna, gotas, chirimiri. **5** pizca, poquito: *a sprinkle of salt = un poquito de sal.*

sprinkler | 'sprɪnklər | *s.c.* **1** aspersor, irrigador. **2** aparato de aspersión automática (en un edificio, contra el fuego).

sprinkling | 'sprɪnklɪŋ | *s.sing.* **1** **[– (of)]** pizca, poquito, gota. **2** pequeño número, cantidad insignificante, pocos: *a sprinkling of visitors = un pequeño número de visitantes.*

sprint | sprɪnt | *v.i.* **1** correr a gran velocidad, hacer esprint (especialmente en

distancias cortas). || *s.sing.* **2** carrera a toda velocidad, esprint.
sprinter | 'sprɪntər | *s.c.* DEP. corredor de distancias cortas, esprinter: *Delgado isn't a sprinter = Delgado no es un sprinter.*
sprite | spraɪt | *s.c.* **1** hada, duende, trasgo. **2** fantasma, aparición. **3** (arc.) alma. **4** INF. sombra, imagen (producida en la pantalla por líneas para dar efecto real al dibujo).
sprocket | 'sprɒkɪt | | 'sprɑːkɪt | *s.c.* **1** (también **sprocket wheel**) rueda de engranaje, rueda de cadena (en una bicicleta). **2** FOT. carrete con dientes de engranaje: *introduce the film in the sprocket = introduce la película en el carrete.* **3** diente de engranaje (de una rueda, de un carrete).
sprout | spraʊt | *v.t.* e *i.* **1 [to – (from /up)]** BOT. brotar, germinar, retoñar (hojas). **2** crecer, dejarse salir, (barba, bigote). **3** surgir, aparecer (edificios). || *v.i.* **4** BOT. echar retoños, echar yemas, retoñar (las patatas). || *s.c.* **5** BOT. brote, retoño, yema, botón, pimpollo. **6** BOT. (brit.) col de bruselas.
spruce | spruːs | *s.c.* e *i.* **1** BOT. abeto, picea. || *adj.* **2** pulcro, emperifollado, engalanado, repulido, aseado, elegante. || *v.t.* e *i.* **3 [to – up]** (fam.) emperifollar(se), engalanar(se), asear(se).
sprucely | 'spruːslɪ | *adv.* pulcramente, elegantemente.
spruceness | spruːsnɪs | *s.i.* pulcritud, engalanamiento, emperifollamiento, elegancia.
sprung | sprʌŋ | *p.p.* y (EE.UU.) *pret.* **1** de **spring.** || *adj.* **2** de muelles, flexible, con resortes: *a sprung seat = un asiento de muelles.*
spry | spraɪ | *adj.* ágil, activo, dinámico, enérgico (una persona mayor): *although he's 80 he's still quite spry = a pesar de tener 80 años aún está bastante ágil.*
spud | spʌd | *s.c.* **1** (fam.) patata, (Am.) papa. **2** escarda (para quitar malas hierbas). || *v.t.* **3** escardar, entresacar (malas hierbas).
spume | spjuːm | *s.i.* **1** (lit.) espuma (de mar). || *v.i.* **2** hacer espuma.
spun | spʌn | *pret.* y *p.p.irreg.* de **spin.**
spunk | spʌnk | *s.i.* **1** (fam.) agallas, valor, coraje, ánimo. **2** (brit.) semen.
spunky | spʌnkɪ | *adj.* (arc. y fam.) con agallas, valeroso, valiente, animoso: *a spunky young girl = una jovencita con agallas.*
spur | spɜː | *s.c.* **1** espuela. **2 [– (to)]** espuela, aguijón, acicate, estímulo, incentivo: *she needed a spur to progress = necesitaba un estímulo para progresar.* **3** GEOG. estribación, espolón, ramal (de montañas). **4** bifurcación, ramificación, vía secundaria. **5** vía muerta (de tren). **6** ZOOL. espolón, garrón. **7** BOT. cornezuelo (del centeno). **8** garfio, trepadera, pincho. **9** rama, brazo, vástago (de un árbol). **10** ARQ. puntal, contrafuerte, machón. **11** BOT. espolón, espuela. || *v.t.* **12 [to – (on)]** espolear, picar con espuelas. **13** (fig.) espolear, estimular, incitar, meter prisa. || **14 on the – of the moment,** impulsivamente, sin reflexionar, sin pensar. **15 to win one's spurs,** (fig.) demostrar lo que uno vale, distinguirse.
spurious | 'spjʊərɪəs | *adj.* (fam.) **1** falso, incorrecto, inexacto (un argumento). **2** falso, simulado (un gesto). **3** TEC. falsificado (un producto).
spuriously | 'spjʊərɪəslɪ | *adv.* **1** falsamente, incorrectamente, inexactamente. **2** falsamente, simuladamente.
spuriousness | 'spjʊərɪəsnɪs | *s.i.* **1** falsedad, inexactitud. **2** simulación. **3** ilegitimidad.
spurn | spɜːn | *v.t.* (form.) rechazar, rehusar, despreciar (con desdén).
spur-of-the-moment | ˌspɜːəfðə'məʊmənt | *adj.* repentino, inesperado, espontáneo, impensado: *a spur-of-the-moment decision = una decisión repentina.*
spurt | spɜːt | *v.t.* e *i.* **1** salir a borbotones, salir a chorro, arrojar a chorro, salir con fuerza (agua, llamas). || *v.i.* **2 [to – (for)]** hacer un esfuerzo, acelerar. || *s.c.* **3** esfuerzo, impulso, ímpetu, arrebato: *a spurt of anger = un arrebato de ira.* **4 [– (of)]** chorro, borbotón; llamarada.
sputter | 'spʌtər | *v.i.* **1** chisporrotear (el fuego). **2** zumbar, hacer explosiones repetidas (un motor). **3** hablar despidiendo saliva, echar perdigones. || *v.t.* e *i.* **4** farfullar, barbotear, tartamudear. || *s.c.* **5** chisporroteo. **6** farfulleo, barboteo. **7** chispeo de saliva.
spy | spaɪ | *s.c.* **1** espía, agente secreto, topo. || *s.i.* **2** espionaje, vigilancia. || *v.i.* **3 [to – (on/upon)]** espiar, trabajar como espía, ser espía. **4 [to – (into/on)]** espiar, trabajar como espía, ser espía. **4 [to – (into/on)]** espiar, escudriñar, acechar. || *v.t.* **5** (lit.) observar, divisar, distinguir, columbrar, notar: *suddenly I spied the bird flying = de repente divisé al pájaro volando.* || **6 to – out,** espiar, husmear, fisgonear (una actividad ilegal). **7 to – out the land,** (fig.) reconocer el terreno, explorar.
sq. | es kjuː | *abreviatura* de **1 square,** cuadrado (en medidas): *20 sq. metres = 20 metros cuadrados.* **2 square,** plaza (en planos, direcciones): *Trafalgar Sq.: Plaza de Trafalgar.*
squabble | 'skwɒbl | *v.i.* **1 [to – (about /over)]** discutir, pelearse, reñir, disputar. || *s.c.* **2** discusión, disputa, pelea, riña.
squad | skwɒd | *s.c.* **1 [– + *v.sing./pl.*]** brigada, equipo, cuadrilla: *a fire-fighting squad = una brigada contra incendios.* **2** MIL. escuadrón, pelotón, patrulla. **3** DEP. equipo atlético. || **4 – car,** (EE.UU.) coche patrulla.
squadron | 'skwɒdrən | | skwɑːdrən | *s.c.* **1 [– + *v.sing./pl.*]** MIL. escuadrón, escuadrilla, escuadra (militar, naval, del aire). || **2 – leader,** (brit.) **a)** MIL. jefe de escuadrón; **b)** AER. comandante de aviación.
squalid | skwɒlɪd | *adj.* **1** miserable, sórdido, sucio. **2** perverso, vil, asqueroso, repulsivo.
squall | skwɔːl | *s.c.* **1** vendaval, borrasca, temporal, tempestad (de aire). **2** (fig.) tempestad, discusión, pelea, follón, griterío: *domestic squalls = peleas domésticas.* || *v.i.* **3** gritar, berrear, chillar.
squalor | 'skwɒlər | *s.i.* escualidez, miseria, penuria, escasez.
squander | 'skwɒndər | *v.t.* **1 [to – (on)]** despilfarrar, dilapidar, derrochar, malgastar. **2** (arc.) desparramar, diseminar, esparcir.
square | skweər | *s.c.* **1** GEOM. cuadrado. **2** cuadro: *the squares are blue and white = los cuadros son azules y blancos.* **3** plaza: *it's in Washington Square = está en la plaza Washington.* **4 [– (of)]** MAT. cuadrado, segunda potencia: *36 is the square of 6 = 36 es el cuadrado de 6.* **5** casilla, escaque (en un tablero de ajedrez). **6** (arc. y jerga) conservador, anticuado, persona chapada a la antigua, persona pasada de moda. **7** TEC. escuadra. || *adj.* **8** [no *comp.*] cuadrado, cuadriculado: *a square box = una caja cuadrada.* **9** cuadrado, rectangular, en escuadra, en ángulo recto: *his square chin = su mandíbula cuadrada.* **10** [no *comp.*] MAT. cuadrado: *143 square metres = 143 metros cuadrados.* **11** [*s.* + – y no *comp.*] en cuadro: *6 metres square = 6 metros en cuadro.* **12 [– (with)]** a nivel, nivelado, recto, derecho, paralelo. **13** saldada, pagada, liquidada (una deuda): *square accounts = cuentas saldadas.* **14** colocado, en su sitio, arreglado, limpio (un lugar). **15** honesto, justo, equitativo, formal (un trato). **16** rotunda, honesta, directa (una respuesta, una negativa). **17** fornido, fuerte, robusto. **18** (arc. y jerga) carca, anticuado, pasado de moda, chapado a la antigua, conservador. **19** DEP. empatado, igualado (en puntos). **20** MAR. cuadrado, de cruz. **21** DEP. en escuadra, en ángulo recto (respecto al bateador en críquet). || *v.t.* **22 [to – (off/up)]** arreglar, colocar, ajustar, enderezar: *he squared everything in front of him = arregló todo lo que había sobre la mesa.* **23** (generalmente pasiva) MAT. cuadrar, elevar al cuadrado. **24 [to – (of)]** cuadricular, dividir en cuadros. **25** DEP. igualar, empatar. **26** (fam.) saldar, pagar, arreglar (cuentas). **27** (fam.) sobornar, comprar (a alguien). || *v.t.* e *i.* **28 [to – (with)]** cuadrar, encajar, ajustar(se). || **29 a – peg in a round hole,** (fam.) forzado, inadecuado, inapropiado, poco apto, poco idóneo (para una actividad). **30 fair and –,** V. **fair. 31 to go back to – one/start again from – one,** (fam.) empezar por el principio, volver al punto de partida. **32 on the –, a)** (fam. y arc.) honestamente, honradamente; **b)** a escuadra, en escuadra. **33 out of –,** fuera de escuadra, desnivelado, no en ángulo recto. **34 – bracket,** (generalmente *pl.*) corchete. **35 – deal,** trato justo; juego limpio. **36 – meal,** comida en toda regla, comida completa. **37 – root,** MAT. raíz cuadrada. **38 to – the circle,** cuadrar el círculo, intentar lo imposible. **39 to – up (with),** (fam.) ajustar cuentas (con), saldar cuentas (con), liquidar cuentas (con). **40 to – up to, a)** hacer frente con valentía a, enfrentarse con determinación a (un problema, una situación); **b)** ponerse en posición de defensa, enfrentarse a (con los puños en alto).
squared | skweəd | *adj.* **1** recto, derecho, en paralelo. **2** cuadrado. **3** cuadriculado.
squarely | 'skweəlɪ | *adv.* **1** directamente en medio, totalmente en el centro: *squarely on top of the house = directamente centrado encima de la casa.* **2**

directamente, sin ambages, de lleno: *we had to look squarely at the problem = tendremos que tratar el problema sin ambages.*

squash | skwɒʃ | | skwɔːʃ | *v.t.* **1** aplastar, machacar, despachurrar. **2** aplastar, acallar, sofocar, suprimir (rumores, una rebelión). || *v.t.* e *i.* **3** apretar(se), apiñar(se), apretujar(se): *we all squashed into the car = todos nos apretujamos dentro del coche.* || *s.sing.* **4** apiñamiento, apretujamiento, aplastamiento. || *s.i.* **5** (también **squash rackets**) (fam.) squash (juego parecido al frontón que se practica en pista cerrada y pequeña). **6** (brit.) refresco de naranja o limón, limonada, naranjada (concentrado que se mezcla con agua). || *s.c.* e *i.* **7** (EE.UU.) BOT. calabaza, calabacín, chayote, cidra.

squashy | skwɒʃɪ | *adj.* blando, blandengue, fofo, esponjoso: *squashy fruit = fruta blandengue.*

squat | skwɒt | [*pret.* y *p.p.* **squatted,** *ger.* **squatting**] *v.i.* **1 [to – (down/on)]** sentarse en cuclillas, ponerse en cuclillas. **2** acurrucarse, agazaparse (un animal). **3 [to – (in/on)]** ocupar sin pagar renta, establecerse ilegalmente, apropiarse sin derecho (en un terreno, en una vivienda). || *s.sing.* **4** postura de una persona en cuclillas, postura de una persona agachada. || *s.c.* **5** (brit.) propiedad vacía que está expuesta a ser ocupada ilegalmente. **6** guarida, madriguera. || *adj.* **7** regordete, achaparrado (una persona, un edificio).

squatter | skwɒtər | *s.c.* **1** intruso, ocupante ilegal (de una vivienda vacía). **2** DER. usucapiente, persona que se establece en terreno público para establecer derecho sobre este.

squaw | skwɔː | *s.c.* india norteamericana, mujer piel roja.

squawk | skwɔːk | *v.i.* **1** graznar, chillar (un ave). **2** (fam.) chillar, montar bronca, quejarse, protestar. || *s.c.* **3** graznido, chillido (de un ave): *the squawks of the parrot = los graznidos del loro.* **4** protesta, queja, bronca.

squeak | skwiːk | *v.i.* **1** chillar (un ratón). **2** chirriar, crujir, rechinar (una puerta). **3** [to – + *adv./prep.*] (fam.) triunfar, ganar, vencer, escapar (por poca diferencia, por los pelos). || *s.c.* **4** chillido. **5** chirrido, crujido.

squeaky | 'skwiːkɪ | *adj.* **1** chirriante, que cruje, que rechina (una puerta). **2** chillona (la voz). || **3 – clean,** (EE.UU. y fam.) **a)** limpio como una patena, como un sol; **b)** (hum.) inmaculado, puro (moralmente).

squeal | skwiːl | *v.i.* **1** chillar, gritar agudamente, dar alaridos. **2** chirriar, crujir. **3 [to – (on)]** (jerga) cantar, revelar, confesar (información a la policía). || *s.c.* **4** chillido, grito agudo, alarido. **5** chirrido (de frenos).

squeamish | 'skwiːmɪʃ | *adj.* **1** melindroso, asustadizo, impresionable, sensible. **2** delicado, propenso a la náusea. **3** susceptible, suspicaz.

squeeze | skwiːz | *v.t.* **1** apretujar, comprimir, prensar. **2** [**to – +** *o.* **+** *adv./prep.*] exprimir, estrujar: *squeeze the juice out these lemons = exprime el zumo de estos limones.* **3** [**to – +** *o.* **+** *adv./prep.*] meter, encajar, hacer un hueco (de tiempo, de espacio): *I may squeeze you at 2.30 = te puedo hacer un hueco a las 2.30.* **4** acosar, agobiar (con demandas, impuestos). **5** exprimir, extorsionar, exigir (dinero). **6** obligar a descartarse (a un adversario en bridge). || *v.t.* e *i.* **7** [**to – +** *adv./prep.*] introducir(se) a presión, comprimir, apiñarse, meterse a la fuerza: *we were squeezed inside = nos metieron a presión.* **8** ganar por los pelos, ganar apuradamente. || *s.c.* **9** compresión, estrujamiento, presión. **10** apretón (de mano). **11 [– (of)]** expresión, gotas, estrujón: *add a squeeze of orange = añade unas gotas de naranja.* **12** ECON. restricción, bloqueo, embargo (de suministros, de créditos). || **13 to put the – on,** (fam.) presionar, apretar las clavijas.

squelch | skweltʃ | *v.i.* **1** chapotear, caminar chapoteando. || *v.t.* **2** despachurrar, aplastar, pisotear. **3** acallar por la fuerza, apabullar. || *s.sing.* **4** chapoteo. **5** réplica grosera, respuesta desconcertante.

squib | skwɪb | *s.c.* **1** petardo, buscapiés (explosivo). **2** pasquín, escrito satírico, libelo (para atacar a un político). || **3 damp –,** (fam.) desastre, ruina, calamidad (un espectáculo).

squid | skwɪd | *s.c.* ZOOL. calamar.

squiffy | 'skwɪfɪ | *adj.* (brit., fam. y arc.) chispa, borracho.

squiggle | 'skwɪgl | *s.c.* (fam.) garabato, línea ondulada (sobre un papel).

squint | skwɪnt | *v.i.* **1** mirar entrecerrando los ojos, cerrar casi los ojos, forzar la vista: *squinting to see the name on the door = forzando la vista para ver el nombre escrito sobre la puerta.* **2** bizquear, tener ojos estrábicos. **3** mirar de lado, mirar de soslayo, mirar por el rabillo del ojo. || *s.c.* **4** estrabismo, mirada bizca. **5** mirada de soslayo, mirada de lado. **6** mirada forzada, mirada entrecerrando los ojos. || *adj.* **7** (fam.) de lado, de soslayo, torcido. **8** desviado, estrábico. || *adv.* **9** de forma ladeada. || **10 to have/take a – at,** (fam.) echar una ojeada, echar un vistazo.

squire | 'skwaɪər | *s.c.* **1** (arc.) propietario, señor, hacendado. **2** (arc.) escudero. **3** (brit. y fam.) señor, caballero (apelativo cariñoso que se da a alguien de clase social superior de quien no se conoce su nombre).

squirm | skwəːm | *v.i.* **1** retorcerse, revolverse, sufrir (de dolor). **2** sentirse violento, avergonzarse. **3** culebrear, serpear (un reptil, un pez). || *s.c.* **4** sufrimiento. **5** contorsión, serpenteo, retorcimiento. **6** vergüenza, bochorno, mal rato.

squirrel | 'skwɪrəl | | 'skwɜːrəl | *s.c.* ZOOL. ardilla.

squirt | skwəːt | *v.t.* e *i.* **1** salir a presión, salir a chorro: *the wine squirted out of a hole = el vino salía a presión por un agujero.* || *v.t.* **2 [to – (with)]** arrojar a chorro: *he squirted us with water from the hose = nos lanzaba chorros de agua con la manguera.* || *s.c.* **3 [– (of)]** chorro, chorretón, chorretada. **4** (arc. y desp.) presumido, engreído, presuntuoso, farolero, persona que se da mucha importancia.

Sr. | 'esɑː | *abreviatura* de **1 Senior,** padre (para distinguirlo del hijo del mismo nombre): *Mike Clayton, Sr. = Mike Clayton, padre.* **2** REL. **Sister,** Hermana. **3** QUIM. **strontium,** estroncio. **4** señor (en Sudamérica).

Sri Lanka | ˌsriː'læŋkə | *s.sing.* Sri Lanka.

Sri Lankan | ˌsriːlæŋkən | *adj.* **1** de Sri Lanka. || *s.c.* **2** habitante de Sri Lanka.

SRN | ˌesɑːr'en | *s.c. abreviatura de* **1** (brit.) **State Registered Nurse,** enfermera cualificada (en títulos): *Susan Fuller, SRN = enfermera Susan Fuller.* **2** (generalmente *sing.*) título de enfermería, carrera de enfermería: *he got his SRN last year = obtuvo su título de enfermero el año pasado.*

ST, STs | ˌes'tiː | *abreviatura* de **sanitary towel,** compresa.

St | sənt | *abreviatura* de **1 Street,** calle (en direcciones). **2 Saint,** [*pl.* **SS.**] santo, san: *St. Martin = San Martín.* **3 (st) stone,** 14 libras (medida de peso). || *sufijo* **4 -st,** terminación de *ord.* que se añade a números que contienen 1: *1st = primero.*

stab | stæb | [**stabbed, stabbing**] *v.t.* e *i.* **1** apuñalar, herir con arma blanca. **2** empujar, hundir, marcar, hurgar; indicar, señalar (con el dedo, con un objeto): *she stabbed at the ground with her finger = señaló hacia el suelo con el dedo.* || *s.c.* **3** puñalada, cuchillada. **4 [– (of)]** punzada, pinchazo: *a stab of pain = un dolor agudo.* **5 [– (at)]** (fam.) intento, tentativa, prueba. || **6 to – someone in the back,** apuñalar a alguien por la espalda, traicionar a alguien. **7 – in the back,** puñalada por la espalda, puñalada trapera, traición. **8 to have /make a –,** hacer un intento, hacer la prueba. **9 – wound,** herida de arma blanca, puñalada.

stabbing | 'stæbɪŋ | *s.c.* **1** apuñalamiento, muerte a puñaladas. **2** punzante, agudo (un dolor).

stability | stə'bɪlɪtɪ | *s.i.* **1** estabilidad, firmeza, equilibrio. **2** integridad, fiabilidad. **3** REL. voto que une de por vida a un monasterio.

stabilize | 'steɪbɪəaɪz | (brit. **stabilise**) *v.t.* e *i.* estabilizar(se), normalizar(se).

stabilization | ˌsteɪbəlaɪ'zeɪʃn | *s.i.* estabilización, normalización.

stabilizer | 'steɪbɪlaɪzər | (brit. **stabiliser**) *s.c.* MEC. **1** estabilizador, plano estabilizador. **2** amortiguador. **3** QUIM. estabilizador.

stable | 'steɪbl | *adj.* **1** estable, constante, fijo, no cambiante: *a stable relationship = una relación estable.* **2** estable, firme, seguro. **3** estable, sereno, juicioso, formal (el carácter). **4** QUIM. estable. || *s.c.* **5** establo, cuadra, caballeriza. **6 [– (of)]** cuadra (organización, grupo de caballos): *he owns one of the best stables = posee una de las mejores cuadras.* **7 [– (of)]** (fig.) grupo (de deportistas, de artistas): *a stable of prizefighters = un grupo de boxeadores profesionales.* || *v.t.* **8** guardar en establo, encerrar en establo, albergar en cuadra. || **9 to shut/close the – door after the horse has bolted,** ser demasiado tarde para prevenir, muerto el burro, la cebada al rabo.

stable-boy | 'steɪblbɔɪ | (también **stable-lad**) *s.c.* mozo de cuadra, mozo de caballeriza.

staccato | stəˈkɑːtəʊ | *adj.* **1** MUS. staccato. **2** entrecortado, quebrado (un ruido, un sonido). || *adv.* **3** en staccato. || *s.pl.* **4** staccato.
stack | stæk | *s.c.* **1** montón, pila, rimero: *a stack of plates = un rimero de platos.* **2** AGR. niara, hacina (de mieses). **3** **[– (of)]** (fam.) montón, mogollón, gran número: *stacks of work = montones de trabajo.* **4** estante, balda (de una librería). **5** INF. pila, lote. **6** MIL. pabellón de fusiles. **7** chimenea (de una casa, de un buque); húmero, cañón (de chimenea). **8** (brit.) 108 pies cúbicos (unidad de medida para carbón y madera). || *v.t.* e *i.* **9** **[to – (up)]** apilar(se), amontonar(se), hacinar(se). || *v.t.* **10** **[to – (with)** y generalmente pasiva] llenar de montones, colocar en montones, apilar: *the pavement was stacked with bricks = la acera estaba llena de montones de ladrillos.* **11** **[to – (against)]** (fam.) hacer trampas, preparar, colocar fraudulentamente (los naipes para tener ventaja). **12** **[to – (up)]** AER. volar en grupo (a la espera de aterrizar un avión). || **13 to – up (against),** (fam.) compararse con. **14 the odds/cards are stacked against,** las circunstancias son desfavorables, el destino está en contra.
stadia | ˈsteɪdjə | *pl.* de **stadium.**
stadium | ˈsteɪdɪəm | [*pl.* **stadiums** o **stadia**] *s.c.* DEP. estadio.
staff | stɑːf | (EE.UU.) | stæf | *s.c.* **1** [– + *v.sing./pl.*] plantilla, personal, empleados, cuerpo administrativo (de una escuela, de una empresa). **2** MIL. plana mayor, estado mayor. **3** [*pl.* **staves**] bastón, palo, estaca, varilla. **4** báculo, bastón de mando, cayado, bordón. **5** asta, palo (de la bandera). **6** MUS. pentagrama. || *v.t.* **7** [**to – (with)** y generalmente pasiva] dotar de personal, proveer de personal. **8** (generalmente pasiva) trabajar en plantilla, ser de plantilla, trabajar, tener un puesto (de una empresa). || **9 – nurse,** enfermera (con rango inferior a la jefa de enfermeras).
staffing | stɑːfɪŋ | *s.i.* empleo, plantilla, personal: *staffing restrictions = restricciones de plantilla.*
stag | stæg | *s.c.* **1** ZOOL. ciervo, venado. **2** ZOOL. (animal) castrado. **3** soltero (varón que asiste solo a reuniones sociales). **4** fiesta de solteros. **5** (brit.) especulador (en bolsa). || *adj.* **6** sólo para hombres, de solteros. || **7 – party,** despedida de soltero.
stage | steɪdʒ | *s.c.* **1** escenario (en un teatro). **2** (fig.) teatro, arte dramático, carrera teatral. **3** plataforma, templete, estrado, tablado. **4** andamio. **5** portaobjeto (de un microscopio). **6** (fig.) escena, acción, acontecimientos: *at the centre of the stage = en el centro de los acontecimientos.* **7** estadio, etapa, fase, punto, paso: *at this first stage = en esta primera fase.* **8** parada de postas, estación. **9** diligencia. **10** etapa, jornada (de un viaje, de una carrera): *he abandoned during the first stage of the cyclist tour = abandonó el primer día de la vuelta ciclista.* **11** nivel, piso, planta (de un edificio). **12** nivel (del agua). **13** AER. piso, etapa, parte (de un cohete). **14** GEOL. era, etapa. **15** ELECTR. paso, etapa. || *v.t.* **16** poner en escena, representar, escenificar, montar (una obra teatral, un espectáculo). **17** organizar, disponer, planificar, llevar a cabo: *they staged a demonstration to complain = organizaron una manifestación de protesta.* || **18 on –/on the –,** actuando, en escena, en el escenario. **19 to set the –,** preparar el camino, sentar la base, hacer posible. **20 – by –,** paso a paso, poco a poco, gradualmente. **21 – direction,** acotación, indicación escénica (en una obra teatral). **22 – door,** entrada de actores. **23 – fright,** miedo al público. **24 – whisper,** cuchicheo, susurro (para que se oiga). **25 the –,** la farándula, el mundo del teatro.
stagecoach | ˈsteɪdʒkəʊtʃ | *s.c.* diligencia.
stagehand | ˈsteɪdʒhænd | *s.c.* tramoyista.
stage-manage | ˌsteɪdʒˈmænɪdʒ | *v.t.* **1** (fam.) preparar de antemano, organizar previamente, orquestar, manipular (de cara al público): *they stage-managed all the campaign against the reforms = manipularon toda la campaña contra las reformas.* **2** dirigir (una obra teatral).
stage-manager | ˌsteɪdʒˈmænɪdʒər | *s.c.* director de escena.
stage-struck | ˈsteɪdʒstrʌk | *adj.* enamorado del teatro, loco por el teatro.
stagger | ˈstægər | *v.i.* **1** **[to – + *adv./prep.*]** tambalearse, hacer eses, oscilar, vacilar, titubear. || *v.t.* **2** asombrar, desconcertar, dejar atónito, dejar perplejo, chocar. **3** escalonar, arreglar a intervalos (las horas de trabajo, las vacaciones). || *s.c.* **4** tambaleo, bamboleo, titubeo, vacilación.
staggered | ˈstægəd | *adj.* asombrado, desconcertado, atónito, perplejo, pasmado.
staggering | ˈstægərɪŋ | *adj.* asombroso, desconcertante, chocante, pasmoso.
staggeringly | ˈstægərɪŋlɪ | *adv.* asombrosamente, desconcertantemente, de forma chocante, de forma pasmosa: *he finished staggeringly early = terminó asombrosamente pronto.*
stagnant | ˈstægnənt | *adj.* **1** estancado, nauseabundo, infecto: *a stagnant pool = una charca infecta.* **2** paralizado, estancado, inmóvil, inactivo, estático: *a stagnant period for sales = un período de inactividad en las ventas.*
stagnate | stægˈneɪt | (EE.UU.) | ˈstægneɪt | *v.i.* estancarse, paralizarse, quedar estancado, vegetar.
stagnation | stægˈneɪʃn | *s.i.* paralización, estancamiento.
stagy | ˈsteɪdʒɪ | *adj.* (desp.) teatral, teatrero, dramático: *a stagy gesture = un gesto teatral.*
staid | steɪd | *adj.* austero, sobrio, formal, serio; carca, conservador (en apariencia, gustos, comportamiento).
stain | steɪn | *v.t.* e *i.* **1** manchar(se), ensuciar(se). || *v.t.* **2** teñir, colorar, pintar: *the pen stained her fingers blue = el bolígrafo le tiñó los dedos de azul.* **3** (generalmente *pasiva*) (form. y fig.) manchar, marcar, mancillar (la reputación). || *s.c.* **4** mancha, marca, lamparón: *blood stains = manchas de sangre.* **5** (fig.) estigma, marca, señal. || *s.c.* e *i.* **6** tinte, tintura, colorante, pintura.
stained | steɪnd | *adj.* **1** manchado, marcado. **2** teñido. | *sufijo* **3 –stained,** [*s.* + – para formar *adj.*] manchado de, marcado con, sucio de: *ink-stained carpet = una alfombra manchada de tinta.* || **4 – glass,** vidrio de colores.
stainless | ˈsteɪnlɪs | *adj.* **1** inoxidable. **2** (lit.) inmaculado, sin mancha, sin tacha. || **3 – steel,** acero inoxidable.
stair | steər | *s.c.* **1** (lit.) escalera, escalinata. **2** peldaño, escalón. **3** piso, tramo de escalera (de una vivienda). || **4 above stairs,** (arc.) arriba, parte de la casa donde viven los dueños. **5 below stairs,** (arc.) zona del servicio (en una casa). **6 flight of stairs,** tramo de escalera. **7 stairs,** escaleras, escalinata.
staircase | ˈsteəkeɪs | *s.c.* escaleras, escalinata.
stairway | ˈsteəweɪ | V. **staircase.**
stairwell | ˈsteəwel | *s.c.* hueco de la escalera.
stake | steɪk | *s.c.* **1** estaca, poste, palo, puntal, rodrigón. **2** (arc.) hoguera, pira, suplicio (de ejecución). **3** **[– (in)]** interés, inversión, participación, cuota (en un negocio, en un asunto). **4** puesta, apuesta (a los caballos). **5** REL. división territorial (de la iglesia mormona). **6** (EE.UU.) avío, adelanto (de dinero que se entrega a un buscador de oro). || *v.t.* **7** **[to – (on)]** apostar, arriesgar, jugar (dinero, bienes). **8** arriesgar, comprometer, exponer (la reputación, la credibilidad). **9** **[to – (up)]** apuntalar, enderezar con estacas, atar a una estaca: *they had to stake the rose trees = tuvieron que atar los rosales a estacas.* **10** **[to – (off /out)]** marcar con estacas, cercar con estacas. **11** ECON. inyectar, financiar (a una empresa). || **12 at –,** en peligro, en juego. **13 burned at the –,** quemado en la hoguera, llevado a la hoguera. **14 to go to the – for something,** arriesgarse por algo, ir al fin del mundo por algo. **15 to – a claim,** hacer una reclamación, reclamar un derecho, afirmar un derecho (sobre un terreno, área de estudio). **16 stakes, a)** premio (de una carrera, una actividad); **b)** [– + *v.sing./pl.*] carrera de caballos en que el dinero del premio se pone entre los dueños de estos a partes iguales. **17 to – out, a)** (EE.UU. y fam.) vigilar durante largo tiempo; **b)** delimitar, establecer los límites. **18 to – somebody to,** (EE.UU.) regalar a alguien, proveer a alguien de (dinero para una adquisición).
stalactite | ˈstæləktaɪt | (EE.UU.) | stəˈlæktaɪt | *s.c.* GEOL. estalactita.
stalagmite | ˈstæləgmaɪt | (EE.UU.) | stəˈlægmaɪt | *s.c.* GEOL. estalagmita.
stale | steɪl | *adj.* **1** rancio, pasado, seco, duro, mohoso (un alimento). **2** viciado (el aire). **3** aburrido, gastado, antiguo, anticuado. **4** estancado, pasado de moda, anticuado, falto de originalidad, viejo, cansado (mentalmente, corporalmente). || *v.i.* **5** ponerse rancio, ponerse duro, estar mohoso. **6** estar anticuado, estar pasado de moda, perder la originalidad.
stalemate | ˈsteɪlmeɪt | *s.c.* e *i.* **1** tablas (en ajedrez). **2** punto muerto, estancamiento, paralización: *the talks have reached a stalemate = las conversaciones han llegado a un punto muerto.*

staleness | steɪlnɪs | *s.i.* **1** enranciamiento,ranciedad, vejez. **2** decadencia, antigüedad.
stalk | stɔːk | *s.c.* **1** BOT. tallo, troncho. **2** BOT. peciolo, pedúnculo. **3** pie (de un vaso). || *v.t.* **4** acechar, cazar al acecho, seguir los pasos (a un animal). || *v.i.* **5** **[to – +** *adv./prep.*] caminar majestuosamente, andar como ofendido, caminar dándose importancia: *she stalked out of the room = salió con aires de ofendido de la habitación.* || *v.t.* e *i.* **6** (lit.) merodear, rondar, andar al acecho: *famine staked the town = el hambre rondaba la ciudad.*
stall | stɔːl | *s.c.* **1** (brit.) puesto, caseta (de venta en el mercado, en la calle): *fruit stalls along the street = puestos de fruta a lo largo de la calle.* **2** cuadra, establo, pesebre. **3** silla del coro, sitial del coro (en una iglesia, catedral). **4** cabina, vestidor, compartimento, cubículo. **5** dedil (para coser). || *s.i.* **6** pérdida de velocidad, pérdida de fuerza, ahogo (de una máquina). || *v.t.* e *i.* **7** ahogar(se), quedar(se), perder velocidad (un motor). **8** AER. entrar en pérdida, caer sin control, perder velocidad. || *v.t.* **9** (fam.) dejar a un lado, posponer, dar largas, ganar tiempo; entretener, distraer (a una persona). **10** encerrar en establo, guardar en establo, estabular. || *v.i.* **11** (fam.) andar con rodeos, dar evasivas, dejarse de evasivas, rehuir, esquivar, vacilar, mostrarse indeciso. || **12 (the) stalls,** (brit.) patio de butacas.
stallholder | 'stɔːlhəuldər | *s.c.* dueño de un puesto (de mercado).
stallion | 'stælɪən | *s.c.* ZOOL. semental, garañón, (Am.) padrillo.
stalwart | 'stɔːlwət | *adj.* **1** (arc. y form.) incondicional, leal. **2** resuelto, decidido, determinado (una persona). **3** robusto, vigoroso, fornido, fuerte. || *s.c.* **4** partidario, incondicional, leal: *the stalwarts of the team = los incondicionales del equipo.*
stalwartly | 'stɔːlwətlɪ | *adv.* **1** incondicionalmente, lealmente. **2** firmemente, resueltamente. **3** vigorosamente.
stalwartness | 'stɔːlwətnɪs | *s.i.* **1** lealtad, fidelidad, adhesión. **2** resolución, decisión, determinación. **3** fortaleza, vigor.
stamen | 'steɪmen | [*pl.* **stamens** o **stamina**] *s.c.* BOT. estambre.
stamina | 'stæmɪnə | *s.i.* **1** resistencia, energía, aguante, vigor. **2** *pl. de* **stamen.**
stammer | 'stæmər | *v.t.* e *i.* **1** tartamudear, tartajear, balbucir. || *s.sing.* **2** tartamudeo, tartajeo, balbuceo. || **3 to – out,** decir tartamudeando, balbucir, decir con dificultad.
stammerer | 'stæmərər | *s.c.* tartamudo.
stammeringly | 'stæmərɪŋlɪ | *adv.* con tartamudeo, tartamudeando, balbuciendo.
stamp | stæmp | *v.t.* e *i.* **1** **[to – +** *adv./prep.*] pisotear, patear, dar un pisotón, golpear con los pies. || *v.t.* **2** sellar, poner un sello, imprimir, marcar, señalar, grabar: *he stamped my passport = me selló el pasaporte.* **3** franquear, poner un sello (de correos), timbrar. **4** **[to – (as)]** identificar, caracterizar, marcar, clasificar, señalar, destacar: *stamped as one of the best European minds = destacado como una de las mejores mentes europeas.* **5** cortar con molde, moldear, troquelar, acuñar. || *s.c.* **6** (también **postage stamp**) sello, timbre, (Am.) estampilla. **7** póliza. **8** (también **trading** –) cupón. **9** tampón, cuño, troquel: *a date stamp = un tampón con la fecha.* **10** sello, marca: *I've got several stamps in my passport = tengo varios sellos en mi pasaporte.* **11** (fig. y form.) marca, huella, signo. **12** pateo, pisotón. **13** (form.) clase, carácter, calaña. || **14 – album,** álbum de sellos. **15 – collecting,** colección de sellos (actividad). **16 to – down,** pisotear, hollar, aplastar. **17 stamped addressed envelope,** sobre con sello y dirección (que se envía al pedir información a una organización para no tener que pagar gastos de envío). **18 stamping ground,** coto privado, lugar favorito, guarida. **19 to – out, a)** erradicar, eliminar, suprimir, extirpar; **b)** acuñar, elaborar con molde, sacar a partir de un molde.
stampede | stæm'piːd | *s.c.* **1** estampida, desbocamiento. **2** (fig.) estampida, pánico, carrera alocada; demanda: *a stampede down the stairs = una estampida escaleras abajo.* || *v.t.* e *i.* **3** **[to – (into)]** salir de estampida, desbocar(se). **4** precipitar(se), presionar.
stance | stæns | *s.sing.* **1** DEP. posición, postura. **2** **[to – (on)]** posición, actitud, punto de vista, postura: *a rigid stance on death penalty = una postura rígida sobre la pena de muerte.*
stanchion | 'stænʃən | (EE.UU.) | 'stæntʃən | *s.c.* puntal, poste, soporte.
stand | stænd | *v.* [*irr.pret.* y *p.p.* **stood**] *i.* **1** estar de pie, mantenerse de pie, levantarse, estar derecho. **2** levantarse, erguirse, tener una altura: *some rose trees stand in the garden = unos rosales se yerguen en el jardín.* **3** **[to – +** *adv./prep.*] estar, quedarse, permanecer (realizando una actividad): *we stood talking for hours = permanecimos hablando horas.* **4** permanecer, estar, encontrarse, hallarse, estar ubicado (sin ser usado, en cierta posición, a cierto nivel): *the bus stood there for months = el autobús permaneció allí durante meses.* **5** reposar, estancarse, sedimentar (un líquido): *leave the cream to stand = deja que la crema repose.* **6** (EE.UU.) detenerse, pararse (por poco tiempo un vehículo). **7** **[to – +** *adv./prep.*] permanecer, mantenerse, perdurar, persistir, quedar (unidos, firmes, etc...). **8** **[to – +** *adv./prep.*] estar, ir (las cosas): *as things stand nowadays = tal y como están las cosas hoy en día.* **9** ser válido, continuar en vigor, quedar en pie: *her offer still stands = su oferta aún es válida.* **10** **[to – +** *inf.*] suponer, estar a punto de, tener posibilidades de: *if you pass, you stand to get the job = si apruebas, tienes posibilidades de conseguir el puesto.* **11** [(brit.) **to – for,** también (EE.UU.) **run**] ser candidato, presentarse a (unas elecciones). **12** MAR. mantener rumbo, poner rumbo. || *t.* **13** [generalmente en *interr.* y *negativas;* **not to – +** *s./o.* + *ger./ger.*] soportar, aguantar, tolerar: *I can't stand alcohol = no aguanto el alcohol; she couldn't stand gossiping = no soportaba el cotilleo.* **14** **[to – +** *o.indirecto* + *o.directo*] invitar, pagar, hacer una invitación, sufragar: *I'll stand you a drink = te invito a una bebida.* **15** pasar, afrontar, aguantar (una prueba). || *t.* e *i.* **16** colocar, poner, situar, ubicar: *we stood the ladder against the wall = colocamos la escalera de mano contra la pared.* **17** levantar(se), elevar(se), alzar(se), izar(se). **18** quedar en pie, permanecer en pie (un edificio, aunque otros caigan). **19** (fig.) poner de relieve. || *s.c.* **20** puesto, caseta, quiosco (callejero, en una feria). **21** estante de exposición, exhibidor. **22** (generalmente en combinación) pedestal, atril, descanso, pie (para colocar algo): *an umbrella stand = un paragüero; a lamp stand = un pie de lámpara.* **23** MIL. resistencia. **24** oposición, antagonismo, resistencia: *a determined stand against nuclear weapons = una resistencia firme contra las armas nucleares.* **25** **[– (on)]** posición, postura, actitud. **26** parada (de taxis). **27** (EE.UU.) DER. estrado, tribuna (de testigos). **28** [también *pl.*] graderías, gradas (en un estadio). || **29 how/where people – on,** como/por donde anda la gente sobre, que piensa la gente sobre: *where do people stand on this subject? = ¿qué piensa la gente sobre este asunto?* **30 it stands to reason,** (fam.) es de cajón, salta a la vista, está claro, es obvio. **31 to know where one stands,** saber por donde anda uno, saber lo que uno piensa. **32 to leave someone standing,** V. **leave. 33 to make one's hair – on end,** V. **hair. 34 not to have a leg to – on,** V. **leg. 35 to – a chance/hope,** tener una posibilidad de. **36 to – corrected,** admitir la equivocación, retractarse, desdecirse, confesar el error. **37 -- and deliver!,** (arc.) ¡manos arriba! (decían los ladrones de diligencias). **38 to – by, a)** estar al lado de, estar cerca de (en la adversidad); **b)** mantener, ser fiel a, tomar partido (una promesa); **c)** mantenerse pasivo, no intervenir. **39 to – by for,** estar atento a, estar alerta a, mantenerse preparado para. **40 to – down, a)** dimitir, ceder el puesto, dimitir en favor de; **b)** DER. abandonar el estrado, retirarse del estrado; **c)** (brit.) MIL. salir de guardia; dar permiso (después de un servicio). **41 to – for, a)** representar, simbolizar, ser la abreviatura de; **b)** permitir, consentir, tolerar; **c)** defender, luchar (por ideas). **42 to – in (for),** sustituir, reemplazar. **43 to – on ceremony,** V. **ceremony. 44 to – on one's dignity,** (desp.) mantenerse digno, ponerse digno (en una discusión). **45 to – on one's own feet,** (fam.) ser independiente. **46 to – one's ground,** V. **ground. 47 to – on one's head/hands,** hacer el pino, ponerse con los pies en alto. **48 to – or fall by,** depender enteramente del éxito de uno (o fracasar). **49 to – out,** resaltar, destacarse, verse a distancia. **50 to – out a mile,** verse a distancia, estar totalmente claro. **51 to – out against,** oponerse a, mantenerse firme contra. **52 to – out from,** sobresalir, destacarse, descollar. **53 to – to,** (brit.) MIL. ocupar un puesto de guardia; enviar a hacer

una guardia. **54 to – someone in good stead,** V. **stead. 55 to – trial,** ser juzgado. **56 standing on one's head,** (fam.) con los ojos cerrados, a ojos cerrados. **57 to – up, a)** levantarse, ponerse en pie; **b)** ser resistente, ser duro, durar mucho, tener buena vejez (un objeto); **c)** sostenerse, mantenerse, salir bien, ser aceptado; **d)** (fam.) dar plantón, dejar plantado. **58 to – up and be counted,** decir lo que se piensa, dar a conocer los puntos de vista de uno (aunque sea peligroso). **59 to – up for,** dar la cara por, ponerse del lado de, defender. **60 to – up to,** hacer frente a, enfrentarse a. **61 to take a – of,** pronunciarse sobre, dar la opinión sobre.

standard | 'stændəd | *s.c.* **1** nivel, grado. **2** regla, norma, criterio, concepto. **3** pauta, patrón, modelo, precepto (moral). **4** patrón (medida de peso, pureza, valor): *gold standard = patrón oro.* **5** estandarte, pabellón, pendón, enseña. **6** soporte, pie, base, palo. **7** BOT. planta, árbol, tronco (derecho). **8** norma, objeto común, objeto de dominio público: *the procedure has become a standard = el procedimiento se ha convertido en algo de dominio público.* **9** MUS. canción popular (que cantan muchos cantantes). || *adj.* **10** estándard, normal, corriente (medida, precio, peso). **11** conocido, recomendado, aceptado, acreditado, clásico (una obra, un texto). **12** estándard, correcto, oficial, ortodoxo (la pronunciación). || **13 – bearer, a)** (fig.) abanderado, adalid (de una organización); **b)** MIL. portaestandarte. **14 – lamp,** (brit.) lámpara de pie. **15 – of living/living –,** nivel de vida.

standardize | 'stændədaɪz | (brit. **standardise**) *v.t.* **1** estandarizar, uniformizar, regularizar, normalizar: *mass media standardize habits = los medios de comunicación de masa estandarizan los hábitos.*

standardization | ˌstændədaɪ'zeɪʃn | (brit. **standardised)** *adj.* estándard, estandarizado, uniforme, unificado.

standby | 'stændbaɪ | *s.c.* **1** recurso, reserva, repuesto: *tins of food are a good standby in the house = las latas de conserva son un buen recurso en la casa.* **2** persona de confianza, persona fiel, paño de lágrimas. || **3 to be on – by,** estar de reserva, estar listo para partir, estar preparado para el momento en que se necesite: *they had some people on standby = tenían gente de reserva.* **4 – ticket,** billete de última hora, entrada de última hora (que sobra y se compra a precio más barato justo antes de partir, de que empiece una obra).

stand-in | 'stændɪn | *s.c.* **1** doble (de un actor en escenas peligrosas, durante una enfermedad). **2** sustituto, suplente.

standing | 'stændɪŋ | *adj.* **1** continuo, permanente, invariable, establecido, arraigado: *a standing habit = un hábito arraigado.* **2** eterno, válido, efectivo. **3** de pie, en pie. **4** erguido, recto, vertical: *a standing ovation = una ovación en pie.* **5** estacionario, estancado, inamovible. || *s.i.* **6** estatus, rango, clase, posición (social). **7** reputación, importancia, categoría. **8** duración, tiempo, antigüedad. || **9 of long –/of five, etc... year's –,** de larga duración, de hace cinco, etc... años. **10 – order/banker's order, a)** (brit.) FIN. orden bancaria de pago (de una cantidad fija mensual); **b)** POL. reglamento vigente. **11 – room,** espacio para permanecer de pie, localidad de pie (en un teatro, en un autobús).

stand-offish | ˌstænd'ɒfɪʃ | *adj.* (fam. y desp.) estirado, reservado, frío, con aires de superioridad.

standpipe | 'stændpaɪp | *s.c.* depósito vertical de agua, torre depósito de alimentación de agua (público).

standpoint | 'stændpɔɪnt | *s.c.* punto de vista, posición.

standstill | 'stændstɪl | *s.sing.* **1** parada, alto, parón. || **2 to bring to a –,** parar, detener (un vehículo, una máquina, una industria). **3 to come to a –,** pararse, detenerse, quedar paralizado.

stand-up | 'stændʌp | *adj.* **1** que se hace o se toma de pie (una actividad, una comida, una pelea). **2** (espectáculo) de un solo cómico en escena contando chistes. **3** alto, rígido: *a stand-up collar = un cuello alto.*

stank | stæŋk | *pret.irreg.* de **stink.**

stanza | 'stænzə | *s.c.* LIT. estrofa, estancia.

staple | 'steɪpl | *s.c.* **1** grapa, (Am.) grapa (para sujetar papel). **2** cibica, laña, patilla. **3** producto de uso cotidiano, producto básico. **4** materia prima. **5** tema central, elemento esencial. || *v.t.* **6** sujetar con grapas o patillas, unir con lañas. || *adj.* **7** básico, principal: *oil as our staple products = el aceite como nuestro principal producto.* **8** común, corriente, cotidiano, establecido. || **9 – diet,** dieta básica. **10 – gun,** máquina grapadora industrial.

stapler | 'steɪplər | *s.c.* grapadora, máquina cosepapeles.

star | stɑːr | *s.c.* **1** estrella, astro. **2** estrella, condecoración, insignia. **3** estrella (que indica forma, categoría, calidad). **4** asterisco (en imprenta). **5** (fig.) estrella, celebridad, figura destacada (del espectáculo). **6** (generalmente *sing.*) (lit.) estrella, suerte, éxito. || *v.t.* **[starred, starring]. 7** presentar como estrella, presentar en el papel principal (en cine, teatro). **8** marcar con asterisco: *we've starred the non available items = hemos marcado con asterisco los productos que no están disponibles.* **9** (generalmente *pasiva.*) decorar con estrellas, adornar con estrellas. || *v.i.* **10 [to – (in)]** protagonizar, hacer el papel protagonista, ser la estrella (en una película, obra de teatro). || *sufijo* **11** de... estrellas (un hotel, los grados de la gasolina): *a three-star hotel = un hotel de tres estrellas.* || **12 to be born under a lucky –,** nacer con buena estrella. **13 to reach for the stars,** V. **reach. 14 stars,** horóscopo. **15 Stars and Stripes,** (fam.) barras y estrellas (nombre popular de la bandera norteamericana). **16 – sign,** signo del Zodíaco. **17 to see stars,** (fam.) ver las estrellas (a causa de un golpe). **18 to thank one's lucky stars,** (fam.) dar las gracias al Dios, estar agradecido a la suerte de uno.

starboard | 'stɑːbɔd | *adj.* MAR. **1** estribor. || *adj.* **2** a estribor, de estribor. || *adv.* **3** a estribor. || *v.t.* **4** poner a estribor, mover a estribor.

starch | stɑːtʃ | *s.c.* e *i.* **1** almidón, fécula, hidratos de carbono (en alimentos). **2** almidón (para la ropa). || *v.t.* **3** almidonar.

starched | stɑːtʃt | *adj.* almidonado.

starchy | stɑːtʃɪ | *adj.* **1** feculento, que engorda, con exceso de hidratos de carbono (un alimento). **2** (fam.) rígido, estricto, ritualista, serio, formalista (una persona).

stardom | 'stɑːdəm | *s.i.* estrellato.

stare | steər | *v.i.* **1 [to – (at)]** mirar fijamente, fijar la vista. **2 [to – + *adv./prep.*]** saltar a la vista, salir de ojo, llamar la atención. || *s.c.* **3** mirada fija. || **4 to – out,** hacer bajar la vista con la mirada, sostener la mirada. **5 to – someone in the face,** (fam.) **a)** saltar a la vista, ser obvio, estar claro; **b)** ser inminente, estar a punto de suceder.

starfish | 'stɑːfɪʃ | *s.c.* ZOOL. estrella de mar.

stark | stɑːk | *adj.* **1** estricto, austero, riguroso (una verdad). **2** (fig.) simple, pelado, escueto, sin adornos, mondo y lirondo (los hechos). **3** desolado, yermo, pelado (un lugar). **4** total, completo, absoluto, claro, obvio: *they lived in stark poverty = vivían en absoluta pobreza.* || *adv.* **5** totalmente, completamente, absolutamente. || **6 – naked,** (fam.) en cueros, completamente desnudo. **7 – raving/staring mad,** (fam. y hum.) como una cabra, loco de atar.

starkly | 'stɑːklɪ *adv.* **1** estrictamente, rigurosamente. **2** escuetamente, al desnudo, claramente, llanamente: *to put it starkly, we have to leave = por decirlo llanamente, tenemos que irnos.* **3** totalmente, completamente.

starkness | 'stɑːknɪs | *s.i.* desnudez, desolación (de un paraje).

starkers | 'stɑːkəz | *adj.* (brit., hum. y fam.) en cueros, como Dios lo trajo al mundo.

starlet | 'stɑːlɪt | *s.c.* **1** aspirante a estrella, estrella joven (de cine, teatro). **2** estrellita, estrella pequeña.

starlight | 'stɑːlaɪt | *s.i.* luz de las estrellas.

starling | 'stɑːlɪŋ | *s.c.* ZOOL. estornino.

starlit | 'stɑːlɪt | *adj.* iluminado por las estrellas.

starry | 'stɑːrɪ | *adj.* **1** estrellado, tachonado de estrellas, plagado de estrellas. **2** en forma de estrella. **3** brillante, fulgurante, rutilante, titilante. **4** estelar.

starry-eyed | ˌstɑːrɪ'aɪd | *adj.* (fam. y desp.) romántico, idealista, ingenuo, cándido, soñador, lleno de esperanzas, emocionado: *starry-eyed about the trip = emocionado con el viaje.*

star-studded | ˌstɑː'stʌdɪd | *adj.* plagado de famosos, lleno de estrellas célebres, estelar: *a star-studded film = una película con un reparto estelar.*

start | stɑːt | *v.t.* e *i.* **1 [to – + *s./inf./ger.*]** empezar, comenzar, iniciar(se), principiar (una acción, un viaje). **2 [to – (up)]** fundar(se), abrir, montar, crear (un negocio): *she's started the family business = ella montó el negocio familiar.* **3** iniciar(se), formar(se), originar(se) (un asunto, un rumor). **4** arrancar, poner(se) en marcha, empezar a funcionar: *the car wouldn't start = el coche no se ponía en marcha.* | *v.i.* **5 [to – (in/on)]**

empezar a trabajar: *can you start next month? = ¿puede empezar a trabajar el mes próximo?* **6 [to – (for/off/out)]** partir, salir, marchar, ponerse en camino: *we dont't have to start early = no tenemos que ponernos en camino temprano.* **7** DEP. tomar parte, iniciar (una competición). **8** (fam.) ponerse pesado, empezar a molestar, empezar a dar la vara: *don't star again! = ¡no empieces a dar la vara otra vez!* **9 [to – (at)]** sobresaltarse, asustarse, espantarse. **10 [to – +** *adv./prep.*] (lit.) saltar, ponerse (de pie) bruscamente: *starting to her feet = poniéndose bruscamente de pie.* || *v.t.* **11** abrir, empezar, comenzar, iniciar (un producto, una nueva vida, un tema de conversación). **12** causar, provocar (una desgracia). || *s.c.* **13** salida, partida, marcha. **14** comienzo, inicio, principio. **15 [the –]** DEP. salida, línea de salida. **16** (generalmente *sing.*) sobresalto, susto, respingo. **17** impulso, arranque, pronto. || *s.c.* e *i.* **18 [– (on/over)]** ventaja, delantera. || **19 false –,** comienzo en falso, mal comienzo. **20 for a –,** en primer lugar, para empezar. **21 from – to finish,** de principio a fin. **22 to get off to a good/bad –,** empezar con buen o mal pie, tener un buen o mal comienzo. **23 to get off to a flying –,** V. **flying. 24 to keep/– the ball rolling,** V. **ball. 25 in fits and starts,** V. **fit. 26 to make a –,** empezar, ponerse manos a la obra. **27 to – a family,** crear una familia. **28 to – from scratch,** empezar de la nada, empezar desde abajo. **29 starting point,** punto de partida (en una discusión, de un viaje). **30 to – off, a)** ponerse en camino, empezar un viaje, partir; **b)** poner a hacer algo (a alguien), poner en marcha, iniciar (en una actividad). **31 to – on,** emprender, comenzar (una actividad). **32 to – out,** partir hacia, salir hacia. **33 to – something,** (fam.) buscar problemas, buscar pelea. **34 to – with, a)** en primer lugar, para empezar; **b)** al principio, en un principio.

starter | 'stɑːtər | *s.c.* **1** DEP. corredor, jinete, competidor, participante. **2** DEP. juez de salida. **3** MEC. motor de arranque. **4** (brit. y fam.) entrante, aperitivo (de una comida). || **5 for starters,** (fam.) lo primero, para empezar.

startle | 'stɑːtl | *v.t.* alarmar, sobresaltar, asustar, dar un susto, sobrecoger: *I was startled by the news = me alarmaron las noticias.*

startled | 'stɑːtld | *adj.* alarmado, sobrecogido, asustado, sobresaltado.

startling | 'stɑːtlɪŋ | *adj.* **1** alarmante, dramático, sorprendente, sobrecogedor, asombroso. **2** chocante, llamativo, chillón, exagerado.

startingly | stɑːtɪŋlɪ | *adv.* alarmantemente, dramáticamente, sorprendentemente, asombrosamente.

starvation | stɑː'veɪʃn | *s.i.* **1** inanición, hambre. **2** (fig.) hambre, privación: *a starvation diet = una dieta de pasar hambre.*

starve | stɑːv | *v.t.* e *i.* **1** morir de hambre, matar de hambre, morir de inanición, privar de alimentos, sufrir hambre. **2 [to – (of)]** privar, sufrir por falta de cariño: *children starving for afection = niños privados de cariño.* || **3 to be starving,** (fig.) estar hambriento, morirse de hambre.

stash | stæʃ | *v.t.* **1 [to – +** *o.* **+** *adv./prep.*] (fam.) esconder, ocultar. || *s.c.* **2** (fam.) escondite, escondrijo. **3** objeto oculto, cosa escondida.

state | steɪt | *s.c.* **1** [– (of)] estado, condición, situación. **2** aspecto, apariencia, naturaleza. **3** POL. estado, nación, territorio. **4** estado, provincia, departamento, cantón. || *s.i.* **5 [(the) –]** estado, gobierno, cuerpo político: *a socialist state = un gobierno socialista.* **6** magnificencia, gala, majestad, fausto, pompa. **7** posición social, rango, dignidad. || *v.t.* **8** declarar, manifestar, exponer, decir, expresar, hacer constar: *please, state whether you were there or not = por favor, manifieste si Vd. estaba allí o no.* **9** especificar, establecer, fijar: *he left the country on the stated date = dejo el país en la fecha establecida.* || *adj.* **10** estatal, del estado, público, de estado: *state secrets = secretos de estado.* **11** ceremonial, de gala, lujoso. || **12 to be in a –/to get into a –,** (brit. y fam.) estar nervioso, ponerse nervioso, inquietarse, estar inquieto. **13 in –,** ceremonialmente, con gran pompa, con gran boato, muy lujosamente. **14 in a – of nature,** (hum.) en cueros, totalmente desnudo. **15 to lie in –,** estar de cuerpo presente, yacer en la capilla ardiente. **16 not to be in a fit –,** no estar en condiciones, no estar capacitado, no estar preparado. **17 State Department,** (EE.UU.) Departamento de Estado, Ministerio de Asuntos Exteriores. **18 State Enrolled Nurse,** V. SEN. **19 – of affairs,** la situación, las circunstancias. **20 – of mind,** humor, estado de ánimo. **21 State Registered Nurse,** V. **SRN. 22 the States,** los Estados Unidos de Norteamérica.

statecraft | 'steɪtkrɑːft | *s.i.* política, arte de gobernar.

stateless | 'steɪtlɪs | *adj.* apátrida, sin nacionalidad.

stateliness | 'steɪtlɪnɪs | *s.i.* majestad, grandeza, esplendor, dignidad.

stately | 'steɪtlɪ | *adj.* **1** imponente, impresionante, majestuoso, sublime, grandioso, formidable. || **2 – home,** (brit.) mansión, casa solariega (generalmente de interés histórico-artístico).

statement | 'steɪtmənt | *s.c.* **1** declaración, afirmación, exposición, aserción, informe. **2** DER. testimonio, declaración. **3** FIN. extracto, informe (bancario), estado de cuenta, cuenta. || *s.i.* **4** (form.) expresión, exposición.

stateroom | 'steɪtrum | *s.c.* **1** MAR. camarote. **2** salón de recepciones (en un palacio).

statesman | 'steɪtsmən | [*pl.* **statesmen**] *s.c.* estadista, hombre de estado.

statesmanship | 'steɪtsmənʃɪp | *s.i.* habilidad de estadista, capacidad de estadista, arte de gobernar.

statesmen | 'steɪtsmən | *pl.irreg.* de **statesman.**

static | 'stætɪk | *adj.* **1** estático, estancado, estacionario, fijo. **2** inactivo, inmóvil. **3** [no *comp.*] ELEC. estático. || *s.i.* **4** RAD. interferencia. || **5 statics,** FIS. estática.

station | 'steɪʃn | *s.c.* **1** estación (de ferrocarril, de autobuses, de metro). **2** observatorio (de investigación). **3** comisaría, cuartel (de policía, de bomberos). **4** gasolinera. **5** MIL. puesto (fronterizo, naval). **6** colegio (electoral). **7** RAD. emisora. **8** rancho de ovejas, granja de ovino, dehesa de ovejas (en Australia). **9** (arc.) clase social, posición social, rango, condición social. || *s.i.* **10** MAR. puesto de servicio (en un buque de guerra). || *v.t.* **11 [to – +** *o.* **+** *adv./prep.* y generalmente *pas.*] MIL. estacionar, apostar, destinar: *the soldiers were stationed in the border = los soldados fueron estacionados en la frontera.* || **12 – house,** (EE.UU.) **a)** comisaría de policía; **b)** cuartel de bomberos. **13 – wagon,** furgoneta, rubia. **14 stations of the Cross,** REL. estaciones del Viacrucis.

stationary | 'steɪʃənrɪ | (EE.UU.) | 'steɪʃənerɪ | *adj.* estacionado, parado, inmóvil, fijo: *a stationary vehicle = un vehículo estacionado.*

stationer | 'steɪʃnər | *s.c.* **1** dueño de papelería, papelero. || **2 the –/stationer's,** papelería.

stationery | 'steɪʃənrɪ | (EE.UU.) | 'steɪʃənerɪ | *s.i.* **1** útiles de papelería, efectos de escritorio. **2** papel de escribir y sobres.

stationmaster | 'steɪʃnˌmɑːstər | *s.c.* jefe de estación (de ferrocarril).

statistic | stə'tɪstɪk | *s.c.* **1** dato, número, cifra (en una estadística). || **2 statistics,** MAT. **a)** estadística (ciencia); **b)** estadísticas, datos estadísticos.

statistical | stə'tɪstɪkl | *adj.* estadístico.

statistically | 'stə'tɪstɪklɪ | *adv.* conforme a la estadística, según las estadísticas.

statistician | ˌstætɪ'stɪʃn | *s.c.* estadístico.

statuary | 'stætjuərɪ | *s.i.* ART. **1** estatuaria, estatuas (grupo, colección). **3** escultura. || *s.c.* **2** escultor.

statue | 'stætʃuː | *s.c.* estatua, escultura.

statuesque | ˌstætju'esk | *adj.* escultural, imponente, impresionante (una mujer).

statuette | ˌstætju'et | *s.c.* estatuilla, figurilla.

stature | 'stætʃər | *s.c.* e *i.* **1** (fig.) estatura, talla, prominencia, importancia, nivel: *a scientist of great stature = un científico de gran prominencia.* **2** estatura, altura, tamaño: *of tall stature = de estatura alta.*

status | 'steɪtəs | | 'stætəs | *s.c.* e *i.* **1** DER. estado, condición: *marital status = estado civil.* || *s.i.* **2** rango, categoría, posición, nivel, prestigio (social, profesional): *social status* = posición social. || *s.c.* **3** estado, situación: *the status of the negociations doesn't seem very promising = el estado de las negociaciones no parece muy prometedor.* || **4 – quo,** statu quo, estado de las cosas. **5 – symbol,** símbolo de prestigio.

statute | 'stætjuːt | *s.c.* **1** (form.) ley. **2** estatuto, reglamento. || **3 (the) – book,** DER. código de leyes. || **4 on the – book,** en funcionamiento (una ley).

statutorily | 'stætjutərɪlɪ | *adv.* legalmente, estatutariamente.

statutory | 'stætjutərɪ | (EE.UU.) | 'stætʃutɔːrɪ | *adj.* **1** estatutario, estatuido, legal, establecido por ley. **2** nominal, elegido a dedo: *there were some statutory members on the committee =*

había algunos miembros en el comité elegidos a dedo.
staunch | stɔːntʃ | *adj.* **1** incondicional, leal, fiel, partidario: *a staunch believer = un fiel creyente.* || *v.t.* **2** (EE.UU.) **stanch,** restañar, detener, contener (la sangre), taponar (una herida).
staunchly | stɔːntʃlɪ | *adv.* incondicionalmente, fielmente, lealmente, firmemente.
stave | steɪv | *s.c.* **1** (también **staff**) MUS. pentagrama. **2** duela (de un barril). **3** peldaño (de una escalera de mano). **4** garrote, estaca, porra. **5** LIT. estrofa, estancia. || *v.t.* [*irr.pret.* y *p.p.* **staved** o **stove**]. **6** romper las duelas. || **7 to – in, a)** romper, abrir un agujero, abrir un boquete, quebrar por golpes; **b)** MAR. desfondarse. **8 to – off,** mantener alejado, evitar, repeler, impedir, detener. **9 staves,** *pl.* **V. staff.**
stay | steɪ | *v.i.* **1** quedar(se), permanecer, estar. **2 [to – +** *adv./prep.***]** permanecer, continuar, seguir, proseguir: *will you stay in teaching? = ¿seguirás como profesor?* **3 [to – (at/with)]** hospedarse, alojarse, estar, residir (poco tiempo, como visitante, invitado): *I stayed at the Cork Hotel for a week = me hospedé en el Hotel Cork durante una semana.* **4** (generalmente *imperativo*) (arc.) esperar, parar: *stay! = ¡un momento!, ¡espera!* **5** aguantar, soportar, resistir. **6** quedarse (en el póker). || *v.t.* **7** parar, detener, frenar, poner freno: *the doctors stayed the desease = los médicos pusieron freno a la epidemia.* **8** posponer, retrasar, demorar, retardar. **9** DER. aplazar, suspender, prorrogar. **10** calmar, apaciguar, serenar (los ánimos). **11** sujetar, sostener, apuntalar. **12** (fig.) resistir, aguantar. || *s.sing.* **13** estancia, visita, permanencia. **14** MAR. estay. **15** soporte, puntal, riostra. || *s.c.* e *i.* **16** DER. aplazamiento, prórroga, suspensión. **17** parada, detención. || *s.i.* **18** (fig.) sostén, alivio, apoyo. || **19 to have come to –/to be here to –,** (fam.) haberse establecido, generalizarse (una moda, un hábito). **20 to – in,** quedarse en casa, no salir. **21 – of execution,** DER. aplazamiento de sentencia. **22 – of proceedings,** DER. sobreseimiento. **23 to – on,** continuar, quedarse. **24 to – out, a)** quedarse fuera de casa, pasar la noche fuera de casa; **b)** permanecer en huelga. **25 to – put,** (fam.) estarse quieto, no moverse. **26 to – the course,** aguantar hasta el final (a pesar de las dificultades). **27 to – up,** quedarse levantado, permanecer despierto.
stay-at-home | 'steɪəthəʊm | *s.c.* (fam. y desp.) persona casera, persona hogareña, persona poco aventurera.
staying power | 'steɪɪŋ,paʊər | *s.i.* aguante, resistencia, fuerza, vigor.
STD | ,es tiː 'diː | *s.i. abreviatura* de **subscriber trunk dialling,** sistema telefónico directo de larga distancia.
stead | sted | *s.c.* **1** lugar, posición. || **2 in someone's –,** en lugar de alguien. **3 to stand someone in good –,** ser de utilidad a alguien, servir a alguien.
steadfast | 'stedfəːst | (EE.UU.) | 'stedfæst | *adj.* (form.) **1** fiel, leal, incondicional, constante. **2** determinado, resuelto, firme.
steadfastly | 'stedfəːstlɪ | *adv.* **1** resueltamente, con determinación. **2** fielmente, incondicionalmente, constantemente.
steadfastness | 'stedfəːstnɪs | *s.i.* **1** fidelidad, constancia. **2** resolución, determinación.
steadily | 'stedɪlɪ | *adv.* **1** firmemente, resistentemente. **2** uniformemente, regularmente, sin parar, continuamente, constantemente: *prices have increased steadily = los precios han subido sin parar.* **3** fijamente, serenamente, tranquilamente, imperturbablemente.
steadiness | 'stedɪnɪs | *s.i.* **1** firmeza, estabilidad, seguridad, resistencia. **2** uniformidad, regularidad, constancia.
steady | 'stedɪ | *adj.* **1** firme, seguro, resistente. **2** uniforme, regular, continuo, constante: *at a steady rhythm = a un ritmo constante.* **3** estable, seguro, fijo: *a steady job = un trabajo estable.* **4** sensato, prudente, juicioso, serio, maduro. **5** tranquilo, sereno, sosegado. || *v.t.* e *i.* **6** estabilizar(se), hacer(se) estable, regularizar(se). **7** tranquilizar(se), serenar(se), calmar(se). || *adv.* **8** regularmente. || **9 to be going –,** salir, ser novios, mantener relaciones. **10 –!/– on!,** ¡cuidado!, ¡calma!, ¡tranquilo! **11 – as a rock,** más firme que una roca.
steak | steɪk | *s.c.* e *i.* **1** filete, bistec. || *s.i.* **2** (brit.) carne en trozos, carne para guisar, carne picada.
steal | stiːl | *v.irr.pret.* **stole,** *p.p.* **stolen,** *t.* e *i.* **1 [to – (from)]** robar, hurtar, quitar. || *v.t.* **2 [to – (from)]** (fig.) robar, obtener, conseguir (por sorpresa, con rapidez): *steal a kiss from a girl = robarle un beso a una chica.* || *v.i.* **3 [to – +** *adv./prep.***]** escabullirse, deslizarse disimuladamente, desaparecer sin ser notado. || *s.sing.* **4** (EE.UU. y fam.) ganga, chollo. || **5 to – a glance,** mirar de soslayo, mirar disimuladamente. **6 to – a march on,** ganar por la mano a, anticiparse a. **7 to – someone's thunder,** (fam.) adelantarse a uno robándole una idea. **8 to – the show,** V. **show.**
stealth | stelθ | *s.i.* **1** (form.) secreto, cautela, cuidado, sigilo. || **2 by –,** a hurtadillas, en secreto, subrepticiamente.
stealthily | 'stelθɪlɪ | *adv.* (form.) furtivamente, subrepticiamente, a hurtadillas, clandestinamente.
stealthy | 'stelθɪ | *adj.* (form.) secreto, furtivo, cauteloso, sigiloso, clandestino.
steam | stiːm | *s.i.* **1** vapor. **2** (fig.) energía, rapidez. **3** vaho: *the room was full of steam = la habitación estaba llena de vaho.* || *v.i.* **4** humear, exhalar vapor. **5 [to – +** *adv./prep.***]** avanzar a vapor, andar a vapor (un medio de transporte). || *v.t.* **6** cocer al vapor. **7 [to – +** *o.* **+** *adj./adv./prep.***]** abrir al vapor, despegar al vapor (un sobre). || *adj.* **8** [no *comp.*] a vapor, de vapor: *a steam car = un coche a vapor.* **9** (brit. y hum.) pasado de moda, del año catapún: *she was wearing a steam dress = llevaba un vestido del año catapún.* || **10 to get/pick up –, a)** tomar velocidad, coger velocidad (un vehículo); **b)** cobrar importancia (un plan, un proyecto); **c)** reunir energías (una persona). **11 to let off –,** (fam. y fig.) desahogarse. **12 to run out of –,** (fam.) estar agotado, acabársele a uno las fuerzas. **13 – iron,** plancha de vapor. **14 to – up, a)** empañarse, tomarse (un cristal); **b)** (fam.) ponerse como un basilisco, enfadarse mucho, ponerse furioso. **15 under one's own –,** (fam.) por su propia cuenta, por sus propios medios, sin ayuda.
steamer | 'stiːmər | *s.c.* **1** buque de vapor, barco de vapor. **2** rejilla, cesta metálica de red (para cocer alimentos al vapor).
steamroller | 'stiːm,rəʊlər | *s.c.* **1** apisonadora de vapor. **2** (fam.) fuerza arrolladora, fuerza incontenible, poder irresistible. || *v.t.* **3** (fam.) arrollar, arrasar, emplear todas las fuerzas para, pasar por encima de (para conseguir algo): *he used to steamroller all his oponents = acostumbraba a pasar por encima de sus oponentes.*
steamy | stiːmɪ | *adj.* **1** húmedo y caluroso, lleno de vapor, empañado por el vapor: *she entered that steamy kitchen = entró en aquella cocina llena de vapor.* **2** (fam.) erótico, picante, apasionado (una película, un libro).
steed | stiːd | *s.c.* (lit.) corcel, alazán.
steel | stiːl | *s.i.* **1** acero: *a steel cutlery = una cubertería de acero.* **2** industria del acero, producción de acero: *the steel negociations = las negociaciones de la industria del acero.* **3** (fig.) acero, bronce: *she has nerves of steel = tiene nervios de acero.* **4** (lit.) arma (blanca), acero, puñal, espada, cuchillo. **5** chaira, piedra de afilar; eslabón (para sacar fuego del pedernal). **6** color gris oscuro. || *v.t.* **7 [to – +** *o.* **+ to** *inf.***]** fortalecer, endurecer, hacerse el duro, hacerse el fuerte, cobrar ánimo: *he steeled himself to talk to her = se hizo el fuerte para hablar con ella.* || *adj.* **8** de acero, como el acero. **9** de color gris oscuro, gris azulado. || **10 – band,** MUS. banda de percusión (muy popular en el Caribe). **11 – wool,** estropajo metálico, estopa metálica.
steelworker | 'stiːlwəːkər | *s.c.* obrero del metal, obrero de la siderurgia.
steelworks | 'stiːlwəːk | *s.c.* **[– +** *v.sing./pl.***]** siderurgia, fábrica de acero, acería.
steely | 'stiːlɪ | *adj.* **1** (fig.) fría, dura, severa (una mirada). **2** inflexible, duro, firme. **3** como el acero, grisáceo, metálico.
steep | stiːp | *adj.* **1** escarpado, pendiente, empinado, abrupto. **2** en picado, fuerte (una subida una bajada de precios). **3** (fam.) exagerado, excesivo, alto, exorbitante (un precio, una demanda). **4** (fam.) ambiciosa, difícil (una tarea). || *v.t.* e *i.* **5** marinar, adobar: *steep the meat in oil, vinegar and mustard = adobar la carne en aceite, vinagre y mostaza.* **6** poner en remojo, empapar, impregnar. || **7 a bit – a)** bastante difícil, poco razonable; **b)** muy caro.
steeped | stiːpt | *adj.* impregnado, empapado: *a place steeped in prejudice = impregnado de prejuicios.*
steeply | 'stiːplɪ | *adv.* **1** abruptamente, escarpadamente. **2** fuertemente, exageradamente.
steepness | 'stiːpnɪs | *s.i.* lo escarpado, lo abrupto, empinamiento.
steeple | 'stiːpl | *s.c.* **1** aguja, chapitel. **2** torre, campanario.
steeplechase | 'stiːpltʃeɪs | *s.c.* DEP. carrera con obstáculos, carrera de vallas.

steeplejack | 'stiːpldʒæk | *s.c.* reparador de torres, tejados, chimeneas.

steer | stɪər | *v.t.* e *i.* **1** guiar, dirigir, conducir, manejar, maniobrar (un vehículo). **2** (fig.) llevar, guiar, conducir (a una persona). **3** (fig.) encauzar, encaminar (una conversación). **4** seguir un curso, dirigir(se), tomar, cambiar (un camino, el rumbo): *they steered a dangerous way = tomaron una ruta peligrosa.* || *v.i.* **5** obedecer al timón, volver el volante, responder el timón: *the car doesn't steer well = el coche no responde bien.* || *s.c.* **6** buey, novillo. **7** (EE.UU.) consejo, aviso, recomendación. || **8 to – clear of,** (fam.) mantenerse alejado de, evitar contacto con.

steering | stɪərɪŋ | *s.i.* **1** MEC. dirección, conducción, gobierno (de un vehículo). || **2 – wheel,** volante.

stellar | 'stelər | *adj.* (form.) **1** estelar, astral. **2** estelar, de estrella de cine. **3** notable, sobresaliente, principal.

stem | stem | *s.c.* **1** BOT. tallo, retoño, tronco; peciolo, pedúnculo. **2** pie (de una copa). **3** cañón (de una pipa, de una pluma). **4** FILOL. raíz, tema (de una palabra). || *v.t.* [*pret.* y *p.p.* **stemmed,** *ger.* **stemming**]. **5** (form.) restañar, taponar, contener, detener (el flujo). **6** (fig.) frenar, detener, hacer frente: *they'll have to stem the tide of protest somehow = tendrán que hacer frente a la avalancha de protestas de algún modo.* || **7 from – to stern,** de proa a popa. **8 to – from,** surgir de, proceder de, provenir de, resultar de.

-stemmed | stemd | *sufijo* [*adj.* + –] de (cierto) tallo, de (cierto) pie, de (cierto) cañón: *a thick-stemmed glass = una copa de pie ancho.*

stench | stentʃ | *s.sing.* (form.) hedor, fetidez, hediondez.

stencil | 'stensl | *s.c.* **1** estarcido, plantilla, patrón picado. **2** cliché (para multicopista). || *v.t.* [(brit.) **stencilled, stencilling,** (EE.UU.) **stenciled, stenciling**]. **3** estarcir, dibujar o pintar con plantilla o patrón picado. **4** sacar un cliché, hacer un cliché.

stenographer | stə'nɒgrəfər | *s.c.* (EE.UU.) estenógrafo, taquígrafo.

stenography | stə'nɔgrəfɪ | *s.c.* taquigrafía.

stentorian | sten'tɔːrɪən | *adj.* estentóreo.

step | step | *s.c.* **1** paso: *three steps forward = tres pasos adelante.* **2** paso, pisada, huella. **3** paso, distancia corta, metro: *the house was a few steps from the beach = la casa estaba a unos pasos de la playa.* **4** peldaño, escalón, grada. **5** paso, medida, gestión: *phoning her should be the first step = llamarla por teléfono debería ser la primera medida.* **6** categoría, grado, esfera. **7** paso (de baile). **8** (EE.UU.) MUS. intervalo. **9** MAR. carlinga. **10** INF. paso, instrucción. || *v.i.* [**stepped, stepping**]. **11** dar un paso, dar pasos. **12** caminar, andar, ir. **13 [to – on]** pisar, tropezar. **14** tratar con indiferencia, mirar por encima del hombro, comportarse arrogantemente. || *v.t.* **15** poner, echar, plantar (el pie): *step foot on land = echar pie a tierra.* **16** medir a pasos (una distancia). **17** escalonar, colocar de trecho en trecho. **18** INF. dar una sola instrucción. **19** MAR. plantar (el mástil). || **20 to break –,** perder el paso (en una marcha). **21 to fall into –,** empezar a llevar el paso. **22 in –, a)** llevando el paso, al paso; **b)** en la misma línea, de acuerdo, conforme (con alguien). **23 out of –, a)** sin llevar el paso, de forma desordenada; **b)** no en la misma línea, en desacuerdo, disconforme. **24 to – aside/down,** apartarse, echarse a un lado, hacerse a un lado. **25 to – back, a)** retroceder, dar un paso atrás; **b)** quedar al margen, quedar a un lado. **26 – by step,** paso a paso, poco a poco, por partes. **27 to – in,** intervenir, tomar parte, meterse (en una discusión, en una situación problemática). **28 to – into the breach,** (fam.) echar una mano (sustituyendo a alguien ausente). **29 to – into someone's shoes,** V. **shoe. 30 to – on, a)** (fam. y fig.) pisar, pisotear (a alguien de menor importancia); **b)** pisar el acelerador, acelerar. **31 to – on it/** (EE.UU.) **to – on the gas,** (fam.) ir más deprisa, acelerar, darse prisa. **32 to – out, a)** (arc.) ir deprisa, acelerar el paso; **b)** (EE.UU.) salir, ir de juerga. **33 to – out of line,** V. **line. 34 steps,** escalera de mano. **35 to – up,** intensificar, aumentar. **36 to take steps,** tomar medidas, dar los pasos necesarios. **37 to watch one's –,** tener cuidado.

stepbrother | 'steptˌbrʌðər | *s.c.* hermanastro.

stepchild | 'steptʃaɪld | [*pl.* **stepchildren**] *s.c.* hijastro, entenado, alnado.

stepchildren | 'stepˌtʃɪldrən | *pl.irreg.* de **stepchild.**

stepdaughter | 'stepˌdɔːtər | *s.c.* hijastra, entenada, alnada.

stepfather | 'stepˌfɑːðər | *s.c.* padrastro.

stepladder | 'stepˌlædər | *s.c.* escalera de mano, escalera plegable, escalera de tijera.

stepmother | 'stepˌmʌðər | *s.c.* madrastra.

stepparent | 'stepˌpeərənt | *s.c.* padrastro, madrastra.

steppe | step | *s.c.* (generalmente *pl.*) GEOG. estepa.

stepped-up | 'steptʌp | *adj.* intensificado, intenso, acelerado, activado, aumentado: *stepped-up production = producción acelerada.*

stepping stone | 'stepɪŋstəun | *s.c.* **1** pasadera, saltana, piedra (para pasar un río). **2 [– (to)]** (fig.) escalón, peldaño, paso adelante, ayuda (para progresar): *a stepping stone in his career = un paso adelante en su carrera.*

stepsister | 'stepˌsɪstər | *s.c.* hermanastra.

stepson | 'stepsʌn | *s.c.* hijastro, alnado, entenado.

stereo | 'sterɪəu | | 'stɪərɪəu | *s.c.* **1** tocadiscos estereofónico, radio estereofónica. || *s.i.* **2** sonido estereofónico. || *adj.* (también **stereophonic**). **3** estereofónico.

stereophonic | ˌsterɪə'fɒnɪk | *adj.* (form.) estereofónico.

stereotype | 'stɪərɪətaɪp | *s.c.* **1 [– (of)]** (desp.) estereotipo, cliché: *the stereotype of a Spaniard dancing flamenco = el cliché de un español bailando flamenco.* || *v.t.* **2** (desp.) estereotipar, encasillar. **3** imprimir, estereotipar.

sterile | 'steraɪl | *adj.* **1** [no *comp.*] estéril, improductivo, infecundo. **2** árido, yermo, baldío. **3** aséptico, esterilizado, desinfectado. **4** (desp. y fig.) estéril, superfluo, vacío, falto de imaginación (el discurso, la vida).

sterility | ste'rɪlɪtɪ | *s.i.* esterilidad, improductividad, infecundidad.

sterilization | ˌsterɪlaɪ'zeɪʃn | (brit. **sterilisation**) *s.i.* esterilización.

sterilize | 'sterəlaɪz | (brit. **sterilise**) *v.t.* **1** esterilizar, castrar, capar, emascular. **2** esterilizar, desinfectar.

sterilized | 'sterəlaɪzd | (brit. **sterilised**) *adj.* esterilizado, desinfectado, aséptico.

sterling | stəːlɪŋ | *s.i.* **1** libra esterlina (sistema monetario): *sterling is going down = está bajando la libra esterlina.* || *adj.* **2** [no *comp.*] (form.) excelente, de grandes cualidades, leal. **3** de ley, puro, fino, verdadero, genuino (la plata, el oro, la moneda): *sterling silver = plata de ley.*

stern | stəːn | *adj.* **1** severo, duro, estricto, férreo, inflexible (una persona, la disciplina, una mirada). **2** desagradable, difícil, laborioso, duro (un trabajo). || *s.c.* **3** MAR. popa. **4** (fam. y hum.) trasero, nalgas. || **5 to be made of sterner stuff,** ser de hierro, tener mucho carácter. **6 from stem to –,** V. **stem.**

sterna | 'stəːnə | *pl.* de **sternum.**

sternly | 'stəːnlɪ | *adv.* severamente, duramente.

sternness | 'stəːnɪs | *s.i.* severidad, austeridad, firmeza, dureza, inflexibilidad.

sternum | 'stəːnm | [*pl.* **sternums** o **sterna**] *s.c.* ANAT. esternón.

steroid | 'stɪərɔɪd | *s.c.* QUIM. esteroide.

stertorous | 'stəːtərəs | *adj.* (lit., hum.) estertoroso, con estertores.

stethoscope | 'steθəskəup | *s.c.* MED. estetoscopio.

stetson | 'stetsn | *s.c.* sombrero de vaquero.

stevedore | 'stiːvɪdɔː | *s.c.* (EE.UU.) estibador, obrero portuario.

stew | stjuː | (EE.UU.) | stuː | *v.t.* e *i.* **1** guisar, estofar, hacer a fuego lento. || *v.i.* **2** (fam.) cocerse, sofocarse, acalorarse, sudar la gota gorda. **3** preocuparse, inquietarse. || *s.c.* e *i.* **4** estofado, guiso, (Am.) puchero. || *s.sing.* **5** (fam.) ansiedad, confusión, agitación mental. **6** lío, follón, apuro. || **7 in a –,** en apuros, muy nervioso, muy preocupado. **8 to let someone – in his own juice,** (fam. y fig.) dejar que alguien se cueza en su propia salsa, dejar que alguien se carcoma por dentro. **9 stewing steak,** carne para guisar. **10 stews,** (arc.) burdel, lupanar.

steward | stjuəd | (EE.UU.) | 'stuːərd | *s.c.m.* **1** AER. ayudante de vuelo, camarero. **2** organizador, director. **3** (arc.) encargado, gerente, administrador, mayordomo.

stewardess | ˌstjuə'des | (EE.UU.) | 'stuːərdəs | *s.c.f.* AER. azafata, camarera.

stewardship | ˌstjuəd'ʃɪp | , (EE.UU.) | 'stuːərdʃɪp | *s.i.* **[– (of)]** (form.) gerencia, administración.

stick | stɪk | *s.c.* **1** palo, vara, astilla: *sticks for a fire = astillas para el fuego.* **2** bastón, cayado, vara. **3** palo, porra, garrote, tranca. **4 [– (of)]** tallo, trozo, barra: *a stick of chalk = una tiza.* **5** DEP.

palo, bate, raqueta. **6** cartucho (de dinamita). **7** (brit., arc. y fam.) tipo, tío: *a boring stick = un tipo aburrido.* **8** (fam.) trasto, telar, pieza, mueble sin valor. **9** (argot) porro de marihuana, cigarrillo de marihuana. **10** AER. palanca de mando. **11** MAR. mástil, palo, verga. **12** MIL. bombas en serie (sobre un objetivo). **13** pinchazo, punzada. **14** dificultad, obstáculo, inconveniente, impedimento. || *s.i.* **15** (brit. y fam.) paliza, leña; rapapolvo, bronca, regañina. **16** adherencia, pegajosidad. || *v.irr.pret.* y *p.p.* **stuck.** *t.* **17 [to – +** *o.* **+** *adv./prep.*] clavar, pinchar, espetar, hincar: *sticking the peas with her fork = pinchando los guisantes con el tenedor.* **18** [**to – +** *o.* + *adv./prep.*] (fam.) poner, echar encima (ropa); introducir, colocar, meter: *stick the record on the self = coloca el disco en el estante.* **19** (generalmente en *interr.* y *negativa*) (brit. y fam.) gustar, soportar, tolerar, aguantar: *I can't stick him = no le puedo soportar.* **20** (brit. y jerga) quedarse con: *you can stick your awful son! = ¡quédese con su espantoso hijo!* || *v.i.* **21** atascarse, quedar atascado, trabarse, engancharse, bloquearse. **22** prenderse, estar prendido (un alfiler). **23** pegarse, quedarse, recordar continuamente: *the tune easily sticks = la tonada se pega fácilmente.* **24** (fam.) persistir, permanecer, quedarse, sostenerse: *they can't make the charges stick = las pruebas no se sostienen.* || *v.t.* e *i.* **25** pegar(se), adherir(se), encolar(se). || **26 to get/get hold of the wrong end of the –,** malinterpretar, coger mal, equivocarse. **27 to get/take –/to give someone –,** (fam.) dar el palo, criticar severamente, poner verde. **28 more than one can shake a – at,** V. **shake. 29 to – about/around,** (fam.) esperar cerca, esperar por ahí. **30 to – at,** continuar trabajando, persistir, no abandonar. **31 to – at nothing,** no tener escrúpulos, intentar cualquier cosa, no pararse en barras. **32 to – by,** (fam.) apoyar, defender, ser fiel. **33 –'em up!,** (fam.) ¡manos arriba! **34 to – in your throat,** V. **throat. 35 – insect,** ZOOL. insecto palo perteneciente al orden de los fármidos. **36 to – out, a)** proyectarse, asomar, sobresalir; **b)** verse a distancia, verse a la legua, ser evidente; **c)** continuar hasta el fin, persistir, no cejar. **37 to – out a mile,** verse a leguas, ser evidente, ser obvio, estar claro. **38 to – out for,** insistir, no ceder, perseverar (para conseguir algo). **39 to – out like a sore thumb,** V. **thumb. 40 to – to,** seguir fiel, continuar con, quedarse con. **41 to – to one's guns,** no dar el brazo a torcer, mantenerse en sus trece. **42 to – together,** (fam.) mantenerse unidos, ser fieles el uno al otro. **43 sticks,** (fam. y desp.) lugar apartado de la civilización, zona rural, donde Cristo perdió el zapato. **44 to – up, a)** pegar, fijar (un cartel); **b)** sobresalir, apuntar hacia arriba; **c)** (fam.) atracar, robar, amenazar con un arma. **45 to – up for,** defender, sacar la cara por. **46 to – with,** estar al lado de, apoyar a, ser leal a. **46 – with it,** continúa, persiste. **47 to – your neck out,** V. **neck.**

sticker | stɪkər | *s.c.* **1** pegatina. **2** etiqueta. **3** (fam.) persona determinada, persona perseverante, persona aplicada. **4** espino, pincho, púa.

sticking plaster | stɪkɪŋˌplɑːstər | *s.c.* tirita, esparadrapo.

stick-in-the-mud | 'stɪkɪnðəmʌd | *s.c.* (fam. y desp.) anticuado, conservador, carca, reaccionario.

stickleback | 'stɪklbæk | *s.c.* ZOOL. pez espinoso.

stickler | 'stɪklər | *s.c.* **1 [– (for)]** (fam.) rigorista, persona insistente, quisquilloso: *a stickler for discipline = un quisquilloso de la disciplina.* **2** dificultad, problema serio.

stick-on | 'stɪkən | *adj.* adhesivo, engomado.

stickpin | 'stɪkpɪn | *s.c.* (EE.UU.) alfiler de corbata.

stick-up | 'stɪkʌp | *s.c.* (fam. y arc.) atraco, robo, asalto.

stickiness | 'stɪkɪnɪs | *s.i.* viscosidad.

sticky | 'stɪkɪ | *adj.* **1** pegajoso, viscoso: *sticky sweets = caramelos pegajosos.* **2** adhesivo, engomado. **3** húmedo y caluroso (el tiempo). **4** (fam.) difícil, embarazosa, penosa, desagradable (una situación). **5 [– (about)]** (fam.) renuente, remiso, reacio (a prestar ayuda). || **6 to come to a – end/to meet a – end,** (fam.) acabar mal, tener un fin dramático. **7 to have – fingers,** (fam. y fig.) pegársele todo a los dedos, tener tendencia al robo. **8 on a – wicket,** (fam.) en situación difícil, en un callejón sin salida, en la boca del lobo.

stiff | stɪf | *adj.* **1** rígido, duro, tieso. **2** agarrotado, tenso, rígido (un músculo, un hueso). **3** denso, espeso, compacto, consistente. **4** formalista, afectado, ceremonioso, frío. **5** (fam.) fuerte, cargado (una bebida alcohólica). **6** fuerte (un viento). **7** duro, severo: *a stiff sentence = una sentencia dura.* **8** difícil, intrincada, laboriosa, ardua, embrollada (una actividad). **9** tenaz, firme (una resistencia). **10** (fam.) inaceptable, excesivo, exorbitante, desmedido (un precio). || *adv.* **11** extremadamente, enormemente: *bored stiff = extremadamente aburrido.* || *s.c.* **12** (jerga) cadáver. **13** formalista, ceremonioso, etiquetero. || **14 to show/keep – upper lip,** conservar la calma, no mostrarse tenso, no amilanarse.

stiffen | 'stɪfn | *v.t.* e *i.* **1** endurecer, atiesar, dar rigidez, poner rígido. **2** dar(se) fuerza, fortalecer(se): *stiffen her resolve = fortalecer su decisión.* || *v.i.* **3** ponerse tieso, ponerse rígido, hacerse el duro: *when she entered the room, he stiffened = cuando ella entró en la habitación él se puso rígido.*

stiffener | 'stɪfənər | *s.c.* endurecedor, atiesador, barilla: *collar stiffeners = barillas para endurecer el cuello.*

stiffening | 'stɪfənɪŋ | *s.i.* entretela, refuerzo.

stiff-necked | ˌstɪf'nekt | *adj.* obstinado, terco, testarudo.

stiffly | 'stɪflɪ | *adv.* **1** rígidamente, de forma tiesa. **2** agarrotadamente, tensamente, rígidamente. **3** afectadamente, ceremoniosamente, fríamente.

stiffness | stɪfnɪs | *s.i.* **1** agarrotamiento, rigidez (de músculos, huesos). **2** formalismo, estiramiento, frialdad, afectación, ceremoniosidad. **3** espesura, densidad, consistencia.

stifle | 'staɪfl | *v.t.* e *i.* **1** asfixiar, ahogar, sofocar. || *v.t.* **2** sofocar, evitar, reprimir: *stifling a cry = ahogando un grito.*

stifling | 'staɪflɪŋ | *adj.* sofocante, asfixiante, bochornoso: *a stifling day = un día de bochorno.*

stigma | 'stɪgmə | [*pl.* **stigmas** o **stigmata**] *s.c.* **1** estigma, deshonor, tacha. **2** BOT. estigma. || **3 stigmata,** estigmas, marcas, huellas (como Cristo).

stigmata | 'stɪgmətə | *pl.* de **stigma.**

stigmatize | 'stɪgmətaɪz | (brit. **stigmatise**) *v.t.* estigmatizar, conceptuar, considerar, calificar, tachar de: *a person stigmatized as a corrupt = una persona conceptuada como corrupta.*

stile | staɪl | *s.c.* peldaño, zanja (en la portilla de un prado para evitar que salga o entre el ganado).

stiletto | stɪ'letəʊ | *s.c.* **1** estilete, punzón. **2** (también **stiletto shoe**) zapato de tacón de aguja.

still | stɪl | *adv.* **1** aún, todavía: *is he still at school? = ¿está él aún en el colegio?* **2** sin embargo, con todo, a pesar de ello, incluso así, no obstante: *it was quite cold, still not enough to take a jacket = hacía bastante frío, sin embargo no lo suficiente para llevar chaqueta.* **3** [para hacer más fuerte la *comp.*] incluso, además, aún más: *she came up with still more lies = se presentó con más mentiras aún.* **4** (lit.) constantemente, siempre, habitualmente. || *adj.* **5** inmóvil, quieto. **6** apacible, en calma: *it was a still night = era una noche apacible.* **7** tranquilo, silencioso, callado. **8** no efervescente, sin gas, sin burbujas, no espumosa (una bebida). || *v.t.* **9** (lit.) silenciar, acallar, calmar, sosegar: *his arrival stilled her cries = la llegada de él acalló sus gritos.* **10** aliviar, mitigar, apaciguar (temores, dudas). || *s.c.* **11** FOT. foto fija, fotografía de escena cinematográfica. **12 [the =N +** *s.sing.* **+ of]** (lit.) quietud, calma, serenidad, paz. **13** alambique, destilador. **14** destilería. || **15 – life,** ART. naturaleza muerta, bodegón. **16 – waters run deep,** del agua mansa me libre Dios (que de la brava me libro yo). **17 the – small voice of conscience,** la voz de la conciencia, el sentido del bien y el mal.

stillbirth | 'stɪlbɜːθ | ˌstɪl'bɜːθ | *s.c.* e *i.* parto de un niño muerto, nacimiento de un feto sin vida.

stillborn | 'stɪlbɔːn | | ˌstɪl'bɔːn | *adj.* **1** nacido muerto (un niño). **2** (fig.) malogrado, fracasado (un plan, una idea).

stillness | 'stɪlnɪs | *s.i.* **1** inmovilidad. **2** calma, silencio, quietud.

stilt | stɪlt | *s.c.* (generalmente *pl.*) **1** zanco. **2** ARQ. pilar, pilote, soporte. **3** ZOOL. cigoñuela. || *v.t.* **4** poner en zancos. **5** levantar sobre pilares, elevar sobre pilotes.

stilted | 'stɪltɪd | *adj.* pomposo, elaborado, formalista, artificial, afectado (el lenguaje, el comportamiento).

stimulant | 'stɪmjʊlənt | *s.c.* **1** estimulante, excitante (una droga, una bebida). **2 [– (to)]** (fig.) estimulante, activador, estímulo, incentivo, aliciente.

stimulate | 'stɪmjʊleɪt | *v.t.* (form.) **1 [to – (to)]** estimular, activar, provocar, ser un acicate. **2** [**to – +** *o.* **+ to** *inf.*] inspirar, animar, avivar, excitar, incitar.

stimulating | 'stɪmjuleɪtɪŋ | *adj.* **1** estimulante, activador. **2** sugerente, sugestivo, inspirador.
stimulation | ˌstɪmju'leɪʃn | *s.i.* **1** estímulo, acicate, inducción. **2** estimulación, excitación.
stimuli | 'stɪmjulaɪ | *pl.* de **stimulus.**
stimulus | 'stɪmjuləs | [*pl.* **stimuli**] *s.c.* **[– (to)] 1** PSIC. estímulo. || *s.c.* e *i.* **2** estímulo, incentivo, acicate.
sting | stɪŋ | *v.irr.pret.* y *p.p.* **stung.** *t.* e *i.* **1** picar, pinchar, punzar. **2** escocer, resquemar, picar: *alcohol makes a wound sting = el alcohol hace que escueza una herida.* **3** (fig.) escocer, herir: *her criticism stung = sus críticas escocían.* **4** remorder (la conciencia). || *v.t.* **5** atormentar, torturar, afligir. **6** aguijonear, espolear, poner en acción. **7 [to – (for)]** (jerga) estafar, clavar: *they stung me for 3.000 pounds = me estafaron 3.000 libras.* || *s.c.* **8** ZOOL. aguijón. **9** pelillo urticante, sustancia que escuece: *some plants have a sting = algunas plantas tienen una sustancia que escuece.* **10** picazón, escozor, dolor agudo: *the sting of a jellyfish = la picadura de una medusa.* **11** picadura, picada. || **12 a – in the tail,** final mordaz (de una historia, de un chiste); gato encerrado, patata caliente: *their promises to change had a sting in the tail = sus promesas de cambio tenían gato encerrado.* **13 to take the – out,** (fig.) sacarse la espina.
stinginess | 'stɪndʒɪnɪs | *s.i.* **1** cicatería, tacañería, avaricia. **2** miseria, insignificancia, pequeñez, insuficiencia.
stinging | 'stɪŋɪŋ | *adj.* **1** desagradable, punzante, que escuece (una crítica). || **2 – nettle,** BOT. ortiga que produce urticaria.
stingray | 'stɪŋreɪ | *s.c.* ZOOL. pastinaca, raya con púa.
stingy | 'stɪndʒɪ | *adj.* **1 [– (with)]** (fam.) tacaño, cicatero, avariento. **2** miserable, escaso, pequeño, insignificante, insuficiente: *a stingy portion = una porción escasa.*
stink | stɪŋk | *v.* [*irr.pret.* **stank,** *p.p.* **stunk**] *i.* **1 [to – (of)],** heder, apestar, atufar, oler mal. **2** (fam. y fig.) oler mal, ser horrible, ser un asco, ser inmoral: *your idea stinks! = ¡tu idea es espantosa!* **3** (fig.) tener mala fama, tener mala reputación. || *s.c.* **4** hedor, hediondez, tufo, mal olor. || **5 to make/create/kick up/raise a –,** armar gresca, armar un alboroto, armar un escándalo. **6 – bomb,** bomba fétida. **7 to – out,** (fam.) **a)** llenar de mal olor, atufar; **b)** ahuyentar (de un lugar) con malos olores.
stinking | stɪŋkɪŋ | *adj.* **1** fétido, hediondo, apestoso. **2** (fam.) desagradable, horrible, espantoso, repugnante. || *adv.* **3** (fam. y desp.) muy, enormemente. || **4 – rich,** (fam.) enormemente rico.
stint | stɪnt | *v.t.* e *i.* **1** (generalmente en *negativa*) privar(se), limitar(se), coartar(se), escatimar, restringir: *don't stint the sugar = no escatimes azúcar.* **2** (arc.) detener, poner fin, desistir. || *s.c.* **3** trabajo, tarea, destajo, labor, obligación. **4** limitación, restricción. || **5 without –,** generosamente, sin limitación, sin restricción.
stipend | 'staɪpend | *s.c.* estipendio, salario, sueldo, remuneración.
stipendiary | staɪ'pendɪərɪ | (EE.UU.) | staɪ'pendɪerɪ | *adj.* **1** estipendiario, asalariado, remunerado. || *s.c.* **2** (también – **magistrate**) estipendiario (un magistrado, un clérigo).
stippled | 'stɪpld | *adj.* granulado, salpicado, moteado, punteado, picado.
stipulate | 'stɪpjuleɪt | *v.t.* (form.) estipular, fijar como condición.
stipulation | ˌstɪpju'leɪʃn | *s.c.* e *i.* estipulación, cláusula, requisito, condición.
stir | stɜː | [*pret.* y *p.p.* **stirred,** *ger. stirring*] *v.t.* **1** revolver, remover, dar vueltas: *stir the soup = remueve la sopa.* **2** atizar, remover (el fuego). **3 [to – (to)]** despertar, fomentar, provocar, excitar (un sentimiento). **4** conmover, afectar, incitar: *stirred by the beauty of the passage = conmovido por la belleza del pasaje.* || *v.t.* e *i.* **5** (lit.) agitar(se), alterar(se), mover(se): *the breeze stirred the grass = la brisa agitó la hierba.* **6** despertar(se), levantar(se), rebullir: *she doesn't stir = no se levanta.* || *v.i.* **7** (fam. y desp.) fomentar descontento, encizañar, meter cizaña. || *s.c.* **8** movimiento, meneo, vuelta. **9 [– (of)** y generalmente *sing.*] revuelo, agitación: *she caused a stir as she entered = causó un revuelo al entrar.* **10** conmoción, alboroto, alegría, júbilo (públicos). || *s.i.* **11** (arc. y jerga) prisión, chirona, maco. || **12 to – in/into,** añadir y remover, agitar, mezclar. **13 to – one's stumps,** (fam.) darse prisa, (fam. y arc.) darse prisa, ir a toda prisa. **14 to – the blood,** hacer bullir la sangre. **15 to – up, a)** remover, revolver; **b)** (desp.) excitar (pasiones), fomentar (rebeliones), armar (problemas).
stir-fry | 'stɜːfraɪ | *v.t.* **1** rehogar, sofreír, freír. || *adj.* **2** rehogado, sofrito: *stir-fry rice = arroz rehogado.*
stirrer | 'stɜːrər | *s.c.* alborotador, camorrista, agitador, revoltoso, liante.
stirring | 'stɜːrɪŋ | *adj.* **1** conmovedor, emocionante, emotivo. **2** inspirador, incitador. **3** turbulento, agitado. || *s.c.* e *i.* **4** movimiento, alteración, conmoción.
stirrup | 'stɪrəp | | 'stɜːrəp | *s.c.* **1** estribo. **2** MAR. estribo de marchapié.
stitch | stɪtʃ | *s.c.* **1** puntada (de costura). **2** punto (en un tejido): *then, drop the stitch = luego, suelta el punto.* **3** MED. punto de sutura. || *s.c.* e *i.* **4** punto (estilo de costura o tejido): *I used two different stitchtches = utilicé dos puntos diferentes.* || *s.sing.* **5** punto de costado, dolor de costado, punzada, pinchazo. **6** (generalmente en *negativa*) (fam.) ropa. || *v.t.* e *i.* **7** coser. **8 [to – (up)]** suturar. || **9 a – in time/a – in time saves nine,** una puntada a tiempo evita un ciento, más vale prevenir que lamentar. **10 to be in stitches,** morirse de risa, desternillarse de risa. **11 not to have a – on,** (fam.) estar en cueros, estar completamente desnudo. **12 to – up,** rematar.
stitching | 'stɪtʃɪŋ | *s.i.* costura.
stoat | stəut | *s.c.* ZOOL. comadreja, armiño europeo.
stock | stɒk | *s.c.* **1 [– (of)** y generalmente *pl.*] provisión, suministro, surtido, existencias. **2** (fig.) colección, acopio, serie: *a stock of good books = una colección de buenos libros.* **3** BOT. tallo, tronco, cepa. **4** BOT. patrón (en que se injerta una planta). **5** culata, caja (del fusil). **6** mango, base, soporte. **7** BOT. alhelí. || *s.c.* e *i.* **8** FIN. capital, valores, papel: *government stock = papel del Estado.* **9** caldo concentrado, extracto (de carne). **10** linaje, estirpe, raza, casta. **11** cálculo, cómputo, estimación. || *s.i.* **12** reputación, popularidad, fama, notoriedad. **13** confianza, credibilidad. **14** ganado, ganadería (de una granja). **15** materia prima. || *v.t.* **16** almacenar, tener almacenado, tener en existencia. **17 [to – (on/with)]** proveer, abastecer, surtir: *a stocked pantry = una despensa abastecida.* || *adj.* **18** (desp.) corriente, cotidiano, vulgar, banal, manido, trillado (un argumento, una respuesta). **19** en existencia, disponible, de surtido: *all the stock sizes = todas las tallas en existencia.* || **20 to be stocked,** estar lleno de peces (un río, un lago). **21 in –,** en existencia, disponible. **22 lock, – and barrel,** V. **lock. 23 on the stocks,** (fig.) en preparación, entre manos. **24 out of –,** agotado. **25 to put –,** dar importancia, valorar. **26 – cube,** pastilla de caldo de carne, cubito de caldo de carne. **27 – exchange,** FIN. bolsa de valores. **28 – market,** FIN. mercado de valores. **29 stocks, a)** MAR. astillero, basada (de construcción); **b)** cepo (de castigo); **c)** potro (que sujeta a un caballo para herrarlo, marcarlo). **30 to – up (on/with),** proveerse de, adquirir existencias de, ir acumulando. **31 to take – (of), a)** evaluar, considerar, analizar (una situación); **b)** inventariar, hacer inventario.
stockade | stɒ'keɪd | *s.c.* **1** empalizada, vallado, estacada. || *v.t.* **2** proteger con una empalizada, vallar con estacas, fortificar.
stockbroker | 'stɒkˌbrəukər | * *s.c.* FIN. corredor de bolsa, agente de bolsa.
stock-car | stɒkkɑːr | *s.c.* **1** coche de carreras de choque (generalmente uno antiguo y modificado). **2** (EE.UU.) vagón para transportar ganado.
stockholder | 'stɒkˌhəuldər | *s.c.* (EE.UU.) FIN. accionista.
stocking | 'stɒkɪŋ | | 'stɑːkɪŋ | *s.c.* **1** media. **2** (arc.) calcetín de caballero. || **3 in one's – feet,** sólo con las medias.
stockinged | 'stɒkɪŋd | *adj.* con medias, calzado con medias o con calcetines.
stock-in-trade | ˌstɒkɪn'treɪd | *s.i.* o *sing.* **1** (fig.) recursos, repertorio: *gesture is part of an actor's stock-in-trade = el gesto forma parte de los recursos de un actor.* **2** útiles, instrumentos (de trabajo).
stockist | 'stɒkɪst | *s.c.* (brit.) COM. distribuidor, representante.
stockpile | 'stɒkpaɪl | | 'stɑːkpaɪl | *s.c.* **1 [– (of)]** reserva, provisión, acopio, acumulación. || *v.t.* **2** almacenar, hacer acopio, acumular.
stockroom | stɒkruːm | *s.c.* almacén, depósito.
stock-still | ˌstɒk'stɪl | *adv.* inmóvil, completamente quieto.
stocktaking | 'stɒkˌteɪkɪŋ | *s.i.* **1** balance, inventario. **2** (fig.) revisión, examen, análisis.
stocky | 'stɒkɪ | *adj.* rechoncho, regordete, robusto.
stodge | stɒdʒ | | stɑːdʒ | *s.i.* **1** (fam. y desp.) comida indigesta, comida pesada. **2** (fig.) literatura aburrida, escrito pesado, obra poco imaginativa.

stodgy | stɒdʒɪ | *adj.* **1** indigesto, pesado (un alimento). **2** pesada, aburrida, difícil (una obra). **3** monótona, corriente, vulgar (una persona). **4** pomposo, afectado, pedante, jactancioso. **5** rechoncho, regordete.

stoic | 'stəuɪk | (también **stoical**) *s.c.* **1** estoico, impasible. **2** FIL. estoico.

stoically | 'stəuɪkəlɪ | *adv.* estoicamente, impasiblemente.

stoicism | 'stəuɪsɪzəm | *s.i.* **1** estoicismo, impasibilidad. **2** FIL. estoicismo.

stoke | stəuk | *v.t.* **1** **[to – (up/with)]** atizar, echar carbón, poner leña, cebar (un fuego, un horno). **2** cargar, llenar (una caldera, un depósito). || **3 to – up, a)** atizar un fuego, cebar el horno, cargar la caldera; **b)** (fig.) comer, cebarse (una persona); **c)** (fig.) echar leña al fuego, activar, excitar (un sentimiento).

stole | stəul | *pret.irreg.* de **steal.** || *s.c.* **2** estola.

stolen | stəulən | *p.p.irreg.* de **steal.**

stolid | 'stɒlɪd | *adj.* (generalmente desp.) impasible, flemático, imperturbable.

stolidly | 'stɒlɪdlɪ | *adv.* impasiblemente, flemáticamente, imperturbablemente.

stomach | 'stʌmək | *s.c.* **1** ANAT. estómago. **2** abdomen, barriga, vientre. || *s.i.* **3** **[– for,** generalmente en *negativa*] intención, ánimo, disposición, humor. **5** (arc.) orgullo, altanería, arrogancia. || *v.t.* **6** [en *interr.* y *negativa*] (fig.) aceptar, soportar, aguantar, tragar. **7** comer, tragar, soportar (alimentos). || **8 to have butterflies in one's –** V. **butterfly. 9 to have no – for,** no tener ganas de, no estar dispuesto a, no tener humor para. **10 – pump,** bomba estomacal. **11 to turn one's –/to make one's – turn,** revolver el estómago a uno, dar asco a uno.

stomach-ache | 'stʌməkeɪk | *s.c.* dolor de estómago.

stomp | stɒmp | | stɔːmp | *v.i.* **1** **[to – *adv./prep.*]** (fam.) pisar fuerte, dar pasos ruidosos. **2** (EE.UU.) pisar, pisotear, dar un pisotón.

stone | stəun | *s.c.* **1** piedra, canto, guijarro, roca. **2** lápida, losa (de una tumba). **3** muela, piedra de moler. **4** piedra de afilar. **5** mojón, hito. **6** gema, piedra (preciosa). **7** [*pl.* **stone** o **stones**] (brit.). 14 libras (medida de peso). **8** (EE.UU. **pit**) BOT. hueso, cuesco, pepita: *a cherry stone = un hueso de cereza.* **9** MED. cálculo, piedra. **10** mesa de componer, piedra (en imprenta). || *s.i.* **11** piedra (material de construcción, un corazón, el mal). || *v.t.* **12** apedrear, lapidar. **13** (EE.UU. **to pit**) deshuesar, despepitar (una fruta). || *adj.* **14** de piedra, pétreo: *a stone pot = un tiesto de piedra.* || **15 a rolling – gathers no moss,** V. **moss. 16 to get blood from a –,** V. **blood. 17 to kill two birds with one –,** V. **bird. 18 to leave no – unturned,** revolver Roma con Santiago, no dejar piedra sin mover. **19 Stone Age,** Edad de Piedra. **20 – deaf,** sordo como una tapia. **21 – the crows/me!,** (brit. y jerga) ¡figúrate!, ¡qué horror!, ¡qué susto! (para expresar sorpresa, susto, disgusto). **22 stone's throw,** a tiro de piedra, una corta distancia, unos pasos.

stonebreaker | 'stəun,breɪkər | *s.c.* máquina apisonadora.

stone-cold | ,stəun'kəuld | *adj.* **1** completamente helado, extremadamente frío. || **2 – sober,** (fam.) completamente sobrio.

stoned | 'stəund | *adj.* (fam.) **1** borracho, ajumado. **2** (argot) ido, colgado, seriamente afectado (por drogas).

stone-ground | 'stəun,graund | *adj.* molido en molino (grano, harina).

stonemason | 'stəun,meɪsn | *s.c.* cantero, asentador, mampostero, albañil.

stonewall | ,stəun'wɔːl | *v.i.* (brit.) **1** utilizar tácticas dilatorias, obstruir la marcha, practicar el obstruccionismo (en una discusión, en el Parlamento); soslayar respuestas, evitar contestar directamente, evitar cooperar. **2** DEP. jugar a la defensiva, emplear la táctica del cerrojo.

stoneware | 'stəunweər | *s.i.* vasijas de gres, cacharros de barro.

stonework | 'stəunwɜːk | *s.i.* cantería, mampostería, trabajo sobre piedra, obra de sillería.

stony | 'stəunɪ | *adj.* **1** pedregoso, cubierto de guijarros, de piedra, pétreo. **2** (fig.) de piedra, cruel, despiadado, desalmado. **3** fría, glacial: *a stony look = una mirada glacial.* **4** rígido, estricto, impasible. **5** paralizante: *stony fear = un temor paralizante.*

stony-broke | 'stəunɪ,brəuk | *adj.* (brit. y fam.) sin blanca, sin un duro, sin un centavo.

stood | stud | *pret.* y *p.p.irreg.* de **stand.**

stooge | stuːdʒ | *s.c.* **1** actor ayudante de un comediante, que es objeto de los chistes del otro en escena. **2** (brit., fam. y desp.) servidor, persona servil, hombre de paja, paniaguado.

stool | stuːl | *s.c.* **1** taburete, banqueta. **2** escabel. **3** inodoro. **4** (form.) MED. heces, defecación, deposición, evacuación de vientre. **5** BOT. cepa, plata madre. || **6 to fall between two stools,** V. **fall.**

stoolpigeon | stuːlpɪdʒən | (EE.UU. **stoollie**) *s.c.* (jerga y desp.) soplón, delator, espía.

stoop | stuːp | *v.i.* **1** inclinarse, agacharse, encorvarse: *stooping over the ironing board = inclinándose sobre la tabla de planchar.* **2** caminar encorvado: *she used to stoop when she was a child = acostumbraba a caminar encorvada cuando era niña.* **3** bajar en picado, abatirse, arrojarse sobre su presa (un ave de rapiña). || *s.c.* **4** encorvamiento, cargazón de espalda. **5** condescendencia, concesión, humillación. **6** (EE.UU.) pórtico, porche. || **7 to – to,** (desp.) rebajarse, degradarse, condescender.

stooping | 'stuːpɪŋ | *adj.* encorvado, cargado de espaldas, inclinado.

stop | stɒp | [*pret.* y *p.p.* **stopped,** *ger.* **stopping**] *v.t.* e *i.* **1** parar(se), detener(se). **2** finalizar, terminar(se), interrumpir(se). || *v.t.* **3** **[to – (from)]** impedir, detener, contener, poner fin, prohibir. **4** **[to – (up)]** bloquear, obstruir, obturar, atascar, tapar, cegar, cortar (un orificio, una carretera). **5** (fig.) tapar, callar: *we'll have to stop his mouth with money = tendremos que taparle la boca con dinero.* **6** empastar (una muela). **7** retener, cancelar, suspender, suprimir (un pago). **8** MUS. pisar, presionar, tapar (las cuerdas, los agujeros de un instrumento). **9** MAR. amarrar. || *v.i.* **10** hacer una pausa, interrumpir: *we stopped for tea = hicimos una pausa para tomar el té.* **11** (brit.) quedarse, permanecer: *I'm stopping home tonight = esta noche me quedo en casa.* || *s.c.* **12** parada, alto, interrupción, pausa. **13** parada, apeadero (de autobús, de tren). **14** estancia, visita. **15** obstrucción. **16** taco, tope, retén. **17** (brit.) GRAM. punto. **18** FOT. abertura (del objetivo). **19** MUS. registro (de un órgano); llave, tecla; agujero (de flauta); traste (de guitarra). **20** (también **plosive**). FON. consonante oclusiva. **21** MAR. amarra. || **22 the buck stops here,** V. **buck. 23 to know where/when to –,** saber controlarse, saber donde o cuando parar. **24 to pull all the stops out,** (fam. y fig.) tocar todas las cuerdas, hacer todo lo posible, desplegar todos los recursos. **25 to put a – to,** acabar con, poner fin a. **26 to – at nothing,** no pararse en barras, no detenerse ante nada, no reparar en nada. **27 to – by,** entrar a hacer una visita, pasar por casa, dejarse caer. **28 to – dead/in one's tracks,** parar en seco, frenar en seco. **29 to – down,** FOT. obstruir el objetivo. **30 to – in/**(EE.UU.) **over, a)** (brit. y fam.) quedarse en casa, no salir; **b)** (fam.) dejarse caer, pasar a ver. **31 to – off,** (fam.) hacer una breve parada, interrumpir el viaje. **32 to – out,** (brit. y fam.) quedarse fuera hasta tarde, regresar tarde a casa. **33 to – over,** pernoctar, pasar la noche, hacer escala. **34 – press,** PER. noticias de última hora. **35 to – short,** V. **short. 36 – thief!,** ¡al ladrón! **37 to – up,** rellenar, **a)** obturar; empastar; **b)** (brit. y fam.) quedarse hasta tarde, irse tarde a la cama.

stopcock | 'stɒpkɒk | (brit.) **turncock.** *s.c.* llave de paso, robinete, grifo, válvula.

stopgap | 'stɒpgæp | *s.c.* sustituto temporal, recurso (persona o cosa).

stopover | 'stɒpəuvər | *s.c.* escala, interrupción de un viaje, parada temporal: *a two day stopover in Paris = una escala de dos días en París.*

stoppage | stɒpɪdʒ | *s.c.* **1** paro, paralización, huelga. **2** interrupción, detención, alto. || *s.c.* e *i.* **3** deducción, impuesto: *he doesn't get much money after all stoppages = no gana mucho dinero una vez hechas todas las deducciones.* **4** suspensión, paralización, cancelación (de pagos, de vacaciones). **5** obstrucción, bloqueo, atasco.

stopper | 'stɒpər | *s.c.* **1** (EE.UU. **plug**) tapón, corcho; tapa, obturador. || *v.t.* **2** tapar, taponar, obturar.

stopwatch | 'stɒpwɒtʃ | *s.c.* cronómetro.

storage | 'stɔːrɪdʒ | *s.i.* **1** almacenamiento, almacenaje: *storage capacity = capacidad de almacenamiento.* **2** almacén, depósito (espacio, coste): *most of the furniture is in storage = la mayor parte de los muebles están en el almacén.*

store | stɔː | *v.t.* **1** **[to – (up)]** almacenar, acumular, hacer acopio, guardar (suministros). **2** **[to – (away)]** almacenar, poner a buen recaudo. **3** INF. archivar (información). || *s.c.* **4** **[– (of)]** almacenamiento, provisión, reserva. **5** (EE.UU.) tienda, comercio, (brit.) almacén. **6** [–

(of)] montón, abundancia, acopio: *a store of old magazines = abundancia de revistas antiguas.* || **7 in –,** aguardando, acumulado: *lots of surprises in store for you = montones de sorpresas te aguardan.* **8 to put great – on/by,** conceder gran importancia a, valorar al máximo. **9 stores,** MIL. equipo, provisiones, suministros, pertrechos. **10 to – up,** almacenar, acumular, guardar (para mejor ocasión).
storefront | stɔːfrʌnt | *s.c.* (EE.UU.) fachada de una tienda, parte frontal de una tienda.
storehouse | 'stɔːhaus | *s.c.* **1 [– (of)]** (fig.) fuente inagotable, colección, mina, tesoro (un lugar, una persona): *a storehouse of information = una fuente inagotable de información.* **2** (EE.UU.) almacén, depósito.
storehouses | 'stɔːhauzɪz | *pl.* de **storehouse.**
storekeeper | 'stɔːˌkiːpər | *s.c.* **1** (EE.UU.) tendero. **2** MIL. encargado de almacén. **3** MAR. encargado de pañol, pañolero.
storeroom | 'stɔːrum | *s.c.* **1** cuarto de almacenaje. **2** despensa, bodega. **3** MAR. pañol.
storey | 'stɔːrɪ | (EE.UU. **story**) *s.c.* piso, planta.
stork | stɔːk | *s.c.* ZOOL. cigüeña.
storm | stɔːm | *s.c.* **1** tormenta, tempestad, temporal, borrasca, vendaval, huracán. **2 [– (of)]** (fig.) torrente, tormenta, vendaval, tempestad: *a storm of protest = un torrente de protestas.* **3 [– of]** polvareda, escándalo, alboroto, revuelo. **4** MIL. ataque, lluvia: *a storm of bullets = una lluvia de balas.* **5** MIL. ataque, asalto. || *v.t.* **6** MIL. asaltar, atacar, tomar por asalto. || *v.i.* **7 [to – + *adv./prep.*]** estallar en cólera, enfurecerse, lanzar improperios: *he stormed out of the house = salió de casa bramando.* || **8 any port in a –,** V. **port. 9 a storm in a teacup,** una tormenta en un vaso de agua. **10 the calm before the –,** V. **calm. 11 the eye of the –,** el ojo del huracán. **12 to ride out/weather the –,** MAR. capear el temporal. **13 – cloud,** nubarrón. **14 – tropper,** MIL. miliciano nazi. **15 to take by –, a)** MIL. tomar por asalto; **b)** cautivar, conquistar, adueñarse de: *the play took the audience by storm = la obra cautivó a la audiencia.*
stormbound | 'stɔːmbaund | *adj.* paralizado por mal tiempo, inmovilizado por tiempo tormentoso (un avión, un barco, los pasajeros).
storming | 'stɔːmɪŋ | *s.i.* MIL. conquista, asalto, toma: *the storming of the Bastille = la toma de la Bastilla.*
stormy | 'stɔːmɪ | *adj.* **1** tormentoso, borrascoso (el tiempo). **2** tempestuoso, violento, turbulento (una relación).
story | 'stɔːrɪ | *s.c.* **1 [– (about)]** historia, cuento, relato, anécdota, chiste. **2** biografía, historia. **3** argumento, trama. **4** historia, rumor, chisme, habladuría. **5 [– (on)]** artículo, noticia (en un periódico). **6** (fam. y euf.) mentira, cuento, embuste. **7** (EE.UU.) piso, planta. || **8 but that's another –,** pero ese es otro tema, eso es harina de otro costal. **9 a cock-and-bull –,** V. **cock. 10 a hard-luck –,** V. **hard. 11 to cut a long – short,** para abreviar, para terminar antes. **12 so the – goes,** la gente dice, andan diciendo que. **13 that's only part of the –/that's not the whole –,** eso no es todo, no le han contado todos los detalles. **14 the same old –/the old old –,** lo de siempre, la misma historia de siempre.
story-book | 'stɔːrɪbuk | *s.c.* **1** (lit.) libro de cuentos. || *adj.* **2** (fig.) cuento de hadas, romántico: *a story-book romance = un amor romántico.*
stout | staut | *adj.* **1** (euf.) corpulento, fuerte, robusto, gordo. **2** (lit.) sólido, macizo, firme, grueso: *a stout table = una mesa sólida.* **3** valiente, osado. **4** tenaz, obstinado, decidido, resuelto, resoluto. **5** vigoroso, enérgico, potente. || *s.i.* **6** cerveza de malta (fuerte y de color oscuro).
stout-hearted | ˌstaut'hɑːtɪd | *adj.* (lit.) valiente, resuelto, determinado, decidido.
stoutly | 'stautlɪ | *adv.* **1** firmemente, tenazmente, decididamente, obstinadamente. **2** sólidamente, fuerte, firme.
stove | stəuv | *pret.* y *p.p.irreg.* **1** de **stave.** || *s.c.* **2** (EE.UU.) hornillo, cocina, fuego. **3** estufa.
stow | stəu | *v.t.* **1 [to – (away)]** guardar, almacenar. **2** MAR. estibar. **3** colocar, instalar, alojar, poner. **4** (fig.) engullir, zampar. || **5 to – away,** MAR. viajar de polizón, viajar clandestinamente, (Am.) viajar de pavo.
stowaway | 'stəuəweɪ | *s.c.* polizón, (Am.) pavo.
straddle | 'strædl | *v.t.* **1** ponerse con una pierna a cada lado de, sentarse a horcajadas, esparrancarse sobre. **2** situarse a ambos lados de, extenderse a un lado y otro de, caer a ambos lados de: *the village straddles the river = el pueblo está situado a uno y otro lado del río.* **3** extenderse por, abarcar, cubrir: *roads straddling the country = carreteras que se extienden por el país.* **4** estar de parte de ambos, nadar entre dos aguas (en una discusión entre dos partes). || *s.c.* **5** postura a horcajadas. **6** posición ambigua (en una discusión). **7** COM. opción de compra y venta (de acciones en bolsa). || **8 to – the fence,** ser neutral (en una discusión).
strafe | strɑːf | *v.t.* **1** bombardear, ametrallar, atacar (desde un avión en vuelo rasante). || *s.c.* **2** bombardeo, ametrallamiento.
straggle | 'strægl | *v.i.* **[to – + *adv./prep.*]** (desp.) **1** extenderse sin orden ni concierto, esparcirse desordenadamente. **2** rezagarse, retrasarse, separarse, andar disperso, extraviarse, perderse (de un grupo principal).
straggly | 'stræglɪ | *adj.* disperso, diseminado, desordenado: *straggly hair = cabello despeinado.*
straight | streɪt | *adj.* **1** recto, derecho. **2** lacio, liso (el pelo). **3** recto, vertical, nivelado: *the painting isn't straight = el cuadro no está vertical.* **4** erguido, derecho, recto. **5** ordenado, en orden, arreglado: *you should leave the room straight = deberías dejar la habitación en orden.* **6 [– (with)]** honesto, honrado, recto, de fiar, franco, directo. **7** correcto, exacto, claro: *I'll put it straight = lo diré claro.* **8** simple, sencillo, sin ambages. **9** consecutivo, continuo, ininterrumpido, seguido: *watching TV por 3 straight hours = viendo TV durante tres horas seguidas.* **10** puro, solo, sin mezcla, sin agua: *a straight whisky = un whisky solo.* **11** serio (el teatro, la expresión). **12** (fam.) en orden, en regla (los asuntos, las cuentas). **13** (jerga) heterosexual. **14** (jerga) abstemio, no consumidor de drogas. **15** convencional, normal, conservador, amante de la ley. **16** fijo, sin descuento (un precio). || *adv.* **17** [– + *adv./prep.*] directamente, en línea recta: *straight in front of him = directamente delante de él.* **18** [– + *adv./prep.*] directamente, derecho, inmediatamente: *I went straight home = fui inmediatamente a casa.* **19** claramente, con claridad, francamente. **20** sin interrupción, ininterrumpidamente, de un tirón, seguido: *she read the whole book straight = se leyó el libro de un tirón.* || *s.sing.* **21** línea recta, recta. **22** (jerga) heterosexual. **23** (jerga) abstemio, persona que no usa drogas. || **24 a – face,** serio, una cara seria. **25 to go –,** ir por el buen camino, estar regenerándose (un criminal). **26 on the – and narrow,** en el buen camino, por el camino recto. **27 to put the record –/to get something –,** poner las cosas en su lugar, hablar claramente. **28 – back,** inmediatamente, directamente. **29 – from the shoulder,** (fam.) sin rodeos, sin ambages. **30 – out,** francamente, sin rodeos. **31 – up,** (brit. y fam.) seguro, cierto, de verdad; sí, claro que sí (en preguntas o respuestas).
straightaway | 'streɪtəweɪ | *adv.* enseguida, ahora mismo, inmediatamente, al instante.
straighten | 'streɪtn | *v.t.* e *i.* **1** enderezar(se), poner(se) recto. **2** alisar (el cabello, una tela). || **3 to – out, a)** resolver, solucionar, organizar, desembrollar (un asunto); **b)** (fam.) aclarar, tranquilizar, sosegar, calmar. **4 to – up, a)** enderezarse, ponerse recto; **b)** arreglar, colocar, poner en orden (una habitación).
straight-faced | 'streɪtˌfeɪst | *adj.* serio, inexpresivo, solemne, con cara de palo.
straightforward | ˌstreɪt'fɔːwəd | *adj.* **1** honesto, honrado, cándido, buena persona, franco. **2** simple, sencillo, fácil (una pregunta). **3** total, completo, sin límite: *a straightforward refusal = un rechazo total.*
straightlaced V. **straitlaced.**
straightway | 'streɪtweɪ | *adv.* (arc.) enseguida, ahora mismo, inmediatamente, al instante.
strain | streɪn | *v.t.* **1** hacer daño, dañar, forzar, violentar (a causa de esfuerzo excesivo). **2** distender, producir un tirón (en un músculo). **3** forzar, cansar (la vista). **4** colar, filtrar, tamizar: *strain the beans before serving them = cuela las alubias antes de servirlas.* **5** pedir demasiado, excederse en, extralimitarse en, propasarse en: *straining his rights = excederse en sus derechos.* **6 [to – + *o.* + to *inf.*]** aguzar (el oído). || *v.i.* **7** esforzarse, hacer grandes esfuerzos. **8 [to – (against)]** (lit.) aferrarse, asirse. || *s.c.* e *i.* **9** tensión, tirantez, presión (de una cuerda). **10** tensión, presión, agotamiento nervioso, fatiga, cansancio. **11** crispación, tensión, tirantez (en una relación). **12** MED. torcedura. || *s.c.* **13 [– (of)]** variedad, raza, cepa (de animales, plantas). || *s.sing.* **14 [– (of)]** (lit.) MUS. son, tonada, melodía, acorde. **15 [– (of)]** rasgo, característica, peculiaridad. **16 [– (of)]** vena

(de locura). **17** (fam.) línea, camino, orientación. || **18 to put a great – on,** exigir un esfuerzo enorme. **19 to – at,** tirar con fuerza, esforzarse tirando. **20 straining at the leash,** (fam.) exigiendo libertad, deseoso de libertad. **21 to – every nerve,** (lit.) intentar con todas las fuerzas, esforzarse al máximo. **22 under the –,** bajo presión, con agotamiento nervioso.

strained | 'streɪnd | *adj.* **1** tenso, poco amistoso, forzado. **2** tensa, tirante, crispada (una relación). **3** cansado, agotado, fatigado.

strainer | 'streɪnər | *s.c.* **1** colador. **2** filtro, tamiz.

strait | streɪt | (también **straits**) *s.c.* **1** GEOG. estrecho. || *adj.* **2** estrecho, angosto, reducido. **3** encerrado, confinado. **4** rígido, estricto, riguroso. || **5 in desperate/dire/financial straits,** en apuros económicos, pasando muchas estrecheces.

straitened | 'streɪtnd | *adj.* **1** (form. y euf.) apurada, difícil, de necesidad (una situación económica). || **2 in – circunstances,** falto de dinero, en situación económicamente apurada.

straitjacket | 'streɪt,dʒækɪt | *s.c.* **1** camisa de fuerza. **2** (desp.) restricción, limitación, cortapisa: *the straitjacket of poverty = las limitaciones de la pobreza.*

straitlaced | ,streɪt'leɪst | *adj.* **1** (desp.) puritano, remilgado, moralista, gazmoño. **2** (arc.) ceñido, apretado, ajustado.

strand | strænd | *s.c.* **1 [– (of)]** hebra, cabo, hilo, filamento. **2** mechón (de cabello). **3** sarta (de perlas). **4** (fig.) hilo, cabo, elemento (de una discusión, de una historia). **5** (lit.) playa, costa, ribera. || *v.t.* **6** MAR. varar, encallar. **7** trenzar, retorcer, unir (cabos para hacer una cuerda). **8** romper un cabo (de una cuerda). || *v.t.* e *i.* **9** abandonar, dejar en la estacada, dejar colgado (en un lugar).

stranded | strændɪd | *adj.* abandonado, en situación poco favorable, desamparado, colgado (en un lugar): *they were left stranded in Rome = les dejaron colgados en Roma.*

strange | streɪndʒ | *adj.* **1** extraño, raro, incomprensible, inusual, sorprendente, peculiar, exótico. **2 [– (to)]** desconocido, poco familiar, extraño (un lugar). **3 [– to]** (form.) no acostumbrado, poco experto, nuevo: *strange to that task = no acostumbrado a esa tarea.* **4** raro, mal, mareado; incómodo, con una sensación extraña: *she felt strange after dinner = se sintió mal después de la cena.* || **5 – to say,** aunque parezca extraño, aunque parezca mentira.

strangely | 'streɪndʒlɪ | *adv.* **1** extrañamente, incomprensiblemente, sorprendentemente, peculiarmente. || **2 – enough,** aunque parezca mentira, sorprendentemente.

strangeness | 'streɪndʒnɪs | *s.i.* extrañeza, rareza, peculiaridad, exotismo, novedad.

stranger | 'streɪndʒər | *s.c.* **1** extraño, desconocido: *it was forbidden to talk to strangers = estaba prohibido hablar con desconocidos.* **2** forastero, nuevo (en un lugar). || **3 to be no – to,** conocer bien, estar acostumbrado a, ser experto en: *he was not a stranger to those problems = conoce bien esos problemas.*

strangle | 'stræŋgl | *v.t.* **1** estrangular, ahogar, asfixiar. **2** (fig.) sofocar, arruinar, ahogar, restringir, inhibir: *financial cuts are strangling development = las restricciones financieras están arruinando el desarrollo.*

strangled | 'stræŋgld | *adj.* sofocado, reprimido, apagado (un grito).

stranglehold | 'stræŋglhəuld | *s.c.* **1** DEP. llave estranguladora, collar de fuerza (en lucha). **2** (fig.) control, dominio, influencia opresiva.

strangler | 'strænglər | *s.c.* estrangulador.

strangulation | ,stræŋgju'leɪʃn | *s.i.* **1** estrangulamiento. **2** control, dominio (generalmente financiero, político).

strap | stræp | *s.c.* **1** correa, banda, tira, trabilla. **2** hombrera, tirante (de un vestido). **3** asidero (en un autobús). **4 [the –]** castigo a base de correazos, azotamiento con correa. **5** asentador (de navaja de afeitar). || *v.t.* **[strapped, strapping]. 6 [to – + *o.* + *adv./prep.*]** atar con correa, sujetar con correa, asegurar con cinturón. **7 [to – (up),** generalmente *pasiva***]** vendar, poner vendajes, fajar.

strapless | 'stræplɪs | *adj.* sin tirantes, sin hombreras (un vestido).

strapping | 'stræpɪŋ | *adj.* **1** (fam.) corpulento, fuerte, fornido, robusto. || *s.i.* **2** correaje.

strata | 'strɑːtə | *pl.* de **stratum.**

stratagem | 'strætɪdʒəm | *s.c.* (form.) estratagema, artimaña, treta.

strategic | strə'tiːdʒɪk | (también **strategical**) *adj.* estratégico, táctico.

strategically | strə'tiːdʒɪkəlɪ | *adv.* estratégicamente, tácticamente.

strategist | 'strætɪdʒɪst | *s.c.* estratega.

strategy | 'strætɪdʒɪ | *s.i.* **1** MIL. estrategia. || *s.c.* **2** estrategia, táctica política, plan: *a strategy to pass the exam = un plan para aprobar el examen.*

stratification | ,strætɪfɪ'keɪʃn | *s.i.* estratificación.

stratified | 'strætɪfaɪd | *adj.* estratificado, en capas, por estratos.

stratosphere | 'stræteu,sfɪər | *s.sing.* estratosfera.

stratum | 'strɑːtəm | [*pl.* **strata**] *s.c.* **1** GEOL. estrato. **2 [– (of)]** (fig.) estrato, capa, nivel (social).

straw | strɔː | *s.c.* e *i.* **1** paja: *a straw hat = un sombrero de paja.* || *s.c.* **2** pajita (para beber). **3** [generalmente *sing.* y en *negativa* o *interr.*] (fig.) paja, insignificancia, bagatela, tontería. || **4 a man of –,** testaferro, un hombre de paja. **5 a – in the wind,** un indicio de lo que puede suceder, una señal de lo que puede pasar. **6 to clutch/grasp at straws,** agarrarse a un clavo ardiendo, echar mano de cualquier cosa. **7 to draw/get the short –,** tocarle a uno la china. **8 to make bricks without –,** no tener los medios adecuados para trabajar. **9 not to care/give a –,** importar un comino. **10 – poll/vote,** votación de tanteo, encuesta pre-electoral. **11 the last/final –,** el colmo. **12 the – that broke the camels back,** la gota que colmó el vaso.

strawberry | 'strɔːbərɪ | (EE.UU.) | 'strɔːberɪ | *s.c.* **1** fresa, fresón. **2** color fresa, color rosa oscuro. || **3 – mark,** antojo, mancha de nacimiento.

straw-coloured | 'strɔː,kʌləd | *adj.* amarillo claro, pajizo, de color paja.

stray | streɪ | *v.i.* **1 [to – (from)]** extraviarse, perderse, descarriarse, apartarse. **2** (fig.) desviarse, apartarse (de un tema, del buen camino). **3** vagar, errar, deambular. || *s.c.* **4** animal callejero. **5** niño abandonado, niño sin hogar, niño vagabundo. **6** (fam.) descarriado, perdido. || *adj.* **7** errante, perdido, extraviado, abandonado. **8** aislado, raro, disperso, esporádico: *stray visits = visitas esporádicas.*

streak | striːk | *s.c.* **1 [– (of)]** línea, banda, tira, raya, lista. **2 [– (of)]** vena (de color). **3 [– (of)]** rayo (de luz). **4 [– (of)]** vena, traza, elemento, rasgo (de locura, de carácter). **5** racha (de suerte). || *v.i.* **6 [to – + *adv./prep.*]** pasar como un rayo, pasar a gran velocidad. **7** relampaguear. **8** correr desnudo a gran velocidad en un lugar público. || *v.t.* **9** marcar, surcar, cubrir, vetear: *marble streaked with grey = mármol veteado de gris.* || **10 a lucky/unlucky/winning –,** una racha de suerte o de mala suerte, una racha de éxito o de mala fortuna. **11 a yellow –,** V. **yellow. 12 like a – of lightning,** (fam.) como un rayo, a gran velocidad.

streaker | 'striːkər | *s.c.* persona que corre desnuda en un lugar público (para atraer la atención).

streaky | 'striːkɪ | *adj.* **1** a rayas, listado, veteado. **2** inestable, variable (de carácter). **3** con suerte, afortunado. || **4 – bacon,** jamón entreverado.

stream | striːm | *s.c.* **1** arroyo, riachuelo. **2 [– (of)]** corriente, flujo, chorro (de líquido, de humo). **3** (generalmente *sing.*) corriente, dirección: *we let ourselves go along with the stream = nos dejamos llevar por la corriente.* **4** (fig.) riada, desfile, oleada, caravana (de gente, de tráfico). **5** (fig.) torrente: *a stream of insults = un torrente de insultos.* **6** (brit.) nivel, clasificación (escolar de un grupo de alumnos). **7** curso (de la historia). || *v.i.* **8 [to – + *adv./prep.*]** brotar, fluir, correr, manar (a borbotones). **9 [to – + *adv./prep.*]** salir o entrar en tropel, moverse en oleadas (la gente). **10 [to – + *adv./prep.*]** ondear, flotar (al viento). **11 [to – (with)]** llorar, lagrimear. || *v.t.* **12** (brit.) clasificar, colocar por niveles (a los niños en la escuela). || **13 to go up/down –,** ir a favor de la corriente o contra corriente. **14 to go/swim against the –/tide,** (fig.) ir contra corriente, ser inconformista. **15 to go/swim with the –/tide,** (fig.) ir con la corriente, ser conformista. **16 on –,** TEC. en funcionamiento: *there'll be a new factory on stream in June = una nueva fábrica entrará en funcionamiento en Junio.*

streamer | 'striːmər | *s.c.* **1** serpentina. **2** gallardete, banderola. **3** rayo, franja (de luz en el horizonte). **4** PER. titular a toda plana.

streaming | 'striːmɪŋ | *s.i.* (brit.) clasificación por niveles (en la escuela).

streamline | 'striːmlaɪn | *v.t.* **1** aerodinamizar, perfilar. **2** modernizar, perfeccionar, hacer más eficaz: *it seems difficult to streamline administration = parece difícil modernizar la administración.* **3** perfilar, simplificar (un texto).

streamlined | 'striːmlaɪnd | *adj.* **1** aerodinámico, perfilado. **2** modernizado, perfeccionado, eficiente, útil.

street | striːt | *s.c.* **1** calle. **2 [the –]** la calle, afuera, el exterior: *lots of noise in the street = mucho ruido afuera.* || **3 to be streets ahead of,** (fam. y fig.) ser superior a, sacar gran ventaja a, ser más aventajado que, ser infinitamente mejor que. **4 to be streets apart,** (fam.) ser totalmente diferentes, no tener nada en común. **5 to be up one's –/right up one's –,** saber mucho sobre el tema, conocer bien el tema, interesar el tema a uno. **6 to be on/walk the streets,** hacer la calle, ser una prostituta. **7 not to be in the same – (as),** (fam.) no estar a la misma altura que. **8 – credibility/cred,** (fam.) aceptación, imagen, credibilidad (entre la gente joven). **9 – value,** valor de venta en la calle (de una droga ilegal). **10 the man in the –/the man or woman in the –,** el hombre de la calle, la gente corriente. **11 walking the streets,** en la calle, sin un lugar en que vivir.
streetcar | 'striːtkɑːr | *s.c.* (EE.UU.) tranvía.
streetlamp | 'striːtlæmp | *s.c.* farol (de alumbrado público).
streetlight | 'striːtlaɪt | *s.c.* V. **streetlamp.**
streetwalker | 'striːtˌwɔːkər | *s.c.* prostituta callejera.
streetwise | 'striːtwaɪz | *adj.* (fam.) que domina la calle, experimentado en vivir en la calle (en grandes ciudades).
strength | streŋθ | *s.c.* e *i.* **1** fuerza, energía, fortaleza, vigor, resistencia. **2** confianza, resolución, coraje. **3** intensidad, potencia, fuerza (del viento, la luz, etc....). || *s.c.* **4 [– (of)]** eficacia, fundamento, base, firmeza (de un plan, de un argumento). || *s.i.* **5** número, fuerza numérica, efectivos. **6** poder, influencia. || **7 at full –/up to full –,** con todos sus componentes presentes, a pleno rendimiento, con el número de gente requerida. **8 to be below/under –,** estar bajo mínimos, tener poco personal. **9 to go from – to –,** prosperar, mejorar, ir cada vez mejor. **10 in –/great –,** en gran número. **11 on the –,** (fam.) miembro (de una organización, del ejército). **12 on the – of,** en base a, en virtud de, influido por, confiado en. **13 with all your –,** con toda su fuerza, duramente, fuertemente.
strengthen | 'streŋθən | | 'strenθən | *v.t.* e *i.* **1** reforzar(se), fortalecer(se), robustecer(se), hacer(se) más fuerte. **2** incrementar, intensificar.
strenuous | 'strenjuəs | *adj.* **1** extenuante, agotador, fatigoso, penoso, arduo: *a strenuous climb = una subida extenuante.* **2** enérgico, vigoroso, activo.
stress | stres | *s.c.* e *i.* **1** tensión, presión, ansiedad: *she suffers from nervous stress = padece tensión nerviosa.* **2** FIS. fuerza, carga, presión, esfuerzo. **3 [– (on)]** FON. acento. **4** acento, énfasis. || *v.t.* **5** subrayar, dar importancia a, dar énfasis a, recalcar. **6** acentuar.
stressed | strest | *adj.* **1** en tensión, nervioso. **2** FIS. forzado, tenso. **3** FON. acentuado.
stressful | 'stresfəl | *adj.* lleno de tensión, agitado, inquieto: *a stressful day = un día lleno de tensión.*
stretch | stretʃ | *v.t.* e *i.* **1** ensanchar(se), dilatar(se), agrandar(se), expandir(se), dar(se) de sí: *wool tends to stretch = la lana tiende a ensancharse.* || *v.t.* **2 [to – (out)]** extender, tender, estirar, alargar: *he stretched his arm to catch it = alargo el brazo para cogerlo.* **3** (fam.) adaptar, hacer una concesión, ir más allá del límite: *let's stretch the rules = adaptemos las reglas.* **4** forzar, exagerar, distorsionar: *stretch the truth = exagerar la verdad.* **5** exigir, requerir (mucho en el trabajo). **6** esforzar, batallar, pugnar. **7** (fam.) caer al suelo por un golpe. || *v.i.* **8 [to – + *adv./prep.*]** extenderse, abarcar, llegar, prolongarse: *the story stretches over generations = la historia abarca generaciones.* **9 [to – (out)]** estirarse, desperezarse, desentumecerse. || *s.c.* **10** estiramiento, estirón, desperezamiento, desentumecimiento. **11 [– (of)]** extensión, zona, parte, paisaje. **12** (generalmente *sing.*) DEP. tramo, recta, trecho, etapa (de una carrera). **13 [– (of)]** período, intervalo: *a two-hour stretch = un intervalo de dos horas.* **14** (generalmente *sing.*) (jerga) condena, pena (en prisión). || *s.i.* **15** elasticidad. || **16 at a –,** sin parar, con continuidad, continuamente, todo seguido. **17 at full –, a)** completamente estirado; **b)** a la máxima potencia, con la mayor energía, con todo el esfuerzo. **18 by any – of the imagination,** con enorme imaginación, con un esfuerzo de la imaginación. **19 to – a point,** hacer una excepción, romper la regla, hacer una concesión. **20 to – one's legs,** estirar las piernas, dar un paseo. **21 to – one's wings,** (fig.) extender alas, hacer algo diferente.
stretcher | stretʃər | *s.c.* **1** camilla, parihuelas. **2** MEC. tensor, ensanchador. **3** bastidor. **4** viga, tirante. **5** ARQ. soga, ladrillos al hilo.
stretcher-bearer | 'stretʃəˌbeərər | *s.c.* camillero.
stretchy | 'stretʃɪ | *adj.* elástico, estirable.
strew | struː | *v.t.* [*pret.* y *p.p.* **strewed** o **strewn**] (lit.) **1** desparramar, esparcir, sembrar, extender, derramar. **2** (fig.) saturar, colmar: *a piece of writing strewn with swear words = un escrito saturado de palabras soeces.*
strewth | struːθ | *interj.* (brit., fam. y arc.) ¡Santo Cielo!, ¡que horror! (expresa sorpresa, alarma).
stricken | 'strɪkən | *adj.* (form.) **1** acongojado, angustiado, destrozado, afligido: *stricken by fear = acongojado de temor.* **2** herido, afectado (por una enfermedad). **3** afectado, debilitado, maltrecho (un negocio, una industria). || *sufijo* **4** [*s.i.* **+ -stricken**] afectado: *terror-stricken = aterrado.*
strict | strɪkt | *adj.* **1 [– (with)]** estricto, riguroso, severo, firme. **2** estricto, preciso, claro, definido, exacto: *very strict rules = reglas muy claras.* **3** terminante, (una orden). **4** escrupuloso, absoluto, total: *a strict vegetarian = un vegetariano escrupuloso.*
strictly | 'strɪktlɪ | *adv.* **1** estrictamente, severamente, rígidamente. **2** rigurosamente, terminantemente: *strictly forbidden = terminantemente prohibido.* **3** exclusivamente, solamente: *strictly for members = exclusivamente para socios.* **4** estrictamente, escrupulosamente. || **5 – speaking,** rigurosamente, en rigor.
strictness | 'strɪktnɪs | *s.i.* **1** severidad, rigor, rigidez. **2** exactitud.
stricture | 'strɪktʃər | *s.c.* (form.) **1 [– (on)** y generalmente *pl.*] condena, censura, reprobación, reproche, crítica, reparo. **2** limitación, restricción. **3** MED. estrechez, constricción.
stridden | 'strɪdn | *p.p.irreg.* de **stride.**
stride | straɪd | *v.i.* [*pret.irreg.* **strode,** *p.p.* **stridden**] **1 [to – + *adv./prep.*]** andar a zancadas, dar zancadas, caminar a trancos. || *s.c.* **2** zancada, paso largo, tranco. || **3 to get into one's –,** empezar a funcionar bien, alcanzar un buen ritmo, tomar confianza (en una actividad). **4 to make strides in,** hacer progresos, avanzar, progresar. **5 to take something in one's –,** tomarse algo bien, hacer algo sin esfuerzo, salir del paso sin esfuerzo.
stridency | 'straɪdənsɪ | *s.i.* estridencia, estrépito.
strident | 'straɪdnt | *adj.* **1** (desp.) estridente, chillona, chirriante. **2** (fig.) clamorosa, fuerte, enérgica, potente (una protesta).
stridently | 'straɪdntlɪ | *adv.* **1** (desp.) estridentemente, de forma chillona, de forma chirriante. **2** clamorosamente, con fuerza, enérgicamente.
strife | straɪf | *s.i.* **1** disensión, desacuerdo, rivalidad, conflicto. **2** pelea, lucha, batalla.
strike | straɪk | *v.* [*pret.* y *p.p.irreg.* **struck**] *t.* **1** (form.) golpear, pegar, dar una bofetada, asestar (un golpe), recibir (un impacto). **2** atacar, asaltar. **3** afligir con, herir en, atacar (una enfermedad). **4** caer sobre (un rayo, una luz): *lightning struck the tree = un rayo cayó sobre el árbol.* **5** MUS. tocar, tañer. **6 [to – + *o.* + *adv./prep.*** y generalmente *pas.*] quedarse de repente, convertirse, dejar: *he was struck dumb = se quedó mudo de repente.* **7 [to – + *o.* + *adv./prep.*]** provocar, causar, penetrar profundamente (un sentimiento). **8** encender, prender, frotar, friccionar: *strike a match = enciende una cerilla.* **9 [to – + *o.* + *adv./prep.*]** (form.) eliminar, borrar, quitar (oficialmente). **10** encontrar, descubrir, hallar, dar con (un material, un lugar, una dificultad). **11** alcanzar, conseguir, lograr (un acuerdo). **12 [to – (as)]** parecer, afectar, impresionar: *it struck me as rather strict = me pareció bastante estricto.* **13** ocurrir(le), parecer(le): *it struck her that he might have left her = se le ocurrió que quizá la había abandonado.* **14** asumir, tomar, adoptar (una postura). **15** TEC. acuñar, imprimir (moneda, una medalla). || *v.i.* **16 [to – (out)]** atacar, golpear, dar golpes. **17 [to – (for)]** ir a la huelga, declararse en huelga. **18** MAR. tocar fondo, encallar (un barco). **19** penetrar, atravesar, entrar, pinchar. **20** BOT. echar raíces, arraigar. || *v.t.* e *i.* **21** dar la hora, indicar la hora (por campanadas): *the clock has just struck five = el reloj acaba de dar las cinco.* **22** morder, picar (una serpiente). **23** enganchar(se) en el anzuelo, morder la carnada (un pez). **24** chocar (con), estrellar(se) (contra), colisionar. **25** arriar, bajar (la bandera). || *s.c.* **26** huelga, paro. **27** ataque aéreo, bombardeo. **28** descubrimiento, hallazgo (de petróleo). **29** mordedura (del pez a la carnada). **30** emisión (de moneda). **31**

DEP. lanzamiento, pasada (en béisbol). **32** DEP. golpe (que derriba 10 bolos de una vez). || **33 to be struck dumb/blind,** quedarse mudo, quedarse ciego. **34 to – a balance,** COM. hacer balance. **35 to – a bargain,** cerrar un trato. **36 to – a blow for,** actuar en favor de, luchar por (un ideal, una causa). **37 to – a chord, a)** identificarse con, causar simpatía, causar buena impresión; **b)** sonarle a uno, recordarle a alguien. **38 to – a note,** dar la impresión. **39 to – at the heart of,** (fig.) golpear directamente al corazón, perjudicar enormemente. **40 to – down,** llevar a la muerte, desaparecer, ser afligido por. **41 to – fear/ter ror into people/their hearts,** sobrecoger de terror a la gente. **42 to – home,** dar en el blanco, producir efecto. **43 to – it rich,** tocar el gordo, descubrir un buen filón, hacerse rico. **44 to – lucky/oil,** (fam.) tener un golpe de suerte, ser muy afortunado. **45 to – off,** borrar, quitar, tachar (de una lista oficial); expulsar (de un colegio profesional por conducta poco ética). **46 to – on/upon, a)** dar con, descubrir, ocurrírsele (una respuesta, una idea); **b)** quedar impresionado (por un plan). **47 to – out, a)** tachar con una raya, borrar con una línea; **b)** moverse resueltamente, caminar a grandes zancadas; nadar con gran energía; **c)** independizarse, obrar por cuenta propia. **48 – pay,** subsidio de huelga (que pagan los sindicatos a los huelguistas). **49 to – the eye,** llamar la atención, impresionar. **50 to – up, a)** iniciarse la música, comenzar a tocar; **b)** trabar, comenzar (una amistad, una conversación). **51 to – while the iron is hot,** V. **iron.**

strike-bound | 'straɪkbaʊnd | *adj.* paralizado por la huelga.

strike-breaker | 'straɪkˌbreɪkər | *s.c.* esquirol.

striker | 'straɪkər | *s.c.* **1** huelguista. **2** DEP. delantero (en fútbol). **3** badajo (de campana), percutor, macillo (en relojería). **4** arpón. **5** arponero.

striking | 'straɪkɪŋ | *adj.* **1** sorprendente, increíble, chocante: *a striking effect = un efecto sorprendente.* **2** impresionante, imponente, escultural, llamativa (una persona). || **3 within – distance,** a tiro de piedra, muy cercano.

strikingly | 'straɪkɪŋlɪ | *adv.* **1** sorprendentemente, increíblemente, de modo chocante. **2** impresionantemente, imponentemente, llamativamente: *a strikingly beautiful girl = una chica llamativamente bella.*

string | strɪŋ | *s.c.* e *i.* **1** cuerda, bramante, cordel. || *s.c.* **2** MUS. cuerda. **3** sarta (de perlas, de mentiras). **4** ristra (de ajos). **5** reata (de animales). **6** procesión, desfile, fila, hilera (de gente). **7** retahíla, serie, montón: *a string of swear words = una retahíla de tacos.* **8** INF. cadena, serie. **9** BOT. fibra, nervio. **10** condición, restricción. || *v.irr.* [*pret.* y *p.p.* **strung**] *t.* **11** encordar, ensartar. **12** atar, apretar, colgar (con cuerda). **13** (fig.) ensartar, unir (una frase con otra). **14** extender, colocar (una cuerda). **15** MUS. tensar (cuerdas). **16** quitar las fibras (a las judías verdes). || *adj.* **17** de cuerda, hecho de cuerda: *a string bag = un bolso de cuerda.* **18** MUS. de cuerda: *a string quartet = un cuarteto de cuerda.* || **19 to have got someone on a –,** tener a alguien en sus manos, tener a alguien en un puño, hacer lo que se quiere de alguien. **20 to have two strings/more than one – to one's bow,** tener varias posibilidades, tener más de una alternativa. **21 to pull strings,** tocar resortes, tocar todos los hilos. **22 to – along,** engañar, embaucar, traer al retortero. **23 to – along with,** (fam.) acompañar, pegarse a, seguir a. **24 – bean,** judía, alubia, vaina. **25 to – out,** extender en fila, poner en una hilera, colocar en fila. **26 strings,** MUS. **a)** instrumentos de cuerda; **b)** orquesta de cuerda, grupo de músicos de cuerda. **27 to – together,** unir, combinar, ensamblar. **28 to – up, a)** colgar, suspender, enganchar; **b)** (fam.) colgar, ahorcar. **29 with no strings attached,** sin condiciones previas, sin condiciones establecidas.

stringed instrument | 'strɪŋgd ɪnstrʊmənt | *s.c.* MUS. instrumento de cuerda.

stringency | 'strɪndʒənsɪ | *s.i.* **1** dificultad, escasez, estrechez (económica). **2** severidad, rigor, rigurosidad (en el cumplimiento de las leyes).

stringent | 'strɪndʒənt | *adj.* **1** severa, rigurosa, estricta (una ley, una regla): *a stringent ban = una prohibición rigurosa.* **2** difícil, estrecho (un período económico).

stringently | 'strɪndʒəntlɪ | *adv.* rigurosamente, severamente, estrictamente.

stringy | 'strɪŋɪ | *adj.* (desp.) **1** fibroso, correoso (un alimento). **2** estropajoso, ratonil (el pelo). **3** largo y delgado (un brazo).

strip | strɪp | [*pret.* y *p.p.* **stripped,** *ger.* **stripping**] *v.t.* **1 [to – (from/of/off)]** despojar, despellejar, desollar. **2 [to – (from /of/off)]** arrancar, quitar, descortezar: *to strip the bark off a tree = descortezar un árbol.* **3** arrancar, raspar, lijar (la pintura, el papel de una pared). **4 [to – (down)]** desmantelar, desmontar (una máquina). **5** MEC. estropear (la caja de cambios). **6** MEC. pasarse de rosca (un tornillo). || *v.t.* e *i.* **7** desnudar(se), desvestir(se), despojar(se) de ropa, quitar(se) la ropa. || *s.c.* **8** franja, zona (de tierra). **9** tira, banda, lista (de material). **10** tira cómica, tira de dibujos. **11** lámina, fleje (de metal). **12** espectáculo de "strip-tease". **13** (brit.) traje, ropa, colores (de un equipo de fútbol). **14** AER. pista de aterrizaje. || **15 to – away/of, a)** despojarse, dejar de lado (hábitos); **b)** desmantelar, despojar de, arrebatar, privar de (objetos de valor, galones). **16 – cartoon,** (brit.) tira cómica, tira de dibujos. **17 – club,** club de "strip-tease". **18 – joint,** (EE.UU. y fam.) club de "strip-tease". **19 – lighting,** ELEC. alumbrado de tubos fluorescentes, alumbrado de banda. **20 to tear a – off,** (fam.) dar una buena regañina, echar una buena reprimenda.

stripe | straɪp | *s.c.* **1** raya, franja, lista, banda: *she wore a skirt with blue stripes = llevaba una falda de rayas azules.* **2** MIL. galón. **3** clase, tipo, calaña. || *s.i.* **4** material de rayas. || **5 stripes,** (fam.) traje a rayas (de prisionero).

striped | straɪpt | *adj.* de rayas, a rayas, listado.

stripling | 'strɪplɪŋ | *s.c.* (hum.) muchacho, joven, imberbe, mozuelo.

stripper | 'strɪpər | *s.c.* **1** (fam.) bailarina de "strip-tease", artista de "strip-tease". **2** espátula, raspador (para quitar pinturas). || *s.i.* **3** QUIM. disolvente.

striptease | 'strɪptiːz | *s.c.* e *i.* "strip-tease", espectáculo en que una bailarina se despoja de la ropa al son de la música.

stripy | straɪpɪ | *adj.* de rayas, de listas.

strive | straɪv | *v.* [*pret.irreg.* **strove,** *p.p.* **striven**] *i.* **[to – (after/against/for)]** (lit.) esforzarse, afanarse, luchar, batallar, porfiar.

striven | 'straɪvn | *p.p.irreg.* de **strive.**

striving | 'straɪvɪŋ | *s.i.* lucha, esfuerzo, batalla, porfía.

strobe | strəʊb (también **strobe lighting**) *s.i.* luz estroboscópica, iluminación estroboscópica (usada en discotecas).

strode | strəʊd | *pret.irreg.* de **stride.**

stroke | strəʊk | *v.t.* **1** acariciar, pasar la mano por. **2** DEP. ser el primer remero. **3** DEP. golpear, dar a (la pelota). || *s.c.* **4** golpe, azote, latigazo. **5** MED. apoplejía, ataque apoplégico. **6** DEP. golpe, jugada, lance, hoyo (en críquet, golf). **7** tacada (en billar). **8** trazo, rasgo, plumazo, pincelada. **9** palada, remada. **10** DEP. brazada; estilo (en natación). **11** campanada, tañido. **12** oblicua, raya oblicua: *note down seven stroke two = anota siete, raya oblicua, dos (= 7/2).* **13** DEP. primer remero, remero mayor. **14** MEC. carrera (de pistón). || *s.sing.* **15 [– (of)]** golpe, racha: *a stroke of luck = un golpe de suerte.* **16 [– (of)]** vena, rasgo, golpe de intuición (de ingenio). || **17 at a single –/in one –,** de un solo golpe, de una sola vez. **18 not to do a –/a – of work,** (fig.) no dar ni golpe, no pegar un palo al agua. **19 to put someone off their –,** distraer a alguien, no dejar concentrarse a alguien.

stroll | strəʊl | *v.i.* **1** pasear, andar, vagar. || *s.c.* **2** paseo, vuelta: *a stroll in the park = un paseo por el parque.*

stroller | strəʊlər | *s.c.* **1** paseante, caminante. **2** (EE.UU.) cochecito de niño, sillita de niño.

strong | strɒŋ | *adj.* **1** fuerte, recio, vigoroso. **2** potente, fuerte, poderoso, influyente (un país, un grupo). **3** resistente, sólido, duro, consistente: *a strong table = una mesa resistente.* **4** fervoroso, ferviente, ardiente, acérrimo (partidario). **5** sano, fuerte, robusto (de constitución): *a strong heart = un corazón sano.* **6** fuerte, impetuoso, violento (el viento, una corriente de agua). **7** intenso, fuerte (un olor, un sabor, una luz, un color, una emoción). **8** fuerte, chillona (una voz). **9** marcado, intenso (un parecido). **10** firme, persuasivo, convincente (un argumento). **11** importante, extraordinario, excepcional, considerable (reparto cinematográfico, una influencia). **12** respetable, con buenas posibilidades (un candidato). **13** marcado, acusado (un rasgo, el acento). **14** fuerte (una droga); cargada, alcohólica (una bebida). **15** franca, definitiva (posibilidad). **16** [*s.* + –] de cierto número (generalmente no se traduce al castellano): *a club of 50 strong = un club de 50 socios.* **17 [– on]** bueno, hábil, diestro (en alguna materia). **18** (fam.) severo, duro, exagerado, inaceptable. **19** [no comp.] GRAM. fuerte, irregular (un verbo). **20** ECON. próspero, en alza, firme. || **21 to come on –, a)** (fam. y desp.) entrar directamente, no andarse por las ramas (en la relación sexual); **b)** ir demasiado lejos, actuar con excesiva severidad. **22 still going –,** (fam.) **a)** en perfecto funcionamiento, en buenas condiciones; **b)** aún popular, en pleno éxito; **c)** con buena salud.

strong-arm | 'strɒŋɑːm | *adj.* de mano dura, represivo, violento (un método, una táctica).

stronghold | 'strɒŋhəuld | *s.c.* **1** (arc.) fuerte, bastión, fortaleza. **2 [– of]** baluarte de, bastión de (actitudes, creencias).

strongly | strɒŋlɪ | *adv.* **1** sólidamente, resistentemente. **2** considerablemente, enormemente. **3** apasionadamente, fervientemente, firmemente: *strongly convinced = fervientemente convencido.* **4** marcadamente, acusadamente: *a strongly American accent = un acento marcadamente americano.* **5** intensamente, fuertemente: *it smelled strongly of gas = olía intensamente a gas.*

strong-minded | ˌstrɒŋ'maɪndɪd | *adj.* decidido, independiente, resuelto, determinado (de carácter).

strong-willed | ˌstrɒŋ'wɪld | *adj.* (desp.) terco, de voluntad fuerte, obstinado, terco.

stroppy | strɒpɪ | *adj.* (brit. y fam.) malhumorado, desabrido, obstinado, de trato difícil (una persona).

strove | strəuv | *pret.irreg.* de **strive.**

struck | strʌk | *pret.* y *p.p.irreg.* de **strike.**

structural | 'strʌktʃərəl | *adj.* **1** estructural, de estructura. **2** GEOL. estructural.

structurally | 'strʌktʃərəlɪ | *adv.* estructuralmente.

structuralism | 'strʌktʃərəlɪzm | *s.i.* estructuralismo.

structuralist | 'strʌktʃərəlɪst | *s.c.* estructuralista.

structure | 'strʌktʃər | *s.i.* **1** estructura, organización, disposición. **2** GEOM. estructura. || *s.c.* **3** estructura, armazón, esqueleto. **4** construcción. **5** entramado, sistema. || *v.t.* **6** estructurar, organizar, diseñar, disponer.

structured | 'strʌktʃəd | *adj.* estructurado, organizado, diseñado: *the company was perfectly structured = la compañía estaba perfectamente estructurada.*

struggle | 'strʌgl | *v.i.* **1** luchar, forcejear, pugnar, batallar, bregar. **2** esforzarse, afanarse, desvivirse, hacer lo imposible. || *s.c.* **3** lucha, pelea, pugna, contienda. **4** (euf.) guerra. **5** esfuerzo, forcejeo: *her struggles to control her tears were patent = sus esfuerzos por dominar las lágrimas eran patentes.* || **6 to – along/on,** avanzar con dificultad, continuar penosamente, sobrevivir con dificultad.

strum | strʌm | **[strummed, strumming]** *v.t.* e *i.* MUS. **1** rasguear, tocar distraídamente. || *s.c.* **2** rasgueo.

strumpet | 'strʌmpɪt | *s.c.* (arc. y desp.) meretriz, ramera, prostituta.

strung | strʌŋ | *pret.* y *p.p.irreg.* de **string.**

strung-out | ˌstrʌŋ'əut | *adj.* **[– (on)]** (argot) enganchado (a una droga).

strung-up | ˌstrʌŋ'ʌp | *adj.* nervioso, tenso, excitado, preocupado, agitado, alterado.

strut | strʌt | [*pret.* y *p.p.* **strutted,** *ger.* **strutting**] *v.i.* **1** (desp.) pavonearse, contonearse, presumir, darse importancia: *she passed by strutting like a peacock = pasó contoneándose como un pavo real.* || *v.t.* **2** apuntalar, reforzar, acodar. || *s.c.* **3** puntal, poste, soporte. **4** pavoneo, contoneo.

strychnine | 'strɪkniːn | | 'strɪknaɪn | *s.i.* QUIM. estricnina.

stub | stʌb | *s.c.* **1** trozo, resto, fragmento, cabo (de lápiz, de vela). **2** tocón, cepa. **3** colilla, (Am.) pucho (de cigarro). **4** matriz (de un talonario). || *v.t.* [*pret.* y *p.p.* **stubbed,** *ger.* **stubbing**]. **5** hacerse daño al tropezar, dar un tropezón, tropezar. **6** arrancar, quitar (malas hierbas). **7** desarraigar (un árbol). || **8 to – out,** apagar aplastando (una colilla).

stubble | 'stʌbl | *s.i.* **1** rastrojo. **2** barba de días.

stubborn | 'stʌbən | *adj.* **1** (desp.) terco, testarudo, porfiado: *a stubborn child = un niño terco.* **2** obstinado, tenaz, resuelto, determinado. **3** firme, arraigado. **4** persistente, difícil de remover: *a stubborn stain = una mancha difícil de sacar.* **5** dificultoso, duro: *stubborn soil = terreno duro.*

stubbornly | 'stʌbənlɪ | *adv.* **1** (desp.) tercamente, con testarudez, porfiadamente, obstinadamente. **2** resueltamente, tenazmente, determinadamente. **3** persistentemente, de forma arraigada.

stubbornness | 'stʌbənnɪs | *s.i.* **1** (desp.) terquedad, testarudez, porfía. **2** obstinación, tenacidad, resolución. **3** persistencia.

stubby | stʌbɪ | *adj.* (desp.) regordete, corto, grueso y romo: *stubby fingers = dedos regordetes.*

stucco | 'stʌkəu | *s.i.* **1** estuco. || *v.t.* **2** estucar. || *adj.* **3** de estuco.

stuck | stʌk | *pret.* y *p.p.* **1** de **stick.** || *adj.* **2** atascado, atollado, pillado. **3** obstruido, atrancado. **4** (fam.) estancado, atascado, paralizado (en un asunto). **5 [– with]** (fam.) atrapado por, cargado con (algo no deseado): *we couldn't leave because we were stuck with the animals = no podíamos irnos a causa de los animales.* **6** abandonado, dejado a su suerte: *they were stuck in Kuwait = estaban en Kuwait abandonados a su suerte.* **7 [– on]** (fam.) enamorado de, loco por, encantado con. || *s.c.* **8 [in –]** (brit. y jerga) problema, lío, dificultad. || **9 to get – in (to),** (brit. y fam.) empezar con grandes ánimos, entusiasmarse con, embelesarse con, ilusionarse con.

stuck-up | ˌstʌk'ʌp | *adj.* (fam. y desp.) engreído, presumido, vanidoso, ensoberbecido.

stud | stʌd | *s.c.* **1** botón de cuello; gemelo. **2** taco, tachuela (en botas, zapatos). **3** taco (de separación en carreteras). **4** tachón, clavo (de adorno). **5** pendiente. **6** yeguada, recua de caballos. **7** (fig. y vulg.) semental (hombre muy activo sexualmente). || *v.t.* [*pret.* y *p.p.* **studded,** *ger.* **studding**] **[to – (with)] 8** poner tacos, poner tachuelas. **9** tachonar, adornar con clavos. **10** (fig.) tachonar, sembrar: *the sky was studded with stars = el cielo estaba tachonado de estrellas.* || **11 – farm,** caballerizas, cuadra de caballos.

studded | stʌdɪd | *adj.* **1** tachonado, decorado con clavos. **2** adornado con piedras preciosas.

student | stjuːdnt | *s.c.* **1** estudiante (de Universidad). **2** alumno, escolar (de secundaria). **3** estudioso, investigador. || **4 students' union,** sindicato de estudiantes (la organización y el edificio en que aloja).

studentship | 'stjuːdntʃɪp | *s.c.* beca.

studied | 'stʌdɪd | *adj.* (generalmente desp.) estudiado, calculado, deliberado (un comportamiento).

studio | 'stjuːdɪəu | *s.c.* **1** TV. estudio. **2** estudio, taller (de un pintor, de un fotógrafo, etc...). **3** academia de baile. || **4 – audience,** audiencia de un programa (de radio, de TV). **5** (brit.) **– flat/**(EE.UU.) **– apartment,** apartamento de una sola habitación, estudio. **6 studios,** estudios cinematográficos.

studious | 'stjuːdɪəs | (EE.UU.) | 'stuːdjəs | *adj.* **1** estudioso, aplicado, amante del estudio. **2** (form.) deliberado, cuidadoso, esmerado: *studious of his way of speaking = esmerado en su modo de hablar.*

studiously | 'stjuːdɪəslɪ | *adv.* cuidadosamente, diligentemente, esmeradamente, deliberadamente.

study | 'stʌdɪ | *s.i.* **1** (form.) estudio, observación. **2** meditación, ensimismamiento. || *s.c.* **3 [– (of)]** estudio, trabajo, análisis, examen, investigación: *a study of the country's economy = un análisis de la economía del país.* **4** asignatura, materia. **5** estudio, despacho, gabinete. **6 [– (of)]** ART. boceto, bosquejo: *a study of the mansion = un boceto de la mansión.* **7** MUS. estudio, ejercicio. || *v.t.* e *i.* **8** estudiar, cursar estudios. | *v.t.* **9** analizar, examinar, observar atentamente, estudiar concienzudamente. || **10 in a brown –,** (fam.) absorto en la meditación.

stuff | stʌf | *s.i.* **1** (fam.) cosa, materia, material, sustancia, líquido, elemento, ingrediente: *you can use some cleaning stuff = puedes usar algún producto de limpieza.* **2** pertenencias, efectos, objetos, bienes (personales). **3** (lit.) esencia, aspecto, cualidad. **4** (arc.) paño, tela, género, tejido. **5** (jerga) tontería, disparate, estupidez, jerigonza. **6** (jerga) arte, maña, habilidad. **7** (jerga) dinero. **8** (jerga) droga dura (heroína, cocaína). || *v.t.* **9 [to – (with)]** rellenar, llenar, atestar, atiborrar. **10 [to – (into)]** meter en desorden, empaquetar deprisa. **11** rellenar (en cocina): *what did you stuff the chicken with? = ¿con qué has rellenado el pollo?* **12** disecar (animales). **13** introducir votos fraudulentos, dar pucherazo. **14** enlustrar, lustrar, encerar (el cuero). **15** (fam. y vulg.) tirarse a (sexualmente). || *v.t.* e *i.* **16** (fam.) atiborrar(se), llenar(se), atracar(se) (de comida). || **17 to do one's –,** mostrar lo que uno sabe, actuar como uno sabe. **18 get stuffed!,** (brit. y jerga) ¡vete a la porra!, ¡que te den morcilla! **19 to know one's –,** conocer perfectamente el oficio de uno, saber lo que uno se trae entre manos. **20 – and nonsense!,** ¡tonterías!, ¡bobadas!, ¡basura!, ¡necedades! **21 to – up,** bloquear, obstruir, atascar. **22 that's**

the –!, (fam.) ¡eso es!, ¡exactamente!, ¡claro!

stuffed | stʌft | *adj.* **1** relleno, lleno, atiborrado. || **2 – shirt,** (fam. y desp.) persona anticuada, persona rimbombante, persona pomposa.

stuffed-up | 'stʌft,ʌp | *adj.* obstruida, congestionada (la nariz a causa del catarro).

stuffing | 'stʌfɪŋ | *s.i.* **1** material para relleno, relleno: *feather stuffing = relleno con plumas.* **2** relleno, mezcla para relleno (en cocina): *bread, egg and onion stuffing = relleno a base de pan, huevo y cebolla.* || **3 to knock the – out of someone,** (fam.) **a)** bajarle a uno los humos; **b)** debilitar, estar bajo de ánimos.

stuffy | stʌfɪ | *adj.* (desp.) **1** cargado, mal ventilado, sofocante (un lugar). **2** congestionada, obstruida (la nariz a causa del catarro). **3** formalista, engolado, chapado a la antigua, remilgado (una persona, una institución).

stultify | 'stʌltɪfaɪ | *v.t.* (form.) **1** entontecer, idiotizar, embrutecer. **2** ridiculizar, hacer parecer estúpido. **3** invalidar, inutilizar. **4** DER. alegar locura.

stultifying | 'stʌltɪfaɪɪŋ | *adj.* entontecedor, idiotizante, embrutecedor: *the stultifying effect of television = el efecto idiotizante de la televisión.*

stumble | 'stʌmbl | *v.i.* **1 [to – (on/over)]** tropezar, dar un traspié. **2 [to – +** *adv./prep.* **(along)]** tambalearse, oscilar, vacilar. **3 [to – (at/over)]** trabarse la lengua, vacilar, titubear (al leer, al hablar). || *s.c.* **4** tropezón, traspié, paso en falso. **5** desliz, titubeo, vacilación. || **6 to – across/on/upon,** tropezarse con, encontrarse inesperadamente con, toparse con.

stumbling block | 'stʌmblɪŋblɒk | *s.c.* obstáculo, dificultad, inconveniente.

stump | stʌmp | *s.c.* **1** tocón, cepa, resto, gancho (de árbol). **2** DEP. estaca, palo (en críquet). **3** fragmento, pedazo, segmento, fracción. **4** raigón (de diente). **5** colilla, (Am.) pucho (de cigarro). **6** cabo, resto, trozo (de vela). **7** ART. difumino, esfumino. **8** muñón. || *v.i.* **9 [to – +** *adv./prep.***]** caminar pesadamente, andar pisando fuerte. **10** cojear, renquear. || *v.t.* **11** (fam.) confundir, aturdir, dejar perplejo, asombrar, dejar sin palabras: *you got me stumped! = ¡me has dejado perplejo!* **12** DEP. eliminar (a un bateador) derribando las estacas con la pelota (en críquet). **13** cortar, cercenar, reducir a un tocón (un árbol). **14** limpiar de tocones, quitar tocones, desarraigar cepas. **15** (EE.UU.) POL. recorrer (una zona) pronunciando discursos. **16** ART. difuminar. **17** (fam.) retar, desafiar. || **18 on the –,** POL. en campaña, por el país pronunciando discursos. **19 to stir one's stumps,** (EE.UU. y fam.) estirar las piernas. **20 to – up,** (brit. y fam.) pagar de mala gana, no querer soltar la pasta.

stumpy | 'stʌmpɪ | *adj.* (fam. y desp.) regordete, pequeño y gordo, achaparrado: *stumpy legs = piernas regordetas.*

stun | stʌn | [*pret.* y *p.p.* **stunned,** *ger.* **stunning**] *v.t.* **1** MED. atontar, dejar inconsciente, aturdir, dejar sin sentido. **2** dejar pasmado, asombrar, sorprender, desconcertar, anonadar: *they were stunned by the war news = estaban anonadados por las noticias de guerra.*

stunned | stʌnd | *adj.* **1** sorprendido, anonadado, pasmado, asombrado. **2** atontado, aturdido, inconsciente, sin sentido.

stung | stʌŋ | **1** *pret.* y *p.p.* de **sting.** || *adj.* **2** ofendido, irritado, picado: *she seemed stung by his remarks = parecía irritada por sus alusiones.*

stunk | stʌŋk | *p.p.irreg.* de **stink.**

stunner | 'stʌnər | *s.c.* (arc. y fam.) belleza, maravilla; persona muy atractiva.

stunning | stʌnɪŋ | *adj.* **1** bellísimo, espléndido, magnífico, maravilloso, fantástico. **2** sorprendente, inesperado, chocante, pasmoso: *stunning revelations = revelations sorprendentes.*

stunningly | stʌnɪŋlɪ | *adv.* **1** espléndidamente, magníficamente, maravillosamente. **2** sorprendentemente, inesperadamente, de un modo pasmoso.

stunt | stʌnt | *v.t.* **1** atrofiar, impedir el crecimiento, impedir el desarrollo. || *v.i.* **2** realizar acrobacias. || *s.c.* **3** proeza, acrobacia, malabarismo (generalmente realizado por un doble en una película). **4** truco, treta, ardid (publicitario). **5** atrofia. || **6 to pull a –,** hacer una tontería, cometer una imprudencia. **7 – man/woman,** especialista (hombre o mujer que realiza los trabajos peligrosos en una película).

stunted | stʌntɪd | *adj.* raquítico, enano: *a stunted child = un niño raquítico.*

stupefaction | ,stjuːpɪ'fækʃn | (EE.UU.) | ,stuːpɪ'fækʃn | *s.i.* **1** estupefacción, cansancio, agotamiento, aburrimiento. **2** estupefacción, sorpresa, asombro, pasmo.

stupefy | 'stjuːpɪfaɪ | (EE.UU.) | 'stuːpɪfaɪ | *v.t.* (generalmente *pasiva*). **1** dejar estupefacto, quedar atónito, sorprender, pasmar, asombrar. **2** entontecer, embrutecer, atontar: *stupefied with drugs = atontado por las drogas.*

stupendous | stjuː'pendəs | (EE.UU.) | stuː'pendəs | *adj.* estupendo, impresionante, asombroso, prodigioso.

stupendously | stjuː'pendəslɪ | (EE.UU.) | stuː'pendəslɪ | *adv.* estupendamente, impresionantemente, asombrosamente, prodigiosamente.

stupid | 'stjuːpɪd | (EE.UU.) | 'stuːpɪd | *adj.* **1** estúpido, imbécil, tonto, infantil, de locos. **2** atontado, adormecido, cansado. **3** (fam.) molesto, fastidioso, dichoso (un objeto): *the stupid door wouldn't open = la dichosa puerta no se abría.*

stupidly | 'stjuːpɪdlɪ | (EE.UU.) | 'stuːpɪdlɪ | *adv.* estúpidamente.

stupidity | stjuː'pɪdɪtɪ | (EE.UU.) | stuː'pɪdɪtɪ | *s.i.* **1** estupidez, locura (comportamiento). || *s.c.* e *i.* **2** estupidez, idiotez, tontería (un acto): *not ideas but stupidities = no eran ideas sino estupideces.*

stupor | 'stjuːpər | (EE.UU.) | 'stuːpə | *s.c.* e *i.* estupor, atontamiento, aturdimiento, sopor, letargo.

sturdy | 'stəːdɪ | *adj.* **1** robusto, vigoroso, fuerte, saludable (una persona). **2** fuerte, sólido (un objeto). **3** tenaz, terco, resuelto, firme, decidido: *a sturdy resistance = una resistencia firme.*

sturdily | 'stəːdɪlɪ | *adv.* **1** robustamente, vigorosamente, fuertemente. **2** tenazmente, firmemente, decididamente, tercamente.

sturdiness | 'stəːdɪnɪs | *s.i.* **1** robustez, vigor, fuerza, salud. **2** solidez. **3** tenacidad, resolución, firmeza, decisión.

sturgeon | 'stəːdʒən | *s.c.* [*pl.* **sturgeon**] ZOOL. esturión, sollo.

stutter | 'stʌtər | *v.t.* e *i.* **1** tartamudear, trastabillar, tartajear. || *v.i.* **2** andar a saltitos, cojear; moverse espasmódicamente, funcionar a golpes (una persona, un motor). || *s.c.* **3** tartamudeo, trastabilleo, tartajeo.

stuttering | 'stʌtərɪŋ | *s.i.* tartamudeo.

sty | staɪ | *s.c.* **1** pocilga, cochiquera, porqueriza. **2** (también **stye**) MED. orzuelo. || *v.t.* e *i.* **3** vivir en una pocilga.

stye | staɪ | *s.c.* MED. orzuelo.

style | staɪl | *s.c.* e *i.* **1** estilo (literario, pictórico, etc...). **2** estilo, moda (en el vestir). **3** estilo (reglas de puntuación, redacción). || *s.c.* **4** estilo, diseño, clase, modelo: *every style of paper = todo tipo de papel.* **5** tratamiento, título: *the style of "Lady" = el tratamiento de "Lady".* **6** estilo, punzón. **7** ELECTR. aguja (de un tocadiscos), estilo, varilla (de un reloj de sol). **8** (lit.) pluma. **9** MED. sonda, cánula. **10** BOT. pistilo. **11** ZOOL. púa, pincho. || *s.sing.* **12** estilo, práctica, costumbre, forma de ser. || *s.i.* **13** elegancia, distinción, gracia, garbo, finura. || *v.t.* **14** diseñar, hacer a la moda, cortar a la moda. **15** dar estilo, dar forma (a un escrito). **16 [to – +** *o.* **+** *s.***]** intitular, dar título de, nombrar: *the Queen styled him Duke = la reina lo nombró duque.* || *sufijo* **17 -styled,** al estilo: *American-style = al estilo americano.* || **18 to cramp someone's –,** V. **cramp.** **19 in –, a)** a la moda; **b)** con gran lujo, elegantemente, a todo confort.

stylised | 'staɪlaɪzd | *adj.* V. **stylized.**

stylish | 'staɪlɪʃ | *adj.* elegante, a la moda, chic, con clase.

stylishly | 'staɪlɪʃlɪ | *adv.* elegantemente, a la moda, con clase.

stylist | 'staɪlɪst | *s.c.* **1** estilista, diseñador: *hair stylist = peluquero.* **2** LIT. estilista.

stylistic | staɪ'lɪstɪk | *adj.* ART. estilístico, de estilo.

stylistically | staɪ'lɪstɪkəlɪ | *adv.* estilísticamente, en cuanto al estilo.

stylistics | staɪ'lɪstɪks | *s.i.* estilística, estudio del estilo.

stylized | 'staɪlaɪzd | (brit. **stylised**) *adj.* estilizado, convencional, artificial.

stylus | 'staɪləs | *s.c.* **1** ELECTR. aguja (de tocadiscos). **2** (arc.) estilete, estilo, punzón.

stymie | 'staɪmɪ | *v.t.* **1** (fam.) dificultar, obstaculizar, bloquear. || *s.c.* **2** obstáculo, obstrucción, dificultad, impedimento. **3** DEP. obstrucción de la línea de juego por la bola del oponente (en golf).

suave | swɑːv | *adj.* **1** encantador, amable, agradable, zalamero. **2** cortés, educado, fino, sofisticado.

suavely | swɑːvlɪ | *adv.* **1** encantadoramente, de forma zalamera. **2** cortésmente, con finura.

sub | sʌb | *s.c.* (fam.) **1** submarino. **2** DEP. sustituto. **3** (brit.) suscripción. **4** (brit.) adelanto de sueldo. **5** PER. redactor, corrector de pruebas. **6** subordinado, subalterno. || [*pret.* y *p.p.* **subbed,** *ger.* **subbing**] *v.i.* **7 [to – (for)]** DEP. sustituir, tomar el puesto de. || *v.t.* **8** pagar un adelanto. **9** PER. corregir, preparar para la prensa. || *prefijo* **10 [sub- +** *s.*] sub: *subdirection = subdirección; subway = paso subterráneo;* (EE.UU.) *metro.* **11 [sub- +** *adj.*] sub, por debajo de, inferior a: *subnormal = subnormal.* || **12 – judice,** sub judice, bajo conocimiento judicial, estudiado por los jueces.

subaltern | 'sʌbltən | (EE.UU.) | sə'bɔːltərn | *s.c.* **1** (brit.) MIL. alférez. **2** subalterno, subordinado. **3** LOG. proposición particular. || *adj.* **4** (brit.) MIL. alférez. **5** subalterno, subordinado. **6** particular (una proposición).

subatomic | ˌsʌbə'tɒmɪk | *adj.* FIS. subatómica (una partícula).

subcommittee | 'sʌbkəˌmɪtɪ | *s.c.* [– + *v.sing./pl.*] subcomisión, subcomité.

subconscious | ˌsʌb'kɒnʃəs | *adj.* **1** [no *comp.*] subconsciente. || *s.sing.* **2** (también **unconscious**) **[the –]** el subconsciente.

subconsciously | ˌsʌb'kɒnʃəslɪ | *adv.* inconscientemente, de forma subconsciente.

subcontinent | ˌsʌb'kɒntɪnənt | *s.c.* GEOG. subcontinente.

subcontract | ˌsʌbkɒn'trækt | *v.t.* **1** subcontratar. || *s.c.* **2** subcontrato.

subcontracting | ˌsʌbkɒn'træktɪŋ | *adj.* subcontratado: *a subcontracting firm = una compañía subcontratada.*

subcontractor | ˌsʌbkɒn'træktər | *s.c.* subcontratista.

subculture | 'sʌbkʌltʃər | *s.c.* **1** subcultura, contracultura. **2** AGR. subcultivo.

subdivide | ˌsʌbdɪ'vaɪd | *v.t.* e *i.* **[to – (into)]** subdividir(se).

subdivision | 'sʌbbɪˌvɪʒn | *s.c.* subdivisión.

subdue | səb'djuː | (EE.UU.) | səb'duː | *v.t.* **1** someter, reprimir, reducir, controlar (una rebelión). **2** vencer, conquistar, dominar, avasallar. **3** calmar, apaciguar, pacificar, serenar (los ánimos, las emociones). **4** suavizar, moderar, amortiguar (la claridad, la voz, el color).

subdued | səb'djuːd | (EE.UU.) | səb'duːd | *adj.* **1** suave, discreto, apagado (un color, una voz). **2** tenue (una luz). **3** deprimido, melancólico, apagado, poco animado, serio.

subeditor | ˌsʌb'edɪtər | (también **sub**) *s.c.* (brit.) PER. corrector de pruebas, redactor.

subgroup | 'sʌbgruːp | *s.c.* subgrupo, subdivisión.

subheading | 'sʌbˌhedɪŋ | *s.c.* subtítulo, título secundario: *the article had several subheadings = el artículo tenía varios subtítulos.*

subhuman | ˌsʌb'hjuːmən | | ˌsʌb'juːmən | *adj.* infrahumano.

subject | səb'dʒɪkt | *s.c.* **1** tema, materia, asunto, contenido (de una obra). **2** tema, tópico, conversación. **3** asignatura, materia: *English is my favorite subject = el inglés es mi asignatura favorita.* **4** GRAM. sujeto. **5** súbdito, ciudadano. **6 [– (for/of)]** (form.) causa, razón, motivo: *the subject of her emotions = la causa de sus emociones.* **7** sujeto, material (de un experimento). **8** MED. caso (de estudio). **9** MUS. tema, frase. || *adj.* **10 [– to]** propenso a, expuesto a, dispuesto a. **11 [– to]** sujeto a, supeditado a, dependiente de, sometido a: *subject to changes of time = sujeto a cambios de horario.* **12** [no *comp.*] (lit.) sometido, subyugado, bajo dominación (un territorio, una persona). || | səb'dʒekt | *v.t.* **13** (lit.) someter, dominar, sojuzgar, subyugar. || **14 to change the –,** cambiar de conversación, cambiar de tema. **15 – matter,** contenido, tema, materia, asunto, tópico. **16 – to,** sujeto a, dependiente de, supeditado a. **17 to – to,** someter a, exponer a, poner a prueba a.

subjection | səb'dʒekʃn | *s.i.* sometimiento, sojuzgamiento, dominación, dependencia.

subjective | səb'dʒektɪv | *adj.* **1** (desp.) subjetivo, personal: *a subjective opinion = una opinión subjetiva.* **2** [no *comp.*] subjetivo, imaginario. **3** GRAM. del sujeto.

subjectively | səb'dʒektɪvlɪ | *adv.* subjetivamente.

subjoin | 'sʌb'dʒɔɪn | *v.t.* adjuntar.

subjugate | 'sʌbdʒʊgeɪt | *v.t.* **1** subyugar, someter, conquistar, avasallar (a un pueblo). **2** someter, subordinar, dominar (un deseo).

subjugation | ˌsʌbdʒʊ'geɪʃn | *s.i.* subyugación, sometimiento, dominación, conquista, avasallamiento.

subjunctive | səb'dʒʌŋktɪv | *s.sing.* **1** (también **subjunctive mood**) GRAM. modo subjuntivo, subjuntivo. || *adj.* **2** subjuntivo.

sublet | ˌsʌb'let | *v.t.* e *i.* [*pret.* y *p.p.* **sublet** o **subletted,** *ger.* **subletting**] subarrendar.

sub-lieutenant | ˌsʌblef'tenənt | *s.c.* MIL. subteniente, alférez.

sublimate | 'sʌblɪmeɪt | *v.t.* **1** sublimar, suplir, sustituir. **2** FIS. sublimar. | 'sʌblɪmət | *s.c.* FIS. sublimado. || *adj.* **3** sublimado.

sublimation | ˌsʌblɪ'meɪʃn | *s.i.* sublimación.

sublime | sə'blaɪm | *adj.* **1** sublime, admirable, incomparable. **2** (fam.) excelente, excepcional, magnífico, maravilloso. **3** (fam. y desp.) completo, absoluto, extremo: *sublime indifference = indiferencia absoluta.* **4** (arc.) arrogante, altivo, altanero. || *s.sing.* **5 [the –]** lo sublime. || *v.t.* **6** sublimar, exaltar. || *v.i.* **7** FIS. sublimar. || **8 to go from the – to the ridiculous,** pasar de lo sublime a lo ridículo.

sublimely | sə'blaɪmlɪ | *adv.* **1** sublimemente. **2** completamente, totalmente, absolutamente, extremadamente.

subliminal | ˌsʌb'lɪmɪnl | *adj.* subliminal.

sub-machine gun | ˌsʌbmə'ʃiːngʌn | *s.c.* metralleta, pistola ametralladora.

submarine | ˌsʌbmə'riːn | (EE.UU.) | sʌbmə'riːn | *adj.* **1** TEC. submarino. || *s.c.* **2** (también **sub**) submarino.

submarine chaser | ˌsʌbmə'riːntʃeɪsər | .

submerge | səb'məːdʒ | *v.t.* e *i.* **1** sumergir(se), introducir(se), hundir(se). || *v.t.* **2** ocultar, esconder, tapar. **3** (fig.) sumir, concentrar, estar inmerso en: *he was all summer submerged in work = estuvo todo el verano sumido en el trabajo.*

submerged | səb'məːdʒd | *adj.* **1** sumergido, bajo el agua. **2** empobrecido, sumido en la miseria. **3** escondido, oculto, tapado.

submergence | səb'məːdʒəns | (también **submersion**) *s.i.* sumersión, sumergimiento, hundimiento.

submersion | səb'məːʃn | (EE.UU.) | səb'məːrʒn | *s.i.* V. **submergence.**

submission | səb'mɪʃn | *s.c.* e *i.* **1** sumisión, rendimiento. **2** presentación (de una solicitud). || *s.i.* **3** (form.) proposición, teoría, opinión. **4 [– (to)]** (form.) obediencia. || *s.c.* **5** petición, proposición, sometimiento a arbitraje.

submissive | səb'mɪsɪv | *adj.* sumiso, obediente, dócil.

submissively | səb'mɪsɪvlɪ | *adv.* sumisamente, obedientemente, dócilmente.

submissiveness | səb'mɪsɪvnɪs | *s.i.* sumisión, docilidad, obediencia.

submit | səb'mɪt | [*pret.* y *p.p.* **submitted,** *ger.* **submitting**] *v.i.* **1 [to – (to)]** rendirse, someterse, resignarse. **2** aceptar, conformarse, dar el brazo a torcer. || *v.t.* **3 [to – (to)]** someter, exponer, presentar (a consideración). **4 [to – (that)/***o.*] DER. aducir, sugerir. **5 [to – (to)]** (form.) aceptar, someterse (a): *I would sumit to your orders = me someteré a tus órdenes.*

subnormal | ˌsʌb'nɔːml | *adj.* **1** subnormal, deficiente (mental). **2** anormal, por debajo de lo corriente: *subnormal temperatures = temperaturas por debajo de lo que es normal.* || *s.pl.* **3 [the –]** los subnormales, los deficientes mentales.

subordinate | sə'bɔːdnɪt | (EE.UU.) | sə'bɔːrdənɪt | *adj.* **1 [– (to)]** subordinado, inferior, de menor importancia, secundario. **2 [– (to)]** subordinado, subalterno. || *s.c.* **3** subordinado, subalterno. || | sə'bɔːdɪneɪt | | sə'bɔːrdə | | neɪt | *v.t.* **4 [to – (to)]** subordinar, someter, sojuzgar. || **5 – clause,** GRAM. oración subordinada.

subordination | səˌbɔːdɪ'neɪʃn | (EE.UU.) | səbɔːrdəneɪʃn | *s.i.* **[– (of/to)]** subordinación, sometimiento.

subpoena | səb'piːnə | | sə'piːnə | *s.c.* **1** DER. citación. || *v.t.* **2** DER. citar, emplazar.

subscribe | səb'skraɪb | *v.i.* **[to – (to)]. 1** donar, hacer una donación, contribuir con dinero. **2** suscribirse, abonarse. || *v.t.* **3** contribuir, dar, entregar (dinero). **4** (form.) firmar, subscribir, poner la firma. || **5 to – for,** (form.) subscribirse (a algo antes de su emisión). **6 to – to,** (generalmente en *interr.*) aprobar, estar de acuerdo con, suscribir (una opinión).

subscriber | səb'skraɪbər | *s.c.* **1** subscriptor. **2** abonado, usuario. **3** firmante, el que suscribe.

subscription | səb'skrɪpʃn | *s.c.* (también **sub**) subscripción, cuota, abono.

subsection | 'sʌbˌsekʃn | *s.c.* apartado, subdivisión.

subsequent | 'sʌbsɪkwənt | *adj.* **1** subsiguiente, siguiente, posterior: *in subsequent years = en años posteriores.* || **2 – to,** después de, con posterioridad a.

subsequently | 'sʌbsɪkwəntlɪ | *adv.* con posterioridad, posteriormente, más tarde.

subservience | səb'səːvjəns | *s.i.* subordinación, sometimiento, servilismo.

subservient | səb'səːvɪənt | *adj.* **1** servil, lacayuno. **2** subordinado, inferior.

subside | səb'saɪd | *v.i.* **1** hundirse, bajar, asentarse, irse al fondo (un edificio). **2** (fig.) dejarse caer, desplomarse. **3** amainar, calmarse (una tempestad). **4** bajar, descender (el nivel del agua, el ruido). **5** disminuir, serenarse, sosegarse (las protestas).

subsidence | səb'saɪdns | | 'sʌbsɪdəns | *s.c.* e *i.* **1** hundimiento, descenso, asentamiento (de un edificio). **2** disminución, calma, apaciguamiento (de una tempestad).

subsidiary | səb'sɪdɪərɪ | (EE.UU.) | səb'sɪdɪərɪ | *adj.* **1** **[– (to)]** subsidiario, secundario, de menor importancia. **2** auxiliar, suplementario. || *s.c.* **3** (también **subsidiary company**) COM. compañía subsidiaria, filial, sucursal. **4** MUS. tema secundario, tema subordinado.

subsidize | 'sʌbsɪdaɪz | (brit. **subsidise**) *v.t.* subvencionar (un producto, una empresa).

subsidized | 'sʌbsɪdaɪzd | (brit. **subsidised**) *adj.* subvencionado (un producto, una empresa).

subsidy | 'sʌbsɪdɪ | *s.c.* e *i.* subvención (estatal a un producto, a una empresa).

subsist | səb'sɪst | *v.i.* **[to – (on)]** subsistir, sobrevivir, sustentarse.

subsistence | səb'sɪstəns | *s.i.* **1** subsistencia, sustentación, supervivencia. **2** sustento, víveres, alimentos, subsistencias.

subsoil | 'sʌbsɔɪl | *s.sing.* **1** subsuelo. || *v.t.* **2** remover el subsuelo, quebrar el subsuelo.

subsonic | ˌsʌb'sɒnɪk | *adj.* FIS. subsónico.

subspecies | 'sʌbˌspiːʃiːz | *s.c.* [*sing./pl.*] BOT. subespecie.

substance | 'sʌbstəns | *s.c.* **1** sustancia, material: *a substance against mice = una sustancia contra los ratones.* || *s.i.* **2** verdad, evidencia, autenticidad, solidez: *rumours without substance = rumores sin evidencia.* **3** **[the – (of)]** (form.) la esencia, la parte esencial, lo sustancioso. **4** (form.) importancia, significación: *matters of substance = asuntos de importancia.* **5** (form.) riqueza, fortuna, bienes. || **6** **a man/woman of –,** un hombre o una mujer acaudalado, importante, influyente. **7** **in –,** esencialmente, sustancialmente.

substandard | ˌsʌb'stændəd | *adj.* inferior, deficiente, de bajo nivel.

substantial | səb'stænʃl | *adj.* **1** sólido, firme, fuerte: *a substantial piece of furniture = un mueble sólido.* **2** sustancial, cuantioso, copioso. **3** sustancial, considerable, importante: *a substantial improvement = una mejora considerable.* **4** (form.) acaudalado, acomodado, rico. **5** esencial, sustancial: *in substantial agreement = de acuerdo en lo esencial.*

substantially | səb'stænʃəlɪ | *adv.* **1** sustancialmente, esencialmente, principalmente. **2** enormemente, considerablemente, en gran medida: *substantially changed = considerablemente cambiado.*

substantiate | səb'stænʃɪeɪt | *v.t.* (form.) confirmar, verificar, probar.

substantive | 'sʌbstəntɪv | *s.c.* **1** GRAM. sustantivo. || | səb'stæntɪv | | 'sʌbstən | | tɪv | *adj.* (form.) **2** significativo, importante, real, actual. **3** GRAM. sustantivo. **4** MIL. permanente, fijo (un rango).

substitute | 'sʌbstɪtjuːt | (EE.UU.) | 'sʌbstɪtuːt | *s.c.* **1** **[– (for)]** sustituto, suplente. **2** sucedáneo. || *v.t.* e *i.* **3** **[to – (for)]** sustituir, reemplazar, suplir. **4** actuar como suplente, hacer de sustituto, ocupar el puesto. || *adj.* **5** suplente, sustituto. **6** sucedáneo. || **7** **to be no –/a poor – for,** no valer como sustituto de, no poderse sustituir por, no tener nada que hacer al lado de (otra cosa).

substitution | 'sʌbstɪtjuːʃn | (EE.UU.) | 'sʌbstɪtuːʃn | *s.c.* e *i.* **[– (for)]** sustitución, suplencia, reemplazo, cambio.

substructure | 'sʌbˌstrʌktʃər | *s.c.* subestructura, infraestructura.

subsume | səb'sjuːm | (EE.UU.) | səb'suːm | *v.t.* **[to – (under)]** (form.) subsumir, incluir (en un grupo, en una categoría).

subsystem | 'sʌbsɪstəm | *s.c.* subsistema, subdivisión.

subtenancy | ˌsʌb'tenənsɪ | *s.c.* e *i.* subarriendo, realquiler.

subtenant | ˌsʌb'tenənt | *s.c.* subarrendado, subarrendador, realquilado.

subterfuge | 'sʌbtəfjuːdʒ | *s.c.* e *i.* subterfugio, evasiva.

subterranean ˌsʌbtə'reɪnɪən | *adj.* (form.) subterráneo.

subtitle | 'sʌbˌtaɪtl | *s.c.* **1** subtítulo. || *v.t.* **2** subtitular. || **3** **subtitles,** subtítulos (en una película).

subtle | 'sʌbtl | *adj.* **1** sutil, delicado, etéreo, tenue, exquisito (un sabor, un olor). **2** leve, liviano, ligero: *a subtle change = un leve cambio.* **3** sutil, astuto, artero, insidioso (un plan). **4** sutil, inteligente, perspicaz, penetrante (una mente).

subtlety | sʌbtltɪ | *s.i.* **1** sutileza, delicadeza, exquisitez, finura, sensibilidad. **2** sagacidad, astucia, argucia, picardía. || *s.c.* **3** (generalmente *pl.*) sutileza, matiz, detalle intrincado.

subtly | 'sʌbtlɪ | *adv.* **1** imperceptiblemente, levemente, ligeramente, apenas. **2** sutilmente, astutamente, ingeniosamente.

substract | səb'strækt | *v.t.* **[to – (from)]** sustraer, restar, deducir.

substraction | ˌsəb'strækʃn | *s.c.* e *i.* sustracción, resta, deducción.

subtropical | ˌsʌb'trɒpɪkl | (también **semitropical**) *adj.* subtropical.

suburb | 'sʌbəːb | *s.c.* periferia, barrio exterior, zona, afueras (especialmente residencial): *she lives in a new suburb = vive en un barrio nuevo.*

suburban | sə'bəːbən | *adj.* **1** (generalmente desp.) de barrio. **2** suburbano. **3** de cercanías (un tren).

suburbia | sə'bəːbɪə | *s.i.* (generalmente desp.) suburbios, afueras, barrios.

subversion | səb'vəːʃn | *s.i.* subversión, alteración.

subversive | səb'vəːsɪv | *adj.* **1** subversivo. || *s.c.* **2** elemento subversivo.

subvert | sʌb'vəːt | *v.t.* (form.) subvertir, minar, demoler, destruir, trastornar (un sistema).

subway | 'sʌbweɪ | *s.c.* **1** pasaje subterráneo, subterráneo. **2** (EE.UU.) metro, (Am.) subte.

succeed | sək'siːd | *v.i.* **1** **[to – (in)]** triunfar, salir bien, tener éxito, conseguir. **2** triunfar, hacerse rico, lograr una posición. || *v.t.* e *i.* **3** suceder, seguir en el puesto; acceder a, heredar (un título); subir (al trono): *she was the one to succeed her father = ella era quien iba a suceder a su padre.* || *v.t.* **4** (form.) suceder, seguir, continuar, proseguir: *a murmur succeeded his words = tras sus palabras hubo un murmullo.*

succeeding | sək'siːdɪŋ | *adj.* **1** subsiguiente, sucesivo, seguido. **2** futuro, próximo.

success | sək'ses | *s.c.* e *i.* **1** **[– (in)]** éxito, logro, triunfo. || *s.i.* **2** prosperidad, progreso. || **3** **a – story,** historia de un triunfo. **4** **to make a – of something,** tener éxito en algo, conseguir un éxito en algo. **5** **nothing succeeds like –,** después de un éxito vienen otros.

successful | sək'səsful | *adj.* **1** **[– (in)]** afortunado, victorioso, (Am.) exitoso: *a successful person = una persona afortunada.* **2** triunfador, próspero, con fortuna: *a successful young man = un joven triunfador.*

successfully | sək'səsfulɪ | *adv.* con éxito, prósperamente.

succession | sək'seʃn | *s.i.* **1** sucesión, continuación, secuencia. **2** **[– (to)]** sucesión, herencia; descendencia. || *s.sing.* **3** **[– (of) +** *v.sing./pl.*] sucesión, procesión, desfile, serie: *after a succession of facts = después de una serie de hechos.* || **4** **in –,** sucesivamente, en serie.

successive | sək'sesɪv | *adj.* sucesivo, consecutivo, siguiente: *during two successive days = durante dos días consecutivos.*

successively | sək'sesɪvlɪ | *adv.* sucesivamente.

successor | sək'sesər | *s.c.* sucesor.

succinct | sək'sɪŋkt | *adj.* sucinto, conciso, breve.

succinctly | sək'sɪŋktlɪ | *adv.* sucintamente, concisamente, brevemente.

succour | 'sʌkər | (EE.UU. **succor**) *s.i.* **1** (lit.) socorro, auxilio, ayuda, asistencia. || *v.t.* **2** (lit.) socorrer, auxiliar, ayudar, prestar asistencia.

succulence | 'sʌkjuləns | *s.i.* suculencia, jugosidad, exquisitez, delicia.

succulent | 'sʌkjulənt | *adj.* **1** suculento, sabroso, jugoso, delicioso. **2** BOT. suculento. || *s.c.* **3** BOT. planta suculenta (como el cactus).

succumb | sə'kʌm | *v.i.* **[to – (to)]** (form.) **1** sucumbir, rendirse. **2** sucumbir, morir.

such | sʌtʃ | *adj.* **1** tal, parecido, semejante, análogo: *I wouldn't write such a story = yo no escribiría semejante historia.* **2** tal, tan: *such a good person = tan buena persona.* || *pron.* **3** (form.) tal, tal cosa, ese, eso, aquello: *the book was boring. Such was his opinion = el libro era aburrido. Eso era lo que él pensaba.* || **4** **and –,** (fam.) y asuntos similares, y gente de ese tipo, y cosas así. **5** **as –,** como tal, per se, en sí mismo. **6** **or some –,** o algo parecido, o algo similar: *a parrot, a parakeet or some such = un loro, un periquito o algo similar.* **7** **– as/– ... as,** tales como ..., por ejemplo ... (para introducir ejemplos). **8** **– ... that/as,** tal ... que: *in such way that = de tal modo que.* **9** **– and –,** tal o cual (lugar, fecha, etc...). **10** **– as it is/there is,** con todos sus inconvenientes, con todos sus problemas, tal y como es.

suchlike | 'sʌtʃlaɪk | *adj.* **1** tal, semejante, similar, por el estilo. || *pron.* **2** (fam.)

gente o cosas de ese tipo, cosas o personas semejantes: *literature, cinema and suchlike = literatura, cine y cosas por el estilo.*
suck | sʌk | *v.t.* e *i.* **1** chupar, sorber, libar. **2** mamar. || *v.t.* **3** [**to – +** *o.* **+** *adv./prep.*] succionar (un remolino). **4** (fig.) absorber, atraer, captar: *sucked into a luxurious life = atraído a una vida de lujo.* || *s.c.* **5** succión, chupada, sorbo. **6** calada (a un cigarro). || **7 to – up,** (brit. y fam.) hacer la pelota, dar jabón, lisonjear.
sucker | 'sʌkər | *s.c.* **1** succionador, chupador, chupón. **2** mamón. **3** ZOOL. ventosa. **4** ventosa, émbolo. **5** BOT. retoño, serpollo. **6** [**– (for)**] (fam.) incauto, ingenuo, primo, bobo. **7** (EE.UU.) chupa-chups, piruleta, pirulí, caramelo. || **8 to be a – for,** no poder resistirse ante, caer fácilmente en: *I'm a real sucker for Indian food = no puedo resistirme fácilmente ante la comida india.* **9 sucking pig,** lechón, cochinillo.
suckle | 'sʌkl | *v.t.* e *i.* **1** amamantar, dar de mamar, dar el pecho, criar. **2** mamar.
suction | 'sʌkʃn | *s.i.* succión, aspiración.
Sudanese | ˌsuːdə'niːz | *adj.* **1** sudanés, del Sudán. || *s.c.* [*sing.* y *pl.*] **2** sudanés.
sudden | 'sʌdn | *adj.* **1** repentino, súbito, inesperado, imprevisto, precipitado: *a sudden trip = un viaje repentino.* || **2 all of a –,** de repente, repentinamente.
suddenness | 'sʌdnnɪs | *s.i.* premura, precipitación, imprevisión, brusquedad.
suds | sʌdz | (también **soapsuds**) *s.pl.* espuma de jabón, pompas de jabón, jabonaduras.
sue | sjuː | *v.t.* e *i.* **1** DER. demandar, entablar un pleito, presentar demanda. || **2 to – for,** (form.) pedir, rogar, suplicar: *they are sueing for peace = están pidiendo un armisticio.*
suede | sweɪd | (también **suède**) *s.i.* ante, gamuza.
suet | sjʊɪt | *s.i.* sebo.
suffer | 'sʌfər | *v.i.* **1** [**to – (for)**] sufrir, padecer (enfermedad, pérdida o dificultades): *he didn't suffer much = no sufrió mucho.* **2** deteriorarse, estropearse, sufrir daño. || *v.t.* **3** sufrir, soportar, aguantar (algo desagradable, doloroso): *he suffered an awful defeat = sufrió una terrible derrota.* **4** (form.) tolerar, aguantar, soportar, aceptar sin protestar. **5** [**to – +** *o.* **+ to** *inf.*] (arc.) permitir, consentir, autorizar, dejar. || **6 not to – fools gladly,** no tener mucha paciencia. **7 to – from,** padecer, sufrir, adolecer; ser víctima de.
sufferance | 'sʌfərəns | *s.i.* **1** capacidad de sufrimiento, tolerancia. **2** paciencia, tolerancia, indulgencia, resignación. **3** permiso, consentimiento. || **4 on –,** por indulgencia, por tolerancia.
sufferer | 'sʌfərər | *s.c.* **1** MED. enfermo, víctima. **2** damnificado, perjudicado.
suffering | 'sʌfərɪŋ | *adj.* **1** doliente, sufridor, sufrido. || *s.i.* **2** sufrimiento, dolor, padecimiento. || **3 sufferings,** sufrimientos, aflicciones, tormentos.
suffice | sə'faɪs | *v.t.* e *i.* **1** (form.) ser suficiente, ser bastante, bastar, alcanzar, llegar. || **2 – it to say,** (form.) basta decir.
sufficiency | sə'fɪʃnsɪ | *s.i.* (form.) **1** suficiencia. || *s.sing.* **2** [**– (of)**] cantidad suficiente.
sufficient | sə'fɪʃnt | *adj.* [**– (for)**] (form.) suficiente, bastante, adecuado.
sufficiently | sə'fɪʃntlɪ | *adv.* suficientemente, adecuadamente, bastante.
suffix | 'sʌfɪks | *s.c.* **1** GRAM. sufijo. || *v.t.* **2** GRAM. añadir un sufijo a.
suffocate | 'sʌfəkeɪt | *v.t.* e *i.* **1** sofocar(se), asfixiar(se), ahogar(se). **2** (fig.) sofocar, dominar, maniatar, impedir: *bureaucracy suffocated commerce = la burocracia impedía el comercio.*
suffocating | 'sʌfəkeɪtɪŋ | *adj.* **1** sofocante, asfixiante. **2** (fig.) sofocante, dominador, que pone impedimentos.
suffocation | sʌ'fəkeɪʃn | *s.i.* sofocación, sofoco, asfixia, ahogo.
suffrage | 'sʌfrɪdʒ | *s.i.* **1** sufragio, voto. **2** oración, súplica, preces. || **3 by universal –,** por sufragio universal.
suffragette | ˌsʌfrə'dʒet | *s.c.* sufragista.
suffuse | sə'fjuːz | *v.t.* (lit.) bañar, inundar, sumergir, cubrir (de luz, color).
sugar | 'ʃʊgər | *s.i.* **1** azúcar. || *s.c.* **2** TEC. azúcar, sacarosa, sacarina. **3** [en *vocativo*] (EE.UU. y fam.) cariño, corazón, amor, encanto. || *v.t.* **4** azucarar, poner azúcar en, endulzar, almibarar, garrapiñar. || **5 Oh, –!,** (fam.) ¡maldita sea!, ¡que horror! (cuando algo va mal). **6 – beet,** remolacha azucarera. **7 – cane,** caña de azúcar. **8 – daddy,** (arc. y fam.) amante viejo y rico, protector viejo y rico (de una joven). **9 – lump,** terrón de azúcar. **10 to – the pill,** dorar la píldora.
sugar-coated | 'ʃʊgəˌkəʊtɪd | *adj.* **1** confitado, recubierto de azúcar. **2** (fig.) azucarada, endulzada (una promesa, unas palabras).
sugared | 'ʃʊgəd | *adj.* **1** (fig.) azucarado, endulzado, agradable (pero poco sincero). || **2 – almond,** almendra garrapiñada.
sugary | 'ʃʊgərɪ | *adj.* **1** azucarado, dulce. **2** (desp.) dulzón, meloso, almibarado, sensiblero (pero poco sincero).
suggest | 'sə'dzest | (EE.UU.) | səg'dʒest | *v.t.* **1** sugerir, proponer, aconsejar, insinuar, plantear. **2** indicar, implicar, mostrar, manifestar: *her words suggested happiness = sus palabras mostraban felicidad.* **3** sugerir, evocar, venir a la mente, ocurrirse (una idea). || **4 I –,** diría yo, pienso yo.
suggestible | sə'dʒestɪbl | (EE.UU.) | səg'dʒestəbl | *adj.* sugestionable.
suggestion | sə'dʒestʃən | (EE.UU.) | səg'dʒestʃən | *s.c.* **1** sugerencia, proposición, planteamiento, insinuación. || *s.i.* **2** sugerencia, sugestión. **3** PSIC. sugestión. || *s.sing.* **4** [**– (of/that);** generalmente en *interr.* y *negativas*] sombra, traza, indicación: *I never saw a suggestion of disagreement = nunca vi una sombra de desacuerdo.*
suggestive | sə'dʒestɪv | (EE.UU.) | səg'dʒestɪv | *adj.* **1** sugerente, insinuante (sexualmente). **2** [**– of**] (form.) sugerente, indicativo.
suggestively | sə'dʒestɪvlɪ | (EE.UU.) | səg'dʒestɪvlɪ | *adv.* sugerentemente, insinuantemente, indecentemente.
suicidal | sʊɪ'saɪdl | | suːɪ'saɪdl | *adj.* **1** [no *comp.*] suicida, con tendencia suicida. **2** suicida, peligroso, aventurado, expuesto: *a suicidal race = una carrera suicida.* **3** destructivo.
suicide | 'sʊɪsaɪd | | 'suːɪsaɪd | *s.c.* e *i.* **1** suicidio. || *s.c.* **2** DER. suicida. || *s.i.* **3** (fig.) suicidio, ruina, destrucción: *economic suicide = ruina económica.* || **4 – pact,** pacto suicida.
suit | suːt | | sjuːt | *s.c.* **1** traje, terno, traje sastre (de hombre o mujer), conjunto (de mujer). **2** armadura. **3** palo (de la baraja). **4** juego (de fichas). **5** vasallaje. **6** galanteo, cortejo. **7** DER. juicio, pleito, litigio. **8** (arc.) pedida, petición de mano (de matrimonio). || *v.t.* **9** convenir, venir bien, satisfacer, agradar: *the time doesn't suit me = la hora no me viene bien.* **10** [no *pasiva*] favorecer, sentar bien, caer bien (un color, una prenda). **11** convenir a, ser apropiado para, acomodarse a, adaptarse a (ciertos requerimientos): *the climate doesn't suit this type of food = el clima no es conveniente para ese tipo de alimentos.* || **12 to file/bring a –,** entablar una demanda, poner un pleito. **13 to follow –,** (fig.) hacer lo mismo; jugar al mismo palo, seguir el palo (en naipes). **14 in one's birthday –,** (fam.) completamente desnudo, como Dios trajo a uno al mundo. **15 one's strongest –,** el punto más fuerte de uno, la mejor cualidad de uno. **16 to – oneself,** (fam.) hacer lo que a uno le da la gana, hacer lo que uno quiere. **17 to – someone down to the ground,** venirle a uno como anillo al dedo, caerle al pelo. **18 to – someone's book,** (fam.) convenir a los planes de uno, ser apropiado para uno. **19 to – to,** (form.) adaptar a, acomodar a, ajustar a.
suitable | 'suːtəbl | | 'sjuːtəbl | *adj.* [**– (for/to)**] adecuado, apropiado, conveniente, idóneo.
suitability | ˌsuːtə'bɪlɪtɪ | | ˌsjuːtə'bɪlətɪ | *s.i.* adecuación, idoneidad.
suitably | 'suːtəblɪ | | 'sjuːtəblɪ | *adv.* convenientemente, apropiadamente, adecuadamente.
suitcase | 'suːtkeɪs | | 'sjuːtkeɪs | *s.c.* maleta.
suite | swiːt | *s.c.* **1** mobiliario, juego de muebles: *a bedroom suite = un dormitorio.* **2** [**– (of)**] suite, apartamento, conjunto de habitaciones (en un hotel). **3** MUS. suite. **4** [**– +** *v.sing./pl.*] séquito, comitiva: *the singer's suite = el séquito de la cantante.* **5** [**– (of)**] INF. serie, colección (de programas, de módulos).
suited | 'suːtɪd | | 'sjuːtɪd | *adj.* adecuado, conveniente, apropiado.
suiting | 'suːtɪŋ | | 'sjuːtɪŋ | *s.i.* tela, paño (para trajes de caballero).
suitor | 'suːtər | | 'sjuːtər | *s.c.* **1** pretendiente, enamorado, galán. **2** DER. demandante. **3** peticionario, aspirante.
sulfur V. **sulphur.**
sulk | sʌlk | *v.i.* **1** estar enfurruñado, estar de mal humor, estar de morros, estar enfadado, estar enrabietado (un niño). || *s.c.* **2** malhumor, enfado, rabieta. || **3 to have the sulks,** tener una rabieta, estar de malhumor, estar enfurruñado.
sulkily | 'sʌlkɪlɪ | *adv.* malhumoradamente, con resentimiento.
sulkiness | 'sʌlkɪnɪs | *s.i.* malhumor, resentimiento, enfurruñamiento.
sulky | 'sʌlkɪ | *adj.* **1** malhumorado, enrabietado, mohíno, enfurruñado, resentido. **2** oscuro, nublado, desagradable (el tiempo).

sullen | 'sʌlən | *adj.* **1** malhumorado, hosco, insociable, reservado, taciturno. **2** (lit.) desagradable, oscuro, plomizo (el tiempo, el cielo). **3** lento, pausado, perezoso: *with a sullen march = con paso lento.*

sullenly | 'sʌlənlɪ | *adv.* malhumoradamente, hoscamente, con resentimiento.

sullenness | 'sʌlənnɪs | *s.i.* malhumor, hosquedad, resentimiento, reserva.

sully | 'sʌlɪ | *v.t.* (form.) **1** manchar, ensuciar. **2** (fig. y lit.) mancillar, manchar (la reputación). || *s.c.* **3** mancha. **4** mancilla, desdoro, deshonra.

sulphur | 'sʌlfər | (EE.UU. **sulfur**) *s.i.* **1** azufre. || *s.c.* **2** ZOOL. mariposa anaranjada.

sultan | 'sʌltən | *s.c.* sultán.

sultana | 'səl'tɑːnə | *s.c.* **1** pasa de Esmirna, uva pasa (usada en cocina). **2** sultana (mujer).

sultry | 'sʌltrɪ | *adj.* **1** bochornoso, sofocante, tórrido (el tiempo). **2** seductor, insinuante, voluptuoso, provocativo, sensual.

sum | sʌm | *s.c.* **1 [– (of)]** suma, cantidad, cuantía. **2** MAT. problema de aritmética, cálculo aritmético. || *s.sing.* **3 [the – (of)]** la suma, el monto, el total: *the sum of it all was $120 = la suma de todo ello ascendía a 120 dólares.* **4 [the – (of)]** el conjunto, la totalidad, la meta: *the sum of her experiences = el conjunto de sus experiencias.* || *v.t.* [*pret.* y *p.p.* **summed,** *ger.* **summing**] **5** sumar, totalizar. || **6 in –,** en suma, en resumen. **7 greater/more than the – of its parts,** mejor que la suma de todas sus partes, mejor en conjunto de lo que cabría esperar individualmente. **8 – total,** total, totalidad, monto. **9 to – up, a)** resumir, compendiar, hacer un resumen; **b)** hacerse una opinión, darse cuenta; **c)** DER. recapitular.

summarily | 'sʌmərɪlɪ | *adv.* sumariamente, brevemente, sucintamente.

summarize | 'sʌməraɪz | (brit. **summarise**) *v.t.* e *i.* resumir, compendiar, hacer un resumen (de), abreviar.

summary | 'sʌmərɪ | *s.c.* **1 [to – (of)]** resumen, síntesis, sumario, esquema. || *adj.* **2** (form.) sumario, breve, sucinto. || **3 in –,** en resumen.

summat | 'sʌmət | *pron.* (brit. y fam.) algo, alguna cosa (dialectal).

summation | sə'meɪʃən | *s.c.* (form.) **1** resumen, compendio, sumario, síntesis, esquema. **2** suma, adición, resultado, total.

summer | 'sʌmər | *s.c.* e *i.* **1** verano, estío. || *s.c.* **2** (lit.) primavera, abril (año de vida): *a woman of 60 summers = una mujer de 60 abriles.* **3** ARQ. viga maestra; dintel. || *v.i.* **4** veranear, pasar el verano. || *v.i.* **5** llevar a pastar, poner a pastar (al ganado durante el verano). || *adj.* **6** de verano, estival, veraniego. || **7 – school,** curso de verano. **8 – time,** horario de verano, hora de verano (para conseguir más largo período de luz).

summerhouse | 'sʌməhaus | *s.c.* cenador.

summertime | 'sʌmətaɪm | *s.i.* verano, estío.

summery | 'sʌmərɪ | *adj.* veraniego, de verano, estival.

summing-up | ˌsʌmɪŋ'ʌp | *s.c.* DER. recapitulación, resumen.

summit | 'sʌmɪt | *s.c.* **1 [– (of)]** cima, cumbre (de una montaña). **2 [the – (of)]** (form. y fig.) cima, cumbre, cúspide (de la fama). **3** conferencia, cima, cumbre (de jefes de gobierno, cargos importantes): *a summit to discuss oil prices = una cumbre para discutir los precios del petróleo.*

summon | 'sʌmən | *v.t.* **1** convocar, requerir, invitar, llamar (oficialmente, a una reunión). **2** (generalmente *pasiva*) DER. citar, notificar. **3** cobrar, reunir (fuerzas, coraje). || **4 to – up, a)** cobrar, reunir (fuerzas, ayuda, recursos); **b)** evocar, despertar (recuerdos).

summons | 'sʌmənz | *s.c.* **1** DER. citación, notificación, requerimiento. **2** orden, invitación, llamamiento. || *v.t.* **3** (generalmente *pasiva*) DER. notificar, entregar una citación.

sump | sʌmp | *s.c.* **1** (brit.) cárter, depósito de aceite, colector de aceite (en un vehículo). **2** sumidero, pozo negro, letrina.

sumptuous | 'sʌmptjuəs | *adj.* suntuoso, lujoso, opulento, magnífico.

sun | sʌn | *s.sing.* **1** sol (astro). **2 [the –]** sol (calor, luz): *sitting in the sun = sentado al sol.* **3** astro, estrella. || *v.t.* **[sunned, sunning] 4** tomar el sol, estar al sol, asolear. || **5 to catch the –, a)** tomar el sol, broncearse ligeramente; **b)** recibir sol, darle el sol (a un lugar). **6 everything under the –,** todo, absolutamente de todo: *calling her everything under the sun = le llamó de todo.* **7 nothing under the –,** absolutamente nada. **8 Sun,** *abreviatura* de **Sunday,** domingo. **9 – lamp,** lámpara de rayos ultravioleta. **10 – lounge,**/(EE.UU.) **parlor,** mirador, solana, galería.

sun-baked | 'sʌnbeɪkt | *adj.* agostado, endurecido al sol.

sunbathe | 'sʌnbeɪð | *v.i.* tomar el sol.

sunbather | 'sʌnbeɪðər | *s.c.* persona que toma el sol: *many sunbathers on the grass = muchas personas tomando el sol en la hierba.*

sunbathing | 'sʌnbeɪðɪŋ | *s.i.* baños de sol: *she spends her time sunbathing = pasa su tiempo tomando el sol.*

sunbeam | 'sʌnbiːm | *s.c.* rayo de sol.

sunbed | 'sʌnbed | *s.c.* tumbona, hamaca (para tomar el sol).

sunbonnet | 'sʌnˌbɒnɪt | *s.c.* gorra o sombrero para el sol, de tela y ala corta.

sunburn | 'sʌnbəːn | *s.i.* **1** quemadura de sol, eritema solar. || *v.t.* e *i.* **2** quemar(se) al sol.

sunburnt | 'sʌnbəːnt | *adj.* **1** quemado por el sol. **2** (brit.) bronceado, tostado por el sol.

sundae | 'sʌdeɪ | *s.c.* copa de helado (con frutas, nueces, crema).

Sunday | 'sʌndɪ | *s.c.* e *i.* **1** domingo. || **2 – best,** las mejores ropas, ropas de domingo, traje dominguero. **3 – school,** catequesis, escuela dominical.

sundeck | 'sʌndek | *s.c.* **1** cubierta superior (de un barco). **2** terraza, balcón, terrado (para tomar el sol).

sundial | 'sʌndaɪəl | *s.c.* reloj de sol.

sundown | 'sʌndaʊn | *s.i.* (EE.UU.) puesta de sol, anochecer, ocaso.

sundrenched | 'sʌndrentʃt | *adj.* inundado de sol, muy soleado.

sundry | 'sʌndrɪ | *adj.* **1** (form.) varios, variados, diversos, múltiples. || *s.pl.* **2** géneros diversos, varios, otros (en una factura). || **3 all and –,** todos y cada uno.

sunflower | 'sʌnˌflaʊər | *s.c.* **1** BOT. girasol, mirasol. **2** color amarillo fuerte. || *adj.* **3** de girasol: *sunflower oil = aceite de girasol.*

sung | sʌŋ | *p.p.irreg.* de **sing.**

sunglasses | 'sʌnˌglɑːsɪz | | 'sʌnˌglæsɪz | *s.pl.* gafas para el sol.

sunhat | 'sʌnhæt | *s.c.* sombrero de sol, pamela.

sunk | sʌŋk | *p.p.irreg.* de **sink.**

sunken | sʌŋkən | *adj.* **1** hundido, sumergido: *a sunken ship = un barco hundido.* **2** hundido, sumido, metido: *her sunken eyes = sus ojos hundidos.* **3** construido a nivel inferior: *a sunken garden = un jardín a un nivel inferior.*

sunless | 'sʌnlɪs | *adj.* sin sol, oscuro.

sunlight | 'sʌnlaɪt | *s.i.* luz del sol, luz solar.

sunlit | 'sʌnlɪt | *adj.* iluminado por el sol.

sunny | 'sʌnɪ | *adj.* **1** soleado, de sol (el tiempo, un día). **2** iluminado por el sol, soleado (habitación, etc.). **3** alegre, jovial, optimista.

sunrise | 'sʌnraɪz | (también fam. **sun-up**) *s.c.* e *i.* salida de sol, alba, amanecer.

sunroof | 'sʌnruːf | *s.c.* techo corredizo (en un automóvil).

sunset | 'sʌnset | *s.i.* (brit.) puesta de sol, anochecer, ocaso.

sunshade | 'sʌnʃeɪd | *s.c.* **1** sombrilla, parasol, quitasol. **2** toldo, marquesina. **3** cortina, persiana.

sunshine | 'sʌnʃaɪn | *s.i.* **1 [the –]** el sol (rayos o calor del sol). **2** alegría, jovialidad, optimismo.

sunstroke | 'sʌnstrəʊk | *s.i.* MED. insolación.

suntan | 'sʌntæn | (también **tan**) *s.c.* bronceado, color moreno, color tostado (por el sol).

sun-tanned | 'sʌntænd | *adj.* bronceado, tostado, moreno.

suntrap | 'sʌntræp | *s.c.* solana, zona muy soleada.

sun-up | 'sʌnʌp | *s.i.* (EE.UU. o fam.) salida del sol.

sup | sʌp | [*pret.* y *p.p.* **supped,** *ger.* **supping**] *v.t.* e *i.* **1** beber a sorbitos, dar pequeños sorbos. || *v.i.* **2 [to – (on/off)]** (arc.) cenar. || *s.c.* **3** sorbo, trago.

super | 'suːpər | | 'sjuːpər | *adj.* **1** (fam.) super, maravilloso, fantástico, excelente, bárbaro: *it's a super idea = es una idea fantástica.* **2** superior, mayor, mejor. || *s.c.* **3** (brit. y fam.) inspector de policía. **4** (fam.) extra, figurante, comparsa (actor). **5** COM. calidad superior, talla extra grande. || *prefijo.* **6** [– + *s./adj.*] super-, sobre-: *superabundant = sobreabundante.*

superabundance | ˌsuːpərə'bʌndəns | | ˌsjuːpərə'bʌndəns | *s.sing.* **[– (of)]** (form.) sobreabundancia, superabundancia, exceso.

superabundant | ˌsuːpərə'bʌndənt | | ˌsjuːpərə'bʌndənt | *adj.* (form.) sobreabundante, superabundante, excesivo.

superannuated | ˌsuːpər'ænjueɪtɪd | | ˌsjuːpər'ænjueɪtɪd | *adj.* (form.) **1** jubilado. **2** obsoleto, anticuado, pasado de moda (un objeto).

superannuation | ˌsuːpərænjʊ'eɪʃən | | ˌsjuːpərænjʊ'eɪʃən | *s.i.* (form.) pensión, jubilación (paga).

superb | sjuː'pəːb | | suː'pəːrb | *adj.* excelente, maravilloso, fantástico, espléndido: *a superb house = una casa fantástica.*

superbly | sjuː'pəːblɪ | | suː'pəːrblɪ | *adv.* excelentemente, maravillosamente, fantásticamente, espléndidamente.

supercilious | ˌsuːpə'sɪlɪəs | | ˌsjuːpə'sɪlɪəs | *adj.* (form. y desp.) desdeñoso, arrogante, altanero.

superciliously | ˌsuːpə'sɪlɪəslɪ | | ˌsjuːpə'sɪlɪəslɪ | *adv.* (form. y desp.) desdeñosamente, arrogantemente, altaneramente.

superciliousness | ˌsuːpə'sɪlɪəsnɪs | | ˌsjuːpə'sɪlɪəsnɪs | *s.i.* desdén, arrogancia, altanería.

super-ego | ˌsuːpər'iːgəʊ | | ˌsuːpər'egəʊ | *s.c.* PSIC. superego, conciencia.

superficial | ˌsuːpə'fɪʃəl | | ˌsjuːpə'fɪʃəl | *adj.* **1** [no *comp.*] superficial, de superficie, externo. **2** superficial, somero, ligero. **3** (desp.) superficial, poco profundo, frívolo, vano.

superficiality | ˌsuːpəfɪʃɪ'ælɪtɪ | | sjuːpəfɪʃɪ'ælətɪ | *s.i.* superficialidad, frivolidad.

superficially | ˌsuːpə'fɪʃəlɪ | | ˌsjuːpə'fɪʃəlɪ | *adv.* superficialmente, aparentemente.

superfluity | ˌsuːpə'fluːɪtɪ | | ˌsjuːpə'fluːɪtɪ | *s.sing.* (form.) superfluidad, demasía, exceso: *a superfluity of details = un exceso de detalles.*

superfluous | suː'pəːfluəs | | sjuː'pəːfluəs | *adj.* superfluo, excesivo, sobrante, demasiado.

superhuman | ˌsuːpə'hjuːmən | | ˌsjuːpə'hjuːmən | *adj.* sobrehumano.

superimpose | ˌsuːpərɪm'pəʊz | | ˌsjuːpərɪm'pəʊz | *v.t.* **[to – (on)] 1** superponer, sobreponer: *you can see this is bigger if you superimpose it on the other = si los superpones, verás que este es mayor.* **2** superponer, añadir.

superintend | ˌsuːpərɪn'tend | | ˌsjuːpərɪn'tend | *v.t.* (form.) inspeccionar, supervisar, estar al cargo de.

superintendent | ˌsuːpərɪn'tendənt | | ˌsjuːpərɪn'tendənt | *s.c.* **1** inspector, subjefe (de policía). **2** superintendente, supervisor, encargado, capataz, vigilante.

superior | suː'pɪərɪər | | sjuː'pɪərɪər | *adj.* **1 [– (to)]** superior, de arriba, más importante: *a superior rank = un rango superior.* **2 [– (to)]** superior, mejor (en calidad, precio, etc...). **3** (desp.) superior, arrogante, desdeñoso, altivo: *with a superior smile = con una sonrisa desdeñosa.* **4** REL. superior, prior (en títulos). || *s.c.* **5** superior, jefe. **6** REL. superior, prior.

superiority | suːˌpɪərɪ'ɒrɪtɪ | | sjuːˌpɪərɪ'ɒrɪtɪ | *s.i.* **1** superioridad, ventaja. **2** superioridad, supremacía, suficiencia, altanería, arrogancia. || **3 – complex,** (fam.) PSIC. complejo de superioridad.

superlative | suː'pəːlətɪv | | sjuː'pəːrlətɪv | *adj.* **1** [no *comp.*] GRAM. superlativo. **2** superlativo, soberbio, supremo: *superlative quality = calidad suprema.* **3** notable, distinguido, excelente (una persona). || *s.c.* **4 [the –]** GRAM. el superlativo. **5** superlativo, exagerado, ponderado.

superlatively | suː'pəːlətɪvlɪ | | sjuː'pəːlətɪvlɪ | *adv.* extremadamente, en grado sumo: *superlative beautiful = extremadamente guapa.*

superman | 'suːpəmæn | | 'sjuːpəmæn | [*pl.irreg.* **supermen**] *s.c.* superhombre.

supermen | suːpəmen | | sjuːpəm | *pl.irreg.* de **superman.**

supernatural | ˌsuːpə'nætʃərəl | | ˌsjuːpə'nætʃərəl | *adj.* **1** sobrenatural. || *s.sing.* **2 [the –]** lo sobrenatural, lo oculto.

superpower | 'suːpəˌpaʊər | | 'sjuːpəˌpaʊər | *s.c.* superpotencia (un país).

supersede | ˌsuːpə'siːd | | ˌsjuːpə'siːd | *v.t.* (generalmente *pasiva*) sustituir, reemplazar, suplantar, desplazar, dejar a un lado: *plastics have been superseded by compact discs = los discos compactos han reemplazado a los de plástico.*

supersonic | ˌsuːpə'sɒnɪk | | ˌsjuːpə'sɒnɪk | *adj.* supersónico.

superstar | 'suːpəstɑːr | | 'sjuːpəstɑːr | *s.c.* super estrella, celebridad.

superstition | ˌsuːpə'stɪʃən | | ˌsjuːpə'stɪʃən | *s.c.* e *i.* superstición.

superstitious | ˌsuːpə'stɪʃəs | | ˌsjuːpə'stɪʃəs | *adj.* supersticioso.

superstructure | 'suːpəˌstrʌktʃər | | 'sjuːpəˌstrʌktʃər | *s.c.* MAR. superestructura.

supervise | 'suːpəvaɪz | | 'sjuːpəvaɪz | *v.t.* e *i.* supervisar, atender, vigilar, inspeccionar.

supervision | ˌsuːpə'vɪʒn | | ˌsjuːpə'vɪʒn | *s.i.* **1** supervisión, atención, vigilancia, inspección. || **2 under –,** bajo supervisión, bajo vigilancia: *working under his father supervision = trabajando bajo la supervisión de su padre.*

supervisory | 'suːpəvaɪzərɪ | | 'sjuːpəvaɪzərɪ | (EE.UU.) | ˌsuːpə'vaɪzərɪ | *adj.* supervisor, de vigilancia, de inspección: *supervisory tasks = tareas de supervisión.*

supine | 'suːpaɪn | | 'sjuːpaɪn | *adj.* (form.) **1** supina (posición). **2** débil, falto de carácter, indolente.

supper | 'sʌpər | *s.c.* e *i.* **1** cena. **2** bocadillo, bocado, pincho.

supplant | sə'plɑːnt | | sə'plænt | *v.t.* suplantar, reemplazar, sustituir (generalmente con malas artes).

supple | 'sʌpl | *adj.* **1** flexible, ágil, en forma: *she keeps supple with exercise = se mantiene ágil a base de ejercicio.* **2** flexible, elástico, plegable, dúctil (un material).

suppleness | 'sʌplnɪs | *s.i.* **1** flexibilidad, agilidad. **2** flexibilidad, elasticidad, ductilidad.

supplement | 'sʌplɪmənt | *s.c.* **1** suplemento, complemento, extra. **2** suplemento, separata, apéndice (de una revista, de un libro). **3** (brit.) complemento, paga complementaria (del Estado, para gente de renta muy baja, ancianos, desempleados): *family supplement = suplemento familiar.* || *v.t.* **4 [to – (by/with)]** complementar, añadir.

supplementary | ˌsʌplɪ'mentərɪ | *adj.* **[– (to)] 1** suplementario, adicional. **2** GEOM. suplementario (un ángulo). || **3 – benefit,** (brit.) complemento, paga complementaria (del Estado, para gente con rentas muy bajas, ancianos, desempleados).

supplicant | 'sʌplɪkənt | *s.c.* (form.) suplicante, persona que ruega.

supplicate | 'sʌplɪkeɪt | *v.t.* e *i.* suplicar, rogar, implorar, hacer súplicas.

supplication | ˌsʌplɪ'keɪʃn | *s.c.* e *i.* súplica, ruego.

supplier | 'sʌplaɪər | (también **suppliers**) *s.c.* proveedor, suministrador, distribuidor, abastecedor.

supply | 'səplaɪ | *v.t.* **1 [to – (to/with)]** proveer, suministrar, abastecer, distribuir. **2 [to – (to/with)]** aprovisionar, surtir, equipar. **3** (form.) satisfacer, saldar, llenar, compensar (una necesidad, una deficiencia). **4** suplir, sustituir, reemplazar (a un cura). || *s.c.* **5 [– (of)** generalmente *sing.*] provisión, suministro, surtido. **6** sustituto, suplente (un cura). || *s.i.* **7 [– (of)]** aprovisionamiento, abastecimiento. **8** COM. oferta. || *adj.* **9** de suministro, de abastecimiento. || **10 in short –,** escaso, poco. **11 supplies, a)** provisiones, víveres, alimentos; **b)** equipo, equipamiento, pertrechos; **c)** COM. artículos; **d)** POL. presupuestos. **12 – teacher,** profesor suplente, profesor de apoyo.

support | sə'pɔːt | *v.t.* **1** sostener, sustentar, apoyar, descansar sobre (un peso). **2** sustentar, sostener, mantener, ayudar: *her son supports the family = su hijo mantiene a la familia.* **3** pagar, aguantar, soportar (un gasto): *a lot of money to support all that luxury = un montón de dinero para pagar ese lujo.* **4** apoyar, secundar, respaldar (una decisión, a un equipo, una teoría). **5** (form.) **[can/cannot –]** soportar, sufrir, aguantar, tolerar. || *s.i.* **6** soporte, apoyo, sujeción: *those flower pots need support = esas macetas necesitan soporte.* **7** aprobación, respaldo, apoyo, ayuda, simpatía: *the idea has all my support = la idea tiene todo mi respaldo.* **8** mantenimiento, sustento, ayuda (económica). **9** soporte, evidencia, pruebas (para una teoría). || *s.c.* **10** soporte, pilar, pilastra, puntal. || **11 in –,** en defensa, en apoyo. **12 means of –,** medios de vida, medios económicos. **13 moral –,** V. **moral.**

supporting | sə'pɔːtɪŋ | *adj.* **1** de apoyo, que prueba: *supporting evidence = testimonio de apoyo.* **2** secundario, corto (un actor, una película): *supporting actors = actores secundarios.*

supporter | sə'pɔːtər | *s.c.* **1** POL. partidario, afiliado, adicto. **2** DEP. hincha, seguidor. **3** defensor, partidario.

supportive | sə'pɔːtɪv | *adj.* de apoyo, de ayuda, que da ánimo (a otros en la desgracia).

suppose | sə'pəʊz | *v.t.* **1 [to – (that)/*o.*]** suponer, imaginar, asumir, figurarse: *I suppose (that) he'll pass his exams = me figuro que aprobará sus exámenes.* **2** [**to – +** *o.* **+ to** *inf./adj.* y generalmente en *pasiva*] (form.) presumir, creer, pensar, dar por sentado: *he was supposed to be in England = se le creía en Inglaterra.* **3** (form.) suponer, presuponer, requerir: *the financial plan supposes a lot of saving = el plan económico presupone mucho ahorro.* || *conj.* **4** (también **supposing**) si solamente, y si, que (sucedería) si (al considerar una situación, al introducir una sugerencia): *suppose he doesn't arrive on time = y si no llega a tiempo.* || **5 you don't –,** crees, no creerás, piensas que (cuando se requiere una opinión): *you don't suppose she is coming after all what's happened? = ¿tú crees que vendrá después de todo lo que ha pasado?* **6 who/what do you – ...?,** ¿quién o qué crees que...? (al contar una historia que requiere imaginación por parte del oyente).

supposed | sə'pəʊzd | *adj.* **1** (desp.) supuesto, hipotético, atribuido, imaginado, pretendido: *her supposed interest wasn't so = su supuesto interés no era tal.* || **2 to be – to, a)** deber, tener por deber, tener como cometido, tocar (hacer algo): *you are supposed to open the door at 3.00 = tu deber es abrir la puerta a las 3, te toca abrir la puerta a las 3;* **b)** tener fama de, tener reputación de, decir que: *it's supposed to be a good novel = dicen que es una buena novela.* **3 what's that – to mean?,** ¡pero que quiere decir eso! (para mostrar enfado, sorpresa).

supposedly | sə'pəʊzɪdlɪ | *adv.* supuestamente, según cabe suponer, tal y como parece, hipotéticamente, presuntamente.

supposition | ˌsʌpə'zɪʃn | *s.i.* **1** suposición, presuposición: *it's just mere supposition = sólo es mera suposición.* || *s.c.* (generalmente *sing.*) **2** (form.) suposición, conjetura, sospecha, hipótesis.

suppress | sə'pres | *v.t.* **1** suprimir (un partido, derechos, etc...). **2** reprimir, acallar, sofocar (una rebelión). **3** reprimir, ahogar, ocultar, contener, disimular: *she tried to suppress her anger = intentó reprimir su ira.* **4** suprimir, prohibir, contener, impedir (una publicación). **5** ocultar (información, un escándalo). **6** contener (una hemorragia).

suppression | sə'preʃn | *s.i.* **[– (of)] 1** supresión, represión, prohibición (de actividades, derechos). **2** ocultamiento, contención, disimulación (de los sentimientos). **3** ocultación (de información, datos). **4** PSIQ. represión, inhibición, eliminación.

suppressor | sə'presər | *s.c.* **1** represor. **2** RAD. dispositivo antiparasitario.

suppurate | 'sʌpjʊəreɪt | *v.i.* supurar.

suppurating | 'sʌpjʊəreɪtɪŋ | *adj.* supurante, que supura.

supremacy | sʊ'preməsɪ | *s.i.* supremacía, hegemonía, superioridad.

supreme | suː'priːm | , | sjuː'priːm | *adj.* **1** supremo, sumo, más alto (en rango, autoridad, poder). **2** supremo, máximo: *with supreme sacrifice = un sumo sacrificio.* **3** magnífico, brillante (una persona). || **4 Supreme Being,** (lit.) Ser Supremo, Dios. **5 Supreme Court,** DER. Tribunal Supremo.

supremely | suː'priːmlɪ | *adv.* sumamente.

Supt. *abreviatura* de **Superintendent,** Inspector, Superintendente (parte de un título en la policía).

surcharge | 'sɜːtʃɑːdʒ | *v.t.* **1 [to – (on)]** sobrecargar, recargar. || *s.c.* **2** sobrecarga, recargo, sobretasa.

sure | ʃʊər | *adj.* **1** seguro, cierto, convencido. **2 [– + to +** *inf.***]** seguro, infalible, inevitable. **3** confiado, seguro. **4** firme, total, absoluto. || *adv.* **5** (EE.UU. y fam.) claro, seguro, por supuesto. || **6 to be –,** admitámoslo, aceptémoslo, efectivamente. **7 be – to,** no te olvides de, no dejes de, recuerda. **8 for –,** (fam.) seguro, con toda seguridad. **9 to make –,** comprobar, cerciorarse, verificar, asegurarse. **10 –/– thing,** claro, naturalmente, sin lugar a dudas. **11 – as/as – as,** cierto como, tan cierto como. **12 – enough,** naturalmente, ciertamente, efectivamente. **13 – of oneself,** seguro de sí mismo.

sure-fire | 'ʃʊəfaɪə | *adj.* (fam.) garantizado, de éxito asegurado, seguro, infalible: *a sure-fire film = una película de éxito asegurado.*

sure-footed | ˌʃʊə'fʊtɪd | *adj.* **1** seguro, de pie firme. **2** (fig.) certero, infalible.

surely | ʃʊəlɪ | *adv.* **1** seguramente, seguro que, por supuesto, sin duda, indudablemente, con toda certeza. **2** con seguridad, de forma segura. **3** (fam.) si, naturalmente, claro. || **4 slowly but –,** lento pero seguro, despacio pero seguro. **5 – to God/goodness,** (fam.) con toda seguridad, lo juro, lo juro por Dios.

surety | 'ʃʊərətɪ | *s.c.* e *i.* **1** DER. fiador, garante, avalista. **2** fianza, aval. **3** garantía.

surf | sɜːf | *s.i.* **1** espuma (de las olas), oleaje. || *v.i.* **2** DEP. hacer surf, practicar con tabla hawaiana.

surface | 'sɜːfɪs | *s.c.* **1** superficie, exterior, faz. **2** firme (de la carretera). **3** superficie (de un líquido). **4 [the –]** (fig.) la superficie, aspecto superficial, exterior. **5** GEOM. superficie. || *v.i.* **6** emerger, salir a la superficie. **7** (fam. y hum.) levantarse, aparecer, asomar la cara: *he always surfaces at 3.00 = siempre aparece a las tres.* || *v.t.* **8** recubrir, revestir (una superficie). **9** alisar, allanar, pulir. || *adj.* **10** exterior, externo, de superficie. **11** de tierra, por tierra; marítimo (el correo). **12** superficial, poco profundo. || **13 below/beneath the –,** bajo la superficie, oculto, encubierto. **14 to come /rise to the –,** salir a la superficie, aflorar, hacerse patente, ser obvio.

surface-to-air | ˌsɜːfɪstə'eər | *adj.* MIL. tierra-aire (un misil).

surfboard | 'sɜːfbɔːd | *s.c.* DEP. tabla de surf, acuaplano, tabla hawaiana.

surfeit | 'sɜːfɪt | *s.sing.* **1 [– (of)]** (form.) exceso, exageración, demasía, sobreabundancia. **2** empacho, indigestión. **3** saciedad, hartazgo, hartura. || *v.t.* e *i.* **4 [to – (with)]** (form.) saciar(se), hartar(se), atracar(se).

surge | sɜːdʒ | *s.sing.* **1 [– (of)]** avalancha, oleada (de gente). **2** (fig.) oleada, arrebato (de ira, de alegría, de entusiasmo). **3** MAR. oleaje, marejada, ola. || *v.i.* **4 [to – +** *adv./prep.***]** abalanzarse, irrumpir en avalancha, entrar en tropel. **5 [to – (up)]** bullir, afluir, surgir, brotar, llenarse: *joy surged within us = nos llenamos de contento.* **6** agitarse, encresparse, embravecer(se) (el mar).

surgeon | 'sɜːdʒən | *s.c.* MED. cirujano.

surgery | 'sɜːdʒərɪ | *s.i.* MED. **1** cirugía, operación. || *s.c.* e *i.* **2** consultorio, gabinete de consulta, clínica, quirófano. || *s.c.* **3** consulta, sesión de consulta. **4** (brit.) POL. hora de visita parlamentaria (en que los votantes de un distrito electoral pueden visitar a su representante).

surgical | 'sɜːdʒɪkl | *adj.* **1** quirúrgico (instrumental, tratamiento). || **2 – spirit,** desinfectante quirúrgico.

surging | sɜːdʒɪŋ | *adj.* encrespado, agitado, embravecido, amenazante: *the surging crowd = la multitud amenazante.*

surly | 'sɜːlɪ | *adj.* malhumorado, hosco, áspero, rudo, desabrido.

surmise | 'sɜːmaɪz | *v.t.* **1 [to – +** *o.* **(that)]** (form.) suponer, presumir, deducir, inferir, sospechar, conjeturar: *I surmise that her help is important = presumo que su ayuda es importante.* || *s.c.* e *i.* **2** (form.) suposición, conjetura, presunción, deducción, inferencia, sospecha.

surmount | sɜː'maʊnt | *v.t.* (form.) **1** superar, salvar, vencer (un obstáculo). **2** (generalmente *pasiva*) remontar, coronar (una altura).

surmountable | sɜː'maʊntəbl | *adj.* superable, batible, remontable.

surname | 'sɜːneɪm | *s.c.* **1** (también **family name**) apellido. **2** sobrenombre, mote. || *v.t.* **3** apellidar.

surpass | sə'pɑːs | *v.t.* **1** (form.) sobrepasar, superar, exceder, eclipsar, ser superior. **2** superar, salvar, vencer (un obstáculo).

surpassing | sə'pɑːsɪŋ | *adj.* (form.) insuperable, incomparable, excelente, sin par.

surplice | 'sɜːplɪs | *s.c.* roquete, sobrepelliz.

surplus | 'sɜːpləs | *s.c.* e *i.* **1** exceso, excedente, superávit, sobrante: *surplus of wheat = excedente de trigo.* || *adj.* **2** sobrante, excedente, superfluo.

surprise | sə'praɪz | *s.i.* **1** sorpresa, asombro, desconcierto. || *s.c.* **2** sorpresa, susto, sobresalto: *it was a nice surprise = fue una agradable sorpresa.* **3** sorpresa (regalo). || *v.t.* **4** sorprender, asombrar, desconcertar. **5** sorprender, coger por sorpresa, pillar, pescar: *they were surprised entering the house = les sorprendieron entrando en la casa.* **6** MIL. atacar por sorpresa. || *adj.atr.* **7** sorpresa, de sorpresa: *a surprise attack = un ataque sorpresa.* || **8 to take by –,** coger por sorpresa.

surprised | sə'praɪzd | *adj.* sorprendido, asombrado, desconcertado.

surprising | sə'praɪzɪŋ | *adj.* sorprendente, asombroso, desconcertante, inesperado.

surprisingly | sə'praɪzɪŋlɪ | *adv.* sorprendentemente, asombrosamente, desconcertantemente, inesperadamente.

surreal | sə'rɪəl | *adj.* surreal, surrealista, extraño, raro.

Surrealism | sə'rɪəlɪzəm | *s.i.* ART. surrealismo.

surrealist | sə'rɪəlɪst | *s.c.* **1** ART. surrealista. || *adj.* **2** ART. surrealista.

surrealistic | sə'rɪəlɪstɪk | *adj.* **1** ART. surrealista. **2** surreal, extraño, raro.

surrender | sə'rendər | *v.t.* e *i.* **1** rendir(se), entregar(se), capitular. **2** (fig.) ceder, entregar(se), abandonar(se). || *v.t.* **3** abandonar, renunciar a (una tentación, un derecho). **4** entregar, dar, dejar: *you must surrender your passport at the reception desk = debe dejar su pasaporte en recepción.*

surreptitious | ˌsʌrəp'tɪʃəs | *adj.* subrepticio, secreto, clandestino, furtivo.
subrrepticiously | ˌsʌrəp'tɪʃəslɪ | *adv.* subrepticiamente, en secreto, clandestinamente, furtivamente.
surrogate | 'sʌrəgeɪt | | 'səːrəgeɪt | *s.c.* (form.) **1** sustituto, suplente. **2** (EE.UU.) DER. juez de testamentaría. **3** REL. vicario, coadjutor. || *adj.* **4** sustituto, suplente. || **5 – mother,** madre de alquiler (en beneficio de otra, incapaz de engendrar).
surround | sə'raʊnd | *v.t.* **1** rodear, cercar, encerrar, circundar: *the house is surrounded by a garden = la casa está rodeada por un jardín.* **2** (fig.) asediar, acorralar. **3** (fig.) concernir, atañer: *many problems surround us = muchos problemas nos atañen.* **4** MIL. sitiar, asediar; acorralar. || *s.c.* **5** marco, reborde, borde (decorativo).
surrounding | sə'raʊndɪŋ | *adj.* **1** circundante, de alrededor. || **2 surroundings,** alrededores, vecindad, cercanías, vecindario.
surtax | 'səːtæks | *s.i.* impuesto adicional, recargo tributario, sobretasa (por ingresos elevados).
surveillance | səː'veɪləns | *s.i.* vigilancia, observación (continua).
survey | 'səːveɪ | *v.t.* **1** observar, examinar, mirar, contemplar. **2** examinar, estudiar, considerar, meditar sobre (una situación). **3** peritar, inspeccionar, examinar, reconocer (una vivienda antes de comprarla). **4** TEC. deslindar, medir (de un área, de una tierra), levantar el plano (de una ciudad). **5** (generalmente pasiva) hacer una encuesta, hacer un estudio (de opinión). || *s.c.* **6** encuesta (de opinión). **7** estudio, investigación. **8** vista de conjunto, visión panorámica (de una situación, de un tema, de un lugar). **9** peritación, inspección, examen, estudio (de una vivienda). **10** TEC. medición, deslinde, apeo.
surveyor | sə'veɪər | *s.c.* perito, agrimensor, topógrafo.
survival | sə'vaɪvl | *s.i.* **1** supervivencia. || *s.c.* **2** reliquia, vestigio: *the radio was a survival from the times she was married = la radio era una reliquia de cuando estaba casada.* || **3 – kit,** equipo de emergencia.
survive | sə'vaɪv | *v.i.* **1** sobrevivir, subsistir, permanecer. || *v.t.* **2** sobrevivir a, aguantar, durar: *will you survive after such a long journey? = ¿aguantarás después de un viaje tan largo?* || **3 to – on,** sobrevivir, subsistir.
survivor | sə'vaɪvər | *s.c.* superviviente.
susceptibility | səˌseptə'bɪlɪtɪ | *s.c.* e *i.* **1 [– (to)]** susceptibilidad, sensibilidad. || **2 susceptibilities,** susceptibilidades, puntos sensibles.
susceptible | sə'septəbl | *adj.* **1** susceptible, influenciable. **2 [– to]** susceptible a, sensible a, propenso a (la enfermedad). **3** impresionable, susceptible. **4 [– of]** DER. susceptible de, sujeto a: *susceptible of change = susceptible de cambio.*
suspect | sə'spekt | *v.t.* **1** sospechar, temer, pensar: *I suspect he is trying to cheat = me temo que está intentando hacer trampa.* **2 [to – (of)]** sospechar (de), desconfiar (de), recelar (de). **3** (fam.) sospechar, imaginarse, figurarse: *we suspected the truth = nos figuramos la verdad.* || | 'sʌspekt | *s.c.* **4** sospechoso. || *adj.* **5** sospechoso, bajo sospecha. **6** sospechoso, cuestionable, dudoso.
suspend | sə'spend | *v.t.* **1** suspender, cesar, interrumpir, finalizar. **2 [to – (from)]** suspender, cesar (en un cargo). **3** [**to – +** *o.* **+** *adv./prep.*] (form.) suspender, colgar. **4** (generalmente *pasiva*) retirar el carnet. **5** (generalmente *pasiva*) QUIM. tener en suspensión, estar en suspensión, dispersar.
suspended | sə'spendɪd | *adj.* **1** suspendido, interrumpido. **2** cesado. **3** suspendido, colgado. **4** sin carnet de conducir. **5** QUIM. disperso, en suspensión. || **6 – animation,** muerte aparente, estado de hibernación. **7 – sentence,** DER. condena condicional (que no se cumple a menos que el criminal reincida).
suspender | sə'spendər | *s.c.* **1** (brit.) liga. || **2 – belt,** liguero, portaligas. **3 suspenders,** (EE.UU.) tirantes (de pantalón).
suspense | sə'spens | *s.i.* **1** suspense, incertidumbre, ansiedad, duda. **2** suspensión. || **3 to keep someone in –,** mantener a alguien en la incertidumbre.
suspension | sə'spenʃn | *s.i.* **1** suspensión. **2** privación, retirada (del carnet de conducir). || *s.c.* **3** QUIM. suspensión. || **4 – bridge,** puente colgante.
suspicion | sə'spɪʃn | *s.c.* e *i.* **1** sospecha, indicio, recelo. **2** sospecha, suposición, conjetura. || *s.sing.* **3 [– (of)]** pizca, fragmento, traza, poquito. || **4 above/beyond –,** por encima de toda sospecha, libre de sospecha. **5 under –,** bajo sospecha, sospechoso.
suspicious | sə'spɪʃəs | *adj.* **1 [– (about /of)]** sospechoso, receloso, suspicaz, desconfiado. **2** sospechoso, dudoso.
suspiciously | sə'spɪʃəslɪ | *adv.* **1** recelosamente, desconfiadamente, suspicazmente. **2** sospechosamente: *acting suspiciously = actuando sospechosamente.*
suspiciousness | sə'spɪʃəsnɪs | *s.i.* recelo, desconfianza, suspicacia.
suss | sʌs | *v.t.* **1** [**to – + (that)/***o.*] (brit. y jerga) descubrir, darse cuenta. || **2 to – out,** (brit.) descubrir, averiguar (algo); calar, desenmascarar: *I got him sussed out = ya le he calado.*
sustain | sə'steɪn | *v.t.* **1** mantener, sustentar, nutrir. **2** mantener, sostener (el ánimo, el interés). **3** (form.) sufrir, padecer, recibir (daño). **4** (form.) sostener, cargar, soportar (un peso). **5** DER. aceptar. **6** MUS. sostener.
sustained | sə'steɪnd | *adj.* sostenido, prolongado, ininterrumpido.
sustenance | 'sʌstɪnəns | *s.i.* (form.) sustento, alimento.
suture | 'suːtʃər | *s.c.* **1** MED. sutura. || *v.t.* **2** MED. suturar, coser.
svelte | svelt | *adj.* esbelto, delgado, grácil.
SW *abreviatura* de **south west,** suroeste.
swab | swɒb | | swɑːb | *s.c.* **1** MED. algodón, tapón, torunda. **2** MED. muestra (recogida en una torunda). **3** estropajo, trapo. || *v.t.* [*pret.* y *p.p.* **swabbed,** *ger.* **swabbing**] **4 [to – (down)]** MED. limpiar con algodón. **5** fregar, limpiar con estropajo.
swaddle | 'swɒdl | *v.t.* **1** envolver en mantillas, empañar, fajar (a un bebé). **2** envolver, enrollar, vendar.
swaddling | 'swɒdlɪŋ | *adj.* **1** de empañar, de fajar. || **2 – clothes,** mantillas, pañales, fajas.
swagger | 'swægər | *v.i.* **1** contonearse, pavonearse, caminar dándose aires. || *s.sing.* **2** pavoneo, contoneo, aires de grandeza.
swain | 'sweɪn | *s.c.* (lit.) **1** mozo, zagal. **2** cortejador, pretendiente, enamorado.
swallow | 'swɒləʊ | *v.t.* **1** tragar, comer, ingerir, pasar. **2** (fam. y fig.) tragar, aceptar pacientemente, tolerar (una impertinencia). **3** (fig.) tragar, contener (el orgullo). || *v.i.* **4** tragar saliva. || *s.c.* **5** trago; bocado. **6** ZOOL. golondrina. || **7 to be swallowed up,** ser absorbido. **8 to – one's pride,** V. **pride. 9 to – one's words,** (fig.) tragarse sus palabras.
swam | 'swæm | *pret.irreg.* de **swim.**
swamp | swɒmp | *s.c.* e *i.* **1** ciénaga, zona pantanosa, marisma. || *v.t.* **2** inundar, agobiar, abrumar (de trabajo). **3** inundar, sumergir, llenar de agua, hacer naufragar.
swampy | swɒmpɪ | *adj.* pantanoso, cenagoso.
swan | swɒn | *s.c.* **1** ZOOL. cisne. || *v.i.* **[swanned, swanning] 2** [**to – +** *adv./prep.*] (fam.) vagar, deambular, pasear, viajar (sin ir un punto fijo). || **3 – song,** (fig.) canto del cisne.
swank | swæŋk | *v.i.* **1** (fam.) presumir, darse tono, fanfarronear, farolear, pavonearse. || *s.i.* **2** (fam.) ostentación, fanfarroneo, faroleo. || *s.c.* **3** farolero, fanfarrón. || *adj.* **4** (también **swanky**) lujoso, elegante y caro, ostentoso: *a swank club = un club lujoso.*
swap | swɒp | (también **swop**) [*pret.* y *p.p.* **swapped,** *ger.* **swapping**] *v.t.* e *i.* **1** (fam.) intercambiar, cambiar, cambalachear, canjear. **2** cambiar, sustituir. || *s.c.* (fam.) **3** cambio, canje, trueque, cambalache (acto, objeto). || **4 to – over/round,** intercambiar el lugar, ocupar el lugar del otro.
swarm | swɔːm | *s.c.* **1** [**– +** *v.sing./pl.*] ZOOL. enjambre. **2** (también **swarms**) **[– (of)]** enjambre, muchedumbre, gentío, multitud. || *v.i.* **3** [**to – +** *adv./prep.*] ir en tropel, salir o entrar en masa, pulular. **4** ZOOL. enjambrar (una colmena). **5** [**to – +** *adv./prep.*] (p.u.) trepar, encaramarse, escalar. || **6 to – with,** bullir de, hervir de, estar plagado de: *fans swarm ing round him = los admiradores estaban como moscas a su alrededor.*
swarthy | 'swɔːðɪ | *adj.* moreno, aceitunado, oscuro.
swashbuckling | 'swɒʃˌbʌklɪŋ | *adj.* bravucón, baladrón, valentón, fanfarrón.
swastika | 'swɒstɪkə | | 'swɑːstɪkə | *s.c.* esvástica, cruz gamada.
swat | swɒt | | swɑːt | **[swatted, swatting]** *v.t.* **1** aplastar con palmeta, matar de un palmetazo, aplastar de un golpe (a un insecto). || *s.c.* **2** palmetazo, golpe. **3** palmeta (para matar moscas).
swath | swɒθ | V. **swathe.**
swathe | sweɪð | (también **swath**) *s.c.* **1** hilera, ringlera (segada). **2** franja, línea, tira: *burnt swathes of land = franjas de tierra quemadas.* **3** tira, lazo, faja, venda (de tela). || *v.t.* **4** [**to – in** y general-

mente *pas.*] (lit.) envolver, rodear, vendar, fajar.
swathed | sweɪðd | *adj.* envuelto, cubierto.
sway | sweɪ | *v.t.* e *i.* **1** mecer(se), balancear(se), bambolear(se), oscilar, mover(se): *branches swaying = ramas que se mecían.* || *v.t.* **2** (generalmente *pasiva.*) inclinar, decidir, influir, persuadir. || *s.c.* **3** vaivén, bamboleo, balanceo, oscilación. || *s.i.* **4** (lit.) poder, mando, dominio. **5** (lit.) influencia, ascendiente. || **6 to hold –,** tener influencia, dominar, ser preponderante.
swear | sweər | *v.irr.* [*pret.irreg.* **swore,** *p.p.* **sworn**] *i.* **1 [to – (at)]** maldecir, decir tacos, blasfemar, decir juramentos. || *v.t.* **2** jurar, prometer, dar palabra, hacer voto. || *v.t.* e *i.* **3 [to – (on)]** jurar, prestar (juramento). || **4 to – blind,** V. **blind. 5 to – by,** (fam.) tener confianza absoluta en, creer ciegamente en. **6 to – somebody in,** tomar juramento a alguien, hacer prestar juramento. **7 to – to, a)** hacer prometer, hacer jurar; **b)** jurar, decir con certeza.
swear-word | 'sweəwɜːd | *s.c.* palabrota, taco, blasfemia, maldición.
sweat | swet | *v.i.* **1** (también **perspire**) sudar, transpirar. **2** resudar, rezumar, fermentar (un producto, una pared). **3** (fam.) sudar, estar nervioso. || *v.t.* **4** (brit.) rehogar en mantequilla, freír en mantequilla lentamente. **5** explotar (a los obreros). || *s.i.* **6** (también **perspiration**) sudor, transpiración. || *s.sing.* **7** (fam.) nervios, apuro, sudor. **8** (fam.) sudor, trabajo aburrido, trabajo penoso. || *s.c.* **9** (arc. y fam.) currante, trabajador experimentado; (brit.) soldado viejo. || **10 to be in a –/to be in a cold –,** estar muy nervioso, estar angustiado. **11 no –!,** sin problemas, no hay problema. **12 to – blood,** (fam.) sudar sangre, sudar la gota gorda. **13 – gland,** ANAT. glándula sudorípara. **14 to – it out, a)** (fam.) sudar la gota gorda, trabajar duro; **b)** aguantarlo, soportarlo (algo desagradable). **15 to – out,** sudar (un catarro).
sweatband | 'swetbænd | *s.c.* **1** badana, tafilete (en el interior del sombrero). **2** banda, tira (que se lleva en la frente o la muñeca contra el sudor).
sweater | swetər | *s.c.* jersey, suéter, (Am.) chompa.
sweatshirt | 'swetʃɜːt | *s.c.* camiseta de deporte, sudadera.
sweatshop | 'swetʃɒp | *s.c.* (desp.) fábrica en que se explota a los obreros, tallerucho.
sweaty | 'swetɪ | *adj.* **1** sudoroso, empapado en sudor. **2** sofocante, que hace sudar (el tiempo extenuante).
swede | swiːd | (también **rutabaga**) *s.c.* e *i.* BOT. rutabaga, nabo sueco. || *s.c.* **2 Swede,** sueco (de origen).
Swedish | 'swiːdɪʃ | *adj.* **1** sueco, de Suecia. || *s.i.* **2** sueco (lengua).
sweep | swiːp | *v.* [*pret.* y *p.p.irreg.* **swept**] *t.* **1** barrer, limpiar; deshollinar (una chimenea). **2** empujar, despejar, limpiar (de un golpe). **3** examinar, escudriñar, recorrer (un espacio con la vista). || *v.t.* e *i.* **4 [to – + *(o.)* + *adv./prep.*]** barrer, arrastrar, transportar, llevar(se): *all the papers were swept by the wind = el viento se llevó todos los papeles.* || *v.i.* **5** precipitarse, entrar o salir precipitadamente, moverse majestuosamente. **6 [to – + *adv./prep.*]** extenderse, llegar hasta, pasar por: *his lands sweep down to the river = sus tierras se extienden hasta el río.* || *s.c.* **7** barrido, barredura, escobazo. **8** golpe, movimiento, vuelo (de un brazo, de un arma). **9** extensión, envergadura, paisaje. **10** (fig.) envergadura, alcance (de un argumento). **11** gama, serie, montón. **12** barrido, recorrido, redada. **13** (fam.) lotería en la que una persona gana todo el dinero apostado (generalmente a un caballo). **14** (fam.) deshollinador. || **15 to make a clean –,** DEP. barrer, ganar todos los partidos. **16 to – aside,** dejar a un lado, apartar, no prestar atención, quitar de en medio. **17 to – away, a)** suprimir, eliminar, borrar (privilegios, vestigios); **b)** (fig.) convencer, persuadir, arrastrar. **18 to – someone off their feet, a)** enamorar, volver loco de amor; **b)** arrastrar, convencer plenamente, persuadir totalmente. **19 to – something under the carpet/rug,** mantener en secreto, esconder (algo vergonzoso). **20 to – the board,** V. **board.**
sweeper | swiːpər | *s.c.* **1** escoba mecánica; aspiradora de mano. **2** barrendero. **3** (brit.) DEP. líbero, defensa libre.
sweeping | swiːpɪŋ | *adj.* **1** abierta (una curva). **2** extenso, amplio, vasto, enorme, significativo. **3** (desp.) general, generalizado, que analiza el detalle (un análisis). || **4 sweepings,** barreduras, basura, polvo.
sweepstake | 'swiːpsteɪk | (también **sweep**) *s.c.* lotería en la que una persona gana todo el dinero apostado (generalmente a un caballo).
sweet | swiːt | *adj.* **1** dulce, azucarado. **2** dulce, melodiosa, romántica (música). **3** suave (un sonido). **4** fresco, limpio, sano, fragante (un olor). **5** dulce, encantador, simpático, agradable, amable, generoso (una persona). **6** mono, majo, lindo, atractivo (una cosa, una persona). || *s.c.* **7** (brit.) caramelo, dulce, bombón, golosina. || *s.c.* e *i.* **8** (brit.) postre. **9** (p.u.) querido, cariño, amor, cielo (usado cariñosamente como vocativo). || **10 to be – on,** (arc. y fam.) estar enamorado de. **11 to go one's own – way/self,** hacer lo que a uno le da la gana. **12 to have a – tooth,** ser muy goloso. **13 to keep someone –,** asegurarse la amistad de un (por medio de regalos, lisonjas). **14 my –,** cariño, mi amor. **15 – corn,** (también **corn**) (EE.UU.) maíz tierno. **16 – nothings,** (hum.) galanterías, palabras cariñosas, zalamerías (susurradas al oído). **17 – pea,** BOT. guisante de olor. **18 – pepper,** pimienta dulce. **19 – potato,** batata, boniato. **20 – shop,** confitería, quiosco.
sweet-and-sour | ˌswiːtən'sauər | *adj.* agridulce (sabor típico de la cocina china).
sweetbread | 'swiːtbred | *s.c.* mollejas (de cordero, de ternera).
sweeten | 'swiːtn | *v.t.* e *i.* **1** endulzar, azucarar. || *v.t.* **2** (fig.) endulzar, dulcificar, suavizar. **3 [to – (up)]** (fam.) sobornar (con regalos). || **4 to – the pill,** V. **pill.**
sweetener | 'swiːtnər | *s.i.* **1** endulzador, dulcificante (una sustancia). **2** (fam.) soborno, regalo, obsequio (para convencer a alguien).
sweetheart | 'swiːthɑːt | *s.c.* (p.u.) **1** novio, amor. **2** cariño, cielo, encanto, amor (usado como vocativo cariñoso).
sweetie | 'swiːtɪ | *s.c.* **1** (brit. y fam.) caramelito, dulce (usado por y con los niños). **2** (fam.) encanto, monería, cielo, amor: *isn't she a sweetie? = ¿no es un encanto?* **3** cariño, cielo, amor (usado como vocativo cariñoso).
sweetish | 'swiːtɪʃ | *adj.* dulzón, dulzarrón, algo dulce.
sweetly | swiːtlɪ | *adv.* **1** dulcemente, melodiosamente. **2** dulcemente, encantadoramente, como un cielo. **3** dulcemente, agradablemente, con dulzura. **4** suavemente, silenciosamente.
sweetmeat | 'swiːtmiːt | *s.c.* (arc.) dulce, pasta; golosina, caramelo; bombón.
sweetness | 'swiːtnɪs | *s.i.* **1** dulzura, dulzor. **2** dulzura, suavidad, encanto, agrado. **3** fragancia.
swell | swel | *v.* [*pret.* **swelled,** *p.p.irreg.* **swollen** o **swelled**] *i.* **1 [to – (up)]** hincharse, inflamarse, entumecerse, dilatarse. **2** (fig.) henchirse (de orgullo). **3** agitarse, encresparse, embravecerse (el mar). || *v.t.* **4** hinchar, abultar, acrecentar, aumentar, engrosar (una cantidad). || *v.t.* e *i.* **5 [to – (out)]** hinchar, expandir, llenar de aire. || *s.c.* **6** marejada, mar de fondo, mar tendida, oleaje. || *s.sing.* **7** MUS. crescendo. **8** hinchazón, bulto, prominencia. || *s.c.* **9** (arc. y fam.) moderno, persona a la última, personaje, personalidad. || *adj.* **10** (EE.UU. y fam.) fantástico, excelente, estupendo, bárbaro.
swelling | 'swelɪŋ | *s.c.* **1** hinchazón, bulto, prominencia. || *s.i.* **2** inflamación, hinchazón.
swelter | 'sweltər | *v.i.* pasar calor, asarse, abrasarse, sudar.
sweltering | 'sweltərɪŋ | *adj.* caluroso, bochornoso, sofocante.
swept | swept | *pret.* y *p.p.irreg.* de **sweep.**
swerve | swɜːv | *v.i.* **1** esquivar, echarse a un lado, desviarse bruscamente, virar con rapidez: *swerving not to run the cat over = virando rápidamente para no atropellar al gato.* **2 [to – (from),** generalmente en *negativas*] cambiar de idea. || *v.t.* **3** DEP. desviar, torcer. || *s.c.* **4** viraje, desvío.
swift | swɪft | *adj.* **1** (lit.) rápido, veloz, acelerado. **2** rápido, diligente, repentino, presto: *a swift reaction = una reacción rápida.* || *s.c.* **3** ZOOL. vencejo, avión.
swiftly | swɪftlɪ | *adv.* **1** rápidamente, velozmente. **2** diligentemente, con presteza, con rapidez; repentinamente, pronto.
swiftness | 'swɪftnɪs | *s.i.* rapidez, velocidad.
swig | swɪg | [*pret.* y *p.p.* **swigged,** *ger.* **swigging**] *v.t.* **1** (fam.) beber a tragantonas, tragar grandes tragos. || *s.c.* **2** (fam.) tragantona, trago.
swill | swɪl | *v.t.* **1 [to – (down/out)]** limpiar con agua, echar cubos de agua. || *v.t.* e *i.* **2** (desp.) beber a tragantonas, beber a gran velocidad. || *s.i.* **3** bazofia, aguachirle (que comen los cerdos).
swim | swɪm | *v.* [*pret.irreg.* **swam,** *p.p.* **swum;** *ger.* **swimming**] *i.* **1** nadar, bañar-

se. **2 [to – (in/with)]** nadar, inundarse, flotar: *they gave us some meat swimming in oil = nos dieron un poco de carne flotando en aceite.* **3** dar vueltas, flotar (la cabeza). || *v.t.* **4** cruzar a nado, pasar a nado, cubrir a nado (una distancia). **5** DEP. nadar (a braza, etc...). || *s.sing.* **6** baño, nadada: *we went for a swim = fuimos a nadar.* || **7 in the –,** (fam.) al corriente, enterado. **8 to sink or –,** V. **sink. 9 to – with/against the tide,** (fig.) ir con o contra corriente.

swimmer | 'swɪmər | *s.c.* nadador, bañista.

swimming | 'swɪmɪŋ | *s.i.* **1** DEP. natación. || **2 – bath,** (brit.) piscina municipal (generalmente cubierta). **3 – costume/ bathing suit,** traje de baño, bañador (de señora). **4 – pool,** piscina. **5 – trunks,** traje de baño, bañador (de caballero).

swimmingly | 'swɪmɪŋlɪ | *adv.* (arc. y fam.) **1** como la seda, sobre ruedas, a las mil maravillas. || **2 to go –,** ir como la seda.

swimsuit | 'swɪmsuːt | *s.c.* traje de baño, bañador (de señora).

swindle | 'swɪndl | *v.t.* **1 [to – (out/of)]** timar, estafar, engañar. || *s.c.* **2** timo, estafa.

swindler | 'swɪndlər | *s.c.* estafador, timador.

swine | swaɪn | *s.c.* **1** [*pl.* **swine**] (arc.) TEC. cerdo, puerco. **2** [*pl.* **swine** o **swines**] (jerga y fig.) cerdo, asqueroso, canalla.

swing | swɪŋ | *v.irr.* [*pret.* y *p.p.* **swung**] *t.* e *i.* **1** balancear(se), bambolear(se), oscilar, mover(se). **2** columpiar(se), mecerse. **3 [to – +** *adv./prep./o.* **+** *adv./prep.***]** girar, virar, hacer una curva. **4 [to – +** *adv./prep./o.* **+** *adv./prep.***]** suspender(se), colgar(se). **5 [to – +** *adv./prep./o.* **+** *adv./prep.***]** dar(se) la vuelta, girar, volver: *he swung round and looked at her = se dio la vuelta y la miró.* **6** (fig.) cambiar, invertir (de opinión, de carácter). || *v.i.* **7 [to – +** *adv./prep.***]** caminar airosamente, andar garbosamente. **8** (fam.) MUS. tocar con swing, tocar con mucho ritmo. **9 [to – (for)]** (arc. y fam.) ser ahorcado, ser colgado. || *v.t.* **10** (fam.) arreglar, colar, solucionar (por medios deshonestos). || *s.c.* **11** balanceo, bamboleo, oscilación, vaivén. **12** columpio. **13** giro, cambio, desplazamiento, viraje. || *s.sing.* **14** MUS. swing, ritmo agradable, ritmo sincopado. **15** DEP. swing (en golf). **16** DEP. golpe, gancho lateral (en boxeo). || *s.i.* **17** música sincopada (de los años 30 y 40). || **18 to get into the –,** (fam.) meterse de lleno, meterse en harina. **19 to go with a –,** (fam.) ir sobre ruedas, marchar bien. **20 in full –,** en pleno desarrollo, en plena actividad. **21 room to – a cat,** (fig.) poquísimo sitio, muy poco espacio. **22 – door,** puerta giratoria. **23 to – into action,** ponerse en acción, ponerse en marcha. **24 to – the lead,** (brit. y fam.) escurrir el bulto, hacerse el loco (para no trabajar). **25 what you lose on the swings you gain on the roundabouts/swings and roundabouts,** (brit. y fam.) lo que se pierde por un lado se gana por otro, lo comido por lo servido.

swingeing | 'swɪndʒɪŋ | *adj.* enorme, exorbitante, desmesurado, abrumador.

swinger | 'swɪŋər | *s.c.* (arc. y fam.) **1** persona mundana, persona a la moda, juerguista. **2** desinhibido.

swinging | 'swɪŋɪŋ | *adj.* (fam.) **1** alegre, divertido, lleno de vida. **2** desinhibido.

swipe | swaɪp | *s.c.* **1** golpe, manotazo. || *v.t.* e *i.* **2** golpear, asestar un golpe, dar un manotazo. **3** (fam.) birlar, guindar. || **4 to take a – at,** (fig.) dar un palo, echar por tierra.

swirl | swəːl | *v.t.* e *i.* **1** formar remolinos, arremolinar(se), girar en desorden. || *s.c.* **2** vuelta, giro, viraje. **3** remolino, torbellino.

swish | swɪʃ | *v.t.* e *i.* **1** zumbar, silbar, hacer sonar (como un látigo). || *v.i.* **2** crujir, sonar (las ropas). || *s.c.* **3** zumbido, silbido, crujido. || *adj.* **4** (fam.) elegante, moderno, caro.

Swiss | swɪs | *adj.* **1** suizo, de Suiza. || *s.c.* **2** suizo.

switch | swɪtʃ | *s.c.* **1** ELEC. interruptor, llave, conmutador. **2** cambio, giro (en un plan). **3** vara, varilla, látigo. **4** postizo, trenza postiza. **5** punta de la cola (de una vaca, de un caballo). **6** agujas, cambio de vía (de un ferrocarril). || *v.t.* e *i.* **7** cambiar, variar, pasar(se) a. || *v.t.* **8** ELEC. conectar, desconectar; conmutar, encender. **9** (fig.) cambiar (de idea, de interés). **10** intercambiar (el puesto, el lugar). || **11 to – off, a)** ELEC. apagar, desconectar; **b)** (fig.) desconectar, dejar de prestar atención. **12 to – on, a)** ELEC. encender, enchufar, conectar; **b)** (fig.) conectar, atraer (la atención). **13 to – over, a)** pasar de un extremo al otro, cambiar totalmente; **b)** ELEC. cambiar de emisora.

switchback | 'swɪtʃbæk | *s.c.* **1** carretera con muchas subidas, bajadas y curvas. **2** montaña rusa.

switchboard | 'swɪtʃbɔːd | *s.c.* **1** centralita telefónica. **2** ELEC. cuadro de distribución.

Switzerland | 'swɪtsələnd | *s.sing.* Suiza.

swivel | 'swɪvl | (brit. **swivell**) *v.t.* e *i.* **1** girar, rotar, dar vueltas. || *s.c.* **2** pivote, eslabón giratorio. || *adj.* **3** giratorio, rotatorio.

swizzle stick | 'swɪzlˌstɪk | *s.c.* palillo para remover cócteles.

swollen | 'swəʊlən | **1** *p.p.* de **swell.** || *adj.* **2** hinchado, inflamado, entumecido, dilatado.

swollen-headed | ˌswəʊlən'hedɪd | *adj.* (brit.) engreído, vanidoso, presumido.

swoon | swuːn | *v.i.* **1** (lit. y fig.) caer, desmayarse (de felicidad): *she swooned into his arms = cayó desvanecida en sus brazos.* **2** (arc.) desmayarse, desvanecerse, perder el conocimiento. || *s.c.* **3** desmayo, desvanecimiento, pérdida de conocimiento.

swoop | swuːp | *v.i.* **1** bajar en picado, lanzarse, saltar, arrojarse. **2 [to – (on)]** (fam.) arremeter, coger, pillar, caer (sobre alguien). || *s.c.* **3** arremetida, lanzamiento, descenso, calada. **4** redada.

swop | swɒp | V. **swap.**

sword | sɔːd | *s.c.* **1** espada. || **2 to cross swords,** reñir, habérselas (con alguien). **3 to put to the –,** (arc. y lit.) pasar a cuchillo.

swordfish | sɔːfɪʃ | [*pl.* **swordfish** o **swordfishes**] *s.c.* ZOOL. pez espada.

swordplay | sɔːpleɪ | *s.i.* DEP. esgrima.

swore | swɔː | *pret.* de **swear.**

sworn | swɔːn | *p.p.* **1** de **swear.** || *adj.* **2** jurado, dado bajo juramento. || **3 – enemies,** enemigos implacables.

swot | swɒt | | swɑːt | (EE.UU. **grind**) *s.c.* **1** (fam. y desp.) empollón. || *v.t.* [**swotted, swotting**] **2 [to – (up)]** (fam. y desp.) empollar.

swum | swʌm | *p.p.* de **swim.**

swung | swʌŋ | *pret.* y *p.p.irreg.* de **swing.**

sycamore | 'sɪkmɔː | *s.c.* BOT. sicomoro.

sycophantic | ˌsɪkəʊ'fæntɪk | *adj.* obsequioso, adulador, servil.

syllable | 'sɪləbl | *s.c.* **1** sílaba. || **2 in words of one –,** simple y llanamente, muy claramente.

syllabus | 'sɪləbəs | *s.c.* programa de estudios (de un curso).

sylvan | 'sɪlvən | *adj.* (lit.) selvático, silvestre, arbolado.

symbiosis | ˌsɪmbɪ'əʊsɪs | *s.i.* BIOL. simbiosis.

symbiotic | ˌsɪmbaɪ'ɒtɪk | *adj.* simbiótico.

symbol | sɪmbl | *s.c.* **[– (of)]** símbolo.

symbolic | sɪmbɒlɪk | *adj.* simbólico.

symbolically | sɪm'bɒlɪkəlɪ | *adj.* simbólicamente.

symbolise V. **symbolize.**

symbolism | 'sɪmbəlɪzəm | *s.i.* simbolismo.

symbolize | 'sɪmbəlaɪz | (brit. **symbolise**) *v.t.* simbolizar, representar, encarnar.

symmetrical | sɪ'metrɪkl | (también **symmetric**) *adj.* simétrico.

symmetrically | sɪ'metrɪkəlɪ | *adv.* simétricamente.

symmetry | 'sɪmɪtrɪ | *s.i.* simetría.

sympathetic | ˌsɪmpə'θetɪk | *adj.* **1** amable, compasivo. **2 [– (to/towards)]** comprensivo, solidario. **3** simpático, agradable, encantador. **4** simpático (un nervio, la tinta).

sympathetically | ˌsɪmpə'θetɪkəlɪ | *adv.* **1** compasivamente, amablemente. **2** comprensivamente.

sympathize | 'sɪmpəθaɪz | (brit. **sympathise**) *v.i.* **[to – (with)]** **1** compadecerse, condolerse. **2** simpatizar, identificarse, solidarizarse, congeniar.

sympathizer | 'sɪmpəθaɪzər | *s.c.* simpatizante, partidario.

sympathy | 'sɪmpəθɪ | *s.i.* **1** lástima, pena, compasión, condolencia. **2** comprensión, simpatía, afinidad. || **3 in –,** en solidaridad.

symphonic | sɪm'fɒnɪk | *adj.* sinfónico.

symphony | 'sɪmfənɪ | *s.c.* **1** MUS. sinfonía. **2** (fig.) sinfonía, armonía. || **3 – orchestra,** orquesta sinfónica.

symposia | sɪm'pəʊzjə | *pl.* de **symposium.**

symposium | sɪm'pəʊzɪəm | [*pl.* **symposia**] *s.c.* **1** simposio, congreso. **2** recolección, recopilación (de artículos, ensayos).

symptom | 'sɪmptəm | *s.c.* **1** síntoma. **2** indicio, indicación, señal.

symptomatic | ˌsɪmptə'mætɪk | *adj.* sintomático, indicativo.

synagogue | 'sɪnəgɒg | | 'sɪnəgɑːg | *s.c.* sinagoga.

sync | sɪŋk | (también **synch**) *s.i.* (fam.) **1** sincronía. || **2 out of –,** sin sincronización, desincronizados.

synchronization | ˌsɪŋkrənaɪ'zeɪʃn | | ˌsɪŋkrənə'zeɪʃn | *s.i.* sincronización.

synchronize | 'sɪŋkrənaɪz | (brit. **synchronise**) *v.t.* e *i.* (form.) sincronizar(se), ir sincrónicamente, coincidir.

syncopate | 'sɪŋkəpeɪt | *v.t.* MUS. sincopar.

syncopation | ˌsɪŋkə'peɪʃn | *s.i.* MUS. síncopa.

syncope | 'sɪŋkəpɪ | *s.i.* **1** MED. síncope. **2** MUS. síncopa.

syndicate | 'sɪndɪkɪt | *s.c.* **1** [– + *v.sing./pl.*] agrupación, grupo (de empresas para fines comunes). **2** agencia periodística. || *v.t.* **3** vender por agencia, distribuir por agencia (un artículo, una fotografía). || *v.t.* e *i.* **4** agruparse, asociar(se) (varias empresas). **5** FIN. concertar (un préstamo).

syndrome | 'sɪndrəʊm | *s.c.* síndrome.

synod | 'sɪnəd | *s.c.* REL. sínodo.

synonym | 'sɪnənɪm | *s.c.* sinónimo.

synonymous | sɪ'nɒnɪməs | | sɪ'nɑːnɪməs | *adj.* **[– (with)]** sinónimo.

synopsis | sɪ'nɒpsɪs | | sɪ'nɑːpsɪs | [*pl.* **synopses**] *s.c.* sinopsis, resumen, síntesis.

synopses | sɪ'nɒpsiːz | *pl.* de **synopsis.**

syntactic | sɪn'tæktɪk | (también **syntactical**) *adj.* GRAM. sintáctico.

syntactical | sɪn'tæktɪkl | V. **syntactic.**

syntax | 'sɪntæks | *s.i.* GRAM. sintaxis.

syntheses | 'sɪnɵɪsiːz | *pl.* de **synthesis.**

synthesis | 'sɪnɵəsɪs | [*pl.* **syntheses**] *s.i.* **[– (of)]** **1** síntesis, resumen, sinopsis. **2** QUIM. síntesis. || *s.c.* **3** síntesis, amalgama.

synthesize | 'sɪnɵəsaɪz | (brit.) **synthesise** *v.t.* sintetizar.

synthesizer | 'sɪnɵɪsaɪzər | *s.c.* MUS. sintetizador.

synthetic | sɪn'ɵetɪk | *adj.* **1** sintético. **2** MUS. electrónico. **3** artificial, poco natural (de carácter).

syphilis | 'sɪfɪlɪs | *s.i.* MED. sífilis.

syphon | 'saɪfn | V. **siphon.**

Syrian | 'sɪrɪən | *adj.* **1** sirio. || *s.c.* **2** sirio.

syringe | 'sɪrɪndʒ | *s.c.* **1** jeringuilla, jeringa. || *v.t.* **2** hacer un lavado, inyectar una lavativa (con jeringuilla).

syrup | 'sɪrəp | *s.i.* almíbar, jarabe.

syrupy | 'sɪrəpɪ | | 'sɜːrəpɪ | *adj.* **1** almibarado. **2** (fig.) almibarado, dulzón, sentimentaloide.

system | 'sɪstəm | *s.c.* **1** sistema, organización, método: *you have to get familiar with the school system = tienes que familiarizarte con el sistema escolar.* **2** MED. organismo. **3** INF. sistema (operativo). **4** ELEC. instalación. || *s.i.* **5** sistema, método, orden, disciplina. || *s.sing.* **6** (fam.) POL. sistema.

systematic | ˌsɪstɪ'mætɪk | *adj.* sistemático, metódico.

systematically | ˌsɪstɪ'mætɪklɪ | *adv.* sistemáticamente.

systematize | 'sɪstɪmətaɪz | (brit. **systematise**) *v.t.* sistematizar, ordenar, organizar.

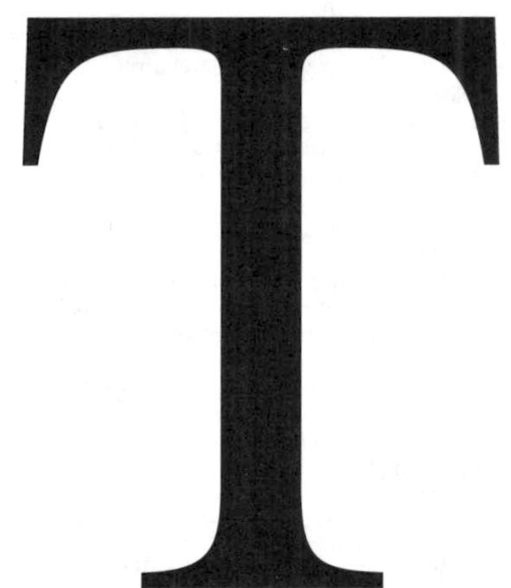

t, T | ti: | *s.c.* **1** t, T (vigésima letra del alfabeto inglés). || **2 to cross the t's,** ser preciso, meticuloso; dar los últimos toques. || **3 to a –/to a tee, a)** así es (él, ella), es típico de (él, ella): *that behaviour is him to a T = ese es su modo de actuar;* **b)** ser el vivo retrato de, ser clavado a; **c)** que ni pintado, ni hecho a medida, de perlas: *it suits me to a T! = ¡es que ni hecho a la medida!*
OBS. Se usa como abreviatura de palabras o nombres que empiezan por "t": *T.V., T.O., T.N.T., ton, tense;* para designar objetos con esa forma o sección: *a T branch, a T joint, a T rail.*

ta | tɑ: | (fam. y brit.) gracias.

tab | tæb | *s.c.* **1** etiqueta, trilla, letrero, rótulo. **2** anilla, lengÅeta (para abrir una lata de bebida). **3** (fam.) tabulador. || **4 to keep the tabs on someone/something,** vigilar, mantener controlado, llevar cuenta de. **5 to pick up the –,** hacerse cargo del gasto, correr con los gastos.

Tabasco | tə'bæskəʊ | *s.i.* GAST. Tabasco (marca registrada).

tabby | 'tæbɪ | *s.c.* gato atigrado.

tabernacle | 'tæbənækl | *s.c.* REL. **1** tabernáculo, sanctasanctórum. **2** tabernáculo, sagrario, trono. **3** templo, tabernáculo, (lugar de culto de los noconformistas y mormones).

table | 'teɪbl | *s.c.* **1** mesa: *Dining table, Kitchen table.* **2** comensales: *the whole table laughed at his jokes = todos los comensales se rieron de sus bromas.* **3** alimento, comida: *they always enjoy a good table = siempre disfrutan con una buena comida.* **4** gráfico, tabla, cuadro (de datos): *there's a table of contents at the end of the book = hay un gráfico con los contenidos al final del libro.* **5** tabla de multiplicar. || *adj.* **6** de mesa: *a table lamp = una lámpara de sobremesa.* || *v.t.* **7** proponer, hacer una propuesta, plantear un tema, poner sobre la mesa. **8** (EE.UU.) posponer, archivar, aparcar, retrasar. **9 to drink someone under the table,** ganar a beber a alguien. **10 on the –, a)** (brit.) (poner) sobre el tapete; **b)** (EE.UU.) quedar sobre el tapete. **11 – manners,** modales en la mesa, formas de comportamiento en la mesa. **12 – wine,** vino de mesa, común, corriente. **13 to turn the tables on someone,** invertir la situación, darle la vuelta a la tortilla, volver las tornas. **14 under the –, a)** bajo mano, soborno; **b)** borracho como una cuba.

tableau | 'tæbləʊ | *s.c.* [pl. **tableaux/tableaus**] **1** retablo, paso, representación teatral. **2** escena: *tableau vivant = escena viviente.* **3** cuadro, espectáculo: *what a tableau! = ¡vaya escenita!*

table centre | 'tæɪbl'sentər | * *s.c.* centro de mesa.

tablecloth | 'teɪblklɒɵ | *s.c.* mantel, tapete.

table d'hôte | ˌtɑ:bl'dəʊt | *s.c.* menú del día, menú turístico.

table-knife | 'teɪblnaɪf | *s.c.* cuchillo de mesa.

table-lamp | 'teɪbllæmp | *s.c.* lámpara de mesa.

table-land | 'teɪbllænd | *s.c.* altiplano, meseta.

table-linen | 'teɪbllɪnɪn | *s.i.* mantelería.

table-mat | 'teɪblmæt | *s.c.* salvamantel.

tablespoon | 'teɪblspu:n | *s.c.* cucharón.

tablespoonful | 'teɪblspu:nfʊl | *s.c.* cucharada.

tablet | 'tæblɪt | *s.c.* **1** MED. tableta, píldora, pastilla, comprimido. **2** pastilla, barra: *a tablet of soap, of chocolate.* **3** HIST. tablilla: *laws were effected in cuneiform on a clay tablet = se promulgaba la ley en escritura cuneiforme en tablillas de arcilla.* **4** lápida, placa conmemorativa.

table-tennis | 'teɪblˌtenɪs | *s.i.* tenis de mesa, ping-pong.

tableware | 'teɪblweər | *s.i.* servicio de mesa.

tabloid | 'tæblɔɪd | *s.c.* **1** tabloide, periódico de formato reducido. **2** sustancia medicamentosa. **3** comprimido, tableta.

taboo | tə'bu: | *s.c.* **1** creencia, tabú: *taboos connected with animals are part of totemism = los tabús que tienen que ver con animales son parte del animismo.* **2** (fig.) prohibición por prejuicios o superstición, tabú. || *adj.* **3** tabú, prohibido, intocable.

tabular | 'tæbjʊlər | *adj.* tabular, en forma de tabla o cuadro.

tabulate | 'tæbjʊleɪt | *v.t.* tabular; poner, esquematizar, resumir, organizar en forma de cuadro o tabla.

tabulation | ˌtæbjʊ'leɪʃn | *s.i.* tabulación.

tabulator | 'tæbjʊleɪtər | *s.c.* tabulador. V. **tab.**

tachograph | 'tækəgrɑ:f | *s.c.* tacógrafo, tacómetro.

tacit | 'tæsɪt | *adj.* tácito, sobreentendido, callado, no verbal o expreso: *a tacit agreement = acuerdo tácito.*

tacitely | 'tæsɪtlɪ | *adv.* tácitamente, de manera tácita.

taciturn | 'tæsɪtə:n | *adj.* taciturno, callado, reticente, silencioso.

taciturnity | ˌtæsɪ'tə:nɪtɪ | *s.i.* taciturnidad.

tack | tæk | *s.c.* **1** tachuela, chincheta. **2** hilván, pespunte, puntada. **3** curso oblicuo, de bolina. **4** modo, método, aproximación, línea de acción; táctica, política. || *v.t.* e *i.* **5** tachonar, clavetear, sujetar con chinchetas. **6** hilvanar, hacer un pespunte. **7** ir de bolina, navegar en zigzag. || **8 on the right/wrong –,** seguir la actuación correcta/equivocada, ir por el buen/mal camino. **9 – something on to something,** (fam.) agregar, incluir, colar de rondón, añadir un cargo extra.

tackle | 'tækl | *s.i.* **1** MAR. aparejo, jarcia de labor. **2** DEP. equipo de deporte, aparejo, aperos, instrumental: *fishing tackle.* **3** presa, blocaje, bloqueo. || *v.* **4** abordar, emprender, atreverse, hacer frente a, vérselas con, arreglárselas con, enfrentarse a. **5** regatear, blocar, interceptar. **6** agarrar y detener, apresar. || **7 – somebody about/over something,** hablar con alguien (de un asunto espinoso).

tacky | 'tækɪ | *adj.* **1** (brit.) pegajoso, húmedo: *the varnish is still tacky = la laca todavía está pegajosa.* **2** (EE.UU., vulg.) raído, viejo, gastado, ajado. V. **shabby.**

tact | tækt | *s.i.* tacto, delicadeza, discreción, prudencia, diplomacia.

tactful | 'tækfl | *adj.* cuidadoso, prudente, discreto, diplomático.

tactfully | 'tækfəlɪ | *adv.* cuidadosamente, prudentemente, discretamente, delicadamente.

tactic | 'tæktɪk | *s.i.* **1** táctica, procedimiento, estratagema. **2** MIL. **tactics,** táctica: *tactics are always largely governed by weapons = la táctica está en su mayor parte regida por las armas.*

tactical | 'tæktɪkl | *adj.* **1** táctico, planificado, estratégico: *it was a clear tactical error = fue un claro error táctico.* **2** MIL. táctico, de corto alcance: *tactical missile.* || **3 – voting,** voto táctico, voto útil.

tactically | 'tæktɪklɪ | *adv.* tácticamente.

tactician | 'tæk'tɪʃn | *s.c.* **1** táctico, estratega. **2** experto.

tactile | 'tæktaɪl | (EE.UU.) | 'tæktəl | *adj.* táctil.

tactless | 'tæktlɪs | *adj.* **1** falto de tacto, insensible, indiscreto. **2** improcedente, impertinente: *a tactless question.*

tactlessly | 'tæktlɪslɪ | *adv.* de modo indiscreto, sin tacto.

tactlessness | 'tæktlɪsnɪs | *s.i.* indiscreción, carencia de tacto.

tadpole | 'tædpaul | *s.c.* renacuajo.

taffeta | 'tæfɪtə | *s.i.* tafetán.

tag | tæg | *s.c.* **1** etiqueta, marbete, letrero: *a price tag = el precio.* **2** herrete, protector al extremo de un cabo. **3** placa de identificación. **4** cliché, cita, frase hecha, lugar común. **5** andrajo, trapo, harapo. V. **rag.** **6** tu-la-llevas (juego infantil). || *v.t.* e *i.* **[tagged]** **7** marcar (un animal mediante una placa). **8** seguir de cerca, pisar los talones. **9** etiquetar.**10** calificar de, tachar de, motejar, colgar el sambenito de: *he was tagged as incompetent = se le colgó el sambenito de incompetente.* || **11 to – along,** proceder con calma. **12 – on,** añadir, agregar. **13 – question,** coletilla, muletilla.

OBS. Las **question tags** se añaden al final de una oración aseverativa bien para confirmar una información, usando entonación ascendente; o con una mera función enfática, entonación descendente. Se usa forma negativa con oraciones afirmativas, y viceversa; si la oración contiene un verbo auxiliar éste se usa en la coletilla, en caso contrario se usa **do.** Hay algunos casos especiales, a saber: **a) I am** tiene como **tag question aren't I; b)** los imperativos usan **will, would, can** o **could; c)** los indefinidos referidos a persona aparecen como **they,** los referidos a cosas, como **it; d)** si el indefinido es negativo la coletilla está en forma afirmativa.

tail | teɪl | *s.c.* **1** ZOOL. cola, rabo, aleta caudal. **2** estela, cola (de un cometa, de un avión, etc.), extremo final, trasera, faldones de la camisa. **3** vigilante. **4** chaqué, frac. **5** cruz (en una moneda). V. **head or tails.** **6** trasero, culo. || *v.t.* **7** seguir de cerca, pisar los talones a, vigilar. || *v.i.* **8** cortar los tallos de una fruta. **9** disminuir progresivamente, desaparecer lentamente, agotarse (las excusas): *as we drove off, the music tailed away = a medida que nos alejábamos.* || **10 head or tails,** V. **head.** **11 one's – between one's legs,** con el rabo entre las piernas, derrotado y humillado, avergonzado. **12 the – is wagging the dog,** estar al capricho del último comparsa, el último mono está moviendo los hilos de la situación. **13 to turn –,** volver la espalda, huir.

tailback | 'teɪlbæk | *s.c.* atasco de tráfico, fila del atasco.

tail end | ˌteɪl'end | *s.sing.* la parte final.

tailgate | 'teɪlgeɪt | *s.c.* (EE.UU.) puerta de carga y descarga, portón del maletero, puerta trasera, quinta puerta.

taillight | 'teɪllaɪt | *s.c.* pilotos traseros, luces traseras.

tail-off | 'teɪlɔf | *s.sing.* bajada, descenso, retroceso, depreciación.

tailor | 'teɪlər | *s.c.* **1** sastre. **2 the – makes the man,** el hábito hace al monje. || *v.t.* **3** ajustar, adaptar, confeccionar, remodelar: *the contract will be tailored to meet your requirements = el contrato se hará según sus deseos.* || **4 the tailor's,** la sastrería.

tailored | teɪləd | *adj.* de sastre, a medida, que ajusta bien.

tailor-made | 'teɪləmaɪd | *adj.* **[to, for]** **1** adaptado a, a la medida de, a propósito, hecho especial para. **2** hecho a medida.

tailpipe | 'teɪlpaɪp | *s.c.* tubo de escape.

tailwind | 'teɪlwɪnd | *s.c.* viento de cola.

taint | teɪnt | *s.sing.* **1** mancha, estigma, rasgo, vena de: *a taint of madness = una vena de locura.* || *v.t.* **2** contaminar, corromper, viciar, inficionar. **3** estropear, hechar a perder.

tainted | 'teɪntɪd | *adj.* **1** pasado: *tainted meat.* || **2** contaminado, teñido, viciado, corrompido, marcado por: *a behaviour tainted with selfishness = una conducta marcada por el egoísmo.*

taintless | 'teɪntlɪs | *adj.* puro, sin mancha, incólume.

take | teɪk | *v.t.* [*pret.irreg.* **took,** *p.p.irreg.* **taken**] **1** acompañar, llevar (a alguien a algún sitio): *I took the children to the cinema yesterday = ayer llevé a los niños al cine.* **2** transportar, coger, llevar (algo a algún sitio): *will you take these chairs to the garden, please? = llevad estas sillas al jardín, por favor.* **3** coger, agarrar, asir: *he took her by the hand = la cogió de la mano.* **4** sacar: *she took a handkerchief out of her handbag = sacó un pañuelo del bolso; the idea was taken from a well-known novel = tomaron la idea de una conocida novela.* **5** llevarse, coger, retirar: *who's taken my pen? = ¿quién ha cogido mi pluma?* **6** restar, sustraer. **7** ganar, conquistar, capturar, tomar, comer (en un juego de tablero: ajedrez...): *the town was taken by the enemy = la ciudad fue tomada por el enemigo.* **8** aceptar, admitir, recibir, seguir (un consejo): *take my advice = sigue mi consejo; will you take a cheque? = ¿acepta un cheque?* **9** caber, tener lugar o cabida para. **10** aceptar, sufrir, soportar, pasar por: *I won't take that behaviour any more = no aceptaré más ese comportamiento.* **11** tomar, tomarse, reaccionar: *she took it badly = se lo tomó a mal.* **12** entender, interpretar, tomar, asumir, suponer, considerar. **13** alquilar, tomar. **14** elegir, comprar. **15** tomar, consumir, comer, beber: *I always take coffee after lunch.* **16** llevar, durar, costar (en tiempo): *it takes me half an hour to get there.* **17** necesitar, ser necesario, requerir: *it took six men to move it = se necesitaron seis hombres para moverlo.* **18** presentarse, hacer un examen; obtener, conseguir, sacar una calificación; estudiar, hacer, seguir: *she took a course in pottery = hizo un curso de cerámica.* **19** anotar, tomar notas, escribir. **20** subirse (a un medio de transporte); tomar, coger (una dirección, un medio de transporte). **21** tomar, hacer, sacar (una fotografía). **22** oficiar (un servicio religioso), dar (una clase), hacerse cargo de: *who takes you for History? = ¿quién os da Historia?* **23** actuar, tomar, resultar eficaz, servir: *the vaccination took = la vacuna hizo su efecto.* **24** picar (un pez). **25** dar, tomar, echar (más un sustantivo que exprese una acción): *take a shower, a walk, a look,* V. **have.** **26** jurar, hacer voto: *they took an oath = hicieron juramento.* **27** usar, ocupar: *take a seat = siéntese.* **28** atraer, encantar, deleitar, interesar: *the novel really took my fancy = la novela me encantó.* **29** hacer el amor. **30** GRAM. regir, llevar: *it takes a singular verb = concuerda en singular.* || *s.c.* **31** toma, vista, escena, secuencia (en una película). **32** parte, porción, cantidad, participación: *he wanted a bigger take.* || **33 hard to –,** demasiado, difícil de aguantar: *his points of view on the subject are rather hard to take = sus opiniones sobre el asunto me parecen difíciles de aguantar.* **34 I – it,** imagino, supongo, entiendo que, doy por sabido que. **35 – my word/– my word for it/– it from me,** ¡palabra!, ¡lo que yo te diga!, ¡créeme, que es así! **36 to – aback,** sorprender mucho, sorprenderse: *I was taken aback at his suggestion = su sugerencia me sorprendió.* **37 to –**

account of/to – something into account, tener en cuenta, tomar en consideración. **38 to – after,** parecerse (a los miembros de la propia familia): *she takes after her father in voice and manner = tiene la voz y las maneras de su padre.* **39 to – against,** estar en contra, ponerse en contra. **40 to – a lot out of somebody/to – it out of somebody,** exigir demasiado, ser mucho esfuerzo. **41 to – apart, a)** desarmar, desmontar, desensamblar; **b)** desmenuzar, analizar cuidadosamente. **42 to – away, a)** hacer perder, retirar, quitar; **b)** restar, sustraer; **c)** restar méritos, quitar importancia; **d)** llevarse a uno a algún sitio, arrestar, encarcelar, encerrar. **43 to – back, a)** devolver, admitir devoluciones; **b)** retirar (lo dicho), disculparse (por un comentario); **c)** recordar, traer a la memoria. **44 to – care,** tener cuidado, prestar atención, cuidar, cuidarse. **45 to – down, a)** bajar; quitar, retirar (de un lugar alto); desmontar (una estructura): *I wonder when that scaffolding is being taken down = me pregunto cuando van a quitar ese andamio;* **b)** tomar por escrito, anotar. **46 to – in, a)** recibir, admitir, aceptar a alguien como huésped; **b)** engañar, hacer creer: *a gullible person can be easily taken in = un simplón es fácil de engañar;* **c)** entender, captar: *she saw it but did not really take it in = lo vio pero no entendió de qué iba;* **d)** encoger, ajustar, meter: *after his illness all his clothes had to be taken in = tras su enfermedad hubieron de ajustarle toda la ropa.* **47 to – off, a)** despegar (un avión); marcharse repentinamente; (fig.) tener éxito; **b)** deducir o retener dinero; reducir, cancelar un servicio; retirar de cartel, quitar un espectáculo; **c)** quitarse (una prenda de vestir); **d)** imitar. **48 to – on, a)** aceptar, asumir (una responsabilidad, un trabajo, un reto, una apuesta); **b)** desarrollar, cambiar: *that word has taken on a new meaning = esa palabra ha cambiado de significado;* **c)** cargar (pasajeros, combustible); **d)** enfadarse, tomárselo a pecho: *I don't know why you take on so about it = no entiendo por qué te lo tomas tan a pecho.* **49 to – out, a)** sacar (algo de algún sitio); obtener, conseguir (un permiso, un préstamo...); **b)** tomarla con: *if you have had a trying day at the office it is not fair to take it out on your wife = si has tenido un día difícil en la oficina, no es justo que lo pague tu mujer;* **c)** invitar a salir, sacar a pasear, acompañar. **50 to – over, a)** apoderarse de, tomar el control de, asaltar; **b)** hacerse responsable de, suceder en un cargo. **51 to – part in,** tomar parte en, participar en. **52 to – place,** tener lugar, ocurrir, suceder. **53 to – somebody by surprise,** sorprender, tomar por sorpresa. **54 to – somebody down a peg or two,** bajarle los humos a alguien, hacer variar a alguien su exagerada opinión de sí mismo. **55 to – somebody out of oneself,** hacer olvidarse de, hacer sentir bien, sentirse transportado. **56 to – something as read,** aceptar, dar por hecho, tomar literalmente. **57 to – something seriously,** tomarse algo en serio. **58 to – to,** gustar, aficionarse, interesarse: *everyone takes to him immediately = enseguida le cae bien a todo el mundo.* **59 to – up, a)** interesarse por, decidirse por; **b)** profundizar en un tema; **c)** coger un trabajo, aceptar una oferta; **d)** ocupar (un lugar), reclamar (tiempo, energías...), adoptar una actitud; **e)** continuar (una tarea donde fue interrumpida por otros); **f)** afincarse, tomar resistencia, instalarse. **60 to – up on,** tomar la palabra, aceptar (una oferta o invitación); pedir explicaciones. **61 to – upon,** actuar bajo la propia responsabilidad. **62 to – up with, a)** comenzar una amistad; **b)** ocupar completamente.

takeaway | 'teɪkˌəweɪ | *s.c.* **1** (brit.) comida para llevar, preparada. **2** establecimiento que prepara ese tipo de comida.

take-home pay | 'teɪkhəʊmpeɪ | *s.i.* salario neto, líquido a percibir (en una nómina), salario en mano, en limpio.

taken | teɪkən | *p.p.* **1** de **take.** || *adj.* **2 [with]** interesado, atraído, encantado con (una idea, una persona, un proyecto).

takeoff | 'teɪkɒf | *s.i.* **1** despegue (de un avión). **2** (fig.) despegue (de un proyecto, de una situación). || *s.c.* **3 [– of]** imitación de.

takeover | 'teɪkˌəʊvər | *s.c.* e *i.* **1** absorción, compra, toma de control (de una compañía, de acciones). **2** toma del poder: *a military takeover = golpe militar.* **3** toma, ocupación (de un organismo).

taker | 'teɪkər | *s.c.* tomador (de una oferta, de una transacción).

take-up | 'teɪkʌp | *s.i.* tasa de cambio, tasa de compra.

takings | 'teɪkɪŋz | *s.pl.* ingresos, la caja.

talc | tælk | *s.i.* (fam.) V. **talcum powder.**

talcum powder | 'tælkəmˌpaʊdər | *s.i.* polvos de talco.

tale | teɪl | *s.c.* **1** cuento, narración breve, historia. **2** cuento, mentira, chisme. || **3 to live to tell the –,** vivir para contarlo, poder contarlo. **4 to tell a –,** decir algo, significar algo: *such a silence tells a tale = tanto silencio es muy significativo.* **5 to tell its own –,** hablar por sí solo. **6 to tell tales, a)** andarse con cuentos, contar chismes, historias: *don't tell tales out of school = no saques los trapos sucios a relucir;* **b)** contar mentiras, contar cuentos: *she was always telling her parents tales = siempre iba con historias a sus padres.*

talent | 'tælənt | *s.i.* **1** talento, aptitud, inteligencia natural. **2** talento (personas). **3** (vulg.) tía buena. **4** HIST. talento (moneda). || *s.c.* **5 talent scout/talent spotter,** buscador de talentos, cazatalentos.

talented | 'tæləntɪd | *adj.* dotado, de talento, talentoso.

talisman | 'tælɪzmən | *s.c.* talismán.

talk | tɔːk | *v.i.* **1** hablar, comunicar, charlar, contar, confiarse a, discutir: *we must talk seriously about that = debemos discutir eso seriamente.* **2 [to/with]** hablar (con alguien). **3 [of/about]** decir, hablar de, mencionar: *talk of the devil and he is sure to appear = en nombrando al ruin de Roma, asoma.* **4** cantar, soltar la lengua, irse de la lengua, largar. **5** dar que hablar, murmurar, cotillear. || *v.t.* **6** hablar, conocer: *he talks Greek = sabe griego.* **7** hablar de, tratar un tema: *they were talking politics = hablaban de política.* || *s.i.* **8** conversación, tema, comentario. **9** ganas de hablar, ganas de darse aires, pompas de jabón. || *s.c.* **10 [on/about]** ponencia, charla, conferencia. || **11 – about...,** como para hablar de que: *talk about Spanish people being fond of eating, the English party beat all I had ever seen = y es como para que digan que los españoles son buenos comedores, el grupo inglés batió todas las marcas.* **12 now you are talking,** ahora empezamos a entendernos, eso ya es más razonable, eso ya es hablar, eso ya es otro cantar. **13 – show,** programa de entrevistas, programa-coloquio. **14 talking of...,** hablando de, a propósito de. **15 talks,** negociaciones, conversaciones. **16 to – back,** responder, contestar de malos modos, replicar. **17 to – down, a)** hacer callar, no dejar hablar; **b)** dar instrucciones, dirigir el aterrizaje de un avión; **c)** ponerse al nivel de (un niño...); hablar con superioridad. **18 to – into,** persuadir, convencer (de que haga algo). **19 to – nonsense /rubbish,** decir tonterías. **20 to – out,** discutir a fondo. **21 to – out of,** disuadir, convencer (de que no se haga algo). **22 to – over,** tratar, hablar un tema. **23 to – round,** darle la vuelta, persuadir, convencer. **24 to – sense,** hablar con sentido, decir algo sensato. **25 to – up,** alabar. **26 you can talk,** ¡mira quién fue a hablar!, ¡pues anda que tú!

talkative | 'tɔːkətɪv | *adj.* hablador, locuaz, que le gusta hablar.

talker | 'tɔːkər | *s.c.* **1** hablador, conversador: *what a poor talker he is! = ¡qué mal hablador es!* **2** charlatán, embaucador: *don't pay any attention to his words, he's just a talker = no hagas caso de lo que dice, no es más que un charlatán.*

talkie | tɔːkɪ | *s.c.* (arc.) película sonora.

talking book | 'tɔːkɪŋbʊk | *s.c.* libro grabado en un cassette.

talking-point | 'tɔːkɪŋpɔɪnt | *s.c.* tema de conversación.

tall | tɔːl | *adj.* **1** alto: *he was quite a tall man = era un hombre muy alto.* **2** de alto, altura, estatura: *how tall is he? = ¿qué estatura tiene?/¿cuánto mide?* || **3 – order,** trabajo difícil, petición excesiva. **4 – story,** un cuento, historia difícil de creer, una de indios. **5 talk –,** jactarse, fanfarronear. **6 to walk –,** caminar con la cabeza bien alta, sentirse orgulloso.

tallish | tɔːlɪʃ | *adj.* (fam.) alto, más bien alto, tirando a alto.

tallow | 'tæləʊ | *s.i.* sebo, grasa animal.

tally | 'tælɪ | *s.c.* **1** cuenta, puntuación, marcador; registro de puntuaciones, cantidades: *i'll keep the tally = ya apunto yo.* **2** etiqueta, letrero. V. **tag.** || *v.i.* **3 [with]** ajustarse a, concordar con, corresponder a, casar con: *the amounts tallied = las cantidades coincidían.* **2** calcular, contar.

Talmud | 'tælmʊd | *s.sing.* Talmud.

talon | 'tælən | *s.c.* ZOOL. garra, garras (de un ave de presa).

tamarind | 'tæmərɪnd | *s.c.* BOT. tamarindo.

tamarisk | 'tæmərɪsk | *s.c.* BOT. tamarisco.

tambour | 'tæmbʊər | *s.c.* **1** ARQ., MUS. tambor. **2** bastidor para bordar. **3** tapa, persiana, cierre articulado de un escritorio.

tambourine | ˌtæmbə'riːn | *s.c.* pandereta.

tame | teɪm | *adj.* **1** domado, domesticado, amansado (un animal). **2** sumiso, condescendiente, complaciente, sin espíritu, dócil (una persona). **3** apagado, aburrido, soso, insulso: *it was a tame play = la obra fue insulsa.* || *v.t.* **4** domar, domesticar, amansar, entrenar. **5** someter, conquistar, apoderarse, ocupar, civilizar: *the wasteland was tamed in a short time = en poco tiempo se ocuparon las tierras baldías.* **6** controlar, contener, dominar, domeñar, reprimir (pasiones, sentimientos...).

tamely | teɪmlɪ | *adv.* sumisamente, dócilmente.

tameness | teɪmnɪs | *s.i.* mansedumbre, insipidez.

tamer | teɪmər | *s.c.* domador: *elephant-tamer = domador de elefantes.*

tammy | tæmɪ | *s.c.* bonete, boina de lana con un pompón.

tam o'shanter | ˌtæmə'ʃæntər | *s.c.* boina escocesa.

tamp | tæmp | *v.t.* **[down] 1** apisonar, retacar, aplastar, asentar. **2** cubrir (un explosivo para aumentar su efecto).

tamper | 'tæmpər | *v.t.* **1** interferir, interceptar, entrometerse, modificar. **2** (fig.) sobornar, (un jurado, un testigo...).

tampon | 'tæmpən | *s.c.* tampón (elemento de higiene femenina).

tan | tæn | *s.sing.* **1** bronceado, moreno. || *adj.* **2** tostado, marrón amarillento. **3** bronceado, moreno. V. **suntanned.** || *v.i.* **4** broncearse, ponerse moreno, tostarse. **5** curtir. || **6 to – somebody's hide,** zurrar la badana, zurrar de lo lindo, dar una paliza.

tandem | 'tændəm | *s.c.* **1** tándem (bicicleta). || **2 in –,** a la vez, juntos, simultáneo. **3 in – with,** en cooperación, conjuntamente, al alimón. **4 to ride –,** circular uno detrás de otro, ir a la zaga.

tandoori | tændʊrɪ | *s.i.* tanduri, forma india de cocinar carne (sobre carbón vegetal en horno de arcilla).

tang | tæŋ | *s.c.sing.* **1** olor penetrante, característico, vaharada: *the tang of the sea = olor a mar.* **2** sabor fuerte, picante.

tangent | 'tændʒənt | *s.c.* **1** GEOM. tangente. || **2 to go off a –,** salirse, escaparse por la tangente, eludir un tema.

tangential | tæn'dʒenʃl | *adj.* tangencial.

tangentially | tæn'dʒenʃəlɪ | *adv.* tangencialmente.

tangerine | tændʒe'rɪːn | *s.c.* mandarina.

tangible | 'tændʒəbl | *adj.* **1** tangible, palpable, que puede ser tocado, percibible por el tacto. **2** material, concreto, claro, real. | **3 – assets,** bienes muebles e inmuebles, propiedades materiales, elementos patrimoniales físicos.

tangibly | 'tændʒeblɪ | *adv.* tangiblemente, obviamente.

tangle | 'tæŋgl | *s.c.* **1** enredo, rebullo, lío, nudo, maraña. **2** caos, confusión, desorden. **3** escaramuza, enfrentamiento. || *v.i.* **4** enredar, enmarañar, liar. **5** (pasiva) enredarse, engancharse; estar o quedar atrapado: *the hedges were tangled with wild rose bushes = los setos estaban entrelazados con rosales silvestres.* **6** discutir, pelearse con. || **7 to – up,** arrugar, arrebullar, arrebujar, enredar.

tangled | 'tæŋgld | *adj.* **1** enredado, enmarañado, liado: *tangled hair.* **2** complicado, liado, confuso.

tango | 'tæŋgəʊ | *s.c.* **1** tango. || *v.i.* **2** bailar el tango.

tangy | 'tæŋgɪ | **[tangier, tangiest]** *adj.* ardiente, picante, penetrante: *a tangly flavour = un sabor fuerte.*

tank | tæŋk | *s.c.* **1** tanque, cisterna, depósito de combustible, contenedor, aljibe. **2** MIL. carro de combate, tanque de guerra. || *v.* **3** llenar el depósito, repostar. || **4 – truk,** (EE.UU.) camión cisterna de gran tonelaje. **5 – wagon,** vagón cisterna. V. **septic tank.**

tankard | 'tæŋkəd | *s.c.* pichel.

tanked up | 'tæŋktʌp | *adj.* **1** borracho, beodo. || **2 to be/get – on,** estar borracho de/emborracharse con.

tanker | 'tæŋkər | *s.c.* **1** avión o barco cisterna: *an oil tanker = petrolero.* **2** camión cisterna. V. **tank 4.**

tanner | 'tænər | *s.c.* **1** curtidor. **2** (fam.) moneda de seis peniques.

tannery | 'tænərɪ | **[tanneries]** *s.c.* tenería, curtiduría.

tannic acid | 'tænɪkˌæsɪd | *s.i.* ácido tánico.

tannin | 'tænɪn | *s.i.* tanino.

tansy | 'tænzɪ | *s.c.* BOT. atanasia, hierba de Santa María, tanaceto, hierba lombriguera. || *s.i.* **2** MED. hojas de estas plantas.

tantalize | 'tæntəlaɪz | (también **tantalise**) *v.i.* atormentar, tentar, incitar, martirizar, hacer sufrir el suplicio de Tántalo.

tantalizing | 'tæntəlaɪzɪŋ | *adj.* atormentador, seductor, tentador.

tantalizingly | 'tæntəlaɪzɪŋlɪ | *adv.* atormentadoramente, tentadoramente: *the fulfilment of his hopes was tantalizingly close = tocaba la realización de sus esperanzas con la punta de los dedos.*

tantamount | 'tæntəmaʊnt | *adj.* **1** equivalente, igual. || **2 to be –,** equivaler, suponer, venir a ser.

tantrum | 'tæntrəm | *s.c.* rabieta, berrinche, pataleta.

Taoism | 'tɑːəʊɪsm | *s.i.* taoísmo.

tap | tæp | *s.c.* **1** grifo, espita. **2** ELEC. derivación, escucha (telefónica). **3** golpe, golpecito, palmada. || *s.i.* **4** zapateado. V. **tap-dancing.** || *v.t.* **5** golpear repetidamente, dar palmadas; tamborilear, llevar el ritmo (golpeando con los dedos, o los pies). **6** aprovechar, explotar (recursos). **7** sonsacar (información), dar un sablazo. **8** intervenir, interceptar, poner una escucha telefónica. **9** sangrar (un árbol). || **10 on –, a)** en el grifo, de barril: *beer on tap;* **b)** a mano, al alcance, listo, disponible. **11 taps,** MIL. (EE.UU.) toque de silencio. **12 tapped out,** sin blanca, ni un duro. **12 to – out,** vaciar, sacar dando golpes; enviar (mensajes en morse), escribir a máquina.

tap-dancer | 'tæpdɑːnsər | *s.c.* bailarín de zapateado.

tap-dancing | 'tæpdɑːnsɪŋ | *s.i.* zapateado.

tape | teɪp | *s.c.* **1** cassette. **2** grabación magnetofónica. **3** cinta, tirilla. **4** (sing.) cinta de llegada (en una carrera). || *s.i.* **5** cinta magnetofónica, de cassette; de tela: *twenty meters of green tape = veinte metros de cinta verde.* **6** cinta adhesiva, esparadrapo. || *v.t.* **7** grabar, impresionar. **8** pegar, adherir, sujetar con cinta adhesiva. | **9 – deck,** grabadora, consola de grabación, pletina. **10** TEC. **– drive,** lector de cintas de ordenador. **11 to be taped,** comprender perfectamente. **12 to have someone/something taped,** tener algo bajo control, tener calado a alguien.

tape-measure | 'teɪpˌmeʒər | *s.c.* cinta métrica.

taper | 'teɪpər | *s.c.* **1** vela, cirio, bujía. **2** disminución, estrechamiento gradual. || *v.i.* **2** estrecharse, reducirse, disminuir de anchura. || **3 to – off,** estrecharse, disminuir, reducirse, decrecer, extinguirse.

tape-record | 'teɪprɪkɔːd | *v.t.* grabar en cinta.

tape-recorder | 'teɪprɪˌkɔːdər | *s.c.* magnetófono, grabadora.

tape-recording | 'teɪprɪˌkɔːdɪŋ | *s.c.* grabación.

tapestry | 'tæpɪstrɪ | *s.c.* e *i.* **1** tapiz. **2** tapicería. **3** (fig.) cuadro, imagen, visión: *the book is a tapestry of life in a big city = el libro es un abigarrado cuadro de la vida en una gran ciudad.*

tapestried | 'tæpɪstrɪd | *adj.* **1** tapizado, cubierto o decorado con tapices: *tapestried walls.* **2** representado, bordado en un tapiz.

tapeworm | 'teɪpwɜːm | *s.c.* tenia, solitaria.

tapioca | tæpɪ'əʊkə | *s.i.* tapioca.

tapir | 'teɪpər | *s.c.* ZOOL. tapir.

tappet | 'tæpɪt | *s.c.* MEC. alzaválvulas, varilla de levantamiento, varilla de empuje, pulsador.

tar | tɑːr | *s.i.* **1** alquitrán, brea. || *v.t.* **[tarred]** **2** alquitranar, embrear. || **3 a touch of the tar-brush,** con algún rasgo negroide, con algo de sangre negra. **4 jack tar,** marinero. **5 to – and feather,** emplumar.
taramasalata | 'tærəməsə'lɑːtə | *s.i.* GAST. crema de marisco.
tarantula | tə'ræntjʊlə | *s.c.* ZOOL. tarántula.
tardily | 'tɑːdɪlɪ | *adv.* tarde, con retraso, con tardanza, tardíamente.
tardiness | 'tɑːdɪnɪs | *s.i.* tardanza, retraso, lentitud.
tardy | 'tɑːdɪ | *adj.* **1** tardío, lento, tardo, atrasado. **2** (EE.UU.) tarde.
target | 'tɑːgɪt | *s.c.* **1** blanco, diana, objetivo. **2** objetivo, meta: *production target = objetivo de producción.* **3** objeto, blanco: *he became the target of scorn = se convirtió en blanco del desprecio.* **4** HIST. rodela, escudo redondo. || **5 on –,** en el punto de mira, en el rumbo previsto.
tariff | 'tærɪf | *s.c.* tarifa, arancel.
tarmac | 'tɑːmæk | *s.i.* (también **tarmacadam**) **1** alquitrán. **2** pista de aterrizaje. || *v.t.* **3** alquitranar.
tarmacadam | 'tɑːmækədəm | V. **tarmac.**
tarn | tɑːn | *s.c.* lago de montaña, ibón.
tarnish | 'tɑːnɪʃ | *v.i.* **1** empañar, manchar, deslustrar, enturbiar, deslucir, volverse opaco (un espejo), opacar, perder el brillo. **2** (fig.) manchar, dañar (una reputación). || *s.c.* e *i.* **3** mancha, mácula, opacidad, pátina.
tarnished | 'tɑːnɪʃt | *adj.* empañado, manchado, dañado, borroso.
tarot | 'tærəʊ | *s.sing.* **[the –]** el Tarot.
tarpaulin | tɑː'pɔːlɪn | *s.c.* e *i.* lona, lona alquitranada, tela asfáltica.
tarragon | 'tærəgən | *s.i.* BOT. estragón.
tarred | tɑːd | *adj.* **1** alquitranado, cubierto de alquitrán. V. **tarry.** || **2 – with the same brush,** cortado con el mismo patrón, de tal palo tal astilla, ser tal para cual.
tarry | 'tærɪ | *v.t.* **1** quedarse, retrasarse, dilatar. || | 'tɑːrɪ | *adj.* **2** alquitranado, embreado. V. **tarred.**
tart | tɑːt | *adj.* **1** ácido, agrio, de sabor fuerte. **2** sarcástico, agresivo, cáustico, desabrido, hiriente. || *s.c.* e *i.* **3** pastel (de frutas), tarta: *apple tart = tarta de manzanas.* **4** (vulg.) coqueta, casquivana, ligera de cascos, furcia. || **5 to – oneself/something up,** emperifollar(se), periponer(se), acicalar(se), arreglar(se), adecentar (un local).
tartan | 'tɑːtən | *s.i.* **1** tartán (tela con un diseño de cuadros). || *s.c.* **2** tartán (diseño emblemático de un determinado clan escocés).
tartar | 'tɑːtər | *s.i.* **1** sarro, tártaro. || *s.c.* **2** tirano, fiera, arpía. || **3 – sauce,** salsa tártara. **4 to catch a –,** toparse con la horma de su zapato.
tartly | 'tɑːtlɪ | *adv.* ásperamente.
task | tɑːsk | *s.c.* **1** tarea, trabajo, faena. **2** misión, cometido, deber. || **3 to take someone to –,** llamar la atención, reprender.
task-force | 'tɑːskfɔːs | *s.c.* **1** MIL. fuerza de choque, destacamento, grupo especial de operaciones. **2** comisión (para solucionar un problema concreto).
taskmaster | 'tɑːsk,mɑːstər | | 'tæsk,mæstər | [*f.* **taskmistress**] *s.c.* **1** amo, capataz, supervisor, encargado. || **2 a hard –,** severo, tirano: *my teacher is a hard taskmaster = mi profesor es un tirano.*
taskmistress | 'tɑːsk,mɪstrɪs | *s.c.* supervisora, encargada.
tassel | 'tæsl | *s.c.* borla.
tasselled | 'tæsld | (EE.UU. **taseled**) *adj.* con borlas.
taste | teɪst | *s.i.* **1** gusto (sentido). **2** gusto estético. || *s.c.* **2** sabor, gusto. **3** muestra, degustación, pizca, sorbo. **4** experiencia, conocimiento. **5 [for]** interés por, gusto por, afición, inclinación. || *v.t.* **6** probar, saborear, degustar, catar. **7** experimentar, saborear, conocer, sufrir. || *v.i.* **8** saber, tener sabor a, notar un sabor. || **9 an acquired –,** gusto adquirido. **10 a – of one's own medicine,** un poco de la propia medicina. **11 each to his own –,** sobre gustos no hay nada escrito. **12 in bad –,** con mucho gusto, de buen gusto. **13 in good –,** con mal gusto, de mal gusto. **14 leave a bad/ bitter/nasty – in the/someone's mouth,** dejar mal sabor de boca. **15 tastes differ/ there is no accounting for –,** sobre gustos no hay nada escrito. **16 to –,** al gusto, a voluntad: *add salt to taste = añadir sal al gusto.*
taste-bud | 'teɪst,bʌd | *s.c.* ANAT. papila gustativa.
tasteful | 'teɪstfʊl | *adj.* elegante, de buen gusto.
tastefully | 'teɪstfəlɪ | *adv.* con buen gusto, con elegancia, elegantemente: *tastefully furnished flat = un piso muy bien amueblado.*
tasteless | 'teɪstlɪs | *adj.* **1** sin sabor, insípido, soso. **2** de mal gusto, sin gusto, vulgar, pobre, poco atractivo.
tastelessly | 'teɪstlɪslɪ | *adv.* con mal gusto, sosamente.
tastelessness | 'teɪstlɪsnɪs | *s.i.* falta de gusto, mal gusto.
taster | teɪstər | *s.c.* **1** catador. **2** catavino, instrumento para catar.
tastily | 'teɪstɪlɪ | *adv.* sabrosamente, apetitosamente.
tastiness | 'teɪstɪnɪs | *s.i.* sabor, gusto.
tasting | 'teɪstɪŋ | *s.c.* **1** degustación: *a wine tasting* || *adj.* **2** de sabor: *sweet-tasting = de sabor dulce.*
tasty | 'teɪstɪ | *adj.* **1** sabroso, apetitoso. **2** (vulg.) sexualmente atractivo, apetecible, apetitoso.
tat | tæt | *s.i.* **1** trastos, chismes, cachivaches, quincalla, morralla. || *v.i.* **2** hacer encaje. **3 tit for –.** V. **tit.**
ta-ta | tæ'tɑː | (fam. y brit.) adiós, abur, hasta luego.
tattered | 'tætəd | *adj.* **1** andrajoso, harapiento, en jirones. **2** desastrado, desaliñado, descuidado. **3** ajetreado, baqueteado.
tatters | 'tætəz | *s.i.* **1** andrajos, jirones, harapos. || **2 in tatters, a)** desgarrado, andrajoso, harapiento; **b)** frustrado, dañado, destrozado, hecho trizas. **3 to be in rags and –,** ir desastrado, desaliñado.
tattle, V. **tittle-tattle.**
tattler | 'tætlər | *s.c.* **1** charlatán, chismoso, hablador. || **2 avoid a questioner, for he's also a –,** no dar tres cuartos al pregonero.
tattoo | tə'tuː | *s.c.* **1** MIL. retreta, desfile militar. **2** redoble, repique de tambor. **3** tatuaje. || *v.t.* **4** tatuar. **5** tamborilear. **6** redoblar, repicar. || **7 beath the devil's –,** tamborilear con los dedos.
tattooed | tə'tuːd | *adj.* tatuado, con tatuajes.
tattooist | tə'tuːɪst | *s.c.* tatuador.
tatty | 'tætɪ | *adj.* ajado, raído, gastado, desaseado, en mal estado.
taught | tɔːt | *pret.* y *p.p.irreg.* de **teach.**
taunt | tɔːnt | *s.c.* **1** burla, insulto, mofa, pulla, sarcasmo. || *v.t.* **2** mofarse, insultar. || **3 – with,** echar en cara, escarnecer: *they taunted him with cowardice = le echaron en cara su cobardía.*
taut | tɔːt | *adj.* tenso, tirante.
tauten | 'tɔːtən | *v.t.* e *i.* tensar.
tautly | 'tɔːtɪ | *adv.* con tensión, tensamente.
tautness | 'tɔːtnɪs | *s.i.* tensión, tirantez.
tautological | tɔːtə'lɒdʒɪkl | *adj.* tautológico.
tautologically | tɔːtə'lɒdʒɪklɪ | *adv.* tautológicamente.
tautology | tɔː'tɒlədʒɪ | *s.i.* (desp.) **1** tautología, redundancia, repetición, retórica: *that villanous tautology of lawyers = esa vil retórica de los abogados.* || *s.c.* **2** pleonasmo, redundancia, tautología.
tavern | 'tævən | *s.c.* taberna, venta.
tawdrily | 'tɔːdrɪlɪ | *adv.* ostentosamente, con cursilería.
tawdriness | 'tɔːdrɪnɪs | *s.i.* ostentosidad, indignidad, vulgaridad.
tawdry | 'tɔːdrɪ | *adj.* **1** cursi, de relumbrón, oropel, ostentoso: *tawdry jewellry = bisutería.* **2** indigno, vergonzoso.
tawny | 'tɔːnɪ | *adj.* leonado.
tax | tæks | *s.c.* **1** impuesto, contribución, tributo, arancel, derecho. **2** carga, esfuerzo: *a tax on one's patience = una prueba para la paciencia.* || *adj.* **3** tributario. || *v.t.* **4** imponer contribuciones, poner impuestos, gravar, tasar. **5** cargar, abrumar, poner a prueba: *he's taxing my patience = está poniendo a prueba mi paciencia.* **6** acusar, tachar de, interrogar: *I was taxed with negligence = se me acusó de negligente.* || **7 – avoidance,** desgravación fiscal. **8 – disc,** (brit.) pegatina del impuesto de circulación. **9 – evasion,** evasión fiscal. **10 – haven,** paraíso fiscal. **11 – relief,** desgravación fiscal. **12 to – with, a)** cargar el sambenito, cargar con las culpas, actuar; **b)** tener una grave responsabilidad. **13 – year,** año fiscal.

taxable | 'tæksəbl | *adj.* imponible, impositivo, sujeto a impuestos: *taxable income = renta imponible.*
taxation | tæk'seɪʃn | *s.i.* **1** impuestos: *direct taxation = impuestos directos.* **2 – system,** sistema tributario.
tax-collector | 'tækskəˌlektər | (también **taxman**) *s.c.* recaudador de impuestos, inspector de hacienda.
tax-deductible | 'tæksdɪˌdʌktɪbl | *adj.* desgravable.
tax-free | ˌtæks'frɪ | *adj.* libre de impuestos.
taxi | 'tæksɪ | *s.c.* **1** taxi. || *v.t.* e *i.* **2** llevar en taxi, rodar un avión por la pista. || **3 – rank/– stand,** parada de taxis.
taxicab | 'tæksɪkæb | *s.c.* taxi.
taxidermist | 'tæksɪdəːmɪst | *s.c.* taxidermista.
taxidermy | 'tæksɪdəːmɪ | *s.i.* taxidermia.
taxi-driver | 'tæksɪˌdraɪvər | *s.c.* taxista.
taxi-man | 'tæksɪˌmən | *s.c.* taxista.
taxing | 'tæksɪŋ | *adj.* difícil, complejo, que exige gran esfuerzo.
taxonomy | tæk'sɒnəmɪ | *s.i.* taxonomía.
taxman | 'tæksmən | *s.c.* V. **tax collector.**
taxpayer | 'tæksˌpeɪər | *s.c.* contribuyente.
TB | ˌtɪː'bɪː | *s.i.* tuberculosis.
tea | tɪː | *s.i.* **1** té, infusión: *camomile tea = infusión de manzanilla.* **2** planta del té. **3** merienda, cena: *high tea = merienda cena.* || **4 for all the – in China,** por todo el oro del mundo, por nada del mundo. **5 not one's cup of –,** no es plato de mi gusto.
tea-bag | 'tiːbæg | *s.c.* bolsa de té.
tea-break | 'tɪːbreɪk | *s.c.* hora del té, descanso para el té.
tea-caddy | 'tiːˌkædɪ | [*pl.* **tea-caddies**] *s.c.* bote para el té.
teacake | 'tɪːkeɪk | *s.c.* bollo de té, pastel de té.
teach | tɪːtʃ | [*pret.* y *p.p.irreg.* **taught**] *v.t.* **1** enseñar, dar clases. || *v.i.* **2** enseñar, dedicarse a la enseñanza, ser profesor. || **3 to – someone a lesson,** (fig.) darle a uno una lección. **4 that'll – you,** ¡así irá aprendiendo!, ¡a ver si así aprendes!
teachable | 'tɪːtʃəbl | *adj.* educable, fácil de enseñar, que aprende fácilmente.
teacher | 'tɪːtʃər | *s.c.* profesor, enseñante, maestro, preceptor: *experience is the best teacher = la experiencia es el mejor maestro.*
tea-chest | 'tɪːtʃest | *s.c.* caja para el té.
teach-in | 'tɪːtʃɪn | *s.c.* reunión, seminario.
teaching | 'tɪːtʃɪŋ | *s.i.* **1** enseñanza. || *adj.* **2** docente, pedagógico. || **3 – hospital,** clínico, hospital universitario. **4 – practice,** período de prácticas, práctica docente, docencia.
teachings | tɪːtʃɪŋz | *s.i.* enseñanzas, doctrinas.
teacloth | 'tɪːkɒθ | (también **tea-towel**) *s.c.* paño de cocina.
tea-cosy | 'tɪːkəuzɪ | *s.c.* (también **tea-cozy**) cubretetera.
teacup | 'tɪːkʌp | *s.c.* **1** taza de té. || **2 a storm in a –,** ahogarse en un vaso de agua.
teak | tɪːk | *s.i.* teca, madera de teca.
teal | tɪːl | *s.c.* ZOOL. cerceta.
tea-leaf | 'tɪːlɪːf | [*pl.* **tea-leaves**] *s.i.* hoja de té, poso.
team | tɪːm | *s.c.* **1** equipo, grupo: *a way team = equipo visitante; home team = equipo de casa.* **2** yunta, tronco, tiro. || *adj.* **3** de equipo, en equipo, en colaboración. || *v.t.* **4** trabajar en equipo, combinar, acompañar. **5** enganchar, uncir. || **6 – spirit,** espíritu de equipo, compañerismo. **7 to – up, a)** agruparse, formar equipo, trabajar en equipo; **b)** conjuntar, ir bien, encajar, combinar: *the tie and the shirt team up very well with your socks = la corbata y la camisa combinan con tus calcetines.*
team-mate | 'tɪːmˌmeɪt | *s.c.* compañero de equipo.
teamster | 'tɪːmstər | *s.c.* camionero.
teamwork | 'tɪːmwəːk | *s.i.* labor de equipo, trabajo en equipo, colaboración, cooperación.
tea-party | 'tɪːˌpɑːtɪ | *s.i.* reunión, tertulia con té.
teapot | 'tɪːpɒt | *s.c.* tetera.
tear | tɪər | , | teər | *s.i.* **1** rasgón, desgarro, rotura. **2** lágrima. || *v.t.* [*pret.irreg.* **tore,** *p.p.irreg.* **torn**]. **3** rasgar, desgarrar, romper, arrancar. || **4 to – around/ about,** dar vueltas sin parar, correr como un loco, moverse continuamente. **5 to – across, a)** rasgar, partir en dos; **b)** cruzar rápidamente. **6 to – along,** correr a toda velocidad a lo largo de. **7 to – apart, a)** separar, apartar, revolver, registrar, desmontar; **b)** desgarrar, echar por tierra; **c)** reprender, regañar, discutir. **8 to – at, a)** afectar, impresionar; **b)** abrir impacientemente, rasgar un envoltorio. **9 to – away, a)** quitar violentamente, arrancar con violencia; **b)** marcharse precipitadamente, salir disparado; **c)** separarse de, apartarse de, librarse de; **d)** descubrir, desenmascarar. **10 to be bored to tears,** muerto de aburrimiento. **11 to be in tears,** llorar. **12 to – between,** dudar entre dos opciones, estar en duda entre dos cosas. **13 to burst into tears,** romper a llorar, estallar en llanto. **14 to – down, a)** correr por; **b)** derribar, demoler; **c)** desmontar, desarmar; **d)** difamar, denigrar. **15 to – from,** apartar violentamente, separar sin contemplaciones. **16 to – in, a)** partir en; **b)** entrar precipitadamente. **17 to – loose,** liberarse, soltarse, escapar. **18 to – off, a)** arrancar, quitar desgarrando; **b)** marcharse apresuradamente, salir disparado; **c)** mostrar la falsedad de; **d)** escribir improvisando. **19 to – one's hair out,** estar nervioso, mesarse los cabellos. **20 to – open,** abrir desgarrando. **21 to – out, a)** arrancar; **b)** marcharse a toda prisa. **22 to shed bitter tears,** derramar lágrimas amargas. **23 to – someone off a strip,** recriminar, regañar, echar la bronca. **24 to – someone's heart out,** conmover, impresionar, afectar. **25 to – someone to pieces/shreds,** criticar despiadadamente, destrozar, ir a por todas. **26 to – up, a)** destrozar, arrancar, hacer pedazos, despedazar; **b)** anular, incumplir, romper (un contrato, acuerdo...); **c)** sacar de raíz, desarraigar.
tearaway | 'teərəweɪ | *s.c.* (brit.) rebelde, gamberro, marginado.
teardrop | 'tɪədrɒp | *s.c.* lágrima.
tear-duct | 'tɪədʌkt | *s.c.* conducto lacrimal.
tearful | 'tɪəfʊl | *adj.* lloroso, lacrimoso, quejumbroso.
tearfully | 'tɪəfəlɪ | *adv.* llorosamente.
tear-gas | 'tɪəgæs | *s.i.* MIL. **1** gas lacrimógeno. || **2 – bomb,** bomba de gas lacrimógeno, bomba lacrimógena.
tearing | 'teərɪŋ | *adj.* **1** desgarrador, lacerante, violento. **2 to be in a – hurry,** tener una prisa loca.
tear-jerker | 'tɪəˌdʒəːkər | *s.c.* obra sentimentaloide, lacrimógena.
tea-room | 'tɪːrʊːm | *s.c.* salón de té.
tease | tɪːz | *s.c.* **1** bromista, burlón, guasón. **2** broma, chanza, pulla. **3** provocativa, provocadora, insinuante. || *v.i.* **4** burlarse, mofarse, reírse, meterse con. **5** incitar, insinuarse, provocar, poner los dientes largos. **6** cardar, perchar, cepillar, cepillar a contrapelo. || **7 to – out,** desenredar, separar, peinar, desenmarañar. **8 to – something out of someone,** entresacar, sonsacar, tirar de la lengua, hacer hablar.
teasel | 'tɪːzl | *s.c.* **1** BOT. cardencha. || *v.i.* **2** cardar.
teaser | 'tɪːzər | *s.c.* **1** pregunta difícil, con truco; problema difícil; rompecabezas. **2** burlón, bromista, guasón.
tea-service | 'tɪːˌsəːvɪs | *s.c.* servicio de té.
tea-set | 'tɪːset | *s.c.* V. **tea-service.**
tea-shop | 'tɪːʃɒp | *s.c.* (brit.) salón de té.
teasing | 'tɪːzɪŋ | *s.i.* **1** bromas pesadas, burlas, guasa. || *adj.* **2** bromista, burlón, de broma, de guasa.
teasingly | 'tɪːzɪŋlɪ | *adv.* en broma, bromeando.
Teasmaid | 'tɪːsmeɪd | *s.c.* tetera con temporizador.
teaspoon | 'tɪːspuːn | *s.c.* cucharilla de té.
tea-strainer | 'tɪːˌstreɪnər | *s.c.* colador de té.
teat | tɪːt | *s.c.* **1** ANAT. pezón, tetilla, teta. **2** tetina de biberón, boquilla, pezón de goma.
tea-table | 'tɪːˌteɪbl | *s.c.* mesa de té.
teatime | 'tɪːtaɪm | *s.i.* hora del té.
tea-towel | 'tɪːtauəl | *s.c.* paño de cocina, paño de secar.
teazel V. **teasel.**
teazle V. **teasel.**
tech | tek | *s.c.* (fam.) colegio técnico.
technical | teknɪkl | *adj.* **1** técnico: *technical language = lenguaje especializado.* || **2 – college,** escuela técnica.
technicality | ˌteknɪ'kælɪtɪ | *s.c.* **1** tecnicismo, aspecto técnico, tecnicidad. || **2**

technicalities, detalles técnicos, procesos técnicos.
technically | 'teknɪkəlɪ | *adv.* técnicamente, estrictamente, en teoría, desde un punto de vista técnico.
technician | tek'nɪʃn | *s.c.* técnico, especialista.
technique | tek'nɪ:k | *s.c.* e *i.* **[– of/for]** técnica de/para, habilidad de/para: *modern techniques of pottery = las técnicas modernas de alfarería.*
technocracy | tek'nɒkrəsɪ | *s.c.* tecnocracia, élite.
technocrat | 'teknəukræt | *s.c.* tecnócrata.
technocratic | teknə'krætɪk | *adj.* tecnocrático.
technological | ˌteknə'lɒdʒɪkl | *adj.* tecnológico, técnico.
technologically | ˌteknə'lɒdʒɪkəlɪ | *adv.* tecnológicamente.
technologist | tek'nɒlədʒɪst | *s.c.* tecnólogo.
technology | tek'nɒlədʒɪ | *s.i.* tecnología.
Ted | ted | *s.c.* V. **Teddy-boy.**
teddy | 'tedɪ | *s.c.* osito, osito de peluche.
teddy-bear | 'tedɪbeər | *s.c.* V. **teddy.**
Teddy-boy | 'tedɪbɔɪ | *s.c.* (brit. años 50) gamberro, roquero.
tedious | 'tɪ:dɪəs | *adj.* tedioso, aburrido.
tediously | 'tɪ:dɪəslɪ | *adv.* tediosamente, aburridamente.
tediousness | 'tɪ:dɪəsnɪs | *s.i.* V. **tedium.**
tedium | 'tɪ:dɪəm | *s.i.* tedio, aburrimiento, fastidio, repugnancia.
tee | tɪ: | *s.c.* **1** tee, soporte de la pelota de golf. **2** área del campo de golf donde se inicia el juego, salida. || **3 – off, a)** empezar, comenzar (en golf); **b)** ponerse en marcha, iniciar una actividad; **c) [– on]** (EE.UU.) quejarse, expresar enfado: *they are always teeing off on the same subject = siempre están quejándose de lo mismo.* **4 teed off,** (EE.UU.) (vulg.) enfadado, cabreado. **5 – up, a)** colocar la pelota en posición de salida (golf); **b)** organizar, arreglar: *if everything has been teed up, let's go = si está todo en orden, vámonos.*
teem | tɪ:m | *v.i.* **1** abundar, pulular, hormiguear, hervir, rebosar. || **2 – down,** caer en cantidad: *the rain is teeming down = está diluviando.* **3 – in,** abundar, haber en cantidad: *good game teems in this area = hay buena caza en esta zona.* **4 – with, a)** abundar, estar lleno de: *the place was teeming with flies = el sitio hervía de moscas;* **b)** diluviar, llover a cántaros: *it's teeming with rain = caen chuzos de punta.*
teeming | tɪ:mɪŋ | *adj.* abundante, que bulle, que hierve, plagado, abarrotado, lleno de, numerosísimo: *teeming streets = calles abarrotadas.*
teenage | 'tɪ:nˌeɪdʒə | (también, **teenaged**) *adj.* joven, adolescente: *teenage fashion = moda joven.*
teenaged | 'tɪ:nˌeɪdʒə | V. **teenage.**
teenager | 'tɪ:nˌeɪdʒər | *s.c.* joven, adolescente.
teens | 'ti:nz | *s.i.* **1** adolescencia. || **2 to be in one's –,** estar en la adolescencia, entre los 13 y los 19 años.
teensy | 'tɪ:nzɪ | *adj.* V. **teeny.**
teensy-weensy | 'tɪ:nzɪˌwɪ:nzɪ | *adj.* V. **teeny.**
teeny | 'tɪ:nɪ | (también **teensy, teeny-weeny, teensy-weensy**) *adj.* (fam.) pequeño, diminuto, chiquitín, minúsculo. V. **tiny.**
teeny-weeny | tɪ:nɪwɪ:nɪ | *adj.* V. **teeny.**
teeny-bopper | 'tɪ:nɪˌbɒpər | *s.c.* (fam.) jovencita, joven adolescente.
tee-shirt V. **T-shirt.**
teeter | 'tɪ:tər | *s.c.* **1** balanceo, vaivén. || **2** *v.i.* balancearse, oscilar, vacilar, titubear. **3** (EE.UU.) columpiarse. || **to – on the edge/on the brink,** bambolearse, tambalearse al borde del abismo.
teeth | ti:θ | *pl.irreg.* de **tooth.**
teethe | tɪ:ð | *v.i.* echar los dientes, dentar, endentecer.
teething | tɪ:ðɪŋ | *s.i.* **1** dentición. || **2 – ring,** mordedor, chupador. **3 – troubles,** problemas iniciales: *they had some teething troubles with the matter = tuvieron problemas para hincarle el diente al asunto.*
teetotal | ti:'təutl | (EE.UU.) | 'ti:təutl | *adj.* **1** abstemio, antialcohol. **2** (EE.UU. y fam.) total, completo.
teetotaler | tɪ:'təutlər | V. **teetotaller.**
teetotalism | tɪ:'təuʃɪzəm | *s.i.* abstinencia.
teetotaller | tɪ:'təutlər | (EE.UU. **teetotaler**) *s.c.* abstemio.
TEFL | tefl | **(Teaching English as a Foreign Language)** *s.i.* enseñanza del inglés como lengua extranjera. V. **TESL.**
telecommunications | 'telɪkəˌmju: | | nɪ'keɪʃn | *s.i.* telecomunicaciones, comunicación a distancia.
telegram | 'telɪgræm | *s.c.* e *i.* telegrama: *let them know by telegram = házselo saber por telegrama.*
telegraph | 'tælɪgrɑ:f | | 'telɪgræf | *s.c.* e *i.* **1** telégrafo. || *adj.* **2** telegráfico. || *v.i.* **3** telegrafiar. || **4 bush –,** radio macuto.
telegrapher | tɪ'legrəfər | *s.c.* telegrafista.
telegraphese | ˌtelɪgrɑ:fɪ:z | *s.i.* estilo telegráfico.
telegraphic | ˌtelɪ'græfɪk | *adj.* telegráfico.
telegraphist | tɪ'legrəfɪst | *s.c.* telegrafista.
telegraphically | ˌtelɪ'græfɪkəlɪ | *adv.* telegráficamente.
telegraphy | tɪ'legrəfɪ | *s.i.* telegrafía.
telemetry | tɪ'lemɪtrɪ | *s.i.* telemetría.
teleology | ˌtelɪ'ɒlədʒɪ | *s.i.* teleología.
telepathic | ˌtelɪ'pæθɪk | *adj.* telepático.
telepathically | ˌtelɪ'pæθɪkəlɪ | *adv.* telepáticamente.
telepathy | tɪ'lepəθɪ | *s.i.* telepatía.
telephone | 'telɪfəun | *s.c.* e *i.* (también fam., **phone**) **1** teléfono. || *adj.* **2** telefónico, de teléfono. || *v.i.* **3** telefonear, llamar por teléfono. || **4 to be on the –,** tener teléfono, estar al teléfono. **5 – book/directory,** guía de teléfonos. **6 – booth/box,** cabina telefónica, locutorio. **7 – call,** llamada telefónica. **8 – exchange,** central telefónica, central de teléfonos, centralita. **9 – in,** comunicar por teléfono: *he telephoned the news in on his way to the hospital = telefoneó para decirlo de camino al hospital.* **10 – number,** número de teléfono. **11 – operator,** telefonista.
telephonist | tɪ'lefənɪst | *s.c.* telefonista.
telephoto lens | ˌtelɪ'fəutəu'lenz | *s.c.* teleobjetivo, objetivo telefotográfico.
teleprinter | 'telɪˌprɪntər | *s.c.* teletipo, teleimpresor.
telescope | 'telɪskəup | *s.c.* **1** telescopio catalejo. || *v.t.* **2** encajar, enchufar; resumir, abreviar, condensar. || *v.i.* **3** encajarse, plegarse como un telescopio, empotrarse. || **4 – into,** abreviar, reducir, hacer caber, encajar, resumir, comprimir, condensar.
telescopic | ˌtelɪ'skɒpɪk | *adj.* telescópico.
teletype | 'telɪtaɪp | *s.c.* teletipo.
televise | 'telɪvaɪz | *v.t.* televisar.
television | 'telɪˌvɪʒn | *s.c.* e *i.* **1** televisión, televisor. || *adj.* **2** de televisión, televisivo. || **3 on –,** en la televisión. **4 – set,** aparato de televisión, televisor. **5 to watch –,** ver la televisión.
telex | 'teleks | *s.c.* **1** télex. || *v.i.* **2** enviar por télex.
tell | tel | [*pret.* y *p.p.irreg.* **told**] *v.t.* e *i.* **1** decir, contar, referir, narrar, informar, comunicar. **2** divulgar, revelar. **3** decir, anunciar, advertir, avisar. **4** indicar, marcar, mostrar, señalar. **5** ordenar, mandar, dirigir. **6** distinguir, diferenciar, identificar, conocer, ver, notar, reconocer. **7** saber, descubrir, deducir. **8** contar, numerar. **9** notarse, causar efecto, hacer mella, influir, dejarse notar: *words that tell = palabras que hacen mella.* || **10 all told,** en total, mirándolo bien, contando todo, todo incluido. **11 I – you/I can – you,** te lo aseguro. **12 I can't – you,** no encuentro palabras para decir. **13 I'll – you what,** ¿sabes el qué...? **14 I told you so,** ¡te lo dije! **15 – me another,** ¡vaya!, ¡ésta sí que es buena!, ¡venga ya! **16 time will –,** el tiempo dirá, si no al tiempo. **17 to – a joke,** contar un chiste. **18 to – a lie,** mentir, decir una mentira. **19 to – about, a)** denunciar, dar parte; **b)** contar, decir acerca de. **20 to – against,** tener algo en contra de alguien, obrar en contra, perjudicar: *your behaviour will tell against you = tu conducta se volverá contra ti.* **21 to – apart,** diferenciar, distinguir. **22 to – between,** diferenciar, distinguir entre (dos cosas). **23 to – by, a)** notarse por, distinguirse por, reconocer por: *if could be told by his face = se le notaba en la cara;* **b)** decir la hora por el reloj, saber la hora. **24 to – from, a)** V. **to – by a); b)** V. **to – apart. 25 to hear – of,** tener oído, tener noticias, se dice que. **26 to – of,** V. **to – about. 27 to – off, a)**

echar la bronca, reprender, reñir; **b)** contar (el número de); **c)** dar órdenes, informar de un cometido, designar para un trabajo. **28 to – on, a)** dejarse notar, afectar, hacer mella; **b)** informar, denunciar, acusar, chivarse. **29 to – over,** contar una y otra vez. **30 to – something to someone's face/teeth,** decírselo a la cara. **31 to – the time,** decir la hora, dar la hora. **32 to – the truth,** decir la verdad. **33 to – to,** decir, hacer saber. **34 to – with,** saber la verdad, saber a qué atenerse. **35 you never can –,** no se puede saber, puede ser tanto lo uno como lo otro, no se puede estar seguro. **36 you're telling me,** ¡qué me vas a decir!, ¡a mí me lo vas a decir!, ¡a quién se lo vas a contar!

teller | 'telər | *s.c.* **1** narrador. **2** cajero. **3** escrutador (persona que cuenta los votos en el Parlamento, en una elección, etc.).

telling | 'telɪŋ | *s.i.* **1** narración, relato, recuento (de votos). || *adj.* **2** eficaz, efectivo, contundente, fuerte, enérgico. **3** expresivo, revelador. || **4 a tale never loses in the –,** las historias son para contarlas. **5 that'd be –,** eso sería hablar de más. **6 there's no –,** no se puede saber, es imposible saberlo.

telling-off | 'telɪŋɒf | *s.c.* reprimenda, regañina, bronca.

telltale | 'telteɪl | *adj.* **1** revelador, delator, indicador. || *s.c.* **2** chivato, soplón, cuentista. **3** MAR. aciómetro.

telly | 'telɪ | *s.c.* e *i.* (fam.) tele, televisión, televisor.

temerity | tɪ'merɪtɪ | *s.i.* temeridad, atrevimiento, osadía.

temp | 'temp | *s.c.* **1** sustituto. || *v.i.* **2** hacer sustituciones.

temper | 'tempər | *s.c.* e *i.* **1** temple, genio, humor: *quick temper = genio vivo.* **2** cólera, rabia, furia, ira, mal genio. || *v.t.* **3** atemperar, moderar, suavizar, hacer tolerable. **4** ART. templar, afinar. || **5 to lose one's –/to fly into a –,** perder el control, salirse de sus casillas, enfadarse, montar en cólera. **6 to – with,** atemperar con, mitigar.

temperament | 'tempərəmənt | *s.c.* e *i.* carácter, disposición, temperamento, manera de ser, excitabilidad.

temperamental | ˌtempərə'mentl | *adj.* temperamental, caprichoso, excitable, inestable, inconstante.

temperamentally | ˌtempərə'mentəlɪ | *adv.* temperamentalmente, por temperamento, por naturaleza.

temperance | 'tempərəns | *s.i.* **1** moderación, templanza, sobriedad, autocontrol. **2** abstinencia de bebidas alcohólicas.

temperate | 'tempərɪt | *adj.* **1** GEOG. templado, moderado (clima). **2** autocontrolado, equilibrado, moderado, morigerado.

temperature | 'temprɪtʃər | *s.i.* **1** temperatura. || *s.c.* **2** fiebre, calentura, temperatura. **3** (fig.) ánimos, ambiente, temperatura: *they were trying to cool down the temperature in the meeting = intentaban apaciguar los ánimos en la reunión.* || **4 to run/have got a –,** tener fiebre. **5 to take someone's –,** tomar la temperatura, medir la fiebre.

tempest | 'tempɪst | *s.c.* tempestad.

tempestuous | tem'pestjuəs | *adj.* **1** (fig.) tempestuoso, agitado, violento: *a tempestuous life = una vida agitada.* **2** tormentoso, como de tormenta, tempestuoso (climatología).

tempestuously | tem'pestjuəslɪ | *adv.* tempestuosamente.

tempi | 'tempiː | V. **tempo.**

template | 'templɪt | *s.c.* plantilla, escantillón.

temple | 'templ | *s.c.* **1** REL. templo. **2** ANAT. sien, pulso. || **3 the Knights of the Temple,** caballeros templarios. || **4 The Temple,** Colegio de Abogados (en Londres).

tempo | 'tempəʊ | [plural **tempos /tempi**] *s.i.* **1** (fig.) tempo, ritmo, paso. **2** MUS. compás, tiempo, tempo, ritmo.

temporal | 'tempərəl | *adj.* **1** temporal, sometido al paso del tiempo. **2** temporal, coyuntural, perecedero, transitorio, limitado a un tiempo. **3** secular, laico, temporal. **4** ANAT. temporal.

temporarily | 'tempərɪlɪ | *adv.* temporalmente, transitoriamente.

temporary | 'tempərərɪ | *adj.* **1** provisional, temporal. **2** no permanente, transitorio, durante un cierto tiempo. **3** interino.

temporise V. **temporize.**

temporize | 'tempəraɪz | (también **temporise**) *v.i.* **1** contemporizar, acomodarse. **2** temporizar, ganar tiempo, dilatar, diferir, retrasar.

tempt | tempt | *v.t.* **1** tentar, atraer, seducir. **2** incitar, inducir, persuadir. **3** poner a prueba, tentar. || **4 to be/feel tempted,** sentirse tentado, tener ganas de. **5 to – from,** apartar, convencer para dejar. || **6 tempting fate/providence,** tentar a Dios, tentar al destino, tentar la suerte. **7 to – into,** inducir, ofrecer, convencer.

temptation | temp'teɪʃn | *s.i.* **1** tentación, incitación, atracción. || *s.c.* **2** impulso, tentación, aliciente, tendencia.

tempting | 'temptɪŋ | *adj.* tentador, atractivo, seductor, apetitoso.

temptingly | 'temptɪŋlɪ | *adv.* atractivamente, tentadoramente, de modo seductor, apetitosamente.

ten | ten | *adj.num.* **1** diez. || **2 tens,** decenas: *to count in tens = contar de diez en diez.* **3 – to one,** doble contra sencillo, muy probable.

tenable | 'tenəbl | *adj.* **1** defendible, plausible, sostenible. **2** ocupable, dispuesto para ser utilizado, tiempo de disfrute.

tenacious | tɪ'neɪʃəs | *adj.* **1** tenaz, firme, porfiado, tozudo, determinado, resuelto. **2** retentiva: *a tenacious memory = una muy buena memoria.* **3** enraizada, arraigada (una idea).

tenaciously | tɪ'neɪʃəslɪ | *adv.* tenazmente, porfiadamente.

tenacity | tɪ'næsɪtɪ | *s.i.* tenacidad, porfía.

tenancy | 'tenənsɪ | *s.i.* tenencia, arrendamiento, alquiler.

tenant | 'tenənt | *adj.* **1** arrendatario, inquilino, ocupante, habitante. || *v.t.* **2** alquilar, tener arrendada, pagar renta de alquiler.

tench | tentʃ | *s.c.* ZOOL. tenca.

tend | tend | *v.i.* **1** tender, inclinarse, tener tendencia, encaminarse, dirigirse, tirar a. || *v.t.* **2** atender, cuidar, ocuparse de, guardar, manejar. **3** cultivar. **4 I –,** estoy por, me siento inclinado a. **5** (EE.UU.) servir. **6 to – to,** cuidar de, cuidar a.

tendency | 'tendənsɪ | *s.i.* tendencia, inclinación, propensión.

tendentious | ten'denʃəs | *adj.* tendencioso.

tender | 'tendər | *s.c.* **1** oferta, propuesta, proposición. **2** cuidador, vigilante. **3** ténder (tren), bote de embarque y suministros. || *adj.* **3** tierno, blando, delicado, afectuoso, cariñoso, sensible, frágil, inmaduro. **4** dolorido, irritado: *the wound is still tender = la herida aún duele.* **5** escrupuloso, espinoso, difícil. || *v.t.* **6** ofrecer, presentar, dar; entregar. || *v.i.* **7** ofertar, hacer una oferta. || **legal –,** moneda de curso legal.

tenderfeet | 'tendəfiːt | *pl.* de **tenderfoot.**

tenderfoot | 'tendəfʊt | [*pl.* **tenderfoots/tenderfeet**] *s.c.* **1** principiante, inexperto, novato. **2** (EE.UU.) recién llegado.

tender-hearted | tendə'hɑːtɪd | *adj.* amable, cariñoso, tierno, de buen corazón, compasivo, bondadoso.

tenderise, V. **tenderize.**

tenderize | 'tendəraɪz | (también **tenderise**) *v.i.* macerar, ablandar.

tenderloin | 'tendəlɔɪŋ | *s.i.* filete.

tenderly | 'tendəlɪ | *adv.* tiernamente, con ternura.

tenderness | 'tendənɪs | *s.i.* ternura, afecto, delicadeza.

tendon | 'tendən | *s.c.* e *i.* ANAT. tendón.

tendril | 'tendrəl | *s.i.* **1** BOT. zarcillo, guedeja. **2** jirón, mechón: *the glossy tendrils of his hair = los brillantes mechones de su pelo.*

tenement | 'tenəmənt | *s.i.* **1** propiedad. || *s.c.* **2** vivienda, casa, piso: *tenement house = bloque de viviendas.*

tenet | 'tenɪt | *s.i.* principio, creencia, dogma, precepto.

tenner | 'tenər | *s.c.* (fam.) billete de diez libras.

tennis | 'tenɪs | *s.i.* **1** DEP. tenis. || **2 – ball,** pelota de tenis. **3 – court,** pista de tenis, cancha. **4 – elbow,** codo de tenista, sinovitis.

tenon | 'tenən | *s.c.* **1** TEC. espiga, almilla, macho, barbilla, muesca. || *v.i.* **2** espigar, ensamblar, entallar, machihembrar.

tenor | 'tenər | *s.c.* **1** curso, contenido, tenor, tono, significado general: *the tenor of the speech = el tono del dis-*

curso. **2** DER. copia conforme, plazo. **3** MUS. tenor. || *adj.* **4** de tenor, tenor: *a tenor saxophone = saxofón tenor.*

tenpence | 'tenpəns | *s.c.* diez peniques.

tenpin | 'tenpɪn | *s.i.* **1** bolos. || *s.c.* **2** bolo. V. **skittle.** || **3 – bowling,** (brit.)/**tenpins,** (EE.UU.) juego de bolos.

tense | tens | *adj.* **1** tenso, nervioso, ansioso. **2** rígido, tieso, tirante, tenso. **3** cargado, tenso, tirante. || *s.c.* **2** GRAM. tiempo verbal. || *v.t.* **3** poner en tensión, tensar, tesar. || **4 tensed up,** tenso, nervioso, en tensión.

tensely | 'tenslɪ | *adv.* tensamente.

tenseness | 'tensnɪs | *s.i.* tensión, ansiedad.

tensile | 'tensaɪl | *adj.* extensible, resistencia, tensor, de tensión.

tension | 'tenʃn | *s.i.* **1** FIS., MED. tensión, tracción, tirantez, voltaje. **2** incomodidad, conflicto, tensión, aprensión.

tent | tent | *s.c.* **1** tienda de campaña. **2** MED. mecha. || *v.t.* **3** alojar en tiendas, suministrar tiendas, cubrir con un toldo. || **4 to pitch one's –,** asentarse, poner casa, instalarse. **5 – peg,** clavija.

tentacle | 'tentəkl | *s.c.* **1** ZOOL. tentáculo. || **2 tentacles,** influencia, ascendiente, dominio, tentáculos.

tentative | 'tentətɪv | *adj.* **1** provisional, de tanteo, indeciso, experimental, vacilante. || *s.c.* **2** tentativa, intento, prueba.

tentatively | tentətɪvlɪ | *adv.* tentativamente, provisionalmente, dubitativamente, de tanteo, de prueba.

tenterhooks | 'tentəhuk | *s.c.* **1** gancho de bastidor. || **2 to be on –,** estar sobre ascuas, ansioso.

tenth | tenθ | *num.ord.* décimo, décima parte, diez (día).

tenuous | 'tenjuəs | *adj.* tenue, fino, sutil, insustancial, ligera.

tenuously | 'tenjuəslɪ | *adv.* de modo tenue, ligeramente.

tenure | 'tenjuər | *s.i.* **1** derecho, dominio. **2** tenencia, posesión, ocupación. **3** (EE.UU.) cargo vitalicio, plaza en propiedad.

tepee | 'tiːpiː | *s.c.* (EE.UU.) tipi, tienda india, wigwam.

tepid | 'tepɪd | *adj.* templado, tibio; poco entusiasmado.

tercentenary | ˌtəːsen'tiːnərɪ | (también **tercentennial**) *adj.* **1** de tres siglos. || *s.c.* **2** tricentenario.

tercentennial V. **tercentenary.**

term | təːm | *s.c.* **1** término, expresión, palabra. **2** sesión, temporada, período, trimestre. **3** período de validez, plazo, mandato, término, finalización, cumplimiento: *born before term = prematuro.* **4** MAT. término numérico, término de una ecuación. || *v.t.* **5** ser llamado, nombrar, denominar, definir, dar nombre, calificar. || **6 to come to terms with,** aceptar, adaptarse, llegar a un acuerdo. **7 in no uncertain terms,** de modo vehemente, de forma inequívoca, claramente. **8 in someone's terms,** según, de acuerdo con: *in her terms = según ella dice.* **9 in... terms, a)** en el terreno; por lo que se refiere a, en términos...: *in economic terms = por lo que respecta a la economía;* **b)** en términos..., de forma...: *in strong terms = de manera contundente.* **10 in terms of,** por lo que se refiere a, en cuanto a... se refiere. **11 in the long/short/medium –,** a largo plazo, a la larga; a corto plazo, en el próximo futuro, a medio plazo: *long term transaction = operación a largo plazo.* **12 on... terms, a)** con condiciones: *I'll do it on my own terms = lo haré a mi modo;* **b)** situación, relaciones: *we are on friendly terms = nos llevamos como amigos.* **13 on the same terms/on equal terms,** en igualdad, sin favoritismos, con justicia, equitativamente. **14 on unfair terms/on unequal terms,** de modo desigual, injustamente, con favoritismos, tendenciosamente. **15 terms,** términos, condiciones, requisitos. **16 terms of reference,** límite de competencias, margen de actuación, margen de maniobra, mandato.

terminal | 'təːmɪnl | *adj.* **1** MED. terminal, fatal, incurable: *a terminal patient = enfermo terminal.* **2** trimestral, final. **3** de demarcación, fronterizo. || *s.c.* **2** terminal, término, final de trayecto. **3** terminal eléctrico, borne, polo, puntos de luz. **4** INF. terminal, teclado y pantalla.

terminally | 'təːmɪnəlɪ | *adv.* fatalmente, terminal.

terminate | 'təːmɪneɪt | *v.t.* e *i.* **1** terminar, acabar, concluir, poner término. **2** llegar hasta, tener parada final en. **3** abortar, poner término.

termini | 'təːmɪniː | V. **terminus.**

terminological | ˌtəːmɪnə'lɒdʒɪkl | *adj.* terminológico, lingÅístico.

terminology | ˌtəːmɪ'nɒlədʒɪ | *s.c.* e *i.* terminología, lenguaje.

terminus | 'təːmɪnəs | [*pl.* **termini/ terminuses**] *s.c.* terminal, estación término, parada final, final de línea. V. **terminal.**

termite | 'təːmaɪt | *s.c.* ZOOL. termita, comején.

tern | təːn | *s.c.* ZOOL. golondrina marina.

terrace | 'terəs | *s.c.* **1** fila de casas adosadas. **2** balcón, terraza, galería, azotea, patio. **3** bancal, rellano, arriate. **4** gradas, graderío. || *v.t.* **5** formar terrazas, arrellanar, aterrazar, disponer en bancales.

terraced | 'terəst | *adj.* **1** en terrazas, formando terrazas, terraplenado, colgante. || **2 – house,** parcela, casa de planta baja, vivienda unifamiliar adosada.

terracotta | ˌterə'kɒtə | *s.i.* **1** terracota, arcilla marrón rojizo sin barnizar. || *adj.* **2** color terracota.

terra firma | ˌterəfəːmə | *s.i.* tierra firme.

terrain | 'tereɪn | *s.i.* terreno.

terrapin | 'terəpɪn | *s.c.* ZOOL. tortuga de agua.

terrestrial | tə'restrɪəl | *adj.* **1** terrestre. || *s.c.* **2** terrícola.

terrible | 'terəbl | *adj.* terrible, malo, desagradable, tremendo, atroz, fatal, malísimo: *his English is terrible = su inglés es muy malo.*

terribly | 'terəblɪ | *adv.* terriblemente, espantosamente, tremendamente, muy, enormemente, extremadamente.

terrier | 'terɪər | *s.c.* terrier.

terrific | te'rɪfɪk | *adj.* **1** terrorífico, terrible. **2** excelente, tremendo, estupendo, fabuloso, bárbaro. **2** enorme, grande.

terrifically | te'rɪfɪklɪ | *adv.* terriblemente, tremendamente, enormemente, muy bien, maravillosamente.

terrified | 'terɪfaɪd | *adj.* aterrorizado, asustado, petrificado.

terrify | 'terɪfaɪ | *v.t.* **1** aterrorizar, asustar, aterrar, petrificar. || **2 to – into,** aterrorizar a alguien para obligarle a hacer algo: *he was terrified into telling everything = lo contó todo bajo la presión del miedo.* **3 to – out of one's mind/wits,** estar fuera de uno de pánico.

terrifying | 'terɪfaɪɪŋ | *adj.* terrible, aterrador, horrible, que horroriza, espantoso: *a terrifying experience = una terrible experiencia.*

terrifyingly | 'terɪfaɪɪŋlɪ | *adv.* espantosamente, horriblemente: *death was terrifyingly close = la muerte estuvo terriblemente cerca.*

territorial | ˌterə'tɔːrɪəl | *adj.* **1** territorial, regional, zonal: *the gods were territorial divinities = los dioses eran divinidades locales.* **2** jurisdiccional. || *s.c.* **3** MIL. soldado reservista. || **4 Territorial Army,** (también **Territorial Force**), MIL. (brit.) segunda reserva, ejército de reservistas. **5 territorial waters,** aguas jurisdiccionales, aguas territoriales, zona marítima nacional.

territoriality | ˌterə'tɔːrɪəlɪtɪ | *s.i.* territorialidad.

territory | 'terɪtərɪ | *s.i.* **1** territorio, dominio. **2** zona, área, región, campo, terreno. **3** competencia, esfera, materia conocida. || *s.c.* **4** provincia, territorio. **5** (EE.UU., HIST) territorio de colonización: *the North Western Territories = los territorios del noroeste.*

terror | 'terər | *s.i.* **1** terror, pánico, miedo, aprensión, espanto. || *s.c.* **2** terror, incordio, molestia, pesadez: *he is a terror of a child = es un incordio de niño.* || **3 to be/live in – of one's life,** temer por la propia vida. **4 to go/live in -- of,** tener miedo de, vivir aterrorizado por. **5 to hold no terrors of,** no tener miedo de, no temer, no asustarse de. **6 reign of terror,** V. **reign. 7 to strike -- into someone's heart,** V. **strike. 8 The Terror,** HIST. el Período del Terror (Revolución Francesa).

terrorise V. **terrorize.**

terrorism | 'terərɪzəm | *s.i.* terrorismo.

terrorist | 'terərɪst | *s.c.* terrorista.

terrorization | ˌterəraɪ'zeɪʃən | (también **terrorisation**) *s.i.* intimidación.

terrorize | 'terəraɪz | (también **terrorise**) *v.t.* aterrorizar, aterrar, llenar de terror, horrorizar, espantar.

terror-stricken | 'terə'strɪkən | *adj.* aterrorizado, espantado, preso de un terror incontrolable, petrificado.
terry | 'terɪ | *s.i.* felpa.
terse | tɜːs | *adj.* abrupto, lacónico, seco, cortante, conciso, sucinto.
tersely | 'tɜːslɪ | *adv.* lacónicamente, con sequedad, de modo cortante, concisamente, bruscamente.
terseness | 'tɜːsnɪs | *s.i.* **1** sequedad, concisión, laconismo, brevedad. **2** brusquedad, aspereza.
tertiary | 'tɜːʃərɪ | *adj.* **1** terciario, en tercer lugar. **2** superior, universitaria: *tertiary education.* **3** MED. de tercer grado, severo, grave: *tertiary burns = quemaduras de tercer grado.* || **The Tertiary,** GEOL. el Terciario.
Terylene | 'terəlɪːn | *s.i.* terilene (tipo de tejido).
TESL | tɪːesel | (fam.) | tesl | **(Teaching English as a Second Language)** *s.i.* Enseñanza del Inglés como Segundo Idioma. V. **TEFL.**
tessellated | 'tesɪleɪtɪd | (EE.UU. **tesselated**) *adj.* **1** teselado, hecho con teselas, de mosaico. || **2 – pavement,** mosaico.
test | test | *s.c.* **1** prueba, experimento, ensayo. **2** prueba, examen, test. **3** prueba, demostración. **4** MED. pruebas, análisis, examen médico. || *v.t.* **5** probar, experimentar, ensayar. **6** probar, examinar, comprobar. **7** probar, intentar. **8** examinar, analizar, estudiar, graduar (la vista). || **9 to put something to –,** poner a prueba, someter a prueba. **10 to stand/withstand the – of time,** resistir el paso del tiempo, pasar la prueba del tiempo. **11 -- match,** ronda, partido. **12 to – the wasters,** sondear opiniones, tantear el terreno, tomar el pulso a la situación.
testament | 'testəment | *s.c.* **1** testimonio, demostración. **2** testamento. || **3 New/Old Testament,** Nuevo/Viejo Testamento. **4 last will and --,** últimas voluntades.
test-case | 'testkeɪs | *s.c.* DER. precedente legal, juicio que sienta jurisprudencia; juicio de ensayo (para la interpretación de una nueva ley).
testicle | 'testɪkl | *s.c.* ANAT. testículo.
testify | 'testɪfaɪ | *v.i.* **1 [for, against, to]** testificar, declarar, prestar declaración, dar fe, atestiguar. **2 [to]** apoyar, demostrar, atestiguar, atestar, ser prueba de, testimoniar.
testimonial | ˌtestɪ'məunɪəl | *s.c.* **1** referencias, certificado, testimonios, recomendación. **2** homenaje, regalo, obsequio testimonial.
testimony | 'testɪmənɪ | *s.c.* e *i.* **1** evidencia, declaración, testimonio. **2** prueba, demostración, testimonio.
testing | testɪŋ | *adj.* de prueba difícil, ardua.
test-pilot | test'paɪlət | *s.c.* AER. piloto de pruebas.
test-tube | 'testjuːb | *s.c.* **1** QUIM. probeta, tubo de ensayo. || **2 – baby,** niño probeta.
testily | 'testɪlɪ | *adv.* con irritación, irritadamente, de mal humor.
testy | 'testɪ | *adj.* irritable, impaciente.
tetanus | 'tetənəs | (también, fam., **lockjaw**) *s.i.* tétanos.
tetchy | 'tetʃɪ | *adj.* irritable, irascible, malhumorado, susceptible.
tether | 'teðər | *s.c.* **1** correa de sujeción, ronzal, atadura, traba. || *v.t.* **2** atar del ronzal, atar con una cuerda. || **3 at the end of one's –,** estar al límite de las propias fuerzas, estar harto.
tethered | 'teðəd | *adj.* atado, sujeto.
text | tekst | *s.c.* **1** texto, tema, escrito, lectura. **2** libro, texto, ejemplar, volumen. **3** extracto, texto. || **4 to stick to one's –,** ceñirse al tema.
textbook | tekstbuk | *s.c.* **1** libro de texto. || *adj.* **2** de texto, de libro, perfecto: *you kiss by the book = besas de modo experto.*
textile | 'tekstaɪl | *s.c.* **1** tejido, tela. || *adj.* **2** textil.
textiles | 'tekstaɪlz | *s.pl.* industrias textiles.
textual | 'tekstjuəl | *adj.* textual, literal.
texture | 'tekstʃər | *s.i.* **1** textura, tacto. **2** contextura, estructura, fábrica. **3** ART. coherencia, combinación, textura.
Thai | taɪ | *s.c.* **1** tailandés, habitante de Tailandia. | *s.i.* **2** tailandés, idioma de Tailandia. || *adj.* **3** de Tailandia, tailandés.
Thailand | taɪlænd | *s.sing.* GEOG. Tailandia.
Thalidomide | θə'lɪdəmaɪd | *s.i.* QUIM. talidomida (marca registrada).
Thames | temz | *s.sing.* **1** GEOG. el Támesis. || **2 to set the – on fire,** (fam. y p.u.) hacer algo grande, hacer algo que se vea.
than | ðæn | *prep./conj.* **1** que: *my brother is older than me = mi hermano es mayor que yo.* **2** de, del que, de la que, de lo que: *I waited for more than half an hour = esperé más de media hora.* **3 [rather/other/sooner]** a, que, antes que, más que: *he likes this one rather than that one = prefiere esta a aquel.* **4** cuando: *hardly had he said it than they arrived = apenas lo había dicho cuando llegaron.* || **5 easier said – done,** V. **easy. 6 less --,** V. **less. 7 more --/no more --,** V. **more. 8 more often -- not,** V. **often.**
thank | θæŋk | *v.i.* **1** agradecer, dar las gracias. **2** sí, gracias; no, gracias: *shall I give you a lift? thank you = ¿te llevo en mi coche? sí, gracias.* || **3 to – for,** dar las gracias por, gracias por, agradecer que: *the blind man thaked me for seeing him across the street = el ciego me agradeció que le ayudase a cruzar la calle.* **4 to give thanks,** dar gracias a Dios. **5 to have someone to – for,** (desp.) tener que agradecer a alguien, ser alguien la causa de algo, culpar, echar la culpa. **6 – God/– goodness/– heavens/etc.** (interj.) ¡gracias a Dios!/¡al cielo!, ¡a Dios gracias!, ¡santo cielo!, ¡Dios mío! **7 to – one's lucky stars,** V. **tar. 8 thanks to,** gracias a, por causa de, debido a. **9 – you/– you very much/etc.,** no, (muchas) gracias.
thankful | 'θæŋkful | *adj.* **1** agradecido, contento, feliz por. || **2 to be –,** alegrarse. || **3 to be – for small mercies,** (fam.) dar las gracias por las cosas pequeñas, por los pequeños favores cotidianos.
thankfully | 'θæŋkfəlɪ | *adv.* **1** con agradecimiento, satisfactoriamente, felizmente. **2** gracias a Dios, afortunadamente.
thankfulness | 'θæŋkfulnɪs | *s.i.* agradecimiento, gratitud.
thankless | 'θæŋklɪs | *adj.* ingrato, desagradecido, desagradable.
thanksgiving | 'θæŋksˌgɪvɪŋ | *s.i.* **1** acción de gracias. || **2 Thanksgiving Day,** (EE.UU.) día de acción de gracias (cuarto jueves de noviembre).
thankyou | θæŋkju | *s.c.* agradecimiento, acto de agradecimiento.
that | ðæt | | ðət | [*pl.* **those** | ðəuz |] *adj./pron.dem.* **1** ese, ése; esa, ésa; eso, aquel, aquél; aquella, aquélla; aquello. **2** el que, la que, lo que, el de, la de. **3** esos que, aquellos que: *those people who... = los que...* || *adv.* **4** tan, así de: *if he's that intelligent, why didn't he pass? = si es tan listo, ¿cómo no aprobó?* || *pron.rel.* **5** que, quien, cual. || *conj.* **6** que: *I said that it was good = dije que era bueno.* **7** para que: *she put the lights out so that he could sleep = apagó las luces para que pudiera dormir.* **8** de que: *I'm happy that you did it = estoy contento de que lo hicieras.* || **9 and all –/and –,** y todo eso, y demás, y tal, y cosas por el estilo. **10 at –,** pero, sin embargo, además de. **11 to come to –,** V. **come. 12 don't give me –,** V. **give. 13 that is/-- is to say,** es decir. **13 -- is it,** así es, exacto; ya está, es todo. **14 -- is --,** eso es todo, no hay más, ya está. **15 that'll be the day,** V. **day. 16 that's (just) the ticket,** V. **ticket. 17 that's the stuff (to give the troops),** V. **stuff. 18 that's torn it!,** ¡ya está echado a perder!. **19 -- would be telling,** V. **telling. 20 this and --,** V. **this.**
OBS. Como demostrativo representa tanto el 2.º como el 3.º grado de proximidad del correspondiente español; puede asociarse a palabras tales como **there, over there,** para matizar el concepto de distancia. Se usa con las oraciones de relativo especificativas, puede suprimirse si no funciona como sujeto, no puede ir regido por una preposición y es especialmente común después de superlativos, indefinidos, cuantificadores, etc. En las oraciones subordinadas nominales y en estilo indirecto puede suprimirse, excepto detrás de verbos poco comunes y formales. En oraciones finales suele ir con **so,** siendo más frecuente que **in order that.**
thatch | θætʃ | *s.c.* **1** techo de paja, de bálago. **2** mata de pelo. || *s.i.* **3** paja, bálago. || *v.t.* **4** cubrir, techar con bálago.
thatched | θætʃt | *adj.* de paja, techado con bálago.

thatcher | 'θætʃər | *s.c.* techador.
thatching | 'θætʃɪŋ | *s.i.* paja, bálago.
that's | ðæts | forma contracta de **that is.**
thaw | ðɔː | *s.c.* **1** deshielo. || *v.i.* **2** fundirse, derretirse. || **3 to – out, a)** deshelar, descongelar; **b)** (fam.) quitarse el frío, templarse; **c)** (fam.) sentirse cómodo, coger confianza, encontrarse a gusto, relajarse.
the | ðə | ante consonantes; | ðɪ | ante vocales; | ðiː | uso enfático. *art.* **1** el, la, lo; los, las. || *adv.* **2** suficiente: *he hasn't got the strength to move it = no tiene bastante fuerza como para moverlo.* **3** cuanto...: *the more, the merrier = cuantos más, mejor.* **4** por, uno: *tomatoes are 30 pence the kilo = los tomates van a 30 peniques el kilo.*
OBS. El artículo determinado no se utiliza al hablar de cosas en plural en sentido general, en caso contrario particularizamos; ahora bien, en singular se usa el artículo para generalizar: *lions are dangerous animals, the lion is a dangerous animal.* Se usa para referirnos a un grupo como un todo; y cuando nos referimos a un nombre especificado por el contexto.
theatre | 'θɪətər | (*brit.*, **theater**) *s.c.* **1** teatro. **2** quirófano, sala de operaciones. **3** MIL. teatro de operaciones, arena, escenario. **4** aula, sala de conferencias. || *s.sing.* **5** el teatro (profesión, medio de vida...). || *s.i.* **6** ART. drama, teatro, representación.
theatergoer | 'θɪətəgəʊər | *s.c.* aficionado al teatro.
theatrical | θɪ'ætrɪkl | *adj.* **1** teatral, de teatro, dramático: *theatrical company = compañía de teatro.* **2** histriónico, teatral, exagerado.
theatricals | θɪ'ætrɪklz | *s.pl.* representaciones teatrales.
theatrically | θɪ'ætrɪkəlɪ | *adv.* dramáticamente, melodramáticamente, histriónicamente, de modo exagerado.
Thebes | θiːbz | Tebas.
thee | ðiː | *pron.pers.* (arc.) **1** te. || **2 with –,** contigo.
OBS. Forma pronominal objetiva arcaica. V. **thou, thy, thine.**
theft | θeft | *s.c.* e *i.* robo, hurto, sustracción.
their | ðeər | *adj.pos.* **1** su, sus (de ellos). **2** Su (con títulos).
theirs | ðeəz | *pron.pos.* **1** (el) suyo, (la) suya; (los) suyos, (las) suyas (de ellos). || **2 of –,** de ellos, suyo: *a friend of theirs = uno de sus amigos.*
theism | 'θiːɪzəm | *s.i.* teísmo.
theist | 'θiːɪst | *s.c.* teísta.
them | ðem | *pron.pers.* los, las; les; ellos, ellas.
thematic | θɪ'mætɪk | *adj.* temático.
theme | θiːm | *s.c.* **1** tema, disertación. **2** MUS. tema, motivo.
themselves | ðəm'selvz | *pron.r.pl.* **1** se, a sí mismo, a sí misma. **2** ellos mismos, ellas mismas; sí mismos, sí mismas. || **3 by –,** solos, sin ayuda. **4 in –,** en sí mismos.
then | ðen | *adv.* **1** entonces, de entonces, en ese momento, en aquel entonces, en aquella época. **2** luego, después. || *adj.* **3** el entonces, de entonces. || *conj.* **4** pues, en ese caso, por tanto, entonces, así que. || **5 now and --,** V. **now. 6 there and --,** V. **there.**
thence | ðens | *adv.* **1** de allí, desde allí. **2** por eso, por consiguiente.
thenceforth | ˌðens'fɔːθ | (también **thenceforward**) *adv.* desde entonces, de allí en adelante, a partir de entonces.
thenceforward | ˌðens'fɔːwəd | V. **thenceforth.**
theocracy | θɪ'ɒkrəsɪ | *s.c.* teocracia.
theocratic | θɪəkrætɪk | *adj.* teocrático.
theodolite | θɪ'ədəlaɪt | *s.c.* teodolito.
theologian | θɪə'ləʊdʒjən | *s.c.* teólogo.
theologic | θɪə'ləʊdʒɪk | V. **theological.**
theological | θɪə'lɒdʒɪkl | *adj.* teológico; religioso: *theological virtues = virtudes teologales.*
theology | θɪ'ɒlədʒɪ | *s.i.* teología, doctrina.
theorem | 'θɪərəm | *s.c.* teorema.
theoretic | ˌθɪə'retɪk | V. **theoretical.**
theoretical | ˌθɪə'retɪkl | *adj.* **1** teórico. **2** supuesto, imaginario.
theoretically | θɪə'retɪkəlɪ | *adv.* teóricamente, en teoría.
theoretician | ˌθɪərə'tɪʃn | *s.c.* teórico.
theorise V. **theorize.**
theorist | 'θɪərɪst | *s.c.* teórico.
theorize | 'θɪəraɪz | (también **theorise**) *v.i.* **1** teorizar. || **2 – about,** especular, formar teorías, sugerir una idea acerca de algo.
theory | 'θɪərɪ | *s.c.* **1** teoría, hipótesis. **2** principios básicos, filosofía. **3** idea, noción, opinión, suposición. || **4 in –,** en teoría, teóricamente.
therapeutic | ˌθerə'pjuːtɪk | V. **therapeutical.**
therapeutical | ˌθerə'pjuːtɪkl | *adj.* terapéutico.
therapist | 'θerəpɪst | *s.c.* terapeuta.
therapy | 'θerəpɪ | *s.i.* **1** terapia, terapéutica. || **2 occupational –,** terapia ocupacional.
there | ðeər | *adv.* **1** allí, allá; ahí. **2** en eso, en ese punto. || *interj.* **2** ¡vaya!, ¡venga!, ¡vamos!: *there, there, take it easy = bien, vale, tranquilo.* || **3 – again,** otra vez, hete aquí que. **4 – and then,** aquí y ahora, enseguida, inmediatamente. **5 is/are,** hay. **6 not all –/not quite –,** no exactamente al tanto. **7 so –,** así pues. **8 – you are, a)** ahí está, es todo, eso es lo que hay; **b)** ¿lo ves?, eso es lo que te decía, ahí lo tienes; **c)** toma, aquí tienes. **9 – you go/– you go again,** ¡ya estamos otra vez!, ¡siempre lo mismo!
thereabouts | ðeərəbaʊts | *adv.* **1** por ahí, allí cerca. **2** más o menos, alrededor de, aproximadamente.
thereafter | ˌðeər'ɑːftər | *adv.* después de, en lo sucesivo, más tarde.
thereby | ˌðeəbaɪ | *adv.* por eso, de ese modo, por esa razón.
therefore | 'ðeəfɔːr | *adv.* por tanto, por lo tanto, por consiguiente: *I think, therefore I am = pienso, luego existo.*
therein | ˌðeər'ɪn | *adv.* **1** allí dentro, en eso, en ese sentido. || **2 – lies,** ahí está el asunto, ahí está el quid.
thereof | ˌðeər'ɒv | *adv.* de eso, de esto, de lo mismo.
thereupon | ˌðeərə'pɒn | *adv.* en eso, con eso; acto seguido, en seguida. **2** por consiguiente, por lo tanto.
therm | θɜːm | *s.c.* termia, unidad térmica.
thermal | 'θɜːml | *adj.* **1** termal. **2** FIS. térmico, calorífico.
thermodynamics | ˌθɜːməudaɪ'næmɪks | *s.i.* termodinámica.
thermometer | θə'mɒmɪtər | *s.c.* termómetro.
thermonuclear | 'θɜːməʊ'njuːklɪər | *adj.* termonuclear, atómico.
thermoplastic | 'θɜːməʊ'plæstɪk | *s.c.* termoplástico.
Thermos | 'θɜːmɒs | *s.c.* **1** termo. || **2 thermos bottle,** (EE.UU.) V. **thermos. 3 thermos flask,** V. **thermos.**
thermostat | 'θɜːməustæt | *s.c.* termostato.
thesaurus | θɪ'sɔːrəs | [*pl.* **thesauruses/ thesauri**] *s.c.* diccionario ideológico, tesoro, compendio.
these | ðiːz | *pl.* de **this.**
theses | 'θiːsiːz | V. **thesis.**
thesis | 'θiːsɪs | [*pl.* **theses** | 'θiːsiːz |] *s.c.* **1** argumento, tesis. **2** tesis de licenciatura, disertación, trabajo de investigación.
thespian | 'θespɪən | *s.c.* **1** (p.u., hum.) actor, actriz. || *adj.* **2** dramático, teatral, trágico. **3** de Tespis.
they | ðeɪ | *pron.pers.* ellos, ellas.
they'd | ðeɪd *contr.* **1 they had. 2 they would.**
they'll | ðeɪəl | *contr.* **they shall/will.**
they're | ðeər *contr.* **they are.**
they've | ðeɪv | *contr.* **they have.**
thick | θɪk *adj.* **1** espeso, grueso, ancho. **2** de ancho, ancho, de espesor, de grueso, de grosor. **3** espeso, cubierto de, apretado, tupido, impenetrable, poblado. **4** en cantidad, montón, espeso. **5** corto, estúpido, tonto, espeso. **6** grueso, de abrigo, gordo. **7** viscoso, condensado, consistente, espeso, denso. **8** oscuro, intenso, nublado, cerrado. **9** cargado, viciado, lleno de. **10** dolor, torpeza, pesadez. **11** voz oscura, pastosa, inteligible. **12** marcado, claro, cerrado, inequívoco. **13** íntimos, uña y carne. || **14 as – as thieves,** uña y carne, inseparables, muy amigos, a partir un piñón. **15 as – as two short planks,** tonto de remate, idiota perdido, más agudo que la punta de un colchón. **16 a – ear,** tirón de orejas, golpe, coscorrón. **17 blood is thicker than water,** los lazos familiares son los más fuertes. **18 in the – of,** de lleno, de pleno, en pleno, en medio, en el ajo, en el fragor de. **19 it's a bit –/that's a bit –,** inaceptable, difícil de tragar, se pasa un poco,

se pasa de castaño oscuro, ¡es el colmo! **20 to lay it on –,** alabar, agradecer en exceso. **21 – and fast,** uno detrás de otro, en cantidad, seguidos, avalancha. **22 – on the ground,** a cientos, a montones. **23 – with,** lleno de, cargado de, a tope de, hasta los topes. **24 through – and thin,** a las crudas y a las maduras, contra viento y marea.

thicken | 'θɪkən | *v.i.* **1** crecer, incrementarse, espesarse. **2** hacerse más denso, aumentar. **3** endurecer, espesar, engordar, trabar. || **4 the plot thickens,** aumentar en complejidad, complicarse, embrollarse, hacerse enrevesado, liarse. **5 – up,** espesar.

thickener | 'θɪkənər | *s.c.* e *i.* espesante, trabador.

thicket | 'θɪkɪt | *s.c.* bosquecillo, espesura.

thickly | 'θɪklɪ | *adv.* **1** espesamente, densamente. **2** en cantidad. **3** ásperamente, torpemente, con voz poco clara.

thickness | 'θɪknɪs | *s.i.* espesor, espesura, densidad.

thickset | ˌθɪk'set | *adj.* **1** robusto, recio. **2** muy poblado, denso.

thick-skinned | ˌθɪk'skɪnd | *adj.* **1** insensible, duro, de piel de elefante. **2** de piel gruesa, de pellejo grueso.

thief | θiːf | [*pl.* **thieves**] *s.c.* **1** ladrón, ratero. || **2 procrastination is the – of time,** la dilación es el ladrón del tiempo. **3 to set a – to catch a –,** la mejor cuña es la de la misma madera; a un pillo, otro pillo.

thieve | θiːv | *v.t.* robar, hurtar.

thieves | θiːvz | *pl.* de **thief.**

thieving | θiːvɪŋ | *s.i.* **1** robo, hurto, latrocinio. || **2** *adj.* ladrón.

thigh | θaɪ | *s.c.* **1** ANAT. muslo. || **2 to smite hip and –,** dar una paliza. **3 thighbone,** fémur.

thimble | 'θɪmbl | *s.c.* dedal.

thimbleful | 'θɪmblfʊl | *s.c.* e *i.* una gota, un dedal, un chorrito, un sorbo, un dedo, una pequeña cantidad.

thin | θɪn | *adj.* **1** delgado, estrecho. **2** delgado, flaco. **3** fino, ligero. **4** escaso, ralo, poco numeroso. **5** débil, flojo, poco consistente. **6** con poca sustancia, aguado. || *v.t.* **7** disminuir, reducir. **8** diluir, aclarar. **9** adelgazar, hacer adelgazar. || *v.i.* **10** dispersarse, reducirse, disiparse. || **11 as – as a rake,** en los huesos, como una raspa, como la caña de la doctrina. **12 a -- time,** momento difícil, época de fracasos. **13 to be thinning/to be getting -- on top,** quedarse calvo, perder pelo, clarear el cabello. **14 to be wearing --,** aburrir, perder interés, tener poco interés, agotarse. **15 disappear/vanish into -- air,** V. **air. 16 to – down,** rebajar, aguar; disminuir en espesor o número. **17 on -- ice,** V. **ice. 18 -- on the ground,** escasos, contados. **19 the – end of the wedge,** el principio de algo peor, el primer paso hacia algo serio. **20 the – red line,** la vanguardia, la primera fila, el frente.

thine | ðaɪn | *pron.pos.sing.* (arc.) tu, tuyo, tuya. V. **thou, thee, thy.**

thing | θɪŋ | *s.c.* **1** cosa. **2** asunto, negocio. **3** chisme, objeto, artículo. **4** cosas, propiedades, ropas, bienes. **5** equipo, algo, nada: *I couldn't say a thing = no pude decir nada.* **6** criatura, ser, monstruo, cosa. || **7 a close –,** casi igual, igualada, justo, por los pelos. **8 a – of the past,** agua pasada. **9 a – or two,** un par de cosas, unas cuantas cosas: *I can still teach him a thing or two = aún tengo algo que enseñarle.* **10 all/other things being equal,** V. **equal. 11 to be all things to all men,** ponerse a la altura de, ponerse en el lugar de, estar para todos y para todo, dar gusto a todos. **12 to be one – (...quite another),** una cosa es (...otra muy diferente), una cosa es predicar (...otra dar trigo). **13 to do one's own –,** hacer lo que a uno le apetece, actuar libremente. **14 to do the... –,** actuar de modo...: *they did de democratic thing = hicieron lo que era democrático.* **15 first –,** V. **first. 16 for one – (...and for another...),** por una razón (...y por otra...), por una parte (...y por otra...), en primer lugar. **17 greatest/best – since sliced bread,** la octava maravilla, el no va más. **18 to have/get a – (about),** tener una fijación/obsesión acerca de, tener manía/tirria a. **19 in all things,** en todo momento. **20 it is just one of those things,** son cosas que pasan, las cosas son así. **21 just the –/the very –,** justo lo que quería, exactamente lo que necesitaba. **22 to know a – or two,** V. **know. 23 last –,** V. **last. 24 little things please little minds,** si se entretienen con eso, no les da para más. **25 to make a – (out of/of),** hacer un monte de. **26 near –,** V. **near. 27 not know the first -- about,** no tener ni noción, no saber por dónde le da a uno el aire. **28 (not) quite the –, a)** (no) es lo adecuado, (no) está bien, (no) es lo que se hace; **b)** el último grito, lo último. **29 of all tings,** V. **all. 30 one -- leads to another,** V. **lead. 31 such a –/no such –,** tal cosa como. **32 the done –,** lo que se hace, lo correcto. **33 the real –,** V. **real. 34 the – is...,** lo que ocurre, lo que pasa.

thingamabob V. **thingummy.**

thingummy | 'θɪŋəmɪ | *s.c.* chisme, cosa, trasto, el-como-se-llame.

thingy | θɪŋɪ | *s.c.* ese como-se-llame.

think | θɪŋk | [*pret., p.p.* **thought**] *v.t.* e *irreg.* **1** pensar, considerar, reflexionar, meditar. **2** creer(se), imaginar(se). **3** razonar, ponderar, sopesar. **4** acordarse: *can you think of her name? = ¿te acuerdas cómo se llama?* **5** concebir, ocurrirse. **6** parecer, opinar. || **7 to – about,** pensar en, considerar, tener en cuenta, opinar. **8 to – again,** reconsiderar. **9 to – ahead,** anticipar, adelantarse. **10 to – aloud,** pensar en voz alta. **11 anybody would think/you would have thought,** cualquiera pensaría. **12 to – away,** pasar meditando. **13 to – back,** acordarse, recordar. **14 to – before,** pensar antes de. **15 to – better of it,** reconsiderar, pensárselo mejor. **16 to – big,** V. **big. 17 can't hear oneself –,** V. **hear. 18 come to – of it/when you – about/thinking about it,** dar en pensar, ocurrirse, pasarse por la cabeza. **19 to – fit,** considerar adecuado. **20 to – for,** pensar. **21 to – for oneself,** tener pensamiento propio, ser independiente. **22 if you – that, you've got another – coming,** si piensas eso, ya puedes ir pensando otra cosa. **23 I wasn't thinking,** no estaba en lo que hacía, no me daba cuenta. **24 just –,** imagina, piensa en que. **25 that's what you /he/etc. –,** esas son tus intenciones. **26 to – nothing of,** no ser nada, no considerar, no parecer. **27 to – of,** pensar, considerar, imaginar, recordar, sugerir, inventar, tener una opinión. **28 to – on,** recordar. **29 to – out,** elaborar, planificar, pensar de antemano. **30 to – over,** considerar, examinar detenidamente, reconsiderar, sopesar. **31 to – the best of,** tener plena confianza, tener la mejor opinión de. **32 to – the world of,** V. **world. 33 to – the worst of,** no tener confianza, tener la peor opinión de. **34 to – through,** pensar hasta los últimos detalles. **35 to – twice,** reconsiderar: *don't think twice, it's alright = no lo pienses más, es así.* **36 to – up,** elaborar, inventar, diseñar, confeccionar, tramar. **37 what was I/were you/etc. thinking of,** ¿en qué estaba/estabas/etc. pensando?

thinker | 'θɪŋkər | *s.c.* pensador.

thinking | 'θɪŋkɪŋ | *adj.* **1** pensante, racional, que piensa, inteligente, serio. || *s.i.* **2** pensamiento, consideración, pensar. || **3 to one's way of –,** a modo de ver de uno, en opinión de uno.

think-tank | θɪŋktæŋk | *s.c.* grupo de expertos, reunión de cerebros.

thinner | θɪnər | *s.i.* disolvente.

thin-skinned | ˌθɪn'skɪnd | *adj.* muy sensible, que se afecta fácilmente, susceptible, de piel fina.

third | θəːd | *num.ord.* **1** tercero. || *s.c.* **2** tercio, tres (día). **3** aprobado. **4** MUS. tercera. || *s.i.* **5** MEC. tercera (marcha). || **6 – degree,** tercer grado, tortura. **6 – degree burn,** quemadura de tercer grado. **7 – party,** tercero, contra terceros, tercera persona: *third party insurance = seguro de terceros.* **8 – person,** GRAM., DER. tercera persona. **9 – time lucky,** a la tercera va la vencida. **10 Third World,** el tercer mundo. **11 – year,** curso tercero, tercer año (escuela).

third-class | θəːdklɑːs | *s.c.* **1** aprobado, apto. || *adj.* **2** tercera clase.

thirdly | θəːdlɪ | *adv.* en tercer lugar.

third-rate | θəːd'reɪt | *adj.* de tercera, de baja calidad.

thirst | θəːst | *s.i.* **1** sed. **2** deseo, afán, pasión, sed. || *v.i.* **3** tener sed, estar sediento. || **4 to – for/after,** desear (ansiosamente), necesitar.

thirstily | 'θəːstɪlɪ | *adv.* con mucha sed.

thirsty | 'θəːstɪ | *adj.* **1** sed, sediento, árido: *to be thirsty = tener sed.* **2** que da sed. **3 to be – for,** estar deseoso, estar sediento de.

thirteen | θəː'tiːn | *num.card.* trece.

thirteenth | θəːtiːnθ | *num.ord.* treceavo, decimotercero, decimotercio, trece (siglo).
thirtieth | 'θəːtɪɪθ | *num.ord.* trigésimo, treintavo, treinta (día).
thirty | 'θəːtɪ | *num.card.* **1** treinta: *the thirties = los años treinta.* || **2 to be in one's thirties,** estar en la treintena.
this | ðɪs | [*pl.* **these**] *adj.* y *pron.dem.* **1** este, esta, esto; éste, ésta. **2** dicha, la cual: *he sent me a note, this note... = me envió una nota, dicha nota...* **3** el próximo, hoy: *this Sunday = este domingo. This is June = estamos en junio.* || *adv.* **4** tan: *this far = así de lejos.* || **5 – and that/--, that and the other,** esto, lo otro y lo de más allá. **6 – is,** éste es, le presento a. **7 – is it, a)** así es; **b)** y aquí estamos, y eso es todo. **8 like –,** así, de este modo. **9 what's all –?,** ¿qué pasa?, ¿qué es esto?
thistle | 'θɪsl | *s.c.* BOT. cardo.
thistledown | 'θɪsldaʊn | *s.i.* BOT. vilano.
thither | 'ðɪðər | *adj.* (arc.) **1** allá. || **2 hither and --,** V. **hither.**
tho | ðəʊ | V. **though.**
thong | θɒŋ | *s.c.* tira, correa.
thoracic | θɔːræsɪk | *adj.* torácico.
thorax | 'θɔːræks | *s.c.* [*pl.* **thoraces/thoraxes**] MED. tórax, pecho.
thorn | θɔːn | *s.c.* BOT. **1** espina. **2** espino. || **3 – in one's flesh/side,** espina en el costado, ser una molestia.
thorny | 'θɔːnɪ | *adj.* **1** espinoso, cubierto de espinas. **2** difícil, erizado de dificultades: *a thorny matter = un asunto peliagudo.*
thorough | 'θʌrə | *adj.* **1** exhaustivo, completo, profundo, total, a fondo, minucioso. **2** meticuloso, concienzudo. **3** correcto, perfecto, adecuado. **4** empedernido, redomado.
thoroughbred | 'θʌrəbred | *s.c.* y *adj.* pura sangre.
thoroughfare | 'θʌrəfeər | *s.c.* **1** calle principal || **2 no –,** calle de circulación prohibida, prohibido el paso.
thoroughgoing | 'θʌrəˌgəʊɪŋ | *adj.* profundo, total, completo, exhaustivo, perfecto: *a thoroughgoing democrat = todo un demócrata.*
thoroughly | 'θʌrəlɪ | *adv.* profundamente, completamente, concienzudamente, minuciosamente, perfectamente.
thoroughness | 'θʌrənɪs | *s.i.* profundidad, perfección, minuciosidad, meticulosidad, escrupulosidad.
those | ðəʊz | *pl.* **1** de **that.** || **2 one of – days,** uno de esos días (en que todo sale mal). **3 – were the days!,** ¡qué tiempos aquellos!
thou | ðaʊ | *pron.pers.* (arc.) **1** tú. || **2 holier-than-thou attitude,** aires de superioridad, estar por encima del bien y del mal. V. **thee, thy, thine.**
though | ðəʊ | (también, **although, tho**) *conj.* **1** aunque, aun, a pesar de que, no obstante que. || *adv.* **2** aun con todo, a pesar de todo, sin embargo. || **2 as –,** como si. **3 – I say it myself/– I say so myself,** aunque no está bien que lo diga. OBS. **Though** es más común que **although** en lenguaje coloquial, **even** suele acompañarlo para enfatizar, mientras que no se puede utilizar con **although;** puede colocarse al final de la oración con el significado de "sin embargo"; en frases largas puede aparecer en otras posiciones, con valor adverbial, y función enfática.
thought | θɔːt | *s.c.* **1** pensamiento, idea, intención, opinión, consideración. || **2 a penny for your thoughts,** V. **penny. 3 as quick as –,** rápido como el pensamiento. **4 food for –,** materia de reflexión, algo que da que pensar. **5 perish the –!,** ¡tiemblo de pensarlo! **6 second thoughts,** V. **second. 7 the wish is father to the –,** creer lo que uno quiere creer, creer lo que a uno le conviene. || V. **think.**
thoughful | 'θɔːtful | *adj.* **1** pensativo, meditabundo, serio, absorto. **2** cuidadoso, atento, pensado. **3** considerado, solícito.
thoughfully | 'θɔːtfəlɪ | *adv.* **1** pensativamente, seriamente. **2** atentamente, cuidadosamente. **3** solícitamente, amablemente.
thoughtfulness | 'θɔːtfulnɪs | *s.i.* **1** meditación, seriedad. **2** atención, cuidado. **3** solicitud, amabilidad.
thoughtless | 'θɔːtlɪs | *adj.* **1** irreflexivo. **2** falto de atención, descuidado. **3** desconsiderado, egoísta.
thoughtlessly | 'θɔːtlɪslɪ | *adv.* **1** irreflexivamente. **2** descuidadamente. **3** desconsideradamente, egoístamente.
thoughtlessness | 'θɔːtlɪsnɪs | *s.i.* **1** irreflexión. **2** descuido, inconsciencia. **3** desconsideración, egoísmo.
thousand | 'θəʊznd | *adj.num.card.* **1** mil. || *s.c.* **2** mil: *by the thousand = a millares.* || **3 a -- and one, one in a thousand,** V. **one.**
thousandth | 'θaʊzntθ | *adj.num.ord.* **1** milésimo. || *s.c.* **2** milésima parte. **3** número mil: *I was the thousandth = yo hacía el número mil.*
thrall | θrɔːl | *s.c.* **1** esclavo. || *s.i.* **2** esclavitud. || *v.t.* **3** esclavizar. || **4 to be /hold in – (to), a)** estar en manos de, bajo el poder de, bajo la influencia de estar esclavizado por; **b)** en vilo, pendiente.
thrash | θræʃ | *s.c.* **1** movimiento. || *v.t.* **2** pegar, golpear, azotar, dar una paliza. **3** derrotar, dar una paliza. || *v.i.* **4 (about)** moverse, agitarse, sacudirse. **5 (out),** discutir en detalle, dar vueltas a un problema.
thrashing | θræʃɪŋ | *s.c.* **1** paliza, tunda, varapalo, zurra, azotaina. **2** paliza, derrota aplastante. **3** AGR. trilla. **4 thrashing floor,** era.
thread | θred | *s.i.* **1** hebra, hilo. **2** voluta. **3** rosca, filete de una tuerca. **4** hilo de una argumentación. || *v.i.* **5** enhebrar, ensartar, enristrar, insertar, hacer pasar. **6** pasar entre, sortear, colarse por. || **7 to hang by a –,** colgar de un hilo, estar pendiente de un hilo. **8 to lose /miss the –,** perder el hilo (de una argumentación). **9 to pick/take/gather up the threads,** retomar, recomenzar, atar cabos. **10 threads,** cabos, tendencias, aspectos.
threadbare | 'θredbeər | *adj.* **1** deshilachado, desgastado, ajado, raído. **2** trillado, flojo, pasado: *a threadbare joke = un chiste viejo.*
threat | θret | *s.c.* **1** amenaza, seria advertencia. **2** riesgo, peligro.
threaten | θretn | *v.t.* e *i.* **1** amenazar, proferir amenazas, advertir. **2** poner en peligro, hacer peligrar, correr el riesgo. **3** estar amenazado, estar bajo/ante la amenaza de.
threatened | 'θretnd | *adj.* amenazado, en peligro.
threatening | 'θretnɪŋ | *adj.* amenazador, amenazante.
threateningly | 'θretnɪŋlɪ | *adv.* amenazadoramente.
three | θrɪː | *adj.num.card.* **1** tres. **2** tri-, de tres: *a three-ring circus = un circo de tres pistas.* || *s.c.* **3** el tres. || **4 by/in twos and threes,** V. **two. 5 – Rs,** las tres disciplinas básicas: **reading,** lectura; **writing,** escritura; **arithmetic,** aritmética.
three-cornered | 'θriː'kɔːnəd | *adj.* triangular, de tres picos: *a three-cornered hat = tricornio, sombrero de tres picos.*
three-dimensional | θriːdɪ'menʃənl | (también, **3-D**) *adj.* **1** tridimensional, de tres dimensiones, sólido. **2** real, auténtico, veraz, creíble (los personajes de una obra, novela, etc...).
three-legged race | 'θrɪː'legdreɪs | *s.c.* carrera de tres piernas, carrera en que los competidores van atados de dos en dos por una pierna.
three-line whip | 'θrɪːləɪn'wɪp | *s.c.* (brit.) nota del líder del partido recordando la obligación de asistir y la disciplina de voto.
three-ply | 'θrɪːplaɪ | *adj.* contrachapado de tres capas, de tres hebras.
three-point turn | 'θrɪːpɔɪnt'təːn | *s.c.* cambio de sentido en la marcha de un vehículo mediante tres maniobras de giro.
three-quarters | 'θrɪː'kwɔːtəz | *adj.* tres cuartos.
threesome | 'θrɪːsəm | *s.c.* trío, grupo de tres, terceto.
three-wheeler | 'θrɪːwɪːlər | *s.c.* coche de tres ruedas.
thresh | θreʃ | *v.t.* e *i.* AGR. trillar, machacar, triturar. V. **thrash.**
threshold | 'θreʃəʊld | *s.c.* **1** umbral, umbrales. **2** punto de partida, puertas. **3** límite, nivel mínimo, nivel umbral. || **4 on the – of,** estar en los umbrales, estar en la antesala de, estar a las puertas de.
threw | θruː | *pret.* de **throw.**
thrice | θraɪs | *adv.* (form.) **1** por tres veces, tres veces. **2** triple: *mine was thrice as old as his = el mío era el triple de antiguo.*
thrift | θrɪft | *s.i.* economía, frugalidad, ahorro.

thrifty | 'θrɪftɪ | *adj.* económico, frugal, ahorrativo.

thrill | θrɪl | *s.c.* **1** emoción, temblor, escalofrío, estremecimiento, excitación. **2** experiencia excitante, sensación. || *v.tr.* **3** emocionar, conmover, hacer ilusión, estremecer, temblar de emoción, excitar. || **4 to – at/to,** emocionarse, estremecerse por/a causa de. **5 big –,** (desp.) ¡que emoción! **6 thrills and spills,** los avatares, los imprevistos, los sobresaltos. **7 to – with,** emocionar con/por medio de, electrizar.

thrilled | θrɪld | *adj.* **1** emocionado, arrobado, embelesado, excitado. || **2 – to bits,** extasiado, cautivado, fuera de sí por la emoción.

thriller | 'θrɪlər | *s.c.* novela, película, etc..., de intriga y misterio.

thrilling | 'θrɪlɪŋ | *adj.* emocionante, escalofriante, sensacional.

thrive | θraɪv | [*pret.reg.*, **thrived;** *irreg.*, **throve,** *p.p.reg.* **thrived;** *irreg.* **thriven**] *v.i.* **1** crecer, desarrollarse. **2** florecer, prosperar, medrar. || **3 to – on/upon,** alimentarse de; disfrutar con, realizarse con: *he thrives on hard work = se siente realizado con mucho trabajo.*

throat | θrəut | *s.c.* **1** ANAT. garganta. **2** cuello, gaznate, pescuezo. **3** GEOG. paso, desfiladero, garganta. || **4 at each other's –,** zarpa a la greña, discutir violentamente. **5 to clear one's –,** V. **clear. 6 to cut/slit one's own –,** crearse/buscarse la propia ruina, (fig.) suicidarse. **7 to have a frog in one's –,** V. **frog. 8 to jump down someone's –,** V. **jump. 9 to lie in one's –,** mentir descaradamente. **10 a lump in one's –,** V. **lump. 11 to ram/force/push something down someone's –,** forzar a aceptar, hacer tragar, obligar a comulgar con ruedas de molino, imponer algo a uno. **12 to stick in someone's –,** tener atragantado, no poder soportar, ser inaceptable, tener cruzado.

thriven | θrɪvn | *p.p.* de **thrive.**

throaty | 'θrəuti | *adj.* gutural, ronca (voz).

throb | θrɒb | *s.c.* **1** latido, pulsación, palpitación. **2** vibración, ruido. || *v.i.* **3** latir, pulsar, palpitar. **4** vibrar. **5** bullir, hervir de actividad (un lugar). || **6 to – away,** doler constantemente.

throbbing | 'θrɒbɪŋ | *s.c.* **1** latido, palpitación, pulsación, vibración. || *adj.* **2** palpitante, vibrante, muy activo, que bulle de actividad.

throes | θrəuz | *s.pl.* **1** dolores de parto. **2** estertores de agonía. || **3 to be in the – of,** estar de lleno en, en pleno; sufrir la incomodidad de.

thromboses | θrɒm'bəusi:z | V. **thrombosis.**

thrombosis | θrɒm'bəusɪs | [*pl.* **thromboses**] *s.c.* e *i.* MED. trombosis.

throne | θrəun | *s.c.* **1** trono, solio, sede, sitial. || *s.sing.* **2** el trono, la realeza, el poder real, la dignidad real.

throng | θrɒŋ | *s.c.* **1** multitud, gentío, tropel, muchedumbre, masa. || *v.t.* **2** atestar, llenar, ocupar. || *v.i.* **3** acudir en masa, venir en tropel. || **4 to – in/into,** entrar en masa. **5 to – out,** salir en masa, abandonar en tropel.

throttle | θrɒtl | *s.c.* e *i.* **1** ANAT. gaznate, cuello. **2** MEC. válvula de admisión. || *v.t.* **3** estrangular, sofocar, ahogar. || **4 to – back/down,** reducir la velocidad, disminuir la marcha, decelerar.

through | θru: | (EE.UU. **thru**) *prep.* **1** a través de, por, de parte a parte de, de un lado a otro de. **2** al otro lado de, por enmedio de, entre. **3** a lo largo y ancho de, por todo. V. **throughout. 4** hasta, durante, a: *Monday through Friday = de lunes a viernes.* **5** a causa de, gracias a, mediante, por medio de. || *adj.* **6** directo, con prioridad: *a through train = tren directo.* **7** acabado, terminado. || *adv.* **8** de parte a parte, totalmente, completamente, de principio a fin: *all the way through = hasta el final*; *half away through = hacia la mitad.* || **9 to be – with,** haber terminado con. **10 to get –, a)** superar, rebasar, pasar; **b)** pasar una llamada, conectar por teléfono. **11 to go –, a)** cruzar, atravesar, recorrer; **b)** aprobar, pasar (una propuesta); **c)** revisar, repasar. **12 – and –,** completamente.

throughout | θru:'aut | *prep.* y *adv.* **1** durante todo, todo a lo largo de, desde principio hasta el fin. **2** por todo, en todas partes, todo a lo largo y ancho de, completamente: *throughout the world = en todo el mundo.*

throughput | 'θru:put | *s.sing.* cantidad de material utilizado o cantidad de información procesada en una unidad de tiempo.

throve | θrəuv | *pret.* de **thrive.**

throw | θrəu | *s.c.* **1** tiro, tirada, jugada. **2** derribo. || *v.t.* e *i.* [*pret.* **threw,** *p.p.* **thrown**] **3** lanzar(se), arrojar(se), tirar(se). **4** empujar, meter. **5** poner, hacer llegar. **6** echar, proyectar. **7** dar, celebrar. **8** encender, apagar. **9** producir, fabricar, tender. **10** sacar. || **11 to – about/around, a)** tirar por ahí, lanzar alrededor, esparcir; **b)** mover, agitar brazos y piernas; **c)** rodear, envolver, echar alrededor. **12 to – a fit,** tener un ataque. **13 to – aside,** echar a un lado, dejar de lado, despreciar. **14 to – a spanner in the works,** estropear a propósito, echar arena en la maquinaria. **15 a stone's –,** V. **stone. 16 to – at,** tirar contra, tirar a dar, dirigir. **17 to – away, a)** librarse de; **b)** desaprovechar, desperdiciar; **c)** deponer. **18 to – back, a)** devolver, retroceder; **b)** retirar, descorrer; **c)** retrasar; **d)** parecerse, tirar a, recordar a. **19 to – back at,** echar en cara, recordarle algo a alguien. **20 to – back on /upon,** hacer depender de, verse forzado a depender de. **21 to – cold water over,** echar un jarro de agua fría, desanimar. **22 to – down, a)** tirar, dejar caer. **23 a)** arrojar, tirarse al suelo; **b)** derrotar, destruir, derrocar. **24 to – down one's arms,** deponer las armas, rendirse. **25 to – down the gauntlet,** V. **gauntlet. 26 to – dust in someone's eyes,** engañar, hacer creer. **27 to – in, a)** tirar de cualquier manera, añadir como regalo; añadir, intercalar un comentario; **b)** dejar, abandonar, sacar de banda. **28 to – in at the deep end,** V. **end. 29 to – in one's lot with,** unirse a, juntarse con. **30 to – in someone's teeth,** acusar, echar la culpa. **31 to – in the towel,** abandonar, aceptar la derrota. **32 to – into, a)** echar dentro de, arrojar dentro de; **b)** poner, hacer ponerse a alguien en; **c)** meter baza, añadir palabra. **33 to – light on,** V. **light. 34 to – mud at,** insultar, hablar ofensivamente. **35 to – off, a)** quitarse de encima, librarse, renunciar, abandonar; **b)** derrotar; **c)** escribir con facilidad, hablar descuidadamente. **36 to – off his balance, a)** hacer perder el equilibrio; **b)** confundir, sorprender. **37 to – on, a)** ponerse rápidamente, echarse encima; **b)** poner, hacer caer o llegar; **c)** culpar, hacer caer la culpa, acusar; **d)** hacerse depender de, crearse una dependencia. **38 to – oneself at someone's head,** hacerse notar, darse a entender. **39 to – oneself at the feet of,** arrojarse a los pies de, pedir perdón humildemente. **40 to – one's hand in,** abandonar todo intento; dejar de jugar. **41 to – one's hat in the air,** estar contento, mostrar alegría. **42 to – one's hat in the ring,** declarar la intención de, tomar parte, manifestarse. **43 to – one's mind back,** recordar, rememorar, traer a la mente. **44 to – one's money about/around,** malgastar, despilfarrar, derrochar. **45 to – one's weight about,** V. **weight. 46 to – open,** abrir violentamente; abrir a todo el mundo, participar libremente. **47 to – out, a)** sacar, dirigir hacia afuera, librarse de algo, expulsar, hacer salir; **b)** rehusar aceptar, echar a perder; **c)** confundir, provocar errores, causar preocupación; **d)** construir. **48 to – over, a)** echar; **b)** poner fin a, terminar, abandonar; **c)** cubrir, tapar. **49 to – overboard,** caer al mar, tirar por la borda, abandonar. **50 to – to,** pasar, echar, lanzar. **51 to – sideways,** sorprender, confundir, tener un efecto negativo. **52 to – someone for a loop,** (EE.UU. y fam.) derrotar, confundir, dejar sin argumentos. **53 to – stones,** atacar, criticar. **54 to – the baby out with the bath water,** V. **baby. 55 to – the book (of rules) at,** acusar de una falta, amenazar con un castigo. **56 the die is thrown/cast,** V. **die. 57 to – to the dogs,** desperdiciar, echar a perder, tirar a los perros, ceder una parte. **58 to – to the lions,** echar a los leones, a las fieras. **59 to – caution to the wind,** V. **wind. 60 to – together,** reunir apresuradamente, componer sin cuidado; juntar, unir. **61 to – up, a)** lanzar hacia arriba, tirar al aire; **b)** echar a perder, dejar de intentar; **c)** vomitar. **62 to – up one's hands,** perder toda esperanza, admitir la derrota. **63 people who live in glass houses should not – stones,** no se deben tirar piedras contra el propio tejado.

throwaway | 'θrəuə,weɪ | *adj.* **1** de usar y tirar, desechable. || *s.c.* **2** prospecto, folleto.
throwback | 'θrəubæk | *s.c.* recuerdo, retroceso, salto atrás.
throw-in | 'θrəuɪn | *s.c.* DEP. saque de banda.
thrown | θrəun | *p.p.* **1** de **throw.** || **2 – in at the deep end,** V. **deep.**
thru V. **through.**
thrum | θrʌm | *v.t.* e *i.* **1** teclear, rasguear, tamborilear. || **2 to – on,** tocar descuidadamente (un instrumento musical).
thrush | θrʌʃ | *s.c.* ZOOL. tordo, zorzal. || *s.i.* **2** MED. afta.
thrust | θrʌst | *s.i.* **1** impulso, propulsión, empuje, ímpetu, empujón. **2** estocada, puñalada, cuchillada. || *s.sing.* **3** tendencia, dirección, corriente. || *v.t.* [*pret.* y *p.p.irreg.* **thrust**] **4** empujar, impeler, impulsar, meter. **5** clavar, hincar. || *v.i.irreg.* **6** seguir, proseguir, avanzar. **7** dar un empujón, abrirse paso, lanzar una estocada. || *v.i.reg.* **8** darse importancia, entrometerse, ofrecerse inmodestamente. || **9 to – against,** apretarse contra. **10 to – aside, a)** rechazar, apartar; **b)** hacer sitio. **11 to – at, a)** asestar un golpe, lanzar una estocada a; **b)** arrojar, poner delante. **12 to – away,** rechazar. **13 to – back,** hacer retroceder. **14 to – down, a)** bajar, lanzar hacia abajo; **b) to – something down someone's throat,** V. **throat. 15 to – forward, a)** avanzar, empujar hacia adelante; **b)** ponerse en evidencia. **16 to – from,** rechazar, retirar, apartar. **17 to – home,** hacer sentir el peso de. **18 to – an/one's advantage home,** aprovechar una oportunidad. **19 to – in/into,** hacer entrar, arrojar al interior, encajar, meter en. **20 to – on/upon,** pegarse a, unirse a. **21 to – out,** sacar, despedir. **22 to – past,** empujar a alguien para pasar, apartar. **23 to – through,** abrirse paso, atravesar. **24 to – towards,** empujar en una dirección, avanzar contra una fuerte oposición. **25 to – up,** crecer.
thud | θʌd | *s.c.* **1** ruido, golpe, sonido sordo. || *v.t.* **2** golpear, dejar caer. || *v.i.* **3** caer con ruido sordo, producir un ruido sordo, sonar. || **4 to – against,** chocar contra algo.
thuggery | 'θʌgərɪ | *s.i.* gamberrismo, bandidaje, brutalidad.
thumb | θʌm | *s.c.* **1** pulgar, dedo pulgar, dedo gordo. || *v.t.* **2** hojear, manosear. **3** hacer auto-stop. || **4 all fingers and thumbs/all thumbs,** manazas, torpe. **5 to – one's nose at,** V. **nose. 6 rule of –,** de modo empírico, a la buena de Dios. **7 to stick out like a sore –,** V. **sore. 8 to – through,** buscar en un libro, pasar las hojas. **9 to twiddle one's thumbs,** V. **twiddle. 10 under someone's –,** estar dominado por.
thumbnail | 'θʌmneɪl | *s.c.* **1** uña del dedo pulgar. || *adj.* **2** breve.
thumbscrew | 'θʌmskru: | *s.c.* empulgueras.
thumbs-down | 'θʌmsdaun | *s.i.* desaprobación.
thumbs-up | 'θʌmsʌp | *s.i.* aprobación, luz verde.
thumbtack | 'θʌmtæk | *s.c.* chincheta.
thump | θʌmp | *s.c.* **1** puñetazo, golpe. **2** ruido sordo. || *v.t.* **3** golpear, dar una paliza, arrojar. || *v.i.* **4** dar golpes, hacer ruido. **5** latir desbocado. || **6 to – out a tune,** tocar música aporreando el piano.
thumping | 'θʌmpɪŋ | *adj.* aplastante, abrumador, tremendo.
thunder | 'θʌndər | *s.i.* **1** trueno. **2** ruido atronador. || *v.i.* **3** tronar, atronar, rugir, resonar. || *v.t.* **4** vociferar, hablar a gritos. || **5 like –/as black as –,** enfadado, estar que trina, estar negro. **6 to steal someone's –,** robar una idea, atraer la atención apropiándose de las ideas de otros.
thunderbolt | 'θʌndəbəult | *s.c.* rayo.
thunderclap | 'θʌndəklæp | *s.c.* trueno.
thundercloud | 'θʌndəklaud | *s.c.* nube de tormenta.
thundering | 'θʌndərɪŋ | *adj.* de trueno, estruendoso, tremendo: *thundering voice = voz de trueno.*
thunderous | 'θʌndərəs | *adj.* **1** ensordecedor, atronador. **2** tremendo, arrollador, violento: *a thunderous attack = un violento ataque.*
thunderstorm | 'θʌndəstɔ:m | *s.c.* tormenta.
thunderstruck | 'θʌndəstrʌk | *adj.* (form. o lit.) sorprendido, atónito, pasmado, asombrado, estupefacto.
thundery | 'θʌndərɪ | *adj.* tormentoso.
Thursday | 'θə:zdɪ | *s.c.* e *i.* jueves.
thus | ðʌs | *adv.* **1** así, de esta manera. **2** por eso, así que, por lo tanto, en consecuencia. || **3 – far,** V. **far.**
thwack | θwæk | *s.c.* **1** golpe fuerte, porrazo. **2** tentativa, intento. || *v.t.* **3** golpear, pegar una paliza, derrotar. **4** (EE.UU.) compartir.
thwart | θwɔ:t | *v.t.* frustrar, desbaratar, impedir, estorbar.
thy | ðaɪ | *adj.pos.* (arc.) tu. V. **thou, thee, thine.**
thyme | taɪm | *s.i.* BOT. tomillo.
thyroid | 'θaɪrɔɪd | *s.c.* **1** ANAT. tiroides. || **2 – gland,** glándula tiroidea.
thyself | ðaɪ'self | *pron.r.* (arc.) te, ti mismo, tú mismo.
tiara | tɪ'ɑ:rə | *s.c.* **1** tiara. **2** diadema.
Tibet | tɪ'bet | *s.sing.* GEOG. El Tibet.
Tibetan | tɪ'betən | *adj.* **1** tibetano. || *s.c.* **2** tibetano, persona del Tibet.
tibia | 'tɪbɪə | [*pl.* **tibias/tibiae**] *s.c.* ANAT. tibia.
tic | tɪk | *s.c.* MED. tic.
tick | tɪk | *s.c.* **1** marca, señal. **2** el tictac del reloj. **3** un segundo, un ratito, un poquitín. **4** ZOOL. garrapata, parásito. || *v.t.* **5** marcar, hacer una señal, señalar. **6** hacer tic-tac. **7** motivar: *I'd like to know what makes you tick = querría saber qué te motiva.* || **8 to – by/away,** pasar el tiempo, transcurrir el tiempo. **9 on –,** a crédito. **10 to – off, a)** marcar; **b)** reprender, echar un rapapolvo; **c)** (EE.UU.) enfadar, hacer enfadar. **11 to – off on one's fingers,** contar con los dedos, enumerar contando con los dedos. **12 to – over, a)** funcionar a marcha lenta, a ralentí; **b)** funcionar despacio con baja producción, hacer lo justo, andar falto de ideas.
ticker | 'tɪkər | *s.c.* (p.u., fam.) corazón.
ticker-tape | 'tɪkəteɪp | *s.i.* cinta perforada.
ticket | 'tɪkɪt | *s.c.* **1** entrada, billete, tiquet. **2** etiqueta, tarjeta: *ration ticket = tarjeta de racionamiento.* **3** multa, comunicación oficial. **4** tema, programa, etiqueta política. || **5 that's the –/that's just the –,** (p.u., fam.) eso es lo que hacía falta. **6 to work one's –,** escurrir el bulto.
ticking | 'tɪkɪŋ | *s.i.* **1** feliz. || **2 – off,** reprimenda, regañina.
tickle | 'tɪkl | *s.sing.* **1** cosquilleo, escozor, picor. || *v.t.* **2** hacer cosquillas, picar. **3** irritar, molestar. **4** entretener, divertir, regalar. || **5 to be tickled pink/to death,** estar encantado, entusiasmado. **6 to – one's fancy/vanity,** divertir, halagar, atraer.
ticklish | 'tɪklɪʃ | *adj.* **1** que tiene cosquillas. **2** quisquilloso, picajoso, irritable. **3** difícil, delicado, espinoso.
tidal | 'taɪdl | *adj.* **1** riada, subida del nivel del agua, marea. **2** mareo-motriz, de marea. **3** cíclico, oleada. **4 – wave,** maremoto, marejada.
tidbit V. **titbit.**
tiddler | 'tɪdlər | *s.c.* (fam. y brit.) pececito.
tiddly | 'tɪdlɪ | *adj.* **1** (fam. y brit.) achispado, entonado. **2** diminuto.
tiddlywink | 'tɪdlɪwɪŋk | *s.i.* **1** juego de la pulga. || *s.c.* **2** ficha del juego de la pulga.
tide | taɪd | *s.sing.* **1** marea, corriente. **2** tendencia, corriente de opinión. **3** oleada, flujo, multitud, cantidad. || **4 to swim/go against the –/current/stream,** nadar/ir contra corriente. **5 to – over,** sacar de un apuro, ayudar a sobrevivir por un tiempo. **6 there is a – in the affairs of men,** hay un momento para cada cosa, la ocasión nunca llega dos veces. **7 time and – wait for no man,** no dejes para mañana lo que puedas hacer hoy, la ocasión la pintan calva.
tideline | 'taɪdlaɪn | *s.c.* línea de la marea.
tidemark | 'taɪdmɑ:k | *s.c.* V. **tideline.**
tidings | 'taɪdɪŋz | *s.pl.* (p.u. y form.) nuevas, noticias.
tidily | 'taɪdɪlɪ | *adv.* ordenadamente, pulcramente, aseadamente.
tidiness | 'taɪdɪnɪs | *s.i.* limpieza, pulcritud, aseo, orden.
tidy | 'taɪdɪ | *adj.* **1** limpio, ordenado, organizado, arreglado. **2** grande, considerable, notable. **3** lógica, metódica. || *s.c.* **4** cajón de sastre, cajón para cacharros. || *v.t.* **5** ordenar, poner en orden, recoger. || **6 to – away,** recoger, retirar,

poner en su sitio. **7 to – out,** clasificar, reorganizar, desechar y ordenar. **8 to – up,** arreglar, limpiar, asear(se).
tie | taɪ | *s.c.* **1** corbata, atadura. **2** unión, enlace, lazo. **3** limitación, atadura, restricción. **4** DEP. empate, partido, ronda. || *v.t.* [*ger.* **tying**] **5** atar, ligar, reunir, rodear, anudar. **6** anudarse, atarse (los zapatos...). **7** unir, vincular. **8** limitar, restringir, atar. || *v.i.* **9** atarse, empatar. || **10 someone's hands are/etc. tied,** no poder hacer nada, estar atado de manos. || **11 to – down,** estar sometido a, estar atado, limitado. **12 to – up, a)** asegurar, atar, anudar, amarrar; **b)** inmovilizar, acaparar, retener; **c)** resolver, solucionar; **d)** ir juntos, estar unidos.
tie-break | 'taɪbreɪk | *s.c.* DEP. juego de desempate en tenis.
tie-breaker | 'taɪbreɪkər | *s.c.* pregunta de desempate.
tied | taɪd | *adj.* anejo.
tied-up | 'taɪdʌp | *adj.* **1** ocupado, atareado. **2** relacionado, implicado.
tie-dye | 'taɪdaɪ | *v.t.* teñir ropa anudada (para obtener tonos varios).
tie-pin | 'taɪpɪn | *s.c.* alfiler de corbata.
tier | tɪər | *s.c.* **1** gradas, fila, hilera. **2** sección, nivel, departamento.
tiff | tɪf | *s.c.* riña, disputa, pelea.
tiger | 'taɪgər | *s.c.* **1** ZOOL. tigre. || **2 – lily,** BOT. tigridia.
tight | taɪt | *adj.* **1** ajustado, apretado. **2** sujetado con fuerza, agarrado. **3** firme, asegurado. **4** tenso, estirado. **5** empaquetado, apretado, nutrido. **6** cerrado, agudo: *a tight turn = un giro cerrado.* **7** estricto, severo, ajustado, riguroso. **8** mal, justo (de dinero). **9** difícil, comprometida (una situación). || **10 to keep a -- rein on,** V. **rein. 12 to sit --,** V. **sit. 13 sleep --,** dormir bien, dormir profundamente. **14 tights,** leotardos.
tighten | 'taɪtn | *v.t.* **1** apretar, asegurar, tensar, agarrar. **2** tensar, endurecer, atirantar. **3** endurecer, estrechar, hacer más riguroso. || **4 to – one's belt,** V. **belt. 5 to – up, a)** apretar, asegurar; **b)** controlar estrictamente, tomar medidas de seguridad.
tight-fisted | 'taɪtfɪstɪd | *adj.* (fam.) avaro, tacaño, roñoso, agarrado.
tightlipped | 'taɪtlɪpt | *adj.* **1** de labios apretados. **2** callado, hermético: *a tightlipped silence = silencio absoluto.*
tightly | 'taɪtlɪ | *adv.* **1** estrechamente, apretadamente, firmemente. **2** de modo compacto, herméticamente. **3** rigurosamente.
tightness | 'taɪtnɪs | *s.i.* **1** estrechez, tensión, tirantez. **2** tacañería.
tightrope | 'taɪtrəʊp | *s.c.* **1** cuerda floja, alambre (circo). || **2 on a –/to walk a –,** en la cuerda floja, en situación difícil. **3 – walker,** equilibrista, funambulista, volatinero.
tigress | 'taɪgrɪs | *s.c.* ZOOL. tigresa.
tilde | tɪld | *s.c.* tilde, vírgula.
tile | taɪl | *s.c.* **1** cubrimiento, plancha. **2** teja, baldosa, azulejo. || *v.t.* **3** tejar, entejar, embaldosar, poner azulejos. || **4 to have a – loose,** tener flojo un tornillo, faltarle a uno una tuerca.
tiled | taɪld | *adj.* embaldosado, de teja, tejado.
till | tɪl | *prep.* **1** hasta. V. **until.** || *conj.* **2** hasta que. || *s.c.* **3** caja del dinero, caja registradora. || *v.t.* **4** labrar, arar, cultivar. || **5 to be caught with one fingers in the –,** coger a alguien con las manos en la masa.
tiller | tɪlər | *s.c.* **1** caña del timón. **2** labrador, agricultor.
tilt | tɪlt | *s.c.* **1** inclinación, ladeo. **2** justa, torneo. || *v.t.* e *i.* **3** inclinar, ladear. **4** influenciar, modificar. || **5 at full –,** a toda velocidad.
timber | 'tɪmbər | *s.i.* **1** madera de construcción, árbol cultivado para madera. || *s.c.* **2** viga, madero, barra de madera. || *v.t.* **3** enmaderar, entibar. || **4 –!,** ¡tronco va!
timbered | 'tɪmbəd | *adj.* **1** con vigas de madera, enmaderado, entibado. **2** arbolado, poblado de árboles, boscoso.
timbre | 'tɪmbə | *s.i.* MUS. timbre.
time | taɪm | *s.i.* **1** tiempo, hora, momento, plazo. **2** período, época, estación, temporada. **3** horas de trabajo, jornada. **4** MAT. por, multiplicado por. **5** MUS. tiempo, duración, compás. || *s.c.* **6** hora, rato, vez, ocasión. || *v.t.* **7** multiplicar. **8** fijar la hora, estar fijado, estar previsto. **9** cronometrar, calcular el tiempo, regular, ajustar, poner en hora. || **10 about –,** ya es hora que. **11 about – too/not before –/etc.,** ya era hora, ya iba siendo hora, ya está bien. **12 – after –/– and again/– and – again,** una y otra vez, continuamente. **13 – and motion study,** estudio de rendimientos. **14 ahead of –,** (llegar) antes de hora. **15 ahead of one's –/in advance of one's –/etc.,** por delante de su tiempo, de ideas avanzadas. **16 all in good –,** a su debido tiempo, a su hora. **17 all the –,** siempre, todo el rato, todo el tiempo. **18 at all times,** en todo momento. **19 at any –,** en cualquier momento. **20 at a –,** a la vez, al mismo tiempo, de una vez. **21 at one –,** en cierta época. **22 at one –/at any one –,** de una vez, de golpe, en total. **23 at the best of times,** en todo momento, en ningún momento, con todo a favor, en los mejores momentos. **24 at the same –, a)** a la vez, al mismo tiempo; **b)** aunque, sin embargo, también. **25 to beat –,** V. **beat. 26 to be doing –,** cumplir condena, estar en prisión. **27 before one's –, a)** antes de nacer uno, antes de lo que uno pueda recordar; **b)** antes de hora, antes de lo que corresponde, muy pronto. **28 behind the times,** anticuado, pasado de moda. **29 behind –,** tarde, retrasado, con retraso, mal de tiempo. **30 for all –,** para siempre, eternamente, permanentemente. **31 for the – being,** de momento, por ahora. **32 from – to –,** de vez en cuando. **33 half the –,** (desp.) la mitad del tiempo, casi siempre. **34 to have no – for,** no caer bien, considerar mal, no poder dedicar tiempo a. **35 high –,** V. **high. 36 in a week's –/in a month's –/etc.,** en una semana, en un mes, dentro de una semana, dentro de un mes. **37 in good –,** a tiempo, a su debido tiempo. **38 in no –/in next to no –/etc.,** en nada, en un momento, inmediatamente, en seguida, de repente. **39 in one's own time,** en horas libres, en el tiempo libre, fuera del trabajo. **40 it is only a matter of –/it is only a question of –,** es sólo cuestión de tiempo. **41 to keep –, a)** ir en punto, ir bien (el reloj); **b)** mantener el ritmo, llevar el compás. **42 to make good/bad/etc. –,** hacer/sacar un buen/mal promedio, costar mucho/poco tiempo, llevar más/menos de la cuenta. **43 to make the – up,** V. **make up. 44 to make up for lost –,** V. **make up. 45 to mark –,** V. **mark. 46 to move with the times,** marchar al ritmo de los tiempos, estar al día, actualizarse. **47 nine times out of ten/ninety times out of a hundred,** nueve veces de cada diez/ noventa veces de cada cien, la mayor parte de las veces, siempre. **48 no – to lose/no – to be lost/etc.,** sin tiempo que perder, no hay tiempo que perder. **49 of all times,** de todos los tiempos. **50 old times,** los viejos tiempos, de otras épocas. **51 once upon a –,** V. **once. 52 on –,** a tiempo, a la hora, en punto, puntualmente, con puntualidad. **53 our –/our times,** de nuestros días, de hoy en día, del momento. **54 – out,** pausa, descanso, intermedio, tiempo libre. **55 out of –,** fuera de compás, desacompasado. **56 to pass the –,** pasar el tiempo, pasar el rato. **57 to pass the – of day,** echar una parrafada, charlar un rato. **58 to play for –,** V. **play. 59 – signal,** señal horaria. **60 – signature,** MUS. compás. **61 someone's – is drawing near/is approaching/is up,** acercarse/llegar la hora de uno, tener los días contados. **62 – switch,** interruptor, temporizador. **63 to take one's –,** tomárselo con calma, tomarse el tiempo que se necesita. **64 to take –,** llevar (un) tiempo, costar tiempo. **65 to tell the –,** V. **tell. 66 the – of one's life,** (pasarlo) en grande/ bomba/estupendamente, etc. **67 -time,** tiempo, jornada, hora de: *full-time job = trabajo de horario completo/dedicación exclusiva; lunch time = hora de comer.* **68 – will tell,** V. **tell. 69 – zone,** huso horario.
time-bomb | 'taɪmbɒm | *s.c.* **1** MIL. bomba de relojería. **2** (fig.) bomba de tiempo: *his behaviour is just a time-bomb, the business will suffer the effects = su conducta es una bomba, el negocio se verá afectado.*
time-consuming | 'taɪmkən'sjuːmɪŋ | *adj.* que requiere/consume mucho tiempo, que cuesta/dura mucho.
timed | taɪmd | *adj.* calculado, de lugar, de hora: *his comments were so badly timed! = ¡sus comentarios estaban fuera de lugar!*
time-honoured | 'təɪm,ɒnəd | *adj.* avalado por el tiempo, tradicional, consagrado, clásico, establecido.

timekeeper | 'taɪmˌkiːpər | *s.c.* **1** reloj cronómetro, cronometrador. **2** persona puntual en el trabajo, cumplidor.
time-lag | 'taɪmlæg | *s.c.* intervalo, intermedio, interín.
timeless | 'taɪmlɪs | *adj.* eterno, intemporal.
time-limit | 'taɪmlɪmɪt | *s.c.* fecha, límite, plazo máximo.
timely | 'taɪmlɪ | *adv.* oportuno.
timepiece | 'taɪmpiːs | *s.c.* (p.u. y form.) reloj.
timer | 'taɪmər | *s.c.* **1** cronometrador. **2** temporizador, cronómetro. **3** MEC. distribuidor de encendido. || **4 -timer, a)** trabajador (por horas): *full/part-timer = trabajador a tiempo completo/parcial;* **b)** medidor del tiempo de: *egg-timer = medidor del tiempo de cocción de huevos.*
time-scale | 'taɪmskeɪl | *s.c.* período de tiempo, espacio de tiempo, lapso de tiempo.
timeserver | 'taɪmsəːvər | *s.c.* **1** contemporizador, chaquetero, acomodaticio, veleta. **2** persona que va al trabajo a pasar el tiempo.
time-share | 'taɪmʃeər | *s.c.* turno, parte de tiempo, porción de tiempo, tiempo que corresponde para el uso o disfrute de una cosa.
time-sharing | 'taɪmʃeərɪŋ | *s.i.* sistema de turnos, distribución o forma de compartir tiempo (para el uso o disfrute de una cosa).
timesheet | 'taɪmʃiːt | *s.c.* registro de permanencia, tarjeta.
timetable | 'taɪmteɪbl | *s.c.* **1** horario, programa; guía de transportes. || *v.t.* **2** planificar, organizar según un horario.
timetown | 'taɪmwɔːn | *adj.* desgastado, gastado, trillado, deteriorado.
timid | 'tɪmɪd | *adj.* **1** tímido, timorato. **2** asustadizo, apocado.
timidity | tɪ'mɪdɪtɪ | *s.i.* timidez.
timidly | 'tɪmɪdlɪ | *adv.* tímidamente.
timing | 'taɪmɪŋ | *s.i.* **1** oportunidad, ritmo, compás. **2** cálculo de tiempos, cronometraje. || *s.sing.* **3** TEC. encendido, distribución, reglaje.
timorous | 'tɪmərəs | *adj.* timorato, apocado, temeroso.
timpani | 'tɪmpənɪ | *s.pl.* MUS. timbales.
timpanist | 'tɪmpənɪst | *s.c.* MUS. timbalista.
tin | tɪn | *s.i.* **1** estaño, hojalata. || *s.c.* **2** lata, bote de conservas. V. **can. 3** molde. || *adj.* **4** de estaño, de hojalata: *tin soldier = soldadito de plomo.* || *v.t.* [*ger.* **tinning,** *pret.* y *p.p.* **tinned**] **5** estañar, enlatar, envasar, conservar. || **6 a little – god,** creído, engreído, diosecillo. **7 to put the – lid on,** poner fin a, dar el cerrojazo. **8 – hat,** MIL. casco de acero. **9 Tin Pan Alley,** mundo de los compositores de música moderna, del espectáculo.
tincture | 'tɪŋktʃər | *s.c.* **1** MED. tintura, disolución. **2** tinte, barniz, matiz. || *v.t.* **3** **[to – with]** teñir de, matizar.
tinder | 'tɪndər | *s.i.* yesca.
tinderbox | 'tɪndəbɒks | *s.c.* yesquero, chisquero.
tine | taɪn | *s.c.* punta, púa, diente (de peine, o tenedor).
tinfoil | 'tɪnfɔɪl | *s.i.* papel de estaño.
ting | tɪŋ | *s.c.* **1** tintineo. **2** tin, clin, tilín, (onomatopeya). || *v.i.* **3** sonar (una campana), tintinear, hacer sonar.
ting-a-ling | ˌtɪŋə'lɪŋ | *adv.* tilín (onomatopeya).
tinge | 'tɪndʒ | *s.c.* **1** tinte, matiz, tono, toque: *with a tinge of indignation = con un tono de indignación.* || *v.t.* **2** **[to – with]** teñir de, matizar.
tinged | 'tɪndʒt | *adj.* **[– with] 1** teñido, matizado. **2** afectado, tener un tono, tocado, cierto: *his voice was tinged with remorse = había un cierto remordimiento en su voz.*
tingle | 'tɪngl | *s.c.* **1** pinchazos, hormigueo, escozor, estremecimiento. || *v.i.* **2** escocer, doler, dar pinchazos. **3** **[to – with]** reventar de, estar lleno de, morirse de, estremecerse de, temblar de: *she was tingling with excitement = no cabía en sí de emoción.*
tingling | 'tɪŋglɪŋ | *s.i.* hormigueo.
tinker | 'tɪŋkər | *s.c.* **1** calderero, hojalatero, quincallero, gitano. **2** pícaro, pillo, malo. **3** un arreglo, un repaso, una revisión. || *v.t.* **4** componer, arreglar, remendar. || *v.i.* **5** **[to – with]** jugar con, entretenerse con, tocar. **6** **[to – about/ around]** enredar con, juguetear con, andar a vueltas con: *to tinker with machines = andar a vueltas con máquinas.* || **7 not to give/care a tinker's cuss/damn,** no importar un bledo/comino.
tinkle | 'tɪŋkl | *s.c.* **1** tintineo. || *v.i.* **2** tintinear. || **3 to give someone a –,** llamar por teléfono, dar un toque, dar un telefonazo.
tinned | tɪnd | *adj.* enlatado: *tinned food = comida en lata.*
tinny | 'tɪnɪ | *adj.* **1** de estaño, de hojalata. **2** metálico, que suena o sabe a lata. **3** cacharro, poco sólido, desvencijado.
tin-opener | 'tɪnəupənər | *s.c.* abrelatas.
tinpot | 'tɪnpɒt | *adj.* insignificante, de pacotilla.
tinsel | 'tɪnsl | *s.i.* oropel.
tint | tɪnt | *s.c.* **1** tinte, tono, matiz. **2** teñido. || *v.t.* **3** teñir.
tinted | 'tɪntɪd | *adj.* coloreado, teñido.
tiny | 'taɪnɪ | *adj.* **1** diminuto, minúsculo. **2** pequeño.
tip | tɪp | *s.c.* **1** punta, extremo, extremidad. **2** advertencia, consejo. **3** propina. **4** pronóstico, confidencia. **5** basurero, vertedero, escombrera. **6** pocilga. || *v.t.* **7** inclinar, ladear, tocar ligeramente. **8** tirar (basura). **9** pronosticar, recomendar, elegir. **10** verter, vaciar, desparramar, volcar. **11** dar propina, dejar una propina. || **12 to be tipped for,** pronosticar para. **13 it is tipping/it is tipping down,** está lloviendo a cántaros. **14 on the – of one's tongue,** en la punta de la lengua. **15 to – off,** advertir, avisar, dar una información, informar, prevenir. **16 to – over,** volcar, vaciar, verter, caerse, hacer caer. **17 the – of the iceberg,** la punta del iceberg. **18 to – someone the wink,** hacer una señal. **19 to – the scales/to – the balance, a)** inclinar la balanza, decidir el resultado; **b)** pesar. **20 to – up,** inclinar, ladear, verter.
tip-off | 'tɪpɒf | *s.c.* advertencia, información, soplo, confidencia.
tipped | tɪpt | *adj.* **1** con contera, con punta. **2** con filtro, emboquillado.
tippet | 'tɪpɪt | *s.c.* esclavina.
tipple | 'tɪpl | *s.c.* **1** bebida, bebida habitual. **2** (EE.UU.) vertedero. || *v.t.* **3** beber más de la cuenta, empinar el codo, soplar.
tippler | 'tɪplər | *s.c.* bebedor, borracho.
tipster | 'tɪpstər | *s.c.* pronosticador.
tipsy | 'tɪpsɪ | *adj.* alegre, achispado, piripi.
tiptoe | 'tɪptəu | *s.i.* **1** punta del pie, puntillas. || *v.i.* **2** andar de puntillas, ir de puntillas. || **3 on –,** de puntillas, sigilosamente.
tip-top | ˌtɪp'tɒp | *adj.* **1** estupendo, excelente, de primera clase, perfecto. || **2 on – form,** en plena forma.
tirade | taɪ'reɪd | *s.c.* diatriba, perorata.
tire | 'taɪər | *v.i.* **1** cansar(se), aburrir(se). || V. **tyre.**
tired | 'taɪəd | *adj.* **1** cansado, fatigado. **2** **[– (of)]** harto, aburrido, cansado. **3** desgastado, viejo: *a tired machine = una máquina que funciona mal.* **4** pasado, tópico, lugar común: *a tired idea = una idea pasada.* || **5 sick and –,** V. **sick. 6 – out,** agotado, exhausto.
tiredness | 'taɪədnɪs | *s.i.* cansancio.
tireless | 'taɪəlɪs | *adj.* incansable, infatigable.
tirelessly | 'taɪəlɪslɪ | *adv.* incansablemente, infatigablemente.
tiresome | 'taɪəsəm | *adj.* irritante, cargante, agotador, pesado.
tiring | 'taɪərɪŋ | *adj.* pesado, cansado.
tiro V. **tyro.**
tissue | 'tɪʃuː | *s.i.* **1** BIOL. tejido. || *s.c.* **2** pañuelo de papel. || **3 – of lies,** sarta de mentiras. **4 – paper,** papel de seda.
tit | tɪt | *s.c.* **1** ZOOL. paro: *blue tit = herrerillo común.* **2** estúpido, gili. **3** (vulg.) teta. || **4 – for tat,** donde las dan las toman.
tits | tɪts | *s.c.* (vulg.) tetas.
titan | 'taɪtn | *s.c.* titán, gigante.
titanic | taɪ'tænɪk | *adj.* titánico, monumental.
titanium | taɪ'teɪnɪəm | *s.i.* titanio.
titbit | 'tɪtbɪt | *s.c.* **1** chisme, cotilleo, escándalo. **2** golosina, bocado de cardenal, manjar exquisito.
titchy | 'tɪtʃɪ | *adj.* diminuto, minúsculo, pequeñísimo.
titfer | 'tɪtfər | *s.c.* (p.u., brit.) sombrero.
tithe | taɪð | *s.c.* contribución, diezmo.
titillate | 'tɪtɪleɪt | *v.t.* excitar, estimular.
titillation | ˌtɪtɪ'leɪʃn | *s.i.* estimulación, excitación.
title | 'taɪtl | *s.c.* **1** título, nombre, letrero. **2** publicación, obra publicada. **3** títu-

lo, tratamiento. **4** escritura, título de propiedad. **5** campeonato. || *s.i.* **6** derecho. || *v.t.* **7** poner título, titular, poner subtítulos, subtitular. || **8 – part/ role,** papel estelar, papel del título.
titled | 'taɪtld | *adj.* con título de nobleza.
title-holder | 'taɪtlhəuldər | *s.c.* campeón, poseedor del título, detentador del título, titular.
titter | 'tɪtər | *s.c.* **1** risita, risa disimulada. || *v.i.* **2** reírse con disimulo.
title-tattle | 'tɪtltætl | *s.i.* charla, conversación informal, cotilleo.
titular | 'tɪtjulər | *adj.* nominal, titular.
tizzy | 'tɪzɪ | *s.i.* **1** excitación, nerviosismo. || **2 to get in/into a –,** ponerse nervioso, liarse, armarse un lío.
TNT | ˌtiːen'tiː | *s.i.* T.N.T.
to | tuː | pronunciación relajada | tə | *prep.* **1** a, para, con destino a. **2** a, hacia, contra: *cheek to cheek = con las mejillas juntas.* **3** en. **4** hasta. **5** menos, para las (reloj). **6** de, con: *kind to her = amable con ella.* **7** por, en honor de: *let's drink to them = bebamos por ellos.* **8** en cada, por: *twenty kilometres to the litre = veinte kilómetros por litro.* **9** según, de acuerdo con. **10** comparado con, en comparación con. || *adv.* **11** cerca: *he closed the door to = volvió la puerta, entornó la puerta.* || *conj.* **12** a, para. || **13 from... to...,** de... a, desde... hasta; de un... a otro, de... en. **14 nothing to it/not much to it,** no es nada, no tiene nada, carece de importancia. **15 to and fro/to-ing and fro-ing,** de un lado a otro, arriba y abajo.
toad | təud | *s.c.* **1** sapo. || **2 toad-in-the-hole,** salchicha rebozada.
toadstool | 'təudstuːl | *s.c.* **1** BOT. seta. **2** hongo venenoso.
toady | 'təudɪ | *s.c.* adulador, pelotillero, lameculos.
toast | təust | *s.i.* **1** tostada. || *s.c.* **2** brindis. || *s.sing.* **3** el orgullo, el héroe. || *v.t.* e *i.* **4** tostar(se). **5** brindar.
toaster | 'təustər | *s.c.* tostadora.
toasting-fork | 'təustɪŋfɔːk | *s.c.* parrilla, tostadera.
toastmaster | 'təustmɑːstər | *s.c.* maestro de ceremonias.
toast-rack | 'təustræk | *s.c.* portatostadas.
tobacco | tə'bækəu | *s.i.* tabaco.
tobacconist | tə'bækənɪst | *s.c.* **1** estanquero, estanquillero, tabaquero. || **2 the tobacconist's,** el estanco, tabaquería.
toboggan | tə'bɒgən | *s.c.* **1** trineo. || *v.i.* **2** (EE.UU.) ir en trineo, deslizarse. **3** (brit.) hacer carreras deslizándose por la nieve.
toccata | tə'kɑːtə | *s.c.* MUS. tocata.
tod | tɒd | (fam., brit.) **on one's tod,** solo.
today | tə'deɪ | *s.c.* **1** hoy: *today is Monday = hoy es lunes.* || *adv.* **2** hoy: *he's coming today = viene hoy.* **3** hoy, hoy en día, actualmente, ahora, en este momento. || **4 better a hen – than a hen tomorrow,** más vale pájaro en mano que ciento volando. **5 here – gone tomorrow,** visto y no visto. **6 never put off till tomorrow what you can do –,** no dejes para mañana lo que puedas hacer hoy.
toddle | 'tɒdl | *v.i.* andar tambaleándose.
toddler | 'tɒdlər | *s.c.* niño que empieza a andar.
toddy | 'tɒdɪ | *s.c.* e *i.* ponche.
to-do | tə'duː | *s.sing.* (fam.) lío, follón, jaleo.
toe | təu | *s.c.* **1** dedo (del pie). **2** puntera, punta (del zapato, del calcetín...). || *v.t.* e *i.* **3** pisar con la punta del pie: *to toe a cigarette out = apagar un cigarrillo pisándolo.* || **4 to keep someone on one's toes,** estar/mantener(se) alerta, atento, al tanto. **5 to – the line/the party line,** comportarse, conformarse, aceptar las normas, someterse. **6 to tread on someone's toes,** V. **tread.**
toecap | 'təukæp | *s.c.* puntera.
toehold | 'təuhəuld | *s.c.* **1** DEP. punto de apoyo para el pie (en escalada). **2** (fig.) proyección, trampolín, pedestal.
toenail | 'təuneɪl | *s.c.* **1** uña del pie **2** clavo oblicuo.
toff | tɒf | *s.c.* (p.u., fam.) rico, noble, elegante.
toffee | 'tɒfɪ |, (EE.UU.) | 'tɒːfɪ | (también **toffy**) *s.c.* e *i.* **1** tofe, caramelo. **2 for –,** en absoluto, en modo alguno; ni idea: *he can't do it for toffee = no tiene ni idea de como hacerlo.*
toffee-apple | 'tɒfɪæpl | *s.c.* manzana con caramelo, pirulí.
toffee-nosed | 'tɒfɪnəuzd | *adj.* engreído, presuntuoso.
toffy V. **toffee.**
tog | tɒg | *s.c.* **1** caloría (medida oficial del calor que proporciona una manta...). || **2 to – up,** vestirse, ataviarse, emperifollarse.
togs | tɒgz | *s.i.* ropa, vestidos.
toga | 'təugə | *s.c.* toga.
together | tə'gəðər | *adv.* **1** junto, juntos, juntamente, a la vez, al mismo tiempo. **2** ininterrumpidamente, sin parar: *days and days together = durante días y días.* || **3 – with,** junto con, conjuntamente.
togetherness | tə'gəðənɪs | *s.i.* espíritu, sentimiento de grupo, familia, etc..., compañerismo, solidaridad.
togged | tɒgd | **– up/out,** perfectamente equipado.
toggle | 'tɒgl | *s.c.* pasador, alamar, cierre.
toil | tɔɪl | *s.i.* **1** trabajo, esfuerzo agotador. || *v.i.* **2** trabajar duro. **3** andar penosamente. || **4 to – at/over,** trabajar mucho algo, dedicar mucha atención a algo. **5 to – away,** trabajar como un esclavo, como un negro. **6 to – and moil,** (p.u., fam.) trabajar a disgusto, descornarse, dejarse la piel. **7 to – up,** escalar con gran esfuerzo.
toilet | 'tɔɪlɪt | *s.c.* **1** taza de retrete, inodoro, letrina. **2** retrete, lavabo, baño, letrina, servicios. **3** arreglo, aseo. || *adj.* **4** de tocador. | **5 to go to the –,** evacuar, defecar, orinar. **6 – paper,** papel higiénico. **7 – roll,** rollo de papel higiénico. **8 – set,** juego de tocador. **9 =N soap,** jabón de tocador. **10 – water,** agua de colonia.
toilet-bag | 'tɔɪlɪtbæg | *s.c.* bolsa de aseo.
toiletries | 'tɔɪlɪtrɪz | *s.i.* artículos de tocador.
toilet-train | 'tɔɪlɪttreɪn | *v.t.* enseñar a controlar los esfínteres.
token | 'təukən | *s.c.* **1** ficha, vale. **2** prueba, muestra. **3** simbólico, nominal. || **4 by the same –,** por la misma razón.
told | təuld | [*pret. p.p.irreg.* **1 tell** || **2 all –,** contando todo, en total.
tolerable | 'tɒlərəbl | *adj.* **1** tolerable, soportable, aceptable. **2** adecuado, razonable, regular, pasable.
tolerably | 'tɒlərəblɪ | *adv.* tolerablemente, aceptablemente.
tolerance | 'tɒlərəns | *s.i.* **1** tolerancia, paciencia, indulgencia. **2** resistencia, aguante. || *s.c.* **2** TEC. resistencia (de un material). **3** MAT. tolerancia, variación, margen de confianza.
tolerant | 'tɒlərənt | *adj.* **1** tolerante, indulgente. **2 [– of]** resistente a.
tolerantly | 'tɒlərəntlɪ | *adv.* con tolerancia, con indulgencia.
tolerate | 'tɒləreɪt | *v.t.* **1** tolerar, aceptar, permitir, admitir, respetar. **2** soportar, aguantar, sufrir: *not to be tolerated = inaguantable.*
toleration | ˌtɒləreɪʃn | *s.i.* tolerancia.
toll | təul | *s.c.* **1** peaje, tasa, pontaje, estación de peaje. **2** bajas, número de víctimas. || *v.t.* **3 [to – (for)]** tañer, tocar, doblar (las campanas): *the bell tolls for thee = las campanas doblan por ti.* || **4 to take a heavy –,** cobrar un alto precio en vidas o daños, infligir muchas bajas. **5 to take a –/to take its –,** se cobra su precio.
tollhouse | 'təulhaus | *s.c.* estación de peaje.
tom | tɒm | *s.c.* gato macho.
tomahawk | 'tɒməhɔːk | *s.c.* tomahawk.
tomato | tə'mɑːtəu | (EE.UU.) | tə'meɪtəu | [*pl.* **tomatoes**] *s.c.* tomate, tomatera.
tomb | tuːm | *s.c.* tumba, sepulcro.
tombola | tɒm'bəulə | *s.c.* e *i.* tómbola, lotería.
tomboy | 'tɒmbɔɪ | *s.c.* (desp.) chicazo, muchachota, marimacho.
tombstone | 'tuːmstəun | *s.c.* lápida sepulcral.
tomcat | 'tɒmkæt | *s.c.* gato macho. V. **tom.**
tome | təum | *s.c.* **1** (form.) volumen. **2** (fam.) librote, libraco.
tomfoolery | ˌtɒm'fuːlərɪ | *s.c.* tonterías, payasadas, estupideces.
tommyrot | ˌtɒmɪ'rɒt | *s.i.* disparates, tonterías, bobadas.
tomorrow | tə'mɒrəu | *adv.* **1** mañana. **2** el mañana, el porvenir. || *s.c.* **3** mañana: *tomorrow is Wednesday = mañana es*

miércoles. || **4 like there is no –,** como si fuera lo último. **5 never put off till – what you can do today,** V. **today. 6 – is another day,** mañana será otro día. **7 – never comes,** mañana es nunca jamás.
tomtit | 'tɒmtɪt | *s.c.* ZOOL. paro carbonero, carbonero común.
tom-tom | 'tɒmtɒm | *s.c.* tam-tam.
ton | tʌn | (también **tonne**) *s.c.* **1** tonelada. || *cuant.* **2** toneladas, montones, kilos. || **3 to come down on someone like a – of bricks,** echar una bronca de mil pares de demonios. **4 to do a –,** (p.u., fam.) ir a toda pastilla, ir a cien. **5 to weigh a –,** pesar mucho, pesar un quintal.
tonal | 'təʊnl | *adj.* tonal.
tonality | təʊ'nælɪtɪ | *s.i.* tonalidad.
tone | təʊn | *s.c.* **1** tono, tonalidad, matiz, modo. **2** MUS. tono, intervalo. || *s.i.* **3** tono, carácter, estilo. || *s.sing.* **4** distinción, buen tono, elegancia, calidad. || *v.i.* **5 [to – with]** armonizar con, conjuntar, ir bien juntos: *do the socks tone in with the tie? = ¿le van los calcetines a la corbata?* || *v.t.* **6** entonar, tonificar. **7** matizar, modificar. **8** FOT. virar. || **9** MUS. afinar, templar. || **10 to – down,** suavizar, rebajar, amortiguar, atenuar. **11 to – up,** resaltar, elevar el tono, avivar.
tone-deaf | ˌtəʊn'def | *adj.* falto de sentido musical, que no tiene oído.
toneless | 'təʊnlɪs | *adj.* monótono, carente de matices, apagado.
tonelessly | 'təʊnlɪslɪ | *adv.* sin matices, apagadamente.
tongs | tɒŋz | *s.pl.* **1** pinzas, tenacillas: *a pair of tongs = unas pinzas.* **2** TEC. tenazas. || **3 hammer and tongs,** V. **hammer.**
tongue | tʌŋ | *s.c.* **1** ANAT. lengua. **2** lengua, lenguaje, idioma. **3** (fig.) lengua, modo de hablar: *he's too free with his tongue = tiene la lengua muy suelta.* **4** lengüeta (zapato...), aguja, badajo. || **5 to feel the rough side/edge of one's –,** sentir la lengua afilada de alguien, recibir una buena bronca. **6 to find one's –,** atreverse a hablar, soltar la lengua. **7 not to get one's – round,** trabarse, enredarse la lengua. **8 to give someone the rough side of one's –,** ser desagradable, descortés con alguien. **9 to have one's – in one's cheek,** irónicamente, burlonamente. **10 to hold/bite one's –,** callarse, morderse la lengua, reprimirse. **11 to keep a civil – in one's head,** ser cortés, mesurado, mantener las formas. **12 to lose one's –/the cat has got one's –,** no tener/haber perdido la lengua, habérsele comido (a alguien) la lengua el gato. **13 on the tip of one's –,** V. **tip. 14 set tongues wagging,** dar que hablar. **15 slip off the –,** lapsus linguae, error, desliz.
tongue-in-cheek | ˌtʌŋɪn'tʃiːk | *adj.* jocoso, irónico, frívolo.
tongue-tied | 'tʌŋtaɪd | *adj.* tímido, que no se atreve a hablar.
tongue-twister | 'tʌŋtwɪstər | *s.c.* trabalenguas.
tonic | 'tɒnɪk | *s.c.* **1** tónico. **2** MUS. tónica. || *s.i.* **3** agua tónica. **4** MED. tonificante, revigorizante: *hair tonic = tónico capilar.* || **5 – water,** agua tónica.
tonight | tə'naɪt | *adv.* **1** esta noche, hoy por la noche. || *s.c.* **2** esta noche: *tonight is New Year's Eve = esta noche es Noche Vieja.*
tonnage | 'tʌnɪdʒ | *s.c.* e *i.* tonelaje.
tonne V. **ton.**
tonsil | 'tɒnsl | *s.c.* ANAT. amígdala, angina.
tonsilitis | ˌtɒnsɪ'laɪtɪs | *s.i.* MED. amigdalitis, anginas.
tonsure | 'tɒnʃər | *s.c.* **1** tonsura. || *v.t.* **2** tonsurar.
too | tuː | *adv.* **1** también. **2** a la vez, al mismo tiempo: *it was nice and sad too = era agradable y triste a la vez.* **3** es más, y lo que es más: *it's very expensive and it's broken too = es muy caro y encima está roto.* **4** por cierto, además: *and very good too = y muy bueno por cierto.* **5** ya está bien, ya era hora. **6** extremadamente, muy: *it's too kind of you = muy amable por su parte.* || *adv./cuant.* **6** demasiado. || **7 all --.../only --...,** demasiado, muy, totalmente. **8 none --,** V. **none. 9 -- bad,** V. **bad. 10 --... by half,** V. **half.**
OBS. Colocación: como adverbio se coloca al final de la frase; con artículo indefinido la siguiente estructura es posible: *it's too warm a day to go out.* Se coloca delante de los adjetivos, y para reforzar su significado puede usarse, **a bit, a little, rather, a lot, much,** o **far;** pero no: **very, fairly, pretty,** o **quite.** Se usa con adjetivo + infinitivo: *too old to travel.* A menudo se utiliza una estructura con **for** después de **too:** *it's too high for you to reach it.* Como cuantificador junto con **much** y **many** para indicar exceso referido a sustantivos incontables y contables respectivamente. **Too much,** puede usarse sin sustantivo con valor adverbial: *that's too much = es demasiado.*
took | tʊk | *pret.irreg.* de **take.**
tool | tuːl | *s.c.* **1** herramienta, útil de trabajo, máquina herramienta, utensilio. **2** (fig.) instrumento. **3** (fig.) marioneta, compañero de viaje. || **4 to down tools,** hacer huelga de brazos caídos. **5 the tools of the trade/the tools of one's trade,** equipo de trabajo, herramientas del oficio.
tool-box | 'tuːlbɒks | *s.c.* caja de herramientas.
tool-kit | 'tuːlkɪt | *s.c.* juego de herramientas.
tool-shed | 'tuːlshed | *s.c.* cobertizo para las herramientas.
toot | tuːt | *s.c.* **1** toque de bocina. || *v.i.* **2** tocar la bocina.
tooth | tuːθ | [*pl.irreg.* **teeth**] *s.c.* **1** ANAT. diente, muela. **2** diente, púa, pico. || **3 a kick in the teeth,** V. **kick. 4 armed to the teeth,** armado hasta los dientes. **5 a sweet –,** V. **sweet. 6 by the skin of one's teeth,** V. **skin. 7 to cut one's teeth on,** ganar experiencia. **8 fed up to the teeth/fed up to the back teeth,** estar harto, hasta las narices, hasta la coronilla. **9 to fight for something – and nail/to fight something tooth and nail,** luchar con uñas y dientes, a brazo partido, como gato panza arriba. **10 to get one's teeth into,** hincarle el diente a algo. **11 to get /take the bit between one's teeth,** V. **bit. 12 to gnash one's teeth at/over,** enfadarse, rechinar los dientes. **13 to grind one's teeth,** V. **grind. 14 to grit one's teeth,** V. **grit. 15 in the teeth of, a)** en pleno, en medio de; **b)** a pesar de. **16 to lie through one's teeth/to lie in some one's teeth,** mentir descaradamente, mentir como un bellaco. **17 long in the tooth,** ser viejo, tener muchos años. **18 to set one's teeth on edge,** V. **edge. 19 to show one's teeth,** enseñar los dientes. **20 to throw/fling/cast in someone's teeth /face,** echar en cara.
toothache | 'tuːθeɪk | *s.i.* dolor de dientes, dolor de muelas.
toothbrush | 'tuːθbrʌʃ | *s.c.* cepillo de dientes.
toothcomb V. **fine-tooth comb.**
toothless | 'tuːθlɪs | *adj.* **1** desdentado. **2** (fig.) inoperante, sin poder.
toothpaste | 'tuːθpeɪst | *s.i.* pasta de dientes, pasta dentífrica.
toothpick | 'tuːθpɪk | *s.c.* palillo de dientes, mondadientes.
toothpowder | 'tuːθpaʊdər | *s.i.* polvos dentífricos.
toothy | 'tuːθɪ | *adj.* dentón, dentudo: *he gave me a toothy smile = me dedicó una sonrisa todo dientes.*
tootle | 'tuːtl | *v.t.* **1** tocar (un instrumento). || *v.i.* **2** andar, ir con calma.
tootsie | 'tuːtsɪ | (también **tootsy**) *s.c.* **1** (EE.UU.) chica, nena, gachí. **2** (fam.) piececito, dedito del pie.
top | tɒp | *s.c.* **1 [the –],** la parte superior, la parte de arriba, parte alta. **2** extremo, final, tejado, techo. **3** tapa, tape, capuchón, capota, tablero. **4** chaqueta, blusa, camiseta, sujetador, sostén. **5** peonza, trompo. **6** cima, cumbre, copa. || *s.i.* **7** MEC. la larga, la directa, la marcha más alta. || *adj.* **8** lo más alto, de arriba, último, extremo, máximo, alto, los mejores, más importante: *top executives = altos ejecutivos.* || *v.t.* **9** alcanzar la cima, coronar, exceder, sobrepasar. **10** superar, mejorar, rematar. **11** cubrir, tapar. || **12 at the – of one's voice,** V. **voice. 13 to be on – of,** dominar. **14 to blow one's –,** perder el control, estallar de furia. **15 to come out on –,** vencer, ponerse a la cabeza. **16 – dressing,** capa de abono o estiércol. **17 from – to bottom,** completamente, totalmente. **18 from – to toe,** de la cabeza a los pies. **19 to get on – of,** superar, desquiciar. **20 – of the tree,** V. **tree. 21 off the – of one's head,** V. **head. 22 on –,** encima. **23 on –/over the –,** por encima, cubriendo. **24 on – of,** además de. **25 on – of the world,** V. **world. 26 over the –,** encima, por encima. **27 thin on –,** V. **thin. 28 –**

and tail, despuntar, cortar los extremos. **27 tops/the tops,** los mejores, los primeros. **28 up –,** tonto, de poco seso.
topaz | 'təʊpæz | *s.c.* topacio.
topcoat | 'tɒpkəʊt | *s.c.* **1** última mano (de pintura). **2** abrigo.
top-drawer | ˌtɒp'drɔːər | *s.c.* de primera, de alta sociedad.
top-hat | ˌtɒp'hæt | *s.c.* sombrero de copa, chistera.
top-heavy | ˌtɒp'hevɪ | *adj.* **1** inestable, mal equilibrado, con mucho peso arriba. **2** con demasiados mandos o altos cargos.
topiary | 'təʊpɪərɪ | *s.i.* TEC. poda artística de setos y arbustos.
topic | 'tɒpɪk | *s.c.* tópico, tema, asunto.
topical | 'tɒpɪkl | *adj.* actual, de actualidad.
topicality | ˌtɒpɪ'kælɪtɪ | *s.i.* actualidad, adecuación.
top-knot | 'tɒpnɒt | *s.c.* moño, copete.
topless | 'tɒplɪs | *adj.* sin sujetador, con el busto desnudo.
top-level | 'tɒplevl | *adj.* del más alto nivel, importante.
topmost | 'tɒpməʊst | *adj.* los más altos.
top-notch | ˌtɒp'nɒtʃ | *adj.* de primera clase, de primera categoría.
topographical | ˌtɒpə'græfɪkl | *adj.* topográfico.
topography | tə'pɒgrəfɪ | *s.i.* topografía.
topped | tɒpt | *adj.* coronado, puesto encima, por encima.
topper | 'tɒpər | *s.c.* sombrero de copa, chistera.
topping | 'tɒpɪŋ | *s.i.* **1** cúspide, copete, cobertura: *the cake had a topping of cream = el pastel tenía una cobertura de nata.* || *adj.* **2** (p.u., fam. y brit.) estupendo, fantástico, bárbaro, extraordinario.
topple | 'tɒpl | *v.t.* **1** hacer caer, derribar. || *v.i.* **2** volcarse, venirse abajo, tambalearse, caerse. || **3 to – down,** caerse, fallar. **4 to – from,** caer desde, derribar de. **5 to – over,** derrumbarse.
top-ranking | ˌtɒp'ræŋkɪŋ | *adj.* dirigente, de altura, de alto cargo.
top-secret | ˌtɒp'siːkrɪt | *adj.* alto secreto, confidencial.
topside | 'tɒpsaɪd | *s.i.* filete de ternera.
topsoil | 'tɒpsɔɪl | *s.i.* capa superficial del suelo.
topsy-turvy | ˌtɒpsɪ'tɜːvɪ | *adj.* patas arriba, revuelto.
top-up | 'tɒpʌp | *s.c.* bebida, otro, otro trago, otra ronda (servida en el mismo vaso): *let's have a top-up = venga, otra de lo mismo.*
torch | tɔːtʃ | *s.c.* **1** linterna eléctrica, lámpara de bolsillo. **2** antorcha, tea, hacha. || **3 to carry a – for,** estar secretamente enamorado de.
torchlight | 'tɔːtʃlaɪt | *s.i.* luz de linterna o antorcha.
tore | tɔːr | *pret.irreg.* de **tear.**
torment | 'tɔːment | *s.c.* **1** tortura, tormento, suplicio. || *s.i.* **2** angustia, agonía. || *v.t.* **3** atormentar, martirizar, torturar. **4** fastidiar, molestar.
tormentor | tɔː'mentər | *s.c.* torturador, atormentador.
torn | tɔːn | *p.p.irreg.* de **tear.**
tornado | tɔː'neɪdəʊ | [*pl.* **tornados** o **tornadoes**] *s.c.* tornado, ciclón.
torpedo | tɔː'piːdəʊ | [*pl.* **torpedoes**] *s.c.* **1** torpedo. || *v.t.* **2** torpedear, atacar con torpedos. **3** (fig.) torpedear, entorpecer, sabotear.
torpid | 'tɔːpɪd | *adj.* letárgico, aletargado, torpe, apático.
torpor | 'tɔːpər | *s.i.* letargo, apatía, sopor.
torque | tɔːk | *s.i.* TEC. momento de torsión, par de torsión.
torrent | 'tɒrənt | *s.c.* **1** torrente. **2** torrente, montón, avalancha.
torrential | tə'renʃl | *adj.* torrencial.
torrid | 'tɒrɪd | *adj.* **1** tórrido. **2** apasionado, ardiente.
torsion | 'tɔːʃn | *s.i.* torsión.
torso | 'tɔːsəʊ | *s.c.* torso, tronco.
tort | tɔːt | *s.c.* e *i.* agravio, daño, falta.
tortilla | tɔː'tiːə | *s.c.* tortilla, tortita, panqueque.
tortoise | 'tɔːtəs | *s.c.* ZOOL. tortuga.
tortoiseshell | 'tɔːtəsʃel | *s.c.* concha de tortuga, carey.
tortuous | 'tɔːtʃʊəs | *adj.* tortuoso, retorcido.
tortuously | 'tɔːtʃʊəslɪ | *adv.* tortuosamente, retorcidamente.
torture | 'tɔːtʃər | *s.c.* **1** tortura, atrocidad. || *s.i.* **2** tormento, tortura, crueldad. || *v.t.* **3** torturar, atormentar, martirizar. **4** sufrir, hacer(se) daño.
torturer | 'tɔːtʃərər | *s.c.* torturador, verdugo.
Tory | 'tɔːrɪ | *s.c.* conservador, miembro del partido Conservador.
toss | tɒs | (EE.UU.) | tɔːs | *s.c.* **1** movimiento, sacudida, caída. **2** lanzamiento, vuelta. || *v.t.* e *i.* **3 [to – (about/ around)]** tirar, lanzar, echar descuidadamente. **4** mover(se), remover(se), dar vueltas. **5** sacudir(se), agitar(se), echar hacia atrás (la cabeza). || **6 to argue the –,** insistir, andar en dimes y diretes, continuar discutiendo. **7 to – a coin,** echarlo a cara o cruz. **8 to – around,** considerar. **9 to – aside, a)** echar a un lado; **b)** dejar a un lado, dar de lado, abandonar. **10 to – away,** desaprovechar. **11 to – back,** beber como un cosaco. **12 to – down,** derribar. **13 to – for,** competir. **14 to – in/into, a)** añadir, agregar, dejar caer; **b)** meter, echar dentro de. **15 not to give a –,** no importar un comino, dar igual. **16 to – off, a)** hacerlo rápidamente, quitárselo de enmedio; **b)** masturbarse. **17 to – one's money about/around,** tirar el dinero, gastar a lo loco. **18 to – one's weight about/ around,** dar órdenes innecesarias, hacer valer la propia autoridad. **19 to – out,** expulsar, librarse de, rechazar. **20 to – together,** reunir, juntar, formar. **21 to – up,** lanzar hacia arriba, desperdiciar, tirar por la borda.
toss-up | 'tɒsʌp | *s.sing.* incertidumbre, duda.
tot | tɒt | *s.c.* **1** nene, crío. || *s.i.* **2** trago, latigazo. || **3 to – up,** sumar, totalizar, calcular: *the bill tots up to... = la factura asciende a...*
total | 'təʊtl | *s.c.* **1** total. || *adj.* **2** global, de conjunto, total. **3** completo, total. || *v.t.* **4** sumar, totalizar, ascender a.
totally | 'təʊtəlɪ | *adv.* totalmente, completamente.
totalitarian | ˌtəʊtælɪ'teərɪən | *adj.* totalitario.
totalitarianism | ˌtəʊtælɪ'teərɪənɪzəm | *s.i.* totalitarismo.
totality | təʊ'tælɪtɪ | *s.i.* totalidad.
tote | təʊt | *s.sing.* **1** totalizador. **2** (fam., brit.) sistema de apuestas. || *v.t.* **3** acarrear, llevar, cargar.
totem | 'təʊtəm | *s.c.* tótem.
totem-pole | 'təʊtəmpəʊl | *s.c.* poste totémico.
totter | 'tɒtər | *v.t.* tambalearse, bambolearse.
toucan | 'tuːkən | *s.c.* tucán.
touch | tʌtʃ | *s.i.* **1** tacto. || *s.c.* **2** toque, roce, contacto. **3** detalle. **4** enfoque, nota, aproximación. **5** pincelada. || *cuant.* **6** poco, pizca. || *v.t.* **7** tocar, rozar. **8** acariciar. **9** sacar, conseguir, dar un sablazo. **10** afectar, conmover, emocionar. **11** tomar, probar. **12** rivalizar, alcanzar, igualar. **13** trastornar, herir, hacer mella. || *v.i.* **14** tocarse, rozarse, lindar. || **15 a finishing –,** V. **finish. 16 a – ...,** en parte, hasta cierto punto. **17 to – and go,** dudoso. **18 to be in –,** estar en contacto. **19 to get in –,** ponerse en contacto. **20 in –,** en contacto. **21 to keep in –,** mantenerse en contacto, mantener relaciones. **22 to lose –,** perder contacto. **23 to – off,** provocar. **24 to – on/upon,** aludir. **25 out of –,** sin contacto. **26 to put someone in –,** poner en contacto. **27 the common –,** V. **common. 28 to – wood,** tocar madera.
touchdown | 'tʌtʃdaʊn | *s.c.* e *i.* AER. aterrizaje, amerizaje.
touché | 'tuːʃeɪ | *interj.* ¡tocado!
touched | tʌtʃt | *adj.* tocado, ido, chiflado.
touchiness | 'tʌtʃɪnɪs | *s.i.* susceptibilidad, irritabilidad.
touching | 'tʌtʃɪŋ | *adj.* conmovedor.
touchingly | 'tʌtʃɪŋlɪ | *adv.* conmovedoramente.
touch-paper | 'tʌtʃpeɪpər | *s.sing.* mecha, rascador.
touchstone | 'tʌtʃstəʊn | *s.c.* piedra de toque, criterio.
touch-type | 'tʌtʃtaɪp | *v.i.* mecanografiar a ciegas, al tacto.
touchy | 'tʌtʃɪ | *adj.* conmovedor.
tough | 'tʌf | *s.c.* **1** duro, gamberro. || *adj.* **2** resistente, fuerte. **3** violento, duro, rudo. **4** correoso, áspero, difícil. || **5 as – as old boots,** duro como una piedra, más basto que la lija. **6 –/– luck,** mala suerte.
toughen | 'tʌfn | *v.t.* **1** endurecer. **2** curtir. || *v.i.* **3** endurecerse.

toughened | ’tʌfnd | *adj.* endurecido.
toughness | ’tʌfnɪs | *s.i.* fuerza.
toupee | ’tu:peɪ | *s.c.* tupé.
tour | tʊər | *s.c.* **1** viaje, excursión, `tour`, circuito. **2** visita turística, recorrido. **3** gira. || *v.t.* **4** viajar por, recorrer. || *v.i.* **5** ir de viaje, hacer una gira. || **6 – de force, a)** obra maestra, actuación inmejorable, demostración; **b)** proeza, hazaña, juego de destreza.
tourism | tʊərɪzəm | *s.i.* turismo.
tourist | ’tʊərɪst | *s.c.* **1** turista. || *adj.* **2** turístico, de viajes, para turistas: *tourist agency = agencia de viajes.* || **2 – class,** clase turista, segunda.
touristy | ’tʊərɪstɪ | *adj.* (fam. y desp.) turístico, para turistas.
tournament | ’tɔ:nəmənt | *s.c.* competición, concurso, torneo.
tourniquet | ’tʊənɪkeɪ | (EE.UU.) | ’tɜ:rnɪkət | *s.c.* torniquete.
tousled | ’taʊzld | *adj.* **1** ajado, desarreglado, desordenado, arrugado. **2** enmarañado, desgreñado, despeinado.
tout | taʊt | *s.c.* **1** revendedor. || *v.t.* **2** revender, vender ilegalmente. **3** acosar, importunar. || *v.i.* **4 to – (for),** solicitar.
tow | təʊ | *s.c.* **1** remolque, sirga. || *v.t.* **2** remolcar, llevar a remolque, arrastrar, llevar a cuestas. || **3 in –,** (fam., fig.) a cuestas, a remolque, arrastras. **4 on –,** a remolque.
towards | tə’wɔ:dz | (EE.UU.) | tɔ:rdz | (también **toward**) *prep.* **1** hacia, a, cerca de. **2** para con, en relación con, con respecto a. **3** a eso de, aproximadamente a las, hacia las, alrededor de. **4** para: *they gave some money towards charity = dieron dinero para caridad.*
towel | ’taʊəl | *s.c.* **1** toalla. || *v.i.* **2** secar con una toalla. || **3 to throw/chuck in the –,** tirar la toalla, darse por vencido.
towelling | ’taʊəlɪŋ | *s.i.* felpa, tejido para hacer toallas.
tower | ’taʊər | *s.c.* **1** torre: *church tower = campanario.* || *v.i.* **2 [to – (above /over)]** elevarse, sobresalir, sobrepasar. || **3 a – of strength,** una gran ayuda. **4 – block,** bloque de pisos, rascacielos, torre.
towering | ’taʊərɪŋ | *adj.* elevado, grande, gigante, masivo, altísimo.
town | taʊn | *s.c.* **1** ciudad, población, pueblo. **2** (fig.) gente, ciudadanos. **3** el centro. || *adj.* **4** urbano, de la ciudad. || **5 to go to –,** tirar la casa por la ventana, no reparar en gastos, poner mucho entusiasmo. **6 on the –/out on the –,** ir de juerga, salir a divertirse. **7 – council,** concejo municipal. **8 – crier,** pregonero. **9 – hall,** ayuntamiento. **10 – house,** casa de ciudad, residencia en la ciudad. **11 – planning,** urbanismo.
townie | taʊ’ni: | *s.c.* (desp.) alguien de ciudad, señorito de ciudad.
townsfolk | ’taʊnsfəʊlk | *s.i.* ciudadanos, gente de la ciudad.
township | ’taʊnʃɪp | *s.c.* municipio, término municipal.
townspeople | ’taʊnspi:pl | *s.i.* ciudadanos, gente de la ciudad.
towpath | ’təʊpɑ:θ | *s.c.* camino de sirga, camino de arrastre.
towrope | ’təʊrəʊp | *s.i.* cable de remolcar, sirga.
toxic | ’tɒksɪk | *adj.* tóxico.
toxicological | ˌtɒksɪkə’lɒdʒɪkl | *adj.* toxicológico.
toxicologist | ˌtɒksɪ’kɒlədʒist | *s.c.* toxicólogo.
toxicology | ˌtɒksɪ’kɒlədʒɪ | *s.i.* toxicología.
toxin | ’tɒksɪn | *s.c.* e *i.* MED. toxina.
toy | tɔɪ | *s.c.* **1** juguete, entretenimiento. || *adj.* **2** de juguete, de jugar. || *v.i.* **[to – with] 3** jugar con, juguetear, acariciar. **4** considerar, acariciar, agradar (una idea). **5** divertirse con, utilizar a (una persona).
trace | treɪs | *s.c.* **1** prueba, pista, huella, rastro. **2** vestigio, señal, resto, indicio. **3** dibujo, diseño. || *v.t.* rastrear, localizar. **4** descubrir, trazar, averiguar, remontar. **5** seguir la pista, describir. **6** buscar, tratar de localizar. **7** calcar, contornear. || **8 without –,** sin (dejar) rastro.
trachea | trə’kɪə | *s.c.* MED. tráquea.
tracing | ’treɪsɪŋ | *s.c.* **1** calco. || **2 – paper,** papel de calco.
track | træk | *s.c.* **1** sendero, senda, camino, pista. **2** vía, estela, ruta, rumbo, curso, trayectoria. **3** rastro, huella, vestigio. **4** pista (de carreras, de disco, de cinta de cassette...): *sound track = banda sonora.* || *v.t.* **5** rastrear, seguir la pista. **6** seguir la trayectoria. || **7 to hide/cover one's tracks,** borrar, eliminar las huellas, no dejar rastro. **8 to keep – of,** seguir la pista, mantenerse informado sobre, mantenerse al tanto de. **9 to lose – of,** perder la pista de, perder de vista, no estar al tanto de. **10 to make tracks,** ponerse en camino, marcharse. **11 off the beaten –,** apartado, perdido. **12 on the right –,** por buen camino. **13 on the – of,** perseguir, (andar) detrás de, sobre la pista de. **14 on the wrong –,** por mal camino, equivocado. **15 to stop dead in one's tracks/to stop one dead in one's tracks,** quedarse helado, pararse en seco, quedarse clavado. **16 tracking station,** estación de seguimiento. **17 – record,** historial. **18 to – up,** dejar huellas, ensuciar con los pies.
tracker | ’trækər | *s.c.* rastreador.
tracksuit | ’træksu:t | *s.c.* chándal.
tract | trækt | *s.c.* **1** panfleto, octavilla, tratado, folleto. **2** territorio, extensión, región, zona. **3** ANAT. aparato, vías, sistema.
tractable | ’træktəbl | *adj.* manejable, tratable.
traction | ’trækʃn | *s.i.* **1** MED. tracción. **2** MEC. fricción, adherencia, tracción. || **3 – engine,** máquina de tracción.
tractor | ’træktər | *s.c.* tractor.
trad | træd | *s.i.* MUS. jazz tradicional.
trade | treɪd | *s.i.* **1** comercio, industria, negocio, transacción. || *s.c.* **2** negocio, trabajo, oficio. || *adj.* **3** comercial, de negocios. *v.t.* e *i.* **4** comerciar, negociar, vender, trocar. || **5 a trick of the –,** truco del oficio. **6 – fair,** feria de muestras. **7 to – in,** dar como entrada. **8 to – on,** aprovecharse, explotar, abusar de. **9 to – off,** trocar. **10 – route,** ruta comercial. **11 – secret, a)** fórmula secreta; **b)** secreto profesional. **12 – union,** sindicato, asociación sindical. **13 – unionism,** sindicalismo. **14 – unionist,** sindicalista, afiliado a un sindicato. **15 to – with,** tener negocios con.
trade-in | ’treɪdɪn | *s.c.* (EE.UU.) intercambio, entrega a cuenta.
trademark | ’treɪdmɑ:k | *s.c.* **1** marca comercial: *registered trademark.* **2** (fig.) sello característico, característica.
trade-name | ’treɪdneɪm | *s.c.* nombre comercial, marca registrada, nombre de mercado, razón social.
trader | ’treɪdər | *s.c.* comerciante, negociante.
tradesman | ’treɪdzmən | *s.c.* tendero, comerciante.
tradesmen | ’treɪdzmən | *pl.irreg.* **1** de **tradesman.** || **2 tradesmen's entrance,** entrada de servicio.
tradespeople | ’treɪdzpi:pl | *s.pl.* comerciantes.
trading | ’treɪdɪŋ | *s.i.* **1** comercio. || *adj.* **2** comercial. || **3 – estate,** zona industrial. V. **industrial estate. 4 – stamp,** vale, bono, cupón, punto.
tradition | trə’dɪʃn | *s.c.* **1** tradición, costumbre, uso, práctica. || *s.i.* **2** folclore, tradición, conjunto de costumbres. || **3 in the – of,** a la manera de, como, según la tradición de, al estilo de.
traditional | trə’dɪʃənl | *adj.* **1** tradicional, establecido, acostumbrado. **2** normal, corriente, consuetudinario, estándar. **3** convencional.
traditionalism | trə’dɪʃənəlɪzəm | *s.i.* tradicionalismo.
traditionalist | trə’dɪʃənəlɪst | *s.c., adj.* tradicionalista, conservador.
traditionally | trə’dɪʃənəlɪ | *adv.* tradicionalmente, según la tradición, de acuerdo con la tradición.
traduce | trə’dju:s | *v.t.* difamar, calumniar.
traffic | ’træfɪk | *s.i.* **1** tráfico, circulación, movimiento de vehículos. **2** tránsito, negocio, comercio. || *adj.* **3** de la circulación, del tráfico. || **4 – circle,** (EE.UU.) glorieta, plazoleta, redondel, encrucijada. **5 – jam,** atasco, embotellamiento, aglomeración: *a three-kilometre traffic jam = una cola de coches de tres kilómetros, una caravana de tres kilómetros.* **6 – light,** semáforo. **7 – warden,** agente de tráfico.
trafficker | ’træfɪkər | *s.c.* traficante, tratante, negociante.
tragedy | ’trædʒɪdɪ | *s.c.* **1** tragedia, desgracia, drama. **2** obra trágica. || *s.i.* **3** LIT. género trágico, tragedia.
tragic | ’trædʒɪk | (también **tragical**) *adj.* trágico.
tragically | ’trædʒɪklɪ | *adv.* trágicamente, dramáticamente.

tragicomedy | ˌtrædʒɪ'kɒmɪdɪ | *s.c.* LIT. tragicomedia.
tragicomic | ˌtrædʒɪ'kɒmɪk | (también, **tragicomical**) *s.c.* tragicómico.
tragicomical V. **tragicomic.**
trail | treɪl | *s.c.* **1** pista forestal, senda, sendero, camino. **2** ruta, circuito, trayecto. **3** pista, rastro, huella, indicios, reguero. || *v.t.* e *i.* **4** seguir el rastro, perseguir, rastrear. **5** arrastrar, tirar de, llevar con, llevar detrás. **6 [to – by]** ir por detrás, a la zaga, estar por debajo de (en una competición, elección, etc.). || **7 to braze a –,** V. **blaze. 8 on someone's/something's –,** (ir) tras la pista de, a la caza de algo o alguien. **9 to – behind, a)** quedar por detrás de, quedar rezagado; seguir (a alguien) lentamente; **b)** quedar o estar por debajo de. **10 to – off/away, a)** perder fuerza gradualmente, desvanecerse, apagarse; **b)** marcharse poco a poco, desfilar. **11 to – over,** extenderse, cubrir.
trailer | 'treɪlər | *s.c.* **1** trailer, remolque, contenedor, caja de camión. **2** avance, anuncio, documental. **3** caravana, casa-remolque.
trailing | 'treɪlɪŋ | *adj.* BOT. trepador, colgante.
train | treɪn | *s.c.* **1** tren. **2** fila, línea, séquito, cortejo, recua. **3** cadena, hilo (de pensamiento), serie, sucesión. **4** cola (de un vestido). || *v.t.* **5** entrenar, adiestrar, amaestrar, educar, enseñar, instruir. **6** apuntar, dirigir. || *v.i.* **7** entrenarse, prepararse, formarse, ejercitarse. || **8 in –,** en marcha, en curso. **9 in its –,** en consecuencia, consigo, en su desarrollo. **10 the gravy –,** V. **gravy.**
trained | treɪnd | *adj.* **1** cualificado, diplomado, especializado, experto. **2** entrenado, preparado, educado, adiestrado.
trainee | treɪ'niː | *s.c.* aprendiz, novato.
trainer | 'treɪnər | *s.c.* **1** entrenador, preparador. **2** (EE.UU.) recluta. || **2 trainers,** zapatillas de deporte, calzado de entrenamiento.
training | 'treɪnɪŋ | *s.i.* **1** entrenamiento, educación física. **2** instrucción, enseñanza, adiestramiento, preparación. || **3 good –,** buena preparación, algo que sirve. **4 in –,** en período de entrenamiento, entrenando. **5 – shoe,** zapatilla de deporte, V. **trainers.**
traipse | treɪps | *v.i.* **1** andar tranquilamente, recorrer, vagar. || **2 to – round,** hacer un recorrido largo y fatigoso.
trait | treɪt | *s.c.* rasgos, características.
traitor | 'treɪtər | *s.c.* **[– (to)]** traidor.
traitorous | 'treɪtərəs | *adj.* traidor, traicionero.
traitress | 'treɪtrɪs | *s.c.* traidora.
trajectory | trə'dʒektərɪ | *s.c.* **1** trayectoria. **2** evolución, desarrollo.
tramcar | 'træmkɑːr | V. **tram.**
tram | træm | (también, **tramcar**) *s.c.* tranvía. V. **streetcar.**
tramline | 'træmlaɪn | *s.c.* **1** vía del tranvía, carriles del tranvía, línea del tranvía. **2** líneas laterales, líneas de dobles (en tenis).
trammel | 'træml | *s.c.* **1** restricción, traba, obstáculo. || *v.t.* **2** poner trabas, obstaculizar, dificultar, impedir.
tramp | træmp | *s.c.* **1** vago, vagabundo. **2** puta, fulana. **3** mercante, barco de carga: *a tramp steamer = vapor de carga sin línea regular.* **4** pasos pesados y regulares, caminata. || *v.i.* **5** andar por, recorrer, caminar. || **6 to go for a –,** ir a dar un largo paseo, hacer una excursión.
trample | 'træmpl | *v.t.* **1 [to – (down)]** pisar, pisotear, aplastar pisando. **2 [to – on/upon]** (fig.) ignorar, despreciar, pisotear, pasar por encima de. **3 to – out, a)** apagar pisando; **b)** pisar (uvas). **4 to – someone to death,** pisotear a alguien hasta matarlo.
trampled | 'træmpld | *adj.* aplastado, escachado, pisoteado.
trampoline | 'træmpəliːn | *s.c.* DEP. cama elástica.
tramway | 'træmweɪ | *s.c.* tranvía, vía del tranvía, carriles del tranvía.
trance | trɑːns | (EE.UU.) | træns | *s.c.* **1** trance, éxtasis, inconsciencia, estado hipnótico, rapto. **2** MED. catalepsia, cataplexia.
tranquil | 'træŋkwɪl | *adj.* tranquilo, sereno, calmado, pacífico.
tranquility V. **tranquillity.**
tranquilize V. **tranquillize.**
tranquilizer V. **tranquillizer.**
tranquillity | træŋ'kwɪlɪtɪ | (EE.UU. **tranquility**) *s.i.* tranquilidad.
tranquillize | 'træŋkwɪlaɪz | (EE.UU. **tranquilize**) *v.t.* e *i.* **1** tranquilizar(se), sedar(se), calmar(se), relajar(se). **2** aplacar, reconciliar.
tranquillizer | 'træŋkwɪlaɪzər | *s.c.* (EE.UU. **tranquilizer**) MED. tranquilizante, sedante, calmante.
trans- | trænz | *pref.* tras-.
OBS. Abreviatura de palabras que empiezan por **trans-**: *transitive, translated, transferred,* etc.
transact | træn'zækt | *v.t.* **[to – with]** llevar a cabo, realizar, negociar, despachar, tramitar, tratar: *I've got some business to transact with him = tengo asuntos que tratar con él.*
transaction | træn'zækʃn | *s.c.* **1** transacción, operación, negociación, tramitación. || **2 transactions,** actas, memorias.
transatlantic | ˌtrænzət'læntɪk | *adj.* trasatlántico.
transcend | træn'send | *v.t.* trascender, ir más allá de, exceder, sobrepasar, estar por encima de, superar, rebasar.
transcendence | træn'sendəns | *s.i.* FIL., REL. trascendencia.
transcendent | træn'sendənt | *adj.* FIL., REL. trascendente.
transcendental | ˌtrænsen'dentl | *adj.* **1** FIL., REL. trascendental, sobrenatural. || **2 – meditation,** meditación trascendental.
transcribe | træn'skraɪb | *v.t.* **1** transcribir, copiar. **2** MUS. transcribir, arreglar, adaptar. **3** RAD. grabar.
transcript | 'trænskrɪpt | *s.c.* transcripción, copia, trasunto.
transcription | træn'skrɪpʃn | *s.c.* **1** transcripción, trasunto, copia. **2** RAD. difusión, grabación. || **3 phonetic –,** pronunciación figurada.
transept | 'trænsept | *s.c.* ARQ. crucero.
transfer | træns'fɜːr | *s.c.* **1** traslado, trasbordo. **2** calcomanía. || *s.i.* **3** transporte, traslado. **4** transferencia bancaria. **5** trasmisión, traspaso, transferencia de titularidad. **6** cambio, entrega de poder. || *v.t.* **7** trasladar. **8** transferir. **9** grabar, transcribir. **10** transmitir, transferir la propiedad. **11** entregar el poder. **12** cambiar, desplazar. || *v.i.* **13** trasladarse.
transferable | træns'fɜːrəbl | *adj.* transferible, transportable, transladable, transmisible: *non transferable = intransferible, inalienable.*
transference | 'trænsfərəns | *s.i.* transferencia, traspaso, traslado.
transfigure | træns'fɪgər | *v.t.* transformarse, transfigurarse.
transfix | træns'fɪks | *v.t.* **1** paralizar, quedar paralizado. **2** atravesar, traspasar, pasar de parte a parte.
transform | træns'fɔːm | *v.t.* **[to – (into)]** transformar, alterar, convertir, cambiar, mejorar, metamorfosear.
transformation | ˌtrænsfə'meɪʃn | *s.c.* e *i.* transformación, cambio, conversión, metamorfosis.
transformer | træns'fɔːmər | *s.c.* ELECTR. transformador.
transfusion | træns'fjuːʒn | *s.c.* **1** MED. transfusión. || **2 to give someone a blood –,** hacer una transfusión de sangre a alguien.
transgress | trænz'gres | *v.t.* **1** traspasar, exceder. **2** infringir, violar, quebrantar, pecar. || *v.i.* **3** pecar, cometer una trasgresión, trasgredir.
transgression | trænz'greʃn | *s.c.* e *i.* transgresión, infracción, pecado.
transience | 'trænzɪəns | *s.i.* brevedad, transitoriedad.
transient | 'trænzɪənt | *s.c.* **1** transeúnte. || *adj.* **2** transitorio, pasajero, efímero, fugaz, de transición, temporal.
transistor | træn'zɪstər | *s.c.* **1** transistor. || **2 – radio,** radio de transistores. **3 transistorized,** transistorizado.
transit | 'trænzɪt | *s.i.* **1** tránsito, paso, transición. || **2 in –,** de paso, de tránsito. **3 – visa,** visado de tránsito.
transition | træn'zɪʃn | *s.c.* e *i.* transición, paso, evolución.
transitional | træn'zɪʃənl | *adj.* de transición, transitorio.
transitive | 'trænzɪtɪv | *adj.* GRAM. transitivo.
transitory | 'trænzɪtrɪ | *adj.* transitorio.
translate | trænz'leɪt | *v.t.* **1 [to – (from /into)]** traducir, trasladar, transferir. **2 [to – (into)]** convertir, transformar. **3** poner en práctica, llevar a cabo, hacer realidad. **4 [to – (as)]** tomar, interpretar, entender.
translation | trænz'leɪʃn | *s.c.* **1** traducción, versión, traslación, retransmisión.

2 ejercicio de traducción. **3** transformación, conversión.
translator | trænz'leɪtər | *s.c.* traductor, intérprete.
translucent | trænz'lu:snt | (también, **translucid**) *adj.* traslúcido.
traslucid V. **translucent.**
transmission | trænz'mɪʃn | *s.i.* **1** traslado, transmisión. **2** traspaso. **3** emisión, retransmisión. || *s.c.* **4** retransmisión. **5** MEC. transmisión.
transmit | trænz'mɪt | *v.t.* **1** transmitir, emitir. **2** distribuir, contagiar. **3** ser conductor, conducir, propagar. **4** comunicar (ideas).
transmitter | trænz'mɪtər | *s.c.* transmisor, emisora.
transmutation | ˌtrænzmju:'teɪʃn | *s.c.* e *i.* **1** transmutación, transformismo. **2** MAT. transformación.
transmute | trænz'mju:t | *v.t.* **[to – (into)]** transmutar, transformar.
transparency | træns'pærənsɪ | *s.i.* **1** transparencia. || *s.c.* **2** FOT. transparencia, diapositiva, proyección.
transparent | træns'pærənt | *adj.* **1** transparente, diáfano, claro, limpio. **2** obvio, que se ve a las claras. **3** que no engaña, patente.
transparently | træns'pærəntlɪ | *adv.* transparentemente.
transpire | træn'spaɪər | *v.t.* **1** transpirar, exudar. **2** revelarse, divulgarse, llegarse a saber. **3** ocurrir, suceder, tener lugar.
transplant | 'trænsplɑ:nt | *s.c.* **1** MED., AGR. transplante. || | træns'plɑ:nt | *v.t.* **2** MED., AGR. transplantar. **3** trasladar, llevar.
transport | 'trænspɔ:t | *s.c.* **1** transporte, vehículo. **2** deportado. || *s.i.* **3** acarreo, arrebato. **4** transporte, servicio de transportes. || | træn'spɔ:t | *v.t.* **5** transportar, llevar, acarrear. **6** deportar. **7** arrebatar, extasiarse, embelesar. || **8 – cafe,** restaurante de carretera.
transportation | ˌtrænspɔ:'teɪʃn | *s.i.* **1** transporte. **2** deportación.
transporter | træns'pɔ:tər | *s.c.* **1** transportista, transportador. **2** camión de transporte. || **3 – bridge,** puente transportador.
transpose | træn'spəuz | *v.t.* **1** transponer, cambiar. **2** MUS. transportar.
transverse | 'trænzvɜ:s | *s.c.* **1** ANAT. músculo transverso. || *adj.* **2** trasverso, transversal.
transvestism | trænz'vestɪzəm | *s.i.* travestismo.
transvestite | trænz'vestaɪt | *s.c.* travestido.
trap | træp | *s.c.* **1** trampa, lazo, celada. **2** ART. escotillón, trampa. **3** ratonera. **4** TEC. sifón, bombillo. || *v.t.* **5** poner trampas, entrampar, coger en una trampa. **6** coger, pillar, atrapar, aprisionar. **7** rodear, cercar, bloquear. **8** retener, detener, controlar. || **9 to shut one's –/to keep one's – shut,** mantener la boca cerrada.
trapdoor | ˌtræp'dɔ:r | *s.c.* **1** trampilla, trampa. **2** ART. escotillón.
trapeze | trə'pi:z | (EE.UU.) | træ'pi:z | *s.c.* trapecio.
trapper | 'træpər | *s.c.* trampero, cazador.
trappings | 'træpɪŋz | *s.i.* adornos, atavíos, galas, arreos.
trash | træʃ | *s.i.* **1** baratija, de baja calidad, trastos viejos. **2** pacotilla, deshechos, desperdicios, basura, porquería. **3** gentuza, gente inútil. || *v.t.* **4** podar, mondar, desbrozar.
trashcan | 'træʃkæn | *s.c.* (EE.UU.) cubo de la basura.
trashy | 'træʃɪ | *adj.* malo, de baja calidad, inútil.
trauma | 'trɔ:mə | (EE.UU.) | 'traumə | *s.c.* MED. trauma.
traumatic | trɔ:'mætɪk | *adj.* traumático.
travel | 'trævl | *s.i.* **1** viajar, viajes. **2** TEC. recorrido, trayecto. || *v.i.* **3** viajar, recorrer, cubrir (una distancia). **4** ir en coche, correr, moverse, desplazarse. || **5 – agency,** agencia de viajes. **6 – agent,** agente de viajes. **7 – bureau,** agencia de viajes.
travelled | 'trævld | *adj.* viajero, que ha viajado mucho.
traveller | 'trævlər | (EE.UU., **traveler**) *s.c.* **1** viajero, viajante. **2** puente de grúa. || **3 traveller's cheque,** cheques de viaje, de viajero.
travelling | 'trævlɪŋ | *s.c.* **1** viajar. **2** ART. travelín. || *adj.* **3** de viaje, ambulante, móvil. || **4 – expenses,** gastos de viaje. **5 – salesman,** viajante de comercio.
travelogue | 'trævəlɒg | (EE.UU., **travelog**) *s.c.* documental de viajes, película, conferencia ilustrada sobre viajes.
travel-sick | 'trævlsɪk | *adj.* mareado.
travel-sickness | 'trævlsɪknɪs | *s.i.* mareo, propensión al mareo.
traverse | træ'vɜ:s | *s.c.* **1** travesía, recorrido, ruta sinuosa, travesaño. **2** MAT. línea quebrada, transversal, traslación. || *adj.* **3** transversal. || *v.t.* **4** atravesar, cruzar, viajar a través, recorrer. **5** examinar detenidamente. || *v.i.* **6** pivotar, girar sobre el eje.
traverser | træ'vɜ:sər | *s.c.* transbordador.
travesty | 'trævəstɪ | *s.c.* **1** parodia, farsa. || *v.t.* **2** parodiar.
trawl | trɔ:l | *s.c.* **1** red de arrastre, barredera. **2** selección. **3** (EE.UU.) palangre. || *v.t.* e *i.* **4** pescar al arrastre, rastrear, dragar. **5** seleccionar. || **4 – net,** red de arrastre.
trawler | 'trɔ:lər | *s.c.* trainera, barco de pesca al arrastre.
trawling | 'trɔ:lɪŋ | *s.i.* pesca de arrastre.
tray | treɪ | *s.c.* **1** bandeja, platillo. **2** FOT., cubeta, cajón.
treacherous | 'tretʃərəs | *adj.* **1** traidor, traicionero, falso, infiel, engañoso, incierto. **2** peligroso: *the treacherous tide = la peligrosa marea.*
treacherously | 'tretʃərəslɪ | *adv.* **1** traicioneramente, falsamente, infielmente, engañosamente, inciertamente. **2** peligrosamente.
treachery | 'tretʃərɪ | *s.i.* traición, perfidia, falsedad, deslealtad.
treacle | 'tri:kl | *s.i.* melaza.
treacly | 'tri:klɪ | *adj.* **1** meloso. **2** voz rica.
tread | tred | *s.c.* **1** paso, pisada, peldaño. **2** andares, modo de andar. **3** huella. **4** suela, dibujo de la llanta. || *v.t.* e *i.* [*pret.irreg.* **trod,** *p.p.irreg.* **trodden**] **5** pisar, andar, hollar, meter el pie, abrir, poner el pie. **6** aplastar, escachar. **7** andar con tiento. || **8 to – on someone's toes/corns,** herir la sensibilidad de, pisotear a alguien, ofender. **9 to – the path of,** seguir el camino de; comportarse, actuar de una determinada manera. **10 to – water,** flotar, mantenerse a flote.
treadle | 'tredl | *s.c.* **1** pedal. || *v.i.* **2** pedalear.
treadmill | 'tredmɪl | *s.c.* rueda de molino, rutina, monotonía.
treason | 'tri:zn | *s.i.* traición.
treasonable | 'tri:zənəbl | *adj.* traicionero, traidor, desleal.
treasure | 'treʒər | *s.i.* **1** tesoro, joya. || *v.t.* **2** valorar, estimar, guardar en la memoria, atesorar, guardar, acumular.
treasurer | 'treʒərər | *s.c.* tesorero.
treasure-trove | 'treʒətrəuv | *s.c.* tesoro descubierto, hallazgo.
treasury | 'treʒərɪ | *s.i.* **1** tesoro, tesorería. **2** antología. || **3 The Treasury,** el Ministerio de Hacienda, el Tesoro, el Erario. **4 Treasury Bench,** escaños del gobierno, primera fila de la Cámara de Diputados. **5 – bond/note,** bono del tesoro.
treat | tri:t | *s.i.* **1** invitación, convite, regalo: *this is my treat = esta ronda la pago yo.* || *v.t.* **2** tratar de. **3** comprar, regalar: *he treated his son to a new football = regaló a su hijo un balón de fútbol.* **4** invitar, convidar: *he treated us to a good dinner = nos invitó a una buena cena.* **5** MED. tratar, curar, asistir, atender. || *v.i.* **6** tratar, manejar. || **7 a Dutch –,** cada uno paga lo suyo. **8 ...a --,** una maravilla, estupendamente.
treatise | 'tri:tɪz | *s.c.* tratado, libro sobre un tema.
treatment | 'tri:tmənt | *s.i.* **1** tratamiento, trato. **2** MUS. interpretación, adaptación. **3** MED. medicación, tratamiento.
treaty | 'tri:tɪ | *s.c.* tratado, acuerdo.
treble | 'trebl | *s.c.* **1** MUS. tiple, soprano. || *adj.* **2** triple. **3** de tiple, de soprano. **4** de sol: *treble clef = clave de sol.* || *v.t.* e *i.* **5** triplicar(se), multiplicar(se) por tres.
tree | tri: | *s.c.* **1** árbol. **2** horma. || *v.t.* **3** refugiarse en un árbol, poner la horma. || **4 at the top of the –,** en lo alto, en la cima del éxito. **5 to bark up the wrong –,** V. **bark. 6 money doesn't grow on trees,** no se atan los perros con longaniza. **7 out of one's –,** loco. **8 up a gum –,** V. **gum.**
treeless | 'tri:lɪs | *adj.* sin árboles, desarbolado, pelado.
tree-lined | 'tri:laɪnd | *adj.* flanqueado de árboles.

treetop | 'triːtɒp | *s.c.* copa del árbol, cima.
tree-trunk | 'triːtrʌŋk | *s.c.* tronco del árbol.
trefoil | 'trefɔɪl | *s.i.* **1** BOT. trébol. **2** ARQ. trifolio.
trek | trek | *s.c.* **1** viaje difícil, expedición, caminata, jornada; migración. || *v.i.* **2** hacer un viaje largo, emigrar, caminar penosamente.
trellis | 'trelɪs | *s.c.* **1** enrejado, soporte para plantas trepadoras, espalderas. || *v.t.* **2** poner un enrejado, emparrar.
tremble | 'trembl | *s.c.* **1** temblor, estremecimiento. || *v.i.* **2** estremecerse, temblar. **3** sacudir, mover.
trembling | 'tremblɪŋ | *adj.* tembloroso.
tremendous | trɪ'mendəs | *adj.* **1** tremendo, enorme, vasto, inmenso. **2** formidable, extraordinario, maravilloso.
tremendously | trɪ'mendəslɪ | *adv.* tremendamente.
tremolo | 'treməlәʊ | *s.c.* e *i.* MUS. trémolo.
tremor | 'tremər | *s.c.* temblor, estremecimiento, vibración.
tremulous | 'tremjʊləs | *adj.* trémulo, tembloroso, febril; tímido.
tremulously | 'tremjʊləslɪ | *adv.* temblorosamente, trémulamente.
trench | trentʃ | *s.c.* **1** zanja, foso. **2** MIL. trinchera, refugio: *the trenches = el campo de batalla.* **3** AGR. acequia. || *v.t.* e *i.* **4** abrir zanjas o trincheras. **5** atrincherar. **6** excavar, remover.
trenchant | 'trentʃənt | *adj.* agudo, mordaz, cáustico, penetrante, incisivo, directo.
trench-coat | 'trentʃkәʊt | *s.c.* trinchera.
trend | trend | *s.i.* **1** tendencia, moda, dirección, curso, orientación. || *v.i.* **2** tender, dirigirse, orientarse. || **3 to set a –,** marcar la pauta.
trend-setter | 'trendsetər | *s.c.* líder, que impone una pauta.
trendy | 'trendɪ | *s.c.* **1** moderno, persona que vive según las últimas tendencias de la moda. || **2** *adj.* elegante, a la última, muy moderno.
trepidation | ˌtrepɪ'deɪʃn | *s.i.* trepidación, inquietud, agitación.
trespass | 'trespəs | *s.c.* **1** delito, entrada ilegal, violación de la ley, infracción, intrusión. || *v.i.* **2** infringir, delinquir, entrar ilegalmente, invadir. **3** REL. pecar contra. || **4 to – upon,** abusar de.
trespasser | 'trespəsər | *s.c.* intruso, delincuente, pecador.
tress | tres | *s.i.* mechón, rizo, trenza, cabellera, melena.
trestle | 'tresl | *s.c.* **1** caballete. || **2 – table,** mesa de caballetes.
tri- | traɪ | *prefijo* **tri-.**
triad | 'traɪәd | *s.c.* **1** tríada, trío. **2** QUIM. trivalente. **3** REL. trinidad.
trial | 'traɪәl | *s.c.* e *i.* **1** prueba, ensayo, experimento, tentativa. **2** dificultad, aflicción, adversidad, molestia, sufrimiento. **3** DER. vista, juicio, proceso. || *adj.* **4** de prueba. || **5 on –,** procesado, a prueba. **6 to stand –,** V. **stand. 7 – and error,** acierto y error. **8 – run,** carrera campo a través. **9 trials,** competición de habilidad.
triangle | 'traɪæŋgl | *s.c.* **1** GEOM. triángulo. **2** escuadra, cartabón. **3** MUS. triángulo. **4** conflicto a tres bandas.
triangular | traɪ'æŋgjʊlər | *adj.* triangular, tripartito.
tribal | 'traɪbl | *adj.* tribal, de tribu.
tribalism | 'traɪbәlɪzәm | *s.i.* sistema tribal, organización en tribu.
tribe | traɪb | *s.c.* **1** tribu. **2** manada, bandada. **3** masa, ralea, tropel.
tribesman | 'traɪbzmәn | [*pl.irreg.* **tribesmen**] *s.c.* miembro de una tribu.
tribesmen | 'traɪbzmәn | *pl.irreg.* de **tribesman.**
tribulation | ˌtrɪbjʊ'leɪʃn | *s.i.* tribulación.
tribunal | traɪ'bjuːnl | *s.c.* tribunal.
tributary | 'trɪbjʊtrɪ | *s.c.* **1** afluente, tributario. || *adj.* **2** tributario.
tribute | 'trɪbjuːt | *s.i.* **1** tributo, homenaje, elogio, ofrenda. **2** mérito. **3** tributo, pago, carga, contribución, gabela.
trice | traɪs | *v.t.* **1** MAR. **[to – up]** izar las velas. || **2 in a –,** en un abrir y cerrar de ojos, en un dos por tres, en un santiamén.
triceps | 'traɪseps | *s.c.* ANAT. tríceps.
trick | trɪk | *s.c.* **1** truco, ardid, engaño, trampa, treta, triquiñuela. **2** astucia, habilidad, maña. **3** tranquillo, truco. **4** broma, travesura, faena. **5** estafa, timo. || *v.t.* **6** engañar, embaucar, estafar, timar. || **7 to do the –,** servir, resolver el problema. **8 never to miss a –,** no perder la oportunidad. **9 – of the light,** ilusión, espejismo. **10 up to one's tricks,** hacer de las suyas. **11 you can't teach an old dog new tricks,** V. **dog.**
trickery | 'trɪkәrɪ | *s.i.* engaño, astucia, superchería, fraude.
trickster | 'trɪkstər | *s.c.* embaucador, embustero, timador.
tricky | 'trɪkɪ | *adj.* **1** difícil, complicado, delicado. **2** hábil, mañoso, astuto, tramposo.
tricolour | 'trɪkәlәr | *adj.* tricolor.
tricycle | 'traɪsɪkl | *s.c.* triciclo.
tried | traɪd | *pret., p.p.* **1** de **try.** || *adj.* **2** probado, experimentado, de confianza, seguro, de garantía.
trier | 'traɪәr | *s.c.* investigador, juez, árbitro.
trifle | 'traɪfl | *s.i.* **1** nadería, fruslería, bagatela, pequeñez, insignificancia, miseria. **2** GAST. tarta. || *v.t.* **2 [to – away]** perder el tiempo, malgastar dinero. || *v.i.* **3 [to – with]** jugar con.
trifling | 'traɪflɪŋ | *s.i.* **1** frivolidad, trivialidad. || *adj.* **2** insignificante, sin importancia. **3** ligero, frívolo, trivial.
trigger | 'trɪgәr | *s.c.* gatillo, disparador, tirador.
trigger-happy | 'trɪgә'hæpɪ | *adj.* gatillo ligero, dispuesto a disparar.
trigonometry | ˌtrɪgә'nɒmɪtrɪ | *s.i.* MAT. trigonometría.
trike | traɪk | *s.c.* (fam.) triciclo.
trilby | 'trɪlbɪ | *s.c.* sombrero flexible.
trill | trɪl | *s.i.* **1** trino, gorjeo. **2** GRAM. vibración, vibrante. || *v.i.* **3** trinar, gorjear. **4** producir una vibración.
trillion | 'trɪlɪәn | *num.card.* **1** trillón. **2** (EE.UU.) billón.
trilogy | 'trɪlәdʒɪ | *s.c.* trilogía.
trim | trɪm | *s.i.* **1** estado, orden, arreglo. **2** marco. **3** orientación, equilibrio. || *adj.* **4** elegante, aseado, cuidado. || *v.t.* **5** arreglar, asear, adornar. **6** recortar, cortar, desbastar, guillotinar. **7** equilibrar, asentar, ordenar, orientar. **8** echar una bronca. || *v.i.* **9** ser oportunista. || **10 in –/in good –,** en forma, en perfecto estado.
trimmed | trɪmd | *adj.* decorado.
trimming | 'trɪmɪŋ | *s.i.* **1** arreglo, orden, adorno, recorte. **2** desbastado, cepillado. **3** orientación, estiba. **4** oportunismo.
trinity | 'trɪnɪtɪ | *s.c.* **1** trío, trinidad. || **2 the Trinity/the Holy Trinity,** REL. la Santísima Trinidad.
trinket | 'trɪnkɪt | *s.c.* dije, baratija, chuchería, bisutería.
trio | 'triːәʊ | *s.c.* trío.
trip | trɪp | *s.c.* **1** viaje, excursión. **2** tropezón, traspié, zancadilla. **4** desliz, tropiezo, error. **5** TEC. disparador. **6** (fam.) viaje, rollo (efecto de estupefacientes). || *v.t.* **7** poner la zancadilla, hacer caer. **8** confundir, coger en falta. **9** MAR. levar anclas, izar. || *v.i.* **10** dar un traspié, tropezar, caer. **11** equivocarse, cometer un error.
tripartite | ˌtraɪ'pɑːtaɪt | *adj.* tripartito.
tripe | traɪp | *s.i.* **1** GAST. callos. **2** (fam.) tonterías, bobadas.
triple | 'trɪpl | *s.c.* **1** triple. || *adj.* **2** triple. **3** MUS. ternario. || *v.t.* e *i.* **4** triplicar(se). || **5 – jump,** triple salto.
triplet | 'trɪplɪt | *s.c.* **1** trío, terceto, trillizo. **2** LIT. terceto. **3** MUS. tresillo.
triplicate | 'trɪplɪkәt | *adj.* **1** triplicado: *in triplicate = por triplicado.* || **2** *v.t.* triplicar, hacer por triplicado.
triplicity | 'trɪplɪsɪtɪ | *s.c.* triplicidad
tripod | 'traɪpɒd | *s.c.* trípode.
tripper | 'trɪpәr | *s.c.* **1** turista, excursionista. **2** TEC. disparador.
triptych | 'trɪptɪk | *s.c.* ART. tríptico.
tripwire | 'trɪpwaɪәr | *s.c.* cable de una trampa.
trite | traɪt | *adj.* trivial, trillado, vulgar.
triumph | 'traɪʌmf | *s.c.* **1** triunfo, éxito, júbilo, regocijo. || *v.i.* **2** triunfar, vencer. **3** alegrarse, regocijarse.
triumphal | traɪ'ʌmfl | *adj.* triunfal.
triumphant | traɪ'ʌmfnt | *adj.* triunfante, victorioso.
triumphantly | traɪ'ʌmfntlɪ | *adv.* triunfantemente.
triumvirate | traɪ'ʌmvɪrәt | *s.c.* triunvirato.
trivia | 'trɪvɪә | *pl.irreg.* **1** de **trivium.** || *s.pl.* **2** trivialidades, banalidades.
trivial | 'trɪvɪәl | *adj.* trivial, banal, insignificante, superficial.

triviality | ˌtrɪvɪ'ælɪtɪ | *s.i.* trivialidad, banalidad.
trivialize | 'trɪvɪəlaɪz | *v.t.* trivializar.
trivium | 'trɪvɪəm | [*pl.* **trivia**] *s.c.* (form.) trívium, trivio.
trod | trɒd | *pret.irreg.* de **tread.**
trodden | 'trɒdn | *p.p.* **1** de **tread.** || *adj.* **2** pisoteado, hollado.
troglodyte | 'trɒglədaɪt | *s.c.* troglodita.
Trojan | 'trəudʒən | *s.c.adj.* **1** troyano. || **2 to work like a –,** trabajar como un negro, trabajar mucho.
troll | trəul | *s.c.* **1** DEP. cucharilla, anzuelo de cuchara. **2** carrete. **3** LIT. trol. **4** canon. || *v.t.* e *i.* **5** cantar en canon. **6** pescar con cucharilla.
trolley | 'trɒlɪ | *s.c.* **1** carretilla, vagoneta, mesita de rueda. **2** teleférico. **3** (EE.UU.) tranvía.
trolley-bus | 'trɒlɪbʌs | *s.c.* trolebús.
trollop | 'trɒləp | *s.c.* ramera, puta.
trombone | trɒm'bəun | *s.c.* MUS. trombón.
trombonist | trɒm'bəunɪst | *s.c.* trombonista.
troop | tru:p | *s.i.* **1** banda, grupo. **2** manada, bandada. **3** MIL. tropa, compañía, escuadrón. **4** ART. compañía. || **5 to – the colour,** (brit.) MIL. ceremonia militar de homenaje a la bandera.
trooper | 'tru:pər | *s.c.* **1** MIL. soldado de caballería, policía montado. **2** barco de transporte militar. || *v.i.* **3** ir en grupos, agruparse, apiñarse. || **4 to swear like a –,** jurar como un carretero.
trophy | 'trəufɪ | *s.c.* trofeo.
tropical | 'trɒpɪkl | *adj.* tropical.
tropics | 'trɒpɪks | *s.pl.* GEOL. trópicos.
trot | trɒt | *s.i.* **1** trote. || *v.t.* **2** hacer trotar, ir al trote. || *v.i.* **3** trotar, correr. || **4 on the –,** seguidos, uno tras otro: *to keep someone on the trot = no dejar parar a uno.*
troth | trəuθ | *s.c.* **1** palabra, promesa. || **2 to plight their –,** dar palabra de matrimonio.
Trotskyst | 'trɒtkɪɪst | *s.c.* trotskista.
Trotskyte, V. **Trotskyst.**
trotter | 'trɒtər | *s.c.* **1** trotón. **2** GAST. mano (de cerdo).
troubadour | 'tru:bədɔ:r | *s.c.* trovador, juglar.
trouble | 'trʌbl | *s.i.* **1** problemas, preocupaciones, inquietudes. **2** apuro, aprieto, dificultad. **3** disgusto, aflicción, pena, angustia, molestia, conflicto, engorro. || *v.t.* e *i.* **4** afligir, preocupar(se), perturbar(se), trastornar(se), molestar, incomodar, importunar. **5** afectar, aquejar. **6** enturbiar. || **7 in –,** en un apuro. **8 more – than it is worth,** muchas molestias para nada. **9 to take the –,** tomarse la molestia.
troubled | 'trʌbld | *adj.* **1** preocupado, agitado. **2** revuelto, turbulento. || **3 to pour oil on – waters,** pacificar, calmar los ánimos.
trouble-free | 'trʌblfri: | *adj.* libre de problemas, sin problemas.
troublemaker | 'trʌblmeɪkər | *s.c.* alborotador, perturbador, camorrista.
troublemaking | 'trʌblmeɪkɪŋ | *s.i.* crear problemas.
troubleshooter | 'trʌblʃu:tər | *s.c.* (EE.UU.) localizador de problemas, árbitro, mediador.
troublesome | 'trʌblsəm | *adj.* molesto, fastidioso, importuno.
trouble-spot | 'trʌblspɒt | *s.c.* lugar conflictivo.
troubling | 'trʌblɪŋ | *adj.* preocupante.
trough | trɒf | *s.c.* **1** pesebre, abrevadero, comedero, bebedero. **2** artesa, amasadera. **3** seno, depresión, hoyo, canal, zona de bajas presiones. **4** MAT. mínimo.
trounce | trauns | *v.t.* **1** dar una paliza, pegar, zurrar. **2** derrotar.
troupe | tru:p | *s.c.* compañía de teatro, "troupe".
trouper | 'tru:pər | *s.c.* actor, miembro de una compañía de teatro.
trouser | 'trauzər | *s.c.* pantalón.
trouser-suit | 'trauzəsu:t | *s.c.* traje de chaqueta.
trousseau | 'tru:səu | [*pl.* **trousseaus, trousseaux**] *s.c.* ajuar, equipo de novia.
trout | traut | *s.c.* ZOOL. trucha.
trowel | 'trauəl | *s.c.* **1** paleta, llana. **1** desplantador, trasplantador. || *v.t.* **3** allanar, pasar la llana. **4** desplantar, trasplantar.
truancy | 'tru:ənsɪ | (fam.) *s.i.* novillos (en la escuela), ausencia sin permiso.
truant | 'tru:ənt | (fam.) *s.c.* **1** alumno que hace novillos, vago, haragán. || *adj.* **2** que hace novillos, vago, perezoso. || **3 to play –,** hacer novillos, pirola.
truce | tru:s | *s.c.* tregua, suspensión.
truck | trʌk | *s.c.* **1** trueque, cambio. **2** trato, pago. **3** vagoneta, carreta; carrito, mesita con ruedas. **4** (EE.UU.) camión. || *v.t.* e *i.* **5** trocar, cambiar, hacer un trueque, un cambio. **6** transportar en camión. || **7 to have no – with,** no tener tratos con, no tener relaciones con.
trucker | 'trʌkər | *s.c.* **1** (EE.UU.) transportista, camionero. **2** hortelano.
truckle | 'trʌkl | *s.c.* **1** rueda, ruedecita. || *v.i.* **2 [to – to]** ser servil con, someterse servilmente.
truckle-bed | 'trʌklbed | *s.c.* cama de ruedas, carriola.
truckload | 'trʌkləud | *s.c.* camión.
truculence | 'trʌkjuləns | *s.i.* truculencia, ferocidad, agresividad, crueldad, salvajismo.
truculent | 'trʌkjulənt | *s.c.* feroz, agresivo, cruel, salvaje.
trudge | trʌdʒ | *s.c.* **1** caminata, paseo. || *v.t.* **2** recorrer una distancia con dificultad.
true | tru: | *adj.* **1** verdadero, de verdad, genuino, verídico, leal, auténtico. **2** MUS. afinado. **3** exacto, centrado, alineado. || *v.t.* **4** corregir, rectificar. **5** centrar. || **6 to come –,** cumplirse, realizarse, hacerse realidad. **7 out of –,** descentrado, no alineado, no aplomado. **7 – north,** norte exacto. **8 – to one's word/promise,** fiel a su palabra.
true-blue | ˌtru:'blu: | *adj.* fiel, leal; legal.
truffle | 'trʌfl | *s.c.* trufa.
trug | trʌg | *s.c.* cesta para herramientas de jardinería.
truism | 'tru:ɪzəm | *s.i.* truismo.
truly | 'tru:lɪ | *adv.* **1** verdaderamente, realmente, fielmente, lealmente. || **2 well an –,** V. **well. 3 yours –,** suyo afectísimo.
trump | trʌmp | *s.c.* **1** triunfo, baza. **2** (fam.) buena persona. || *v.t.* **3** perder la baza, fallar; forjar, inventar, falsificar. || **4 – card,** triunfo, baza. **5 to turn/come up trumps,** resultar bien, salir bien.
trumped-up | 'trʌmptʌp | *adj.* imaginado, inventado, forjado.
trumpet | 'trʌmpɪt | *s.c.* **1** MUS. trompeta, trompetista. **2** trompetilla. || *v.t.* **3** tocar la trompeta. **4** barritar, bramar. || *v.i.* **5** anunciar al son de la trompeta, pregonar. || **6 to blow one's own –,** darse bombo.
trumpeter | 'trʌmpɪtər | *s.c.* trompetista.
truncate | trʌŋ'keɪt | *v.t.* truncar.
truncheon | 'trʌntʃən | *s.c.* porra.
trundle | 'trʌndl | *s.c.* **1** ruedecita. **2** cama con ruedas. **3** carretilla. || *v.t.* e *i.* **4** rodar, hacer rodar. **5** empujar, llevar.
trunk | trʌŋk | *s.c.* **1** BOT. tronco. **2** ANAT. tórax, tronco. **3** ZOOL. trompa. **4** línea interurbana; línea principal. **5** baúl. **6** ARQ. fuste. **7** TEC. conducto, cañería. **8** bañador, pantalón corto. **9** (EE.UU.) maleta, maletero, portaequipajes. || **10 – call,** conferencia, llamada interurbana.
truss | trʌs | *s.c.* **1** MED. braguero. **2** BOT. racimo. **3** ARQ. modillón. || *v.t.* **4** atar, liar, espetar. **5** ARQ. apuntalar.
trust | trʌst | *s.i.* **1** confianza, cargo. **2** deber, obligación. **3** depósito. || *v.t.* e *i.* **4** confiar en, fiarse de, esperar. || **5 in –,** en fideicomiso. **6 to take on –,** aceptar, creer a ojos cerrados. **7 – fund,** depósito de confianza. **8 to – someone to do something,** encomendar.
trustee | trʌ'sti: | *s.c.* **1** fideicomisario. **2** administrador, síndico.
trustful | 'trʌstfl | *adj.* confiado.
trusting | 'trʌstɪŋ | *adj.* confiado.
trustingly | 'trʌstɪŋlɪ | *adv.* confiadamente.
trustworthy | 'trʌstwə:θɪ | *adj.* digno de confianza, fidedigno.
trusty | 'trʌstɪ | *adj.* digno de confianza, fiel, leal.
truth | tru:θ | *s.i.* **1** verdad, veracidad, sinceridad. **2** exactitud. || **3 in –/in all –,** en verdad. **4 to tell you the –/– to tell,** decir la verdad.
truthful | 'tru:θfl | *adj.* **1** veraz, verídico. **2** parecido (retrato).
truthfully | 'tru:θfəlɪ | *adv.* verdaderamente, fielmente.
truthfulness | 'tru:θflnɪs | *s.i.* **1** veracidad, verdad. **2** parecido.
try | traɪ | *s.c.* **1** prueba, intento, tentativa. **2** DEP. ensayo. || *v.t.* **3** probar, intentar, tratar. **4** ensayar, poner a prueba. **5** probar, saborear, catar. **6** hacer sufrir,

afligir, fatigar, cansar. || *v.i.* **7** esforzarse, hacer un intento. || **8 to – one's hand at,** V. **hand. 9 to – one's luck/to – one's fortunes,** intentar, probar, probar suerte. **10 to – one's patience,** poner a prueba la paciencia de alguien.

trying | 'traɪɪŋ | *adj.* molesto, penoso, cansado, difícil.

try-out | 'traɪaʊt | *s.c.* **1** prueba de aptitud. **2** ART. audición.

tryst | trɪst | *s.c.* **1** cita. || **2 – place,** lugar de la cita.

tsar | zɑːr | *s.c.* zar.

tsarina | zɑː'riːnə | *s.c.* zarina.

tsarist | zɑːrɪst | *s.c.* zarista.

tsetse-fly | 'tsetsɪflaɪ | *s.c.* ZOOL. mosca tse-tsé.

T-shirt | 'tiːʃəːt | *s.c.* camiseta.

tub | tʌb | *s.c.* **1** bañera, baño. **2** tina, cubo, bote, barreño. || *v.t.* e *i.* **4** tomar un baño, bañar(se), lavar(se) en un barreño o tina.

tuba | 'tjuːbə | *s.c.* MUS. tuba.

tubby | 'tʌbɪ | *adj.* rechoncho.

tube | tjuːb | *s.c.* **1** tubo. **2** el Metro. **3** ANAT. trompa, tubo. **4** túnel. **5** (EE.UU.) lámpara, válvula. **6** cámara neumática. || *v.t.* **7** entubar, meter en tubos. **8** ir en metro. || **8 Fallopian –,** ANAT. trompa de Falopio.

tubeless | 'tjuːblɪs | *adj.* sin cámara (neumáticos).

tuber | 'tjuːbər | *s.c.* **1** ANAT., MED. tubérculo, tuberosidad. **2** BOT. tubérculo.

tubercular | tjuː'bəːkjulər | *s.c.adj.* tubercular, tuberculoso.

tuberculosis | tjuːˌbəːkju'ləusɪs | *s.i.* MED. tuberculosis.

tubing | 'tjuːbɪŋ | *s.i.* **1** tubería, tubos. **2** MED., TEC. entubado.

tubular | 'tjuːbjulər | *adj.* tubular.

tuck | tʌk | *s.i.* **1** pliegue, alforza. **2** comestibles, provisiones, chucherías, caramelos. **3** comida. || *v.t.* **4** meter, remeter, hacer pliegues. **5** devorar, zampar. || *v.i.* **6** comer con apetito, caber.

tuck-shop | tʌkʃɒp | *s.c.* confitería, bombonería.

Tuesday | 'tjuːzdɪ | *s.c.* martes: *on Tuesday = el martes.*

tuft | tʌft | *s.c.* **1** penacho, mechón, cresta, mata. **2** borla, copo (de algodón). || *v.t.* **3** poner un penacho, una borla; acolchar.

tufted | 'tʌftɪd | *adj.* copetudo.

tug | tʌg | *s.c.* **1** tirón, estirón, tracción. **2** tirante. **3** remolcador. || *v.t.* **4** tirar, arrastrar, remolcar. || *v.i.* **5** tirar, dar un estirón fuerte. **6** MAR. remolcar. || **6 – boat,** remolcador.

tug-of-love | ˌtʌgəu'lʌv | *adj.* intento de conseguir la custodia de un hijo, rapto del hijo bajo la custodia del otro cónyuge (en un divorcio).

tug-of-war | ˌtʌgəu'wɔːr | [*pl.* **tugs-of-war**] *s.c.* **1** juego de la cuerda. **2** lucha. **3** tira y afloja.

tuition | tjuː'ɪʃn | *s.i.* **1** enseñanza, instrucción, educación. **2** clases particulares. **3** (EE.UU.) matrícula.

tulip | 'tjuːlɪp | *s.c.* BOT. tulipán.

tulle | tjuːl | *s.i.* tul.

tumble | 'tʌmbl | *s.c.* **1** caída, voltereta. **2** revoltijo. || *v.t.* **3** derribar, abatir, tumbar, desordenar, arrugar, despeinar, deshacer. **4** derrocar. || *v.i.* **5** caerse, dar volteretas, retozar, tropezar, tambalearse. || **6 to – down,** derribar, venirse abajo, derrumbarse. **7 to – into,** tropezar con, echarse en. **8 to – on,** dar con, tropezarse con. **9 to – to,** caer en, darse cuenta, caer en la cuenta, comprender.

tumbled | 'tʌmbld | *adj.* revuelto, desordenado.

tumbledown | 'tʌmbldaun | *adj.* ruinoso, destartalado.

tumble-dryer | 'tʌmbldraɪər | *s.c.* secador.

tumbler | 'tʌmblər | *s.c.* **1** vaso, cubilete. **2** acróbata. **3** TEC. tambor. **4** MEC. balancín.

tumbler-dryer | 'tʌmblədraɪər | *s.c.* tambor secador.

tumbling | 'tʌmblɪŋ | *s.i.* caída, acrobacia.

tumbrel | 'tʌmbrəl | *s.c.* volquete, carreta.

tumescent | tjuː'mesnt | *adj.* MED. tumescente, tumefacto.

tummy | 'tʌmɪ | *s.c.* (fam.) barriga, tripa, vientre.

tumour | 'tjuːmər | *s.c.* MED. tumor.

tumult | 'tjuːmʌlt | *s.c.* tumulto.

tumultuous | tjuː'mʌltʃuəs | *adj.* tumultuoso.

tun | tʌn | *s.c.* cuba, tonel.

tuna | tjuːnə | *s.c.* **1** ZOOL. atún. **2** tuna, nopal, chumbera.

tundra | 'tʌndrə | *s.i.* GEOG. tundra.

tune | tjuːn | *s.c.* **1** MUS. aire, melodía, tono; armonía. **2** sintonización. || *v.t.* e *i.* **3** afinar, templar, sintonizar, armonizar, adaptar. || **4 to call the –,** pedir la canción. **5 to change one's –/to sing a different –,** cambiar de tono. **6 to dance to someone's –,** bailar al son que tocan. **7 in tune,** sintonizado, afinado. **8 out of –,** desafinado. **9 to the – of,** por la cantidad de, por la friolera de. **10 tuned in,** sintonizado. **11 tuning fork,** MUS. diapasón.

tuneful | 'tjuːnfl | *adj.* melodioso, armonioso, sonoro.

tuneless | 'tjuːnlɪs | *adj.* discordante, disonante, mudo.

tunelessly | 'tjuːnlɪslɪ | *adv.* discordantemente, silenciosamente.

tuner | 'tjuːnər | *s.c.* **1** afinador. **2** RAD. sintonizador.

tungsten | 'tʌŋstən | *s.i.* QUIM. tungsteno.

tunic | 'tjuːnɪk | *s.c.* ANAT. túnica.

Tunisia | tjuː'nɪzɪə | *s.sing.* Túnez.

Tunisian | tjuː'nɪzɪən | *s.c.adj.* tunecino.

tunnel | 'tʌnl | *s.c.* **1** túnel. **2** MIN. galería. || *v.t.* **3** cavar, hacer un túnel. **4** hacer galerías. || **5 light at the end of the –,** V. **light. 5 – vision,** ceguera, cerrazón.

tuppence | 'tʌpəns | *s.c.* **1** dos peniques. || **2 not to care –,** no importar un comino, dar igual.

tuppenny | 'tʌpənɪ | *adj.* de dos peniques.

turban | 'təːbən | *s.c.* turbante.

turbaned | 'təːbənd | *adj.* con turbante.

turbid | 'təːbɪd | *adj.* denso, espeso, turbio, confuso, túrbido.

turbine | 'təːbaɪn | *s.c.* TEC. turbina.

turbo | ˌtəːbəu | *pret.* turbo.

turbocharged | ˌtəːbəu'tʃɑːdʒt | *adj.* equipado con turbo.

turbot | 'təːbət | *s.c.* ZOOL. rodaballo (pez).

turbulence | 'təːbjuləns | *s.c.* **1** turbulencia, desorden, disturbios. **2** GEOG. turbulencia.

turbulent | 'təːbjulənt | *adj.* **1** turbulento, tumultuoso. **2** revoltoso.

turbulently | 'təːbjuləntlɪ | *adv.* **1** turbulentamente, tumultuosamente. **2** revoltosamente.

turd | təːd | *s.c.* **1** (vulg.) mierda. **2** desagradable, indeseable.

tureen | tə'riːn | *s.c.* sopera, salsera.

turf | təːf | [*pl.* **turfs/turves**] *s.c.* **1** césped. **2** turba. **3** deporte hípico, carreras de caballos. || *v.t.* **4** poner césped. || **5 – accountant,** corredor de apuestas hípicas.

turgid | 'təːdʒɪd | *adj.* **1** MED. turgente, túrgido, hinchado. **2** (fam.) ampuloso, hinchado.

Turk | təːk | *s.c.* **1** turco, musulmán. **2** tirano.

turkey | 'təːkɪ | *s.c.* **1** ZOOL., GAST. pavo. || **2 to talk –,** no andarse con rodeos, no tener pelos en la lengua. **3 Turkey,** GEOG. Turquía.

Turkish | 'təːkɪʃ | *adj.* **1** turco. || **2 – bath,** baño turco. **3 – coffee,** café turco. **4 – delight,** delicia turca.

turmeric | 'təːmərɪk | *s.i.* BOT. cúrcuma.

turmoil | 'təːmɔɪl | *s.i.* confusión, desorden, alboroto, tumulto.

turn | təːn | *s.c.* e *i.* **1** vuelta, revolución, viraje, giro. **2** curva, recodo, espira. **3** movimiento, turno, vez, oportunidad. **4** cambio, sesgo, cariz, aspecto. **5** susto, vahído, desmayo, crisis, ataque. || *v.t.* **6** hacer girar, dar vueltas, dar la vuelta. **7** volver, torcer, doblar. **8** desviar, apartar, desechar, eludir. **9** rechazar, rebasar. **10** echar a perder, agriar, poner rancio, cortar. **11** tornear, moldear, labrar. || *v.i.* **12** girar, volver, regresar, torcer, virar. **13** cambiar, convertir, volverse, ponerse. **14** echarse a perder, cortarse. **15** dedicarse, recurrir. || **16 a bad –,** una faena, una mala jugada. **17 a good –,** un favor, una buena acción. **18 at every –,** a cada paso. **19 by turns,** por turnos. **20 done to a –, 21 to give one a –,** dar un susto. **22 in –,** uno tras otro, cada uno a su vez. **23 on the –,** iniciarse o terminarse la marea. **24 out of –,** fuera de turno. **25 to take turns/to take it in turns,** turnarse, alternarse. **26 to – about,** dar la vuelta. **27 to – a blind eye,** V. **blind. 28 to – against,** poner en contra, enemistar. **29 to turn and turn about,** dar vueltas y más vueltas. **30 to – around,** dar la vuelta, desvirtuar. **31 to – aside,** apartar. **32 to – away,** volver, apartar la vista. **33 to – back,** volver, volverse. **34 to – down,** bajar, mitigar, rechazar. **35 to – from,** apartarse de, apartar. **36 to – in,** estar vuelto, presentar, entregar. **37 to – into,** transformar en, convertir en. **38 to – off,** cerrar, apagar, quitar. **39 to – on,** encender, poner, abrir, conectar. **40 to – out,** apagar, cerrar, volver hacia fuera. **41 turned out,** rechazado. **42 to – one's back on,** V. **back. 43 to – one's hand to,** V. **hand. 44 to – over,** dar la vuelta a, volverse, volcar. **45 to – round,** dar la vuelta a, volverse. **46 to – tail,** V. **tail. 47 to – the tables on,** V. **table. 48 to – to,** empezar. **48 to – up,** poner más fuerte, subir. **49 to – ...upside down,** dar la vuelta, poner cabeza abajo.

turnabout | 'tɜːnəbaʊt | (también **turnaround**) *s.c.* **1** vuelta, cambio. **2** (EE.UU.) tiovivo.

turnaround | 'tɜːnəraʊnd | V. **turnabout.**

turncoat | 'tɜːnkəʊt | *s.c.* renegado, veleta.

turning | 'tɜːnɪŋ | *s.c.* vuelta, ángulo, recodo, curva, viraje.

turning-point | 'tɜːnɪŋpɔɪnt | *s.c.* viraje, momento crucial, hito, coyuntura, punto decisivo.

turnip | 'tɜːnɪp | *s.c.* **1** nabo. **2** reloj de bolsillo.

turn-off | 'tɜːnɒf | *s.c.* **1** desvío. **2** (EE.UU.) bocacalle.

turn-on | 'tɜːnɒn | *s.c.* alguien o algo que excita sexualmente.

turnout | 'tɜːnaʊt | *s.i.* **1** asistentes, concurrencia, público, entrada. **2** producción, atuendo. **3** limpieza, reorganización.

turnover | 'tɜːnəʊvər | *s.c.* volumen de venta, facturación.

turnpike | 'tɜːnpaɪk | *s.c.* **1** barrera. **2** (EE.UU.) autopista de peaje.

turnround | 'tɜːnraʊnd | *s.i.* período de carga y descarga.

turnstile | 'tɜːnstaɪl | *s.c.* torniquete.

turntable | 'tɜːnteɪbl | *s.c.* plataforma giratoria.

turn-up | 'tɜːnʌp | *s.c.* **1** vuelta. **2** (fam.) pelea, trifulca. || *adj.* **3** nariz respingona. **4** alto. || **5 a – for the book /books,** ser algo inesperado.

turpentine | 'tɜːpəntaɪn | *s.i.* trementina.

turpitude | 'tɜːpɪtjuːd | *s.i.* bajeza, infamia, vileza.

turps | tɜːps | *s.i.* trementina, aguarrás.

turquoise | 'tɜːkwɔɪz | *s.i.adj.* **1** GEOL. turquesa. || **2 – blue,** azul turquesa.

turret | 'tʌrɪt | *s.c.* **1** ARQ. torreón, torre, torrecilla. **2** MIL. torreta. **3** TEC. portaherramientas.

turtle | 'tɜːtl | *s.c.* **1** ZOOL. tortuga marina. || *v.i.* **2** cazar tortugas. || **3 to turn –,** dar una vuelta de campana, zozobrar.

turtledove | 'tɜːtldʌv | *s.c.* ZOOL. tórtola.

turtleneck | 'tɜːtlnek | *s.c.* cuello alzado, cuello vuelto.

tusk | tʌsk | *s.c.* **1** colmillo. **2** TEC. espiga.

tussle | 'tʌsl | *s.c.* **1** pelea, agarrada, riña. || *v.i.* **2** pelearse.

tussock | 'tʌsək | *s.c.* mata de hierba.

tut | tʌt | *interj.* **1** ¡vaya!, ¡vamos! || *v.i.* **2** hacer un gesto de desaprobación, de disgusto.

tutelage | 'tjuːtɪlɪdʒ | *s.i.* tutela.

tutor | 'tjuːtər | *s.c.* **1** tutor, preceptor, profesor particular. **2** ayo. **3** método de aprendizaje. **4** DER. tutor. || *v.t.* e *i.* **5** dar clases privadas, enseñar, instruir. **6** ser tutor de, tutelar.

tutorial | tjuː'tɔːrɪəl | *s.c.* **1** clases prácticas. || *adj.* **2** tutorial, tutelar.

tutti-frutti | ˌtuːtɪ'fruːtɪ | *s.i.* **1** tuttifrutti. || **2 – ice-cream,** helado de tuttifrutti.

tut-tut | ˌtʌt'tʌt | *interj.* **1** chasquido de desaprobación. || *v.i.* **2** quejarse, mostrar desaprobación.

tutu | 'tuːtuː | *s.c.* falda de bailarina, tutú.

tuxedo | tʌk'siːdəʊ | *s.c.* (EE.UU.) esmoquin.

TV | ˌtiː'viː | *s.c.* TV, televisión.

twaddle | 'twɒdl | *s.i.* **1** tonterías. || *v.i.* **2** decir tonterías.

twain | tweɪn | *s.c.adj.* **1** dos. || **2 and never the – shall meet,** sin que el uno se acerque al otro, sin que tengan nada en común.

twang | twæŋ | *s.i.* **1** tañido, punteado, ruido, sonido de cuerda. || *v.t.* **2** MUS. puntear. **3** disparar (una flecha).

tweak | twiːk | *s.c.* **1** pellizco. || *v.t.* **2** pellizcar.

twee | twiː | *s.i.* mezcla de lana.

tweed | twiːd | *s.i.* tejido de lana, tweed.

tweedy | 'twiːdɪ | *adj.* parecido al tweed.

tweet | twiːt | *s.c.* **1** altavoz para alta frecuencia. || *v.i.* **2** piar.

tweezers | 'twiːzəz | *s.pl.* pinzas.

twelfth | twelfθ | *num.ord.* **1** duodécimo, decimosegundo, dozavo; duodécima parte. || **2 – Night,** Epifanía, Noche de Reyes.

twelve | twelv | *num.card.* doce.

twelve-month | 'twelvmʌnθ | *s.* año.

twentieth | 'twentɪəθ | *num.ord.* **1** vigésimo, veinteavo, vigésima parte. **2** veinte (día).

twenty | 'twentɪ | *num.ord.* **1** veinte. || **2 – odd,** veintitantos.

twenty-first | 'twentɪfɜːst | *s.i.* mayoría de edad.

twerp | twɜːp | *s.c.* (vulg.) tío, individuo, tipo, imbécil.

twice | twaɪs | *adj.* **1** dos veces. || **2 once or –,** V. **once. 3 to think –,** V. **think. 4 – over,** V. **over. 5 – the man/ woman,** superior, mejor. **6 – the man he was/– the woman she was,** mejorados, mucho mejor.

twiddle | 'twɪdl | *s.i.* **1** vuelta. || *v.t.* **2** girar, hacer girar, jugar con, dar vueltas a. || **3 to – one's thumbs,** dar vueltas a los pulgares.

twig | twɪg | *s.i.* **1** ramita, leña menuda. **2** ANAT. vaso capilar. || *v.t.* **3** comprender, caer en la cuenta.

twilight | 'twaɪlaɪt | *s.c.* **1** crepúsculo, medialuz, ocaso. || *adj.* **2** crepuscular. **3** decadente.

twilit | 'twaɪlɪt | *adj.* **1** oscuro, grisáceo. **2** sombrío.

twill | twɪl | *s.i.* tela cruzada, asargada.

twin | twɪn | *adj.* **1** gemelo, mellizo. || *s.c.* **2** gemelo, hermano gemelo, doble, parecido. || *v.t.* **3** hermanar, tener una ciudad hermanada, ligar, vincular. || *v.i.* **4** dar a luz mellizos. || **5 – beds,** camas separadas, gemelas. **6 – tub,** máquina secadora-lavadora.

twin-bedded | ˌtwɪn'bedɪd | *adj.* doble (habitación en un hotel).

twine | twaɪn | *s.* **1** guita, hilo, bramante. **2** torcimiento, enmarañamiento, enredo. **3** GEOG. meandro. || *v.t.* **4** retorcer, torcer, trenzar, tejer, ceder, enrollar, ceñir, rodear. || *v.i.* **5** enroscarse, enrollarse, trepar, entrelazarse, serpentear.

twinge | twɪndʒ | *s.i.* **1** punzada, dolor agudo. **2** arrebato, acceso, remordimiento. || *v.t.* e *i.* **3** dar punzadas, remorder.

twinkle | 'twɪŋkl | *s.i.* **1** centelleo, parpadeo, brillo, guiño. || *v.i.* **2** titilar, centellear, parpadear, brillar. **3** moverse rápidamente.

twinkling | 'twɪŋklɪŋ | *adj.* **1** centelleante, titilante. **2** risueño, brillante, rápido. || *s.i.* **3** centelleo, parpadeo, brillo. || **4 in the – of the eye,** en un abrir y cerrar de ojos, en un santiamén.

twin-set | 'twɪnset | (también **twinset**) *s.i.* conjunto.

twirl | twɜːl | *s.i.* **1** vuelta, giro, rasgo, pirueta. || *v.t.* **2** girar rápidamente, dar vueltas rápidas a, voltear. **3** atusarse. || *v.i.* **3** hacer piruetas.

twirp V. **twerp.**

twist | twɪst | *s.c.* **1** retorcimiento, vuelta, rollo, pliegue, trenza, mecha. **2** movimiento giratorio. **3** giro, cambio, variación. **5** twist (baile). || *v.t.* e *i.* **6** girar, torcer(se), retorcer, contorsionar(se). **7** enrollar. **8** dar vueltas, serpentear. **9** distorsionar. **10** bailar el twist. || **11 round the –,** (fam., brit.) chalado, fuera de sus cabales. **12 twists and turns,** vueltas y revueltas. **13 to – someone round one's little finger,** tener dominado, tener en el bolsillo. **14 to – someone's arm,** convencer, hacer dar el brazo a torcer.

twisted | 'twɪstɪd | *adj.* **1** retorcido, contorsionado. **2** de mente retorcida, de malas intenciones, perverso.

twister | 'twɪstər | *s.c.* **1** deshonesto, defraudador, embaucador, tramposo, estafador. **2** (fam.) rompecabezas, problema difícil. **3** (EE.UU.) tornado.

twisty | 'twɪstɪ | *adj.* serpenteante, retorcida.

twit | twɪt | (fam.) *s.c.* **1** rollo, pesado, plomo: *he's a twit = es un rollo.* || *v.t.* **2** tomar el pelo, gastar bromas, burlarse.

twitch | twɪtʃ | *s.c.* **1** tirón, punzada, sacudida, contracción. || *v.t.* **2** dar un tirón, crispar. || *v.i.* **3** crisparse, dar un tirón a.
twitchy | 'twɪtʃɪ | *adj.* nervioso, ansioso, excitado.
twitter | 'twɪtər | *s.i.* **1** gorjeo. **2** agitación, inquietud, nerviosismo. || *v.i.* **2** gorjear. **3** ponerse nervioso. **4** temblar, agitarse.
two | tuː | *num.card.* **1** dos. || *s.c.* **2** dos (cartas,...). || **3 to kill – birds with one stone,** V. **bird. 4 to put – and – together,** atar cabos, deducir, llegar a la conclusión. **4 – a penny,** V. **penny. 5 two's company, three's a crowd,** V. **company.**
two-dimensional | ˌtuːdaɪ'menʃənəl | *adj.* de dos dimensiones.
two-edged | ˌtuː'edʒt | *adj.* de doble filo.
two-faced | ˌtuː'feɪst | *adj.* **1** de dos caras. **2** (fig.) falso, hipócrita.
twofold | 'tuːfəuld | *adj.* **1** doble. || *adv.* **2** dos veces.
two-handed | ˌtuː'hændɪd | *adj.* de dos manos, ambidextro.
two-piece | ˌtuː'piːs | *adj.* de dos piezas.
two-ply | 'tuːplaɪ | *adj.* de dos cabos.
twosome | 'tuːsəm | *s.c.* pareja.
two-way | ˌtuː'weɪ | *adj.* **1** de doble dirección. **2** TEC. de doble paso.
tycoon | taɪ'kuːn | *s.c.* magnate.
tyke | taɪk | *s.c.* **1** niño travieso, pícaro. **2** (fam.) chucho.
type | taɪp | *s.c.* **1** tipo, clase. || *v.t.* **2** mecanografiar, imprimir. || **3 not one's –,** no es mi tipo. **4 to – away,** escribir mucho rato. **5 to – up,** escribir definitivamente, hacer la copia definitiva.
typecast | 'taɪpkɑːst | *adj.* **1** encasillado. || *v.t.* **2** encasillar.
typeface | 'taɪpfeɪs | *s.i.* TEC. tipo, carácter.
typescript | 'taɪpskrɪpt | *s.c.* e *i.* texto mecanografiado.
typewriter | 'taɪpraɪtər | *s.c.* **1** mecanógrafo. **2** máquina de escribir.
typewritten | 'taɪprɪtn | *adj.* mecanografiado, escrito a máquina.
typhoid | 'taɪfɔɪd | *s.i.* **1** MED. fiebre tifoidea. || *adj.* **2** tifoideo.
typhoon | taɪ'fuːn | *s.c.* GEOG. tifón.
typical | 'tɪpɪkl | *adj.* típico, característico.
typically | 'tɪpɪklɪ | *adv.* típicamente.
typify | 'tɪpɪfaɪ | *v.t.* **1** simbolizar. **2** tipificar, caracterizar.
typing | 'taɪpɪŋ | *s.i.* mecanografía.
typist | 'taɪpɪst | *s.c.* mecanógrafo.
typographical | ˌtaɪpə'græfɪkl | *adj.* tipográfico.
typography | taɪ'pɒgrəfɪ | *s.i.* tipografía.
tyrannical | tɪ'rænɪkl | *adj.* tiránico.
tyrannize | 'tɪrənaɪz | *v.t.* tiranizar.
tyranny | 'tɪrənɪ | *s.c.* e *i.* tiranía, dictadura, opresión.
tyrant | 'taɪərənt | *s.c.* tirano, dictador, opresor.
tyre | 'taɪər | *s.c.* neumático.
tyro | 'taɪrəu | *s.c.* aprendiz, principiante.
tzar V. **tsar.**
tzarina V. **tsarina.**
tzarist V. **tsarist.**
tzetze-fly V. **tsetse-fly.**

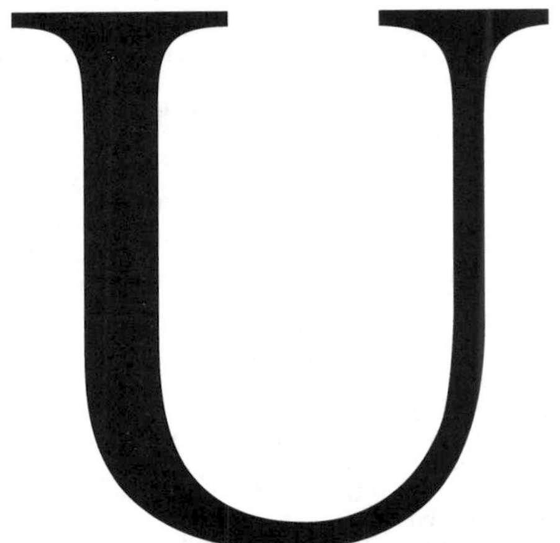

u, U *s.c.* **1** u, U (vigésima primera letra del alfabeto inglés). **2** *abreviatura* de **uranium, unit, united, University. 3** cualquier objeto en forma de U: *a U-shaped kitchen = una cocina en forma de U.* || *adj.* **4** propio de clase alta, típico de clase social alta (lenguaje, comportamiento). **5** en forma de U.

UAE | ˌjuːeɪ'iː | (**United Arab Emirates**) Emiratos Arabes Unidos.

ubiquitous | juː'bɪkwɪtəs | *adj.* ubicuo, omnímodo, omnipresente.

ubiquity | juː'bkwɪtɪ | *s.i.* ubicuidad, omnipresencia.

U-boat | 'juːbəut | *s.c.* MAR. submarino alemán.

udder | 'ʌdər | *s.c.* ubre, mama (de un animal).

UFO | ˌjuːef'əu | (**Unidentified flying object**) objeto volante no identificado.

Uganda | juː'gændə | *s.* Uganda.

Ugandan | juː'gændən | *adj.* **1** ugandés. || *s.c.* **2** ugandés.

ugh | ux | | əg | *interj.* ¡uf!, ¡pufff! (indica asco, horror).

ugli | 'ʌglɪ | *s.c.* ugli (cítrico tropical caribeño, híbrido de pomelo y mandarina).

ugliness | 'ʌglɪnɪs | *s.i.* fealdad, afeamiento, monstruosidad, repugnancia.

ugly | 'ʌglɪ | *adj.* **1** feo, repulsivo, horrible: *an ugly face = un rostro repulsivo.* **2** fea, desagradable, peligrosa (una situación). **3** ofensivo, desagradable, violento, amenazador, peligroso. **4** malo, perverso (moralmente). **5** desapacible, horrible: *an ugly morning = una mañana desapacible.* || **6 an – duckling,** (fam.) un patito feo (persona que va mejorando en belleza, inteligencia, etc.). **7 as – as a sin,** (fam.) más feo que un pecado, feísimo.

UHF | ˌjuːeɪtʃ'ef | (**ultra high frequency**) frecuencia ultraelevada.

uh-huh | ʌˌhʌ | *interj.* (fam.) ¡ajá!, ¡sí! (sonido que se utiliza para afirmar).

UK | ˌjuː'keɪ | (**United Kingdom**) Reino Unido.

ukelele | juːkə'leɪlɪ | *s.c.* MUS. ukelele, guitarra hawayana.

ulcer | 'ʌlsər | *s.c.* MED. úlcera, llaga.

ulcerated | 'ʌlsəreɪt | *adj.* MED. ulcerado, llagado.

ulceration | ˌʌlsə'reɪʃn | *s.i.* MED. ulceración.

ulcerous | 'ʌlsərəs | *adj.* MED. ulceroso.

ulna | 'ʌlnə | [*pl.* **ulnae** o **ulnas**] *s.c.* ANAT. cúbito.

ulterior | ʌl'tɪərɪər | *adj.* **1** oculto, escondido, latente: *ulterior motives = motivos ocultos.* **2** ulterior, posterior, subsiguiente. **3** ulterior, remoto, lejano (lugar).

ultimate | 'ʌltɪmɪt | *adj.* **1** último, final (de una serie): *the ultimate part = la parte final.* **2** fundamental, básico, elemental, primordial. **3** (fam.) máximo, mayúsculo, superlativo: *it was an ultimate mistake = fue un error mayúsculo.* || **4 the – in,** lo último en, lo más avanzado en: *the ultimate in technology = lo último en tecnología.*

ultimately | 'ʌltɪmɪtlɪ | *adv.* **1** finalmente, por último, a la larga. **2** básicamente, fundamentalmente.

ultimata | ˌʌltɪ'meɪtə | V. **ultimatum.**

ultimatum | ˌʌltɪ'meɪtəm | [*pl.* **ultimatums** o **ultimata**] *s.c.* ultimátum.

ultramarine | ˌʌltrəmə'riːn | *adj.* **1** (form.) azul ultramarino, azul fuerte. **2** ultramarino, del otro lado del mar. || *s.i.* **3** color azul fuerte, color azul ultramarino.

ultrasonic | ˌʌltrə'sɒnɪk | *adj.* ultrasónico, ultrasonoro.

ultrasound | 'ʌltrəˌsaund | *s.i.* ultrasonido.

ultraviolet | ˌʌltrə'vaɪəlɪt | *adj.* FIS. ultravioleta.

ululate | 'juːljuleɪt | *v.i.* (form.) ulular, gritar, aullar, bramar, rugir.

ululation | ˌjuːlju'leɪʃn | *s.i.* ululato, aullido, bramido, rugido.

um | ʌm | | əm | *interj.* er, ummm... (muestra indecisión, duda).

umber | 'ʌmbər | *adj.* **1** (form.) ocre oscuro, marrón oscuro, pardo oscuro. || *s.i.* **2** tierra de sombra (en pintura). **3** color ocre oscuro.

umbilical | ʌm'bɪlɪkl | *adj.* **1** ANAT. umbilical. || **2 – cord, a)** ANAT. cordón umbilical; **b)** ASTRON. conexión eléctrica de un proyectil antes del lanzamiento; cable de conexión de un astronauta con la nave nodriza.

umbilicus | ʌm'bɪlɪkəs | *s.c.* ANAT. ombligo.

umbra | 'ʌmbrə | [*pl.* **umbrae** o **umbras**] *s.i.* **1** ASTR. cono de sombra, (en un eclipse total). **2** sombra.

umbrae | 'ʌmbriː | *pl.* de **umbra.**

umbrage | 'ʌmbrɪdʒ | *s.i.* **1** resentimiento, ofensa, agravio. **2** (arc.) sombra, umbría. || *s.c.* **3** indicación, insinuación, aviso, señal. || **4 to give/take –,** (form.) ofenderse, resentirse, tomarse a mal (algo).

umbrella | ʌm'brelə | *s.c.* **1** paraguas; sombrilla, parasol. **2** (fig.) protección, amparo, cobertura, patrocinio: *under the umbrella of the President = bajo la protección del Presidente.* **3** MIL. cobertura aérea. **4** ZOOL. umbrela (de una medusa).

umlaut | 'umlaut | *s.c.* **1** diéresis. **2** FON. metafonía, cambio de sonido vocálico. || *v.t.* **3** modificar un sonido vocálico. **4** poner diéresis.

umpire | 'ʌmpaɪər | *s.c.* **1** DEP. árbitro (en tenis, críquet, etc.). **2** juez, árbitro (de una discusión). **3** DER. juez. || *v.t.* e *i.* **4** DEP. arbitrar.

umpteen | ˌʌmp'tiːn | *adj.* (fam.) innumerables, incontables, muchísimos: *he told me umpteen times = me lo dijo muchísimas veces.*

umpteenth | ˌʌmp'tiːnθ | *adj.* enésimo: *for the umpteenth time = por enésima vez.*

'un | ʌn | *pron.* (fam.) uno, ejemplar, sujeto, tipo: *a bad 'un = un mal tipo.*

UN | ˌjuːˈen | **(United Nations)** Naciones Unidas.

unabashed | ˌʌnəˈbæʃt | *adj.* desenvuelto, desenfadado, confiado en sí mismo, sereno.

unabated | ˌʌnəˈbeɪtɪd | *adj.* (form.) exacto, como al principio, intenso, sin disminución, sin cambios: *the wind continued unabated = el viento continuó con la misma intensidad.*

unable | ʌnˈeɪbl | *adj.* (form.) incapaz, imposibilitado, impotente.

unabridged | ˌʌnəˈbrɪdʒd | *adj.* íntegro, completo, no resumido: *an unabridged article = un artículo íntegro.*

unacceptable | ˌʌnəkˈseptəbl | *adj.* inaceptable, intolerable.

unacceptably | ˌʌnəkˈseptəblɪ | *adv.* inaceptablemente, intolerablemente.

unaccompanied | ˌʌnəˈkʌmpənɪd | *adj.* **1** solo, sin compañía: *she was unaccompanied = estaba sola.* **2** MUS. sin acompañamiento.

unaccountable | ˌʌnəˈkaʊntəbl | *adj.* **1** inexplicable, incomprensible, inaudito, desconocido, misterioso. **2** (form.) falto de responsabilidad, falto de compromiso.

unaccountably | ˌʌnəˈkaʊntəblɪ | *adv.* inexplicablemente, incomprensiblemente, misteriosamente.

unaccounted | ˌʌnəˈkaʊntɪd | *adj.* **1** inexplicado, no encontrado. || **2 – for,** perdido, extraviado, sin noticias: *two of the boys were unaccounted for = sin noticias de dos chicos.*

unaccustomed | ˌʌnəˈkʌstəmd | *adj.* **1** no habituado, poco familiarizado: *unaccustomed to high-heeled shoes = poco habituada a los zapatos de tacón.* **2** poco común, inusitado, insólito, inusual: *an unaccustomed voice = una voz insólita.*

unacknowledged | ˌʌnəkˈnɒlɪdʒd | *adj.* despreciado, no tomado en cuenta, no reconocido, ignorado: *as a poet he was unacknowledged = no fue reconocido como poeta.*

unacquainted | ˌʌnəˈkweɪntɪd | *adj.* **[– (with)]** poco familiarizado, poco versado, desconocedor de: *unacquainted with technology = poco familiarizado con la tecnología.*

unadopted | ˌʌnəˈdɒptɪd | *adj.* (brit.) que es de responsabilidad vecinal, y no de las autoridades locales (una carretera).

unadorned | ˌʌnəˈdɔːnd | *adj.* sin adornos, no decorado, sencillo, simple.

unadulterated | ˌʌnəˈdʌtəreɪtɪd | *adj.* **1** puro, no adulterado, sin aditivos, natural. **2** (fig. y fam.) completo, puro, total: *unadulterated rubbish = pura basura.*

unaffected | ˌʌnəˈfektɪd | *adj.* **1** no afectado, no influido, insensible, indiferente: *unaffected by war = no afectados por la guerra.* **2** sin afectación, sincero, franco.

unafraid | ˌʌnəˈfreɪd | *adj.* sin temor, sin miedo, seguro de sí, impertérrito.

unaided | ˌʌnˈeɪdɪd | *adj.* **1** sin ayuda, solo. || *adv.* **2** sin ayuda.

unalloyed | ˌʌnəˈlɔɪd | *adj.* (lit.) puro, sin mezcla, sin impurezas.

unalterable | ʌnˈɔːltərəbl | *adj.* inalterable, invariable, inmutable.

unalterably | ʌnˈɔːltərəblɪ | *adv.* inalterablemente, inmutablemente, invariablemente.

unaltered | ˌʌnˈɒːltəd | *adj.* inalterado, sin cambio.

unambiguous | ˌʌnæmˈbɪgjʊəs | *adj.* sin ambigüedad, claro, inequívoco.

unambiguously | ˌʌnæmˈbɪgjʊəslɪ | *adv.* inequívocamente, con claridad, sin ambigüedades.

unambitious | ˌʌnæmˈbɪʃəs | *adj.* falto de ambición, poco ambicioso, poco emprendedor, falto de aspiraciones.

un-American | ˌʌnˈəmerɪkən | *adj.* antiamericano, antinorteamericano.

unanimity | ˌjuːnəˈnɪmɪtɪ | *s.i.* (form.) unanimidad.

unanimous | juːˈnænɪməs | *adj.* unánime.

unanimously | juːˈnænɪməslɪ | *adv.* unánimemente.

unannounced | ˌʌnəˈnaʊnst | *adj.* no anunciado, no avisado, no notificado: *an unnounced visit = una visita no anunciada.*

unanswerable | ˌʌnˈɑːnsərəbl | *adj.* **1** incontestable, sin respuesta. **2** irrefutable, irrebatible (un argumento).

unanswered | ˌʌnˈɑːnsəd | *adj.* sin respuesta, sin contestación.

unappealing | ˌʌnəˈpiːlɪŋ | *adj.* poco atractivo, desagradable.

unappetizing, unappetising | ˌʌnˈæpɪtaɪzɪŋ | *adj.* poco apetecible, poco apetitoso, repugnante.

unapproachable | ˌʌnəˈprəʊtʃəbl | *adj.* inaccesible, inasequible, intratable, lejana (persona).

unarguable | ˌʌnˈɑːgjʊəbl | *adj.* indiscutible, incuestionable, irrefutable, irrebatible.

unarguably | ˌʌnˈɑːgjʊəblɪ | *adv.* indiscutiblemente, incuestionablemente.

unarmed | ˌʌnˈɑːmd | *adj.* **1** desarmado, sin armas. **2** BIOL. inerme, sin espinos. || **3 – combat,** combate sin armas.

unashamed | ˌʌnəˈʃeɪmd | *adj.* sinvergüenza, desvergonzado, descarado.

unashamedly | ˌʌnəˈʃeɪmdlɪ | *adv.* desvergonzadamente, descaradamente.

unasked | ˌʌnˈɑːskt | (EE.UU. | ˌʌnˈæskt |) *adj.* **1** no mencionado, no solicitado, no preguntado, no formulado: *unasked questions = preguntas que no han sido formuladas.* **2** no invitado, no querido: *they came unasked = vinieron sin ser invitados.* || *adv.* **3** voluntariamente, espontáneamente. || **4 – for,** no solicitado, no requerido, voluntario: *unasked for help = ayuda no requerida.*

unassailable | ˌʌnəˈseɪləbl | *adj.* **1** inexpugnable, inatacable. **2** (fig.) irrebatible, incuestionable, claro (un argumento).

unassisted | ˌʌnəˈsɪstɪd | *adj.* sin ayuda, sin asistencia, por sí mismo.

unassuming | ˌʌnəˈsjuːmɪŋ | *adj.* modesto, discreto, recatado.

unassumingly | ˌʌnəˈsjuːmɪŋlɪ | *adv.* modestamente, discretamente, recatadamente.

unattached | ˌʌnəˈtætʃt | *adj.* **1** soltero, no comprometido, libre. **2 [– (to)]** sin conexión, suelto, desligado, independiente. **3** DER. no pignorado, no embargado.

unattainable | ˌʌnəˈteɪnəbl | *adj.* inalcanzable, inasequible, imposible, irrealizable: *unattainable aims = objetivos inalcanzables.*

unattended | ˌʌnəˈtendɪd | *adj.* **1** desatendido, sin vigilancia, descuidado, solo: *unattended belongins = pertenencias desatendidas.* **2** sin personal, solo, desatendido (un negocio).

unattractive | ˌʌnəˈtræktɪv | *adj.* poco atractivo, desagradable, feo.

unauthorized | ˌʌnˈɔːθəraɪzd | (brit.) **unauthorised.** *adj.* desautorizado.

unavailable | ˌʌnəˈveɪləbl | *adj.* **1** agotado, acabado, no disponible (un producto en el mercado). **2** inasequible, que no puede atender a uno: *she was unavailable when I arrived = ella no pudo atenderme cuando llegué.*

unavailing | ˌʌnəˈveɪlɪŋ | *adj.* (lit.) fútil, inútil, vano, infructuoso (un intento).

unavoidable | ˌʌnəˈvɔɪdəbl | *adj.* inevitable, ineludible.

unavoidably | ˌʌnəˈvɔɪdəblɪ | *adv.* inevitablemente, ineludiblemente.

unaware | ˌʌnəˈweər | *adj.* **[– (of)]** ignorante, desconocedor, ajeno, inconsciente: *he was unaware of the problems = desconocía los problemas.*

unawareness | ˌʌnəˈweənɪs | *s.i.* **[– (of)]** desconocimiento, inconsciencia.

unawares | ˌʌnəˈweəz | *adv.* **1** inesperadamente, por sorpresa, de improviso. **2** (form.) inconscientemente, sin darse cuenta. || **3 to catch/take somebody –,** coger a alguien desprevenido.

unbalance | ˌʌnˈbæləns | *v.t.* **1** desequilibrar, volver loco, trastornar. **2** desequilibrar, desestabilizar, perturbar, alterar. || *s.i.* **3** desequilibrio, perturbación, alteración.

unbalanced | ˌʌnˈbælənst | *adj.* **1** desequilibrado, trastornado, perturbado, irracional, fuera de su sano juicio. **2** COM. desequilibrado, que no cuadra (cuentas). **3** no equilibrado, poco objetivo (un comentario).

unbar | ˌʌnˈbɑːr | *v.t.* **1** desatrancar, quitar la tranca o barra (de una puerta). **2** (form. y fig.) abrir, franquear: *unbar the way to dialogue = abrir camino al diálogo.*

unbearable | ʌnˈbeərəbl | *adj.* insoportable, inaguantable, insufrible, intolerable.

unbearably | ʌnˈbeərəbl | *adv.* insoportablemente, inaguantablemente, insufriblemente, intolerablemente.

unbeatable | ˌʌn'biːtəbl | *adj.* imbatible, inigualable, inmejorable.
unbeaten | ˌʌn'biːtn | *adj.* **1** imbatido, invicto, insuperado (récord, ejército, equipo). **2** no pisado, no frecuentado (lugar).
unbecoming | ˌʌnbɪ'kʌmɪŋ | *adj.* (arc.) **1** poco elegante, que sienta mal (la ropa). **2** impropio, indigno, incorrecto (el comportamiento).
unbelief | ˌʌnbɪ'liːf | *s.i.* (form.) incredulidad, descreimiento, escepticismo (generalmente religioso).
unbelievable | ˌʌnbɪ'liːvəbl | *adj.* **1** increíble, inverosímil, inaudito, extraño. **2** increíble, sorprendente, extraordinario.
unbelievably | ˌʌnbɪ'liːvəblɪ | *adv.* increíblemente, sorprendentemente, extraordinariamente.
unbeliever | ˌʌnbɪ'liːvər | *s.c.* no creyente, ateo, descreído.
unbelieving | ˌʌnbɪ'liːvɪŋ | *adj.* incrédulo, escéptico, desconfiado.
unbend | ˌʌnbənd | *v.t.* e *i.* [*irr.pret.* y *p.p.* **unbent**] **1** suavizar(se), ablandar(se), volverse afable. **2** (fig.) relajarse, tranquilizarse. **3** MAR. desenvergar, soltar, aflojar (amarras, velas). **4** enderezar, desencorvar.
unbending | ˌʌn'bendɪŋ | *adj.* **1** (desp.) inflexible, inamovible, rígido, inconmovible (actitud, creencia). **2** poco afable.
unbiased, unbiassed | ˌʌn'baɪəst | *adj.* imparcial, justo, objetivo, neutral.
unbidden | ˌʌn'bɪdn | *adj.* (lit.) inesperado, espontáneo, no solicitado, sin querer: *his name came unbidden to my memory = su nombre me acudía sin querer a la memoria.*
unbind | ˌʌn'baɪnd | *v.t.* [*irr.pret.* y *p.p.* **unbound**] **1** desatar, desanudar, desligar, soltar, desamarrar. **2** liberar, dejar libre.
unblemished | ˌʌn'blemɪʃt | *adj.* inmaculado, sin tacha, intacto, sin destrozos, no averiado: *the walls were unblemished = las paredes no tenían destrozos.*
unblinking | ˌʌn'blɪŋkɪŋ | *adj.* imperturbable, sin pestañear, fijo.
unblinkingly | ˌʌn'blɪŋkɪŋlɪ | *adv.* imperturbablemente, fijamente, sin pestañear.
unblushing | ˌʌn'blʌʃɪŋ | *adj.* (form.) desvergonzado, insolente.
unblushingly | ˌʌn'blʌʃɪŋlɪ | *adv.* (form.) desvergonzadamente, descaradamente, insolentemente.
unborn | ˌʌn'bɔːn | *adj.* **1** nonato, aún no nacido (niño, animal). **2** futuro, venidero, por venir (generaciones).
unbound | ˌʌn'baʊnd | **1** *pret.* y *p.p.* de **unbind.** || *adj.* **2** suelto, desatado. **3** sin encuadernar, en hojas sueltas (un libro).
unbounded | ˌʌn'baʊndɪd | *adj.* (lit.) ilimitado, infinito, inmenso, incalculable.
unbowed | ˌʌn'baʊd | *adj.* erguido, orgulloso, no vencido, no domado.
unbreakable | ˌʌn'breɪkəbl | *adj.* irrompible, indestructible, inquebrantable.
unbridled | ˌʌn'braɪdld | *adj.* **1** (lit.) desenfrenado, incontrolado, desatado, desquiciado, imprudente. **2** sin brida.
unbroken | ˌʌn'brəʊkən | *adj.* **1** intacto, entero, perfecto, íntegro. **2** inviolada, no infringida (una ley). **3** continuo, ininterrumpido, prolongado: *a long and unbroken speech = un discurso largo y sin interrupción.* **4** indómito, no domado (espíritu, animal). **5** no desordenado, no desorganizado. **6** imbatido, no sobrepasado (récord).
unbuckle | ˌʌn'bʌkl | *v.t.* aflojar la hebilla, deshebillar.
unburden | ˌʌn'bəːdn | *v.t.* (form. y fig.) desahogar, confiarse a, abrirse a, liberarse de, confesar: *she unburdened herself of the secret = confesó el secreto.*
unbusinesslike | ˌʌn'bɪznɪslaɪk | *adj.* poco práctico, poco metódico; inexperto, ineficaz (en los negocios).
unbutton | ˌʌn'bʌtn | *v.t.* **1** desabotonar, desabrochar. || *v.i.* **2** (fig.) volverse más amable, relajarse.
unbottoned | ˌʌn'bʌtnd | *adj.* **1** desabrochado, abierto, suelto. **2** (fig.) relajado, afable.
uncalled-for | ˌʌn'kɔːldfɔː | *adj.* impertinente, gratuito, injustificado, innecesario.
uncannily | ʌn'kænɪlɪ | *adv.* de forma extraña, misteriosamente, extraordinariamente, sobrenaturalmente.
uncanny | ʌn'kænɪ | *adj.* **1** extraño, inexplicable, misterioso, extraordinario, sobrenatural. **2** pavoroso, horripilante, espantoso, no natural.
uncared-for | ˌʌn'keədfɔːr | *adj.* abandonado, descuidado, desamparado, mal atendido, desaseado.
uncaring | ʌn'keərɪŋ | *adj.* (desp.) insensible, indiferente, frío, poco afectuoso.
unceasing | ʌn'siːsɪŋ | *adj.* incesante, constante, persistente, continuo.
unceasingly | ʌn'siːsɪŋlɪ | *adv.* incesantemente, constantemente, persistentemente, continuamente.
unceremonious | 'ʌnˌserɪ'məʊnɪəs | *adj.* **1** descortés, desatento, brusco, abrupto, rudo: *in an unceremonious way = de forma brusca.* **2** informal, sin ceremonia, familiar.
unceremoniously | 'ʌnˌserɪ'məʊnɪəslɪ | *adv.* **1** (desp.) descortésmente, bruscamente, rudamente. **2** informalmente, familiarmente.
uncertain | ʌn'səːtn | *adj.* **1** [**– (of)**] no seguro, dudoso, sin certeza: *he's uncertain of the results = no está seguro de los resultados.* **2** indeciso, vacilante, dubitativo. **3** incierto, poco seguro, nebuloso: *uncertain plans = planes inciertos.* **4** variable, cambiante, inconstante: *uncertain weather = tiempo variable.* **5** fluctuante, intermitente: *an uncertain light = una luz intermitente.* || **6 in no – terms,** V. **term.**
uncertainly | ʌn'səːtnlɪ | *adv.* con dudas, de forma vacilante, con titubeos, inciertamente.
uncertainty | ʌn'səːtntɪ | *s.c.* e *i.* incertidumbre, inseguridad, duda, conjetura, indecisión.
unchain | ˌʌn'tʃeɪn | *v.t.* desencadenar, libertar.
unchallenged | ʌn'tʃælɪndʒd | *adj.* **1** indisputable, incuestionable. **2** libremente, sin restricción, sin (ser) preguntado, sin comprobación: *he went, unchallenged, past the guard = pasó libremente por delante de la guardia.*
unchangeable | ˌʌn'tʃeɪndʒəbl | *adj.* inmutable, inalterable, invariable (porque no admite variación).
unchanged | ˌʌn'tʃeɪndʒd | *adj.* inalterado, invariado, estable, fijo.
unchanging | ˌʌn'tʃeɪndʒɪŋ | *adj.* constante, inalterable, invariable, inmutable.
uncharacteristic | ˌʌŋkærəktər'ɪstɪk | *adj.* poco característico, inusual, poco común, poco corriente: *an uncharacteristic strength = una fuerza inusual.*
uncharacteristically | 'ʌŋkærəktər'ɪs | tɪklɪ | *adv.* inusualmente, poco corrientemente: *uncharacteristically violent = inusualmente violento.*
uncharitably ,| ˌʌntʃærɪtəblɪ | *adj.* poco caritativo, severo, áspero, duro, poco amable.
uncharitably | ʌn'tʃærɪtəblɪ | *adv.* sin benevolencia, severamente, ásperamente, duramente.
uncharted | ˌʌn'tʃɑːtɪd | *adj.* **1** (lit.) inexplorado, desconocido: *uncharted lands = tierras inexploradas.* || **2 – waters/seas/oceans,** (fig.) aguas desconocidas, situaciones poco familiares, extrañas.
unchecked | ˌʌn'tʃekt | *adj.* **1** (desp.) libre, sin restricción: *an unchecked growth = un crecimiento sin restricción.* **2** no comprobado, no examinado: *unchecked results = resultados no comprobados.* || *adv.* **3** libremente, sin restricción: *expenses went on unchecked = los gastos continuaron sin restricción.*
unchristian | ˌʌn'krɪstɪən | *adj.* (form.) poco cristiano, poco caritativo, poco generoso, poco amable.
uncivil | ˌʌn'sɪvl | *adj.* incivil, maleducado, grosero, rudo, descortés.
uncivilly | ˌʌn'sɪvəlɪ | *adv.* groseramente, descortésmente, rudamente.
uncivilized | ˌʌn'sɪvlaɪzd | (brit. **uncivilised**) *adj.* **1** incivilizado, salvaje, primitivo. **2** bárbaro, inhumano (comportamiento). **3** (fam.) excesivamente temprana: *an uncivilized hour = una hora excesivamente temprana.*
unclaimed | ˌʌn'kleɪmd | *adj.* sin reclamar, sin dueño, no reclamado.
unclasp | ˌʌn'klɑːsp | *v.t.* separar, soltar (las manos entrelazadas, al aplaudir un abrazo).
unclassified | ˌʌn'klæsɪfaɪd | *adj.* sin clasificar, no clasificado.
uncle | 'ʌŋkl | *s.c.* **1** tío (pariente). **2** (argot) prestamista. || **3 bob's your –,** V. **bob. 4 to cry/say –,** (EE.UU. y fam.) rendirse, darse por vencido, admitir la derrota. **5 to talk like a Dutch –,** decirle (a

uno) cuatro verdades, cantarle (a uno) las cuarenta. **6 Uncle Sam,** el Tío Sam, los Estados Unidos. **3 Uncle Tom,** (EE.UU., fam. y desp.) Tío Tom (negro que se comporta servilmente con los blancos).

unclean | ˌʌn'kliːn | *adj.* **1** sucio, inmundo, impuro. **2** sucio, poco casto (moralmente).

unclear | ˌʌn'klɪər | *adj.* **1** poco claro, poco evidente, oscuro. **2** confuso, ininteligible, incomprensible.

unclothed | ˌʌn'kləuðd | *adj.* (form.) desnudo.

uncluttered | ˌʌn'klʌtəd | *adj.* despejado, libre de estorbos, desocupado, abierto.

uncoil | ˌʌn'kɔɪl | *v.t.* e *i.* desenroscar(se), desenrollar(se), desanillar(se), desovillar(se).

uncoloured | ˌʌn'kʌləd | (EE.UU. **uncolored**) *adj.* **1** sin color, no coloreado. **2** (fig.) objetivo, imparcial: *an uncoloured opinion = una opinión objetiva.*

uncombed | ˌʌn'kəumd | *adj.* despeinado.

uncomfortable | ʌn'kʌmfətəbl | (EE.UU. | ʌn'kʌmfərtəbl |) *adj.* **1** incómodo, poco confortable (físicamente). **2** preocupado, molesto, intranquilo, inquieto. **3** embarazosa, preocupante, desagradable, difícil (una situación). **4** penoso, desagradable (un hecho).

uncomfortably | ʌn'kʌmfətəblɪ | *adv.* **1** incómodamente. **2** con inquietud, con preocupación; embarazosamente.

uncommitted | ˌʌnkə'mɪtɪd | *adj.* no comprometido, sin tomar partido, neutral, no alineado.

uncommon | ʌn'kɒmən | *adj.* **1** poco común, poco frecuente, inusual, raro. **2** (form.) excepcional, extraordinario, notable, insólito.

uncommonly | ʌn'kɒmənlɪ | *adv.* (form.) notablemente, extraordinariamente, enormemente.

uncommunicative | ˌʌnkə'mjuːnɪkətɪv | *adj.* poco comunicativo, reservado, taciturno.

uncomplaining | ˌʌnkəm'pleɪnɪŋ | *adj.* resignado, impasible, paciente, sin protestar, sin quejarse.

uncomplainingly | ˌʌnkəm'pleɪnɪŋlɪ | *adv.* resignadamente, pacientemente, impasiblemente.

uncomplicated | ˌʌn'kɒmplɪkeɪtɪd | *adj.* poco complicado, simple, fácil.

uncomprehending | ʌnˌkɒmprɪ'hendɪŋ | *adj.* desconcertado, confuso, sin entender, con asombro.

uncomprehendingly | ʌnˌkɒmprɪ'hendɪŋlɪ | *adv.* desconcertadamente.

uncompromising | ʌn'kɒmprəmaɪzɪŋ | *adv.* intransigente, inflexible, firme.

uncompromisingly | ʌn'kɒmprə | | maɪzɪŋlɪ | *adv.* intransigentemente, inflexiblemente, firmemente.

unconcealed | ˌʌnkən'siːld | *adj.* no disimulado, abierto.

unconcern | ˌʌnkən'səːn | *s.i.* (desp.) desinterés, indiferencia, apatía, despreocupación.

unconcerned | ˌʌnkən'səːnd | *adj.* **1** indiferente, apático, falto de interés, no interesado. **2** tranquilo, despreocupado.

unconcernedly | ˌʌnkən'səːnɪdlɪ | *adv.* indiferentemente, despreocupadamente, apáticamente.

unconditional | ˌʌnkən'dɪʃənl | *adj.* incondicional, sin condiciones.

unconditionally | ˌʌnkən'dɪʃnəlɪ | *adv.* incondicionalmente.

unconditioned | ˌʌnkən'dɪʃnd | *adj.* **1** PSIC. no condicionado, no aprendido, instintivo, espontáneo. **2** incondicional.

unconfirmed | ˌʌnkən'fəːmd | *adj.* no confirmado (rumor).

uncongenial | ˌʌnkən'dʒiːnɪəl | *adj.* **1** inhóspito, desagradable (lugar). **2** incompatible, que no congenia. **3** inapropiado, inadecuado.

unconnected | ˌʌnkə'nektɪd | *adj.* **1 [– (with)]** desconectado, desligado, desunido. **2** inconexo, incoherente.

unconscionable | ʌn'kɒnʃnəbl | *adj.* **1** (lit.) irrazonable, desmedido, excesivo. **2** falto de escrúpulos.

unconscionably | ʌn'kɒnʃnəblɪ | *adv.* **1** desmedidamente, excesivamente. **2** sin escrúpulos.

unconscious | ʌn'kɒnʃəs | *adj.* **1** inconsciente, sin conocimiento, sin sentido, desmayado. **2 [– (of)]** inconsciente, ignorante. **3** no intencionado, involuntario. || *s.sing.* **4 [the –]** PSIC. el inconsciente, el subconsciente.

unconsciously | ʌn'kɒnʃəslɪ | *adv.* **1** inconscientemente, sin darse cuenta. **2** involuntariamente, sin intención.

unconsciousness | ʌn'kɒnʃəsnɪs | *s.i.* inconsciencia, pérdida del conocimiento.

unconsidered | ˌʌnkən'sɪdəd | *adj.* **1** irreflexivo, impulsivo, imprudente. **2** (form.) desatendido, descuidado, inadvertido.

unconstitucional | 'ʌnˌkɒnstɪ'tjuːʃənl | *adj.* inconstitucional.

uncontrollable | ˌʌnkən'trəuləbl | *adj.* **1** incontrolable, incontenible, irrefrenable. **2** incontrolable, ingobernable, indomable.

uncontrollably | ˌʌnkən'trəuləblɪ | *adv.* incontrolablemente, imprevisiblemente, irrefrenablemente.

uncontrolled | ˌʌnkən'trəuld | *adj.* **1** incontrolado, incontenido, libre. **2** incontrolado, no vigilado.

unconventional | ˌʌnkən'venʃənl | *adj.* poco convencional, inconformista, extravagante, informal.

unconverted | 'ʌnkənvəːtɪd | *adj.* no convertido.

unconvinced | ˌʌnkən'vɪnst | *adj.* poco convencido, dudoso.

unconvincing | ˌʌnkən'vɪnsɪŋ | *adj.* poco convincente, poco creíble.

unconvincingly | ˌʌnkən'vɪnsɪŋlɪ | *adv.* sin convencer.

uncooked | ˌʌn'kukt | *adj.* sin cocer, crudo, sin hacer (un alimento).

uncooperative | ˌʌnkəu'ɒpərətɪv | *adj.* poco cooperativo, poco colaborador.

uncoordinated | ˌʌnkəu'ɔːdɪneɪtɪd | *adj.* descoordinado, no coordinado.

uncork | ˌʌn'kɔːk | *v.t.* descorchar, abrir, destapar.

uncount noun | ˌʌn'kauntˌnaun | *s.c.* GRAM. nombre incontable.

uncouple | ˌʌn'kʌpl | *v.t.* desenganchar, separar (vagones de tren).

uncouth | ʌn'kuːθ | *adj.* **1** (arc.) grosero, rudo, de mala educación, poco refinado. **2** patoso, tosco, falto de gracia. **3** (arc.) extraño, poco familiar.

uncouthness | ʌn'kuːθnɪs | *s.i.* **1** grosería, rudeza, mala educación, falta de refinamiento. **2** tosquedad, falta de gracia.

uncover | ʌn'kʌvər | *v.t.* **1** descubrir, destapar, dejar al descubierto: *uncovering her knees = dejando al descubierto sus rodillas.* **2** descubrir, revelar, dejar patente: *uncover the truth = descubrir la verdad.* **3** desenterrar, excavar. || *v.i.* **4** descubrirse, quitarse el sombrero.

uncovered | ʌn'kʌvəd | *adj.* **1** descubierto, expuesto, destapado. **2** con la cabeza descubierta, sin sombrero. **3** COM. descubierto.

uncritical | ˌʌn'krɪtɪkl | *adj.* (desp.) acrítico, falto de sentido crítico.

uncritically | ˌʌn'krɪtɪkəlɪ | *adv.* acríticamente, sin cuestionar nada.

uncrossed | ˌʌn'krɒst | (EE.UU. | ˌʌn'kɔːst |) *adj.* (brit.) sin cruzar (un cheque).

uncrowned | ˌʌn'kraund | *adj.* **1** no coronado, sin corona. || **2 the – king /queen of,** (fig.) el rey o reina de.

unction | 'ʌŋkʃn *s.i.* **1** REL. extremaunción, unción. **2** halago, adulación, zalamería, devoción (fingido). **3** ungüento, bálsamo.

unctuous | 'ʌŋktjuəs | *adj.* **1** (form.) adulador, zalamero, meloso. **2** untuoso, aceitoso, grasiento. **3** moldeable, rico en materia orgánica (arcilla).

unctuously | 'ʌŋktjuəslɪ | *adv.* aduladoramente, melosamente, afectadamente, hipócritamente.

unctuousness | 'ʌŋktjuəsnɪs | *s.i.* untuosidad, zalamería, adulación, halago (fingido).

uncultivated | ˌʌn'kʌltɪveɪtɪd | *adj.* **1** no cultivado, yermo, baldío. **2** inculto, (Am.) adocenado.

uncultured | ˌʌn'kʌltʃəd | *adj.* (desp.) inculto, iletrado, (Am.) adocenado.

uncurl | ˌʌn'kəːl | *v.t.* e *i.* enderezar(se), estirar(se), desrizar(se).

uncut | ˌʌn'kʌt | *adj.* **1** íntegro, completo, sin censurar (libro). **2** sin recortar los bordes (en imprenta). **3** sin cortar, sin segar (hierba). **4** en bruto, sin tallar (piedra).

undamaged | ˌʌn'dæmɪdʒd | *adj.* intacto, indemne, sin desperfectos.

undated | 'ʌndeɪtɪd | *adj.* sin fecha.

undaunted | ˌʌn'dɔːntɪd | *adj.* no desanimado, inmutable, impertérrito.

undeceive | ˌʌndɪ'siːv | *v.t.* (form.) desengañar, desilusionar.
undecided | ˌʌndɪ'saɪdɪd | *adj.* indeciso, irresoluto, poco convencido, dudoso.
undeclared | ˌʌndɪ'kleəd | *adj.* no declarado (en aduana).
undemanding | ˌʌndɪ'mɑːndɪŋ | *adj.* **1** que requiere poco esfuerzo (trabajo). **2** fácil de agradar, poco exigente (persona).
undemocratic | ʌnˌdemə'krætɪk | *adj.* poco democrático.
undemonstrative | ˌʌndɪ'mɒnstrətɪv | *adj.* poco efusivo, poco expresivo, reservado.
undeniable | ˌʌndɪ'naɪəbl | *adj.* **1** innegable, irrefutable, indiscutible. **2** excelente, sobresaliente.
undeniably | ˌʌndɪ'naɪəblɪ | *adv.* innegablemente, indiscutiblemente.
under | 'ʌndər | *prep.* **1** debajo de, bajo: *under the cupboard = debajo del armario.* **2** por debajo de, menos de, inferior a: *it costs under ú 10 = cuesta menos de 10 libras; people under 26 = gente de menos de 26 años.* **3** bajo, por debajo de (un control, una autoridad): *workers under him = los trabajadores bajo su control.* **4** bajo, durante, en la época de, en tiempos de: *under the Republic = en tiempos de la República.* **5** por, bajo, en: *check under "M" = comprueba en la "M".* **6** conforme a, con arreglo a, según: *under the contract = según el contrato.* **7** bajo, en estado de: *under construction = en construcción; under his influence = bajo su influencia.* **8** en proceso de, bajo: *under examination = en proceso de examen.* || *adv.* **9** debajo, bajo, abajo: *she stayed under = ella permaneció abajo.* **10** menos: *if you are 18 or under = si tienes 18 años o menos.* || *adj.* **11** inferior, subalterno. **12** inferior, bajo: *the under parts = las partes inferiores.* **13** (fam.) inconsciente, drogado, anestesiado. || *prefijo.* **14** **[– *adj.*]** insuficientemente, poco, sub: *underdeveloped = subdesarrollado.* **15** **[– *s.*]** bajo: *undercurrent = corriente submarina.* **16** **[– *s.*]** inferior, subalterno: *undercook = pinche de cocina.*
underachieve | ˌʌndərə'tʃiːv | *v.i.* (euf.) rendir menos de lo esperado, rendir por debajo de sus posibilidades (un estudiante).
underachiever | ˌʌndrə'tʃiːvər | *s.c.* alumno de bajo rendimiento escolar.
underact | ˌʌndər'ækt | *v.t.* e *i.* actuar mal, representar mal, no dar el tono, no dar de sí (en teatro).
underarm | 'ʌndərɑːm | (también **underhand**) *adj.* **1** (euf.) de axila, de sobaco: *underarm deodorants = desodorantes de axila.* **2** DEP. por debajo del brazo, ejecutado por debajo del hombro (movimiento). || *adv.* **3** por debajo del hombro. || *s.c.* **4** axila, sobaco.
underbelly | 'ʌndəˌbelɪ | *s.c.* **1** **[the – (of)]** (lit.) la parte más débil, la parte más vulnerable: *the underbelly of our plan = la parte más vulnerable de nuestro plan.* **2** parte inferior (de un animal).
underbid | ˌʌndə'bɪd | *v.t. irr.pret.* y *p.p.* **underbid, underbidding.** **1** ofrecer menor precio que (en una subasta). || *v.t.* e *i.* **2** declarar menos que lo que uno tiene (en bridge).
underbrush | 'ʌndəbrʌʃ | *s.i.* (EE.UU.) maleza, hierbajos, broza, monte bajo.
undercarriage | 'ʌndəˌkærɪdʒ | (también **landing gear**) *s.c.* **1** AER. tren de aterrizaje. **2** MEC. chasis, estructura metálica, bastidor.
undercharge | ˌʌndə'tʃɑːdʒ | *v.t.* e *i.* **1** cobrar de menos. **2** MIL. cargar con poca pólvora, con insuficiente carga (un arma). || *s.i.* **3** precio menor, precio insuficiente. **4** MIL. carga insuficiente.
underclothes | ˌʌndəkləʊðz | (también **underclothing**) *s.pl.* **1** ropa interior. || **2 in one's –,** en paños menores.
underclothing | 'ʌndəˌkləʊðɪŋ | *s.i.* (form.) V. **underclothes.**
undercoat | 'ʌndəkəʊt | *s.c.* e *i.* primera capa, base (de pintura).
undercover | 'ʌndəˌkʌvər | *adj.* **1** secreto, clandestino, reservado, confidencial, subrepticio (trabajo, método). || **2 – agent,** agente secreto, espía.
undercurrent | 'ʌndəˌkʌrənt | *s.c.* **1** corriente submarina, corriente subfluvial. **2** **[– (of)]** contracorriente, tendencia contraria; insinuación, indirecta.
undercut | ˌʌndə'kʌt | *v.t.* [*irr. pret.* y *p.p.* **undercut,** *ger.* **undercutting**] **1** vender a menor precio que (un competidor), rebajar los precios; trabajar por un salario menor. || *v.t.* e *i.* **2** socavar, minar (esfuerzos, popularidad). **3** cincelar, grabar, tallar, burilar. **4** DEP. dar un golpe oblicuo (en golf, béisbol), cortar (en tenis).
underdeveloped | ˌʌndədɪ'veləpt | *adj.* subdesarrollado, en desarrollo.
underdog | ˌʌndə'dɒg | *s.c.* **1** poco favorecido, débil, endeble, desamparado (persona, país). **2** DEP. el que tiene las de perder, el que va perdiendo.
underdone | ˌʌndə'dʌn | *adj.* (desp.) poco hecho, soasado (alimento).
underemployed | ˌʌndərɪm'plɔɪd | *adj.* **1** subempleado, empleado a tiempo parcial (trabajador). **2** infrautilizado (objeto, fábrica).
underemployment | ˌʌndərɪm'plɔɪmənt | *s.i.* **1** subempleo, empleo a tiempo parcial. **2** infrautilización (de un objeto).
underestimate | ˌʌndər'estɪmɪt | *v.t.* e *i.* **1** infravalorar, tasar por debajo de su precio, presupuestar en menos de lo que vale (un coste). || *v.t.* **2** subestimar, menospreciar, tener en menos de lo que es (a una persona). || *s.i.* **3** valoración inferior al coste, infravaloración.
underestimation | ˌʌndər'estɪmeɪʃn | *s.c.* e *i.* **1** valoración inferior al coste, infravaloración, presupuesto bajo. **2** menosprecio, subestimación.
underexpose | ˌʌndərɪk'spəʊz | *v.t.* (generalmente pasiva) exponer insuficientemente (en fotografía).
underexposure | ˌʌndərɪk'spəʊʒər | *s.i.* exposición insuficiente (en fotografía).
underfed | ˌʌndə'fed | *adj.* desnutrido, subalimentado, famélico.
underfelt | 'ʌndəfelt | *s.c.* e *i.* fieltro (que va bajo la moqueta).
underfloor | ˌʌndə'flɔːr | *adj.* oculto bajo el suelo, situado bajo el suelo (calefacción, cables).
underfinanced | ˌʌndəfaɪ'nænst | *adj.* infradotada económicamente (institución, organización).
underfoot | ˌʌndə'fʊt | *adv.* **1** debajo de los pies, en el suelo: *the surface underfoot was soft = la superficie bajo los pies era blanda.* **2** en medio, molestando, estorbando: *they are always underfoot = siempre están estorbando.* || **3 to trample /crush –,** pisotear, pisar.
undergarment | 'ʌndəˌgɑːmənt | *s.c.* (form.) prenda de ropa interior.
undergo | ˌʌndə'gəʊ | *v.t.* [*irr.pret.* **underwent,** *p.p.* **undergone**] **1** someterse a, pasar por (algo desagradable): *she is undergoing a painful treatment = está sometida a un tratamiento doloroso.* **2** estar sujeto a, experimentar, sufrir (cambios, reparaciones).
undergone | ˌʌndə'gɒn | *p.p.* **V. undergo.**
undergraduate | ˌʌndə'grædjʊɪt | (también **undergrand**) *s.c.* estudiante universitario (no licenciado).
underground | ˌʌndə'graʊnd | *adv.* **1** bajo tierra. **2** (fig.) clandestinamente, secretamente, confidencialmente. || | 'ʌndəgraʊnd | *adj.* **3** subterráneo. **4** ART. de vanguardia, no convencional. **5** POL. clandestino, ilegal. || *s.sing.* **6** **[the –]** (también brit. fam. **tube,** EE.UU. **subway**) metro, suburbano. **7** **[the – *v.sing./pl.*]** movimiento de vanguardia, movimiento no convencional (en arte, cine en los años 60-70). **8** POL. movimiento de resistencia, movimiento clandestino.
undergrowth | 'ʌndəgrəʊð | *s.i.* maleza, broza, matas (de hierba), monte bajo.
underhand | ˌʌndə'hænd | *adj.* **1** (desp.) poco limpio, deshonesto, fraudulento (negocio, persona). **2** DEP. ejecutado con la mano por debajo del hombro (un movimiento). || *adv.* **3** bajo cuerda, solapadamente, secretamente. **4** DEP. con la mano por debajo del hombro.
underlay | 'ʌndəleɪ | **1** *pret.* de **underlie.** || *s.c.* e *i.* **2** material de base, material aislante (debajo de la moqueta). || *v.t.* **3** colocar una base, colocar un aislante. **4** reforzar, realzar (en imprenta).
underlie | ˌʌndə'laɪ | *v.t.* [*irr.pret.* **underlay,** *p.p.* **underlain**] **1** subyacer, estar oculto, ser la base de, ser el fundamento de. **2** estar debajo, extenderse por debajo de. **3** FIN. preceder como garantía, comprender como garantía.
underline | 'ʌndəlaɪn | (también **underscore**) *v.t.* **1** subrayar. **2** (fig.) acentuar,

recalcar, enfatizar, subrayar. || *s.c.* **3** raya, línea.

underling | 'ʌndəlɪŋ | *s.c.* (desp.) subalterno, empleado, subordinado, dependiente.

underlip | 'ʌndəlɪp | *s.c.* ANAT. labio inferior.

underlying | ˌʌndə'laɪɪŋ | *adj.* **1** subyacente, implícito, esencial. **2** (form.) inferior, del suelo. **3** FIN. precedente, anterior (reclamación).

undermanned | ˌʌndə'mænd | *adj.* infradotado de personal, falto de personal (empresa); falto de tripulación (barco).

undermentioned | ˌʌndə'menʃnd | *adj. (brit. y form.)* **1** abajo mencionado, abajo citado: *please send the undermentioned items = por favor, envíen los artículos abajo citados.* || *s.pl.* **2 [the –]** lo anteriormente citado, lo previamente mencionado.

undermine | ˌʌndə'maɪn | *v.t.* **1** minar, socavar, desgastar. **2** (fig.) socavar, minar, destruir, debilitar.

underneath | ˌʌndə'niːθ | *prep.* **1** por debajo de, bajo: *underneath the blanket = bajo la manta.* || *adv.* **2** debajo, bajo, por dentro: *she was wearing a jumper underneath = llevaba un jersey debajo.* || *s.sing.* **3 [the –]** (fam.) la parte inferior, la superficie inferior. || *adj.* **4** inferior, de abajo.

undernourished | ˌʌndə'nʌrɪʃt | *adj.* desnutrido, famélico, mal alimentado.

undernourishment | ˌʌndə'nʌrɪʃmənt | *s.i.* desnutrición.

underpaid | ˌʌndə'peɪd | *adj.* mal pagado, mal retribuido.

underpants | 'ʌndəpænts | *s.pl.* **1** calzoncillos. || **2 in one's –,** en paños menores.

underpass | 'ʌndəpɑːs | (EE.UU. | 'ʌndəpæs |) *s.c.* paso subterráneo.

underpay | ˌʌndə'peɪ | *v.t. irr.pret.* y *p.p.* **underpaid,** pagar mal, pagar un sueldo bajo (menor de lo merecido).

underpin | ˌʌndə'pɪn | *v.t.* **1** apuntalar, asegurar, afianzar, sujetar (una pared). **2** (fig.) sostener, sustentar, dar fuerza a (un argumento, una teoría).

underpinning | ˌʌndə'pɪnɪŋ | *s.c.* e *i.* **1** base, soporte, sustento (de una teoría). **2** apuntalamiento, sujeción (de un edificio). || **3 underpinnings,** (fam.) piernas.

underplay | ˌʌndə'pleɪ | *v.t.* **1** minimizar, dar poca importancia, quitar importancia. || *v.t.* e *i.* **2** actuar mal, hacer una mala interpretación, estar flojo (en teatro). || **3 to – one's hands,** (fig.) esconder cartas en la manga, no dejar clara la jugada.

underpopulated | ˌʌndə'pɒpjʊleɪtɪd | *adj.* con poca densidad de población.

underprivileged | ˌʌndə'prɪvɪlɪdʒd | *adj.* **1** (euf.) necesitado, desamparado, menesteroso. || *s.pl.* **2 [the –]** los desamparados, los menesterosos, los desvalidos.

underrate | ˌʌndə'reɪt | *v.t.* minusvalorar, infravalorar, menospreciar, subestimar.

underrated | ˌʌndə'reɪtɪd | *adj.* subestimado, infravalorado, minusvalorado, menospreciado.

underscore | ˌʌndə'skɔː | V. **underline.**

undersea | ˌʌndəsiː | *adj.* **1** submarino. || *adv.* **2** bajo la superficie del mar.

underseal | ˌʌndəsiːl | (EE.UU. **undercoat**) *s.i.* petroleado (de protección para motores).

under-secretary | ˌʌndə'sekrətərɪ | *s.c.* POL. subsecretario.

undersell | ˌʌndə'sel | *v.t.* [*irr.pret.* y *p.p.* **undersold**] **1** malvender, vender a bajo precio. **2** (fig.) malvenderse, ofrecerse a bajo precio, no darse la debida importancia (una persona).

undersexed | ˌʌndə'sekst | *adj.* inapetente sexual, sexualmente frío.

undershirt | ˌʌndəʃəːt | *s.c.* (EE.UU.) camiseta.

underside | 'ʌndəsaɪd | *s.c.* parte baja, parte inferior, lado de abajo.

undersigned | ˌʌndə'saɪnd | *adj.* **1** (form.) abajo firmado, subscrito. || *s.pl.* **2 [the –]** los abajo firmantes.

undersized | ˌʌndəsaɪzd | (también **undersize**) *adj.* (desp.). **1** más pequeño de lo normal, mínimo, muy pequeño. **2** bajito, enano, sietemesino.

underslung | ˌʌndəslʌŋ | *adj.* **1** colgante, suspendido, colgado. **2** suspendido del eje (el chasis de un vehículo).

undersold | ˌʌndə'səʊld | V. **undersell.**

understaffed | ˌʌndə'stɑːft | *adj.* infradotado, falto de personal.

understand | ˌʌndə'stænd | *v.* [*irr.pret.* y *p.p.* **understood**] *t.* e *i.* **1** entender, comprender, captar el significado. **2** comprender, entender de, saber: *do you understand about finances? = ¿entiendes algo de finanzas?* || *t.* **3** comprender, conocer, entender, ser comprensivo: *I understand you = te comprendo.* **4** (form.) darse cuenta, presuponer, presumir, estar enterado de (que), tener entendido, inferir: *I understand you are divorced = tengo entendido que está usted divorciado.* **5** juzgar, interpretar, colegir: *as I understand... = según colijo...* **6** (generalmente pasiva) sobreentender, dar por supuesto, dar por sentado. || **7 to give someone to –,** dar a entender a uno. **8 it is understood,** se sobreentiende, se da por supuesto. **9 to make oneself understood,** hacerse entender, hacerse comprender. **10 –?/you –?/is that understood?,** ¿vale?, ¿comprendido?

understandable | ˌʌndə'stændəbl | *adj.* **1** comprensible, que se comprende. **2** comprensible, razonable, natural.

understandably | ˌʌndə'stændəblɪ | *adv.* comprensiblemente, razonablemente, naturalmente.

understanding | ˌʌndə'stændɪŋ | *s.i.* **1** entendimiento, inteligencia, raciocinio. **2** conocimiento, noción: *little understanding of Maths = pocas nociones de Matemáticas.* **3 [– (of)]** interpretación, análisis. **4** comprensión, simpatía, cooperación, armonía. || *s.c.* (generalmente *sing.*) **5** acuerdo, pacto, convenio, arreglo. || *adj.* **6** comprensivo, tolerante; compasivo. || **7 on the – that,** a condición de que.

understate | ˌʌndə'steɪt | *v.t.* **1** disminuir, quitar importancia, aminorar, reducir: *understating his age = quitándose años.* **2** exponer modestamente, expresar sin énfasis.

understated | ˌʌndə'steɪtɪd | *adj.* **1** subestimado, atenuado, que se le ha quitado importancia (a un problema). **2** modesto, recatado.

understatement | ˌʌndə'steɪtmənt | *s.c.* e *i.* juicio modesto, declaración sin énfasis, estimación insuficiente: *it's an understatement to say that the book is bad = decir que el libro es malo es una estimación insuficiente.*

understood | ˌʌndə'stʊd | *pret.* y *p.p.* de **understand.**

understudy | ˌʌndəˌstʌdɪ | *s.c.* **1** actor suplente, doble, actor sustituto (en teatro). **2** suplente, sustituto. || *v.t.* **3** aprender un papel teatral (para suplir a otro actor). **4** actuar como actor suplente.

undertake | ˌʌndə'teɪk | *v.t. irr.pret.* **undertook,** *p.p.* **undertaken.** (form.) **1** acometer, emprender, iniciar (una tarea). **2 [to – (to** *inf.*)] prometer, quedar en, ofrecerse a, garantizar, comprometerse a: *he undertook to do it = se ofreció a hacerlo.*

undertaken | ˌʌndə'teɪkən | *p.p.* de **undertake.**

undertaker | ˌʌndə'teɪkər | *s.c.* dueño de una funeraria, director de pompas fúnebres.

undertaking | ˌʌndə'teɪkɪŋ | *s.c.* **1** tarea, empresa, responsabilidad, obligación, exigencia. **2** (form.) promesa, garantía, compromiso. || *s.i.* **3** profesión de empresario de funeraria, pompas fúnebres.

underthings | ˌʌndə'θɪŋz | *s.pl.* (fam.) ropa interior.

undertone | ˌʌndətəʊn | *s.c.* **1** voz baja, sonido suave. **2 [– (of)]** matiz de fondo, tono, tendencia subyacente. **3** color apagado, tono mortecino.

undertook | ˌʌndə'tʊk | *pret.* de **undertake.**

undertow | ˌʌndətəʊ | *s.c.* e *i.* MAR. resaca, corriente de fondo.

underused | ˌʌndə'juːst | *adj.* infrautilizado.

under-utilized | ˌʌndə'juːtɪlaɪzd | *adj.* (form.) infrautilizado.

undervalue | ˌʌndə'væljuː | *v.t.* infravalorar, subestimar, menospreciar.

underwater | ˌʌndə'wɔːtər | *adj.* **1** subacuático, submarino. || *adv.* **2** bajo el agua.

underway | ˌʌndə'weɪ | *adj.* en movimiento, iniciado, comenzado.

underwear | ˌʌndəweər | (también **under-clothes,** (form.) **underclothing**). *s.i.* ropa interior.

underweight | ˌʌndə'weɪt | *adj.* bajo de peso, de poco peso, por debajo del peso legal.

underwent | ˌʌndə'went | *pret.* de **undergo.**
underworld | ˌʌndəwɜːld | *s.sing.* **1** infierno, inframundo. **2 [the Underworld]** el Hades (en la mitología griega). **3 [the –]** el hampa, los bajos fondos. **4** antípodas. **5 [the –]** (arc.) la tierra, el mundo terrenal.
underwrite | ˌʌndəraɪt | *v.t.* **1** FIN. asegurar, avalar, cubrir, garantizar, asumir financieramente (pérdidas, generalmente marítimas). **2** respaldar, apoyar, avalar (financieramente un proyecto).
underwriter | ˌʌndəˌraɪtər | *s.c.* FIN. asegurador, empresa aseguradora.
undeserved | ˌʌndɪ'zɜːvd | *adj.* inmerecido, injustificado.
undeservedly | ˌʌndɪ'zɜːvɪdlɪ | *adv.* inmerecidamente, injustificadamente.
undesirable | ˌʌndɪ'zaɪərəbl | *adj.* **1** (form.) indeseable. **2** inaguantable, desagradable (persona). || *s.c.* **3** (form. y desp.) persona indeseable, persona inaguantable.
undesirably | ˌʌndɪ'zaɪərəblɪ | *adv.* de forma no deseada.
undetected | ˌʌndɪ'tektɪd | *adj.* no detectado, inadvertido, no descubierto.
undeterred | ˌʌndɪ'tɜːd | *adj.* no intimidado, no asustado, no amilanado.
undeveloped | ˌʌndɪ'veləpt | *adj.* **1** subdesarrollado, no desarrollado (país). **2** inmaduro (persona). **3** verde, poco madura (fruta). **4** FOT. no revelada, sin revelar.
undid | ˌʌn'dɪd | *pret.* de **undo.**
undies | 'ʌndɪz | *s.pl.* (fam. y hum.) prendas íntimas, paños menores (especialmente de mujer).
undignified | ʌn'dɪgnɪfaɪd | *adj.* **1** poco digno, indecoroso (postura). **2** embarazoso, vergonzoso (acto).
undiluted | ˌʌndaɪ'ljuːtɪd | *adj.* **1** puro, limpio, no adulterado (sentimiento). **2** no diluido, concentrado.
undischarged | ˌʌndɪs'tʃɑːdʒd | *adj.* **1** no pagado, no liquidado, no cargado en cuenta (deuda). **2** incumplido (deber). **3** endeudado. **4** no descargado, no desembarcado.
undisciplined | ʌn'dɪsɪplɪnd | *adj.* indisciplinado, malcriado.
undisguised | ˌʌndɪs'gaɪzd | *adj.* abierto, franco, no disimulado.
undismayed | ˌʌndɪs'meɪd | *adj.* (lit.) impávido, imperturbable, impertérrito.
undisputed | ˌʌndɪ'spjuːtɪd | *adj.* indisputable, incuestionable.
undistinguished | ˌʌndɪ'stɪŋgwɪʃət | *adj.* poco distinguido, mediocre, vulgar, común.
undisturbed | ˌʌndɪ'stɜːbd | *adj.* **1** tranquilo, sin ruidos, sosegado (lugar). **2** no molestado, no interrumpido, en paz. **3** no tocado, no movido, no usado.
undivided | ˌʌndɪ'vaɪdɪd | *adj.* **1** indiviso, completo, íntegro. **2** total, entero, todo. || **3 to give/have/take one's/somebody's – attention,** escuchar con toda atención.
undo | ˌʌn'duː | *v.t.* [*irr.pret.* **undid,** *p.p.* **undone**] **1** desatar, desabrochar, desabotonar. **2** abrir, desenvolver, deshacer (un paquete). **3** anular, eliminar, invalidar, destruir. **4** (generalmente pasiva) (arc.) descomponer, trastornar: *he was absolutely undone = estaba absolutamente trastornado.*
undoing | ˌʌn'duːɪŋ | *s.i.* (form.) **1** ruina, perdición, destrucción, fracaso. **2** anulación, cancelación. **3** aflojamiento, acto de desabrochar.
undone | ˌʌn'dʌn | *adj.* **1** desatado, desabrochado, desabotonado. **2** no hecho, pendiente, no realizado. **3** (lit.) perdido, arruinado, destruido, asolado (persona).
undoubted | ʌn'daʊtɪd | *adj.* indudable, evidente, innegable, incuestionable.
undoubtedly | ʌn'daʊtɪdlɪ | *adv.* indudablemente, evidentemente, innegablemente.
undreamed-of | ʌn'dremtɒv | (también **undreamt-of**) *adj.* inimaginado, no soñado, jamás pensado: *an undreamed-of joy = una dicha jamás imaginada.*
undreamt-of | ʌn'dremtɒv | *adj.* V. **undreamed.**
undress | 'ʌndres | *v.t.* e *i.* **1** desvestir(se), desnudar(se). || *s.i.* **2** desnudez, falta de ropa. **3** ropa de casa, ropa informal. || **4 in a state of –,** desnudo, sin ropa.
undressed | ˌʌn'drest | *adj.* **1** desnudo, sin vestir, sin ropa. || **2 to get –,** desnudarse, desvestirse.
undrinkable | ˌʌn'drɪŋkəbl | *adj.* no potable, no bebible.
undue | ˌʌn'djuː | (EE.UU. | ˌʌn'duː |) *adj.* excesivo, desmedido, inmoderado, innecesario.
undulate | ˌʌndjʊleɪt | (EE.UU. | 'ʌndʒʊ-leɪt |) *v.i.* (form.) ondular, ondear.
undulation | ˌʌndjʊ'leɪʃn | (EE.UU. | ˌʌndʒʊ'leɪʃn |) *s.c.* e *i.* ondulación, ondeo.
unduly | ˌʌn'djuːlɪ | *adv.* excesivamente, inmoderadamente, desmedidamente, innecesariamente.
undying | ʌn'daɪɪŋ | *adj.* eterno, imperecedero, indestructible.
unearned | ˌʌn'ɜːnd | *adj.* **1** no devengado, no ganado. **2** inmerecido. || **3 – income,** renta de capital.
unearth | ˌʌn'ɜːθ | *v.t.* **1** desenterrar, exhumar, excavar. **2** (form. y fig.) desvelar, sacar a la luz, descubrir.
unearthly | ˌʌn'ɜːθlɪ | *adj.* **1** no terrenal, sobrenatural, misterioso. **2** (fam.) intempestivo, inconveniente, nefasto (hora). **3** (fam.) horrible, estruendoso (ruido).
unease | ʌn'iːz | *s.i.* (lit.) ansiedad, nerviosismo, preocupación, inquietud, tensión.
uneasily | ʌn'iːzɪlɪ | *adv.* ansiosamente, nerviosamente, inquietamente.
uneasiness | ʌn'iːzɪnɪs | *s.i.* inquietud, preocupación, desasosiego, intranquilidad.
uneasy | ʌn'iːzɪ | *adj.* **1** angustiado, intranquilo, tenso, nervioso. **2** inquietante, intranquilizador, perturbador. **3** desasosegado, inquieto, agitado.
uneatable | ˌʌn'iːtəbl | *adj.* incomible, no comestible.
uneconomic | 'ʌnˌiːkə'nɒmɪk | *adj.* antieconómico, poco lucrativo (negocio).
uneconomical | 'ʌnˌɪːkə'nɒmɪkl | *adj.* ineficiente, antieconómico, no rentable (método).
uneconomically | 'ʌnˌɪːkə'nɒmɪklɪ | *adv.* ineficientemente, sin rentabilidad.
uneducated | ˌʌn'edjʊkeɪtɪd | *adj.* inculto, ignorante, ineducado, iletrado.
unemotional | ˌʌnɪ'məʊʃənl | *adj.* (desp.) frío, reservado, indiferente.
unemotionally | ˌʌnɪ'məʊʃənəlɪ | *adv.* fríamente, indiferentemente.
unemployable | ˌʌnɪm'plɔɪbl | *adj.* inútil para un trabajo, incapacitado para desempeñar un empleo.
unemployed | ˌʌnɪm'plɔɪd | *adj.* **1** desempleado, parado, en paro. || *s.pl.* **2 [the –]** los parados, los desempleados.
unemployement | ˌʌnɪm'plɔɪmənt | *s.i.* **1** desempleo, paro. || **2 – benefit,** subsidio de desempleo.
unending | ʌn'endɪŋ | *adj.* que no tiene fin, interminable, eterno, inacabable.
unendurable | ˌʌnɪn'djʊərəbl | *adj.* (form.) intolerable, insoportable, inaguantable, insufrible, fastidioso.
unenviable | ʌn'envɪəbl | *adj.* poco envidiable.
unequal | ˌʌn'iːkwəl | *adj.* **1 [– (to)]** desigual, distinto, diferente. **2** (desp.) discriminatorio, desequilibrado: *unequal wages = sueldos discriminatorios.* **3 [– (to)]** (form.) inadecuado, incapaz, no capacitado (para un trabajo).
unequalled | ˌʌn'iːkwəld | *adj.* inigualable, sin par, sin rival, sin parangón.
unequally | ˌʌn'iːkwəlɪ | *adv.* desigualmente, de manera diferente, desproporcionadamente.
unequivocal | ˌʌnɪ'kwɪvəkl | *adj.* (form.) **1** inequívoco, claro, indudable. **2** categórico, preciso, terminante.
unequivocally | ˌʌnɪ'kwɪvəkəlɪ | *adv.* **1** inequívocamente, indudablemente. **2** categóricamente, terminantemente, con precisión.
unerring | ˌʌn'ɜːrɪŋ | *adj.* infalible, seguro.
unerringly | ˌʌn'ɜːrɪŋlɪ | *adv.* infaliblemente, con toda seguridad.
UNESCO | juː'neskəʊ | (**United Nations Educational, Scientific and Cultural Organization**) Organización de las Naciones Unidas para la Educación, la Ciencia y la Cultura.
unescorted | ˌʌnɪ'skɔːtɪd | *adj.* no escoltado, que no lleva compañía, acompañante.
unethical | ʌn'eθɪkl | *adj.* poco ético, inmoral.
unethically | ʌn'eθɪkəlɪ | *adv.* de forma poco ética, con inmoralidad, inmoralmente.

uneven | ˌʌn'iːvn | *adv.* **1** desigual, poco uniforme, accidentado, ondulado, torcido, escabroso: *an uneven surface = una superficie irregular.* **2** irregular, inconstante. **3** irregular, con altibajos: *a very uneven period of his life = un período de su vida con muchos altibajos.* **4** desequilibrado, desigual, injusto: *an uneven match = un partido desigual.* **5** impar (un número).

unevenness | ˌʌn'iːvnnɪs | *s.i.* **1** desigualdad, irregularidad, ondulación. **2** inconstancia. **3** desequilibrio, desigualdad, injusticia.

uneventful | ˌʌnɪ'ventfʊl | *adj.* sin acontecimientos, sin novedad, sin incidentes, tranquilo.

uneventfully | ˌʌnɪ'ventfʊlɪ | *adv.* plácidamente, tranquilamente.

unexceptionable | ˌʌnɪk'sepʃnəbl | *adj.* (form.) enteramente satisfactorio, irreprochable, intachable.

unexceptionably | ˌʌnɪk'sepʃnəblɪ | *adv.* irreprochablemente, intachablemente.

unexceptional | ˌʌnɪk'sepʃənl | *adj.* (form.) ordinario, nada excepcional, común, vulgar.

unexceptionally | ˌʌnɪk'sepʃənlɪ | *adv.* ordinariamente, vulgarmente.

unexciting | ˌʌnɪk'saɪtɪŋ | *adj.* aburrido, tedioso, trivial.

unexpected | ˌʌnɪk'spektɪd | *adj.* **1** inesperado, imprevisto, casual, accidental. || *s.i.* **2** **[the –]** acontecimiento inesperado.

unexpectedly | ˌʌnɪk'spektɪdlɪ | *adv.* inesperadamente, casualmente, accidentalmente.

unexpectedness | ˌʌnɪk'spektɪdnɪs | *s.i.* casualidad, accidente.

unexplained | ˌʌnɪk'spleɪnd | *adj.* inexplicado, poco claro.

unfailing | ʌn'feɪlɪŋ | *adj.* (form.) **1** continuo, constante, incesante, inagotable. **2** infalible.

unfailingly | ʌn'feɪlɪŋlɪ | *adv.* **1** continuamente, constantemente, incesantemente, inagotablemente. **2** infaliblemente.

unfair | ˌʌn'feər | *adj.* **1** injusto, inmerecido, indebido. **2** injusto, parcial, exagerado, poco amable (comentario). **3** injusto, no equitativo, desigual (sistema). **4** desleal, poco ética (competencia). **5** sucio (juego).

unfairly | ˌʌn'feəlɪ | *adv.* **1** injustamente, inmerecidamente, indebidamente. **2** exageradamente, de manera poco amable, suciamente. **3** de forma poco ética, poco honestamente, de forma contraria a las reglas.

unfairness | ˌʌn'feənɪs | *s.i.* **1** injusticia, desigualdad, falta de equidad. **2** deshonestidad, suciedad, incorrección.

unfaithful | ˌʌn'feɪθfʊl | *adj.* **1** infiel, adúltero: *he's an unfaithful lover = es un amante infiel.* **2** (p.u.) desleal, engañador, no cumplidor.

unfaithfully | ˌʌn'feɪθfʊlɪ | *adv.* **1** infielmente, adúlteramente. **2** deslealmente.

unfaithfulness | ˌʌn'feɪθfʊlnɪs | *s.i.* infidelidad, perfidia.

unfamiliar | ˌʌnfə'mɪljər | *adj.* **1** poco familiar, desconocido, extraño: *his name is unfamiliar to me = su nombre no me resulta familiar.* **2** **[– (with)]** (form.) desconocedor, ignorante, poco familiarizado: *I'm unfamiliar with the topic = estoy poco familiarizado con el tema.*

unfamiliarity | 'vnfəˌmɪlɪ'ærɪtɪ | *s.i.* desconocimiento.

unfashionable | ˌʌn'fæʃnəbl | *adj.* pasado de moda, poco elegante.

unfasten | ˌʌn'fɑːsn | *v.t.* e *i.* desabrochar, soltar, aflojar, desatar: *you can unfasten your seat belts = pueden desabrocharse los cinturones de seguridad.*

unfathomable | ʌn'fæðəməbl | *adj.* (lit.) insondable, indescifrable.

unfavourable | ˌʌn'feɪvərəbl | (EE.UU. **unfavorable**) *adj.* **[– (for/to)]** desfavorable, contrario, negativo, adverso, desventajoso.

unfavourably | ˌʌn'feɪvərəblɪ | (EE.UU. **unfavorably**) *adv.* desfavorablemente, negativamente, adversamente, desventajosamente.

unfeeling | ʌn'fiːlɪŋ | *adj.* insensible, cruel, desalmado, despiadado.

unfeelingly | ʌn'fiːlɪŋlɪ | *adv.* insensiblemente, cruelmente, despiadadamente.

unfeigned | ʌn'feɪnd | *adj.* genuino, sincero, verdadero, auténtico.

unfeignedly | ʌn'feɪnɪdlɪ | *adv.* genuinamente, sinceramente, verdaderamente, auténticamente.

unfettered | ˌʌn'fetəd | *adj.* (form.) libre, sin trabas, exento.

unfinished | ˌʌn'fɪnɪʃ | *adj.* inacabado, inconcluso, por terminar.

unfit | ˌʌn'fɪt | *adj.* **1** en baja forma, poco saludable, en pésimas condiciones físicas o psíquicas. **2** **[– (for)]** poco cualificado, inadecuado, no apto, inapropiado. || *v.t.* e *i.* **3** incapacitar, invalidar, inhabilitar.

unflagging | ˌʌn'flægɪŋ | *adj.* incansable, infatigable, incesante.

unflaggingly | ˌʌn'flægɪŋlɪ | *adv.* incansablemente, infatigablemente, incesantemente.

unflappable | ˌʌn'flæpəbl | *adj.* (brit. y fam.) inmutable, imperturbable, impasible, flemático.

unflattering | ˌʌn'flætərɪŋ | *adj.* poco atractivo, poco halagador: *an unflattering image = una imagen poco halagadora.*

unflinching | ʌn'flɪntʃɪŋ | *adj.* (lit.) firme, resuelto, determinado, osado, impávido.

unflinchingly | ʌn'flɪntʃɪŋlɪ | *adv.* (lit.) sin temor, firmemente, resueltamente, con determinación, con osadía.

unfocused, unfocussed | ʌn'fəʊkəst | *adj.* **1** perdida, vaga, abstraída, (mirada). **2** no centrado, no específico (deseo, objetivo).

unfold | ʌn'fəʊld | *v.t.* e *i.* **1** desdoblar(se), desplegar(se), extender(se), desenrollar(se) (algo doblado). **2** clarificar(se), desvelar(se), dar a conocer, descubrir(se) (un plan, un secreto).

unforeseen | ˌʌnfɔː'siːn | *adj.* inesperado, imprevisto, repentino.

unforgettable | ˌʌnfə'getəbl | *adj.* inolvidable.

unforgettably | ˌʌnfə'getəblɪ | *adv.* inolvidablemente.

unforgivable | ˌʌnfə'gɪvəbl | *adj.* imperdonable, inexcusable.

unforgiving | ˌʌnfə'gɪvɪŋ | *adj.* implacable, despiadado, inhumano.

unformed | ˌʌn'fɔːmd | *adj.* **1** inmaduro (carácter). **2** no formado, imperfecto, no desarrollado, informe.

unfortunate | ʌn'fɔːtʃnɪt | *adj.* **1** infortunado, desgraciado, infeliz, desdichado. **2** desafortunado, deplorable, lamentable, desastroso. **3** (euf.) rudo, inoportuno, torpe, falto de tacto (comentario). || *s.c.* **4** desgraciado, desafortunado.

unfortunately | ʌn'fɔːtʃnɪtlɪ | *adv.* desgraciadamente, desdichadamente, desafortunadamente.

unfounded | ˌʌn'faʊndɪd | *adj.* **1** infundado, sin fundamento, sin base. **2** no fundado, no establecido.

unfreeze | ˌʌn'friːz | *v.* [*irr.pret.* **unfroze**, *p.p.* **unfrozen**] *t.* e *i.* **1** descongelar, deshelar. || *t.* **2** FIN. liberar (la economía). **3** descongelar (salarios, precios).

unfrequented | ʌnfrɪ'kwentɪd | *adj.* poco frecuentado, desierto, solitario.

unfriendly | ˌʌn'frendlɪ | *adj.* **1** poco amistoso, hostil. **2** desfavorable, poco propicio.

unfrock | ʌn'frɒk | (también **defrock**) *v.t.* (generalmente pasiva) expulsar, privar de sus funciones (a un sacerdote).

unfrocked | ʌn'frɒkt | *adj.* destituido, expulsado, privado (de sus funciones un sacerdote).

unfruitful | ˌʌn'fruːtfʊl | *adj.* **1** infructuoso, improductivo, ineficaz. **2** sin fruto, yermo, infecundo.

unfulfilled | ˌʌnfʊl'fɪld | *adj.* **1** incumplido, no cumplido: *unfulfilled promises = promesas incumplidas.* **2** insatisfecho, frustrado.

unfurl | ˌʌn'fəːl | *v.t.* desenrollar, desplegar, desdoblar (velas, banderas, mapas).

unfurnished | ˌʌn'fəːnɪʃt | *adj.* sin amueblar, desamueblado.

ungainliness | ʌn'geɪnlɪnɪs | *s.i.* torpeza, falta de garbo, desmaña.

ungainly | ʌn'geɪnlɪ | *adj.* torpe, patoso, desmañado, desgarbado.

ungenerous | ʌn'dʒenərəs | *adj.* (form.) **1** poco generoso, egoísta, cicatero, avariento. **2** falto de tacto, desconsiderado.

ungetatable | ˌʌnget'ætəbl | *adj.* (fam.) inaccesible, de difícil acceso.

ungodly | ˌʌn'gɒdlɪ | *adj.* **1** (lit.) impío, irrespetuoso, irreligioso, blasfemo. **2** (fam.) inverosímil, atroz, poco razonable, nefasto. **3** pecaminoso, malvado, vil.

ungovernable | ˌʌn'gʌvənəbl | *adj.* ingobernable, incontrolable.
ungracious | ˌʌn'greɪʃəs | *adj.* **1** desagradable, descortés, maleducado, grosero. **2** inaceptable, poco atractivo. **3** (arc.) malvado, demoniaco.
ungraciously | ˌʌn'greɪʃəslɪ | *adv.* descortésmente, groseramente.
ungrammatical | ˌʌngrə'mætɪkl | *adj.* gramaticalmente incorrecto.
ungrammatically | ˌʌngrə'mætɪkəlɪ | *adv.* incorrectamente, sin corrección.
ungrateful | ʌn'greɪtfʊl | *adj.* **1** desagradecido, ingrato: *an ungrateful person = una persona desagradecida.* **2** (form.) desagradable, ingrato, fastidioso (trabajo).
unguarded | ˌʌn'gɑːdɪd | *adj.* **1** inoportuno, de descuido, de indiscreción, poco prudente (momento). **2** franco, sincero, sin ambages. **3** no vigilado, desprotegido, vulnerable (lugar, objeto).
unhampered | ˌʌn'hæmpəd | *adj.* libre, sin trabas, sin estorbo.
unhappily | ʌn'hæpɪlɪ | *adv.* **1** tristemente, desconsoladamente. **2** desgraciadamente, lamentablemente.
unhappiness | ʌn'hæpɪnɪs | *s.i.* infelicidad, desdicha, desconsuelo.
unhappy | ʌn'hæpɪ | *adj.* **1** infeliz, desgraciado, desdichado, triste. **2 [– (about/ at)]** preocupado, intranquilo, desasosegado, inquieto. **3** (form.) inoportuno, desacertado (momento, elección). **4** desgraciado, desafortunado: *an unhappy accident = un desafortunado accidente.*
unharmed | ˌʌn'hɑːmd | *adj.* ileso, indemne, intacto, sin daño.
unhealthily | ʌn'helθɪlɪ | *adv.* sin salud, enfermizamente, insalubremente.
unhealthiness | ʌn'helθɪnɪs | *s.i.* insalubridad, falta de salud.
unhealthy | ʌn'helθɪ | *adj.* **1** enfermizo, poco sano (persona). **2** insalubre, insano, nocivo, perjudicial (condiciones, un lugar). **3** (desp.) morboso, malsano, enfermizo (interés).
unheard | ˌʌn'hɜːd | *adj.* **1** desatendido, desoído, sin escuchar, sin tomar en cuenta. || **2 – of, a)** poco corriente, inaudito, sin precedentes; **b)** ofensivo, chocante; **c)** desconocido, sin fama.
unheeded | ˌʌn'hiːdɪd | *adj.* despreciado, desoído, desatendido.
unhelpful | ʌn'helpfʊl | *adj.* inútil, inservible.
unhelpfulness | ʌn'helpfʊlnɪs | *s.i.* inutilidad, incapacidad, ineptitud.
unheralded | ʌn'herəldɪd | *adj.* no anunciado, sin previo aviso.
unhesitating | ʌn'hezɪteɪtɪŋ | *adj.* decidido, pronto, listo, resuelto, firme, sin vacilación.
unhesitatingly | ʌn'hezɪteɪtɪŋlɪ | *adv.* decididamente, resueltamente, firmemente.
unhinge | ˌʌn'hɪndʒ | *v.t.* desequilibrar, alterar, perturbar, trastornar (la mente).
unhinged | ˌʌn'hɪndʒd | *adj.* desequilibrado, perturbado, trastornado.
unholiness | ˌʌn'həʊlɪnɪs | *s.i.* maldad, impiedad, perversidad.
unholy | ˌʌn'həʊlɪ | *adj.* **1** perverso, malvado, impío. **2** (fam.) ultrajante, terrible, espantoso, desagradable, atroz. **3** preocupante, no deseable (alianza, unión).
unhook | ˌʌn'hʊk | *v.t.* **1** desenganchar, descolgar. **2** desabrochar (un vestido).
unhoped-for | ʌn'həʊptfɔːr | *adj.* inesperado, imprevisto, casual.
unhurried | ʌn'hʌrɪd | *adj.* pausado, tranquilo, relajado, parsimonioso.
unhurriedly | ʌn'hʌrɪdlɪ | *adv.* pausadamente, tranquilamente, relajadamente, parsimoniosamente.
unhurt | ˌʌn'hɜːt | *adj.* ileso, indemne.
unhygienic | 'ʌnhaɪ'dʒiːnɪk | *adj.* antihigiénico.
unicellular | ˌjuːnɪ'seljʊlər | *adj.* BIOL. unicelular.
UNICEF | 'juːnɪsef | (**United Nations Children's Fund**) Fondo de las Naciones Unidas para la Infancia (UNICEF).
unicorn | 'juːnɪkɔːn | *s.c.* unicornio.
unidentifiable | ˌʌnaɪ'dentɪ'faɪəbl | *adj.* no identificable, difícil de identificar.
unidentified | ˌʌnaɪ'dentɪfaɪd | *adj.* **1** no identificado, sin identificar, poco familiar. **2** no identificado, anónimo. || **3 – flying object,** V. **UFO.**
unification | ˌjuːnɪfɪ'keɪʃn | *s.i.* unificación.
uniform | 'juːnɪfɔːm | *s.c.* e *i.* **1** uniforme. || *adj.* **2** uniforme, igual, idéntico; regular. || *v.t.* **3** uniformar.
uniformed | 'juːnɪfɔːmd | *adj.* uniformado.
uniformity | 'juːnɪfɔːmɪtɪ | *s.i.* uniformidad, regularidad, igualdad.
uniformly | 'juːnɪfɔːmlɪ | *adv.* uniformemente, regularmente.
unify | 'juːnɪfaɪ | *v.t.* [*pret.* y *p.p.* **unified**] **1** unificar, unir. **2** uniformar, igualar.
unifying | 'juːnɪfaɪɪŋ | *adj.* unificante, unificador.
unilateral | ˌjuːnɪ'lætərəl | *adj.* **1** unilateral. || **2 – disarmament,** desarme unilateral.
unilaterally | ˌjuːnɪ'lætərəlɪ | *adv.* unilateralmente.
unilateralism | 'juːnɪ'lætərəlɪsm | *s.i.* unilateralidad.
unilateralist | 'juːnɪ'lætərəlɪst | *adj.* unilateralista.
unimaginable ,| ˌʌnɪ́mædʒɪnəbl | *adj.* inimaginable, inconcebible.
unimaginative | ˌʌnɪ'mædʒɪnətɪv | *adj.* poco imaginativo, falto de imaginación.
unimpaired | ˌʌnɪm'peəd | *adj.* intacto, no disminuido, no mermado: *Greta Garbo's unimpaired fame = la fama intacta de Greta Garbo.*
unimpeachable | ˌʌnɪm'piːtʃəbl | *adj.* (form.) indudable, incuestionable, intachable, fidedigno, irreprochable.
unimpeachably | ˌʌnɪm'piːtʃəblɪ | *adv.* (form.) indudablemente, incuestionablemente, intachablemente, irreprochablemente.
unimpeded | ˌʌnɪm'piːdɪd | *adj.* ininterrumpido, incesante, constante.
unimportant | ˌʌnɪm'pɔːtənt | *adj.* poco importante, insignificante, trivial, menor.
unimpressed | ˌʌnɪm'prest | *adj.* poco impresionado, no sorprendido.
unimpressive | ˌʌnɪm'presɪv | *adj.* poco impresionante, insignificante, trivial.
uninformed | ˌʌnɪn'fɔːmd | *adj.* **1** desinformado. **2** ignorante, inculto.
uninhabitable | ˌʌnɪn'hæbɪtəbl | *adj.* inhabitable.
uninhabited | ˌʌnɪn'hæbɪtɪd | *adj.* deshabitado, despoblado, desierto.
uninhibited | ˌʌnɪn'hɪbɪtɪd | *adj.* desinhibido, sin inhibiciones.
uninitiated | ˌʌnɪ'nɪʃɪəɪtɪd | *adj.* **1** no acostumbrado, desconocedor, sin experiencia. || *s.pl.* **2 [the –]** (form.) no iniciado, profano.
uninspired | ˌʌnɪn'spaɪəd | *adj.* sin inspiración, tedioso, soso, aburrido.
uninspiring | ˌʌnɪn'spaɪərɪŋ | *adj.* poco interesante, poco imaginativo.
unintelligent | ˌʌnɪn'telɪdʒənt | *adj.* poco inteligente, estúpido.
unintelligible | ˌʌnɪn'telɪdʒəbl | *adj.* ininteligible, incomprensible.
unintelligibly | ˌʌnɪn'telɪdʒəblɪ | *adv.* ininteligiblemente, incomprensiblemente.
unintended | ˌʌnɪn'tendɪd | *adj.* no intencionado, no planeado, casual, involuntario.
unintentional | ˌʌnɪn'tenʃənl | *adj.* sin intención, sin querer, no deliberado.
unintentionally | ˌʌnɪn'tenʃənəlɪ | *adv.* de manera no intencionada, sin querer, no deliberadamente.
uninterested | ˌʌn'ɪntrɪstɪd | *adj.* **1 [– (in)]** no interesado, desinteresado. **2** falto de interés, indiferente, sin prestar atención.
uninteresting ˌʌn'ɪntrɪstɪŋ | *adj.* poco interesante, aburrido, soso, insípido.
uninterrupted | 'ʌnˌɪntə'rʌptɪd | *adj.* sin interrupción, ininterrumpido, continuo.
uninvited | ˌʌnɪn'vaɪtɪd | *adj.* no invitado, sin invitación.
uninviting | ˌʌnɪn'vaɪtɪŋ | *adj.* **1** desagradable, poco atractivo. **2** poco apetitoso (un alimento).
union | 'juːnjən | *s.c.* **1 [–** *v.sing./pl.*] unión, sociedad, asociación. **2 [–** *v.sing./pl.*] sindicato, gremio. **3** unión, confederación, coalición, alianza (de estados, partidos). **4** MEC. unión, tuerca de unión. **5** emblema (en una bandera). || *s.i.* **6** unión, cohesión, armonía. **7** (lit.) unión, enlace, matrimonio. || **8 the Union,** la Unión, los Estados Unidos de América. **9 the Union/Jack/Flag,** la bandera del Reino Unido.
unionism | 'juːnjənɪzəm | *s.i.* **1** sindicalismo, gremialismo. **2 Unionism,** POL. unionismo, conservadurismo (principios de los conservadores de Irlanda del Norte).

unionist | 'juːnjənɪst | *adj.* **1** sindicalista, gremialista. **2 Unionist,** POL. conservador (de Irlanda del Norte).

unionization | 'juːnjənaɪzeɪʃən | *s.i.* sindicación.

unionize | 'juːnjənaɪz | (brit. **unionise**) *v.t.* e *i.* sindicar(se), agremiar(se).

unique | juː'niːk | *adj.* [no *comp.*] **1** único, solo (en su especie). **2** (fam.) poco corriente, inusual, excepcional, extraordinario. **3 [– to]** exclusivo, especial, único: *problems unique to teachers = problemas exclusivos de los profesores.*

uniquely | juː'niːklɪ | *adv.* **1** excepcionalmente, extraordinariamente. **2** exclusivamente, especialmente.

uniqueness | juː'niːknɪs | *s.i.* unidad, singularidad, originalidad.

unisex | 'juːnɪseks | *adj.* unisexual, para ambos sexos (ropas, peinados).

unison | 'juːnɪzn | *s.i.* **1** armonía, uniformidad, concordancia. **2** MUS. unisonancia. || **3 in –, a)** simultáneamente, al unísono, al mismo tiempo; **b)** de acuerdo, en armonía.

unit | juːnɪt | *s.c.* **1 [–** *v.sing./pl.***]** unidad (grupo de cosas, personas): *the family unit = la unidad familiar.* **2 [– (of)]** unidad: *a unit of length = una unidad de longitud.* **3** unidad, pieza, elemento, mueble: *a kitchen units = muebles de cocina.* **4** unidad didáctica, lección, tema. **5** MEC. unidad, grupo (de máquinas). **6** MAT. unidad. || **7 – trust/**(EE.UU.) **mutual fund,** ECON. fondo de inversiones.

unite | juː'naɪt | *v.t.* e *i.* **1** unir(se), juntar(se), anexionar(se). **2** casar(se), unir(se) en matrimonio. **3 [to – (in/for/against)]** unir(se), asociar(se), aliarse (en, para o contra un propósito, interés). **4 [to – (with)]** reunir, combinar: *he units intelligence with humour = reúne inteligencia y humor.*

united | juː'naɪtɪd | *adj.* **1** unido. || **2 the United Kingdom,** el Reino Unido. **3 the United Nations,** las Naciones Unidas. **4 the United States,** los Estados Unidos.

unity | 'juːnɪtɪ | *s.c.* e *i.* **1** unidad. || *s.i.* **2** unión, unanimidad, armonía, concordia. **3** cohesión, coherencia. **4** MAT. unidad, número uno.

universal | ˌjuːnɪ'vəːsl | *adj.* **1** universal, global, cósmico. **2** general, absoluto, colectivo, total: *a universal rejection = un rechazo general.* || *s.c.* **3** FIL. concepto universal, principio general. **4** LOG. proposición universal. || **5 – joint/coupling,** MEC. articulación universal, acoplamiento universal.

universality | ˌjuːnɪvəː'sælɪtɪ | *s.i.* universalidad.

universally | ˌjuːnɪ'vəːsəlɪ | *adv.* **1** universalmente, generalmente, unánimemente, colectivamente. **2** mundialmente, en todas partes.

universe | ˌjuːnɪ'vəːs | *s.c.* **[the –]** el universo, el cosmos, el orbe, el mundo.

university | ˌjuːnɪ'vəːsɪtɪ | *s.c.* e *i.* Universidad.

unjust | ˌʌn'dʒʌst | *adj.* **1** (desp.) injusto, arbitrario, parcial. **2** (arc.) deshonesto, desleal.

unjustly | ˌʌn'dʒʌstlɪ | *adv.* injustamente, arbitrariamente, parcialmente.

unjustifiable | ʌn'dʒʌstɪfaɪəbl | *adj.* injustificable, inexcusable.

ujustifiably | ʌn'dʒʌstɪfaɪblɪ | *adv.* injustificadamente, inexcusablemente.

unjustified | ʌn'dʒʌstɪfaɪd | *adj.* injustificado, infundado.

unkempt | ˌʌn'kempt | *adj.* **1** sucio, desaseado, mugriento, sin arreglar. **2** despeinado, desgreñado. **3** (arc.) maleducado, grosero, rudo.

unkind | ʌn'kaɪnd | *adj.* **1** desagradable, despiadado, poco amable, duro, cruel. **2** malo, riguroso, inclemente (el tiempo).

unkindly | ʌn'kaɪndlɪ | *adv.* poco amablemente, desagradablemente, duramente, cruelmente.

unkindness | ʌn'kaɪndnɪs | *s.i.* falta de amabilidad, crueldad, dureza.

unknowable | ˌʌn'nəuəbl | *adj.* inescrutable, difícil de conocer, insondable, impenetrable.

unknowing | ˌʌn'nəuɪŋ | *adj.* desconocedor, inconsciente, ignorante, que no se da cuenta.

unknowingly | ˌʌn'nəuɪŋlɪ | *adv.* (lit.) sin darse cuenta, sin saberlo, inconscientemente.

unknown | ˌʌn'nəun | *adj.* **1 [– (to)]** desconocido, ignorado, no reconocido, no identificado. || *s.c.* **2** desconocido. **3 [the –]** lo misterioso, lo desconocido. || **4 – quantity, a)** (fig.) incógnita: *the new system is still an unknown quantity = el nuevo sistema es aún una incógnita;* **b)** MAT. incógnita, x.

unlace | ˌʌn'leɪs | *v.t.* desenlazar, soltar, desatar (un cordón).

unladen | ˌʌn'leɪd | *adj.* sin carga, descargado, vacío.

unlawful | ˌʌn'lɔːful | *adj.* **1** ilegal, ilícito, contra la ley. **2** ilegítimo (un hijo).

unlawfully | ˌʌn'lɔːfəlɪ | *adv.* ilegalmente, ilícitamente.

unlearn | ˌʌn'ləːn | *v.t.* desaprender, olvidar lo aprendido, desacostumbrarse a.

unleash | ʌn'liːʃ | *v.t.* **1 [to – (on/upon)]** (fig.) descargar, desencadenar, liberar (un sentimiento). **2** desatar, aflojar, dejar libre.

unleavened | ˌʌn'levnd | *adj.* ácimo, sin levadura.

unless | ən'les | *conj.* **1** a menos que, a no ser que, si no: *don't do it unless you're told = no lo hagas a menos que te lo digan.* || *prep.* **2** excepto, salvo, con excepción de.

unlettered | ˌʌn'letəd | *adj.* (form.) **1** iletrado, ignorante, ineducado. **2** analfabeto. **3** sin letras, desprovisto de letras.

unlike | ˌʌn'laɪk | *prep.* **1** a diferencia de, no como: *unlike him, she didn't leave = a diferencia de él, ella no se fue.* **2** no característico de, impropio de: *it's unlike her to say so = no es propio de ella decir eso.* || *adj.* **3** (form.) diferente, distinto, disímil, opuesto.

unlikely | ʌn'laɪklɪ | *adj.* **1** improbable, difícil, remoto: *it's unlikely to happen = es poco probable que suceda.* **2** inverosímil, poco creíble (una historia).

unlimited | ʌn'lɪmɪtɪd | *adj.* ilimitado, indefinido, infinito, incalculable.

unlined | ʌn'laɪnd | *adj.* **1** sin forrar, sin forro. **2** sin rayar, sin rayas (el papel). **3** sin arrugas, terso (el rostro).

unlisted | ˌʌn'lɪstɪd | *adj.* **1** FIN. no cotizable (acciones). **2** (EE.UU.) no registrado, que no figura en lista (telefónica).

unlit | ˌʌn'lɪt | *adj.* **1** apagado, no encendido (el fuego). **2** oscuro, sin luz, sin alumbrado.

unload | ˌʌn'ləud | *v.t.* **1** descargar, aligerar (de peso). **2 [to – (on)]** (fam.) deshacerse de, inundar el mercado con, vender en grandes cantidades. || *v.t.* e *i.* **3** desembarcar, descargar. **4** descargar, vaciar (un arma, una cámara fotográfica).

unlock | ˌʌn'lɒk | *v.t.* **1** abrir (con llave). **2** (fig.) descubrir, revelar, resolver (problemas, secretos). **3** dejar en libertad, liberar, desencadenar.

unlooked-for | ʌn'luktfɔːr | *adj.* inesperado, imprevisto, casual.

unloose | ˌʌn'luːs | *v.t.* **1** (fig.) desencadenar, liberar, desatar, descargar (un sentimiento). **2** soltar, aflojar, liberar, desatar.

unlovable | ʌn'lʌbəbl | *adj.* antipático, difícil de amar.

unlovely | ʌn'lʌvlɪ | *adj.* poco atractivo, feo, desagradable, poco seductor.

unluckily | ʌn'lʌkɪlɪ | *adv.* desgraciadamente, desafortunadamente.

unlucky | ʌn'lʌkɪ | *adj.* **1** desafortunado, infortunado, con mala suerte. **2** de mal agüero, nefasto, aciago. **3** decepcionante, desilusionante.

unmade | ˌʌn'meɪd | *adj.* **1** deshecha, sin hacer, desarreglada (cama). **2** (brit.) sin terminar, sin acabar (carretera).

unman | ˌʌn'mæn | *v.t.* **1** (lit. y arc.) desanimar, descorazonar, quitar el ánimo, acobardar. **2** castrar, emascular.

unmanageable | ʌn'mænɪdʒəbl | *adj.* poco manejable, incontrolable, ingobernable, intratable.

unmanly | ˌʌn'mænlɪ | *adj.* **1** afeminado, impropio de un hombre. **2** cobarde, miedoso, tímido. **3** degradante, poco honorable.

unmanned | ˌʌn'mænd | *adj.* **1** AER. no tripulado, sin tripulación. **2** no entrenado (un halcón).

unmannerly | ʌn'mænəlɪ | *adv.* (form. y desp.) rudo, tosco, maleducado, grosero.

unmarked | ˌʌn'mɑːkt | *adj.* **1** ileso, sin marcas. **2** sin letrero, sin distintivo, sin identificación.

unmarried | ˌʌn'mærɪd | *adj.* soltero, célibe.

unmask | ˌʌn'mɑːsk | (EE.UU.) | ˌʌn'mæsk | *v.t.* e *i.* **1** desenmascarar(se), quitar(se) la máscara, descubrir(se). || *v.t.* **2** (fig.) desenmascarar, revelar, descubrir.

unmatched | ˌʌn'mætʃt | *adj.* único, incomparable, sin par, sin rival.
unmentionable | ʌn'menʃnəbl | *adj.* **1** inmencionable, indescriptible, inenarrable. || **2 unmentionables,** (arc. euf. y hum.) prendas íntimas, bragas.
unmerciful | ʌn'mɜːsɪful | *adj.* despiadado, cruel, desalmado.
unmercifully | ʌn'mɜːsɪfulɪ | *adv.* despiadadamente, brutalmente, cruelmente.
unmindful | ʌn'maɪndful | *adj.* (form.) desconsiderado, descuidado, sin darse cuenta, olvidadizo.
unmistakable | ˌʌnmɪ'steɪkəbl | *adj.* inconfundible, patente, manifiesto, inequívoco, obvio.
unmistakably | ˌʌnmɪ'steɪkəblɪ | *adv.* inconfundiblemente, manifiestamente, inequívocamente, obviamente.
unmitigated | ʌn'mɪtɪgeɪtɪd | *adj.* **1** inexcusable, total, absoluto, completo, redomado. **2** no aliviado, no mitigado.
unmolested | ˌʌnməʊ'lestɪd | *adj.* sin interferencias, sin ser molestado.
unmoved | ˌʌn'muːvd | *adj.* **1** impasible, indiferente, frío. **2** tranquilo, sin preocupaciones, inalterado.
unmusical | ˌʌn'mjuːzɪkl | *adj.* **1** falto de oído para la música, falto de gusto musical. **2** MUS. discordante, inarmónico.
unnamed | ˌʌn'neɪmd | *adj.* **1** no mencionado, no nombrado. **2** sin nombre.
unnatural | ʌn'nætʃrəl | *adj.* **1** inusual, inesperado, raro, peculiar. **2** (desp.) antinatural, anómalo, anormal. **3** insincero, forzado, afectado, falto de naturalidad.
unnaturally | ʌn'nætʃrəlɪ | *adv.* **1** inusualmente, peculiarmente, extrañamente. **2** afectadamente, de forma forzada. || **3 not –,** naturalmente, de forma natural.
unnecessarily | ʌn'nesəsərɪlɪ | *adv.* innecesariamente, inútilmente.
unnecessary | ʌn'nesɪsərɪ | *adj.* innecesario, superfluo, inútil.
unnerve | ˌʌn'nɜːv | *v.t.* asustar, poner nervioso, sobrecoger, alarmar, desconcertar, acobardar.
unnerving | ˌʌn'nɜːvɪŋ | *adj.* alarmante, desconcertante, perturbador, desalentador.
unnervingly | ˌʌn'nɜːvɪŋlɪ | *adv.* alarmantemente, desconcertantemente, desalentadoramente.
unnoticed | ˌʌn'nəʊtɪst | *adj.* inadvertido, desapercibido.
unnumbered | ˌʌn'nʌmbəd | *adj.* **1** sin número, sin numeración, no numerado. **2** innumerable, incontable.
UNO | 'juːnəʊ | (**United Nations Organization**) Organización de las Naciones Unidas (ONU).
unobserved | ˌʌnəb'zɜːvd | *adj.* desapercibido, inadvertido.
unobtainable | ˌʌnəb'teɪnəbl | *adj.* inasequible, imposible de conseguir.
unobtrusive | ˌʌnəb'truːsɪv | *adj.* discreto, prudente, callado, poco llamativo, apenas visible.
unobtrusively | ˌʌnəb'truːsɪvlɪ | *adv.* discretamente, prudentemente, de forma poco llamativa.
unoccupied | ˌʌn'ɒkjupaɪd | *adj.* **1** desocupado, vacío, vacante. **2** despoblado, deshabitado. **3** MIL. no ocupado (un país, un territorio). **4** ocioso, inactivo, sin ocupación (persona).
unofficial | ˌʌnə'fɪʃl | *adj.* **1** extraoficial, no oficial. **2** informal, privado.
unofficially | ˌʌnə'fɪʃəlɪ | *adv.* **1** extraoficialmente. **2** informalmente, en privado.
unopened | ˌʌn'əupənd | *adj.* cerrado, sin abrir.
unorthodox | ˌʌn'ɔːθədɒks | *adj.* poco ortodoxo, poco convencional, heterodoxo.
unpack | ˌʌn'pæk | *v.t.* e *i.* **1** deshacer, vaciar (el equipaje), desembalar, desempacar. || *v.t.* **2** INF. desempaquetar (un formato).
unpaid | ˌʌn'peɪd | *adj.* **1** no asalariado, no retribuido (una persona, un trabajo). **2** no pagado, sin pagar: *an unpaid bill = una cuenta sin pagar.*
unpalatable | ʌn'pælɪtəbl | *adj.* **1** incomible, intragable, indigesto, vomitivo. **2** (fig.) desagradable, inaceptable, difícil de asimilar (una idea).
unpalatably | ʌn'pælətəblɪ | *adv.* desagradablemente, inaceptablemente.
unparalleled | ʌn'pærəleld | *adj.* inigualable, incomparable, sin par.
unpardonable | ʌn'pɑːdˌnəbl | *adj.* imperdonable, inaceptable, inexcusable, inadmisible.
unparliamentary | 'ʌnˌpɑːlə'mentərɪ | *adj.* antiparlamentario, contrario a las normas parlamentarias.
unpick | ˌʌn'pɪk | *v.t.* descoser.
unplaced | ˌʌn'pleɪst | *adj.* DEP. no colocado (fuera de tiempo en una carrera).
unplayable | ˌʌn'pleɪəbl | *adj.* **1** MUS. intocable, difícil de tocar. **2** DEP. difícil de golpear, imposible de devolver (una pelota). **3** impracticable, inutilizable (un terreno deportivo).
unpleasant | ʌn'pleznt | *adj.* **1** desagradable, repugnante. **2** antipático, poco amistoso, grosero.
unpleasantly | ʌn'plezntlɪ | *adv.* **1** desagradablemente, repugnantemente. **2** de forma antipática, groseramente.
unpleasantness | ʌn'plezntnɪs | *s.c.* e *i.* **1** desagrado, antipatía, molestia. **2** disgusto, enfado, enojo.
unplug | ˌʌn'plʌg | *v.t.* desenchufar, desconectar.
unpolluted | ˌʌnpə'luːtɪd | *adj.* no contaminado, impoluto, puro, limpio.
unpopular | ˌʌn'pɒpjulər | *adj.* impopular.
unpopularity | 'ʌnˌpɒpju'lærɪtɪ | *s.i.* impopularidad.
unpractised | ʌn'præktɪst | *adj.* inexperto, no cualificado.
unprecedented | ʌn'presɪdəntɪd | *adj.* sin precedentes, inaudito, jamás oído, inusual.
unpredictability | ˌʌnprɪ'dɪktə'bɪlɪtɪ | *s.i.* incertidumbre, imprevisibilidad.
unpredictable | ʌnprɪ'dɪktəbl | *adj.* **1** imprevisible, impredecible. **2** caprichoso, inestable, voluble: *an unpredictable person = una persona voluble.*
unpredictably | ˌʌnprɪ'dɪktəblɪ | *adv.* **1** imprevisiblemente. **2** caprichosamente, de forma voluble.
unprejudiced | ˌʌn'predʒudɪst | *adj.* sin prejuicios, imparcial.
unpremeditated | ˌʌnprɪ'medɪteɪtɪd | *adj.* no premeditado, inpremeditado, no deliberado.
unprepared | ˌʌnprɪ'peəd | *adj.* no preparado, desprevenido.
unprepossessing | 'ʌnˌpriːpə'zesɪŋ | *adj.* poco atractivo.
unpretentious | ˌʌnprɪ'tenʃəs | *adj.* poco pretencioso, sencillo, modesto.
unprincipled | ʌn'prɪnsɪpld | *adj.* sin principios, inmoral, poco escrupuloso, poco ético.
unprintable | ˌʌn'prɪntəbl | *adj.* imposible de repetir, ofensivo, grosero, obsceno (lenguaje).
unproductive | ˌʌnprə'dʌktɪv | *adj.* improductivo, infructuoso.
unprofessional | ˌʌnprə'feʃənl | *adj.* (desp.) poco profesional, poco ético.
unprofessionally | ˌʌnprə'feʃnəlɪ | *adv.* poco profesionalmente, poco éticamente.
unprofitable | ˌʌn'prɒfɪtəbl | *adj.* **1** improductivo, poco lucrativo. **2** improductiva, poco constructiva, inútil (una conversación).
unprompted | ˌʌn'prɒmptɪd | *adj.* (form.) espontáneo.
unpronounceable | ˌʌnprə'naunsəbl | *adj.* impronunciable, difícil de pronunciar.
unprotected | ˌʌn'prə'tektɪd | *adj.* **1** desprotegido, indefenso, desvalido. **2** descubierto, sin protección.
unprovided | ˌʌnprə'vaɪdɪd | *adj.* **1 [– with]** (form.) desprovisto, desabastecido. **2 [– for]** desamparado, desvalido.
unprovoked | ˌʌnprə'vəukt | *adj.* no provocado, sin provocación, espontáneo.
unpublished | ˌʌn'pʌblɪʃt | *adj.* inédito, no publicado, no editado.
unpunished | ˌʌn'pʌnɪʃt | *adj.* impune, sin castigo.
unputdownable | ˌʌnput'daunəbl | *adj.* (fam.) imposible de dejar, de mucha intriga, muy absorbente: *an unputdownable novel = una novela difícil de dejar.*
unqualified | ˌʌn'kwɒlɪfaɪd | *adj.* **1** no cualificado, sin título, sin licencia. **2** incompetente, inepto. **3** ilimitado, incondicional, total, completo, entero: *my unqualified aproval = mi aprobación incondicional.*
unquestionable | ʌn'kwestʃənəbl | *adj.* incuestionable, indisputable, indiscutible.
unquestionably | ʌn'kwestʃənəblɪ | *adv.* incuestionablemente, indisputablemente, indiscutiblemente.

unquestioned | ʌn'kwestʃənd | *adj.* **1** incuestionable, que no se cuestiona, indisputable. **2** no interrogado.
unquestioning | ʌn'kwestʃənɪŋ | *adj.* incondicional, total, ciego: *unquestioning faith = fe ciega.*
unquestioningly | ʌn'kwestʃənɪŋlɪ | *adv.* incondicionalmente, ciegamente.
unquiet | ʌn'kaɪət | *adj.* (lit.) **1** intranquilo, alterado, inquieto, desasosegado. **2** turbulento, agitado, desordenado (época).
unquote | ʌn'kwəʊt | *adv.* **1** fin de la cita, se cierran las comillas (palabra utilizada al final de una cita). || *v.t.* e *i.* **2** cerrar comillas.
unravel | ʌn'rævl | (brit. **unravell**) *v.t.* e *i.* **1** deshilar(se), deshilachar(se), abrir(se) (los hilos de un tejido). || *v.t.* **2** desenmarañar, desentrañar, descifrar (un misterio).
unread | ˌʌn'red | *adj.* **1** sin leer, no leído (un libro). **2** poco leído, ignorante (persona).
unreadable | ˌʌn'riːdəbl | *adj.* **1** (desp.) que no merece la pena leerlo, poco útil, malo. **2** ilegible. **3** incomprensible, oscuro, difícil de leer.
unreal | ˌʌn'rɪəl | *adj.* irreal, imaginario, ficticio, ilusorio.
unrealistic | ˌʌnrɪə'lɪstɪk | *adj.* poco realista, poco práctico.
unrealistically | ˌʌnrɪə'lɪstɪklɪ | *adv.* de forma poco realista, de forma poco práctica.
unreality | ˌʌnrɪ'ælɪtɪ | *s.i.* irrealidad.
unreasonable | ʌn'riːznəbl | *adj.* **1** irrazonable, injusto, exagerado. **2** abusivo, excesivo (un precio).
unreasonably | ʌn'riːznəblɪ | *adv.* **1** irrazonablemente, injustamente, exageradamente. **2** abusivamente, excesivamente.
unreasoning | ʌn'riːznɪŋ | *adj.* (form.) irracional, ilógico (un sentimiento, una creencia).
unrecognizable | ˌʌn'rekəgnaɪzəbl | (brit. **irrecognisable**) *adj.* irreconocible.
unrecognized | ˌʌn'rekəgnaɪzd | (brit. **irrecognised**) *adj.* **1** no reconocido, ignorado (persona, cosa). **2** no reconocido, no apreciado (obra).
unrecorded | ˌʌnrɪ'kɔːdɪd | *adj.* no registrado, no anotado, no inscrito.
unreel | ˌʌn'riːl | *v.t.* e *i.* desenrollar, desenroscar.
unrefined | ˌʌnrɪ'faɪnd | *adj.* **1** no refinado (producto). **2** (desp.) poco refinado, vulgar, tosco (persona).
unrehearsed | ˌʌnrɪ'həːst | *adj.* improvisado, no planeado.
unrelated | ˌʌnrɪ'leɪtɪd | *adj.* sin conexión, inconexo.
unrelenting | ˌʌnrɪ'lentɪŋ | *adj.* imparable, implacable, riguroso, inflexible, tenaz, porfiado.
unrelentingly | ˌʌnrɪ'lentɪŋlɪ | *adv.* sin parar, implacablemente, inflexiblemente, tenazmente, porfiadamente.
unreliability | 'ʌnrɪˌlaɪə'bɪlɪtɪ | *s.i.* desconfianza, falta de credibilidad.
unreliable | ˌʌnrɪ'laɪəbl | *adj.* **1** poco fiable, poco serio, informal (persona). **2** de poca confianza, que funciona mal (máquina).
unrelieved | ˌʌnrɪ'liːvd | *adj.* continuo, monótono, total, no mitigado: *unrelieved anxiety = ansiedad no mitigada.*
unremarkable | ˌʌnrɪ'mɑːkəbl | *adj.* sin importancia, poco notorio, ordinario, vulgar, corriente.
unremarked | ˌʌnrɪ'mɑːkt | *adj.* desapercibido, inadvertido, que no se nota.
unremitting | ˌʌnrɪ'mɪtɪŋ | *adj.* (form.) que no remite, persistente, sostenido, continuo, incesante.
unremittingly | ˌʌnrɪ'mɪtɪŋlɪ | *adv.* sostenidamente, continuamente, incesantemente.
unrepeatable | ˌʌnrɪ'piːtəbl | *adj.* **1** irrepetible, que no se da con frecuencia. **2** irrepetible, que no puede repetirse, obsceno, ofensivo.
unrepentant | ˌʌnrɪ'pentənt | *adj.* impenitente, empedernido, contumaz.
unrepresentative | ˌʌnreprɪ'zentətɪv | *adj.* poco representativo, poco característico, atípico.
unrepresented | ˌʌnreprɪ'zentɪd | *adj.* no representado.
unrequited | ˌʌnrɪkwaɪtɪd | *adj.* (lit.) no correspondido (amor).
unreserved | ˌʌnrɪ'zəːvd | *adj.* **1** (form.) incondicional, total, absoluto, completo. **2** no reservado, sin reserva, libre (una plaza, un asiento). **3** cándido, abierto, poco reservado.
unreservedly | ˌʌnrɪ'zəːvɪdlɪ | *adv.* **1** incondicionalmente, absolutamente, completamente. **2** abiertamente, cándidamente, francamente.
unresolved | ˌʌnrɪ'zɔlvd | *adj.* (form.) no resuelto, pendiente de resolución.
unresponsive | ˌʌnrɪ'spɒnsɪv | *adj.* (desp.) indiferente, insensible.
unrest | ˌʌn'rest | *s.i.* **1** insatisfacción, desasosiego, desazón, intranquilidad, inquietud. **2** disturbio, desorden.
unrestrained | ˌʌnrɪ'streɪnd | *adj.* desenfrenado, incontrolado, ilimitado, libre.
unrestrainedly | ˌʌnrɪ'streɪnɪdlɪ | *adv.* desenfrenadamente, incontroladamente, ilimitadamente, libremente.
unrestricted | ˌʌnrɪ'strɪktɪd | *adj.* sin restricción, ilimitado.
unrewarded | ˌʌnrɪ'wɔːdɪd | *adj.* no recompensado, sin recompensa.
unrewarding | ˌʌnrɪ'wɔːdɪdŋ | *adj.* infructuoso, inútil, inservible, (Am.) inoficioso.
unripe | ˌʌn'raɪp | *adj.* verde, no madura (una fruta).
unrivalled | ʌn'raɪvld | *adj.* sin rival, sin par, incomparable.
unroll | ˌʌn'rəʊl | *v.t.* e *i.* **1** desenrollar(se), desenroscar(se), desplegar(se). **2** (fig.) desplegar(se), descubrir, extender(se) (ante los ojos).
unruffled | ˌʌn'rʌfld | *adj.* tranquilo, sereno, sin preocupaciones.
unruly | ʌn'ruːlɪ | *adj.* **1** revoltoso, díscolo, indisciplinado, rebelde. **2** despeinado, incontrolable (el pelo).
unsaddle | ˌʌn'sædl | *v.t.* **1** desensillar (a un animal). **2** derribar, descabalgar, desarzonar (a un jinete).
unsafe | ˌʌn'seɪf | *adj.* **1** peligroso, inseguro, arriesgado (edificio, lugar). **2** peligro, inseguro (persona).
unsaid | ˌʌn'sed | *adj.* que no se ha dicho, pronunciado, expresado: *lots of things were left unsaid = muchas cosas quedaron sin decir.*
unsaleable | ˌʌn'seɪləbl | (EE.UU. **unsalable**) *adj.* invendible.
unsanitary | ˌʌn'sænɪtərɪ | *adj.* insalubre, antihigiénico.
unsatisfactory 'ʌnˌsætɪs'fæktərɪ | *adj.* insatisfactorio, inadecuado, inaceptable.
unsatisfied | ˌʌn'sætɪsfaɪd | *adj.* insatisfecho, descontento.
unsatisfying | ˌʌn'sætɪsfaɪɪŋ | *adj.* poco satisfactorio, insuficiente, deficiente.
unsaturated | ʌn'sætʃəreɪtɪd | *adj.* **1** no saturado, no lleno. **2** QUIM. no saturado.
unsavoury | ˌʌn'seɪvərɪ | (EE.UU. **unsavory**) *adj.* **1** despreciable, repugnante, repulsivo, inmoral (una persona). **2** desagradable, insípido.
unsay | ˌʌn'seɪ | *v.t.* desdecirse de, retractarse de.
unscathed | ˌʌn'skeɪθd | *adj.* ileso, intacto, sano y salvo.
unscheduled | ˌʌn'ʃedjuːld | *adj.* imprevisto, no planeado.
unscientific | ʌnˌsaɪən'tɪfɪk | *adj.* (desp.) acientífico, poco científico, poco objetivo.
unscramble | ˌʌn'skræmbl | *v.t.* **1** descifrar (un mensaje). **2** desenredar, desenmarañar.
unscrew | ˌʌn'skruː | *v.t.* **1** desatornillar, destornillar. **2** desenroscar, quitar (un tapón).
unscripted | ʌn'skrɪptɪd | *adj.* improvisado, sin guión (charla).
unscrupulous | ʌn'skruːpjʊləs | *adj.* (desp.) poco escrupuloso, inmoral, que no tiene escrúpulos, principios.
unscrupulously | ʌn'skruːpjʊləslɪ | *adv.* poco escrupulosamente, inmoralmente.
unscrupulousness | ʌn'skruːpjʊləsnɪs | *s.i.* falta de escrúpulos, falta de principios.
unseasonable | ʌn'siːznəbl | *adj.* **1** fuera de temporada, inapropiado para la época del año (tiempo, ropa, comida). **2** a destiempo, inoportuno.
unseasonably | ʌn'siːznəblɪ | *adv.* **1** inapropiadamente. **2** inoportunamente.
unseat | ˌʌn'siːt | *v.t.* **1** (también **unsaddle**) derribar, descabalgar, desarzonar (a un jinete). **2** destituir, deponer, separar (de un puesto).
unseeing | ˌʌn'siːɪŋ | *adj.* (lit.) abstraída, vaga, perdida (la mirada).
unseeingly | ˌʌn'siːɪŋlɪ | *adv.* abstraídamente, de forma vaga, con la mirada perdida.
unseemliness | ʌn'siːmlɪnɪs | *s.i.* (form.) indecencia, falta de decoro.

unseemly | ʌn'siːmlɪ | *adj.* indecoroso, indigno, indecente, impropio.
unseen | ˌʌn'siːn | *adj.* **1** invisible, que no se ve. **2** oculto, misterioso, desconocido, secreto. **3** inadvertido, desapercibido, sin ser notado. **4** hecho a primera vista (traducción). || *s.c.* **5** traducción a primera vista: *a German unseen = una traducción a primera vista del alemán.* || **6 sight –,** V. **sight.**
unselfish | ˌʌn'selfɪʃ | *adj.* generoso, desinteresado, altruista.
unselfishly | ˌʌn'selfɪʃlɪ | *adv.* generosamente, desinteresadamente, de forma altruista.
unselfishness | ˌʌn'selfɪʃnɪs | *s.i.* generosidad, desinterés, altruismo.
unsentimental | 'ʌnˌsentɪ'mentl | *adj.* poco sentimental, falto de sentimientos, poco afectivo.
unserviceable | ˌʌn'səːvɪsəbl | *adj.* (form.) inservible, inútil, no reparable (un objeto).
unsettle | ˌʌn'setl | *v.t.* **1** desazonar, alterar, inquietar, trastornar. **2** desordenar, descomponer.
unsettled | ˌʌn'setld | *adj.* **1** pendiente, no resuelto, en suspenso. **2** incierto, nebuloso, indeterminado (un plan). **3** variable, inestable (el tiempo). **4** intranquilo, inquieto, alterado, agitado. **5** revuelto, mal (el estómago). **6** pendiente, no pagado (cuenta). **7** despoblado, no colonizado (territorio). **8** que no ha sentado cabeza (persona).
unsettling | ˌʌn'setlɪŋ | *adj.* inquietante, perturbador.
unshaded | ˌʌn'ʃeɪdɪd | *adj.* sin pantalla, descubierta (bombilla).
unshakable, unshakeable | ʌn'ʃeɪkəbl | *adj.* inquebrantable, firme, inconmovible.
unshakably, unshakeably | ˌʌn'ʃeɪkəblɪ | *adv.* inquebrantablemente, firmemente, de forma inconmovible.
unshaken | ˌʌn'ʃeɪkən | *adj.* firme, sólido, sin quebrantar (una idea, una creencia).
unshaven | ˌʌn'ʃeɪvn | *adj.* no afeitado.
unshockable | ʌn'ʃɒkəbl | *adj.* tolerante, comprensivo, que no se sorprende fácilmente.
unsightliness | ʌn'saɪtlɪnɪs | *s.i.* fealdad, repugnancia.
unsightly | ʌn'saɪtlɪ | *adj.* desagradable, feo, repugnante, repulsivo.
unsigned | ˌʌn'saɪnd | *adj.* sin firma, sin firmar.
unskilled | ˌʌn'skɪld | *adj.* no cualificado, inexperto.
unsmiling | ʌns'maɪlɪŋ | *adj.* serio, grave, seco.
unsmilingly | ʌns'maɪlɪŋlɪ | *adv.* seriamente, gravemente, secamente.
unsociable | ʌn'səʊʃəbl | *adj.* (desp.) antisocial, insociable, reservado, huraño.
unsocial | ʌn'səʊʃl | *adj.* **1** insociable, huraño. **2** poco conveniente, de noche: *he works unsocial hours = trabaja de noche.*
unsold | ˌʌn'səʊld | *adj.* no vendido.
unsolicited | ˌʌnsə'lɪsɪtɪd | *adj.* no solicitado, no pedido.
unsolved | ˌʌn'sɒlvd | *adj.* no solucionado, no resuelto.
unsophisticated | ˌʌnsə'fɪstɪkeɪtɪd | *adj.* poco sofisticado, sencillo, simple, infantil, cándido.
unsound | ˌʌn'saʊnd | *adj.* **1** débil, poco saludable, enfermizo (persona). **2** poco sólido, poco resistente, defectuoso. **3** falso, erróneo, falaz, insostenible (sistema, conclusión). || **4 of – mind,** demente, que no está en su sano juicio.
unsparing | ʌn'speərɪŋ | *adj.* **1** generoso, espléndido, pródigo. **2** incansable, infatigable. **3** despiadado, desalmado, cruel.
unsparingly | ʌn'speərɪŋlɪ | *adv.* generosamente, espléndidamente. **2** despiadadamente, cruelmente.
unspeakable | ʌn'spiːkəbl | *adj.* indecible, inenarrable, irrepetible, espantoso, terrible.
unspeakably | ʌn'spiːkəblɪ | *adv.* inenarrablemente, irrepetiblemente, espantosamente.
unspecified | ˌʌn'spesɪfaɪd | *adj.* no especificado, que está sin especificar, sin determinar.
unspectacular | ˌʌnspek'tækjələ | *adj.* poco espectacular, corriente, normal.
unspoiled, unspoilt | ˌʌn'spɔɪlt | *adj.* **1** intacto, no estropeado. **2** no mimado (un niño).
unspoken | ˌʌn'spəukən | *adj.* **1** no expresado, no mencionado (un pensamiento). **2** tácito (un acuerdo).
unsporting | ˌʌn'spɔːtɪŋ | *adj.* antideportivo, falto de deportividad.
unstable | ˌʌn'steɪbl | *adj.* **1** inestable, inseguro, poco firme. **2** inestable, desequilibrado (psicológicamente). **3** imprevisible, fluctuante. **4** QUIM. inestable. **5** FIS. radioactivo.
unstated | ˌʌns'teɪtɪd | *adj.* no mencionado, no especificado.
unsteadily | ˌʌnstedɪlɪ | *adv.* inestablemente, con inseguridad, de forma desequilibrada.
unsteadiness | ˌʌn'stedɪnɪs | *s.i.* inestabilidad, inseguridad, desequilibrio.
unsteady | ʌn'stedɪ | *adj.* **1** inseguro, tambaleante, inestable, poco firme. **2** tembloroso, irregular, no uniforme (un movimiento). **3** fluctuante, inconstante.
unstick | ˌʌn'stɪk | *v.t.* [*irr.pret.* y *p.p.* **unstuck**] despegar, desprender, soltar (algo pegado).
unstinting | ˌʌns'tɪntɪŋ | *adj.* (form.) generoso, desinteresado, abundante.
unstintingly | ˌʌns'tɪntɪŋlɪ | *adv.* generosamente, desinteresadamente.
unstop | ˌʌn'stɒp | [**unstopped, unstopping**] *v.t.* **1** destapar, destaponar, desobstruir. **2** descorchar, destapar, abrir (una botella).
unstoppable | ˌʌn'stpəbl | *adj.* imparable, incontenible.
unstrap | ˌʌn'stræp | [**unstrapped, unstrapping**] *v.t.* desabrochar, quitar (correas, cinturones).
unstructured | ʌns'trʌktʃəd | *adj.* no estructurado.
unstuck | ˌʌn'stʌk | *adj.* **1** flojo, suelto, separado. || **2 to come –,** (fam.) **a)** despegarse, soltarse, aflojarse; **b)** fracasar, venirse abajo, fallar, sufrir un revés.
unstudied | ˌʌn'stʌdɪd | *adj.* (form.) no estudiado, sin afectación, natural: *unstudied charm = encanto natural.*
unsubstantiated | ʌnsəbs'tæʃɪəɪtɪd | *adj.* no confirmado, no probado (historia, acusación).
unsuccessful | ˌʌnsək'sesfʊl | *adj.* falto de éxito, fracasado, desafortunado, ineficaz.
unsuccessfully | ˌʌnsək'sesfəlɪ | *adv.* infructuosamente, desafortunadamente.
unsuitable | ˌʌn'suːtəbl | *adj.* inadecuado, inconveniente, inservible, no válido, poco apto.
unsuitably | ˌʌn'suːtəblɪ | *adv.* inadecuadamente, inconvenientemente, sin validez, sin aptitud.
unsuited | ˌʌn'suːtɪd | *adj.* **1** impropio, inadecuado, no apto. **2** incompatible, opuesto, discordante: *they are not suited to each other = no son el uno para el otro.*
unsullied | ˌʌn'sʌlɪd | *adj.* (lit.) puro, no corrompido, impoluto.
unsung | ˌʌn'sʌŋ | *adj.* no alabado, no celebrado, poco famoso, desconocido, anónimo: *an unsung work = un trabajo anónimo.*
unsupported | ˌʌnsə'pɔːtɪd | *adj.* **1** que no tiene apoyo, ayuda, respaldo; solo: *an unsupported party = un partido sin respaldo.* **2** que no tiene base, datos, pruebas.
unsure | ˌʌn'ʃʊəːr | *adj.* **1** inseguro (de sí mismo). **2** inseguro, indeciso.
unsurpassed | ˌʌnsə'pɑːst | *adj.* insuperado, sin par, sin rival.
unsurprising | ˌʌnsə'praɪsɪŋ | *adj.* poco sorprendente, previsible, probable.
unsurprisingly | ˌʌnsə'praɪsɪŋlɪ | *adv.* de manera poco sorprendente, previsiblemente, probablemente.
unsuspected | ˌʌnsə'spektɪd | *adj.* insospechado.
unsuspecting | ˌʌnsə'spektɪŋ | *adj.* confiado, crédulo, poco suspicaz, inocente, incauto.
unsweetened | ˌʌn'swiːtnd | *adj.* sin azúcar, no azucarado.
unswerving | ʌn'swəːvɪŋ | *adj.* firme, incondicional, inquebrantable.
unsympathetic | 'ʌnˌsɪmpə'θetɪk | *adj.* **1** poco compasivo, poco comprensivo, indiferente, que no tiene corazón. **2 [– to]** enemigo de, hostil a, contrario a.
untamed | ˌʌn'teɪmd | *adj.* indomado, salvaje, no domesticado.
untangle | ˌʌn'tæŋgl | *v.t.* **1** desenredar, desenmarañar. **2** (fig.) desentrañar, descifrar, resolver.
untapped | ˌʌn'tæpt | *adj.* **1** que no ha sido explotado, no utilizado: *untapped resources = recursos sin explotar.* **2** sin descorchar, sin abrir (botella).

untenable | ˌʌn'tenəbl | *adj.* **1** insostenible, indefendible. **2** inhabitable, difícil de ocupar.
untested | ʌn'testɪd | *adj.* no probado, no comprobado.
unthinkable | ˌʌn'θɪŋkəbl | *adj.* **1** impensable, inconcebible, inimaginable, inaceptable. || **2 the –**, lo impensable.
unthinking | ˌʌn'θɪŋkɪŋ | *adj.* irreflexivo, inconsciente, alocado, imprudente, impulsivo, irresponsable.
unthinkingly | ˌʌn'θɪŋkɪŋlɪ | *adv.* irreflexivamente, inconscientemente, imprudentemente, de forma impulsiva, irresponsablemente.
untidily | ʌn'taɪdɪlɪ | *adv.* **1** descuidadamente, desaliñadamente. **2** en desorden, desorganizadamente.
untidiness | ʌn'taɪdɪnɪs | *s.i.* **1** desaliño, desaseo. **2** desorden, desorganización.
untidy | ʌn'taɪdɪ | *adj.* **1** desaliñado, desaseado, mal arreglado. **2** desordenado, desorganizado, sin método.
untie | ˌʌn'taɪ | *v.t.* desatar, desanudar.
untied | ˌʌn'taɪd | *adj.* desatado, desanudado.
until, till | ən'tɪl | *prep.* **1** hasta (un tiempo, un lugar): *we waited until 7.00 = esperamos hasta las siete; he went on reading until Madrid = estuvo leyendo hasta llegar a Madrid.* || *conj.* **2** hasta que: *wait until I arrive = espera hasta que llegue yo.* || **3 up –**, (fam.) hasta: *up until Saturday = hasta el sábado.*
untimeliness | ʌn'taɪmlɪnɪs | *s.i.* inoportunidad, inconveniencia.
untimely | ʌn'taɪmlɪ | *adj.* **1** prematuro, anticipado, intempestivo. **2** inapropiado, inoportuno. || *adv.* **3** prematuramente, con anticipación, intempestivamente. **4** inoportunamente, inapropiadamente.
untiring | ʌn'taɪərɪŋ | *adj.* incansable, infatigable.
untiringly | ʌn'taɪərɪŋlɪ | *adv.* incansablemente, infatigablemente.
unto | 'ʌntu | *prep.* (arc. y lit.) **1** a, hacia, para: *speaking unto me = hablándome.* **2** hasta: *unto her arrival = hasta que ella llegó.*
untold | ˌʌn'təuld | *adj.* (lit.) **1** innumerable, incalculable, incontable. **2** no contado, jamás dicho, jamás revelado.
untouchable | ʌn'tʌtʃəbl | *adj.* [no *comp.*] **1** intocable, inatacable, imposible de criticar. **2** imposible de conseguir. **3** desagradable al tacto. **4** intocable (casta inferior del sistema hindú). || *s.c.* **5** intocable, intangible (casta hindú).
untouched | ˌʌn'tʌtʃt | *adj.* **1** intacto, que no ha sido modificado, indemne; íntegro, entero. **2** inconmovible, no afectado, insensible.
untoward | ˌʌntə'wɔːd | (EE.UU.) | ʌn'tɔːd | *adj.* **1** (form.) adverso, infortunado, inesperado, desfavorable, indeseable, extraño. **2** obstinado, incontrolable, ingobernable. **3** (arc.) impropio, inadecuado.
untrained | ˌʌn'treɪnd | *adj.* **1** no cualificado, no especializado, que no tiene formación. **2** no entrenado, no acostumbrado, no adiestrado. **3** que no ha sido amaestrado (un animal).
untrammelled | ʌn'træməld | (EE.UU. **untrammeled**) *adj.* (lit.) libre, sin trabas, independiente, emancipado.
untreated | ʌn'triːtɪd | *adj.* **1** no tratado, que no ha sido tratado (una enfermedad). **2** que no ha sido tratado, no procesado, natural (un producto).
untried | ˌʌn'traɪd | *adj.* **1** DER. no juzgado, no procesado, no visto (un preso, una causa). **2** no probado, no experimentado.
untroubled | ˌʌn'trʌbld | *adj.* no preocupado, tranquilo, sereno, relajado.
untrue | ˌʌn'truː | *adj.* **1** falso, incorrecto, inexacto. **2** desleal, infiel, pérfido.
untrustworthy | ˌʌn'trʌstˌwəːθɪ | *adj.* poco fiable, indigno de confianza.
untruth | ˌʌn'truːθ | *s.c.* **1** (euf.) mentira, infundio, calumnia. **2** infidelidad, deslealtad, felonía.
untruthful | ˌʌn'truːθful | *adj.* mentiroso, calumniador, falso, mendaz.
untruthfully | ˌʌn'truːθfəlɪ | *adv.* falsamente.
unturned | ˌʌn'təːnd | *adj.* **1** no vuelto, que no se le ha dado la vuelta (a algo). || **2 to leave no stone –**, V. **leave.**
untutored | ˌʌn'tʃjuːtəd | (EE.UU.) | ˌʌn'tʃuːtəd | *adj.* (form.) poco instruido, poco sofisticado, poco refinado, ineducado.
unusable | ʌn'juːzəbl | *adj.* inservible, inútil.
unused | ˌʌn'juːzd | *adj.* **1** no utilizado, no usado, que no ha sido estrenado. | ˌʌn'juːst | **2 [– to]** no acostumbrado, no familiarizado, no habituado.
unusual | ʌn'juːʒuəl | *adj.* raro, insólito, poco común, extraordinario.
unusually | ʌn'juːʒuəlɪ | *adv.* extraordinariamente, sorprendentemente, excepcionalmente.
unutterable | ʌn'ʌtərəbl | *adj.* (form.) increíble, indecible, terrible, espantoso, intenso.
unuterably | ʌn'ʌtərəblɪ | *adv.* increíblemente, indeciblemente, espantosamente, terriblemente, intensamente.
unvarnished | ˌʌn'vɑːnɪʃt | *adj.* **1** no barnizado. **2** sencillo, simple y llano, sin adornos (la verdad, una historia).
unvarying | ʌn'veərɪɪŋ | *adj.* invariable, constante.
unveil | ˌʌn'veɪl | *v.t.* **1** quitar el velo. **2** (fig.) desvelar, descubrir, mostrar.
unveiling | ˌʌn'veɪlɪŋ | *s.i.* ceremonial al descubrir una estatua, una placa, etc...
unversed | ˌʌn'vəːst | *adj.* **[– in]** (form.) no versado en, poco ducho en.
unvoiced | ˌʌn'vɔɪst | *adj.* **1** no expresado. **2** FON. sordo.
unwaged | ˌʌn'weɪdʒd | *adj.* (brit. y euf.) en paro, parado, desempleado.
unwanted | ˌʌn'wɒntɪd | *adj.* no querido, no deseado.
unwarrantable | ʌn'wɒrəntəbl | (EE.UU.) | ʌn'wɔːrəntəbl | *adj.* (form.) injustificable, insostenible.
unwarranted | ʌn'wɒrəntɪd | (EE.UU.) | ʌn'wɔːrəntɪd | *adj.* (form.) **1** injustificado, no autorizado. **2** no garantizado, sin garantía.
unwarily | ʌn'weərɪlɪ | *adv.* imprudentemente, incautamente.
unwariness | ʌn'weərɪnɪs | *s.i.* imprudencia, falta de precaución, falta de cautela.
unwary | ʌn'weərɪ | *adj.* **1** imprudente, falto de precaución. || **2 the unwary,** los ingenuos, los incautos.
unwavering | ʌn'weɪvərɪŋ | *adj.* inquebrantable, firme.
unwelcome | ʌn'welkəm | *adj.* **1** mal recibido, no querido, inoportuno. **2** embarazosa, inconveniente, molesta, desagradable (una situación).
unwelcoming | ʌn'welkəmɪŋ | *adj.* **1** frío, poco amistoso, hostil. **2** poco acogedor, inhóspito, inhabitable (un lugar).
unwell | ˌʌn'wel | *adj.* enfermo, malo, indispuesto.
unwholesome | ˌʌn'həulsəm | *adj.* **1** malsano, perjudicial, nocivo. **2** indecente, desagradable, indeseable.
unwieldiness | ʌn'wiːldɪnɪs | *s.i.* pesadez, dificultad de manejo, dificultad de movimiento.
unwieldy | ʌn'wiːldɪ | *adj.* **1** pesado, abultado, difícil de manejar, difícil de mover. **2** ineficiente, incontrolable, desorganizado (un sistema).
unwilling | ˌʌn'wɪlɪŋ | *adj.* reacio, contrario, reticente, poco dispuesto.
unwillingly | ˌʌn'wɪlɪŋlɪ | *adv.* reticentemente, de mala gana.
unwillingness | ˌʌn'wɪlɪŋnɪs | *s.i.* reticencia, renuencia, mala gana.
unwind | ˌʌn'waɪnd | *v.* [*irr.pret.* y *p.p.* **unwound**] *t.* e *i.* **1** desenrollar(se), desenvolver(se), desenroscar(se). || *i.* **2** (fam.) relajarse, tranquilizarse, serenarse.
unwise | ˌʌn'waɪz | *adj.* imprudente, estúpido, insensato, desatinado, poco aconsejable.
unwisely | ˌʌn'waɪzlɪ | *adv.* imprudentemente, insensatamente, desatinadamente.
unwitting | ʌn'wɪtɪŋ | *adj.* (form.) inconsciente, no intencionado, sin intención, sin darse cuenta.
unwittingly | ʌn'wɪtɪŋlɪ | *adv.* inconscientemente, no intencionadamente, inadvertidamente.
unwonted | ʌn'wəuntɪd | *adj.* **1** (form.) raro, insólito, anormal, poco usual, desacostumbrado. **2** (arc.) no acostumbrado, poco familiarizado.
unworkable | ˌʌn'wəəkəbl | *adj.* impracticable, imposible de hacer.
unworldliness | ˌʌn'wəːldlɪnɪs | *s.i.* **1** espiritualidad. **2** ingenuidad, simplicidad, sencillez.
unworldly | ˌʌn'wəːldlɪ | *adj.* **1** espiritual, poco mundano, poco realista. **2** ingenuo, simple, sencillo.
unworthily | ʌn'wəːθɪlɪ | *adv.* indignamente.
unworthiness | ʌn'wəːθɪnɪs | *s.i.* indignidad, falta de mérito.

unworthy | ʌn'wɜːθɪ | *adj.* **1** indigno, no merecedor, que no tiene mérito. **2** inaceptable, innoble, vil.
unwound | ˌʌn'waʊnd | *pret.* y *p.p.* de **unwind.**
unwritten | ˌʌn'rɪtn | *adj.* **1** no escrito, no registrado. **2** tradicional, oral. **3** tácito, sobreentendido. || **4 – law/rule,** DER. derecho consuetudinario; ley tácita, costumbre.
unyielding | ʌn'jiːldɪŋ | *adj.* inflexible, firme, inexorable, inconmovible, obstinado.
unzip | ʌn'zɪp | **[unzipped, unzipping]** *v.t.* bajar una cremallera (de), (Am.) abrir un cierre relámpago de (una prenda).
up | ʌp | *adv.* **1** hacia arriba, para arriba; allá, hacia el norte (posición): *come up and tell me = sube y dímelo; up to Scotland = allá en Escocia.* **2** en pie, de pie, derecho: *could you stand up? = ¿puedes ponerte de pie?* **3** más, arriba, hacia arriba (un precio, una cantidad): *prices have gone up = los precios han subido.* **4 [to be –]** levantado, en pie, sin acostarse: *we were up at 7.00 = nos levantamos a las siete.* **5** hasta, hacia (un punto): *we walked up to the shop = fuimos andando hasta la tienda.* **6** más alto, en alto, más fuerte (en sonido, en peso): *speak up = habla más alto.* **7** totalmente, enteramente, completamente, bien, absolutamente todo; en pedazos: *eat all up = cómetelo absolutamente todo; the vase was broken up = el jarrón estaba hecho pedazos.* **8** firmemente, muy apretado, fuertemente: *she fastened up her laces = se ató fuertemente los cordones.* **9** juntamente, en total: *add these figures up = suma estos números.* **10** en consideración, sobre la mesa, a relucir: *he brought up a delicate subject = sacó a relucir un tema delicado.* || *prep.* **11** hacia arriba de, en lo alto de, encima de: *the cat's up the tree = el gato está en lo alto del árbol.* **12** arriba, subiendo hacia, más arriba, a lo largo de: *up the road on the left = subiendo la calle a la izquierda.* **13** contra, en contra de (la corriente, el viento). **14** (brit.) a, hasta, hacia; en: *he's up Mary's = está en casa de Mary.* || *adj.* no *comp.* **15** ascendente, que sube (una escalera), que va hacia el norte (un tren). **16** en reparación, en obras; en mal estado (una carretera). **17** INF. en funcionamiento, en uso. **18** levantado (de la cama); erecto, erguido. **19** (fam.) DER. inculpado, acusado, en los tribunales. **20** (fam.) eufórico, excitado, muy animado. **21** agitado, acelerado. **22 [– in/on]** (fam.) informado sobre, al tanto de (una materia). **23** acabado, terminado (un período de tiempo). || *v.t.* **(upped, upping)** (fam.) **24** subir, elevar, incrementar. || *v.i.* **25** ponerse de repente a, actuar con rapidez. || **26 all – with,** todo ha terminado entre. **27 not – to much,** (fam.) no muy bueno, nada especial: *the film is not up to much = la película no es ninguna maravilla.* **28 on the – and –,** (fam.) cada vez mejor, subiendo como la espuma. **29 something is –,** (fam.) algo está pasando, algo va mal, algo marcha mal. **30 – against,** tener que hacer frente a, tener que vérselas con. **31 upped,** de repente, sin más: *he upped and started to shout = y sin más empezó a gritar.* **32 ups and downs,** altibajos, vicisitudes, peripecias. **33 – yours!,** (vulg.) ¡tu madre!, ¡que te den morcilla!, ¡vete al cuerno! **34 what's –?,** ¿qué pasa?, ¿qué ocurre?
up-and-coming | ˌʌpən'kʌmɪŋ | *adj.* prometedor, halagüeño.
upbeat | 'ʌpbiːt | *adj.* (fam.) alegre, optimista, feliz.
upbraid | ʌp'breɪd | *v.t.* (form.) recriminar, reprender, reprochar, censurar, reñir.
upbringing | 'ʌpˌbrɪŋɪŋ | *s.i.* educación, crianza.
upcountry | ˌʌp'kʌntrɪ | *adv.* **1** del interior, de tierra adentro: *they travelled upcountry = viajaron hacia el interior.* || *adj.* **2** interior, profundo, recóndito (lugar). **3** pueblerino, del campo.
update | ˌʌp'deɪt | *v.t.* modernizar, renovar, actualizar; poner al día.
upend | ˌʌp'end | *v.t.* **1** poner boca abajo, volcar, poner al revés. **2** (fam.) derribar, tirar al suelo (de un puñetazo).
up-front | ˌʌp'frʌnt | *adj.* (fam.) directo, franco, sin doblez.
upgrade | ˌʌp'greɪd | *v.t.* **1** ascender, subir (de rango), promover. **2** mejorar (una raza por medio de selección). || *s.c.* **3** rampa, pendiente, cuesta. || *adj.* **4** ascendente, pendiente, en cuesta. || *adv.* **5** cuesta arriba. || **6 on the –,** mejorando, prosperando.
upheaval | ʌp'hiːvl | *s.c.* e *i.* **1** cataclismo, confusión, trastorno. **2** levantamiento (político). **3** GEOL. levantamiento (de la corteza terrestre).
upheld | ʌp'held | *pret.* y *p.p.* de **uphold.**
uphill | ˌʌp'hɪl | *adj.* **1** pendiente, en cuesta, ascendente. **2** arduo, difícil, laborioso, penoso. || *adv.* **3** cuesta arriba, pendiente arriba. **4** penosamente, arduamente, con dificultad.
uphold | ʌp'həʊld | *v.t.* [*irr.pret.* y *p.p.* **upheld**] (form.) **1** mantener, sostener, defender (un derecho, un principio). **2** apoyar, confirmar, ratificar.
upholder | ʌp'həʊldər | *s.c.* defensor, protector.
upholster | ʌp'həʊlstər | *v.t.* tapizar (muebles).
upholstered | ʌp'həʊlstəd | *adj.* **1** tapizado. || **2 well –,** (fig. y hum.) gordinflón, cebón.
upholstery | ʌp'həʊlstərɪ | *s.i.* tapicería, tapizado.
upkeep | 'ʌpkiːp | *s.i.* mantenimiento, conservación (de un edificio).
upland | 'ʌplənd | *s.c.* **1** altiplano, meseta. || *adj.* **2** mesetario, del altiplano. || **3 the uplands,** las tierras altas.
uplift | ʌp'lɪft | *v.t.* **1** (form.) elevar, edificar, exaltar (social o moralmente). **2** elevar, subir, alzar. || | 'ʌplɪft | *s.i.* **3** elevación. **4** exaltación, encumbramiento, edificación. **5** GEOL. levantamiento.
uplifted | ʌp'lɪftɪd | *adj.* elevado, en alto, alzado, prominente: *uplifted hands = manos en alto.*
uplifting | ʌp'lɪftɪŋ | *adj.* edificante, enriquecedor.
upmarket | ʌp'mɑːkɪt | *adj.* (fam.) exclusivo, elegante, lujoso, caro.
upmost | 'ʌpməʊst | V. **uppermost.**
upon | ə'pɒn | *prep.* (form.) **1** sobre, en, encima de: *it is upon the table = está encima de la mesa.* **2** después de, una vez que: *upon swimming = después de nadar.* **3** por: *upon his advice = por consejo suyo.* **4** y: *miles upon miles = millas y millas, muchísimas millas.*
upper | 'ʌpər | *adj.* **1** superior, de arriba, más elevado, de encima (de posición, rango). **2** GEOG. alto, superior: *the upper Nile = el Alto Nilo.* **3** interior; del norte. || *s.c.* **4** pala, cara (del calzado). **5** (fam.) litera superior (de un camarote, de un coche cama). **6** (argot) droga estimulante (especialmente anfetamina). || **7 to be on one's uppers,** (arc. y fam.) estar sin blanca, no tener un duro. **8 the – hand,** el control; la ventaja, la delantera. **9 – case,** caja alta, mayúscula (en imprenta). **10 – class,** clase alta. **11 – crust,** (fam.) clase alta. **12 – lip,** ANAT. labio superior. **13 uppers,** (fam.) dentadura postiza superior.
upper-cut | 'ʌpəkʌt | *s.c.* DEP. gancho de abajo a arriba (en boxeo).
uppermost, upmost | 'ʌpəməʊst | *adj.* **1** más alto, hacia arriba, más elevado, encima. **2** obvio, preponderante, sobresaliente, principal. || *adv.* **3** en primer lugar, en primera posición. **4** principalmente, predominantemente. ||**5 – in one's mind,** el primer lugar en la mente de uno.
uppish | 'ʌpɪʃ | *adj.* (desp. y arc.) orgulloso, soberbio, altanero, arrogante, presumido.
uppity | 'ʌpətɪ | *adj.* (EE.UU.) V. **uppish.**
uprised | ʌ'preɪzd | *adj.* levantado, en alto, elevado, izado.
upright | 'ʌpraɪt | *adj.* **1** erecto, erguido, recto, derecho. **2** vertical, de pie: *an upright freezer = un congelador vertical.* **3** (fig.) honesto, justo, recto, probo, responsable. || *adv.* **4** verticalmente, sin doblar. **5** rectamente, con justicia, responsablemente. || *s.c.* **6** poste, viga, montante (de apoyo). || **7 – piano,** piano vertical.
uprightness | 'ʌpˌraɪtnɪs | *s.i.* rectitud, honestidad, responsabilidad.
uprising | 'ʌpˌraɪzɪŋ | *s.c.* levantamiento, rebelión, revuelta.
up-river | ˌʌp'rɪvər | *adv.* río arriba, aguas arriba, contra corriente.
uproar | 'ʌprɔːr | *s.i.* **1** alboroto, algarabía, bulla, vocerío, escándalo, protesta. **2** controversia, polémica, debate.
uproarious | ʌp'rɔːrɪəs | *adj.* **1** ruidoso, escandaloso, bullicioso. **2** animadísimo, divertidísimo, hilarante.

uproariously | ʌp'rɔːrɪəslɪ | *adv.* **1** ruidosamente, escandalosamente, bulliciosamente. **2** extremadamente (divertido), para morirse de risa.

uproot | ʌp'ruːt | *v.t.* **1** arrancar de raíz, desarraigar, sacar de cuajo. **2** erradicar, suprimir, extirpar. **3** (fig.) desarraigar, separar, arrancar: *she was uprooted from her home = fue separada de su hogar.*

upset | 'ʌpset | *v.t.* [*irr.pret.* y *p.p.* **upset**] **1** volcar, hacer caer, derramar: *upset a glass of wine = derramar un vaso de vino.* **2** trastocar, trastornar, desbaratar, dar al traste con (un plan). **3** disgustar, entristecer, enfadar, molestar, trastornar, acongojar. **4** MED. alterar, afectar a, revolver, poner fatal (el estómago): *drinks upset my stomach = las bebidas me ponen el estómago fatal.* **5** MEC. recalcar, achatar (con martillo). || *s.c.* e *i.* **6** trastorno estomacal, alteración del estómago. **8** DEP. resultado inesperado. **9** MEC. recalco, tas. || *adj.* **10** disgustado, triste, trastornado, acongojado. **11** MED. alterado, mal (el estómago). || **12 to – the apple cart,** V. **apple cart. 13 – price,** precio mínimo, precio de salida (en subasta).

upsetting | ʌp'setɪŋ | *adj.* tremendo, terrible, para volver loco.

upshot | 'ʌpʃɒt | *s.sing.* resultado, balance, conclusión.

upside-down | ˌʌpsaɪd'daʊn | *adj.* **1** al revés, invertido. **2** desordenado, confuso, hecho un lío. || *adv.* **3** con lo de arriba abajo, boca abajo, patas arriba.

upstage | ˌʌp'steɪdʒ | *adj.* **1** localizado al fondo del escenario. **2** (fam.) arrogante, engreído. || *adv.* **3** hacia el fondo del escenario. || *v.t.* **4** robar la escena (a un actor más importante), captar la atención (en detrimento de otro actor). **5** (fam.) tratar con arrogancia, comportarse altaneramente.

upstairs | ˌʌp'steəz | *adv.* **1** arriba, al piso superior: *go upstairs = vete arriba.* **2** a nivel superior, a un puesto superior: *promoted upstairs = elevado a un nivel superior.* || *adj.* **3** de arriba, del piso superior: *an upstairs bedroom = una habitación de arriba.* || *s.i.* **4 [the –]** el piso de arriba, el piso superior.

upstanding | ˌʌp'stændɪŋ | *adj.* **1** (form. y hum.) respetable, honrado, íntegro. **2** buen mozo, gallardo, garboso.

upstart | 'ʌpstɑːt | *s.c.* **1** (desp.) arribista, advenedizo, nuevo rico. || *adj.* **2** arribista, advenedizo. **3** presuntuoso, fatuo, jactancioso.

upstream | ˌʌp'striːm | *adv.* contra corriente, aguas arriba, río arriba.

upsurge | 'ʌpsɜːdʒ | *s.sing.* **1** ascenso, incremento, aumento, subida vertiginosa. || *v.i.* **2** subir vertiginosamente, incrementar.

upswing | 'ʌpswɪŋ | *s.c.* **1 [– (in)]** subida, recuperación. **2** COM. mejora, alza, curva ascendente.

uptake | 'ʌpteɪk | *s.sing.* **1** entendimiento, comprensión. || *s.c.* e *i.* **2** captación, aceptación. || *s.c.* **3** tubo de ventilación, chimenea. || **4 quick on the –,** muy listo, inteligente. **5 slow on the –,** torpe.

uptight | 'ʌptaɪt | *adj.* **1** (argot) tenso, nervioso, inquieto. **2** molesto, enojado, enfadado. **3** indigente, menesteroso, que no tiene un duro. **4** (EE.UU.) rígido, convencional, formalista, ceremonioso.

up-to-date | ˌʌptə'deɪt | *adj.* **1** moderno, de última hora. **2** muy al día, puesto al día, actualizado, informado, muy al corriente.

up-to-the-minute | ˌʌptəðə'mɪnɪt | *adj.* **1** muy moderno, a la última moda. **2** con la más reciente información, muy al día.

uptown | ˌʌp'taʊn | *adj.* (EE.UU.) **1** en las afueras, en la zona residencial. || *adv.* **2** hacia las afueras, hacia la zona residencial.

upturn | ʌp'tɜːn | *s.c.* **1** alza, mejora, aumento, cambio a mejor. || *v.t.* e *i.* **2** volver(se) hacia arriba. **3** volcar(se), derramar(se), caer(se).

upturned | ʌp'tɜːnd | *adj.* **1** respingona, vuelta hacia arriba (nariz). **2** volcado, derribado.

upward | 'ʌpwəd | V. **upwards.**

upwards | 'ʌpwədz | (EE.UU. **upward**) *adv.* **1** hacia arriba, para arriba: *facing upwards = mirando hacia arriba.* || *adj.* **2** ascendente, hacia arriba: *an upward movement = un movimiento ascendente.* **3** ascendente, en alza (un precio). || **4 – mobility,** cambio a una clase social más alta. **5 – of,** (fam.) más de: *upwards of 30 = más de 30.*

upwardly | 'ʌpwədlɪ | *adv.* **1** ascendentemente. || **2 – mobile,** trepador, con posibilidad para el ascenso a otra clase social.

upwind | ʌp'wɪnd | *adj.* **1** contrario al viento. || *adv.* **2** contra el viento.

uranium | jʊ'reɪnɪəm | *s.i.* QUIM. uranio.

urban | 'ɜːbən | *adj.* urbano, de ciudad.

urbane | ɜː'beɪn | *adj.* educado, fino, cortés, de buenas maneras.

urbanity | ɜː'bænɪtɪ | *s.i.* urbanidad, corrección, cortesía.

urbanization | ˌɜːbənaɪ'zeɪʃn | *s.i.* urbanización.

urbanize | 'ɜːbənaɪz | (brit. **urbanise**) *v.t.* (generalmente pasiva) urbanizar.

urchin | 'ɜːtʃɪn | *s.c.* **1** (arc.) rapazuelo, pilluelo, golfillo. **2** travieso, diablillo. **3** ZOOL. erizo de mar; erizo.

Urdu | 'ʊəduː | *s.i.* **1** urdu (lengua oficial de Pakistán). || *adj.* **2** urdu.

urea | 'jʊəriə | , (EE.UU.) | 'jʊrɪə | *s.i.* BIOQ. urea.

ureter | ˌjʊə'riːtər | *s.c.* ANAT. uréter.

urethra | ˌjʊə'riːθrə | [*pl.* **urethrae** o **urethras**] *s.c.* ANAT. uretra.

urge | ɜːdʒ | *v.t.* **1** urgir, apremiar, acuciar, compeler. **2** instar, alentar, incitar, exhortar. **3 [to – on]** recomendar encarecidamente, abogar, aconsejar, propugnar (medidas). || *v.t.* e *i.* **4** obligar, forzar, empujar, impeler. || *s.c.* **5** deseo, instinto, impulso, vehemencia.

urgency | 'ɜːdʒənsɪ | *s.i.* urgencia, prontitud, premura.

urgent | 'ɜːdʒənt | *adj.* **1** urgente, apremiante. **2** insistente, desesperado.

urgently | 'ɜːdʒəntlɪ | *adv.* **1** urgentemente, apremiantemente. **2** insistentemente, desesperadamente.

urinal | jʊə'raɪnl | , (EE.UU.) | 'jʊərɪnl | *s.c.* **1** orinal. **2** urinario.

urinary | jʊə'raɪnərɪ | , (EE.UU.) | 'jʊərɪnerɪ | *adj.* urinario, de las vías urinarias.

urinate | 'jʊərɪneɪt | *v.i.* orinar.

urine | 'jʊərɪn | *s.i.* orina, orines.

urn | ɜːn | *s.c.* **1** urna. **2** cafetera, tetera (para grandes cantidades y utilizada en bares).

us | ʌs | | əs | *pron.* (*o.* de **we**). **1** nos, a nosotros, nosotros: *he told us to go = dijo que nos fuéramos.* **2** (brit. y fam.) me, a mí: *give us a biscuit = danos una galleta.*

US | ˌjuː'es | (**Unites States**) Estados Unidos.

USA | ˌjuːes'eɪ | (**United States of America**) Estados Unidos de América.

usable | 'juːzəbl | *adj.* usable, utilizable, aprovechable, servible.

usage | 'juːsɪdʒ | 'juːzɪdʒ | *s.c.* e *i.* **1** uso, empleo, utilización (de la lengua, de una palabra). **2** manejo, empleo, uso (de un objeto). **3** costumbre, usanza.

use | juːz | *v.t.* **1** usar, utilizar, emplear, aprovechar. **2** (fam.) tomar, utilizar: *I could use a cup of tea = me tomaría una taza de té.* **3** consumir, gastar, derrochar: *we are using a lot of paint = estamos consumiendo mucha pintura.* **4** utilizar, explotar, aprovecharse de (una persona, una situación). **5 [to – +** *o.* **+** *adv./prep.***]** (form.) tratar, portarse con: *she had been badly used = ha sido muy mal tratada.* || *v.i.* [sólo se usa en pret. y la contracción negativa es **usedn't**; expresa hábitos pasados] | juːst | **6** acostumbrar, soler: *I used to drive to work = solía ir en coche a trabajar.* || *s.i.* **7 [– (of)]** uso, utilización, empleo. **8** DER. usufructo, derecho de utilización: *I've got the use of her boat = tengo el usufructo de su barco.* **9** utilidad, provecho, ventaja, finalidad: *was it any use? = ¿te sirvió de algo?* || *s.c.* e *i.* **10** uso, aplicación, servicio: *the machine has many uses = la máquina tiene muchas aplicaciones.* **11** costumbre, práctica, usanza, uso. **12** liturgia, culto, rito. || **13 for ... –/for – as,** para usar como..., para usar de... **14 for the – of,** para uso de (alguien en particular). **15 to have its uses,** tener sus ventajas. **16 in –,** en uso, funcionando. **17 it is no –/there is no –,** no vale la pena, no sirve de nada. **18 to make – of,** utilizar, hacer uso de, valerse de. **19 of –,** útil, válido, aprovechable, servible. **20 out of –,** fuera de uso, en desuso. **21 to – up,** agotar, terminar, gastar. **22 what is the –?/what – is there?,** ¿para qué sirve?, ¿de qué vale?

used | juːst | *adj.* **1** usado, desgastado, de segunda mano. **2** habituado, acos-

tumbrado. || **3 to be – to,** estar acostumbrado a, estar habituado a. **4 to get – to,** acostumbrarse a, habituarse a.
useful | 'ju:sful | *adj.* **1** útil, ventajoso, provechoso. **2** servicial, competente, capaz. **3** (brit. y fam.) satisfactorio, excelente. || **4 to come in –,** venir bien, hacer el avío.
usefully | 'ju:sfəlɪ | *adv.* útilmente, ventajosamente, provechosamente.
usefulness | 'ju:sfulnɪs | *s.i.* utilidad, provecho, validez, ventaja.
useless | 'ju:slɪs | *adj.* **1** inútil, inservible. **2** vano, ineficaz (un esfuerzo). **3** incompetente, torpe, inepto.
uselessly | 'ju:slɪslɪ | *adv.* inútilmente, ineficazmente, vanamente.
uselessness | 'ju:slɪsnɪs | *s.i.* ineficacia, inutilidad, ineptitud.
user | 'ju:zər | *s.c.* usuario.
user-friendly | 'ju:zə'frendlɪ | *adj.* de fácil manejo (una máquina).
usher | 'ʌʃər | *s.c.* **1** ujier, portero, conserje; alguacil (en un juzgado). **2** acomodador. **3** anunciador, presentador (en actos oficiales). **4** (arc.) profesor auxiliar. || *v.t.* **5 [to –** *o.* **+** *adv./prep.***]** acomodar, acompañar, aposentar. **6 [to – in]** (fig.) anunciar, pronosticar, ser el comienzo de.
usherette | ˌʌʃə'ret | *s.c.* acomodadora.
USSR | ˌju:eses'ɑ: | *s.* **(Union of Soviet Socialist Republics)** Unión de Repúblicas Socialistas Soviéticas.
usual | 'ju:ʒuəl | *adj.* **1** usual, habitual, normal, corriente, acostumbrado. || **2 as –,** como de costumbre, como siempre. **3 business as –,** todo va como de costumbre, todo sigue igual. **4 the –,** lo de costumbre.
usually | 'ju:ʒuəlɪ | *adv.* **1** usualmente, habitualmente, normalmente, por lo general, por regla general. || **2 more than –,** más que nunca, increíblemente.
usurer | 'ju:ʒərər | *s.c.* usurero.
usurp | ju:'zə:ə | *v.t.* (form.) usurpar, arrebatar, despojar.
usurpation | ˌju:zə:'peɪʃn | *s.i.* usurpación.
usurper | ju:'zə:pər | *s.c.* usurpador.
usury | 'ju:ʒurɪ | *s.i.* usura.
utensil | ju:'tensl | *s.c.* (form.) utensilio, implemento.
uterine | 'ju:təraɪn | *adj.* uterino, del útero.
uterus | 'ju:tərəs | [*pl.* **uteres**] *s.c.* ANAT. útero.
utilitarian ,| ju:tɪlɪ́tɜərɪən | *adj.* **1** (desp.) funcional, utilitario (un mueble). **2** FIL. utilitarista.
utility | ju:'tɪlɪtɪ | *s.i.* **1** (form.) utilidad, provecho, rendimiento. || *s.c.* **2** servicio, prestación (público). || **3 – room,** cuarto de lavado y plancha, trascocina, despensa. **4 utilities,** empresa de servicios.
utilization | ˌju:tɪlaɪ'zeɪʃn | *s.i.* utilización, explotación, aprovechamiento.
utilize | 'ju:tɪlaɪz | (brit.) **utilise.** *v.t.* (form.) usar, utilizar, explotar, aprovechar.
utmost, uttermost | 'ʌtməust | *adj.* (form.) **1** sumo, supremo, máximo: *of the utmost importance = de primerísima importancia.* || *s.sing.* **2 [the –]** lo sumo, lo máximo: *the utmost we could to help = lo máximo que pudimos para ayudar.*
utopia | ju:'təupɪə | *s.c.* e *i.* utopía.
utopian | ju:'təupɪən | *adj.* **1** utópico, idealista. || *s.c.* **2** utópico, idealista.
utter | 'ʌtər | *adj.* **1** completo, absoluto, total: *that's utter rubbish! = ¡eso es una absoluta basura!* || *v.t.* **2** (form.) articular, pronunciar, proferir. **3** poner en circulación (moneda falsa). **4** publicar, editar (un libro). **5** (arc.) vender, repartir (mercancía).
utterance | 'ʌtərəns | *s.i.* (form.) **1** pronunciación, articulación, expresión. || *s.c.* **2** declaración, afirmación, expresión, opinión. **3** fin, muerte, último suspiro.
utterly | 'ʌtəlɪ | *adv.* absolutamente, totalmente, completamente.
uttermost | 'ʌtəməust | V. **utmost.**
U-turn | 'ju:tə:n | *s.c.* **1** viraje en U. **2** (fam. y desp.) cambio total, viraje total: *he has done a U-turn = ha dado un vuelco total.*
uvula | 'ju:vjələ | [*pl.* **uvulae** o **uvulas**] *s.c.* ANAT. úvula.
uxorious | ʌk'sɔ:rɪəs | *adj.* (form. y hum.) demasiado amoroso con la propia esposa.

v, V | viː | *s.c.* **v, V** **1** v (vigésimo-segunda letra del alfabeto inglés). || *abreviatura* **2** de **verse, very, verb, versus, volt and volume.** || *número romano* **3** cinco.

vac | væk | (brit. y fam.) *abreviatura* **1** de **vacation. 2** de **vacuum.**

vacancy | 'veɪkənsɪ | *s.c.* **1** plaza libre, habitación disponible (hostelería): *no vacancies = completo (hotel, etc.).* **2** empleo, puesto vacante (oferta): *vacancy for receptionist = puesto de recepcionista vacante.* || *s.i.* **3** vacío, ausencia, vaguedad (de mente, mirada, ideas, etc.).

vacant | 'veɪkənt | *adj.* **1** libre, desocupado, disponible (lavabo, puesto de trabajo, habitación, etc.). **2** vacío, en blanco, distraído, perdido, necio (mirada, mente, etc.). **3** libre, sin hacer nada (tiempo). || **4 – possession,** (casa, piso, etc.) lista para ocupar; llave en mano (lenguaje publicitario).

vacantly | 'veɪkəntlɪ | *adv.* distraídamente, vagamente, neciamente.

vacate | və'keɪt | (EE.UU.) | 'veɪkeɪt | *v.t.* (form.) **1** dejar libre (empleo, puesto). **2** desalojar, evacuar, desocupar (lugar, posición).

vacation | və'keɪʃn | (EE.UU.) | veɪ'keɪʃn | *s.c.* **1** vacaciones (en la Universidad, Magistratura, etc.). **2** (EE.UU.) vacaciones: *to take a vacation = tomarse unas vacaciones.* || *s.i.* **3** (form.) desalojo, evacuación (de un lugar o posición). || *v.i.* **4** (EE.UU.) pasar las vacaciones, estar de vacaciones: *vacationing in the mountains = de vacaciones en la sierra.*

vaccinate | 'væksɪneɪt | *v.t.* **[to – (against)]** vacunar.

vaccination | ˌvæksɪ'neɪʃn | *s.c.* e *i.* vacunación.

vaccine | 'væksiːn | (EE.UU.) | vaek'siːn | *s.c.* e *i.* vacuna.

vacillate | 'væsɪleɪt | *v.i.* **[to – (between)]** (form.) vacilar, dudar, oscilar.

vacillating | 'væsɪleɪtɪŋ | *adj.* vacilante, dudoso, indefinido.

vacillation | ˌvæsɪ'leɪʃn | *s.c.* e *i.* (form.) vacilación, duda.

vacua | 'vækjuə | *pl.irreg.* de **vacuum.**

vacuity | væ'kjuːɪtɪ | *s.i.* (form.) vacío, vacuidad, vaguedad, banalidad (de expresión, mirada, ideas, etc.).

vacuous | 'vækjuəs | *adj.* (form.) vacuo, vago, superficial, banal, inconsistente (expresión, ideas, etc.).

vacuously | 'vækjuəslɪ | *adv.* (form.) vagamente, superficialmente.

vacuum | 'vækjuəm | *s.sing.* **1** vacío, ausencia, hueco: *power vacuum = vacío de poder.* **2** FIS. vacío. || *s.c.* **3** (fam.) aspiradora. **4** (fam.) pasada (de aspiradora). || *v.t.* e *i.* **5** limpiar con aspiradora, pasar la aspiradora. || **6 in a –,** en el vacío, aislado.

vacuum-bottle | 'vækjuəmˌbɒtl | *s.c.* (EE.UU.) termo.

vacuum-cleaner | 'vækjuəmˌkliːnər | *s.c.* aspiradora.

vacuum-flask | 'vækjuəmflɑːsk | *s.c.* (brit.) termo.

vacuum-packed | 'vækjuəmpækt | *adj.* envasado al vacío.

vacuum-pump | 'vækjuəmpʌmp | *s.c.* bomba neumática.

vacuum-tube | 'vækjuəmtjuːb | *s.c.* tubo al vacío.

vade-mecum | ˌveɪdɪ'miːkum | *s.c.* vademécum.

vagabond | 'vægəbɒnd | *s.c.* (arc.) vagabundo; (Am.) lambarero.

vagary | 'veɪgərɪ | *s.c.* (form.) capricho, variación, extravagancia.

vagina | vədʒaɪnə | *s.c.* ANAT. vagina.

vaginal | və'dʒaɪnl | *adj.* vaginal.

vagrancy | 'veɪgrənsɪ | *s.i.* vagancia, vagabundeo; (Am.) vagabundería.

vagrant | 'veɪgrənt | *s.c.* **1** vagabundo, vago, holgazán; (Am.) perdido. || *adj.* **2** errante, nómada: *vagrant tribes = tribus nómadas.*

vague | veɪg | *adj.* **1** vago, superficial, inconcreto (respuesta, petición, noción, etc.). **2** vago, impreciso, inexacto, confuso, ambiguo (descripción, exposición, etc.). **3** vago, inseguro, indeciso, incierto (necesidad, intención, etc.). **4** vago, ausente, distraído (expresión, mirada, gesto). **5** borroso, oscuro, confuso, indeterminado: *vague figures in the shadows = figuras borrosas en la oscuridad.* **6** ligero, inconcreto (sensaciones, sentimientos): *vague pains all over the body = ligeros dolores en todo el cuerpo.*

vaguely | 'veɪglɪ | *adv.* vagamente, indecisamente, ligeramente.

vagueness | 'veɪgnɪs | *s.i.* vaguedad, imprecisión, indecisión, indeterminación.

vain | veɪn | *adj.* **1** vano, inútil: *a vain attempt = intento vano.* **2** vanidoso, presumido, presuntuoso, creído; (Am.) entonado. **3** (lit.) vano, vacuo: *vain promises = vanas promesas.* || **4 in =N,** en vano. **5 to take someone's name in –,** hablar de alguien con poco respeto (estando ausente el aludido).

vainglorious | ˌveɪn'glɔːrɪəs | *adj.* (lit.) presumido, presuntuoso.

vainglory | veɪn'glɔːrɪ | *s.i.* (lit.) vanagloria, vanidad, presunción.

vainly | 'veɪnlɪ | *adv.* **1** vanidosamente, presuntuosamente. **2** vanamente, inútilmente.

vainness | 'veɪnnɪs | *s.i.* vanidad, inutilidad, presuntuosidad.

valance | 'væləns | (también **valence**) *s.c.* cenefa, doselera, faldilla.

vale | veɪl | *s.c.* (lit.) *valle: vale of tears = valle de lágrimas.*

valediction | vælɪ'dɪkʃn | *s.c.* (from.) discurso de despedida, palabras de adiós.

valedictorian | vælɪk'tɔːrɪən | *s.c.* (EE.UU.) universitario recién graduado (pronunciando el discurso de despedida).

valedictory | ɪvælɪ'dɪktərɪ | *atr.* **1** (from.) de despedida, de adiós: *a valedictory gift = regalo de despedida.* ||

s.c. **2** (EE.UU.) discurso de despedida (de un graduado universitario).
valence | 'veɪləns | *s.i.* QUIM. valencia.
valency | 'veɪlənsɪ | *s.c.* (brit.) QUIM. valenia.
valentine | 'væləntaɪn | *s.c.* **1** novio, estinatario e una tarjeta de San Valentín. **2** tarjeta de San Valentín. || **3 -- card,** tarjeta de San Valentín.
valerian | və'lɪərɪən | *s.i.* BOT. valeriana
valet | 'vælɪt | *s.c.* **1** ayuda de cámara, mozo. || *v.t.* **2** limpiar, cepillar, reparar (ropa, tapicería), || *v.i.* **3** servir como ayuda de cámara.
valetudinarian | vælɪtjuːdɪneərɪən | *s.c.* (form.) aprensivo, hipocondríaco.
valiant | 'vælɪənt | *adj.* valiente, bravo, arrojado, decidido, (Am.) chirote, (Am.) agalludo.
valiantly | 'vælɪəntlɪ | *adv.* valientemente, bravamente, ecididamente.
valid | 'vælɪd | *adj.* **1** válido, legal (documento, contrato, etc.). **2** válido, lógico, razonable, firme, serio (argumento, razón, exusa, etc.).
validate | 'vælɪdeɪt | *v.t.* (from.) validar, ratificar, corroborar, confirmar.
validation | vælɪ'deɪʃn | *s.i.* validación, atificación, confirmación.
validity | və'lɪdɪtɪ | *s.i.* **1** validez, legalidad (de un documento, contrato, etc.). **2** lógica, seriedad, firmeza (de un argumento, razón, exusa, etc.).
valise | və'liːz | *s.c.* maletín.
Valium | 'vælɪəm | *s.c.* e *i.* [*pl.* **Valium**]Valium (marca registrada).
valley | 'vælɪ | *s.c.* valle.
valour | 'vælər | (EE.UU. **valor**) *s.i.* **1** (lit.) valor, valentía, coraje. || **2 discretion is the better part of –,** la prudencia no está reñida con el valor.
valuable | 'væljuəbl | *adj.* **1** valioso, precioso, estimable, útil (ayuda, consejo, etc.). **2** valioso, costoso, de mucho valor (objetos). || **3 valuables,** objetos de valor (joyas, principalmente).
valuation | ˌvælju'eɪʃn | *s.c.* e *i.* **1 [– (on/of)]** valoración, tasación (de bienes). **2** juicio, valoración, estima (de personas o cosas). || **3 to take/accept someone at their own –,** fiarse de lo que alguien dice de sí mismo.
value | 'væljuː | *s.i.* **1** valor, ayuda, importancia, utilidad: *the value of regular exercise = el valor del ejercicio constante.* **2** valor, precio: *the value of the dollar = el valor del dólar.* **3** valor (especificado): *the news value of a royal romance = el valor noticiable de un romance real.* || *s.c.* **4** MAT. valor. **5** MUS. valor (de una nota). || *v.t.* **6** valorar, apreciar, estimar: *to value health above all else = valorar la salud por encima de todo.* **7** valorar, tasar (objetos). || **8 to be/give good –/– for money,** estar muy bien de precio. **9 of –,** de valor, de interés, de importancia. **10 to put/place a high – on something,** darle a algo mucho valor o importancia. **11 to take something at face –,** aceptar algo sin pararse en mientes. **12 – added tax,** V. **VAT. 13 – judgement,** (desp.) opinión, juicio de valor (basado en el crédito de alguien, no en hechos probados). **14 values,** valores, principios morales (de un individuo o de una comunidad).
valued | 'væljuːd | *adj.* apreciado, estimado.
valueless | 'væljulis | *adj.* inútil, sin valor.
valuer | 'væljuər | *s.c.* tasador.
valve | vælv | *s.c.* **1** ANAT. válvula. **2** MEC. válvula.
vamoose | və'muːs | *v.i.* (EE.UU. y fam.) largarse, desaparecer (usado en imperativo, principalmente).
vamp | væmp | *s.c.* **1** (arc.) vampiresa. **2** empella (de zapato). || *s.c.* **3** engatusar, conseguir (sirviéndose una mujer de su encanto femenino). || **4 to – something up,** (fam.) renovar, actualizar, hacer una nueva versión (literatura, música, etc.).
vampire | 'væmpaɪər | *s.c.* **1** vampiro (en relatos o películas de terror). **2** (fam.) vampiro, aprovechado, chupón. **3** (también **vampire bat**) ZOOL. vampiro (murciélago de América del Sur).
van | væn | *s.c.* **1** furgoneta. **2** vagón, furgón (de ferrocarril destinado al correo, equipaje, etc.). || *abreviatura* **3** (form.) de **vanguard.** || **4 in the –,** a la vanguardia, a la cabeza.
vandal | 'vændl | *s.c.* vándalo, gamberro.
vandalise V. **vandalize.**
vandalism | 'vændəlɪzəm | *s.i.* vandalismo.
vandalize | 'vændəlaɪz | (también vandalise) *v.t.* destruir, destrozar, arrasar, saquear.
vane | veɪn | *s.c.* **1** veleta. **2** MEC. aspa, aleta, álabe.
vanguard | 'vængaːd | *s.sing.* **1** vanguardia (de un ejército). **2** vanguardia, cabeza (de progreso, movimiento, revolución, etc.): *in the vanguard of industrial progress = a la cabeza del desarrollo industrial.*
vanilla | və'nɪlə | *s.i.* vainilla.
vanish | 'vænɪʃ | *v.i.* **1** desaparecer, extinguirse, dejar de existir. || **2 vanishing point, a)** punto en el infinito (donde dos paralelas parecen juntarse); **b)** punto, estadio en que algo se da por perdido.
vanity | 'vænɪtɪ | *s.i.* **1** vanidad, presuntuosidad, orgullo. **2** (form.) trivialidad, insignificancia, caducidad, lo trivial, lo caduco, etc.: *the vanity of wordly goods = lo caduco de los bienes mundanos.* || **3 – bag/case,** neceser de maquillaje.
vanquish | 'væŋkwɪʃ | *v.t.* (lit.) vencer, batir, derrotar.
vantage | 'vɑːntɪdʒ | (EE.UU.) | 'vaen↓tɪdʒ | *s.i.* **1** situación de ventaja, posición de superioridad. || *s.c.* **2** DEP. ventaja (en tenis). || **3 – point, a)** lugar estratégico, mirador, atalaya; **b)** situación de ventaja, perspectiva.
vapid | 'væpɪd | *adj.* (form.) insípido, insustancial, soso, superficial.
vapidly | 'væpɪdlɪ | *adv.* (form.) insípidamente, sin vida.
vapidity | væ'pɪdɪtɪ | *s.i.* (form.) **1** sosería, aburrimiento, superficialidad. || *s.c.* **2** estupidez, banalidad.
vapor | 'veɪpər | V. **vapour.**
vaporize | 'veɪpəraɪz | (también **vaporise**) *v.t.* e *i.* vaporizar, volatilizar, evaporar.
vaporization | ˌveɪpəraɪ'zeɪʃn | *s.i.* vaporización, evaporación.
vaporous | 'veɪpərəs | *adj.* (lit.) vaporoso, brumoso.
vapour | 'veɪpər | (EE.UU. **vapor**) *s.i.* **1** vapor. **2** FIS. estado gaseoso. || **3 the vapours,** (arc.) sensación repentina de mareo.
vapour-trail | 'veɪpətreɪl | *s.c.* estela de vapor (producida por un reactor).
variability | ˌveərɪə'bɪlɪtɪ | *s.i.* variabilidad.
variable | 'veərɪəbl | *adj.* **1** variable, inestable, irregular. **2** variable, adaptable, ajustable. || *s.c.* **3** variable, factor (con influencia en una situación o proyecto). **4** MAT. variable.
variance | 'veərɪəns | *s.c.* **1** disparidad. || **2 to be at =N (with someone/ something),** (form.) estar en desacuerdo con alguien o algo.
variant | 'veərɪənt | *s.c.* **1** variante, forma distinta, alternativa. || *adj.* **2** distinto, diferente, alternativo, otro.
variation | ˌveərɪ'eɪʃn | *s.c.* e *i.* **1 [– (in/of)]** variación, cambio. **2** MUS. **[–(on)]** variación.
varicose | 'værɪkəus | *adj.* **1** varicoso. || **2 – veins,** MED. varices.
varied | 'veərɪd | *pret.* y *p.p.* **1** de **vary.** || *adj.* **2** variado, diverso.
variegated | 'veərɪgeɪtɪd | *adj.* **1** jaspeado, abigarrado, variopinto, multicolor. **2** (form.) diversificado, complejo (producto, sistema).
variegation | ˌveərɪ'geɪʃn | *s.i.* coloración irregular, abigarramiento.
variety | və'raɪətɪ | *s.i.* **1** variedad, diferencia, diversidad. **2** (brit.) variedades, revista. || *s.c.* **3 [– (of)]** tipo, especie, clase. **4** variedad, gama, surtido. **5** BIOL. variedad, subespecie. || **6 – store,** (EE.UU.) tienda barata que vende de todo.
various | 'veərɪəs | *adj.* **1** vario, diverso, diferente: *ties in various designs = corbatas con diferente dibujo.* **2** bastante, múltiple: *for various reasons = por múltiples razones.*
variously | 'veərɪəslɪ | *adv.* (form.) diversamente, de distinto modo.
varnish | 'vɑːnɪʃ | *s.i.* **1** barniz. **2** (brit.) esmalte (de uñas). || *v.t.* **3** barnizar, esmaltar. || **4 to – something over,** disimular el lado negativo de algo.
varnished | 'vɑːnɪʃt | *adj.* barnizado, esmaltado.
varsity | 'vɑːsɪtɪ | *s.c.* **1** (brit. y fam.) Universidad (Oxford y Cambridge, generalmente). **2** (EE.UU.) equipo, selección (de un centro docente, en competiciones deportivas).
vary | 'veərɪ | *v.t.* e *i.* **1** variar, diferir: *opinions vary on this point = las opi-*

niones difieren en este punto. **2** variar, cambiar, alterarse: *prices vary with the seasons = los precios cambian según la temporada.* || *v.t.* **3** cambiar, alterar (hábitos de conducta, programas, etc.).
vascular | 'væskjʊlər | *adj.* ANAT. vascular.
vase | vɑːz | (EE.UU.) | veɪs | *s.c.* florero, jarrón.
vasectomy | væ'sektəmɪ | *s.c.* MED. vasectomía.
Vaseline | 'væsɪliːn | *s.i.* vaselina, crema.
vassal | 'væsl | *s.c.* **1** vasallo (en la sociedad feudal). **2** (fig.) vasallo (persona o nación sometida a otra).
vassalage | 'væsəlɪdʒ | *s.i.* vasallaje.
vast | vɑːst | *adj.* vasto, amplio, extenso, grande, inmenso, enorme.
vastly | 'vɑːstlɪ | *adv.* ampliamente, enormemente, inmensamente, sumamente.
vastness | 'vɑːstnɪs | *s.i.* amplitud, inmensidad, enormidad.
vat | væt | *s.c.* barrica, cuba, tonel.
VAT | ˌviː eɪ 'tiː | | væt | *siglas* (de **value added tax**) IVA (impuesto del valor añadido).
Vatican | 'vætɪkən | *s.sing.* **1** Vaticano. || *adj.* **2** vaticano.
vatman | 'vætmən | *s.sing.* (brit.) (fam.) el hombre del IVA (negociado administrativo que controla el IVA).
vaudeville | 'vəʊdəvil | *s.i.* (EE.UU.) variedades, revista, comedia.
vault | vɔːlt | *s.c.* **1** cámara acorazada (de un banco). **2** cripta, panteón, tumba. **3** bóveda. **4** sótano, bodega. **5** salto (de pértiga). || *v.i.* **6 [to – (over)]** saltar (sirviéndose de las manos o pértiga).
vaulted | 'vɔːltɪd | *adj.* abovedado.
vaulting | 'vɔːltɪŋ | *s.i.* **1** techo de bóveda, abovedado. || *adj.* **2** (lit.) dirigido a lo más alto, desmedido, sin límites: *vaulting ambition = ambición sin límites.* || **3 – horse,** plinto (instrumento gimnástico).
vaunt | vɔːnt | *v.t.* (form.) jactarse, alardear, presumir, hacer ostentación: *to vaunt one's success = alardear de éxito.*
vaunted | 'vɔːntɪd | *adj.* alardeado, cacareado.
VC | ˌviː 'siː | (Brit.) *siglas* (de **Victoria Cross**) medalla al valor en combate.
VCR | ˌviː siː 'ɑː | *siglas* (de **video cassette recorder**) vídeo.
VD | ˌviː 'diː | *siglas* (de **venereal disease**) enfermedad venérea.
VDU | ˌviː diː 'juː | *siglas* (de **visual display unit**) INF. terminal de información.
've | v | | əv | *abreviatura* de **have,** como verbo auxiliar; (lenguaje hablado).
veal | viːl | *s.i.* carne de ternera.
vector | 'vektər | *s.c.* **1** FIS. vector. **2** AER. rumbo.
veer | vɪər | *v.i.* **1** virar, girar, torcer (vehículos). **2** cambiar, variar (de opinión, conversación, postura, etc.). **3** cambiar (la dirección del viento).
veg | vedʒ | *s.pl.* (abreviatura de **vegetable**) (brit. y fam.) verduras, legumbres, hortalizas: *he sells fruit and veg = vende fruta y hortalizas.*
vegan | 'viːgən | | 'viːdʒən | *s.c.* **1** vegetariano. || *adj.* **2** vegetariano: *vegan diet = dieta vegetariana.*
vegetable | 'vedʒtəbl | *s.c.* **1** hortaliza, legumbre, verdura. **2** (fam.) vegetal (persona que ha perdido toda actividad cerebral). | *adj.* **3** vegetal (reino, origen, etc.). || **4 – marrow,** BOT. calabacín.
vegetarian | ˌvedʒɪ'teərɪən | *s.c.* **1** vegetariano. || *adj.* **2** vegetariano.
vegetarianism | ˌvedʒɪ'teərɪənɪzəm | *s.i.* vegetarianismo.
vegetate | 'vedʒɪteɪt | *v.i.* vegetar, no hacer nada.
vegetated | 'vedʒɪteɪtɪd | *adj.* que tiene vegetación.
vegetation | ˌvedʒɪ'teɪʃn | *s.i.* vegetación.
vehemence | 'viːɪməns | *s.i.* vehemencia, pasión, ferocidad.
vehement | 'viːɪmənt | *adj.* vehemente, apasionado, enérgico, violento.
vehemently | 'viːɪməntlɪ | *adv.* vehementemente, apasionadamente, violentamente.
vehicle | 'viːɪkl | *s.c.* **1** (form.) vehículo (de motor). **2** vehículo, medio, instrumento: *a vehicle of communication = un medio de comunicación.*
vehicular | vi'hikjʊlər | *adj.* (form.) de vehículos, rodado (tráfico).
veil | veɪl | *s.c.* **1** velo. **2** velo, halo, bruma, oscuridad, niebla (que oculta o desfigura la realidad). || *v.t.* **3** ocultar, disimular (una situación, sentimientos, etc.). || **4 to draw a – over something,** (form.) correr un tupido velo sobre algo. **5 to take the –,** (lit.) tomar el hábito, meterse a monja. **6 under a – of secrecy,** (form.) en el mayor secreto.
veiled | veɪld | *adj.* **1** cubierto con velo: *a veiled Muslim woman = musulmana cubierta con velo.* **2** velado, indirecto (comentario, crítica, excusa, etc.). **3** (lit.) oculto, escondido, disimulado (expresión, pensamientos, sentimientos, etc.).
vein | vein | *s.c.* **1** vena. **2** veta, filón (de mineral). **3** fibra, hebra, vena (madera). **4** (fig.) rasgo, sombra, toque, tendencia (como característica diferencial): *a vein of melancholy in his character = un toque de melancolía en su carácter.* **5** vena, sentido, clave (estilo de discurso o escrito): *in a humorous vein = en clave de humor.* **6** BIOL. vena.
veined | 'veɪnd | *adj.* **1** de venas muy marcadas. **2 [– (with)]** veteado, jaspeado.
velar | 'viːlər | *adj.* FON. velar.
veldt | velt | | felt | (también **veld**) *s.sing.* llanura, páramo, sabana (en Sudáfrica).
vellum | 'veləm | *s.i.* vitela, pergamino.
velocity | vi'lɒsɪtɪ | *s.c.* e *i.* velocidad.
velour | və'lʊər | *s.i.* fieltro, veludillo.
velvet | 'velvit | *s.i.* **1** terciopelo. || **2 to have an iron fist/hand in a – glove,** esconder un carácter muy fuerte bajo suaves maneras.
velvety | 'velviti | *adj.* **1** aterciopelado. **2** (fig.) suave, dulce (voz).
venal | 'viːnl | *adj.* (form.) venal, sobornable, corrupto.
venality | viː'nælɪti | *s.i.* venalidad, corrupción.
venally | 'viːnəlɪ | *adv.* venalmente.
vend | vend | *v.t.* **1** (form.) vender (pequeños artículos en lugares públicos). **2** DER. vender (fincas, inmuebles, etc.).
vendetta | ven'detə | *s.c.* vendetta, venganza, odio, enemistad.
vending-machine | 'vendiŋ mæˌtʃiːn | *s.c.* máquina expendedora.
vendor | 'vendər | *s.c.* **1** vendedor (en puesto callejero, quiosco, etc.). **2** DER. vendedor (de fincas, inmuebles, etc.).
veneer | və'nɪər | *s.sing.* **1** (fig.) barniz, apariencia, máscara, fachada: *a veneer of scientific objectivity = un barniz de objetividad científica.* || *s.i.* **2** chapeli, contrachapado.
venerable | 'venərəbl | *adj.* **1** venerable, respetable, digno (persona). **2** venerable, admirable, histórico (objetos). **3** REL. venerable.
venerate | 'venəreɪt | *v.t.* (form.) venerar, respetar, reverenciar.
veneration | ˌvenə'reɪʃn | *s.i.* (form.) veneración, reverencia.
venereal | və'nɪərɪəl | *adj.* **1** venéreo. || **2 – disease** (también **VD**), enfermedad venérea.
Venetian blind | veˌniːʃn'blaind | *s.c.* persiana veneciana.
vengeance | 'vendʒəns | *s.i.* **1** venganza. || **2 to take – on someone,** vengarse de alguien. **3 with a –,** (fam.) (producirse algo) con una fuerza o proporción inusual.
vengeful | 'vendʒfl | *adj.* (lit.) vengativo.
vengefully | 'vendʒfəlɪ | *adv.* (lit.) vengativamente.
venial | 'viːniəl | *adj.* (form.) venial, perdonable.
venison | 'venzn | *s.i.* carne de venado.
venom | 'venəm | *s.i.* **1** veneno (de serpientes, escorpiones, arañas, etc.). **2** (fig.) veneno, malicia, intención (en dicho).
venomous | 'venəməs | *adj.* **1** venenoso. **2** (fig.) envenenado, malintencionado, maligno (expresión, conducta, etc.).
venomously | 'venəməslɪ | *adv.* envenenadamente, maliciosamente.
venous | 'viːnəs | *adj.* BIOL. venoso.
vent | vent | *s.c.* **1** respiradero, salida (de gas, humo, etc.). **2** orificio, grieta, escape (de lava, gas, etc.). **3** BIOL. cloaca. || **4 to give (full) – to something, a)** expresar algo (sentimientos) con toda libertad; **b)** desahogarse.
ventilate | 'ventɪleɪt | *v.t.* **1** ventilar. **2** (fig.) (form.) airear, soltar, tratar en público (las propias ideas, sentimientos, etc.).
ventilation | ˌventɪ'leiʃn | *s.i.* ventilación, sistema de ventilación.
ventilator | 'ventɪleɪtər | *s.c.* ventilador.
ventricle | 'ventrɪkl | *s.c.* **1** ANAT. ventrículo.

ventriloquism | ven'trilәkwɪzәm | *s.i.* ventriloquia.
ventriloquist | ven'trilәkwɪst | *s.c.* ventrílocuo.
venture | 'ventʃәr | *s.c.* **1** aventura (empresa difícil, negocio nuevo, viaje arriesgado, etc.). || *v.t.* e *i.* **2** aventurarse, arriesgarse: *to venture into the water = aventurarse a meterse en el agua.* **3** aventurar (una opinión, un juicio, etc.). **4** aventurarse, arriesgarse, atreverse (a hacer algo desagradable): *to venture to visit the doctor = aventurarse a visitar al médico.* **5** aventurar, hacer (una apuesta). || **6 nothing –, nothing gain /win,** quien no se arriesga no pasa la mar. **7 to – on/upon something,** emprender algo arriesgado.
venturesome | 'ventʃәsәm | *adj.* (lit.) arriesgado, atrevido, audaz.
venue | 'venjuː | *s.c.* lugar (de un acontecimiento, reunión, etc.).
veracious | vә'reɪʃәs | *adj.* (form.) veraz, sincero.
veraciously | vә'reɪʃәslɪ | *adv.* (form.) verazmente.
veracity | vә'ræsɪtɪ | *s.i.* (form.) veracidad, sinceridad.
veranda | vә'rændә | (también **verandah**) *s.c.* porche, terraza.
verb | vәːb | *s.c.* GRAM. verbo.
verbal | 'vәːbl | *adj.* **1** verbal (referido a las palabras): *a verbal reasoning test = prueba de razonamiento verbal.* **2** verbal, de palabra: *a verbal attack = una agresión verbal.* **3** literal, palabra por palabra: *a verbal translation = una traducción literal.* **4** GRAM. verbal, del verbo: *the verbal group = el grupo verbal.*
verbally | 'vәːbәlɪ | *adv.* verbalmente, de palabra.
verbalise V. **verbalize.**
verbalize | 'vәːbәlaiz | (también **verbalise**) *v.t.* e *i.* (form.) expresar, decir (con palabras).
verbatim | vәː'beɪtɪm | *adv.* **1** palabra por palabra, al pie de la letra, literalmente. || *adj.* **2** literal, palabra por palabra: *a verbatim quotation = una cita literal.*
verbiage | 'vәːbiidʒ | *s.i.* (form.) verbosidad, palabrería, (Am.) palabrerío.
verbose | vәː'bәʊs | *adj.* (form.) verboso, prolijo, farragoso.
verbosity | vәː'bɒsɪtɪ | *s.i.* (form.) verbosidad; (Am.) palabrerío.
verdant | 'vәːdәnt | *adj.* (lit.) frondoso, verde, fresco.
verdict | 'vәːdɪkt | *s.c.* **1** veredicto, sentencia, fallo (de un jurado). **2** (fig.) opinión, juicio, resolución (tras ponderado examen, experimentación, etc.).
verdigris | 'vәːdɪgrɪs | *s.i.* cardenillo, verdete.
verdure | 'vәːdʒәr | *s.c.* (lit.) verdor, verdura.
verge | vәːdʒ | *s.c.* **1** borde, margen, orilla: *we walked along the grass verge = caminábamos por el borde de la carretera.* || **2 on the – of,** a punto de, a un paso de. **3 to – on/upon something,** bordear, rayar, estar cercano, rozar: *the situation verges on the chaotic = la situación roza lo caótico.*
verger | 'vәːdʒәr | *s.c.* **1** sacristán (en la Iglesia Anglicana). **2** (brit.) macero.
verifiable | 'verɪfaɪәbl | *adj.* verificable, comprobable.
verification | ˌverɪfɪ'keɪʃn | *s.i.* comprobación, verificación, confirmación.
verify | 'verɪfaɪ | *v.t.* comprobar, verificar, confirmar.
verily | 'verәlɪ | *adv.* (arc.) verdaderamente, ciertamente.
verisimilitude | ˌverɪsɪ'mɪlɪtjuːd | *s.i.* (form.) verosimilitud.
veritable | 'verɪtәbl | *adj.* (form.) auténtico, verdadero: *a veritable disaster = un auténtico desastre.*
verity | 'verɪtɪ | *s.i.* **1** (arc.) verdad. || *s.c.* **2** (form.) verdad, fundamento, principio básico (admitido como cierto): *the eternal verities = las verdades eternas.*
vermicelli | ˌvәːmɪ'selɪ | *s.i.* fideos.
vermilion | vә'mɪlɪәn | *s.i.* **1** bermellón. || *adj.* **2** bermejo.
vermin | 'vәːmɪn | *s.pl.* **1** bichos, sabandijas. **2** (fig.) sabandijas, peste (personas): *football hooligans are vermin = los hinchas alborotadores son una peste.*
verminous | 'vәːmɪnәs | *adj.* infestado (de parásitos), piojoso, pulgoso.
vermouth | 'vәːmәθ | *s.i.* vermut.
vernacular | vә'nækjʊlәr | *s.c.* **1** lengua vernácula, idioma local. **2** arquitectura popular, construcción sencilla. || *adj.* **3** vernáculo, local, ordinario, corriente, vulgar.
vernal | 'vәːnl | *adj.* (lit.) primaveral, de primavera.
veronica | vә'rɒnikә | *s.c.* e *i.* BOT. verónica.
verruca | vә'ruːkә | *s.c.* verruga, callo, papiloma.
versatile | 'vәːsәtaɪl | *adj.* **1** polifacético, habilidoso, flexible. **2** multiuso, polivalente, adaptable (máquina, objeto).
versatility | ˌvәːsә'tɪlɪtɪ | *s.i.* polivalencia, habilidad, multiuso.
verse | vәːs | *s.i.* **1** verso, poesía. || *s.c.* **2** verso, línea (de un poema o canción). **3** versículo (de la Biblia).
versed | vәːst | *adj.* **[– (in)]** (form.) versado, entendido, experto.
versification | ˌvәːsɪfɪ'keɪʃn | *s.i.* versificación.
versifier | 'vәːsɪfaɪәr | *s.c.* versificador.
versify | 'vәːsɪfaɪ | *v.t.* e *i.* versificar, poner en verso.
version | 'vәːʃn | *s.c.* **1** versión, copia, variante: *the original version of a play = la versión original de una comedia.* **2** versión, adaptación: *the film version of a novel = la versión cinematográfica de una novela.* **3** versión, descripción (de un hecho): *contradictory versions of an event = versiones contradictorias de un hecho.* **4** traducción, versión.
verso | 'vәːsәʊ | *s.c.* (form.) verso, página par.
versus | 'vәːsәs | *prep.* contra, en oposición a, frente a.
vertebra | 'vәːtɪbrә | *s.c.* [*pl.irreg.* **vertebrae**] ANAT. vértebra.
vertebrae | 'vәːtɪbriː | *pl.irreg.* de **vertebra.**
vertebral | 'vәːtɪbrәl | *adj.* vertebral.
vertebrate | 'vәːtɪbrɪt | *s.c.* **1** BIOL. vertebrado. || *adj.* **2** vertebrado.
vertex | 'vәːteks | *s.c.* [*pl.* **vertexes** o **vertices**] GEOM. vértice.
vertical | 'vәːtɪkl | *adj.* **1** vertical. **2** vertical, jerárquico, autoritario (estructura, organización, etc.). || *s.c.* **3** vertical.
vertically | 'vәːtɪkәlɪ | *adv.* verticalmente.
vertices | 'vәːtɪsiːz | *pl.irreg.* de **vertex.**
vertiginous | vәː'tɪdʒɪnәs | *adj.* (form.) vertiginoso, de vértigo, que causa vértigo: *vertiginous heights = alturas de vértigo.*
vertigo | 'vәːtɪgәʊ | *s.i.* vértigo.
verve | vәːv | *s.i.* brío, vigor, fuerza (de obra artística).
very | 'verɪ | *adv.* **1** muy. **2** muy, realmente: *he seemed very English = parecía realmente inglés.* **3** **[– *super.*]** (para dar énfasis): *the very best quality = la mejor calidad.* || *adj.* **4** absoluto, exacto, mismo, del todo: *from the very top = desde arriba del todo.* **5** exacto, preciso, mismo, textual: *they're his very words = son sus mismas palabras.* || **6 not –,** no en absoluto, ni mucho menos. **7 of one's – own,** de uno mismo, auténticamente suyo. **8 (someone) cannot – well do something, a)** no poder realmente hacer una cosa; **b)** no estar bien hacer una cosa. **9 the – thing,** justo lo que se buscaba, necesitaba, etc. **10 – good,** (form.) muy bien, de acuerdo. **11 – high frequency,** V. **VHF. 12 – much so,** así es, pues sí. **13 – well,** muy bien, de acuerdo, como usted quiera.
vesicle | 'vesɪkl | *s.c.* MED. vesícula, ampolla.
vespers | 'vespәz | *s.pl.* REL. vísperas.
vessel | 'vesl | *s.c.* **1** (form.) barco, buque, embarcación. **2** (lit.) vaso, cuenco, vasija. **3** vaso (sanguíneo o de savia).
vest | vest | *s.i.* **1** (brit.) camiseta. **2** (EE.UU.) chaleco. || *v.i.* **3** pertenecer (por derecho): *that power vested in the Church = esa potestad perteneció a la Iglesia.* **3** REL. ponerse los ornamentos sagrados.
vestal | 'vestl | *adj.* **1** vestal. || **2 – virgin, a)** vestal; **b)** (fam. y desp.) mujer que renuncia al sexo.
vested | 'vestɪd | *adj.* **1** **[– (in)]** concedido, depositado, encomendado (derecho, autoridad, responsabilidad): *the authority vested in him by the government = la autoridad que le tiene encomendada el gobierno.* || **2 – interest(s),** intereses creados.
vestibule | 'vestɪbjuːl | *s.c.* vestíbulo, zaguán.
vestige | 'vestɪdʒ | *s.c.* (dorm.) vestigio, rastro, resto.

vestigial | ve'stɪdʒɪəl | *adj.* (form.) **1** preservado, residual. **2** atrofiado, rudimentario, inútil.
vestments | 'vestmənts | *s.pl.* ornamentos (sagrados).
vestry | 'vestrɪ | *s.c.* sacristía.
vet | vet | *s.c.* **1** (también **veterinary surgeon**) (brit. y fam.) veterinario. **2** (EE.UU. y fam.) veterano (de guerra). || *v.t.* **[vetted, vetted] 3** revisar, examinar, comprobar. **4** someter a prueba (para funciones militares o políticas).
vetch | vetʃ | *s.i.* BOT. arveja, algarroba, (Am.) guisante.
veteran | 'vetərən | *s.c.* (también EE.UU. **vet**) veterano, licenciado (de guerra o de las fuerzas armadas), ex combatiente. **2** antiguo, ex-: *a veteran blood donor; ex donante de sangre.* **3** veterano, experimentado, avezado: *a veteran politician = político experimentado.* || **4 – car,** (brit.) coche antiguo (fabricado antes de 1916).
veterinarian | ˌvetəri'neəriən | *s.c.* (EE.UU.) veterinario.
veterinary | 'vetərinəri | *adj.* **1** veterinario: *veterinary studies = estudios veterinarios.* || **2 – surgeon,** (form.) veterinario.
veto | 'viːtəu | *s.c.* e *i.* [*pl.irreg.* **vetoes**] **1** veto, derecho de veto. || *v.t.* **[vetoed, vetoes, vetoing]** vetar, prohibir.
vetting | 'vetɪŋ | *s.i.* examen, prueba (para ejercer funciones de seguridad).
vex | veks | *v.t.* (form.) molestar, irritar, contrariar.
vexation | vek'seɪʃn | *s.c.* e i. (form.) molestia, irritación, aflicción.
vexed | vekst | *adj.* **1** molesto, enfadado, contrariado. **2** difícil, controvertido, inquietante (problema, pregunta, etc.).
vexing | 'veksɪŋ | *adj.* molesto, desagradable, sorprendente.
v.g. | viː 'dʒiː | *abreviatura* (de **very good**) muy bien (en ejercicios escolares escritos).
VHF | ˌviː eɪtʃ 'ef | *siglas* (de **very high frequency**) RAD. VHF, frecuencia muy alta.
via | 'vaɪə | *prep.* vía, a través de, por medio de.
viable | 'vaɪəbl | *adj.* **1** viable, posible, realizable. **2** BIOL. viable (feto, embrión, etc.).
viability | ˌvaɪə'bɪlɪtɪ | *s.i.* viabilidad, posibilidad.
viaduct | 'vaɪədʌkt | *s.c.* viaducto.
vial | 'vaɪəl | *s.c.* (form.) frasco, ampolla, redoma.
viands | 'vaɪəndz | *s.pl.* (arc.) viandas.
vibes | vaɪbz | *s.pl.* (fam.) **1** vibraciones, emociones, sensaciones (de uno consigo mismo o con lo que le rodea): *to get good vibes = tener buenas vibraciones* (sentirse bien). **2** vibráfono (jazz).
vibrancy | 'vaɪbrənsɪ | *s.i.* brío, vitalidad, energía, empuje.
vibrant | 'vaɪbrənt | *adj.* **1** vibrante, vivo, dinámico, apasionante. **2** vibrante, resonante (voz, sonido). **3** vibrante, vivo, brillante (luz, color).
vibraphone | 'vaɪbrəfəun | *s.c.* MUS. vibráfono.
vibrate | vaɪ'breɪt | (EE.UU.) | 'vaibreit | *v.i.* vibrar.
vibration | vaɪ'breɪʃn | *s.c.* e *i.* vibración.
vibrato | vi'brɑːtəu | *s.c.* e *i.* MUS. vibrato.
vibrator | vaɪ'breɪtər | *s.c.* vibrador.
vicar | 'vɪkər | *s.c.* **1** párroco, cura (Iglesia Anglicana). **2** vicario, delegado, representante.
vicarage | 'vɪkərɪdʒ | *s.c.* casa del cura, vicaría.
vicarious | vɪ'keərɪəs | (EE.UU.) | vai'-keəriəs | *adj.* **1** delegado, indirecto, experimentado por otro, sucedáneo: *vicarious pleasure = placer sentido ante el que otro experimenta.* **2** dado, sentido, experimentado, etc. (en el lugar de otra persona): *vicarious punishment = castigo sufrido por otro.*
vicariously | vɪ'keərɪəslɪ | *adv.* indirectamente, de rebote, en lugar de otro, por cuenta ajena.
vice | vaɪs | *s.i.* **1** vicio, corrupción, inmoralidad: *a campaign against vice and violence = campaña contra el vicio y la violencia.* || *s.c.* **2** vicio, falta, debilidad: *her main vice is smoking = su mayor vicio es fumar.* **3** (EE.UU. **vise**) MEC. tornillo de banco. || **4 vice-,** vice- (seguido de un rango, título, cargo, etc.). **5 – squad,** brigada antivicio. **6 – versa,** viceversa, al revés
vice-chancellor | ˌvaɪs'tʃɑːnsələr | *s.c.* rector (de una universidad británica).
viceroy | 'vaɪsrɔɪ | *s.c.* virrey.
vicinity | vɪ'sɪnɪtɪ | *s.sing.* **1** vecindad, proximidad, cercanía, alrededores, barrio. || **2 in the – of,** (form.) cerca de, entorno a.
vicious | 'vɪʃəs | *adj.* **1** cruel, violento, desalmado, malintencionado (acción, mirada, comentario, etc.). **2** vicioso, depravado: *a vicious life = una vida depravada.* **3** salvaje, fiero, feroz, peligroso (animales). **4** (fam.) violento, terrible, severo: *a vicious wind = un viento terrible.* || **5 – circle,** círculo vicioso. **6 – spiral,** espiral (de violencia, de inflación, etc.).
viciously | 'vɪʃəslɪ | *adv.* cruelmente, violentamente, salvajemente.
viciousness | 'vɪʃəsnɪs | *s.i.* crueldad, violencia, depravación.
vicissitudes | vɪ'sɪsɪtjuːdz | (EE.UU.) | vɪ'sɪsɪtuːdz | *s.pl.* (form.) vicisitudes, peripecias, altibajos.
victim | 'vɪktɪm | *s.c.* **1** víctima (de un accidente, agresión, etc.). || **2 to fall – of something,** caer víctima de algo, sucumbir.
victimise V. **victimize.**
victimize | 'vɪktɪmaɪz | (también **victimise**) *s.c.* hacer víctima, castigar, perseguir, tomarla con alguien.
victimization | ˌvɪktɪmaɪ'zeɪʃn | *s.i.* persecución, castigo, malos tratos.
victor | 'vɪktər | *s.c.* (arc.) vencedor, héroe (de guerra).
Victorian | vɪk'tɔːrɪən | *adj.* **1** victoriano. || *s.c.* **2** victoriano.
Victoriana | vɪkˌtɔrɪ'ɑːnə | *s.i.* antigüedades de la época victoriana.
victorious | vɪk'tɔːrɪəs | *adj.* victorioso, vencedor, triunfante.
victoriously | vik'tɔːrɪəslɪ | *adv.* victoriosamente, triunfantemente.
victory | 'vɪktərɪ | *s.c.* e *i.* victoria (en batalla, competición, juego).
victual | 'vɪtl | *v.t.* e *i.* **1** abastecer, avituallar. || **2 victuals,** (arc.) víveres, provisiones, vitualla.
video | 'vidiəu | *s.i.* **1** vídeo, grabación, proyección (de material de vídeo). || *s.c.* **2** vídeo, aparato de vídeo, cinta de vídeo. || *v.t.* **3** grabar en vídeo. || **4 – cassette,** cassette de vídeo. **5 – recorder/– cassette recorder,** aparato de vídeo, grabadora de vídeo. **6 – game,** vídeo juego. **7 video nasty,** (fam.) vídeo con imágenes violentas.
video-tape | 'vɪdɪəuˌteɪp | *s.c.* e *i.* **1** cinta de vídeo. || *v.t.* **2** grabar en vídeo.
vie | vaɪ | *v.i.* [*ger.* **vying**] **[to – (with)]** (form.) competir, disputar: *rivals vying with each other for the first place = rivales disputándose el primer puesto.*
view | vjuː | *s.i.* **1** vista, visión: *the sun disappear from view = el sol desapareció de la vista.* | *s.c.* **2** vista, panorama, paisaje: *a marvellous view from the window = una vista preciosa desde la ventana.* **3** opinión, parecer, sentir, visión: *that's my view on the problem = ésa es mi opinión.* **4** visión, observación, inspección: *a private view of the jewels = una visión privada de las joyas.* || *v.t.* **5** (form.) ver, considerar, mirar, contemplar: *he views the future with interest = ve el futuro con interés.* **6** mirar, observar: *he viewed the battle from the top = observó la batalla desde lo alto.* **7** ver, inspeccionar (con idea de comprar). **8** (form.) ver (un programa de televisión, un vídeo, etc.). || **9 to come into –,** ponerse a la vista, aparecer. **10 in full –,** bien visible. **11 in my –,** (form.) en mi opinión. **12 in –, a)** a la vista, visible; **b)** en perspectiva, en proyecto; **c)** como objetivo, pensando en. **13 in – of,** a la vista de, considerando. **14 on –,** expuesto. **15 to take a dim/poor – of something,** (fam.) desaprobar, condenar algo. **16 to take the long –,** mirar a largo plazo. **17 to take the – that,** creer, dar por cierto que. **18 with a – to (doing something),** (form.) con la intención/la esperanza de (hacer algo).
viewer | vjuːər | *s.c.* **1** televidente, espectador, observador. **2** visor de aumento (para diapositivas).
viewfinder | 'vjuːˌfaɪndər | *s.c.* visor de imagen.
viewpoint | 'vjuːpɔɪnt | *s.c.* **1** punto de vista, opinión. **2** mirador.
vigil | 'vɪdʒɪl | *s.c.* vigilia, vela, guardia.
vigilance | 'vɪdʒɪləns | *s.i.* (form.) vigilancia.
vigilant | 'vɪdʒɪlənt | *adj.* (form.) vigilante, alerta.

vigilante | ˌvɪdʒi'læntɪ | *s.c.* vigilante, patrullero (espontáneo).
vignette | vɪ'njet | *s.c.* viñeta, ilustración.
vigor V. **vigour.**
vigorous | 'vɪgərəs | *adj.* **1** vigoroso, decidido, enérgico (acción). **2** activo, vivo, entusiasta, acalorado (actividad, campaña, etc.). **3** fuerte, robusto (persona). **4** entusiasta, convencido, apasionado (persona).
vigorously | 'vɪgərəslɪ | *adv.* enérgicamente, decididamente, con vigor.
vigour | 'vɪgər | (EE.UU. **vigor**) *s.i.* energía, vigor, entusiasmo, vitalidad.
Viking | 'vaɪkɪŋ | *s.c.* **1** vikingo. || *adj.* **2** vikingo.
vile | vaɪl | *adj.* vil, horrible, detestable, asqueroso.
vilely | 'vaɪlɪ | *adv.* vilmente, horriblemente, detestablemente.
vilification | ˌvɪlɪfɪ'keɪʃn | *s.i.* (form.) vilipendio, difamación.
vilify | 'vɪlɪfaɪ | *v.t.* (form.) vilipendiar, difamar.
villa | 'vɪlə | *s.c.* chalet, quinta, casa de campo, villa.
village | 'vɪlɪdʒ | *s.c.* pueblo, aldea.
villager | 'vɪlɪdər | *s.c.* aldeano.
villain | 'vɪlən | *s.c.* **1** villano, malvado. **2** (fam.) malhechor, criminal (lenguaje policial). **3** (fam.) canalla, bribón. **4** malo, villano, antagonista (novela, teatro, etc.). || **5 the – of the piece,** (hum.) el malo de la película.
villainous | 'vɪlənəs | *adj.* malvado, perverso, vil, horrible.
villainously | 'vɪlənəslɪ | *adv.* malvadamente, vilmente, horriblemente.
villainy | 'vɪlənɪ | *s.c.* e *i.* villanía, maldad, vileza, perversidad.
villein | 'vɪlɪn | *s.c.* villano (medieval).
vim | vɪm | *s.i.* (arc.) energía, vigor.
vinaigrette | ˌvɪneɪ'gret | *s.i.* vinagreta.
vindicate | 'vɪndɪkeɪt | *v.t.* (form.) vindicar, justificar, resarcir.
vindication | ˌvɪndɪ'keɪʃn | *s.i.* vindicación, justificación.
vindictive | vɪn'dɪktɪv | *adj.* vengativo, rencoroso.
vindictively | vɪn'dɪktɪvlɪ | *adv.* vengativamente, rencorosamente.
vindictiveness | vɪn'dɪktɪvnɪs | *s.i.* deseo de venganza, rencor.
vine | vaɪn | *s.c.* **1** vid, parra. **2** parra, planta (de tallos trepadores).
vinegar | 'vɪnɪgər | *s.i.* vinagre.
vinegary | 'vɪnɪgəri | *adj.* **1** avinagrado. **2** irritable, colérico, malhumorado, malhablado.
vineyard | 'vɪnjəd | *s.c.* viña, viñedo, majuelo.
vintage | 'vɪntɪdʒ | *s.c.* **1** vendimia. **2** cosecha, añada: *a rare vintage = cosecha extraordinaria.* || *adj.* **3** selecto, de buena añada, de crianza (vino). **4** (fig.) de solera, típico, clásico, de lo mejor: *a vintage Chaplin film = una película de lo mejor de Chaplin.* **5** (brit.) de los años veinte (coche).
vintner | 'vɪntnər | *s.c.* vinatero.
vinyl | 'vaɪnɪl | *s.i.* **1** vinilo. || *atr.* **2** de vinilo.
viola | vɪ'əʊlə | *s.c.* MUS. viola.
violate | 'vaɪəleɪt | *v.t.* **1** violar, quebrantar, infringir (acuerdo, ley, promesa, etc.). **2** violar, invadir, perturbar (paz, privacidad, etc.). **3** violar, violentar, saquear (tumbas). **4** (form.) violar (a una persona).
violation | ˌvaɪə'leɪʃn | *s.c.* e *i.* violación, infracción, perturbación.
violator | 'vaɪəleɪtər | *s.c.* violador.
violence | 'vaɪələns | *s.i.* **1** violencia (acciones que matan o hieren). **2** violencia, furia, rabia (dichos o hechos motivados por el enfado). **3** violencia, daño, agresión (de palabra o hecho). || **4 to do – to something,** (form.) violentar, ser contrario a algo: *it would do violence to my principles = sería contrario a mis principios.*
violent | 'vaɪələnt | *adj.* **1** violento, agresivo, brutal. **2** violento, doloroso, anormal (muerte). **3** violento, vehemente, apabullante (discurso, argumentación). **4** violento, repentino, paralizante, sobrecogedor. **5** violento, fuerte, intenso, brutal (sensación, emoción, etc.). **6** violento, radical, drástico (cambio). **7** chillón (color). **8** desapacible, tormentoso (tiempo).
violently | 'vaɪələntlɪ | *adv.* violentamente, brutalmente.
violet | 'vaɪəlɪt | *s.i.* **1** violeta, violado, violáceo (color). || *s.c.* **2** BOT. violeta. || *adj.* **3** violeta, violado, violáceo. || **4 a shrinking –,** (fam.) mosquita muerta (mujer, generalmente).
violin | ˌvaɪə'lɪn | *s.c.* violín.
violinist | 'vaɪəlɪnɪst | *s.c.* violinista.
VIP | ˌviː aɪ 'piː | *siglas* (de **very important person**) VIP, persona famosa o influyente.
viper | 'vaɪpər | *s.c.* **1** víbora. **2** (form.) víbora, traidor.
viperish | 'vaɪpərɪʃ | *adj.* viperino, malvado (lengua, dicho).
virago | vɪ'rɑːgəʊ | *s.c.* (arc.) arpía, fiera.
viral | 'vaɪərəl | *adj.* vírico.
virgin | 'vɜːdʒɪn | *s.c.* **1** virgen (mujer, generalmente). **2** REL. (la) Virgen. || *adj.* **3** virgen. **4** virgen, nuevo, original, natural, puro (lana, nieve, etc.). **5** virgen, salvaje, sin explorar, sin cultivar (tierra).
virginal | 'vɜːdʒɪnl | *adj.* **1** virginal, puro, casto, incólume. **2** prístino, nuevo, intacto. || *s.c.* **3** MUS. virginal.
virile | 'vɪraɪl | (EE.UU.) | 'vɪrəl | *adj.* **1** viril. **2** varonil, fuerte, enérgico, de hombres.
virility | vɪ'rɪlɪtɪ | *s.i.* virilidad, hombría.
virology | ˌvaɪə'rɒlədʒɪ | *s.i.* virología.
virtual | 'vɜːtʃʊəl | *adj.* virtual, efectivo.
virtually | 'vɜːtʊəlɪ | *adv.* virtualmente, prácticamente, casi.
virtue | 'vɜːtjuː | | 'vɜːtʃuː | *s.i.* **1** virtud, bondad, moralidad. **2** (hum.) castidad, reputación (femenina). || *s.c.* **3** virtud, ventaja, tanto a favor. || **4 by – of,** (form.) en virtud de, debido a. **5 to make a – of necessity,** hacer de buena gana la obligación. **6 – is its own reward,** en la virtud está la recompensa.
virtuosi | ˌvɜːtjʊ'əʊziː | *pl.* de **virtuoso.**
virtuoso | ˌvɜːtjʊ'əʊzəʊ | *s.c.* [pl. **virtuosos** o **virtuosi**] virtuoso, experto, maestro (de un instrumento musical, principalmente).
virtuosity | ˌvɜːtju'ɒsɪtɪ | *s.i.* virtuosismo.
virtuous | 'vɜːtʃʊəs | *adj.* **1** virtuoso, bueno, justo. **2** (desp.) virtuoso (pagado de su virtud). **3** (arc.) virtuoso, casto, púdico (mujer).
virulence | 'vɪrʊləns | *s.i.* **1** (form.) virulencia, hostilidad. **2** arraigo, fortaleza, pervivencia (para seguir causando daño). **3** virulencia, agresividad, gravedad (enfermedad, veneno, etc.).
virulent | 'vɪrʊlənt | *adj.* **1** virulento, hostil, enconado (acción, dicho o sentimiento). **2** virulento, maligno, grave (enfermedad, veneno, etc.). **3** agresivo, fuerte, llamativo, desagradable (color).
virulently | 'vɪrʊləntlɪ | *adv.* virulentamente, hostilmente, gravemente.
virus | 'vaɪərəs | *s.c.* **1** virus. **2** (fig.) virus (idea, escrito, etc. que puede causar daño).
visa | 'viːzə | *s.c.* visado.
visage | 'vɪzɪdʒ | *s.c.* (form.) semblante, rostro.
vis-à-vis | 'viːzəːviː | *prep.* con relación a, respecto de.
viscera | 'vɪsərə | *s.pl.* ANAT. vísceras.
visceral | 'vɪsərəl | *adj.* instintivo, irracional, visceral (sentimiento).
viscose | 'vɪskəʊz | *s.i.* QUIM. viscosa.
viscosity | vɪ'skɒsɪtɪ | *s.i.* viscosidad.
viscount | 'vaɪcaʊnt | *s.c.* vizconde.
viscountess | 'vaɪkaʊntɪs | *s.c.* vizcondesa.
viscous | 'vɪskəs | *adj.* viscoso, espeso, glutinoso.
vise | vaɪs | V. **vice.**
visibility | ˌvɪzɪ'bɪlɪtɪ | *s.i.* visibilidad.
visible | 'vɪzəbl | *adj.* visible, detectable, evidente, obvio.
visibly | 'vɪzəblɪ | *adv.* visiblemente, evidentemente, obviamente.
vision | 'viʒn | *s.i.* **1** vista. **2** visión, perspectiva (de futuro). **3** visión, imagen (televisión). || *s.c.* **4** visión, idea, imagen: *the vision of a new nation = la visión de una nación nueva.* **5** visión, aparición, alucinación. **6** (lit.) persona, paisaje bello.
visionary | 'vɪʒnərɪ | *s.c.* **1** visionario, sabio. || *adj.* **2** imaginativo, carismático. **3** fantástico, etéreo, soñado.
visit | 'vɪzɪt | *v.t.* **1** visitar (lugares, personas). **2** visitar, consultar (a profesionales). **3** visitar (pacientes, clientes, etc.). **4** visitar, inspeccionar, examinar (de forma oficial). **5** [pasiva] (arc.) afectar, atormentar: *he was visited by a terrible dream = le atormentó un sueño espantoso.* **6** [pasiva] (arc.) recaer, afec-

tar (como herencia negativa). || *s.c.* **7** visita, consulta. **8** viaje, visita: *a brief visit to the U.S. = un rápido viaje a EE.UU.* **9** (EE.UU. y fam.) charla. || **10 visiting card,** (brit.) tarjeta de visita. **11 visiting hours,** horas de visita (hospital). **12 visiting professor,** profesor visitante. **13 to – with someone,** (EE.UU.) visitar a alguien y quedarse algún tiempo.

visitation | ˌvɪzɪ'teɪʃn | *s.c.* **1** (form.) visita, inspección. **2** (fam.) visita (no deseada). **3** (form.) castigo (por los pecados).

visitor | 'vɪzɪtər | *s.c.* visitante, turista, huésped.

visor | 'vaɪzər | *s.c.* visera (de motorista, de coche, etc.).

vista | 'vɪstə | *s.c.* **1** (lit.) visita, panorama. **2** visión, perspectiva, horizonte, posibilidad.

visual | 'vɪzjuəl | *adj.* **1** visual: *visual arts = artes visuales.* || **2 – aid(s),** material instrumental visual (para transmitir información). **3 – display unit, V. VDU.**

visualisation V. **visualization.**

visualization | ˌvɪzjuəlaɪ'zeɪʃn | (EE.UU.) | ˌvɪzjuəlɪ'zeɪʃn | (también **visualisation**) *s.i.* visualización.

visualize | 'vɪzjuəlaɪz | *v.t.* (también **visualise**) visualizar.

visually | 'vɪzjuəlɪ | *adv.* visualmente.

vital | 'vaɪtl | *adj.* **1** vital, crucial, esencial, trascendental, decisivo. **2** activo, dinámico, vital. || **3 the vitals,** (arc.) **a)** partes vitales (del cuerpo); **b)** genitales. **4 – statistics, a)** estadísticas demográficas; **b)** (brit. y fam.) medidas corporales (de una mujer).

vitality | vaɪ'tælɪtɪ | *s.i.* **1** vitalidad, energía, vigor. **2** vida, existencia, continuidad (de una institución).

vitally | 'vaɪtəlɪ | *adv.* vitalmente, crucialmente, esencialmente.

vitamin | 'vɪtəmɪn | (EE.UU.) | 'vaɪtəmɪn | *s.c.* vitamina.

vitiate | 'vɪʃɪeɪt | *v.t.* (form.) **1** viciar, debilitar, rebajar (calidad, eficacia). **2** quitar valor, dejar sin efecto (contratos, reclamaciones, teorías, etc.).

viticulture | 'vɪtɪkʌltʃər | *s.i.* viticultura.

vitreous | 'vɪtrɪəs | *adj.* vítreo.

vitriol | 'vɪtrɪəl | *s.i.* **1** (arc.) QUIM. vitriolo. **2** (fig.) comentario corrosivo, crítica mordaz.

vitriolic | ˌvɪtrɪ'ɒlɪk | *adj.* vitriólico, hostil, corrosivo, mordaz.

vituperate | vɪ'tjuːpəreɪt | (EE.UU.) | vaɪ'tuːpəreɪt | *v.i.* **[to – (against)]** (form.) vituperar, hacer comentarios injuriosos.

vituperation | vɪˌtjuːpə'reɪʃn | (EE.UU.) | vaɪˌtuːpə'reɪʃn | *s.i.* (form.) vituperio, baldón, afrenta.

vituperative | vi'tjuːpərətiv | (EE.UU.) | vaɪ'tuːpərətɪv | *adj.* (form.) injurioso, insultante.

viva | 'vaɪvə | *s.c.* (también **viva voce**) **1** examen oral (en universidad). || | 'viːvə | *interj.* **2** ¡viva!

vivacious | vɪ'veɪʃəs | *adj.* vivaz, atractivo, alegre, animoso (mujer).

vivaciously | vɪ'veɪʃəslɪ | *adv.* vivazmente, alegremente, animosamente.

vivacity | vɪ'væsɪtɪ | *s.i.* vivacidad, animación, atractivo.

vivid | 'vɪvɪd | *adj.* **1** fuerte, brillante, deslumbrante (luz, color). **2** vivo, brillante, portentoso (memoria, imaginación). **3** intenso, vivo, gráfico.

vividly | 'vɪvɪdlɪ | *adv.* vivamente, intensamente, brillantemente.

vividness | 'vɪvɪdnɪs | *s.i.* vivacidad, intensidad.

vivisection | ˌvɪvɪ'sekʃn | *s i.* vivisección.

vivisectionist | ˌvɪvɪ'sekʃnɪst | *s.c.* **1** viviseccionador. **2** partidario de la experimentación en animales.

vixen | 'vɪksn | *s.c.* **1** ZOOL. zorra. **2** (fig. y arc.) arpía.

viz | vɪz | *abreviatura* (del latín *videlicet*) a saber.

vizier | vɪ'zɪər | *s.c.* visir.

V-neck | viː'nek | *s.c.* **1** cuello en uve (jersey). || *atr.* **2** de cuello en uve.

vocabulary | vəʊ'kæbjulərɪ | *s.c.* e *i.* vocabulario.

vocal | 'vəʊkl | *adj.* **1** vocal, de la voz: *the vocal organs = los órganos vocales.* **2** chillón, gritón, ruidoso: *a small but vocal minority = una exigua pero ruidosa minoría.* **3** de voz, vocal: *the vocal range of a singer = la extensión de voz de un cantante.* || *s.c.* **4** voz, canto, parte cantada: *who's singing lead vocals? = ¿quién canta la voz principal?* **5 – cords/chords,** cuerdas vocales.

vocalist | 'vəʊkəlɪst | *s.c.* cantante, vocalista.

vocalize | 'vəʊkəlaɪz | (también **vocalise**) *v.t.* e *i.* (form.) decir, vocalizar, pronunciar.

vocally | 'vəʊkəlɪ | *adv.* vocalmente, ruidosamente, a voces.

vocation | vəʊ'keɪʃn | *s.c.* e *i.* **1** vocación (sentimiento de llamada, aptitud para una actividad): *little vocation for teaching = poca vocación para la enseñanza.* **2** vocación, profesión, carrera: *you've missed your vocation = te has equivocado de carrera.*

vocational | vəʊ'keɪʃənl | *adj.* profesional.

vocationally | vəʊ'keɪʃnəlɪ | *adv.* profesionalmente.

vocative | 'vɒkətɪv | *s.c.* GRAM. vocativo.

vociferate | vəʊ'sɪfəreɪt | *v.t.* e *i.* (form.) vociferar.

vociferous | vəʊ'sɪfərəs | *adj.* vociferante, vocinglero, ruidoso, chillón.

vociferously | vəʊ'sɪfərəslɪ | *adv.* a gritos, clamorosamente.

vodka | 'vɒdkə | *s.i.* vodka.

vogue | vəʊg | *s.c.* **1** boga, moda, actualidad, aceptación popular. || **2 to be all the –,** (fam.) estar de moda. **3 in –,** en boga, de actualidad.

vogue-word | 'vəʊgwəːd | *s.c.* palabra de moda.

voice | vɔis | *s.c.* **1** voz. **2** voz, habla (capacidad de hablar). **3** voz (calidad musical). **4** voz, opinión, parecer. **5** voz, derecho a opinar. **6** voz, autoridad, influencia. **7** (lit.) voz, murmullo, ruido (del mar, del viento). **8** GRAM. voz. || *v.t.* **9** vociferar, gritar, decir a voces. || **10 at the top of one's –,** gritando todo lo que uno puede. **11 to find one's –,** vencer los obstáculos (miedo, nervios, etc.) que impiden hablar. **12 to have no – in a matter,** no tener voz en un asunto. **13 to give – (to something),** (form.) manifestar (sentimientos, preocupación) en voz alta. **14 to keep one's – down,** hablar bajo. **15 to lower one's –,** bajar la voz (para no ser oído). **16 to raise one's –, a)** elevar la voz (por enfado, generalmente); **b)** hacer pública una opinión. **17 with one –,** (form.) a una voz, unánimemente, todos de acuerdo.

voiced | vɔist | *adj.* FON. sonoro.

voiceless | 'vɔɪslɪs | *adj.* **1** sin voz, mudo, afónico. **2** FON. sordo.

voice-over | 'vɔisəʊvər | *s.c.* narración en off (en películas).

void | 'vɔid | *s.c.* **1** vacío, hueco, espacio. **2** vacío, desolación, tristeza (por pérdida, muerte, etc.). **3** vacío, desocupado, desprovisto. **6** DER. sin valor, sin efecto, nulo (contrato, acuerdo, etc.). || *v.t.* **7** (form.) evacuar (el intestino). **8** DER. invalidar, anular.

voile | vɔil | *s.i.* gasa.

vol | vɒl | *abreviatura* (de **volume**) vol., volumen.

volatile | 'vɒlətaɪl | *adj.* **1** inestable, mudable, volátil (situación). **2** inconstante, imprevisible, volátil, voluble (persona). **3** QUIM. volátil.

volatility | ˌvɒlə'tiːlɪtɪ | *s.i.* volatilidad, mudabilidad, inestabilidad.

vol-au-vent | 'vɒləuvaːŋ | *s.c.* pastelillo de hojalre relleno de carne, pescado, etc.

volcanic | vɒl'kænɪk | *adj.* **1** volcánico. **2** (fig.) violento, repentino.

volcano | vɒl'keɪnəʊ | *s.c.* [*pl.* **volcanoes**] volcán.

vole | vəʊl | *s.c.* ZOOL. campañol.

volition | vəʊ'lɪʃn | *s.i.* (form.) **1** deseo, voluntad. || **2 of one's own –,** por propia voluntad.

volley | 'vɒlɪ | *s.c.* **1** descarga, ráfaga, salva. **2** salva, lluvia (de objetos lanzados). **3** torrente, retahíla (de palabras, preguntas, etc.). **4** DEP. volea (tenis, fútbol). || *v.t.* **5** DEP. golpear de volea, volear.

volleyball | 'vɒlɪbɔːl | *s.i.* balonvolea.

volt | vəult | *s.c.* voltio.

voltage | 'vəʊltidʒ | *s.c.* e *i.* voltaje.

volte-face | ˌvɒlt'fɑːs | *s.sing.* (lit.) cambio total (de parecer).

volubility | ˌvɒlju'bɪlɪtɪ | *s.i.* fluidez, locuacidad, palabrería.

voluble | 'vɒljubl | *adj.* **1** locuaz, palabrero, parlanchín, (Am.) labioso. **2** entusiasta, fogoso, atropellado (discurso).

volubly | 'vɒljʊblɪ | *adv.* locuazmente, fogosamente, con soltura.

volume | 'vɒljuːm | (EE.UU.) | 'vɒljəm | *s.c.* **1** volumen, tomo. **2** volumen

(colección de revistas o periódicos encuadernados). || *s.i.* **3** volumen, espacio. **4** volumen, cantidad, nivel, amplitud (de protesta, adhesión, etc.). **5** volumen, cantidad, monto (de exportación, importación, ventas, etc.). **6** RAD. volumen (control de sonido). || **7 to speak volumes,** aportar abundante información.
voluminous | və'lju:mɪnəs | *adj.* (form.) **1** amplio, holgado, de talla superior (prendas). **2** voluminoso, abundante, largo, prolijo (correspondencia, escrito, obra, etc.).
voluminously | və'lju:mɪnəslɪ | *adv.* voluminosamente, abundantemente.
voluntarily | 'vɒləntərɪlɪ | (EE.UU.) | ˌvɒlən'terəlɪ | *adv.* voluntariamente, libremente, sin remunerar.
voluntary | 'vɒləntərɪ | *adj.* **1** voluntario, espontáneo, libre. **2** voluntario, no remunerado, desinteresado (trabajo, colaboración, etc.). **3** voluntario, de iniciativa privada, no subvencionado (institución). **4** voluntario, controlado (movimiento de músculos). || *s.c.* **5** MUS. solo (generalmente de órgano, anterior o posterior al servicio religioso).
volunteer | ˌvɒlən'tɪə*r* | *s.c.* **1** voluntario, trabajador voluntario, colaborador desinteresado. **2** MIL. voluntario. || *atr.* **3** voluntario, de voluntarios: *volunteer groups = grupos de voluntarios.*
voluptuary | və'lʌptʃuərɪ | *adj.* (form.) hedonista, voluptuoso.
voluptuous | və'lʌptʃuəs | *adj.* **1** voluptuoso, sensual, atractivo, excitante (persona, cosa). **2** (form.) sensual, placentero, hedonista (conducta, vida, etc.).
voluptuously | və'lʌptʃuəslɪ | *adv.* voluptuosamente, sensualmente.
voluptuousness | və'lʌptʃuəsnɪs | *s.i.* voluptuosidad, sensualidad.
vomit | 'vɒmɪt | *v.t.* e *i.* **1** vomitar, devolver. || *s.i.* **2** vómito.
vomiting | 'vɒmɪtɪŋ | *s.i.* vómito, vomitona.
voodoo | 'vu:du: | *s.i.* vudú.
voracious | və'reɪʃəs | *adj.* (lit.) **1** voraz, insaciable. **2** (fig.) ávido (de información, conocimiento, etc.).
voraciously | və'reɪʃəslɪ | *adv.* vorazmente, insaciablemente, ávidamente.
voraciousness | və'reɪʃəsnɪs | *s.i.* voracidad, insaciabilidad.
voracity | və'ræsɪtɪ | *s.i.* voracidad, insaciabilidad.
vortex | 'vɔ:teks | *s.c.* [*pl.* **vortexes** o **vortices**] **1** vórtice, remolino, torbellino. **2** (fig. y lit.) torbellino, vorágine.
vote | vəut | *s.c.* **1** voto, sufragio. **2** voto, votación (elección, decisión, expresión de voluntad): *to hold a vote on the motion = someter la propuesta a votación.* **3** voto, papeleta: *the votes in the ballot box = los votos de la urna.* **4** voto, votantes: *the opposition vote = el voto de la oposición.* **5** voto, derecho al voto: *when the women got the vote = cuando la mujer logró el derecho al voto.* || *v.t.* e *i.* **[to – (for/against/on)] 6** votar. **7** votar, proponer. **8** votar (una opción): *to vote Liberal = votar a los liberales.* **9** nombrar/destituir cargos (por votación). **10** asignar, destinar, aprobar (presupuestos, fondos, obras, etc., por votación). **11** (fam.) proclamar, declarar, considerar (de forma unánime). || **12 to be voted down,** ser rechazado en votación (personas, propuestas, etc.). **13 one man one vote,** un hombre un voto. **14 to – in,** elegir, dar el poder, decidir una votación: *pensioners can vote a party in = los pensionistas pueden dar el poder a un partido.* **15 – of censure,** voto de censura. **16 – of confidence/no confidence,** voto de confianza/desconfianza. **17 – of thanks,** voto, expresión pública de agradecimiento. **18 to – out,** rechazar, retirar del poder (por votación). **19 to – with one's feet,** abandonar un lugar en señal de rechazo.
voter | 'vəutə*r* | *s.c.* votante.
votive | 'vəutiv | *adj.* votivo.
vouch | vautʃ | *v.t.* **1** confirmar, garantizar, atestiguar, hacerse responsable. || **2 to – for someone,** responder por, hacerse responsable de alguien (o por la conducta de alguien). **3 to – for something,** garantizar, asegurar, atestiguar algo.
voutcher | 'vautʃə*r* | *s.c.* **1** (brit.) vale, bono. **2** comprobante, justificante, resguardo, factura.
vouchsafe | vautʃ'seɪf | *v.t.* (form.) **1** regalar, ofrecer, otorgar. **2** asegurar, garantizar.
vow | vau | *v.t.* **1** jurar, hacer votos, prometer solemnemente. || *s.c.* **2** voto, promesa solemne. || **3 vows,** votos (de casados o de religiosos).
vowel | vauəl | *s.c.* **1** vocal. || *atr.* **2** vocálico.
voyage | 'vɔiidʒ | *s.c.* **1** viaje (más bien largo, por mar o por aire). || *s.i.* **2** (form.) viajar (por mar).
voyager | 'vɔiədʒə*r* | *s.c.* viajero (afrontando ciertos riesgos): *the first space voyagers = los primeros viajeros del espacio.*
voyeur | vwɑ:'jɜ:*r* | *s.c.* voyeur, mirón.
vs versus.
V-sign | vi:'saɪn | *s.c.* **1** (brit.) signo de uve (con el interior de la mano hacia el propio ejecutor. Signo vulgar y ofensivo). **2** signo de la victoria (dorso de la mano hacia el ejecutor).
VSO | ˌvi: es 'əu | **Voluntary Service Overseas** (brit.) servicio de voluntarios en países en vías de desarrollo.
vulcanisation V. **vulcanization.**
vulcanise V. **vulcanize.**
vulcanite | 'vʌlkənait | *s.i.* QUIM. vulcanita, ebonita.
vulcanization | ˌvʌlkənai'zeɪʃn | (también **vulcanisation**) *s.i.* vulcanización, vulcanizado.
vulcanize | 'vʌlkənaiz | (también **vulcanise**) *v.t.* vulcanizar.
vulgar | 'vʌlgə*r* | *adj.* **1** vulgar, malo, feo, cursi, de mal gusto. **2** vulgar, desvergonzado, indecente, obsceno. **3** vulgar, ordinario, barriobajero. || **4 – fraction,** (EE.UU.) MAT. fracción, número quebrado.
vulgarity | vʌl'gærɪtɪ | *s.i.* **1** vulgaridad, ordinariez, cursilería, indecencia. || *s.c.* **2** ordinariez, indecencia (acto o expresión).
vulgarly | 'vʌlgəlɪ | *adv.* vulgarmente, de mal gusto, indecentemente.
vulnerability | ˌvʌlnərə'bɪlɪtɪ | *s.i.* vulnerabilidad, desprotección.
vulnerable | 'vʌlnərəbl | *adj.* **[– (to)]** vulnerable, débil, desprotegido.
vulnerably | 'vʌlnərəblɪ | *adv.* vulnerablemente, débilmente.
vulpine | 'vʌlpaɪn | *adj.* vulpino.
vulture | 'vʌltʃə*r* | *s.c.* **1** (fig.) buitre, carroñero, aprovechado. **2** ZOOL. buitre.
vulva | 'vʌlvə | *s.c.* [*pl.* **vulvas** o **vulvae**] ANAT. vulva.
vulvae | 'vʌlvi: | *pl.* de **vulva.**
vying | 'vaɪɪŋ | *ger.* de **vie.**

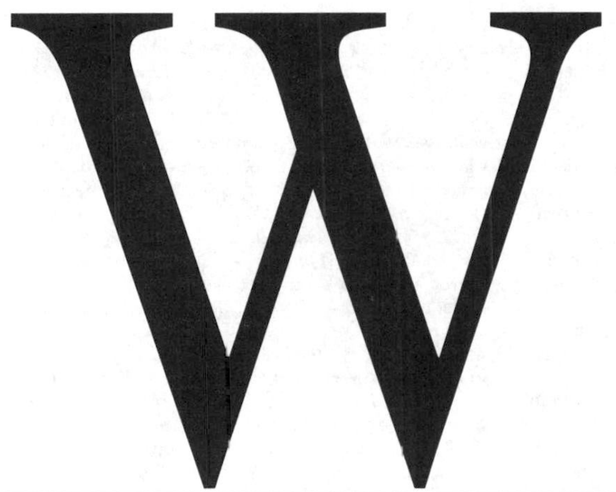

w, W | 'dʌblju: | *s.c.* **1** w, W (vigésimotercera letra del alfabeto inglés). **2** abreviatura de **west** o **watt**, oeste, vatio.

wacky | 'wækɪ | (también **whacky**) *adj.* (EE.UU. y fam.) tonto, bobo, chiflado, disparatado, divertido.

wad | wɒd | *s.c.* **1** taco, rollo, tapón (de materia suave y blanda): *she put wads of cotton in her ears = se puso tapones de algodón en los oídos.* **2** fajo, paquete (de documentos o papeles): *a wad of bank notes = un fajo de billetes.* **3** (brit. y fam.) bollo, pasta. || *v.t.* **4** embalar, envolver, empaquetar, rellenar, proteger (con tacos o rollos de materia blanda). **5** enguatar, forrar (prendas de vestir con algodón o lana): *a wadded jacket = una chaqueta enguatada.*

wadding | 'wɒdɪŋ | *s.i.* **1** guata, forro (de seda o lana). **2** relleno, acolchado, aislante, material de protección (en embalaje).

waddle | 'wɒdl | *v.i.* **1** (desp.) andar, moverse (como un pato), contonearse: *she came waddling along = venía contoneándose.* || *s.sing.* **2** contoneo, andares de pato.

wade | weɪd | *v.t.* e *i.* **1** vadear: *to wade across a river = vadear un río.* || **2 to – in, a)** (fam.) iniciar con energía y determinación una tarea costosa, ponerse manos a la obra: *the job was hard, so they waded in = la empresa era ardua, por lo que se pusieron manos a la obra.* **b)** interrumpir con energía (una argumentación): *he waded in with his opinion = interrumpió con su opinión.* **3 to – into,** (fam.) atacar con energía: *she really waded into her critics = atacó enérgicamente a sus críticos.* **4 to – through,** (fam.) hacer un trabajo costoso y pesado: *to wade through pages of boring statistics = revisar páginas de aburridas estadísticas.* **5 wading bird,** ave zancuda. **6 wading pool,** (EE.UU.) piscina (de poco fondo, para niños).

wader | 'weɪdər | *s.c.* **1** ave zancuda. || **2 waders,** botas altas de goma (aptas para vadear).

wadi | 'wɒdɪ | *s.c.* lecho de un río seco (en el Norte de Africa y Arabia).

WAF | ˌdʌblju:eɪ'ef | | wæf | (EE.UU.) (Women in the Air Force) mujeres en las Fuerzas Aéreas.

wafer | 'weɪfər | *s.c.* **1** oblea, barquillo, cucurucho (de helado). **2** sello (de documento oficial). **3** REL. forma, hostia.

wafer-thin | ˌweɪfə'θɪn | *adj.* muy delgado, muy estrecho, de poco contenido: *a wafer-thin majority = una mayoría muy estrecha.*

waffle | 'wɒfl | *s.c.* e *i.* **1** bollo, buñuelo. **2** palabrería, palabras, paja: *the report is only waffle = el informe es pura palabrería.* || *v.i.* **3** (brit. y fam.) decir palabras y palabras, meter mucha paja, alargarse excesivamente (en discurso o escrito): *he waffled on but nobody was listening = siguió hablando pero nadie escuchaba.*

waft | wɑ:ft | (EE.UU.) | wæft | *v.i.* (lit.) moverse, avanzar, flotar en el aire: *cooking smells wafted up = flotaban en el aire olores de guiso.* || *s.c.* **2** soplo, ráfaga (de olor): *a waft of perfume = un soplo de perfume.*

wag | wæg | *v.t.* e *i.* [*ger.* **wagging,** *pret.* y *p.p.* **wagged**] **1** menear, agitar, mover: *the dog wagged its tail = el perro meneaba la cola.* **2** (fig.) hablar, murmurar. || *s.c.* **3** meneo, movimiento rápido: *a wag of tail = un meneo de cola.* **4** (fam.) bromista, zumbón, guasón. || **5 tongues –,** dicen las malas lenguas.

wage | weɪdʒ | *s.c.* **1** salario, jornal, paga (semanal, generalmente): *wages are paid on Fridays = el salario se abona los viernes.* || *v.t.* **2** declarar, entablar, librar (guerras): *to wage a war against sex discrimination = declarar la guerra a la discriminación sexual.* || **3 – freeze,** congelación salarial. **4 – rise,** subida salarial. **5 – slave,** (hum.) currito. **6 to – war (on/against),** declarar la guerra.

wage-claim | 'weɪdʒkleɪm | *s.c.* demanda de mejoras salariales (promovida por los sindicatos).

wage-earner | 'weɪdʒɜ:nər | *s.c.* asalariado, trabajador a sueldo.

wage-packet | 'weɪdʒpækɪt | *s.c.* sobre de la paga.

wager | 'weɪdʒər | *v.t.* e *i.* **1 [to – (on)]** (form.) apostar, jugarse (dinero o cosas de valor): *to wage money on a horse = apostar dinero a un caballo.* || **2** (form.) apuesta: *to take up a wager = aceptar una apuesta.*

waggish | 'wægɪʃ *adj.* (p.u.) divertido, chistoso, de broma, chusco: *a wag gish remark = un comentario chusco.*

waggishly | 'wægɪʃlɪ | *adv.* divertidamente, chistosamente, en broma.

waggishness | 'wægɪʃnɪs | *s.i.* (p.u.) broma, guasa.

waggle | 'wægl | *v.t.* e *i.* **1** mover, menear: *he can waggle his ears = sabe mover las orejas.* || *s.c.* **2** movimiento, meneo.

waggon V. **wagon.**

waggoner V. **wagoner.**

wagon | 'wægən | (brit. **waggon**) *s.c.* **1** carro, carreta, carromato. **2** (brit.) vagón de ferrocarril (abierto y de mercancías). **3** (EE.UU.) carro, carretilla (para el transporte de alimentos). || **4 to be/go on the –,** (fam.) estar resuelto a apartarse del alcohol.

wagoner | 'wægənər | (brit. **waggoner**) *s.c.* carrero, carretero, guía.

wagon-lit | ˌwægɒn'li: | [*pl.* **wagons-lits**] *s.c.* coche-cama (en transporte de ferrocarril).

wagonload | 'wæganləud | *s.c.* carretada.

wagtail | 'wægteɪl | *s.c.* ZOOL. aguzanieves, lavandera.

waif | weɪf | *s.c.* **1** (lit.) persona sin hogar, niño abandonado. **2** objeto o animal sin dueño. || **3 waifs and strays,** desamparados, sin dueño.

wail | weɪl | *v.i.* **1** gemir, lamentarse: *she cried and wailed but did nothing =*

lloraba y se lamentaba sin hacer nada. || *s.c.* **2** gemido, lamento.
wailing | 'weɪlɪŋ | *s.i.* gemido, lamento, lamentación.
wainscot | 'weɪnskət | *s.c.* zócalo, entablado, revestimiento de madera.
waist | weɪst | *s.c.* **1** cintura, talle. **2** talle (en prendas de vestir). **3** parte media, cintura (de aparatos, instrumentos musicales, etc.). **4** MAR. combés.
waistband | 'weɪstbænd | *s.c.* cintura, cinturón, refuerzo de cintura (en prendas de vestir).
waistcoat | 'weɪstkəut | *s.c.* chaleco.
waisted | 'weɪstɪd | *adj.* entallado, ajustado (prendas de vestir).
-waisted | weɪstɪd | *adj.* de cintura o talle (determinados, según el *adj.* de la primera parte del compuesto): *slim-waisted = de cintura fina; high-waisted = de talle alto.*
waistline | 'weɪstlaɪn | *s.c.* **1** línea, cintura, talle: *no sweets, I'm watching my waistline = nada de dulces, guardo la línea.* **2** talle, línea de talle (en prendas de vestir).
wait | weɪt | *v.i.* **1 [to – (for)]** esperar, aguardar: *wait for me = espérame.* **2 [to – (until)]** esperar, permanecer (sin efecto, inactivo o silenciado): *the news can't wait until tomorrow = la noticia no puede esperar a mañana.* **3** estar listo, a punto, servido: *your supper's waiting = tu cena está lista.* || *v.t.* **4** esperar, aguardar: *just wait your turn = espere su turno.* **5** (fam.) retrasar, posponer: *don't wait supper for me, I'll be late = no retraséis la cena por mí, llegaré tarde.* || *s.c.* **6** espera. || **7 to – about/around,** esperar sin hacer nada, pasar el tiempo. **8 to – a moment/minute/second, a)** un momento, espere un momento; **b)** un momento (para interrumpir a alguien o detenerse a pensar). **9 to – and see,** esperar a ver qué pasa. **10 to – at table,** (brit. y form.) trabajar como camarero. **11 to – behind,** esperar (a que todos se vayan), quedarse el último: *he waited behind to speak to her in private = se quedó el último para hablar con ella a solas.* **12 – for it, a)** quietos, atentos (al dar una señal de salida): *ready, steady, wait for it-go! = preparados, listos, atentos, ¡ya!* **b)** ¡te va a hacer reír!, por gracioso que parezca. **13 to – in,** quedarse en casa a la espera. **14 to – in the wings,** V. **wing. 15 to – on, a)** (EE.UU.) servir comida (en restaurantes); **b)** estar a la espera: *we're still waiting on the results = estamos aún a la espera de los resultados.* **16 to – on someone hand and foot,** servir a alguien a cuerpo de rey. **17 – until/just you wait,** espera y verás, ya verás lo que te espera. **18 to – up,** permanecer levantado (a la espera). **19 to – upon (someone),** (arc.) hacer una visita de cortesía.
waiter | 'weɪtər | *s.c.* camarero.
waiting | 'weɪtɪŋ | *adj.* **1** de espera, a la espera, esperando: *a waiting period of one month = período de espera de un mes.* || **2 – game,** broma (de esperar), tiempo de espera deliberado: *the waiting game has ended = se acabó la broma de esperar.* **3 – list,** lista de espera.
waiting-room | 'weɪtɪŋrum | *s.c.* sala de espera.
waitress | 'weɪtrɪs | *s.c.* camarera.
waive | weɪv | *v.t.* (form.) suspender, dejar sin efecto, renunciar, ignorar, no exigir (un derecho, el cumplimiento de una ley, etc.): *to waive a rule = dejar sin efecto una norma.*
waiver | 'weɪvər | *s.c.* DER. documento de renuncia, de suspensión, de derogación, etc.
wake | 'weɪk | *v.t.* e *i.* [*pret.* **woke** o **waked,** *p.p.* **woken** o **waked**] **1** despertar, despertarse: *I usually wake (up) early = suelo despertarme temprano.* **2 [to – (to)]** (fig.) despertar, abrir los ojos, tomar conciencia: *to wake to the dangers of a war = abrir los ojos a los peligros de guerra.* || *s.c.* **3** estela: *the wake of a ship = la estela de un barco.* **4** velatorio. || **5 in one's –,** tras de sí, al paso de uno: *they left a trail of rubbish in their wake = dejaron un rastro de basura a su paso.* **6 in the – of,** como resultado de. **7 to – up, a)** despertar; **b)** despertar, estimular, animar: *the exercises woke him up = el ejercicio físico le estimuló;* **c)** despertar, abrir los ojos, tomar conciencia.
wakeful | 'weɪkful | *adj.* **1** despierto, desvelado, en vela, insomne. **2** (form.) vigilante, alerta.
wakefully | 'weɪkfulɪ | *adv.* sin dormir, desvelado, en vela.
wakefulness | 'weɪkfulnɪs | *s.i.* desvelo, insomnio.
waken | 'weɪkən | *v.t.* e *i.* (lit.) despertar.
wakey wakey | ˌweɪkɪ'weɪkɪ | *interj.* (brit. y hum.) ¡despierta!
waking | 'weɪkɪŋ | *adj.* despierto, de vigilia: *waking hours = las horas de vigilia (las no dedicadas al sueño).*
Wales | weɪlz | *s.sing.* Gales.
walk | wɔːk | *v.i.* **1** andar, caminar. **2** (p.u.) aparecer, salir a la luz, manifestarse (espíritus, fantasmas, etc.). || *v.t.* **3** andar, recorrer a pie: *to walk the fields looking for flowers = recorrer los campos en busca de flores.* **4** acompañar (andando): *I'll walk you to the bus stop = te acompaño hasta la parada del autobús.* **5** pasear, sacar a pasear o a tomar el aire (animales): *she's walking the dog = está paseando al perro.* **6** mover (objetos pesados simulando pasos): *let's walk the ladder = movamos la escalera.* || *s.c.* **7** paseo, caminata: *he's gone for a walk = se ha ido de paseo.* **8** ruta, sendero, paraje (de paseo): *pleasant walks in the forest = deliciosos parajes en el bosque.* **9** actividad, condición, tipo: *people from every walk of life = gentes de toda condición.* || *s.sing.* **10** paso, ritmo (al andar): *a brisk walk = paso vivo.* **11** distancia a pie: *the station is ten minutes' walk = la estación está a diez minutos (a pie).* **12** andar, andares: *she's got an odd walk = tiene andares raros.* **13** paso, marcha (al paso): *after running, he went on walking = tras una carrera, siguió al paso.* || **14 to – away from someone/something, a)** salir ileso o con heridas sin importancia de un accidente; **b)** (EE.UU. y fam.) vencer con facilidad, distanciarse (en carreras, competiciones, etc.): *No. 5 walked away from the others = el número 5 se distanció de los demás.* **15 to – before one can run,** dominar lo fácil antes de acometer lo difícil. **16 to – into something,** (fam.) **a)** caer atrapado (por descuido): *he walked into the trap = cayó en la trampa;* **b)** conseguir algo sin esfuerzo alguno: *after graduating, she walked into the job = consiguió el empleo apenas graduarse;* **c)** chocar con algo o alguien por despiste. **17 to – off/away with something,** (fam.) **a)** llevarse algo; **b)** ganar fácilmente (en competiciones). **18 – of life,** ocupación, condición humana. **19 to – on air,** V. **air. 20 to – one's leg off,** (fam.) estar roto de tanto caminar. **21 to – out,** (fam.) **a)** abandonar (una sala, reunión, etc.); **b)** ponerse en huelga. **22 to – out on someone/something,** (fam.) dejar abandonado: *he walked out on his wife and children = dejó abandonados a su mujer e hijos.* **23 to – out with someone,** salir, mantener relaciones con alguien. **24 to – over someone,** (fam.) **a)** derrotar totalmente a alguien (en competiciones); **b)** emplear malos modos con alguien: *don't let him walk over you like that = no le consientas que te trate así.* **25 to – someone off his feet,** (fam.) dejar a alguien exhausto de tanto caminar. **26 to – tall,** V. **tall. 27 to – the plank,** V. **plank. 28 to –/tread a tightrope, a)** hacer ejercicio de, aplicarse al funambulismo; **b)** (fig.) verse en una situación delicada. **29 – up! – up!,** (fam.) pasen y vean (en espectáculos). **30 to – up (to someone/something),** llegar, acercarse: *a stranger walked up to her = un extraño se le acercó.*
walkabout | 'wɔːkəbaut | *s.c.* **1** andanzas, correrías (de un aborigen australiano). **2** (brit. y fam.) paseo (de una personalidad entre la gente). || **3 to go –,** patear (el campo, la ciudad, etc.). **4 to go –/to do a –,** dar un paseo (una personalidad para comunicarse con la gente).
walkaway | 'wɔːkəweɪ | *s.c.* (EE.UU. y fam.) victoria fácil, paseo (en competiciones).
walker | 'wɔːkər | *s.c.* **1** paseante, caminante, peatón, andarín. **2** pollera.
walkies | 'wɔːkɪz | *s.pl.* (brit. y fam.) paseo (del perro): *to go walkies with the dog = sacar de paseo al perro.*
walkie-talkie | ˌwɔːkɪ'tɔːkɪ | *s.c.* aparato emisor-receptor portátil.
walk-in | 'wɔːkɪn | *adj.* (EE.UU.) **1** amplio, espacioso: *a walk-in wardrobe = un armario espacioso.* **2** fácil (victoria, éxito): *a walk-in victory.*
walking | 'wɔːkɪŋ | *adj.* **1** de paseo, de marcha, de caminar: *walking shoes = zapatos de caminar.* **2** a pie, pedestre: *a*

walking tour = excursión a pie. **3** (fam.) humano, viviente, andante: *he is a walking encyclopaedia = es una enciclopedia viviente.* || *s.i.* **4** senderismo. || **5 – papers,** (EE.UU.) (fam.) despido (de un trabajo). **6 – rein,** correa, guía de niño (para controlar sus pasos).

walking-stick | 'wɔːkɪŋstɪk | *s.c.* bastón (de caminar).

walkman | 'wɔːkmən | *s.c.* cassette personal con auriculares.

walk-on | 'wɔːkɒn | *adj.* figurante (en teatro): *a walk-on part = papel de figurante.*

walk-out | 'wɔːkaʊt | *s.c.* **1** abandono, retirada (de una reunión u organización en señal de desaprobación). **2** huelga de trabajadores.

walk-over | 'wɔːkəʊvər | *s.c.* **1** paseo triunfal, victoria fácil (en competiciones). **2** adelanto (de un programa deportivo por incomparecencia del rival).

walk-up | 'wɔːkʌp | *s.c.* (EE.UU. y fam.) **1** piso, oficina, etc. (en edificio alto y sin ascensor): *he lives in a 4th floor in a walk-up = vive en un cuarto piso sin ascensor.* **2** edificio alto sin ascensor.

walkway | 'wɔːkweɪ | *s.c.* pasadizo, pasaje peatonal.

wall | wɔːl | *s.c.* **1** pared, muro: *a stone wall = un muro de piedra.* **2** pared (interior): *a picture on the wall = un cuadro en la pared.* **3** muralla: *the city walls = las murallas de la ciudad.* **4** pared, cara interior (de envases, conductos, etc.): *the walls of a blood vessel = las paredes de un vaso sanguíneo.* **5** (fig.) muro, barrera: *a wall of silence = una barrera de silencio.* || *v.t.* **6** amurallar, cercar, poner una pared. || **7 to bang one's head against a brick –,** darse contra un muro, no avanzar pese al esfuerzo hecho. **8 to come up against a brick –,** estancarse ante un obstáculo insalvable. **9 to drive/push someone to the –,** poner a alguien contra la pared, en situación difícil. **10 to drive/send someone up the –,** (fam.) enfadar, sacar de quicio a alguien. **11 to go to the –,** ir al fracaso, a la ruina. **12 to go up the –,** (fam.) subirse por las paredes, estar muy enfadado. **13 to have one's back to the –,** (fam.) estar en apuros y no ver salida. **14 the writing is on the –,** hay signos de que se aproxima el final (para un negocio, empresa, etc.). **15 to – in,** rodear, cercar, emparedar: *walled in by mountains = rodeado de montañas.* **16 to – off (from),** separar (con pared): *the living area is walled off from the rest = la zona habitada está separada del resto.* **17 walls have ears,** (fam.) las paredes oyen. **18 Wall Street,** Wall Street (centro bursátil y financiero de Nueva York). **19 to – up,** cegar, cerrar con pared: *the window was walled up = cegaron la ventana.*

wallaby | 'wɒləbɪ | *s.c.* ZOOL. canguro pequeño (Australia).

wallchart | 'wɔːltʃɑːt | *s.c.* mural.

walled | wɔːld | *adj.* amurallado, cercado, pared que tiene una característica especial (determinado por la primera parte del compuesto): *a mud-walled hut = cabaña de paredes de barro.*

wallet | 'wɒlɪt | *s.c.* **1** cartera, billetera. **2** (EE.UU.) monedero, portamonedas. **3** carpeta, cartera.

wall-eyed | 'wɔːlaɪd | *adj.* de ojos desviados (hacia fuera).

wallflower | 'wɔːlˌflaʊər | *s.c.* **1** alhelí. **2** (fig.) persona que no baila (por ser tímida o porque nadie la saca).

wallop | 'wɒləp | (fam.) *v.t.* **1** golpear contundentemente. **2 [to – (at)]** derrotar abrumadoramente, barrer (en el juego): *she walloped him at chess = lo barrió al ajedrez.* || *s.c.* **3** golpe fuerte.

walloping | 'wɒləpɪŋ | (fam.) *s.c.* **1** paliza, zurra, castigo. **2** derrota total. || *adj.* **3** grande, descomunal, colosal.

wallow | 'wɒləʊ | *v.i* **1** revolcarse, remozarse, sumirse (en la suciedad): *to wallow in the mud = revolcarse en el fango.* **2** sumirse, permanecer, quedarse (en un estado o situación negativos): *don't just wallow in self-pity = no te quedes ahí lamentándote.* **3** zozobrar (un barco). || *s.sing.* **4** inmersión, baño. || *s.c.* **5** barrizal, fango, lodazal, arroyo.

wallpaper | 'wɔːlˌpeɪpər | *s.i.* **1** papel (de pared o de empapelar). || *v.t.* **2** empapelar (paredes).

wall-to-wall | ˌwɔːltə'wɔːl | *adj.* **1** de pared a pared: *wall-to-wall carpeting = enmoquetado de pared a pared.* **2** (fam.) continuo, intenso, envolvente, completo: *a wall-to-wall stereo sound = un sonido estéreo envolvente.*

wally | 'wɒlɪ | *s.c.* (brit. y fam.) estúpido, imbécil, inútil, (Am.) maleta, quiebra.

walnut | 'wɔːlnʌt | *s.c.* e *i.* **1** nuez. **2** nogal (árbol, madera). || **3 – tree,** BOT. nogal.

walrus | 'wɔːlrəs | *s.c.* **1** ZOOL. morsa. || **2 – moustache,** (fam.) bigote a lo morsa (con las guías hacia abajo).

waltz | wɔːls | , (EE.UU.) | wɔːlts | *s.c.* **1** vals. || *v.t.* e *i.* **2** bailar el vals. **3** moverse en una dirección (alegremente, bailando): *she waltzed up to us and said she was off = se nos acercó bailando y dijo que se iba.* || **4 to – off,** (fam.) capturar, coger, echar el guante: *the police waltzed him off to jail = la policía lo cogió y lo encerró.* **5 to – off with something,** (fam.) **a)** robar, llevarse algo; **b)** ganar fácilmente (premios, competiciones, etc.).

wampum | 'wɒmpəm | *s.i.* conchas en ristras o cinturones (usadas como dinero u ornamentación por tribus indias norteamericanas).

wan | wɒn | *adj.* [*comp.* **wanner,** *super.* **wannest**] (lit.) pálido, triste, débil, desmejorado, desvaído, tenue: *a wan smile = una débil sonrisa.*

wand | wɒnd | *s.c.* **1** varita mágica (de magos y brujas). **2** INF. lápiz fotoeléctrico (lector de código de barras).

wander | 'wɒndər | *v.t.* e *i.* **1 [to – (about)]** vagar, errar, deambular, andar de aquí para allá: *the child was wandering about = el niño andaba de aquí para allá.* **2** recorrer, patear: *nomadic tribes wander the desert = tribus nómadas recorren el desierto.* **3** (fig.) serpentear (ríos, caminos, etc.). **4 [to – (from/ off)]** apartarse, desviarse, distraerse: *don't wander off the point = no te desvíes del asunto.* **5** desvariar, delirar: *his mind often wanders = a menudo desvaría.*

wanderer | 'wɒndərər | *s.c.* viajero, nómada, vagabundo.

wandering | 'wɒndərɪŋ | *adj.* errante, nómada, ambulante: *wandering tribes = tribus nómadas.*

wanderings | 'wɒndərɪŋz | *s.pl.* andanzas, viajes: *his experience comes from his wanderings = su experiencia le viene de sus andanzas.*

wanderlust | 'wɒndəlʌst | *s.i.* pasión de viajar, inquietud viajera.

wane | weɪn | *v.i.* **1** disminuir, decaer, declinar, desfallecer, disiparse: *her enthusiasm often wanes = su entusiasmo decae con facilidad.* **2** menguar, estar en cuarto menguante (la luna): *a waning moon = luna en cuarto menguante.* || **3 on the –,** en declive, en retroceso: *unemployment is on the wane = el desempleo está en retroceso.* **4 to wax and –,** V. **wax.**

wangle | 'wæŋgl | *v.t.* **1 [to – (into/out of)]** (fam.) conseguir, agenciarse, convencer, persuadir: *he always wangles the easy jobs out of the manager = siempre consigue del encargado los trabajos fáciles.* || **2 to – one's way (into/out of),** conseguir algo ventajoso, superar una dificultad (gracias a la maña propia).

wank | wæŋk | (brit. y vulg.) *v.i.* **1** masturbarse, meneársela. || *s.c.* **2** masturbación, paja, (Am.) puñeta.

wanker | 'wæŋkər | *s.c.* (brit. y vulg.) **1** estúpido, inútil. **2** persona que se masturba.

wanly | 'wɒnlɪ | *adv.* (lit.) pálidamente, tristemente, débilmente.

wanness | 'wɒnnɪs | *s.i.* (lit.) palidez, languidez, tristeza, debilidad.

want | wɒnt | *v.t.* **1** querer, desear. **2** querer ver, preguntar (por alguien) requerir (la presencia de alguien): *somebody wants the manager = alguien quiere ver al encargado.* **3 [to – (for)]** buscar (por la policía): *he is wanted for murder = se le busca por asesinato.* **4** (fam.) necesitar, pedir, exigir: *this wants doing at once = se necesita hacerlo al momento.* **5** (fam.) deber, ser preciso: *you don't want to work so hard = no deberías trabajar tanto.* **6** (form.) carecer, sufrir carencia: *many people want food = mucha gente carece de alimento.* **7** (EE.UU. y fam.) querer (entrar, salir): *the cat wants in = el gato quiere entrar.* **8** desear (sexualmente). || *s.c.* e *i.* **9** ausencia, carencia, insuficiencia, necesidad: *want of water = insuficiencia de agua.* **10** (form.) carestía absoluta, estado de necesidad, pobreza: *a policy fighting want and deprivation*

= *una política que combata la pobreza.* || **11 for – of,** a falta de: *for want of anything better to do = a falta de algo mejor que hacer.* **12 in – of,** (arc.) necesitar: *the house is in want of repair = la casa necesita un arreglo.* **13 – ads,** (EE.UU. y fam.) anuncios por palabras. **14 to – for nothing,** (lit.) no faltar de nada, tener todo lo necesario: *those children want for nothing = a esos niños no les falta de nada.* **15 to – out (of something),** (EE.UU. y fam.) cancelar compromisos, dejar de estar implicado (en planes, proyectos, etc.): *I was afraid and so I wanted out = tenía miedo y quise dejar de estar implicado.* **16 wants,** necesidades, las cosas que uno necesita para vivir: *a man of few wants = hombre de pocas necesidades.*

wanting | 'wɒntɪŋ | *adj.* **1** (form.) deficiente, defectuoso, inadecuado: *he found the test wanting = encontró la prueba inadecuada.* **2 [– (in)]** (form.) carente, falto: *he's wanting in team spirit = está falto de espíritu de equipo.* **3** (euf.) corto, torpe.

wanton | 'wɒntən | *adj.* **1** injustificable, inexplicable (de una mala acción): *a wanton waste of money = un derroche de dinero injustificable.* **2** (form.) impropio, insinuante (actitud lasciva): *wanton glances = miradas insinuantes.* **3** (form.) incontrolado, desordenado: *wanton growth of weeds = crecimiento incontrolado de hierbas.* **4** (lit.) extravagante, extraño (conducta).

wantonly | 'wɒntənlɪ | *adv.* (form.) injustificablemente, sin recato, desordenadamente, extrañamente; sin motivo, gratuitamente.

wantonness | 'wɒntənnɪs | *s.i.* (form.) injustificabilidad, descaro, extravagancia, descontrol.

war | wɔːr | *s.c.* e *i.* **1** guerra, conflicto bélico. **2** situación, época de guerra: *between the two World Wars = entre las dos guerras mundiales.* **3** guerra, lucha, batalla (entre fuerzas opuestas o por un fin determinado): *the war against inflation = la guerra contra la inflación.* || *v.i.* **4** guerrear, estar en guerra: *they warred in the past = estuvieron en guerra en el pasado.* || **5 to be at –,** estar en guerra. **6 to go to –,** ir a la guerra, declarar la guerra, entrar en guerra. **7 to have been in the wars,** (fam.) haber participado en una situación donde se ha repartido leña: *you've been in the wars, haven't you? = ha habido leña, ¿eh?* **7 – chest,** (EE.UU.) fondos recogidos para la guerra. **8 – clouds,** amenaza de guerra. **9 – crime,** crimen de guerra. **10 – of nerves,** guerra de nervios. **11 – widow,** viuda de guerra.

warble | 'wɔːbl | *v.i.* **1** trinar, gorjear. || *s.sing.* **2** trino, gorjeo.

warbler | 'wɔːblər | *s.c.* **1** pájaro canoro. **2** (hum.) cantante femenina.

war-cry | 'wɔːkraɪ | *s.c.* grito de guerra, lema, eslogan.

ward | wɔːd | *s.c.* **1** sala, sección, ala (de un hospital): *maternity ward = sección de maternidad.* **2** distrito electoral urbano. **3** pupilo, protegido, niño en custodia (de un protector o institución). **4** diente, guarda (de una llave). || **5 a – in chancery,** (brit.) niño dependiente del Tribunal Tutelar de Menores. **6 wards of court,** niños bajo la tutela del estado. **7 to – someone/something off,** ahuyentar, evitar, mantener a salvo (de peligros, enfermedades, etc.): *regular exercises may ward off disease = el ejercicio físico continuado puede evitar enfermedades.*

ward | wəd | (también **-wards**) *adj./adv.* hacia, en la dirección (señalada en la primera parte del compuesto): *homeward = hacia casa.*

war-dance | 'wɔːdɑːns | *s.c.* danza de guerra (realizada por tribus guerreras antes de la batalla o tras la victoria).

warden | 'wɔːdn | *s.c.* **1** guarda, guardián, supervisor. **2** presidente, director (de algunas instituciones académicas). **3** (EE.UU.) alcaide, director (de una prisión).

warder | 'wɔːdər | *s.c.* (brit.) guardián, carcelero.

wardress | 'wɔːdrɪs | *s.c.* guardiana, carcelera.

wardrobe | 'wɔːdrəʊb | *s.c.* **1** armario, guardarropa. **2** guardarropía, ropa: *a winter wardrobe = ropa de invierno.* **3** vestuario (de actores de teatro). || **4 – master/mistress,** encargado/encargada del vestuario (en una compañía teatral).

wardroom | 'wɔːdrʊm | *s.c.* MAR. sala de oficiales.

wards | wədz | V. **-ward.**

ware | weər | *s.i.* **1** productos, artículos (del tipo especificado en la primera parte del compuesto): *ironware = productos de hierro.* **2** cerámica, porcelana (del tipo o finalidad determinados): *earthenware = cerámica de barro cocido.*

warehouse | 'weəhaʊs | *s.c.* almacén, depósito.

wares | weəz | *s.pl.* (lit.) baratijas, artículos de venta (en puestos callejeros o en mercados).

warfare | 'wɔːfeər | *s.i.* **1** guerra (tipo, clase): *guerrilla warfare = guerra de guerrillas.* **2** guerra, confrontación (entre tribus, pandillas, etc.).

warhead | 'wɔːhed | *s.c.* MIL. cabeza explosiva (de un misil o torpedo).

war-horse | 'wɔːhɔːs | *s.c.* **1** caballo de combate. **2** (fig.) soldado o político experimentado. **3** (fam.) algo muy visto.

warily | 'weərəlɪ | *adv.* cautelosamente, precavidamente, cuidadosamente.

wariness | 'weərɪnɪs | *s.i.* cautela, precaución.

warlike | 'wɔːlaɪk | *adj.* belicoso, guerrero, agresivo, hostil.

warlock | 'wɔːlɒk | *s.c.* brujo, mago (en literatura fantástica).

warlord | 'wɔːlɔːd | *s.c.* (lit.) comandante en jefe.

warm | wɔːm | *adj.* **1** caliente (sin exceso): *a baby's food should be warm, not hot = la comida de los niños debe estar caliente, pero sin quemar.* **2** caliente, que tiene o hace sentir calor: *are you warm enough? = ¿tienes suficiente calor?* **3** de abrigo: *warm clothes = ropa de abrigo.* **4** sentido, sincero: *warm feelings of gratitude = sincero sentimiento de gratitud.* **5** cálido, entusiasta, de corazón: *warm applause = aplauso cálido.* **6** alegre, sugestivo, cálido (color, sonido, voz, etc.): *furnished in warm colours = amueblado en tonos alegres.* **7** fresco, reciente (rastro seguido en caza). **8** caliente (en adivinanzas y otros juegos infantiles). || *v.t.* **9** calentar, hacer entrar en calor: *this will warm you (up) = esto te hará entrar en calor.* || *v.i.* **10** calentarse (cosas): *the soup is warming in the pot = la sopa se está calentando en la cazuela.* || *s.sing.* **11** calor, ambiente de calor: *come into the warm = ven al calor.* || **12 as – as a toast,** (fam.) estar bien calentito. **13 to get –,** entrar en calor. **14 to keep someone's seat/post/etc. – (for him),** (fam.) calentar la silla/el puesto a alguien. **15 to make it/things – for someone,** (fam.) **a)** crearle problemas a alguien; **b)** castigar a alguien. **16 – front,** FIS. frente cálido. **17 to – someone/something up, a)** (brit.) recalentar (comida); **b)** calentar, ponerse a punto (antes de entrar en competición); **c)** motivar, cautivar el ánimo (de una audiencia, clase, etc.); **d)** (fam.) animar, dar vida (reuniones, fiestas, etc.). **18 to – something over,** (EE.UU.) **a)** calentar; **b)** recalentar (comida); **c)** repetir ideas, argumentos, etc. (sin añadir nada nuevo). **19 to – the cockles of someone's heart,** V. **cockle. 20 to – to/towards someone,** empezar a gustar o apreciar a alguien, caer bien: *they warmed to the new boss at once = el nuevo jefe les cayó bien al momento.* **21 to – to/towards something,** interesarse, entusiasmarse más por algo: *he warmed to his walk as he went on = a medida que avanzaba, se iba entusiasmando más con su paseo.*

warm-blooded | ˌwɔːm'blʌdɪd | *adj.* de sangre caliente, de temperatura corporal alta.

warm-hearted | ˌwɔːm'hɑːtɪd | *adj.* afectivo, cariñoso, atento, agradable.

warmly | 'wɔːmlɪ | *adv.* cálidamente, con entusiasmo, con simpatía.

warmonger | 'wɔːˌmʌŋgər | *s.c.* belicista, guerrero, agitador, pendenciero.

warmongering | 'wɔːˌmʌŋgərɪŋ | *s.i.* **1** belicismo, agitación. || *adj.* **2** belicista.

warmth | wɔːmθ | *s.i.* **1** calor: *the warmth of the sun.* **2** calor, abrigo, protección: *blankets of little warmth = mantas de poco abrigo.* **3** entusiasmo, calor: *he answered with no warmth = respondió sin entusiasmo alguno.*

warm-up | 'wɔːmʌp | *s.c.* preparación, puesta a punto, calentamiento (previos a una competición).

warn | wɔːn | *v.t.* e *i.* **1 [to – (of/ against)]** avisar, advertir, aconsejar, prevenir: *I warned you against going out at night = te aconsejé no salir de noche.* **2** avisar, informar: *warn the police if you're going away = avisa a la policía si te vas a ausentar.* || **3 to – someone off/away,** advertir a alguien que se mantenga alejado: *his doctor warned him off drink = el médico le advirtió que se mantuviera alejado de la bebida.*

warning | 'wɔːnɪŋ | *s.c.* **1** advertencia, aviso: *a warning against drugs = advertencia contra la droga.* **2** consejo (de no hacer algo): *the warning not to come back late = el consejo de no volver tarde.* **3** aviso previo, información: *she left without any warning = se marchó sin avisar.* **4** signo, señal, gesto, acción de aviso: *to make warning faces at somebody = avisar a alguien con gestos de la cara.*

warningly | 'wɔːnɪŋlɪ | *adv.* como advertencia, en señal de aviso.

warp | wɔːp | *v.i.* **1** alabearse, torcerse, combarse, barquearse (madera): *this wood warps easily = esta madera se alabea fácilmente.* || *v.t.* **2** (fig.) afectar, condicionar, influir: *warped by his bad experience = afectado por su experiencia negativa.* || *s.sing.* **3** alabeo, comba, desnivel. **4** alteración, deformación (de carácter o personalidad). **5** urdimbre (tejido). **6** maroma, cable de arrastre (en barcos de pesca).

war-paint | 'wɔːpeɪnt | *s.i.* **1** pintura, maquillaje de guerra (empleados por tribus primitivas antes de entrar en combate). **2** (hum.) maquillaje.

warpath | 'wɔːpɑːθ | *s.c.* **1** senda de guerra. || **2 on the –, a)** en disposición de guerra (tribus indias norteamericanas); **b)** (fam.) enfadado, dispuesto a emprenderla con alguien.

warped | wɔːpt | *adj.* **1** alabeado, combado, barqueado: *a warped plank = una tabla alabeada.* **2** (fig.) retorcido, pervertido: *thoughts of warped minds = pensamientos de mentes retorcidas.*

warrant | 'wɒrənt | (EE.UU.) | 'wɔːrənt | *s.c.* e *i.* **1** (form.) justificación, derecho, autorización: *he had no warrant for doing that = no tenía derecho a hacerlo.* **2** DER. autorización, mandato, orden (escrita): *a search warrant = orden de registro.* **3** COM. título, garantía, derechos: *a warrant for dividends on shares = derechos para percibir dividendos.* || *v.t.* **4** (form.) justificar, autorizar, dar derecho: *nothing warrants such punishment = nada justifica semejante castigo.* **5** (form.) garantizar: *to warrant that the product is authentic = garantizar que el producto es auténtico.* **6** (arc.) prometer, asegurar: *I warrant nobody will bother you = te aseguro que nadie te molestará.* || **6 I('ll) – you,** (arc.) te lo aseguro.

warranted | 'wɒrəntɪd | (EE.UU.) | 'wɔːrəntɪd | *adj.* autorizado, garantizado, justificado.

warrantee | ˌwɒrən'tiː | (EE.UU.) | ˌwɔːrən'tiː | *s.c.* poseedor, titular, beneficiario (de una autorización, garantía o derecho).

warrant-officer | 'wɒrəntˌɒfɪsər | *s.c.* **1** MIL. suboficial. **2** MAR. contramaestre.

warrantor | 'wɒrəntɔːr | *s.c.* persona que otorga una autorización, garantía o derecho.

warranty | 'wɒrəntɪ | (EE.UU.) | 'wɔːrəntɪ | *s.c.* e *i.* **1** (form.) autoridad, derecho (para hacer algo). **2** COM. garantía: *the car is still under warranty = el coche está en garantía todavía.*

warren | 'wɒrən | (EE.UU.) | 'wɔːrən | *s.c.* **1** madriguera, conejera. **2** (fig.) colmena (humana), laberinto de calles.

warring | 'wɔːrɪŋ | *adj.* enfrentado, en guerra, opuesto, contrario, encontrado: *warring families = familias enfrentadas; warring interests = intereses opuestos.*

warrior | 'wɒrɪər | (EE.UU.) | 'wɔːrɪər | *s.c.* (form.) guerrero, combatiente.

warship | 'wɔːʃɪp | *s.c.* barco, buque de guerra.

wart | wɔːt | *s.c.* **1** verruga. || **2 warts and all,** (fam.) sin ocultar defectos o partes negativas: *the whole account of her life, warts and all = toda la historia de su vida, defectos incluidos.*

warthog | wɔːthɒg | *s.c.* ZOOL. jabalí africano.

warty | 'wɔːtɪ | *adj.* cubierto de verrugas, verrugoso.

wartime | 'wɔːtaɪm | *s.i.* guerra, tiempo de guerra.

wary | 'weərɪ | *adj.* **[– (of)]** cauto, cauteloso, desconfiado, receloso: *wary of strangers = desconfiado de los extraños.*

was | wɒz | , | wəz | *pret.* de **be.**

wash | wɒʃ | , (EE.UU.) | wɔːʃ | *v.t.* e *i.* **1** lavar. **2** lavarse. **3** lavar (objetos): *this detergent washes well = este detergente lava bien.* **4** llevar, arrastrar (el agua): *to wash ashore = arrastrar hacia la orilla.* **5 [to – (against/over)]** (lit.) avanzar, chapotear, romper, batir (el agua): *waves washing against the boat = olas chapoteando contra el barco.* **6 [to – (with)]** (fam.) ser creíble, convencer, servir, colar: *that excuse won't wash with me = esa excusa no me sirve.* **7** lavar, cribar (arenas fluviales en busca de oro). **8** dar una capa de pintura líquida. || *s.c.* **9** lavado (de uno mismo): *I'll have a wash = me daré un lavado.* **10** (EE.UU.) lavado, colada. **11** lugar, establecimiento de lavado (de coches): *car wash = lavado de coches.* **12** baño, chapoteo (de las olas). **13** capa de pintura (líquida y fina). || *s.i.* **14** comida para cerdos (hecha de desperdicios). || *adj.* **15** (EE.UU.) lavable: *wash cotton = algodón lavable.* || **16 to come out in the –,** (fam.) **a)** aparecer al final; **b)** hacerse público algo oculto y vergonzoso; **c)** resultar bien finalmente. **17 in the –,** con la ropa sucia, dispuesto para ser lavado. **18 the –, a)** lavado de ropa (el proceso): *all my shirts are in the wash = todas mis camisas se están lavando;* **b)** ropa para lavar: *there is a large wash = hay mucha ropa para lavar;* **c)** ruido de agua o viento (al chocar contra un vehículo en movimiento); **d)** olas y espuma (producidos por el paso de un barco). **19 to – away,** arrasar, destruir, arrastrar (el agua descontrolada): *the flood washed the bridge away = la crecida arrastró el puente.* **20 to – down (with something) a)** lavar (con manguera o chorro de agua): *to wash down a car = lavar un coche;* **b)** beber para pasar la comida, regar (la comida): *we washed our meal down with claret = regamos la comida con clarete.* **21 to – off,** limpiar, quitar, eliminar (manchas): *ink stains are hard to wash off = las manchas de tinta se quitan mal.* **22 to – one's dirty linen in public,** V. **linen. 23 to – one's hands of something,** lavarse las manos, no querer saber nada. **24 to – out, a)** limpiar, quitar manchas: *it will wash out in the rain = se quitará con la lluvia;* **b)** limpiar la parte interior de algo: *to wash out empty bottles = limpiar botellas;* **c)** interrumpir, suspender (acontecimientos a causa de la lluvia): *the match was completely washed out = el encuentro se suspendió a causa de la lluvia.* **25 to – over someone,** (fam.) resbalarle, no afectarle a uno: *the criticism seemed to wash over him = la crítica pareció resbalarle.* **26 to – up, a)** (brit.) fregar (los cacharros): *I hate washing up at night = odio fregar por la noche;* **b)** (EE.UU.) lavarse (el cuerpo); **c)** sacar a tierra (las olas del mar): *things washed up from a wrecked ship = restos de un naufragio sacados a tierra.* **27 ... won't/wouldn't –,** no se quita (mancha).

washable | 'wɒʃəbl | *adj.* lavable, que se lava fácilmente.

washbasin | 'wɒʃˌbeɪsn | *s.c.* lavabo, palangana, jofaina.

washbowl | 'wɒʃˌbəul | *s.c.* (EE.UU.) lavabo, palangana, jofaina.

washcloth | 'wɒʃklɒθ | *s.c.* (EE.UU.) manopla, paño para lavarse.

washday | 'wɒʃdeɪ | *s.c.* día de colada.

wash-drawing | 'wɒʃˌdrɔːɪŋ | *s.c.* e *i.* dibujo (de pintura líquida y monocolor).

washed-out | ˌwɒʃt'aut | *adj.* **1** descolorido, gastado (tras varios lavados). **2** cansado, rendido, exhausto: *washed-out after hard work = rendido tras un duro trabajo.*

washed-up | ˌwɒʃt'ʌp | *adj.* (fam.) acabado, roto, arruinado, vencido, derrotado, fracasado: *their marriage was already washed-up = su matrimonio estaba ya roto.*

washer | 'wɒʃər | (EE.UU.) | 'wɔːʃər | *s.c.* **1** arandela, zapata. **2** (fam.) lavadora, lavandera. **3** (EE.UU.) lavadora.

washing | 'wɒʃɪŋ | (EE.UU.) | 'wɔːʃɪŋ | *s.c.* e *i.* **1** lavado: *it has shrunk after the first washing = ha encogido tras el primer lavado.* **2** ropa sucia, ropa para lavar o ya lavada, colada: *a pile of dirty washing = un montón de ropa para lavar.* || **3 – powder,** jabón, detergente (para lavar). **4 – soda,** sosa cáustica (para desatascar tuberías).

washing-machine | 'wɒʃɪŋmə,ʃiːn | *s.c.* lavadora.
washing-up | 'wɒʃɪŋ'ʌp | *s.i.* (brit. y fam.) **1** fregado, fregar: *who is doing the washing-up? = ¿quién va a fregar?* **2** platos, cacharros sucios, fregadero. || **3 – liquid,** detergente, jabón líquido (de fregar).
washout | 'wɒʃaʊt | *s.c.* (fam.) fracaso, ruina.
washroom | 'wɒʃrʊm | *s.c.* (EE.UU.) lavabo, servicio, aseo.
washstand | 'wɒʃtænd | *s.c.* (arc.) lavabo (mueble de dormitorio).
wasn't | 'wɒznt | *pret.* de **to be,** (*contr.* de **was not**), V. **be.**
wasp | wɒsp | *s.c.* ZOOL. avispa.
WASP, Wasp | wɒsp | *s./adj.* (EE.UU. y desp., **white Anglo-Saxon Protestant) 1** de origen anglosajón. **2** de la clase social influyente.
waspish | 'wɒspɪʃ | *adj.* mordaz, sarcástico, puntilloso, irascible.
waspishness | 'wɒspɪʃnɪs | *s.i.* mordacidad, sarcasmo, irascibilidad.
wastage | 'weɪstɪdʒ | *s.i.* **1** derroche, despilfarro, dispendio, desperdicio: *a wastage of energy = un despilfarro de energía.* **2** bajas, pérdidas (por causas naturales).
waste | weɪst | *s.i.* **1** derroche, despilfarro, pérdida, dispendio: *a waste of time = pérdida de tiempo; a waste of money = un derroche de dinero.* **2** residuos, desperdicios: *industrial waste = residuos industriales; radioactive waste = residuos radiactivos.* || *v.t.* **3 [to – (on)]** derrochar, despilfarrar, malgastar, tirar: *he's wasting his talents = está malgastando sus cualidades.* **4** desperdiciar, dejar pasar (oportunidades). **5** (form.) debilitar, consumir, perder, hacer perder (energía, vitalidad): *a wasting disease = una enfermedad que consume.* **6** desaprovechar, hacer inútil, no saber apreciar: *fine clothes are wasted on her = no sabe apreciar la ropa elegante.* || *adj.* **7** inútil, gastado, de tirar: *waste material = material inútil.* **8** de desagüe, de desecho: *waste pipes = tuberías de desagüe.* **9** perdido, abandonado, desolado: *a waste ground = descampado, terreno abandonado.* || **10 to go to –,** desperdiciar, dejar sin aprovechar. **11 to lay to –/to lay – to,** (lit.) aniquilar, destruir totalmente: *to lay waste to a civilization = aniquilar una civilización.* **12 to – away,** decaer, languidecer (la salud). **13 to – no time in doing something,** ponerse manos a la obra al momento. **14 – not, want not,** ahorremos que ya vendrán tiempos peores. **15 to – one's breath,** (fam.) gastar saliva inútilmente. **16 wastes,** (lit.) perdidos, páramos salvajes e improductivos.
wastebasket | 'weɪstbɑːskɪt | *s.c.* (EE.UU.) papelera.
wasted | 'weɪstɪd | *adj.* **1** innecesario, inútil: *a wasted journey = un viaje innecesario.* **2** cansado, débil, de aspecto enfermizo: *you look absolutely wasted = pareces muy cansado.*
wasteful | 'weɪstfʊl | *adj.* **1** derrochador, despilfarrador, antieconómico (hábitos, métodos, procesos, etc.). **2** excesivo, pródigo, extravagante: *wasteful expenditure = gastos excesivos.*
wastefully | 'weɪstfəlɪ | *adv.* derrochadoramente, antieconómicamente, pródigamente, excesivamente.
wastefulness | 'weɪstfʊlnɪs | *s.i.* despilfarro, derroche, prodigalidad.
wasteland | 'weɪstlænd | *s.c.* **1** yermo, tierra baldía: *an industrial wasteland = yermo a causa del desarrollo industrial.* **2** (fig.) experiencia inútil (cultural o espiritualmente).
waste paper | ,weɪst'peɪpər | *s.i.* **1** papeles, basura. || **2 wastepaper basket/bin,** papelera.
waster | 'weɪstər | *s.c.* (desp.) **1** despilfarrador, derrochador, manirroto. **2** descuidado, vago, inútil.
wasting | 'weɪstɪŋ | *adj.* que consume o debilita poco a poco, devastador, destructor: *a wasting disease = una enfermedad que consume poco a poco.*
wastrel | 'weɪstrəl | *s.c.* (lit.) derrochador, despilfarrador, descuidado, manirroto.
watch | wɒtʃ | *v.t.* e *i.* **1** mirar, observar, contemplar: *we were just watching = sólo mirábamos.* **2** ver (televisión, deportes, etc.): *I never watch TV = nunca veo la televisión.* **3** vigilar, cuidar: *she watches her weight = ella vigila su peso.* **4** vigilar, ser responsable: *let her watch the baby = déjala que vigile al niño.* **5** cuidar, prestar atención: *watch what you say = cuida lo que dices.* **6 [to – (at)]** (p.u.) estar despierto y vigilante. || *s.c.* **7** reloj (de pulsera). **8** guardia, vigilancia: *the sentry keeps watch = el centinela hace guardia.* **9** turno de servicio (en la tripulación de un buque). || *s.sing.* **10** (arc.) ronda, patrulla de vigilancia nocturna. || **11 to keep – (for someone/ something),** vigilar, mantener vigilancia. **12 on the – (for someone/something),** estar en guardia. **13 on –,** de servicio (la tripulación de un buque). **14 the watches,** horas de vigilia durante la noche. **15 under –,** sometido a vigilancia (por razones de protección). **16 to – at someone/something,** permanecer en vela al cuidado de alguien o algo. **17 to – for,** esperar, buscar: *she watched for her chance to go = esperó su oportunidad para irse.* **18 -watching,** observación de personas, animales, etc. (según determine la primera parte del compuesto) para su estudio: *bird-watching = observación de pájaros.* **19 – it!,** (fam.) ten cuidado. **20 to – one's step,** (fam.) ir con tiento, andarse con cuidado. **21 – out!,** ¡cuidado!, ¡en guardia! **22 to – out for someone/something, a)** buscar; **b)** tener cuidado: *watch out for his temper = ten cuidado con su genio.* **23 to – over someone/something,** guardar, proteger. **24 to – the clock,** (fam.) estar deseando que algo acabe. **25 to – the time,** estar pendiente de la hora. **26 – this space,** (fam.) espera nueva información. **27 to – the world go by,** observar lo que pasa alrededor. **28 you –,** ya lo verás: *he'll be punished, you watch = le castigarán, ya lo verás.*
watchband | 'wɒtʃbænd | *s.c.* (EE.UU.) correa, pulsera de reloj.
watch-chain | 'wɒtʃtʃeɪn | *s.c.* cadena de reloj (de bolsillo).
watchdog | 'wɒtʃdɒg | *s.c.* **1** perro guardián. **2** (fig.) vigilante, inspector, auditor.
watcher | 'wɒtʃər | *s.c.* **1** espectador, observador, mirón. || **2 -watcher,** observador, estudioso de personas o animales (según se determine en la primera parte del compuesto) para su estudio: *he is a serious bird-watcher = es un concienzudo estudioso de los pájaros.*
watchful | 'wɒtʃfʊl | *adj.* **[– (for)]** vigilante, observador, atento: *he was watchful for any changes = se mantenía atento a cualquier cambio.*
watchfully | 'wɒtʃfəlɪ | *adv.* vigilantemente, observadoramente, atentamente.
watchfulness | 'wɒtʃfʊlnɪs | *s.i.* vigilancia, atención, desvelo.
watchmaker | 'wɒtʃ,meɪkər | *s.c.* relojero.
watchman | 'wɒtʃmən | *s.c.* vigilante, guardián (de un edificio o área edificada).
watchstrap | 'wɒtʃstræp | *s.c.* correa, pulsera de reloj.
watchtower | 'wɒtʃ,taʊər | *s.c.* atalaya, vigía.
watchword | 'wɒtʃwəːd | *s.c.* consigna, lema.
water | 'wɔːtər | *s.i.* **1** agua. **2** agua (corriente, doméstica): *turn the water off = cierra el agua.* **3** masa de agua (río, lago, etc.): *he fell in the water = cayó al agua.* **4** estado de la marea (pleamar, bajamar): *the boat left a high water = el barco partió en pleamar.* || *v.t.* **5** regar: *to water the plants = regar las plantas.* **6** abrevar, dar a beber (a animales): *to water the horses = abrevar a los caballos.* **7** aguar, añadir agua: *to water the wine = aguar el vino.* **8** surcar, regar (ríos). || *v.i.* **9** llorar (los ojos): *the smoke makes my eyes water = el humo me hace llorar los ojos.* **10** hacerse agua (la boca): *the smell of food makes his mouth water = el olor a comida le hace la boca agua.* || **11 above –,** (fam.) fuera de graves dificultades (económicas principalmente). **12 be in/get into hot –,** (fam.) estar/meterse en dificultades. **13 to break waters,** romper aguas. **14 to fish out of,** V. **fish. 15 to hold –,** (fam.) ser sólido, válido, capaz de someterse a prueba (argumentos, teorías, excusas, etc.). **16 in deep –,** en graves dificultades. **17 to keep one's head above,** no tener deudas, aunque no sobre el dinero. **18 like a duck to –,** V. **duck. 19 like –,** (fam.) a manos llenas: *to spend money like water = gastar dinero a manos llenas.* **20 (like) – off a duck's back,** V. **duck. 21 to make/pass –,** (fam.) orinar. **22 to make –,** hacer agua (barcos). **23 of the first –,** de lo mejor, de pri-

merísima calidad. **24 to pour/throw cold – on (suggestions/ideas/plans),** echar un jarro de agua fría, mostrar tibia acogida. **25 to pour oil on troubled waters,** tratar de apaciguar una desavenencia o disputa acalorada. **26 still waters run deep,** las apariencias engañan; hondas emociones se esconden a menudo detrás de una apariencia de tranquilidad. **27 to test the water(s),** tantear el terreno antes de aventurarse en mayores complicaciones. **28 under –, a)** bajo el agua: *to swim under water = nadar bajo el agua;* **b)** inundado: *the field is under water = la parcela está inundada.* **29 – on the brain/on the knee,** líquido en el cerebro, la rodilla, etc., como resultado de enfermedad. **30 – under the bridge,** agua pasada que ya no mueve molinos.

waterbed | 'wɔːtəbed | *s.c.* colchón de agua.

water-bird | 'wɔːtəbɜːd | *s.c.* ave acuática.

water-biscuit | 'wɔːtə,bɪskɪt | *s.c.* galleta de harina y agua (para ser acompañada de mantequilla y queso).

water-blister | 'wɔːtə,blɪstər | *s.c.* ampolla de agua.

waterborne | 'wɔːtəbɔːn | *adj.* **1** transportado en barco (mercancía). **2** contagiado, transmitido por el agua (enfermedad).

water-bottle | 'wɔːtə,bɒtl | *s.c.* **1** botella de vidrio (para beber agua). **2** (brit.) cantimplora.

water-buffalo | 'wɔːtə,bʌfələu | *s.c.* ZOOL. búfalo asiático (empleado como animal de labor).

water-butt | 'wɔːtəbʌt | *s.c.* tubo, cañón (para recoger el agua del tejado).

water-cannon | 'wɔːtə,kænən | *s.c.* propulsor de agua (usado para dispersar grupos de personas).

water-chestnut | 'wɔːtə,tʃesnʌt | *s.c.* tallo de planta china (empleado como ingrediente culinario).

water-closet | 'wɔːtə,klɒzɪt | *s.c.* (arc.) lavabo, aseo, retrete, servicio.

watercolour | 'wɔːtə,kʌlər | (EE.UU. **watercolor**) *s.c.* **1** acuarela. || **2 watercolours,** pinturas para ser mezcladas con agua.

watercourse | 'wɔːtəkɔːs | *s.c.* corriente de agua, canal.

watercress | 'wɔːtəkres | *s.i.* BOT. berro, mastuerzo.

watered-down | 'wɔːtəd,daun | *adj.* (desp.) aguado, rebajado, devaluado.

waterfall | 'wɔːtəfɔːl | *s.c.* cascada, catarata, salto de agua.

waterfowl | 'wɔːtəfaul | *s.c.* aves acuáticas.

waterfront | 'wɔːtəfrʌnt | *s.c.* zona lindera con el agua, puerto, dársenas.

waterhole | 'wɔːtəhəul | *s.c.* charco, charca.

water-ice | 'wɔːtəraɪs | *s.c.* e *i.* (brit.) sorbete, helado.

watering-can | 'wɔːtərɪŋkæn | *s.c.* regadera.

watering-hole | 'wɔːtərɪŋhəul | *s.c.* **1** charco. **2** (hum.) taberna.

water-jump | 'wɔːtədʒʌmp | *s.c.* DEP. obstáculo con agua (competiciones deportivas).

waterless | 'wɔːtəlɪs | *adj.* árido, seco, sediento.

waterlily | 'wɔːtə,lɪlɪ | *s.c.* BOT. nenúfar.

waterline | 'wɔːtəlaɪn | *s.c.* **1** línea de flotación (de embarcaciones). || **2 the light –,** línea de flotación en vacío. **3 the load –,** línea de flotación con carga.

waterlogged | 'wɔːtəlɒgd | , (EE.UU.) | 'wɔːtəlɔːgd | *adj.* empapado, saturado, inundado, anegado.

water-main | 'wɔːtəmeɪn | *s.c.* tubería principal (del abastecimiento de agua).

watermark | 'wɔːtəmɑːk | *s.c.* **1** marca del papel (visible al contraluz). **2** marca, señal del nivel del agua.

water-meadow | 'wɔːtə,medəu | *s.c.* vega.

watermelon | 'wɔːtə,melən | *s.c.* e *i.* sandía.

watermill | 'wɔːtəmɪl | *s.c.* molino de agua.

water-pistol | 'wɔːtə,pɪstl | *s.c.* pistola de agua.

water-polo | 'wɔːtə,pəuləu | *s.i.* DEP. waterpolo.

water-power | 'wɔːtə,pauər | *s.i.* energía hidráulica.

waterproof | 'wɔːtəpruːf | *adj.* **1** impermeable, a prueba de agua. || *s.c.* **2** impermeable. || *v.t.* **3** impermeabilizar.

water-rat | 'wɔːtəræt | *s.c.* ZOOL. rata de agua.

water-rate | 'wɔːtə,reɪt | *s.c.* (brit.) factura del agua.

water-resistant | 'wɔːtərɪ,zɪstənt | *adj.* resistente al agua, a prueba de agua.

waters | 'wɔːtəz | *s.pl.* **1** aguas territoriales: *fishing in Spanish waters = pescando en aguas territoriales españolas.* **2** aguas fluviales: *the waters of the Thames = las aguas del Támesis.* **3** aguas medicinales: *to take the waters = tomar las aguas.*

watershed | 'wɔːtəʃed | *s.c.* **1** vertiente, línea divisoria de aguas. **2** (fig.) cambio profundo, rumbo nuevo.

waterside | 'wɔːtəsaɪd | *s.sing.* **1** orilla, ribera. || *atr.* **2** ribereño.

water-ski | 'wɔːtəskiː | *s.c.* esquí (de esquí acuático): *a pair of skis.*

water-skiing | 'wɔːtəskiːɪŋ | *s.i.* DEP. esquí acuático.

water-softener | 'wɔːtə,sɒfnər | *s.c.* e *i.* suavizante de agua.

water-soluble | 'wɔːtə,sɒljubl | *adj.* soluble, diluible en agua.

waterspout | 'wɔːtəspaut | *s.c.* tormenta marina.

water-supply | 'wɔːtəsə,plaɪ | *s.c.* e *i.* **1** abastecimiento de agua. **2** agua embalsada, reserva de agua (para abastecer una población).

water-table | 'wɔːtə,teɪbl | *s.c.* nivel de los acuíferos subterráneos.

watertight | 'wɔːtətaɪt | *adj.* **1** hermético, seguro, de cierre perfecto. **2** (fig.) irrecusable, lógico, cuidadoso, minucioso (plan, coartada, excusa, etc.).

water-tower | 'wɔːtə,tauər | *s.c.* depósito de agua elevado.

water-vole | 'wɔːtə,vəul | *s.c.* ZOOL. rata de agua.

waterway | 'wɔːtəweɪ | *s.c.* vía fluvial, canal navegable.

waterwheel | 'wɔːtəwiːl | *s.c.* rueda hidráulica.

water-wings | 'wɔːtə,wɪŋz | *s.pl.* flotadores, nadaderas.

waterworks | 'wɔːtəwɜːks | *s.pl.* **1** sistema de abastecimiento de agua. **2** (brit. y euf.) sistema urinario humano. || **3 to turn on the –,** (fam.) romper a llorar.

watery | 'wɔːtərɪ | *adj.* **1** (desp.) aguado, acuoso, ligero, claro: *watery coffee = café ligero.* **2** de color pálido: *a watery sun = un sol pálido.* **3** húmedo, que amenaza lluvia: *a watery sky = cielo que amenaza lluvia.* **4** (lit.) en el agua, ahogado: *a watery grave = muerte en el agua (ahogado).*

watt | wɒt | *s.c.* vatio.

wattage | 'wɒtɪdʒ | *s.i.* vatiaje.

wattle | 'wɒtl | *s.c.* e *i.* **1** zarzo. **2** carúncula, barba (del pavo o del gallo). **3** BOT. acacia australiana.

wattle-and-daub | ,wɒtlən'dɔːb | *s.i.* mezcla de zarzo y barro (usada antiguamente en la construcción de paredes).

wave | weɪv | *s.c.* **1** ola. **2** ademán, movimiento de mano (de saludo, despedida, etc.). **3 [– (of)]** oleada, corriente (de algún tipo de sentimiento, conducta, etc.): *a wave of enthusiasm = ola de entusiasmo; a cold wave = ola de frío.* **4** onda (de transmisión de energía): *sound waves = ondas sonoras.* **5** cabello ondulado (natural o artificialmente). || *v.t.* e *i.* **6 [– (at)]** agitar la mano (en señal de saludo, despedida, etc.): *he waved at us as he left = agitaba su mano hacia nosotros al partir.* **7** expresar saludo/despedida (moviendo la mano): *she waved us goodbye = nos decía adiós con la mano.* **8** dirigir, ordenar, organizar (con la mano): *the policeman waved the car on = el policía ordenó que el coche avanzara.* **9** ondear (la bandera). **10** ondular, ser/crecer ondulado (el pelo): *her hair waves naturally = su pelo es ondulado.* || **11 in waves,** en oleadas: *the invaders came in waves = los invasores llegaron en oleadas.* **12 the waves,** (form.) el mar. **13 to – along/away/ on/etc.,** indicar con la mano, seguir una dirección determinada: *he waved them away = les indicó que se retiraran.* **14 to – aside,** rechazar (ideas, sugerencias, etc.) como irrelevantes: *his plan was waved aside = rechazaron su plan.* **15 to – down,** indicar a alguien con la mano que se detenga: *he waved the driver down = indicó al conductor que detuviera el coche.*

waveband | 'weɪvbænd | *s.c.* FIS. banda de onda.

wavelength | 'weɪvleŋθ | *s.c.* **1** FIS. longitud de onda. || **2 on the same –,** en la misma longitud de onda, en sintonía.

waver | 'weɪvər | *v.i.* **1** desfallecer, flaquear, debilitarse: *his courage never wavered = su valor nunca flaqueó.* **2** vacilar, dudar, oscilar: *to waver betwe-*

en two points of view = dudar entre dos puntos de vista. **3** debilitarse, parpadear (luz, llama, etc.).
wavering | 'weɪvərɪŋ | *adj.* indeciso, vacilante, inseguro, irresoluto, tembloroso (personas, pasos, voz, etc.).
wavily | 'weɪvɪlɪ | *adv.* onduladamente, ondulantemente.
waviness | 'weɪvɪnɪs | *s.i.* ondulación.
wavy | 'weɪvɪ | *adj.* ondulado, ondulante, curvo: *a wavy line = línea curva.*
wax | wæks | *s.i.* **1** cera, cerumen. || *v.t.* **2** encerar, dar cera. || *v.i.* **3** (lit.) estar en cuarto creciente (la luna). **4 [to -- + *adj.*]** (arc.) ponerse, convertirse, hacerse: *he waxed sad as he told the story = se puso triste al contar la historia.* || **5 to – and wane,** crecer y decrecer en importancia, brillar y extinguirse: *empires have waxed and waned = los imperios han brillado para luego extinguirse.* **6 wax(ed) paper,** papel encerado.
waxen | 'wæksən | *adj.* (form.) pálido: *a waxen complexion = aspecto pálido.* **2** (arc.) de cera.
waxwork | 'wækswɔːk | *s.c.* **1** figura de cera (de tamaño y aspecto naturales). || **2 waxworks,** museo de cera.
waxy | 'wæksɪ | *adj.* pálido, como la cera: *waxy skin = piel pálida.*
way | weɪ | *s.c.* **1** camino, ruta (a seguir): *is this the way out? = ¿es ésta la salida (camino hacia fuera)?* **2** dirección: *which way is the station? = ¿en qué dirección está la estación?; come this way = por aquí.* **3** manera, modo, forma (de hacer algo): *cook it this way = cocínalo de este modo (así).* **4** distancia (cerca, lejos, etc.): *a long way from home = lejos de casa.* **5** forma, estilo, aire (característico de conducta): *he smiles in a superior way = sonríe con aires de superioridad.* **6** aspecto, punto de vista, ángulo: *there are two ways to look at it = hay dos aspectos a considerar.* **7** opción (entre dos o más alternativas): *they're deciding which way to cast their vote = están decidiendo a qué opción votar.* **8** opinión, actitud: *she still feels the same way = mantiene la misma opinión.* || **9 across/over the –,** cerca, en frente, al otro lado de la calle: *we just live across the way = vivimos ahí enfrente.* **10 all the –/most of the –/half the –,** todo/la mayor parte/la mitad del camino o trecho. **11 a long –/quite a –/a little –,** lejos/bastante lejos/un poco lejos. **12 always the –,** (fam.) como siempre, para no variar (de algo negativo). **13 as is the –/that's the way,** típico, como suele suceder. **14 to be on one's –,** estar de camino, haber comenzado ya el viaje. **15 to be on the –/on its –,** estar a punto de llegar, estar próximo a aparecer: *the book is on its way = el libro va a aparecer próximamente.* **16 to be well on one's way (to something),** tener mucho camino andado, estar ya cerca de conseguir algo. **17 by a long –,** con mucho, sin comparación: *that's my favourite program by a long way = ése es con mucho mi programa favorito.* **18 by the –,** a propósito. **19 by – of, a)** a modo de, a guisa de: *he told us a joke by way of introduction = nos contó un chiste a modo de introducción;* **b)** por, pasando por, vía: *we came by way of Paris = vinimos pasando por París.* **20 to come one's –,** encontrarse con algo sin esfuerzo, salirle a uno al paso: *opportunities came my way = las oportunidades me salieron al paso.* **21 either –,** de una u otra forma, en cualquier caso. **22 to get/have one's –,** conseguir hacer las cosas de la manera que uno quiere: *he always gets his way = siempre consigue hacer las cosas a su manera.* **23 to get in the –,** estar en medio, estorbar, obstaculizar. **24 to get into/out of the – of (doing) something,** habituarse/perder el hábito de hacer algo. **25 to give –,** romperse, hundirse, ceder (por efecto del peso). **26 to give – (to someone/something), a)** ceder el paso (tráfico): *give way to traffic from the right = ceda el paso al tráfico de la derecha;* **b)** ceder, rendirse: *to give way to despair = rendirse a la desesperación;* **c)** hacer concesiones: *to give way to demands = hacer concesiones a reivindicaciones;* **d)** dar paso, abrirse: *the storm gave way to bright sunshine = la tormenta dio paso a un sol brillante.* **27 to go one's own –,** hacer lo que uno quiere al margen de los demás. **28 to go on one's –,** continuar el viaje de uno. **29 to go out of one's – to do something,** relegar a un lado lo habitual por atender algo imprevisto. **30 to have a – of doing something,** hacer algo frecuentemente. **31 to have a – with one,** tener el don de atraer o persuadir a otros. **32 to have a – with someone/something,** tener una mano especial, dársele bien a uno: *she has a way with difficult children = tiene una mano especial con los niños difíciles.* **33 to have it all/everything one's own –,** resultar todo como uno quiere. **34 to have it one's (own) –,** hacer algo como a uno le gusta (aunque lo acepten mal): *Have it your way = Hazlo como te plazca.* **35 to have one's evil/wicked – with a woman,** (arc. y fam.) seducir y acostarse con una mujer. **36 in a big/ small –,** a gran/pequeña escala: *he went into business in a big way = se introdujo en los negocios a lo grande.* **37 in a good/bad –,** en buen/mal estado. **38 in a –/in some ways/in many ways/in every –,** en uno/algunos/muchos/todos los aspectos. **39 in more ways than one,** en más de un sentido. **40 in on –/not in any –,** en absoluto: *I wasn't put off in any way = en absoluto me hicieron desistir.* **41 in one's (own) –,** a su manera, sólo en algún aspecto: *in his own way he was an actor = a su manera, fue un actor.* **42 in the same –,** del mismo modo. **43 in the – of,** en concepto de, en cuanto, a : *he got very little in the way of wages = consiguió muy poco en concepto de sueldo.* **44 in the – that/in a – that,** de forma tal, como: *it affected her in a way that nothing had done = le afectó como nada lo había hecho.* **45 to keep out of someone's –,** evitar a alguien. **46 to know/to have learned one's – about/around,** saber por dónde anda uno. **47 to lose one's –,** no saber qué dirección tomar. **48 to make one's – (somewhere),** (form.) ir, dirigirse, trasladarse. **49 to make –,** ceder/dejar sitio, ahuecar. **50 no two ways about it,** sin duda alguna al respecto. **51 no –,** (fam.) no, ni hablar. **52 one – or another/the other,** de todas formas, en cualquier caso. **53 on one's –,** en el camino o viaje, durante el camino o viaje: *they spoke very little on their way back = hablaron muy poco en su viaje de vuelta.* **54 on the –/along the –, a)** durante el viaje; **b)** en el transcurso, durante el proceso (de un acontecimiento, gestión, aventura, etc.): *of course, there were some problems along the way = por supuesto, surgieron problemas durante el proceso.* **55 on the – out,** pronto a desaparecer o ser reemplazado (personas, cargos). **56 out of one's –,** a trasmano. **57 to see one's – clear,** (fam.) no tener grandes dificultades a la vista para llevar algo a cabo. **58 to see/realize the error of one's ways,** admitir los errores propios. **59 (something is) out of the –/to have something out of the –,** quedar algo resuelto, no constituir problema. **60 to take the easy – out,** hacer lo fácil y no lo que es debido. **61 that's the –,** estupendo, me alegro (de que estés bien o de que te vayan bien las cosas). **62 that's the – the cookie crumbles,** (EE.UU. y fam.) así es la cosa y de nada sirve darle vueltas. **63 that –/this –,** así, de esa/esta manera. **64 the other (a)round,** al revés. **64 there's no –/there isn't any –,** no hay manera, no hay posibilidad alguna. **66 the – of all flesh,** la muerte, que a todos iguala: *to go the way of all flesh = morir, como todo el mundo/sufrir el mismo trato que los demás.* **67 the – of the world,** la conducta de la mayoría de la gente. **68 to my – of thinking,** en mi opinión. **69 under –,** en proceso, realizándose. **70 – of life, a)** forma de ser (de una persona, grupo, etc.): *the American way of life = la forma de ser de los norteamericanos;* **b)** talante: *being a teacher is a way of life rather than a job = la enseñanza es más un talante que una profesión.* **71 -way,** dirección, banda, parte, etc. (según determine el numeral de la primera parte del compuesto): *a two-way radio = radio de doble dirección; a three-way conversation = conversación a tres bandas; a four-way split = división en cuatro partes.* **72 ways, a)** destinos, vidas, trayectorias, caminos: *their ways led apart = sus destinos se separaron;* **b)** partes, porciones: *the money was divided three ways = se dividió el dinero en tres partes;* **c)** costumbres, manías: *we all have our funny little ways = todos tenemos nuestras pequeñas manías;* **d)** (EE.UU.) camino, trecho, distancia: *we're a long ways to go yet = todavía nos queda un buen trecho.* **73 you can't have it both ways,** o una cosa o la otra.

wayfarer | 'weɪˌfeərər | *s.c.* (lit.) caminante.
waylay | weɪ'leɪ | *v.t.* [*pret.* y *p.p.irreg.* **waylaid**] (arc.) abordar (personas): *to waylay somebody on the street = abordar a alguien en la calle.*
way-out | weɪ'aʊt | *adj.* (arc. y fam.) pasado, pasado de moda, raro: *way-out clothes = ropa pasada de moda.*
wayside | 'weɪsaɪd | *s.c.* (arc.) **1** lado, borde de la carretera. || **2 to fall by the –,** fracasar en el intento de conseguir algo.
wayward | 'weɪwəd | *adj.* voluble, egoísta, porfiado, díscolo.
w.c. | ˌdʌblju:'si: | *s.c.* (abreviatura de **water closet**) servicio, lavabo, aseo (usado en publicidad de viviendas, principalmente).
we | wi: | *pron.pers.suj.* **1** nosotros (hablante y otro/otros): *we study English = (nosotros) estudiamos inglés; we went by car = (nosotros) fuimos en coche.* **2** nosotros (el escritor y sus lectores, el profesor y sus alumnos, etc.): *we saw in chapter I... = vimos en el capítulo I...* **3** (form.) nos (mayestático). **4** (form.) nosotros (los humanos, la gente, en general): *do we have the right to spoil wild life? = ¿tenemos derecho a deteriorar la vida salvaje?* **5** (fam.) nosotros (referido a niños, enfermos, ancianos, etc.): *and how are we feeling today? = ¿qué, cómo nos sentimos hoy?*
OBS. El sujeto pronominal, **we** en este caso, va siempre expreso en la frase inglesa, por carecer el verbo inglés de marca de persona en la mayoría de sus tiempos. En español, por el contrario, el pronombre personal en funciones de sujeto no suele ir expreso, a no ser que esté enfatizado.
weak | wi:k | *adj.* **1** débil, flojo: *weak after illness = débil tras enfermedad.* **2** blando (de carácter): *a weak leader = un líder blando.* **3** claro, poco cargado: *weak tea = té poco cargado.* **4** flojo, deficiente, imperfecto, defectuoso (sentidos): *weak eyes/sight = vista deficiente.* **5** tenue, mortecino: *a weak light = una luz mortecina.* **6** inconsistente, poco convincente (excusas, argumentos, etc.): *weak evidence = prueba inconsistente.* **7** limitado, corto, sin atractivo (ideas, movimientos, corrientes, etc.): *the movement proved weak internationally = el movimiento resultó falto de atractivo internacional.* || **8 a – moment,** un momento de debilidad o descuido. **9 the –,** los débiles: los pobres, enfermos, marginados, etc. (presas fáciles de explotación). **10 – at the knees,** (fam.) flojo en momentos en que hay que demostrar fortaleza. **11 – in the head,** (fam.) retrasado mental, bobo, ingenuo.
weaken | 'wi:kən | *v.t.* e *i.* **1** debilitar, debilitarse, flaquear, desfallecer. **2** ablandarse, ceder (a ruegos, presiones, etc.). **3** bajar, perder valor (la moneda): *the dollar could weaken further = el dólar podría seguir bajando.* **4** debilitar, reducir (la fuerza de una postura o un argumento): *they tried to weaken the position of the strikers = trataron de debilitar la postura de los huelguistas.*
weak-kneed | ˌwi:k'ni:d | *adj.* (fam.) débil, inconstante, sin voluntad.
weakling 'wi:klɪŋ | *s.c.* **1** ser delicado, persona enfermiza. **2** cobarde.
weakly | 'wi:klɪ | *adv.* débilmente, flojamente, tenuemente, deficientemente.
weakness | 'wi:knɪs | *s.i.* **1** debilidad, inconsistencia, desvalorización. || *s.c.* **2** punto flaco, debilidad: *food is one of her weaknesses = la comida es una de sus debilidades.*
weal | wi:l | *s.c.* contusión, moratón, verdugón, cicatriz, señal.
wealth | welθ | *s.i.* **1** riqueza, fortuna (dinero, propiedades, etc.): *a man of wealth = un hombre de gran fortuna.* || *s.sing.* **2 [– of]** (form.) riqueza de, abundancia de, profusión de: *a book with a wealth of illustrations = libro con profusión de ilustraciones.*
wealthy | 'welθɪ | *adj.* **1** rico, adinerado, acaudalado, hacendado (personas). **2 [– (in)]** rico, abundante, pródigo (lugares, pueblos, etc.): *a country wealthy in historic monuments = un país rico en monumentos históricos.* || **3 the –,** los ricos, (Am.) los amonedados.
wean | wi:n | *v.t.* **1** destetar (personas, animales). **2 [to – (from/off)]** desacostumbrar, deshabituar, apartar, alejar: *to wean people from smoking = deshabituar del tabaco.* || **3 to – someone on something,** crear/desarrollar una fuerte dependencia: *children are being weaned on TV = se está creando en los niños una fuerte dependencia de la televisión.*
weaning | 'wi:nɪŋ | *s.i.* destete.
weapon | 'wepən | *s.c.* **1** arma. **2** (fig.) arma, aliado, recurso, instrumento: *humour is his best weapon = el humor es su mejor arma.*
weaponry | 'wepənrɪ | *s.i.* armamento, armas.
wear | weər | *v. t.* [*pret.irreg.* **wore**, *p.p.irreg.* **worn**] **1** llevar puesto, vestir, lucir (ropa, complementos, adornos, etc.): *he wears expensive clothes = viste ropa cara; she wore dark glasses = llevaba gafas oscuras.* **2** (lit.) lucir, manifestar, exteriorizar (determinadas expresiones): *she wore a bright look = lucía una expresión radiante.* **3** (brit. y fam.) aceptar, tragar, aguantar, pasar por ello: *he wanted to buy the flat but his wife wouldn't wear it = él quería comprar el piso, pero su mujer no tragaba.* || *i.* **4** gastarse, envejecer, llevar (mal) la edad: *he has worn badly = ha envejecido mucho.* **5** durar, aguantar (el tiempo): *this carpet wears well = esta moqueta aguanta bien.* || *s.i.* **6** uso (de ropa): *a suit for everyday wear = un traje para uso diario.* **7** desgaste, deterioro (por el uso): *your trousers show signs of wear = tus pantalones están ya muy usados (muestran signos de desgaste).* **8** vida, (capacidad de) uso: *there's still a lot of wear left in these tyres = aún les queda mucha vida a estas ruedas.* **9** ropa: *men's wear = ropa de caballero; evening wear = ropa de noche.* || **10 the worse for –,** (fam.) cansado, gastado, deteriorado, roto (por exceso de trabajo o uso). **11 – and tear,** uso, desgaste por el uso. **12 to – off,** remitir, debilitarse, desaparecer progresivamente: (sentimientos, sensaciones, etc.): *eventually the pain wore off = finalmente desapareció el dolor.* **13 to – on,** transcurrir, alargarse, prolongarse: *the evening was wearing on = iba transcurriendo la tarde.* **14 to – one's heart on one's sleeve,** (fam.) ser incapaz de guardar los sentimientos. **15 to – (something) away,** gastar, deteriorar, borrar, erosionar, desaparecer: *the inscription has worn away = la inscripción se ha gastado.* **16 to – something/someone down, a)** gastar; **b)** reducir, debilitar: *our insistence wore their opposition down = nuestra insistencia debilitó su oposición.* **17 to – something /someone out, a)** gastar, destrozar, dejar para el arrastre: *I wore out two pairs of shoes in a week = destrocé dos pares de zapatos en dos semanas;* **b)** cansar, dejar molido: *the children are wearing me out = los niños me están dejando molido.* **18 to – the trousers,** (fam.) llevar los pantalones, mandar. **19 to – thin,** estar a punto de acabarse, perder utilidad o interés, dejar de convencer: *his excuses are wearing a bit thin = sus excusas ya no convencen.*
wearable | 'weərəbl | *adj.* que se puede llevar o poner, decente, en buen uso.
wearer | 'weərər | *s.c.* usuario, el que viste (ropa, calzado, etc.).
wearied | 'wɪərɪd | *adj.* (form.) muy cansado, harto.
wearily | 'wɪərɪlɪ | *adv.* cansadamente, fatigadamente, aburridamente.
weariness | 'wɪərɪnɪs | *s.i.* cansancio, fatiga, abatimiento, aburrimiento.
wearing | 'weərɪŋ | *adj.* **1** cansado, pesado, agotador, molesto: *a wearing job = un trabajo agotador.* **2** perjudicial, nocivo (por debilitar, gastar, etc.): *it is very wearing on the teeth = es nocivo para los dientes.*
wearisome | 'wɪərɪsəm | *adj.* (form.) cansado, pesado, agotador, frustrante.
weary | 'wɪərɪ | *adj.* **1** cansado, exhausto, roto, hastiado. **2** aburrido, desinteresado. **3** (form.) cansado, fatigoso, agotador, pesado, fastidioso, aburrido. || (form.) *v.i.* **4** cansarse, hartarse, estar harto: *I was beginning to weary = comenzaba a estar harto.* || *v.t.* **5** cansar, fatigar, aburrir: *she wearies you with her questions = cansa con sus preguntas.*
weasel | 'wi:zl | *s.c.* **1** ZOOL. comadreja. || **2 to – out (of),** (EE.UU. y fam.) eludir responsabilidades, escurrir el bulto.
weather | 'weðər | *s.i.* **1** tiempo (atmosférico): *what's the weather like? = ¿qué tiempo hace?* || *v.t.* **2** aguantar, hacer frente, superar: *to weather a cri-*

sis = superar una crisis. || *v.i.* **3** erosionarse, curarse o secarse (la madera), curtirse (la piel): *wood weathers better if it is treated = la madera cura mejor si se la trata.* || **4 a – eye on (something),** alerta para evitar contratiempos. **5 in all weathers,** haga frío o haga sol. **6 to make heavy – (of something),** complicar las cosas, hacer algo más difícil de lo que es. **7 under the –,** (fam.) ligeramente indispuesto. **8 – forecast,** pronóstico meteorológico. **9 – forecaster,** pronosticador del tiempo. **10 – station,** estación meteorológica.

weatherbeaten | 'weðə,biːtn | *adj.* curtido por el tiempo (la cara).

weathercock | 'weðəkɒk | *s.c.* veleta.

weatherman | 'weðəmæn | *s.c.* hombre del tiempo.

weatherproof | 'weðəpruːf | *adj.* a prueba de intemperie.

weather-vane | 'weðəveɪn | *s.c.* veleta.

weave | wiːv | *v. t.* [*pret.irreg.* **wove,** *p.p.irreg.* **woven**] **1** tejer. **2** urdir, tramar: *to weave a complicated plan = urdir un plan complicado.* **3** entramar, entrelazar: *he wove some branches together for the roof = entrelazó unas ramas para hacer el techo.* **4** entretejer, trenzar: *when birds weave their nests = cuando los pájaros entretejen sus nidos.* || *i.* [*pret.* y *p.p.* **eaved**]. **5** abrirse paso, avanzar (sorteando obstáculos): *he weaved his way through the crowd = se abrió paso entre la multitud.* || *s.c.* **6** tejido, textura: *a tight weave = textura prieta.* || **7 to get weaving,** (brit. y fam.) aplicarse a la tarea.

weaver | 'wiːvər | *s.c.* tejedor.

weaving | 'wiːvɪŋ | *s.i.* tejido, tejeduría.

web | web | *s.c.* **1** tela, tejido, telaraña, red. **2** entramado, maraña: *a complex web of reasons = una compleja maraña de razones.* **3** membrana (palmípedos).

webbed | webd | *adj.* palmeado.

webbing | 'webɪŋ | *s.i.* lona, cincha, correa, banda trenzada.

wed | wed | *v.t.* e *i.* [*pret. y p.p.* **wedded** o **wed**] (lit.) casarse, unirse en matrimonio: *they wed in April = se casaron en abril.*

we'd | wɪd | *contr.* **1** we had: *we'd been there before = habíamos estado allí antes.* **2 we would:** *the questions we'd like to ask = las preguntas que nos gustaría hacer.*

wedded | 'wedɪd | *adj.* (form.) **1** casado, legítimo. **2 [– (to)]** comprometido, empeñado: *wedded to her ideas = comprometida con sus ideas.* **3 [– (to)]** relacionado, vinculado, aferrado, inseparable: *beauty wedded to simplicity = la belleza inseparable de la sencillez.*

wedding | 'wedɪŋ | *s.c.* boda, casamiento, enlace matrimonial.

wedge | wedʒ | *s.c.* **1** cuña, calce, calza. **2** tronco, porción, pedazo (de queso o tarta). || *v.t.* **3** acuñar, calzar, fijar con cuñas: *to wedge a window = fijar una ventana con cuñas.* **4** meter a presión, encajar, apretarse: *he was wedged between two other passengers = estaba apretado entre otros dos pasajeros.* || **5 to drive a – (between people),** enemistar a terceras personas entre sí para beneficio propio. **6 the thin end of the –,** el principio de muchos males, aunque no lo parezca.

wedlock | 'wedlɒk | *s.i.* **1** (form.) matrimonio, estado de casado. || **2 born in –,** nacido dentro del matrimonio, legítimo. **3 born out of –,** ilegítimo (hijo).

Wednesday | 'wenzdɪ | *s.c.* e *i.* miércoles.

wee | wiː | *adj.* **1** (fam.) pequeño, diminuto, pequeñito (Escocia): *a wee fishing place = un pequeñito enclave pesquero.* || *s.i.* **2** (fam.) meado, orín, meada. || *v.i.* **3** (vulg.) mear.

weed | wiːd | *s.c.* **1** mala hierba. **2** ova. **3** (brit. y juv.) enclenque, pasmarote. **4** (fam.) tabaco, marihuana. || *v.t.* e *i.* **5** quitar hierba. || **6 weeds,** (arc.) (ropa de) luto: *she wears her widow's weeds = viste el luto de viuda.* **7 to – someone/something out,** deshacerse de los incompetentes o de otros obstáculos para que un negocio rinda más.

weeding | 'wiːdɪŋ | *s.i.* escarda, desherbaje, limpieza de hierbas.

weed-killer | 'wiːd,kɪlər | *s.c.* herbicida.

weedy | 'wiːdɪ | *adj.* **1** perdido, cubierto de hierbas. **2** escuálido, enclenque, inerte.

week | wiːk | *s.c.* **1** semana. **2** (fam.) semana laboral, días laborables: *I never cook during the week = nunca cocino en días laborables.* || **3 a – last Monday/yesterday/etc.,** el lunes/ayer/etc. hizo ocho días. **4 for weeks on end,** durante largo tiempo. **5 from – to –,** de una semana para otra, en cuestión de semanas. **6 today/tomorrow/Monday/etc. –,** desde hoy/mañana/el lunes/etc. en ocho días. **7 – after –,** semana tras semana. **8 – by –,** todas las semanas, continuamente. **9 – in, – out,** una semana sí y la otra también.

weekday | 'wiːkdeɪ | *s.c.* día laborable, día entre semana.

weekend | ,wiːk'end | (EE.UU.) | 'wiːkend | *s.c.* **1** fin de semana. || *v.i.* **2** pasar el fin de semana: *they're weekendling in the country = están pasando el fin de semana en el campo.* || **3 long –,** puente.

weekender | ,wiːk'endər | *s.c.* residente de fin de semana.

weekly | 'wiːklɪ | *adj.* **1** semanal: *a weekly newspaper = periódico semanal; weekly earnings = haberes semanales.* || *adv.* **2** semanalmente, a la semana, por semana: *we meet weekly = nos reunimos semanalmente.* || *s.c.* **3** semanario, publicación semanal: *they control three weeklies = controlan tres semanarios.*

weeny | 'wiːnɪ | *adj.* (fam.) pequeñito, diminuto, poquito.

weep | wiːp | [*pret.* y *p.p.irreg.* **wept**] *i.* (lit.) **1** llorar. **2** rezumar, supurar (heridas): *the wound is no longer weeping = la herida ya no supura.* || *t.* **3** llorar, derramar (lágrimas): *she was weeping tears of joy = lloraba de alegría.* || *s.sing.* **4** llanto, llantina: *they had a little weep together = compartieron el llanto un rato.* || **5 weeping willow,** BOT. sauce llorón.

weepy | 'wiːpɪ | *adj.* **1** lloroso, de lágrima fácil. || *s.c.* **2** (fam.) película o historia sentimental.

weevil | 'wiːvɪl | *s.c.* ZOOL. gorgojo.

wee-wee | 'wiːwiː | *s.i.* (fam.) orín (balbuceo de niños).

weft | weft | *s.sing.* trama, red (tejido).

weigh | weɪ | *v.t.* e *i.* **1** pesar: *it weighs two tons = pesa dos toneladas.* **2** pesar (en báscula): *to weigh a baby = pesar a un niño.* **3** pesar, sopesar (los pros y los contras): *all the factors have to be weighed = hay que sopesar todos los puntos.* **4** pesar, importar, influir. || **5 to be weighed down (by/with something), a)** estar rendido o vencido: *the branch was weighed down with the apples = la rama estaba vencida por las manzanas;* **b)** estar oprimido por algún tipo de dificultad: *weighed down by the burdon of state secrets = oprimido por el peso de los secretos de estado.* **6 to – anchor,** V. **anchor. 7 to – a ton,** (fam.) pesar mucho: *these cases weigh a ton = estas maletas pesan un montón.* **8 to – in (at something),** dar un peso determinado (un jinete, un boxeador, etc., antes de una competición). **9 to – in (with something),** (fam.) terciar de forma convincente y eficaz en una discusión o argumentación. **10 to – one's words,** elegir cuidadosamente las palabras para expresarse con precisión. **11 to – on someone/something,** pesar sobre alguien/ algo: *the worries weigh heavily on him = las preocupaciones pesan sobre él.* **12 to – someone/something down,** impedir que alguien se mueva ágilmente por el exceso de peso: *the luggage weighed him down = el equipaje le impedía moverse con agilidad.* **13 to – something out,** pesar cosas: *she weighed out a kilo of oranges = pesó un kilo de naranjas.* **14 to – someone up,** estudiar a alguien (para hacerse una idea cabal): *there they stood weighing each other up = allí estaban estudiándose mutuamente.* **15 to – something up,** sopesar los pros y los contras.

weighbridge | 'weɪbrɪdʒ | *s.c.* báscula de puente.

weigh-in | 'weɪɪn | *s.c.* pesaje (de deportistas antes de una competición).

weight | weɪt | *s.c.* e *i.* **1** peso: *ten kilos in weight = diez kilos de peso.* **2** pesa: *a five-kilo weight = una pesa de cinco kilos.* **3** peso, cosas pesadas: *you shouldn't lift weights = no debes levantar pesos.* **4** peso (sistema convencional): *tables of weights and measures = tablas de pesos y medidas.* **5 [– (on/off)]** peso, carga, preocupación: *a weight off one's mind = el peso que uno se quita de encima.* **6** peso, valor, importancia, influencia, relieve: *don't give much weight to rumours = no des mucho valor a los rumores.* **7** FIS. peso, fuerza de atracción. || *v.t.* **8** poner, añadir peso: *fishing nets are weighted = a las redes de pesca se les añade peso.* || **9 a – off one's mind,** V. **mind. 10 to carry –,** V. **carry. 11 to lose –,** perder peso. **12 to pull one's –,** arrimar el hombro. **13 to put on/gain –,** aumentar peso, poner peso. **14 to take the – off one's feet,** (fam.) sentarse a descansar. **15 to throw one's – about,** actuar agresivamente y con abuso de autoridad. **16 to throw one's – behind (someone),** emplear todos los medios al alcance para apoyar a alguien. **17 to – someone/something down (with),** ir rendido por el peso, cargar de forma que dificulte el movimiento: *she was weighted down with parcels = iba rendida por el peso de los paquetes.* **18 worth one's – in gold,** (valer) su peso en oro, muy útil, inestimable.

weighted | 'weɪtɪd | *adj.* **[– in favour of]** inclinado, favorable, del lado de: *a law weighted in favour of the wealthy = una ley favorable a los ricos.*

weightily | 'weɪtɪlɪ | *adv.* pesadamente, gravosamente, seriamente.

weightiness | 'weɪtɪnɪs | *s.i.* pesadez, gravosidad, seriedad, importancia.

weighting | 'weɪtɪŋ | *s.i.* (brit.) gratificación, plus, bonificación (por trabajar en una ciudad cara): *a London weighting allowance = bonificación por trabajar en Londres.*

weightless | 'weɪtlɪs | *adj.* ingrávido, muy liviano, no sometido a la gravedad: *in weightless conditions = en condiciones no sometidas a la gravedad.*

weightlessness | 'weɪtlɪsnɪs | *s.i.* ingravidez.

weightlifter | 'weɪtlɪftər | *s.c.* DEP. levantador de peso.

weightlifting | 'weɪtlɪftɪŋ | *s.i.* DEP. levantamiento de peso.

weighty | 'weɪtɪ | *adj.* **1** pesado, gravoso. **2** (form.) serio, grave, importante (asuntos, decisiones, etc.).

weir | wɪər | *s.c.* **1** vertedero, vertedor (de embalse). **2** dique, tapia de contención (para pequeñas recogidas de agua).

weird | wɪəd | *adj.* **1** extraño, peculiar, misterioso, inquietante. **2** (brit. y fam.) raro, anormal, extravagante, llamativo: *he's certainly weird but not mad = es raro, ciertamente, pero no está loco.*

weirdie | 'wɪədɪ | V. **weirdo.**

weirdly | 'wɪədlɪ | *adv.* extrañamente, misteriosamente, inquietantemente.

weirdness | 'wɪədnɪs | *s.i.* rareza, peculiaridad, misterio, originalidad.

weirdo | 'wɪədəʊ | (también **weirdie**) *s.c.* (fam.) persona excéntrica, ser extraño.

welch | welʃ | V. **welsh.**

welcome | 'welkəm | *v.t.* **1** dar la bienvenida, saludar, acoger, recibir. **2** aceptar, admitir: *we always welcome people from outside = siempre admitimos gente de fuera.* || *adj.* **3** bienvenido: *all suggestions are welcome = todas las sugerencias son bienvenidas.* **4** bienvenido, grato, agradable, deseable: *welcome news = noticias gratas.* || *s.c.* **5** bienvenida, recibimiento, acogida: *a warm welcome = un cálido recibimiento.* || *interj.* **6** ¡bienvenido!: *welcome back! = ¡bienvenido de vuelta!* || **7 to make someone –,** hacer que alguien se sienta bien recibido. **8 to outstay/overstay one's –,** abusar de la hospitalidad (prolongando la estancia como invitado). **9 to – with open arms,** recibir con los brazos abiertos. **10 you're welcome,** (EE.UU.) de nada, no hay de qué.

welcoming | 'welkəmɪŋ | *adj.* acogedor, cordial.

weld | weld | *v.t.* **1** soldar. **2** (form. y fig.) unir, ensamblar, mantener unido (grupos, asociaciones, etc.): *to weld soldiers into an operating whole = unir a los soldados en un conjunto operativo.* || *s.c.* **3** soldadura.

welder | 'weldər | *s.c.* soldador.

welfare | 'welfeər | *s.i.* **1** bienestar, bien, prosperidad, confort, salud, felicidad: *a life devoted to the child's welfare = una vida dedicada al bienestar del niño.* **2** asistencia social, beneficencia pública: *welfare service = servicio de asistencia social.* **3** (EE.UU.) fondos públicos asistenciales: *to live on welfare = vivir de fondos públicos asistenciales.* || **4 – state,** estado del bienestar, estado benefactor.

welkin | 'welkɪn | *s.sing.* (lit.) firmamento, cielo.

well | wel | *adv.* [*comp.* **better,** *super.* **best**] **1** bien, satisfactoriamente: *the job was well done = se hizo bien el trabajo.* **2** bien, completamente, totalmente: *the eggs must be well beaten = los huevos han de estar bien batidos.* **3** bien, sabiamente, sensatamente, debidamente: *you did well to tell me = obraste debidamente diciéndomelo.* **4 [– +** *prep.***]** bien, mucho, muy, bastante: *make your reservations well in advance = hagan sus reservas con bastante antelación.* **5 [– +** *p.p.***]** bien, muy, en gran medida, a un nivel considerable: *a well-educated family = una familia muy culta.* **6 [how –]** qué tal, cómo: *how well are they doing? = ¿qué tal les va?* **7 [– +** *adj.***]** ciertamente, absolutamente, bien, muy: *well aware of our limitations = absolutamente conscientes de nuestras limitaciones.* **8** muy bien, posiblemente, probablemente: *their water supplies may well last several years = sus reservas de agua pueden muy bien durar años.* || *interj.* **9** bueno, vaya (expresión de asombro: *well, you do surprise me! = ¡vaya!, realmente me sorprendes.* **10** bueno (alivio): *well, here we are at last! = ¡bueno!, por fin estamos aquí.* **11** bueno (resignación): *oh well, it can't be helped = bueno, es inevitable.* **12** bien, bueno, vale (acuerdo): *very well, then, I'll take it = muy bien, me lo quedo.* **13** bien, bueno (tras pausa o cambiando de conversación): *well, as I was saying = bien, como iba diciendo.* **14** bueno (duda): *well, I'm not sure = bueno, no estoy seguro.* || *adj.* [*comp.* **better,** *super.* **best**] **15** bien, sano, saludable, de buena salud: *I'm well, thank you = estoy bien, gracias; he's not a well man = no es hombre de buena salud.* **16** (lit.) bien, correcto, satisfactorio: *all well at home, I hope? = en casa todo bien, supongo.* || *s.c.* **17** pozo: *well water = agua de pozo; oil well = pozo petrolífero.* **18** hueco (de la escalera, del ascensor, etc.). **19 [– (of)]** (form. y fig.) fuente: *a well of information = fuente de información.* **20** (brit.) estrado de los abogados (en salas de juicios). || *v.i.* **21 [– (out/up)]** fluir, manar: *blood was welling out from the wound = manaba sangre de su herida.* || **22 all is –/(things are) going –,** todo marcha bien. **23 all very –,** V. **well. 24 as –,** también, asimismo: *her reading is good, and her writing as well = su lectura es buena, y también su escritura.* **25 as – as,** además de, tanto como, al igual que: *it has symbolic as well as economic significance = tiene una significación tanto simbólica como económica.* **26 as – someone/something might/may,** y motivo hay para ello, y no es para menos: *he was puzzled, as well he might = estaba perplejo, y no era para menos.* **27 to be – in (with),** (fam.) llevarse muy bien, ser muy amigo: *they're well in with the people next door = se llevan muy bien con los de al lado.* **28 to be – out (of),** no tener ya nada que ver: *I'm glad to be well out of it = me alegro de no tener ya nada que ver en ello.* **29 to do – to (do something),** V. **do. 30 perfectly/jolly/damn/etc. –,** bien, estupendamente, la mar de bien: *we managed perfectly well without you = nos las arreglamos estupendamente sin vosotros.* **31 pretty –,** V. **pretty. 32 someone may/might as – (do something),** también (aunque con reservas): *I might as well go = también podría ir yo.* **33 (something) is just as –,** por fortuna: *she doesn't have to do any typing, which is just as well = no tiene que escribir a máquina, por fortuna (para ella).* **34 to speak/think – (of),** manifestar/tener buena opinión (de personas o cosas). **35 very –,** V. **very. 36 – and good,** estupendo, mejor que mejor: *if they turn up earlier, well and good = si se presentan antes, mejor que mejor.* **37 – and truly,** del todo, completamente: *that way of thinking is well and truly gone = esas ideas están del todo trasnochadas.* **38 – enough,** bastante, bastante bien: *I like it well enough = me gusta bastante.* **39 to – over,** rebasar. **40 to – up,** manar (sangre de heridas, lágrimas de los ojos).

we'll | wiːl | *contr.* de **we will** o **we shall** (lenguaje hablado).

well-adjusted | ˌweləˈdʒʌstɪd | *adj.* integrado, a gusto (socialmente).

well-advised | ˌweləd'vaɪzd | *adj.* sensato, prudente, inteligente.

well-aimed | ˌwel'eɪmd | *adj.* certero, atinado.

well-appointed | ˌwelə'pɔɪntɪd | *adj.* (form.) bien amueblado, bien equipado.

well-balanced | ˌwel'bælənst | *adj.* **1** estable, sensato, equilibrado. **2** equilibrado, justo, variado (alimentación, dieta).
well-behaved | ˌwelbɪ'heɪvd | *adj.* **1** formal, educado. **2** manso, obediente, noble (animal).
well-being | ˌwel'biːŋ | *s.i.* bienestar, prosperidad, bien, felicidad.
well-born | ˌwel'bɔːn | *adj.* de buena familia, de buena cuna.
well-bred | ˌwel'bred | *adj.* educado, cortés.
well-brought-up | ˌwel'brɔːtʌp | *adj.* educado, respetuoso (niños).
well-built | ˌwel'bɪlt | *adj.* fuerte, robusto, fornido, bien construido.
well-chosen | ˌwel'tʃəuzn | *adj.* acertado, atinado, bien elegido (palabras).
well-connected | ˌwelkə'nektɪd | *adj.* bien relacionado.
well-defined | ˌweldɪ'faɪnd | *adj.* claro, preciso, bien definido.
well-disposed | ˌweldɪ'spəuzd | *adj.* favorable, entusiasta, bien dispuesto.
well-done | ˌwel'dʌn | *adj.* bien hecho, bien pasado (carne).
well-dressed | ˌwel'drest | *adj.* bien vestido.
well-earned | ˌwel'əːnd | *adj.* merecido, bien ganado, bien trabajado.
well-established | ˌwele'stæblɪʃt | *adj.* firme, asentado, bien establecido.
well-fed | ˌwel'fed | *adj.* bien alimentado.
well-founded | ˌwel'faundɪd | *adj.* bien fundado, documentado, demostrable.
well-groomed | ˌwel'gruːmd | *adj.* pulcro, fino, limpio.
well-grounded | ˌwel'graundɪd | *adj.* **1** bien fundado, acertado, documentado. **2** bien entrenado, bien instruido.
well-heeled | ˌwel'hiːld | *adj.* (fam.) rico, acomodado, pudiente, (Am.) amonedado.
well-informed | ˌwelɪn'fɔːmd | *adj.* bien informado, enterado, instruido.
wellington | 'welɪŋtən | *s.c.* bota de goma: *a pair of wellingtons = un par de botas de goma.*
well-intentioned | ˌwelɪn'tenʃnd | *adj.* bienintencionado, de buen corazón, noble.
well-kept | ˌwel'kept | *adj.* bien cuidado, bien conservado (lugar, edificio).
well-known | ˌwel'nəun | *adj.* bien conocido, famoso, célebre.
well-mannered | ˌwel'mænəd | *adj.* educado, cortés, culto.
well-meaning | ˌwel'miːnɪŋ | *adj.* bienintencionado, de buen corazón, noble.
well-meant | ˌwel'ment | *adj.* bienintencionado.
well-nigh | 'welnaɪ | *adv.* (form.) casi, prácticamente, poco menos que.
well-off | ˌwel'ɒf | *adj.* [*comp.* **better-off,** *super.* **best-off**] **1** rico, acomodado, pudiente. **2 [– (for)]** bien surtido: *we're well-off for shops here = estamos bien surtidos de tiendas aquí.* || **3 not to know when one is –,** ser feliz y no saberlo, no saber apreciar lo afortunado que uno es. **4 the –,** los ricos.
well-oiled | ˌwel'ɔɪld | *adj.* (fam.) cargado, bebido, trompa.
well-paid | ˌwel'peɪd | *adj.* bien pagado, bien retribuido (personas, trabajos).
well-preserved | ˌwelprɪ'səːvd | *adj.* bien conservado, de buen aspecto.
well-read | ˌwel'red | *adj.* muy leído, culto, instruido, documentado.
well-rounded | ˌwel'raundɪd | *adj.* **1** (euf.) gordito, rellenito. **2** amplio, variado, completo, rico (experiencia, formación): *a well-rounded education = una amplia formación.*
well-spoken | ˌwel'spəukən | *adj.* bienhablado, de habla culta.
well-thought-of | ˌwel'θɔːtəv | *adj.* admirado, respetado, considerado.
well-thought-out | ˌwel'θɔːtaut | *adj.* bien planificado, bien diseñado.
well-thumbed | ˌwel'θʌmd | *adj.* manoseado, muy usado, muy hojeado (libro, revista, etc.).
well-timed | ˌwel'taɪmd | *adj.* oportuno, a su debido tiempo.
well-to-do | ˌweltə'duː | *adj.* **1** rico, acomodado, pudiente. || **2 the –,** los ricos.
well-tried | ˌwel'traɪd | *adj.* experimentado, comprobado, de buenos resultados.
well-turned | ˌwel'təːnd | *adj.* (p.u.) **1** escogido, agradable, favorable (comentario, juicio, etc.). **2** elegante, atractivo, bien hecho.
well-versed | ˌwel'vəːst | *adj.* **[– (in)]** versado, impuesto, ducho, experimentado.
wellwisher | 'welˌwɪʃər | *s.c.* persona amiga, leal y sincera.
well-worn | ˌwel'wɔːn | *adj.* **1** gastado, viejo, pasado, impresentable (objetos, prendas de vestir, etc.). **2** visto, poco original, repetido, sin interés (comentario, frase, etc.).
welly | 'welɪ | *s.c.* (brit. y fam.) bota de goma.
Welsh | welʃ | *adj.* **1** galés. || *s.i.* **2** galés (lengua). || **3 the –,** los galeses. **4 – rarebit** (también **– rabbit**), pan tostado con queso derretido.
welsh | welʃ | (también **welch**) *v.i.* (desp.) **[to – (on)] 1** no pagar deudas (de juego, principalmente): *to welsh on one's debts = no pagar las propias deudas.* **2** dejar de cumplir promesas.
welsher | 'welʃər | *s.c.* deudor, incumplidor.
Welshman | 'welʃmən | *s.c.* [*pl.irreg.* **Welshmen**] galés.
Welshmen | 'welʃmən | V. **Welshman.**
Welshwoman | 'welʃwumən | *s.c.* [*pl.irreg.* **Welshwomen**] galesa.
Welshwomen | 'welʃwɪmɪn | V. **Welshwoman.**
welt | welt | *s.c.* **1** verdugo, verdugón, herida, roncha. **2** vira (de zapato).
welter | 'weltər | *s.sing.* (form.) mezcla, revoltijo, mescolanza.
welterweight | 'weltəweɪt | *s.c.* DEP. welter, peso welter.
wench | wentʃ | *s.c.* (p.u.) **1** chica, moza, sirvienta. **2** puta, fulana. || *v.i.* **3** acostarse con putas.
wend | wend | *v.i.* (lit.) **1** encaminarse. || **2 to – one's way,** (hum.) dirigir los pasos, irse, avanzar (lentamente).
went | went | *pret.irreg.* de **go.**
wept | wept | *pret.irreg.* de **weep.**
were | wəːr | (forma relajada | wə |) *pret.irreg.* de **be.**
we're | wɪə | *contr.* de **we are** (lenguaje hablado).
weren't | wəːnt | *contr.* de **were not** (lenguaje hablado).
werewolf | 'wɪəwulf | *s.c.* [*pl.irreg.* **werewolves**] hombre lobo.
werewolves | 'wɪəwulvz | *pl.irreg.* de **werewolf.**
wesleyan | 'wezlɪən | *adj./s.c.* metodista.
wesleyanism | 'wezlɪənɪzəm | *s.c.* metodismo.
west | west | (también **West**) *s.sing.* **1** oeste, occidente, poniente: *the west of the country = el oeste del país.* || *adj.* **2** oeste, occidental: *the west side of the city = el lado occidental de la ciudad.* **3** de poniente (viento): *a west wind = un viento de poniente.* || *adv.* **4** hacia el oeste, dirección oeste: *they're travelling west = viajan en dirección oeste.* || **5 to go –,** (hum.) **a)** morirse; **b)** malograrse, irse al garete. **6 the West, a)** Occidente (Europa occidental y América); **b)** Occidente (Europa en contraste con los países orientales); **c)** las tierras del oeste norteamericano. **7 West Country,** (brit.) el suroeste de Inglaterra. **8 West End,** (brit.) centro comercial y de entretenimiento de Londres. **9 West German,** germano-occidental. **10 West Indian,** antillano.
westbound | 'westbaund | *adj.* hacia el oeste, en dirección oeste, con destino al oeste: *westbound traffic = tráfico en dirección oeste.*
westerly | 'westəlɪ | *adj.* **1** oeste, occidental (localización, dirección, etc.): *the most westerly point of the country = el punto más occidental del país.* **2** del oeste, de poniente (viento): *a westerly breeze = una brisa de poniente.*
western | 'westən | (también **Western**) *adj.* **1** occidental, del oeste (localización geográfica): *the western regions = las regiones occidentales.* **2** occidental (mundo occidental): *the impact of western technology = el impacto de la tecnología occidental.* || *s.c.* **3** película o novela del oeste (norteamericano).
westerner | 'westənər | (también **Westerner**) *s.c.* **1** occidental: *westerners in Japan = occidentales en Japón.* **2** (EE.UU.) habitante o nativo del oeste norteamericano.
westernization | 'westənaɪzeɪʃn | (también **westernisation**) *s.i.* occidentalización.
westernize | 'westənaɪz | (también **westernise**) *v.t.* occidentalizar (formas de ser, comportamientos, etc.).
westernmost | 'westənməust | *adj.* más occidental, más al oeste: *the westernmost tip of the island = el punto más occidental de la isla.*

westward | 'westwəd | *adj.* **1** oeste, hacia el oeste: *in a westward direction = en dirección oeste.* || *adv.* (también **westwards**) **2** hacia el oeste, rumbo oeste: *they sailed westward = navegaron rumbo oeste.*
westwards | 'westwədz | V. **westward.**
wet | wet | *adj.* [*comp.* **wetter,** *super.* **wettest**] **1** húmedo, mojado: *my hair is still wet = tengo el pelo húmedo todavía.* **2** húmedo, lluvioso, de lluvia: *it was a wet day = hizo un día lluvioso.* **3** húmedo, fresco, reciente (pintura, tinta, cemento, etc.): *the paint is wet = la pintura está reciente.* **4** lloroso, cubierto de lágrimas, húmedo: *her eyes were red and wet = tenía los ojos rojos y llorosos.* **5** húmedo, mojado, cubierto de orines (bebés, ropa de bebé). **6** fresco (pescado). **7** (fam.) débil, flojo, apagado, inseguro (personas). || *s.c.* e *i.* **8** lluvia: *let's get in out of the wet = entremos y cobijémonos de la lluvia.* **9** humedad: *don't go through the wet = no andes por la humedad.* **10** (brit. y fam.) moderado (políticamente): *the Tory wets = los moderados del partido conservador.* || *v.t.* [*pret.* y *p.p.* **wetted** o **wet**] **11** humedecer: *he wetted his lips = se humedeció los labios.* **12** mojar, humedecer, orinarse: *the child wet his bed = el niño mojó la cama.* || **13 – behind the ears,** (fam.) novato, pipiolo, inexperto, pardillo. **14 – blanket,** (fam.) aguafiestas. **15 to – one's whistle,** V. **whistle. 16 – through,** empapado: *your clothes are wet through = tienes la ropa empapada.*
wetly | 'wetlı | *adv.* húmedo, húmedamente, débilmente, inseguramente.
wetness | 'wetnıs | *s.i.* humedad.
wet-nurse | 'wetnə:s | *s.c.* nodriza, ama de cría.
wet-suit | 'wetsu:t | *s.c.* traje de submarinista.
we've | wi:v | *contr.* de **we have** (lenguaje hablado).
whack | wæk | | hw' | (fam.) *v.t.* **1** golpear, pegar, zurrar, (Am.) chicotear. || *s.c.* **2** golpe (seco y ruidoso): *I heard a sudden whack = oí un golpe seco.* **3 [– (at)]** tentativa, intentona: *let's have a whack at it = hagamos una intentona.* **4** parte, lo que corresponde: *you'll all have your whack = todos tendréis lo que os corresponde.*
whacked | wækt | | hw' | *adj.* (fam.) exhausto, roto, hecho polvo.
whacking | 'wækıŋ | | 'hw' | (fam.) *s.c.* **1** (arc.) zurra, paliza. || *adj.* **2** enorme, descomunal, soberano: *a whacking lie = una enorme mentira.* || *adv.* **3** enormemente, desmesuradamente.
whacky V. **wacky.**
whale | weıl | | hw' | *s.c.* **1** ZOOL. ballena. || **2 to have a – of a time,** (fam.) pasarlo la mar de bien.
whalebone | 'weılbəun | | 'hw' | *s.i.* (p.u.) ballena, lámina (córnea y elástica).
whaler | 'weılər | | 'hw' | *s.c.* ballenero (barco o persona dedicada a la captura de ballenas).
whaling | 'weılıŋ | | 'hw' | *s.i.* **1** pesca de ballena. || *atr.* **2** ballenero, de ballena: *the whaling industry = la industria ballenera.*
wham | wæm | | hw' | *interj.* **1** (fam.) ¡zas!: *wham! the car hit the wall = ¡zas! el coche chocó contra la pared.* || *s.c.* **2** estruendo, golpe.
wharf | wɔ:f | | hw' | *s.c.* [*pl.* **wharfs** o **wharves**] muelle, embarcadero.
wharves | wɔ:vz | | hw' | *pl.* de **wharf.**
what | wɒt | | hw' | *pron.interr.* **1** qué, cuál: *what do you think? = ¿qué piensas?* **2** qué (en preguntas indirectas): *not to know what to do = no saber qué hacer.* **3** (fam.) qué, sí, dime: *dad? – what? – can I have your car? = papá -- ¿qué? -- ¿me dejas tu coche?* **4** (fam.) qué, cómo, ¿eh?: *more coffee? – what? do you want more coffee? = ¿más café? -- ¿eh? -- ¿quieres más café?* || *pron.rel.* **5** lo que (al comienzo de frase): *what you need is rest = lo que necesitas es descanso.* **6** lo que (en referencias generales a la calidad, naturaleza, etc. de algo): *he mixes what is true with what is untrue = mezcla lo que es cierto con lo que no lo es.* || *adj.interr.* **7** qué (en preguntas): *what time is it? = ¿qué hora es?* **8** qué (en preguntas indirectas): *I didn't know what bus to get = no sabía qué autobús tomar.* || *adj.ind.* **9** cuanto, todo cuanto: *I've spent what money I had = he gastado cuanto dinero tenía.* || *interj.* **10** ¡cómo!, ¡vaya! (en expresiones de sorpresa, incredulidad, etc.): *What, another book about Cromwell? = ¡cómo! ¿otro libro sobre Cromwell?* **11** qué (para enfatizar opiniones, reacciones, etc.): *what a good question! = ¡qué buena pregunta!* **12** bueno, veamos (en expresiones de cálculo, tanteo, etc.): *he's been a member for, what, something like 20 years = lleva de socio, veamos, unos veinte años.* || *adv.* **13** qué: *and what does it matter? = ¿y qué importa?* || **14 and I don't know –/and God knows –,** y quién sabe qué: *the chickens are injected with antibiotics and God knows what = a los pollos se les inyecta antibióticos y Dios sabe qué.* **15 to give someone – for,** V. **give. 16 guess –/do you know –,** ¿te imaginas? (como introducción a una noticia sorprendente): *guess what, she's got the prize = ¿te lo imaginas? ha alcanzado el premio.* **17 I tell you –/I know –,** (fam.) lo que yo te diga/ya sé: *tell you what, we'll start again = ya sé, comenzaremos de nuevo.* **18 or –?,** (fam.) o qué: *do you want to come or what? = ¿quieres venir o qué?* **19 so –?/– of it?,** (fam.) y ¿qué? (para restar importancia a un hecho): *yes, I wrote it. What of it? = sí, yo lo escribí, y ¿qué?* **20 – about/– of...?,** y qué hay de/qué pasa con...: *and what about your promise? = y ¿qué hay de tu promesa?* **21 – have you,** y demás: *the needs, physical, cultural, what have you, of those people = las necesidades, físicas, culturales y demás, de esas gentes.* **22 – if...?,** y si...: *what if nobody's waiting? = ¿y si nadie está esperando?* **23 – is it?/what's the matter?,** (fam.) ¿cuál es el problema?/¿qué pasa? **24 – is called/– amounts to...,** (form.) lo que se ha dado en llamar/lo equivalente a...: *we're here during what amounts to our holidays = estaremos aquí lo equivalente a nuestras vacaciones.* **25 what's more,** V. **more. 26 what's someone's name,** (fam.) como quiera que se llame: *where's what's his name? = ¿dónde está como quiera que se llame?* **27 what's –,** (fam.) lo principal, lo importante, lo que hay que...: *she certainly knows what's what = sabe ciertamente lo que hay que saber.* **28 – with (something),** entre (una cosa) y (la otra): *what with the weather and my poor health... = entre el mal tiempo y mi mala salud...* **29 you/he/she/etc. what?,** tú/ él/ella/etc. ¿qué? (sorpresa, incredulidad): *I'm going to be an actor, You what? = voy a ser actor, tú ¿qué?*
whatever | wɒt'evər | | hw' | *pron.ind.* **1** todo lo que, cualquier cosa que: *I read whatever I could find = leí todo lo que pillé.* **2** lo que (pase lo que pase, en cualquier circunstancia, etc.): *I'll call you whatever happens = te llamaré pase lo que pase.* **3** lo que (sea lo que sea, por no conocerse o no importar la identidad, el significado, el valor, etc.): *she wants to have cocido, whatever that is = quiere comer cocido, sin importarle lo que sea.* || *pron.interr.* **4** qué, cuál (con expresión de sorpresa y énfasis): *whatever is the matter? = pero ¿qué es lo que pasa?* | *adj.ind.* **5** todo, cualquier: *he gave up whatever hopes he might have = abandonó cualquier esperanza que pudiera tener.* **6** cualquiera, no importa cómo: *he's always there, whatever the weather = siempre está ahí no importa cómo haga.* || *adv.* **7** absolutamente, en absoluto (en expresión de énfasis en una proposición negativa): *there can be no doubt whatever about it = no puede haber absolutamente ninguna duda.* || **8 or –,** (fam.) o algo parecido/por el estilo: *take any sport: basketball, tennis, swimming or whatever = coge un deporte cualquiera: baloncesto, tenis, natación o alguno por el estilo.* **9 – you say/– you think/etc.,** lo que usted diga, como a usted le parezca, a mandar.
whatnot | 'wɒtnɒt | | 'hw' | *s.c.* e *i.* **1** chisme, cualquier cosa: *she puts those whatnots in her hair = se pone todos esos chismes en el pelo.* **2** (p.u.) estante, estantería. || **3 and/or –,** (fam.) y tal, o cosas por el estilo.
what's | wɒts | | hw' | *contr.* de **what is** o **what has,** siendo **has,** en el segundo caso, verbo auxiliar, generalmente (lenguaje hablado).
whatsoever | ˌwɒtsəu'evər | | 'hw' | *adv.* absolutamente, en absoluto (en expresión de énfasis en una proposición negativa): *he has no social life whatsoever = no hace vida social en absoluto.*

wheat | wiːt | | hw' | *s.i.* **1** trigo (grano, cereal, planta). || **2 (to separate) the – from the shaff,** (separar) el trigo de la paja.
wheatgerm | 'wiːtdʒəːm | | 'hw' | *s.i.* esencia de trigo, corazón de trigo.
wheatmeal | 'wiːtmiːl | | 'hw' | *s.i.* harina de trigo.
wheedle | 'wiːdl | | 'hw' | *v.t.* e *i.* **[to – (out of/into)]** engatusar, convencer; sacar, conseguir (con halagos): *she wheedled money out of him = le sacó bien el dinero.*
wheedling | 'wiːdlɪŋ | | 'hw' | *adj.* halagador, engatusador, zalamero, mimoso, (Am.) pechichoso.
wheel | wiːl | | hw' | *s.c.* **1** rueda. **2** volante (de un vehículo). **3** timón (de una embarcación). **4** torno (de alfarero). **5** (lit.) rueda, ciclo (de la moda, fortuna, etc.). **6** MIL. vuelta (instrucción de orden cerrado). || *v.t.* e *i.* **7** rodar, llevar, empujar (un carro, una silla de ruedas, etc.): *to wheel a trolley = llevar un carrito.* **8** girar, virar, volverse. **9** volar en círculo (pájaros). || **10 at/behind the –,** al volante (de un vehículo). **11 Ferris –,** noria (de feria o parque de atracciones). **12 to oil the wheels,** V. **oil. 13 on wheels,** (provisto) de ruedas para un fácil desplazamiento. **14 to put one's shoulder to the –,** V. **shoulder. 15 to take/grab the –,** ponerse al volante (haciendo turnos). **16 wheeling and dealing,** (desp.) intrigas que preceden a negocios importantes: *there was a lot of wheeling and dealing before the agreement = abundaron las intrigas antes del acuerdo.* **17 wheels, a)** (fam.) coche, (Am.) carro: *these are my new wheels, man = aquí mi nuevo carro, tío;* **b)** maquinaria, engranaje (de un reloj). **18 to – something out,** (brit. y fam.) emprender negocios, acciones, etc. generalmente censurables. **19 wheels within wheels,** influencias, circunstancias, etc., generalmente desconocidas, que pesan negativamente en una situación.
wheelbarrow | 'wiːlˌbærəʊ | | 'hw' | *s.c.* carretilla.
wheelbase | 'wiːlbeɪs | *s.c.* distancia entre ejes (en vehículos).
wheelchair | ˌwiːl'tʃeər | | ˌhw' | *s.c.* silla de ruedas.
wheeled | 'wiːld | | 'hw' | *adj.* **1** (provisto) de ruedas: *wheeled vehicles = vehículos de ruedas.* **2** rodado: *wheeled transport = transporte rodado.* || **3 -wheeled,** de un número determinado de ruedas (según se concrete en el numeral de la primera parte del compuesto): *a sixteen-wheeled lorry = un camión de dieciséis ruedas.*
wheeler-dealer | ˌwiːlə'diːlər | | ˌhw' | *s.c.* (desp.) ventajista, intrigante, (Am.) mazamorrero.
wheelhouse | 'wiːlhaʊs | | 'hw' | *s.c.* cabina del timonel (en un barco).
wheelwright | 'wiːlraɪt | | 'hw' | *s.c.* carretero, ruedero.
wheeze | wiːz | | hw' | *v.i.* **1** respirar con dificultad, resollar, jadear (por vejez o enfermedad). || *s.c.* **2** resuello, jadeo, respiración ruidosa. **3** (brit. y fam.) treta, truco, golpe de ingenio.
wheezily | 'wiːzɪlɪ | | 'hw' | *adv.* jadeantemente, sibilantemente.
wheeziness | 'wiːzɪnɪs | | 'hw' | *s.i.* jadeo, dificultad respiratoria.
wheezy | 'wiːzɪ | | 'hw' | *adj.* jadeante, ruidoso, pesado (respiración).
whelk | welk | | hw' | *s.c.* ZOOL. buccino.
whelp | welp | | hw' | *s.c.* **1** cachorro (de la especie canina). **2** (arc.) trasto (niño o joven travieso). || *v.i.* **3** (form.) parir (animal).
when | wen | | hw' | *adv.interr.* **1** cuándo: *when has she come? = ¿cuándo ha llegado?; I don't know when he died = no sé cuándo murió.* || *adv.rel.* **2 [time/day/month/etc. –]** cuando, en que: *it is the day when nobody comes = es el día en que nadie viene.* **3** cuando, coincidiendo con, con ocasión de (añadiendo más información): *years ago, when the war broke out = años atrás, cuando estalló la guerra.* || *conj.* **4** cuando: *he left school when he was eleven = dejó el colegio a los once años.* **5** cuando, siempre que: *when visiting London I like to travel by bus = cuando voy a Londres me gusta desplazarme en autobús.* **6** cuando, si, considerando que (como explicación de una opinión): *How can I get the job when I've forgotten everything? = ¿cómo puedo conseguir el empleo cuando he olvidado todo?*
whence | wens | | hw' | *adv., pron., conj.* (arc. y form.) **1** de donde: *he returned to the land whence he came = volvió a la tierra de donde vino.* **2** de dónde: *whence came the stranger? = ¿de dónde vino el forastero?*
whenever | wen'evər | | hw' | *conj.* **1** siempre que, cuando, cuando quiera que: *it leaks whenever it rains = se hacen goteras siempre que llueve.* || *adv.interr.* **2** cuándo (con expresión de sorpresa): *whenever do you find time to do all that? = ¿cuándo encuentras el tiempo para hacer todo?* || **3 or –,** (fam.) o así, o por ahí: *I started work in June or whenever = comencé a trabajar en junio o así.*
where | weər | | hw' | *adv.interr.* **1** dónde: *where do you live? = ¿dónde vives?; ask him where he comes from = pregúntale de dónde viene.* || *adv.rel.* **2** donde (en oración especificativa): *that's where I last saw him = ahí es donde lo vi por última vez.* **3** donde (en oración explicativa): *that was in Chester, where we lived for ten years = eso fue en Chester, donde vivimos diez años.* || *conj.* **4** donde: *put it where we can all see it = póngalo donde todos podamos verlo.*
whereabouts | 'weərəbaʊts | | 'hw' | *s.c.* **1** localización, paradero, por donde uno anda, lugares que uno frecuenta: *nobody knows her whereabouts = nadie sabe su paradero.* || *adv.interr.* **2** dónde, por dónde: *whereabouts are you going in the U.S.A.? = ¿por dónde andarás en los EE.UU.?*
whereas | weər'æz | | hw' | *conj.* (form.) **1** pero, por el contrario, mientras: *they want a flat, whereas we're looking for a house = ellos quieren un piso, nosotros, por el contrario, buscamos una casa.* **2** DER. considerando que (principio de párrafo).
whereby | weə'baɪ | | hw' | *adv.rel.* (form.) por donde, con el que, de acuerdo con el cual: *a plan whereby they might save money = un plan con el que ahorrarían dinero.*
wherefore | 'weəfɔːr | | 'hw' | (form.) *adv.interr.* **1** por qué. || *conj.* **2** de ahí que, en consecuencia. || **3 the whys and wherefores,** las razones, el por qué y el para qué.
wherein | weər'ɪn | | hw' | (arc.) *adv.interr.* **1** dónde, en qué: *wherein lies the problem? = ¿dónde está el problema?* || *adv.rel.* **2** en donde, en el que: *a forest wherein dangers lurk = un bosque en donde el peligro acecha.*
whereof | weər'ɒv | | hw' | (arc.) *adv.rel.* del que, de los cuales, de donde: *ten cats, six whereof were black = diez gatos, seis de los cuales eran negros.*
whereupon | weərʌp'ɒn | | hw' | (form.) *conj.* después de lo cual, como consecuencia de lo cual: *he went to bed late, whereupon he overslept next morning = se acostó tarde, como consecuencia de lo cual se despertaría tarde.*
wherever | weər'evər | | hw' | *conj.* **1** dondequiera que, no importa dónde: *find him, wherever he may be = encuéntrenlo dondequiera que se halle.* || *adv.interr.* **2** dónde (diablos): *wherever have you been? = ¿dónde (diablos) te has metido?* || **3 or –,** (fam.) o donde sea: *a house in Ealing or wherever = una casa en Ealing o donde sea.*
wherewithal | 'weəwɪðɔːl | | 'hw' | *s.sing.* (fam.) medios, recursos: *I need a new car, but I haven't got the wherewithal = necesito un coche nuevo, pero no tengo medios.*
whet | wet | hw' | *v.t.* [*pret.* y *p.p.* **whetted,** *ger.* **whetting**] **1** estimular, despertar, avivar (apetito, interés, etc.): *good books whet one's appetite for reading = los buenos libros avivan el deseo de leer.* **2** (form.) afilar, amolar (cuchillos, armas, etc.).
whether | 'weðər | | 'hw' | *conj.* **1** si (en expresiones de duda o alternativas): *I'm not sure whether I like it or not = no estoy seguro de si me gusta o no.* **2** si (como introducción de preguntas indirectas): *he was asked whether he agreed = se le preguntó si estaba de acuerdo.* **3** si, tanto si, aunque (en enunciados que se cumplirán al margen de variables o en todas ellas): *we'll play on Saturday whether it rains or not = jugaremos el sábado tanto si llueve como si no.*
whetstone | 'wetstəʊn | | 'hw' | *s.i.* piedra de afilar.

whew | hwjuː | (también **phew**) *interj.* ¡uf!, ¡vaya!

whey | weɪ | | hwˈ | *s.i.* suero (derivado lácteo).

which | wɪtʃ | | hwˈ | *adj.interr.* **1** qué, cuál (al principio de frases interrogativas, estableciendo elección entre un número determinado de posibilidades): *which way is quicker, by bus or by train? = ¿cómo (qué medio) es más rápido, en autobús o en tren?* **2** qué, cuál (en interrogativas indirectas, y estableciendo elección): *ask him which bus is the right one = pregúntale qué autobús es el apropiado.* || *pron.interr.* **3** qué, cuál, quién (en frases interrogativas, estableciendo elección entre un número limitado de posibilidades): *which of the boys is tallest? = ¿cuál de los chicos es el más alto?* **4** qué, cuál, quién (en interrogativas indirectas): *I don't know which fits better = no sé cuál sienta mejor.* || *pron.rel.* **5** que, el cual, al cual (en oraciones especificativas): *the awful conditions which exist in some prisons = las malas condiciones que se dan en algunas cárceles.* **6** que, el cual, al cual (en oraciones explicativas): *his best film, which won several awards, was about Gandhi = su mejor película, que ganó varios premios, trataba de Gandhi.* **7** lo cual (referido a lo previamente dicho o sugerido): *it takes me an hour, which is not bad = tardo una hora, lo cual no está nada mal.* || *adj.rel.* **8** (form.) que, cuyo: *he comes back at 6 in the morning, at which time I am asleep? = llega a las seis de la mañana, hora en que yo estoy dormida.*

whichever | wɪtʃ'evər | | hwˈ | *adj.ind.* **1** cualquier (entre un número limitado de posibilidades): *take whichever seat you like = tome cualquier asiento que le guste.* || *pron.ind.* **2** cualquiera que: *whichever of you comes first will get a prize = cualquiera de vosotros que llegue el primero se llevará un premio.* || *adj.* o *pron.interr.* **3** cuál (con expresión de sorpresa o énfasis ante un número limitado de posibilidades): *whichever of these is your car? = pero bueno, ¿cuál de éstos es tu coche?*

whiff | wɪf | | hwˈ | *s.c.* **1 [– (of)]** soplo, bocanada; chupada, calada; olorcillo: *a little whiff of perfume = un soplo de perfume.* **2** (fig.) indicio, señal, pista (de peligro, escándalo, sospecha, etc.).

Whig | wɪg | *s.c.* (brit.) Whig (partido político británico que propugnaba mayores poderes para el Parlamento y que se convertiría en el Partido Liberal).

while | waɪl | | hwˈ | *s.sing.* **1** rato, tiempo: *we had no news of him for a long while = bastante tiempo no supimos nada de él.* || *conj.* (también **whilst**). **2** mientras, cuando: *she arrived while we were shopping = llegó mientras estábamos de compras.* **3** (form.) aunque, aun cuando: *while I admit that I did it, I don't agree it was on purpose = aunque admito que lo hice yo, no estoy conforme en que fuera aposta.* **4** mientras que, pero: *some children were working, while others were playing = algunos niños trabajaban, pero otros jugaban.* || *v.t.* **5** pasar, entretener (el tiempo). || **6 all the –/the whole –,** todo el tiempo, mientras tanto. **7 to make it worth one's –,** V. **worth. 8 once in a –,** V. **once. 9 to – (something) away,** pasar, entretener (el tiempo): *we whiled away the time in a museum = entretuvimos el tiempo en un museo.* **10 – one's about it,** V. **about.**

whilst | waɪlst | | hwˈ | (form.) *conj.* V. **while.**

whim | wɪm | | hwˈ | *s.c.* e *i.* capricho, antojo, (Am.) retobo.

whimper | 'wɪmpər | | 'hwˈ | *v.i.* **1** lloriquear, gemir, sollozar, quejarse (niños, animales, etc.). || *v.t.* **2** decir lloriqueando. || *s.c.* **3** lloriqueo, gemido, sollozo.

whimsey | 'wɪmzɪ | | 'hwˈ | V. **whimsy.**

whimsical | 'wɪmzɪkl | | 'hwˈ | *adj.* caprichoso, original, curioso, extraño.

whimsy | 'wɪmzɪ | | 'hwˈ | (también **whimsey**) *s.c.* e *i.* capricho, antojo, (Am.) retobo.

whine | waɪn | | hwˈ | *v.i.* **1** gañir (animales), chirriar, silbar: *the dog was whining in pain = el perro gañía de dolor.* **2** (desp.) gimotear, lloriquear, quejarse (por causas triviales). || *s.c.* **3** gañido, chirrido, silbido, gemido, lloriqueo, queja.

whinge | wɪndʒ | | hwˈ | *v.i.* (fam.) quejarse.

whining | 'waɪnɪŋ | | 'hwˈ | *s.i.* gimoteo, gemido, lloriqueo.

whinny | 'wɪnɪ | | 'hwˈ | *s.c.* **1** relincho (suave). || *v.i.* **2** relinchar (suavemente).

whip | wɪp | | hwˈ | *s.c.* **1** látigo, fusta, zurriago. **2** (brit.) llamada a los diputados (para votación). **3** mezcla dulce de huevos y fruta. || [*ger.* **whipping,** *pret.* y *p.p.* **whipped**] *v.t.* **4** dar latigazos, azotar. **5** batir (salsas, pastas, huevos, etc.). **6** (fam.) batir, derrotar, barrer (en competiciones deportivas). **7** (brit. y fam.) quitar, afanar, birlar. **8** golpear, sacudir (el viento, principalmente): *the wind whipped my face = el viento me sacudía en la cara.* **9** mover, excitar, empujar, despertar (sentimientos de emoción, odio, etc.): *he whipped his men into excitement = despertó en sus hombres el entusiasmo.* || *v.i.* **10** ondear, blandir, agitarse (por acción del viento): *flags whipping in the wind = banderas ondeando al viento.* || **11 a fair crack of the –,** V. **crack. 12 to have/get the – hand (over someone),** tener dominado a alguien. **13 to – someone/something on, a)** arrear animales con un látigo; **b)** obligar a personas a ir más aprisa o trabajar más. **14 to – something/someone up, a)** comunicar, despertar sentimientos de entusiasmo, odio, etc.; **b)** levantar, producir (polvo, olas, etc.); **c)** batir huevos, salsas, etc.; **d)** (fam.) preparar algo (una comida, por ejemplo) en un santiamén.

whiplash | 'wɪplæʃ | | 'hwˈ | *s.c.* **1** tralla. || **2 – injury,** lesión cervical (por sacudida brusca del cuello).

whipped | wɪpt | | hwˈ | *adj.* batido: *whipped cream = crema batida.*

whippersnapper | 'wɪpəˌsnæpər | | 'hwˈ | *s.c.* (fam. y desp.) carota, mequetrefe.

whippet | 'wɪpɪt | | 'hwˈ | *s.c.* perro lebrel.

whipping | 'wɪpɪŋ | | 'hwˈ | *s.c.* **1** flagelación, azotaina, paliza, derrota. || **2 a – boy,** cabeza de turco, el que paga los platos rotos. **3 – cream,** crema batida. **4 – top,** peonza, trompo.

whippy | 'wɪpɪ | | 'hwˈ | *adj.* flexible, elástico.

whip-round | 'wɪpraund | | 'hwˈ | *s.c.* (brit. y fam.) colecta.

whir | wəːr | hwˈ | V. **whirr.**

whirl | wəːl | | hwˈ | *v.t.* e *i.* **1** girar, dar vueltas, rotar: *the leaves whirled as they fell = las hojas giraban al caer.* **2 [– (away/off)]** llevar, arrancar (a toda velocidad): *the car whirled them off = el coche se los llevó a toda velocidad.* **3** (lit.) estar confuso o excitado (la mente, el ánimo): *my head's whirling with the impression = tengo la mente confusa de la impresión.* || *s.c.* **4** giro, vuelta, rotación. **5** ritmo vertiginoso: *we got into a whirl of activity = nos metimos en un vertiginoso ritmo de trabajo.* || **6 to give it a –,** (fam.) hacer una prueba, someter algo a experimentación. **7 in a –,** (lit.) confuso, conturbado, excitado.

whirlpool | 'wəːpuːl | | 'hwˈ | *s.c.* **1** remolino, torbellino (en aguas fluviales o marinas). **2** ritmo loco, vorágine, espiral: *a whirlpool of violence = una espiral de violencia.*

whirlwind | 'wəːlwɪnd | | 'hwˈ | *s.c.* **1** torbellino, manga (en tierra o en mar). || *adj.* **2** de torbellino, muy rápido, fugaz: *a whirlwind love affair = una fugaz relación amorosa.*

whirr | wəːr | | hwˈ | (también **whir**) *v.i.* **1** zumbar, ronronear, rechinar, batir alas. || *s.c.* **2** zumbido (de insectos o de motores eléctricos), aleteo (de aves).

whisk | wɪsk | | hwˈ | *v.t.* **1** mover, sacudir (con energía): *the horse whisked its tail = el caballo sacudió la cola.* **2** agitar, batir (huevos). **3 [to – (away/off)]** llevar, trasladar, retirar (con un objetivo preciso): *the waiter whisked our dishes away = el camarero se llevó nuestros platos.* | *s.c.* **4** batidor (de huevos). **5** sacudida, movimiento (de la cola de un animal). **6** escobilla (para sacudir las moscas).

whisker | 'wɪskər | | 'hwˈ | *s.c.* **1** barba, bigote (de gatos, ratones, etc.). **2** patilla. || **3 by a –,** (fam.) por una ínfima diferencia, por muy poco. **4 whiskers, a)** bigotes (de gatos, ratones, etc.); **b)** patillas.

whiskered | 'wɪskəd | | 'hwˈ | *adj.* **1** bigotudo (animal). **2** patilludo, de abundantes patillas (persona).

whiskery | 'wɪskərɪ | | 'hwˈ | *adj.* bigotudo, barbudo, patilludo.

whiskey V. **whisky.**
whisky | 'wɪskɪ | | 'hw' | (EE.UU. e Irlanda **whiskey**) *s.i.* **1** whisky. || *s.c.* **2** whisky (vaso o copa).
whisper | 'wɪspər | | 'hw' | *v.t.* e *i.* **1** susurrar, cuchichear. **2** (lit.) susurrar, murmurar (el viento, las hojas de los árboles, etc.). **3** insinuar, comunicar (información secreta). || *s.c.* **4** susurro, cuchicheo, voz baja: *to speak in whispers = hablar en voz baja.* **5** susurro, murmullo (viento, hojas, etc.). **6** rumor: *the whisper that he's resigning = el rumor de que va a dimitir.*
whist | wɪst | | hw' | *s.i.* **1** whist (juego de naipes similar al bridge). || **2 – drive,** competición de whist.
whistle | 'wɪsl | | 'hw' | *s.c.* **1** silbido, silbo. **2** pito, silbato: *the referee blew his whistle = el árbitro tocó su silbato.* || *v.t.* e *i.* **3** silbar (una melodía, o como expresión de asombro). **4** silbar, zumbar (el viento, el tren de vapor, las balas, etc.): *the wind whistled through a crack = el viento silbaba por una rendija.* **5** silbar, piar (algunos pájaros). **6** pitar: *the referee whistled for the end of the match = el árbitro pitó el final del partido.* || **7 to blow the – (on someone/something),** denunciar, informar de algo incorrecto. **8 to – for (something),** (fam.) esperar sentado: *if he expects to get his money back, he can whistle for it = si espera recuperar el dinero, puede esperar sentado.* **9 to wet one's –,** (fam.) remojar el gaznate, echar un trago. **10 to – in the dark,** tratar de vencer el miedo o la indecisión en una situación comprometida.
whistle-stop | 'wɪslstɒp | | 'hw' | *s.c.* **1** (EE.UU.) localidad de poca monta (donde el tren no tiene parada fija). **2** (fig.) recalada de un político en campaña electoral. || **3 – tour,** excursión rápida (visitando muchos lugares).
whit | wɪt | | hw' | *s.sing.* **1** (arc.) lo más mínimo, en absoluto, ápice: *the place hasn't changed a whit = el lugar no ha cambiado lo más mínimo.* || **2 not a –/no –,** (arc.) nada, ni un ápice. **3 Whit,** (fam.) V. **Whitsun.**
white | waɪt | | hw' | *adj.* **1** blanco. **2** blanco (raza, color de piel): *they live in a white area = viven en una zona de blancos.* **3 [– (with)]** blanco, pálido, lívido: *he was white with anger = estaba blanco de ira.* **4** con leche (café, té): *two white coffees = dos cafés con leche.* **5** blanco (vino). || *s.c.* e *i.* **6** blanco: *a woman dressed in white = mujer vestida de blanco.* **7** blanco (raza, color de piel): *whites attacking blacks = blancos atacando a negros.* **8** clara (de huevo). **9** blanco (del ojo). || **10 as – as a sheet,** pálido como un muerto. **11 to bleed (someone) –,** V. **bleed.** **12 – blood cell,** ANAT. glóbulo blanco. **13 – Christmas,** Navidades blancas (nevadas). **14 whited sepulchre,** (lit.) sepulcro blanqueado (persona hipócrita). **15 – elephant,** algo costoso e inútil. **16 – ensign,** (brit.) enseña blanca (que ondea en los buques de la Armada Británica). **17 – goods,** electrodomésticos de línea blanca. **18 – horses,** V. **whitecaps.** **19 White House, a)** la Casa Blanca (residencia oficial del Presidente de EE.UU.); **b)** el Presidente de EE.UU. y sus colaboradores. **20 – lie,** mentira piadosa. **21 – meat,** carne blanca (pollo, cerdo, etc.). **22 White Paper,** Libro Blanco. **23 – pepper,** pimienta blanca. **24 whites,** vestimenta deportiva blanca (como la exigida en la práctica del críquet y otros deportes). **25 – sauce,** salsa blanca. **26 – spirit,** (brit.) aguarrás. **27 – wedding,** boda por lo eclesiástico con novia vestida de blanco.
whitebait | 'waɪtbeɪt | | 'hw' | *s.pl.* pescaditos variados, morralla.
whitecaps | 'waɪtkæps | | 'hw' | *s.c.* olas de cresta blanca.
white-collar | ˌwaɪt'kɒlər | | ˌhw' | *adj./atr.* de cuello blanco, de oficina: *white-collar work = trabajo de oficina.*
white-haired | ˌwaɪt'heəd | | ˌhw' | *adj.* de pelo blanco, canoso.
Whitehall | ˌwaɪt'hɔːl | | ˌhw' | *s.sing.* **1 Whitehall** (calle londinense donde se asienta gran parte del aparato administrativo). **2** (fig.) el Gobierno Británico.
white-hot | ˌwaɪt'hɒt | | ˌhw' | *adj.* candente, incandescente.
whiten | 'waɪtn | | 'hw' | *v.t.* e *i.* blanquear.
whiteness | 'waɪtnɪs | | 'hw' | *s.i.* blancura, claridad (deslumbrante).
whitening | 'waɪtnɪŋ | | 'hw' | *s.i.* blanqueador, blanco (de zapatos).
whiteout | 'waɪtaʊt | | 'hw' | *s.c.* nevada, luminosidad de nieve.
whitewash | 'waɪtwɒʃ | | 'hw' | *s.i.* **1** cal (líquida), jalbegue. **2** maquillaje, justificación (de acciones erróneas). || *v.t.* **3** encalar, enjalbegar. **4** encubrir, maquillar, disculpar, justificar (errores).
whither | 'wɪðər | | 'hw' | *adv.* (arc.) adónde, hacia donde.
whiting | 'waɪtɪŋ | | 'hw' | *s.c.* e *i.* **1** blanqueador, blanco (de zapatos). **2** ZOOL. pescadilla.
whitish | 'waɪtɪʃ | | 'hw' | *adj.* blanquecino, blancuzco.
Whitsun | 'wɪtsn | | 'hw' | (también **Whit**) *s.i.* REL. Pentecostés.
whittle | 'wɪtl | | 'hw' | *v.t.* e *i.* **1** modelar, rebajar, cortar (madera con una navaja). || **2 to – (something) away/to – away (at something),** reducir, debilitar, llevarse: *inflation whittled their savings away = la inflación se llevó sus ahorros.* **3 to – (something) down, a)** achicar, desgastar (con navaja); **b)** acortar, reducir (gradualmente): *workers are being whittled down = se está reduciendo la mano de obra.*
whiz V. **whizz.**
whizz | wɪz | | 'hw' | (fam.) *v.i.* **1** zumbar, silbar, pasar zumbando: *the cars whizzed along = los coches pasaban zumbando.* || *s.c.* **2** zumbido. **3 [– (at)]** diestro, especialista, experto, genio: *he's a whizz at computers = es un genio en informática.*
whizz-kid | 'wɪzkɪd | | 'hw' | *s.c.* (fam.) joven de éxito, triunfador, ganador.
who | huː | *pron.interr.* **1** quién (en preguntas directas): *who told you? = ¿quién te lo dijo?; who was he with? = ¿con quiénes estaba?* **2** quién (en preguntas indirectas): *he didn't know who I was = él no sabía quién era yo.* || *pron.rel.* **3** que, quien (en función especificativa): *the people who live next door = las personas que viven al lado.* **4** que, quien, el cual (en función explicativa): *my wife, who is out at the moment, will phone you later = mi mujer, que ahora no está, le llamará más tarde.*
WHO | ˌdʌbljuːeɪtʃ'əʊ | *siglas* **World Health Organization**, OMS, Organización Mundial de la Salud.
whoa | wəʊ | *interj.* ¡so!
who'd | huːd | *contr.* de **who had** (**had** en función de *v. auxiliar,* generalmente) o **who would** (lenguaje hablado).
whodunit | ˌhuː'dʌnɪt | (también **whodunnit**) *s.c.* (fam.) historia policíaca (narración, película o comedia, donde la intriga se centra en la identificación del criminal).
whoever | huː'evər | *pron.ind.* **1** quienquiera que, cualquiera que, el que: *whoever says that is a liar = quienquiera que diga eso es un mentiroso.* **2** quienquiera que sea el que, sea quien sea quien: *whoever wants me on the phone, tell them I'm busy = quienquiera que sea el que me llame por teléfono, dile que estoy ocupado.* **3** no importa quién, independientemente de quién: *whoever wins this war, we'll lose it = no importa quién gane esta guerra, nosotros la perderemos.* || *pron.interr.* **4** quién (en expresión de sorpresa): *whoever heard of such a thing! = ¡y quién ha oído tal cosa!* || **5 or –,** (fam.) o quien sea: *I spoke to the director or manager or whoever = hablé con el director, con el encargado o con quien fuera.*
whole | həʊl | *adj.* **1** todo, completo: *he ate the whole cake = se comió toda la tarta.* **2** todo, todo a lo largo de: *he was sleeping the whole way back = estuvo dormido todo el camino de vuelta.* **3** completo, intacto, sano: *there wasn't a glass left whole, after the party = no quedó un vaso sano tras la fiesta.* || *s.sing.* **4** todo: *the whole of the morning was wasted = se perdió toda la mañana.* **5** todo, conjunto: *the three parts make a whole = las tres partes hacen un todo.* || *adv.* **6** entero, enteramente, completamente: *a snake can swallow a small rat whole = una serpiente puede tragarse entera una rata pequeña.* || **7 as a –, a)** como un todo: *the collection is sold as a whole = la colección se vende como un todo;* **b)** en general: *the country as a whole is for it = el país en general está a favor.* **8 on the –,** en general, en conjunto: *on the whole it's a hard task = es una empresa difícil en conjunto.* **9 – note,** (EE.UU.) MUS. redonda. **10 – number,** MAT. número entero.

wholefood | 'həʊlfu:d | *s.c.* e *i.* **1** alimento integral, alimento natural. || *atr.* **2** integral, basado en alimentos naturales: *a wholefood diet = dieta integral.*
wholehearted | ˌhəʊl'hɑ:tɪd | *adj.* entusiasta, incondicional, total, sin reservas: *a wholehearted support = un apoyo incondicional.*
wholeheartedly | ˌhəʊl'hɑ:tɪdlɪ | *adv.* de todo corazón, incondicionalmente, totalmente, sin reservas.
wholemeal | 'həʊlmi:l | *s.i.* **1** harina integral. || *atr.* **2** integral (pan, harina, etc.): *wholemeal bread = pan integral.*
wholeness | 'həʊlnɪs | *s.i.* (form.) totalidad, integridad, unidad.
wholesale | 'həʊlseɪl | *atr.* **1** al por mayor: *wholesale trade = comercio al por mayor; wholesale price = precio al por mayor.* **2** (desp.) masivo, indiscriminado, a gran escala, desmedido: *a wholesale slaughter of innocent people = una matanza masiva de inocentes.* || *adv.* **3** al por mayor: *to buy wholesale = comprar al por mayor.*
wholesaler | 'həʊlˌseɪlər | *s.c.* mayorista.
wholesome | 'həʊlsəm | *adj.* **1** sano, saludable, positivo, consciente: *to have a wholesome appearance = tener aspecto saludable.* **2** sano, nutritivo (alimento).
wholewheat | 'həʊlwi:t | (EE.UU.) *s.i.* **1** harina integral. || **2** integral (pan, harina, etc.): *wholewheat bread = pan integral.*
who'll | hu:l | *contr.* de **who will** (lenguaje hablado).
wholly | 'həʊlɪ | *adv.* totalmente, completamente, del todo, absolutamente.
whom | hu:m | (form.) *pron.interr.* **1** a quién: *whom do you represent? = ¿a quién representa usted?* **2 [***prep.* **+ –]** quién (precedido de *prep.*): *to whom should I deliver the message? = ¿a quién he de enviar el recado?* || *pron.rel.* **3** a quien, al cual (en función especificativa): *the writer whom we admire so much = el escritor a quien tanto admiramos.* **4** a quien, al cual (en función explicativa): *my parents, whom you have already met = mis padres, a quienes ya conoces.* **5 [***prep.* **–]** quien, el cual (precedido de *prep.*, en función especificativa o explicativa): *the women to whom we had just talked = las mujeres con las que acabamos de hablar.*
OBS. **Whom** queda fuera del uso ordinario de la lengua, siendo **who** la forma más empleada en funciones de *o.d.*, principalmente en preguntas: *who do you represent? = ¿a quién representa usted?* Gramaticalmente se haría necesario el uso del *interr.* **whom,** precedido de *prep.*: *to whom should I give the message? = ¿a quién he de dar el recado?*, pero se impone una fórmula más familiar: *who should I give the message to?*
whoop | hu:p | | hwᵋ | *v.i.* **1** (lit.) gritar (de alegría). || *s.c.* **2** (lit.) grito (de alegría). || **3 to – it up,** (fam.) divertirse o celebrarlo ruidosamente. **4 whoops,** (fam.) **a)** ¡uf!, ¡vaya!, ¡menos mal! **b)** ¡ay! lo siento (tras decir algo indebido).
whoopee | 'wupɪ: | | 'hwᵋ | (fam.) *interj.* **1** ¡yupi! || *s.i.* **2** fiesta, celebración ruidosa.
whooping-cough | 'hu:pɪŋkɒf | *s.i.* tos ferina.
whoosh | wuʃ | (fam.) *s.sing.* **1** zumbido, bufido (de aire o agua a presión). || *v.i.* **2** pasar zumbando. || *interj.* **3** ¡buf!, ¡zas!
whop | wɒp | | hwᵋ | *v.t.* (EE.UU. y fam.) golpear, castigar, derrotar.
whopper | 'wɒpər | | 'hwᵋ | (fam.) *s.c.* **1** gran mentira, trola, (Am.) bolada. **2** pieza, ejemplar: *you caught that fish? What a whopper! = ¿capturaste ese pez? ¡menuda pieza!*
whopping | 'wɒpɪŋ | | 'hwᵋ | *adj.* (fam.) enorme, descomunal, grandísimo.
whore | hɔ:r | *s.c.* puta, prostituta.
who're | 'hu:ər | *contr.* de **who are** (lenguaje hablado).
whorehouse | 'hɔ:haus | *s.c.* (fam.) casa de putas, burdel.
whorl | wɜ:l | | hwᵋ | *s.c.* **1** (lit.) espiral, espira. **2** BOT. verticilo.
who's | hu:z | *contr.* de **who has** (**has** como auxiliar generalmente) o **who is;** (lenguaje hablado).
whose | hu:z | *pron.interr.* **1** de quién: *whose book is this? = ¿de quién es este libro?; I don't know whose fault is it = no sé de quién es la culpa.* || *pron.rel.* **2** cuyo (en función especificativa): *the people whose situation is desperate = la gente cuya situación es desesperada.* **3** cuyo (en función explicativa): *he reads aloud to his mother, whose eyesight is poor = lee alto a su madre, cuya vista es defectuosa.*
whosoever | ˌhu:səu'evər | *pron.ind.* (arc.) (form.) quienquiera que, cualquiera que, todo el que.
who've | hu:v | *contr.* de **who have** (**have** como auxiliar, generalmente); (lenguaje hablado).
why | waɪ | | hwᵋ | *adv.* **1** por qué: *Why were you late? = ¿por qué llegaste tarde?* **2 [– (not)]** por qué (no) (en sugerencias): *why don't we all go? = ¿por qué no vamos todos?* || *conj.* **3** por qué: *tell me why you did it = dime por qué lo hiciste.* || *pron.rel.* **4 [(reason) –]** (razón) por la que: *the reasons why the measures were taken = las razones por las que se tomaron las medidas.* || *interj.* **5** (EE.UU.) cómo, toma, si: *why, there were five of us! = ¡si éramos cinco!* || *s.c.* **6** porqué: *there are so many whys = hay tantos porqués.* || **7 the whys and wherefores,** V. **wherefores. 8 – not,** por qué no, claro.
WI | ˌdʌblju:'aɪ | *siglas* **1 West Indies,** Indias Occidentales, Antillas. **2** (brit.) **Women's Institute,** Instituto de la Mujer.
wick | wɪk | *s.c.* **1** mecha, pábilo (de una vela, antorcha, candil, etc.). || **2 to get on one's –,** (brit. y fam.) fastidiar continuamente.
wicked | 'wɪkɪd | *adj.* **1** malo, malvado, inicuo, perverso, malintencionado. **2** (fig.) mordaz, cruel, retorcido (ingenio, comentario, etc.). **3** (fam.) horrible, desagradable, molesto, mortificante, inaguantable (situación).
wickedly | 'wɪkɪdlɪ | *adv.* mal, malintencionadamente, maliciosamente, cruelmente, horriblemente.
wickedness | 'wɪkɪdnɪs | *s.i.* malicia, perversidad, iniquidad, crueldad.
wicker | 'wɪkər | *s.i.* **1** mimbre. || *atr.* **2** de mimbre: *a wicker chair = silla de mimbre.*
wickerwork | 'wɪkəwɜ:k | *s.i.* **1** cestería, artesanía del mimbre, artículos de mimbre. || *atr.* **2** de mimbre: *wickerwork furniture = muebles de mimbre.*
wicket | 'wɪkɪt | DEP. *s.i.* **1** rastrillo (juego de palos hacia donde se lanza la pelota en críquet). **2** zona de hierba entre los dos rastrillos (críquet). || **3 –gate,** (arc.) postigo, portillo.
wicketkeeper | 'wɪkɪtˌki:pər | *s.c.* DEP. jugador de críquet colocado tras el rastrillo (encargado de detener la pelota).
wide | waɪd | *adj.* **1** ancho: *a wide river = río ancho.* **2** amplio, vasto, extenso: *a man with wide experience of industry = hombre de amplia experiencia en la industria.* **3** de ancho: *a plank five inches wide = una tabla de cinco pulgadas de ancho.* **4** completamente abierto (ojos): *to watch with wide eyes = mirar con ojos completamente abiertos (de sorpresa, terror, etc.).* **5** amplio, grande, general, importante (situación, aspecto, estado, etc.): *the wider political issues = los asuntos políticos más importantes.* **6** errado, fallido, desatinado (tiro, golpe): *the shot went wide = el tiro salió errado.* || *adv.* **7** completamente, del todo: *legs wide apart = piernas completamente abiertas; eyes wide open = ojos completamente abiertos (como platos).* **8 [– (of)]** lejos, desviado: *it went wide of the target = fue lejos del blanco.* || *s.c.* **9** DEP. pelota desviada (lejos del rastrillo, en cricket). || **10 far and –,** V. **far. 11 -wide,** todo a lo ancho de, en todo el (según el significado de la otra parte del compuesto): *a worldwide influence = influencia en todo el mundo (mundial).* **12 – of the mark,** V. **mark.**
wide-angle | ˌwaɪd'æŋgl | *adj.* **1** de amplio espectro, de gran ángulo (objetivo, lente, etc.). | **2 – lens,** V. **lens.**
wide-awake | ˌwaɪdə'weɪk | *adj.* despierto, avisado, consciente, despabilado.
wide-eyed | ˌwaɪd'aɪd | *adj.* **1** de ojos muy abiertos (de sorpresa o pánico). **2** inexperto, ingenuo, sin malear.
widely | 'waɪdlɪ | *adv.* ampliamente, extensamente, considerablemente.
widen | 'waɪdn | *v.t.* e *i.* **1** ensanchar, ampliar, extender: *to widen a road = ensanchar una carretera.* **2** abrir, aumentar: *the gap between the rich and the poor widens = la diferencia entre ricos y pobres aumenta.*

wide-ranging | ˌwaɪd'reɪndʒɪŋ | *adj.* amplio, variado, de amplio alcance, importante, trascendente.
widespread | 'waɪdspred | *adj.* amplio, extenso, generalizado, difundido.
widow | 'wɪdəʊ | *s.c.* **1** viuda. || *v.t.* **2** [en *pas.* generalmente] enviudar, quedar viuda: *she was widowed at an early age = enviudó muy joven.*
widowed | 'wɪdəʊd | *adj.* viudo: *his widowed mother = su viuda madre.*
widower | 'wɪdəʊər | *s.c.* viudo.
widowhood | 'wɪdəʊhʊd | *s.i.* viudez, viudedaz.
width | wɪdθ | *s.i.* **1** anchura, extensión, amplitud, envergadura. || *s.c.* **2** ancho (de una ventana, piscina, etc.): *she can swim a width = puede nadar un ancho.*
widthways | 'wɪdθweɪz | *adv.* a lo ancho.
wield | wiːld | *v.t.* **1** manejar, empuñar, blandir, enarbolar (herramientas, armas, etc.). **2** ejercer (el poder).
wife | waɪf | *s.c.* [*pl.irreg.* **wives**] esposa, mujer.
wifely | 'waɪflɪ | *adj.* de mujer casada, de esposa: *wifely duty = obligaciones de esposa.*
wig | wɪg | *s.c.* peluca.
wigged | wɪgd | *adj.* con peluca, que lleva peluca, tocado de peluca.
wigging | 'wɪgɪŋ | *s.sing.* (brit. y fam.) regañina, reprimenda.
wiggle | 'wɪgl | *v.t.* **1** mover, menear: *he can wiggle his ears = es capaz de mover las orejas.* || *s.c.* **2** meneo, movimiento (rápido): *the wiggle of hips = el meneo de caderas.*
wigwam | 'wɪgwæm | *s.c.* tienda de indio norteamericano (de piel animal).
wild | waɪld | *adj.* **1** salvaje, en libertad: *wild animals = animales salvajes.* **2** silvestre: *wild flowers = flores silvestres.* **3** salvaje, deshabitado, agreste, sin cultivar (tierra): *the wilder parts of Scotland = las regiones más salvajes de Escocia.* **4** salvaje, sin civilizar (cultura, persona, etc.): *wild tribes = tribus salvajes.* **5** revuelto, desapacible, tormentoso, bravo (mar, tiempo, etc.): *a February wild day = un día desapacible de febrero.* **6** largo, descuidado (pelo). **7** fiero, feroz, desencajado, fuera de sí (mirada, aspecto). **8** frenético, histérico: *the audience went wild = el público se puso histérico.* **9** (fam.) furioso, descontrolado, fuera de sí (conductas, sentimientos, etc.). **10** (fam.) estupendo, insuperable: *it was a really wild party = fue una fiesta insuperable.* **11** **[- about]** loco por: *he's wild about racing cars = está loco por los coches de carreras.* **12** descabellado, fantasioso, original (idea, proyecto, etc.). **13** impulsivo, desesperado, enérgico (reacción, movimiento, ataque, etc.). **14** irracional, ilógico, improbable (cálculo, conjetura, etc.). || *s.sing.* **15** ambiente, entorno, hábitat natural (de los animales salvajes). || **16 beyond one's wildest dreams,** del todo imprevisto, fuera de toda lógica. **17 in the –,** en su entorno natural, salvaje, en libertad. **18 not to be – about,** (fam.) no gustarle a uno, molar poco. **19 to run –, a)** vivir como salvajes (niños); **b)** campar por sus respetos. **20 to sow one's – oats, a)** llevar una vida disoluta; **b)** echar una canita al aire. **21 – boar,** ZOOL. jabalí. **22 – flower,** flor silvestre. **23 wilds,** tierra virgen, lugares remotos apartados de la civilización, yermo. **24 – West,** el salvaje Oeste americano (antes de que imperase la ley).
wildcat | 'waɪldkæt | *s.c.* **1** ZOOL. gato montés. || *adj.* **2** salvaje, repentino, ilegal (huelga). **3** osado, arriesgado, loco (plan, proyecto, negocio).
wildebeest | 'waɪldbiːst | , | 'vɪldə | *s.c.* [*pl.* **wildebeest** o **wildebeests**] ZOOL. ñu.
wilderness | 'wɪldənɪs | *s.c.* **1** desierto, tierra salvaje, yermo: *the arctic wilderness = el desierto ártico.* || **2 in the –,** retirado a su vida privada (político o persona pública).
wildfire | 'waɪldfaɪər | *s.sing.* **1** fuego incontrolado. || **2 to spread like –,** propagarse como la pólvora.
wildfowl | 'waɪldfaʊl | *s.pl.* aves salvajes (patos, generalmente).
wild-goose chase | ˌwaɪld'guːstʃeɪs | *s.c.* esfuerzo inútil, pérdida de tiempo, búsqueda de algo inexistente.
wildlife | 'waɪldlaɪf | *s.i.* vida salvaje (animales y plantas en su entorno natural).
wildly | 'waɪldlɪ | *adv.* salvajemente, violentamente, frenéticamente, locamente, desordenadamente, insensatamente, totalmente.
wildness | 'waɪldnɪs | *s.i.* turbulencia, desenfreno, descontrol, furia, frenesí.
wiles | waɪlz | *s.pl.* tretas, estratagemas, engaños, ardides.
wilful | 'wɪlfʊl | *adj.* (desp.) **1** intencionado, deliberado, premeditado. **2** testarudo, de ideas fijas.
wilfully | 'wɪlfəlɪ | *adv.* intencionadamente, deliberadamente, a posta.
wilfulness | 'wɪlfʊlnɪs | *s.i.* intencionalidad, voluntariedad, testarudez.
will | wɪl | *v.modal* **1** (como auxiliar para construir el futuro): *it will be good for you = será bueno para ti.* **2** **[I/we –]** (intencionalidad, determinación del hablante): *I will never betray you = nunca te traicionaré.* **3** (en preguntas sobre el futuro): *where will you be tomorrow? = ¿dónde estará usted mañana?* **4** (en preguntas sobre la intencionalidad del interlocutor): *will you be coming to the party? = ¿vendrás a la fiesta?* **5** (en peticiones): *will you do me a favour? = ¿me quiere hacer un favor?* **6** (en órdenes): *you will forget this conversation = ni una palabra de esta conversación.* **7** (en expresión de capacidad): *the car won't go = el coche no va.* **8** (para expresar que una situación suele repetirse): *don't worry, these things will happen = no te preocupes, suele suceder.* **9** (para enfatizar una conducta reprochable): *he will always leave the door open = siempre tiene que dejar la puerta abierta.* **10** (en expresión de presunción, suposición, sospecha, etc.): *I suspect you will already have told her = sospecho que ya se lo habrás dicho.* || *v.t.* **11** hacer, conseguir (que algo suceda): *he willed his trembling legs to walk straight = consiguió caminar recto con sus vacilantes piernas.* **12** (form.) querer, desear: *I never willed this outcome = nunca deseé este resultado.* **13** legar, dejar en herencia: *he willed all his money to charities = legó todo su dinero a obras de caridad.* || *s.c.* e *i.* **14** voluntad, ganas: *the team lacked will and ambition = el equipo careció de ganas y ambición.* **15** fuerza de voluntad, carácter, amor propio: *she has a will of her own = tiene mucho amor propio.* **16** deseo, voluntad (de alguien investido de poder o autoridad): *the will of the majority = el deseo de la mayoría.* **17** testamento, últimas voluntades, legado. || **18 against one's –,** contra la voluntad de alguien. **19 at –,** como a uno le plazca. **20 where there's a –, there's a way,** querer es poder. **21 with a –,** con mucho entusiasmo y energía.
willie | 'wɪlɪ | V. **willy.**
willing | 'wɪlɪŋ | *adj.* **1** dispuesto, resuelto, listo: *willing to help = dispuesto a ayudar.* **2** voluntarioso, entusiasta, diligente, aplicado, favorable: *willing students = estudiantes aplicados.*
willingly | 'wɪlɪŋlɪ | *adv.* voluntariamente, de buena gana, diligentemente.
willingness | 'wɪlɪŋnɪs | *s.i.* buena disposición, buena gana, diligencia.
will-o'-the-wisp | ˌwɪləðə'wɪsp | *s.c.* quimera, ilusión, fuego fatuo.
willow | 'wɪləʊ | *s.c.* **1** BOT. sauce. || **2 – tree,** sauce.
willowy | 'wɪləʊɪ | *adj.* esbelto, espigado, juncal, grácil.
will-power | 'wɪlˌpaʊər | *s.i.* fuerza de voluntad, carácter, amor propio.
willy | 'wɪlɪ | (también **willie**) *s.c.* **1** (fam.) colita, pilila, pene. || **2 to give someone the willies,** (fam.) causarle horror a alguien.
willy-nilly | ˌwɪlɪ'nɪlɪ | *adv.* a la fuerza, se quiera o no se quiera.
wilt | wɪlt | *v.t.* e *i.* **1** marchitarse, debilitarse, decaer, ponerse mustio (plantas). **2** debilitar, languidecer, perder la contextura, perder moral.
wily | 'waɪlɪ | *adj.* astuto, mañoso, artero, taimado.
wimp | wɪmp | *s.c.* (fam.) hombre cortado, gallina, pasmarote.
wimpish | 'wɪmpɪʃ | *adj.* (fam.) cortado, tímido, cobarde.
wimple | 'wɪmpl | *s.c.* toca, griñón.
win | wɪn | *v.t.* e *i.* [*pret.* y *p.p.irreg.* **won**] **1** ganar (competiciones, batallas, disputas, apuestas, etc.). **2** ganar, vencer, derrotar. **3** ganar, conseguir, alcanzar (premios, medallas, escaños, apoyo, libertad, etc.). || *s.c.* **4** victoria, triunfo (competiciones, apuestas, etc.). || **5 (someone) can't –,** (fam.) tener la batalla perdida, tenerlo crudo. **6 to – hands down,** (fam.) vencer fácilmente. **7 to –**

someone over/round, ganarse, convencer, persuadir a alguien. **8 to – something back,** recuperar, volver a ganar algo (mediante el propio esfuerzo). **9 to – the day,** V. **day. 10 to – through/out,** (fam.) alcanzar al fin el triunfo. **11 you –, tú ganas** (para terminar una discusión o porfía).

wince | wɪns | *v.i.* **1 [to – (at)]** estremecerse, quedarse pasmado, retroceder, (ante algo desagradable). || *s.c.* **2** estremecimiento, mueca de dolor.

winch | wɪntʃ | *s.c.* **1** cabrestante, torno (de rescate). || *v.t.* **2** rescatar, levantar (con cabrestante).

wind | wɪnd | *s.c.* e *i.* **1** viento. **2** aliento, respiración, resuello: *he needed to regain his wind = necesitaba recuperar su aliento.* **3** (fam.) gases, flatulencia. **4** (lit.) aire, viento (de cambio, novedad, etc.). **5** rastro: *the dogs got the wind = los perros cogieron el rastro.* **6** (fam.) tontería, fanfarronada, trola. **7** MUS. viento, sección de viento (de una orquesta). || *v.t.* **8** (pasiva) dejar sin respiración: *I was winded by a blow to the stomach = un golpe en el estómago me dejó sin respiración.* **9** olfatear, seguir el rastro. || **10 to break –,** (form.) ventosear. **11 to get the – up,** (fam.) entrarle a uno miedo, amilanarse. **12 to get – of,** (fam.) llegar a enterarse de algo. **13 in the –,** (fam.) en preparación, estarse cociendo. **14 to put the – up someone,** (fam.) meterle a uno el miedo en el cuerpo. **15 to sail close to the –,** correr demasiados riesgos. **16 to take the – out of somebody's sails,** hacer que alguien pierda la seguridad en sí mismo. **17 to throw caution to the –,** ignorar los riesgos (de una acción). **18 which way the – is blowing,** qué cariz tomarán las cosas. **19 – instrument,** MUS. instrumento de viento.

wind | waɪnd | *v.i.* [*pret.* y *p.p.irreg.* **wound**] **1** serpentear, zigzaguear: *the river winds down the valley = el río serpentea en el valle.* || *t.* **2** enrollar, envolver, liar, bobinar. **3** dar cuerda (reloj), girar (llave, mango). **4** (lit.) soplar, hacer sonar (cuerno). || *s.c.* **5** giro, vuelta. || **6 to – back,** rebobinar (cintas). **7 to – down, a)** bajar (la ventanilla de un coche). **b)** reducir la marcha hasta pararse (aparatos mecánicos); **c)** reducir (volumen de negocio, plantilla laboral, etc.); **d)** (fam.) relajarse, descansar. **8 to – forward,** avanzar (cintas). **9 to – up, a)** terminar, concluir, liquidar (una actividad, negocios, etc.); **b)** acabar en (una situación o lugar); **c)** dar cuerda (reloj), girar (llave, mango, etc.); **d)** levantar (la ventanilla de un coche); **e)** (fam.) injuriar, ofender (de palabra y deliberadamente); **f)** (fam.) burlarse, quedarse con alguien. **10 wound up,** tenso, rígido, agarrotado, nervioso.

windbag | 'wɪndbæg | *s.c.* (fam.) charlatán, cencerro, (Am.) lengüeta.

wind-blown | 'wɪnd,bləʊn | *adj.* llevado, zarandeado por el viento.

windbreak | 'wɪndbreɪk | *s.c.* barrera, protección contra el viento.

winded | 'wɪndɪd | *adj.* falto de aire, sin respiración, sin resuello.

windfall | 'wɪndfɔːl | *s.c.* **1** lluvia de dinero, golpe de fortuna, herencia inesperada. **2** fruta caída del árbol.

winding | 'waɪndɪŋ | *adj.* **1** tortuoso, sinuoso, serpenteante, zigzagueante. **2** de caracol (escalera).

windlass | 'wɪndləs | *s.c.* polea, cabrestante.

windless | 'wɪndlɪs | *adj.* (lit.) sin viento, calmoso, sereno.

windmill | 'wɪnmɪl | *s.c.* molino de viento.

window | 'wɪndəʊ | *s.c.* **1** ventana, ventanilla. **2** escaparate. || **3 out of the window,** desaparecido completamente.

window-box | 'wɪndəʊbɒks | *s.c.* jardinera (de ventana).

window-dresser | 'wɪndəʊ,dresər | *s.c.* escaparatista.

window-dressing | 'wɪndəʊ,dresɪŋ | *s.i.* **1** decoración de escaparate. **2** (desp.) fachada, maquillaje, falsedad.

window-frame | 'wɪndəʊ,freɪm | *s.c.* marco de ventana.

window-pane | 'wɪndəʊ,peɪn | *s.c.* cristal, panel de cristal (de ventana).

window-seat | 'wɪndəʊ,siːt | *s.c.* asiento de ventana (tren, autocar, avión).

window-shop | 'wɪndəʊ,ʃɒp | *v.i.* [*pret.* y *p.p.* **window-shopped,** *ger.* **window-shopping**] mirar escaparates.

window-sill | 'wɪndəʊ,sɪl | *s.c.* alféizar.

windpipe | 'wɪndpaɪp | *s.c.* ANAT. tráquea.

windscreen | 'wɪndskriːn | (brit.) *s.c.* **1** parabrisas. || **2 – wiper,** limpiaparabrisas.

windshield | 'wɪndʃiːld | *s.c.* **1** protector transparente (en motocicletas). **2** (EE.UU.) parabrisas.

windsock | 'wɪndsɒk | *s.c.* indicador de viento.

windstorm | 'wɪndstɔːm | *s.c.* tormenta de viento, huracán.

windsurfer | 'wɪnd,sɜːfər | *s.c.* **1** tabla con vela. **2** navegante de tabla y vela.

windsurfing | 'wɪnd,sɜːfɪŋ | *s.i.* **1** DEP. windsurfing. || **2 to go –,** hacer windsurfing.

windswept | 'wɪndswept | *adj.* **1** barrido por el viento, abierto, desprotegido (lugar). **2** despeluchado, desaseado (persona).

wind-up | 'waɪndʌp | *atr.* **1** de cuerda, que se da cuerda (mecanismo). **2** (fam.) provocador: *a wind-up artist = un artista provocador.* || *s.c.* **3** (fam.) provocación.

windward | 'wɪndwəd | *adj./adv.* **1** contra el viento, con el viento de cara. **2** MAR. de barlovento. || *s.i.* **3** MAR. barlovento.

windy | 'wɪndɪ | *adj.* **1** ventoso, desapacible, azotado por el viento. **2** (fam.) pomposo, inflado, huero (discurso, escrito). **3** que produce gases (en el estómago). **4** (brit. y fam.) asustado, nervioso.

wine | waɪn | *s.i.* **1** vino. **2** vino, licor (de fruta): *apple wine = licor de manzana.* || **3 to – and dine,** invitar o agasajar a alguien en un buen restaurante. **4 – red,** del color del vino tinto. **5 wining and dining,** buena mesa.

wine-bar | 'waɪnbɑːr | *s.c.* (brit.) taberna, bar.

wine-glass | 'waɪnglɑːs | *s.c.* vaso para vino.

wing | wɪŋ | *s.c.* **1** ala (de aves, insectos o aeroplanos). **2** ala, extensión (de un edificio). **3** ala, sector, facción (de un grupo o partido político). **4** (brit.) guardabarros. **5** DEP. ala, alero (jugador que juega por las alas). || *v.t.* e *i.* **6** volar (aeroplano). **7** herir en brazo o ala. || **8 on the –,** (lit.) en vuelo, mientras vuela (pájaro). **9 to spread one's wings, a)** remontar el vuelo; **b)** acometer empresas más difíciles. **10 to take –,** (lit.) echar a volar, emprender el vuelo. **11 to wait in the wings,** estar listo y a la espera. **12 – commander,** (brit.) teniente coronel de aviación. **13 wings, a)** bastidores (escenario teatral); **b)** alas (insignia de piloto).

winged | wɪŋd | *adj.* alado, con alas.

winger | 'wɪŋər | *s.c.* **1** DEP. ala, alero, extremo. || **2 -winger,** perteneciente al ala especificada en la primera parte del compuesto.

wingspan | 'wɪŋspæn | *s.c.* e *i.* envergadura (de aves, insectos, etc.).

wink | wɪŋk | *v.t.* e *i.* **1** guiñar, hacer guiños, parpadear, pestañear. **2** (lit.) centellear, parpadear, titilar, hacer reflejos (la luz). || *s.c.* **3** guiño, parpadeo, pestañeo. || **4 a nod is as good as a –,** a buen entendedor pocas palabras. **5 to have/take forty winks,** (fam.) echar una cabezadita, descabezar un sueño. **6 not to sleep/get a –,** no pegar ojo. **7 to tip someone the –,** V. **tip. 8 to – at something,** (arc.) hacer la vista gorda (a actos reprochables).

winkle | 'wɪŋkl | *s.c.* **1** ZOOL. bigarro, litorina. || **2 to – (information) out of someone,** (fam.) arrancar información de alguien. **3 to – someone out,** (fam.) echar a alguien (de algún lugar).

winner | 'wɪnər | *s.c.* **1** ganador, vencedor, triunfador. **2** (fam.) éxito.

winning | 'wɪnɪŋ | *adj.* **1** ganador, vencedor, victorioso (competidor, equipo, etc.). **2** atractivo, decisivo, irresistible, determinante (acciones o cualidades de personas). || **3 winnings,** ganancias (de competiciones o apuestas).

winnow | 'wɪnəʊ | *v.t.* aventar.

winsome | 'wɪnsəm | *adj.* (lit.) atractivo, fascinante, encantador.

winter | 'wɪntər | *s.c.* e *i.* **1** invierno. || *v.i.* **2** (form.) invernar. || **3 – sports,** deportes de invierno.

wintertime | 'wɪntətaɪm | *s.i.* invierno, estación invernal.

wintry | 'wɪntrɪ | *adj.* **1** invernal, frío, glacial. **2** frío, distante, adusto (expresión o trato de una persona).

wipe | waɪp | *v.t.* **1** limpiar, pasar un paño. **2** secar, enjugar (con un paño, con la mano, etc.): *to wipe the dishes = secar los platos, to wipe one's tears =*

secarse las lágrimas. **3** borrar, grabar encima (cintas). || *s.c.* **4** limpieza. || **5 to – at something,** limpiar algo. **6 to – away/off,** quitar, limpiar (con un paño). **7 to – down,** limpiar, secar completamente (superficies). **8 to – out,** (fam.) barrer, eliminar, destruir violentamente (lugares, gente). **9 to – the floor with someone,** (fam.) derrotar a alguien (en competición o disputa). **10 to – the grin/smile/etc. off someone's face,** (fam.) cortar en seco el regocijo de alguien. **11 to – up, a)** limpiar la suciedad (con un paño); **b)** (brit. y arc.) secar (la vajilla con un paño).

wiper | 'waɪpər | *s.c.* limpiaparabrisas.

wire | waɪər | *s.c.* e *i.* **1** alambre. **2** cable (electricidad, teléfono, etc.). **3** (EE.UU.) telegrama. || *v.t.* **4** unir, atar (con alambre). **5 [to – (up)]** conectar, instalar (un sistema electrónico). **6** (EE.UU.) enviar un telegrama. **7** (EE.UU.) girar dinero (telegráficamente). || **8 – wool,** estropajo metálico.

wired | waɪəd | *adj.* **1** protegido, reforzado (con alambre). **2** provisto de alarma, conectado a alarma. **3** vigilado microfónicamente.

wireless | 'waɪəlɪs | *s.c.* e *i.* **1** (arc.) radio, radiofonía. || *atr.* **2** por radio, radiofónico. || **3 – (set), a)** aparato de radio; **b)** equipo de radiofonía.

wire-tap | 'waɪətæp | *v.t.* **1** espiar, pinchar (teléfono). || *s.c.* **2** pinchado de teléfono.

wire-tapping | 'waɪəˌtæpɪŋ | *s.i.* escucha telefónica (mediante pinchado).

wiring | 'waɪərɪŋ | *s.i.* cableado, instalación eléctrica (de un edificio).

wiry | 'waɪərɪ | *adj.* **1** duro como el alambre. **2** tieso, tenso, áspero.

wisdom | 'wɪzdəm | *s.i.* **1** sabiduría, conocimiento (por tradición, experiencia o estudio). **2** rectitud de juicio, sensatez, prudencia. **3** (form.) opinión, parecer, sentir (de un grupo o casta autorizados): *The prevailing Wall Street wisdom is that... = el sentir de Wall Street se decanta por...* || **4 – tooth,** muela del juicio.

wise | waɪz | *adj.* **1** sabio, juicioso, prudente (persona, acción, dicho, etc.). || **2 to get – to,** (EE.UU. y fam.) descubrir, averiguar algo secreto. **3 in no –,** (p.u.) de ninguna manera, en absoluto. **4 no /none the/not any the wiser,** no saber/ entender más que antes: *even after his explanation I'm none the wiser = aun con su explicación, sigo sin entenderlo.* **5 to put someone – to,** (EE.UU. y fam.) poner a alguien al tanto. **6 ...would be – to,** habría que, lo mejor es. **7 -wise, a)** en el sentido de, según, conforme a (lo especificado en la primera parte del compuesto): *start clockwise = comiéncese en el sentido de las manillas del reloj;* **b)** en cuanto a: *we're at a disadvantage profitwise = estamos en desventaja en cuanto a beneficios.* **8 to – up,** (EE.UU. y fam.) caer en la cuenta (de algo desagradable).

wisecrack | 'waɪzkræk | (fam.) *s.c.* **1** broma, chiste, cuchufleta. || *v.i.* **2** bromear, hacerse el gracioso.

wish | wɪʃ | *s.c.* **1** deseo, esperanza. **2** deseo (objeto de deseo): *she got her wish = alcanzó su deseo.* **3** deseo (expresión de deseo): *close your eyes and make three wishes = cierra los ojos y formula tres deseos.* || *v.t.* e *i.* **4** (form.) desear, querer: *they wish to marry = desean casarse.* **5** desear (expresar el deseo de felicidad, bienestar, que alguien cumpla años, etc.). **6 [to – (for)]** expresar deseos (en forma ritual): *she closed her eyes and wished for a new doll = cerró los ojos y expresó el deseo de tener una nueva muñeca.* **7 [to – + *v.* en *pret.*]** desear (algo improbable o imposible), ojalá (algo se realizara): *I wish I knew = ojalá lo supiera yo.* || **8 I don't – to be rude/to interrupt/etc. but...,** no quiero ser descortés/interrumpir/etc. pero... **9 not to – something on (a person),** (fam.) no desear algo (desagradable) a alguien: *I wouldn't wish it on my worst enemy = no se lo desearía a mi peor enemigo.* **10 wishes (for), a)** saludos (en cartas); **b)** votos, deseos (de bienestar, felicidad, etc.).

wishbone | 'wɪʃbəun | *s.c.* hueso de los deseos (hueso de ave en forma de uve).

wishful thinking | ˌwɪʃful'θɪŋkɪŋ | *s.i.* buenos deseos, ilusiones.

wishy-washy | 'wɪʃɪˌwɒʃɪ | *adj.* **1** ligero, aguado, sin consistencia (caldo, bebida, etc.). **2** (fam.) sin convicción, sin entusiasmo, indeciso (ideas, creencias, etc.).

wisp | wɪsp | *s.c.* **1** brizna, matojo (de hierba), mechón, mata (de pelo). **2** columna (de humo), jirón (de nube). **3** (lit.) rastro, pista, eco, sombra (de algo que apenas se ve, oye o percibe).

wispy | 'wɪspɪ | *adj.* delgado, ralo, tenue, sutil.

wisteria | wɪ'stɪərɪə | (también **wistaria**) *s.i.* BOT. vistaria.

wistful | 'wɪstful | *adj.* triste, melancólico, meditabundo.

wistfully | 'wɪstfəlɪ | *adv.* tristemente, melancólicamente, pensativamente.

wistfulness | 'wɪstfulnɪs | *s.i.* tristeza, melancolía, indolencia.

wit | wɪt | *s.c.* e *i.* **1** ingenio, gracia, agudeza. **2** persona ingeniosa: *his reputation as a wit = su fama de persona ingeniosa.* **3** inteligencia, talento. **4** intuición, agilidad mental: *her wits to bluff her enemies = su agilidad mental para confundir a sus enemigos.* || **5 at one's wits' end,** al borde de la ofuscación. **6 battle of wits,** V. **battle. 7 to collect/gather one's wits,** tratar de recuperar el control de uno mismo (tras una experiencia traumática). **8 to have/keep one's wits about oneself,** estar alerta para controlar una situación difícil. **9 to live by/on one's wits,** V. **live. 10 to pit one's wits,** V. **pit. 11 to scare/terrify someone out of their wits/to frighten the wits out of someone,** dar a alguien un susto de muerte. **12 to sharpen one's wits,** avivar el ingenio. **13 to wit,** (form.) a saber.

witch | wɪtʃ | *s.c.* **1** bruja, maga, hechicera. **2** bruja (mujer de aspecto desagradable).

witchcraft | 'wɪtʃkrɑːft | *s.i.* brujería.

witch-doctor | 'wɪtʃˌdɒktər | *s.c.* hechicero.

witch-hazel | 'wɪtʃˌheɪzl | *s.i.* ungüento medicinal.

witch-hunt | 'wɪtʃhʌnt | *s.c.* **1** caza de brujas. **2** persecución de personas subversivas.

witch-hunting | 'wɪtʃhʌntɪŋ | *s.i.* caza de brujas, represión de personas subversivas.

with | wɪð | | wɪθ | *prep.* **1** con (compañía): *she's with her parents = está con sus padres.* **2** con (acuerdo, asociación, etc.): *a treatry with U.S.A. = un tratado con EE.UU.* **3** con (lucha, riña, competición): *an argument with my sister = una discusión con mi hermana.* **4** con (proximidad, complemento, guarnición): *meat with potatoes = carne con patatas.* **5** con, a (relación estrecha): *risks associated with nuclear power = riesgos asociados a la energía nuclear.* **6** con (medio, instrumento): *to cut with a knife = cortar con un cuchillo.* **7** con, de (en posesión de ciertas características personales): *the man with a beard = el hombre de barba.* **8** con (detalles que matizan una acción): *she greeted us with a smile = nos saludó con una sonrisa.* **9** con (dando detalle de una conversación): *she broke in with, "I don't agree" = saltó con un "no estoy de acuerdo".* **10** con (forma de realizar una acción): *done with great accuracy = hecho con gran precisión.* **11** de, a causa de: *he was turning blue with cold = se estaba volviendo morado del frío.* **12** con, con respecto a, en cuanto a: *inflexible with shopping = inflexible con la compra.* **13** con (simultaneidad de acciones): *she went out, with the cat following her = salió, con el perro siguiéndola.* **14** con, a la vista de (punto de argumentación en discurso): *with unemployment growing, work conditions... = con un desempleo en aumento, las condiciones laborales...* **15** con, protagonizado por: Moby-Dick, *with Gregory Peck.* **16** con, aquejado de: *in bed with flu = en cama con gripe.* **17** con, a favor de, en el sentido de: *sailing with the wind = navegando a favor del viento; swimming with the tide = nadando a favor de la corriente.* **18** con, de, etc. (como régimen de algunos verbos): *to agree with = estar de acuerdo con; fill the bowl with water = llena el cuenco de agua; to break with someone = romper con alguien.* **19** con, de, en, etc. (como régimen de algunos adjetivos): *busy with her homework = enfrascada en sus deberes... unhappy with the results = insatisfecho de los resultados.* **20** de (en algunas expresiones muy comunes): *fed up with washing up = harta de fregar; in love with a diplomat = enamorada de un diplomático.* || **21 to be – someone,** (fam.)

seguir, entender una explicación: *I'm not quite with you = no le sigo.* **22 to get – it,** (fam.) ponerse a la última. **23 in –,** V. **in. 24 to start –,** V. **start. 25 what –,** V. **what. 26 – it,** (fam.) al loro.

withdraw | wɪð'drɔː | (form.) *v.t.* e *i.* [*pret.* **withdrew,** *p.p.* **withdrawn**] **1** retirar, sacar (dinero del banco). **2** marcharse, abandonar un lugar. **3** retirar, retirarse (tropas de una posición). **4** abandonar, desistir, renunciar, causar baja (competición, programa conjunto, etc.). **5** retirar (algo dicho previamente).

withdrawal | wɪð'drɔːəl | (form.) *s.c.* e *i.* **1** retirada, renuncia, abandono (de una actividad o lugar). **2** retirada (de comentario, juicio, etc.). **3** reintegro, retirada de fondos (del banco). **4** retiro, aislamiento (voluntario o por enfermedad). **5** retirada (de tropas). || **6 – symptoms,** síndrome de abstinencia.

withdrawn | wɪð'drɔːn | *p.p.* **1** de **withdraw.** || *adj.* **2** introvertido, reservado, callado.

withdrew | wɪð'druː | *pret.* de **withdraw.**

wither | 'wɪðər | *v.i.* **[to – (away)] 1** debilitarse, decrecer, difuminarse, desaparecer. **2** debilitarse, marchitarse, secarse (plantas). || **3 withers,** cruz (de algunos animales).

withered | 'wɪðəd | *adj.* **1** seco, muerto (plantas, hojas, etc.). **2** arrugado, viejo, ajado (aspecto de persona). **3** deformado, tullido, débil, marchito (brazo, pierna, etc.).

withering | 'wɪðərɪŋ | *adj.* desdeñoso, de desprecio, humillante.

withhold | wɪð'həuld | *v.t.* e *i.* negar, denegar, rehusar, mantener para sí.

within | wɪ'ðɪn | *prep.* **1** dentro de: *within the city walls = dentro del recinto amurallado.* **2** dentro de (una sociedad, sistema, grupo, etc.): *the main forces within society = las fuerzas principales dentro de la sociedad.* **3** dentro de (unos límites establecidos): *to keep within the budget = mantenerse dentro del presupuesto.* **4** dentro de (una distancia determinada): *within ten miles around = dentro de diez millas a la redonda.* **5** dentro de (una distancia convencional): *within sight = dentro de donde alcanza la vista.* **6** dentro de (un espacio de tiempo): *any day within the week = cualquier día dentro de la semana.* **7** dentro de (otra cosa similar): *a play within a play = una obra de teatro dentro de otra.* || *adv.* **8** dentro: *the noise came from within = el ruido venía de dentro.* **9** (lit.) internamente: *he felt a sort of hatred within = sintió internamente una suerte de odio.* || **10 inquire –,** infórmese dentro.

without | wɪ'ðaut | *prep.* **1** sin (la cosa o cualidad mencionada): *two long days without food = dos interminables días sin alimento.* **2** sin (un tipo de sentimientos o conducta concretos): *done without any ambition = hecho sin ambición alguna.* **3** sin (una persona o cosa concreta, algo negativo se derivaría): *without a leader, the team would not work = sin un líder, el equipo no rendiría.* **4 [– (-ing)]** sin (la acción que se especifica): *without making mistakes = sin cometer errores.* **5** (arc.) fuera: *without the city walls = fuera de las murallas.* || *adv.* **6** sin: *if there's no sugar, we'll have to manage without = si no hay azúcar, tendremos que pasar sin él.* || **7 to do –,** V. **do. 8 to go –,** V. **go. 9 – so much as,** sin siquiera: *off he went, without so much as a goodbye = partió sin un adiós siquiera.*

withstand | wɪð'stænd | *v.t.* [*pret.* y *p.p.irreg.* **withstood**] (form.) aguantar, resistir.

witless | 'wɪtlɪs | (form.) *adj.* **1** estúpido, tonto, (Am.) nefasto. || **2 to scare someone –,** darle a uno un susto de muerte.

witness | 'wɪtnɪs | *s.c.* **1** testigo (de un hecho, ante un tribunal, etc.). **2 [– (to)]** (form.) testigo, testimonio, signo: *her smile is a witness to her happiness = su sonrisa es testimonio de su dicha.* || *v.t.* **3** (form.) observar, ser testigo: *two people witnessed the accident = dos personas fueron testigos del accidente.* **4** ver, presenciar, vivir: *we are witnessing deep political changes = estamos viviendo profundos cambios políticos.* **5** firmar como testigo (un documento oficial). **6** (form.) considerar, tener en cuenta (como apoyo de una argumentación): *witness the number of mistakes... = téngase en cuenta la cantidad de errores...* || *v.i.* **7 [to – (to)]** ser testigo, hacer de testigo. || **8 to bear – to,** dar testimonio. **9 to be – to something,** (form.) ver, presenciar algo.

witness-box | 'wɪtnɪsbɒks | *s.c.* tribuna de testigos (en el juzgado).

witness-stand | 'wɪtnɪsˌstænd | V. **witness-box.**

witter | 'wɪtər | *v.i.* (fam.) decir tonterías, gastar saliva.

witticism | 'wɪtɪsɪzəm | *s.c.* (form.) agudeza, gracia, ocurrencia.

wittily | 'wɪtɪlɪ | *adv.* ingeniosamente, agudamente, con gracia, sutilmente.

wittingly | 'wɪtɪŋlɪ | *adv.* (form.) a sabiendas, conscientemente.

witty | 'wɪtɪ | *adj.* ingenioso, agudo, sutil, gracioso, salado.

wives | waɪvz | *pl.* de **wife.**

wizard | 'wɪzəd | *s.c.* **1** mago (literatura fantástica). **2** genio, experto.

wizardry | 'wɪzədrɪ | *s.i.* magia, brujería, ingenio, talento.

wizened | 'wɪznd | *adj.* seco, ajado, marchito, arrugado.

woad | wəud | *s.i.* tinte azul (usado en la antigüedad como maquillaje).

wobble | 'wɒbl | *v.i.* tambalear, bambolear, vacilar, balancear.

wobbly | 'wɒblɪ | *adj.* inestable, inseguro, tembloroso, torcido.

wodge | wɒdʒ | *s.c.* (brit. y fam.) buen trozo, porción grande.

woe | wəu | (lit.) *s.c.* e *i.* **1** pesar, aflicción, infortunio, desgracia, cuita. || *interj.* **2** ay, oh, horror. || **3 – betide/– to (someone),** ¡ay de...!

woebegone | 'wəubɪgɒn | *adj.* (form.) triste, angustiado, apesadumbrado.

woeful | 'wəuful | (form.) *adj.* **1** triste, afligido, angustiado (persona). **2** horrible, indeseable, lamentable (cosa, acción, etc.).

woefully | 'wəufəlɪ | *adv.* tristemente, angustiadamente, horriblemente.

wog | wɒg | *s.c.* (desp.) negro.

wok | wɒk | *s.c.* sartén (cocina china).

woke | wəuk *pret.irreg.* de **wake.**

woken | wəukən | *p.p.irreg.* de **wake.**

wolf | wulf | *s.c.* [*pl.irreg.* **wolves**] **1** ZOOL. lobo. || *v.t.* **2** devorar, zampar, comer vorazmente. || **3 to cry –,** gritar el lobo, pedir auxilio sin necesidad (de forma que cuando aquél es necesario nadie lo presta). **4 to keep the – from the door,** (fam.) ganar lo necesario. **5 lone –,** persona solitaria. **6 to throw someone to the wolves,** cortar un traje a alguien, poner a alguien de vuelta y media (o permitir que esto suceda). **7 – cub,** lobezno. **8 – in sheep's clothing,** lobo con piel de cordero. **9 to – something down,** devorar, zamparse algo.

wolfhound | 'wulfhaund | *s.c.* ZOOL. perro lobo.

wolfram | 'wulfrəm | *s.i.* QUIM. volframio.

wolf-whistle | 'wulfˌwɪsl | *v.t.* **1** silbar admirativamente (especialmente a una mujer que pasa cerca). || *s.c.* **2** silbido admirativo (dirigido a mujeres, principalmente).

wolves | wulvz | *pl.* de **wolf.**

woman | 'wumən | *s.c.* [*pl.irreg.* **women**] **1** mujer. **2** (fam.) mujer (en afirmaciones de carácter genérico): *only a woman can stand it = sólo una mujer puede soportarlo.* **3** mujer, sirvienta, asistenta: *a daily woman does his room = una asistenta le hace la habitación.* **4** (delante de sustantivos de profesiones, principalmente, para expresar el femenino): *women drivers = las conductoras; a woman teacher = profesora.* **5** (p.u.) mujer, esposa, amante. **6** señora (mujer de determinada profesión o cometido): *the publicity woman told me = la señora de la publicidad me lo dijo.* **7** (fam.) mujer (en determinadas órdenes): *for God's sake, woman, be quiet! = ¡por Dios, mujer, cállate!* || *s.i.* **8** mujer (en sentido general): *woman lives longer than man = la mujer vive más que el hombre.* **9 [the –]** (fam. y desp.) la mujer (en contextos que parecen exigir el *pron.pers.* más pertinentemente): *I haven't even met the woman = ni siquiera conozco a la mujer.* || **10 as one –,** como una sola mujer, todas a la vez. **11 to be her own –,** ser una mujer independiente. **12 my good –,** (arc.) mi dócil mujer. **13 to a –,** como una sola mujer. **14 -woman, a)** mujer de una determinada nacionalidad o procedencia (según la primera parte del compuesto): *Welshwoman = galesa; Yorkshirewoman = mujer de Yorkshire;* **b)** de un número determinado de mujeres (según el numeral que precede): *a four-*

woman band = una banda de cuatro mujeres. **15 – to –,** de mujer a mujer, sin tapujos.
womanhood | 'wʊmənhʊd | *s.i.* **1** ser mujer, madurez de la mujer. **2** las mujeres, el mundo femenino.
womanish | 'wʊmənɪʃ | *adj.* (desp.) afeminado.
womanize | 'wʊmənaɪz | (también **womanise**) *v.i.* (desp.) tener relaciones sexuales con muchas mujeres (un hombre).
womanizer | 'wʊmənaɪzər | (también **womaniser**) *s.c.* (desp.) mujeriego, conquistador, ligón.
womanizing | 'wʊmənaɪzɪŋ | (también **womanising**) *s.i.* (desp.) promiscuidad.
womankind | 'wʊmənkaɪnd | *s.i.* (form.) las mujeres, el sexo femenino.
womanly | 'wʊmənlɪ | *adj.* de mujer, femenino.
womb | wuːm | *s.c.* ANAT. matriz, útero.
wombat | 'wɒmbæt | *s.c.* ZOOL. wombat (marsupial australiano).
women | 'wɪmɪn | *pl.irreg.* **1** de **woman.** || **2 women's group,** grupo de mujeres (que se reúnen con cierta regularidad). **3 Women's Lib,** (fam.) Liberación de la Mujer. **4 Women's Libber,** (fam.) militante del Movimiento de la Liberación de la Mujer. **5 Women's Liberation,** Liberación de la Mujer, Feminismo. **6 women's movement,** movimiento feminista.
won | wʌŋ | *pret.* y *p.p.irreg.* de **win.**
wonder | 'wʌndər | *v.t.* e *i.* **1** preguntarse: *I wondered where to go = me preguntaba adónde ir.* **2 [to – (if/whether)]** preguntarse (petición muy cortés): *I wonder if you'd mind speaking louder? = ¿podría usted quizá hablar más alto?* **3 [to – (that)]** sorprenderse: *I don't wonder that she didn't come = no me sorprende que no viniera.* **4 [to – (at)]** maravillarse, extrañarse: *I wondered at his slowness = me extrañó su lentitud.* **5** dudar, poner en duda: *do you mean it? I just wonder = pongo en duda que sea ésa tu intención.* || *s.i.* **5** extrañeza, sorpresa, admiración: *they gazed at the snow in wonder = miraron con sorpresa la nieve.* || *s.c.* **6** maravilla: *the seven wonders of the world = las siete maravillas del mundo.* **7** prodigio, portento, maravilla (persona o cosa): *the wonders of modern medicine = los prodigios de la medicina moderna.* || **8 nine days' –,** interés o importancia pasajera. **9 no –/little –/small –/etc.,** poco/nada/etc. es de extrañar. **10 wonders will never cease,** (fam.) bienvenida la sorpresa. **11 to work/do wonders, a)** hacer maravillas; **b)** sentar muy bien (al cuerpo).
wonderful | 'wʌndəfʊl | *adj.* maravilloso, admirable, impresionante, estupendo.
wonderfully | 'wʌndəfəlɪ | *adv.* maravillosamente, admirablemente, estupendamente.
wonderland | 'wʌndəlænd | *s.c.* e *i.* **1** país de las maravillas (literatura fantástica). **2** mundo maravilloso.
wonderment | 'wʌndəmənt | *s.i.* sorpresa, admiración.
wondrous | 'wʌndrəs | *adj.* (lit.) maravilloso, sorprendente, fascinante.
wonky | 'wɒŋkɪ | *adj.* **1** flojo, desajustado, inseguro. **2** cojo (mesa).
wont | wəʊnt | (arc.) *adj.* **1 [– (to)]** habituado, acostumbrado. || **2 as is one's –,** como de costumbre.
won't | wəʊnt | *contr.* de **will not** (lenguaje hablado).
woo | wuː | *v.t.* **1** atraer, ganarse (apoyo, votos, amistad, etc.). **2** (arc.) pretender, cortejar.
wood | wʊd | *s.i.* **1** madera, leña. **2** madera, barrica, barril (proceso de elaboración del vino). || *s.c.* **3** bosque, monte, soto. **4** cualquiera de los bastones de cabeza de madera (golf). || **4 ... can't see the – for the trees,** las ramas impiden ver el bosque. **5 not out of the woods,** (fam.) el peligro, la dificultad no están aún soslayados. **6 to touch –,** V. **touch.** **7 – pulp,** pulpa de madera, lignocelulosa.
wood-carving | 'wʊdkɑːvɪŋ | *s.c.* e *i.* tallado de madera, escultura de madera, talla de madera.
woodcock | 'wʊdkɒk | *s.c.* ZOOL. chocha (perdiz), becada.
woodcutter | 'wʊdˌkʌtər | *s.c.* leñador.
wooded | 'wʊdɪd | *adj.* arbolado, boscoso.
wooden | 'wʊdn | *adj.* **1** de madera, de palo. **2** (desp.) inexpresivo, rutinario, desanimado, soso, aburrido (expresión, actitud, etc.). || **3 to get the – spoon,** (fam.) llegar el último (en una competición). **4 – spoon,** cuchara de madera (usada para cocinar).
wooden-headed | ˌwʊdn'hedɪd | *adj.* (fam.) estúpido, abobado, descerebrado.
woodenly | 'wʊdnlɪ | *adv.* inexpresivamente, aburridamente, sin vida.
woodland | 'wʊdlənd | *s.c.* e *i.* **1** bosque, monte, soto, zona boscosa. || *adj.* **2** de los bosques, silvestre.
woodlice | 'wʊdlaɪs | *pl.irreg.* de **woodlouse.**
woodlouse | 'wʊdlaʊs | [*pl.irreg.* **woodlice**] *s.c.* ZOOL. cochinilla.
woodpecker | 'wʊdpekər | *s.c.* ZOOL. pito, pájaro carpintero.
woodpile | 'wʊdpaɪl | *s.c.* montón de madera, hacina de leña.
woodshed | 'wʊdʃed | *s.c.* leñera, almacén de leña.
woodwind | 'wʊdwɪnd | *s.c.* **1** instrumento musical de madera y viento. **2** sección de madera y viento (en una orquesta).
woodwork | 'wʊdwəːk | *s.i.* **1** (brit.) carpintería, ebanistería, trabajo de madera. **2** (fam.) carpintería (puertas, ventanas, etc.). || **3 to crawl out of the –,** (desp.) salir a flote, dar la cara.
woodworm | 'wʊdwəːm | *s.i.* **1** carcoma. || *s.c.* **2** ZOOL. carcoma.
woody | 'wʊdɪ | *adj.* leñoso.
wooer | wʊər | *s.c.* (arc.) pretendiente.
woof | wuːf | *s.c.* **1** (fam.) guau-guau, perro (lenguaje infantil). **2** trama (tejido).
wool | wʊl | *s.i.* **1** lana, material de lana. || **2 to pull the – over someone's eyes,** (fam.) sacar ventaja mediante engaño.
woolen | 'wʊlən | V. **woollen.**
wool-gathering | | *s.i.* soñar despierto, (estar) en Babia.
woollen | 'wʊlən | (EE.UU. **woolen**) *adj.* **1** de lana, de punto. || **2 woollens,** ropa de lana, géneros de punto.
woolly | 'wʊlɪ | (EE.UU. **wooly**) *adj.* **1** de lana. **2** (desp.) oscuro, confuso, vago (ideas, planes, etc.). || *s.c.* **3** (fam.) prenda de lana, jersey.
woolly-minded | ˌwʊlɪ'maɪndɪd | *adj.* (desp.) vago, oscuro, confuso (ideas, planes, etc.).
wooly | 'wʊlɪ | V. **woolly.**
woozy | 'wuːzɪ | *adj.* (fam.) débil, mareado, aturdido, indispuesto.
wop | wɒp | *s.c.* (desp.) italiano (insulto).
word | wəːd | *s.c.* **1** palabra. **2** (fam.) palabras, conversación: *I had a little word with him = tuve una pequeña conversación con él.* **3** palabra, cualquier cosa dicha, comentario, frase: *I didn't say a word = no dije palabra.* **4** palabra, consejo, aviso, advertencia: *here's a word in your ear = he aquí mi consejo para ti.* **5** palabra, mensaje (no entendido): *he didn't understand a word = no entendió ni palabra.* **6** palabra, noticia, anuncio: *he brought them word of her visit = les llevó el anuncio de su visita.* **7** palabra dada, promesa: *to keep one's word = mantener la palabra dada.* **8** palabra, orden: *he gave the word to move on = dio la orden de avanzar.* **9** REL. palabra, mensaje, enseñanza (contenidos en la Biblia). || *v.t.* **10** expresar con palabras, redactar. || **11 a man/woman of few words,** hombre/mujer de pocas palabras. **12 a man/woman of his/her –,** hombre/mujer de palabra. **13 as good as one's –,** cumplir lo que se promete. **14 to bandy word with someone,** V. **bandy.** **15 by/through – of mouth,** de palabra (no escrito). **16 to get a – in edgeways,** V. **edgeways.** **17 to have/exchange a few words (with),** mantener una breve conversación. **18 to have to eat one's words,** tenerse que tragar uno las palabras (por cometer imprudencia en lo dicho). **19 to have words with someone,** mantener una conversación acalorada. **20 in a –,** en una palabra. **21 in one's own words,** en las mismas palabras de uno, en sus propias palabras. **22 in other words,** con otras palabras. **23 in so many words,** lisa y llanamente. **24 mark my words,** (fam.) fíjate bien lo que te digo. **25 my –!/upon my –!,** (arc.) ¡santo cielo! (sorpresa y maravilla). **26 never to have a good – to say for someone/something,** no salirle jamás a uno una palabra de elogio. **27 not in so many words,** de forma indirecta, con rodeos. **28 not to know the meaning of the –,** no saber lo que alguien se dice, no tener ni idea. **29 not to mince one's words,** V. **mince.** **30 to pass the –,**

pasar el recado que uno ha recibido. **31 to put in a –/good – for someone, a)** hablar favorablemente de alguien; **b)** recomendar a alguien. **32 to put words into someone's mouth,** poner cosas no dichas en la boca de alguien. **33 to say the –,** dar aprobación (para que algo comience). **34 to send –,** V. **send. 35 take my – for it,** puedes fiarte de mi palabra. **36 to take someone at their –,** tomar literalmente lo que alguien dice (cuando el sentido puede ser distinto). **37 to take the words out of one's mouth,** adelantarse a lo que otro va a decir, adivinar el pensamiento. **38 the last –,** la última palabra (que termina una discusión, porfía, etc.). **39 the operative –,** V. **operative. 40 the printed –,** V. **print. 41 there's no other – for it/that's the only – for it,** ésa es la palabra exacta (por extraño que parezca). **42 too silly/stubborn/etc. for words,** de lo más estúpido/cabezota/etc. **43 – class,** GRAM. clase de palabra, parte de la oración. **44 – for –,** palabra por palabra, literalmente. **45 words, a)** palabras (dichas o escritas en una ocasión concreta): *my father's words ring in my head = tengo grabadas las palabras de mi padre;* **b)** hablar, expresión de ideas, sentimientos, etc.: *there is no need for words = no se necesita hablar;* **c)** palabras (por oposición a hechos): *words, words... results we want = palabras, palabras... resultados es lo que queremos;* **d)** letra, texto (de una canción). **46 words fail me,** (la emoción/la sorpresa/el dolor/etc.) me embarga.

word-blind | 'wɜːdblaɪnd | *adj.* disléxico, con dificultades de lectura.

word-blindness | 'wɜːdˌblaɪndnɪs | *s.i.* disfunción lectora, dislexia.

wordbook | 'wɜːdbuk | *s.c.* vocabulario.

wording | 'wɜːdɪŋ | *s.i.* redacción, fraseología, estilo.

wordless | 'wɜːdlɪs | (lit.) *adj.* **1** callado, silencioso, mudo, sin palabras. **2** inarticulado, ininteligible (sonido, ruido).

word-perfect | ˌwɜːd'pɜːfɪkt | *adj.* de prodigiosa memoria, exacto, fiel, que sabe perfectamente su papel.

wordplay | 'wɜːdpleɪ | *s.i.* juego de palabras.

word-processing | 'wɜːdˌprəʊsɪsɪŋ | *s.i.* INF. procesamiento de texto.

word-processor | 'wɜːdˌprəʊsesər | *s.c.* INF. procesador de texto.

wordy | 'wɜːdɪ | *adj.* prolijo, farragoso, verboso, difuso.

wore | wɔːr | *pret.* de **wear.**

work | wɜːk | *s.i.* **1** trabajo, actividad remunerada, tarea, empleo, ocupación. **2** trabajo (tipo, actividad, etc.): *what work do you do? = ¿qué trabajo haces?* **3** trabajo (lugar): *I can't leave work till 8 = no puedo dejar el trabajo hasta las ocho.* **4** trabajo (objeto concreto, material, etc.): *I often take some work home = con frecuencia me llevo trabajo a casa.* **5** obra, trabajo (resultado del trabajo): *that must be the work of a madman = debe de ser la obra de un loco.* **6** trabajo, estudio, investigación: *a lot of work is being done on this subject = se está realizando mucha investigación en esta disciplina.* **7** trabajo, actividad, esfuerzo (no impuesto): *that work on the car has given me an appetite = ese trabajo en el coche me ha abierto el apetito.* **8** FIS. trabajo. || *s.c.* **9** obra, trabajo (literario, musical, etc.): *the latest work of an artist = la última obra de un artista.* || *v.t.* e *i.* [*pret.* y *p.p.* **worked,** (arc.) **wrought**]. **10** trabajar (en empleo o actividad remunerada). **11** funcionar (máquinas): *it works by electricity = funciona por electricidad.* **12** poner en funcionamiento, hacer que una máquina trabaje, trabajar: *the boy who works the milking machine = el mozo que trabaja en la ordeñadora.* **13** exigir, hacer trabajar: *they work us very hard here = aquí nos hacen trabajar mucho.* **14** funcionar, tener éxito (ideas, sistemas, espectáculos, etc.): *I don't think that plan will work = no creo que ese plan funcione.* **15** hacer, surtir efecto (medicamentos): *let's hope the medicine works = esperemos que la medicina surta efecto.* **16** trabajar (materiales: metal, piedra, piel, etc.): *I watched him work the stone = vi cómo trabajaba la piedra.* **17 [to – (in/with)]** trabajar (en/con materiales): *to work with steel = trabajar con acero.* **18 [to – (with)]** trabajar (con, en ayuda de necesitados): *to work with the handicapped = trabajar con disminuidos.* **19** trabajar, cubrir (una zona: vendedores, repartidores, etc.): *who works that area? = ¿quién cubre esa zona?* **20** trabajar, cultivar (la tierra). **21** operar, jugar (a favor, en contra): *those factors may work against you = esos factores pueden jugar en tu contra.* **22** [**to –** *(adj.)*] producir, operar (el efecto señalado por el adjetivo): *the ropes worked loose = las sogas se fueron aflojando.* **23** hacer, abrir (camino o paso, con esfuerzo): *he worked his way in the jungle = se abrió camino en la selva.* **24** mover (el cuerpo, parte del cuerpo): *his eyes worked expressively = sus ojos se movieron expresivamente.* **25** calcular: *to work a percentage = calcular un porcentaje.* || **26 all in a day's –,** que puede hacerse sin grandes dificultades. **27 at – (on), a)** ocupado, realizando un trabajo; **b)** que afecta o ejerce influencia (en su entorno). **28 to give someone/something the works,** (fam.) **a)** entregar o decir todo; **b)** dar el mejor trato; **c)** (hum.) despedir con cajas destempladas. **29 to go/ set/get to –,** ponerse manos a la obra. **30 to gum up the works/to bung up the works,** evitar que algo se produzca en la forma prevista. **31 to have one's – cut out (to do something),** ponerse muy difícil llevar a cabo una tarea. **32 to make short/light – of something,** realizar un trabajo sin grandes dificultades. **33 to put/set someone to –,** dar trabajo a alguien. **34 to throw a spanner in the works,** V. **spanner. 35 - work,** trabajo, obra, artículo, etc. (hechos de una materia concreta, o de la forma especificada en la primera parte del compuesto): *wicker-work = artículo de mimbre; woodwork = trabajo en madera; needlework = costura, bordado.* **36 – basket,** cesta o caja de costura. **37 to – like a Trojan,** V. **Trojan. 38 – of art, a)** obra de arte; **b)** tarea complicada llevada a cabo brillantemente. **39 to – one's fingers to the bone,** V. **bone. 40 to – on someone,** tratar de convencer o influir en alguien. **41 to – out, a)** transcurrir, resultar, desarrollarse (de un modo determinado); **b)** entrenar, hacer ejercicio físico. **42 to – out at (something),** sumar, ascender, dar como resultado. **43 works, a)** obras (de un artista); **b)** mecanismo, piezas (de un reloj, motor, etc.); **c)** (fam.) de todo (lo relacionado con un objeto o situación): *we had coffee, bacon, eggs... the works! = tomamos café, bacon, huevos... ¡de todo!;* **d)** fábrica, lugar (donde se fabrica algo determinado o se desarrolla un proceso industrial): *a brick works = fábrica de ladrillos; a printing works = imprenta;* **e)** obras (civiles o públicas): *roads works = obras de carretera.* **44 to – someone out,** entender el carácter de alguien. **45 to – someone over,** (fam.) atizar bien a alguien. **46 to – something in/into, a)** añadir una sustancia a otra, mezclar dos sustancias; **b)** incluir, insertar algo (olvidado antes). **47 to – something off, a)** saldar (un préstamo) con esfuerzo; **b)** descargar en los demás (el mal humor, el enfado, etc.). **48 to – something out, a)** calcular algo; **b)** resolver (un problema), descifrar (un código), etc.; **c)** concebir, diseñar (planes, proyectos, etc.): *a well worked-out plan = plan bien concebido;* **d)** agotar (construcción pasiva): *a worked-out gold mine = mina de oro agotada.* **49 to – something up, a)** despertar, promover, causar (sentimientos, reacciones, etc.); **b)** desarrollar, mejorar algo gradualmente; **c)** revisar, completar, perfeccionar (un escrito, una destreza, etc.). **50 – surface,** V. **worktop. 51 to – to something,** seguir, atenerse (a un plan, a un programa, etc.): *to work to the budget = atenerse al presupuesto.* **52 to – towards something,** esforzarse, afanarse (por conseguir un objetivo).

workable | 'wɜːkəbl | *adj.* práctico, factible, utilizable, útil, laborable.

workaday | 'wɜːkədeɪ | *adj.* ordinario, rutinario, prosaico, gris.

workaholic | ˌwɜːkə'hɒlɪk | *s.c.* (fam.) persona excesivamente celosa en el trabajo, adicto al trabajo.

workbook | 'wɜːkbuk | *s.c.* libro de trabajo, cuaderno de ejercicios.

workday | 'wɜːkdeɪ | *s.c.* **1** jornada laboral. **2** día laborable.

worker | 'wɜːkər | *s.c.* **1** trabajador, empleado, obrero, operario. **2** trabajador especializado (que realiza un trabajo concreto): *a research worker = investigador.* **3** obrera (de la especie de

las abejas o avispas): *a worker bee = abeja obrera.*
workforce | 'wəːkfɔːs | *s.c.* **1** población en edad laboral. **2** mano de obra, personal asalariado, parte social (de una empresa).
workhorse | 'wəːkhɔːs | *s.c.* **1** caballo de labor. **2** (fig.) animal de carga, esclavo (persona que hace el trabajo que otros eluden).
workhouse | 'wəːkhaus | *s.c.* (arc.) asilo (de menesterosos, que debían trabajar a cambio de sustento y cobijo).
work-in | 'wəːkın | *s.c.* ocupación y gestión de una empresa por los obreros (como protesta contra el cierre).
working | 'wəːkıŋ | *adj.* **1** trabajador, laboral: *working mothers = madres trabajadoras; working conditions = condiciones laborales.* **2** laborable, de trabajo (día): *working day = día laborable.* **3** laboral, activo (edad, población, situación). **4** de trabajo, de faena (ropa). **5** laboral (relación). **6** de explotación, por negocio (actividad empresarial, granja, etc.). **7** suficiente, práctico, para manejarse (conocimiento, v.g. de idiomas). **8** provisional, práctico, funcional (teoría, definición, etc.). || **9 in – order,** en pleno funcionamiento. **10 – capital,** capital en efectivo, disponible. **11 – class,** clase obrera. **12 – group/– party,** comisión de investigación (sobre un problema o situación). **13 workings, a)** mecánica, forma de operar (una organización, un sistema, etc.); **b)** trabajos de excavación (en una mina).
workload | 'wəːkləud | *s.c.* carga laboral, volumen de trabajo asignado (a personas o máquinas).
workman | 'wəːkmən | *s.c.* [*pl.irreg.* **workmen**] trabajador, obrero.
workmanlike | 'wəːkmənlaık | *adj.* eficiente, hábil, correcto (trabajo).
workmanship | 'wəːkmənʃıp | *s.i.* hechura, realización, acabado, obra; destreza, habilidad.
workmate | 'wəːkmeıt | *s.c.* (fam.) compañero, colega.
workmen | 'wəːkmən | *pl.irreg.* de **workman.**
workout | 'wəːkaut | *s.c.* entrenamiento, ejercicio físico.
workpeople | 'wəːkˌpiːpl | *s.pl.* personal asalariado, mano de obra, trabajadores (de una empresa o negocio).
workshop | 'wəːkʃɒp | *s.c.* **1** taller (de carpintería o metalurgia, principalmente). **2** taller, grupo de trabajo o estudio (con intercambio de experiencias).
work-shy | 'wəːkʃaı | *adj.* perezoso, vago, holgazán, gandul.
worktop | 'wəːktɒp | *s.c.* encimera (de muebles de cocina).
work-to-rule | ˌwəːktə'ruːl | *s.c.* huelga de celo.
world | wəːld | *s.sing.* **1** mundo, tierra, planeta: *to travel round the world = viajar por todo el mundo.* **2** mundo, reino, grupo (de cosas vivientes): *the animal world = el reino animal.* **3** mundo, países, naciones (con una característica común): *the industrialized world = el mundo industrializado.* **4** mundo (sección o faceta dentro de la actividad humana): *the world of show business = el mundo del espectáculo.* **5** mundo, público, la gente: *the world waited for the outcome = el mundo estaba pendiente del resultado.* **6** mundo, vida, experiencia: *she doesn't know much about the world = sabe poco de la vida.* **7** (form.) mundo (por oposición al espíritu): *to renounce the world = renunciar al mundo.* **8** mundo, sociedad: *he left the world to enter a convent = dejó el mundo para entrar en un convento.* || *s.c.* **9** mundo, planeta, galaxia: *strange creatures from another world = seres extraños de otro mundo.* **10** mundo, esfera, reino, plano: *a world of hypothesis and speculation = un mundo de hipótesis y especulación.* || *adj.* **11** mundial, de primer orden: *a world power = potencia mundial; a world figure = una personalidad mundial.* || **12 a man/woman of the –,** un hombre/una mujer de mundo. **13 to be all the – (to someone)/to mean the – (to someone),** ser lo más importante y querido del mundo (para alguien). **14 to bring children into the –,** (form.) traer hijos al mundo. **15 to come into the –,** (lit.) venir al mundo. **16 dead to the –,** V. **dead. 17 to do someone a/the – of good,** (fam.) hacerle a alguien sentirse mucho mejor (una medicina, una buena noticia). **18 for all the – as if/like (something was the case),** (fam.) exactamente como si (ése fuera el caso): *he bosses everyone about, for all the world as if he owns the company = va dando órdenes como si fuera el amo.* **19 to go/come down in the –,** tener menos dinero que antes, bajar de posición. **20 to go/come up in the –,** enriquecerse, subir de posición. **21 in the –, a)** en el mundo, absolutamente: *nothing in the world will stop him = absolutamente nada le detendrá;* **b)** demonios (en preguntas con expresión de sorpresa, enfado, etc.): *what in the world were you doing there? = ¿qué demonios hacías allí?* **c)** del mundo (con superlativos): *the best in the world = lo mejor del mundo;* **d)** del mundo (enfatizando una expresión de cantidad): *to have all the time in the world = tener todo el tiempo del mundo.* **22 to live in a – of one's own,** vivir encerrado en el mundo de uno. **23 (not to do something) for the –,** (fam.) no hacer algo por nada del mundo. **24 on top of the –,** (fam.) inmensamente feliz. **25 out of this –,** (fam.) estupendo, sensacional. **26 to set the – on fire,** (fam.) comerse el mundo, tener mucho éxito. **27 the (John Smiths/ etc.) of this –,** (fam.) los tipos como (J. Smith etc.): *the Ben Pitts of this world always do well = a los tipos como Pitts siempre les va bien.* **28 there is a – of difference,** hay un abismo, ni punto de comparación. **29 to think the – (of someone/something),** apreciar, admirar mucho. **30 the – is one's oyster,** V. **oyster. 31 the – over,** en todas partes: *speculators are the same the world over = los especuladores son iguales en todas partes.* **32 worlds apart,** completamente distinto, como de la noche al día (dos personas o cosas). **33 – war,** guerra mundial.
world-class | ˌwəːld'klɑːs | *adj.* de primera clase, de categoría mundial.
world-famous | ˌwəːld'feıməs | *adj.* mundialmente conocido, famoso.
worldliness | 'wəːldlınıs | *s.i.* mundo, conocimiento práctico, experiencia.
worldly | 'wəːdlı | *adj.* **1** mundano, terrenal. **2** (form.) material: *wordly goods = bienes materiales.* **3** mundano, experimentado, práctico (persona).
worldly-wise | ˌwəːdlı'waız | *adj.* de mucho mundo, experimentado.
world-weary | ˌwəːdl'wıərı | *adj.* cansado de la vida, hastiado, apático.
worldwide | ˌwəːld'waıd | **1** *adj.* mundial, universal. || *adv.* **2** en todo el mundo.
worm | wəːm | *s.c.* **1** gusano, lombriz. **2** (desp.) gusano, vil, cobarde, canalla. **3** rosca (de un tornillo). || *v.t.* **4** purgar, desinfectar (de gusanos o lombrices). || *v.i.* **5** arrastrarse, deslizarse, trepar. **6** (desp.) introducirse (con malas artes). || **7 the – in the apple/bud,** (lit.) el gusano en la manzana. **8 the – will turn,** el más dócil se rebela cuando está harto. **9 – cast,** agujero de gusano (en la superficie de la tierra). **10 to – one's way (along/ forward),** avanzar lentamente (con cautela o por la dificultad). **11 to – one's way into (someone's confidence, affection),** (desp.) ganarse astutamente la confianza, el afecto, etc. de alguien. **12 to – something out (of someone),** obtener información (con paciencia o con estratagemas).
worm-eaten | 'wəːmˌiːtn | *adj.* carcomido (mueble), apolillado (ropa), podrido (fruta, etc.).
wormwood | 'wəːmwud | *s.i.* **1** (fig.) hiel, amargura, pesar, resentimiento. **2** BOT. ajenjo.
wormy | 'wəːmı | *adj.* lleno de gusanos, infectado de gusanos, carcomido.
worn | wɔːn | *p.p.* **1** de **wear.** || *adj.* **2** gastado (por ser viejo o por el uso). **3** viejo, demacrado, cansado.
worn-out | ˌwɔːn'aut | *adj.* **1** gastado, estropeado, inservible, para tirar: *a worn-out sofa = un sofá gastado.* **2** muy cansado, exhausto, rendido, roto, para el arrastre.
worried | 'wʌrıd | *adj.* **1** preocupado, inquieto, desasosegado. || **2 to have someone –,** (fam.) inquietar, asustar a alguien (por error o por broma): *oh good, you had me worried = ah bueno, me habías asustado.* **3 not –,** (fam.) sin cuidado, da igual, sin especial predilección (en una situación de elección).
worriedly | 'wʌrıdlı | *adv.* inquietamente, desasosegadamente.
worrier | 'wʌrıər | *s.c.* aprensivo, pesimista, depresivo.
worrisome | 'wʌrısəm | *adj.* (arc.) preocupante, inquietante, alarmante.

worry | 'wʌrɪ | *v.t.* e *i.* **1** preocupar, alarmar: *that's what worries me most = eso es lo que más me preocupa.* **2 [to – (about/over)]** preocuparse, inquietarse: *don't worry about my diet = no te preocupes de mi régimen.* **3** molestar: *why worry her when it's all over? = ¿a qué molestarla cuando todo ha pasado ya?* **4** molestar, desagradar: *his bossiness didn't worry her unduly = su afán de mando no la molestaba en exceso.* **5** asustar, perseguir, ladrar (el perro a las ovejas). || *s.i.* **6** preocupación, inquietud, desasosiego. **7** responsabilidad, problema, deber (aceptado por una persona): *sorry, but that's my worry = perdone pero ése es problema mío.* || *s.c.* **8** problema, preocupación: *I don't have any worries = no tengo preocupación alguna.* || **9 to have enough to – about,** tener ya bastantes problemas. **10 nothing to – about,** nada de que preocuparse, todo bajo control. **11 not to –,** tranquilo, no te preocupes. **12 to – at something, a)** darle vueltas (a un problema); **b)** estar ocupado (el perro con un hueso).

worrying | 'wʌrɪɪŋ | *adj.* preocupante, inquietante, molesto, desagradable.

worryingly | 'wʌrɪɪŋlɪ | *adv.* inquietantemente, desagradablemente.

worse | wɜːs | *adj.comp.* de **bad 1** peor, más desagradable, de peor calidad, más bajo: *his marks are getting worse = sus notas son cada vez peores.* **2** peor, más enfermo: *stay in bed or you'll get worse = quédate en cama o te pondrás peor.* || *adv.comp.* de **badly. 3** peor: *some children swam worse = algunos niños nadaban peor.* || **4 for better or –,** V. **better. 5 for the –,** a peor (cambios). **6 to go from bad to –,** V. **bad. 7 to make matters –,** V. **matter. 8 ... might do – than,** no estaría mal que, sería bueno que... **9 none the – (for something),** sin ser peor (por ello). **10 someone's bark is – than their bite,** V. **bark. 11 the – for wear,** V. **wear. 12 – luck,** V. **luck. 13 – off,** menos rico, en peor situación económica.

worsen | 'wɜːsn | *v.t.* e *i.* empeorar, poner peor, deteriorar, agravar, dificultar.

worsening | 'wɜːsnɪŋ | *s.i.* empeoramiento, agravamiento, deterioro.

worship | 'wɜːʃɪp | *s.i.* **1** culto, adoración, veneración (de Dios): *freedom of worship = libertad de cultos.* **2** culto, veneración, adoración (de personas o cosas): *an object of worship = objeto de veneración.* || *v.t.* [(brit.) *pret.* y *p.p.* **worshipped,** *ger.* **worshipping**] **3** adorar, venerar, rendir culto (a Dios). **4** adorar, rendir culto, venerar, admirar (personas o cosas): *a society that worships money = una sociedad que rinde culto al dinero.* || **5 Worship,** (brit. y form.) Señoría, Excelencia (tratamiento de alcaldes o magistrados).

worshipful | 'wɜːʃɪpful | *adj.* reverente, respetuoso, devoto, ferviente.

worshipper | 'wɜːʃɪpər | (EE.UU. **worshiper**) *s.c.* **1** creyente, fiel, devoto, adorador. **2** devoto, admirador, adorador (de personas o cosas).

worst | wɜːst | *adj.sup.* de **bad. 1** el peor, el más duro, el más desagradable (persona, cosa, situación): *the worst winter for years = el peor invierno en mucho tiempo.* **2** el peor, el de menor calidad, el de menor éxito (persona o cosa): *I was the worst swimmer = yo era el peor nadador.* **3** el peor, el más afectado (en una situación desfavorable): *the handicapped are the worst victims = los minusválidos son las víctimas más afectadas.* || *adv.sup.* de **badly. 4** peor: *foreigners are the worst treated = los extranjeros son los peor tratados.* || *s.c.* **5** peor (persona, cosa, situación, etc.): *the worst is over = lo peor ha pasado.* || *v.t.* **6** (arc.) vencer, derrotar (en competición). || **7 at –/at the –,** en el peor de los casos, a lo peor. **8 if the – comes to the –,** si las cosas se ponen muy feas.

worsted | 'wustɪd | *s.i.* estambre.

worth | wɜːθ | *adj.* **1** de un valor (determinado), valorado: *the red car is worth a lot more = el coche rojo es de un valor superior.* **2** valorado (la fortuna de una persona): *he's worth at least ú1,000,000 = su fortuna está valorada en un millón de libras como poco.* **3** que merece, que vale (la pena, el esfuerzo, etc.): *the city is well worth a visit = la ciudad bien merece una visita.* || *s.i.* **4** (form.) valía, mérito, importancia, valor (que se atribuye a personas o cosas): *to judge people for their worth = juzgar a las personas por su valía.* || **5 to be – it,** valer la pena. **6 to be – someone's while,** merecerle a alguien la pena. **7 for all it is –/for what it's –, a)** con todo el esfuerzo de que uno es capaz: *I tried for all I was worth = puse mi mayor esfuerzo;* **b)** por si sirve de algo: *I've brought the report, for what it's worth = he traído el informe, por si sirve de algo.* **8 to get one's money's –,** V. **money. 9 to make it – someone's while,** hacer que a alguien le valga la pena, recompensar a alguien. **10 to make life – living,** hacer la vida agradable. **11 not – the paper it's written on,** V. **paper. 12 the game is not – the candle,** V. **candle. 13 – one's weight in gold,** valer su peso en oro.

OBS. Desde el punto de vista gramatical, se puede considerar a **worth** como preposición, en lugar de como adjetivo, y así se trata en numerosas gramáticas, sin que su significado se vea alterado.

worthily | 'wɜːðɪlɪ | *adv.* dignamente, merecedoramente, respetablemente.

worthiness | 'wɜːðɪnɪs | *s.i.* dignidad, respetabilidad, merecimiento.

worthless | 'wɜːθlɪs | *adj.* carente de valor, despreciable, inútil (cosas, personas).

worthlessly | 'wɜːθlɪslɪ | *adv.* inútilmente, sin valor.

worthlessness | 'wɜːθlɪsnɪs | *s.i.* inutilidad, carencia de valor.

worthwhile | 'wɜːθwaɪl | *adj.* bueno, valioso, útil, que vale la pena.

worthy | 'wɜːðɪ | *adj.* **1 [– (of)]** digno, meritorio, justo: *a worthy winner = digno ganador.* **2** digno, respetable, honrado, meritorio, esforzado. || *s.c.* **3** (form.) personalidad, notable.

wot | wɒt | *pron.interr.* **1** (fam.) qué (usado en lenguaje escrito para representar **what**). || *v.i.* **2 [to – (of)]** (arc.) saber, conocer.

would | wud | | wəd | *v.modal* **1** (en lugar de **will** en enunciados de estilo indirecto): *he said he would come later = dijo que vendría más tarde.* **2** (en expresiones de condiciones improbables): *I'd be surprised if he came = me sorprendería que viniera.* **3** (en expresiones de actitud favorable/desfavorable): *some would do more for a dog than for a fellow = algunos harían más por un perro que por el prójimo.* **4** (referido a una actitud contraria y continuada): *she whouldn't go, though she was asked to = no se marchó, aunque se lo pidieron.* **5** (referido al deseo de que algo suceda): *I wouldn't mind having a day off = no me importaría tener un día libre.* **6** (en ofertas corteses): *Would you like a drink? = ¿te apetece tomar algo?* **7** (en peticiones corteses): *would you do me a favour? = ¿me quieres hacer un favor?* **8** (para expresar una opinión no del todo segura): *you'd expect it to happen, wouldn't you? = era de esperar que pasara ¿no?* **9** (fam.) (sugiriendo un consejo): *I wouldn't take it, if I were you = yo en tu lugar no lo aceptaría.* **10** (para expresar acciones repetidas en el pasado): *she would often go without a word = se iba a veces sin decir palabra.* **11** (referido a circunstancias que pudieran haberse dado): *it would have been useless to complain = de nada hubiera servido quejarse.* **12** (referido al deseo de que algo hubiera sucedido de distinta forma): *I would have liked to stay longer = me hubiera gustado estar más tiempo.* **13** (en expresión de suposiciones o deducciones referidas al pasado): *he wouldn't have heard it: he was a bit deaf = no lo habría oído: estaba un poco sordo.* || **14 – rather,** V. **rather. 15 – that (something were the case),** (form.) ojalá (que fuera así).

OBS. El verbo **would** no tiene correspondencia directa con ningún verbo castellano. Como verbo modal, ayuda a formar el condicional o potencia de los verbos y a expresar muchos de los matices referidos a tiempos pasados, algunos de los cuales se expresan en castellano mediante el subjuntivo.

would-be | 'wudbiː | *adj.* futuro, en ciernes, aspirante.

wouldn't | 'wudnt | *contr.* de **would not** (lenguaje hablado).

would've | 'wudəv | *contr.* de **would have,** siendo **have** verbo auxiliar (lenguaje hablado).

wound | waund | *pret.* y *p.p.irreg.* de **wind.**

wound | wuːnd | *s.c.* **1** herida (producida por arma blanca, armas de fuego etc.). **2** (lit.) herida, daño, mal (produci dos por una mala experiencia). || *v.t.* **3** herir (con arma blanca, armas de fuego, etc.). **4** (pasiva) herir (sentimientos, reputación, etc.): *she felt wounded by his words = se sintió herida por sus palabras.* || **5 to lick one's wounds,** V. **lick. 6 to open old wounds,** (lit.) abrir viejas heridas, traer al recuerdo experiencias negativas. **7 to rub salt in the –,** V. **salt. 8 wound up,** V. **wind.**

wounded | wuːndɪd | *adj.* **1** herido (por arma blanca, de fuego, etc.). **2** herido (en sentimientos, reputación, etc.). || **3 the –,** los heridos (de guerra, generalmente).

wounding | wuːndɪŋ | *adj.* hiriente, mordaz, cruel.

wove | wəʊv | *pret.irreg.* de **weave.**

woven | wəʊvən | *p.p.irreg.* de **weave.**

wow | waʊ | *interj.* (fam.) ¡huau! (expresión de sorpresa o regocijo).

wrack | ræk | V. **rack.**

wraith | reɪɵ | *s.c.* (lit.) fantasma, aparición, espectro.

wrangle | 'ræŋgl | *v.i.* **1 [to – (over)]** discutir, reñir: *he was wrangling with another boy over a toy = reñía con otro niño por un juguete.* || *s.c.* **2** riña, altercado, disputa.

wrangling | 'ræŋglɪŋ | *s.i.* riña, disputa, discusión.

wrap | ræp | *v.t.* [*ger.* **wrapping,** *pret.* y *p.p.* **wrapped**] **1 [to – (in)]** envolver: *she wrapped the book in brown paper = envolvió el libro en papel marrón.* **2 [to – (round)]** enrollar, poner alrededor: *a bandage was wrapped around his arm = tenía una venda puesta en el brazo.* **3** envolver, arropar, abrigar: *they were wrapped in thick clothes = se abrigaban con ropa gruesa.* **4** rodear; poner, echar alrededor (brazos, piernas, etc.): *he wrapped his arms round her = la rodeó con sus brazos.* || *s.c.* **5** (arc.) prenda (sobre los hombros: bufanda, chal, bata, etc.). || **6 to keep something under wraps,** (fam.) mantener algo secreto, bien guardado. **7 the wraps come off,** se acaban los secretos, se descubren los secretos. **8 to – (it) up,** (fam.) callarse, cerrar el pico (en imperativos, generalmente). **9 wrapped up (in something),** absorbido, dedicado completamente: *we're wrapped up in the baby = estamos absorbidos por el niño.* **10 to – (someone/oneself) up,** abrigar(se), arrebujar(se). **11 to – (something) up, a)** envolver bien; **b)** (fam.) cerrar (un trato), dar por terminado (un trabajo, un debate, etc.); **c)** desviar, complicar, enmarañar (con palabras).

wrap-around | 'ræpəˌraund | *adj.* abierto, superpuesto (falda).

wrapper | 'ræpər | *s.c.* envoltura, cobertura, sobrecubierta.

wrapping | 'ræpɪŋ | *s.i.* **1** envoltura, envase. || **2 – paper,** papel de envolver (artículos de regalo).

wrath | rɒɵ | *s.i.* (form.) ira, cólera.

wreak | riːk | (form.) *v.t.* **1** causar, provocar, desencadenar (catástrofes, desastres, etc.). **2** tomar (venganza).

wreath | riːɵ | *s.c.* corona de flores, guirnalda.

wreathe | riːð | (lit.) *v.t.* **1** envolver, rodear, cubrir (de neblina, humo, etc.): *the sun was wreathed in mist = el sol aparecía envuelto en neblina.* **2** decorar (con flores, guirnaldas, etc.). || *v.i.* **3** subir, elevarse (en espirales: humo, niebla, etc.). || **4 wreathed in smiles,** radiante de felicidad.

wreck | rek | *v.t.* **1** romper, destruir, estropear, arruinar. **2** (pasiva) hundir, naufragar (barcos): *the vessels were wrecked on the rooks = las naves naufragaron contra las rocas.* || *s.c.* **3** siniestro, accidente (de aeroplanos, automóviles, etc.). **4** vehículo afectado en siniestro. **5** naufragio, hundimiento (de un barco). **6** (fam.) ruina, carcamal. || **7 wrecking service,** servicio de grúa (para vehículos averiados).

wreckage | 'rekɪdʒ | *s.i.* **1** restos, ruinas (de un accidente aéreo o de vehículos, hundimiento de un edificio, etc.). **2** restos, despojos (de planes, ideas, etc. fracasados).

wrecker | 'rekər | *s.c.* **1** destructor, destrozón, ruina. **2** (EE.UU.) grúa, remolcador (de vehículos averiados).

wren | ren | *s.c.* ZOOL. chochín, reyezuelo.

wrench | rentʃ | *v.t.* e *i.* **1** soltar(se), liberar(se) (mediante tirón o giro violento). **2** torcer, retorcer (brazo, pierna, articulación). **3** retirar, apartar (la vista, la mente, etc., con gran esfuerzo). || *s.c.* **4** tirón, sacudida (para abrir, coger o liberar algo). **5** pena, lástima, dolor (de desprenderse de alguien o algo). **6** MEC. (EE.UU.) llave de tuercas.

wrest | rest | *v.t.* (form.) **1** arrancar, arrebatar, llevarse. **2** usurpar, llevarse (con esfuerzo).

wrestle | 'resl | *v.t.* e *i.* **1 [to – (with)]** luchar (físicamente). **2** luchar, esforzarse, tratar de controlar, resolver (problemas, situaciones complicadas). **3** luchar, tener dificultades (para manejar, controlar, etc. cosas demasiado voluminosas): *he was wrestling with the map = luchaba por controlar el mapa.*

wrestler | 'reslər | *s.c.* DEP. luchador (de lucha libre).

wrestling | 'reslɪŋ | *s.i.* DEP. lucha libre.

wretch | retʃ | *s.c.* **1** desgraciado, malvado, canalla. **2** infeliz, pobre diablo: *a poor half-starved retch = un pobre infeliz muerto de hambre.*

wretched | retʃɪd | *adj.* pobre, desgraciado, miserable, desdichado, lastimoso (personas). **2** horrible, malo, enfermo: *I was in bed feeling wretched = estaba en cama sintiéndome horrible.* **3** malo, miserable, pobre, impresentable (cosas): *the house was wretched = la casa era miserable.* **4** (fam.) maldito, dichoso, de las narices: *he's always ready to tell his wretched story = siempre está presto a largar su maldita historia.*

wretchedly | retʃɪdlɪ | *adv.* pobremente, miserablemente, horriblemente.

wretchedness | retʃɪdnɪs | *s.i.* miseria, desgracia, desdicha, decaimiento, abatimiento.

wriggle | 'rɪgl | *v.t.* e *i.* **1** menear, revolver, cambiar de postura. **2** avanzar culebreando, deslizarse, colarse: *we wriggled under the fence = nos deslizamos por debajo de la tapia.* || *s.c.* **3** meneo, movimiento ligero. || **4 to – out of something/doing something,** (fam.) evitar, eludir algo desagradable (con excusas).

wring | rɪŋ | *v.t.* [*pret.* **wrung,** *p.p.* **wrung**] **1** sacar, extraer, lograr, conseguir (con esfuerzo): *to wring the utmost from a situation = sacar el máximo de una situación.* **2** escurrir (ropa húmeda). **3** retorcer(se) (las manos con ansiedad). **4** (p.u.) estrechar, apretar fuerte (al saludar). **5** retorcer (el pescuezo de un ave para sacrificarla). || **6 wringing wet,** (fam.) empapado (persona, cosa). **7 to – one's heart/soul/etc.,** encoger el corazón/el alma/etc., dar mucha pena. **8 to – someone's neck,** (hum.) retorcer el cuello a alguien, castigarlo (amenaza). **9 to – something out,** exprimir el agua, escurrir.

wringer | 'rɪŋər | *s.c.* **1** escurridor. || **2 to put someone through the –,** (fam.) poner a alguien en aprietos.

wrinkle | 'rɪŋkl | *s.c.* **1** arruga (en la piel). **2** arruga, pliegue (en tela, papel, etc.). **3** (fam.) sugerencia, indicación, dato práctico. || *s.c.* e *i.* **4** arrugarse, plegarse. **5** arrugar (la cara, la frente, etc.).

wrinkled | 'rɪŋkld | *adj.* arrugado, lleno de arrugas.

wrist | rɪst | *s.c.* ANAT. muñeca.

wristwatch | 'rɪstwɒtʃ | *s.c.* reloj de pulsera.

writ | rɪt | *s.c.* **1** escrito, oficio, escritura, orden, mandato, decreto, autorización. || **2 – large,** (form.) **a)** claro y evidente; **b)** en versión corregida y aumentada: *the old conservatism writ large = el viejo conservadurismo en versión corregida y aumentada.*

write | raɪt | *v.t.* e *i.* [*pret.* **wrote,** *p.p.* **written**] **1** escribir: *learning to read and write = aprendiendo a leer y escribir.* **2** escribir (cartas, libros, etc.): *she wrote me a letter = me escribió una carta.* **3** (EE.UU.) escribir (a alguien): *write me soon = escríbeme pronto.* **4** escribir, poner por escrito: *to write a report = escribir un informe.* **5** escribir, ser escritor, dedicarse a escribir: *she said she wanted to write = dijo que quería dedicarse a escribir.* **6** escribir, completar, rellenar (documentos, impresos, etc.). **7** hacer, escribir, extender (cheques, facturas, prescripciones, etc.). || **8 nothing to – home about,** V. **home. 9 to – away/off (to someone for something),** escribir a alguien pidiendo algo. **10 to – back (to someone),** escribir a vuelta de correo, contestar carta. **11 to – in (to someone),** escribir a una institución dando una opinión. **12 to – in (to someone for something),** hacer un pedido a una compañía por escrito. **13 to – someone out (of something),** retirar (a un actor) de una obra o serie. **14 to – someone/ something off, a)** considerar a alguien/algo un fracaso; **b)** satisfacer, cancelar una deuda; **c)** declarar a algo como siniestro total: *the car was completely written off = declararon al coche como siniestro total.* **15 to – someone/something off as,** despachar a alguien como: *it's easy to write him off as just an old bore = es fácil despacharle como un aburrido.* **16 to – something down, a)** apuntar, tomar nota de algo; **b)** COM. reducir el valor nominal de bienes. **17 to – something into something,** incluir algo como parte de (un acuerdo, contrato, etc.). **18 to – something out, a)** escribir (un informe, un trabajo, un cheque, etc.) en su versión definitiva, completarlo; **b)** copiar algo (como castigo, también). **19 to – something up, a)** redactar un escrito (a partir de notas); **b)** poner al día (un diario); **c)** hacer la reseña, crítica, etc. de una obra (para un periódico, por ejemplo).

write-in | 'raɪtɪn | *s.c.* (EE.UU.) voto por correo (elecciones).

write-off | 'raɪtɒf | *s.c.* (brit.) siniestro total.

writer | 'raɪtər | *s.c.* **1** escritor. **2** escritor, autor (de un determinado escrito). || **3 writer's cramp,** agujetas de mano (de tanto escribir).

write-up | 'raɪtʌp | *s.c.* crítica, reseña (de un hecho cultural, producto comercial, etc.).

writhe | raɪð | *v.i.* retorcerse, agitarse, debatirse (de dolor).

writing | 'raɪtɪŋ | *s.i.* **1** escritura, escrito. **2** escritura, oficio de escritor. **3** texto literario. **4** letra, escritura a mano. || **5 in –,** por escrito: *can I have what you say in writing? = ¿puede darme lo que usted dice por escrito?* **6 the – on the wall,** V. **wall. 7 – materials,** material de escritura, recado de escribir. **8 writings,** obras (de un escritor, o de varios escritores sobre una disciplina).

writing-desk | 'raɪtɪŋˌdesk | *s.c.* escritorio.

writing-paper | 'raɪtɪŋˌpeɪpər | *s.i.* papel de escribir.

written | 'rɪtn | *p.p.* **1** de **write.** || *adj.* **2** escrito (examen, trabajo, acuerdo, garantía, confirmación, ley, norma, etc.). || **3 the – word, a)** la palabra escrita: *the power of the written word = el peso de la palabra escrita;* **b)** literatura. **4 – all over one's face/on one's face,** escrito en la cara, pregonado.

wrong | rɒŋ | *adj.* **1** mal, fuera de lo normal, extraño, chocante: *it was in a mess; something was wrong = estaba todo revuelto; algo extraño pasaba.* **2 [– (with)]** defectuoso, que falla, que no va bien, que pasa algo: *what's wrong with the engine? = ¿qué pasa con el motor?* **3** inaceptable, inadecuado (en una situación): *the timing is wrong = el tiempo registrado es inaceptable.* **4** incorrecto, erróneo, que no se ajusta a los hechos: *the information he got was wrong = la información obtenida no se ajusta a los hechos.* **5** desacertado, que no tiene razón: *I still have to be proved wrong = falta aún por demostrar que no tengo razón.* **6** equivocado, reprochable, imperdonable (en una situación dada): *you were wrong not to let me know first = es imperdonable que no me lo dijeras a mí primero.* **7** injusto, punible, que es delito: *it is wrong to steal = robar es un delito.* **8** erróneo, equivocado, confundido: *they took the wrong bus = cogieron un autobús equivocado.* **9** inconveniente, inadecuado (socialmente): *they took her to the wrong school = la llevaron a un colegio inadecuado.* **10** del revés, el revés (en prendas de vestir): *the wrong side of a jumper = el revés de un jersey.* || *adv.* **11** mal, erróneamente, equivocadamente, inadecuadamente, por error. || *s.i.* **12** mal, lo malo, lo que está mal, lo injusto: *he can't tell between right and wrong = no sabe distinguir lo que está bien de lo que está mal.* || *s.c.* **13** error, injusticia: *the rights and wrongs of their policy = los aciertos y los errores de su política.* || *v.t.* **14** tratar, juzgar (injusta o inadecuadamente): *he felt he had been wronged = tenía la sensación de haber sido injustamente tratado.* || **15 to be barking up the – tree,** V. **bark. 16 to be the – side of (a particular age),** superar (la edad mencionada). **17 to be wronged,** ser tratado injustamente. **18 don't get me –,** no me malinterprete. **19 to get hold of the – end of the stick,** V. **stick. 20 to get something –,** entender mal algo. **21 to go –, a)** equivocarse (en lo que uno está haciendo); **b)** salir, resultar algo mal; **c)** dejar de funcionar adecuadamente (motor, mecanismo, etc.); **d)** (arc.) actuar inmoralmente. **22 to have/get the – number,** marcar un número de teléfono equivocado. **23 in the –,** culpable, responsable. **24 to say the – thing,** decir lo que no se debe. **25 to start off on the – foot,** V. **foot. 26 the – way round,** al revés (lo de atrás adelante). **27 two wrongs don't make a right,** de nada sirve pagar con la misma moneda (dicho popular).

wrongdoer | 'rɒŋduːər | *s.c.* malhechor, facineroso, pecador.

wrongdoing | 'rɒŋduːɪŋ | *s.c.* e *i.* maldad, perversidad, fechoría, pecado.

wrong-foot | ˌrɒŋ'fʊt | *v.t.* **1** sorprender, pillar en renuncio, poner en ridículo. **2** DEP. sorprender, pillar con el paso cambiado.

wrongful | 'rɒŋfʊl | *adj.* injusto, ilegal, inmoral.

wrongfully | 'rɒŋfʊlɪ | *adv.* injustamente, ilegalmente.

wrong-headed | ˌrɒŋ'hedɪd | *adj.* malpensado, equivocado, errado, de juicio apresurado, obstinado.

wrongly | 'rɒŋlɪ | *adv.* mal, equivocadamente, erróneamente, injustamente.

wrote | rəʊt | *pret.irreg.* de **write.**

wrought | rɔːt | *pret.* y *p.p.* **1** (arc.) de **work.** || *v.t.* **2** (en pasado) (lit.) producir, operar, causar: *the change that time has wrought = el cambio que el tiempo ha producido.* || *adj.* **3** labrado, hecho a mano, decorado (metal): *wrought silver = plata labrada.*

wrought-iron | ˌrɔːt'aɪən | *s.i.* hierro forjado.

wrung | rʌŋ | *pret.* y *p.p.* de **wring.**

wry | raɪ | *adj.* **1** burlón, malicioso, avieso (gesto, aspecto). **2** irónico, retorcido, zumbón (humor).

wrily | raɪlɪ | *adv.* burlonamente, maliciosamente, irónicamente.

wrought-iron | ˌrɔːt'aɪən | *s.i.* hierro forjado.

wrung | rʌŋ | *pret.* y *p.p.* de **wring.**

wry | raɪ | *adj.* **1** burlón, malicioso, avieso (gesto, aspecto). **2** irónico, retorcido, zumbón (humor).

wrily | raɪlɪ | *adv.* burlonamente, maliciosamente, irónicamente.

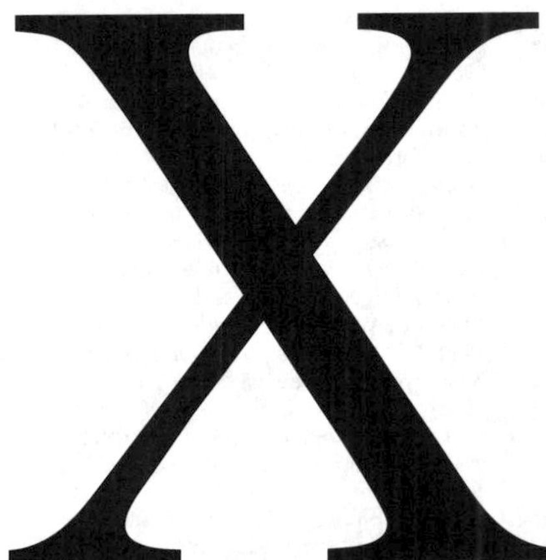

x, X | eks | *s.c.* **1** x, X. (vigesimocuarta letra del alfabeto inglés). **2** x (lugar, persona, etc. desconocidos o mantenidos en secreto). **3** x (número indeterminado de cosas). **4** x (señal de localización en un mapa). **5** x (símbolo de beso al final de una carta o mensaje). **6** X (número romano: 10). **7** MAT. x (incógnita). || **8 X chromosome,** BIOL. cromosoma X.

xenophobia |ˌzenə'fəubɪər| *s.i.* (form.) xenofobia.

xenophobic | ˌzenə'fəubɪk | *adj.* (form.) xenofóbico.

Xerox | 'zɪərɒks | *s.c.* **1** fotocopiadora. **2** fotocopia. || *v.t.* **3** fotocopiar.

Xmas | 'krɪsməs | | 'eksməs | *abreviatura* (de **Christmas**) Navidad (en tarjetas, principalmente).

X-ray | ˌeks'reɪ | *s.c.* **1** rayos x. **2** radiografía. **3** (fam.) rayos (exploración médica por medio de rayos x). || *atr.* **4** de rayos x, radiológico: *an X-ray examination = una exploración radiológica.* || *v.t.* **5** radiografiar, mirar por rayos x, hacer radiografías: *he was X-rayed = le hicieron radiografías.*

OBS. Como sustantivo, **X-ray** suele usarse en plural, excepto en función atributiva.

xylophone | 'zaɪləfəun | *s.c.* MUS. xilófono.

y ,Y | waɪ | *s.c.* y, Y **1** vigesimoquinta letra del alfabeto inglés. **2** MAT. y (incógnita). || **3 Y chromosome,** BIOL. cromosoma Y.

yacht | jɒt | *s.c.* yate, balandro.

yachting | 'jɒtɪŋ | *s.i.* **1** navegación en yate. **2** DEP. vela, balandrismo.

yachtsman | 'jɒtsmən | *s.c.* [*pl.irreg.* **yachtsmen**] navegante de yate, aficionado al deporte de la vela.

yachtswoman | 'jɒtswʊmən | *s.c.* [*pl. irreg.yachtswomen*] mujer navegante de yate, aficionada al deporte de la vela.

yack | jæk | (fam.) *v.i.* **1** charlar, parlotear, rajar. || *s.c.* **2** charla, parrafada, cháchara.

yackety-yack | ˌjækətɪ'jæk | *s.i.* (fam.) cháchara.

yahoo | jɑ'huː | *s.c.* bruto, patán.

yak | jæk | *s.c.* ZOOL. yac.

yam | jæm | *s.c.* BOT. batata, ñame.

yammer | 'jæmər | *v.i.* (fam.) **1** lloriquear, gemir. **2** aullar, dar alaridos (el perro).

yank | jæŋk | *s.c.* **1** (brit. y fam.) yanqui. **2** tirón. || *v.t.* e *i.* **3** (fam.) tirar, dar un tirón: *he yanked on the rope and it broke = dio un tirón a la soga y ésta se rompió.*

Yankee | 'jæŋkɪ | *s.c.* **1** (brit. y fam.) yanqui. **2** (EE.UU.) yanqui, norteamericano (del Noreste de EE.UU. principalmente). **3** yanqui (soldado federal en la guerra civil norteamericana). || *atr.* **4** yanqui, norteamericano.

yap | jæp | *v.i.* **1** gañir, aullar (el perro). **2** (fam.) darle a la lengua, no parar de hablar.

yard | jɑːd | *s.c.* **1** (también **yd**) yarda (91,4 cm.). **2** patio, taller, almacén, corral. **3** MAR. verga.

yardage | 'jɑːdɪdʒ | *s.c.* e *i.* medida en yardas.

yardarm | 'jɑːdɑːm | *s.c.* MAR. verga, penol.

yardstick | 'jɑːdstɪk | *s.c.* criterio, norma, canon.

yarn | jɑːn | *s.i.* **1** hilo, hilaza. || *s.c.* **2** (fam.) cuento, historia (de viajes, a veces exagerados o inventados). || *v.i.* **3** (fam.) contar historias. || **4 to spin some one a –,** (fam.) venir a alguien con cuentos.

yarrow | 'jærəʊ | *s.c.* e *i.* BOT. milenrama.

yashmak | 'jæʃmæk | *s.c.* velo (de mujer musulmana).

yaw | jɔː | MAR. *v.i.* **1** guiñar, hacer una guiñada, desviar el rumbo. || *s.c.* **2** guiñada.

yawl | jɔːl | *s.c.* yola.

yawn | jɔːn | *v.i.* **1** bostezar. **2** estar abierto, resquebrajado. || *s.c.* **3** bostezo. **4** (fam.) aburrimiento, bodrio, ladrillo (libro, película, etc.).

yd V. **yard.**

ye | jiː | | jɪ | (arc.) *pron.pers.* **1** vosotros, vosotras (lenguaje poético o religioso). || *art.* **2** el, la, los, las (en nombres de tiendas o establecimientos públicos).

yea | jeɪ | *adv.* **1** (form.) sí, de acuerdo. **2** (arc.) sí, en efecto (forma bíblica de yes). || **3 – or nay,** sí o no, estar de acuerdo o en desacuerdo (al solicitar respuesta a una oferta).

yeah | jeə | (fam.) *adv.* **1** sí (variante gráfica y prosódica de yes). || **2 oh –?,** ¿ah sí? (con sentido de incredulidad).

year | jɪər | | jː | *s.c.* **1** año. **2** año, curso académico (en centros escolares: *his final year at University = su último curso en la universidad.* **3** alumno (del curso especificado): *she teaches the first years = da clase a los alumnos de primero.* **4** año, ejercicio (en los negocios, finanzas, etc.). || **5 all (the) – round,** durante todo el año. **6 donkey's years,** V. **donkey. 7 for a man of his years/for a woman of her years,** para un hombre /mujer de sus años (estableciendo comparación con la edad). **8 to put years on someone,** (fam.) ponerle a uno años encima, hacerle a uno parecer más viejo (ropa, sufrimiento, trabajo, etc.). **9 to take years off someone,** (fam.) quitarle a uno años de encima (forma de vestir, fin de penalidades, etc.). **10 – after –,** año tras año, de forma regular y continuada. **11 – by –,** progresivamente, cada año más (en relación con cosas que cambian a un ritmo determinado). **12 – in – out,** año tras año, un año sí y el otro también. **13 -year-old/-year-olds,** de los años o edad (señalados por el numeral con el que forma compuesto): *a class of eight-year-olds = una clase de niños de ocho años.* **14 years, a)** años, mucho tiempo: *I haven't seen her for years = hace años que no la veo;* **b)** años (transcurridos en una actividad o en un lugar señalados): *no accident in all my years with lions = sin accidentes en todos mis años entre leones.* **15 years old/years of age,** años (de edad o de existencia): *rocks over 600 million years old = rocas de más de seiscientos millones de años.*

yearbook | 'jɪəbʊk | *s.c.* libro del año anterior.

yearling | 'jɪəlɪŋ | *s.c.* potro (de entre uno y dos años).

year-long | ˌjiə'lɒŋ | *adj.* que dura todo el año, de duración anual: *a year-long course = un curso de duración anual.*

yearly | 'jɪəlɪ | *adj.* **1** anual. || *adv.* **2** anualmente, todos los años.

yearn | jəːn | *v.i.* **[to – (for)]** suspirar, ansiar, anhelar: *she yearned for home = suspiraba por volver a casa.*

yearning | 'jəːnɪŋ | *s.c.* e *i.* ansia, anhelo: *yearning for power = anhelo de poder.*

yearningly | 'jəːnɪŋlɪ | *adv.* **1** ansiosamente, anhelantemente. **2** tiernamente.

year-round | ˌjiə'raund | *adj.* de todo el año, continuo.

yeast | jiːst | *s.i.* levadura.

yeasty | 'jiːstɪ | *adj.* amargo, fermentado (olor, sabor).

yell | jel | *v.i.* **1 [to – (at)]** gritar, decir a gritos, vociferar. **2** chillar, quejarse, protestar (un niño pequeño). || *v.t.* **3** decir a gritos. || *s.c.* **4** grito, chillido, alarido. **5** (EE.UU.) grito de ánimo (de colegiales hacia su equipo). || **6 to – out,** gritar, decir a gritos, vociferar.

yellow | 'jeləʊ | *adj.* **1** amarillo (color). **2** amarillo (chino, japonés). **3** (fam.) cobarde, cortado, (Am.) vilote. || *s.i.* **4** amarillo. || *v.t.* e *i.* **5** amarillear, poner amarillo, volverse amarillo. || **6 – card,** tarjeta amarilla (en fútbol). **7 – fever,** MED. fiebre amarilla. **8 – flag,** bandera amarilla (barco, hospital, etc., en cuarentena). **9 – line(s),** línea o líneas amarillas (para regular el aparcamiento en el lateral de la calzada). **10 – pages,** páginas amarillas. **11 – press,** prensa amarilla (sensacionalista).

yellowed | 'jeləʊd | *adj.* amarilleado, amarillento.

yellowing | 'jeləʊɪŋ | *adj.* amarillento, descolorido.

yellowish | 'jeləʊɪʃ | *adj.* amarillento, tirando a amarillo.

yellowness | 'jeləʊnɪs | *s.i.* amarillez.

yellowy | 'jeləʊɪ | *adj.* amarillento, tirando a amarillo.

yelp | jelp | *v.i.* **1** gañir, aullar (el perro). **2** gritar (de miedo o dolor). || *s.c.* **3** gañido, grito.

Yemen | 'jemən | *s.sing.* Yemen (Norte o Sur).

Yemeni | 'jeməni | *adj.* **1** yemenita, del Yemen. || *s.c.* **2** yemenita.

yen | jen | *s.c.* [*pl.* **yen**] **1** yen (unidad monetaria japonesa). **2 [– to *inf.*/for]** (fam.) deseo, anhelo, ilusión: *the yen to visit far-off countries = el anhelo de visitar países lejanos.*

yeoman | 'jəʊmən | *s.c.* [*pl.irreg.* **yeomen**] (brit. y arc.) **1** terrateniente, dueño de su tierra. **2** voluntario (al servicio de un noble: Edad Media). || **3 Yeoman of the Guard,** alabardero de la Casa Real. **4 – service,** (lit.) largo y meritorio esfuerzo.

yeomanry | 'jəʊmənrɪ | *s.c.* (brit.) **1** (lit.) terratenientes. **2** fuerza de caballería (reclutada entre campesinos voluntarios: Edad Media).

yeomen | 'jəʊmən | *pl.irreg.* de **yeoman.**

yes | jes | *adv.* **1** sí (en respuesta a una pregunta). **2** sí (como aceptación de una oferta). **3** sí (respuesta a una petición). **4** sí (como acuerdo con lo dicho). **5** sí (como disposición positiva a responder a la puerta, el teléfono, etc.). **6** sí, por favor/gracias (como respuesta a una invitación). **7** sí (como muestra de atención y seguimiento en la conversación). **8** ¿sí? (como respuesta a una interpelación). **9** ¿sí? (en el sentido de "¿en qué puedo servirle?"). **10** ¿sí? (para sugerir al interlocutor que continúe informando). **11** sí, pero (para introducir cortésmente una objeción). **12** sí, por supuesto (para señalar lo erróneo de una negación o sugerencia). **13** ¿ah sí? (muestra de duda o desacuerdo con lo escuchado). **14** sí, bueno (para responder avanzando una opinión). **15** ah, sí (al recordar súbitamente lo que uno iba a decir). **16** sí, eso es (para confirmar y enfatizar la idea expresada). || *s.c.* **17** sí (respuesta afirmativa, voto o persona que ha respondido afirmativamente). || **18 – and no,** sí y no, depende de cómo se mire.

yes-man | 'jesmæn | *s.c.* [*pl.irreg.* **yes-men**] pelotillero, cobista, lameculos.

yesmen | 'jesmən | *pl.irreg.* de **yes-man.**

yesterday | 'jestədəɪ | | 'jestədeɪ | *adv.* **1** ayer: *he arrived yesterday = llegó ayer.* || *s.c.* **2** ayer: *this is yesterday's paper = éste es el periódico de ayer.* **3** ayer, pasado: *all our yesterdays = nuestro pasado (recuerdos del pasado).* || **4 the day before –,** anteayer. **5 – afternoon,** ayer por la tarde. **6 – morning,** ayer por la mañana. **7 – week,** hace una semana.

yesteryear | 'jestəjɪər | *s.i.* (arc.) antaño, viejos tiempos.

yet | jet | *adv.* **1** todavía, aún (en frases negativas): *he hasn't arrived yet = no ha llegado todavía.* **2** ya (en frases interrogativas): *have you had your breakfast yet? = ¿has desayunado ya?* **3** todavía, hasta ahora, de momento (en frase con superlativo): *he is the best yet = es el mejor hasta ahora.* **4** todavía, aún (quedan aún posibilidades de que algo determinado suceda): *your case may yet be revised again = es posible todavía que se revise su caso.* **5** todavía (para enfatizar la duración de una acción): *we'll have him around for a long while yet = le tendremos que soportar bastante todavía.* **6** todavía, aún (con insinuación de sorpresa, lamentación, disgusto, etc.): *a just society has yet to be established = aún queda por instaurar una sociedad justa.* **7** todavía, aún (enfatizando a comparativos o superlativos): *the dole queues might grow longer yet = podría crecer más aún el número de los que viven del paro.* **8** todavía, aún, encima (para enfatizar que algo rebasa lo esperado): *work, work and yet more work = trabajo, trabajo y más trabajo encima.* || *conj.* **9** sin embargo, no obstante, pero (para introducir un comentario de sorpresa): *they criticize the state, yet get money from it = critican al estado, y sin embargo reciben dinero de él.* || **10 as –,** (form.) todavía, hasta ahora, de momento (en frases negativas): *no one, as yet, is suspicious = ninguno sospecha todavía.* **11 not –,** todavía no. **12 – again,** una vez más: *yet again we'll wait for the results = una vez más esperaremos a los resultados.*

yeti | 'jetɪ | *s.c.* yeti, abominable hombre de las nieves.

yew | juː | *s.c.* **1** (también **yew tree**) BOT. tejo. || *s.i.* **2** madera de tejo.

YHA | ˌwaɪ eitʃ 'eɪ | *siglas* (de **Youth Hostel Association**) Organización de Albergues de Juventud.

yid | jɪd | *s.c.* (fam. y desp.) judío (palabra ofensiva).

Yiddish | 'jɪdɪʃ | *s.i.* yiddish, lengua judía internacional (mezcla de hebreo y alemán).

yield | jiːld | *v.t.* **1** producir, proporcionar (frutos, ganancias, resultados): *trees that no longer yield fruit = árboles que ya no producen.* **2** rendir, dejar (beneficios): *investment accounts yielding high interest = inversiones que rinden un alto interés.* **3** (form.) ceder, entregar, rendir (responsabilidad, control): *they yielded their position to the enemy = rindieron su posición al enemigo.* || *v.i.* **[to – (to)] 4** ceder, entregarse, rendirse, someterse: *he yielded to public pressure = cedió ante la presión pública.* **5** (form.) dejar paso, sucumbir, ser sustituido: *will radio yield to television? = ¿sucumbirá la radio ante la televisión?* **6** ceder, vencerse, venirse abajo: *the shelf is beginning to yield = el estante está empezando a ceder.* **7** (EE.UU.) ceder el paso (tráfico). || *s.c.* **8** fruto, producción, producto, rendimiento: *a yield of 12% = un rendimiento del 12% ... a high yield of wheat = alta producción de trigo.* || **9 to – up secrets,** (form.) revelar secretos.

yielding | 'jiːldɪŋ | *adj.* **1** flexible, elástico, blando (material). **2** dócil, complaciente, flexible, (persona).

yieldingly | 'jiːldɪŋlɪ | *adv.* flexiblemente, dócilmente.

yippee | 'jɪpiː | *interj.* ¡yupi!, ¡estupendo!

YMCA | ˌwaɪ em siː 'eɪ | *siglas* (de **Young Men's Christian Association). 1** Asociación Cristiana de Jóvenes. **2** albergue de esta asociación.

yob | jɔb | (también **yobbo**) *s.c.* (brit. y fam.) gamberro, alborotador, pendenciero, (Am.) rechelero.

yobbo | 'jɒbəʊ | V. **yob.**

yodel | 'jəʊdl | (también **yodle**) *v.i.* **1** cantar a la manera tirolesa. || *s.c.* **2** canto tirolés.

yoga | 'jəʊgə | *s.i.* yoga.

yoghurt | 'jaʊgət | (también **yogurt** o **yoghourt**) *s.i.* yogur.

yogi | 'jəʊgɪ | *s.c.* yogui.

yogurt V. **yoghurt.**

yoke | jəʊk | *s.c.* **1** yugo. **2** [*pl.* **yoke**] yunta, pareja (de animales en posición de tiro): *three yoke of oxen = tres yuntas de bueyes.* **3** balancín (en cuyos extremos se puede transportar peso). **4** canesú. **5** (form.) yugo, dominio, autoridad, carga: *the yoke of tyrany = el yugo de la tiranía.* || *v.t.* **6** uncir, enganchar (animales en posición de tiro). **7 [to – (together/to)]** (form.) unir, ligar, vincular: *yoked together in marriage = unidos en matrimonio.*

yokel | 'jəʊkl | *s.c.* (desp.) paleto, palurdo, patán.

yolk | jəʊk | *s.c.* e *i.* yema (de huevo).

Yom Kippur | ˌjɒm'kɪpər | *s.i.* Yom Kippur (festividad judía dedicada al ayuno y oración).

yon | jɒn | (arc.) *adj.* ese, esa, esos, esas.

yonder | 'jɒndər | (arc.) *adv.* y *adj.* allí, aquel.

yonks | jɒŋks | *s.i.* (fam.) mucho tiempo, la tira (de tiempo): *I haven't seen her for yonks = hace la tira que no la veo.*

yore | jɔːr | *s.i.* (arc. y lit.) pasado, antaño, épocas remotas: *in days of yore = en épocas muy remotas.*

Yorkshire pudding | ˌjɔːkʃə'pʊdɪŋ | *s.c.* e *i.* pudin de Yorkshire (mezcla al horno de harina, leche y huevos, para servir con la ternera asada).

you | juː | *pron.pers.* **1** tú, vosotros, vosotras; usted, ustedes (como sujeto en la frase): *you've come very early = habéis llegado muy pronto.* **2** te, os, usted, ustedes (como objeto): *he loves you = os quiere.* **3** ti, vosotros, vosotras, usted, ustedes (como objeto preposicional): *we do it for you = lo hacemos por ustedes.* **4** eh tú, vosotros, vosotras, usted, ustedes (en interpelaciones directas o con sustantivos o adjetivos): *you there! = ¡eh! ¡usted!; you girls, stop giggling = ¡eh! chicas, dejad de reíros.* **5** (fam.) se, tú, uno (referido impersonalmente a situaciones generales, forma de hacer cosas, etc.): *it's hard, but you get used to it = es duro pero uno se hace a ello.* || **6 – and yours,** tú y los tuyos, usted y los suyos, vosotros y los vuestros.

you-all | 'juːɔːl | *pron.pers.* (EE.UU.) vosotros, vosotras, ustedes: *are you-all ready? = ¿están ustedes listos?*

you'd | juːd | *contr.* **1** de **you had** (siendo **'d** verbo auxiliar). **2** de **you would** (lenguaje hablado).

you'll | juːl | *contr.* de **you will** (lenguaje hablado).

young | jʌŋ | *adj.* **1** joven (de poca edad). **2** joven, juvenil (de aspecto, movimientos, etc.): *she's very young in her tastes = es muy juvenil en sus gustos.* **3** joven, en sus comienzos: *the evening is still young = la noche es joven todavía.* **4** joven, juvenil, de jóvenes: *young fashion = moda joven.* **5** (arc.) joven, hijo (precediendo a un nombre de persona que puede resultar impreciso): *young Bates is just like his father = Bates hijo es exacto al padre.* || **6 to be with –,** estar preñada (animal). **7 the young, a)** los jóvenes, la juventud, gente joven. **b)** crías (de animal). **8 the younger,** (form.) el joven, el hijo (delante o detrás de nombre de persona que necesita mayor precisión): *the younger Pitt/Pitt the younger = Pitt, el joven.* **9 – at heart,** de espíritu joven. **10 – in (something),** inexperto, de poca práctica. **11 – lady, a)** señorita, joven: *a young lady wants to talk to you = una señorita quiere hablar con usted.* **b)** (arc.) novia. **12 – man, a)** joven; **b)** (arc.) novio.

youngish | 'jʌŋiʃ | *adj.* bastante joven, tirando a joven (en aspecto, modales, etc.).

youngster | 'jʌŋstər | *s.c.* (fam.) joven, jovencito.

your | jʊər | , (EE.UU.) | jʊər | *adj.pos.* **1** tu, tus, vuestro/s, vuestra/s, su, sus (de usted/es): *your book = su libro; your parents = tus padres.* **2** (fam.) tu, tus, vuestro, etc. (dentro de una apostilla de humor, ironía, etc.): *here's your English weather = he aquí vuestro tiempo inglés.* **3** (fam.) de uno, tu, tus (en sentido general y despersonalizado): *if you face north, east is on your right = mirando al norte, el este queda a la derecha (de uno).* **4** su, vuestra (con títulos y tratamientos).

OBS: El adjetivo posesivo inglés, lo mismo que el pronombre, concuerda con el poseedor; no con el objeto poseído, como sucede en castellano.

you're | jʊər | | jɔːr | *contr.* de **you are** (lenguaje hablado).

yours | jʊəz | , (EE.UU.) | jʊərz | *pron.pos.* **1** tuyo/s, tuya/s, vuestro/s, vuestra/s, suyo/s (de usted/es): *the future is yours = el futuro es tuyo; is she a friend of yours? = ¿es una amiga tuya?* **2** (form.) le saluda atentamente, suyo afectísimo, etc. (junto a **faithfully, sincerely** o **truly** en la despedida convencional de una carta). **3** (fam.) tuyo, un abrazo, etc. (como despedida de carta informal). || **4 – truly,** (fam.) el menda, el que suscribe.

yourself | jɔː'self | , (EE.UU.) | jʊər'self | *pron.r.* [*pl.* **yourselves**] **1** te, ti mismo/a; os, vosotros/as mismos/as; se, usted/es mismo/s (como objeto directo o preposicional): *stop torturing yourself = deja de atormentarte; help yourselves to cheese = servíos queso.* **2** tú mismo/a, vosotros/as mismos/as, etc. (en función de énfasis del sujeto de la frase): *you yourself told me = tú mismo me lo dijiste.* **3** tú solo, por ti mismo: *did you make them yourself? = ¿los hiciste tú solo?* || **4 by –/yourselves, a)** solo/s, sola/s: *how long have you been by yourself? = ¿cuánto tiempo llevas sola?* **b)** solo, sola, etc. (sin ayuda de nadie).

yourselves | jəː'selvz | *pl.irreg.* de **yourself.**

youth | juːθ | *s.i.* **1** juventud (época en la vida de una persona): *I went there in my youth = fui allí en mi juventud.* **2** (form.) juventud (vitalidad, idealismo, inmadurez, etc.): *she's full of youth = rebosa juventud.* || *s.c.* **3** joven, adolescente, chaval, chico: *a long queue of youths and girls = una larga cola de chicos y chicas.* **4** juventud, jóvenes, gente joven, población joven: *the youth of the country = la población joven del país.* || **5 – club,** club de jóvenes. **6 – hostel,** albergue de juventud. **7 – hostelling,** alojamiento en albergues de juventud.

youthful | 'juːθfʊl | *adj.* joven, juvenil, de aspecto joven.

youthfully | 'juːθfʊlɪ | *adv.* juvenilmente.

youthfulness | 'juːθfʊlnɪs | *s.i.* juventud, vitalidad.

you've | juːv | *contr.* de **you have** (siendo **'ve** verbo auxiliar); (lenguaje hablado).

yowl | jaʊl | *v.i.* **1** aullar, ulular, dar alaridos. || *s.c.* e *i.* **2** aullido, alarido, ulular: *the yowl of emergency sirens = el ulular de las sirenas de emergencia.*

yowling | 'jaʊlɪŋ | *s.i.* aullido, alarido.

yo-yo | 'jəʊjəʊ | *s.c.* yo-yó.

yr [*pl.* **yrs**] abreviatura de **year.**

yuan | juːæn | *s.c.* [*pl.* **yuan**] yuan (unidad monetaria de la República Popular China).

yucca | 'jʌkə | *s.c.* BOT. yuca.

Yugoslav | ˌjuːgəʊ'slɑːv | *adj.* **1** yugoslavo. || *s.c.* **2** yugoslavo.

Yugoslavia | ˌjuːgəʊ'slɑːvɪə | *s.sing.* Yugoslavia.

Yugoslavian | ˌjuːgəʊ'slɑːvɪən | *adj.* yugoslavo.

yuk | jʌk | *interj.* (fam.) ¡uaj!

Yule | juːl | *s.i.* (arc.) navidad.

Yuletide | 'juːltaɪd | *s.i.* (arc.) Navidad, época de Navidad.

yummy | 'jʌmɪ | *adj.* (fam.) de rechupete, de chuparse los dedos.

YWCA | ˌwaɪ dʌbljuː siː 'eɪ | *siglas* (de **Young Women's Christian Association**). **1** Asociación Cristiana de Jóvenes Mujeres. **2** albergue de esta asociación.

z, Z | zed | (EE.UU.) | zi: | *s.c.* **1** z, Z (vigesimosexta letra del alfabeto inglés). || **2 from A to Z,** V. **a.**

zany | zeɪnɪ | *adj.* (fam.) extraño, estrafalario, loco, disparatado.

zap | zæp | *v.t.* e *i.* (fam.) **1** liquidar, matar. **2 [to – (into/through)]** ir pitando, hacer (algo) pitando.

zeal | zi:l | *s.i.* celo, ardor, pasión, fanatismo.

zealot | zelət | *s.c.* fanático, extremista, radical, intransigente.

zealous | zeləs | *adj.* apasionado, fanático, acérrimo, convencido.

zebra | zi:brə | | ebrə | *s.c.* **1** ZOOL. cebra. || **2 – crossing,** (brit.) paso de cebra, paso de peatones.

Zen | zen | *s.i.* Zen (variante japonesa del budismo).

zenith | zenɪθ | *s.sing.* **1** cenit, cima, cúspide (de una civilización, país, carrera humana, etc.). **2** ASTR. cenit.

zephyr | zefər | *s.c.* (lit.) céfiro, brisa, marea.

zero | ziərəu | *num.* [*pl.* **zeros** o **zeroes**] **1** cero, el punto más bajo, nada: *the economic growth is at zero = el crecimiento económico está en cero.* **2** cero, punto de congelación: *ten below zero = diez grados bajo cero.* || *adj.* **3** (EE.UU.) (fam.) cero, ningún, nulo: *we went on in zero visibility = seguimos adelante con visibilidad nula.* || **4 – growth,** ECON. crecimiento cero. **5 to – in on (a target),** apuntar/dirigirse un proyectil (hacia un blanco). **6 to – in on (a problem/subject), etc.,** centrar la atención en un problema/asunto/etc.

zero-hour | ziərəu 'uər | *s.c.* MIL. hora cero.

zero-rated | ziərəu 'eɪtɪd | *adj.* libre de impuestos (coste de bienes).

zest | zest | *s.i.* **1 [– (for)]** entusiasmo, gusto, ganas, interés: *her terrific zest for life = su tremendo interés por la vida.* || **2** cáscara de naranja o limón (como ingrediente de tartas o bebidas).

zestful | zestful | *adj.* entusiasta, apasionado.

zestfully | zestfəlɪ | *adv.* con ganas, con entusiasmo, apasionadamente.

zigzag | zigzæg | *s.c.* **1** zigzag, línea en zigzag. || *adj.* **2** zigzagueante, en zigzag, con curvas a derecha e izquierda (línea, ruta, etc.). || *v.i.* **3 [zigzagged, zigzagging]** zigzaguear, avanzar en zigzag.

zillion | ziljən | *s.c.* (EE.UU.) (fam.) **[– (of)]** cantidad enorme, tropecientos.

zinc | zɪŋk | *s.i.* QUIM. cinc.

zing | zɪŋ | *s.i.* (fam.) chispa, garra, salero, marcha.

Zionism | zaiənɪzəm | *s.i.* sionismo.

Zionist | zaiənɪst | *s.c.* **1** sionista. || *adj.* **2** sionista.

zip | zɪp | *s.c.* **1** (brit.) cremallera. || *v.t.* **2** cerrar la cremallera, echar la cremallera, unir con cremallera. || **3 – code,** (EE.UU.) código postal. **4 – fastener,** (brit.) (cierre de) cremallera. **5 to – someone up,** subirle la cremallera a alguien. **6 to – up,** subir la cremallera (en prendas de vestir).

zipper | zɪpər | *s.c.* (EE.UU.) cremallera.

zippy | zɪpɪ | *adj.* (fam.) vivo, brioso, marchoso.

zither | zɪðər | *s.c.* MUS. cítara.

zodiac | zəudiæk | *s.sing.* zodiaco.

zombie | zɒmbɪ | *s.c.* **1** zombie, cadáver resucitado. **2** (fig.) autómata.

zonal | zəunl | *adj.* zonal.

zone | zəun | *s.c.* **1** zona, región (con características distintas de las demás). **2** área, zona, enclave (con una peculiaridad propia): *a nuclear-free zone = zona desnuclearizada.* || *v.t.* **3** dividir en zonas. **4 [to – (as/for)]** asignar, destinar, dedicar (una zona a un cometido concreto).

zoning | zəunɪŋ | *s.i.* distribución en zonas.

zonked | zɒŋkt | *adj.* (fam.) cansado, exhausto, roto.

zoo | zu: | *s.c.* zoo.

zoological | zəuə'lɒdʒɪkl | *adj.* **1** zoológico. || **2 – gardens,** (form.) parque zoológico.

zoologically | zəuə'lɒdʒɪkəlɪ | *adv.* zoológicamente.

zoologist | zəu'ɒlədʒɪst | *s.c.* zoólogo.

zoology | zəu'ɒlədʒɪ | *s.i.* zoología.

zoom | zu:m | *v.i.* **1** ir zumbando. **2** (fam.) dispararse, subir muy deprisa (los precios). || *s.i.* **3** zumbido. **4** AER. subida vertical, empinadura. || **5 to – in (on something),** FOT. agrandar un objeto mediante zoom. **6 – lens,** FOT. zoom, objetivo de distancia focal variable. **7 to – out,** FOT. distanciar un objeto mediante zoom.

zucchini | zu:ki:nɪ | *s.c.* [*pl.* **zucchini**] (EE.UU.) calabacín.

Zulu | zu:lu: | *s.c.* **1** zulú. || *s.i.* **2** zulú (lengua). || *adj.* **3** zulú.

English Grammar

Gramática inglesa

EL ARTÍCULO

Indeterminado: **a/an**.
La forma **a** se utiliza ante palabras que comienzan por sonidos consonánticos (*a coat*). La forma **an**, ante las que comienzan por sonidos vocálicos (*an idea*; *an hour*). Es invariable en género.

Se utiliza:

- ante sustantivos contables en singular, ya sean masculinos o femeninos.
- ante nombres de profesiones, religiones, clases o nacionalidades: *he's a doctor and a catholic, but a fool.*
- en ciertas expresiones de medida, precio o peso: *it took a hundred miles an hour*; *a dozen eggs*; *a hundred pounds.*
- ante nombres de enfermedades: *to have a toothache.*
- en frases exclamativas que comienzan por **what**: *what a pity!*
- detrás de **quite** y de **such**: *it's quite a good book*; *we had such a nice time.*
- delante o detrás de **rather**: *it's rather an/a rather interesting job.*

No se utiliza:

- ante sustantivos contables en plural.
- ante sustantivos incontables, salvo los dichos anteriormente.
- tras el verbo **turn**.

Determinado: **the**.
Es invariable en género y número. Se pronuncia | ðiː | ante palabras que comienzan por sonidos vocálicos: *the idea* | ðiːaɪ'dɪə |; *the hour* |ðiː'aʊə |.

Se utiliza:

- ante sustantivos contables masculinos y femeninos, en singular o en plural.
- cuando acompaña a un sustantivo único: *the moon.*
- ante sustantivo seguido de nombre propio: *the planet Earth.*

No se utiliza:

- ante nombres abstractos, nombres de materiales o de comidas o sustantivos plurales, usados en sentido general: *Freedom is a preciated thing*; *coal is very much used*; *I'm having lunch*; *you can get magazines at the newsagent's.*
- ante nombres de lugares, cuando uno se refiere a su función: *Mary goes to school* (para aprender).

EL SUSTANTIVO

Sustantivos contables: hacen mención a cosas que se pueden contar. Tienen singular y plural.
Sustantivos incontables: son nombres de sustancias o cosas abstractas, que no se pueden contar pero sí medir o hablar de su cantidad, intensidad, etc. No tienen forma plural.

Formación del plural

La mayoría de los sustantivos forman el plural añadiendo **s** al singular: *girl, girls*; *photo, photos*. Sin embargo, hay algunas normas particulares, algunas excepciones:

- se añade **es** al singular en los sustantivos terminados en **ch, s, sh** o **x**, y en algunos terminados en **o**: *church, churches*; *dish, dishes*; *glass, glasses*; *box, boxes*; *tomato, tomatoes*; *potato, potatoes*; *hero, heroes*.
- la **y** se convierte en **ies** en los terminados en **y** precedida de consonante: *lady, ladies*.
- algunos terminados en **f** o **fe** pierden esta terminación y añaden **ves**: *wife, wives*; *leaf, leaves*; *proof, prooves*.
- el plural de los sustantivos compuestos se forma sobre la segunda palabra: *schoolgirl, schoolgirls*.

Concordancias

- Los sustantivos colectivos (people, cattle, police, public, etc.) concuerdan con el verbo en plural.
- Lo mismo ocurre con expresiones que indican pluralidad (a number of, a group of, etc.): *a number of houses were demolished*.
- Los sustantivos singulares, aunque acaben en **s**, concuerdan con el verbo en singular (mathematics, physics, billiards, etc.).

EL ADJETIVO

Es invariable en género, número, persona y caso. En cuanto a su situación en la frase, se pone delante el sustantivo; cuando se utilizan varios, se sigue el siguiente orden:

tamaño + edad + forma + color + origen + material + propósito + sustantivo

Algunos sustantivos pueden hacer de adjetivo, anteponiéndolos al sustantivo: *a garden chair*; *some garden chairs*.

Otros, se convierten en adjetivo añadiéndoles determinados sufijos (**-y, -ly, -ful, -en, -ous, -able, -some, -ic, -ed, -like, -al, -an, ian, ical, ish**):

cloudy, friendly, useful, golden, luxurious, childlike, atomic, ...

En otros casos, con la anteposición de prefijos se forman adjetivos negativos (**un-, in-, im-, ir-, il-, is-**): *unhappy, inaccurate, impossible, disagreeable*. La misma función cumple el sufijo **-less**: *careless*.

EL ADVERBIO

Adverbios de modo: salvo algunas excepciones (*all, high, near, etc.*), acaban en **-ly**: easily, beautifully, quickly, etc. Suelen ir al final de la frase, o tras el objeto directo.

Adverbios de tiempo y de lugar: tanto las expresiones adverbiales como los adverbios de lugar (**here, everywhere, around, across, below, down, etc.**) o de tiempo (**tomorrow, yesterday, early, today, soon, etc.**) van, normalmente, al final o al principio de la frase. Cuando hay de lugar y de tiempo, suele ir primero el de lugar, y ambos al final de la frase: *I'll see you at the pub tomorrow*. Sin embargo, algunos adverbios de tiempo (**soon, already, now, just, then, still**) suelen colocarse en el centro de la frase: *I've just seen him*. **Yet** se utiliza solamente en frases interrogativas y negativas y va al final de la frase: *have you done the shopping yet?*; *no, not yet*.

Adverbios de frecuencia: (**always, never, ever, often, sometimes, usually, generally, etc.**): aunque, igual que en los casos anteriores, no se puede decir que haya normas fijas, suelen ir en posición intermedia dentro de la frase: *we frequently go to Rome*. Hay algunos (**sometimes, usually, normally** y **occasionally**) que van, sistemáticamente, al principio o al final: *sometimes we see good plays*: *we go to the theatre occasionally*.

Adverbios de grado o modificadores: (**very, so, too, enough, rather, pretty, fairly, quite, etc.**): salvo en el caso de **enough**, que va detrás (*it isn't big enough*), suelen ir delante de la palabra a la que modifican: *it's extremely hot*; *the boy is too tall*.

Adverbios de probabilidad: (**certainly, definitely, probably, obviously, etc.**): van delante de los verbos léxicos o detrás de los auxiliares: *they probably know each other*; *we are obviously not going*. En las frases negativas se colocan delante de la negación: *she definitely didn't do it*.

FORMACIÓN DE COMPARATIVOS Y SUPERLATIVOS

Como norma general, si el adjetivo o el adverbio tienen menos de tres sílabas, se añade **er** para formar el comparativo y **est**, para el superlativo: *tall, taller, tallest*.

Cuando acaban en **e**, solo se añade **r** o **st**: *brave, braver, bravest*.

Si acaban en **consonante + y**, la **y** se convierte en **ier** o **iest**: *funny, funnier, funniest*.
Los de más de tres sílabas, y algunos de dos, forman el comparativo anteponiéndole **more** y el superlativo anteponiéndole **the most**: *more intelligent, the most intelligent*.

Comparativos y superlativos irregulares:

good, better, best.	**bad, worse, worst.**
well, better, best.	**badly, worse, worst.**
little, less, least.	**old, older/elder, oldest/eldest.**
much/many, more, most.	**far, farther/further, farthest/furthest.**

Comparativo de superioridad:
Se forma con el **comparativo + than**: *John is older than Anne*; *this lock is more expensive than that one*.
Se utiliza **comparativo + and + comparativo** para expresar que algo aumenta o decrece: *petrol is getting more and more expensive these days*; *he drove faster and faster*.
Para expresar que dos cosas cambian al mismo tiempo, o que una depende de la otra, se utiliza **the + frase de comparativo + the + frase de comparativo**: *the harder you work, the easier it is to pass*.

Comparativo de igualdad:
Se usa la estructura **as + adjetivo/adverbio + as**: *John is as tall as Mary*; *I'm driving as fast as I can*.
En frase negativas, **not as + adjetivo + as**, o **not so + adjetivo + as**: *John isn't as/so tall as Mary*.

LOS PRONOMBRES PERSONALES

De sujeto: **I, you, he/she/it; we, you, they**: *she likes Peter*.
I = yo; you = tú, usted, vosotros, ustedes; he = él (hombre, niño, o animal macho); **she = ella** (mujer, niñas, o animal hembra); **it** se emplea cuando el sujeto es una cosa o un animal cuyo sexo se desconoce, y en frases impersonales: *it's raining*; **we = nosotros; they = ellos, ellas**.

De objeto: **me, you, him/her/it; us, you, them**: *I don't like it*; *he'll write to us*.
ME = **me, a mí** (*give me*; *wait for me*; *speak to me*); YOU = **te, se, os, se, a tí/usted/vosotros/ustedes**; HIM = **le, a él**; HER = **le, a ella**; IT = **se, a ello**; US = **nos, a nosotros**; THEM = **les, a ellos/ellas**.

PRONOMBRES INTERROGATIVOS

What ...?	= ¿qué ...?	**Who ...?**	= ¿quién ...?
Where ...?	= ¿dónde ...?	**When ...?**	= ¿cuándo ...?
How ...?	= ¿cómo ...?	**Why ...?**	= ¿por qué ...?
Whose ...?	= ¿de quién ...?	**Which ...?**	= ¿cuál ...?

PRONOMBRES RELATIVOS

Introduce oraciones de relativo. Son los siguientes: **who, whom, which, that**.
Otros pronombres pueden ser también considerados como **relativos** cuando cumplen esa función: **where, when, why, whose, what**.

LOS REFLEXIVOS

Myself, yourself, himself, itself, ourselves, yourselves, themselves: *I'm preparing myself/yourself/... a cup of coffee = estoy haciéndome/haciéndote/haciéndole/... una taza de café.*

Estos pronombres, utilizados como ENFÁTICOS se colocan al final o directamente detrás de la frase nominal a que se refieren: *my sister did it herself.*

LOS INDEFINIDOS

Son los siguientes: **some, any, no** y **every** (y sus compuestos); **all, one, none, other, another, much, less, (a) few, (a) little, enough, each, more, most, half, either** y **neither**.

Salvo NONE, A LOT y HALF, funcionan como adjetivos y van delante del sustantivo: *some milk.* Excepto NO y EVERY, pueden usarse antes de + **the/your/her/this, etc.** + **sustantivo**: *some of them went home.* **Some** y **any** se utilizan con sustantivos contables en plural (*some books*), o con incontables para hablar de una cantidad indefinida (*some milk*). Normalmente, **some** se usa en frases afirmativas y **any** en interrogativas y negativas. Pero cuando se hace una petición o una oferta, o se espera que la respuesta sea afirmativa, se usa **some**.

Much y **many**, excepto cuando se espera respuesta afirmativa (que se utiliza **a lot of/a lots of**), se usan en frases negativas e interrogativas. **A lot/lots of**, en afirmativas y algunas interrogativas.

Every, con sustantivos en singular, se usa para hablar de un número indeterminado de personas o cosas y equivale a "todos sin excepción". **Each**, cuando se habla individualmente de personas o cosas. **All** se utiliza en el mismo caso que **each**, pero con sustantivos en plural.

Either (= el uno o el otro) y **neither** (= ni el uno ni el otro) van con sustantivos contables en singular. **Both** (= el uno y el otro), con sustantivos contables en plural. Los tres, seguidos de **of** + **adjetivo o artículo**, se usan con sustantivos contables en plural: *either of my friends ...*; *neither of these boxes ...*; *both of the books were really good.* También van delante de pronombre objeto en plural: *neither of us can ...*

Las mismas normas de uso sirven para los compuestos de estos indefinidos formados con **thing, body, one** y **where**: **something, anybody, everyone, nowhere, etc.**

LOS POSESIVOS

Adjetivos: **my, your, his/her/its, our, your, their**: *is this my/your/... book? = ¿es este mi/tu/su/nuestro/vuestro/su ... libro?*

Pronombres: **mine, yours, his, hers, ours, yours, theirs**: *no, it isn't mine/yours/... = no, no es... el mío, el tuyo, el suyo, el nuestro, el vuestro, el suyo.*

LOS DEMOSTRATIVOS

This = *este, esta, esto*; **these** = *estos, estas.*
That = *ese, esa, eso, aquel, aquella, aquello*;
those = *esos, esas, aquellos, aquellas.*

LAS CONJUNCIONES

Damos a continuación la tabla de conjunciones agrupadas por el tipo de oraciones subordinadas que suelen unir:

Oraciones subordinadas	conjunciones
de tiempo	**after, as soon as, before, since, when, whenever, while, until, till.**
de lugar	**where, whenever.**
explicativas	**as, because, since.**
finales	**in order to, so that.**
resultativas	**so and so, therefore, such, so + adj. + that.**
concesivas	**although, though, even though, despite, however, while, whereas, in spite of.**
modales	**as, as if, (in) the way.**

LAS PREPOSICIONES

De lugar: **in, at, on**.

De lugar y movimiento: **about, above, across, against, along, among, at, by, before, behind, below, beneath, beside, between, beyond, down, from, in, inside, into, near, off, on, over, past, round, through, to, towards, under, underneath, up, at the back (front, top, side, bottom) of, at the beginning of, at the end of, away from, far from, in front of, in the middle of, out of.**

De tiempo: **about, after, at, by, before, between, during, for, from, in, on, since, till, through, throughout, to, at the beginning (end) of, at the time of, in the middle (midst) of, down to, up to.**

Generalmente, **at, by** y **on** se utilizan cuando se habla de un momento concreto: *at 4 o'clock*; *by 3.30*; *on Saturday*; *on the 13th of July*. **After, before, by, in, since, till** y **until**, cuando de un período de tiempo; *after Christmas*; *before Sunday*, ... **For** y **during** indican duración.

For + un período de tiempo se usa para expresar una cantidad de tiempo (cuánto): *I've been waiting for 2 hours*. **During + sustantivo**, para expresar cuándo ocurrió algo: *he worked as a gardener during the summer*.

EL VERBO

Los VERBOS REGULARES forman el **pretérito** y el **participio pasado** añadiéndole **ed** al infinitivo: *walk*, *walked*. Si el infinitivo acaba en **e**, se añade **d**: *like*, *liked*; si terminan en consonante + **y**, esta se convierte en **ied**: *carry*, *carried*. Los monosílabos que acaban en consonante precedida de vocal, salvo los acabados en **y** o **w**, duplican la consonante: *stop*, *stopped*.

Las formas **interrogativas** y **negativas** se construyen con el verbo **to do**: *do you want to go? I don't like it*. Los demás *tiempos verbales* se forman como se indica a continuación:

El **presente** tiene la misma forma que el infinitivo sin **to**, salvo la tercera persona del singular, que añade una **s**: *I/you/we/they/* **like**, he/she/it **likes**. Si el infinitivo acaba en **ch, sh, s** o **x**, se añade **es**: *fix*, *fixes*.

El **gerundio** se forma añadiendo **ing** al infinitivo: *go*, *going*. Si acaba en **e**, la pierde: *drive*, *driving*. Si es monosílabo terminado en consonante, ocurre lo mismo que con la formación del p. pasado: *stop*, *stopping*.

Presente continuo: presente de to be + gerundio: *I'm driving*.

Pasado continuo: pasado de to be + gerundio: *I was driving*.

Futuro simple: la primera persona (de singular y de plural), con **shall** + el infinitivo sin to: *we shall drive*; el resto, con **will** + infinitivo sin *to*: *you will speak*.

Futuro simple continuo: shall/will + be + gerundio: *I shall be driving*, *they will be driving*.

Futuro perfecto: shall/will + presente de *to* have + p. pasado: *I shall have driven*.

Futuro perfecto continuo: shall/will + presente de *to* have + been + gerundio: *he will have been driving*.

Pretérito perfecto: presente de *to* have + p. pasado: *he has driven*.

Pretérito perfecto continuo: presente de *to* have + been + gerundio: *they have been driving*.

Pretérito pluscuamperfecto: had + p. pasado: *she had driven*.

Pretérito pluscuamperfecto continuo: had been + gerundio: *I had been driving*.

Imperativo: infinitivo sin to: *drive*.

Los VERBOS IRREGULARES tienen pretérito y participio pasado específicos (ver la tabla siguiente). Para la formación de los tiempos verbales se siguen las mismas normas que en los regulares.

English Irregular Verbs

Verbos irregulares ingleses

Infinitive	Past Tense	Past Participle
abide	abode, abided	abode, abided
arise	arose	arisen
awake	awoke	awaked, awoke
be	was	been
bear	bore	borne, born
beat	beat	beaten
become	became	become
befall	befell	befallen
beget	begot	begotten
begin	began	begun
behold	beheld	beheld
bend	bent	bent, bended
bereave	bereaved, bereft	bereaved, bereft
beseech	besought	besought
beset	beset	beset
bet	bet, betted	bet, betted
betake	betook	betaken
bethink	bethought	bethought
bid	bade, bid	bidden, bid
bide	bode, bided	bided
bind	bound	bound
bite	bit	bitten, bit
bleed	bled	bled
blend	blended, blent	blended, blent
bless	blessed, blest	blessed, blest
blow	blew	blown
break	broke	broken
breed	bred	bred
bring	brought	brought
broadcast	broadcast, broadcasted	broadcast, broadcasted
build	built	built
burn	burnt, burned	burnt, burned
burst	burst	burst
buy	bought	bought
cast	cast	cast
catch	caught	caught
chide	chid	chidden, chid
choose	chose	chosen
cleave	clove, cleft	cloven, cleft
cling	clung	clung
clothe	clothed	clothed
come	came	come
cost	cost	cost
creep	crept	crept
crow	crowed, crew	crowed
cut	cut	cut
dare	dared, durst	dared
deal	dealt	dealt
dig	dug	dug
dive	dived: (US) dove	dived
do	did	done
draw	drew	drawn
dream	dreamed, dreamt	dreamed, dreamt
drink	drank	drunk
drive	drove	driven
dwell	dwelt	dwelt
eat	ate	eaten
fall	fell	fallen
feed	fed	fed
feel	felt	felt
fight	fought	fought
find	found	found
flee	fled	fled
fling	flung	flung
fly	flew	flown
forbear	forbore	forborne
forbid	forbade, forbad	forbidden
forecast	forecast, forecasted	forecast, forecasted
foreknow	foreknew	foreknown
foresee	foresaw	foreseen
foretell	foretold	foretold
forget	forgot	forgotten
forgive	forgave	forgiven
forsake	forsook	forsaken
forswear	forswore	forsworn
freeze	froze	frozen
gainsay	gainsaid	gainsaid
get	got	got, (US) gotten

Infinitive	Past Tense	Past Participle
gild	gilded, gilt	gilded, gilt
gird	girded, girt	girded, girt
give	gave	given
go	went	gone
grave	graved	graven, graved
grind	ground	ground
grow	grew	grown
hamstring	hamstringed, hamstrung	hamstringed, hamstrung
hang	hung, hanged	hung, hanged
have	had	had
hear	heard	heard
heave	heaved, hove	heaved, hove
hew	hewed	hewed, hewn
hide	hid	hidden, hid
hit	hit	hit
hold	held	held
hurt	hurt	hurt
inlay	inlaid	inlaid
keep	kept	kept
kneel	knelt	knelt
knit	knitted, knit	knitted, knit
know	knew	known
lade	laded	laden, laded
lay	laid	laid
lead	led	led
lean	leant, leaned	leant, leaned
leap	leapt, leaped	leapt, leaped
learn	learnt, learned	learnt, learned
leave	left	left
lend	lent	lent
let	let	let
lie	lay	lain
light	lighted, lit	lighted, lit
lose	lost	lost
make	made	made
mean	meant	meant
meet	met	met
melt	melted	melted, molten
miscast	miscast	miscast
misdeal	misdealt	misdealt
misgive	misgave	misgiven
mislay	mislaid	mislaid
mislead	misled	misled
misspell	misspelt	misspelt
misspend	misspent	misspent
mistake	mistook	mistaken
misunderstand	misunderstood	misunderstood
mow	mowed	mown, (US) mowed
outbid	outbade, outdid	outbidden, outbid
outdo	outdid	outdone
outgo	outwent	outgone
outgrow	outgrew	outgrown
outride	outrode	outridden
outrun	outran	outrun
outshine	outshone	outshone

Infinitive	Past Tense	Past Participle
overbear	overbore	overborne
overcast	overcast	overcast
overcome	overcame	overcome
overdo	overdid	overdone
overhang	overhung	overhung
overhear	overheard	overheard
overlay	overlaid	overlaid
overleap	overleapt, overleaped	overleapt, overleaped
overlie	overlay	overlain
override	overrode	overridden
overrun	overran	overrun
oversee	oversaw	overseen
overset	overset	overset
overshoot	overshot	overshot
oversleep	overslept	overslept
overtake	overtook	overtaken
overthrow	overthrew	overthrown
overwork	overworked	overworked, overwrought
partake	partook	partaken
pay	paid	paid
prove	proved	proved, proven
put	put	put
read	read	read
rebind	rebound	rebound
rebuild	rebuilt	rebuilt
recast	recast	recast
redo	redid	redone
relay	relaid	relaid
remake	remade	remade
rend	rent	rent
repay	repaid	repaid
rerun	reran	rerun
reset	reset	reset
retell	retold	retold
rewrite	rewrote	rewritten
rid	rid, ridded	rid, ridded
ride	rode	ridden
ring	rang	rung
rise	rose	risen
rive	rived	riven, rived
run	ran	run
saw	sawed	sawn, sawed
say	said	said
see	saw	seen
seek	sought	sought
sell	sold	sold
send	sent	sent
set	set	set
sew	sewed	sewn, sewed
shake	shook	shaken
shave	shaved	shaved, shaven
shear	sheared	shorn, sheared
shed	shed	shed
shoe	shod	shod
shoot	shot	shot
show	showed	shown, showed

Infinitive	Past Tense	Past Participle
shred	shredded, shred	shredded, shred
shrink	shrank, shrunk	shrunk, shrunken
shrive	shrove, shrived	shriven, shrived
shut	shut	shut
sing	sang	sung
sink	sank	sunk, sunken
sit	sat	sat
slay	slew	slain
sleep	slept	slept
slide	slid	slid, slidden
sling	slung	slung
slink	slunk	slunk
slit	slit	slit
smell	smelt, smelled	smelt, smelled
smite	smote	smitten
sow	sowed	sown, sowed
speak	spoke	spoken
speed	sped, speeded	sped, speeded
spell	spelt, spelled	spelt, spelled
spend	spent	spent
spill	spilt, spilled	spilt, spilled
spin	spun, span	spun
spit	spat	spat
split	split	split
spoil	spoilt, spoiled	spoilt, spoiled
spread	spread	spread
spring	sprang	sprung
stand	stood	stood
stave	staved, stove	staved, stove
steal	stole	stolen
stick	stuck	stuck
sting	stung	stung
stink	stank, stunk	stunk
strew	strewed	strewn, strewed
stride	strode	stridden, strid
strike	struck	struck, stricken
string	strung	strung
strive	strove	striven

Infinitive	Past Tense	Past Participle
sunburn	sunburned, sunburnt	sunburned, sunburnt
swear	swore	sworn
sweep	swept	swept
swell	swelled	swollen, swelled
swim	swam	swum
swing	swung	swung
take	took	taken
teach	taught	taught
tear	tore	torn
tell	told	told
think	thought	thought
thrive	throve, thrived	thriven, thrived
throw	threw	thrown
thrust	thrust	thrust
tread	trod	trodden, trod
unbend	unbent	unbent
unbind	unbound	unbound
underbid	underbid	underbidden, underbid
undergo	underwent	undergone
understand	understood	understood
undertake	undertook	undertaken
undo	undid	undone
upset	upset	upset
wake	woke, waked	woken, waked
waylay	waylaid	waylaid
wear	wore	worn
weave	wove	woven, wove
wed	wedded	wedded, wed
weep	wept	wept
win	won	won
wind	winded, wound	winded, wound
withdraw	withdrew	withdrawn
withhold	withheld	withheld
withstand	withstood	withstood
work	wrought	wrought
wring	wrung	wrung
write	wrote	written

Verbos auxiliares

To do, como auxiliar, se utiliza para formar la interrogativa y la negativa en presente simple (**o, does:** *do you like fish?*) y en pasado simple (**did:** *did you work yesterday?*) También en las respuestas cortas: *yes, I do.*

To be sirve para formar:

a) los tiempos continuos (**to be** + **participio de presente/gerundio**): *he is telephoning at the moment.*
b) la voz pasiva (**to be** + **participio pasado**): *she was taken to hospital very ill.*

To have se utiliza para formar los tiempos de perfecto (**to have** + **participio pasado**): *she had read the whole book.*

Conjugación de verbos auxiliares

to be		**to have**	
presente	*pasado*	*presente*	*pasado*
I am (I'm)	I was	I have (I've)	I had
you are (you're)	your were	you have	you had
he is (he's)	he was	he has	he had
she is (she's)	she was	she has (she's)	she had
it is (it's)	it was	it has	it had
we are	we were	we have	we had
you are	you were	you have	you had
they are	they were	they have	they had

Aclaraciones:

- hemos indicado las contradicciones más frecuentes.
- **to be** suele contraerse también en la tercera persona de singular del presente cuando el sujeto es un sustantivo: *his mother's making a cake.*
- **to have** se contrae cuando va seguido de **got**: *I've got.*
- la **interrogativa** se construye poniendo la forma verbal antes que el pronombre: *am I?*; *are you?*; *have you got?*
- la **negativa**, añadiendo **not**: *I was not.* Esta forma también admite contracciones: *he isn't*; *he wasn't*; *they weren't*; *they aren't*; *he hasn't* (*got*); *they haven't* (*got*).
- la **interrogativa negativa**, invirtiendo el orden de la negativa: *wasn't he?*

Verbos auxiliares modales
Son los verbos **can, may, shall** y **will**.
Sirven como auxiliares de otros verbos, y expresan duda, certeza, posibilidad, disposición, habilidad, obligación, consejo y permiso: *she may bring the book we need?*
No experimentan variación en ninguna persona: *I can, you can, she can, we can, ...*
Las formas **interrogativa** y **negativa** se construyen como en los verbos auxiliares: *could you come tomorrow?*; *I can't swim.*

La voz pasiva se construye en inglés utilizando el tiempo correspondiente del verbo **to be** + el p. pasado del verbo en cuestión: *the house is painted by Mr. X.*

Las oraciones condicionales se introducen con **if**. La relación entre los tiempos variables en este tipo de oraciones es la siguiente:

- **if** + **presente ... futuro simple**: *if I go to London I'll bring you a present.*
- **if** + **pret. perfecto ... verbo modal** (can, may): *if she has already gone, we can use the house.*
- **if** + **presente continuo ... imperativo**: *if he is working, don't disturb him.*
- **if** + **pasado simple ... would** + **infinitivo**: *if I won the lotery, I would travel round the world.*
- **if** + **pret. pluscuamperfecto ... would have** + **p. pasado**: *if I had talked to her, this wouldn't have happened.*

En ciertas ocasiones se utilizan oraciones condicionales que no van introducidas por **if**. En estos casos se usan palabras como **unless** (= if ... not), **as/so long as/provided/providing ... that** (= únicamente si ...), **suppose/supposing** (= si ...).

American and British Abbreviations

Abreviaturas americanas y británicas

Each entry contains an expansion of the English abbreviation, and wherever possible the equivalent Spanish abbreviation with its expansion in parentheses.

A

AA *Automobile Association equivalente de* Real Automóvil Club *m* de España.
abbr. *abbreviated* abreviado; *abbreviation* abreviatura *f.*
ABC *American Broadcasting Company Compañía americana de radiotelevisión.*
A/C *account* (*current*) c.ta (c.te) (cuenta *f* [corriente]).
AC *alternating current* c.a. (corriente *f* alterna).
acc(t). *account* c.ta, cta (cuenta *f*).
AEC *Atomic Energy Commission* Comisión *f* de la Energía Atómica.
AFL-CIO *American Federation of Labor and Congress of Industrial Organizations Confederación general de los sindicatos de EE.UU.*
AIDS *acquired immune-deficiency syndrome* SIDA (síndrome *m* de inmunidad deficiente adquirida).
Ala *Alabama Estado de EE.UU.*
Alas *Alaska Estado de EE.UU.*
a.m. *ante meridiem* (*Latin* = *before noon*) de la mañana, antes del mediodía.
AP *Am. Associated Press Agencia de información.*
Apr. *April* abril *m.*
ARC *American Red Cross* Cruz *f* Roja Americana.
Ariz *Arizona Estado de EE.UU.*
Ark *Arkansas Estado de EE.UU.*
arr. *arrival* Ll. (llegada *f*).
Aug. *August* agosto *m.*
Ave. *Avenue* avenida *f.*

B

BA 1. *Bachelor of Arts* Lic. en Fil. y Let. (Licenciado [a *f*] *m* en Filosofía y Letras); **3.** *British Airways Compañía británica de aviación.*
BBC *British Broadcasting Corporation* BBC *f* (*Radiotelevisión nacional de Gran Bretaña*).
BE *bill of exchange* letra *f* de cambio.
BL 1. *bill of lading* conocimiento *m*; **2.** *Bachelor of Law* Licenciado (a*f*) *m* en Derecho.
Blvd. *Boulevard* Bulevar *m.*
BM 1. *British Museum* Museo *m* Británico; **2.** *Bachelor of Medicine* Licenciado (a *f*) *m* en Medicina.
BOT *Board of Trade* Ministerio *m* de Comercio (*británico*).
BR *British Rail Ferrocarriles británicos.*
Br(it). 1. *Britain* Gran Bretaña *f*; **2.** *British* británico.
Bros. *brothers* Hnos. (hermanos *m/pl.*).
BS *British Standard norma* (*industrial*) *británica.*
BS *Am.*, **B.Sc.** *Bachelor of Science* Licenciado (a *f*) *m* en Ciencias.
Bucks. *Buckinghamshire Condado inglés.*

C

c. 1. *cent(s)* céntimo(s) *m(pl.)* (*moneda americana*); **2.** *circa* h. (hacia); aproximadamente; **3.** *cubic* cúbico.
C. *Celsius, centigrade termómetro centigrado.*
C/A *current account* c/c (cuenta *f* corriente).
CAD *Computer-aided design* DAO (*diseño m asistido por ordenador*).
Cal(if) *California Estado de EE.UU.*
Cambs. *Cambridgeshire condado inglés.*
Can. 1. *Canada* (el) Canadá; **2.** *Canadian* canadiense.
CC *continuous current* c.c. (corriente *f* continua).
CD *compact disc* disco *m* compacto.
cf. *confer* comp. (compárese).
Ches. *Cheshire Condado inglés.*
CIA *Central Intelligence Agency* CIA (Servicio *m* Secreto de Información *de EE.UU.*).
CID *Criminal Investigation Department Departamento de Investigación Criminal* (*británico*), *eqivalente de* Brigada *f* Criminal.
c.i.f. *cost, insurance, freight* c.i.f., c.s.f. (costo, seguro, flete).
Co. 1. *Company* C., Cía. (compañía *f*); **2.** *county* condado *m* (*en EE.UU. e Irlanda*).
c/o. *care of* c/d (en casa de); a/c (al cuidado de).
COD *cash* (*Am. collect*) *on delivery* cóbrese a la entrega, contra re(e)mbolso.
Col *Colorado Estado de EE.UU.*
Conn *Connecticut Estado de EE.UU.*
Corp. *Corporation* S.A. (sociedad *f* anónima).
cp. *compare* comp. (compárese).
CPI *Consumer Price Index* IPC (índice *m* de precios al consumo).
c.w.o. *cash with order* pago *m* al contado.
cwt. hundredweight (= *50,8 kg.*) *approx.* quintal *m.*

D

DA 1. *deposit account approx.* cuenta *f* de ahorro; **2.** *Am. District Attorney* fiscal *m* de distrito.
DC 1. *direct current* c.c. (corriente *f* continua); **2.** *District of Columbia Washington, capital de EE.UU., y sus alrededores.*
Dec. *December* diciembre *m.*
Del *Delaware Estado de EE.UU.*
dep. *departure* S. (salida *f*).
Dept. *Department* dep. (departamento *m*).
Derby. *Derbyshire Condado inglés.*
disc(t). *discount* d.to (descuento *m*).

doz. *dozen* d.^{na} (docena *f*).
DST *Daylight Saving Time* hora *f* de verano.
Dur(h.) *Durham Condado inglés.*
dz. *dozen* d.^{na} (docena *f*).

E

E. 1. *east(ern)* E (este [*m*]); **2.** *English* inglés.
ECE *Economic Commission for Europe* Comisión *f* Económica para Europa (*de las Naciones Unidas*).
ECOSOC *Economic and Social Council* Consejo *m* Económico y Social (*de las Naciones Unidas*).
ECU *European Currency Unit* Unidad *f* de cuenta europea
Ed., ed. 1. *edition* ed. (edición *f*); **2.** *editor* director *m*, editor *m*, redactor *m*; **3.** *edited* editado.
EEC *European Economic Community* CEE (Comunidad *f* Económica Europea).
e.g. *exempli gratia* (*Latin* = *for example*) p.ej. (por ejemplo).
enc(l). *enclosure(s)* adjunto; anexo(s) *m(pl.)*.
Esq. *Esquire* D. (Don); (*Esq., en el sobre después del apellido*).
EU *European Union* UE (Unión *f* Europea).

F

f. 1. *fathom* (= *1,8288 m.*) braza *f*; **2.** *female, feminine* f. (femenino); **3.** *following* sgte. (siguiente).
F(ahr). *Fahrenheit termómetro Fahrenheit.*
FAO *Food and Agriculture Organization* OAA (Organización *f* de Agricultura y Alimentación).
FBI *Federal Bureau of Investigation Departamento de Investigación Criminal, equivalente de* Brigada *f* Criminal.
FC *Football Club* CF (Club *m* de Fútbol).
Feb. *February* febrero *m*.
Fla *Florida Estado de EE.UU.*
fo(l). *folio* f^{o}, fol. (folio *m*).
f.o.b. *free on board* f.a.b. (franco a bordo).
f.o.r. *free on rail* libre en la estación ferroviaria.
fr. *franc(s)* franco(s) *m(pl.)*.
Fri. *Friday* viernes *m*.
ft. *foot, pl. feet* (= *30,48 cm.*) pie(s) *m(pl.)*.

G

g. *gram(me[s])* gr(s). (gramo[s] *m[pl.]*).
Ga *Georgia Estado de EE.UU.*
gal. *gallon* (= *4,546 litros, Am. 3,785 litros*) galón *m*.
GB *Great Britain* Gran Bretaña *f*.
GI *Am. government issue* propiedad *f* del Estado; *por extensión, el soldado raso americano.*
Glos. *Gloucestershire Condado inglés.*
GMT *Greenwich Mean Time* T.M.G. (Tiempo *m* Medio de Greenwich).
GNP *Gross National Product* PNB (producto *m* nacional bruto).
GOP *Am. Grand Old Party* Partido *m* Republicano.
Govt. *Government* gob.^{no} (gobierno *m*).
GPO *General Post Office* Oficina *f* Central de Correos.
gr. *gross* bruto.

H

h. *hour(s)* hora(s) *f(pl.)*.
Hants. *Hampshire Condado inglés.*
Herts. *Hertfordshire Condado inglés.*
hf. *half medio.*
HI *Hawaii(an Islands)* (Islas *f/pl.*) Hawai.
HM *His (Her) Majesty* S.M. (Su Majestad).
HMS 1. *His (Her) Majesty's Ship (Steamer)* buque *m* ([buque *m* de] vapor *m*) de Su Majestad; **2.** *His (Her) Majesty's Service* servicio *m* (de Su Majestad); ✉ oficial.
HO *head office* oficina *f* central.
Hon. *Honourable Título de la nobleza británica.*
h.p. *horse-power approx.* c.v. (caballo[s] *m[pl.]* de vapor).
HQ *Headquarters* Cuartel *m* General.
HR *Am. House of Representatives* Cámara *f* de Representantes (= *Diputados*).
HRH *His (Her) Royal Highness* S A.R. (Su Alteza Real).
hrs. *hours* horas *f/pl.*

I

Ia *Iowa Estado de EE.UU.*
ICAO *International Civil Aviation Organization* OACI (Organización *f* de Aviación Civil Internacional)
ICU *intensive care unit* UVI (unidad *f* de vigilancia intensiva).
Id *Idaho Estado de EE.UU.*
i.e. *id est* (*Latin* = *that is*) es decir.
Ill *Illinois Estado de EE.UU.*
ILO *International Labour Organization* OIT (Organización *f* Internacional del Trabajo).
IMF *International Monetary Fund* FMI (Fondo *m* Monetario Internacional).
in. *inch(es)* (= *2,54 cm.*) pulgada(s) *f(pl.)*.
Inc. *Am. Incorporated* S.A. (Sociedad *f* Anónima).
Ind *Indiana Estado de EE.UU.*
inst. *instant* cte (corriente, de los corrientes).
IOC *International Olympic Committee* COI (Comité *m* Olímpico Internacional).
IOU *I owe you* pagaré.
IQ *Intelligence Quotient* cociente *m* intelectual.
Ir. 1. *Ireland* Irlanda *f*; **2.** *Irish* irlandés.
IRA *Irish Republican Army* Ejército *m* Republicano Irlandés.
IRC *International Red Cross* Cruz *f* Roja Internacional.
IT *information technology* informática *f*.

J

Jan. *January* enero *m*.
JP *Justice of the Peace* juez *m* de paz.
Jr., Jun(r). *junior* hijo.
Jul. *July* julio *m*.
Jun. *June* junio *m*.

K

Kans *Kansas Estado de EE.UU.*
kg *kilogram* kg (kilogramo *m*).
KO 1. *knock-out* k.o. (fuera *m* de combate); **2.** *knocked out* k.o. (fuera de combate).
Ky *Kentucky Estado de EE.UU.*

L

l. 1. *left* izquierdo; a la izquierda; **2.** *liter* l. (litro *m*).
La *Louisiana Estado de EE.UU.*
LA *Los Angeles* Los Ángeles.
Lancs. *Lancashire Condado inglés.*
lb. *pound* (= *453,6 gr.*) libra *f*.
LC *letter of credit* carta *f* de crédito.
Leics. *Leicestershire Condado inglés.*
Lincs. *Lincolnshire Condado inglés.*
LP 1. *long-playing* (de) larga duración *f*; **2.** *long-playing record* LP, elepé *m* (disco *m* de larga duración).
Ltd. *Limited* S. A. (Sociedad *f* Anónima).

M

m. 1. *male, masculine* m. (masculino); **2.** *meter* m. (metro *m*); **3.** *mile* (= *1609,34 m.*) milla *f*; **4.** *minute* m. (minuto *m*).

MA *Master of Arts* Maestro *m* en Artes.
Mar. *March* marzo *m.*
Mass *Massachusetts Estado de EE.UU.*
MD *medicinae doctor* (*Latin* = *Doctor of Medicine*) Doctor *m* en Medicina.
Md *Maryland Estado de EE.UU.*
Me *Maine Estado de EE.UU.*
mi. *mile* (= *1609,34 m.*) milla *f.*
Mich *Michigan Estado de EE.UU.*
Middx. *Middlesex Condado inglés.*
min. *minute* minuto *m.*
Minn *Minnesota Estado de EE.UU.*
Miss *Mississippi Estado de EE.UU.*
Mo *Missouri Estado de EE.UU.*
MO *money order* giro *m* postal.
Mon. *Monday* lunes *m.*
Mont *Montana Estado de EE.UU.*
MP 1. *Member of Parliament* miembro *m* del Parlamento; **2.** *Military Police* policía *f* militar.
m.p.h. *miles per hour* millas por hora.
Mr *Mister* Sr. (Señor *m*).
Mrs ['misiz] Sra. (Señora *f*).
Ms [mɪz] *prefijo de nombre para mujeres casadas y solteras.*
MS 1. *manuscript* MS (manuscrito *m*); **2.** *motorship* motonave *f.*
Mt. *Mount* montaña *f*, monte *m.*

N

n. 1. *neuter* neutro; **2.** *noun* sustantivo *m*; **3.** *noon* mediodía *m.*
N. *North*(*ern*) N (norte [*m*]).
NASA *National Aeronautics and Space Administration* NASA (Administración *f* Nacional de Aeronáutica y del Espacio).
NATO *North Atlantic Treaty Organization* OTAN (Organización *f* del Tratado del Atlántico Norte).
NBC *National Broadcasting Company Compañía americana de radiotelevisión.*
NC *North Carolina Estado de EE.UU.*
ND(ak) *North Dakota Estado de EE.UU.*
NE *northeast*(*ern*) NE (noreste [*m*]).
Neb(r) *Nebraska Estado de EE.UU.*
Nev *Nevada Estado de EE.UU.*
NF *Newfoundland* Terranova *f.*
NH *New Hampshire Estado de EE.UU.*
NHS *National Health Service* Servicio *m* Nacional de Sanidad.
NJ *New Jersey Estado de EE.UU.*
NMex *New Mexico Estado de EE.UU.*
Norf. *Norfolk Condado inglés.*
Northants. *Northamptonshire Condado inglés.*
Northumb. *Northumberland Condado inglés.*
Notts *Nottinghamshire Condado inglés.*
Nov. *November* noviembre *m.*
nt. *net* n.º (neto).
NW *northwest*(*ern*) NO (noroeste [*m*]).
NY *New York Estado de EE.UU.*
NYC *New York City* Cuidad *f* de Nueva York.

O

O *Ohio Estado de EE.UU.*
o/a *on account* (*of*) a/c. (de) (a cuenta [de]).
OAS *Organization of American States* OEA (Organización *f* de los Estados Americanos).
OECD *Organization for Economic Cooperation and Development* OCDE (Organización *f* para la Cooperación y el Desarrollo Económico).
Okla *Oklahoma Estado de EE.UU.*
OPEC *Organization of Petroleum Exporting Countries* OPEP (Organización *f* de los Países Exportadores de Petróleo).
Ore(g) *Oregon Estado de EE.UU.*
Oxon. *Oxfordshire Condado inglés.*
oz. *ounce* onza *f* = *28,35 gr.*

P

p. *page* página *f.*
Pa *Pennsylvania Estado de EE.UU.*
p.a. *per annum* (*Latin* = *yearly*) por año.
PAU *Panamerican Union* Unión *f* Panamericana.
PC *police constable* guardia *m.*
p.c. 1. *per cent* P%, %, p. c. (por cien[to]); **2.** *postcard* tarjeta *f* postal.
pd. *paid* pagado.
PEN Club *Poets, Playwrights, Editors, Essayists and Novelists* PEN (*Asociación internacional de escritores, etc.*).
Penn(a) *Pennsylvania Estado de EE.UU.*
per pro(c). *per procurationem* (*Latin* = *by proxy*) p.o. (por orden), p.p. (por poder).
Ph.D. *philosophiae doctor* (*Latin* = *Doctor of Philosophy*) Doctor *m* en Filosofía.
PIN *personal identification number* NPI (número *m* personal de identificación)
Pl. *Place* plaza *f.*
PLO *Palestine Liberation Organization* OLP (Organización *f* para la Liberación de Palestina).
p.m. *post meridiem* (*Latin* = *after noon*) de la tarde.
PO 1. *Post Office* (Oficina *f* de) Correos *m*/*pl.*; **2.** *postal order* giro *m* postal.
POB *Post Office Box* apartado *m.*
p.o.d. *pay on delivery* (contra) re(e)mbolso.
POW *prisoner of war* prisionero *m* de guerra.
p.p. 1. *v. per pro*(*c*); **2.** *past participle* participio *m* del pasado.
PS *postscript* PD (posdata *f*).
PTO *please turn over* véase al dorso.

Q

quot. *quotation* cotización *f.*

R

r. *right* derecho, a la derecha.
RAF *Royal Air Force* Fuerzas *f*/*pl.* Aéreas Británicas.
RAM *random access memory* memoria *f* de acceso aleatorio.
Rd. *road* carretera *f*; c. (calle *f*).
ref. (*in*) *reference* (*to*) (con) referencia (a).
regd. *registered* certificado.
reg.tn. *register ton* tonelada *f* de arqueo.
resp. *respective*(*ly*) respectivamente.
ret. *retired* retirado.
Rev. *Reverend* R., Rdo (Reverendo).
RI *Rhode Island Estado de EE.UU.*
RN *Royal Navy* Marina *f* Real.
ROM *read only memory* memoria *f* de sola lectura.
RP *reply paid* CP (contestación *f* pagada).
r.p.m. *revolutions per minute* r.p.m. (revoluciones *f*/*pl.* por minuto).
RR *Am. railroad* f.c. (ferrocarril *m*).
RSVP *répondez s'il vous plaît* = *please reply* S.R.C. (se ruega contestación)
RV *recreational vehicle* caravana *f.*
Ry. *railway* f.c. (ferrocarril *m*).

S

s. 1. *second*(*s*) segundo(s) *m*(*pl.*); **2.** *shilling*(*s*) chelin(es) *m*(*pl.*).

S. *south(ern)* S (sur [*m*]).
Sa 1. *South Africa* Africa *f* del Sur; **2.** *South America* América *f* del Sur; **3.** *Salvation Army* Ejército *m* de Salvación.
SALT *Strategic Arms Limitation Talks* SALT (Conversaciones *f/pl.* para la limitación de las armas estratégicas).
Sat. *Saturday* sábado *m.*
SC 1. *South Carolina Estado de EE.UU.*; **2.** *Security Council* Consejo *m* de Seguridad (*de las Naciones Unidas*).
SD(ak) *South Dakota Estado de EE.UU.*
SE 1. *southeast(ern)* SE (sudeste [*m*]); **2.** *Stock Exchange* Bolsa *f.*
SEATO *South East Asia Treaty Organization* OTASE (Organización *f* del Tratado de Asia de Sudeste).
sec. *second* segundo *m.*
Sept. *September* setiembre *m.*
SJ *Society of Jesus* C. de J. (Compañía *f* de Jesús).
Soc. *Society* sociedad *f.*
Som. *Somerset Condado inglés.*
Sq. *square* plaza *f.*
sq. *square* cuadrado.
Sr. *senior* padre.
SS *steamship* vapor *m.*
St. 1. *Saint* S. (San[ta]); **2.** *Street* calle *f*; **3.** *station* estación *f.*
Staffs. *Staffordshire Condado inglés.*
St. Ex. *Stock Exchange* Bolsa *f.*
stg. *sterling* moneda *f* esterlina.
Suff. *Suffolk Condado inglés.*
Sun. *Sunday* domingo *m.*
suppl. *supplement* suplemento *m.*
SW *southwest(ern)* SO (suroeste [*m*]).

T

t. *ton(s)* tonelada(s) *f(pl.).*
Tenn *Tennessee Estado de EE.UU.*
Tex *Texas Estado de EE.UU.*
Thurs. *Thursday* jueves *m.*
TU *Trade Union* sindicato *m.*
Tue. *Tuesday* martes *m.*

U

UFO *unidentified flying object* OVNI (objeto *m* volante no identificado).
UK *United Kingdom* RU (Reino *m* Unido: *Inglaterra, Escocia, Gales e Irlanda del Norte*).
UMW *Am. United Mine Workers* Sindicato *m* de Mineros.
UN *United Nations* NU, NN.UU. (Naciones *f/pl.* Unidas).
UNESCO *United Nations Educational, Scientific and Cultural Organization* UNESCO (Organización *f* de las Naciones Unidas para la Educación, la Ciencia y la Cultura).
UNICEF *United Nations (International) Children's (Emergency) Fund* UNICEF (Fondo *m* Internacional de Emergencia de las Naciones Unidas para la Infancia).
UNO *United Nations Organization* ONU (Organización *f* de las Naciones Unidas).
UPI *United Press International Agencia de información americana.*
US(A) *United States (of America)* EE.UU. (Estados *m/pl.* Unidos [de América]).
USAF(E) *United States Air Force (Europe)* Fuerzas *f/pl.* Aéreas de Estados Unidos (en Europa).
USN *United States Navy* Marina *f* Estadounidense.
UT *Utah Estado de EE.UU.*

V

v. 1. *verse* verso *m*; estrofa *f*; (*biblical*) vers.º (versículo *m*); **2.** *versus* (*Latin = against*) contra; **3.** *vide* (*Latin = see*) v. (véase), vid. (vide); **4.** *volt* v. (voltio *m*).
Va *Virginia Estado de EE.UU.*
VAT *value-added tax* IVA (impuesto *m* sobre el valor añadido).
VCR *video cassette recorder* videograbadora *f.*
VHF *very high frequency* MF (modulación *f* de frecuencia).
VIP *very important person* personaje *m* importante.
viz. *videlicet* (*Latin = namely*) v.gr. (verbigracia).
Vt *Vermont Estado de EE.UU.*
v.v. *vice versa* (*Latin = conversely*) viceversa.

W

W. *west(ern)* O (oeste [*m*]).
War. *Warwickshire Condado inglés.*
Wash *Washington Estado de EE.UU.*
Wed. *Wednesday* miércoles *m.*
WHO *World Health Organization* OMS (Organización *f* Mundial de la Salud).
WI *West Indies* Antillas *f/pl.*
Wilts. *Wiltshire Condado inglés.*
Wis *Wisconsin Estado de EE.UU.*
wt. *weight* peso *m.*
WVa *West Virgina Estado de EE.UU.*
Wyo *Wyoming Estado de EE.UU.*

X

Xmas *Christmas* Navidad *f.*

Y

yd. *yard(s)* (= *91,44 cm.*) yarda(s) *f(pl.).*
YMCA *Young Men's Christian Association* Asociación *f* Cristiana para los Jóvenes.
Yorks. *Yorkshire Condado inglés.*
yr(s). *year(s)* año(s) *m(pl.).*
YWCA *Young Women's Christian Association* Asociación *f* Cristiana para las Jóvenes.

American and British Proper Names

Nombres propios americanos y británicos

A

Ab·er·deen [æbər'di:n] *Ciudad de Escocia.*

Ad·am ['ædəm] Adán.

Ad·e·laide ['ædəleid] **1.** *Ciudad de Australia*; **2.** Adelaida.

A·den ['eidn] Adén.

Ad·i·ron·dacks [ˌædɪ'rondæks] *Montañas en el Estado de Nueva York.*

Ad·olf ['ædɔlf], **A·dol·phus** [ə'dɔlfəs] Adolfo.

Af·ghan·i·stan [æf'gænistæn] Afganistán *m.*

Af·ri·ca ['æfrikə] Africa *f.*

Ag·nes ['ægnis] Inés.

Al·a·bam·a [ælə'bæmə] *Estado de EE.UU.*

A·las·ka [ə'læskə] *Estado de EE.UU.*

Al·ba·ni·a [æl'beinjə] Albania *f.*

Al·bert ['ælbərt] Alberto.

Al·ber·ta [æl'bə:rtə] *Provincia de Canadá.*

Aleutian [ə'lu:ʃən] **Islands** Islas Aleutianas.

Al·ex·an·der [ælig'zændər] Alejandro.

Al·fred ['ælfrid] Alfredo.

Al·ge·ri·a [æl'dʒiriə] Argelia *f.*

Al·ice ['ælis] Alicia.

Alps [ælps] *pl.* Alpes *m/pl.*

Am·a·zon ['æməzn] Amazonas *m.*

A·mer·i·ca [ə'merikə] América *f.*

An·des ['ændi:z] *pl.* Andes *m/pl.*

An·drew ['ændru:] Andrés.

Ann(e) [æn] Ana.

An·nap·o·lis [ə'næpəlis] *Capital del Estado de Maryland. Sede de la Academia de Marina.*

An·tho·ny ['æntəni] Antonio.

An·til·les [æn'tili:z] *pl.* Antillas *f/pl.*

Ap·pa·lach·i·ans [æpə'lei(t)ʃənz] *pl.* Apalaches *m/pl.*

A·ra·bia [ə'reibjə] Arabia *f.*

Ar·gen·ti·na [ɑ:rdʒən'ti:nə], *the* **Ar·gen·tine** ['ɑ:rdʒəntin] (la) Argentina.

Ar·i·zo·na [ærə'zounə] *Estado de EE.UU.*

Ar·kan·sas ['ɑ:rkənsɔ:] *Estado, y* [ɑ:r'kænzəs] *Río de EE.UU.*

As·cot ['æskət] *Pueblo de Inglaterra con hipódromo de fama.*

A·sia ['eiʃə] Asia *f*; ~ *Minor* asia *f* Menor.

Ath·ens ['æθənz] Atenas.

At·lan·tic (**O·cean**) [ət'læntik ('ouʃn)] (Océano *m*) Atlántico *m.*

Auck·land ['ɔ:klənd] *Puerto de Nueva Zelanda.*

Aus·tra·lia [ɔ:s'treiljə] Australia *f.*

Aus·tri·a ['ɔ:striə] Austria *f.*

A·von ['eivən, 'ævən] *Río de Inglaterra.*

Az·er·bai·jan [ˌæzəbaɪ'dʒɑ:n] Azerbaiyán *m.*

A·zores [ə'zɔ:rz] *pl.* Azores *f/pl.*

B

Ba·ha·mas [bə'hɑ:məz] *pl.* Islas *f/pl.* Bahama, las Bahamas.

Ba·le·ar·ic Is·lands [bæli'ærik 'ailəndz] *pl.* Islas *f/pl.* Baleares.

Bal·kans ['bɔ:lkənz] Balcanes *m/pl.*

Bal·ti·more ['bɔ:ltəmɔ:r] *Puerto en la costa oriental de EE.UU.*

Bat·on Rouge [ˌbætən'ru:ʒ] *Capital del Estado de Luisiana.*

Be·a·trice ['biətris] Beatriz.

Bel·fast ['belfæst] *Capital de Irlanda del Norte.*

Bel·gium ['beldʒəm] Bélgica *f.*

Bel·grade [bel'greid] Belgrado.

Bel·o·rus·sia [ˌbelou'rʌʃə] Bielorusia *f.*

Ben·ja·min ['bendʒəmin] Benjamín.

Ben Ne·vis [ben'nevis] *Pico más alto de Gran Bretaña (1343 m).*

Ber·lin [bə:r'lin] Berlín.

Ber·mu·das [bər'mju:dəz] Islas *f/pl.* Bermudas.

Bess(y) ['bes(i)] Isabelita.

Beth·le·hem ['beθlihem] Belén.

Bet·ty ['beti] Isabelita.

Bhu·tan [bu:'tɑ:n] Bután *m.*

Bill, Bil·ly ['bil(i)] *nombre cariñoso de William.*

Bir·ming·ham ['bə:rmiŋhæm] *Ciudad industrial de Inglaterra; Ciudad de Alabama.*

Bis·cay ['bisk(e)i]: *Bay of* ~ Golfo *m* de Vizcaya.

Bob(·by) ['bɔb(i)] *nombre cariñoso de Robert.*

Bo·liv·i·a [bə'livjə] Bolivia *f.*

Bos·nia ['bɑzniə] Bosnia *f.*

Bos·ton ['bɔstən] *Ciudad de EE.UU. con la Universidad de Harvard en el barrio de Cambridge.*

Bra·zil [brə'zil] (el) Brasil.

Bridg·et ['bridʒit] Brígida.

Brit·ain ['britn] Gran Bretaña *f.*

Bronx [broŋks] *Barrio de Nueva York.*

Brook·lyn ['bruklin] *Barrio de Nueva York.*

Brus·sels ['brʌslz] Bruselas.

Bul·gar·i·a [bʌl'geriə] Bulgaria *f.*

Bur·ma ['bə:rmə] Birmania *f.*

C

Cal·i·for·nia [kæli'fɔ:rnjə] California *f* (*Estado de EE.UU.*).

Cam·bo·dia [kæm'bəudiə] Camboya *f.*

Cam·bridge ['keimbridʒ] *Ciudad universitaria inglesa; v. Boston*; **~shire** ['~ʃər] *Condado inglés.*

Can·a·da ['kænədə] (el) Canadá.

Can·ar·y Is·lands [kə'neri 'ailəndz] Islas *f/pl.* Canarias.

Can·ter·bur·y ['kæntərbəri] Cantórbery.

Cape Ca·nav·er·al [keɪpkə'nævərəl] Cabo *m* Cañaveral

Cape Horn [keip'hɔ:rn] Cabo *m* de Hornos.

Cape of Good Hope ['keɪpəvgud'həʊp] Cabo *m* de Buena Esperanza.

Car·diff ['kɑ:rdif] *Capital de Gales.*

Ca·rib·be·an (**Sea**) [kæri'bi:ən ('si:)] (Mar *m*) Caribe *m.*

Car·o·li·na [kærə'lainə]: *North* ~ Carolina *f* del Norte; *South* ~ Carolina *f* del Sur (*Estados de EE.UU.*).

Cath·e·rine, Cath·a·rine ['kæθərin] Catalina.

Cey·lon [si'lɔn] Ceilán *m.*

Chan·nel Is·lands ['tʃænl 'ailəndz] *pl.* Islas *f/pl.* Normandas.

Charles [tʃɑ:rlz] Carlos.

Charles·ton ['tʃɑ:lstən] *Capital del Estado de Virgina del Oeste.*

Char·lotte ['ʃɑ:rlət] Carlota.

Chey·enne [ʃɑɪ'æn] *Capital del Estado de Wyoming.*

Chech·nya ['tʃetʃnjə] Chechenia *f.*

Chi·ca·go [ʃi'kɑ:gou] *Ciudad industrial de EE.UU.*

Chil·e ['tʃili] Chile *m.*

Chi·na ['tʃainə] China *f.*

Christ [kraist] Cristo.

Chris·to·pher ['kristəfər] Cristóbal.

Cin·cin·na·ti [sinsi'næti] *Ciudad de EE.UU.*

Cleve·land ['kli:vlənd] *Ciudad industrial y de comercio de EE.UU.*
Co·lom·bi·a [kə'lʌmbiə] Colombia *f.*
Col·or·a·do [kɔlə'rædou] Colorado *m* (*Nombre de dos ríos y de un Estado de EE.UU.*).
Co·lum·bi·a [kə'lʌmbiə] *Capital del Estado de Carolina del Sur.*
Co·lum·bus [kə'lʌmbəs] Colón.
Con·nect·i·cut [kə'netikət] *Río y Estado de EE.UU.*
Co·pen·ha·gen [koupn'heign] Copenhague.
Cor·do·va ['kɔ:rdəvə] Córdoba.
Corn·wall [''kɔrnwəl] Cornualles *m.*
Co·sta Ri·ca ['kɔstə 'ri:kə] Costa Rica *f.*
Cov·en·try ['kʌvəntri] *Ciudad industrial de Inglaterra.*
Crete ['kri:t] Creta *f.*
Cro·a·tia [krou'eɪʃɪə] Croacia *f.*
Cu·ba ['kju:bə] Cuba *f.*
Cyp·rus ['saiprəs] Chipre *f.*
Czech Re·pub·lic [ˌtʃekri'pʌblɪk] República Checa.

D

Da·ko·ta [də'koutə]: *North* ~ Dakota *f* del Norte; *South* ~ Dakota *f* del Sur (*Estados de EE.UU.*).
Dan·iel ['dænjəl] Daniel.
Da·nube ['dænju:b] Danubio *m.*
Da·vid ['deivid] David.
Del·a·ware ['deləwer] *Río y Estado de EE.UU.*
Den·mark ['denmɑ:rk] Dinamarca *f.*
Den·ver ['denvə] *Capital del Estado de Colorado.*
Des Moines [dɪ'mɔɪn] *Capital del Estado de Iowa.*
De·troit ['di'trɔit] *Ciudad industrial de EE.UU.*
Di·a·na [dai'ænə] Diana.
Dick [dik] *nombre cariñoso de Richard.*
Do·mi·ni·can Re·pub·lic [də'minikən ri'pʌblik] República *f* Dominicana.
Do·ver ['douvər] *Puerto en el sur de Inglaterra.*
Down·ing Street ['dauniŋ 'stri:t] *Calle de Londres con la sede del Primer Ministro.*
Dub·lin ['dʌblin] Dublín (*Capital de Irlanda*).
Dun·kirk [dʌn'kə:rk] Dunquerque.

E

Ec·ua·dor ['ekwədɔ:] Ecuador *m.*
Ed·in·burgh ['ed(i)nbərə] Edimburgo (*Capital de Escocia*).
E·gypt ['i:dʒipt] Egipto *m.*
Ei·re ['eərə] *Nombre irlandés de Irlanda.*
E·li·za·beth [i'lizəbəθ] Isabel.
El Sal·va·dor [el 'sælvədɔ:r] El Salvador.
E·m(m)a·nu·el [i'mænjuəl] Manuel.
Eng·land ['iŋglənd] Inglaterra *f.*
Ep·som ['epsəm] *Pueblo inglés donde se verifican célebres carreras de caballos.*
Es·sex ['esiks] *Condado inglés.*
Es·to·nia [e'stəʊnjə] Estonia *f.*
E·thi·o·pi·a [i:θi'oupiə] Etiopía *f.*
E·ton ['i:tn] *Pueblo inglés con colegio del mismo nombre.*
Eu·gene ['ju:dʒ:n] Eugenio.
Eu·rope ['jurəp] Europa *f.*
Eve [i:v] Eva.
Ever·glades ['evəgleidz] *Pantano en el Estado de Florida.*

F

Falk·land Is·lands ['fɔ:klənd 'ailəndz] (Islas *f/pl.*) Malvinas *f/pl.*
Fer·di·nand ['fə:rdinənd] Fernando.
Fin·land ['finlənd] Finlandia *f.*
Flor·i·da ['flɔridə] *Península y Estado de EE.UU.*
France [fræns] Francia *f.*
Fran·ces ['frænsis] Francisca.
Fran·cis ['frænsis] Francisco.
Frank [fræŋk] Paco.
Fred·e·rick ['fredrik] Federico.

G

Ga·za Strip [gɑ:zəstrɪp] *Franja de Gaza.*
Ge·ne·va [dʒi'ni:və] Ginebra.
Gen·o·a ['dʒenouə] Génova.
George [dʒɔ:rdʒ] Jorge.
Geor·gia ['dʒɔ:rdʒə] *Estado de EE.UU.*
Ger·ma·ny ['dʒərməni] Alemania *f.*
Get·tys·burg ['getizbərg] *Pueblo del Estado de Pensilvania* (*EE.UU.*).
Gib·ral·tar [dʒib'rɔltər] Gibraltar; *Rock of* ~ Peñón *m* de Gibraltar; *Straits of* ~ *pl.* Estrecho *m* de Gibraltar.
Giles [dʒailz] Gil.
Glas·gow ['glæsgou] *Puerto de Escocia.*
Glouces·ter ['glɔstər] *Ciudad de Inglaterra*; **~·shire** ['~ʃər] *Condado inglés.*
Grand Can·yon [grænd 'kæniən] Gran Cañón *m del río Colorado* (*EE.UU.*).
Great Brit·ain ['greit 'britn] Gran Bretaña *f.*
Greece [gri:s] Grecia *f.*
Green·land ['gri:nlənd] Groenlandia *f.*
Green·wich ['grinidʒ] *Barrio de Londres*; ~ *Village* ['~'vilidʒ] *Barrio de los artistas de Nueva York.*
Gua·te·ma·la [gwɑ:tə'mɑ:lə] Guatemala *f.*
Guern·sey ['gə:rnzi] Guernesey *m.*
Gui·a·na [gai'ænə] Guayana *f.*
Guin·ea ['gini] Guinea *f.*
Guy [gai] Guido.

H

Hague [heig]: *The* ~ La Haya.
Hai·ti ['heiti] Haití *m.*
Har·lem ['hɑ:ləm] *Barrio de Nueva York.*
Har·ry ['hæri] Enrique.
Har·vard U·ni·ver·si·ty ['hɑ:rvərd ju:ni'və:rsiti] *Universidad de fama de los EE.UU.*
Ha·van·a [hə'vænə] La Habana.
Ha·wai·i [hɑ:'waii:] (Islas *f/pl.*) Hawai.
Heb·ri·des ['hebridi:z] *pl.* Hébridas *f/pl.*
Hel·en ['helin] Elena.
Hen·ry ['henri] Enrique.
Hol·ly·wood ['hɔliwud] *Ciudad de California y centro de la industria del cine de EE.UU.*
Hon·du·ras [hɔn'durəs] Honduras *f.*
Ho·no·lu·lu [ˌhɑnə'lu:lu:] *Capital del Estado de Hawai.*
Hud·son ['hʌdsn] *Río en el este de EE.UU.*
Hugh [hju:] Hugo.
Hun·ga·ry ['hʌŋgəri] Hungría *f.*
Hu·ron ['hjurən]: *Lake* ~ el lago Hurón.
Hyde Park ['haid 'pɑ:rk] *Parque público de Londres.*

I

I·be·ri·an Pen·in·su·la [aɪ'bɪərɪən pɪ'nɪnsjʊlə] *Península Ibérica.*
Ice·land ['aislənd] Islandia *f.*
I·da·ho ['aidəhou] *Estado de EE.UU.*
Il·li·nois [ili'nɔi] *Río y Estado de EE.UU.*
In·dia ['indjə] (la) India.
In·di·an·a [indi'ænə] *Estado de EE.UU.*
In·dian O·cean ['indjən 'ouʃn] Océano *m* Indico.
In·dies ['indiz] Indias *f/pl.*
In·do·ne·sia [indəu'ni:ʒə] Indonesia *f.*
I·o·wa ['aiouə, 'aiəwə] *Estado de EE.UU.*
I·ran [i'rɑ:n, i'ræn] (el) Irán.
I·raq [i'rɑ:k, i'ræk] (el) Irak.
Ire·land ['aiərlənd] Irlanda *f.*
Is·rael ['izriəl] Israel *m.*
It·a·ly ['it(ə)li] Italia *f.*
I·vo·ry Coast ['aivəri 'koust] Costa *f* de Marfil.

J

Jack [dʒæk] Juan(ito).
Jack·son ['dʒæksn] *Capital del Estado de Misisipi.*
Ja·mai·ca [dʒə'meikə] Jamaica *f.*
James [dʒeimz] Diego; Jaime.
Jane [dʒein] Juana.
Ja·pan [dʒə'pæn] (el) Japón.
Jef·fer·son Cit·y [ˌdʒefəsn 'sɪtɪ] *Capital del Estado de Misuri.*
Jer·e·my ['dʒerəmi] Jeremías.
Jer·ome [dʒə'roum] Jerónimo.
Jer·sey ['dʒə:rzi] *Isla británica de las islas Normandas*; **~ City** *Ciudad a orillas del Hudson* (*EE.UU.*).
Je·ru·sa·lem [dʒə'ru:sələm] Jerusalén.
Je·sus ['dʒi:zəs] Jesús; *Jesus Christ* ['dʒi:zəs 'kraist] Jesucristo.
Jim(·my) ['dʒim(i)] *nombre cariñoso de James.*
Joan [dʒoun] Juana.
Joe [dʒou] Pepe.
John [dʒɔn] Juan.
Jor·dan ['dʒɔ:rdn] (*river*) Jordán *m*; (*country*) Jordania *f.*
Jo·seph ['dʒouzif] José.

Jo·se·phine ['dʒouzifi:n] Josefina.
Ju·lian ['dʒu:ljən] Juliano.
Ju·neau ['dʒu:nəʊ] *Capital del Estado de Alaska.*

K

Kan·sas ['kænzəs] *Río y Estado de EE.UU.*
Kate [keit] *nombre cariñoso de Catherine.*
Ken·tuck·y [ken'tʌki] *Río y Estado de EE.UU.*
Ken·ya ['kenjə] Kenia.
Kit(·ty) ['kit(i)] *nombre cariñoso de Catherine.*
Ko·re·a [kə'riə] Corea *f.*

L

Lab·ra·dor ['læbrədɔ:r] Labrador *m* (*Canadá*).
La·os [laʊs] Laos *m.*
Lap·land ['læplənd] Laponia *f.*
Lat·in A·mer·i·ca ['lætn ə'merikə] América *f* Latina.
Lat·via ['lætvɪə] Letonia *f.*
Leb·a·non ['lebənən] Líbano *m.*
Lew·is ['lu:is] Luis.
Lib·y·a ['libiə] Libia *f.*
Lin·coln ['lɪŋkən] *Capital del Estado de Nebraska.*
Lis·bon ['lizbən] Lisboa.
Lith·u·a·nia [lɪθju:'eɪnjə] Lituania *f.*
Little Rock ['litlrok] *Capital del Estado de Arkansas.*
Liv·er·pool ['livərpu:l] *Puerto y ciudad industrial de Inglaterra.*
Lon·don ['lʌndən] Londres.
Los An·ge·les [lɔs 'ændʒələs] Los Angeles (*Ciudad de EE.UU.*).
Lou·i·si·an·a [lui:zi'ænə] Luisiana *f* (*Estado de EE.UU.*).
Luke [lu:k] Lucas.
Lux·em·bourg ['lʌksəmbərg] Luxemburgo *m.*

M

Ma·dei·ra [mə'dirə] Madera *f.*
Mad·i·son ['mædisn] *Capital del Estado de Wisconsin* (*EE.UU.*).
Ma·gel·lan [mə'gelən] Magallanes; ~ *Straits pl.* Estrecho *m* de Magallanes.
Maine [mein] *Estado de EE.UU.*
Ma·jor·ca [mə'dʒɔ:rkə] Mallorca *f.*
Man·ches·ter ['mæntʃestər] *Ciudad industrial de Inglaterra.*
Man·hat·tan [mæn'hætn] *Isla y centro de la ciudad de Nueva York.*
Man·i·to·ba [mæni'toubə] *Provincia de Canadá.*
Mar·ga·ret ['mɑ:rgərit] Margarita.
Mark [mɑ:rk] Marcos.
Mar·tin·ique [mɑ:rtn'i:k] Martinica *f.*
Mar·y ['meri] María.
Mar·y·land ['merilənd] *Estado de EE.UU.*
Mas·sa·chu·setts [mæsə'tʃu:səts] *Estado de EE.UU.*
Mat·thew ['mæθju:] Mateo.
Mau·rice ['mɔ:rəs] Mauricio.
Mau·ri·tius [mɔ:'riʃəs] Mauricio *m* (*isla*).
Med·i·ter·ra·ne·an (Sea) [meditə'reinjən (si:)] (mar *m*) Mediterráneo *m.*
Mel·bourne ['melbərn] Melburne (*Australia*).
Mem·phis ['memfis] *Ciudad en el Estado de Tennessee*; *ciudad en Egipto.*
Mex·i·co ['meksikou] Méjico *m,* México *m.*
Mi·am·i [mai'æmi] *Ciudad en el Estado de Florida* (*EE.UU.*).
Mich·ael ['maikl] Miguel.
Mich·i·gan ['miʃigən] *Estado de EE.UU.*; *Lake* ~ el lago Michigan (*el tercero de los cinco Grandes Lagos de Norteamérica*).
Min·ne·ap·o·lis [mini'æpəlis] *Ciudad en el Estado de Minnesota* (*EE.UU.*).
Min·ne·so·ta [mini'soutə] *Estado de EE.UU.*
Mi·nor·ca [mi'nɔ:rkə] Menorca *f.*
Mis·sis·sip·pi [misi'sipi] Misisipí *m* (*Estado y río de EE.UU.*).
Mis·sou·ri [mi'zuri] Misuri *m* (*Río y Estado de EE.UU.*).
Mo·ham·med [mou'hæmed] Mahoma.
Mon·tan·a [mɔn'tænə] *Estado de EE.UU.*
Mont·re·al [mɔntri'ɔ:l] *Ciudad de Canadá.*
Mo·roc·co [mə'rɔkou] Marruecos *m.*
Mos·cow ['mɔskou] Moscú.
Mo·ses ['mouziz] Moisés.
Mount Ev·er·est [ˌmaʊnt'evərɪst] *Pico más alto del mundo.*
Mount McKin·ley [ˌmaʊntmə'kɪnlɪ] *Pico más alto de EE.UU.*

N

Nash·ville ['næʃvil] *Capital del Estado de Tennessee.*
Ne·bras·ka [ni'bræskə] *Estado de EE.UU.*
Ne·pal [nɪ'pɔ:l] Nepal *m.*
Neth·er·lands ['neðərləndz] *pl.* (los) Países *m/pl.* Bajos.
Ne·vad·a [nə'vædə] *Estado de EE.UU.*
New Bruns·wick [ni(j)u: 'brʌnzwik] *Provincia de Canadá.*
New Eng·land [n(j)u: 'iŋglənd] Nueva Inglaterra *f.*
New·found·land ['n(j)u:fəndlənd] Terranova *f.*
New Guin·ea [n(j)u: 'gini] Nueva Guinea *f.*
New Hamp·shire [n(j)u: 'hæmpʃər] *Estado de EE.UU.*
New Jer·sey [n(j)u: 'dʒərzi] *Estado de EE.UU.*
New Mex·i·co [n(j)u: 'meksikou] *Estado de EE.UU.*
New Or·le·ans [n(j)u: 'ɔ:rli:nz] Nueva Orleans *f.*
New South Wales ['n(j)u:'sauθ'weilz] Nueva Gales *f* del Sur (*Australia*).
New York [n(j)u: 'jɔ:rk] Nueva York (*Ciudad y Estado de EE.UU.*).
New Zea·land [n(j)u:'zi:lənd] Nueva Zelanda *f.*
Ni·ag·a·ra [nai'ægərə] Niágara *m.*
Nic·a·ra·gua [nikə'rɑ:gwə] Nicaragua *f.*
Nice [ni:s] Niza.
Nich·o·las ['nikələs] Nicolás.
Ni·ge·ri·a [nai'dʒi:riə] Nigeria *f.*
Nile [nail] Nilo *m.*
No·ah ['nɔ:ə] Noé.
North Car·o·li·na [ˌnɔ:θkærə'laɪnə] *Estado de EE.UU.*
North Da·ko·ta [ˌnɔ:θdə'kəʊtə] *Estado de EE.UU.*
North·ern Ire·land ['nɔ:rðərn 'aiərlənd] Irlanda *f* del Norte.
North Sea ['nɔ:rθ'si:] Mar *m* del Norte.
Nor·way ['nɔ:rwei] Noruega *f.*
No·va Sco·tia ['nouvə'skouʃə] Nueva Escocia *f* (*Provincia de Canadá*).

O

O·hi·o [ou'haiou] Ohío *m* (*Río y Estado de EE.UU.*).
O·kla·ho·ma [ouklə'houmə] *Estado de EE.UU.*
O·lym·pia [əʊ'lɪmpɪə] *Capital del Estado de Washington.*
On·tar·i·o [ɔn'teriou] *Provincia de Canadá*; *Lake* ~ el lago Ontario.
Or·e·gon ['ɔrigən] *Estado de EE.UU.*
Ork·ney Is·lands ['ɔ:rkni 'ailəndz] *pl.* (las) Orcadas *f/pl.* (*Archipiélago situado al norte de Escocia*).
Ot·ta·wa ['ɔtəwə] *Capital de Canadá.*
Ox·ford ['ɔksfərd] *Ciudad universitaria inglesa.*

P

Pa·cif·ic (O·cean) [pə'sifik ('ouʃn)] (Océano *m*) Pacífico *m.*
Pa·ki·stan [pæki'stæn] Pakistán *m.*
Pal·es·tine ['pælistain] Palestina *f.*
Pan·a·ma [pænə'mɑ:] Panamá *m.*
Par·a·guay ['pærəgwai] (el) Paraguay.
Par·is ['pærɪs] París.
Pat·rick ['pætrik] Patricio.
Paul [pɔ:l] Pablo.
Pearl Har·bor ['pə:rl 'hɑ:rbər] *Puerto cerca de Honolulú, Hawai.*
Penn·syl·va·nia [pensil'veinjə] Pensilvania *f* (*Estado de EE.UU.*).
Pe·ru [pə'ru:] (el) Perú.
Pe·ter ['pi:tər] Pedro.
Phil·a·del·phi·a [filə'delfjə] Filadelfia (*Gran ciudad de EE.UU.*).
Phil·ip ['filip] Felipe.
Phil·ip·pines ['filipi:nz] *pl.* Filipinas *f/pl.*
Phoe·nix ['fi:niks] *Capital de Arizona* (*EE.UU.*).
Pic·ca·dil·ly [pikə'dili] *Avenida principal en la parte occidental de Londres.*
Pitts·burgh ['pitsbərg] *Ciudad de EE.UU.*
Pi·us ['paɪəs] Pío.
Plym·outh ['liməθ] **1.** *Puerto de Inglaterra*; **2.** *Ciudad de EE.UU.*
Po·land ['poulənd] Polonia *f.*
Ports·mouth ['pɔ:rtsməθ] *Puerto de Inglaterra.*
Por·tu·gal ['pɔ:rtʃigəl] Portugal *m.*

Po·to·mac [pə'toumək] *Río de EE.UU.*
Prague [prɑːg] Praga.
Puer·to Ri·co ['pwertə 'riːkou] Puerto Rico *m.*
Pyr·e·ness [pirə'niːz] Pirineos *m/pl.*

Q

Que·bec [kwi'bek] *Provincia y ciudad de Canadá.*

R

Ra·phael ['ræfiəl] Rafael.
Rhine [rain] Rin *m.*
Rhode Is·land [roud'ailənd] *Estado de EE.UU.*
Rhone [roun] Ródano *m.*
Rich·ard ['ritʃərd] Ricardo.
Rich·mond ['ritʃmənd] **1.** *Capital de Virgina* (*EE.UU.*); **2.** *Barrio de Nueva York*; *barrio de Londres.*
Rob·ert ['rɔbərt], **Rob·in** ['rɔbən] Roberto.
Rock·y Moun·tains ['rɔki'mauntnz] *pl.* Montañas *f/pl.* Rocosas (*Sierra principal en el oeste de EE.UU.*).
Rome [roum] Roma.
Rose [rouz] Rosa.
Ru·ma·ni·a [ruː'meinjə] Rumania *f.*
Rus·sia ['rʌʃə] Rusia *f.*
Rwan·da [rʊ'ændə] Ruanda *f.*

S

Sac·ra·men·to [sækrə'mentəʊ] *Capital del Estado de California.*
Sa·har·a [sə'hɑːrə] Sáhara *m.*
Sa·lem ['sɑləm] *Capital del Estado de Oregon.*
Salt Lake Cit·y [ˌsɔːltleɪk'sɪtɪ] *Capital del Estado de Utah.*
Sam [sæm] *nombre cariñoso de Samuel.*
Sam·u·el ['sæmjəl] Samuel.
San Fran·cis·co [sænfrən'siskou] San Francisco (*EE.UU.*).
San·ta Fe [ˌsæntə'feɪ] *Capital del Estado de New Mexico.*
Sa·ra·gos·sa [særə'gɔsə] Zaragoza.
Sar·di·nia [sɑːr'dinjə] Cerdeña *f.*
Sas·katch·e·wan [səs'kætʃiwən] *Río y provincia de Canadá.*
Sau·di A·ra·bia ['sɔːdi ə'reibjə] Arabia *f* Saudita.
Scan·di·na·via [skændi'neivjə] Escandinavia *f.*
Scot·land ['skɔtlənd] Escocia *f*; *New ~ Yard Oficina central de la policía de Londres.*
Se·at·tle [si'ætl] *Puerto en el noroeste de EE.UU.*
Seine [sein] Sena *m.*
Ser·bia ['sɜːbɪə] Serbia *f.*
Se·ville ['səvil] Sevilla.
Si·be·ri·a [sai'biriə] Siberia *f.*
Sic·i·ly ['sisili] Sicilia *f.*
Si·er·ra Le·one [si'erəli'oun] Sierra *f* Leona.
Si·er·ra Ne·va·da [si'erə ni'vɑːdə] Sierra Nevada *en España y California.*
Si·mon ['saimən] Simón.
Sin·ga·pore [siŋgə'pɔːr] Singapur.
Slo·ve·nia [sləʊ'vina] Eslovenia *f.*
Slo·va·kia [sləʊ'vækɪə] Eslovaguia *f.*
South Af·ri·ca: Re·pub·lic of ~ [ri'pʌblik əvsauθ'æfrikə] República *f* Sudafricana.
South A·mer·i·ca ['sauθ ə'merikə] América *f* del Sur.
South·amp·ton [sauθ'æmptən] *Puerto en Inglaterra.*
South Car·o·li·na [ˌsauθkærə'laɪnə] *Estado de EE.UU.*
South Da·ko·ta [ˌsauθdə'kəutə] *Estado de EE.UU.*
Spain [spein] España *f.*
Sri Lan·ka [sriː'lɑŋkə] Sri Lanka *m.*
Staf·ford·shire ['stæfərdʃər] *Condado inglés.*
Ste·phen ['stiːvn] Esteban.
St. Lou·is [seint 'luːəs] *Ciudad industrial de EE.UU.*
St. Paul [seint'pɔːl] *Capital del Estado de Minnesota.*
Stock·holm ['stɔkhɔlm] Estocolmo.
Stras·bourg ['stræzbərg] Estrasburgo.
Strat·ford ['strætfərd] *Nombre de varias poblaciones de Inglaterra y de EE.UU.*; *~-on-Avon Lugar de nacimiento de Shakespeare.*
Stu·art ['st(j)uːərt] Estuardo.
Su·dan [suː'dæn] Sudán *m.*
Su·ez Ca·nal ['suːez kə'næl] Canal *m* de Suez.
Su·san ['suːzn] Susana.
Swe·den ['swiːdn] Suecia *f.*
Swit·zer·land ['switsərlənd] Suiza *f.*
Syd·ney ['sidni] *Puerto y ciudad industrial de Australia.*
Sy·ri·a ['siriə] Siria *f.*

T

Ta·gus ['teigəs] Tajo *m.*
Ta·hi·ti [taː'hiːtɪː] Tahiti *m.*
Tal·la·has·see [tælə'hæsɪ] *Capital del Estado de Florida.*
Tan·gier [tæn'dʒiər] Tánger.
Tan·za·nia [ˌtænzə'nɪːə] Tanzania *f.*
Ten·nes·see [tenə'siː] *Río y Estado de EE.UU.*
Tex·as ['teksəs] Tejas *m* (*Estado de EE.UU.*).
Thai·land ['tailænd] Tailandia *f.*
Thames [temz] Támesis *m.*
Thom·as ['tɔməs] Tomás.
To·kyo ['toukjou] Tokio.
Tom(·my) ['tɔm(i)] *nombre cariñoso de Thomas.*
Ton·y ['touni] *nombre cariñoso de Anthony.*
To·ron·to [tə'rɔntou] *Ciudad de Canadá.*
Tra·fal·gar [trə'fælgər] *Promontorio cerca de Gibraltar.*
Tu·nis ['tuːnəs] Túnez.
Tur·key ['təːrki] Turquía *f.*

U

U·kraine [juː'krein] Ucrania *f.*
Ul·ster ['ʌlstər] *Provincia de Irlanda.*
U·nit·ed King·dom [juː'naitid 'kiŋdəm] (el) Reino Unido (*Gran Bretaña e Irlanda del Norte*).
U·nit·ed States (of A·mer·i·ca) [juː'naitid 'steits (əvə'merikə)] *pl.* (los) Estados *m/pl.* Unidos (de América).
U·ru·guay ['urugwai] (el) Uruguay.
U·tah ['juːtɑː] *Estado de EE.UU.*

V

Van·cou·ver [væn'kuːvər] *Isla y ciudad en la costa occidental de Canadá.*
Vat·i·can ['vætikən] Vaticano *m.*
Ven·e·zue·la [vene'zweilə] Venezuela *f.*
Ven·ice ['venis] Venecia.
Ver·mont [vər'mɔnt] *Estado de EE.UU.*
Ver·sailles [ver'sai] Versalles.
Vi·en·na [vi'enə] Viena.
Viet·nam ['vjet'næm] Vietnam *m.*
Vir·gin·ia [vər'dʒinjə] *Estado de EE.UU.*

W

Wales [weilz] Gales *f.*
Wall Street ['wɔːlstriːt] *Calle de Nueva York y centro financiero de EE.UU.*
War·saw ['wɔːrsɔː] Varsovia.
War·wick(·shire) ['wɔrik(ʃər)] *Condado inglés.*
Wash·ing·ton ['wɔʃiŋtən] **1.** *Estado de EE.UU.*; **2.** *Capital federal y sede del gobierno de EE.UU.*
Wel·ling·ton ['weliŋtən] *Capital y puerto principal de Nueva Zelanda.*
West In·dies ['west 'indiz] *pl.* Antillas *f/pl.*
West·min·ster ['westminstər] *Barrio de Londres.*
West Vir·gin·ia [ˌwestvə'dʒɪnjə] *Estado de EE.UU.*
White·hall ['wait'hɔːl] *Calle de Londres con edificios del gobierno inglés.*
White House ['wait 'haus]: *the ~* la Casa Blanca (*sede oficial y residencia del presidente de EE.UU.*).
Wight: Isle of ~ [wait] *Isla en la costa meridional de Inglaterra.*
Will [wil], **Will·iam** ['wiljəm] Guillermo.
Wim·ble·don ['wimbldən] *Barrio de Londres* (*campeonatos de tenis*).
Wis·con·sin [wis'kɔnsn] *Estado de EE.UU.*
Wy·o·ming [wai'oumiŋ] *Estado de EE.UU.*

Y

Yale U·ni·ver·si·ty ['jeil juːni'vəːrsiti] Universidad de Yale (*en el Estado norteamericano de Connecticut*).
Yel·low·stone ['jeloustoun] *Río y parque nacional de EE.UU.*
York [jɔːrk] *Ciudad y sede arzobispal en Inglaterra.*
York·shire ['jɔːrkʃər] *Condado inglés.*
Yo·sem·i·te [jou'semiti] *Valle y parque nacional de EE.UU.*

Z

Zaire [zɑː'ɪə] Zaire *m.*
Zam·bia ['zæmbɪə] Zambia *f.*
Zim·bab·we [zɪm'bɑːbwɪ] Zimbabwe.

Numerals – Numerales

Cardinal Numbers - Números cardinales

0 nought *cero*
1 one *uno, una*
2 two *dos*
3 three *tres*
4 four *cuatro*
5 five *cinco*
6 six *seis*
7 seven *siete*
8 eight *ocho*
9 nine *nueve*
10 ten *diez*
11 eleven *once*
12 twelve *doce*
13 thirteen *trece*
14 fourteen *catorce*
15 fifteen *quince*
16 sixteen *dieciséis*
17 seventeen *diecisiete*
18 eighteen *dieciocho*
19 nineteen *diecinueve*
20 twenty *veinte*
21 twenty-one *veintiuno*
22 twenty-two *veintidós*
30 thirty *treinta*
31 thirty-one *treinta y uno*
40 forty *cuarenta*
50 fifty *cincuenta*
60 sixty *sesenta*
70 seventy *setenta*
80 eighty *ochenta*
90 ninety *noventa*
100 a (*o* one) hundred *cien(to)*
101 a hundred and one *ciento uno*
110 a hundred and ten *ciento diez*
200 two hundred *doscientos -as*
300 three hundred *trescientos -as*
400 four hundred *cuatrocientos -as*
500 five hundred *quinientos -as*
600 six hundred *seiscientos -as*
700 seven hundred *setecientos -as*
800 eight hundred *ochocientos -as*
900 nine hundred *novecientos -as*
1000 a thousand *mil*
1959 nineteen hundred and fifty-nine *mil novecientos cincuenta y nueve*
2000 two thousand *dos mil*
1 000 000 a (*o* one) million *un millón (de)*
2 000 000 two million *dos millones (de)*

Ordinal Numbers – Números ordinales

1 first *primero*
2 second *segundo*
3 third *tercero*
4 fourth *cuarto*
5 fifth *quinto*
6 sixth *sexto*
7 seventh *séptimo*
8 eighth *octavo*
9 ninth *noveno, nono*
10 tenth *décimo*
11 eleventh *undécimo*
12 twelfth *duodécimo*
13 thirteenth *decimotercero, decimotercio*
14 fourteenth *decimocuarto*
15 fifteenth *decimoquinto*
16 sixteenth *decimosexto*
17 seventeenth *decimoséptimo*
18 eighteenth *decimoctavo*
19 nineteenth *decimono(ve)no*
20 twentieth *vigésimo*
21 twenty-first *vigésimo prim(er)o*
22 twenty-second *vigésimo segundo*
30 thirtieth *trigésimo*
31 thirty-first *trigésimo prim(er)o*
40 fortieth *cuadragésimo*
50 fiftieth *quincuagésimo*
60 sixtieth *sexagésimo*
70 seventieth *septuagésimo*
80 eightieth *octogésimo*
90 ninetieth *nonagésimo*
100 hundredth *centésimo*
101 hundred and first *centésimo primero*
110 hundred and tenth *centésimo décimo*
200 two hundredth *ducentésimo*
300 three hundredth *tricentésimo*
400 four hundredth *cuadringentésimo*
500 five hundredth *quingentésimo*
600 six hundredth *sexcentésimo*
700 seven hundredth *septingentésimo*
800 eight hundredth *octingentésimo*
900 nine hundredth *noningentésimo*
1000 thousandth *milésimo*
2000 two thousandth *dos milésimo*
1 000 000 millionth *millonésimo*
2 000 000 two millionth *dos millonésimo*

En inglés, los números ordinales suelen abreviarse **1**st., **2**nd., **3**rd., **4**th., **5**th., etc.

Fractions and other Numerals – Números quebrados y otros

$^1/_2$ one (*o* a) half *medio, media*;
1$^1/_2$ one and a half *uno y medio*;
2$^1/_2$ two and a half *dos y medio*;
$^1/_2$ h. half an hour *media hora*;
1$^1/_2$ m. one and a half miles *milla y media*

$^1/_3$ one (*o* a) third *un tercio*; $^2/_3$ two thirds *dos tercios*

$^1/_4$ one (*o*) quarter *un cuarto*; $^3/_4$ three quarters *tres cuartos*; $^1/_4$ h. (a) quarter of an hour *un cuarto de hora*; **1**$^1/_4$ h. one and a quarter hours *hora y cuarto*

$^1/_5$ one (*o* a) fifth *un quinto*; **3**$^4/_5$ three and four fifths *tres y cuatro quintos*

$^1/_{11}$ one (*o* an) eleventh *un onzavo*

$^5/_{12}$ five twelfths *cinco dozavos*

$^{75}/_{100}$ seventy-five hundredths *setenta y cinco centésimos*

$^1/_{1000}$ one (*o* a) thousandth *un milésimo*

single *simple*
double *doble, duplo*
treble, triple, threefold *triple*
fourfold *cuádruplo*
fivefold *quíntuplo etc.*

once *una vez*
twice *dos veces*
three times *tres veces etc.*
seven times as big *siete veces más grande*;
twice more *dos veces más*

firstly *en primer lugar*
secondly *en segundo lugar etc.*

7 + 8 = 15 seven and eight are fifteen *siete y ocho son quince*

10 − 3 = 7 three from ten leaves seven *diez menos tres igual siete, de tres a diez van siete*

2 × 3 = 6 two times three are six *dos por tres son seis*

20 ÷ 4 = 5 twenty divided by four is five *veinte dividido por cuatro es cinco.*

American and British Weights and Measures

Pesos y medidas americanos y británicos

1. Linear measures – Medidas de longitud

1 inch (in.) = 2,54 cm.
1 foot (ft.) = 12 inches = 30,48 cm.
1 yard (yd.) = 3 feet = 91,44 cm.

2. Distance and surveyors' measures – Medidas de distancia y de agrimensura

1 link (li., l.) = 7.92 inches = 20,12 cm.
1 rod (rd.), pole *o* **perch (p.)** = 25 links = 5,029 m.
1 chain (ch.) = 4 rods = 20,12 m.
1 furlong (fur.) = 10 chains = 201,17 m.
1 (statute) mile (mi.) = 1,760 yards = 1609,34 m.

3. Nautical measures – Medidas náuticas

1 fathom (fm.) = 6 feet = 1,83 m.
1 cable('s) length = 100 fathoms = 183 m. *Am.* 120 fathoms = 219 m.
1 nautical mile (n. m.) = 10 cables' length = 1852 m.

4. Square measures – Medidas cuadradas

1 square inch (sq. in.) = 6,45 cm².
1 square foot (sq. ft.) = 144 square inches = 929,03 cm².
1 square yard (sq. yd.) = 9 square feet = 0,836 m².
1 square rod (sq. rd.) = 30.25 square yards = 25,29 m².
1 rood (ro.) = 40 square rods = 10,12 áreas.
1 acre (a.) = 4 roods = 40,47 áreas.
1 square mile (sq. mi.) = 640 acres = 2,59 km².

5. Cubic measures – medidas de cubicación

1 cubic inch (cu. in.) = 16,387 cm³.
1 cubic foot (cu. ft.) = 1728 cubic inches = 0,028 m³.
1 cubic yard (cu. yd.) = 27 cubic feet = 0,765 m³.
1 register ton (reg. tn.) = 100 cubic feet = 2,832 m³.

6. British measures of capacity – Medidas de capacidad (Gran Bretaña)

Dry and liquid measures – Medidas para áridos y líquidos

1 British *o* **Imperial gill (gi., gl.)** = 0,142 l.
1 British *o* **Imperial pint (pt.)** = 4 gills = 0,568 l.
1 British *o* **Imperial quart (qt.)** = 2 Imp. pints = 1,136 l.
1 British *o* **Imp. gallon (Imp. gal.)** = 4 Imp. quarts = 4,546 l.

Dry measures – Medidas para áridos

1 British *o* **Imperial peck (pk.)** = 2 Imp. gallons = 9,087 l.

1 Brit. *o* **Imp. bushel (bu., bsh.)** = 4 Imp. pecks = 36,36 l.

1 Brit. *o* **Imperial quarter (qr.)** = 8 Imp. bushels = 290,94 l.

Medida para líquidos – Liquid measure

1 Brit. *o* **Imp. barrel (bbl., bl.)** = 36 Imp. gallons = 1,636 Hl.

7. Medidas de capacidad (EE.UU.) – Measures of capacity (U.S.A.)

Medidas para áridos – Dry measures

1 U.S. dry point = 0,550 l.

1 U.S. dry quart = 2 dry pints = 1,1 l.

1 U.S. peck = 8 dry quarts = 8,81 l.

1 U.S. bushel *(granos) = 4 pecks = 35,24 l.*

Medidas para líquidos – Liquid measures

1 U.S. liquid gill = 0,118 l.

1 U.S. liquid pint = 4 gills = 0,473 l.

1 U.S. liquid quart = 2 liquid pints = 0,946 l.

1 U.S. gallon = 4 liquid quarts = 3,785 l.

1 U.S. barrel = $31^1/_2$ gallons = 119 l.

1 U.S. barrel petroleum = 42 gallons = 158,97 l.

8. Medidas de boticario – Apothecaries' fluid measures

1 minim (min., m.) = 0,0006 dl.

1fluid drachm, *Am.* **dram (dr. fl.)** = 60 minims = 0,0355 dl.

1 fluid ounce (oz. fl) = 8 fluid dra(ch)ms = 0,284 dl.

1 pint (pt.) = 20 fluid ounces =0,568 l. *Am.* 16 fluid ounces = 0,473 l.

9. Peso Avoirdupois – Avoirdupois weight

1 grain (gr.) = 0,0648 gr.

1 drachm, *Am.* **dram (dr. av.)** = 27.34 grains = 1,77 gr.

1 ounce (oz. av.) = 16 dra(ch)ms = 28,35 gr.

1 pound (lb. av.) = 16 ounces = 0,453 kg.

1 stone (st.) = 14 pounds = 6,35 kg.

1 quarter (qr.) = 28 pounds = 12,7 kg. *Am.* 25 pounds = 11,34 kg.

1 hundredweight (cwt.) = 112 pounds = 50,8 kg. (*a.* long hundredweight: cwt. l.) *Am.* 100 pounds = 45,36 kg. (*a.* short hundredweight: cwt. sh.)

1 ton (tn., t.) = 2240 pounds (= 20 cwt. l) = 1016 kg. (*a.* long ton: tn. l.) *Am.* = 2000 pounds (= 20 cwt. sh.) = 907,18 kg (*a.* short ton: tn. sh.)

10. Peso Troy y de boticario – Troy and apothecaries' weight

1 grain (gr.) = 0,0648 gr.

1 scruple (s. ap.) = 20 grains = 1,296 gr.

1 pennyweight (dwt.) = 24 grains = 1,555 gr.

1 dra(ch)m (dr. t. *o* **dr. ap.)** = 3 scruples = 3,888 gr.

1 ounce (oz. ap.) = 8 dra(ch)ms = 31,104 gr.

1 pound (lb. t. *o* **lb. ap.)** = 12 ounces = 0,373 kg.

Notes

Notes

Notes

Notes

Notes